All Music Guide

THE DEFINITIVE GUIDE

TO POPULAR MUSIC

4TH EDITION

Edited by

Vladimir Bogdanov

Chris Woodstra

Stephen Thomas Erlewine

AMG
All Media Guide

Backbeat Books

AMG
All Media Guide **All Media Guide** has created the world's largest and most comprehensive information databases for music, videos, DVDs, and video games. With coverage of both in-print and out-of-print titles, the massive AMG archive includes reviews, plot synopses, biographies, ratings, images, titles, credits, essays, and thousands of descriptive categories. All content is original, written expressly for AMG by a worldwide network of professional staff and freelance writers specializing in music, movies, and games. The AMG databases—**All Music Guide®**, **All Movie Guide®**, and **All Game Guide™**—are licensed by major retailers and Internet content sites and are available to the public through its websites (www.allmusic.com, www.allmovie.com, www.allgame.com) and through its series of books: *All Music Guide, All Music Guide to Rock, All Music Guide to Country, All Music Guide to Jazz, All Music Guide to Blues,* and *All Music Guide to Electronica.*

All Media Guide 301 E. Liberty Street, Suite 400, Ann Arbor, MI 48104
T: 734/887-5600 F: 734/827-2492
www. allmediaguide.com email: feedback@allmediaguide.com

Published by Backbeat Books
600 Harrison Street, San Francisco, CA 94105
www.backbeatbooks.com
Email: books@musicplayer.com
An imprint of Music Player Network
United Entertainment Media, Inc.
Publishers of MusicPlayer.com

Distributed to the book trade in the U.S and Canada by Publishers Group West, 1700 Fourth Street, Berkeley, CA 94710

Distributed to the music trade in the U.S. and Canada by Hal Leonard Publishing, P.O. Box 13819, Milwaukee, WI 53213

Cover Design: Wagner Design, Ann Arbor, MI
AMG—All Music Guide Founder: Michael Erlewine
Text Composition: Graphic Composition, Inc., Athens, GA

Library of Congress Cataloging-in-Publication Data

All music guide : the definitive quide to popular music / edited by Vladimir Bogdanov, Chris Woodstra, Stephen Thomas Erlewine.—4th ed.
p. cm.
ISBN 0-87930-627-0
1. Sound recordings—Reviews. 2. Popular music—Discography. 3. Music—Discography. I. Bogdanov, Vladimir, 1965- II. Woodstra, Chris. III. Erlewine, Stephen Thomas.

ML156.9 .A38 2001
016.78026'6—dc21

Printed in the United States of America
01 02 03 04 05 5 4 3 2 1

Dedication

This book is dedicated to Cub Koda, a rock & roll wildman and true believer whose warmth, humor, knowledge and wisdom was an inspiration to all of us at *All Music Guide.* Without him, our publications would have been very different, and his spirit lives on not just through his records and writing, but in this book.

How to Use This Book

ARTIST NAME

VITAL STATISTICS: For groups, **f.** indicates date and place of formation; **db.** indicated date disbanded. For individual performers, date and place of birth (**b.**) and death (**d.**), if known, are given.

PERFORMER(S) / STYLE: Indicates a group, musician, DJ, or producer, followed by the styles of music associated with the performer or group.

BIOGRAPHY: A quick view of the artist's life and musical career. For major performers, proportionately longer biographies are provided.

ALBUM REVIEWS: These are the albums selected by our editors and contributors.

KEY TO SYMBOLS: ● ☆ ★

☆ESSENTIAL RECORDINGS: Albums marked with a star should be part of any good collection of the genre. Often, these are also a good first purchase (filled star). By hearing these albums, you can get a good overview of the entire genre. These are must-hear and must-have recordings. You can't go wrong with them.

●★FIRST PURCHASE: Albums marked with either a filled circle or a filled star should be your first purchase. This is where to begin to find out if you like this particular artist. These albums are representative of the best this artist has to offer. If you don't like these picks, chances are this artist is not for you. In the case of an artist who has a number of distinct periods, you will find an essential pick marked for each period. Albums are listed chronologically when possible.

ALBUM TITLE: The name of the album is listed in bold as it appears on the original when possible. Very long titles have been abbreviated, or repeated in full as part of the comment, where needed.

DATE: The year of an album's first recording or release, if known.

RECORD LABEL: Record labels indicate the current (or most recent) release of this recording. Label numbers are not included because they change frequently.

ALBUM RATINGS: ✦ TO ✦✦✦✦✦ In addition to the stars and circles used to distinguish exceptional noteworthy albums, as explained above, all albums are rated on a scale from one to five diamonds.

REVIEWERS: The name of each review's author are given at the end of the review.

Crosby, Stills & Nash (And Young)

f. 1968, Laurel Canyon, CA

Group / Pop/Rock, Folk-Rock, Singer/Songwriter

The musical partnership of David Crosby, Stephen Stills and Graham Nash–with and without Neil Young–not only was one of the most successful touring and recording acts of the late '60s,'70s, and early '80s; with the colorful, contrasting nature of the members' characters and their connection to the political and cultural upheavals of the time, it was the only American-based band to approach the overall societal impact of the Beatles. The group was a second marriage for all the participants when it came together in 1968: Crosby had been a member of the Byrds, Nash was in the Hollies, and Stills had been part of Buffalo Springfield. By the time of their first tour (which included the Woodstock festival), they had added Young, also a veteran of Buffalo Springfield, who maintained a solo career. The first CSNY album, *Deja Vu*, was a chart-topping hit in 1970, but the group split acrimoniously after a summer tour. In 1974, CSNY reformed for a summer stadium tour without releasing a new record. Nevertheless, the compilation *So Far* became their third straight number one. Crosby, Stills and Nash reformed without Young in 1977 for the album *CSN*, another giant hit. The trio remains a popular live act. *–William Ruhlmann*

☆**Deja Vu / Mar. 11, 1970 / Atlantic ✦✦✦✦✦**

The first of the group's albums to include Neil Young, *Deja Vu* is the CSNY aggregate's most consistent and lovely LP. Not only does Young's recruitment bring an idiosyncratic new dimension to the group's shimmering harmonies, but the addition of his guitar skills greatly broadens their musical scope; at the same time, his prodigious songwriting gifts seem to have spurred the original CSN line-up to new creative heights–the material on *Deja Vu* is uniformly excellent, ranging from the gorgeous "Helpless" to the ambitious title cut. The star of the record is Graham Nash, who delivers a pair of classics, the country-inflected "Teach Your Children" and "Our House," written for Joni Mitchell; speaking of Mitchell, she also penned the record's centerpiece, the perennial "Woodstock," a sweeping celebration of counterculture values. *–Jason Ankeny*

Four Way Street / Apr. 7, 1971 / Atlantic ✦✦✦✦✦

This 1992 expanded version of the original double live album (originally released on April 7, 1971) by CSNY is now an indispensible part of any collection, with additional Neil Young and Graham Nash material (and even a version of "King Midas in Reverse," the old Hollies tune) that any serious listener will want. Some of the extended guitar jams between Stills and Young ("Southern Man") go on longer than strict musical sense would dictate, but it seemed right at the time, and they capture a form that was far more abused in other hands after this group broke up. *–Bruce Eder*

● **So Far / Aug. 1974 / Atlantic ✦✦✦✦✦**

Released to coincide with CSNY's 1974 reunion tour, this compilation remains the best representation of the group's early work, featuring such hits as "Teach Your Children" and "Suite: Judy Blue Eyes." It also put the one-off single "Ohio/Find the Cost of Freedom" (CSNY's response to the shooting of four anti-war student protestors at Kent State University) on an album for the first time. *–William Ruhlmann*

Daylight Again / Jun. 21, 1982 / Atlantic ✦✦✦

Originally a Stills and Nash project, but with the drug-addled Crosby added virtually in name only for commercial reasons (Timothy Schmit and Art Garfunkel provide many of the harmonies), this turned out better than expected, featuring Nash's reflective "Wasted on the Way" and Stills' "Southern Cross," both hits and respectable additions to the CSN repertoire. *–William Ruhlmann*

Table of Contents

Introduction

Since the first edition of *All Music Guide* was published in 1992, much has changed in the world of record collecting and record guides. At that time, there weren't many guides on the shelves and only a handful of those attempted to navigate the turbulence of the CD revolution. Now it's hard to imagine a situation like that. Scores of record guides were published throughout the {apos}90s, and, more importantly, the internet made all of this information, in much greater detail, instantly available, as well.

So, there was once a deficit of guides and now, in 2001, there is an abundance. That's a good thing. Given the never-ending stream of new releases and reissues, there needs to be some guide through the wilderness. *All Music Guide*'s website, which covers much more than any print edition ever could, is that guide, and, considering its existence, it may be reasonable to ask, why publish a new general guide when it's already on the net? Well, not only are there still many avid music fans that have no internet access, but there is a certain magic to a guide. Record collectors love assembling lists and guides are like an uber-list—a series of highlights to collect and discover.

The internet has liberated the assembly of the print edition of the *All Music Guide.* There is a place to display complete discographies, extensive biographies, in-depth reviews, and formalized data, thereby freeing space in the print edition. And with that extra space, we're able to offer a true generalist guide—a guide that will allow music fans to find the best recordings, not just from the usual suspects, but also by cult figures that have a lot to offer the average music fan.

Now, for the big question—how did we decide what to include? For each genre, the obvious choices—the Beatles, Miles Davis, Hank Williams, and others of their ilk—have been surrounded by popular favorites (acts that have scored well on either the charts or the critics lists), acts that define their era, and, happily, artists that exist *outside* of their era. Music that will interest listeners with voracious appetites and wide taste. There will be albums you know, but maybe there will be something you haven't heard of before—and it could be a new compilation or a brand-new artist. Inevitably, there will be artists missing, perhaps one of your favorite artists. This is the nature of this kind of guide—cuts have to be made and sometimes they are painful and sometimes they may even be misguided. We have set out to make a guide that will appeal to listeners that want to know about everything from Louis Armstrong to Radiohead.

There's actually a trickier question of inclusion—what albums to include? During the {apos}90s, two phenomenons happened—countless compilations, from box sets to *Millennium Series,* were released and veteran acts of all genres continued to record at a steady pace. Practically, it is impossible to list and review each of these albums within a book, so we made cuts. Only the best compilations are listed. More controversially, some artists are represented by long discographies, others have a handful of albums, others are summarized with collections. The goal is to find the best way of listening to an artist, whether it's through actual albums, boxes, or hits collections. Though we have tried to ensure most of our listings are in print at the time of publication (particularly for compilations), we have listed several out of print albums. These are records that are worth the search—and, with any luck, they will go into print again. Also, another blessing of the Internet is that it's much easier to find rare recordings and imports, whether it's on an auction on Ebay or on any of the e-commerce sites. Because of this, we have not hesitated to list and recommend these recordings—the savvy listeners will no doubt be able to find what they're looking for (whether they're willing to pay for it is another question entirely).

Finally, if any artist is missing, or if you want to see reviews for albums not featured in the book—say, for instance, reviews of the reunited Lynyrd Skynyrd's albums—please go to allmusic.com, which contains thousands of reviews and biographies.

Call us old-fashioned, but even in an age where music is traded in digital files, we have a love for proper albums, old records, compilations, and compact discs. We like collecting, we like searching for new music. This is to help you on your own search. —*Stephen Thomas Erlewine*

Contributors

All Music Guide Editors

Vladimir Bogdanov, President
Chris Woodstra, Vice President of Content Development
Stephen Thomas Erlewine, Director of Content, Pop Music
John Bush, Senior Editor, Pop Music

AMG Pop Editors

Al Campbell
Steve Huey
Zac Johnson
Joslyn Layne
Heather Phares
Diana Potts
Stacia Proefrock
Sean Westergaard
MacKenzie Wilson

Contributors

Nitsuh Abebe
Iván Adaime
Bret Adams
Greg Adams
David R. Adler
Steve Aldrich
Mark Allan
Aric Laurence Allen
Rick Allen
Rick Anderson
Robert Aniento
Jason Ankeny
Jennifer Ansbach
William Ashford
Glenn Astarita
Jon Azpiri
Aaron Badgley
Jonathan Ball
Toby Ball
Brian Bartolini
Ashley S. Battel
George Bedard
Larry Belanger
Shaun Belcher
Jason Birchmeier
Roxanne Blanford
Dacia Blodgett-Williams
Lee Bloom
Michael Blostein
Vladimir Bogdanov
Myles Boisen
Ross Boissoneau
Gina Boldman
Drago Bonacich
John Book
Rob Bowman
Michael Breece
Sandra Brennan
Deanne Briggs
Brian Briscoe
Rick A. Bueche
Scott Bultman
Jeff Burger
John Bush
Nathan Bush
Bryan Buss
Blake Butler
Becky Byrkit
Al Campbell
Rachel Campbell
Matthew Carlin
Dean Carlson
Matt Carlson
Danny Carnahan
Bil Carpenter
Troy Carpenter
Sean Carruthers
Phil Carter
Bill Cassel
Kenneth M. Cassidy
Marc Castellani
Darryl Cater
Evan Cater
Tom Chandler
James Chrispell
David Cleary
Paul Collins
Matt Conaway
Stephen Constantelos
Stephen Cook
Dan Cooper
Sean Cooper
William Cooper
Kristi Coulter
François Couture
Jeff Crooke
Dan Cross
Susan Cruickshank
Rosalind Cummings-Yeates
Joanna Curzon
Michael Cusanelli
Bill Dahl
Jason Damas
Mike DaRonco
Hank Davis
Michael P. Dawson
Paul de Barros
Mike DeGagne
Tom Demalon
Mark Deming
Caleb Deupree
Michael Di Bella
Tim DiGravina
Charlotte Dillon
Kirk Dombek
Chuck Donkers
Charles Donovan
Jim Dorsch
John Dougan
Ken Dryden
John Duffy
David Dwyer
Doug Dwyer
Paula Edelstein
Bruce Eder
Brian Christopher Egan
Jason Elias
Iotis Erlewine
Meredith Erlewine
Michael Erlewine
Sarah Erlewine
Stephen Thomas Erlewine
Alan Esher
Todd Everett
Banning Eyre
Peter Fawthrop
Inigo C. Figuracion
Matt Fink
Phil Fink
Sigmund Finman
Mike Fleischer
Brian Flota
John Floyd
Luke Forrest
Dan Forte
John Franck
Niles J. Frantz
Michael Freedberg
David Freedlander
Michael Frey
Tracy Frey
Michael Gallucci
Alex S. Garcia
James A. Gardner
Alexander Gelfand
Bob Gendron
Yuri German
Maya Geryk
Marc Gilman
Cary Ginell
Richard Ginell
Geoff Ginsberg
Dan Gizzi
Ryan Randall Goble
John Gonsalves
Robert Gordon
Bob Gottlieb
Mary Grady
Thom Granger
Tom Graves
Adam Greenberg
Matthew Greenwald
Ted Greenwald
Mark C. Gridley
Tim Griggs
Jason Gross
Scot Hacker
Char Ham
Andrew Hamilton
Chris Handyside
Shawn Haney
Jeff Hannusch
James Harley
Spencer Harrington
Craig Harris
Brett Hartenbach
Kelvin Hayes
Ralph Heibutzki
Dan Heilman
Alex Henderson
Nick Herman
Matthew Hilburn
Don Hill
Melinda Hill
Bob Hinkle
Terri Hinte
Tavia Hobart
Larry Hoffman
Steve Hoffman
Ed Hogan
Hal Horowitz
David Howell
Stephen Howell
Carl Hoyt
Robert Hubbard
Steve Huey
Eddie Huffman
Mark A. Humphrey
Jason Hundey
Ken Hunt
Jaime Ikeda
Bruce Ishikawa
Lee (Jack) Isles
Vik Iyengar
Leon Jackson
Qa'id Jacobs
Steve James
Alonso Jasso
Dale Jensen
Zac Johnson
Blair Johnston
Liana Jonas
Thom Jurek

Michael Katz
Jason Kaufman
Claire Keaveney
Kurt Keefner
Andy Kellman
Chris Kelsey
Nick Kemper
Kit Kiefer
Cub Koda
Linda Kohanov
Paul Kohler
Maria Konicki
Jeffrey Konkel
Paul Kott
Stuart Kremsky
Todd Kristel
Philip Krumm
Peter Kurtz
Steve Kurutz
Ronnie D. Lankford, Jr.
Larry Lapka
Sanz Lashley
Peggy Latkovich
Theresa LaVeck
David Lavin
Joslyn Layne
Jack Leaver
Robert Leaver
Roberto Ledesma
Nick Leggatt
Jonathan Lewis
Richard Lieberson
Les Line
Steven Loewy
John Lomax
Kip Lornell
Steven Losey
Robert Lovering
John Lowe
John Lupton
Dave Lynch
Craig Lytle
Dennis MacDonald
Daniel Malich
Brian Mansfield
Derrick Mathis
Steve Matteo
David L. Mayers
Michael McCall
Kieran McCarthy
Kelly McCartney
Wilson McCloy
Steven McDonald
Kembrew McLeod
Steve McMullen
Richard Meyer
David A. Milberg
Mark Miller
Ted Mills
Martin Monkman
Jeri Montesano
Stansted Montfichet
Mark Morgenstein
Dan Morgenstern
Brian Musich
Michael G. Nastos
Dave Nathan
Opal Louis Nations
J. Neal
Alvaro Neder
Neufeld
Jim Newsom
Chris Nickson
Ed Nimmervoll
Ben O'Connor
Michael Ofjord
Alex Ogg
Christine Ohlman
Brian Olewnick
J.P. Ollio
Jim O'Neal
Buz Overbeck
Pat Padua
Roch Parisien
Chris Parker
Archie Patterson
John Patterson
Dan Pavlides
Douglas Payne
Barry Lee Pearson
Paul Pearson
Jana Pendragon
Keith Pettipas
Heather Phares
Richard Pierson
Lindsay Planer
Matthew Plichta
J. Poet
Bob Porter
Diana Potts
Larry Powell
Jim Powers
Greg Prato
Stacia Proefrock
Jose Promis
Bruce Boyd Raeburn
Brian Raftery
Ned Raggett
Stephen Raiteri
Chip Renner
Jamie Renton
Michael Ribas
Maurice Rickard
Ed Rivadavia
Pemberton Roach
Joel Roberts
John Storm Roberts
Matthew Robinson
Tom Roland
Janet Rosen
Gregg Rounds
Arthur Rowe
Marjorie Ellen Ruhlmann
William Ruhlmann
David Rumpler
Bob Rusch
Raissa St. Pierre
Bob Sakomano
Mtume Salaam
Max Salazar
Jeremy Salmon
Cliff Samaniego
Mary K. Scanlan
Gene Scaramuzzo
Steven Spaz Schnee
Tom Schulte
Steven Schwartz
Lisa Schwartzman
Tim Sendra
Joshua David Shanker
Douglas Shannon
Allan Shaw
Tim Sheridan
Earl Simmons
Richard Skelly
Chris Slawecki
Dave Sleger
Craig Robert Smith
David Ross Smith
Edwin Smith
Jim Smith
Michael Smith
Leo Stanley
Roger Steffens
Peter Stepek
Don Stevens
Joseph Stevenson
Freddy Stidean
Alex Stimmel
Doug Stone
Ned Sublette
Denise Sullivan
Kim Summers
P.J. Swift
Stanton Swihart
David Szatmary
Jeff Tamarkin
Bob Tarte
Robert Taylor
Bryan Thomas
Lang Thompson
William Tilland
Jim Todd
Bradley Torreano
Chris True
Greg Turner
Blue Gene Tyranny
Jeremy Ulrey
Neal Umphred
Richie Unterberger
John Vallier
Andrew Vance
Marc van der Pol
Philip Van Vleck
Joe Viglione
David Vinopal
Lynn Vought
Brian Wahlert
Robert Walker
Rick Watrous
Michael Waynick
Barry Weber
Sean Westergaard
Ann Wickstrom
Jonathan Widran
Tony Wilds
MacKenzie Wilson
Steve Winick
Billy C. Wirtz
Christopher Witt
Charles S. Wolfe
Carlo Wolff
Kurt Wolff
Cary Wolfson
Jan Mark Wolkin
Chris Woodstra
Jim Worbois
Carol Wright
Ron Wynn
Scott Yanow
Curtis Zimmermann

AMG Technical Editors

Jonathan Ball
George Davis
Mark Schaub-Donkers
Heather Humphrey
Jack LV Isles
Andy Kellman
Don Kline
Tim Sendra
Rob Theakston
Chris True

AMG Copy Editors

Jason Birchmeier
Kerri Covey
Elizabeth Erlewine
Margaret Erlewine
Benjamin Goldstein
Jennifer Jones
David Lynch
Karen Paik
Stephanie Somerville

Rock

Rock & roll, in its loosest definition, is popular music that was made after 1955. It includes rock & roll, to be certain, but also R&B, soul, pop, folk-rock, heavy metal, country-rock, glam, psychedelia, pub rock, arena rock, disco, punk, hardcore, new wave, synth-pop, jangle pop, industrial, acid jazz, house music, alternative, lo-fi, grunge, Brit-pop, techno, and any variation or fusion of any number of subgenres. Given the vast array of styles that can be classified under "rock & roll," it is nearly impossible to provide a comprehensive overview of the genre. Nevertheless, the rock section of *The All Music Guide* offers a concise and effective introduction to the music, from Little Richard and Elvis Presley to Prince and Pavement.

The rock section of *The All Music Guide* does not attempt to tell the history of rock & roll—it offers a guide to the genre's essential performers and their recordings. The intent is not to draw comparisons between the artists, but to judge each artist on their own terms.

Given our space limitations, worthy artists had to be excluded, yet we included a broad range of musicians reflecting the wide range of stylistic variations rock & roll has taken over the years. All of the major artists from every decade and subgenre have been included. So have cult artists of all genres and eras, just to give a suggestion of the vast variety of styles that make rock & roll endlessly fascinating.

What makes rock & roll so interesting is the sheer amount of variety it offers. It's been a long road from Bo Diddley and Jerry Lee Lewis to Nirvana and Oasis, and all the detours have something interesting to offer. It may be the songcraft of Neil Diamond or it could be the trance-inducing electronics of the Orb. It could be the direct rock & roll of Bob Seger and John Mellencamp or the minimalist approaches of the Ramones, AC/DC and Unrest, who all take simplicity in different sonic directions. Is it all rock & roll? No, in the conventional three-chord sense it's not, but it is all popular music that owes its existence to rock & roll. There's not an obvious link between Sonic Youth and Chuck Berry, yet there are links between Chuck Berry and the Velvet Underground, and the Velvet Underground and Sonic Youth.

The All Music Guide tries to explain Sonic Youth to Chuck Berry fans and, just as importantly, Chuck Berry to Sonic Youth fans. In the meantime, it explores subgenres like garage and surf rock that rarely get space in conventional rock histories. It also spotlights cult figures from the Celibate Rifles to Scott Walker that may have never gotten popular recognition, yet they had a small impact in shaping popular music—or they simply made intriguing, interesting music.

As the decades have passed, the music has changed and so have the recording formats. For the past decade, the compact disc has been the dominant medium, replacing the long-playing album. However, in the early years of rock & roll, the single was the primary method of recording. Artists like Elvis Presley, Chuck Berry, Fats Domino, Buddy Holly, the Everly Brothers, and Jerry Lee Lewis didn't think in terms of making cohesive full-length albums—they were making their next hit single. Around 1966, long-playing albums became the dominant musical format in rock & roll, with British Invasion bands like the Beatles and the Kinks making records that were tied together by both lyrical and musical themes. Soon, artists were putting more thought into making cohesive albums. Initially, this meant "concept albums"—records like the Who's *Tommy*, the Kinks' *Arthur*, or the Moody Blues' *Days of Future Passed*—that told specific stories with their songs. Concept albums gave way to a wave of progressive rock bands that wrote music that could only be told over the course of a full-length album, as well as psychedelic bands like the Grateful Dead and Jefferson Airplane, and hard rock bands like Led Zeppelin that didn't have hit singles, they had hit albums. Ever since the late '60s, bands have been concentrating their creative efforts on full-length albums, and have had long, successful careers without the benefit of hit singles. Consequently, albums were more important to the careers of '70s rockers like David Bowie and Queen than they were to Duane Eddy or the Ventures. That explains why Bowie and Queen have more albums listed than Eddy or the Ventures—it's not a critical judgment about which band is more important, it's a reflection of their particular era.

Furthermore, due to limitations in space, it was impossible to offer comprehensive discographies for each artist. Instead, selected recordings that offer a sense of the artist's history are listed. For some, that will mean just compilation, for others it means a fairly thorough listing of albums. On the other hand, musicians like James Brown and Elvis Presley have simply released too many albums for each album to be reviewed. In this case, their major records have been included, along with some interesting minor albums that help to showcase the depth of their artistry. Even when records haven't been reviewed, they have been rated, providing a guideline, if not a description.

The goal of the rock section in *The All Music Guide* is not to draw comparisons between the Carpenters and Mötley Crüe albums, or pit the Beatles against the Clash. Rather, the intent is to provide a guide for a particular artist, offering a biography and description of the music, as well as to capsule reviews of their albums. Within each entry, to the right of the album's title, is a rating for the album itself, on a scale from one to five. These ratings are based on the artist, not on their overall worth (for instance, a four-star Whitney Houston album is not necessarily the same as a four-star Black Sabbath album). The only global rating in the book is a star, which signals an album that is the best of its genre—in other words, it's essential listening.

A more complete listing and exploration of rock & roll is available in *The All Music Guide to Rock*, but this section offers an excellent overview of the music and all of its subgenres. Hopefully, it will alert you to some terrific music you may not have heard before. —*Stephen Thomas Erlewine and Chris Woodstra*

Rock Styles

ACID HOUSE—Acid house falls somewhere between the insistent beats of house and the jazzy, free-form experimentations of acid jazz.

ACID JAZZ—Incorporating jazzy samples and hip-hop beats, acid jazz was an outgrowth of the house music scene of the late '80s. As the music progressed in the early '90s, it moved closer to its jazz roots, especially when rappers created a fusion of jazz and hip-hop and when jazz instrumentalists began performing live with a hip-hop beat. Nevertheless, acid jazz is distinguished by its thick beats, rubbery bass grooves, and its samples of bebop and soul jazz.

ACID ROCK—Acid rock was the heaviest, loudest variation of psychedelic rock. Drawing from the overblown blues improvisations of Cream and Jimi Hendrix, acid rock bands relied on distorted guitars, trippy lyrics, and long jams. Acid rock didn't last too long—it evolved and imploded within the lifespan of psychedelia—and the bands that didn't break up, became heavy metal bands.

ADULT CONTEMPORARY—Adult contemporary is a soft-rock, easy listening genre that came into existence in the early '70s. Essentially, it is post-Beatles pop music with slight rock and soul influences. It is highly polished, without much of an edge but with a lot of melody and production. Throughout the '70s, there were string-laden easy listening bands like the Carpenters and Bread. In the '80s, synthesizers replaced strings and artists that had been relatively harder in their early careers—Elton John, Billy Joel, and Sting, for instance—began to become calmer and softer. Along with pseudo-soul singers like Michael Bolton, they became the staples of adult contemporary radio in the '80s and '90s.

ALTERNATIVE COUNTRY-ROCK—Alternative country-rock keeps the sound of Gram Parsons and Neil Young alive. Though the bands are all rock & roll, their dedication to replicating the sound of Parsons and Young made them more traditionalist than either the alternative rock bands of the late '80s and '90s or the country bands of the same era. Though alternative country-rock bands occasionally have louder, grungier guitars than their idols, they are traditional in their sense of songwriting and dedication to keeping the actual sound of the early '70s alive, through the use of vintage instruments. Occasionally, some alternative country-rock bands stretch the boundaries of the form, but most are simply revivalists.

ALTERNATIVE METAL—At its core, alternative metal uses the same conventions that heavy metal always has—loud guitars, bludgeoning riffs—but it subverts the genre with post-punk concepts. Instead of adhering to the traditional lightweight lyrical topics that dominate mainstream metal, alternative metal bands tackle weightier matters, much like Metallica but without the insanely fast tempos, intricate guitar solos, and hoarse, bellowed vocals. Musically, the bands tended to be more atonal than traditional metal, but that all changed after Nirvana became popular in the early '90s and grunge became the dominant form of hard rock. After Nirvana, alternative metal ranged from the grinding, dissonant Helmet to the big riffs of Stone Temple Pilots, who closely followed the formula of '70s hard-rock acts. Soon, many new metal bands were packaged as alternative acts, though there was little besides visual presentation and a trademark fuzzy distortion to distinguish them from conventional metal bands.

ALTERNATIVE POP-ROCK—Alternative pop/rock is essentially a catch-all term for post-punk bands from the mid-'80s to the mid-'90s. Though there are a variety of musical styles within alternative rock, they are all tied together because they existed outside of the mainstream. In some ways, there are two waves of alternative bands, with Nirvana's success in 1991 acting as a dividing point. In the '80s, most alternative bands were on independent labels; if they were on majors, they didn't receive as much support as most of the label's mainstream acts. During the '80s, alternative included everything from jangle pop, post-hardcore punk, funk-metal, punk-pop, and experimental rock. After Nirvana's success in the '90s, alternative included all of these subgenres, but many of the edges were sanded off because the music was now being marketed as part of the mainstream. Hard rock and punk-derived music were more commercially successful than the left-of-center pop that dominated late '80s alternative pop/rock, so alternative lost some of its quirkier tendencies in the '90s. Strangely, experimental bands were relegated to indie rock.

ARENA ROCK—Arena rock developed in the mid-'70s, when hard-rock and heavy-metal bands began to gain popularity. The music became more commercially-oriented and radio-friendly, boasting slick productions and anthemic choruses, both on their hard rock numbers and their sweeping power ballads. Most of these bands earned their following through saturation airplay on FM radio and through constant touring. Bands like Journey, REO Speedwagon, Boston, Foreigner, and Styx became some of the most popular bands of the mid- to late '70s through this circuit.

ART ROCK/PROGRESSIVE ROCK—Art rock and progressive rock incorporate elements of European and classical music to rock & roll music, resulting in long, complex instrumental passages and dramatic, grandiose flourishes. Though the movement was sparked by the Beatles' Sgt. Pepper, art rock bands tend to write compositions, not songs; instrumental prowess is also emphasized. Primarily, art rock and progressive rock are album-oriented, not single-oriented. The album format gives the bands freedom to experiment musically and expand their ideas over the course of a side. Another tendency of art rock bands is to tell stories—frequently, their albums are structured as rock operas. The difference between art rock and progressive rock is slight, but important. Art rock bands tend to draw more heavily on classical influences and show a tendency toward medieval and mystical lyrical imagery. Progressive rockers do have some classical elements to their music, but they also have more overt jazz and psychedelic influences, and they have a greater tendency to improvise.

BLUE-EYED SOUL—Blue-eyed soul refers to soul and R&B music performed and sung by White musicians. The term first came into play during the mid-'60s, when acts like the Righteous Brothers had hits with soulful songs like "You Lost that Loving Feeling." Throughout the late '60s, blue-eyed soul thrived, as acts like the Rascals, the Boxtops, Mitch Ryder, Tony Joe White, and Roy Head had a series of hits. During the '70s, blue-eyed soul continued to be successful as acts like Hall & Oates, Robert Palmer, Average White Band, Boz Scaggs, and David Bowie updated the blue-eyed soul formula.

BLUES-ROCK—Though much early rock & roll was based in the blues, blues-rock didn't fully develop into a sub-genre until the late-'60s. Blues-rock emphasized two specific things—the traditional, three-chord blues song and instrumental improvisation. Borrowing the idea of an instrumental combo and loud amplification from rock & roll, the original blues-rockers—bands like Cream, that grew out of the Alexis Korner and John Mayall tradition of British blues, as well as American bands like Paul Butterfield Blues Band and Canned Heat—also attempted to play long, involved improvisations which were commonplace on jazz records, as well as live blues shows. The hybrid became quite popular and the bands that immediately followed them were louder and more riff-oriented. Out of this approach came heavy metal and Southern rock, both of which used basic blues riffs and featured extended solos. In the early '70s, the lines between blues-rock and hard rock were barely visible, as boogie-based bands like ZZ Top employed album-rock production techniques that tended to obscure their blues roots. However, blues-rock soon backed away from hard rock, and there was a set number of acts that continued to play (and re-write) blues standards as well as write their own songs in the same idiom. In the '80s and '90s, blues-rock was more roots-oriented than in the '60s and '70s, even when artists like Fabulous Thunderbirds and Stevie Ray Vaughan flirted with rock stardom. By the '80s, blues-rock had become an accepted tradition, much like the blues.

BOOGIE ROCK—Boogie rock is an off-shoot of the heavy blues rock of the late '60s. Instead of emphasizing instrumental improvisation like the original blues-rock bands (Cream, Jimi Hendrix, Yardbirds, Led Zeppelin), boogie rockers concentrated on the groove, working a steady, choogling backbeat. While nearly every boogie-rock band played the same 4/4 tempo, the main distinction between the groups was their instrumental attack— some groups, like Foghat, played heavier than others.

BRILL BUILDING POP—The Brill Building sound applied the concept of professional songwriters in traditional pop to rock & roll. Numerous teams of professional songwriters worked at the Brill Building—a block of music publishing houses in New York City—writing songs for artists as diverse as the Coasters, the Drifters, the Shangri-las, the Ronettes, Neil Sedaka, and Connie Francis. The songs were indebted not only to rock & roll and R&B, but also Tin Pan Alley pop, as the sophisticated lyrics and melodies proved. The productions on these early '60s records were also more sophisticated than most rock & roll records, featuring orchestras and bands with large rhythm and guitar sections. Though it fell out of favor after the British Invasion, both British and American pop-rock demonstrated an enormous debt to the Brill Building sound for years to come.

BRIT-POP—Brit-pop evolved in the early '90s, somewhat as a response to American grunge and the anti-rock stars dominating the British-techno and indie-rock scenes. Brit-pop revived the idea of rock stars and pop songs with big, catchy melodies and hooks. Though the bands differed greatly in styles—they ranged from the massive guitar roar of Oasis and the defiantly British pop of Blur to the disco/glam-rock pastiche of Pulp—they were tied together by attitude. All of the groups were dedicated to the concept of a pop single, as well as the glamour of being a pop star. Some of the bands managed to cross over to the American market, but there had never been a generation of British rock musicians that had been less concerned with American success.

BRITISH INVASION—The British Invasion occurred in the mid-'60s, when a wave of English rock & roll bands crossed over into the American market after the breakthrough success of the Beatles. Though not all of the bands sounded similar—they ranged from the hard rock of the Rolling Stones and Kinks to the sweet pop of Gerry & the Pacemakers and Herman's Hermits—each group was heavily influenced by American rock & roll, blues, and R&B. British Invasion bands were either blues-based rockers or pop-rockers with ringing guitars and catchy hooks and melodies. Between 1964 and 1966, the British bands dominated the U.S. charts, as well as the charts in the U.K. In that time, there was a second wave of British Invasion bands—such as the Who and the Zombies—which were indebted to both American rock and British Invasion pop. By the late '60s, many of the bands had become rock icons, but a greater number didn't survive the transition into the post-Sgt. Pepper era.

BRITISH METAL—British metal, in an odd way, is as much a reaction to the lumbering arena heavy-metal groups of the mid-'70s as punk rock. Taking their cue from the grimy riffs of Black Sabbath, British metal groups were faster, tougher, harder, and louder than their predecessors. Frequently dressed in leather and playing fast, pounding riffs, they stood apart from the AOR-oriented metal bands that dominated hard rock since the early-'70s. Judas Priest, Iron Maiden, and Motörhead were the leaders of the movement and they gained a dedicated following in both Europe and America, even though they didn't cross over into the mainstream. Nevertheless, they set the tone for all the metal bands that followed, from thrash to death metal.

BRITISH MUSICHALL—In terms of rock & roll, British musichall derives from the music of Noel Coward and Anthony Newley, who performed pop standards and vaudevillian comedy numbers. It is characterized by kitschy dramatics, sing-along-choruses, horns, tinkling pianos, and either stomping beats or smooth crooning. During the '60s, the Beatles, the Kinks, and the Small Faces were some of the first bands to incorporate this style of British music into rock & roll, followed quickly by the whimsical psychedelia of Syd Barrett-era Pink Floyd and early David Bowie. Throughout the next three decades of rock & roll history, a number of British artists dabbled in this tradition, from pub rockers like Ian Dury to ska revivalists like Madness and Brit-poppers like Blur.

BUBBLEGUM—Bubblegum is lightweight, catchy pop music that was a significant commercial force in the late '60s and early '70s. Bubblegum was targeted at a pre-teen audience whose older siblings had been raised on rock & roll. It was simple, melodic, and light as feather—neither the lyrics or the music had much substance. Bubblegum was a manufactured music, created by record producers that often hired session musicians to play and sing the songs. Frequently, the session musicians were given a fake band name, to give the illusion that they were a real group. Apart from acts like the Partridge Family and Tommy Roe, most Bubblegum groups were one-hit wonders. Appropriately, the genre also had a short life span, lasting roughly five years. As the pre-teens that Bubblegum was created for grew up, they left the music behind and the following generation found other records. However, the genre had a surprisingly long legacy, as musicians that grew up with Bubblegum created songs that reflected the sunny, catchy simplicity of the music.

DANCE/CLUB-DANCE—Dance music comes in many different forms, from disco to hip-hop. Though there have been various dance crazes throughout the history of popular music, dance music became its own genre in the mid-'70s, as soul mutated into disco and whole clubs were devoted to dancing. In the late '70s, dance clubs played disco, but by the end of the decade, disco was mutating into a number of different genres. All of the genres were collected under the catch-all term "dance," though there were distinct differences between dance-pop, hip-hop, house, and techno, among other subgenres. What tied them all together was their emphasis on rhythm—in each dance subgenre, the beat remains all-important.

COUNTRY-ROCK—Essentially, country-rock is rock bands playing country music. It is country music informed by rock's counter-culture ideals, as well as its reliance on loud amplification, prominent back-beat, and pop melodies. The first country-rock bands—Flying Burrito Brothers, Gram Parsons, the Byrds, Neil Young—played straight country, as inspired by the Bakersfield sound of Merle Haggard and Buck Owens, as well as honky tonkers like Hank Williams. As the genre moved into the '70s, the rougher edges were smoothed out as the Eagles, Poco, Pure Prairie League, and Linda Ronstadt made music that was smoother and more laid-back. This became the predominant sound of country-rock in the '70s. In the late '80s, a small group of alternative rock bands began to revive the spartan sound of the original sound of Gram Parsons and Neil Young.

DANCE-POP—Dance-pop was an outgrowth of disco. Over a pounding, dance-club beat, there are simple, catchy melodies—dance-pop has more fully-formed songs than pure dance music. Dance-pop is primarily a producer's medium. The producer writes the songs and constructs the tracks, picking an appropriate vocalist to sing the songs. These dance divas become stars, but frequently the artistic vision is the producer's. Naturally, there are some major exceptions—Madonna and Janet Jackson have had control over the sound and direction of their records—but dance-pop is music that is about image, not substance. It is music of the moment.

DEATH METAL—Death metal grew out of the thrash metal in the late '80s. Taking the gritty lyrics and morbid obsessions of thrash to extremes, death metal was—as its name suggests—solely about death, pain, and suffering. These relentlessly bleak lyrics were set to loud, heavy riffs that owed as much to the lumbering metal of Black Sabbath as it did to Metallica. Death metal bands also owed a debt to the complex song structures of '70s art rockers, though most of these winding, intricate compositional methods were learned through Metallica. Death metal never attracted a wide audience, but to some diehard heavy-metal fans, it was a preferable alternative to Metallica and Guns N' Roses, who were selling millions of records in the late '80s and early '90s, or the pop-metal of Poison. It kept a small, dedicated cult throughout the '90s.

DISCO—Disco marked the dawn of dance-based popular music. Growing out of the increasingly groove-oriented sound of early '70s and funk, disco emphasized the beat above anything else, even the singer and the song. Disco was named after discotheques, clubs that played nothing music for dancing. Most of the discotheques were gay clubs in New York, and the DJs in these clubs specifically picked soul and funk records that had a strong, heavy groove. After being played in the disco, the records began receiving radio play and sold well. Soon, record companies and producers were cutting records created specifically for discos. Naturally, these records also had strong pop hooks, so they could have crossover success. Disco albums frequently didn't have many tracks—they had a handful of long songs that kept the beat going. Similarly, the singles were issued on 12-inch records, which allowed for extended remixes. DJs could mix these tracks together, matching the beats on each song since they were marked beats per minute. In no time, the insistent, pounding disco beat dominated the pop charts and everyone from rockers like the Rolling Stones and Rod Stewart, to pop acts like the Bee Gees and new wave artists like Blondie got in on the act. There were disco artists that became stars—Donna Summer, Chic, Village People, and KC & the Sunshine Band—but the music was primarily a producer's medium, since they created the tracks and wrote the songs. Disco lost momentum as the '70s became the '80s, but it didn't die—it mutated into a variety of different dance-based genres, ranging from dance-pop and hip-hop to acid house and techno.

DOO WOP—Doo wop was one of the most popular genres of rock & roll and R&B in the late '50s. Doo-wop artists were vocal groups, with each singer in the group taking a different part that interwove with the other singers. Frequently, the backing vocalists sang nonsense words as rhythm, and the genre's name derives from this trait. Most of the doo-wop groups started as a cappella bands, performing without instrumental accompaniment. The hit doo-wop singles inspired countless teenagers to form their own a cappella groups, though many of them were never recorded. Despite its a cappella origins, few doo-wop records were made without instrumental backing. Doo wop faded away in the early '60s, though its influence was felt throughout popular music in the following decades.

EURO-DANCE—Euro-dance is much like Europop. It is lightweight, studio-constructed pop, with catchy melodies and an insistent, repetitive beat. Euro-dance draws heavily from disco, but it makes it more mechanical and synthesized.

EUROPOP—As the name suggests, Europop is pop music that is made in Europe. The music is primarily lightweight pop confections, constructed in the studio by behind-the-scenes producers. ABBA defined the sound in the '70s, and hundreds of acts followed.

EXPERIMENTAL—Experimental rock owes as much to the avant garde as it does to rock & roll. Like progressive rock, experimental rock consciously pushes the boundaries by incorporating elements of classical music, avant garde, electronics, noise, etc. Not all experimental bands sound the same, but they are tied together by a willingness to be adventurous and expand the lexicon of rock & roll.

FOLK-POP—Folk-pop falls into two categories. Either it is folk songs with large, sweeping pop arrangements or pop songs given intimate, acoustic-based folk arrangements. Folk-pop began to evolve in the early '60s, but it came into full force after folk-rock became a sensation in the mid-'60s. Folk-pop doesn't have ringing guitars and those rougher edges of folk-rock. Instead, it is softer and gentler, and more pop-oriented.

FOLK-ROCK—Folk-rock takes the simple, direct songwriting style of folk music and melds it to a prominent rock & roll backbeat. One of the most distinctive elements of folk-rock is the chiming, ringing guitar hooks, coupled with clear vocal harmonies. Folk-rock was pioneered in the mid-'60s by the Byrds, who played Bob Dylan songs as if they were from the British Invasion. The Byrds established the blueprint that many bands followed. As the '60s wound down, more folk-rock groups emphasized the acoustic origins of folk and backed away from the ringing electric arpeggios of the Byrds. In the next three decades, both the acoustic and electric folk-rock sounds were commonplace in rock & roll.

FUNK—As soul began to experiment with rock textures in the late '60s, funk emerged. Funk kept the groove of soul but made it deeper. It also added a greater reliance on improvisation, much like the blues-rock and psychedelia of the era. James Brown and Sly Stone were the godfathers of funk—Brown's funk was stripped-down and spare, while Stone's was wilder and drew more from rock & roll. George Clinton, the leader of Parliament and Funkadelic, was the next great funkster. Clinton expanded Stone's blueprint, adding wild conceptual fantasies derived from the psychedelia of Sgt. Pepper and the counterculture humor of Frank Zappa. But the main signature of Clinton's music was how he kept working one groove, how he kept jamming over a deep bass line and adding instrumental breaks. Most of the funk bands of the '70s picked up on the groove, not the concepts, though funk and hip-hop groups in the '80s and '90s would expand on both the sound and the concept.

FUNK-METAL—Funk-metal takes the loud guitars and riffs of heavy metal and melds them to the popping bass lines and syncopated rhythms of funk. Funk-metal evolved in the mid-'80s when alternative bands like the Red Hot Chili Peppers and Fishbone began playing the hybrid with a stronger funk underpinning than metal. The bands that followed relied more on metal than funk, though they retained the wild bass lines. Like heavy metal, the genre became a way to showcase instrumental prowess.

GARAGE ROCK—Garage rock was a simple, raw form of rock & roll created by a number of American bands in the mid-'60s. Inspired by British Invasion bands like the Beatles, Kinks, and Rolling Stones, these midwestern American groups played a variation on British Invasion rock. Since they were usually young and amateurish, the results were much cruder than their inspirations but that is what made the sound exciting. Most of the bands emphasized their amateurishness, playing the same three chords, bashing their guitars, and growling their vocals. In many ways, the garage bands were the first wave of do-it-yourself punk rockers. Hundreds of garage bands popped up around America and a handful of them—the Shadows of Knight, the Count 5, the Seeds, the Standells—had hits, but most were destined for obscurity. In fact, nearly all of the bands were forgotten in the early '70s, but the Nuggets compilation brought them back to the spotlight. In the '80s, there was a garage rock revival that saw a number of bands earnestly trying to replicate the sound, style, and look of the '60s garage bands.

GIRL GROUP—Falling somewhere between traditional pop and R&B, the sound of the girl groups was one of the most popular rock & roll genres in the early '60s. Though there were strong elements of rock & roll and R&B in the music, girl groups were decidedly more polished than earlier forms of rock & roll. It was driven by producers and songwriters, who helped guide the groups and gave them material to sing. The vocalists had roots in gospel and R&B, while the songwriters and producers were schooled in traditional pop, which resulted in an exciting hybrid. The songs were innocent and yearning, with sweet, catchy melodies and driving backbeats. Though the girl groups faded away in the mid-'60s, they had a profound influence on pop-rock, particularly British Invasion acts like the Beatles.

GLAM ROCK—Glam rock combined the hard rock crunch of heavy metal with bubblegum pop melodies and a glitzy flair for theatrical dramatics. In the early '70s, it was one of the most popular styles of rock & roll in Britain, as T. Rex, David Bowie, and several other similar artists dominated the charts. Though it never crossed over into the American market, it had a lasting effect on rock & roll, as both heavy metal and post-punk in the late '70s and '80s demonstrated a massive debt to the riffs and look of glam rock.

GOTH ROCK—Goth rock grew out of the bleak post-punk rock of the Cure and Joy Division. As the name implies, goth rock had grand, baroque arrangements performed with gloomy synthesizers and processed guitars. Lyrically, goth was equally dark, featuring a lot of cryptic, morbid poetry. Almost as remarkable as its sound was goth's image. The bands and the fans usually dressed in black and wore heavy makeup. Primarily, goth rock was a mid-'80s British sensation—it was one of several fringe genres that occupied the space between new wave and alternative. Nevertheless, certain musical elements of goth lingered into the '90s, even if it didn't capture the imagination of alternative audiences like it did before.

GRINDCORE—Grindcore is an offspring of heavy metal and industrial music that has a fast, grinding tempo, bleak lyrics, and relentlessly loud distorted guitars.

GRUNGE—Using the sludgy, murky sound of the Stooges and Black Sabbath as a foundation, grunge was a hybrid of heavy metal and punk. Though the guitars were straight from early '70s metal, the aesthetic of grunge was far from metal. Both the lyrical approach and musical attack of grunge were adopted from punk, particularly the independent ideals of early '80s American hardcore. The first wave of grunge bands—Green River, Mudhoney, Soundgarden—were heavier than the second, which began with Nirvana. Nirvana was more melodic than their predecessors, and they also had signature stop-start dynamics, which became a genre convention nearly as recognizable as fuzzy, distorted guitars. After Nirvana crossed over into the mainstream, grunge lost many of its independent and punk connections and became the most popular style of hard rock in the '90s.

HAIR METAL—Hair metal is a derisive term applied to the slick, pretty, and pop-oriented heavy-metal and hard-rock bands of the late '80s. These bands expanded the approach of the loud but safe arena-rock bands, only they had a more distinctive visual image because they were living in the post-MTV era. Wearing flashy clothing, heavy makeup, and large, teased hair, the bands had an appearance that was more distinctive than their music, though both their look and their sound became a curse in the early '90s. After Nirvana brought grunge and alternative music to the top of the charts in 1991, hair metal bands quickly died, losing all of their popular support. Some tried to change their sound, others struggled on with their trademark sound to no avail. Though some bands still survived in the mid-'90s, they had adopted a harder sound than they had in the '80s, but their fondness for pop hooks and melodies had not faded away.

HARD ROCK—Hard rock evolved in the late '60s, as psychedelia and blues rock began pushing the boundaries of amplification and blues-based riffs. Hard rock tends to rely less on improvisation than blues-rock, and it isn't as loud as heavy metal, though it still has distorted guitars and long solos. Throughout the '70s and '80s, hard rock stayed essentially the same, though there were slight changes in production technique. At its core, hard rock is simple, loud, anthemic, and macho, and it always stayed that way, no matter what decade it was.

HARDCORE PUNK—Hardcore punk was the most rigid and extreme variation of punk rock. Emerging in the early '80s, hardcore took the ideals of punk as far as it could go. The music was impossibly fast, the vocals were shouted, the riffs were simple, and the records looked (and sounded) like they were made in someone's basement. Most of the bands sounded incredibly similar to each other, but there were a handful of distinctive bands; they usually developed musically quite quickly, leaving the sound of hardcore behind, but not its ideals. Hardcore punk was primarily an American sensation, concentrated in Los Angeles and New York, but there were small, individual scenes scattered across the country. Hardcore kept going into the '90s without breaking into the mainstream, though bands influenced by the hardcore aesthetic—including Nirvana and Green Day—became major rock stars, and former hardcore punkers like Bob Mould, Henry Rollins, Mike Watt, Ian McKaye, and Dinosaur Jr.'s J Mascis became alternative icons.

HARDCORE TECHNO—Hardcore techno is distinguished by high-power, impossibly fast beats that rarely fall below 190 beats per minute. Hardcore techno is all-instrumental, performed on synthesizers and drum machines. There's not much variety within the genre, but the differences mainly lie in the arrangements of the rhythm, since there is no melody to the music.

HEAVY METAL—Heavy metal derived from the shatteringly loud blues-rock and psychedelia of the late '60s. Metal sanded away most of the blues influences, leaving the powerful, loud guitar riffs. In the early '70s, heavy metal established itself as one of the most commercially successful forms of rock & roll. In the next three decades, metal adapted itself to the times and never completely disappeared from the charts. At its core, heavy metal is an adolescent experience; teenagers —primarily white males—form the majority of its audience. Some critics dismiss metal as simplistic primal pounding. Certainly, a fair share of heavy metal is nothing but three-chord riffing, yet most metal bands place a premium on technical skill. Metal guitarists have always been innovators in technique, speed, and skill. In every subgenre of heavy metal, the guitar is the center of the music. The songs are assembled around the riff, with the guitar solo taking prominence. By and large, heavy metal is rock & roll with all of the roll stripped away—the blues remains, but it doesn't swing. All the rhythms are fairly rigid, almost military in origin. Bombast is the key—from the drums to the guitars, it's about being as loud as possible.

HI-NRG—Hi-Nrg is a fast variation of disco that evolved in the '80s. Driven by a fast drum machine and synthesizers, Hi-Nrg is essentially a dance-oriented music with only slight hints of pop. There are a few hooks—generally sung by disembodied vocalists wailing in the background—but the emphasis of the music, like most dance music, is in the beat. Hi-Nrg is a predecessor to techno and house, which drew from its beats in decidedly different ways. House has a funkier, soulful rhythm while techno expanded with the mechanical beats of Hi-Nrg.

HOUSE MUSIC—House music grew out of the post-disco dance club culture of the early '80s. After disco became popular, certain urban DJs—particularly those in gay communities—altered the music to make it less pop-oriented. The beat became more mechanical and the bass grooves became deeper, while elements of electronic synth-pop, Latin soul, dub reggae, rap, and jazz were grafted over the music's insistent, unvarying four-four beat. Frequently, the music was purely instrumental, and when there was vocalists, they were faceless female divas that often sang wordless melodies. By the late '80s, house had broken out of underground clubs in cities like Chicago, New York, and London and had begun making inroads on the pop charts, particularly in England and Europe, but also in America under the guise of artists like M/A/R/R/S and Madonna, as well as producers like David Cole and Robert Clivilles. At the same time house was breaking into the pop charts, it fragmented into a number of subgenres, including acid house (a fusion of house and acid jazz), hip house (rap and house), and, most significantly, ambient, and techno. During the '90s, house ceased to be a cutting-edge music, yet it remained popular within clubs throughout Europe and America.

INDIE ROCK—There have always been independent labels in the history of rock & roll, but indie rock refers to the independent rock music of the early '90s. After Nirvana inadvertently brought alternative music into the Top Ten in 1991, many alternative bands resisted the fact that their music was becoming popular, so they went further underground. They refused to sign to major labels and adhered to their independent, punk ideals. Not all of the music sounds the same, but nearly every indie-rock band is based in the post-punk guitar rock of the '80s.

INDUSTRIAL—Industrial music was a dissonant, abrasive genre that grew out of the electronic experiments of post-punk bands like Cabaret Voltaire. The music was largely electronic, with fast, pounding drum machines and samples. It was named industrial because it sounds like giant machinery, cranking away. Though industrial sometimes flirts with hard rock—Ministry and Nine Inch Nails, in particular, subvert hard rock formulas with their music—it always has experimental and dance underpinnings that keep it from falling into traditional rock & roll conventions.

JANGLE POP—Jangle pop was an American post-punk movement of the mid-'80s which marked a return to the chiming guitars and pop melodies of the '60s. Sparked by the arrival of R.E.M., jangle-pop also had some folk-rock overtones, but it was essentially a pop-based format. But it wasn't mainstream music—the bands' lyrics were often deliberately cryptic and their sound was raw and amateurish, bearing all the signs of do-it-yourself productions. Jangle pop was a major force between 1984 and 1987, not only were thereSouthern-pop bands like R.E.M. and Let's Active, there were the Paisley Underground bands on the west coast who were more psychedelic, and there were numerous bands scattered throughout the mid-west. In the late '80s, the sound fell out of favor, mainly because there were so many bands that sounded similar and were indistinguishable from each other. Though R.E.M. managed to cross over into the mainstream—in fact, become one of the most popular rock bands in the world—many of the groups (including Uncle Green and Miracle Legion) simply ran out of steam by the early '90s and disbanded.

JAZZ-ROCK—Unlike fusion, which is jazz played with rock influences, jazz-rock is essentially rock-based songs played with jazz flourishes and jazzy improvisations. When the two genres first developed in the late '60s, they were nearly identical; during the early '70s they began to branch away from each other and jazz-rock became known as a slightly more commercial version of fusion.

JUNGLE—Based almost entirely in England, jungle is a permutation of hardcore techno that emerged in the early '90s. Jungle is the most rhythmically complex of all forms of techno, relying on extremely fast polyrhythms and breakbeats. Usually, jungle is entirely instrumental—it is among the hardest of all hardcore techno, consisting of nothing but fast drum machines and deep bass. As its name implies, jungle does have more overt reggae, dub, and R&B influences than most hardcore—and that is why some critics claimed that the music was the sound of Black techno musicians and DJs reclaiming it from the White musicians and DJs who dominated the hardcore scene. Nevertheless, jungle never slows down to develop a groove—it just speeds along. Like most techno genres, jungle is primarily a singles-genre designed for a small, dedicated audience, although the crossover success of Goldie and his 1995 debut *Timeless* suggest that the music may have a broader appeal and more musical possibilities than other forms of techno.

KRAUTROCK—Krautrock refers to the legions of German bands of the early '70s that expanded the sonic possibilities of art and progressive rock. Instead of following in the direction of their British and American counterparts, who were moving toward jazz and classical-based compositions and concept albums, the German bands became more mechanical and electronic. Working with early synthesizers and splicing together seemingly unconnected reels of tape, bands like Faust, Can, and Neu created a droning, pulsating sound that owed more to the avant garde than to rock & roll. Although the bands didn't make much of an impact while they were active in the '70s, their music anticipated much of the post-punk of the early '80s, particularly industrial rock. Krautrock also came into vogue in the '90s, when groups like Stereolab and Tortoise began incorporating the hypnotic rhythms and electronic experiments of the German art rock bands into their own, vaguely avant garde indie rock.

LO-FI—During the late '80s and early '90s, lo fidelity became not only a description of the recording quality of a particular album, but it also became a genre onto itself. Throughout rock & roll's history, recordings were made cheaply and quickly, often on substandard equipment. In that sense, the earliest rock & roll records, most of the garage rock of the '60s, and much of the punk rock of the late '70s could be tagged as lo-fi. However, the term came to refer to a breed of underground indie rockers that recorded their material at home on four-track machines. Most of this music grew out of the American underground of the '80s, including bands like R.E.M., as well as a handful of British post-punk bands and New Zealand bands like the Chills and the Clean. Often, these lo-fi bands fluctuated from simple pop and rock songs to free-form song structures to pure noise and arty experimentalism. Even when the groups kept the songs relatively straightforward, the thin quality of the recordings, the layers of tape distortion and hiss, as well as the tendency toward abstract, obtuse lyrics made the music sound different and left-of-center. Initially, lo-fi recordings were traded on home-made tapes, but several indie labels—most notably K Records, which was run by Calvin Johnson, who led the lo-fi band Beat Happening—released albums on vinyl. Several groups in the late '80s, like Pussy Galore, Beat Happening, and Royal Trux, earned small cult followings within the American underground. By 1992, groups like Sebadoh and Pavement had become popular cult acts in America and Britain with their willfully noisy, chaotic recordings. A few years later, Liz Phair and Beck helped break the lo-fi aesthetic into the mainstream, albeit in a more streamlined fashion.

MOD—Technically, mod refers to a lifestyle and fashion more than music itself. During the early '60s, legions of teenagers in Great Britain began dressing in stylish, neo-Italian fashions and listening to American R&B, particularly Motown. Soon, these teens were dubbed "mods." The original mod bands were all R&B cover bands, but soon they began writing their own material which was generally in the vein of their influences. Mod bands played R&B harder and faster than the original recordings—it was relentless, amphetamine-driven rock & roll. Many of the mod bands were barely heard outside of the U.K. since the lifestyle was primarily a British phenomenon. Two bands—the Small Faces and the Who—were able to crossover to the U.S. market, but that was after both bands began developing and expanding their R&B-based sound. By the time psychedelia came around in the late '60s, mod had died out in Britain. However, mod—both the music and the lifestyle—came back in full force in the late '70s, thanks to the Jam.

MOD REVIVAL—In the late '70s, a group of British punk rockers inspired by the Jam brought back the mod styles and sound of mid-'60s London. The mod revivalists stuck to the R&B-informed rock & roll that distinguished the original '60s mods, but the sound was harder and more frenetic, and often only implied the music's R&B roots. Since the original wave of mod bands in the '60s only included a few bands—the Small Faces, the Who, the Creation, and the Action, as well as a handful of others—there were actually more mod groups in the revival than there were in the '60s. Furthermore, since most of the original mods only performed in cover bands (with the exception of the aforementioned groups) or simply danced to Motown records, the revival was the first wave of mod bands to rely on original material. Nevertheless, the mod revival only produced a handful of popular bands. The Jam were the most popular band in Britain during the late '70s and early '80s, but groups like the Lambrettas, the Merton Parkas, Squire, and Purple Hearts managed to cultivate cult followings and occasionally have pop hits. The mod revival lasted as long as the Jam's career—after Paul Weller disbanded the trio to form the Style Council, most of the mod revivalists either split up or became new romantics, which usually resulted in a breakup as well. Despite its brief time in the spotlight, the mod revival had a lasting impact on British pop music, as many of the most popular English rock bands of the '80s and '90s—from the Smiths to Blur and Oasis—were indebted either to the Jam or to the movement in general.

MOTOWN—Motown is one of the few record labels that created a sound and style so distinct that it became known as a genre onto itself. For most R&B and pop fans, the sound of Motown is instantly identifiable—strong backbeat, supported with bouncy bass lines, and soulful vocals. It was R&B, but with a pop production and written with a sense of pop craftsmanship.

NEO-PSYCHEDELIA—Neo-psychedelia represents all the legions of bands that have adapted, replicated, or interpreted the original sounds of psychedelic years after the fact. The first wave of neo-psychedelic bands who arrived in the mid-'80s was largely influenced by the psychedelic sounds of the mid-'60s and generally sounded quite similar to bands like the Beatles, the Byrds, Pink Floyd, and countless garage bands. Neo-psychedelic bands in the late '80s and '90s have tended to be more experimental and jam-oriented, much like how the first wave of psychedelia slowly evolved into the free-form jams of the late '60s.

NEW JACK R&B—New jack R&B evolved in the late '80s, when urban contemporary soul artists began incorporating hip-hop rhythms, samples, and production techniques into their sound. Some songs simply had hip-hop beats, others had rapped sections and sung choruses, but the overall result was an edgier, more street-oriented sound that seamlessly blended both the melodic qualities of soul and the funky rhythms of rap. It paved the way for the '90s soul, where the dividing line between rap and R&B was frequently indistinguishable.

NEW ROMANTIC—The new romantics were a peculiar subgenre of new wave. Wearing heavy makeup and dressed in stylish clothing, the new romantics took not only their visual cues from David Bowie and Roxy Music, but also their musical cues. Drawing from latter-day Roxy and Station to Station- and Low-era Roxy Music, new romantics created a sleek, synthesized, and danceable form of pop that was designed to be fashionable and transient. More than any other post-punk genre, new romantics relied on style and glamour. Duran Duran was the ultimate new romantic group, and they were the only one to become superstars. New romantic had died out by 1984, but it had a brief revival in the mid-'90s by the Melody Maker-sponsored, non-movement Romo.

NEW WAVE—During the late '70s and early '80s, "new wave" was a catch-all term for the music that directly followed punk rock; often, the term encompassed punk itself, as well. In retrospect, it's become clear that the music that followed punk could be divided, more or less, into two categories—post-punk and new wave. Where post-punk was arty, difficult, and challenging, new wave was pop music, pure and simple. It retained the fresh vigor and irreverence of punk music, as well as a fascination with electronics, style, and art. Therefore, there was a lot of stylistic diversity to new wave. It meant the nervy power-pop of bands like XTC and Nick Lowe, but it also meant synth-rockers like Gary Numan, or rock revivalists like Graham Parker and Rockpile. There were edgy new wave songwriters like Elvis Costello, pop bands like Squeeze, tough rock & rollers like the Pretenders, pop-reggae like the Police, mainstream rockers like the Cars, and ska revivalists like the Specials and Madness. As important as these major artists were, countless one-hit wonders that emerged during early new wave. These one-hit groups were as diverse as the major artists, but they all shared a love of pop hooks, modernist, synthesized production, and a fascination for being slightly left of center. By the early '80s, new wave described nearly every new pop/rock artist, especially those that used synthesizers like the Human League and Duran Duran. New wave received a boost in the early '80s by MTV, who broadcast endless hours of new wave videos in order to keep themselves on the air. Therefore, new wave got a second life in 1982, when it probably would have died out. Instead, 1982 and 1983 were boom years for polished, MTV-radio new wave outfits like Culture Club, Adam Ant, Spandau Ballet, Haircut 100, and A Flock of Seagulls. New wave finally died out in 1984, when established artists began to make professional videos and a new crop of guitar-oriented bands like the Smiths and R.E.M. emerged to capture the attention of college-radio and underground rock fans. Nevertheless, new wave proved more influential than many of its critics would have suspected, as the mid-'90s were dominated by bands, from Blur to Weezer, that were raised on the music.

NO WAVE—No wave was one of the first post-punk genres to emerge in the late '70s. It was an atonal, dissonant, and experimental group of bands that was consciously pushing the limits of rock music; in that sense, it was more like performance art than music. Though the movement didn't exist outside of New York, it managed to worm its way into alternative music in the mid-'80s through the feedback-laden, sonic experimentations of Sonic Youth.

PAISLEY UNDERGROUND—The Paisley Underground was the most distinctive subgenre of jangle pop in the mid-'80s. Like jangle pop, the bands in the Paisley Underground revived the clean, chiming textures of folk-rock, but they had a more psychedelic bent to their sound. Jangle-pop bands weren't necessarily revivalists—they updated the ringing guitars and melodies of '60s guitar pop for the '80s—but the Paisley Underground was determined to keep the sound of the '60s alive, through their music and their appearance. The Paisley Underground gained a dedicated following in the American underground during the mid-'80s, but their audience declined in the late '80s and the scene soon disappeared.

PHILLY SOUL—Philly soul was one of the most popular forms of soul music in the early '70s. Building on the steady groove of Hi Records and Stax/Volt singles, Philly soul added sweeping strings, seductive horns, and lush arrangements to the deep rhythms. As a result, it was much smoother—even slicker—than the deep soul of the late '60s, but the vocals remained as soulful as any previous form of R&B. Philly soul was primarily a producer's medium, as Kenny Gamble & Leon Huff and Thom Bell created the instrumental textures that came to distinguish the genre. That isn't to short change the vocalists, since the Spinners, the O'Jays, Harold Melvin & the Blue Notes, and the Stylistics were among fine soul singers with distinctive voices, but the sonic elements that made Philly soul distinctive were the creation of the producers. Gamble & Huff worked with the Delfonics, Archie Bell, Harold Melvin & the Blue Notes, and the O'Jays; Bell produced the Spinners and the Stylistics, among others. The highly-produced sound of Philly soul paved the way for the studio constructions of disco and urban contemporary R&B.

POST-GRUNGE—Post-grunge emerged in the early '90s, after alternative music had broken into the mainstream. Where nearly all of the original grunge bands had strong ties to the indie-rock scene of the '80s, the post-grunge groups built on the angst-ridden, heavy sound of Seattle grunge. Most post-grunge was released on major labels and was consequently slicker and more polished than grunge itself—it was merely informed by the same lyrical themes, heavy instrumental attack, and visual style of grunge. Post-grunge isn't strictly grunge—it tends to draw from sources as varied as jangle pop and AOR—but all of the groups are tied together by their polished, radio-ready productions, a reliance on canned distorted guitars, and self-consciously introspective lyrics.

POST-PUNK—After the punk revolution of 1977, a number of bands formed. They were all inspired by the independent spirit of punk, as well as its raw sound. Instead of replicating the sound of the Sex Pistols, many of these bands forged into more experimental territory, taking cues from Roxy Music, David Bowie, and T. Rex in addition to punk rock. The result was a group of bands tied together by their counter-culture spirit and defiance of accepted rock conventions. Many of these groups—like Joy Division or the Cure—created dark, bleak soundscapes that employed both synthesizers and guitars. Others had a lighter musical approach, but their lyrics and music were off-kilter and subverted traditional pop/rock song structures. Post-punk eventually evolved into alternative pop/rock in the '80s.

POST-ROCK/EXPERIMENTAL—Post-rock was an experimental, avant-garde movement that emerged in the mid-'90s. Most post-rock was droning and hypnotic, drawing from ambient, free-form jazz, avant garde, and electronic music more than rock. The majority of post-rock groups were like Tortoise, a Chicago-based band with a rotating lineup. Tortoise viewed their music not as songs, but as ever-changing compositions that they improvised nightly. Most of post-rock was defiantly anti-mainstream and anti-indie rock in the vein of Tortoise. However, there were certain groups—like Stereolab—that essentially worked in a pop and indie-rock format, but touched on the experimental and avant- garde tendencies of Tortoise.

POWER POP—Power pop is a cross between the crunching hard rock of the Who and the sweet melodicism of the Beatles and the Beach Boys, with the ringing guitars of the Byrds thrown in for good measure. Although several bands of the early '70s—most notably the Raspberries, Big Star, and Badfinger—established the sound of power pop, it wasn't until the late '70s that a whole group of like-minded bands emerged. Most of these groups modeled themselves on the Raspberries (since they were the only power-pop band of their era to have hit singles), or they went directly back to the source and based their sound on stacks of British Invasion records. What tied all of these bands together was their love of the three-minute pop single. Power-pop bands happened to emerge around the same time of punk, so they were swept along with the new wave because their brief, catchy songs fit into the post-punk aesthetic. Out of these bands, Cheap Trick, the Knack, the Romantics, and Dwight Twilley had the biggest hits, but the Shoes, the Records, the Nerves, and 20/20, among many others, became cult favorites. During the early '80s, power pop died away as a hip movement, and nearly all of the bands broke up. However, in the late '80s, a new breed of power pop began to form. The new bands, who were primarily influenced by Big Star, blended traditional power pop with alternative-rock sensibilities and sounds; in the process, groups like Teenage Fanclub, Material Issue, and the Posies became critical and cult favorites. While these bands gained the attention of hip circles, many of the original power-pop groups began recording new material and releasing it on independent labels. In the early '90s, the Yellow Pills compilation series gathered together highlights from these re-activated power poppers, as well as new artists that worked in a traditional power-pop vein. Throughout the early and mid-'90s, this group of independent, grass roots power-pop bands gained a small, but dedicated, cult following in the U.S.

PROTO-PUNK—Proto-punk is a loose gathering of artists that never quite fit into the mainstream rock & roll of the late '60s and early '70s. From the sonic experimentations and deceptively gentle folk-rock of the Velvet Underground to the wild, gender-bending hard rock of the New York Dolls and the song poetry of Patti Smith, proto-punk covers a diverse array of sounds and styles, but they are all tied together by an edgy, artsy attempt to subvert, ignore, and rewrite rock conventions. In the process, the spirit—if not always the music—of these artists sowed the seeds of the punk revolution of the late '70s.

PSYCHEDELIC—Psychedelic rock emerged in the mid-'60s, as British Invasion and folk-rock bands began expanding the sonic possibilities of their music. Instead of confining themselves to the brief, concise verse-chorus-verse patterns of rock & roll, they moved toward more free-form, fluid song structures. Just as important—if not more so—the groups began incorporating elements of Indian and Eastern music and free-form jazz to their sound, as well as experimenting with electronically altering instruments and voices within the recording studio. Initially, around 1965 and 1966, bands like the Yardbirds and the Byrds broke down the boundaries for psychedelia, creating swirling layers of fuzz-toned guitars, sitars, and chanted vocals. Soon, numerous groups followed their pattern, including the Beatles and the Rolling Stones, who both recorded psychedelia in 1966. In no time, groups on both sides of the Atlantic embraced the possibilities of the new genre and the differences were notable. In Britain, psychedelia tended to be whimsical and surrealistic. Nevertheless, bands—most notably Pink Floyd and Traffic—played extended instrumentals that relied on improvisation as much as their American contemporaries the Grateful Dead, the Doors, Love, and Jefferson Airplane. In other corners of America, garage bands began playing psychedelic rock without abandoning their raw, amateurish foundation of three-chord rock—they just layered in layers of distortion, feedback, and effects. Eventually, psychedelic evolved into acid rock, heavy metal, and art rock, but there continued to be revivals of psychedelia in the decades that followed, most notably in the American underground of the mid-'80s.

PUB ROCK—In some ways, the British phenomenon of pub rock in the early '70s wasn't much more than roots rock, since it basically consisted of bar bands that played rock & roll, country-rock, and the blues. But there were some crucial differences, particularly in approach. If pub rock is anything, it is loose and unpretentious—these were guys that played music for the hell of it. The members of the major pub-rock bands—Brinsley Schwarz, Ducks Deluxe, Bees Make Honey, Ace, Dr. Feelgood—came from a variety of musical backgrounds, including folk-rock, blues, country-rock, and traditional rock & roll. This kind of rootsy music stood in direct contrast to the glam-rock, hard rock, and progressive rock that dominated the British charts. Consequently, the groups had trouble finding places to play, and they had to create their own circuit by playing hidden-away pubs throughout England. In no time, the unconventional venues and their defiantly good-time, back-to-basics rock & roll became a rallying cry for pub rockers. None of the pub-rock bands became stars or had hits, but their do-it-yourself attitude and stripped-down sound—as well as the creation of the pub-rock circuit itself—paved the way for punk rock. Indeed many pub rockers—including Brinsley Schwarz's Nick Lowe, the 101ers' Joe Strummer, Flip City's Elvis Costello, Kilburn & the High Roads' Ian Dury and Graham Parker—became important figures in punk and new wave just a few years after the pub-rock scene faded away in the mid-'70s.

PUNK—Punk rock returned rock & roll to the basics—three chords and a simple melody. It just did it louder and faster and more abrasively than any other rock & roller in the past. Although there had been several bands to flirt with what became known as punk rock—including the garage rockers of the '60s and the Velvet Underground, the Stooges, and the New York Dolls—it wasn't until the mid-'70s that punk became its own genre. On both sides of the Atlantic, young bands began forsaking the sonic excesses that distinguished mainstream hard rock and stripping the music down to its essentials. In New York, the first punk band was the Ramones; in London, the first punk band was the Sex Pistols. Although the bands had different agendas and sounds—the Ramones were faster and indebted to bubblegum, while the Pistols played Faces riffs sloppier and louder than the Faces themselves—the direct approach of the bands revolutionized music in both the U.K. and the U.S. In America, punk remained an underground sensation, eventually spawning the hardcore and indie-rock scenes of the '80s, but in the U.K., it was a full-scale phenomenon. In the U.K., the Sex Pistols were thought of as a serious threat to the well-being of the government and monarchy, but more importantly, they caused countless bands to form. Some of the bands stuck close to the Pistols original blueprint, but many found their own sound, whether it was the edgy pop of the Buzzcocks, the anthemic reggae-informed rock of the Clash, or the arty experiments of Wire and Joy Division. Soon, punk splintered into post-punk (which was more experimental and artier than punk), new wave (which was more pop-oriented), and hardcore, which simply made punk harder, faster, and more abrasive. Throughout the '80s, punk was identified with the hardcore scenes in both America and England. In the early '90s, a wave of punk revivalists—led by Green Day and Rancid—emerged from the American underground. The new wave of punk rockers followed the same template as the original punks, but they tended to incorporate elements of heavy metal into their sound.

PUNK REVIVAL—During the early '90s—nearly 20 years after punk happened—the U.S. had its first punk rock hit albums and singles, as a wave of bands raised on '80s hardcore and '70s punk worked its way into the American mainstream. Essentially, these bands were all traditionalists, keeping alive the styles of groups like the Sex Pistols, the Stooges, the Jam, the Exploited, Black Flag, Dead Kennedys, the Descendants, and countless other punk and hardcore bands. Since hardcore mutated into speed-metal in the late '80s, it wasn't surprising that these punk traditionalists were heavier than their initial influences, but that is partially what made the music appealing to a mass audience in America. The first punk revivalists to break into the American mainstream were Green Day and the Offspring, and their success helped solidify cult followings for groups like Rancid, NOFX, Pennywise, and Pansy Division, as well as bring the spotlight to neglected '80s punk bands like Bad Religion and underground punk genres like the third wave of ska revival.

R&B—Evolving out of jump blues in the late '40s, R&B laid the groundwork for rock & roll. R&B kept the tempo and the drive of jump blues, but its instrumentation was sparer and the emphasis was on the song, not improvisation. It was blues chord changes played with an insistent backbeat. During the '50s, R&B was dominated by vocalists like Ray Charles and Ruth Brown, as well as vocal groups like the Drifters and the Coasters. Eventually, R&B evolved into soul, which was funkier and looser than the pile-driving rhythms of R&B.

RAVE—Rave is more of an event than a genre of music. Raves were underground parties where acid house and hardcore records were played and large quantities of hallucinogens, particularly ecstasy, were consumed. Most of the music played at raves had a psychedelic quality, even before hallucinogens became a major element of the scene. DJs played at the raves, mixing stacks of house, acid jazz, and techno singles; the DJs, not the recording artists themselves, became the most recognizable names in the scene. Raves were primarily an English phenomenon during the late '80s and early '90s. They were conducted in large venues, particularly abandoned warehouses and open fields. Eventually, the British government became concerned that raves were a dangerous, anti-social phenomenon that had to be shut down, but the parties never disappeared, especially since word of the events were usually passed through word-of-mouth and handmade fliers. In the U.S., raves began to make some inroads in the early '90s, but they never gained a large audience, even by underground standards. Throughout the '90s, bands that were directly influenced by rave culture—particularly "baggy" bands like the Stone Roses, Happy Mondays, and Charlatans, Brit-pop acts like Pulp and Oasis, and techno artists like the Prodigy—made their way into the mainstream, and the culture continued to capture the attention of British youth into the late '90s.

RIOT GRRRL—Riot Grrrl is a subgenre of early '90s indie rock and punk rock that is distinguished by its radical feminist lyrics and its raw, willfully amateurish musical attack. Although Riot Grrrl received a lot of press, most of it was misguided, identifying such acts as Hole and PJ Harvey as riot grrrls. All genuine Riot Grrrl bands—most notable Bikini Kill, Bratmobile, and Huggy Bear—never broke into the mainstream, mainly because their music was too abrasive for general consumption, even after alternative music broke into the mainstream.

ROCK & ROLL—In its purest form, rock & roll has three-chords, a strong, insistent back beat, and a catchy melody. Early rock & roll drew from a variety of sources, primarily blues, R&B, and country, but also gospel, traditional pop, jazz, and folk. All of these influences combined in a simple, blues-based song structure that was fast, danceable, and catchy. The first wave of rock & rollers—Chuck Berry, Elvis Presley, Little Richard, Jerry Lee Lewis, Buddy Holly, Bo Diddley, Bill Haley, Gene Vincent, the Everly Brothers, Carl Perkins, among many others—set the template for rock & roll that was followed over the next four decades. During each decade, a number of artists replicated the sound of the first rockers, while others expanded that definition, and still others completely exploded the constrictions of the genre. From the British Invasion, folk-rock and psychedelia, through hard rock, heavy metal, glam rock, and punk, most subgenres of rock & roll initially demonstrated an allegiance to the basic structure of rock & roll. Once these permutations emerged, traditional rock & roll faded away from the pop charts, yet there were always artists that kept the flame alive. Some, like the Rolling Stones and the Faces, adhered to the basic rules of traditional rock & roll but played the music fast and loose. Others, like proto-punk rockers the Velvet Underground, the New York Dolls, and the Stooges, kept the basic song structure, but played it with more menace. Still others, like Dave Edmunds and Graham Parker, became rock & roll traditionalists, writing and recording music that never wavered from the sound of the late '50s and early '60s. Although the term "rock & roll" came to refer to a number of different musics in the decades following its inception, the essential form of the music never changed.

ROCKABILLY—Rockabilly was one of the earliest forms of rock & roll and it has proved to be one of the most enduring. Where rock & rollers like Chuck Berry, Little Richard, Jerry Lee Lewis, and Fats Domino emphasized the blues, R&B, and pop roots of rock & roll, rockabilly was backwoods hillbilly music played to boogie beat. The form emerged in the mid-'50s and it stayed the same for the next four decades, with new performers occasionally adding contemporary flairs but essentially sticking to the basic rockabilly formula.

ROOTS ROCK—During the mid-'80s, a generation of bands reacted to the slick, pop-oriented sounds of new wave by reverting back to the traditional rock & roll values of the '50s and '60s. By bringing rock back to its roots—whether that was rock & roll, blues, or country—the group managed to sound like a fresh alternative, which brought them critical praise and heavy airplay from American college radio stations. Most of the leading bands of the era—such as the Beat Farmers, Del Lords, Long Ryders, and the Del Fuegos—filtered much of their traditional values through the music of Creedence Clearwater Revival, but there were an equally large number of groups that simply worked in a "rootsy" fashion, without any direct influence outside of the concept of traditional rock and blues. In the late '80s, roots rock ceased to be a hip music in the American underground, but most of the bands continued to record and perform into the '90s. Throughout the '90s, a small number of new roots rockers emerged, although they weren't afforded the same exposure as their predecessors.

SHOEGAZING—Shoegazing is a genre of late '80s and early '90s British indie rock, named after the band's motionless performing style, where they stood on stage and stared at the floor while they played. But shoegazing wasn't about visuals—it was about pure sound. The sound of the music was overwhelmingly loud, with long, droning riffs, waves of distortion, and cascades of feedback. Vocals and melodies disappeared into the walls of guitars, creating a wash of sound where no instrument was distinguishable from the other. Most shoegazing groups worked off the template My Bloody Valentine established with their early EPs and their first full-length album, Isn't Anything, but Dinosaur Jr., the Jesus & Mary Chain, and Cocteau Twins were also major influences. Bands that followed—most notably Ride, Lush, Chapterhouse, and the Boo Radleys—added their own stylistic flourishes. Ride veered close to '60s psychedelia, while Lush alternated between straight pop and the dream pop of the Cocteau Twins. None of the shoegazers were dynamic performers or interesting interviews, which prevented them from breaking through into the crucial U.S. market. In 1992—after the groups had dominated the British music press and indie charts for about three years—the shoegazing groups were swept aside by the twin tides of American grunge and Suede, the band to initiate the wave of Brit-pop that ruled British music during the mid-'90s. Some shoegazers broke up within a few years (Chapterhouse, Ride), while other groups—such as the Boo Radleys and Lush—evolved with the times and were able to sustain careers into the late '90s.

SINGER/SONGWRITER—Although many vocalists sang their own songs, including early rock & rollers like Chuck Berry and Buddy Holly, the term "singer/songwriter" refers to the legions of performers that followed Bob Dylan. Most of the original singer-songwriters performed alone with an acoustic guitar or a piano. Their lyrics were personal, although they were often veiled by layers of metaphors and obscure imagery. Singer/songwriters drew primarily from folk and country, although certain writers like Randy Newman and Carole King incorporated the songcraft of Tin Pan Alley pop. The main concern for any singer-songwriter was the song itself, not necessarily the performance. However, most singer/songwriter records have a similar sound, which is usually spare, direct, and reflective, which places the emphasis on the song itself. James Taylor, Jackson Browne, and Joni Mitchell were the quintessential singer/songwriters of the '70s and most of the songwriters that followed them based themselves on their styles, or Dylan. Singer/songwriters were at the height of their popularity in the early '70s, and although they faded away from the pop chart, they never disappeared. In the late '70s, Rikki Lee Jones and Joan Armatrading crossed over into the pop charts, as did Suzanne Vega and Tracy Chapman in the late '80s. Throughout the '80s and '90s, a number of songwriters—like John Gorka and Bill Morrissey—kept the tradition alive through a series of independently-released albums.

SKA REVIVAL—Ska evolved in the early '60s, when Jamaicans tried to replicate the sound of the New Orleans R&B they heard over their radio. Instead of mimicking the sound of the R&B, the first ska artists developed a distinctive rhythmic and melodic sensibility, which eventually turned into reggae music. In the late '70s, a number of young British bands began reviving the sound of original ska, adding a nervous punk edge to the skittish rhythms. Furthermore, the ska revivalists were among the only bands of the era to feature racially integrated lineups, which was a bold political statement for the time. Indeed, ska revival was more implicitly political than any of its British-punk and new-wave contemporaries. The leading ska revivalist band was the Specials, who formed their own independent label, 2--Tone. Led by Jerry Dammers and fronted by Terry Hall, the Specials established the sound and approach for all of the bands that followed, and were an immediate hit in England. Through 2-Tone and a variety of tours, the Specials helped cultivate an active ska-revival scene—the group offered support for all of the major ska revivalists that followed, including Madness, the (English) Beat, and Selecter. Throughout the early '80s, ska-revival bands, particularly Madness, were very popular in the U.K. The groups didn't make much headway in the U.S. until 1982 and 1983, when MTV aired videos by all of the important (and many of the lesser) bands. By that time, most of the bands had run their peak, and it was just a matter of months before the Specials, Madness, the (English) Beat, and Selecter all broke up. Although the ska-revival bands never became stars outside of the UK, they did become major cult figures in the U.S. and inspired several generations of musicians to form similar bands. This wave of ska revivalists was equally inspired by hardcore punk and heavy metal, thereby stripping out much of the R&B groove that informed the original ska and 2-Tone artists. Nevertheless, these bands—including Rancid, Mighty Mighty Bosstones, and No Doubt—became quite popular in America during the mid-'90s. In the U.K., ska revivalists influenced both Brit-pop bands like Blur and trip-hop artists like Tricky.

SKIFFLE—This refers to a mixture of jazz and country blues often played on a mixture of basically simple instruments such as the guitar, harmonica, jug, kazoo, and washtub bass. Although the term "skiffle" was originally used in the U.S. in the '30s to describe mixtures of blues, boogie-woogie, and other popular Black music, the skiffle revival of the '50s—as typified by Lonnie Donegan's recording of "Rock Island Line"—was most pronounced the U.K. where it remained popular until the style was replaced by rock & roll at the end of the decade. Major skiffle artists include Chris Barber and Ken Colyer.

SOFT ROCK—Soft rock emerged in the early '70s, partially as a reaction to the extreme sounds of the late '60s. Soft rock was commercial and inoffensive, taking the sound of singer/-songwriter and pop/rock but smoothing out all the edges. Bands like Bread, the Carpenters, and Chicago relied on simple, melodic songs with big, lush productions. Throughout the '70s, soft rock dominated the airwaves, and it eventually evolved into the synthesized sounds of adult contemporary in the '80s.

SOUL—Soul music was the result of the urbanization and commercialization of rhythm and blues in the '60s. Soul came to describe a number of R&B-based music. From the bouncy, catchy acts at Motown to the horn-driven, gritty soul of Stax/Volt, there was an immense amount of diversity within soul. During the first part of the '60s, soul music remained close to its R&B roots. However, musicians pushed the music in different directions; usually, different regions of America produced different kinds of soul. In urban centers like New York, Philadelphia, and Chicago, the music concentrated on vocal interplay and smooth productions. In Detroit, Motown concentrated on creating a pop-oriented sound that was informed equally by gospel, R&B, and rock & roll. In the south, the music became harder and tougher, relying on syncopated rhythms, raw vocals, and blaring horns. All of these styles formed soul, which ruled the Black music charts throughout the '60s and also frequently crossed over into the pop charts. At the end of the '60s, soul began to splinter apart, as artists like James Brown and Sly Stone developed funk and other artists developed slicker forms of soul. Although soul music evolved, it never went away—not only did the music inform all of the R&B of the '70s, '80s, and '90s, there were always pockets of musicians around the world that kept performing traditional soul.

SOUTHERN ROCK—Southern rock drew from the heavy blues-rock of the late '60s, as well as honky tonk and Bakersfield country, creating a distinctive fusion of the genres. Throughout the early '70s, Southern-rock bands formed a major part of the American hard-rock band. The first Southern-rock band was the Allman Brothers, who elaborated on the improvisational tendencies and loudness of Cream and the Grateful Dead while staying closer to rock & roll's blues and country roots. They were followed shortly afterward by Lynyrd Skynyrd, who played heavier and louder than the Allman Brothers; in the process, they set the template for all the Southern-rock bands that followed them. Skynyrd had three lead guitarists, so they naturally indulged themselves in long jams. They also had a sharp songwriter in Ronnie Van Zandt, who was able to fuse traditional music with contemporary rock & roll and also had a gift for perceptive lyrics. The bands that followed Skynyrd often lacked a songwriter the stature of Van Zandt, but they were able to replicate the group's heavy boogie and long jams. Several bands took the music closer to its country or blues roots, while others, like the Dixie Dregs, developed skilled improvisational technique. Still, the dominant sound of Southern rock was its loose fusion of several rootsy genres and its fondness for heavy boogie jams. The genre died out in the early '80s, after Molly Hatchet, the Marshall Tucker Band, and .38 Special experienced a string of AOR hits, but the spirit of the music lived on in '90s bands like the Black Crowes and Widespread Panic.

SPEED METAL—In the mid-'80s, speed metal became the most popular form of heavy metal in the American underground. Crossing the new wave of British heavy metal with hardcore punk, speed metal was extremely fast, abrasive, and technically demanding—the bands played fast, but their attack was precise and clean. In that sense, speed metal always remained true to its metal roots. But what it borrowed from hardcore—namely, insanely fast tempos and a defiant, do-it-yourself attitude—was equally important, since it gave the band not only a unique musical approach but also an attractive image for legions of alienated suburban youths. Led by Metallica, Megadeth, and Anthrax, this new wave of metal bands stood in direct contrast with the pop-oriented metal that dominated the charts during the '80s (Ratt, Poison, and Mötley Crüe, among countless others), but the groups managed to cultivate dedicated cult followings that would eventually allow them to go platinum with no support from mainstream media, radio, or MTV. Eventually, speed metal fractured into a number of different subgenres, most notably thrash, grindcore, and black metal.

SURF—Surf rock was one of the most popular forms of American rock & roll of the early '60s. Distinguished by reverb-drenched guitar, rolling instrumentals that were designed to sound like crashing waves, and simple, three-chord songs, the music may sound similar on the surface, but it was revolutionary for its time, exploring sonic territories previously unheard in rock music. The first wave of surf rock was kicked off by Dick Dale and his single "Let's Go Trippin." The single was a local hit in California, but it inspired countless bands to form, such as the Chantays and Surfaris, who had national hits ("Pipeline" and "Wipe Out," respectively). Nearly all of these groups were one-hit wonders that struggled to produce a second hit single. The second wave of surf rock was led by the Beach Boys, who added Four Freshmen-style pop harmonies to the basic Chuck Berry rhythms of surf rock. Groups like Jan & Dean and Ronny & the Daytonas followed, but the Beach Boys remained the ultimate surf band for many listeners, simply because they put the appeal of the beach and surfing into words instead of conveying it with impressionistic music. Nevertheless, the sounds of the instrumental surf rock echoed throughout the sonic experimentations of '60s guitarists and the genre remained popular into the '90s, thanks to the efforts of several generations of surf-rock revivalists.

SYNTH-POP—Synth-pop was one of the most distinctive subgenres of new wave. In the early '80s, a number of bands—primarily British and heavily influenced by Roxy Music and David Bowie—adapted the electronic innovations of bands like Kraftwerk for pop songs. Initially, in the hands of artists like Gary Numan, the Human League, and Depeche Mode, the sound was eerie, sterile, and vaguely menacing, since the electronics droned on relentlessly without any change in inflections. However, these first stabs at synth-pop were transformed into danceable, synthesized pop by Duran Duran, who made the synthesized hooks warmer and catchier by grafting them onto a dance beat. Soon, a flood of bands followed Duran Duran's lead, and although some of the groups weren't as infectious as that band, they nevertheless relied on the conventions of three-minute pop. Duran Duran became stars, while most other synth-pop groups were lucky to have more than one hit. There were some exceptions—Human League and Eurythmics had several hits, as did Howard Jones—but the field was mainly occupied by one-hit wonders like A Flock of Seagulls. By 1984, synth-pop had begun to die out, but the music had helped establish the synthesizer as a primary instrument in mainstream pop music during its time in the spotlight.

TECHNO—Techno had its roots in the electronic house music made in Detroit in the mid-'80s. Where house still had explicit connection to disco even when it was entirely mechanical, techno was strictly electronic music, designed for a small, specific audience. The first techno DJs—Kevin Suanderson, Juan Atkins, Derrick May, among others—emphasized the electronic, synthesized beats of electro-funk artists like Afrika Bambatta and synth-rock units like Kraftwerk. In the U.S., techno was strictly an underground phenomenon, but in the U.K., it broke into the mainstream in the late '80s. In the early '90s, techno began to fragment into a number of subgenres, including hardcore, ambient, and jungle. In hardcore techno, the beats-per-minute on each record were sped up to ridiculous, undanceable levels—it was designed to alienate a broad audience. Ambient took the opposite direction, slowing the beats down and relying on watery electronic textures—it was used as come-down music, when ravers and club-goers needed a break from the acid house and hardcore techno. Jungle was nearly as aggressive as hardcore, combining driving techno beats with breakbeats and dancehall reggae—essentially. All subgenres of techno often were initially designed to be played in clubs, where they would be mixed by DJs. Consequently, most of the music was available on 12-inch singles or various artists compilations, where the songs could run for a long time, providing the DJ with a lot of material to mix into his set. In the mid-'90s, a new breed of techno artists—most notably ambient acts like the Orb and Aphex Twin, but also harder-edged artists like the Prodigy and Goldie— began constructing albums that didn't consist of raw beats intended for mixing. Not surprisingly, these artists—particularly the Prodigy— became the first recognizable stars in techno.

TEEN IDOL—It took rock & roll a few years before they had a group of attractive young vocalists to claim as their own teen idols. Most of the teen idols of the late '50s and early '60s owed more to traditional pop than rock & roll. They didn't have the raw sexuality of Elvis Presley, nor did they have his instinctive vocal talents. The teen idols were carefully groomed and given inoffensive, catchy material to sing. Pat Boone was the first of the teen idols of the late '50s. Boone primarily covered rock & roll and R&B hits, but his clean-cut good looks and smooth vocals set the stage for singers like Paul Anka, who primarily sang ballads that were given contemporary pop/rock productions. Ricky Nelson emerged at the same time as Anka and out of all the teen idols, his music remained the closest to rock & roll—Nelson performed rockabilly, R&B, and rock & roll, but he played with professional studio musicians who helped give the music a cleaner attack. After Anka and Nelson, the golden age of teen idols emerged, as a number of vocalists with limited vocal skills but good looks became stars. These vocalists—like Fabian and Frankie Avalon—sang songs written by professional songwriters. Frequently, this material hearkened back to the Tin Pan Alley and traditional pop that dominated the early '50s, but the records were given rock & roll productions. Teen idols continued to be popular throughout the early '60s and the genre went through a number of fads, including a string of teenage television actors who turned into singers, as well as a wave of melodramatic songs about tragic teenage deaths. Rockers like Gene Pitney, Dion, and Del Shannon were packaged as teenage idols, but their music was substantial enough to essentially sustain the death of teen idols in 1963. Furthermore, there were a number of British teen idols—such as Cliff Richard and Adam Faith—who dominated the charts in the same era with similar music, but they all faded away upon the arrival of the Beatles in 1963. During the '70s, the term "teen idol" came to describe a number of AM-pop artists like the Bay City Rollers and Shaun Cassidy, who essentially updated the lightweight approach of '60s teen idols for the '70s.

TEX-MEX—Tex-Mex is a unique fusion of rock & roll, blues, country, and various strains of Latin music, particularly conjunto. As far as rock & roll is concerned, Tex-Mex emerged in the '60s, when garage rock bands like the Sir Douglas Quintet and vocalists like Freddy Fender began pounding out rock & roll that was spiced with south-of-the-border flourishes. During the '70s, these conjunto, country, and blues roots became more pronounced and by the '80s, Tex-Mex was established as a unique genre of its own that fell between the cracks of rock, country, and Latin music.

THIRD WAVE SKA REVIVAL—The third wave of ska revival emerged in the late '80s, when certain members of the American punk underground began returning to the sounds of British ska revival and infusing it with a hardcore punk attack. During the early '80s, this third wave continued to grow—more bands continued to pop up across the country, but many of the most popular were based in California. As time wore one, the hardcore influences eventually mutated into heavy metal, much like hardcore punk itself. Eventually, the third wave of ska revivalists broke into the American mainstream, thanks to the success of fellow Californian punk revivalists Green Day and the Offspring. The first third wave band to break big was Rancid, but they were quickly followed by groups like No Doubt, Goldfinger, Sublime, and Dancehall Crashers; the Mighty Mighty Bosstones, who were one of the leading figures of the scene in the early '90s, just missed the commercial bandwagon. Most of the bands that followed Rancid into the charts emphasized metal over ska, but some—like No Doubt—drew from new wave pop roots as well, while Rancid themselves managed to stay true to both ska revival and punk. During 1996, the third wave of ska revival became one of the most popular forms of alternative music in the U.S.

THRASH—Thrash is an outgrowth of hardcore punk and speed metal. Where speed metal remained true to the technical precision of heavy metal, thrash was closer to punk. By retaining the speed of hardcore but adding the relentless loudness and heaviness of metal, thrash appealed more to punks than metal fans, but it did play to the same audience of disaffected suburban adolescents. Thrash didn't evolve musically like speed metal, nor did it produce any stars—Suicidal Tendencies was the most recognizable name to emerge from the genre. During the late '80s, thrash began to die out, but certain groups kept it alive in the U.S. underground.

TRANCE—Trance is a subgenre of techno music that emerged in the early '90s. Similar to ambient in that it emphasizes sonic textures instead of insistent beats, the difference between the two genres is that, unlike ambient, trance is still danceable. Even though it could be danced to, trance is primarily used as come down music—it is more hypnotic and soothing than the various strands of hardcore techno that usually dominate the dance floor.

TRIP-HOP—Trip-hop is a hybrid of hip-hop, soul, dub, pop, and experimental. The beats are slow and the music is atmospheric, with sampled guitars and strings. Massive Attack was the first trip-hop band, but the genre was popularized by Portishead and Tricky.

URBAN—Urban is the soul of the '80s and '90s, music that followed the smooth stylings of quiet storm. It demonstrated a debt to pop music, particularly in its polished production techniques. By the late '80s, that sheen had been dulled, thanks to the gritty sounds of hip-hop. After hip-hop, urban had a broader sonic palette, which was reflected in the music of the '90s.

URBAN FOLK—Urban folk was a movement of singer/songwriters in the '80s that grew out of punk rock. Urban-folk musicians were initially inspired by punk rock, but they performed solo, either with an acoustic or electric guitar. Urban folk was extremely political—the songs were ways of conveying the message, so they had basic melodies and direct, angry lyrics. Though there was only a small handful of urban-folk musicians, they made a significant impact in the mid-'80s.

Artist Reviews

ABBA

f. 1971, Stockholm, Sweden, **db.** 1983

Group / Swedish Pop/Rock, Euro-Dance, Pop/Rock, Europop

The most commercially successful pop group of the 1970s, ABBA comprised singer Agnetha Faltskog, keyboardist/vocalist Benny Andersson, guitarist/ vocalist Bjorn Ulvaeus, and singer Anni-Frid Lyngstad. In 1972, the duo of Andersson and Ulvaeus had scored a massive international hit with "People Need Love," which featured Faltskog and Lyngstad on backing vocals. The record's success earned them an invitation to enter the Swedish leg of the 1973 Eurovision song contest, where, under the unwieldy name of Bjorn, Benny, Agnetha, & Frida, they submitted "Ring Ring," which proved extremely popular with audiences but placed only third in the judges' ballots. The next year, rechristened ABBA (an acronym of the members' first names), the quartet submitted the single "Waterloo," and became the first Swedish act to win the Eurovision competition. In 1975, ABBA issued "S.O.S.," a smash not only in America and Britain but also in non-English speaking countries such as Spain, Germany and the Benelux nations, where the group's success was fairly unprecedented. A string of hits followed, including "Mamma Mia," "Fernando," and "Dancing Queen" (ABBA's sole U.S. chart-topper), further honing their lush, buoyant sound. ABBA's popularity continued in 1977, when both "Knowing Me, Knowing You" and "The Name of the Game" dominated airwaves. A year later, Andersson and Lyngstad married, as had Ulvaeus and Faltskog in 1971, although the latter couple separated a few months later; in fact, romantic suffering was the subject of many songs on the quartet's next LP, 1979's *Voulez-Vous*. Shortly after the release of 1980's *Super Trouper*, Andersson and Lyngstad divorced as well, further straining the group dynamic; *The Visitors*, issued the following year, was the final LP of new ABBA material, and the foursome officially disbanded in late 1982. *—Jason Ankeny*

Ring Ring / 1973 / Polygram ✦✦

Waterloo / 1974 / Polygram ✦✦✦

ABBA / 1975 / Polygram ✦✦✦
ABBA appears on the cover of this album sitting in the back of a limousine and drinking champagne, which may have been intended as an ironic comment on their one-hit wonder status at the time but became an apt reflection of their status after this record's success. The lead-off track is the irresistible "Mamma Mia," their second U.K. chart topper and a U.S. Top 40 hit, and also included are the equally catchy "S.O.S" (Top Ten in Britain, Top 40 in America) and the minor U.K. hit "I Do, I Do, I Do, I Do, I Do," which actually did better in the U.S. *— William Ruhlmann*

Arrival / Jan. 1977 / Polygram ✦✦✦✦✦
ABBA's fourth album of new material appeared after the group had "arrived" as major stars. It featured "Dancing Queen," a tame disco number that went to number one in both the U.S. and U.K., as well as "Knowing Me, Knowing You" (another U.K. number one that hit the Top 40 in the U.S.) and a third single, "Money Money Money." The 1999 remastered edition (part of Polydor's *The ABBA Remasters* series) in 24-bit digital audio is a significant improvement over earlier CD or LP editions, bringing out not only stunning richness and radiance in the vocals by Faltskog and Lyngstadt, but also Rutger Gunnarsson's especially muscular bass playing throughout the album and the rich texture of Bjorn Ulvaeus' acoustic guitar on "When I Kissed the Teacher," Lasse Wellander's acoustic rhythm guitar on "Dum Dum Diddle," and the rippling electric guitar and keyboard textures of "Knowing Me, Knowing You"—Wellander's power chords over the chorus of the latter song is one of those dramatic musical effects that this group played for maximum effect and gave their music a raw power that their detractors usually overlooked. Some of this clarity is wasted on disco numbers that now seem to have relatively little point, though they are catchy and have relentless beat, but that's what the group was about at this point in their history—and the sheer presence of the bass drums behind the choruses on "Tiger" will be pretty impressive to any noise freaks. *— William Ruhlmann/Bruce Eder*

The Album / Feb. 1978 / Polygram ✦✦✦✦
ABBA's fifth album continued its phenomenal international success, featuring the U.K. number ones "The Name of the Game" and "Take a Chance on Me" and achieving ABBA's highest ever showing in the U.S. LP charts: it reached the Top 20 and sold a million copies in six months. *The Album* was unusually progressive by the standards of this group, opening with the decidedly dramatic, six-minute long synthesizer-dominated "Eagle" (almost an art-rock track), before giving way to the hit "Take a Chance on Me." Even the latter, with its luminous a cappella opening, was rather bold in its exploiting of the group's established strengths. Despite its hit status, "The Name of the Game" was never as strong or interesting a cut as "Take a Chance on Me," and there are better tracks surrounding it, including "Move On," which has a better beat and more impressive harmonizing, and "Hole in Your Soul" (which is a rare guitar showcase for Lasse Wellander's lead electric playing). "Girl With the Golden Hair" shows ABBA move into the realm of Broadway-style material, courtesy of Andersson and Ulvaeus's aspirations to compose in that direction: "Thank You for the Music" became a popular stage number, but is rather flat as a studio recording; "I Wonder" is rather dullish; and "I'm a Marionette" seems like an attempt (only partly successful) to recast the vague influence of Kurt Weill in a hard-rock mode. *— Bruce Eder & William Ruhlmann*

Voulez-Vous / Jun. 1979 / Polygram ✦✦

Super Trouper / Dec. 1980 / Polygram ✦✦✦✦
Always pop-savvy, ABBA took account of the passing of disco with this release and moved back toward the pop/rock sound more typical of their early albums with this, their seventh. They were rewarded with their last big U.S. hit, "The Winner Takes It All," plus two more American chart entries and an uptick in album sales. In the U.K., they continued to roll along, with the title track becoming their final #1 single. *— William Ruhlmann*

The Visitors / 1981 / Polygram ✦✦✦✦
ABBA's swan song was also perhaps their most musically sophisticated album. Although it was short on big hits ("The Visitors" and "When All Is Said and Done" charted in the U.S., "One of Us" and "Head Over Heels" in the U.K., with only "One of Us" making the Top Ten), it was a consistent record imbued with a sense of the pressures that were splitting the group (the title track was subtitled "Crackin' Up"). *— William Ruhlmann*

ABBA Live / 1986 / Polygram ✦✦✦✦

★ **Gold: Greatest Hits** / Aug. 9, 1993 / Polygram ✦✦✦✦✦
This 19-song collection was the first hits compilation prepared specifically for the CD format by the 1970s supergroup, and, appearing after a period of several years in which ABBA's music had been off the market, was a welcome addition to the catalog. It is still the simplest and most straightforward collection of the group's material that it is possible to buy, but there is a negative consideration—for reasons best understood by their record label, in contrast to virtually the entire rest of the group's CD catalog (even the Spanish-language compilation *Oro: Grand Exitos* and the live album), it has never been remastered to modern standards. Thus, the songs that most fans and casual listeners want to hear—all of the worldwide international hits—are present, but don't sound remotely as good as they do on the upgraded individual CDs (in cases where they appear on those CDs). And lest anyone think that considerations of 24-bit sound aren't too important with a group like this, most of ABBA's songs featured meticulous productions, arrangements, and playing, and very strong singing, all of which are enhanced on the remasterings that have surfaced. *— Bruce Eder*

Thank You for the Music / Apr. 18, 1995 / Polygram ✦✦✦✦✦
Released in Europe in October 1994 and in the U.S. six months later, *Thank You for the Music* is the ABBA box-set retrospective, tracing their ten years of record making, 1972-1982, including 52 previously released tracks on the first three discs, plus a fourth disc of rarities. Listening to all the singles, plus scattered album tracks and B-sides, provides a clear picture of the group's development. Early on, there is considerable stylistic experimentation, as these pop dabblers ape everything from Phil Spector's "Wall of Sound" rock to big-band swing. But after "Dancing Queen," they find their niche in disco, and the second disc is loaded with hit songs anchored to the familiar bass-heavy walking beat and swooping synths-meant-to-sound-like-strings that defined that most '70s of genres. On the third disc, covering their last years, ABBA returns to the more propulsive pop/rock of early classics like "S.O.S" and "Mamma Mia," revving up the tempo in acknowledgment of the arrival of new wave. Wracked by romantic discord, they also achieve somewhat more meaningful lyrics before calling it a day. In the album's liner notes, the band members register mild protest at the inclusion of unreleased material on the fourth disc—what they finished and liked, they released, they note. Fair warning. Most prominent in a collection of alternate takes, miscellaneous B-sides, foreign-language recordings, and TV soundtracks is the 23-and-a-half-minute "ABBA Undeleted," a medley of 15 song fragments and Swedish studio chatter that suggests ABBA had a few more hits in them if they had found the time to finish them off. Nevertheless, this remains fan-only material. (This album is not to be confused with the 1983 compilation of the same title released by Epic Records in the U.K.) *— William Ruhlmann*

AC/DC

f. 1973, Sydney, Australia
Group / Aussie Rock, Album Rock, Arena Rock, Heavy Metal, Hard Rock
AC/DC's mammoth power-chord roar became one of the most influential hard-rock sounds of the '70s. In its own way, it was a reaction against the pompous art rock and lumbering stadium rock of the early '70s. AC/DC's rock was minimalist—no matter how huge and bludgeoning the guitar chords were, there was a clear sense of space and restraint. Combined with Bon Scott's larynx-shredding vocals, the band spawned countless imitators over the next two decades. AC/DC was formed in 1973 in Australia by guitarist Malcolm Young, with his younger brother Angus as lead guitarist. When Scott joined in 1974 (the year the group released its first album in Australia), he helped cement the group's image as brutes—he had several convictions on minor criminal offenses and was rejected by the Australian army for being "socially maladjusted." And AC/DC *was* socially maladjusted. Throughout their career, they favored crude double entendres and violent imagery, all spiked with a mischievous sense of fun. What really broke the doors down for the band was 1979's *Highway to Hell*, which became their first million-seller. However, AC/DC's train was nearly derailed when Bon Scott died on February 20, 1980. The official coroner's report stated that he had "drunk himself to death." The band quickly replaced Scott with Brian Johnson and recorded *Back in Black*, which would prove to be their biggest album, selling over ten million copies in the U.S. alone. For the next few years, AC/DC was one of the biggest rock bands in the world, with *For Those About to Rock We Salute You* topping the charts in the U.S. After 1983's *Flick of the Switch*, the band's commercial standing began to slip; they were able to reverse their slide with 1990's *The Razor's Edge*, which spawned the hits "Moneytalks" and "Thunderstruck." While they haven't proved to be the commercial powerhouse they were during the late '70s and early '80s, the '90s have seen them maintain their status as a top international concert draw, and they continued to record into the new millennium. *— Stephen Thomas Erlewine*

High Voltage / Oct. 1976 / Atco ✦✦✦✦✦
AC/DC's debut album, *High Voltage*, is a stripped-down collection of loud, raw, rude rockers, mostly odes to rock & roll and its attendant hard-partying lifestyle—to paraphrase the lead-off track "It's a Long Way to the Top (If You Wanna Rock & Roll)," getting drunk, stoned, beat up, and laid. The band reveled in its own macho obnoxiousness, particularly Bon Scott; at the end of the gleefully sexist, double-entendre-filled "The Jack," Scott grandiosely thanks a hostile, booing dubbed-in crowd. While their sense of humor and clever wordplay made early AC/DC a great deal of sleazy, infectious fun, the band's revolutionary musical attack could not be overlooked—Angus Young's manic guitar solos overlaid a series of simple, basic boogie grooves delivered with ferocious power and volume, a sound that made the band a popular attraction at British punk clubs around this same time. The formula would be refined on subsequent albums, but *High Voltage* proves that AC/DC was already in the big leagues. *— Steve Huey*

Let There Be Rock / Jun. 1977 / Atco ✦✦✦✦✦
Let There Be Rock kicks up the energy level a notch from its predecessor, making for a bracing hard-rock record of blasting guitar and basic, aggressive grooves. While slightly more metallic, AC/DC's sound was still bluesier than it would be by the time of their commercial breakthrough. Appealing in spite of himself, Bon Scott delivers his leering double entendres and humorous asides with typical panache, while the Young brothers' guitars bite, kick, and scratch behind him. While the music still meanders on occasion, the songwriting is overall a bit more memorable; AC/DC classics on hand include "Problem Child," "Whole Lotta Rosie," and "Bad Boy Boogie." *— Steve Huey*

Powerage / May 1978 / Atco ✦✦✦

If You Want Blood You've Got It / Dec. 1978 / Atco ✦✦✦

☆ **Highway to Hell** / Aug. 1979 / Atco ✦✦✦✦✦
Given that Bon Scott's hard-partying, sex-booze-and-brawls lifestyle tragically caught up with him some six months after *Highway to Hell* was released, the album-opening title track—one of hard rock's all-time classics—now takes on an eerie resonance. It's not just a snotty, nihilistic party anthem, but a moment of unrepentant self-recognition from a rowdy ruffian who, for better or worse, exulted in what he was. The rest of the songs on *Highway to Hell* don't lend themselves to any deep readings, but of course, that's not the point. *Highway to Hell* distilled all the virtues of AC/DC's signature minimalism—loud, simple, pounding riffs and grooving backbeats—into the tightest batch of songs the group had written to that point, barreling along at a take-no-prisoners rate and producing a handful of gems ("Girl's Got Rhythm," "If You Want Blood (You've Got It)") along the way. *Highway to Hell* is not only a fitting epitaph for Bon Scott, it's also a classic rock & roll album. *— Steve Huey*

★ **Back in Black** / Aug. 1980 / Atco ✦✦✦✦✦
Bon Scott's alcohol-related death in early 1980 couldn't have come at a worse time for AC/DC; the band was poised for worldwide breakthrough success, as their last album, *Highway to Hell*, was Angus and company's first gold-certified stateside release. Their next album was already written, with Scott even having lyrics penned. But shortly after his death, the

remaining members decided to scrap Scott's work and carry on with a new singer. They made an excellent choice in selecting Brian Johnson as their new vocalist; while he had the same bluesy edge as Scott, Johnson sang with more power and conviction. The first album from the new group, *Back in Black*, was issued only five months after Scott's passing but immediately rocketed up the charts, eventually becoming one of rock's all-time classics. By 1997, it had sold an astounding 16 million copies in the U.S. alone. Musically, the band hadn't changed much, although producer "Mutt" Lange helped the group focus their high voltage rock. The result was such perennial rock anthems as the stomping title track, the eerie "Hell's Bells," the melodic "Shoot to Thrill," the album-closing battle cry "Rock and Roll Ain't Noise Pollution," and one of AC/DC's best and most recognizable tracks, "You Shook Me All Night Long." Not a single weak track is included, even the lesser-known album tracks are strong ("Have a Drink on Me," "Shake a Leg,"). *Back in Black* is the ultimate example of a band turning a career-threatening negative into a remarkable positive and stands alongside such landmark albums as *Van Halen*, *Led Zeppelin II*, *Are You Experienced?*, and *Paranoid* as hard rock's greatest achievements. Rock music rarely gets better than *Back in Black*. *— Greg Prato*

☆ **Dirty Deeds Done Dirt Cheap** / Apr. 1981 / Atco ✦✦✦✦✦
Originally released in 1975, *Dirty Deeds Done Dirt Cheap* did not hit the U.S. until 1981, when AC/DC became rock icons the previous year and fans were growing hungry for more material featuring the band's late singer, Bon Scott. Overall, the record is worth the wait, even if there is absolutely no reason to place "Problem Child" on the album since it was placed on *Let There Be Rock*. The title track became a concert staple for the band, but *Dirty Deeds'* most well-known track is arguably "Big Balls," a sleazy, ambiguous number that would become one of the band's most well-recognized songs. The album's greatest artistic moment, however, comes in the form of "Ride On," where AC/DC experiments with a slow, rhythmic blues ballad. The song, highlighted by the Keith Richards-inspired licks of Angus Young and the haunting, melancholy lyrics of Bon Scott, shows AC/DC in a rare sensitive form yet manages to retain the raw power that has since become the band's trademark ("Ride On" would be the only Bon Scott-era song to be placed on the 1986 compilation *Who Made Who*). On the whole, *Dirty Deeds* is a fine album with some nice treats for diehards. Though it may not be as well-crafted as the in-memory-of-Bon classic *Back in Black*, *Dirty Deeds Done Dirt Cheap* is another fitting eulogy to one of hard rock's most influential vocalists. *— Barry Weber*

For Those About to Rock We Salute You / Nov. 1981 / Atco ✦✦✦

Flick of the Switch / Aug. 1983 / Atco ✦✦

Who Made Who / May 1986 / Atco ✦✦✦

Blow Up Your Video / Feb. 1988 / Atco ✦✦✦

The Razor's Edge / Sep. 1990 / Atco ✦✦✦
Although AC/DC's popularity had decreased by the early '90s, the band still had a lot of life left in it. Arguably the Australian headbangers' strongest album in over half a decade, *Razor's Edge* is quintessential AC/DC—rowdy, abrasive, unapologetically fun metal full of blistering power chords, memorable hooks, and testosterone-driven lyrics. Lead singer Brian Johnson sounds more inspired than he had since 1983's *Flick of the Switch*, and lead guitarist Angus Young isn't about to take any prisoners on such hard-hitting material as "Shot of Love," the menacing title song and the appropriately titled "Got You by the Balls." Although not quite in a class with *Back in Black*, *Highway to Hell* or *Let There Be Rock*—all of which would, for novices, serve as fine introductions to the distinctive band—*Razor's Edge* was a welcome addition to AC/DC's catalogue. *— Alex Henderson*

AC/DC Live / Oct. 27, 1992 / Atco ✦✦✦

Ballbreaker / Sep. 26, 1995 / East West ✦✦✦

Bonfire / Nov. 11, 1997 / East West ✦✦✦

Stiff Upper Lip / Feb. 29, 2000 / East West ✦✦✦

Bryan Adams

b. Nov. 5, 1959, Kingston, Ontario, Canada
Vocals, Guitar / Pop/Rock, Adult Contemporary, Rock & Roll
Bryan Adams was one of the most popular mainstream rock & rollers to emerge in the '80s, producing a series of platinum albums and Top Ten hits. Adams wasn't an innovator on the level of Bruce Springsteen, or even John Cougar Mellencamp. He followed in their footsteps, smoothing out their rougher edges while retaining a down-to-earth earnestness in both his straightforward rock & roll and his husky voice. At the beginning of his career, he relied more on rock than pop, but as his career progressed, he became known for his ballads. But both his rockers and his slow numbers were the result of his craftsmanship, both as a writer and a performer—Adams never let anything obscure a good hook. *— Stephen Thomas Erlewine*

You Want It, You Got It / 1981 / A&M ✦✦✦

Cuts Like a Knife / Jan. 1983 / A&M ✦✦✦✦✦

Reckless / 1984 / A&M ✦✦✦✦✦

Into the Fire / Mar. 1987 / A&M ✦✦

Waking Up the Neighbours / Sep. 1991 / A&M ✦✦✦

● **So Far So Good** / Nov. 2, 1993 / A&M ✦✦✦✦✦
Throughout the 1980s and early '90s, few contemporary rock artists were able to come up with as many lighthearted, guilty pleasures as Bryan Adams. This is especially evident through *So Far So Good*, which neglects all album fillers and compiles many of his most noteworthy songs, from such rockers as "Summer of '69," "Run to You," and "Cuts Like a Knife" to the equally popular power ballads "Heaven" and "(Everything I Do) I Do It for You." Also included is the all-new "Please Forgive Me," one of his best power ballads yet. It's not quite a perfect compilation, however; in particular, his Top 20 hits "She's Only Happy When She's Dancin" and "Thought I'd Died and Gone to Heaven" are overlooked. These are only minor flaws, though. There is no better introduction to Bryan Adams to date than *So Far So Good*. *— Barry Weber*

Live! Live! Live! / 1995 / A&M ✦✦

18 'til I Die / Jun. 1996 / A&M ✦✦

MTV Unplugged / Dec. 9, 1997 / A&M ✦✦✦

On a Day Like Today / Oct. 27, 1998 / A&M ✦✦

Aerosmith

f. 1970, Boston, MA
Group / Pop-Metal, Album Rock, Arena Rock, Heavy Metal, Pop/Rock, Hard Rock
Aerosmith was one of the most popular hard-rock bands of the '70s, setting the style and sound of hard rock and heavy metal for the next two decades with their raunchy, bluesy swagger. The Boston-based quintet—singer Steven Tyler, guitarists Joe Perry and Brad Whitford, bassist Tom Hamilton, and drummer Joey Kramer—found the middle ground between the menace of the Rolling Stones and the campy, sleazy flamboyance of the New York Dolls, developing a lean, dirty riff-oriented boogie that was loose and swinging and as hard as a diamond. In the meantime, they developed a prototype for power ballads with "Dream On," a piano ballad that was orchestrated with strings and distorted guitars. Aerosmith's ability to pull off both ballads and rock & roll made them extremely popular during the mid-'70s, when they had a string of gold and platinum albums. By the early '80s, the group's audience had declined as the band fell prey to drug and alcohol abuse. However, their career was far from over—in the late '80s, Aerosmith pulled off one of the most remarkable comebacks in rock history, returning to the top of the charts with a group of albums that equalled, if not surpassed, the popularity of their '70s albums. *— Stephen Thomas Erlewine*

Aerosmith / Jan. 1973 / Columbia ✦✦✦
Over the years, Aerosmith has voiced dissatisfaction with its 1973 self-titled debut. While the songwriting may not be as exceptional as future releases, and Steven Tyler's singing style wasn't fully developed yet, the album succeeds on the band's raw, loose, and bluesy performance. The now legendary quintet was unfairly labeled as a Stones/N.Y. Dolls rip-off at the time, but Aerosmith was more technically proficient at their instruments than the Dolls, and was much more hard rock-based than the Stones (i.e. Led Zeppelin, Yardbirds, etc.). *Aerosmith* spawned one of the first true rock ballads ever, the reflective "Dream On" (a hit single when re-released in 1976), while the rocking "Mama Kin" was one of the band's best early anthems, receiving further attention after Aero-disciples Guns N' Roses covered it on 1989's *G n' R Lies*. Other tracks, such as "Make It," "Somebody," "One Way Street," "Write Me," and "Walking the Dog" serve as the perfect snapshot of the young band finding their foothold, while the oft-overlooked, long-and-winding storyteller, "Movin' Out," remains one of Aerosmith's all-time best. *Aerosmith* is one of their most underrated records. *— Greg Prato*

Get Your Wings / Mar. 1974 / Columbia ✦✦✦✦✦
Due to the commercial underachievement of Aerosmith's 1973 self-titled debut, the young band was nearly dropped by their record label. But a rigorous touring schedule helped strengthen their songwriting and tightened their playing even further, so after Columbia wisely decided to back the band again, the classic, *Get Your Wings*, was released. It didn't prove to be the sudden commercial breakthrough that Tyler and company hoped for, but it did go gold one year after it's release and set the stage perfectly for 1975's *Toys in the Attic*, which would propel Aerosmith into the rock & roll stratosphere. Comparing *Get Your Wings* to the 1973 debut is like night and day; it sounds almost like a completely different band—the playing is more aggressive, the songwriting succinct, and singer Steven Tyler had almost fully perfected his instantly recognizable yowl. But the sleaze and grit remained—"Same Old Song and Dance" combines a nasty blues groove with a tale of a drug deal gone bad, both "S.O.S. (Too Bad)" and "Lord of the Thighs" are straight-up rockers, and "Seasons of Wither" remains the band's most haunting ballad. But the best known song is their cover of "Train Kept a' Rollin'," which would soon become a perennial showstopper in concert. *Get Your Wings* also marked the first time that producer Jack Douglas worked with the band, he would remain on the controls on nearly all of their future '70s hits. *— Greg Prato*

☆ **Toys in the Attic** / Apr. 1975 / Columbia ✦✦✦✦✦
After nearly getting off the ground with *Get Your Wings*, Aerosmith finally perfected their mix of Stonesy raunch and Zeppelin-esque riffing with their third album, *Toys in the Attic*. The success of the album derives from a combination of an increased sense of songwriting skills and purpose. Not only does Joe Perry turn out indelible riffs like "Walk This Way," "Toys in the Attic," and "Sweet Emotion," but Steven Tyler has fully embraced sleaziness as his artistic muse. Taking his cue from the old dirty blues "Big Ten Inch Record," Tyler writes with a gleeful impishness about sex throughout *Toys in the Attic*, whether it's the teenage heavy petting of "Walk This Way," the promiscuous "Sweet Emotion," or the double entendres of "Uncle Salty" and "Adam's Apple." The rest of Aerosmith, led by Perry's dirty, exaggerated riffing, provide an appropriately greasy backing. Before *Toys in the Attic*, no other hard-rock band sounded like this. Sure, Aerosmith cribbed heavily from the records of the Rolling Stones, New York Dolls, and Led Zeppelin, but they didn't have any of the menace of their influences, nor any of their mystique. Aerosmith was a gritty, street-wise hard-rock band who played their blues as blooze and were in it for a good time; *Toys in the Attic* crystalizes that attitude. *— Stephen Thomas Erlewine*

★ **Rocks** / May 1976 / Columbia ✦✦✦✦✦
Few albums have been so appropriately named as Aerosmith's 1976 classic, *Rocks*. Despite hard drug use escalating among it's bandmembers, Aerosmith produced a superb follow-up to their masterwork, *Toys in the Attic*, nearly topping it in the process. Many Aero-fans will point to *Toys* as the band's quintessential album (it contained two radio/concert standards after all, "Walk This Way" and "Sweet Emotion"), but out of all their albums, *Rocks* did the best

job of capturing Aerosmith at their most raw and rocking. Like it's predecessor, a pair of songs have become their most renown—the menacing, hard-rock, cowboy-stomper "Back in the Saddle," as well as the downright viscous funk groove of "Last Child." Again, even the lesser-known tracks prove essential to the make up of the album, such as the stimulated "Rats in the Cellar" (a response of sorts to "Toys in the Attic"), the Stonesy "Combination," and the forgotten riff-rocker, "Get the Lead Out." Also included is the apocalyptic "Nobody's Fault," the up-and-coming rock star tale of "Lick and a Promise," and the album closing ballad, "Home Tonight." With *Rocks*, Aerosmith appeared to be indestructible, but this would not prove to be the case for long. *—Greg Prato*

Draw the Line / Dec. 1977 / Columbia ♦♦♦
Renting out an abandoned convent on the outskirts of New York City to record the follow-up to the hellacious *Rocks* may not of been the best idea, but 1977's *Draw the Line* still managed to be another down and dirty Aerosmith release. While it wasn't as awe inspiring as their last two albums—the members have said that the music suddenly got "cloudy" around this time (due to in-band fighting/ego-clashes, excessive living, etc.)– *Draw the Line* catches fire more times than not. Unlike their most recent album successes, the band shies away from studio experimentry and dabbling in different styles, instead they return to simple, straight-ahead, hard rock. The album opening title track features a gloriously abrasive Joe Perry slide guitar riff and has been featured in concert ever since, while the punk-esque "Bright Light Fright" featured Perry's first ever lead vocal spot on an Aerosmith record. Other highlights include a re-working of the blues obscurity, "Milk Cow Blues," which Perry's pre-Aerosmith group, the Jam Band, played live, as well as "I Wanna Know Why," "Critical Mass," "Get It Up," "Kings and Queens," and "Sight for Sore Eyes." *Draw the Line* would turn out to be the last true studio album from Aerosmith's original line-up for nearly a decade. *—Greg Prato*

Live Bootleg / Oct. 1978 / Columbia ♦♦

Night in the Ruts / Nov. 1979 / Columbia ♦

★ **Greatest Hits** / Oct. 1980 / Columbia ♦♦♦♦♦
Aerosmith's *Greatest Hits* remains one of the most popular and enduring best-of collections by any rock band, selling nearly ten million copies in the U.S. alone since it's release. But when it was issued in 1980, the band had just about reached its nadir. With original guitarist Joe Perry gone (and Brad Whitford soon to follow), Aerosmith had turned into a directionless, time-consuming ghost of it's former self. Since there would be a three-year gap between 1979's *Night in the Ruts* and 1982's *Rock in a Hard Place*, *Greatest Hits* was assembled, more or less, to fill the void and buy the band some time. With the album clocking in at only 37-and a-half minutes, many Aero-classics are not included, such as what many consider the band's quintessential track, their cover of "Train Kept a' Rollin." The only poor selection is the forgettable "Remember (Walking in the Sand)," but nine out of ten are bonafide classics—"Dream On," "Same Old Song and Dance," "Sweet Emotion," "Walk this Way," "Last Child," "Back in the Saddle," and "Draw the Line." Also featured is their venomous cover of the Beatles' "Come Together," previously only available as a single and on the soundtrack to the 1978 movie, *Sgt. Pepper's Lonely Hearts Club Band*. For the casual fan, *Greatest Hits* will do the job, as well as it's sister-album, 1988's *Gems*. *—Greg Prato*

Rock in a Hard Place / Aug. 1982 / Columbia ♦

Done with Mirrors / Nov. 1985 / Geffen ♦♦♦♦

Classics Live / Apr. 1986 / Columbia ♦♦

Classics Live 2 / Jun. 1987 / Columbia ♦♦♦

Permanent Vacation / Aug. 1987 / Geffen ♦♦♦♦
The much-ballyhooed reunion of the original Aerosmith lineup had pretty much fallen flat on its face after 1985's hit-and-miss *Done With Mirrors*. Realizing that the band simply couldn't do it alone, A&R guru John Kalodner capitalized on the runaway success of Run-D.M.C.'s cover of "Walk This Way" and decided to draft in the day's top hired hands, including knob-twiddler extraordinaire Bruce Fairbairn and career-revitalizing song doctors Desmond Child and Jim Vallance. Together, they would help craft *Permanent Vacation*, the album which would reinvent Aerosmith as '80s and '90s superstars. Yet, despite the mostly stellar songwriting, which makes it a strong effort overall, some of the album's nooks and crannies haven't aged all that well because of Fairbairn's overwrought production, featuring an exaggerated sleekness typical of most mid-'80s pop- metal albums. Furthermore, Desmond Child's pedantic writing often compromises the timeliness of even the best material. On the other hand, pre-fab radio gems like "Rag Doll" and "Dude (Looks like a Lady)" remain largely unassailable from a "delivering the goods" perspective. But remember kids, this *is* Aerosmith, so that can only mean one thing: a guaranteed number of incredible tracks for any time and place. These include the earthy voodoo blues of "St. John" and the excellent hobo-harmonica fable of "Hangman Jury." And, although some of the remaining cuts lean to the filler side, both the awkwardly Caribbean title track and the cover of the Beatles' "I'm Down" are well executed. Finally, the crowd-pleasing schmaltz of "Angel" showcases the band at the peak of their power-ballad cheese. A valiant effort, this album proved to be the crucial catalyst in reintroducing Aerosmith to the masses, but if you're looking for an even better example of the band's renewed strength, check out *Pump* first. *—John Franck & Ed Rivadavia*

Gems / 1988 / Columbia ♦♦♦♦♦

Pump / Sep. 1989 / Geffen ♦♦♦♦♦
Where *Permanent Vacation* seemed a little overwhelmed by its pop concessions, *Pump* revels in them without ever losing sight of Aerosmith's dirty hard-rock core. Which doesn't mean the record is a sellout—"What It Takes" has more emotion and grit than any of their other power ballads; "Janie's Got a Gun" tackles more complex territory than most previous songs; and "The Other Side" and "Love in an Elevator" rock relentlessly, no matter how many horns and synths fight with the guitars. Such ambition and successful musical eclecticism make *Pump* rank with *Rocks* and *Toys in the Attic*. *—Stephen Thomas Erlewine*

Get a Grip / Apr. 1993 / Geffen ♦♦♦

● **Big Ones** / Nov. 1, 1994 / Geffen ♦♦♦♦♦
Big Ones serves up the hits and nothing but the hits; Aerosmith's excellent debut for Geffen, *Done With Mirrors*, is conveniently overlooked. So what's left is some of the finest mainstream hard rock of the late '80s and early '90s—the fruits of one of the most remarkable comebacks in rock & roll history. Unfortunately, there's precious little of the classic Aerosmith raunch; in fact, the two new tracks are the hardest, slinkiest tracks here. Otherwise, the uptempo tracks bog down in overproduction ("Love in an Elevator"), and the frequently embarrassingly overwrought power ballads ("Angel" and "Crazy") dominate too much of the album. So what's left? The band's best stab at social commentary ("Janie's Got a Gun"), a sublime slinky throwaway ("Deuces Are Wild"), deliciously sleazy blues-rockers ("Rag Doll," "(Dude) Looks Like a Lady"), and their best ballads ("What It Takes" and "Cryin' "). *—Stephen Thomas Erlewine*

Nine Lives / Mar. 18, 1997 / Columbia ♦♦♦

A Little South of Sanity / Oct. 20, 1998 / Geffen ♦♦♦

Afghan Whigs

f. 1986, Hamilton, OH, **db.** 2001
Group / Indie Rock, Alternative Pop/Rock
Evolving from a garage-punk band in the vein of the Replacements, Dinosaur Jr. and Mudhoney to a literate, pretentious, soul-inflected post-punk quartet, the Afghan Whigs were one of most critically acclaimed alternative bands of the early '90s. Although the band never broke into the mainstream, they developed a dedicated cult following, primarily because of lead singer/songwriter Greg Dulli's tortured, angst-ridden tales of broken relationships and self-loathing. The Afghan Whigs were one of the few alternative bands around in the late '90s to acknowledge R&B, attempting to create a fusion of soul and post-punk. A 1988 debut with good word-of-mouth led to a record contract with the influential Seattle-based independent Sub Pop, and Afghan Wigs earned many positive reviews for their third, 1992's *Congregation*. Signed to the major label Elektra, the band released *Gentlemen* one year later; "Debonair," the first single pulled from the album, received major play from MTV, and all of the reviews were positive. Nevertheless, the band wasn't able to ascend past cult status, and the critical praise even engendered a backlash. An extended break during 1994 preceded the release of *Black Love* in 1996. Again, the album received positive reviews but the band failed to break out of their cult status. *1965*, their first effort for new label Columbia, followed two years later, but it would prove to be their last—the band called it quits in February of 2001, citing geographical separation. *—Stephen Thomas Erlewine*

Big Top Halloween / 1988 / Ultrasuede ♦♦

Up in It / 1990 / Sub Pop ♦♦♦

Congregation / Aug. 1991 / Sub Pop ♦♦♦♦♦
The grunge era's most overlooked masterpiece, *Congregation* was the Afghan Whigs' breakthrough album, an incendiary and insidious set which bridges the gap between the noisy aggression of the band's early releases and the soulful swagger of their later work. Slipping with ominous ease into the sinister, self-obsessed lothario guise which would serve him so well from here on out, Greg Dulli announces his arrival as a truly magnetic presence—by turns predator ("Tonight") and prey ("I'm Her Slave"), he's the guy your parents always warned you about, delivering each syllable of his remarkable lyrics with equal measures of innuendo and venom. Equally startling is the Whigs' musical growth—while still unmistakably a member of the Sub Pop stable, there's a greater maturity and depth to their sinewy sound, with a new-found grasp of mood and nuance on tracks like the opening "Her Against Me" and "Let Me Lie to You"—the wah-wah guitar which dominates "Turn on the Water," meanwhile, offers the first taste of the funk ambitions to follow. It was hardly a surprise when the Whigs jumped to Elektra soon after—*Congregation* was clearly their ticket to the big leagues. *—Jason Ankeny*

Uptown Avondale / 1992 / Sub Pop ♦♦♦♦

● **Gentlemen** / Oct. 5, 1993 / Elektra ♦♦♦♦♦
The Afghan Whigs' sound was growing larger by the release during the days on Sub Pop, so the fact that *Gentlemen* turned out the way it did wasn't all that surprising as a result ("cinematic" was certainly the word the band were aiming for, what with credits describing the recording process as being "shot on location" at Ardent Studios). While *Gentlemen* is no monolith, it is very much of a piece at the start. While "If I Were Going" opens things on a slightly moodier tip, it's the crunch of "Gentlemen," "Be Sweet," and "Debonair" that really stands out, each of which features a tightly wound R&B punch that rocks out as much as it grooves, if not more so. Dulli's lyrics immediately set about the task of emotional self-evisceration at the same time, with lines like "Ladies, let me tell you about myself/I got a dick for a brain" being among the calmer points. The album truly comes into its own with "When We Two Parted," though, as sad countryish guitars chime over a slow crawling rhythm and Dulli's quiet-then-anguished detailing of an exploding relationship. From there on in, things surge from strength to greater strength, sometimes due to the subtlest of touches—the string arrangement on "Fountain and Fairfax" or the unexpected, resigned lead vocal from Scrawl's Marcy Mays on "My Curse," for instance. Other times, it's all the much more up front, as "What Jail Is Like," with its heartbroken-and-fierce combination of piano, feedback, and drive building to an explosive chorus. Dulli's blend of utter abnegation and masculine swagger may be a crutch, but when everything connects, as it does more often than not on *Gentlemen*, both he and his band are unstoppable. *—Ned Raggett*

Black Love / Mar. 12, 1996 / Elektra ♦♦♦

1965 / Oct. 27, 1998 / Columbia ♦♦♦♦♦
With *1965*, the Afghan Whigs have finally made the gritty soul record just always out of their reach—seamlessly integrating the R&B aspirations which have textured the band's sound since the beginning, the music simmers with raw energy, its deep, dark grooves not so much white-boy as simply white-hot. Recorded in New Orleans, the album is plainly the product of its environment—sultry, sleazy, and more than a little menacing; here more than ever, Greg Dulli is the frontman you love to hate, strutting and swaggering his way through stand-

out tracks like "Something Hot," "Uptown Again," and "John the Baptist" with predatory aggression. (Who else would deliver a lyric like "I got the devil in me, girl" as though it were a pickup line?) Still, for all its cocksure arrogance, *1965* is neverthless a sincere tribute to the classic music recalled by the album's title—lyrics aside, even if Dulli did sell his soul, he's somehow managed to get it all back. *—Jason Ankeny*

Christina Aguilera

b. Dec. 18, 1980

Vocals / Teen Pop, Adult Contemporary, Dance-Pop

Teen pop diva Christina Aguilera was born December 18, 1980 in Staten Island, NY; the careers of her military father and musician mother ensured that the family traveled the globe before finally settling in Wexford, PA, where the youngster first began performing in area talent shows. At age eight, Aguilera appeared on the syndicated television series *Star Search;* four years later, she landed a regular role on Disney's *The New Mickey Mouse Club,* co-starring with future luminaries including Britney Spears, 'N Sync's JC Chasez and Justin Timberlake, and *Felicity*'s Keri Russell. Aguilera's first pop-music success came in Japan thanks to "All I Wanna Do," a smash duet with Keizo Nakanishi; she returned to the U.S. in 1998 to record the song "Reflection" for the soundtrack of the animated film *Mulan,* that same week signing to RCA. Releasing her self-titled debut album the following year, Aguilera topped the pop charts with the single "Genie in a Bottle." *Christina Aguilera* sold over ten million copies worldwide in just under a year and turned its namesake into a superstar. She followed this successs with performances at the Super Bowl XXXIII Halftime Show and for President Clinton, and won a Best New Artist Grammy. Just over a year after she released her debut album, Aguilera released *Mi Reflejo,* a collection of Spanish-language songs, as well as *My Kind of Christmas,* a holiday album. *—Jason Ankeny*

● **Christina Aguilera** / Aug. 24, 1999 / RCA ♦♦♦♦

Since Christina Aguilera is the third and last of *The New Mickey Mouse Club* alumni to hit the charts in the mid-'90s—following two members of 'N Sync and Britney Spears—it's easy for cynical observers to assume that she was the lesser of the three talents since she arrived last after everyone scaled the charts. That's not the case at all. If anything, Aguilera is the best of the three, blessed with a rich voice that's given the material it deserves. Her eponymous debut remains firmly within the teen-oriented dance-pop genre, but unlike Spears' album, this is done right. The songwriting is strong—the ballads are engaging, the dance numbers are catchy—the production is clean and uncluttered, letting Aguilera's voice take the foreground. Most impressively, she not only has charisma, she can actually sing, bringing conviction to these love and heartbreak songs. So, *Christina Aguilera* may be lightweight, but it's lightweight in the best possible sense—breezy, fun, engaging, and enjoyable on each repeated listen. Out of the deluge of teen-pop albums in 1999, this feels like the best of the lot. *—Stephen Thomas Erlewine*

Mi Reflejo / Sep. 12, 2000 / RCA International ♦♦♦

Arthur Alexander

b. 1942, Florence, AL, **d.** Jun. 9, 1993, Nashville, TN

Vocals / Deep Soul, Southern Soul, Country-Soul, Soul

Arthur Alexander was one of the first true singing/songwriting stars of country-soul, a genre that wed Southern Black R&B singers to songs written in a country format and played basically by White musicians. Alexander's "You Better Move On" was the first hit to come out of Rick Hall's fledgling Muscle Shoals studio. His work was immediately appreciated by his peers in the business; those who have covered his tunes (self-penned or otherwise) read like a *Who's Who* from both sides of the Atlantic—"Anna" (Beatles); "Soldiers of Love" (Beatles and Marshall Crenshaw); "Burning Love" (Elvis Presley); "Set Me Free" (Joe Tex, Esther Phillips, Percy Sledge). The Rolling Stones' cover of "You Better Move On" led to valuable contacts for Rick Hall, and the resulting business enabled him to build the new FAME studio. It was the start of the whole Muscle Shoals sound, and Alexander's career was one of its cornerstones. He went on, after a brief retirement, to record for both Warner Brothers and Buddah. "Anna (Go to Him)," one of Alexander's best-known tunes, epitomizes the anguished, haunting tone of his music. From the onset, the heavily echoed piano and tortured vocal set a mood that is soulful, mysterious, a little spooky, and totally mesmerizing. His work is essential to any country-soul collection. *—Christine Ohlman*

★ **The Ultimate Arthur Alexander** / Jun. 15, 1993 / Razor & Tie ♦♦♦♦♦

Alexander's songs are better known in versions by the Beatles, Elvis Presley, and the Rolling Stones, but no one recorded better versions than Alexander himself. *The Ultimate Arthur Alexander* truly lives up to its title, gathering together the best songs (including "Anna (Go to Him)," "You Better Move On," and "Soldiers of Love") from Alexander's remarkably influential and underrated career. Absolutely essential for any R&B and soul collection. *—Stephen Thomas Erlewine*

Rainbow Road / Apr. 26, 1994 / Warner Archives ♦♦♦♦♦

Songwriter and vocalist Arthur Alexander was sorely neglected during his lifetime, despite possessing a stark, compelling voice and being among pop and soul's greatest storytellers. He remained on the outside, coming close but never attaining stardom. This CD features 15 fantastic songs, most from the great 1972 Warner Bros. album recorded in Memphis that Alexander thought would finally earn him that elusive smash. There are also some singles cut in Nashville as companion records to the Memphis session. The 15 tracks range from the hypnotic title cut and "In the Middle of It All" to the uptempo burners "You Got Me Knockin'" and "Burning Love." There's also a moving gospel number, "Thank God He Came." This disc is a wonderful tribute to an unjustly ignored artist. *—Ron Wynn*

Alice in Chains

f. 1987, Seattle, WA

Group / Alternative Metal, Grunge, Heavy Metal, Alternative Pop/Rock

In many ways, Alice in Chains was the definitive heavy-metal band of the early '90s. Drawing equally from the heavy riffing of post-Van Halen metal and the gloomy strains of post-punk, the band developed a bleak, nihilistic sound that balanced grinding hard rock with subtly textured acoustic numbers. They were hard enough for metal fans, yet their dark subject matter and punky attack placed them among the front ranks of the Seattle-based grunge bands. While this dichotomy helped the group soar to multi-platinum status with their second album, 1992's *Dirt,* it also divided them. Guitarist Jerry Cantrell always leaned toward the mainstream, while vocalist Layne Staley was fascinated with the seamy underground. Such tension drove the band towards stardom in their early years, but following *Dirt,* Alice in Chains suffered from near-crippling internal tensions that kept the band off the road for the remainder of the '90s, and, consequently, the group never quite fulfilled their potential. *—Stephen Thomas Erlewine*

Facelift / Aug. 1990 / Columbia ♦♦♦

Sap / Feb. 1992 / Columbia ♦♦♦♦

Upon its release, *Sap* was a revelation, a seemingly tossed-off EP of four mostly acoustic ballads (augmented with a goofy bonus track) that threw Alice in Chains' melodic gifts into stunning relief while exposing a gentler, more melancholy side of their sound, something that *Facelift* never even hinted at. The mood is still bleak, but not affectedly so, as was sometimes the case on *Facelift.* There's a newfound maturity in the subtlety and confessional introspection of the first four songs, whose somber beauty is unfortunately dispelled by the bonus track (in a different context, it might be idiotic fun, but it really doesn't fit here). Still, *Sap* served notice that there was a great deal more depth to Alice in Chains than their debut had let on, hinting at the potential that would be realized with *Dirt.* *—Steve Huey*

● **Dirt** / Oct. 1992 / Columbia ♦♦♦♦♦

Dirt is Alice in Chains' major artistic statement and the closest they ever came to recording a flat-out masterpiece. It's a primal, sickening howl from the depths of Layne Staley's heroin addiction, and one of the most harrowing concept albums ever recorded. Not every song on *Dirt* is explicitly about heroin, but Jerry Cantrell's solo-written contributions (nearly half the album) effectively maintain the thematic coherence—nearly every song is imbued with the morbidity, self-disgust, and/or resignation of a self-aware yet powerless addict. Cantrell's technically limited but inventive guitar work is by turns explosive, textured, and queasily disorienting, keeping the listener off balance with atonal riffs and off-kilter time signatures. Staley's stark confessional lyrics are similarly effective, and consistently miserable. Sometimes he's just numb and apathetic, totally desensitized to the outside world; sometimes his self-justifications betray a shockingly casual amorality; his moments of self-recognition are permeated by despair and suicidal self-loathing. Even given its subject matter, *Dirt* is monstrously bleak, closely resembling the cracked, haunted landscape of its cover art. The album holds out little hope for its protagonists (aside from the much-needed survival story of "Rooster," a tribute to Cantrell's Vietnam-vet father), but in the end, it's redeemed by the honesty of its self-revelation and the sharp focus of its music. [Some versions of *Dirt* feature "Down in a Hole" as the next-to-last track rather than the fourth.] *—Steve Huey*

Jar of Flies / Jan. 25, 1994 / Columbia ♦♦♦♦

Written and recorded in about a week, *Jar of Flies* solidified Alice in Chains' somewhat bizarre pattern of alternating full-length hard-rock albums with mostly acoustic, ballad-oriented EPs. That quirk aside, *Jar of Flies* is a low-key stunner, achingly gorgeous and harrowingly sorrowful all at once. In a way, it's a logical sequel to *Dirt*—despite the veneer of calm, the songs' voices still blame only themselves. But where *Dirt* found catharsis in its unrelenting darkness and depravity, *Jar of Flies* is about living with the consequences, full of deeply felt reflections on loneliness, self-imposed isolation, and lost human connections. The mood is still hopelessly bleak, but the poignant, introspective tone produces a sense of acceptance that's actually soothing, in a funereal sort of way. Jerry Cantrell's arrangements keep growing more detailed and layered; while there are a few noisy moments, most of *Jar of Flies* is bathed in a clean, shimmering ambience whose source is difficult to pin down, but is well served by Cantrell's varied guitar tones and even occasional string arrangements. And coming on the heels of *Dirt,* the restraint and subtlety of *Jar of Flies* are nothing short of revelatory—though it was written and recorded in about a week, it feels much more crafted and textured than *Sap.* Perhaps *Jar of Flies* would have gotten more credit if it had been a full-length album; as it stands, the EP is a leap forward and a major work in the Alice in Chains catalog. *—Steve Huey*

Alice in Chains / Nov. 21, 1995 / Columbia ♦♦♦

Dispelling rumors of their demise due to Layne Staley's heroin addiction, *Alice in Chains* is a sonically detailed effort that ranks as their best-produced record, and its best moments are easily some of their most mature music. *Alice in Chains* relies less on metallic riffs and more on melody and texturally varied arrangements than the group's previous full-length albums, finally integrating some of the more delicate acoustic moods of their EPs. The lyrics deal with familiar AIC subject matter: despair, misery, loneliness, and disappointment, but in a more understated fashion, and the lyrics take on more uplifting qualities of toughness and endurance, which were missing from much of their previous work. The consistent visceral impact *Alice In Chains* lacks in comparison to that previous work is partially made up for by the skilled production and songs like "Grind," "Brush Away," "Over Now," and the hit ballad "Heaven Beside You," which are among the band's best work. Still, in spite of its many virtues, it's hard not to feel a little frustrated with the record, as though, given those qualities, it should have turned out better than it did—there are some slow spots where the songs are undercrafted and not especially memorable, and those moments can make the band sound uncommitted and distracted. That, in turn, can make the defiance of songs like "Grind" ("you'd be well advised/not to plan my funeral "fore the body dies") sound more like denial; just when Alice in Chains' music was finally beginning to emerge from the dark side, the intra-band problems became too much to bear and made *Alice in Chains* likely the last collection of new material the band will ever release. *—Steve Huey*

Unplugged / Jul. 1996 / Columbia ♦♦♦

Nothing Safe: Best of the Box / Jun. 29, 1999 / Columbia ♦♦♦♦

Music Bank / Oct. 26, 1999 / Columbia ✦✦✦✦

Live / Dec. 5, 2000 / Columbia ✦✦✦

The Allman Brothers Band

f. 1969, Macon, GA, **db.** 1982

Group / Slide Guitar Blues, Album Rock, Boogie Rock, Southern Rock, Hard Rock, Blues-Rock

The story of the Allman Brothers Band is one of triumph, tragedy, redemption, dissolution, and a new redemption. Over nearly 30 years, they've gone from being America's single most influential band to a has-been group trading on past glories, to reaching the 1990s as one of the most respected rock acts of their era. For the first half of the 1970s, the Allman Brothers Band was the most influential rock group in America, redefining rock music and its boundaries. The band's mix of blues, country, jazz, and even classical influences, and their powerful, extended onstage jamming altered the standards of concert performance—other groups were known for their onstage jamming, but when the Allman Brothers—guitarist Duane Allman, his singer/organist brother Gregg, guitarist Dickey Betts, bassist Berry Oakley, and drummers Butch Trucks and Jaimoe in their most celebrated incarnation—stretched a song out for 30 or 40 minutes, at their best they were exciting, never self-indulgent. They gave it all a distinctly Southern voice and, in the process, opened the way for a wave of '70s rock acts from south of the Mason-Dixon Line, including the Marshall Tucker Band, Lynyrd Skynyrd, and Blackfoot, whose music, at least initially, celebrated their roots. And for a time, almost single-handedly, they also made Capricorn Records into a major independent label. *—Bruce Eder*

The Allman Brothers Band / 1969 / Polydor ✦✦✦✦✦

This might be the best debut album ever delivered by an American blues band, a bold, powerful, hard-edged, soulful essay in electric blues with a native Southern ambience. Some lingering elements of the psychedelic era then drawing to a close can be found in "Dreams," and along with the template for the group's onstage workouts with "Whipping Post," and a solid cover of Muddy Waters' "Trouble No More." There isn't a bad song here, and only the fact that the group did even better the next time out keeps this from getting the highest possible rating. *—Bruce Eder*

☆ **Idlewild South** / 1970 / Polydor ✦✦✦✦✦

The best studio album in the group's history, electric blues with an acoustic texture, virtuoso lead, slide, and organ playing, and a killer selection of songs, including "Midnight Rider," "Revival," "Don't Keep Me Wonderin," and "In Memory of Elizabeth Reed" in its embryonic studio version, which is pretty impressive even at a mere six minutes and change. They also do the best white cover of Willie Dixon's "Hoochie Coochie Man" anyone's ever likely to hear. *—Bruce Eder*

☆ **Live at Fillmore East** / Mar. 1971 / Polydor ✦✦✦✦✦

Whereas most great live rock albums are about energy, *Live at Fillmore East* is like a great live jazz session, where the pleasure comes from the musicians' interaction and playing. The great thing about that is, the original album that brought the Allmans so much acclaim is as notable for its clever studio editing as it is for its performances. Producer Tom Down skillfully trimmed some of the performances down to relatively concise running time (edits later restored on the double-disc set *The Fillmore Concerts*), at times condensing several performances into one track. Far from being a sacrilege, this tactic helps present the Allman's in their best light, since even if the music isn't necessarily concise (three tracks run over ten minutes, with two in the 20-minute range), it does showcase the group's terrific instrumental interplay, letting each member (but particularly guitarist Duane and keyboardist/vocalist Gregg) shine. Even after the release of the unedited concerts, this original double album (single CD) remains the pinnacle of the Allman's and Southern rock at its most elastic, bluesy, and jazzy. *—Stephen Thomas Erlewine*

★ **Eat a Peach** / 1972 / Polydor ✦✦✦✦✦

A tribute to the dearly departed Duane, *Eat a Peach* rambles through two albums, running through a side of new songs, recorded post-Duane, spending a full album on live cuts from the *Fillmore East* sessions, then offering a round of studio tracks Duane completed before his death. On the first side, they do suggest the mellowness of the Dickey Betts-led *Brothers and Sisters*, particularly on the lovely "Melissa," and this stands in direct contrast with the monumental live cuts that dominate the album. They're at the best on the punchier covers of "One Way Out" and "Trouble No More," both proof of the group's exceptional talents as a roadhouse blues-rock band, but Duane does get his needed showcase on "Mountain Jam," a sprawling 33-minute jam that may feature a lot of great playing, but is certainly a little hard for anyone outside of diehards to sit through. Apart from that cut, the record showcases the Allmans at their peak, and it's hard not to feel sad as the acoustic guitars of "Little Martha" conclude the record, since this tribute isn't just heartfelt, it offers proof of Duane Allman's immense talents and contribution to the band. *—Stephen Thomas Erlewine*

☆ **Beginnings** / 1973 / Polydor ✦✦✦✦✦

This is where the group's CD release history gets complicated. *Beginnings* was originally put together by Atco as a double-LP to encourage new fans who'd missed them to buy the group's first two album, and proved so successful that it was kept in print on CD by Polydor when it acquired the group's catalog. Polydor's single-CD version of this double-LP, however, was substandard in audio quality, digitized from an LP production master, and their individual CDs of *The Allman Brothers Band* and *Idlewild South* were far superior. But when Capricorn got the library back in 1997, they remastered *Beginnings* along with the rest of the library, and the Capricorn version of this CD is one of the better bargains going *—Bruce Eder*

Brothers and Sisters / 1973 / Polydor ✦✦✦✦

The group's first new studio album in two years shows off a leaner, brand of musicianship, which, coupled with a pair of serious crowd-pleasers, "Ramblin' Man" and "Jessica," helped drive it to the top of the charts for a month and a half, and platinum record sales. This was the first album to feature the group's new lineup, with Chuck Leavell on keyboards and Lamar Williams on bass, as well as Dickey Betts' emergence as a singer alongside Gregg Allman. The tracks appear on the album in the order in which they were recorded, and the first three, up through "Ramblin' Man," feature Berry Oakley—their sound is rock hard and crisp. The subsequent songs with Williams have the bass buried in the mix, and an overall muddier sound. The interplay between Leavell and Betts is beautiful on some songs, and Betts' slide on "Pony Boy" is a dazzling showcase that surprised everybody. Despite its sales, *Brothers and Sisters* is not quite a classic album (although it was their best for the next 17 years), especially in the wake of the four that had appeared previously, but it served as a template for some killer stage performances, and it proved that the band could survive the deaths of two key members. Capricorn's 1997 reissue has a brighter sound than the older PolyGram CD, but the Mobile Fidelity audiophile disc has the best sound, a richer, broader tone. *—Bruce Eder*

Win, Lose or Draw / 1975 / Polydor ✦✦

Wipe the Windows, Check the Oil, Dollar Gas / 1976 / Polydor ✦✦✦

Enlightened Rogues / 1979 / Polydor ✦✦✦

The group's best studio album since *Brothers and Sisters* is a loud, brash, hard-rocking collection of consistently solid if not first-rate songs. The singing is some of the best since *Idlewild South*, and although they would do better once they brought in Warren Haynes, the dual guitar lineup of Dickey Betts and Dan Toler is a reminder of what the group had been missing since Duane Allman's death. The music isn't earth-shattering, but it is exciting through and through. *—Bruce Eder*

Reach for the Sky / 1980 / Razor & Tie ✦✦

Brothers of the Road / 1981 / Razor & Tie ✦✦

Dreams / Jun. 1989 / Polydor ✦✦✦✦✦

Spanning four discs and nearly 100 tracks, *Dreams* is one of those rare box sets that tells a story while delivering the definitive word on its subject. Its success has a lot to do with its status as Polygram/Bill Levinson's sequel to the acclaimed hit *Crossroads*, which summarized Eric Clapton's winding career perfectly. They follow the same approach here, gathering pre-Allman's recordings from the clan, including cuts by the Allman Joys, selecting the hits from the classic years, adding stray cuts by solo projects to the mix. It's a smart move, and it results in a terrific box that truly offers the definitive word on one of the longest-running dramas in Southern rock. Yes, the Allmans reunited rather successfully after this box, so none of that material is here, but it's not missed—this is the story of the band. *—Stephen Thomas Erlewine*

Seven Turns / Oct. 1990 / Epic ✦✦✦✦✦

Live at Ludlow Garage: 1970 / 1991 / Polydor ✦✦✦✦✦

Shades of Two Worlds / Jul. 1991 / Epic ✦✦✦✦

A Decade of Hits 1969-1979 / Oct. 1991 / Polydor ✦✦✦✦

Where It All Begins / May 3, 1994 / Epic ✦✦✦

Mycology: An Anthology / Jun. 9, 1998 / Epic ✦✦✦

Mycology: An Anthology collects highlights from the Allman Brothers' '90s recordings for Epic Records. Although these latter-day recordings didn't quite reach the heights of the group's '70s heyday, they were surprisingly strong, and *Mycology* is the best way for the curious fan to discover that. By rounding up the best moments from *Seven Turns, Shades of Two Worlds, An Evening with the Allman Brothers*, and *Where it All Begins*, the collection offers a good distillation of an underrated portion of the group's career, thereby making it of equal interest to casual and hardcore fans alike. *—Stephen Thomas Erlewine*

Peakin' at the Beacon / Nov. 14, 2000 / Epic ✦✦✦

America

f. 1967, London, England

Group / Pop/Rock, Soft Rock, Adult Contemporary

America was a light folk-rock act of the early '70s who had several Top Ten hits, including the number ones "A Horse with No Name" and "Sister Golden Hair." Formed around Dewey Bunnell, Dan Peak, and Gerry Beckley, the group landed a contract with a prominent promoter and opened for several major artists. America soon signed with Warner Bros. Records. Debut single "A Horse with No Name"—which strongly recalled the acoustic numbers of Neil Young—hit number three in the U.K. and number one in the U.S. Two straight Top Ten singles ("I Need You" and "Ventura Highway") followed, though the hits stopped coming fairly soon—they had only one minor Top 40 hit in 1973. One year later, *Holiday* returned America to the top of the charts, peaking at number three and launching the hit singles "Tin Man" and "Lonely People." "Sister Golden Hair," pulled from 1975's *Hearts*, became their second number one single. The group's audience began to decline in 1976, though they returned to the Top Ten in 1982 with "You Can Do Magic," an adult-contemporary pop number that featured synthesizers along with their trademark harmonies. After releasing *America in Concert* in the summer of 1985, the group continued to tour successfully into the '90s, resurfacing in 1998 with *Human Nature*. *—Stephen Thomas Erlewine*

● **History: Greatest Hits** / 1975 / Warner Brothers ✦✦✦✦✦

Even decades after its original release, *History: Greatest Hits* remains the definitive America retrospective. All of the group's blockbusters are here, from "A Horse with No Name" to "Ventura Highway" to "Sister Golden Hair," and the trio's luminous folk-pop sound and lush harmonies still capture the imagination all these years later. *—Chuck Donkers*

Encore: More Greatest Hits / Jul. 1991 / Rhino ✦✦✦✦✦

This follow-up to their *Greatest Hits* contains "The Border," "Right Before Your Eyes," "Today's the Day," and "You Can Do Magic." The rest of the tracks are album sides or previously unreleased material. *—AMG*

Highway: 30 Years of America / Jul. 18, 2000 / Rhino ✦✦✦✦✦

America may be best-known for "A Horse With No Name," but they had a number of hits right into 1982. These weren't just Top 100 hits, but songs that remained staples of soft- rock and oldies stations for years: "I Need You," "Ventura Highway," "Tin Man," "Lonely People," "Sister Golden Hair," and "You Can Do Magic," all well-crafted, melodic, memorable gems. Rhino's three-disc box set *Highway: 30 Years of America* proves that much, but if that's all that it did, it wouldn't be recommended over a hits collection. To some, a single-disc collection still may be preferable (although no single-disc set has all the hits), yet this is an ideal box. *Highway* contains all the charting singles, selected album tracks, alternate mixes, single edits, and demos, but the key to its success is that it plays as smoothly as a well-sequenced studio album. The compilers did a terrific job, selecting nearly every noteworthy track from America's albums, so there is no discernable drop-off in quality until the very end of the collection when the demos and latter-day recordings are hauled out. This box reveals a band that may have been indebted to Crosby, Stills, Nash & Young and the Beatles, but still wound up developing their own voice, rising to the forefront of soft rock. As *Highway* moves from one well-constructed, charming cut to another, it's hard not to admire America's skill at crafting appealing pop tunes that were folky, but not folk-rock, soft but not shapeless, melodic and memorable. Make no mistake—America is decidedly uncool, yet anyone with a fondness for easy, melodic soft rock will certainly find much to treasure on this superb set. —*Stephen Thomas Erlewine*

Tori Amos

b. Aug. 22, 1963, Newton, NC

Vocals, Keyboards, Piano/Adult Alternative Pop/Rock, Alternative Pop/Rock, Singer/Songwriter

Tori Amos was one of several female singer/songwriters who combined the stark lyrical attack of alternative rock with a distinctly '70s musical approach. Her music falls between the orchestrated meditations of Kate Bush and the stripped-down poetics of Joni Mitchell. In addition to reviving the singer/songwriter traditions of the '70s, Amos revived the piano as a rock & roll instrument. With her 1992 album *Little Earthquakes,* Amos built a dedicated following that continued to expand with subsequent albums. The daughter of a methodist preacher, Amos began writing her own songs as a child and studied at Baltimore's Peabody Conservatory. After becoming infatuated by rock & roll, particularly the music of Led Zeppelin, she began performing in local bars and later moved to Los Angeles. Signed to Atlantic in 1987, Amos debuted with an uninspired pop-metal album called *Y Kant Tori Read.* By 1990, Amos had adopted a new approach, singing spare, haunting semiconfessional piano ballads. *Little Earthquakes,* Amos' first album as a singer/songwriter, was released in late 1991 and sold well in both the U.S. and the U.K. Her second album, *Under the Pink,* was a bigger hit and and launched the minor hit singles "God" and "Cornflake Girl." Two years later she released *Boys for Pele,* her most ambitious and difficult record to date. *From the Choirgirl Hotel* followed in 1998. —*Stephen Thomas Erlewine*

● **Little Earthquakes** / 1991 / Atlantic ✦✦✦✦✦

With her haunting solo debut *Little Earthquakes,* Tori Amos carved the template for the female singer/songwriter movement of the '90s. Amos' delicate, prog-rock piano work and confessional, poetically quirky lyrics invited close emotional connection, giving her a fanatical cult following and setting the stage for the Lilith Fair legions. But *Little Earthquakes* is no mere style-setter or feminine stereotype—its intimacy is uncompromising, intense, and often far from comforting. Amos' musings on major personal issues—religion, relationships, gender, childhood—were just as likely to encompass rage, sarcasm, and defiant independence as pain or tenderness; sometimes, it all happened in the same song. The apex of that intimacy is the harrowing "Me and a Gun," where Amos strips away all the music, save for her own voice, and confronts the listener with the story of her own real-life rape; the free-associative lyrics come off as a heart-wrenching attempt to block out the ordeal. *Little Earthquakes* isn't always so stomach-churning, but it never seems less than deeply cathartic; it's the sound of a young woman (like the protagonist of "Silent All These Years") finally learning to use her own voice—sort of the musical equivalent of Mary Pipher's *Reviving Ophelia.* That's why Amos draws strength from her relentless vulnerability, and that's why the constantly shifting emotions of the material never seem illogical—Amos simply delights in the frankness of her own responses, whatever they might be. Though her subsequent albums were often very strong, Amos would never bare her soul quite so directly (or comprehensibly) as she did here, nor with such consistently focused results. *Little Earthquakes* is the most accessible work in Amos' catalog, and it's also the most influential and rewarding. —*Steve Huey*

Crucify / 1992 / Atlantic ✦✦✦

Under the Pink / Dec. 7, 1994 / Atlantic ✦✦✦✦✦

The proper follow-up to *Little Earthquakes* finds Amos stretching her compositions out a bit, expanding her arrangements, and playing up the prog-rock influence of Kate Bush. Overall, *Under the Pink* is slightly less consistent than its predecessor; the intimacy is there, but not quite so stunning, and some of her poetic imagery is a bit more obscure. However, these are minor complaints; *Under the Pink* is still compelling and necessary for anyone who enjoyed *Little Earthquakes.* —*Steve Huey*

Boys for Pele / Jan. 23, 1996 / Atlantic ✦✦✦

Highly ambitious, challenging, idiosyncratic, and confounding, *Boys for Pele* expands on the more experimental and progressive tendencies of *Under the Pink.* Amos frequently discards traditional song structures and employs wide-ranging, eclectic instrumentation in her music, while her lyrics seem to grow even more obscure, giving the album a very impressionistic feel. While there are certainly worthwhile moments, her experiments don't always work; some of the songs fail to stick, and it takes a few plays before many start to sink in. Ultimately, *Boys for Pele* is polarizing: Some Amos fans will only admire her more for taking the risks she does, while others may find to their disappointment that the intimacy and personal connection that helped Amos build her fan base are too difficult to detect. —*Steve Huey*

From the Choirgirl Hotel / May 5, 1998 / Atlantic ✦✦✦✦

Shortly before she began work on *From the Choirgirl Hotel,* Tori Amos suffered a miscarriage. While she was recording the album, she married her long-term boyfriend. As expected, both events cryptically wind their way into the album, which arguably has Amos' most personal lyrics since *Little Earthquakes.* The surprise is, *From the Choirgirl Hotel* is considerably more accessible than its immediate predecessor, *Boys for Pele.* Tori has opened up her sound by working live with a full band, bringing an immediacy to her sound that has never been heard before. Added to that are samples and drum loops, ballads supported by eerie, sweeping strings and heavy guitars—everything she played with on *Pele* has come to fruition here. All the while, she's kept the perversely cryptic, convoluted lyrics that have always marked her work, yet the lines that connect have more power and savage wit than ever. Besides, Amos' songs have an interior logic of their own. Until now, it only seemed that she could only deliver them on her own, supported by her piano, a guitar or strings. With *From the Choirgirl Hotel,* she proves that with a little aural experimentation and muscle, she's as potent and powerful as any modern-rock artist. —*Stephen Thomas Erlewine*

To Venus and Back / Sep. 21, 1999 / Atlantic ✦✦✦

The Angels

f. 1961, Orange, NJ

Group / Girl Group, Pop

The Angels' 1963 number one hit, "My Boyfriend's Back," is one of the half-dozen or so archetypal girl-group classics. Handclap beats, sassy vocals, slightly campy lyrics, and an arrangement paced by wailing horns and street-corner harmonies—it was a surefire hit and one that the group could never live up to, although they continued to record for some time. The Angels had actually been around for a while before "My Boyfriend's Back," making the Top 20 in 1961 with the ballad "Till," and the Top 40 with a follow-up, "Cry Baby Cry." In 1963, they hooked up with the songwriting/production team of Feldman-Goldstein-Gottehrer, who penned and produced material more in line with the Spectorian "wall of sound" gracing the airwaves at the peak of the girl-group era. "My Boyfriend's Back" was originally cut as a demo that music publishers hoped to shop to the Shirelles, but it turned out so well that it was released as an Angels single. Surprisingly, they would never make the Top 20 again, although they had minor hits with "Thank You and Goodnight," "I Adore Him," and "Wow Wow Wee (He's the Boy for Me)." —*Richie Unterberger*

● **The Best of the Angels** / Jun. 18, 1996 / Polygram ✦✦✦✦✦

Twenty-one-song anthology of cuts from the early and mid-'60s, with all the hits, including the pre-"My Boyfriend's Back" charters "Till" and "Cry Baby Cry." Despite the spirited vocals, accomplished production, and occasional highlights like "Why Don't the Boy Leave Me Alone?," "World Without Love" (not the Lennon-McCartney song), the ska-flavored "Jamaica Joe," and the James Bond riffs of "Boy from Crosstown," nothing here lights up the room like "My Boyfriend's Back." It's certainly the best collection, though, for those who want to hear more from the group than what's available on various-artist oldies compilations. —*Richie Unterberger*

The Animals

f. 1964, Newcastle, England, **db.** 1968

Group / British Blues, Psychedelic, British Invasion, Blues-Rock, Rock & Roll

One of the most important bands originating from England's R&B scene during the early '60s, the Animals were second only to the Rolling Stones in influence among R&B-based bands in the first wave of the British Invasion. A studio session in February 1964 yielded their Columbia debut single, "Baby Let Me Take You Home" (adapted from "Baby Let Me Follow You Down"). For years, it has been rumored incorrectly that the Animals got their next single, "House of the Rising Sun," from Bob Dylan's first album, but more recently it has been revealed that, like "Baby Let Me Take You Home," the song came to them courtesy of Josh White. In any event, the song—given a new guitar riff by Hilton Valentine and a soulful organ accompaniment devised by Alan Price—shot to the top of the U.K. and U.S. charts early that summer. This success yielded their first long-playing record, *The Animals.* Their third single, "I'm Crying," rose to number eight on the British charts. The group compiled an enviable record of Top Ten successes, including "Don't Let Me Be Misunderstood" and "We've Gotta Get Out of This Place," along with a second album, *Animal Tracks.* However, the group was growing increasingly unhappy with the material they were being given to record by manager Mickie Most. Not only were the majority of these songs much too commercial for their taste, but they represented a false image of the band, even if many were successful. "It's My Life," a number seven British hit and a similar smash in America, caused the Animals to terminate their association with Most and with EMI Records. They moved over to Decca/London Records and came up with a more forceful, powerful sound on their first album for the new label, *Animalisms.* Finally, in 1969, frontman Eric Burdon pulled the plug on the Animals. He hooked up with a Los Angeles-based group called War, and started a subsequent solo career that continues to this day. —*Bruce Eder*

The Best of Eric Burdon & the Animals, Vol. 2 / 1969 / MGM ✦✦✦

Actually the third Animals hits LP to be released by MGM in the 1960s, this collection is the work of lead singer Eric Burdon with the backup group he assembled upon the breakup of the original Animals. The recordings all come from 1967 and 1968, Burdon's psychedelicized period, when he was penning praises of *The Monterey Pop Festival* ("Monterey," number 15) and San Francisco ("San Franciscan Nights," number nine). The only other Top 40 hit on the album was the antiwar epic "Sky Pilot" (number 15), in its full seven-and-a-half-minute glory. Burdon had come a long way from his Manchester roots and his blues records, and this was the last album in his second phase; in fact, the New Animals had split by the time it was released. —*William Ruhlmann*

★ **The Best of the Animals** / 1988 / ABKCO ✦✦✦✦✦

The original Animals' American hits, including "House of the Rising Sun," "Don't Let Me Be Misunderstood," "It's My Life," and "We Gotta Get Out of This Place," in a compilation originally released in 1965. The lineup of songs is strong, but the sound is indifferent—the British *Complete Animals* covers the same territory and a lot more to much greater effect, at only twice the cost with three times the music and infinitely superior sound and notes. *—Bruce Eder*

Inside Looking Out: The 1965-1966 Sessions / 1990 / Sequel ✦✦✦✦✦
Together with the double-CD *The Complete Animals, Inside Looking Out* forms a complete retrospective of the great British Invasion band. This 22-song compilation features all of the essential recordings cut by the group in 1965 and 1966 after they broke with their original producer Mickie Most, and before Eric Burdon dissolved the core of the original lineup to pursue solo stardom with an Animals group featuring entirely different musicians. These tracks were perhaps more soul-oriented than their previous recordings, but the group still burns on the hits "Inside Looking Out" and "Don't Bring Me Down." Despite the absence of original keyboardist Alan Price, the group continued to showcase Burdon's passionate vocals and burning, vibrant organ (by Price's replacement Dave Rowberry) on both renowned and obscure R&B tunes, with an occasional original thrown in. Besides the entirety of their final British LP *Animalisms* (from 1966) and the above-mentioned singles, the CD includes the hits "Help Me Girl" and "See See Rider" (credited to "Eric Burdon and the Animals," these were possibly Burdon solo records). The four tracks from their first release, an independently released 1963 EP featuring primitive R&B standards, are small but noteworthy bonus cuts that close this collection. *—Richie Unterberger*

☆ **The Complete Animals** / Jul. 1990 / EMI ✦✦✦✦✦
The title is a bit of a misnomer; this double CD does include the complete sessions that the Animals recorded with producer Mickie Most in 1964 and 1965. The 40 songs capture the band at their peak, including most of their best and biggest hits: "House of the Rising Sun," "Don't Let Me Be Misunderstood," "Bring It on Home to Me," "We Gotta Get Out of This Place," "I'm Crying," "It's My Life," and "Boom Boom." Most of the rest of the tunes don't match the excellence of these smashes, though they're solid. The great majority of them are covers of vintage R&B/rock tunes by Chuck Berry, Fats Domino, and the like, which aren't quite as durable as reinterpretations from the same era by the Stones and Yardbirds. When they hit the mark, though, the Animals produced some great album tracks that have been mostly forgotten by time, such as "I'm Mad Again" (originally by John Lee Hooker), "Worried Life Blues," and "Bury My Body." After leaving Most, the group would maintain their peak for another year or so (this period is represented on the fine import collection *Inside Looking Out*) despite the departure of one of rock's all-time finest organists, Alan Price. This compilation has everything that Price recorded with the group, including four previously unreleased cuts and the non-LP Eric Burdon original on the B-side of "It's My Life," "I'm Gonna Change the World." *—Richie Unterberger*

Paul Anka

b. Jul. 30, 1941, Ottawa, Ontario, Canada
Vocals / Brill Building Pop, Teen Idol, Pop
Paul Anka was one of the biggest teen idols of the late '50s, and a successful songwriter, music businessman, and recording artist well into the 1990s. After gaining an audition with ABC in 1957, his ode to a former babysitter, "Diana," hit number one on both sides of the Atlantic later that year and eventually sold a reported ten million copies. His biggest American hit however, was "Lonely Boy" from the 1959 film *Girls Town*. As the teen idol craze cooled off in the early '60s, Paul Anka moved to RCA, acquired the rights to his own AB masters, made a fortune on reissues alone, and began moving toward a nightclub background (he was one of the first pop singers to do shows in Las Vegas). Anka also wrote the theme to *The Tonight Show* and the lyrics to Frank Sinatra's trademark "My Way," and also wrote Tom Jones' biggest hit, "She's a Lady." Although he had hit the Top 40 only once since 1963, Paul Anka stormed the number one slot in 1974 with "(You're) Having My Baby," a duet recorded with his singing protege, Odia Coates. Anka continued to chart into the early '80s, continuing his many casino and international appearances while recording sparingly but continually. *—John Bush*

● **30th Anniversary Collection** / Oct. 1989 / Rhino ✦✦✦✦✦
Not many artists can claim a 20-year run of hits, much less be credited with writing the majority of them as well, but Paul Anka can. Starting out as a sawed-off Canadian teen idol, he rocketed to the top of the charts with fare like "Diana," "Put Your Head on My Shoulder," "Lonely Boy," and "Puppy Love" before moving into the '70s with more adult fare like "You're Having My Baby" and "My Way." Pop enthusiasts will appreciate this package, even if rock & roll fans shun his work to the very end. *—Cub Koda*

The Very Best of Paul Anka / Oct. 24, 2000 / RCA ✦✦✦
The Very Best of Paul Anka concentrates on his early RCA recordings, as well as the re-recorded, stereo versions of his first hits that he cut when he switched labels. The revamped versions of "Diana," "You Are My Destiny," "Put Your Head on My Shoulder," and "Puppy Love" are mixed with later singles like "A Steel Guitar and a Glass of Wine," "Remember Diana," "Eso Beso (That Kiss)," and "It Doesn't Matter Any More." Though it doesn't quite live up to its title, *The Very Best of Paul Anka* is still a decent and fairly comprehensive collection of his '60s sound. *—Heather Phares*

Adam Ant (Goddard, Stuart)

b. Nov. 3, 1954, London, England
Vocals, Keyboards / Post-Punk, Pop/Rock, New Wave
One of the seminal figures of new wave, Adam Ant initially explored darkly angular, jagged post-punk with his group Adam & the Ants. After releasing their debut, *Dirk Wears White Sox*, in 1979, Malcolm McLaren became the group's manager, and after he convinced the group to revamp their style and sound, he lured the core of the band away to form Bow Wow Wow. Ant and his faithful guitarist/collaborator Marco Pirroni regrouped, carrying through on their newly revamped image. Dressing up in pirates outfits, streaking their faces with makeup and using thunderous Burundi drumming as an anchor, they developed an infectious, silly, glam-speckled blend of pop and post-punk sensibilities. The group had enormous success in England with their second album, 1980's *Kings of the Wild Frontier*. Over the next few years, Adam & the Ants had several hits, such as "Ant Music" and "Stand and Deliver," and as their popularity grew, their sound got increasingly streamlined and pop-oriented, culminating in Adam Ant's first official solo album, 1982's *Friend or Foe*. This record proved to be his breakthrough to the American pop mainstream, thanks in large part to the clever videos for the title track and "Goody Two Shoes," which were heavily aired on MTV. With 1985's *Viva Le Rock*, the slickness outweighed the substance, and his sales dropped dramatically. Ant turned to acting, releasing his next album, *Manners & Physique*, in 1990, which faded away after a moderately successful single in "Room at the Top." As Ant again concentrated on acting, a new generation of bands, such as Nine Inch Nails and Elastica, built on his influence. During this revival, Ant released the understated 1995's *Wonderful*. It did respectable business, yet Ant again retreated from music until 2000 when he released the triple-disc retrospective, *Antbox*. *—Stephen Thomas Erlewine*

Dirk Wears White Sox / Dec. 1979 / Epic ✦✦✦✦✦
The original Ants line-up released only one LP, *Dirk Wears White Sox* for Do It in 1979. The album finds a young Adam Ant exploring the sometimes-awkward fusion of punk, glam, and minimalist post-punk with bizarre images and disturbing tales of alienation, sex, and brutality. And while the somewhat pretentious, overly-arty lyrics and inexperienced playing are a drawback, the album offers a fascinating look at the Ants' formative years, capturing a raw energy that would be sacrificed for more polish on subsequent releases. [At the height of Antmania, Adam Ant acquired the rights to the album, re-mixing it, dropping a few tracks, and adding a couple of early tracks for reissue in 1983 with a different cover for Epic. In 1995, Sony Music U.K. released a hybrid version for CD, restoring the cover art, original mixes, and the previously dropped tracks but retaining the additions and running order of the reissue. Epic chose to keep the re-mixed version for CD release in the U.S.] *—Chris Woodstra*

Kings of the Wild Frontier / 1980 / Epic ✦✦✦✦✦
Combining pounding tom-toms (from two drummers and drum kits), a guitar style adapted from Ennio Morricone movie soundtracks and a visual motif borrowed from pirates and Native Americans, Adam & the Ants had a brief run as Britain's top band in the wake of the punk/power-pop days of the late '70s. This second album was their apex, featuring the signature tune "Antmusic." *—William Ruhlmann*

Prince Charming / 1981 / Epic ✦✦✦
The final album with the Ants is bland in comparison to the brilliant *Kings of the Wild Frontier* with the band drifting dangerously close to "new romantic" territory. While "Stand and Deliver" is one of the high points of the band's career, the cringe-worthy "Ant Rap" is certainly the low point. The essential tracks can all be found on *Antics in the Forbidden Zone* so only completists need bother. *—Chris Woodstra*

Friend or Foe / 1982 / Epic ✦✦✦
As a solo artist, Adam Ant struck gold in the U.S. with this album, which adopts the same musical style as that of the Ants and features the hit "Goody Two Shoes" and a version of the Doors' "Hello, I Love You." *—William Ruhlmann*

Strip / Nov. 1983 / Epic ✦✦

Vive Le Rock / 1985 / Epic ✦✦

Manners & Physique / Feb. 1990 / MCA ✦✦

● **Antics in the Forbidden Zone** / Oct. 1990 / Epic ✦✦✦✦✦
The most comprehensive overview of the band. In 22 tracks, all of the hits are represented as well as key album cuts and a rare B-side, "Beat My Guest." An essential part of any new wave collection. *—Chris Woodstra*

B-Side Babies! / Sep. 27, 1994 / Epic/Legacy ✦✦✦✦

Wonderful / Mar. 7, 1995 / Capitol ✦✦✦

Antbox / Nov. 2000 / Epic ✦✦✦✦✦
There are some that will scoff at the very idea of a comprehensive, three-disc box set overview of Adam Ant's career, dismissing him as nothing more than a New Wave fad. Let 'em laugh, since *Antbox* proves that he, along with trusty guitarist sidekick Marco Pirroni, was a post-punk heavyweight, adept at creating claustrophobic dark angular tunes and giddy glam revivals with equal. *Antbox* gives room to both sides of the equation, and it's one of the rare boxes that succeeds precisely because of its rarities, which not only add depth and dimension, they fill in gaps in his history—particularly on the first disc, which is devoted entirely to pre-*Kings of the Wild Frontier* material, including demos, singles, BBC sessions, and rejected audition tapes for Decca. This is the cream of the crop of literally hundreds of unreleased songs from the *Dirk Wears White Sox* era ,and the amazing thing is, they more than hold their own with what actually made the cut. The high quality is maintained on the second disc, which contains all the blockbusters, sometimes duplicated in alternate versions which are interesting, not excessive. If the quality dips dramatically on the last disc, despite a few good unreleased cuts plus the absence of *Manners & Physique* (MCA/Universal wouldn't license the recordings), it still is the best way to listen to these years and "Wonderful" remains a career-capping return to form. Yes, three discs is a bit much for most listeners, especially three discs filled with rarities, but this is the truest testament to Adam Ant's gifts as a musician. Any serious post-punk/New Wave fan will find this a fascinating, revelatory set. *—Stephen Thomas Erlewine*

Anthrax

f. Jun. 1981, New York, NY
Group / Rap-Metal, Speed Metal, Heavy Metal, Thrash
Nearly as much as Metallica or Megadeth, Anthrax was responsible for the emergence of speed and thrash metal; combining the speed and fury of hardcore punk with the prominent guitars and vocals of heavy metal, they helped create a new subgenre of heavy metal on their early albums. Original guitarists Scott Ian and Dan Spitz were a formidable pair, spitting out lightning fast riffs and solos that never seemed masturbatory. Unlike Metallica or Megadeth, they had the good sense to temper their often serious music with a healthy dose of humor

and realism. After their first album, *Fistful of Metal*, singer Joey Belladonna joined the lineup; he helped take the band further away from conventional metal clichés, and over the next five albums (with the exception of 1988's *State of Euphoria*, where the band sounded like they were in a creative strait-jacket), Anthrax arguably became the leaders of speed metal. As the '80s became the '90s, they also began to increase their experiments with hip-hop, culminating in a tour with Public Enemy in 1991 and a joint re-recording of PE's classic "Bring the Noise." *—Stephen Thomas Erlewine*

Fistful of Metal / 1984 / Megaforce ✦✦

Armed and Dangerous / 1985 / Megaforce ✦✦✦
An EP featuring the debut of vocalist Joey Belladonna and bassist Frank Bello, *Armed and Dangerous* is mostly composed of songs originally recorded for the band's debut, *Fistful of Metal*. As such, the band sounds better, but were still in the process of coming up with quality material and truly hitting their stride. *—Steve Huey*

Spreading the Disease / 1985 / Megaforce/Island ✦✦✦✦
Anthrax's first album with vocalist Joey Belladonna is a huge leap forward, featuring strongly rhythmic, pounding riffs and vocals that alternate between hardcore-type shouting and surprising amounts of melody. Two tracks left over from the Lilker days are here as well. The traditional metal lyrical fare is more original, while also introducing a penchant for paying tribute to favorite fictional characters and pop-culture artifacts ("Lone Justice" and "Medusa" are prime examples). One of Anthrax's best efforts. *—Steve Huey*

Among the Living / 1987 / Megaforce/Island ✦✦✦✦✦
Generally considered the band's best album, *Among the Living* broadened the scope of Anthrax's subject matter with socially conscious lyrics addressing prejudice, violence, drug abuse ("Efilnikufesin [N.F.L.]," a rip on John Belushi), and the hollowness of the music business, as well as a politically correct ode to the "Indians." However, the band refuses to take itself too seriously, also recording tributes to Stephen King and Judge Dredd. Musically, the band delivers a powerful, aggressive roar driven by impossibly fast riffing, changing tempos, and collectively shouted vocals of hardcore, especially on the classic "Caught in a Mosh." The brutal rhythm guitar work of Scott Ian and the explosive drumming of Charlie Benante relentlessly pushes the songs along while still maintaining a solid groove, and more than makes up for some lyrical awkwardness. *Among the Living* remains arguably Anthrax's foremost achievement. *—Steve Huey*

I'm the Man / 1987 / Megaforce/Island ✦✦✦✦
This EP features three versions of the title track, the group's pioneering fusion of rap and heavy metal, plus a cover of Black Sabbath's "Sabbath, Bloody Sabbath" and live performances of *Among the Living*'s "Caught in a Mosh" and "I Am the Law." While artists like the Beastie Boys and Run-D.M.C. had experimented with rock/rap fusion, Anthrax was the first band on the rock side of the equation to do so, and their take was naturally harder and heavier than anything that came before. Of course, the experiment wouldn't have worked if Anthrax's music hadn't already relied on strongly rhythmic grooves, and their playful sense of humor didn't hurt either. A must-hear. *—Steve Huey*

State of Euphoria / 1988 / Megaforce/Island ✦✦✦
The proper follow-up to *Among the Living* was somewhat disappointing in its inconsistency. While there are some good moments—"Be All, End All" is one of the band's most melodic moments, and several other tracks catch fire—the best thing here is a cover of Trust's "Antisocial," and it doesn't bode well when covers outshine original material. The lyrics continue the self-consciously intellectual, P.C. approach begun on *Among the Living*, but about half of the album is surprisingly dull. *—Steve Huey*

Persistence of Time / Aug. 1990 / Megaforce/Island ✦✦✦✦

Attack of the Killer B's / Jun. 1991 / Island ✦✦✦✦

Sound of White Noise / May 1993 / Elektra ✦✦✦

Live—the Island Years / Apr. 5, 1994 / Island ✦✦✦

Stomp 442 / Oct. 24, 1995 / Elektra ✦✦

● **Return of the Killer A's: The Best of Anthrax** / Nov. 23, 1999 / Beyond ✦✦✦✦

Any Trouble

f. 1975, Manchester, England, **db.** Dec. 1984
Group / Pub Rock, New Wave
Any Trouble was an underappreciated bright spot on Stiff Records, a label which had no shortage of talented artists. Bandleader Clive Gregson's appearance, hardened love songs, and vocal style may have led to comparisons to Elvis Costello, but they were no second-rate rip-off—each of their four albums revealed a songwriter of unique talent and a more-than-capable band to execute the songs. Manchester native Gregson formed the original band in 1975 as a folky trio; by 1976, Any Trouble was a four-piece rock group, speeding up their repertoire in response to the punk movement. They built a strong following playing the pub circuit and signed with Stiff Records by 1980. Any Trouble's first album, *Where Are All the Nice Girls?*, had all the makings of a new wave classic. It was met with some rave reviews, but failed to rack up the big sales that were expected of it. *Wheels in Motion* (1981), while certainly more accomplished, lacked the spark of the first album and simply didn't catch on in the U.K. Halfway through a small stateside tour, the band heard by word-of-mouth that they had been dropped by Stiff and were left stranded in America. Eventually they found their way back, but the stress of the situation broke up the band temporarily. A new deal was arranged with EMI-America, and what was essentially a new band behind Gregson recorded *Any Trouble* in 1983. Again, the same story—the reviews were good, but the band's cult status didn't change. Gregson, knowing the band couldn't last much longer, decided to stretch out for *Wrong End of the Race*, a sprawling double album that allowed the band to show their diversity and influences. In December of 1984, the band played their last gig and called it quits. Gregson went on to a distinguished, though still underappreciated, career both as a solo artist and as a collaborator with Christine Collister. *—Chris Woodstra*

● **Where Are All the Nice Girls?** / 1980 / Compass ✦✦✦✦✦
Where Are All the Nice Girls? is a pure pub/pop/rock gem. Leading off with the infectious "Second Choice" (one of the great "should have been hits") and ending up with the unlikely ABBA cover "Name of the Game," Gregson and company run though 12 tunes, almost all obsessed with love gone wrong. A cult favorite. [In 1997, Compass Records reissued *Where Are All the Nice Girls?* on CD, dropping the ABBA cover in favor of adding the single "Yesterday's Love" and "Honolulu" (a track originally dropped from the U.S. edition).] *—Chris Woodstra*

Live at the Venue / 1981 / Line ✦✦✦✦✦
Originally released as a promo for radio, this live show from 1980 finds the band in its natural setting. Playing with higher energy than in the studio, this provides the best picture of the band at its peak. *—Chris Woodstra*

Wheels in Motion / Aug. 1981 / Stiff ✦✦✦
The playing on their sophomore effort is more sophisticated and the production is cleaner but it lacks some of the bite of the first album. Gregson's now-standard obsession makes an appearance on the album's highlight, "Trouble with Love." *—Chris Woodstra*

Any Trouble / 1983 / EMI ✦✦✦

Wrong End of the Race / 1984 / BGO ✦✦✦
Wrong End of the Race compiles unnecessary re-recordings of previously released songs, some new tracks, and a few interesting covers. Knowing that this would be their final album, Gregson attempted to assemble material that would show the band's diversity and their wide variety of influences. And while this does reveal some interesting sides to the band, ultimately, the exercise misses more often than it hits. *—Chris Woodstra*

Aphex Twin (Richard D. James)

b. Aug. 18, 1971
Producer / IDM, Drill'n'bass, Experimental Jungle, Experimental Techno, Electronica, Ambient-Techno, Acid Techno, Trance, Techno
Exploring the experimental possibilities inherent in acid and ambience, the two major influences on home-listening techno during the late '80s, Richard D. James' recordings as Aphex Twin brought him more critical praise than any other electronic artist during the 1990s. Though his first major single "Didgeridoo" was a piece of acid thrash designed to tire dancers during his DJ sets, ambient stylists and critics later took him under their wing for *Selected Ambient Works 85-92*, a sublime touchstone in the field of ambient-techno. James' reaction to the exposure portrayed an artist unwilling to become either pigeonholed or categorizable. His second Aphex Twin album, *Selected Ambient Works, Vol. 2*, was so minimal as to be barely conscious—in what appeared to be an elaborate joke on the electronic community. Follow-ups showed James gradually returning to his hardcore and acid roots, even while his stated desire to crash the British Top Ten (and perform on *Top of the Pops*) resulted in a series of cartoonish pop songs whose twisted genius was near-masked by their many absurdities. His iconoclastic behavior surprisingly aligned with MTV audiences turned on to end-of-the-millennium nihilist-pop along the lines of Marilyn Manson and Nine Inch Nails. *—John Bush*

★ **Selected Ambient Works 85-92** / 1993 / Apollo ✦✦✦✦✦
Selected Ambient Works is a desperately sparse album: thin percussion and several haunted-synth lines are the only components on most songs, and Richard D. James added only one vocal sample on the entire album ("We are the music makers, and we are the dreamers of dreams"). Also, the sound quality is relatively poor; it was recorded direct to cassette tape and reportedly suffered a mangling job by a cat. All this belies the status of *Selected Ambient Works* as a watershed of ambient music. It reveals no influences and sounds unlike anything that preceded it, due in large part to the effects James managed to wrangle from his supply of home-manufactured contraptions. *—John Bush*

Selected Ambient Works, Vol. 2 / Mar. 8, 1994 / Sire ✦✦✦
Selected Ambient Works, Vol. 2 is a more difficult and challenging album than the Aphex Twin's previous collection. The music is all texture; there are only the faintest traces of beats and forward movement. Instead, all of these untitled tracks are long, unsettling electronic soundscapes, alternately quiet and confrontational; although most of the music is rather subdued, it is never easy listening. While some listeners may find this double-disc album dull (both discs run over 70 minutes), many listeners will be intrigued and fascinated by the intricately detailed music of the Aphex Twin. *—Stephen Thomas Erlewine*

Classics / 1995 / R&S ✦✦✦

I Care Because You Do / Apr. 25, 1995 / Sire ✦✦✦✦
James' most consistent work, *I Care Because You Do* fuses his earlier hardcore techno days with the smooth rhythm and atmosphere of his ambient work, often on the same song. "Ventolin" is one of the harshest singles ever recorded; the orchestrated closer "Next Heap With" is the highlight of the album. *—John Bush*

Richard D. James Album / Nov. 4, 1996 / Elektra ✦✦✦✦✦
Perhaps inspired by the experimental drum'n'bass being created by Squarepusher (a recent signee to his Rephlex label), Richard D. James' third major-label album as Aphex Twin was his first to work with jungle—though, to his credit, he had released the breakbeat EP *Hangable Auto Bulb* almost a year earlier. Contemporaries Orbital and Underworld were beginning to incorporate moderate use of drum'n'bass in their work as well, but this album was more extreme than virtually all jungle being made at the time. The beats are jackhammer quick and even more jarring considering what is—for the most part—laid over the top: the same fragile, slow-moving melodies that characterized Aphex Twin's earlier ambient works. Most overtly disturbing is "Milkman," the first straight-ahead vocal track from Aphex Twin; the song is a child-like ode that gradually deteriorates into a bizarre fantasy concerning the milkman's wife. With all the Aphex Twin's curious idiosyncracies, though, *Richard D. James Album* is a very listenable record and a worthy follow-up to *I Care Because You Do*. [The American issue features the English EP "Girl/Boy."] *—John Bush*

Come to Daddy EP / Oct. 6, 1997 / Warp ♦♦♦♦

Fiona Apple

b. 1977

Vocals / Adult Alternative Pop/Rock, Alternative Pop/Rock, Singer/Songwriter

Singer/songwriter Fiona Apple gained a recording contract in 1995 as one in a crop of mid-'90s female artists, but her confessional writing and throaty vocals made the teenager sound like much more than just the latest flavor. Born in 1977 in New York to singer Diana McAfee and actor Brandon Maggart, Fiona Apple began playing the piano at the age of eight and started composing her own songs just four years later, after the separation of her parents and her own brutal rape. After leaving high school at the age of 16, she journeyed to Los Angeles to see her father and make a demo tape of her songs. After several months of tape-passing, Sony Music signed Apple in 1995. After recording *Tidal* with producer Andrew Slater, she released the album in mid-1996 and began touring. Constant videoplay of the single "Shadowboxer" on both MTV and VH1 brought *Tidal* into the upper reaches of the album charts. The long-awaited *When the Pawn Hits the Conflicts He Thinks Like a King What He Knows Throws the Blows When He Goes to the Fight and He'll Win the Whole Thing' 'Fore He Enters the Ring There's No Body to Batter When Your Mind Is Your Might So When You Go Solo, You Hold Your Own Hand and Remember That Depth Is the Greatest of Heights and if You Know Where You Stand, Then You Know Where to Land and if You Fall It Won't Matter, 'Cuz You'll Know That You're Right*—the album's full title—followed in 1999. *—John Bush*

Tidal / Jul. 23, 1996 / Clean Slate/Epic ♦♦♦♦

Fiona Apple demonstrates considerable talent on her debut album *Tidal*, but it is unformed, unfocused talent. Her voice is surprisingly rich and supple for a teenager, and her jazzy, sophisticated piano playing also belies her age. Given the right material, such talents could have flourished, but she has concentrated on her own compositions, which are nowhere near as impressive as her musicianship. Most of *Tidal* is comprised of confessional singer/-songwriter material, and while they strive to say something deep and important, much of the lyrics settle for cliches. Apple does have a handful of impressive songs on *Tidal*, like the haunting "Shadowboxer" and "Sullen Girl," but the gap between her performing talents and songwriting skills is too large to make the album anything more than a promising, and very intriguing, debut. *—Stephen Thomas Erlewine*

● **When the Pawn Hits the Conflicts He Thinks Like a King . . .** / Nov. 9, 1999 / Clean Slate/Epic ♦♦♦♦♦

Fiona Apple may have been grouped in with the other female singer/songwriters who dominated the pop charts in 1996 and 1997, but she stood out by virtue of her grand ambitions and considerable musical sophistication. Even though her 1996 debut *Tidal* occasionally was hampered by naïvéte, it showcased a gifted young artist in the process of finding her voice. Even so, the artistic leap between *Tidal* and its long-awaited 1999 sequel *When the Pawn Hits . . .* is startling. It's evident that not only have Apple's ambitions grown, so has her confidence—few artists would open themselves up to the ridicule that comes with having a 90-word poem function as the full title, but that captures the fearless feeling of the record. Apple doesn't break from the jazzy pop of *Tidal* on *Pawn*, choosing instead to refine her sound and then expand its horizons. Although there are echoes of everything from Nina Simone to Aimee Mann on the record, it's not easy to spot specific influences, because this is truly an individual work. As a songwriter, she balances her words and melodies skillfully, no longer sounding self-conscious as she crafts highly personal, slightly cryptic songs that never sound precocious or insular. With producer Jon Brion, she created the ideal arrangements for these idiosyncratic songs, finding a multi-layered sound that's simultaneously elegant and carnivalesque. As a result, *Pawn* is immediately grabbing, and instead of fading upon further plays, it reveals more with each listen, whether it's a lyrical turn of phrase or an unexpected twist in the arrangement; what's more, Apple has made it as rich emotionally as it is musically. That's quite a feat for any album, but it's doubly impressive since it is the only the second effort by a musician who is only 22 years old. *—Stephen Thomas Erlewine*

The Art of Noise

f. Jan. 1984, London, England

Group / Experimental Rock, New Wave, Synth-Pop

Anne Dudley, Gary Lanagan, and J.J. Jeczalik were members of producer Trevor Horn's in-house studio band in the early '80s before they formed Art of Noise, a techno-pop group whose music was an amalgam of studio gimmickry, tape splicing, and synthesized beats. The Art of Noise took material from a variety of sources: hip-hop, rock, jazz, R&B, traditional pop, found sounds, and noise all worked their way into the group's distinctly post-modern soundscapes. The trio signed with Trevor Horn's ZTT label, releasing their first EP, *Into Battle with the Art of Noise*, in 1983. The following year, they released the full-length *(Who's Afraid Of?) The Art of Noise!*, which featured the hit single "Close (To the Edit)." 1986's *In Visible Silence* included the U.K. Top Ten hit "Peter Gunn," which featured Duane Eddy on guitar. *In No Sense? Nonsense!*, released in 1987, saw the band experimenting with orchestras and choirs, as well as horns and rock bands. *Below the Waste* (1990) captured the band experimenting with world music; it received a lukewarm critical and commercial reception. *—Stephen Thomas Erlewine*

Into Battle with the Art of Noise / 1983 / ZTT/Island ♦♦♦

(Who's Afraid Of?) The Art of Noise! / 1984 / ZTT/Island ♦♦♦♦♦

Art of Noise's first full album consolidated the future shock of the earlier EPs and singles in one entertaining and often frightening and screwed-up package. Rarely has something aiming for modern pop status also sought to destroy and disturb so effectively. The most legendary song is still "Close (To the Edit)," benefiting not merely from the innovative video but from its strong funk groove and nutty sense of humor in the mostly lyric-less vocals, not to mention the "Hey!" vocal hook the Prodigy would sample for "Firestarter." Its close cousin, the title track, brilliantly blends a nagging bass synth, echoed drum, and percussion fills and constantly shifting vocal cut-ups, random noises, and strange melodies. They're just two highlights on this prescient release, though. Part of the thrill of *Who's Afraid* is the sense of juxtaposition and playing around, something still not very common in music and even less so in the pop music genre. The blunt political protest of "A Time for Fear (Who's Afraid)" and the more abstract "How to Kill," achieved via appropriate sampling, slams right up against the rough beat sonics and serene orchestration. If such material had appeared on Rephlex or even DHR in the mid- to late '90s, few would have been surprised. Things aren't all dour and gloomy, though; "Beat Box" captures heavy grooves from said source with quirky vocal bits and soft vibes. Patented Trevor Horn orchestral stabs surface throughout, while Anne Dudley's knack for gentler shadings and dramatic arrangements also comes through clearly, something that would surface ever more strongly in her freelance production career. The full ten-minute version of "Moments in Love" is perhaps her triumph here, a seemingly pretty instrumental turned increasingly strange. *—Ned Raggett*

In Visible Silence / 1986 / China/Chrysalis ♦♦♦

Daft / 1987 / Uptown/Universal ♦♦♦♦

● **The Best of the Art of Noise** / 1988 / China/Polydor ♦♦♦♦♦

As an overview of Art of Noise's brief output, this best-of can't be beat, though it does inadvertently track their slide from forerunners to recyclers and cultural panderers. The 1-2-3 rush of "Beat Box," "Moments in Love," and "Close (To the Edit)" make this CD worth the money already—at the time of their release, these singles swiped electronic music back from America (by way of Germany) and cut the whole thing up with ridiculous samples (a car starting, the omnipresent orchestral hit) and enjoyable art school posturing. It was like Dada had invaded the charts, circa 1984. But soon, after their break with ZTT and joining China Records, it wasn't long until they were parodying themselves and trying to score pop hits with a recognizable "sound." Singles featured older pop stars trying to score a hit again (Duane Eddy on "Peter Gunn," Tom Jones on "Kiss"), current celebrities riding their own popularity wave (Max Headroom), or cover songs gussied up with a few more car starting sounds (the made-for-hire "Dragnet '88," used in the regrettable film remake). Only "Legs," which even then still borrows all its drum sounds from "Close (To the Edit)," sounds like a real follow up, and—no pun intended—can stand on its own feet. The vinyl version contains the (sometimes preferable) single mixes; the CD and cassette contain 12" remixes, good for the collector, bad on the patience. A similarly covered CD, only in pink (and released two years later), is also called "The Best Of" but focuses more on the group's album tracks. *—Ted Mills*

The Seduction of Claude Debussy / Jun. 15, 1999 / ZTT/Universal ♦♦

Frankie Avalon (Francis Avallone)

b. Sep. 18, 1939, Philadelphia, PA

Vocals / Teen Idol, Pop

Frankie Avalon was the first of the manufactured teen idols, before Fabian and Bobby Rydell and the myriads of other pretenders to the throne who worked the turf with tight black pants and red, red sweaters to the fore while Elvis cooled his heels in Germany. In the late '50s and early '60s, post-Twist and pre-Beatles, these generally untalented pretty boys were the cardboard no-threat remnants of a post-Elvis age. But Avalon had a real musical background to go with the pretty boy looks. He broke into show business as a child prodigy trumpeter, and made a few early records for a subsidiary of RCA Victor. Later on, a local impresario became more impressed with his vocals than his trumpet playing and signed him. His third single, "De De Dinah," became a Top Ten hit and with 1959's "Venus," Avalon placed his first number one. He gradually eased into more "adult" fare, and though his chart domination ended in 1962, Avalon reinvented himself as a clean-cut surfer in a wildly successful batch of *Beach Party* movies with Annette Funicello that got him through the '60s in far better shape than most of his colleagues. Though he quit recording, he continued to perform and appeared on an oldies revival show with Bobby Rydell and Fabian into the 1990s. *—Cub Koda*

● **The Best of Frankie Avalon** / Apr. 11, 1995 / Varese Sarabande ♦♦♦♦♦

The definitive compilation: the original versions of 18 songs from 1958-1962, all but one of them a chart hit of some sort. Has all the Top Ten smashes and a bunch of minor post-1959 singles that found him swinging toward pop crooner material with barely any relation to rock & roll whatsoever. *—Richie Unterberger*

Kevin Ayers

b. Aug. 16, 1945, Herne Bay, Kent, England

Vocals, Guitar, Bass / Canterbury Scene, British Psychedelia, Prog Rock/Art Rock

Kevin Ayers is one of rock's oddest and more likable enigmas, even if often he's seemed not to operate at his highest potential. Perhaps that's because he's never seemed to have taken his music too seriously—one of his essential charms *and* most aggravating limitations. Since the late '60s, he's released many albums with a distinctly British sensibility, making ordinary lyrical subjects seem extraordinary with his rich low vocals, inventive wordplay, and bemused, relaxed attitude. Apt to flavor his songs with female backup choruses and exotic island rhythms, the singer/songwriter inspires the image of a sort of progressive rock beach bum, writing about life's absurdities with a celebratory, relaxed detachment. Yet he is also one of progressive rock's more important (and more humane) innovators, helping to launch the Soft Machine as their original bassist, and working with noted European progressive musicians like Mike Oldfield, Lol Coxhill, and Steve Hillage. *—Richie Unterberger*

Joy of a Toy / Nov. 1969 / BGO ♦♦♦

As the Soft Machine's first bassist and original principal songwriter, Kevin Ayers was an overlooked force behind the group's groundbreaking recordings in 1967 and 1968. This, his solo debut, is so tossed-off and nonchalant that one gets the impression he wanted to take it easy after helping pilot the manic innovations of the Softs. Laissez-faire sloth has always been part of Ayers' persona, and this record's intermittent lazy charm helped establish it. That doesn't get around the fact, however, that this set of early progressive rock does not feature extremely strong material. Ayers' command of an assortment of instruments is impressive, and his deep bass vocals and playful, almost goofy song-sketches are affecting, but they don't really stick with the listener. It's no accident that some of the tracks recall early Soft Machine: Robert Wyatt drums on most of the songs, and "Song for Insane Times" is virtually a bona fide Soft Machine performance, featuring actual backing from the group itself. A likable but slight album that is at its best when Ayers is at his folkiest. *—Richie Unterberger*

Shooting at the Moon / Mar. 1970 / BGO ✦✦

Whatevershebringswesing / Jan. 1971 / BGO ✦✦✦✦✦
This album of songs about melancholy and solitude may, at first, seem like a disparate collection. After listening a few times, the essence of the song cycle becomes clear. The near-hit "Stranger in Blue Suede Shoes" and "Song from the Bottom of a Well" are among the standout tracks. *—Jim Powers*

Bananamour / May 1973 / BGO ✦✦✦
A solid, enjoyable collection of songs written from the point of view of Kevin Ayers' own particular brand of existentialism—self-conscious individualism sustained by plenty of wine. The American version of this album contains the near-hit "Caribbean Moon," as well as the Syd Barrett tribute "Oh Wot a Dream." *—Jim Powers*

Sweet Deceiver / Mar. 1975 / BGO ✦✦✦
One of Ayers' more mainstream efforts. Any album that has Elton John playing piano on a few tracks can't be too weird. That's not to say, though, that this is exactly mainstream in and of itself. Ayers continues to play his offhandedly charming miniatures, with occasional Caribbean rhythms and trademark droll, bemused lyrics. The problem is that while this has its charm while you're listening, little of it sticks or incites you to return. By this point in his career, Ayers was in danger of catching on a treadmill, restating his idiosyncratic concerns in familiar ways without amplifying them. *—Richie Unterberger*

Odd Ditties / 1976 / Harvest ✦✦✦✦✦
It is indeed an oddity that, for all the considerable ambition of his albums, this collection of singles and unreleased outtakes may be Ayers' most satisfying LP. Why? Perhaps because when he's constrained within the 45 format, he taps his strongest and most endearing qualities: easygoing, singalong melodies, droll, nonchalant (even non sequitur) lyrics, good-natured sotto voce vocals, even female backup harmonies. There's little trace of the inaccessible, difficult (usually instrumental) passages that occupy much of the space on his early albums. Spanning 1969 to 1973, this includes eight tracks that wound up on flop singles, as well as six outtakes from the albums he recorded during this period, though there were no obvious reasons for their exclusion (too pop oriented, perhaps?). These are, indeed, "odd ditties": catchy, with occasional Caribbean rhythms and French lyrics, but way too goofball to be taken to heart by a mass audience, at times sounding like a more together Syd Barrett. Needless to say, none of these nifty tunes were anything close to hits. But if they had been, the world would have been a better place. *—Richie Unterberger*

Yes We Have No Mañanas / Jul. 1976 / BGO ✦✦✦

Rainbow Takeaway / Apr. 1978 / BGO ✦✦

● **Kevin Ayers Collection** / 1983 / See For Miles ✦✦✦✦✦
This hour-long chronological sampling of Ayers' Harvest and Island discs features several rare single sides (like "Puis-Je?," the French version of "May I?") in addition to some of his best album cuts. With an extensive biographical essay in the liner notes, this is the ideal place to get acquainted with Ayers' work. *—Jim Powers*

Too Old to Die Young: BBC Live 1972-76 / Sep. 22, 1998 / Hux ✦✦✦

The B-52's

f. Oct. 1976, Athens, GA, **db.** 1994
Group / College Rock, Post-Punk, New Wave, Alternative Pop/Rock
The first of many acts to cement the college town of Athens, GA as a hotbed of alternative music, the B-52's took their name from the Southern slang for the mile-high bouffant wigs sported by singers Kate Pierson and Cindy Wilson, a look emblematic of the band's campy, thrift-store aesthetic. The group formed in the mid-1970s after a drunken evening at a Chinese restaurant; the band members had little or no previous musical experience, and performed most of their earliest shows with taped guitar and percussion accompaniment. After pressing up a few thousand copies of the single "Rock Lobster," the B-52's travelled to the famed Max's Kansas City club for their first paying gig. Subsequent appearances at CBGB's brought the group to the attention of the New York press, and in 1979, they issued their self-titled debut album, a collection of manic, bizarre, and eminently danceable songs which scored an underground club hit with a reworked version of "Rock Lobster." The following year, they issued *Wild Planet*, which reached the Top 20 on the U.S. album charts. 1989's *Cosmic Thing* was their most commercially successful effort to date—marked by club-friendly production from Don Was and Nile Rodgers, the album launched several hit singles, including the party smash "Love Shack," "Roam," and "Deadbeat Club." *—Jason Ankeny*

★ **The B-52's** / Jul. 1979 / Warner Brothers ✦✦✦✦✦
Even in the weird, quirky world of new wave and post-punk in the late '70s, the B-52's' eponymous debut stood out as an original. Unabashed kitsch mavens at a time when their peers were either vulgar or stylish, the Athens quintet celebrated all the silliest aspects of pre-Beatles pop culture—bad hairdos, sci-fi nightmares, dance crazes, pastels, and anything else that sprung into their minds—to a skewed fusion of pop, surf, avant-garde, amateurish punk and white funk. On paper, it sounds like a cerebral exercise, but it played like a party. The jerky, angular funk was irresistibly danceable, winning over listeners dubious of Kate Pierson and Cindy Wilson's high-pitched, shrill close harmonies and Fred Schneider's campy, flamboyant vocalizing, pitched halfway between singing and speaking. It's all great fun, but it wouldn't have resonated throughout the years if the group hadn't written such incredibly infectious, memorable tunes as "Planet Claire," "Dance This Mess Around," and, of course, their signature tune "Rock Lobster." These songs illustrated that the B-52's' adoration of camp culture wasn't simply affectation—it was a world view capable of turning out brilliant pop singles and, in turn, influencing mainstream pop culture. It's difficult to imagine the endless kitschy retro fads of the '80s and '90s without the B-52's pointing the way, but *The B-52's* isn't simply an historic artifact—it's a hell of a good time. *—Stephen Thomas Erlewine*

Wild Planet / Sep. 1980 / Warner Brothers ✦✦✦
Conventional wisdom has it that all the B-52's' subsequent releases are highly inferior to their debut. While *Wild Planet* is not the rarefied wonder their first platter is, it's still darned good. The songs here are generally faster, tighter, and punchier than previously, though production values are not as wonderfully quirky and detailed; fewer songs here are as over-the-top crazy as the first album's "Rock Lobster" or "52 Girls." These formless selections continue to exhibit a cunning mix of girl-group, garage band, surf, and television theme song influences, all propelled along by an itchy dance beat. "Give Me Back My Man" allows Cindy Wilson a unique opportunity to croon a broad, expressive melodic line. Fred Schneider parades his inimitably nervous vocals on chucklesome ditties like "Quiche Lorraine" and "Strobe Light." The best songs here are "Private Idaho," a wonderfully jittery number that employs a variant on the famous melodic snippet from the *Twilight Zone* theme music, and "Devil In My Car," a delightfully loopy hoot that lays the craziness on very thickly. Performances and sound quality are fine. This album is well worth hearing and recommended. *—David Cleary*

Whammy! / Apr. 1983 / Warner Brothers ✦✦✦
Following the botched collaboration with David Byrne on *Mesopotamia*, the B-52's decided to craft their fourth album as return to the pop-culture funk explosion of their debut. Smartly, they decided to not simply replicate the skewed Southern funk of that album, choosing to update their signature sound with drum machines and new wave synths. As a result, it now sounds a little forced and dated, but the best moments—"Legal Tender," "Whammy Kiss," "Butterbean," "Song for a Future Genartion"—rank as B-52's classics, and the entire record is certainly entertaining, even with its faults. [*Whammy!* was originally released with a cover of Yoko Ono's "Don't Worry." When the time came to reissue the CD in 1989, the group ran into copyright troubles with Ono and the song was pulled, replaced by "Moon 83."] *—Stephen Thomas Erlewine*

Cosmic Thing / Jun. 1989 / Reprise ✦✦✦✦
Many observers were prepared to write the B-52's off after the release of *Bouncing off the Satellites*. Granted, the album was completed in the wake of Ricky Wilson's death, but the group appeared bereft of new musical ideas and were sounding rather stale. In other words, the last thing anyone expected was a first-class return to form, which is what they got with *Cosmic Thing*. Working with producers Don Was and Nile Rodgers, the B-52's updated their sound with shiny new surfaces and deep, funky grooves—it was the same basic pattern as before, only refurbished and contemporized. Just as importantly, they had their best set of songs since at least *Wild Planet*, possibly since their debut. "Cosmic Thing" and "Channel Z" were great uptempo rockers; "Roam" had a groovy beat blessed with a great Cindy Wilson vocal; and "Deadbeat Club" was one of their rare successful reflective numbers. Then there was "Love Shack," an irresistible dance number with delightfully silly lyrics and hooks as big as a whale that unbelievably gave the group a long-awaited Top Ten hit. The thing is, *Cosmic Thing* would already have been considered a triumphant return without its commercial success. The big sales were just the icing on the cake. *—Stephen Thomas Erlewine*

Party Mix/Mesopotamia / Feb. 1991 / Warner Brothers ✦✦

Good Stuff / Jun. 23, 1992 / Reprise ✦✦

● **Time Capsule** / May 26, 1998 / Warner Brothers ✦✦✦✦✦
Time Capsule: Songs for a Future Generation is an excellent, 18-track collection that offers a comprehensive overview of the B-52's' career, from their kitschy post-punk beginnings to their unexpected chart success in the early '90s. Along the way, all the big songs—"Planet Claire," "Rock Lobster," "Private Idaho," "Quiche Lorraine," "Summer of Love" (in its original mix), "Channel Z," "Deadbeat Club," "Love Shack," "Roam," "Good Stuff"—are here, making this an ideal choice for casual fans. For collectors, there are two new cuts ("Debbie," "Hallucinating Pluto") which are fine, but not particularly noteworthy outside of the fact they're only available on this disc. Then again, the very idea behind *Time Capsule* is to provide a concise introduction for the curious, and on that level, it works perfectly. *—Stephen Thomas Erlewine*

Party Mix / Jul. 1981 / Warner Brothers ✦✦

Bouncing Off the Satellites / Sep. 1986 / Warner Brothers ✦✦

Best of the B-52's: Dance This Mess Around / 1990 / Island ✦✦✦✦
Released only in the U.K., Japan, and various parts of Europe in 1990, *The Best of the B-52's: Dance This Mess Around* was designed to capitalize on the unexpected success of *Cosmic Thing*. It's an excellent summation of the group's late-'70s/early-'80s heyday, featuring such staples as "Wig," "Give Me Back My Man," "Song for a Future Generation," "52 Girls," "Private Idaho," "Strobe Light," "Devil in My Car," "Planet Claire," and "Rock Lobster," as well as remixes of "Party Out of Bounds" and "Dance This Mess Around." Even though it ignores the group's most commercially successful period (because it was *released* during that era), it still is arguably the best compilation of the group's work, since it has a focus and doesn't contain the chaff (namely, the new songs) that weighs down *Time Capsule*. Anyone looking for a far-reaching overview of the group's career should stick with *Time Capsule*, but *Dance This Mess Around* is a first-rate survey of the band's best (and most groundbreaking) years. *—Stephen Thomas Erlewine*

Babyface (Kenneth Edmonds)

b. Apr. 10, 1959, Indianapolis, IN
Vocals, Keyboards, Producer / Quiet Storm, Club/Dance, Adult Contemporary, Urban
With his friend Antonio Reid, Babyface formed a Cincinnati-based band, the Deele, in the early '80s. They were introduced by members of Midnight Star to Solar Records executive Dick Griffey, who put them to work producing music for Carrie Lucas, the Whispers, and Dynasty. Since then, they've produced hits for Sheena Easton, Pebbles, Paula Abdul, and others. During the '90s, Babyface's dominance has extended beyond the production arena and into the performing circle. A series of hit releases depicting him simultaneously as a vulner-

able romantic and accomplished lover turned Babyface into arguably this decade's biggest urban male vocalist. *Tender Lover* crossed him over into pop territory and eventually sold more than two million copies, ending any doubts that Babyface would be a major solo star. The singles "Whip Appeal" and "It's No Crime" were Top Ten R&B and pop hits, and remain staples on urban radio. He followed that with *A Closer Look* in 1991, and *For the Cool in You* earned another platinum certification and ranked among 1993's biggest R&B/urban albums. Babyface hit his peak in 1995, as he produced hits for artists like Boyz II Men, Madonna, and Whitney Houston and coordinated the *Waiting to Exhale* soundtrack. *—Bil Carpenter*

Tender Lover / Jul. 1989 / Epic/Legacy ✦✦✦✦✦
Babyface's second solo album yielded the first number one R&B hit of the 1990s while establishing Edmonds as a major personality and performer. He wrote or co-wrote much of the material and even played several instruments. It was a combination of slick production and nicely sung sentimental tributes and heartache ballads. [The 2001 CD reissue adds historical liner notes and three bonus tracks: a "Dub L.A." version of "Tender Lover," a 12" version of "Whip Appeal," and a 12" version of "My Kinda Girl."] *—Ron Wynn*

Lovers / Sep. 1989 / Epic/Legacy ✦✦✦

A Closer Look / Nov. 19, 1991 / Solar/Epic ✦✦✦✦
Babyface has established himself as both a performing and production star in the '90s. His alternately innocent, hurt, and disillusioned vocals are this decade's equivalent of the soul/love songs of the '70s and '80s. He can sing sentimental material, tender tunes, or seem angry and confused. His lyrics get overly coy, but they've struck many responsive chords among women in particular. It's not soul, but it's what many who never heard Sam Cooke think it is. *—Ron Wynn*

For the Cool in You / Aug. 1993 / Epic/Legacy ✦✦✦✦

The Day / Oct. 29, 1996 / Epic/Legacy ✦✦✦✦✦
The Day was the first album Babyface released after being elevated into a virtually guaranteed hitmaker in the mid-'90s through his work with Whitney Houston, Boyz II Men, Madonna, and Mariah Carey, among many others. The album confirms his skill for subtle, inventive songwriting and accessible, polished yet soulful production. Babyface can straddle the line between hip-hop and traditional soul better than nearly any other artist, as evidenced by the hits he has orchestrated for other artists. On his own, he is still compelling—his voice is as smooth as silk, and nearly as seductive—but it doesn't quite have the force of personality as his greatest productions. Nevertheless, *The Day* qualifies as state-of-the-art mid-'90s soul, featuring a handful of terrific songs, and a lot of extremely pleasurable filler. [The 2001 CD reissue adds historical liner notes and three bonus tracks: remixes of "Everytime I Close My Eyes," "This Is for the Lover in You," and "Everytime I Feel the Groove," the last of which was previously unreleased and not found on the original album in any form.] *—Leo Stanley*

MTV Unplugged NYC 1997 / Nov. 25, 1997 / Epic ✦✦✦

● **A Collection of His Greatest Hits** / Nov. 14, 2000 / Epic ✦✦✦✦✦

Burt Bacharach

b. May 12, 1928, Kansas City, MO
Piano, Producer, Composer, Arranger, Strings / Baroque Pop, Film Music, Brill Building Pop, Pop
With a hit-single track record spanning four decades, Burt Bacharach became one of the most important composers of popular music in the 20th century, almost equal to such classic tunesmiths as George Gershwin or Irving Berlin. His sophistocated yet breezy productions borrowed from cool jazz, soul, Brazilian bossa-nova, and traditional pop to virtually define and undoubtedly transcend the staid forms of Brill Building adult-pop during the 1960s. His first hit came from Marty Robbins in late 1957 when Robbins took "The Story of My Life" to the American Top 20 and the number one spot in England. The single was also notable for its co-composer, Hal David, who became Bacharach's songwriting partner and collaborated on most of his big hits. By late 1962, Bacharach and David began focusing most of their composing energy on singer Dionne Warwick, who was the recipient of 15 Top 40 singles from 1962 to 1968 (including the Top Tens "Anyone Who Had a Heart," "Walk on By," "I Say a Little Prayer," and "Do You Know the Way to San Jose?"). The duo also remained dominant in England, where Frankie Vaughan, Cilla Black, Sandie Shaw, the Walker Brothers, and Herb Alpert all hit number one with Bacharach/David compositions. If their schedule wasn't busy enough throughout the '60s, the songwriters contributed film scores for *What's New Pussycat?, Alfie, Casino Royale,* and *Butch Cassidy and the Sundance Kid.* Bacharach and David began working on the musical *Promises, Promises* in the late '60s; it won a Tony and a Grammy Award (for cast album) during a popular three-year Broadway run. At the beginning of the '70s, three of his closest partners—Hal David, Dionne Warwick, and his second wife Angie Dickinson—left him. Bacharach's next hit was over a decade in coming; finally in 1981, he collaborated with Christopher Cross, Carol Bayer Sager, and Peter Allen on the Oscar-winning "Arthur's Theme." Once Bacharach resumed composing he began to hit, and 1986 was one of his finest years, with two American number ones: "That's What Friends Are For" and "On My Own." By the mid-1990s, many alternative bands began name-checking the hit-maker as an influence, and a three-disc retrospective of his compositions was released by Rhino in 1998. That same year he collaborated with Elvis Costello on the acclaimed *Painted from Memory,* and was celebrated at an all-star concert at Radio City Music Hall which later formed the basis for the LP *One Amazing Night.* *—John Bush*

★ **Look of Love: The Burt Bacharach Collection** / Nov. 3, 1998 / Rhino ✦✦✦✦✦
While this three-CD, 75-song box set only has a half-dozen tracks credited to Burt Bacharach, it's certainly the best representation of his music likely to ever be assembled. Spanning the late '50s to a 1996 duet with Elvis Costello, this is the cream of his work as a composer (and, frequently, producer), properly concentrating mostly on the 1960s hit versions of his songs (usually, though not always, co-written with Hal David) by Dionne Warwick, the Drifters, Chuck Jackson, Dusty Springfield, and many others. Classics like "Baby It's You," "Walk on By," and "Wishin' and Hopin'" are here, of course. What really makes this exceptional, however, is the deft intermingling of smash hits with interesting minor hits and rarities. There are four cuts by the unknown Lou Johnson, who has been described as the male counterpart to Dionne Warwick; intriguing obscurities by Gene Pitney, Jackie DeShannon, and others that even fans of the artists might not have heard; rare original versions of familiar classics (Tommy Hunt's "I Just Don't Know What to Do With Myself"); hits by artists who only benefited grandly from the magic Bacharach-David touch once (Bobby Vinton's "Blue on Blue," Jack Jones' "Wives and Lovers"); and just plain off-the-wall things like the Five Blobs' novelty "The Blob," Manfred Mann's "My Little Red Book," Bobby Goldsboro's "Me Japanese Boy I Love You," and TV actor Richard Chamberlain's "Blue Guitar." Aficionados may find some things to carp about, particularly the absence of some small hits and the track choice when several singers made worthy versions; sometimes the big hit is used, sometimes it's a rare original version, sometimes it's a rare rendition that was neither the original nor the biggest hit. For a rich but manageable anthology of his best work, though, it could hardly be bettered. *—Richie Unterberger*

Bachman-Turner Overdrive

f. 1972, Winnipeg, Canada, **db.** 1979
Group / Album Rock, Boogie Rock, Arena Rock, Hard Rock
Following his 1970 departure from the Guess Who, guitarist Randy Bachman recorded a solo album (*Axe*) before forming Bachman-Turner Overdrive in 1972. Originally called Brave Belt, the metal group was comprised of singer/guitarist Bachman, fellow Guess Who alum Chad Allan, bassist C.F. "Fred" Turner, and Randy's brother, drummer Robbie; after a pair of LPs (*Brave Belt I* and *Brave Belt II*), Allan was replaced by another Bachman brother, guitarist Tim, and in homage to the trucker's magazine *Overdrive,* the unit became BTO. While their self-titled 1973 debut caused little impact in the U.S. or the band's native Canada, *Bachman-Turner Overdrive II* was a smash, netting a hit single with the anthemic "Taking Care of Business." 1974's *Not Fragile* was a chart-topping success, and notched a number one single with "You Ain't Seen Nothin' Yet." After two more albums—*Four Wheel Drive* and *Head On,* both issued in 1975—Randy Bachman left the group for a solo career. *—Jason Ankeny*

● **The Best of BTO (Remastered Hits)** / May 19, 1998 / Mercury ✦✦✦✦✦
Best of BTO (Remastered Hits) is essentially a remastered version of the 1976 compilation *Best of BTO (So Far),* augmented by three bonus tracks: "Four Wheel Drive," "Free Wheelin," and "Down to the Line," which was previously only available as a single. The sound is better than on the initial issue, and the album remains an effective summary of BTO's career, the perfect choice for anyone looking for just one album from the hard-rocking Canadians. *—Stephen Thomas Erlewine*

Backstreet Boys

f. 1992
Group / Teen Pop, Euro-Dance, Europop, Adult Contemporary, Dance-Pop
Paradoxical in many ways, the Backstreet Boys were white Americans that sang a hybrid of R&B and dance-pop and found their first success in Europe and Canada. While their 1996 debut album made the Top ten in nearly every European country, it took another two years for them to succeed in the U.S.

The group featured cousins and Lexington, KY natives Kevin Richardson and Brian Littrell, who sang doo wop and new-jack R&B at local events, and Orlando, FL residents Howie Dorough and A.J. McLean, who met each other—and the fifth Backstreeter, transplanted New Yorker Nick Carter—through TV and theater auditions. When Richardson moved to Orlando, he met the trio through one of his Disney World co-workers. The four formed a group, naming themselves after an Orlando flea market; they invited Littrell to make the band a quintet.

Record producer Louis J. Pearlman, found them managers Donna and Johnny Wright, who invited A&R reps to see the Boys perform; Jive Records signed the group in 1994. In late 1995, the Backstreet Boys released their eponymous debut in continental Europe, where it spent several weeks near the top of the charts and featured the international hits "We've Got It Goin' On" and "I'll Never Break Your Heart." Success also greeted the album's 1996 Canadian and U.K. releases; however hits eluded them in the U.S. until the release of the American version of *Backstreet Boys.* A mix of their singles with tracks from their album *Backstreet's Back,* it sold over 13 million copies and featured platinum-selling singles like "Quit Playin' Games (With My Heart)" and "Everybody (Backstreet's Back.)" Despite setbacks in 1998 like their royalties lawsuits against Pearlman and their other managers, the Boys persevered; Pearlman remained their manager and they worked on their follow-up album, *Millennium.* It debuted at number one in the summer of 1999, selling over a million copies its first week and ended up with sales of over 12 million. Later that year they released a *Christmas Album* and issued *Black & Blue* in fall 2000. *—Stephen Thomas Erlewine*

Backstreet Boys / 1996 / Jive ✦✦✦✦
The Backstreet Boys' eponymous debut album was released in America nearly a full year after its original European release, and the wait proved to be a blessing in disguise. In that year, light dance-pop—such as the Spice Girls and Hanson—returned to the top of the American charts, paving the way for the frothy pleasures of *Backstreet Boys.* Like those groups, the Backstreet Boys divide their time between catchy, uptempo dance numbers and syrupy ballads, and they are as reliant on their personality as they are their talent. As a result, there are a couple of slow spots on the record, but each of the singles, plus a handful of album tracks, are potent combinations of professional hooks and personal charm that make *Backstreet Boys* a thoroughly enjoyable affair. *—Stephen Thomas Erlewine*

● **Millennium** / May 18, 1999 / Jive ✦✦✦✦
The Backstreet Boys finally broke (and broke big) in America during 1998, as if by design. They had been Euro sensations for a couple of years, but it wasn't until *Backstreet's Back* was unleashed in the U.S. in 1997 that they had a presence in the States, and it was no small presence, either—after selling over ten million copies, the album remained in the Top 40 on the eve of the release of its sequel, *Millennium.* And sequel is the appropriate word—*Millen-*

nium has no pretense of being anything other than an album for the moment, delivering more of everything that made *Backstreet's Back* a blockbuster. There's a familiar blend of ballads and dance-pop, a similar shiny production, a reliance on the Boys' charisma that brings to mind the debut. If *Millennium* were anything other than big, glossy mainstream pop, such calculation may be a little unseemly, but in this context, it can be rather fun. True, the album doesn't pack as much punch as its predecessor—there's a number of good songs, but more filler than before, and the Backstreet sound isn't as fresh as it was the first time around—but it does deliver what fans want: more of the same. And since there are singles as infectious as "I Want It That Way" and a handful of good ballads, that will be enough to satisfy anyone craving more, more, more. *—Stephen Thomas Erlewine*

Black & Blue / Nov. 21, 2000 / Jive ✦✦✦
When 'N Sync usurped the Backstreet Boys' record of number of albums sold in a single week early in 2000, it had to hurt the Backstreets, since it was played in the press as if they had lost the teen pop throne. By the time the group released their third album, *Black & Blue*, Thanksgiving week 2000, 'N Sync was still popular, but the arc of *No Strings Attached* illustrated that they were weak where the Backstreets were strong—namely, they couldn't really deliver the seductive mid-tempo pop tunes and ballads that were the backbone of the Boys' crossover success. Songs like "Shape of My Heart," which flows as gracefully as "I Want It That Way," prove that the Backstreet Boys do teen-pop ballads better than anyone, but what's interesting about *Black & Blue* is how aggressively they protect their territory. Of course, it's relative protection, since they, like 'N Sync and Britney Spears, work with Max Martin, the man behind the biggest hits by all three artists. Consequently, it's not a coincidence that "Get Another Boyfriend" is a dead ringer for "It's Gonna Be Me" crossed with "Baby One More Time," but what gives *Black & Blue* character is that it's clear that the Backstreets want to remain kings of their world. So, the ballads are smoother than ever, and their dance numbers hit harder, all in an attempt to keep their throne. It works, even if it takes a couple spins before the singles stand out, since the Backstreets' material and voices are stronger than that of their peers, adding up to state of the art teenpop. *—Stephen Thomas Erlewine*

Bad Brains

f. 1979, Washington, D.C., **db.** 1995
Group / Hardcore Punk, Alternative Pop/Rock
By melding punk with reggae, Bad Brains became one of the definitive American hardcore punk groups of the early '80s. Although the group released only a handful of records during their peak, including the legendary cassette-only debut *Bad Brains*, they developed a dedicated following, many of whom would later form their own hardcore and alternative bands. Inspired by both the amateurish rage of the Sex Pistols and the political reggae of Bob Marley, guitarist Dr. Know formed Bad Brains in 1979. Realizing that the lines between punk and reggae were already blurred in the U.K., he set out to replicate that situation in the U.S., recruiting several similarly minded musicians—vocalist H.R., bassist Darryl Aaron Jenifer and drummer Earl Hudson—to prove his point. Poor distribution and erratic touring prevented the band from breaking out of the hardcore scene until their third album *I Against I* appeared in 1986 on SST. In the wake of the alternative rock boom of the early '90s, Bad Brains moved to the major label Epic in 1993 for *Rise*, though the album failed and the group was dropped. Maverick Records signed Bad Brains two years later for the band's next album, *God of Love*, though it also performed poorly. *—Stephen Thomas Erlewine*

Bad Brains / Feb. 1982 / ROIR ✦✦✦✦✦
For fans of hardcore, many would agree that the holy-grail of the genre is the Bad Brains' self-titled album, originally released back in 1982 as a cassette-only release on ROIR. Although it was available on CD on the now-defunct In Effect label in the late 80's (then titled *Attitude, The ROIR Sessions* with a different album cover), it's been remastered and re-released (on ROIR) with it's original cover, as well as an untitled bonus track added at the end. The ensuing years after its initial release haven't dulled the album's fury and rage in the least, and it's still impressive how the band can switch gears from red-hot hardcore to cool reggae dubs in the blink of an eye. All the classics are here: "Sailin' On," "Banned in D.C.," "Pay to Cum," "Right Brigade," as well as one of their strongest reggae tunes, "I Luv I Jah." The back of the album boasts a quote from the Beastie Boys' Adam Yauch, which sums up the proceedings simply, "the best punk/hardcore album of all time." *—Greg Prato*

Rock for Light / 1983 / Caroline ✦✦✦✦
After the tinny sound quality of the band's debut, the second Bad Brains album came as a real blast of sonic fresh air. Producer Ric Ocasek is largely responsible, but the increased tightness and focus are also a function of maturation. This band was a weird bundle of contradictions from day one: black, Rastafarian instrumental virtuosos playing hard-core punk, formerly the exclusive domain of white, aggressively atheist musical amateurs. That last contradiction would come to full musical flower on *I Against I*, but *Rock for Light* shows the band at the height of its punk energy. *P.M.A., Joshuaís Song*, and *Coptic Times* are typical examples of Bad Brains' unique blend of punk velocity and Rasta ideology. When they suddenly swing into mellow reggae (on *I and I Survive, The Meek, Rally ëRound Jah Throne*, and the dubwise instrumental *Jam*) the effect is like some kind of pleasant musical whiplash. The 1990 CD reissue of this album was remixed by Ocasek and bassist Darryl Jennifer, and it includes several bonus tracks. *—Rick Anderson*

● **I Against I** / 1986 / SST ✦✦✦✦✦
This album was for Bad Brains what *London Calling* was for the Clash—the band's first fully mature work, one which successfully brought together all of its diverse influences while at the same time showcasing a singular vision. Also like *London Calling*, it was to be the band's masterpiece, in the original sense of that term—a creative pinnacle which they would not reach again. The album opens with the title track, a blistering and musically exhilarating deploration of violence, and then moves directly into "House of Suffering," teasily the most complex and yet viscerally compelling song the band ever produced. Singer HR digs deep into his bag of voices and pulls them all out, one by one: the frightening nasal falsetto that was his signature in the band's hardcore days, an almost bel canto baritone, and a declamatory speed-rap chatter that spews lyrics with the mechanical precision of a machine gun. He positively croons on the surprisingly melodic "Secret 77" and "Let Me Help." But his voice isn't even the best thing happening here. It's the incredibly tight, funky, and tonally rich interplay between guitarist Dr. Know, bassist Darryl Jenifer and drummer Earl Hudson that gives this album its deeply satisfying texture. The stop/start rhythms of "Secret 77" and "Sacred Love," the gorgeous guitar hook on "She's Calling You," Dr. Know's completely counter-intuitive ability to meld the raw directness of hardcore punk with an almost supernatural virtuosity without sacrificing the power of either approach—this is music-making of an order not usually seen in rock & roll. *—Rick Anderson*

Live / 1988 / SST ✦✦✦

Quickness / Sep. 1989 / Caroline ✦✦✦

Rise / Aug. 1993 / Epic ✦✦

God of Love / May 23, 1995 / Maverick ✦✦

Black Dots / 1996 / Caroline ✦✦

Bad Company

f. 1973, England
Group / Album Rock, Arena Rock, Hard Rock, Blues-Rock
Formed in 1973, the British hard-rock outfit Bad Company was a supergroup comprised of ex-King Crimson bassist Boz Burrell, former Mott the Hoople guitarist Mick Ralphs, and singer Paul Rodgers and drummer Simon Kirke, both onetime members of Free. Powered by Rodgers' muscular vocals and Ralphs' blues-based guitar work, Bad Company was the first group signed to Led Zeppelin's vanity label Swan Song; their eponymously-titled 1974 debut was an international hit which topped the U.S. album charts and scored a number one single with "Can't Get Enough of Your Love." *Straight Shooter*, issued the following year, was another major success, notching the hit "Feel Like Makin' Love," while 1976's *Run With the Pack* was Bad Company's third consecutive million-selling record. After 1977's *Burnin' Sky*, the group recorded 1979's *Desolation Angels*, which embellished their sound with synthesizers and strings; a three-year hiatus followed before the release of *Rough Diamonds*, the group's final LP in its original incarnation. *—Jason Ankeny*

Bad Company / Jun. 1974 / Swan Song ✦✦✦✦✦

Straight Shooter / Apr. 1975 / Swan Song ✦✦✦

Run With the Pack / Jan. 1976 / Swan Song ✦✦

Burnin' Sky / Mar. 1977 / Swan Song ✦✦✦

Desolation Angels / Mar. 1979 / Swan Song ✦✦✦

● **10 From 6** / Dec. 1985 / Swan Song/Atlantic ✦✦✦✦✦
10 From 6 means ten songs from six albums—namely, Bad Company's first six records, all of which were big hits on album-rock radio. This brief yet very effective collection gathers all of the group's best-known songs ("Can't Get Enough," "Feel Like Makin' Love," "Shootin' Star," "Bad Company," "Rock & Roll Fantasy," "Ready for Love") in one place. Although most album-oriented hard-rock acts are better heard on the original albums, Bad Company's records tended to be more uneven than those of their peers, making *10 From 6* a valuable collection for the group's casual fans, who will want to bypass the cluttered studio albums and just get the cream of the crop. *—Stephen Thomas Erlewine*

Original Bad Company Anthology / Mar. 23, 1999 / Elektra ✦✦✦✦✦
Somehow or other, Bad Company got lumped in with other '70s rock dinosaurs. In a way they were—not because their music was excessive or dated, but because when Bad Company walked the earth, the ground shook. Featuring the voice of Paul Rodgers, one of rock's greatest singers, the thoroughly excellent *Original Bad Company Anthology* re-establishes Bad Company as a force in the music world. The 33-song, two-CD set contains all the classic songs that made the band a top-selling recording and concert attraction, as well as four brand new songs and six B-sides and outtakes. The new songs are (surprise!) awesome. All four tracks (two by Mick Ralphs, two by Paul Rodgers) sound like they could be on the band's classic early albums. The first single, "Hey Hey," is a blustery rocker; "Tracking Down a Runaway," a totally exhilarating number, sounds like a future hit. The rarities include "Easy on My Soul," a remade Free song from the *Straight Shooter* sessions—complete with Paul Rodgers' signature piano—that blows the Free version out of the water, and might just be the best track Bad Company has ever done. Other highlights include "Superstar Woman," a soulful outtake from the first LP sessions, and "Smokin' 45" from the *Burnin' Sky* sessions. "Little Miss Fortune," with its cool lyrics and groove, is a former B-side finally seeing the light of day in the CD age. The set draws from all of their albums, emphasizing the first two, but the band even found two good tracks from the utterly pathetic *Rough Diamonds;* if those songs are good you can be sure the rest kicks some serious butt as well. *—Geoff Ginsberg*

Bad Religion

f. 1980, Los Angeles, CA
Group / L.A. Punk, Hardcore Punk, Alternative Pop/Rock, Punk
Out of all of the Southern Californian hardcore punk bands of the early '80s, Bad Religion stayed around the longest. For over a decade, they retained their underground credibility without turning out a series of indistinguishable records that all sounded the same. Instead, the band refined their attack, adding inflections of psychedelia, heavy metal, and hard rock along the way, as well as a considerable dose of melody. Between their 1982 debut and their first major-label record, 1993's *Recipe for Hate*, Bad Religion stayed vital in the hardcore community by tightening their musical execution and keeping their lyrics complex and righteously angry. Formed around guitarist Brett Gurewitz and vocalist Greg Graffin, Bad Religion debuted with 1983's *Into the Unknown*, released on Gurewitz's label Epitaph. After a lengthy hiatus, *Suffer* followed in 1988 and re-established the group as prominent players in the American hardcore scene. By the time of 1993's *Recipe for Hate*, alternative rock had become such a mainstream commodity that the group signed to Atlantic. The label re-

released *Recipe for Hate*, then new album *Stranger Than Fiction*, the album that proved to be Gurewitz's last (his label's unexpected hit, the Offspring's *Smash*, caused Gurewitz to spend more time on business matters). Bad Religion followed with *The Gray Race* in 1996, and *No Substance* two years later. *—Stephen Thomas Erlewine*

Into the Unknown / 1983 / Epitaph ♦♦♦♦♦
At a time when most L.A. bands were playing extremely fast, stripped-down rock, Bad Religion released this chunk of '70s-styled hard rock that anticipated the '70s revival by about a decade. It's a bit off-putting at first blush, mainly because the tempos are slower and more deliberate, and because of the use of swirling organs and pianos. But it's a terrific record that was perhaps more daring than anyone realized at the time of its release. An extremely influential and interesting record, one that any fan of hard rock should own. *—John Dougan*

Back to the Known / 1984 / Epitaph ♦♦

Suffer / 1988 / Epitaph ♦♦♦♦♦

No Control / Dec. 1989 / Epitaph ♦♦♦♦♦

Against the Grain / 1990 / Epitaph ♦♦♦♦
After reuniting in 1988, Bad Religion went on a recording binge that saw the release of three records in two years. All are good, with *No Control* hands-down the best of the three. What's crucial at this point in their career is that the band was concerned with simply being a good rock band and less concerned with being aging punks. As a result the music doesn't sound retrograde or tossed-off, and Graffin, Gurewitz, and Co. never come off like a pathetic bunch of middle-age punks desperately attempting to sound young. This music takes maturity head-on and deals with it in a way that gets to the roots of living in society as opposed to dying before you get old—the former being much tougher than the latter. But, even from the start Bad Religion's music was never about taking the easy way out, and these three releases are a testament to that attitude. *—John Dougan*

80-85 / 1990 / Epitaph ♦♦♦
A tremendous collection of early Bad Religion that covers most of their hardcore and early post-hardcore period, including their debut record, *How Could Hell Be Any Worse*. Graffin's snarl is prominently displayed, and the band rages through this anthology's 28 tracks, which includes three takes of their signature theme "Bad Religion." Lots of tracks are suffused with a quasi-liberal, populist message (e.g., "Politics," "World War III," and "Oligarchy") and are more lyrically sophisticated than one might assume. An excellent introduction. *—John Dougan*

Generator / Mar. 13, 1992 / Epitaph ♦♦♦

Recipe for Hate / Sep. 21, 1993 / Epitaph ♦♦♦
Although it doesn't sound all that different from what X was doing ten years ago (and fairly close to the music they were making, too), the seminal L.A. punk rockers gained a larger audience with *Recipe for Hate*. Featuring guest spots from Eddie Vedder and Johnette Napolitano from Concrete Blonde, *Recipe for Hate* features a smoother version of punk. All of the trademark anger and guitars are still present, but some of the melodies, harmonies, and riffs lean toward mainstream rock & roll. Fortunately, this all works in Bad Religion's favor—their music is more accessible, but it doesn't lack integrity. *—Stephen Thomas Erlewine*

Stranger Than Fiction / Aug. 30, 1994 / Atlantic ♦♦♦

• **All Ages** / Nov. 7, 1995 / Epitaph ♦♦♦♦♦
A best-of collection from Bad Religion's latter-period Epitaph years, *All Ages* has a pretty good selection of the standout tracks from their 1988 to 1992 period (*Suffer* to *Generator*) with just a couple of songs predating 1985 (including a live version of "Fuck Armageddon ... This Is Hell"). It's a consistently fine, often exhilarating selection, boasting such enduring tracks as "Flat Earth Society," "21st Century Digital Boy," and others. The title, incidentally, is a salute to the Southern Californian hardcore scene's determination to play venues where alcohol was not on sale (and thus allow entry to under-21s). Alongside the *80-85* compilation issued in 1991, it provides a comprehensive introduction to one of the few hardcore bands with the legs to take relevance and social critique into a second decade of existence. *—Alex Ogg*

Gray Race / Feb. 27, 1996 / Atlantic ♦♦

No Substance / May 5, 1998 / Atlantic ♦♦♦

The New America / May 9, 2000 / Atlantic ♦♦♦♦

Badfinger

f. 1968, England, **db.** 1983
Group / Album Rock, Pop/Rock, Power Pop, Soft Rock
There are few bands in the annals of rock music as star-crossed in their history as Badfinger. Pegged as one of the most promising British groups of the late '60s, and the one world-class talent ever signed to the Beatles' Apple Records label that remained with the label, Badfinger enjoyed the kind of success in England and America that most other bands could only envy—and a string of memorable hit singles, "Come and Get It," "No Matter What," "Day After Day," and "Baby Blue"—yet saw almost no reward from that success. Instead, four years of hit singles and international tours precipitated the suicide of its two creative members and legal proceedings that left lawyers as the only ones enriched by the group's work. Originally known as the Iveys and comprised of Pete Ham, Joey Molland, Tom Evans, and Mike Gibbons, Badfinger earned a Top Ten hit in Britain and America with the Paul McCartney composition "Come and Get It." In 1970, they released their debut, *Magic Christian Music*, and *No Dice*, the latter yielding an original song ("Without You") that was turned into a monster worldwide hit by Harry Nilsson. One year later, *Straight Up* produced two huge singles, "Day After Day" and "Baby Blue," plus an FM hit in the form of "Name of the Game." Their final Apple album, entitled *Ass*, was released in 1973, just as the label was nearing the end of its existence as a viable company. Badfinger's debut for Warner Bros., 1974's *Wish You Were Here*, should have been a triumphant comeback for the group, though financial troubles necessitated its withdrawal just weeks after release. The group was dropped from their Warner Bros. contract in 1975, and later that year, Pete Ham hanged himself. Though 1979's *Airwaves* and 1983's *Say No More* tried to revive the Badfinger name, the suicide of Tom Evans in 1983 ended the band's career. *—Bruce Eder*

Magic Christian Music / Feb. 16, 1970 / Capitol ♦♦♦
If Badfinger's debut album *Magic Christian Music* sounds patchy, there's a reason why: It was assembled from three different sources. Although the title suggests that the record is a soundtrack to *The Magic Christian* it isn't. It's a hodgepodge, containing the group's three contributions to the film, six highlights from the band's pre-Badfinger album *Maybe Tomorrow* (released when they were known as the Iveys), an alternate take from *Maybe Tomorrow*, and four new songs. It's little wonder that it doesn't hold together, and winds up as a document of Badfinger's unharnessed potential. Since their breakthrough hit "Come and Get It" was written by Paul McCartney, Badfinger was dogged by comparisons to the Beatles, but they were hardly copyists. Elements of the Hollies, the Kinks and very mild psychedelia are discernable throughout *Magic Christian Music*, all part of the band's search for their own voice. Apart from the lovely pop tune "Dear Angie" and Tom Evans' stately, yearning "Maybe Tomorrow," the Iveys numbers aren't particularly distinguished pop but they are, by and large, pleasant period pieces. On the newer material, Badfinger sounds stronger and their craftsmanship surfaces. Pete Ham emerges as a fine songsmith, with the convincing rocker "Midnight Sun" and the gentle "Walk Out in the Rain." Still, the true standouts among the newer songs are "Crimson Ship" and "Carry on Till Tomorrow," both co-written by Ham and Evans. They're two sides of the same coin—dreamy post-psych pop tunes driven by strong hooks and harmonies. They might not always deliver on that promise on *Magic Christian Music*, but with its appealing melodies, lite psychedelic flourishes and, yes, Beatlesque harmonies, it's an enjoyable artifact of its time. *—Stephen Thomas Erlewine*

No Dice / Nov. 9, 1970 / Capitol ♦♦♦♦♦
Badfinger's second album *No Dice* kicks off with "I Can't Take It," a rocker that signaled even if Badfinger still played pop and sang ballads, they considered themselves a rock band. What gave Badfinger character is they blended their desire to rock with their sensitive side instead of compartmentalizing. Even when they rock on *No Dice*, it's never earthy, like, say, the Stones. Badfinger's very sensibility and sound is modeled after the early British Invasion, where bands sang catchy, concise love songs. Yet there's a worldliness to their music absent from that of their forefathers, partially because Badfinger styled themselves as classicists, adapting the sound of their idols and striving to create a similar body of work. *No Dice* bears this out, boasting old-fashioned rockers, catchy pop tunes, and acoustic ballads. On the surface, there's nothing special about such a well-crafted, sharply-produced, straight-ahead pop record, but the pleasure of a power-pop album is in the craft. *No Dice* is not without flaws—a byproduct of an all-writing, all-singing band is that some songs don't measure up—but it does achieve the right balance of craft, fun, and emotion, due in no small part to Pete Ham's songwriting. Ham dominates the record, providing note-perfect openers and closers, along with the centerpiece singles "No Matter What" and "Without You," the latter a yearning, painful ballad co-written with Tom Evans. Collaborating with new guitarist Joey Molland, Evans wrote two other excellent songs ("I Don't Mind", "Better Days"), while Molland's own "Love Me Do" chugs along with nice momentum. Still, the heart of the album lies in Ham's work. He proves that songcraft is what separates great power pop from good, and it's what makes *No Dice* a superb pop record. *—Stephen Thomas Erlewine*

Straight Up / Dec. 13, 1971 / Capitol ♦♦♦♦♦
Straight Up winds up somewhat less dynamic than *No Dice*, largely because that record alternated its rockers, pop tunes, and ballads. Here, everything is at a similar level, as the ballads are made grander and the rockers have their melodic side emphasized. Consequently, the record sounds more unified than *No Dice*, which had a bit of a split personality. Todd Rundgren's warm, detailed production makes each songwriter sound as if he was on the same page, although the bonus tracks—revealing the abandoned original Geoff Emerick productions—prove that the distinctive voices on *No Dice* were still present. Frankly, the increased production is for the best, since Badfinger sounds best when there's as much craft in the production as there is in the writing. Here, there's absolutely no filler and everybody is in top form. Pete Ham's "Baby Blue" is textbook power pop—irresistibly catchy fuzz riffs and sighing melodies—and with its Harrison-esque slide guitars, "Day After Day" is so gorgeous it practically aches. "Perfection" is an unheralded gem, while "Name of the Game" and "Take It All" are note-perfect pop ballads. Tom Evans isn't as prolific here, but the one-two punch of "Money" and "Flying" is the closest *Straight Up* gets to *Abbey Road*, and "It's Over" is a fine closer. Still, what holds the record together is Joey Molland's emergence as a songwriter. His work on *No Dice* is enjoyable, but here, he comes into his own with a set of well-constructed songs. This fine songwriting, combined with sharp performances and exquisite studio craft, make *Straight Up* one of the cornerstones of power pop, a record that proved that it was possible to make classic guitar pop after its golden era had passed. *—Stephen Thomas Erlewine*

Ass / Nov. 26, 1973 / Apple ♦♦♦

Badfinger / Feb. 1974 / Warner Brothers ♦♦♦

Wish You Were Here / Nov. 1974 / Warner Brothers ♦♦♦♦
Wish You Were Here is a glistening, powerful rock record that stays true to power pop while sounding as contemporary as any mainstream rock band of the mid-'70s. It was the kind of record that could have been a hit, but due to a series of legal and managerial entanglements, it was pulled from stores before it had a chance to find its audience. Despite its relative obscurity, most diehard Badfinger fans maintain that the group shines brilliantly on *Wish You Were Here* and they're correct. For one, it's easily the most cohesive album the group ever recorded—a nice by-product of working with one talented producer (in this case, Chris Thomas) for an entire album instead of piecing a record together. Also, the album showcases each band member at a peak of songwriting. As the band's most prolific and gifted composer, Ham naturally has the strongest presence, and while each of his songs stands as proof that he was a consummate pop craftsman—particularly the elegant "Dennis," the hard-hitting "Just a Chance," and the *Abbey Road*-esque "Meanwhile Back at the Ranch." Joey Molland

has a strong showing with the stately ballad "Love Time" and "Should I Smoke," his complement to "Ranch." What is surprising is that Mike Gibbins' two contributions are of the same caliber, as is Tom Evans' electric-piano laden "King of the Load," since they were in a bit of a slump prior to this album. Thomas ties the record together with a clean, professional production that keeps the rockers energetic without losing their melodic edge, while preventing the sentimental numbers from seeming syrupy. All of this results in a classy, catchy pop record, possibly the best Badfinger ever released. It could have been a hit, too, but we'll never know. *—Stephen Thomas Erlewine*

Airwaves / Mar. 1979 / Elektra ✦✦

Say No More / 1981 / Real Music ✦✦

● **The Very Best of Badfinger** / Sep. 12, 2000 / Capitol ✦✦✦✦✦
The difference between 2000's *The Very Best of Badfinger* and 1995's *Come and Get It: The Best of Badfinger* is a simple one—the 1995 collection concentrated on the group's Apple recordings, where the 2000 collection runs all the way until 1974's *Wish You Were Here*, the band's final album with Pete Ham. Not only does the collection benefit from the expanded timeline, but it has a sharp selection of songs from the classic Apple years—yes, "Flying" is absent and *Ass* is bypassed (perhaps understandably so), but "We're for the Dark" is a more than welcome addition. The 19 tracks may not be in chronological order, but the sequencing packs a real punch and, in this context, the best of the Warner material more than holds its own with the Apple cuts. Inevitably, there are some fan favorites missing, but apart from "Flying," all the classics are here and this compilation is unquestionably the most thorough (and arguably the best) overview of Badfinger's entire career yet assembled. *—Stephen Thomas Erlewine*

Head First / Nov. 14, 2000 / Artisan/Snapper Music Group ✦✦✦✦

LaVern Baker

b. Nov. 11, 1929, Chicago, IL, **d.** Mar. 10, 1997, New York, NY [Manhattan]
Vocals / Jump Blues, R&B
LaVern Baker was one of the sexiest divas gracing the mid-'50s rock & roll circuit, boasting a brashly seductive vocal delivery tailor-made for belting the catchy novelties "Tweedlee Dee," "Bop-Ting-A-Ling," and "Tra La La" for Atlantic Records during rock's first wave of prominence. Baker made her recording debut with RCA Victor in 1949 and signed to Atlantic four years later, debuting with the incendiary "Soul on Fire." The coy, Latin-tempoed "Tweedlee Dee" was a smash in 1955 on both the R&B and pop charts, and her follow-ups "Bop-Ting-A-Ling," "Play It Fair," "Still," and the rocking "Jim Dandy" all vaulted into the R&B Top Ten over the next couple of years. She also hit big in 1958 with the ballad "I Cried a Tear," adopted a pseudosanctified bellow for the rousing Leiber & Stoller-penned gospel sendup "Saved" in 1960, and cut a Bessie Smith tribute album before leaving Atlantic in 1964. A brief stop at Brunswick Records preceded a late-'60s jaunt to entertain the troops in Vietnam. Baker became seriously ill after the trip and was hospitalized, eventually settling far out of the limelight in the Philippines for over 20 years. She finally returned in 1988, starring in the Broadway musical *Black & Blue* and making a nice comeback disc for DRG (*Woke Up This Mornin'*). She died in 1997. *—Bill Dahl*

Sings Bessie Smith / Jan. 27, 1958 / Atlantic ✦✦✦✦✦
This is an album that should not have worked. LaVern Baker (a fine R&B singer) was joined by all-stars from mainstream jazz (including trumpeter Buck Clayton, trombonist Vic Dickenson, tenor-saxophonist Paul Quinichette, and pianist Nat Pierce) for twelve songs associated with the great '20s blues singer Bessie Smith. Despite the potentially conflicting styles, this project is quite successful and often exciting. The arrangements by Phil Moore, Nat Pierce, and Ernie Wilkins do not attempt to re-create the original recordings, Baker sings in her own style (rather than trying to emulate Bessie Smith), and the hot solos work well with her vocals. *—Scott Yanow*

★ **Soul on Fire: The Best of LaVern Baker** / 1991 / Rhino/Atlantic ✦✦✦✦✦
The cream of this vivacious 1950s R&B belter's Atlantic catalog comprises this 20-track hits collection. Includes Baker's bouncy "Tweedlee Dee," and the storming rockers "Jim Dandy" and "Bop-Ting-a-Ling," the pseudo-gospel raveup "Saved," and Baker's torchy blues ballads "Soul on Fire" and "I Cried a Tear." She imparts "See See Rider" with a lighthearted reading that contrasts starkly with Chuck Willis' Atlantic smash of a few years before. *—Bill Dahl*

Hank Ballard

b. Nov. 18, 1936, Detroit, MI
Vocals / R&B
Though born in Detroit, Ballard moved down to Alabama at an early age, to stay with relations after his father died. He was back in Detroit by the age of 15, forming a doo-wop group called the Royals one year later. He signed to King Records in early 1953. Mid-size chart hits followed, and the group's name was changed to the Midnighters to avoid confusion with labelmates the Five Royales when "Work with Me Annie" became a national hit. Banned because of "explicit" lyrics, the song spawned a flurry of answer records (some by Ballard himself), most of them hitting the R&B charts as well. The hits kept coming throughout the early '60s, but the flipside of one of them became a national hit when Chubby Checker re-recorded "The Twist," spawning a national craze. Ballard's best records are informed by gospel-style harmonies and gritty guitar work, usually played by Alonzo Tucker. *—Cub Koda*

★ **Sexy Ways: The Best of Hank Ballard & the Midnighters** / Nov. 16, 1993 / Rhino ✦✦✦✦✦
Hank Ballard & the Midnighters were the 2 Live Crew of the early '50s, burning up the airwaves and black jukeboxes with lascivious-for-the-time period tunes like "Work with Me Annie," "Annie Had a Baby," and the title track. Although Ballard would go on to write dance hits, including the original version of "The Twist," the Midnighters at their best ("Open Up the Back Door") were Black doo wop at the end of a dark alley. Forget all previous compilations on these guys, this is the one you want. *—Cub Koda*

Dancin' and Twistin' / Oct. 31, 2000 / Ace ✦✦✦

The Band

f. 1967, Toronto, Ontario, Canada, **db.** Nov. 1976
Group / Album Rock, Folk-Rock, Country-Rock, Rock & Roll
The Band were arguably the most important North American rock band of the late '60s, leading a retreat from psychedelia and a return roots music, blending folk, country, blues, and rock & roll into a warm, freewheeling sound. The Band first coalesced as rockabilly wildman Ronnie Hawkins' supporting band in the early '60s. In 1965, they were hired as Bob Dylan's backing band for his 1965/66 tour. Drummer Levon Helm left shortly afterward, yet it was an artistically productive relationship, extending to a series of sessions recorded in Woodstock after the tour's completion—recordings that became known as the Basement Tapes. Around this time, Helm returned to the group, and they signed to Capitol, releasing their debut, *Music From Big Pink*, in summer 1968. It sent shockwaves throughout rock, earning praise in the underground press and the respect of peers. Their second album, *The Band*, appeared in 1969, was their commercial breakthrough, reaching the Top Ten. As their sales increased, the spotlight shifted to guitarist/songwriter Robbie Robertson, causing tensions within the group that escalated during the Todd Rundgren-produced sessions for *Stage Fright*. Their fourth album, 1971's *Cahoots*, was poorly received and failed to crack the Top 20. The Band took a bit of a break in 1972, releasing the double-live *Rock of Ages*, then a covers album, 1973's *Moondog Matinee*. They supported Dylan on his 1973 *Planet Waves* LP and its supporting tour, which was captured on *Before the Flood*. *Northern Lights, Southern Cross*, the Band's first album of new material in four years, appeared in 1975. One final studio album, 1977's *Islands*, was turned out before they called it a day, commemorating their final concert with a triple-album set and Martin Scorsese documentary called *The Last Waltz*. The Band minus Robertson reunited occasionally in the '80s until pianist Richard Manuel took his own life in 1986. Helm, bassist Rick Danko and organist Garth Hudson assembled a new Band in 1993, releasing *Jericho*, followed by 1996's *High on the Hog*. The Band continued to work until Danko's death in 1999. *—Stephen Thomas Erlewine*

☆ **Music From Big Pink** / Jul. 1, 1968 / Capitol ✦✦✦✦✦
None of the Band's previous work gave much of a clue about how they would sound when they released their first album in July 1968. As it was, *Music From Big Pink* came as a surprise. At first blush, the group seemed to affect the sound of a loose jam session, alternating emphasis on different instruments, while the lead and harmony vocals passed back and forth as if the singers were making up their blend on the spot. In retrospect, especially as the lyrics sank in, the arrangements seemed far more considered and crafted to support a group of songs that took family, faith, and rural life as their subjects and proceeded to imbue their values with uncertainty. Some songs took on the theme of declining institutions less clearly than others, but the points were made musically as much as lyrically. Tenor Richard Manuel's haunting, lonely voice gave the album much of its frightening aspect, while Rick Danko and Levon Helm's rough-hewn styles reinforced the songs' rustic fervor. The dominant instrument was Garth Hudson's often icy and majestic organ, while Robbie Robertson's unusual guitar work further destabilized the sound. The result was an album that reflected the turmoil of the late '60s in a way that emphasized the tragedy inherent in the conflicts. *Music From Big Pink* came off as a shockingly divergent musical statement only a year after the ornate productions of *Sgt. Pepper*, and initially attracted attention because of the three songs Bob Dylan had either written or co-written. Soon, however, as "The Weight" became a minor singles chart entry, the album and the group made their own impact, influencing a movement toward roots styles and country elements in rock. Over time, *Music From Big Pink* came to be regarded as a watershed work in the history of rock, one that introduced new tones and approaches to the constantly evolving genre. *—William Ruhlmann*

★ **The Band** / Sep. 22, 1969 / Capitol ✦✦✦✦✦
The Band's first album, *Music From Big Pink*, seemed to come out of nowhere, with its ramshackle musical blend and songs of rural tragedy. *The Band*, the group's second album, was a more deliberate and even more accomplished effort, partially because the players had become a more cohesive unit and partially because guitarist Robbie Robertson had taken over the songwriting, writing or co-writing all 12 songs. Though a Canadian, Robertson focused on a series of American archetypes from the union worker in "King Harvest (Has Surely Come)" and the retired sailor in "Rockin' Chair" to, most famously, the Confederate Civil War observer Virgil Cane in "The Night They Drove Old Dixie Down." The album effectively mixed the kind of mournful songs that had dominated *Music From Big Pink*, here including "Whispering Pines" and "When You Awake" (both co-written and sung by haunting tenor Richard Manuel), with rollicking uptempo numbers like "Rag Mama Rag" and "Up on Cripple Creek" (both sung by Levon Helm and released as singles, with "Up on Cripple Creek" making the Top 40). As had been true of the first album, it was the Band's sound that stood out the most, from Helm's (and occasionally Manuel's) propulsive drumming to Robertson's distinctive guitar fills and the endlessly inventive keyboard textures of Garth Hudson, all topped by the rough, expressive singing of Manuel, Helm, and Rick Danko that mixed leads with harmonies. The arrangements were simultaneously loose and assured, giving the songs a timeless appeal, while the lyrics continued to paint portraits of 19th century rural life (especially Southern life, as references to Tennessee and Virginia made clear), its sometimes less savory aspects treated with warmth and humor. The 2000 CD reissue featured seven bonus tracks. *—William Ruhlmann*

Stage Fright / Aug. 17, 1970 / Capitol ✦✦✦✦
Stage Fright, the Band's third album, sounded on its surface like the group's first two releases, *Music From Big Pink* and *The Band*, employing the same dense arrangements, with their mixture of a deep bottom formed by drummer Levon Helm and bassist Rick Danko, penetrating guitar work by Robbie Robertson, and the varied keyboard work of pianist Richard Manuel and organist Garth Hudson, with Helm, Danko, and Manuel's vocals on top. But the songs this time around were far more personal, and, despite a nominal complacency, quite troubling. Only "All La Glory," Robertson's song about the birth of his daughter, was fully positive. "Strawberry Wine" and "Sleeping" were celebrations of indolence, while "Time to Kill," as its title implied, revealed boredom while claiming romantic contentment. Several of the album's

later songs seemed to be metaphors for trouble the group was encountering, with "The W.S. Walcott Medicine Show" commenting on the falseness of show business, "Daniel and the Sacred Harp" worrying about a loss of integrity, and the title song talking about the pitfalls of fortune and fame. "The Shape I'm In" was perhaps the album's most blatant statement of panic. The Band was widely acclaimed after its first two albums; *Stage Fright* seemed to be the group's alarmed response, which made it their most nakedly confessional. It was certainly different from their previous work, which had tended toward story songs set in earlier times, but it was hardly less compelling for that. The 2000 expanded edition was the first CD reissue containing the mixes that had been used on the original LP. *—William Ruhlmann*

Cahoots / Sep. 15, 1971 / Capitol ✦✦✦
In comparison to its predecessors, *Cahoots*, the Band's fourth album, may be characterized as an essentially minor effort that nevertheless contains a few small pleasures. These pleasures begin with the leadoff track "Life Is a Carnival," a song that continues the theme of *Stage Fright* by emphasizing the false nature of show business and its impact on reality. The song features a lively Dixieland horn chart courtesy of Allen Toussaint. "When I Paint My Masterpiece," a Bob Dylan song making its recorded debut here as the second selection, is another welcome track, buoyed by mandolin and accordion in a charming arrangement appropriate to its tale of an odd trip to Europe. "4% Pantomime" is a duet between the Band's Richard Manuel and Van Morrison that is entertaining to hear, even if the song itself is slight. Unfortunately, that just about completes the list of the album's attractions. Annotator Rob Bowman claims that the overriding theme of the songs is "extinction and the sadness that accompanies the passing of things that once were held to be of great value"; actually, there is no overriding theme to the minor songs written by Robbie Robertson. Several of the songs' lyrics come across as half-baked film scenarios, but they fail to be evocative, and they are paired to music lacking in structure. The failure is solely in the writing; the Band sounds as good as ever playing the songs, with singers Manuel, Levon Helm, and Rick Danko all performing effectively and primary instrumentalist Garth Hudson filling in the arrangements cleverly. It's just that the material is not strong enough, particularly in comparison to the three impressive albums the Band had released previously. By adding four good bonus tracks, the 2000 reissue significantly strengthens the collection. *—William Ruhlmann*

Rock of Ages / Aug. 15, 1972 / Capitol ✦✦✦✦✦
Recorded on New Year's Eve 1971/1972, this was the Band's last gig for a year and a half. Allen Toussaint was brought in again to write horn arrangements for many of their classics. The results were inspired. Highlights are many, but of particular note are a cover of Marvin Gaye's "Baby Don't Do It" and a live recording of a track that had earlier been relegated to B-side status only, "Get Up Jake." *—Rob Bowman*

Moondog Matinee / Oct. 15, 1973 / Capitol ✦✦

Northern Lights,Southern Cross / Nov. 1, 1975 / Capitol ✦✦✦✦
The first studio album of Band originals in four years, in many respects *Northern Lights, Southern Cross* was viewed as a comeback. It also can be seen as a swan song. The album was the Band's finest since their self-titled sophomore effort. Totaling eight songs in all, on this album the Band explores new timbres, utilizing for the first time 24 tracks and what was (then) new synthesizer technology. "Acadian Driftwood" stands out as one of Robertson's finest compositions, the equal to anything else the Band ever recorded. *—Rob Bowman*

Islands / Mar. 15, 1977 / Capitol ✦✦

The Last Waltz / Apr. 1978 / Warner Brothers ✦✦✦✦
The Band's farewell gig was held at Winterland in San Francisco on Thanksgiving 1976. Guests from all periods of their career were invited to participate. The luminaries included Bob Dylan, Van Morrison, Neil Young, Joni Mitchell, Muddy Waters, Eric Clapton, and Paul Butterfield. The four-hour concert was one of the most spectacular in rock history. Two hours of it were released on this three-LP (now two-CD) set. Utilizing horns one more time, this was the gig of the Band's life and one of the greatest in rock history. *—Rob Bowman*

Greatest Hits / Sep. 26, 2000 / Capitol ✦✦✦✦✦
The Band was a very album-oriented group, and only had two Top 40 hit singles. So one could argue that a single-disc greatest hits compilation, or best-of anthology as this might more properly be called, is not the optimum way to dig into their repertoire. But if you're limiting yourself to one Band collection and your budget or patience does not stretch for the two-CD *To Kingdom Come* set, this 18-song program hits all the famous buttons, including "The Weight," "Chest Fever," "Up on Cripple Creek," "The Night They Drove Old Dixie Down," "The Shape I'm In," "Stage Fright," and "When I Paint My Masterpiece." Naturally, it leans most heavily on their first two albums, which supply four songs each. Good, lengthy liner notes by Rob Bowman are a nice bonus, considering that single-disc career-spanning overviews often dispense with such frills. Strange, though, that "Don't Do It," their one Top 40 hit single other than "Up on Cripple Creek," isn't here; in fact, there's nothing from their live *Rock of Ages*. *—Richie Unterberger*

The Bangles

f. 1981, Los Angeles, CA
Group / Jangle Pop, Paisley Underground, Pop/Rock, New Wave
The all singing/all performing four-woman Bangles formed in 1981 and sprung from the L.A. Paisley Underground scene. Later they traded their garage band roots for a slick, heavily-produced pop sound that turned them into one of the most successful chart groups of either gender during the '80s. Sisters Debbi and Vicki Peterson (drums and bass, respectively) and singer/guitarist Susanna Hoffs formed the group, and released an EP on IRS before signing to Columbia. For their second album, 1985's *Different Light*, the band was aided by Prince with his song "Manic Monday," which charted at number two and paved the way for the follow-up smash, "Walk Like an Egyptian," which went to number one and sent the album to the top of the charts. Their next single, a cover of Simon and Garfunkel's "Hazy Shade of Winter," from the *Less Than Zero* soundtrack, reached number one in 1987. The follow-up album *Everything* spawned another number one, "Eternal Flame," in 1988. One year later, the band broke up. Hoffs recorded two solo albums after the band's break-up, *When You're a Boy* in 1991 and a self-titled record in 1996. *—Denise Sullivan*

All Over the Place / May 1984 / Columbia ✦✦✦✦
The Bangles' major label debut is an essential album in the band's catalog. Guitarist and vocalist Vicki Peterson penned most of the '60s and early '70s guitar-rock songs, like the minihit "Hero Takes a Fall" (it was rumored the hero in the title was Dream Syndicate's Steve Wynn). The record also includes covers of the obscure Merry Go Round hit "Live" and ex-Soft Boy Kimberley Rew's "Going Down to Liverpool." The band was polished a bit by producer David Kahne and the release capitalized on the pretty, all-girl-group angle rather than the band's actual raw talent, which might otherwise have been too rough and retro for radio at the time. Nonetheless, the band retained enough of the original spunk that made them appealing in the first place. *—Denise Sullivan*

Different Light / Jan. 1986 / Columbia ✦✦✦
The band's second album went to number one on the strength of the first single, "Manic Monday," written especially for the band by Prince, and its follow-up, "Walk Like an Egyptian," penned by '80s hit-making giant Liam Sternberg. Though even more polished than the debut, *Different Light* is a testament to the mid-'80s sound, replete with synthesizers (Mitchell Froom assisted); even on Jules Shear's magnificent "If She Knew What She Wants" and Alex Chilton's standard "September Gurls," the band's vocal strengths shine through the gloss, and their pop sensibilities are not completely lost. *—Denise Sullivan*

Everything / Oct. 1988 / Columbia ✦✦

• **Greatest Hits** / May 1990 / Columbia ✦✦✦✦✦
Weighing in at 14 tracks, *Greatest Hits* is a good, basic collection of the Bangles' biggest singles, containing all the hits, including the previously non-LP "Hazy Shade of Winter," plus a couple of album tracks and, for the dedicated, a new cover of the Grass Roots' "Where Were You When I Needed You." It may be easy to carp about fine album tracks from *All Over the Place* and *Different Light* that should have been included, yet this is a fine sampler/introduction that might not necessarily capture the Bangles' best—in this context, their ties to the Paisley Underground and college rock seem nonexistent—but still finds them as masters of irresistible pop singles. *—Stephen Thomas Erlewine*

The Bar-Kays

f. 1966, Memphis, TN
Group / Instrumental Rock, Funk, Soul
Even though four group founders were killed in a 1967 plane crash along with Otis Redding, the Bar-Kays came back to reign as one of the top R&B outfits of the '70s. The original Bar-Kays were a Memphis instrumental combo that scored an R&B hit in 1967 on Volt with the rousing "Soul Finger." Guitarist Jimmy King, organist Ronnie Caldwell, drummer Carl Cunningham, and saxist Phalon Jones perished with Redding, leaving trumpeter Ben Cauley and bassist James Alexander to re-form the group. After honing their chops with session work at Stax, the new Bar-Kays kicked off a long string of R&B smashes in 1976 with "Shake Your Rump to the Funk" on Mercury. *—Bill Dahl*

• **Best of the Bar-Kays [Stax]** / 1988 / Stax ✦✦✦✦✦
Stax's *The Best of the Bar-Kays* inexplicably leaves off "Soul Finger," as well as "Knucklehead" and "Give Everybody Some," concentrating instead on the group's early-'70s incarnation as a funk band. Although it is missing their soul instrumentals from the late '60s, the compilation remains a good overview of their early-'70s work for Stax/Volt, featuring such songs as "Montego Bay," "Humpin'," "A.J. the Housefly" and the Top Ten R&B hit "Son of Shaft." *—Stephen Thomas Erlewine*

The Best of the Bar-Kays [Mercury] / May 18, 1993 / Mercury ✦✦✦✦✦
When the Bar-Kays joined Mercury Records in 1976, they shifted musical styles slightly, veering away from the goofy yet funky soul instrumentals that defined their Stax singles and concentrating on loose, wild funk driven by fat bass lines and whining synthesizers. Mercury's *The Best of the Bar-Kays* captures the majority of the highlights from their '70s recordings for the label. Over the course of 16 tracks, the compilation features the majority of their Top Ten R&B hits—including "Shake Your Rump to the Funk," "Too Hot to Stop," "Move Your Boogie Body," and "Hit and Run"—as well as several fine album tracks like "Freakshow on the Dance Floor," "Shut the Funk Up" and "Sexomatic," which illustrate the depth of the group's musical skills. *—Stephen Thomas Erlewine*

The Best of Bar-Kays, Vol. 2 / May 21, 1996 / Mercury ✦✦✦
Another scoop of mid-'70s-mid-'80s material from the Mercury era, for those with an interest in the band's slicker phase. It's pretty formulaic, but does include several R&B hits, such as "Spellbound," "Do It," "Boogie Body Land," "Let's Have Some Fun," "Dirty Dancer," "Your Place or Mine," "Sexomatic," and "She Talks to Me with Her Body," whose thematic concerns can be easily gleaned from the titles. *—Richie Unterberger*

Barenaked Ladies

f. 1990
Group / Adult Alternative Pop/Rock, Post-Grunge, Alternative Pop/Rock
Barenaked Ladies is a pop quintet from Toronto founded by Ed Robertson (guitar, vocals) and Steven Page (guitar, vocals) in 1988. Completing the band are Tyler Stewart (drums) and brothers Jim (bass) and Andrew Creeggan (keyboards). They released a successful independent EP, *Be My Yoko Ono*, in 1990, and their debut album, *Gordon*, was a substantial hit in Canada in 1992. Their second album, *Maybe You Should Drive*, was released in 1994; *Born on a Pirate Ship* followed two years later, promoted by the group's appearance on the popular drama *Beverly Hills 90210*. Barenaked Ladies resurfaced in 1998 with *Stunt*, also co-headlining that year's H.O.R.D.E. tour. 2000 saw the release of *Maroon*, which was produced by Don Was. *—William Ruhlmann*

• **Gordon** / Mar. 1992 / Sire ✦✦✦✦
Gordon contains re-recordings of key tracks from their Indy cassette that outsold many a "big

star" major-label release in Canada, and that cemented BNL's witty, gosh-darn reputation: "Brian Wilson," "If I Had a Million Dollars," and "Be My Yoko Ono." New numbers "Box Set"—poking fun at music industry excess—and "New Kid (On The Block)"—poking fun at different music industry excesses—carry on the tradition. But... surprise surprise... the group has decided it doesn't want to be typecast as a cute, cuddly, novelty-tune act. *Gordon* also contains several serious moments, notably "The Flag"'s metaphor for abusive relationships, and the poignant, "it's tough growing up in a complicated world" ballad "What a Good Boy." *—Roch Parisien*

Maybe You Should Drive / 1994 / Sire ✦✦✦
Barenaked Ladies are a little less interested in the quirky and comic on their second album, perhaps recognizing that They Might Be Giants have that niche covered. Instead, though, they are showing their sensitive folk-pop roots, which makes them winning, if a little wet. (XTC, anyone?) But one thing they aren't is "alternative," a matter dealt with in the chorus of the song "Alternative Girlfriend," when they sing, "There's nothing left that won't cross over." Well put, and present company included. *— William Ruhlmann*

Born on a Pirate Ship / Mar. 19, 1996 / Reprise ✦✦✦

Rock Spectacle / Nov. 19, 1996 / Reprise ✦✦✦

Stunt / Jul. 7, 1998 / Warner Brothers ✦✦✦✦
By trying to mask their smart-assed humor in a big pop production, the Barenaked Ladies attempt to set themselves up for the big crossover that they nearly achieved with such past singles as "Be My Yoko Ono" and "Brian Wilson." Nothing on *Stunt*, the group's fourth studio album, is so clearly jokey (although "Alcohol" comes close), but they still rely on clever satire. That may irritate some listeners who would otherwise be won over by the group's increased musical skill. Never before has the band been able to pull off so many different styles, from jangly pop and alt-country to loungey bossa nova, so well. Musically, it could convince the doubters who have written off Barenaked Ladies as novelty pranksters, but the lyrics still will stand in the way of trad-rockers predisposed to this style of music. Of course, listeners who are a little less uptight will find *Stunt* to be a fine collegiate party record and one of the best albums the Barenaked Ladies have released. *—Stephen Thomas Erlewine*

Maroon / Sep. 12, 2000 / Warner Brothers ✦✦✦

Syd Barrett

b. Jan. 6, 1946, Cambridge, England
Vocals, Guitar / British Psychedelia, Psychedelic, Prog Rock/Art Rock
Like a supernova, Roger "Syd" Barrett burned briefly and brightly, leaving an indelible mark upon psychedelic and progressive rock as the founder and original singer, songwriter, and lead guitarist of Pink Floyd. He was responsible for most of their brilliant first album, 1967's *The Piper at the Gates of Dawn*, but left and/or was fired from the band in early 1968 after his erratic behavior had made him too difficult to deal with; Pink Floyd never recaptured the playful humor and mad energy of their work with Barrett. After a period of hibernation, he re-emerged in 1970 with a pair of albums, *The Madcap Laughs* and *Barrett*, which featured considerable support from his former bandmates. Barrett's eccentric humor, sly wordplay, and infectious melodies range from brilliant to chaotic on his solo work. Lacking the taut power of his recordings with the Floyd in 1967, they nevertheless remain fascinating and moving glimpses into a creative psyche gone awry after (it is theorized) too much fame and too many drugs too early. With increasing psychological problems, Barrett withdrew into near-total reclusion after these albums. He never released any more material, and these days rarely appears in public, let alone to play music. *—Richie Unterberger*

● **The Madcap Laughs** / Jan. 3, 1970 / Capitol ✦✦✦✦✦
While this collection bears similarities to the songs found on *The Piper at the Gates of Dawn*, the only Pink Floyd album Barrett contributed to significantly, it nevertheless comes across more as a session of run-throughs and demos than as a finished record. Its very roughness is its charm, undercutting the whimsy of the songs with Barrett's ultimate strangeness. *—William Ruhlmann*

Barrett / Nov. 1970 / Capitol ✦✦✦
On his second solo album, Barrett was joined by Humble Pie drummer Jerry Shirley and Pink Floyd members Rick Wright (organ) and Dave Gilmour (guitar). Gilmour and Wright acted as producers as well. Instrumentally, the result is a bit fuller and smoother than the first album, although it's since been revealed that Gilmour and Wright embellished these songs as best they could without much involvement from Barrett, who was often unable or unwilling to perfect his performance. The songs, however, are just as fractured as on his debut, if not more so. "Baby Lemonade," "Gigolo Aunt," and the nursery rhyming "Effervescing Elephant" rank among his peppiest and best-loved tunes. Elsewhere, the tone is darker and more meandering. It was regarded as something of a charming but unfocused throwaway at the time of its release, but Barrett's singularly whimsical and unsettling vision holds up well. *—Richie Unterberger*

● **Opel** / Apr. 1989 / Capitol ✦✦✦
For several years, the existence of "lost" material by Barrett had been speculated on by the singer's vociferous cult, fueled by numerous patchy bootlegs of intriguing outtakes. The release of *Opel* lived up to, and perhaps exceeded, fans' expectations. With 14 tracks spanning 1968 to 1970, including six alternate takes and eight songs that had never been officially released in any form, it is equally as essential as his two 1970 LPs. The tone is very much in keeping with his pair of solo albums; ragged, predominantly acoustic, melodic, and teetering on the edge of dementia. At the same time, it's charming and lyrically pungent, with Barrett's inimitable sense of childlike whimsy. The production is generally more minimal than on his other albums, even bare-bones at times, but if anything, this adds to the music's stark power. Highlights are the lengthy brooding title track, the multi-layered swirl of "Swan Lee," the alternate take of "Dark Globe" (with much better, more restrained vocals than the previous version), and the exuberant, infectious "Milky Way." Meticulous liner notes and excellent sound complete this lovingly archival package. *—Richie Unterberger*

Crazy Diamond / Apr. 19, 1994 / Harvest/EMI ✦✦✦✦✦
A three-CD box set that enshrines Barrett's complete recorded legacy as a solo artist. Besides including his two 1970 albums, this collection includes the 1989 compilation of unreleased material, *Opel*. The chief attraction of this set for Barrett fans is no less than 19 previously unreleased alternate takes from throughout his quite brief solo career. All of those alternate takes, it's important to note, are alternate versions of songs that appear on the three previously available albums; no entirely unheard compositions were unearthed. Nonetheless, these alternate takes are more interesting listening than you might expect, for a couple of reasons. First, Barrett was so mercurial (and occasionally unfocused) in the studio that it was difficult to get him to play a song the same way twice. Second, the alternate takes are usually starker and more acoustic in nature than the official versions; they're not better, but have interesting different slants. With some of the songs repeated two, three, or even four times, this is definitely for the hardcore fan. But it's a beautifully produced document, with a meticulously detailed booklet, of a uniquely primitive visionary, and has many moments of charming and chilling power. It includes everything salvageable that he produced, with the exception of the *Peel Sessions*. It doesn't match his work with the original Pink Floyd, but the music continues to influence and be emulated (most notably by Robyn Hitchcock), though never equaled. *—Richie Unterberger*

Dave Bartholomew

b. Dec. 24, 1920, Edgard, LA
Vocals, Trumpet / New Orleans R&B, Rock & Roll, R&B
Dave Bartholomew is the multi-talented figure behind a majority of classic New Orleans R&B of the '50s and the self proclaimed inventor of the "Big Beat." Bartholomew has over 4000 songs in his enormous catalog and is responsible for arranging and producing timeless records by Shirley & Lee, Lloyd Price, Smiley Lewis, and especially Fats Domino. Bartholomew was born in Edgard, LA, on December 24, 1920. His first instruments were tuba and trumpet. He fronted several bands in the Crescent City before being drafted into the army. His military time brought scoring and arranging experience which came in handy following World War II. After his stint in the service, Bartholomew returned to New Orleans and put together a group of musicians that would comprise the bedrock of R&B in the city, including saxophonists Alvin "Red" Tyler, Lee Allen, and drummer Earl Palmer. This became the band that backed up the majority of solo talent traveling through New Orleans. Bartholomew led his first studio session under his own name in 1947 for Deluxe, but the label went out of business shortly thereafter and the sessions went unnoticed. In 1949, Bartholomew met Lew Chudd who was forming a new label, Imperial Records. Chudd hired Bartholomew as house arranger, bandleader, and talent scout, and he immediately started cranking out numerous hits through the '50s for Fats Domino, Shirley & Lee, Smiley Lewis, Earl King, Chris Kenner, Tommy Ridgely, Frankie Ford, Robert Parker, and a host of others. Bartholomew stayed with Imperial until the hits dried up in the mid-'60s, followed by short stays at Trumpet, Mercury, and his own Broadmoor label. In the '70s and '80s, he took various behind-the-scenes musical jobs while living off his many song royalties and formed a Dixieland jazz band that continues to play around the Crescent City. The '90s found Bartholomew being inducted into the Rock and Roll Hall of Fame in 1991 and releasing two discs: *Dave Bartholomew and the Maryland Jazz Band* in 1995 and *New Orleans Big Beat* three years later. *—Al Campbell*

★ **The Spirit of New Orleans: The Genius of Dave Bartholomew** / 1993 / EMI ✦✦✦✦✦
A two-disc set featuring 50 tracks and several different artists (including Fats Domino, Smiley Lewis, T-Bone Walker, Shirley & Lee, and Earl King), *The Spirit of New Orleans* effectively conveys Bartholomew's groundbreaking achievements in R&B and rock & roll. *—Stephen Thomas Erlewine*

Fontella Bass

b. Jul. 3, 1940, St. Louis, MO
Vocals, Piano / Chicago Soul, Pop-Soul, Northern Soul, Soul
An explosive gospel and soul singer, Fontella Bass is the daughter of the great vocalist Martha Bass and sister of David Peaston, as well as ex-wife of Art Ensemble of Chicago trumpeter Lester Bowie. But none of that family history means as much as her own skills, which include a tremendous voice, great range, and distinctive delivery. Bass first sang in several church choirs but later moved into R&B, singing in Oliver Sain's band and working with Little Milton in the early '60s. Bass teamed with Bobby McClure for two duets on Checker in 1965. "Don't Mess up a Good Thing" reached number five on the R&B charts and inched into the pop Top 30, while "You'll Miss Me When I'm Gone" got into the R&B Top 30. Bass' debut single as a solo act was her greatest; "Rescue Me" topped the R&B charts for a month, peaked at number four on the pop charts, and was among the era's finest soul singles. The follow--up, "Recovery," was better than it has been credited, and reached number 13. Bass never again attained soul stardom, but has remained busy in the ensuing years. She later sang with Bowie's group, the Art Ensemble of Chicago, and was also part of the gospel group From the Root to the Source. *—Ron Wynn*

Free / 1972 / Varese ✦✦✦
An expanded version of her 1972 Paula album *Now That I Found a Good Thing*, Fontella Bass' *Free* adds a new version of her classic "Rescue Me" along with four B-sides: "It Sure Is Good," "I'm Leaving the Choice to You," "Home Wrecker," and "It's Hard to Get Back In." Bass wrote most of the songs included here herself—along with a few collaborative efforts with her then-husband Lester Bowie—and all the tracks showcase her dynamic, dramatic approach to soul. *—Heather Phares*

● **Rescued: The Best of Fontella Bass** / Mar. 10, 1992 / Chess/MCA ✦✦✦✦✦
"Rescue Me" might have been her only big hit, but Fontella Bass was a terrific gospel-influenced soul vocalist who cut several great sides for Checker/Chess Records in the mid-

'60s. They might not have gotten the attention they deserved when they were released, but they have held up very well over the years. *Rescued: The Best of Fontella Bass* collects 16 of her finest tracks, including "Rescue Me," three duets with Bobby McClure, and a previously unreleased song; it makes a convincing case that she should have had more hit singles than she did. *— Stephen Thomas Erlewine*

Bauhaus

f. 1978, Northampton, Northamptonshire, England, **db.** 1987

Group / Post-Punk, Goth Rock, Alternative Pop/Rock

Bauhaus is made up of the founding fathers of goth rock, creating a minimalistic, overbearingly gloomy style of post-punk rock driven by jagged guitar chords and cold, distant synthesizers. Throughout their brief career, the band explored all the variations on their bleak musical ideas, adding elements of glam rock, experimental electronic rock, funk, and heavy metal. While their following never expanded beyond a cult, they kept that cult alive well into the '90s. Guitarist/vocalist Daniel Ash, bassist/vocalist David J, and drummer Kevin Haskins had played together before forming Bauhaus in Northampton, England with vocalist Peter Murphy. In August of 1979, the group released their debut single "Bela Lugosi's Dead"; although it did not make the pop charts, it became the de facto goth-rock anthem, staying in the U.K. independent charts for years. In October of 1980, following a couple more singles, they released their debut album, *In the Flat Field,* whose success led to their first hits on the pop charts the following year. 1981's *Mask* revealed a more ambitious musical direction; elements of metal and electronic textures made the music more accessible without abandoning its dark, foreboding core, and it was a commercial success. In the fall of 1982, the group had a number 15 hit with their version of David Bowie's "Ziggy Stardust." The success of the single propelled their third album, *The Sky's Gone Out,* to number four. Peter Murphy contracted pneumonia at the beginning of 1983, which prevented him from participating in the recording sessions for Bauhaus' fourth album, *Burning from the Inside.* Consequently, the record featured substantial contributions from Daniel Ash and David J, who both pursued more personal and atmospheric directions; the album was another hit. In July, Bauhaus split up. Murphy pursued a solo career; Ash, Haskins, and J formed the successful Love and Rockets in 1985 after a proposed Bauhaus reunion fell apart. More than a decade later, Bauhaus re-formed for a full-blown tour in 1998; the two-disc *Gotham* documented the reunited group's performance in New York. *— Stephen Thomas Erlewine*

In the Flat Field / Dec. 1980 / 4AD/Beggars Banquet ✦✦✦✦

Few debut albums ever arrived so nearly perfectly formed; that *In the Flat Field* practically single-handedly invented what remains for many as the stereotype of goth music—wracked, at times spindly vocals about despair and desolation of many kinds, sung over mysterious and moody music—demonstrates the *sui generis* power of both the band and its work. This said, perhaps the best thing about the album isn't what it's supposed to sound like, but what it actually does—an awesomely powerful, glam-inspired rock band firing on all fours, capable of both restraint and complete overdrive, fronted by a charismatic, storming frontman. Starting with the challenging angst of "Double Dare," with shattering guitar over a curious but fierce stop-start rhythm while Murphy rages ever more strongly over the top, *In the Flat Field* contains a wide variety of inspirations and ideas. The astonishingly precise rhythm section of David J and Haskins pulls off a variety of jaw-dropping performances, including the high-paced tension of the title track and the brooding crawl from "Spy in the Cab." Ash, much like his longtime hero Mick Ronson, turns out to be a master of turning relatively simple guitar parts into apocalyptic explosions, from the background fills on "St. Vitus Dance" to the brutal descending chords of "Stigmata Martyr." Murphy, meanwhile, channels as much Iggy Pop as he does Bowie, proving to be no simple copyist of either, able to both maniacally sing-shout and take a somewhat lighter touch throughout. Concluding with the seven-minute "Nerves," an aptly titled piece that alternates between understated energy and unleashed power toward a dramatic ending, *In the Flat Field* started off Bauhaus' album career with a near-perfect bang. *— Ned Raggett*

Mask / Oct. 1981 / Beggars Banquet ✦✦✦✦

Managing the sometimes hard-to-negotiate trick of expanding their sound while retaining all the qualities which got them attention to begin with, on *Mask* the members of Bauhaus consciously stretched themselves into newer areas of music and performance, resulting in an album that was arguably even better than the band's almost flawless debut. More familiar sides of the band were apparent from the get-go; opening number "Hair of the Dog," one of the band's best songs, starts with a double-tracked squalling guitar solo before turning into a stomping, surging flow, carefully paced by sudden silences and equally sudden returns to the music, while Murphy details cases of mental addictions in pithy phrases. The energy wasn't all just explosive angst and despair, though; the one-two punches of "Kick in the Eye" and "In Fear of Fear" have as much hip-shaking groove and upbeat swing to them as portentous gloom (Ash's sax skronk on the latter, as well as on the similarly sharp "Dancing," is a particularly nice touch). Elsewhere, numerous flashes of the band's quirky sense of humor—something often missed by both fanatical followers and negative critics both—make an appearance; perhaps most amusing is the dry spoken-word lyric beginning "Of Lillies and Remains," as David J details a goofily grotesque situation as much Edward Gorey as Edgar Allen Poe. Add to that three of the most dramatic things the band ever recorded—the charging, keyboard-accompanied "The Passion of Lovers," the slow, dark fairy-tale-gone-wrong "Hollow Hills," and the wracked, trudging title track, where the sudden appearance of an acoustic guitar turns a great song into a near-perfect blend of ugliness and sheer beauty—and the end result was a perfect trouncing of the sophomore-slump myth. *— Ned Raggett*

Press the Eject and Give Me the Tape / 1982 / Atlantic ✦✦✦

The Sky's Gone Out / Oct. 1982 / A&M ✦✦✦

Burning from the Inside / Jul. 1983 / A&M ✦✦✦

1979-1983: Volume One / 1986 / Beggars Banquet ✦✦✦✦✦

If all single-artist compilations were like this, the world would be a much better place—while lacking liner notes, or even specific references as to what songs come from where, *Volume One,* drawing mostly from *In the Flat Field* and *Mask* does a frankly smashing job at capturing the many early high points of Bauhaus' recording career. No real obscurities appear—singles tracks like "Dark Entries" and "Terror Couple Kill Colonel" had been available on EP and would soon be reissued with the *Field* CD—while the version of "Bela Lugosi's Dead" in fact was the live take from the *Press the Eject* album. As an overview, though, it's just flat-out great, covering many of the band's different facets, from aggressive thrash ("Double Dare," "In the Flat Field," "Hair of the Dog") to mysterious, arty shades ("God in an Alcove," "Spy in the Cab," "Mask") and more. While one could argue over including other worthwhile tracks—the nutty humor of "Of Lillies and Remains" would have demonstrated the band's reach even more—*Volume One* remains as near perfect a starting place for a neophyte listener as any. *— Ned Raggett*

1979-1983: Volume Two / 1986 / Beggars Banquet ✦✦✦✦

Understandably complementing *Volume One, Two* is as similarly bereft of any sort of packaging notes as its predecessor, but is also as successful at pulling together many of Bauhaus' best moments from its later career into one knock-your-socks-off release. More *Mask* numbers crop up here—two funk-heavy groovers ("In Fear of Fear" and "Kick In the Eye"), counterpointed by the slow, haunting "Hollow Hills." *The Sky's Gone Out* is cherry-picked for some of its best moments, including "Swing the Heartache" and "All We Ever Wanted Was Everything," though the version of "Spirit" is the less effective single re-recording rather than the dramatic album take. Rather tellingly, only three songs from *Burning from the Inside* are included—"She's in Parties," the David J-sung "Who Killed Mr. Moonlight," and the Daniel Ash number "Slice of Life." Added to all of this are the peerless covers of "Ziggy Stardust" and "Third Uncle," a couple of ringers from earlier in the band's career ("Satori" and "Crowds"), stand-alone singles "Lagartija Nick" and "The Sanity Assassin," and one honest-to-goodness rarity, "Paranoia Paranoia," a radical dub reworking of "Silent Hedges" that's just as good as the original in its own unique way. In all, a great overview of the latter years of a great band, at least in its original career. *— Ned Raggett*

Swing the Heartache: The BBC Sessions / Jul. 1989 / Beggars Banquet ✦✦✦

● **Crackle** / Jul. 7, 1998 / Beggars Banquet ✦✦✦✦✦

To celebrate their twentieth anniversary, Bauhaus reunited for a tour and released the *Crackle* compilation in the U.S. The band initially claimed that *Crackle* was an American edition of *1979-1983: Vol. 2,* which was never released in the U.S., but less than half of the songs appear on both collections. Which means, of course, that *Crackle* shouldn't be viewed as a compilation for collectors—instead, it's an excellent single-disc overview of the group's brief career, containing all of their essential songs, from "In the Flat Field" and "Bela Lugosi's Dead" to "Ziggy Stardust" and "Burning from the Inside." Hardcore fans may wish there was something special about the comp—the only thing new is the perfectly adequate remastering—but it's nice that there's finally a thorough single-disc retrospective of the groundbreaking goth quartet. *— Stephen Thomas Erlewine*

Bay City Rollers

f. 1967, Edinburgh, Scotland, **db.** 1978

Group / Pop/Rock, Power Pop

The Bay City Rollers were a Scottish pop/rock band of the '70s with a strong following among teenage girls. Adopting their name again by pointing at random to a spot on a map of the United States and hitting Bay City, MI, their first hit was a cover of the Gentrys' "Keep on Dancing," which reached number nine in the U.K. in September 1971. After flopping with three singles, they finally hit the Top Ten again in February 1974 with a cover of the Shangri-Las' "Remember (Walking in the Sand)." At this point, the Rollers became a teen sensation in Great Britain, with their good looks and tartan knickers, and they scored a series of Top Ten U.K. hits over the next two and a half years: "Shang-a-Lang," "Summerlove Sensation," "All of Me Loves All of You," "Bye Bye Baby" (a cover of the Four Seasons hit that went to number one), "Give a Little Love" (another number one), "Love Me Like I Love You," and "I Only Wanna Be with You" (a cover of the Dusty Springfield hit). Their albums *Rollin' and Once Upon a Star* topped the charts as well. They scored their first U.S. hit with "Saturday Night," which reached number one in January 1976. It was followed by the Top Ten hits "Money Honey" and "You Made Me Believe in Magic." *— William Ruhlmann*

● **The Definitive Collection** / Feb. 8, 2000 / Arista ✦✦✦✦

The Beach Boys

f. 1961, Hawthorne, CA

Group / Sunshine Pop, Psychedelic Pop, Pop/Rock, Surf, Psychedelic, Pop, Rock & Roll

The Beach Boys are the most successful and important American band of the rock era. They were formed in 1961 in Hawthorne, CA, around the three Wilson brothers: Brian, Dennis, and Carl. Additional members were Mike Love, the Wilsons' cousin, and Al Jardine. From the start, the focus of the group's music was Brian Wilson, who combined a fascination with vocal harmony in the Four Freshmen mold with a love of Chuck Berry-derived rock & roll. Added to that was the subject matter of middle-class teenage life in Southern California—surfing, cars, and girls. The result was massive popular success for the group during the first half of the 1960s, starting with their first chart entry, "Surfin'," in 1962. Soon, Brian Wilson, who was composing nearly all of the material, had taken over production of the group's records as well. Given the accelerated recording schedule of the day, it was an awesome task when coupled with his onstage performing duties. The strain of all that work caught up with Brian Wilson, however, and at the end of 1964, he retired from onstage work with the Beach Boys, retaining his composing and producing duties. The group eventually settled on Bruce Johnston as his replacement. Such recordings as "California Girls" gave evidence of the expansion of Brian Wilson's musical imagination, which found him taking longer to make records that were more ambitious than the group's early teen anthems. 1966's *Pet Sounds* LP was universally hailed as one of the greatest rock albums of all time; Wilson trumped it with the number one gold single "Good Vibrations." By this point, he was being hailed as a genius in the media, as he prepared a new album tentatively titled *Smile*. The album never appeared, however. A single, "Heroes and Villains," offered tantalizing clues to what would become a legendary unheard, unfinished masterpiece. But Brian Wilson, whether because of the pressure to top himself and compete with the Beatles and others, internal disagreements within the group, psychological problems, or drug abuse, ceded leadership of the Beach Boys, and their next album, *Smiley Smile* (September 1967), was produced by the group as a whole. The Beach Boys returned to prominence in the mid-'70s on a wave of nostalgia and a potent concert act that focused on their early hits. *—William Ruhlmann*

Surfin' Safari / Oct. 29, 1962 / Capitol ✦✦

Surfin' U.S.A. / Mar. 25, 1963 / Capitol ✦✦✦✦
The real breakthrough, as Brian Wilson asserts himself in the studio as both songwriter and arranger on a set of material that was much stronger than *Surfin' Safari*. Besides the hit title track and its popular drag-racing flip side ("Shut Down"), this has a lovely, heartbreaking ballad ("Lonely Sea") and a couple of strong Brian Wilson originals ("The Noble Surfer" and "Farmer's Daughter"). There are also a surprisingly high quotient of instrumentals (five) that demonstrate that, before session musicians took over most of the parts, the Beach Boys could play respectably gutsy surf rock as a self-contained unit. Indeed, the album as a whole is the best they would make, prior to the late '60s, as a band that played most of their instruments, rather than as a vehicle for Brian Wilson's ideas. The LP was a huge hit, vital to launching surf music as a national craze, and one of the few truly strong records to be recorded by a self-contained American rock band prior to the British Invasion. A 1990 Capitol CD combines this and *Surfin' Safari* onto one disc, with the addition of three rare bonus cuts from the same era. *—Richie Unterberger*

Surfer Girl / Sep. 23, 1963 / Capitol ✦✦✦
Capitol pushed the Beach Boys for too much material in too short a time for the group to maintain as much quality control as would have been desirable. Consequently, most of their pre-1965 albums contain a high degree of filler, and thus stack up poorly next to those of such contemporaries as the Beatles, who were able to maintain high standards on almost all of their tracks. *Surfer Girl* does have some great tunes, including the title song, the hot rod ditty "Little Deuce Coupe," and "Catch a Wave" (which could have been a substantial hit single on its own merits). Most significant of all is the gorgeous ballad "In My Room," which anticipated future Beach Boys releases both in its sophisticated production (strings, organ, dense harmonies) and its personal, solipsistic lyrics. The rest is surprisingly mediocre filler, especially as at this point they were restricting their lyrical themes to beach culture almost exclusively; "Your Summer Dream," with its unusual harmonies, is about the most interesting of the obscure tracks. If you're not a dedicated Beach Boys fan, though, you should pass, as you can find the first-rate tracks on best-of anthologies. A 1990 Capitol CD combines this and *Shut Down, Vol. 2* onto one disc, adding the 45 version of "Fun, Fun, Fun," a German version of "In My Room," and the previously unreleased Brian Wilson composition "I Do." *—Richie Unterberger*

Little Deuce Coupe / Oct. 21, 1963 / Capitol ✦✦

Shut Down, Vol. 2 / Mar. 23, 1964 / Capitol ✦✦✦
Another erratic early album from the Beach Boys; few other rock LPs have such a wide gap between the best and worst material. On the good side, you have absolute classics in the Chuck Berry-ish "Fun, Fun, Fun" and its superb B-side, "Don't Worry Baby," one of the most advanced pop productions of 1964 with its breathtaking harmonies and unusual lyric. "The Warmth of the Sun" is one of the most melodic (and melancholic) ballads they ever recorded, and "Why Do Fools Fall in Love" is one of their best oldies covers. Yet the rest reduces the oceanic scale of the classics to dishwater, whether they're throwaway hot rod tunes and instrumentals, innocuous high school romantic ditties, or a soulless cover of "Louie Louie." When this album hit the racks in early 1964, the Beatles were proving that you could make LPs that were all killer, no filler; the Beach Boys would soon be forced to up their ante. A 1990 Capitol CD combines this and *Surfer Girl* into one disc, adding the 45 version of "Fun, Fun, Fun," a German version of "In My Room," and the previously unreleased Brian Wilson composition "I Do." *—Richie Unterberger*

All Summer Long / Jul. 13, 1964 / Capitol ✦✦✦
The best pre-1965 Beach Boys album featured their brilliant number one single "I Get Around," and as well as other standout cuts in the beautifully sad "Wendy," "Little Honda" (one of their best hot rod tunes, covered by the Hondells for a hit), and their remake of the late-'50s doo-wop classic "Hushabye." The nostalgic "All Summer Long," another great production, seemed (whether intentionally or not) like a sort of farewell to the frivolous California beach culture that had supplied the lyrical grist for most of their music up to this point, with a longing, regretful chorus that was totally at odds with the bouncy arrangement. Other relatively little-known treasures are the sumptuous ballad "Girls on the Beach," with some of their best early harmonizing, and "Don't Back Down," with uncommonly anxious lyrics. You can't give a high rating, however, to an album that also contained such disposable filler as the "Our Favorite Recording Sessions" comedy bit and "Do You Remember?," and a "let's-pay-tribute-to-rock's-early-days" number with a shit-eating grin wide enough to qualify as an oldies radio ID jingle. A 1990 Capitol CD combines this and *Little Deuce Coupe* onto one disc, adding the 45 version of "Be True to Your School," alternate takes of "Little Honda" and "Don't Back Down," and the previously unreleased "All Dressed Up for School." *—Richie Unterberger*

Beach Boys Concert / Oct. 19, 1964 / Capitol ✦✦✦

The Beach Boys Today! / Mar. 8, 1965 / Capitol ✦✦✦✦✦
Brian Wilson's retirement from performing to concentrate on studio recording and production reaped immediate dividends with *Today!*, the first Beach Boys album that is strong almost from start to finish. "Dance, Dance, Dance" and "Do You Wanna Dance" were upbeat hits with Spector-influenced arrangements, but Wilson began to deal with more sophisticated themes on another smash 45, "When I Grow Up," on which these eternal teenagers looked forward to the advancing years with fear and uncertainty. Surf/hot rod/beach themes were permanently retired in favor of late adolescent-early adult romance on this album, which included such decent outings in this vein as "She Knows Me Too Well," "Kiss Me Baby," and "In the Back of My Mind." The true gem is "Please Let Me Wonder," one of the group's most delicate mid-'60s works, with heartbreaking melodies and harmonies. Be aware that the version of "Help Me, Rhonda" found here is an inferior, earlier, and slower rendition; the familiar hit single take was included on their next album, *Summer Days (And Summer Nights!!)*. A 1990 Capitol CD combines this and *Summer Days (And Summer Nights!!)* onto one disc, adding alternate takes of "Dance, Dance, Dance," "I'm So Young," and "Let Him Run Wild," as well as a previously unreleased studio version of "Graduation Day." Most significantly, it also adds the non-LP single from late 1965, "The Little Girl I Once Knew," which looked forward to *Pet Sounds* in its studio experimentation and lyrical themes. *—Richie Unterberger*

Summer Days (And Summer Nights!!) / Jul. 5, 1965 / Capitol ✦✦✦✦
Summer Days (And Summer Nights!!) was a bit of a regression from the success of *Today*, lapsing back into that distressing division between first-rate cuts and lightweight also-rans that characterized their pre-1965 albums. The difference is that the very best tracks were operating on a more sophisicated level than the 1962-1964 classics. "Help Me, Rhonda" was a number one single and would be their last Top 40 exercise in sheer fun for a while. More impressive was "California Girls," with its symphonic arrangement, glorious harmonies, and archetypal statement of Californian lifestyle. On the other hand, subpar efforts like "Amusement Park U.S.A." and "Salt Lake City," throwbacks to the emptyheaded summer filler of previous days, will necessitate that the CD remote button remains close at hand. The covers of "The Girl From New York City" and "Then I Kissed Her" are well done but don't break new ground. Yet a couple of cuts are among their most essential LP-only efforts. "Let Him Run Wild" is a soulful ballad with a great Brian Wilson falsetto vocal. "Girl Don't Tell Me," with its gorgeous melody, fine lead vocal debut from Carl Wilson, and subtle depiction of romantic rejection and disappointment, may be *the* best obscure pre-*Pet Sounds* Beach Boys track. A 1990 Capitol CD combines this and *The Beach Boys Today!* onto one disc, adding alternate takes of "Dance, Dance, Dance," "I'm So Young," and "Let Him Run Wild," as well as a previously unreleased studio version of "Graduation Day." Most significantly, it also adds the non-LP single from late 1965, "The Little Girl I Once Knew," which looked forward to *Pet Sounds* in its studio experimentation and lyrical themes. *—Richie Unterberger*

Beach Boys Party! / Nov. 8, 1965 / Capitol ✦✦✦✦

☆ **Pet Sounds** / May 16, 1966 / Capitol ✦✦✦✦✦
The best Beach Boys album, and one of the best of the 1960s. The group here reached a whole new level in terms of both composition and production, layering tracks upon tracks of vocals and instruments to create a richly symphonic sound. Conventional keyboards and guitars were combined with exotic touches of orchestrated strings, bicycle bells, buzzing organs, harpsichords, flutes, the theremin, Hawaiian-sounding string instruments, Coca-Cola cans, barking dogs, and more. It wouldn't have been a classic without great songs, and this has some of the group's most stunning melodies, as well as lyrical themes that evoke both the intensity of newly born love affairs and the disappointment of failed romance (add in some general statements about loss of innocence and modern-day confusion as well). The spiritual quality of the material is enhanced by some of the most gorgeous upper-register male vocals (especially by Brian and Carl Wilson) ever heard on a rock record. "Wouldn't It Be Nice," "God Only Knows," "Caroline No," and "Sloop John B" are the well-known hits, but equally worthy are such cuts as "You Still Believe in Me," "Don't Talk," "I Know There's an Answer," and "I Just Wasn't Made for These Times." It's often said that this is more of a Brian Wilson album than a Beach Boys recording (session musicians played most of the parts), but it should be noted that the harmonies are pure Beach Boys (and some of their best). Massively influential upon its release (although it was a relatively low seller compared to their previous LPs), it immediately vaunted the band into the top level of rock innovators among the intelligentsia. The 1990 CD reissue added a few interesting but inessential outtakes, and a 1999 reissue added a new stereo version of the entire album to the original mono program. *—Richie Unterberger*

Smile [Not Released] / May 1967 / Capitol ✦✦✦
In 1966, Brian Wilson began work on the *Smile* LP, which was intended as the ultimate pop/progressive/psychedelic record. Many vocal and instrumental tracks were recorded, but the project was abandoned in 1967 due to accumulated pressures from Wilson's family, fellow Beach Boys, and the record company, combined with Wilson's own fragile and sensitive ego. In the ensuing years, *Smile* was accorded status as the most legendary unreleased album of all time, although the record was, in fact, never close to being finished. Many, though by no means all, of the tracks in progress were bootlegged in the 1980s; many, though by no means all, of these, in turn, finally surfaced on Capitol's *Good Vibrations* box set. Several bootlegs of the *Smile* sessions are still easily available, most featuring tracks which still haven't been officially released, or alternate takes and mixes of ones that did surface. A lot of these are interesting, to say the least, including the "Fire" part of the legendary "Elements" suite, the downright avant-garde "George Fell Into His French Horn," and extended snippets of "Good Vibrations" and "Heroes and Villains" as works in progress. There are numerous exquisitely beautiful passages, great ensemble singing, and brilliant orchestral pop instrumentation to be found on these outtakes, but the fact is that Wilson somehow lacked the discipline needed to combine them into a pop masterpiece that was both brilliant and commercial. Search for the double-CD compilation versions of these outtakes, which, though expensive, are more thorough than the various single-disc versions available. In 1999, the bootleg label Vigotone released an expansive four-disc set of *Smile* sessions, the fourth disc of which functions as Vigotone's best guess at an LP running order. *—Richie Unterberger*

Smiley Smile / Sep. 18, 1967 / Capitol ✦✦✦✦
After the much-discussed, uncompleted *Smile* project—which was supposed to take the innovations of *Pet Sounds* to even grander heights—collapsed, the Beach Boys released *Smiley Smile* in its place. (To clarify much confusion: *Smiley Smile* is an entirely different piece of work than *Smile* would have been, although some material that ended up on *Smiley Smile*

would have most likely been used on *Smile.* Also, much of *Smiley Smile* was in fact recorded *after* the *Smile* sessions had ceased.) For fans expecting something along the lines of *Sgt. Pepper* (and there were many of them), *Smile* was a major disappointment, replacing psychedelic experimentation with spare, eccentric miniatures. Heard now, outside of such unrealistic expectations, it's a rather nifty, if rather slight, effort that's plenty weird—in fact, often downright goofy—despite Brian Wilson's retreat from both avant-pop and active leadership of the group. "Wind Chimes," "Wonderful," "Vegetables," and much of the rest are low-key psychedelic quirkiness, with abundant fine harmonies and unusual arrangements. The standouts, nonetheless, were two recent hit singles in which Brian Wilson's ambitions were still intact: the inscrutable mini-opera "Heroes and Villains," and the number one hit "Good Vibrations," one of the few occasions where the group managed to be recklessly experimental and massively commercial at the same time. A 1990 Capitol CD combines this and *Wild Honey* onto one disc, adding previously unreleased in-progress versions of "Good Vibrations" and "Heroes and Villains," the a cappella B-side "You're Welcome," a 1967 version of "Their Hearts Were Full of Spring," and an excellent outtake, "Can't Wait Too Long." *—Richie Unterberger*

Wild Honey / Dec. 18, 1967 / Capitol ✦✦✦✦
After the *Smile* sessions shut down, the Beach Boys became much more of a *band* than they had been in the mid-'60s. They began playing most of their own instruments on record for the first time since 1963, and Brian Wilson was no longer nearly as dominant a production mastermind. The problem was, as Wilson increasingly withdrew from a leadership role (and, subsequently, from the real world altogether), the Beach Boys were revealed as a group that, although capable of producing some fine and interesting music, were no longer innovators on the level of the Beatles and other figureheads. *Wild Honey* had a looser, funkier feel than any previous Beach Boys effort, at times approaching a kind of bleached-out white soul. The resulting music was often quite pleasant, for the great harmonies if nothing else, but the material and arrangements were quite simply thinner than they had been for a long time. The record does feature a nice Top 20 hit in "Darlin'" (even if it was a rewrite of a song that had been composed four years earlier, and recorded by Sharon Marie). The small hit single "Wild Honey," with its seductive theremin lines, was also a highlight, and "Here Comes the Night" (a group original, not the Them hit) also had a lot of appeal. But much of the rest was pleasing but inessential. A 1990 Capitol CD combines this and *Smiley Smile* onto one disc, adding previously unreleased in-progress versions of "Good Vibrations" and "Heroes and Villains," the a cappella B-side "You're Welcome," a 1967 version of "Their Hearts Were Full of Spring," and an excellent outtake, "Can't Wait Too Long." *—Richie Unterberger*

Friends / Jun. 24, 1968 / Capitol ✦✦✦
Released when Cream and Jimi Hendrix were at their apex, the low-key pleasantries of *Friends* seemed downright irrelevant in mid-1968. Today it sounds better, but it's certainly one of the group's more minor efforts, as the members started to divide the songwriting more or less evenly among themselves, rather than letting Brian Wilson provide most of the material. The title track was a charming, if innocuous, minor hit. The bossa nova "Busy Doin' Nothin'" was a subtly subversive piece of rock Muzak, though hindsight reveals a rather worrisome indolencey in the lyrics, as penned by Wilson, who was starting to withdraw into his own world. The production and harmonies remained pleasantly idiosyncratic, but there was little substance at the heart of most of the songs. The irony was that *Smile* had collapsed, in part, because some of the Beach Boys felt that Wilson's increasingly avant-garde leanings would lose their pop audience; yet by the time of *Friends,* the Beach Boys had done a pretty good job of losing most of their audience by retreating to a less experimental, more group-based approach. A 1990 Capitol CD combines this and *20/20* onto one disc, adding five bonus tracks also cut in the late '60s, highlighted by the minor hit "Break Away," Dennis Wilson's oddly spacy "Celebrate the News," and a cover of "Walk on By." *—Richie Unterberger*

Stack-O-Tracks / Aug. 1968 / Capitol ✦✦

20/20 / Feb. 3, 1969 / Capitol ✦✦✦
20/20 was not a proper album, being compiled from singles and leftovers in order to fulfill contractual obligations to Capitol. Nonetheless, it's one of their better post-*Pet Sounds* records, with a couple of good medium-sized late-'60s hit singles, "Do It Again" and "I Can Hear Music," that were fun retro sort of exercises. "Time to Get Alone," with its unusually shifting, jazzy melody, was one of Brian Wilson's last outstanding compositions. "Never Learn Not to Love" is far more notorious, not for the music (which is average), but for the fact that it was, according to some sources, composed by Charles Manson (although the song is credited to Dennis Wilson). The highlights, however, were a couple of *Smile*-session era tunes, especially "Cabinessence," a suite-like collaboration between Brian Wilson and Van Dyke Parks that gives some idea of the complex directions that were being explored during that ill-fated project. Therein lay the group's dilemma: as hard as they were trying to establish their identity as an integrated band in the late '60s, their new recordings were overshadowed by the bits and pieces of *Smile* that emerged at the time. A 1990 Capitol CD combines this and *Friends* onto one disc, adding five bonus tracks also cut in the late '60s, highlighted by the minor hit "Break Away," Dennis Wilson's oddly spacy "Celebrate the News," and a cover of "Walk On By." *—Richie Unterberger*

Sunflower / Aug. 21, 1970 / Caribou ✦✦✦✦✦
After Reprise rejected what was to be their debut album for the label, the Beach Boys re-entered the studio to begin work on what would become a largely different set of songs. The results signaled a creative rebirth for the band, a return to the beautiful harmonies and orchestral productions of their classic mid-'60s material. Though the songwriting didn't quite reach the high quality of "California Girls" or "God Only Knows," *Sunflower* showed the Beach Boys truly working as a band, and doing so better than they ever had in the past (or would in the future). Many of the songs were co-compositions, and the undeniable songwriting and performance talents of Dennis Wilson and Bruce Johnston were finally allowed to flourish: Dennis contributed "Slip on Through," "Forever," and "Got to Know the Woman," while Bruce wrote "Deirdre" and "Tears in the Morning." After a succession of spare, unadorned lead vocals on rock-oriented albums like *Wild Honey* and *20/20, Sunflower* returned the Beach Boys to gorgeous vocal harmonies on the tracks "Add Some Music to Your Day," "Cool, Cool Water," and "This Whole World." And the arrangements, tight and inventive, showed Brian Wilson once again back near the top of his game (though the production is credited to the entire band). *Sunflower* is also a remarkably cohesive album, something not seen from the Beach Boys since *Pet Sounds.* As with that album, *Sunflower* earned critical raves in Britain but was virtually ignored in America. *—John Bush*

Surf's Up / Aug. 30, 1971 / Caribou ✦✦✦✦
The Beach Boys' catalog is littered with forgotten 1970s LPs that barely scraped the charts upon release but matured into solid fan favorites despite—and occasionally, because of—their many and varied eccentricities. *Surf's Up* could well be the most definitive, beginning with the cloying "Don't Go Near the Water" and ending a bare half-hour later with the baroque majesty of the title track (originally written in 1966). The LP is a virtual laundry list of each uncommon intricacy that made the Beach Boys' forgotten decade such a bittersweet thrill—the fluffy yet endearing pop (od)ditties of Brian Wilson, quasi-mystical white-boy soul from brother Carl, and the downright laughable songwriting on tracks charting Mike Love's devotion to Buddhism and Al Jardine's social/environmental concerns.

Those songs are enjoyable enough, but the last three tracks are what make *Surf's Up* such a masterpiece. The first, "A Day in the Life of a Tree," is simultaneously one of Brian's most deeply touching *and* bizarre compositions; he is the narrator and object of the song (though not the vocalist; co-writer Jack Rieley lends a hand), lamenting his long life amidst the pollution and grime of a city park while the somber tones of a pipe organ build atmosphere. The second, "'Til I Die," isn't the love song the title suggests; it's a haunting, fatalistic piece of pop surrealism that appeared to signal Brian's retirement from active life. The album closer, "Surf's Up," is a masterpiece of baroque psychedelia, probably the most compelling track from the *Smile.* period. Carl gives a soulful performance despite the surreal wordplay, and Brian's coda is one of the most stirring moments in his catalog. Wrapped up in a mess of contradictions, *Surf's Up* defined the Beach Boys' tumultuous career better than any other album. *—John Bush*

Carl and the Passions-So Tough / May 15, 1972 / Brother ✦✦✦
With the addition of drummer Ricky Fataar and guitarist Blondie Chaplin to the lineup, the Beach Boys entered a period of surprisingly earthy arrangements, obviously based on what they'd been hearing on cooler outlets like FM radio and AOR. Kicking off with the rough Carl Wilson rocker "You Need a Mess of Help to Stand Alone," *Carl and the Passions—So Tough* cycles through all manner of roots-based rock; Fataar and Chaplin lead the band through a bluesy number ("Here She Comes") and a country song complete with steel guitar ("Hold on Dear Brother"), while Mike Love exercises his spiritual side on the gospel-inspired "He Came Down." The songwriting was neither as solid as 1970's *Sunflower* nor as idiosyncratic as 1971's *Surf's Up* though, and the few fans left from the '60s were undoubtedly turned off—if not by the weak songs, then certainly by the muddy sound. Still, there are a few moments of beauty: Brian's "Marcella" is a midtempo gem, and side two ends with three excellent ballads, "All This Is That," "Make It Good," and "Cuddle Up" (the latter two featuring heart-wrenching performances by Dennis). *—John Bush*

Holland / Jan. 8, 1973 / Caribou ✦✦✦
The surprisingly weak result of a concerted effort by both band and label to push the Beach Boys back into the Top 40 (they succeeded, barely), *Holland* continued the muddy sound of *Carl and the Passions—So Tough.* The highlights here—Carl's "The Trader," Brian's "Sail on Sailor" and "Funky Pretty"—are marginally better than their immediate predecessors, though "Leavin' This Town" (from recent addition Blondie Chaplin) is rather tiresome. Also, Al Jardine and Mike Love's three-part "California Saga" shows the effects of their environmentalist spirituality left to bake in the sun a few minutes too long (though the conclusion, "California," is a solid return to the harmony-laden sun-and-surf '60s). Dennis' sole lead-vocal contribution, "Only With You," is yet another tender ballad given an excellent reading by the most underutilized member of the group. *—John Bush*

The Beach Boys in Concert / Nov. 19, 1973 / Caribou ✦✦✦

☆ **Endless Summer** / Jun. 24, 1974 / Capitol ✦✦✦✦✦
This was the album by which millions of sons of late baby boomers (and sons and daughters of the early ones) first really discovered the Beach Boys, beyond hearing the occasional oldie on the radio. It was the summer of 1974, and the Beach Boys were still trying to get themselves back on track commercially after a seven-year commercial dry spell, when this double LP of their 1963-66 material (all but one cut pre-dating *Pet Sounds*) came along and did the job. *Endless Summer,* which was assembled in consultation with Mike Love, soared to number one and charted high over two subsequent summers (spending three years on the charts, the longest of any of the group's albums), and attracted the enthusiastic attention of millions of listeners too young to have bought their singles back when. The programming was a little thin, not even running an hour total, spread among two LPs, but most of the group's best loved singles were represented—no notes, not a word of historical context, just a great collection of songs that proved irresistible to many shoppers. The packaging was nigh perfect, a simple, celebratory sun-lit graphic that spoke volumes about the music. Although it's been supplanted by other compilations (including the British *20 Golden Greats*), on LP and CD alike, *Endless Summer* was a sentimental favorite for many listeners, sufficient to justify not only a standard CD release but a re-sourced, re-compiled audiophile disc as well from DCC Records. *—Bruce Eder*

15 Big Ones / Jul. 5, 1976 / Caribou ✦✦✦

Love You / Apr. 11, 1977 / Caribou ✦✦✦✦
Judging by the title and the quilted design on the cover, *Love You* would appear to be an album of ballads or romantic tracks, maybe '70s remakes of "Surfer Girl" or "In My Room." But from the brutal synthesizer stabs and Carl Wilson's throaty yell, "Harrahhh!," on the opening track, it's clear this is no ordinary Beach Boys LP. Besides several hard-charging pop songs ("Honkin' Down the Highway," "Roller Skating Child," "Let Us Go on This Way"), there are

a couple of baffling but ultimately endearing tracks whose titles ("Johnny Carson," "Solar System," "Ding Dang") are good indicators of the amateurish lyrics and subject matter.
What makes *Love You* one of the best Beach Boys LPs of the 1970s, though, is the return to an uncommonly Brian Wilson sense of romantic naivete and "adult child" wonder at the world. "The Night Was So Young," "I'll Bet He's Nice," and "Let's Put Our Hearts Together" form a suite during the middle of side two that rivals *Pet Sounds* for breadth of emotional attachment. Originally slated to be a Brian Wilson solo album (titled *Brian Loves You*), it shows the aging genius with many of his pop smarts intact, his wildly eccentric lifestyle tweaking his sense of songcraft in an intriguing direction. *—John Bush*

M.I.U. Album / Sep. 25, 1978 / Caribou ✦✦

L.A. (Light Album) / Mar. 16, 1979 / Caribou ✦✦

Keepin' the Summer Alive / Mar. 17, 1980 / Caribou ✦

The Beach Boys / Jun. 1985 / Sessions ✦✦

Summer in Paradise / Aug. 3, 1992 / Brother ✦

☆ **Good Vibrations: Thirty Years of the Beach Boys** / Jun. 21, 1993 / Capitol ✦✦✦✦✦
A five-CD box set, containing a whopping 142 tracks and covering the group's entire career, that manages to feel like too much and not enough at the same time. True, all of the key hits and most of their finest album tracks are here. The group's decline after 1966—and very sharp decline after 1970—is inescapable, and even though most of the material here is from the 1960s, the fourth disc especially (spanning the early 1970s to the late 1980s) is very rough sailing indeed. It's true that about 50 of these tracks are previously unreleased, but be warned that many of them are demos, backing tracks, and alternate versions of well-known songs that aren't a great deal different from the officially released versions. Also, some of the unreleased "tracks" are radio spots. That's not to say that these rare items aren't interesting for the fan; they are. It's just that it's too overwhelming a package for the non-fanatic, and a rather expensive, spotty one for the devoted fan (who will undoubtedly already have at least half the contents). By far, the most interesting unreleased tracks date from the legendary *Smile* sessions (nearly an album's worth). Never actually completed, they aren't quite the masterpiece that some have claimed, but are extremely interesting, often beautiful excursions into psychedelic production and songwriting that often resemble sound paintings more than songs. Comes with a 60-page booklet by Beach Boy historian David Leaf. *—Richie Unterberger*

Stars & Stripes, Vol. 1 / Aug. 20, 1996 / A&M ✦

Pet Sounds 30th Anniversary Box Set / Nov. 4, 1997 / Capitol ✦✦✦
There's little arguing that *Pet Sounds* is one of the greatest albums in rock & roll, and its cult, if anything, has only grown in the 30 years since its intial release. Part of the fascination with *Pet Sounds* lies in its detailed, multi-layered arrangements, in which all the parts blend together into a symphonic whole. The richness of the music is one of the reasons hardcore fans have desired a set like *The Pet Sounds Sessions*, a four-disc box that presents an abundance of working mixes, alternate takes, instrumental tracks, and rarities, as well as the first true stereo mix of the album. Certainly, a set this exacting is only of interest to serious fans, and even they might find the endless succession of work tracks tedious. Nevertheless, there's something fascinating about hearing the album broken down to its individual parts; after hearing horn lines, vocals, and percussion tracks out of their original context, the scope and originality of Brian Wilson's vision becomes all the more impressive. (Make no mistake about it, *Pet Sounds* is entirely Wilson's project, despite what Mike Love states in his self-serving liner notes.) The original mono mix of *Pet Sounds* (included here in a minature, cardboard record sleeve) remains the best way to appreciate Wilson's gifts, but for fans already convinced of his genius, *The Pet Sounds Sessions* is a fascinating, educational listen, even if it's not necessarily indispensable. *—Stephen Thomas Erlewine*

Endless Harmony / Aug. 11, 1998 / Capitol ✦✦✦✦

★ **Greatest Hits, Vol. 1** / Sep. 21, 1999 / Capitol ✦✦✦✦✦
With the *Absolute Best* collections out of print at the end of the '90s and the *20 Good Vibrations: The Greatest Hits* missing about as many great singles as it included, Capitol's release of two generous Beach Boys *Greatest Hits* discs in 1999 was welcome. Unfortunately, they got it only half-right. Since the Beach Boys had too many hits to fit onto one 20-track collection, it made sense to have two separate 20-track discs, but the dividing line is arbitrary. For its three quarters, *Greatest Hits, Vol. 1* appears to be a straight chronological trawl through the hits, beginning with "Surfin' Safari" and running through "Barbara Ann." Upon close inspection, a number of major songs—"Surfin'," "Shut Down," "In My Room," "Don't Worry Baby"—are missing, yet that portion of the album plays very well. The last five songs are a bit problematic. True, there's a good selection of *Pet Sounds*-era highlights, but the late '60s and '70s are skipped in favor of "Kokomo," which has never sounded more out of place than it does here. Of course, to some casual fans, this will seem like nitpicking since *Greatest Hits, Vol. 1* does have the lion's share of the Beach Boys' popular material, and it is nice to have these songs on one disc, even if "Do It Again," "Caroline No," and "Heroes and Villains" are missing, along with the previously mentioned cuts. What is here qualifies as a top-notch introduction, yet it's hard not to wish that the two *Greatest Hits* were chronological, with *Vol. 1* ending before *Pet Sounds* and the second volume tying up the remaining Capitol recordings. *—Stephen Thomas Erlewine*

☆ **Greatest Hits, Vol. 2** / Sep. 21, 1999z / Capitol ✦✦✦✦✦
Since Capitol's two-volume 1999 *Greatest Hits* only seemed to be chronological—they followed a rough timeline, but *Vol. 1* had many curious omissions from the early years, yet it basically stopped after *Pet Sounds*—there were many early hits that should have fit on the first volume that were saved for the second. In other words, if you were wondering where "In My Room," "Warmth of the Sun," "Don't Worry Baby," "All Summer Long," "Wendy," "Little Honda," "When I Grow up to Be a Man," and "Caroline No" all were, the answer is, they're here on the first half of *Vol. 2* ("Surfin'" is still curiously absent from these collections). The second half of the disc rounds up highlights from the Beach Boys' late-'60s recordings for Capitol—"Heroes and Villains," "Wild Honey," "Darlin'," "Friends," "Do It Again," "I Can Hear Music"—stopping when they switched to Reprise in 1970. Combined with *Vol. 1*, this offers an excellent portrait of the Beach Boys as a singles band, which was always their strength in the '60s. It would have been nice if the two volumes complemented each other chronologically, yet they still work very well together; as they stand, they're the best available collection of the Beach Boys' hits. *—Stephen Thomas Erlewine*

Greatest Hits, Vol. 3: The Best of the Brother Years / Feb. 1, 2000 / Capitol ✦✦✦✦
Long out of print but often treasured by collectors and particularly obsessive fans, the Beach Boys' work from the '70s and early '80s also enjoyed a growing cachet with music cognoscenti during the '90s. Finally, in 2000, Capitol reissued the group's later catalog on a series of two-fers. *The Greatest Hits, Vol. 3: Best of the Brother Years* preceded the reissues with a 20-track overview of the years 1970 through 1986, from the first Brother single ("Add Some Music to Your Day") to the last ("California Dreamin'"). Besides the inclusion of '70s classics like "Surf's Up" and "'Til I Die," there are a few engaging Brian Wilson rockers ("Honkin' Down the Highway," "Good Timin'") and the many classic R&B standards ("Rock and Roll Music," "Peggy Sue," "Come Go With Me") pointing the way to the county-fair oldies act the Beach Boys were soon to become. On the whole, the track selection is solid but rather unappealing: *Greatest Hits, Vol. 3* may have taken a lot of singles from the Brother years, but it didn't take all of the best songs. And the short shrift given to Dennis Wilson is *very* disappointing. The tender ballads Dennis delivered at the end of albums like *Carl and the Passions—So Tough* and *Holland* were excellent, and among the most affecting work of the Beach Boys' career. For listeners curious about the quality of the '70s years, this probably isn't the best compilation: the group just wasn't a singles act anymore, and the most entertaining Beach Boys albums of the decade—*Sunflower, Surf's Up, The Beach Boys Love You*—are best heard in their entireties. *—John Bush*

Beat Happening

f. 1982, Olympia, WA
Group / Twee Pop, Indie Rock, Alternative Pop/Rock
Beat Happening was among the truly seminal and influential American bands of the post-punk era, a paragon of pop minimalism, rebellious innocence and indie defiance. The linchpin of the Olympia, Washington-based International Pop Underground, members Calvin (Johnson), Heather (Lewis), and Bret (Lunsford) expressed simple truths and simple emotions with simple music, favoring off-key, tuneless vocals and three-chord primitivism over slick, processed packaging; implicit in their work was also a rejection of major-label trappings, as the group steadfastly remained with K Records, Calvin's self-owned imprint and a model of D.I.Y. indie success. After several EPs and many shows around Olympia, Beat Happening's 1985 eponymous full-length debut brought the trio their first widespread exposure, as well as a number of comparisons to the burgeoning British twee-pop scene spearheaded by the Pastels. With the release of 1991's *Dreamy*, the group's influence on the indie community and the blossoming cuddle-core movement became increasingly pronounced. The sublime *You Turn Me On* followed, but the band spent much of the decade in limbo as Calvin focused on his Dub Narcotic Sound System project as well as the Halo Benders. Despite their absence from the stage and the studio, the trio maintained that they had not disbanded, and reportedly continued practicing on a monthly basis. *—Jason Ankeny*

Beat Happening / 1985 / K ✦✦✦
Beat Happening can't be given credit for *creating* the indie pop genre, but they certainly gave it life in America. This, their first album, is indie-pop in its purest form: fuzzy bedroom recordings of simplistic, cutesy songs, with intentionally innocent and juvenile lyrics, which Calvin Johnson belts out with one of the most endearingly bad voices in music history. Their later albums sport better songwriting and are more listenable from a production standpoint, but *Beat Happening* is as twee and charming as this type of music can get. *1983-85*, its CD reissue (with a few live songs and early recordings added), is for *devoted* indie-pop fans only. *—Nitsuh Abebe*

Jamboree / 1988 / Sub Pop/K ✦✦✦✦✦
Co-produced by Steve Fisk and the Screaming Trees' Mark Lanegan and Gary Lee Conner, Beat Happening's brief, brilliant sophomore effort significantly expands the trio's horizons without sacrificing any of their naive charm. Sporting a fuller, more intricate sound and stronger songs than their debut, *Jamboree* crystallizes the trio's love-rock aesthetic in its embryonic stages; veering sharply from the idyllic drones of the perennial "Indian Summer" to the poignant crush-pop of "Cat Walk" to the indie-party classic "Midnight A Go-Go," each cut is a marvel of innocence and ingenuity. *—Jason Ankeny*

Black Candy / 1989 / Sub Pop/K ✦✦✦
As evidenced by its title, *Black Candy* is Beat Happening's darkest, most delirously ominous album; clearly influenced by the Cramps, the record is dominated by Calvin Johnson's coffin-creak vocals, with Heather Lewis' breathy sweetness rarely in earshot to lighten the mood. A less developed batch of compositions than the previous *Jamboree*, it strives to evoke the mood of a grade-Z teen horror flick soundtrack, with faux-creepy songs ("Pajama Party in a Haunted Hive," "Gravedigger Blues," "Bonfire") and primal, drum-dominated production; less eclectic and nuanced than the trio's other LPs, *Black Candy* quickly grows tiresome, although the oft-covered highlight "Cast a Shadow" is a treat. *—Jason Ankeny*

1983-85 / 1990 / K ✦✦✦✦✦
1983-85 compiles 27 early Beat Happening tracks, spanning the trio's eponymous debut LP, the *Three Tea Breakfast* EP, a handful of compilation appearances, singles, and a wealth of unreleased material. A portrait of the group at their most primitive, the fidelity is often poor, but the kinetic energy of the early sessions is palpable, and the wide-eyed charm of gems like "Look Around," "Foggy Eyes," "fourteen," and the classic "Bad Seeds" is undeniable. *—Jason Ankeny*

Dreamy / 1991 / Sub Pop/K ✦✦✦✦✦
A stunning return to form, *Dreamy* reprises the dark aggression of the preceding *Black Candy*, but brings to the table a significantly stronger and more assured collection of songs.

Measuring Calvin Johnson's increasingly menacing lead turns with Heather Lewis' more wistful contributions, the album strikes a careful balance between maturity and naivete; for all of their ragged minimalism, tracks like "Collide," "Revolution Come and Gone" and "Me Untamed" are remarkably sophisticated and assured. And in addition to the newfound sexiness of cuts like "Nancy Sin" and "Red Head Walking," there's also a renewed sense of emotional urgency—Heather's beguiling "Fortune Cookie Prize" is one of the group's most buoyant love songs, while the mournful "Cry for a Shadow" exposes the tenderness beneath Calvin's tough-guy veneer. *—Jason Ankeny*

● **You Turn Me On** / Oct. 2, 1992 / Sub Pop ✦✦✦✦✦
Beat Happening's (possibly) final LP is also their best: concluding the emotional and musical progression begun with the minimalist innocence of their earliest work, *You Turn Me On* is a mature record of tremendous breadth and complexity. Where once the trio's songs were brief and bouncy, the nine tracks here are epic (several top out at over six minutes) and ambitious; produced in part by ex-Young Marble Giant Stuart Moxham (an obvious influence), the record's full, deep sound belies its bare-bones performances—"Teenage Caveman" sports booming, primal drums perfectly suited to its title, while the propulsive "Noise" manufactures the illusion of a bassline where none ever existed. The most democratic record in an output founded on egalitarian ideals, *You Turn Me On* offers Heather Lewis' strongest songs ever—her hypnotic nine-minute "Godsend" is the LP's heart and soul—and she and Calvin Johnson even trade verses on the closing "Bury the Hammer." As for Calvin himself, his solo contributions are exceptional—the spartan opener "Tiger Trap" is an evocative heartbreaker, and the title track is a fire-breathing corker. A masterpiece. *—Jason Ankeny*

The Beatles

f. 1960, Liverpool, England, **db.** 1970
Group / British Psychedelia, Pop/Rock, Folk-Rock, Merseybeat, Psychedelic, British Invasion, Rock & Roll
The Beatles were the most popular and influential rock act of all time, but their significance cannot solely be measured in sales records (as impressive as those are). John Lennon, Paul McCartney, George Harrison and Ringo Starr synthesized all that was good about early rock and roll, and changed it into something original and even more exciting. They established the prototype for the self-contained rock group that wrote and performed their own material. As composers, their craft and melodic inventiveness were second to none, and key to the evolution of rock from its blues/R&B-based forms into a style that was far more eclectic, but equally visceral. As singers, both Lennon and McCartney were among the best and most expressive vocalists in rock; the group's harmonies were intricate and exhilarating. As performers, they were exciting and photogenic; when they retreated into the studio, they were instrumental in pioneering advanced techniques and multi-layered arrangements. They were also the first British rock group to achieve worldwide prominence, launching a British Invasion that made rock truly an international phenomenon. With their unmatched songwriting savvy, brash guitar-oriented attack and wildly enthusiastic vocals, they were the embodiment of the youthful flair of their generation, ready to dispense with post-war austerity and claim a culture of their own. The Beatles were also unsurpassed in their eclecticism, willing to borrow from blues, popular standards, gospel, folk, or whatever seemed suitable for their musical vision. Producer George Martin was the perfect foil for the group, refining their ideas without tinkering with their essence. During the last half of their career, he was indispensable for his ability to translate their concepts into arrangements that required complex orchestration, innovative applications of recording technology, and an ever-widening array of instruments. Just as crucially, the Beatles were never ones to stand still and milk formulas. All of their albums and singles would show remarkable artistic progression (though never at the expense of a damn catchy tune). *—Richie Unterberger*

☆ **Please Please Me** / Mar. 22, 1963 / Capitol ✦✦✦✦✦
Once "Please Please Me" rocketed to number one, the Beatles rushed to deliver a debut album, bashing out *Please Please Me* in a day. Decades after its release, the album still sounds fresh, precisely because of its intense origins. As the songs rush past, it's easy to get wrapped up in the sound of the record itself without realizing how the album effectively summarizes the band's eclectic influences. Naturally, the influences shine through their covers, all of which are unconventional and illustrate the group's superior taste. There's a love of girl groups, vocal harmonies, sophisticated popcraft, schmaltz, R&B and hard-driving rock & roll, which is enough to make *Please Please Me* impressive, but what makes it astonishing is how these elements converge in the originals. "I Saw Here Standing There" is one of their best rockers, yet it has surprising harmonies and melodic progressions. "Misery" and "There's a Place" grow out of the girl group tradition without being tied to it. A few of their originals, such as "Do You Want to Know a Secret" and the pleasantly light "PS I Love You," have dated slightly, but endearingly so, since they're infused with cheerful innocence and enthusiasm. And there is an innocence to *Please Please Me.* The Beatles may have played notoriously rough dives in Hamburg, but the only way you could tell that on their first album was how the constant gigging turned the group into a tight, professional band that could run through their set list at the drop of a hat with boundless energy. It's no surprise that Lennon had shouted himself hoarse by the end of the session, barely getting through "Twist and Shout," the most famous single-take in rock history. He simply got caught up in the music, just like generations of listeners did. *—Stephen Thomas Erlewine*

☆ **With the Beatles** / Nov. 22, 1963 / Capitol ✦✦✦✦✦
With the Beatles is a sequel of the highest order—one that betters the original by developing its own tone and adding depth. While it may share several similarities with its predecessor—there is an equal ratio of covers-to-originals, a familiar blend of girl group, Motown, R&B, pop, and rock, and a show tune that interrupts the flow of the album— *With the Beatles* is a better record that not only rocks harder, it's considerably more sophisticated. They could deliver rock & roll straight ("I Wanna Be Your Man") or twist it around with a little Latin lilt ("Little Child," one of their most underrated early rockers); Lennon and McCartney wrote sweet ballads (the achingly gorgeous "All I've Got to Do") and sprightly pop/rockers ("All My Loving") with equal aplomb; and propulsive rockers ("It Won't Be Long") were as richly melodic as slower songs ("Not a Second Time"). Even George Harrison's first recorded song, "Don't Bother Me," is a standout, with its wonderfully foreboding minor-key melody. Since the Beatles covered so much ground with their originals, their covers pale slightly in comparison, particularly since they rely on familiar hits (only "Devil in Her Heart" qualifies as a forgotten gem). But for every "Roll Over Beethoven," a surprisingly stiff reading of the Chuck Berry standard, there is a sublime moment, such as Lennon's soaring interpretation of "You Really Got a Hold on Me," and the group always turns in thoroughly enjoyable performances. Still, the heart of *With the Beatles* lies not in the covers, but the originals, where it was clear that, even at this early stage, the Beatles were rapidly maturing and changing, turning into expert craftsmen and musical innovators. *—Stephen Thomas Erlewine*

☆ **A Hard Day's Night** / Jul. 10, 1964 / Capitol ✦✦✦✦✦
A Hard Day's Night is not only was the de-facto soundtrack for their movie, not only was it filled with nothing but Lennon-McCartney originals, but it found the Beatles truly coming into their own as a band. All of the disparate influences on their first two albums had coalesced into a bright, joyous, original sound, filled with ringing guitars and irresistible melodies. *A Hard Day's Night* is where the Beatles became mythical, but this is the sound of Beatlemania in all of its giddy glory. Decades after its original release, its punchy blend of propulsive rhythms, jangly guitars and infectious, sing-along melodies is remarkably fresh. There's something intrinsically exciting in the *sound* of the album itself, something to keep the record vital years after it was recorded. Even more impressive are the songs themselves. Not only are the melodies forceful and memorable, but Lennon and McCartney have found a number of variations to their basic Merseybeat style, from the brash "Can't Buy Me Love" and "Any Time At All" through the gentle "If I Fell" to the tough folk-rock of "I'll Cry Instead." It's possible to hear both songwriters develop their own distinctive voices on the album, but overall, *A Hard Day's Night* stands as a testament to their collaborative powers—never again did they write together so well or so easily, choosing to pursue their own routes. John and Paul must have known how strong the material is—they threw the pleasant trifle "I'm Happy Just to Dance with You" to George and didn't give anything to Ringo to sing. That may have been a little selfish, but it hardly hurts the album, since everything on the record is performed with genuine glee and excitement. It's the pinnacle of their early years. *—Stephen Thomas Erlewine*

☆ **Beatles for Sale** / Dec. 4, 1964 / Capitol ✦✦✦✦✦
It was inevitable that the constant grind of touring, writing, promoting, and recording would grate on the Beatles, but the weariness of *Beatles for Sale* comes as something of a shock. Only five months before, the group released the joyous *A Hard Day's Night.* Now, they sound beaten, worn, and, in Lennon's case, bitter and self-loathing. His opening trilogy ("No Reply," "I'm a Loser," "Baby's in Black") is the darkest sequence on any Beatles record, setting the tone for the album. Moments of joy pop up now and again, mainly in the forms of covers and the dynamic "Eight Days a Week," but the very presence of six covers after the triumphant all-original *A Hard Day's Night* feels like an admission of defeat or at least a regression. (It doesn't help that Lennon's cover of his beloved obscurity "Mr. Moonlight" winds up as arguably the worst thing the group ever recorded.) Beneath those surface suspicions, however, there are some important changes on *Beatles for Sale,* most notably Lennon's discovery of Bob Dylan and folk-rock. The opening three songs, along with "I Don't Want to Spoil the Party," are implicitly confessional and all quite bleak, which is a new development. This spirit winds up overshadowing McCartney's cheery "I'll Follow the Sun" or the thundering covers of "Rock & Roll Music," "Honey Don't," and "Kansas City/Hey, Hey, Hey Hey," and the weariness creeps up in unexpected places—"Every Little Thing," "What You're Doing," even George's cover of Carl Perkins' "Everybody's Trying to Be My Baby"—leaving the impression that Beatlemania may have been fun but now the group is exhausted. That exhaustion results in the group's most uneven album, but its best moments find them moving from Merseybeat to the sophisticated pop/rock they developed in mid-career. *—Stephen Thomas Erlewine*

☆ **Help!** / Aug. 6, 1965 / Capitol ✦✦✦✦✦
Considering that *Help!* functions as the Beatles' fifth album and as the soundtrack to their second film—while filming, they continued to release non-LP singles on a regular basis—it's not entirely surprising that it still has some of the weariness of *Beatles for Sale.* Again, they pad the album with covers, but the Bakersfield bounce of "Act Naturally" adds new flavor (along with an ideal showcase for Ringo's amiable vocals) and "Dizzy Miss Lizzie" gives John an opportunity to flex his rock & roll muscle. George is writing again and if his two contributions don't touch Lennon and McCartney's originals, they hold their own against much of their British pop peers. Since Lennon wrote *a third* more songs than McCartney, it's easy to forgive a pair of minor numbers ("It's Only Love," "Tell Me What You See"), especially since they're overshadowed by four great songs. His Dylan infatuation holds strong, particularly on the plaintive "You've Got to Hide Your Love Away" and the title track, where the brash arrangement disguises Lennon's desperation. Driven by an indelible 12-string guitar, "Ticket to Ride" is another masterpiece and "You're Going to Lose That Girl" is the kind of song McCartney effortlessly tosses off—which he does, with the jaunty "The Night Before" and "Another Girl," two very fine tunes that simply update his melodic signature. He did much better with "I've Just Seen a Face," an irresistible folk-rock gem, and "Yesterday," a simple, beautiful ballad whose arrangement—an acoustic guitar supported by a string quartet—and composition suggested much more sophisticated and adventurous musical territory, which the group immediately began exploring with *Rubber Soul.* *—Stephen Thomas Erlewine*

☆ **Rubber Soul** / Dec. 3, 1965 / Capitol ✦✦✦✦✦
While the Beatles still largely stuck to love songs on *Rubber Soul,* the lyrics represented a quantum leap in terms of thoughtfulness, maturity, and complex ambiguities. Musically, too, it was a substantial leap forward, with intricate folk-rock arrangements that reflected the increasing influence of Dylan and the Byrds. The group and George Martin were also beginning to expand the conventional instrumental parameters of the rock group, using a sitar on "Norwegian Wood," and Greek-like guitar lines on "Michelle" and "Girl," fuzz bass on "Think

for Yourself," and a piano made to sound like a harpsichord on the instrumental break of "In My Life." While John and Paul were beginning to carve separate songwriting identities at this point, the album is full of great tunes, from "Norwegian Wood" and "Michelle" to "Girl," "I'm Looking Through You," "You Won't See Me," "Drive My Car," and "Nowhere Man" (the last of which was the first Beatle song to move beyond romantic themes entirely). George Harrison was also developing into a fine songwriter with his two contributions, "Think for Yourself" and the Byrdsish "If I Needed Someone." *—Richie Unterberger*

☆ **Revolver** / Aug. 5, 1966 / Capitol ♦♦♦♦♦
All the rules fell by the wayside with *Revolver,* as the Beatles began exploring new sonic territory, lyrical subjects, and styles of composition. It wasn't just Lennon and McCartney, either—Harrison staked out his own dark territory with the tightly wound, cynical rocker "Taxman"; the jaunty yet dissonant "I Want to Tell You"; and "Love You To," George's first and best foray into Indian music. Such explorations were bold, yet they were eclipsed by Lennon's trippy kaleidoscopes of sound. His most straightforward number was "Doctor Robert," an ode to his dealer, and things just got stranger from there, as he buried "And Your Bird Can Sing" in a maze of multi-tracked guitars, gave Ringo a charmingly hallucinogenic slice of childhood whimsy in "Yellow Submarine," and then capped it off with a triptych of bad trips: the spiraling "She Said She Said"; the crawling, druggy "I'm Only Sleeping"; and "Tomorrow Never Knows," a pure nightmare where John sang portions of the *Tibetan Book of the Dead* into a suspended microphone over Ringo's thundering, menacing drumbeats and layers of overdubbed, phased guitars and tape loops. McCartney's experiments were formal, as he tried on every pop style from chamber pop to soul, and when placed alongside Lennon and Harrison's outright experimentations, McCartney's songcraft becomes all the more impressive. The biggest miracle of *Revolver* may be that the Beatles covered so much new stylistic ground and executed it perfectly on one record, or it may be that all of it holds together perfectly. Either way, its daring sonic adventures and consistently stunning songcraft set the standard for what pop/rock could achieve. Even after *Sgt. Pepper, Revolver* stands as the ultimate modern pop album and it's still as emulated as it was upon its original release. *—Stephen Thomas Erlewine*

☆ **Sgt. Pepper's Lonely Hearts Club Band** / Jun. 1, 1967 / Capitol ♦♦♦♦♦
With *Revolver,* the Beatles made the Great Leap Forward, reaching a previously unheard-of level of sophistication and fearless experimentation. *Sgt. Pepper,* in many ways, refines that breakthrough, as the Beatles consciously synthesized such disparate influences as psychedelia, art-song, classical music, rock & roll and music hall, often in the course of one song. Not once does the diversity seem forced—the genius of the record is how the vaudevillian "When I'm 64" seems like a logical extension of "Within You Without You" and how it provides a gateway to the chiming guitars of "Lovely Rita." There's no discounting the individual contributions of each member or their producer George Martin, but the preponderance of whimsy and self-conscious art gives the impression that Paul McCartney is the leader of the Lonely Hearts Club Band. He dominates the album in terms of compositions, setting the tone for the album with his unabashed melodicism and deviously clever arrangements. In comparison, Lennon's contributions seem fewer, and a couple of them are a little slight but his major statements are stunning. "With a Little Help from My Friends" is the ideal Ringo tune, a rolling, friendly pop song that hides genuine Lennon anguish, ala "Help;!" "Lucy in the Sky with Diamonds" remains one of the touchstones of British psychedelia; and he's the mastermind behind the bulk of "A Day in the Life," a haunting number that skillfuly blends Lennon's verse and chorus with McCartney's bridge. It's possibly to argue that there are better Beatles albums, yet no album is as historically important as this. After *Sgt. Pepper,* there were no rules to follow—rock and pop bands could try anything, for better or worse. Ironically, few tried to achieve the sweeping, all-encompassing embrace of music as the Beatles did here. *—Stephen Thomas Erlewine*

☆ **Magical Mystery Tour** / Nov. 27, 1967 / Capitol ♦♦♦♦♦
The U.S. version of the soundtrack for their ill-fated British television special embellished the six songs that were found on the British *Magical Mystery Tour* double EP with five other cuts from their 1967 singles. (The CD version of the record has now been standardized worldwide as the 11 tracks found on the American version.) The psychedelic sound is very much in the vein of *Sgt. Pepper,* and even spacier in parts (especially the sound collages of "I Am the Walrus"). Unlike *Sgt. Pepper,* there's no vague overall conceptual/thematic unity to the material, which has made *Magical Mystery Tour* suffer slightly in comparison. Still, the music is mostly great, and "Penny Lane," "Strawberry Fields Forever," "All You Need Is Love," and "Hello Goodbye" were all huge, glorious, and innovative singles. The ballad "The Fool in the Hill," though only a part of the *Magical Mystery Tour* soundtrack, is also one of the most popular Beatle tunes from the era. *—Richie Unterberger*

☆ **The Beatles [White Album]** / Nov. 22, 1968 / Capitol ♦♦♦♦♦
Each song on the sprawling double album *The Beatles* is an entity to itself, as the band touches on anything and everything they can. This makes for a frustratingly scattershot record or a singularly gripping musical experience, depending on your view, but what makes the White Album interesting is its mess. Never before had a rock record been so self-reflective, or so ironic; the Beach Boys send-up "Back in the USSR" and the British blooze parody "Yer Blues" are delivered straight-faced, so it's never clear if these are affectionate tributes or wicked satires. Lennon turns in two of his best ballads with "Dear Prudence" and "Julia"; scours the Abbey Road vaults for the musique concrete collage "Revolution 9"; pours on the schmaltz for Ringo's closing number, "Good Night"; celebrates the Beatles cult with "Glass Onion"; and, with "Cry Baby Cry," rivals Syd Barrett. McCartney doesn't reach quite as far, yet his songs are stunning—the music-hall romp "Honey Pie", the mock country of "Rocky Raccoon", the ska-inflected "Ob-La-Di, Ob-La-Da" and the proto-metal roar of "Helter Skelter." Clearly, the Beatles' two main songwriting forces were no longer on the same page, but neither were George and Ringo. Harrison still had just two songs per LP, but it's clear from "While My Guitar Gently Weeps," the canned soul of "Savoy Truffle," the haunting "Long Long Long," and even the silly "Piggies" that he had developed into a songwriter who deserved wider exposure. And Ringo turns in a delight with his first original, the lumbering country-carnival stomp "Don't Pass Me By." None of it sounds like it was meant to share album space together, but somehow *The Beatles* creates its own style and sound through its mess. *—Stephen Thomas Erlewine*

Yellow Submarine / Jan. 13, 1969 / Capitol ♦♦♦
The only Beatles album that could really be classified as inessential, mostly because it wasn't really a proper album at all, but a soundtrack that only utilized four new Beatles songs. (The rest of the album was filled out with "Yellow Submarine," "All You Need Is Love," and a George Martin score that held little appeal to rock listeners.) What's more, the four new tracks were little more than pleasant throwaways that had been recorded during 1967 and early 1968. These aren't all that bad; "All Together Now" is a kiddieish singalong, "Hey Bulldog" has some mild Lennon nastiness, and Harrison's "It's All Too Much" is highlighted by some tidal waves of feedback guitar. It would have been far better value if it had been released as a four-song EP (an idea the Beatles even considered at one point, with the addition of a bonus track in "Across the Universe," but ultimately discarded). *—Richie Unterberger*

☆ **Abbey Road** / Sep. 26, 1969 / Capitol ♦♦♦♦♦
The last Beatles album to be recorded (although *Let It Be* was the last to be released), *Abbey Road* was a fitting swan song for the group, echoing some of the faux-conceptual forms of *Sgt. Pepper,* but featuring stronger compositions and more rock-oriented ensemble work. The group were still pushing forward in all facets of their art, whether devising some of the greatest harmonies to be heard on any rock record (especially on "Because"), constructing a medley of songs/vignettes that covered much of side two, adding subtle touches of Moog synthesizer, or crafting furious guitar-heavy rock ("The End," "I Want You (She's So Heavy)," "Come Together"). George Harrison also blossomed into a major songwriter, contributing the buoyant "Here Comes the Sun" and the supremely melodic ballad "Something," the latter of which became the first Harrison-penned Beatles hit. Whether *Abbey Road* is the Beatles' best work is debatable, but it's certainly the most immaculately produced (with the possible exception of *Sgt. Pepper*) and most tightly constructed. *—Richie Unterberger*

☆ **Let It Be** / May 8, 1970 / Capitol ♦♦♦♦♦
The only Beatles album to occasion negative, even hostile reviews, there are few other rock records as controversial as *Let It Be.* First off, several facts need to be explained: Although released in May 1970, this was *not* their final album, but largely recorded in early 1969, way before *Abbey Road.* Phil Spector was enlisted in early 1970 to do some post-production mixing and overdubs, but he did *not* work with the band as a unit. And, although his use of strings has generated much criticism, by and large he left the original performances to stand as is: only "The Long and Winding Road" and (to a lesser degree) "Across the Universe" and "I Me Mine" get the wall-of-sound treatment. The main problem was that the material wasn't uniformly strong, and that the Beatles themselves were in fairly lousy moods due to inter-group tension. All that said, the album is on the whole underrated, even discounting the fact that a substandard Beatles record is better than almost any other group's best work. McCartney in particular offers several gems: the gospelish "Let It Be," which has some of his best lyrics; "Get Back," one of his hardest rockers; and the melodic "The Long and Winding Road," ruined by Spector's heavy-handed overdubs. The folky "Two of Us," with John and Paul harmonizing together, was also a highlight. Most of the rest of the material, by contrast, was going through the motions to some degree, although there are some good moments of straight hard rock in "I've Got a Feeling" and "Dig a Pony." As flawed and bumpy as it is, it's an album well-worth having, as when the Beatles were in top form here, they were as good as ever. *—Richie Unterberger*

1962-1966 / Apr. 2, 1973 / Capitol ♦♦♦♦♦

1967-1970 / Apr. 2, 1973 / Capitol ♦♦♦♦♦

☆ **Past Masters, Vol. 1** / Mar. 7, 1988 / Capitol ♦♦♦♦♦
When Capitol decided to release the original British editions of the Beatles' albums instead of the bastardized American versions, they were left with a bit of a quandary. Since the Beatles had an enormous number of non-LP singles, some of their greatest hits—from "I Want to Hold Your Hand" through "Hey Jude"—would not be included on disc if Capitol simply served up straight reissues. They had two options: They could add the singles as bonus tracks to the appropriate CDs, or they could release a compilation of all the non-LP tracks. It should come as no surprise that they chose the latter. In fact, they took it one further, issuing two separate compilations of non-LP tracks, which is fairly appropriate since the Beatles released far more singles and EPs in the first two years of their recording career than they did in the last five. *Past Masters, Vol. 1* covers those first two years and, to be fair, there are some cuts that are unnecessary for anyone outside of the hardcore—only a handful of people will be able to spot the difference in the alternate "Love Me Do," while German versions of "I Want to Hold Your Hand" and "She Loves You" aren't even good for a chuckle. Still, the sheer number of astounding singles makes this essential, even with its faults. These 17 songs capture the exuberance of Beatlemania while confirming their talents as pop craftsmen ("This Boy," "Yes It Is") and proving that they could rock really, really hard ("I Feel Fine," "She's a Woman," the peerless "I'm Down"). Apart from the cuts that are merely rarities, this is a near-perfect compilation that captures the energy and spirit of the Beatles' early years. *—Stephen Thomas Erlewine*

☆ **Past Masters, Vol. 2** / Mar. 7, 1988 / Capitol ♦♦♦♦♦
Picking up in 1965 where *Past Masters, Vol. 1* left off, *Past Masters, Vol. 2* collects the 15 non-LP tracks that the Beatles released in the last five years of their career (not counting the singles that were released on *the Magical Mystery Tour*). If *Vol. 2* is more eclectic than its predecessor, it isn't quite as thematically consistent, but it does hit greater highs with a greater frequency. Indeed, some of the greatest singles in pop history are here: "Day Tripper," "We Can Work It Out," "Paperback Writer," "Rain," "Lady Madonna," "Hey Jude," "Revolution," "Don't Let Me Down," and "The Ballad of John and Yoko." All of the aforementioned are staples in the Lennon/McCartney canon and while George Harrison's two contributions aren't as familiar, "The Inner Light" is arguably his best Indian excursion and "Old Brown Shoe" is a charmingly jaunty tune that points toward his solo career. In the middle of all this,

single versions of "Get Back" and "Let It Be" appear (the former is stiffer than the LP version, the latter is better than its counterpart), along with the alternate (and superior) "Across the Universe" and the silly yet strangely irresistible "You Know My Name (Look Up the Number)." Overall, the compilation feels a little disjointed, mainly because it covers so much ground so quickly, but that takes nothing away from the quality of the music, since many of these songs rank among the best, most inventive recordings of the pop-rock era. *—Stephen Thomas Erlewine*

Live at the BBC / Dec. 1994 / Apple/Capitol ♦♦♦♦♦
From 1962 to 1965, the Beatles made 52 appearances on the BBC, recording live-in-the-studio performances of both their official releases and several dozen songs that they never issued on disc. This magnificent two-disc compilation features 56 of these tracks, including 29 covers of early rock, R&B, soul, and pop tunes that never appeared on their official releases, as well as the Lennon-McCartney original "I'll Be on My Way," which they gave in 1963 to Billy J. Kramer rather than record it themselves. These performances are nothing less than electrifying, especially the previously unavailable covers, which feature quite a few versions of classics by Chuck Berry, Little Richard, Carl Perkins, and Elvis Presley. There are also off-the-beaten-path tunes by the Everly Brothers and Buddy Holly, on down to obscurities by the Jodimars, Chan Romero (a marvelous "Hippy Hippy Shake"), Eddie Fontaine, and Ann-Margret. The greatest gem is probably their fabulous version of Arthur Alexander's "Soldier of Love," which (like several of the tracks) would have easily qualified as a highlight of their early releases if they had issued it officially. Restored from existing tapes of various quality, the sound is mostly very good and never less than listenable. Unfortunately, they weren't able to include every single rarity that the Beatles recorded for the BBC; the absence of Carl Perkins' "Lend Me Your Comb," which has circulated on bootlegs in a high-fidelity version, is especially mystifying. Minor quibbles aside, these performances, available on bootlegs for years, compose the major missing chapter in the Beatles' legacy, and it's great to have them easily obtainable in a first-rate package. *—Richie Unterberger*

Anthology 1 / Nov. 21, 1995 / Apple/Capitol ♦♦♦
The first in a series of three double-CD sets of previously unreleased and rare Beatles material, released in conjunction with the mammoth *Anthology* video documentary. This covers the late '50s to the end of 1964, mixing studio outtakes, live performances, primitive recordings from the Quarrymen/Silver Beatles days, excerpts from the famous 1962 Decca audition, the most notable 1961 Tony Sheridan-era recordings, and brief spoken bits from interviews. Although this material is undeniably of vast historical importance, it can't be placed in the same company as the Beatles' proper albums, in either cohesion or quality. While the studio outtakes (many never even heard on bootleg) are the most enticing items, these are almost exclusively alternate versions of songs they placed on their official releases (the most notable exceptions being the 1964 R&B cover "Leave My Kitten Alone," the 1962 demo "How Do You Do It," and the unimpressive 1964 Harrison original "You Know What to Do"). Sometimes the differences are quite interesting (a much more electric-oriented version of "And I Love Her," for example), but the alternates also illustrate how the group were virtually unerring in selecting the best arrangement and take of their songs for the final versions. The pre-1962 items are sometimes taken from private rehearsal tapes of primitive fidelity and are really of archival value only. One could go on at great length about the many curiosities and finds unearthed by this compilation, but for most general consumers, two observations may suffice. It does not stand up to the Beatles' fully conceived albums (even *Live at the BBC*), but the Beatles' scraps and leavings are more interesting than over 95 percent of other performers' best work. By that standard, this must be judged a worthwhile collection, especially (but not solely) for dedicated Beatles fans. *—Richie Unterberger*

Anthology 2 / Mar. 19, 1996 / Apple/Capitol ♦♦♦
As expected, the second installment of the *Anthology* series reflects the Beatles' increasing use of the studio-as-laboratory during their "middle years." Some live material from 1965 to 1966 appears on the first disc, and the second "reunion" single ("Real Love") leads off the set. But the emphasis is upon alternate takes from early 1965 to early 1968, during which time the group rapidly evolved from post-Merseybeat through folk-rock to psychedelia. As with the first volume, this is nearly always interesting but perhaps thinner on revelations that some might expect. The *Help!*-era outtakes "If You've Got Troubles" and "That Means a Lot" are on the light side but very fun, especially the latter, which Paul and the group perform much better than P.J. Proby (who covered the song shortly afterward). Some of the alternate takes are extremely different and excellent performances on their own merits: the funkier version of "I'm Looking Through You" and the less mellow arrangement of "Norwegian Wood," a wall-of-drugs reverb for "Tomorrow Never Knows," a very Byrds-like approach to "And Your Bird Can Sing" (with giggle-laden vocals), and an acoustic demo of "Fool on the Hill." The earlier, much more acoustic version of "Strawberry Fields Forever" is the most notable gem. On the other hand, much of the material differs from the official cuts in fairly minute gradations and will be of greater interest to scholars than general listeners (although discoveries like a different solo on "Penny Lane" are fascinating). The seven live tracks on disc one, from the waning days of Beatlemania, are better than many would have assumed, showing the group still capable of generating heat onstage. *—Richie Unterberger*

Anthology 3 / Oct. 29, 1996 / Apple/Capitol ♦♦♦♦
The final installment of the *Anthology* series has two discs of previously unreleased material from the *White Album* era through the group's demise in early 1970. In terms of sheer listenability, this may be the strongest volume of the three, if only because it focuses almost solely upon studio recordings, rather than mixing live concerts/broadcasts and outtakes. Also, by this time the Beatles had perfected their approach to recording, meaning that even the early/alternate versions of many of their cuts were often of outstanding quality. There's some prime stuff here: "unplugged" *White Album* demos from mid-'68, radically different versions of "While My Guitar Gently Weeps" and "Helter Skelter," a stringless "The Long and Winding Road," three beautifully sung and played Harrison solo demos from early 1969, and several songs the Beatles never released, like "All Things Must Pass," "Not Guilty," "Teddy Boy," "Come and Get It," and "Junk." Not everything here is so great that the casual consumer will be fascinated, of course. As on previous *Anthology* sets, some of these alternates are only very slightly different from the official versions; the oldies covers from the *Let It Be* era are off-the-cuff jams that aren't up to the group's usual level of brilliance. It's still a fascinating collection, both for the insight it affords us into the group's creative process at the end of their career, and for the considerable excellence of the music itself. *—Richie Unterberger*

Yellow Submarine [Songtrack] / Sep. 14, 1999 / Apple/Capitol ♦♦♦
Admittedly, the soundtrack to *Yellow Submarine* wasn't one of the highlights in the Beatles' catalog, so providing an official alternate version of it is no big deal. It only contained four new songs—two of which were written by Harrison, which indicates how seriously Lennon and McCartney took the project, if their enjoyable throwaways ("Hey Bulldog" and "All Together Now," respectively) didn't provide enough of a clue—plus two previously released songs ("All You Need Is Love," "Yellow Submarine") and a side of George Martin instrumentals from the film's score. The Beatles never assembled a slighter album while they were active, so it wasn't a sacrilege when their organization decided to assemble a "songtrack"—a soundtrack that featured only the songs in the film, not any of the instrumentals—to coincide with the re-release of the film in 1999. In a way, it's an improvement on the soundtrack since it eliminates dead weight and strengthens the original six songs with nine songs featured in the movie ("Eleanor Rigby," "Lucy in the Sky With Diamonds," "Sgt. Pepper," etc.). It's a little jarring not to hear the songs from the soundtrack in a different order on the songtrack, but ultimately the record is entertaining, if a bit familiar. That's not the case with the sound, though. The Beatles (or their managers or their company, since the three surviving members feel as curiously uninvolved with the songtrack as they did with the soundtrack) have decided to make this the first remixed CD in their catalog instead of simply producing a new remastered tape. The differences are slight but never really an improvement, making this an enjoyable but unnecessary addition to the group's catalog. *—Stephen Thomas Erlewine*

● **The Beatles One** / Nov. 14, 2000 / Apple/Capitol ♦♦♦♦♦
Apparently, there was a gap in the Beatles' catalog, after all—all the big hits weren't on one tidy, single-disc compilation. It's not the kind of gap you'd necessarily notice—it's kind of like realizing you don't have a pair of navy blue dress socks—but it was a gap all the same, so the group released *Beatles 1* late in 2000, coinciding with the publication of their official autobiography, the puzzlingly titled *Anthology*. The idea behind this compilation is to have all the number one singles the Beatles had, either in the U.K. or U.S., on one disc, and that's pretty much what this generous 27-track collection is. It's easy, nay necessary, to quibble with a couple of the judgment calls—look, "Please Please Me" should be here instead of "From Me to You," and it's unforgivable to bypass "Strawberry Fields Forever" (kick out "Yellow Submarine" or "Eleanor Rigby")—but there's still no question that this is all great music, and there is a bit of a rush hearing all these dazzling songs follow one after another. If there's any complaint, it's that even if it's nice to have something like this, it's not really essential. There's really no reason for anyone that owns all the records to get this too—if you've lived happily without the red or blue albums, you'll live without this. But, if you give this to any six- or seven-year-old, they'll be pop fans, even fanatics, for life. And that's reason enough for it to exist. *—Stephen Thomas Erlewine*

The Beau Brummels

f. 1964, San Francisco, CA, **db.** 1968
Group / Folk-Rock, Pop, Country-Rock
While they only had two big hits, the Beau Brummels were one of the most important and underrated American groups of the 1960s. They were the first US unit of any sort to successfully respond to the British Invasion. They were arguably the first folk-rock group, even predating the Byrds, and also anticipated some key elements of the San Francisco psychedelic sound with their soaring harmonies and exuberant melodies. Before they finally reached the end of the string, they were also among the first bands to record country-rock in the late '60s. After signing to the Autumn label in 1964, they made the Top 20 right off the bat with "Laugh, Laugh," and hit the Top Ten with "Just a Little." The Beau Brummels made a couple of fine albums in 1965, dominated by strong original material and featuring the band's ringing guitars and multipart, mournful harmonies. The band was losing ground commercially though, partially because Autumn lacked promotional muscle. The label was sold in 1966 to Warner, who made the lunkheaded move of forcing the band to record an entire album of Top 40 covers—ignoring the fact that original material was one of the Brummels' primary fortes. Regrouping as a trio, the group recorded a more experimental album in 1967, *Triangle*. Their last Warner LP, *Bradley's Barn*, found the group branching into country-rock, a year or so before it became trendy. *—Richie Unterberger*

Introducing the Beau Brummels / Apr. 1965 / Sundazed ♦♦♦♦♦
A much stronger debut than the norm for the era. Ten of the 12 cuts are Ron Elliott originals, including the hits "Laugh Laugh," "Still in Love with You Baby," and "Just a Little." The hard-rocking numbers are the weakest, but "Stick Like Glue" and "I Would Be Happy" are fine Beatlesque numbers, and "They'll Make You Cry" is a first-rate moody folk-rocker. The CD reissue adds two bonus tracks, a demo of "Just a Little" and the single "Good Time Music." *—Richie Unterberger*

The Beau Brummels, Vol. 2 / Aug. 1965 / Sundazed ♦♦♦

Beau Brummels '66 / Jul. 1966 / Warner Brothers ♦♦

Triangle / Jul. 1967 / Warner Brothers ♦♦♦♦

Bradley's Barn / Oct. 1968 / Edsel ♦♦♦♦
After taking the Beau Brummels to the pop/folk psychedelic edge, producer Lenny Waronker took the band to Nashville, literally. Possibly influenced by the Byrds *Sweetheart* experiments, the group (now down to just Sal Valentino on vocals and Ron Elliott on guitars) wedded with Nashville's finest, including guitarist Jerry Reed and drummer Kenneth A. Buttrey, both veterans of Dylan's Nashville sessions. These players were not just good musicians, but *smart* musicians, easily embellishing the Elliott/Valentino duo as if they had been playing

with the two for years, not days. The resulting masterpiece, no doubt due to the awesome Brummels original songs (especially "Cherokee Girl," "Turn Around," and "Deep Water"), is a virtual tapestry in country and rock. *—Matthew Greenwald*

- **The Best of the Beau Brummels: Golden Archive Series** / 1987 / Rhino ✦✦✦✦✦
Probably the best (and best-sounding) anthology covering their golden years, although it lacks their brilliant, later country-based work at its best. *—Bruce Eder*

Autumn of Their Years / 1994 / Big Beat ✦✦✦

San Fran Sessions / Jun. 11, 1996 / Sundazed ✦✦✦

The Beautiful South

f. 1989, Hull, England
Group / Adult Alternative Pop/Rock, Pop/Rock, Alternative Pop/Rock
Following the disbandment of the British indie-pop group the Housemartins in 1989, vocalist Paul Heaton and drummer David Hemmingway formed the Beautiful South. Where their previous group relied on jazzy guitars and witty, wry lyrics, the Beautiful South boasted a more sophisticated, jazzy pop sound, layered with keyboards, R&B-inflected female backing vocals and, occasionally, light orchestrations. Often, the group's relaxed, catchy songs often contradicted the sarcastic, cyncial thrust of the lyrics. Nevertheless, the band's pleasant arrangements often tempered whatever bitterness there was in Heaton's lyrics, and that's part of the reason why the Beautiful South became quite popular within its native Britain during the '90s. Though the group never found a niche in America—by the middle of the decade, their records weren't even being released in the U.S.—their string of melodic jazz-pop singles made them one of the most successful, if one of the least flashy, bands in Britain. Their popularity was confirmed by the astonishing success of their 1994 singles compilation, *Carry on Up the Charts,* which became one of the biggest-selling albums in British history. *—Stephen Thomas Erlewine*

Welcome to the Beautiful South / Oct. 1989 / Go! Discs ✦✦✦✦✦
The difference between the catchy light pop that constitutes the Beautiful South's music and the bitter, pessimistic lyrics innocently sung by Paul Heaton is so great it constitutes a kind of malevolent seduction. But that's the point. Released in the U.S. in January 1990. *—William Ruhlmann*

Choke / Nov. 1990 / Go! Discs ✦✦✦
The Beautiful South's second album conceals its bitter, mean cynicism in layers of lush, jazz-tinged pop, making all of the bile go down easily. *—Stephen Thomas Erlewine*

0898 / Apr. 1992 / Go! Discs ✦✦✦
There are no big poses or walls of crunchy guitars on *0898.* Instead, the group—which includes three lead vocalists—deals in fragile melodies and harmonies, soulful but low-key instrumentation, and lyrics full of subtle social commentary and humor. In North America, where mainstream audiences have been well trained to salivate to very obvious musical bells, the Beautiful South may be too clever for its own good. At times, the group even couches itself in the guise of a smooth lounge act, rebelling against current trends by having something to say while not making a racket about it. Producer John Kelly (Peter Gabriel) has contributed an incisive and full-bodied production to *0898,* a great improvement over the rather thin sound of the group's previous *Choke.* *—Roch Parisien*

Miaow / 1994 / Go! Discs ✦✦✦
The Beautiful South expanded upon the sound of *0898* with *Miaow,* another expertly crafted set of sophisticated, jazzy pop. Even with the addition of new vocalist Jacqueline Abbot, the band has not changed much between the two albums and what is different is subtle—the arrangements are more intricate and the melodies are more graceful. Though the album is slightly uneven, much of the music is excellent, highlighted by "Prettiest Eyes" and a cover of Fred Neil's "Everybody's Talkin'." *—Stephen Thomas Erlewine*

- **Carry on up the Charts: The Best of the Beautiful South** / Oct. 9, 1995 / Go! Discs ✦✦✦✦✦
Carry On Up the Charts: The Best of the Beautiful South was the surprise British hit of 1994, going quintuple platinum five times between its late fall release and the summer of 1995. The success was surprising, because while the band had been modestly popular, their last few albums were sliding down the charts. However, their hits collection, *Carry On Up the Charts,* flew to number one and stayed there for weeks. It's nothing more than all their singles, yet compiled together they make the most convincing case for the Beautiful South's sly, cynical sophisticated pop. *Carry On Up the Charts* was finally released in the United States in the fall of 1995. *—Stephen Thomas Erlewine*

Blue is the Colour / Nov. 5, 1996 / Ark 21 ✦✦✦✦

Quench / Nov. 17, 1998 / Mercury ✦✦✦

Painting It Red / Oct. 31, 2000 / Ark 21 ✦✦✦

Beck (Beck Hansen)

b. Jul. 8, 1970, Los Angeles, CA
Vocals, Guitar / Experimental Rock, Alternative Dance, Indie Rock, Lo-Fi, Club/Dance, Alternative Pop/Rock, Singer/Songwriter
With his portastudio, keyboard, drum machine, and guitar, singer/songwriter Beck (b. Beck Hansen) created music that celebrated the junk culture of the '90s. Beck's music drew from hip-hop, folk, experimental rock, psychedelia, pop, and rock & roll, recycling everything into a colorful, messy and willfully diverse brand of post-modern rock, filled with warped, satiric imagery and clumsy poetry. With all of his rootless eclecticism, Beck is distinctly a product of the '90s; all of his influences were processed through television and records, not real-life experiences. But that trashy, disposable quality is what makes his music unique.

Beck came to national attention in early 1994, when his folky hip-hop single "Loser" began to receive airplay on alternative rock stations across America. "Loser" was originally released independently on a Californian label in late 1993. The single became a club hit and quickly spread to underground and alternative radio stations. Beck became the center of a major-label bidding war; he eventually signed with DGC Records. Beck released his debut album, *Mellow Gold,* in early 1994. *Mellow Gold* received rave reviews and became a gold record as "Loser" climbed into the Top Ten. Beck's contract with DGC allowed him to release records that he and the company deem as uncommercial on indie labels. Consequently, the singer/songwriter released two new records by the summer of 1994, which were both recorded roughly around the same time as *Mellow Gold. Stereopathetic Soul Manure* was a noisy, more experimental album than his debut and was released on Flipside Records. *One Foot in the Grave* accentuated his folk roots and was released on K Records. Neither album sold on the level of *Mellow Gold,* but they sold respectably.

As he prepared his second album for DGC, Beck toured with Lollapalooza Five in the summer of 1995. Beck's second major-label album, *Odelay,* finally appeared in the summer of 1996; it was released to overwhelmingly positive reviews. Throughout 1996, word-of-mouth began to spread on *Odelay,* and earned Album of the Year status from most major critic's polls and, even more surprisingly, it received several Grammy Nominations, including Album of the Year. Originally slated for release on indie label Bong Load, *Mutations* instead became *Odelay*'s "unofficial" follow-up when it was released on DGC in the autumn of 1998; the soul-influenced *Midnite Vultures* followed a year later. *—Stephen Thomas Erlewine*

☆ **Mellow Gold** / Mar. 1994 / DGC ✦✦✦✦✦
From its kaleidoscopic array of junk-culture musical styles to its assured, surrealistic wordplay, Beck's debut album *Mellow Gold* is a stunner. Throughout the record, Beck plays as if there are no divisions between musical genres, freely blending rock, rap, folk, psychedelia, and country. Although his inspired sense of humor occasionally plays like he's a smirking, irony-addled hipster, his music is never kitschy, and his wordplay is constantly inspired. Since *Mellow Gold* was pieced together from home-recorded tapes, it lacks a coherent production, functioning more as a stylistic sampler: there are the stoner raps of "Loser" and "Beercan," the urban folk of "Pay No Mind (Snoozer)," the mock-industrial onslaught of "Motherf—er," the garagey "F—-in With My Head," the trancy acoustic "Blackhole," and the gently sardonic folk-rock of "Nitemare Hippy Girl." It's a dizzying demonstration of musical skills, yet it's all tied together by a simple yet clever sense of songcraft and a truly original lyrical viewpoint, one that's basic yet as colorful as free verse. By blending boundaries so thoroughly and intoxicatingly, *Mellow Gold* established a new vein of alternative rock, one that was fueled by ideas instead of attitude. *—Stephen Thomas Erlewine*

Stereopathetic Soul Manure / Apr. 1994 / Flipside ✦✦

One Foot in the Grave / Aug. 1994 / K ✦✦✦✦
One Foot in the Grave appeared not long after the noisy freak-out of *Stereopathetic Soulmanure,* and its quiet, folky textures couldn't be more different than its predecessor, or the genre-bending *Mellow Gold,* for that matter. Recorded before *Mellow Gold,* the record showcases Beck as a post-modern folkie, and the results are revelatory. Stripped of the intoxicating production that dominated *Mellow Gold,* Beck's songs prove to be wonderful, vibrant tunes, teeming with emotion, haunting wordplay and simple, memorable melodies. It's alternately haunting and jubilant, and Calvin Johnson's occasional harmonies lend the record an intimate warmth. It's a gentle record, and its collection of small gems are every bit as impressive as the songs on *Mellow Gold* or its 1996 follow-up, *Odelay.* *—Stephen Thomas Erlewine*

★ **Odelay** / Jun. 18, 1996 / DGC ✦✦✦✦✦
Beck's debut, *Mellow Gold,* was a glorious sampler of different musical styles, careening from lo-fi hip-hop to folk, moving back through garage rock and arty noise. It was an impressive album, but the parts didn't necessarily stick together. The two albums that followed within months *Mellow Gold*—*Stereopathetic Soul Manure* and *One Foot in the Grave*—were specialist releases that disproved the idea that Beck was simply a one-hit wonder. But *Odelay,* the much-delayed proper follow-up to *Mellow Gold,* proves the depth and scope of his talents. *Odelay* fuses the disparate strands of Beck's music—folk, country, hip-hop, rock & roll, blues, jazz, easy listening, rap, pop—into one dense sonic collage. Songs frequently morph from one genre to another, seemingly unrelated genre—bursts of noise give way to country songs with hip-hop beats, easy listening melodies transform into a weird fusion of pop, jazz, and cinematic strings; it's genre-defying music that refuses to see boundaries. All of the songs on *Odelay* are rooted in simple forms—whether it's blues ("Devil's Haircut"), country ("Lord Only Knows," "Sissyneck"), soul ("Hotwax"), folk ("Ramshackle"), or rap ("High 5 (Rock the Catskills)," "Where It's At")—but they twist the conventions of the genre. "Where It's At" is peppered with soul, jazz, funk, and rap references, while "Novacane" slams from indie rock to funk and back to white noise. With the aid of the Dust Brothers, Beck has created a dense, endlessly intriguing album overflowing with ideas. Furthermore, it's an album that completely ignores the static, nihilistic trends of the American alternative/independent underground, creating a fluid, creative, and startlingly original work. *—Stephen Thomas Erlewine*

Mutations / Nov. 3, 1998 / Geffen ✦✦✦✦
According to party line, neither Beck nor Geffen ever intended *Mutations* to be considered as the official follow-up to *Odelay,* his Grammy-winning breakthrough. It was more like *One Foot in the Grave,* designed to be an off-kilter, subdued collection of acoustic-based songs pitched halfway between psychedelic country-blues and lo-fi folk. The presence of producer Nigel Godrich, the man who helmed Radiohead's acclaimed *OK Computer,* makes such claims dubious. Godrich is not a slick producer, but he's no Calvin Johnson, either, and *Mutations* has an appropriately clean, trippy feel. There's little question that with the blues, country, psych, bossa nova, and folk that comprise it, *Mutations* was never meant to be a commercial endeavor—there's no floor-shaker like "Where It's At," and it doesn't it trade in the junk culture that brought *Odelay* to life. Recording with his touring band—marking the first time he has entered the studio with a live band—does result in a different sound, but it's not so much a departure as it is a side road that is going in the same direction. None of the songs explore new territory, but they're rich, lyrically and musically. There's an off-the-cuff wit to the songwriting, especially on "Cancelled Check" and "Bottle of Blues," and the

performances are natural, relaxed, and laid-back, without ever sounding complacent. In fact, one of the nifty tricks of *Mutations* is how it sounds simple upon the first listen, then reveals more psychedelic layers upon each play. Beck is not only a startling songwriter—his best songs are simultaneously modern and timeless—he is a sharp record maker, crafting albums that sound distinct and original, no matter how much they may borrow. In its own quiet, organic way, *Mutations* confirms this as much as either *Mellow Gold* or *Odelay*. *—Stephen Thomas Erlewine*

Midnite Vultures / Nov. 16, 1999 / Interscope ✦✦✦
By calling the muted psychedelic folk-rock, blues, and tropicalia of *Mutations* a stopgap, Beck set expectations for *Midnight Vultures* unreasonably high. Ironically, *Midnite Vultures* doesn't feel like a sequel to *Odelay*—it's a genre exercise, like *Mutations*. This time, Beck delves into soul, funk, and hip-hop, touching on everything from Stax/Volt to No Limit but using Prince as his home base. He's eschewed samples, more or less, but not the aesthetic. Even when a song is reminiscent of a particular style, it's assembled in strange, exciting ways. As it kicks off with "Sexx Laws," it's hard not to get caught up in the rush, and "Nicotine & Gravy" carries on the vibe expertly, as does the party jam "Mixed Bizness" and the full-on electro workout "Get Real Paid," an intoxicating number that sounds like a *Black Album* reject. So far, so good—the songs are tight, catchy, and memorable, the production dense. Then comes "Hollywood Freaks". The self-conscious gangsta goof is singularly irritating, not least because of Beck's affected voice. It's the first on *Midnite Vultures* to feel like a parody, and it's such an awkward, misguided shift in tone that it colors the rest of the album. Tributes now sound like send-ups, allusions that once seemed affectionate feel snide, and the whole thing comes off as a little jive. Musically, *Midnite Vultures* is filled with wonderful little quirks, but these are undercut by the sneaking suspicion that for all the ingenuity, it's just a hipster joke. Humor has always been a big part of Beck's music, but it was gloriously absurd, never elitist. Here, it's delivered with a smug smirk, undercutting whatever the joy the music generates. *—Stephen Thomas Erlewine*

Jeff Beck

b. Jun. 24, 1944, Wallington, Surrey, England
Guitar (Electric), Guitar, Bass / Album Rock, Guitar Virtuoso, British Blues, Fusion, Hard Rock, Blues-Rock, Rock & Roll

While he was as innovative as Jimmy Page, as tasteful as Eric Clapton and nearly as visionary as Jimi Hendrix, Jeff Beck never achieved the same commercial success as any of his contemporaries, primarily because of the haphazard way he approached his career. After Rod Stewart left the Jeff Beck Group, Beck never worked with a charismatic lead singer who could have helped sell his music to a wide audience. Furthermore, he was simply too idiosyncratic, moving from heavy metal to jazz-fusion within a blink of an eye. All the while, Beck retained the respect of fellow guitarists, who found his reclusiveness all the more alluring.

Jeff Beck began his musical career as the Yardbirds' lead guitarist, following the departure of Eric Clapton. He stayed with the band for nearly two years, then formed the Jeff Beck Group in 1967 with a lineup including vocalist Rod Stewart and bassist Ron Wood. With their crushingly loud reworkings of blues songs and vocal/guitar interplay, 1968's *Truth* and 1969's *Beck-Ola* became early templates for heavy metal. After Stewart and Wood left to join the Faces in 1970, Beck recorded two more albums with a new version of the group before releasing a lone LP as the head of a power trio including former Vanilla Fudge members Tim Bogert (bass) and Carmine Appice (drums). He moved from hard rock to jazz-rock with 1975's *Blow by Blow* and 1976's *Wired*, but recorded only three studio albums during the next 15 years. (One of which, the slick 1985 LP *Flash*, featured Beck's only hit single, "People Get Ready.") In 1993, he recorded the Gene Vincent tribute *Crazy Legs*, but then remained quiet for over five years before resurfacing in 1999 with *Who Else!* *—Stephen Thomas Erlewine*

☆ **Truth** / Aug. 1968 / Epic ✦✦✦✦✦
Despite being the premiere of heavy metal, Jeff Beck's *Truth* has never quite carried its reputation the way the early albums by Led Zeppelin did, or even Cream's two most popular LPs, mostly as a result of the erratic nature of the guitarist's subsequent work. Time has muted some of its daring, radical nature, elements of which were appropriated by practically every metal band (and most arena rock bands) that followed. *Truth* was almost as groundbreaking and influential a record as the first Beatles, Rolling Stones, or Who albums. Its attributes weren't all new—Cream and Jimi Hendrix had been moving in similar directions—but the combination was: the wailing, heart-stoppingly dramatic vocalizing by Rod Stewart, the thunderous rhythm section of Ron Wood's bass and Mickey Waller's drums, and Beck's blistering lead guitar, which sounds like his amp is turned up to 13 and ready to short out. Beck opens the proceedings in a strikingly bold manner, using his old Yardbirds hit "Shapes of Things" as a jumping-off point, deliberately rebuilding the song from the ground up so it sounds closer to Howlin' Wolf. There are lots of unexpected moments on this record: a bone-pounding version of Willie Dixon's "You Shook Me"; a version of Jerome Kern's "Ol' Man River" done as a slow electric blues; a brief plunge into folk territory with a solo acoustic guitar version of "Greensleeves" (which was intended as filler but audiences loved); the progressive blues of "Beck's Bolero"; the extended live "Blues Deluxe"; and "I Ain't Superstitious," a blazing reworking of another Willie Dixon song. It was a triumph—a number 15 album in America, astoundingly good for a band that had been utterly unknown in the U.S. just six months earlier—and a very improbable success. *—Bruce Eder*

Beck-Ola / Jun. 1969 / Epic ✦✦✦✦
A year after Jeff Beck recorded *Truth*, he came back with the even heavier *Beck-Ola*. Although the songwriting seems diluted, and the addition of Nicky Hopkins on piano added spice in all the wrong places, *Beck-Ola* is still a gut-slamming good time. Notable tracks include "Spanish Boots" and "Plynth (Water Down the Drain)." *—Tom Graves*

Rough and Ready / Oct. 1971 / Epic ✦✦✦
Recouping after a car crash and faced with the loss of Rod Stewart and Ron Wood, Jeff Beck redefined what the Jeff Beck Group was about, deciding to tone down the bluesy bombast, adding keyboardist Max Middleton for a jazz edge, then having Bob Tench sing to give it an overblown early-'70s AOR edge. As expected, these two sides are in conflict and Tench can be a little overbearing, but there are moments here that bring out the best in Beck. Namely, these are the times when the group ventures into extended, funk-inflected, reflective jazzy instrumental sections. These are the moments that point the way toward the success of *Blow by Blow*, yet this remains an unabashed rock record of its time, and it falls prey to many of its era's excesses, particularly lack of focus. Still, there are moments that are as fine as anything Beck played here. *—Stephen Thomas Erlewine*

Jeff Beck Group / Apr. 1972 / Epic ✦✦✦

Blow by Blow / Mar. 1975 / Epic ✦✦✦✦✦
When Jeff Beck announced that he was working on an all-instrumental album, few but his legion of guitar fans could have predicted the far-reaching impact of this pivotal jazz-rock fusion album. Teamed with the Beatles' ex-producer George Martin, Beck singlehandedly created a new subtext for rock & roll. With his virtuosity and taste at an all-time peak, Beck let loose with such unforgettable tracks as the Roy Buchanan-inspired "Cause We've Ended as Lovers" and the percolating "Freeway Jam." This is one of rock's great instrumental works. *—Tom Graves*

Wired / May 1976 / Epic ✦✦✦✦✦
Nearly *Blow by Blow*'s equal, although Beck doesn't venture any further musically. Charles Mingus' "Goodbye Pork Pie Hat" is worth the price alone. *—Tom Graves*

Jeff Beck with the Jan Hammer Group Live / Mar. 1977 / Epic ✦✦

There & Back / Jun. 1980 / Epic ✦✦✦

Flash / Jul. 1985 / Epic ✦✦✦
Produced by Nile Rodgers and Arthur Baker, *Flash* is Beck's surprisingly successful stab at a pop album, featuring a fine performance with Rod Stewart on "People Get Ready." *—Stephen Thomas Erlewine*

Jeff Beck's Guitar Shop / Oct. 1989 / Epic ✦✦✦✦

Beckology / Nov. 19, 1991 / Epic/Legacy ✦✦✦✦✦
Jeff Beck is a genius, arguably the greatest rock guitarist of his generation (and, yes, that includes Hendrix), but never has such a gifted musician had such a spotty discography. Beck did some of his best work on his solo albums, yet he only cut a few terrific albums, with the rest of the albums being remarkably uneven. Often, he had inspired work as a sideman or as part of a band, such as the Yardbirds. This means that even the dedicated fans have had to sort through a lot of dreck, not to mention the casual fans that wanted a way to explore his vast, at times, confusing discography. The triple-disc box set *Beckology* performs its duty exceedingly well, drawing a history from his earliest recordings with his first band, the Tridents, right up to 1992's *Jeff Beck's Guitar Shop*. Some great moments are missing (there always are on a box), but it's impossible to argue with what's here, which not only offers everything essential he recorded, but winds up summarizing his career brilliantly. This is the one necessary Beck album, the one that makes the case that he is indeed a genius. *—Stephen Thomas Erlewine*

Frankie's House / Jan. 5, 1992 / Epic ✦✦

Crazy Legs / Jun. 29, 1993 / Epic ✦✦

● **The Best of Beck** / Aug. 15, 1995 / Epic ✦✦✦✦✦
Basically this record exists because the record company wanted to have some product on the shelf while Beck was touring. The 14 tracks do contain some of his most often-played (by radio, at any rate) recordings, including "Shapes of Things," "Plynth," and "Beck's Bolero" from the original Jeff Beck Group days in the late '60s, and the vocoder showcase "She's a Woman" and fusion landmark "Freeway Jam" from *Blow by Blow*. It may do for casual listeners who only want one Beck CD, although more serious fans would be better off with the *Beckology* box. *—Richie Unterberger*

Who Else! / Mar. 16, 1999 / Epic ✦✦✦✦
Jeff Beck has never shied away from following trends, at least as far as the musical styles he uses to back up his signature guitar sound. Back in 1969, in a sleeve note on *Beck-Ola*, he noted that he hadn't come up with "anything totally original," and instead made an album "with the accent on heavy music" at a time when the "heavy music" of the Jimi Hendrix Experience and Led Zeppelin was all the rage. In 1975, at the height of the jazz fusion movement, he made a jazz fusion album, and a good one, too. In both cases, however, the fashionable genres only provided a contemporary-sounding context in which his playing could flourish. If anyone has ever needed to be inspired to work, it's this recluse. So on his first regular studio album of new material in ten years, Beck, on at least a few tracks, solos over heavily percussive techno tracks reminiscent of Prodigy. But whether he's piercing such a rhythmic wall, rearranging the blues on the live "Blast from the East," or floating over an ambient soundscape on "Angel (Footsteps)," it's the same old Beck, with his stinging and sustained single-note melodies, his harmonics, his contrasting tones, his drive. And the man who played "Greensleeves" straight on *Truth* in 1968 is the same one who is faithful to the Irish air "Declan" here. Older fans who haven't been spending time at raves in recent years may want to program their CDs to avoid the electronica, but they should at least give those tunes a listen—are they any heavier than the "heavy music" of 1969? *—William Ruhlmann*

The Bee Gees

f. 1958, Brisbane, Australia
Group / Psychedelic Pop, Pop/Rock, Soft Rock, Adult Contemporary, Disco

No popular music act of the 1960s, 1970s, 1980s, and 1990s experienced more ups and downs in their popularity than the Bee Gees, or drew more of a varied audience. Beginning in the mid-to-late '60s as a kind of Beatles-lite ensemble, Barry Gibb and his fraternal twin brothers Robin and Maurice quickly developed as songwriters in their own right and perfected a strange mix of progressive-pop music. "New York Mining Disaster 1941," released in 1967, made the Top 20 in England and America, and established the pattern of the group's work for the next several years. "Massachusetts" was a chart-topper in England and, after a temporary break-up, 1970's "Lonely Days" became the group's first number one hit in America. Then, after hitting a trough in their popularity in the early '70s, the Bee Gees reinvented themselves with a heavily Americanized, R&B-flavored sound that emphasized high harmonies and funk rhythms. "Jive Talkin'" became their second American number one in 1975, and two years later, the group's soundtrack of a forthcoming movie called *Saturday Night Fever* led to three chart-topping hits: "Stayin' Alive," "How Deep Is Your Love,", and "Night Fever." It didn't last, nor did the Bee Gees' second wave of success. The group may have helped contribute to the end of the party with their own excesses, in particular their contribution to a multi-million dollar film called *Sergeant Pepper's Lonely Hearts Club Band*, "inspired" (if that's the word) by the Beatles' album and songs. The youngest Gibb brother, Andy Gibb, had emerged as a star in his own right late in the 1970s and he fell even harder when the decade ended, eventually losing his life in 1988 at the end of a downward personal spiral. The Bee Gees were virtually invisible for most of the mid-'80s as recording artists, though 1987's *ESP* received a good reception around the world and the title track of 1989's *One* even generated a Top Ten U.S. single. Their induction into the Rock 'n Roll Hall of Fame in 1997 led to the release of *Still Waters*, and in 1998, they issued the second live album in their history, cut at their first concert appearance in ten years. *—Bruce Eder*

The Bee Gee's 1st / Jul. 1967 / Polydor ✦✦✦
The debut long-player by the Bee Gees may shock anyone who only remembers them for their mid- to late-'70s disco mega-hits, or their quirky early-'70s romantic balladry. Up until 1966, they'd shown a penchant for melodic songs and rich, high harmonies, in the process becoming Australia's answer to the Everly Brothers. When the brothers arrived in London late in 1966, however, they proved quick studies in absorbing and assimilating progressive pop and rock sounds around them. In one fell swoop, they became competitors to the likes of veteran rock bands such as the Hollies and the Tremeloes, and their debut long-player is more of a rock album than the group usually got credit for generating. Parts of it do sound very much like the Beatles circa *Revolver*, but there was far more to their sound than that. The three hits off of *Bee Gees 1st*, "To Love Somebody," "New York Mining Disaster," and "Holiday," were gorgeous but relatively somber, thus giving *Bee Gees 1st* a melancholy cast, but much of the rest is relatively upbeat psychedelic pop. "In My Own Time" may echo elements of "Dr. Robert" and "Taxman," but it's difficult to dislike a song with such delicious rhythm guitars and a great beat, coupled to the trio's soaring harmonies; "Every Christian Lion-Hearted Man Will Show You" was closer in spirit to the Moody Blues of this era, opening with a Gregorian chant backed by a Mellotron, before breaking into a strangely spaced-out, psychedelic main song body. Robin Gibb's lead vocals veered toward the melodramatic and poignant, and the orchestra did dress up some of the songs a little sweetly, yet overall the group presented themselves as a proficient rock ensemble who'd filled their debut album with a full set of solid, refreshingly original songs. *—Bruce Eder*

Horizontal / Jan. 1968 / Polydor ✦✦✦
The group's second album, cut late in 1967 amid their first major British success, is less focused than their first, but also presents a more majestic sound than its predecessor. The opening track, "World," is a poignant, even somber yet gorgeous ballad filled with clever lyrics, and highlighted by a quavering Mellotron accompaniment, a very close grand piano sound (anticipating elements of the *Odessa* album), and twangy fuzz-tone guitar. "And the Sun Will Shine" is an even more serious, regretful ballad that is bearable because it is also prettier than "World." The enigmatically titled "Lemons Never Forget" breaks up the mood with a harder rocking sound, just the group without any orchestra, dominated by a pounding piano and volume-pedal guitar. The most interesting aspect of "Really and Sincerely"—a song that descends into an even more emotionally melodramatic mood than "And the Sun Will Shine"—is its opening, which contains a musical phrase that seems to anticipate the group's disco-era "Nights on Broadway." "Birdie Told Me" is another tale of lost love that offers the variety of some leaner and tasteful electric guitar accompaniment. Side two of the original LP was more upbeat, opening with the group's catchy chart-topping British hit, "Massachusetts," followed by the cheerful "Harry Braff." "The Earnest of Being George" and "The Change Is Made" are attempts at a harder rock sound, featuring heavy guitar on both and an attempt at bluesy feel on the latter, while the title track is a trippy psychedelic number that closes the album on an upbeat note. *—Bruce Eder*

' / Aug. 1968 / Polydor ✦✦✦

Odessa / Jan. 1969 / Polydor ✦✦✦✦✦
Though it was recorded during times of great stress, *Odessa* was one of the Bee Gees' finest achievements. Originally conceived as a concept album, the record became a double album tied together only by its lavish sound. While the album failed to spin off any major hit singles, most of the songs on the record are excellent, highlighted by "Odessa (City on the Black Sea)," "Melody Fair," and "Black Diamond." *—Stephen Thomas Erlewine*

★ **The Best of the Bee Gees, Vol. 1** / Jun. 1969 / Polydor ✦✦✦✦✦
If anyone needs conclusive proof that the brothers Gibb weren't always the chest-medallion-flashing kings of mainstream disco or, since about 1980 on, meaningless AOR washouts, the nearly 40-minute collection of the Bee Gees' earliest hits will suffice in spades. At their (perhaps, in hindsight) surprising best, the threesome, along with capable if generally unremarkable rhythm section members Melouney and Colin Peterson, created a slew of tender, affecting, and quite lovely hits. While the Stones/proto-metal crowd of the time probably thought them unbearably wimpy, their songwriting acumen, combined with their harmonies, fine production by Robert Stigwood, and ace orchestral/band arrangements by Bill Shephard, holds up astonishingly well. For all that the band clearly was often following the lead of the more elaborate Beatles songs of the same time—consider the watery piano line opening "Words" as one example of many—the Bee Gees didn't so much ape as they did come up with their own flavor. Considering that everyone from Catherine ("Every Christian Lion-Hearted Man Will Show You") and Jimmy Somerville ("To Love Somebody") to Low ("I Started a Joke") and Jose Feliciano ("I've Gotta Get a Message to You") has covered something from this collection is testimony to the songs' continuing influence. Other times the connections to the future are subtler but still present—"I Can't See Nobody," sonically and lyrically, has the same deep blue/string-backed feeling as Verve's "History." Sometimes the line between emotion and deep schmaltz is pretty fine, admittedly. However, when Robin's lead vocal on "I Started a Joke" hits the high notes while his brothers add soft backup as the music swells, it's just one example of many why the Bee Gees deserved their long overdue induction into the Rock & Roll Hall of Fame. *—Ned Raggett*

Cucumber Castle / Apr. 1970 / Polydor ✦✦✦
An overlooked work in the Brothers Gibb catalog, *Cucumber Castle* is an excellent album that plays to the Bee Gees' strengths of melody, arrangement, and craftsmanship. Though at times one may miss the distinctive trembling vocals of Robin Gibb (the brothers had split up at this point), Barry and Maurice carry on with 12 cuts that continue in the tradition of their distinctive pop sound. Orchestral arrangements and Mellotrons abound, and the sound tends toward full productions, especially in "Then You Left Me" and "I Lay Down and Die." One can also hear country influences ("Sweetheart"), gospel ("Bury Me Down by the River"), and light jazz ("My Thing"). What sets this album above others is that there is not a bad cut on the album, and Barry's vocals are particularly strong and heartfelt. Although most of the cuts deal with the usual subject of love and particularly love lost, superb eye for detail in the arrangements of the songs give them added life. Adding a few songs with classic singalong melodies ("Sweetheart" and "Don't Forget to Remember") certainly doesn't hurt the cause. All in all, this is a fine album that cements the Brothers Gibb's reputation as superior pop songwriters and craftsmen. *—Michael I. Offord*

2 Years On / Jan. 1971 / Polydor ✦✦✦✦
The Bee Gees split apart in the wake of a dispute regarding the single to be released from their album *Odessa*, spent a year with Barry and Maurice Gibb recording together (and doing a television special) while Robin Gibb cut music on his own, and fighting a lawsuit in which their ex-drummer tried to claim the name "the Bee Gees." Finally, they regrouped with *2 Years On* and surprised everyone with their biggest selling single to date, "Lonely Days," and a surprisingly hard edged accompanying album, on which the supposed Beatles influences of their earlier days were pushed aside (it also didn't hurt that the Beatles were now history). The music is somewhat less fey and more progressive here, and at times they sound like a lighter-weight version of the Moody Blues of the same era, with sharper vocals. The surprises on this album, apart from the overall tone and quality, include the sprightly title track, which was one of the first Bee Gees songs to feature surreal lyrics that weren't downbeat, and "Back Home," with the loudest guitar ever heard on a Bee Gees record. The quality of the recording itself was also improved over their earlier releases, with a much wider range and less compression, and between that and the song selection, the Bee Gees suddenly found themselves right back in the thick of popular music, and as close to the cutting edge of pop/rock as they'd ever been. *—Bruce Eder*

Trafalgar / Sep. 1971 / Polydor ✦✦✦✦
The Bee Gees had entered the early '70s with a roaring success in the guise of "Lonely Days" and its accompanying album, which established their sound as a softer pop variant on the Moody Blues' brand of progressive rock. *Trafalgar*, which followed, carried the process further on what was their longest single LP release, clocking in at 47 minutes. The music all sounded meaningful, much of it displaying the same kind of faux-grandeur that the Moody Blues affected on their music of this era, the core group (playing pretty hard) accompanied by either Mellotron-generated orchestra or the real thing, with the group's soaring harmonies and Robin Gibb's quavaring lead vocals all over the place. As with *2 Years On*'s "A Man for All Seasons," there was also one title ("Lion in Winter," featuring a startling falsetto performance) lifted from a recently popular film and play having to do with English history. It was all very beautifully produced and, propelled into record-store racks by the presence of "How Can You Mend a Broken Heart," the group's first No. 1 single, *Trafalgar* shipped very well initially. Nothing else on the record was remotely as memorable as the single, however, and its sales were limited. *Trafalgar* was also the handsomest and most elaborately designed of their albums, its cover reprinting Pocock's painting "The Battle of Trafalgar" and the interior gateful containing a shot of the brothers enacting the scene of the death of Lord Nelson. It all imparted the sense of a concept album, though nothing in the music said so, except perhaps the finale, "Walking Back to Waterloo." Despite the hit single, the album showed the limits of the Bee Gees' talents as songwriters and of their appeal as album artists. *—Bruce Eder*

To Whom It May Concern / 1972 / Polydor ✦✦✦
The next to last of the Bee Gee's "old-style" albums is one of their most fully realized works, with pleasing and memorable songs from beginning to end, and for a change this time, it's the single ("Run to Me"), rather than the surrounding tracks, that suffers from predictability. Another in a string of haunting ballads, it has a more plaintive, whining quality, and less of an ethereal feel than its predecessor, "How Can You Mend a Broken Heart"—not that "Run to Me" isn't a lovely song, but it was possible to tire of hearing it on the radio faster than their prior singles. By contrast, the album's other tracks are all intensely melodic and varied enough in tempo and texture to make for very satisfying listening, "You Know It's for You" calling to mind Paul McCartney at his most accessible; the group plunges into relatively hard rock, with a heavy guitar sound, on "Bad Bad Dreams," and a country-ish sound on "Road to Alaska," before returning to a kind of post-psychedelic mode in "Sweet Song of Summer." The Bee Gees were pushing their credibility as a cohesive band more than ever, emphasizing Barry Gibb and Maurice Gibb's contributions to their instrumental sound and retaining guitarist Alan Kendall, who had debuted with them on the *Trafalgar* album and who would play with them for the next two decades. As it turned out, *To Whom It May Concern* was also the commercial swan song for the trio in this phase of their career, and the last of their albums to be released by Atlantic Records in the United States, something of an artistic peak before a period of massive change in their sound and future. *—Bruce Eder*

Life in a Tin Can / Jan. 1973 / Polydor ✦✦

The Best of the Bee Gees, Vol. 2 / Jul. 1973 / Polydor ✦✦✦✦✦
This volume spans from 1970-1973. Although the hits aren't as abundant as *The Best of the Bee Gees*, there is still plenty of strong material on this edition. The hits include "Run To Me,"

"Lonely Days," and "How Can You Mend A Broken Heart," but some of the best songs are among the non-hits, including "Morning Of My Life," "Man For All Seasons,"and "Let There Be Love." Prior to the disco years, The Bee Gees were excellent songwriters, composing some of the finest introspective and soul searching songs of the late sixties and early seventies. As this volume features material from the brothers' brief breakup, there is also some weaker material, such as the reggae-tinged "I.O.I.O", the country ballad "Don't Forget To Remember", and Robin Gibb's solo single "Saved By The Bell", which was a huge hit in Britain. However, despite these mediocre tracks, the album is still a worthwhile addition to a collection of some of the best pop music of its era. *—Jim Powers*

Mr. Natural / May 1974 / Polydor ✦✦

Main Course / May 1975 / Polydor ✦✦✦✦✦
On *Main Course* the Bee Gees began incorporating soul into their well-constructed sound, inching the group closer to their watershed disco years. Like most Bee Gees' albums, the material is fairly inconsistent, yet the strongest moments—including the hit singles "Jive Talkin'" and "Nights on Broadway"—rank with the group's best work. *—Stephen Thomas Erlewine*

Children of the World / Sep. 1976 / Polydor ✦✦

Bee Gees Gold, Vol. 1 / Oct. 1976 / Polydor ✦✦✦✦✦
The Bee Gees Gold, Vol. 1 compiles the group's biggest singles from their first five years of hit records, beginning with 1967's "New York Mining Disaster 1941" and ending with 1971's "How Can You Mend a Broken Heart." Although the compilation isn't presented in chronological order, it does contains all of their biggest hits ("To Love Somebody," "Holiday," "Lonely Days," "I've Got to Get a Message to You," "I Started a Joke"), making it a fine overview of the group's first heyday. *—Stephen Thomas Erlewine*

☆ **Saturday Night Fever** / Nov. 1977 / RSO ✦✦✦✦✦
One of the biggest-selling albums of all time, this double-disc soundtrack features the Bee Gees hits "Stayin' Alive," "Night Fever," and "How Deep Is Your Love"; Yvonne Elliman's "If I Can't Have You"; and a selection of popular disco hits by Tavares, K.C. & the Sunshine Band, and others. This wasn't only the soundtrack to a film, it was the soundtrack to an era. That era is over, but it's evoked by the music. *—William Ruhlmann*

Spirits Having Flown / Jan. 1979 / Polydor ✦✦✦✦✦
How does one follow up a phenomenal success? Well, that was the question the Bee Gees faced after their contributions catapulted them into the disco stratosphere. They appeared they could do no wrong, writing hits not only for themselves, but for many others as well. However, *Spirits Having Flown*, while a solid effort, did not catch fire with the public. This time out, there were no memorable hooks to grab the listener, or even the dancer. Who knows? Perhaps they tried too hard. The tracks "Too Much Heaven," "Tragedy" and "Love You Inside and Out" were all number one hits, but the public didn't bite the way they had before. Good music, but a bit dated. Reminders of polyester jumpsuits abound. *—James Chrispell*

● **Greatest** / Oct. 1979 / Polydor ✦✦✦✦✦
Greatest is a double-album, 20-song retrospective of the Bee Gees' late '70s hits. All of the band's biggest disco-era hits—"Jive Talkin'," "Nights on Broadway," "Fanny (Be Tender with My Love)," "You Should Be Dancing," "Love So Right," "How Deep Is Your Love," "Stayin' Alive," "Night Fever," "Too Much Heaven," "Tragedy," "Love You Inside Out"—are included, as well as several fine album tracks and the group's version of Andy Gibb's "(Our Love) Don't Throw It All Away." Although it's a a little too long for some casual fans, it remains an excellent overview of the Bee Gees' most commercially successful era. *—Stephen Thomas Erlewine*

Living Eyes / 1981 / RSO ✦✦

Staying Alive / Jun. 1983 / RSO ✦✦✦

E.S.P. / Sep. 1987 / Warner Brothers ✦✦

One / Jul. 25, 1989 / Warner Brothers ✦✦✦

Tales from the Brothers Gibb / Oct. 1990 / Polydor ✦✦✦
Although the Bee Gees were a singles band, and consequently their hits compilations were frequently more consistent than their actual albums, the four-disc box set *Tales from the Brothers Gibb* is an example of a wasted opportunity. While all of the big hits are featured over the course of 71 tracks, the set is unevenly balanced, featuring more latter-day material than their generally more interesting early recordings. Also, it doesn't choose particularly well from the group's albums, overlooking several key tracks in favor of bland cuts from '80s records, and the rarities, including several live tracks and a demo of "E.S.P.," aren't of much worth. Consequently, *Tales from the Brothers Gibb* neither appeals to the collector, who will have the bulk of this material, nor the casual fan, since it contains too much mediocre material for them to sift through. *—Stephen Thomas Erlewine*

High Civilization / Apr. 1991 / Warner Brothers ✦✦

Size Isn't Everything / Nov. 1993 / Polydor ✦✦✦

Still Waters / May 6, 1997 / Polydor ✦✦✦

Brilliant from Birth / Apr. 27, 1999 / Festival ✦✦✦

Archie Bell

b. Sep. 1, 1944, Henderson, TX
Vocals / Philly Soul, Disco, Soul
Few groups offered good-time soul music as enjoyable, danceable, and high-spirited as Archie Bell & the Drells. The singer (from Houston, as he was eager to proclaim in the middle of some of his uptempo hits) had a left-field number one smash with the limb-loosening "Tighten Up," which took off right after Bell was drafted. In 1968, Bell (who was able to fit in some recording and performing duties until his stint in the army was over) teamed with emerging Philadelphia soul mavens Kenneth Gamble and Leon Huff, who produced and wrote his material over the next couple years. With sophisticated arrangements and punchy horn charts, dance hits like "I Can't Stop Dancing," "(There's Gonna Be a) Showdown," and "Do the Choo Choo" were instrumental in establishing the sound of Philadelphia as an artistic force. After a fallow period in the early '70s, Bell reunited with Gamble and Huff on the Philadelphia International for a run of successful, discofied dance soul in the mid-'70s. *—Richie Unterberger*

● **Tightening It Up: The Best of Archie Bell & the Drells** / Aug. 16, 1994 / Rhino ✦✦✦✦✦
Twenty of the group's big and small hits, charting their course from Southern-fried soul through the sound of Philadelphia and disco. *—Richie Unterberger*

Chris Bell

b. Jan. 12, 1951, Memphis, TN, **d.** Dec. 27, 1978, Memphis, TN
Vocals, Guitar / Power Pop, Singer/Songwriter
Chris Bell was one of the unsung heroes of American pop music; despite a life marked by tragedy and a career crippled by commercial indifference, the singer/songwriter's slim body of recorded work proved massively influential on the generations of indie rockers who emerged in his wake. With high-school friend Alex Chilton, Bell formed Big Star, whose debut album, 1972's *1 Record*, eventually earned mythic status as an underground classic (though it was deemed a commercial failure at the time of release). Crushed, Bell became suicidal and left the band. Though he continued working on music, his depression worsened; to help revitalize his career, his brother David led him to France, where a batch of demos were cut for a planned album (the songs wer mixed with Beatles engineer Geoff Emerick). The completed tracks were roundly rejected however, and Bell soon dropped out of music. In 1977 however, the remarkable single "I Am the Cosmos" was issued on the tiny Car label; its positive reception spurred him to form a new band. But in late 1978, Bell was killed in a car crash. Over the course of the following decade, the legendary stature of Big Star continued to grow exponentially, and finally, Bell's long-unreleased demos were released as *I Am the Cosmos*. *—Jason Ankeny*

I Am the Cosmos / Feb. 21, 1992 / Rykodisc ✦✦✦✦✦
Unreleased for over 15 years, *I Am the Cosmos* is nevertheless an enduring testament to the brilliance of Chris Bell; lyrically poignant and melodically stunning, this lone solo album is proof positive of his underappreciated pop mastery. While cuts like "Get Away," "I Got Kinda Lost," and "Fight at the Table" recall the glowing, energetic power-pop of Bell's earlier work, the majority of the songs on *I Am the Cosmos* are more reflective and deeply personal; the title track is a harrowingly schizophrenic tale of romantic despair, while other cuts like the lurching "Better Save Yourself" and the lovely "Look Up" are infused with a spiritual power largely missing from his Big Star material. The album's highlight, "You and Your Sister"—which features backing vocals from none other than Bell's Big Star mate Alex Chilton—is simply one of the great unknown love songs in the pop canon, a luminous and fragile ballad almost otherworldly in its beauty. *—Jason Ankeny*

William Bell (William Yarborough)

b. Jul. 16, 1937, Memphis, TN
Vocals, Piano / Northern Soul, Soul
A principal architect of the Stax-Volt sound, singer/composer William Bell remains best known for his classic "You Don't Miss Your Water," one of the quintessential soul records to emerge from the Memphis scene. Born William Yarborough on July 16, 1939, he cut his teeth backing Rufus Thomas, and in 1957 recorded his first sides as a member of the Del Rios. After joining the Stax staff as a writer, in 1961 Bell made his solo debut with the self-penned "You Don't Miss Your Water," an archetypal slice of country-soul and one of the label's first big hits. A two-year armed forces stint effectively derailed his career, however, and he did not release his first full-length album, *The Soul of a Bell*, until 1967, generating a Top 20 hit with the single "Everybody Loves a Winner"; that same year, Albert King also scored with another classic Bell composition, the oft-covered "Born Under a Bad Sign."

Bell's next solo hit, 1968's "A Tribute to a King," was a poignant farewell to the late Otis Redding; the R&B Top Ten hit "I Forgot to Be Your Lover" soon followed, and a series of duets with Judy Clay, most notably "Private Number," also earned airplay. In 1969 he relocated to Atlanta and set up his own label, Peachtree; the hits dried up as the next decade opened, but in 1977 Bell capped a major comeback with "Trying to Love Two," which topped the R&B charts. In 1985 he founded another label, Wilbe, and issued *Passion*, which found its most receptive audiences in the UK (although "I Don't Want to Wake Up Feeling Guilty," a duet with Janice Bullock, was a minor US hit). In addition to subsequent LPs including 1989's *On a Roll* and 1992's *Bedtime Stories*, in 1987 Bell was inducted into the Georgia Music Hall of Fame, that same year receiving the Rhythm & Blues Foundation's R&B Pioneer Award. *—Jason Ankeny*

● **The Best of William Bell** / 1988 / Stax ✦✦✦✦✦
Post-Atlantic work from the late '60s and early '70s, it includes Bell's playful duets with Judy Clay. *—Bill Dahl*

Wow . . . /Bound to Happen / Apr. 1, 1997 / Stax ✦✦✦✦✦

Phases of Reality/Relating / 1999 / Stax ✦✦✦

Belle & Sebastian

f. 1995, Glasgow, Scotland
Group / Indie Pop, Twee Pop, Chamber Pop, Alternative Pop/Rock
A band named for a French children's television series about a boy and his dog would almost have to be precious, and Glasgow's Belle & Sebastian certainly is—but in the good way; they make gorgeous, delicate melodies sound full-bodied. Their penchant for whimsical, unsettling lyrical details mirrors their quirky approach to being a band, which includes publicity photos with fake band members and performances in odd venues like homes, church halls and libraries. Belle & Sebastian's idiosyncratic career isn't surprising, given the group's unusual beginnings. Vocalist/guitarist Stuart Murdoch formed the band as the final

project for a music business course at his university. He chose band members by instinct at a local cafe in late 1995, eventually assembling Sarah Martin (violin), Stevie Jackson (guitar), Chris Geddes (keyboards), Stuart David (bass), Richard Colburn (drums) and Isobel Campbell (cello). All of them agreed that the band was to stay on a small scale; they even assumed they would release two albums and break up. But in May 1996 their self-released debut album *Tigermilk* became a sensation, earning terrific word of mouth even though only 1000 copies of the LP were released. Six months later, *If You're Feeling Sinister* earned the band widespread critical acclaim and a large cult following in the in the U.K. Some of this buzz reached the US, where *If You're Feeling Sinister* was released by the EMI subsidiary Enclave just before it closed shop. The band's cult continued to build in 1997 helped by three EPs—*Dog on Wheels, Lazy Line Painter Jane* and *3, 6, 9 Seconds of Light*...—all of which were well-received by critics and indie fans alike. By the year's end, the group finalized an American deal with Matador Records, who issued *The Boy with the Arab Strap* in 1998 and re-released *Tigermilk* in 1999. After completing 2000's *Fold Your Hands Child, You Walk Like a Peasant,* Stuart David left the group for his solo project, Looper. *—Stephen Thomas Erlewine*

Tigermilk / May 1996 / Matador ✦✦✦✦

Belle & Sebastian's first album, *Tigermilk,* was initially pressed in a quantity of 1000 on their own label, Electric Honey Recordings. The record was intended to be the end result of Stuart Murdoch's music business school course, but it became an unexpected word-of-mouth sensation in England, and the LP quickly disappeared from shops. As a result, once the group's second album, *If You're Feeling Sinister,* became a hit, there were no copies of *Tigermilk* available for newly converted fans and it remained unheard by the majority of the group's audience. Those that have heard it say it is quite similar stylistically to *If You're Feeling Sinister* and the songs match that record's high standard. *Tigermilk* was re-released in 1999 to the delight of the often cultish fans of Belle & Sebastian. *—Stephen Thomas Erlewine*

● **If You're Feeling Sinister** / Nov. 18, 1996 / Matador ✦✦✦✦✦

Belle & Sebastian's second record was, for all intents and purposes, really its first, since their debut in 1997 was not heard outside of privileged inner circles, due to its status as a self-released pseudo-class project. And it really did have quite a bit of an impact upon its release in 1997, largely because during the first half of the '90s, the whimsy and preciousness that had been an integral part of alternative music was suppressed by grunge. Whimsy and preciousness is an integral part of *If You're Feeling Sinister,* along with clever wit and gentle, intricate arrangements—a wonderful blend of the Smiths and Simon & Garfunkel, to be reductive. Even if its firmly within the college, bed-sit tradition, and is unabashedly retrogressive, that gives *Sinister* a special, timeless character that's enhanced by Stuart Murdoch's wonderful, lively songwriting. Blessed with an impish sense of humor, a sly turn of phrase, and an alluringly fey voice, he gives this record a real sense of backbone, in that its humor if far more biting than the music appears and the music is far more substantial that it initially seems. *Sinister* plays like this record has a real sense of backbone, in that its humor is far more biting than the music appears and the music is far more substantial that it initially seems. *Sinister* plays like a great forgotten album, couched in '80s indie, '90s attitude, and '60s, folk-pop—it's beautifully out of time and even if other Belle & Sebastian albums sound like it, this is where they achieved a sense of grace. *—Stephen Thomas Erlewine*

The Boy With the Arab Strap / Sep. 8, 1998 / Matador ✦✦✦✦✦

Belle & Sebastian quietly built a dedicated following after the release of their second album, *If You're Feeling Sinister,* as word of mouth spread from indie kids to record collectors to store clerks to critics. By the end of 1997, the Scottish septet had developed a following every bit as passionate as the Smiths at their peak, which is only appropriate since leader Stuart Murdoch is as wittily literate as Morrissey. *If You're Feeling Sinister* proved this, as did the three excellent EPs that followed, rising expectations for *The Boy With the Arab Strap.* Even if the album doesn't match the peerless *If You're Feeling Sinister* or break new ground for Belle & Sebastian, it's not a sophomore slump. From the Motown stomp of "Dirty Dream No. 2" to the Paul Simon shuffle of the title track, there is more musical texture on *Boy* than *Sinister,* but much of this was already explored on the EPs, which means *Arab Strap* essentially consolidates the group's talents. Murdoch recedes from the spotlight on occasion, letting Steve Jackson deliver two music-biz spiels and giving Isobel Campbell space to shine with the lilting "Is It Wicked Not to Care." All three songs are highlights, but Murdoch's songs still attract the most attention. His vicious wit, often overlooked in favor of his poetic narratives, surfaces on the title track, while "It Could Have Been a Brilliant Career" summarizes his effortless gift for elegant melancholia. Such small, precious gems are what Belle & Sebastian are all about, and *The Boy With the Arab Strap* offers another round of timeless, endlessly fascinating pop-folk treasures. *—Stephen Thomas Erlewine*

Lazy Line Painter Jane / Mar. 7, 2000 / Matador ✦✦✦✦✦

Fold Your Hands Child, You Walk Like a Peasant / Jun. 5, 2000 / Matador ✦✦✦

When Belle and Sebastian cancelled several dates on their 1998 North American tour after cellist Isobel Campbell fell ill, many fans cried foul; couldn't the rest of the group have gone on without her? Of course not—Belle and Sebastian is a band in the most democratic sense of the word, a point reinforced by *Fold Your Hands Child, You Walk Like a Peasant,* their fourth and most ambitiously eclectic album to date. Nominal frontman Stuart Murdoch recedes into the background even more than on *The Boy with the Arab Strap,* allowing bandmates like Campbell and Stevie Jackson to take on a greater share of the writing and vocal duties. Also like its predecessor, *Fold Your Hands Child* opts for a subtle, intimate palette that reveals its charms only in its own sweet time. It may be too subtle for its own good; even after repeated listens it fails to connect on any meaningful level. The record has many intriguing ideas (like the delicate "Beyond the Sunrise," which evokes the classic duets of Nancy Sinatra and Lee Hazlewood, and the vaguely rootsy "The Wrong Girl"), but few of the concepts seem fully developed. For better or worse, *Fold Your Hands Child*'s best moments are those which hew most closely to the classic Belle and Sebastian sound—i.e., Stuart Murdoch songs. Though there's little advancement in his contributions, they capture the band's past glories. The radiant "Woman's Realm" is a dead ringer for *The Boy With the Arab Strap*'s title cut, while "The Model" retreads so much lyrical and musical ground it could be a self-parody. Still, the album provokes an intriguing question: Belle and Sebastian may be a band, not Stuart Murdoch's solo project, but is that a good thing? *—Jason Ankeny*

Pat Benatar (Pat Andrzejewski)

b. Jan. 10, 1953, Brooklyn, NY

Vocals / Album Rock, Arena Rock, Pop/Rock, Hard Rock

Pat Benatar's polished mainstream pop/rock made her one of the more popular female vocalists of the early '80s. Although she came on like an arena rocker with her power chords, tough sexuality and powerful vocals, her music was straight pop/rock underneath all the bluster. Benatar signed with Chrysalis Records in 1979, releasing her debut album, *In the Heat of the Night,* that same year. The record launched her string of hit singles with the number 23 "Heartbreaker." Featuring the Top Ten hit "Hit Me with Your Best Shot," Benatar's second album, 1980's *Crimes of Passion* was a greater success, selling over four million copies and winning the Grammy for Best Female Rock Vocal Performance. Her third album, *Precious Time* (1981), reached number one on the album charts; a single from the album called "Fire and Ice" won Benatar another Grammy. Benatar released a live album, *Live from Earth,* in 1983; it contained one of her biggest hits, "Love Is a Battlefield." Although 1984's *Tropico* contained her biggest hit "We Belong" (number five), the album was her lowest-charting to date. "Invincible" (1985), taken from *The Legend of Billie Jean* soundtrack, was her last Top Ten hit. Even though it included the hit single "Sex as a Weapon," Benatar's *Seven the Hard Way* (1985) became her first album not to go platinum—it didn't even go gold. *—Stephen Thomas Erlewine*

● **Best Shots** / Nov. 1989 / Chrysalis ✦✦✦✦✦

Several compilations have appeared in the years since it first hit the shelves, but *Best Shots* remains the finest Pat Benatar collection yet assembled, largely because it is the most concise. True, there may be a few lesser hits missing in favor of a couple newly recorded songs—"Sex as a Weapon," "Treat Me Right," "I Need a Lover," "Promises in the Dark," "Little Too Late," and "Looking for a Stranger" all could have made the cut instead of "Painted Desert" and "Outlaw Blues"—but the remainder of the disc is nearly flawless, delivering arena-rock staples such as "Hit Me with Your Best Shot," "Fire and Ice," "Heartbreaker," "We Belong," "Invincible," and "All Fired Up" one after another. It may not be perfect, but it delivers enough thrills to make it all worthwhile. *—Stephen Thomas Erlewine*

Brook Benton (Benjamin Franklin Peay)

b. Sep. 19, 1931, Camden, SC, **d.** Apr. 9, 1988, New York, NY

Vocals / R&B, Soul

Silky smooth: that was Brook Benton's byword from his first record to his very last, as the singer parlayed his rich baritone pipes into seven number one R&B hits and eight Top Ten items. Stints on the gospel circuit preceded Benton's first secular session for Okeh in 1953, but his career didn't begin to take off until he teamed with writer/producer Clyde Otis. Benton cowrote and sang hundreds of demos for other artists before frequent collaborator Otis signed his friend to Mercury; together they pioneered a lush, violin-studded variation on the standard R&B sound, which beautifully showcased Benton's intimate vocals.

Benton crashed the top spot on the R&B charts in early 1959 with his moving "It's Just a Matter of Time," then rapidly encored with three more R&B chart-toppers—"Thank You Pretty Baby," "So Many Ways," and "Kiddio." Pairing with Mercury labelmate Dinah Washington, their delightful repartee on "Baby (You've Got What It Takes)" and "A Rockin' Good Way" paced the R&B lists in 1960.

The early '60s were a prolific period for Benton, but he left Mercury a few years later and bounced between labels before reemerging with the atmospheric Tony Joe White ballad "Rainy Night in Georgia" on Cotillion in 1970. Benton later made a halfhearted attempt to cash in on the disco craze, but his hitmaking reign was at an end long before his death in 1988. *—Bill Dahl*

Anthology / 1986 / Rhino ✦✦✦✦✦

Rhino's Brook Benton *Anthology* is a 23-track collection that hits all of the high points, not only including songs from his tenure with Mercury—"It's Just a Matter of Time," "So Many Ways," "Kiddio," "Baby (You've Got What It Takes)," "A Rockin' Good Way (To Mess Around and Fall in Love)," "The Boll Weevil Song," "Hotel Happiness"—but also his later hits on Cotillion Records, including "Rainy Night in Georgia." It's the only collection that covers such a wide range of material—the terrific *40 Greatest Hits* only features his Mercury recordings, which admittedly are his best work—and thereby gives a good overview of his entire career. However, Rhino never released *Anthology* on compact disc due to licensing reasons, and ten years after its 1986 release, there was no compilation encompassing Benton's entire career available on disc. Of course, since *40 Greatest Hits* did its job so well, this turns out to be just a minor complaint, but Rhino's *Anthology* remains the only thoughtfully compiled retrospective of Benton's entire career. *—Stephen Thomas Erlewine*

40 Greatest Hits / 1989 / Mercury ✦✦✦✦✦

● **Endlessly: The Best of Brook Benton** / Jun. 16, 1998 / Rhino ✦✦✦✦✦

Twelve years after they released *Anthology,* arguably the definitive career-spanning Brook Benton collection, Rhino adapted the compilation for CD, releasing *Endlessly: The Best of Brook Benton. Endlessly* features three tracks less than *Anthology,* yet it doesn't suffer—it remains a nearly flawless overview of Benton's career, featuring all of his big hits plus many terrific lesser-known singles. Every one of his great singles—from "It's Just a Matter of Time," "Baby (You've Got What It Takes)," and "Kiddio" to "The Boll Weevil Song" and "Rainy Night in Georgia"—are here, in a more concise and accessible form than Mercury's double-disc *40 Greatest Hits.* That double-disc set remains an ideal choice for collectors, but less dedicated fans will find *Endlessly* to be essential. *—Stephen Thomas Erlewine*

Chuck Berry (Charles Edward Anderson Berry)

b. Oct. 18, 1926, St Louis, MO
Vocals, Guitar (Electric), Guitar / Rock & Roll
Of all the early breakthrough rock & roll artists, none is more important to the development of the music than Chuck Berry. He is its greatest songwriter, the main shaper of its instrumental voice, one of its greatest guitarists and one of its greatest performers. Quite simply, without him, there would be no Beatles, Rolling Stones, Beach Boys, Bob Dylan nor a myriad others. There would be no standard 'Chuck Berry guitar intro,' the instrument's clarion call to get the joint rockin' in any setting. The clippety clop rhythms of rockabilly would not have been mainstreamed into the now standard 4/4 rock & roll beat. There would be no obsessive wordplay by modern-day tunesmiths; in fact, the whole history (and artistic level) of rock & roll songwriting would have been much poorer without him. Like Brian Wilson said, he wrote "all of the great songs and came up with all the rock&roll beats." Those who do not claim him as a seminal influence or profess a liking for his music and showmanship show their ignorance of rock's development as well as his place as the music's first great creator. Elvis may have fueled rock & roll's imagery, but Chuck Berry was its heartbeat and original mindset. *—Cub Koda*

After School Session / 1958 / Chess ✦✦✦✦✦
While Chuck Berry's first album, *After School Session*, featured only one hit single, the Top Ten "School Day," and several of the songs became rock & roll standards, including "Too Much Monkey Business," "No Money Down," and "Brown Eyed Handsome Man." *After School Session* also featured a couple of stylistic variations, including the calypso-flavored "Havana Moon" and the straight blues of "Wee, Wee Hours." *—Stephen Thomas Erlewine*

One Dozen Berrys / 1958 / Chess ✦✦✦✦✦

☆ **Chuck Berry Is on Top** / 1959 / Chess ✦✦✦✦✦
If you had to sweat all of Chuck Berry's early albums on Chess (and some, but not all, of all his subsequent greatest-hits packages), this would be the one to own. The song lineup is exemplary, cobbling together classics like "Maybellene," "Carol," "Sweet Little Rock & Roller," "Little Queenie," "Roll Over Beethoven," "Around and Around," "Johnny B. Goode," and "Almost Grown." With the addition of the Latin-flavored "Hey Pedro," the steel guitar workout "Blues for Hawaiians," "Anthony Boy," and "Jo Jo Gunne," this serves as almost a mini-greatest hits package in and of itself. While this may be merely a collection of singles and album ballast (as were most rock & roll LPs of the 1950s and early '60s), it ends up being the most perfectly realized of Chuck Berry's career. *—Cub Koda*

☆ **St. Louis to Liverpool** / 1964 / Chess ✦✦✦✦✦
This album puts the lie to the popular myth that Chuck Berry's music started to fade away around the same time that the Beatles, the Rolling Stones, et al. emerged covering his stuff. His songwriting is as strong here as ever—side one is packed with now-familiar fare like "Little Marie" (a sequel to "Memphis, Tennessee"), "No Particular Place to Go," "Promised Land," and "You Never Can Tell," but even filler tracks like "Our Little Rendezvous" and "You Two" are among Berry's better album numbers, the latter showing off the slightly softer pop/R&B side to his music that many listeners forget about. Side two includes a bunch of tracks, including the hard-rocking "Go Bobby Soxer" and the even better "Brenda Lee," the slow blues "Things I Used to Do" (with a killer guitar break), and the instrumentals "Liverpool Drive" and "Night Beat," one fast and the other slow, that never get reissued or compiled anywhere. The sound on the 1984 reissue LP is excellent, and it's a lot easier to find than an original album. *—Bruce Eder*

Chuck Berry's Golden Hits / 1967 / Mercury ✦

Live at the Fillmore Auditorium / 1967 / Mercury ✦✦✦

The London Sessions / 1972 / Chess ✦✦✦
One-half of this album is a studio recording featuring Ian McLagan and Kenny Jones of the Faces. The other half is a live recording from the *Lancaster Arts Festival* in Coventry, England, featuring performances of "My Ding-a-Ling" and "Reelin' and Rockin'" that, in edited form, became the first hit singles for Chuck Berry in many years. ("My Ding-a-Ling" went gold and hit number one.) This gold-selling, Top Ten album represents Berry's commercial, if not artistic, peak. *— William Ruhlmann*

★ **The Great Twenty-Eight** / 1982 / Chess ✦✦✦✦✦
This is the place to start listening to Chuck Berry. *The Great Twenty-Eight* was a two-LP, single CD compilation that emerged during the early '80s, amid a brief period in which the Chess catalog was in the hands of the Sugar Hill label, a disco-oriented outfit that later lost the catalog to MCA. It has proved to be one of the most enduring of all compilations of Berry's work. Up until the release of this disc, every attempt at a compilation had either been too sketchy (the 1964 *Greatest Hits* album on Chess) or too demanding for the casual listener (the three *Golden Decade* double-LP sets), and this was the first set to find a happy medium between convenience and thoroughness. Veteran listeners will love this CD even if they learn little from it, while neophytes will want to play it to death. All of the cuts come from Berry's first nine years in music, including all of the major singles as well as relatively minor hits such as "Come On" (which was more significant in the history of rock & roll in its cover version performed by the Rolling Stones as their debut release). The sound is decent throughout (surprisingly, except for "Come On," which has some considerable noise), although it is considerably outclassed by the most recent round of remasterings. In the decades since its release, there have been more comprehensive collections of Berry's work, but this is the best single disc, if one can overlook the relatively lo-fi digital sound. *—Bruce Eder*

Rock & Roll Rarities / 1986 / Chess ✦✦✦✦✦
On this follow-up to *The Great Twenty-Eight*, the songs are familiar, but the versions are not. Delving into the Chess Records archives, producer Steve Hoffman has come up with 20 tracks, many in unreleased or unusual versions. Some are demos, some are stereo recordings of songs usually heard in mono. Hoffman has remixed many of them, bringing up the '50s and '60s sound quality to near-'80s standard. Start with *The Great Twenty-Eight*, but come to this collection for interesting new ways to hear the old Berry favorites. *— William Ruhlmann*

More Rock 'n Roll Rarities from the Golden Era of Chess Record / Aug. 1986 / Chess ✦✦✦
This second volume of producer Steve Hoffman's discoveries in the Chess Records vaults features some less prominent Chuck Berry tunes, again in the form of demos, unreleased alternate takes, and stereo remixes. We are getting into collector territory here, but there are still some enjoyable examples of the Berry repertoire. *— William Ruhlmann*

☆ **The Chess Box** / 1988 / Chess ✦✦✦✦✦
Over the course of three compact discs, *The Chess Box* contains all the highlights from Chuck Berry's career, including all of the hit singles. In addition to the familar items, which are all included here, there are numerous tracks that are lesser-known but equally as good. That's particularly true on the stellar first two discs, where album tracks, B-sides, and forgotten singles like "Dowbound Train," "Drifting Heart," "Havana Moon," "Betty Jean," "Bye Bye Johnny," "Down the Road a Piece," and "The Thirteen Question Method" get equal space with "Maybellene," "Thirty Days," "No Money Down," "Roll Over Beethoven," "Too Much Monkey Business," "Brown Eyed Handsome Man," "School Day," "Rock & Roll Music," "Sweet Little Sixteen," "Johnny B. Goode," and "Carol." Toward the end of the set, the quality of the material begins to sag a bit, but there are still forgotten gems like "Tulane" that prove that Berry's songwriting hadn't completely dried up. *The Great Twenty Eight* remains the definitive hits collection, but *The Chess Box* is an absolutely essential item for any serious fan, either of Chuck Berry or rock & roll. *—Stephen Thomas Erlewine*

Missing Berries / Jul. 1990 / Chess ✦✦✦

★ **His Best, Vol. 1** / Mar. 25, 1997 / Chess ✦✦✦✦✦
Strictly focusing on his single tracks in a chronological manner, this first of two volumes in MCA's Chess 50th Anniversary collection hits all the high spots of Chuck's career up to 1958. It also serves as the first compilation to really showcase Berry's development as a songwriter over the first three years of his massive crossover success, including the seldom-anthologized "Downbound Train" (perhaps the darkest and most demonic ditty he ever recorded) juxtaposed against his car songs ("Maybellene," "You Can't Catch Me"), his calculated and carefully crafted instant classics for the 1950s teenage market ("Reelin' and Rockin'," "Sweet Little Sixteen," "School Day") and his celebrations of the music itself ("Rock and Roll Music," "Johnny B. Goode," "Roll Over Beethoven"). There's a ton of great music here (with a second companion volume to complete the picture) and for a big chunk of what makes Chuck Berry perhaps rock & roll's original triple-threat package (singer, songwriter and its first guitar hero), there's much here to tip the scales in its favor to recommend this volume as a first-time purchase. Note: This collection and its companion volume now take the place of the single disc *The Great Twenty Eight*, which is now out of print. *—Cub Koda*

☆ **His Best, Vol. 2** / May 20, 1997 / Chess ✦✦✦✦✦
Picking up where the first volume left off, *His Best, Vol. 2* runs through Chuck Berry's best-known singles in 1958 with "Sweet Little Rock and Roller" and runs through 1972, when he inexplicably had his first number one record with "My Ding-A-Ling." In addition to hits like "Let It Rock," "Little Queenie," "Almost Grown," "Nadine," "No Particular Place to Go," "You Never Can Tell," and "Promised Land," there are lesser-known gems like "Jo Jo Gunne," making it more than just a rote greatest-hits collection. No matter how good the two-part *His Best* series is—and for fans that don't want to spring for *The Chess Box*, it's the best way to assemble a reasonably comprehensive Chuck collection—it's still a shame that Chess decided to delete the flawless single-disc compilation *The Great 28* in favor of this series. *—Stephen Thomas Erlewine*

★ **Anthology** / Jun. 27, 2000 / Chess ✦✦✦✦✦
Falling squarely between the 71-track triple-disc *Chess Box* and numerous single-album distillations of Chuck Berry's hits, most notably *The Great Twenty-Eight*, is this 2000-released, chronologically compiled double-disc set. Its 50 tunes include all of Berry's seminal Chess hits plus key album tracks like "Beautiful Delilah," "Jo Jo Gunne," and "Jaguar & Thunderbird" that were influential but never cracked the charts. The 20-page booklet features a fascinating, extensive essay that provides crucial insights into Berry's work as well as rare pictures and track-by-track personnel listing. Since virtually all of Berry's essential work was done for the Chess label, now part of the Universal empire, there's no reason to decry the lack of anything from Berry's Mercury years, even though those tracks are now owned by the same company and could have been included, especially tacked onto disc two that times out at a relatively conservative 64 minutes. But with a lineup like this, who's complaining? Berry is the undisputed father of rock & roll and his music, much of it blues based and in a few cases like "Havana Moon" even Caribbean inspired, remains timeless as well as inspirational decades after it was recorded. The joys of discovering forgotten, relatively obscure cuts like "Come On" or "I'm Talking About You," both of which are easily on par with any of his more popular hits, is one of life's little bonuses. Berry's lyrics remain intriguingly descriptive, and the remastered sound brings these songs alive with every instrument, especially Willie Dixon's dynamic, jazzy stand-up bass clearly defined. The savvy track selection makes this a better, more consistent listen than the bulky box and stands as the best introduction to one of the most significant pop musicians on 20th century music and the single most important rock & roller ever. *—Hal Horowitz*

The Beta Band

f. 1997, Edinburgh, Scotland
Group / Experimental Dub, Electronica, Neo-Electro, Indie Rock, Trip-Hop
Their sound veering from post-grunge balladry to funk and ambient breakbeat to Madchester acid-house, the Beta Band emerged on the British scene as (nominally) a pop group with few similarities to any other act going. Formed around three friends originally from Edinburgh—vocalist Stephen Mason, drummer Robin Jones and DJ/sampler John Maclean—the group later added bassist Richard Greentree. Scant months after forming, the Beta Band gained a formidable ally in gaining exposure: manager Brian Cannon, the designer responsible for virtually every Oasis sleeve released to that point. The group's first EP, 1997's *Champion Versions*, featured mixing by the Verve's Nick McCabe. Two additional EPs followed in early 1998, *The Patty Patty Sound* and *Los Amigos del Beta Bandidos*. After collecting all

three EPs on an album, the Beta Band began recording for their proper debut, a self-titled effort released in 1999. *—John Bush*

● **The 3 E.P.'s** / Sep. 28, 1998 / Astralwerks ♦♦♦♦♦
This grouping of the Beta Band's first recordings—three EPs, four tracks each—is a collection of practically indescribabe songs. In fact, many of the tracks are only nominally pop songs; the group ranges from Kraut and avant-rock musings to heavy funk and hip-hop without the feeling of force that it's being done for the sake of critics. *—John Bush*

The Beta Band / Jun. 15, 1999 / Astralwerks ♦♦♦♦
Though dismissed by the group themselves as "fucking awful" and "the worst record made this year," the Beta Band's self-titled album otherwise defies simple criticism—seemingly infinite in its sonic complexities, it's an album of remarkable density and detail, a brashly schizophrenic freak-out which weaves its way throughout the history of rock & roll. Pop, blues, folk, psychedelia, hip-hop—they're all here, sometimes even colliding within the same song; the disc somehow sounds almost completely different with each successive listen, consistently revealing new layers and possibilities. It all constantly runs the risk of collapsing into complete self-indulgence, but in its way the Beta Band's genius is their wanton disregard for niceties like verses, choruses, and melodies; rejecting musical theory in favor of the chaos theory, the album's neither a masterpiece nor a mess, but both. *—Jason Ankeny*

The Big Bopper (Jiles Perry Richardson)

b. Oct. 24, 1930, Sabine Pass, TX, **d.** Feb. 3, 1959, Clear Lake, IO
Vocals / Rock & Roll
Legendary as one of the three rock greats to die in the tragic 1959 Clear Lake, IA, plane crash that also claimed the lives of Buddy Holly and Ritchie Valens, the Big Bopper (born Jiles Perry Richardson) had just established himself as a rock hitmaker with the rollicking "Chantilly Lace." Born in the heart of Texas, Richardson grew up in Beaumont and changed his first name to Jape. He broke into show biz as a DJ over KTRM radio, where he coined the nickname "The Big Bopper." He began recording for Mercury in 1957, his animated baritone scaling pop playlists the next year with "Chantilly Lace"—easily his top seller—and the equally raucous novelty "Big Bopper's Wedding." Richardson wrote "White Lightning," a huge country hit for George Jones, and Johnny Preston's number one smash "Running Bear." *—Bill Dahl*

● **Hellooo Baby!: Best of the Big Bopper, 1954-1959** / 1989 / Rhino ♦♦♦♦♦
Hellooo Baby!: Best of the Big Bopper, 1954-1959 is a single-CD compilation of the Bopper's finest, including "Chantilly Lace," "Little Red Riding Hood," and "The Big Bopper's Wedding." It's wild and fun. *—Cub Koda*

Big Brother & the Holding Company

f. 1965, San Francisco, CA, **db.** 1972
Group / Album Rock, Acid Rock, Psychedelic, Blues-Rock
Big Brother are primarily remembered as the group that gave Janis Joplin her start. There's no denying both that Joplin was by far the band's most striking asset, and that Big Brother would never have made a significant impression if they hadn't been fortunate enough to add her to their lineup shortly after forming. But Big Brother also occupy a significant place in the history of San Francisco psychedelic rock, as one of the bands that best captured the era's loosest, reckless, and indulgent qualities in its high-energy mutations of blues and folk-rock. Soon after Joplin joined the lineup in mid-1966, it became evident to both band and audience that Joplin's fiery wail—mature and emotionally wrenching, even at that early stage—had to be spotlighted to make Big Brother a contender.

The band's legendary performance at 1967's Monterey Pop Festival catapulted themselves into national attention, though an ill-advised contract with the tiny Mainstream label forced them to record one album before accepting any of major-label bids rolling in. After signing with Columbia, the one Big Brother album that featured Joplin, *Cheap Thrills*, went to number one when it was released. By the end of 1968 though, Joplin had decided to go solo, a move that totally knocked the wind out of the band's sails. Although they did re-form for a while in the early '70s with different singers (indeed, they continue to perform in watered-down variations today), nothing would ever be the same. *—Richie Unterberger*

Big Brother & the Holding Company / 1967 / Columbia ♦♦♦
Big Brother's debut album was not recorded under optimum circumstances. The sessions were too rushed, and the sound thinner than the band would have liked, especially given how much more powerful some of the material (such as "Down on Me") would sound in later concerts. Still, it's not the useless throwaway some critics have portrayed it as, and it decently conveys the band's loose, sometimes reckless blend of blues, folk-rock, and psychedelia. Janis Joplin sings with soulful intensity on "Down on Me" and "Call on Me"; Peter Albin's "Light Is Faster Than Sound" is good wacked-out early Haight-Ashbury psychedelic rock; and the rock cover of Moondog's "All Is Loneliness" is spookily imaginative. The 1999 CD reissue adds the worthy single "Coo Coo"/"The Last Time" (good Eastern-influenced guitar work on the former, a good hurt hard rock vocal from Joplin on the latter) and previously unreleased alternate takes of "Call on Me" and "Bye, Bye Baby." *—Richie Unterberger*

★ **Cheap Thrills** / Aug. 1968 / Columbia ♦♦♦♦♦
Cheap Thrills, the major-label debut of Janis Joplin, was one of the most eagerly anticipated, and one of the most successful, albums of 1968. Joplin and Big Brother had earned extensive press notice ever since they played *the Monterey Pop Festival* in June 1967, but their only recorded work was a poorly produced, self-titled Mainstream album, and they spent a year getting out of their contract with Mainstream in order to sign with Columbia while demand built. When *Cheap Thrills* appeared in August 1968, it shot into the charts, reaching number one and going gold within a couple of months, and "Piece of My Heart" became a Top 40 hit. Joplin, with her ear- (and vocal cord-) shredding voice, was the obvious standout. Nobody had ever heard singing as emotional, as desperate, as determined, as loud as Joplin's, and *Cheap Thrills* was her greatest moment. Big Brother's backup, typical of the guitar-dominated sound of San Francisco psychedelia, made up in enthusiasm what it lacked in precision. But everybody knew who the real star was, and Joplin played her last gig with Big Brother while the album was still on top of the charts. Neither she nor the band would ever equal it. Heard today, *Cheap Thrills* is a musical time capsule and remains a showcase for one of rock's most distinctive singers. The 1999 CD reissue adds the previously unreleased outtakes "Roadblock" and "Flower in the Sun" from the *Cheap Thrills* sessions, along with previously unreleased live March 1968 versions of "Catch Me Daddy" and "Magic of Love." *—William Ruhlmann*

Be a Brother / Oct. 1970 / Columbia ♦♦

Cheaper Thrills / Apr. 1984 / Acadia ♦♦

Live at Winterland '68 / 1998 / Columbia/Legacy ♦♦♦
Recorded live in San Francisco on April 12 and April 13, this set is a snapshot of the band—with fine sound—reaching the peak of their form. All of the well-known songs from their first two albums are present: "Ball and Chain," "Down on Me," "Piece of My Heart," "Summertime," "Combination of the Two," and "Light Is Faster Than Sound," for starters. There isn't a single song that isn't available in some form on either the *Janis* box or the *Farewell Song* compilation, though. Also, these versions aren't remarkably different or better than the familiar ones, although they tend to run longer, particularly on the seven-minute "Light Is Faster Than Sound" and the ten-minute "Ball and Chain." A treat for fans to hear, with a 24-page booklet that has lots of comments from the band. *—Richie Unterberger*

Big Star

f. 1971, Memphis, TN, **db.** 1975
Group / Proto-Punk, Pop/Rock, Power Pop
The quintessential American power pop band, Big Star remains one of the most mythic and influential cult acts in all of rock & roll. Originally led by the singing and songwriting duo of Alex Chilton and Chris Bell, the Memphis-based group fused the strongest elements of the British Invasion era—the melodic invention of the Beatles, the whiplash guitars of the Who, and the radiant harmonies of the Byrds—into a ramshackle but poignantly beautiful sound which recaptured the spirit of pop's past even as it pointed the way toward the music's future. Although creative tensions, haphazard distribution, and marketplace indifference conspired to ensure Big Star's brief existence and commercial failure, the group's three studio albums nevertheless remain unqualified classics, and their impact on subsequent generations of indie bands on both sides of the Atlantic is surpassed only by that of the Velvet Underground.

Big Star came together in 1971, with Chilton (the onetime Box Tops vocalist) and Bell plus bassist Andy Hummel and drummer Jody Stephens. After a brilliant debut, 1972's *#1 Record*, Bell and Chilton began butting heads over Big Star's direction. In 1972 Bell finally left the band—his subsequent attempts to mount a solo career proved largely fruitless, with only a spectacular solo single, "I Am the Cosmos," receiving official release prior to his untimely death in a 1978 car crash. Big Star temporarily disbanded but returned with 1974's *Radio City*, a record that remains their masterpiece. Sessions for a planned third album proved disastrous, and then Big Star was no more. After finally earning release overseas in 1978, the third Big Star album earned a significant cult following, and countless alternative rock bands cited the band's enormous influence in the years to follow. In 1993, Chilton and Stephens appeared at a reunion gig that was captured on the *Columbia* live disc, although no new studio recordings were forthcoming. *—Jason Ankeny*

☆ **Third/Sister Lovers** / 1978 / Rykodisc ♦♦♦♦♦
A shambling wreck of an album, Big Star's *Third/Sister Lovers* ranks among the most harrowing experiences in pop music; impassioned, erratic and stark, it's the slow, sinking sound of a band falling apart. Recorded with their label, Stax, poised on the verge of bankruptcy, the album finds Alex Chilton at the end of his rope, sabotaging his own music long before it can ever reach the wrecking crew of poor distribution, indifferent marketing and disinterested pop radio; his songs are haphazardly brilliant, a head-on collision between inspiration and frustration. The album is a kind of self-fulfilling prophecy, each song smacking of utter defeat and desperation; the result is either one of the most vividly emotional experiences in pop music or a completely wasted opportunity, and while the truth probably lies somewhere in between, there's no denying *Third*'s magnetic pull—it's like an undertow. Although previously issued on a variety of different labels, Rykodisc's 1992 release is the definitive edition of this unfinished masterpiece, its 19 tracks most closely appoximating the original planned running order while restoring the music's intended impact; in addition to unearthing a blistering cover of the Kinks' "At the End of the Day" and a haunting rendition of Nat King Cole's "Nature Boy," it also appends the disturbing "Dream Lover," which distills the album's messiest themes into less than four minutes of psychic torment. *—Jason Ankeny*

Big Star Live / Feb. 21, 1992 / Rykodisc ♦♦♦
Recorded in the wake of the release of *Radio City, Big Star Live* documents a freewheeling radio date originally broadcast in 1974. Spotlighting the strongest material from the group's first two LPs, the mood is both lighthearted and world-weary, the attitude of a band fully cognizant of the fact that the music they're creating is exceptional, yet dumbfounded by their almost complete lack of commercial success. A cover of Loudon Wainwright's "Motel Blues" is wholly indicative of Alex Chilton's mindset at this point in the game; already a battle-scarred veteran of the music industry, his frustration is palpable, lending even greater urgency to remarkable songs like "September Gurls," "The Ballad of El Goodo," "O My Soul," and "Thirteen." While certainly not the best starting point for new fans, *Big Star Live* is essential stuff for the converted. *—Jason Ankeny*

★ **#1 Record/Radio City** / Jun. 10, 1992 / Fantasy ♦♦♦♦♦
A two-fer combining Big Star's first and second albums, *#1 Record/Radio City* remains a definitive document of early-'70s American power pop and a virtual blueprint for much of the finest alternative rock that came after it. The lone Big Star record to merit the full participation of founder Chris Bell, the brightly produced *#1 Record* splits the songwriting credits evenly between him and Alex Chilton (in the tradition of Lennon-McCartney). But from the beginning, the group is tearing apart at the seams: Bell and Chilton's relationship seems less a working partnership than a battle of wills, and each possesses his own distinctive vision. The purist, Bell crafts electrifying and melodic classic pop like "Feel" and "In the Street," while

Chilton, the malcontent, pens luminous, melancholy ballads like "The Ballad of El Goodo" and "Thirteen." Ultimately, their tension makes *#1 Record* brilliant. However, *Radio City* shifts gears dramatically: Bell is largely absent (though he guests, uncredited, on a few tracks, including the wonderful "Back of a Car"), allowing Chilton's darker impulses free reign. From the raucous opener "O My Soul" onward, the new Big Star is noisier, edgier, and even more potent. Erratic mixing, spotty production, shaky performances—by all rights, *Radio City* should be a failure, yet Chilton is at his best when poised on the brink of disaster, and the songs hang together seemingly on faith and conviction alone. Each track recalls pop's glory days, from the Kinks-ish snarl of "Mod Lang" to the Byrds-like guitar glow that adorns "Way Out West." The much-celebrated "September Gurls" is indeed a classic—everything right and good about pop music distilled down to three minutes of pure genius. *—Jason Ankeny*

Columbia: Live at Missouri University / Sep. 14, 1993 / Zoo/Volcano ✦✦

Nobody Can Dance / Mar. 16, 1999 / Norton ✦✦✦

The Birthday Party

f. 1977, Melbourne, Australia, **db.** 1983

Group / No Wave, Post-Punk

The Birthday Party was one of the darkest and most challenging post-punk groups to emerge in the early '80s, creating bleak and noisy soundscapes that provided the perfect setting for vocalist Nick Cave's difficult, disturbing stories of religion, violence, and perversity. Under the direction of Cave and guitarist Rowland S. Howard, the band tore through reams of blues and rockabilly licks, spitting out hellacious feedback and noise at an unrelenting pace. As the band's career progressed, Cave's vision got darker and their songs alternated between dirges to blistering sonic assaults. Originally, the Australian band was called the Boys Next Door; after moving to London and switching their name to the deceptively benign Birthday Party, the group's demented, knotty post-punk began to gel. Cave had the most successful solo career, recording a series of albums in the '80s and '90s that maintained his status as a popular cult figure. *—Stephen Thomas Erlewine*

Prayers on Fire / 1981 / 4AD ✦✦✦✦✦

Junkyard / 1982 / 4AD ✦✦✦

● **Hits** / Oct. 13, 1992 / 4AD ✦✦✦✦✦

As an album title, *Hits* is an intentionally ironic misnomer for one of Australia's most influential rock bands of the late '70s and early '80s. Having "hits" was the furthest thing from the Birthday Party's collective mind over the course of five tumultuous years that followed the group's move to England from Down Under; the members reviled anything that hinted at mainstream acceptance. Ten years on, the intensity of this music is still frightening. It's a dense, mutant hybrid that evolved from punk, progressive rock, funk, and improvisational jazz, without directly owning up to any of these base materials. Vocalist Nick Cave (who has gone on to an equally creative solo career) didn't just sing about society's dark, depraved underbelly, he lived the experience right there on disc and on stage. *—Roch Parisien*

Mutiny!/The Bad Seed / Feb. 11, 1997 / Thirsty Ear ✦✦✦✦✦

Collecting the two EPs onto one disc, this release also includes two rough mixes from the *Mutiny* sessions as a bonus. "The Six Strings That Drew Blood," also later recorded by Cave's Bad Seeds, is a quick brawler like many a past Party classic, Cave hitting a strangled falsetto at points as the group rips along. "Pleasure Avalanche" works on the slow grind trip; Cave husks his vocals over a nicely creepy arrangement from the rest, calling for the titular situation in question with increasing desperation. *—Ned Raggett*

Live, 1981-1982 / Apr. 20, 1999 / 4AD ✦✦✦✦

Björk (Björk Guðmundsdóttir)

b. Nov. 21, 1965, Reykjavik, Iceland

Vocals, Keyboards / Electronica, Alternative Dance, Trip-Hop, Club/Dance, Alternative Pop/Rock

Björk first came to prominence as one of the lead vocalists of the avant-pop Icelandic sextet the Sugarcubes, but when she launched a solo career after the group's 1992 demise, she quickly eclipsed her old band's popularity. Instead of following in the Sugarcubes' arty guitar-rock pretentions, Björk immersed herself in dance and club culture, working with many of the biggest names in the genre, including Nellee Hooper, Underworld and Tricky. *Debut*, her first solo effort (except for an Icelandic-only smash released when she was just eleven years old) not only established her new artistic direction, but it became an international hit, making her one of the '90s most unlikely stars.The first result of her partnership with Hooper was "Human Behaviour," which became a Top 40 hit in the UK, setting the stage for the surprising number three debut of the full-length album, *Debut.* Throughout 1993, Björk had hit UK singles—including "Venus as a Boy" and "Big Time Sensuality"—as well as modern rock radio hits in the US and in both countries, she earned rave reviews. "Army of Me," the first single from Björk's forthcoming album, was released as a teaser single in the spring of 1995; it debuted at number 10 in the UK and became a moderate alternative rock hit in the US. *Post*, her second album, was released in June of 1995 to positive reviews and yielding the British hit singles "Isobel," "It's Oh So Quiet," and "Hyperballad." Late in 1996, Björk released *Telegram*, an album comprised of radical remixes of the entire *Post* album; *Telegram* was released in America in January of 1997. *Homogenic*, her most experimental studio effort to date, followed later that same year. *—Stephen Thomas Erlewine*

★ **Debut** / Jul. 1993 / Elektra ✦✦✦✦✦

Freed from the Sugarcubes' confines, Bjork takes her voice and creativity to new heights on *Debut*, her first work after the group's breakup. With producer Nellee Hooper's help, she moves in an elegantly playful, dance-inspired direction, crafting highly individual, emotional electronic pop songs like the shivery, idealistic "One Day" and the bittersweet "Violently Happy." Despite the album's swift stylistic shifts, each of *Debut*'s tracks are distinctively Bjork. "Human Behaviour"'s dramatic percussion provides a perfect showcase for her wide-ranging voice; "Aeroplane" casts her as a yearning lover against a lush, exotica-inspired backdrop; and the spare, poignant "Anchor Song" uses just her voice and a brass section to capture the loneliness of the sea. Though *Debut* is just as arty as anything she recorded with the Sugarcubes, the album's club-oriented tracks provide an exciting contrast to the rest of the album's delicate atmosphere. Bjork's playful energy ignites dance-pop-like "Big Time Sensuality," and turns the genre on its head with "There's More to Life Than This." Recorded live at *the Milk Bar Toilets*, it captures the dancefloor's sweaty, claustrophobic groove, but her impish voice gives it an almost alien feel. But the album's romantic moments may be its most striking; "Venus As a Boy" fairly swoons with twinkly vibes and lush strings, and Bjork's vocals and lyrics—"His wicked sense of humor/suggests exciting sex"—are sweet and just the slightest bit naughty. With harpist Corki Hale, she completely reinvents "Like Someone in Love," making it one of her own ballads. Possibly her prettiest work, Bjork's horizons expanded on her other releases, but the album still sounds fresh, which is even more impressive considering electronic music's whiplash-speed innovations. *Debut* not only announced Bjork's remarkable talent, it suggested she had even more to offer. *—Heather Phares*

Post / Jun. 13, 1995 / Elektra ✦✦✦✦✦

After *Debut*'s success, the pressure was on Björk to surpass that album's creative, tantalizing electronic pop. She more than delivered with 1995's *Post;* from the menacing, industrial-tinged opener "Army of Me," it's clear that this album is not simply *Debut* redux. The songs—especially the epic, modern fairy tale "Isobel"—production, and arrangements all aim for, and accomplish, more. *Post* also features *Debut* producer Nellee Hooper, 808 State's Graham Massey, Howie B., and Tricky, who help Björk incorporate a spectrum of electronic and orchestral styles into songs like "Hyperballad," which sounds like a love song penned by Aphex Twin. Meanwhile, the bristling beats on the volatile, sensual "Enjoy" and the fragile, weightless ballad "Possibly Maybe" nod to trip-hop without being overwhelmed by it. As on *Debut*, Björk finds new ways of expressing timeworn emotions like love, lust, and yearning in abstractly precise lyrics like "Since you went away/I'm wearing lipstick again/I suck my tongue in remembrance of you," from "Possibly Maybe." But *Post*'s emotional peaks and valleys are more extreme than *Debut*'s. "I Miss You"'s exuberance is so animated, it makes perfect sense that *Ren & Stimpy*'s John Kricfalusi directed the song's video. Likewise, "It's Oh So Quiet"—which eventually led to Björk's award-winning turn as Selma in *Dancer in the Dark*—is so cartoonishly vibrant, it could have been arranged by Warner Bros. musical director Carl Stalling. Yet Björk sounds equally comfortable with an understated string section on "You've Been Flirting Again." "Headphones" ends the album on an experimental, hypnotic note, layering Björk's vocals over and over till they circle each other atop a bubbling, minimal beat. The work of a constantly changing artist, *Post* proves that as Björk moves toward more ambitious, complex music, she always surpasses herself. *—Heather Phares*

Telegram / Nov. 25, 1996 / Elektra ✦✦✦✦

☆ **Homogenic** / Sep. 22, 1997 / One Little Indian ✦✦✦✦✦

By the late '90s, Björk's playful, unique worldview and singular voice became as confining as they were defining. With its surprising starkness and darkness, 1997's *Homogenic* shatters her "Icelandic pixie" image. Possibly inspired by her failed relationship with drum'n'bass kingpin Goldie, Björk sheds her more precious aspects, displaying more emotional depth than even her best previous work indicated. Her collaborators—LFO's Mark Bell, Mark "Spike" Stent, and *Post* contributor Howie B.—help make this album not only her most emotionally brave work, but her most sonically adventurous as well. A seamless fusion of chilly strings (courtesy of the Icelandic String Octet), stuttering, abstract beats, and unique touches like accordion and glass harmonica, *Homogenic* alternates between dark, uncompromising songs such as the icy opener "Hunter" and more soothing fare like the gently percolating "All Neon Like." The noisy, four-on-the-floor catharsis of "Pluto" and the raw vocals and abstract beats of "5 Years" and "Immature" reveal surprising amounts of anger, pain and strength in the face of heartache. "I dare you to take me on," Björk challenges her lover in "5 Years," and wonders on "Immature," "How could I be so immature/To think he would replace/The missing elements in me? "Bachelorette," a sweeping, brooding cousin to *Post*'s "Isobel," is possibly *Homogenic*'s saddest, most beautiful moment, giving filmic grandeur to a stormy relationship. Björk lets a little hope shine through on "Joga," a moving song dedicated to her homeland and her best friend, and the reassuring finale "All Is Full of Love." "Alarm Call"'s uplifting dance-pop seems out of place with the rest of the album but, as its title implies, *Homogenic* is her most holistic work. While it might not represent every side of Björk's music, *Homogenic* displays some of her most impressive heights. *—Heather Phares*

Selmasongs: Music from the Motion Picture Dancer in the Dark / Sep. 19, 2000 / Elektra ✦✦✦✦

Selmasongs: Music From the Motion Picture Soundtrack Dancer in the Dark is, and is not, a Björk album. While it's filled with rampant creativity, startling emotional leaps, and breathtaking vocals and arrangements, it isn't as playful as her other albums, even 1997's relatively dark *Homogenic.* Instead, it presents Björk as Selma, her character from Lars VonTrier's *Dancer in the Dark:* a Czech factory worker who is going blind but finds hope and refuge in the musicals she watches at the cinema. (VonTrier wanted to work with Björk after seeing Spike Jonze's musical-inspired video for "It's Oh So Quiet.") She acts through the music she composed, performed, and produced with conductor/arranger Vincent Mendoza and her longtime collaborators Mark "Spike" Stent and Mark Bell. Selma's unsinkable optimism and tragic end are telegraphed through songs like the irrepressible, cartoonish "Cvalda" to the sad, starry lullaby "Scatterheart." *Selmasongs*' best tracks are poignant, inventive expressions of Björk's talent and Selma's daydreams and suffering. "In the Musicals" shows how easy it is for Selma to slip into one of her Technicolor reveries: "There is always someone to catch me," Björk sighs as clouds of strings, harps, and xylophones rise up to meet her. "New World" reprises the simultaneously hopeful and ominous melody of "Overture," adding striking vocals and shuffling, industrial beats that reflect Selma's life in the factory as well as Björk's distinctive style. *Selmasongs* also succeeds as a soundtrack, sketching in details of Selma's story. "I've Seen It All," a duet with Thom Yorke, captures her stunted romance with a co-worker, while the tense "107 Steps" takes the listener to her journey's end. Intimate and theatrical, innovative and tied to tradition, *Selmasongs* paints a portrait of a woman losing her sight, but it maintains Björk's unique vision. *—Heather Phares*

The Black Crowes

f. 1984, Atlanta, GA

Group / Jam Bands, American Trad Rock, Southern Rock, Hard Rock

At the time of their 1990 debut, the kind of rock & roll the Black Crowes specialize in was out of style. Only Guns N' Roses came close to approximating a vintage Stones-style raunch, but they were too angry and jagged to pull it off completely. The Black Crowes replicated that Stonesy swagger and Faces boogie perfectly. Vocalist Chris Robinson appropriated the sound and style of vintage Rod Stewart while guitarist Rich Robinson fused Keith Richards' lean attack with Ron Wood's messy rhythmic sense. At their best, the Black Crowes echo classic rock without slavishly imitating their influences. "Jealous Again," the first single from their 1990 debut *Shake Your Money Maker,* was a moderate hit, but it was the band's cover of Otis Redding's "Hard to Handle" that made the group a multi-platinum success. The acoustic ballad "She Talks to Angels" became their second Top 40 hit in the spring of 1991. The Black Crowes delivered their second album, *The Southern Harmony and Musical Companion,* in the spring of 1992. It entered the charts at number one, but it didn't have as many hit singles as the debut; none of the singles cracked the Top 40 and only "Remedy" and "Thorn in My Pride" made the Top 100. *Amorica* debuted in the Top Ten, but none of the singles from the album made the charts; even though the record went gold, it slipped off the charts in early 1995. *—Stephen Thomas Erlewine*

Shake Your Money Maker / Jan. 1990 / American ✦✦✦✦

The Black Crowes' debut album, *Shake Your Money Maker,* may borrow heavily from the bluesy hard-rock grooves of the Rolling Stones and Faces (plus a bit of classic soul), but the band gets away with it due to sharp songwriting and an ear for strong riffs and chorus melodies, not to mention the gritty, muscular rhythm guitar of Rich Robinson and brother Chris's appropriate vocal swagger. Unlike their later records, the Crowes don't really stretch out and jam that much on *Money Maker,* but that helps distill their virtues into a handful of memorable singles ("Jealous Again," "She Talks to Angels," a cover of Otis Redding's "Hard to Handle"), and most of the album tracks maintain an equally high standard. *Shake Your Money Maker* may not be stunningly original, but it doesn't need to be; it's the most concise demonstration of the fact that the Black Crowes are a great, classic rock & roll band. *—Steve Huey*

The Southern Harmony and Musical Companion / May 12, 1992 / American ✦✦✦✦✦

The addition of the more technically gifted guitarist Marc Ford and a full-time organist gives the Black Crowes room to stretch out on *The Southern Harmony and Musical Companion,* perhaps the band's finest moment. Using Rich Robinson's descending chord progressions as a base, the band grooves its way through a remarkably fresh-sounding collection of Faces-like rockers and ballads, tearing into the material with flair and confidence and really coming into its own as a top-notch rock & roll outfit. But while the focus is undeniably on the band's musical chemistry, *Southern Harmony* also boasts a strong collection of songs, striking a perfect balance between the concise *Shake Your Money Maker* and their later, more jam-oriented records. While there aren't as many obvious singles as on their debut album, *The Southern Harmony and Musical Companion* is the best expression of the Crowes' ability to take a classic, tried-and-true sound and make it their own. *—Steve Huey*

Amorica / Nov. 1, 1994 / American ✦✦✦✦✦

On *Amorica,* the Black Crowes finally come into their own, taking their cue from the most relaxed, groove-oriented tracks on their previous album. While the album contains no immediately obvious singles, the songs are the best the band has ever written, stretching out into a hard, jam-oriented, funky blues-rock. The Black Crowes' influences are still discernable—no band celebrates the glory days of rock culture quite as enthusiastically—but they use the music of the Stones, the Faces, and Little Feat much the same way the Stones used the music of Chuck Berry: it's a starting point that leads the band into a new direction, incorporating different musical genres and making the music original. That sense of reinterpretation is what keeps *Amorica* fresh. *—Stephen Thomas Erlewine*

Three Snakes & One Charm / Jul. 23, 1996 / American ✦✦✦

By Your Side / Jan. 12, 1999 / American ✦✦✦✦

Between *Shake Your Moneymaker* and *Three Snakes & One Charm,* the Black Crowes evolved from a muscular, Stonesy hard rock outfit to full-fledged modern-day Southern rockers, drawing from a wealth of blues, country, folk, and rock styles to create a sprawling, fluid sound that was simultaneously traditional and distinctive. The problem was, their loose-limbed grooves tended to connect better in concert than on record, especially since they were sacrificing songs for the sake of sound, which in turn was decreasing their audience. Aware of the situation, the Crowes went back to their roots with *By Your Side.* Armed with a string of concise, energetic rockers, the Crowes hit harder than they have since their debut, yet they retain the sonic detail that reared its head on *Amorica,* adding pianos, choirs and scores of other flourishes throughout the record. It's a back-to-basics set performed with all of the knowledge they have gained over the years, and the result is a thoroughly enjoyable record, their most satisfying and accessible effort since *The Southern Harmony and Musical Companion.* Not that it's necessarily in that league—it lacks the parade of great songs that elevate that album above all their other records—but it does find the Crowes in lean fighting form for the first time in years, proving that they're possibly the best straight-ahead rock & roll band of the '90s. *—Stephen Thomas Erlewine*

● **Greatest Hits 1990-1999: A Tribute to a Work in Progress** / Jun. 20, 2000 / American/Columbia/Legacy ✦✦✦✦✦

Black Flag

f. 1977, Los Angeles, CA, **db.** 1986

Group / American Punk, L.A. Punk, Hardcore Punk

In many ways, Black Flag were the definitve Los Angeles hardcore punk band. Although their music flirted with heavy metal and experimental noise and jazz more than that of most hardcore bands, they defined the image and the aesthetic. Through their ceaseless touring, the band cultivated the American underground punk scene—every year, Black Flag played in every area of the U.S., influencing countless numbers of bands. Although their recording career was hampered by a draining lawsuit, which was followed by a seemingly endless stream of independently released records, the band was unquestionably one of the most influential American post-punk bands. A full decade and a half before the fusion of punk and metal became popular, Black Flag created a ferocious, edgy and ironic amalgam of underground aesthetics and gut-pounding metal. Their lyrics alluded to social criticism and a political viewpoint, but it was all conveyed as seething, cynical angst, which was occasionally very funny. Furthermore, Black Flag demonstrated an affection for bohemia—both in terms of musical experimentation and a fondness for poetry—that reiterated the band's underground roots and prevented it from becoming nothing but a heavy metal group. And it didn't matter who was in the band—throughout the years, the lineup changed numerous times—because the Black Flag name and four-bar logo became punk institutions. *—Stephen Thomas Erlewine*

★ **Damaged** / 1981 / SST ✦✦✦✦✦

Perhaps the best album to emerge from the quagmire that was early-'80s California hardcore punk, the visceral, intensely physical presence of this record has yet to be equaled, although many bands have tried. Although Black Flag had been recording for three years prior to this release, the fact that Henry Rollins was now their lead singer made all the difference. His furious bellow and barely contained ferocity was the missing piece the band needed to become great. Also, guitarist/mastermind Greg Ginn wrote a slew of great songs for this record that, while suffused with the usual punk conceits (alienation, boredom, disenfranchisement), were capable of making one laugh out loud, especially the proto-slacker satire "TV Party." Extremely controversial when it was released, *Damaged* endured the slings and arrows of outrageous criticism (some reacted as though this record alone would cause the fall of America's youth) to become and remain an important document of its time. *—John Dougan*

Everything Went Black / 1983 / SST ✦✦✦

When it was first released in 1983, Black Flag was in the middle of a backbreaking legal dispute with Unicorn Records. As a result of litigation, the band was prevented from using the Black Flag name on any records. Hence the original packaging for this album, which listed only the names of individual band members on the cover (this was rectified on subsequent issues). It's a double album (on vinyl) compilation of previously released material and outtakes—though the European edition features a wholly different running order. The material, dating from 1978 to 1981, is excellent in places, average in others. However, only obsessives need track it down—as signified by the inclusion of two versions of several songs (including stalwarts "Damaged" and "Police Story"). The fourth side of the original vinyl issue also included a sequence of radio spots discussing forthcoming Black Flag gigs, which is entertaining stuff, but it's more useful as a historical document than a listening experience. *—Alex Ogg*

Family Man / 1984 / SST ✦✦✦

The First Four Years / 1984 / SST ✦✦✦

The best collection of pre-Rollins era Black Flag. Much of *The First Four Years* finds the band in developmental mode, but the sonic anarchy and political vituperation met head-on more than once, creating a ferociously good time. Not simply for completists, this is an important recording of the then-burgeoning L.A. hardcore scene. *—John Dougan*

Live '84 / 1984 / SST ✦✦

My War / 1984 / SST ✦✦

Slip it In / 1984 / SST ✦✦✦

Slip It In followed *My War* almost immediately, and while a bit better (fewer mega-volume angst drones), the band still wanders a bit, experimenting with expanding the breadth of hardcore into a newer hard rock/punk sound. This is especially true of Greg Ginn's guitar playing, which was becoming increasingly avant-garde and exciting. Rather than simply coughing up one cliched solo after another, he wandered harmolodically up and down the fretboard as a jazz player like Blood Ulmer would, making the material more interesting than what most Black Flag-influenced bands were playing. *—John Dougan*

In My Head / 1985 / SST ✦✦✦✦✦

Hot on the heels of the live record came *Loose Nut* and *In My Head* which showed significant improvement over *My War* and *Slip It In.* Rollins and Ginn were exploring by-now standard lyrical themes: hate, paranoia, loneliness, anomie, and violence, but framing them around music that was demanding, powerful and exciting. *In My Head* is the slightly better of the two, primarily because it's a little edgier and uncontrolled, but at this juncture, Black Flag was making some of the best contemporary rock music extant. *—John Dougan*

Loose Nut / 1985 / SST ✦✦✦

One of three LPs released by Black Flag in 1985, *Loose Nut* suffers from its creators' rampant profligacy. Too much of the record is under-rehearsed and under-ripe, yet when the group hits its stride, as on Rollins's brutal "This Is Good," it's hard to deny the group's trademark, adrenaline-rush appeal. Other highlights include "Annihilate This Week" and "Bastard in Love." *—Alex Ogg*

Who's Got the 10? / 1986 / SST ✦✦✦✦✦

Black Flag's second live album, recorded at a 1985 Portland show with the Kira/Martinez rhythm section, is about what you'd expect the late period of the band to sound like live. A couple of older songs crop up—"Slip It In" and "Gimmie Gimmie Gimmie" are transformed into a great fifteen-minute medley with Rollins getting in some audience-baiting that explains the album title—but mostly this is from *Loose Nut,* its songs sounding generally better here than on that release. Rollins is in typically fiery form throughout; whatever dissatisfactions with the band he spoke of in future years evidently didn't keep him from forgetting how to put on a show. It's interesting to realize how much of the vaunted Rollins attitude comes from singing lyrics written mostly by Ginn, but the singer definitely makes those words his own regardless. Certainly his generally terse spoken-word bits practically drip with the man's essence—talking about "Annihilate": "This is a song about killing yourself to live." Ginn's blend of straight-ahead punk riffage and ponderous if still exciting open-ended sludge tones and soloing matches Rollins just fine, while Kira and Martinez do their job well enough. Kira adds some deadpan backing vocals at points as well. Strong numbers include "Bastard in Love," given a tight performance and an almost sweet touch of guitar jangle at points, and smoking takes on "The Best One Yet" and their inimitable version of "Louie, Louie." The CD version is the one to get, with a further half-hour of music from the show than on the vinyl version. *—Ned Raggett*

Wasted . . . Again / 1987 / SST ✦✦✦✦✦
Wasted . . . Again is a posthumous release that is an essential career summation. For those hearing the ear-searing sounds of early-'80s SoCal hardcore punk for the first time, *Wasted . . . Again* is an essential purchase. *—John Dougan*

Black Sabbath

f. 1969, Birmingham, England
Group / Album Rock, British Metal, Heavy Metal
No other band has come closer to embodying heavy metal than Black Sabbath. Over the years, their lineup may have changed, but their music hasn't—it has remained the same loud, methodical guitar-based heavy rock that it was in the early '70s. Their slow, sludgy attack was part design and part accident. Because of an accident that cut the tips of his fingers, Tony Iommi played with strings that were slightly slack—the lower tuning made his mammoth riffs sound heavier. Bassist Geezer Butler's lyrics reveled in black magic, fantasy, drugs, mental illness, and the occult, but never sex; Ozzy Osbourne sang them in a flat, almost tuneless, banshee wail. Taken together, the primitive musicianship, bad poetry, obsessive fantasy world, crawling tempos, and overpowering volume simultaneously represents everything good and bad about heavy metal. Of course, after Black Sabbath hit their peak, they stuck around way too long. Each of their first six albums had, at the very least, something to recommend them. Osbourne hung around for two more records before jumping ship for good. After former Rainbow lead vocalist Ronnie James Dio replaced him in 1979, band members kept shifting throughout the '80s, with Iommi the only original remaining throughout. With Butler rejoining in 1991, Black Sabbath continued to lurch forward (sometimes with Osbourne back in the fold), oblivious of the criticism and declining record sales. *—Stephen Thomas Erlewine*

Black Sabbath / May 1970 / Warner Brothers ✦✦✦✦✦
Black Sabbath's debut album is given over to lengthy songs and suite-like pieces where individual songs blur together and riffs pound away one after another, frequently under extended jams. There isn't much variety in tempo, mood, or the band's simple, blues-derived musical vocabulary, but that's not the point; Sabbath's slowed-down, murky guitar rock bludgeons the listener in an almost hallucinatory fashion, reveling in its own dazed, druggy state of consciousness. Songs like the apocalyptic title track, "N.I.B.," and "The Wizard" make their obsessions with evil and black magic seem like more than just stereotypical heavy metal posturing because of the dim, suffocating musical atmosphere the band frames them in. This blueprint would be refined and occasionally elaborated upon over the band's next few albums, but there are plenty of metal classics already here. *—Steve Huey*

★ **Paranoid** / Jan. 1971 / Warner Brothers ✦✦✦✦✦
Paranoid was not only Black Sabbath's most popular record (it was a number one smash in the U.K., and "Paranoid" and "Iron Man" both scraped the U.S. charts despite virtually nonexistent radio play), it also stands as one of the greatest and most influential heavy metal albums of all time. *Paranoid* refined Black Sabbath's signature sound—crushingly loud, minor-key dirges loosely based on heavy blues-rock—and applied it to a newly consistent set of songs with utterly memorable riffs, most of which now rank as all-time metal classics. Where the extended, multi-sectioned songs on the debut sometimes felt like aimless jams, their counterparts on *Paranoid* have been given focus and direction, lending an epic drama to now-standards like "War Pigs" and "Iron Man" (which sports one of the most immediately identifiable riffs in metal history). The subject matter is unrelentingly, obsessively dark, covering both supernatural/sci-fi horrors and the real-life traumas of death, war, nuclear annihilation, mental illness, drug hallucinations, and narcotic abuse. Yet Sabbath makes it totally convincing, thanks to the crawling, muddled bleakness and bad-trip depression evoked so frighteningly well by their music. Even the qualities that made critics deplore the album (and the group) for years increase the overall effect—the technical simplicity of Ozzy Osbourne's vocals and Tony Iommi's lead guitar vocabulary; the spots when the lyrics sink into melodrama or awkwardness; the lack of subtlety and the infrequent dynamic contrast. Everything adds up to more than the sum of its parts, as though the anxieties behind the music simply demanded that the band achieve catharsis by steamrolling everything in its path, including its own limitations. Monolithic and primally powerful, *Paranoid* defined the sound and style of heavy metal more than any other record in rock history. *—Steve Huey*

☆ **Master of Reality** / Aug. 1971 / Warner Brothers ✦✦✦✦✦
With *Paranoid*, Black Sabbath perfected the formula for their lumbering heavy metal. On its followup, *Masters of Reality*, the group merely repeated the formula, setting the stage for a career of recycling the same sounds and riffs. But on *Masters of Reality* Sabbath still were fresh and had a seemingly endless supply of crushingly heavy riffs to bludgeon their audiences into sweet, willing oblivion. If the album is a showcase for anyone, it is Tony Iommi, who keeps the album afloat with a series of slow, loud riffs, the best of which—"Sweet Leaf" and "Children of the Grave" among them—rank among his finest playing. Taken in tandem with the more consistent *Paranoid*, *Masters of Reality* forms the core of Sabbath's canon. There are a few stray necessary tracks scattered throughout the group's other early '70s albums, but *Masters of Reality* is the last time they delivered a consistent album and its influence can be heard throughout the generations of heavy metal bands that followed. *—Stephen Thomas Erlewine*

Black Sabbath, Vol. 4 / Sep. 1972 / Warner Brothers ✦✦✦✦✦
Vol. 4 is just a cut below its two undisputedly classic predecessors, as it begins to run out of steam—and memorable riffs—toward the end. However, it finds Sabbath beginning to experiment successfully with its trademark sound on tracks like the ambitious, psychedelic-tinged, multi-part "Wheels of Confusion," and the concise, textured "Tomorrow's Dream," and the orchestrated piano ballad "Changes" (even if the latter's lyrics cross the line into triteness). But the classic Sabbath sound is still very much in evidence; the crushing "Supernaut" is one of the heaviest tracks the band ever recorded. *—Steve Huey*

Sabbath, Bloody Sabbath / Dec. 1973 / Warner Brothers ✦✦✦✦✦
With 1973's *Sabbath, Bloody Sabbath* (their fifth masterpiece in four years), Black Sabbath made a concerted effort to raise their creative stakes and dispensed unprecedented attention to the album's production, arrangements, and even the cover artwork. While faithful to the band's signature compositional style and sound, brilliant songs such as the title track, "A National Acrobat," and "Killing Yourself to Live" also displayed a newfound sense of finesse and maturity. The introduction of keyboards and synthesizers, on the other hand, meets with mixed results. Erstwhile Yes keyboard wizard Rick Wakeman makes a positive contribution to "Sabbra Cadabra," but "Who are You" definitely suffers from synth overkill. Still, "Spiral Architect" benefits from its tasteful background orchestration, and the gentle "Fluff" is the first truly memorable solo instrumental from guitarist Tony Iommi, whose previous attempts often seemed pointless and haphazard. Simply put, this album is essential to any heavy metal collection. *—Ed Rivadavia*

Sabotage / Aug. 1975 / Warner Brothers ✦✦✦✦✦
Heavy metal gods Black Sabbath's impeccable recording legacy finally began to unravel with 1975's *Sabotage*, which attempted to continue the evolution begun with 1973's *Sabbath, Bloody Sabbath*, but somewhat lacked its focus. The plodding rhythm of "Hole in the Sky" and the guitar interlude that is "Don't Start (Too Late)" merely serve as tasters for the album's tour de force, "Symptom of the Universe," arguably Sabbath's last great classic, despite its rather pointless acoustic outro. The group treads familiar but compelling ground with "Thrill of It All" and the multipart epics "The Writ" and "Megalomania," but problems emerge when they attempt to stretch creatively. While they were largely successful with the experiments on *Sabbath, Bloody Sabbath*, the band goes so far overboard on the peculiar "Supertzar" (basically an instrumental overlayed with wordless, chorused vocals), and the obvious hit single fiasco "Am I Going Insane (Radio)" that the result is virtually unrecognizable as Black Sabbath. Unfortunately, subsequent efforts would see the band continue this reckless attempt to evolve at the expense of their original identity. *—Ed Rivadavia*

We Sold Our Soul for Rock and Roll / Feb. 1976 / Warner Brothers ✦✦✦✦✦
We Sold Our Soul for Rock and Roll is a good single-disc collection of many—but not all—of Black Sabbath's best tracks from the Ozzy Osbourne era, drawing about half of its material from the group's first two albums, *Black Sabbath* and *Paranoid*. That makes it ideal for the fan who only wants one Black Sabbath disc, but those who want to dig deeper should be advised that all six LPs from the Osbourne period contain high-quality items not present here, especially the underrepresented *Masters of Reality* and *Vol. 4*. Still, there's no quibbling with what is here. *—Steve Huey*

Technical Ecstasy / Oct. 1976 / Warner Brothers ✦✦

Never Say Die! / Oct. 1978 / Warner Brothers ✦✦

Heaven & Hell / May 1980 / Warner Brothers ✦✦✦✦✦
Many had left Black Sabbath for dead at the dawn of the '80s, and with good reason—the band's last few albums were not even close to their early classics, and original singer Ozzy Osbourne had just split from the band. But the Sabs had found a worthy replacement in former Elf and Rainbow singer Ronnie James Dio, and bounced back to issue their finest album since the early '70s, 1980's *Heaven and Hell*. The band sounds reborn and re-energized throughout. Several tracks easily rank among Sabbath's all-time best, such as the vicious album opener, "Neon Knights," the moody, mid-paced epic "Children of the Sea," and the title track, which features one of Tony Iommi 's best guitar riffs. With *Heaven and Hell*, Black Sabbath were obviously back in business. Unfortunately, the Dio-led version of the band would only record one more studio album before splitting up (although Dio would return briefly in the early '90s). One of Sabbath's finest records. *—Greg Prato*

The Mob Rules / Nov. 1981 / Warner Brothers ✦✦✦✦

Live Evil / Dec. 1982 / Vertigo ✦✦

Born Again / Oct. 1983 / Warner Brothers ✦

Seventh Star / Jan. 1986 / Warner Brothers ✦✦✦

The Eternal Idol / Dec. 1987 / Warner Brothers ✦✦✦

Headless Cross / Apr. 1989 / IRS ✦✦✦✦

Reunion / Oct. 20, 1998 / Epic ✦✦✦

Frank Black

b. 1965, Long Beach, CA
Vocals, Guitar / Indie Rock, Alternative Pop/Rock
Inverting his stage name from Black Francis to Frank Black, the former Pixies lead singer/songwriter embarked on a solo career after he broke up the band in early 1993; actually, he began recording his solo album *before* he told the band the news. Working with former Pere Ubu member Eric Drew Feldman, Black occasionally heads into the ferocious post-punk guitar territory that marked such landmark albums as *Surfer Rosa* and *Doolittle*, but more frequently he plays up his considerably underrated melodic side. His self-titled 1993 debut album was an adventurous sketchbook of pop styles ranging from surf rock to heavy metal, from Beatlesque pop to new wave. Black's second album, 1994's *Teenager of the Year*, was a sprawling and diverse album that amplified all the best points of *Frank Black*. He released his first album for American and Sony, the hard-rocking *The Cult of Ray*, in January of 1996. It hardly found the wide audience Black had hoped for, selling considerably less than his two previous efforts. *—Stephen Thomas Erlewine*

Frank Black / Mar. 1993 / 4AD/Elektra ✦✦✦✦✦
Underneath their noise and weirdness, the Pixies had a thorough knowledge of rock history,

spanning '50s and '60s surf-rock, '70s punk's menacing energy and '80s college rock's quirkiness. After dismantling the band, Black Francis inverted his name, collaborated with Captain Beefheart / Pere Ubu sideman Eric Drew Feldman and let his inner rock historian loose on *Frank Black*. Much of the album nods Black's inspirations, but his own gifts still shine through. The chugging Iggy Pop homage "Ten Percenter" borrows the Stooges' primitive grind, while the arty, dissonant UFO convention tale "Parry the Wind High, Low" recalls Bowie's Berlin era. However, "I Heard Ramona Sing"—a Ramones tribute—is an airy, jangly pop number that sounds nothing like its subject; the Beach Boys' "Hang On To Your Ego" gets a new wave makeover with crunchy guitars and shiny keyboards. Despite his efforts to escape the Pixies' sound, many of *Frank Black*'s songs would have fit on *Trompe Le Monde*. "Los Angeles" builds on that album's spacy, metallic feel; with its thrashy choruses and dreamy coda, it almost caricatures the Pixies' extreme dynamics. However, whimsical vignettes like "Brackish Boy" and "Two Spaces" sound more like They Might Be Giants—one of Black's favorite groups—than his old band, while softer songs like "Adda Lee" and "Every Time I Go Around Here" reveal more emotional depth. *Frank Black* also boasts an unabashedly big, polished sound; keyboards and brass embellish "Places Named After Numbers" and the epic surf-rock instrumental "Tossed." Just a few years later, new wave-inspired punk-pop bands like Weezer, the Rentals, and even No Doubt ruled alternative rock, proving that even if his solo career wasn't as influential as his Pixies years, Frank Black was still ahead of his time. *—Heather Phares*

● **Teenager of the Year** / May 24, 1994 / 4AD/Elektra ✦✦✦✦✦
A sprawling double album, Frank Black's *Teenager of the Year* builds on the clever, carefully crafted pop he forged on his solo debut and moves even farther away from the Pixies' sound. It feels like the album Black wanted to make since *Bossanova:* "Whatever Happened To Pong?" and "Thalassocracy" are a one-two blast of energetic fun, but the tight songwriting and detailed arrangements on the strummy "Headache" and gentle, piano-driven "Sir Rockaby" are more interesting. Despite its 22-song length, most of *Teenager Of the Year*'s tracks are keepers; the first nine rank among Black's catchiest songs with or without the Pixies. "I Want to Live on an Abstract Plain" and "The Vanishing Spies" mix sweet straightforward melodies with spacy keyboards, and Black delivers a creative love song in "Speedy Marie"; the first letter of each line in the song's second half spells out his girlfriend's name. The driving, anthemic "Freedom Rock" is one of the album's more ambitious tracks, along with the catchy, educational "Ole Mulholland," a musical history lesson about William Mulholland, the developer and planner of Los Angeles' municipal water system. *Teenager*'s beginning is so consistent, it's not surprising that its second half isn't quite as essential, but it's still interesting. the spacy, ska-tinged "Fiddle Riddle," the cryptic "Superabound" and the sprightly final track "Pie In The Sky"—which sounds strangely like a punk version of Gary U.S. Bonds' hit "A Quarter to Three"—all add to the album's individuality. Even less-developed songs like "Fazer Eyes" and "The Hostest with the Mostest" are still worthwhile. Though his later albums took a sparer, simpler approach, *Teenager Of The Year*'s ambition and quirkiness begin Black's evolution into a cult artist who makes the music he wants to, regardless of whether or not it's fashionable. *—Heather Phares*

The Cult of Ray / Jan. 30, 1996 / American ✦✦✦

Frank Black & The Catholics / May 1998 / spinART ✦✦✦

Pistolero / Mar. 23, 1999 / spinART ✦✦✦

Dog in the Sand / Jan. 30, 2001 / What Are? ✦✦✦✦

The Blasters

f. 1979, Los Angeles, CA
Group / College Rock, Roots Rock, Rock & Roll
The all-American roots music band, the Blasters were principally brothers Dave and Phil Alvin, whose first hand experience with blues masters shaped their sound and turned them both into contemporary singer-songwriters whose interest in roots rock has never waned. Their musical education involved hanging out with musicians like Lee Allen, Marcus Johnson and T-Bone Walker, all of whom tipped the band to the ways of blues and R&B. Ironically, by the time they were ready to work in Los Angeles clubs, the punk rock explosion was in full swing, and they found an audience for their rough and ready sound among the punks, particularly fans of X with whom they frequently shared the bill. *American Music* (1980) was a collection of roots covers and originals. Amazingly, their self-titled 1981 album reached number 36 on the charts. Less focused on rockabilly revivalism, Dave Alvin had become the band's chief cook and songwriter, and *The Hard Line* in 1985 was even more polished. The band called it a day after that, but continue to perform live. *—Denise Sullivan*

American Music / 1980 / Hightone ✦✦✦✦✦
Right from the beginning, with Dave Alvin's title song, the Blasters made their statement, that basic rock & roll was as contemporary in 1980 as it had been in the mid-1950s. The other 12 tracks, which mixed Dave and Phil Alvin originals with covers like "I Wish You Would" and "Never No More Blues," reiterated the opening remark, re-creating the feel of a biker bar after a couple of tall ones. Actually, the Blasters didn't have much to say beyond this record, of which only a couple of thousand copies were pressed, but they went on to a few years with Warner Bros. After 17 years, the debut was released on CD with six bonus tracks, all covers, and that statement seemed just as valid as it had at first. *—William Ruhlmann*

The Blasters / 1981 / Slash ✦✦✦✦✦
You might have thought the Blasters had been in suspended animation for 25 years when their major-label debut turned up in late 1981 sounding for all the world like something cut in the Sun Studios in Memphis in 1956. Dave Alvin knew all the licks and his brother Phil had the R&B/country wail down. Best of all, you couldn't tell the oldies from Dave's newly written classics. Welcome to the birth of rock & roll, all over again. *—William Ruhlmann*

Over There / Oct. 1982 / Slash ✦✦✦

Non Fiction / 1983 / Slash ✦✦✦✦

Hard Line / 1985 / Slash ✦✦

● **The Blasters Collection** / Mar. 12, 1991 / Slash ✦✦✦✦✦
The Slash years are compiled here, along with three previously unreleased tracks, forming the perfect overview of the Blasters' short recording career devoted to blues, country, and R&B. From the outset of their career, from "Marie Marie" to "Border Radio," it was clear Dave Alvin would be a songwriter to be reckoned with—one for the ages. Tracing his development through "Long White Cadillac" (later recorded by Dwight Yoakam), "Trouble Bound" (with the Jordanaires on vocals), and the hard country of "Dark Night," brother Phil Alvin brings the necessary heart, soul, and authenticity to the work, and the band is a master of their form. Few work or rock harder. *—Denise Sullivan*

Mary J. Blige

b. Jan. 11, 1971, New York, NY [The Bronx]
Vocals / Contemporary R&B, Club/Dance, Urban, Hip-Hop
Crowned the new "Queen of Hip-Hop Soul," Mary J. Blige enjoyed a breakout year in 1992 with *What's the 411?* Such singles as "Reminisce" and "Real Love" thrust the Atlanta-born singer into the spotlight at age 21. She was raised in Yonkers and performed in local groups before making her debut for the Uptown label. The album went platinum, and a remixed version was later issued. The single "Reminisce" had a second life when it was reworked and re-done in a rap version by the duo of Pete Rock and C.L. Smooth. After 1994's *My Life*, she released *Share My World* in 1997. *The Tour* appeared a year later, and in 1999 she returned with *Mary*. *—Ron Wynn*

● **What's the 411—** / 1992 / Uptown/MCA ✦✦✦✦✦
Mary J. Blige's debut album, *What's the 411?*, was a revolution in disguise. Like her new-jack predecessors, Blige combined R&B with hip-hop, but unlike Guy and Bobby Brown, her music was more seductive and sly. More importantly, she sounds grittier and more real than most new jack swingers or female R&B vocalists. Blige can slip between singing and rapping with ease, which is partially the reason why *What's the 411?* is so successful. It doesn't hurt that her collaborators, from Grand Puba to Sean "Puffy" Combs, help construct backing tracks that are both melodic, relentlessly funky, and sexy. *—Stephen Thomas Erlewine*

My Life / 1994 / Uptown/MCA ✦✦✦✦
Perhaps the single finest moment in Sean "Puffy" Combs' musical career has been the production on this, Mary J. Blige's second proper album. The production is not exactly original, and there is evidence here of him borrowing wholesale from other songs. The melodic sources this time around, though, are so expertly incorporated into the music that they never seem to be intrusions, instead playing like inspired dialogues with soulsters from the past, connecting past legacies with a new one. This certainly isn't your parents' (or grandparents') soul. But it is some of the finest modern soul of the '90s, backing away to a certain extent from the hip-hop/soul consolidation that Blige introduced on her debut album. The hip-hop part of the combination takes a few steps into the background, allowing Blige's tortured soul to carry the album completely, and it does so with heartwrenching authority. *My Life* is, from beginning to end, a brilliant, wistful individual plea of desire. Blige took a huge leap in artistry by penning almost everything herself (the major exception being Norman Whitfield's "I'm Going Down") in collaboration with co-producers Combs and multi-instrumentalist Chucky Thompson, and everything seems to leap directly from her gut. Blige's strain is sleekly modern and urban, and the grit in it comes from being streetwise and thoroughly realistic about the travails of life. *My Life*, nevertheless, emanates from some deep, dark place where both sadness and happiness cohabitate and turn into one single, beautiful sorrow. *—Stanton Swihart*

Share My World / Apr. 22, 1997 / MCA ✦✦✦✦

The Tour / Jul. 28, 1998 / MCA ✦✦✦

Mary / Aug. 17, 1999 / MCA ✦✦✦✦

Blind Faith

f. May 1969, England, **db.** Nov. 1969
Group / Album Rock, British Blues, Hard Rock, Blues-Rock
Blind Faith was either the culmination of a decade's efforts by three legendary musicians, or a disaster of monumental proportions, symbolizing everything that had gone wrong with the business of rock at the close of the '60s. They generated some great songs and sold hundreds of thousands of concert tickets and perhaps a million more albums, all in under seven months together. The initial spark for Blind Faith came from ex-Cream guitarist Eric Clapton and ex-Traffic leader Steve Winwood, who began jamming together in early 1969. The notion of forming a band took a more immediate turn when Cream drummer Ginger Baker sat in, even though Clapton was not looking forward to the expectations that their link up would engender. By the time tours were booked (with millions of dollars promised), the group was known as Blind Faith, a slyly cynical reference to the fact that they'd barely had any time to work out songs. Despite being under-rehearsed, all the quartet had to do to please the crowds was show up, and riots ensued at several American venues. By the time the tour ended in late August, the self-titled album—which ran into controversy over its cover, a topless pre-pubescent girl—had been out for almost a month, and had already sold more than half a million copies in America alone. There was very good music on *Blind Faith*, but there wasn't a lot of it—six songs didn't constitute a repertory. The band had left its members a bit shell shocked, and by October, it became official that there would be no second Blind Faith album. Blind Faith's short life span made them a symbol of the tail end of the '60s: too much too soon in that overheated environment, even for the prodigious talents and personalities involved, resulting in a quick burnout. *—Bruce Eder*

● **Blind Faith** / Jul. 1969 / Polydor ✦✦✦✦
Blind Faith's first and last album, more than 30 years old and counting, remains one of the jewels of the Eric Clapton, Steve Winwood, and Ginger Baker catalogs, despite the crash-and-burn history of the band itself, which scarcely lasted six months. As much a follow-up to Traffic's self-titled second album as it is to Cream's final output, it merges the soulful blues of the

former with the heavy riffing and outsized song lengths of the latter for a very compelling sound unique to this band. Not all of it works—between the virtuoso electric blues of "Had to Cry Today," the acoustic-textured "Can't Find My Way Home," the soaring "Presence of the Lord" (Eric Clapton's one contribution here as a songwriter, and the first great song he ever authored) and "Sea of Joy," the band doesn't do much with the Buddy Holly song "Well All Right"; and Ginger Baker's "Do What You Like" was a little weak to take up 15 minutes of space on an LP that might have been better used for a shorter drum solo and more songs. Unfortunately, the group was never *that* together as a band and evidently had just the 42 minutes of new music here ready to tour behind. *—Bruce Eder*

Blondie

f. Aug. 1974, New York, NY, **db.** Oct. 1982

Group / American Punk, New York Punk, Club/Dance, Pop/Rock, New Wave, Punk

Blondie was the most commercially successful band to emerge from the much vaunted punk/new wave movement of the late '70s. Formed by singer Deborah Harry and guitarist Chris Stein, the group released a self-titled album in 1976, then signed to Chrysalis for their second album, *Plastic Letters*. Blondie broke commercially in the UK in 1978, when their singles "Denis" and "(I'm Always Touched by Your) Presence, Dear" became Top Ten hits. Third album *Parallel Lines* broke them worldwide, with the disco-influenced "Heart of Glass" hitting number one in both the UK and the US. Two more transatlantic chart toppers ("Call Me" and "The Tide Is High") followed in 1980, though the band began breaking apart one year later, helped along by Harry's gold-selling solo album, *KooKoo*. *The Hunter*, Blondie's sixth and last new album, was a commercial disappointment. At the same time, Stein became seriously ill with the genetic disease pemphigus. As a result, Blondie broke up in October 1982, with Deborah Harry launching a part-time solo career while caring for Stein, who eventually recovered. In 1998, the original line-up reunited to tour Europe, their first series of dates in 16 years; a new LP, *No Exit*, followed early the next year. *— William Ruhlmann*

Blondie / Dec. 1976 / Chrysalis ✦✦✦✦✦

If new wave was about reconfiguring and re-contextualizing simple pop/rock forms of the '50s and '60s in new, ironic, and aggressive ways, then Blondie, which took the girl group style of the early and mid-'60s and added a '70s archness, fit right in. True punksters may have deplored the group early on (they never had the hip cachet of Talking Heads or even the Ramones), but Blondie's secret weapon, which was deployed increasingly over their career, was a canny pop straddle—they sent the music up and celebrated it at the same time. So, for instance, songs like "X Offender" (their first single) and "In the Flesh" (their first hit, in Australia) had the tough-girl-with-a-tender-heart tone of the Shangri-Las (Brill Building songwriter Ellie Greenwich even sang backup on the latter), while going one step too far into hard-edged decadence—that is, if you chose to see that. The whole point was that you could take Blondie either way. *— William Ruhlmann*

Plastic Letters / Oct. 1977 / Chrysalis ✦✦✦✦✦

Blondie's second album was a less distinctive version of its first, matching the first record's bright, sharp production (courtesy of Richard Gottehrer), but marking a fall-off in songwriting. The two best tracks—both UK hits—were "Denis," a remake of an oldie, and "(I'm Always Touched By Your) Presence, Dear," written by departed bass player Gary Valentine, and that didn't bode well. Nevertheless, those songs were enough to assure the album's British success and to make some noise in the U.S. But Blondie would take a distinctly different approach next time out. *— William Ruhlmann*

☆ **Parallel Lines** / Sep. 1978 / Chrysalis ✦✦✦✦✦

Blondie turned to British pop producer Mike Chapman for their third album, on which they abandoned any pretensions to new wave legitimacy (just in time, given the decline of the new wave) and emerged as a pure pop band. But it wasn't just Chapman that made *Parallel Lines* Blondie's best album; it was the band's own songwriting, including Deborah Harry, Chris Stein, and James Destri's "Picture This," and Harry and Stein's "Heart of Glass," and Harry and new bass player Nigel Harrison's "One Way or Another," plus two contributions from non-band-member Jack Lee, "Will Anything Happen?" and "Hanging on the Telephone." That was enough to give Blondie a number one on both sides of the Atlantic with "Heart of Glass" and three more UK hits, but what impresses is the album's depth and consistency—album tracks like "Fade Away and Radiate" and "Just Go Away" are as impressive as the songs pulled for singles. The result is state-of-the-art pop-rock circa 1978, with Harry's tough-girl glamour setting the pattern that would be exploited over the next decade by a host of successors led by Madonna. *— William Ruhlmann*

Eat to the Beat / Oct. 1979 / Chrysalis ✦✦✦✦✦

Just as Blondie's second album, *Plastic Letters*, was a pale imitation of their debut, *Blondie*, *Eat to the Beat*, their fourth album, was a secondhand version of their breakthrough third album, *Parallel Lines*: one step forward, half a step back. There was an attempt, on such songs as "The Hardest Part" and "Atomic," to recreate the rock-disco fusion of the group's one major U.S. hit, "Heart of Glass," without similar success, and elsewhere, the band just tried to cover too many stylistic bases. The British, who had long since been converted, made *Eat to the Beat* another chart-topper, but in the U.S., which still saw Blondie as a slightly comic one-hit wonder, the album was greeted for what it was—slick corporate rock without the tangy flavor that had made *Parallel Lines* such ear candy. *— William Ruhlmann*

Autoamerican / Nov. 1980 / Chrysalis ✦✦✦

★ **The Best of Blondie** / 1981 / Chrysalis ✦✦✦✦✦

Although Blondie made several first-rate albums, most of their best songs were released as singles, which makes *The Best of Blondie* an essential collection. *The Best of Blondie* glosses over their punk roots—very little from the first album, apart from the vicious "Rip Her to Shreds" and the seductive "In the Flesh"—but the band's pop hits are among the finest of their era and encapsulate all of the virtues of new wave. Apart from genuine chart hits like "Heart of Glass," "One Way or Another," "Dreaming," "Call Me," "Atomic," "The Tide Is High," and "Rapture," *Best of Blondie* picks up several of the group's best album tracks, like "(I'm Always Touched By Your) Presence, Dear" and "Hanging on the Telephone." *The Best of Blondie* isn't all you need to know, but it is an excellent introduction to one of the best new wave bands. *— Stephen Thomas Erlewine*

The Hunter / Jul. 1982 / Chrysalis ✦✦

Blonde & Beyond / Nov. 16, 1993 / Chrysalis ✦✦✦

Platinum Collection / Nov. 1, 1994 / Capitol ✦✦✦✦✦

A double-CD, 47-track collection built around Blondie's singles, including every one of their U.S. and U.K. A-sides and B-sides. Not a definitive best-of, as it excludes album tracks from consideration, but pretty close. Serious fans will be most interested in five 1975 demos, recorded before the band's first LP. Bootlegged in the past, these include "Once I Had a Love," and an early version of "Heart of Glass," and a cover of the Shangri-Las' "Out in the Streets." Also of interest to fanatics are the extensive liner notes, including a detailed family tree and lengthy comments from everyone in the band except Harry and Stein. *— Richie Unterberger*

No Exit / Feb. 23, 1999 / Beyond ✦✦✦

Blood, Sweat & Tears

f. 1967, New York, NY

Group / Album Rock, Jazz-Rock, Pop/Rock, Psychedelic

For a brief period at the end of the '60s and the start of the '70s, Blood, Sweat & Tears, which fused a rock & roll rhythm section to a horn section, held out the promise of a jazz-rock fusion that could storm the pop charts. The eight-piece band signed to Columbia Records and released their debut album *Child Is Father to the Man* in February 1968. Singer David Clayton-Thomas was added for BS&T's self-titled second album, released in January 1969. It was a runaway hit, spawning three gold-selling Top Ten singles, "You've Made Me So Very Happy," "Spinning Wheel," and "And When I Die," selling three million copies and winning the Grammy Award for Album of the Year. It was also their highwater mark, as BS&T increasingly became a backup group for Clayton-Thomas. Nevertheless, the third album, *Blood, Sweat & Tears 3* (1970), and the fourth, *Blood, Sweat & Tears 4* (1971), were substantial hits. Clayton-Thomas went solo in early 1972, but returned in 1974. Numerous other personnel changes took place, as the group's commercial fortunes gradually declined. *— William Ruhlmann*

Child Is Father to the Man / Feb. 1968 / Columbia/Legacy ✦✦✦✦✦

This is keyboard player/singer/arranger Al Kooper's finest work, an album on which he moves the folk-blues-rock amalgamation of the Blues Project into even wider pastures, taking in classical and jazz elements (including strings and horns), all without losing the pop essence that makes the hybrid work. This is one of the great albums of the eclectic post-*Sgt. Pepper* era of the late '60s, a time when you could borrow styles from Greenwich Village contemporary folk to San Francisco acid rock and mix them into what seemed to have the potential to become a new American musical form. It's Kooper's bluesy songs, such as "I Love You More Than You'll Ever Know" and "I Can't Quit Her," and his singing that are the primary focus, but the album is an aural delight; listen to the way the bass guitar interacts with the horns on "My Days Are Numbered" or the charming arrangement and Steve Katz' vocal on Tim Buckley's "Morning Glory." Then Kooper sings Harry Nilsson's "Without Her" over a delicate, jazzy backing with flügelhorn/alto saxophone interplay by Randy Brecker and Fred Lipsius. This is the sound of a group of virtuosos enjoying themselves in the newly open possibilities of pop music. Maybe it couldn't have lasted; anyway, it didn't. [Columbia/Legacy's 1994 gold Mastersound edition reissue, and the 2000 regular-line Columbia/Legacy reissue, add three bonus tracks from their November 1967 audition: the instrumental "Refugee From Yuhupitz" and alternate versions of "I Love You More Than You'll Ever Know" and "The Modern Adventures of Plato, Diogenes and Freud."] *— William Ruhlmann*

Blood, Sweat & Tears / Jan. 1969 / Columbia/Legacy ✦✦✦✦✦

Arguably, the Blood, Sweat & Tears that made this self-titled second album, consisting of five of the eight original members and four newcomers, including singer David Clayton-Thomas, was really a different group from the one that made the debut album, *Child Is Father to the Man*, largely under the direction of singer/songwriter/keyboard player/arranger Al Kooper. They had certain similarities to the original: the musical mixture of classical, jazz, and rock elements was still apparent, and the interplay between the horns and the keyboards was still occurring, even if those instruments were being played by different people. Kooper was even still present as an arranger on two tracks, notably the initial hit "You've Made Me So Very Happy." But the second BS&T, under the aegis of producer James William Guercio, was a less adventurous unit, and, as fronted by Clayton-Thomas, a far more commercial one. Not only did the album contain three songs that neared the top of the charts as singles—"Happy," "Spinning Wheel," and "And When I Die"—but the whole album, including an arrangement of "God Bless the Child" and the radical rewrite of Traffic's "Smiling Phases," was wonderfully accessible. It was a repertoire to build a career on, and they did exactly that, although they never came close to equaling this album. [The 2000 CD reissue on Columbia/Legacy adds previously unreleased live versions of "More and More" and "Smiling Phases," recorded in August 1968 at New York's *Cafe Au Go Go*.] *— William Ruhlmann*

Blood, Sweat & Tears 3 / Jun. 1970 / Columbia ✦✦✦

Blood, Sweat & Tears 4 / Jun. 1971 / Columbia ✦✦

What Goes Up: The Best of Blood, Sweat & Tears / Nov. 7, 1995 / Columbia ✦✦✦✦

Blood, Sweat & Tears' 11-track *Greatest Hits* album, released in February 1972, contained all of the group's six Top 40 singles, plus notable tracks from its two best albums, *Child Is Father to the Man* and *Blood, Sweat & Tears*. Almost 24 years later came this 32-track, 138-minute, double-CD expansion, much of it extraneous. Where *Greatest Hits* contained the single edits of songs like "You've Made Me So Very Happy" and "And When I Die," here "all titles are original album versions," as the back cover noted, which means the jazzy interludes, frequently having nothing to do with the rest of the song, remained. There were a couple of unreleased tracks, and otherwise the bloated running time was filled out by, for example, four tracks from the 1972 stiff *New Blood*, which didn't even feature singer David Clayton-Thomas. Legacy would have better served consumers by either expanding the original 41--minute *Greatest Hits* to proper CD length with a few bonus tracks or reissuing the first two albums in a double-disc set, again with a few bonus tracks to fill up the time. This compilation did not enhance the band's reputation. And the error-filled liner notes are less than worthless. *— William Ruhlmann*

- **Blood, Sweat & Tears' Greatest Hits** / Feb. 23, 1999 / Columbia ✦✦✦✦✦
While no substitute for the remastered version of the *Child Is Father to the Man* album or the Mobile Fidelity version of *Blood, Sweat & Tears*, this disc is a good idea since it has remastered versions of tracks from the later, non-upgraded albums. Columbia/Legacy went back and recompiled this multimillion selling album (previously available as a fairly lackluster 40-minute, 11-song CD), adding two songs ("So Long Dixie" and "More and More") that were previously available only on singles from 1972 and 1968, respectively, and upgrading the sound. It's more compact and much less pricey than the double-CD *What Goes Up: The Best of Blood, Sweat & Tears*. Using the single edits—as on the old CD edition and the original LP—would have made it perfect, but the producers chose to use the extended album versions instead. To serious fans, it's still sort of Blood, Sweat & Tears-lite, but at least the tracks now sport state-of-the-art sound—hard, upfront bass and drums, horns that pour out of the speakers, and close and intimate singing from David Clayton-Thomas (or, on two tracks here, Al Kooper and Steve Katz). The new release also recreates the packaging of the original LP, with reviewers' quotes across the band's prime years (1968-1972) and a time line history, as well as release and production information on each song. The two additional numbers and the use of the LP cuts bring the running time up to 48 minutes. *—Bruce Eder*

The Blue Nile

f. 1981, Glasgow, Scotland
Group / College Rock, Sophisti-Pop, Dream Pop, Adult Alternative Pop/Rock
The Scottish folk-ambient band the Blue Nile has enjoyed a mystique contrived by its inaccessibility and the infrequency of its recordings, but it has also made a series of critically acclaimed discs. The group was formed by three Glasgow natives who had graduated from university there: singer/songwriter/guitarist Paul Buchanan, bassist Robert Bell, and keyboardist Paul Joseph Moore. (Engineer Callum Malcolm and drummer Nigel Thomas have worked with the trio consistently, to the point of being considered secondary band-members.) (The Blue Nile is the title of Alan Moorehead's 1962 sequel to *The White Nile*, the two books making up a history of the Nile River.) They recorded their own single, "I Love This Life," which was distributed by Robert Stigwood's RSO Records just before the company closed its doors. They were then signed by Linn Products, which released their debut album, *A Walk Across the Rooftops*, in 1984. (A&M handled it in the U.S.) Since the company was small and the band did not tour, the album took some time to find its audience, though it briefly reached the U.K. charts and led to high expectations for a second album. This came in 1989 with *Hats*, which reached the British Top 20, throwing off three chart singles, "The Downtown Lights," "Headlights on the Parade," and "Saturday Night." The album also made the lower reaches of the American charts as the Blue Nile embarked on its first tour, a 30--date journey taking place in the British Isles and the U.S. In the ensuing years, the band members switched record labels, signing to Warner Bros., and contributed to recordings by Robbie Robertson and Julian Lennon. They finally emerged with their third album, *Peace at Last*, in June 1996. Another critically acclaimed release, it placed in the U.K. Top 20, but failed to chart in the U.S. *— William Ruhlmann*

A Walk Across the Rooftops / May 1984 / A&M ✦✦✦✦
The Blue Nile's debut LP is an oblique, supremely enigmatic work which immediately establishes the Glaswegian trio as a force to be reckoned with; while *A Walk Across the Rooftops* doesn't iron all the wrinkles out of the group's spaciously atmospheric sound, its thoughtful and original use of electronic textures nevertheless makes for compelling listening, an experience furthered by Paul Buchanan's keen sense of compositional dynamics on such highlights as "Tinseltown in the Rain" and "Stay." *—Jason Ankeny*

- **Hats** / Oct. 1989 / A&M ✦✦✦✦✦
Five long years in the making, the Blue Nile's stellar *Hats* was well worth the wait; sweeping and majestic, it's a triumph of personal vision over the cold, remote calculations of technology. While created almost solely without benefit of live instruments, it is nevertheless an immensely warm and human album; Paul Buchanan's plaintive vocals and poignant songs are uncommonly moving, and his deployment of lush synth washes and electronic percussion is never gratuitous, each song instead crafted with painterly precision. Impressionistic and shimmering, tracks like "The Downtown Lights" and "From a Late Night Train" are perfectly evocative of their titles: Rich in romantic atmosphere and detail, they conjure a nocturnal fantasy world lit by neon and shrouded in fog, leaving *Hats* an intensely cinematic experience as well as a masterpiece of musical obsession. *—Jason Ankeny*

Peace at Last / Jul. 1996 / Warner Brothers ✦✦✦

Blue Öyster Cult

f. 1967, Long Island, NY
Group / Album Rock, Arena Rock, Heavy Metal, Hard Rock
Blue Öyster Cult was the thinking man's heavy-metal group. Put together on a college campus by a couple of rock critics, it maintained a close relationship with a series of literary figures (often in the fields of science fiction and horror), while turning out some of the more listenable metal music of the early and mid '70s. Formed by Sandy Pearlman and Richard Meltzer with guitarist Donald "Buck Dharma" Roeser, the group later added vocalist Eric Bloom and released two albums (one as Soft White Underbelly, another as Oaxaca) before debuting as Blue Öyster Cult in 1972. Their fourth studio album, *Agents of Fortune*, included the Top 40 hit single "(Don't Fear) the Reaper" (featured in the classic John Carpenter horror film *Halloween*). The group continued recording albums popular with hard rock audiences during the late '70s before a series of lineup changes curtailed their career during the '80s. After being dropped from Columbia 1988, BÖC scored the movie *Bad Channels* in 1992 and, two years later, released an album of rerecorded favorites (*Cult Classic*), in connection with the use of their music in the TV miniseries of horror novelist Stephen King's *The Stand*. *— William Ruhlmann*

Blue Öyster Cult / Jan. 1972 / Columbia ✦✦✦✦✦
Blue Öyster Cult's debut album provided the missing link between the heavy, blues-based rock of the late '60s and the bombastic heavy metal of the '70s and beyond. You could hear major influences like Steppenwolf, with its melodic, aggressive rock, the Rolling Stones (post-1965), and even boogie bands like Canned Heat in their sound. But BOC streamlined the approach, picked up the tempo, overlaid the guitars, brought the rhythm section up in the mix, and de-emphasized the blues, giving the music a machinelike propulsion. Manager/co-producer Sandy Pearlman (who co-wrote five songs) and lyricist Richard Meltzer (who co-wrote two) may have seen the group as a vehicle for their "clever" (in fact, pretentious) lyrics, but in fact lead vocalist Eric Bloom was the weakest element in the band, and you couldn't make out much of what he had to say over guitarist Donald "Buck Dharma" Roeser's furious power chording. What you could seemed to express some sort of mythology—or demonology; future metal bands would fill their songs with just such half-baked philosophies. *Blue Öyster Cult* was not quite full-fledged heavy metal: the production was too compressed, the playing too light and energetic. But it was the sound of something new and different in the world of hard rock. *— William Ruhlmann*

Tyranny & Mutation / Feb. 1973 / Columbia ✦✦✦✦✦
Co-producers Murray Krugman and Sandy Pearlman achieved a far sharper, more spacious production on Blue Öyster Cult's second album than they had in the cramped sound of its first, twinning, for instance, the high, ringing tone of Donald Roeser's lead guitar to Albert Bouchard's cymbals or Alan Lanier's keyboards and adding echo to give presence to Eric Bloom's still barely (or not quite) discernable vocals. In a sense, it's remarkable that albums like this have been categorized as heavy metal: despite the fullness of the aural attack, the fast tempos and raunchy sound give it much more the feel of old rockabilly or punk-rock-to-come. *— William Ruhlmann*

Secret Treaties / Apr. 1974 / Columbia ✦✦

On Your Feet or on Your Knees / Feb. 1975 / Columbia ✦✦

Agents of Fortune / May 1976 / Columbia ✦✦✦✦✦
Nothing Blue Öyster Cult had produced previously prepared listeners for its infectious mid-tempo hit, "(Don't Fear) the Reaper," which propelled it into a higher commercial orbit and caused (or reflected) a change in the balance of power in the group. The song was written by guitarist Donald "Buck Dharma" Roeser and was an indication that the band was now largely doing its own songwriting; co-producer Sandy Pearlman earned only one co-writing credit on the record, while drummer Albert Bouchard had five. Poetess Patti Smith, meanwhile, not only co-wrote two tracks, but also performed on one, "The Revenge of Vera Gemini." The result was a record much more in a pop-rock vein than the vaunted metal of the first three albums and BÖC's biggest hit ever. *— William Ruhlmann*

Spectres / Oct. 1977 / Columbia ✦✦✦
On the all-important follow-up to its commercial breakthrough with *Agents of Fortune*, Blue Öyster Cult introduced some enjoyable additions to its repertoire in "Godzilla" and "R.U. Ready 2 Rock," but did not come up with a song as memorable as "(Don't Fear) the Reaper," despite trying the same formula with "Fireworks" and "Nosferatu." Instead of consolidating its success, the group seemed to be, as one of the better songs had it, "Goin' Through the Motions," seemingly unable to follow through on the pop aspirations of the previous album and unwilling to retreat to the metal pretensions of its early records. Talk about being caught between a rock and a hard place—just when Blue Öyster Cult should have been conquering, they seemed ready to retreat. *— William Ruhlmann*

Some Enchanted Evening / Sep. 1978 / Columbia ✦✦

Mirrors / Jun. 1979 / Columbia ✦✦✦
Blue Öyster Cult tried a new producer on *Mirrors*, replacing longtime mentor Sandy Pearlman with Tom Werman, a CBS staffer who had worked with Cheap Trick and Ted Nugent. The result is an album that tried to straddle pop and hard rock just as those acts did, emphasizing choral vocals (plus female backup) and a sharp, trebly sound. But this approach appeared to displease longtime metal-oriented fans without attracting new ones: "In Thee" became a minor singles-chart entry, but the album broke BÖC's string of five gold or platinum albums in a row. The real reason simply may have been that the songs weren't distinctive enough. Much of this was generic hard rock that could have been made by any one of a dozen '70s arena bands. *— William Ruhlmann*

Cultosaurus Erectus / Jun. 1980 / Columbia ✦✦✦
Signing on with Deep Purple/Black Sabbath producer Martin Birch, Blue Öyster Cult made more of a guitar-heavy hard-rock album in *Cultosaurus Erectus*, after flirting with pop ever since the success of *Agents of Fortune*. (They also promoted this album by going out on a co-headlining tour with Sabbath.) Gone are the female backup singers, the pop hooks, the songs based on keyboard structures, and they are replaced by lots of guitar solos and a beefed-up rhythm section. But the band still was not generating strong enough material to compete with their concert repertoire, so they found themselves in the bind of being a strong touring act unable to translate that success into record sales. *— William Ruhlmann*

Fire of Unknown Origin / Jun. 1981 / Columbia ✦✦✦
Just when Blue Öyster Cult was nearly written off after a series of mediocre albums, the band came roaring back with *Fire of Unknown Origin*, their best record in five years, on which they found the appropriate mixture of metal, rock and pop that had eluded them since "(Don't Fear) the Reaper." With Sandy Pearlman, Richard Meltzer, and Patti Smith, among others, back in the writing credits, the Cult sounded like they'd been listening hard to their first two albums and *Agents of Fortune* for inspiration. Images of fire, darkness, and war were everywhere, the guitar riffs were inventive, and the melodies compelling. There was a new hit single in the Top 40 "Burnin' for You," but the overall song quality was unusually high.

Somehow, BÖC had recaptured the trashy gothic appeal of its best work, and the result was a gold-selling album that seemed to put the band's career back on track. *—William Ruhlmann*

Extraterrestrial Live / Apr. 1982 / Columbia ✦✦✦

The Revolution by Night / Oct. 1983 / Columbia ✦✦

Club Ninja / Jan. 1986 / Koch International ✦✦

Imaginos / Jul. 1988 / Columbia ✦✦✦
Blue Öyster Cult went out with a bang as a major-label recording act on their 14th and last new Columbia album, *Imaginos*. The idea for this concept album came as early as *Secret Treaties*, on which some of its music appeared, and the recording took place over a six-year period. (As a result, album credits give the erroneous impression that the original band had reformed.) The story line, which is easier to appreciate in the liner notes than on the record, concerns a mysterious, protean 19th century figure who has a talent for turning up at key moments in history and influencing them for the worse. This is perhaps BÖC's most consistent album, certainly its most uncompromising (none of its usual nods to pop accessibility), and also the closest thing to a real heavy-metal statement from a band that never quite fit that description. Unfortunately, this ambitious work came out as BÖC was dropping out of the frontline of the music business, so the album that comes closest to defining Blue Öyster Cult turned into its creative swan song. *—William Ruhlmann*

Workshop of the Telescopes / Sep. 26, 1995 / Columbia/Legacy ✦✦✦✦✦
Blue Öyster Cult was long in need of a thorough career retrospective, and this is it. Thirty-two tracks filling up two discs with a total running time of 154:46, *Workshop of the Telescopes* traces BÖC through 14 years as the kings of lite metal, 1972-1986. Actually, as annotator Arthur Levy notes, there are at least two phases in that era. The first, running through 1974, includes the classic first two albums, *Blue Öyster Cult* and *Tyranny & Mutation*, when BÖC was one of the few acts in those pre-punk days bucking the trend toward soft rock without indulging in the more grotesque aspects of heavy metal. This material takes up disc one. Disc two leads off with "(Don't Fear) the Reaper," which launched the second phase of the band's career, when it sought to balance its hard rocking approach (heard especially in concert) with pop accessibility. Since this period was marked by uneven material, it is ripe for compiling, and the selection here is good. (We could have used a bit more from *Agents of Fortune*, but that's a quibble.) On the whole, *Workshop of the Telescopes* lives up to Levy's description of it as "the ultimate BÖC anthology." It's about time. *—William Ruhlmann*

● **Don't Fear The Reaper: The Best of Blue Oyster Cult** / Feb. 8, 2000 / Columbia/Legacy ✦✦✦✦✦
With 16 cuts spanning 1971-83, this is a briefer, single-disc counterpart to the 1995 double-CD *Workshop of the Telescopes* compilation. This has taken care—perhaps too much care—to draw evenly from all of their first nine studio albums, with one or two songs from each (except for *Spectres*, which is represented by three). The early years are a little underrepresented, with just a tune apiece from *Blue Oyster Cult* and *Tyranny and Mutation*. For listeners on a tight budget, this might be satisfactory, but otherwise it's a considerably inferior value to the much more comprehensive *Workshop of the Telescopes*. *—Richie Unterberger*

The Blues Brothers

Group / Retro-Soul, Soul
Whether celebrated as a sincere tribute or derided as a tongue-in-cheek put-on, the Blues Brothers—Joliet Jake and his silent brother Elwood—was among the most popular groups of the late '70s; what started as a skit on the hit NBC television sketch comedy series *Saturday Night Live* quickly snowballed to become a true phenomenon, complete with hit records, a sold-out concert tour and even a feature film. Clad in vintage black suits, narrow ties, fedoras, and omnipresent wrap-around sunglasses, the Blues Brothers delivered spirited renditions of classic soul hits in the tradition of the signature Stax-Volt sound; purists may still cringe, but if nothing else the group deserves credit for introducing any number of soul and blues classics to a new generation of listeners while also allowing some of the most gifted session men in the business a chance to shine on stage and screen. In reality, vocalist Jake and harpist Elwood were music lovers John Belushi and Dan Aykroyd, two of *SNL*'s brightest stars who created their respective aliases in early 1976 to warm up crowds before performances of the hit series. The Blues Brothers made their national TV debut with Belushi and Aykroyd outfitted in the bee costumes they often wore for another sketch, performing (naturally enough) Slim Harpo's "I'm a King Bee," and in the months to follow they grew in popularity, releasing a series of hit albums and starring in a 1980 film prior to Belushi's 1982 death from an accidental drug overdose. —Jason Ankeny

Briefcase Full of Blues / Dec. 1978 / Atlantic ✦✦✦✦
"The Blues Brothers" began as an affectionate joke-cum-tribute to R&B music, and taken in that spirit it retained its entertainment value, even after this live album topped the charts, sold two million copies, and produced hit singles in "Rubber Biscuit" and "Soul Man." The guardians of popular music have always been entirely too reverent and humorless, however, and it wasn't long before they were leveling charges of rip-off against the Brothers and complaining that John Belushi couldn't sing as well as Otis Redding. So what? No one seems to have noticed that Belushi was as obsessive about citing his sources as Frank Sinatra is about naming his arrangers—you'd have thought those critics would have appreciated the footnotes. The beneficiaries of Belushi's encomiums didn't mind the increased exposure or the renewed royalty checks ("I suggest you buy as many blues albums as you can," Belushi told the audience), and even today, what comes across in these performances is the sincerity of feeling—that and some tasty playing from a top-notch band. *—William Ruhlmann*

Blues Brothers [Original Soundtrack] / Jun. 1980 / Atlantic ✦✦✦
Comic actors John Belushi and Dan Aykroyd received a lot of flak for their Blues Brothers shtick—mostly for the albums, not 1980's beloved classic film. But they should be given credit for exposing many people—including this reviewer—to the music of blues and R&B veterans. *The Blues Brothers* soundtrack was released on Atlantic Records. On the surface this doesn't seem unusual, since the Blues Brothers' Atlantic debut, *Briefcase Full of Blues*, was a number one album; but the movie was released by Universal, and its parent company, MCA, passed on the soundtrack. The rollicking remake of the Spencer Davis Group's "Gimme Some Lovin'" was a hit, featuring an arrangement notable for the horn section that replaces Steve Winwood's rumbling organ work. Ray Charles has a good time with "Shake a Tail Feather," and he's helped out by Jake and Elwood Blues (Belushi and Aykroyd, respectively). The cover of Solomon Burke's "Everybody Needs Somebody to Love" is a lot of fun, thanks to the great overall rhythm and Elwood's lightning-fast stage rap, while James Brown and the Reverend James Cleveland Choir provide a blast of gospel music on "Old Landmark." Aretha Franklin's "Think" is explosive, and Cab Calloway's "Minnie the Moocher" is slyly irresistible. Charles, Brown, Franklin, and Calloway all have small roles in the film, yet so does John Lee Hooker, but he's not represented here. *—Bret Adams*

The Best of the Blues Brothers / Dec. 1981 / Atlantic ✦✦✦

● **The Definitive Collection** / 1992 / Atlantic ✦✦✦✦

The Blues Project

f. 1965, New York, NY, **db.** 1972, New York, NY
Group / Folk-Rock, Blues-Rock, Modern Electric Blues
One of the first album-oriented, "underground" groups in the United States, the Blues Project offered an electric brew of rock, blues, folk, pop, and even some jazz, classical, and psychedelia during their brief heyday in the mid-'60s. It's not quite accurate to categorize them as a blues-rock group, although they did plenty of that kind of material; they were more like a Jewish-American equivalent to British bands like the Yardbirds, who used a blues and R&B base to explore any music that interested them. Erratic songwriting talent and a lack of a truly outstanding vocalist prevented them from rising to the front line of '60s bands, but they recorded plenty of interesting material over the course of their first three albums, before the departure of their most creative members took its toll. *—Richie Unterberger*

Live at the Cafe Au-Go-Go / May 1966 / Verve/Forecast ✦✦✦
Although Tommy Flanders (who'd already left the band by the time this debut hit the streets) is credited as sole vocalist, four of the then-sextet's members sang; in fact, Danny Kalb handles as many leads as Flanders (four each), Steve Katz takes center stage on Donovan's "Catch the Wind," and Al Kooper is featured on "I Want to Be Your Driver." The band could be low-down when appropriate (Kalb's reading of "Jelly, Jelly"), high energy (Muddy Waters' "Goin' Down Louisiana" sounds closer to Chuck Berry or Bo Diddley), and unabashedly eclectic (tossing in Donovan or Eric Andersen with no apologies). Kalb's moody take on "Alberta" is transcendent, and the up-tempo arrangement of "Spoonful" is surprisingly effective. *—Dan Forte*

Projections / Nov. 1966 / Verve/Forecast ✦✦✦✦✦
Produced by Tom Wilson (Dylan, Zappa), the Blues Project's second effort was their finest hour. In less than a year the enthusiastic live band had matured into a seasoned studio ensemble. Steve Katz's features are lightweight folk but Al Kooper reworks two gospel themes ("Wake Me, Shake Me," "I Can't Keep from Crying") into ambitious blues-rock compositions, and Danny Kalb proves he's no mere folkie on extended versions of "Two Trains Running" and "Caress Me Baby." Bassist Andy Kulberg switches to flute and Kalb gets psychedelic on the jazzy "Flute Thing," penned by Kooper. *—Dan Forte*

The Best of the Blues Project [Rhino] / 1966-1967 / Rhino ✦✦✦✦✦
With the exception of a live version of "Flute Thing" from the Blues Project's 1973 reunion concert included only on the CD version, this compilation is culled entirely from the albums *Live at the Cafe Au-Go-Go*, *Projections*, and *The Blues Project Live at Town Hall*, all recorded and released in the period 1966-1967. Just as those individual albums do, it confirms the acclaim accorded the Blues Project at the time. The group's sophistication and ability to create a hybrid of musical styles keeps the music from sounding dated. In fact, this music not only stands as among the best of its time, but it continues to appeal where much of the music made simultaneously fails to escape its era. (Not to be confused with *Best of the Blues Project*, Verve Forecast FTS 3077 [1969 07], which is an earlier compilation with a different selection of songs.) *—William Ruhlmann*

Live at Town Hall / Sep. 1967 / One Way ✦✦✦
Released just after Al Kooper left the band, one imagines that neither he nor the other members of the group were pleased with this LP. According to Kooper, it was a pastiche of studio outtakes and a few live performances, and only one of the songs was actually recorded at New York City's *Town Hall*. Anyway, this has a meandering, ten-minute "Flute Thing" and decent live versions of "Wake Me Shake Me" and "I Can't Keep from Crying" which, despite a somewhat rawer feel, are not necessary supplements to the fine studio takes. "Where There's Smoke, There's Fire" and the great "No Time Like the Right Time" had already been released as singles; to hear them without canned applause, you only need to turn to Rhino's first-rate *Best of the Blues Project* instead. That compilation also contains the other cut of note on this album, an outtake-sounding cover of Patrick Sky's "Love Will Endure." *—Richie Unterberger*

Best of the Blues Project [Forecast] / Jul. 1969 / Verve/Forecast ✦✦✦✦

● **Anthology** / Jan. 28, 1997 / Polygram ✦✦✦✦✦
The most complete Blues Project collection ever assembled, the two-disc *Anthology* compiles 36 tracks taken from their three albums on Verve and their two records on Capitol as well as rare singles, previously unreleased songs and alternate versions, and material from solo projects. *—Jason Ankeny*

Blues Traveler

f. 1988
Group / Jam Bands, American Trad Rock, Pop/Rock, Blues-Rock
A New York-based blues-rock quartet formed in 1988 by singer/harmonica player John Popper, guitarist Chan Kinchla, bassist Bobby Sheehan, and drummer Brendan Hill, Blues Trav-

eler was part of a revival of the extended jamming style of '60s and '70s groups like the Grateful Dead and Led Zeppelin. Signed to A&M, they released their first album, *Blues Traveler,* in May 1990 and followed it with *Travelers & Thieves* in September 1991. Popper was in a serious car accident in 1992, leaving him unable to perform for a number of months. Fortunately, he recovered, yet he still had to perform in a wheelchair for a period of time. In April 1993, Blues Traveler released its third album, *Save His Soul,* which became its first to make the Top 100. Blues Traveler's aptly named fourth album, *Four,* released in September 1994, at first looked like a sales disappointment, but it rebounded in 1995 when "Run-Around," a single taken from it, became the group's first chart hit. "Run-Around" became one of the biggest singles of 1995, spending nearly a full year on the charts and sending *Four* into quintuple platinum status.

As the group prepared the followup to *Four,* Blues Traveller released the live double-album *Live from the Fall* in the summer of 1996. The group returned in the summer of 1997 with its fifth studio album, *Straight on Till Morning.* After completing his 1999 debut solo effort *Zygote,* Popper—who'd been experiencing chest pains for months—was forced to undergo an angioplasty; weeks later, tragedy struck on August 20, 1999, when Sheehan was found dead in his New Orleans home. He was just 31 years old. *—William Ruhlmann*

● **Blues Traveler** / May 1990 / A&M ✦✦✦✦✦
Blues Traveler's loose jam structures on basic blues riffs mark them as a band in the tradition of such predecessors as The Grateful Dead. Unlike that communal effort, however, this group has a distinct focal point in virtuoso harmonica player and vocalist John Popper, who keeps things from meandering too much. *—William Ruhlmann*

Travelers & Thieves / Sep. 1991 / A&M ✦✦✦
"I have my moments," John Popper declares, and many of them, as harmonica player, singer, and lyricist are here, on an album that finds Blues Traveler stretching out much as they do onstage. Popper is a man with a lot on his mind, but when he reaches "The Best Part," his verbosity approaches a Walt Whitman-like exuberance, and guitarist Chan Kinchla is right with him, contributing sweet fills here, Pete Townshend-style strumming there. And as for the rhythm work of bassist Bobby Sheehan and drummer Brendan Hill, as Popper says, "It's all in the groove." *—William Ruhlmann*

Save His Soul / Apr. 1993 / A&M ✦✦✦

Four / Sep. 13, 1994 / A&M ✦✦✦✦
Lacking the rootsier edge of *Save His Soul, Four* finds Blues Traveler retreating to their standard blues-boogie formula, with mixed results. Of course, there are some fine songs here—including their breakthrough hit single "Run-Around"—but too often the band sounds like they're coasting. *Four* is a solid record, but it shows signs that the band's formula may be wearing thin. *—Stephen Thomas Erlewine*

Live from the Fall / Jul. 1996 / A&M ✦✦✦✦✦

Straight on Till Morning / Jul. 1, 1997 / A&M ✦✦✦✦

Blur

f. 1989, Colchester, England
Group / Indie Pop, Alternative Dance, Britpop, Pop/Rock, Alternative Pop/Rock
Initially, Blur were one of the multitude of British bands that appeared in the wake of the Stone Roses, mining the same swirling, psuedo-psychedelic guitar-pop, only with louder guitars. Following an image makeover in the mid-'90s, the group emerged as the most popular band in the U.K., establishing themselves as the heir to the English guitar-pop tradition of the Kinks, the Small Faces, the Who, the Jam, Madness, and the Smiths. In the process, the group broke down the doors a new generation of guitar bands that became labelled as Brit-pop. With Damon Albarn's wry lyrics and the group's mastery of British pop tradition, Blur were the leaders of Brit-pop, but they quickly became confined by the movement; since they were its biggest band, they nearly died when the movement itself died. Through some reinvention, Blur reclaimed their position as an art-pop band in the late '90s by incorporating indie-rock and lo-fi influences, which finally gave them their elusive American success in 1997. But the band's legacy remained in Britain, where they helped revitalize guitar-pop by skillfully updating the country's pop traditions and bringing it into the '90s. *—Stephen Thomas Erlewine*

Leisure / Aug. 27, 1991 / SBK ✦✦✦
"She's So High" and "There's No Other Way" were auspicious debut singles, alternately trancy and melodic, suggesting how shoegazing and baggy beats could be incorporated into pop song structures. Both songs suggested that Blur was capable of a striking debut album, but *Leisure* wasn't it. Mired by directionless soundscapes and incomplete songwriting, *Leisure* was nevertheless full of promise. Whenever the group tread close to the warped psychedelia of Syd Barrett, their compositions sprang to life, and "Sing" was an eerie, entrancing minor-key drone reminiscent of the Velvet Underground's "Venus in Furs." Those moments, however, were few and far between on *Leisure,* since much of the record was devoted to either naïve pop like "Bang" or washes of feedback and effects. From *Leisure,* it appeared that Blur was only capable of a pair of fine singles, which is what made the complete reinvention of *Modern Life Is Rubbish* such a surprise. [For the American release of *Leisure,* SBK Records lopped off one of the album's best songs, "Sing," and shuffled the running order for no apparent reason other than having "She's So High" and "There's No Other Way" appear first.] *—Stephen Thomas Erlewine*

Modern Life Is Rubbish / May 10, 1993 / SBK ✦✦✦✦✦
As a response to the dominance of grunge in the U.K. and their own decreasing profile in their homeland—and also as a response to Suede's sudden popularity—Blur reinvented themselves with their second album, *Modern Life is Rubbish,* abandoning the shoegazing and baggy influences that dominated *Leisure* for traditional pop. On the surface, *Modern Life* may appear to be an homage to the Kinks, David Bowie, the Beatles and Syd Barrett, yet it isn't a restatement, it's a revitalization. Blur use British guitar-pop from the Beatles to My Bloody Valentine as a foundation, spinning off tales of contemporary despair. If Damon Albarn wasn't such a clever songwriter, both lyrically and melodically, *Modern Life* could have sunk under its own pretensions, and the latter half does drag slightly. However, the record teems with life, since Blur refuse to treat their classicist songs as museum pieces. Graham Coxon's guitar tears each song open, either with unpredictable melodic lines or layers of translucent, hypnotic effects, and his work creates great tension with Alex James' kinetic bass. And that provides Albarn a vibrant background for his social satires and cutting commentary. But the reason *Modern Life is Rubbish* is such a dynamic record and ushered in a new era of British pop is that nearly every song is carefully constructed and boasts a killer melody, from the stately "For Tomorrow" and the punky "Advert" to the vaudeville stomp of "Sunday Sunday" and the neo-psychedelic "Chemical World." Even with its flaws, it's a record of considerable vision and excitement. [The American version of *Modern Life is Rubbish* substitutes the demo version of "Chemical World" for the studio version on the British edition. It also adds the superb single "Pop Scene" before the final song, "Resigned."] *—Stephen Thomas Erlewine*

★ **Parklife** / Apr. 25, 1994 / Food/SBK ✦✦✦✦✦
Modern Life Is Rubbish established Blur as the heir to the archly British pop of the Kinks, Small Faces, and the Jam, but its follow-up *Parklife* revealed the depth of that transformation. Relying more heavily on Ray Davies' seriocomic social commentary, as well as new wave, *Parklife* runs through the entire history of post-British Invasion Brit-pop in the course of 16 songs, touching on psychedelia, synth-pop, disco, punk, and musichall along the way. Damon Albarn intended these songs to form a sketch of British life in the mid-'90s, and it's startling how close he came to his goal; not only did the bouncy, disco-fied "Girls & Boys" and singalong chant "Parklife" become anthems in the U.K., but they inaugurated a new era of Brit-pop and lad culture, where British youth celebrated their country and traditions. The legions of jangly, melodic bands that followed in the wake of *Parklife* revealed how much more complex Blur's vision was. Not only was their music precisely detailed—sound effects and brilliant guitar lines pop up all over the record—but the melodies elegantly interweaved with the chords, as in the graceful, heartbreaking "Badhead." Surprisingly, Albarn, for all of his cold, dispassionate wit, demonstrates compassion that gives these songs three dimensions, as on the pathos-laden "End of a Century," the melancholy Walker Brothers tribute "To the End," and the swirling, epic closer "This Is a Low." For all of its celebration of tradition, *Parklife* is a thoroughly modern record in that it bends genres and is self-referential (the mod anthem of the title track is voiced by none other than Phil Daniels, the star of *Quadrophenia*). And, by tying the past and the present together, Blur articulated the mid-'90s zeitgeist and produced an epoch-defining record. *—Stephen Thomas Erlewine*

The Great Escape / Sep. 11, 1995 / Virgin ✦✦✦✦✦
In the simplest terms, *The Great Escape* is the flipside of *Parklife.* Where Blur's breakthrough album was a celebration of the working class, drawing on British pop from the '60s and reaching through the '80s, *The Great Escape* concentrates on the suburbs, featuring a cast of characters all trying to cope with the numbing pressures of modern life. Consequently, it's darker than *Parklife,* even if the melancholia is hidden underneath the crisp production and catchy melodies. Even the bright, infectious numbers on *The Great Escape* have gloomy subtexts, whether it's the disillusioned millionaire of "Country House," and the sycophant of "Charmless Man," or the bleak loneliness of "Globe Alone" and "Entertain Me." Naturally, the slower numbers are even more despairing, with the acoustic "Best Days," the lush, sweeping strings of "The Universal" and the stark, moving electronic ballad "Yuko and Hiro" ranking as the most affecting work Blur has ever recorded. However, none of this makes *The Great Escape* a burden or a difficult album. The music bristles with invention throughout, as Blur delves deeper into experimentation with synthesizers, horns and strings; guitarist Graham Coxon twists out unusual chords and lead lines, and Damon Albarn spits out unexpected lyrical couplets filled with wit and venemous intelligence in each song. But Blur's most remarkable accomplishment is that it can reference the past—the Scott Walker homage of "The Universal," the Terry Hall/Fun Boy Three cop on "Top Man," the skittish, XTC-flavored pop of "It Could Be You," and Albarn's devotion to Ray Davies—while still moving forward, creating a vibrant, invigorating record. *—Stephen Thomas Erlewine*

Blur / Feb. 10, 1997 / Virgin ✦✦✦✦✦
The Great Escape, for all of its many virtues, painted Blur into a corner and there was only one way out—to abandon the Brit-pop that they had instigated by bringing the weird strands that always floated through their music to the surface. *Blur* may superficially appear to be a break from tradition, but it is a logical progression, highlighting the band's rich eclecticism and sense of songcraft. Certainly, they are trying for new sonic territory, bringing in shards of white noise, gurgling electronics, raw guitars, and druggy psychedelia, but these are just extensions of previously hidden elements of Blur's music. What makes it exceptional is how hard the band tries to reinvent themselves within their own framework, and the level of which they succeed. "Beetlebum" runs through the *White Album* in the space of five minute; "M.O.R." reinterprets Berlin-era Bowie; "You're So Great," despite the corny title, is affecting lo-fi from Graham Coxon; "Country Sad Ballad Man" is a bizarrely affecting, strangled lo-fi psychedelia; "Death of a Party" is an affecting resignation; "On Your Own" is an incredible slice of singaalong pop spiked with winding, fluid guitar and synth eruptions; while "Look Inside America" cleverly subverts the traditional Blur song, complete with strings. And "Essex Dogs" is a six-minute slab of free verse and rattling guitar noise. *Blur* might be self-consciously eclectic, but Blur is at their best when they are trying to live up to their own pretensions, because Damon Albarn's exceptional sense of songcraft and the band's knack for detailed arrangements that flesh out the song to its fullest. There might be dark overtones to the record, but the band sounds positively joyous, not only in making noise but wreaking havoc with the expectations of their audience and critics. *—Stephen Thomas Erlewine*

13 / Mar. 15, 1999 / Virgin ✦✦✦✦
Blur's penitence for Brit-pop continues with the aptly named *13,* which deals with star-crossed situations like personal and professional breakups with Damon Albarn's longtime girlfriend, Justine Frischmann of Elastica, and the group's longtime producer, Stephen Street. Building on *Blur*'s un-pop experiments, the group's ambitions to expand their musical and

emotional horizons result in a half-baked baker's dozen of songs, featuring some of their most creative peaks and self-indulgent valleys. Albarn has been criticized for lacking depth in his songwriting, but his ballads remain some of Blur's best moments. When Albarn and crew risk some honesty, *13* shines: on "Tender," Albarn is battered and frail, urged by a lush gospel choir to "get through it." His confiding continues on "1992," which alludes to the beginning—and ending—of his relationship with Frischmann. On "No Distance Left to Run," one of *13*'s most moving moments, Albarn addresses post-breakup ambivalence, sighing, "I hope you're with someone who makes you feel safe while you sleep." While these songs reflect Albarn's romantic chaos, "Mellow Song," "Caramel," and "Trimm Trabb" express day-to-day desperation. Musically, the saddest songs on *13* are also the clearest, mixing electronic and acoustic elements in sleek but heartfelt harmony. However, "B.L.U.R.E.M.I." is a by-the-numbers rave-up, and the blustery "Swamp Song" and "Bugman" nick Blur's old punky glam pop style but sound misplaced here. "Trailerpark" veers in yet another direction, a too-trendy trip-hop rip-off that emphasizes the band's musical fog, proving that William Orbit's kitchen-sink production doesn't serve the songs'—or the band's—best interests. *13*'s strange, frustrating combination of expert musicianship and self-indulgence reveals the sound of a band trying to find itself. With some closer editing, this could have been the emotionally deep, sonically wide album Blur yearns to make. *—Heather Phares*

The Best of Blur / Nov. 21, 2000 / Virgin ✦✦✦✦

Michael Bolton (Michael Bolotin)

b. Feb. 26, 1954, New Haven, CT

Vocals / Adult Contemporary

Singer/songwriter Michael Bolton had an extensive, though not very successful, career under his real name, Michael Bolotin, before emerging in the mid-'80s as a major soft-rock balladeer. He first turned up on RCA Records in the mid-'70s, then later became the lead singer in Blackjack, a heavy-metal band. In 1983, he changed his name to Michael Bolton, signed to Columbia Records as a solo act, and relaunched his career.

Michael Bolton was released in April 1983 and made the Top 100 bestsellers. His real breakthrough began with his third album, *The Hunger,* released in September 1987. On this album, Bolton abandoned the more hard-rock aspects of his style to concentrate on blue-eyed soul singing. *Soul Provider,* released in July 1989, turned Bolton into a superstar, reaching the Top Ten, selling four million copies, spawning five Top 40 singles, and earning him a Grammy. *Time, Love & Tenderness,* released in April 1991, was even more successful, hitting number one, selling six million copies, and featuring four Top 40 hits, including "Love Is a Wonderful Thing" (later the subject of a successful plagiarism suit brought against Bolton by the Isley Brothers.)

Bolton won another Grammy Award in 1992 for "When a Man Loves a Woman." Bolton's next album of original material, *The One Thing,* came in November 1993. It hit the Top Ten and sold three million copies. *All That Matters,* his first album of new material since *The One Thing,* came in the fall of 1997. Instead of continuing his success, it was a surprise flop. Its lack of success didn't stop Bolton from turning his attention to *My Secret Passion,* a collection of opera and arias that he released in January 1998. By classical standards, the album was a hit, and the record received a great deal of press and surprisingly good reviews. *—William Ruhlmann*

● **Greatest Hits 1985-1995** / Sep. 19, 1995 / Columbia ✦✦✦✦

Although he has always been a favorite target of rock critics, Michael Bolton amassed a large number of hit singles in the late '80s and early '90s, including seven Top Ten hits and two number one singles ("How Am I Supposed to Live Without You" and "When a Man Loves a Woman"). With the notable exception of "Love Is a Wonderful Thing," all of his big hits are collected on *Greatest Hits 1985-1995,* as well as a handful of new tracks that aren't quite as successful as the older hits. Nevertheless, *Greatest Hits 1985-1995* is the one definitive Michael Bolton album. *—Stephen Thomas Erlewine*

Bon Jovi

f. 1983, Sayreville, NJ

Group / Pop-Metal, Album Rock, Arena Rock, Hair Metal, Heavy Metal, Pop/Rock, Hard Rock

Few bands embodied the era of pop-metal like Bon Jovi. By merging Def Leppard's loud but tuneful metal with Bruce Springsteen's working-class sensibilities, the New Jersey-based quintet developed an ingratiatingly melodic and professional variation of hard-rock—one that appealed as much to teenagers as to housewives. Bon Jovi skillfully employed professional songwriters to give their songs, especially their power ballads, an appropriately commercial sheen, inaugurating a trend that dominated mainstream hard rock and metal for the next decade. They also made simple performance videos that emphasized lead singer Jon Bon Jovi's photogenic good looks, and these clips helped propel 1986's *Slippery When Wet* and 1988's *New Jersey* into multi-platinum status around the world. Both records were criticized for being more pop than metal, as well as being targeted toward teenyboppers, yet the group managed to subtly change their image in the early '90s, moving away from metal and concentrating on straightforward arena-rock and big ballads. The shift in style worked, and Bon Jovi were the only American pop-metal band of the '80s to retain a sizable audience in the '90s. *—Stephen Thomas Erlewine*

Bon Jovi / Jan. 1984 / Mercury ✦✦✦

7800 Fahrenheit / Apr. 1985 / Mercury ✦✦✦

Slippery When Wet / Aug. 1986 / Mercury ✦✦✦✦✦

It is probably true that Bon Jovi's breakthrough success with *Slippery When Wet,* their third album, had more to do with lead singer Jon Bon Jovi's mop of curls and winning smile than with anything in the grooves of the record. Nevertheless, the album contained competent contemporary pop/rock, from its Eddie Van Halen-inspired guitar solos to the singer's enthusiastic, husky wail (which owed a lot to Bruce Springsteen). Jon Bon Jovi, guitarist Richie Sambora, and songwriter-for-hire Desmond Child had little more on their minds than girls and rock-as-mythology (even the working-class anthem "Livin' on a Prayer" featured a character who was forced to hock his "six string"), but that may only mean they had identified their audience—young white adolescent males—and were targeting it accurately. *—William Ruhlmann*

New Jersey / Sep. 1988 / Mercury ✦✦✦✦✦

Bon Jovi had perfected a formula for hard pop/rock by the time of this album, concentrating on sing-along choruses sung over and over again, frequently by a rough, extensively overdubbed chorus, producing an effect not unlike what these songs sounded like in the arenas and stadiums where they were most often heard. The lyrics had that typical pop twist—although they nominally expressed romantic commitment, sentiments such as "Lay Your Hands on Me" and "I'll Be There for You" worked equally well as a means for the band and its audience to reaffirm their affection for each other. The only thing that marred the perfection of this communion was Jon Bon Jovi's continuing obsession with a certain predecessor from his home state; at times, he seemed to be trying to recreate *Born to Run* using cheaper materials. *—William Ruhlmann*

Keep the Faith / Nov. 1992 / Mercury ✦✦✦

After being missing in action for nearly four years, Bon Jovi returns with *Keep the Faith,* an update on their trademark pop-metal sound. Because the rules had changed since *New Jersey,* the band knew they had to shake things up a bit. Bon Jovi wants to be taken seriously this time around—hence, epics like the ten-minute "Dry County" and stabs at significance like "Fear" (plus the new short haircuts). Most of these grand statements fall flat, but there are songs here ("Bed of Roses," "Keep the Faith") that nearly match the glory days. *—Stephen Thomas Erlewine*

● **Cross Road** / Oct. 4, 1994 / Mercury ✦✦✦✦✦

While Bon Jovi always managed to stick a couple of killer album tracks on their records, their main strength has always been singles. *Cross Road* collects all of their biggest hits, adding a couple of new songs and Jon Bon Jovi's solo hit, "Blaze of Glory," for good measure. Even the band's detractors may not be able to resist the constant flow of big guitars, big hooks, and sweet melodies that pour out on *Cross Road.* After all, this is what state-of-the-art mainstream hard rock was all about in the late '80s. *—Stephen Thomas Erlewine*

These Days / 1995 / Mercury ✦✦✦

Crush / Jun. 13, 2000 / Mercury ✦✦✦✦

Even if it was classified as pop-metal, Bon Jovi never really was much of a metal band, relying on big, catchy melodies and not guitar riffs to make their songs memorable. That's why, in 2000, they're able to make an album like *Crush,* which strays far enough into pop/rock to actually stand a chance of getting airplay (which it did, with the hit lead single "It's My Life"). The guitar crunch on the uptempo numbers keeps Bon Jovi from becoming a full-fledged pop/rock band, but in addition to the typical hard rockers, there are nods to heartland rock, Bryan Adams-style adult contemporary balladry ("Thank You for Loving Me"), the Beatles (the surprisingly effective "Say It Isn't So"), and even British glam à la T. Rex or David Bowie ("Captain Crash and the Beauty Queen From Mars"). Occasionally, it sounds like the band is attempting to cover as many bases as possible for multi-format appeal, but for the most part, the variety—coupled with the consistently polished songcraft—makes for a surprisingly listenable album. The production is a little more electronic-tinged, but not obtrusively high-tech, so the band doesn't come off as desperate to sound contemporary. Aside from a couple of missteps (the soppy, aforementioned "Thank You for Loving Me" and the mawkish posturing of "Save the World"), *Crush* is a solidly crafted mainstream rock record that's much better than most might expect. Even if *Crush* is more measured than Bon Jovi's early work, "Just Older" sums up the band's acceptance of their status nicely: "The skin I'm in is all right with me/It's not old, just older." *—Steve Huey*

Graham Bond (Graham John Clifton Bond)

b. Oct. 28, 1937, Romford, Essex, England, **d.** May 8, 1974, London, England

Vocals, Saxophone, Organ / British Blues, British Invasion, Blues-Rock

An important, underappreciated figure of early British R&B, Graham Bond is known in the U.S., if at all, for heading the group that Jack Bruce and Ginger Baker played in before they joined Cream. He met Bruce and Baker in 1962 after joining Alexis Koerner's Blues Incorporated, and the trio formed their own band one year later, with Bond on the Hammond organ, as well as handling the lion's share of the vocals. In its prime, the Graham Bond Organization played rhythm and blues with a strong jazzy flavor, emphasizing Bond's demonic organ and gruff vocals. The band performed imaginative covers and fairly strong original material, and Bond was also perhaps the very first rock musician to record with the Mellotron synthesizer. Hit singles, though, were necessary for British bands to thrive in the mid-'60s, and Bond's group began to fall apart in 1966, when Bruce and Baker formed Cream with Eric Clapton. After struggling on with the Organization for a few years, he moved to the US in the late '60s to record a few albums, then moved back to Britain to form the band Holy Magick. Bond's demise was more tragic than most: he developed serious drug and alcohol problems, and committed suicide by throwing himself into the path of a London Underground train in 1974. *—Richie Unterberger*

● **The Sound of 65** / Mar. 1965 / Edsel ✦✦✦✦✦

Although the Organization's first album was recorded a mere year or two before Cream's debut, it bears little resemblance to Cream's pioneering hard blues-rock. Instead, it's taut British R&B with a considerable jazz influence. That influence comes not so much from the rhythm section as saxophonist Dick Heckstall-Smith and lead singer/organist Bond himself. This LP is not as exciting or rock-oriented as those of contemporaries like the Rolling Stones or John Mayall, but is respectably gritty, mostly original material, with an occasionally nasty edge. There are some obscure treasures of the British R&B explosion to be found here, including the original version of "Train Time" (later performed by Cream), the thrilling bass runs on "Baby Be Good to Me," and the group's hardboiled rearrangements of such traditional standards as "Wade in the Water" and "Early in the Morning." Even their blatant stab at commercialism (the ballad "Tammy") has its charm. *—Richie Unterberger*

There's a Bond Between Us / Nov. 1965 / Edsel ♦♦♦♦♦
Bond's second album stakes out similar territory as his debut in a more polished but slightly less exciting fashion. Some of the covers are a bit routine and hackneyed, and the original material isn't quite as strong (or frequent) as on the first effort. On a few tunes, the group expands from rave-ups to mellower, jazzier ballads that retain an R&B base. Highlights include the early Jack Bruce composition "Hear Me Calling Your Name" (to which he also contributes a fine lead vocal) and the excellent Bond tune "Walkin' in the Park," which holds up to the best early British R&B numbers. The album is also notable for being one of the very first rock LPs to feature the Mellotron, which Bond uses subtly and well. *—Richie Unterberger*

Gary "U.S." Bonds (Gary Anderson)

b. Jun. 6, 1939, Jacksonville, FL
Vocals / Rock & Roll, R&B
After moving to the Norfolk, VA, area in the mid '50s, young Gary Anderson began plying his vocal wares, first in church, later with a local group called the Turks. When he was not yet 21, he was approached by local record producer Frank Guida to join his tiny Legrand label. Guida changed Anderson's name to US Bonds, hoping the first release would get extra airplay by disc jockeys mistaking it for a public-service announcement. The result was the classic "New Orleans," combining rock-combo raunch with impassioned, scorched soul-singing that set the stage for all that would follow. Guida double- and triple-tracked Bonds' voice, and the resulting murky production gave all the hits (including "Quarter to Three," "School Is Out," and "Dear Lady Twist") a party-in-outer-space quality all their own. Though he has kept recording, making a couple of excellent solo albums in the early '80s with the help of Bruce Springsteen, Bonds is best seen today dotting the landscape of oldies shows the world over, singing the songs that made him famous. *—Cub Koda*

Dedication / Apr. 1981 / Razor & Tie ♦♦♦
Bruce Springsteen played guitar, sang a duet, wrote three songs, and co-produced and co-arranged four on Gary U.S. Bonds' comeback album, recorded 20 years after his heyday. Springsteen also lent his backup group, The E Street Band, while E Street guitarist Miami Steve (Van Zandt) also contributed a song and produced the bulk of the record. The result, naturally, sounds like a Bruce Springsteen and the E Street Band album with lead vocals by Gary U.S. Bonds. Bonds' elastic tenor, heard in much greater clarity than it ever was in his early years, has just enough grit to be soulful, and he puts across the pop-soul tunes Springsteen and Van Zandt have constructed for him effectively. He also tackles the Beatles' "It's Only Love" and Bob Dylan's "From a Buick 6," and sings Jackson Browne's "The Pretender" as if the lyric was devoid of irony. It's an enjoyable album that does nothing to change the notion that Bonds as a recording artist essentially conforms himself to the intentions of his producer, whether that's Frank Guida, Jerry Williams, Jr., or Bruce Springsteen. *—William Ruhlmann*

On the Line / Jun. 1982 / Razor & Tie ♦♦♦
On The Line, Gary U.S. Bonds' second comeback album under the sponsorship of Bruce Springsteen, was even more of a Springsteen record than its predecessor. This time, Springsteen wrote seven of the 11 songs, co-produced all of them with Miami Steve (Van Zandt) and again lent the E Street Band for the sessions. While there were no Springsteen masterpieces here, the rock & roll revival style of the material, similar to that on *Dedication*, made it, in effect, the follow-up to Springsteen's *The River* album, albeit with a different vocalist. And that vocalist was, if anything, more expressive than the author—on a song like "Out of Work," one of Springsteen's blue-collar anthems, Bonds sang with the conviction of a journeyman who knows what work is and what it's like not to have it. *—William Ruhlmann*

The School of Rock & Roll: Best of Gary U.S. Bonds / Apr. 1990 / Rhino ♦♦♦♦♦

● **The Very Best of Gary "U.S." Bonds: Original Legrand Masters** / Aug. 11, 1998 / Varese ♦♦♦♦♦
The title to this 16-track collection has more than its share of quirks and wrinkles. 14 tracks are duplicated with Rhino's 1990's *Best of Gary U.S. Bonds*, making it a negligible buy for anyone who already owns the latter compilation. All the chart hits are here, including "New Orleans," "Quarter to Three," "School Is Out" (again with the original intro clipped off, same as the Rhino comp), "School Is In," "Twist Twist Senora," and "Dear Lady Twist." New to this collection are the inclusion of "Gettin' a Groove," "Copy Cat," and "I Dig This Station." The latter two items grazed the bottom of the charts, hence their inclusion, but leaving off strong album and single material like "Trip to the Moon," "I Know Why Dreamers Cry," "Mixed Up Faculty" and "Cecelia" to make room for the second go round of non-charters like "Take Me Back to New Orleans," "Having So Much Fun," "Where Did the Naughty Little Girl Go," and "I Want To Holler (But the Town's Too Small)" makes this a less than stellar supplement to the Rhino package. But it's a decent alternative, leaving a half of a compilation's worth of material between the two best-of's. *—Cub Koda*

The Boo Radleys

f. 1988, Liverpool, England, **db.** Feb. 1, 1999
Group / Indie Pop, Dream Pop, Britpop, Shoegazing, Alternative Pop/Rock
Initially wannabe shoegazers, the English dream-pop group the Boo Radleys developed a dedicated cult following in the early '90s before edging into the mainstream a few years later. Formed in Liverpool in 1988, The Boo Radleys consisted of guitarist/songwriter Martin Carr, vocalist/guitarist Sice, bassist Timothy Brown, and drummer Steve Hewitt. They released their debut *Ichabod and I*, on a local independent label in 1990; Rob Cieka replaced Hewitt after record's release. British disc jockey John Peel's support helped the band sign with Rough Trade Records, who released the 1991 EP *Every Heaven*, which was a minor UK chart success. Soon after, Rough Trade folded and the Boo Radleys moved to Creation Records, releasing *Everything's Alright Forever* in 1992. Columbia released the album in the U.S., but it didn't gain much attention. In England, it received favorable reviews and the group began building a fan base. Topping several Best-of-the-Year lists, including *Melody Maker*'s, 1993's *Giant Steps* was a critical success in England and sold respectably. In America, the record launched the minor alternative-rock hit "Lazarus" and led to a second-stage spot on Lollapalooza '94.

1995's Britpop-influenced *Wake Up!* was the band's commercial breakthrough, debuting at number one. The bright, brassy single "Wake Up Boo" entered in the Top Ten and stayed on the charts until the early summer, preventing the follow-up single "Find the Answer Within" from charting higher than the Top 30. Columbia did little to promote *Wake Up!* when they released it in America in the fall of 1995; they dropped the band in early 1996.

The Boo Radleys returned that fall with *C'Mon Kids*, a self-consciously arty album designed to shake off the band's newfound pop fans. It worked—the album debuted in the Top 10 but soon fell off the charts, despite overwhelmingly positive reviews. Early in 1997, the band finalized an American contract with Mercury, and *C'Mon Kids* was released in March, a half a year after its initial British release. *Kingsize* followed in late 1998, though the group officially broke up just months later. *—Stephen Thomas Erlewine*

Ichabod & I / Jul. 1990 / Action ♦♦

Everything's Alright Forever / Aug. 1992 / Columbia ♦♦♦

Giant Steps / Aug. 31, 1993 / Columbia ♦♦♦♦♦
Titling an album after John Coltrane's masterpiece may well seem the height of pretension, but heck, it never stopped the Replacements from a similar move vis-a-vis the Rolling Stones. As it is, the title is perfectly justified—Carr, a Coltrane aficionado among many other things, here finally leads his band from the promising to the truly inspired. With the inventive, groundbreaking *Lazarus* EP as a touchstone (the title track is included here in an unfortunately abbreviated form), the Boos self-produce themselves to new heights. The genius of the Boos definitely lies in their ability to adapt many a different touch and make it their own, taking what are often straightforward, hooky pop songs and turning them into something more, an ability *Giant Steps* shows in spades. The old fuzz blast is here, but less beholden to the likes of My Bloody Valentine, instead drawing on Carr's wide-ranging tastes (Beach Boys, psych-pop, Human League/New Order-inspired arrangements) to reach different, individual conclusions. From the near free-noise wash of "Run My Way Runway" to the soaring pop blast of "Barney (...and Me)," a poignant, nostalgiac lyric backed by a thrilling overall performance, the band does little wrong. Brown and Cjeka effectively incorporate dub/reggae rhythms, as "Lazarus" itself showed they could do, blending in loping, funky skank to "Upon 7th and Fairchild" and the fantastic "Butterfly McQueen." Carr's guitar work is much more distinctly his own throughout the album, with often volcanic, inspired soloing adding a huge, echoed sound to many of the songs. A number of guest performers help, notably Steve Kitchen on brass; his trumpet and flugelhorn parts and flourishes add jazzy touches throughout, at times reminiscent of Miles Davis' work on *Sketches of Spain*. *—Ned Raggett*

● **Wake Up!** / Sep. 12, 1995 / Columbia ♦♦♦♦♦
With their third album, the Boo Radleys abandoned the overt noise that obscured the pop sensibilities of their early work and scaled back the ambitions of *Giant Steps*. The result is *Wake Up!*, a glorious, brightly colored gem of a pop record. From the Beach Boy harmonies and trumpet fanfares of the opening "Wake Up Boo!" to the closing epic, McCartney-styled ballad "Wilder," the group winds through many styles of British pop. Much of the darkness—both musically and lyrically—of their previous music has been lifted; in its place is a sterling piece of pure pop, with all the big choruses, bright melodies, and simple hooks that word implies. *Giant Steps* had elements of this grand pop, yet it tried too hard. *Wake Up!* doesn't try for as much, and in doing so, it achieves more, both musically and commercially—upon the release of the album and the "Wake Up Boo!" single, the Boos became genuine Top Ten pop stars in England. The Boo Radleys were always a band with ambitions. The only difference with *Wake Up!* is that they finally fulfilled them. *—Stephen Thomas Erlewine*

C'mon Kids / Sep. 9, 1996 / Mercury ♦♦♦♦
Wake Up! brought the Boo Radleys pop success that they weren't sure what to do with. After embracing the album's number one success, the group eventually recoiled from the spotlight and Martin Carr wrote *C'mon Kids* as a direct response to the group's celebrity status in the UK. Simply put, *C'mon Kids* is an attempt to scare away any of the fellow travelers who welcomed the sunny-sounding pop of *Wake Up!* It's a gnarled, twisted and disorted album, as dense as *Giant Steps* and as loud as the Boos' early EPs. And, if you can make it through the murky guitars, fragments of songs, altered vocals and tape effects, there's a number of melodies and creatively crafted songs that make the album nearly as rewarding as *Giant Steps* or *Wake Up!* However, it takes time to get into *C'mon Kids*, though. At first, it's disarming to hear Sice scream his vocals and the Boos play heavy riffs. After a while the melodies begin to reveal themselves, as do the clever song structures and inversions of the band's psychedelic hooks and folk tendecies. *C'mon Kids* might not be as accessible as even *Giant Steps* but it displays a feverish sense of purpose and a perverse willfullness to refashion their sound that makes it an easy album to admire, if not love. *—Stephen Thomas Erlewine*

Kingsize / Oct. 1998 / Creation ♦♦

Booker T. & the MG's

f. 1962, Memphis, TN, **db.** 1971
Group / Southern Soul, Instrumental Rock, R&B, Soul
As the house band at Stax Records in Memphis, Booker T. & the MG's may have been the single greatest factor in the lasting value of that label's soul music—not to mention Southern soul as a whole. Their tight, impeccable grooves can be heard on classic hits by Otis Redding, Wilson Pickett, Carla Thomas, Albert King, and Sam & Dave, just to name the very most prominent examples. For that reason alone, they would deserve their spot in rock & roll's hall of fame. But in addition to their formidable skills as a house band, on their own they were one of the top instrumental outfits of the rock era, cutting classics like "Green Onions," "Time Is Tight," and "Hang 'em High." The anchors of the Booker T. sound were Steve Cropper, whose slicing, economic riffs influenced tons of other guitar players, and Booker T. Jones himself, who provided much of the groove with his floating organ lines. In

1960, Jones started working as a session man for Stax; there he met Cropper, who had been in the Mar-Keys, whose 1961 instrumental hit "Last Night" laid out the protoype for much of the MG's (and indeed Memphis soul's) sound with its organ-sax-guitar combo. The band's first and biggest hit, "Green Onions" (number three, 1962), came about by accident. Jamming in the studio while fruitlessly waiting for Billy Lee Riley to show up for a session, they came up with a classic minor-key, bluesy soul instrumental, distinguished by its nervous organ bounce and ferocious bursts of guitar. For the next five years, they'd have trouble recapturing its commercial success, though the standard of their records remained fairly high, and Stax's dependence upon them as the house band ensured a decent living. In the late '60s, the MG's really hit their stride with "Hip Hug-Her," "Groovin'," "Soul-Limbo," "Hang 'em High," and "Time Is Tight," all of which were Top 40 charters between 1967 and 1969. *—Richie Unterberger*

Green Onions / Oct. 1962 / Atlantic ✦✦✦✦✦
There's not a note or a nuance out of place anywhere on this record, which was 35 of the most exciting minutes of instrumental music in any category that one could purchase in 1962 (and it's no slouch four decades out, either). "I Got a Woman" is the single best indicator of how superb this record is and this band was—listening to this track, it's easy to forget that the song ever had lyrics or ever needed them, Booker T. Jones' organ and Steve Cropper's guitar serving as more-than-adequate substitutes for any singer. Their version of "Twist and Shout" is every bit as satisfying. Even "Mo' Onions," an effort to repeat the success of "Green Onions," doesn't repeat anything from the earlier track except the tempo, and Jones and Cropper both come up with fresh sounds within the same framework.

"Behave Yourself" is a beautifully wrought piece of organ-based blues that gives Jones a chance to show off some surprisingly nimble-fingered playing, while "Stranger on the Shore" is transformed into a piece of prime soul music in the group's hands. "Lonely Avenue" is another showcase for Jones' keyboard dexterity, and then there's the group's cover of Smokey Robinson's "One Who Really Loves You", with a ravishing lead performance by Jones on organ and Cropper's guitar handling the choruses. Just when it seems like the album has turned in all of the surprises in repertory that it could reasonably deliver, it ends with "Comin' Home Baby," a killer jazz piece on which Steve Cropper gets to shine, his guitar suddenly animated around Jones' playing, his quietly trilled notes at the crescendo some of the most elegant guitar heard on an R&B record up to that time. *—Bruce Eder*

The Best of Booker T. & the MG's [Stax] / 1986 / Stax ✦✦✦
Somewhat confusingly, this disc is titled identically to a CD on Atlantic that concentrates on their earlier material. This 17-cut disc draws from 1967-1971, and includes three of their four Top 20 pop hits: "Soul Limbo," "Hang 'em High," and "Time Is Tight." This perhaps lacks a bit of the edge of their mid-'60s recordings, concentrating on loping, relaxed grooves more than biting, incisive chops. The standard remains pretty high, though, with the interplay between Steve Cropper's guitar, Booker T. Jones' organ, and the rhythm section never less than telepathic. Most of the material is original, but even on the covers of period pop hits—including unlikely versions of "Something," "Eleanor Rigby," and "Mrs. Robinson"—the group is soulful and tight. This is perhaps better music for background and party listening than anything else, but within those confines it's quite good. *—Richie Unterberger*

★ **The Very Best of Booker T. & the MG's** / Jun. 21, 1994 / Rhino ✦✦✦✦✦
This 16-song CD, clocking in at 46 minutes, is the second-best, and the handiest and most easily affordable, compilation available on Booker T. & the MG's. It's not remotely as comprehensive as Fantasy Records' three-CD set (although this disc does have two tracks, "Booker-Loo" and "Slum Baby," that don't appear on the triple-CD set) but is more comprehensive and better representative of their work (and offers better sound) than either Fantasy's single-disc best-of or the old Atlantic Records' best-of compilation. The collection does jump around a bit across history in the course of covering the years 1963-1971, bouncing between late-'60s singles and album tracks and odd early/middle-'60s tracks. "Booker-Loo," one of the pieces unique to this set, features some very crunchy rhythm guitar and flamboyant organ work in its intro, before Steve Cropper takes center stage with an unusually flashy lead guitar solo spot. "Slum Baby," from three years later, features a much smoother and funkier sound. "Slim Jenkins' Place" shows off Booker T. Jones's piano skills as well as his organ playing, and all of it is marked by virtuoso playing. The collection also makes a strong case for the band's members as composers—hits like "Hang 'Em High" come off beautifully, especially in the crisply remastered version presented here, which brings out every nuance in the organ and guitar-dominated rendition of Dominic Frontiere's theme from the Clint Eastwood movie of that name. But originals like the majestic, soaring "Time Is Tight" and the lyrical, playful "Soul-Limbo" are great pieces of pop-soul composition as well, and stand up just as well to repeated listening. Buy the triple-disc set if it's in your budget, but at less than one-third of the cost, this collection shouldn't be dismissed for its compactness and range. *—Bruce Eder*

Time Is Tight / Oct. 6, 1998 / Stax ✦✦✦✦✦
A three-CD, 65-song box set that includes all their hits from 1962 and 1971, in addition to numerous LP tracks and failed singles; the third disc is devoted entirely to previously unreleased live material (most from 1992-94) and rarities. Greatest-hits compilations will serve the needs of all but intense Booker T. and Stax fans. However, if you really dig their instrumental sound, this is a fine package. It might skip an odd worthy track from their catalog, but basically has just about everything deserving of attention, concentrating more on their original compositions than their covers. Some of the more obscure selections, like their jazzy 1967 LP cut "Pigmy" and their inventive 1969 cover of "Lady Madonna," are overlooked standouts. A number of sides here, like "Burnt Biscuits," "Fannie Mae," "Sunday Sermon," "MG Party," and the moody, dignified "Meditation," were never on album before. Other oddities fans will want to know about is a live medley of James Brown material from 1968, Albert King doing "Born Under a Bad Sign" with them live (also from 1968), a hit 1965 single ("Hole in the Wall") released under the name "the Packers," and "Booker's Theme," which was only available on the 1969 Stax various-artists sampler *Soul Explosion*. The 1992-94 live cuts (all previously unreleased), with various drummers in place of the late Al Jackson, show the band in decent though not amazing form, including a ten-minute jam on "Time Is Tight" and a version of "(Sittin' On) The Dock of the Bay" with Neil Young on vocals. The booklet contains extensive liner notes by Stax Records authority Rob Bowman. *—Richie Unterberger*

The Boomtown Rats

f. 1975, Dun Laoghaire, Ireland, **db.** 1986
Group / New Wave, Punk
The Boomtown Rats were an Irish rock band that scored a series of British hits between 1977 and 1980 and were led by singer Bob Geldof, who organized the Ethiopian relief efforts Band Aid and Live Aid. After moving from Ireland to London in late 1976, the group became associated with punk rock and released their debut single, "Lookin' After No. 1." It was the first of nine straight singles to make the UK Top 15. The Boomtown Rats' second album, 1978's *A Tonic for the Troops*, featured a number one hit in "Rat Trap" and spawned an American contract with Columbia Records. "I Don't Like Mondays" became their second straight British number one (and their only US chart entry), though the band slipped from the charts soon after. Shades of the end came in 1983, when Columbia rejected the Boomtown Rats' sixth album *In the Long Grass* (eventually released by Ensign). One year later, Geldof formed the star-studded Band Aid group to record his song "Do They Know It's Christmas?" for Ethiopian relief, resulting in the biggest selling single in UK history. He then organized the two Live Aid concerts. Despite a belated US release of *In the Long Grass*, the Boomtown Rats folded soon after and Geldof launched a solo career. *— William Ruhlmann*

The Boomtown Rats / Sep. 1977 / Mercury ✦✦✦
Anyone who heard the Boomtown Rats' debut single, "Lookin' After No. 1," with its rapid drum beat, slashing guitars, and aggressive singing about impatience with the dole queue, would think of the group as a particularly tight, standard punk rock band on the London scene in 1977. The Rats' debut album also featured the leering "Mary of the Fourth Form," their second single, but the rest of the album revealed more traditional rock influences. "Joey's on the Street Again" sounded like the sort of street opera Bruce Springsteen was aiming for on *The Wild, the Innocent & the E Street Shuffle*. "I Can Make It If You Can" was the sort of ballad the Rolling Stones favored in the mid-'70s. Overall, there were enough power chords and snotty sentiments to justify the punk tag, but it was already clear that the Rats aspired to the mainstream. *— William Ruhlmann*

Tonic for the Troops / Jun. 1978 / Columbia ✦✦✦

The Fine Art of Surfacing / Oct. 1979 / Columbia ✦✦✦

Mondo Bongo / Feb. 1981 / Columbia ✦✦

V Deep / Apr. 1982 / Columbia ✦✦

In the Long Grass / May 1985 / Columbia ✦✦✦

The Greatest Hits / 1987 / Columbia ✦✦✦✦

● **Great Songs of Indifference: The Best of Bob Geldof & the Boomtown Rats** / Apr. 22, 1997 / Columbia ✦✦✦✦✦
Great Songs of Indifference: The Best of Bob Geldof & the Boomtown Rats is the first comprehensive collection compiled on not only the Boomtown Rats, but also Bob Geldof's solo career. All of the group's biggest hits, including "I Don't Like Mondays," "Looking After Number One," and "Banana Republic," are here, as are a handful of solo tracks; while those aren't as strong as the Rats cuts, they neverthless sum up Geldof's post-Boomtown career quite effectively. In other words, it's a definitive retrospective. *—Stephen Thomas Erlewine*

Boston

f. 1971, Boston, MA
Group / Album Rock, Arena Rock, Pop/Rock, Hard Rock
The arena-rock group behind one of the fastest-selling debut albums in history, Boston was essentially the vehicle of studio wizard Tom Scholz. A rock fan and songwriter even while earning a master's degree at MIT, he joined a local band led by guitarist Barry Goudreau and constructed his own 12-track recording studio in his basement. Along with vocalist Brad Delp, bassist Fran Sheehan and drummer John "Sib" Hashian, the group—now dubbed Boston—earned a contract with Epic. The 1976 release of *Boston* (consisting largely of Scholz's original basement tapes) spawned three hit singles ("More Than a Feeling," "Long Time," and "Peace of My Mind"), shot immediately to the top of the charts, and became the best-selling pop debut in history. Scholz spent over two years working on the follow-up, 1978's number one hit *Don't Look Back*. The third Boston album, *Third Stage*, didn't appear until 1986, at which time only Scholz and Delp remained. During the '80s, Scholz was sued by Goudreau, who alleged that Scholz had damaged his solo career (they settled out-of-court) and Epic, who claimed Boston had reneged on their contract by taking so long between releases (he won). When the band resurfaced again in 1994 with *Walk On*, Scholz was the lone remaining member; Delp and Goudreau had reunited in 1992 as RTZ, releasing the album *Return to Zero*. In addition to his fame as a musician, Scholz also found success as an inventor and businessman. *—Jason Ankeny*

● **Boston** / Sep. 1976 / Epic ✦✦✦✦✦
Boston is one of the best-selling albums of all time, and deservedly so. Because of the rise of disco and punk, FM rock radio seemed all but dead until the rise of acts like Boston, Tom Petty, and Bruce Springsteen. Nearly every song on Boston's debut album can still be heard on classic rock radio today due to the strong vocals of Brad Delp and unique guitar sound of Tom Scholz. Tom Scholz, who wrote most of the songs, was a studio wizard and used self-designed equipment such as 12-track recording devices to come up with an anthemic "arena rock" sound before the term was even coined. The sound was hard rock, but the layered melodies and harmonics reveal the work of a master craftsman. While much has been written about the sound of the album, the lyrics are often overlooked. There are songs about their rise from a bar band ("Rock and Roll Band") as well as fond remembrances of summers gone by ("More Than a Feeling"). *Boston* is essential for any fan of classic rock, and the album marks the re-emergence of the genre in the 1970s. *— Vik Iyengar*

Don't Look Back / Aug. 1978 / Epic ♦♦♦

Third Stage / Oct. 1986 / MCA ♦♦♦

Walk On / Jun. 7, 1994 / MCA ♦♦

Greatest Hits / Jun. 3, 1997 / Epic ♦♦♦♦
Since Tom Scholz is such a slow worker, there were only four Boston albums between the group's 1976 debut and this *Greatest Hits* collection in 1997. That may mean that there isn't much music to compile, as the reliance on their biggest-selling album *Boston* suggests, but that doesn't matter for most casual fans, since *Greatest Hits* gathers all of their best songs, from "More than a Feeling" to "Amanda," on one compact disc. For the collector, the record isn't quite as appealing, even if it contains three new songs as bait. Given that the likelihood of another Boston album in the 20th century seems slim at the time of *Greatest Hits'* 1997 release, these three songs could be the only new tracks fans hear for years, and they simply don't deliver the melodic punch or guitar crunch that distinguishes the group's best work. It's nice to hear original vocalist Brad Delp on "Higher Power," but "Tell Me" is slight, and an instrumental version of "The Star Spangled Banner" is nearly an insult. So, for the devoted, *Greatest Hits* is a mixed bag, but for less dedicated listeners, it may be all the Boston they need. *—Stephen Thomas Erlewine*

Bow Wow Wow

f. 1980, London, England, **db.** 1983
Group / New Wave
Bow Wow Wow was a quartet organized by U.K. manager Malcolm McLaren (best known as the mastermind behind the Sex Pistols) at the start of the '80s. McLaren matched the trio of musicians who had constituted Adam Ant's Ants—Matthew Ashman (b. 1962) on guitar, Leigh Gorman (b. 1961) on bass, and David Barbarossa (b. 1961) on drums—with teenage singer Annabella Lwin (b. Oct. 31, 1965), retaining the earlier group's African-derived drum sound. In 1983, Lwin quit the group for a solo career, and the remaining three changed their name to the Chiefs of Relief. Both Lwin and the Chiefs issued their own albums. In 1995, Ashman passed away due to diabetes. Headed by Lwin and Gorman, a reformed Bow Wow Wow resurfaced in 1998 with *Wild in the U.S.A.*, which featured both remixes and concert performances from the reunion tour; guitarist Dave Calhoun and drummer Eshan Khadaroo filled the other slots. *—William Ruhlmann*

● **The Best of Bow Wow Wow** / Oct. 29, 1996 / RCA ♦♦♦♦♦
The Best of Bow Wow Wow is a thorough overview of Malcolm McLaren's manufactured new wave pop group, featuring all the highlights of the group's albums and EPs—including, of course, "I Want Candy," but also "Go Wild in the Country," "W.O.R.K." and "Do You Want to Hold Me"—as well as the previously unreleased "Where's My Snake." Since the group didn't make consistent albums, *The Best of Bow Wow Wow* is the best way to listen to the band, since it features every one of their worthwhile tracks, plus good liner notes. *—Stephen Thomas Erlewine*

David Bowie (David Robert Jones)

b. Jan. 8, 1947, Brixton, England
Vocals, Saxophone, Keyboards, Guitar / Experimental Rock, Blue-Eyed Soul, Proto-Punk, Pop/Rock, Glam Rock, Prog-Rock/Art Rock, Hard Rock
The cliche about David Bowie says he's a musical chameleon, adapting himself according to fashion and trends. While such a criticism is too glib, there's no denying that Bowie demonstrated remarkable skill for perceiving musical trends at his peak in the '70s. After spending several years in the late '60s as a mod and as an all-around music-hall entertainer, Bowie reinvented himself as a hippie singer/songwriter. Prior to his breakthrough in 1972, he recorded a proto-metal record and a pop-rock album, eventually redefining glam-rock with his ambiguously sexy Ziggy Stardust persona. Ziggy made Bowie an international star, yet he wasn't content to continue to churn out glitter-rock. By the mid-'70s, he developed an effete, sophisticated version of Philly soul that he dubbed "plastic soul," which eventually morphed into the eerie avant-pop of 1976's *Station to Station*. Shortly afterward, he relocated to Berlin, where he recorded three experimental electronic albums with Brian Eno. At the dawn of the '80s, Bowie was still at the height of his powers, yet following his blockbuster dance-pop album *Let's Dance* in 1983, he slowly sank into mediocrity before salvaging his career in the early '90s. Even when he was out of fashion in the '80s and '90s, it was clear that Bowie was one of the most influential musicians in rock, for better and for worse. Each one of his phases in the '70s sparked a number of subgenres, including punk, new wave, goth-rock, the New Romantics, and electronica. Few rockers ever had such lasting impact. *—Stephen Thomas Erlewine*

Space Oddity / 1969 / Virgin ♦♦♦
Originally released as *Man of Words/Man of Music*, *Space Oddity* was David Bowie's first successful reinvention of himself. Abandoning both the mod and Anthony Newley fascinations that marked his earlier recordings, Bowie delves into a lightly psychedelic folk-rock, exemplified by the album's soaring title track. Bowie actually attempts a variety of styles on *Space Oddity*, as if he were trying to find the ones that suited him best. As such, the record isn't very cohesive, but it is charming, especially in light of his later records. Nevertheless, only "Wild Eyed Boy From Freecloud" and "Memory of a Free Festival" rank as Bowie classics, and even those lack the hooks or purpose of "Space Oddity." *—Stephen Thomas Erlewine*

The Man Who Sold the World / 1970 / Virgin ♦♦♦♦♦
Even though it contained no hits, *The Man Who Sold the World*, for most intents and purposes, is the beginning of David Bowie's classic period. Working with guitarist Mick Ronson and producer Tony Visconti for the first time, Bowie developed a tight, twisted heavy guitar rock that appears simple on the surface, but sounds more gnarled upon each listen. The mix is off-center, with the fuzz-bass dominating the compressed, razor-thin guitars and Bowie's strangled, affected voice. The sound of *The Man Who Sold the World* is odd, but the music is bizarre itself, with Bowie's bizarre, paranoid futuristic tales are melded to Ronson's riffing and the band's relentless attack. Musically, there isn't much innovation on *The Man Who Sold the World*—it is almost all hard blues-rock or psychedelic folk-rock—but there's an unsettling edge to the band's performance, which makes the record one of Bowie's best albums. [Rykodisc's 1990 CD reissue includes four bonus tracks, including the previously unreleased "Lightning Frightening," and the single "Holy Holy," and both sides of the 1971 "Arnold Corns" single, "Moonage Daydream" and "Hang on to Yourself," which are early and inferior versions of songs that would later appear on *Ziggy Stardust*.] *—Stephen Thomas Erlewine*

☆ **Hunky Dory** / 1972 / Virgin ♦♦♦♦♦
After the freakish hard rock of *The Man Who Sold the World*, David Bowie returned to singer/songwriter territory on *Hunky Dory*. Not only did the album boast more folky songs ("Song for Bob Dylan," "The Bewlay Brothers"), but he again flirted with Anthony Newley-esque dancehall music ("Kooks," "Fill Your Heart"), seemingly leaving heavy metal behind. As a result, *Hunky Dory* is a kaleidoscopic array of pop styles, tied together only by Bowie's sense of vision: a sweeping, cinematic mélange of high and low art, ambiguous sexuality, kitsch, and class. Mick Ronson's guitar is pushed to the back, leaving Rick Wakeman's cabaret piano to dominate the sound of the album. The subdued support accentuates the depth of Bowie's material, whether it's the revamped Tin Pan Alley of "Changes," the Neil Young homage "Quicksand," the soaring "Life on Mars?," the rolling, vaguely homosexual anthem "Oh! You Pretty Things," or the dark acoustic rocker "Andy Warhol." On the surface, such a wide range of styles and sounds would make an album incoherent, but Bowie's improved songwriting and determined sense of style instead made *Hunky Dory* a touchstone for reinterpreting pop's traditions into fresh, postmodern pop music. *—Stephen Thomas Erlewine*

☆ **The Rise & Fall of Ziggy Stardust** / 1972 / Virgin ♦♦♦♦♦
Borrowing heavily from Marc Bolan's glam rock and the future shock of *A Clockwork Orange*, David Bowie reached back to the heavy rock of *The Man Who Sold the World* for *The Rise & Fall of Ziggy Stardust and the Spiders From Mars*. Constructed as a loose concept album about an androgynous alien rock star named Ziggy Stardust, the story falls apart quickly, yet Bowie's fractured, paranoid lyrics are evocative of a decadent, decaying future, and the music echoes an apocalyptic, nuclear dread. Fleshing out the off-kilter metallic mix with fatter guitars, genuine pop songs, string sections, keyboards, and a cinematic flourish, *Ziggy Stardust* is a glitzy array of riffs, hooks, melodrama, and style and the logical culmination of glam. Mick Ronson plays with a maverick flair that invigorates rockers like "Suffragette City," "Moonage Daydream," and "Hang Onto Yourself," while "Lady Stardust," "Five Years," and "Rock and Roll Suicide" have a grand sense of staged drama previously unheard of in rock & roll. And that self-conscious sense of theater is part of the reason why *Ziggy Stardust* sounds so foreign. Bowie succeeds not in spite of his pretensions but because of them, and *Ziggy Stardust*—familiar in structure, but alien in performance—is the first time his vision and execution met in such a grand, sweeping fashion. *—Stephen Thomas Erlewine*

Aladdin Sane / 1973 / Virgin ♦♦♦♦♦
Ziggy Stardust wrote the blueprint for Bowie's hard-rocking glam, and *Aladdin Sane* essentially follows the pattern, for both better and worse. A lighter affair than *Ziggy Stardust*, *Aladdin Sane* is actually a stranger album than its predecessor, buoyed by bizarre lounge-jazz flourishes from pianist Mick Garson and a handful of winding, vaguely experimental songs. Bowie abandons his futuristic obsessions to concentrate on the detached cool of New York and London hipsters, as on the compressed rockers "Watch That Man," "Cracked Actor," and "The Jean Genie." Bowie follows the hard stuff with the jazzy, dissonant sprawls of "Lady Grinning Soul," "Aladdin Sane," and "Time," all of which manage to be both campy and avant-garde simultaneously, while the sweepingly cinematic "Drive-In Saturday" is a soaring fusion of sci-fi doo wop and melodramatic teenage glam. He lets his paranoia slip through in the clenched rhythms of "Panic in Detroit," as well as on his oddly clueless cover of "Let's Spend the Night Together." For all the pleasures on *Aladdin Sane*, there's no distinctive sound or theme to make the album cohesive; it's Bowie riding the wake of *Ziggy Stardust*, which means there's a wealth of classic material here, but not enough focus to make the album itself a classic. *—Stephen Thomas Erlewine*

Pin-Ups / 1973 / Virgin ♦♦♦

David Live / 1974 / RCA ♦♦

Diamond Dogs / 1974 / Virgin ♦♦♦
David Bowie fired the Spiders from Mars shortly after the release of *Pin-Ups*, but he didn't completely leave the Ziggy Stardust persona behind. *Diamond Dogs* suffers precisely because of this—he doesn't know *how* to move forward. Originally conceived as a concept album based on George Orwell's *1984*, *Diamond Dogs* evolved into another one of Bowie's paranoid future nightmares. Throughout the album, there are hints that he's tired with the Ziggy formula, particularly in the disco underpinning of "Candidate" and his cut-and-paste lyrics. However, it's not enough to make *Diamond Dogs* a step forward, and without Mick Ronson to lead the band, the rockers are too stiff to make an impact. Ironically, the one exception is one of Bowie's very best songs—the tight, sexy "Rebel Rebel." The song doesn't have much to do with the theme, and the ones one he does throw to further the story, they usually fall flat. *Diamond Dogs* isn't a total waste, with "1984," "Candidate," and "Diamond Dogs" all offering some sort of pleasure, but it is the first record since *Space Oddity* where Bowie's reach exceeds his grasp. *—Stephen Thomas Erlewine*

Young Americans / 1975 / Virgin ♦♦♦
Bowie had dropped hints during the *Diamond Dogs* tour that he was moving toward R&B, but the full-blown blue-eyed soul of *Young Americans* came as a shock. Surrounding himself with first-rate sessionmen, Bowie comes up with a set of songs that approximate the sound of Phillie-soul and disco, yet remain detached from their inspirations; even at his most passionate, Bowie sounds like a commentator, as if the entire album was a genre exercise. Nevertheless, the distance doesn't hurt the album—it gives the record its own distinctive flavor, and its plastic, robotic soul helped inform generations of synthetic British soul. What does hurt the record is a lack of strong songwriting. "Young Americans" is a masterpiece, and

"Fame" had a beat funky enough that James Brown ripped it off, but only a handful cuts ("Win," "Fascination," "Somebody Up There Likes Me") come close to matching their quality. As a result, *Young Americans* is more enjoyable as a stylistic adventure, than as a substantive record. [The 1991 CD has three bonus tracks, including the terrific outtake "Who Can I Be Now?"] *—Stephen Thomas Erlewine*

Station to Station / 1976 / Virgin ✦✦✦✦✦
Taking the detached plastic soul of *Young Americans* to an elegant, robotic extreme, *Station to Station* is a transitional album that creates its own distinctive style. Abandoning any pretense of being a soulman, yet keeping rhythmic elements of soul, Bowie positions himself as a cold, clinical crooner and explores a variety of styles. Everything from epic ballads and disco to synthesized avant-pop is present on *Station to Station*, but what ties it together is Bowie's cocaine-induced paranoia and detached musical persona. At its heart, *Station to Station* is an avant-garde, art rock album, most explicitly on "TVC15" and the epic sprawl of the title track, but also on the cool crooning of "Wild Is the Wind" and "Word on a Wing," as well as the disco stylings of "Golden Years." It's not an easy album to warm to, but its epic structure and clinical sound were an impressive, individualistic achievement, as well as a style that would prove enormously influential on post-punk. *—Stephen Thomas Erlewine*

☆ **Heroes** / 1977 / Virgin ✦✦✦✦✦
Repeating the formula of *Low*'s half-vocal/half-instrumental structure, *Heroes* develops and strengthens the sonic innovations Bowie and Eno explored on their first collaboration. The vocal songs are fuller, boasting harder rhythms and deeper layers of sound. Much of the harder-edged sound of *Heroes* is due to Robert Fripp's guitar, which provides a muscular foundation for the electronics, especially on the relatively conventional rock songs. Similarly, the instrumentals on *Heroes* are more detailed, this time showing a more explicit debt to German synth-pop and European experimental rock & roll. Essentially, the difference between *Low* and *Heroes* lies in the details, but the record is equally challenging and groundbreaking. [The CD reissue includes the previously unreleased instrumental "Abdulmajid" and a remix of "Joe the Lion."] *—Stephen Thomas Erlewine*

☆ **Low** / 1977 / Virgin ✦✦✦✦✦
Following through with the avant-garde inclinations of *Station to Station*, yet explicitly breaking with Bowie's past, *Low* is a dense, challenging album that confirmed Bowie's place at rock's cutting edge. Driven by dissonant synthesizers and electronics, *Low* is divided between brief, angular songs and atmospheric instrumentals. Throughout the record's first half, the guitars are jagged and the synthesizers drone with a menacing robotic pulse, while Bowie's vocals are unnaturally layered and overdubbed. During the instrumental half, the electronics turn cool, which is a relief after the intensity of the preceding avant-pop. Half the credit for *Low*'s success goes to Brian Eno, who explored similar ambient territory on his own releases. Eno functioned as a conduit for Bowie's ideas, and in turn Bowie made the experimentalism of not only Eno, but of the German synth group Kraftwerk and the post-punk group Wire, respectable, if not quite mainstream. Though a handful of the vocal pieces on *Low* are accessible—"Sound and Vision" has a shimmering guitar hook, and "Be My Wife" subverts soul structure in a surprisingly catchy fashion—the record is defiantly experimental and dense with detail, providing a new direction for the avant-garde in rock & roll. *—Stephen Thomas Erlewine*

Stage / 1978 / Rykodisc ✦✦✦

Lodger / 1979 / Virgin ✦✦✦✦✦
On the surface, *Lodger* is the most accessible of the three Berlin-era records Bowie made with Brian Eno, simply because there are no instrumentals and there are a handful of concise pop songs. Nevertheless, *Lodger* is still gnarled and twisted avant-pop; what makes it different is how it incorporates such experimental tendencies into genuine songs, something that *Low* and *Heroes* purposely avoided. "D.J.," "Look Back in Anger," and "Boys Keep Swinging" have strong melodic hooks which are subverted and strengthened by the layered, dissonant productions, while the remainder of the record is divided between similarly effective avant-pop and ambient instrumentals. *Lodger* has an edgier, more minimalistic bent than its two predecessors, which makes it more accessible for rock fans, as well as giving it a more immediate, emotional impact. It might not stretch the boundaries of rock like *Low* and *Heroes*, but it arguably utilizes those ideas in a more effective fashion. *—Stephen Thomas Erlewine*

☆ **Scary Monsters (And Super Creeps)** / 1980 / Virgin ✦✦✦✦✦
Bowie returns to relatively conventional rock & roll with *Scary Monsters*, an album that effectively acts as an encapsulation of all his '70s experiments. Reworking glam rock themes with avant-garde synth flourishes, and reversing the process as well, Bowie creates dense but accessible music throughout *Scary Monsters*. Though it doesn't have the vision of his other classic records, it wasn't designed to break new ground—it was created as the culmination of Bowie's experimental genre-shifting of the '70s. As a result, *Scary Monsters* is Bowie's last great album. While the music isn't far removed from the post-punk of the early '80s, it does sound fresh, hip, and contemporary, which is something Bowie lost over the course of the '80s. [Rykodisc's 1992 reissue includes re-recorded versions of "Space Oddity" and "Panic in Detroit," the Japanese single "Crystal Japan," and the British single "Alabama Song."] *—Stephen Thomas Erlewine*

Let's Dance / 1983 / Virgin ✦✦✦
After summing up his maverick tendencies on *Scary Monsters*, David Bowie aimed for the mainstream *Let's Dance*. Hiring Chic bassist Nile Rodgers as a co-producer, Bowie created a stylish, synthesized post-disco dance music that was equally informed by classic soul and the emerging New Romantic subgenre of New Wave, which was ironically heavily inspired by Bowie himself. *Let's Dance* comes tearing out of the date, propulsed by the skittering "Modern Love," the seductively menacing "China Girl" and the brittle funk of the title track. All three songs became international hits, and for good reason—they are catchy, accessible pop songs that have just enough of an alien edge to make them distinctive. However, that careful balance is quickly thrown off by a succession of pleasant but unremarkable plastic soul workouts. "Cat People" and a cover of Metro's "Criminal World" are relatively strong songs, but the remainder of the album indicates the Bowie was entering a songwriting slump. However, the three hits were enough to make the album a massive hit, and their power hasn't diminished over the years, even if the rest of the record sounds like an artifact. *—Stephen Thomas Erlewine*

Tonight / 1984 / Virgin ✦✦

Never Let Me Down / 1987 / Virgin ✦✦

Sound + Vision / Sep. 1989 / Rykodisc ✦✦✦✦✦
Sound + Vision is a triple-disc box set designed to introduce Rykodisc's extensive reissue program of David Bowie's RCA albums. As a result, it has a number of idiosyncrasies that prevent it from becoming a definitive box set. Conceptually, the set was intended to showcase Rykodisc's remastering expertise, as well as the rarities lying in the vaults. Consequently, the song selection is targeted toward hardcore Bowie fans, ignoring such hits as "Jean Genie," "Starman," "Golden Years," and "Fame," among many others. However, there is an abundance of terrific rare material, including the demo for "Space Oddity," the *Man Who Sold the World* outtake "London Bye Ta-Ta," an alternate "John, I'm Only Dancing," the soulful *Young Americans* outtake "After Today," and a single version of "Rebel Rebel," which arguably is better than the more familiar version. However, such rarities and unpredictable selections ("Red Sails" but not "DJ" from *Lodger*, live versions of "Sufragette City," "Station to Station," and "Breaking Glass") mean that the set is neither a good introduction or compliment to *Changesbowie*. Instead, it's a good, if frustrating, curio piece for collectors. [The initial pressings of *Sound + Vision* included a bonus disc which contained a CD-video of "Ashes to Ashes," as well as three live tracks. It was replaced in 1995 with a CD-ROM of the same material.] *—Stephen Thomas Erlewine*

★ **Changesbowie** / Mar. 1990 / Rykodisc ✦✦✦✦✦
Changesbowie is CD greatest hits collection that revamps the original *Changesonebowie* by adding selections from Bowie's late '70s and early '80s albums. Consequently, it functions as a definitive single-disc introduction to David Bowie, featuring all of his major hits from "Space Oddity," "Changes," "Ziggy Stardust," "Jean Genie," and "Rebel Rebel" to "Heroes," "Ashes to Ashes," "Let's Dance," "Modern Love," and "Blue Jean." One complaint: it wasn't necessary to substitute the "Fame '90" remix for the original to hook completists, since it is inferior and was already issued as a separate single. *—Stephen Thomas Erlewine*

Early On (1964-1966) / 1991 / Rhino ✦✦

Black Tie White Noise / Oct. 1993 / Virgin ✦✦✦

☆ **Singles: 1969-1993** / Nov. 16, 1993 / Rykodisc ✦✦✦✦✦
Taking *Changesbowie* one step further, *Singles 1969-1993* collects all of David Bowie's biggest hits while picking up such overlooked gems as "Drive-In Saturday" and "Loving the Alien." The comprehensiveness and quality of the songs make *Singles* the best Bowie compilation available; fans will be pleased with the inclusion of the complete lyrics to all of the songs on this two-disc set. *—Stephen Thomas Erlewine*

Outside / Sep. 26, 1995 / Virgin ✦✦✦

The Deram Anthology 1966-1968 / 1997 / Deram ✦✦✦
Polygram's *The Deram Anthology 1966-1968* is the best packaging of Bowie's Anthony Newley-esque music-hall material in the CD era. The disc contains 27 tracks, including the infamous "The Laughing Gnome" and three tracks from the *Love You Till Tuesday* soundtrack that have previously gone unissued on CD, and it's lavishly assembled, with detailed liner notes and remastered sound. *—Stephen Thomas Erlewine*

Earthling / Feb. 11, 1997 / Virgin ✦✦✦

● **Best of David Bowie: 1969-1974** / Oct. 7, 1997 / Virgin ✦✦✦✦
Early in 1997, David Bowie sold the rights to his RCA catalog to EMI, and the first release to appear under the new agreement was *The Best of 1969-1974*, which was part of EMI's limited-edition 100th Birthday series. Instead of playing it straight, the 20-track set offers both the predictable classics—"The Jean Genie," "Space Oddity," "Starman," "Drive In Saturday," "Ziggy Stardust," "Suffragette City," "Changes," "Sorrow," "The Man Who Sold the World"—and relative obscurities, like the B-side "Velvet Goldmine," Bowie's version of "All the Young Dudes" and alternate takes of "John, I'm Only Dancing" and "The Prettiest Star." There are also album tracks like "Oh! You Pretty Things" and "Life on Mars" that have become classics, making *The Best of 1969-1974* an impressive, reasonably thorough overview of Bowie's glam years. *—Stephen Thomas Erlewine*

● **Best of David Bowie: 1974-1979** / Apr. 1998 / Virgin ✦✦✦✦
Picking up where EMI's first compilation, *The Best of David Bowie: 1969-74*, left off, *The Best of David Bowie: 1974-79* is an excellent 18-track overview of what are arguably Bowie's most creative years. During these five years, he moved from the stylized "Plastic Soul" of *Young Americans* to the cold, synthesized Berlin collaborations with Brian Eno, turning out some classic singles along the way ("Sound and Vision," "Golden Years," "Fame," "Young Americans," "TVC 15," "DJ," "Boys Keep Swinging," "Heroes"). Those hits, along with some strong album tracks, the discofied "John I'm Only Dancing (Again)" and the rarity "It's Hard to Be a Saint in the City," are all here. Unfortunately, the compilation wasn't sequenced in chronological order—although his range is impressive, it's even more astonishing when it's placed in the proper sequence. Nevertheless, *The Best of David Bowie: 1974-79* is a good summation of those five years and a nice companion piece to its predecessor, even if the double-disc *Singles* set or the concise *Changesbowie* are better career overviews. [Although *The Best of David Bowie: 1969-74* was released initially in the U.S., then in the U.K., this volume was released in Britain and not in America.] *—Stephen Thomas Erlewine*

Hours / Oct. 5, 1999 / Virgin ✦✦✦

Bowie at the Beeb: The Best of the BBC Radio Sessions / Sep. 26, 2000 / EMI ✦✦✦✦✦
Some collectors might complain that the double-disc *Bowie at the Beeb*, the first official collection of David Bowie's BBC Radio sessions, isn't complete, yet they likely have bootlegs of this material. All other fans are in for a real treat. Spanning from 1968 and 1972, these recordings find Bowie, if not in his prime, at least at a peak, as he developed from a swing-

ing Carnaby Street pop crooner to swaggering glam rock star. *Bowie at the Beeb* makes this era come alive. Opening with the lovely, florid "In the Heat of the Morning," the sessions spend time with David the Dandy before he delves into his dramatic heavy rock of the early '70s. That's where guitarist Mick Ronson made his public debut with Bowie at the session that comprises the middle of disc one. This is lean, powerful, terrific music, not as pummeling as *The Man Who Sold the World*, but it's slightly overshadowed by the session that concludes the first disc. It contains the bulk of rarities here, including the never-released "Looking for a Friend," a rollicking cover of Chuck Berry's "Almost Grown," a version of "It Ain't Easy" where Bowie trades verses with Geoffery Alexander and George Underwood, and a performance of the exquisite "Bombers." After a pair of songs by just Bowie and Ronson, the second disc finds the Spiders of Mars forming and quickly hitting its stride. Since this disc is largely devoted to recordings from 1972, it's a bit more consistent than the first, and it results in a live Spiders album better than any yet officially released. This may not be revelatory, yet this set is filled with wonderful music that deepens appreciation of Bowie's first great blast of creativity. Any true fan needs it in their collection. *—Stephen Thomas Erlewine*

The Box Tops

f. 1966, Memphis, TN, **db.** Feb. 1970

Group / Sunshine Pop, Blue-Eyed Soul, Pop

If you forget about the Rascals and the Righteous Brothers, the Memphis-based Box Tops are the finest blue-eyed soul group. Lead singer (and former Big Star honcho) Alex Chilton had a tough, swaggering voice that belied his teenage years, sounding at times as if he were in a cutting match with the young Steve Winwood. Producers Chips Moman and Dan Penn surrounded Chilton with a crack American studio band, giving the music more muscle and deep funk than you'll ever find in "Mary Mary."

Instead of knocking off pimply, lightweight teen-fodder, the Box Tops managed to add another link in the Memphis soul chain, mixing blues, Beatlesque pop, and the sound of Stax, Hi, and Goldwax. And unlike the Monkees, the Box Tops benefited from top-notch material: Dan Penn and Spooner Oldham's "Cry Like a Baby" and "I Met Her in Church"; Wayne Thompson's "The Letter" and "Soul Deep"; and the occasional Chilton-penned nugget, such as "I Must Be the Devil." The group's heyday was brief—two years, tops—but their music remains a staple on oldies stations and has retained its vitality for over two decades. *—John Floyd*

● **The Best of the Box Tops: Soul Deep** / Oct. 1, 1996 / Arista ✦✦✦✦✦

This compilation boasts "20-bit digital mastering from the original master tapes," if that matters to you. Audiophile considerations aside, it's the best anthology of the group, the 18 songs including all of the hits and their best LP-only tracks. Their credentials as the best pop-oriented blue-eyed soul group fly high, with occasional glimpses of something rootsier, especially the bluesy, Chilton-penned "I Must Be the Devil," which has one of his grittiest vocals. Another high-caliber Chilton original, "(The) Happy Song," affords a glimpse of his lighter, poppier aspirations. *—Richie Unterberger*

Boyz II Men

f. 1988, Philadelphia, PA

Group / New Jack Swing, Club/Dance, Adult Contemporary, Urban

Under the guidance of Michael Bivins of Bell Biv Devoe, the four-man vocal group Boyz II Men became a pop sensation in 1992. Although they call their music "hip-hop doo wop," there's very little traditional doo wop in it. Instead, they bring the sound of '60s and early-'70s R&B vocal groups into the '90s, adding a little New Jack swing to that timeless sound. Their 1991 debut, *Cooleyhighharmony*, featured a massive hit single, "Motownphilly" which exemplifies the best of their dance work. Their second single, a ballad called "It's So Hard to Say Goodbye," was an even bigger hit; its success paved the way for "The End of the Road" (taken from the *Boomerang* soundtrack), the group's follow-up single, which broke Elvis Presley's record for the most weeks spent at number one. After releasing a Christmas album in 1993, Boyz II Men went to work on their second album, which appeared in the fall of 1994. *II* proved to be even more successful than its predecessor, selling over seven million copies by summer of 1995 and spawning the record-breaking hit "I'll Make Love to You." *Evolution* followed in 1997 and their long-awaited fourth album *Nathan Michael Shawn Wanya* was issued three years later. *—Stephen Thomas Erlewine*

Cooleyhighharmony / Nov. 2, 1993 / Motown ✦✦✦✦✦

Boyz II Men's retro sound dominated the 1991 pop and R&B marketplaces, with their singles "It's So Hard to Say Goodbye to Yesterday" and "Motownphilly" hitting the Top Ten on both charts. The album eventually sold over five million copies and put Boyz II Men at the forefront of a movement returning the emphasis in Black popular music to vocal harmonies and a cappella interaction. *—Ron Wynn*

● **II** / Aug. 30, 1994 / Motown ✦✦✦✦✦

With their second album, Boyz II Men assured their place at the top of the charts, as well as history. "I'll Make Love to You," the album's first single, stayed on the top of the charts for over two months, only to be unseated by "On Bended Knee," the album's second single. Not surprisingly, *II* is a carefully constructed crowd pleaser, accentuating all of the finest moments from their hit debut. While there are some high-energy dance tracks, the album's main strength is its slower numbers, where the group's vocals soar. *—Stephen Thomas Erlewine*

Evolution / Sep. 23, 1997 / Motown ✦✦✦

Nathan Michael Shawn Wanya / Sep. 12, 2000 / Uptown/Universal ✦✦✦✦

Billy Bragg

b. Dec. 20, 1957, Barking, Essex, England

Vocals, Guitar / College Rock, Alternative Folk, British Folk, Alternative Pop/Rock, Singer/Songwriter, Urban Folk

Finding inspiration in the righteous anger of punk rock and the socially conscious folk tradition of Woody Guthrie and Bob Dylan, Billy Bragg was the leading figure of the anti-folk movement of the '80s. For most of the decade, Bragg bashed out songs alone on his electric guitar, singing about politics and love. While his lyrics were bitingly intelligent and clever, they were also warm and humane, filled with detail and wit. Even though his lyrics were carefully considered, Bragg never neglected to write melodies for songs that were strong and memorable. His first LP, 1984's *Brewing Up with Billy Bragg*, climbed to number 16 in the charts and Bragg soon became a minor celebrity in Britain, appearing at leftist political rallies, strikes, and benefits across the country. Featuring some subtle instrumental additions of piano and horns, 1986's *Talking to the Taxman About Poetry* reached the UK Top Ten. The singer recorded with a full band for the first time on 1988's *Workers Playtime* and three years later, again worked with a full band to record his most pop-oriented and accessible set of songs, *Don't Try This at Home* (featuring the hit single, "Sexuality"). Bragg took several years off but returned in 1996 with *William Bloke*. In 1998, he teamed with the American alternative country band Wilco to record *Mermaid Avenue*, a collection of performances based on unreleased songs originally written by Woody Guthrie. *—Stephen Thomas Erlewine*

Life's a Riot with Spy Vs Spy / 1983 / Go! Discs/Utility ✦✦✦✦✦

Brewing Up / 1984 / Go! Discs ✦✦✦✦✦

Between the Wars / 1985 / Go! Discs ✦✦✦✦✦

Talking with the Taxman About Poetry / 1986 / Go! Discs/Elektra ✦✦✦✦✦

Bragg's one-man approach is fleshed out on *Talking with the Taxman About Poetry*, his second long-player. "Levi Stubb's Tears" and "The Marriage" include subtle percussion and horn flourishes; "Greetings to the New Brunette" is cushioned in layers of overdubbed acoustic guitars. That makes it Bragg's most satisfying album musically, but the witty, plaintive songs listed above—in addition to "Ideology" and "The Warmest Room"—make it a stirring and evocative lyrical statement as well. *—John Floyd*

● **Back to Basics** / 1987 / Go! Discs/Elektra ✦✦✦✦✦

This disc brings together Bragg's first three releases (*Life's a Riot with Spy vs. Spy, Brewing Up with Billy Bragg*, and the *Between the Wars* EP) and offers the best introduction to his confessional songwriting and uncompromising politics. Highlights include "A New England" and "A Lover Sings." *—John Floyd*

Workers Playtime / 1988 / Go! Discs/Elektra ✦✦✦

Bragg's first attempt at working with a full band could be better—most of the songs are mopey and depressing, and some of his socialist manifestos are tiresome and dogmatic. Still, cuts like "She's Got a New Spell," "Must I Paint You a Picture," and "Little Time Bomb" are excellent, and "Waiting for the Great Leap Forward" is a humble and humorous explanation of Bragg's motives and intentions, both political and emotional. *—John Floyd*

The Internationale / Jun. 1990 / Utility/Elektra ✦✦

Don't Try This at Home / Sep. 17, 1991 / Go! Discs/Elektra ✦✦✦✦✦

With full-blown production by the likes of Johnny Marr, and with musical assistance from R.E.M., this would seem like a blatant stab at the post-modern marketplace. Maybe so, but the thrust of his band turns "Accident Waiting to Happen" and "North Sea Bubble" into throttling rockers and makes "Sexuality" his best single. There are also several gorgeous ballads, "Tank Park Salute" and "Wish You Were Here" among them. *—John Floyd*

William Bloke / Sep. 9, 1996 / Elektra ✦✦✦

Following the release of *Don't Try This At Home*, Billy Bragg went into seclusion for five years, as he raised his young child. *William Bloke* reflects a newfound maturity for Bragg, as he tones down his attack and returns to simple, acoustic-based arrangements. Though there are a few songs that are infused with his trademark leftist politics, most of *William Bloke* is comprised of songs about fatherhood and maturity, which are warm, compassionate and melodic. In short, it's the sound of urban folk settling into adulthood without dreading its responsibilities. *—Stephen Thomas Erlewine*

Mermaid Avenue / Jun. 23, 1998 / Elektra ✦✦✦✦

During the spring of 1995, Woody Guthrie's daughter Nora contacted British urban folk troubadour Billy Bragg about writing music for a selection of completed Guthrie lyrics. This was no minor task—Guthrie left behind over a thousand sets of complete lyrics written between 1939 and 1967 that had no music other than a vague stylistic notation. Bragg chose a number of songs to finish, as did Jeff Tweedy of the alt-country band Wilco (often with bandmate Jay Bennett). Nora Guthrie impressed a common goal upon them: Rather than recreating Guthrie tunes, they should write as if they were collaborating with Woody, creating new, vital music for the lyrics. Both artists completed more songs than could fit on *Mermaid Avenue*, which is neatly split between Bragg and Wilco, with Bragg taking lead on eight of the 15 songs. The results are almost entirely a delight, mainly because all involved are faithful to Guthrie's rowdy spirit—it's a reverent project that knows how to have fun. There are many minor, irresistible gems scattered throughout the album, and most of them come from Bragg. Where Wilco's fine contributions sound inextricably tied to the '90s, both for better and for worse, Bragg's music sounds contemporary while capturing Guthrie's folk traditions. That's not to say Wilco's contributions are failures—it's just hard to imagine Guthrie singing the plaintive "California Stars" or the plodding "Christ for President," neither of which quite fit the lyrics. Nevertheless, their hearts are in the right place; more often than not, they come close to the target, and their joyous playing invigorates *Mermaid Avenue*. The blend of Bragg's traditionalist sensibility and Wilco's contemporary style ultimately illustrates that Guthrie's words, ideals, and aesthetics remain alive in the '90s. It's a remarkable record that deserves a sequel. *—Stephen Thomas Erlewine*

Reaching to the Converted / Aug. 31, 1999 / Rhino ✦✦✦✦

Rhino's *Reaching to the Converted* collects 17 non-LP cuts Billy Bragg released between 1985 and 1997, including singles, B-sides, and compilation album contributions, along with the previously unreleased "Shirley," a 1992 re-recording of "Greetings to the New Brunette," which features Johnny Marr. Some hardcore fans will have nearly all of the material presented here, yet they'll still want this collection, not only because it provides a bunch of rarities in a simple package, but because it is a thoroughly engaging and entertaining listen. —*Stephen Thomas Erlewine*

Mermaid Avenue, Vol. 2 / May 30, 2000 / Elektra ✦✦✦
Like many sequels, *Mermaid Avenue, Vol. 2* isn't the equal of its predecessor—that felt fully realized, where this feels a little patchwork—yet it is still satisfying on many levels. As on the first, the Billy Bragg-written and sung music is the most convincing since he captures the cadences and spirit of Guthrie's music. They sound like classic, weathered folk songs whereas Wilco's numbers are modern inventions, splicing music that is clearly theirs with Guthrie's words. The chasm between the two artists was apparent on the first, but it's more evident this time around, largely due to the fact that several of Wilco's songs were recorded without Bragg after the release of *Mermaid Avenue*. This gives the record a strangely disjointed feel that isn't helped by the guest appearances by Natalie Merchant on "I Was Born" and Corey Harris whose vocals overpower "Aginst th' Law." Since Bragg and Wilco are pursuing slightly different directions in the first place, the guest artists only add to the patchwork quality of the record. Still, even with its weaknesses, there are plenty of worthwhile things here from both sides of the spectrum. If Wilco occasionally is a little too somber or introspective, they do have moments where everything aligns perfectly. But, as on the first, it's the Bragg-led numbers that truly catch fire, feeling every bit as warm, funny, and vibrant as Guthrie's best work. His contributions go a long way to making *Mermaid Avenue, Vol. 2* a pleasing sequel. —*Stephen Thomas Erlewine*

Toni Braxton

b. Oct. 7, 1967
Vocals / Contemporary R&B, Adult Contemporary, Urban
Toni Braxton made her vocal debut with the single "Love Shoulda Brought You Home" from the *Boomerang* soundtrack. She issued her first full album in 1993, and it soared to the top of both the pop and R&B charts. Braxton eventually earned two Grammy and two Soul Train awards, saw her self-titled release go platinum, and also reaped both critical and commercial plaudits for such singles as "Love Shoulda Brought You Home" and "Just Another Sad Love Song." In the summer of 1996, Braxton released her second album, *Secrets*, which entered the charts at number two and produced the number one single, "You're Makin' Me High." *Heat* followed in the spring of 2000. —*Ron Wynn*

● **Toni Braxton** / Jul. 1993 / La Face ✦✦✦✦✦
Toni Braxton is both an elegant and earthy songstress, nicely balancing those seemingly divergent sentiments on her self-titled debut disc. Braxton's husky, enticing voice sounds hypnotic on "Breathe Again," dismayed on "Another Sad Love Song" and disillusioned on "Love Shoulda Brought You Home." But she's never out of control, indignant or so anguished and hurt that she fails to retain her dignity. It's a sign of how great the Babyface/L.A. Reid production team was that they didn't settle for a defining mood; they presented Braxton with enough diverse emotional settings to hold the interest of urban contemporary males and females. —*Ron Wynn*

Secrets / Jun. 18, 1996 / La Face ✦✦✦✦✦
Toni Braxton's second album, *Secrets*, follows through on the promise of her eponymous debut. Like her first album, the majority of *Secrets* was co-produced by Babyface and his partner L.A. Reid, while the material is divided between songs written by outside songwriters like R. Kelly, Tony Rich, and Diane Warren and originals by Braxton and Babyface. Braxton and Babyface's collaborations are the highlights of the album, combining rich melodies and gorgeous choruses with subtle, clever lyrics that are never laced with clichés. Nearly equalling the original numbers are contributions by Tony Rich ("Come On Over Here") and R. Kelly ("I Don't Want To"); with these tracks, both musicians demonstrate why they are considered two of the top songwriters in '90s R&B and soul. *Secrets* does have a couple of weak moments. The numbers produced by David Foster are too predictable in their slick commercial appeal, but Braxton manages to infuse the songs with life and passion that elevates them beyond their generic confines. And her vocal talent is what unites *Secrets* and makes it into a first-rate contemporary R&B collection. Braxton is a singer who can cross over into the smooth confines of adult contemporary radio without losing or betraying the soul that lies at the foundation of her music, and her talent burns at its brightest on *Secrets*. —*Stephen Thomas Erlewine*

The Heat / Apr. 25, 2000 / La Face ✦✦✦✦
Toni Braxton went through a lot in the years separating her star-making *Toni* and her 2000 comeback *The Heat*. Yes, she became a star, but she also went through a painful bankruptcy that delayed her sequel for years. Fortunately, you wouldn't be able to tell that there was so much behind-the-scenes drama from *The Heat*—it's a confident, assured, sexy effort that reaffirms Braxton's status as one of the finest contemporary mainstream soul singers. She may not be as street-smart as Mary J. Blige, nor does she push the boundaries of the genre the way TLC does, but she has a full, rich voice that instantly lends her songs a sense of maturity and sensuality, especially since she never, ever over-sings or misjudges her material. And, while that material can occasionally be a little generic, much of *The Heat* is built on solid ballads and smoldering, midtempo dance numbers. Producers as diverse as Babyface, Rodney Jerkins, Daryl Simmons, Teddy Bishop, and David Foster are responsible for various tracks on the album, which is typical for a big-budget, superstar release like this, but rarely are the tracks quite as consistent and cohesive as they are here. The skittering beats of "He Wasn't Man Enough" and "Gimme Some" are every bit as effective as the simmering title track or ballads "I'm Still Breathing" and "Spanish Guitar"—or "Just Be a Man About It," an instant classic telephone break-up song, with Dr. Dre playing the wayward lover breaking the news to Ms. Braxton. True, *The Heat* slightly runs out of momentum toward the end, but there aren't many dull spots on the record—it's all stylish, sultry, seductive, appealing urban contemporary soul that confirms Braxton's prodigious talents. —*Stephen Thomas Erlewine*

Bread

f. 1968, Los Angeles, CA, **db.** 1977
Group / Soft Rock
Bread was one of the most popular pop groups of the early '70s, earning a string of well-crafted, melodic soft-rock singles, all of which were written by keyboardist/vocalist David Gates. Gates met guitarist/vocalist James Griffin in 1968, and recorded a self-titled debut for Elektra by the end of the year. Their second album, *On the Waters*, established Bread as hit-makers with the number one single "Make It with You" and the Top Ten hit "It Don't Matter to Me" (actually taken from *Bread*). In 1971, *Manna* launched another Top Ten single with "If," but the group then hit with "Baby I'm-A Want You," which peaked at number three. At the beginning of 1973, Bread disbanded after a songwriting dispute between Gates and Griffin, but reunited three years later with one last Top Ten hit, "Lost Without Your Love." After Griffin left in 1977, Gates assembled a new version of Bread, leading to a lawsuit over the name that wasn't resolved until 1984. Both pursued solo careers, with Gates gaining the upper hand courtesy of a Top 20 hit, 1978's "Goodbye Girl." —*Stephen Thomas Erlewine*

The Best of Bread / 1972 / Elektra ✦✦✦✦
As *The Best of Bread* unfolds, its 12 tracks begin to tell a tale of two different types of bands. The first half dozen songs, all of which were composed by leader David Gates, are each studies in soft pop perfection. On these two- and three-minute gems, Gates crafts soaring, evocative melodies that can stand against rock's finest. And though these songs' lyrics tend toward sentimentality, the band offers enough tasteful instrumentation to prevent them from slipping into easy listening melodramatics. Though there are no such concerns for the album's second half, Bread's more aggressive approach is not nearly as compelling. Certainly, tunes like "Mother Freedom" are appealing, middle-of-the-road rockers, but they lack the polished, melodic sophistication of their gentler counterparts. —*Brian Christopher Egan*

● **Anthology** / 1985 / Elektra ✦✦✦✦✦
This is the definitive collection for these soft rock giants of the early '70s. Contained within are all of their hits, plus some delectable gems unknown to those familiar with Bread only from the radio. This set begins with "Make It with You," and which hit the number one spot in 1970, and ends with the group's last Top Ten hit, "Lost Without Your Love" from their reunion album of 1977. Other Top Ten hits include "If," "Baby I'm-a Want You," "Everything I Own," "It Don't Matter to Me," and "Guitar Man," which reached number 11. The popular songs have held up well, but perhaps the most interesting cuts here are the lesser-known ones, like "Dismal Day," "Down on My Knees," and "The Last Time." David Gates and company had quite a run, and this anthology shows why. —*Jim Newsom*

Retrospective / Jul. 1996 / Rhino ✦✦✦✦✦
Retrospective is the definitive compilation of Bread, perhaps the definitive soft-rock group of the '70s. If anything, it may be too comprehensive for most listeners. Covering the entire course of Bread's career, plus selected highlights from David Gates in the late '70s and early '80s, the compilation spans two very full compact discs. For those who want more than the hits but are unwilling to delve into individual albums, the collection is ideal. Listeners who want the hits might find the album tracks a little tedious. Then again, the presence of Gates' solo hits like "The Goodbye Girl" is enticing for even casual fans, since he lacks a solo compilation and there are no sets that cover both his solo career and Bread. Since *Retrospective* does cover all the Bread hits plus solid obscurities and Gates' solo highlights, it does qualify as the definitive collection. In fact, it's hard to imagine how another set could be as thorough as this. —*Stephen Thomas Erlewine*

The Breeders

f. 1988, Dayton, OH
Group / Indie Rock, Alternative Pop/Rock
One of alternative rock's most promising—and frustrating—groups, the Breeders began as a way for Pixies' bassist Kim Deal and Throwing Muses' guitarist Tanya Donelly to escape their second-banana status. After Donelly left to form Belly, the group achieved massive success with the hit "Cannonball," but the group seemed stuck in limbo during the late '90s, playing a handful of dates and releasing even fewer songs. Deal, Donelly, Perfect Disaster's Josephine Wiggs, and Slint's Britt Walford played on 1990's *Pod*, their critically acclaimed debut album. Donelly left after 1992's *Safari* EP and was replaced by Kim's sister Kelley; the EP also featured drummer Jim MacPherson, who was billed as "Mike Hunt." In 1993, the Pixies split and the Breeders released *Last Splash*, which featured the breakthrough single "Cannonball." *Last Splash* earned platinum sales and the band played 1994's *Lollapalooza*, but as quickly they became stars, the Breeders went on hiatus, exhausted by their sudden fame and extensive touring. Late in 1994, Kelley was arrested for drug possession and went to a Minnesota rehab clinic. Wiggs formed the Josephine Wiggs Experience, and Kim returned to Dayton with MacPherson and formed the Amps. After rehab, Kelley formed the Kelley Deal 6000, and Kim played and recorded under the Breeders name again. Kelley rejoined the band in 1998; the only song to surface from their sessions was a cover of 3 Degrees' "Collage," which appeared on *The Mod Squad* soundtrack. In 2000, the Deals recorded with Steve Albini and played a secret show in Los Angeles. A new Breeders record was expected sometime in 2001 but seemed unlikely, given the group's unpredictable history. —*Stephen Thomas Erlewine & Heather Phares*

● **Pod** / 1990 / 4AD/Elektra ✦✦✦✦✦
On their 1990 debut album *Pod*, the Breeders—led by the Pixies' Kim Deal and Throwing Muses' Tanya Donelly—prove that they have more potential, and more fun, than the average side project. In fact, thanks to the album's creative songwriting, immediate production (courtesy of *Surfer Rosa* producer Steve Albini), and clever arrangements, *Pod* is a fresher and more successful work than the Pixies' *Bossanova* and the Muses' *Hunkpapa*, their main projects' releases from around that time. Though the album doesn't feature as many of Donelly's contributions as was originally planned—which was part of the reason she formed Belly a few years later—songs like "Iris" and "Lime House" blend the best of the Pixies' elliptical punk and the Muses' angular pop. *Pod* reaffirms what a distinctive

songwriter Deal is, and how much the Pixies missed out on by not including more of her material on their albums. With their unusual subjects—"Hellbound" is about a living abortion—and quirky-but-direct sound, songs like "Opened" and "When I Was a Painter" could have easily fit on *Doolittle* or *Bossanova.* But the spare, sensual "Doe," "Fortunately Gone," and "Only in Threes" are more lighthearted and good-natured than the work of Deal's other band, pointing the way to the sexy, clever alternative pop she'd craft on *Last Splash.* A vibrantly creative debut, *Pod* remains the Breeders' most genuine moment. —*Heather Phares*

Safari / 1992 / 4AD/Elektra ♦♦♦

Last Splash / Aug. 31, 1993 / 4AD/Elektra ♦♦♦♦
Thanks to good timing and some great singles, the Breeders' second album, *Last Splash,* turned them into the alternative rock stars that Kim Deal's former band, the Pixies, always seemed on the verge of becoming. Building on *Safari*'s driving, polished sound, *Last Splash* is half-brilliant singles and half-unfinished, uninspired ideas. When it's good, it's very, very good: "Cannonball"'s instantly catchy collage of bouncy bass, rhythmic stops and starts, and singsong vocals; the sweetly sexy "Divine Hammer"; and swaggering "Saints" are among the Breeders' finest moments, and deserved all of the airplay they received. And the charming country-pop of "Drivin' on 9," "I Just Wanna Get Along"'s spiky punk-pop, and the bittersweet "Invisible Man" proved *Last Splash* had a bit of depth. But underdeveloped snippets such as "Roi" and "No Aloha" drag down the album's momentum; likewise, the band tries to stretch their range on the rambling, cryptic "Mad Lucas" and "Hag," but neither quite comes together as a full-fledged song. Though instrumentals such as "S.O.S." and "Flipside" showcase the Breeders' chops and some nifty production tricks, they feel like filler; worst of all, *Last Splash* features an inferior, plodding new version of *Safari*'s soaring "Do You Love Me Now" that emphasizes the album's unevenness. One of the definitive alternative rock albums of the '90s, *Last Splash* is equally inspired and infuriating; that it was the Breeders' last album of that decade makes it even more frustrating. —*Heather Phares*

Brinsley Schwarz

f. Oct. 1969, England, **db.** 1975
Group / Pub Rock, Country-Rock, Rock & Roll
Pub rock, the English roots-rock movement of the early '70s, would never have earned a cult following if it wasn't for Brinsley Schwarz. Initially, Brinsley Schwarz was a rambling, neo-psychedelic folk-rock band, who borrowed heavily from Crosby, Stills & Nash and the Grateful Dead. Following a disaterous publicity stunt to promote their debut album, the band went into seclusion outside of London and developed a laid-back, rootsy sound inspired by Eggs Over Easy, an American band who had been playing a mixture of originals and covers in English pubs. Following their conversion to pub rock, the Brinsleys ditched their pretensions of stardom and became a down-to-earth, self-effacing rock & roll band. Between 1971 and 1974, Brinsley Schwarz toured England innumerable times, playing pubs across the country. Along the way, they established a circuit for similar bands like Dr. Feelgood and Ducks Deluxe to follow. Though the group was nominally guitarist Brinsley Schwarz's band, bassist/lead vocalist Nick Lowe provided the bulk of the group's songs. Lowe developed a distinctive songwriting voice—conversational, melodic, off-beat, and funny—and the band was infused with his skewed sense of humor. Despite strong reviews and a dedicated fan base, the Brinsleys never managed to escape cult status, yet they influenced a legion of other artists, creating an underground, back-to-basics movement that laid the foundation for punk rock. —*Stephen Thomas Erlewine*

Brinsley Schwarz / 1970 / One Way ♦♦♦
Brinsley Schwarz's eponymous debut is the stuff of rock legend because it is the punch line to a great story. It arrived after a disastrous publicity blitz, where the band's management arranged for prominent British journalists to cross the ocean to hear the Brinsleys' showcase performance at the *Fillmore East.* In a series of mishaps that would shame Spinal Tap, the band arrived in New York hours before their show and the journalists, who dipped heavily into the courtesy bar when their plane nearly crashed, arrived minutes before the concert. The press was underwhelmed to say the least and savaged the band and the record. Listening to *Brinsley Schwarz,* it's easy to see why they weren't turned on by the Brinsleys: this is a bizarre, naïve blend of Crosby, Stills & Nash, Dylan & the Band, and Buffalo Springfield, with a heavy dose of early Yes. It's filled with awkward steps and bad judgments, fueled by the group's romanticized view of Californian hippies. Consequently, it's hard not cringe or chuckle by their hippie affectations, whether it's the lyrics ("she was my lady/had no plans to make her my wife") or the a cappella folk-rock harmonies that come out of nowhere on "Lady Constant" (it doesn't help that they sing "colored serpent coiled around your waist") or the bongo solo that ends "Shining Brightly." But, amidst all this hippie posturing, there some weird touches, like the multi-octave chromatic guitar break on "Hymn to Me" or the heavy prog jam of "What Do You Suggest?" and "Ballad of a Has-Been Beauty Queen" that illustrates how English the Brinsleys still were at this stage. All of this adds up to a debut that's decidedly uneven and unsure, but in retrospect, it's easy for sympathetic listeners to be charmed by their eccentricities. —*Stephen Thomas Erlewine*

Despite It All / 1970 / Liberty ♦♦♦
Brinsley Schwarz was hit hard by the terrible performance of their debut, so they rented a communal house and concentrated on becoming a real, organic band. They also recorded a second album swiftly, releasing *Despite It All* by the end of 1970. As soon as the folksy, fiddle-driven "Country Girl" amiably ambles out of the gates, the difference between the two records is apparent. They tried this kind of rootsy country-rock before, but it sounded awkward. Here, it rings true, not just because the songwriting is stronger, but because the band knows what they're doing, adding real grit and passion to the performances. *Despite It All* benefits from this looser playing, and for a while, it sounds like the group accomplished everything it wanted to do, since the first three songs are all early Nick Lowe masterpieces—"Country Girl," the fine ballad "The Slow One" and the flat-out terrific "Funk Angel," which is the first real flowering of his gifts as a pop tunesmith and sly humorist. After this, the record doesn't go off the rails, but it slowly loses its momentum, deteriorating to pleasant aping of CSN and Band plus the prog-inflected jams that were the bane of their debut. Some of this works—"Love Song" is a sweet tune, "Ebury Down" has a campfire charm—but when it ends with the drawn-out "Old Jarrow" (which does boasts the timeless question "why don't you financially back her?" in its refrain) it's clear that the group is still in the process of finding of its voice. Their stumbles are brought into perspective by those three wonderful songs that begin the album, which not only make the record, but prove that the group does indeed have greatness in them. —*Stephen Thomas Erlewine*

☆ **Nervous on the Road** / 1972 / United Artists ♦♦♦♦♦
Silver Pistol wrote the blueprint for Brinsley Schwarz's pub rock, but *Nervous on the Road* perfected their sound, becoming the definitive pub rock band in the process. *Nervous on the Road* has a fuller, more detailed production than its predecessor, as well as a looser feeling—even with the smooth production, it sounds like the band was captured on a good night at the *Tally Ho.* But what really makes the record is its excellent selection of songs, almost all of which are written by Nick Lowe. "Happy Doing What We're Doing," "Surrender to the Rhythm," and "Nervous on the Road" are all great rock & roll songs about rock & roll, spiked with an off-kilter sense of humor. "Don't Lose Your Grip on Love" is Lowe's first great ballad, while Ian Gomm's "It's Been So Long" is one of his best songs. And the covers of "I Like It Like That" and "Home In My Hand" are wonderful pub-rockers, and help give the album the feeling of an excellent concert. Nevertheless, what makes *Nervous on the Road* such a fine record is the combination of empathatic performances, unpredictable songwriting and a charming unpretentiousness, all of which help make the album one of the great forgotten rock & roll records. —*Stephen Thomas Erlewine*

Silver Pistol / 1972 / Edsel ♦♦♦♦♦
Silver Pistol isn't the definitive pub rock album, but it is the first great record to surface from the scene. Like much of the first wave of pub rock, *Silver Pistol* is quiet, laid-back, and low-key—with its warm, rustic sound and a gentleness that infuses even the rockers, this is the closest to the Band that the Brinsleys got. There are some major differences, most of them coming from Nick Lowe. That's not to denigrate new guitarist/songwriter Ian Gomm, since his four numbers (particularly "Dry Land" and "Range War") reveal a fine songwriter with a keen sense of melody and a knack for synthesizing country, rock, and folk into something distinctive, but Lowe really hits his stride with this record. This is in to some degree due to the influence of Jim Ford, a renegade American roots-rocker who Brinsley Schwarz backed on an unreleased and subsequently lost 1971 album. The group covers two of his songs, "Niki Hoeke Speedway" and "Ju Ju Man," on *Silver Pistol,* and these numbers reveal the appealingly off-kilter sense of humor and pop hooks that would form the foundation of Lowe's style. Those sensibilities are just beginning to creep into his songwriting on *Silver Pistol,* on the Beatles-meets-Band "Unknown Number," the lovely "Nightingale," the wonderful pop tune "The Last Time I Was Fooled," and the epic "Silver Pistol." His other two songs are sturdy country-rock numbers a notch below Gomm's best on the record, but still very good, and it all adds up to an endearing low-key roots rock album that doesn't just find Brinsley Schwarz coming into their own, it stands as one of the most appealing records of its kind. —*Stephen Thomas Erlewine*

Please Don't Ever Change / 1973 / Edsel ♦♦♦♦
Released in 1973 as Brinsley Schwarz were busy touring and recording the followup to *Nervous on the Road, Please Don't Ever Change* is a collection of singles, live cuts, and radio sessions from the early '70s. The odds-and-sods nature of the record actually works in its favor, since it accentuates the group's ramshackle nature. Sure, there's a fair amount of filler on the record—their ill-advised reggae excursion "The Version (Hypocrite)" is simply mystifying—but unevenness was part of the Brinsley's charm, and the simply enjoyable cuts make the best tracks feel like classics. And some of them are definitive Brinsley cuts. "I Worry ('bout You Baby)" is a revamped R&B number, the live "Home in My Hand" speeds along with a relentless energy, the cover of Goffin/King's "Don't Ever Change" indicates Nick Lowe's latent pop roots, "Down in Mexico" is a hysterical travelogue and "Play That Fast Thing (One More Time)" is among the classic pub rock singles, distilling the essence of pub rock into one piledriving song. —*Stephen Thomas Erlewine*

New Favourites of Brinsley Schwarz / 1974 / United Artists ♦♦♦♦♦
With their final album, Brinsley Schwarz turn in their most pop-oriented record, filled with infectious gems like "The Ugly Things," "Trying to Live My Life Without You," and "(What's So Funny 'bout) Peace, Love and Understanding." Lowe's songs were the best he had ever written and show that his ambitions were beginning to conflict with those of the rest of the band. Nevertheless, there isn't a weak song or uninspired performance on *New Favourites,* making it an excellent farewell album. —*Stephen Thomas Erlewine*

★ **Nervous on the Road/The New Favourites of Brinsley Schwarz** / 1975 / BGO ♦♦♦♦♦

☆ **Surrender to the Rhythm** / 1991 / EMI ♦♦♦♦♦
The 20-track compilation *Surrender to the Rhythm* is an excellent retrospective of Brinsley Schwarz's career. The compilation is culled from each of the group's albums, touching lightly on their earlier records and drawing heavily from *Silver Pistol, Nervous on the Road,* and *The New Favourites,* which is appropriate, since they were the stronger records. Although *Nervous on the Road* remains a necessary album, *Surrender to the Rhythm* compiles nearly every one of the Brinsleys' greatest tracks, including "Country Girl," "Ju Ju Man," "Down in Mexico," "Play That Fast Thing (One More Time)," "Happy Doing What We're Doing," "Don't Lose Your Grip on Love," "The Ugly Things," a ripping live version of "Home in My Hand," and the original version of Nick Lowe's classic "(What's So Funny 'Bout) Peace, Love and Understanding." *Surrender to the Rhythm* offers convincing evidence that Brinsley Schwarz is one of the great underrated bands of the early '70s, while essentially summing up the spirit of pub rock. —*Stephen Thomas Erlewine*

The Brothers Johnson

f. 1975, Los Angeles, CA
Group / Pop/Rock, Funk, Soul
Led by guitarist/vocalist George Johnson and bassist/vocalist Louis Johnson, in 1973 the Brothers Johnson were hired by Quincy Jones to play on his LP *Mellow Madness;* Jones also recorded four of their songs, including "Is It Love That We're Missing?" and "Just a Taste of Me." Jones also took them on a Japanese tour, then produced their debut LP, *Look Out for Number 1,* after they signed with A&M, which was also his label at the time (1976). They scored a number-one R&B and number-three pop hit with "I'll Be Good to You," and enjoyed R&B chart toppers in 1977 and 1980 respectively with "Strawberry Letter 23" and "Stomp!," while sustaining a consistent hit presence via such songs as "Get the Funk Out Ma Face" and "Runnin' for Your Lovin." The Brothers earned platinum records for *Look Out for Number 1* and *Right on Time.* The group produced its single "The Real Thing" in 1981. It reached number 11 on the R&B charts, and the Brothers had another hit with "Welcome to the Club" in 1982. *—Ron Wynn*

● **Greatest Hits** / Jun. 18, 1996 / A&M ✦✦✦✦
Greatest Hits contains all of the Brothers Johnson's biggest singles, including the gold singles "I'll Be Good to You" and "Strawberry Letter 23." In addition to all the familiar hits, there are some lesser-known singles that are nearly as good, making this single-disc compilation the definitive retrospective. *—Stephen Thomas Erlewine*

Arthur Brown

b. Jun. 24, 1944, Whitby, Yorkshire, England
Vocals / British Psychedelia, Psychedelic
One of the most electrifying one-shot artists of the '60s, British singer Arthur Brown briefly set the charts alight in 1968, as well as thrilling audiences with his theatrical performances, which saw him wearing helmets of fire and outlandish costumes. His debut album was surely one of the most left-field commercial successes of the late '60s, if not of rock history. Besides topping the British charts (and reaching number two in the U.S.) with his brilliantly demonic single "Fire," the self-proclaimed god of hellfire actually scored a Top Ten LP with his 1968 debut. Unveiling Arthur's demented, fire-obsessed lyrical visions and swooping, theatrical vocals, it showcased his band's manic, agitated psychedelic sound, which was anchored by incendiary drumming, Pete Townshend's production, and an organist who could be best described as Jimmy Smith on acid. Brown's original band broke up in early 1969; in the early '70s, he released several albums with Kingdom Come, which saw him pursuing a maddeningly obscure, and less exciting, brand of arty rock. He's recorded off and on since, but his last flash of fame was his role as a priest in the film version of *Tommy.* *—Richie Unterberger*

● **Crazy World of Arthur Brown** / 1968 / Polydor ✦✦✦✦✦
Though a bit over-the-top, this album was still powerful and surprisingly melodic, and managed to be quite bluesy and soulful even as the band overhauled chestnuts by James Brown and Screamin' Jay Hawkins. "Spontaneous Apple Creation" is a willfully histrionic, atonal song that gives Captain Beefheart a run for his money. Though this one-shot was not (and perhaps could not ever) be repeated, it remains an exhilaratingly reckless slice of psychedelia. The CD reissue includes both mono and stereo versions of five of the songs. Although the mono mixes lack the full-bodied power of the stereo ones, they're marked by some interesting differences, especially in the brief spoken and instrumental links between tracks. *—Richie Unterberger*

Strangelands / 1988 / Reckless ✦✦

Bobby Brown

b. Feb. 5, 1969, Boston, MA
Vocals / New Jack Swing, Club/Dance, Urban, Dance-Pop
At the end of the '80s, former New Edition member Bobby Brown made the album that made new-jack swing a dominant force not only on the urban charts, but on the pop charts as well. Brown's first album, *King of the Stage,* wasn't that remarkable but 1988's *Don't Be Cruel* is the definitive new-jack album, thanks to L.A. Reid's and Babyface's massive production and songs, including the hits "Don't Be Cruel," "Every Little Step," and "Roni." While recording the follow-up album, Brown married pop star Whitney Houston and they had a child; their marriage has been plagued with tabloid-fueled rumors. In 1992, Brown released *Bobby,* a follow-up record that didn't have the commercial success of *Don't Be Cruel,* mainly because it lacked the focused songs and production that made that album such a huge success. *—Stephen Thomas Erlewine*

Don't Be Cruel / 1988 / MCA ✦✦✦✦
Don't Be Cruel was to Bobby Brown what *Control* was to Janet Jackson—a tougher, more aggressive project that shed his "bubble gum" image altogether and brought him to a new artistic and commercial plateau. With "My Prerogative" and the title song, Brown became a leader of "new-jack swing"—a forceful, high-tech blend of traditional soul singing and rap/hip-hop that's also associated with Guy and Brown's New Edition colleagues, Bell Biv DeVoe. Brown had been a strong advocate of rap since his days with New Edition, and on *Cruel,* he did even more rapping than before. But for all the tough-mindedness he exhibited on his "new-jack" hits, the charismatic Bostonian hadn't lost his love of sentimental, old-fashioned R&B romanticism—and he definitely excels in that area on his hits "Every Little Step," "Roni" and "Rock Wit' Cha." Much of *Cruel* was produced by the ubiquitous production/songwriting duo L.A. & Babyface, who've often been accused (and rightly so) of taking a formulaic, cookie-cutter approach to R&B. But here, their work is never less than inspired. *—Alex Henderson*

● **Greatest Hits** / Sep. 26, 2000 / MCA ✦✦✦✦
Although the bulk of Bobby Brown's most important work is featured on *Don't Be Cruel,* he was a fairly consistent singles artist throughout most of his solo career (that is, when he actually recorded). *Greatest Hits* doesn't feature anything from 1997's lackluster *Forever,* but that's entirely forgivable; the 14 tracks that are here include an amazing 11 Top Ten R&B hits, six of which went to number one, and eight of which also reached the pop Top Ten. Brown's hit duets with Glenn Medeiros ("She Ain't Worth It") and wife Whitney Houston ("Something in Common") are also included, although there's nothing from his first or second go-rounds with New Edition. However, there doesn't need to be—the body of work presented on *Greatest Hits,* while not completely uniform in style or production, is arguably the catchiest urban pop-soul of its time. There are a few silky ballads, but Brown's real bread and butter is slamming, up-tempo new jack dance-pop. On those numbers, Brown is the total urban contemporary package, able to stick with the melody, improvise around it, or throw in credible raps that complement the hard-hitting hip-hop-derived beats. He may not be a technical master, but Brown's understanding of how to construct a tight, catchy single makes *Greatest Hits* an essential purchase for even the most casual fans of late-'80s/early-'90s R&B. *—Steve Huey*

James Brown

b. May 3, 1933, Macon, GA
Vocals, Piano, Organ, Arranger / Blaxploitation, R&B, Funk, Soul
Soul Brother Number One, the Godfather of Soul, the Hardest Working Man in Show Business, Mr. Dynamite—those are mighty titles, but no one can question that James Brown has earned them more than any other performer. Other singers were more popular, others were equally skilled, but no other African-American musician has been so influential on the course of popular music in the past several decades. And no other musician, pop or otherwise, put on a more exciting, exhilarating stage show—Brown's performances were marvels of athletic stamina and split-second timing. Through the gospel-impassioned fury of his vocals and the complex polyrhythms of his beats, Brown was a crucial midwife in not just one, but two revolutions in American Black music. He was one of the figures most responsible for turning R&B into soul; he was, most would agree, the figure most responsible for turning soul music into the funk of the late '60s and early '70s. Since the mid-'70s, he's done little more than tread water artistically; his financial and drug problems eventually got him a controversial prison sentence. Yet in a sense his music is now more influential than ever, as his voice and rhythms are sampled on innumerable rap and hip-hop recordings, and critics have belatedly hailed his innovations as among the most important in all of rock or soul. *—Richie Unterberger*

Please, Please, Please / 1959 / Polygram ✦✦✦

Try Me! / 1959 / King ✦✦✦

Think / 1960 / Polygram ✦✦✦

★ **Live at the Apollo [1963]** / Jan. 1963 / Polydor ✦✦✦✦✦
An astonishing record of James and the Flames tearing the roof off the sucker at the mecca of R&B theatres, New York's *Apollo.* When King Records owner Syd Nathan refused to fund the recording, thinking it commercial folly, Brown single-mindedly proceeded anyway, paying for it out of his own pocket. He had been out on the road night after night for a while, and he knew that the magic that was part and parcel of a James Brown show was something no record had ever caught. Hit follows hit without a pause—"I'll Go Crazy," "Try Me," "Think," "Please Please Please," "I Don't Mind," "Night Train," and more. The affirmative screams and cries of the audience are something you've never experienced unless you've seen the Brown Revue in a Black theater. If you have, I need not say more; if you haven't, suffice to say that this should be one of the very first records you ever own. *—Rob Bowman*

Say It Loud, I'm Black and I'm Proud / Mar. 1969 / Polydor ✦✦✦
Although historical evaluations of Brown's work during the last half of the '60s tend to focus on the innovative funk of his biggest hit singles, his repertoire—both live and on record—in fact remained pretty versatile. Like his other '60s studio albums, *Say It Loud* is more R&B/pop-conscious than a lot of listeners would expect, mixing the funky monsters "Say It, Loud I'm Black and I'm Proud" and "Licking Stick" with soul ballads. It's a notch above similar albums from earlier in the decade, however, in that the slow numbers are usually gritty slow burns that eschew syrupy orchestration. Reissued on CD in 1996, it includes a couple of minor hits ("Goodbye My Love" and "I Guess I'll Have to Cry, Cry, Cry") that don't turn up on the *Star Time* box set. Reissued on CD in 1996. *—Richie Unterberger*

Sex Machine / Aug. 1970 / Polydor ✦✦✦✦✦
A double live outing from Brown's seminal 1970 JBs lineup, including Bootsy Collins, Clyde Stubblefield, Fred Wesley, Maceo Parker, Bobby Byrd, and many more. While it's a cut below *Love Power Peace* in documenting this lineup live, Brown and his band still smoke, tearing into extended versions of funk classics like "Sex Machine" (nearly eleven minutes), "Brother Rapp," "Give It Up Or Turnit-a Loose," and "Mother Popcorn," plus a healthy quotient of earlier soul material sprinkled in between. *—Steve Huey*

Revolution of the Mind / Dec. 1971 / Polydor ✦✦✦

There It Is / Jun. 1972 / Polydor ✦✦✦✦✦
Brown's Polydor debut, *Hot Pants,* was nothing more than the inferior remake of the title track baited with a batch of half-baked vamps. *There It Is,* his second Polydor studio album, was a marked improvement. Not that he put much into this one either. This 1972 effort collected five of his best early-'70s tracks and mixed in minimal filler. "Talking Loud and Saying Nothing" and "There It Is (Parts 1 and 2)," with its bebop style horns, were both innovative and hard driving to a fault. The hilarious "I'm a Greedy Man," with its hypnotic bass and help from Bobby Byrd, has Brown firing off such witticisms as "I'm a greedy man/yes I are" and "Taking care of my business/now run tell that." Brown wasn't all fun and games on this one. "King Heroin," an eerie, laid-back jazz offering, has him reciting chilling poetry about the ills of the drug. "Public Enemy *1 (Pt. 1)*" attempts to re-create the same message. By "Public Enemy *2 (Pt. 2)*" he is doing nothing but connecting the same dots and screaming himself hoarse to little effect. Although by this point Brown was best known for his dance tracks, he still had a way with a ballad. "Who am I," a song that had been kicking around his oeuvre for aeons, gets a strong arrangement and has Brown giving an impassioned performance. Like many of his '70s albums, *There It Is* was out of circulation for close to 20 years until it was reissued on CD in mid-'90s. It's well worth picking up. *—Jason Elias*

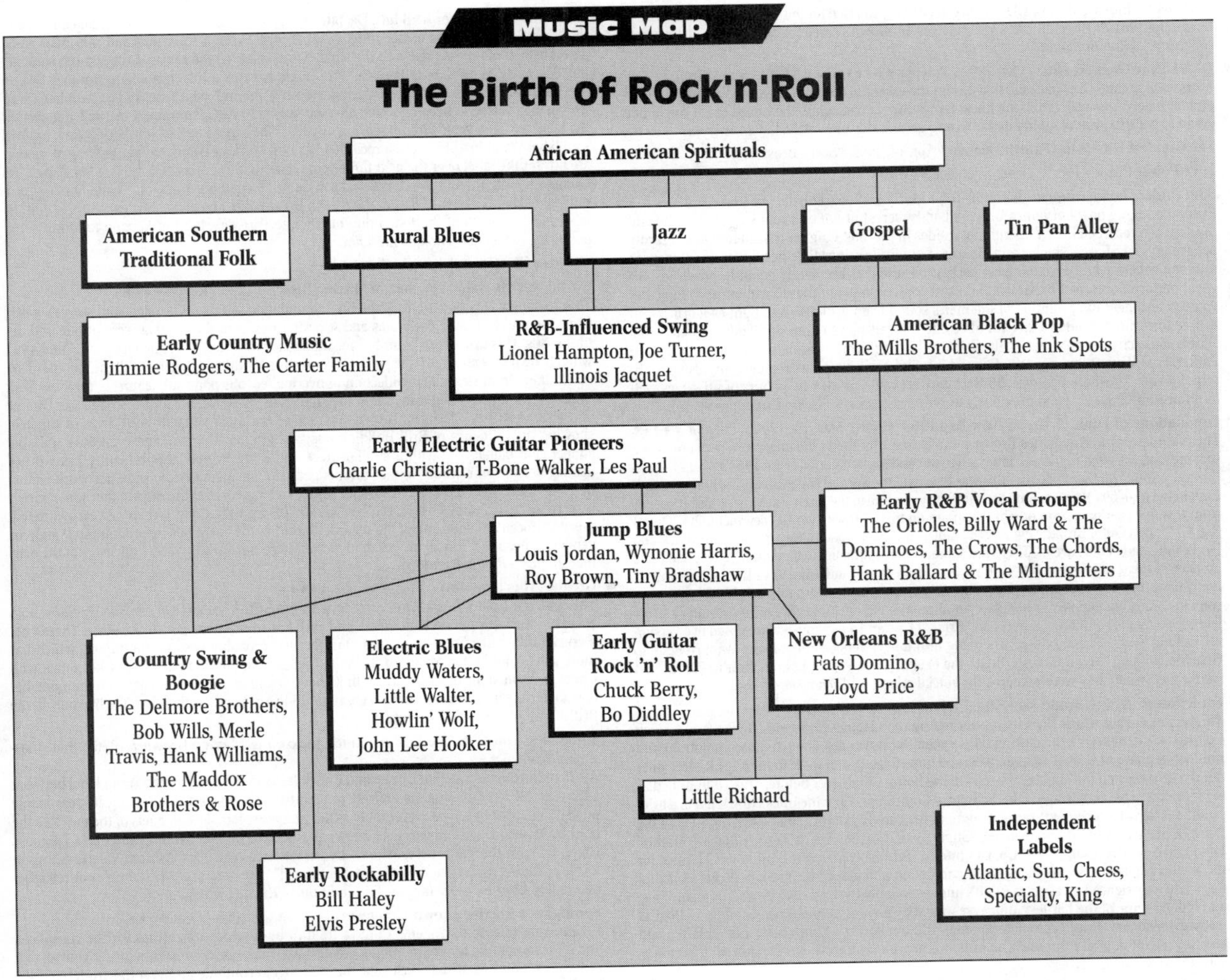

Get on the Good Foot / Nov. 1972 / Polydor ✦✦✦✦

Black Caesar / Feb. 1973 / Polydor ✦✦✦

The Payback / Dec. 1973 / Polydor ✦✦✦✦✦

Hell / Jul. 1974 / Polydor ✦✦✦✦✦

Roots of a Revolution / 1984 / Polydor ✦✦✦✦✦
A double-CD retrospective of 1956-1964 recordings that charts Brown's progress from doo wop and Little Richard-influenced R&B to the verge of his groundbreaking mid-'60s funk. It doesn't include his biggest hits of the era (which are found on *Star Time*), but these are by and large equally exciting. Many fine overlooked R&B hits and B-sides like "Shout and Shimmy," "I've Got Money," the gospel-influenced "Oh Baby Don't You Weep," and "Maybe the Last Time," which inspired the Rolling Stones' "The Last Time." *—Richie Unterberger*

In the Jungle Groove / 1986 / Polydor ✦✦✦✦✦
In the Jungle Groove was one of the first (and still one of the best) collections of James Brown's transitional and hard-hitting soul/funk workouts from 1969-1971. While the first few numbers here feature Brown sidemen who were in on his mid-'60s hits, the majority feature the original JBs outfit that helped the singer forge several extended and funk-defining sides during 1970. Faced with a walkout by his old band, Brown partially formed the JBs out of the New Dapps from Cincinnati, taking aboard brothers Phelps "Catfish" Collins on guitar and William "Bootsy" Collins on bass; many of those ex-band members, namely drummer Clyde Stubblefield, guitarist Clair St. Pinckney, and trombonist Fred Wesley, would eventually return to flesh out the JBs lineup. The one constant was vocalist and organist Bobby Byrd, who had been with Brown since the singer's start in 1956. The incredible grooves Bootsy Collins and Stubblefield laid down here would become manna for hip-hop DJs over 15 years later, with the album's "Funky Drummer (Bonus Beat Reprise)" becoming one of the supreme breakbeats of all time. Filling out the collection are the very soulful pre-JBs tracks "It's a Brand New Day" (tenor saxophonist Maceo Parker's only appearance on the disc) and the original "Funky Drummer," as well as the post-Bootsy cut "Hot Pants (She's Got to Use What She's Got to Get What She Wants)." All the numbers here are as in the pocket as you will ever hear in soul and funk. And while many of these tracks are found on various packages like Polydor's *Funk Power* and *Foundations of Funk*, *In the Jungle Groove* has the upper hand with its unequaled coverage of Brown's transformation from soul brother number one to funk originator. *—Stephen Cook*

Messing with the Blues / 1991 / Polydor ✦✦✦
Although he is most famous for his innovations in soul and funk music, James Brown never lost sight of his blues and R&B roots. His albums often placed surprisingly rootsy covers of old chestnuts alongside his groundbreaking polyrhythmic workouts. This double CD compiles thirty of the bluesiest items from his vast recorded legacy. Cut between 1957 and 1985, most of the tracks actually date from the '60s; many of these, in turn, were laid down in the early part of the decade, when J.B. was gradually evolving from his more conventional beginnings. The artists whose songs are covered here read like a *Who's Who* of R&B pioneers: Louis Jordan, Roy Brown, Memphis Slim, Ivory Joe Hunter, Fats Domino, Chuck Willis, Little Willie John, Billy Ward, Guitar Slim, and Bobby Bland. It's quite an instructive insight into Brown's not-always-visible roots. It would be fair to say that this does not rank among his most exciting material, finding him in a smoother and more conventional style than his most innovative work. It is nonetheless always entertaining and accomplished, with Brown's love for this material shining through strongly in his committed interpretations. Especially intriguing are an 11-minute cover of Chuck Willis' "Don't Deceive Me" and a two-part, blues-based rap vamp from the early '70s, "Like It Is, Like It Was (The Blues)." The disc includes several unreleased cuts, alternate takes, and unedited versions of previously released songs. *—Richie Unterberger*

☆ **Star Time** / Jun. 1991 / Polydor ✦✦✦✦✦
One of the great box sets of all time; over four CDs, Brown's recorded legacy is traced from "Please Please Please" in 1956 through his 1984 duet with Afrika Bambaataa, "Unity Pt. 1." With 71 tracks in all, the set places the number one R&B artist ever in his proper perspective as the prime progenitor of funk, one of the architects of soul, and the Godfather of Rap. To have done any one of these things would have been a bid for immortality; having done all

three makes him a god. Four CDs at once is virtually too rich for one sitting. The well-written liner notes provide three different perspectives on Brown's career. A cornerstone of any great collection. *—Rob Bowman*

★ **20 All-Time Greatest Hits!** / Oct. 1991 / Polydor ✦✦✦✦✦
A first-rate greatest-hits package that covers the essential soul singles and some of the funk-period material as well. While the finest James Brown package is the boxed set, if you're not going to get that, you wouldn't be far wrong getting this one instead. *—Ron Wynn*

The Greatest Hits of the Fourth Decade / Apr. 14, 1992 / Scotti Bros. ✦✦✦

Love Power Peace / Jun. 23, 1992 / Polydor ✦✦✦✦✦

Soul Pride: The Instrumentals (1960-69) / Mar. 23, 1993 / Polydor ✦✦✦✦✦
Everyone knows how hot James Brown's bands were, but not everyone's aware that he and his sidemen recorded lots of instrumental sides in the '60s. Originally scattered haphazardly over many out-of-print singles and albums, *Soul Pride* brings together the best of this work into one cohesive and chronological package. These cuts are nearly equal in power to J.B.'s vocal performances. Not only does the band cook on most of these insinuating vamps, but you can also hear the evolution of the man's sound from gritty R&B to tight-as-a-drum soul to free-form funk. Soul Brother number one himself plays organ and adds unpredictable shouts and screams on most of these tracks. But the chief stars are sidemen like Maceo Parker, Fred Wesley, and Pee Wee Ellis, who broke new ground with their compulsive counterpoint riffs. This fiery two-disc, 36-track box set contains over two hours of music, as well as a few non-LP B-sides and previously unreleased tracks. *—Richie Unterberger*

☆ **Foundations of Funk: A Brand New Bag,1964-1969** / Mar. 19, 1996 / Polydor ✦✦✦✦✦
There are several worthy James Brown compilations. But this is the one, more than any other, that presents his most fertile and innovative soul and funk material. From 1964's "Out of Sight" through 1969's "Mother Popcorn," this was Brown at the apex of his creativity, turning soul into funk in the mid-'60s, then pushing the rhythm even more to the forefront. Most of his hit singles from this five-year explosion of white heat are on this 27-track, two-CD set, including "Out of Sight," "Papa's Got a Brand New Bag," "I Got You (I Feel Good)," "Say It Loud, I'm Black and I'm Proud," and "Cold Sweat." There are some minor omissions that could be questioned (the absence of the studio version of "Bring It Up," for instance), and big James Brown fans will already have the lion's share of tracks, on the *Star Time* box and other releases. It does, however, contain minor but significant bonuses: an alternate take of "Cold Sweat," a previously unreleased live medley of "Out of Sight" and "Bring It Up," and a previously unreleased live version of "Licking Stick—Licking Stick." There are also longer versions of "I Don't Want Nobody to Give Me Nothing" (ten minutes!), "I Got the Feelin'," "The Popcorn," and "Brother Rapp" that were edited when they were prepared for official release. *—Richie Unterberger*

Funk Power 1970: A Brand New Thang / Jun. 4, 1996 / Polydor ✦✦✦✦✦
The period during which Brown was backed by the original J.B.'s (with Bootsy and Catfish Collins) was extremely brief, lasting only a year. But it was also an extremely important and influential phase of Brown's career, when he moved from soul-funk to hard funk, stretching out the grooves and putting more stress on the bottom than ever before. This 78-minute disc is the cream of his recordings from the Bootsy Collins era. The nine tracks (the tenth is a brief public-service annoncement) include some of his core funk workouts—"Get Up I Feel Like Being a Sex Machine" (two versions), "Super Bad," "Give It Up or Turn It Loose," "Talkin' Loud and Sayin' Nothing," "Get Up, Get Into It, Get Involved," and "Soul Power." It's not for those who find Brown's funk phase too monotonous, and indeed the grooves do get a bit similar when experienced all at once. But it's unquestionably the best of Brown's '70s recordings, and indeed some of the hardest funk ever waxed by anyone at any time. As a bonus, the CD has previously unreleased complete versions of "Soul Power" (12 minutes) and "Talkin' Loud and Sayin' Nothing" (14 minutes), as well as a previously unreleased version of "There Was a Time." *—Richie Unterberger*

Make It Funky—*The Big Payback: 1971-1975* */ Jul. 23, 1996 / Polydor* ✦✦✦✦✦
While the first half of the 1970s saw Brown's sales and art start to slowly decline, at their best he and the JB's remained capable of generating a lot of heat. Record-wise it was a very erratic period, especially on his albums, which makes this two-and-a-half-hour double-disc compilation of his best material from the era especially welcome. Besides his biggest hits from the time ("Make It Funky," "Get on the Good Foot," "The Payback," "Funky President"), it has a number of high-charting R&B 45s that didn't make it onto the *Star Time* box. Familiar hits are sometimes presented in their full unedited mega-versions (12 minutes of "Make It Funky," 14 of "Papa Don't Take No Mess"), and there are also a few previously unreleased outtakes and alternate versions. It's only a disappointment relative to the towering accomplishments of his 1960s and early-'70s classics. On its own terms, it's excellent funk, if rather homogenous taken all at once, with occasional departures from the formula, like "Down and Out in New York City," with its poppy woodwinds. *—Richie Unterberger*

★ **JB40: 40th Anniversary Collection** / Oct. 8, 1996 / Polydor ✦✦✦✦✦
Brown's catalog was in a shambles for years, but the CD age has reversed the situation to such an extent that you now have a wide variety of greatest-hits options to choose from. On the whole, this might be the best buy, cramming 40 of his biggest hit singles from 1956-1979 onto two discs. It's perhaps a little too weighted toward the '70s (which comprise all of disc two), and some decent moderate-size hits are omitted, like "Oh Baby Don't You Weep," "Bring It Up," and "Get It Together." But it does have the core classics. If you don't want to spring for the *Star Time* box, but want more than a single-disc collection, this is the one to have. *—Richie Unterberger*

Dead on the Heavy Funk / May 12, 1998 / Polydor ✦✦✦

Maxine Brown

b. Apr. 27, 1932, Kingstree, SC
Vocals / Uptown Soul, Pop-Soul, R&B, Soul
Although she never had many hits, Maxine Brown was one of the most underrated soul and R&B vocalists of the '60s, releasing a series of singles with only a couple of songsmanaging to become either pop or R&B hits. Despite her lack of hits, Brown is acknowledged as one of the finest R&B vocalists of her time, capable of delivering soul, jazz and pop with equal aplomb. In 1960, she signed with the small Normar label, who released the smooth soul ballad "All in My Mind" late in the year. The single became a hit, climbing to number two on the R&B charts, and it was quickly followed by "Funny," which peaked at number three. Brown was poised to become a star, and she moved to ABC-Paramount in 1962, but she left the label within a year, without scoring any hits. She signed to the New York-based, uptown soul label Wand in 1963. Brown recorded her best work at Wand, having a string of moderate hits for the label over the next three years. Among these were "Oh No Not My Baby," "It's Gonna Be Alright," and the Chuck Jackson duets "Something You Got," "Hold On I'm Coming," and "Daddy's Home." Part of the reason Brown didn't receive much exposure is that the label focused much of their attention on Dionne Warwick, leaving Maxine to toil in semi-obscurity. *—Stephen Thomas Erlewine*

Greatest Hits [Wand] / 1967 / Wand ✦✦✦✦

● **Oh No Not My Baby: The Best of Maxine Brown** / 1990 / Kent ✦✦✦✦✦
This 28-song CD is undoubtedly the best compilation of this underrated soul singer's work, featuring many of her '60s singles and several tunes from the era that were unreleased until the '80s. This disc draws from her recordings for the Wand label between 1963 and 1967, when Brown was at her artistic peak. Of course the hit title track is a highlight, but there are no clunkers in this excellent collection of overlooked '60s pop-soul, featuring the New York "uptown" production that also graced the records of fellow Wand/Scepter artists like Dionne Warwick and Chuck Jackson. Brown was one of the most versatile soul divas of the '60s, showing the influence of Brill Building pop, girl groups, Motown, and even Stax soul and supper-club ballads. As with a similar artist like Betty Everett, this versaility has worked against her in some ways. Neither full-fledged pop nor unabashedly soul, her work cannot be easily pigeonholed into a certain soul genre, and has cost her the respect that some purists reserve for "deep" soul singers. But her work holds up well. Collectors should be aware that this disc doesn't include any of the records she cut in the early '60s before joining Wand; the version of her 1961 Top 20 hit "All in My Mind" here is from a live 1964 release, not the original single. *—Richie Unterberger*

● **Greatest Hits [Tomato]** / 1995 / Tomato ✦✦✦✦✦
This 23-track best-of has a lot of overlap with the British import *Oh No Not My Baby;* both cover her mid-'60s period with Wand, and each has some songs not on the other. There's not a crucial difference between the pair, but the nod probably goes to the import, which has more songs and better sound. In its favor, this compilation includes five of her duets with Chuck Jackson, none of which are on the other CD (although the duets don't rank among her best material). It also has a studio version of "All in My Mind," rather than the live one on the British anthology. *—Richie Unterberger*

Something You Got: The Best of Chuck Jackson & Maxine Brown / 1996 / Soul Classics/Ichiban ✦✦✦
All 20 of the duet tracks that Brown and Chuck Jackson recorded for the Wand label between 1965 and 1967, comprising the entirety of their two albums for the company. It's reasonable pop/soul, but not nearly as memorable as the best male-female soul duets of the era (like the ones by Marvin Gaye and various Motown partners, or by Otis Redding and Carla Thomas). Highlights are the early compositions by the Jo Armstead-Nick Ashford-Valerie Simpson team, including a version of "Let's Go Get Stoned" that was recorded (though not released) before Ray Charles' more famous hit rendition. *—Richie Unterberger*

Spotlight on Maxine Brown/Greatest Hits / Aug. 29, 2000 / Kent ✦✦✦✦
A confusing release that seems to have tried to both sweep up rarities for the completist and offer something approximating a greatest-hits package, the result being, of course, that everyone's a bit unsatisfied. Basically, the idea was to combine all the songs from her 1965 LP *Spotlight* (actually largely a collection of 1963-65 singles) and her 1967 LP *Greatest Hits* (which duplicated five tracks from *Spotlight*) onto one CD, adding eight rare bonus tracks. Those additional cuts are taken from non-LP mid-'60s recordings and a couple of previously unissued items. There are two problems with that concept. The first is that no less than 15 of the 28 tracks also appear on another Kent release, the fine anthology *Oh No Not My Baby: The Best of Maxine Brown,* which many of the people considering buying any Brown reissue are likely to have already. The second is that this CD actually does not include "All in My Mind" and "Funny," which—if the cover art of *Greatest Hits,* complete with track listing, reproduced on the cover of this two-fer is to be believed—were on the original 1967 *Greatest Hits* LP. That's an uncommon gaffe for Ace/Kent to make, but from all appearances that's what happened. Now, certainly this is still a fine pop-soul disc from one of the best pop-soul vocalists. Of the material on *Spotlight On/Greatest Hits* not on that other Kent collection, it ranges from good—the bluesy "You Upset My Soul," an odd cover of the Beatles' "We Can Work It Out," the brassy 1966 single "Anything You Do Is Alright," a nice interpretation of the pop standard "When I Fall in Love"—to unmemorable. *—Richie Unterberger*

Ruth Brown

b. Jan. 12, 1928, Portsmouth, VA
Vocals / Jump Blues, R&B
They called Atlantic Records "the house that Ruth built" during the 1950s, and they weren't referring to the Sultan of Swat. Ruth Brown's regal hitmaking reign from 1949 to the close of the '50s helped tremendously to establish the New York label's predominance in the R&B field. After performing with bandleaders including Lucky Millinder, she signed to the fledgling Atlantic label in 1948 and found a hit with her first single, the torch ballad "So Long."

Brown's seductive vocal delivery shone incandescently on her Atlantic smashes "Teardrops in My Eyes," "I'll Wait for You," "I Know," "5-10-15 Hours," the seminal "(Mama) He Treats Your Daughter Mean," "Oh What a Dream," and "Mambo Baby." After an even two dozen R&B chart appearances for Atlantic that ended in 1960, Brown faded from view. After raising her two sons and working a nine-to-five job, Brown began to rebuild her musical career in the mid-'70s. There were more records for Fantasy, notably 1991's jumping *Fine and Mellow*. Her pipes are mellowed but not frayed by the ensuing decades that have seen her rise to stardom not once, but twice. *—Bill Dahl*

Sweet Baby of Mine (1949-1956) / Apr. 6, 1949-Mar. 2, 1956 / Route 66 ♦♦♦♦♦
Excellent collection covering blues and R&B songs Brown did prior to becoming a huge hit artist for Atlantic in the late '50s. These were R&B gems, but such artists as Patti Page and Georgia Gibbs were covering them for the white market and Brown was locked out until 1957. But she enjoyed 11 Top 10 R&B hits, which are contained on this anthology. *—Ron Wynn*

★ **The Best of Ruth Brown** / May 25, 1949-May 1959 / Rhino ♦♦♦♦♦
For those who want a cheaper and more concise collection of her best Atlantic cuts than the two-CD *Miss Rhythm*, this superb 23-track CD has the cream of her '50s work, including no less than 19 Top Ten R&B singles. Charting her evolution from her jazzy debut, "So Long," through jump blues and early rock&roll, it also adds a bonus of two previously unissued live cuts from 1959. *—Richie Unterberger*

☆ **Miss Rhythm (Greatest Hits and More)** / May 25, 1949-Aug. 30, 1960 / Rhino/Atlantic ♦♦♦♦♦
Before Aretha Franklin was exalted as the Queen of Soul, Ruth Brown was dubbed "Miss Rhythm"—and with good reason. A gritty, aggressive belter with an impressive range and a powerhouse of a voice, Brown was the top female R&B singer of the early-to-mid-'50s, and would directly or indirectly have an influence such greats as Etta James and LaVern Baker. A two-CD set ranging from Brown's early hits to engaging obscurities and rarities, *Miss Rhythm* offers a fine overview of her Atlantic years. Early hits like "Mama, He Treats Your Daughter Mean," "Teardrops from My Eyes," "Mambo Baby" and "5-10-15 Hours" point to the fact that a lot of early R&B was essentially blues at a fast tempo. The set also reminds us of early R&B's connection to jazz—in fact, classics like 1949's "So Long" (her first single) and "Have a Good Time" are examples of first-class torch singing. There are numerous Brown albums that are well worth acquiring, but for those interested in exploring her early music for the first time, *Miss Rhythm* is an excellent place to start. *—Alex Henderson*

Jackson Browne

b. Oct. 9, 1948, Heidelberg, Germany
Vocals, Keyboards, Piano, Guitar / Pop/Rock, Folk-Rock, Soft Rock, Singer/Songwriter
In many ways, Jackson Browne was the quintessential sensitive Californian singer-songwriter of the early '70s. Only Joni Mitchell and James Taylor ranked alongside him in terms of influence, but neither artist tapped into the post-'60s zeitgeist like Browne. While the majority of his classic '70s work was unflinchingly personal, it nevertheless provided a touchstone for a generation of maturing baby boomers coming to terms with adulthood. Not only did his introspective, literate lyrics strike a nerve, but his laid-back folk-rock set the template for much of the music to come out of California during the '70s. With his first four albums, Browne built a loyal following that helped him break into the mainstream with 1976's *The Pretender*. During the late '70s and early '80s, he was at the height of his popularity, as each of his albums charted in the Top 10. Midway through the '80s, Browne made a series of political protest records which caused his audience to gradually shrink, but when he returned to introspective songwriting with 1993's *I'm Alive*, he made a modest comeback. *—Stephen Thomas Erlewine*

☆ **Jackson Browne** / Jan. 1972 / Asylum ♦♦♦♦♦
An auspicious debut that doesn't sound like a debut: although only 23, Browne had kicked around the music business for several years and developed an unusual use of language, studiedly casual yet full of striking imagery, and a post-apocalyptic viewpoint to go with it. He sang with a calm certainty over spare, discretely placed backup that highlighted the songs and always seemed about to disappear. In song after song, Browne described the world as a desert in need of moisture: in "Doctor My Eyes," the album's most propulsive song and a Top Ten hit, he sang, "Doctor, my eyes/Cannot see the sky/Is this the prize/For having learned how not to cry?" If Browne's outlook was cautious, its expression was original. His conditional optimism seemed to reflect hard experience, and in the early 1970s, a lot of his listeners shared that perspective. Like any great artist, Browne articulated the tenor of his times. But the album has long since come to seem a timeless collection of reflective ballads touching on still-difficult subjects—suicide (explicitly), depression and drug use (probably), spiritual uncertainty and desperate hope—all in calm, reasoned tones, and all with an amazingly eloquent sense of language. *Jackson Browne*'s greater triumph is that, having perfectly expressed its times, it transcended them as well. *—William Ruhlmann*

For Everyman / Oct. 1973 / Asylum ♦♦♦♦♦
Jackson Browne faced the nearly insurmountable task of following a masterpiece in making his second album. Having cherry-picked years of songwriting the first time around, he turned to some of his secondary older material, which was still better than most people's best and, ironically, more accessible—notably such songs as "These Days," and which had been covered six times already, dating back to Nico's *Chelsea Girl* album in 1967, and "Take It Easy," a co-composition with the Eagles' Glenn Frey, which had been a Top 40 hit for the group in 1972. Browne unsuccessfully looked for another hit single with the uptempo "Red Neck Friend," reminisced about meeting his wife and starting a family in the coy "Ready or Not," and, at the end, finally came up with a new song to rank with those on the first album in the philosophical title track, which reportedly was his more positive reply to Crosby, Stills, Nash & Young's "Wooden Ships." (David Crosby sang harmony.) Musically, the album was still restrained, but not as austere as *Jackson Browne*, as the singer had hooked up with multi-instrumentalist David Lindley, who would introduce interesting textures to his music on a variety of stringed instruments for the next several years. All of which is to say that *For Everyman* was a less consistent collection than Browne's debut album. But Browne's songwriting ability remained impressive. *—William Ruhlmann*

★ **Late for the Sky** / Sep. 1974 / Asylum ♦♦♦♦♦
On his third album, Jackson Browne returned to the themes of his debut record (love, loss, identity, apocalypse), and, amazingly, delved even deeper into them. "For a Dancer," and a meditation on death like the first album's "Song for Adam," is a more eloquent eulogy; "Farther On" extends the "moving on" point of "Looking Into You"; "Before the Deluge" is a glimpse beyond the apocalypse evoked on "My Opening Farewell" and the second album's "For Everyman." If Browne had seemed to question everything in his first records, here he even questioned himself. "For me some words come easy, but I know that they don't mean that much," he sang on the opening track, "Late for the Sky," and added in "Farther On," "I'm not sure what I'm trying to say." Yet his seeming uncertainty and self-doubt reflected the size and complexity of the problems he was addressing in these songs, and few had ever explored such territory, much less mapped it so well. "The Late Show," the album's thematic center, doubted but ultimately affirmed the nature of relationships, while by the end, "After the Deluge," if "only a few survived," the human race continued nonetheless. It was a lot to put into a pop music album, but Browne stretched the limits of what could be found in what he called "the beauty in songs," just as Bob Dylan had a decade before. *—William Ruhlmann*

The Pretender / Nov. 1976 / Asylum ♦♦♦
On *The Pretender*, Jackson Browne took a step back from the precipice so well defined on his first three albums, but doing so didn't seem to make him feel any better. Employing a real producer, Jon Landau, for the first time, Browne made what sounded like a real contemporary rock record, but this made his songs less effective; the ersatz Mexican arrangement of "Linda Paloma" and the bouncy second half of "Daddy's Tune," with its horn charts and guitar solo, undercut the lyrics. The man who had delved so deeply into life's abyss on his earlier albums was in search of escape this time around, whether by crying ("Here Come Those Tears Again"), sleeping ("Sleep's Dark and Silent Gate"), or making peace with estranged love ones ("The Only Child," "Daddy's Tune"). None of it worked, however, and when Browne came to the final track—traditionally the place on his albums where he summed up his current philosophical stance—he delivered "The Pretender," a cynical, sarcastic treatise on moneygrubbing and the shallow life of the suburbs. Primarily inner directed, the song's defeatist tone demands rejection, but it is also a quintessential statement of its time, the post-Watergate '70s; dire as that might be, you had to admire that kind of honesty, even as it made you wince. *—William Ruhlmann*

Running on Empty / 1977 / Asylum ♦♦♦
Having acknowledged a certain creative desperation on *The Pretender*, Jackson Browne lowered his sights (and raised his commercial appeal) considerably with *Running on Empty*, which was more a concept album about the road than an actual live album, even though its songs were sometimes recorded on stage (and sometimes on the bus or in the hotel). Although unlike most live albums, it consisted of previously unrecorded songs, Browne had less creative participation on this album than on any he ever made, solely composing only two songs, co-writing four others, and covering another four. And he had less to say—the title song and leadoff track neatly conjoined his artistic and escapist themes. Figuratively and creatively, he was out of gas, but like "the pretender," still had to make a living. The songs covered all aspects of touring, from Danny O'Keefe's "The Road," which detailed romantic encounters, and "Rosie" (co-written by Browne and his manager Donald Miller), in which a soundman pays tribute to auto-eroticism, to, well, "Cocaine," to the travails of being a roadie ("The Load-Out"). Audience noises, humorous asides, loose playing—they were all part of a rough-around-the-edges musical evocation of the rock & roll touring life. It was not what fans had come to expect from Browne, of course, but the disaffected were more than outnumbered by the newly converted. (It didn't hurt that "Running on Empty" and "The Load-Out"/"Stay" both became Top 40 hits.) As a result, Jackson Browne's least ambitious, but perhaps most accessible, album ironically became his biggest seller. But it is not characteristic of his other work: for many, it will be the only Browne album they will want to own, just as others always will regard it disdainfully as "Jackson Browne Lite." *—William Ruhlmann*

Hold Out / 1980 / Asylum ♦♦

Lawyers in Love / 1983 / Asylum ♦♦
Jackson Browne's messages had always seemed so important that one tended to overlook the sheer songwriting craft that went into his work, craft that was apparent, for example, on his 1982 single "Somebody's Baby," awhich became his biggest hit ever (and which appears on none of his albums, only being available on the soundtrack to *Fast Times at Ridgemont High*), and on songs like "Downtown," a street-life portrait on his seventh album, *Lawyers in Love*. The craft seemed all the more important because Browne was so intent on turning his back on the conundrums that had obsessed him in the past. On "Cut it Away," he sang of his desire to remove his "desperate heart" (a phrase he had used before), to rid himself of "this crazy longing for something more/This question that I don't have the answer for." In place of such ambitions, Browne substituted the beginnings of social concern ("Say It Isn't True") and, most imaginatively, a humorous look at contemporary trash culture in the title track, one of the more exhilaratingly silly moments in Browne's generally dour catalog. But the craft, and the familiar tightness of Browne's veteran studio/live band, couldn't hide the essentially retread nature of much of this material. *—William Ruhlmann*

Lives in the Balance / 1986 / Asylum ♦♦♦
Usually among the most introspective of songwriters, Jackson Browne cast his gaze on the world outside on *Lives in the Balance* and did not like what he saw. Beginning with "For America," and he lamented his previous indifference to social issues—"I went on speaking of the future/While other people fought and bled"—but immediately tried to make up for lost time. The album's context, of course, was five years of Ronald Reagan's presidency, with what the Left saw as an indifference to the plight of the poor at home and a dangerously aggressive policy against insurgent movements in the Central American countries of El Salvador and Nicaragua they feared would lead to a Vietnam-like war. Without naming those places, Browne wrote and sang passionately against poverty in the songs "Soldier of Plenty" and "Lawless Avenues" and against war in "For America," "Lives in the Balance," and "Till I Go Down." Elsewhere, his more familiar themes of romantic ("In the Shape of a Heart") and philosophical ("Black and White") disillusionment also made appearances. But, from its hard rock sound and forceful singing to its frankly agitprop lyrics, "For America" remained pri-

marily a political statement, and if Browne sounded more involved in his music than he had in some time, the specificity of its approach inevitably limited its appeal and its long-term significance. — *William Ruhlmann*

World in Motion / Jun. 1989 / Elektra ✦✦

I'm Alive / Oct. 1993 / Elektra ✦✦✦

Looking East / Feb. 1996 / Elektra ✦✦✦

The Next Voice You Hear: The Best of Jackson Browne / Sep. 23, 1997 / Elektra ✦✦✦
Theoretically, assembling a Jackson Browne greatest-hits collection would be easy, but *The Next Voice You Hear: The Best of Jackson Browne* proves that isn't necessarily the case. Boasting 13 tracks, plus two new songs, *The Next Voice You Hear* contains some of Browne's biggest hits— "Doctor My Eyes," "Running on Empty," "Somebody's Baby," "Tender is the Night"—but it leaves just as many off, including "Rock Me on the Water," "Here Come Those Tears Again," "Stay," "Boulevard," "Lawyers in Love," and "For America." Of course, singles only told half the story with Browne, and many of his greatest songs were only available as album tracks. Therefore, it makes sense that album cuts like "These Days," "Late for Sky," and "The Pretender" are present, but there are still a number of equally good, if not better, cuts that are left off. As a result, *The Next Voice You Hear* is merely adequate for casual Browne fans, but it's nowhere near definitive. — *Stephen Thomas Erlewine*

Brownsville Station

f. 1969, Ann Arbor, MI, **db.** 1979
Group / Detroit Rock, Boogie Rock, Hard Rock, Rock & Roll
A Detroit-area rock & roll band formed in 1969 by guitarist Cub Koda. Original members also included Mike Lutz (guitar), T.J. Cronley (drums), and Tony Driggins (bass). Initially influenced by Chuck Berry, Bo Diddley, Jerry Lee Lewis, and other '50s rockers, their early albums included inspired covers and genre-faithful originals, all presented in Marshall stack, double-bass-drum bigness. Far more effective as a live act (with Koda's onstage banter influencing everyone from J. Geils' Peter Wolf to Alice Cooper), the group finally hit paydirt in late 1973 with their number-three hit, the Koda-penned "Smokin' in the Boys' Room." After disbanding the group in 1979, Koda went on to a career as a solo recording artist (see separate entry) and as a journalist for several music magazines. — *Stephen Thomas Erlewine*

No B.S. / 1970 / Warner Brothers ✦✦✦✦✦
Their debut album, featuring pedal-to-the-metal renditions of "Road Runner," "Rumble," and "Be Bop Confidential." — *Stephen Thomas Erlewine*

Brownsville Station [Palladium] / 1971 / Palladium ✦✦✦✦

A Night on the Town / 1972 / Big Tree ✦✦✦

Yeah! / 1973 / Big Tree ✦✦✦✦✦
With ten great songs, *Yeah!* is an album that lives up to its name—quite possibly the only fully realized LP the band ever made. Eight covers, all given the treatment, and two originals—one of which sold two million copies. *Yeah!* is the quintessential "nice little record"—it won't take up a lot of your time, and it's got a very friendly vibe to it. The cover songs span a wide variety of musical styles, which isn't that surprising, considering that guitarist/vocalist Cub Koda has a deep knowledge of music history. From Hoyt Axton's "Lightning Bar Blues" to then-unknown Jimmy Cliff's "Let Your Yeah Be Yeah" to Lou Reed's "Sweet Jane," the band pumps out all of its songs in a chugging, lighthearted manner that ends up being nothing but fun. Lead vocals were previously the exclusive domain of bassist Michael Lutz, but Koda emerges as a singer as well; Lutz may have been the more prototypical rock singer, but it was Koda's sleazy, nasal snarl that worked to perfection on the classic hit single "Smokin' In the Boys Room." While the success of "Smokin" opened a lot of doors for the band, it also pigeonholed them in such a way as to render them almost un-arrestable only a couple of years later. Between their wild onstage antics and the fact that the follow-up album, *School Punks*, was a blatant attempt at cashing in, the band lost a lot of the credibility they had earned by playing straight-ahead rock & roll. Although Brownsville Station would never again capture the magic here, *Yeah!* easily stands the test of time—it's truly delightful. — *Geoff Ginsberg*

School Punks / 1974 / Big Tree ✦✦✦

Motor City Connection / 1975 / Big Tree ✦✦

Brownsville Station [Private Stock] / 1977 / Private Stock ✦✦✦

Air Special / 1980 / Epic ✦✦

● **Smoking in the Boys' Room: The Best of Brownsville Station** / Dec. 14, 1993 / Rhino ✦✦✦✦✦
A roaring romp through the Brownsville Station's back pages compiled by Cub Koda himself, *Smokin' in the Boys' Room* makes a convincing case that these Ann Arbor, Michigan garage punks were one of the most underrated rock & roll bands of the 1970s. — *Stephen Thomas Erlewine*

Lindsey Buckingham

b. Oct. 3, 1948, Palo Alto, CA
Vocals, Guitar (Electric), Guitar, Producer / Pop/Rock
Before he joined Fleetwood Mac, Lindsey Buckingham was sketching out his brand of Brian Wilson-influenced pop with Stevie Nicks in the folkie duo Buckingham/Nicks. Mick Fleetwood invited the duo to join his band in late 1974. After Buckingham joined, the band's pop tendencies flowered under his direction. Not only did he provide the group with some brilliant, surprisingly dark pop songs, he sharpened the other members' songs with his production, arrangements, and breathtaking guitar-playing. Buckingham left the band after their 1987 album, *Tango in the Night*, to concentrate on his solo work.

While Buckingham's solo albums are deceptively simple and calm on the surface, there are complex arrangements and emotions beneath the smooth production. None of them have sold anything approaching the level of *Rumours*—or even *Tango in the Night*—yet they are rich, layered pop albums; his first solo record, *Law & Order*, had a hit single with "Trouble." — *Stephen Thomas Erlewine*

Buckingham Nicks / 1973 / Polydor ✦✦✦

Law and Order / Oct. 1981 / Asylum ✦✦✦✦✦
Lindsey Buckingham's talents as guitarist, arranger, and producer were particularly well suited to Fleetwood Mac, a band in which he was only one among three songwriters whose material complemented each other's. As a solo artist, Buckingham retains his strengths, but he encounters a form-over-substance problem. The seven songs he wrote for his debut album come across as sketches, musical pieces for which he has constructed interesting guitar riffs and the occasional sonic effect, plus a lyric tag—"Trouble," "That's How We Do It in L.A." But they have not been fleshed out into full-fledged songs, perhaps because Buckingham hasn't much interest in lyrics, or because he declines to use more than one or two of his ideas per tune. On the eclectic choice of covers ("September Song," "A Satisfied Mind"), Buckingham at least has fully composed and written pieces to work with, but he embalms them in his production techniques. As such, *Law and Order* comes off as a high-quality demo of largely unfinished material. (Nevertheless, "Trouble" became a Top Ten single.) — *William Ruhlmann*

Go Insane / Jul. 1984 / Asylum ✦✦✦
Lindsey Buckingham's second album, like his first, *Law and Order*, was a triumph of studio wizardry over songwriting craft. Buckingham's work was ear-catching, but once he'd gotten your attention with some gimmicky sound effect or busy arrangement, he had very little to tell you. The exception was the album's most ambitious piece, the closing track, "D.W. Suite," on which Buckingham, always strongly influenced by the Beach Boys, took on what sounded like an elaborate tribute to Beach Boy Dennis Wilson, who died while the album was being made. The title track, which also had massed choral sounds (all made by Buckingham) reminiscent of a Fleetwood Mac track, became a Top 40 hit, but the album lacked the accessibility to make it more than a moderate seller, and at least at this point it appeared that Buckingham's solo albums were going to serve as laboratory experiments in which he tried out new musical ideas before bringing them to greater popular attention through Fleetwood Mac. — *William Ruhlmann*

● **Out of the Cradle** / Jun. 16, 1992 / Reprise ✦✦✦✦✦
Lindsey Buckingham quit Fleetwood Mac after the release of their *Tango in the Night* album in 1987 and spent the subsequent five years working on his first post-Mac solo album, *Out of the Cradle*. Perhaps because he was now focused on his solo career, Buckingham reined in the experimental style of his first two albums, producing more conventional, accessible material, much of it similar to his later work with Fleetwood Mac. The inventiveness this time was heard largely in Buckingham's electro-acoustic guitar style, which combined the power of a rock guitarist with the delicacy and precision of a classical nylon-string player. Perhaps the biggest difference from his previous solo work, however, was that Buckingham actually wrote a group of songs that were about something, not just riffs full of aural tricks. Unfortunately, Buckingham had never fully established himself in the public mind as a separate entity apart from Fleetwood Mac, so taking eight years between solo albums made *Out of the Cradle* a tough sell. Which means that, although this is his most listenable solo album, not many people heard it. — *William Ruhlmann*

Jeff Buckley

b. Nov. 17, 1966, Orange County, CA, **d.** May 29, 1997
Vocals, Guitar, Organ / Adult Alternative Pop/Rock, Alternative Pop/Rock, Singer/Songwriter
Since he was the son of cult songwriter Tim Buckley, Jeff Buckley faced more expectations and pre-conceived notions than most singer/songwriters. Perhaps it wasn't surprising that Buckley's music was related to his father's by only the thinnest of margins. His voice was grand and sweeping, which fit with the mock-operatic grandeur of his Van Morrison-meets-Led Zeppelin music. Buckley first surfaced in Gods & Monsters with the experimental guitarist Gary Lucas; The band became a hip name, yet their life-span was short. Buckley began a solo career playing clubs and coffeehouses, building up a considerable following. Soon, he signed a record deal with Columbia Records, releasing the *Live at Sin-e* EP in November of 1993. It received good reviews, yet they didn't compare to the raves Buckley's full-length debut, 1994's *Grace*, received. A long hiatus followed as Buckley worked on material for his follow-up effort, provisionally titled *My Sweetheart, the Drunk*. He finally began work on the record in Memphis during the late spring of 1997; tragically, that May 29, he drowned in the Mississippi River. A collection of unreleased recordings, *Sketches (For My Sweetheart the Drunk)*, appeared in 1998. — *Stephen Thomas Erlewine*

Live at Sin-E [EP] / 1993 / Columbia ✦✦✦

● **Grace** / Aug. 23, 1994 / Columbia ✦✦✦✦✦
Jeff Buckley was many things, but humble wasn't one of them. *Grace* is an audacious debut album, filled with sweeping choruses, bombastic arrangements, searching lyrics and, above all, the richly textured voice of Buckley himself, which resembled a cross between Robert Plant, Van Morrison, and his father Tim. And that's a fair starting point for his music: *Grace* sounds like a Led Zeppelin album written by an ambitious folkie with a fondness for lounge jazz. At his best—the soaring title track, "Last Goodbye," and the mournful "Lover, You Should've Come Over"—Buckley's grasp met his reach with startling results; at its worst, *Grace* is merely promising. — *Stephen Thomas Erlewine*

Sketches (For My Sweetheart the Drunk) / May 26, 1998 / Columbia ✦✦✦✦

Mystery White Boy / May 9, 2000 / Columbia ✦✦✦

Tim Buckley

b. Feb. 14, 1947, Washington, D.C., **d.** Jun. 29, 1975, Santa Monica, CA
Vocals, Guitar / Jazz-Rock, Folk-Jazz, Folk-Rock, Singer/Songwriter
One of the great rock vocalists of the 1960s, Tim Buckley drew from folk, psychedelic rock, and progressive jazz to create a considerable body of adventurous work in his brief lifetime.

His multi-octave range was capable of not just astonishing power, but great emotional expressiveness, swooping from sorrowful tenderness to anguished wailing. His restless quest for new territory worked against him commercially: By the time his fans had hooked into his latest album, he was onto something else entirely, both live and in the studio. In this sense he recalled artists such as Miles Davis and David Bowie, who were so eager to look forward and change that they confused and even angered listeners who wanted more stylistic consistency. However, his eclecticism has also ensured a durable fascination with his work that has engendered a growing posthumous cult for his music, often with listeners who were too young (or not around) to appreciate his music while he was active. *—Richie Unterberger*

● **Tim Buckley** / 1966 / Asylum ✦✦✦✦✦
Buckley's 1966 debut was the most straightforward and folk-rock-oriented of his albums. The material has a lyrical and melodic sophistication that was astounding for a 19-year-old. The pretty, almost precious songs are complemented by appropriately baroque, psychedelic-tinged production. If there was a record that exemplified the '60s Elektra folk-rock sound, this may have been it, featuring production by Elektra owner Jac Holzman and Doors producer Paul Rothchild, Love and Doors engineer Bruce Botnick, and string arrangements by Jack Nitzsche. That's not to diminish the contributions of the band, which included his long-time lead guitarist Lee Underwood and Van Dyke Parks on keyboards. Buckley was still firmly in the singer-songwriter camp on this album, showing only brief flashes of the experimental vocal flights, angst-ridden lyrics, and soul influences that would characterize much of his later work. It's not his most adventurous outing, but it's one of his most accessible, and retains a fragile beauty. *—Richie Unterberger*

Goodbye & Hello / 1967 / Asylum ✦✦✦✦✦
Often cited as the ultimate Tim Buckley statement, *Goodbye and Hello* is indeed a fabulous album, but it's merely one side of Tim Buckley's enormous talent. Recorded in the middle of 1967 (in the afterglow of *Sgt. Pepper*), this album is clearly inspired by *Pepper's* exploratory spirit. More often than not, this helps to bring Buckley's awesome musical vision home, but occasionally falters. Not that the album is overrated (it's not), it's just that it is only one side of Buckley. The finest songs on the album were written by him alone, particularly "Once I Was" and "Pleasant Street." Buoyed by Jerry Yester's excellent production, these tracks are easily among the finest example of Buckley's psychedelic/folk vision. A few tracks, namely the title cut and "No Man Can Find the War," were co-written by poet Larry Beckett. While Beckett's lyrics are undoubtedly literate and evocative, they occasionally tend to be too heavy-handed for Buckley. However, this is a minor criticism of an excellent and revolutionary album that was a quantum leap for both Tim Buckley and the audience. *—Matthew Greenwald*

Dream Letter: Live in London / Jul. 1968 / Rhino/Bizarre ✦✦✦✦✦

Blue Afternoon / 1969 / Rhino/Bizarre ✦✦✦✦✦
On these alternately dark and romantic ballads with a brooding intensity, Buckley's fine vocal and acoustic guitar work is backed up capably by Lee Underwood (guitar, piano), David Friedman (vibes), John Miller (bass), and Jimmy Madison (drums). Songs include "Chase the Blues Away," "Cafe," "So Lonely," "Blue Melody," and "The Train." *—Roundup Newsletter*

Happy Sad / 1969 / Asylum ✦✦✦✦✦
Easily Tim Buckley's most underrated album, *Happy/Sad* was another departure for the eclectic Southern California-based singer/songwriter. After the success of the widely acclaimed *Goodbye and Hello*, Buckley mellowed enough to explore his jazz roots. Sounding like Fred Neil's Capitol-era albums, Buckley and his small, acoustic-based ensemble weave elegant, minimalist tapestries around the six Buckley originals. The effect is completely mesmerizing. On "Buzzin' Fly" and "Strange Feelin'," you are slowly drawn into Buckley's intoxicating vision. The extended opus in the middle of the record, "Love from Room 109," is an intense, complex composition. Lovingly underproduced by Jerry Yester and Zal Yanovsky, this is one of the finest records of the late '60s. *—Matthew Greenwald*

Lorca / 1970 / Asylum ✦✦✦
Buckley stunned and, to a rare degree, alienated fans with the dissonant, at times wearying, avant-garde exercises in vocal gymnastics that took up the entire first side of this LP. Side two was far more accessible, though Buckley's fusion of folk instrumentation with jazzy improvisation on extended compositions continued to take him further away from his folk-rock roots. *—Richie Unterberger*

Starsailor / 1970 / Rhino/Bizarre ✦✦✦✦✦
After his beginnings as a gentle, melodic baroque folk-rocker, Buckley gradually evolved into a downright experimental singer/songwriter who explored both jazz and avant-garde territory. *Starsailor* is the culmination of his experimentation and alienated far more listeners than it exhilarated upon its release in 1970. Buckley had already begun to delve into jazz fusion on late-'60s records like *Happy Sad*, and explored some fairly "out" acrobatic, quasi-operatic vocals on his final Elektra LP, *Lorca*. With former Mother of Invention Bunk Gardner augmenting Buckley's group on sax and alto flute, Buckley applies vocal gymnastics to a set of material that's as avant-garde in its songwriting as its execution. At his most anguished (which is often on this album), he sounds as if his liver is being torn out—slowly. Almost as if to prove he can still deliver a mellow buzz, he throws in a couple of pleasant jazz-pop cuts, including the odd, jaunty French tune "Moulin Rouge." Surrealistic lyrics, heavy on landscape imagery like rivers, skies, suns, and jungle fires, top off a record that isn't for everybody, or even for every Buckley fan, but endures as one of the most uncompromising statements ever made by a singer/songwriter. *—Richie Unterberger*

Greetings from L.A. / 1972 / Rhino/Bizarre ✦✦✦✦
Stepping back from the swooping avant-garde touches of *Starsailor* for a fairly greasy, funky, honky tonk set of songs, the opening lines of *Greetings from L.A.* set the tone: "I went down to the meat rack tavern/And I found myself a big ol' healthy girl." Sassy backing vocalists, honking sax, and more add to the atmosphere, while Tim Buckley himself blends his vocal acrobatics with touches not unfamiliar to fans of Mick Jagger or Jim Morrison. The studio band backing him up might not be the equal to, say, War, but in their own way they do the business; extra touches like the string arrangement on "Sweet Surrender" help all the more. The argument that this was all somehow a compromise or sellout doesn't seem to entirely wash. While no doubt there were commercial pressures at play, given Buckley's constant change from album to album it seems like he simply found something else to try, which he did with gusto. "Get On Top," one of his best numbers, certainly doesn't sound like something aimed for the charts. The music may have a solid groove to it (Kevin Kelly's organ is worth a mention), but Buckley's frank lyrics and improv scatting both show it as him following his own muse. *—Ned Raggett*

Sefronia / 1973 / Manifesto ✦✦

Look at the Fool / 1974 / Manifesto ✦

Live at the Troubadour 1969 / Mar. 22, 1994 / Rhino/Bizarre ✦✦✦

Once I Was / 1999 / Varese ✦✦✦

Works in Progress / 1999 / Rhino Handmade ✦✦✦

Buffalo Springfield

f. 1966, Los Angeles, CA, **db.** 1968
Group / Folk-Rock, Country-Rock, Rock & Roll
Few American groups have produced a wealth of talent like that of Buffalo Springfield. The group's formation is the stuff of legend: driving on Sunset Boulevard in Los Angeles, Stephen Stills and Richie Furay spotted a hearse that Stills was sure belonged to Neil Young, a Canadian he had crossed paths with earlier. Indeed it was, and with the addition of fellow hearse passenger and Canadian Bruce Palmer on bass and ex-Dillard Dewey Martin on drums, the cluster of ex-folkies determined, as the Byrds had just done, to become a rock & roll band. Over a 19-month period, during 1967 and 1968, Buffalo Springfield released three impressive albums. Their debut, including their sole big hit (Stills' "For What It's Worth"), established them as the best folk-rock band in the land barring the Byrds, though the Springfield were a bit more folk and country oriented. The second, *Again*, is their masterpiece, as the group expanded their folk-rock base into tough hard rock and psychedelic orchestration. *—Rick Clark & Richie Unterberger*

Buffalo Springfield / 1967 / Atco ✦✦✦✦
The band themselves were displeased with this record, feeling that the production did not capture their onstage energy and excitement. Yet to most ears, this debut sounds pretty great, featuring some of their most melodic and accomplished songwriting and harmonies, delivered with a hard-rocking punch. "For What It's Worth" was the hit single, but there are several other equally stunning treasures. Stills' "Go and Say Goodbye" was a pioneering country-rock fusion; his "Sit Down I Think I Love You" was the band at their poppiest and most early Beatlesque; and his "Everybody's Wrong" and "Pay the Price" were tough rockers. Although Neil Young has only two lead vocals on the record (Richie Furay sang three other Young compositions), he's already a songwriter of great talent and enigmatic lyricism, particularly on "Nowadays Clancy Can't Even Sing," "Out of My Mind," and "Flying on the Ground is Wrong." The entire album bursts with thrilling guitar and vocal interplay, with a bright exuberance that would tone down considerably by their second record. A 1997 CD reissue presents both mono and stereo mixes of the album, and includes "Baby Don't Scold Me" (which was on the first pressing of the record, but soon replaced by "For What It's Worth"). *—Richie Unterberger*

☆ **Buffalo Springfield Again** / 1967 / Atco ✦✦✦✦✦
Due in part to personnel problems which saw Bruce Palmer and Neil Young in and out of the group, Buffalo Springfield's second album did not have as unified an approach as their debut. Yet it doesn't suffer for that in the least—indeed, the group continued to make major strides in both their songwriting and arranging, and this record stands as their greatest triumph. Stills' "Bluebird" and "Rock & Roll Woman" were masterful folk-rockers that should have been big hits (although they did manage to become small ones); his lesser-known contributions "Hung Upside Down" and the jazz-flavored "Everdays" were also first-rate. Young contributed the Rolling Stones-derived "Mr. Soul," as well as the brilliant "Expecting to Fly" and "Broken Arrow," both of which employed lush psychedelic textures and brooding, surrealistic lyrics that stretched rock conventions to their breaking point. Furay (who had not written any of the songs on the debut) takes tentative songwriting steps with three compositions, although only "A Child's Claim to Fame," with its memorable dobro hooks by James Burton, meets the standards of the material by Stills and Young; the cut also anticipates the country-rock direction of Furay's post-Springfield band, Poco. Although a slightly uneven record that did not feature the entire band on several cuts, the high points were so high and plentiful that its classic status cannot be denied. *—Richie Unterberger*

Last Time Around / 1968 / Atco ✦✦✦
The internal dissension that was already eating away at the group's dynamic on their second album came home to roost on their third and final effort. This was in some sense a Buffalo Springfield album in name but not in spirit, as the songwriters sometimes did not even play on cuts written by other members of the band. Young's relatively slight contribution was a particularly tough blow. He wrote only two of the songs (though he did help Furay write "It's So Hard to Wait"), both of which were outstanding: the plaintive "I Am a Child" and the bittersweet "On the Way Home" (sung by Furay, not Young, on the record). The rest of the ride was bumpier: Stills' material in particular was not as strong as it had been on the first two LPs, though the lovely Latin-flavored "Pretty Girl Why," with its gorgeous guitar work, is one of the group's best songs. Furay was developing into a quality songwriter with the orchestrated "The Hour of Not Quite Rain" and his best Springfield contribution, the beautiful ballad "Kind Woman," which became one of the first country-rock standards. But it was a case of not enough, too late, not only for Furay, but for the group as a whole. *—Richie Unterberger*

★ **Best of Buffalo Springfield . . . Retrospective** / 1969 / Atco ✦✦✦✦✦
Best of Buffalo Springfield . . . Retrospective may not be definitive, but it's a good, basic overview of the group's career, containing most of the group's biggest hits and signature

songs. Yes, there several worthy album cuts are missing, but as a sampler, this works quite well, offering a nice introduction to the group. *—Stephen Thomas Erlewine*

Buffalo Tom

f. 1986, Boston, MA

Group / Adult Alternative Pop/Rock, Alternative Pop/Rock

When they released their first album in 1989, the Boston-based trio Buffalo Tom was written off as Dinosaur Jr. junior. Admittedly, their debut was in debt to J Mascis' thundering guitar and folk-tinged songs and it didn't help that Mascis produced the record, either. Over time, Buffalo Tom stripped away their grungier influences and developed into a straightahead rock group of the early '90s, capable of throttling rockers and beautiful ballads.

Comprised of guitarist/vocalist Bill Janovitz, bassist/vocalist Chris Colbourn, and drummer Tom Maginnis, Buffalo Tom began to develop their own style with their second album, 1990's *Birdbrain*, which featured a noticeable improvement in songwriting. In 1992, Buffalo Tom released *Let Me Come Over*, a gritty set of driving rock and achingly melancholy ballads; several of its tracks became alternative-radio staples, including the gorgeous ballad "Taillights Fade." Despite an increased amount of critical praise and some radio airplay, the album didn't sell. The follow-up, 1993's *Big Red Letter Day*, featured a more polished, radio-ready production, but the album received only a small push from radio and MTV. "Soda Jerk," the first single from the album, became a minor alternative-radio and MTV hit. After a year-long tour, the group returned in the summer of 1995 with *Sleepy Eyed*, a return to the more direct sound of *Let Me Come Over*. *Smitten* followed in 1998, and two years later the best-of, *Asides From Buffalo Tom*, arrived. *—Stephen Thomas Erlewine*

Buffalo Tom / 1989 / Beggars Banquet ✦✦✦

Birdbrain / Nov. 1990 / Beggars Banquet ✦✦✦

Birdbrain is a transitional record which marks the beginnings of Buffalo Tom's move away from the guitar-drenched sound which earned them the perjorative nickname Dinosaur Jr. Junior into leaner, more acoustically-driven pop-rock. While Dinosaur's J. Mascis is still on as producer, his influence is measurably diminished this time out, as evidenced on the tense, delicate "Enemy" and an acoustic cover of the Psychedelic Furs' "Heaven." And speaking of psychedelia, *Birdbrain* draws on elements of '60s acid-rock too, as well as the feedback that defined the Buffalo Tom of yore. *—Jason Ankeny*

Let Me Come Over / Mar. 10, 1992 / Beggars Banquet ✦✦✦✦✦

With *Let Me Come Over*, Buffalo Tom comes into its own, producing a remarkably strong album filled with exceptional songwriting. The Dinosaur Jr. comparisons are no longer accurate; now, the band sounds slightly like R.E.M. crossed with the Replacements, but that's just a starting point—the band has carved out its own brand of guitar-heavy rock & roll, somewhere between college-rock and traditional, classic rock. Buffalo Tom proves equally adept at pulling off the driving "Staples" and "Mountains of Your Head," the majestic folk-rock of "Mineral," the ballads "Larry," "Frozen Lake," and the gorgeous "Taillights Fade," which is a masterpiece. *Let Me Come Over* is the breakthrough album from one of America's best rock & roll bands of the 1990s. *—Stephen Thomas Erlewine*

Big Red Letter Day / Nov. 2, 1993 / Beggars Banquet ✦✦✦✦

Produced by the Robb Brothers (Kristen Barry), the Boston-based trio released album number four in 1993 to more critical acclaim but tepid sales and airplay. A more polished effort than previous efforts, *Big Red Letter Day* still manages to maintain the band's D.I.Y. charm. The set alternates musically between upbeat, driving rock and slower, more introspective cuts with equal aplomb. The single "Sodajerk" kicks thinks off in style with its ultra-melodic guitar and things continue on an upward curve. The multi-layered "Tree House" features some lovely harmonies by Julia and Maxine Waters and "Dry Land" is bracing, highlighted by a raucous guitar solo from Bill Janovitz. *Big Red Letter Day* is a sonic delight right through the resilience of the closing track "Anything That Way." *—Tom Demalon*

Sleepy Eyed / Jul. 11, 1995 / East West ✦✦✦

Lead singer Bill Janovitz and company followed 1993's *Big Red Letter Day* with another collection of engaging power pop with an alternative twist. *Sleepy Eyed* found the band producing themselves with John Agnello and, although they break no new ground, there's plenty here to please fans of both melody and lyrical depth. Backed by bassist Chris Colbourn and drummer Tom Maginnis, Janovitz leads Buffalo Tom through 14 tracks that range from the leadoff rocker "Tangerine" and the mid-tempo "Kitchen Door," which features Coulbourn taking the vocal lead. Other noteworthy cuts include the propulsive kick of the playful "Your Stripes," the soul-searching "When You Discover," and the spacy guitar on "Crueler," which starts out gently before erupting. Not the band's best but still well worth repeated listens. *—Tom Demalon*

Smitten / Sep. 29, 1998 / Polydor ✦✦

• **A-Sides from 1988-1999** / Aug. 22, 2000 / Beggars Banquet ✦✦✦✦✦

Buffalo Tom began life as a trio of pre-grunge, neo-psychedelic guitar maulers owing a heavy debt to Dinosaur Jr. (though one might argue that on *Birdbrain* they actually beat J. Mascis at his own game), but over the next dozen years they matured into a considerably more dynamic and intelligent band, capable of generating crunching rockers or acoustic ballads with equal precision, all of which possessed heart, soul, and a compassionate intelligence. *A-sides From 1988-1999* compiles most of the band's best-known songs, including the top sides of their singles, radio emphasis tracks, a few fan favorites, and a cover of the Jam's "Going Underground" from a 1999 tribute album. While the album isn't sequenced chronologically, which would have made a greater case for their growth over time, it does a superb job of capturing the many sides of their musical personality, and it is both a fine summation of their first 11 years as a recording act and great introduction to one of the better bands to rise from the alt-rock scene in the 1990s. *A-sides From 1988-1999* also features excellent and enlightening liner notes from the three members of the band, Bill Janovitz, Chris Colbourn, and Tom Maginnis. *—Mark Deming*

Jimmy Buffett

b. Dec. 25, 1946, Pascogoula, MS

Vocals, Guitar / Pop/Rock, Singer/Songwriter, Country-Rock

Singer/songwriter Jimmy Buffett has translated his easy-going Gulf Coast persona into more than just a successful recording career—he has expanded into clothing, nightclubs, and literature. But the basis of his business empire is undeniably music. After recording in Nashville during the early '70s, Buffett moved to Key West, Florida, where he gradually evolved the beach bum character and tropical folk-rock style that would endear him to millions. Signed to ABC-Dunhill, Buffett achieved notoriety but not much else with his second album, 1973's *White Sport Coat & A Pink Crustacean*, which featured a song called, "Why Don't We Get Drunk" ("...and screw?," goes the chorus). It took the 1977 Top Ten song "Margaritaville" and the album in which it was featured, *Changes in Latitudes, Changes in Attitudes*, to capture his tropical worldview and, for a while, turn him into a pop star. By the '80s, a steadily growing core of Sun Belt fans he dubbed "Parrotheads" began making his concerts into successful, Mardi Gras-like affairs. His recording career, meanwhile, languished, though a hits compilation, a 1990 live album and a 1992 box-set retrospective were quite successful. Buffett finally returned to the studio for 1994's *Fruitcakes;* the album became one of his fastest-selling records. It was followed in 1995 by *Barometer Soup* and *Banana Wind* in 1996. After a short-lived Broadway venture, he returned in 1999 with *Beach House on the Moon*. *—William Ruhlmann*

• **Songs You Know By Heart** / Oct. 1985 / MCA ✦✦✦✦✦

Combining aloof humor with a laid-back, devil-may-care island attitude, Jimmy Buffet sang songs about alcohol consumption, lazing around in the sun, and the freedom of not having to work for a living. *Songs You Know By Heart* is a solid offering of Buffet's greatest hits, pulling together his truly strongest material and avoiding the unnecessary filler that appears on his albums. His claim to fame, "Margaritaville," is the jewel in the crown here, which still harbors that tropical feel thanks to its Caribbean-styled rhythm and relaxed flow. "Come Monday" picks up where "Margaritaville" leaves off, only this ballad plays out with subdued sincerity and has Buffet sounding strangely serious, and romantic. Most of the songs from Buffet are centered around his frolicking lifestyle, like the comical "Cheeseburger in Paradise" or the naughtiness of "Why Don't We Get Drunk," an ode to his party-filled outlook on life. Buffet's voice shines on the clever "Changes in Latitudes, Changes in Attitudes," which again spotlights his love of living without concern, especially in someplace warm. The catchy and whimsical "Fins" is lifted by a contagious pace with a smart chorus and serves as one of the highlights of this collection. As a compilation, this bunch of Jimmy Buffet's most famous tunes contains just the right amount of tracks. Any less would be inconsistent and any more would be deemed as overkill. *—Mike DeGagne*

Boats, Beaches, Bars & Ballads / May 1992 / MCA ✦✦✦✦✦

Most listeners will be satisfied with the excellent Jimmy Buffett summary *Songs You Know By Heart*, but anyone that wants to dig deeper should bypass the albums (there are several that are first-rate, yet many are spotty) and pick up the four-disc, 72-track box set, *Boats, Beaches, Bars & Ballads*. Assembled thematically, with each disc devoted to one of the words in the title, this rounds up not just every Buffett hit, but pretty much every one of his noteworthy album tracks, plus a couple of rarities and unreleased cuts. For some, this much Buffett may cause sunstroke, yet this proves that he had some fine moments that weren't singles, and even those that aren't Parrotheads will be impressed by the consistency of his music—if you like Jimmy, he usually delivers what you like. *—Stephen Thomas Erlewine*

The Buggles

f. 1979, England, **db.** 1980

Group / New Wave, Synth Pop

As the answer to the trivia question "What was the first act ever played on MTV?," the Buggles assured their place in pop music history. Vocalist and bassist Trevor Horn and keyboardist Geoff Downes formed the electro-pop duo in England in 1979 after meeting two years prior as session musicians. Their first single, "Video Killed the Radio Star," hit number one in the U.K. in late 1979; when MTV went on the air in 1981, the prophetically-titled record's video was the first ever broadcast on the fledgling cable network.

Although the Buggles enjoyed three more British hits—"The Plastic Age," "Clean Clean" and "Elstree"—both Horn and Downes were more interested in production than performing; in 1980, they helmed Yes' *Drama*, and later joined the group as replacements for Rick Wakeman and Jon Anderson. After Yes' break-up, Downes signed on with Asia, while Horn formed ZTT Records and produced hits for the likes of Frankie Goes to Hollywood and ABC. *—Jason Ankeny*

• **The Age of Plastic** / 1980 / Island ✦✦✦✦✦

The fun, quirky single "Video Killed the Radio Star" garnered The Buggles international attention in 1980, but it was just one of *The Age of Plastic*'s fascinating, futuristic visions. From the title track's opening strains,Trevor Horn and Geoff Downes transform your living room into a world of *Jetson*-like proportions. It's a world, though, where technology is seen for what it is—full of both promise and frightening implications. On "I Love You Miss Robot," a metaphorical love affair with a robot explores modern man's relationship to, and dependence on, technology. "Kid Dynamo"'s spirited tempo, biting lyrics, and menacing vocal track questions the loss of imagination plaguing the mass media age. For the most part, *The Age of Plastic* is a fun record doesn't need to be taken too seriously, though a subtle sense of loss is woven throughout. Variety is the constant and tracks vary from the giddy "Video," to the dark and pulsating "Johnny on the Monorail." The vision here is so beautifully articulated that the superb musicianship and production wizardry is easily overlooked. Paradoxically, Horn and Downes employed electronic devices (which were considered new and cutting edge in the late seventies) to create an album which, at times, spoke eloquently about their drawbacks. With *The Age of Plastic*, Horn and Downes stamped an indelible image in the collective pop psyche. What is equally impressive is the sound of this disc given its analog origins and 1980-release date. While hiss can be heard in some of the quieter passages, it would be difficult to find a record from this era that sounds half as good. Pop rarely reaches these heights. *—Jeri Montesano*

Adventures in Modern Recording / Feb. 1982 / EMI ✦✦✦✦

Sonny Burgess

b. May 28, 1931, Newport, AR

Vocals, Guitar / Rockabilly

Sonny Burgess is one of the wildest rockers to record for the legendary Sun label in Memphis. He and his band the Pacers came out of Newport, Arkansas, with a hard-rocking style that, unlike that of most rockabillies, owed little to nothing in the way of a stylistic debt to country music. With his red-dyed hair, matching stage suit and guitar, and wild stage performances, Burgess and the Pacers made mincemeat of the competition on many of the early-'50s rock & roll package tours. Though his Sun releases never brought him much in the way of commercial success, his recordings nonetheless remain landmarks of the early rockabilly style. Currently touring and recording with other Memphis alumni in the Sun Rhythm Section, the rockin' flame that is Sonny Burgess refuses to be snuffed out. *—Cub Koda*

● **We Wanna Boogie** / 1990 / Rounder ✦✦✦✦✦

If you want a fairly definitive compilation of the Sun material by this minor rockabilly figure, but don't want to go the whole nine yards for the expensive import double CD on Bear Family, this domestic anthology is a recommended alternative. The 13 tracks contain six sides from his '50s singles (including the most noted, "Red Headed Woman" and "My Bucket's Got a Hole in It"), and seven other cuts from the '50s that were unissued at the time. *—Richie Unterberger*

The Classic Recordings 1956-1959 / Jul. 1991 / Bear Family ✦✦✦✦✦

Sonny's complete output for Sun spread over two CDs. Wild and crazed, featuring Burgess' spitfire guitar and booming vocals and the relentless drive of the Pacers in support. *—Cub Koda*

Solomon Burke

b. 1936, Philadelphia, PA

Vocals / Deep Soul, Southern Soul, Soul

While Solomon Burke never made a major impact upon the pop audience—he never, in fact, had a Top Twenty hit—he was an important early soul pioneer. On his 1960s singles for Atlantic, he brought a country influence into R&B with emotional phrasing and intricately constructed, melodic ballads and mid-tempo songs. At the same time, he was surrounded with sophisticated "uptown" arrangements, and provided with much of his material, by his producers, particularly Bert Berns. The combination of gospel, pop, country, and production polish was basic to the recipe of early soul. While Burke wasn't the only one pursuing this path, not many others did so as successfully. He began recording gospel and R&B sides for Apollo in the mid-to-late '50s, and was molded into a more secular direction when he signed with Atlantic in the 1960s. Burke had a wealth of high-charting R&B hits in the early half of the '60s, which crossed over to the pop listings in a mild fashion as well. "Just out of Reach," "Cry to Me," "If You Need Me," "Got to Get You off My Mind," "Tonight's the Night," and "Goodbye Baby (Baby Goodbye)" were the most successful. He left Atlantic in the late '60s, and spent the next decade hopping between various labels, getting his biggest hit with a cover of Creedence Clearwater Revival's "Proud Mary" in 1969. *—Richie Unterberger*

Home in Your Heart / Apr. 21, 1992 / Rhino ✦✦✦✦✦

Home in Your Heart—The Best of Solomon Burke is a 41-track two-disc set that covers Burke's Atlantic recordings from 1961 to 1968. Seventeen of those tracks charted. All are superior examples of country-soul and gospel-soul. *—Rob Bowman*

★ **The Very Best of Solomon Burke** / Feb. 3, 1998 / Rhino ✦✦✦✦✦

The Very Best of Solomon Burke is an excellent 16-track collection that features his biggest hits from 1961-1968, including "Just Out of Reach (Of My Two Open Arms)," "Cry to Me," "Down in the Valley," "I'm Hanging Up My Heart for You," "If You Need Me," "You're Good for Me," "Goodbye Baby (Baby Goodbye)," and "Everybody Needs Somebody to Love." All of his best-known songs in their hit versions are available on this concise, affordable disc, not always in strict release order but still an education in and of themselves—the tracks all come from the first generation original single masters, many of which were remixed or even shunted aside in favor of re-recorded versions for his albums during the 1960s, including his greatest-hits and best-of collections. The producers spent the time to track down those long-unused and forgotten originals for this, their first authentic representation on CD. Additionally, the 16th song is a true diamond among the R&B treasures here—the June 1968 single "Soul Meeting" cut by the Soul Clan, which consisted of Burke, Arthur Conley, Don Covay, Ben E. King, and Joe Tex, the super-session product of a short-lived experiment in raising money for the black community. This is the only appearance of this Don Covay-authored track on CD, and makes this release essential even for those who already own the 1992 double-CD set *Home In Your Heart*. *—Stephen Thomas Erlewine & Bruce Eder*

Proud Mary: The Bell Sessions / Jul. 18, 2000 / Sundazed ✦✦✦

This is a somewhat spruced-up version of Burke's 1969 *Proud Mary* album, containing all of the songs from that LP, and adding seven bonus cuts from 1969-70 singles and outtakes. Burke kept pace with changing soul and rock trends fairly well on *Proud Mary*, which has a funkier, bluesier deep soul feel than his more famous early- and mid-1960s Atlantic material. That feel didn't come about by total accident, of course; the record was recorded at Muscle Shoals, where he could sing with the area's esteemed session musicians, rather than the uptown New York players he'd worked with at Atlantic. There's a bit of a sense of Burke following the crowd rather than blazing his own path, and the song selection is a bit unimaginative (not that this was an unusual happenstance on soul albums). Still, even those are given respectable readings, and Burke also tackles a couple of songs Dan Penn co-penned, in addition to waxing one of his own, "How Big a Fool (Can a Fool Be)," which has that thin electric sitar-guitar hybrid sound peculiar to some pop-soul discs of the era. The bonus tracks are pretty interesting, including previously unissued covers of Bob Dylan's "The Mighty Quinn" and Sam Cooke's "Change Is Gonna Come," along with some non-LP singles that showed Burke absorbing (as he had on the *Proud Mary* album) some contemporary rock influences. His own "The Generation of Revelations," a 1969 single, made some fashionable lyrical bows to the counterculture; an odd 1970 single matched a post-Elvis Presley cover of "In the Ghetto" with the gospel rock of "God Knows I Love You," written by the unusual songwriting team of Delaney Bramlett and "In the Ghetto" composer Mac Davis. *—Richie Unterberger*

Bush

f. 1992

Group / Post-Grunge, Grunge, Alternative Pop/Rock

Led by guitarist/vocalist Gavin Rossdale, Bush became the first post-Nirvana British band to hit it big in America. Of course, they became a hit by playing by the grunge rules—they had loud guitars, guttural vocals, stop-start rhythms, and extreme dynamics. Bush landed an American record deal before they had a British label; *Sixteen Stone*, their debut album, was released in late 1993 by Interscope Records. By the end of December, Bush's "Everything Zen" video had landed in MTV's Buzz Bin and the album began to take off; by spring of 1995, the record had gone gold, despite a stack of bad reviews. Over the course of 1995, *Sixteen Stone* became a major hit in the US, with "Little Things" reaching number four on the modern rock charts in the spring; later that year "Comedown" and "Glycerine" both reached number one on the modern rock charts, as well as crossing over into the pop Top 40. Despite their success, Bush received scathing reviews from the press and many alternative-rock insiders, who believed the group was manufactured. To counter such charges, the band asked Steve Albini—notorious for his abrasive productions for not only Pixies, Nirvana and PJ Harvey, but also countless indie bands—to helm their second album, *Razorblade Suitcase*. *—Stephen Thomas Erlewine*

● **Sixteen Stone** / Dec. 5, 1994 / Trauma/Interscope ✦✦✦✦

Bush's grunge-by-the-numbers is certainly well produced. Under the guidance of Clive Langer and Alan Winstanley—the kings of early-'80s British pop—Bush turns in album that follows all the rules and sounds of American hard rock, specifically Nirvana and Pearl Jam. Their songwriting isn't original, nor is it particularly catchy. What makes "Everything Zen" and "Little Things" memorable is the exact reproduction of all of Nirvana's trademarks, only with a more professional execution—in other words, all the guitars keep rhythm perfectly and Gavin doesn't shred his throat when he sings, he projects from his diaphragm. As far as pop craftmanship goes, it's actually quite impressive. It would be even more so if they had songs to accompany their sounds. *—Stephen Thomas Erlewine*

Razorblade Suitcase / Nov. 19, 1996 / Trauma/Interscope ✦✦✦

The Science of Things / Oct. 26, 1999 / Trauma/Interscope ✦✦✦

Kate Bush

b. Jul. 30, 1958, Bexleyheath, Kent, England

Vocals, Keyboards, Piano / College Rock, Prog-Rock/Art Rock, Alternative Pop/Rock

One of the most successful and popular solo female acts of the past 20 years to come out of England, Kate Bush is also one of the most unusual, with her keening vocals and unusually literate and complex body of songs. By the time Bush was 16, she had signed to EMI Records, though the company made the decision to bring her along slowly. In 1977, her debut single "Wuthering Heights" rose to number one on the British charts. By the beginning of the 1980s, Bush was established as one of the most challenging and eccentric artists ever to have achieved success in rock music, with a range of sounds and interests that constantly challenged listeners. Her third album *Never for Ever* hit number one, as did her fifth, *Hounds of Love*. The latter remained on top for a full month, and soon after, the single "Running Up That Hill" gave Bush her long-awaited American breakthrough, reaching number 30 on *Billboard's* charts. In October of 1989, Bush's first new album in almost four years, *The Sensual World*, reached the British number two spot. Bush's next album, *The Red Shoes* (1993), debuted in the American Top 30, the first time one of her albums had ever charted that high. *—Bruce Eder*

The Kick Inside / Feb. 17, 1978 / EMI America ✦✦✦✦✦

Bush's first album is her most unabashedly romantic, the sound of an impressionable and highly precocious teenage singer/songwriter spreading her wings for the first time. "Wuthering Heights" was a monster hit everywhere in the world except America, and it's still an impressive debut nearly 20 years later, but Bush would do better work than this. *—Bruce Eder*

Lionheart / Nov. 13, 1978 / EMI America ✦✦✦

Bush's second album was something of a disappointment, lacking the depth and certainty of direction of her debut. The title track is an enigmatic paean to her mother country, "Wow" is a strong vocal workout but somewhat on the obscure side, and the rest is enjoyable and teasing but nowhere near what Bush is capable of. *—Bruce Eder*

Never for Ever / Sep. 8, 1980 / EMI America ✦✦✦

Kate Bush returned to form on her third album, which is steeped in images of violence and anger ("Babooshka," "The Wedding List") but also includes fascinating references to classical music ("Delius"). Very finely produced as well. *—Bruce Eder*

The Dreaming / Sep. 13, 1982 / EMI America ✦✦

Hounds of Love / 1985 / EMI America ✦✦✦✦✦

Bush's strongest album to date marked her breakthrough into the American charts, and yielded a set of dazzling videos. The material ranges from the sensual ("Hounds of Love," "Running Up That Hill"—the latter one of the most sensual recordings ever made) to the mystical ("Hello Earth," "The Morning Fog"). This was also the first album produced by Bush entirely at her own home studio, and the results are spellbinding, the layered instruments recalling the Beatles at the most ornate, but also displaying an exquisite timbral range, bringing out the richness of the individual instruments. Note: The British edition of this and Bush's earlier albums all have significantly better sound than their American editions and are worth finding as imports. [In 1997, as a part of EMI's 100th Anniversary, *Hounds of Love* was reissued, augmented with a bunch of rare singles, B-sides, outtakes etc. from the same period.] *—Bruce Eder*

● **The Whole Story** / Nov. 10, 1986 / EMI America ✦✦✦✦✦
Bush's first best-of is an excellent compilation/overview, encompassing all her best-known songs (including "Wuthering Heights" with an improved, re-recorded vocal track) up through the major tracks off of *Hounds of Love* and her follow-up single, the haunting and dramatic "Experiment IV." *—Bruce Eder*

The Sensual World / Oct. 1989 / Columbia ✦✦✦✦✦
The follow-up to *Hounds of Love* is almost its match, a collection of material devoted to Bush's perceptions of love and sensuality. The best track, however, is "This Woman's Work," from a now-forgotten feature film, a beautiful and poignant look at the female psyche at its most gentle and giving. *—Bruce Eder*

This Woman's Work (1978-1990) / 1990 / EMI ✦✦✦✦✦
Excellent box collecting all of Bush's work, including obscure B-sides, odd mixes, and other rarities in one place. The notes are skimpy, and some people who already own some of her individual CDs will be unhappy having to duplicate their purchases, but the rarities are fascinating, and because this set is from England, it uses the superior British masters on the 1978-1985 albums. (British import) *—Bruce Eder*

The Red Shoes / Nov. 2, 1993 / Columbia ✦✦

Jerry Butler

b. Dec. 8, 1939, Sunflower, MS
Vocals / Chicago Soul, Uptown Soul, Pop-Soul, Northern Soul, R&B, Soul
Jerry Butler's career spans four decades; he's recorded more than 50 albums and his voice is one of the most distinguished voices in all of music. As soulful as ever, yet smooth as ice, his nickname "The Iceman" epitomizes his demeanor—and sound. Butler scored his first hit with the Impressions in 1958 with the timeless ballad "For Your Precious Love." That same year he began his solo career. Butler had his first hit as a solo artist with "He Will Break Your Heart." The single popped the top of the charts at number one and stayed there for seven consecutive weeks. In 1961 Butler bounced back with two top ten singles: "Find Another Girl" and "I'm a Telling You." In 1967 Butler signed with Mercury and teamed up with the production duo of Kenny Gamble and Leon Huff. His work with these two master producers and songwriters resulted in some classic recordings, including the outstanding album *Ice Man Cometh*. The album featured one superb track after another, including the number one singles "Hey, Western Union Man" and "Only the Strong Survive." Always known for being a crooner, "Hey, Western Union Man" revealed to many that Butler was more than capable of singing uptempo songs. In 1971 Gamble and Huff formed their own label and subsequently Butler formed a creative workshop to help provide material for his forthcoming albums. He continued his hit-making tradition with "Ain't Understanding Mellow," a classic soul-ballad duet with Brenda Lee Eager that peaked at number three on the Billboard R&B charts. The timeless single remains a Quiet Storm jewel. "(I'm Just Thinking About) Cooling Out" was his last top 20 hit. *—Craig Lytle*

★ **The Best of Jerry Butler [Rhino]** / 1987 / Rhino ✦✦✦✦✦
The primary value of this 14-song collection is that it includes material from both the Vee-Jay and Mercury eras. Butler fans are much better advised to get the compilations that cover his output for each label in much greater depth (*The Ice Man* for Vee-Jay, *Iceman: The Mercury Years* for Mercury). For the casual fan, though, it might be the best buy, as it's the only best-of spanning both labels, and includes all of his biggest hits. *—Richie Unterberger*

The Best of Jerry Butler [Vee-Jay] / 1987 / Vee-Jay ✦✦✦✦✦
Almost the same thing can be said for this one as for many other Jerry Butler hit sets, except that it's probably still available and has been issued on CD. The usual hits are here, and it's a good starting point. *—Ron Wynn*

☆ **Iceman: The Mercury Years** / Feb. 4, 1992 / Mercury ✦✦✦✦✦
A glorious 44-song double-disc set, it collects Butler's best Mercury sides, with several previously unreleased songs and alternate mixes. The liner notes are crummy, though. *—John Floyd*

The Butthole Surfers

f. 1982, San Antonio, TX
Group / College Rock, Experimental Rock, Noise-Rock, Alternative Pop/Rock
Arguably the most infamously named band in the annals of popular music—for years, radio found their moniker unspeakable, and the press deemed it unprintable—the Butthole Surfers long reigned among the most twisted and depraved acts ever to bubble up from the American underground. Masters of calculated outrage, the group fused the sicko antics of shock-rock with a distinct and chaotic mishmash of avant-garde, hardcore and Texas psychedelia which seemed destined to guarantee the Buttholes little more than a lifetime of cultdom. Yet, by the mid-'90s, they were left-field Top 40 hitmakers, success perhaps their ultimate subversion of mainstream ideals. Gibby Haynes and Paul Leary founded the band and in 1981 signed to Alternative Tentacles for their hallucinatory eponymous debut. The Surfers' lineup stabilized with the 1983 addition of drummers King Coffey and Theresa Nervosa and a move to the Chicago-based indie Touch and Go precipitated a turn towards even greater thematic offensiveness, as evidenced by 1985's *Psychic... Powerless... Another Man's Sac*. Following a series of late-'80s albums, they remained uncharacteristically silent until 1991's uneven *Pioughd*, recorded for the Rough Trade label. One year later, the group signed with major label Capitol, which released 1993's *Independent Worm Saloon*. The Butthole Surfers returned in 1996 with *Electriclarryland*, scoring a major chart hit with the trip-hop-flavored "Pepper." *—Jason Ankeny*

Brown Reason to Live [EP] / 1983 / Alternative Tentacles ✦✦✦✦

Psychic . . . Powerless . . . Another Man's Sac / 1985 / Latino Bugger Veil ✦✦✦✦
The Surfers' Touch and Go debut remains their highlight for many fans, an inspired blast of ugly noise, knowing idiocy, drugged-out insanity and some backhanded surprises. Haynes is still relatively interpretable here; the vocal distortion are only on a few songs, like the opening "Concubine," and what one can't quite understand one can still sense. The band's self-production, brings out the mighty rumbles of drummers Coffey and Nervosa and Leary's avant-junkyard guitar work with clarity and a big, thick punch. Leary begins with screwy blues and gentle strums, then cranks up the amps and lets fly. The band also officially recorded their semi-theme song "Butthole Surfer," after which they were accidentally named; the bizarro backing vocals and sudden sped-up shifts at the end are just part of the oddities on display. "Negro Observer" is one of the most straightforward, calmest songs of the bunch, and even that's saying something, with Haynes going off about the title characters—described as aliens coming to "count heads in singles bars"—like a barely stable street crazy, insane laughter and all. When it comes to full-on craziness, though, nothing beats the obscene "Lady Sniff," which sounds like an amped-up blues act fronted by a 100-year-old man, and the hallucinatory "Mexican Caravan," with Haynes raving about "that heroin BROWN!" The nods to rock history are subtle but present, from the Black Sabbath-quoting (specifically "Children of the Grave") opening rhythm of "Dum Dum" to the fried Tex/Mex-ranting of "Gary Floyd," written about the legendary Dicks bandleader. However, the Surfers' crazy blend is completely distinctive, taking punk and the inspiration of their acid-addled Texas forebears new heights. *—Ned Raggett*

Rembrandt Pussyhorse / 1986 / Latino Bugger Veil ✦✦✦✦
Everything seems to start almost normally on *Pussyhorse* with "Creep in the Cellar," even with the rather gone violin line—Haynes is intelligible, the piano part is quiet serene. Then again, Haynes is talking about the creep in question doing things like taking off his skin, so clearly all is still at least somewhat tweaked in Surferland. The rest of the album makes that pretty clear; if not quite as strong as *Psychic... Powerless*, *Pussyhorse* is still a strong slice of homegrown art/psychedelia gone to a murky hell. Gentler songs like "Sea Ferring" still have a distinct queasiness to them, its sea chanty feeling undercut by the nagging bass line and Haynes' yelps. When the group goes totally nuts, as on a drum-blasting, squiggly voiced cover of the Guess Who's "American Woman" that makes the later Lenny Kravitz version seem like the redundant slice of nostalgia it is, no prisoners are taken. "Perry" is another definite nutter, with Haynes or somebody talking about this and that to his "baby" over a slow, organ-heavy groove. This said, the trick about *Pussyhorse*, and arguably why it's slightly lesser than *Psychic... Powerless*, is its overall subtlety in comparison. Things are more dark and gloomy throughout, downright gothic, even, with the organ start and whispery lyrics of "Strangers Die Everyday" being a good example. Leary keeps his playing low and strange throughout, fitting in with new bassist Pinkus rather well as a result. Get past the slight surprise of not always hearing the Surfers going near-all out most of the time, though, and *Pussyhorse* is still mighty fine, whether talking about the drony guitar weirdness opening "Whirling Hall of Knives" or the echo-treated reprise of "In the Cellar." CD versions of *Pussyhorse* conveniently include the *Cream Corn From the Socket of Davis* EP. *—Ned Raggett*

● **Locust Abortion Technician** / 1987 / Latino Bugger Veil ✦✦✦✦✦
By the time *Locust Abortion Technician* came out, the Surfers were well-established as a hugely popular affair in the American indie rock scene, with albums as notorious as its bacchanalian concerts, which often featured things like penile surgery films projected over the band's monstrous performances. From the start, *Locust* was the perfect aural equivalent to such insanity. The hilarious opening segment—later sampled by Orbital—sounds like something from a '50s morality film: a friendly, fatherly voice explains the nature of regret before concluding, "And by the way son, if you see your mother, tell her... SATAN! SATAN!" Then the band kicks into "Sweat Loaf," which uses Black Sabbath's ode to weed "Sweet Leaf" as a starting point, mixing a massive, crunching version of the original with Haynes', looped, flanged vocals, which send the song spiraling off into the netherworld with even more weirdness. The remainder of *Locust* (a very quick album, barely over half an hour long) maintains the high standard with all sorts of rampant production trickery, resulting in a step up from the fine but somewhat subdued *Rembrandt Pussyhorse*. Haynes sounds like Satan after a series of drug injections, while Leary's guitar goes equally nuts with squalling solos, screeching noises and all sorts of general weirdness (particularly on "O-Men"). Pinkus and Coffey lay down the rhythms in finest death-march tradition. Not everything is total doom and snarl, though; "22 Going on 23" closes things out on a weirdly ambiguous note, with a live found-sound interview of a sexual assault victim playing over a slow, deliberate crunch and a final, soaring Leary solo, provides some fun variety among the mayhem. *—Ned Raggett*

Hairway to Steven / 1988 / Latino Bugger Veil ✦✦✦✦✦
The final album for the Surfers' legendary run on Touch and Go got a reception probably not even the band figured on—lead reviews in major music magazines, increasingly higher profiles, and more. As it is, though, *Hairway* is actually a touch lazy in comparison to the previous releases, sometimes sounding almost all too normal. When it connects, though, *Steven* works wonders, whether continuing in the punk/psychedelic fusion vein of the past or exploring a gentler, tuneful side. The lengthy opener "Jimi" is the album's high note, and as one might guess from the title it's something of a tribute to Hendrix—at least, if "Third Stone From the Sun" sounded like it was recorded in a sewer tunnel and was even more gone than it already was. Haynes' alternately deep and hyper-high-pitched vocals work perfectly against Leary's searing, crazed guitar noises, while the Pinkus/Coffey rhythm section lays down a massive beat. Everything concludes with deceptive peacefulness: acoustic guitar, tweeting birds, sounds of bowling, and the like. Other highlights include "I Saw an X-Ray of a Girl Passing Gas," a relatively straightforward, mostly acoustic-plus-rhythm section number sung clearly (!) by Haynes, and the mock live recording "John E. Smokes," with Haynes often sounding like a rural preacher gone mad. The humming guitar buzz of "Backass" and the quick blast of "Fart Song" concludes *Steven* with vim. As a final note, the song titles themselves can't be found anywhere on the release—instead, and quite notoriously, a series of car-

toon drawings stand in for them. Some are fairly calm, but most show things like nude women displaying their butts and rabbits taking dumps on deer. Juvenile? Of course, but the Butthole Surfers never pretended to be nice and sweet. *—Ned Raggett*

Pioughd / 1991 / Capitol ✦✦

Independent Worm Saloon / Mar. 23, 1993 / Capitol ✦✦✦
After *Pioughd*'s semi-misfire and Rough Trade's subsequent collapse, the Surfers were in a surprising position. Not only were they courted and signed to Capitol thanks to the Nirvana-led alternative explosion, they also got high-profile arranger and Led Zeppelin legend John Paul Jones to produce the new album. When *Saloon* surfaced in early 1993, some accused the band of basically cloning Haynes' memorable collaboration with Ministry, "Jesus Built My Hot Rod," for the entire album. It's true that "Some Dispute Over T-Shirt Sales," simply takes the lyrics from that number and grafts it onto a quick rip from the band, but *Saloon* is far from a clone of Ministry or anything else. More energetic than the straggling *Pioughd* and benefiting from Jones' brilliant ear and tight, crisp arrangements, *Saloon* starts with the fierce "Who Was In My Room Last Night?"; from there, the Surfers tear through hilarious and strong numbers. Creating radio-friendly unit shifters was clearly the last thing on the band's mind, as numbers like "The Annoying Song," with Haynes sounding like what a radar dish would do if it could sing, and the wittily solemn acoustic ditty "The Ballad of Naked Man" demonstrate. The Surfers' taste for rude grostequerie surfaces throughout—the foul "Chewin' George Lucas' Chocolate," the series of vomit sounds that conclude the record after "Clean It Up"'s heavy trudge and the extremely disturbing artwork are just a few examples. Combined with numerous examples of Surfer-mania at its finest—the dipsomaniacal rager "Alcohol," the electric country hoedown "You Don't Know Me" and more—and *Saloon* is that rarest of records, a major-label debut that surpasses the indie release preceding it. *—Ned Raggett*

Hole Truth . . . And Nothing Butt / Mar. 27, 1995 / Trance Syndicate ✦✦✦

Electriclarryland / Apr. 1996 / Capitol ✦✦✦

The Buzzcocks

f. 1975, Manchester, England
Group / British Punk, Punk
With their crisp melodies, driving guitars, and guitarist Pete Shelley's biting lyrics, the Buzzcocks were one of the best, most influential punk bands. Inspired by the Sex Pistols' energy, the Buzzcocks didn't copy the Pistols' angry political stance; they brought that intense, brilliant energy to the three-minute pop song. Shelly's alternately funny and anguished lyrics about adolescence and love were some of the best of his era, and their melodies and hooks were pointed and memorable. Their punk-pop proved to be enormously influential, with echoes of their music being apparent in everyone from Hüsker Dü to Nirvana.

Shelleyand Howard Devoto formed the Buzzcocks in Manchester in early 1976, adding bassist Steve Diggleand drummer John Maher. In January 1977, the group released their debut EP, *Spiral Scratch*, the first independently released record of the punk era. Shortly after its release, Devoto quit the group; he later formed Magazine. Following Devoto's departure, Shelley became lead vocalist. The Buzzcocks signed with United Artists September 1977, releasing their debut single, "Orgasm Addict," a month later. Their first album, *Another Music in a Different Kitchen* appeared in March 1978; the second, *Love Bites*, arrived six months later. Their rapid recording and performing schedules had effects on the group, and their third album, 1979's *A Different Kind of Tension*, displayed some signs of wear and tear. EMI bought out UA in 1980 and the new label prevented the Buzzcocks from recording their fourth album until the compilation *Singles Going Steady* was released in the U.K. Shelley decided to break up the band instead of fight the label. In 1989, the group re-formed and toured the United States. By 1990, the reunion had become permanent, albeit with a new lineup of Shelley, Diggle, bassist Tony Barber, and drummer Phil Barker; this incarnation debuted on 1993's *Trade Test Transmission*. Throughout the rest of the '90s, the Buzzcocks continued to tour and record at a steady pace. *—Stephen Thomas Erlewine*

Another Music in a Different Kitchen / 1978 / United Artists ✦✦✦
General judgment holds the Buzzcocks' peerless singles, the definition of punk-pop at its finest, as the best expression of their work. However, while the singles showcased one particular side of the band, albums like the group's long-playing debut *Another Music* showcased the foursome's other influences, sometimes brilliantly. The big secret is Shelley's worship of Krautrock's obsessive focus on repetition and rhythm, which transforms what would be 'simply' basic punk songs into at-times monstrous epics. The ghost of Can particular hovers even on some of the shorter songs—unsurprising, given Shelley's worship of that band's guitarist Michael Karoli. "Moving Away From the Pulsebeat" is the best instance of this, with a rumbling Maher rhythm supporting some trancelike guitar lines. As for the sheer rush of pop craziness, *Another Music* is simply crammed with stellar examples. Lead-off track "Fast Cars" starts with the opening of *Spiral Scratch*'s "Boredom"'s intentionally hilarious two-note solo intact, before ripping into a slightly bemusing critique of the objects in question. Most of the similar tracks on the album may be more distinct for their speed, but Shelley in particular always seems to sneak in at least one astonishing line per song, sometimes on his own and sometimes thanks to Devoto via older cowritten tunes redone for the record. One favorite standout: "All this slurping and sucking—it's putting me off my food!" on "You Tear Me Up." Top all this off with any number of perfect moments—the guitar work during the breaks on "Love Battery," the energizing yet nervous coda of "Fiction Romance," the soaring angst throughout "I Don't Mind"—and *Another Music* flat out succeeds. *—Ned Raggett*

Love Bites / Sep. 22, 1978 / United Artists ✦✦✦
More musically accomplished, more obsessively self-questioning, and with equally energetic yet sometimes gloomy performances, *Love Bites* finds the Buzzcocks coming into their own. With Devoto and his influence now fully worked out of the band's system, Shelley is the clearly predominant voice, with the exception of Diggle's first lead vocal on an album track, the semi-acoustic, perversely sprightly "Love is Lies." Though the song received even further acclaim on *Singles Going Steady*, "Ever Fallen in Love," for many the band's signature song, appears here. With its note-perfect blend of romance gone wrong, a weirdly catchy, treated lead guitar line, and Shelley's wounded singing deserves its instant classic status, but it's only one of many highlights. The opening "Real World" is one of the band's strongest: a chunky, forceful yet crisp band performance leads into a strong Shelley lyric about unrequited love and life. "Nostalgia"'s strikingly mature, inventive lyrics about where one's life can lead, and the sometimes charging, sometimes quietly tense, heartbroken "Nothing Left" are two other standouts. The group's well-seasoned abilities, the members' increasing reach and Martin Rushent's excellent production make *Love Bites* shine. The Garvey/Maher rhythm section is especially fine; Maher's fills and similar small but significant touches take the music to an even higher level. His undisputed highlight is the terribly underrated concluding instrumental "Late for the Train." Originally done for a John Peel radio session and rerecorded with even more a dramatic sweep here, it gives the group's motorik/Krautrock new power. Not far behind it is "E.S.P.," a strong rock burn that only fades out at the end very slowly and subtly. *—Ned Raggett*

★ **Singles Going Steady** / Sep. 1979 / IRS ✦✦✦✦✦
If *Never Mind the Bollocks* and *London Calling* are held up as punk masterpieces, then there's no question that *Singles Going Steady* belongs alongside them. In fact, the slew of astonishing seven-inches collected on *Steady* and their influence on future musicians—punk or otherwise—sometimes even betters more famous efforts. The title and artwork alone (the latter itself partially inspired by the Beatles' *Let it Be*) have been parodied or referred to by Halo of Flies and Don Caballero, which titled its own singles comp *Singles Breaking Up*. As for the music, anybody who ever combined full-blast rock, catchy melodies and romantic and social anxieties owes something to what the classic quartet did here. The deservedly well-known masterpiece "Ever Fallen in Love" appears along with *Love Bites*' "Just Lust," but the remaining tracks originally appeared only as individual A and B-sides, making this collection all the more essential. The earlier numbers showcase a band bursting with energy and wicked humor—the tongue-in-cheek "Orgasm Addict," details the adventures of a sex freak with a ridiculous fake orgasm vocal break to boot. However, the slightly more serious but no less frenetic singles are equally enthralling. "What Do I Get?" with its pained cry about lacking love, the deeply cynical "Everybody's Happy Nowadays" and Diggle's roaring "Harmony in My Head" are just three highlights on an album made of them. The final songs show the band incorporating their more adventuresome side into their singles, as with the slower, very Can-inspired "Why Can't I Touch It?," the semi-jokey stop-start thrash "Noise Annoys," and the Murphy's Law worries of "Something's Gone Wrong Again." *—Ned Raggett*

A Different Kind of Tension / Jan. 1980 / IRS ✦✦✦
The final album of the Buzzcocks' first phase of existence is the most fragmented of the three, with increasingly ambitious songs fighting for time with tracks that sound much like the group's earliest efforts. Said songs are often quite good, like the opening "Paradise" or the great romantic angst of "You Say You Don't Love Me," but one can sense the band working to avoid the trap the Ramones fell into by simply offering up yet more soundalikes. Diggle makes a definite mark on this album, as on the slow crawl then fast thrash "Sitting Round at Home," a highlight of *Tension* that also features his electronically distorted vocals. "Mad Mad Judy" is a slightly more straightforward blitz, but with energy to spare and a spacious feel (credit again to producer Rushent). As the album closes, the sense of slight schizophrenia resolves itself as the group embraces all-out experimentation, producing some of the Buzzcocks' all-time best songs. "Hollow Inside" shows the band's knack for disguising scalpel-sharp sentiments with seeming simplicity, and the title track's contradictory slogans demands disturbing robot vocals and nagging beat and melody up the ante even further. "I Believe" concludes things (aside from the fake found-sound snippet "Radio Nine") on the highest possible note. Shelley's slightly bemused recitation of all the things he believes in is suddenly interrupted by the line "There is no love in this world anymore," turned and electronically distorted into an obsessive, anthemic mantra as the band charges along with him up and out. An invigorating blast of, indeed, tension and angst, it alone makes *Tension* worth investigating. *—Ned Raggett*

Parts 1, 2, 3 / Feb. 1981 / IRS ✦✦✦

Lest We Forget / 1988 / ROIR ✦✦

Product / 1989 / Restless ✦✦✦✦✦
Product is a triple-disc box set that contains all of the Buzzcocks' studio recordings—totalling three LPs and 12 singles—following the departure of Howard Devoto, as well as one outtake and eight live songs taken from a 1978 concert. Collecting all of the Buzzcocks' major music in one place confirms the influence and depth of the band's tense, nervy music and Pete Shelley's terse, melodic songwriting. Though the bulk of this material is available individually, the set is essential for hardcore Buzzcocks fans, especially since it contains a detailed, definitive band history. *—Stephen Thomas Erlewine*

Operator's Manual / Nov. 12, 1991 / IRS ✦✦✦✦✦
A 25-song set, it duplicates 11 songs from the *Singles* album. It also contains the best of their three albums, only one of which was released in the US, and showcases a different side of the band. *—John Floyd*

Entertaining Friends / Nov. 3, 1992 / IRS ✦✦✦

Trade Test Transmission / Jun. 2, 1993 / Caroline ✦✦✦

All Set / Apr. 1996 / IRS ✦✦✦

Modern / Sep. 7, 1999 / Go Kart ✦✦✦

The Byrds

f. 1964, Los Angeles, CA, **db.** 1973
Group / Folk-Rock, Psychedelic, Country-Rock
Although they only attained the huge success of the Beatles, Rolling Stones, and the Beach Boys for a short time in the mid-'60s, time has judged the Byrds to be nearly as influential as those groups in the long run. They were not solely responsible for devising folk-rock, but

they were certainly more responsible than any other single act (Dylan included) for melding the innovations and energy of the British Invasion with the best lyrical and musical elements of contemporary folk music. The jangling, 12-string guitar sound of leader Roger McGuinn's Rickenbacker was permanently absorbed into the vocabulary of rock. They also played a vital role in pioneering psychedelic rock and country-rock, the unifying element being their angelic harmonies and restless eclecticism. Often described in their early days as a hybrid of Dylan and the Beatles, the Byrds in turn influenced Dylan and the Beatles almost as much as Bob and the Fab Four had influenced the Byrds. The Byrds' innovations have echoed nearly as strongly through subsequent generations, in the work of Tom Petty, R.E.M., and innumerable alternative bands of the post-punk era that feature those jangling guitars and dense harmonies. *—Richie Unterberger*

☆ **Mr. Tambourine Man** / 1965 / Columbia/Legacy ✦✦✦✦✦
One of the greatest debuts in the history of rock, *Mr. Tambourine Man* was nothing less than a significant step in the evolution of rock & roll itself, demonstrating that intelligent lyrical content could be wedded to compelling electric guitar riffs and a solid backbeat. It was also the album that was most responsible for establishing folk-rock as a popular phenomenon, its most alluring traits being McGuinn's immediately distinctive 12-string Rickenbacker jangle and the band's beautiful harmonies. The material was uniformly strong, whether they were interpreting Dylan (on the title cut and three other songs, including the hit single "All I Really Want to Do"), Pete Seeger ("The Bells of Rhymney"), or Jackie DeShannon ("Don't Doubt Yourself, Babe"). The originals were lyrically less challenging, but equally powerful musically, especially Gene Clark's "I Knew I'd Want You," "I'll Feel a Whole Lot Better," and "Here Without You"; "It's No Use" showed a tougher, harder-rocking side and a guitar solo with hints of psychedelia. The CD reissue adds six less impressive (but still satisfying) bonus tracks and alternate takes from the same era. *—Richie Unterberger*

Turn! Turn! Turn! / 1966 / Columbia/Legacy ✦✦✦✦✦
The group's second album was only a disappointment in comparison with *Mr. Tambourine Man.* They couldn't maintain such a level of consistent magnificence, and the follow-up was not quite as powerful or impressive. It was still quite good, however, particularly the ringing number one title cut, a classic on par with the "Mr. Tambourine Man" single. Elsewhere they concentrated more on original material, Gene Clark in particular offering some strong compositions with "Set You Free This Time," "The World Turns All Around Her," and "If You're Gone." A couple more Dylan covers were included as well, and "Satisfied Mind" was their first foray into country-rock, a direction they would explore in much greater depth throughout the rest of the '60s. The CD adds seven decent alternate takes and bonus tracks, the most interesting being a version of Dylan's "It's All Over Now, Baby Blue," and an enigmatic Gene Clark song, "The Day Walk (Never Before)." *—Richie Unterberger*

Fifth Dimension / Jul. 18, 1966 / Columbia/Legacy ✦✦✦✦✦
Although *Fifth Dimension* was wildly uneven, its high points were as innovative as any rock music being recorded in 1966. Immaculate folk-rock was still present in their superb arrangements of the traditional songs "Wild Mountain Thyme" and "John Riley." For the originals, they devised some of the first and best psychedelic rock, often drawing from the influence of Indian raga in the guitar arrangements. "Eight Miles High," with its astral lyrics, pumping bass line, and fractured guitar solo, was a Top 20 hit, and one of the greatest singles of the '60s. The minor hit title track and the country-rock-tinged "Mr. Spaceman" are among their best songs; "I See You" has great 12-string psychedelic guitar solos; and "I Come and Stand at Every Door" is an unusual and moving update of a traditional rock tune, with new lyrics pleading for peace in the nuclear age. At the same time, the R&B instrumental "Captain Soul" was a throwaway, "Hey Joe" not nearly as good as the versions by the Leaves or Jimi Hendrix, and "What's Happening?!?!" the earliest example of David Crosby's disagreeably vapid hippie ethos. These weak spots keep *Fifth Dimension* from attaining truly classic status. The CD reissue has six notable bonus tracks, including the single version of the early psychedelic cut "Why" (the B-side to "Eight Miles High"), a significantly different alternate take of "Eight Miles High," "I Know My Rider" (with some fine McGuinn 12-string workouts), and a much jazzier, faster instrumental version of "John Riley." *—Richie Unterberger*

☆ **Younger than Yesterday** / 1967 / Columbia/Legacy ✦✦✦✦✦
Younger than Yesterday was somewhat overlooked at the time of its release during an intensely competitive era that found the Byrds on a commercial downslide. However, time has shown it to be the most durable of the Byrds' albums, with the exception of *Mr. Tambourine Man.* Crosby, McGuinn, and especially Hillman come into their own as songwriters on an eclectic but focused set blending folk-rock, psychedelia, and early country-rock. The sardonic "So You Want to Be a Rock & Roll Star" was a terrific single; "My Back Pages," also a small hit, was the last of their classic Dylan covers; "Thoughts and Words," the flower-power anthem "Renaissance Fair," "Have You Seen Her Face," and the bluegrass-tinged "Time Between" are all among their best songs. The jazzy "Everybody's Been Burned" may be David Crosby's best composition, although his "Mind Gardens" is one of his most excessive. The CD reissue has six bonus tracks, including the fine Crosby-penned single "Lady Friend" and notably different alternate versions of "Mind Gardens" and "My Back Pages." *—Richie Unterberger*

The Notorious Byrd Brothers / Jan. 3, 1968 / Columbia/Legacy ✦✦✦✦✦
The recording sessions for the Byrds' fifth album were conducted in the midst of internal turmoil that found them reduced to a duo by the time the record was completed. That wasn't evident from listening to the results, which showed the group continuing to expand the parameters of their eclecticism, while retaining their hallmark guitar jangle and harmonies. With assistance from producer Gary Usher, they took more chances in the studio, enhancing the spacy quality of tracks like "Natural Harmony" and Goffin-King's "Wasn't Born to Follow" with electronic phasing. Washes of Moog synthesizer formed the eerie backdrop for "Space Odyssey," and the songs were craftily and unobtrusively linked with segues and fades. But the Byrds did not bury the essential strengths of their tunes in effects: "Goin' Back" (also written by Goffin-King) was a magnificent and melodic cover, with the expected tasteful 12-string guitar runs, that should have been a big hit. "Tribal Gathering" has some of the band's most effervescent harmonies; "Draft Morning" is a subtle and effective reflection of the horrors of the Vietnam War; and "Old John Robertson" looks forward to the country-rock that would soon dominate their repertoire. The CD reissue adds six bonus tracks, including different versions of "Goin' Back" and "Draft Morning," a few instrumentals, and David Crosby's controversial "Triad"; unlisted on the sleeve is a rehearsal outtake which captures comically vitriolic arguments among the band. *—Richie Unterberger*

★ **Sweetheart of the Rodeo** / Aug. 1968 / Columbia/Legacy ✦✦✦✦✦
The Byrds' *Sweetheart of the Rodeo* was not the first important country-rock album (Gram Parson managed that feat with The International Submarine Band's debut *Safe at Home*), and The Byrds were hardly strangers to country music, dipping their toes in the twangy stuff as early as their second album. But no major band had gone so deep into the sound and feeling of classic country (without parody or condescension) as The Byrds did on *Sweetheart;* at a time when most rock fans viewed country as a musical "L'il Abner" routine, The Byrds dared to declare that C&W could be hip, cool, and heartfelt. Though Gram Parsons had joined the band as a pianist and lead guitarist, his deep love of C&W soon took hold, and Roger McGuinn and Chris Hillman followed his lead; significantly, the only two original songs on the album were both written by Parsons (the achingly beautiful "Hickory Wind" and "One Hundred Years From Now"), while on the rest of the set classic tunes by Merle Haggard, The Louvin Brothers, and Woody Guthrie were sandwiched between a pair of twanged-up Bob Dylan compositions. While many cite this as more of a Gram Parsons album than a Byrds set, given the strong country influence of McGuinn and Hillman's later work, it's obvious Parsons didn't impose a style upon this band so much as he tapped into a sound that was already there, waiting to be released. If The Byrds didn't do country-rock first, they did it brilliantly, and few albums in the style are as beautiful and emotionally effecting as this. Columbia's 1997 CD reissue of the album improves on the masterpiece by adding eight strong bonus tracks, including four cuts with Gram Parsons singing lead trimmed from the original release for legal reasons. *—Mark Deming*

Dr. Byrds & Mr. Hyde / 1969 / Columbia/Legacy ✦✦✦
Chris Hillman, Gram Parsons, and Kevin Kelley all left The Byrds in wake of the release of *Sweetheart of the Rodeo,* leaving Roger McGuinn to assemble a new band from scratch. *Dr. Byrds & Mr. Hyde,* the first album with McGuinn as unquestioned leader (and sole founding member), was an interesting but uneven set that saw him attempting to bring together the psych-tinged rock of the group's early period with the pure country that Parsons had brought to *Sweetheart.* The new line-up on this album was as strong as any the band would ever have, with guitarist Clarence White sounding revelatory whenever he opens up, and Gene Parsons and John York comprising a strong and sympathetic rhythm section. But while everyone on board was a great musician, they don't always sound like a band just yet, and the strain to come up with new material seems to have let them down; McGuinn contributes a few strong originals (especially "King Apathy III" and "Drug Store Truck Drivin' Man," the latter written with Parsons before his departure from the group), but the two songs he penned for the movie *Candy* are just short of disastrous, and the closing medley of "My Back Pages" and "Baby What You Want Me to Do" sounds like padding. *Dr. Byrds & Mr. Hyde* proved there was still life left in The Byrds, but also suggested that they hadn't gotten back to full speed yet. *—Mark Deming*

The Ballad of Easy Rider / Feb. 1969 / Columbia/Legacy ✦✦✦✦
If *Dr. Byrds and Mr. Hyde* found Roger McGuinn having to recreate The Byrds after massive personnel turnovers (and not having an easy time of it), *Ballad of Easy Rider* was the album where the new lineup really hit its stride. Gracefully moving back and forth between serene folk rock (the title cut, still one of McGuinn's most beautiful melodies), sure-handed rock & roll ("Jesus Is Just All Right"), heartfelt country-rock ("Oil In My Lamp" and "Tulsa County"), and even a dash of R&B (the unexpectedly funky "Fido," which even features a percussion solo), *Ballad of Easy Rider* sounds confident and committed where *Dr. Byrds and Mr. Hyde* often seemed tentative. The band plays sounds tight, self-assured, and fully in touch with the music's emotional palate, and Clarence White's guitar work is truly a pleasure to hear (if Roger McGuinn's fabled 12-string work seems to take a back seat to White's superb string bends, it is doubtful that any but the most fanatical fans would think to object). While not generally regarded as one of the group's major works, in retrospect this release stands alongside *Untitled* as the finest work of The Byrds' final period. *—Mark Deming*

Live at the Fillmore West February 1969 / Feb. 1969 / Columbia/Legacy ✦✦✦

Untitled / 1970 / Columbia/Legacy ✦✦✦✦
This two-CD set contains the Byrds' 1970 *Untitled* album (originally a double LP) on disc one, and 14 previously unissued alternate versions, studio recordings, and live performances on disc two. This was not the Byrds' most exciting era, but a lot of extra material existed, and *Untitled* was going to be reissued either way. *Untitled* itself was one of the Byrds' better late efforts, with an album of live material (built around updates of their most famous tunes) sharing space with uneven new studio recordings in the expected country/folk-rock mode, highlighted by "Chestnut Mare" and "Just a Season." Listeners will be most interested in this expanded reissue for the disc of previously unreleased stuff, which is not remarkable, but is okay for those who enjoyed *Untitled.* There are alternate studio versions of two songs from *Untitled*'s studio portion ("Yesterday's Train" and a more jangly "All the Things"); a studio alternate of "Kathleen's Song," without the orchestration that would be added when it was redone for *Byrdmaniax;* a studio version of "Lover of the Bayou" (done live on *Untitled*); the instrumental "White's Lightning Pt. 2"; and Lowell George's "Willin'" (different from the version that appears on the Byrds' box set). Then you get eight previously unavailable 1970 live recordings, much in the style of what's heard on the live part of *Untitled,* and including such favorites as "It's Alright Ma (I'm Only Bleeding)," "Ballad of Easy Rider," "My Back Pages," and "Jesus Is Just Alright." An unindexed bonus track, an a cappella studio rendition of "Amazing Grace," ends the set. *—Richie Unterberger*

Byrdmaniax / 1971 / Columbia/Legacy ✦✦

Farther Along / 1972 / Columbia/Legacy ✦✦✦
One thing The Byrds had in common with most of their fans was that they weren't espe-

cially happy with the absurd overproduction that had been inflicted upon *Byrdmaniax* in their absence. As a response, the group quickly cut *Farther Along* in 1971, producing the sessions themselves and getting the album into stores a mere six months after its predecessor. It's certainly a significant improvement, but something short of a triumphant return; the band sounds a bit tired in spots, as if they were starting to run out of gas—which quickly proved to be the case as The Byrds split up a few months after the album's release. However, Roger McGuinn and Clarence White were nothing if not professionals, and if *Farther Along* doesn't always sound inspired, it's never less than well-played, really connecting when the group can get their enthusiasm up; the tough rockin' "Tiffany Queen" and the pensive "Bugler" are the late-period Byrds at the top of their game, and "Bristol Steam Convention Blues" features some superb bluegrass picking from White. This is hardly the rousing conclusion the The Byrds' story that some fans might have hoped for, but it's a strong and well-crafted set from a band that inarguably gave it their all right up to the finish line. *—Mark Deming*

The Byrds [1973] / 1973 / Asylum ✦✦

In the Beginning / 1988 / Rhino ✦✦✦

Never Before / 1989 / Murray Hill ✦✦✦

☆ **The Byrds [Box Set]** / Oct. 1990 / Columbia ✦✦✦✦✦
The value of the four-disc box set *The Byrds* as a rarities set has diminished somewhat, as much of the truly rare items later appeared on Columbia/Legacy's excellent reissues as bonus tracks, but this set remains a good overview of the group's career. Although the remastering and rarities are prominent enough to draw in the hardcore, the main strength of this compilation is that it tells the story exceedingly well, capturing the scope of their career. Very few (if any) great songs are missing, and if it dwells a little bit too long on the fourth disc, such is the nature of box sets. The rest of the record is remarkably well-balanced, containing all their hits and key album tracks, making it a nice, thorough retrospective. *—Stephen Thomas Erlewine*

★ **Greatest Hits [Expanded Edition]** / Mar. 30, 1999 / Columbia/Legacy ✦✦✦✦✦
Without question, the Byrds were one of the great bands of the '60s and one of the few American bands of their time to continually turn out inventive, compelling albums. As they were recording a series of fine records, they released a number of classic singles that defined their era. *The Byrds' Greatest Hits* does an excellent job of chronicling the peak years of their popularity before they went country-rock on 1968's *Sweetheart of the Rodeo*. Columbia/Legacy's expanded 1999 reissue added the three minor hits missing from the original collection, which means that *Greatest Hits* now contains all of the group's hit singles—from 1965's "Mr. Tambourine Man" to 1967's "Have You Seen Her Face." That's an impressive collection indeed, and it also includes "All I Really Want to Do," "Turn! Turn! Turn! (To Everything There Is a Season)," "It Won't Be Wrong," "Set You Free this Time," "Eight Miles High," "5D (Fifth Dimension)," "Mr. Spaceman," "So You Want to Be a Rock N' Roll Star," and "My Back Pages." Yes, some great songs were left behind on the albums, but important cuts like "I'll Feel a Whole Lot Better," "The Bells of Rhymney," and "Chimes of Freedom" are included, making this pretty close to a definitive single-disc summary of the Byrds' prime. *—Stephen Thomas Erlewine*

The Cadillacs

f. 1953, Harlem, NY, **db.** 1962
Group / Doo Wop
Equally adept at polished ballads or torrid rockers, the Cadillacs were one of New York's top doo wop groups. The Harlem quintet signed with Josie in 1954 and debuted with the beautiful "Gloria," but with Earl Carroll's prominent energetic lead vocals, the Cadillacs became known for humorous jump material and hot choreography after "Speedoo" hit big for them in 1956. Tapping into the novelty R&B market pioneered by the Coasters, the Cadillacs cut a load of great rockers during the late '50s, such as "Peek-a-Boo" and "Please, Mr. Johnson," and performed in the quickie flick *Go, Johnny, Go!* in 1959. Carroll left to join the Coasters in 1958 but the group persevered, eventually signing with Mercury. Carroll has re-formed the Cadillacs in recent years. *—Bill Dahl*

★ **The Best of the Cadillacs** / 1990 / Rhino ✦✦✦✦✦
Although completists will have to have the multi-disc set on Collectables, for the rest of their listeners, this seldom championed but nonetheless superlative single-disc compilation will more than fill the bill. At 18 tracks, a few collectors' favorites are understandably absent ("Wishing Well," "Jaywalkin'"), but *all* of the major and minor hits are well aboard, clearly showcasing the groups' ability to tackle everything from beautiful ballads ("Gloria," "The Girl I Love") to jump numbers ("Speedo," "My Girl Friend") to Coaster-style novelties ("Peek-a-Boo," "Please, Mr. Johnson") and do it all with style, grace, and choreography that *burned*. Covering their stint with Josie Records from 1954 to 1960 in a straight chronological fashion with excellent liner notes from John Neilson, this particular compilation offers great value for the bread and should be one of your very first stops in assembling a definitive doo wop collection. The Cadillacs were one of the first and one of the very best, and here's where you go to dig their basic message before proceeding further. *—Cub Koda*

The Complete Josie Sessions / 1995 / Bear Family ✦✦✦✦✦
This box is really the CD descendant of Murray Hill Records' early-'80s-era LP set, which included lots of outtakes. It seems like complete and absolute overkill to put out four CDs on a vocal quintet that only ever charted two songs ("Speedoo," "Peek-A-Boo") nationally, and, yet . . . it works. But, if you like '50s R&B, doo wop music, or generally just good singing, there's so much here to listen to that will delight you that the package suddenly seems reasonable. The Cadillacs' secret was the sheer variety of their music—they started out working in a slow romantic vein, and eventually hit it big with one of the fastest-rocking vocal numbers od the period, but they also sang blues (with solid backing, including some fine guitar work) like "(That's) All I Need." Their last sides are still finely sung, but aren't romantic—rather, they began moving toward comedic and satiric pieces such as "Please Mr. Johnson" and "Jaywalker." The diversity is entertaining in itself, and the only real objection that one could have is the presence of different versions of the same songs. Even these are very interesting, such as the slower alternate version of "Speedo," which would never have been a hit but does reveal more about the song itself. The sessionography is also a big help in sorting out precisely who was in the group at any given moment after their early sides. *—Bruce Eder*

J.J. Cale

b. Dec. 5, 1938, Oklahoma City, OK
Vocals, Guitar / Singer/Songwriter, Blues-Rock
Notorious for his laidback, rootsy style, J.J. Cale (b. Jean Jacques Cale) is bestknown for writing "After Midnight" and "Cocaine," songs that Eric Clapton later made into hits. But Cale's influence wasn't only through songwriting—his distinctly loping sense of rhythm and shuffling boogie became the blueprint for the adult-oriented roots-rock of Clapton and Mark Knopfler, among others. Cale's refusal to vary the sound of his music over the course of his career caused some critics to label him as a one-trick pony, but he managed to build a dedicated cult following with his sporadically released recordings.

Raised in Tulsa, OK, Calearrived in Los Angeles in 1964. After a short stint with Delaney and Bonnie he began a solo career in 1965, cutting the first version of "After Midnight," which would become his most famous song. Cale returned to Tulsa in 1967. Within a year, he had recorded a set of demos which led to a deal with the fledgling Shelter Records in 1969. The following year, Eric Clapton recorded "After Midnight," taking it to the American Top 20. In December of 1971, Cale released his debut album, *Naturally* which was followed by *Really* later that same year. *Okie*, his third album, appeared in 1974. Two years later, he released *Troubadour*, which yielded "Cocaine," a song that Clapton later covered. Following 1979's *Number Five*, he signed with MCA, where released only one album, 1981's *Shades*. The next year, he moved to Mercury Records, releasing *Grasshopper*, which was followed by *8* in 1983. The album became his first not to chart. After its release, Cale left Mercury and entered a long period of seclusion, reappearing in late 1989 with *Travelog*. He released *Number 10* in 1992, an album that failed to chart but re-established his status as a cult artist. He moved to Virgin in 1994, releasing *Close to You* the same year; it was followed by *Guitar Man* in 1996. *—Stephen Thomas Erlewine*

Naturally / Dec. 1971 / Mercury ✦✦✦
J.J. Cale's debut album, *Naturally*, was recorded after Eric Clapton made "After Midnight" a huge success. Instead of following Slowhand's cue and constructing a slick blues-rock album, Cale recruited a number of his Oklahoma friends and made a laid-back country-rock record that firmly established his distinctive, relaxed style. Cale included a new version of "After Midnight" on the album, but the true meat of the record lay in songs like "Crazy Mama," which became a hit single, and "Call Me the Breeze," which Lynyrd Skynyrd later covered. On these songs and many others on *Naturally*, Cale effortlessly captured a lazy, rolling boogie that contradicted all the commercial styles of boogie, blues and country rock at the time. Where his contemporaries concentrated on solos, Cale worked the song and its rhythm, and the result was a pleasant, engaging album that was in no danger of raising anybody's temperature. *—Thom Owens*

Really / Dec. 1972 / Mercury ✦✦✦
Cale's guitar work manages to be both understated and intense here. The same is true of his seemingly offhand singing, which finds him drawling lines like "You get your gun, I'll get mine" with disarming casualness. But he has trouble coming up with original material as strong as that on his debut, and for some, his approach will be too casual; there are many times, when the band is percolating along and Cale is muttering into the microphone, that the music seems to be all background and no foreground. You may find yourself waiting for a payoff that never comes. *—William Ruhlmann*

Okie / May 1974 / Mercury ✦✦✦

Troubadour / Sep. 1976 / Mercury ✦✦✦✦✦
Producer Audie Ashworth introduced some different instruments, notably vibes and what sound like horns (although none are credited), for a slightly altered sound here. But Cale's albums are so steeped in his introspective style that they become interchangeable. If you like one of them, chances are you'll want to have them all. This one is notable for introducing "Cocaine," which Eric Clapton covered on his *Slowhand* album a year later. *—William Ruhlmann*

5 / Aug. 1979 / Mercury ✦✦

Grasshopper / Mar. 1982 / Mercury ✦✦

8 / 1983 / Mercury ✦✦

Special Edition / 1984 / Mercury ✦✦✦✦✦
Sinuous rhythms, conversational singing, and, most of all, intricate, bluesy guitar playing characterize Cale's performances of his own songs. This compilation, covering 11 years of recording, includes the songs Eric Clapton, who borrowed heavily from Cale's style in his 1970s solo work, made famous: "After Midnight" and "Cocaine." *—William Ruhlmann*

Travel Log / Feb. 1990 / Silvertone ✦✦✦✦✦
Cale's first album in six years finds him taking a more aggressive stance in terms of tempos and playing, although he remains a man with a profound sense of the groove and, especially as a singer, a minimalist. But as he says, "Shuffle or die." *—William Ruhlmann*

10 / Nov. 10, 1992 / Silvertone ✦✦✦

Guitar Man / Jun. 25, 1996 / Virgin ✦✦✦

Anyway the Wind Blows: The Anthology / Jun. 17, 1997 / Mercury ✦✦✦✦✦
Although it is a little too extensive for casual fans, the double-disc, 50-track *Anyway the Wind Blows—The Anthology* is a definitive retrospective of J.J. Cale's career, featuring all the highlights from his career. Cale's albums often sounded similar, but they were remarkably uneven in terms of quality, which is what makes *Anyway the Wind Blows* essential for both neophytes and collectors. Not only is it a perfect introduction, containing such essentials as

"Cocaine," "Call Me the Breeze," and "After Midnight," but it is one of his most consistently listenable and enjoyable discs. *—Stephen Thomas Erlewine*

- **The Very Best of J.J. Cale** / Jun. 9, 1998 / Mercury ✦✦✦✦✦
The Very Best of J.J. Cale is an excellent single-disc collection of the music from one of the most influential singer-songwriters that emerged out of America during the 1970s. Just as Townes Van Zandt and Guy Clark define Texas songwriting, Cale is the epitome of the Oklahoma writers. Although most people know him as the writer of Eric Clapton's hit "Cocaine," Cale constantly offered up other quality material that could only be defined by his vocal style, which can accurately be described as "reclining in the groove." Popular tunes such as "Call Me the Breeze," "Hey Baby," and "Crazy Mama" have a deceptively laid-back intensity that to a large degree influenced such rockers as Lowell George of Little Feat and the previously mentioned Clapton. Cale's guitar work proved to be influential as well (again on Clapton), but also popular swamp-rockers such as Delaney Bramlett. *The Very Best of J.J. Cale* offers a comprehensive collection from Cale's early-'70s recordings in Nashville, to Muscle Shoals in Alabama, to his later work on Hollywood. If you're going to explore Cale's groove, this is the place to start. *—Matthew Greenwald*

Camper Van Beethoven

f. 1983, Santa Cruz, CA, **db.** 1990
Group / College Rock, Jangle Pop, Indie Rock, Alternative Pop/Rock
At the time of their 1985 debut, Camper Van Beethoven's merging of punk, folk, ska and world musics was truly a revelation. Self-described as "surrealist absurdist folk," the band was formed by singer-songwriter David Lowery, with his dry humor and valley-boy voice (sometimes confused for a faux English accent), and boyhood friends Chris Molla and Chris Pedersen. The 1985 re-release of their debut *Telephone Free Landslide Victory* did well with critics, and on their second album, *II & III*, they went for a purer indie-rock sound with touches of country. The band deftly switched modes from punk to ska to rock on alternate takes, and the eponymous third album continued the thread. For their Virgin Records debut, subsequent with the label's US re-launch in 1988, the band took a more serious tack for *Our Beloved Revolutionary Sweetheart*. For *Key Lime Pie*, the band's final release in 1989, they took it as far as it could go. Pedersen's side-project Monks of Doom soon turned into a full-time job, while Lowery later formed Cracker. *—Denise Sullivan*

- **Telephone Free Landslide Victory** / 1985 / IRS ✦✦✦✦✦
They say "never say never," but it's still extremely unlikely something so goofily low-key, inventive, and fun will ever achieve cult status so quickly again, especially in terms of musical range on display. Not simply a rock group but not anything else, Camper Van Beethoven pulled off a series of entertaining fusions throughout its debut record, as the opening song "Border Ska" indicates by name along. Eastern European folk, tropical grooves, post-punk atmospherics, country laid-back good times, psych/garage band aesthetics, lyrics about Mao, Greece, and more—a lot of stuff went into the Santa Cruz band's brew, and most of it came up trumps on *Telephone*. Lowery's lead vocals aren't much like what his more famous work in Cracker would indicate, being more speak-singing through shaggy dog stories (even one about Lassie) of all stripes. Hearing his tale of woe on "Wasted"—"I was a punker, and I had a Mohawk/I was so gnarly and I drove my dad's car"—delivered in a "yeah dude" tone of voice is pretty darn funny. Segel's keyboards and violins color the arrangements with a fun touch, while rhythm team Krummenacher and then recently departed drummer Anthony Guess try out nearly everything at least once. The production is eminently suited for the proceedings, sounding a bit like the thick, fuzzy flow of many Shimmy-Disc releases but with just enough of a crisp edge. When it comes to humor, it's everywhere—for instance, the plaintively sung chorus of "Where the Hell Is Bill?," not to mention the various speculative answers ("Maybe he went to get a Vespa scooter"). Or, of course, the song that kick started the band's reputation, "Take the Skinheads Bowling," two and a half minutes of chiming, goofy nonsense with references to Jah and incomplete rhymes. *—Ned Raggett*

II & III / Jan. 1986 / IRS ✦✦✦
Admittedly, it's understandable to see why CVB's sense of humor rubbed some people the wrong way. Titling a second album *II & III* and sprinkling it with songs titled "ZZ Top Goes to Egypt" and "No Kruggerands for David" sounds more like a parody of rock rather than rock itself. That never stopped Pavement, though, and on *II & III*, CVB sounds as inventive and unexpectedly inspired as before, mashing its influences together into a delightful brew. However, this time the band sounds a touch more straightforward; new member Chris Pederson's drumming sounds stronger, providing a good pace throughout and pumping up the energy on "Down And Out." Wigginess abounds musically and lyrically—"Cowboys from Hollywood" sounds like an amped-up honky-tonk, and following it with the on-the-level country of "Sad Lovers Waltz" fit whatever master plan there was. Lowery doesn't sing lead as much this time out; he's still the primary singer, but often is accompanied by most of the rest of the band as well. But as always, Segel is the wild card with violin and nutty keyboards ahoy. There's some refreshing iconoclasm at play—years before Sonic Youth became "the legendary Sonic Youth," CVB took that group's "I Love Her All the Time" and transformed its New York art angst into a kick-up-your-heels bit of yee-haw ska. It's worth hearing for Lowery and company's vocal drawls alone. The album concludes with the hilarious "No More Bullshit," mixing wanky solos with repetitive punk-rock slogans and strange comments "Elvis Presley died! And no-one knows why!" *—Ned Raggett*

Camper Van Beethoven / Aug. 1986 / IRS ✦✦✦
CVB's self-titled third album generally differs little from *II & III*, continuing the blend of wistfully weird lyrics, any number of musical touches from all over the map and good-time vibes. The opening "Good Guys & Bad Guys" proves that much, with reggae, folk, country, and more stewed together as Lowery plaintively sings about lawyers and the people in Russia and the like. From there on in it's another collection of generally short and generally fun ditties, but with a few more tweaks here and there. The bandmembers definitely have more fun with the studio this time out, thus a lot of tape manipulation and semi-psychedelic oddity sprinkled around the album. Something of a Led Zeppelin fascination seems to crop up throughout, perhaps not too surprising considering that band's similar fondness for many musical influences and Jimmy Page's more acoustic numbers. Lowery drawls "Has anyone seen the bridge?" on "Joe Stalin's Cadillac," the following song is "Five Sticks," while later on in the album one gets "Stairway to Heavan (sic)," most definitely not a remake of the referenced song in question. Not to say there aren't reinterpretations here: an obscure sixties track, "Lulu Land," lets CVB fool around with a bit of twinkly jauntiness, while early Pink Floyd gets the band treatment with an impressive, strong version of "Interstellar Overdrive." Then there's the catchy pop salute to a certain Mr. Garcia of the Grateful Dead, "We Saw Jerry's Daughter," the sitars and kicks on "Still Wishing to Course," the concluding 90-second long "Shut Us Down" and more to fill out this album's corners well. *—Ned Raggett*

Our Beloved Revolutionary Sweetheart / 1988 / Virgin ✦✦✦✦✦
With Lowery's by-now more sharply sung words up front and Segel's multi-instrumental abilities helping to lead the way, the quintet came up trumps more often than not. "Eye of Fatima (pt. 2)," for instance, could have easily fit in on most of the group's earlier records at the start. Even so, the addition of some screaming Lisher guitar solos on top of the measured reggae/hard rock/folk stew cooked up didn't feel anything like, say, Eddie Van Halen's drop-in on "Beat It." Distinctly nonrock tempos and touches run merrily rampant as always, as a listen to the fiddle, dub and brass revamp of the traditional number "O Death" demonstrates. However, the fivesome can pump it up when needed—the group's appreciation of Led Zeppelin certainly hasn't dimmed any, based on the majestic stomp of "Waka." When CVB aim to create something possibly more radio-friendly, the members pull it off in their own way rather than anyone else's. Thus, the almost anthemic "She Divines Water," with some great Segel violin work, or the gentler groove of "One of These Days." Add in multitudes of other joys like the fun romp "My Path Belated" and Bruce Licher's clever cover art—at one point you see Bob Dylan looking towards a Turkish music combo in another photo with resignation—and once again CVB create an enjoyable, not-easily-pegged down listening experience. *—Ned Raggett*

Key Lime Pie / Sep. 1989 / Virgin ✦✦✦✦✦
Our Beloved Revolutionary Sweetheart closed with Lowery singing about how "Life Is Grand" in pointed response to "those of you who have appointed yourselves to expect us to say something darker." So when *Key Lime Pie* came out, its moodier music and imagery, not to mention that soon after the fact that the band fell apart on the tour for the album, led more than one person to think those darker times had finally arrived. As it is, the group had already gone through one major shake-up between the two albums—founding member Segel had taken a powder to concentrate on other efforts, with Morgan Fichter brought in as a replacement violinist. Her abilities were certainly praiseworthy, as the album-starting instrumental "Opening Theme" shows quite well. However, it's definitely not the same band that did *Telephone Free Landslide Victory* a mere four years previous—things are more straightforwardly rock here most of the time, perhaps not too surprising in light of Lowery's subsequent work in Cracker. As it is, though, it's excellently conceived rock, with space, moodiness, and more to spare. Consider "Jack Ruby," with its wordless backing vocals, tense rhythms, and thick soloing, or "Laundromat" and its steady but unnerving crunch. It's not all potential melancholia, though—"June" in particular is an underrated number, celebrating the early summer with sweetness and love (at least up to the increasingly stranger ending). Lowery's singing is his best yet, perhaps a little less prone to wackiness but an emergent, distinct voice all the same, and certainly prone to sing a quirky lyric or two still. The oddest thing of all was that the band actually gained a little mainstream attention on MTV and radio via a cover of Status Quo's psych-era nugget "Pictures of Matchstick Men." *—Ned Raggett*

Camper Vantiquities / Mar. 23, 1993 / IRS ✦✦✦

Canned Heat

f. 1966, Los Angeles, CA
Group / Boogie Rock, Blues-Rock, Modern Electric Blues
A hard-luck blues band of the '60s, Canned Heat was founded by blues historians and record collectors Alan Wilson and Bob Hite. They seemed to be on the right track and played all the right festivals (including Monterey and Woodstock, making it very prominently into the documentaries about both) but somehow never found a lasting audience. Canned Heat's debut album—released shortly after their appearance at Monterey—was every bit as deep into the roots of the blues as any other combo of the time mining similar turf, with the exception of the original Paul Butterfield band. Hite was nicknamed "The Bear" and stalked the stage in the time-honored tradition of Howlin' Wolf and other large-proportioned bluesmen. Wilson was an extraordinary harmonica player, with a fat tone and great vibrato. His work on guitar, especially in open tunings, gave the band a depth and texture that most other rhythm players could only aspire to. Canned Heat's breakthrough moment occurred with the release of their second album, establishing them with hippie ballroom audiences as the "kings of the boogie." After two big chart hits with "Goin' up the Country" and an explosive version of Wilbert Harrison's "Let's Work Together," Wilson died under mysterious (probably drug-related) circumstances in 1970, and Hite carried on with various reconstituted versions of the band until his death just before a show in 1981, from a heart seizure. *—Cub Koda & Bruce Eder*

- **The Best of Canned Heat [EMI]** / 1972 / EMI America ✦✦✦✦✦

Uncanned! The Best of Canned Heat / May 17, 1994 / EMI America ✦✦✦✦✦
Uncanned! The Best of Canned Heat is exactly what it claims to be—the definitive portrait of the blues-soaked hippie boogie band. Spreading 41 tracks (including numerous rarities, alternate takes, and Levi commercials) over two CDs, the set is perfect for the hardcore Canned Heat collector. For casual fans, the collection simply contains too much music; they would be better served by the single-disc collection, *The Best of Canned Heat*. *—Stephen Thomas Erlewine*

Freddy Cannon

b. Dec. 4, 1940, Lynn, MA
Vocals / Rock & Roll
No one would claim that Freddy Cannon was one of the great early rock & roll singers. His throaty rasp rated much higher for enthusiasm than impressive chops, and his 17 hit singles

were often repetitious variations of his most successful tunes: "Tallahassee Lassie," "Way Down Yonder in New Orleans," and "Palisades Park." Yet he did his own small part to keep the rock & roll spirit burning in the late '50s and early '60s, a time at which it sometimes seemed in danger of being extinguished. He was an unabashed rock & roller, for one thing, even when he was fed ancient Tin Pan Alley standards to retool for teenagers. And he was not one to let the lack of top-notch skills stand in the way of putting his heart into his vocals for all he was worth. His enthusiasm is infectious, though much of his material cannot be rescued by enthusiasm alone. Sometimes categorized as a teen idol, he was in fact too raw to fit comfortably into that mold (not to mention not quite good-looking enough). As ludicrous as it sounds, he was something of an early prototype of rock & roller as Everyman, where spirit and fun counted more than conventional skill. *—Richie Unterberger*

● **The Best of Freddy "Boom Boom" Cannon** / Nov. 21, 1995 / Rhino ✦✦✦✦✦
The definitive collection. Twenty tracks, 17 of them Top 100 singles, including "Tallahassee Lassie," "Way Down Yonder in New Orleans," "Palisades Park," "Abigail Beecher," and "Action," as well as a rare 1958 single by Spindrift. The other selections really aren't up to the level of the best hits, despite occasional raw detours like "Buzz Buzz A-Diddle-It" and the odd novelty "If You Were a Rock and Roll Record," with the immortal line, "If you were a rock and roll record, I know they'd sell a million of you." *—Richie Unterberger*

Captain Beefheart (Don Van Vliet)

b. Jan. 15, 1941, Glendale, CA
Vocals, Keyboards, Harmonica, Guitar / Experimental Rock, Proto-Punk, Experimental, Psychedelic, Prog-Rock/Art Rock, Blues-Rock
Born Don Van Vliet, Captain Beefheart was one of modern music's true innovators. The owner of a remarkable four-and-one-half octave vocal range, he employed idiosyncratic rhythms, absurdist lyrics and an unholy alliance of free jazz, Delta blues, latter-day classical music and rock & roll to create a singular body of work virtually unrivalled in its daring and fluid creativity. While he never came even remotely close to mainstream success, Beefheart's impact was incalculable, and his fingerprints were all over punk, New Wave and post-rock. In their original incarnation, Captain Beefheart and His Magic Band were a blues-rock outfit which became staples of the teen-dance circuit; they quickly signed to A&M Records, where the success of the single "Diddy Wah Diddy" earned them the opportunity to record a full-length album. Label president Jerry Moss rejected the completed record as "too negative," however, and a crushed Beefheart went into seclusion. After producer Bob Krasnow radically remixed 1968's hallucinatory *Strictly Personal* without Beefheart's approval, he again retired. At the same time, however, longtime friend Frank Zappa formed his own Straight Records, and he soon approached Van Vliet with the promise of complete creative control; a deal was struck, and after writing 28 songs in a nine-hour frenzy, Beefheart recorded the seminal 1969 double album *Trout Mask Replica*. After 1982's *Ice Cream for Crow*, Van Vliet again retired from music, this time for good; he returned to the desert, took up residence in a trailer and focused on painting. In 1985, he mounted the first major exhibit of his work, done in an abstract, primitive style reminiscent of Francis Bacon. Like his music, his art won wide acclaim, and some of his paintings sold for as much as $25,000. In the 1990s Van Vliet dropped completely from sight when he fell prey to multiple sclerosis. *—Jason Ankeny*

☆ **Safe as Milk** / 1967 / Buddha ✦✦✦✦✦
Beefheart's first proper studio album is a much more accessible, pop-inflected brand of blues-rock than the efforts that followed in the late '60s—which isn't to say that it's exactly normal and straightforward. Featuring Ry Cooder on guitar, this is blues-rock gone slightly askew, with jagged, fractured rhythms, soulful, twisting vocals from Van Vliet, and more doo wop, soul, straight blues, and folk-rock influences than he would employ on his more avant-garde outings. "Zig Zag Wanderer," "Call on Me," and "Yellow Brick Road" are some of his most enduring and riff-driven songs, although there's plenty of weirdness on tracks like "Electricity" and "Abba Zaba." [Buddha's 1999 reissue of *Safe as Milk* contained restored artwork and seven bonus tracks.] *—Richie Unterberger*

☆ **Trout Mask Replica** / 1969 / Reprise ✦✦✦✦✦
Trout Mask Replica is Captain Beefheart's masterpiece, a fascinating, stunningly imaginative work that still sounds like little else in the rock & roll canon. Given total creative control by producer and friend Frank Zappa, Beefheart and his Magic Band rehearsed the material for this 28-song double album for over a year, wedding minimalistic R&B, blues, and garage rock to free jazz and avant-garde experimentalism. Atonal, sometimes singsong melodies; jagged, intricately constructed dual-guitar parts; stuttering, complicated rhythmic interaction—all of these elements float out seemingly at random, often without completely interlocking, while Beefheart groans his surrealist poetry in a throaty Howlin' Wolf growl. The disjointedness is perhaps partly unintentional—reportedly, Beefheart's refusal to wear headphones while recording his vocals caused him to sing in time with studio reverberations, not the actual backing tracks—but by all accounts, the music and arrangements were carefully scripted and notated by the Captain, which makes the results even more remarkable. As one might expect from music so complex and, to many ears, inaccessible, the influence of *Trout Mask Replica* was felt more in spirit than in direct copycatting, as a catalyst rather than a literal musical starting point. However, its inspiring reimagining of what was possible in a rock context laid the groundwork for countless future experiments in rock surrealism, especially during the punk/new wave era. *—Steve Huey*

Lick My Decals Off, Baby / 1970 / Bizarre/Straight ✦✦✦✦✦
Produced by Captain Beefheart himself, *Lick My Decals Off, Baby* was a further refining and exploration of the musical ideas posited on *Trout Mask Replica*. As such, the imaginative fervor of *Trout Mask* is toned down somewhat, but in its place is an increased self-assurance; the tone of *Decals* is also a bit darker, examining environmental issues in some songs rather than simply concentrating on surreal wordplay. Whatever the differences, the jagged, complex rhythms and guitar interplay continue to amaze. Those wanting to dig deeper after the essential *Trout Mask Replica* are advised to begin doing so here (be warned: *Decals* has tended to flutter in and out of print). *—Steve Huey*

Mirror Man / 1970 / Castle ✦✦✦

Clear Spot / 1972 / Reprise ✦✦✦✦
Producer Ted Templeman was a bit of a surprising choice given his firmly mainstream production credits, with the Doobie Brothers already under his belt and Van Halen lurking in the near future. As it turned out, such a combination led to a better-working fusion than might be expected, making one wonder why in the world *Clear Spot* wasn't more of a commercial success than it was. The sound is great throughout, and the feeling is of the coolest bar-band in town, not to mention one that could eat all the patrons for breakfast if it felt like it. Fans of the fully all-out side of Beefheart might find the end result not fully up to snuff as a result, but those less concerned with pushing back all borders all the time will enjoy his unexpected blend of everything tempered with a new accessibility. "Nowadays a Woman's Got to Hit a Man," besides having a brilliant title, shows the balance perfectly—Van Vliet serves up his rough asides with all his expected wit and sass, while the Magic Band trade off notes here and there just so. At the same time, the track is strong blues-rock that doesn't pander, with a particularly fierce solo thanks to Zoot Horn Rollo. "My Head Is My Only House Unless It Rains" is a great love song, the softer arrangement saved from being too off by Beefheart's delivery. Other winners include the title track, a sharp combination of an off-kilter arrangement for a straightforward melody, the great shaggy-dog story of "Golden Birdies," and "Big Eyed Beans from Venus," a fantastically strange piece of aggression. *—Ned Raggett*

The Spotlight Kid / 1972 / Reprise ✦✦✦✦
Released mere months after *Clear Spot*, on *Spotlight* Beefheart took over full production duties. Rather than returning to the artistic aggro of *Trout Mask/Decals* days, *Spotlight* takes things lower and looser, with a lot of typical Beefheart fun crawling around in weird, strange ways. Consider the ominous opening cut "I'm Gonna Booglarize You Baby" it isn't just the title and Beefheart's breathy growl, but Rockette Morton's purring bass, Zoot Horn Rollo's snarling guitar, Ed Marimba's brisk fade on the cymbals again and again, and more. The overall atmosphere is definitely relaxed and fun, maybe one step up from a jam. Marimba's vibes and other percussion work—including, of course, the marimba itself—stand out quite a bit here as a result, perhaps, brought out from behind the drums and the more straightforward work on *Clear Spot*. Consider "When It Blows Its Stacks," with its unexpected breaks into more playful parts, or "Alice in Blunderland"'s admittedly more aimless approach, but vibing along well nonetheless. Sometimes things do sound maybe just a little too blasé, but Beefheart at his worst still has something more than most groups at their best. *Spotlight* does have one stone-cold Beefheart classic—"Grow Fins," an understated number with fine harmonica and a brilliant lyric about getting so tired of his woman that the best option is to take to the sea and fall in love with a mermaid. Another song, though, does have an all-time great title—"There Ain't No Santa Claus on the Evenin' Stage." Definite fun touch—the cover photo of Beefheart looking great in a classic Nudie suit, outlined in yellow light to boot. *—Ned Raggett*

Bluejeans & Moonbeams / 1974 / Blue Plate ✦✦

Unconditionally Guaranteed / 1974 / Blue Plate ✦✦

Shiny Beast (Bat Chain Puller) / Jan. 1978 / Bizarre/Straight ✦✦✦✦✦
So titled because the original album, simply titled *Bat Chain Puller*, had to be ditched and rerecorded after a legal tuzzle involving Frank Zappa's manager, *Shiny Beast* turned out to be manna from heaven for those feeling Beefheart had lost his way on his two Mercury albums. Then again, what else could be assumed with a song titled "Tropical Hot Dog Night" that sounds like what happened when Beefheart encountered Miami disco and decided to make something of it? When it comes to singing, though, he's still the atypical growler, snarler and more of lore, conjuring up more wonderfully odd lyrical stories than can easily be measured, while the album as a whole gets steadily more and more bent. "You Know You're a Man" is at once straightforward and incredibly weird when it comes to love and gender, while other standouts include "Bat Chain Puller," a steady chugger that feels like a goofy death march, and the nervy freak of "Owed T'Alex." As for the Magic Band in general, keyboardist Eric Drew Feldman, guitarists Jeff Tepper and Richard Redus and drummer Robert Williams lay down the business with appropriately gone aplomb, as a listen to "Suction Prints" will demonstrate. *—Ned Raggett*

Doc at the Radar Station / 1980 / Blue Plate ✦✦✦✦✦

Ice Cream for Crow / 1982 / Blue Plate ✦✦✦✦✦

Mirror Man Sessions / Jun. 1, 1999 / Buddha ✦✦✦
The Mirror Man Sessions features the complete remastered contents of *Mirror Man*, albeit in a resequenced running order, and fills out the rest of the CD with a number of bonus tracks taken from additional recordings, both finished and unfinished, made around the same time for what would have been a *double* album titled *It Comes to You in a Plain Brown Wrapper*. As a listening experience, the package will appeal more to those who value the instrumental Beefheart; the *Mirror Man* album is, of course, essentially a 50-plus-minute jam session, containing as it does only four songs, and the bonus tracks—many of which appeared on the One Way label's reissue of *Safe as Milk*—mostly consist of jams and instrumentals which push the boundaries of conventional blues-rock, with a Beefheart vocal tossed in here and there. Some may miss Beefheart's surreal poetry, gruff vocals, and/or free jazz influence, while others may find it fascinating to hear the Magic Band simply letting go and cutting loose. *—Steve Huey*

● **The Dust Blows Forward: An Anthology** / Aug. 17, 1999 / Rhino ✦✦✦✦✦
Leaving alone the obvious condition that Captain Beefheart's numerous experimental albums aren't as prime for a "best of" treatment as the discographies of most artists are, this is a pretty good overview of career highlights. The two CDs span his 1966 "Diddy Wah Diddy" single to his final album (1982's *Ice Cream for Crow*), each disc weighing in at about 75 minutes. With so much material to draw from (not even counting that mammoth five-CD box set of unreleased stuff), there will be inevitable disagreements among fans as to which songs were selected; there are seven from *Clear Spot*, for instance, but only two from *Safe as Milk*. Every period is sampled, however, and his weakest albums (*Unconditionally Guaran-*

teed and *Bluejeans & Moonbeams*) are judiciously represented by just one cut each. A few rarities do crop up, including a quite good and bluesy previously unreleased *Clear Spot* outtake ("Little Scratch"), "Hard Workin' Man" (from the soundtrack to *Blue Collar*), and the 1982 instrumental B-side "Light Reflected off the Oceands [sic] of the Moon." There are also little detours from Beefheart's albums for two tracks from 1966 singles and two collaborations with Frank Zappa from Zappa's *Bongo Fury*. It's not for the collector, but it's a decent package for someone who wants to get familiar with the Captain or doesn't need more than a few of his regular albums. Comprehensive notes in a 60-page booklet offer a good straightforward cruise through his oft-confusing history and shifting Magic Band personnel. *—Richie Unterberger*

Grow Fins: Rarities (1965-1982) / 1999 / Revenant ♦♦♦
An unprecedented project in the rock field: a five-CD box set of unreleased material by a cult artist that never had anything close to a chart hit. Of course Captain Beefheart is the ultimate cult artist, and one with a following so rabid (if limited) that the compilation has a wider audience than many would anticipate. Despite the impressive chronological span and variety of demos, live performances, backing tracks, and outtakes, be cautioned that this is *not* a best-of or ad hoc career overview. A good deal of the tracks (some of which have long been available on bootleg) are of slightly substandard or low fidelity, and Beefheart's most significant work is ultimately contained on his numerous official releases. However, this is an important addition to his catalog, and one that many of his fanatics will find essential, though it won't do much to convert the casual fan due to the difficult nature of much of the material. Disc one, with 1966-67 live cuts and demos that include a few songs recorded on *Safe as Milk* is certainly the most interesting and accessible of the quintet. Disc two is more shambling and experimental, with its assortment of 1968 live performances. Disc three is for the hardcore: home-recorded (though in okay fidelity) run-throughs of *Trout Mask Replica* material from 1969, without vocals. Disc four is for the harder core: twelve more minutes of *Trout Mask* home sessions, plus enhanced-CD live-performance footage from 1968-73. CD five is an interesting, erratic assortment of live, radio, demo, and worktape material from 1969-82, fidelity varying from good to poor. The liner notes are exceptionally detailed, with many first-hand quotes by band members and much historical narrative by frequent Magic Band drummer John French. *—Richie Unterberger*

The Cardigans

f. 1992, Jonkoping, Sweden
Group / Swedish Pop/Rock, Indie Pop, Ambient Pop, Twee Pop, Adult Alternative Pop/Rock, Alternative Pop/Rock
One of the most pleasing pop groups of the '90s, the Cardigans' sugary confections would grow annoying very quickly if they weren't backed by great musicianship and clever arrangements. The band's 1995 breakout album *Life* reflected the Cardigans at their most saccharine—the sunny disposition of vocalist Nina Persson being the major argument in favor—and critics inserted the group into the space-age pop revivalist camp. The Cardigans later proved that they were more difficult to pigeonhole, however. They released their debut album *Emmerdale* in May 1994. The single "Rise & Shine" became a hit on Swedish radio soon after the release of the LP, and a readers poll in Sweden's *Slitz* magazine voted *Emmerdale* the best album of 1994. A satirical response to their moody debut, *Life* showed the band at their most upbeat, including an angelic picture of Nina in an ice-skating outfit for the cover. Released in March 1995, the album eventually sold one and a half million copies worldwide and became especially popular in Japan, where it achieved platinum status. American major labels began to notice the attention, and Mercury signed them soon after. *First Band on the Moon*, released in September 1996, de-emphasized the pure pop in favor of abstract arrangements and some rather violent themes. Nevertheless, the infectious single "Lovefool" became a radio hit by early 1997. *—John Bush*

Emmerdale / 1994 / Minty Fresh ♦♦♦

● **Life** / 1995 / Minty Fresh ♦♦♦♦♦
With tongue firmly in cheek, the Cardigans decided to play up the candyfloss arrangements of their debut for second album *Life*. Where *Emmerdale* studied an introverted melancholy, *Life* is undiminished in both its independent-minded exuberance ("Hey! Get Out of My Way") and zest to enjoy life with others ("Daddy's Car," "Gordon's Gardenparty"). The incredible production and quality of arrangement from the debut is here also, even more strikingly crisp and spot-on. (Over 50 instruments were used on the 14 songs included on the Minty Fresh American release.) Though the Cardigans planned *Life* as something of a joke, it became one of the finest pop albums of the '90s. *—John Bush*

First Band on the Moon / Sep. 17, 1996 / Mercury ♦♦♦♦♦
For listeners who had caught up with the Cardigans on their breakout album *Life*, the group's third album was a confusing pastiche which included several conventional pop songs, but also added tracks with left-field arrangements and some (comparatively) disturbing lyrics. In reality, however, the group had simply returned to the mood and feel of their debut album. On *Emmerdale*, the melancholy was personal and solitary in nature, but here depression is focused on unfaithful lovers—in both the songs which vocalist Nina Persson helped out with lyrics and those written by the rest of the band ("Choke," "Step on Me," "The Great Divide"). Even the single "Lovefool" is a depressing lament of unrequited affection, and the presence of another Black Sabbath cover ("Iron Man") certainly isn't an immediate upper. Still, *First Band on the Moon* is saved by the Cardigans' core strengths: Persson's vocals and Svensson's arrangements. *—John Bush*

Gran Turismo / Nov. 3, 1998 / Mercury ♦♦♦

Mariah Carey

b. Mar. 27, 1970, New York, NY
Vocals / Club/Dance, Adult Contemporary, Urban, Dance-Pop
The best-selling female performer of the 1990s, Mariah Carey rose to superstardom on the strength of her stunning five-octave voice; an elastic talent who moved easily from glossy ballads to hip-hop-inspired dance-pop, she earned frequent comparison to rivals Whitney Houston and Celine Dion, but did them both one better by composing all of her own material. Signed to Columbia before she turned 20, Carey found a chart-topping smash with her self-titled debut album, launching no less than four number one singles— "Vision of Love," "Love Takes Time," "Someday," and "I Don't Wanna Cry." Expectations were high for Carey's follow-up, 1991's *Emotions*. The album did not disappoint, as the title track reached number one—a record fifth consecutive chart-topper. Carey's next release was 1992's *MTV Unplugged* EP, which generated a number one cover of the Jackson 5's "I'll Be There." Her third full-length effort, *Music Box*, was her best selling record to date. Two more singles, "Dreamlover" and "Hero," reached the top spot on the charts. 1995's *Daydream* reflected a new artistic maturity; the singles "Fantasy" and "One Sweet Day" both hit the top of the charts (the latter for 16 weeks). Carey returned in 1997 with *Butterfly*, another staggering success and her most hip-hop-flavored recording to date. *—Jason Ankeny*

Mariah Carey / May 1990 / Columbia ♦♦♦
This extremely impressive debut is replete with smooth-sounding ballads and uplifting dance/R&B cuts. Carey convincingly seizes many opportunities to display her incredible vocal range on such memorable tracks as the popular "Vision of Love" (featured during her television debut on *The Arsenio Hall Show*, an appearance noted by many as her formal introduction to stardom), the energetic "Someday," and the moody sounds of the hidden treasure "Vanishing." With this collection of songs acting as a springboard for future successes, Carey establishes a strong standard of comparison for other breakthrough artists of this genre. *—Ashley S. Battel*

Emotions / Sep. 1991 / Columbia ♦♦♦

MTV Unplugged EP / Mar. 1992 / Columbia ♦♦♦

Music Box / Sep. 1993 / Columbia ♦♦♦♦
Mariah Carey has been stung by critical charges that she's all vocal bombast and no subtlety, soul or shading. Her solution was to make an album in which her celebrated octave-leaping voice would be downplayed and she could demonstrate her ability to sing softly and coolly. Well, she was partly successful; she trimmed the volume on *Music Box*. Unfortunately, she also cut the energy level; Carey sounds detached on several selections. She scored a couple of huge hits, "Hero" and "Dreamlover," where she did inject some personality and intensity into the leads. Most other times, Carey blended into the background and let the tracks guide her, instead of pushing and exploding through them. It was wise for Carey to display other elements of her approach, but sometimes excessive spirit is preferable to an absence of passion. *—Ron Wynn*

Daydream / Oct. 3, 1995 / Columbia ♦♦♦♦♦
Mariah Carey certainly knows how to construct an album. Positioning herself directly between urban R&B with tracks like "Fantasy" and adult contemporary with songs like "One Sweet Day," a duet with Boyz II Men, Carey appeals to both audiences equally because of the sheer amount of craft and hard work she puts into her albums. *Daydream* is her best record to date, featuring a consistently strong selection of songs and a remarkably impassioned performance by Carey. A few of the songs are second-rate—particularly the cover of Journey's "Open Arms"—but *Daydream* demonstrates that Carey continues to perfect her craft and that she has earned her status as an R&B/pop diva. *—Stephen Thomas Erlewine*

Butterfly / Sep. 16, 1997 / Columbia ♦♦♦♦
Upon its release, *Butterfly* was interpreted as Mariah Carey's declaration of independence from her ex-husband (and label president) Tommy Mottola, and to a certain extent, that's true. *Butterfly* is peppered with allusions to her troubled marriage and her newfound freedom, and the music is supposed to be in tune with contemporary urban sounds instead of adult contemporary radio. Nevertheless, it feels like a Mariah Carey album, which means that it's a collection of hit singles surrounded by classy filler. What is surprising about *Butterfly* is the lack of uptempo dance-pop. Apart from the Puffy Combs-produced "Honey," *Butterfly* is devoted to ballads, and while they are all well-crafted, many of them blend together upon initial listening. Subsequent plays reveal that Carey's vocals are sultrier and more controlled than ever, and that helps "Butterfly," "Break Down," "Babydoll," and the Prince cover "The Beautiful Ones" rank among her best; also, the ballads do have a stronger urban feel than before. Even though *Butterfly* doesn't have as many strong singles as *Daydream*, it's one of her best records, illustrating that Carey is continuing to improve and refine her music, which makes her a rarity among her '90s peers. *—Stephen Thomas Erlewine*

● **#1's** / Nov. 17, 1998 / Columbia ♦♦♦♦♦
Protest as she may—and she does, claiming in the liner notes that *#1's* is "not a greatest hits album! It's too soon, I haven't been recording long enough for that!"—it's hard to view *#1's*, Mariah Carey's first compilation, as anything other than a greatest-hits album. Carey was fortunate enough to have nearly every single she released top the pop charts. Between 1990's "Vision of Love" and 1998's "My All," all but four commercially released singles ("Anytime You Need a Friend," "Can't Let Go," "Make It Happen," "Without You") hit number one, with only a handful of radio-only singles ("Butterfly," "Breakdown") making the airwaves, not the charts. That leaves 12 big hits on *#1's*, all number ones. Since Carey's singles always dominated her albums, it comes as no surprise that *#1's* is her best, most consistent album, filled with songs that represent state-of-the-art '90s adult contemporary and pop-oriented urban soul. That said, it isn't a perfect overview—a couple of good singles are missing because of the self-imposed "1 rule"; plus, the Ol' Dirty Bastard mix of "Fantasy" is strong, but fans familiar with the radio single will be disappointed that the chorus is completely missing on this version. The album is also padded with a personal favorite (her Brian McKnight duet "Whenever You Call," taken from *Butterfly*) and three new songs—the Jermaine Dupri-produced "Sweetheart," the Whitney Houston duet "When You Believe" (taken from *The Prince of Egypt* soundtrack), and "I Still Believe," a remake of a Brenda K. Starr tune—which are all fine, but not particularly memorable. Still, that's hardly enough to bring down a thoroughly entertaining compilation that will stand as her best record until the "official" hits collection is released. *—Stephen Thomas Erlewine*

Rainbow / Nov. 2, 1999 / Columbia ♦♦♦

The Carpenters

f. 1968, New Haven, CT, **db.** 1983

Group / Soft Rock, Pop

With their light, airy melodies and meticulously crafted, clean arrangements, the Carpenters stood in direct contrast with the excessive, gaudy pop/rock of the '70s, yet they became one of the most popular artists of the decade, scoring 12 Top Ten hits, including three number one singles. Karen Carpenter's calm, pretty voice was the most distinctive element of their music, settling in perfectly amidst the precise, lush arrangements provided by her brother Richard. The duo's sound drew more from pre-rock pop than rock & roll, but that didn't prevent the Carpenters from appealing to a variety of audiences, particularly Top 40, easy listening and adult contemporary. While their popularity declined during the latter half of the '70s, they remained one of the most distinctive and recognizable acts of the decade produced.

Offering, the Carpenters' first album, was released in November 1969 but failed to make a big impression. However, the Carpenters' fortunes changed with their second single, a version of Burt Bacharach and Hal David's "(They Long to Be) Close to You," which became the group's first number one, spending four weeks on the top of the U.S. charts. "Close to You" became an international hit, beginning a five-year period where the duo was one of the most popular recording acts in the world. During that period the Carpenters won two Grammy Awards, including Best New Artist of 1970, and had an impressive string of Top Ten hits, including "Rainy Days and Mondays," "Superstar," "Hurting Each Other," "Goodbye to Love," "Yesterday Once More," and "Top of the World." After 1975's number four hit "Only Yesterday," the group's popularity began to decline. On February 4, 1983, Karen was found unconscious at her parents' home in New Haven; she died in the hospital that morning from a cardiac arrest, which was caused by a long battle with anorexia. *—Stephen Thomas Erlewine*

● **The Singles (1969-1973)** / Nov. 1973 / A&M ✦✦✦✦✦

There's a certain inherent sadness listening to this concise 12-song collection of the duo's early hits, especially as it opens with "We've Only Just Begun," with its hopeful, dreamy lyrics—for it was never supposed to be definitive, just the first of at least two such collections. But changes in the public's taste and a slackening (though never a disappearance) of hits for the duo, and Karen Carpenter's death in 1983, made this the first and only real mass choice for a Carpenters' collection. Ten of the duo's dozen Top Ten hits are present, from "Close to You" to "Top of the World," with their gorgeous and original slow ballad interpretation of "Ticket to Ride" and their cover of Carole King's "It's Going to Take Some Time" thrown in to offer a slightly wider perspective. Listening to this material, it's easy to accuse the Carpenters of being hopelessly retro even in their own time—bear in mind that "We've Only Just Begun" and "Superstar" being contemporaneous with the Allman Brothers' *At the Fillmore* and *Eat a Peach* and you get the idea. But the lush melodies brought out in Richard Carpenter's arrangements and Karen's singing are justification in themselves—additionally, the 1999 reissue in A&M "Remastered Classics" series (82839-3601-2) has a closer, toughened but warmer sound; yes, the strings are brighter, to the point of glistening, but the rhythm section (Joe Osborn on bass, Hal Blaine on drums) has more impact as well. Moreover, the full original notes from the insert are now included, explaining how each song came to be discovered and recorded. *—Bruce Eder*

Yesterday Once More / May 1985 / A&M ✦✦✦✦✦

This double-CD set was probably too much of the Carpenters for the average fan, but just the same, it touches bases that *The Singles* misses, and it is rewarding. The 1998 remastering (catalog number 31454 1000-2) is doubly attractive, as a mid-priced item with 24-bit remastered sound and new notes by Paul Grein. The 28 songs, totaling more than 110 minutes of music, still have a few holes, like their cover of "Beechwood 4-5789" and the deeply atmospheric "Crescent Noon," but every one of their albums is represented from *Ticket to Ride* on up. The remastering makes all of the difference in the enjoyment of the songs, presenting Karen Carpenter's voice and Richard Carpenter's arrangements in close, rich detail and intimacy; it all makes the care that was put into the original performances completely worth the effort. The duo's music never sounded less like recordings and more like performances, a fact—brought home by the crystalline tones of Joe Osborn's bass—that may distress those who merely want to relive their memories of hearing these songs on the radio. There will also be a few worthwhile surprises even for the casual listener, including the melodic dance number "(Want You) Back in My Life Again" from their final album and the rhapsodic "I Just Fall in Love Again" from *Passage.* This set is a decent compromise between the superficiality of *The Singles* and the deep but awkward construction of the four-CD boxed set, made more valuable by the remastering, which renders its sound superior to that of the same material on the box. *—Bruce Eder*

James Carr

b. Jun. 13, 1942, Memphis, TN

Vocals, Sax (Tenor) / Deep Soul, Southern Soul, Soul

Considered to be among the very greatest of "deep" Southern male soul singers, James Carr's succession of R&B hits on the Memphis Goldwax label were all gems of "country" soul, that wonderful '60s marriage of Southern Black R&B vocalists with songs written in a country format and played mostly by White musicians. Carr's dark, gospel-inflected style, marked by a subtle, rich voice that is almost frightening in its intensity and range, has been compared to that of Otis Redding and Percy Sledge; many reviewers would class him above even these formidable peers. "At the Dark End of the Street," the first songwriting collaboration between Dan Penn and Chips Moman, is Carr's undisputed masterpiece. Also recorded by Aretha Franklin, Clarence Carter, Linda Ronstadt, and Ry Cooder, it is the quintessential country-soul take on adulterous love.

Carr's career initially was short; Goldwax ceased operation in 1969, and Carr cut only one other single for Atlantic in 1971; however, he has recently emerged from retirement with a new album on Goldwax. His work stands at the apex of '60s soul—with Aretha, Otis, Percy, and Wilson—essential stuff! *—Christine Ohlman*

● **The Essential James Carr** / Feb. 21, 1995 / Razor & Tie ✦✦✦✦✦

When the soul era of the mid-'60s was in full bloom, for a period of three years James Carr was the maker of some of its mightiest music. His warm, soulful voice could make the reading of virtually anything he touched (even his version here of the Bee Gees' "To Love Somebody") a transcendent event. He is also the mystery man of the genre, unlettered and imbued with an almost childlike innocence, disappearing for a decade after these recordings were made with charges of mental instability cropping up whenever his name is mentioned. But music this special doesn't come without a price and certainly Carr paid that price, not unlike the gospel singers who influenced him who sometimes sang themselves to death right on stage. But the music will always win out, because personal problems aside, the music James Carr made is as deep as Southern soul music gets, on an equal par with the best of a Sam Cooke or an Otis Redding. Tracks like "You've Got My Mind Messed Up," "Pouring Water on a Drowning Man," and his masterpiece, "The Dark End of the Street" are all justifiable classics of the genre, and this 20-track collection is where you go to get the big picture on an artist who deserves a much wider hearing. *—Cub Koda*

The Cars

f. 1976, Boston, MA, **db.** 1988

Group / Album Rock, Pop/Rock, New Wave

Blondie may have had a string of number one hits and Talking Heads may have won the hearts of the critics, but the Cars were the most successful American New Wave band to emerge in the late '70s. With their sleek, mechanical pop-rock, the band racked up a string of platinum albums and Top 40 singles that made them one of the most popular American rock & roll bands of the late '70s and early '80s. While they were more commercially-oriented than their New York peers, the Cars were nevertheless inspired by proto-punk, garage rock and bubblegum pop. The difference was in packaging. Where their peers were as equally inspired by art as music, the Cars were strictly a rock & roll band, and while their music occasionally sounded clipped and distant, they had enough attitude to crossover to album rock radio, which is where they made their name. Nevertheless, the Cars remained a New Wave band, picking up cues from the Velvet Underground, David Bowie and Roxy Music. Ric Ocasek and Ben Orr's vocals uncannily recalled Lou Reed's dead-pan delivery, while the band's insistent, rhythmic pulse was reminiscent of Berlin-era Iggy Pop. Furthermore, the group followed Roxy Music's lead and had artist Alberto Vargas design sexy illustrations of pinups for their record sleeves. These airbrushed drawings were the group's primary visual attraction until 1984, when the group made a series of striking videos to accompany the singles from *Heartbeat City.* The videos for "You Might Think," "Magic," and "Drive" became MTV staples, sending the Cars to near-superstar status. Instead of following through with their success, the Cars slowly faded away, quietly breaking up after releasing one final album in 1987. *—Stephen Thomas Erlewine*

The Cars / May 1978 / Elektra ✦✦✦✦✦

The Cars' 1978 self-titled debut, issued on the Elektra label, is a genuine rock masterpiece. The band jokingly referred to the album as their "true greatest-hits album," but it's no exaggeration—all nine tracks are new wave/rock classics, still in rotation on rock radio. Whereas most bands of the late '70s embraced either punk/new wave or hard rock, the Cars were one of the first bands to do the unthinkable—merge the two styles together. Add to it bandleader/songwriter Ric Ocasek's supreme pop sensibilities, and you had an album that appealed to new wavers, rockers, and Top 40 fans. One of the most popular new wave songs ever, "Just What I Needed," is an obvious highlight, as are such familiar hits as "Good Times Roll," "My Best Friend's Girl," and "You're All I've Got Tonight." But like most consummate rock albums, the lesser-known compositions are just as exhilarating—"Don't Cha Stop," "Bye Bye Love," "All Mixed Up," and "Moving In Stereo," the latter featured as an instrumental during a steamy scene in the popular movie *Fast Times at Ridgemont High.* With flawless performances, songwriting, and production (courtesy of Queen alumni Roy Thomas Baker), the Cars' debut remains one of rock's all-time classics. *—Greg Prato*

Candy-O / Jun. 1979 / Elektra ✦✦✦

Panorama / Aug. 1980 / Elektra ✦✦

Shake It Up / Nov. 1981 / Elektra ✦✦✦

By augmenting their sound with more synthesizers, electronics, and drum machines, the Cars' fourth release, *Shake It Up* (1981, Elektra), helped bridge their hard rock-based early work (1978's *The Cars*) with the futuristic-pop direction of 1984's *Heartbeat City.* The band's sound may have been evolving with each succeeding album, but Ric Ocasek was still writing compelling new wave compositions despite all the change, many of which would ultimately become rock & roll standards. The up-tempo title track remains a party favorite to this day (reaching number four on the singles charts), while the melancholic "Since You're Gone" remains one of Ocasek's best-ever tales of heartbreak. Intriguing videos were made for both songs, officially introducing the band to the MTV/video age. Like it's predecessor, 1980's *Panorama,* filler is present ("This Could Be Love," "Maybe Baby"), but many lesser-known album tracks prove to be highlights: the almost entirely synth-oriented tracks "Think It Over" and "A Dream Away," the rocking "Cruiser," plus the more pop-oriented "I'm Not the One" and "Victim of Love." Although *Shake It Up* was another resounding commercial success, their next album would be the one that made the Cars one of the rock quintessential acts of the '80s. *—Greg Prato*

Heartbeat City / Mar. 1984 / Elektra ✦✦✦✦✦

MTV had become a major marketing tool by 1984, and the Cars were one of the first bands to use the new video medium to their advantage. The band's fifth album, *Heartbeat City* (Elektra), spawned several imaginative and memorable videos, which translated into massive chart and commercial success, making it one of the biggest releases of the year. Produced by hitmaker John "Mutt" Lange (AC/DC, Def Leppard), the album included two Top Ten singles—the ballad "Drive" and the charismatic "You Might Think," plus an additional two that landed in the Top 20—the summer anthem "Magic," and the eccentric "Hello Again." But it didn't just stop there, plenty of other tracks could have been hits as well, such as the sparse rocker "It's Not the Night" and the breezy pop of "Looking for Love." Other highlights included the ethereal title track, the melodic rocker "Stranger Eyes," and the moderately paced love song "Why Can't I Have You." Although the Cars experienced their greatest success yet with *Heartbeat City,* it would unfortunately not last for long—after just one more studio album (1987's spotty *Door to Door*), the band split up. *—Greg Prato*

- **Greatest Hits** / Oct. 1985 / Elektra ✦✦✦✦✦

The Cars were responsible for some of rock's most recognizable radio hits by the mid- '80s, so when the band took an extended break after their successful tour for *Heartbeat City,* 1985's *Greatest Hits* (Elektra) was assembled. Mixed in with the familiar selections was a brand new track, the playful "Tonight She Comes" (which became a Top Ten hit), as well as a remix of the overlooked "Shake It Up" ballad, "I'm Not the One." And while most of the expected hits are represented ("Just What I Needed," "Let's Go," "Drive," "Shake It Up," etc.), some of the selections prove questionable—why was the title track from *Heartbeat City* (an unsuccessful single) included instead of the 1984 Top 20 hit "Hello Again"? Other missing radio staples include "You're All I've Got Tonight," "It's All I Can Do," and the title track from *Candy-O,* which would have made the collection definitive (all are included on the more extensive *Just What I Needed: Cars Anthology* from 1995). But for the casual fan, *Greatest Hits* will do the trick. *—Greg Prato*

Door to Door / Aug. 1987 / Elektra ✦

Just What I Needed: The Cars Anthology / Nov. 7, 1995 / Rhino ✦✦✦✦✦

While casual admirers of the Cars can stick with their 1985 *Greatest Hits* collection, more serious fans should go right to the more thorough two-CD set, *The Cars Anthology: Just What I Needed.* Whereas *Greatest Hits* stuck more or less with their singles, *The Cars Anthology* contains strong album cuts, non-album B-sides, demos and unreleased takes, as well as all the expected hits (and a 27-page booklet crammed with rare photos and the band's bio). Just about every rock fan is long familiar with such tracks as "Just What I Needed," "Shake It Up," "Magic," and "Let's Go" (to name a few), but the collection's main attraction is it's abundance of unfamiliar material. Such previously-released album tracks as "Dangerous Type," "Gimme Some Slack," and "Cruiser" are highlights, as are the rarities "Cool Fool" (one of their hardest rocking tracks ever), "That's It," a cover of Iggy Pop's "Funtime" and a pair of album-closing early demos ("Leave or Stay" and "Ta Ta Wayo Wayo"). At nearly two and a half hours long, *The Cars Anthology: Just What I Needed* is the ultimate Cars collection, which only confirms their standing as one of the finest bands of the new wave era. *—Greg Prato*

Clarence Carter

b. Jan. 14, 1936, Montgomery, AL

Vocals, Keyboards, Guitar / Deep Soul, Southern Soul, Soul

A blind soul singer whose numerous hits of the late '60s and early '70s epitomized the Muscle Shoals rhythm & blues sound, Carter hit the big time with his Atlantic single "Patches" (1970) and won a lasting place in the annals of Southern soul with others like "Slip Away" and "Too Weak to Fight." In 1981 Carter broke out of a dry spell with the Venture album *Let's Burn,* featuring a track called "Workin' (On a Love Building)," which set the theme for much of what was to follow: robust, lascivious lovemaking boasts. More recent tracks such as his salacious reworking of Tampa Red's "Love Me with a Feeling" and the jukebox favorite "Strokin'" (too risque for some radio stations) further solidified the carnal Carter image. Still primarily a soul/R&B singer, Carter has incorporated more hard blues elements in his music recently than in the Muscle Shoals days, despite his new and unblues-minded penchant for playing and programming all the instruments on his albums. *—Jim O'Neal*

- **Snatchin' It Back** / 1992 / Rhino ✦✦✦✦✦

Snatchin' It Back—The Best of Clarence Carter is a great compilation, spotlighting Carter's stellar guitar work and trademark vocals on classics like "Slip Away," "Too Weak to Fight," and "Lookin' for a Fox." His great "Tell Daddy" (covered by Etta James as "Tell Mama") is included. Dave Marsh contributes the liner notes. Soul music at its funky best, and the compilation to own if you're a Carter fan. *—Christine Ohlman*

Catherine Wheel

f. Apr. 1990, Great Yarmouth, England

Group / Shoegazing, Alternative Pop/Rock

By using their influences as a mere launching pad and consistently developing their many strengths, Catherine Wheel was able to outlast all of their early peers. With their initial singles and first album, the band from East Anglia fit snugly with the remainder of bands that the British press eventually labeled as shoegazers, a short-lived sub-scene of bands that were characterized by an inactive stage presence, loads of effects pedals, and buried vocals. However, the always tuneful Catherine Wheel survived by refusing to repeat themselves and remaining accessible to their constantly swelling fanbase through touring like dogs. The band's extensive discography plays like a how-to guide for bands that aspire to do most things imaginable within the domain of bass/drum/guitar/vocals with enthusiasm and sharp skill. They might not have reached the level of popularity that they aimed for, but their career was one that most bands would commit felonies to experience.

Formed by Rob Dickinson (vocals and guitar), Brian Futter (guitar), Dave Hawes (bass), and Neil Sims (drums) in 1990, Catherine Wheel debuted on the tiny Norwich independent label Wilde Club with the She's My Friend and Painful Thing singles. Though inspired by the likes of Echo and the Bunnymen and the House of Love, even the band's earliest recordings strayed from being derivative. Those singles earned them a spot on John Peel's BBC show. One listener was famed producer and ìnon-musicianî Brian Eno, who was delighted enough by what he heard to phone the band's manager up and express admiration. Eno, who had his Opal label at the time, threw his hat into the ring of people wanting to release the band's future material. Since the tiny Opal imprint didn't fit into the big plans the band had for themselves, they declined to sign on with the bald wonder. Creation boss Alan McGee was another interested major figure. Since McGee was about to become knee-deep in debt, thanks to the extensive costs of My Bloody Valentine's *Loveless,* the band passed on the pre-Oasis label. Fontana had the ability to market the band on a wider scale and the label's licensing deal with Mercury in the U.S. made them more attractive.

Signed to Fontana, the band set about wrangling a producer for their debut full-length. Being huge fans of Talk Talk's sonically expansive records, they contacted the band's associate, Tim Friese-Greene. To their pleasant surprise, Friese-Greene had bought the Wild Club singles and needed no convincing to work with them. Friese-Greene became the fifth Wheel as much as he was the fifth member of Talk Talk, playing a crucial role in sound development, production, and adding his trademark keyboards when necessary. Ferment gained the band a small following in their native land and abroad on the strength of the epic "Black Metallic," which remained the band's most recognized song throughout their career.

The cinematic Chrome followed in 1993, toughening the band's sound and providing increased exposure on U.S. alternative radio through "Crank." Dickinson's increased confidence as a singer allowed them more emotional depth. Another strong alliance was forged with engineer Gil Norton during the recording sessions. As always, extensive touring ensued and the band's heavier edge on stage was captured on 1995's Happy Days, which hardcore fans dismissed for being too flat-out rock for their tastes. Neo-metal single "Waydown" was the radio staple in the U.S., giving the band more exposure than ever. At this point, the band was criticized for abandoning Britain, which was something of a fallacy. Although they would routinely circle the U.S. multiple times while touring, only in relative terms did it appear that they were neglecting their homeland.

Meanwhile, Catherine Wheel had been stockpiling spectacular B-sides that only rabid collectors and those who would listen to their tales of depleted wallets knew about. To provide a stop-gap between albums, Like Cats and Dogs was released in 1996, which only contained a small fraction of those extras. Ingeniously, those that were selected were sequenced in a manner that resembled a regular studio album; the immediacy and experimentalism of the hodgepodge made for the band's best full-length in the eyes of several fans.

Peeling back from the aural onslaught of Happy Days, the band exposed more of their atmospheric knack for 1997's Adam and Eve (released by Chrysalis in the U.K.), which was also designed to play as a single piece. Frustrated with the current generation's aversion to listening to a single record through its entirety, they went so far as to bring in Bob Ezrin to give it a classic front-to-back feel; they obviously liked the result of Like Cats and Dogs and the result of Adam and Eve was just as pleasing. Despite having numerous radio friendly songs on the album, sales for the record stalled outside of the usual pack and those catching on by word of mouth and more gigging. Not pleased with Mercury, Catherine Wheel abandoned ship prior to the bloodshed that ensued when Mercury's distributor Polygram merged with Universal.

Creatively stalled by not knowing where to go next, it took a while for Catherine Wheel to come up with 2000's Wishville, which found release through the band's new label, Columbia. Dave Hawes was relieved of his bass duties prior to recording sessions; since he was the most accessible and affable member of the group (and an excellent musician), the announcement of his departure was met with much scrutiny by their fans. The band had their reasons in sacking Hawes and the bass lines for Wishville were handled by Dickinson, Futter, and Friese-Greene. Ben Ellis was eventually brought on as full-time bassist. Wishville gained noticeable play on alternative radio, but it translated into the usual amount of sales that the band was accustomed to. Frustrated with having all the tools to be a huge platinum act for nearly a decade, the band went on hiatus after touring. *—Andy Kellman*

Ferment / Jun. 9, 1992 / Fontana ✦✦✦✦✦

Centered around re-recorded versions of four songs from the band's two Wilde Club singles and the seven minute lovelorn "Black Metallic"—which was referred to as the "Like a Hurricane" of the '90s—the deeply rich *Ferment* firmly established Catherine Wheel amongst the shoegaze contingent of the early '90s. The band would proceed to denounce the shoegaze tag, but it was a fitting one, at least with everything they released prior to 1993's harder edged *Chrome.* Along with bands like Lush, Ride, and Slowdive, Catherine Wheel buried their sing-along melodies in wafts of distortion and blurry production values. Rob Dickinson had yet to find comfort as a lead singer, so his somewhat fey and dazed emoting blended perfectly with Tim Friese-Greene's comfy production. A fair amount of the bands thrown into the same category as Catherine Wheel were criticized for lacking knowledge of their instruments, but a couple listens to *Ferment* should prove that they were hardly amateurish. The employment of numerous guitar pedals didn't serve as a smoke-and-mirrors ruse, and Friese-Greene knew enough to allow room for bassist Dave Hawes and drummer Neil Sims to flex their able muscles. Dickinson and lead guitarist Brian Futter were immensely skilled and complementary to each other from the band's inception; certainly they were one of the most unrecognized guitar duos of their stylistic brethren. Like all fine debuts, *Ferment* is varied emotionally, ranging from lust ("I Want to Touch You") to bliss ("Shallow" and "Salt"). It's a record that makes you want to crawl inside its sleeve and remain. It's as welcoming as it is insular and sheltered. *—Andy Kellman*

- **Chrome** / Jul. 20, 1993 / Fontana ✦✦✦✦✦

The biggest change in Catherine Wheel's sound, whether from Gil Norton's production or the decision of the band as a whole, is in *Chrome*'s general aggressiveness: not brutish, but definitely more in your face, even as Dickinson's lyrics and singing call to mind emotional calamities and internal collapses as much as exultation. The edges are a touch sharper, the sound bursts from the speakers, and Futter in particular earns his deserved guitar god reputation, peeling off powerful rhythms and brilliant, non-wanky solos in profusion. "I Confess" is a great example of how the two work well together, Dickinson taking advantage of a quieter passage to softly sing, "Took too many drugs, popped too many pills" before a massive, charging crash back into the song. Other strong numbers include the snarling title track, one of the band's angriest and most passionate, and the anthemic up-and-out surge of "Ursa Major Space Station," named after a guitar pedal and yet anything but cold technical ability. The real ringer is at the end, the poppy burst of "Show Me Mary," which slightly hints at where *Happy Days* would end up. When it comes to the absolute highlight, though, it's "Pain." While it has similar loud/soft dynamics as "Black Metallic," the shifts are crisper and the deep ache conveyed by the lyrics all that much more powerful. Add on some simply stunning guitar in the mid-song break, and it's another example of the Wheel's abilities. —*Ned Raggett*

Happy Days / May 1995 / Fontana/Mercury ✦✦✦

Like Cats and Dogs / Sep. 9, 1996 / Mercury ✦✦✦✦

Adam and Eve / Jul. 29, 1997 / Mercury ✦✦✦✦
With Catherine Wheel's records getting heavier, harder, and more bloated in succession, it came as great relief that their fourth proper record would provide a change. From the opening atonal plink of Brian Futter's guitar on "Future Boy," it is apparent that they're focusing more than ever on the use of sublime atmospherics, an arrow in the band's quiver that had only been exposed briefly during prior outings on their full-lengths and largely shelved for use as B-sides until then. Prior comparisons to Pink Floyd didn't make a great deal of sense, but here they did. The solemn, dusky edge to the likes of "Future Boy" and "Ma Solituda" recalls parts of *Wish You Were Here* and *Animals*, although leaning toward pop and removing most strains of gargoyle rock. Furthermore, when was the last time a song was closed off with the sound of a car door being slammed?

The references don't end there. The constant, repetitive drum pattern from Neil Sims that forms the basis of the ten-times gorgeous "Thunderbird" is lifted from Talk Talk's "After the Flood." Much more than a batch of smart references, *Adam and Eve* is a cold splash of water in the face of the pessimistic and cynical. Even in the most melancholy of *Adam and Eve*'s songs, there's an uplifting quality that carries throughout, extracting most of the emotional detritus that seeped through the band's earlier work. Not everything is windswept atmospherics, either. The romping "Delicious" catches Rob Dickinson at his most randy, imagining he's Bruce Lee and Michael Caine. "Broken Nose" and "Satellite" are dynamic, muscular modern rock at its finest. Anyone finding that some of this material errs on the side of sappiness or boldness really needs more sunshine in their life. —*Andy Kellman*

Wishville / May 2000 / Columbia ✦✦

Nick Cave (Nicholas Edward Cave)

b. Sep. 22, 1957, Warracknabeal, Australia
Vocals, Piano, Organ / Post-Punk, Alternative Pop/Rock, Singer/Songwriter
After goth pioneers the Birthday Party called it quits in 1983, singer/songwriter Nick Cave assembled the Bad Seeds, a post-punk supergroup featuring former Birthday Party guitarist Mick Harvey on drums, ex-Magazine bassist Barry Adamson, and Einsturzende Neubauten guitarist Blixa Bargeld. With the Bad Seeds, Cave continued to explore his obsessions with religion, death, love, America, and violence with a bizarre, sometimes self-consciously eclectic hybrid of blues, gospel, rock, and arty post-punk, although in a more subdued fashion than his work with the Birthday Party. Cave also allowed his literary aspirations to come to the forefront; the lyrics are narrative prose, heavy on literary allusions and myth-making and taking some inspiration from Leonard Cohen. Cave's gloomy lyrics, dark musical arrangements, and deep baritone voice recall the albums of Scott Walker, who also obsessed over death and love with a frightening passion. However, Cave brings a hefty amount of post-punk experimentalism to Walker's epic dark pop. —*Stephen Thomas Erlewine & Steve Huey*

From Her to Eternity / 1984 / Restless/Mute ✦✦✦

The Firstborn Is Dead / 1985 / Mute ✦✦✦✦
The blues had long been a potent undercurrent in the Birthday Party's music, so it wasn't all that surprising that Nick Cave embraced the sound and feeling of rural blues on his second album with the Bad Seeds, *The Firstborn Is Dead*. What was startling was how well Cave and his bandmates—Barry Adamson, Mick Harvey, and Blixa Bargeld—were able to absorb and honor the influences of artists like Skip James and Charley Patton while creating a sound that was unmistakably their own. The moody obsessions of rural blues—trains, floods, imprisonment, sin, fear, and death—seemed made to order for Cave, and he was able to tap into the doomy iconography of this music with potent emotional force; on "Tupelo," he makes a sweeping and disturbing epic of the rain-swept night when Elvis Presley was born, and "Knocking on Joe" is a tale of life on the work gang that communicates the pain of the spirit as clearly as the ache of the body. Also, the blues helped transform Cave's music as well as his lyrics; the brutal sonic pummel of the Birthday Party here gave way to a more subtle and dynamic approach that still made effective use of dissonance and bare-wired electric guitar noise while proving the balance of loud and soft only made each side deeper and more resonant. (The stark, barely there guitar and drums of "Blind Lemon Jefferson" are as startling and malignantly fascinating as anything in the Birthday Party's catalog.) *The Firstborn Is Dead* proved Nick Cave's musical palate was significantly broader than his debut album suggested and pointed to a path (channeling the sounds and emotions of American roots music) he would return to on many of his albums that followed. —*Mark Deming*

Kicking Against the Pricks / 1986 / Mute/Elektra ✦✦✦✦
Besides being noteworthy as an astonishingly good all-covers album, *Kicking Against the Pricks* is notable for the arrival of a new key member for the Seeds, drummer Thomas Wydler. Besides being a fine percussionist, able to perform at both the explosive and restrained levels Cave requires, Wydler also allowed Harvey to concentrate on adding guitar and keyboards live as well as in the studio, a notable bonus. Race reappears briefly to add some guitar while former Birthday Party cohorts Rowland Howard and Tracy Pew guest as well, the latter on some of his last tracks before his untimely death. The selection of songs is quite impressive, ranging from old standards like "Long Black Veil" to everything from John Lee Hooker's "I'm Gonna Kill That Woman" and Gene Pitney's pop aria "Something's Gotten Hold of My Heart." Matching the range of material, the Seeds are well on their way to becoming the rock/cabaret/blues showband of Cave's dreams, able to conjure up haunting, winsome atmospheres ("Sleeping Annaleah") as much as higher-volume takes (Roy Orbison's "Running Scared," the Velvet Underground's "All Tomorrow's Parties"). The version of Leadbelly's "Black Betty" is particularly grand, Harvey's drumming driving the track with ominous power. This said, often holding everything back is the key, as the creepout build of "Hey Joe" demonstrates. Even more striking is how Cave's own vocals rebut the charges that all he ever does is overdramatize everything he sings—consider the husky, purring delivery on Johnny Cash's "The Singer." Other winners include a masterful version of Jimmy Webb's "By the Time I Get to Phoenix" and the stately, album-closing "The Carnival Is Over," originally a mid-'60s hit for the Seekers. —*Ned Raggett*

Your Funeral . . . My Trial / 1986 / Mute/Elektra ✦✦✦

The Good Son / Oct. 1990 / Mute ✦✦✦

Henry's Dream / May 12, 1992 / Mute ✦✦✦✦

Let Love In / Apr. 19, 1994 / Mute ✦✦✦✦✦
Keeping the same line-up from *Henry's Dream*, Nick Cave and company turn in yet another winner with *Let Love In*. Compared to *Henry's Dream*, *Let Love In* is something of a more produced effort—longtime Cave boardsman Tony Cohen oversees things, and from the first track, one can hear the subtle arrangements and carefully constructed performances. Love, unsurprisingly, takes center stage of the album. Besides concluding with a second part to "Do You Love Me?," two of its stronger cuts are the (almost) title track "I Let Love In," and "Loverman," an even creepier depiction of lust's throttling power so gripping that Metallica ended up covering it. On the full-on explosive front, "Jangling Jack" sounds like it wants to do nothing but destroy sound systems, strange noises and overmodulations ripping throughout the song. The Seeds can always turn in almost deceptively peaceful performances as well, of course—standouts here are "Nobody's Baby Now," with a particularly lovely guitar/piano line, and the brooding drama of "Ain't Gonna Rain Anymore." The highlight of the album, though, has little to do with love and everything to do with the group's abilities at music noir. "Red Right Hand" depicts a nightmarish figure emerging on "the edge of town," maybe a criminal and maybe something more demonic. Cave's vicious lyric combines fear and black humor perfectly, while the Seeds' performance redefines "cinematic," a disturbing organ figure leading the subtle but crisp arrangement and Harvey's addition of a sharp bell ratcheting up the feeling of doom and judgment. —*Ned Raggett*

Murder Ballads / Feb. 1996 / Mute/Reprise ✦✦✦

The Boatman's Call / Mar. 4, 1997 / Mute/Reprise ✦✦✦✦✦
Murder Ballads brought Nick Cave's morbidity to near-parodic levels, which makes the disarmingly frank and introspective songs of *The Boatman's Call* all the more startling. A song cycle equally inspired by Cave's failed romantic affairs and religious doubts, *The Boatman's Call* captures him at his most honest and despairing—while he retains a fascination for Gothic, Biblical imagery, it has little of the grand theatricality and self-conscious poetics that made his albums emotionally distant in the past. This time, there's no posturing, either from Cave or the Bad Seeds. The music is direct, yet it has many textures, from blues to jazz, which offers a revealing and sympathetic bed for Cave's best, most affecting songs. *The Boatman's Call* is one of his finest albums and arguably the masterpiece he has been promising throughout his career. —*Stephen Thomas Erlewine*

● **The Best of Nick Cave & the Bad Seeds** / May 26, 1998 / Mute/Reprise ✦✦✦✦✦
Nick Cave is unquestionably an album artist. Each of his records has a specific mood and theme, standing as an individual work. That said, his albums also have been notoriously uneven. Sometimes, as on *From Her to Eternity* or *The Boatman's Call*, he has delivered near-masterpieces, while on other albums, only a handful of songs have hit the mark accurately, which is why *The Best of Nick Cave* is a welcome addition to his catalog. Granted, the title is a bit odd (it's better than "Greatest Hits", however), but the compilation itself is as good as it could possibly be. All the major songs—"Red Right Hand," "Straight to You," "Nobody's Baby Now," "Into My Arms," "Do You Love Me?," "Henry Lee," "Where the Wild Roses Grow," "From Her to Eternity"—are on this 16-track collection, along with several strong album cuts. Some hardcore fans will find a couple of favorites missing, and the disc should have been sequenced in chronological order, but *The Best of Nick Cave and the Bad Seeds* is nevertheless a terrific single-disc overview of his rewarding, occasionally inaccessible work with the Bad Seeds; it's ideal for both the curious and the casual fan. [Collectors will be interested in the initial British pressings of *The Best of Nick Cave & the Bad Seeds*, which contained a bonus disc, *Live at the Royal Albert Hall*. The bonus live album was recorded in May of 1997 and contains such songs as "Lime Tree Arbour," "Stranger Than Kindness," "The Weeping Song," "Red Right Hand" and "Where the Wild Roses Grow."] —*Stephen Thomas Erlewine*

Chad & Jeremy

f. 1964, London, England, **db.** 1969
Group / Sunshine Pop, British Invasion, Pop
The American success of the folkish duo of Chad Stuart (b. Dec. 10, 1943, Durham, England) and Jeremy Clyde (b. Mar. 22, 1944, Buckinghamshire, England) pointed up the impact of the British Invasion led by the Beatles in February 1964. Chad & Jeremy charted only once in their native country, but their single "Yesterday's Gone," released in May 1964, was the first of 11 U.S. chart hits they achieved through 1966. The biggest of these, and their only Top Ten, was "A Summer Song" (July 1964). Adopting a lighter approach than many of their Mersey Beat contemporaries, Chad & Jeremy focused on pop revivals such as "Willow, Weep for Me" and songs from Broadway shows, such as "I Have Dreamed" from *Carousel*, both Top 40 hits for them. Having moved to Hollywood, they were frequent television guests, both on music shows such as "Hullabaloo" and series like "Batman." Their commercial progress was complicated after 1965, when they signed to Columbia Records, while Capitol Records continued to issue their earlier recordings (previously issued on the World Artists label), such that they were forced to compete with themselves. They recorded the musically ambitious *Of Cabbages and Kings* (September 1967) in the wake of the Beatles' *Sgt. Pepper's Lonely Hearts Club Band*. They broke up after the commercial failure of its equally ambitious follow-up, *The Ark* (September 1968). Jeremy Clyde established himself as a British stage actor. The duo reunited for a new album in 1983; *Of Cabbages & Kings* was re-released in 1999. —*William Ruhlmann*

● **Very Best of Chad & Jeremy** / Mar. 7, 2000 / Varese ✦✦✦✦✦
Although this 18-song best-of duplicates much of what was on the best previous Chad & Je-

remy CD compilation (One Way's *The Best of Chad & Jeremy*), this release is definitely the superior option. Its most crucial edge is the inclusion of four songs from 1965-1966 Columbia singles, as the One Way disc was limited to the material they released on World Artists. In addition, the Varese Sarabande anthology has comprehensive liner notes, songwriting credits, and original release date info, whereas the One Way disc had none of those things at all. This CD still concentrates on the World Artists sides from 1964-1965, including all of the hit singles. Some of the inessential covers of hits and standards from the One Way compilation are axed, but decent original tunes like "My How the Time Goes By" are retained. The four Columbia sides include the three Top 40 hits "Before and After" and "I Don't Wanna Lose You Baby" (both written by Van McCoy), and "Distant Shores" (by future Chicago and Blood, Sweat & Tears producer James Guercio). Oddest of all, though, is the 1966 single "Teenage Failure," a satirical folk-rocker in which writer Jeremy Clyde does a middling parody of protest singers in the sub-Bob Dylan mold. As British Invasion duos performing folk music with a folk-rock tinge go, Peter & Gordon definitely still have the edge; nonetheless, Chad & Jeremy make for pleasant if undemanding listening. Speaking of which, a photo of the somewhat similar-looking Peter & Gordon was apparently mistaken for Chad & Jeremy and snuck past quality control into page three of these liner notes (with no accompanying label to indicate that it was *not* Chad & Jeremy), unless this was an inside joke on someone's part. *—Richie Unterberger*

The Chairmen of the Board

f. 1969, Detroit, MI, **db.** 1976
Group / Pop-Soul, Soul
Best-known for the stuttering hit single "Give Me Just a Little More Time," the Chairmen of the Board were one of the smoothest and most popular soul acts to emerge from Detroit in the early '70s. Although their time at the top of the R&B charts was brief—their first Top 10 arrived in 1970, their last in 1973—they recorded a handful of '70s soul classics, all distinguished by the high, trembling vocals of General Norman Johnson, who also wrote the bulk of the group's material. Formed by Johnson after he signed to the fledgling Invictus label of former Motown producers and songwriters Holland-Dozier-Holland, the Chairmen of the Board found an instant hit with their debut single "Give Me Just a Little More Time," which reached number three on the pop charts. Though they managed only one more major hit on the pop charts ("Pay to the Piper"), Johnson's songs became hits for the likes of Clarence Carter ("Patches"), Freda Payne ("Bring the Boys Home") and Honey Cone, who had no less than three hits—"Want Ads," "Stick Up," "One Monkey Don't Stop No Show"—with his compositions. After a temporary break-up in 1971, the Chairmen of the Board continued touring and releasing albums until 1976, when they disbanded (with each member releasing solo albums). Johnson and group-member Danny Woods reunited as the Chairmen in the early '80s and regularly toured the Southeast to much success. *—Stephen Thomas Erlewine*

• **Greatest Hits** / Jan. 9, 1992 / Fantasy ✦✦✦✦✦
When hit songwriters/producers Holland/Dozier/Holland left Motown Records and founded Hot Wax/Invictus, there was plenty of cause for optimism. And, to be sure, the labels had their share of Motown-ish "uptown soul" hits courtesy of the Honey Cone, 100 Proof (Aged in Soul), Freda Payne and Laura Lee. Another one of the company's strong points was the Chairmen of the Board, a vocal harmony group that, like the Four Tops at Motown, could be gritty and sweet at the same time. Lead singer General Norman Johnson, in fact, had a Levi Stubbs-like quality. Though not quite on a par with HDH's work with the Tops, enjoyably Detroit-sounding hits like "Dangling on a String," "Give Me Just a Little More Time" and "Pay to the Piper" showed that the team's knack for finding memorable, hook-laded soul/pop hadn't gone away. The group gets away from its Four Tops-influenced approach on the arresting "Try My Love on for Size" and the surprisingly bluesy "Chairman of the Board," a moderate hit. Unfortunately, the Chairmen's success—like that of Hot Wax/Invictus—was short-lived. *—Alex Henderson*

The Chambers Brothers

f. 1954, Lee County, MS, **db.** 1972
Group / Psychedelic, Soul
Like their West Coast contemporaries Sly and the Family Stone, the Chambers Brothers shattered racial and musical divides to forge an incendiary fusion of funk, gospel, blues, and psychedelia which reached its apex with the perennial 1968 song "Time Has Come Today." The Chambers siblings—bassist George, guitarist Willie, harpist Lester, and guitarist Joe, all of whom contributed vocals—were born and raised in Lee County, MS; the products of an impoverished sharecropping family, the brothers first polished their vocal harmonies in the choir of their Baptist church, a collaboration which ended after George was drafted into the army in 1952. Following his discharge he relocated to Los Angeles, where the other Chambers brothers soon settled as well; the foursome began performing gospel and folk throughout Southern California in 1954, but remained virtually unknown until appearing in New York City in 1965. The addition of white drummer Brian Keenan not only made the Chambers Brothers an interracial group, but pushed their music closer to rock & roll; a well-received appearance at the Newport Folk Festival further enhanced their growing reputation, and they soon recorded their debut LP, *People Get Ready.*

As the Chambers Brothers toured rock clubs (including the famed *Fillmore* in San Francisco) and R&B venues (most notably *the Apollo Theatre*) alike, their music increasingly embraced elements of both; after recording 1968's *Shout!* for the Vault label, the group signed to Columbia to issue *Time Has Come Today,* scoring a major pop hit with the title track, an 11-minute psychedelic soul epic in its original album incarnation. The follow-up, *A New Time—A New Day,* yielded another Top 40 hit, a cover of the Otis Redding's classic "I Can't Turn You Loose," but subsequent efforts including 1969's *Love, Peace and Happiness* and 1970's *Live at Fillmore East* failed to maintain the commercial momentum. Upon completing 1972's *Oh My God!,* the Chambers Brothers disbanded, only to reunite two years later for *Unbonded. Right Move* appeared in 1975, and although no new studio records were forthcoming, the group regularly performed live in the decades to follow, with the brothers also pursuing individual projects; the Chambers Family Choir, a gospel group including the siblings' own children, remained a priority as well. *—Jason Ankeny*

• **Time Has Come: The Best of the Chambers Brothers** / Oct. 15, 1996 / Columbia/Legacy ✦✦✦✦✦
As the Chambers Brothers' albums could be erratic and/or excessive, this 16-track best-of, covering their 1966-70 prime, is a most welcome distillation of their career highlights. Focusing mostly on their late-'60s singles (some of them non-LP), it also includes a live rendition of "Wade in the Water" and a rejected, even more psychedelicized, 1966 version of their signature tune, "Time Has Come Today." By concentrating on the band's most economic and soulful outings, this disc is the most effective compilation of their gospel-soul-psychedelia. *—Richie Unterberger*

Gene Chandler (Eugene Dixon)

b. Jul. 6, 1937, Chicago, IL
Vocals / Brown Eyed Soul, Chicago Soul, Pop-Soul, Northern Soul, Soul
Chandler is remembered by the rock & roll audience almost solely for the classic novelty and doo wop-tinged soul ballad "Duke of Earl"; the unforgettable opening chant of the title leading the way, the song was a number one hit in 1962. He's esteemed by soul fans as one of the leading exponents of the '60s Chicago soul scene, along with Curtis Mayfield and Jerry Butler. Born Eugene Dixon, he was a member of the doo wop group the Dukays, and "Duke of Earl" was actually a Dukays recording; Dixon was renamed Gene Chandler, and the single bore his credit as a solo singer. Chandler never approached the massive pop success of that chart-topper (although he occasionally entered the Top 20), but he was a big star with the R&B audience with straightforward mid-tempo and ballad soul numbers in the mid-'60s, many of which were written by Curtis Mayfield and produced by Carl Davis. Chandler's success became more fitful after Mayfield stopped penning material for him, although he enjoyed some late '60s hits, and had a monster pop and soul smash in 1970 with "Groovy Situation." His last successes were the far less distinguished disco and dance-influenced R&B hits "Get Down" (1978) and "Does She Have a Friend?" (1980). *—Richie Unterberger*

Just Be True / 1964 / Collectables ✦✦✦
Led by the title track, Gene Chandler's biggest hit of the '60s after "Duke of Earl," *Just Be True* is a set of period soul tracks including "You Threw a Lucky Punch" (an answer record to Mary Wells' "You Beat Me to the Punch") and the lame "Duke of Earl" knockoff "Walk On With the Duke." Chandler's wonderful voice raises all this material to a level unimagined by any but the half-dozen best soul singers out there. The Collectables reissue includes four bonus tracks. *—John Bush*

• **Nothing Can Stop Me: Gene Chandler's Greatest Hits** / Aug. 30, 1994 / Varese Sarabande ✦✦✦✦✦
This 20-track CD is the only collection that has all of his most popular recordings, from "Duke of Earl" through his soul hits for Constellation, Vee Jay, Checker, Mercury, and Chi-Sound, spanning 1962 to 1980 (all but three tracks were released before 1968). Some fans might prefer *The Duke of Earl,* which focuses on his Vee Jay years, but this has a much wider breadth, and includes "Groovy Situation." Curtis Mayfield wrote eight of the songs, although they frankly don't fully measure up to the Chicago soul he was writing for his own group, the Impressions, at the time. *—Richie Unterberger*

Duke of Soul: The Brunswick Years / Oct. 27, 1998 / Diablo ✦✦✦✦
Edsel's 20-track summation of Gene Chandler's short career at Brunswick Records (1966 through 1969) hits all of the obvious high points: "Nothing Can Stop Me," "(Gonna Be) Good Times," "Here Comes the Tears," "There Was a Time," "Those Were the Good Old Days," "Cowboys to Girls," and "You Can't Hurt Me No More." Perhaps wisely, the compilers completely bypassed his inferior final album for Brunswick, *The Two Sides of Gene Chandler.* Though there's still a lot of quality material from the period for which space didn't allow, *Duke of Soul: The Brunswick Years* is an excellent study of one of the most underrated soul singers of the '60s. (Since the two-disc set—*The Brunswick Years 1966-69,* also known as *The Girl Don't Care/There Was a Time/Two Sides of Gene Chandler*—includes all three of Chandler's original Brunswick LPs, and can be found at a relatively inexpensive price, some listeners may find it worthwhile to bypass this greatest-hits volume and spring for the complete set instead.) *—John Bush*

The Brunswick Years: 1966-1969 / Oct. 26, 1999 / West Side ✦✦✦✦✦
Give this high marks for definitiveness—it's the most comprehensive assemblage of Gene Chandler's Brunswick sides ever, and includes six duets with Barbara Acklin all on two shiny, durable compact discs. Chandler's solo sides represent three complete albums fattened with a few singles that didn't make it to an LP. The Acklin duets are the best from their album together. High notes include "Nothing Can Stop Me," "I'm Just a Fool for You," "Here Come the Tears," "Good Times," "The Girl Don't Care," and remakes of James Brown's "There Was a Time," and the Intruders' "Cowboys to Girls." This is the best of the many compilations of Chandler's Brunswick sides on the market. *—Andrew Hamilton*

The Best of Gene Chandler: The Duke of Earl / Oct. 17, 2000 / Collectables ✦✦✦✦
Early Gene Chandler sides, many recorded with the Dukays, including the immortal "Duke of Earl." Feature tracks include "Walk on With the Duke," which was a total bust although it is interesting in retrospect, as it was the answer to "Duke of Earl"; the original studio cut of "Rainbow"; the stark and magnificent "Man's Temptation"; an answer to Mary Wells' "You Beat Me to the Punch" via "You Threw a Lucky Punch"; a remake of the Temptations' "Check Yourself," where Chandler outdoes Paul Williams who led the original; and a whole slew of Dukays tracks when Chandler toiled with them. *—Andrew Hamilton*

Bruce Channel

b. Nov. 28, 1940, Jacksonville, TX
Vocals / Rock & Roll
Bruce Channel's "Hey Baby"—a classic one-shot, number one hit from 1962—is one of the many records proving that, during a period in which rock has sometimes been characterized

as near death, the form was continuing to evolve in unexpected and delightful ways. An irresistible mid-tempo shuffle from the first few bars of homespun harmonica (played by Delbert McClinton), it was a seemingly effortless blend of rock, blues, country, and Cajun beats, featuring Channel's lazy, drawling vocals and an instantly catchy tune. It was perhaps too much of a natural—Channel could never recapture the organic spontaneity of the track, failing to re-enter the Top 40 despite many attempts.

The Texan had written "Hey Baby" around 1959 with his friend Margaret Cobb, and had already been performing the tune for a couple of years before recording it amidst a series of demos for Fort Worth producer Major Bill Smith. First released locally on Smith's label, it was picked up for national distribution by Smash. Channel would continue to write most of his own material (sometimes in collaboration with Cobb) for a series of moderately enjoyable follow-ups that echoed the riffs of "Hey Baby" too closely.

McClinton played his immediately identifiable harmonica on several of these, and made his own contribution to rock history in 1962, when he was touring as a member of Channel's band in Britain. On one of their shows, they were supported by a then-unknown Liverpool group, the Beatles, who had yet to cut their first record. John Lennon was smitten by McClinton's style of playing, and picked up some pointers that he put to use on the Beatles' very first single, "Love Me Do"; in fact, McClinton's influence can be easily detected in Lennon's harmonica playing on many early Beatles tracks from 1962 and 1963.

Channel did get another Top 20 hit in Britain in 1968, "Keep On," which was written by Wayne Carson Thompson (famous for penning the Box Tops' "The Letter"). Nothing else clicked in a big way on either side of the ocean, and by the late '70s he was working in Nashville as a songwriter. *—Richie Unterberger*

Hey Baby! [Teenager] / 1990 / Teenager ✦✦✦✦
Nineteen of his vintage sides, many mining the same Cajun-Tex-Mex-shuffle groove as "Hey Baby," sometimes simply rewriting the song sideways by inserting or mildly modifying its key riffs. It's still highly enjoyable stuff, just too derivative of his one great hit to qualify him as a true original. McClinton plays harmonica on several of the tracks, and also wrote one of them, "My Baby"; the LP also includes his 1968 British hit, "Keep On." The sound and liner notes aren't that great; this interesting early exponent of Southern swamp rock deserves a more carefully packaged retrospective on CD. *—Richie Unterberger*

● **Hey! Baby [Collectables]** / Apr. 24, 1995 / Collectables ✦✦✦✦
Here's Bruce's original Smash album, recorded hot on the heels of the title hit, along with the bonus of the follow-up single, "Number One Man." The album filler all features Delbert McClinton's harmonica, which added the signature sparkle to "Hey! Baby" (the track that made John Lennon want to pick up a harp), with credible renditions of "Baby, It's You," "Chantilly Lace," Jivin' Gene's "Breakin' Up Is Hard to Do," "Ain't Got No Home," Roy Orbison's "Dream Baby," and Elvis' "Love Me," probably all staples of his then-current stage act. For a quickie album, this is a marvelously cohesive-sounding effort, and a nice souvenir of early-'60s Texas rock & roll/pop. *—Cub Koda*

The Chantels

f. 1956, New York, NY [The Bronx], **db.** 1970
Group / Girl Group, Doo Wop, R&B
One of the very first girl groups, the Chantels are best-known for their 1957 hit "Maybe." Between 1957 and 1963, the trio racked up a number of hit singles, but none of them was ever as popular as "Maybe," which came to be regarded as one of the definitive singles of the genre. All five members of the Chantels met as children, and sang in the choir of a Bronx-area school. Arlene Smith, the leader of the quintet, wrote all of the group's early material including their second single, "Maybe." A smash hit, it peaked at number two on the R&B charts and number 15 on the pop charts in early 1958. Two hit singles—"Every Night (I Pray)" and "I Love You So"—followed on End Records, but the label dropped them soon after. In 1961, the Chantels signed with Carlton Records, where they had two minor pop hits: "Look in My Eyes" and "Well, I Told You." Carlton dropped the group the following year and the band moved to Ludix, where they had a minor hit with "Eternally" in the spring of 1963. Though the Chantels officially disbanded in 1970, Arlene Smith later re-formed the group with a new lineup and continued to lead various incarnations into the '90s. *—Stephen Thomas Erlewine*

● **The Best of the Chantels** / May 1990 / Rhino ✦✦✦✦✦
The Chantels were rock & roll's first great female group. This 18-track best-of gathers all of their important recordings for George Goldner's End label, along with some rarities amongst the hits. In addition to the smashes "Maybe," "He's Gone," and "Every Night," the set also includes their work with Richard Barrett and their one-off single backing Willie Wilson, issued as the Tunemasters. An interesting chapter of the distaff side of rock & roll history. *—Cub Koda*

We Are the Chantels/There's Our Song Again / Jun. 9, 1998 / West Side ✦✦✦✦
This combines the first two Chantels albums recorded for End Records between 1957 and 1961. The track listing for the group's first album consists of little more than both sides of the first six singles the girls recorded for the label. As such, it's almost a greatest-hits package, as it includes "Maybe," "Every Night" and "I Love You So," all very big hits for the group. Their second album, *There's Our Song Again,* was issued in 1962 and completes the package, featuring "I," "Believe Me (My Angel)" and tracks from their two extended play (EP) 45s released in front of this album. The transfers are clear and crisp, and the cover art depicts the rare original "plantation girls" cover to their first album. *—Cub Koda*

Harry Chapin

b. Dec. 7, 1942, Greenwich Village, NY, **d.** Jul. 16, 1981, Jericho, NY
Vocals, Guitar / Folk-Rock, Soft Rock, Singer/Songwriter
Harry Chapin's career as a popular singer/songwriter was cut short by an auto accident in 1981, yet he left behind a series of recordings that his fans continue to treasure well over a decade after his death. Accused of over-sentimentalizing his subjects and attaching heavy-handed morals to his socially aware story-songs, Chapin was never a critically acclaimed singer/songwriter. Nevertheless, he earned a devoted audience during the '70s, through his music and his charity work as a social activist.

After pursuing a career as a documentary filmmaker, Chapin switched gears and recruited a backing band through an ad in the *Village Voice.* The group began performing in various clubs around New York and the singer/songwriter was soon signed to Elektra records.

Heads and Tails, Chapin's first album, was released in the summer of 1972 and became a success thanks to the hit single "Taxi," which soon became the songwriter's signature tune. After recording *Verities and Balderdash* in 1974, Chapin began work on his musical *The Night that Made America Famous.* While he was working on the musical, *Verities and Balderdash* became his biggest hit, peaking at number four on the U.S. charts and becoming a gold record.

The Night that Made America Famous opened on February 26, 1975 and earned two Tony nominations. That spring, the singer/songwriter also co-founded World Hunger Year, a charity designed to raise money to fight international famine.

Greatest Stories—Live, a double album released in the spring of 1976, became the singer/songwriter's second gold album. .In 1980, he signed with Boardwalk records, releasing *Sequel* that fall; the title track of the album was a sequel to his first hit single, "Taxi," and became his last Top 40 hit.

On July 16, 1981, Chapin was killed in an auto accident near Jericho, New York. A memorial fund was established in his name following his death, supporting a variety of social causes that were close to his heart. *—Stephen Thomas Erlewine*

● **Anthology of Harry Chapin** / 1985 / Elektra ✦✦✦✦✦
Anthology of Harry Chapin is a fine 11-track collection that contains the cream of the inconsistent singer-songwriter's career, including "Taxi," "Sunday Morning Sunshine," "She Is Always Seventeen," "WOLD," "I Wanna Learn a Love Song," "Better Place to Be" and "Cat's in the Cradle." *—Stephen Thomas Erlewine*

Story of a Life: The Harry Chapin Box / Oct. 19, 1999 / Rhino ✦✦✦✦
Harry Chapin was always a bit of a polarizing figure, attracting many dedicated fans but never earning much critical respect. Rhino's comprehensive three-disc box set *Story of a Life* doesn't really offer an opportunity for re-evaluation, nor does it even try to win over doubters. Instead, it tells a thorough history of Chapin's career, not missing a single hit or major song along the way. There are some rarities scattered throughout the set, mostly live tracks, but also the Chapin Brothers' 1966 single "Someone Keeps Callin' My Name." However, the box shouldn't be seen as a treasure trove of unreleased material; instead, it's a journey through Chapin's career, providing an exhaustively detailed travelogue. Really, it contains too much material for anyone but the die-hard fan. But that's where *Story of a Life* is a success—it's a loving tribute to Chapin, made with the cooperation of his estate and designed for his loving fans. It works quite well on that level, even if it's far too much for the average fan who just likes "Taxi" and "Cat's in the Cradle." *—Stephen Thomas Erlewine*

Tracy Chapman

b. Mar. 20, 1964, Cleveland, OH
Vocals, Guitar / College Rock, Alternative Folk, Contemporary Folk, Adult Alternative Pop/Rock, Singer/Songwriter
Tracy Chapman helped restore singer-songwriters to the spotlight in the '80s. The multi-platinum success of Chapman's eponymous 1988 debut was unexpected, and it had lasting impact. Although Chapman was working from the same confessional singer-songwriter foundation that had been popularized in the '70s, her songs were fresh and powerful, driven by simple melodies and affecting lyrics. At the time of her first album, there were only a handful of artists performing such a style successfully, and her success ushered in a new era of singer-songwriters that lasted well into the '90s. Furthermore, her album helped usher in the era of political correctness—along with 10,000 Maniacs and R.E.M., Chapman's liberal politics proved enormously influential on American college campuses in the late '80s. Of course, such implications meant that Chapman's subsequent recordings were greeted with mixed reactions, but after several years out of the spotlight, she managed to make a very successful comeback in 1996 with her fourth album, *New Beginning,* thanks to the Top Ten single "Give Me One Reason." *—Stephen Thomas Erlewine*

★ **Tracy Chapman** / 1988 / Elektra ✦✦✦✦✦
Arriving with little fanfare in the spring of 1988, Tracy Chapman's eponymous debut album became one of the key records of the Bush era, providing a touchstone for the entire PC movement while reviving the singer/songwriter tradition. And *Tracy Chapman* is firmly within the classic singer/songwriter tradition, sounding for all the world as if it was recorded in the early '70s—that is, if all you paid attention to were the sonics, since Chapman's songs are clearly a result of the Reagan revolution. Even the love songs and laments are underscored by a realized vision of trickle-down modern life—listen to the lyrical details of "Fast Car" for proof. Chapman's impassioned liberal activism and emotional resonance enlivens her music, breathing life into her songs even when the production is a little bit too clean. Still, the juxtaposition of contemporary themes and classic production precisely is what makes the album distinctive—it brings the traditions into the present. At the time, it revitalized traditional folk ideals of social activism and the like, kickstarting the PC revolution in the process, but if those were its only merits, *Tracy Chapman* would sound dated. The record continues to sound fresh because Chapman's writing is so keenly observed and her strong, gutsy singing makes each song sound intimate and immediate. *—Stephen Thomas Erlewine*

Crossroads / Sep. 1989 / Elektra ✦✦✦
Tracy Chapman's self-titled debut album of 1988 was an incredibly tough act to follow, but the folk-rocker delivered an inspired sophomore effort with *Crossroads.* While it falls short of the excellence of her stunning debut, *Crossroads* is a heartfelt, honest offering that's well

worth obtaining. Dedicated to South African freedom fighter Nelson Mandela, the anthemic "Freedom Now" is one of Chapman's best protest songs. Equally compelling is "Subcity," a lament for the poor, disenfranchised underclass that stands on the outside of the American Dream looking in. Much of the time, however, Chapman isn't going for immediacy—introspective and subtle, songs like "Bridges," "Be Careful of My Heart" and "All That You Have is Your Soul" require at least several listenings in order to be fully appreciated. *—Alex Henderson*

Matters of the Heart / Apr. 28, 1992 / Elektra ✦✦

New Beginning / Nov. 14, 1995 / Elektra ✦✦✦
One might assume that the difference between Tracy Chapman's third album, which spent less than three months in the charts and failed to go gold after her first two albums had sold in the millions, and her fourth, which restored her to substantial commercial success, was the album's hit single, "Give Me One Reason." In fact, after a disappointing start, *New Beginning* turned around and started selling a few months after its release and before the single took off. It went gold the week that "Give Me One Reason" hit the charts. Of course, having a hit single helps, too, but since "Give Me One Reason" is a nearly generic blues song that isn't particularly characteristic of Chapman or of the album, it may have brought in an audience that didn't get what it expected. Though she has added a backup band, Chapman continues to take a simple musical approach that focuses attention on her voice and to sing lyrics that alternate between intimate emotional portraits and broad political generalizations that seem more felt than deeply thought out. Three songs here, "Heaven's Here on Earth," "The Rape of the World," and the title cut, are about the state of the whole world, which is viewed in either excessively sunny or gloomy terms. As such, Chapman's relationship songs, though they too can be a little vague, register more powerfully because they are so personal. As the title suggests, Chapman is adopting a more open and hopeful posture in both her feelings and her politics on *New Beginning*, and while the surprise success of "Give Me One Reason" is heartening from a career perspective, that's the real news here. *—William Ruhlmann*

Telling Stories / Feb. 15, 2000 / Elektra ✦✦✦
Forget that Tracy Chapman's fourth album shares a title with the Charlatans [UK]'s fifth album (and sole masterpiece) *Telling Stories*—as far any fan knows, Chapman probably isn't even aware of the Madchester group's existence. Instead, it should be viewed as what it is—the sequel to *New Beginning*, the album that reaffirmed Chapman's status as a fine singer/songwriter to a wide audience. That record became a hit thanks to a bluesy, hooky cut called "Give Me One Reason." *Telling Stories*, as the title suggests, leans toward narratives, but not necessarily in the conventional sense of the term. There are no story songs, in the way that "Fast Car" was a story. Instead, they are emotional, poetic snapshots—sort of like the musical equivalent of a dense, impressionistic short story. Chapman's songs on *Telling Stories* may not be as packed with detail as, say, Raymond Carver's work, but they certainly have a way of creating impressionistic lyrics, making short lines mean a lot. Also, the last album taught her a valuable lesson: her lyrics can be rich, but her compositions won't work collectively as a record if she doesn't craft melodic songs and warm productions. That's exactly what she delivers on *Telling Stories*. Some may think she does this to a fault—it's easy to coast on the sound of the record without digging into the lyrics—but the end result is basically the same: a strong, appealing collection of sturdy, tuneful, and evocative songs. This album may not sparkle with genius, as her debut did, nor is it as direct as its predecessor, but it's a strong, solid record that maintains Chapman's reputation as a reliably intriguing and substantive singer/songwriter. *—Stephen Thomas Erlewine*

The Charlatans

f. 1966, **db.** 1970
Group / Folk-Rock, Psychedelic
No relation to the British alternative rock band, the Charlatans, this San Francisco group has been widely credited as starting the Haight/Ashbury psychedelic scene. In retrospect, their contribution was more of a social one, planting seeds of a rock counterculture with their unconventional, at times outrageous dress and attitudes. While they occasionally delved into guitar distortion and fractured, stoned songwriting, the Charlatans' music was rooted in good-time jug-band blues, not psychedelic freakouts. That's not to say their records didn't have a low-key, easygoing charm, although they didn't match the innovations of the Jefferson Airplane and other peers. Cutting demos for a couple labels in 1966, most of the material they recorded at this time was unissued, and the commercial explosion of San Francisco rock passed them by. The band eventually did release a nationally distributed album in the late '60s, by which time personnel changes had diluted some of the crazy energy of the original lineup, although the LP has its engaging moments. *—Richie Unterberger*

The Charlatans / 1969 / One Way ✦✦✦
The word is that this album failed to capture the group's essence, but it has its share of good stuff. Their good-timey sound is balanced by an engaging sincerity and folky, melodic compositions reminiscent of very early Jefferson Airplane, although there are a couple ho-hum jug-band tunes. But the production and performances are too complacent and tame, lacking the spaced-out recklessness of the San Francisco scene that groups like the Airplane captured so well on record. *—Richie Unterberger*

Alabama Bound / 1970 / Eva ✦✦✦✦✦
Mid-1966 demos, recorded by Lovin' Spoonful producer Erik Jacobsen. Featuring blues, good-time music, and tentative psychedelia, it doesn't sound as crazy as one might have thought, but remains the only glimpse into the band at their most original during their early days. Also includes a live, ten-minute 1969 recording of the title track. *—Richie Unterberger*

● **The Amazing Charlatans** / Sep. 17, 1996 / Big Beat ✦✦✦✦✦
After almost 30 years, there's finally a definitive document of one of the first San Francisco psychedelic groups—or, at least, as definitive a document as surviving tapes allow. This compilation assembles 23 tracks from their demos for the Kama Sutra and Autumn labels, as well as a couple of later sessions recorded at San Francisco area studios. Much of this material has been bootlegged previously, on both vinyl and tape, but here it appears in its best fidelity to date by far. Those expecting psychedelic fireworks will be surprised. There's some acid-soaked folk-rock here (most notably "We're Not on the Same Trip" and "I Saw Her," the two best cuts), but on the whole it's much more of a travelog of roots music, with White blues, jugband, folk, country, and music hall influences much more to the fore. Sure the Charlatans never really got the opportunity to flex their muscles in the studio, but it's also true that they didn't possess either the songwriting or instrumental chops to rival the Jefferson Airplane or Moby Grape. If you gear your expectations to the appropriate level, there's plenty of good-time mid-to-late-'60s Bay Area rock to savor here. Big Beat's meticulous packaging and programming also ensures that an important chapter in psychedelic/San Francisco music has been properly presented for the first time. *—Richie Unterberger*

Charlatans UK

f. 1989, Manchester, England
Group / Madchester, British Trad Rock, Britpop, Alternative Pop/Rock
For many years, the Charlatans [U.K.] were perceived as the also-rans of Madchester, the group that didn't capture the zeitgeist like the Stone Roses or the band that failed to match the mad genre-bending of the Happy Mondays. Of course, they were more traditional than either of their peers. Working from a Stonesy foundation, the Charlatans added dance-oriented rhythms and layers of swirling organs straight out of '60s psychedelia. At first, the Charlatans had great promise, and their initial singles—including "The Only One I Know"—were hits, but as Madchester and "baggy" faded away, the group began to look like relics. It was commonly assumed that their third album, 1994's *Up to Our Hips*, was the end of the line. However, the Charlatans made a remarkable comeback in 1995 with their eponymous fourth album, which found them embracing not only the flourishing Brit-pop movement, but also underground dance and techno, as well as their mainstay of classic rock. *The Charlatans* debuted at number one, and the group was hailed as survivors. Unfortunately, few knew how literal that term was—as the band was recording its follow-up album in 1996, organist Rob Collins, who had defined the band's sound, died in a car crash. The Charlatans decided to continue as a quartet, and their subsequent album, *Tellin' Stories*, debuted at number one upon its 1997 release, suggesting that they had become one of the great British journeyman bands of the '90s. *—Stephen Thomas Erlewine*

Some Friendly / 1990 / Beggars Banquet ✦✦✦✦
Emerging out of semi-nowhere—well, Norwich—the Charlatans UK were saddled with a name that lent itself to jibes about their quality, perceived bandwagon jumping and the burden of being a one-hit wonder with "The Only One I Know." Then *Some Friendly*, the group's debut, planted itself at the top of the UK charts; while the rest of the '90s were up-and-down for the band, this album set the band on its way. Drawing on Blunt's background in mod and psych outfits, Collins' outrageously funky keyboards and Burgess' unexpected star quality—even if his voice wasn't the strongest—*Some Friendly* is just that, a friendly and fun vibe. Some of the lyrics betray Burgess' sharp-tongued punk background—"You're Not Very Well," the opener, expresses anything but sunny sentiments—but otherwise *Some Friendly* delivers everything from '60s beat groove to Madchester bagginess with verve. True, the group was still following in the Roses/Mondays slipstream—"Fool's Gold" was the blueprint for much of the album—but the individual delights of the slow trance "Opportunity," "Polar Bear"'s upfront rhythms and "Flower"'s slightly ominous funk all show the band's abilities well. "The Only One I Know" remains the best-known cut, Blunt's crisp bass and Collins' Deep Purple-inspired keyboards providing its charge. But *Some Friendly*'s hidden masterpiece comes at the very end— "Sproston Green," a monster jam based on Collins' supreme keyboard work, with Burgess' soaring lyric matching the massive surge of the music. It remains the concluding number of the band's sets to this day for good reason. *—Ned Raggett*

Between 10th and 11th / Apr. 14, 1992 / Beggars Banquet ✦✦✦✦
A few songs aside, the Charlatans generally regard this release as their least successful album, considering it recorded at a personal and professional crossroads (Baker's departure, Rob Collins' conviction, and so forth). Criticism within and without settled on Flood's production style as well, his crisp, technically sharp abilities seem to go against the band's natural flow. In hindsight, though, *Between* is much stronger than its reputation, with many fans proclaiming it their favorite. It's partly due to Burgess' more up-front vocals—his singing is still some of the calmest one will ever hear at the front of such a band, but his performance maintains *Some Friendly*'s loose flow of while sounding more compelling. Similarly, Blunt's bass sounds stronger and Rob Collins' keyboards stand out more, either shading or leading the songs perfectly. "Weirdo," the album's lead single and strongest point, has a brilliant lead organ break from Collins and series of great funk stabs that became his strongest performance ever. Equally fine is the electric piano start to "Tremolo Song," leading to a deep Blunt bass and sassy flow of a song. Brookes and Mark Collins also fill out their parts equally well, with Flood's production strengthening and creating excellent arrangements for everyone as a whole. His numerous touches are really something, from the sudden shift to buried/flanged production on "Ignition" to "Subtitle"'s atmospheric mixing and burbling bass. Other highlights include the string-laden charge of "Can't Even Be Bothered" and the concluding "No One (Not Even the Rain)." *—Ned Raggett*

Up to Our Hips / Mar. 22, 1994 / Beggars Banquet ✦✦✦✦
Having experienced initial fame and its retreat, the Charlatans (perhaps somewhat self-consciously) set out to create a series of classic-rock-inspired albums, fusing everything from Dylan and the Stones to whatever else caught their fancy. *Up to Our Hips*, the first result, was produced by Steve Hillage, who made a career ranging from wacked-out hippie ramblings in Gong to the clean, inspired synth/Krautrock surge suffusing his production for Simple Minds. One thing he contributed to the Charlatans was more active percussion. While Flood didn't hide the drums on *Between*, on "Come In Number 21" Brookes' work feels strong and punchy for the first time. While production was a touch more straightforward than on *Between*, Hillage otherwise let the Charlatans be the Charlatans; where changes are apparent, it's more in the name of atmosphere than attention-getting, especially on the echoed, rumbling funk instrumental "Feel Flows" (excellent Blunt bass and Rob Collins

clavinet on this one). The band stretches with the lovely, acoustic stomp "Autograph"; Mark Collins' guitar work was, increasingly, a larger part of the band's sound than Rob Collins' Hammond, but both worked well together. The laid-back lead single "Can't Get Out of Bed"'s lazy *Exile on Main Street* vibe and the equally groovy "Patrol" and "Jesus Hairdo" showcased both of their work to good effect, especially on the breaks between chorus and verse. Rob Collins certainly still has his moments—witness the opening build to the title track, another great effort with Blunt. Burgess sounds his strongest yet; while his singing still lurks in the mix more than anything else, he never disappears entirely. *—Ned Raggett*

The Charlatans [UK] / Sep. 12, 1995 / Beggars Banquet ♦♦♦♦
The Charlatans demonstrated signs of a revival on *Up to Our Hips*, yet that record in no way suggested the full-fledged return to form of *The Charlatans [UK]*, the group's most ambitious, focused and successful album. The group hasn't changed its sonic approach, yet their music has deepened, incorporating heavy dance elements without losing their core sound. Occasionally, the album relies too heavily on trippy dance instrumentals, but those are funkier and wilder than ever before, and they fit neatly next to the group's Stonesy pop, which are consistently catchy this time around. *The Charlatans [UK]* illustrates how a working rock & roll band can balance between traditional rock and modern, post-acid house music, and the results are frequently glorious. *—Stephen Thomas Erlewine*

Tellin' Stories / Apr. 21, 1997 / MCA ♦♦♦♦♦
The Charlatans made a surprising comeback in 1995, turning in an eponymous album that earned them their best reviews and sales ever. *Tellin' Stories*, the follow-up to *The Charlatans*, should have been triumphant, but tragedy struck midway through its recording, when keyboardist Rob Collins was killed in a car accident. Collins was an integral part of the band's lineup, creating a distinctive, swirling, neo-psychedelic sound, and it seemed unlikely that the band could carry on without him, much less record a record as earthy and warm as *Tellin' Stories*. Primal Scream's Martin Duffy volunteered to help the band complete the album, which was bascially written before Collins' death, and that might explain why there are no overt refrrences to his absence anywhere on the album. Instead, *Tellin' Stories* is another collection of classicist rock & roll spiked with dance beats, much like any other Charlatans album. Where its predecessor was more informed by mechanicized beats, the rhythms are more organic, which perfectly suits the rolling "North Country Boy," the sweeping "One to Another" and the heart-tugging "How Can You Leave Us?" And, like any other Charlatans album, it doesn't quite hold together, falling apart with instrumentals and ill-conceived songs toward the end. On the whole, however, *Tellin' Stories* is more consistent than their earlier records, and the best songs showcase the band at their strongest, which is quite an achievement considering the traumas the Charlatans underwent during its recording. More than anything, that's a fitting salute to Rob Collins. *—Stephen Thomas Erlewine*

● **Melting Pot** / Jun. 9, 1998 / Beggars Banquet ♦♦♦♦♦

Us and Us Only / Oct. 19, 1999 / Uptown/Universal ♦♦♦♦
Us and Us Only picks up where *Tellin' Stories* left off and twists that album's virtues around. Where that record was essentially a stripped-down, straight-ahead collection, *Us and Us Only* dresses up the band's continually impressive songcraft in a moody atmosphere, borrowed in equal parts from *Blonde on Blonde*, *Beggars Banquet*, and the Chemical Brothers. The album unfolds in a haze of keyboards and subdued beats, and this murky veil never really lifts throughout the record, even as harmonics and acoustic guitars break through the mist every once and a while. Consequently, the album can initially seem a little amorphous, albeit intriguingly amorphous, filled with deep grooves and tantalizing sonic textures. Repeated plays reveal that *Us and Us Only* is merely a step below their previous high point of *Tellin' Stories*. If nothing is as immediately grabbing as "North Country Boy" or "One to Another," that's not a problem, since nearly every song works its charms with subtle grace and considerable muscle. "Forever" soon reveals itself as a minor masterpiece of swirling menace and swagger, while the Dylan inflections of "A House Is Not a Home" and "My Beautiful Friend" seem natural instead of grandstanding. Soon, it becomes apparent that, unlike most of their trad rock contemporaries, the Charlatans figured out how to make their music sound both timeless and modern by quietly adding influences and changing their attack each time around, while remaining true to their core sound, much like the Stones did in their prime. The Charlatans may not be as innovative or as song-oriented as the Stones, but after a decade of recording, they're turning out to be nearly as consistent as the Stones were at the same point in their career, which is no small accomplishment. *—Stephen Thomas Erlewine*

Ray Charles (Ray Charles Robinson)

b. Sep. 23, 1930, Albany, GA
Vocals, Piano / Pop-Soul, Country-Soul, Jazz Blues, Pop, Urban Blues, Piano Blues, R&B, Soul

Ray Charles was the musician most responsible for developing soul music. Singers like Sam Cooke and Jackie Wilson also did a great deal to pioneer the form, but Charles did even more to devise a new form of Black pop by merging '50s R&B with gospel-powered vocals, adding plenty of flavor from contemporary jazz, blues, and (in the '60s) country. Then there is his singing—his style is among the most emotional and easily identifiable of any 20th-century performer, up there with the likes of Elvis and Billie Holiday. He's also a superb keyboard player, arranger, and bandleader. The brilliance of his 1950s and 1960s work, however, can't obscure the fact that he's made few classic tracks since the mid-'60s, though he's recorded often and tours to this day. Blind since the age of six (from glaucoma), by the late '40s he was recording in a smooth pop/R&B style derivative of Nat "King" Cole and Charles Brown. He got his first Top Ten R&B hit with "Baby, Let Me Hold Your Hand" in 1951. It was at Atlantic Records that Ray truly found his voice with "I Got a Woman," a number two R&B hit in 1955. This is the song most frequently singled out as his pivotal performance, on which Charles first truly let go with his unmistakable gospelish moan, backed by a tight, bouncy horn-driven arrangement. Throughout the '50s, Charles ran off a series of R&B hits that, although they weren't called "soul" at the time, did a lot to pave the way for soul by presenting a form of R&B that was sophisticated without sacrificing any emotional grit. "This Little Girl of Mine," "Drown in My Own Tears," "Hallelujah I Love Her So," "Lonely Avenue," and "The Right Time" were all big hits. But Charles didn't really capture the pop audience until "What'd I Say," which caught the fervor of the church with its pleading vocals, as well as the spirit of rock & roll with its classic electric piano line. It was his first Top Ten pop hit, and one of his final Atlantic singles, as he left the label at the end of the '50s for ABC. One of the chief attractions of the ABC deal for Charles was a much greater degree of artistic control of his recordings. He put it to good use on early-'60s hits like "Unchain My Heart" and "Hit the Road Jack," which solidified his pop stardom with only a modicum of polish attached to the R&B he had perfected at Atlantic. In 1962, he surprised the pop world by turning his attention to country & western music, topping the charts with the "I Can't Stop Loving You" single, and making a hugely popular album (in an era in which R&B/soul LPs rarely scored high on the charts) with *Modern Sounds in Country and Western Music*. *—Richie Unterberger*

Genius & Soul: The 50th Anniversary Collection / Feb. 1949-1993 / Rhino ♦♦♦♦♦
As the first comprehensive, multi-label box set assembled on Ray Charles, the five-disc, 101-song *Genius & Soul: The 50th Anniversary Collection* is an extensive overview of one of the greatest musicians of the 20th century. Charles produced a body of work so rich and diverse that even five CDs only scratches the surface of his accomplishments. None of his instrumentals are on *Genius & Soul*, nor are his jazz and traditional pop efforts spotlighted. Instead, the box traces the evolution of his career, as he moves from an R&B pioneer to a mainstream pop crooner to a country-pop vocalist to a contemporary soul singer. Charles was a gripping, captivating vocalist, capable of making even bland music sound vital, but the fact is, his '70s and '80s recordings pale in comparison to his seminal '50s and '60s sides. Which means that the set becomes less compelling as it reaches the fifth disc, but the first three and a half discs are filled with timeless music that remains exciting, vital and altogether wondrous. *—Stephen Thomas Erlewine*

The Early Years / 1949-1952 / Tomato ♦♦♦
In the late '40s and early '50s, Charles recorded several dozen sides for the Swingtime/Downbeat label, 30 of which are presented here. As has been noted many times by critics, these usually found Charles in a Nat "King" Cole swing-blues groove that was much smoother than the gritty R&B/soul he'd record for Atlantic in the later '50s; the influence of urban blues balladeer Charles Brown is also evident. Some critical essays, in fact, may lead you to believe that this work is trivial, but while it's undeniably derivative, it's enjoyable on its own terms, and not without strong hints of the searing soulfulness that was to come. Some of the selections are delivered with such refined polish that it doesn't even sound like Charles. But on the more anguished and fast-tempoed cuts in particular, you can hear him starting to arrive at the phrasing and emotion that would flower in the mid-'50s. Unfortunately, like most Tomato reissues, the sound is substandard; even assuming that the master tapes can't be located, a better job was probably possible, and a couple of cuts even duplicate skips from the vinyl. Exact dates and songwriting credits are also missing, although Pete Welding's essay does at least discuss the material on the discs in some detail, unlike many of Tomato's liner notes. *—Richie Unterberger*

Blues + Jazz / May 26, 1950-Jun. 26, 1959 / Rhino/Atlantic ♦♦♦♦♦
Another easy access point for Charles' seminal Atlantic catalog. This two-disc set is evenly split between his bluesiest sides on the first disc and a selection of his greatest jazz sides on disc two (gorgeously showcasing the sax work of David "Fathead" Newman on several pieces). Charles was a masterful blues purveyor; his "I Believe to My Soul" is simultaneously invested with heartbreak and humor, while the earlier "Sinner's Prayer," "The Sun's Gonna Shine Again," and the gospel-based "A Fool for You" emanate both hope and deep pain. *—Bill Dahl*

★ **The Best of Atlantic** / 1951-1961 / Rhino ♦♦♦♦♦
The 20-track compilation (only 12 tracks on cassette) *The Best of Atlantic* compiles all of Ray Charles' Top Ten R&B hits for Atlantic Records, from "I've Got A Woman" and "This Little Girl of Mine" to "Drown in My Own Tears," "Halleujah I Love Her So," "Lonely Avenue," "(Night Time Is) The Right Time," and "What'd I Say (Part 1)." In addition to the big hits, there are minor hits that nevertheless showcase Charles at his peak, like "Swanee River Rock" and "Just for a Thrill." For fans that only want the hits and don't want to invest in the splendid three-disc set *The Birth of Soul*, *The Best of Atlantic* is an essential purchase. *—Stephen Thomas Erlewine*

☆ **The Birth of Soul** / 1951-1959 / Atlantic ♦♦♦♦♦
The title isn't just hype—this absolutely essential three-disc box is where soul music first took shape and soared, courtesy of Ray Charles' church-soaked pipes and bedrock piano work. Brother Ray's formula for inventing the genre was disarmingly simple: he brought gospel intensity to the R&B world with his seminal "I Got a Woman," "Hallelujah I Love Her So," "Leave My Woman Alone," "You Be My Baby," and the primal 1959 call-and-response classic "What'd I Say." There's plenty of brilliant blues content within these 53 historic sides: Charles' mournful "Losing Hand," "Feelin' Sad," "Hard Times," and "Blackjack" ooze after-hours desperation. No blues collection should be without this boxed set, which comes with well-researched notes by Robert Palmer, a nicely illustrated accompanying booklet, and discographical info aplenty. *—Bill Dahl*

The Genius After Hours / 1956 / Rhino ♦♦♦♦♦

The Great Ray Charles / 1956 / Atlantic ♦♦♦
This set is rather unusual, for it is strictly instrumental, allowing Ray Charles a rare opportunity to be a jazz-oriented pianist. Two selections are with a trio (bassist Oscar Pettiford joins Charles on "Black Coffee"), while the other six are with a septet taken from his big band of the period. Key among the sidemen are David Newman (soloing on both tenor and alto) and trumpeter Joseph Bridgewater; highlights include Quincy Jones' "The Ray," "My Melancholy Baby," "Doodlin'," and "Undecided." Ray Charles should have recorded in this setting more often in his later years. *—Scott Yanow*

The Genius Hits the Road / 1956-1972 / Rhino ♦♦♦
In keeping with his jazz/pop crossover ambitions, Charles decided to record a concept album

of sorts with a dozen songs devoted to various parts of the U.S.—"Alabamy Bound," "Georgia On My Mind," "Moonlight in Vermont," "California, Here I Come," "Blue Hawaii," etc. The crossover vibe is further heightened by the brassy big-band arrangements, and material from the likes of Al Jolson and Hoagy Carmichael. It sounds a bit corny now, with an in-your-face gung-ho cheer. But it did what Charles wanted it to do, reaching the Top Ten of the album charts, and spinning off a big hit with "Georgia On My Mind." The 1997 CD reissue on Rhino adds seven bonus tracks from 1956-1972 that also had a travel/geographic theme, and the best of these are actually the highlights of the record, most notably "Hit the Road Jack," "Lonely Avenue," and his cover of Hank Snow's "I'm Movin' On." *—Richie Unterberger*

Ray Charles at Newport / Jul. 5, 1958 / Atlantic ♦♦♦♦♦
For his appearance at the *Newport Jazz Festival* on July 5, 1958, Charles pulled out all the stops, performing raucous versions of "The Right Time," "I Got a Woman," and "Talkin' 'bout You." (This album was reissued in 1973 as a two-record set, packaged with *Ray Charles in Person* under the title *Ray Charles Live* [Atlantic SD 2-503].) *—William Ruhlmann*

The Genius of Ray Charles / 1959 / Atlantic ♦♦♦♦♦

Genius + Soul Jazz/My Kind of Jazz / Dec. 26, 1960-1970 / Rhino ♦♦♦♦♦

Ray Charles & Betty Carter / Jun. 13, 1961-1966 / ABC/Paramount ♦♦♦♦
This pairing of two totally idiosyncratic vocalists acquired legendary status over the decades in which it had been out of print. But the proof is in the listening, and frankly it doesn't represent either artist's best work. There is certainly a powerful, often sexy rapport between the two—Charles in his sweet balladeering mode, Carter with her uniquely keening, drifting high register—and they definitely create sparks in the justly famous rendition of "Baby, It's Cold Outside." The main problem is in Marty Paich's string/choir arrangements, which too often cross over the line into treacle, whereas his charts for big band are far more listenable. Moreover, Charles' sweetness can get a bit cloying too, although some of the old grit emerges on "Takes Two To Tango." On the CD reissue—remixed by Charles himself—Dunhill adds the great, rare B-side to the "Unchain My Heart" single, "But On The Other Hand Baby," and two excellent if unrelated album cuts, "I Never See Maggie Alone" (1964) and "I Like To Hear It Sometime" (1966). —Richard S. Ginell

Greatest Hits, Vol. 1 / 1961-1965 / DCC ♦♦♦♦♦
The first of two DCC compilations to collect the best of Brother Ray's 1960s stint at ABC-Paramount Records, when he flew off in a dozen different stylistic directions. Included on this 20-track disc are Charles' immortal rendering of "Georgia on My Mind," and the sinuously bluesy "Unchain My Heart," the Latin-beat instrumental "One Mint Julep," personalized remakes of the country standards "Born to Lose," "Your Cheating Heart," and "Crying Time," and his exultant rendition of the soulful "Let's Go Get Stoned." *—Bill Dahl*

Greatest Hits, Vol. 2 / 1961-1965 / DCC ♦♦♦♦♦
More seminal performances from the '60s ABC catalog of the Genius (DCC split the classics evenly between the two discs, making both of them indispensable). His beloved "Hit the Road Jack" (one of several Percy Mayfield copyrights dotting Charles' repertoire), the daring country crossover "I Can't Stop Loving You," an electric-piano powered "Sticks and Stones," a wise "Them That Got," and a wonderfully mellow "At the Club" rank with the 20-song disc's standouts (though versions of the Beatles' "Yesterday" and the corny "Look What They Done to My Song, Ma" end the set on a bummer note). *—Bill Dahl*

☆ **Modern Sounds in Country & Western Music** / 1961-1962 / Rhino ♦♦♦♦♦
Modern Sounds in Country & Western Music is historically important, and considered by most critics to be a classic, but some have mixed feelings about it. Charles' interpretations of songs previously recorded by Hank Williams, Eddy Arnold, Floyd Tillman, and Don Gibson are superb, but so often the arrangements by Marty Paich, Gerald Wilson, and Gil Fuller threaten to drown him in a sea of lachrymose bric-a-brac. "I Can't Stop Loving You" and "You Don't Know Me" were Top Ten pop and R&B. *—Rob Bowman*

☆ **Modern Sounds in Country & Western, Vol. 2** / 1962 / Rhino ♦♦♦♦♦

Ingredients in a Recipe for Soul/Have a Smile with Me / 1963-1964 / Rhino ♦♦♦
A two-for-one pairing of albums from 1963 (*Ingredients in a Recipe for Soul*) and 1964 (*Have a Smile with Me*), with the addition of historical liner notes. Neither rate among his better albums—both are inconsistent mixtures of hard-edged jazz/pop/soul and mainstream pop standards. Each, though, has some fine cuts, notably the Top Ten hit "Busted" (on *Recipe*) and a jazzy cover of Hank Williams' "Move It On Over" (on *Have a Smile With Me*). The CD also adds two bonus tracks: both parts of the orchestral pop "Without a Song" single from 1965. *—Richie Unterberger*

Sweet & Sour Tears / Mar. 1964 / Rhino ♦♦♦

Anthology / 1989 / Rhino ♦♦♦♦♦
Perhaps the best single CD collection of Ray Charles' '60s and '70s ABC-Paramount material. They've also been issued on two separate anthologies, but for someone who only wants the essential items, this disc has them all over its 20 tracks. *—Ron Wynn*

Soul Brothers/Soul Meeting / 1989 / Atlantic ♦♦♦♦♦
This brings together all of the extant takes recorded for two albums that Milt Jackson made with Ray Charles for Atlantic in 1957 and 1958. With Oscar Pettiford, Connie Kay, and Kenny Burrell in the various lineups, this is bluesy jazz in a laid-back manner; it surprised many hardcore R&B fans when these albums were originally issued. Jackson moves from vibes to piano, and even guitar (on "Bag's Guitar Blues"), while Ray jumps between piano and alto sax on these sessions. A rare glimpse of Charles' jazz soul coming up for air. *—Cub Koda*

Complete Country & Western Recordings 1959-1986 / Oct. 27, 1998 / Rhino ♦♦♦♦
Ray Charles' explorations into country music were no mere dalliance. They have their genesis in "I'm Movin' On," the last record he made for Atlantic before moving on to ABC Paramount in 1960. But it was with the enormously successful *Modern Sounds in Country & Western* series of albums in 1962 (and the career making single, "I Can't Stop Lovin' You") that made their mark, crossing over genre boundaries that were unthinkable at the time. An African-American doing hillbilly music was not a first, nor was uptown arrangements of hillbilly songs but here was the Genius of Soul validating the music of the white working class, plain and simple. He was putting his own spin to it (hence the *Modern Sounds*), not merely a black voice singing Gene Autry songs, investing them with pain, emotion and sorrow. It was an unprecedented achievement, both commercially and artistically, and now—decades later—it's viewed as just another genre-bender in the grand Ray Charles tradition. But this 92-track, four CD box set is the first to gather them all in one place and view it as a consistent piece of work spread over a career as a stylist that's second to none. The first disc combines both volumes of the *Modern Sounds* albums; the rest of the anthology moving through singles, various returns to the concept over the years and stray tracks from his later stretch at Columbia to spice it all it all up. This multi-disc set contains some very special music, nicely packaged, a moment in American music well worth investigating. *—Cub Koda*

The Very Best of Ray Charles / Mar. 14, 2000 / Rhino ♦♦♦♦
This 16-track budget package hits all the high notes of Brother Ray's rise to greatness. Starting in the '50s with classic Atlantic sides like "I've Got a Woman," "Hallelujah I Love Her So," "Night Time (Is the Right Time)," and "What'd I Say," the set also includes his landmark ABC country sides of the '60s ("I Can't Stop Loving You," "Georgia on My Mind"), finishing up with a duet with Willie Nelson on "Seven Spanish Angels." A perfect introduction to an American musical treasure. *—Cub Koda*

Genius After Hours/Great Ray Charles / Rhino/Atlantic ♦♦♦

Cheap Trick

f. 1975, Rockford, IL
Group / Album Rock, Arena Rock, Pop/Rock, Power Pop, New Wave, Hard Rock
Combining a love for British guitar-pop songcraft with crunching power chords and a flair for the absurd, Cheap Trick provided the necessary links between '60s pop, heavy metal, and punk. The band's early albums were filled with highly melodic, well-written songs that drew equally from the crafted pop of the Beatles, the sonic assault of the Who, and the tongue-in-cheek musical eclecticism and humor of the Move. Their sound provided a blueprint for both power-pop and arena rock, plus influenced alternative and heavy-metal bands of the '80s and '90s.

Although beloved by fans and acclaimed in some quarters, Cheap Trick's first three albums, didn't reach anything larger than a cult audience in the late '70s. These same recordings made them virtual superstars in Japan, something the band realized when they toured the country in 1978. They recorded their sold-out shows at Budokan Arena, and the album, *At Budokan*, appeared after 1978's *Heaven Tonight* made headway on the pop charts. *At Budokan* turned into a smash, reaching number four, staying on the charts for over year, giving them their first Top 10 hit with "I Want You to Want Me" and eventually selling over three million copies. *Dream Police*, their fourth album, followed it into the Top 10. Following the recording of 1980's George Martin-produced *All Shook Up*, Petersson left the group. *All Shook Up* performed respectably, as did 1982's *One on One*, yet they soon hit a commercial slump that lasted over five years. Petersson rejoined the band in 1988, as the band began work on *Lap of Luxury*. Thanks to the number one power ballad "The Flame," the album was a genuine comeback, reaching the Top 20. Its followup, *Busted*, stalled on the charts. During the '90s, they never had a hit, yet they were held in high regard by a new generation of rockers who embraced the group's early records. Toward the end of the decade, the group released two acclaimed independent records—1997's *Cheap Trick* plus the 1999 live LP, *Music For Hangovers*. *—Stephen Thomas Erlewine*

☆ **Cheap Trick** / 1977 / Epic/Legacy ♦♦♦♦♦
Cheap Trick's eponymous debut is an explosion fusion of Beatlesesque melodic hooks, Who-styled power, and a twisted sense of humor partially borrowed from the Move. But that only begins to scratch the surface of what makes *Cheap Trick* a dynamic record. Guitarist Rick Nielsen has a powerful sense of dynamics and arrangments, which gives the music an extra kick, but he also can write exceptionally melodic and subversive songs. Nothing on *Cheap Trick* is quite what it seems. While the songs have hooks and attitude that arena-rock was sorely lacking in the late '70s, they are also informed by a bizarre sensibility, whether it's the driving "He's a Whore," the dreamy "Mandocello," or the thumping Gary Glitter perversion "ELO Kiddies." "The Ballad of TV Violence" is about mass murder, while "Daddy Should Have Stayed in High School" concerns pedophiles. All of it is told with a sense of humor, but it doesn't come off as cheap or smirking because of the group's hard-rocking drive and Robin Zander's pop-idol vocals. Even "Oh, Candy," apparently a love song on first listen, is an affecting tribute to a friend who committed suicide. In short, Cheap Trick revels in taboo subjects with abandon, devoting themselves to the power of the hook, as well as sheer volume and gut-wrenching rock & roll—though the record was more musically accomplished than punk rock, it shared the same aesthetic. The combination of off-kilter humor, bizarre subjects and blissful power-pop made *Cheap Trick* one of the defining albums of its era, as well as one of the most influential. *—Stephen Thomas Erlewine*

In Color / 1977 / Epic/Legacy ♦♦♦♦♦
Though Cheap Trick's second album *In Color (And In Black and White)* draws from the same stockpile of Midwestern barroom favorites as their debut album, it was produced by Tom Werman, who had the band strip away their raw attack and replace it with a shiny, radio-ready sound. Consequently, *In Color* doesn't have the visceral attack of its predecessor, but it still has the same sensibility and a similar set or spectacular songs. From the druggy psychedelia of "Downed" and the bubblegum sing-a-long "I Want You to Want Me" to the "California Girls" homage of "Southern Girls," the album has the same encyclopedic knowledge of rock & roll, as well as the good sense to subvert it with a perverse sense of humor. Portions of the album haven't dated well, simply due to the glossy production, but the songs and music on *In Color* are as splendid as the debut. *—Stephen Thomas Erlewine*

☆ **Heaven Tonight** / 1978 / Epic/Legacy ♦♦♦♦♦
Heaven Tonight, like *In Color*, was produced by Tom Werman, but the difference between the two records is substantial. Where *In Color* often sounded emasculated, *Heaven Tonight* regains the powerful, arena-ready punch of *Cheap Trick*, but crosses it with a clever radio-

friendly production that relies both on synthesizers and studio effects. Even with the fairly slick production, Cheap Trick sounds ferocious throughout the album, slamming heavy metal, power-pop and hard rock together in a humongous sound. "Surrender," the definitive Cheap Trick song, opens the album with a tale about a kid whose parents are hipper than himself, and the remainder of the record is rollercoaster ride, peaking with the sneering "Auf Wiedersehen," the dreamily psychedelic title track, the roaring rocker "On Top of the World," the high-stepping, tongue-in-cheek "How Are You" and the pulverizing cover of the Move's "California Man." *Heaven Tonight* is the culmination of the group's dizzying early career, summing up the strengths of their first two albums, their live show and their talent for inverting pop conventions. They were never quite as consistently thrilling on record ever again. *—Stephen Thomas Erlewine*

★ **Live at Budokan** / Feb. 1979 / Epic ♦♦♦♦♦
While their records were entertaining and full of skillful pop, it wasn't until *Live at Budokan* that Cheap Trick's vision truly gelled. Many of these songs, like "I Want You to Want Me" and "Big Eyes," were pleasant in their original form, but seemed more like sketches compared to the roaring versions on this album. With their ear-shatteringly loud guitars and sweet melodies, Cheap Trick unwittingly paved the way for much of the hard-rock of the next decade, as well as a surprising amount of alternative rock of the 1990s, and it was *Live at Budokan* that captured the band in all of its power. *—Stephen Thomas Erlewine*

Dream Police / Oct. 1979 / Epic ♦♦♦♦♦
At the Budokan unexpectedly made Cheap Trick stars, largely because "I Want You to Want Me" had a tougher sound than its original studio inclination. Perversely—and most things Cheap Trick have done are somehow perverse—the band decided *not* to continue with the direct, stripped-down sound of *Live at Budokan,* which would have been a return to their debut. Instead, the group went for their biggest, most elaborate production to date, taking the synthesized flourishes of *Heaven Tonight* to extremes. While it kept the group in the charts, it lessened the impact of the music. Underneath the gloss, there are a number of songs that rank among Cheap Trick's finest, particularly the paranoid title track, the epic rocker "Gonna Raise Hell," the tough "I Know What I Want," the simpy pop of "Voices" and the closer "Need Your Love." Still, *Dream Police* feels like a let-down in comparison to its predecessors, even though it would later feel like one of the group's last high-water marks. *—Stephen Thomas Erlewine*

All Shook Up / 1980 / Epic ♦♦

One on One / 1982 / Epic ♦♦♦

Next Position Please / 1983 / Epic ♦♦♦
Perhaps sensing something was going wrong, Cheap Trick hired superstar producer Todd Rundgren for *Next Position Please.* Rundgren helped the band return to the appealing pop-rock of their *In Color* days, albiet stamping it with his heavy-handed production. However, Cheap Trick do benefit from Rundgren's control, since it gives them a sense of focus lacking on *All Shook Up* and *One on One.* Though the record was hampered somewhat by Epic's insistence of adding a bad cover of the Motors' terrific "Dancin' the Night Away" and the lightweight "You Say Jump," *Next Position Please* is effectively a return to form for Cheap Trick, boasting their most consistent set of songs since *Heaven Tonight.* "I Can't Take It," "Borderline," "Younger Girls," "Heaven's Falling" and "Invaders of the Heart" may not quite reach the heights of the first three albums, but they come within shooting distance, making *Next Position Please* Cheap Trick's last satisfying record. *—Stephen Thomas Erlewine*

Standing on the Edge / 1985 / Epic ♦♦

The Doctor / 1986 / Epic ♦

Lap of Luxury / 1988 / Epic ♦♦♦
Cheap Trick's comeback album is by no means a return to the creativity and vitality of their glory days. But even though *Lap of Luxury* is largely formulaic, the band's strongest collection of material in some time fills that late-'80s pop/metal formula quite well. Combining grandly romantic power ballads ("Ghost Town") with catchy hard rockers ("Never Had a Lot to Lose"), *Lap of Luxury* consistently delivers strong hooks and well-crafted songs, proving that Cheap Trick was still capable of outdoing many of the bands they helped inspire. The album produced two Top Five singles in a cover of Elvis Presley's "Don't Be Cruel" and the band's first number one hit, "The Flame." *—Steve Huey*

Busted / Jun. 1990 / Epic ♦♦

Greatest Hits / 1991 / Epic ♦♦♦♦♦
The greatest failing of *Greatest Hits* is the fact that much of Cheap Trick's best material didn't come near the charts. "I Want You to Want Me," "Surrender," and "Dream Police," either climbed the charts or scraped them, as did the fine singles "Ain't That a Shame," "Voices," "If You Want My Love," and "She's Tight," but many of their stone-cold classics—including "He's a Whore," "Oh, Candy," "Downed," "Southern Girls," "Auf Wiedersehen"—weren't successes. What were successes were pleasant arena-rockers and power ballads like "Tonight It's You," "The Flame," and "Don't Be Cruel," and that's what forms the basis of *Greatest Hits,* along with an extraneous new rendition of the Beatles' "Magical Mystery Tour." Casual fans who only want the hits will be satiated by this collection, but the album misses the point of Cheap Trick, and thereby doesn't work as either an introduction or retrospective. *—Stephen Thomas Erlewine*

Woke up with a Monster / Mar. 22, 1994 / Warner Brothers ♦♦♦

Sex, America, Cheap Trick / Aug. 1996 / Epic/Legacy ♦♦♦
Sex, America, Cheap Trick is a classic example of a botched box set. Spanning four discs and 64 songs, the box contains nearly all of the group's hit singles and an amazing amount of rarities—a grand total of 30 outtakes, live tracks, demos, single versions, soundtrack songs, and B-sides. Despite all of the abundance of material, there are still a lot of essential items missing, as well as several odd inclusions. Many of the group's biggest hits and concert staples are present, but Cheap Trick classics like "He's a Whore," "Downed," "Come On, Come On," "Taxman, Mr. Thief," "California Man," and several others are inexplicably absent. Furthermore, the final two discs bog down with slick radio-ready pop, even though they rescue all the highlights from the band's decidedly uneven '80s recordings. Still, the rarities—particularly single versions of early tracks like "Oh, Candy" and "Southern Girls," demos like "Fan Club," and a ripping live set—are usually worthy, even if they might have been better showcased on a double-disc rarities set. *—Stephen Thomas Erlewine*

Cheap Trick at Budokan: The Complete Concert / Apr. 21, 1998 / Epic/Legacy ♦♦♦♦♦
At Budokan was the pivotal album for Cheap Trick, the one that made them stars. The louder, harder-rocking versions of such Rick Nielsen classics as "I Want You to Want Me" and "Come On, Come On" connected with a wide audience in a way the studio recordings didn't and the record consequently became a smash. Given its enduring popularity, it wasn't surprising that Epic and Cheap Trick celebrated its 20th anniversary by releasing *The Complete Concert,* a double-disc set that contains all of the 19 songs the band had performed. Much of this material was released on *Budokan II,* but this set restores all the music to its original running order, making it an entirely unique album in its own right. There's no question that the music is terrific and it certainly is interesting to hear all of this the way it was actually performed, but *The Complete Concert* doesn't have the punch of the original album, which hit hard at only 10 tracks. The length of this set might make it frustrating for some fans, but any hardcore Trick fan will need this comprehensive, detailed document of the band's most celebrated concert. *—Stephen Thomas Erlewine*

Music for Hangovers / Jun. 15, 1999 / Cheap Trick Unlimited ♦♦♦♦

Authorized Greatest Hits / Aug. 29, 2000 / Epic/Legacy ♦♦♦♦
This is an "authorized" greatest hits collection in the sense that the band picked the selections themselves. It's preferable to the 1992 *Greatest Hits* comp for its slightly greater length (16 songs) and better choice of material; the single version of "Southern Girls" makes it on this time around, for instance. Still, like that other album with "Greatest Hits" in the title, it misses a number of rockers that fans might rate among their best work. The only previously unreleased item is a live 1988 performance of "The Flame"; a live version of "I Can't Take It" and their rendition of "That 70's Song (In the Street)," the latter famed for its use as a television theme, are the only tracks recorded after 1990. *—Richie Unterberger*

Chubby Checker (Ernest Evans)

b. Oct. 3, 1941, Philadelphia, PA
Vocals / Rock & Roll, R&B
Chubby Checker was the unrivaled king of the rock & roll dance craze; although most of the dances his records promoted—the Pony, the Fly and the Hucklebuck, to cite just three—have long since faded into obscurity, his most famous hit, "The Twist," remains the yardstick against which all subsequent dancefloor phenomena are measured. Signed to Philadelphia's Cameo-Parkway in 1959, he recorded a number of minor novelty hits before 1960's "The Twist" (a cover of a 1958 Hank Ballard & the Midnighters B-side) rocketed to number one in 1960 and again in 1961. After "The Twist" first made Checker a superstar, he returned to the top in 1961 with "Do the Pony"; that same year, he also reached the Top Ten with "Let's Twist Again," which assured the dance's passage from novelty to institution. In addition to 1961's "The Fly," Checker's other Top Ten hits included three 1962 smashes—"Slow Twistin'," "Limbo Rock" and "Popeye the Hitchhiker." In total, Checker notched 32 chart hits before the bubble burst in 1966. From the 1970s onward, he was a staple of oldies revival tours. In 1988, Checker returned to the Top 40 for the first time in a quarter century when he appeared on the Fat Boys' rap rendition of "The Twist." *—Jason Ankeny*

● **Chubby Checker's Greatest Hits** / Nov. 1972 / London ♦♦♦♦♦
In 1972, when nostalgia for late-'50s and early-'60s rock & roll was bringing Chuck Berry and others back into the charts, Allen Klein's ABKCO Records obtained the rights to reissue Chubby Checker's Cameo-Parkway singles on this 15-track hits LP. Checker actually had many more hits than just "The Twist" and "Let's Twist Again," and this LP presents both his other dance tunes—"Pony Time," "The Fly," "Limbo Rock"—and several of his later, less successful singles when he was trying to branch out into a sort of Harry Belafonte-style folk approach. But the heart of the collection is still the early-'60s dance tunes, which demonstrate that, while Checker was not a great rocker, he still, like Freddy Cannon and Gary U.S. Bonds, was one of the people keeping the flame of rock & roll flickering between the time Buddy Holly's plane went down in Iowa and the day the Beatles flew in from London. (Released on LP, this album is long out of print, and it is listed as Checker's "pick" album because, as of 1995, there is no in-print album containing his original hits.) *—William Ruhlmann*

The Chemical Brothers

f. 1989, Manchester, England
Group / Big Beat, Funky Breaks, Electronica, Trip-Hop, Club/Dance
The act with the first arena-sized sound in the electronica movement, the Chemical Brothers united such varying influences as Public Enemy, Cabaret Voltaire and My Bloody Valentine to create a dance-rock-rap fusion which rivalled the best old-school DJs on their own terms—keeping a crowd of people on the floor by working through any number of groove-oriented styles featuring unmissable samples, from familiar guitar riffs to vocal tags to various sound effects. And when the duo (Tom Rowlands and Ed Simons) decided to supplement their DJ careers by turning their bedrooms into recording studios, they pioneered a style of music (later termed big beat) remarkable for its lack of energy-loss from the dancefloor to the radio. Chemical Brothers albums were less collections of songs and more hour-long journeys, chock full of deep bomb-studded beats, percussive breakdowns and effects borrowed from a host of sources. All in all, the duo proved one of the few exceptions to the rule that intelligent dance music could never be bombastic or truly satisying to the seasoned rock fan; it's hardly surprising that they were one of the few dance acts to enjoy simultaneous succes in the British/American mainstream and in critical quarters. *—John Bush*

Exit Planet Dust / Aug. 15, 1995 / Astralwerks ♦♦♦♦♦
The former Dust Brothers make oblique reference to litigation averted on their debut full-length. The Brothers' sound is big on bombast, replete with screeching guitar samples and

lots of sirens and screaming divas. A breakthrough album of sorts, *Exit* was, upon its release, one of the few European post-techno albums to make any sort of headway into the stateside market. *—Sean Cooper*

★ **Dig Your Own Hole** / Apr. 7, 1997 / Astralwerks ✦✦✦✦✦
Taking the swirling eclecticism of their post-techno debut, *Exit Planet Dust*, to the extreme, the Chemical Brothers blow all stylistic boundaries down with their second album, *Dig Your Own Hole*. Bigger, bolder, and more adventurous than *Exit Planet Dust, Dig Your Own Hole* opens with the slamming cacophony of "Block Rockin' Beats," where hip-hop meets hardcore techno, complete with a Schoolly D sample and an elastic bass riff. Everything is going on at once in "Block Rockin' Beats," and it sets the pace for the rest of the record, where songs and styles blur into a continuous kaleidoscope of sound. It rocks hard enough for the pop audience, but it doesn't compromise either the Chemicals' sound or the adventurous, futuristic spirit of electronica—even "Setting Sun," with its sly homages to the Beatles' "Tomorrow Never Knows" and Noel Gallagher's twisting, catchy melody, doesn't sound like retro psychedelia; it sounds vibrant, unexpected, and utterly contemporary. There are no distinctions between different styles, and the Chemicals sound as if they're having fun, building *Dig Your Own Hole* from fragments of the past, distorting the rhythms and samples, and pushing it forward with an intoxicating rush of synthesizers, electronics, and layered drum machines. The Chemical Brothers might not push forward into self-consciously arty territories like some of their electronic peers, but they have more style and focus, constructing a blindingly innovative and relentlessly propulsive album that's an exhilarating listen—one that sounds positively new but utterly inviting at the same time. *—Stephen Thomas Erlewine*

Brothers Gonna Work It Out / Sep. 22, 1998 / Astralwerks ✦✦✦

Surrender / Jun. 22, 1999 / Astralwerks ✦✦✦✦

Cher (Cherilyn Sarkasian LaPier)

b. May 20, 1946, El Centro, CA
Vocals / Girl Group, Pop/Rock, Folk-Rock, Soft Rock, Pop, Adult Contemporary, Dance-Pop
Cher has had three careers that place her indelibly in the public consciousness, and two have been in association with her then-husband, composer/producer/singer Salvatore "Sonny" Bono. She charted major hit records in the 1960s and 1970s, working in idioms ranging from early '60s girl group-style ballads to Jackie Deshannon folk-influenced pop, to adult pop in the manner of later Dusty Springfield. She also embarked on an acting career, initially in the late 1960s in association with her work as part of Sonny and Cher but later on her own, which led to a series of increasingly polished and compelling performances in *Silkwood, Mask* and *Moonstruck*, for which she won the Academy Award(tm) for Best Actress. Since the mid-1970s, Cher has been known more for her acting than for her music, although she has continued to record for numerous labels, including Columbia, and in 1998 scored an international chart-topping smash with the club-friendly single "Believe." *—Bruce Eder*

The Best of the Casablanca Years / Apr. 1996 / Casablanca/Chronicles ✦✦
Cher's *The Best of the Casablanca Years* collects all of her hit singles from the late '70s, and there weren't that many. Only three singles charted in the Top 100 and only one—the number eight "Take Me Home"—cracked the Top 40. So, the rest of the collection is padded with album tracks, making the disc into a mammoth, 17-track compilation. Nearly everything she released on the label is included and it all sounds similar—it's all insistent, mildly catchy disco. During this era, Cher didn't work with particularly gifted producers or songwriters, which meant her disco tracks were undistinguished. Occasionally, such as "Take Me Home," she had a strong song, but she was more likely to cut a wealth of mediocre material, throwing in a few genuinely embarassing tracks along the way. And that means *The Best of the Casablanca Years* is an artifact of the late '70s that is only of use for dedicated Cher fans. It's a well-produced and thorough collection, but no one but the most devoted fan needs to own this music *—Stephen Thomas Erlewine*

Bang Bang: The Early Years / May 18, 1999 / Capitol ✦✦✦
Released in the spring of 1999, *Bang Bang: The Early Years* arrived at the perfect time. After years in exile—she hadn't had a hit single or movie in over five years—Cher returned to the spotlight in early 1998 under tragic circumstances, delivering a moving eulogy at Sonny Bono's funeral. It served as a reminder to a mass audience that she was alive and well, and within a year, she had a huge hit single with "Believe" and a hit movie with *Tea with Mussolini*. All in all, it was the perfect opportunity for a collection that spotlighted her recordings for Imperial from the mid-'60s. There had been many compilations focusing on her duets with Sonny, but *Bang Bang* was the first in many years to focus directly on her solo recordings, and at a generous 18 tracks, it ranks among the best of its kind ever assembled. All seven of her charting singles for Imperial—"All I Really Want to Do," "Where Do You Go," "Bang Bang (My Baby Shot Me Down)," "Alfie," "Behind the Door," "Hey Joe," "You Better Sit Down Kids"—are here, along with most of the B-sides and selected album tracks. There may be a personal favorite or two missing, but overall this is as close as it comes to a definitive collection of Cher's early solo recordings. Overall, the songs aren't quite as strong as those she recorded with Sonny, but it's still very good indeed. *—Stephen Thomas Erlewine*

20th Century Masters—*The Millennium Collection: The Best of Cher* / *Jan. 25, 2000 / MCA* ✦✦✦
You might have thought that, since the 1998 merger of MCA and PolyGram, creating Universal Music, brought the hits Cher scored in the 1970s and '80s for Kapp, MCA, Casablanca, and Geffen under one roof, the next time they got around to doing a best-of they would combine all those catalogs. No such luck. In the wake of Cher's 1999 comeback with "Believe," Geffen issued its own comp, *If I Could Turn Back Time: Cher's Greatest Hits*. So, when MCA came to compile *The Best of Cher* as part of the midline-priced 20th Century Masters/The Millennium Collection series, they simply took the 1974 MCA *Greatest Hits* album, stripped off two B-sides, and added the 1979 Casablanca disco hit "Take Me Home" and the 1971 Sonny & Cher hit "All I Ever Need Is You." The result is an improvement on the still-in-print and also discount-priced *Greatest Hits* that really should be called "The Best of Cher in the '70s". But, with the '80s hits on the Geffen set and Cher's '60s hits belonging to Warner EMI, anyone looking for a comprehensive single-disc compilation on the artist remains frustrated. *—William Ruhlmann*

● **The Way of Love: The Cher Collection** / Nov. 21, 2000 / MCA ✦✦✦✦✦

The Chi-Lites

f. 1959, Chicago, IL, **db.** 1983
Group / Smooth Soul, Chicago Soul, Soul
One of the most popular smooth soul groups of the early '70s didn't hail from Philadelphia or Memphis, the two cities known for sweet, string-laden soul. Instead, the Chi-Lites were from Chicago, a town better-known for its gritty urban blues and driving R&B. Led by vocalist Eugene Record, the Chi-Lites had a lush, creamy sound distinguished by their four-part harmonies and layered productions. During the early '70s, they racked up 11 Top 10 R&B singles, ranging from the romantic ballads "Have You Sween Her" and "Oh Girl" to protest songs like "(For God's Sake) Give More Power to the People" and "There Will Never Be Any Peace (Until God Is Seated at The Conference Table)." All the songs featured Record's warm, pleading tenor and falsetto, and the majority of the group's hits were written by Record, often in collaboration with other songwriters like his wife, Barbra Acklin. *—Stephen Thomas Erlewine*

★ **Greatest Hits [Brunswick]** / 1972 / Brunswick ✦✦✦✦✦
The Chi-Lites were one of the most influential and skilled vocal groups of the late '60s to the mid-'70s. Producer and lead singer Eugene Record always crafted interesting tracks that made the group stand out in a genre that was full of competition. *Greatest Hits* assembles 16 of their best 1969-1972 tracks. Early songs, "I Like Your Lovin'" and "Are You My Woman," still are a little cluttered and unfocused. This package proves that Record more than caught on. The well produced "(For God's Sake) Give More Power to the People" accurately depicts the problems of early '70s America without being preachy. The astute "We're Are Neighbors" is a production gem with its blaring horns and fuzz/acid guitar. As polemic tracks began to play out, the Chi-Lites began to concentrate more on ballads. Classics "Oh Girl" and "Have You Seen Her" both have retained their melancholy strength and lyrical prowess. Perhaps the most interesting thing about *Greatest Hits* is the breadth of their work. From the not too bright protagonist of the "I'm Ready If I Don't Get to Go" to the unintentionally hilarious "Living in the Footsteps of Another Man," the group simply covered more lyrical ground than most of their contemporaries. *Greatest Hits* also includes the Chi Lites and Record's most ambitious work. The dreary yet skilled "Coldest Days of My Life" certainly attains the sense of loneliness and isolation that Record often covered in his work. Other anthologies covering their work certainly came after this 1972 set, but *Greatest Hits* may be most desired by their fans. *—Jason Elias*

☆ **Greatest Hits [Rhino]** / 1992 / Rhino ✦✦✦✦✦
All of the Chi-Lites' best songs and biggest hits—including "Oh Girl," "(For God's Sake) Give More Power to the People" and "Stoned Out of My Mind"—are collected on the definitive single-disc retrospective *Greatest Hits*. *—Stephen Thomas Erlewine*

Greatest Hits, Vol. 2 [Rhino] / Oct. 15, 1996 / Rhino ✦✦✦
Greatest Hits, Vol. 2 picks up where Rhino's first volume of Chi-Lites' *Greatest Hits* left off, compiling all of the group's lesser-known R&B hit singles. The compilation contains recordings that the group made between 1968 and 1981 for the record labels Dakar, Brunswick, Mercury, and Chi-Sound. Though there are a few gems on the record—including "I Like Your Lovin' (Do You Like Mine)," "A Lonely Man," and "You Got to Be the One"—the material on *Greatest Hits, Vol. 2* by and large pales to the songs on the first collection, yet fans of the group's smooth soul sound will find several cuts to treasure on this album. *—Stephen Thomas Erlewine*

The Very Best of the Chi-Lites / May 26, 1998 / Music Club ✦✦✦✦

Chic

f. 1977, New York, NY
Group / Disco, Funk
Chic was the best and most influential disco band of the latter half of the '70s, earning hits with both their own records and the outside productions of co-leaders Nile Rodgers and Bernard Edwards. Atlantic picked it up their demo for "Dance Dance Dance" in late 1977 after a series of rejections from other record labels; the single sold a million copies in one month, catapulting Chic into the forefront of the disco scene. Chic's biggest hits—"Le Freak" (number one), "I Want Your Love" (number seven), and the "Good Times" (number one)—came in 1978-1979, and as disco started to fade, so did the group's popularity. Still, Chic's influence was apparent throughout the '80s; "Good Times" alone spawned Queen's hit "Another One Bites the Dust" (a complete rip-off), and Sugarhill Gang used the record as the foundation for "Rapper's Delight," arguably the first rap single. Rodgers was one of the most successful producers of the early '80s, scoring hits with David Bowie's *Let's Dance*, Madonna's *Like a Virgin*, and Mick Jagger's solo debut, *She's the Boss*. Chic re-formed in 1992, but failed to recapture the fire of its glory days. *—Stephen Thomas Erlewine*

Chic / 1977 / Atlantic ✦✦

C'est Chic / 1978 / Atlantic ✦✦✦

Risque / 1979 / Atlantic ✦✦✦

Dance Dance Dance: Best of Chic / Nov. 5, 1991 / Atlantic ✦✦✦✦✦
You think disco was nothing more than assembly line funk and freeze-dried beats— Then you need to step into the crisp grooves and walloping boogie found on this stunning collection of Chic's '70s recordings. Such hits as "Good Times," "Dance Dance Dance," and "Le Freak" used the stylistic innovations of James Brown and Sly Stone as a blueprint for a new era of funk. Bernard Edwards' bass lines are so provocative they seem to talk, while Nile Rodgers' skeletal guitar runs hark back to Steve Cropper's slashing style. Sure, the songs don't say much. Sure, the dance mixes collected here ramble on after about six minutes. But once you step into these grooves—grooves that influenced an entire generation of artists

from David Byrne to Prince—you will realize that these were indeed good times. —*John Floyd*

The Best of Chic, Vol. 2 / Nov. 10, 1992 / Rhino ✦✦✦✦✦

★ **The Very Best of Chic** / Mar. 14, 2000 / Rhino ✦✦✦✦✦
To the rock critics who dismissed Chic's music as disposable and mindless back in the late '70s: it might seem like a stretch to say that Nile Rogers and Bernard Edwards had as great an impact as Gamble & Huff, George Clinton, and the folks at Stax Records. But in fact, Chic's music *was* that influential—and its disco/funk/soul innovations would be having an impact long after the '70s ended. From Madonna, Change, and Queen, to Duran Duran, Soul II Soul, and ABC—new wave, hip-hop, house, European Hi-NRG, Latin freestyle, and acid jazz—you could write a book about all the artists who have been influenced by Chic. This collection, which came out in 2000 and spans 1977-1982, is full of grooves that prove to be anything but disposable. Most of Chic's essential hits are provided, including "Good Times," "Le Freak," "Dance, Dance, Dance," "I Want Your Love," and "Everybody Dance." Less than essential, but still likable and decent, are early '80s recordings such as "Rebels Are We" from *Real People*, and "Stage Fright" from *Take It Off*. By 1980, Chic wasn't having as many hits and was feeling the sting of the death-to-disco movement. But disco never really died—it simply changed its name to dance music and evolved into such forms as Hi-NRG, Latin freestyle and house. When that happened, Chic's long-lasting influence was impossible to miss—you could say that Chic's influence lasted a lot longer than Chic itself. For those who need a concise introduction to Chic's legacy and want to hear some of R&B's most influential grooves, *The Very Best of Chic* is highly recommended. —*Alex Henderson*

Chicago

f. Feb. 15, 1967, Chicago, IL
Group / Jazz-Rock, Pop/Rock, Soft Rock, Adult Contemporary
Chicago is second only to the Beach Boys as the most successful American rock band of all time. The group formed officially on February 15, 1967, in the city from which it eventually would take its name. The band members intended to launch a rock group with a fully integrated horn section (a novel idea at the time); initially, they did without a bass player, but in December 1967, bassist/vocalist Peter Cetera joined from rival band the Exceptions. Under the guidance of manager/producer James William Guercio, who initially named them Chicago Transit Authority (the name was shortened after the real C.T.A. objected), the group moved to Los Angeles and signed to Columbia Records, recording its debut album, *Chicago Transit Authority*, in January 1969. It sold over two million copies and spawned four chart singles, beginning a string of massive hits that lasted to the end of the decade, with each album cover sporting a variation on the Chicago logo and a sequential title with a roman numeral. Chicago's music was a mixture of styles, from hard rock to light pop, incorporating elements of jazz and classical, but after Cetera's "If You Leave Me Now" became a gold-selling number one hit in 1976, the group became more identified with romantic ballads than anything else. Chicago went into decline after a split with Guercio in 1977, but rebounded in 1982 with "Hard to Say I'm Sorry" and the million-selling *Chicago 16*, and was able to sustain its renewed popularity despite Cetera's departure for a solo career in 1985. After several years of hits, Chicago's popularity began to decline in the early '90s, as the group retired to the oldies circuit. —*William Ruhlmann*

Chicago Transit Authority / Apr. 1969 / Chicago ✦✦✦✦
The first rock & roll band to integrate a horn section into its sound successfully, Chicago Transit Authority (later Chicago), fresh from years on the Midwest bar circuit, demonstrated a wide versatility on its debut album. The band seemed capable of playing everything from lounge music to hard rock, and here it mixed ballad material with gritty funk and psychedelic guitar, often on the same song. This time capsule of the varying strands of popular music in the late '60s features the hits "Does Anybody Really Know What Time It Is?," "Beginnings," and "Questions 67 and 68." —*William Ruhlmann*

Chicago II / Jan. 1970 / Chicago ✦✦✦✦
With its second double album (now on one CD), Chicago became even more ambitious and even more successful, mounting the extended "Suite for a Girl in Buchannon," from which were excerpted the hit singles "Make Me Smile" and "Color My World." "25 or 6 to 4" is also featured on this album. —*William Ruhlmann*

Chicago III / Jan. 1971 / Chicago ✦✦

At Carnegie Hall, Vols. 1-4 (Chicago IV) / Oct. 1971 / Chicago ✦

Chicago V / Jul. 1972 / Chicago ✦✦✦
The group's avant-garde roots are explored on the set-opening "A Hit by Varese," while the album also includes the autobiographical "Alma Mater" and the hits "Saturday in the Park" and "Dialogue." —*William Ruhlmann*

Chicago VI / Jun. 1973 / Chicago ✦✦✦
Chicago demonstrates all its strength here, turning in one of its great ballads in "Just You 'N' Me" and one of its great rockers in "Feelin' Stronger Every Day." Elsewhere, the group takes on its negative reviews in "Critics' Choice" and acknowledges the impact of L.A. stardom on a bunch of Midwestern kids in "Something in This City Changes People." —*William Ruhlmann*

Chicago VII / Mar. 1974 / Chicago ✦✦

Chicago VIII / Mar. 1975 / Chicago ✦✦

● **Greatest Hits (Chicago IX)** / Nov. 1975 / Chicago ✦✦✦✦✦
The biggest hits of Chicago's first five years of recording, including "Just You 'N' Me," "Feelin' Stronger Every Day," "Wishing You Were Here," "Call On Me," and "(I've Been) Searchin' So Long." —*William Ruhlmann*

Chicago X / Jun. 1976 / Chicago ✦✦

Chicago XI / Sep. 1977 / Chicago ✦✦

Hot Streets / Sep. 1978 / Chicago ✦✦

Chicago 13 / Aug. 1979 / Chicago ✦

Chicago XIV / Jul. 1980 / Chicago ✦

Chicago's Greatest Hits, Vol. 2 / 1981 / Chicago ✦✦✦
This album chronicles Chicago's gradual transformation in the second half of the '70s into a group that produced big ballads, usually sung by Peter Cetera. And here they are, starting with "If You Leave Me Now" and continuing with "Baby, What a Big Surprise" and the nostalgic "Old Days." —*William Ruhlmann*

If You Leave Me Now / 1982 / Chicago ✦✦

Chicago 16 / Jun. 1982 / Full Moon/Warner Brothers ✦✦

Chicago 17 / May 1984 / Full Moon/Warner Brothers ✦✦✦
With sales of four million, this is the biggest-selling regular studio album Chicago has made. That's what happens when you really go for the ballads: "Stay the Night," "Hard Habit to Break," "You're the Inspiration," and "Along Comes a Woman" all fit into that category; all featured Peter Cetera, and all made the Top 40. Not surprisingly, Cetera decamped soon after. —*William Ruhlmann*

Chicago 18 / Sep. 1986 / Full Moon/Warner Brothers ✦✦

Chicago 19 / Jun. 1988 / Full Moon/Reprise ✦✦

Greatest Hits: 1982-1989 / Nov. 1989 / Full Moon/Reprise ✦✦✦✦
Chicago returned from a career dip in 1982 with "Hard to Say I'm Sorry" and continued to hit with power ballads, among them "Hard Habit to Break" and "You're the Inspiration," all sung by Peter Cetera. But the streak continued after Cetera departed in 1985, as Jason Scheff stepped in and Chicago went on to score hits like "Will You Still Love Me?," "I Don't Wanna Live Without Your Love," and "Look Away," which are all heard here. —*William Ruhlmann*

Group Portrait / 1991 / Chicago ✦✦✦✦✦
Weighing in at four discs and 63 songs, *Group Portrait* offers an excellent, comprehensive overview of Chicago's prime period. Be forewarned: this does not dip into the group's early-'80s hits or post-Peter Cetera recordings, choosing to end the story before their 1982 comeback. Although this music is missed, this isn't a fatal flaw, since instead of telling the band's story, this box sketches a portrait of the group at their creative peak. And it works very well indeed. Chicago most certainly made albums, yet those albums, no matter if they were intended conceptually, really played better as a series of moments. This collects those moments, whether they're hits or album tracks, spotlighting Chicago at their very best. Is it for everybody— No, since most casual listeners will be content with the fine hits collections, and some hardcore fans will still swear by the albums—yet for the audience that wants all of prime '70s Chicago in one set, this box set couldn't be better. —*Stephen Thomas Erlewine*

Twenty 1 / Jan. 1991 / Full Moon/Warner Brothers ✦✦

The Chiffons

f. 1960, New York, NY [The Bronx], **db.** 1972
Group / Brill Building Pop, Girl Group, Pop
One of the best early-'60s New York girl groups, combining sassiness and innocence on several of the style's greatest classics. The Chiffons had some singles under their belt when they reached number one with "He's So Fine," whose classic "doo-lang, doo-lang" riff was appropriated by George Harrison in 1970 for his own chart-topper, "My Sweet Lord" (Harrison was subsequently ordered to pay substantial damages to the original publishers, though he always claimed the resemblance was unintentional). Their follow-up, Goffin-King's "One Fine Day," was just as good, featuring killer piano riffs from King herself. Actually cut as a Little Eva track, the Chiffons' vocal was substituted, resulting in a Top Five hit. There were a couple other memorable hits, "I Have a Boyfriend" and the Motown-influenced "Sweet Talkin' Guy," and interesting misfires like the Martha & the Vandellas-inspired "The Real Thing," as well as some singles issued under an alter ego, the Four Pennies. The group recorded quite a bit of material during the '60s, much of it derivative; the hits are their best tracks by far. —*Richie Unterberger*

● **16 Golden Classics** / Collectables ✦✦✦✦✦

Alex Chilton

b. Dec. 28, 1950, Memphis, TN
Vocals, Guitar / College Rock, Roots Rock, Rock & Roll
In a business that reinvents itself at every turn, Alex Chilton has managed to survive for three decades with a three-fold career as well—his early recordings with the Box Tops, the three albums he did with Big Star in the mid-'70s and the spate of cool, but chaotic, solo albums he's recorded since then. To some, he's a classic hit-maker from the '60s. To others, he's a genius British-style pop musician and songwriter. To yet another audience, he's a doomed and despairing artist who spent several years battling the bottle, delivering anarchistic records and performances while thumbing his nose at all pretenses of stardom, a quirky iconoclast whose influence has spawned the likes of the Replacements and Teenage Fanclub. With the Box Tops, he cut "The Letter," a record that sounded White enough to go number one on the pop charts and yet Black enough to track on R&B stations, too. Chilton was still in his teens, but armed with a strong conception of how pop and R&B vocals should be handled. The hits kept coming, with "Cry like a Baby," "Soul Deep" and "Sweet Cream Ladies" all showing visible chart action. After a few errant solo sessions, Chilton next found himself in Big Star with singer/guitarist Chris Bell. Their blend of ethereal harmonies, quirky lyrics and Beatlesque song structure appeared to be radio-friendly, but distribution for their label, Ardent Records, spelled disaster. Around 1976, Chilton started producing a wild cross-section of solo outings for various foreign and American independent labels, all featuring his love for obscure material, barbed-wire guitar playing, howling feedback and bands who sounded barely familiar with the material. —*Cub Koda*

Bach's Bottom / 1975 / Razor & Tie ✦✦✦

Recorded during one of Chilton's more chaotic periods, *Bach's Bottom* is an interesting document of misguided talent. It's not so much the music as it is the sense of what is going on around the music that makes this 1975 outing fascinating. Chilton's dismemberment of "Free Again," "Take Me Home and Make Me Like It," the Beatles' "I'm So Tired," and "Jesus Christ" are pretty funny, while his great self-productions of "Bangkok" and the Seeds' "Can't Seem to Make You Mine" reveal his penchant for making something special happen at times when everything seems to be falling apart. *—AMG*

Like Flies on Sherbert / 1979 / Peabody ✦

Live in London / 1982 / Varese ✦✦

● **19 Years: A Collection** / Feb. 1991 / Rhino ✦✦✦✦
Collecting tracks from, indeed, 19 years of Chilton's career, *19 Years* remains the best place to get a sampling of his widely varied work. Big Star is represented (perhaps a bit too strongly) by five tracks from *3rd/Sister Lovers*, which at that time had not been re-released in America by Rykodisc, including such masterpieces of desolation as "Kanga Roo" and "Holocaust." Otherwise, this is Chilton solo getting the focus, starting with "Free Again," an infectious country-rock cut from his then unreleased debut album away from the Box Tops, *1970*, and concluding with cuts from his 1987 release *High Priest*. Even Chilton's fans admit to—or perhaps can't easily take or understand—his almost willful stylistic jumps and sidesteps, making a full encapsulation of his interests and detours impossible, but *19 Years* comes pretty close. Both sides of his one-off single from 1977, "Bangkok"/"Can't Seem to Make You Mine," make the grade, the former being one of the better punk-influenced tunes by older musicians out there. If the sound is more quavering Marc Bolan meets rockabilly, why not? The latter serves up a Seeds cover with folk-rocky panache and more than a few strange noises. Ragged tracks from *Like Flies on Sherbert* capture the half-engaging, half-troubling points of his late-'70s life, while cuts from the *Feudalist Tarts* and *No Sex* EPs show him exploring his rootsier, New Orleans-tinged side with low-key fire. The addition of a Troggs cover, "With a Girl Like You," from a French compilation gives *19 Years* a nice little bonus. Detailed liner notes from Darcy Sullivan trace the strange course of his career, not shying away from acknowledging periods where his drinking and other problems disrupted any kind of regular career flow, while the remastering and presentation is up to Rhino's usual standard. *—Ned Raggett*

Cliches / Feb. 11, 1994 / Ardent ✦✦✦

Feudalist Tarts/No Sex / May 1, 1994 / Razor & Tie ✦✦✦✦✦
Since Alex Chilton seems to have had trouble coming up with an LP's worth of tunes at one time since re-emerging as an active performer in the 1980s, he's released a number of EPs, and this CD reissue pairs up two of his best. 1985's *Feudalist Tarts* was Chilton's first studio release since 1979; after spending most of the 1970s as one of the few rock acts from the Deep South who displayed almost no visible R&B influence, Chilton belatedly embraced the pleasures of vintage soul music after moving to New Orleans and giving up alcohol, and *Feudalist Tarts* is dominated by covers of Slim Harpo's "Ti Ni Nee Ni Noo" and Carla Thomas's "B-A-B-Y," with bare-wired originals like "Lost My Job" along for good measure. Cut in a single day, *Feudalist Tarts* is a bit rough around the edges, but Chilton's guitar playing is solid, and the band of veteran Southern studio players give Chilton as good as he gets (if not better). The following year, Chilton released the three-song *No Sex* 12"; the title tune is the best song he's written since Big Star's breakup, a witty but ominous meditation on the consequences of the AIDS pandemic (which, given his reputation as a ladies' man, has doubtless been a matter of great concern to Chilton). *Feudalist Tarts* and *No Sex* don't do much to fill out a CD together—their combined length is less than 33 minutes—but they are two of the most solid records of Chilton's mid-'80s "comeback" period. *—Mark Deming*

High Priest/Black List / May 1, 1994 / Razor & Tie ✦✦✦
1987's *High Priest* was Alex Chilton's first full-length studio album since the fascinatingly disastrous *Like Flies on Sherbert* in 1979. While it certainly wasn't the return to pure-pop form some fans were hoping for from the former leader of Big Star, it at least showed Chilton to be in firm command of his faculties again, and fronting a solid band of Memphis/New Orleans studio heavyweights. *High Priest* boasted only four original songs from Chilton, the best being the mildly sleazy "Thing for You" (though the just-plain-weird "Dalai Lama" has a certain perverse charm), but he dug up a handful of worthwhile covers, including the good-and-greasy "Make a Little Love" and a fine, obscure Carole King number, "Let Me Get Close to You." While Chilton's vocals betray a certain inscrutable irony, he's in fine voice throughout, and his wildly underrated guitar work is very much in evidence. *Black List*, a six-song EP Chilton released in 1989, is featured on this CD release as a bonus; it works on the same level as *High Priest*, only with six songs instead of 12. It does include that modern rarity, a noteworthy original Alex Chilton song ("Guantanamerika," a witty meditation on right-wing politics and Tammy Faye Bakker) and a solid version of the R&B chestnut "I Will Turn You Money Green." In addition, Razor and Tie have dug up unreleased tunes from the sessions for each record that, for a change, are actually worth hearing; "Magnetic Field," a leftover from *Black List*, is a frantic old-school rocker written by Chilton, while his superb cover of Charlie Rich's "Lonely Weekends" is an outtake from *High Priest* that's better than most of what made the cut. *—Mark Deming*

A Man Called Destruction / Sep. 12, 1995 / Ardent ✦✦✦

1970 / Apr. 1996 / Ardent ✦✦✦
1970 comprises the sessions that would have formed Alex Chilton's first solo album. As the title suggests, Chilton recorded these songs after he left the Box Tops but right before he joined Big Star—appropriately, the music sounds caught between the Box Tops' blue-eyed soul and Big Star's jangly power-pop. In that respect, it has more in common with his numerous solo recordings than either of his bands. And like his solo records, *1970* is wildly uneven and lacks focus. It careens between charming tributes to R&B and pop (a medley of the Archies' "Sugar, Sugar" and James Brown's "There Was a Time"), and his originals, which only hint at the heights he would reach with Big Star. If *1970* does anything, it illustrates that Chilton needs a strong collaborative force like Chris Bell to bring out the best in his music. *—Stephen Thomas Erlewine*

Set / Feb. 22, 2000 / Bar/None ✦✦✦

The Chocolate Watchband

f. 1965, Los Altos, California, **db.** 1968
Group / Garage Rock, Psychedelic
The Chocolate Watchband never charted a record nationally. Indeed, ask most casual 1960s rock fans about them and you'll probably get little more than a blank stare. Most will remember their AVI Records labelmates the Standells more clearly, because they actually managed to chart a few singles. Alas, the Watchband had the disadvantage of being a punkier band than the Standells, and suffering continual lineup changes. The Chocolate Watchband was a mod-outfitted garage punk unit par excellence, their sound founded on English-style R&B with a special fixation on the Rolling Stones at their most sneering. After hooking up with producer Ed Cobb, a former member of the 1950s vocal ensemble the Four Preps, the group released *No Way Out* in mid-1967, though the Watchband had already begun breaking up. A new incarnation carried them through 1967, though the band's existence as a viable performing unit were all but over. The group's producers had other ideas, however, releasing two more albums (*The Inner Mystique*, *One Step Beyond*) in 1968, sporting the band's name but not too much else associated with the group. That would probably have been the end of the group's story, but in the early '80s, record buyers and, more particularly, young musicians discovered the Watchband. A set of Australian reissues of the group's albums quickly found a market in America and Europe. Thus, it was no surprise when, in 1994, Sundazed Records reissued the complete Watchband catalog on compact disc. *—Bruce Eder*

● **The Best of the Chocolate Watchband** / 1983 / Rhino ✦✦✦✦✦
The first CD-era collection of this hard-luck band's work was also the best compilation of the band's work, but it was a good idea done a little too early. The sound is deficient compared with Rhino's usual standard, and the notes were later outdone by Sundazed Records' reissue of the band's complete catalog. It's still a good starter, however, if one can find it. *—Bruce Eder*

Lou Christie (Lugee Alfredo Giovanni Sacco)

b. Feb. 19, 1943, Glen Willard, PA
Vocals / Bubblegum, Pop
While Lou Christie's shrieking falsetto was among the most distinctive voices in all of pop music, he was also one of the first solo performers of the rock era to compose his own material, generating some of the biggest and most memorable hits of the mid-1960s. Born Lugee Alfredo Giovanni Sacco in Glen Willard, Pennsylvania on February 19, 1963, he won a scholarship to Moon Township High School as a teen; there he studied music and vocal technique, later joining a group dubbed the Classics. Between 1959 and 1962, in collaboration with a variety of Pittsburgh-area bands, he cut a series of records for small local labels, adopting the stage name Lou Christie along the way. Eventually he made the acquaintance of Twila Herbert, a classically trained musician and self-proclaimed mystic some 20 years his senior; they became songwriting partners, and in 1962 penned "The Gypsy Cried," which he recorded on two-track in his garage. The single became a local phenomenon, and was eventually licensed for national release by the Roulette label, peaking at number 24 on the pop charts in 1963.

After relocating to New York and landing session work as a backing vocalist, Christie wrote and recorded a follow-up, "Two Faces Have I"; it landed in the Top Ten, but shortly after its release he began a two-year stint in the Army. He returned to action in 1966, picking up right where he left off with his biggest hit yet—the lush, chart-topping "Lightnin' Strikes." Christie's next smash, 1966's "Rhapsody in the Rain," was notorious for being among the more sexually explicit efforts of the period. After brief stays with Colpix and Columbia, he next moved to the Buddah label, scoring one last Top Ten hit in 1969 with "I'm Gonna Make You Mine." Drug problems plagued Christie during the early 1970s, and after getting clean at a London rehab clinic, he dropped out of music, working variously as a ranch hand, offshore oil driller and carnival barker; by the 1980s, he was making the occasional appearance on oldies package tours, and in 1997 issued *Pledging My Love*, his first new material in over a quarter-century. *—Jason Ankeny*

● **Enlightnin'ment: The Best of Lou Christie** / 1991 / Rhino ✦✦✦✦✦

The Church

f. 1980, Sydney, Australia
Group / College Rock, Neo-Psychedelia, Alternative Pop/Rock
Best known for the shimmering "Under the Milky Way," their lone Top 40 hit, the Australian band the Church combined the jangling guitar-pop of '60s icons like the Byrds with the opaque wordplay of frontman Steve Kilbey to create a lush, melancholy brand of neo-psychedelia rich in texture and melody. Their 1981 debut *Of Skin and Heart* was an evocative collection highlighted by the ringing "The Unguarded Moment," a major success down under; the group resurfaced in 1982 with *The Blurred Crusade*, a stunning effort featuring mature standouts like "Almost With You" and "When You Were Mine." After moving to Arista, the Church teamed with famed session guitarists Danny Kortchmar and Waddy Wachtel to record 1988's *Starfish*, their most artistically and commercially successful effort to date. Highlighted by "Under the Milky Way," the album also featured the minor hits "Reptile" and "Spark," a marvelous pop blast penned by guitarist Marty Willson-Piper. The follow-up, 1988's *Gold Afternoon Fix*, failed to repeat the success of its predecessor as the single "Metropolis" garnered only minor airplay. *—Jason Ankeny*

Of Skins and Heart / 1981 / Arista ✦✦✦✦✦
On their debut, *Of Skin and Heart*, the Church play a straightforward pop/rock firmly rooted in new wave, though owing no small debt to '60s pop. Edgier and more direct than their later work, it also ranks among their finest for that very reason. None of the excesses and ambi-

tions that would sometimes get out of hand on later releases are present, though much of the band's basic formula was laid down—Steve Kilbey's cool, detached vocals and slightly surrealistic lyrics combined with some outstanding pop hooks, nice harmonies, and layers of ringing guitar. The classic "Unguarded Moment" (arguably one of the greatest singles of the '80s) overshadows much of the material on the album, but there is really no shortage of great songs here. [The album was originally released in the U.S. as *The Church* with some tracks dropped in favor of three tracks from singles released around the same time. In 1988, Arista released *Of Skin and Heart* on CD in its original form with the added tracks from *The Church* tacked on to the end.] *—Chris Woodstra*

The Blurred Crusade / 1982 / Arista ✦✦✦✦✦
After such a fine debut as *Of Skins and Heart,* creating a follow-up might have been a burden for the Church—and maybe it was, but the end result was well worth it. Perhaps even better than their first, *Blurred Crusade* captures what for many remains the classic early Church sound, blending both the various strains of '60s inspiration and postpunk drive detected from the start with an even more elegant melancholy. Musically, both Willson-Piper and Koppes are just fantastic, their combination of guitar playing running the range from sparkling post-Byrds chime to sharp power. If the group doesn't fully explode here as much as later albums would demonstrate, especially on *Heyday,* that perhaps can be laid at producer Bob Clearmountain's feet. Consider the slow but steady build up of "When You Were Mine," guitar lines and notes setting the scene before fully kicking into the main riff and the clever but not forced production on the vocals on some of the middle verses. Add on the fantastic solo about four minutes in, and this is great rock music, period, deeply impressive coming on a sophomore album. Highlights are plentiful throughout *Blurred,* but the best numbers are perhaps the opening "Almost With You," a note-perfect combination of hooks and downbeat but not morose atmosphere, and the lengthy, powerful "You Took." Willson-Piper's lead vocal number "Field of Mars" and the brief, concluding "Don't Look Back" are further songs of note. *—Ned Raggett*

Seance / 1983 / Arista ✦✦✦
The cover may have looked like something of a goth record of the era, though then again not many goths would have used pink as the dominant color of an album. On this, the band's third full album, the band consolidated the advances of *Blurred Crusade* well; if *Seance* isn't as immediately striking as the first two albums, it still has its share of winners, starting with the opening "Fly." Its string-synth touched, stripped-down arrangement almost sounded like something from the Chameleons' quieter moments, but the following "One Day" returned the Church to more familiar ringing-yet-forceful guitar territory. One very curious thing about this song and many of the others on the album has to with the drumming—while Ploog very much remains the key credited drummer, here and on many other cuts nearly everything sounds produced by a particularly muffled drum machine. Whether or not one was used, the result is at once stiff and more than a little underwhelming, making what should be stronger songs sound more run of the mill than they are. Even the otherwise excellent remastering of the early catalog when the albums were reissued on Arista can't save some of the problems. Aside from this major flaw, *Séance* keeps at the understated guitar groove that the Church rapidly made its own, containing marvelous songs like "Disappear?" and the nicely paced "Electric Lash." Experimenting with keyboards more provides some nice results, as the Kilbey-and-synth introduction to the lovely "It's No Reason" shows. Meanwhile, the interplay between Willson-Piper, Koppes, and Kilbey on their respective instruments remains strong, with many noted strong points: the dramatic, tense build of "Travel By Thought," the low-key combination on "Electric" bursting into keyboard-touched life on its choruses, and the quick, punchy "Dropping Names." *—Ned Raggett*

Remote Luxury / 1984 / Arista ✦✦✦✦
Collecting the contents of two separate EPs into a full-length album for American purposes, *Remote Luxury* actually makes for a reasonable release, avoiding the miserable drum sound that plagued *Séance.* The band are hardly so groansome, mixing the light synth touches evident on *Séance* with a tight, sharp postpunk groove. While the comparisons to bands like R.E.M. were sometimes stretched a bit, there's no denying the similar love of brisk, economic velocity which crops up on many of these songs, including the steady beat of "Violet Town" and the crisp flow on "Into My Hands." "No Explanation" perhaps fits the R.E.M. likeness best after a brief instrumental beginning, a shimmering, strummed gem with a great main melody. Kilbey again handles the vocals with his usual mix of low-key singing and sometimes clever, sometimes obscure lyrics, while the band as a whole keep things moving. Willson-Piper, who handles lead vocals for "10,000 Miles" and "Volumes," and Koppes by now show their excellent guitar abilities almost at every turn, their avoidance of pointless flash in favor of compelling hooks and a little extra shading when needed always coming through. "A Month of Sundays" and "Shadow Cabinet" are just two highlights of their abilities, beautiful and hummable all at once. An interesting if slightly atypical effort on the disc is "Maybe These Boys," with a relentless keyboard hook that almost sounds like a military fanfare leading into the full band performance, though with further keyboards still prominent. Kilbey's vocals are eventually contrasted with a Vocodered treatment of the same words, making for a strange, unsettling ending. *—Ned Raggett*

Heyday / 1986 / Arista ✦✦✦✦✦
Whether it was the assistance of Peter Walsh on production, a decision to bear down and see what could be done, or some further combination of that and other factors, the Church came up with its best release since *The Blurred Crusade* with the powerful *Heyday.* Not changing anything in the basic Church sound but presenting both a brilliant slew of songs and some fantastic performances, the quartet created a flat-out fantastic record. The first side alone almost reads like a greatest-hits collection, with one highlight following hard on the other. "Myrrh," leading things off with a careful build up to the main part of the song much like "When You Were Mine," has a strange chorus that almost shouldn't work but does. It's only two lines long and sung in harmony by the full band, all while Willson-Piper and Koppes' guitars keep things moving. "Tristesse" begins with a playful guitar line before shifting into another mid-paced, just dreamy enough effort. "Already Yesterday," with a fine, low-key backing choir, the dramatic "Columbus" and the gentle, string-touched instrumental "Happy Hunting Ground" continue the mood, one lovely moment after another. The second side kicks off with a barnstormer, "Tantalized," easily the band's most aggressive and upfront song since its earliest days. With horns and bells adding to the rushed feel, Kilbey delivers quickly sung verses and staccato choruses, the music continuing to soar along as Willson-Piper and Koppes turn in brilliant guitar work. Add to that further horn and string orchestrations on songs like the wistful "Youth Worshipper" and "Night of Light," and *Heyday* is a total success. *—Ned Raggett*

Starfish / 1988 / Arista ✦✦✦✦✦
Signing to Arista might have seemed an unusual move to start with, getting produced by L.A. studio types like Waddy Wachtel even more so. But for the Church the rewards were great—if sometimes too clean around the corners in comparison to the song-for-song masterpiece *Heyday, Starfish* set up the band's well-deserved breakthrough in the States. The reason was "Under the Milky Way," still one of the most haunting and elegant songs ever to make the Top 40. As Kilbey details a lyric of emotional distance and atmosphere, the band executes a quietly beautiful—and as is so often the case with the Church, astonishingly well-arranged—song, with mock bagpipes swirling through the mix for extra effect. That wasn't the only strong point on an album with more than a few; the lead-off track "Destination" was as strong an album opener as "Myrrh," if slower paced and much more mysterious, piano blending through the song's steady pace. The rest of the first side has its share of highlights, such as the quietly threatening edge of "Blood Money" and the confident, restrained charge of "North, South, East and West." Willson-Piper gets to lead off the second side with "Spark," a vicious, tight rocker that captures some of the best '60s rock edge and gives it a smart update. Equally strong is Kilbey's "Reptile," with an appropriately snaky guitar line and rhythm punch offset against weirdly soothing keyboards. Koppes has an okay vocal to his credit on "A New Season," but the stronger tracks are Kilbey's other contributions, the strong guitar waltz of "Antenna" (with great guest mandolin from David Lindley) and the closing charge (and very Church-like title) of "Hotel Womb." Performances throughout are at the least fine and at the most fantastic. *—Ned Raggett*

Gold Afternoon Fix / Feb. 1990 / Arista ✦✦✦

Priest Aura / Mar. 10, 1992 / Arista ✦✦✦✦

Sometime Anywhere / May 24, 1994 / Arista ✦✦✦✦

● **Under the Milky Way: The Best of the Church** / Sep. 28, 1999 / Buddha ✦✦✦✦✦
Buddha's *Under the Milky Way: Best of the Church* is a terrific, comprehensive anthology, tracing their career from their 1981 debut *Of Skin and Heart* to 1994's *Sometime Anywhere.* Some hardcore fans may notice some personal favorites missing, but all their best-known songs—"The Unguarded Moment," "Tear it All Away," "Month of Sundays," "Myrrh," "Under the Milky Way," "Reptile," "Metropolis," "Ripple"—are here, along with an excellent, representative sampling of album tracks. It's an ideal record for casual fans, along with being a great introduction for the curious and neophytes. *—Stephen Thomas Erlewine*

Cibo Matto

f. 1994, New York, NY
Group / Shibuya-Kei, Alternative Dance, Indie Rock, Trip-Hop, Alternative Pop/Rock
A Japanese-born duo relocated to New York and christened with an Italian band name, Cibo Matto's music mirrored the melting-pot aesthetics of their origins, resulting in a heady brew of funk samples, hip-hop rhythms, tape loops and fractured pop melodies all topped off by surreal narratives sung in a combination of French and broken English. Cibo Matto comprised vocalist Miho Hatori and keyboardist/sampler Yuka Honda, a pair of expatriate Japanese women who arrived in the U.S. independently: After meeting in 1994, they first teamed in the Boredoms-inspired noise outfit Leitoh Lychee (translated as "frozen lychee nut"); after that band's breakup, the duo formed Cibo Matto, Italian for "food madness" (their love of culinary delights quickly becoming the stuff of legend). After a pair of acclaimed 1995 independent singles, "Birthday Cake" and "Know Your Chicken," Cibo Matto signed to Warner Bros., surfacing in 1996 with *Viva! La Woman,* a delirious, stunningly inventive record celebrating love, food, and love of food. The EP *Super Relax* followed in 1997; bassist Sean Lennon, percussionist Duma Love and drummer Timo Ellis were installed as full-time members for the follow-up, 1999's *Stereotype A. —Jason Ankeny*

● **Viva! La Woman** / Jan. 16, 1996 / Warner Brothers ✦✦✦✦✦
Fresh and funky, female and Japanese, the trip-hop/rap duo Cibo Matto has been the recipient of a lot of hype. Fortunately, it's well-founded; all trendiness aside, *Viva! La Woman* is an innovative and catchy mix of eclectic samples and stream-of-consciousness lyrics. The likes of Paul Weller, Ennio Morricone, and Duke Ellington combine with observations like "My weight is three hundred pounds/my favorite is beef jerky" (from "Beef Jerky") and "Shut up and eat! You know my love is sweet!" from ("Birthday Cake") in a fun and refreshing way. The tone of the album varies with each song; on tracks like "Sugar Water" and "Artichoke," Cibo Matto plays it spooky and ethereal, while "Birthday Cake" and the single "Know Your Chicken" find them as a couple of cryptic Beastie Girls, tossing off wacky non sequiturs over found soundscapes. Cibo Matto cooks up a tasty appetizer of their talent with *Viva! La Woman.* Like their tongue-in-cheek cover of "The Candy Man," Cibo Matto makes everything they bake satisfying and delicious. A diverse and entertaining album, *Viva! La Woman* leaves the listener hungry for more of their crazy food for thought. *—Heather Phares*

Super Relax / Jan. 28, 1997 / Warner Brothers ✦✦✦✦

Stereo Type A / Jun. 8, 1999 / Warner Brothers ✦✦✦
Cibo Matto's eagerly anticipated second album, *Stereo Type A,* reflects growth and change in the band's lineup and sound. Joining the core duo of Yuka Honda and Miho Hatori are new band member Sean Lennon and guests like Arto Lindsay, Caetano Veloso, Sebastian Steinberg of Soul Coughing, and John Medeski and Billy Martin of Medeski, Martin & Wood. The new additions reflect the changing sound of Cibo Matto: Relying less on samples and more on their latent funk and jazz elements, *Stereotype A* sounds like summer in New York—eclec-

tic, hot, and funky. Hatori's vocals are her most fluid and assured yet, and Honda's harmonies, particularly on "Moonchild," add a dreamy undercurrent to the sound. Though the hip-hop of "Sci-Fi Wasabi" and filmic quality of "Spoon" (which originally appeared on the *Super Relax* EP) hearken back to old-school Cibo Matto, *Stereotype A*'s overall sound is more direct and less fanciful than of their debut album *Viva! La Woman*. Tracks like "Clouds" and "Morning" reflect a nice fusion of the group's old and new sounds, while the brassy "Speechless" and thrash metal of "Blue Train" round out a delightfully sunny collection from this diverse group. *—Heather Phares*

Eric Clapton (Eric Patrick Clapp)

b. Mar. 30, 1945, Ripley, England

Vocals, Guitar (Electric), Guitar / Album Rock, British Blues, Pop/Rock, Adult Contemporary, Hard Rock, Blues-Rock

By the time Eric Clapton launched his solo career with the release of his self-titled debut album in August 1970, he was long established as one of the world's major rock stars due to his group affiliations—the Yardbirds, John Mayall's Bluesbreakers, Cream, and Blind Faith—affiliations that had demonstrated his claim to being the best rock guitarist of his generation. That it took Clapton so long to go out on his own, however, was evidence of a degree of reticence unusual for one of his stature. And his debut album, though it spawned the Top 40 hit "After Midnight," was typical of his self-effacing approach: It was, in effect, an album by the group he had lately been featured in, Delaney & Bonnie & Friends. Clapton did not launch a sustained solo career until July 1974, when he released *461 Ocean Boulevard*, which topped the charts and spawned the number one single "I Shot the Sheriff." The persona Clapton established over the next decade was less that of guitar hero than arena rock star with a weakness for ballads. *Slowhand* (November 1977), which featured both the powerful "Cocaine" (written by J.J. Cale, who had also written "After Midnight") and the hit singles "Lay Down Sally" and "Wonderful Tonight," was a million-seller, and its follow-ups were all big sellers. Clapton's popularity waned somewhat in the first half of the '80s, but he was buoyed up by the release of the boxed set retrospective *Crossroads* (April 1988), which seemed to remind his fans of how great he was. On March 20, 1991, Clapton's four-year-old son was killed in a fall. While he mourned, he prepared a movie soundtrack, *Rush* (January 1992). The soundtrack featured a song written for his son, "Tears in Heaven," that became a massive hit single. In March 1992, Clapton recorded a concert for *MTV Unplugged* that, when released on an album in August, became his biggest-selling record ever. Two years later, Clapton returned with a blues album, *From the Cradle*, which became one of his most successful albums, both commerically and critically. *—William Ruhlmann*

Eric Clapton / Jul. 1970 / Polydor ✦✦✦✦✦

Eric Clapton's eponymous solo debut was recorded after he completed a tour with Delaney & Bonnie. Clapton used the core of the duo's backing band and co-wrote the majority of the songs with Delaney Bramlett—accordingly, *Eric Clapton* sounds more laidback and straightforward than any of the guitarist's previous recordings. There are still elements of blues and rock & roll, but they're hidden beneath layers of gospel, R&B, country, and pop flourishes. And the pop element of the record is the strongest of the album's many elements—"Blues Power" isn't a blues song and only "Let It Rain," the album's closer, features extended solos. Throughout the album, Clapton turns out concise solos that de-emphasize his status as guitar god, even when they display astonishing musicality and technique. That is both a good and a bad thing—it's encouraging to hear him grow and become a more fully rounded musician, but too often the album needs the spark that some long guitar solos would have given it. In short, it needs a little more of Clapton's personality. *—Stephen Thomas Erlewine*

461 Ocean Boulevard / Jul. 1974 / Polydor ✦✦✦✦✦

461 Ocean Boulevard is Eric Clapton's second studio solo album, arriving after his side project of Derek & the Dominos and a long struggle with heroin addiction. Although there are some new reggae influences, the album doesn't sound all that different from the rock, pop, blues, country, and R&B amalgam of *Eric Clapton*. However, *461 Ocean Boulevard* is a tighter, more focused outing that enables Clapton to stretch out instrumentally. Furthermore, the pop concessions on the album—the sleek production, the concise running times—don't detract from the rootsy origins of the material, whether it's Johnny Otis' "Willie and the Hand Jive," the traditional blues "Motherless Children," Bob Marley's "I Shot the Sheriff," or Clapton's emotional originals, "Let It Grow" and "Better Make It Through Today" (the latter included only on several reissues of the album). With its relaxed, friendly atmosphere and strong bluesy roots, *461 Ocean Boulevard* set the template for Clapton's '70s albums. Though he tried hard to make an album exactly like it, he never quite managed to replicate its charms. *—Stephen Thomas Erlewine*

There's One in Every Crowd / Mar. 1975 / Polydor ✦✦

E.C. Was Here / Aug. 1975 / Polydor ✦✦✦

No Reason to Cry / Aug. 1976 / Polydor ✦✦✦

Slowhand / Nov. 1977 / Polydor ✦✦✦✦✦

After the guest-star-drenched *No Reason to Cry* failed to make much of an impact commercially, Eric Clapton returned to using his own band for *Slowhand*. The difference is substantial—where *No Reason to Cry* struggled hard to find the right tone, *Slowhand* opens with the relaxed, bluesy shuffle of J.J. Cale's "Cocaine" and sustains it throughout the course of the album. Alternating between straight blues ("Mean Old Frisco"), country ("Lay Down Sally"), mainstream rock ("Cocaine," "The Core"), and pop ("Wonderful Tonight"), *Slowhand* doesn't sound schizophrenic because of the band's grasp of the material. This is laid-back virtuosity—although Clapton and his band are never flashy, their playing is masterful and assured. That assurance and the album's eclectic material make *Slowhand* rank with *461 Ocean Boulevard* as Eric Clapton's best album. *—Stephen Thomas Erlewine*

Backless / Nov. 1978 / Polydor ✦✦✦

Having made his best album since *461 Ocean Boulevard* with *Slowhand*, Eric Clapton followed with *Backless*, which took the same authoritative, no-nonsense approach. If it wasn't quite the masterpiece, or the sales monster, that *Slowhand* had been, this probably was because of that usual Clapton problem—material. Once again, he returned to those Oklahoma hills for another song from J.J. Cale, but "I'll Make Love to You Anytime" wasn't quite up to "Cocaine" or "After Midnight." Bob Dylan contributed two songs, but you could see why he hadn't saved them for his own album, and Clapton's own writing contributions were mediocre. Clapton did earn a Top Ten hit with Richard Feldman and Roger Linn's understated pop shuffle "Promises," but it was not one of his more memorable recordings. Of course, Clapton's blues playing on the lone obligatory blues cut, "Early in the Morning" (presented in its full eight-minute version on the CD reissue), was stellar. (*Backless* was his last album to feature the backup group that had been with him since 1974.) *—William Ruhlmann*

Just One Night / Apr. 1980 / Polydor ✦✦✦✦✦

Although Eric Clapton has released a bevy of live albums, none of them have ever quite captured the guitarist's raw energy and dazzling virtuosity. The double-live album *Just One Night* may have gotten closer to that elusive goal than most of its predecessors, but it is still lacking in many ways. The most notable difference between *Just One Night* and Clapton's other live albums is his backing band. Led by guitarist Albert Lee, the group is a collective of accomplished professionals that have managed to keep some grit in their playing. They help push Clapton along, forcing him to spit out crackling solos throughout the album. However, the performances aren't consistent on *Just One Night*—there are plenty of dynamic moments like "Double Trouble" and "Rambling on My Mind," but they are weighed down by pedestrian renditions of songs like "All Our Past Times." Nevertheless, more than any other Clapton live album, *Just One Night* suggests the guitarist's in-concert potential. It's just too bad that the recording didn't occur on a night when he *did* fulfill all of that potential. *—Stephen Thomas Erlewine*

Another Ticket / Feb. 1981 / Polydor ✦✦✦

Time Pieces: Best of Eric Clapton / May 1982 / Polydor ✦✦✦✦✦

Time Pieces is a good single-disc collection of Eric Clapton's solo hits—including "I Shot the Sheriff," "After Midnight," "Wonderful Tonight," Derek & the Dominos' "Layla," and "Cocaine"—that has since been supplanted by the more thorough *The Cream of Eric Clapton*, which combines his solo work with selections of his Cream and Blind Faith work. Nevertheless, the compilation still provides a good introduction for neophyte Clapton fans, especially those that just want copies of his '70s hits. *—Stephen Thomas Erlewine*

Money and Cigarettes / Feb. 1983 / Reprise ✦✦✦✦

Time Pieces, Vol. 2: Live in the '70s / 1985 / Polydor ✦✦✦

Behind the Sun / Mar. 1985 / Reprise ✦✦✦

August / Nov. 1986 / Reprise ✦✦

☆ **Crossroads** / Apr. 1988 / Polydor ✦✦✦✦✦

A four-disc box set spanning Eric Clapton's entire career—running from the Yardbirds to his '80s solo recordings—*Crossroads* not only revitalized Clapton's commerical standing, but it established the rock & roll multi-disc box set retrospective as a commercially viable proposition. Bob Dylan's *Biograph* was successful two years before the release of *Crossroads*, but Clapton's set was a bonafide blockbuster. And it's easy to see why. *Crossroads* manages to sum up Clapton's career succinctly and thoroughly, touching upon all of his hits and adding a bevy of first-rate unreleased material (most notably selections from the scrapped second Derek & the Dominos album). Although not all of his greatest performances are included on the set—none of his work as a session musician or guest artist is included, for instance—every truly essential item he recorded is present on these four discs. No other Clapton album accurately explains why the guitarist was so influential, or demonstrates exactly what he accomplished. *—Stephen Thomas Erlewine*

Journeyman / Nov. 1989 / Reprise ✦✦✦✦✦

For most of the '80s, Eric Clapton seemed rather lost, uncertain of whether he should return to his blues roots or pander to AOR radio. By the mid-'80s, he appeared to have made the decision to revamp himself as a glossy mainstream rocker, working with synthesizers and drum machines. Instead of expanding his audience, it only reduced it. Then came the career retrospective *Crossroads*, which helped revitalize his career, not only commercially, but also creatively, as *Journeyman*—the first album he recorded after the success of *Crossroads*—proved. Although *Journeyman* still suffers from an overly slick production, Clapton sounds more convincing than he has since the early '70s. Not only is his guitar playing muscular and forceful, his singing is soulful and gritty. Furthermore, the songwriting is consistently strong, alternating between fine mainstream rock originals ("Pretending") and covers ("Before You Accuse Me," "Hound Dog"). Like any of Clapton's best albums, there is no grandstanding to be found on *Journeyman*—it's simply a laidback and thoroughly engaging display of Clapton's virtuosity. On the whole, it's the best studio album he's released since *Slowhand*. *—Stephen Thomas Erlewine*

24 Nights / Oct. 8, 1991 / Reprise ✦✦✦

Unplugged / Aug. 18, 1992 / Reprise ✦✦✦✦✦

Clapton's *Unplugged* was responsible for making acoustic-based music, and *Unplugged* albums in particular, a hot trend in the early '90s. Clapton's concert was not only one of the finest *Unplugged* episodes, but was also some of the finest music he had recorded in years. Instead of the slick productions that tainted his '80s albums, the music was straightforward and direct, alternating between his pop numbers and traditional blues songs. The result was some of the most genuine, heartfelt music the guitarist has ever committed to tape. And some of his most popular—the album sold over seven million copies in the U.S. and won several Grammies. *—Stephen Thomas Erlewine*

From the Cradle / Sep. 13, 1994 / Reprise ✦✦✦✦✦

For years, fans craved an all-blues album from Clapton; he waited until 1994 to deliver *From the Cradle*. The album manages to recreate the ambience of postwar electric blues, right down to the bottomless thump of the rhythm section. If it wasn't for Clapton's labored vocals, everything would be perfect. As long as he plays his guitar, he can't fail—his solos are white-hot and evocative, original and captivating. When he sings, Clapton loses that sense of originality, choosing to mimic the vocals of the original recordings. At times, his overemotive singing is painful; he doesn't have the strength to pull off Howlin' Wolf's growl or the confidence to replicate Muddy Waters' assured phrasing. Yet, whenever he plays, it's easier to forget his vocal shortcomings. Even with its faults, *From the Cradle* is one of Clapton's finest moments. *—Stephen Thomas Erlewine*

● **The Cream of Clapton** / Mar. 7, 1995 / Polydor ✦✦✦✦✦
Eric Clapton was contracted to Polydor Records from 1966 to 1981, first as a member of Cream, then Blind Faith, and later as a solo artist and as the leader of Derek and the Dominos. This 19-track, 79-minute disc surveys his career, presenting an excellent selection from the period, including the Cream hits "Sunshine of Your Love," "White Room," and "Crossroads"; "Presence of the Lord," Clapton's finest moment with Blind Faith; "Bell Bottom Blues" and "Layla" from Derek and the Dominos; and 11 songs from Clapton's solo work, among them the hits "I Shot The Sheriff," "Promises," and "I Can't Stand It." The selection is thus broader and better than that found on 1982's *Time Pieces* collection, and with excellent sound and liner notes by Clapton biographer Ray Coleman, *The Cream of Clapton* stands as the single-disc best-of to own for Clapton's greatest recordings. (Not to be confused with the popular 1987 Polydor [U.K.] compilation *The Cream of Eric Clapton*, which has since been retitled *The Best of Eric Clapton*.) *—William Ruhlmann*

Eric Clapton's Rainbow Concert [Expanded] / Jul. 25, 1995 / Polydor ✦✦✦
In these days of CD expansion, it is not unusual for a record company to reissue an old album with a bonus track or two. This reconstruction of the January 13, 1973, comeback concert by Eric Clapton is something else again, however. The original six-track LP ran less than 27 minutes; the new 14-track CD runs almost 74 minutes. The eight additions—"Layla," "Blues Power," "Bottle of Red Wine," "Bell Bottom Blues," "Tell the Truth," "Key to the Highway," "Let It Rain," and "Crossroads"—make the disc an effective recapitulation of Clapton's career over the previous seven years, including his solo work and his appearances with John Mayall's Bluesbreakers, Cream, and Derek and the Dominos. Despite the addiction that had kept him largely homebound for almost two years, Clapton played well, though the all-star backup band was as ragged as it was spirited. The loose feel of the evening was brought out in the stage announcements, many by Pete Townshend, who even mentioned a social disease just before introducing "Presence of the Lord." This still isn't a great Eric Clapton show, but it has been transformed from a historical curiosity to a historical document. *—William Ruhlmann*

Crossroads 2: Live in the Seventies / Apr. 2, 1996 / Polydor Chronicles ✦✦✦

Pilgrim / Mar. 10, 1998 / Reprise ✦✦

Clapton Chronicles: Best of 1981-1999 / Oct. 12, 1999 / Reprise ✦✦✦✦
Clapton Chronicles ignores Clapton's 1983 Reprise debut, *Money and Cigarettes* (which sounded more like an RSO album, anyway), starting with the pair of Phil Collins-produced mid-'80s albums, *Behind the Sun* and *August*. Though these had a pop sheen, they were album-rock holdovers. Clapton didn't get the balance between hard rock and commercial gloss right until 1989's *Journeyman*, whose featured songs—"Before You Accuse Me," "Bad Love," and "Pretending"—form the heart of this compilation. *Journeyman* was overshadowed by the phenomenal success of "Tears in Heaven" and 1992's *Unplugged*. Not only did *Unplugged* go platinum ten times, it established a new public image—classy, stylish, and substantial. That's the image that prevails on *Clapton Chronicles*. His triple-platinum blues album *From the Cradle* is written out of the picture, with songs from movie soundtracks taking its place. Apart from the Babyface-produced "Change the World," these tunes are a little too self-conscious and subdued, as are selections from 1998's *Pilgrim*. However, this deliberate move to paint Clapton's '80s and '90s recordings as adult-contemporary fare is accurate. Clapton's musical journey from 1985 to 1999 was taken mostly in the middle of the road, and *Clapton Chronicles* certainly captures that journey, missing no major hits from the late '80s and '90s. Whether it's a necessary addition to a Clapton collection is a matter of taste. It's certainly an excellent compliment to *Unplugged* and *Time Pieces*, his two most popular and pop-oriented albums, but that might not be what every fan wants. *—Stephen Thomas Erlewine*

Riding with the King / Jun. 13, 2000 / Reprise ✦✦✦✦
The potential for a collaboration between B.B. King and Eric Clapton is enormous, of course, and the real questions concern how it is organized and executed. This first recorded pairing between the 74-year-old King and the 55-year-old Clapton was put together in the most obvious way: Clapton arranged the session using many of his regular musicians, picked the songs, and co-produced with his partner Simon Climie. That ought to mean that King would be a virtual guest star rather than earning a co-billing, but because of Clapton's respect for his elder, it nearly works the other way around. The set list includes lots of King specialties—"Ten Long Years," "Three O'Clock Blues," "Days of Old," "When My Heart Beats Like a Hammer"—as well as standards like "Hold on I'm Coming" and "Come Rain or Come Shine," with some specially written and appropriate recent material thrown in, so King has reason to be comfortable without being complacent. The real danger is that Clapton will defer too much; though he can be inspired by a competing guitarist such as Duane Allman, he has sometimes tended to lean too heavily on accompanists such as Albert Lee and Mark Knopfler when working with them in concert. That danger is partially realized; as its title indicates, *Riding With the King* is more about King than it is about Clapton. But the two players turn out to have sufficiently complementary, if distinct, styles that Clapton's supportive role fills out and surrounds King's stinging single-string playing. (It's also worth noting that there are usually another two or three guitarists on each track.) The result is an effective, if never really stunning, work. *—William Ruhlmann*

The Dave Clark Five

f. 1961, Tottenham, London, England, **db.** 1970
Group / British Invasion
For a very brief time in 1964, it seemed that the biggest challenger to the Beatles phenomenon was the Dave Clark Five. The quintet had the fortune to knock "I Want to Hold Your Hand" off the top of the British charts with "Glad All Over," and were championed (for about 15 minutes) by the British press as the Beatles' most serious threat. They were the first British Invasion band to break in a big way in the States after the Beatles, though the Rolling Stones and others quickly supplanted the DC5 as the Fab Four's most serious rivals. The Dave Clark Five reached the Top 40 seventeen times between 1964 and 1967 with memorable hits like "Glad All Over," "Bits and Pieces," "Because," and a remake of Bobby Day's "Over and Over," as well as making more appearances on *The Ed Sullivan Show* than any other English act. The DC5 were distinguished from their British contemporaries by their larger-than-life production, Clark's loud stomping drum sound, and Mike Smith's leathery vocals. Though accused by detractors of lacking finesse and hipness, they had a solid ear for melodies and harmonies, and wrote much of their early material, the best of which has endured quite well, although their albums were fairly weak. *—Rick Clark & Richie Unterberger*

● **History of the Dave Clark Five** / Aug. 3, 1993 / Hollywood ✦✦✦✦✦
For many years, the Dave Clark Five were one of the few major groups of the 1960s whose work was unavailable on compact disc. This two-disc, 50-track reissue not only rectifies that situation but arguably includes more than all but devoted fans will want to hear. All of the band's mammoth mid-'60s hits —"Glad All Over," "Bits and Pieces," "Because," "Catch Us If You Can," "Any Way You Want It," and others—are included, and while they don't rival the work of British Invasion heavyweights like the Beatles, Stones, and Kinks, they still burst with exuberant melodies, harmonies, and dense production. This compilation also features worthy lesser-known hits like "Try Too Hard" and "Everybody Knows," as well as obscure but commendable beat ballads and raveups from their B-sides and albums. Nonetheless, there is a fair amount of filler, and their post-1966 work is undistinguished by either artistic growth or the hooks and heavy beat of their early material. But at their peak, the DC5 captured the joie de vivre of the British Invasion with a lasting power that cannot be dismissed. This reissue includes a comprehensive booklet featuring recollections from Dave Clark himself. *—Richie Unterberger*

Dee Clark (Delecta Clark)

b. Nov. 7, 1938, Blythesville, AR, **d.** Dec. 7, 1990, Smyrna, GA
Vocals / R&B, Soul
Dee Clark was a solid R&B vocalist who had some huge hits in the late '50s and early '60s. The Arkansas-born singer moved to Chicago as a child and was in the Hambone Kids with Sammy McGrier and Ronny Strong. They recorded for Okeh in 1952; the next year Clark sang with the Goldentones. This group later became the Kool Gents, then recorded as the Delegates for Vee-Jay in 1956. Clark went solo in 1957 and in 1958 enjoyed his first smash with "Nobody for You," an Abner release that reached number three R&B and just missed the Top 20 on the pop charts. He continued a string of R&B winners with "Just Keep It Up," "Hey Little Girl," and "How About That" for Abner in 1959 and 1960. Clark teamed with guitarist Phil Upchurch to write "Raindrops" in 1961, his signature tune. The song peaked at number three R&B and number two pop, and was his last major hit. Clark continued performing through the '60s,'70s, and '80s, but never again was a factor, though "Raindrops" remains a staple on oldies radio. *—Ron Wynn*

● **Rain Drops** / 1994 / Vee-Jay ✦✦✦✦✦
Dee Clark was one of the most adaptable R&B vocalists of the '50s and early '60s, as this 25-song reissue shows. He did songs in a Little Richard mode, an Afro-Latin setting, and also performed ballads, novelty tunes ("Kangaroo Hop"), and covers ("Cupid"). Clark's gem was "Raindrops," a song with enough drama, hooks, and appeal to nearly top both the pop and R&B charts. It was his biggest hit, but not his only fine number. There are many cuts, such as "Nobody but You," "What Kind of Fool," and the newly issued "Bring Back My Heart," that equal or even top the tune that made him famous. *—Ron Wynn*

Golden Classics / Nov. 5, 1996 / Collectables ✦✦✦✦
Not exactly a greatest-hits package, but an interesting blend of three of Dee's biggest hits on Vee-Jay (a nice stereo mix of "Raindrops" kicks things off) with a generous helping of his later sides for Constellation. These sides capture Clark moving toward a proto-soul style, with tracks like "Crossfire Time," "I'm Going Home," "Warm Summer Breezes," and "Heartbreak" showing the depth of Clark's vocal range on ballads, soul grinders, and jazz-tinged material. Lots of great Vee-Jay sides MIA on this, but a nice companion once you track the earlier sides down. *—Cub Koda*

Take Care of Business / Aug. 11, 1998 / West Side ✦✦✦
Subtitled "The Constellation Masters, 1963-1966," and this picks up the second phase of Clark's solo career after his hit-making days at Vee-Jay. These sides find him moving in a more soulful direction, making hard Southern and Motown-inflected soul with the best of them on "Crossfire Time," "I'm Going Home," "Come Closer" and "That's My Girl." Although material like "Heartbreak," "I Ain't Gonna Be a Fool," "Warm Summer Breezes," and "I Don't Need (Nobody Like You)" were top-flight, Clark couldn't score a hit during his three years with Constellation chronicled here. But the lack of hits still yields a 17-track feast of brand-name mid-'60s Chicago soul music, played and sung with a professional flair that's unmistakably Dee Clark. Other highlights include "T.C.B.," "She's My Baby," "Hot Potato" and a live two-part workout on "Nobody But You" that makes a fitting closer to this set. *—Cub Koda*

Gene Clark (Harold Eugene Clark)

b. Nov. 17, 1944, Tipton, MO, **d.** May 24, 1991, Sherman Oaks, CA
Vocals, Guitar / Folk-Rock, Singer/Songwriter, Country-Rock, Progressive Bluegrass
Very few musicians had as much influence in creating new styles of music as Gene Clark. As co-founder of the Byrds, he helped pioneer what was to become known as folk-rock. Clark and Bob Dylan were the most prolific songwriters of the genre. After leaving the group, he and banjoist Doug Dillard invented newgrass, a progressive blend of traditional bluegrass instrumentation augmented by electronics, drums, piano and even harpsichord. The fusion of country and rock on Clark's first solo album predated the Byrds' *Sweetheart of the Rodeo* by nearly two years and the first Flying Burrito Brothers album by three years. A member of the New Christy Minstrels as early as 1962, Clark later moved to Los Angeles and formed

the Byrds though he left the group in 1966 to pursue a solo career on *Gene Clark with the Gosdin Brothers* in 1967. The following year *The Fantastic Expedition of Dillard and Clark* heralded the dawning of newgrass. Two solo albums followed, *White Light* and *Roadmaster* (the latter featured the original Byrds on two tracks and foreshadowed a brief Byrds reformation). Clark recorded two more solo albums in the '70s, then joined Roger McGuinn and Chris Hillman for two albums as McGuinn, Clark and Hillman. He died in 1991, just a few short months after he and the Byrds were inducted into the Rock and Roll Hall of Fame. *—Dan Pavlides*

Echoes / 1967 / Columbia/Legacy ♦♦♦♦♦
This is Gene Clark's debut album, *Gene Clark & The Gosdin Brothers.* The Byrds comparison is really unavoidable: it's both Clark's best solo work, and not coincidentally, the one which resembles The Byrds most strongly. Indeed, this could easily pass for a somewhat less-than-average vintage Byrds album, with actual Byrds Chris Hillman and Michael Clarke forming the rhythm section, and Vern and Rex Gosdin on guitar (hence the title). To be brutal, it doesn't measure up to Clark's best songs from his Byrds days, but it's fairly strong, melodic '60s folk-rock nonetheless, perhaps with a bit of a more countrified, laidback, generic feel. "So You Say You Lost Your Baby," "Echoes," and especially "Tried So Hard" are standouts. The CD adds three interesting previously unreleased outtakes from the era, as well as six of the best early Byrds songs graced by Clark's songwriting and vocals. *—Richie Unterberger*

Gene Clark with the Gosdin Brothers / 1967 / Edsel ♦♦♦♦
The first album that Gene Clark released after his departure from the Byrds followed very closely on the model of his earlier efforts on the Byrds' first two albums. His backing musicians included ex-bandmates Chris Hillman and Michael Clarke, as well as future Byrd Clarence White and Clark collaborator Doug Dillard; not to mention the Gosdin brothers, whose harmonies resembled a rockier Everly Brothers and brought the sound very close to the Byrds'. The album contains a number of fine pop-oriented tunes and stellar folk-rock/country-rock numbers (a year before the Byrds' *Sweetheart of the Rodeo,* which employed both White and Dillard) and established Gene Clark as a major songwriter, rivaling his old band and often coming close to the fabness of the Beatles. Still, despite such solid songs and backing musicians, *Gene Clark With the Gosdin Brothers* failed to make much of an impact, perhaps due to its being released in the same week as the Byrds' *Younger Than Yesterday,* itself a *tour de force* that cemented their influence. However, in the realm of Clark's recorded output, this album stands as the one of the best, if not the best, example of how powerful a singer, writer, and bandleader Gene Clark was. *—Alex Stimmel*

Roadmaster / 1972 / Demon ♦♦♦♦♦
Gene Clark, record business bad news. Case in point, this album. Or masterpiece, you could say. After two brilliant Dillard & Clark albums, A&M signed Clark to a solo deal. Okay, fair enough—so far. In 1972, he delivered perhaps the finest album of his career, *Gene Clark,* (also known as *White Light*). Excellent reviews in all the top magazines, including *Rolling Stone.* Guess what? Almost zero sales. Now, here's the follow up, almost—if not more—brilliant. Released only in Holland. Aside from containing some of Clark's finest tracks like "In a Misty Morning" and "Full Circle Song," this record contains two gems recorded with the willing participation of the other original Byrds. "One in a Hundred" and "She's the Kind of Girl" are so good that they would have easily stood out on *The Byrds* box set, had McGuinn elected to include them. Oh well, the music is still here—an example of an artist who couldn't quite get in on with commerce. What a disaster. The man should be mentioned in the same breath as Neil Young. *Roadmaster* is one of the many reasons why. *—Matthew Greenwald*

White Light / 1972 / A&M ♦♦♦♦♦

No Other / 1974 / Line ♦♦♦

Firebyrd / 1987 / Takoma ♦♦♦

American Dreamer / Feb. 11, 1997 / Raven ♦♦♦♦♦
Kudos to Australia's Raven for assembling this fine 24-track overview of Gene's most fertile period. Included are three Clark-penned Byrds stunners, two of the best from his first solo album, six from the Dillard and Clark albums (the Velvet Crush-covered "Why Not Your Baby" is unfortunately overlooked), a Flying Burritos-backed gem, two ersatz Byrds-reunion cuts from *Road Master,* a whopping six from *White Light,* "Full Circle" from the otherwise tepid 1973 Byrds reunion, and two selections from *No Other* (though not the This Mortal Coil-covered "Strength of Strings"). An interesting early mix of "Full Circle" is included as a bonus. For the uninitiated, this is a great place to start, but even a fanatic will be pleased by the inclusion of the hard-to-find *White Light* cuts and Sid Griffin's fannish liner notes. *—Michael Ribas*

● **Flying High** / 1998 / A&M ♦♦♦♦♦
When someone mentions the Byrds in conversation, the names of McGuinn, Crosby, and maybe Hillman pop up, but hardly anyone mentions Gene Clark, the Byrds' first original songwriter and lead singer until a fear of flying caused him to leave the band and strike out on his own. With *Flying High,* all of that should be put to rest, because the spotlight is finally on Clark and his many contributions to both rock and country. Starting with Byrds cuts like "Feel a Whole Lot Better" and "She Don't Care About Time," this two-disc set moves through Clark's early solo career into his fine collaboration with Doug Dillard on to more mature solo work while attempting to reunite the Byrds on "One In a Million" and "She's the Kind of Girl," which never quite got off the ground. Added here are some otherwise unreleased cuts, such as "Winter In," "That's Alright By Me" and Dylan's "I Pity the Poor Immigrant," which show that Clark had more talent than was released to the public in his lifetime. And while disc two does have waning interest and fewer cuts, it does show that Clark never gave up on trying to restart his career, even if the chips appeared to be down; of special note is his sensitive cover of Phil Ochs' "Changes." Compiled and reproduced for disc by Sid Griffin, *Flying High* is a fine spotlight on an underappreciated artist. With liner notes by Griffin and Chris Hillman, this has just about everything one needs to know about Gene Clark. *—James Chrispell*

Petula Clark

b. Nov. 15, 1932, Epsom, England
Vocals / Sunshine Pop, British Invasion, Pop
The most commercially successful female singer in British chart history, Petula Clark embarked on a stage career at the age of seven, began hosting her own radio show four years later and made her film debut soon after. By the dawn of the 1950s she was a superstar throughout the UK, with a Top 20 single by 1954 and her first chart-topper, "Sailor," in 1960. Riding the wave of the British Invasion, Clark was finally able to penetrate the US market in 1964 with the Grammy-winning "Downtown," the first single by a British woman ever to reach number one on the American pop charts. It was also the first in a series of American Top Ten hits (most written and arranged by Tony Hatch) which also included "I Know a Place," "I Couldn't Live Without Your Love" and the number one smash "My Love." In addition to hosting her own BBC series, she also starred in the 1968 NBC television special *Petula.* As the 1960s drew to a close, Clark's commercial stature slipped. In 1968 she revived her film career by starring in *Finian's Rainbow,* followed a year later by *Goodbye, Mr. Chips.* In later years Clark focused primarily on international touring and her stage career. *—Jason Ankeny*

The Classic Collection / Mar. 23, 1999 / Pulse/Castle ♦♦♦♦♦
Four-CD, 80-song box set of Clark's '60s material contains all of her big U.S. and U.K. hits, numerous singles that were only hits in other countries (usually France), and a bunch of interesting covers, B-sides, and LP tracks, some quite rare. If you're enough of a fan to want more than what you'll find on the usual thorough hits anthology, but not enough of a fan to want everything she ever did, this is perfect. It's got all of the classics, serviceable (although not terribly extensive) liner notes, and a host of interesting items that aren't well-known. These include a 1963 version of "Please Please Me" (sung in French) that was most likely one of the very first Lennon-McCartney covers; a French-sung cover of "Nobody I Know," the Lennon-McCartney tune never done by the Beatles, although Peter & Gordon had a hit with it; the original versions of "I Will Follow Him" (in English and French), covered for a chart-topper by Little Peggy March in the U.S.; yet another French-sung British Invasion cover, of the Kinks' "Well Respected Man," that was a hit in Canada; and "You're the One" (covered for a hit by the Vogues in the States). Best of all is the mid-'60s B-side "Heart" (covered by the Remains in America), a Clark original that's her hardest-rocking cut, and proof that she could muster the energy to sing rock & roll convincingly on occasion. *—Richie Unterberger*

● **Downtown: The Greatest Hits of Petula Clark** / Oct. 12, 1999 / Buddha ♦♦♦♦♦
Although it's a little skimpy at 12 tracks—especially compared with GNP's import *The Greatest Hits of Petula Clark,* which features 16 cuts—Buddha's *Downtown: The Greatest Hits of Petula Clark* is nevertheless an excellent, concise chronicle of her peak hit-making years. All of her American Top Ten hits are here—"Downtown," "I Know a Place," "My Love," "I Couldn't Live Without Your Love," "This Is My Song," "Don't Sleep in the Subway"—plus the majority of her Top 40 singles, including "You'd Better Come Home," "A Sign of the Times," "Colour My World," "Kiss Me Goodbye," and "Who Am I?" They've all been perfectly remastered, sounding clean and vibrant, yet still of their era. All of this makes *Downtown* an ideal choice for most fans, especially casual listeners. It may not be as comprehensive as some collections, but it's concise, delivering everything you need in terrific sound. *—Stephen Thomas Erlewine*

Anthology: Downtown to Sunset Boulevard / Feb. 15, 2000 / Uptown/Universal ♦♦♦♦♦
Here's a two-disc set of every last great Petula Clark side you'll need for a collection. Truly an anthology, this includes all of the hits and rarities that make up an artist's career, taking it right through to present time 2000. It's all big-band pop appended with strident rock & roll beats; the best songs are immediately recognizable and immensely hummable. Clark wrote her own notes for the inside booklet, commenting on each of the 41 songs included. As the best bang for your buck, this is the one to get. *—Cub Koda*

The Clash

f. 1976, London, England, **db.** 1986
Group / British Punk, Hard Rock, Punk
The Sex Pistols may have been the first British punk rock band, but the Clash were the definitive British punk rockers. Where the Pistols were nihilistic, the Clash were fiery and idealistic, charged with righteousness and a leftist political ideology. From the outset, the band was more musically adventurous, expanding their hard rock & roll with reggae, dub, and rap rockabilly among other roots musics. Furthermore, they were blessed with two exceptional songwriters in Joe Strummer and Mick Jones, each with a distinctive voice and style. The Clash copped heavily from classic outlaw imagery, positioning themselves as rebels with a cause. As a result, they won a passionately devoted following on both sides of the Atlantic. While they became rock & roll heroes in the UK, second only to the Jam in terms of popularity, it took the Clash several years to break into the American market and when they finally did in 1982, they imploded several months later. Though the Clash never became the superstars they always threatened to become, they restored passion and protest to rock & roll. For a while, they really did seem like "the only band that mattered." *—Stephen Thomas Erlewine*

☆ **The Clash [UK]** / Apr. 8, 1977 / Epic/Legacy ♦♦♦♦♦

Give 'em Enough Rope / Nov. 10, 1978 / Epic ♦♦♦♦♦
For their second album, the Clash worked with the American hard rock producer Sandy Pearlman, best-known for his work with Blue Oyster Cult and the Dictators. The teaming was quite controversial within the punk community, and the sound of *Give 'Em Enough Rope* is considerably cleaner, yet the more direct sound hardly tamed the Clash. While the record doesn't burn with the same intense, amateurish energy of *The Clash,* it does have a big, forceful sound that is nearly as powerful. What keeps *Give 'Em Enough Rope* from being a classic is its slightly inconsistent material. Many of the songs are outright classics, particularly the first half of the record ("Safe European Home," "English Civile War," "Tommy Gun," "Julie's in the Drug Squad") and "Stay Free," but the group loses some momentum toward

the end of the record. Even with such flaws, *Give 'Em Enough Rope* ranks as one of the strongest albums of punk era. [In 2000 Columbia/Legacy reissued and remastered *Give 'Em Enough Rope — Stephen Thomas Erlewine*

☆ **The Clash [US]** / Jul. 1979 / Epic ✦✦✦✦✦
Never Mind the Bollocks may have appeared revolutionary, but the Clash's eponymous debut album was pure, unadultarated rage and fury, fueled by passion for both rock & roll and revolution. Though the cliché about punk rock was that the bands couldn't play, the key to the Clash is that although they gave that illusion, they really could play—*hard.* The charging, relentless rhythms, primitive three-chord rockers, and the poor sound quality give the album a nervy, vital energy. Joe Strummer's slurred wails perfectly compliment the edgy rock, while Mick Jones' clearer singing and charged guitar breaks make his numbers righteously anthemic. Even at this early stage, the Clash were experimenting with reggae, most notably on the Junior Murvin cover "Police and Thieves" and the extraordinary "White Man in Hammersmith Palais," which was one of five tracks added to the American edition of *The Clash.* "Deny," "Protex Blue," "Cheat," and "48 Hours" were removed from the British edition and replaced for the U.S. release with the British-only singles "Complete Control," "White Man in Hammersmith Palais," "Clash City Rockers," "I Fought the Law," and "Jail Guitar Doors," all of which were stronger than the items they replaced. Though the sequencing and selection were slightly different, the core of the album remained the same, and each song retained its power individually. In 2000, Columbia/Legacy re-issued and re-mastered the album to include the UK songs. Few punk songs expressed anger quite as bracingly as "White Riot," "I'm So Bored With the U.S.A.," "Career Opportunities," and "London's Burning," and their power is all the more incredible today. Rock & roll is rarely as edgy, invigorating, and sonically revolutionary as *The Clash. — Stephen Thomas Erlewine*

★ **London Calling** / Dec. 14, 1979 / Epic ✦✦✦✦✦
Give 'Em Enough Rope, for all of its many attributes, was essentially a holding pattern for the Clash, but the double album *London Calling* is a remarkable leap forward, incorporating the punk aesthetic into rock & roll mythology and roots music. Before, the Clash had experimented with reggae, but that was no preparation for the dizzying array of styles on *London Calling.* There's punk and reggae, but there's also rockabilly, ska, New Orleans R&B, pop, lounge jazz, and hard rock; and while the record isn't tied together by a specific theme, its eclecticism and anthemic punk function as a rallying call. While many of the songs—particuarly "London Calling," "Spanish Bombs," and "The Guns of Brixton"—are explicitly political, by acknowledging no boundaries the music itself is political and revolutionary. But it is also invigorating, rocking harder and with more purpose than most albums, let alone double albums. Over the course of the record, Strummer and Jones (and Paul Simonon, who wrote "The Guns of Brixton") explore their familiar themes of working-class rebellion and anti-establishment rants, but they also tie them in to old rock & roll traditions and myths, whether it's rockabilly greasers or "Stagger Lee," as well as mavericks like doomed actor Montgomery Clift. The result is a stunning statement of purpose and one of the greatest rock & roll albums ever recorded. [In 2000 Columbia/Legacy reissued and remastered *London Calling*] *— Stephen Thomas Erlewine*

Sandinista! / Dec. 12, 1980 / Epic ✦✦
The Clash sounded like they could do anything on *London Calling.* For its triple-album followup, *Sandinista!,* they tried do *everything,* adding dub, rap, gospel and even children's choruses to the punk, reggae, R&B and roots-rock they already were playing. Instead of presenting a band with a far-reaching vision, like *London Calling* did, *Sandinista!* plays as a messy, confused jumble, which means that its numerous virtues are easy to ignore. Amid all the dub experiments, backward tracks, unfinished songs and instrumentals, there's a number of classic Clash songs which rank among their best, including "Police on My Back," "The Call-Up," "Somebody Got Murdered," "Charlie Don't Surf," "Hitsville U.K.," and "Lightning Strikes (Not Once, But Twice)," yet it's difficult for anyone but the most dedicated listeners to find them. A few of the failed ideas were worth exploring, but even more—like the children's choir version of "Career Opportunities" or the Terry Doggs song "Lose This Skin"—weren't even pursuing. As the cliche says, there's a great single album within these three records, and those songs make *Sandinista!* worthwhile. Nevertheless, it's sloppy attack is disheartening after the tour-de-force of *London Calling* and the focused agression of *The Clash.* [In 2000 Columbia/Legacy reissued, remastered, and restored the artwork for *Sandinista!*] *— Stephen Thomas Erlewine*

Combat Rock / May 14, 1982 / Epic ✦✦✦
On the surface of things, *Combat Rock* appears to be a retreat from the sprawling stylistic explorations of *London Calling* and *Sandinista!* The pounding arena-rock of "Should I Stay or Should I Go?" makes the Clash sound like an arena rock band, and much of the album boasts a muscular, heavy sound courtesy of producer Glyn Johns. But things aren't quite that simple. *Combat Rock* contains heavy flirtations with rap, funk and reggae, and it even has a cameo by poet Allen Ginsberg—if this album is, as it has often been claimed, the Clash's sell-out effort, it's a very strange way to sell-out. Even with the infectious, dance-inflected New Wave pop of "Rock the Casbah" leading the way, there aren't many overt attempts at crossover success, mainly because the group is tearing in two separate directions. Mick Jones wants the Clash to inherit the Who's righteous arena rock stance and Joe Strummer wants to forge ahead into Black music. The result is an album that is nearly as inconsistent as *Sandinista!,* even though its finest moments—"Should I Stay or Should I Go," "Rock the Casbah," "Straight to Hell"—illustrate why the Clash were able to reach a larger audience than ever before with the record. [In 2000 Columbia/Legacy reissued and remastered *Combat Rock.*] *— Stephen Thomas Erlewine*

Cut the Crap / 1985 / Epic/Legacy ✦✦

Story of the Clash, Vol. 1 / Mar. 1988 / Epic/Legacy ✦✦✦✦
In some ways, the double-disc, 28-track compilation *The Story of the Clash, Vol. 1* does its job quite well—if the job is indeed presenting a relatively thorough overview for casual fans. The great majority of the band's hits and signature tunes are here, including album tracks and such non-LP singles as "Bank Robber," "Armagideon Time," and "Capital Radio," albeit in non-chronological order. While there may be many worthy tunes missing, nothing here is undeserving of inclusion, and its expansive method of operation works in its favor, since it hints at the richness of the Clash's music. After all, it's no great loss to have such official singles as "Hitsville U.K." missing, since there are some extraordinary album tracks included. Still, the compilation is a little problematic. Not because the music isn't great—it's so great that the rather bewildering sequencing does nothing to dilute its power—but because it's hard to tell who needs this compilation, apart from complete neophytes. Granted, in 1988, it marked the first CD release of this music, but since the appearance of *The Singles, Super Black Market Clash,* and the comprehensive box set *Clash on Broadway,* no diehard need own it, unless they need the otherwise unavailable edits of such songs as "The Magnificent Seven" that are included here in lieu of the full-length originals. For novices, it's not a bad introduction at all, but it's sort of like a set of training wheels on a bicycle. Still, as training wheels go, it's about the best Clash compilation out there, since it draws a fuller picture than *The Singles* and is more manageable than *Clash on Broadway.* Of course, jumping in with *The Clash* or *London Calling* is just as effective an introduction. *— Stephen Thomas Erlewine*

The Singles / 1991 / Epic/Legacy ✦✦✦✦
The Singles is exactly what the title says—a collection of the Clash's U.K. single A-sides. This approach can hardly result in a definitive compilation, since the Clash's albums were such cohesive, important works in their own right, and even more erratic LPs like *Sandinista!* and *Combat Rock* had their share of fine album tracks. Nevertheless, the collection does have some value, particularly for more casual fans who don't want to spend the time or money sifting through those uneven albums. And because the best way to hear the Clash is on their original albums, *The Singles* can also be useful for fans who already own those albums and don't want to purchase the three-disc *Clash on Broadway,* thereby duplicating a good portion of their collection. *The Singles* does illustrate the progression of the Clash's music from raw, energetic punk to eclectic dabblings in rockabilly, reggae, and dance-rock (even if it doesn't do so as seamlessly as *London Calling*), and so far, it is the only single-disc Clash comp to feature the original version of the non-LP single "Bankrobber" (the one on *Super Black Market Clash* is a dub version with most of the lyrics missing). So, the utility of *The Singles* all depends on how deeply you want to dig into the Clash, and how much tolerance you have for duplication in the compilations necessary for supplementing the original albums (if your tolerance is high, stick with the more thorough *Clash on Broadway*). [While *The Singles* is only available as a British import, it *can* be found at a reasonable price—avoid retailers charging exorbitant sums.] *— Steve Huey*

Clash on Broadway / Nov. 19, 1991 / Epic/Legacy ✦✦✦✦✦
Clash on the Broadway is a fine triple-disc, 63-song box set covering the Clash's entire career. Although there are very few rarities, it does included all of the band's important songs, including cuts that were only available on EPs, singles and B-sides. As a result, it's a useful box set even for dedicated fans, presenting their evolution in a logical fashion. Nevertheless, compilations don't always suit the Clash well, because *The Clash* and *London Calling* were powerful individual works in their own right, and hearing them cut up in this fashion alters their impact. Even so, anyone looking for one set illustrating why the Clash were a great, important and influential band, *Clash On Broadway* explains exactly why. *— Stephen Thomas Erlewine*

Super Black Market Clash / 1994 / Epic/Legacy ✦✦✦✦
An expanded version of the *Black Market Clash* EP, *Super Black Market Clash* adds assorted singles and remixes to the original recording. A couple of tracks aren't that interesting, but the majority of the disc is splendid, featuring some of the band's best, but unfortunately overlooked tracks, including "Armagideon Time," "The Prisoner," "Gates of the West," and "Capital Radio One." *— Stephen Thomas Erlewine*

George Clinton

b. Jul. 22, 1940, Kannapolis, NC
Vocals, Keyboards, Synthesizer, Producer / Urban, Funk
The mastermind of the Parliament/Funkadelic collective during the 1970s, George Clinton broke up both bands by 1981 and began recording solo albums, occasionally performing live with his former bandmates as the P.Funk All-Stars. Clinton became interested in doo wop while living in New Jersey during the early '50s. He formed the Parliaments in 1955, based out of a barbershop back-room where he straightened hair. The group had a small R&B hit during 1967, but Clinton began to mastermind the Parliaments' activities two years later. Recording both as Parliament and Funkadelic, the group revolutionized R&B during the '70s, twisting soul music into funk by adding influences from several late-'60s acid heroes: Jimi Hendrix, Frank Zappa, and Sly Stone. The Parliament/Funkadelic machine ruled black music during the '70s, capturing over 40 R&B hit singles (including three number ones) and recording three platinum albums. His first solo album, 1982's *Computer Games,* contained the Top 20 R&B hit "Loopzilla." Several months later, the title track from Clinton's *Atomic Dog* EP hit number one on the R&B charts; it stayed at the top spot for four weeks. During the latter half of the '80s Clinton's reputation as a true forefather of rock was disintegrating; by the end of the decade, however, a generation of rappers reared on P-Funk were beginning to name-check him. *—John Bush*

● **Computer Games** / Nov. 5, 1982 / Capitol ✦✦✦✦✦
In the late '70s George Clinton helmed a massive empire bound to eventually decline—which it did, in a rather ugly manner. Once he finally distanced himself in the early '80s from the massive kinetic force that was Parliament/Funkadelic and signed a solo contract with Capitol, he suddenly seemed rejuvenated in terms of creativity and enthusiasm. This freewheeling disposition comes across clearly on *Computer Games,* his first solo album. Of course, calling this a true solo album isn't exactly true, since Bootsy, Gary Shider, and Walter "Junie" Morrison all play a role in the album's success. Still, you get the sense that Clinton is firmly in control of this album, something you can't honestly say about the latter-day Parliament and Funkadelic records, and this sense makes the album quite revealing. Above anything, Clinton turns here to the early-'80s vogue for synthesizers and drum machines that would

later become staples of hip-hop and techno production. This fetish for new studio technology still in its primitive stage gives the album a slightly stiff feeling, as the humans are replaced by machines, a very different style of funk. It's this proto-techno funk that colors the album's better moments, particularly "Atomic Dog," "Loopzilla," and the title track. If you're expecting the freewheeling style of his earlier work, you may be disappointed by the confined feeling of Clinton's '80s work. Ultimately, this album ends up being by far the best of Clinton's solo career, with nearly every song having its own character and its own strengths, while latter albums struggled to come up with anything as inventive or effective. Furthermore, no successive album has anything remotely as catchy as "Atomic Dog," a song that Clinton himself could never duplicate no matter how hard he tried on his next three albums. *—Jason Birchmeier*

You Shouldn't-Nuf Bit Fish / Dec. 1983 / Capitol ♦♦♦

Some of My Best Jokes Are Friends / Jul. 1985 / Capitol ♦♦♦

R&B Skeletons in the Closet / Apr. 1986 / Capitol ♦♦♦♦♦
A definite improvement over the uneven *Some of My Best Jokes Are Friends*, the considerably more focused and confident *R&B Skeletons in the Closet* is one of George Clinton's strongest solo efforts. The P-Funkster continues using technology extensively, but this time, his blend of technology and "real instruments" sounds much more natural. Though not quite in a class with Parliament classics like *Mothership Connection* or *Funkentelechy Vs. the Placebo Syndrome* or Funkadelic treasures ranging from *Cosmic Slop* to *Uncle Jam Wants You, Skeletons* is a superb collection that's well worth acquiring. The CD kicks into high gear with the wildly infectious "Hey Good Lookin'" and maintains that high level of excitement on such driving, sweaty funk treasures as "Do Fries Go With That Shake?" and the appropriately titled "Intense" and the title song. Clinton's eccentricity and outrageous sense of humor serve him well on "Electric Pygmies" and "Mix-Master Suite," an unorthodox, quirky, and cinematic ode to hip-hop drawing on everything from jazz to classical music to Western movies. Many of Clinton's longtime associates are on hand to help make this album the artistic success it is, including saxman Maceo Parker, trombonist Fred Wesley, and the ever-amusing Bootsy Collins. *—Alex Henderson*

The Cinderella Theory / Aug. 1989 / Paisley Park ♦♦♦

Hey Man, Smell My Finger / Oct. 1993 / Paisley Park ♦♦♦♦

T.A.P.O.A.F.O.M. [The Awesome Power of a Fully Operational Mothership] / Jun. 1996 / 550 Music/Epic ♦♦

Greatest Hits / May 9, 2000 / Right Stuff/Capitol ♦♦♦♦
George Clinton's solo output of the 1980s and 1990s wasn't as consistent as his work with Parliament/Funkadelic in the 1970s—nonetheless, the P-Funk innovator has had his share of inspired moments as a solo artist, and some of his best solo recordings are united on this collection. Released in 2000, *Greatest Hits* spans 1976-1986 and draws on such solo albums as *Computer Games, You Shouldn't-Nuf Bit Fish, Some of My Best Jokes Are Friends*, and *R&B Skeletons in the Closet*. The oldest recording is the bonus track, a live Parliament/Funkadelic medley of "Let's Take It to the Stage" and "Do That Stuff" from a 1976 Houston show; most of the selections, however, come from Clinton's Capitol solo albums of 1982-1986. Not surprisingly, the CD opens with "Atomic Dog," Clinton's best-known and most essential solo hit. And The Right Stuff's other choices are also wise ones, including "Do Fries Go With That Shake?," "Cool Joe," "Loopzilla," "Hey Good Lookin'," and the quirky rap item "Nubian Nut." *Greatest Hits* isn't the last word on George Clinton's solo career, but if you need a concise introduction to the funkmeister's Capitol efforts of the 1980s, it's the logical place to go. *—Alex Henderson*

The Clovers

f. 1946, Washington, D.C.
Group / Doo Wop, R&B
One of the earliest doo wop vocal groups, formed in the late '40s in Washington, DC. Original members were Buddy Bailey Matthew McQuater, Hal Lucas, Jr., and Harold Winley. Bobby Mitchell replaced Bailey by the time the group was signed to the fledgling Atlantic label in 1950. The Clovers racked up 13 Top Ten R&B hits between 1951 to 1954, all showcasing their solid harmonies and unerring rhythmic verve.

Before the early '50s, most non-gospel Black vocal groups were in the smooth pop vein of the Inkspots and Mills Brothers. Then the Clovers burst on the scene in 1951 with "Don't You Know I Love You," and things would never be the same.

Under the influence of Atlantic Records' Ahmet Ertegun (who wrote and produced most of their early songs), the Clovers combined quartet harmony, the big dance beat of the R&B jump bands, and the rawer sounds of urban blues into an exciting new blend that caught on with the young Black audience and put them consistently at the top of the R&B charts in the early '50s.

Going beyond this, just as their contemporary B.B. King was doing for blues, lead singers Buddy Bailey and later Charlie White brought a gospel influence to Ertegun's bluesy R&B songs—helping to lay the foundation for the soul music to come. *—George Bedard & Cub Koda*

☆ **Down in the Alley: The Best of the Clovers** / Oct. 1, 1991 / Rhino/Atlantic ♦♦♦♦♦
This 21-song compilation covers the six-year history of one of history's most important R&B groups at Atlantic Records. All of the Clovers' charting singles are represented (albeit not in release order), along with notes indicating their chart history. For the uninitiated, this is where rhythm & blues started as a popular phenomenon, from a group that was incredibly consistent for its six years on the label. The material is representative of rhythm & blues as it sounded at its point of origin, and at its most well-defined and powerful, an unerring jump band beat melded with elements of urban blues and superb quartet singing, all of which were a new musical phenomenon when the Clovers brought it to the charts in 1951. Moreover, one hears the basis in these early tracks for Atlantic's subsequent move into R&B vocals with the Drifters and the Coasters, the sound of these early sides highlighted by very powerful sax and electric guitar accompaniment and the stomping beat one would expect out of a roadhouse band. From "Don't You Know I Love You" through "Ting-A-Ling," "Crawlin'," "Hey, Miss Fannie," and "Lovey Dovey," right into the middle of the decade, this CD moves from one jewel-like R&B-cum-rock & roll classic to the next, and the only complaint that one could reasonably have is that there isn't a complete compilation of the Clovers' work on Atlantic, from Rhino, Collectables, or Sequel. *—Bruce Eder*

Love Potion No. 9 / the Best of the Clovers / 1991 / EMI America ♦♦♦♦♦
The Best of the Clovers—Love Potion No. 9 features their later sides for United Artists including the classic title track. *—Cub Koda*

★ **Very Best of the Clovers** / Feb. 3, 1998 / Rhino ♦♦♦♦♦
The Very Best of the Clovers is an excellent 16-track collection that features his biggest hits from 1951-1959, including "Don't You Know I Love You," "Fool, Fool, Fool," "One Mint Julep," "Ting-A-Ling," "I Played the Fool," "Hey, Miss Fannie," "Good Lovin'," "Lovey Dovey," "Little Mama," "Your Cash Ain't Nothin' But Trash," "Blue Velvet," "Devil or Angel" and "Love Potion No. 9." All of the group's best-known songs in their hit versions are available on this concise, affordable disc, which makes for an ideal introduction to this legendary R&B group. *—Stephen Thomas Erlewine*

The Coasters

f. Feb. 1956, Los Angeles, CA, **db.** 1972
Group / Doo Wop, Rock & Roll, R&B
Possibly the most popular doo wop group of the '50s, the Coasters started on the West Coast as the Robins, scoring hits under the writing-and-production helm of Jerry Leiber and Mike Stoller. When Atlantic signed Leiber and Stoller as a production team, the group split into two factions; the core of the group became the Coasters and moved to New York to record, while the Robins continued on the West Coast to diminishing acclaim. The Coasters' hits, some of the most finely crafted, well written, and hilarious in the genre, continued throughout the rest of the decade. The sly leads of Carl Gardner and bass singing by Will "Dub" Jones defined their sound through numerous personnel changes. When their time on the charts came to an end a number of "Coasters" groups suddenly proliferated (much like the Drifters), many of them still dotting the landscape of a million oldies shows and still singing those classic songs. *—Cub Koda*

☆ **50 Coastin' Classics: Anthology** / Nov. 24, 1992 / Rhino ♦♦♦♦♦
Although it may well be too much for the casual fan, this double CD is easily the best Coasters retrospective ever assembled. Besides featuring every one of their hits, it also contains nine strong tunes cut in the mid-'50s by the Robins, who evolved into the Coasters after some personnel changes. As for the enticing obscurities, "Three Cool Cats" and "Besame Mucho" were cut by the Beatles on unreleased recordings in the early '60s, and "Ain't That Just like Me" would be a small hit for the Searchers. "Down in Mexico" and "Brazil" are cool R&B/Latin melodramas, and "Shoppin' for Clothes," "What About Us," and "That Is Rock & Roll" are half-forgotten vignettes of youthful independence that stack up against the best songs of Jerry Leiber and Mike Stoller, who wrote most of the group's material. Indeed, there's little difference in quality between the hits and the B-sides on this comp, either in the group's matchless ensemble R&B/comedy vocals or Leiber/Stoller's witty songwriting. The accompanying booklet features comments on most of the tracks by Leiber and Stoller themselves. *—Richie Unterberger*

★ **The Very Best of the Coasters** / 1993 / Rhino ♦♦♦♦♦
The Coasters were the 1950s' (and early rock's) dominant novelty/comic R&B ensemble, benefiting from Jerry Leiber and Mike Stoller's lyrical wit and inspired production. They weren't simply proficient clowns; the Coasters were a skilled vocal unit whose talents were utilized on slice-of-life narratives, prophetic youth manifestos, and even an occasional teen anthem, as well as the prototype humorous vehicles "Yakety Yak" and "Poison Ivy." Although Rhino has already given them the deluxe two-disc treatment, consumers who either don't want that much Coasters material or prefer only the hits are nicely served by this 18-track anthology. It contains every major release, plus valuable lesser-known selections such as "Shoppin' for Clothes" and "What About Us." *—Ron Wynn*

Eddie Cochran

b. Oct. 3, 1938, Oklahoma City, OK, **d.** Apr. 17, 1960, Wiltshire, England
Vocals, Guitar (Electric), Drums, Guitar, Bass / Rockabilly, Rock & Roll
Somehow, time has not accorded Eddie Cochran quite the same respect as other early rockabilly pioneers like Buddy Holly, or even Ricky Nelson or Gene Vincent. This is partially attributable to his very brief lifespan as a star: he only had a couple of big hits before dying in a car crash during a British tour in 1960. He was in the same league as the best rockabilly stars, though, with a brash, fat guitar sound that helped lay the groundwork for the power chord. He was also a good songwriter and singer, celebrating the joys of teenage life—the parties, the music, the adolescent rebellion—with an economic wit that bore some similarities to Chuck Berry. Cochran was more lighthearted and less ironic than Berry, though, and if his work was less consistent and not as penetrating, it was almost always exuberant. Cochran had his first Top 20 hit in early 1957, "Sittin' in the Balcony," with an echo-chambered vocal reminiscent of Elvis. That single was written by John D. Loudermilk, but Eddie would write much of his material, including his only Top Ten hit, "Summertime Blues." A definitive teenage anthem with hints of the overt protest that would seep into rock music in the 1960s, it was also a technical tour de force for the time: Cochran overdubbed himself on guitar to create an especially thick sound. That, disappointingly, was the extent of Cochran's major commercial success in the U.S. "C'mon Everybody," a chugging rocker that was almost as good as "Summertime Blues," made the Top 40 in 1959, and also gave Eddie his first British Top Tenner. *—Richie Unterberger*

Box Set / 1988 / Liberty ♦♦♦
This six-LP import—which still, somehow, manages not to include every track Cochran recorded—is excessive for the non-fanatic. Nevertheless, it does include quite a few obscure,

interesting pre-fame performances from the mid-'50s (some as part of the Cochran Brothers). Other bonuses include a live 1960 British TV broadcast, an album's worth of sessions and his work as a producer, and entire sides of instrumentals and stereo versions, as well as a 32-page booklet. *—Richie Unterberger*

The Early Years / 1988 / Ace ✦✦✦
Compilation of 16 tracks from the mid-'50s, most or all dating from before Cochran's breakthrough to national recognition with "Twenty-Flight Rock." Some were recorded when Eddie was half of the Cochran Brothers, with (the unrelated) Hank Cochran; there are also tracks credited to Jerry Capehart and Albert Stone, which Eddie most likely had a prominent role on, as session man or producer (the liner notes are resolutely unhelpful on providing exact details). Most of this is pretty solid rockabilly, not much below the standards of Cochran's best releases. There are also a couple of hot instrumentals, and ballad-type numbers on which Eddie employs a husky, echoed Elvisoid delivery. A decent release, but assembled in a scattershot fashion. Also, if you're interested enough in Cochran to want to track this down, you may well also be interested enough in him to spring for a box set, and most or all of these are also contained on whatever box set you manage to locate. *—Richie Unterberger*

★ **Somethin' Else: The Fine Lookin' Hits of Eddie Cochran** / Feb. 24, 1998 / Razor & Tie ✦✦✦✦✦
Eddie Cochran hasn't been unaccounted for in the reissue sweepstakes since the rockabilly revival of the late 1970s/early '80s—quite the contrary. His greatest hits have been around the block a few times, and his voluminous amount of session work has all resurfaced on myriads of foreign collector labels. This 1998 best-of on Razor & Tie duplicates 15 of the 20 tracks on EMI's *Legendary Masters Series* compilation from 1990. Hits *are* hits, after all, and Cochran's best is hardly open to debate. What distinguishes this package is the inclusion of "Tired and Sleepy" from the Cochran Brothers, an early swipe at "Long Tall Sally," the instrumental "Guybo," "Cherished Memories" and the almost pop-folk "Boll Weevil." Great liner notes from Colin Escott and top-flight sound also make this disc highly recommended. If you're looking to start your Eddie Cochran collection, this makes an excellent first purchase. *—Cub Koda*

Bruce Cockburn

b. May 27, 1945, Pembroke, Ontario, Canada
Vocals, Guitar, Dulcimer / Contemporary Folk, Singer/Songwriter
Immensely popular in his native Canada, singer/songwriter Bruce Cockburn has found only cult success south of the border, in spite of a rich, varied body of work and considerable critical nods. He has won numerous Juno Awards and has kept the quality control on most of his albums at a high level. Cockburn's first decade of work (1970-1979) is largely literate, singer/songwriter folk-rock, often with a strong Christian tone and mystical, devotional lyrics. In 1979, Cockburn had his only major U.S. single, "Wondering Where the Lions Are," which peaked at number 21. The accompanying album, *Dancing in the Dragon's Jaw*, saw him augmenting his music with worldbeat rhythms, an approach he would continue over his next few albums. Cockburn toned down his Christian viewpoint for much of the 1980s, partially as a way of disconnecting himself from the American religious right, which he found antithetical to his own spiritual beliefs, and partially to concentrate on more humanitarian, political subject matter. In 1984 Cockburn produced an AOR hit, "If I Had a Rocket Launcher," whose accompanying video depicted conditions in war-torn Central America and gained a fair amount of MTV play. Cockburn's later 1980s work took on a more streamlined rock sound, and his political agenda was weighted towards environmental concerns, as well as oppression. In the 1990s, Cockburn has returned to a more introspective feel recalling his earlier work. *—Steve Huey*

Bruce Cockburn / 1971 / Columbia ✦✦

High Winds White Sky / 1971 / Columbia ✦✦

Sunwheel Dance / 1972 / Columbia ✦✦

Night Vision / 1973 / Columbia ✦✦

Salt, Sun and Time / 1974 / Columbia ✦✦✦

Joy Will Find a Way / 1975 / Columbia ✦✦✦

In the Falling Dark / 1976 / Columbia ✦✦✦✦
With every album he released during the first half of the '70s, Bruce Cockburn continued to evolve and show signs of greatness, and with his seventh, *In the Falling Dark*, he makes good on these promises. As a whole, this record trumps anything that its predecessors had to offer, almost to the point where it's difficult to imagine that it followed the release of *Joy Will Find a Way* by only a year. The sound that was merely suggested on his previous recordings is fully realized here: check out the flute and trumpet interplay on the jazz inflected instrumental "Giftbearer," the hypnotic "I'm Gonna Fly Someday" with its irresistible flute, horn, and voice line, and Fred Stone's flügelhorn on & "Silver Wheels." Furthermore, the songwriting is without a doubt his most consistent; & "Lord of the Starfields" and the evocative title track are the pinnacle of his Christian mysticism, whereas the aforementioned "Silver Wheels" is one of his keenest social observations to date. There's still the occasional slide into the sort of hippie-ish sentiments that have plagued his recordings from time to time, but even at its most mawkish, there's a sweetness and warmth to the material. His first U.S. release since 1972, *In the Falling Dark* may not have made Bruce Cockburn a household name, but it did mark his emergence as an important artist. *—Brett Hartenbach*

Circles in the Stream / 1977 / True North ✦✦✦

Further Adventures of Bruce Cockburn / 1978 / True North ✦✦✦
Further Adventures Of, though it may contain Bruce Cockburn's usual mix of beautifully intricate acoustic work and pastoral mysticism, along with the occasional touches of anger and irony, continues the growth that was so evident on his last studio outing *In the Falling Dark*. And while it may lack anything quite as powerful as "Lord of the Starfields" or the title song from that record, the use of his electric guitar, which is at the forefront on a couple of tracks, brings a bit more of an edge to the proceedings. Lyrically, his odes to God and nature can still at times be as soft as his social relevance can be heavy-handed, but cuts such as the joyful & "Rainfall," the bilingual "Pernons La Mer," and the Eastern meditation & "Nanzen Ji" get by on their sheer beauty, while & "A Montreal Song" and the pensive & "Outside a Broken Phone Booth With Money in My Hand" are sharp and effective. The latter, with its lyrical urgency and effected electric guitar, shows a toughness in his songwriting, as well as the direction of his sound, both of which would become even more prevalent in the coming years. Like much of Cockburn's earlier output, *Further Adventures Of*, though not a major work in his catalog, shows flashes of brilliance among some fairly ordinary material that's distinguished only by his excellent guitar. Beyond this, it serves as another steppingstone to what would be the most impressive period of his career—including the gorgeous *Dancing in the Dragon's Jaws* (1979) and his stunning work of the early '80s—and is worth a listen. *—Brett Hartenbach*

Dancing in the Dragons Jaws / 1979 / Columbia ✦✦✦✦
After nearly a decade spent in relative obscurity outside of his native Canada, Bruce Cockburn finally made a dent in the US market with the Top 40 hit "Wondering Where the Lions Are" from 1979's *Dancing in the Dragon's Jaws*. The album continues the jazz-inflected folk he had been pursuing on his past several releases, but with a heavier emphasis on the worldbeat rhythms that would play a larger part in his music in the years to come. This album is the gentler side of Bruce Cockburn, beautiful and searching, with his acoustic guitar once again at the forefront; his intricate, yet melodic patterns the perfect backdrop for his poetic ruminations on spirituality and nature. From the opener, "Creation Dream," his vision of the Earth's genesis to the meditative & "No Footprints" Cockburn is overcome by the wonderment of God's work. Even amidst the "concrete vortex" and "people looking ill-at-ease," there's a sense of peace and overwhelming faith that runs throughout. Only "Incandescent Blue" (coincidentally the only song written outside of Canada) exhibits the kind of urban tension and consciousness that would become so evident in his work throughout the next decade; although he still finds a sort of respite in the chorus with its "white birds... [soaring] away free." *Dancing in the Dragon's Jaws*, though it can't match the sheer power of his next few releases, may be his most beautiful record, as well as an excellent culmination of his '70s work. *—Brett Hartenbach*

● **Humans** / Nov. 1980 / Columbia ✦✦✦✦✦
Bruce Cockburn asks, "You see the extremes, of what humans can be?" in "Rumours of Glory," which works as an excellent summation of *Humans*, his 11th album. Between the opener & "Grim Travellers" and the beautifully contemplative final track & "The Rose Above the Sky," he examines these "extremes" not only in others, but also in himself. Along the way, Cockburn attempts to make sense of his own spirituality and faith in a world of imperialism, greed, urban violence, and even his own divorce. However, he questions himself as thoroughly as he does the world around him. Although he'd often touched on social issues in the past, he'd never dealt with them quite so acutely, or on such a grand scale as he does here. Cockburn also seemed to understand that the U.S. Top 40 success of & "Wondering Where the Lions Are" from the previous year, though a pleasant surprise, was somewhat of a fluke, and continued to progress without necessarily trying to duplicate the feat. There's a toughness here, both musically and lyrically, at which he had merely hinted before. More than any of his prior releases, *Humans* is able to convey, not only the love and mercy of his Christian beliefs, but also the anger and frustration of trying to live in a world of "gutless arrogance and rage..." where people are treated as if they were "...so many cattle." In the late '70s, Cockburn's music began to change and grow to a great degree, and with *Humans* it reaches fruition and remains one of the most important recordings in his extensive catalog. *—Brett Hartenbach*

Inner City Front / 1981 / Columbia ✦✦✦✦
Inner City Front continues the urban toughness that moved to the forefront on Bruce Cockburn's previous release, *Humans*. Furthermore, like that record, there's an uneasiness that runs throughout, from the jazz-tinged opener, & "You Pay Your Money and You Take Your Chance," to the disquieting & "Loner," which closes the album. Even a love song like & "Wanna Go Walking," one of the most straightforward rockers he's ever recorded, reflects the weight of the outside world. Only the jazzy instrumental & "Radio Shoes" and the joyful & "And We Dance" remain free of this underlying tension. Musically, moody synths, violin, and woodwinds on *Inner City Front* underscore the dark, reflective nature of the material, which like its predecessor, deals with the "paradox and contrast" in the human condition, from personal relationships to world affairs. Also, for the second consecutive recording, Cockburn eschews the folkier, acoustic leanings of his '70s work and places both feet squarely into the jazz and worldbeat rock that dominated the majority of *Humans*. One track, & "The Strong One," is even given a slow, brooding, techno treatment. Since the release of *In the Falling Dark*, Cockburn was gaining creative momentum with each release, and *Inner City Front* continues that trend. *—Brett Hartenbach*

The Trouble with Normal / 1983 / Columbia ✦✦✦✦
Like his two previous efforts in the '80s, *The Trouble With Normal* places Bruce Cockburn yet another step further from his days as Canada's resident mystic folky. And while he had touched on similar musical themes on earlier recordings, the eclectic blend of folk, rock, and world music here is much more defined and realized. The use of synths, electric guitar, violin, and Chapman Stick, along with the occasional keyboard and drum sequences, complement the weighty, ominous nature of his lyrical concerns, which seem to paint a picture of a world, though teetering on the edge, still filled with beauty ("Hoop Dancer"), hope ("Put Our Hearts Together"), and contentment ("Waiting for the Moon to Show"). Amidst the "chaos" and "fashionable fascism," Cockburn's message, though cloaked in frustration and cynicism, and not nearly as overt as it has been in the past, is still one of faith and love. There is the tendency to get heavy-handed at times, but still, *The Trouble With Normal* contains some of Cockburn's most beautifully imagistic writing to date and is another strong effort. The U.S. release contains an alternate, yet inferior take of the title track, which makes the Canadian (True North) version preferable. *—Brett Hartenbach*

Stealing Fire / 1984 / Columbia ✦✦✦✦✦
After visiting Central America, Bruce Cockburn recorded *Stealing Fire,* part of which passionately and eloquently details what he'd seen while in Nicaragua and Guatemala. With the opening track, the terse rocker "Lovers in a Dangerous Time," Cockburn conveys both a sense of urgency and uncertainty. There's a brief calm as the second half begins, before a triad of songs written about his time spent in Central America brings the record to a sober conclusion. These three tunes, which, like the majority of the album, sport a tight, worldbeat, folk and rock flavor, are the true highlights of *Stealing Fire,* and Cockburn at his very best. The first, "Nicaragua," is part observation, part commentary, and part tribute to the Sandinista-led revolution in that country. "If I Had a Rocket Launcher" follows, and is arguably Cockburn's most powerful merging of personal and political feelings. Written after witnessing Guatemalan refugees being chased across the border by gun-wielding helicopters, "Rocket Launcher" evokes not only the pain and suffering of the people, but the conflict between Cockburn's pacifist leanings, and the vengeful anger and hatred incited by such a horrific sight. The Nicaraguan, road-inspired "Dust and Diesel" closes the record with a portrait of a country whose daily contrast of beauty and violence is summed up by the images of people who are proud, hopeful, passionate, afraid, and tired. *Stealing Fire,* despite a few less than compelling tracks, is the work of an artist at his peak. It also contains some of the most intensely significant material by a singer/songwriter in the 1980s. *—Brett Hartenbach*

World of Wonders / 1986 / Columbia ✦✦✦

- **Waiting for a Miracle (Singles 1970-1987)** / Jan. 1987 / Gold Castle ✦✦✦✦
Waiting for a Miracle, with two discs spanning 17 years and 22 songs, is the third and by far most comprehensive of three Bruce Cockburn retrospectives released in a six-year period. Still, because it's centered around his Canadian singles, it lacks the sort of impact a best-of collection should have from someone such as Cockburn, who could never be mistaken for a "singles" artist. On the other hand, if you're looking for an overview of his career, *Waiting for a Miracle,* which also has a sprinkling of new songs and alternate takes to lure fans, isn't a bad place to start. The chronological order of the tracks makes it easy to see the progression of his career, from mystic folky, to outspoken, left-wing, worldbeat rocker. It also shows Cockburn's growth as both a writer and performer, although the choices included here from his early records are good ones. *Waiting for a Miracle* may not be a perfect representation of Cockburn's work, but until something better comes along, it will have to do. *—Brett Hartenbach*

Big Circumstance / 1989 / Columbia ✦✦✦

Nothing but a Burning Light / Nov. 5, 1991 / Columbia ✦✦✦

Dart to the Heart / Mar. 1, 1994 / Columbia ✦✦✦

Charity of Night / Feb. 4, 1997 / Rykodisc ✦✦

Breakfast in New Orleans Dinner in Timbuktu / Sep. 14, 1999 / Rykodisc ✦✦✦

Joe Cocker

b. May 20, 1944, Sheffield, Yorkshire, England
Vocals / Pop/Rock, Soft Rock, Adult Contemporary, Blues-Rock
After starting out as an unsuccessful pop singer, Joe Cocker found his niche singing rock and soul in the pubs of England with his superb backing group, the Grease Band. He hit number one in the UK in November 1968 with his version of the Beatles' "A Little Help from My Friends." His career really took off after he sang that song at the Woodstock festival in August 1969. A second British hit came with a version of Leon Russell's "Delta Lady" in the fall of 1969 (by then, Russell was Cocker's musical director) and both of his albums, *With a Little Help from My Friends* and *Joe Cocker!,* went gold in America. In 1970, his cover of the Box Tops' hit "The Letter" became his first US Top Ten. Cocker's first peak of success came when Russell organized the "Mad Dogs & Englishmen" tour of 1970, featuring Cocker and over 40 others, and resulting in a third gold album and a concert film. Subsequent efforts were less popular, and problems with alcohol (both on stage and off) reduced Cocker's once-powerful voice to a croaking rasp. But he returned to the US Top Ten with the romantic ballad "You Are So Beautiful" in 1975 and topped the charts in a duet with Jennifer Warnes on "Up Where We Belong," the theme from the 1982 film *An Officer and a Gentleman.* He has survived, still charting into the '90s, albiet with less frequency than he did in the '70s and '80s. *—Cub Koda & William Ruhlmann*

With a Little Help from My Friends / Apr. 1969 / A&M ✦✦✦✦✦
The album that foisted Joe Cocker on an unsuspecting public is full of tasteful, raucous covers, Cocker's trademark hysterical vocals, and outstanding studio backing by pros like Jimmy Page and Steve Winwood. *—Tom Graves*

Joe Cocker! / Oct. 1969 / A&M ✦✦✦✦✦
The rare sophomore effort that was an improvement over the first, it features great tracks (and vocals) like "Delta Lady" and "She Came in Through the Bathroom Window." Arguably, it's Cocker's most soulful album. *—Tom Graves*

Mad Dogs & Englishmen / Aug. 1970 / A&M ✦✦✦✦✦
A superb document of Cocker's high-energy 1970 tour, it included about a zillion musicians and hangers-on. All the goods are here, and many consider this Cocker's last great moment. *—Tom Graves*

I Can Stand a Little Rain / Aug. 1974 / A&M ✦✦✦

Jamaica Say You Will / Aug. 1975 / A&M ✦✦

Stingray / Apr. 1976 / A&M ✦✦✦

The Best of Joe Cocker / Mar. 16, 1993 / Capitol ✦✦✦✦✦
Although Cocker's Capitol material wasn't as consistent as his A&M work, this compilation successfully distills the highlights, including the splendid "When the Night Comes," onto a single CD. *—Stephen Thomas Erlewine*

Long Voyage Home / Nov. 21, 1995 / A&M ✦✦✦✦✦
Long Voyage Home: The Silver Anniversary Collection is nearly the definitive Joe Cocker anthology, covering his recording career from the late '60s to the mid-'90s, featuring material from all the labels he recorded for—*A&M,* Elektra, Island, and Capitol. After an early single from 1965 (a version of the Beatles' "I'll Cry Instead"), the set skips ahead to his late-'60s recordings with his Mad Dogs & Englishmen troupe. From there, the collection doesn't miss many of Cocker's greatest hits or favorite album tracks. In addition to the familiar tracks, there are a handful of unreleased cuts that are tantalizing for the collector; casual fans will find them of marginal interest. *—Stephen Thomas Erlewine*

- **The Anthology** / Aug. 17, 1999 / A&M ✦✦✦✦✦
A&M's double-disc *Anthology* may be too much for casual fans that just want the hits, but anyone else will find this exhaustive 37-track chronicle of Joe Cocker's prime years definitive. The first disc concentrates on his first three albums, buttressed by a rare 1964 single of the Beatles' "I'll Cry Instead" and his 1970 non-LP single "The Letter"/"Space Captain." Disc two features highlights of all the albums he recorded between 1972 and 1982, selecting not only hits, but key album tracks. The end result is a collection that is concise and definitive. It may be missing such latter day hits as "When the Night Comes" and doesn't cover as much ground as the box set *Long Voyage Home,* but anyone looking for a comprehensive collection of Cocker's classic recordings will be satisfied by *Anthology. —Stephen Thomas Erlewine*

Super Hits / Feb. 15, 2000 / 550/Legacy ✦✦✦

Cocteau Twins

f. 1979, Grangemouth, Scotland, **db.** 1997
Group / Ambient Pop, Dream Pop, Post-Punk, Alternative Pop/Rock
A group whose distinctly ethereal and gossamer sound virtually defined the enigmatic image of their record label 4AD, the Cocteau Twins were originally formed by guitarist Robin Guthrie and bassist Will Heggie and later rounded out by Guthrie's girlfriend Elizabeth Fraser, an utterly unique performer whose swooping, operatic vocals relied less on any recognizable language than on the subjective sounds and textures of verbalized emotions. In 1982, the trio signed to 4AD and debuted with *Garlands,* which offered an embryonic taste of their rapidly-developing, atmospheric sound, crafted around Guthrie's creative use of distorted guitars, tape loops and echo boxes and anchored in Heggie's rhythmic bass as well as an omnipresent Roland 808 drum machine. Shortly after the release of the *Peppermint Pig* EP, Heggie left the group, and Guthrie and Fraser cut 1983's *Head Over Heels* as a duo; nonetheless, the album largely perfected the Cocteaus' gauzy formula, and established the foundation from which the group would continue to work for the duration of its career. In late 1983, bassist Simon Raymonde joined the band to record the EP *The Spangle Maker.* After 1990's *Heaven or Las Vegas,* the Cocteaus severed their long-standing relationship with 4AD; notably, the album also found Fraser's vocals offering the occasional comprehensible turn of phrase, a trend continued on 1993's *Four-Calendar Cafe. —Jason Ankeny*

Garlands / Jun. 1982 / 4AD ✦✦

Head Over Heels / Aug. 1983 / 4AD ✦✦✦✦✦
Losing original member Heggie might at first have seemed a troubling blow, but in fact it allowed the duo of Fraser and Guthrie to transcend the darkened one-note gloom of *Garlands* with *Head Over Heels.* The album introduces a variety of different shadings and approaches to the incipient Cocteaus sound, pointing the band towards the exultant, elegant beauty of later releases. Opening number "When Mama Was Moth" demonstrates the new musical range nicely; Fraser's singing is much more upfront, while Guthrie creates a bewitching mix of dark guitar notes and sparkling keyboard tones, with percussion echoing in the background. Other songs, like the sax-accompanied "Five Ten Fiftyfold" and "The Tinderbox (Of a Heart)" reflect the more elaborate musical melancholy of the group, while still other cuts are downright sprightly. "Multifoiled" in particular is a charm, a jazzily-arranged number that lets Fraser do a bit of scatting (a perfect avenue for her lyrical approach!), while "In the Gold Dust Rush" mixes acoustic guitar drama into Fraser's swooping singing. Perhaps the two strongest numbers of all are: "Sugar Hiccup," mixing the mock choir effect the band would use elsewhere with both a lovely guitar line and singing; and "Musette and Drums," a massive, powerful collision of Guthrie's guitar at its loudest and most powerful and Fraser's singing at its most intense. *—Ned Raggett*

- **Treasure** / Oct. 1984 / 4AD ✦✦✦✦✦
The opening two numbers are simply flawless, starting with "Ivo," where gently strummed guitar and low bass support Fraser's singing; then suddenly added, astonishing chimes and steady percussion build up to a jaw-dropping Guthrie guitar solo. Topping that would be hard for anyone, but in "Lorelei," the Twins do it, with an introductory, breathtaking guitar surge leading into one of Fraser's best vocals, compelling in both its heavenly and earthly tones and rolls. Not a word may be understandable, but it isn't necessary, while the music, driven on by a pounding rhythm, is as perfect a justification of digital delay pedals and the like as can be found. As *Treasure* continues, the accomplished variety is what stands out the most, whether it be the gentle, futuristic-medieval pluckings on "Beatrix," the understated moody washes and Fraser whispers on "Otterley," the upbeat guitar lines of "Aloysius," or the slightly jazzy touches on "Pandora." The concluding number ends the record on the peak with which it began. "Donimo" starts with a mysterious mix of mock choir sounds, ambient echoes and noises, and Fraser's careful singing before finally exploding into one last heavenly wash of powerful sound; Guthrie's guitar, Raymonde's steady bass, and drum machine smashes provide the perfect bed for Fraser's final, exultant vocals. *Treasure* lives up to its title and then some as a thorough and complete triumph. *—Ned Raggett*

Victorialand / Apr. 1986 / 4AD ✦✦✦

Blue Bell Knoll / Oct. 1988 / 4AD ✦✦✦
The first Cocteaus album to feature a full-band lineup since *Treasure* was also their first full studio record released in America, resulting from the group's stateside deal with Capitol. Much to longtime fans' surprise, the Twins in fact were much more content with Capitol than

4AD, hinting at their eventual full departure from that label. This was all well and good, but the trio's new inspiration didn't fully translate into their work, unfortunately. While *Blue Bell Knoll* has some striking moments that are pure Cocteaus at their best—the opening title track is especially lovely with a keyboard loop leading into Fraser's ever-wonderful vocals, a light rhythm, and a great final Guthrie solo—it's still the band's least noteworthy release since *Garlands*. The feeling throughout is of a group interested in dressing up older approaches that have served them well, but aren't as distinct; the quite-lush arrangements by Guthrie are fine but the songs are a touch more pedestrian. *Blue Bell Knoll* has enough initial steam, however, to ensure that there are reasons to listen, happily. "Athol-Brose" has the inspirational feel that the Twins can easily create. "Carolyn's Fingers," the clear album standout, is perhaps the strongest individual Cocteau song since "Aikea-Guinea," with Fraser singing against herself over a rough, hip-hop-inspired rhythm while Guthrie peels off a fantastic main guitar melody and Raymonde contributes some supple bass work. After that amazing opening, things slowly but surely slide back a bit; most of the rest sounds okay enough to listen to, but the heartgripping intensity that defines the Twins at their best isn't present. *—Ned Raggett*

Heaven or Las Vegas / Sep. 1990 / 4AD ✦✦✦✦✦
Deciding to scale back the overly pretty sound on *Blue Bell Knoll* while experimenting with more accessibility, the Twins ended up creating their best album since *Treasure*. From the start, *Heaven…* is simply fantastic: on "Cherry-Coloured Funk", Guthrie's inimitable guitar work chimes leading a low-key but forceful rhythm, while Raymonde's grand bass work fleshes it out. Fraser simply captivates; her vocals are the clearest, most direct they've ever been, purring with energy and life. Many songs have longer openings and closings; rather than crashing fully into a song and then quickly ending, instead the trio carefully builds up and eases back. These songs are still quite focused, though, almost sounding like they were recorded live instead of being assembled in the studio. Due credit has to be given to the Cocteaus' drum programming; years of working with the machines translated into the detailed work here, right down to the fills. "Fifty-Fifty Clown," starting with an ominous bass throb, turns into a lovely showcase Fraser's singing and Guthrie's more restrained playing. But the Twins don't completely turn their back on *Knoll*'s sound; "Iceblink Luck," has the same lush feeling and a newfound energy—the instrumental break is almost a rave-up!—and everything pulses to a fine conclusion. There are many moments of sheer Cocteaus beauty and power, including the title track, with its great chorus, and two spotlight Guthrie solos: "Fotzepolitic," a powerful number building to a rushing conclusion, and the album-ending "Frou Frou Foxes in Midsummer Fires." Possessing the same climactic sense of drama past disc-closers as "Donimo" and "The Thinner the Air," it's a perfect way to end a near-perfect album. *—Ned Raggett*

Four-Calendar Cafe / Nov. 1993 / Capitol ✦✦✦
The Cocteau Twins' first release following their exodus from the 4AD stable, *Four-Calendar Cafe* is also, tellingly, their most earthbound effort; as with *Heaven or Las Vegas*, the emphasis here is on substance as much as style—"Evangeline," "Bluebeard" and "Know Who You Are at Every Age" continue the trio's advance into more accessible melodic and lyrical ground without sacrificing even an ounce of their trademark ethereality. *—Jason Ankeny*

Milk & Kisses / Mar. 1996 / Capitol ✦✦✦

BBC Sessions / Oct. 12, 1999 / Rykodisc ✦✦✦✦
Cocteau Twins have always been a love'em-or-hate'em kind of band—to some, Elizabeth Fraser's cool, chirpy warble, the shimmering multi-layered guitars and bass of Simon Raymonde and Robin Guthrie, and the affectless electronic percussion that always accompanies them combine to approximate the music of the spheres. To others, it's all frosting and no cake. This two-disc compilation of live and radio studio recordings (some of which are previously unreleased) probably won't change anyone's mind either way, but if there was ever any doubt of Fraser's vocal virtuosity, that doubt can be laid to rest now: imagine a cross between Emmylou Harris (without any twang) and Sinéad O'Connor (with discipline). The program proceeds chronologically, from the relatively tuneless "Wax and Wane" and "Garlands" through "Ivo" and "Otterley" (two luscious melodies from the band's aptly titled *Treasure*) and several almost equally pretty tracks from 1996. At their best, no one can match Cocteau Twins for sheer, swooning, inscrutable elegance, and they're frequently at their best on this fine collection. *—Rick Anderson*

Leonard Cohen

b. Sep. 21, 1934, Montreal, Quebec, Canada
Vocals, Guitar / Folk-Rock, Singer/Songwriter
One of the most interesting and enduring, if not the most successful singer-songwriters of the late 1960s, Leonard Cohen has retained a substantial following for more than 30 years, along with the attention of critics who long since ceased worrying about new works by most of his contemporaries. Cohen was born nearly a decade earlier than the Beatles or the Rolling Stones, and a year before Elvis Presley, but his personal, social and intellectual background couldn't be more different from *any* rock stars of any generation, nor can he be easily compared even with any members of the generation of folksingers that came of age in the 1960's—he didn't start performing or recording until he was in his mid-30's, after he had already written several books. As an established novelist and poet, his literary accomplishments far exceed those of Bob Dylan, though as a performer, his rather monotone voice is less appealing than Dylan's singing. *—Bruce Eder*

★ **The Songs of Leonard Cohen** / 1968 / Columbia ✦✦✦✦✦
A breathtaking and perfect debut, *Songs of Leonard Cohen* marked the emergence of one of the most enduring, unique and brilliant voices in popular music. Led off by the gorgeous "Suzanne," previously a hit for both Judy Collins and Noel Harrison, the album is an exposed nerve, a Fellini-esque parade of losers, victims and fallen angels. Brittle and unforgiving, tracks like "So Long, Marianne," "Winter Lady" and "Sisters of Mercy" are unflinchingly honest and desolate; the subdued beauty of the songs' spartan backdrop only adds to their force—Cohen takes acoustic folk, for so long a musical expression of empowerment and hope, and bleeds it dry of all its redemptive qualities. A masterpiece of perversity and pain. *—Jason Ankeny*

Songs from a Room / 1969 / Columbia ✦✦✦✦✦
Somehow even darker and more melancholy than *Songs of Leonard Cohen*, *Songs From a Room* is an emotionally claustrophobic set produced with austere beauty by Bob Johnston. The arrangements are eerily spare, heightening the impact of Cohen's weary vocals; the intermittent and idiosyncratic appearance of a Jew's harp only adds to the record's overwhelming sense of disorientation. While not as uniformly strong as its predecessor, *Songs From a Room* does contain a number of Cohen's finest compositions, including "Bird on the Wire," "Lady Midnight" and "Story of Isaac." *—Jason Ankeny*

Songs of Love and Hate / 1971 / Columbia ✦✦✦✦✦
Songs of Love and Hate is one of Leonard Cohen's most emotionally intense albums—which, given the nature of Cohen's body of work, is no small statement. While the title *Songs of Love and Hate* sums up the album's themes accurately enough, it's hardly as simple as that description might lead you to expect—in these eight songs, "love" encompasses the physical ("Last Year's Man"), the emotional ("Famous Blue Raincoat"), and the spiritual ("Joan of Arc"), and the contempt in songs like "Dress Rehearsal Rag" and "Avalanche" is the sort of venom that can only come from someone who once cared very deeply. The sound of the album is clean and uncluttered, and for the most part the music stays out of the way of the lyrics, which dominate the songs. Thankfully, Cohen had grown noticeably as a singer since his first two albums, and if he hardly boasts a range to rival Roy Orbison here, he is able to bring out the subtleties of "Joan of Arc" and "Famous Blue Raincoat" in a way his previous work would not have led you to expect. And while Bob Johnston's production is spare, it's spare with a purpose, letting Cohen's voice and guitar tell their stories and using other musicians for intelligent, emotionally resonant punctuation (Paul Buckmaster's unobtrusive string arrangements and the use of a children's chorus are especially inspired). And *Songs of Love and Hate* captured Cohen in one of his finest hours as a songwriter, and the best selections (especially "Famous Blue Raincoat," "Joan of Arc," and "Love Calls You by Your Name") rank with the most satisfying work of his career. If *Songs of Love and Hate* isn't Cohen's best album, it comes close enough to be essential to anyone interested in his work. *—Mark Deming*

New Skin for the Old Ceremony / 1974 / Columbia ✦✦✦✦✦
Leonard Cohen was a poet long before he decided to pick up a guitar. Despite singing in a dry baritone over spare arrangements, Cohen is a gifted lyricist who captivates the listener. *New Skin for the Old Ceremony* may be Leonard Cohen's most musical album, as he is accompanied by violas, mandolins, banjos, and percussion that give his music more texture than usual. The fact that Cohen does more real singing on this album can be seen as both a blessing and a curse—while his voice sounds more strained, the songs are delivered with more passion than usual. Furthermore, he has background vocalists including Janis Ian that add significantly to create a fuller sound. It is no surprise, however, that he generally uses simple song structures to draw attention to the words ("Who By Fire"). The lyrics are filled with abstract yet vivid images, and the album primarily uses the metaphor of love and relationships as battlegrounds ("There Is a War," "Field Commander Cohen"). Cohen is clearly singing from the heart, and he chronicles his relationship with Janis Joplin in "Chelsea Hotel No. 2." This is one of his best albums, although new listeners should start with *Songs of Leonard Cohen*. *— Vik Iyengar*

☆ **The Best of Leonard Cohen** / 1975 / Columbia ✦✦✦✦✦
The Best of Leonard Cohen samples 12 of the many highlights from the singer's first four studio LPs. With a heavy emphasis on the debut *Songs of Leonard Cohen* and its follow-up *Songs From a Room*, the set includes such masterpieces as "Suzanne," "So Long, Marianne" and "Bird on the Wire," as well as later efforts including "Chelsea Hotel" and "Famous Blue Raincoat." *—Jason Ankeny*

Death of a Ladies' Man / 1977 / Columbia ✦✦
While not the unmitigated disaster conventional wisdom holds it to be, *Death of a Ladies' Man* remains one of Leonard Cohen's least successful efforts. In a 180-degree turn from the spare, muted settings of most of Cohen's work, the record is produced by Phil Spector, whose trademark Wall of Sound swallows the singer whole; Cohen's songs are up to snuff, and Spector's vision remains as awe-striking as ever, but the two artists are simply incompatible—apart from a few bright spots ("True Love Leaves No Traces," "Paper Thin Hotel"), *Death of a Ladies' Man* is an ambitious failure. *—Jason Ankeny*

Recent Songs / 1979 / Columbia ✦✦✦

Various Positions / 1985 / Columbia ✦✦✦
Recorded with vocalist Jennifer Warnes (who later cut the album *Famous Blue Raincoat*, a collection of Cohen compositions), *Various Positions* is a stunning return to form—Cohen's strongest work since *New Skin for the Old Ceremony*. Cryptic and spartan, the set continues in the eclectic vein of recent efforts, but with greater clarity and focus, resulting in a intriguingly diffuse collection ranging from the Serge Gainsbourg-esque pop of "Dance Me to the End of Love" to the boozy, country-inflected "The Captain." *—Jason Ankeny*

I'm Your Man / 1988 / Columbia ✦✦✦✦✦
A stunningly sophisticated leap into modern musical textures, *I'm Your Man* re-establishes Leonard Cohen's mastery. Against a backdrop of keyboards and propulsive rhythms, Cohen surveys the global landscape with a precise, unflinching eye: the opening "First We Take Manhattan" is an ominous fantasy of commercial success bundled in crypto-fascist imagery, while the remarkable "Everybody Knows" is a cynical catalog of the landmines littering the surface of love in the age of AIDS. *—Jason Ankeny*

The Future / Nov. 10, 1992 / Columbia ✦✦✦✦
On his latest recording, Canada's poet-musician laureate has glimpsed *The Future*, and it's not a pretty sight. Cohen's apocalyptic vision takes us through a morbid roll-call that includes torture, environmental destruction, drug abuse, abortion, sexual abuse, murder, Stalin,

Charles Manson, Hiroshima, and (shudder) lousy poets. And that's just the title track. Instrumental backings focus mostly on unobtrusive textures—synths, strings, female backing vocals, and the occasional flavor of pedal steel guitar, mandolin, fiddle, and horns. *—Roch Parisien*

More Best of Leonard Cohen / Oct. 7, 1997 / Columbia ♦♦♦♦♦

Lloyd Cole

b. Jan. 31, 1961, Buxton, England

Vocals, Guitar / College Rock, Alternative Pop/Rock, Singer/Songwriter

Through both his lauded work fronting the Commotions and his more eclectic solo efforts, Lloyd Cole established himself as one of the most articulate and acute songwriters of the postpunk era. The uncommon quality of Cole's writing earned the Commotions a contract with British Polydor in 1984, and they debuted with *Rattlesnakes,* a wry, heartfelt record of jangling guitar pop heralded by the shimmering single "Perfect Skin," which reached the U.K. Top 30. 1985's *Easy Pieces* was a slicker effort that included the singles "Lost Weekend" and "Brand New Friend," both of which earned significant airplay on alternative radio outlets. Following the release of 1987's *Mainstream,* Cole disbanded the Commotions and moved to New York City to establish himself as a solo performer. His eponymously-titled 1990 solo debut continued much in the vein of his work with the Commotions, but 1991's *Don't Get Weird on Me, Babe* marked a major artistic shift, as the entire second half of the album explored lush, string-sweetened cabaret music. Commercial success continued to elude Cole, however, and it took 1993's *Bad Vibes*—a diverse effort touching upon psychedelia and electronics—a year to find U.S. distribution. By the time of 1995's *Love Story,* his sound had come full circle, with a return to the more minimalist, folk-rock inspired work of the Commotions. *—Jason Ankeny*

Rattlesnakes / Oct. 1984 / Capitol ♦♦♦♦♦

The Commotions' debut is also their peak moment; while Cole's ambitions and pretentions would occasionally overwhelm his later work, the fresh-scrubbed *Rattlesnakes* easily skirts such pitfalls. Couched in a sparkling folk-rock setting, Cole's songs drop all the right names (Norman Mailer, Arthur Lee, Simone de Beauvoir), reference all the right films (*Jules and Jim, On the Waterfront*), and touch all the right emotional bases (wounded heartbreak, unrequited love, arch flippancy). Similarly, his vocals strike the perfect balance between clinical distance and complete romantic submission; for all of the literate polish *Rattlesnakes,* possesses, it never loses touch with its humanity. *—Jason Ankeny*

Easy Pieces / Nov. 1985 / Capitol ♦♦♦

Producers Clive Langer and Alan Winstanley, as is their wont, created a shimmering pop surface for Lloyd Cole & the Commotions' second album, sweetening the tracks with string and brass countermelodies and emphasizing the chiming highs of the guitar and keyboards for an attractive sound that echoed the earnestness of British bands like the Hollies and Herman's Hermits, circa 1966. It was, of course, like sugar coating cyanide capsules, given Lloyd Cole's pleasantly sung lyrics, which detailed philosophical disillusionment, romantic discord, and, yes, at least attempted suicide. In the U.K., *Easy Pieces* was a Top Ten hit. But although the album saw something like a proper release in the U.S. and the Commotions toured extensively, no American breakthrough materialized. *— William Ruhlmann*

Mainstream / Sep. 1987 / Capitol ♦♦

● **1984-1989** / Jun. 1989 / Capitol ♦♦♦♦♦

The lush, facile simplicity of Lloyd Cole's music is brimmed with cushioned harmonies and soft-spoken choruses, and more often than not deals with the complexity of love. Accompanied by the bright jangle of guitar that's hitched to palatable pop tempos, his work with backup band the Commotions produced a number of melody-ridden songs that are best accessed on *1984-1989,* a collection of their finest material. Not unlike Orange Juice or the Blue Nile, Cole's music used polished instrumentation behind elements of subdued '80s Euro-pop, best exemplified in songs like "Perfect Skin" and "You Will Never Be No Good." As an enduring and enjoyable compilation, *1984-1989* really does gather the cream of their music, and each song relinquishes a clean, robust sound. Some of the more beautiful tracks include the friendly candor of "Are You Ready to Be Heartbroken?" or the irregularity between the lines of "Jennifer She Said." "Brand New Friend" glimmers with Cole's vocal resilience, as does the pristine bounce of "Lost Weekend." All three of Lloyd Cole & the Commotions' albums contribute songs to this best-of, with the stronger pieces coming from 1984's *Rattlesnakes.* Cole's music strays from sounding contrived or overlapped and sports comparisons to the Beautiful South in that they share the same lyrical wit and appeal. Relatively unknown in North America, Lloyd Cole & the Commotions contributed to some of the finest music to ever hover with pop ease, and this compilation lines up his best work all in one place. *—Mike DeGagne*

Lloyd Cole / Feb. 1990 / Capitol ♦♦♦

In the two and a half years following the release of *Mainstream,* Lloyd Cole signed to Capitol Records for the U.S., split from the Commotions, and moved to New York. For his first solo album, he assembled a team consisting of two New York band veterans—drummer/co-producer Fred Maher and guitarist Robert Quine, both of whom had played in Richard Hell's Voidoids and Lou Reed's backup group—plus bassist Matthew Sweet and Commotions keyboard player Blair Cowan. As a result, *Lloyd Cole* boasts a tougher, harder sound than the Commotions' records. Cole's vocals, meanwhile, have become more direct and less stylized. Cole's lyrics are also less adorned, and he has lightened up somewhat. Much of *Lloyd Cole* is musically astringent in a way Cole hasn't managed previously, even if the album is far less ambitious than his first two records. *— William Ruhlmann*

Don't Get Weird on Me Babe / Sep. 16, 1991 / Capitol ♦♦♦

Bad Vibes / Oct. 1993 / Rykodisc ♦♦♦

Love Story / Oct. 3, 1995 / Rykodisc ♦♦♦

Lloyd Cole & The Negatives / Nov. 14, 2000 / Indigo ♦♦♦

Phil Collins

b. Jan. 31, 1951, Chiswick, London, England

Vocals, Drums, Percussion / Pop/Rock, Soft Rock, Adult Contemporary

Phil Collins' ascent to the status of one of the most successful pop and adult-contemporary singers of the '80s and beyond was probably as much of a surprise to him as it was to many others. Balding and diminutive, Collins was almost 30 years old when his first solo single, "In the Air Tonight," became a number two hit in his native U.K. (the song was a Top 20 hit in the U.S.). Between 1984 and 1990, Collins had a string of 13 straight U.S. Top Ten hits. He got his first break in music at the end of his teens, when he was chosen to be a replacement drummer in the British art-rock band Genesis in 1970. When frontman Peter Gabriel abruptly left in 1974, Genesis auditioned 400 singers without success, then decided to let Collins have a go. The result was a gradual simplifying of Genesis' sound and an increasing focus on Collins's expressive, throaty voice. Collins made his debut solo album *Face Value* in 1981, which turned out to be a bigger hit than any Genesis album. It concentrated on Collins' voice, often in stark, haunting contexts such as the piano-and-drum dirge "In the Air Tonight." During the '80s, Collins balanced his continuing solo work with Genesis with enormous success. *— William Ruhlmann*

Face Value / 1981 / Atlantic ♦♦♦♦♦

Collins proves himself a passionate singer (and distinctive drummer) with a gift for both deeply felt ballads and snarling rockers. His debut album transformed him from the frontman of Genesis to a solo star who happened to be in Genesis, too. Contains "In the Air Tonight" and "I Missed Again." *— William Ruhlmann*

Hello, I Must Be Going / 1982 / Atlantic ♦♦♦

As his hit cover of "You Can't Hurry Love" demonstrates, Collins began to inject his highly melodic pop songwriting with more soul and R&B influences on his second solo album. While some of the material was successful, much of it showed that he was still coming to grips with how to incorporate R&B techniques into his style; in retrospect, *Hello, I Must Be Going* laid the groundwork for his breakthrough album, *No Jacket Required. — Stephen Thomas Erlewine*

No Jacket Required / 1985 / Atlantic ♦♦♦♦♦

From ballads like the number one "One More Night" to uptempo funk like the #1 "Sussudio," another tour de force in what was by now one of the most identifiable styles in pop music. The 1985 Grammy winner for Album of the Year. *— William Ruhlmann*

But Seriously / Nov. 1989 / Atlantic ♦♦♦

This chart-topping fourth album contains "Another Day in Paradise," "I Wish It Would Rain Down," "Do You Remember?," and "Something Happened on the Way to Heaven," all Top Five hits. *— William Ruhlmann*

Serious Hits . . . Live! / 1990 / Atlantic ♦♦

Both Sides / Nov. 9, 1993 / Atlantic ♦♦♦

Dance into the Light / Oct. 22, 1996 / Atlantic ♦♦♦

● **Hits** / Oct. 6, 1998 / Atlantic ♦♦♦♦♦

If *Hits* seems a little inadequate, even though it weighs in at 16 tracks, that's because Phil Collins had such a long, productive run. Also, to casual listeners (and possibly even some fans), it's hard to tell which singles by Genesis and which ones are solo cuts. So, it's almost a certainty that listeners will find something missing from this disc—and not just because Genesis cuts are absent, but because there's not enough space to fit all of Collins' solo hits, especially since the compilers decided to include a couple of lesser, latter-day hits at the expense of some earlier, bigger ones, while adding his non-LP cover of Cyndi Lauper's "True Colors" to entice hardcore fans. Thus, there are only 13 hits, which means some other big hits and good songs are absent—"I Missed Again," "I Don't Care Anymore," "Don't Lose My Number," "Do You Remember?" are all MIA. A few of these omissions are quite regrettable, but in the end, *Hits* is nevertheless a representative and pretty entertaining collection. The sequencing is not chronological, so it doesn't develop a nice flow (although "Take Me Home" is admittedly the ideal closer), but the chief strength of this collection is that it puts all of the big hits—including "Easy Lover," "Against All Odds," "In the Air Tonight," "Sussudio," "One More Night" and "Separate Lives"—in one place. No, it's not perfect—and it's hard not to wish that it was—but *Hits* still contains the majority of Collins' solo smashes, and that alone makes it a nice addition to his catalog. *— Stephen Thomas Erlewine*

Shawn Colvin

b. Jan. 10, 1956, Vermillion, SD

Vocals, Guitar / Contemporary Folk, Adult Alternative Pop/Rock, Singer/Songwriter

Shawn Colvin is one of the bright spots of the so-called "new folk movement" that began in the late '80s. And though she grew out of the somewhat limited "woman with a guitar" school, she has managed to keep the form fresh with a diverse approach, avoiding the clichéd sentiments and all-too-often formulaic arrangements that have plagued the genre. In less than a decade of recording, Colvin has emerged as a songcraftsman with plenty of pop smarts, which has earned her a broad and loyal following. She played in several bands while growing up, and began building a following on New York's singer/songwriter scene after moving there in 1983. Her work appeared in *Fast Folk Magazine,* and she got her first break in 1987 singing backup on Suzanne Vega's hit "Luka." A live tape sold at gigs gained her a contract with Columbia, and Colvin's major-label debut *Steady On* won the Grammy for Best Contemporary Folk Recording. Her 1992 follow-up, the more pop-oriented *Fat City,* earned her considerable critical praise and a growing crossover audience. The single "I Don't Know Why" became a big adult contemporary hit. Colvin's 1996 album *A Few Small Repairs* slowly became a hit over the course of 1997, thanks to strong word of mouth and the single "Sunny Came Home," which won a Grammy for Song of the Year. *— Chris Woodstra*

Steady On / Oct. 1989 / Columbia ♦♦♦♦♦

Sonically, *Steady On* is a triumph, with its emotional intimacy captured with smooth precision. Vocally, Colvin's tender, sometimes whisper-like performances are astonishing and haunting, provocative and seductive all at once. Then there are the songs that flow so effortlessly into one another that to remove even one would seemingly upset the entire balance of the cosmos as we know it. The sly Colvin adeptly plays with words, beats, phrasing, and rhymes, focusing not just on the meaning, but also the feel and rhythm of the lyrics to great effect. Having once claimed that she tends to write about the "positive side of the painful experience," this album proves her point, for even if you do listen amidst gray skies and drizzles, you will be soothed to the point of contentment. The opening strains of the wistful title track set the mood and ease you into Colvin's head and heart, as you embark on this journey with her to discover countless souls and their heretofore untold truths. On a album full of great songs, "Shotgun Down the Avalanche" still stands as one of her finest compositions, with its metaphoric imagery of riding an out of control emotional tide as one would cascade helplessly down a mountain of snow. The requisite troubadour-on-the-road tune, "Ricochet in Time," is made ever more poignant by Colvin's sleepy vocal track, bringing home the weariness that is a very large part of being an artist on tour. *Steady On* is a must have for anyone who loves acoustic music created in the grand tradition of Joni Mitchell and James Taylor, two legends Colvin now counts as contemporaries. *—Kelly McCartney*

Fat City / Oct. 1992 / Columbia ✦✦✦✦
For her second album, Shawn Colvin took a temporary break from longtime collaborator and producer John Leventhal, teaming up instead with Larry Klein. And while the strongest songs—"Tennessee," "Climb On (A Back That's Strong)" and "Object of My Desire"—are Colvin/Leventhal collaborations, credit should be given to Klein, who incorporated a glossy, more dynamic production and top-notch session players for a stronger and more accessible album. In addition to turning in a strong batch of songs, Colvin shows much more diversity, tackling everything from rootsy rockers to more sensitive folk ballads with equally passionate delivery. "I Don't Know Why" (the first song she wrote) and "Round of Blues" both found considerable success in adult contemporary radio formats, adding to her growing fan base. *—Chris Woodstra*

Cover Girl / Aug. 23, 1994 / Columbia ✦✦

Live '88 / Oct. 1995 / Plump ✦✦✦✦✦

● **A Few Small Repairs** / Oct. 1, 1996 / Columbia ✦✦✦✦✦
A Few Small Repairs, the proper follow-up to *Fat City,* was recorded on the heels of Colvin's divorce. And while the album is certainly a response, she avoids the obvious clichés in dealing with the aftermath, revealing instead the complex thought processes and complete range of human emotion, from anger, sadness, confusion, yearning, and disillusionment to resolve and recovery. Colvin has always been a songwriter of note, but with *A Few Small Repairs,* she reaches new heights, painting hauntingly vivid images that address not only relationships but also life in general with great insight. The subject matter predictably gives a generally dark mood to the album, but musically, the album is both diverse and irresistibly catchy. The album marks a reunion with former collaborator/producer John Leventhal, and the two have found a perfect blend between words, music, and tasteful, organic arrangements for Colvin's finest effort to date. *—Chris Woodstra*

Commander Cody

f. Jul. 19, 1944, Ann Arbor, MI
Group / Western Swing Revival, Country-Rock, Rock & Roll
Commander Cody and the Lost Planet Airmen were equally adept at stripped-down basic rock & roll, R&B, and gritty country-rock. Commander Cody's country-rock rocked harder than the Eagles or Poco—essentially, the group was a bar band. Much like English pub rock bands like Brinsley Schwarz and Ducks Deluxe, Commander Cody resisted the overblown and bombastic trends of early-'70s rock, preferring a basic, no-frills approach. Commander Cody and the Lost Planet Airmen never had the impact of the British pub rockers, yet their straightforward energy gave their records a distinguishing drive; they could play country, western swing, rockabilly, and R&B, and it all sounded convincing. In 1972, the group scored a fluke Top Ten hit with "Hot Rod Lincoln," taken from their second album, *Hot Licks, Cold Steel and Trucker's Favourites.* Commander Cody was never able to capitalize on the single's success, partially because their albums never completely captured their live energy. *—Stephen Thomas Erlewine*

Lost in the Ozone / 1971 / MCA ✦✦✦
This is the monumental debut by one of insurgent country's pioneer bands. Playing with electric instruments, including the all important steel and fiddle, and a good dose of irreverence, allowed the band to adhere to their own agenda. This first release was only a taste of the things to come. A combination of original tunes and some dusty covers, Cody & His Airmen were at the head of a parade that continues on through the '90s. Songs by Billy C. Farlow like "Daddy's Gonna Treat You Right" and the ever popular "Lost in the Ozone" were instant hits with the country-rock and hippy crowds. But, the rednecks loved them too and this was an amazing social phenomenon. Cody, whose real name is George Frayne, partnered with Farlow on a number of songs from this first collection that still pack a wallop. "Wine Do Yer Stuff" and the tearful "Seeds and Stems (Again)" left no doubt where these boys were coming from. A strong honky tonk album that swings, *Lost In the Ozone* is a viable recording. Cover tunes performed with energy and humor won crowds over everywhere. "Hot Rod Lincoln" is still played on outlaw country radio stations as is "20 Flight Rock," a boogie number that lets everything hang out. With not a single cut wasted, this is one of the buried gems of modern country music that displays guitarman Bill Kirchen at his wildest and Bruce Barlow, Lance Dickerson, Andy Stein, John Tichy, Bobby Black, West Virginia Creeper, Farlow and Commander Cody comin' out of the shoot ready to change the world for the better. *—Jana Pendragon*

Hot Licks, Cold Steel & Truckers' Favorites / 1972 / MCA ✦✦✦

Country Casanova / 1973 / MCA ✦✦✦

Commander Cody & His Lost Planet Airmen / 1975 / Warner Brothers ✦✦✦

We've Got a Live One Here / 1976 / Warner Brothers ✦✦✦✦✦
This is really the final hurrah for the band inspite of the fact that there were more recordings to follow. This is a two-record set from their 1976 tour of Europe with most of the original members still on board. After this tour, George Frayne, aka Commander Cody, broke up the band which now included Norton Buffalo. While this live recording is just as powerful as the preceding, *Live Deep in the Heart of Texas,* it is obvious that some of their fire is burning mighty low. Still, this bunch always did their best work on stage and they never failed to satisfy. Full of old standards, some new favorites and plenty of wattage to make it all work just right, the stand out tunes here are the Commander Cody classics like "Seeds and Stems," "Too Much Fun" and "Lost in the Ozone." Other numbers that bring back the good old days include the Airmen's version of "Milkcow Blues" and "San Antonio Rose." Trucker songs, big with the Continental crowd, are "Semi Truck," "Lookin' at the World Through a Windshield" and "18 Wheels." Other numbers of note are "One of Those Nights," written by Farlow, Frayne and Kirchen, as well as the Commander's send ups of "Smoke! Smoke! Smoke!," "Riot in Cell Block 9" and "Hot Rod Lincoln." Always extraordinary, the era of Commander Cody & His Lost Planet Airmen was a special moment in time that created a place for hipsters, cosmic cowboys, rednecks and the working class to all come together and enjoy some real American music. Never will there be another band like this one or recordings like the ones they made between 1971 and 1976. They ended this project with "Lost in the Ozone," bringing the band and its audience full circle. *—Jana Pendragon*

● **Too Much Fun: Best of Commander Cody** / Oct. 1990 / MCA ✦✦✦✦✦
Not only could they play the hell out of their instruments, but C.C. and his Lost Planet Airmen were a virtual melting pot of American music—country, R&B, rockabilly, Western swing. And always too much fun. *—Jeff Tamarkin*

The Best of Commander Cody & His Lost Planet Airmen / Aug. 8, 1995 / Relix ✦✦✦✦✦

The Commodores

f. 1967, Tuskegee, AL
Group / Quiet Storm, Urban, Funk, Soul
Formed by a group of friends from Tuskeegee Institute in Alabama, the Commodores were one of the top bands during their long tenure at Motown. Known for such hits as "Just to Be Close to You," "Easy," "Brickhouse," to name a few, the group is credited with seven number one songs and a host of other top ten numbers on the Billboard charts. They also have a vast music catalog that has generated more than 50 albums, and the recordings continue to be in demand. Initially formed to simply play music as a pastime and to meet girls, the line-up consisted of William King (trumpet), Thomas McClary (guitar), Ronald LaPread (bass), Walter "Clyde" Orange (drums), Lionel Richie (saxophone) and Milan Williams (keyboards). After attaining regional success performing, the band moved to New York City, where gigs at Smalls led to being invited to tour with the Jackson 5. That tour ultimately solidified a deal with Motown which would last until the mid '80s. In 1982, Lionel Richie left the band and the group courted the talents of tenor J.D. Nicholas (formerly of Heatwave) and would go on to release its biggest hit, "Nightshift" in 1985. Soon after, however, the group left Motown and signed with Polydor, producing their final top ten hit, "Goin' to the Bank," before the end of the year. *—Craig Lytle*

Anthology: The Best of the Commodores / Feb. 7, 1995 / Motown ✦✦✦✦✦
The revamped 1995 edition of *Anthology* includes all of the group's hit singles, as well as significant album tracks and singles that didn't chart, making it the definitive portrait of the popular, groundbreaking urban contemporary group. *—Sara Sytsma*

● **Ultimate Collection** / Mar. 25, 1997 / Motown ✦✦✦✦✦
The various stages of the Commodores' tenure on Motown are summarized on the excellent *Ultimate Collection,* which features 13 Top Ten hits including the monumental "Brick House," "Machine Gun," "Slippery When Wet," "Sweet Love," "Just to Be Close to You," "Fancy Dancer," "Easy," "Too Hot Ta Trot," "Three Times a Lady," "Still," "Lady (You Bring Me Up)" and "Nightshift." *—Jason Ankeny*

The Contours

f. 1958, Detroit, MI
Group / Frat Rock, Motown, R&B, Soul
One of Berry Gordy's earliest discoveries at Motown, the hard-rocking Contours cultivated a new generation of fans when their "Do You Love Me" was featured in the 1987 hit movie *Dirty Dancing.* Led by gravelly-voiced Billy Gordon, the quintet scored an R&B chart-topper in 1962 with the rollicking "Do You Love Me" on Gordy's label, then smoothed out their sound just a bit for the mid-'60s soul classics "First I Look at the Purse" and "Just a Little Misunderstanding." Dennis Edwards, who joined the group well after "Do You Love Me," was recruited to replace David Ruffin as lead of the Temptations in 1968. *—Bill Dahl*

The Very Best of the Contours [Motown] / Mar. 23, 1999 / Motown ✦✦✦✦
The first CD best-of compilation for the Contours actually takes the exact same ten tracks that were available on the *Do You Love Me* album and adds five more, most of which are of secondary interest. Regardless, it's a decent overview of a minor but good Motown act. "Do You Love Me" will always be their calling card, but "Shake Sherry," "First I Look at the Purse," "It Must Be Love" and "Can You Do It" are well worth hearing for anyone who wants to hear the Motown sound at its rawest and most raucous. Smokey Robinson's "That Day When She Needed Me" and the 1961 doo wop single "Funny" show an unexpectedly mellow side of the group. The 1966-67 sides, "Just a Little Misunderstanding" and "It's So Hard Being a Loser" find them being steered toward a slicker, Temptations-like direction; indeed, future Temp, Dennis Edwards, sings lead on the latter cut. *—Richie Unterberger*

Ry Cooder

b. Mar. 15, 1947, Los Angeles, CA
Slide Guitar, Vocals, Mandolin, Guitar / Slide Guitar Blues, Cuban Pop, Contemporary Blues, Roots Rock, Worldbeat, Ethnic Fusion, Country-Rock, Blues-Rock, Modern Electric Blues
Whether serving as a session musician, solo artist, or soundtrack composer, Ry Cooder's chameleon-like fretted instrument virtuosity, songwriting, and choices of material encom-

pass an incredibly eclectic range of North American musical styles, including rock & roll, blues, reggae, Tex-Mex, Hawaiian, Dixieland jazz, country, folk, R&B, gospel, and vaudeville. The 16-year-old Cooder began his career in 1963 in a blues band with Jackie DeShannon and then formed the short-lived Rising Sons in 1965 with Taj Mahal and Spirit drummer Ed Cassidy. During his subsequent career as a session musician, Cooder's trademark slide guitar work graced the recordings of such artists as Captain Beefheart, Randy Newman, Little Feat, Van Dyke Parks, the Rolling Stones and Gordon Lightfoot. Cooder made his debut as a solo artist in 1970; the follow-up, *Into the Purple Valley,* introduced longtime cohorts Jim Keltner on drums and Jim Dickinson on bass, and it and *Boomer's Story* largely repeated and refined the syncopated style and mood of the first. In 1974, Cooder produced what is generally regarded as his best album, *Paradise and Lunch;* its follow-up, *Chicken Skin Music,* showcased a potent blend of Tex-Mex, Hawaiian, gospel, and soul music, and featured contributions from Flaco Jimenez and Gabby Pahinui. In 1979, *Bop till You Drop* was the first major-label album to be recorded digitally. In the early '80s, Cooder began to augment his solo output with extensive soundtrack work. *—Steve Huey*

Ry Cooder / 1970 / Reprise ✦✦✦
His debut serves as a neat prototype, with its Sleepy John Estes and Woody Guthrie covers. It also introduces a most talented musician in its leader. But it's still a prototype; the best was yet to come. *—Jeff Tamarkin*

Into the Purple Valley / 1971 / Reprise ✦✦✦✦✦

Boomer's Story / 1972 / Reprise ✦✦✦✦✦
Largely laidback and bluesy, this album features a number of paeans to an America long lost. *—Jeff Tamarkin*

● **Paradise & Lunch** / 1974 / Reprise ✦✦✦✦✦
Working with an intriguing collection of veteran musicians, the master musician and archivist turns in a stunning set of timeless remakes and new compositions. *—Jeff Tamarkin*

Chicken Skin Music / 1976 / Reprise ✦✦✦✦✦
Hawaiian traditional music meets Leadbelly and Ben E. King on Cooder's gospelization of rock & soul. *—Jeff Tamarkin*

Showtime / 1976 / Reprise ✦✦✦
Recorded live in 1976, Cooder cooks and struts his stuff on this grand tour of his abilities. The great Flaco Jimenez is on accordion. *—Jeff Tamarkin*

Jazz / 1978 / Reprise ✦✦✦
A tribute to Dixieland, with a stopover at the blues hotel. Joseph Byrd's arrangements on tunes by Bix Beiderbecke, Joseph Spence, et al., are inspired. *—Jeff Tamarkin*

Bop Till You Drop / 1979 / Reprise ✦✦

Borderline / 1980 / Reprise ✦

The Slide Area / 1982 / Reprise ✦✦

Get Rhythm / 1987 / Reprise ✦✦✦

Meeting by the River / 1993 / Waterlily Acoustics ✦✦✦✦✦

Music by Ry Cooder / Jul. 11, 1995 / Reprise ✦✦✦✦✦
Since he's a limited vocalist with erratic songwriting skills, one could justifiably argue that the soundtrack medium is the best vehicle for Cooder's talents, allowing him to construct eclectic, chiefly instrumental pieces drawing upon all sorts of roots music and ethnic flavors (often, but not always, employing his excellent blues and slide guitar). This two-CD, 34-song compilation gathers excerpts from eleven of the soundtracks he worked on between 1980 and 1993 (three of the cuts, from the 1981 film *Southern Comfort,* are previously unreleased). As few listeners (even Cooder fans) are dedicated enough to go to the trouble of finding all of his individual soundtracks, this is a good distillation of many of his more notable contributions in this idiom, although it inevitably leaves out some fine moments. Still, it's well programmed and evocative, often conjuring visions of ghostly landscapes and funky border towns. *—Richie Unterberger*

Sam Cooke

b. Jan. 22, 1931, Clarksdale, MS, **d.** Dec. 11, 1964, Los Angeles, CA
Vocals / R&B, Soul

A performer whose sophisticated, crystalline vocal delivery and alchemical fusion of pop and gospel laid the foundations for the rise of modern soul music, Sam Cooke was a singer of remarkable spiritual resonance, a supreme talent whose vision transcended all barriers of race and faith. A champion of creative rights who wrote much of his own material and even established his own business empire to better realize his far-reaching musical ambitions, Cooke was also a champion of civil rights who utilized his stature as a performer to break down the color lines separating blacks from whites; a major crossover success, his brilliant career was tragically brief, but his shadow looms large over the generations of artists who emerged in his wake. As a teen, Cooke became a member of the gospel group the Highway QCs, and in 1950, he joined the Soul Stirrers. 1957's "You Send Me," a majestic soul confection which sold some two million copies, made him a secular pop star. A series of hits—most of them light romantic ballads and novelty tunes—followed over the next two years, most notably the Top 40 hits "Wonderful World," "Only Sixteen" and "Everybody Likes to Cha Cha." As the 1960s dawned, Cooke began taking an active interest in the music business, founding his own independent label, SAR; upon his arrival at RCA, his music adopted a grittier, more gospel-influenced feel, and his gifts reached their full potential as he reeled off a string of early 1960s hits ranging from the bluesy "Sad Mood" to the gospel-pop of "Bring It on Home to Me," through to the smooth soul of "Another Saturday Night" and the buoyant R&B of "Twisting the Night Away." As his reputation as a performer grew, Cooke established fervent fan bases in both the pop and R&B markets, and eventually he graduated from the so-called "chitlin' circuit" of black-owned venues to Las Vegas casino stages and white nightclubs, emerging as a crossover superstar. Cooke was murdered on December 11, 1964; "A Change Is Gonna Come," a posthumous 1965 smash, was his epitaph—a thoughtful, spiritually charged assessment of the then-current state of American race relations, it presaged the ascendent civil rights movement with remarkable clarity. *—Jason Ankeny*

Night Beat / Aug. 1963 / ABKCO ✦✦✦✦✦
Intense, spiraling uptempo numbers, gripping ballads, and simply marvelous performances by a legend who sadly wouldn't be around much longer. Originally released in August 1963, *Night Beat* [RCA 2709] was reissued on CD on June 6, 1995 [ABKCO 1124]. *—Ron Wynn*

Sam Cooke at the Copa / Oct. 1964 / ABKCO ✦✦✦
Cooke's classic live album is a mixed bag—he was playing to a White supper-club audience and altered his sound accordingly, favoring ballads and folk songs over most of his celebrated classic soul numbers. The voice is there, and the style, but he never does cut loose completely, and the backing band is too clean. *—Bruce Eder*

Two Sides of Sam Cooke / 1970 / Specialty ✦✦✦✦✦
This 12-song release, a straight-up reissue of the original vinyl album from 1970, splits its time between Cooke's early gospel sides as a member of the Soul Stirrers ("The Last Mile of the Way," "Were You There," "Touch the Hem of His Garment") and his early attempts at crossing over into pop music, including "Lovable," which was originally issued under the name of Dale Cooke to avoid upsetting his gospel fans. A major highlight is "Jesus Gave Me Water," Sam's first recording, done when he was 19 years old. Top-notch liner notes from Barret Hansen (aka Dr. Demento) make this a great little package well worth checking out. *—Cub Koda*

☆ **Live at the Harlem Square Club** / Jun. 1985 / RCA ✦✦✦✦✦
Long believed lost, this live album—rejected for release in 1963 by Cooke's managers, who wanted to broaden his appeal to White listeners—captures Cooke playing to a largely Black crowd, and it couldn't be more different from his *At the Copa* live album. A hot, sweaty performance, with Cooke and a proper band luxuriating in his most soulful material in its most wrenching and impassioned form. *—Bruce Eder*

★ **The Man & His Music** / Feb. 1986 / RCA ✦✦✦✦✦
The ultimate Sam Cooke collection, and really the only one worth owning, covering his post-1957 career from his pop music breakthrough ("You Send Me") to his final impassioned soul statement, "A Change Is Gonna Come" (which is included in its seldom-heard uncut version). Few stones are left unturned, the sound is clean and sharp, and the tragedy of Cooke's early death is recalled with each play of this collection. *—Bruce Eder*

His Earliest Recordings / 1991 / Specialty ✦✦✦✦✦
A superb collection of 25 of the earliest recordings made by Sam Cooke, including "Touch the Hem of His Garment." *—Stephen Thomas Erlewine*

The SAR Records Story / 1994 / ABKCO ✦✦✦✦✦
Sam Cooke's SAR Records Story is a double-disc set presenting material recorded for the legendary soul singer's own SAR label from 1959-1965, much of it produced by Cooke himself and including a few of his rough, unreleased demos. The first disc covers the label's religious side, with a multitude of cuts from Cooke's former group the Soul Stirrers (now with Jimmie Outler on lead vocals), plus a generous helping of songs by R.H. Harris & His Gospel Paraders and the Womack Brothers. The second disc covers essentially the same gospel-derived soul territory but with a secular bent, featuring future stars Bobby Womack (with the Valentinos), Billy Preston, and Johnnie Taylor, plus L.C. Cooke, Johnnie Morisette, the Simms Twins, and Mel Carter. All in all, it's an excellent look at a lesser-known portion of Cooke's career, and there's some great, underappreciated music to boot. *—Steve Huey*

Rhythm and the Blues / Oct. 24, 1995 / RCA ✦✦✦✦
From the title, you might infer that this 20-track compilation—taken from early-'60s sessions, and principally composed of LP-only cuts—aims to showcase Cooke's most soulful side. That's true to some degree, but this isn't his funkiest stuff; for that, look to *Live at the Harlem Square Club 1963,* or even his most uptempo singles. Most of this is in fact suave pop/R&B, the emphasis sometimes falling on the pop, with lightly swinging, jazzy arrangements and some orchestration. Cooke didn't write most of the material here, and while "Little Red Rooster" (a hit single) represents the earthiest extreme that the CD touches upon, there are also quite a few songs that were originally performed by jazz/popsters from the '20s, '30s, and '40s. Certainly these are decent offerings; Cooke's a great singer and interpreter, and the arrangements are smooth without being overdone. But it's neither Cooke at his very best (the hits compilation *Man and His Music* is much better) or his grittiest (that honor belongs to *Harlem Square*). It does restore much of his better obscure material to wide availability and is recommended to those who have the above-mentioned albums and want more Cooke, although the 1963 LP *Night Beat* (reissued on CD in 1995) is a bluesier and better one to check out first. *—Richie Unterberger*

★ **Greatest Hits** / Feb. 24, 1998 / RCA ✦✦✦✦✦
Although it isn't as sublime as the definitive *The Man and His Music, Greatest Hits* still does a good job of rounding up the majority of Sam Cooke's biggest pop hits. Ironically, it doesn't have enough gospel or R&B cuts, skipping over such essentials as "Touch the Hem of His Garment," "Ain't That Good News" and "A Change Is Gonna Come" in favor of such pop hits as "Sugar Dumpling." However, it has just enough songs that aren't on *The Man and His Music* to make it worth exploring for fans who haven't been able to hear some of this material before, since some of these songs have been out of print for years. Nevertheless, the curious and the novice should be aware that this is not a good introduction to Sam Cooke, because it doesn't provide a full portrait of his career and it overlooks too many necessary songs. *—Stephen Thomas Erlewine*

☆ **The Man Who Invented Soul** / Sep. 26, 2000 / RCA ✦✦✦✦✦
This set is near essential to fans of Sam Cooke, despite the fact that it contains none of his gospel recordings for Specialty Records or any of the work from the final year of his career (owned by ABKCO Records). Scattered every few minutes across this four-disc collection are reminders of just how far ahead of all existing musical forms Cooke was, creating sounds that stretched the definitions of song genres as they were understood and created completely new categories. Indeed, he was so successful that it's easy to underestimate the impact and

importance of many of his early triumphs. "You Send Me," which opens this set, may seem today like the safest, tamest pop music, but in 1957 it was a genre-bending single, a new kind of R&B/pop music hybrid and one that quietly shook the foundations of the music business when it hit number one.

Disc one offers a fresh appreciation of the best of the early Keen Records sides, drawing on the best of nearly two years of singles and the strongest of Cooke's LP tracks in the best account to date of his early career in popular music. Disc two begins Cooke's RCA years, and the quality of his singles, which clearly and easily bridge the gap between genres, races, and generations, improves dramatically. The development of Cooke's writing and singing and his growing confidence and range culminate with disc four, which encompasses the *Night Beat* album and Cooke's live performance from *the Harlem Square Club*. The sound is extraordinary throughout, expansive, rich-textured, and vividly detailed; a choice earlier CD release, *The Man and His Music*, by comparison, sounds thin and tinny. *—Bruce Eder*

Elvis Costello (Declan Patrick McManus)

b. Aug. 25, 1955, Liverpool, England

Vocals, Keyboards, Guitar / College Rock, British Punk, Adult Alternative Pop/Rock, Pub Rock, New Wave, Singer/Songwriter

Elvis Costello emerged from the punk explosion of 1977, soon proving that he was a singer/songwriter and musician of extraordinary talent. Throughout his career, musical eclecticism has distinguished Costello's records as much as his fiercely literate lyrics, confirming his place as one of the best singer-songwriters to emerge since Bob Dylan.

Costello began his career toiling away in folk clubs and leading a pub-rock group called Flip City. Still performing under his given name Declan McManus, took his demo tapes to the fledgling British independent Stiff Records. Impressed with what they heard, they signed him, encouraging him to change his name to Elvis Costello. His Nick Lowe-produced debut *My Aim is True* appeared in 1977 to great critical acclaim. That year, he assembled the Attractions, who were showcased to great effect on the scathing *This Year's Model*, which became a British Top 10 hit. Costello began to diversify on 1979's *Armed Forces*, a glimmering pop record that gave him his American breakthrough. Despite some press controversies, he continued his momentum with the soul-influenced of 1980's *Get Happy* and 1981's *Trust*. Costello stretched with 1981's *Almost Blue*, a country album produced by Nashville legend Billy Sherrill. He followed in 1982 with the lush, ambitious *Imperial Bedroom;* although it was highly acclaimed, it stalled on the charts. Costello then tried for a hit with the streamlined *Punch the Clock*, a moderate success followed by the tired *Goodbye Cruel World*. He bounced back with a pair of masterpieces in 1986, the Americana album *King of America* and the tough *Blood and Chocolate*. He then signed with Warner, put the Attractions on hiatus and took three years off. He returned in 1989 with *Spike*, a wildly eclectic affair that gave him a hit with "Veronica," yet signaled how erratic his Warner years would be. Throughout the '90s, Costello worked consistently, trying something new each time out, whether it was avant-pop, classical chamber pop or a reunion with the Attractions, appealing only to his cult. In 1998, he began his time at Mercury with *Painted from Memory*, a collaboration with Burt Bacharach that earned his strongest reviews and sales in years, even if it failed to turn into a genuine hit. *—Stephen Thomas Erlewine*

★ **My Aim Is True** / Aug. 1977 / Rykodisc ✦✦✦✦✦

Elvis Costello was as much a pub-rocker as he was a punk-rocker and nowhere is that more evident than on his debut, *My Aim Is True*. It's not just that Clover, a San Franciscan rock outfit led by Huey Lewis (absent here), back him here, not the Attractions, it's that his sensibility is borrowed from the pile-driving rock & roll and folksy introspection of pub-rockers like Brinsley Schwarz, adding touches of cult singer/songwriters like Randy Newman and David Ackles. Then, there's the infusion of pure nastiness and cynical humor, which is pure Costello. That blend of classicist sensibilities and cleverness make this collection of shiny roots rock a punk record—it informs his nervy performances his prickly songs. Of all classic punk debuts, this remains perhaps the most idiosyncratic because it's not cathartic in sound, only in spirit. Which, of course, meant that it could play to a broader audience, and Linda Ronstadt did indeed cover the standout ballad "Alison." Still, there's no mistaking this for anything other than a punk record, and it's a terrific one at that, since even if he buries his singer/songwriter inclinations, they shine through as brightly as his cheerfully mean humor and immense musical skill; he sounds as comfortable with a '50s knockoff like "No Dancing" as he does on the reggae-inflected "Less Than Zero." Costello went onto more ambitious territory fairly quickly, but *My Aim Is True* is a phenomenal debut, capturing a songwriter and musician whose words were as rich and clever as his music. [Ryko/Demon's 1993 reissue contained several bonus tracks, including the country B-sides "Radio Sweetheart" and "Stranger in the House," plus demos of his first group, Flip City.] *—Stephen Thomas Erlewine*

☆ **This Year's Model** / Jul. 1978 / Rykodisc ✦✦✦✦✦

Where *My Aim Is True* implied punk rock with its lyrics and stripped-down production, *This Year's Model* sounds like punk. Not that Costello's songwriting has changed—*This Year's Model* is comprised largely of leftovers from *My Aim Is True* and songs written on the road. It's the music that changed. After releasing *My Aim Is True*, Costello assembled a backing band called the Attractions, which were considerably tougher and wilder than Clover, who played on his debut. The Attractions were a rock & roll band, which gives *This Year's Model* a reckless, careening feel. It's nervous, amphetamine-fueled, nearly paranoid music—the group sounds like they're spinning out of control as soon as they crash in on the brief opener, "No Action," and they never get completely back on track, even on the slower numbers. Costello and the Attractions speed through *This Year's Model* at a blinding pace, which gives his songs—which were already meaner than the set on *My Aim Is True*—a nastier edge. "Lipstick Vogue," "Pump It Up," and "(I Don't Want to Go to) Chelsea" are all underscored with sexual menace, while "Night Rally" touches on a bizzare fascination with fascism that would blossom on his next album, *Armed Forces*. Even the songs that sound relatively lighthearted—"Hand in Hand," "Little Triggers," "Lip Service," "Living in Paradise"—are all edgy, thanks to Costello's breathless vocals, Steve Nieve's carnivalesque organ riffs, and Nick Lowe's bare-bones production. Of course, the songs on *This Year's Model* are typically catchy and help the vicious sentiments sink into your skin, but the most remarkable thing about the album is the sound—Costello and the Attractions never rocked this hard, or this vengefully, ever again. *—Stephen Thomas Erlewine*

☆ **Armed Forces** / 1979 / Rykodisc ✦✦✦✦✦

After releasing and touring the intense *This Year's Model*, Elvis Costello quickly returned to the studio with the Attractions to record his third album, *Armed Forces*. In contrast to the stripped-down pop and rock of his first two albums, *Armed Forces* boasted a detailed and textured pop production, but it was hardly lavish. However, the more spacious arrangements—complete with ringing pianos, echoing reverb, layered guitars and harmonies—accent Costello's melodies, making the record more accessible than his first two albums. Perversely, while the sound of Costello's music was becoming more open and welcoming, his songs became more insular and paranoid, even though he cloaked his emotions well. Many of the songs on *Armed Forces* use politics as a metaphor for personal relationships, particularly fascism, which explains its working title, *Emotional Fascism*. Occasionally, the lyrics are forced, but the music never is—the album demonstrates the depth of Costello's compositional talents and how he can move from the hook-laden pop of "Accidents Will Happen" to the paranoid "Goon Squad" with ease. Some of the songs, like the light reggae of "Two Little Hitlers" and the impassioned "Party Girl," build on his strengths, while others like the layered "Oliver's Army" take Costello into new territories. It's a dense but accessible pop record and ranks as his third masterpiece in a row. *—Stephen Thomas Erlewine*

☆ **Get Happy!!** / 1980 / Rykodisc ✦✦✦✦✦

Get Happy was born as much from sincere love for soul as it was for Costello's desire to distance himself from an unfortunate verbal faux-pas where he insulted Ray Charles in an attempt to get Stephen Stills' goat. Either way, it resulted in a 20-song blue-eyed soul tour-de-force, where Elvis doesn't just want to prove his love, he wants to prove his knowledge. So, he tries everything, starting with Motown and Northern Soul, then touching on smooth uptown ballads and gritty southern soul, even finding common ground between the two by recasting Sam & Dave's "I Can't Stand Up (For Falling Down)" as a careening stomper. What's remarkable is that this approach dovetails with the pop carnival essayed by *Armed Forces*, standing as a full-fledged Costello record instead of a genre exercise. As it furiously flits through 20 songs, Costello's cynicisms, rage, humor and misanthropic sensibility gel remarkably well. Some songs may not quite hit their target, but that's part of the album's charm—it moves so fast, its lesser songs rush by on the way to such full-fledged masterpieces as "New Amsterdam," "High Fidelity" and "Riot Act." *Get Happy* bursts with energy and invention, standing as a testament to how Costello, the pop encyclopedia, can reinvent the past in his own image. [The Ryko/Demon reissue contains no less than 10 bonus tracks, including such Costelo essentials as "Girls Talk," "So Young," "Getting Mighty Crowded," "Hoover Factory," "Dr. Luther's Assistant" and "Just a Memory," written for Dusty Springfield.] *—Stephen Thomas Erlewine*

☆ **Trust** / Feb. 1981 / Rykodisc ✦✦✦✦✦

Following the frenzied pop-soul of *Get Happy*, Elvis Costello & the Attractions quickly returned to the studio and recorded *Trust*, their most ambitious and eclectic album to date. As if he was proving his stylistic diversity and his sophistication after the concentrated genre experiment of *Get Happy*, Costello assembled *Trust* as a stylistic tour-de-force, packing the record with a wild array of material. "Clubland" has jazzy flourishes, "Lovers' Walk" rolls to a Bo Diddley beat, "Luxembourg" is rockabilly-redux, "Watch Your Step" is soul-pop, "From a Whisper to a Scream" rocks as hard as anything since *This Year's Model*, "Shot With His Own Gun" is Tin Pan Alley pop, "Different Finger" is the first country song he put on an official album. And that's not even counting highlights like "New Lace Sleeves" and "White Knuckles," which essentially stick to Costello's signature pop but offer more complex arrangements and musicianship than before. In fact, both "complexity" and "sophistication" are keywords to the success of *Trust*—without delving into the minutely textured arrangements that would dominate his next pop album, *Imperial Bedroom*—Costello & the Attractions demonstrate their musical skill and savvy by essentially sticking to their direct sound of their four-piece band. In the process, they recorded arguably their most impressive album, one that demonstrates all sides of Costello's songwriting and performing personality without succumbing to pretentiousness. *—Stephen Thomas Erlewine*

Almost Blue / Nov. 1981 / Rykodisc ✦✦✦

Costello's "country record" is usually written off as a vanity project, but *Almost Blue* is quite a bit more than that. It's one of the most entertaining cover records in rock & roll, simply because of its enthusiasm. The album begins with a roaring version of Hank Williams' "Why Don't You Love Me" and doesn't stop. Costello sings with conviction on the tear-jerking ballads, as well as barn burners like "Tonight the Bottle Let Me Down." It's clear that Costello knows this music, and it's also clear who he learned it from—Gram Parsons. Costello covers Parsons' "Hot Burrito No. 1" and "How Much I Lied," and all of the music on *Almost Blue* recalls Parsons' taste for hardcore honky-tonk and weepy ballads. It's to Costello's credit that he made a record relying on emotion to pay tribute. *—Stephen Thomas Erlewine*

☆ **Imperial Bedroom** / Jul. 1982 / Rykodisc ✦✦✦✦✦

Having gotten country out of his system with *Almost Blue*, Elvis Costello returned to pop music with *Imperial Bedroom*—and it was *pop* in the classic, Tin Pan Alley sense. Costello chose to hire Geoff Emerick, who engineered all of the Beatles' most ambitious records, to produce *Imperial Bedroom* which indicates what it sounds like—it's traditional pop with a post-*Sgt. Pepper* production. Essentially, the songs on *Imperial Bedroom* are an extension of Costello's jazz and pop infatuations on *Trust*. Costello's music is complex and intricate, yet it flows so smoothly, it's easy to miss the bitter, brutal lyrics. The interweaving layers of "Beyond Belief" and the whirlwind intro are the most overtly dark sounds on the record, with most of the album given over the orchestrated, melancholy torch songs and pop singles. Never once do Costello and the Attractions deliver a rock & roll song—the album is all about sonic detail, from the accordion on "The Long Honeymoon" to the lilting strings on "Town Cryer." Of course, the detail and the ornate arrangements immediately peg *Imperial Bedroom* as Costello's most ambitious album, but that doesn't mean it's his absolute masterpiece.

Imperial Bedroom remains one of Costello's essential records because it is the culmination of his ambitions and desires—it's where he proves that he can play with the big boys, both as a songwriter and a record-maker. It may not have been a commercial blockbuster, but it certainly earned the respect of legions of musicians and critics who would have previously disdained such a punk rocker. And, perhaps, that's also the reason that he abandoned this immaculately crafted style of work on his next album, *Punch the Clock*. *—Stephen Thomas Erlewine*

Punch the Clock / 1983 / Rykodisc ✦✦✦
Perhaps frustrated by the lack of commercial success *Imperial Bedroom* encountered, Elvis Costello enlisted British hitmakers Clive Langer and Alan Winstanley to produce its followup, *Punch the Clock*. The difference between the two records is immediately noticeable. *Punch the Clock* has a slick, glossy surface, complete with layered synthesizers, horns, studio effects and the backup vocals of Afrodisiac. The approach isn't necessarily a misguided one, since Costello is as much a pop musician as he is a singer/songwriter and many of the best moments on the record—"Everyday I Write the Book," "Let Them All Talk"—work well as shiny pop singles. However, the problem with *Punch the Clock* is that Costello is entering a fallow songwriting period; it his least consistent of original songs to date. The best moments, the anti-war ballad "Shipbuilding" and the eerie pseudo-rap "Pills and Soap," are as articulate and effective as any of his past work, but frequently Costello falls short of meeting his standards, particularly when he's trying to write a song in the style of his older songs. Nevertheless, the sheen of the Langer & Winstanley production makes *Punch the Clock* a pleasurable listen. Costello's uneven writing means that only portions of the album are memorable. *—Stephen Thomas Erlewine*

Goodbye Cruel World / 1984 / Rykodisc ✦✦

King of America / Jan. 1986 / Rykodisc ✦✦✦✦✦
Stripping away much of the excess that cluttered *Punch the Clock* and *Goodbye Cruel World*, Elvis Costello returned to his folk-rock and pub-rock roots with *King of America*, creating one of his most affecting and personal records. Costello literally took the album as a return to roots, billing himself by his given name Declan MacManus and replacing the Attractions with a bunch of L.A. session men (although his old band appears on one cut), who give the album a rootsy but sleek veneer which sounds remarkably charged after the polished affectations of his Langer/Winstanley productions. And not only does the music sound alive, but so do his songs, arguably his best overall set since *Trust*. Working inside the limits of country, folk and blues, Costello writes literate, introspective tales of loss, heartbreak and America that are surprisingly moving—he rarely got better than "Brilliant Mistake," "Glitter Gulch," "American Without Tears," "Big Light" and "Indoor Fireworks." What separates *King of America* from the underrated *Almost Blue* is that Costello's country now sounds lived-in and worn, bringing a new emotional depth to the music, and that helps make it one of his masterpieces. *—Stephen Thomas Erlewine*

Blood & Chocolate / Feb. 1986 / Rykodisc ✦✦✦✦
Costello returned to the Attractions as quickly as he abandoned them, hiring the band and old producer Nick Lowe to record *Blood & Chocolate*, his second record in the span of one year. Where *King of America* was a stripped-down, roots-rock affair, *Blood & Chocolate* is a return to the harder rock of *This Year's Model*. Occasionally, there are hints of country and folk, but the majority of the album is straight-ahead rock & roll—the opener, "Uncomplicated," only has two chords. The main difference between the reunion and the Attractions' earlier work is the tone—*This Year's Model* was tense and out-of-control, where *Blood & Chocolate* is controlled viciousness. "Tokyo Storm Warning," "I Hope You're Happy Now" and "I Want You" are the nastiest songs he has ever recorded, both lyrically and musically—Costello snarls the lyrics and the Attractions bash out the chords. *Blood & Chocolate* doesn't retain that high-level of energy throughout the record and to lose momentum toward the end of the album. Still, it's a lively and frequently compelling reunion, even if it is a rather mean-spirited one. *—Stephen Thomas Erlewine*

Out of Our Idiot / 1987 / Demon ✦✦✦

Girls Girls Girls / 1989 / Columbia ✦✦✦

Spike / 1989 / Warner Brothers ✦✦
Following a pair of near-masterpieces in 1986, Elvis Costello went into semi-seclusion, separating from the Attractions (once again) and Columbia records, emerging three years later on Warner Brothers with *Spike*. Mockingly billing himself as "the Beloved Entertainer" on the album's front cover, there's nevertheless a real sense of showbiz pizzazz here, as he tries on a little bit of everything. You like Costello, the soul singer— Try "Deep Dark Truthful Mirror," recorded with the Dirty Dozen Brass Band. Costello the pop sophisticate— How about the torch song "Baby Plays Around" or "God's Comic," a tune that mocks Andrew Lloyd Webber, while aching to eclipse him. The angry young man— There's "Tramp the Dirt Down," perhaps the nastiest anti-Thatcher song ever waxed. Costello, the witty wordsmith— Well, there's "Pads, Paws and Claws," a rockabilly tune overflowing with labored puns. Costello, the gifted pure pop tunesmith— There's plenty of that here, from "This Town" with Roger McGuinn and Paul McCartney and the lovely "Veronica," a tune co-written with McCartney that became one of his biggest hits. So, there's a lot here—everything except focus, actually. And Costello certainly likes to indulge himself here, throwing in the awkward "Chewing Gum" and the instrumental "Stalin Malone" for good measure. There are some moments that work quite well, but there's nothing connecting them, and if anything, he's trying way too hard—and, for all of the overarching ambition of his early-'80s recordings, that criticism never applied before. Certainly, there are cuts for cultists to enjoy, but *Spike's* sprawl works against it, resulting in a maddeningly diffuse listen. *—Stephen Thomas Erlewine*

Mighty Like a Rose / May 14, 1991 / Warner Brothers ✦✦
If *Spike* seemed frustratingly incoherent, it's nothing compared to *Mighty Like a Rose*, a deliberately dense, difficult record that is easily the most impenetrable Elvis Costello ever cut. With producers Mitchell Froom and Kevin Killen, Costello made a record with no easy entrances, even if the sparkling Beach Boys-esque "The Other Side of Summer" and the lovely "So Like Candy" would have been accessible with different production. And, certainly, production is the most notable thing about this record. Filled with clattering production, spongy bass, cardboard guitars, studio white noise, and layers upon layers of tracks, there's so much going on that it's hard to get to the core of the songs. Not that Costello makes it any easier for the listener, either, since only a few songs (the aforementioned pair, plus "All Grown Up" and "Playboy to a Man") don't seem self-satisfied in their own construction. And his performances are nearly as affected as the songs, as he over-sings (albeit for effect) and contributes to the muddy wall of sound. Yes, this is "interesting," but it takes many plays before you realize all those "interesting" effects lead nowhere—only to the strangest record Costello ever cut (and that's not a compliment, unfortunately). *—Stephen Thomas Erlewine*

The Juliet Letters / Jan. 19, 1993 / Warner Brothers ✦✦✦
Looking back on it, it's remarkable that Warner didn't sue Elvis Costello for making deliberately noncommercial, non-representative records, the way Geffen did with Neil Young in the '80s. After all, it's not just that he made a record as anti-pop as *Mighty Like a Rose*, it's that he followed it with a full-fledged classical album, *The Juliet Letters*—"a song sequence for string quartet and voice," recorded with the Brodsky Quartet. It's inspired by a Verona professor that responded to letters addressed to Juliet, of Romeo and Juliet fame, too. Given this history, it's little wonder that the record didn't storm the charts, but it is remarkable that Warner, even with their reputation for being an artist's label, decided to release it, since this just doesn't fit anywhere—not within pop (especially in the grunge-saturated 1993) and not within classical, either. Of course, that's precisely what's interesting about the record, and if interesting didn't signify any rewards with *Mighty*, it does here. This is a distinctive, unusual affair that, at its best, effectively marries chamber music with Beatlesque art pop. And there are a number of moments that work remarkably well on the record, such as "I Almost Had a Weakness" and "Jacksons, Monk and Rowe." True, these are the songs closest to straight-ahead Costello songs, yet they're still nice, small gems, and even if the rest of the record can be a little arch and awkward, it's not hard to admire what Costello and the Brodskys set out to do. And that's the problem with the record—it's easy to intellectualize, even appreciate, what it intends to be, but it's never compelling enough to return to. More experiment than effective, then. *—Stephen Thomas Erlewine*

Brutal Youth / Mar. 8, 1994 / Warner Brothers ✦✦✦
Perhaps realizing that *The Juliet Letters* was one step too far, especially after the willfully eclectic pair of *Spike* and *Mighty Like a Rose*, Elvis Costello set out to make a straight-ahead rock & roll record with *Brutal Youth*, reuniting with the Attractions (though Bruce Thomas appears on only five tracks) and Nick Lowe (who plays bass on most of the rest). Unfortunately, all this nostalgia and good intentions are cancelled by the retention of producer Mitchell Froom, whose junkyard, hazily cerebral productions stand in direct contrast to the Attractions' best work. Likely, Froom's self-conscious production appealed to Costello, since it makes *Brutal Youth* look less like a retreat, but it severely undercuts the effectiveness of the music, since it lacks guts, no matter how smugly secure it is in its tempered "experimentation." Costello certainly had the raw elements for a dynamic little record here—the band, when they can be heard, sounds good, and many songs (highlighted by "Pony St.," "Kinder Murder," "13 Steps Lead Down," "You Tripped at Every Step," and "20% Amnesia") are fresh, effective evocations of his classic work—but it needed to be punchier to succeed. He needed to be produced by Lowe, instead of just having him sit in on bass. *—Stephen Thomas Erlewine*

● **The Very Best of Elvis Costello & the Attractions** / Oct. 25, 1994 / Rykodisc ✦✦✦✦✦
A solid complement to Ryko's Costello reissue series if you don't want to pick up each individual album. Of course, the 22 tracks (drawn from his first 11 eleven albums and, according to the liner notes, "hand-picked by Elvis himself") also sport the crisply remastered sound featured on the rest of the series. "The Very Best Of" halts abruptly at 1986's *Blood and Chocolate*, his last release for Columbia. *—Roch Parisien*

Kojak Variety / May 9, 1995 / Warner Brothers ✦✦

All This Useless Beauty / May 14, 1996 / Warner Brothers ✦✦✦
Following his second covers album, *Kojak Variety*, Elvis Costello set out to assemble a collection of songs he had written for other artists, but he never recorded himself—sort of a reverse covers album. As it turned out, that idea was only used as a launching pad—the resulting album, *All This Useless Beauty*, is a mixture of nine old and three new songs. Given its origins, it's surprising that the record holds together as well as it does. The main strength of *All This Useless Beauty* is the quality of the individual songs—each song can stand on its own as an individual entity, as the music is as sharp as the lyrics. Although the music is certainly eclectic, it's accessible, which wasn't the case with *Mighty like a Rose*. Furthermore, the production is more textured and punchier than Mitchell Froom's botched job on *Brutal Youth*. *All This Useless Beauty* doesn't quite add up to a major statement, but the simple pleasures it offers makes it one of the more rewarding records of the latter part of Costello's career. *—Stephen Thomas Erlewine*

Extreme Honey: The Very Best of Warner Brothers Years / Oct. 21, 1997 / Warner Brothers ✦✦✦✦

Painted from Memory / Sep. 29, 1998 / Mercury ✦✦✦✦✦
Elvis Costello teamed with Burt Bacharach first collaborated on "God Give Me Strength," a sweeping ballad that functioned as the centerpiece in Allison Anders' *Grace of My Heart*. It was a stunning song in the tradition of Bacharach's classic '60s work and it was successful enough that the composers decided to collaborate on a full album, *Painted from Memory*. Wisely, they chose to work within the stylistic parameters of Bacharach's '60s material, but *Painted from Memory* never sounds like a stylistic exercise. Instead, it's a return to form for both artists. Bacharach hasn't written such graceful, powerful melodies since his glory days, and Costello hasn't crafted such a fully realized album since *King of America*. It's a testament to both that even if the album is clearly in Bacharach's territory, it feels like a genuine collaboration. Often, the music not only evokes the spirit of Dionne Warwick, it's reminiscent of Elvis' torchy ballads for *Trust*. Costello keeps Bacharach from his schmaltzier tendencies,

and Bacharach keeps Costello from overwriting. With its lush arrangements, sighing brass and strings, gentle pianos and backing vocals, it's clearly a classicist album, yet it sounds utterly timeless. Its melodies are immediate, its emotions subtle, its impact lasting —and, in doing so, *Painted from Memory* illustrates that craft can not only be its own reward, but it can be genuinely moving. *—Stephen Thomas Erlewine*

Count Five

f. 1965, San Jose, CA, **db.** 1967
Group / Acid Rock, Garage Rock, Psychedelic
The definitive one-hit wonders, the Count Five failed to make much of a lasting impression—but just play that one hit, "Psychotic Reaction," and almost any audience will want to hear more. Their one fault was that they could never generate more—they tried but never issued another record half as good. The Count Five started life in San Jose, California in the early '60s, still in their mid-teens and specializing in surf instrumental music before trying to pick up on the British Invasion sound. At about the time the group changed its name to the Count Five, guitarist Sean Byrne put the finishing touches on a song he'd been outlining in his head, ultimately called "Psychotic Reaction." It became a showcase for the band's abilities, and the crescendo of their stage act. A local deejay eventually got the song and the group placed with L.A.-based Double Shot Records. A chugging, fuzz-tone laden piece of punk defiance with more than a few signature licks and phrasings borrowed from Bo Diddley and the Yardbirds, plus a punk attitude worthy of the Standells, the record eventually made No. 5 nationally. An album was rushed out, containing some ill-conceived originals, but nothing that the group did after "Psychotic Reaction" seemed to work. The strain of maintaining music careers while attending college—which was essential to the members keeping their draft deferments—took its toll, as did the dwindling bookings; by the end of 1967, the Count Five ceased to exist. Their story might have ended there, but for the 1972 release of *Nuggets*, Lenny Kaye's original '60s garage/psychedelic punk compilation. Suddenly a new generation discovered the Count Five, and demand for their album resulted in several rounds of reissues on vinyl and CD. In the decades since, the group has rated at least a mention in most histories of garage rock and psychedelic punk, and "Psychotic Reaction" is a standard of the genre, still potent and enjoyable on its own terms. *—Bruce Eder*

● **Psychotic Reaction: The Very Best of Count Five** / Mar. 23, 1999 / Collectables ✦✦✦✦✦
Re-release of the earlier Count Five compilation from Performance, with new packaging and notes. There's a considerable range of material here, all of it pretty punk oriented, though very little as rewarding as the title track, a number five hit nationally that managed to incorporate the best elements of the Yardbirds' and Bo Diddley's music. The other highlights include "Pretty Big Mouth" and a very animated cover of the Who's "My Generation." The sound is ridiculously good as well, and the biographical notes are highly informative. *—Bruce Eder*

Counting Crows

f. Aug. 1991
Group / American Trad Rock, Adult Alternative Pop/Rock, Alternative Pop/Rock
With their angst-filled hybrid of Van Morrison, the Band, and R.E.M., Counting Crows became an overnight sensation in 1994. Only a year earlier, the band was a group of unknown musicians, filling in for the absent Van Morrison at the Rock & Roll Hall of Fame ceremony; they were introduced by an enthusiastic Robbie Robertson. Early in 1993, the band recorded their debut album, *August & Everything After*, with T-Bone Burnett; it was released in the fall. It was a dark, somber record, driven by the morose lyrics and expressive vocals of Adam Duritz; the only up-tempo song, "Mr. Jones," became their ticket to stardom. What made Counting Crows was how they were able to balance Duritz's tortured lyrics with the sound of the late '60s and early '70s; it made them one of the few alternative bands to appeal to listeners who thought that rock & roll died in 1972. *Recovering the Satellites* followed in 1996, and in 1998 they issued the two-disc *Across a Wire—Live in New York*. Counting Crows' third studio album, *This Desert Life*, appeared in 1999. *—Stephen Thomas Erlewine*

● **August and Everything After** / Sep. 14, 1993 / Geffen ✦✦✦✦
When the prevailing guitar jingle of "Mr. Jones" cascaded over radio in the early nineties, it was a sure sign that The Counting Crows were a musical force to reckoned with. Their debut album *August and Everything After* burst at the seams with both dominant pop harmonies and rich, hearty ballads, all thanks to lead singer Adam Duritz. The lone guitar work of "Mr. Jones coupled with the sweet, in-front pull of Duritz's voice kicked off the album in full force. The starkly beautiful and lonely sounding "Round Here" captured the band's honest yet subtle talent for singing ballads, while "Omaha" is lyrically reminiscent of a Springsteen tune. The fusion of hauntingly smooth vocals with such instruments as the Hammond B-3 organ and the accordion pumped new life into the music scene, and their brisk sound catapulted them into stardom. On "Rain Kings", the piano takes over as it's aloof flair dances behind Duritz with elegant crispness. The slower paced "Raining In Baltimore" paints a perfectly grey picture and illustrates the band's ease at conveying mood by eliminating the tempo. Most of the songs here engage in overly contagious hooks that won't go away, making for a solid bunch of tunes. Containing the perfect portions of instrumental and vocal conglomeration, The Counting Crows showed off their appealing sound to it's full extent with their very first album. *—Mike DeGagne*

Recovering the Satellites / Oct. 15, 1996 / Geffen ✦✦✦✦

Across a Wire: Live in New York / Jul. 14, 1998 / Geffen ✦✦✦

This Desert Life / Nov. 2, 1999 / Interscope ✦✦✦✦
It's likely that critics and listeners will consider Counting Crows' long-delayed third album, *This Desert Life*, another retro effort by a traditionalist band, but it's actually their most individual and finest album yet. All the familiar elements are in place, from Adam Duritz's impassioned vocals and cryptic lyrics to the jangling instrumentation, but the laments gel better than ever before. Part of it undoubtedly has to do with David Lowery and Dennis Herring's organic production, which keeps the rough edges in place, helping the music to breathe, but the real success of the record is due to the band themselves, who have matured gracefully. They may have spent a long time recording this album, but the music feels natural and immediate. Upon closer inspection, the craft really shines through. The songs are tight, with strong hooks on the choruses, and nice, memorable melody lines; the arrangements may be earthy, but they're never cluttered. Most importantly, Duritz has reigned in his tendency to overwrite and over-emote, turning his best sets of songs to date. But the best thing about *This Desert Life* is that it holds together as a cohesive album while providing the best individual songs in the band's catalog. And that just doesn't mean the best singles, although "Hanginaround" is their finest uptempo number to date; the album tracks are consistently compelling, ranging from the winding narrative of "Mrs. Potter's Lullaby" to the measured ballad "Speedway." These subtle differences—the confident performances, cohesion, and assured songwriting—add up Counting Crows' strongest album to date. They may still recall rock giants, but only in the best possible way—by crafting an album that ebbs and flows like the best classic rock records. *—Stephen Thomas Erlewine*

Don Covay (Donald Randolph)

b. Mar. 24, 1938, Orangeburg, SC
Vocals / Deep Soul, Southern Soul, Soul
An R&B and soul songwriting great, Don Covay compositions have been recorded by everyone from the Rolling Stones to Jimi Hendrix, Gladys Knight to Wilson Pickett, and many others. Covay joined the Rainbows alongside Marvin Gaye, John Berry, and Billy Stewart in the '50s. He also performed as a solo singer with Little Richard, who recorded Covay as "Pretty Boy" on the Atlantic release "Bip Bop Bip." Covay had moderate success with the single "Pony Time," which he co-wrote with Berry, for the Arnold label in 1960. He began to hit his stride in 1964 with "Mercy Mercy," "Sookie Sookie," and "See Saw," and had tunes recorded by Gene Chandler and Aretha Franklin. Covay did both blues and soul numbers for Janus and Mercury labels in the '70s. His most electrifying number was 1973's "I Was Checkin' Out While She Was Checkin' In," which made it to number six. Covay made one LP for Gamble and Huff's Philadelphia International label in 1976, but *Travelin' in Heavy Traffic* proved a disappointment. Covay recorded for Newman in 1980, and got his last chart single with "Badd Boy." *—Ron Wynn*

● **Mercy Mercy: The Definitive Don Covay** / Oct. 19, 1994 / Razor & Tie ✦✦✦✦✦
Mercy Mercy: The Definitive Don Covay compiles 23 tracks from throughout the soul singer's career. Encompassing everything from the R&B stomp of "Bip Bop Bip" and "Pony Time" to the seductive soul of "I Was Checkin' Out While She Was Checkin' In" and "No Tell Motel," the disc makes a convincing argument that Covay was one of the great overlooked R&B/soul artists of the '60s. *—Stephen Thomas Erlewine*

Cowboy Junkies

f. 1985, Toronto, Ontario, Canada
Group / College Rock, Adult Alternative Pop/Rock, Alternative Country-Rock, Alternative Pop/Rock
Although it was solely a way to gain attention, the Cowboy Junkies' name goes a long way in describing the Canadian band's sound. At its core, the group's music is based in country and folk traditions, except their tempos are slow and lethargic, their guitars are languid, and Margo Timmins' vocals are lovely, yet hauntingly detached. The group recorded their first album, *Whites off Earth Now!!*, in 1986, releasing it on a Canadian independent label. Two years later, they recorded *The Trinity Sessions* in an abandoned church, using only one microphone. The album may have only cost $250 to record, but it sparked a small sensation, with the band's reworkings of "Blue Moon," "I'm So Lonesome I Could Cry," "Walking After Midnight," and "Sweet Jane" earning them a diverse and dedicated cult following. *The Caution Horses* didn't earn as much press as their previous album, yet they maintained a sizable cult, which stuck by the band through their next two records, *Black-Eyed Man* (1992) and *Pale Sun, Crescent Moon* (1993). *—Stephen Thomas Erlewine*

Whites off Earth Now!! / 1986 / RCA ✦✦✦
Featuring only one original song, the Cowboy Junkies' debut *Whites Off Earth Now!!* captures the band forming their own sound through covers, including songs by Robert Johnson and Bruce Springsteen. It's not as captivating as their later releases, but it's fascinating to hear their signature country-on-valium sound develop. Margo Timmins sings beautifully. *—Stephen Thomas Erlewine*

● **The Trinity Sessions** / 1988 / RCA ✦✦✦✦✦
Recorded in a one-night session at a Toronto church using only a DAT recorder, *Trinity Sessions* turned into the Junkies' American breakthrough thanks to the fluke success of "Sweet Jane," a cover of the Velvet Underground classic. Lou Reed himself praised it due to its inclusion of the lost verse about "heavenly wine and roses," and the four-piece do it all proud, with Margo Timmins' lovely, haunted vocal and the band's quietly narcotic performance in perfect sync. As a whole, *Trinity Sessions* captures that entire mood throughout, building on the sound established on *Whites Off Earth Now!* to create a perfect balance between older inspirations and a newer, hushed dramatic edge. The album is split evenly between covers and new cuts, with the former showing the group's many gifts at creating its own interpretations and the latter its abilities to come up with equally fine cuts. Among the originals, "Misguided Angel" is perhaps the best, a lengthy, sweetly beautiful piece that showcases the abilities of guest performers Jaro Czerwinec on accordion and Jeff Bird on mandolin and harmonica. The core quartet just nails the main performance to a T, and the end result is wondrous. As for the covers, while some of the choices are well known—Hank Williams' "I'm So Lonesome I Could Cry," Patsy Cline's "Walking After Midnight"—the Junkies effectively turn each take into their own. *—Ned Raggett*

The Caution Horses / Feb. 1990 / RCA ✦✦

Black-Eyed Man / Feb. 11, 1992 / RCA ✦✦✦
The Cowboy Junkies' *Black Eyed Man* is an excellent return to form following their disappointing third LP, *The Caution Horses*. Where Michael Timmins' songwriting was stilted and

overly self-conscious on the previous record, here his character studies are literate and finely-etched; like Robbie Robertson before him, Timmins' Canadian roots allow him to view the rural American experience with unique objectivity, and narratives like the opening "Southern Rain" and "Murder, Tonight, in the Trailer Park" are told with compassion and cinematic detail. *Black Eyed Man* also broadens the Junkies' musical horizons: "If You Were the Woman and I Was the Man," a duet with John Prine, is like a Fifties-era love song intercepted from an alternate reality, while tracks like the lilting "A Horse in the Country" push the group closer to the folk-pop territory of 10, 000 Maniacs. At the same time, their country roots are further reinforced by a pair of outstanding Townes Van Zandt covers, "Cowboy Junkies Lament" and "To Live Is to Fly;" sandwiched between them is Timmins' own tribute, "Townes' Blues." *—Jason Ankeny*

Pale Sun, Crescent Moon / Nov. 23, 1993 / RCA ✦✦✦✦✦
A refreshed, revitalized sound that doesn't sacrifice the delicate touches that first made them unique; rugged, but still pristine. Much of the new spark emanates from the strings of honorary Junkie Ken Myhr, who peals out intense, biting lead guitar throughout. Especially prominent is his incendiary slide work on "Seven Years" and a spectacular cover of Dinosaur Jr.'s "The Post." Still, it's hard to imagine a ballad instrument more haunting and ethereal than Margo Timmins' voice. *—Roch Parisien*

200 More Miles, Live Performances 1985-1994 / Oct. 10, 1995 / RCA ✦✦✦

Lay It Down / Feb. 27, 1996 / Geffen ✦✦✦

Studio: Selected Studio Recordings 1986-1995 / Nov. 12, 1996 / RCA ✦✦✦✦✦

Miles from Our Home / Jun. 30, 1998 / Geffen ✦✦✦
Working with producer John Leckie on *Miles from Our Home* has enlivened the Cowboy Junkies' trademark lackadaisical style somewhat. Replacing the group's calm, minimalist sound with a polished production, Leckie manages to make the record sound unlike anything else in the band's catalog. That's not to say that there's no trace of the old style—he has simply updated their sound, bringing it in line with adult alternative pop that they played a part in establishing in the late '80s. If the results aren't as magical as *The Trinity Sessions*, they're far from disappointing. Margo Timmins' voice remains as enchanting as ever and her brother Michae Timmin's songs are sturdy. There might not be any masterpieces on *Miles from Our Home*, but there aren't any misfires, either—it's simply a solid album from a reliable band. *—Stephen Thomas Erlewine*

Rarities, B-Sides and Slow, Sad Waltzes / Oct. 12, 1999 / Valley ✦✦✦

Cracker

f. 1991
Group / American Trad Rock, Adult Alternative Pop/Rock, Alternative Pop/Rock
While he was the frontman for Camper Van Beethoven, it seemed that it would take nothing short of a miracle to make guitarist/singer David Lowery a favorite of mainstream rockers, but that's what he and his second band, Cracker, have become. Led by Lowery and guitarist Johnny Hickman, Cracker is much more straightforward than Camper; Cracker concentrates on rock and country, creating a twisted, rootsy rock & roll that sounds like a post-punk Rolling Stones or Little Feat. While their self-titled 1992 debut had moments of raw brilliance, Cracker's second album, 1993's *Kerosene Hat*, fulfilled their promise. Powered by the hit single "Low," the album was a hard-rocking meeting of traditional rock and post-punk sensibilities. Like Camper Van Beethoven's albums, it deserved to be heard by a wide audience; this time Lowery found a larger audience—*Kerosene Hat* eventually went gold.

Cracker released their third album, *The Golden Age*, in the spring of 1996. The album didn't repeat the success of its predecessor, falling off the charts within three months of its release. *Gentleman's Blues* followed in 1998. *—Stephen Thomas Erlewine*

Cracker / Mar. 10, 1992 / Virgin ✦✦✦✦
Apart from David Lowery's tendency to slip in some smug, self-serving lyrics, Cracker's debut is a terrific rock & roll record, full of energetic three-chord bashers and surprisingly moving ballads. *—Stephen Thomas Erlewine*

Kerosene Hat / Aug. 24, 1993 / Virgin ✦✦✦✦
With their second album, Cracker have lost the smarmy self-righteousness that plagued their otherwise fine debut, replacing it with a surprisingly solid, rocking core. *Kerosene Hat* is David Lowery's least affected album yet—its humor is no stranger than "Dead Flowers" by the Stones or "Fat Man in a Bathtub" by Little Feat, two groups that Cracker strongly recall throughout the album. *Kerosene Hat* is more blues- and country-based than their debut, but it sounds natural, since their songwriting has improved and they've grown tighter as a unit. *—Stephen Thomas Erlewine*

The Golden Age / Apr. 2, 1996 / Classic Compact Disc ✦✦✦

Gentleman's Blues / Aug. 25, 1998 / Virgin ✦✦✦

● **Garage d'Or** / Mar. 14, 2000 / Virgin ✦✦✦✦
Garage d'Or chronicles Cracker's rise and fall, choosing to cut corners where it better suits the band's legacy. For instance, "I Hate My Generation" is nowhere to be found on the 16-track disc, but a cover of the Flamin' Groovies' "Shake Some Action" (from the *Clueless* soundtrack) is. Why, you ask? Because *Garage D'Or* is designed for Cracker's core audience—not the people who requested "Low" every hour on the hour, but those who understood all the musical references, jokes, and lyrical allusions, and cherished each little detail. Consequently, it may not be "comprehensive," in the traditional sense of the word, but there's little question that it is definitive, capturing the wry essence of the band. Based on these 16 tracks, including all their modern rock radio hits, Cracker might not have been the great overlooked band of the '90s, but they were still quite good. They still may not be for every listener. Fans of Camper Van Beethoven will find this a little too obvious, though they'll certainly treasure such bizarre, little gems as the priceless travelogue "Euro-Trash Girl" (originally a "hidden" bonus track at the end of *Kerosene Hat*, and arguably their finest moment). Trad rock fans who might be receptive to the the general sound of the band may find the lyrical irony a little quirky for their tastes. That was their problem in a nutshell: Despite being musically accessible, they didn't appeal to everyone. Naturally, that's what makes them more lovable in the eyes of hardcore fans, and *Garage D'Or* goes a long way to proving that those fans just may be right. *—Stephen Thomas Erlewine*

The Cramps

f. 1976, New York, NY
Group / Psychobilly, Rockabilly Revival, Post-Punk, Alternative Pop/Rock
The Cramps' unique sound synthesizes classic rockabilly, touches of psychedelia, and lyrical fare devoted mostly to monster movies and sleazy sex into an infectious, gloriously tasteless conglomeration of American trash culture. While their subject matter may verge on offensive to some, their obvious sense of humor and the fun, disposable feel of their best work prevent the listener from ever taking things more seriously than they should. The group was formed by vocalist Erick "Lux Interior" Purkhiser and guitarist Kirsty "Poison Ivy Rorschach" Wallace, who met in Sacramento and found they shared an affinity for obscure '50s rockabilly and surf records and junk culture. The Cramps eventually went to the legendary Sun studio with cult icon Alex Chilton producing to record several singles, later released on the *Gravest Hits* EP. Chilton also produced their minimalistic 1980 debut album, *Songs the Lord Taught Us*. Following the 1983 live EP *Smell of Female*, the Cramps sued I.R.S. for lack of support; the case was settled out of court and resulted in the band being released from the label. Nothing more was heard from them in the way of new material for years; their only new album prior to 1990, 1986's *A Date with Elvis*, was not released in the U.S. until four years later. *—Steve Huey*

Gravest Hits / Jul. 1979 / Illegal ✦✦✦
This first release by the Cramps shows the group laying out many of the aspects of their curious style in rudimentary fashion. Raw, slashing guitar playing derived mostly from rockabilly and somewhat from psychedelic and 1960s garage pop (the group would have no bass player until the mid-'80s) and primitive drumming provide the platform for Lux Interior's eccentric singing, which is best described as a hyper-crazed, reverb-drenched, exhibitionist rockabilly style complete with groaning, shouting, growling, and hiccuping effects. The only song written by the band here is "Human Fly," a skulking mid-tempo fuzz-guitar number with monster movie lyrics; the line "I got 96 tears/And 96 eyes" is a sly reference to the ? and the Mysterians garage band hit. The other selections are covers of classic 1950s and 1960s songs; these include a bizarre version of the Ricky Nelson crooning hit "Lonesome Town" that peppers the musical texture with stray guitar interjections, and a rip-snorting version of the Trashmen song "Surfin' Bird" that ends with a long, noisy improvisation section of doubtful tonal focus. The cavernous sound quality here lends a certain bleak feel to the music here, but distortions on the vocal in "Human Fly" and drums on "Lonesome Town" merely sound poor. This unpolished but effective release is worth hearing. *—David Cleary*

Songs the Lord Taught Us / May 1980 / IRS ✦✦✦✦
Continuing the spooked-out and raging snarls of *Gravest Hits*, the Cramps once again worked with Alex Chilton on the group's full-album debut, *Songs the Lord Taught Us*. The jacket reads "file under: sacred music," but only if one's definition includes the holy love of rockabilly sex-stomp, something which the Cramps fulfill in spades. Having spent *Gravest Hits* mostly doing revamps of older material, the foursome tackled a slew of originals like "The Mad Daddy" and "TV Set" this time around, creating one of the few neo-rockabilly records worthy of the name. Years later *Songs* still drips with threat and desire both, testament to both the band's worth and Chilton's just-right production. "Garbageman" surfaced as a single in some areas, a wise choice given the at-once catchy roll of the song and downright frightening guitar snarls, especially on the solo. The covers of the Sonics' "Strychnine" and Billy Burnette's "Tear It Up"—not to mention the concluding riff on "Fever"—all challenge the originals. Interior has the wailing, hiccuping, and more down pat, but transformed into his own breathless howl, while Ivy and Gregory keep up the electric fuzz through more layers of echo than legality should allow. Knox helms the drums relentlessly; instead of punching through arena rock style, Chilton keeps him the rushed rhythm running along in the back, increasing the sheer psychosis of it all. *—Ned Raggett*

Psychedelic Jungle / May 1981 / IRS ✦✦✦✦
Here, Kid Congo Powers and Ivy form just as fine a team as she and Gregory did on earlier releases, and if things aren't always as flat-out fried as on *Gravest Hits* and *Songs*, the same atmosphere of swampy, trashy, rockabilly-into-voodoo ramalama reigns supreme. The song titles alone show the band hasn't really changed its sights any: the opening two cuts are covers, "Green Fuz" and "Goo Goo Muck," while originals include "Caveman," "Can't Find My Mind," and the brilliant "The Natives Are Restless." Then there's "Don't Eat Stuff Off the Sidewalk," which almost sounds worthy of a Frank Zappa freakout (at least lyrically). Other legendary tracks like "Primitive" and "Green Door" get the Cramps makeover this time out, with the proper mix of respect and hot-wired energy, while "The Crusher" sounds like Interior's on the verge of going completely insane. The Cramps themselves take over the production this time out, resulting in a cleaner, crisper sound (especially when it comes to Knox's drums) that isn't quite as wired, for better or for worse. As commanding showmen, though, the quartet's style comes through big time, with Interior throwing in appropriate yells, yipes, and other sounds where appropriate; his antics at the end of "Goo Goo Muck" are especially gone. If anything, the moodier strutting throughout increases the creepiness of what's afoot; if things aren't psychedelic in the commonly accepted sense, it's certainly not easy listening. Interior sometimes sounds almost normal, but with the sense that something strange is lurking just around the corner, and Ivy is still one of the best guitarists around, her snarling reverb worth a thousand fret-shredders. *—Ned Raggett*

Smell of Female / 1983 / Capitol/Enigma ✦✦✦
One gets the feeling from the title and cover art alone that if the Cramps could have released this live document in Glorious Smell-o-rama they would have jumped at the chance. Even without it one can almost sense the whiffs of perspiration and energy the group was cooking up; recorded at New York's *Peppermint Lounge* with Powers on guitar, the quartet slams

out a then mostly entirely new set of songs with, as expected, appropriate covers as needed. The wonderfully profane take on Hasil Adkins' "She Said" surfaces here, with Interior sounding like he's about to die more than once. The Count Five's "Psychotic Reaction" and the perfectly appropriate "Faster Pussycat," taken from the legendary Russ Meyer film of the same name, also give the band more than a little something to chew on. As for the originals, the usual mess of swampy rockabilly and industrial strength noise comes together in just the right way from the start. "Thee Most Exalted Potentate of Love" gives Interior the chance to do his undead but still wired loveman thang right from the start, while Ivy and Powers hit the twang hard and Knox keeps everything going just right. "Call of the Wighat" is another highpoint, Knox showing that he's up to more involved pounding and percussion when the need arises. A studio cut, "Surfin' Dead," surfaces as a ringer at the end; if not quite the Cramps go Beach Boys, it arguably forecasts the Jesus and Mary Chain's "Kill Surf City" just enough. *—Ned Raggett*

● **Bad Music for Bad People** / 1984 / IRS ✦✦✦✦
An extremely skimpy compilation, *Bad Music* is only 31 minutes long. Still, this dog's breakfast of material, assembled upon the Cramps' departure from IRS, was the only place for a variety of B-sides and rarities, at least for a long while. The most well-known is "New Kind of Kick," covered later by the the Jesus and Mary Chain. It isn't as out there sonically as that band, but it has plenty of attitude to burn, with Interior getting lyrically rude more than once and Ivy turning in some fierce, screeching guitar. Another winner is the sassy "Drug Train," originally the B-side to "Garbageman," which celebrates debauchery with the expected gusto. Knox gets to show his command for steady but right drumming on this one, while Interior and Ivy go crazy with the usual vim. The usual selection of covers of rockabilly and garage rarities surfaces, most memorably with a ripping redo of rock & roll wildman Hasil Adkins' "She Said." The rave-up qualities are brought out in a full-bodied performance, while Interior sounds like he's been either dug up from a grave or a swamp. More semi-hits like "Human Fly" and "Goo Goo Muck" surface as well, making the whole release a fine if overly short overview of the Cramps' vision of the universe. Production at points ventures into the totally primitive—all the more appropriate for the band in question, admittedly—giving everything the necessarily rough-and-ready atmosphere for the group's own brand of scummy sleaze. The artwork is notable in its own right, with the fleshless big-haired ghoul on the cover having turned into an icon for the Cramps and goth/rockabilly music worldwide. *—Ned Raggett*

Date with Elvis / 1986 / Restless ✦✦✦

Stay Sick! / Jan. 1990 / Capitol/Enigma ✦✦

Look Mom No Head! / Nov. 1991 / Restless/Enigma ✦✦

Flamejob / Oct. 11, 1994 / Medicine Label/Warner Brothers ✦✦✦

Big Beat from Badsville / Sep. 23, 1997 / Epitaph ✦✦✦

The Cranberries

f. 1990
Group / Celtic Rock, Adult Alternative Pop/Rock, Alternative Pop/Rock
Combining the melodic jangle of post-Smiths indie-guitar-pop with the lilting, trance-inducing sonic textures of late '80s dream-pop and adding a slight Celtic tint, the Cranberries became one of the more successful groups to emerge from the pre-Britpop UK indie scene of the early '90s. Led by vocalist Dolores O'Riordan, whose keening, powerful voice is the most distinctive element of the group's sound, the group initially made little impact in the United Kingdom. It wasn't until the lush ballad "Linger" became an American hit in 1993 that the band also achieved mass success in the UK. Following the success of "Linger," the Cranberries quickly became international stars, as both their 1993 debut album, *Everybody Else Is Doing It, So Why Can't We* and its 1994 follow-up, *No Need to Argue*, sold millions of copies and produced a string of hit singles. By the time of their third album, 1996's *To the Faithful Departed*, the group had added distorted guitars to its sonic pallete and attempted to make more socially significant music, which resulted in a downturn in the band's commercial fortunes. *—Stephen Thomas Erlewine*

● **Everybody Else Is Doing It, So Why Can't We—** / Apr. 20, 1993 / Island ✦✦✦✦✦
Title aside, what the Cranberries *were* doing wasn't that common at the time, at least in mainstream pop terms; grunge and G-funk had done their respective big splashes via Nirvana and Dr. Dre when *Everybody* came out first in the U.K. and then in America some months later. Lead guitarist Noel Hogan is in many ways the true center of the band at this point, co-writing all but three songs with O'Riordan and showing an amazing economy in his playing, and having longtime Smiths/Morrissey producer Stephen Street behind the boards meant that the right blend of projection and delicacy still held sway. One can tell he likes Johnny Marr and his ability to do the job just right: check out the quick strums and blasts on "Pretty" or the concluding part of the lovely "Waltzing Back." O'Riordan herself offers up a number of romantic ponderings and considerations lyrically (as well as playing perfectly fine acoustic guitar), and her undisputed vocal ability suits the material perfectly. The two best cuts were the deserved smashes: "Dreams," a brisk, charging number combining low-key tension and full-on rock, and the melancholic, string-swept break-up song "Linger." If *Everybody* is in the end a derivative pleasure—and O'Riordan's vocal acrobatics would never again be so relatively calm in comparison—a pleasure it remains nonetheless, the work of a young band creating a fine little synthesis. *—Ned Raggett*

No Need to Argue / 1994 / Island ✦✦✦✦✦
With their surprise success behind them, the Cranberries went ahead and essentially created a sequel to *Everybody Else is Doing It, Why Can't We* with only tiny variations, with mixed results. The fact that the album is essentially a redo of previously established stylistic ground isn't apparent in just the production, handled again by Stephen Street, or the overall sound, or even that one particularly fine song is called "Dreaming My Dreams." *Everybody* wasn't a laugh riot, to be sure, but *No Need To Argue* starts to see O'Riordan take a more commanding and unfortunately much more self-conscious role that ended up not standing the band in good stead later. Lead single "Zombie" is the worst offender in this regard—the heavy rock trudge isn't immediately suited for the band's strengths (notably, O'Riordan wrote this without Noel Hogan)—while the subject matter—the continuing Northern Ireland tensions—ends up sounding trivialized. Opening cut "Ode to My Family" is actually one of the band's best, with a lovely string arrangement created by O'Riordan, but her overdubbed vocals start showing her distinct vocal tics becoming a bit more gimmicky at the expense of the performance. Where *No Need* succeeds best is when the Cranberries stick at what they know, resulting in a number of charmers like "Twenty One," the uilleann pipes-touched "Daffodil's Lament," which has an epic sweep that doesn't overbear like "Zombie," and the evocative "Disappointment." *—Ned Raggett*

To the Faithful Departed / Apr. 30, 1996 / Island ✦✦

Bury the Hatchet / Apr. 27, 1999 / Island ✦✦✦

Cream

f. 1966, England, **db.** 1969, London, England
Group / British Psychedelia, British Blues, Psychedelic, Hard Rock, Blues-Rock
Although Cream were only together for a little more than two years, their influence was immense, both during their late-'60s peak and in the years following their breakup. Cream were the first top group to truly exploit the power-trio format, in the process laying the foundation for much blues-rock and hard rock of the 1960s and '70s. It was with Cream, too, that guitarist Eric Clapton truly became an international superstar. Critical revisionists have tagged the band as overrated, citing the musicians' emphasis upon flash, virtuosity, and showmanship at the expense of taste and focus. This was sometimes true of their live shows in particular, but in reality The best of their studio recordings were excellent fusions of blues, pop, and psychedelia, with concise original material outnumbering the bloated blues jams and overlong solos.

Clapton had established himself as a guitar hero with the Yardbirds, and later with John Mayall's Bluesbreakers, while bassist/singer Jack Bruce and drummer Ginger Baker had both been in the British R&B combo the Graham Bond Organisation. At first Cream's focus was electrified and amped-up traditional blues, which dominated their first album, 1967's *Fresh Cream.* Originals like "N.S.U." and "I Feel Free" gave notice that the band were capable of moving beyond the blues, and they truly found their voice on *Disraeli Gears* in late 1967. The album broke the band bigtime in the States, generating their first big U.S. hit single, "Sunshine of Your Love." With the double album *Wheels of Fire*, Cream topped the American charts in 1968, though the record itself was an erratic affair dogged by the decision to present separate discs of studio and live material. Their decision to disband later that year—at a time when they were seemingly on top of the world—came as a shock to most of the rock audience. In 1969, a posthumous album featuring both studio and live material, *Goodbye*, made number two. Clapton and Baker would quickly resurface in 1969 as half of another short-lived supergroup, Blind Faith, and Clapton of course went on to one of the longest and most successful careers of anyone in the rock business. *—Richie Unterberger*

Fresh Cream / Dec. 1966 / Polydor ✦✦✦
Cream's debut album was largely rooted in the blues, and included here highly charged versions of such standards as Willie Dixon's "Spoonful," and Muddy Waters' "Rollin' and Tumblin'," and bassist Jack Bruce's "N.S.U."—which took on a whole new life on stage. On this record they sound somewhat flat and uninspired. *—Rob Bowman*

Disraeli Gears / Nov. 1967 / Polydor ✦✦✦✦
The threesome of Jack Bruce, Peter Brown, and legendary guitarist Eric Clapton forming the band Cream was a monumental effort of jazz, blues, and psychedelic rock during the British rock period of the late 1960s. Cream, with their raw fury of intense sound, was renowned for their rare talent of taking songs of complex arrangements and making them an act of spontaneous beauty during live shows. *Disreali Gears*, their second release, was an essential landmark recording that brought listeners to the direction they were soon to take with *Wheels of Fire.* Taking on a circus-spinning arsenal of sounds and effects, Cream's fashionable art is a blend of highly sustained drenched distortion, rampant percussion, and a kaleidoscope of various musical textures and colors, both in melody and rhythm. Each of the Disreali Gears' list of 11 tunes is original in format, containing it own unique brands of dashing blues-laden guitar riffs by Clapton, as well as thick bass lines and smashing drum leads. Highlights of the record feature Clapton's awe-inspiring and soul-gripping guitar leads, including hits such as "Sunshine of Your Love" and "Tales of Brave Ulysses." The latter is a magical poem laced into a line of mesmerizing chordal changes. Disreali Gears is a definitive staple of early British rock and a sensational addition to the avid classic rock listener. *—Shawn Haney*

Wheels of Fire / Jun. 1968 / Polydor ✦✦✦✦
Wheels of Fire was a two-album set, one disc recorded in the studio, the second disc recorded on stage in San Francisco. Side three contains the definitive live version of what became Clapton's signature piece, Robert Johnson's "Crossroads," plus a version of "Spoonful" that clocks in just short of 17 minutes. On such pieces, Cream approached blues-based rock with a jazz aesthetic, using the song as a framework to begin and end a performance. The strength of the performance is in the improvisation. When it worked, as it does on "Spoonful," they were brilliant. When it didn't, as on "Traintime" and "Toad," the band became excess incarnate. The studio disc contained their second Top Ten single, Jack Bruce's "White Room," as well as a stunning cover of Albert King's "Born Under a Bad Sign." Other tracks, particularly those written by Ginger Baker, do not hold up. *—Rob Bowman*

Goodbye / Jan. 1969 / Polydor ✦✦✦
As the title implies, this is Cream's farewell. By the time it was issued, the band had broken up. Three studio recordings that were left were coupled with extended live versions of "I'm So Glad," "Politician," and "I'm Sitting on Top of the World." The live tracks burn. Clapton, Bruce, and Baker each take credit for one of the studio tracks. Clapton's cut, "Badge," was co-written by George Harrison and remains what was surely the prettiest melody to ever grace a Cream recording. *—Rob Bowman*

Live Cream, Vol. 1 / Apr. 1970 / Polydor ♦♦♦

Live Cream, Vol. 2 / Mar. 1972 / Polydor ♦♦♦

★ **The Very Best of Cream** / May 9, 1995 / Polydor/Chronicles ♦♦♦♦♦
There have been many compilations drawn from the four albums Cream originally released between 1966 and 1969. But the one most commonly available since the early 1980s was the ten-track *Strange Brew: The Very Best of Cream* (1983) (Polydor 811 639), a bare-bones collection focusing on the group's hit singles. Note, then, that this album, despite the similar title, is a newly compiled 1995 CD/cassette containing all of the recordings on *Strange Brew,* plus ten more. It is thus the most comprehensive Cream anthology on the market, including all the group's essential tracks on a single disc with superior sound in a package containing good annotations. *—William Ruhlmann*

Those Were the Days / Sep. 23, 1997 / Polydor ♦♦♦♦
Those Were the Days is an ambitious four-disc, 63-track box set that divides Cream's career into two halves. The first two discs feature every studio track the group ever released, plus a handful of unreleased cuts, alternate takes and rarities. The other two discs are devoted to live material, which is segued together in an attempt to recreate the "ideal" Cream concert. It's a remarkably comprehensive collection, complete with an extensive booklet and remastered sound, yet it doesn't reveal any new insights about Cream, nor does it offer any invaluable rarities. Therefore, it's only for diehard collectors or listeners wanting to acquire the entire Cream catalog at once; casual fans will be satisfied with individual albums or greatest-hits collections. *—Stephen Thomas Erlewine*

The Creation

f. 1966, Middlesex, England, **db.** 1968
Group / Freakbeat, British Psychedelia, Mod, Psychedelic, British Invasion, Rock & Roll
No other band came closer to emulating the feedback-ridden autodestruction of the early Who than the Creation, who had a couple minor British hit singles in 1966 with "Making Time" and "Painter Man." The sonic resemblance is hardly surprising; the Creation were produced by Shel Talmy, who also produced the Who's earliest records, and lead guitarist Eddie Phillips was even asked by Pete Townshend to join the Who as second guitarist. Phillips' feedback freakouts were grounded by solid mod power chords and British Invasion harmonies. The Creation produced several interesting singles between 1966 and 1968, and although they achieved brief stardom in Germany, they never made it big in the U.K. Ronnie Wood was briefly a member before the group disbanded in 1968. *—Richie Unterberger*

• **How Does It Feel to Feel?** / 1982 / Edsel ♦♦♦♦♦
Unquestionably the best of the several Creation repackages floating around. Includes virtually all of their 1966-68 singles and a few other stray tracks of interest from the same period. *—Richie Unterberger*

• **Our Music Is Red With Purple Flashes** / *May 5, 1998 / Diablo* ♦♦♦♦♦
Our Music Is Red with Purple Flashes doesn't improve on the definitive Creation collection *How Does It Feel to Feel,* nor is it any worse. Instead, it's a comprehensive, well-produced 24-track compilation that contains every one of the group's major songs, plus a couple of interesting covers, lesser-known singers and album tracks. Like *How Does It Feel to Feel* it offers a generous retrospective of the underappreciated Mod quartet and if you don't have that compilation, it's a worthwhile acquisition. If you already have that other excellent collection, *Our Music Is Red with Purple Flashes* isn't necessary. *—Stephen Thomas Erlewine*

Complete Collection, Vol. 1: Making Time / Oct. 13, 1998 / Retroactive ♦♦♦♦
Along with its companion volume (*Biff Bang Pow!*), this collects everything available by the Creation: all of their officially released tracks, rare mono and stereo mixes, and a smattering of live German TV show appearances. General fans should continue to stick with Edsel's *How Does It Feel to Feel,* a well-chosen anthology of their best 20 tracks. However, a cult band such as the Creation tends to attract fans who *do* want everything, and this two-volume series is exemplary in that regard, although much of the rare material is slightly different stereo mixes, rather than entirely new versions. The most interesting rarities on this disc are the live TV broadcasts from 1966 (including covers of "I'm a Man" and "That's How Strong My Love Is," which they never recorded in the studio), and an entirely unreleased instrumental. It also has several of their most renowned official tracks ("Making Time," "Try and Stop Me," "How Does It Feel to Feel," "Nightmares"), and the package is made more enticing with extensive liner notes by Mike Stax. *—Richie Unterberger*

Complete Collection, Vol. 2: Biff Bang Pow / Oct. 13, 1998 / Retroactive ♦♦♦♦
Together with its companion volume *Making Time,* this 20-track disc collects everything by the Creation. It's just as worthy as the first installment, featuring several of their most well-known tunes ("Painter Man," "Biff Bang Pow," "Life Is Just Beginning," "Through My Eyes") and a bunch more alternate stereo mixes. Tracks such as "Sweet Helen," "Like a Rolling Stone," and the instrumental "Sylvette" have been hard to find over the years, although they don't rate among their better efforts. There are also a couple of German TV show performances circa 1967 of "Painter Man" and "Try and Stop Me." By the way, the two *Complete Collection* discs don't have the rare mid-'60s singles by the Mark Four (who evolved into the Creation), some of which were quite good; for those you'll need to look for Eva's *The Mark Four/The Creation.* *—Richie Unterberger*

Creedence Clearwater Revival

f. 1967, El Cerrito, CA, **db.** Oct. 1972
Group / Rock & Roll
At a time when rock was evolving further and further away from the forces that had made the music possible in the first place, Creedence Clearwater Revival brought things back to their roots with their concise synthesis of rockabilly, swamp pop, R&B, and country. Though CCR were very a much a group in their tight, punchy arrangements, their vision was very much singer, songwriter, guitarist, and leader John Fogerty's. Fogerty's classic compositions for Creedence both evoked enduring images of Americana and reflected burning social issues of the day. The band's genius was their ability to accomplish this with the economic, primal power of a classic rockabilly ensemble. On their first album in 1968, the group played it both ways, offering extended, quasi-psychedelic workouts of the '50s classics "I Put a Spell on You" and "Suzy Q." The latter song became their first big hit, but the band didn't really bloom until "Proud Mary," a number-two single in early 1969 that demonstrated John's talent at tapping into Southern roots music and imagery with a natural ease. It was the start of a torrent of classic hits from the gritty, Little Richard-inspired singer over the next two years, including "Bad Moon Rising," "Green River," "Down on the Corner," "Travelin' Band," "Who'll Stop the Rain," "Up Around the Bend," and "Lookin' out My Back Door." *—Richie Unterberger*

Creedence Clearwater Revival / Jul. 1968 / Fantasy ♦♦♦♦
Released in the summer of 1968—a year after the summer of love, but still in the thick of the age of Aquarius—Creedence Clearwater Revival's self-titled debut album was gloriously out-of-step with the times, teeming with John Fogerty's Americana fascinations. While many of Fogerty's obsessions and CCR's signatures are in place—weird blues ("I Put a Spell on You"), Stax R&B (Wilson Pickett's "Ninety-Nine and a Half"), rockabilly ("Susie Q"), winding instrumental interplay, the swamp sound, and songs for "The Working Man"—the band was still finding their way. Out of all their records (discounting *Mardi Gras*), this is the one that sounds the most like its era, thanks to the wordless vocal harmonies toward the end of "Susie Q," the backward guitars on "Gloomy," and the directionless, awkward jamming that concludes "Walking on the Water." Still, the band's sound is vibrant, with gutsy arrangements that borrow equally from Sun, Stax, and the swamp. Fogerty's songwriting is a little tentative. Not for nothing were two of the three singles pulled from the album were covers (Dale Hawkins' "Susie Q", Screamin' Jay Hawkins' "I Put a Spell on You")—he wasn't an accomplished tunesmith yet. Though "The Working Man" isn't bad, the true exception is that third single, "Porterville," an exceptional song with great hooks, an underlying sense of menace, and the first inkling of the working-class rage that fueled such landmarks as "Fortunate Son." It's the song that points the way to the breakthrough of *Bayou Country,* but the rest of the album shouldn't be dismissed, because judged simply against the rock & roll of its time, it rises above its peers. *—Stephen Thomas Erlewine*

Bayou Country / Jan. 1969 / Fantasy ♦♦♦♦♦
Opening slowly with the dark, swampy "Born on the Bayou," *Bayou Country* reveals an assured Creedence Clearwater Revival, a band that has found its voice between their first and second album. It's not just that "Born on the Bayou" announces that CCR has discovered its sound—it reveals the extent of John Fogerty's myth-making. With this song, he sketches out his persona; it makes him sound as if he crawled out of the backwoods of Louisiana instead of being a native San Franciscan. He carries this illusion throughout the record, through the ominous meanderings of "Graveyard Train" through the stoked cover of "Good Golly Miss Molly" to "Keep on Chooglin'," which rides out a southern-fried groove for nearly eight minutes. At the heart of *Bayou Country,* as well as Fogerty's myth and Creedence's entire career, is "Proud Mary." A riverboat tale where the narrator leaves a good job in the city for a life rolling down the river, the song is filled with details that ring so true that it feels autobiographical. The lyric is married to music that is utterly unique yet curiously timeless, blending rockabilly, country, and Stax R&B into something utterly distinctive and addictive. "Proud Mary" is the emotional fulcrum at the center of Fogerty's seductive imaginary Americana, and while it's the best song here, his other songs are no slouch, either. "Born on the Bayou" is a magnificent piece of swamp-rock, "Penthouse Pauper" is a first-rate rocker with the angry undertow apparent on "Porterville" and "Bootleg" is a minor masterpiece, thanks to its tough acoustic foundation, sterling guitar work, and clever story. All the songs add up to a superb statement of purpose, a record that captures Creedence Clearwater Revival's muscular, spare, deceptively simple sound as an evocative portrait of America. *—Stephen Thomas Erlewine*

☆ **Green River** / Aug. 1969 / Fantasy ♦♦♦♦♦
If anything, CCR's third album *Green River* represents the full flower of their classic sound initially essayed on its predecessor, *Bayou Country.* One of the differences between the two albums is that *Green River* is tighter, with none of the five-minute-plus jams that filled out both their debut and *Bayou Country,* but the true key to its success is a peak in John Fogerty's creativity. Although CCR had at least one cover on each album, they relied on Fogerty to crank out new material every month. He was writing so frequently that the craft became second-nature. He was writing so often that he laid his emotions and fears bare, perhaps unintentionally. Perhaps that's why *Green River* has fear, anger, dread, and weariness creeping on the edges of gleeful music. This was a band that played rock & roll so joyously that they masked the, well, "sinister" undercurrents in Fogerty's songs. "Bad Moon Rising" has the famous line "Hope you've got your things together/Hope you're quite prepared to die," but that was only the most obvious indication of Fogerty's gloom. Consider all the other dark touches: the "Sinister Purpose knocking at your door;" the chaos of "Commotion"; the threat of death in "Tombstone Shadow"; you only return to the idyllic "Green River" once you get lost and realize the "world is smolderin'." Even the ballads have a strong melancholy undercurrent, highlighted by "Lodi", where Fogerty imagines himself stuck playing in dead-end towns for the rest of his life. Not the typical thoughts of a newly-famous rock & roller, but certainly an indication of Fogerty's inner tumult. For all its darkness, *Green River* is ultimately welcoming music, since the band rocks hard and bright and the melancholy feels comforting, not alienating. *—Stephen Thomas Erlewine*

☆ **Willy & the Poor Boys** / Nov. 1969 / Fantasy ♦♦♦♦♦
Make no mistake, *Willie & the Poor Boys* is a *fun* record, perhaps the breeziest album CCR ever made. Apart from the eerie minor-key closer "Effigy" (one of John Fogerty's most haunting numbers), there is little of the doom that colored *Green River.* Fogerty's rage remains, blazing to the forefront on "Fortunate Son," a working-class protest song that cuts harder than any of the explicit Vietnam protest songs of the era, which is one of the reasons that it hasn't aged where its peers have. Also, there's that unbridled vocal from Fogerty and the ferocious playing on *CCR,* which both sound fresh as they did upon release. "Fortunate Son"

is one of the greatest, hardest rock & rollers ever cut, so it might seem to be out of step with an album that is pretty laid-back and friendly, but there's that elemental joy that by late '69 was one of CCR's main trademarks. That joy runs throughout the album, from the gleeful single "Down on the Corner" and the lazy jugband blues of "Poorboy Shuffle" through the great slow blues jam "Feelin' Blue" to the great rockabilly spiritual "Don't Look Now," one of Fogerty's overlooked gems. The covers don't feel like throwaways, either, since both "Cotton Fields" and "The Midnight Special" have been overhauled to feel like genuine CCR songs. It all adds up to one of the greatest pure rock & roll records ever cut. *—Stephen Thomas Erlewine*

☆ **Cosmo's Factory** / Jul. 1970 / Fantasy ✦✦✦✦✦
Throughout 1969 and into 1970, CCR toured incessantly and recorded nearly as much. Appropriately, *Cosmo's Factory*'s first single was the working band's anthem "Travelin' Band," a funny, piledriving rocker with a blaring horn section—the first indication their sonic palette was broadening. Two more singles appeared prior to the album's release, backed by John Fogerty originals that rivaled the A-side or paled just slightly. When it came time to assemble a full album, Fogerty had only one original left, the claustrophobic, paranoid rocker "Ramble Tamble." Unlike some extended instrumentals, this was dramatic and had a direction—a distinction made clear by the meandering jam that brings CCR's version of "I Heard It Through the Grapevine" to 11 minutes. Even if it wanders, their take on the Marvin Gaye classic isn't unpleasant, and their faithful, exuberant takes on the Sun classics "Ooby Dooby" and "My Baby Left Me" are joyous tributes. Still, the heart of the album lays in those six fantastic songs released on singles. "Up Around the Bend" is a searing rocker, one of their best, balanced by the menacing murkiness of "Run Through the Jungle." "Who'll Stop the Rain"'s poignant melody and melancholy undertow has a counterpart in Fogerty's dope song, "Lookin' out My Back Door" a charming, bright shuffle, filled with dancing animals and domestic bliss—he had never been as sweet and silly as he is here. On "Long as I Can See the Light," the record's final song, he again finds solace in home, anchored by a soulful, laid-back groove. It's hits a comforting, elegiac note, the perfect way to draw *Cosmo's Factory*—an album made during stress and chaos, filled with raging rockers, covers, and intense jams—to a close. *—Stephen Thomas Erlewine*

Pendulum / Dec. 1970 / Fantasy ✦✦✦✦
During 1969 and 1970, CCR was dismissed by hipsters as a bubblegum pop band and the sniping had grown intolerable, at least to John Fogerty, who designed *Pendulum* as a rebuke to critics. He spent time polishing the production, bringing in keyboards, horns, even a vocal choir. His songs became self-consciously serious and tighter, working with the aesthetic of the rock underground—*Pendulum* was constructed as a proper album, contrasting dramatically with CCR's previous records, all throwbacks to joyous early rock records where covers sat nicely next to hits and overlooked gems tucked away at the end of the second side. To some fans of classic CCR, this approach may feel a little odd since only "Have You Ever Seen the Rain" and maybe its B-side "Hey Tonight" sound undeniably like prime Creedence. But, given time, the album is a real grower, revealing many overlooked Fogerty gems. Yes, it isn't transcendent like the albums they made from *Bayou Country* through *Cosmo's Factory,* but most bands never even come close to that kind of hot streak. Instead, *Pendulum* finds a first class songwriter and craftsman pushing himself and his band to try new sounds, styles and textures. His ambition results in a stumble—"Rude Awakening 2" portentously teeters on the verge of prog-rock, something CCR just can't pull off—but the rest of the record is excellent, with such great numbers as the bluesy groove "Pagan Baby," the soulful vamp "Chameleon," the moody "It's Just a Thought" and the raver "Molina." Most bands would kill for this to be their best stuff, and the fact that it's tucked away on an album that even some fans forget illustrates what a tremendous band Creedence Clearwater Revival was. *—Stephen Thomas Erlewine*

Mardi Gras / Apr. 1972 / Fantasy ✦✦

★ **Chronicle, Vol. 1** / 1976 / Fantasy ✦✦✦✦✦
Chronicle, Vol. 1 contains every one of Creedence Clearwater Revival's original 19 hit singles—including "Proud Mary," "Bad Moon Rising," "Green River," "Down on the Corner," "Travelin' Band," "Up Around the Band," and "Have You Ever Scene the Rain"—plus "I Heard It Through the Grapevine," which became a hit at the same time this double-record compilation was released. It's a lean, concise collection that tells you everything you need to know about Creedence. Several of the band's individual albums are essential, but *Chronicle* is not only an excellent introduction to the group, it offers definitive proof that group was one of the definitive singles bands of the late '60s. Rarely has a greatest hits collection has been so well-assembled. (The compact disc edition is hampered by the inclusion of the full-length, eleven-minute album version of "I Heard It Through the Grapevine;" its presence slows down the momentum of the collection considerably). *—Stephen Thomas Erlewine*

The Concert / 1980 / Fantasy ✦✦✦✦

Chronicle, Vol. 2 / 1986 / Fantasy ✦✦✦✦✦
Chronicle, Vol. 2 effectively compiles all of the highlights from Creedence Clearwater Revival's career that weren't on the first volume. All of the singles were included on *Chronicle,* so *Chronicle, Vol. 2* is comprised solely of album tracks. That doesn't mean these are lesser items. On the contrary, the majority of these songs—"Born on the Bayou," "Tombstone Shadow," "Wrote a Song for Everyone," "It Came out of the Sky," "Midnight Special"—rank among their best performances. Of course, a couple of great tracks remain on CCR's individual albums, notably "Bootleg," but *Chronicle, Vol. 2* is an ideal choice for listeners that want a little more than the hits but are unwilling to delve into the proper albums. *—Stephen Thomas Erlewine*

Marshall Crenshaw

b. Nov. 11, 1953, Detroit, MI
Vocals, Guitar / College Rock, Pop/Rock, Power Pop, New Wave
Singer/songwriter Marshall Crenshaw has built up an impressive body of work over the course of his careers, showing a fine craft for everything he approaches while stubbornly following his own creative muse to reach that end. To say that Crenshaw has had an interesting career so far would be putting it mildly. He's been in the movies and he's been in the road show version of *Beatlemania.* His songs have been plastered all over the soundtracks to several hit movies and covered by artists as diverse as Robert Gordon, Bette Midler, Kelly Willis, Marti Jones and the Gin Blossoms. He got a bunch of his like-minded show business acquaintances together and put out a book on all the great and lousy rock & roll movies in existence called *Hollywood Rock & Roll.* He's put together comps of his own for record companies (most notably *Hillbilly Music, Thank God!* for the short lived Bug Music label) and has contributed chapters to books on vintage guitar collecting. Crenshaw is a true rock & roll renaissance man while still remaining the everyman. *—Cub Koda*

★ **Marshall Crenshaw [1982]** / Apr. 28, 1982 / Warner Brothers ✦✦✦✦✦
On the cover of his self-titled LP, Marshall Crenshaw—complete with crew-cut, thick glasses and unfashionable suit—looks like nothing so much as the second coming of Buddy Holly, or possibly an Americanized Elvis Costello; listening to the record itself does little to alter those first impressions, and even if his subsequent LPs failed to live up to such immense promise there's no doubting this debut release's enduring greatness. Working without any kind of smoke or mirrors, Crenshaw delivers simple, straightforward pop music invested with remarkable melodic ingenuity; his material is timeless and fresh—gems like "Someday, Someway," "She Can't Dance" and "Not for Me" are the kinds of songs which would fit like a glove on both oldies radio and contemporary Top 40 playlists in any era. Witty, assured and utterly infectious, *Marshall Crenshaw* remains among the finest debuts of its day. *—Jason Ankeny*

Field Day / 1983 / Warner Brothers ✦✦✦✦
Following his critically acclaimed 1982 debut and successful single "Someday, Someway," Marshall Crenshaw returned with the following year's greatly anticipated *Field Day.* Crenshaw doesn't fall prey to the sophomore jinx, delivering nine more brilliantly crafted pop/rock originals and a terrific cover of the Jive Five's & "What Time Is It?" Though the record meets the high standard that Crenshaw, his brother Robert Crenshaw (drums) and bassist Chris Donato, set with the first album, many had trouble warming up to producer Steve Lillywhite's dense, more muscular production, especially Robert's explosive snare and bass drum. But while it may lack its predecessor's immediate sparkle and charm, *Field Day* is equally infectious. It also shows a newfound depth and maturity in Crenshaw's writing, which Lillywhite's sound reinforces. Like *Marshall Crenshaw,* the majority of *Field Day* deals with time-honored themes of loves lost and found, albeit from a slightly less innocent viewpoint, much like the lyrical growth of the Beatles in late 1964, early 1965, or Buddy Holly's "True Love Ways" and "Learning the Game." Previously, he would move on and "find someone better" or "feel the need to go "Rockin' Around in N.Y.C." Now, he's willing to "try with all [his] heart every day," seeing a night on the town as a "duty" that must be done before slipping back into comfortable domesticity and responsibility. Crenshaw realizes now that even true love "makes demands" amidst the fun and summer evening walks. This album brims with deceptively simple, pure pop pleasures that continue to unfold with repeated listens. Though *Field Day* didn't match the commercial promise of the first album, it was the perfect second step in Marshall Crenshaw's artistic evolution. *—Brett Hartenbach*

Downtown / 1985 / Warner Brothers ✦✦✦✦
Marshall Crenshaw entered the studio to begin work on his third album, *Downtown,* but for the first time, he was without the familiar backing of Chris Donato on bass and brother Robert Crenshaw on drums (though he does appear on two tracks). Following the dense, sonic thunder of the commercially disappointing *Field Day,* this album employed the services of various studio pros, and returned him to the roomier, more traditional tone of his first effort. Along with co-producers T-Bone Burnett and Larry Hirsch (and Mitch Easter on one track), Crenshaw, creates an old-fashioned rock & roll record with the inviting warmth of '60s pop and the swing and recklessness of the '50s. And though he doesn't do anything radically new or different here, the results are once again never less than fresh or stirring. Tracks like the irresistible "Little Wild One (No. 5)," the primal beat of "Yvonne," and "(We're Gonna) Shake Their Minds," with it's syncopated guitar and drum interplay, are first-rate rockers, while Ben Vaughn's "I'm Sorry (But So Is Brenda Lee)" and Crenshaw's own "Like a Vague Memory" have the feel of classic '50s pop tunes. Though *Downtown* did little to reverse the downward slide of Marshall Crenshaw's market value, it does complete a brilliant triad of releases going back to his 1982 debut. *—Brett Hartenbach*

Mary Jean & 9 Others / 1987 / Warner Brothers ✦✦✦
Marshall Crenshaw's first three records, though each with their own distinct personality, were an irresistible combination of masterful pop and vibrant, timeless rock & roll. His fourth effort, *Mary Jean & 9 Others,* has many of these same ingredients, while at the same time lacking the impact of its predecessors. And though there isn't really a bad cut here, there isn't much that would make you think of Crenshaw as much more than a craftsman. Even the best of the originals, including the title track and "Somebody Crying," seem to lumber along, never really delivering on their promise. This may be partially due to Don Dixon's production that, though not out of place with Crenshaw's material, lacks the freshness of the first album, the allure and depth of *Field Day,* and the spirit of *Downtown.* Overall, it's the beautiful closer, "They Never Will Know," and Peter Case's "Steel Strings" that are most successful in this setting. Like the rest of Crenshaw's mid-'80s, early-'90s catalog, *Mary Jean* is difficult to find, but of this period, *Downtown,* which is also on Warner Bros., and *Life's Too Short,* his only release for MCA, are preferred. *—Brett Hartenbach*

Good Evening / Jun. 1989 / Warner Brothers ✦✦✦

Life's Too Short / May 14, 1991 / MCA ✦✦✦✦

Live: My Truck Is My Home / Sep. 20, 1994 / Razor & Tie ✦✦✦

The 9 Volt Years: Battery Powered Home Demos & Curios / 1998 / Razor & Tie ✦✦✦✦✦
Far from the collection of scraps and throw-aways its humble title would suggest, *The 9 Volt Years: Battery Powered Home Demos & Curios (1979-198?)* is instead a showcase for Marshall Crenshaw at his most engaging and refreshing. Whereas some of his studio LPs have suffered

from overproduction, the bare-bones ambience of these 15 cuts—home recordings, live performances and the stray studio date—allows his songs' melodic smarts and impeccable craftsmanship to truly shine. Familiar tracks like "Someday, Someway," "Rockin' Around in NYC" and "Vague Memory" are dramatically revitalized in these spartan settings, while lost gems like "Run Back to You," "Everyone's in Love with You" and the classic B-side "You're My Favorite Waste of Time" assume their rightful place alongside Crenshaw's best work. The end result is not only a must-have for fans, but also an ideal introduction to one of the best singer/songwriters around, captured here at his purest, loosest and most honest. *—Jason Ankeny*

#447 / Sep. 28, 1999 / Razor & Tie ✦✦✦✦
Crenshaw's first album since 1998's wonderful home demo collection, *The 9 Volt Years* (and his first studio album since 1996's *Miracle of Science*), *#447* finds the singer/songwriter constructing the kind of clever pop gems that have become his trademark. "Dime a Dozen Guy," for example, is as witty a song about being cheated on as you'll ever find, with Crenshaw sarcastically repeating "I've been passed over for a dime a dozen guy" to form the hook. The singer also employs a string section to masterful use to create the melodic hook of "Television Light" and experiments with Dobro for the country & western-sounding "Glad Goodbye." Though the latter half of the album strays a bit from Crenshaw's three-minute pop gem style, favoring jazzier bass lines and chord progressions, *#447* is still a strong addition to this underrated artist's recorded work. *—Steve Kurutz*

The Best of Marshall Crenshaw: This Is Easy / Aug. 15, 2000 / Rhino ✦✦✦✦✦
Co-compiler Gary Stewart and project assistant David Gorman waste no time at all before addressing the question that has plagued rock critics and fans since 1981: "how can we rationalize the continued underappreciation of Marshall Crenshaw?" It's not just that Crenshaw is a cult favorite and critics' pet; he's also steeped in rock & roll traditions that date back to Buddy Holly and Gene Vincent, and his records are such ear candy that you'd figure they would attract a big audience. Instead, only three of Crenshaw's previous ten albums have even reached the charts, along with just one single; Stewart and Gorman hope this compilation will "set things right." If only it could. Running from 1981 to 1996, the 22-track collection gathers four tracks each from Crenshaw's first three albums, as well as his first indie single "Something's Gonna Happen," the exceptional B-side "You're My Favorite Waste of Time," and assorted tracks from four subsequent albums. Crenshaw doesn't so much write songs as he makes records, at least as interested in guitar textures and what echo is placed on his vocal as what he's singing about. For all the surface pleasure his work provides, the only depth it reveals is one of craft; one is more impressed than really involved. And yet, it would be hard for a rock & roll fan not to enjoy this record, which cherry-picks Crenshaw's albums, diminishing, for example, the inappropriately bombastic production Steve Lillywhite brought to *Field Day*. The tracks are all pop gems, and they do, as Stewart and Gorman claim, induce the fantasy of a world in which classic, 1965-vintage pop/rock was still on top 20 years later. It's a nice dream for rock & roll fans; with this album they can close their eyes and, for 75 minutes, pretend it's true. *—William Ruhlmann*

The Crests

f. 1956, **db.** 1960
Group / Doo Wop
One of the most successful integrated doo wop groups, the Crests waxed the classic ballad "16 Candles" in 1959. Formed in 1956, they began recording the next year for Joyce, where they inched onto the pop lists with "Sweetest One." Moving to the brand-new Coed logo, Johnny Maestro's (b. May 7, 1930) warm tenor made "16 Candles" a national smash, and pop/R&B hybrids like "The Angels Listened In" and "Step by Step" also did well. Maestro went solo in 1960, scoring the next year with "Model Girl" on Coed, while the Crests attempted to survive on their own. Maestro eventually reclaimed stardom as leader of Brooklyn Bridge, an 11-piece aggregation that hit with "Worst That Could Happen" in 1968. *—Bill Dahl*

● **The Best of the Crests Featuring Johnny Maestro** / 1990 / Rhino ✦✦✦✦✦

Jim Croce

b. Jan. 10, 1943, Philadelphia, PA, **d.** Sep. 20, 1973, Natchitoches, LA
Vocals, Guitar / Soft Rock, Singer/Songwriter
Arguably the worst tragedy that can befall a recording artist is to die when he or she is just beginning to break through on a national level. One such artist was Jim Croce, a songwriter with a knack for both upbeat, catchy singles and empathetic, melancholy ballads. Croce appealed to fans as a common man, and it was not a gimmick—he was a father and husband who went through a series of blue-collar jobs. And whether he used dry wit, gentle emotions or sorrow, Croce sang with a rare form of honesty and power. Few artists have ever been able to pull off such down-to-earth storytelling as convincingly as Croce. After a failed first album recorded with wife Ingrid in 1969, Jim juggled several jobs, including singing for radio commercials. Eventually he was noticed and signed by the ABC/Dunhill label, and released his second album, *Life and Times*, in 1973. The record spawned three hits: "You Don't Mess Around With Jim," "Operator (That's Not the Way It Feels)" and "Bad, Bad Leroy Brown." The latter would become Croce's breakthrough hit, shooting all the way to number one on the *Billboard* charts. Unfortunately, just two months after it did so, Croce's plane crashed in Natchitoches, Lousiana; he and the four other passengers were killed instantly. Ironically, Croce's career peaked after his death. In 1974, the album *I Got A Name* surfaced, containing the hit "Time in a Bottle," which would become his second #1 single. Shortly afterwards, "I'll Have to Say I Love You in a Song" reached the Top Ten. Several albums were released posthumously, most notably the greatest-hits collection *Photographs and Memories*, which became a best-seller. One cannot help but wonder how far Croce's extraordinary talents could have taken him; unfortunately, such a question may only be looked at rhetorically, but Jim Croce lives on in the impressive catalog of songs he left behind. *—Barry Weber*

● **Photographs & Memories: His Greatest Hits** / 1974 / Atlantic ✦✦✦✦✦
Though Jim Croce produced a handful of hit singles before his death, one can nonetheless argue that Croce was and is a rather underrated songwriter. This is especially evident in listening to his album tracks, many of which are remarkably potent and arguably could have been hits themselves. The numerous double-disc collections that have been released echo this factor, but for casual fans who merely want the radio favorites, the single-disc *Photographs and Memories* will suffice. All of Croce's biggest singles are here, including "Bad Bad Leroy Brown," "Time in a Bottle," and "Operator," as well as overlooked album tracks such as "New York's Not My Home" and "Lovers Cross." This is far from a perfect compilation; the album barely clocks in over 40 minutes, leaving time for numerous tracks that could have easily been added onto the same disc during the record's move from vinyl to CD. Still, it's hard to argue with what's here. While Croce's more devoted followers would prefer with the double-disc *50th Anniversary Collection*, casual listeners merely in search of Croce's well-known songs would be best suited with *Photographs and Memories*. *—Barry Weber*

Time in a Bottle/Greatest Love Songs / 1977 / Atlantic ✦✦✦✦✦
Since it contains only his love ballads, fans who prefer his sweetly sentimental songs like "Operator" and "Time in a Bottle" to story-songs like "Bad, Bad Leroy Brown" and "You Don't Mess Around With Jim," will find *Time in a Bottle* the essential compilation; despite the amount of good material here, *Photographs and Memories* remains a better collection, because it presents both sides of the popular singer/songwriter. *—Stephen Thomas Erlewine*

The 50th Anniversary Collection / Sep. 22, 1992 / Saja ✦✦✦✦✦
For those who want to dig a little deeper into Croce's music than just his well-known songs, the double-CD set *The 50th Anniversary Collection* is a fine buy. The 49-track collection, released in 1992 to commemorate what would have been Croce's 50th birthday, includes all of his radio singles as well as many of the noteworthy album tracks that the single-disc *Photographs and Memories* overlooks. It's not quite a flawless compilation; both discs have a substantial amount of filler, but that doesn't stop the *50th Anniversary Collection* from being a great retrospective on a career that was silenced far too soon. *—Barry Weber*

Crosby, Stills & Nash (And Young)

f. 1968, Laurel Canyon, CA
Group / Pop/Rock, Folk-Rock, Singer/Songwriter
The musical partnership of David Crosby, Stephen Stills and Graham Nash—with and without Neil Young—not only was one of the most successful touring and recording acts of the late '60s,'70s, and early '80s; with the colorful, contrasting nature of the members' characters and their connection to the political and cultural upheavals of the time, it was the only American-based band to approach the overall societal impact of the Beatles. The group was a second marriage for all the participants when it came together in 1968: Crosby had been a member of the Byrds, Nash was in the Hollies, and Stills had been part of Buffalo Springfield. The resulting trio, however, sounded like none of its predecessors and was characterized by a unique vocal blend and a musical approach that ranged from acoustic folk to melodic pop to hard rock. By the time of their first tour (which included the Woodstock festival), they had added Young, also a veteran of Buffalo Springfield, who maintained a solo career. The first CSN*Y* album, *Deja-vu*, was a chart-topping hit in 1970, but the group split acrimoniously after a summer tour. In 1974, CSN*Y* reformed for a summer stadium tour without releasing a new record. Nevertheless, the compilation *So Far* became their third straight number one. Crosby, Stills and Nash reformed without Young in 1977 for the album *CSN*, another giant hit. The trio remains a popular live act. *—William Ruhlmann*

☆ **Crosby, Stills & Nash** / May 29, 1969 / Atlantic ✦✦✦✦✦
The Crosby, Stills and Nash triumvirate shot to immediate superstardom with the release of their self-titled debut LP, a sparkling set immortalizing the group's amazing close high harmonies. While elements of the record haven't dated well—Nash's Eastern-influenced musings on the hit "Marrakesh Express" now seem more than a little silly, while the anti-war sentiments of *"Wooden Ships,"* though well-intentioned, are rather hokey—the harmonies are absolutely timeless, and the best material remains rock-solid. Stills' gorgeous opener *"Suite: Judy Blue Eyes,"* in particular, is an epic love song remarkable in its musical and emotional intricacy, Nash's *"Pre-Road Downs"* is buoyant folk-pop underpinned by light psychedelic textures, and Crosby's "Long Time Gone" remains a potent indictment of the assassination of Robert Kennedy. A definitive document of its era. *—Jason Ankeny*

☆ **Deja Vu** / Mar. 11, 1970 / Atlantic ✦✦✦✦✦
The first of the group's albums to include Neil Young, *Deja-Vu* is the CSNY aggregrate's most consistent and lovely LP. Not only does Young's recruitment bring an idiosyncratic new dimension to the group's shimmering harmonies, but the addition of his guitar skills greatly broadens their musical scope; at the same time, his prodigious songwriting gifts seem to have spurred the original CSN line-up to new creative heights—the material on *Deja-Vu* is uniformly excellent, ranging from the gorgeous "Helpless" to the ambitious title cut. The star of the record is Graham Nash, who delivers a pair of classics, the country-inflected "Teach Your Children" and "Our House," awritten for Joni Mitchell; speaking of Mitchell, she also penned the record's centerpiece, the perennial "Woodstock," a sweeping celebration of counterculture values. *—Jason Ankeny*

Four Way Street / Apr. 7, 1971 / Atlantic ✦✦✦✦✦
This 1992 expanded version of the original double live album (originally released on April 7, 1971) by CSN*Y* is now an indispensible part of any collection, with additional Neil Young and Graham Nash material (and even a version of "King Midas in Reverse," the old Hollies tune) that any serious listener will want. Some of the extended guitar jams between Stills and Young ("Southern Man") go on longer than strict musical sense would dictate, but it seemed right at the time, and they capture a form that was far more abused in other hands after this group broke up. *—Bruce Eder*

● **So Far** / Aug. 1974 / Atlantic ✦✦✦✦✦
Released to coincide with CSN*Y*'s 1974 reunion tour, this compilation remains the best representation of the group's early work, featuring such hits as "Teach Your Children" and "Suite: Judy Blue Eyes." It also put the one-off single "Ohio/Find the Cost of Freedom"

(CSNY's response to the shooting of four anti-war student protestors at Kent State University) on an album for the first time. *— William Ruhlmann*

CSN / Jun. 17, 1977 / Atlantic ✦✦✦✦
The times had certainly changed since *Déjà-vu's* release in 1970. Nevertheless, there was a hunger in the musical audience for a return to the harmony-soaked idealism with which this trio had catapulted to popularity, and *CSN* consequently reached number two on the charts, behind Fleetwood Mac's mega-success *Rumours*. The music here is very good, though probably not up to the hard-to-match level of *Crosby, Stills & Nash* or *Déjà-vu*. Still, the songs showed a great deal of lyrical maturity and compositional complexity compared to those earlier albums from a far more innocent time. "Just a Song Before I Go" was the latest of Graham Nash's radio-friendly acoustic numbers, and was a Top Ten single. "See the Changes" and "Dark Star" rank with the best of Stephen Stills' work, while David Crosby contributes three classics from his distinctive oeuvre: "Shadow Captain," "Anything at All," and the beautiful "In My Dreams." Nash's multi-part "Cathedral," a recollection of an acid trip taken in Winchester Cathedral on his 32nd birthday, became a staple of the group's live repertoire. *CSN* was this trio's last fully realized album. It was also the last recording on which the three principals handled all the vocal parts without the sweetening of additional voices. It has held up remarkably well, both as a memento of its time, and as a thoroughly enjoyable musical work. *— Jim Newsom*

Daylight Again / Jun. 21, 1982 / Atlantic ✦✦✦
Originally a Stills and Nash project, but with the drug-addled Crosby added virtually in name only for commercial reasons (Timothy Schmit and Art Garfunkel provide many of the harmonies), this turned out better than expected, featuring Nash's reflective "Wasted on the Way" and Stills' "Southern Cross," both hits and respectable additions to the CSN repertoire. *— William Ruhlmann*

Allies / Jun. 6, 1983 / Atlantic ✦✦

American Dream / Nov. 3, 1988 / Atlantic ✦✦

Live It Up / Jun. 11, 1990 / Atlantic ✦✦

Crosby, Stills & Nash / Oct. 1991 / Atlantic ✦✦✦✦✦
Seventy-seven tracks make up this four-CD boxed set retrospective of the various permutations of Crosby, Stills and Nash (and Young) from 1968 to 1990. The set is dotted with unreleased tracks from abortive album sessions (CSNY may have recorded only two studio albums, but they sure tried a lot of other times), and there are also good choices from both solo work and the well-known material. For a neophyte, it may be on the long side, but seasoned fans can welcome this lavish tribute. *— William Ruhlmann*

After the Storm / Aug. 16, 1994 / Atlantic ✦✦

Looking Forward / Oct. 26, 1999 / Reprise ✦✦✦

Sheryl Crow

b. Feb. 11, 1962
Singer, Vocals, Guitar / American Trad Rock, Adult Alternative Pop/Rock, Pop/Rock, Singer/Songwriter

Of all the singer-songwriters that emerged during the much-publicized "women in rock" explosion of the mid-'90s, Sheryl Crow was the traditionalist of the bunch, revitalizing classic rock. Her first album, 1993's *Tuesday Night Music Club*, slowly became a hit, thanks to the bouncy "All I Wanna Do," yet she found her voice over her next two albums, consolidating her fan base, earning strong reviews and winning Grammys.

Crow began her professional music career as a backing vocalist for both Don Henley and Michael Jackson. After landing a couple of original songs on other artist's records, she scored a record deal with A&M. Her first attempt at a solo album was recorded with producer Hugh Padgham. The resulting record was glossy, streamlined and calculated—enough so that she and the label shelved it. Crow headed back into the studio with producers Kevin Gilbert and Bill Botrell. They used music played during a local LA jam session called "Tuesday Night Music Club" as the inspiration for the record, eventually taking the title for her 1993 album. Initially, the record didn't make much of an impact, but the next year "All I Wanna Do" became a smash hit, sending the album into blockbuster territory. Her success was not without controversy, as members of the Music Club, led by David Baerwald, claimed that Crow took too much credit for what was essentially a collaborative effort. Determined to shed these criticisms, Crow largely abandoned the Club for her eponymous 1996 album, relying on Tchad Blake as her primary collaborator. Though it was still classicist in many ways, it was considerably more ambitious lyrically and musically, a determinedly modern record. It was another smash success, thanks to singles like "Every Day Is a Winding Road." She returned to fairly straightforward territory for 1998's *The Globe Sessions*. While it wasn't quite as popular as its two predecessors, it nevertheless went platinum. She bought time in 1999 with her fourth album, *Sheryl Crow and Friends: Live in Central Park*. *— Stephen Thomas Erlewine*

Tuesday Night Music Club / Aug. 3, 1993 / A&M ✦✦✦
Sheryl Crow earned her recording contract through hard work, gigging as a backing vocalist for everyone from Don Henley to Michael Jackson before entering the studio with Hugh Padgham to record her debut album. As it turned out, things didn't go entirely as planned. Instead of adhering to her rock & roll roots, the record was a slick set of contemporary pop, relying heavily on ballads. Upon hearing the completed album, Crow convinced A&M not to release the album, choosing to cut a new record with producer Bill Bottrell. Along with several Los Angeles-based songwriters and producers, including David Baerwald, David Ricketts, and Brian McLeod, Bottrell was part of a collective dubbed "the Tuesday Night Music Club." Every Tuesday, the group would get together, drink beer, jam, and write songs. Crow became part of the Club and, within a few months, she decided to craft her debut album around the songs and spirit of the collective. It was, for the most part, an inspired idea, since *Tuesday Night Music Club* has a loose, ramshackle charm that her unreleased debut lacked. At its best—the opening quartet of "Run, Baby, Run," "Leaving Las Vegas," "Strong Enough," and "Can't Cry Anymore," plus the deceptively infectious "All I Wanna Do"—are remarkable testaments to their collaboration, proving that roots rock can sound contemporary and have humor. That same spirit, however, also resulted in some half-finished songs, and the preponderance of those tracks make *Tuesday Night Music Club* better in memory than it is in practice. Still, even with the weaker moments, Crow manages to create an identity for herself—a classic rocker at heart but with enough smarts to stay contemporary. And that's the lasting impression *Tuesday Night Music Club* leaves. *— Stephen Thomas Erlewine*

● **Sheryl Crow** / Sep. 24, 1996 / A&M ✦✦✦✦✦
Hiring noted roots experimentalists Tchad Blake and Mitchell Froom as engineer and consultant, respectively, Sheryl Crow took a cue from their Latin Playboys project for her second album—she kept her roots rock foundation and added all sorts of noises, weird instruments, percussion loops, and off-balance production to give *Sheryl Crow* a distinctly modern flavor. And, even with the Stones-y grind of "Sweet Rosalyn" or hippie spirits of "Love Is a Good Thing," it is an album that couldn't have been made any other time than the '90s. As strange as it may sound, *Sheryl Crow* is a post-modern masterpiece of sorts—albeit a *mainstream*, post-alternative, post-modern masterpiece. It may not be as hip or innovative as, say, the Beastie Boys' *Paul's Boutique*, but it is as self-referential, pop-culture obsessed, and musically eclectic. Throughout the record, Crow spins out wild, nearly incomprehensible stream-of-consciousness lyrics, dropping celebrity names and products every chance she gets ("drinking Falstaff beer/Mercedes Ruehl and a rented Leer"). Often, these litanies don't necessarily add up to anything specific, but they're a perfect match for the mess of rock, blues, alt-rock, country, folk, and lite hip-hop loops that dominate the record. At her core, she remains a traditionalist—the songcraft behind the infectious "Change Would Do You Good," the bubbly "Everyday Is a Winding Road," and the weary "If It Makes You Happy" helped get the singles on the radio—but the production and lyrics are often at odds with those instincts, creating for a fascinating and compelling (and occasionally humorous) listen and one of the most individual albums of its era. *— Stephen Thomas Erlewine*

The Globe Sessions / Sep. 29, 1998 / A&M ✦✦✦✦
Since her dense, varied, post-modernist eponymous second album illustrated that Sheryl Crow was no one-album wonder, she wasn't left with as much to prove the third time around. Having created an original variation on roots rock with *Sheryl Crow*, she was left with the dilemma of how to remain loyal to that sound without repeating herself on her third album, *The Globe Sessions*. To her credit, she never plays lazy, not when she's turning out Stones-y rockers ("There Goes the Neighborhood") or when she's covering Dylan (the remarkable "Mississippi," an outtake from *Time Out of Mind*). However, she has decided to abandon the layered, yard-sale production and pop-culture fixations that made *Sheryl Crow* a defining album of the mid-'90s. *The Globe Sessions*, instead, is the work of a craftsman, one who knows how to balance introspective songs with pop/rockers, one who knows how to exploit their signature sound while becoming slightly more eclectic. In that sense, the album is a lot like a latter-day album from her idols, the Stones—it finds pleasures within the craft and the signature sound themselves. That means that there are no surprises (apart from the synthesized handclaps, of course)—the Celtic homage "Riverwide" may be new, but it's not unexpected, much like how the whiplash transition in "Am I Getting Through" isn't entirely out of the blue—but that's not necessarily a bad thing, since *The Globe Sessions* has a strong set of songs. Since it lacks the varied sonics, humor, and flat-out weirdness of *Sheryl Crow*, it's never quite as compelling a listen as its predecessor, yet it is a strong record, again confirming Crow's position as one of the best roots-rockers of the '90s. *— Stephen Thomas Erlewine*

Sheryl Crow and Friends: Live in Central Park / Dec. 7, 1999 / A&M ✦✦

Crowded House

f. Jul. 1985, **db.** Jun. 1996
Group / College Rock, New Zealand Rock, Adult Alternative Pop/Rock, Pop/Rock

An institution in their homeland, a two-hit wonder in the U.S. and, during the last half of their ten-year career, bonafide stars in the U.K. and most of Europe, Crowded House recorded some of the best pop music of the late '80s and early '90s. Leader Neil Finn's carefully crafted songs, meticulous eye for lyrical detail and gift for melody are matched by few other songwriters.

Crowded House formed in the ashes of Split Enz in 1985 when Neil Finn shifted to a stripped down, back-to-basics combo featuring ex-Enz drummer Paul Hester, bassist Nick Seymour. The group headed to Los Angeles, eventually signing with Capitol Records and after several name changes, settled on Crowded House, a reflection of their living conditions in L.A. Their self-titled debut didn't gain much attention upon its release in the summer of 1986, but the band created a buzz in North America by taking an unorthodox, low-profile tour of odd venues like ethnic restaurants. On the talk-show circuit, they won over audiences with their charm and wit. By early 1987, the album eventually peaked at number 12, spawning the number two hit single "Don't Dream It's Over" and number seven "Something So Strong." In their homeland, multi-platinum success followed. 1988's *Temple of Low Men* showcased a notable progression in Finn's songcraft but the album's slightly darker tone failed to spark the interest of pop audiences. *Woodface*, released in 1991, featured several collaborations from Neil's brother (and temporary member of the band) Tim. The album certainly represents their finest recorded moments, and the smash hit "Weather with You" eventually made the band stars in the U.K. and Europe. In early 1993, they recorded their fourth album, adding American guitarist Mark Hart. *Together Alone* was released in 1993 to unanimously positive reviews. Paul Hester left the band in 1994.

Following a Finn Brothers album, Neil officially broke up Crowded House in June 1996. That same month, *Recurring Dream: The Very Best of Crowded House* was released, entering the U.K. and Australian charts at number one. After a handful of "final shows" in various locations, on Sunday November 24, 1996, Crowded House played their official farewell show at the Sydney Opera House to 100,000 fans.

By 1997, Paul Hester formed a new band, Largest Living Things, releasing two EPs and playing regular gigs in Australia. Neil Finn made his debut as a solo artist in 1998 with *Try Whistling This.* In December 1999, *Afterglow,* an album's worth of Crowded House leftovers and rarities, was issued. *—Chris Woodstra*

Crowded House / Jun. 1986 / Capitol ✦✦✦
Split Enz needed to end, particularly since founding member Tim Finn found his little brother Neil's growth spurt uncomfortable, but also because Neil was no longer writing tunes that made sense within the context of a band that ran the gamut from art rock to eccentric new wave. Neil Finn was now writing songs that were undeniably totems of popcraft, but infused with the spirit and introspection of a singer/songwriter. This formula would later become quite popular with artists from Matthew Sweet to the legions of basement auteurs in the pop underground, but this sensibility was relatively unheard of in the mid-'80s—hence the birth of Crowded House. Neil Finn retained Paul Hester from Enz, added Nick Seymour for the trio, and recorded one abandoned attempt at an album before joining with Mitchell Froom for the band's eponymous debut. At the time, Froom's clean production seemed refreshing, almost rootsy, compared to the synth-pop dominating the mainstream and college scenes at the time, but in retrospect it seems a little overreaching and fussy, particularly in its addition of echo and layers of keyboards during particularly inappropriate moments. But Finn at his best overshadowed this fairly stilted production with his expert songcraft. As it happened, the record was blessed by good timing, and the majestic ballad "Don't Dream It's Over" became an international hit, while its follow-up, the breezy "Something So Strong," also turned into a hit. Both revealed different sides of Finn's talents, with the first being lyrical and the second being effervescent, but perhaps the truest testaments to his talents are "Mean to Me," "World Where You Live," and "Now We're Getting Somewhere," songs where the lyrics meld with the melody in a way that is distinctive, affecting, and personal. If the rest of the record doesn't reach those heights, it's still good, well-constructed pop, and these aforementioned highlights point the way to *Temple of Low Men,* where Crowded House (and particularly Neil Finn) came into its own. *—Stephen Thomas Erlewine*

Temple of Low Men / Jul. 1988 / Capitol ✦✦✦✦✦
Following the success of Crowded House's debut and the band's gruelling promotion schedule, Neil Finn was clearly showing signs that he was no longer happy being New Zealand's zany ambassador to the U.S. While the material on *Temple of Low Men* demonstrates great leaps in quality over its predecessor, it is a darkly difficult album, especially for those expecting *Crowded House, Pt. 2*—in short, there are no immediately accessible singles. Instead, Finn digs into the depths of his emotional psyche with obsessive detail, crafting a set of intense, personal songs that range from the all-too-intimate look at infidelity of "Into Temptation" to the raucous exorcism of "Kill Eye." Through all of this introspective soul searching, Finn reveals most of all his true mastery of melody. *—Chris Woodstra*

Woodface / Jul. 2, 1991 / Capitol ✦✦✦✦✦
Where Crowded House's previous album, *Temple of Low Men,* showcased the often dark side of a man alone with his thoughts, *Woodface* represents the joy of reunion and the freedom of a collaborative effort—more than half of the album was originally conceived as a Finn Brothers project, which was Tim and Neil's first crack at writing together. The songs are easily their finest to date, combining flawless melodies and the outstanding harmonies of the brothers' perfectly matched voices. *—Chris Woodstra*

Together Alone / Oct. 18, 1993 / EMI-Capitol Special Markets ✦✦✦
More experimental and musically varied than any of their previous releases, *Together Alone* finds Crowded House branching out into traditional Maori music and heavy guitars, as well as the shining pop songcraft that is Neil Finn's trademark. Picking up a new guitarist and adding the production skills of ex-Killing Joke member Youth, Crowded House energizes their sound without losing sight of Neil Finn's classic pop songwriting, as "Locked Out" and "Distant Sun" prove. *—Stephen Thomas Erlewine*

• **Recurring Dream: The Very Best of Crowded House** / Jun. 24, 1996 / Capitol ✦✦✦✦✦
Recurring Dream is a 19-track collection which assembles most of the band's singles and adds three new studio tracks to entice fans—"Not the Girl You Think You Are," "Instinct" and "Everything Is Good for You." As a career summary, the collection works fairly well, though the nonchronological sequencing makes for a slightly confusing listen. Nevertheless, for a band with no shortage of great material (there's not a bad album in the bunch), *Recurring Dream* is a good place to get aquainted with them. Initial pressings also came with a second disc which compiles highlights from the band's always entertaining live shows. Maybe a disc of non-album rarities and B-sides would have been a better choice, but for fans this is an essential addition. *—Chris Woodstra*

Afterglow / Dec. 7, 1999 / Capitol ✦✦✦
Like any band, Crowded House had some unfinished business after their split. Namely, they had a number of very good songs that never appeared on an official album. These weren't rejects, per se—they were tunes that didn't have a home, so they popped up on B-sides, soundtracks and live shows, where Crowded House regularly aired unreleased and rare songs. These often became fan favorites yet they weren't readily available until the appearance of the rarities, B-sides, and "orphans" collection, *Afterglow.* Not every non-LP song made the cut, but everything here is quite strong and the album gels very well, sounding a bit like a lost album, even if the tracks were recorded between 1985 and 1994. Is it an essential collection? Well, for hardcore fans—the kind that know that with the existence of *Afterglow* they can now piece together the running order of the original *Woodface*—it certainly is. But it's not just for them, since casual fans will find several gems here. Perhaps Paul Hester's endearingly silly "My Telly's Gone Bung" will rub them the wrong way, but such gems as the pre-Crowded House tune "Recurring Dream" and the gorgeous "I Love You Dawn" rank among the group's finest, proving that Neil Finn became an exceptional songsmith during the time he led Crowded House. They, along with several other tunes, mean *Afterglow* isn't just appealing for Crowded House diehards, but for anyone with a taste for fine, well-crafted pop. *—Stephen Thomas Erlewine*

The Crystals

f. 1961, Brooklyn, NY, **db.** 1966
Group / Girl Group
This Brooklyn female vocal group had R&B roots, but the Crystals were really a pop ensemble whose best songs perfectly expressed the romantic innocence of the early '60s. Barbara Alston, Lala Brooks, Dee Dee Kennibrew, Mary Thomas, and Patricia Wright were the original lineup; the remarkable producer Phil Spector heard them rehearsing and eventually signed them to his Philles label, where they had several classic songs. "There's No Other like My Baby" got things started in 1961; "Uptown" cracked the R&B and pop Top 20, and then came "He's a Rebel," arguably their finest song and one of the era's landmarks. Darlene Love was lead vocalist, and both it and the successful follow-up "He's Sure the Boy I Love" featured Love and the Blossoms but were credited to the Crystals. The actual Crystals returned in 1963 and had two more huge hits, "Da Doo Ron Ron (When He Walked Me Home)" and "Then He Kissed Me" in 1963, each one making the Top Ten on both the R&B and pop lists. But the party ended in 1964, as their final two singles for Philles both flopped and relations between them and Spector degenerated. Various editions of the Crystals have been plentiful on the oldies circuit, but at last account, only Kennibrew was still involved out of the originals. *—Ron Wynn*

• **The Best of the Crystals** / Sep. 22, 1992 / ABKCO ✦✦✦✦✦
All of the Crystals' biggest hits are included on this comprehensive collection, which also features many forgotten singles and album tracks; while some of the lesser-known material might not match the standards of the classic singles, many songs do come close. *—Stephen Thomas Erlewine*

The Cult

f. 1984, Bradford, W. Yorks, England, **db.** 1995
Group / Heavy Metal, Alternative Pop/Rock, Hard Rock
Following a succession of name and stylistic changes, the Cult emerged in 1984 as one of England's leading heavy metal revivalists. Picking up the pseudo-mysticism and native American obsessions of the Doors, the guitar-orchestrations of Led Zeppelin and the three-chord crunch of AC/DC, while adding touches of post-punk goth-rock, the Cult gained a dedicated following in their native Britain with mid-'80s singles like "She Sells Sanctuary" before breaking into the American metal market in the late '80s with "Love Removal Machine."

The origins of the Cult lie in the Southern Death Cult, a goth-rock outfit formed by vocalist Ian Astbury in 1981. Though it was popular, Astbury soon pulled the plug on the band, recruited guitarist Billy Duffy and bassist Jamie Stewart, and renamed it Death Cult. After recording just one EP, the group became the Cult and moved into heavy hard rock with slight psychedelic flourishes. Their debut album, 1984's *Dreamtime,* performed well and the follow-up *Love* amplified the hard rock direction with a break-out single, "She Sells Sanctuary." For their third album, the Cult hired Rick Rubin as producer and recorded *Electric,* their hardest record to date. In 1988, *Sonic Temple* became the Cult's most successful album, propelled into the American Top Ten by the hit single "Fire Woman." By the time they recorded their follow-up to *Sonic Temple* though, infighting and substance abuse had begun tearing up the band. With Astbury and Duffy the only continuing members of the band, *Ceremony,* was released in the fall of 1991 to weak reviews and disappointing sales. *The Cult* appeared in 1994, though by the following year the Cult had disbanded, with Ian Astbury forming the Holy Barbarians later in 1995. *—Stephen Thomas Erlewine*

Love / 1985 / Sire ✦✦✦
1985's *Love* displayed a marked improvement over the Cult's early material, and though it remains underappreciated in America (worldwide it was a smash), this exceptional record has actually aged better than the band's more notorious (and equally important) releases: *Electric* and *Sonic Temple.* Equal parts psychedelic hard rock and new wave-goth, the songs on *Love* emanate a bright guitar sheen, tight arrangements, crisp drumming, and a command performance from vocalist Ian Astbury, who, as usual says a lot more with less than most singers. Overall, the album benefits from a wonderful sense of space, thanks in large part to guitarist Billy Duffy (who is much more subdued here than on future releases), whose restraint is especially notable on "Revolution" and the remarkably uncluttered title track. Duffy also provides compelling melodies ("Hollow Man," "Revolution"), driving riffs ("Nirvana," "The Phoenix"), and even a U2-like intro to "Big Neon Glitter." Also on offer is the near-perfect "She Sells Sanctuary" and the smash hit "Rain," quite possibly the band's most appealing single ever. Considering the musical schizophrenia that would plague each subsequent Cult release, *Love* just may be the band's purest moment. *—Ed Rivadavia*

Electric / 1987 / Beggars Banquet ✦✦✦✦✦
The roots of *Electric* lay in another album entirely, *Peace,* which was recorded with *Love* producer Steve Brown in a series of sessions that the band found increasingly pressure-filled and fraught with tension. A chance meeting with Def Jam supremo Rick Rubin at an American awards ceremony turned out to be the charm, resulting in the saucy chest-baring stomp of *Electric.* Rubin chucked all the old recordings for a series of new sessions, stripping everything down and essentially transforming Duffy into the logical successor to AC/DC's Angus Young. Thankfully Astbury decided not to become Brian Johnson, and while his macho yells can't help being cartoonish, he's clearly having fun throughout. Though both band and album caught a lot of flack for its perceived wallowing in dinosaur sounds and styles, the end result is still a fist-punching yelp of energy that demands to be heard at maximum volume in arenas, with a brusque punch in Les Warner's drums to match Duffy's power-chord action. "Love Removal Machine" is still the album's calling card, another in the series of instantly catchy Cult singles. "Li'l Devil" is almost as worthy, while other cuts like "Wild Flower" and "King Contrary Man" would have sounded good in 1973 and sound just as good in a new century. There are a couple of missteps—"Peace Dog" starts good but ends up being what happens when the Doors are used as a model in the wrong way, while the version of the Steppenwolf classic "Born to Be Wild" should be taken out and shot. Otherwise, an enjoyable

pleasure from start to finish—even if Astbury sings "Plastic fantastic lobster telephone" at one point. *—Ned Raggett*

Sonic Temple / 1989 / Beggars Banquet ♦♦♦
More varied than its predecessor, *Electric, Sonic Temple* finds the Cult trying several different metal styles, from crunchy *Electric*-era '70s grooves and the fuzzy, noisy psychedelia of *Love* to mellow ballads and commercial '80s hard rock. Not all of the experiments work, as some of the songs lean toward ponderousness, but enough of them did to send *Sonic Temple* into the *Billboard* Top Ten, due to the exposure provided by the hit single "Fire Woman." *—Steve Huey*

Ceremony / Sep. 24, 1991 / Beggars Banquet ♦♦

Pure Cult: The Best of the Cult (For Rockers, Ravers, Lovers & Sinners) / Feb. 16, 1993 / Polygram International ♦♦♦♦♦

Cult / 1994 / Beggars Banquet ♦♦♦

High Octane Cult / Nov. 5, 1996 / Beggars Banquet/Sire/Reprise ♦♦♦♦♦

● **Pure Cult: The Singles 1984-1995** / Jun. 6, 2000 / Beggars Banquet ♦♦♦♦♦
Say what you want about the Cult—a band which will certainly go down as one of the most schizophrenic in rock history—but singer Ian Astbury and guitarist Billy Duffy could sure write a great tune. Just glance at a few titles included on this greatest-hits collection *Pure Cult:* "Edie (Ciao Baby)," "Love Removal Machine," "She Sells Sanctuary," "Wild Flower," "Fire Woman," "Rain," "Lil' Devil," and "Sun King." Spread haphazardly across the disc (rather than in chronological order), each track's uniqueness is even more evident, further showcasing the Cult's fearless creativity. Early songs such as "Spiritwalker" and "Resurrection Joe" will surprise most fans with their class and maturity, while later cuts like "Wild Hearted Son" and "Heart of Soul" (from the disappointing *Ceremony* album) show new life when viewed on their own merits. And for those seeking some added collector's value, the band offered a fine later track in the industrial-tinged "The Witch." [After languishing for several years in an import release, Beggars Banquet released a virtually similar version of *Pure Cult* for American audiences in 2000.] *—Ed Rivadavia*

Best of Rare Cult / Oct. 17, 2000 / Beggars Banquet ♦♦♦

Culture Club

f. 1981, London, England, **db.** 1986
Group / Blue-Eyed Soul, Pop/Rock, New Wave
Few New Wave groups were as popular as Culture Club. During the early '80s, the group racked up seven straight Top 10 hits in the UK and six Top 10 singles in the US with their light, infectious pop-soul. Though their music was radio-ready, what brought the band stardom was Boy George, the group's charismatic, cross-dressing lead singer. George dressed in flamboyant dresses and wore heavy makeup, creating a disarmingly androgynous appearanence that created a sensation on early MTV. George also had a biting wit and frequently came up with cutting quips that won Culture Club heavy media exposure in both America and Britain. Although closely aligned with the New Romantics—they were both inspired by Northern Soul and fashion—Culture Club had sharper pop sense than their peers and they consequently had a broader appeal. However, their time in the spotlight was brief. Not only could they not withstand the changing fashions of MTV, but the group was fraught with personal tensions, including Boy George's drug addiction. By 1986, the group had broken up, leaving behind several singles that rank as classics of the New Wave era. *—Stephen Thomas Erlewine*

Kissing to Be Clever / 1982 / Virgin ♦♦♦♦♦

Colour by Numbers / 1983 / Virgin ♦♦♦♦♦

Waking Up with the House on Fire / 1984 / Virgin ♦♦

From Luxury to Heartache / 1986 / Virgin ♦♦

● **At Worst . . . The Best of Boy George and Culture Club** / Nov. 2, 1993 / Virgin ♦♦♦♦♦
The success of "The Crying Game" marked a comeback for Boy George, especially in the U.S., where his solo career had never taken hold beyond the dance clubs, and SBK (distributor of his label, Virgin) took advantage of his resurgence by compiling this 75-minute, 19-track album, which combines his former group Culture Club's biggest hits with selections from his solo work. The ten Culture Club tracks are of a piece, from 1982's "Do You Really Want to Hurt Me" (which here leads off with an ominous voice intoning, "Popularity breeds contempt") to "Love Is Love," which wasn't a hit, but is a better choice than the missing "The War Song," which was. The solo tracks are a more mixed batch, and not only because Top 40 U.K. hits like "Keep Me in Mind," "Sold," and "To Be Reborn" are missing. They often rely on loud percussion tracks that strand Boy George's tender tenor somewhere in the distance. He remains most effective on rhythmic ballads, whether "Do You Really Want to Hurt Me," "Everything I Own" (his chart-topping first U.K. solo hit), or "The Crying Game." *—William Ruhlmann*

VH-1 Storytellers/Greatest Moments / Aug. 11, 1998 / Virgin ♦♦♦♦

The Cure

f. 1976, Crawley, England
Group / College Rock, Post-Punk, Goth Rock, New Wave, Alternative Pop/Rock
Out of all the bands that emerged in the immediate aftermath of punk rock in the late '70s, the Cure was one of the most enduring and popular. Led through numerous incarnations by guitarist/vocalist Robert Smith, the band became notorious for their slow, gloomy dirges and Smith's ghoulish appearance. But the public image often hid the diversity of the Cure's music. At the outset, they played jagged, edgy pop songs and they slowly evolved into a more textured outfit. As one of the bands that laid the seeds for goth-rock, the group created towering layers of guitars and synthesizers, but by the time goth caught on in the mid-'80s, the Cure had moved away from the genre. By the end of the '80s, the Cure had crossed over into the mainstream not only in their native England, but also in the United States and in various parts of Europe. *—Stephen Thomas Erlewine*

Three Imaginary Boys / Jun. 1979 / Fiction ♦♦♦♦♦
Bursting with high-energy playing and bare-bones production, the band's first album showcases Robert Smith's most concise songwriting. Smith's now common themes of isolation, alienation and despair are present, this time presented in perfect three-minute form with a more aggressive stance. *Three Imaginary Boys* ends up sounding like a slightly more tuneful version of Wire's *Pink Flag* and quite unlike anything else they would record later on. *—Chris Woodstra*

Boys Don't Cry / Jan. 1980 / Elektra ♦♦♦♦♦
Boys Don't Cry combines the finer moments of *Three Imaginary Boys* with the singles released around the same time—the title track, "Jumping Someone Else's Train," and the often misinterpreted "Killing an Arab," as well as "Plastic Passion." The adding of the singles makes this the perfect encapsulation of the band's early days. *—Chris Woodstra*

Seventeen Seconds / May 1980 / Elektra ♦♦♦
Still capturing the more accessible pop elements and angular post-punk leanings of *Three Imaginary Boys, Seventeen Seconds* marks a move toward the despair for which the band would become best known. The tempos are slowed down considerably, and the addition of subtle synthesizers to minimalist arrangements builds a darkly evocative atmosphere of depression. *—Chris Woodstra*

Faith / Sep. 1981 / Elektra ♦♦♦
Continuing the trend set by *Seventeen Seconds, Faith* is an even darker affair. Smith sings with suicidal resignation through eight somber epics of gloom typified by the title track and "The Funeral Party," raising the funeral march tempo only for the single "Primary." The atmosphere created is chilling, though very few of the songs stand out. That's probably not the point anyway—as a mood-setting piece, *Faith* is quite effective. *—Chris Woodstra*

Pornography / 1982 / Elektra ♦♦♦
Pornography is the culmination of the band's gloom-and-doom period. It's not that they've changed their mood much since *Faith*—this is still pretty bleak stuff—but this album marks a more aggressive stance, incorporating faster, near-tribal rhythms and layers of heavy, distorted guitars that serve to bring out Smith's echoed vocals and doom-laden lyrics like "It doesn't matter if we all die." *Pornography* isn't their most interesting album—much of it suffers from same-sounding monotony—but it did manage to crack the U.K. Top Ten and was undoubtedly influential in the emerging goth-rock movement. *—Chris Woodstra*

Concert: The Cure Live / 1984 / Fiction ♦♦

Japanese Whispers / 1984 / Sire ♦♦♦
After reaching the depths of gloom, Smith recast himself as something of a British pop eccentric, releasing three singles—"The Walk," "Let's Go to Bed," and "The Lovecats"—that revealed an accessible and upbeat, nearly bubbly, side. *Japanese Whispers* collects those singles, along with their slightly less interesting b-sides. The singles were compiled on the more comprehensive *Standing on a Beach* collection, but as a collection of Smith's brief period of whimsy, there is no better collection than *Japanese Whispers. —Chris Woodstra*

The Top / 1984 / Sire ♦♦
Where their previous albums were gloomy and depressing, *The Top* is downright scary in places. The opener, "Shake Dog Shake," doesn't sound too dissimilar to the songs found on *Pornography,* but the album quickly shifts gears from that point on, with rapid style and mood changes that go from manic to nightmarish near-psychedelia with disturbing themes and a swirl of odd sounds. Ultimately, *The Top* is the band's least consistent album and their most difficult listen, but it is an interesting study in paranoid chaos, and it provides a fascinating look at a band (and more specifically, leader Robert Smith) spinning out of control. *—Chris Woodstra*

The Head on the Door / 1985 / Elektra ♦♦♦♦♦
The Cure refocused and ultimately hit their stride with *Head On the Door,* producing an album which not only more effectively depicted gloom, but also showed enough pop smarts to make it memorable (and even danceable). The band scored a hit with the infectious, New Order-ish "In Between Days" (which managed to beat New Order at their own game) and the highly memorable "Close to Me," but the album's outstanding trait is its diversity—they managed to combine a wide variety of influences, not only that of contemporary dance-floor peers, but also incorporating rhythms from the Far East and South America to fine effect. The Cure made more accomplished albums later on and had bigger hits, but none combined artistic ambition with really catchy songs as well as *Head On the Door. —Chris Woodstra*

★ **Staring at the Sea: The Singles** / 1986 / Elektra ♦♦♦♦♦
Staring at the Sea: The Singles collects all of the Cure's biggest UK hits and best-known songs from the late '70s and early '80s. Spanning from "Killing an Arab" and "Boys Don't Cry" to "The Lovecats," "Inbetween Days," and "Close to Me," *Staring at the Sea* captures some of the finest—and most influential—post-punk music. At their best, the Cure were nervy, intellectual, catchy and foreboding all at once. No matter how carefully crafted the Cure's individual albums were, their finest moments occured on singles like these, when they distilled their essence into surprisingly catchy, but decidedly left-of-center, pop singles. *Standing on a Beach* not only selects highlights from their uneven early albums, it collects many of the group's terrific non-LP singles. It's a definitive retrospective of the Cure and is one of the finest albums of the '80s. [The cassette version of *Staring at the Sea* was titled *Standing on a Beach* and included several B-sides.] *—Stephen Thomas Erlewine*

Kiss Me, Kiss Me, Kiss Me / 1987 / Elektra ♦♦♦
Simultaneously more accessible and ambitious than any of the Cure's previous albums, the double-album *Kiss Me, Kiss Me, Kiss Me* finds Robert Smith expanding his pop vocabulary by tentatively adding bigger guitars, the occasional horn section, lite-funk rhythms and string sections. It's eclectic, to be sure, but it's also a mess, bouncing from idea to idea and refusing to develop some of the most intriguing detours. Even if *Kiss Me* doesn't quite gel, its

best moments—including the deceptively bouncy "Why Can't I Be You?" and the stately "Just Like Heaven"—are remarkable and help make the album one of the group's very best. *—Stephen Thomas Erlewine*

Disintegration / May 1989 / Elektra ✦✦✦✦✦
Expanding the latent arena-rock sensibilities that peppered *Kiss Me, Kiss Me, Kiss Me* by slowing them down and stretching them to the breaking point, the Cure reached the peak of their popularity with the crawling, darkly seductive *Disintegration*. It's a hypnotic, mesmerizing record, comprised nearly entirely of epics like the soaring, icy "Pictures of You." The handful of pop songs, like the concise and utterly charming "Love Song," don't alleviate the doomy atmosphere. The Cure's gloomy soundscapes have rarely sounded so alluring, however, and the songs—from the pulsating, ominous "Fascination Street" to the eerie, string-laced "Lullaby"—have rarely been so well-constructed and memorable. It's fitting that *Disintegration* was their commercial breakthrough, since, in many ways, the album in the culmination of all the musical directions the Cure were pursuing over the course of the '80s. *—Stephen Thomas Erlewine*

Mixed Up / Oct. 19, 1990 / Elektra ✦✦

Wish / Apr. 21, 1992 / Elektra ✦✦✦

Paris / Oct. 26, 1993 / Elektra ✦✦

Show / Nov. 23, 1993 / Elektra ✦✦

Wild Mood Swings / May 21, 1996 / Fiction/Elektra ✦✦✦
After the relatively straightforward pop of *Wish*, the Cure moved back toward stranger, edgier territory with *Wild Mood Swings*. Actually, that's only part of the truth. As the title suggests, there's a vast array of textures and emotions on *Wild Mood Swings*, from the woozy mariachi lounge horns of "The 13th" to the perfect pop of "Mint Car" and the monolithic dirge of "Want." In between the extremes, Robert Smith and the Cure—which now features a radically reworked lineup, with several key players from *Wish* now missing—explore some simpler territory, from contemplative acoustic numbers tinged with strings to swooning neo-psychedelia. But what ties it all together is conviction—Smith sounds more content than he ever has, but he sings with more passion than he has for a number of years. Of course, the Cure haven't significantly changed their sound—tinny synthesizers and guitar effects that haven't appeared on an album since 1988 are in abundance throughout the record—but the variety of sounds and strength of performance offers enough surprises to make *Wild Mood Swings* more than just another Cure record. *—Stephen Thomas Erlewine*

Galore / Oct. 28, 1997 / Fiction/Elektra ✦✦✦✦✦
It's ironic that the Cure, a band whose albums have always seemed like definitive artistic statements, were at their best as a singles band. On the group's singles, Robert Smith's ideas reached their full potential, since they captured not only the group's off-kilter pop sense, but also the haunting melancholy and wacky humor that interlaced Smith's songs. *Galore* rounds up the singles from the second part of the Cure's career, beginning with "Why Can't I Be You?" from 1987's *Kiss Me Kiss Me Kiss Me* and ending with "Gone!" from 1996's *Wild Mood Swings*. Between those two are 15 more songs, nearly every one of which is a gem. The Cure were never a repetitive singles band, and there's a dizzying array of styles here, from infectious jangle-pop ("Friday I'm In Love," "Mint Car") and monolithic, chilly goth-rock ("Fascination Street," "Pictures of You," "Just Like Heaven") to jaunty, clever dance-club pop (the remix of "Close to Me"), eerie crawls ("Lullaby"), neo-mariachi madness ("The 13th") and even love songs ("Catch," "Lovesong"). There are a couple of missteps along the way—the pounding dance and pseudo-rap of "Hot Hot Hot!!!" sound dated, as does the ill-conceived Madchester diversion "Never Enough"—but *Galore* emphatically confirms the Cure's status as one of the best and most adventurous alternative bands of the '80s. And the new song, "Wrong Number," is pretty good, too. *—Stephen Thomas Erlewine*

Bloodflowers / Feb. 15, 2000 / Elektra ✦✦✦
The Cure edged into new territory with *Wild Mood Swings*, but nevertheless drew scorn from certain quarters because it eschewed goth rock for pop, both pure and twisted. For 2000's *Bloodflowers*, Robert Smith decided to give the people what they wanted: a classic Cure album, billed as the third part of a trilogy begun with *Pornography* and continued with *Disintegration*. That turns out to be more or less true, since *Bloodflowers* boasts all of the Cure's signatures: stately tempos, languid melodies, spacious arrangements, cavernous echoes, morose lyrics, keening vocals, long running times. If that's all you're looking for, *Bloodflowers* delivers in spades. If you want something transcendent, you're out of luck, since the album falls short of the mark, largely because it sounds too self-conscious. As one song segues into the next, it feels like Smith is striving to make a classic Cure record, putting all the sounds in place before he constructs the actual songs. That makes for a good listening experience, especially for fans of *Disintegration*, but it never catches hold the way that record did, for two simple reasons: there isn't enough variation between the songs for them to distinguish themselves, nor are there are enough sonic details to give individual tracks character. While *Disintegration* had goth monoliths, it also had pristine pop gems and elegant neo-psychedelia; with a couple of exceptions, the songs on *Bloodflowers* all feel like cousins of "Pictures of You." The album is certainly well made, and even enjoyable; however, its achievement is a bit hollow, since it never seems like Smith is pushing himself or the band. Nobody else can come close to capturing the Cure's graceful gloom, but it's hard to shake the suspicion that *Bloodflowers* could have been something grand if he had shaken up the formula slightly. *—Stephen Thomas Erlewine*

D'Angelo

b. Feb. 11, 1974, Richmond, VA
Vocals / Contemporary R&B, Urban
A self-taught pianist who began playing at the age of three, D'Angelo took his soul influences (Marvin Gaye, Al Green, Stevie Wonder, Prince) and parlayed them into a EMI contract when he was 18 years old. He wrote and co-produced "U Will Know," from the soundtrack for *Jason's Lyric*. The single featured D'Angelo with Tony Toni Tone, Boyz II Men, Tevin Campbell, Gerald Levert, R. Kelly, After 7 and others. His debut, *Brown Sugar*, appeared on EMI in 1995. *Live at the Jazz Cafe* followed in 1998, and two years later D'Angelo returned with *Voodoo*. *—John Bush*

● **Brown Sugar** / 1995 / Capitol ✦✦✦✦✦
By the mid-'90s, most urban R&B had become rather predictable, working on similar combinations of soul and hip-hop, or relying on vocal theatrics on slow seductive numbers. With his debut album, *Brown Sugar*, the 21 year-old D'Angelo crashed down some of those barriers. D'Angelo concentrates on classic versions of soul and R&B, but unlike most of his contemporaries, he doesn't cut and paste older songs with hip-hop beats; instead, he attacks the forms with a hip-hop attitude, breathing new life into traditional forms. Not all of his music works—there are several songs that sound incomplete, relying more on sound than structure. But when he does have a good song—like the hit "Brown Sugar," Smokey Robinson's "Cruisin'," or the bluesy "Shit, Damn, Motherfucker," among several others—D'Angelo's wild talents are evident. *Brown Sugar* might not be consistently brilliant, but it is one of the most exciting debuts of 1995, giving a good sense of how deep D'Angelo's talents run. *—Stephen Thomas Erlewine*

Live at the Jazz Cafe / Jun. 30, 1998 / EMI ✦✦✦

Voodoo / Jan. 11, 2000 / Virgin ✦✦✦✦
Five years after his *Brown Sugar* album helped launch contemporary R&B, D'Angelo finally returned with his sophomore effort, *Voodoo*. His soulful voice is just as sweet as it was on *Brown Sugar*, though D'Angelo stretches out with a varied cast of collaborators, including trumpeter Roy Hargrove and guitarist Charlie Hunter, fellow neo-soul stars Lauryn Hill and Raphael Saadiq, and hip-hop heads like DJ Premier, Method Man & Redman, and Q-Tip. It must have been difficult to match his debut (and the frequent delays prove it was on his mind), but *Voodoo* is just as rewarding a soul album as D'Angelo's first. *—John Bush*

Daft Punk

f. 1992, Paris, France
Group / Electronica, Club/Dance, House
In similar company with new-school French progressive dance artists such as Motorbass, Air, Cassius and Dimitri from Paris, Parisian duo Daft Punk have quickly risen to acclaim by adapting a love for first-wave acid house and techno to their younger roots in pop, indie rock, and hip-hop. The combined talents of DJs Guy-Manuel De Homem-Christo and Thomas Bangalter, Daft Punk released their debut single, "The New Wave," in 1993 on the celebrated Soma label. Instantly hailed by the dance music press as the work of a new breed of house innovators, the single was followed by "Da Funk," the band's first true hit (the record has sold 30,000 copies worldwide and seen thorough rinsings by everyone from Kris Needs to the Chemical Brothers). The group eventually signed with Virgin, with their first long-player, *Home Work*, appearing early the following year. As with the earlier singles, the group's sound is a brazen, dancefloor-oriented blend of progressive house, funk, electro, and techno, with sprinklings of hip-hop-styled breakbeats and excessive, crowd-firing samples, similar to other anthemic dance-fusion acts such as the Chemical Brothers and Monkey Mafia. *—Sean Cooper*

● **Homework** / Jan. 20, 1997 / Virgin ✦✦✦✦✦
Daft Punk's full-length debut is a funk-house hailstorm, giving real form to a style of straightahead dance music not attempted since the early fusion days of on-the-one funk and dance-party disco. Thick, rumbling bass, vocoders, choppy breaks and beats, and a certain brash naivete permeate the record from start to finish, giving it the edge of an almost certain classic. While a few fall flat, the best tracks make this one essential. *—Sean Cooper*

Dick Dale

b. May 4, 1937
Guitar / Surf Revival, Surf, Instrumental Rock
The father of surf music, guitarist Dick Dale to a large degree invented and defined the form in the early '60s with his pioneering use of Fender reverb, dazzling staccato playing, and thundering instrumentals that incorporated Middle Eastern and Latin melodic influences. Playing guitars strung for right-handers with his left hand (as Hendrix would years later), he had an agreement with Fender instruments to "road test" new amplification equipment before it was manufactured for the general public, and found that its hollow, sustained tones evoked the mood of surfing, then catching on in a big way in his Southern California stomping grounds. Dale's impact was largely limited to Southern California, but his influence was vast, helping ignite surf music and contributing several of the genre's most enduring classics, especially "Let's Go Trippin'" and "Miserlou" (both of which were covered by the Beach Boys on their early albums). In the 1990s, Dale made an unexpectedly successful comeback with newly recorded material that closely echoed his vintage sides. *—Richie Unterberger*

★ **King of the Surf Guitar: The Best of Dick Dale** / Aug. 4, 1989 / Rhino ✦✦✦✦✦
King of the Surf Guitar: Best of Dick Dale is the definitive compilation of the father of surf-rock, containing 18 of his best-known songs, including all of his biggest hits ("Miserlou," "Let's Go Trippin'"), all presented in their original versions and in excellent audio. In addition to showcasing the roots of surf, *King of the Surf Guitar* demonstrates what a skilled and eclectic guitarist Dale was. Dale was one of the first guitarists in rock & roll to rely on studio and guitar effects and fuse elements of world musics to his sound, and every one of his experiments is captured on this disc. It's a definitive retrospective. *—Stephen Thomas Erlewine*

Better Shred than Dead: The Dick Dale Anthology / Jun. 10, 1997 / Rhino ✦✦✦✦
The big picture on Dick Dale—the inventor of surf music, the Godfather of Loud, precursor of heavy metal, the first high-energy power guitarist (all titles being proffered from the man himself to describe his contributions)—gets told in a real fine way on this two-disc, 39-track anthology. Although single-disc best-of's exist, this is the first one to cross-license from various labels. Dick started as a vocalist who just happened to be able to furnish his own guitar

solos, and it's here that the compilation starts. But by track four on the first disc, "Let's Go Trippin'," the Dick Dale story begins in earnest. The sopping-wet "surf" sound hadn't been invented yet, but the staccato picking, heavy twang and hard attack were already in place. The outboard Fender reverb tank that became part of Dale's signature found its first workout on "Miserlou" (although Dale claims otherwise), and what followed was the beginning of surf music, pure and simple. Most of the groundbreaking recordings were featured on Dick's debut disc, *Surfer's Choice*, hands down *the* surf album that started it all. From this classic comes "Shake-N-Stomp," "Take It Off" and the one that made him a California legend, "Surf Beat." The rest of the first disc carries us through his later Capitol recordings while the second starts with the second half of Dale's career in 1983 with live tracks from his *The Tigers Loose* album and steers us through duets with Stevie Ray Vaughan, tributes to Hendrix, and best of all, documenting his own resurrection in the '90s, totally viable and still his own man. Transfers sound a bit buzzier in an over-EQ'd way on some of the early tracks, but overall, this is one really great tribute to an original pioneer. *—Cub Koda*

The Damned

f. 1976, England, **db.** 1989

Group / British Punk, Goth Rock, Punk

The Damned usurped the Sex Pistols, working behind their backs to become the first British punk band to release a record, the first to have a hit single (the epochal "New Rose") and the first to tour America. That, in a nutshell, is the appeal of the Damned—they weren't revolutionaries, they were drunken louts who would do anything for a prank. Like many of their first-generation punk peers, the band were rooted in pub-rock, playing simple three-chord pounders, but the group played fast, loose and sloppy, often sounding like everything was about to fall apart. Their 1977 debut *Damned Damned Damned* epitomized this sound, and they never quite captured it again, partially because of their limited talent and partially because of their defiant, boundless stupidity. Following the debut, the Damned released a pair of similar records that weren't quite as successful before delving into a bizarre affair with goth-rock for several years in the early '80s. By the time that was worked out of their system, several key members had left the band and the group had nothing more than a cult following, yet they still managed the odd hit single in the U.K. until the late '80s, when the Damned decided to call it a day. But that wasn't the end of the story. During the '90s, the band continually reunited in various incarnations, playing concerts across England and functioning as a sort of bizarre punk nostalgia act. *—Stephen Thomas Erlewine*

★ **Damned Damned Damned** / Apr. 16, 1977 / Frontier ✦✦✦✦✦

While the Sex Pistols will always have a prominent place in the story of U.K. punk, the Damned did nearly everything first, including the first single, the smoking "New Rose," and the first album, namely, this stone classic of rock & roll fire. At just half an hour long, *Damned Damned Damned* is a permanent testimony to original guitarist Brian James' songwriting (ten of the 12 tracks are his) and the band's take no prisoners aesthetic. Starting with Captain Sensible's sharp bass line for "Neat Neat Neat," which rapidly explodes into a full band thrash, the Damned left rhetoric for the theoreticians and political posing for the the Clash. All the foursome wanted to do was rock, and that they do here. Vanian already has his spooky-voiced theatrics down cold; "Feel the Pain" indulges his Alice Cooper fascination while the band creates some creepy fun behind him. Most of the time, he's yelping with the best of them, but with considerably more control than most of the era's shouters. Scabies' considerable reputation as a drummer starts here; comparisons flew thick and fast to Keith Moon, and not just for onstage antics (of which there were plenty). His sense of stop-start rhythm and fills is simply astounding, whether on "So Messed Up" or in his own one-minute goof, "Stab Yer Back." Though the Captain doesn't get his full chance to shine on bass, he's more than adequate, while James just cranks the amps and lets fly. Concluding with a version of the Stooges' "1970" which sounds hollower than the original but no less energetic, *Damned Damned Damned* is and remains rock at its messy, wonderful best. *—Ned Raggett*

Music for Pleasure / Nov. 1977 / Demon ✦✦

Machine Gun Etiquette / Dec. 1979 / Roadrunner ✦✦✦✦✦

Rejoining forces without James, who pursued his own interests from then on (only hooking up with the band again for a late-'80s "farewell" show), the remaining three brought in young Saints veteran Ward on bass, recorded an album, and hoped for the best. That best proved much better than expected; while singles ended up on the charts, *Etiquette* itself was deservedly hailed as another classic from the band. Over time, its reputation has grown to equal the original *Damned Damned Damned;* while no less strong than that record, the Damned here bring in a wide variety of touches and influences to create a record that most of their contemporaries could never have approached. The group's wicked way around witty punk hadn't ebbed a bit; the opening cut, "Love Song," is a hilarious trashing of romantic clichés (sample lyric: "I'll be the rubbish, you'll be the bin!") that barely lasts two minutes, while "Noise, Noise, Noise" and "Liar" work in the same general vein. These, however, only scratch the surface. "Melody Lee," written by the Captain for a favorite comic character, starts with a lovely piano intro, whereas the celebratory angst of "I Just Can't Be Happy Today" chugs along with garagey élan and keyboards á la the Electric Prunes. Other prime standouts include "Plan 9 Channel 7," a Grand Guignol of an epic about James Dean and Vampira with a fantastic Vanian vocal; the merry mayhem of "These Hands" (belonging to a killer circus clown, with appropriate carnival music, of course); and a great rip through the MC5's "Looking at You." The best moment was saved for last, though: "Smash It Up," a two-part number divided between an affecting instrumental tribute to longtime supporter and Captain hero Marc Bolan, and a perfect trash-the-rules-and-party pop/punk/R&B scorcher. *—Ned Raggett*

The Black Album / Dec. 1980 / Chiswick ✦✦✦

The fact that one of its songs is called "Hit or Miss" is quite appropriate for the double-vinyl *Black Album;* while not perfect, it's definitely got some high points on it. Given the intentionally parodic reference to the Beatles' own two-disc sprawler, perhaps the schizophrenia is perfectly intentional. Some of the numbers show the band following their original punk vein, but by this point the four (joined here by a new bassist, Paul Gray) were leaving straight, three-chord thrash to the cul-de-sac revivalists. The album begins with a Damned classic, "Wait for the Blackout," a dramatic psych/punk surge infected with Vanian's glorious croon, celebrating the joys of the night while steering clear of overtly-serious goth affectations. After that, things start to vary, but tracks of note are still thick on the ground, including the Sensible-sung "Lively Arts," a nicely barbed take on culture with some harpsichord to match, and the goofy but still enjoyable "Drinking About My Baby." Regardless, things get a bit restful at points, and while Vanian often steps forward to continue carrying it along, sometimes even the band isn't happy with the results. "History of the World (Part One)" has always carried the credit "overproduced by Hans Zimmer" because they felt the guest synth player did just that! However, the final two studio tracks are doozies: "Therapy," a Sensible/Vanian-sung romp with a great chorus, and the sidelong "Curtain Call," perhaps the most unlikely thing the Damned ever did. That said, it's still a surprisingly good blast, a tour de force for Vanian particularly and a chance for the band to try everything from straightforward rock to gentler atmospherics. *—Ned Raggett*

Strawberries / 1982 / Castle ✦✦✦

Phantasmagoria / 1985 / Off Beat ✦✦✦✦

By the time the Damned found themselves on a major label after nine years of ups, downs, and all arounds, a big change had taken place: Captain Sensible, with both his own solo successes and other pressures coming to bear, decided to depart. Keyboardist Roman Jugg took over the guitar, while Bryn Merrick remained on bass and Vanian and Scabies continued doing their thing. The first fruit of this new Damned, *Phantasmagoria,* doesn't match up to the excellent variety and performance level on *Strawberries,* but still has a lot to show while at the same time exploring new territory for the group. The cover and artwork seem to ally the Damned even more closely with goth rock than before, but Vanian thankfully has never seen fit to simply ape those clichés, steering his own powerful path. Similarly the music can be moody but never without its own distinct energy and fire—more a Cramps sense (if not sound) of loving the dark than anything, but with a clean, modern sheen and just enough Hammer horror. "Street of Dreams" makes for a powerful, anthemic opener, with some fine Scabies drumming. "Is It a Dream," the one song with a Sensible co-writing credit, is yet another fantastic Vanian vocal showcase in a career of many. The really killer tracks include "Shadow of Love," a semi-Morricone style mood-out quick shuffle with haunting guitar from Jugg, and "Grimly Fiendish," a funny bit of spooky psychedelia not all that far off from where the Dukes of Stratosphear would end up a couple of years later. *Phantasmagoria* concludes with the surging instrumental "Trojans," a strong number that showed the Damned had lots of life in them yet. *—Ned Raggett*

Anything / 1986 / MCA ✦

The Light at the End of the Tunnel / 1987 / MCA ✦✦✦✦✦

Anyone expecting a fully organized compilation from this double-disc effort will be sorely disappointed; while the years for release dates are mentioned, the sources for many of the releases aren't, leaving neophytes to the Damned a bit high and dry. Happily, an appreciative and detailed essay from one Herb Feinstein (more likely Chiswick label boss Roger Armstrong writing under a pseudonym, as he did in the liner notes to the CD version of *Machine Gun Etiquette*) helps. Even without the chronological organization, *Light* is still a great overview of the first ten years of the band's career, especially given the sheer amount of labels that they'd been on over the years (at least five, if not more!). The selection is, for the most part, quite on the money; while those who feel the group fell off dramatically with the *Phantasmagoria* and *Anything* albums will think them over-represented, it's still definitely the Damned at their best from track to track. Early punk breakouts like "Neat Neat Neat" and "New Rose" as well as turn of the '80s standards as "Plan 9 Channel 7," "Smash It Up," and "I Just Can't Be Happy Today" make a case for the band's early days. *The Black Album* is mostly ignored, but the sidelong "Curtain Call" thankfully is included, giving Vanian his well-deserved showcase. Later numbers like "Ignite," "Lovely Money," "Grimly Fiendish," and the smash single "Eloise" demonstrate that far from fading away, the Damned just found other ways to make their mark. Add to this a slew of rarities—the studio cover of the Beatles' "Help!," "Rabid (Over You)," "Disco Man," and some alternate mixes of other numbers—and *Light* remains the best place for those new to the Damned to start. Comprehensive and perfectly entertaining all at once. *—Ned Raggett*

Tales from the Damned / Aug. 13, 1993 / Cleopatra ✦✦✦✦✦

The Damned's period on Ace/Chiswick Records in the late seventies and early eighties was one of the band's busiest, with a slew of EPs and side projects surfacing. Some tracks and B-sides were captured on the CD reissues of albums like *Machine Gun Etiquette,* but most remained out of print in the digital age until this fantastic collection surfaced. Commissioned for Cleopatra, *Tales from the Damned* is a detailed, thorough and fantastic sounding collection with fine liner notes to boot. Three cuts—the hilarious rip into "Disco Man," an anti-holiday standard, "There Ain't No Sanity Clause" and a live version of "Looking At You"—had received the digital treatment before. Otherwise, it was lost classics—and non-classics!—ahoy. Starting with the great rough pop/punk gem "Burglar"—with sore-throat vocals from either Captain Sensible or then-bassist Algy Ward—*Tales* covers everything from a collaborative smash with Motorhead through that band's "Over the Top" to a surprisingly faithful cover of the Rolling Stones' "Citadel." The humorous side of the band comes out on a lot of these cuts, whether it's the semi-skit that concludes "Burglar," the intentionally moronic "I'm So Bored," or the wonderfully profane "Anti-Pope," appearing in its rare violin-tinged alternate version. A fair number, though, are straightforward and all the better for it -the keyboard-touched, strong pop ballad "The Limit Club," one of Vanian's best vocal showcases, the wonderful "Teenage Dream" and the moody instrumental "Seagulls," a chance for the band to relax in a calm, reflective way. *—Ned Raggett*

Sessions of the Damned / Mar. 4, 1994 / Varese ✦✦✦✦

Neat Neat Neat / Nov. 19, 1996 / Demon Duplicate ✦✦✦

Danzig

f. 1987

Group / Alternative Metal, Heavy Metal

After the demise of Samhain, ex-Misfits vocalist Glenn Danzig formed his own eponymous heavy metal band in 1987, which would prove a more effective vehicle for his obsession with the dark side. But there's more than meets the eye—Danzig obviously relishes casting himself as the archetypally evil, menacing heavy metal frontman, and his theatricality often seems to indicate that his posturing is tongue-in-cheek. The darkness of Danzig's vision increasingly expressed itself over the band's career in a romanticized, gothic sensibility, more quietly sinister and darkly seductive than aggressively threatening, and the group's music has progressed from simple, blues-based metal riffs to more atmospheric, coldly haunting textures that attempt to sonically replicate the feel of the lyrics. Their self-titled debut for Rick Rubin's Def American label found Glenn Danzig playing the Satanic metal singer role to the hilt, even if the band's songs sounded much the same. *Danzig II: Lucifuge* followed in 1990, and it expanded on the simple blues riffs of the debut with more extensive forays into that style. *Danzig III: How the Gods Kill* marked a full-fledged entry into the realm of gothic romanticism, working to create moods rather than pounding heavy metal aggression. Glenn Danzig next released a solo project, *Black Aria*, a quasi-operatic attempt at classical instrumentals. The band broke through into the mainstream in 1993, when a live video for "Mother," a song originally released on Danzig, became an inescapable smash on MTV and even charted as a single, nearly cracking the *Billboard* Top 40. The more experimental *Danzig 4* was released in 1994 and entered the charts at number 29, but its moody, atmospheric subtlety didn't find as much favor with the band's new audience as the anthemic "Mother." Following the supporting tour, Danzig broke up the band and assembled another version more in line with his new direction. Though increasingly ignored by the press and the public, Danzig continued to release records into the new millennium. *—Steve Huey*

Danzig / 1988 / American ✦✦✦

Danzig debuts with a record of simple, pounding, bluesy metal featuring lead singer Glenn Danzig's trademark Elvis-meets-Jim Morrison bellow and outlandishly dark, evil lyrics. There isn't a great deal of musical variety or complexity here, but the band powers its way through such signature tunes as "Twist of Cain," "Am I Demon," and the (future) hit "Mother" with a primal energy. Plus, Danzig's tongue-in-cheek posturing as the ultimate unholier-than-thou heavy metal frontman gives the record a definite appeal, even if one is not inclined to view his theatrics as dangerous or threatening. *—Steve Huey*

Danzig II: Lucifuge / Jun. 1990 / American ✦✦✦✦

Danzig's second release is also their most diversified. They explore their blues roots with a couple of boogies, a slow shuffle, and a slide number, throwing in a '50s-reminiscent ballad in waltz time for good measure. Glenn Danzig's theatrical vocals don't prevent these numbers from working surprisingly well (except when he attempts a Mississippi-delta accent on "Killer Wolf"), demonstrating his talents and range of expression as a vocalist. The simple, somewhat standard blues-metal riffs of their debut are here ("Snakes of Christ" is a flat-out rewrite of *Danzig*'s "Twist of Cain"), but not as plentiful, making the record more interesting and listenable. "Her Black Wings" ranks with the band's best songs. *—Steve Huey*

• **Danzig III: How the Gods Kill** / Jul. 14, 1992 / American ✦✦✦✦

Featuring disturbing cover art from H.R. Giger, Danzig's third album continues to expand the band's musical range; rather than pounding away at simple blues riffs, the atmospheric title track (yet another rewrite of "Twist of Cain," this time at a slower tempo) and the haunting ballad "Sistinas" attempt to match their music with the darkness of Glenn Danzig's lyrics, resulting in two of the album's high points. Danzig's vocals are more subtle in places, and John Christ's guitar work continues to improve. Arguably the definitive Danzig album. *—Steve Huey*

Black Aria / 1993 / Phonographie ✦

Thrall: Demonsweatlive / May 25, 1993 / American ✦✦✦

Danzig 4 / Dec. 1994 / American ✦✦✦

Danzig's experiments with using texture and atmosphere to evoke their trademark mood of darkness and evil come to the forefront on their fourth full-length album, with John Christ contributing more effects and fuller chord voicings. The band has also started to craft their songs, using different instruments and a few industrial sounds in the background of some tracks. Not all of the experiments are successful or interesting, partially due to inconsistent songwriting, but out of all their releases, the music here comes the closest to reflecting the darkness of Glenn Danzig's lyrics. Some, however, may miss their more energetic earlier albums. *—Steve Huey*

Blackacidevil / Oct. 29, 1996 / Phonographie ✦✦✦

Terence Trent D'Arby

b. Mar. 15, 1962, New York, NY

Vocals, Saxophone, Keyboards, Drums, Guitar / Contemporary R&B, Adult Alternative Pop/Rock, Pop/Rock, Urban

Terence Trent D'Arby emerged in 1987 amid a storm of publicity. Claiming his debut record was the best since *Sgt. Pepper*, his brash arrogance captured headlines throughout the U.K., eventually winding their way back to America. D'Arby's first single, "If You Let Me Stay," rocketed into the U.K. Top Ten upon its release. Its accompanying album, *Introducing the Hardline According to Terence Trent D'Arby*, was also a massive success, hitting number one and spending over a year in the top half of the chart. D'Arby didn't have a major hit in the U.S. until 1988, when the sparse funk of "Wishing Well" hit number one. All of the success—both commercial and critical—had D'Arby poised as a major act, artistically and popularly. His mix of soul, rock, pop and R&B recalled Prince in its scope and sound, yet his sensibility was grittier and earthier. At least they were at first. By the time of his second album, 1989's *Neither Fish nor Flesh*, his ambitions were more nakedly pretentious, and the album dropped off the charts quickly, without so much as one hit single. *Terence Trent D'Arby's Symphony or Damn*—an album containing many of the same ideas as *Neither Fish Nor Flesh*, only better executed—was released in 1993 to favorable reviews, as well as some airplay on modern rock radio stations and MTV. It was enough for D'Arby to regain some credibility, yet it wasn't enough to make the album a hit. Two years later, he released *TTD's Vibrator*, which received the same fate as *Symphony or Damn*. *—Stephen Thomas Erlewine*

Introducing the Hardline According to Terence Trent D'Arby / 1987 / Columbia ✦✦✦✦

Introducing the Hardline According to Terence Trent D'Arby is a strong debut by this young, cocky Black British singer, who wrote virtually every note, played a multitude of instruments, and claimed that his was the most important album since the Beatles' *Sgt. Pepper.* Hits included "If You Let Me Stay," "Dance Little Sister," "Sign Your Name," and the number one "Wishing Well." His first album is a curious mixture of old and new styles. Although the production is quite modern, D'Arby shows his roots in the work of older artists, borrowing a page or two from Michael Jackson and Stevie Wonder, while James Brown appears to have had the strongest influence on D'Arby's stage presence. *—Rob Bowman*

Neither Fish Nor Flesh / Oct. 1989 / Columbia ✦✦✦

Following the major success of his debut, Terence Trent D'Arby made the always-difficult sophomore effort more difficult. In addition to the brash declarations that preceded his first record, D'Arby made ultimately self-sabotaging demands upon his label, concerning *Neither Fish Nor Flesh*'s promotion and release (to coincide with the competitive Christmas market). The challenging nature of the album didn't help matters. *Neither Fish Nor Flesh* is a sprawling, overly ambitious work that incorporates Middle Eastern flavorings and even more of a gospel influence into his gritty mix of rock, R&B, and funk. Lyrically, D'Arby's pretensions run a bit wild, but the man does possess a voice that is a force to be reckoned with. Songs like the rousing, soulful "I'll Be Alright" and the sexy "To Know Someone Deeply Is to Know Someone Softly" are masterful. Other highlights include the breezy, Motown vibe of "Billy Don't Fall" (a song actually about AIDS) and the skeletal, fiery "This Side of Love." *Neither Fish Nor Flesh* crashed upon release, but the album remains a compelling, if flawed, effort from a musician that has been one of the more baffling unfulfilled talents in recent memory. *—Tom Demalon*

• **Terence Trent D'Arby's Symphony or Damn** / May 11, 1993 / Columbia ✦✦✦✦✦

Falling halfway between the modern R&B of *Introducing the Hardline* and the extravagent *Neither Fish nor Flesh*, *Symphony or Damn* is Terence Trent D'Arby's most ambitious album yet. It's also his best, because it takes the fine songwriting of his debut and melds it to the sonic excesses of *Fish.* Sure, some of it is embarassing (it's hard not to cringe during the "Welcome to My Monasteryo" declaration at the beginning of the album), but more often than not, D'Arby's experimentations succeed, and succeed grandly, at that. *—Stephen Thomas Erlewine*

TTD's Vibrator / Jun. 1, 1995 / Work ✦✦✦

Bobby Darin

b. May 14, 1936, New York, NY [The Bronx], **d.** Dec. 20, 1973, Los Angeles, CA

Vocals / Traditional Pop, Brill Building Pop, Folk-Rock, Pop

There's been considerable discussion about whether Darin should be classified as a rock-'n'roll singer, a Vegas hipster cat, an interpreter of popular standards, or even a folk-rocker. He was all of these and none of these. Throughout his career he made a point out of not becoming committed to any one style at the exclusion of others; at the height of his nightclub fame he incorporated a folk set into his act. When it appeared he could have gone on indefinitely as a sort of junior version of Frank Sinatra, he would periodically record pop-rock and folk-rock singles whose principal appeal lay outside of the adult pop market. At one point he started calling himself Bob Darin and recorded songs with vague anti-establishment overtones that could be said to be biting the largely bourgeois hands that fed his highest-paying gigs. It may be most accurate to say that Darin was, above all, a *singer* who wanted to do a lot of things, rather than make his mark as a particular stylist. That may have cost him some points as far as making it to the very top of certain genres, but also makes his work more versatile than almost any other vocalist of his era. *—Richie Unterberger*

• **The Ultimate Bobby Darin** / Jun. 1988 / Warner Brothers ✦✦✦✦✦

The Ultimate Bobby Darin remains the most thorough single-disc retrospective of the legendary singer to date, effectively capturing the stunning range of his unique musical vision. Each of its 17 songs is a gem, although the cream of the crop includes "Splish Splash," "Dream Lover," "Mack the Knife" and "Beyond the Sea." *—Chuck Donkers*

Capitol Collectors Series / 1989 / Capitol ✦✦✦✦✦

A compilation of Darin's mid-'60s singles, which showcase Darin's diversity even if the majority of the set leans heavily on his pop material. Comprehensive liner notes, intelligent track selection, and great fidelity make this worth picking up. *—Stephen Thomas Erlewine*

As Long as I'm Singing: The Bobby Darin Collection / Nov. 21, 1995 / Rhino ✦✦✦✦✦

A four-CD box set spanning several styles, labels, and eras, this will stand as the most thorough retrospective of Darin's eclectic career, though not necessarily the best. There's a lot of material here—96 songs, including not only the hits, but obscure flops, B-sides, album cuts, and 11 previously unreleased tracks. Because Darin covered a lot of different genres, it's not programmed chronologically, but by style—one disc for "The Rock'n'Roll Years" (which, truth be told, were often closer to pop than rock), two to his pop sides, and one to his folk and country outings. In hindsight (and in the enclosed 64-page book), much has been made of Darin's versatility. But while it's true he could handle a range of genres competently, versatility does not automatically equate with quality. Just as a baseball player who can play all the positions is not necessarily a great player, Darin's unusual eclecticism did not mean that he was as great a singer as some legends who concentrated only on rock, or only on pop, or only on folk. There are some neat surprises here—the mid-'60s protest folk-rock of "We Didn't Ask to Be Brought Here," the full-bodied pop of "When I Get Home," the fine rendition of "Nature Boy," and the reasonably cogent and sincere late-'60s folk-rock. But a lot of it is not more than competent, and some of it (especially the slighter rock efforts) are less than that. And the almost diametrically opposed range of sounds (it's a long way from "Splish Splash" to "Mame" and "If I Were a Carpenter," after all) means that not many listeners except Darin fanatics will be able to get through the whole set without skipping over a lot of the tracks. —*Richie Unterberger*

The Very Best of Bobby Darin: 1966-1969 / Sep. 14, 1999 / Varese ✦✦✦✦
It's easy to criticize Bobby Darin as a shameless follower of trends who shifted from rock & roll to mainstream pop patterned after Frank Sinatra, when rock appeared to be on the wane at the end of the '50s. In this sense, his mid-'60s embrace of folk-rock protest music looks like just another example of opportunism. When Darin returned to Atlantic Records in 1966, he released nearly unknown folk-rock singer/songwriter Tim Hardin's "If I Were a Carpenter" as a single. Though it soared into the Top Ten, Darin didn't just become Tim Hardin's popularizer; as this collection demonstrates, he also tried the music of the Lovin' Spoonful and obtained a contribution from Alan Gordon and Gary Bonner, writers of the Turtles' hit "Happy Together." But a greater indication of the sincerity of Darin's conversion was his own songwriting. Always an excellent writer, he turned his attention to more personal and political topics. In 1968, he left Atlantic to form his own Direction Records label; by 1969, he had grown a mustache, taken to wearing blue jeans, and started calling himself Bob Darin. It didn't last. Darin's new approach was not taken to by the hippies, and it was soundly rejected by his old audience. Since Darin's death, his period as a folk-rocker has been nearly forgotten, but this album demonstrates that it contained some of his best writing and performances. Few pop vocalists were inclined or able to make music in the serious style that became popular in the mid-'60s; Bobby Darin was one of them, and it is a tribute to his talent and courage as an artist that he did. —*William Ruhlmann*

The Spencer Davis Group

f. 1963, Birmingham, England, **db.** 1986
Guitar / Blue-Eyed Soul, British Invasion
His ferocious soul-drenched vocals belying his tender teenage years, Stevie Winwood powered the Spencer Davis Group's three biggest US hits during their brief life span as one of the British Invasion's most convincing R&B-based combos.

Guitarist Davis formed the band with Winwood on organ, his brother Muff Winwood on bass, and drummer Peter York. Signing on with producer Chris Blackwell, the quartet got their first hit (the blistering "Keep on Running") from another of Blackwell's acts, West Indian performer Jackie Edwards. After topping the British charts in 1965, the song struggled on the lower reaches of the US Hot 100.

The group's two hottest sellers were self-penned projects. "Gimme Some Lovin'" and "I'm a Man" were searing showcases for the adolescent Winwood's gritty vocals and blazing keyboards and the band's pounding rhythms. Although they burned up the charts even on this side of the ocean in 1967, the quartet never capitalized on their fame with an American tour. At the height of their power, Winwood left to form Traffic, leaving Davis without his dynamic front man. The bandleader focused on producing other acts, including a Canadian ensemble called the Downchild Blues Band during the early 80s. —*Bill Dahl*

Their First LP / 1965 / Fontana ✦✦✦
The group's first album is basically a reflection of their early repertoire and very heavy on the R&B/soul standards. Dominated by covers of Ike & Tina Turner, the Coasters, John Lee Hooker, Little Walter, Brenda Holloway, and others, only three of the tunes are original. Two of these are written by Stevie Winwood, the other by Spencer Davis; Winwood's mid-tempo soul number "It Hurts Me So" is easily the best of them. Winwood is in fine voice and the group is energetic, but this is neither as good as their best work nor nearly as good as the best British R&B albums of the era by competitors like Them and the Rolling Stones. Includes their first two British singles, "Dimples" and "I Can't Stand It." —*Richie Unterberger*

Autumn 66 / 1966 / Fontana ✦✦✦
At the peak of their popularity, the Spencer Davis Group's albums were considerably less impressive than their hits and a bit thin on imagination, although they were never less than competent. This, their third LP, relies heavily on soul covers, as well as a few oft-covered blues standards ("Midnight Special," "Mean Woman Blues," "Dust My Blues"). Highlights are their second British number one hit "Somebody Help Me," the decent group original "High Time Baby," Winwood's organ-based instrumental "On the Green Light," and "When I Get Home," which (like "Somebody Help Me") was a hit in Britain, but not the U.S. —*Richie Unterberger*

Best of the Spencer Davis Group [Island Masters] / 1967 / Island ✦✦✦✦✦
Anyone who has suffered through Capitol Records' domestic *Best of the Spencer Davis Group*, and also doesn't want to spring for the double-CD import, should look to this 14-song collection from British Island Records. All of the best-known songs are here—"I'm a Man," "Gimme Some Lovin'," "Every Little Bit Hurts," "Keep on Running," "When I Come Home," "This Hammer," etc.—in loud, robust, and richly textured sound. The organ, piano, drums, and guitars fairly leap out at you, and Winwood's vocals never sounded better or closer than they do on this CD. The double CD is a better deal and sounds superior to this collection, but it also has a lot more dross on it. The real crime is that there isn't a decent-sounding domestic best-of, but this one will do. —*Bruce Eder*

● **Best of the Spencer Davis Group [EMI]** / 1985 / EMI America ✦✦✦✦✦
Somehow the same label issued two albums with the same name in the same year. This one, with 15 tracks, is vastly preferable to its 10-song counterpart. Both releases hit the high points with the irresistible "Gimme Some Lovin'," "I'm a Man," and others. With half as many tunes, though, this album includes the minor hit "Strong Love" and "Goodbye Stevie," written by the group to commemorate the departure of sensational singer and multi-instrumentalist prodigy Steve Winwood. "Waltz for Lumumba" presages the jazzier turns he would take with Traffic. —*Mark Allan*

Taking Out Time 1967-1969 / 1994 / RPM ✦✦

Eight Gigs a Week: The Steve Winwood Years / Apr. 22, 1996 / Island/Chronicles ✦✦✦✦✦
This two-CD, 51-song set covers virtually everything the group recorded with Steve Winwood in the lineup from 1964-1967. The gap between the band's best and worst material was considerable; quite a few of their R&B covers are surprisingly routine, and the occasional cuts that don't have Winwood on lead vocals are downright pedestrian. Because of this inconsistency, the general fan's better off with the Rhino best-of, if it can be found. If you want to get more, though, this is the first and last place to go, with all the hit singles, everything from their three albums, an early EP, some B-sides, and a couple of previously unissued tracks. And some of the obscure material is really good, whether in a straight R&B/blues or more soulful vein. Be aware that the version of "Gimme Some Lovin'" here is the less dynamic, original British mix, minus some backup vocals and percussion. —*Richie Unterberger*

Mulberry Bush / Jan. 11, 2000 / RPM ✦✦✦

The dB's

f. 1978
Group / College Rock, Jangle Pop, Power Pop, Alternative Pop/Rock
Along with Let's Active, the dB's defined the Southern power-pop/jangle-pop movement of the early-to-mid-'80s. The band's music was a quirky blend of smart pop and psychedelia crossed with the more experimental side of new wave. Though they never received widespread recognition outside of critical acclaim, they provided a key link between Big Star and '80s alternative guitar acts such as R.E.M. Formed in 1978 in Winston-Salem, NC, the original lineup of the band featured Chris Stamey (guitar, vocals, keyboards), Gene Holder (bass), and Will Rigby (drums). After relocating to New York, the dBs released their debut single, "(I Thought) You Wanted to Know," for Stamey's Car label. Guitarist/vocalist/keyboardist Peter Holsapple joined the band by the end of 1978. Holsapple and Stamey shared the songwriting chores during the band's early years. The dB's were unable to secure a U.S. recording contract, so they signed to the British Albion label. They released two albums on Albion: *Stands for Decibels* (1981) and *Repercussions* (1982). Both records received rave reviews but little sales. Stamey left in 1983 to resume a solo career. With Holsapple fronting the group, they signed to Bearsville in 1984 and released *Like This*, a more conventional jangle-pop album with strong country leanings. Bearsville's internal problems doomed the album despite its obvious hit potential. They eventually left to sign with I.R.S. Records in 1987, where they released *The Sound of Music*. By the end of 1988, the band decided to break up. —*Chris Woodstra*

● **Stands for Decibels** / 1981 / IRS ✦✦✦✦✦
On their debut, the dB's combined a reverence for British pop and arty, post-punk leanings that alternate between minimalism and a love of quirky embellishment, odd sounds, and unexpected twists; *Stands for Decibels* is clearly a collegiate pop experiment, but rarely is experimentation so enjoyable and irresistibly catchy. Singing and songwriting duties are shared equally by Chris Stamey and Peter Holsapple—Stamey, more quirky and psychedelic-leaning with a winsome, pure-pop whine, is nicely balanced by Holsapple's more earthy drawl and straightforward approach. The album stands not only as a landmark power-pop album but also as a prototype for much of the Southern jangle that would follow. [*Stands for Decibels* remained criminally unavailable in the U.S. for years. When IRS reissued it on CD in 1989, Holsapple's "Judy" was added as a bonus track.] —*Chris Woodstra*

● **Stands for Decibels/Repurcussion** / 1981 / Line ✦✦✦✦✦

Repercussion / 1982 / IRS ✦✦✦✦✦
Repercussion is very much of a piece with the debut, repeating much of the same formula that made *Stands for Decibels* great—terrific harmonies, winning melodies and catchy hooks with subtle quirks thrown into the mix. This time, they feature a fuller, more polished sound, but the impact of the songs isn't diminished. Stamey left shortly after *Repercussion* to pursue a solo career. ["pH Factor" was added as a bonus track to the IRS CD reissue in 1989.] —*Chris Woodstra*

Like This / 1984 / Rhino ✦✦✦
From the opening notes of "Love Is for Lovers," this is obviously no ordinary dB's record. The group, now pared down to a trio fronted by Peter Holsapple, have stripped away the arty quirks of the first two albums, opting instead for straight-ahead, rootsy rockers and country-rock romps. Amid the more muscular, guitar-based sound, Holsapple turns in his same instantly endearing melodies, especially on the album highlight, "Lonely Is as Lonely Does," this most beautiful song to date. [Rhino's CD reissue adds an unnecessary extended remix of "A Spy in the House of Love."] —*Chris Woodstra*

The Sound of Music / 1987 / IRS ✦✦✦
What Peter Holsapple calls "the band's most blatant attempt to make a commercial album" sounds like it—but it's also very enjoyable. There's some tremendous merges of melody and lyrics here, from the satiny pop of "I Lie," the funny kick of "Working for Somebody Else," and the folky Holsapple-Syd Straw duet, "Never Before and Never Again." —*Kit Kiefer*

Ride the Wild Tom Tom / Aug. 17, 1993 / Rhino ✦✦✦
In his liner essay for *Ride the Wild Tom-Tom*, former dB's member Peter Holsapple jokingly describes this collection as "the equivalent of our *Basement Tapes*," and that statement actually describes the contents fairly well, especially when one remembers that Bob Dylan's *Basement Tapes* were mostly recorded as a goof. A collection of rehearsal tapes, demos, early single sides, and inside jokes, *Ride the Wild Tom-Tom* is hardly a definitive portrait of The dB's, but anyone looking for a ragged-but-right look at the band's formative days during Chris Stamey's tenure with the band will eat it up. Along with early versions of "Soul Kiss," "Modern Boys and Girls," and "A Spy in the House of Love," *Ride The Wild Tom-Tom* features a highly individual cover of The Grassroots' "Let's Live for Today," a commercial jingle for the East Coast music magazine *New York Rocker* (the band was using their offices as a rehearsal space), and the mock-punk onslaught "Hardcore Judy." Committed dB's fans will find this to be hoot, and while it's hardly the best introduction to the band's music, the quality of Chris Stamey and Peter Holsapple's songwriting shines through on even the jokiest numbers. —*Mark Deming*

Paris Avenue / Oct. 4, 1994 / Monkey Hill ✦✦

Dead Kennedys

f. 1978, **db.** 1987

Group / Anarchist Punk, American Punk, L.A. Punk, Hardcore Punk

The Dead Kennedys merged revolutionary politics with hardcore punk music and, in the process, became one of the defining hardcore bands. Often, they were more notable for their politics than their music, but that was part of their impact. The Kennedys were more inspired by British punk and the fiery, revolutionary-implied politics of the Sex Pistols than the artier tendencies of New York punk rockers. Under the direction of lead vocalist Jello Biafra, the Dead Kennedys became the most political and—to the eyes of many observers, including Christians and right-wing politicians—the most dangerous band in hardcore. Within a year of their formation, the band had released two of their most well-known singles, "California Uber Alles" and "Holiday in Cambodia." After releasing their debut album *Fresh Fruit for Rotting Vegetables*, Dead Kennedys formed their own label, Alternative Tentacles. One year later, the group released their second full-length album, *Plastic Surgery Disasters*. Following a three-year hiatus, 1985's *Frankenchrist* precipitated a bitter legal battle (regarding an allegedly pornographic poster included with copies of the album) that revealed Biafra as one of the most articulate advocates for free speech and vocal opponents of the PMRC (the case ended with a hung jury and was dismissed). Just before the prosecution began in 1986, the band released *Bedtime for Democracy*, which turned out to be their last official album. Biafra embarked on a solo career, releasing musical and spoken word recordings sporadically over the next decade and a half. *—Stephen Thomas Erlewine*

★ **Fresh Fruit for Rotting Vegetables** / 1980 / Alternative Tentacles ♦♦♦♦♦

A hyper-speed blast of ultra-polemical, left-wing hardcore punk and bitingly funny sarcasm, *Fresh Fruit for Rotting Vegetables* stands as the Dead Kennedys' signature statement. As one of the first hardcore albums, it was a galvanizing influence on the musical and attitudinal development of the genre, also helping to kickstart the fertile California scene. The record's tactics are not subtle in the least; Jello Biafra's odd warble and spat-out lyrics leave no doubt as to what he thinks, baiting his targets of conservatism, violence, overbearing authority, and capitalist greed with a viciously satirical sarcasm that keeps his unflinchingly political outlook from becoming too didactic. The thin production dilutes some of the music's power, but the ragged speed-blur still packs a wallop, and the hooks cribbed from surf and rockabilly give it a gonzo edge. The songwriting isn't consistent all the way through the album, but classics like "Kill the Poor," "Let's Lynch the Landlord," "Chemical Warfare," "California Über Alles," and "Holiday In Cambodia" helped define the hardcore genre and, thus, must be heard. *—Steve Huey*

In God We Trust, Inc. / Feb. 1981 / Alternative Tentacles ♦♦♦

Plastic Surgery Disasters / 1982 / Alternative Tentacles ♦♦♦♦♦

Having proved themselves masters of the quick, vicious smash and bash, on their second album the Kennedys continued in that vein while finding other effective ways to express their all-encompassing message of resistance and satire. Absolutely nobody is safe, whether it's the more expected targets of conservative society, or those who claim to follow what the Kennedys and punk promised but only ended up acting like idiots. For the most part, though, it's a well-deserved smackdown of all the jerks the early '80s produced, set to some fantastic music. Bookended by random noise jams—the first one with a wonderfully dismissive spoken-word analysis on societal programming for The Good Life—*Plastic Surgery Disasters* shows East Bay Ray, Klaus Fluoride and D.H. Peligro turning into an even more awesome unit than before. Ray's sheet-metal intense guitar may once or twice get slammed into too much treble for its own good, but his spaghetti-western-cranked-to-ten playing is fantastic stuff at its best. The others have their moments, like Peligro's rolling drum breaks on "Government Mechanic." When the band aims for subtlety, the results are grand—the sudden silences on "Trust Your Mechanic," the goofy hipswing start to "Forest Fire." Unsurprisingly, Biafra is still at the center of it all; once again, the song titles make it clear what's at play. "Terminal Preppie," rips into an example of the type with gusto, and the wonderfully sneering "Winnebago Warrior" is just the tip of the iceberg. The real highlight can be found at the end—"Moon Over Marin," with a soaring, anthemic surf-rock line from Ray offsetting Biafra's semi-apocalyptic vision of the Bay Area's snooty region. *—Ned Raggett*

Frankenchrist / 1985 / Alternative Tentacles ♦♦♦

Released after a three-year studio hiatus, this album picks up right where *Plastic Surgery Disasters* left off. As always, the lyrics are among the most literate and angry in all of rock & roll. "Goons of Hazard" scores the culture of guns and the rednecks who love them, utilizing full-textured hard rock to set the verses. "Soup Is Good Food" lacerates the concept of disposable people in disposable jobs, pairing this idea with repeated guitar-riff-based music that suggests a nightmare version of 1960s songs. "Jock-O-Rama" excoriates organized sports and macho attitudes; musically, the outer sections wed rockabilly and hardcore influences, sandwiching a slow middle section that spoofs martial numbers like Barry Sadler's "Ballad of the Green Berets." "This Could Be Anywhere" has critical lyrics about racism and classism set to music highly reminiscent of the Sex Pistols. "Hellnation" has garbled, wide-range, muckracking verses set to stun-speed punk that recalls numbers from *In God We Trust Inc.* The excellent "MTV—Get Off the Air" lambasts the corporate influences on rock and roll; musically, the song exhibits a tripartite structure, using a vacuously poppy opening, a speed hardcore central section, and a midtempo rocking finale that prominently features trumpet (a very brief coda reprise of hardcore ends the number). The finest selection on this album (and perhaps in the whole Dead Kennedys' canon) is the anthemic "Stars and Stripes of Corruption." This number also utilizes a three-part construct, consisting here of a hard-rocking midsection flanked by faster, punk-oriented material. The verses here are stunningly detailed, describing what the band believes is wrong with the United States and what the solutions should be. This wonderful and challenging album is very highly recommended. *—David Cleary*

Bedtime for Democracy / 1986 / Alternative Tentacles ♦♦

Give Me Convenience or Give Me Death / 1987 / Alternative Tentacles ♦♦♦♦♦

Hounded by political enemies and reaching their personal breaking point, the Kennedys bowed with a retrospective of some of their fiercest, finest moments. If one needs a starting point for the band's fierce, funny assault on any level of complacency imaginable, *Give Me Convenience* is indeed as convenient as it gets. Focusing for the most part on non-album cuts or various rarities, it appeals to hardcore Dead Kennedys fans as well as neophytes. The collection includes some of the band's earliest greats, like the legendary rant "Too Drunk to Fuck," as withering a depiction of getting trashed and stupid as any. While the definitive "California Uber Alles" and "Holiday in Cambodia" make the cut from the first album, there are also plenty of more obscure and unknown goodies. The second half features live tracks like the hilarious "Pull My Strings," which vivisects typical rock star pomposity (knowingly quoting the Knack's "My Sharona") before shifting into an even nuttier chorus. Another screamingly funny number is the improv "Night of the Living Rednecks," done "while Ray was changing strings" at an Oregon date in 1979. After threatening to play the theme from the *Dinah Shore* show, the remaining three members light into something resembling a beat/'50s hep groove, only with Biafra recalling a tale of idiots encountered during a previous visit to Portland. Meanwhile, there's a version of "I Fought the Law," which easily trumps the Clash's version, helped by a lyric change or two along the way. Messy, nutty, and fun, *Convenience* is a treat and a half. *—Ned Raggett*

The Dead Milkmen

f. 1983, Philadelphia, PA

Group / College Rock, Comedy Rock, Alternative Pop/Rock, Novelty

Philadelphia pop-punk quartet featuring vocalist Rodney Anonymous (who sometimes adds "Amadeus" or "Mellencamp" to his name), guitarist Joe Jack Talcum, bassist Dave Blood, and drummer Dean Clean. The Milkmen are renowned for their dumb, obnoxious sense of humor, which they frequently focus on pop culture. Some critics love them, some critics hate them, but all agree that The Milkmen are sophomoric and snotty. "Bitchin' Camaro," from their debut, *Big Lizard In My Backyard*, was a minor alternative-radio hit. The band got a small measure of publicity when Detroit Tiger infielder Jim Walewander praised them in interviews, and had a minor MTV hit with *Beelzebubba*'s "Punk Rock Girl." Unfortunately, they were never as consistently funny as they tried to be, and wound up dropped from Enigma after *Metaphysical Graffiti*. Their subsequent releases found them trying to learn how to be serious, and their popularity had almost disappeared by the time they broke up in the mid-'90s. *—Steve Huey*

Big Lizard in My Backyard / 1985 / Enigma/Restless ♦♦♦♦♦

It may not be deathless, but 1984's *Big Lizard in My Backyard* is that rarest of beasts (as a random listen to any Barenaked Ladies disc will show): a collection of rock & roll silliness that outlives one playing. That mid-'80s' favorite "Bitchin' Camaro," already demonstrated that ability plenty of times over. Portraying two guys yammering about Doors cover bands and "going down to the Shore" before finally getting to the main point—the way-cool car of the title—it somehow finds the lost gap between pseudo-jazz grooves and punky snottiness. As left field a fluke hit single as it gets, its mix of bad taste, rock-star mockery and stoner humor still works well. As a whole, the album shows that the Milkmen know their rock & roll history, whether tackling serious issues with sarcasm or just aiming for straight-up silliness. The opening track "Tiny Town," is a quick thrash-and-scream about small minds in small towns and the blatant idiocy of "Takin' Retards to the Zoo," which is about just what it says it is, find the Milkmen's tongues planted firmly in their cheeks. The reggae-tinged "Gorilla Girl"is about a choice in sweethearts that meets with parental disapproval, while the tense, nervous bite of "Right Wing Pigeons," trashes the Reagan administration with style and smirks. Semi-seriousness crops up on the wistfully poppy "Dean's Dream" about "a girl with long blonde hair" or the instrumental finale "Tugena," which shows that when they want to, the Milkmen can rock out with the best of them. Never too heavy but deeper than expected, *Big Lizard* captures these disaffected class clowns getting it out of their system with energy. *—Ned Raggett*

Eat Your Paisley / 1986 / Enigma/Restless ♦♦♦

Bucky Fellini / 1987 / Enigma/Restless ♦♦♦♦♦

A step up from the good but not great *Eat Your Paisley, Bucky Fellini* begins with a parody of the bandmember introductions from Sweet's "Ballroom Blitz" and raises another fun and funny stink. The most entertaining and ridiculous thing the band ever did takes deserved center stage—"Instant Club Hit (You'll Dance to Anything)." Consisting of drum machine fills, intentionally basic bass lines and Rodney Anonymous' instantly recognizable sneer, it's a hilarious, all-too-knowing rip on '80s new wave/dance culture. With lines like "Oh, baby, look at you, don't you look like Siouxsie Sioux" and "I met Andy Warhol at a really chic party/Blow it out your hair, dude, cuz you work at Hardee's!" it's hilarity personified (and bizarrely enough won them an appearance on an MTV dance show, where they encouraged a bout of stage diving). Nothing equals that song's sublime satire, but the Milkmen still stir things up with a touch more fire and sass than before. Naming a song "I Am the Walrus" that has absolutely nothing to do with the Beatles song proves that the jokers are in full effect. The goofy, country-tinged "Watching Scotty Die," features Joe Jack Talcum's surprisingly good Dobro playing. In honor of the album's Texas recording locale, some native sons are honored via covers. Daniel Johnston's "Rocketship" keeps its charm in a full-band arrangement, while the LeRoi Brothers' "Big Time Operator" gets an appropriate rave-up that also trashes Lone Star blowhards like Stevie Ray Vaughn and Charlie Sexton. Add in songs trashing Graceland and titles like "(Theme From) Blood Orgy of the Atomic Fern," and the result is another successful batch of silliness. *—Ned Raggett*

Beelzebubba / 1988 / Enigma/Restless ♦♦♦

Having built up a sizeable cult with surprising mainstream exposure here and there, the Milkmen got as close as they ever would to high-profile success with *Beelzebubba*. The basic formula and approach of the band hadn't changed a lot, but they did get it all together to create another near-perfect single, "Punk Rock Girl." Sprightly and catchy, it mixes the unexpectedly tender, sweet side of the band with the usual drawling humor from Anonymous—everything from accordion to utterly random Beach Boys (or is that the Mamas and the Papas?) references crop up. Beyond that splash, it was Milkmen time as usual: over the top, sarcastic, and more. Production was the clearest and most radio-friendly it ever was. The band's eternal hatred for trendoids, poseurs, and morons unsurprisingly continued to flourish from the first song in: "Brat in the Frat" targets the title character in question but spends some time demolishing the radical wannabe as well. Similarly amusing slams and smackdowns crop up throughout: "Bad Party," the snarky "Everybody's Got Nice Stuff But Me," and so forth. As an album through and through, *Beelzebubba* suffers from the same problem as *Eat Your Paisley* in many ways—a load of potentially inspiring ideas that often don't add up in the end. "RC's Mom" is a good example; if the music is meant to parody funk, it doesn't do it as well as, say, Led Zeppelin's "The Crunge," and if it's a celebration, it's pretty obvious and boring. As for the vocals, well, never mind. But so long as songs like "My Many Smells" and "Born to Love Volcanoes" are around, there's still hope yet. *—Ned Raggett*

Metaphysical Grafitti / Apr. 1990 / Enigma/Restless ✦✦

Soul Rotation / Apr. 14, 1992 / Hollywood ✦✦

Not Richard But Dick / Oct. 12, 1993 / Hollywood ✦✦

Stoney's Extra Stout (Pig) / Nov. 7, 1995 / Restless ✦

● **Death Rides a Pale Cow** / Nov. 11, 1997 / Restless ✦✦✦✦✦
Death Rides a Pale Cow is an excellent, 22-track overview of the Dead Milkmen's career, containing all of their cult classics—"Bitchin' Camaro," "Instant Club Hit (You'll Dance to Anything)," "Punk Rock Girl," "Smokin' Banana Peels"—plus the previously unreleased "Labor Day" and "Milkmen Stomp," which was previously only available on a self-released cassette. For the curious or the casual fan, this contains everything you'd need, and it provides a fine, thorough introduction to the group's warped humor and amateurish punk rock. *—Stephen Thomas Erlewine*

Deep Purple

f. 1968, Hertford, England
Group / British Metal, Arena Rock, Heavy Metal, British Invasion, Hard Rock
Deep Purple survived a seemingly endless series of lineup changes and a dramatic mid-career shift from grandiose progressive rock to ear-shattering heavy metal to emerge as a true institution of the British hard rock community. The group, first assembled as a session band, fused rock and classical elements on their early LPs, though guitarist Ritchie Blackmore soon took creative control of the band, steering it towards a heavier, guitar-dominated approach. Deep Purple's most enduring hit, the AOR staple "Smoke on the Water," featured on the 1973 multi-platinum classic *Machine Head* and positioned the group among rock's elite.

Long-simmering creative differences soon pushed vocalist Ian Gillan and bassist Roger Glover out of the band, the former replaced by David Coverdale. After completing 1974's *Stormbringer,* Blackmore himself left (to form Rainbow) and was replaced by Tommy Bolin. Following a 1976 tour, the group completely dissolved, with Coverdale going on to form Whitesnake and Bolin dying from a drug overdose later in the year. Most of the classic lineup reunited in 1984 for the platinum smash *Perfect Strangers,* and though Gillan again exited the group, he returned for 1992's *The Battle Rages On*... Blackmore quit the group next, replaced temporarily by Joe Satriani and later by Steve Morse. The revitalized group returned to the studio for 1996's *Purpendicular,* which proved a success among the Purple faithful. *—Jason Ankeny*

Shades of Deep Purple / 1968 / Spitfire ✦✦✦✦✦
This is worthwhile mainly for their psychezilla cover of Joe South's "Hush," which pits Ritchie Blackmore's flame-throwing guitar bursts against Jon Lord's chugging organ. *—Tom Graves*

The Book of Taliesyn / 1969 / Spitfire ✦✦✦

Concerto for Group and Orchestra / 1969 / Warner Brothers ✦✦✦

Deep Purple in Rock / 1970 / Warner Brothers ✦✦✦✦✦
After satisfying all of their classical music kinks with keyboard player Jon Lord's overblown *Concerto for Group and Orchestra,* Deep Purple's soon-to-be classic Mark II lineup made their proper debut on 1970's awesome *In Rock.* The cacophony of sound (led by Ritchie Blackmore's blistering guitar solo), which introduces the opener "Speed King," makes it immediately obvious that the band is no longer fooling around. The slightly less intense "Bloodsucker" allows for some breathing room before the band embarks on the album's epic, ten-minute tour de force "Child in Time." In what is arguably his greatest performance, singer Ian Gillan leads the band on a series of crescendos, from the song's gentle beginning through to its ear-shattering climax, and back again to an even more intense encore. With searing power chords, "Flight of the Rat" is another example of the band's new hard-rock stance; though at nearly eight minutes, it too finds room for some extended soloing from Blackmore and Lord. "Into the Fire" and "Living Wreck" are more concise but equally appealing, and despite the closer "Hard Lovin' Man," which waffles on a bit before descending into feedback, this is still an essential album. *—Ed Rivadavia*

Fireball / 1971 / Warner Brothers ✦✦✦✦✦
One of Deep Purple's three essential albums, 1971's *Fireball* finds the band taking the no-holds-barred, hard-rock direction of the previous year's *In Rock* to new creative heights. Metal machine noises introduce the sizzling title track, which is an explosively tight group effort with Jon Lord's organ truly shining. The somewhat repetitive "No No No" threatens to drop the ball, but the fantastic "Strange Kind of Woman" picks things up again. The innuendo-encrusted hilarity of "Anyone's Daughter" features one of singer Ian Gillan's best lyrics, and guitarist Ritchie Blackmore shows his range with one of his most uncharacteristic, bluesier performances. "The Mule" is perhaps the band's finest instrumental and they flirt with progressive rock on "Fools," which probably could have been done without the rather boring, drawn-out middle section. Closing the album is the exceptional "No One Came," which sounds so fresh that its plausible that the band improvised it on the spot. Their intertwining instrumental lines lock together beautifully, and Gillan weaves a comic, semi-autobiographical story that is equal parts rooted in fact and *Monty Python.* *—Ed Rivadavia*

★ **Machine Head** / 1972 / Warner Brothers ✦✦✦✦✦
Led Zeppelin's fourth album, Black Sabbath's *Paranoid,* and Deep Purple's *Machine Head* stand as the Holy Trinity of English hard rock. These recordings provide the blueprint followed by virtually every heavy rock & roll band since the mid-'70s. Though probably the least celebrated of the three, *Machine Head* contains the mother of all guitar riffs in "Smoke on the Water," a song that needs no further explanation. The album also features the classic "Highway Star," which epitomizes all of Deep Purple's intensity and versatility, while featuring perhaps the greatest soloing duel ever between guitarist Ritchie Blackmore and organist Jon Lord. Also in top form is singer Ian Gillan (simply one of the finest singers of his generation, bar none), who explodes with amazing power and range throughout. His presence is sorely missed on the instrumental "Lazy," which would nonetheless evolve into an incredible live jam. The plodding shuffle of "Maybe I'm a Leo" shows some signs of age, but "Pictures of Home" and "Never Before" remain vital, displaying Purple at their melodic best. Another tremendous Blackmore riff drives the marvelous "Space Truckin'," a fitting end to one of the essential hard-rock albums of all time. *—Ed Rivadavia*

Who Do We Think We Are / Jan. 1973 / Warner Brothers ✦✦✦
The last gasp for the classic Deep Purple lineup, *Who Do We Think We Are* isn't as rock-solid as their previous records, but its best moments, including the deliriously stupid "Woman from Tokyo," are bludgeoning hard rock of the highest order. *—Stephen Thomas Erlewine*

Made in Japan / Apr. 1973 / Warner Brothers ✦✦✦✦✦
Not only could they kick ass in the studio, they could stir up a hornet's nest on stage, too. This double-album (one CD) set recorded in Japan includes most of their best material ("Highway Star," "Smoke on the Water") and pushes the metal envelope even further. Ritchie Blackmore is in peak form throughout. *—Tom Graves*

Burn / 1974 / Warner Brothers ✦✦✦

Stormbringer / 1974 / Warner Brothers ✦✦

Come Taste the Band / 1975 / Warner Brothers ✦✦✦
When Ritchie Blackmore departed Deep Purple in the mid-'70s and formed Elf (which evolved into Blackmore's Rainbow and featured Ronnie James Dio), his replacement was Tommy Bolin. To be sure, Blackmore was a darn tough act to follow, but Bolin proved himself to be a fine guitarist in his own right on *Come Taste The Band,* his first album with Purple. But unfortunately, Bolin didn't have exceptional material to work with—decent and likable, but hardly exceptional. While sweaty yet melodic cuts like "Dealer," "Lady Luck" and "You Keep On Moving" are far from bad, nothing here is in a class with "Smoke On The Water" or "Highway Star." Purple's more hardcore devotees will want this album (reissued on CD in the early 1990s), though it's far from the best representation of their '70s work. *—Alex Henderson*

Made in Europe / 1976 / Warner Brothers ✦✦✦

When We Rock, We Rock & When We Roll, We Roll / 1978 / Warner Brothers ✦✦✦✦✦

Perfect Strangers / 1984 / Mercury ✦✦

The House of Blue Light / 1987 / Mercury ✦✦✦

Nobody's Perfect / 1988 / Mercury ✦✦

Knocking at Your Back Door: The Best Of Deep Purple in the 80's / 1992 / Mercury ✦✦

Shades 1968-1998 / Mar. 16, 1999 / Rhino ✦✦✦✦✦
A lot of care went into the track selection and mastering on this four-CD set, devoted to 30 years in the history of Deep Purple—though for most listeners, discs one through three, devoted to the band's first eight years, are what will really count. Deep Purple recorded significant bodies of work in several styles, but the years 1968 through 1974, when they evolved out of psychedelia and into heavy metal, are the vitally important ones. The first disc is a treat not only for Deep Purple fans but '60s British rock completists, highlighted by two previously unissued tracks dating from a time when the band was apparently still known officially as Roundabout.

The band's chart singles and a beautifully lyrical and reflective version of the Beatles' "Help" open the first disk, and it's hard not to love those early singles. And then comes "Hallelujah (I Am the Preacher)," which opens the group's classic heavy metal era and heralds the arrival of Ian Gillan on lead vocals and Roger Glover on bass. From there on, and for most of the next two-and-a-half CDs, this set threatens to fry any speakers or ears in its presence. Disc two is from the core of the group's prime years, from the spring of 1971 through the end of that year. The *Fireball* and *Machine Head* albums are well represented, and some of this music is surprisingly durable. Disc three covers the peak years, closing out in 1975 at the end of the Tommy Bolin/Glenn Hughes lineup, and Disc four picks up with the 1984 reunion. The packaging is slightly awkward, but it comes with a 55-page booklet giving just about the fullest easily available account of the band's impact and importance. *—Bruce Eder*

● **The Very Best of Deep Purple** / May 9, 2000 / Rhino ✦✦✦✦✦
The Very Best of Deep Purple collects 15 live performances, singles, and album tracks from the group's inception in 1968 to 1984, when the Mark II lineup (featuring vocalist Ian Gillan) reunited. Hits like "Hush," "Smoke on the Water," "Woman From Tokyo," "Kentucky Woman," and "Knocking at Your Backdoor" anchor the set, while "Black Night," "Demon's Eye," "Burn," and other staples of Deep Purple's body of work add depth to the collection. Designed to complement, not compete with, the four-disc box set *Shades (1968-1998)* that Rhino released in 1999, *The Very Best of Deep Purple* gathers the definitive tracks from one of hard rock and heavy metal's most popular and influential bands. *—Heather Phares*

Def Leppard

f. 1977, Sheffield, Yorkshire, England
Group / New Wave of British Heavy Metal, Pop-Metal, British Metal, Hair Metal, Heavy Metal, Pop/Rock, Hard Rock
Def Leppard, in many ways, was the definitive hard rock band of the '80s. There were many bands that rocked harder, and were more dangerous, than the Sheffield quintet, but few others captured the spirit of the times quite as well. Emerging in the late '70s as part of the New

Wave of British Heavy Metal, the group actually owed more to the glam-rock and metal of the early '70s—their sound was equal parts T. Rex, Mott the Hoople, Queen and Led Zeppelin. By toning down their heavy riffs and emphasizing melody, Def Leppard were poised for crossover success by 1983's *Pyromania*, but skillfully used the fledgling MTV network to their advantage. The group was already blessed with photogenic good looks, but they also crafted a series of innovative, exciting videos, which made them into stars. They intended to follow *Pyromania* quickly, but were derailed when their drummer lost an arm in a car accident, the first of many problems that plagued the group's career. Def Leppard managed to pull through such tragedies and they even expanded their large audience with 1987's blockbuster *Hysteria*. As the '90s began, mainstream hard rock shifted away from Leppard's signature pop-metal and towards edgier, louder bands, yet the group maintained a sizable audience into the late '90s and were one of only a handful of '80s metal groups to survive the decade more or less intact. *—Stephen Thomas Erlewine*

On Through the Night / 1980 / Mercury ♦♦♦

High 'n' Dry / 1981 / Mercury ♦♦♦
Def Leppard's second album, *High 'N' Dry*, continues in the vein of the anthemic, working-class hard rock of their debut. While still opting for a controlled musical attack and melodies as big-sounding and stadium-ready as possible, the band opens up its arrangements a bit more on *High 'N' Dry*, letting the songs breathe and groove, and the rhythm section and guitar riffs play off one another. MTV helped break the album in the U.S. with its heavy rotation of the video for the unabashedly dramatic rock ballad "Bringin' On the Heartbreak." *—Steve Huey*

☆ **Pyromania** / 1983 / Mercury ♦♦♦♦♦
While Def Leppard had obviously wanted to write big-sounding anthems on their previous records, *Pyromania* was where the band's vision coalesced and jelled into something more. More than ever before, the band's songs on *Pyromania* are driven by catchy, shiny melodic hooks instead of heavy guitar riffs, although the latter do pop up once in a while. But it wasn't just this newly intensified focus on melody and consistent songwriting (and heavy MTV exposure) that made *Pyromania* a massive success and the catalyst for the '80s pop-metal movement; Robert John "Mutt" Lange's buffed-to-a-sheen production—polished drum and guitar sounds, multi-tracked layers of vocal harmonies, a general sanding of any and all musical rough edges, and a perfectionistic attention to detail—set the style for much of the melodic hard rock that followed. It wasn't a raw or spontaneous sound, but the performances were still energetic and committed. Leppard's quest for huge, transcendent hard rock perfection on *Pyromania* was surprisingly successful; their reach never exceeded their grasp, which makes the album an enduring (and massively influential) classic. *—Steve Huey*

☆ **Hysteria** / 1987 / Mercury ♦♦♦♦♦
Where *Pyromania* had set the standard for polished, catchy pop-metal, *Hysteria* only upped the ante. *Pyromania*'s slick, layered Mutt Lange production turned into a painstaking obsession with dense sonic detail on *Hysteria*, with the result that some critics dismissed the record as a stiff, mechanized pop sell-out (perhaps due in part to Rick Allen's new, partially electronic drum kit). But Leppard's music had always employed big, anthemic hooks, and few of the pop-metal bands who had hit the charts in the wake of *Pyromania* could compete with Leppard's sense of craft; certainly none had the pop songwriting savvy to produce seven chart singles from the same album, as the stunningly consistent *Hysteria* did. Joe Elliott's lyrics owe an obvious debt to his obsession with T. Rex, particularly on the playfully silly anthem "Pour Some Sugar On Me" and the British glam-rock tribute "Rocket," while power ballads like "Love Bites" and the title track lack the histrionics or gooey sentimentality of many similar offerings. The strong pop hooks and "perfect"-sounding production of *Hysteria* may not appeal to diehard heavy metal fans, but it isn't heavy metal—it's pop-metal, and arguably the best pop-metal ever recorded. Its blockbuster success helped pave the way for a whole new second wave of hair-metal bands, while proving that the late-'80s musical climate could also be very friendly to veteran hard rock acts, a lead many would follow in the next few years. *—Steve Huey*

Adrenalize / Dec. 24, 1992 / Mercury ♦♦♦
After two straight blockbusters that delivered the goods both musically and commercially, anticipation ran high for Def Leppard's follow-up to *Hysteria*, in spite of the tragic death of guitarist Steve Clark. Unfortunately, *Adrenalize* sounds somewhat tired, formulaic, and bland, qualities absent from the band's best pop-metal work. Perhaps somewhat understandably, Leppard doesn't sound like its heart is really in the party anthems, and their ballads sound more calculated and generic. But most of all, the songs don't really have the effortlessly anthemic feel Leppard achieved so well on its past two albums, even though they try mightily. *Adrenalize* is competent, workmanlike, and impeccably produced, but not much more. *—Steve Huey*

Retro Active / Oct. 5, 1993 / Mercury ♦♦♦

● **Vault: Def Leppard's Greatest Hits** / Oct. 31, 1995 / Mercury ♦♦♦♦♦
Def Leppard was untouchable in the '80s. Over the course of four albums, the band established themselves as one of the best and most popular hard-rock/heavy-metal groups of the decade, scoring a long list of hit singles. *Vault: Def Leppard's Greatest Hits—1980-1995* compiles the biggest of those hits, as well as selections from their first album of the '90s, *Adrenalize*, and the outtakes collection *Retro Active*. Essentially, Def Leppard's legacy rests on two albums, 1983's *Pyromania* and 1987's *Hysteria*. On both records, the group created a sleek, shiny brand of hard rock powered by huge, catchy melodies and guitar hooks that owed more to Mott the Hoople and T. Rex than Deep Purple and Black Sabbath. It was a polished but potent sound, whether the band turned out rockers ("Photograph," "Rocket") or ballads ("Bringin' on the Heartbreak," "Love Bites"). *Vault* has all of the necessary items, from "Pour Some Sugar on Me" to "Rock of Ages." It's not a perfect collection—it's not sequenced chronologically, it includes too much material from *Adrenalize*, and the new "When Love & Hate Collide" is simply average—but that doesn't stop *Vault* from being a great greatest hits collection. *—Stephen Thomas Erlewine*

Slang / May 14, 1996 / Mercury ♦♦♦

Euphoria / Jun. 8, 1999 / Mercury ♦♦♦♦

The Del-Vikings

f. 1955, Pittsburgh, PA, **db.** 1965
Group / Doo Wop
The story of the Dell-Vikings (or Del Vikings, or Del-Vikings) is one of the most glorious, complicated and frustrating of any successful doo wop group in music history. With two major national hits ("Come Go With Me," "Whispering Bells") to their credit—one more hit than most other successful doo wop groups ever had—they had a jump on virtually all of their competition. Just as they were ascending those heights of fame and success, however, internal fractures and some greed and misdirected ambition helped destroy any chance they had of making a lasting place for themselves at the top of their profession. They left behind two hits and a large body of very good records that weren't nearly as well known, as well as a reputation as one of the few successful integrated vocal groups of their era. *—Bruce Eder*

For Collectors Only / 1992 / Collectables ♦♦♦♦♦
This really isn't for collectors only—it is the only single collection of the group's stuff that shows the full range of this sadly underrated vocal group. As it is, its mere existence as a mid-priced double CD, alongside the presence of the two best-of compilations from MCA and Mercury, makes collecting the best Dell Vikings material extremely complicated. Collectables Records got access to the complete recordings that the original group made for Fee Bee Records, which covers their history from 1956 through 1957, overlapping with the history of the Mercury version of the group. This includes the hit version of "Come Go With Me," as well as "Whispering Bells" (both of which appear on MCA's best-of in those very same versions) and their other early tracks. Collectables also got access to an extraordinary body of outtakes—a magnificent fast version of "I'm Spinning" that's completely different from the version that appears on both the MCA and Mercury best-of discs. We get distinctive outtakes of "Willette" and oddities such as the Joey Briscoe single "What Made Maggie Run," on which the group sang backup in a hurried attempt to get them out before the public again after that first hit. More important are tracks like "Uh Uh Baby," a fast jump number that shows the group at about its rockingest and nimblest, with a killer guitar solo courtesy of the late Joe Lopes. Other highlights include radiant outtakes of "Girl, Girl" and "Cold Feet" (done a cappella), little snippets of session chatter (amazing the stuff survived 40 years), and rehearsal and audition versions of the group's songs and generally the fullest account possible of the history of the Fee Bee Records version of the group that we'll ever see. *—Bruce Eder*

The Best of the Del-Vikings: The Mercury Years / Jul. 16, 1996 / Mercury ♦♦♦
Read the title carefully, because the Dell-Vikings' two great doo wop hits—"Come Go with Me" and "Whispering Bells"—were *not* recorded for Mercury, and so are not contained on this compilation. This disc has 22 sides they recorded for Mercury in 1957-58, with a lineup that had some but not all of the members that recorded "Come Go with Me" and "Whispering Bells." (To make matters more confusing, a different Dell-Vikings, led by Kripp Johnson, who had sung lead on "Whispering Bells," kept recording for a different label.) The Mercury Dell-Vikings did have a Top 20 hit right out of the box, "Cool Shake" (included here), but never had a big single again. Most of this is routine doo wop that's below the standards of their Dot sides, sometimes clouded by inadvisable attempts at pop-oriented material and production. It's only of value to hard-core doo wop bugs, who will appreciate the inclusion of many tracks only available on rare EPs, singles, and compilations, as well as one previously unissued in the U.S. The intro to "The Bells," by the way, bears a close similarity to the famous wordless scats that kicked off the Marcels' classic "Blue Moon" several years later. *—Richie Unterberger*

★ **Come Go With Me: The Best of the Del-Vikings-The Dot/ABC Recordings** / Jun. 17, 1997 / Hip-O ♦♦♦♦♦
As one of the first interracial vocal groups of the rock & roll era—and the first to score a Top Ten million-selling record on their very first try—the Dell Vikings seemed poised for very big things indeed. But when "Come Go With Me" became a national hit, the spoils of war caused the Dell Vikings to split into two separate groups. Recording at various times with almost the same name, sometimes utilizing interchangeable group members as the two groups released follow-up singles both Dot and Mercury simultaneously (with errant tracks showing up a couple of years later on a third label, Luniverse), this put the brakes on the groups' success in a most confusing manner, raising the ire of disc jockeys and radio station programmers alike. This 16-track compilation from Hip-O subsidiary is subtitled "the Dot-ABC Recordings" and does a better than average job of cherry-picking through their sides for that label. Their big hit, "Come Go With Me," kicks things off, followed by the A- and B-sides of five early Fee-Bee, Dot and ABC-Paramount singles. Filling out the compilation are the top sides of four more ABC singles. Oddly enough, the follow-up to "Come Go With Me," a two-sided rocker ("What Made Maggie Run" and "Little Billy Boy"), isn't here, making this collection somewhat incomplete. But as a basic hits primer, this tells the story of the "original Dell Vikings" in a thoroughly digestible way. *—Cub Koda*

The Delfonics

f. 1965, Philadelphia, PA, **db.** 1974
Group / Smooth Soul, Pop-Soul, Quiet Storm, Philly Soul, Soul
The Delfonics were one of the first groups to sing in the sleek, soulful style that became popularized (thanks to producer Thom Bell) as the "Philadelphia sound." Their roots go back to doo-wop singing at school dances in the early 60s. They were well-known in the Philly area for their supple, airtight harmonies talent that brought them to the attention of record producers eventually landing them a contract with Cameo-Parkway. While their early records brought them little if any notice, it did bring them to the attention of producer/arranger Thom Bell who signed the band to his soon-to-be influential soul label Philly Groove. Right from the start this was a perfect match as the band released the classic "La La Means I Love You" in 1968 a song that began a string of hits lasting into the mid-70s. The sound that Bell

created for the Delfonics was the antithesis of the soul sound that came from Stax in Memphis and Muscle Shoals in Alabama. He sandpapered away the grit, lightened up on the backbeat, brought in string sections, and created a smooth, airy, sound—Bell and the Delfonics were setting the stage for a different kind of groove where subtlety and nuance reigned. —*John Dougan*

● **La, La Means I Love You: The Definitive Collection** / Aug. 26, 1997 / Arista ♦♦♦♦♦
A lush collection of classy Delfonics tracks. The trio had a more soulful sound than the Stylistics whom Thom Bell (who produced the lion's share of these tracks) later produced. Initially flooring the world with "La, La Means I Love You," the Harts, William & Wilbert, Randy Cain, and later Major Harris churned out delightful ear candies for years. "I'm Sorry," "Break Your Promise," "Ready or Not Here I Come," and "You Got Yours I'll Get Mine," included here, were as potent as "La, La." But, it took the eloquent, French-horn embellished "Didn't I Blow Your Mind This Time," however, to put them on top again. "Somebody Loves You" is a luscious B-side featuring Williams' sweet falsetto and harmonies that run over. Later, less successful recording's provide the most thrills: "Over & Over," "Lying to Myself," "Think It Over," and "I Told You So" are as smooth and as creamy as whipped cream. "Hey Love," an exquisite slow jam, featuring Wilbert Hart's heavier tenor, has shown an amazing longevity for a flip side. Not quite definitive, they could have omitted the awkward "Funny Feeling," and "Loving Him"—a B-side, for "I Gave to You" and "Can You Remember." But this is still fantastic, and more than enough Delfonics for most; you'll want two copies—one for the car and one for the crib. —*Andrew Hamilton*

More Best of the Delfonics / May 18, 1999 / M.I.L. Multimedia ♦♦♦♦
MIL Multimedia's *More Best of the Delfonics* is a budget-priced, double-disc set that concentrates on the smaller singles and lesser-known tracks from the Delfonics. For fans who already have the obvious hits, this is a good (albeit imperfect) way to dig a little deeper, since it contains a number of very fine songs—"Lying to Myself," "I Told You So," "Seventeen (And in Love)," "The Phoney," "Start All Over Again"—plus the previously unreleased song "Don't Leave Me." The set could have benefited from a little editing, so that it could all fit onto one disc, but there's enough prime material to make it a bargain. —*Stephen Thomas Erlewine*

The Dells

f. 1952, Chicago, IL, **db.** 1986
Group / Smooth Soul, Chicago Soul, Pop-Soul, Northern Soul, Doo Wop, R&B, Soul
After nearly four decades of recording an incredible legacy of hits, the Dells have made only one personnel change in their entire professional career. Perhaps that's why the venerable R&B vocal group can boast such a remarkably consistent track record.

The quintet from Chicago's south suburbs has weathered stylistic shifts from doo wop and soul to disco and urban contemporary, and every permutation in between. Their harmony remains as striking as ever, with Marvin Junior's earthshaking lead enduring as the group's focal point.

Signing with Vee-Jay in 1955, their creamy vocal blend on "Oh, What a Night" gave the Dells their first major R&B hit the next year, but it would be nearly a decade before they returned to the winner's circle with another dreamy classic, "Stay in My Corner." By then Chicago's R&B sound had changed drastically—doo wop was dead and soul was king—but the Dells adapted effortlessly, regularly scaling the charts for the Chess subsidiary Cadet with "There Is," "Always Together," "Give Your Baby a Standing Ovation," and a marathon remake of "Stay in My Corner" that afforded Junior's booming baritone room to roam.

Seemingly an indestructible force (turning up on the R&B charts as recently as 1984), the succinct harmonies of the Dells span entire generations of R&B history. —*Bill Dahl*

☆ **On Their Corner** / Mar. 10, 1992 / Chess ♦♦♦♦♦
Excellent compilation of their late-'60s sides, like "Oh What a Night," "Stay in My Corner, " "The Love We Had Stays on My Mind," and "Give Your Baby a Standing Ovation." —*Stephen Thomas Erlewine*

Dreams of Contentment / Nov. 17, 1993 / Vee-Jay ♦♦♦♦♦
The Dells never made it over the hump while at Vee-Jay, despite making many impressive singles. They were a top-flight doo wop group, but they couldn't find a way to advance beyond the R&B margins. Only when they moved to Chess, changed their style, and made Marvin Junior the lead singer did they enjoy the success they deserved. Still, as this 24-track reissue shows, there wasn't anything wrong with their Vee-Jay output. They experimented on such numbers as "Lil Darlin'," "It's Not for Me to Say," and "It's Not Unusual" with jazz/pop harmonies and covers. In addition, songs like "Now I Pray" and "Pain in My Heart" are wonderfully sung and harmonized, even if they weren't huge sellers. —*Ron Wynn*

Passionate Breezes: The Best of the Dells 1975-1991 / Oct. 1995 / Mercury ♦♦♦
By the last half of the '70s, the Dells had already gone through two phases in their career, transforming themselves from an R&B vocal group into a smooth soul outfit and scoring hits in both incarnations. During the late '70s and '80s, the group continued to perform, usually in the same vein as their early-'70s hits. Even if the strength of their voices hadn't diminished, their audience had. Nevertheless, much of the material they recorded during this era was fine, as *Passionate Breezes: Best of 1975-1991* proves. It's not as compulsively listenable as the group's doo wop hits or their early-'70s material, but there is still enough first-rate music here to satisfy fans. —*Stephen Thomas Erlewine*

★ **Anthology** / Sep. 28, 1999 / Hip-O ♦♦♦♦♦
The Dells were one of the few groups that rode the transition from doo wop to smooth soul without missing a beat and without falling off the charts. Just as remarkably, the group did so without declining much in quality, as Hip-O's definitive double-disc *Anthology* proves. Throughout these 36 tracks, the music changes, from street-corner R&B to string-drenched disco-soul, but in all their incarnations, the Dells always sound wonderful. There are a handful of minor hits missing, but all the big singles—including both the Vee-Jay and Cadet versions of "Oh, What a Nite" and "Stay in My Corner"—are here, assembled chronologically. As such, it tells an epic story of a group whose history mirrored the story of R&B vocal groups from the '50s through the '70s. The latter-day material may pale somewhat in comparison to the band's early classics, but it holds up well against other '70s soul. The final cut, the group's surprise 1991 hit "A Heart Is a House for Love"—their contribution to Robert Townsend's *The Five Heartbeats*, which was a loose tribute to the Dells themselves—illustrates that the group sounded terrific well into their third decade of performing, which is a true sign of greatness. *Anthology* is a testament to their greatness, offering solid proof that they were one of the greatest vocal R&B groups of their time. —*Stephen Thomas Erlewine*

John Denver (Henry John Deutchendorf)

b. Dec. 31, 1943, Roswell, NM, **d.** Oct. 12, 1997
Vocals, Guitar / Folk-Rock, Soft Rock, Singer/Songwriter
One of the most popular recording artists of the 1970s, country-folk singer/songwriter John Denver's gentle, environmentally conscious music established him among the most beloved entertainers of his era; wholesome and clean-cut, his appeal extended to fans of all ages and backgrounds, and led to parallel careers as both an actor and a humanitarian. After moving to Los Angeles in 1964, he joined the Chad Mitchell Trio and helped resuscitate the group on the strength of his songwriting skills. Denver finally began a solo career in 1969 that gained him a degree of fame as the songwriter of "Leaving on a Jet Plane," an international chart-topper for Peter, Paul & Mary. Finally, with 1971's *Poems, Prayers and Promises*, he achieved superstardom as an artist, thanks to the million-selling hits "Take Me Home, Country Roads" and "Sunshine on My Shoulders." By 1974, he was firmly established as America's best-selling performer; his greatest-hits collection that year sold over ten million copies worldwide. In 1977, he moved into film but drastically curtailed his recording output as a result. In the '80s, Denver's popularity waned as he turned his focus more towards humanitarian work. He made more news for a 1993 drunk-driving arrest than he did for records like 1991's *Different Directions*. Tragedy struck in 1997 when his experimental aircraft suddenly crashed, killing him instantly. —*Jason Ankeny*

● **Greatest Hits** / 1973 / RCA ♦♦♦♦♦
Released in 1973, *Greatest Hits* only sums up a handful of years of hitmaking for John Denver, but what years those were. Between 1971 and 1973, Denver actually didn't have that many hits, but they were songs that defined him—"Take Me Home, Country Roads"; "Rocky Mountain High"; and "Sunshine on My Shoulders." Those three songs, along with "Leaving on a Jet Plane"—which he wrote but Peter Paul & Mary made into a standard—are all here, along with seven other early songs recorded between 1969 and 1973 that may not be familiar to the average casual fan, and all capture Denver's warm folk-pop at its best. There may be more hits on *Greatest Hits, Vol. 2*, but this collection is every bit as engaging as that record. —*Stephen Thomas Erlewine*

Greatest Hits, Vol. 2 / 1977 / RCA ♦♦♦♦♦
Greatest Hits, Vol. 2 captures the hitmaking years, containing many of John Denver's most beloved songs: "Annie's Song," "Back Home Again," "Thank God I'm a Country Boy," "I'm Sorry," "Calypso," "Fly Away," "Grandma's Feather Bed" and "This Old Guitar." These are also the songs that found Denver enhancing his pop leanings, crafting endearingly catchy, sweet folk-pop songs that sounded more suited for airplay than singalongs around the campfire. And while the songs on the first *Greatest Hits* volume are perhaps more organic, these are impeccably crafted songs that justifiably turned Denver into a superstar. —*Stephen Thomas Erlewine*

Greatest Hits, Vol. 3 / 1985 / RCA ♦♦♦♦
By the end of the '70s, John Denver was still a star, but he didn't have many hits. That situation didn't improve in the early '80s, as his records started sliding slowly down the charts. This is the era that *Greatest Hits, Vol. 3* covers—one that found Denver's popularity fading, but not necessarily his skills. Sure, his songs don't sound as effortless or charming as they used to, but the best moments from these years (most of which are captured on this compilation) illustrate that he was still capable of crafting ingratiating folk-pop songs. It's not for every listener, but fans of Denver's classic years that want to dig a little deeper may find some gems here. —*Stephen Thomas Erlewine*

The Rocky Mountain Collection / Apr. 1996 / RCA ♦♦♦♦♦
The Rocky Mountain Collection is a double-disc, 39-track collection that features all of John Denver's greatest hits—"Leaving on a Jet Plane," "Sunshine on My Shoulders," "Take Me Home Country Roads," "Rocky Mountain High," "Annie's Song," "Thank God I'm a Country Boy," "Back Home Again," "Sweet Surrender," "Fly Away," "I'm Sorry"—plus several lesser-known but equally fine songs from throughout his career. For those who want to dig deeper than the *Greatest Hits* collections, or want to pass by those individual volumes in favor of one set, *The Rocky Mountain Collection* is an ideal purchase. —*Stephen Thomas Erlewine*

Greatest Country Hits / Mar. 24, 1998 / RCA ♦♦♦♦♦
To the hardcore, John Denver was never really country, as evidenced by Charlie Rich's infamous protest at the Country Music Awards. Nevertheless, he was a country-pop star, scoring a number of hits on the country charts during the '70s and early '80s. *Greatest Country Hits* is a superb 18-track collection of those hits, and it's nearly as good as any of his greatest-hits collections. A few big songs, such as "Rocky Mountain High" and "Calypso," are missing, but all the familiar songs—"Take Me Home, Country Roads," "Sunshine On My Shoulders," "Annie's Song," "Back Home Again," "Sweet Surrender," "Thank God I'm a Country Boy," "I'm Sorry"—are here, along with such latter-day country hits as "Some Days Are Diamonds (Some Days Are Stone)" and "Dreamland Express." Furthermore, it's a generous, attractively packaged collection that is one of the best compilations RCA has yet assembled on John Denver, and it hopefully bodes well for upcoming reissues from the label. —*Stephen Thomas Erlewine*

Depeche Mode

f. 1980, Basildon, England
Group / Alternative Dance, Club/Dance, Post-Punk, Alternative Pop/Rock, Synth Pop
Originally a product of Britain's New Romantic movement, Depeche Mode went on to become the quintessential electro-pop band of the 1980s; one of the first acts to establish a mu-

sical identity based completely around the use of synthesizers, the group began their existence as a bouncy dance-pop outfit but gradually developed a darker, more dramatic sound which ultimately positioned them as one of the most successful alternative bands of their era. After building a following on the London club scene, Depeche Mode scored their first major hit with "Just Can't Get Enough," and their 1981 debut LP *Speak and Spell* was also a success. Just as the group appeared poised for a major commercial breakthrough, however, principal songwriter Vince Clarke abruptly exited to form Yazoo; keyboardist Martin Gore grabbed the reins, and his ominous compositions grew more assured and sophisticated by the time of 1983's *Construction Time Again*. *Some Great Reward* was Depeche Mode's artistic and commercial breakthrough, as Gore's dark, kinky preoccupations with spiritual doubt ("Blasphemous Rumours") and psychosexual manipulation ("Master and Servant") came to the fore; the egalitarian single "People Are People" was a major hit on both sides of the Atlantic, and typified the music's turn towards more industrial textures. Still, despite an enormous fan base, the group was considered very much an underground cult phenomenon prior to the release of 1990's *Violator*, a Top Ten smash which spawned the hits "Enjoy the Silence," "Policy of Truth" and "Personal Jesus." *—Jason Ankeny*

Speak & Spell / 1981 / Sire ✦✦✦✦
Though probably nobody fully appreciated it at the time—perhaps least of all the band!—Depeche Mode's debut is at once both a conservative, functional pop record and a groundbreaking release. While various synth pioneers had come before—Gary Numan, early Human League, late-'70s Euro-disco, and above all Kraftwerk all had clear influence on *Speak and Spell*—Depeche became the undisputed founder of straight-up synth-pop with the album's 11 songs, light, hooky, and danceable numbers about love, life, and clubs. For all the claims about "dated" '80s sounds from rock purists, it should be noted that the basic guitar/bass/drums lineup of rock is almost 25 years older than the catchy keyboard lines and electronic drums making the music here. That such a sound would eventually become ubiquitous during the Reagan years, spawning lots of crud along the way, means the band should no more be held to blame for that than Motown and the Beatles for inspiring lots of bad stuff in the '60s, for instance. Credit for the album's success has to go to main songwriter Vince Clarke, who would extend and arguably perfect the synth-pop formula with Yaz and Erasure; the classic early singles "New Life," "Dreaming of Me," and "Just Can't Get Enough," along with numbers ranging from the slyly homoerotic "Pretty Boy" to the moody thumper "Photographic," keep everything moving throughout. Gahan undersings about half the album, and Gore's two numbers lack the distinctiveness of his later work, but *Speak and Spell* remains an undiluted joy. *—Ned Raggett*

A Broken Frame / 1982 / Sire ✦✦✦

Construction Time Again / 1983 / Sire ✦✦✦

People Are People / 1984 / Sire ✦✦✦

Some Great Reward / 1984 / Sire ✦✦✦✦✦
The peak of the band's industrial-gone-mainstream fusion, and still one of the best electronic music albums yet recorded, *Reward* still sounds great, with the band's ever-evolving musical and production skills matching even more ambitious songwriting from Gore. "People Are People" appears here, but finds itself outclassed by some of Depeche's undisputed classics, most especially the moody, beautiful "Somebody," a Gore-sung piano ballad that mixes its wit and emotion skillfully; "Master and Servant," an amped-up, slamming dance track that conflates sexual and economic politics to sharp effect; and the closing "Blasphemous Rumors," a slow-building anthemic number supporting one of Gore's most cynical lyrics, addressing a suicidal teen who finds God only to die soon afterward. Even lesser-known tracks like the low-key pulse of "Lie to Me" and the weirdly dreamy "It Doesn't Matter" showcase an increasingly confident band. Wilder's arrangements veer from the big to the stripped down, but always with just the right touch, such as the crowd samples bubbling beneath "Somebody" or the call/response a cappella start to "Master and Servant." With *Reward*, Gahan's singing style found the metier it was going to stick with for the next ten years, and while it's never gone down well with some ears, it still has a compelling edge to it that suits the material well. *—Ned Raggett*

Catching Up with Depeche Mode / 1985 / Sire ✦✦✦✦✦
Like its predecessor, *People Are People*, *Catching Up With Depeche Mode* attempts to fill in gaps in the group's extensive discography by compiling singles and album tracks taken from their four previous studio LPs. Dating back to the band's Vince Clarke-penned hits ("Just Can't Get Enough," "Dreaming of Me"), the set culminates with tracks like "Master and Servant" and "Blasphemous Rumours," which bear the full fruit of Martin Gore's dark obsessions; a preview of *Black Celebration* is even offered via "Fly on the Windshield." *—Jason Ankeny*

● **The Singles 81–85** / 1998 / Sire ✦✦✦✦✦
Replacing the original *Catching Up with Depeche Mode* compilation, *81-85* subtracts two tracks—the lightweight curiosity "Flexible" and "Fly on the Windscreen," which surfaced to better effect on *Black Celebration*—and adds two, the full six-minute remix of "Just Can't Get Enough" and the original version of "Photographic," Depeche's recording debut on a 1980 compilation album. The overall collection remains the same, though, namely, a run through the peerless singles that kept the band on the charts in the U.K. and elsewhere, as well as building up their increasing cult following in America. It's an embarrassment of riches, from such bouncy early hits as "New Life," "Just Can't Enough," and "The Meaning of Love" to the increasingly heavier sound of "Everything Counts," "People Are People," and "Blasphemous Rumors." Nearly all the tracks appear in the original single mixes, some quite different from their album versions, others essentially the same (the one subtle difference in "Somebody" is an echoey percussion pattern buried in the mix, for instance). Two otherwise unavailable singles also appear here: "It's Called a Heart" is pleasant enough, but "Shake the Disease" is great, an obsessive love lyric matched to a wonderful, slow dance melody and an excellent pairing of Gahan's more aggressive and Gore's gentler vocals. As an introduction to Depeche's brilliant knack for catchy tunes evolving over time into a more challenging but no less popular collection of songs, at once defining and expanding the boundaries of synth-pop, look no further. *—Ned Raggett*

Black Celebration / 1986 / Sire ✦✦✦✦
Whether the band felt it was simply the time to move on from its most explicit industrial pop fusion days, or whether increased success and concurrently larger venues pushed the music into different avenues, Depeche Mode's fifth studio album saw the group embarked on a path that in many ways defined their sound to the present: emotionally extreme lyrics matched with amped-up tunes, as much anthemic rock as they are compelling dance, along with stark, low-key ballads. The slow, sneaky build of the opening title track, with a strange distorted vocal sample providing a curious opening hook, sets the tone as Gahan sings of making it through "another black day" while powerful drums and echoing metallic pings carry the song. *Black Celebration* is actually heavier on the ballads throughout, many sung by Gore—the most per album he has yet taken lead on—with notable dramatic beauties including "Sometimes," with its surprise gospel choir start and rough piano sonics, and the hyper-nihilistic "World Full of Nothing." The various singles from the album remain definite highlights, such as "A Question of Time," a brawling, aggressive number with a solid Gahan vocal, and the romantic/physical politics of "Stripped," featuring particularly sharp arrangements from Alan Wilder. However, with such comparatively lesser-known but equally impressive numbers as the quietly intense romance of "Here Is the House" to boast, *Black Celebration* is solid through and through. *—Ned Raggett*

Music for the Masses / 1987 / Sire ✦✦✦✦✦
Initially the title must have sounded like an incredibly pretentious boast, except that Depeche Mode then went on to do a monstrous world tour, score even more hits in America and elsewhere than ever before, and pick up a large number of name checks from emerging house and techno artists on top of all that. As for the music the masses got this time around, the opening cut "Never Let Me Down Again" started things off wonderfully: a compressed guitar riff suddenly slamming into a huge-sounding percussion/keyboard/piano combination, anchored to a constantly repeated melodic hook, ever-building synth/orchestral parts at the song's end, and one of Gahan's best vocals (though admittedly singing one of Gore's more pedestrian lyrics). It feels huge throughout, like they taped Depeche recording at the world's largest arena show instead of in a studio. Other key singles "Strangelove" and the (literally) driving "Behind the Wheel" maintained the same blend of power and song skill, while some of the quieter numbers as "The Things You Said" and "I Want You Now" showed musical and lyrical intimacy could easily co-exist with the big chart-busters. Add to that other winners like "To Have and to Hold," with its Russian radio broadcast start and dramatic, downward spiral of music accompanied by Gahan's subtly powerful take on a desperate Gore love lyric, and the weird, wonderful choral closer "Pimpf," and Depeche's massive success becomes perfectly clear. *—Ned Raggett*

101 / 1989 / Sire ✦✦✦✦

Violator / Feb. 1990 / Sire ✦✦✦✦✦
In a word, stunning. Perhaps an odd word to use given that *Violator* continued in the general vein of the previous two studio efforts by Depeche Mode: Gore's upfront lyrical emotional extremism and knack for a catchy hook filtered through Wilder's ear for perfect arrangements, ably assisted by top English producer Flood. Yet the idea that this record would both dominate worldwide charts, while song for song being simply the best, most consistent effort yet from the band could only have been the wildest fantasy before its release. The opening two singles from the album, however, signaled something was up. First was "Personal Jesus," at once perversely simplistic, with a stiff, arcane funk/hip-hop beat and basic blues guitar chords, and tremendous, thanks to sharp production touches and Gahan's echoed, snaky vocals. Then "Enjoy the Silence," a nothing-else-remains-but-us ballad pumped up into a huge, dramatic romance/dance number, commanding in its mock orchestral/choir scope. Follow-up single "Policy of Truth" did just fine as well, a low-key Motown funk number for the modern day with a sharp love/hate lyric to boot. To top it all off, the album itself scored on song after song, from the shuffling beat of "Sweetest Perfection" (well sung by Gore) and the ethereal "Waiting for the Night" to the guilt-ridden and loving it "Halo," building into a string-swept pounder. "Clean" wraps up *Violator* on an eerie note, all ominous bass notes and odd atmospherics carrying the song. Goth without ever being stupidly hammy, synth without sounding like the clinical stereotype of synth music, rock without ever sounding like a "rock" band, Depeche here reached astounding heights indeed. *—Ned Raggett*

Songs of Faith & Devotion / Mar. 23, 1993 / Sire ✦✦✦✦
In between *Violator* and *Songs of Faith & Devotion*, a lot happened: Nirvana rewrote the ideas of what "alternative" was supposed to be, while Nine Inch Nails, hit the airwaves as the most clearly Depeche-influenced new hit band around. In the meantime, the band went through some high-profile arguing as Gahan turned into a long-haired, leather-clad rocker and pushed for a more guitar-oriented sound. Yet the odd thing about *Songs of Faith & Devotion* is that it sounds pretty much like a Depeche Mode album, only with some new sonic tricks courtesy of Alan Wilder and co-producer Flood. Perhaps even odder is the fact that it works incredibly well all the same. "I Feel You," opening with a screech of feedback, works its live drums well, but when the heavy synth bass kicks in with the wailing backing vocals, even most rockers might find it hard to compete. Gore's lyrical bent, as per the title, ponders relationships through distinctly religious imagery; while the gambit is hardly new, on songs like the centerpiece "In Your Room," the combination of personal and spiritual love blends perfectly. Outside musicians appear for the first time, including female backing singers on a couple of tracks, most notably the gospel-flavored "Condemnation" and the uilleann pipes on "Judas," providing a lovely intro to the underrated song (later covered by Tricky). "Rush" is the biggest misstep, a too obvious sign that Nine Inch Nails was a recording-session favorite to unwind to. But with other numbers such as "Walking in My Shoes" and "The Mercy in You" to recommend it, *Songs of Faith & Devotion* continues the Depeche Mode winning streak. *—Ned Raggett*

Songs of Faith & Devotion Live / May 1993 / Sire ✦✦

Ultra / Apr. 15, 1997 / Reprise ✦✦✦

● **The Singles 86–98** / Oct. 6, 1998 / Reprise ✦✦✦✦✦
It took Depeche Mode only four years to assemble their first singles compilation, but 12 to release *The Singles 86–98.* Appropriately, the second set was much more ambitious than *The Singles 81-85,* spanning two discs and 20 songs, plus a live version of "Everything Counts." *The Singles 86–98* was an album that many fans, both casual and hardcore, waited patiently for, and for good reason—Depeche Mode was always more effective as a singles band than as album artists. That's not to say that the double-disc compilation is perfect. DM's output fluctuated wildly during those 12 years, as the group hit both career highs and lows. It's possible to hear it all on this set, from "Strangelove" and "Never Let Me Down Again," through "Personal Jesus" and "Enjoy the Silence," to "I Feel You" and "Barrel of a Gun." It's possible that some casual listeners will find that the collection meanders a bit too much for their tastes, but the end result is definitive and, along with *The Singles 81-85,* ranks as Depeche Mode's best, most listenable album. *—Stephen Thomas Erlewine*

Derek & the Dominos

f. 1970, New York, NY, **db.** 1971
Group / Album Rock, British Blues, Hard Rock, Blues-Rock
Derek & the Dominos was a group formed by guitarist/singer Eric Clapton with other former members of Delaney & Bonnie & Friends, in the spring of 1970. From late August to early October, they recorded the celebrated double album *Layla and Other Assorted Love Songs* with guitarist Duane Allman sitting in. They then returned to touring in England and the U.S., playing their final date on December 6. The *Layla* album was successful in the U.S., where "Bell Bottom Blues" and the title song charted as singles in abbreviated versions, but it did not chart in the U.K. The Dominos reconvened to record a second album in May 1971, but split up without completing it. Clapton then retired from the music business, nursing a heroin addiction. In his absence, and in the wake of Allman's death in a motorcycle accident on October 29, 1971, the Dominos and *Layla* gained in stature. Rereleased as a single at its full, seven-minute length in connection with the compilation album *History of Eric Clapton,* "Layla" hit the Top Ten in the U.S. and the U.K. in the summer of 1972. Time has only added to the renown for the group, which is now rated among Eric Clapton's most outstanding achievements. *—William Ruhlmann*

★ **Layla & Other Assorted Love Songs** / Nov. 1970 / Polydor ✦✦✦✦✦
Wishing to escape the superstar expectations that sank Blind Faith before it was launched, Eric Clapton retreated with several sidemen from Delaney & Bonnie to record the material that would form *Layla & Other Assorted Love Songs.* From these meager beginnings grew his greatest album. Duane Allman joined the band shortly after recording began, and his spectacular slide guitar pushed Clapton to new heights. Then again, Clapton may have gotten there without him, considering the emotional turmoil he was in during the recording. He was in hopeless, unrequited love with Patti Boyd, the wife of his best friend, George Harrison, and that pain surges throughout *Layla,* especially on its epic title track. But what really makes *Layla* such a powerful record is that Clapton, ignoring the traditions that occasionally painted him into a corner, simply tears through these songs with burning, intense emotion. He makes standards like "Have You Ever Loved a Woman" and "Nobody Knows You (When You're Down and Out)" into his own, while his collaborations with Bobby Whitlock—including "Any Day" and "Why Does Love Got to Be So Sad?"—teem with passion. And, considering what a personal album *Layla* is, it's somewhat ironic that the lovely coda "Thorn Tree in the Garden" is a solo performance by Whitlock, and that the song sums up the entire album as well as "Layla" itself. *—Stephen Thomas Erlewine*

The Layla Sessions: 20th Anniversary Edition / Sep. 1990 / Polydor ✦✦✦

Live at the Fillmore / Feb. 22, 1994 / Polydor ✦✦✦

Descendents

f. 1979
Group / College Rock, L.A. Punk, Punk-Pop, Hardcore Punk
Fueled by "rejection, food, coffee, girls, fishing and food," the Descendents sprang up during the halcyon days of the Los Angeles punk scene; fusing the blind rage of hardcore with an unexpectedly wry, self-deprecating wit and a strong melodic sensibility which set them distinctly apart from their West Coast brethren, they gradually emerged as one of the most enduring and adored bands of their time. Formed in 1979, the Descendents' first lineup consisted of vocalist/guitarist Frank Navetta, vocalist/bassist Tony Lombardo and drummer Bill Stevenson; initially sporting an edgy power-pop sound inspired by the Buzzcocks, the group issued a debut single, "Ride the Wild," and then promptly vanished from sight.

When the Descendents resurfaced in 1981, they were a four-piece fronted by vocalist Milo Auckerman, a beloved figure within the hardcore community who infused the group's identity with both unmitigated teen angst and a healthy dose of goofball humor. Amid a relentless, caffeine-powered touring schedule, the Descendents found time to record the 1981 EP *Fat,* a collection spotlighting both Auckerman's affection for fast food ("Weinerschnitzel," "I Like Food") and distaste for parental guidance ("My Dad Sucks"). A year later, the group issued their debut LP, *Milo Goes to College;* despite the considerable levity of tracks like "Bikeage" and "Suburban Home," the title was no joke—Auckerman was indeed headed off to study biochemistry, and when Stevenson joined the ranks of Black Flag, the Descendents went on sabbatical.

In 1985, the group re-formed, with SWA alum Ray Cooper replacing Navetta on guitar; after the release of the more pop-flavored album *I Don't Want to Grow Up,* ex-Anti bassist Doug Carrion assumed Lombardo's duties. A sunnier perspective informed 1986's *Enjoy!,* as evidenced by the inclusion of a cover of the Beach Boys' "Wendy," but after 1987's lackluster *All,* the group split again; after Stevenson formed a new group, also dubbed All, the only Descendents products to appear for a number of years were a pair of live releases, 1987's *Liveage!* and 1989's *Hallraker.* Somewhat surprisingly, Auckerman and Stevenson re-formed the Descendents in 1996 with All bassist Karl Alvarez and guitarist Stephen Egerton; in addition to mounting a tour, the group recorded a new album, *Everything Sucks. —Jason Ankeny*

Fat / 1981 / SST ✦✦✦

Milo Goes to College / 1982 / SST ✦✦✦✦✦

I Don't Want to Grow Up / 1985 / SST ✦✦✦✦

Enjoy / 1986 / SST ✦✦

All / 1987 / SST ✦✦✦✦

Liveage / 1987 / SST ✦✦✦

● **Somery** / Jul. 16, 1991 / SST ✦✦✦✦✦
Somery is an overview of the Descendents' SST records, drawing equally from each record. Although this means a handful of great songs from their best albums are missing, *Somery* nevertheless selects the highlights from their occasionally uneven records, making it a useful and comprehensive retrospective. *—Stephen Thomas Erlewine*

Jackie DeShannon

b. Aug. 21, 1944, Hazel, KY
Vocals, Guitar / Brill Building Pop, Folk-Rock, Pop, Singer/Songwriter
Few performers have enjoyed as versatile a career as Jackie DeShannon, and although she made a couple of well-remembered Top Ten pop hits in the '60s, she's never achieved the level of success or artistic recognition she deserves. One of the first established rock figures to see the potential for crossbreeding rock and folk, she was a crucial midwife to the birth of folk-rock, with the wonderful singles "Needles and Pins" and "When You Walk in the Room." DeShannon's famous affiliations and success as a songwriter have sometimes obscured her own enormous talents. She's a superb singer, capable of both sweet ballads and (more satisfyingly) a gutsy, soulfully husky delivery. She performed her own material with an honest, vulnerable, intelligent intensity that pre-figured the singer/songwriter movement by several years, and demonstrated command of pop, soul, hard rock, girl group, and country styles. Her greatest success, however, came not with her own material, but with Bacharach-David's "What the World Needs Now Is Love," which made the Top Ten in 1965. The soft-rock "Put a Little Love in Your Heart" gave her another Top Ten hit in 1969, and she made some well-received singer/songwriter albums in the 1970s. One of the songs from her '70s LPs, "Bette Davis Eyes," became a number one hit for Kim Carnes in 1981. *—Richie Unterberger*

● **Pop Princess** / 1981 / EMI Australia ✦✦✦✦✦
Rhino and EMI have come out with fairly extensive CD compilations of DeShannon's work, but this 23-song Australian album—if it can be found—is probably the best. It concentrates almost solely on her '60s recordings (one 1959 track is included), which remains her most fertile era. It also has a few excellent singles that didn't make it onto either compilation. These include the early-'60s girl group-type efforts "It's Love Baby," "Baby (When Ya Kiss Me)," "I Won't Turn You Down," and "Should I Cry?"—most written by DeShannon, all flops, and all worth hearing. Later, more mainstream efforts like "A Proper Girl" and Jim Webb's "The Girls' Song" are also not included on other reissues, and also worth a listen. The gatefold package contains informative liner notes, photos, and an exhaustive discography which also lists dozens of songs she wrote for other performers. *—Richie Unterberger*

● **What the World Needs Now . . . : The Definitive Collection** / Jul. 26, 1994 / EMI ✦✦✦✦✦
DeShannon's work is actually too diverse to be satisfactorily captured on an anthology, even one that includes 28 tracks, as this one does. Still, considering how hard the one DeShannon anthology that might be better than this one is to find (the Australian import *Pop Princess*), this has to be cited as the recommended first purchase. Focusing on her output for Liberty between 1959 and 1970, it has all the essentials: her two Top Ten hits, the minor hits like "A Lifetime of Loneliness," and the original versions of "Needles and Pins" and "When You Walk in the Room," and a host of fine girl group, ballad, folk-rock, and singer/songwriter flop singles. From the collector's viewpoint, the most interesting songs are the rarities. The six previously unreleased tracks include the exuberant "Breakaway," a hit for Irma Thomas; the rocker "Dream Boy," cut in 1964 in Britain with Jimmy Page on guitar; and a cover of Tim Hardin's "Reason to Believe." A couple of interesting rarities are "For Granted" (from the little-seen movie *C'mon, Let's Live a Little*) and the 45 version of "Splendor in the Grass," a somewhat sloppy folk-rock performance on which DeShannon was backed by the Byrds. *—Richie Unterberger*

Destiny's Child

f. 1990, Houston, TX
Group / Teen Pop, Urban
Destiny's Child is an R&B girl group from Houston, signed to Columbia and first premiered on *Men in Black: The Album* with their song "Killing Time." Early in 1998, the group released their self-titled debut album, featuring the single "No, No, No (Part II)" featuring Wyclef Jean. The quartet, including Beyoncé Knowles, Kelly Rowland (Beyonce's cousin), La Tavia Roberson and Le Toya Luckett, also toured with Wyclef Jean. The album, *The Writing's on the Wall* followed in 1999. In March of 2000, before shooting a video for the single "Say My Name," Columbia Records announced Roberson and Luckett left the group. Though details remain hazy, the two cited that the group's manager, Beyonce's father, showed confict of interest. The two were replaced by similar looking, 18-year-old Farrah Franklin and 19-year-old Michelle Williams. Five months after her addition, Franklin announced she was leaving. The group remained a trio thereafter *—John Bush*

Destiny's Child / Feb. 17, 1998 / Columbia ✦✦✦✦
Destiny's Child isn't quite just another debut album from an R&B girl-group. The quartet worked with Wyclef Jean and Jermaine Dupri among others, and their voices sound beautiful together, but much of the album sounds indistinguishable fom all the other female groups out there. When Destiny's Child does sound different, as on the single "No, No, No (Part II)," they're more than competent. *—John Bush*

● **The Writing's on the Wall** / Jul. 27, 1999 / Columbia ✦✦✦✦
With their second album, *Writing's on the Wall,* Destiny's Child still suffers from slightly un-

even songwriting, but it's nevertheless an assured step forward from the girl group. Not only are they maturing as vocalists, they are fortunate to work with such skilled, talented producers as Kevin "She'kspere" Biggs, Rodney Jerkins, Dwayne Wiggins, Chad Elliot, Daryl Simmons and Missy Elliott, who all give the quartet rich, varied music upon which to work their charm. So, even when the album fails to deliver memorable songs, it always sounds alluring, thanks to the perfect combination of vocalists and producers. *—Stephen Thomas Erlewine*

Devo

f. 1972, Akron, OH, **db.** 1991

Group / College Rock, American Punk, Post-Punk, New Wave, Synth Pop

One of new wave's most innovative and (for a time) successful bands, Devo was also perhaps one of its most misunderstood. Formed in Akron, Ohio in 1972 by Kent State art students Jerry Casale (bass) and Mark Mothersbaugh (vocals), along with Bob Casale (guitar), Bob Mothersbaugh (lead guitar), and Alan Myers (drums), Devo took its name from their concept of "de-evolution"—the idea that instead of evolving, mankind has actually regressed, as evidenced by the dysfunction and herd mentality of American society. Their music echoed this view of society as rigid, repressive, and mechanical, with appropriate touches—jerky, robotic rhythms; an obsession with technology and electronics (the group was among the first non-art-rock bands to make the synthesizer a core element); and often atonal melodies and chord progressions—all filtered through the perspectives of geeky misfits. After attracting the attention of luminaries like David Bowie and Iggy Pop through their soundtrack work for the short film *The Truth About De-Evolution*, Devo recorded its 1978 debut, *Q: Are We Not Men? A: We Are Devo!* under the auspices of pioneering producer Brian Eno. The record was a cult sensation, helped in part by the band's concurrent emphasis on its highly stylized visuals—videos, costumes which made the band members look alike, etc. Their third album, *Freedom of Choice*, featured a smash single in "Whip It," and the fledgling MTV network made the accompanying video into a staple. However, following those first three albums, the group began to run out of ideas, both musical and conceptual; their simple, basic electronic sound had proven very influential, and other bands were already expanding on some of Devo's ideas. After a series of largely uninteresting albums, the band called it quits early in the '90s. Casale and Mothersbaugh concentrated on other projects until a brief reunion for several dates at 1996's Lollapalooza tour. *—Steve Huey*

Q: Are We Not Men— A: We Are Devo! / Jul. 1978 / Warner Brothers ✦✦✦✦✦

Produced by Brian Eno, *Q: Are We Not Men? A: We Are Devo!* was a seminal touchstone in the development of American new wave. It was one of the first pop albums to use synthesizers as an important textural element, and although they mostly play a supporting role in this guitar-driven set, the innovation began to lay the groundwork for the synth-pop explosion that would follow very shortly. *Q: Are We Not Men* also revived the absurdist social satire of the Mothers of Invention, claiming punk rock's outsider alienation as a home for freaks and geeks. While Devo's appeal was certainly broader, their sound was tailored well enough to that sensibility that it still resonates with a rabid cult following. It isn't just the dadaist pseudo-intellectual theories, or the critique of the American mindset as unthinkingly, submissively conformist. It was the way their music reflected that view, crafted to be as mechanical and robotic as their targets. Yet Devo hardly sounded like a machine that ran smoothly. There was an almost unbearable tension in the speed of their jerky, jumpy rhythms, outstripping Talking Heads, XTC, and other similarly nervy new wavers. And thanks to all the dissonant, angular melodies, odd-numbered time signatures, and yelping, sing-song vocals, the tension never finds release, which is key to the album's impact. It also doesn't hurt that this is arguably Devo's strongest set of material, though several brilliant peaks can overshadow the remainder. Of those peaks, the most definitive are the de-evolution manifesto "Jocko Homo" (one of the extremely few rock anthems written in 7/8 time) and a wicked deconstruction of "(I Can't Get No) Satisfaction," which reworks the original's alienation into a spastic freak-out that's nearly unrecognizable. But *Q: Are We Not Men?* also had a conceptual unity that bolstered the consistent songwriting, making it an essential document of one of new wave's most influential bands. *—Steve Huey*

Duty Now for the Future / Jul. 1979 / Warner Brothers ✦✦✦✦

While the most obvious flaw of Devo's *Duty Now For The Future* is that the material simply isn't as good as on their debut, their second album also captures the group in the midst of a significant stylistic shift. On their first album, for all their herky-jerky rhythms and electronic accents, Devo were pretty much a standard guitars/bass/drums rock band, albeit one with more than their share of eccentricities. *Duty Now For The Future* found them bringing the keyboards that were used as punctuation on their earlier material into the forefront, adding a new level of irony to their "little minds through big technology" philosophy. While Devo would later learn to use electronics with confidence and wit, they were still learning how to integrate them into their sound on *Duty Now*, and the results lacked the strength and coherence of their debut. Of course, it also helped that the first album had better songs; the two instrumentals on side one are merely filler, "Pink Pussycat" and "Clockout" are jokes that just aren't funny, and "Triumph Of The Will" embraces fascism as a satirical target without bothering to make it sound as if they disapprove. But "Secret Agent Man" is a wittier devolved cover than "Satisfaction," the band rarely sounded as cheerfully creepy as on "The Day My Baby Gave Me A Surprize," and the side two rave up, "Smart Patrol/Mr. DNA" is superbly potent (for all their progressive trappings, Devo were formalists enough to know you make a big rock move near the end of side two.) *Duty Now For The Future* is hardly a bad album, but it isn't as strong as what Devo had already brought to the table—or would offer later on. *—Mark Deming*

Freedom of Choice / Jul. 1980 / Warner Brothers ✦✦✦✦✦

With *Freedom of Choice*, Devo completed their transition into a full-fledged synth-pop group, producing arguably their most musically cohesive effort in the process. Synthesizers are now fully integrated into the band's sound, frequently dominating the arrangements and at least sharing equal time with the guitars. Everything is played with a cool, polished precision that mirrors the stylized uniformity of the band's visuals; the dissonance is more subdued than in the past, and the uptight rhythms are no longer jarring, instead locking the band into a rigidly even keel. Oddly, even though the music is the least human-sounding Devo had yet produced, their social observations were growing less insular and more sympathetic. Several tunes—like the oft-covered "Girl U Want"—have a geeky (but pragmatic) romantic angst that was new to Devo albums, although the band's view of relationships is occasionally colored by their cultural themes of competition and domination. Those preoccupations also inform their breakthrough hit single, "Whip It," but elsewhere, they're finding enough connection with the rest of the world to moderate their cynicism, at least a little bit. Songs like "Gates of Steel," "Planet Earth," and the title track reveal a frustrated idealism under their irony, one that can't quite understand why Americans don't use more of their freedom to search for happiness. Altogether, there's a little less of the debut's energy, and a little less variety as well. But the songwriting is a match for consistent quality, and moreover, the music on *Freedom of Choice* is the sound that defines Devo in the minds of many. In the end, that makes it the band's only other truly necessary album. *—Steve Huey*

New Traditionalists / 1981 / Warner Brothers ✦✦✦

Oh, No! It's Devo / 1982 / Warner Brothers ✦✦✦

Total Devo / 1988 / Enigma ✦

The Greatest Hits / Dec. 1990 / Warner Brothers ✦✦✦✦

While *Greatest Hits* contains all of the truly necessary items, it also tends to overlook some of the better album tracks from Devo's early period (easily their best work) in favor of a more balanced overview, which means that later albums receive more exposure than they really deserve. The import collection *Hot Potatoes: The Best of Devo* has stronger selections and is the preferred single-disc overview of Devo's career, but if you can't find it and only want one Devo disc, this will do. *—Steve Huey*

● **Pioneers Who Got Scalped: The Anthology** / May 9, 2000 / Rhino ✦✦✦✦

Heading into the new millennium, there was no truly definitive Devo compilation on the market, so Rhino attempted to remedy the situation with the double-disc *Pioneers Who Got Scalped: The Anthology*—and did a pretty good job, without quite pulling it off. When faced with a choice, the compilation takes the collector-oriented route by including the rarer version; as a result, buyers get a couple of early Booji Boy-label recordings, and several single and dance remixes. More problematic, though, is the anthology's attempt to present a balanced overview of Devo's career. While admirable in intent, the fact is that the group's oeuvre grew steadily weaker as time passed, and since Disc One runs all the way through their first (and best) four albums, Disc Two is a pretty bumpy ride. Not that it's worthless—devotees will be thrilled with the inclusion of quite a few songs that had only previously appeared on movie soundtracks, and it also rescues a few worthwhile singles from obscurity. But it pales next to the first disc in terms of songwriting, musical invention, and edgy humor; plus, where the band's early covers reinvented rock standards as comments on alienation, latter-day items like "Bread and Butter" and "Itsy Bitsy Teenie Weenie Yellow Polka Dot Bikini" are nothing more than novelties. So the bottom line is, you've got to be a hardcore Devo enthusiast to fully appreciate *Pioneers Who Got Scalped*. If you are, it's a fantastic package; if you want a more basic overview, you're better off with the somewhat disorganized *Greatest Hits* or the import collection *Hot Potatoes*. It's kind of a shame, though, that in spite of the generally fine job done compiling *Pioneers*, there still isn't a Devo anthology that distills *all* the best moments from their crucial early years, and throws in just the right (small) number of later singles. *—Steve Huey*

Dexys Midnight Runners

f. Jul. 1978, Birmingham, England, **db.** 1986

Group / Blue-Eyed Soul, Post-Punk, New Wave

When Dexys Midnight Runners were at their peak in the early '80s, U.K. critics hailed their lead singer/songwriter Kevin Rowland as a genius, capable of fusing soul, pop, Irish folk, new wave, and rock into one seamless, unique mix. Although the band wasn't able to fulfill their promise, the best of their music was remarkable. On their first album, *Searching for the Young Soul Rebels*, the group featured scores of horns along with accomplished songwriting from Rowland. It became a sensation in England, although it didn't dent the charts in America. After the album's release, three members of the band split and formed the Bureau, leaving Rowland to refashion Dexy's Midnight Runners. What he came up with was a departure from the debut, although it shared the same spirit. Instead of soul, the band was rooted in folk and celtic music on their second album, *Too-Rye-Ay*, which produced the enormous international hit, "Come on Eileen." Rowland seemed lost in the wake of his success, lacking a new idea for his music; the last Dexy's album was bland and directionless, as was his solo album, 1988's *The Wanderer*. Following the album's release, Rowland entered a period of seclusion. In early 1997, he signed with Creation Records and was scheduled to deliver an album by the end of the year. *—Stephen Thomas Erlewine*

● **Searching for the Young Soul Rebels** / Jul. 1980 / EMI ✦✦✦✦✦

The crackling stations being switched on the radio and the gang shout followed by the spoken injunction to "burn it down" sound like they should be starting off a Sham 69 record. Then "Burn It Down" actually starts, with its horn section, Hammond organ and Kevin Rowland's utterly unconventional soul vocals. The cult of Dexy's, and this album in particular, were worshipped as the return of "soul" to English rock music at the dawn of Thatcherism. Exploring the myth that this album holds, especially in Brit music terms, can be a strange prospect: 20 years on it doesn't sound revolutionary, it just sounds good. And good it is, quite good, compared to where Paul Weller ended up, i.e., too reverential by half. This is vibrant, alive, and unconcerned with perfection. Rowland takes a role that Morrissey would have in 1985 and Jarvis Cocker in 1995—the unexpected but perfect voice to capture a time and moment in the U.K. His slightly strangled wail and sly, wry lyrics and song titles ("Tell Me When My Light Turns Green," "Thankfully Not Living in Yorkshire It Doesn't Apply") make this album in many ways. Musically, the group lays down R&B grooves and brassy hooks with aplomb, as on the brilliant "Seven Days Too Long" and the number one single "Geno," but throw in film noir touches, John Barry-writing-for-James Bond fare and more just as ably. The liner notes have a fun description of the group's origins and brief notes for most of the tunes—the best for the finale, "There, There, My Dear": "P.S. Old clothes do not make a tortured artist." The 2000 reissue contains a slew of extra tracks and B-sides, making it the version to find. *—Ned Raggett*

Too-Rye-Ay / Aug. 1982 / Mercury ✦✦✦✦✦
For one brief moment, Dexy's exploded into America's consciousness—and what a song to do it with! "Come on Eileen" combines ramalama rock & roll, soul delivery, and Celtic/country flavor into a perfect musical fusion and an irresistible U.K. and U.S. number one hit. Both the song and its video were such hits that years later, ska/punk band Save Ferris made a minor splash with its own version of the tune, while Garth Brooks appeared in a *Saturday Night Live* skit dressed as the capering, bedraggled Rowland. The rest of the album is nearly as successful, with quite a few numbers that should have matched "Come on Eileen"'s fame. Given that song's obvious debt to Van Morrison's similar fusions, it's no surprise that Dexy's tipped their hat with a great cover of Morrison's "Jackie Wilson Said," another big British single. Throughout the album, Rowland's distinct, unique voice takes the fore, but the revamped Dexy's lineup proves it was the original version's equal, if not better. Given that only trombonist Big Jimmy Patterson remained, and even then only for two tracks, recruiting a new band able to create the "Celtic soul" Rowland dreamed about turned out to be exactly the right move. Excellently produced by Rowland and the legendary Clive Langer/Alan Winstanley production team, *Too-Rye-Ay* sounds like an old soul revue recorded on stage, no doubt an intentional goal. Other highlights include the opening jaunt "The Celtic Soul Brothers," which just about says it all both in title and delivery; the slow swirl of "All in All"; and the vicious ballad "Liars A to E." 1996's reissue is recommended, with eight extra tracks, including some fantastic live cuts like a seven-minute "Come on Eileen," and an appreciative and thorough essay. *—Ned Raggett*

Don't Stand Me Down / Sep. 1985 / Mercury ✦✦

The Very Best of Dexy's Midnight Runners / 1991 / Mercury ✦✦✦✦

Neil Diamond

b. Jan. 24, 1941, Brooklyn, NY
Vocals, Guitar / Pop/Rock, Soft Rock, Pop, Adult Contemporary
Neil Diamond built a career, first as a pop songwriter, and then as a pop singer, that has withstood the changing fashions of music, especially rock, over more than 25 years. Diamond was writing and recording in New York in his teens, and in 1965, he signed to Bang Records as an artist while also working as a songwriter. In 1966, he reached the Top Ten with his "Cherry, Cherry," while the Monkees took his "I'm a Believer" to number one. "Cherry, Cherry" was the first of five straight Top 20 hits, among them "Girl, You'll Be a Woman Soon." Diamond began to develop into more of an individual writer in the mold of Bob Dylan and Paul Simon in the late '60s, and this led to his move to Uni Records in 1968, where he continued to score hits like "Sweet Caroline," "Holly Holy," and "Cracklin' Rosie," in a pop/rock style laced with gospel and country influences. His 1976 album, *Beautiful Noise*, was produced by Robbie Robertson of the Band; it was his first album to go platinum. In 1980, Diamond starred in a remake of the film *The Jazz Singer*. Its soundtrack was another million-seller for him. Diamond had developed into a dynamic live performer over the years, and his concert recordings were among his most successful. In the late '80s and early '90s, while updating his sound, he faded from the singles charts though his albums continued to sell consistently and his shows continued to sell out. *—William Ruhlmann*

Velvet Gloves & Spit / 1968 / MCA ✦✦✦
Most of Neil Diamond's albums are cluttered with filler, but few of his records were as flat-out strange as *Velvet Gloves & Spit*. Apart from "Two Bit Manchild," the album is comprised of lesser-known material, some of it quite good ("Modern Day Version of Love," "Honey-Drippin' Times"), and some of it just weird. The unintelligible "Knackelflerg" is one thing, but "The Pot Smoker's Song" is something else entirely. With its trippy, spoken-word testimonials about the dangers of drugs (including one addict that claims to shoot heroin into his spine) punctuated by Neil's ridiculous, sing-song chorus ("Pot, pot / Gimme some pot/ Forget who you are / You can be who you're not"), it's anti-drug pontificating at its worst, but it's a strangely fascinating artifact and helps distinguish *Velvet Gloves & Spit* from Diamond's catalog of uneven albums. *—Stephen Thomas Erlewine*

Touching You, Touching Me / 1969 / MCA ✦✦✦✦✦
Diamond's first regular album release to sell in substantial numbers, *Touching You, Touching Me* contains the gold Top Ten single "Holly Holy," and a Diamond composition, but is mostly notable for its covers of standards by other songwriters: "Everybody's Talkin'," "Mr. Bojangles," "Both Sides Now," and the chart entry "Until It's Time for You to Go." These helped signal that Diamond was thinking of himself less as a Brill Building hack than as a peer of Fred Neil, Jerry Jeff Walker, Joni Mitchell, and Buffy Sainte-Marie. *—William Ruhlmann*

Tap Root Manuscript / 1970 / MCA ✦✦✦✦✦
The follow-up to *Touching You, Touching Me* was an ambitious set of songs, all originals except for a Top 20 cover of "He Ain't Heavy... He's My Brother," including the side-long suite "The African Trilogy" (which featured the hit "Soolaimon"), the number one hit "Cracklin' Rosie" and "Done Too Soon." Going gold within two months, this album confirmed Diamond's breakthrough as a recording star. *—William Ruhlmann*

Hot August Night / 1972 / MCA ✦✦✦✦✦
This is the ultimate Neil Diamond record. Not necessarily the best—he's at his most appealing crafting in the studio—but certainly the ultimate, capturing all the kitsch and glitz of Neil Diamond, the showman. And that also means that it's not just loaded with flair, but with filler, songs like "Porcupine Pie," "Soggy Pretzels," and "And the Grass Won't Pay No Mind"—attempts to write grand, sweeping epics that collapse under their own weight. Still, that's part of the charm of Diamond and while it can sound unbearable on studio albums, it makes some sense here, surrounded by his pomp and circumstance. That spectacle is the great thing about the record, since it inflates not just his great songs, it gives the weaker moments character. And while this does wind up being a little much—21 songs, 24 on the 2000 reissue—it nevertheless is the one record for casual Neil fans, after the hits collections, since this shows Diamond the icon in full glory. *—Stephen Thomas Erlewine*

Jonathan Livingston Seagull / Oct. 1973 / Columbia ✦✦✦
Columbia Records' multi-million-dollar signing of Diamond was questioned by industry-ites who felt president Clive Davis had paid too high a price. Davis had left the company by the time this, Diamond's first Columbia album, was released in October 1973, but it was posthumous vindication. The soundtrack to a forgettable film based on a trivial best-seller, *Jonathan Livingston Seagull*, sold two million copies, spinning off the singles "Be" and "Skybird," even if, in retrospect, it is not one of Diamond's more consistent efforts. *—William Ruhlmann*

Serenade / Oct. 1974 / Columbia ✦✦

Beautiful Noise / 1976 / Columbia ✦✦✦

Love at the Greek / Jan. 1977 / Columbia ✦✦

I'm Glad You're Here with Me Tonight / Feb. 1977 / Columbia ✦✦

You Don't Bring Me Flowers / 1978 / Columbia ✦✦✦
Reprising "You Don't Bring Me Flowers" from *I'm Glad You're Here With Me Tonight*, Neil Diamond constructed his finest late-'70s record with *You Don't Bring Me Flowers*. Although the glossy production will be a little too sterile for some listeners, the shiny, radio-ready sound is appealing, and the songs—including the title track and "Forever in Blue Jeans"—are consistently entertaining, even if they are a little similar. *—Stephen Thomas Erlewine*

September Morn / 1979 / Columbia ✦✦

The Jazz Singer / 1980 / Columbia ✦✦✦✦✦
Diamond's only notable screen appearance was his starring role in this remake of the 1927 movie that was Hollywood's first real talkie and originally featured Al Jolson. Diamond wrote a new score, featuring his biggest latter-day hits, "Love on the Rocks," "Hello Again," and "America," and as a result this soundtrack album became his biggest seller ever—five million copies and counting. *—William Ruhlmann*

Heartlight / 1982 / Columbia ✦✦

12 Greatest Hits, Vol. 2 / May 1982 / Columbia ✦✦✦✦✦
Keying off the title of an earlier hits collection on another label, Columbia's *12 Greatest Hits Volume II* summed up Neil Diamond's first eight years with the label, 1973-1981, as well as his successful 1980 soundtrack for *The Jazz Singer* on Capitol Records. Five of the 12, "Longfellow Serenade," "You Don't Bring Me Flowers" (with Barbra Streisand), "Love on the Rocks," "Hello Again," and "America," were Top Ten hits. Another six, "Be," "If You Know What I Mean," "Desiree," "Forever in Blue Jeans," "September Morn," and "Yesterday's Songs," made the Top 40, and the last, "Beautiful Noise," was the title track of Diamond's best album of the period. The songs shared a catchiness that belied Diamond's shallow philosophizing and thinly veiled lust, and they made for a consistent collection out of what had been a series of uneven albums. And, since Diamond only made the Top Ten one more time, the album capped his hit-making days. This is the record to buy instead of investing in the Columbia catalog. *—William Ruhlmann*

★ **Classics: The Early Years** / 1983 / Columbia ✦✦✦✦✦
Classics: The Early Years rounds up 12 highlights from Neil Diamond's recordings for Bang Records. These, of course, were Diamond's earliest recordings and for many fans they remain among his very best work, and it's easy to see why—not only are these terrific songs, but the productions don't oversell the songs. Even when strings grace the productions, there's a dark, brooding vibe to the ballads and a crisp feeling to the pop songs. And while some of the songs won't be instantly recognizable, most of them will, because these are the tunes that made Diamond's reputation as a songwriter and performer: "Kentucky Woman," "Cherry, Cherry," "Solitary Man," "Thank the Lord for the Night Time," "I'm a Believer," "Girl, You'll Be a Woman Soon," "Shilo" and "Red, Red Wine." Diamond occasionally matched these peaks later in his career, but never again did he deliver so many great songs at such a frequency—and *Classics* conveniently collects them all in one place. *—Stephen Thomas Erlewine*

Primitive / 1984 / Columbia ✦✦

Headed for the Future / 1986 / Columbia ✦✦

Hot August Night 2 / 1987 / Columbia ✦✦

The Best Years of Our Lives / 1988 / Columbia ✦✦✦

Lovescape / Aug. 27, 1991 / Columbia ✦✦

The Greatest Hits (1966-1992) / May 19, 1992 / Columbia ✦✦✦✦
Columbia has been Diamond's label since 1973, and it acquired the rights to his Bang material of 1966-1968. But MCA still controls the recordings from 1968-1973. That's why (although you won't find out by reading the album cover) this two-disc, 37-track retrospective consists of the original versions of such hits as "Cherry, Cherry" (1966) and "You Don't Bring Me Flowers" (1978) but covers the middle period with re-recordings and live renditions of 13 of Diamond's biggest hits. As such, this collection gets only a qualified recommendation. *—William Ruhlmann*

Glory Road: 1968 to 1972 / Jun. 30, 1992 / MCA ✦✦✦✦✦
A fine two-disc retrospective of Diamond's late-'60s and early-'70s tracks, it includes some of his biggest hits—"Cracklin' Rosie," "Sweet Caroline," and "Song Sung Blue," among others. If *His Twelve Greatest Hits* doesn't offer enough material, *Glory Road* is the definitive retrospective of his years with Uni/MCA. *—AMG*

Up on the Roof: Songs from the Brill Building / Sep. 28, 1993 / Columbia ✦✦✦

Live in America / 1995 / Columbia ✦✦✦

Tennessee Moon / Feb. 1996 / Columbia ✦✦✦

In My Lifetime / Oct. 29, 1996 / Columbia ✦✦✦✦✦
In My Lifetime is a triple-disc, 71-track box set spanning Neil Diamond's entire career, from his early Bang hits, through his heyday at MCA to his latter-day adult contemporary hits for Columbia. Demos, alternate takes, and live cuts are interspersed throughout the box. Not all of Diamond's greatest songs are here—obscurities like "Two-Bit Manchild" would have been welcome—but all of the classics are present. Aside from the flimsy book-style packaging, the only real problem with the set are the rarities. While the songwriting demos from the beginning of his career are of interest to both dedicated and casual fans, latter-day demos and alternate takes are only of interest to hardcore collectors and break the rhythm of the set. Nevertheless, if anyone wants just one Neil Diamond album, *In My Lifetime* is the one to get—it has all the songs you know plus several great lesser-known gems, presented in crisp, clear sound and with an excellent biography and discography. *—Stephen Thomas Erlewine*

The Movie Album: As Time Goes By / Oct. 27, 1998 / Columbia ✦✦

★ **The Neil Diamond Collection** / Nov. 23, 1999 / MCA ✦✦✦✦✦
Not as comprehensive an anthology of Neil Diamond's eight-album, four-year affiliation with MCA as 1992's 38-track double *Glory Road, Collection* is a definitive single disc recap of one of his extensive career's most influential periods. At 17 songs, it's less than half as long as the two-disc set; oddly, the two live albums Diamond recorded during these years are ignored. Only a hot version of "Cherry, Cherry" from *Hot August Night*, at the time his most successful album and even one these liner notes tout it as "one of the strongest live albums ever recorded," is included. *Neil Diamond Gold* is completely absent, but since it primarily consisted of inferior versions of his Bang material, that's not unusual. Instead, it's a beautifully remastered, non-chronologically arranged 67 minutes of studio highlights from Diamond's most ambitious, if not his most commercially successful years. Only his version of "He Ain't Heavy, He's My Brother," the disc's lone cover, is a questionable choice, but since it charted at number 20 in 1970, its inclusion is justified. Otherwise, this non-stop, hit-filled collection shifts from one radio standard to another, easily replacing the existing and rather anemic *12 Greatest Hits* with its sound quality, depth and breadth. Dramatic, classic mini pop-operas like "Brother Love's Traveling Salvation Show," "Cracklin' Rosie," and "Holly Holy" are as much a part of the late '60s singer/songwriter rubric as work from the era's more feted artists. The thoughtfully compiled 16-page booklet includes detailed track documentation, an extensive essay, and some rare pictures of the young artist, making this the essential single-disc representation of Neil Diamond's short, yet significant, MCA tenure. *—Hal Horowitz*

The Dictators

f. 1974, **db.** 1978
Group / American Punk, New York Punk, Proto-Punk, Hard Rock
Formed in 1974, NYC's Dictators were one of the finest and most influential proto-punk bands to walk the earth. Alternately reveling in and satirizing the wanton excesses of a rock & roll lifestyle and lowbrow culture (e.g., wrestling, TV, fast food), the Dictators played loud, fast rock & roll fueled by a love of '60s American garage rock, British Invasion pop, and the sonic onslaught of the Who. Driven by the guitar barrage of Scott "Top Ten" Kempner and Ross "the Boss" Funichello and fronted by indefatigable ex-roadie and wrestler Handsome Dick Manitoba (aka Richard Blum), it seemed that nothing stood in the way of the Dictators and mega-popularity. But that's not what happened. There were complications with record companies, personnel changes, radio hated them, critical response was lukewarm, and lots of audiences didn't get the jokes; supporters remained loyal and vociferous, but it didn't turn into anything tangible. Ironically, what didn't help at all was the rise of the New York punk scene, which only diverted attention away from them and onto bands they influenced (e.g., the Ramones). They did manage to release three fine albums, but by 1978, it was over, and the Dictators broke up in the face of the public apathy and overstated accusations of sellout that greeted what was to be their final album, *Bloodbrothers*. *—John Dougan*

• **The Dictators Go Girl Crazy** / Mar. 1975 / Epic ✦✦✦✦✦
In 1976, when punk rock and heavy metal were two opposing camps who barely who acknowledged each other's existence, The Dictators' first album, *The Dictators Go Girl Crazy!*, found New York's finest trying to bring both sides together in a brave, prescient, and (at least at the time) futile gesture. The band's "smart guys who like dumb stuff" humor, junk-culture reference points, and 60's cheeze rock covers ("California Sun" AND "I Got You Babe" on one album) would seem tailor made for the crowd at *CBGB* digging The Ramones and The Dead Boys, but their sludgy and stripped down hard rock (and Ross "The Boss" Funichello's neo-metal guitar solos) were something else altogether. And at a time when the arena rock audience had not yet embraced the less-than-subtle humor and theatrics of Sparks or Cheap Trick, The Dictators ahead-of-their-time enthusiasm for wrestling, White Castle hamburgers, and television confused more kids than it converted. Heard today, the album is a hoot and a half; if the tempos could often stand to be a bit livelier, Adny Shernoff's songs are still great (especially the absurdly anthemic "Two Tub Man", "I Live For Cars and Girls", and "Weekend"), the jokes still register (while the contemporary Political Correctness brigade might blanch at "Back To Africa" or "Master Race Rock", they're merely absurd in the *Mad Magazine* tradition), and "secret weapon" Handsome Dick Manitoba was truly a find. Dozens of groups borrowed wholesale from *The Dictators Go Girl Crazy!* later on down the line, but the original is still the greatest... and the funniest. *—Mark Deming*

Manifest Destiny / 1977 / Asylum ✦✦✦
By this time, Manitoba was considered the full-time lead singer (although Shernoff and Kempner sing plenty) and the band was hitting its stride. Despite a longish dud track that closes Side One ("Disease"), *Manifest Destiny* shows off the Dictators' strong (and often tender) pop smarts, especially on Shernoff's "Sleepin' With the Television On" and Kempner's "Hey Boys." Also, there's a fast and furious cover of the Stooges' "Search & Destroy." *—John Dougan*

Bloodbrothers / 1978 / Dictators Multimedia ✦✦✦

New York, New York / Oct. 27, 1998 / ROIR ✦✦✦

Bo Diddley (Ellas Otha Bates McDaniels)

b. Dec. 30, 1928, McComb, MS
Vocals, Guitar (Electric), Violin, Guitar / Rock & Roll, R&B
He only had a few hits in the 1950s and early '60s, but as Bo Diddley sang, "You Can't Judge a Book by Its Cover." You can't judge an artist by his chart success, either, and Diddley produced greater and more influential music than all but a handful of the best early rockers. The Bo Diddley beat—bomp, ba-bomp-bomp, bomp-bomp—is one of rock & roll's bedrock rhythms, showing up in the work of Buddy Holly, the Rolling Stones, and even pop-garage knockoffs like the Strangeloves' 1965 hit "I Want Candy." Diddley's hypnotic rhythmic attack and declamatory, boasting vocals stretched back as far as Africa for their roots, and looked as far into the future as rap. His trademark otherwordly vibrating, fuzzy guitar style did much to expand the instrument's power and range. But even more important, Bo's bounce was fun and irresistibly rocking, with a wisecracking, jiving tone that epitomized rock & roll at its most humorously outlandish and freewheeling. *—Richie Unterberger*

Bo Diddley in the Spotlight / 1960 / Chess ✦✦✦✦
As with Bo Diddley's first five albums (except *Have Guitar Will Travel*), the most important cuts (but not all the good ones) off of this album have been included on *The Chess Box* from MCA, which doesn't mean that this record isn't a good separate issue, just somewhat redundant if you have the box. There are surprises from these 1960-vintage recordings, including the languid, Caribbean-sounding "Limber"; the soft, romantic "Love Me"; the doo wop-style "Deed and Deed I Do"; the loping "Walkin' and Talkin'"; upbeat, gospel-tinged rockers such as "Let Me In" interspersed with the hot and raunchy "Road Runner," "The Story of Bo Diddley," "Craw-Dad" (a genuine diamond in the rough), and "Signifying Blues"; and solid instrumentals like "Scuttle Bug" (really "Live My Life" with the vocals removed and Otis Spann overdubbed on piano) that make this record more than worthwhile. *—Bruce Eder*

Have Guitar, Will Travel / 1960 / Chess ✦✦✦✦
Amazingly, Bo Diddley's third album—containing classics such as "Cops and Robbers," "Run Diddley Daddy," and "Mona (I Need You Baby)"—has only been reissued on vinyl, and even that's out of print. More than one British Invasion band learned what they needed to know about American rock & roll from the songs on this record (the Stones cut "Cops and Robbers" at their earliest recording session, and later released a killer version of "Mona," though the most interesting British version of the latter was done by an all-girl band with an attitude called the Liverbirds). This record is every bit as raunchy as Diddley's first two albums (the guitars may even be crunchier, and the singing shows more range), and has more than enough to recommend it to collectors and fans. This is the album that began the funny cover photos on Diddley's records. *—Bruce Eder*

Bo Diddley Is a Lover / 1961 / Checker ✦✦✦✦
There's not a bad song on this long-forgotten album; in fact, it's all good, and so little of it has been reissued that it's a crime. There are a lot of familiar moments here: Diddley slips most effectively into his "Say Man" groove on "Bo's Vacation"; plays some serious Chicago blues on "Call Me (Bo's Blues)" and makes it count; invades Chuck Berry territory by way of Howlin' Wolf on the window-rattling "Hong Kong Mississippi" (a track so riveting and funny, and so rippling in superb guitar work, it makes this album worthwhile on its own); bounces back to his signature beat on the title song, the hysterically funny autobiographical "Bo Diddley Is Loose," "Quick Draw," "Back Home," and "Not Guilty" (a song that deserves enshrinement as one of Diddley's best); and slips into a romantic groove on "You're Looking Good." Find it, buy it, and savor it. *—Bruce Eder*

Bo Diddley Is a Gunslinger / 1963 / Chess ✦✦✦✦
Not only does it sport one of the most striking album covers of its era (Diddley decked out in cowboy finery, about to get the drop on some unfortunate varmint with one of his fieriest guitars lying at his feet), this 1963 album contains some fine music. The title track continues the legend of you-know-who, while "Ride on Josephine" and "Cadillac" rock like hell (and Ed Sullivan must have been glad to see that Diddley finally learned "Sixteen Tons"). Two bonus cuts, "Working Man" and "Do What I Say," make this one a must. *—Bill Dahl*

Bo Diddley's Beach Party / 1963 / Checker ✦✦✦✦✦
A blistering live album, especially in genuine mono (the re-channeled stereo is barely passable)—and quite simply the finest live rock & roll album of its era, cut live by Diddley and band at Myrtle Beach, SC, on July 5 and 6, 1963. From the opening track (erroneously listed as "Memphis" and credited to Chuck Berry as composer) to the final note, this is some of the loudest, raunchiest guitar-based rock & roll ever preserved. It also bears an uncanny resemblance to the sound that the Rolling Stones achieved on their own *Got Live If You Want It*, which only shows how much the Stones learned from Diddley. Highlights include "Gunslinger," "Hey Bo Diddley," "Road Runner," and "I'm All Right." The sound doesn't necessarily translate ideally to compact disc, but that shouldn't dissuade anyone. Currently out of print but well worth the search. *—Bruce Eder & Cub Koda*

☆ **Bo Diddley/Go Bo Diddley** / 1986 / Chess ✦✦✦✦✦
There are precious few weak tracks on this combination of Bo Diddley's first two late-'50s albums for Chess/Checker, which boasts a plethora of classics ("Bo Diddley," "I'm a Man," "Before You Accuse Me," "Crackin' Up," "Little Girl," even his electric violin workout "The Clock Struck Twelve"). The only drawback: someone failed to notice that "Dearest Darling" was on both LPs, so... it's on here twice! *—Bill Dahl*

☆ **The Chess Box** / Jul. 26, 1990 / Chess ✦✦✦✦✦
Not every single track you'll ever want or need by the legendary shave-and-a-haircut rhythm R&B/rock pioneer, but a great place to begin. Two discs (45 songs) in a great big box with a nice accompanying booklet contain the groundbreaking introduction "Bo Diddley" (never again would he be referred to as Ellas McDaniel), its swaggering flipside "I'm a Man," the killer follow-ups "Diddley Daddy," "I'm Looking for a Woman," "Who Do You Love?," and "Hey Bo Diddley;" signifying street-corner humor ("Say Man"), piledriving rockers ("Road Runner," "She's Alright," "You Can't Judge a Book by Its Cover"), and numerous stunning examples of his daringly innovative guitar style. *—Bill Dahl*

Rare & Well Done / Sep. 10, 1991 / Chess ✦✦✦✦
Sixteen extreme rarities from the deepest recesses of the Chess vaults that date from 1955-1968. The grinding "She's Fine, She's Mine" and snarling "I'm Bad" are comparatively well known, at least to collectors; far more obscure are the previously unissued "Heart-O-Matic Love," "Cookie-Headed Diddley," and "Moon Baby." *—Bill Dahl*

Bo's Blues / 1993 / Ace ✦✦✦✦✦
Twenty-two of Bo Diddley's best blues-oriented sides from the Chess catalog, including some rare stuff—the rip-roaring 1959 outing "Run Diddley Daddy," a jive-loaded "Cops and Robbers" from 1956 that features maraca shaker Jerome Green more than Diddley, and a surging "Down Home Special." If you think that everything Bo Diddley ever made has that same shave-and-a-haircut beat, this collection will set you straight! *—Bill Dahl*

★ **His Best (Chess 50th Anniversary Collection)** / Apr. 8, 1997 / Chess ✦✦✦✦✦
With his various hits and anthology packages all out of print and the multi-disc deluxe box set out of pocketbook reach for most casual consumers, MCA finally comes up with a 20-track compilation that hits the bullseye and makes this rock pioneer's best and most influential work available to everyone. The song list reads like a primer for '60s British rhythm & blues and '90s blues bands: "Bo Diddley," "I'm a Man," "Diddley Daddy," "Pretty Thing," "Before You Accuse Me," "Hey! Bo Diddley," "Who Do You Love," "Mona" and "Roadrunner" are the tracks that made the legend and put his sound on the map worldwide. The transfers used on this set are exemplary, the majority of them utilizing masters that have a few extra seconds (or more) appended to the fades, which will cause even hardliners to hear these old standards with fresh ears; especially revelatory are the "long versions" of "I Can Tell" and "You Can't Judge a Book By Its Cover." If the box set is too big a trigger to pull and you want all of Bo's influential sides in one package, this one should be first-stop shopping of the highest priority. *—Cub Koda*

Ani DiFranco

b. Sep. 23, 1970
Vocals, Guitar / Alternative Folk, Indie Rock, Alternative Pop/Rock, Singer/Songwriter, Urban Folk
A folkie in punk's clothing, Ani DiFranco battled successfully against the Goliath of corporate rock to emerge as one of the most influential and inspirational cult heroines of the 1990s. A resolute follower of D.I.Y. ethos, DiFranco released her records through her own indie label, slowly but steadily building a devout grass-roots following on the strength of a relentless tour schedule; an ardent feminist and an open bisexual, her songs tackled issues like rape, abortion and sexism with insight and compassion, the music's empowering attitude and anger tempered by the poignant candor of singer-songwriter confessionalism. By the age of 19 DiFranco had written over 100 original songs, later relocating to New York City to further her musical aspirations. After recording a demo tape for sale at her shows, she founded Righteous Babe in 1990 to better distribute her recordings. As albums like 1992's *Imperfectly* and 1993's *Puddle Dive* expanded her musical ambitions as well as her following, DiFranco became the subject of considerable major-label interest, yet she steadfastly rejected all offers. She exploded with 1995's *Not a Pretty Girl,* which garnered notice from outlets ranging from CNN to the *New York Times. Dilate* even debuted in the Top 100 album charts upon released in 1996, and 1998's *Little Plastic Castle* became her highest-charting album to date, setting the stage for the release of *Up Up Up Up Up Up* the following year. *—Jason Ankeny*

Ani DiFranco / 1989 / Righteous Babe ✦✦✦✦
"I am a work in progress," appropriately announces Ani DiFranco on her debut album. Though her lyrics have the rambling style of free-form poetry and she sounds like she learned her spare, percussive style of guitar playing by listening to Suzanne Vega albums, she defines a distinct persona, that of a self-possessed, assertive woman in a tough, urban landscape who feels the need to lash out first (usually in reference to heterosexual romantic relationships) and then turn vulnerable. She justifies her chip-on-the-shoulder attitude with some telling observations and turns of phrase, even if individual lines are sometimes better than whole songs, and puts the songs across with her elastic phrasing and sheer conviction even when they're not really about much of anything. When she has a real subject, however, notably on the album's best composition, "Lost Woman Song," which concerns abortion, it all comes together and she displays a writing and performing talent that is as thrilling as it is affecting. *—William Ruhlmann*

Not So Soft / 1991 / Righteous Babe ✦✦✦

Imperfectly / 1992 / Righteous Babe ✦✦✦✦
Ani DiFranco continued to expand her musical palette gradually on her third album, using outside musicians on some tracks to support her acoustic guitar with bass and drums, and adding individual instruments—trumpet, viola—for color on certain tunes. But the focus was still on the evolving persona depicted in her lyrics, one who continued to flirt with lesbianism consciously on "In or Out" and "If It Isn't Her," and, perhaps unconsciously, in the what-does-she-see-in-him sentiment of "Fixing Her Hair." The larger theme of the album, also suggested in "In or Out," was the artist's inability to "fit in," either because of her sexuality, her politics, or, most tellingly, her occupation as an itinerant musician. In "Every State Line," she reflected on the difficulties of shoestring travel, and in "Good, Bad, Ugly" and "The Waiting Song," the difficulties of long-distance relationships shaped both the songwriter's anger and her self-doubt. She had not tended to question herself before this, but from its title, *Imperfectly,* on, DiFranco deconstructed her persona, asking, "What If No One's Watching" in one song and declaring, "I'm No Heroine" in another. At the same time, she upped the ante of her sexual politics, expanding from criticizing individual men to berating a culture she saw as dominated by male views in everything from the music business to architecture ("Who says I like right angles?"). But if *Imperfectly* presented the singer at her most doctrinaire, it also displayed surprising warmth for individuals, notably the uncharacteristically forgiving "Served Faithfully." *Imperfectly* was the work of a still-growing, still passionate, sometimes confused artist whose personal story in song was proving to be fascinating. *—William Ruhlmann*

Puddle Dive / 1993 / Righteous Babe ✦✦✦

Like I Said: Songs 1990-91 / Jul. 26, 1994 / Righteous Babe ✦✦✦

Out of Range / Jul. 26, 1994 / Righteous Babe ✦✦✦✦

Not a Pretty Girl / Jul. 18, 1995 / Righteous Babe ✦✦✦
On her relatively spare sixth album (which features only one other musician, percussionist/vocalist Andy Stochansky, and, on one song, singer Kate Fenner), Ani DiFranco takes on a few expected topics, such as abortion ("Tiptoe"), capital punishment ("Crime for Crime"), and why she isn't on a major label ("The Million You Never Made"). But much of the disc is given over to introspective ruminations on personal life and love. As usual, the singer is not shy (despite a song of that title) about offering criticism of the person or persons she's addressing, but she is also self-critical and even, on "Sorry I Am," apologetic. The songs do not add up to the complete story of a relationship, but there are some deeply felt portraits here, especially "Light of Some Kind" in which the singer seems to be confessing to a man that she has been unfaithful to him with a woman. As usual, the imagery is urban and gritty; DiFranco is the kind of writer who likes to tell us that she's got last night's underwear in her back pocket as she rides home on the subway on the afternoon following an assignation. But the sometimes messy details are in the service of her view of reality, an unflinching one in which everything can faced, even the songwriter's emotional torment. *—William Ruhlmann*

Dilate / May 21, 1996 / Righteous Babe ✦✦✦✦

Living in Clip / Apr. 22, 1997 / Righteous Babe ✦✦✦✦✦
For all of their cult popularity, Ani DiFranco's studio albums were frequently hampered by mannered performances, which is precisely what her live shows were not. In concert, DiFranco plays her songs with infectious energy, frequently twisting the melody lines and digressing into rambling, entertaining stories and jokes. That side of Ani DiFranco is finally captured in the double-disc live album, *Living in Clip.* Supported by bassist Sara Lee and drummer Andy Stochansky, she runs through 32 songs, including the previously unreleased "Gravel," plus all of her best-known songs, occasionally spinning off stories and humorous anecdotes and illustrating exactly why a rabid cult following developed around her appealingly edgy persona and songs. *—Thom Owens*

Little Plastic Castle / Feb. 17, 1998 / Righteous Babe ✦✦✦✦
Little Plastic Castle posed an unusual challenge for Ani DiFranco. She released this record after spending a year promoting her first live CD (*Living In Clip*) by repeatedly admitting to reporters that her studio albums lack the vitality of her concert performances. Rock critics agreed en masse, and their praise for the live album helped to propel DiFranco to a new level of mainstream stardom—but it also heightened the scrutiny on her next studio recording. Fortunately, she managed to dodge several of the pitfalls ofher previous albums. Her excellent band had plenty of time to jell on the road, and their performances here are as tight, driven and intense as they've ever been. Vocally, DiFranco is somewhat less affected than on previous albums, where the unnatural isolation of the studio sometimes led her to unnatural mannerisms. Her songwriting, however, is not quite up to par. While her melodies have almost never been exactly catchy, they have usually been perfect vessels for her terrifically smart lyrics. This time, the lyrical tail seems to be wagging the melodic dog willy-nilly. That's especially damaging when her songs are wallowing too comfortably in angst ("Independence Day," "Glass House"). Nonetheless, this is the most creatively produced Ani DiFranco album to date, combining her distinctively frenetic acoustic fingerstyle with computer samples, dance rhythms, mariachi brass and full-band rock jams. The result is colorful—almost cartoony—but almost never overshadows the emotional content. When Jon Hassel contributes a gorgeous jazz trumpet solo on the album's final track (the fourteen-minute "Pulse"), it blends in so perfectly that one has to remind oneself that DiFranco is one of the biggest talents in *folk* music. *—Darryl Cater*

Up Up Up Up Up Up / Jan. 19, 1999 / Righteous Babe ✦✦✦

To the Teeth / Nov. 16, 1999 / Righteous Babe ✦✦✦
With the release of *To the Teeth,* it has been ten studio albums of original material in ten years for Ani DiFranco, and she sounds tired. The singer/songwriter has always had ample reserves of anger and criticism, some of which she has directed at herself, but here her self-questioning is unusually intense. As usual, a couple of songs deal with political topics, but much of the album is given over to songs in which the singer looks at her life and career unhappily. "Going Once" and "Swing" are in the third person, though the characters seem self-identified, with the "she" in the former wondering "how did I get here/Without even knowing where I was going?," while in the latter "she" speaks of weariness, dread, and nagging voices inside her head that say "You suck." "Freakshow," a metaphor for the performer's life, is almost unrelentingly critical, its only relief coming from the comfort that the life of a traveling entertainer is better than being stuck in a hometown. The culmination of all this comes with "Wish I May," which she closes by singing, "I don't think I am strong enough/To do this much longer." She also says she wishes the song were longer, and that wish may have been expressed in the album's musical arrangements. Employing horns (including Maceo Parker's saxophone) and other embellishments, DiFranco has written a series of downbeat riff tunes and stretched them out, in some cases to six or seven minutes, often with extended instrumental codas after the lyrics have been sung. As usual, she gives her audience a warts-and-all portrait of her current view of herself and the world. Longtime fans will find the result compelling (while perhaps fearing for their favorite's future), but this is probably not the place to start your Ani DiFranco collection. *—William Ruhlmann*

Dinosaur Jr.

f. 1983, Amherst, MA
Group / Indie Rock, Alternative Pop/Rock
Dinosaur Jr. was largely responsible for returning lead guitar to indie-rock and, along with their peers the Pixies, they injected late-'80s alternative rock with monumental levels of pure guitar noise. As the group's career progressed, it turned into a vehicle for J. Mascis' songwriting and playing, which had the ultimate result of turning Dinosaur's albums into largely

similar affairs. Over time, Mascis shed his hardcore punk roots and revealed himself to be a disciple of Neil Young, crafting simple songs that were delivered at a crushing volume and spiked with shards of feedback. Consequently, Dinosaur Jr.'s '90s albums—when the group was essentially a front for Mascis—don't sound particularly revolutionary, even with their subtle sonic innovations, yet their original '80s records for SST were a different matter. On their early records, Dinosaur lurched forward, taking weird detours into free-form noise and melodic soloing before the songs are brought back into relief by Mascis' laconic whine. Dinosaur's SST Records laid the foundation for alternative rock's commercial breakthrough in the early '90s, and while the band's profile was raised substantially in the wake of Nirvana's success, they never really became much bigger than highly respected cult figures. *—Stephen Thomas Erlewine*

Dinosaur / 1985 / Homestead ♦♦♦

★ **You're Living All Over Me** / 1987 / SST ♦♦♦♦♦
A blitzkrieg fusion of hardcore punk, Sonic Youth-style noise freak-outs, heavy metal and melodic hard rock in the vein of Neil Young, *You're Living All Over Me* was a turning point in American underground rock & roll. With its thin, unbalanced mix, the album sounds positively menacing and edgy—Lou Barlow's bass barrels forward over Murph's clanking drums, with J. Mascis guitar twisting pummeling riffs and careening, occasionally atonal solos. It established guitar heroics as a part of indie-rock, bringing the noise of Sonic Youth into more conventional song structures. Also, Mascis' laconic, self-absorbed whine was a distinct departure from the furious post-hardcore rants or the mumbling Michael Stipe imitations that dominated indie-rock. While the songwriting is occasionally uneven, the best moments of *You're Living All Over Me*—"Little Fury Things," "Raisans," "In a Jar" and Barlow's proto-Sebadoh "Poledo"—retain their power, and it's possible to hear the record's influence throughout alternative rock. *—Stephen Thomas Erlewine*

Bug / 1988 / SST ♦♦♦♦♦
Relatively cleaner-produced and more accessible than *You're Living All Over Me, Bug* expanded on the strengths of its predecessor and established Dinosaur Jr. as a major band in the American underground. Although the majority of the album is firmly situated in the sprawling, noisy metallic fusion of hard rock and avant-noise, *Bug* also demonstrates that J. Mascis has a talent for winding folk-rock, particularly on "The Post" and "Pond Song." Like its predecessor, the songs on *Bug* are quite uneven, but it does represent a major step forward for Mascis, particularly on the masterpiece of the record, "Freak Scene," a surprisingly catchy song encapsulating the appeal and pitfalls of indie-rock within three minutes. *—Stephen Thomas Erlewine*

Green Mind / Feb. 1991 / Blanco y Negro/Sire ♦♦♦♦♦
Many consider *Green Mind* to be a weak, uninspired effort, but Dinosaur Jr.'s major-label debut is a strong, varied album, featuring some of J. Mascis' best songwriting, as well as some of his best, most fluid guitar work. Essentially a solo effort by Mascis (Murph only appears on three tracks), *Green Mind* finds him stretching and expanding his traditional sonic assault with more acoustic guitars and tighter melodies. With its gentle Mellotron and lovely, sighing melody, "Thumb" stands as one of Mascis' finest songs; "Muck" is a surprisingly enjoyable stab at funk, "How'd You Pin That One on Me" is a great guitar workout, "Puke & Cry" and "I Live for That Look" are impressive folk-punk, and "The Wagon" rivals "Freak Scene" in its depiction of the underground scene. *—Stephen Thomas Erlewine*

Fossils / Aug. 1991 / SST ♦♦♦♦
A brief, eight-song compilation of the group's SST singles, *Fossils* effectively sums up the power and vision of Dinosaur Jr.'s early work. Not only does it contain the two masterpieces from *You're Living All Over Me* and *Bug*—"Little Fury Things" and "Freak Scene," respectively—but it also gathers several excellent B-sides, including sardonic covers of Peter Frampton's "Show Me the Way" and the Cure's "Just Like Heaven," making it an excellent retrospective of Dinosaur's influential and erratic indie recordings. *—Stephen Thomas Erlewine*

Whatever's Cool with Me / Oct. 22, 1991 / Blanco y Negro/Sire ♦♦♦♦

Where You Been / Feb. 9, 1993 / Blanco y Negro/Sire ♦♦♦♦
By the time *Where You Been* surfaced, Seattle had completely exploded, and given that Dinosaur Jr.'s sound, attitude and more were as proto-slacker as could be, the temptation must have been great to cash in. But Mascis stuck to his guns, and there's little about *Where You Been* that would have seemed out of place on *Green Mind* or even some earlier records. Recorded with a full band throughout, Johnson and Murph lay down does-the-job rhythm tracks while Mascis tackles almost everything else, *Where You Been* is occasionally moody and dark but otherwise is more rough fun. Opening track "Out There" is one of the mournful most things Mascis has recorded, with an especially yearning chorus, but his fiery solo still makes it classic Dinosaur Jr. "Start Choppin" immediately follows, its quick, catchy lead riff helping to make it as close to a radio hit as the band ever had—and, of course, a big ol' solo or two adding to the fun of it all. From there on in it's a pureed blast of punk, classic rock and more. It may business as usual, but it's good business just the same, whether it's the gentle "Not the Same," on which Mascis does his best Neil Young impersonation, or the stuttering feedback snorts and rips on "Hide," on which he borrows a bit back from disciple Kevin Shields. Other highlights include "Get Me," a melancholic, steady cruncher with another trademark solo of the gods, and the unjustly ignored "What Else is New," which sounds like a mid-seventies rock ballad with louder volume and none of the crud, right down to the concluding string section. *—Ned Raggett*

Without a Sound / Aug. 23, 1994 / Blanco y Negro/Sire ♦♦

Hand It Over / Mar. 25, 1997 / Blanco y Negro/Sire ♦♦♦♦
Bouncing back from the staid *Without a Sound,* J. Mascis turns in his most eclectic album since *Green Mind* with Dinosaur Jr.'s *Hand It Over.* Dinosaur's bedrock sound hasn't changed—it's still a sprawling, electric mess of hard rock filtered through folk-rock song structures—but Mascis plays with the arrangements, adding strings, trumpets and, on a handful of tracks, My Bloody Valentine's slippery guitar orchestrations and vocals (Kevin Shields and Blinda Butcher both sing on the album). These additions make the music sound fresh, but they would only be window-dressing if Mascis' songs weren't as strong as they are. Again, his progressions are subtle, but songs like "I Don't Think," "Nothin's Goin' On," "Can't We Move This" and "Sure Not Over You" are fine additions to his catalog, and help make *Hand It Over* one of Dinosaur Jr.'s most consistent and best records. *—Stephen Thomas Erlewine*

Dion

b. Jul. 18, 1937, New York, NY [The Bronx]
Vocals / Teen Idol, Folk-Rock, Doo Wop, Rock & Roll
Bridging the era between late-'50s rock and the British Invasion, Dion DiMucci was one of the top White rock singers of his time, blending the best elements of doo wop, teen idol, and R&B styles. Some revisionists have tried to cast him as a sort of early blue-eyed soul figure, although he was probably more aligned with pop-rock, at first as the lead singer of the Belmonts, and then as a solo star. Formed by a group of friends that sang on Bronx street corners, Dion and the Belmonts recorded a few hits including "I Wonder Why" and "A Teenager in Love," the latter pointing the way for the slightly self-pitying, pained odes to adolescence and early adulthood that would characterize much of his solo work. Dion finally made the move in 1960, handling himself with a suave, cocky ease on hits like "The Wanderer" and "Runaround Sue." After battling heroin for several years, he re-emerged in 1968 as a gentle folk-rocker with a number four hit single, "Abraham, Martin and John." He continued recording for the LP market during the '70s, reunited with the Belmonts in 1972, and cut a disappointing record with Phil Spector as producer. He's been recording and performing fairly often over the last two decades, sometimes singing Christian music. *—Richie Unterberger*

Lovers Who Wander / 1962 / The Right Stuff ♦♦♦♦
A better-than-average early-'60s effort. Besides the oft-anthologized singles "Lovers Who Wander," "Little Diane," "Sandy," and "(I Was) Born to Cry," it has some hot covers ("The Twist," "Stagger Lee," and "Shout") that Dion makes his own. The haunting "Lost for Sure," which Dion co-wrote, is one of his best obscure Laurie-era tracks. *—Richie Unterberger*

Dion / 1968 / The Right Stuff ♦♦♦♦♦
Featuring his Top Five comeback single "Abraham, Martin and John," athis folk-rock and blues-flavored effort remains his most fully realized album. In addition to the impressive anti-war original "He Looks a Lot Like Me," it contains mature interpretations, arranged both acoustically and with strings, of songs by Fred Neil, Joni Mitchell, Leonard Cohen, Bob Dylan, and Lightnin' Hopkins (though the florid version of Jimi Hendrix's "Purple Haze" is embarrassing). The CD reissue adds the highly sought-after non-LP B-side "Daddy Rollin'," a Dion original that ranks as his most country-blues-influenced performance. *—Richie Unterberger*

★ **24 Golden Greats** / 1983 / Arista ♦♦♦♦♦
24 Golden Greats contains all of Dion & the Belmonts' biggest hits, plus all of Dion's solo hits from the late '60s and early '70s, making it the definitive compilation of the vocalist's long, successful career. *—Stephen Thomas Erlewine*

Bronx Blues: The Columbia Recordings / Feb. 2, 1991 / Columbia ♦♦♦♦♦
After many hit singles with the Belmonts, Dion went solo and became one of the first rock & roll stars signed to the Columbia label. Although he was only with the label for four years, Dion recorded some of his most adventurous music during this period. *Bronx Blues* chronicles this phase in his career, and is the best single-disc compilation of his mid-'60s work. The first singles released were similar in style to the Belmont's recordings ("Donna the Prima Donna") and demonstrated his continued love for doo wop as he covers older songs such as the Drifters' "Ruby Baby," which peaked at number two. While the first half of this album is strong, the second half is truly revelatory; it shows Dion, who had just been exposed to the music of Robert Johnson, infusing the bravado of his streetwise persona into the blues. The results don't always work (he doesn't have the deep, powerful voice required to sing Willie Dixon's "Spoonful"), but the results are magic when he hits the mark. The best example is his own "Two Ton Feather," a song that's not pure blues, but blues interpreted by a newly converted fan of the genre. In that respect, it's not surprising that his style is similar to Bob Dylan's. In fact, the highlight of the album, and perhaps Dion's best recording ever, is his previously unreleased version of Dylan's "Baby, I'm in the Mood for You" in which he brings out all the snarl and attitude of the tune. While these years are often considered a transition period for Dion, this compilation is essential in showcasing his songwriting talents and restless spirit. *—Vik Iyengar*

The Road I'm On: A Retrospective / Feb. 18, 1997 / Columbia/Legacy ♦♦♦♦♦
Dion's mid-'60s Columbia period was a strange and rather mysterious one. After notching up some solid hits that were more or less in his early '60s rock style ("Ruby Baby," "Donna the Prima Donna"), he dove into blues, folk, and folk-rock with varying degrees of success. Although the results were usually pretty interesting, commercially he seemed to have disappeared (a situation not helped by either his heroin problems or the failure of some of the material to get released). This is a good, if imperfect, two-CD overview of the Columbia years, moving from the expected early hits to quite a few tasty surprises, including covers of Woody Guthrie, Chuck Berry, Willie Dixon, "Work Song" (penned by Nat Adderley and Oscar Brown), Tom Paxton, and Bob Dylan's "It's All Over Now, Baby Blue." There are also a number of pretty fair self-penned originals in a folk-rock, slightly Dylanish style, unsurprising considering that Dion was recording with one-time Dylan producer Tom Wilson in late '65. It doesn't make a 100% convincing argument that Dion would have matured into a top-rank blues-folk-rocker if not for his drug problems, but it has integrity, and the material is usually well-sung, whether pop or not. About half a dozen of the tracks were previously unreleased; there are also a couple of new recordings from 1996. This does not, by the way, make the 1991 *Bronx Blues* CD (much of it drawn from the same era) redundant. Almost half of the tracks from that disc don't appear, the most serious omission being the cover of Dylan's "Baby, I'm in the Mood for You," which was probably Dion's best mid-'60s recording of all. *—Richie Unterberger*

Deja Nu / Jul. 25, 2000 / Ace ✦✦✦✦✦

- **King of the New York Streets** / Dec. 5, 2000 / Capitol ✦✦✦✦✦

Although Dion's career wasn't over when *King of the New York Streets* appeared, this three-CD package is likely to be the most thorough overview of his output to be heard in one place. "Most thorough" is not synonymous with "best music of his career," however, and while this box contains much of major significance, it really does slide downhill after the early '70s. That point is reached around the middle of the second disc, so that leaves about half of this material as average, or duller than average, stuff. In its favor, the box set has all the familiar hits from the salad days, from the Belmonts' "I Wonder Why" through "Abraham, Martin and John," as well as a number of fine cuts that are largely known only to collectors. Those include his hard-rocking 1965 cover of the obscure Bob Dylan song "Baby, I'm in the Mood for You"; the folk-rock version of Tom Paxton's "I Can't Help but Wonder Where I'm Bound" from the same era; the little-heard 1966 ABC single "My Girl the Month of May" (with the Belmonts); the bluesy B-side "Daddy Rollin'"; and the anti-drug "Your Own Backyard." The post-early-'70s tracks do have their high points, like "(I Used to Be a) Brooklyn Dodger," but they're just not remotely on the same level as what precedes them. Anyone wanting to focus on Dion's best music can get more of it, in more concentrated doses and for about the same amount of money, by purchasing several other less extensive compilations that target a specific period of his work. *—Richie Unterberger*

Complete Dion & The Belmonts / Collectors' Choice Music ✦✦✦✦✦

Celine Dion

b. Mar. 30, 1968, Charlemagne, Quebec, Canada
Vocals / Adult Contemporary

Rising from humble beginnings in the small town of Charlemagne, Quebec, Celine Dion became one of the biggest international stars in pop music history, selling more than 100 million albums worldwide. The youngest in a family of 14 children, her parents and siblings were important figures in the early development of her singing career. By the age of 12 she had written one of her first songs, "Ce N'etait Qu'un Rêve" ("It Was Only a Dream"), which she recorded with the help of her mother and brother and shipped off to a manager named Rene Angelil, who mortgaged his house to pay for her first two albums and became a driving force in the career that would make her an international star.

1990's *Unison* was her breakthrough album, but it was her duet with Peabo Bryson on the theme song of Disney's *Beauty and the Beast* that was her true breakthrough. The song reached number one on the pop charts and won both a Grammy and an Academy award. It was also featured on her second English album, 1992's *Celine Dion,*

During this time there were also important developments in Dion's personal life. In 1988 Angelil crossed the line from manager to romantic partner when he kissed Dion one night after a show in Dublin. Fearful that fans would find the 26-year difference in their ages unsettling, the couple kept their relationship a secret for several years, eventually marrying in 1994.

Dion recorded six albums between 1992 and 1996, when *Falling Into You* took her to a new level of stardom. Dion's longest tenure on the pop charts would come the following year, however, when she recorded "My Heart Will Go On," the theme song for James Cameron's blockbuster movie *Titanic.*

The continuing popularity of her recordings and live performances made her 1999 sabbatical seem like a tragedy to her fans, but Dion needed a break after more than a decade and a half of breakneck pace. After undergoing fertility treatments, she announced her pregnancy in June, 2000, declaring "There is no hiding happiness... the dream dearest to our hearts has come true." *—Stacia Proefrock*

Unison / Aug. 21, 1990 / Epic ✦✦✦

Celine Dion / Mar. 31, 1992 / Epic ✦✦✦✦

The Colour of My Love / Nov. 9, 1993 / 550 Music/Epic ✦✦✦

Falling into You / Mar. 12, 1996 / 550 Music/Epic ✦✦✦✦

Celine Dion's *Falling into You* returned the Canadian vocalist to the top of the American charts, and for good reason. Although the album is formulaic, it is a well-executed, stylish, and catchy formula, accentuating her natural vocal charm. Dion shines on ballads like "Because You Love Me" and mock-epics like Jim Steinman's "It's All Coming Back to Me Now." Between those two peaks, she tackles dance-pop and love songs with grace; that effortless elegance saves the mediocre material on the album from being tedious. Though there are a couple of weak tracks, *Falling Into You* a remarkably well-crafted set of adult contemporary pop and Dion's best album. *—Stephen Thomas Erlewine*

Let's Talk About Love / Nov. 18, 1997 / 550 Music ✦✦✦✦

Falling Into You finally established Celine Dion as a superstar in America, so its sequel, *Let's Talk About Love,* was designed to consolidate her position as a newly-minted star. The album was constructed as a blockbuster, featuring Dion's trademark melodramatic ballads, some carefully-tailored dance-pop, a bevy of duets with the likes of Barbra Streisand and the Bee Gees and production and songs from adult contemporary gurus David Foster, Jim Steinman and Walter Afanasieff. Given that so many talented craftsmen worked on *Let's Talk About Love,* it makes sense that a number of the cuts succeed according to adult contemporary terms—they are predictably sweeping showcases for Dion's soaring, technically skilled voice. As usual, the singles (including the Streisand duet "Tell Him" and the *Titanic* love theme "My Heart Will Go On") shine the most brilliantly, but even the filler is immaculately produced. If the end result doesn't quite gel as an album, that shouldn't be surprising—this is music by committee, a product that was made to appeal to the widest possible audience. Such a calculated execution guarantees that anyone that liked one of the singles shouldn't be disappointed by *Let's Talk About,* but it doesn't necessarily mean they'll remember all of the record after it's finished playing. *—Stephen Thomas Erlewine*

- **All the Way: A Decade of Song** / Nov. 16, 1999 / 550 Music ✦✦✦✦

There aren't a lot of greatest-hits albums with seven new songs, which is exactly what *All the Way: A Decade of Song* is. There are just nine hits on this hits collection, and of those, only a handful—"If You Asked Me To," "Beauty and the Beast," "The Power of Love," "Because You Loved Me," "It's All Coming Back to Me Now," and "My Heart Will Go On"—were huge hits in the U.S. Her first American hit, "Where Does My Heart Beat Now," isn't here, nor is her duet with Barbra Streisand, "Tell Him." Naturally, this means it's not a definitive collection, but rather an unsatisfying album that feels suspiciously like a piece of product. The best of the hits, like the Meat Loaf-ian epic "It's All Coming Back to Me Now" and "My Heart will Go On," are certainly among the best adult contemporary songs of the decade, and the new stuff would pale in comparison, even if it was very good—which, by and large, it is not. Two numbers, the danceable "That's the Way it Is" and the pretty ballad "If Walls Could Talk," work, but the cover of "The First Time Ever I Saw Your Face" falls flat and "All the Way," complete with old vocals from Sinatra, is a disaster. The remaining three aren't bad, but they're not particularly memorable, especially compared to the hits. And that's the problem with *All the Way*—if it had been a straight hits collection, with "That's the Way it Is" and "If Walls Could Talk" added to the end, it would have been fine, but padding it with nearly a full album worth of new material hurts it. *—Stephen Thomas Erlewine*

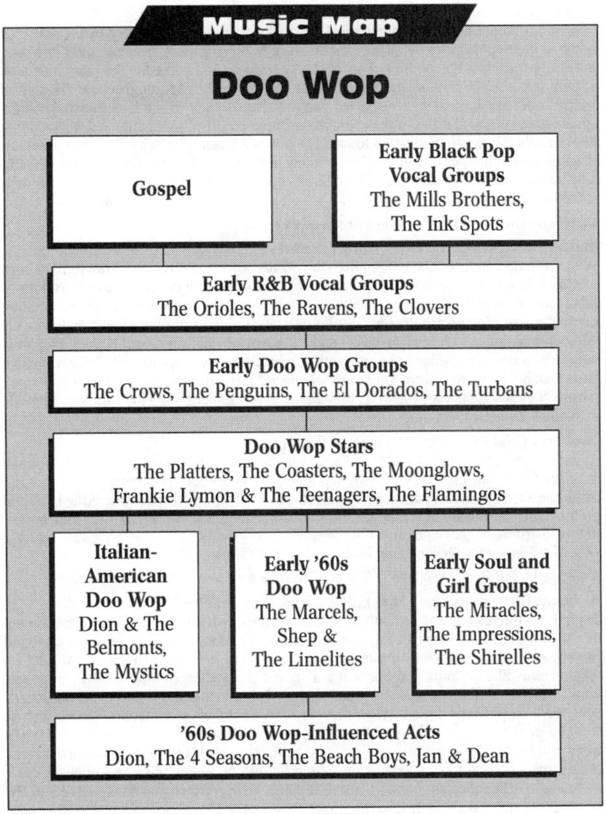

The Collector's Series, Vol. 1 / Oct. 24, 2000 / 550 Music ✦✦

Dire Straits

f. 1977, London, England, **db.** 1995
Group / Album Rock, Pop/Rock

Dire Straits emerged during the post-punk era of the late '70s, and while their sound was minimalistic and stripped-down, they owed little to punk. If anything, the band was a direct outgrowth of the roots-revivalism of pub rock, but where pub rock celebrated good times, Dire Straits were melancholy. Led by guitarist/vocalist Mark Knopfler, the group built their sound upon the laid-back blues-rock of J.J. Cale, but they also had jazz and country inflections, occasionally dipping into the epic song structures of progressive rock. The band's music was offset by Knopfler's lyrics, which approximated the winding, stream-of-conscious narratives of Bob Dylan. As their career progressed, Dire Straits became more refined and their new maturity happened to coincide with the rise of MTV and the compact disc. These two musical revolutions from the mid-'80s helped make Dire Straits' sixth album, *Brothers in Arms,* an international blockbuster. The band—along with Eric Clapton, Phil Collins, and Steve Winwood—become one of the leaders of a group of self-consciously mature veteran rock & rollers in the late '80s that designed their music to appeal to aging baby boomers. Despite the band's international success, they couldn't sustain their stardom, waiting a full six years to deliver a followup to *Brothers in Arms,* by which time their audience had shrunk significantly. *—Stephen Thomas Erlewine*

Dire Straits / Oct. 1978 / Warner Brothers ✦✦✦✦
Dire Straits' minimalistic interpretation of pub-rock had already crystallized by the time they released their eponymous debut. Driven by Mark Knopfler's spare, tasteful guitar lines and his husky warbling, the album is a set of bluesy rockers. And while the bar-band mentality of pub-rock is at the core of Dire Straits—even the group's breakthrough single, "Sultans of Swing," offered a lament for a neglected pub-rock band—their music is already beyond the simple boogies and shuffles of their forefathers, occasionally dipping into jazz and country. Knopfler also shows an inclination toward Dylanesque imagery, which enhances the smoky, low-key atmosphere of the album. While a few of the songs fall flat, the album is remarkably accomplished for a debut, and Dire Straits had difficulty surpassing it throughout their career. *—Stephen Thomas Erlewine*

Communiqué / Jun. 1979 / Warner Brothers ✦✦✦

Making Movies / Oct. 17, 1980 / Warner Brothers ✦✦✦✦✦
Without second guitarist David Knopfler, Dire Straits began to move away from its roots-rock origins into a jazzier variation of country-rock and singer-songwriter folk-rock. Naturally, this means that Mark Knopfler's ambitions as a songwriter are growing, as the storytelling pretensions of *Making Movies* indicate. Fortunately, his skills are increasing, as the lovely "Romeo and Juliet," "Tunnel of Love" and "Skateaway" indicate. And *Making Movies* is helped by a new wave-tinged pop production, which actually helps Knopfler's jazzy inclinations take hold. The record runs out of steam toward the end, closing with the borderline offensive "Les Boys," but the remainder of *Making Movies* ranks among the band's finest work. *—Stephen Thomas Erlewine*

Love over Gold / Sep. 1982 / Warner Brothers ✦✦✦✦
Adding a new rhythm guitarist, Dire Straits expands its sounds and ambitions on the sprawling *Love Over Gold.* In a sense, the album is their prog-rock effort, containing only five songs, including the 14-minute opener "Telegraph Road." Since Mark Knopfler is a skilled, tasteful guitarist, he can sustain interest even throughout the languid stretches, but the long atmospheric instrumental passages aren't as effective as the group's tight blues-rock, leaving *Love Over Gold* only a fitfully engaging listen. *—Stephen Thomas Erlewine*

Twisting by the Pool / Feb. 1983 / Warner Brothers ✦✦✦

Alchemy: Dire Straits Live / Mar. 1984 / Warner Brothers ✦✦✦
There is an interesting contrast on this 94-minute double-disc live album (recorded at London's Hammersmith Odeon in July 1983) between the music, much of which is slow and moody, with Mark Knopfler's muttered vocals and large helpings of his fingerpicking on what sounds like an amplified Spanish guitar, and the audience response. The arena-size crowd cheers wildly and claps and sings along, when given half a chance, as though each song were an uptempo rocker. When they do have a song of even medium speed, such as "Sultans of Swing" or "Solid Rock," they are in ecstasy. That Dire Straits' introspective music loses much of its detail in a live setting matters less than that it gains presence and a sense of anticipation. Alan Clark's keyboards help to fill out the sound and give Knopfler's spare melodies a certain majesty, but Dire Straits remains an overgrown pub band with a Bob Dylan fixation, and that's exactly how the crowd likes it. (The CD version of the album contains one extra track, "Expresso Love," which adds a needed change of pace to the otherwise slow-moving first disc.) *—William Ruhlmann*

Brothers in Arms / May 1985 / Warner Brothers ✦✦✦✦
Brothers in Arms brought the atmospheric, jazz-rock inclinations of *Love Over Gold* into a pop setting, resulting in a surprise international best-seller. Of course, the success of *Brothers in Arms* was helped considerably by the clever computer-animated video for "Money for Nothing," and a sardonic atttack on MTV. But what kept the record selling was Knopfler's increased sense of pop songcraft—"Money for Nothing" had an indelible guitar riff, "Walk of Life" is a catchy uptempo boogie variation on "Sultans of Swing," and the melodies of the bluesy "So Far Away" and downtempo Everly Brothers-style "Why Worry" were wistful and lovely. Dire Straits had never been so concise or pop-oriented, and it wore well on them. Though they couldn't maintain that consistency through the rest of the album—only the jazzy "Your Latest Trick" and the flinty "Ride Across the River" make an impact—*Brothers in Arms* remains one of their most focused and accomplished albums and, in its succinct pop sense, it is distinctive within their catalog. *—Stephen Thomas Erlewine*

Money for Nothing / Oct. 1988 / Warner Brothers ✦✦✦✦
Released in late 1988, as everyone was waiting for the follow-up for *Brothers in Arms,* the 12-track *Money for Nothing* does an adequate job of summarizing hits and highlights from Dire Straits. Since the group only released one studio album after this compilation, and that really didn't produce any blockbusters, *Money for Nothing* winds up being a pretty good career summary. Far from perfect, though: too many album rock hits, such as "Expresso Love" and "Skateaway," are missing, plus there's two live cuts and the new cut "Where Do You Think You're Going?" doesn't go anywhere. Discounting these, the remainder of the compilation does hit many of the big songs, relying heavily on *Brothers in Arms. Sultans of Swing,* the post-*On Every Street* collection, is a better overview, yet this still has enough of the best-known tracks to satisfy the majority of casual fans. *—Stephen Thomas Erlewine*

On Every Street / Sep. 1991 / Warner Brothers ✦✦

On the Night / May 11, 1993 / Warner Brothers ✦✦

Live at the BBC / Jun. 26, 1995 / Warner Brothers ✦✦✦

● **Sultans of Swing: The Very Best of Dire Straits** / Nov. 10, 1998 / Warner Brothers ✦✦✦✦
Exactly ten years after Dire Straits' first compilation, *Money for Nothing,* appeared in the stores, their second, *Sultans of Swing: The Very Best of Dire Straits,* was released. Though a decade is a significant span of time, Dire Straits had released just two subsequent albums—1991's *On Every Street* and 1993's *On the Night,* a live album culled from tapes of the record's supporting tour. Not quite enough material for a new greatest-hits album, but it had been years since Dire Straits had released an album of any sort (a compilation of BBC sessions snuck into the stores in 1995)—hence the birth of *Sultans of Swing.* Unsurprisingly, it covers much of the same ground as *Money for Nothing,* containing all the essentials ("Sultans of Swing," "Romeo and Juliet," "Tunnel of Love," "Private Investigations," "Twisting by the Pool," "Money for Nothing," "Brothers in Arms," "Walk of Life"), with the exception of "Telegraph Road," which was left on the earlier compilation. A live "Love Over Gold," "Lady Writer" and "So Far Away" replace "Down to the Waterline," "Where Do You Think You're Going" and a live "Portobello Belle," which is really just a trade-off, since they're all equal in quality. Then there are the three hits from *On Every Street* ("Calling Elvis," "Heavy Fuel," "On Every Street"), all of which are pleasant recreations of the *Brothers in Arms* sound; a live version of "Your Latest Trick" from *On the Night,* and, inexplicably, Mark Knopfler's "Wild Theme (Theme from Local Hero)." Fine tunes all, but none of them are reason enough to replace *Money for Nothing* with *Sultans of Swing.* For casual fans or curious listeners looking for an introduction/sampler, it's the better choice, simply because it covers more ground and contains more music while remaining quite listenable and entertaining. *—Stephen Thomas Erlewine*

DJ Shadow (Josh Davis)

b. 1973, Hayward, CA
DJ, Producer / Turntablism, Electronica, Ambient Breakbeat, Trip-Hop, Hip-Hop
DJ Shadow's Josh Davis is widely credited as a key figure in developing the experimental instrumental hip-hop style associated with the London-based Mo'Wax label. His early singles for the label, including "In/Flux" and "Lost and Found (S.F.L.)," were all-over-the-map mini-masterpieces combining elements of funk, rock, hip-hop, ambient, jazz, soul, and used-bin incidentalia. Although he'd already done a scattering of original and production work (during 1991-92 for Hollywood Records) by the time Mo'Wax's James Lavelle contacted him about releasing "In/Flux" on the fledgling imprint, it wasn't until his association with Mo'Wax that his sound began to mature and cohere. Mo'Wax released his longest work to date in 1995—the 40-minute single in four movements, "What Does Your Soul Look Like," which topped the British indie charts—and Davis has gone on to co-write, remix, and produce tracks for labelmates DJ Krush and Doctor Octagon. Shadow's first full-length, *Endtroducing,* was released in late 1996. *—Sean Cooper*

★ **Endtroducing . . .** / Nov. 19, 1996 / Mo' Wax/ffrr ✦✦✦✦✦
As a suburban Californian kid, DJ Shadow tended to treat hip-hop as a musical innovation, not as an explicit social protest, which goes a long way toward explaining why his debut album *Endtroducing...* sounded like nothing else at the time of its release. Using hip-hop, not only its rhythms but its cut-and-paste techniques, as a foundation, Shadow created a deep, endlessly intriguing world on *Endtroducing,* one where there are no musical genres, only shifting sonic textures and styles. Shadow created the entire album from samples, almost all pulled from obscure, forgotten vinyl, and the effect is that of a hazy, half-familiar dream—parts of the record sound familiar, yet it's clear that it only suggests music you've heard before, and that the multi-layered samples and genres create something new. And that's one of the keys to the success of *Endtroducing*—it's innovative, but it builds on a solid historical foundation, giving it a rich, multi-faceted sound. It's not only a major breakthrough for hip-hop and electronica, but for pop music. *—Stephen Thomas Erlewine*

Preemptive Strike / Jan. 13, 1998 / Mo' Wax/ffrr/London ✦✦✦✦

Dr. Feelgood

f. 1971
Group / Pub Rock, Rock & Roll
Dr. Feelgood was the ultimate working band. From their formation in 1971 to lead vocalist Lee Brilleaux's untimely death in 1994, the band never left the road, playing hundreds of gigs every year. Throughout their entire career, Dr. Feelgood never left simple, hard-driving rock & roll behind, and their devotion to the blues and R&B earned them a devoted fan base. That following first emerged in the mid-'70s, when Dr. Feelgood became the leader of the second wave of pub-rockers. Unlike Brinsley Schwarz, the laidback leaders of the pub-rock scene, Dr. Feelgood was devoted to edgy, Stonesy rock & roll, and their sweaty live shows—powered by Brilleaux's intense singing and guitarist Wilko Johnson's muscular leads—became legendary. While the group's stripped-down, energetic sound paved the way for English punk rock in the late '70s, their back-to-basics style was overshadowed by the dominance of punk and new wave, and the group had retreated to cult status by the early '80s. *—Stephen Thomas Erlewine*

Down by the Jetty / Jan. 1975 / Grand ✦✦✦✦✦
The CD reissue of this album is a must-own release, even for those who already have one of the Dr. Feelgood anthologies currently available, neither of which has more than three of the 13 tracks here. The 1975 album, a magnificent first album, recorded in pure mono, has been transferred to CD in exemplary form, a clean, sharp, crunchy, close sound that recalls the sonic textures of the Rolling Stones' first album, even as they cross swords with the Stones' arch-rivals of the era, the Animals, with a superb version of "Boom Boom." Released amid the burgeoning radio presence of acts like Thin Lizzy, Blue Oyster Cult, and Kansas, and the growing self-conscious profundity of Bruce Springsteen, *Down by the Jetty* was as refreshingly lean as anything the headline-grabbing '70s punks would later loose on the world, and as stripped down as the most basic roots-rock. Lee Brilleaux's singing could go up against Eric Burdon's or Cyril Davies, and even take on elements of a thick rasp vaguely reminiscent of Howlin' Wolf (listen closely to "Roxette"), certainly better than Mick Jagger ever did; and guitarist Wilko Johnson could play Jimmy Reed, Chuck Berry, or Bo Diddley licks with equally imposing (and seemingly effortless) virtuosity. This record was one of the great '70s rock & roll albums, right up there with the Groovies' *Shake Some Action* and anything CCR left us, and ran circles around the Rolling Stones' post-*Exile on Main Street* output. The final cut, a killer live medley of ""Bonie Maronie"/"Tequila" with guests Brinsley Schwarz and Bob Andrews blowing saxes, was a taste of what they did on stage with astonishing regularity, and could have sent the Ramones back to the drawing board if the Queens-based quartet had heard it. *—Bruce Eder*

• **Malpractice** / Feb. 1975 / Columbia ✦✦✦✦✦
Guitarist Wilko Johnson's songs shine against such inspired covers as "Riot in Cell Block *9*." And his Stonesy playing takes no prisoners. *—Bruce Eder*

Stupidity / 1976 / Grand ✦✦✦✦✦
Comprised of recordings taken from 1975 tours, the live *Stupidity* finally captures the relentless, hard-driving energy of Dr. Feelgood at their peak. All the music on *Stupidity* is presented raw and without overdubs, making it clear that the dynamic friction between guitarist Wilko Johnson and vocalist Lee Brilleaux could propel the band toward greatness. While many of the versions here don't differ in form from the original studio versions, these unvarnished performances are considerably more exciting, revealing the Johnson originals "She Does It Right" and "All Through the City" as minor rock & roll classics. *—Stephen Thomas Erlewine*

Be Seeing You / 1977 / Grand ✦✦✦✦
The Nick Lowe-produced *Be Seeing You*, Dr. Feelgood's first album with guitarist John Mayo, was only slightly weaker than the group's previous records. Although Mayo was still working his way into the band's sound, Dr. Feelgood retained their tough, hard-rocking appeal. *—Stephen Thomas Erlewine*

Sneakin' Suspicion / 1977 / Grand ✦✦✦✦
Wilko Johnson's last album with Dr. Feelgood continues to be dominated by his tough guitar playing, although fewer of his songs are heard. *—Bruce Eder*

Dr. John (Mac Rebennack)

b. Nov. 21, 1940, New Orleans, LA
Vocals, Keyboards, Piano, Guitar / New Orleans R&B, Piano Blues, Rock & Roll, R&B
Although he didn't become widely known until the 1970s, Dr. John had been active in the music industry since the late '50s, when the teenager was still known as Mac Rebennack. A formidable boogie and blues pianist with a lovable growl of a voice, his most enduring achievements have fused New Orleans R&B, rock, and Mardi Gras craziness to come up with his own brand of "voodoo" music. He's also quite accomplished and enjoyable when sticking to purely traditional forms of blues and R&B. On record, he veers between the two approaches, making for an inconsistent and frequently frustrating legacy that often makes the listener feel as if the Night Tripper (as he's nicknamed himself) has been underachieving. Rebennack renamed himself Dr. John the Night Tripper when he recorded his first album, *Gris-Gris*. According to legend, this was hurriedly cut with leftover studio time from a Sonny & Cher session, but it never sounded hastily conceived. In fact, its mix of New Orleans R&B with voodoo sounds and a tinge of psychedelia was downright enthralling, and may have resulted in his greatest album. He began building an underground following with both his music and his eccentric stage presence, which found him conducting ceremonial-type events in full Mardi Gras costume.

Dr. John was nothing if not eclectic, and his later albums were granted mixed critical receptions because of their unevenness and occasional excess. *—Richie Unterberger*

Gris-Gris / 1968 / Collectors' Choice Music ✦✦✦✦✦
The most exploratory and psychedelic outing of Dr. John's career, a one-of-a-kind fusion of New Orleans Mardi Gras R&B and voodoo mysticism. Great rasping, bluesy vocals, soulful backup singers, and eerie melodies on flute, sax, and clarinet, as well as odd Middle Eastern-like chanting and mandolin runs. It's got the setting of a strange religious ritual, but the mood is far more joyous than solemn. *—Richie Unterberger*

Babylon / 1969 / Atco ✦✦✦
Dr. John's ambition remained undiminished on his second solo album, *Babylon*, released shortly after the groundbreaking voodoo-psychedelia-New Orleans R&B fusion of his debut, *Gris-Gris*. The results, however, were not nearly as consistent or impressive. Coolly received by critics, the album nonetheless is deserving of attention, though it pales a bit in comparison with *Gris-Gris*. The production is sparser and more reliant on female backup vocals than his debut. Dr. John remains intent on fusing voodoo and R&B, but the mood is oddly bleak and despairing, in comparison with the wild Mardi Gras-gone-amok tone of his first LP. The hushed, damned atmosphere and after-hours R&B sound a bit like Van Morrison on a bummer trip at times, as peculiar as that might seem. "The Patriotic Flag-Waiver" (sic), in keeping with the mood of the late '60s, damns social ills and hypocrisy of all sorts. An FM underground radio favorite at the time, its ambitious structure remains admirable, though its musical imperfections haven't worn well. To a degree, you could say the same about the album as a whole. But it has enough of an eerie fascination to merit investigation. *—Richie Unterberger*

Dr. John's Gumbo / Apr. 1972 / Atco ✦✦✦✦✦
Gumbo bridged the gap between post-hippie rock and early rock & roll, blues and R&B, offering a selection of classic New Orleans R&B, including "Tipitina" and "Junko Partner," updated with a gritty, funky beat. There aren't as many psychedelic flourishes as there were on his first two albums, but the ones that are present enhance his sweeping vision of American roots music. And that sly fusion of styles makes *Gumbo* one of Dr. John's finest albums. *—Stephen Thomas Erlewine*

Mos' Scocious: Anthology / Oct. 19, 1993 / Rhino ✦✦✦✦✦
Over his 35 years of recording, Mac "Dr. John" Rebennack has worn many hats, from '50s greasy rock & roller to psychedelic '70s weirdo to keeper of the New Orleans music flame. All of these modes, plus more, are excellently served up on this two-disc anthology. From the early New Orleans sides featuring Rebennack's blistering guitar work ("Storm Warning" and "Morgus the Magnificent") to the fabled '70s sides as the Night Tripper to his present day status as repository of the Crescent City's noble musical tradition, this is the one you want to have for the collection. *—Cub Koda*

Cut Me While I'm Hot: The Sixties Sessions / 1995 / Magnum ✦✦✦
The liner notes for this 19-song compilation are brief, but at least have the honesty to admit that "the precise details of the circumstances surrounding these recordings may be lost forever." It speculates that the first half of the outtake-sounding program was cut in New Orleans during the first half of the 1960s, while the latter part dates from L.A. sessions from 1965-1967. It actually sounds like much of this postdates the mid-'60s, with a feeling not unlike his early-'70s work. Most of the titles are self-penned, and there are also a few Professor Longhair covers. The material isn't really up to the level of his better early records, and the earlier tracks boast muffled audio (though fidelity is listenable throughout). At the same time, if you like vintage Dr. John, this is not much worse than the official stuff, the jiving throaty vocals, humorous songwriting, and distinctive keyboard playing all in place. It's low on outstanding compositions, but isn't bad at all, meaning there's no need to rush out and buy it, but also that committed fans won't mind having it around. *—Richie Unterberger*

• **The Very Best of Dr. John** / Apr. 25, 1995 / Rhino ✦✦✦✦✦
The Very Best of Dr. John compiles the best moments from the comprehensive double-disc *Anthology*, making it a more effective, and cheaper, introduction for casual fans. *—Stephen Thomas Erlewine*

Anutha Zone / Aug. 11, 1998 / Virgin ✦✦✦✦

Medical School: The Early Sessions of Mac "Dr. John" Rebennaack / Jun. 22, 1999 / Music Club ✦✦✦✦
Dr. John's early work as a producer, sessionman, and songwriter for Ace Records is legendary, not only among fans of Mac Rebennack but among devotees of New Orleans R&B. Unfortunately, there was no easy way to hear this material until Music Club's 1999 release, *Medical School: The Early Sessions of Mac "Dr. John" Rebennack*. Clocking in at 18 tracks, the disc isn't complete, but it is definitive—all the best-known cuts are here, along with a generous selection of little-known gems. To anyone but scholars and aficionados, most of the names on the compilation will not be familiar (The Ends, Al Reed, Ronnie & the Delinquents, Sugar Boy Crawford, Bobby Hebb, among others), and many of these cuts have never been well-circulated, or even released, but that's what makes the compilation so special. Not only are these lost classics from Dr. John, but these are lost gems from the prime period of New Orleans R&B. And this is not hyperbole—listening to *Medical School*, it's hard not to escape the feeling that almost every song is a hit you've never heard or have forgotten about. The instrumentals are not weak, the novelties (such as "Morgus the Magnificent") are fun, and cuts like "It Ain't No Use," "Bad Neighborhood," "You Don't Leave Me No Choice," and "Keeps Dragging Me On" are simply fantastic, sounding for all the world like classics, not throwaways. And that's the reason why *Medical School* isn't simply a necessary addition to Dr. John's catalog—it's an essential addition to any New Orleans R&B library. *—Stephen Thomas Erlewine*

Thomas Dolby

b. Oct. 14, 1958, Cairo, Egypt
Vocals, Keyboards, Guitar, Synthesizer / New Wave, Synth Pop
Though he never had many hits, Thomas Dolby became one of the most recognizable figures of the synth-pop movement of early-'80s new wave. Largely, this was due to his skillful marketing. Dolby promoted himself as a kind of mad scientist, an egghead that had successfully harnassed the power of synthesizers and samplers, using them to make catchy pop and light electro-funk. Before he launched a solo career, Dolby had worked a studio musician, technician, and songwriter; his most notable work as a songwriter was "New Toy," which he wrote for Lene Lovich, and Whodini's "Magic's Wand." In 1981, he launched a solo career, which resulted in a number of minor hits and two big hits—"She Blinded Me with Science" (1982) and "Hyperactive" (1984). Following "Hyperactive," his career faded away, as he began producing more frequently, as well as exploring new synthesizer and computer technology. Dolby continued to record into the '90s, but by that time, he was strictly a cult act. *—Stephen Thomas Erlewine*

The Golden Age of Wireless / Mar. 1983 / Capitol ✦✦✦✦✦
Talk to anyone who was the right age in the early '80s for both pop radio and the dawn of MTV and "She Blinded Me With Science" will inevitably come up. The most famous song from the reissued version of the album, it's a defiantly quirky, strange number that mixes its pop hooks with unusual keyboard melodies pitched very low and a recurrent spoken-word interjection ("Science!") from guest vocalist/video star Magnus Pike. To Dolby's credit, the rest of the album isn't simply that song over and over again, making *Golden Age of Wireless* an intriguing and often very entertaining curio from the glory days of synth-pop. Part of the album's overall appeal is the range of participating musicians, no doubt thanks in part to Dolby's own considerable range of musical work elsewhere. "She Blinded Me With Science" itself features Kevin Armstrong on guitar, Matthew Seligman on bass, megaproducer Robert "Mutt" Lange on backing vocals, and co-production with Tim Friese-Greene. Elsewhere, Andy Partridge contributes harmonica, Mute Records founding genius Daniel Miller adds keyboards, and Lene Lovich adds some vocals of her own. The overall result is still first and foremost Dolby's, with echoes of David Bowie's and Bryan Ferry's elegantly wasted late-'70s personae setting the stage. If anything, *Golden Age of Wireless* is the friendlier, peppier flip side of fellow Bowie obsessive Gary Numan's work, where the melancholy is gentle instead of harrowing. Dolby's melodies are sprightly without being annoyingly perky, his singing warm, and his overall performance a pleasant gem. Especially fine numbers include the amusing romp "Europa and the Pirate Twins" and the nostalgia-touched, just-mysterious-enough "One of Our Submarines." *—Ned Raggett*

The Flat Earth / Feb. 1984 / Capitol ✦✦✦✦✦
A departure from the style of his debut, this moody and atmospheric album adds jazz and Joni Mitchell-esque elements to warm his synth textures. Only "White City" and the single, "Hyperactive!," feature the hard dance beats of his early hits. *—Scott Bultman*

Aliens Ate My Buick / Apr. 1988 / EMI-Manhattan ✦✦

Gate to the Mind's Eye / Oct. 18, 1994 / Giant ✦✦✦✦✦

• **The Best of Thomas Dolby: Retrospectacle** / Apr. 4, 1995 / Capitol ✦✦✦✦✦
After what had seemed like a promising start with "She Blinded Me With Science" in 1983,

Thomas Dolby only charted with two other singles in the U.S. (though he had nine chart singles in his native U.K., 1981-1992). This 16-track compilation, embracing both his Capitol/EMI and Warner Bros. recordings, demonstrates that Dolby deserved better. His synthesizer-based songs are consistently catchy and clever, and especially notable are early songs like "Urges" and "Leipzig" that have not previously appeared on a U.S. album. "One of Our Submarines," Dolby's cover of Dan Hicks' "I Scare Myself," and "Hyperactive!" all hold up well. Some of the later (non-hit) material from the albums *Aliens Ate My Buick* and *Astronauts & Heretics* is less impressive; a better choice could have been made from those records. But for the most part, this is an efficient collection that justifies its name. *—William Ruhlmann*

Fats Domino (Antoine Domino)

b. Feb. 26, 1928, New Orleans, LA

Vocals, Piano / New Orleans R&B, Piano Blues, Rock & Roll, R&B

The most popular exponent of the classic New Orleans R&B sound, Fats Domino sold more records than any other Black rock & roll star of the 1950s. His relaxed, lolling boogie-woogie piano style and easygoing, warm vocals anchored a long series of national hits from the mid-'50s to the early '60s. Through it all, his basic approach rarely changed. He may not have been one of early rock's most charismatic, innovative, or threatening figures, but he was certainly one of its most consistent. Domino's first single, 1949's "The Fat Man," is one of the dozens of tracks that have been consistently singled out as a candidate for the first rock & roll record. The record made number two on the R&B charts, sold a million copies, and established a vital production partnership between Fats and Imperial A&R man Dave Bartholomew. Domino didn't really cross over into the pop charts in a big way until 1955, when "Ain't That a Shame" made the Top Ten. Between 1955 and 1963, he racked up an astonishing 35 Top 40 singles, the best (and best-remembered) of which was probably 1956's "Blueberry Hill." Although an active performer in the ensuing decades, his career as an important artist was essentially over in the mid-'60s. He did stir up a bit of attention in 1968 when he covered the Beatles' "Lady Madonna" single, which had been an obvious homage to Fats' style. *—Richie Unterberger*

Fats Is Back / 1968 / Bullseye Blues ✦✦✦

Like many of the early legends of rock & roll, Fats Domino didn't command a lot of attention in the late '60s. Not only had the British Invasion pushed Fats, Chuck, Little Richard and their contemporaries off the charts, but post-1965 developments like psychedelia and folk-rock made straightforward rock & roll and rolling New Orleans R&B sound a little old-fashioned. In other words, it was time for the first generation to stage a comeback. Producer Richard Perry never neglects the essentials of Fats' music—he retains the easygoing charm and endearing shuffles, just updating it slightly. In retrospect, *Fats Is Back* feels like Perry's blueprint for Ringo Starr's starstudded extravaganzas of the mid-'70s—he selects an impeccable set of songs, nearly all covers but not just relying on obvious selections, assembles a first-rate cast of musicians and then puts on a show. After all, this is an album that begins with a roll-call of Domino's greatest hits and then ends with "One More Song for You"—it's intended to be spectacular and it comes damn close to being one. Part of the reason *Fats Is Back* works is that it's designed to entertain but never oversells itself—sort of like the man himself, actually. Fats delivers tailor-made new songs, Barbara George's "I Know," a remake of his classic "I'm Ready" and two Beatles covers (McCartney's Fats tribute "Lady Madonna" and "Lovely Rita") with equal gusto. Years on from its initial release, *Fats Is Back* still sounds like a sly, endearing update of the classic Domino sound. It may not match his classic Imperial recordings, yet it will no doubt please anyone wishing to dig a little deeper. *—Stephen Thomas Erlewine*

☆ **My Blue Heaven: The Best of Fats Domino** / Jul. 30, 1990 / EMI America ✦✦✦✦✦

For the budget-minded fan, this 20-track single-disc compilation of Fats Domino's Imperial smashes will serve nicely. Not much of his early pre-rock stuff—"The Fat Man" and "Please Don't Leave Me" are all that are here—but there's plenty of his hit-laden output from 1955 on—"Ain't It a Shame," "Blue Monday," "I'm in Love Again," "Blueberry Hill," "I'm Ready," among others. One small but substantial difference between this set and the larger packages: It uses non-sped-up masters of his mid-'50s material (some of his hits from this era were mastered slightly faster than true pitch). Even if they're not historically correct, these versions actually sound better. *—Bill Dahl*

☆ **They Call Me the Fat Man: The Legendary Imperial Recordings** / Oct. 22, 1991 / EMI America ✦✦✦✦✦

If you can't quite finance the Bear Family box, this four-disc compilation is the next best thing; an even 100 of the best Imperial sides, including a great many from 1958 on that turn up in crystal-clear stereo (as they also do on the Bear Family package). All the hits are aboard, along with a nice cross section of the important non-hits. The saxes (usually including Herb Hardesty and sometimes Lee Allen) roar with typical Crescent City power, Fats rolls the ivories, and magic happens—over and over again! Another nice booklet with plenty of photos (but a less detailed discography without sideman credits). *—Bill Dahl*

Out of New Orleans / 1993 / Bear Family ✦✦✦✦✦

An amazing piece of work—a massive eight-disc boxed set that contains every one of Fats Domino's 1949-1962 Imperial waxings. That's a tremendous load of one artist, but the legacy of Domino and his partner Dave Bartholomew is so consistently innovative and infectious that it never grows tiresome for a second. From the clarion call of "The Fat Man," Domino's 1949 debut, to the storming "Dance with Mr. Domino" in 1962, he typified everything charming about Crescent City R&B, his Creole patois and boogie-based piano a non-threatening vehicle for the rise of rock & roll. A thick, photo-filled book accompanies the disc, and there's an exhaustive discography that makes sense of Domino's many visits to Cosimo Matassa's studios. If you care about Fats Domino, this is the package to purchase! *—Bill Dahl*

Fat Man: 25 Classic Performances / Aug. 20, 1996 / Capitol ✦✦✦✦

Ostensibly replacing the compact disc *My Blue Heaven* as the definitive single-disc collection of Fats Domino's biggest hits singles, *Fat Man: 25 Classic Performances* features most of Fats Domino's biggest hits, but it inexplicably neglects such hits as "Walking to New Orleans," "Be My Guest" and "I'm Gonna Be a Wheel Someday." The only justification for the omission of so many hits is that the intent of the collection is to portray Fats Domino as the R&B heavyweight that he undoubtedly is, but seldom receives credit for being. Nevertheless, *Fat Man* masquerades as a greatest hits collection, billing itself as "25 Classic Performances," which leads you to believe that it is simply another hits collection. As an R&B compilation, *Fat Man* is strong—and, like any proper R&B collection, it presents the singles at the speed they were recorded at, not the sped-up versions that became hits—but because it lacks these hits, *My Blue Heaven* remains a preferable collection and introduction to Fats. *—Stephen Thomas Erlewine*

★ **Legends of the 20th Century** / Nov. 2, 1999 / Capitol ✦✦✦✦✦

Released as part of Capitol/EMI's *Legends of the 20th Century* series, this single-disc collection is an excellent summary of Fats Domino's legendary singles. Technically, it doesn't have all the hits—it's missing such gold singles as "Bo Weevil," "It's You I Love," and "Wait and See"—but it has every classic: "The Fat Man," "Ain't It a Shame," "I'm In Love Again," "My Blue Heaven," "Blueberry Hill," "Blue Monday," "I'm Walkin'," "Whole Lotta Loving," "I'm Ready," "I Want to Walk You Home," "I'm Gonna Be a Wheel Some Day," "Be My Guest," "Walking to New Orleans," "My Girl Josephine," and "Let the Four Winds Blow," among others. Yes, it's essentially the same as many of the other greatest hits collection, but it's done well, sounds good, and, at 25 tracks, is quite generous, making it an ideal choice for most listeners. *—Stephen Thomas Erlewine*

Lonnie Donegan (Anthony James Donegan)

b. Apr. 29, 1931, Glasgow, Scotland

Vocals, Guitar, Banjo / British Folk, Rockabilly, Skiffle

To look at Lonnie Donegan today, in pictures taken 40 years ago when he was topping the British charts and hitting the top Ten in America, dressed in a suit, his hair cut short and strumming an acoustic guitar, he looks like a musical non-entity. But in 1954, before anyone (especially anybody in England) knew what rock 'n roll was, Donegan was cool, and his music was hot. He's relatively little remembered outside of England, but Donegan shares an important professional attribute with Elvis Presley, Bill Haley, the Beatles, the Rolling Stones, and the Sex Pistols—he invented a style of music, skiffle, that completely altered the pop culture landscape and the youth around him, and for a time completely ruled popular music through that new form. What's more, his music, like that of Presley and Haley, was vital to the early musical careers and future histories of the Beatles, the Stones, and hundreds of other groups. And he did it in 1954, before Elvis was known anywhere outside of Memphis and before Bill Haley was perceived as anything but a western swing novelty act. *—Bruce Eder*

● **The EP Collection** / 1992 / See For Miles ✦✦✦✦✦

In England, before the Beatles and the Rolling Stones came along, EPs (four-song extended play singles) outsold albums. This compilation of the best of Donegan's EPs is the definitive Lonnie Donegan collection, eclipsing any album or CD that existed previously on his work. It is certainly the best hits compilation there ever has been on him, containing the 1956 hit "Rock Island Line" and its B-side, "Digging My Potatoes," plus 23 more fairly hard-rocking tracks dating up through 1962, all very crisply remastered, with original artwork represented and a very detailed biography. *—Bruce Eder*

More Than "Pie in the Sky" / 1993 / Bear Family ✦✦✦✦✦

Eight CDs, and nearly 10 hours of music may seem like overkill to most onlookers, but this is a boxed set that truly justifies itself, once you've listened to it. What is here is amazing—this set presents Lonnie Donegan as the prodigious musical talent he actually was, a white bluesman extraordinaire and a country, rockabilly, and gospel singer of no small merit as well. No, he didn't have Elvis Presley's voice, or his way with the girls, but Donegan had musical talent by the ton—his blues stylings on songs like the previously unreleased alternate take of Lonnie Johnson's "I've Got Rocks In My Bed" or Leroy Carr's "Hoe Long How Long Blues" will astonish anyone who thinks that British blues began with the Rolling Stones or even with Alexis Korner (who had never been anywhere near a recording studio when Donegan cut some of this stuff); his covers of numbers by Cole Porter (in a blues style, no less) and Bob Dylan (from Donegan's final Pye album) will amaze anyone who never got past "Rock Island Line." And the unedited live set from Conway Hall in 1957 will delight anyone who likes great, exciting concert recordings. And most of the rest is of as high quality as these rarities. The only drawback is the $180 price-tag, but that's the cost of quality. The profusely annotated and illustrated booklet is an added bonus. *—Bruce Eder*

The EP Collection, Vol. 2 / 1994 / See For Miles ✦✦✦✦

Donovan (Donovan Phillip Leitch)

b. May 10, 1946, Glasgow, Scotland

Vocals, Harmonica, Guitar / British Psychedelia, Psychedelic Pop, British Folk, Folk-Rock, Psychedelic, British Invasion, Singer/Songwriter

Upon his emergence during the mid-'60s, Donovan was anointed "Britain's answer to Bob Dylan," a facile but largely unfounded comparison which compromised the Scottish folk-pop troubadour's own unique vision. Where the thrust of Dylan's music remains its bleak introspection and bitter realism, Donovan fully embraced the wide-eyed optimism of the flower-power movement, his ethereal, ornate songs radiating a mystical beauty and childlike wonder. For better or worse, his recordings remain quintessential artifacts of the psychedelic era, capturing the peace-and-love idealism of their time to perfection. Born in Glasgow in 1946, Donovan Leitch was tapped as a regular on the television pop showcase *Ready, Steady, Go!* He soon issued his debut single "Catch the Wind," earning the first round of Dylan comparisons with his ramshackle folk sound and ragamuffin look. Signing with Epic in 1966, he released his breakthrough album, *Sunshine Superman,* which in its exotic arrangements and pointedly psychedelic lyrical outlook heralded a major shift from his previous work; the title track topped the charts on both sides of the Atlantic, with the enigmatic "Mellow Yellow" reaching the number two spot a few months later. Donovan remained a chart fixture throughout 1967, generating a series of hits including "Epistle to Dippy," "There Is a Mountain," and "Wear Your Love Like Heaven." In 1968 Donovan scored a Top Five smash with the hallucinatory title cut of *The Hurdy Gurdy Man.* He retreated to Ireland in 1970, and California in 1974, living quietly and emerging only occasionally. In 1996, Donovan released his comeback LP, Sutras, helmed by producer-du-jour Rick Rubin. *—Jason Ankeny*

Catch the Wind / Jun. 1965 / Castle ✦✦

Fairytale / Nov. 1965 / Castle ✦✦

Sunshine Superman / Sep. 1966 / Epic ✦✦✦✦✦
The release of this audiophile version of *Sunshine Superman* gives consumers a real choice, as well as an opportunity to hear this record the way it was meant to be heard. Remastered by EMI in 1996 using state-of-the-art technology, it sounds even brighter and sharper than the 1994 remastering used in the EMI Donovan box. But it also offers nothing in the way of notes or historical background, which the box does. The sound here is about the best you'll ever hear on a recording of this vintage, however, and puts the domestic Epic CD to shame and then some—indeed, it completely transforms the album from a somewhat dullish acoustic psychedelic piece into a pretty, rich sound painting, built around the sounds of acoustic and electric guitar (the latter mostly by Jimmy Page), sitar (played by Shawn Phillips), harpsichord, and tabla, and the occasional overdubbed string group and reed players ("Legend of a Girl Child Linda"), all of which leaps out at the listener. "Season of the Witch" and the title track are completely transformed and superior to the versions on the domestic Sony Donovan set. (British import) *—Bruce Eder*

Mellow Yellow / Jan. 1967 / Epic ✦✦✦✦
Mellow Yellow is actually more diverse in its sounds than *Sunshine Superman,* drawing on some of the same era's better follow-up material but also reaching back somewhat further for repertory. It was, as one could rightly guess, a by-product of the late-1966 hit title track, but the songs dated back in some instances as much as a year, to a point prior to Donovan's having made the leap from folk to pop artist. "Mellow Yellow" itself was cut after "Sunshine Superman" and boasted one of the earliest arrangements by John Paul Jones to achieve international recognition (although not without some resistance from Donovan himself), with its broad, biting brass sound. The next two tracks, however, reached back to the singer-songwriter's earlier acoustic/folk songbag, and a very different point in his career—the reflective, somber "Writer in the Sun" was written in Greece during the spring of 1966, when it looked as though Donovan's career was in danger of ending due to legal problems. By contrast, the hauntingly beautiful "Sand and Foam" dated from a somewhat happier visit to Mexico. "The Observation" manages to quote the album's title tune obliquely in its bass-line, even as the singer veers close to a beat-style poetry recital. "Museum," which sounds at times almost like an artier sequel to "Sunshine Superman" and a precursor to "There Is a Mountain" in its word pattern, breaks up the succession of blues settings on the album's second side, as does the jazz-flavored "Hampstead Incident". The album ends with "Sunny South Kensington," an upbeat number driven by radiant (albeit name-dropping) lyrics, Eric Ford's crunchy guitar (emulating his contribution to "Sunshine Superman"), Shawn Phillips' sitar, and an economical arrangement by John Cameron (who also plays the harpsichord). *—Bruce Eder*

For Little Ones / Dec. 1967 / Epic ✦✦

Wear Your Love Like Heaven / Dec. 1967 / Epic ✦✦✦
Donovan's double album *A Gift from a Flower to a Garden* was simultaneously released as two single albums as well. This is the first, a psychedelic pop album containing the title track single and other like selections. *—William Ruhlmann*

A Gift from a Flower to a Garden / Dec. 1967 / Collectors' Choice Music ✦✦✦✦✦
Rock music's first two-LP box set has been reissued on one CD. Even better, enough time has passed that the music has overcome its original shortcomings and now stands out as a prime artifact of the flower-power era that produced it. The music still seems a bit fey, and overall more spacy than the average Moody Blues album of this era, but the sheer range of subjects and influences make this a surprisingly rewarding work. Essentially two albums recorded simultaneously in the summer of 1967, the electric tracks include Jack Bruce among the session players. The acoustic tracks represent an attempt by Donovan to get back to his old sound and depart from the heavily electric singles ("Sunshine Superman," etc.) and albums he'd been doing—it is folkier and bluesier (in an English folk sense) than much of his recent work. *—Bruce Eder*

Hurdy Gurdy Man / Oct. 1968 / Epic ✦✦✦
For this performer, this is a hard-rocking album, driven by some loud electric guitar subbing for sitar, which dresses up the plainer folk melodies and turns the title tune into a near-classic. *—Bruce Eder*

Barabajagal / Aug. 11, 1969 / Epic ✦✦✦✦✦
Donovan was moving beyond his hippie-dippie phase by this point, collaborating with the Jeff Beck Group on the title track, protesting the Vietnam War with "Susan on the West Coast Waiting," adapting the epic style of Beatles songs like "Hey Jude" on the hit "Atlantis" (which features Paul McCartney) and turning in two of his most charming, childlike songs in "Happiness Runs" and "I Love My Shirt." Overall, this may be Donovan's strongest collection of original songs, other than his compilations. *—William Ruhlmann*

Open Road / 1970 / Epic ✦✦✦

Troubadour: The Definitive Collection 1964-1976 / Aug. 4, 1992 / Epic/Legacy ✦✦✦✦✦
This two-disc, 44-track retrospective album (initially released as a boxed set) chronicles Donovan's decade-long career at Epic Records, with the few folk hits he recorded before joining the label and a couple of early demos added. All the hippie hits of the '60s are included, plus a judicious selection of the less successful '70s recordings. Good liner notes by Brian Hogg and Derek Taylor. *—William Ruhlmann*

Sutras / Oct. 15, 1996 / American ✦✦✦

★ **Greatest Hits [Expanded Edition]** / Mar. 30, 1999 / Epic/Legacy ✦✦✦✦✦
Epic/Legacy's 1999 reissue of *Greatest Hits* improves on the original 1969 collection in a number of ways. First of all, the original Hickory versions of "Catch the Wind" and "Colours" are included instead of re-recordings, which is enough to make this new version preferable, but the compilers have also chosen to include the original mono version of these hits instead of the stereo cuts that were on the first edition. Plus, they've added four excellent bonus tracks: "Atlantis," "To Susan on the West Coast Waiting," "Barabajagal" and "Riki Tiki Tavi." All of that means that this expanded and updated *Greatest Hits* is a near-perfect single-disc summary of Donovan's most popular material and hit singles. As these songs prove, Donovan and producer Mickie Most could craft irresistible folk-rock and psychedelic-pop singles. Some of the sounds and sentiments may sound a little dated, but the productions and the songs—"Sunshine Superman," "Jennifer Juniper," "Wear Your Love Like Heaven," "Season of the Witch," "Mellow Yellow," "Hurdy Gurdy Man," "Epistle to Dippy," "There Is a Mountain," "Lalena," plus the aforementioned bonus tracks—have proven to be classics of the era, and this is the best place to get them all on one collection. *—Stephen Thomas Erlewine*

Summer Day Reflection Songs / Apr. 25, 2000 / Castle ✦✦✦✦✦
In 1965, before Donovan's U.S. contract was transferred to Epic, he made 30-plus recordings for Pye in the U.K., all in an acoustic folk mold (with occasional additional instruments and percussion). It would not seem to be such a heroic feat to gather all of that material in one place, but prior to this double-CD compilation, that had never occurred. This is the anthology to rectify that gap permanently. The two CDs contain all 34 known songs from this era, including a few rarities: the original single versions of "Catch the Wind" and "Colours," an alternate take of "The Ballad of a Crystal Man," and "Every Man Has His Chain," which during the '60s only showed up on a French EP. These rarities aren't so amazing that you necessarily need to shell out if you already have most of the cuts, but for historical completism's sake their presence is most satisfying. The historical liner notes, covering the pre-"Sunshine Superman" period almost exclusively, are thorough and excellent. And the music is fine, quite consistent folk or pre-folk-rock that should permanently put an end to all the unwarranted dismissals of his early work as twee Dylan imitation. Donovan was his own man, even at this young age, and hard to beat as far as tuneful yet meaningful mid-'60s folk went. *—Richie Unterberger*

Mellow Yellow/Wear Your Love Like Heaven / Jan. 16, 2001 / Collectables ✦✦✦

The Doobie Brothers

f. Mar. 1970, San Jose, CA, **db.** 1982
Group / Album Rock, Blue-Eyed Soul, Boogie Rock, Pop/Rock, Soft Rock
As one of the most popular Californian pop/rock bands of the '70s, the Doobie Brothers evolved from a mellow, post-hippie boogie band to a slick, soul-inflected pop band by the end of the decade. Along the way, the group racked up a string of gold and platinum albums in the US. Driven by the singles "Listen to the Music" and "Jesus Is Just Alright," 1972's *Toulouse Street* became the group's breakthrough. *The Captain and Me* (1973) was even more successful, spawning the Top 10 hit "Long Train Runnin'" and "China Grove," while 1974's *What Once Were Vices Are Now Habits* launched their first number one single, "Black Water."

Baxter officially joined the Doobie Brothers for 1975's *Stampede.* Prior to the release of 1975's *Stampede,* singer/guitarist Tom Johnston was hospitalized with a stomach ailment, and was replaced for the supporting tour by keyboardist/vocalist Michael McDonald. Although it peaked at number four, *Stampede* wasn't as commercially successful as its three predecessors, and the group decided to let McDonald and ex-Steely Dan member Jeff "Skunk" Baxter, who were now official Doobies, revamp the band's light country-rock and boogie. The new sound was showcased on 1976's *Takin' It to the Streets,* a collection of light funk and jazzy pop that resulted in a platinum album. In 1977, the group released *Livin' on the Fault Line,* which was successful without producing any big hits. Johnston left the band after the album's release to pursue an unsuccessful solo career. Following his departure, the Doobies released their most successful album, *Minute By Minute* (1979) which spent five weeks at number one on the strength of the number one single "What a Fool Believes." *—Stephen Thomas Erlewine*

The Doobie Brothers / Apr. 1971 / Warner Brothers ✦✦✦

Toulouse Street / Jul. 1972 / Warner Brothers ✦✦✦✦✦
After a promising but ill-formed debut, The Doobie Brothers returned with *Toulouse Street,* a better-written and more energetically performed effort that became a platinum record on the strength of its catchy single, "Listen to the Music." *—Stephen Thomas Erlewine*

The Captain & Me / Mar. 1973 / Warner Brothers ✦✦✦✦✦

What Were Once Vices Are Now Habits / Feb. 1974 / Warner Brothers ✦✦✦

Stampede / May 1975 / Warner Brothers ✦✦

Takin' It to the Streets / Mar. 1976 / Warner Brothers ✦✦✦✦✦
Jeff "Skunk" Baxter left after *Stampede* and keyboardist/vocalist Michael McDonald—who also recorded with Steely Dan—joined the band. Under McDonald's direction, the group departed from their trademark bluesy country-rock on *Takin' It to the Streets,* taking a laidback pop-soul that touched on jazz and White funk. The result was a commercial and artistic success, providing a blueprint for the band's next two records. *—Stephen Thomas Erlewine*

● **Best of the Doobies** / Nov. 1976 / Warner Brothers ✦✦✦✦✦
Featuring 11 of the group's best-known songs from their first five albums (from 1971's *The Doobie Brothers* to 1976's *Takin' it to the Streets*), *The Best of the Doobie Brothers* contains the boogie-rock band's very best songs, including the big hits "Listen to the Music," "Jesus Is Just Alright," "Long Train Runnin'," "China Grove," "Black Water," "Takin' It to the Streets." For most casual fans, *The Best of the Doobie Brothers* is the perfect summation of the group's early career, before they turned into a slick, jazzy blue-eyed soul band in the late '70s. *—Stephen Thomas Erlewine*

Livin' on the Fault Line / Aug. 1977 / Warner Brothers ✦✦✦

Minute by Minute / Dec. 1978 / Warner Brothers ✦✦✦✦✦
Due to health problems, founding member Tom Johnson departed after *Livin' on the Fault Line*, leaving Michael McDonald as the leader of The Doobie Brothers. McDonald, in turn, wrote his finest set of songs for *Minute by Minute*, highlighted by the number one single "What a Fool Believes." *—Stephen Thomas Erlewine*

One Step Closer / Oct. 1980 / Warner Brothers ✦✦

Best of the Doobies, Vol. 2 / Nov. 1981 / Warner Brothers ✦✦✦✦✦

Long Train Runnin' 1970-2000 / Sep. 14, 1999 / Rhino ✦✦✦✦
There's little question that the four-disc box set *Long Train Runnin' 1971-2000* is only for hardcore Doobie Brothers fans, since it not only spans 79 tracks, but it also contains a full disc of rarities. The sheer abundance of material makes it unnecessary for anyone that isn't already a dedicated fan, either of the Doobies or of album rock, and even those listeners may find *Long Train Runnin'* a little long. After all, the Doobies' hit-making years end around the end of disc two, even though a few hits spill over to the beginning of disc three. That means the first half of the box is essentially an expanded greatest hits, featuring all the '70s singles—from "Listen to the Music" to "Dependin' on You"—balanced by a handful of album tracks. There is some elaboration of these years on disc four, but it takes a while to get there, since disc three chronicles the '80s and beyond. In the early '80s, the Doobies had only one Top Ten hit with "Real Love" before going on hiatus. They reunited in 1989 and continued to tour and record throughout the '90s. Those two decades comprise disc three and while it has its moments, it pales considerably next to the Doobies' prime material. The rarities disc is similarly uneven, but more interesting because much of the music dates from the '70s. Also, the mix of solo songs, alternate mixes, and demos illuminates those classic years somewhat, throwing out a handful of gems along the way. It's a nice bonus for the dedicated, but they really are the only audience for this set. *—Stephen Thomas Erlewine*

The Doors

f. Jul. 1965, Los Angeles, CA, **db.** 1973
Group / Album Rock, Proto-Punk, Psychedelic, Rock & Roll
The Doors, one of the most influential and controversial rock bands of the 1960s, were formed by UCLA film students Ray Manzarek and Jim Morrison with drummer John Densmore, and guitarist Robby Krieger. The group never added a bass player, and their sound was dominated by Manzarek's electric organ work and Morrison's deep, sonorous voice, with which he sang and intoned his highly poetic lyrics. The group signed to Elektra Records in 1966 and released its first album, *The Doors*, featuring the hit "Light My Fire," in 1967. Blending blues, classical, Eastern music, and pop into sinister but beguiling melodies, the band sounded like no other. From the start, the Doors' focus was the charismatic Morrison, who proved increasingly unstable over the group's brief career. In 1969, Morrison was arrested for indecent exposure during a concert in Miami, an incident that nearly derailed the band. Nevertheless, the Doors managed to turn out a series of successful albums and singles through 1971, when, upon the completion of their final album, *L.A. Woman*, Morrison decamped for Paris. He died there, apparently of a drug overdose. The three surviving Doors tried to carry on without him, but ultimately disbanded. In 1991, director Oliver Stone made *The Doors*, a feature film about the group starring Val Kilmer as Morrison. *—William Ruhlmann & Richie Unterberger*

☆ **The Doors** / Jan. 1967 / Elektra ✦✦✦✦✦
A tremendous debut album, and indeed one of the best first-time outings in rock history, introducing the band's fusion of rock, blues, classical, jazz, and poetry with a knockout punch. The lean, spidery guitar and organ riffs interwove with a hypnotic menace, providing a seductive backdrop for Jim Morrison's captivating vocals and probing prose. "Light My Fire" was the cut that would top the charts and establish the group as stars, but most of the rest of the album is just as impressive, including some of their best songs: the propulsive "Break On Through" (their first single), the beguiling Oriental mystery of "The Crystal Ship," the mysterious "End of the Night," "Take It As It Comes" (one of several tunes besides "Light My Fire" that also had hit potential), and the stomping rock of "Soul Kitchen" and "Twentieth Century Fox." The eleven-minute Oedipal drama "The End" was the group at their most daring and, some would contend, overambitious. It was nonetheless a haunting cap to an album whose nonstop melodicism and dynamic tension would never be equaled by the group again, let alone bettered. *—Richie Unterberger*

Strange Days / Oct. 1967 / Elektra ✦✦✦
Many of the songs on *Strange Days* had been written around the same time as the ones that appeared on *The Doors*, and with hindsight one has the sense that the best of the batch had already been cherry-picked for the debut album. For that reason, the band's second effort isn't as consistently stunning as their debut, though overall it's a very successful continuation of the themes of their classic album. Besides the hit "Strange Days," highlights included the funky "Moonlight Drive," the eerie "You're Lost Little Girl," and the jerkily rhythmic "Love Me Two Times," which gave the band a small chart single. "My Eyes Have Seen You" and "I Can't See Your Face In My Mind" are minor but pleasing entries in the group's repertoire that share a subdued Eastern psychedelic air. The eleven-minute "When the Music's Over" would often be featured as a live showstopper, yet it also illustrated their tendency to occasionally slip into drawn-out bombast. *—Richie Unterberger*

Waiting for the Sun / Jul. 1968 / Elektra ✦✦✦
The Doors' 1967 albums had raised expectations so high that their third effort was greeted as a major disappointment. With a few exceptions, the material was much mellower, and while this yielded some fine melodic ballad-rock in "Love Street," "Wintertime Love," "Summer's Almost Gone," and "Yes the River Knows," and there was no denying that the songwriting was not as impressive as it had been on the first two records. On the other hand, there were first-rate tunes such as the spooky "The Unknown Soldier," with anti-war lyrics as uncompromisingly forceful as anything the band did, and the compulsively riff-driven "Hello, I Love You," which nonetheless bore an uncomfortably close resemblance to the Kinks' "All Day and All of the Night." The flamenco guitar of "Spanish Caravan," the all-out weirdness of "Not to Touch the Earth" (which was a snippet of a legendary abandoned opus, "The Celebration of the Lizard"), and the menacing closer "Five to One" were also interesting. In fact, time's been fairly kind to the record, which is quite enjoyable and diverse, just not as powerful a full-length statement as the group's best albums. *—Richie Unterberger*

The Soft Parade / Jul. 1969 / Elektra ✦✦✦
The weakest studio album recorded with Morrison in the group, partially because their experiments with brass and strings on about half the tracks weren't entirely successful. More to the point, though, this was their weakest set of material, lowlights including filler like "Do It" and "Runnin' Blue," a strange bluegrass-soul blend that was a small hit. On the other hand, about half the record is quite good, especially the huge hit "Touch Me" (their most successful integration of orchestration), the vicious hard-rock riffs of "Wild Child," the overlooked "Shaman's Blues," and the lengthy title track, a multi-part suite that was one of the band's best attempts to mix rock with poetry. "Tell All the People" and "Wishful Sinful," both penned by Robby Krieger, were uncharacteristically wistful tunes that became small hits, but were not all that good, and not sung very convincingly by Morrison. *—Richie Unterberger*

Morrison Hotel / 1970 / Elektra ✦✦✦✦✦
The Doors returned to crunching, straightforward hard rock on an album that, despite yielding no major hit singles, returned them to critical favor with hip listeners. An increasingly bluesy flavor began to color the songwriting and arrangements, especially on the party and booze anthem "Roadhouse Blues." Airy mysticism was still present on "Waiting for the Sun," "Queen of the Highway," and "Indian Summer"; "Ship of Fools" and "Land Ho!" struck effective balances between the hard rock arrangements and the narrative reach of the lyrics. "Peace Frog" was the most political and controversial track, documenting the domestic unrest of late-'60s America before unexpectedly segueing into the restful ballad "Blue Sunday." "The Spy," by contrast, was a slow blues that pointed to the direction that would fully blossom on *L.A. Woman*. *—Richie Unterberger*

Absolutely Live / Sep. 1970 / Elektra ✦✦

L.A. Woman / Apr. 1971 / Elektra ✦✦✦✦✦
The final album with Morrison in the lineup is by far their most blues-oriented, and the singer's poetic ardor is undiminished, though his voice sounds increasingly worn and craggy on some numbers. Actually, some of the straight blues items sound kind of turgid, but that's more than made up for by several cuts that rate among their finest and most disturbing work. The seven-minute title track was a car-cruising classic that celebrated both the glamour and seediness of Los Angeles; the other long cut, the brooding, jazzy "Riders on the Storm," was the group at their most melodic and ominous. It and the far bouncier "Love Her Madly" were hit singles, and "The Changeling" and "L'America" count as some of their better little-heeded album tracks. An uneven but worthy finale from the original quartet. *—Richie Unterberger*

★ **The Best of the Doors** / 1985 / Elektra ✦✦✦✦✦
Ideally, one would avoid compilations of the Doors' work, except perhaps for the hit singles and moments when one wanted very light listening. This was a band that took itself very seriously, almost to the point of self-parody at times, and their music ought to be discovered in the setting and context in which it was intended, but assuming that one needs a Doors anthology, this 18-track collection (19 on CD) is the place to start. It started life during the quadrophonic era as a single LP of the same title, with programming intended to combine the concepts behind two earlier compilations, *13* and *Weird Scenes Inside the Goldmine*, under one cover. In 1985, the two-LP version, the fourth compilation of the group's work, and the most comprehensive, was released, providing a good overview to the most obvious different sides of the group's output, and in 1991 this was remastered for CD with improved sound and an extra track. Good as it is, the compilation misleads somewhat by removing the material from its original context and also shuffling the order, so that songs off of *The Soft Parade* bump up against tracks from *L.A. Woman*. The hits can stand on their own, but overall the music lacks the broader impact that it was intended to have when heard juxtaposed with the other tracks on their respective original albums. The 1996 *Greatest Hits* CD, with its remastered sound, and the remastering of their individual albums that began in the year 2000, also renders this collection somewhat less attractive than it was on its initial release. *—Bruce Eder*

In Concert / May 21, 1991 / Elektra ✦✦✦

Greatest Hits / Oct. 15, 1996 / Elektra ✦✦✦✦✦

The Doors Box Set / Oct. 28, 1997 / Elektra ✦✦✦
Fans of the Doors waited many years for *The Doors Box Set* to be released, and when it finally arrived in the fall of 1997, it was a bit of a mixed blessing. The classic conundrum for box sets is how much rare and unreleased material to showcase, and in this case, the producers opted for three discs of rarities, devoting the last disc to "band favorites," instead of hits. This means, of course, that the casual fan is not going to be well-served by the box, since it not only doesn't contain studio versions of such staples as "Five to One," but it doesn't even have versions of "People are Strange" and "Touch Me." Furthermore, die-hards might very well be frustrated by the quality of the rarities. The first disc and third disc are peppered with live cuts, outtakes and the legendary 1965 demos for Columbia Records. The quality of the music is uneven—the demos are interesting but mainly from a historical standpoint, the live cuts vascillate in sonic and performance quality, and outtakes like the plodding, 17-minute "Rock Is Dead" encapsulate much of what was wrong with the band—but much of it is worth hearing once, unlike the second disc, "Live in New York," which is startlingly similar to *Alive She Cried*. In the end, the sheer abundence of rare material makes the set of interest to diehard fans, but they might find that the collection falls short of their expectations. Listeners that have a passing interest in the Doors are advised to stick to the double disc set, *The Best of the Doors*. *—Stephen Thomas Erlewine*

Complete Studio Recordings / Nov. 9, 1999 / Elektra ✦✦✦✦

Essential Rarities / Jun. 20, 2000 / Elektra ✦✦✦

Lee Dorsey

b. Dec. 24, 1924, New Orleans, LA, **d.** Dec. 1, 1986, New Orleans, LA

Vocals / New Orleans R&B, R&B, Soul

The effervescent approach of Lee Dorsey perfectly summarizes the infectious charm of early-'60s New Orleans R&B. Dorsey specialized in good-humored music with a touch of second-line funk thrown in to make it all the more irresistible. Although he had already waxed a couple of singles, Dorsey caught the country by total surprise in 1961 with his deceptively simply nursery-rhyme-style "Ya Ya" on Bobby Robinson's Fury label. Arranged by prolific New Orleans pianist Allen Toussaint, the track proved an R&B chart-topper and a major pop hit to boot.

Dorsey's laconic vocal charms served him well on "Ya Ya" and the Earl King-penned follow-up "Do Re Mi," and the mid-'60s found him working with Toussaint on the funky smashes "Ride Your Pony" and "Working in the Coal Mine," this time for Amy Records. It's little remembered that Dorsey was responsible for the original 1970 version of Toussaint's "Yes We Can," revived to much greater acclaim by the Pointer Sisters (who tacked on an extra "Can"). From all accounts, Dorsey remained an exceedingly humble R&B star who preferred tinkering with cars to extensively touring the country. He died of emphysema in 1986. *—Bill Dahl*

The New Lee Dorsey / 1966 / Sundazed ♦♦♦

Less than a year had passed between this and Dorsey's previous LP *Ride Your Pony,* and Allen Toussaint was again the prime creative force, writing material and co-producing. The sound, however, had definitely taken a step in a funkier direction. It's still lighthearted, though not lightweight, soul music with a New Orleans bounce, paced by the Top Ten hit "Working in a Coal Mine" and also including the Top 30 follow-up "Holy Cow." Other than those hit singles, the songs, though not exactly throwaways, aren't up to the same level. The original LP duplicated four songs from *Ride Your Pony,* and the 2000 Sundazed CD reissue has taken intelligent liberties with the track sequence. It removes the four duplicated songs and replaces them with rare singles from the era, most notably the uncommonly moody 1967 45 "Rain Rain Go Away." Furthermore, an additional dozen tunes are added as bonus tracks, most taken from rare 1968-1970 singles, with a couple of previously unissued cuts and a 1968 recording ("Lottie Mo '68") that didn't show up until 1997. These bonus items are on the whole more worthy of investigation than the slightly earlier rarities that fill out Sundazed's *Ride Your Pony* CD, as Dorsey and Toussaint (who was, still, writing virtually everything) venturing into deeper funk, sometimes with backup by the Meters. Maybe you don't need the five-minute reading of "What Now My Love," but "Little Ba-By," the self-fulfilling prophecy "Everything I Do Gonh Be Funky (From Now On)," and "What You Want (Is What You Get)" are decent soul-funk. Of the previously unavailable songs, "A Mellow Good Time Pt. 2" is an instrumental continuation of one of the songs on *The New Lee Dorsey,* while "I'm the One" is a serviceable 1970 Toussaint number. *—Richie Unterberger*

Ride Your Pony / 1966 / Sundazed ♦♦♦

Aside from the title track and the oft-covered, ultra-funky "Get out of My Life, Woman," none of the 12 songs on this early 1966 album are familiar to most listeners. As it turns out it's a quality full-length bridging early-'60s New Orleans R&B with soul, even if the songs tend to be on the light partying side. That's part of the main draw of much New Orleans music, of course, and few were better at projecting a relaxed sense of fun than Dorsey. It helped that all but two of the songs were written by co-producer Allen Toussaint; the Crescent City giant doesn't get nearly as much attention as Smokey Robinson, but as with Smokey, one wonders if Toussaint ever slept in the 1960s, so prolific and generally fine was his output. The Sundazed CD reissue is recommended even if you have the (by now hard to find) original LP, since it nearly doubles the length with almost a dozen tracks from rare 1966-1968 singles. These are more rare than exciting, to be honest, but Toussaint wrote all of these (sharing songwriting credit on one tune, "My Old Car"), and they're more good-time New Orleans soul with gradually modernizing production, even if the tunes weren't memorable enough to reach classic status. Certainly the most interesting is the two-part 1968 45 "Four Corners," an unabashed "Tighten Up" takeoff with bits of James Brown and the Meters rattling around the corners; there's also a 1967 duet single with Betty Harris. *—Richie Unterberger*

★ **Wheelin' and Dealin'** / Aug. 26, 1997 / Arista ♦♦♦♦♦

The EP Collection / Mar. 21, 2000 / See For Miles ♦♦♦♦♦

Nick Drake

b. Jun. 19, 1948, Rangoon, Burma, **d.** Nov. 25, 1974, Tanworth-in-Arden, England

Vocals, Piano, Guitar / British Folk-Rock, Baroque Pop, Progressive Folk, British Folk, Folk-Rock, Singer/Songwriter

A singular talent who passed almost unnoticed during his brief lifetime, Nick Drake produced several albums of chilling, somber beauty. With hindsight, these have come to be recognized as peak achievements of both the British folk-rock scene and the entire rock singer/songwriter genre. Sometimes compared to Van Morrison, Drake in fact resembled Donovan much more in his breathy vocals, strong melodies, and the acoustic-based orchestral sweep of his arrangements. His was a much darker vision than Donovan's, however, with disturbing themes of melancholy, failed romance, mortality, and depression lurking just beneath, or even well above, the surface. Ironically, Drake has achieved a far greater stature in the decades following his death, with an avid cult following that grows by the year. In the manner of the young romantic poets of the 19th century who died before their time, Drake is revered by many listeners today, with a following that spans generations. Baby boomers who missed him the first time around found much to revisit once they discovered him, and his pensive loneliness speaks directly to contemporary alternative rockers who share his sense of morose alienation. *—Richie Unterberger*

★ **Five Leaves Left** / 1969 / Hannibal ♦♦♦♦♦

It's little wonder why Drake felt frustrated at the lack of commercial success his music initially gathered, considering the help he had on his debut record. Besides fine production from Joe Boyd and assistance from folks like Fairport Convention's Richard Thompson and his unrelated bass counterpart from Pentangle, Danny Thompson, Drake also recruited school friend Robert Kirby to create most of the just-right string and wind arrangements. His own performance itself steered a careful balance between too-easy accessibility and maudlin self-reflection, combining the best of both worlds while avoiding the pitfalls on either side. The result was a fantastic debut appearance, and if the cult of Drake consistently reads more into his work than is perhaps deserved, *Five Leaves Left* is still a most successful effort. Having grown out of the amiable but derivative styles captured on the long-circulating series of bootleg home recordings, Drake assays his tunes with just enough drama—world-weariness in the vocals, carefully paced playing, and more—to make it all work. His lyrics capture a subtle poetry of emotion, as on the pastoral semi-fantasia of "The Thoughts of Mary Jane," which his soft, articulate singing brings even more to the full. Sometimes he projects a little more clearly, as on the astonishing voice-and-strings combination "Way to Blue," while elsewhere he's not so clear, suggesting rather than outlining the mood. Understatement is the key to his songs and performances' general success, which makes the combination of his vocals and Rocki Dzidzornu's congas on "Three Hours" and the lovely "'Cello Song," to name two instances, so effective. Danny Thompson is the most regular side performer on the album, his bass work providing subtle heft while never standing in the way of the song—kudos well deserved for Boyd's production as well. *—Ned Raggett*

☆ **Bryter Layter** / 1970 / Hannibal ♦♦♦♦♦

With even more of the Fairport Convention crew helping him out—including bassist Dave Pegg and drummer Dave Mattacks along with, again, a bit of help from Richard Thompson—as well as John Cale and a variety of others, Drake tackled another excellent selection of songs on his second album. Demonstrating the abilities shown on *Five Leaves Left* didn't consist of a fluke, *Bryter Layter* featured another set of exquisitely arranged and performed tunes, with producer Joe Boyd and orchestrator Robert Kirby reprising their roles from the earlier release. Starting with the elegant instrumental "Introduction," as lovely a mood-setting piece as one would want, *Bryter Layter* indulges in a more playful sound at many points, showing that Drake was far from being a constant king of depression. While his performances remain generally low-key and his voice quietly passionate, the arrangements and surrounding musicians add a considerable amount of pep, as on the jazzy groove of the lengthy "Poor Boy." The argument could be made that this contravenes the spirit of Drake's work, but it feels more like a calmer equivalent to the genre-sliding experiments of Van Morrison at around the same time. Numbers that retain a softer approach, like "At the Chime of a City Clock," still possess a gentle drive to them. Cale's additions unsurprisingly favor the classically trained side of his personality, with particularly brilliant results on "Northern Sky." As his performances on keyboards and celeste help set the atmosphere, Drake reaches for a perfectly artful reflection on loss and loneliness and succeeds wonderfully. *—Ned Raggett*

☆ **Pink Moon** / 1972 / Hannibal ♦♦♦♦♦

After two albums of tastefully orchestrated folk-pop, albeit some of the least demonstrative and most affecting around, Drake chose a radical change for what turned out to be his final album. Not even half-an-hour long, with 11 short songs and no more—he famously remarked at the time that he simply had no more to record—*Pink Moon* more than anything else is the record that made Drake the cult figure he remains. Specifically, *Pink Moon* is the bleakest of them all; that the likes of Belle and Sebastian are fans of Drake may be clear enough, but it's doubtful they could ever achieve the calm, focused anguish of this album, as harrowing as it is attractive. No side musicians or outside performers help this time around—it's simply Drake and Drake alone on vocals, acoustic guitar, and a bit of piano, recorded by regular producer Joe Boyd but otherwise untouched by anyone else. The lead-off title track was eventually used in a Volkswagen commercial nearly 30 years later, giving him another renewed burst of appreciation—one of life's many ironies, in that such an affecting song, Drake's softly keened singing and gentle strumming, could turn up in such a strange context. The remainder of the album follows the same general path, with Drake's elegant melancholia avoiding sounding pretentious in the least thanks to his continued embrace of simple, tender vocalizing. Meanwhile, the sheer majesty of his guitar playing—consider the opening notes of "Radio" or "Parasite"—makes for a breathless wonder to behold. If anyone needs confirmation as to why artists like Mark Eitzel, Elliot Smith, Lou Barlow, or Robert Smith hold Drake close to their hearts, it's all here, still as beautiful as the day it was released. *—Ned Raggett*

☆ **Fruit Tree** / 1986 / Hannibal ♦♦♦♦♦

Fruit Tree is a four-disc box set featuring all three of Nick Drake's studio albums (*Five Leaves Left, Bryter Layter, Pink Moon*) and the rarities collection *Time of No Reply.* In other words, it contains every known recording Drake made during his brief lifetime, and listening to the set, the depth of his talent becomes abundantly clear. And the four discs are *not* overkill. The quality of Drake's songs was startlingly high, and anyone who purchases one disc will eventually need the other three albums, making *Fruit Tree* a logical way to acquire all of the records at once. *—Stephen Thomas Erlewine*

Time of No Reply / 1986 / Hannibal ♦♦♦

Released in the mid-'80 during one of the many Drake revivals over the years, combining tracks from the original *Fruit Tree* box set and other outtakes unreleased until then, *Time of No Reply* is a fine coda to Drake's all too brief recording career. A collection of outtakes and alternate versions of more familiar songs, it parallels *Pink Moon* in that all songs but two are simply Drake on his own, his guitar and his voice doing all that needs to be done. The majority of the recordings come from the late '60s, from the slew of sessions and home recordings predating the release of *Five Leaves Left.* They still show Drake working in a touch more traditional mode, but his unmistakable vocal approach is well in place throughout. The title track itself is a gem, raising the question as to why Drake thought it unworthy for initial release, with a softly catchy chorus and sweet, reflective lyrical cast. The takes on "Man in a Shed" and "The Thoughts of Mary Jane," with Richard Thompson adding electric guitar on the latter, make for an intersting contrast to their more familiar studio incarnations. The release concludes with the "final session," four last songs recorded two years after *Pink Moon,* shortly before his death. The songs included on *Time of No Reply* should be considered demos and experiments, but there's no questioning Drake's power for understated exploration of darker moments and emotions remained. *—Ned Raggett*

- **Way to Blue: an Introduction to Nick Drake** / Oct. 4, 1994 / Hannibal ✦✦✦✦
A selection of 16 tracks from all three of his studio albums and the *Time of No Reply* collection, compiled by Drake's producer, Joe Boyd. Of course the music is excellent, but Drake's albums stand so well on their own that this collection of piecemeal offerings hardly works as the best way to experience his distinctively haunting brand of folk-rock. *—Richie Unterberger*

The Dramatics

f. 1962, Detroit, MI, **db.**
Group / Smooth Soul, Quiet Storm, Soul
Before assuming the name the Dramatics, the vocal sextet that was comprised of Rob Davis, Ron Banks, Larry Reed, Robert Ellington, Larry "Squirrel" Demps and Elbert Wilkens initially released two singles as the Dynamics on the Wingate imprint that saw no chart action. The group became a quintet upon Ellington's exit, and also changed their name to the Dramatics. They migrated to the Sport label and in 1967 released their first single to hit the charts, "All Because of You," which peaked at number 42 on the *Billboard* R&B charts. However, in spite of the of the exposure and limited record sales, some group members became discouraged, which facilitated a major personnel change. William "Wee Gee" Howard replaced lead singer Reed, and Willie Ford of the Capitols replaced bass Rob Davis. Also during this time, the Dramatics had signed with producer Don Davis' productions company.

The group wouldn't see a major hit for four years until "Watcha See Is Watcha Get." was released, peaking at number three on the Billboard R&B charts, and sustaining chart action for 15 weeks. That single was followed by the R&B Top Ten single "Get Up and Get Down." Several other hits followed, including "In the Rain."

In 1973 Larry "L.J." Reynolds replaced Howardand Lenny Mayes replacedWilkens. Wilkensformed his own band under the same name, which led the original Dramatics to be briefly known as Ron Banks and the Dramatics while the legal battles ensued.

The Dramatics' success continued with mainly R&B Top 20 hits during the heyday of disco, cracking the R&B Top Ten just once more with "Welcome Back Home" in 1980. In 1981, Reynolds went solo and the group disbanded after Banks' exit in 1983. *—Craig Lytle*

- **The Best of the Dramatics** / 1976 / Stax ✦✦✦✦✦
In the 1960s, Stax Records was best known for raw southern soul that rejected the type of sleekness and pop sensibilities favored by the northern soulsters at Motown. But by the early '70s, Memphis soul was losing its popularity, and Stax's A&R department started to emphasize northern and so-called "uptown" soul in order to stay competitive. One of Stax/Volt's biggest sellers was the Dramatics, a Detroit group that, like the Temptations at Motown and the O'Jays in the Gamble & Huff camp, effectively combined gritty soul belting with a sleek production style. Thanks to major hits ranging from the delightfully funky "Whacha See Is Whacha Get" to slow jams and ballads like "Hey You! Get Off My Mountain," "Toast to the Fool" and the melancholy "In the Rain," the Dramatics were on quite a roll in the early-to-mid-'70s. All of those gems are included on the hour-long CD, *The Best of the Dramatics,* which offers a fine overview of the quintet's Stax/Volt years. Many Dramatics albums are worth owning, but if a listener were allowed to own only one Dramatics CD, this would be it. *—Alex Henderson*

ABC Years 1974-1980 / Nov. 21, 1995 / Soul Classics ✦✦✦
The Dramatics were one of the best soul groups of the early '70s, scoring a series of hits for Volt Records. After leaving Volt, they went to ABC Records in 1974 and stayed there until the end of the decade. The hits began to become a little bit smaller, and that's partially because they were either covering other people's hits ("Me and Mrs. Jones") or lacked solid material. *ABC Years 1974-1980* collects their biggest hits from this period. While the music on the collection isn't as consistently thrilling as their early '70s hits, there are a couple of gems buried in these 11 tracks that makes the album worthwhile for dedicated fans. *—Stephen Thomas Erlewine*

The Shake It Well: The Best of the Dramatics 1974-1980 / Oct. 20, 1998 / MCA ✦✦✦
A nice collection of this Detroit-based group's best records for the Cadet and ABC-MCA labels between 1974-1980. Besides the title track (a number five R&B hit that crossed over to the pop charts), highlights include "I Can't Get Over You,""Be My Girl," "You're Foolin' You," "Love Is Missing From Our Lives," "Don't Make Me No Promises" and the pop crossover smash "Do What You Want, Be What You Are." Although their earlier sides for Wingate, Sport and Volt aren't on here (thus leaving off their biggest hit, "Whatcha See Is What You Get"), this is still a nice collection of tunes by one of the '70s' most prolific and dependable R&B acts. *—Cub Koda*

Ultimate Collection / Sep. 19, 2000 / Hip-O ✦✦✦✦
Spanning their biggest singles from the '70s and '80s, the Dramatics' *Ultimate Collection* includes staples like "In the Rain," "Whatcha See Is Whatcha Get," and "Be My Girl." "You're Fooling You," "Welcome Back Home," "I'm Going By the Stars in Your Eyes," and "Me and Mrs. Jones" are some of the other notable tracks from this retrospective, which covers the group's years with Stax, ABC, and Volt. Though it doesn't go into as much depth as some previous Dramatics collections, *Ultimate Collection* does a good job of presenting highlights from the majority of the group's career. *—Heather Phares*

Dream Syndicate

f. 1981, Los Angeles, CA, **db.** 1989
Group / College Rock, Jangle Pop, Paisley Underground, Alternative Pop/Rock
Dream Syndicate are at the foundation (alongside the Velvet Underground, the Stooges and R.E.M.) of contemporary alternative music sheerly because at the time when most bands were experimenting with new technology, the Syndicate deigned to bring back the guitar. Fronted by Steve Wynn, the band debuted with a self-titled, unbelievably Velvet Underground-like EP on Wynn's own Down There label. It was shortly off to Ruby/Slash for *Days of Wine and Roses,* the most lauded record on the college charts that year. The record has been cited as influential from artists as diverse as Kurt Cobain to the Black Crowes' Chris Robinson. Live, they had developed into an assaultive guitar band prone to jamming which helped earn them the tag as leaders of L.A.'s Paisley Underground movement. 1984's *Medicine Show* was met with mixed response by the college crowd. Wynn took his cues from Neil Young and Crazy Horse on the record rather than Lou Reed (who was considered a preferable source at the time), and the rootsier sound caused a backlash with the fan base. In 1986, a new lineup and a flailing morale, as the band label-hopped, spawned *Out of the Grey* and the Elliot Mazer-produced *Ghost Stories* in 1989. *—Denise Sullivan*

The Days of Wine & Roses / 1982 / Slash ✦✦✦✦✦
On the one hand, where the Dream Syndicate came from was so obvious that it almost hurt. The Velvet Underground was a clear touchstone (if not quite the original LaMonte Young ensemble the band name referred to), as were the Doors, the Byrds, and any number of blues and country traditions and more. Had they been around in the late '60, one might have wondered whether they would have garnered much attention in comparison. But the early '80s was the band's time and place, and their fusions of all the above and more via punk-inspired energy achieved its own level of deserved attention. Capturing the original killer Wynn/Precoda/Smith/Duck lineup performing with inspiration throughout, *The Days of Wine and Roses* trumps the "paisley underground" tag the band was saddled with by being a great rock record, full on. While Wynn received the lion's share of attention thanks to his ghost-of-Lou Reed vocals and frontman status, arguably it's Precoda who is the real reason to listen in. Both his rave-ups and gentler shadings are phenomenal, as a random listen of songs like "Definitely Clean" and the sweet, Smith-sung "Too Little, Too Late" show. The Smith/Duck rhythm section grooves along fairly enough, at its best on the Krautrock-inspired chug of Precoda's composition "Halloween." Highlights include the romping "Then She Remembers," with a much more direct Wynn vocal that makes for good in-your-face fun, and the mid-tempo moodout of "When You Smile," Precoda's screeching feedback playing around the mix's edges. Concluding with the epochal title track, which builds to a frenetic climax not once but twice, *The Days of Wine and Roses* is a grand treat. *—Ned Raggett*

Medicine Show / 1984 / A&M ✦✦✦✦✦
More Neil Young and Crazy Horse than the previous Lou Reed and the Velvet Underground-inspired album, the Syndicate rip through eight fairly traditional (save for the feedback) rock songs. The CD reissue includes *This Is Not the Dream Syndicate Album... Live!,* five songs performed from the album. "The Medicine Show" and the similar "John Coltrane Stereo Blues" are the keepers, and check the guitar on "Bullet With My Name on It." The record wrestles with American roots music in a way college rockers probably weren't familiar with, and thus it was almost universally hated at the time. Wynn admits in the liner notes to the CD reissue that this is his favorite release with the band. *—Denise Sullivan*

Out of the Grey / 1986 / Atavistic ✦✦✦
Like nearly everything released that year, *Out of the Grey* suffered from a touch of the post-new wave flu. But "50 in a 25 Zone" has that old, bluesy Syndicate spirit, as does "Now I Ride Alone," and Steve Wynn is still an exceptional vocal stylist, bringing heart and meaning to every word he writes. *—Denise Sullivan*

Ghost Stories / 1988 / Restless ✦✦✦
Opening with the self-referential "The Side I'll Never Show," and produced by Neil Young and Crazy Horse vet Elliot Mazer, Wynn and Co. mine the dark and rusty terrain of folk and blues-rock that they ultimately made work to their advantage on this very straight-ahead rock album. Wynn's vocal style and forthright lyrics never really connected with the masses at the time, but years later, it's clear he was making music for the ages. *—Denise Sullivan*

- **Tell Me When It's Over: The Best of Dream Syndicate** / Jun. 23, 1992 / Rhino ✦✦✦✦✦
While the Dream Syndicate's 1982 debut album, *The Days of Wine and Roses,* made them an immediate sensation on the post-punk underground scene, their subsequent body of work rarely received the same degree of attention, partly because of the band's deliberate swing away from noisy neo-Velvet Underground jamming after the departure of guitarist Karl Precoda and partly because most of their subsequent albums lacked the sonic and thematic consistency of their debut. The shame of this was that leader Steve Wynn grew steadily as a songwriter through the band's career, and even their patchiest albums had at least two or three cuts worth hearing. Thankfully, *Tell Me When It's Over: The Best of the Dream Syndicate* sets the record straight about this misunderstood band's career, offering about half of *The Days of Wine and Roses* (and a cut from the band's first self-released EP) alongside nine neglected gems like "Merrittville," "Now I Ride Alone," and "Loving the Sinner, Hating the Sin"; there's also a hard rocking cover of Eric Clapton's "Let It Rain" thrown in for good measure. Anyone wanting a crash course in the Dream Syndicate's challenging body of work could hardly do better than to give *Tell Me When It's Over* a listen. *—Mark Deming*

The Drifters

f. May 1953, New York, NY
Group / Doo Wop, R&B, Soul
Originally a backup group formed around the soaring vocal talents of Clyde McPhatter, the Drifters—like their '50s counterparts, the Platters and the Coasters—have turned out to be one of the most enduring "franchises" in rock & roll. Though it's been years since any of the original members have been involved (almost all of them being long deceased), chances are if there's an oldies but goodies stage show happening somewhere tonight, there's a 50-50 shot that some form of the Drifters will be up on that stage, singing the hits that made the original group a legend. Unlike other groups who lost key members along the way and never regained their artistic or commercial footing, the various incarnations of the Drifters produced distinctly memorable material every step of the way. Depending on what time frame you come in on during their 40-plus years as a group, you'll discover that they turned from a hard rhythm and gospel doo wop aggregation to one of the smoothest and most romantic ever to grace an AM radio. One of the first Black R&B groups to utilize a string section on their records ("There Goes My Baby," 1959), their middle period sound defined universal love and the good life as seen through the eyes of the ghetto, an arresting combination that won

them crossover appeal. That they not only moved, but prospered, with the times is testimony enough to their rightly deserved longevity. *—Cub Koda*

☆ **All-Time Greatest Hits & More: 1959-1965** / 1988 / Rhino/Atlantic ✦✦✦✦✦
If Rhino's *Very Best of the Drifters* is a fine R&B snack, then *All-Time Greatest Hits & More: 1959-1965* is a three-course gourmet meal with dessert built on the same ingredients. Forget about the higher price and the fact that 40 songs might seem to be more Drifters than most casual listeners would want—*All-Time Greatest Hits & More: 1959-1965* is a towering and magnificent collection of some of the best popular R&B ever done this side of Sam Cooke. And, as with Sam Cooke, the beautiful part of the Drifters' work during this period is that any look beyond and behind their hits reveals a lot more songs that were every bit as good as those hits. There's not even a slightly weak track anywhere on *All-Time Greatest Hits & More,* which contains the biggest hits Ben E. King, Rudy Lewis, and Johnny Moore sang for the group. "There Goes My Baby," "This Magic Moment," "Save the Last Dance for Me," "Sweets for My Sweet," "I Count the Tears," "Some Kind of Wonderful," "Up on the Roof," "On Broadway," and "Under the Boardwalk" are all here, mastered in surprisingly good sound for the late '80s. There's a lot more than that, however—the producers have also included killer B-sides (such as "Let the Music Play") that hadn't been in print since the mid-'60s, and they've dug even deeper to throw in finished tracks that were left in the vaults until the '70s. The notes by Colin Escott are an added bonus, displaying his usual command for historical detail. *—Bruce Eder*

☆ **Let the Boogie-Woogie Roll: Greatest Hits 1953-1958** / 1988 / Rhino/Atlantic ✦✦✦✦✦
This is a repackaged and resequenced version of the similarly titled 1988 Atlantic double CD, containing the 40 songs recorded by the early Drifters in their Clyde McPhatter, David Baughan, and Johnny Moore eras—and it's as fine a body of rhythm & blues-cum-rock & roll as you'll ever find. The work runs from the ethereal, soulful balladry ("Gone") to bluesy laments ("Don't Dog Me") and distinctive reinterpretations of classic songs ("White Christmas," "The Bells of St. Mary's") to out and out rock & roll ("Money Honey," "Let The Boogie Woogie Roll," "Bip Bam"), with lots of classic moments and songs. Certainly Clyde McPhatter never cut better music than the 20 tracks he did with the Drifters, all laid out on Disc One. Their string of hits was unbroken by the arrival of Johnny Moore, so the second disc in this set is as enjoyable as the first. The improvement to this set over the original include a bigger type-face for the notes, and the altered sequencing, which puts everything in order of recording, not release, thus presenting the way the group evolved, step by step and song by song. The sound, in addition to showing off the group's extraordinary vocal prowess, also highlights the playing of guitarist Mickey Baker and saxman Sam "The Man" Taylor. *—Bruce Eder*

★ **The Very Best of the Drifters** / Apr. 20, 1993 / Rhino ✦✦✦✦✦
This mid-priced 16-song collection is the successor to the old Atlantic Records *Drifters Golden Hits,* covering the group's very best songs from "There Goes My Baby" in 1959 on up through 1964 in a more comprehensive way. Very pleasingly remastered and handy on its own terms, *The Very Best of the Drifters* also provides just a taste of what the post-1958 group had to offer, even in terms of singles. No one will dislike anything about it, but those who have heard even part of the two-CD package *All-Time Greatest Hits & More* will recognize *The Very Best of the Drifters* as nothing but a superficial sampler of what the Ben E. King/Rudy Lewis/Johnny Moore version of the group left behind. *The Very Best of the Drifters* is a great place to start, but the leap from this material to the rest of the Drifters' best is such a short one that, unless time or budgetary limitations dictate otherwise, it can be bypassed in favor of Atlantic's double-disc *All-Time Greatest Hits & More.* *—Bruce Eder*

Rockin' & Driftin': The Drifters Box / 1996 / Rhino ✦✦✦✦✦
A three-CD, 79-song box spanning all incarnations of the group, from 1953 to 1976 (although only six of the tracks date from after 1966). Sure, there's a lot of classic music here: All of the big hits, and many interesting flops and B-sides. Assuming, however, that the audience for this set is mostly limited to serious Drifters fans, it's likely that many or most of the listeners falling into that category already have the *Let the Boogie Woogie Roll* and *All-Time Greatest Hits & More* compilations, which covers just about all of the essential cuts from the box. If you already own those CDs, you may well want to pass this up, but if you have yet to build a serious Drifters collection, this will supply virtually everything you need. And, frankly, then some; some of this is pretty extraneous, particularly the '70s cuts. A significant bonus is their previously unreleased 1963 version of "Only in America," a song which was ultimately given to Jay & the Americans (who had a hit with it) because it was deemed too controversial for a Black group to release. *—Richie Unterberger*

Ducks Deluxe

f. 1972, **db.** 1975
Group / Pub Rock, Rock & Roll
If the old scientific adage is true—that for every action there is an equal and opposite reaction—than British pub-rockers Ducks Deluxe were purely and simply a reaction. With the mid-'70s English pop scene dominated by glitter/glam-rockers like Gary Glitter, Sweet or blustery, chops-heavy art-rockers like Yes, Tull, Genesis, etc., then Ducks Deluxe represented none of the above. One of the first pub-rock bands, the Ducks played basic American-style blues and boogie with remarkable panache and thorough disregard for the whims of the zeitgeist. They never were hugely popular, but the unpretentious, do-it-yourself, working-class attitude they and their contemporaries (most notably seminal pub-rockers Dr. Feelgood) exuded influenced the English punk scene that was right around the corner. With friends like Dave Edmunds producing their records, the Ducks (guitarist/vocalist Sean Tyla, guitarist Martin Belmont, bassist Nick Garvey, and keyboardist Andy McMasters) came up with engaging, though not life-changing, records that celebrated the simple joys of rock & roll. Sure, much of it sounds like recycled Chuck Berry, but there's an infectious enthusiasm that the fan in you, who simply wants to hoist a pint of lager and hear some Little Richard, will love. Ironically, to get the biggest promotional boost in America, the Ducks Deluxe LP was released three years after they'd split up. This little bit of shift marketing came as a result of ex-Ducks going on to more prominent bands like the Motors, the Rumour and the Tyla Gang. *—John Dougan*

● **Ducks Deluxe/Taxi to the Terminal Zone** / 1974 / Edsel ✦✦✦✦✦
Both of the group's albums, *Ducks Deluxe* and *Taxi to the Terminal Zone,* compiled on one CD with one song from each removed to fit the format's time restriction—really a best-of, and worth any three Led Zeppelin albums. *—Bruce Eder*

Don't Mind Rockin' Tonite / 1978 / RCA ✦✦✦
After RCA failed to do much for the band when the label released their self-titled debut record in 1974, the powers that be decided that this collection of material from their two previous LPs, along with some outtakes and B-sides, would engender more interest in the band now that they had some punk/new wave credibility. Well, it was a good thought, but it didn't work. Marketing avarice notwithstanding, this is a fine, loose-limbed, fast, and funky record chock full of guitar bombs from Martin Belmont and some macho growling from Sean Tyla. The pure pop of "Love's Melody" (written by McMasters) is jarring in juxtaposition to all the blues-based grunting, but nothing detracts from the good vibe this record and the Ducks produced in their short existence. *—John Dougan*

The Dukes of Stratosphear

f. 1985
Group / College Rock, British Psychedelia, Neo-Psychedelia, Psychedelic, Alternative Pop/Rock
In 1985, the British pop band XTC recorded an EP of affectionate parodies of '60s psychedelia and guitar-pop called *25 O'Clock.* Instead of releasing the EP under their own name, they released the record under the name the Dukes of Stratosphear. Working with producer John Leckie, all three members of the group adopted pseudonyms—Andy Partridge was Sir John Johns, Colin Moulding was the Red Curtain and David Gregory was Lord Cornelius Plum. For this one project Gregory's brother Ian joined the band under the nameIan E.I.E.I. Owen. The EP was released without mention of XTC's name anywhere on the record, and the group claimed they had nothing to do with the project.

Two years after the appearance of *25 O'Clock,* the Dukes of Stratosphear released a full album, *Psonic Psunspot.* By the time *Psonic Psunspot* appeared in 1987, XTC were beginning to admit in interviews that they were indeed the Dukes of Stratosphear. Later in 1987, both the EP and album were released on a single compact disc, *Chips from the Chocolate Fireball.* *—Stephen Thomas Erlewine*

● **Chips from the Chocolate Fireball** / 1987 / Geffen ✦✦✦✦✦
During the mid-'80s, XTC developed a deep fascination with '60s psychedelia that manifested itself on their late-1986 masterpiece *Skylarking.* While *Skylarking* was filled with lush pop reminiscent of the Beatles and Beach Boys, it was generally a sober affair, since they decided to leave many of the lighter songs off the album for B-sides and future albums. During this time, they decided to develop their alter egos of the Dukes of Stratosphear, a way to let all of their infatuation with psychedelia flourish. Both the EP *25 O'Clock* and the full-length *Psonic Psunspot,* collected on the single-disc *Chips From the Chocolate Fireball,* capture the sound of '60s psychedelia remarkably well. All of the sonic details, from the fuzz guitars to the cavernous echoes and sound effects, are in place, as are the self-consciously trippy lyrics. But what makes the Dukes of Stratosphear far more than a comedy band are the songs, which happen to be some of the best pure pop tunes XTC ever wrote: "My Love Explodes" has a tense, spiraling guitar line and melody; "Little Lighthouse" and "You're My Drug" are wonderful pastiches; "The Mole From the Ministry" is a devilish homage to "I Am the Walrus" and Bowie; and the group rarely wrote a song as infectious as the bright, jangling "Vanishing Girl." Despite the clever craftsmanship, XTC has never sounded so carefree or effortless, been quite as immediately catchy or consistent—*Chips From the Chocolate Fireball* is too good to be overlooked as a side-project folly, because it truly is some of the best music XTC ever made. And, coincidentally, it's some of the best psychedelic pop ever recorded as well. *—Stephen Thomas Erlewine*

Duran Duran

f. 1978, Birmingham, England
Group / New Romantic, Pop/Rock, New Wave, Synth Pop, Dance-Pop
Duran Duran personified New Wave for much of the mainstream audience. And for good reason, too. Duran Duran's reputation was built through music videos, which accentuated their fashion-model looks and glamourous sense of style. Without music videos, it is likely that the band's pop-funk—described by the group as the Sex Pistols meets Chic—would never have made the group international pop stars. While Duran Duran did have sharper pop sensibilities than their New Romantic contemporaries like Spandau Ballet and Ultravox, none of their peers exploited MTV and music video like the Birmingham-based quintet. Each video the group made was distinctive, incorporatin a number of cinematic styles to showcase the band as either part of the jet-setting elite ("Rio") or as worldly adventurers ("Hungry Like the Wolf"). While early videos like "Girls on Film" and "The Chaffeur" sparked controversy in England over their sexual content, their best-known clips were often based on hit contemporary movies. "Hungry Like the Wolf" uncannily recalled *Raiders of the Lost Ark,* while "Union of the Snake" and "The Wild Boys" brought to mind *The Road Warrior.* The clever videos helped make Duran Duran's rise to popularity remarkably swift. Between 1982 and 1984, they rocketed from underground British post-punk sensations to teen idols. But their fall from grace was equally fast. By the late '80s, the group's lineup had fragmented, and the remaining members had trouble landing hist singles. Nevertheless, the group pulled off a surprising, if short-lived, comeback in the early '90s as a sophisticated soft-rock trio. *—Stephen Thomas Erlewine*

Duran Duran [First] / 1981 / Capitol ✦✦✦✦✦
Duran Duran's self-titled debut effectively established their slick, catchy synth-pop sound. Featuring the decadent "Girls on Film" and "Planet Earth," the album set the pace for scores of new wave bands in the early '80s, which were subsequently dubbed the new romantics. *—Stephen Thomas Erlewine*

Rio / 1982 / Capitol ✦✦✦✦✦
From its Nagel cover to the haircuts and overall design—and first and foremost the music—*Rio* is as representative of the eighties as it gets, at its best. The original Duran Duran's high point, and just as likely the band's as a whole, its fusion of style and substance ensures that even two decades after its release it remains as listenable and danceable as ever. The quintet integrates its sound near-perfectly throughout, the John and Roger Taylor rhythm section providing both driving propulsion and subtle pacing. For the latter, consider the lush semi-tropical sway of "Save a Prayer" or the closing paranoid creep of "The Chauffeur," a descendant of Roxy Music's equally affecting dark groover "The Bogus Man." Andy Taylor's muscular riffs provide fine rock crunch throughout, Rhodes' synth wash adds perfect sheen, and Le Bon tops it off with sometimes overly cryptic lyrics that still always sound just fine in context courtesy of his strong delivery. *Rio's* two biggest smashes burst open the door in America for the New Romantic/synth rock crossover. & "Hungry Like the Wolf" blended a tight, guitar-heavy groove with electronic production and a series of instant hooks, while the title track was even more anthemic, with a great sax break from guest Andy Hamilton adding to the soaring atmosphere. Lesser known cuts like "Lonely In Your Nightmare" and "Last Chance on the Stairway" still have pop thrills a-plenty, while "Hold Back the Rain" is the sleeper hit on *Rio*, an invigorating blast of feedback, keyboards and beat that doesn't let up. From start to finish, a great album that has outlasted its era. *—Ned Raggett*

Seven and the Ragged Tiger / 1983 / Capitol ✦✦✦
Seven and the Ragged Tiger was released at the height of Duran Duran-mania and it shows. Throughout the album, the group replicates the sound of *Rio*, yet they have failed to write strong material. Although they are catchy, the singles "Union of the Snake" and "The Reflex" aren't on par with "Hungry like the Wolf" and "Rio." Only the brooding "New Moon on Monday" matches the inspired pop-craft of *Rio*. *—Stephen Thomas Erlewine*

Arena / 1984 / Capitol ✦✦

Notorious / 1986 / Capitol ✦✦✦

Big Thing / 1988 / Capitol ✦✦

Decade: Greatest Hits / Nov. 15, 1989 / Capitol ✦✦✦✦✦
Decade is an excellent singles compilation, featuring all of the highlights from Duran Duran's heyday—"Planet of Earth," "Girls on Film," "Rio," "Is There Something I Should Know," "Union of the Snake," "The Reflex," "The Wild Boys," "Save a Prayer," "A View to a Kill"—plus late-'80s hits like "Notorious," "Skin Trade," "I Don't Want Your Love" and "All She Wants Is." By juxtaposing their stylish new wave pop against their latter-day lite-funk experiments, the group's decline becomes shockingly evident, but no other Duran Duran album sums up their appeal like *Decade*, and it's hard to imagine another compilation working the same ground as effectively. *—Stephen Thomas Erlewine*

Liberty / Aug. 13, 1990 / Capitol ✦

Duran Duran [The Wedding Album] / 1993 / Capitol ✦✦✦✦
Duran Duran came back out of nowhere in early 1993 with a new album and a huge hit, "Ordinary World." The group sounds more relaxed and mature than it did during their glory days, but not all that much has changed; instead of personifying the days of early-'80s synthesized dance-pop, the music is smooth dance-pop for the '90s. Taken on its own terms, *Duran Duran* works every bit as well as *Duran Duran, Rio* or *Seven and the Ragged Tiger*. "Ordinary World" and "Come Undone" are wonderful pop singles that sit between some passable album tracks and the occasional embarrassment, namely the wretched cover of The Velvet Underground's "Femme Fatale." In other words, Duran Duran are back and as good as they ever were. *—Stephen Thomas Erlewine*

Thank You / Apr. 1995 / Capitol ✦

Medazzaland / Oct. 14, 1997 / Capitol ✦✦✦

● **Greatest** / Nov. 3, 1998 / Capitol ✦✦✦✦✦
Although it doesn't play as well as the chronologically-arranged *Decade, Greatest* features all of its 14 tracks and adds, most significantly, the minor hit "New Moon on Monday" and the comeback smashes "Ordinary World" and "Come Undone." The drab packaging is a disappointment, and one could do probably do without "Electric Barbarella" and "Serious," but *Greatest* is currently the best (and only) portrait of one of the great pop bands of the '80s. *—Jim Smith*

Pop Trash / Jun. 13, 2000 / Hollywood ✦✦

Ian Dury

b. May 12, 1942, Upminster, Essex, England, **d.** Mar. 27, 2000
Vocals / British Punk, Pub Rock, New Wave, Punk, Disco
Rock & roll has always been populated by fringe figures, cult artists that managed to develop a fanatical following because of their outsized quirks, but few cult rockers have ever been quite as weird, or beloved, as Ian Dury. As the leader of the underappreciated and ill-fated pub-rockers Kilburn & the High Roads, Dury cut a striking figure—he remained handicapped from a childhood bout with polio, yet stalked the stage with dynamic charisma, spitting out music-hall numbers and rockers in his thick Cockney accent. Dury was 28 at the time he formed Kilburn, and once they disbanded, conventional wisdom would have suggested that he was far too old to become a pop star, but conventional wisdom never played much of a role in Dury's career. Signing with the fledgling indie label Stiff in 1978, Dury developed a strange fusion of music-hall, punk rock and disco that brought him to stardom in his native England. Driven by a warped sense of humor and a pulsating beat, singles like "Hit Me With Your Rhythm Stick," "Sex & Drugs & Rock & Roll" and "Reasons to Be Cheerful (Part 3)" became Top Ten hits in the U.K., yet Dury's most distinctive qualities—his dry wit and wordplay, thick Cockney brogue, and fascination with music-hall—kept him from gaining popularity outside of England. After his second album, Dury's style became formulaic, and he faded away in the early '80s, turning to an acting career instead. *—Stephen Thomas Erlewine*

New Boots & Panties!! / 1977 / Repertoire ✦✦✦✦✦
Ian Dury's primary appeal lies in his lyrics, which are remarkably clever sketches of British life delivered with a wry wit. Since Dury's accent is thick and his language dense with local slang, much of these pleasures aren't discernable to casual listeners, leaving the music to stand on its own merits. On his debut album, *New Boots and Panties!*, Dury's music is at its best, and even that is a bizarrely uneven fusion of pub rock, punk rock, and disco. Still, Dury's off-kilter charm and irrepressible energy make the album gel, with the disco pulse of "Wake Up and Make Love With Me" making perfect sense next to the gentle tribute "Sweet Gene Vincent," the roaring punk of "Blockheads," and the revamped musichall of "Billericay Dickie" and "My Old Man." [Repertoire's 1996 CD reissue adds five essential singles—"Sex and Drugs and Rock and Roll," "Razzle in My Pocket," "You're More Than Fair," "England's Glory," "What a Waste"—that nearly make the disc a Dury best-of.] *—Stephen Thomas Erlewine*

Do It Yourself / 1979 / Repertoire ✦✦✦✦
Ian Dury's music always bordered on the functional, since it was used as a backdrop for his wry vignettes and stories, but on his second album *Do It Yourself*, that aspect came to the fore. Largely abandoning the punk inflections that were scattered throughout *New Boots and Panties!*, *Do It Yourself* is a record of mid-tempo pub rock disco—competently played, but rarely engaging. Dury's stories are all wonderful, filled with humor and penetrating detail, but only a handful of tracks, such as the terrific "Inbetweenies," are married to actual hooks, and by the end of the record, the steady disco throb has become a little numbing. Even with these faults, *Do It Yourself* remains one of Dury's very best records, since his lyrical facility throughout the album is simply amazing. [Repertoire's 1996 CD reissue of *Do It Yourself* improves the album considerably by adding several singles—"Hit Me With Your Rhythm Stick," "There Ain't Half Been Some Clever Bastards," "Reasons to Be Cheerful, Part 3," "Common As Muck," "I Want to Be Straight"—that are far more successful disco/pub rock fusions than anything on the album.] *—Stephen Thomas Erlewine*

Laughter / 1980 / Stiff ✦✦✦
Working with lead guitarist Wilko Johnson (Dr. Feelgood), Ian Dury gradually moves away from disco with his third album, *Laughter*. The steady dance pulse is still apparent, but it's balanced by rockers and pub singalongs that give the album more depth. That doesn't necessarily make it a better album, however. Dury's humor is at its most basic, as the titles of "Uncoolohol," "Take Your Elbow out of the Soup You're Sitting on the Chicken," "Oh Mr. Peanut," and "Fucking Ada" indicate, and his lyrics aren't quite as stunningly fluid as before. Still, the record is fun, and "Superman's Big Sister," "Yes & No (Paula)," and "Over the Points" are pretty infectious, but the record can't help but illustrate that Dury's peak period is over. *—Stephen Thomas Erlewine*

Lord Upminster / Nov. 1981 / Polydor ✦✦✦

● **Sex & Drugs & Rock 'n' Roll: Best of Ian Dury and the Blockheads** / Apr. 28, 1992 / Rhino ✦✦✦✦✦
Ian Dury could make wonderful albums (and sometimes did, most notably the inarguable classic *New Boots and Panties!!*), but he saved many of his finest moments for his singles, which justifiably made him a legend in his native England between 1977 and 1980. With the most notable exception of Ray Davies and Paul Weller, few U.K. rockers embraced their Britishness with greater fervor than Dury, and he mined his for a wit, gleeful eccentricity, and street-smart intelligence no one could touch. And his band, the Blockheads, were as musos stronger than anyone to emerge during the British new wave explosion (their years of slogging it out on the pub circuit certainly paid off), but their curiously refreshing light funk also boasted an oddball good humor and cleverness that was the equal of their leader (no small feat). *Sex & Drugs & Rock & Roll: The Best of Ian Dury and the Blockheads* collects 18 superb sides from the band's glory days, and while the bigger hits like "Hit Me With Your Rhythm Stick," "Reasons to Be Cheerful, Part 3," and the title cut are just as good as you remember, there are plenty of pearly lesser-knowns on board, such as the childhood tale of daring "Razzle in My Pocket," the charming "Common As Muck," the hilariously anthemic "I Want to Be Straight," and the odd but captivating prognostication of "You'll See Glimpses." While Dury made plenty of other records worth investigating, if you're only going to own one Ian Dury album, this is certainly the one to get, and it truly does capture the man's singular magic at its best. *—Mark Deming*

Bob Dylan (Robert Allen Zimmerman)

b. May 24, 1941, Duluth, MN
Vocals, Keyboards, Piano, Harmonica, Guitar / Album Rock, Folk-Rock, Singer/Songwriter, Country-Rock, Rock & Roll
Bob Dylan's influence on popular music is incalculable. As a songwriter, he pioneered several different schools of pop songwriting, from confessional singer/songwriter to winding, hallucinatory, stream-of-conscious narratives. As a vocalist, he broke down the notions that in order to perform, a singer had to have a conventionally good voice, thereby redefining the role of vocalist in popular music. As a musician, he sparked several genres of pop music, including electrified folk-rock and country-rock. And that just touches on the tip of his achievements. Dylan's force was evident during his height of popularity in the '60s—the Beatles' shift toward introspective songwriting in the mid-'60s never would have happened without him—but his influence echoed throughout several subsequent generations. Many of his songs became popular standards, and his best albums were undisputed classics of the rock & roll canon. Dylan's influence throughout folk music was equally powerful, and he marks a pivotal turning point in its 20th-century evolution, signifying when the genre moved away from traditional songs and toward personal songwriting. Even when his sales declined in the '80s and '90s, Dylan's presence was calculable. *—Stephen Thomas Erlewine*

Bob Dylan / Mar. 19, 1962 / Columbia ✦✦✦
Somewhat dismissed in comparison to the overwhelming quality of what followed, Bob Dylan's eponymous debut is nevertheless a wonderful modern folk record, capturing a singer of considerable skill and a writer of enormous potential. The record is primarily devoted to covers, but these are largely imaginative choices and the interpretations are equally so, particu-

larly on "Pretty Peggy-O," "Baby Let Me Follow You Down," "House of the Risin' Sun," and "In My Time of Dyin'." These songs find Dylan giving idiosyncratic, yet inviting performances and certainly stand among the finest folk revival of the time. Still, what's really impressive about the album are the two originals, "Talkin' New York" and "Song to Woody," which reveal Dylan already possesses a remarkable sense of songcraft, relying on tradition but opening it up, personalizing it. He would soon expand these gifts, but this charming record remains revelatory in how it illustrates exactly where he's coming from. *—Stephen Thomas Erlewine*

★ **The Freewheelin' Bob Dylan** / May 27, 1963 / Columbia ♦♦♦♦♦
It's hard not to overestimate the importance of *Freewheelin' Bob Dylan*, the record that firmly established Bob Dylan as an unparalleled songwriter, one of considerable skill, imagination, and vision. At the time, folk had been quite popular on college campus and bohemian circles, making headway onto the pop charts in diluted form, and while there certainly were a number of gifted songwriters, nobody had transcended the scene as Dylan did with this record. There are a couple (very good) covers, with "Corrina Corrina" and "Honey Just Allow Me One More Chance," but they pale with the originals here. At the time, the social protests received the most attention, and deservedly so, since "Blowin' in the Wind," "Masters of War," and "A Hard Rain's A-Gonna Fall" weren't just specific in their targets, they were gracefully executed and even melodic. Although they've proven resilient throughout the years, if that's all *Freewheelin'* had to offer, it wouldn't have had its seismic impact, but this also revealed a songwriter who could turn out whimsy ("Don't Think Twice, It's All Right"), gorgeous love songs ("Girl From the North Country"), and cheerfully absurdist humor ("Bob Dylan's Blues," "Bob Dylan's Dream") with equal skill. This is rich, imaginative music, capturing the sound and spirit of America as much as that of Louis Armstrong, Hank Williams, or Elvis Presley. Dylan, in many ways, recorded music that equaled it, but he never topped it. *—Stephen Thomas Erlewine*

The Times They Are A-Changin' / Jan. 13, 1964 / Columbia ♦♦♦♦♦
If *The Times They Are A-Changin'* isn't a marked step forward from *The Freewheelin' Bob Dylan*, even if it is his first collection of all originals, it's nevertheless a fine collection all the same. It isn't as rich as *Freewheelin'*, and Dylan has tempered his sense of humor considerably, choosing to concentrate on social protests in the style of "Blowin' in the Wind." With the title track, he wrote an anthem that nearly equaled that song, and "With God on Our Side" and "Only a Pawn in Their Game" are nearly as good, while "Ballad of Hollis Brown" and "The Lonesome Death of Hattie Carroll" are remarkably skilled re-castings of contemporary tales of injustice. His absurdity is missed, but he makes up for it with the wonderful "One Too Many Mornings" and "Boots of Spanish Leather," two lovely classics. If there are a couple of songs that don't achieve the level of the aforementioned songs, that speaks more to the quality of those songs than the weakness of the remainder of the record. And that's also true of the album itself—yes, it pales next to its predecessor, but it's terrific by any other standard. *—Stephen Thomas Erlewine*

☆ **Another Side of Bob Dylan** / Aug. 8, 1964 / Columbia ♦♦♦♦♦
The other side of Bob Dylan referred to in the title is presumably his romantic, absurdist and whimsical sides—anything that wasn't featured on the staunchly folky, protest-heavy *Times They Are A-Changing*, really. Because of this, *Another Side of Bob Dylan* is a more varied record and it's more successful, too, since it captures Dylan expanding his music, turning in imaginative, poetic performance on love songs and protest tunes alike. This has an equal number of classics to its predecessor, actually, with "All I Really Want to Do," "Chimes of Freedom," "My Back Pages," "I Don't' Believe You," and "It Ain't Me Babe" standing among his standards, but the key to the record's success are the album tracks, which are graceful, poetic, and layered. Both the lyrics and music have gotten deeper and Dylan's trying more things—this, in its construction and attitude, is hardly strictly folk, it encompasses far more than that. The result is one of his very best records, a lovely intimate affair. *—Stephen Thomas Erlewine*

☆ **Bringing It All Back Home** / Mar. 22, 1965 / Columbia ♦♦♦♦♦
With *Another Side of Bob Dylan*, Dylan began pushing past folk, and with *Bringing It All Back Home*, he exploded the boundaries, producing an album of boundless imagination and skill. And it's not just that he went electric, either, rocking hard on "Subterranean Homesick Blues," "Maggie's Farm," and "Outlaw Blues," it's that he's exploding with imagination throughout the record. After all, the music on its second side—the nominal folk songs—derive from the same vantage point as the rockers, leaving traditional folk concerns behind and delving deep into the personal. And this isn't just introspection, either, since the surreal paranoia on "It's Alright, Ma (I'm Only Bleeding)" and the whimsical poetry of "Mr. Tambourine Man" are individual, yet not personal. And that's just the tip of the iceberg, really, as he writes uncommonly beautiful love songs ("She Belongs to Me," "Love Minus Zero/No Limit") which sit along side uncommonly funny fantasias ("On the Road Again," "Bob Dylan's 115th Dream"). This is the point where Dylan eclipses any conventional sense of folk and rewrites the rules of rock, making it safe for personal expression and poetry, not only making words mean as much as the music, but making the music an extension of the words. A truly remarkable album. *—Stephen Thomas Erlewine*

★ **Highway 61 Revisited** / Aug. 30, 1965 / Columbia ♦♦♦♦♦
Taking the first, electric side of *Bringing It All Back Home* to its logical conclusion, Bob Dylan hired a full rock & roll band, featuring guitarist Michael Bloomfield, for *Highway 61 Revisited*. Opening with the epic "Like a Rolling Stone," *Highway 61 Revisted* careens through nine songs that range from reflective folk-rock ("Desolation Row") and blues ("It Takes a Lot to Laugh, It Takes a Train to Cry") to flat-out garage rock ("Tombstone Blues," "From a Buick 6," "Highway 61 Revisted"). Dylan had not only changed his sound, but his persona, trading the folk troubadour for a streetwise, cynical hipster. Throughout the album, he alternates between druggy, surreal imagery, which can either have a sense of menace or beauty, and the music reflects that, jumping between soothing melodies to hard, bluesy rock. And that is the most revolutionary thing about *Highway 61 Revisited*—it proved that rock & roll needn't be collegiate and tame in order to be literate, poetic and complex. *—Stephen Thomas Erlewine*

☆ **Blonde on Blonde** / May 16, 1966 / Columbia ♦♦♦♦♦
If *Highway 61 Revisited* played as a garage rock record, the double album *Blonde on Blonde* inverted that sound, blending blues, country, rock and folk into a wild, careening and dense sound. Replacing the fiery Michael Bloomfield with the intense, weaving guitar of Robbie Robertson, Dylan led a group comprised of his touring band the Hawks and session musicians through his richest set of songs. *Blonde on Blonde* is an album of enormous depth, providing endless lyrical and musical revelations on each play. Leavening the edginess of *Highway 61* with a sense of the absurd, *Blonde on Blonde* is comprised entirely of songs driven by inventive, surreal and witty wordplay, not only on the rockers but also on winding, moving ballads like "Visions of Johanna," "Just Like a Woman," and "Sad Eyed Lady of the Lowlands." Throughout the record, the music matches the inventiveness of the songs, filled with cutting guitar riffs, liquid organ riffs, crisp pianos and even woozy brass bands ("Rainy Day Women 12 & 35"). It's the culmination of Dylan's electric rock & roll period—he would never release a studio record that rocked this hard, or had such bizarre imagery, ever again. *—Stephen Thomas Erlewine*

★ **Bob Dylan's Greatest Hits** / Mar. 27, 1967 / Columbia ♦♦♦♦♦
Arriving in 1967, *Greatest Hits* does an excellent job of summarizing Dylan's best-known songs from his first seven albums. At just ten songs, it's a little brief, and the song selection may be a little predictable, but that's actually not a bad thing, since this provides a nice sampler for the curious and casual listener, as it boasts standards from "Blowin' in the Wind" to "Like a Rolling Stone." And, for collectors, the brilliant non-LP single "Positively Fourth Street" was added, which provided reason enough for anybody that already owned the original records to pick this up. This has since been supplanted by more exhaustive collections, but as a sampler of Dylan at his absolute peak, this is first-rate. *—Stephen Thomas Erlewine*

☆ **John Wesley Harding** / Dec. 27, 1967 / Columbia ♦♦♦♦♦
Bob Dylan returned from exile with *John Wesley Harding*, a quiet, country-tinged album that split dramatically from his previous three albums. A calm, reflective album, *John Wesley Harding* strips away all of the wilder tendencies of Dylan's rock albums—even the then-unreleased *Basement Tapes* he made the previous year—but it isn't a return to his folk roots. If anything, the album is his first serious foray into country, but only a handful of songs, such as "I'll Be Your Baby Tonight," are straight country songs. Instead, *John Wesley Harding* is informed by the rustic sound of country, as well as many rural myths, with seemingly simple songs like "All Along the Watchtower," "I Dreamed I Saw St. Augustine" and "The Wicked Messenger" revealing several layers of meanings with repeated plays. Although the lyrics are somewhat enigmatic, the music is simple, direct and melodic, providing a touchstone for the country-rock revolution that swept through rock in the late '60s. *—Stephen Thomas Erlewine*

☆ **Nashville Skyline** / Apr. 9, 1969 / Columbia ♦♦♦♦♦
John Wesley Harding suggested country with its textures and structures, but *Nashville Skyline* was a full-fledged country album, complete with steel guitars and brief, direct songs. It's a warm, friendly album, particularly since Dylan is singing in a previously unheard gentle croon—the sound of his voice is so different it may be disarming upon first listen, but it suits the songs. While there are a handful of lightweight numbers on the record, at its core are several excellent songs—"Lay Lady Lay," "To Be Alone With You," "I Threw It All Away," "Tonight I'll Be Staying Here With You," as well as a duet with Johnny Cash on "Girl from the North Country"—that have become country-rock standards. And there's no discounting that *Nashville Skyline*, arriving in the spring of 1969, established country-rock as a vital force in pop music, as well as a commercially viable genre. *—Stephen Thomas Erlewine*

Self Portrait / Jun. 8, 1970 / Columbia ♦♦
There has never been a clearer attempt to shed an audience than *Self-Portrait*. At least, that's one way of looking at this baffling double album, a deliberately sprawling affair that runs the gamut from self-portrait to self-parody, touching on operatic pop, rowdy *Basement Tapes* leftovers, slight whimsy, and covers of wannabe Dylans from Paul Simon to Gordon Lightfoot. To say the least, it's confusing, especially arriving at the end of a decade of unmitigated brilliance, and while the years have made it easier to listen to, it still remains inscrutable, an impossible record to unlock. It may not be worth the effort, either, since this isn't a matter of deciphering cryptic lyrics or interpreting lyrics, it's all about discerning intent, figuring out what the hell Dylan was thinking when he was recording—not trying to decode a song. There are times where it's quite clearly played for a laugh—if his shambling version of "The Boxer" isn't a pointed parody of Paul Simon, there was no reason to cut it—but he's poker-faced elsewhere, and the songs (apart from such earthed gems as "Mighty Quinn," which aren't presented in their best versions) are simply not worth much consideration. But, in a strange way, *Self Portrait* is, because decades have passed and it still doesn't make much sense, even for Dylanphiles. That doesn't necessarily mean that it's worth the time to figure it out—you're not going to find an answer, anyway—but it's sort of fascinating all the same. *—Stephen Thomas Erlewine*

New Morning / Oct. 21, 1970 / Columbia ♦♦♦♦♦
Dylan rushed out *New Morning* in the wake of the commercial and critical disaster *Self Portrait*, and the difference between the two albums suggests that its legendary failed predecessor was intentionally flawed. *New Morning* expands on the laidback country-rock of *John Wesley Harding* and *Nashville Skyline* by adding a more pronounced rock & roll edge. While there are only a couple of genuine classics on the record ("If Not for You," "One More Weekend"), the overall quality is quite high, and many of the songs explore idiosyncratic routes Dylan had previously left untouched, whether it's the jazzy experiments of "Sign on the Window" and "Winterlude," the rambling spoken-word piece "If Dogs Run Free" or the Elvis parable "Went to See the Gypsy." Such offbeat songs make *New Morning* a charming, endearing record. *—Stephen Thomas Erlewine*

☆ **Bob Dylan's Greatest Hits, Vol. 2** / Nov. 17, 1971 / Columbia ♦♦♦♦♦
Where Dylan's first *Greatest Hits* took its title literally, *Greatest Hits, Vol. 2* is a greatest hits album only in the loosest sense of the term. While the double album does contain several genuine hits—"Lay Lady Lay," "Tonight I'll Be Staying Here With You," the non-LP "Watching the River Flow"—it is largely comprised of album tracks which became classics, either through Dylan's own version or through covers. These include "Don't Think Twice, It's All Right," "All I Really Want to Do," "My Back Pages," "Maggie's Farm," "She Belongs to Me," "If Not for You," and "Just Like Tom Thumb's Blues," among many others. There are also a num-

ber of rarities scattered throughout the 21 songs, including a live version of "Tomorrow Is a Long Time" from 1963, a live take of "The Mighty Quinn (Quinn, the Eskimo)" and the *Basement Tapes* songs "I Shall Be Released," "Down in the Flood" and "You Ain't Goin' Nowhere." While some of the cuts may not be immediately familiar to some listeners, *Greatest Hits, Vol. 2* in many ways is a more accurate picture of the depth and breadth of Dylan's talents, making it an excellent introduction. And it's not just for casual fans, because the rarities and sequencing are revealing for even devoted Dylan fans. [*Greatest Hits, Vol. 2* was reissued with 24-bit remastering in the summer of 1999.] *—Stephen Thomas Erlewine*

Pat Garrett & Billy the Kid [Soundtrack] / Jul. 13, 1973 / Columbia ✦✦

Dylan / Nov. 16, 1973 / Columbia ✦

Planet Waves / Jan. 17, 1974 / Columbia ✦✦✦
Re-teaming with the Band, Bob Dylan winds up with an album that recalls *New Morning* more than *The Basement Tapes*, since *Planet Waves* is given to a relaxed intimate tone—all the more appropriate for a collection of modest songs about domestic life. As such, it may seem a little anticlimactic, since it has none of the wildness of the best Dylan and the Band music of the '60s—just an approximation of the homespun rusticness. Considering that the record was knocked out in the course of three days, its unassuming nature shouldn't be a surprise, and sometimes it's as much a flaw as a virtue, since there are a several cuts that float into the ether. Still, it still is a virtue in places, as there are moments—"On a Night Like This," "Something There Is About You," the lovely "Forever Young"—where it just gels, almost making the diffuse nature of the rest of the record acceptable. *—Stephen Thomas Erlewine*

Before Flood / Jun. 20, 1974 / Columbia ✦✦✦✦✦
Bob Dylan and the Band both needed the celebrated reunion tour of 1974, since Dylan's fortunes had been floundering since *Self Portrait* and the Band stumbled with 1971's *Cahoots*. The tour, with its attendant publicity, definitely returned both artists to center stage, and it definitely succeeded, breaking box office records and earning great reviews. *Before the Flood*, a double-album souvenir of the tour, suggests that these were generally dynamic shows, but not because they were reveling in the past, but because Dylan was fighting the nostalgia of his audience—nostalgia, it must be noted, that was promoted as the very reason behind these shows. Yet that's what gives this music such kick—Dylan reworks, rearranges, reinterprets these songs in ways that are still disarming, years after its initial release. He could only have performed interpretations this radical with a group as sympathetic, knowing of his traits as the band, whose own recordings here are respites from the storm. And this is a storm—the sound of a great rocker, surprising his band and audience by tearing through his greatest songs in a manner that might not be comforting, but it guarantees it to be one of the best live albums of its time. Ever, maybe. *—Stephen Thomas Erlewine*

☆ **Blood on the Tracks** / Jan. 17, 1975 / Columbia ✦✦✦✦✦
Following on the heels of an album where he repudiated his past with his greatest backing band, *Blood on the Tracks* finds Bob Dylan, in a way, retreating to the past, recording a largely quiet, acoustic-based album. But this is hardly nostalgia—this is the sound of an artist returning to his strengths, what feels most familiar, as he accepts a traumatic situation, namely the breakdown of his marriage. This is an album alternately bitter, sorrowful, regretful, and peaceful, easily the closest he ever came to wearing his emotions on his sleeve. That's not to say that it's an explicitly confessional record, since many songs are riddles or allegories, yet the warmth of the music makes it feel that way. The original version of the album was even quieter—first takes of "Idiot Wind" and "Tangled Up in Blue," available on *The Bootleg Series, Vols. 1-3*, are hushed and quiet (excised verses are quoted in the liner notes, but not heard on the record)—but *Blood on the Tracks* remains an intimate, revealing affair, since these harsher takes let his anger surface the way his sadness does elsewhere. As such, it's an affecting, unbearably poignant record, not because it's a glimpse into his soul, but because the songs are remarkably clear-eyed *and* sentimental, lovely and melancholy at once. And, in a way, it's best that he was backed with studio musicians here, since the professional, understated backing lets the songs and emotion stand at the forefront. Dylan made albums more influential than this, but he never made one better. *—Stephen Thomas Erlewine*

☆ **The Basement Tapes** / Jun. 26, 1975 / Columbia ✦✦✦✦✦
The official release of *The Basement Tapes*—which were first heard on a 1968 bootleg called *The Great White Wonder*—plays with history somewhat, as Robbie Robertson overemphasizes the Band's status in the sessions, making them out to be equally active to Dylan, adding in demos not cut at the sessions and overdubbing their recordings to flesh them out. As many bootlegs (most notably the complete five-disc series) reveal, this isn't entirely true and that the Band were nowhere near as active as Dylan, but that ultimately is a bit like nitpicking, since the music here (including the Band's) is astonishingly good. The party line on *the Basement Tapes* is that it is Americana, as Dylan and the Band pick up the weirdness inherent in old folk, country, and blues tunes, but it transcends mere historical arcana by being lively, humorous, full-bodied performances. Dylan never sounded as loose, nor was he ever as funny as he is here, and this positively revels in its weird, wild character. For all the apparent antecedents—and the allusions are sly and obvious in equal measures—this is truly Dylan's show, as he majestically evokes old myths and creates new ones, resulting in a crazy quilt of blues, humor, folk, tall tales, inside jokes, and rock. The Band pretty much pick up where Dylan left off, even singing a couple of his tunes, but they play it a little straight, on both their rockers and ballads. Not a bad thing at all, since this actually winds up providing context for the wild, mercurial brilliance of Dylan's work—and, taken together, the results (especially in this judiciously compiled form; expert song selection, even there's a bit too much Band) rank among the greatest American music ever made. *—Stephen Thomas Erlewine*

Desire / Jan. 16, 1976 / Columbia ✦✦✦✦✦
If *Blood on the Tracks* was an unapologetically intimate affair, *Desire* is unwieldy and messy, the deliberate work of a collective. And while Dylan directly addresses his crumbling relationship with his wife, Sara, on the final track, *Desire* is hardly as personal as its predecessor, finding Dylan returning to topical songwriting and folk tales for the core of the record. It's all over the map, as far as songwriting goes, and so is is musically, capturing Dylan at the beginning of the Rolling Thunder Revue era, which was more notable for its chaos than its music. And, so it's only fitting that *Desire* fits that description, as well, as it careens between surging folk-rock, mideastern dirges, skipping pop, and epic narratives. It's little surprise that *Desire* doesn't quite gel, yet it retains its own character—really, there's no other place where Dylan tried as many different style, as many weird detours, as he does here. And, there's something to be said for its rambling, sprawling character, which has a charm of its own. Even so, the record would have been assisted by a more consistent set of songs; there are some masterpieces here, though—"Hurricane" is the best-known, but the effervescent "Mozambique" is Dylan at his breeziest, "Sara" at his most nakedly emotional, and "Isis" is one of his very best songs of the '70s, a hypnotic, contemporarized spin on a classic fable. This may not add up to a masterpiece, but it does result in one of his most fascinating records of the '70s and '80s—more intriguing, lyrically and musically, than most of his latter-day affairs. *—Stephen Thomas Erlewine*

Hard Rain / Sep. 10, 1976 / Columbia ✦✦

Street-Legal / Jun. 15, 1978 / Columbia ✦✦✦
Arriving after the twin peaks of *Blood on the Tracks* and *Desire*, *Street Legal* seemed like a disappointment upon its 1978 release, and it still seems a little subpar, years after its release. Perhaps thats because Dylan was uncertain himself, not just writing a set of songs with no connecting themes, but replacing the sprawl of the Rolling Thunder Revue with a slick, professional big band, featuring a horn section and several backing vocalists. The interesting thing about this is that the music and slick production doesn't jibe with the songs, which are as dense as anything Dylan has written since before his motorcycle accident. So, *Street Legal* becomes an interesting dichotomy, filled with songs that deserve close attention but recorded in arrangements that discourage such listening. As such, *Street Legal* is fascinating just for that reason—in another setting, these are songs that would have been hailed as near-masterpieces, but covered in gloss, they seem strange. Consequentially, it's not surprising that there are factions of Dylanphiles that find this worth the time, while just as many consider it a missed opportunity. *—Stephen Thomas Erlewine*

At Budokan / 1979 / Columbia ✦✦

Slow Train Coming / Aug. 20, 1979 / Columbia ✦✦✦
Perhaps it was inevitable that Dylan would change direction at the end of the '70s, since he had dabbled in everything from full-on repudiation of his legacy to a quiet embrace of it, to dipping his toe into pure showmanship. Nobody really could have expected that he would turn to Christianity, embracing a born-again philosophy with enthusiasm. He has no problem in believing in a vengeful god—you gotta serve somebody, after all—and this is pure brimstone and fire throughout the record, even on such lovely testimonials as "I Believe in You." The unexpected side-effect of his conversion is that it gave Dylan a focus he hadn't had since *Blood on the Tracks*, and his concentration carries over to the music, which is lean and direct in a way that he hadn't been since, well, *Blood on the Tracks*. Focus isn't necessarily the same thing as consistency, and this does suffer from being a bit too dogmatic, not just in its religion, but in its musical approach. Still, it's hard to deny that Dylan doesn't sound revitalized here and the result is a modest success that at least works on its own terms. *—Stephen Thomas Erlewine*

Saved / Jun. 20, 1980 / Columbia ✦✦

Shot of Love / Aug. 12, 1981 / Columbia ✦✦

Infidels / Nov. 1, 1983 / Columbia ✦✦✦✦
Infidels is the first secular record Bob Dylan recorded since *Street Legal*, and it's far more like a classicist Dylan album than that, filled with songs that are evocative in their imagery and direct in their approach. This is lean, much like *Slow Train Coming*, but its writing is closer to the peak of the mid-'70s, and some of the songs here—particularly on the first side—are minor classics, capturing him reviving his sense of social consciousness and his gift for poetic, elegant love songs. For a while, *Infidels* seems like a latter-day masterpiece, but toward the end of the record it runs out of steam, preventing it from being a triumph. Still, in comparison to everything that arrived in the near-decade before it, *Infidels* is a triumph, finding Dylan coming tantalizing close to regaining all his powers. *—Stephen Thomas Erlewine*

Real Live / Dec. 3, 1984 / Columbia ✦✦✦

Empire Burlesque / Jun. 8, 1985 / Columbia ✦✦✦✦✦
Say what you want about *Empire Burlesque*—at the very least, it's the most consistent record Bob Dylan has made since *Blood on the Tracks*, even if it isn't quite as interesting as *Desire*. However, it is a better set of songs, all deriving from the same place and filled with subtle gems—the most obvious being "Tight Connection to My Heart (Has Anybody Seen My Love?)," but also "Emotionally Yours" and "Dark Eyes"—proving that his powers are still there. The rest of the album may not be as graceful, but it's still well-crafted songwriting that never fails to be interesting. The record's biggest flaw is its state-of-the-art production; this is every bit as slick as *Street Legal*, but now sounds more focused and more of its time—thanks to a reliance on synthesizers and mildly sequenced beats—than it did upon its original release. All this makes *Empire Burlesque* seem more transient than it actually is, since—discounting the production—this is as good as Dylan gets in his latter days. *—Stephen Thomas Erlewine*

☆ **Biograph** / Oct. 28, 1985 / Columbia ✦✦✦✦✦
Historically, *Biograph* is significant not for what it did for Dylan's career, but for establishing the box set, complete with hits and rarities, as a viable part of rock history. Following *Biograph*, multi-disc box sets for veteran rockers became accepted and almost the norm, but that doesn't discount this set's strengths as a summary of Dylan's career, using the familiar and the rare to draw a fully rounded portrait of his strengths as a songwriter, musician, and record-maker in a way that conventional choices alone couldn't achieve. Certainly, the chief attraction of this set, even years after its initial release, is its smattering of rarities that aren't just rare, but revealing—ranging from forgotten rock B-sides and singles to demos, alternate takes, and unreleased songs that rival official releases. But *Biograph* is really remarkable for weaving these songs into a fabric that reveals the true trajectory of Dylan's career, offering as much to the curious as it

does to the dedicated. That sets a standard for box sets that has rarely been matched, making *Biograph* all the more impressive in retrospect. *—Stephen Thomas Erlewine*

Knocked Out Loaded / Aug. 8, 1986 / Columbia ✦✦

Dylan & the Dead / Feb. 6, 1989 / Columbia ✦

Oh Mercy / Sep. 22, 1989 / Columbia ✦✦✦
Oh Mercy was hailed as a comeback, not just because it had songs noticeably more meaningful than anything Dylan had recently released, but because Daniel Lanois' production gave it cohesion. There was cohesion on *Empire Burlesque*, of course, but that cohesion was a little too slick, a little too commercial, whereas this record was filled with atmospheric, hazy production—a sound as arty as most assumed the songs to be. And Dylan followed suit, giving Lanois significant songs—palpably social works, love songs, and poems—that seemed to connect with his past. And, at the time, this production made it seem like the equivalent of his '60s records, meaning that its artiness was cutting edge, not portentious. Over the years, *Oh Mercy* hasn't aged particularly well, seeming as self-conscious as such other gauzy Lanois productions as *So* and *The Joshua Tree*, even though it makes more sense than the ersatz pizzazz of *Burlesque*. Still, the songs make *Oh Mercy* noteworthy; they find Dylan quietly raging against the materialism of Reagan and accepting maturity, albeit with a slight reluctance. So, *Oh Mercy* is finally more interesting for what it tries to achieve than for what it actually does achieve. At its best, this is a collection of small, shining moments, with the best songs shining brighter than their production or the album's overall effect. *—Stephen Thomas Erlewine*

Under the Red Sky / Sep. 11, 1990 / Columbia ✦✦

Bootleg Series, Vols. 1-3: Rare & Unreleased, 1961-1991 / Mar. 26, 1991 / Columbia ✦✦✦✦✦
This three-disc box set is what Dylanphiles have been waiting for, sitting patiently for years, even decades. And, even after its 1991 release, it retains the feeling of being a special, shared secret among the hardcore, since—no matter the acclaim—it's the kind of record that only the hardcore will seek out. Of course, the great irony is that even casual Dylan fans will find much to treasure in this three-disc set of unreleased material. They'll find songs as good as anything that made the records (sometimes surpassing the official releases, especially on the last disc), plus alternate versions (including original versions of songs on *Blood on the Tracks*) and long-fabled songs, from the incomplete "She's Your Lover Now" to songs cut from *The Freewheelin' Bob Dylan*. This doesn't just function as an alternate history of Dylan, but as an expansion of Dylan's history, enriching what is already known about the greatest songwriter of his era—after all, every song here would qualify as the best song on anybody else's album. And that's no exaggeration. *—Stephen Thomas Erlewine*

Good as I Been to You / Oct. 27, 1992 / Columbia ✦✦✦

World Gone Wrong / Oct. 28, 1993 / Columbia ✦✦✦

Greatest Hits, Vol. 3 / Nov. 15, 1994 / Columbia ✦✦✦✦
Dylan's first greatest hits album was released in 1967, and his second in 1971. Twenty-three years later comes his third, and it's a reasonable compilation of the better-known songs he has produced over the period, notably standards like "Knockin' on Heaven's Door" and "Forever Young," Dylan chart hits like "Tangled Up in Blue" and "Hurricane," songs that have been covered extensively by other singers, such as "Ring Them Bells," and some of the better album tracks, such as "Changing of the Guard" and "Brownsville Girl." In an effort to span the period, a few lesser, later songs, such as "Silvio" and "Under the Red Sky" are included, while some stronger, earlier songs are not ("Simple Twist of Fate," "Senor," "Emotionally Yours," and "Everything Is Broken"). But on the whole, the selection is excellent, and this is the album to get for that Dylan fan who stopped listening to him at the end of the '60s. (Includes the previously unreleased 1989 track "Dignity.") *—William Ruhlmann*

MTV Unplugged / Apr. 25, 1995 / Columbia ✦✦

Time Out of Mind / Sep. 30, 1997 / Columbia ✦✦✦✦
After spending much of the '90s touring and simply not writing songs, Bob Dylan returned in 1997 with *Time Out of Mind*, his first collection of new material in seven years. Where *Under the Red Sky*, his last collection of original compositions, had a casual, tossed-off feel, *Time Out of Mind* is carefully considered, from the densely detailed songs to the dark, atmospheric production. Sonically, the album is reminiscent of *Oh Mercy*, the last album Dylan recorded with producer Daniel Lanois, but *Time Out of Mind* has a grittier foundation—by and large, the songs are bitter and resigned, and Dylan gives them appropriately anguished performances. Lanois bathes them in hazy, ominous sounds, which may suit the spirit of the lyrics, but are often in opposition to Dylan's performances. Consequently, the album loses a little of its emotional impact, yet the songs themselves are uniformly powerful, adding up to Dylan's best overall collection in years. It's a better, more affecting record than *Oh Mercy*, not only because the songs have a stronger emotional pull, but because Lanois hasn't sanded away all the grit. As a result, the songs retain their power, leaving *Time Out of Mind* as one of the rare latter-day Dylan albums that meets his high standards. *—Stephen Thomas Erlewine*

☆ **Bootleg Series, Vol. 4: Live 1966—*Royal Albert Concert*** / *Oct. 13, 1998 / Columbia/Legacy* ✦✦✦✦✦
The most famous bootleg in rock history, with the possible exception of Dylan's own *Basement Tapes*, finally makes its official appearance 32 years after the event, and nearly 30 years after it started circulating in the underground. Although often identified as a *Royal Albert Hall* show, this May 17, 1966 concert, in which Dylan played electric material in front of a British audience, was actually recorded in Manchester (hence the unwieldy title with quotes around "Royal Albert Hall"). Even those who've owned this recording for many a year might be tempted by this official package, as it's been expanded into a two-CD set that not only includes the eight electric rock songs from the original bootleg, but also the seven solo acoustic performances that comprised the first half of the show. It's all in very good fidelity, about as good as any copies you could find through unofficial sources. More importantly, the electric half in particular is an important document of rock history. It captures the point at which Dylan was at his most controversial and hard-rocking as he blazes through mid-'60s classics such as "Like a Rolling Stone" and "Ballad of a Thin Man," radical electric arrangements of songs that had originally been recorded acoustically ("One Too Many Mornings," "I Don't Believe You"), and the hard rocker "Tell Me, Momma," which Dylan never recorded in the studio. The acoustic disc is not as epochal, but on par with the electric half in the quality of material and performance. On top of everything else there's a 56-page booklet with a fine essay by Dylan's friend Tony Glover (a notable folk musician in his own right). It's not just an interesting adjunct to Dylan's '60s discography; it's as worthy of attention as anything else he recorded during that decade. *—Richie Unterberger*

● **Essential Bob Dylan** / Oct. 31, 2000 / Columbia ✦✦✦✦✦
A double-disc set released for the holiday season of 2000, *The Essential Bob Dylan* is a fine choice for the casual listener that just wants all the songs they know on one collection—it's Dylan's equivalent of *Beatles One*. Outside of the remastering and the previously non-LP (and very good) "Things Have Changed," there's nothing here for collectors, but, then again, that's not who this was designed for. This collection is for the listener that wants "Blowin' in the Wind," "Like a Rolling Stone," "All Along the Watchtower," "Quinn the Eskimo," "Lay Lady Lay," and "Tangled Up in Blue" in one tidy place. Yes, it's easy to find great songs missing, but for those casual fans, and for those looking for a fairly comprehensive yet concise entry point, *The Essential Bob Dylan* comes close to living up to its title. *—Stephen Thomas Erlewine*

The Eagles

f. 1971, Los Angeles, CA, **db.** 1982
Group / Album Rock, Pop/Rock, Folk-Rock, Soft Rock, Country-Rock
The Eagles were among the most successful rock groups of the '70s, and their blend of country, folk, and rock continues to sell well in catalog. The group's four original members—Glenn Frey, Bernie Leadon, Randy Meisner and Don Henley—were Los Angeles session veterans assembled as backup musicians for Linda Ronstadt. Signed to Ronstadt's Asylum label, they found a couple of Top 40 hits with their eponymous 1972 debut. The third Eagles LP, 1974's *On the Border*, was their breakthrough record; it went gold in three months and produced the number one hit "Best of My Love." The follow-up, *One of These Nights*, was the first of four straight albums to top the charts. The Eagles' 1976 greatest-hits album became the best-selling hits record of all time, now standing at 22 million sales. Soon after, they suffered the loss of Leadon, who was replaced by Joe Walsh. At the end of the year, the Eagles released *Hotel California*, including hits with the ominous title track, "New Kid in Town" and "Life in the Fast Lane." After Meisner left, he was replaced by Timothy B. Schmit. It took the group until the fall of 1979 to complete *The Long Run*, another million-seller featuring the chart-topper "Heartache Tonight." By 1981, the Eagles had split up. A dozen years later, the group reunited for a summer stadium tour and recorded an album for *MTV Unplugged*. Released in 1994, *Hell Freezes Over* debuted at number one and sold over six million copies. *—William Ruhlmann*

The Eagles / Jun. 1, 1972 / Asylum ✦✦✦
Balance is the key element of the Eagles' self-titled debut album, a collection that contains elements of rock & roll, folk, and country, overlaid by vocal harmonies alternately suggestive of doo-wop, the Beach Boys, and the Everly Brothers. If the group kicks up its heels on rockers like "Chug All Night," "Nightingale," and "Tryin'," it is equally convincing on ballads like "Most of Us Are Sad" and "Train Leaves Here This Morning." The album is also balanced among its members, who trade off on lead vocal chores and divide the songwriting such that Glenn Frey, Bernie Leadon, and Randy Meisner all get three writing or co-writing credits. (Fourth member Don Henley, with only one co-writing credit and two lead vocals, falls a little behind, while Jackson Browne, Gene Clark, and Jack Tempchin also figure in the writing credits.) The album's overall balance is worth keeping in mind because it produced three Top 40 hit singles (all of which turned up on the massively popular *Eagles: Their Greatest Hits 1971-1975*) that do not reflect that balance. "Take It Easy" and "Peaceful Easy Feeling" are similar-sounding mid-tempo folk-rock tunes sung by Frey that express the same sort of laid-back philosophy, as indicated by the word "easy" in both titles, while "Witchy Woman," a Henley vocal and co-composition, initiates the band's career-long examination of supernaturally evil females. These are the songs one remembers from *Eagles*, and they look forward to the eventual dominance of the band by Frey and Henley. But the complete album from which they come belongs as much to Leadon's country-steeped playing and singing and to Meisner's melodic rock & roll feel, which, on the release date, made it seem a more varied and consistent effort than it did later, when the singles had become overly familiar. *—William Ruhlmann*

Desperado / Apr. 17, 1973 / Asylum ✦✦✦
If Don Henley was the sole member of the Eagles underrepresented on their debut album, *Eagles*, with only two lead vocals and one co-songwriting credit, he made up for it on their follow-up, the "concept" album *Desperado*. The concept had to do with Old West outlaws, but it had no specific narrative. On *Eagles*, the group had already begun to marry itself to a Southwest sound and lyrical references, from the Indian-style introduction of "Witchy Woman" to the Winslow, AZ, address in "Take It Easy." All of this became more overt on *Desperado*, and it may be that Henley, who hailed from Northeast Texas, had the greatest affinity for the subject matter. In any case, he had co-writing credits on eight of the 11 selections and sang such key tracks as "Doolin-Dalton" and the title song. What would become recognizable as Henley's lyrical touch was apparent on those songs, which bore a serious, world-weary tone. Henley had begun co-writing with Glenn Frey, and they contributed the album's strongest material, which included the first single, "Tequila Sunrise," and "Desperado" (strangely never released as a single). But where *Eagles* seemed deliberately to balance the band's many musical styles and the talents of the band's members, *Desperado*, despite its overarching theme, often seemed a collection of disparate tracks—"Out of Control" was a raucous rocker, while "Desperado" was a painfully slow ballad backed by strings—with other band members' contributions tacked on rather than integrated. Randy Meisner was down to two co-writing credits and one lead vocal ("Certain Kind of Fool"), while Bernie Leadon's two songs, "Twenty-One" and "Bitter Creek," seemed to come from a different record entirely. The result was an album that was simultaneously more ambitious and serious-minded than its predecessor and also slighter and less consistent. *—William Ruhlmann*

On the Border / Mar. 22, 1974 / Asylum ♦♦♦
The Eagles began recording their third album in England with producer Glyn Johns, as they had their first two albums, but abandoned the sessions after completing two acceptable tracks. Johns, it is said, tended to emphasize the group's country elements and its harmonies, while the band, in particular Glenn Frey and Don Henley, wanted to take more of a hard rock direction. They reconvened with a new producer, Bill Szymczyk, who had produced artists like B.B. King and, more significantly, Joe Walsh. But the resulting album is not an outright rock effort by any means. Certainly, Frey and Henley got what they wanted with "Already Gone," the lead-off track, which introduces new band member Don Felder as one part of the twin guitar solo that recalls the Allman Brothers Band; "James Dean," a rock & roll song on the order of "Your Mama Don't Dance"; and "Good Day in Hell," which is strongly reminiscent of Joe Walsh songs like "Rocky Mountain Way." But the album also features the usual mixture of styles typical of an Eagles album. For example, "Midnight Flyer," sung by Randy Meisner, is modern bluegrass; "My Man" is Bernie Leadon's country-rock tribute to the recently deceased Gram Parsons; and "Ol' 55" is one of the group's well-done covers of a tune by a singer-songwriter labelmate, in this case Tom Waits. The title track, meanwhile, points the band in a new R&B direction that was later pursued more fully. Like most successful groups, the Eagles combined many different elements, and their third album, which looked back to their earlier work and anticipated their later work, was a transitional effort that combined even more styles than most of their records did. *—William Ruhlmann*

One of These Nights / Jun. 10, 1975 / Asylum ♦♦♦♦
The Eagles recorded their albums relatively quickly in their first years of existence, their albums succeeding each other by less than a year. *One of These Nights*, their fourth album, was released in June 1975, more than 14 months after its predecessor. Anticipation had been heightened by the belated chart-topping success of the third album's "The Best of My Love"; taking a little more time, the band generated more original material, and that material was more polished. More than ever, the Eagles seemed to be a vehicle for Don Henley (six co-writing credits) and Glenn Frey (five), but at the same time Randy Meisner was more audible than ever, his two lead vocals including one of the album's three hit singles, "Take It to the Limit," and Bernie Leadon had two showcases, among them the cosmic-cowboy instrumental "Journey of the Sorcerer" (later used as the theme music for the British television series *The Hitchhiker's Guide to the Galaxy*). Nevertheless, it was the team of Henley and Frey that stood out, starting with the title track, a number one single, which had more of an R&B—even disco—sound than anything the band had attempted previously, and continuing through the ersatz Western swing of "Hollywood Waltz" to "Lyin' Eyes," one of Frey's patented folk-rock shuffles, which became another major hit. *One of These Nights* was the culmination of the blend of rock, country, and folk styles the Eagles had been making since their start; there wasn't much that was new, just the same sorts of things done better than they had been before. In particular, a lyrical stance—knowing and disillusioned, but desperately hopeful—had evolved, and the musical arrangements were tighter and more purposeful. The result was the Eagles' best-realized and most popular album so far. *—William Ruhlmann*

★ **Their Greatest Hits (1971-1975)** / Feb. 17, 1976 / Asylum ♦♦♦♦♦
On their first four albums, the Eagles were at pains to demonstrate that they were a group of at least near-equals, each getting a share of the songwriting credits and lead vocals. But this compilation drawn from those albums, comprising the group's nine Top 40 hits plus "Desperado," demonstrates that this evenhandedness did not extend to singles—as far as those go, the Eagles belong to Glenn Frey and Don Henley. The tunes are melodic, and the arrangements—full of strummed acoustic guitars over a rock rhythm section often playing a shuffle beat, topped by tenor-dominated harmonies—are immediately engaging. There is also a lyrical consistency to the songs, which often concern romantic uncertainties in an atmosphere soaked in intoxicants. The narrators of the songs usually seem exhausted, if not satiated, and the loping rhythms are appropriate to these impressions. All of which means that, unlike the albums from which they come, these songs make up a collection consistent in mood and identity, which may help explain why *Eagles: Their Greatest Hits 1971-1975* works so much better than the band's previous discs and practically makes them redundant. No wonder it was such a big hit out of the box, topping the charts and becoming the first album ever certified platinum. Still, there must be more to it, since the album wasn't just a big hit, but one of the biggest ever, becoming one of the very few discs to cross the threshold of 20 million copies and competing for the title of best-selling album of all time. There may be no explaining that, really, except to note that this was the pervasive music of the first half of the 1970s, and somehow it never went away. *—William Ruhlmann*

☆ **Hotel California** / Dec. 8, 1976 / Asylum ♦♦♦♦♦
The Eagles took 18 months between their fourth and fifth albums, reportedly spending eight months in the studio recording *Hotel California*. The album was also their first to be made without Bernie Leadon, who had given the band much of its country flavor, and with rock guitarist Joe Walsh. As a result, the album marks a major leap for the Eagles from their earlier work, as well as a stylistic shift toward mainstream rock. An even more important aspect, however, is the emergence of Don Henley as the band's dominant voice, both as a singer and a lyricist. On the six songs to which he contributes, Henley sketches a thematic statement that begins by using California as a metaphor for a dark, surreal world of dissipation; comments on the ephemeral nature of success and the attraction of excess; branches out into romantic disappointment; and finally sketches a broad, pessimistic history of America that borders on nihilism. Of course, the lyrics kick in some time after one has appreciated the album's music, which marks a peak in the Eagles' playing. Early on, the group couldn't rock convincingly, but the rhythm section of Henley and Meisner has finally solidified, and the electric guitar work of Don Felder and Joe Walsh has arena-rock heft. In the early part of their career, the Eagles never seemed to get a sound big enough for their ambitions; after changes in producer and personnel, as well as a noticeable growth in creativity, *Hotel California* unveiled what seemed almost like a whole new band. It was a band that could be bombastic, but also one that made music worthy of the later tag of "classic rock," music appropriate for the arenas and stadiums the band was playing. The result was the Eagles' biggest-selling regular album release, and one of the most successful rock albums ever. *—William Ruhlmann*

The Long Run / Sep. 24, 1979 / Asylum ♦♦♦
Three years in the making (which was considered an eternity in the '70s), the Eagles' follow-up to the massively successful, critically acclaimed *Hotel California* was a major disappointment, even though it sold several million copies and threw off three hit singles. Those singles, in fact, provide some insight into the record. "Heartache Tonight" was an old-fashioned rock & roll song sung by Glenn Frey, while "I Can't Tell You Why" was a delicate ballad by Timothy B. Schmit, the band's newest member. Only "The Long Run," a conventional pop/rock tune with a Stax Records R&B flavor, bore the stamp and vocal signature of Don Henley, who had largely taken the reins of the band on *Hotel California*. Henley also dominated *The Long Run*, getting co-writing credits on nine of the ten songs, singing five lead vocals, and sharing another two with Frey. This time around, however, Henley's contributions were for the most part painfully slight. Only "The Long Run" and the regret-filled closing song, "The Sad Café," showed any of his usual craftsmanship. The album was dominated by second-rank songs like "The Disco Strangler," "King of Hollywood," and "Teenage Jail" that sounded like they couldn't have taken three hours much less three years to come up with. (Joe Walsh's "In the City" was up to his usual standard, but it may not even have been an Eagles recording, having appeared months earlier on the soundtrack to *The Warriors* where it was credited as a Walsh solo track.) Amazingly, *The Long Run* reportedly was planned as a double album before being truncated to a single disc. If these were the keepers, what can the rejects have sounded like— *—William Ruhlmann*

Eagles Live / Nov. 7, 1980 / Asylum ♦♦♦

The Eagles Greatest Hits, Vol. 2 / Oct. 1982 / Asylum ♦♦♦♦
With the Eagles having officially disbanded in May 1982, leaving behind eight Top 40 hits that followed the release of the spectacularly successful *Eagles: Their Greatest Hits 1971-1975*, Asylum Records naturally compiled a second hits collection for fall 1982 release. Seven of those hits were included (the exception being the seasonal "Please Come Home for Christmas"), along with three LP tracks, one each from *One of These Nights*, *Hotel California*, and *The Long Run*. Disdained by longtime fans and by the Eagles themselves, the collection was perfect for listeners who knew the band through number one radio hits like "New Kid in Town," "Hotel California," and "Heartache Tonight." It also spared them having to buy mediocre albums like *The Long Run* and *Eagles Live* just to have copies of the best-known songs from those releases. No wonder, then, that over the years *Eagles Greatest Hits, Vol. 2* achieved multi-platinum status. *—William Ruhlmann*

Hell Freezes Over / Nov. 8, 1994 / Geffen ♦♦♦

Selected Works: 1972-1999 / Nov. 14, 2000 / Elektra ♦♦♦♦
The relative sonic neglect suffered by the Eagles' catalog was the fault of the band's consistent success—with the original albums and hits collections still selling year after year, why bother to upgrade— Finally, however, longtime Eagles producer Bill Szymczyk remastered their albums in 1999, and the band put together a box set. Including most of their hits (the exception is "Seven Bridges Road") and lots of album tracks, the four-CD set regroups the Eagles' material into three categories: "The Early Days," which consists of 13 tracks from their first four albums; "The Ballads"; and "The Fast Lane," i.e., rhythm songs. The fourth disc is drawn from their millennium concert at *the Staples Center* in Los Angeles. While their early albums balanced the contributions of their members, "The Early Days" is dominated by Glenn Frey and Don Henley; that means a few worthy efforts are missing, but the selection is generally good. "The Ballads" is a straightforward collection of popular slow songs. Along with their more uptempo hits, "The Fast Lane" contains what little unreleased material there is, but anyone hoping for greatness is going to be disappointed. The Eagles have gone out of their way in "The Millennium Concert" to perform songs out of their usual repertoire, including several solo hits and both sides of their 1978 seasonal single, "Please Come Home for Christmas" and "Funky New Year." Much of this is minor or atypical material, but at least the unusually animated band members were trying (though it sounds like there was plenty of studio overdubbing). The overall result is a nearly four-hour collection that is something of a hodgepodge. There are enough rarities to bait the hook for hardcore Eagles fans, but not really satisfy them, and casual fans will probably be better off with the two single-disc hits collections. *—William Ruhlmann*

Earth, Wind & Fire

f. 1969, Chicago, IL
Group / Blaxploitation, Smooth Soul, Quiet Storm, Urban, Disco, Funk, Soul
Earth, Wind & Fire was the most successful R&B group of the second half of the '70s. Founded by Maurice White and his brother Verdine in Chicago in 1969, they released their self-titled debut album on Warner Brothers in 1970. EWF encapsulated many strains of Black pop from before their time—their high-pitched harmony vocals called to mind groups such as the Temptations, while their funkiness was reminiscent of Sly and the Family Stone, and their horn section sometimes evoked the work of James Brown and others. Over this, Maurice White laid his own brand of African-inspired kalimba music for a thorough synthesis that nonetheless bore a particular musical stamp unique to Earth, Wind & Fire. The band began to break through with its fourth album, *Head to the Sky*, in 1973. Their first R&B Top Ten hit was "Mighty Mighty," from their first gold album, *Open Your Eyes*, which also contained the R&B hit "Kalimba Story." EWF's breakthrough to a mass audience, however, came in 1975 with the release of *That's the Way of the World*, the soundtrack to a film in which the group appeared. Led by its gold-selling number one single, "Shining Star," the album topped the pop charts. After the relative failure of *Electric Universe* in 1983, EWF disbanded. It re-formed for the 1987 release *Touch the World*. *—William Ruhlmann and Ron Wynn*

Earth, Wind & Fire / 1971 / Warner Brothers ♦♦♦

The Need of Love / 1971 / Warner Brothers ♦♦♦

Last Days & Time / 1972 / Columbia ✦✦✦

Head to the Sky / May 1973 / Columbia ✦✦✦

Open Our Eyes / Mar. 1974 / Columbia ✦✦✦

That's the Way of the World / Mar. 1975 / Columbia ✦✦✦✦✦

Gratitude / Dec. 1975 / Columbia ✦✦✦✦✦
With *That's the Way of the World* having made Earth, Wind & Fire one of the best selling soul bands of the 1970s, Maurice White & Co. had no problem filling large arenas. As dynamic as EWF was on stage, it's a shame that there isn't more documentation of the band's live show. Only one live EWF album was released by a major label in America, the superb *Gratitude*. First a two-LP set and later reissued on CD, *Gratitude* brilliantly captures the excitement EWF generated on stage at its creative peak. Neither hardcore EWF devotees nor more casual listeners should deprive themselves of the joys of the live versions of "Shining Star" and "Yearnin', Learnin'." Maurice White is magnificent throughout, and Philip Bailey truly soars on extended versions of "Reasons" (which boasts a memorable alto sax solo by guest Don Myrick) and "Devotion." The album also introduced some excellent new studio songs, including the haunting "Can't Hide Love" and the uplifting "Sing a Song." One could nitpick and wish for live versions of "Evil," "Keep Your Head to the Sky" and "Kalimba Song," but the bottom line is that *Gratitude* is one of EWF's finest accomplishments. *—Alex Henderson*

Spirit / Sep. 1976 / Columbia ✦✦✦✦✦
With *That's the Way of the World* having enjoyed multi-platinum success, Earth, Wind & Fire had a lot to live up to when the time came for another studio project. And the soul powerhouse didn't let us down (either commercially or creatively) on the outstanding *Spirit*, which boasted hits ranging from the optimistic "On Your Face" and the passionate funk classic "Getaway" to the poetic ballad "Imagination." Philip Bailey is as charismatic as ever on "Imagination" and the gorgeous title song. Maurice White's message and vision (an interesting blend of Afro-American Christianity and Eastern philosophy) was as positive and uplifting as ever, and as always, EWF expressed this positivity without being Pollyanna-ish or corny. And even if one didn't take EWF's calls for unity, hard work, self-respect and faith in God to heart, they had no problem with their solid grooves. *—Alex Henderson*

All 'n All / Nov. 1977 / Columbia ✦✦✦✦
Earth, Wind & Fire's artistic and commercial winning streak continued with its ninth album, *All 'n All*, the diverse jewel that gave us major hits like "Serpentine Fire" and the dreamy "Fantasy." Whether the visionary soul men are tearing into the hardest of funk on "Jupiter" or the most sentimental of ballads on "I'll Write a Song for You" (which boasts one of Philip Bailey's many soaring, five-star performances), *All 'n All* was a highly rewarding addition to EWF's catalogue. Because EWF had such a clean-cut image and fared so well among pop audiences, some may have forgotten just how sweaty its funk could be. But "Jupiter"—like "Mighty, Mighty," "Shining Star" and "Getaway"—underscores the fact that EWF delivered some of the most intense and gutsy funk of the 1970s. The 1999 CD reissue adds three bonus tracks: "Would You Mind" (a demo version of "Love's Holiday"), the "original Hollywood mix" of "Runnin'," and a live version of "Brazilian Rhyme," recorded live in 1980. *—Alex Henderson*

☆ **The Best of Earth, Wind & Fire, Vol. 1** / Nov. 1978 / Columbia ✦✦✦✦✦
Best of Earth, Wind & Fire, Vol. 1 contains the bulk of their hits from the mid-'70s, including "Shining Star," "September," "Got to Get You into My Life," "Sing a Song," "Getaway" and several other hits. The 1999 CD reissue has a bonus track, the late 1990s dance-mixed EWF hit medley "Mega Mix 2000," along with a radio edit of the same. *—Stephen Thomas Erlewine*

I Am / Jun. 1979 / Columbia ✦✦✦

Faces / Oct. 1980 / Columbia ✦✦✦

Raise! / Oct. 1981 / Columbia ✦✦

Powerlight / Feb. 1983 / Columbia ✦✦✦✦

The Best of Earth, Wind & Fire, Vol. 2 / 1988 / Columbia ✦✦✦✦✦
The second collection covering hit singles from the '70s top funk and soul band, Earth, Wind & Fire. This anthology has recently been supplanted by a box set covering virtually all of their big Columbia singles and some early Warners material. If you enjoyed their disco and late '70s cuts more than the early tracks, this anthology is worth getting. The 2000 CD reissue has two bonus tracks: the moderate 1973 hit "Keep Your Head to the Sky" and "I'll Write a Song for You," from the 1977 album *All 'n All*. *—Ron Wynn & Richie Unterberger*

The Eternal Dance / Sep. 8, 1992 / Columbia/Legacy ✦✦✦✦✦
Covering three discs and including all the hits, as well as a healthy selection of rarities, *The Eternal Dance* is not designed for the casual listener; only hardcore fans will remain enthralled through the numerous rarities. Most listeners will be content with the two greatest hits collections, but this comprehensive box set remains essential for hardcore Earth, Wind & Fire fans. *—Stephen Thomas Erlewine*

★ **Greatest Hits** / Nov. 17, 1998 / Columbia ✦✦✦✦✦
Columbia's 1998 collection of Earth, Wind & Fire's *Greatest Hits*, in many ways, stands as the group's definitive compilation. Even though there have been more extensive overviews of the group's work, such as the triple-disc set *The Eternal Disc*, this is the first collection to contain all of the group's biggest hits on one disc. All but one ("Love Music") of the ten songs from 1978's *The Best of Earth, Wind & Fire* are included, while six of the ten songs from *The Best Of, Vol. 2* are featured; the remaining two cuts on the 17-track collection are the minor early single "Kalimba Story" and the album cut "Gratitude." These are fine additions to the album, but the true meat of the collection lies in the hits—"Shining Star," "That's the Way of the World," "Sing a Song," "Getaway," "Got to Get You Into My Life," "September," "Boogie Wonderland," "After the Love Has Gone," "Let's Groove" and so many others. They might not be presented in chronological order (the only flaw in this otherwise flawless collection), but it's a sheer delight to have all of the hits on one terrifically entertaining and valuable disc. *—Stephen Thomas Erlewine*

The Easybeats

f. 1963, Sydney, Australia, **db.** 1970
Group / British Invasion, Pop, Rock & Roll
The most successful Australian rock group of the 1960s, the Easybeats were nearly as popular as the Beatles in their homeland in the mid-'60s. In 1965 and 1966, they ran off a rapid string of seven Top Ten singles in Australia with peppy variations on the early Beatle and Merseybeat sound. With a nervous energy that featured staccato guitar lines, unexpected tempo changes, and strong original material, they also betrayed strong debts to the Kinks, Who, and Small Faces, although their songs were generally cheerier and more lightweight. Like all of the aforementioned bands, the Easybeats stand as one of the earliest and foremost exponents of pure power-pop. In late 1966, the Easybeats moved to London and hooked up with legendary producer Shel Talmy (Who, Kinks) in an attempt to crack the international pop market. Against all the odds, they did so the first time out with the classic "Friday on My Mind," which hit the British Top Ten and the American Top 20. Some ill-chosen follow-ups, however, deflated their momentum, although the group—led by the increasingly adventurous combination songwriting/production team of guitarists George Young and Harry Vanda—were keeping up with the tenor of their times by expanding the scope of their lyrics and arrangements. *—Richie Unterberger*

Aussie Beat That Shook the World: The Definitive Anthology / 1996 / Repertoire ✦✦✦✦✦
Two-CD, 56-song anthology is an excellent value even at an import price. It contains all their Australian hits, lots of album tracks, and some rarities that don't show up very often, like the 1965 B-side "The Old Oak Tree." It may be too lengthy an introduction or overview for some, though; some of their LP tracks weren't memorable, and one gets the feeling that some of the rarities and cover versions were put on here because they were rare, not because of their musical quality. In addition, all of the Easybeat rarities you could want have been placed on Repertoire's reissues of individual Easybeats albums as bonus tracks. The 48-page booklet does have interview material with Harry Vanda, including comments on each song in the set. *—Richie Unterberger*

● **Gonna Have a Good Time** / Apr. 20, 1999 / Retroactive ✦✦✦✦✦

Echo & the Bunnymen

f. Sep. 1978, Liverpool, England
Group / College Rock, Dream Pop, Neo-Psychedelia, Post-Punk, Alternative Pop/Rock
Echo & the Bunnymen's dark, swirling fusion of gloomy post-punk and Doors-inspired psychedelia brought the group a handful of British hits in the early '80s, while attracting a cult following in the United States. Formed around vocalist Ian McCulloch and guitarist Will Sergent, the group's debut album, 1980's *Crocodiles*, reached number 17 on the UK charts. The more ambitious and atmospheric *Heaven Up Here* (1981) became their first UK Top Ten album, and two years later, *Porcupine* appeared, becoming the band's biggest hit (peaking at No. 2 on the U.K. charts) and launching the Top Ten single, "The Cutter." "The Killing Moon" became the group's second Top Ten hit at the beginning of 1984, and the album *Ocean Rain* was the Bunnymen's first album to chart in the US Top 100. Just after their eponymous 1987 album became their biggest American hit, peaking at number 51, McCulloch left for a solo career while the band continued on for one more album before quitting. McCulloch and Sergeant reunited for a 1995 album as Electrafixion, then re-formed Echo and the Bunnymen two years later, issuing two LPs in the late '90s. *—Stephen Thomas Erlewine*

Heaven Up Here / Jul. 1981 / Sire ✦✦✦
While darker and more intense than *Crocodiles*, Echo and the Bunnymen's sophomore effort lacks the immediacy of their debut; the songs are subpar, relying too much on atmosphere and texture instead of substance. Although a few of the tracks, including "A Promise" and "All I Want," are keepers, the vast majoirity of *Heaven Up Here* is too self-indulgent and ridiculously gloomy to warrant serious consideration among the group's most enduring work. *—Jason Ankeny*

Porcupine / 1983 / Sire ✦✦✦
The group's third album is a solid outing, a noticeably better listen than its predecessor, *Heaven Up Here*. Songs are intriguing and elaborate, often featuring swooping, howling melodic lines. Arrangements here owe a lot to 1960s psychedelia and feature lots of reverb, washed textures, intricate production touches, and altered guitar sounds. Ian McCulloch's vocals are yearning, soaring, and hyper-expressive here, almost to the point of being histrionic, most notably on "Clay," "Ripeness," and the title track. Driving bass and drums lend the songs urgency and keep the music from collapsing into self-indulgence. Parallels between the group's U.S. contemporaries such as Translator, Wire Train, and R.E.M. can be drawn, though all seem to have developed aspects of this style at about the same time—and none utilize it as flamboyantly as the Bunnymen do. Highlights here include "Back of Love" (with its galloping drumbeat and fragmented, yet ardent vocal line) and "Gods Will Be Gods" (which gradually speeds up from beginning to end, working itself into a swirling frenzy). This album is well worth hearing. *—David Cleary*

Ocean Rain / 1984 / Sire ✦✦✦✦✦
Ocean Rain more or less continues the basic yearning 1960s-oriented approach of prior Bunnymen releases, though there are some important differences. In general, the arrangements here are cleaner, less swirlingly cluttered, though production values are still interesting and imaginative. The songs are a bit more focused and straightforward than on immediately preceding albums; some selections, such as "Silver," "Seven Seas," and "My Kingdom" contain memorable melodic hooks. Under such circumstances, Ian McCulloch's vocals often sound overwrought and forced, most noticeably on "My Kingdom" and "Thorn of Crowns." The latter song is unusual, based on a Bo Diddley-influenced rhythmic pattern. "Crystal Days" and "Silver" show more R.E.M.-oriented guitar work than before. And the curious "Nocturnal Me," with its gypsy-like tremolo guitar, jittery strings, oboe-and-piano-colored texture, and darkly affected vocals has a distinct Roxy Music flavor. While not one of the group's better releases, this platter is not a bad listen. *—David Cleary*

- **Songs to Learn & Sing** / 1985 / Sire ✦✦✦✦✦

Liverpool's favorite lads Echo & the Bunnymen battled the cathartic reign of the Smiths and the enigmatic synth-pop of Depeche Mode and New Order throughout the '80s movement of redesigned post-punk, and they became a staple image as well. *Songs to Learn & Sing* marked the Bunnymen's cemented place in new wave and relished the crooning ambience of frontman Ian McCulloch. This collection recalls the rise and steadfast career of the band, highlighting the Bunnymen's work between 1980 and 1985 and collecting the most prominent tracks that made the band the waxed poetics the British press hailed them to be (specifically on older cuts like "Do It Clean" and "Rescue"). Frequent use of the band's classic drum machine or "echo" was also a major feature in Bunnymen tracks, especially on the vibrant dance cuts "Never Stop" and "Back of Love." With various production work from Lightning Seeds' Ian Broudie and Chameleons and Zoo labelmates David Balfe and Bill Drummond (the KLF), Echo & the Bunnymen achieved great cult status throughout the '80s stream of U.K. pop music. *Songs to Learn & Sing* is a solid and comprehensive collection of the band's material, also introducing the previously unissued album track "Bring on the Dancing Horses," which was featured on the soundtrack to the Molly Ringwald film *Pretty in Pink* (1986). *—MacKenzie Wilson*

Echo & the Bunnymen / 1987 / Sire ✦✦✦

This fine release (not to be confused with the self-titled 1983 EP) is the Bunnymen's best since their debut, *Crocodiles*. The album catches the group at a fortuitous career juncture; the clutch of songs here is among the hookiest and most memorable the band would ever write, while the arrangements are noticeably clean and punchy, mostly eliminating strings and similar clutter to focus almost exclusively on guitars, keyboards, drums, and occasional percussion touches. The warmly expressive "All My Life," and which might perhaps have received an overheated arrangement on prior albums, benefits especially from this approach. The band rocks out convincingly on other selections, such as "Satellite" and "All in Your Mind." Pete DeFreitas' solid drumming at times veers toward the danceable on tracks like "Lost and Found," "Lips Like Sugar," and the overtly Doors-influenced "Bedbugs and Ballyhoo." Surprisingly, vocalist Ian MuCulloch appears to have rediscovered the maxim "less is more"; his singing is comparatively restrained and tasteful here, resulting in a more natural, unforced emotiveness that is extremely effective. Production values are excellent, with many subtle touches that do not detract from the album's overall directness. In short, doing it clean really pays off here; this energetic, top-notch album is highly recomended. *—David Cleary*

Evergreen / Jul. 1, 1997 / London ✦✦✦

What Are You Going to Do with Your Life / Jun. 1, 1999 / London ✦✦✦✦

Eddie & the Hot Rods

f. 1975

Group / British Punk, Pub Rock, Power Pop, New Wave, Punk

Arriving during the waning days of pub rock, Eddie & the Hot Rods helped usher in punk rock in the United Kingdom. Working from the same bluesy, Stonesy three-chord foundation as contemporaries like Dr. Feelgood, the Hot Rods were faster, tougher, wilder and louder than any other pub-rock band. They also celebrated adolescent abandon, unlike their peers, who usually concentrated on working-class subjects. Developing a substantial cult following by touring the pub circuit relentlessly, Eddie & the Hot Rods, with their fast, tough rock & roll, made the pub-rock taverns more willing to book wilder acts like the Damned and the Sex Pistols, thereby firing the first shot in the U.K. punk revolution. They also made some inroads on the pop charts with their 1976 debut EP *Live at the Marquee* and the singles "Teenage Depression" and "Do Anything You Wanna Do," but by the time the latter reached the Top Ten in the summer of 1977, Eddie & the Hot Rods and their bar-band demeanor had already begun to appear outdated. The group's following declined sharply over the next two years, and they disbanded in 1980. Although they never wound up as stars, the band undeniably made an impact in the birth of punk rock. *—Stephen Thomas Erlewine*

Live at the Marquee / Aug. 1976 / Island ✦✦✦✦✦

Teenage Depression / Dec. 1976 / Captain Oi! ✦✦✦

Life on the Line / 1977 / Captain Oi! ✦✦✦✦✦

Thriller / 1977 / Island ✦✦

- **End of the Beginning: The Best of Eddie & the Hot Rods** / 1994 / Island ✦✦✦✦✦

A nearly flawless collection, *End of the Beginning* documents the band's golden period of 1976-1979 with the infectious singles, inspired live workouts, album tracks and a rarity or two for the collectors. This is an important, though unfortunately overlooked, part of British punk rock's roots that shouldn't be missed. *—Chris Woodstra*

Duane Eddy

b. Apr. 26, 1938, Corning, NY

Guitar / Instrumental Rock, Rock & Roll

If Duane Eddy's instrumental hits from the late '50s can sound unduly basic and repetitive (especially when taken all at once), he was vastly influential. Perhaps the most successful instrumental rocker of his time, he may have also been the man most responsible (along with Chuck Berry) for popularizing the electric rock guitar. His distinctively low, twangy riffs could be heard on no less than 15 Top Forty hits between 1958 and 1963. He was also one of the first rock stars to successfully crack the LP market. It was his second single, "Rebel Rouser," that really broke him as a national star, reaching the Top Ten in 1958. Opening with a down-and-dirty, heavily echoed guitar riff, it remains the tune with which he's most often identified. Eddy's phenomenally successful run of hits over the next few years was to some extent a variation on the "Rebel Rouser" theme. Duane would have his biggest hit, however, in 1960, when he sweetened the twang with strings for the movie theme "Because They're Young." After Eddy signed with RCA in 1962, his albums—often based on loose themes, like *A Million Dollars Worth of Twang, Twisting with Duane Eddy,* and *Surfing with Duane Eddy*—kept him afloat to some degree, though his style doggedly refused evolution. Paul McCartney, George Harrison, Ry Cooder, and Jeff Lynne all helped produce a 1987 album. *—Richie Unterberger*

★ **Twang Thang: Anthology** / May 18, 1993 / Rhino ✦✦✦✦✦

Duane Eddy was America's first bona-fide rock & roll guitar hero, playing minimalistic riffs that any kid with a pawnshop guitar could aspire to with a little determination and elbow grease. This two-CD anthology offers the finest retrospective of his career available, with all facets of his career being well documented, from the early hits to later collaborations with the famous rockers he initially inspired. Featuring just enough rarities to keep it from being merely a greatest-hits package, this truly showcases Duane at his best. *—Cub Koda*

Dave Edmunds

b. Apr. 15, 1944, Cardiff, Wales

Vocals, Keyboards, Guitar, Bass / Pub Rock, New Wave, Roots Rock, Rock & Roll

Roots-rockers are seldom as purist as Dave Edmunds. Throughout his career, he stayed true to '50s and '60s rock & roll—for Edmunds, rock & roll history stopped somewhere in 1963, after the Beach Boys' first singles but before the Beatles' hits. After establishing himself as a hotshot lead guitarist in the blues-rockers Love Sculpture, he launched his solo career by painstakingly re-creating oldies in his own studio, usually recording every track by himself. Through all of his efforts, he learned how to uncannily replicate the sound of Sun, Chess and Phil Spector records, which not only helped him garner several U.K. hits in the early '70s, but also led to successful production work with artists like the Flamin' Groovies and Brinsley Schwarz. In the late '70s, he hit the peak of his career when he teamed up with former Schwarz bassist Nick Lowe to form Rockpile. For several years, Edmunds recorded albums with Rockpile and toured relentlessly with the band, which resulted in a string of hit U.K. singles. After the group imploded in the early '80s, he slowly disappeared from the mainstream, even as he made his most commercial music with producer Jeff Lynne; Edmunds eventually retreated to cult status in the '90s. *—Stephen Thomas Erlewine*

Rockpile / 1972 / Mamou ✦✦✦✦

Dave Edmunds' debut album *Rockpile* established his sound—not only his revivalist tendencies, but also his method of meticulously recreating the sound and style of classic early rock & roll, R&B, and country records. Edmunds plays nearly every instrument on the album, with bassist John Williams being the only full-time collaborator. As a result, the record doesn't sound "live," it has a pinched, precise quality that may contradict the spontaneity that was at the core of the original singles, but it does offer an otherworldly quality that makes the record distinctive. Take the hit "I Hear You Knocking," which has a mechanical rhythm and a weird, out-of-phase vocal that qualifies as an original interpretation, unlike his by the book take on Chuck Berry's "The Promised Land," which suffers from the stiff rhythms. Still, the best moments on *Rockpile* come from songs like "Down, Down, Down," an obscure gem that manages to recreate not only the sound, but the feeling of classic rock & roll, perhaps because Edmunds wasn't concerned with recreating one of his beloved singles. *—Stephen Thomas Erlewine*

Subtle as a Flying Mallet / 1975 / One Way ✦✦✦

Taking the one-man band aesthetic to an extreme, Dave Edmunds recorded nearly all of his second album *Subtle As A Flying Mallet* on his own, hiring a bassist and a drummer for only a pair of tracks. Edmunds took several years to complete the record, probably because it took a considerable amount of effort to recreate these songs so throughly—he spends so much attention on detail that he refuses to change the sex on "Da Doo Ron Ron." Alternating between Spector classics, the Everly Brothers, Chuck Berry, and a variety of R&B, country and pop numbers, Edmunds hits on all the styles of the late '50s and early '60s, but he spends so much time on duplicating the sound that he sucks the joy out of the music; it is positively eerie to hear these songs performed by one man, who spent weeks overdubbing himself to sound like his own wall of sound. And the main problem with *Subtle As A Flying Mallet* is that these are not reintrpretations, they are recreations, and there's little point in hearing a one-man version of rock classics if he offers new ideas. When Edmunds works with obscure material, like the Chordettes' "Born to Be With You," or with newer items like Nick Lowe's "She's My Baby," the results are better, because the songs are less familiar, which makes his painstaking production exciting, but his isolation makes *Subtle As A Flying Mallet* sound less like a revival and more like a creepy science experiment. *—Stephen Thomas Erlewine*

Get It / 1977 / Swan Song ✦✦✦✦✦

Get It marks a significant departure from Dave Edmunds' early records, as it is the first time he's backed by a full band. Most of *Get It* was recorded with a fledgling version of Rockpile, with other session men filling in when necessary, and the live band gives the album a lively feel which he had previously ignored. Just as importantly, the song selection is more carefully-considered than before, containing only a handful of classics and obscure rock & roll, and concentrating on pub rock staples ("Get Out of Denver," "Back to School Days," "JuJu Man") and songs written or co-written by Nick Lowe, which gives the album a freshness lacking on his early records. Lowe's homages to the Everly Brothers ("Here Comes the Weekend"), Chuck Berry ("I Knew the Bride") and Phil Spector ("Little Darlin'") are more appealing than Edmunds' recreations of the originals, because Nick's songs are lyrically and musically clever. But Dave knows how to make them sound like forgotten classics, and that's why *Get It* is one of his very best albums. *—Stephen Thomas Erlewine*

Tracks on Wax 4 / 1978 / Swan Song ✦✦✦✦✦

Tracks on Wax 4 is the first official Rockpile collaboration and its hard-driving, unified sound make it one of Dave Edmunds' very best records. Like *Get It, Tracks on Wax 4* relies primarily on originals and contemporary pub rock songs, leaving behind the classic oldies; the older songs on the record are obscurities like Chuck Berry's "It's My Own Business" and Jan & Dean's "Thread Your Needle." Built on such fine songs as the rockabilly tinged "Trouble Boys," the Everly-esque "Never Been in Love," "Television," "Readers Wives," and "Deborah," *Tracks on Wax 4* is a tight, snappy rock & roll record that is only derailed by a version of Nick Lowe's classic "Heart of the City," where Lowe's original vocal is stripped away and replaced by a new take by Edmunds. Only then does the record recall Edmunds' perfectionist nature. *—Stephen Thomas Erlewine*

Repeat When Necessary / 1979 / Swan Song ✦✦✦✦✦
Recorded simultaneously with Nick Lowe's *Labour of Lust, Repeat when Necessary* continues the winning streak of *Get It* and *Tracks on Wax 4* simply by sticking to the formula. Though Rockpile's sound is a little cleaner here than before, nothing's changed but the songs, which are uniformly excellent. Culled primarily from pub-rock contemporaries (and containing no Lowe songs whatsoever), the record contains four classics: Elvis Costello's galloping "Girls Talk," and Graham Parker's relentless "Crawling from the Wreckage," the funny (a rarity of Edmunds) "Creature from the Black Lagoon," and the country-rocker "Queen of Hearts," which would later become a hit for Juice Newton in exactly the same arrangement. A few songs come close to meeting this high standard, but they are occasionally hampered by a tightness similar to the pinched rhythms of *Subtle As A Flying Mallet.* In particular, the early Huey Lewis song "Bad Is Bad" and the old Brinsley Schwarz number "Home In My Hand" are hurt by this. But these are minor flaws—*Repeat When Necessary* is an energetic, old-fashioned rock & roll record that ranks as Edmunds last great album. *—Stephen Thomas Erlewine*

The Best of Dave Edmunds / 1981 / Swan Song ✦✦✦✦✦
The Best of Dave Edmunds is a terrific single-disc retrospective picking highlights from Edmunds' best albums, which were all recorded with Rockpile. While Edmunds' tight-assed covers of "Singin' the Blues" and John Fogerty's "Almost Saturday Night" should never have been included, the rest of the album captures the rock revivalist at his best, containing nearly all of his finest moments ("Deborah," "Girls Talk," "I Knew the Bride," "Here Comes the Weekend," "Trouble Boys," "Crawling from the Wreckage," "JuJu Man," "Queen of Hearts"). *—Stephen Thomas Erlewine*

Twangin' / 1981 / Swan Song ✦✦✦
Twangin' was recorded as Rockpile was in the process of breaking up, and the record suffered as a result. Where the previous Rockpile collaborations were loose and rocking, *Twangin'* is tight and precise, as if Edmunds recorded it on his own. Only on "The Race Is On" does the record truly cut loose, and he's backed by the Stray Cats on that one. Still, there are a number of fine moments on the record, particularly in the pseudo-new wave pulse of John Hiatt's "Something Happens," the pub rock of Mickey Jupp's "You'll Never Get Me Up (In One of Those)," and the gorgeous Everly-esque "(I'm Gonna Start) Living Again If It Kills Me." The rest of the record is pleasant filler which could have used some of the old Rockpile spark. *—Stephen Thomas Erlewine*

D.E. 7th / 1982 / Columbia ✦✦✦
Dave Edmunds assembled a self-consciously eclectic root-rock album for *D.E. 7th,* his first post-Rockpile effort. Instead of returning to a one-man band status, Edmunds hired a new band, which prevented him from returning to the studied perfectionism of his early work. Nevertheless, *D.E. 7th* lacks the pop sensibilities that made early Edmunds a guilty pleasure, concentrating instead on roots-musics. While that occasionally means there's mis-steps like "Deep in the Heart of Texas," tbut it also means the wonderful bluegrass-stomp "Warmed Over Kisses (Left Over Love)," the country-rocker "Bail You Out," the cajun-tinged "Louisiana Man" and the excellent Springsteen cover "From Small Things (Big Things One Day Come)." The rest of *D.E. 7th* is uneven, but there a few enjoyable cuts, and compared to what came later, it's certainly more fun. *—Stephen Thomas Erlewine*

Information / 1983 / Columbia ✦✦

Riff Raff / 1984 / Columbia ✦✦

Dave Edmunds Band Live: I Hear You Rockin' / 1987 / Columbia ✦✦✦

Closer to the Flame / 1990 / Capitol ✦✦

The Early Edmunds / 1991 / EMI ✦✦✦✦

● **The Anthology (1968-1990)** / Apr. 20, 1993 / Rhino ✦✦✦✦✦
A double-disc set covering Dave Edmunds' entire career, the 41-song *Anthology (1968-1990)* does a fine job of capturing his musical evolution, even if it is not without its faults. To a certain extent, *Anthology* is a definitive compilation, since it begins with Love Sculpture's infamous "Sabre Dance" and runs through his early solo recordings ("I Hear You Knocking"), before hitting Rockpile ("Trouble Boys," "Deborah," "Girls Talk," "Crawling from the Wreckage," "Queen of Hearts") and Edmunds' overly-synthesized recordings with Jeff Lynne, adding a couple of rarities like the excellent Carlene Carter duet "Baby Ride Easy" along the way. However, the track selection is uneven, including far too many Love Sculpture songs and Lynne collaborations, which tends to dilute the spirit of Edmunds best music. Still, *Anthology* is the best overview of Edmunds' entire career, even if the single-disc *The Best of Dave Edmunds* may be better, more consistent introduction for many listeners. *—Stephen Thomas Erlewine*

Plugged In / Jul. 19, 1994 / Forward/Rhino ✦✦

Electric Flag

f. Apr. 1967, Chicago, IL, **db.** 1974
Group / Jazz-Rock, Psychedelic, Blues-Rock
When guitarist Mike Bloomfield left the Paul Butterfield Blues Band in 1967, he wanted to form a band that combined blues, rock, soul, psychedelia, and jazz into something new. The ambitious concept didn't come off, despite some interesting moments; maybe the Electric Flag was *too* ambitious to hold all that weight. Oddly, before even playing any live concerts, the group recorded the soundtrack for the 1967 psychedelic exploitation movie, *The Trip,* which afforded them the opportunity to experiment with some of their ideas without much pressure. *A Long Time Comin'* was an erratic affair, predating Blood, Sweat & Tears and Chicago as a sort of attempt at a big band rock sound. Calling it an early jazz-rock outing is not exactly accurate; it was more like late '60s soul-rock-psychedelia that sometimes (but not always) employed prominent horns. Indeed, it sometimes didn't always sound like the work of the same band—or, at least, you could say that it seemed torn between blues-rock, soul-rock, and California psychedelic influences. *—Richie Unterberger*

The Trip [Original Soundtrack] / 1967 / Curb ✦✦✦

A Long Time Comin' / 1968 / Columbia ✦✦✦✦✦
Ex-Butterfield Band guitarist/drummer Miles and others put this soul-rock band together in 1967. This debut is a testament to their ability to catch fire and keep on burnin'. *—Jeff Tamarkin*

● **Old Glory: The Best of Electric Flag** / Oct. 1995 / Columbia/Legacy ✦✦✦✦✦
The Electric Flag was Michael Bloomfield's doomed-from-the-start musical vision of an American Music band that played it all and sometimes mixed it all up together. This 17-track set brings together all the highlights from their two albums (with and without Bloomfield), some unissued demos, and a pair of live tracks from the group's debut at *the Monterey Pop Festival* in 1967. A nice collection that serves their musical legacy well, with great notes from Jeff Tamarkin to recommend it. *—Cub Koda*

Electric Light Orchestra

f. Oct. 1970, Birmingham, England, **db.** 1988
Group / Album Rock, Pop/Rock, Prog-Rock/Art Rock
The Electric Light Orchestra's ambitious yet irresistible fusion of Beatlesque pop, classical arrangements, and futuristic iconography rocketed the group to massive commercial success throughout the 1970s. ELO was formed in Birmingham, England in the autumn of 1970 from the ashes of the eccentric art-pop combo the Move, reuniting frontman Roy Wood with guitarist/composer Jeff Lynne, bassist Rick Price, and drummer Bev Bevan; announcing their intentions to "pick up where *'I Am the Walrus'* left off," the quartet embellished their engagingly melodic rock with classical flourishes for their self-titled debut LP (issued as *No Answer* in the US). *Electric Light Orchestra* sold strongly, buoyed by the success of the UK Top Ten hit "10538 Overture." Wood soon left ELO to form Wizzard, taking two members with him. Bevan and Lynne restructured the group; Lynne assumed vocal duties, with his Lennonesque tenor proving the ideal complement to his increasingly sophisticated melodies. With 1973's *ELO II,* the group returned to the Top Ten with their grandiose cover of the Chuck Berry chestnut "Roll Over Beethoven"; the record was also their first American hit, with 1974's *Eldorado* yielding their first US Top Ten, the lovely "Can't Get It Out of My Head." Despite Electric Light Orchestra's commercial success, the band remained relatively faceless; the lineup changed constantly, with sole mainstays Lynne and Bevan preferring to let their elaborate stage shows and omnipresent spaceship imagery instead serve as the group's public persona. 1975's *Face the Music* went gold, while the follow-up, *A New World Record,* sold five million copies internationally thanks to standouts like "Livin' Thing."

The platinum-selling double-LP, *Out of the Blue,* appeared in 1977. Beginning with 1979's *Discovery,* the group launched their own Jet imprint. In the wake of ELO's best-selling *Greatest Hits* compilation, Lynne wrote several songs for the soundtrack of the Olivia Newton-John film *Xanadu,* including the hit title track. *Time* (1980) generated their final Top Ten hit, "Hold on Tight." Following 1983's *Secret Messages,* Bevan left the group to join Black Sabbath, although he returned to the fold for 1986's *Balance of Power,* which received little interest from fans and media alike. *—Jason Ankeny*

No Answer / 1972 / Jet ✦✦✦✦
Electric Light Orchestra's debut album is an astonishing creation in its own right, but neophyte listeners should be aware that it bears very little resemblance to the sound for which ELO would become known on its subsequent records. *No Answer,* as it ended up being called in America through a miscommunication with ELO's U.S. label, is a minimalist work by comparison with anything on the band's later albums. The core trio of Roy Wood, Jeff Lynne, and Bev Bevan, augmented by one horn player and a violinist, approaches the music alternately like a hard rock band attacking a song and a string ensemble playing a chamber piece. Filled with surprisingly loose playing and sounds throughout, and with a psychedelic aura hovering over most of the music, *No Answer* is unique in ELO's output. Written and sung by Lynne, "10538 Overture" is the opener and the best song on the album. Wood's "Look at Me Now," by comparison, plays like a sweet, melodic follow-up to "Beautiful Daughter" from the Move's *Shazam,* with some digressions on the oboe and a cello and violin subbing for the guitars.

The rest moves from period-style popular songs to strangely cinematic conceptual pieces, on which the rock elements almost disappear in favor of quasi-classical playing by all concerned. A beautiful acoustic guitar workout by Wood, "1st Movement" also features the song's composer on the oboe, while "Mr. Radio," an exercise in 1920s nostalgia written and sung by Lynne, digresses for a moment into 1940s-style classical piano pyrotechnics. His "Whisper in the Night" ends the album with a lean and textured acoustic sound that, ironically, disappeared from ELO's repertory when he exited the lineup following these sessions. *—Bruce Eder*

Electric Light Orchestra II / Feb. 1973 / Jet ✦✦
Cut during the fall of 1972, *Electric Light Orchestra II* was where Jeff Lynne started building (or, more correctly, rebuilding) the sound of Electric Light Orchestra following the departure of Roy Wood from the original lineup. It was as personal an effort as Lynne had ever made in music, showcasing his work as singer, songwriter, guitarist, sometime synthesizer player, and producer, and it is somewhat more focused than its predecessor but also retains some of the earlier album's lean textures. Lynne, drummer Bev Bevan, bassist Mike D'Albberquerque, and keyboardist Richard Tandy comprise the basic core of the band, with two cellists and a violinist sawing away around them. There were holes in their sound that made the group seem somewhat ragged, as on the pounding "In Old England Town (Boogie 2)"; Lynne's singing would also have to develop, and some of the material also showed the need of an editor. On the other hand, "From the Sun to the World (Boogie 1)" was a succinct progressive rock workout, and "Kuiama" was a decent showcase for the different sides of the group that worked about as well as any 11-minute progressive rock track of the period. But the very fact that the group's cover of "Roll Over Beethoven" was the hit off of this album also showed how far Lynne had to go as a songwriter—there's nothing else here one-quarter as good as that as a song, and the fact that the band attacked it like a buzzsaw made it one of the most

bracing pieces of progressive rock to make the charts. As a patchwork job, the album holds up well, and it and the single did go a long way toward getting them the beginnings of an audience in America. *—Bruce Eder*

On the Third Day / Dec. 1973 / Jet ✦✦✦
The group's third album showed a marked advancement, with a fuller, more cohesive sound from the band as a whole and major improvements in Jeff Lynne's singing and songwriting. This is where Electric Light Orchestra took on its familiar sound, Lynne's voice suddenly showing an attractive expressiveness reminiscent of John Lennon in his early solo years, and also sporting a convincing white British soulful quality that was utterly lacking earlier. The group also plugged the holes that made its work seem so close to being ragged on those earlier records. "Showdown" and "Ma-Ma-Ma Belle" (the latter featuring Marc Bolan on double lead guitar with Lynne) became AM radio fixtures while "Daybreaker" became a concert opener for the group and, along with "In the Hall of the Mountain King," kept the group's FM/art rock credentials in order. *—Bruce Eder*

☆ **Eldorado** / Oct. 1974 / Jet ✦✦✦✦✦
This is the album where Jeff Lynne finally found the sound he'd wanted since co-founding ELO three years earlier. Up to this point, most of the group's music had been self-contained—Lynne, Richard Tandy, et al. providing whatever was needed, vocally or instrumentally, even if it meant overdubbing their work layer upon layer. Lynne saw the limitations of this process, however, and opted for the presence of an orchestra—it was only 30 pieces, but the result was a much richer musical palette than the group had ever had to work with, and their most ambitious and successful record up to that time. Indeed, *Eldorado* was strongly reminiscent in some ways of *Sgt. Pepper's Lonely Hearts Club Band*. Not that it could ever have the same impact or be as distinctive, but it had its feet planted in so many richly melodic and varied musical traditions, yet made it all work in a rock context, that it did recall the Beatles classic. It was a very romantic work, especially on the opening "Eldorado Overture," which was steeped in a wistful 1920s/1930s notion of popular fantasy (embodied in movies and novels like James Hilton's *Lost Horizon* and Somerset Maugham's The Razor's Edge) about disillusioned seekers. It boasted Lynne's best single up to that time, "Can't Get It out of My Head," which most radio listeners could never get out of their respective heads, either. The integration of the orchestra would become even more thorough on future albums, but *Eldorado* was notable for mixing the band and orchestra (and a choir) in ways that did no violence to the best elements of both. The album has appeared on CD twice as of early 2001, from Sony Music, and from DCC in a gold-plated audiophile CD, with significantly better sound. *—Bruce Eder*

Face the Music / Oct. 1975 / Jet ✦✦✦✦
The group's more modest follow-up to *Eldorado* is a very solid album, if not as bold or unified. It was also their first recorded at Musicland in Munich, which became Jeff Lynne's preferred venue for cutting records. At the time, he was also generating songs at a breakneck pace and had perfected the majestic, quasi-Beatles-type style (sort of high-wattage *Magical Mystery Tour*) introduced two albums earlier. The sound is stripped down a bit on *Face the Music*, Louis Clark's orchestral contributions generally more subdued than on *Eldorado*, even when they compete with the band, as on "Strange Magic." The soulful "Evil Woman" was one of the most respectable chart hits of its era, and one of the best songs that Lynne ever wrote (reportedly in 30 minutes), while "Strange Magic" showed off his writing in a more ethereal vein. "One Summer Dream," which is written in a similar mode, also has a touchingly wistful mood about it but is a somewhat lackluster finale compared to the albums that preceded and followed this one. The requisite rock & roll number, "Poker," is a quicker tempo than anything previously heard from the band, the guitar is pumped up louder than ever. And "Down Home Town," an experiment in achieving a country & western sound, is fresh at this point and more interesting than the equivalent material of *Out of the Blue*. *—Bruce Eder*

Ole' ELO / 1976 / Jet ✦✦✦✦✦
The early hits, marred only by the unnecessary cutting of "Roll over Beethoven." *—Bruce Eder*

A New World Record / Nov. 1976 / Jet ✦✦✦✦✦
Jeff Lynne reportedly regards this album and its follow-up, *Out of the Blue*, as the high-points in the band's history. One might be better off opting for *A New World Record* over its successor, however, as a more modest-sized creation chock full of superb songs that are produced even better. Opening with the opulently orchestrated "Tightrope," which heralds the perfect production found throughout this album, *A New World Record* contains seven of the best songs ever to come out of the group. The Beatles influence is present, to be sure, but developed to a very high degree of sophistication and on Lynne's own terms, rather than being imitative of specific songs. "Telephone Line" might be the best Lennon-McCartney collaboration that never was, lyrical and soaring in a way that manages to echo elements of *Revolver* and *The Beatles* without ever mimicking them. The original LP's second side opened with "So Fine," which seems like the perfect pop synthesis of guitar, percussion, and orchestral sounds, embodying precisely what Lynne had first set out to do with Roy Wood at the moment the ELO was conceived. From there, the album soars through stomping rock numbers like "Livin' Thing" and "Do Ya," interspersed with lyrical pieces like "Above the Clouds" (which makes striking use of pizzicato bass strings). The album was a jewel on vinyl, especially coming out at a time when disco was starting to undermine the airwaves. "Do Ya," in particular, was a breath of fresh air. The album has held up well on CD and, along with the rest of ELO's catalog, is slated for upgrading on CD in the year 2001, with the addition of extra songs. Any version of this album is worth hearing, however, if only to savor the production, which recalls the glory days of psychedelic pop/rock. *—Bruce Eder*

Out of the Blue / Nov. 1977 / Jet ✦✦✦
The last ELO album to make a major impact on popular music, *Out of the Blue* was of a piece with its lavishly produced predecessor, *A New World Record*, but it's a much more mixed bag as an album. For starters, it was a double LP, a format that has proved daunting to all but a handful of rock artists, and was no less so here. The songs were flowing fast and freely from Jeff Lynne at the time, however, and well more than half of what is here is very solid, at least as songs if not necessarily as recordings. "Sweet Talkin' Woman" and "Turn to Stone" are among the best songs in the group's output, and much of the rest is very entertaining. The heavy sound of the orchestra, however, as well as the layer upon layer of vocal overdubs, often seem out of place. All in all, the group was trying too hard to generate a substantial sounding double LP, complete with a suite, "Concerto for a Rainy Day." The latter is the nadir of the album, an effort at conceptual rock that seemed archaic even in 1977. Another chunk is filled up with what might best be called art-rock mood music ("The Whale"), before you finally get to the relief of a basic rocker like "Birmingham Blues." Even here, the group couldn't leave well enough alone—rather than ending it on that note, they had to finish the album with "Wild West Hero," a piece of ersatz movie music that adds nothing to what you've heard over the previous 65 minutes. In its defense, *Out of the Blue* was massively popular and did become the centerpiece of a huge worldwide tour that earned the group status as a major live attraction for a time. *—Bruce Eder*

● **ELO's Greatest Hits** / 1979 / Jet ✦✦✦✦✦
Most of ELO's biggest and best hits—"Evil Woman," "Rockaria," "Telephone Line"—are included on this solid but slightly skimpy collection. *—Stephen Thomas Erlewine*

Discovery / Jun. 1979 / Jet ✦✦

Xanadu / Jul. 1980 / MCA ✦

Time / Aug. 1981 / Jet ✦✦

Secret Messages / Jun. 1983 / Jet ✦✦

Balance of Power / Mar. 1986 / Epic ✦✦

Afterglow / Jun. 1990 / Epic ✦✦✦✦
Although it contains all the hits and the remastering sounds superb, the three-disc box set *Afterglow* is likely to be more ELO than anyone but the most devoted fans would want from an anthology. *—Stephen Thomas Erlewine*

Strange Magic: The Best of Electric Light Orchestra / Apr. 11, 1995 / Epic Associated/Legacy ✦✦✦✦✦

Flashback / Nov. 21, 2000 / Epic/Legacy ✦✦✦✦✦
The very fact that Electric Light Orchestra released a second three-disc box set is a tacit admission that, yes, 1987's *Afterglow* wasn't everything it should be. Happily, 2000's *Flashback* is. Assembled with the cooperation of Jeff Lynne, *Flashback* covers all the bases, featuring all the hits, a good selection of album tracks, and seven previously unreleased tracks, two alternate mixes and "After All," previously unavailable on CD. The sequencing is roughly chronological, with each of the three discs spotlighting a different era, then sequenced for maximum listenability within that—so "10538 Overture" segues to "Showdown" and "Ma-Ma-Ma Belle" then doubles back to the first album. It's a gambit that works, since *Flashback* winds up flowing as gracefully as ELO's best albums. And, make no mistake, this is one of their best albums, a rare box set that satisfies the needs of both casual and mildly dedicated fans, while offering the hardcore not just a bunch of rarities but an enjoyable album with its own character. So, it trumps *Afterglow* in every possible way, then, and thereby eliminates the need for yet another three-disc ELO box. *—Stephen Thomas Erlewine*

Emerson, Lake & Palmer

f. 1970, Bournemouth, Dorset, England, **db.** Dec. 1978
Group / Album Rock, Prog-Rock/Art Rock
Emerson, Lake & Palmer were progressive rock's first supergroup. They succeeded in broadening the audience for progressive rock from hundreds of thousands into tens of millions of listeners, creating a major radio phenomenon as well. Their flamboyance on record and in the studio proved that classical rockers could compete for that arena-scale audience, paving the way for bands like Yes. Upon officially teaming in 1970, keyboardist Keith Emerson (formerly of the Nice) and singer/bassist Greg Lake (ex-King Crimson) auditioned several drummers before they approached Carl Palmer, a former member of the Crazy World of Arthur Brown. The group's self-titled debut album was released in November 1970 and was an instant success. The title track of their second album, 1971's *Tarkus*, was an extended suite that ultimately defined the ELP sound as most people understood it—loud, dense, and bombastic, somewhat gloomy in its lyrical tone, and exultant in its instrumental power. After *Tarkus* hit number one on the English charts and reached the Top Ten in America, a concert featuring the group's adaptation of Mussorgsky's *Pictures at an Exhibition* was recorded for release, and became another major hit. 1972's *Trilogy* found each member taking an equal share of musical responsibility. *Brain Salad Surgery* was released in 1973 on their own record label, Manticore. Their string of successes came to a halt with 1977's *Works;* at the time, each member was feeling constrained by the presence of the others, and the resulting album consisted of three solo sides and a collaborative fourth side. *Works* fared poorly and destroyed ELP's unity, and their main motivation for recording seemed only to be their contractual obligations. Plus, the public's taste was changing—extended suites, conceptual rock albums and classical-rock fusion seemed hopelessly ponderous and pretentious with the rise of punk rock and disco. ELP split up in 1979, but reunited in 1991 for an album called *Black Moon*, followed by a fairly successful tour. However, Emerson developed of a repetitive stress disorder in one hand which required surgery and restricted the group's ability to record or perform. *—Bruce Eder*

Emerson, Lake & Palmer / 1970 / Rhino ✦✦✦✦✦
Lively, ambitious, almost entirely successful debut album, made up of keyboard-dominated instrumentals ("The Barbarian," "Three Fates") and romantic ballads ("Lucky Man") showcasing all three members' very daunting talents. This album, which reached the Top 20 in America and got to number four in England, showcased the group at its least pretentious and most musicianly—with the exception of a few moments on "Three Fates" and perhaps "Take a Pebble," there isn't much excess, and there is a lot of impressive musicianship here. "Take a Pebble" might have passed for a Moody Blues track of the era, but for the fact that none of the Moodies' keyboardmen could solo like Keith Emerson. Even here, in a relatively balanced

collection of material, the album shows the beginnings of a dark, savage, imposingly Gothic edge that had scarcely been seen before in so-called "art-rock," mostly courtesy of Emerson's larger-than-life organ and synthesizer attacks. Greg Lake's beautifully sung, deliberately archaic "Lucky Man" had a brush with success on FM radio, and Carl Palmer became the idol of many thousands of would-be drummers based on this one album (especially for "Three Fates" and "Tank"), but Emerson emerged as the overpowering talent here for much of the public. The reissues of this album on either the Victory or Rhino labels are much superior in sound and graphics to the older Atlantic compact disc. *—Bruce Eder*

Tarkus / Jun. 14, 1971 / Rhino ✦✦✦
This album nearly broke the trio up, but instead its title track delivered the first definitive ELP composition, an apocalyptic piece that gave most listeners their first experience of the full range of the Moog synthesizer. The rest is pretty forgettable, and since the title track also appears on the group's box set, owners of the latter may skip this release. The Mobile Fidelity, Victory, or Rhino versions are all worth owning, however, over the Atlantic version. *—Bruce Eder*

Pictures at an Exhibition / Jan. 1972 / Rhino ✦✦✦
One of the seminal documents of the progressive rock era, a record that made its way into the collections of millions of high school kids who never heard of Mussorgsky and knew nothing of Russia's Nationalist "Five." It does some violence to Mussorgsky, but it is also the most energetic and well-realized live release in the trio's catalog, and it makes a fairly compelling case for adapting classical pieces in this way. At the time, it introduced "classical rock" to millions of listeners, including the classical community, most of whose members regarded this record as something akin to an armed assault. The early-'70s live sound is a little crude by today's standards, but the tightness of the playing (Palmer is especially good) makes up for any sonic inadequacies. Emerson is the dominant musical personality here, but Lake and Palmer get the spotlight enough to prevent it from being a pure keyboard showcase. *—Bruce Eder*

Trilogy / Jul. 6, 1972 / Rhino ✦✦✦✦
The first real group effort once ELP was established, a very romantic-sounding album, with a very restrained use of the synthesizer, which stands in for an orchestra here, rather than setting new boundaries in electronic sound. Mobile Fidelity, Victory, and Rhino each has an excellent version of this disc out. *—Bruce Eder*

Brain Salad Surgery / Nov. 19, 1973 / Rhino ✦✦✦✦✦
The trio's most successful and well-realized album (after their first), and their most ambitious as a group, as well as their loudest, is also their most electronic sounding one. The main focus, thanks to the three-part "Karn Evil 9" is sci-fi rock, approached with a volume and vengeance that stretched the art-rock audience's tolerance to its outer limit, but also managed to appeal to the metal audience in ways that little of *Trilogy* did. Indeed, "Karn Evil 9" is the piece and the place where Emerson and his keyboards finally matched in both music and flamboyance the larger-than-life guitar sound of Jimi Hendrix. Pete Sinfield's lyrics, while not up to his best King Crimson-era standard, were better than anything the group had to work with previously, and Lake pulled out all the stops on his heaviest singing voice in handling them, coming off a bit like Peter Gabriel in the process. The songs (except for the throwaway "Benny the Bouncer") are also among their best work—the group's arrangement of Sir Charles Hubert Parry's setting of William Blake's "Jerusalem" manages to be reverent yet rocking, while Emerson's adaptation of Alberto Ginastera's music in "Tocatta" outstrips even "The Barbarian" and "Knife Edge" from the first album as a distinctive and rewarding reinterpretation of a piece of serious music. Lake's "Still... You Turn Me On" is his last great ballad with the group, possessing a melody and arrangement sufficiently pretty to forgive the presence of the rhyming triplet "everyday a little sadder/a little madder/someone get me a ladder." The Rhino CD is to be preferred over all other domestic reissues, as it features an improved remastering, an interview, and packaging with a very cool 3-D cover design. *—Bruce Eder*

Ladies & Gentlemen (Welcome Back My Friends to the Show That Never Ends) / 1974 / Manticore ✦✦

Works, Vol. 1 / Mar. 17, 1977 / Rhino ✦✦✦✦
Though no one talked about it at the time of its release, this album reflected a growing split within the group. Originally, the trio's members, tired of sublimating their musical identities within the context of ELP, each intended to do a solo album of his own. Reason prevailed, however, probably aided by the group's awareness that the combined sales of the solo albums issued by the five members of Yes the previous year were a fraction of the sales of Yes' most recent records. The result was this double LP; essentially three solo sides and one group side, it is the most complex and demanding of the group's albums. Keith Emerson's "Piano Concerto" is on the level of a good music-student piece, without much original language. Where Emerson, in conjunction with his conductor and co-orchestrator, John Mayer, succeeds admirably is in writing beautiful virtuoso passages for the piano. Greg Lake's romantic songs mark the final flowering of his work in this vein—and perhaps its going to seed, since "C'Est la Vie," the featured single, says little that "Still... You Turn Me On," from their previous album, didn't say better and shorter. Carl Palmer's side is the most accessible of the three solo sides for casual rock listeners, rocking hard on the classical adaptations and featuring Joe Walsh on lead guitar for one song. The group's two tracks, "Fanfare for the Common Man" and "Pirates," cover a lot of old ground, albeit in ornate and stylish fashion. Having used Copland's "Hoedown" as a concert showstopper for four years, the trio takes "Fanfare" to new heights of indulgence, and it actually works, up to a point—like CCR's extended version of "Heard It Through the Grapevine," this is just a little too much of a good thing. *—Bruce Eder*

Works, Vol. 2 / Nov. 10, 1977 / Rhino ✦✦✦
After the relentlessly dull *Works, Vol. 1,* the highly underrated *Works, Vol. 2* is a godsend. *Works Vol. 1* took their pompous, bombastic, keyboard-driven prog rock epics to the limit; had it been stripped of its excesses and coupled with the strongest cuts from *Works Vol. 2,* the band may have had an enormous success with critics and fans alike. *Volume 2*'s brief, eclectic compositions cover an array of musical styles, combining stimulating originals and handsomely orchestrated renditions of "Maple Leaf Rag," "Honky Tonk Train Blues," and "Show Me the Way to Go Home." Lake peppers the tunes with guitar and bass flourishes, resulting in some of his most challenging instrumental work, and both he and Palmer deliver incredibly strong performances. Meanwhile,Peter Sinfield contributes some of his most mature and accomplished lyrics. Emerson's work is solid and creative, but sounds a bit dated, which is part of why the band couldn't endure. Unlike some ELP albums, *Volume 2*'s brief pieces sustain interest; there really isn't a weak tune in the set. The five instrumentals are highlighted by two short prog rock tunes, including the jazzy "Bullfrog", which features Lake's brief jazz bass solo and Palmer's fluid, versatile drumming. "Barrelhouse Shakedown" and "Maple Leaf Rag" showcase Emerson's superb ragtime and barrelhouse piano playing, and Palmer's jazz fusion/marching band piece, "Close but Not Touching," features horns and Lake's psychedelic electric guitar lines.

The vocal pieces are equally interesting. "Brain Salad Surgery" is progressive jazz-rock that bears some resemblance to King Crimson's "Cat Food," unsurprising since each features Lake singing Sinfield's lyrics. And, of course, there is the hit "I Believe in Father Christmas," a beautiful Lake/Sinfield composition that highlights Lake's strong voice and vibrant acoustic guitar. *—David Ross Smith*

Love Beach / Nov. 18, 1978 / Rhino ✦

In Concert / Oct. 1979 / Atlantic ✦

Black Moon / Jun. 27, 1992 / Rhino ✦✦

The Atlantic Years / Jul. 14, 1992 / Atlantic ✦✦✦✦✦
This double-disc set is a solid two-and-a-half hours' overview of ELP's career highlights, including "The Endless Enigma (Parts 1 & 2)," "Fugue," "Knife-Edge," "Take a Pebble," "Lucky Man," "From the Beginning," "Fanfare for the Common Man," "Still... You Turn Me On," Greg Lake's "Father Christmas," and excerpts from *Pictures at an Exhibition.* *—AMG*

The Return of the Manticore / Nov. 16, 1993 / Rhino ✦✦✦✦✦
It's hard not to mention progressive rock without bringing up Emerson, Lake & Palmer. Ever since their first major live gig at The Isle of Wight Festival in 1970, they've been a staple in symphonic rock history. *The Return of the Manticore* is a beautifully packaged four-disc set that gathers essential tracks, covering E.L.P.'s best albums and offering up some re-recorded favorites as well. The first disc begins with an alternate version of 1986's "Touch and Go" that emphasizes Carl Palmer's presence. The disc also includes a cover of "Hang on to a Dream," originally by Keith Emerson's former band The Nice, and King Crimson's pièce de résistance "21st Century Schizoid Man." A new recording of the Crazy World of Arthur Brown's "Fire" rounds out Disc 1's novelties. The remaining discs overflow with E.L.P.'s greatest creations, pleasing the most avid fan and saturating the curious beginner. A new, extended recording of "Pictures at an Exhibition" is a must-hear, accompanied by a choir and recorded in full surround sound. A stunning unreleased version of "Rondo" and a bizarrely entertaining adaptation of "Bo Diddley" are also highlights. The improved, remastered sound stands out on "Karn Evil 9," "Fanfare for the Common Man," and "Knife Edge." "Prelude And Fugue", previously unreleased, finds Emerson molesting the piano, releasing all its unbridled energy. An excellent collection, *Return of the Manticore* bridges E.L.P.'s symphonic work with their classical work, and unites their dazzling electronic pieces with their ragtime and blues efforts. The band's essence, as well as each member's individual talents, stands out on every song, defining the sole purpose of a box set. *—Mike DeGagne*

● **The Best of Emerson, Lake & Palmer** / 1994 / Rhino ✦✦✦✦
Serves up a more digestible portion than the box set, focusing mostly on key early material. 14 tracks isn't skimpy in the ELP context; "Tarkus" is represented, for instance, in all of its 20-minute glory. The set also includes the original single version of "I Believe In Father Christmas." *—Roch Parisien*

The Emotions

f. 1968, Chicago, IL, **db.** 1986
Group / Smooth Soul, Quiet Storm, Disco, Soul
A trio of sisters with a strong gospel base, the Emotions were one of the leading female R&B acts of the '70s. Lead singer Sheila Hutchinson and her sisters Wanda and Jeanette were only teenagers when they crashed the soul charts in 1969 with the engaging "So I Can Love You," but they sang gospel as children and enjoyed secular fame locally before signing with Memphis-based Volt and working with producers Isaac Hayes and David Porter. When Stax folded in 1975, the group hooked up with Maurice White of Earth, Wind & Fire, an association that led to the number one pop/R&B hit "Best of My Love" in 1977. Two years after, White and the Emotions collaborated on "Boogie Wonderland," which was both a number two R&B and number six pop hit. They issued three more albums on White's ARC label from 1979 to 1981, but were unable to duplicate their earlier success. *—Bill Dahl and Ron Wynn*

● **Best of My Love: The Best of the Emotions** / Mar. 12, 1996 / Columbia/Legacy ✦✦✦✦✦
This 16-track, 69-minute disc surveys the Emotions' five-year, five-album stay on Columbia Records (and the custom label ARC), which was the group's most successful period, featuring the gold number one hit "Best of My Love" and the gold Top Ten hit "Boogie Wonderland" (on which the Emotions backed their mentors, Earth, Wind & Fire), both of which are heard here, along with four other songs that saw action on the pop charts. Surprisingly, the Emotions' five singles that only made the R&B charts are excluded in favor of album tracks. Unlike their earlier period at Stax, at Columbia the Emotions essentially were an adjunct to EWF and its leader, Maurice White, and since EWF featured tenor and falsetto vocals, the similarity was often heightened, especially on "Boogie Wonderland." Nevertheless, the sisters sang well over the horns and disco rhythms that characterized the pop/R&B music of the period. *—William Ruhlmann*

En Vogue

f. Jul. 18, 1988

Group / New Jack Swing, Club/Dance, Urban

The female vocal quartet En Vogue was conceived and put together by the production team of Denzil Foster and Thomas McElroy, both former members of Club Nouveau. Foster and McElroy wanted a vocal group who could exude sultriness and intelligence in addition to vocal proficiency, and as producers, they wanted material that would fuse R&B and girl-group traditions with hip-hop and New Jack Swing rhythms. The two held auditions and settled on a membership of former Miss Black California Cindy Herron, Maxine Jones, Dawn Robinson, and Terry Ellis. The producers crafted an image of them as stylish, sophisticated, and sexy. En Vogue's debut album, *Born to Sing*, appeared in 1990 and launched the pop crossover smash "Hold On," which peaked at number two and helped the album go platinum. When En Vogue returned in 1992 with *Funky Divas*, critical and commercial response was overwhelming. The album's wide array of styles, from pop, rock, and R&B to rap, rock, and reggae, were lauded in print; the first three singles—"My Lovin' (You're Never Gonna Get It)," "Giving Him Something He Can Feel" (both covers of songs written by Curtis Mayfield), and "Free Your Mind" —reached the Top Ten, and the album went multiplatinum. As En Vogue was recording its third album, Dawn Robinson left the group. *—Steve Huey*

● **Best of En Vogue** / Jun. 1, 1999 / Elektra ✦✦✦✦✦

En Vogue did make some fine albums, but they always shone on singles. As a matter of fact, the best of their hits—"My Lovin' (You're Never Gonna Get It)," "Whatta Man," "Runaway Love," "Free Your Mind," "Hold On," "Don't Let Go (Love)"—were among the very best singles of the '90s, regardless of genre. That's why *The Best of En Vogue* is such a welcome addition to their catalog. Serious and casual fans alike will find this 14-track collection a captivating listen, since there's a certain intoxicating thrill in hearing each great single flow into the next. It can be argued that the high quality of the material makes this En Vogue's best record, but at the very least, *The Best of En Vogue* is a dynamite, definitive compilation. *—Stephen Thomas Erlewine*

The English Beat

f. 1978, Birmingham, England, **db.** 1983

Group / College Rock, Ska Revival, New Wave

One of the earliest and most important ska-revivalist groups, Birmingham's the Beat formed in 1978 (the band had to change their name to the English Beat in the U.S. to avoid confusion with Paul Collins' band of the same name). The multiracial band carved a distinct sound through the use of alternating lead vocals by guitarist Dave Wakeling and punk-toaster/rapper Ranking Roger, while the addition of 50-year-old saxophonist Saxa, who originally played with Prince Buster and Desmond Dekker, gave the band credibility and fleshed out its sound. Signing to 2-Tone, they released the hit single "Tears of a Clown," a wonderful version of the Smokey Robinson classic. In 1980, the band decided to form their own 2-Tone inspired label, Go-Feet. A string of hit singles followed in the U.K., including "Mirror in the Bathroom." Their debut LP, *I Just Can't Stop It*, combined the early hits with other pop/ska-oriented material. "Stand Down Margaret," with its anti-Thatcher stance, found the band moving in a more political direction. Musically, the Beat slowed down the tempo for a more traditional reggae sound showcased on 1981's *Wha'ppen*. Featuring a more pop-oriented approach, 1982's *Special Beat Service* helped the band increase its U.S. fan base through MTV exposure of "Save It for Later" and "I Confess," but the band members decided to call it quits later that same year. Wakeling and Ranking Roger went on to form General Public, and guitarist Andy Cox and bassist Dave Steel formed Fine Young Cannibals. *—Chris Woodstra*

☆ **I Just Can't Stop It** / Oct. 1980 / Sire ✦✦✦✦✦

The Beat's debut is a true landmark of the period, perfectly blending intense politics with a playful, yet driving dance beat. While the sound could be mimicked by other revivalists, the top-notch songwriting represented on this album is what set them apart. *I Just Can't Stop It* plays like a *Greatest Hits* album (most of their hits are found here) and still holds up today. *—Chris Woodstra*

Wha'ppen— / Jun. 1981 / Sire ✦✦✦

After the nearly perfect debut, The Beat seem somewhat directionless on *Wha'ppen?* No longer instantly danceable, the tunes have slowed to sub-Reggae tempo with more political content (though less focused this time around). The two unmemorable singles, "Drowning" and "Doors of Your Heart," failed to make an impact in the charts and only "Dreamhome in N.Z." leaves any lasting impression. *—Chris Woodstra*

Special Beat Service / 1982 / Sire ✦✦✦✦✦

The final Beat album focuses less on politics and more on the subject of personal relationships. Their most polished effort, the band leaves behind their early ska influences in favor of jangly pop that, at times, delves into African and Latin rhythms. Includes the flawless singles "Save It for Later" and "I Confess." *—Chris Woodstra*

● **What Is Beat—** / 1983 / IRS ✦✦✦✦✦

Little surprise that the Beat (or English Beat, depending on what country the band found itself in) quickly achieved a cult status that has yet to die. A perfect blend of Madness' warm, winning spin on ska and the early Specials' tenser, darker sound, the septet created pop/rock/ska fusions that were instantly memorable and rewarded repeated listens. This compilation showcases many of the band's strongest points, including its two biggest American hits in the incipient alternative scene. "Mirror in the Bathroom" is a crisp, to-the-point picture of self-doubt with great, unnerving sax on the breaks, while "Save It for Later" remains one of the few pop songs about holding off on sex instead of taking the plunge. The latter appears in its fine 12" remix version, one of several rarities making *What is Beat?* of interest to hardcore fans. Most are U.K.-only singles that never appeared on any of the group's three albums, including the almost sprightly "What's Your Best Thing" and "Too Nice to Talk To"'s just-dark-enough nervous dance. Two other remixes turn up: the cover of "Can't Get Used to Losing You" moves with moody, string-touched atmosphere, while noted early-'80s dance producer John "Jellybean" Benitez does a salsa-tinged revamp of "I Confess." More familiar cuts include the captivating remake of Smokey Robinson and the Miracles' "Tears of a Clown," the shuddering "Twist and Crawl," and "Doors of Your Heart," which features Ranking Roger's toasting skills quite nicely. The album wraps up with a fiery live medley of "Get a Job" and "Stand Down Margaret," recorded in Boston in late 1982, a bonus that captures the band at a definite highpoint. *—Ned Raggett*

Brian Eno

b. May 15, 1948, Woodbridge, Suffolk, England

Vocals, Keyboards, Synthesizer, Producer, Arranger / Experimental Rock, Proto-Punk, Experimental, Glam Rock, Prog-Rock/Art Rock, Ambient, Electronic

Ambient pioneer, glam-rocker, hit producer, multimedia artist, technological innovator, worldbeat proponent and self-described non-musician—over the course of his long, prolific and immensely influential career, Brian Eno was all of these things and much, much more. Eno championed theory over practice, serendipity over forethought, and texture over craft; in the process, he forever altered the ways in which music is approached, composed, performed and perceived, and everything from punk to techno to new age bears his unmistakable influence. In 1971 he rose to prominence as a member of the seminal glam band Roxy Music, playing the synthesizer and electronically treating the band's sound. A flamboyantly decked-out enigma, his presence threatened the focal dominance of frontman Bryan Ferry, and he exited after just two LPs. Eno's first solo project, the frenzied and wildly experimental *Here Come the Warm Jets*, reached the U.K. Top 30 in 1973. A 1975 car accident left Eno bedridden for several months and resulted in perhaps his most significant innovation, the creation of ambient music. Unable to move to turn up his stereo to hear above the din of a rainstorm, he realized that music could blend thoroughly into its given atmosphere without upsetting the environmental balance. Heralded by 1975's minimalist *Another Green World*, Eno plunged completely into ambient with the instrumental *Discreet Music*. After returning to pop structures for 1977's *Before and After Science*, Eno continued his ambient experimentation with albums like 1979's *Music for Airports;* concurrently, he became a much-sought-after collaborator and producer, including a landmark teaming with David Bowie. In 1978, he began a long, fruitful union with Talking Heads; friction with David Byrne's bandmates hastened Eno's departure, but in 1981 he and Byrne reunited for *My Life in the Bush of Ghosts*, which fused electronic music with a pioneering use of Third World percussion. His collaboration with Acadian producer Daniel Lanois would emerge as one of the most commercially successful production teams of the 1980s, most notably helming records for U2. Eno remained dedicated to his solo work, and frequently ventured into other realms of media as well. *—Jason Ankeny*

☆ **Here Come the Warm Jets** / Jan. 1974 / EG ✦✦✦✦✦

Eno's solo debut, *Here Come the Warm Jets*, is a spirited, experimental collection of unabashed pop songs on which Eno mostly reprises his Roxy Music role as "sound manipulator," taking the lead vocals but leaving much of the instrumental work to various studio cohorts (including ex-Roxy mates Phil Manzanera and Andy Mackay, plus Robert Fripp and others). Eno's compositions are quirky, whimsical, and catchy, his lyrics bizarre and often free-associative, with a decidedly dark bent in their humor ("Baby's on Fire," "Dead Finks Don't Talk"). Yet the album wouldn't sound nearly as manic as it does without Eno's wildly unpredictable sound processing; he coaxes otherworldly noises and textures from the treated guitars and keyboards, layering them in complex arrangements or bouncing them off one another in a weird cacophony. Avant-garde yet very accessible, *Here Come the Warm Jets* still sounds exciting, forward-looking, and densely detailed, revealing more intricacies with every play. *—Steve Huey*

☆ **Taking Tiger Mountain (By Strategy)** / Nov. 1974 / EG ✦✦✦✦✦

Continuing the twisted pop explorations of *Here Come the Warm Jets*, Eno's sophomore album, *Taking Tiger Mountain (By Strategy)*, is more subdued and cerebral, and a bit darker when he does cut loose, but it's no less thrilling once the music reveals itself. It's a loose concept album—often inscrutable, but still playful—about espionage, the Chinese Communist revolution, and dream associations, with the more stream-of-consciousness lyrics beginning to resemble the sorts of random connections made in dream states. Eno's richly layered arrangements juxtapose very different treated sounds, yet they blend and flow together perfectly, hinting at the directions his work would soon take with the seamless sound paintings of *Another Green World*. Although not quite as enthusiastic as *Here Come the Warm Jets*, *Taking Tiger Mountain* is made accessible through Eno's mastery of pop song structure, a form he would soon transcend and largely discard. *—Steve Huey*

★ **Another Green World** / Nov. 1975 / EG ✦✦✦✦✦

A universally acknowledged masterpiece, *Another Green World* represents a departure from song structure and toward a more ethereal, minimalistic approach to sound. Despite the stripped-down arrangements, the album's sumptuous tone quality reflects Eno's growing virtuosity at handling the recording studio as an instrument in itself (à la Brian Wilson). There are a few pop songs scattered here and there ("St. Elmo's Fire," "I'll Come Running," "Golden Hours"), but most of the album consists of deliberately paced instrumentals which, while often closer to ambient music than pop, are both melodic and rhythmic; many, like "Sky Saw," "In Dark Trees," and "Little Fishes," are highly imagistic, like paintings done in sound which actually resemble their titles. Lyrics are infrequent, but when they do pop up, they follow the free-associative style of albums past; this time, though, the humor seems less bizarre than gently whimsical and addled, fitting perfectly into the dreamlike mood of the rest of the album. Most of *Another Green World* is like experiencing a soothing, dream-filled slumber while awake, and even if some of the pieces have dark or threatening qualities, the moments of unease are temporary, like a passing nightmare whose feeling lingers briefly upon waking but whose content is forgotten. Unlike some of his later, full-fledged ambient work, Eno's gift for melodicism and tight focus here keep the entirety of the album in the forefront of the listener's consciousness, making it the perfect introduction to his achievements even for those who find ambient music difficult to enjoy. *—Steve Huey*

Discreet Music / Dec. 1975 / EG ✦✦✦✦✦
Taking a cue from Satie's idea of "musique d'ameublement" (furniture music), music that just exists like furnishings in an apartment, played so as not to draw attention to itself (not really Muzak, a company which seeks to produce a more intentional work-product effect), Eno created several albums of what he termed "ambient music" which combined a softer style of pattern music (influenced by Bryars, Nyman, Harold Budd) with environmental noises. *Discreet Music* is probably the best of these, using an Oliveros-style tape delay arrangement to slowly change patterns of repeating sounds. —"Blue" Gene Tyranny

☆ **Before and After Science** / 1977 / EG ✦✦✦✦✦
Before and After Science is really a study of "studio composition" whereby recordings are created by deconstruction and elimination: tracks are recorded and assembled in layers, then selectively subtracted one after another, resulting in a composition and sound quite unlike that at the beginning of the process. Despite the album's pop format, the sound is unique and strays far from the mainstream. Eno also experiments with his lyrics, choosing a sound-over-sense approach. When mixed with the music, these lyrics create a new sense or meaning, or the feeling of meaning, a concept inspired by abstract sound poet Kurt Schwitters (epitomized on the track "Kurt's Rejoinder," on which you actually hear samples from Schwitters' "Ursonate"). *Before and After Science* opens with two bouncy, upbeat cuts: "No One Receiving," featuring the offbeat rhythm machine of Percy Jones and Phil Collins (Eno regulars during this period), and "Backwater." Jones' analog delay bass dominates on the following "Kurt's Rejoinder," and he and Collins return on the mysterious instrumental "Energy Fools the Magician." The last five tracks (the entire second side of the album format) display a serenity unlike anything in the pop music field. These compositions take on an occasional pastoral quality, pensive and atmospheric. Cluster join Eno on the mood-evoking "By This River," but the album's apex is the final cut, "Spider and I." With its misty emotional intensity, the song seems at once sad yet hopeful. The music on *Before and After Science* at times resembles *Another Green World* ("No One Receiving") and *Here Come the Warm Jets* ("King's Lead Hat") and ranks alongside both as the most essential Eno material. *—David Ross Smith*

☆ **Ambient 1: Music for Airports** / 1978 / EG ✦✦✦✦✦
Four subtle, slowly evolving pieces grace Eno's first conscious effort at creating ambient music. The composer was in part striving to create music that approximated the effect of visual art. Like a fine painting, these evolving soundscapes don't require constant involvement on the part of the listener. They can hang in the background and add to the atmosphere of the room, yet the music also rewards close attention with a sonic richness absent in standard types of background or easy-listening music. *—Linda Kohanov*

Music for Films / Oct. 1978 / EG ✦✦✦
Recorded intermittently between 1975 and 1978, *Music for Films* compiles moody, instrumental electronic pieces intended as soundtrack material for imaginary motion pictures; the songs are brief and fragmentary, ranging from the haunting "Sparrowfall" to the luminous, densely layered "Quartz." *—Jason Ankeny*

After the Heat / 1978 / Sky ✦✦✦

My Life in the Bush of Ghosts / Feb. 1981 / Sire ✦✦✦✦✦
A pioneering work for countless styles connected to electronics, ambience, and third-world music, *My Life in the Bush of Ghosts* expands on the fourth-world concepts of Hassell/Eno work with a whirlwind 45 minutes of worldbeat/funk-rock (with the combined talents of several percussionists and bassists including Bill Laswell, Tim Wright, David van Tieghem, and Talking Heads' Chris Frantz) that's also heavy on the samples—from radio talk-show hosts, Lebanese mountain singers, preachers, exorcism ceremonies, Muslim chanting, and Egyptian pop, among others. It's also light years away from the respectful, preservationist angles of previous generations' field recorders and folk song gatherers. The songs on *My Life in the Bush of Ghosts* present myriad elements from around the world in the same jumbled stew, without regard for race, creed, or color. As such, it's a tremendously prescient record for the future development of music during the 1980s and '90s. *—John Bush*

Ambient 4: On Land / Apr. 1982 / EG ✦✦✦✦

Apollo: Atmospheres & Soundtracks / 1983 / EG ✦✦✦✦✦
An exquisite experiment, *Apollo* takes Eno's spacescapes from albums like *Another Green World* and arranges them with some heavenly pedal steel guitar by Daniel Lanois. The recording engulfs the listener, and captures the feel of space travel, weightlessness, and other sensations vividly. It's also perhaps Eno's warmest record ever. In the end, it comes off sounding not unlike a Grateful Dead experiment, with Lanois' lazy pedal steel sounding quite similar to Jerry Garcia's playing on David Crosby's "Laughing." An excellent nighttime vehicle. *—Matthew Greenwald*

Begegnungen / 1984 / Gyroscope ✦✦✦✦

Begegnungen II / 1985 / Gyroscope ✦✦✦✦

Desert Island Selection / 1986 / EG ✦✦✦✦✦
A CD-only survey of Eno's first four albums, with songs hand-picked and annotations written by Eno himself. *—John Floyd*

Wrong Way Up / Oct. 1990 / Opal ✦✦✦✦✦
Both Eno and Cale have always flirted with conventional pop music throughout their careers, while reserving the right to go off on less accessible experiments, which means they've always held out the promise that they would make something as attractive as this synthesizer-dominated collection, on which Eno comes as close to the mainstream as he has since *Another Green World* and Cale is as catchy as he's been since *Honi Soit*. The result is one of the best albums either one has ever made. *— William Ruhlmann*

Nerve Net / Sep. 1992 / Opal ✦✦✦

The Shutov Assembly / Oct. 1992 / Opal ✦✦✦

Neroli / Aug. 3, 1993 / Gyroscope ✦✦✦

Eno Box II: Vocals / Nov. 16, 1993 / Virgin ✦✦✦✦✦
The first of two retrospective box sets devoted to the groundbreaking work of Brian Eno, *Eno Box II* concentrates on his pop and vocal material, including some selections from the unreleased *My Squelchy Life*. Although his music still makes the most sense in the context of his albums, *Eno Box II* is solid crash-course introduction to his work, which remains as revolutionary today as it was when it was released. *—Stephen Thomas Erlewine*

Eno Box I: Instrumentals / Mar. 22, 1994 / Virgin ✦✦✦✦✦
This is one of the nicest box sets released in a while, from the outer box to the design of the accompanying booklet. The selection of tracks covers everything from Eno's earliest instrumental explorations through to an assortment of collaborations with artists such as David Bowie and Jon Hassell. This is a great set for owners of CD changers—the structure of these three discs allows a continuous performance in which the music develops over a period of almost four hours. Despite the ambient nature of some of the material, it's never boring. An excellent job. *—Steven McDonald*

The Drop / Jul. 7, 1997 / Thirsty Ear ✦✦✦

Erasure

f. 1985, London, England
Group / College Rock, Alternative Dance, Club/Dance, Alternative Pop/Rock, House, Dance-Pop
Following the disbandment of the short-lived synth-pop group Yazoo, former Depeche Mode member Vince Clarke formed Erasure in 1985 with singer Andy Bell. Like Yaz and Depeche Mode (both formed by Clarke), Erasure was a synth-based group, but they had stronger dance inclinations, as well as a sharper, more accessible sense of pop songcraft, than either of Clarke's previous bands. Furthermore, Erasure had the flamboyantly eccentric Andy Bell as its focal point. One of the first openly gay performers in pop music, his keening, high voice and exaggerated sense of theatrically became the band's defining image. After a failed debut album, Erasure followed with the single "Sometimes," a number two hit in Britain. *The Innocents*, Erasure's third album, became their first number one album in Britain upon its release in 1988. The album also featured the group's first American hits, the Top 20 entries "Chains of Love" and "A Little Respect." Subsequent albums *Wild!* and *Chorus* both topped British charts, and their tribute EP *Abba-Esque* became their first number one single. The duo's its fifth album, *I Say, I Say, I Say*, featured "Always," their first American hit since 1988. Erasure's eponymous sixth album was released in the fall of 1995. It was followed in the spring of 1997 by *Cowboy*. *—Stephen Thomas Erlewine*

Wonderland / May 1986 / Sire ✦✦✦✦✦
The duo's full debut was a sparkling collection of synth-pop tunes that made up in enthusiasm and immediate catchiness what it lacked in overall variety or any sense of artistic progression from Clarke's past. Though the production, one of Flood's earliest high-profile efforts, is detailed and often lush, anyone who had followed Clarke's career wouldn't be surprised by anything on *Wonderland*. Bell's vocals merely tie the connections to the past further, his at-times too-shrill-for-comfort falsetto inevitably echoing Yaz' Alison Moyet as well as one-time Assembly vocalist Feargal Sharkey. Allowing for all these inevitable reminders, though, still means *Wonderland* is well worth a listen. The key reason is the smash UK single "Oh l'Amour," which rapidly became a staple for American modern rock stations as well. A lovely a cappella opening and instantly catchy hook, not to mention sprightly performances from Clarke and Bell both (the latter wisely undersings rather than pushing the flamboyance, letting loose more on the chorus), ensured its classic status. The two other singles, "Who Needs Love like That" and "Heavenly Action," aren't quite as strong but work in the general formula quite well regardless. Other album cuts are a touch more scattered in quality; nothing is awful, but there are some definite highlights. The slightly slower "Cry So Easy" has a great chorus, giving Bell a chance to show his chops, while "March on Down the Line" moves with a fine positive energy, an anthem without calling attention to itself as such. "Say What" is an interesting mostly instrumental, aside from a gang shout or two of the title, letting Clarke's compositional abilities come to the fore on their own. *—Ned Raggett*

The Circus / Mar. 1987 / Sire ✦✦✦

The Two Ring Circus / Dec. 1987 / Sire ✦✦

The Innocents / Apr. 1988 / Sire ✦✦✦✦✦
Having built up a strong fan base and back catalogue in just a couple of years, Erasure turned into a full-blown pop phenomenon thanks to *The Innocents*, winning the British equivalent of the Grammy for album of the year and spawning a big American hit single, "Chains of Love." Stephen Hague took over as producer from Flood, perhaps smoothing out some points for a more general mainstream appeal but otherwise letting the strengths of the songs speak for themselves. It begins with another single and stone-cold classic, "A Little Respect," with a charging beat/acoustic guitar/synth arrangement and a flat-out fantastic performance from Bell, especially on the ascending chorus. Guest performances help flesh out a number of songs quite well. Wheeler and others reappear on "Yahoo!," a gospel-touched (musically and lyrically) number, while noted session performers the Kick Horns add just that to the "please come back" punch of "Heart of Stone." On their own, though, the duo continues in the same general vein of earlier releases while the Erasure formula of dance/synth/soul was now clearly established through and through, thankfully the combination of slight variety and overall performance prevents the album from dragging. *The Innocents*' ballads are perhaps a touch prettier than the lyrics would make them out to be, but if the sheen of songs like "Hallowed Ground" cuts away from the sometimes blunt images of poverty and hopelessness Bell calls up, the music still has a solid power. The CD version adds a fine original, "When I Needed You," and a fun cover of the Phil Spector/Ike and Tina Turner classic "River Deep, Mountain High." *—Ned Raggett*

Wild! / Oct. 1989 / Sire ✦✦

Chorus / Oct. 1991 / Sire ✦✦

● **Erasure Pop!: The First 20 Hits** / Nov. 24, 1992 / Sire ✦✦✦✦✦
On a roll from its U.K. chart-topping success with the *Abba-esque* EP, Erasure celebrated with

the baldly titled *Pop!* While scant in terms of general info, as a no-frills hit-for-hit collection *Pop!* lives up to its considerable brief. Taken out of context from the various albums, hearing one straight-up smash after enough becomes a pure delight. It's intriguing to hear how the pure synth-pop/soul fusions of the earliest years give way to a more fluid style, almost as if the notoriously hard-to-stay-satisfied Clarke, having finally found a perfect partner in Bell, found the time and inclination to explore other options. As for Bell, hearing his evolution from an all-too-obvious clone of Clarke's Yaz partner Alison Moyet into his own English soul style makes for a treat. Picking out highlights from already powerful material almost begs the question, but hearing the stretch of brilliant songs from the soothing jump of "Oh L'Amour" to the explosive, infectious energy of "Stop!" makes for great listening, Clarke's arrangements and Bell's passionate vocals hitting everything song for song. Calling a straightforward, chronologically organized singles collection one of "hits" would be arrogant if it weren't for the fact that it was also true, almost every number a Top 40 placer at home, more than half hitting the Top Ten—and it's never hard to hear why. There is one wryly funny and informative bonus in the liner notes—without explanation, though unquestionably written by self-confessed gearhead Clarke, a list of classic keyboards he's used on Erasure's hits appears with this note: "This is a general list of synthesizers you may or may not be interested in. It is not a product endorsement." *—Ned Raggett*

I Say I Say I Say / May 17, 1994 / Mute/Elektra ✦✦✦
I Say I Say I Say, Erasure's sixth full-length album, was something of a new start for the group following its successful EP of ABBA covers and greatest hits compilation. And it earned them their long-awaited third U.S. Top 40 hit with "Always." But while the group maintained a mass following in Britain and a dance following in America, Erasure still seemed like proponents of a style that had long since peaked and passed into decline, which may have accounted for the wistful, vaguely spiritual tone of Andy Bell's lyrics. Early on, Erasure had seemed to represent a radical change in the sound of pop music, but nine years, six albums, and several EPs later, they just seemed like another weightless British pop band who happened to use synthesizers a lot. *—William Ruhlmann*

Erasure / Oct. 24, 1995 / Elektra ✦✦✦

Cowboy / Apr. 22, 1997 / Elektra ✦✦✦

Loveboat / Oct. 31, 2000 / Mute ✦✦✦✦

Gloria Estefan

b. Sep. 1, 1957, Havana, Cuba
Vocals / Tropical, Club/Dance, Adult Contemporary, Latin Pop, Dance-Pop
As one of the biggest new stars to emerge during the mid-1980s, singer Gloria Estefan predated the coming Latin pop explosion by a decade, scoring a series of propulsive dance hits rooted in the rhythms of her native Cuba before shifting her focus to softer, more ballad-oriented fare. Born Gloria Fajardo in Havana on September 1, 1957, she was raised primarily in Miami, FL . In the fall of 1975, Fajardo and her cousin Merci Murciano auditioned for the Miami Latin Boys, a local wedding band headed by keyboardist Emilio Estefan; with their addition, the group was rechristened Miami Sound Machine, and four years later, Fajardo and Estefan were wed. As Miami Sound Machine began composing their own original material, their fusion of pop, disco and salsa earned a devoted local following, eventually bursting onto the national stage.

The band recorded several albums, each progressively giving more credit to Gloria until 1989's *Cuts Both Ways* was credited to Estefan alone. Unfortunately while touring in support of the album, on March 20, 1990 her bus was struck by a tractor-trailer, resulting in a broken vertebrae which required extensive surgery and kept her off the road for over a year. She resurfaced in 1991 with *Into the Light,* again topping the charts.

With 1993's *Mi Tierra,* Estefan returned to her roots, recording her first Spanish-language record in close to a decade and earning a Grammy Award for Best Tropical Latin Album. Another all-Spanish effort, *Abriendo Puertas,* earned the Grammy as well. In1999, she also made her feature film debut alongside Meryl Streep in *Music of the Heart,* recording the film's title song as a duet with 'N Sync and scoring both a massive pop hit and an Oscar nomination in the process. A new Spanish-language album, *Alma Caribeña,* followed in the spring of 2000. Several months later, Estefan was awarded a Grammy for Best Music Video for "No Me Dehes De Querer at the first annual Latin Grammy Awards. *—Jason Ankeny*

● **Greatest Hits** / Oct. 6, 1992 / Epic ✦✦✦✦✦
All of Gloria Estefan's hits, with and without the Miami Sound Machine, are here, making *Greatest Hits* the best Estefan CD available. *—AMG*

Melissa Etheridge

b. May 29, 1961, Leavenworth, KS
Vocals, Guitar / Heartland Rock, Adult Alternative Pop/Rock, Singer/Songwriter
Melissa Etheridge's gutsy electric blues-rock has earned her favorable comparisons to Rod Stewart and Janis Joplin, as well as a considerable fan base across America. Not only is she a solid live performer, but she has written several songs that have became AOR favorites since the late '80s, including "Bring Me Some Water" and "Similar Features." Although she earned some fans with her debut in 1988, her audience has increased with each new album. When she revealed that she is a lesbian in 1992, her commercial fortunes were not hurt at all; in fact, her audience continued to grow. Because it is rooted in the heart-break and turmoils of everyday life, Etheridge's music has a widespread appeal that makes her one of the top concert draws and AOR acts of the '90s. *—Stephen Thomas Erlewine*

● **Melissa Etheridge** / 1988 / Island ✦✦✦✦✦
This was one of the most stunning debut albums of the 1980s. Given the domination of synthesizer pop on the radio, Melissa Etheridge was a breath of fresh air when she burst out of the gate with this roots rock album sung with a sensitive bravado often compared to Janis Joplin. Although the passionate vocal deliveries are similar, the comparisons end there: Etheridge is a Midwesterner who was clearly influenced by classic rock artists such as Bruce Springsteen and John Cougar Mellencamp. The main theme explored is the emotional complexity of relationships, and throughout the album she sings about the hunger for affection, the pain of unrequited love, and the fire of obsessive romance. While the limited scope of the songwriting requires the listener to enter her world and exorcise the demons of relationships past, the album is full of infectious, up-tempo songs that propel the album forward. Etheridge's true talent, however, is reconciling uncontrollable emotions such as jealousy with a strong and fiercely independent spirit ("Similar Features," "Like the Way I Do"). Perhaps that's why Etheridge became a role model for a generation of young women who found her to be an uncompromising artist unafraid to expose (and celebrate) her strengths and weaknesses. This is a fine introduction to Melissa Etheridge, and it is one of her most enjoyable albums. *—Vik Iyengar*

Brave & Crazy / Sep. 1989 / Island ✦✦✦
Not a trace of the dreaded sophomore curse was to be found on Melissa Etheridge's second album. On *Brave and Crazy,* the throaty singer/guitarist/composer is slightly more reflective than on her first release, but no less confident. Nor is she is any less rootsy. Etheridge's earthiness is a large part of her appeal, and she uses it most advantageously on the gutsy rockers "Skin Deep" and "Let Me Go," as well as more reflective pieces such as "Testify," "You Used to Love to Dance" and "You Can Sleep While I Drive" (which, like a lot of Bruce Springsteen's songs, equates long drives with freedom and liberation). As introspective as things get on this CD, Etheridge never becomes wimpy or self-pitying. For all its vulnerability, *Brave and Crazy* is the work of someone who comes across as a survivor. *—Alex Henderson*

Never Enough / Mar. 17, 1992 / Island ✦✦✦

Yes I Am / Sep. 21, 1993 / Island ✦✦✦✦
Melissa Etheridge wasn't out of the closet when she released *Yes I Am* in 1993, yet it's hard not to notice the defiant acclamation in the album's title. This barely concealed sense of sexual identity seeps out from the lyrics, and it informs the music as well, which is perhaps the most confident she has ever been. It's also the most professional she's ever been (perhaps not a coincidence), as she belts out these unapologetically anthemic numbers with a sense of finesse that's suited to lifestyle newspaper pages, not rock & roll, thereby setting herself up for her bout with celebrity during the second half of the '90s. *Yes I Am* wouldn't have been as convincing if it wasn't so slick, though; her Springsteen-isms and Janis tributes are tempered by songs that work as album rock favorites, even if they aren't as epic or passionate as their inspirations. She may not have songs as great as she did the first time out—"Somebody Bring Me Some Water" remains her finest moment—but she has a sense of purpose and identity that suits her well. And that identity wound up being the touchstone for the rest of her career. *—Stephen Thomas Erlewine*

Your Little Secret / Nov. 14, 1995 / Island ✦✦

Breakdown / Oct. 5, 1999 / Island ✦✦✦

Eurythmics

f. 1980, London, England, **db.** 1990
Group / Pop/Rock, New Wave, Synth Pop
Eurythmics were one of the most successful duos to emerge in the early '80s. Where most of their British synth-pop contemporaries disappeared from the charts as soon as new wave faded away in 1984, Eurythmics continued to have hits until the end of the decade, making vocalist Annie Lennox a star in her own right, as well as establishing intstrumentalist Dave Stewart as a successful, savvy producer and songwriter. Originally, the duo channelled the eerily detached sound of electronic synthesizermusic into pop songs driven by robotic beats. By the mid-'80s, singles like "Sweet Dreams (Are Made of This)" and "Here Comes the Rain Again" had made the group into international stars and the group had begun to experiment with their sound, delving into soul and R&B. As the decade wore on, the duo's popularity eroded somewhat—by the late '80s, they were having trouble cracking the Top 40 in America, although they stayed successful in the UK. During the early '90s, Eurythmics took an extended hiatus, as both Lennox and Stewart pursued solo careers. *—Stephen Thomas Erlewine*

In the Garden / 1981 / RCA ✦✦✦

Sweet Dreams (Are Made of This) / Jan. 1983 / RCA ✦✦✦✦✦
The Eurythmics' breakthrough album is a deft mix of electronic thrills, new wave chills, and sultry R&B, the latter supplied by Annie Lennox's warm tenor. Pretty much relying on themselves, Lennon and Dave Stewart slip past the music's usual coldness and into a territory all their own. It can be smug (the new wave here is served with a side of irony) and a tad dull (the long, operatic pieces serve little purpose), but the payoffs—"Love Is a Stranger" and, especially, the magnificent title tune—are among the finest the genre has to offer. *—Michael Gallucci*

Touch / Nov. 1983 / RCA ✦✦✦✦✦
The follow-up to the success of *Sweet Dreams* showed a more confident Lennox and Stewart, ready to expand their stylistic range. It contains the Top 40 hits "Here Comes the Rain Again," "Who's That Girl," and "Right by Your Side." *—Scott Bultman*

1984 (For the Love of Big Brother) / Nov. 1984 / RCA ✦✦

Be Yourself Tonight / May 1985 / RCA ✦✦✦✦

Revenge / Jul. 1986 / RCA ✦✦✦
On their fifth album, Eurythmics moved away from the austere synth-pop of their previous work and toward more of a neo-'60s pop/rock stance. "Missionary Man" (which went Top 40 as a single in the U.S. and charted in the U.K.) featured a prominent harmonica solo, while "Thorn in My Side" had a chiming guitar riff reminiscent of the Searchers and a fat sax solo. Of course, the primary element in the group's sound remained Annie Lennox's distinctive alto voice, which was still impressive even if the material was slightly less so. *Revenge* was a successful album, reaching the Top Ten in the U.K. and going gold in the U.S., but it was a disappointment compared to their last three albums. And creatively, it was a step down as

well—there was nothing here that they hadn't done a little better before. —*William Ruhlmann*

Savage / Nov. 1987 / RCA ✦✦

We Too Are One / Sep. 1989 / Arista ✦✦✦
Switching to Arista Records in the U.S., Eurythmics made their last album together with *We Too Are One*, and they went out in style. Calling upon a broad pop range, their seventh album was their best since *Be Yourself Tonight* in 1985. The sound was varied, the melodies were strong, and the lyrics were unusually well-crafted. In retrospect, the album can be seen as a dry run for Annie Lennox's debut solo album, *Diva* (1992); songs like "Don't Ask Me Why" (which grazed the U.S. Top 40) serve as precursors to the dramatic ballads to come. There is, however, an air of romantic resignation throughout *We Too Are One*, appropriate to its valedictory nature. The disc spawned four chart singles in the U.K. and returned Eurythmics to number one in the album charts, but it did not substantially improve Eurythmics' reduced commercial standing in the U.S., confirming that it was time for Lennox and Dave Stewart to pursue other opportunities. —*William Ruhlmann*

● **Greatest Hits** / May 1991 / Arista ✦✦✦✦✦
It may have taken them a little while to get going, but when the Eurythmics hit their stride with their second album *Sweet Dreams (Are Made of This)*, they began a hit streak that defined them as one of the most commercially successful and musically satisfying new wave bands of the '80s. For six years, the group was reliable, turning out at least one great single on each album, none of which sounded identical, yet all were recognizable as the work of Dave Stewart and Annie Lennox. *Greatest Hits* summarizes those glorious years and while it misses a couple of hits—a bad thing when the sublime "Right by Your Side" is concerned, but not when "Sexcrime (Nineteen Eighty-Four)" is—it remains an excellent collection. It might not follow a strict chronological order, but it flows nicely, revealing that the band that produced such chilly synth-pop classics as "Sweet Dreams," "Here Comes the Rain Again," "Love Is a Stranger," and "Who's that Girl?" were capable of delivering equally captivating light pop and ballads ("There Must Be an Angel (Playing With My Heart)," "Don't Ask Me Why," "Thorn in My Side"), ersatz soul ("Sisters Are Doin' It for Themselves"), and hard-driving rock & roll ("Missionary Man," "I Need a Man"). Few of their contemporaries were capable of such range and *Greatest Hits* proves that the best of the Eurythmics' work were undeniable pop classics. —*Stephen Thomas Erlewine*

Live 1983-1989 / Nov. 15, 1993 / Arista ✦✦

Peace / Oct. 19, 1999 / Arista ✦✦✦

Everclear

f. 1992, Portland, OR
Group / Grunge, Alternative Pop/Rock, Hard Rock
Though Everclear's Northwestern grunge-punk style was hardly revolutionary when the band became popular in 1995, the band's superb songs and Art Alexakis' us-against-them lyrics were taken to heart by bored Gen-X teens. Also elemental to Everclear's success is their obsessive touring schedule and agressive self-promotion. The death of both his brother and girlfriend by drug overdoses convinced Alexakis' to kick his own cocaine habit in the mid-'80s, and he later formed a country-punk band named Colorfinger In 1992, he met Craig Montoya and Everclear's first drummer, Scott Cuthbert; the trio recorded a demo EP that was released on Portland, OR's Tim/Kerr label. Alexakis grew frustrated with the company's lack of promotion, so he hired an independent promoter to push the EP and personally mailed copies to media outlets and distributors. Everclear then added several songs to the EP and released it as *World of Noise* in 1993. During 1994, the group toured relentlessly, replaced Cuthbert with Greg Eklund, and signed to Capitol in June. Second album *Sparkle and Fade* appeared in 1995, and alternative radio quickly picked up on the singles "Santa Monica" and "Heroin Girl." *So Much for the Afterglow* followed in 1997. —*John Bush*

World of Noise / 1995 / Capitol ✦✦✦

Sparkle & Fade / May 23, 1995 / Capitol ✦✦✦✦

● **So Much for the Afterglow** / Oct. 7, 1997 / Capitol ✦✦✦✦
Sparkle & Fade became a surprise hit thanks to "Santa Monica," a gritty, infectious grunge hit that captured Everclear at their best. Like many grunge and post-grunge rockers, however, Everclear's leader Art Alexakis felt constrained by his modest success and its implications, deciding to take his band in new experimental directions for their follow-up album, *So Much for the Afterglow*. As the title suggests—as well as song titles like "One Hit Wonder," "White Men in Black Suits" and "Everything to Everyone"—Alexakis is feeling a bit ambivalent about his success, believing that it's only a transient thing. He may be right—*So Much for the Afterglow* lacks anything as catchy as "Santa Monica." He attempts to compensate by adding a more elaborate production, complete with Beach Boys harmonies and guest musicians. The result sounds cluttered, not symphonic, and distracts from Everclear's strength as a straight-ahead grunge trio. There are several songs on the album that do showcase the group at their best, but they aren't enough to excuse the confused attempts at progression that make *So Much for the Afterglow* a muddled affair. —*Stephen Thomas Erlewine*

Songs from an American Movie, Vol. 1: Learning How to Smile / Jul. 11, 2000 / Capitol ✦✦✦✦
If the two-part title wasn't a tip-off, let's make this clear: *Songs From an American Movie, Vol. 1: Learning How to Smile* is a concept album, based on Everclear leader Art Alexakis' divorce. Many pop musicians have mined this territory before, but Alexakis pulls off an ingenious move by dividing his divorce album in two parts and two records, separating falling in love from the fallout. *Learning How to Smile* is the courtship album, painting a picture of when everything was wonderful. He goes back further than that, returning to his childhood, specifically the sparkling, catchy late-'60s and '70s pop that provided the soundtrack to his coming of age. It's all innocent, from the sounds and melodies to the aesthetic; at first, it's hard to tell that this music was made in the wake of a divorce. As the album unfolds, certain themes of regret, sadness, and longing run to the surface, but they're all coated in glittering pop melodies and big rock riffs that mask the emotions of the songs. And, make no mistake, Alexakis is digging deep into his psyche, especially at the end of the record as the romance begins to fall apart. What makes *Learning to Smile* work—and an album this ambitious could easily have collapsed under its own weight—is that the songs are strong and smart, and are given savvy productions that make them sound even smarter. Very few of Everclear's peers could have pulled off an album that skillfully balances such an arty concept with such strong, strikingly revealing songs. *Songs From an American Movie, Vol. 1* is their best, most consistent effort to date—and certainly whets the appetite for the sequel. —*Stephen Thomas Erlewine*

Songs From an American Movie, Vol. 2: Good Time for a Bad Attitude / Nov. 21, 2000 / Capitol ✦✦✦
Everclear separated their double album into two different albums, isolating the poppier songs (thematically, the courtship songs) onto the first album, leaving *Songs From an American Movie, Vol. 2: Good Time for a Bad Attitude* as the hard rock record (thematically, the divorce songs, or, as Art Alexakis puts it, "When It All Goes Wrong Again"). This may have concentrated their talents a little bit too much, but it does result in two pretty dynamic, effective records—albums whose connections only become apparent through close listening, which is a compliment. If *Good Time* pales slightly to its predecessor, it's because it isn't as sonically varied as *Vol. 1*, even if it's still quite catchy even it its most metallic. And this is the great thing about Everclear's advanced age, compared to their peers—they not only have a greater musical reach, they are stronger craftsman, not afraid to give their big riffs big melodies, and pacing the record well, even if it winds up being heavy on hard-rockers. Yes, sometimes they seem a little out of step—the Spike character on "Babytalk" seemed just as out of date when Tom Petty wrote about him on 1986's *Southern Accents*—but this is still a stronger post-grunge record than most, heavy on heavy rock, fine songcraft, and lyrics. If Alexakis occasionally delves into inadvertent misogyny, he balances it with sharp wit and warm humanity, plus fine riffs and melodies. —*Stephen Thomas Erlewine*

Betty Everett

b. Nov. 23, 1939, Greenwood, MS, **d.** Aug. 17, 2001
Vocals, Piano / Pop-Soul, Soul
Betty Everett sang gospel growing up in Greenwood, MS, before relocating to Chicago and moving into secular music. She began recording for Cobra in 1958, then joined Vee-Jay in the early '60s and started to land hit records. Her original version of "You're No Good," though sung with fire and verve, didn't make much impact until it was turned into a number one pop hit by Linda Ronstadt in 1975. Her next single, "The Shoop Shoop Song (It's in His Kiss)," was her first major release, peaking at number six pop in 1964. Her next success was the duet "Let it Be Me" with Jerry Butler, a soul version of the Everly Brothers tune that reached number five R&B that same year. Everett's finest song as a solo act was 1969's "There Comes a Time," which reached number two on the R&B charts and also cracked the pop Top 30 at number 26. Everett was now on Uni, where she remained until 1970. She continued recording for Fantasy until 1974 and made one other record for United Artists in 1978. —*Ron Wynn*

There'll Come a Time / 1969 / Varese Sarabande ✦✦✦✦✦
Everett made her best records for Vee-Jay in the mid-'60s, but this album, originally released on Uni in 1969, isn't far behind in merit. Featuring her number two R&B single (and Top 40 pop hit) "There'll Come a Time," this has much more of a sweet soul flavor than her Vee-Jay sides, at times blending the trademarks of her brassy native Chicago scene with a Philadelphia influence. It's far from too sweet, though, with strong material, punchy arrangements, and Everett's always dependably energetic and warm vocals. Also contains the R&B hit "I Can't Say No to You"; the CD reissue adds three valuable 1969-1970 singles that were previously unavailable on album, including the Top 20 R&B hit "It's Been a Long Time," arranged by Donny Hathaway and written by Kenny Gamble, Leon Huff, and Jerry Butler. —*Richie Unterberger*

● **The Shoop Shoop Song** / Nov. 22, 1993 / Vee-Jay ✦✦✦✦✦
Though sometimes classified as a girl group singer because of the Top Ten success of "The Shoop Shoop Song," Betty Everett's main thrust was much more in the R&B/soul vein. This excellent 25-track anthology of her 1963-1965 material shows her facility with various soul, R&B, and pop styles. She had three other minor hits—the original hit version of "You're No Good," the energetic Goffin/King pop/rocker "I Can't Hear You," and Van McCoy's soulful "Gettin' Mighty Crowded"—all of which are featured here. But most of the other material is equally enjoyable, including other early efforts by McCoy, Valerie Simpson, and Nick Ashford, and even P.F. Sloan (whose "Can I Get to Know You" is presented in a much earthier, slower version here than the Turtles' rendition several years later). This CD doesn't include her hit duets with fellow Chicago soulster Jerry Butler, but is a consistently enjoyable retrospective of an underrated singer who straddled the soul and pop worlds. —*Richie Unterberger*

The Fantasy Years / Oct. 3, 1995 / Fantasy ✦✦✦
For the first half of the 1970s, Everett recorded updated soul-pop for the Fantasy label with mixed but generally positive results. This 18-track compilation features cuts from two mid-'70s LPs, as well as various singles from the early '70s, including the R&B hits "I Got to Tell You," "Ain't Nothing Gonna Change Me," and "Sweet Dan." Not nearly as pop-oriented as her more famous mid-'60s recordings, this finds Everett in fine, expressive voice, but somewhat at the mercy of the quality of the material, which is variable. The selections from the 1975 *Happy Endings* album are kind of anonymous, but much of the rest is good, gutsy '70s soul. Johnny "Guitar" Watson helps out on a few numbers, as co-producer, guitarist, and occasional songwriter, and a couple were cut in Memphis with the Hi Rhythm Section. —*Richie Unterberger*

● **The Shoop Shoop Song (It's in His Kiss)** / Jun. 20, 2000 / Collectables ✦✦✦✦✦

The Everly Brothers

f. 1954, **db.** 1973

Vocals / Close Harmony, Folk-Rock, Pop, Rockabilly, Country-Rock, Rock & Roll

The Everly Brothers were not only among the most important and best early rock & roll stars, but also among the most influential rockers of any era. They set unmatched standards for close, two-part harmonies, and infused early rock & roll with some of the best elements of country and pop music. Their legacy was and is felt enormously in all rock acts that employ harmonies as prime features, from the Beatles, Simon & Garfunkel, and legions of country-rockers to modern-day roots rockers like Dave Edmunds and Nick Lowe (who once recorded an EP of Everlys songs together). 1957's "Bye Bye Love" began a phenomenal three-year string of classic hit singles for Cadence, including "Wake Up Little Susie," "All I Have to Do Is Dream," "Bird Dog," "('Til) I Kissed You," and "When Will I Be Loved." The Everlys sang of young love with a heart-rending yearning and compelling melodies. The harmonies owed audible debts to Appalachian country music, but were imbued with a keen modern pop sensibility that made them more accessible without sacrificing any power or beauty. They were not as raw as the wild rockabilly men from Sun Records, but they could rock hard when they wanted. In 1960, the Everlys left Cadence for a lucrative contract with the then-young Warner Brothers label (though it's not often noted, the Everlys would do a lot to establish Warners as a major force in the record business). It's sometimes been written that the duo never recaptured the magic of their Cadence recordings, but actually Phil and Don peaked both commercially and artistically with their first Warners releases. "Cathy's Clown," their first Warners single, was one of their greatest songs and a number one hit. The hits kept coming for a couple of years, some great ("Walk Right Back," "Temptation"), some displaying a distressing, increasing tendency toward soft pop and maudlin sentiments ("Ebony Eyes," "That's Old Fashioned"). In the late '60s, they also helped pioneer country-rock with the 1968 album *Roots*, their most sophisticated and unified full-length statement. *—Richie Unterberger*

The Everly Brothers / 1958 / Rhino ✦✦✦✦✦

Although the Everlys hadn't quite fully matured as artists, their debut is a fine, consistent effort divided between original material and respectably energetic covers of early rockers by Little Richard, Gene Vincent, and Ray Charles. Besides their first few hits, it includes some superb, underappreciated tracks that are nearly as good, like "Should We Tell Him" and "I Wonder If I Cared as Much." *—Richie Unterberger*

Songs Our Daddy Taught Us / 1959 / Rhino ✦✦✦

The Everlys had reached their commercial peak when they made this album of sparsely arranged traditional songs, a concept that was quite a surprise from a top rock & roll act, and considerably ahead of its time. It's actually not as enduring as their early rockers and pop ballads, but the singing is superb on their interpretations of standards like "Barbara Allen" and "Kentucky." *—Richie Unterberger*

The Fabulous Style of the Everly Brothers / 1960 / Rhino ✦✦✦✦✦

The best of their original Cadence albums, packed with hits ("Bird Dog," "All I Have To Do Is Dream," "When Will I Be Loved," "'Til I Kissed You") and other classic tracks ("Devoted to You," "Let It Be Me," "Since You Broke My Heart," "Like Strangers"). Almost all of the songs show up on their greatest hits collections, so it might be a superfluous purchase for all but serious fans, despite its top-drawer quality. *—Richie Unterberger*

It's Everly Time / 1960 / Warner Brothers ✦✦✦✦✦

While the Everlys' sound was diluted by more elaborate production in the '60s, that's not at all true on this LP, which is one of their very best. Not a stiff among the twelve tracks, most of which are barely known outside of serious Everly fans. Includes six stellar contributions by Boudleaux and Felice Bryant, one of Don Everly's best compositions ("So Sad"), and incredible harmony singing throughout. *—Richie Unterberger*

A Date with the Everly Brothers / 1961 / Warner Brothers ✦✦✦✦✦

Although the material is not on the killer level of *Everly Time*, there are some very fine songs on their second Warner LP. Includes "Cathy's Clown," their raucous cover of Little Richard's "Lucille," "Love Hurts" (which preceded Roy Orbison's hit version), and "So How Come" (covered by The Beatles in 1963 on the BBC). *—Richie Unterberger*

The Very Best of the Everly Brothers / Aug. 1964 / Warner Brothers ✦

The operative word here is: beware. This does indeed have 12 of their biggest hits, but half of them are re-recorded versions of Cadence-era material. It's not that they're bad or radically different (after all, they were recorded only a few years later). But why settle for these when only the originals will do? *—Richie Unterberger*

Gone, Gone, Gone / 1965 / Warner Brothers ✦✦

Two Yanks in England / 1966 / Demon ✦✦✦

At first glance, this seems like a cash-in on the British Invasion. Recorded in London in 1966, no less than eight of the 12 songs were written by the Hollies (who released their own versions of many of the tunes). There are also covers of hits by the Spencer Davis Group and Manfred Mann. With a harder rock guitar sound (though not overdone or inappropriate) than previous Everlys discs, the duo's interpretations are actually worth hearing in their own right. The harmonies are fabulous, and indeed, the Everlys improve a few of the Hollies' songs substantially. "So Lonely" and "Hard Hard Year," in particular, have a lot more force, transforming the tunes from decent Hollies album tracks to excellence. Because so much of the material is non-original, this couldn't be placed in the top rank of Everly Brothers recordings. But it is a good effort that shows them, almost ten years after "Bye Bye Love," still at the top of their game and still heavily committed to a rock & roll sound. This was a bold contrast to other '50s white rock & rollers with roots in country, most of who had retreated to tamer country-oriented sounds by the mid-'60s. *—Richie Unterberger*

Roots / 1968 / Warner Brothers ✦✦✦✦✦

Considered one of the finest early country-rock albums, this showed The Everlys, unlike virtually every other top rock & roll act of the '50s, keeping abreast of contemporary rock and pop trends. In the manner of their 1958 LP *Songs Our Daddy Taught Us*, the concept was to cover songs by performers and composers that had been influential on the duo, including Jimmie Rodgers, Merle Haggard, traditional standards, and a couple of numbers by Ron Elliott of The Beau Brummels. Although this laidback, tasteful, acoustic-oriented recording isn't as outstanding as their classic early hits, the vocals are superb, conveying qualities of innocence tempered by experience. *—Richie Unterberger*

All They Had to Do Was Dream / 1985 / Rhino ✦✦✦

Alternate takes of much of their strongest material from the Cadence era, cut between 1957 and 1960. A bit more tentative than the familiar renditions, these aren't as good as the versions that ended up on official releases, but are enjoyable and fascinating glimpses of works in progress, and the singing is excellent throughout. Includes different versions of hits like "Wake Up Little Susie," "All I Have to Do Is Dream," "'Til I Kissed You," and "When Will I Be Loved." *—Richie Unterberger*

★ **Cadence Classics: Their 20 Greatest Hits** / 1986 / Rhino ✦✦✦✦✦

The single-disc collection *Cadence Classics: Their 20 Greatest Hits* compiles all of the Everly Brothers' hits, plus many terrific album tracks, from the duo's recordings for Cadence Records in the late '50s. Every one of the Everlys' biggest hits, including "Bye Bye Love," "I Wonder If I Care As Much," "Wake Up, Little Susie," "This Little Girl of Mine," "All I Have to Do Is Dream," "Claudette," "Bird Dog," "Devoted to You," "Problems," "Message to Mary," "('Til) I Kissed You," "Let It Be Me," and "When Will I Be Loved." *Cadence Classics* misses no essential track, making it a definitive collection and the perfect introduction to the duo's sound. *—Stephen Thomas Erlewine*

Hidden Gems from the Warner Years / 1989 / Ace ✦✦✦✦✦

This collects 14 songs that originally appeared on non-hit singles between 1962 and 1965; many of them had never been on LP. This material strongly counters the view that the Everlys faded artistically after "Cathy's Clown." The writing credits for these strong compositions read a bit like a who's who of early-'60s pop/rock, with contributions from Gerry Goffin, Mann/Weill, Doc Pomus and Mort Shuman, Sonny Curtis, Boudleaux and Felice Bryant, and the Everlys themselves. The singing is fabulous, and the arrangements still strong, rock-oriented, and tastefully produced. Tracks like "Nancy's Minuet" (1963), a great Don Everly original and one of their best paeans to lovelorn melancholia, and "You're the One I Love" (1964), a fine, brooding mid-tempo rocker, stand with their very best work. Only three of these appear on the '60s Everlys anthology *Walk Right Back*, making this a necessary purchase for Everlys fans. *—Richie Unterberger*

Classic Everly Brothers / 1992 / Bear Family ✦✦✦✦✦

The three-disc box set *Classic Everly Brothers* collects all of their Cadence recordings, including alternate takes, as well as several early radio shows and the four tracks the duo recorded for Columbia in 1955. While this music is the most essential the brothers ever made, the disc of rarities is only of interest to devoted fans. Nevertheless, the sound on the box is stellar, the liner notes are excellent, and the whole package is wonderful; for hardcore fans, the set is worth the money. *—Stephen Thomas Erlewine*

The Mercury Years / Jul. 20, 1993 / Mercury ✦✦✦✦

☆ **Walk Right Back: The Everly Brothers on Warner Bros.** / Sep. 14, 1993 / Warner Archive ✦✦✦✦✦

This two-CD, 50-track compilation assembles the Everly Brothers' most memorable recordings of the 1960s. Although their work from this period has sometimes been criticized as inferior to their classic '50s recordings for Cadence, the best of these songs are a match for anything the duo recorded. As it happens, the strongest of these tunes are drawn from their first two albums for Warners in the 1960s, including the hits "Cathy's Clown" and "So Sad." In the following years, their material suffered from increasing inconsistency and ill-suited production. Yet the Brothers continued to intermittently hit the mark squarely—not only with early-'60s hits like "Crying in the Rain" and "Temptation," but neglected flop singles like "Nancy's Minuet" and "You're the One I Love," as well as the hard-rocking minor 1964 hit "Gone Gone Gone" (their last Top 40 single). They also showed a willingness to incorporate the hard-rocking beat of the British Invasion into their work that was not shared by any of the other major stars of the '50s. This compilation misses a number of fine B-sides and non-hit singles from the early and mid-'60s (check the Ace import collection *Hidden Gems* for those), and perhaps leans too heavily on their tepid late-'60s country-rock. But it's a good overview of a body of work that is often unfairly overlooked. *—Richie Unterberger*

☆ **Heartaches & Harmonies** / Oct. 18, 1994 / Rhino ✦✦✦✦✦

This four-CD, 102-song set includes all of their key performances, as well as many overlooked ones, dating from a previously unreleased 1951 radio performance of "Don't Let Our Love Die" to a 1990 live rendition of the very same tune. Opening with a disc's worth of classic Cadence performances, most of the next three CDs are given over to their largely overlooked Warner Bros. '60s output, including many interesting flop singles and album tracks, as well as top-notch rarities like an alternate version of the supremely moody "Nancy's Minuet" and the mid-'60s outtake "And I'll Go." Fine liner notes with detailed comments from the Everlys themselves, but it still manages to miss some great tunes (like the 1964 single "You're the One I Love" and various tracks from their late-'50s and early-'60s LPs), and shouldn't be considered a definitive collection of all their great performances. And the hard fact is, a lot of their post-1966 material (which comprises some of disc three and all of disc four) is kind of boring. *—Richie Unterberger*

● **All-Time Original Hits** / Nov. 2, 1999 / Rhino ✦✦✦✦✦

Rhino's 16-track collection *All-Time Original Hits* provides a useful service by compiling the Everly Brothers' greatest hits from both Cadence and Warner onto one disc. This, of course, means that many great songs are missing, particularly from the Cadence era, since only the A-sides of Top 10 singles were chosen for inclusion (which means such classics as "I Wonder if I Care As Much," "This Little Girl of Mine," "Claudette," "Poor Jenny," and "Like Strangers" are absent). Still, it's nice to have "Bye Be Love," "Wake Up Little Susie," "Bird Dog," "('Til) I Kissed You," "When Will I be Loved," "Cathy's Clown," "Ebony Eyes," "Walk Right Back," and "Crying in the Rain" on one disc, which may make it preferable to *Cadence Classics* and *Walk*

Right Back: The Everly Brothers on Warner Bros. for some casual fans. One caveat: the mixes on *All-Time Original Hits* sound wrong, with the voices pushed too far up in the mix and the instruments a little bit muted. At times, these mixes are disarming enough to distract from the actual music, at least to listeners well-acquainted with other mixes that are closer to the originals. *—Stephen Thomas Erlewine*

Everything But the Girl

f. 1982, Hull, England
Group / College Rock, Alternative Dance, Club/Dance, Alternative Pop/Rock
Originating at the turn of the 1980s as a leader of the lite-jazz movement, Everything But the Girl became an unlikely success story more than a decade later, emerging at the vanguard of the fusion between pop and electronica. The duo of Tracey Thorn and Ben Watt debuted in 1982 and hit the British Top 40 two years later with the single "Each and Every One." The jazz-pop confections of the group's early work gave way to shimmering jangle-rock and occasional subtle country influences. The 1988 single "I Don't Want to Talk About It" became the pair's biggest hit to date, landing at the number three spot on the British charts. After the slick, L.A.-recorded *The Language of Life* and a return to pop textures for 1991's *Worldwide,* Everything But the Girl released *Acoustic,* the results of a series of club performances which presaged the coming ascendancy of the "Unplugged" concept. In 1994, EBTG collaborated with dub-trance innovators Massive Attack on their LP *Protection;* Thorn's vocal turn highlighted the hit title track, and the cinematic Massive Attack sound clearly informed Everything But the Girl's own 1994 effort *Amplified Heart.* In 1995 the soulful single "Missing" was innovatively remixed by Todd Terry, and soon became a club sensation and major international hit, reaching the number two position on the US pop charts. With 1996's brilliant *Walking Wounded,* Everything But the Girl dove headfirst into electronica, crafting sophisticated, assured excursions into trip-hop, drum 'n' bass and jungle. *—Jason Ankeny*

Everything But the Girl / 1984 / Blanco y Negro/Sire ✦✦✦

Love Not Money / Apr. 1985 / Blanco y Negro/Sire ✦✦✦

Baby, the Stars Shine Bright / Aug. 1986 / Blanco y Negro/Sire ✦✦✦

Idlewild / Feb. 1988 / Blanco y Negro/Sire ✦✦✦✦✦
Thorn and Watt made a couple of albums with a cocktail-jazz backup and one with strings before trying a small unit for the intimate songs of their most accessible recording. The setting is perfect for such moving compositions as "Love Is Here Where I Live" and "Apron Strings." Start here, then go on to the rest of this remarkable group's catalog. *—William Ruhlmann*

The Language of Life / Jan. 1990 / Atlantic ✦✦

Worldwide / Sep. 1991 / Atlantic ✦✦✦
Ben Watt and Tracey Thorn returned to the direct record-making style of their first two albums on *Worldwide.* Here, the music was carried largely by Watt's bank of keyboards. But the duo's lyrical concerns reflected their recent frenetic lifestyle. Sooner or later, every group that lasts makes a road album, and this was the one for Everything But the Girl, its songs nostalgically reminiscing about childhood back in England, along with reflections on the big-time touring life in America. Happily, there was still room for a few of Everything But the Girl's complicated adult love songs, notably Thorn's "Understanding," though even that one talked about how love "depends on geography." The breezy subject matter contrasted with the more contemplative music. *—William Ruhlmann*

Acoustic / Jun. 1992 / Atlantic ✦✦✦

Amplified Heart / Jul. 19, 1994 / Atlantic ✦✦✦✦✦
Despite its title, *Amplified Heart* is one of Everything But the Girl's more acoustic works. A simple instrumentation of guitars and keyboards, augmented here and there by British folk-rock veterans like Richard Thompson, Danny Thompson, and Dave Mattacks, serves to set up a series of songs of romantic disillusionment. Declaring "My life is just an image of a roller coaster, anyway" and "I don't understand anything," among other things, over and over the songs speak of confusion and disappointment deriving from failed love affairs. The approach is much more introspective than that taken on the group's last new original album, *Worldwide,* but Tracey Thorn and Ben Watt's musical restraint supports it well. This is an album to listen to when you've just broken up with your lover, or even when you're just in the mood to think about lost lovers from long ago—self-pity set to music. *—William Ruhlmann*

● **Walking Wounded** / May 21, 1996 / Atlantic ✦✦✦✦✦
With *Walking Wounded,* Everything but the Girl puts an acceptable face on trip-hop, jungle, and techno, opening up the world of experimental dance music to a new audience. At its core, Everything but the Girl is a pop group, which means they automatically abandon the free-form song structures that characterize most of trip-hop and techno. In a sense, that dilutes the impact of the music, but the duo found a way around that by seamlessly incorporating the rhythms into carefully crafted songs. They work the same ground as Massive Attack, but their songwriting is more accessible and less adventurous than the groundbreaking Bristol group. Furthermore, Everything but the Girl never approaches the tarnished glamour of Portishead, the kineticism of Björk, or the brilliantly evocative soundscapes of Tricky. Essentially, the beats are used as window dressing—the group's music hasn't changed that much. *—Stephen Thomas Erlewine*

Temperamental / Sep. 28, 1999 / Atlantic ✦✦✦✦✦

Faces

f. Mar. 1969, London, England, **db.** Sep. 1975
Group / Album Rock, Proto-Punk, Hard Rock, Rock & Roll
When Steve Marriott left the Small Faces in 1969, the three remaining members brought in guitarist Ron Wood and lead singer Rod Stewart to complete the lineup and changed their name to the Faces, which was only appropriate since the group now only slightly resembled the mod-pop group of the past. Instead, the Faces were a rough, sloppy rock & roll band, able to pound out a rocker like "Had Me a Real Good Time," a blues ballad like "Tell Everyone," or a folk number like "Richmond" all in one album. Stewart, already becoming a star in his own right, let himself go wild with the Faces, tearing through covers and originals with abandon. Notorious for their hard-partying, boozy tours and ragged concerts, the Faces lived the rock & roll life-style to the extreme. They never sold that many records and were never considered as important as the Stones, yet their music has proven extremely influential over the years. Many punk rockers in the late '70s learned how to play their instruments by listening to Faces records; in the '80s and '90s, guitar-rock bands from the Replacements to the Black Crowes took their cue from the Faces as much as the Stones. Their reckless, loose and joyous spirit has stayed alive in much of the best rock & roll of the past two decades. *—Stephen Thomas Erlewine*

First Step / 1970 / Warner Brothers ✦✦✦✦✦
On their first album, the Faces established the pattern they would follow throughout their four albums—a ragged mix of breakneck rockers ("Shake, Shudder"), sensitive yet gritty ballads ("Devotion"), folk songs ("Stone"), revelatory covers (Bob Dylan's "Wicked Messenger"), and relaxed, friendly rockers ("Three Button Hand Me Down"). Although two instrumentals on the second side is one too many (Ron Wood's "Pineapple and the Monkey" is pretty great), the Faces seldom got better than the first half of *First Step.* *—Stephen Thomas Erlewine*

☆ **Long Player** / 1971 / Warner Brothers ✦✦✦✦✦
With their second effort, the Faces grew more muscular and loose, rocking with loose abandon on "Bad N' Ruin" and "Had Me a Real Good Time," two of their best songs. At the same time, their ballads also improved, with Stewart's "Tell Everyone" and Lane's "Richmond" rivaling each other for the most touching number on the album. Out of the two live tracks, "I Feel So Good" goes on a little too long, but "Maybe I'm Amazed" is tremendous—the Faces tear into the song, transforming it from a McCartney ballad to a heartfelt cry of devotion. *Long Player* is a sloppy, terrific record; although it may have a couple of weak moments, it has the heart and soul of the band. *—Stephen Thomas Erlewine*

☆ **A Nod Is As Good As a Wink . . . To A Blind Horse** / 1971 / Warner Brothers ✦✦✦✦✦
Boasting "Stay With Me," the only hit the Faces ever had, *A Nod is As Good As a Wink* is their most consistent record, and arguably their best. "Stay With Me" and "Miss Judy's Farm" showcase the band at their best—they're all over the place, threatening to fall apart altogether before they snap it all back into place. Nobody rocked better than this, and the album is full of such terrific moments, including a rollicking cover of Chuck Berry's "Memphis." As with all of the Faces' albums, it's a little messy, but it is a classic rock & roll band at the top of their form. *—Stephen Thomas Erlewine*

Ooh La La / 1973 / Warner Brothers ✦✦✦
Although it's routinely lambasted as an uninspired effort or a sell-out, *Ooh La La* is a tight rock & roll album, with its best moments—"Cindy Incidentally" and "Borstal Boy"—ranking among the Faces' best songs. *—Stephen Thomas Erlewine*

★ **The Best of Faces: Good Boys When They're Asleep** / Aug. 17, 1999 / Rhino ✦✦✦✦✦
Twenty years after their breakup, the Faces remained one of the most beloved bands in rock history, but it wasn't until 1999 that they were rewarded with a genuine collection, one that worked as an introduction while satisfying the dedicated with a truly listenable, terrific album. Not that the 19-track *Best of Faces: Good Boys When They're Asleep* contains everything worthwhile from the band—the absence of the extraordinary live version of Paul McCartney's "Maybe I'm Amazed" is the most egregious omission, and there's a number of remarkable songs missing as well—but it's hard to quibble with anything that is here. As a matter of fact, listening to *Good Boys When They're Asleep* is quite a thrilling ride, since it emphasizes their two sides—the rowdy, party-addled rockers and the melancholy ballads. Collectors will be happy to have the previously unreleased "Open to Ideas," along with the non-LP selections "Pool Hall Richard" and "You Can Make Me Dance, Sing or Anything," but the real news about the disc is that it offers a genuine retrospective that's every bit as good as the band itself, while arguably being a better, more cohesive record than any of the original albums. For longtime fans, as well as neophytes who have read about the Faces but never dived into the records, it's an album that's worth the wait. *—Stephen Thomas Erlewine*

Donald Fagen

b. Jan. 10, 1948, Passaic, NJ
Vocals, Keyboards, Synthesizer / Jazz-Rock, Pop/Rock, Soft Rock
Donald Fagen was one of the two masterminds behind Steely Dan, the seminal jazz-pop band of the '70s. Fagen's solo work has been a continuation of the band's work of the early '80s—carefully constructed and arranged, intricately detailed pop songs that are more substantial than their stylish surface may indicate. His 1982 solo debut, *The Nightfly,* was the best album he had made in years; it covered the same ground as the last two Steely Dan albums, yet surpassed it in terms of ambition and achievement.

After the success of *The Nightfly,* Fagen suffered a case of writer's block; for the rest of the decade he contributed music to the occasional film and briefly wrote a column for *Premiere* magazine in the mid-'80s. In the early '90s, he toured with the New York Rock & Soul Revue as he finished the material for his second album. With his former Steely Dan partner Walter Becker producing, 1993's *Kamakiriad* sounded like *Aja* recorded with '90s technology. It had some success on the adult-contemporary charts, but it was overshadowed by the duo's decision to re-form Steely Dan and tour for the first time in nearly 20 years; the tour was a massive success. *—Stephen Thomas Erlewine*

● **The Nightfly** / Oct. 1982 / Warner Brothers ✦✦✦✦✦
A portrait of the artist as a young man, *The Nightfly* is a wonderfully evocative reminiscence of Kennedy-era American life; in the liner notes, Donald Fagen describes the songs as representative of the kinds of fantasies he entertained as an adolescent during the late Fifties and early Sixties, and he conveys the tenor of the times with some of his most personal and least obtuse material to date. Continuing in the smooth pop-jazz mode favored on the final Steely Dan records, *The Nightfly* is lush and shimmering, produced with cinematic flair by Gary Katz; romanticized but never sentimental, the songs are slices of suburbanite soap opera, tales of space-

age hopes (the hit "I.G.Y.") and Cold War fears (the wonderful "The New Frontier," a memoir of fallout-shelter love) crafted with impeccable style and sophistication. *—Jason Ankeny*

Kamakiriad / May 25, 1993 / Reprise ✦✦✦
After eleven years, Donald Fagen delivered his second album, *Kamakiriad*, in the summer of 1993. Where the sophisticated eclecticism of *The Nightfly* was warm and welcoming, *Kamakiriad* is insular; it takes several listens before all of the pieces fall into place. While all of the album *sounds* terrific, the melodies are subtler and tend to get buried under the meticulous arrangements. However, the hooks and melodies emerge after a couple of plays, as do Fagen's wry, witty lyrics. *—Stephen Thomas Erlewine*

Fairport Convention

f. 1967
Group / British Folk-Rock, Progressive Folk, British Folk, Folk-Rock
The best British folk-rock band of the late '60s, Fairport Convention did more than any other act to develop a truly British variation on the folk-rock prototype by drawing upon traditional material and styles indigenous to the British Isles. While the revved-up renditions of traditional British folk tunes drew the most critical attention, the group were also (at least at the outset) talented songwriters as well as interpreters. They were comfortable with conventional harmony-based folk-rock as well as tunes that drew upon more explicitly traditional sources, and boasted some of the best singers and instrumentalists of the day. A revolving door of personnel changes, however, saw the exit of their most distinguished talents, and basically changed the band into a living museum piece after the early '70s, albeit an enjoyable one with integrity. Fairport didn't reach their peak until 1968 and the addition of singer Sandy Denny, whose penetrating, resonant style qualified her as the best British folk-rock singer of all time and provided the band with the best vocalist they would ever have. *What We Did on Our Holidays* (1968) and *Unhalfbricking* (1969) are their best albums, mixing strong originals, excellent covers of contemporary folk-rock songs by the likes of Joni Mitchell and Bob Dylan, and imaginative revivals of traditional folk songs that mixed electric and acoustic instruments with a beguiling ease. With *Liege and Lief* (1969), critical thought diverges; some insist that this is unequivocally their peak, marking a final escape from their '60s folk-rock influences into a much more original style. This school of thought severely underestimates their songwriting talents, and others feel that they were at their best when mixing original and outside material, and contemporary and traditional styles, in fact becoming more predictable and derivative when they opted to concentrate on British folk chestnuts. *—Richie Unterberger*

Fairport Convention / Jun. 1968 / Polydor ✦✦✦✦✦
By far the most rock-oriented of Fairport's early albums, this was recorded before Denny joined the band (Judy Dyble handles the female vocals). Unjustly overlooked by listeners who consider the band's pre-Denny output insignificant, this is a fine folk-rock effort that takes far more inspiration from West Coast '60s sounds than traditional British folk. Good originals and excellent covers of a variety of obscure tunes by Joni Mitchell, Dylan, Emmitt Rhodes, and Jim & Jean. *—Richie Unterberger*

What We Did on Our Holidays / Jan. 1969 / Hannibal ✦✦✦✦✦
Sandy Denny's haunting, ethereal vocals give Fairport a big boost on her debut with the group. A more folk-based album than their initial effort, divided between original material and a few well-chosen covers. This contains several of their greatest moments: Sandy Denny's "Fotheringay," and Richard Thompson's "Meet on the Ledge," the obscure Joni Mitchell composition "Eastern Rain," the traditional "She Moves Through the Fair," and their version of Dylan's "I'll Keep It with Mine." *—Richie Unterberger*

★ **Unhalfbricking** / Jul. 1969 / Hannibal ✦✦✦✦✦
Richard Thompson and Sandy Denny shine throughout this record, which is considered by some to be their Fairport peak together. The second album by a tragically short-lived Fairport Convention line-up. It seems top-heavy with Dylan tunes, three of them included, but they're done with such verve and freshness that they seem perfectly appropriate. As for the rest, Denny's performance on "Autopsy" is outshone only by her work on the apocalyptic nine-minute "A Sailor's Life," which is one of the great English folk-rock showcases ever recorded, a rival to such works as Phil Ochs' "Crucifixion" and Bob Dylan's "Desolation Row," as a song that just makes the listener "white out" inside, mouth open, when its over. Also highlighted by the definitive Denny recording of "Who Knows Where The Time Goes." And take in the powerhouse drumming, and realize what the band lost when Martin Lamble died. *—William Ruhlmann & Bruce Eder*

☆ **Liege and Lief** / Dec. 1969 / A&M ✦✦✦✦✦
For their fourth album, Fairport Convention released what is regarded by many as not only the best record in their history but also one of the seminal English folk-rock albums of all time. This was also the album that marked the transformation of the group from, essentially, a rock band that utilized folk music (in tandem with modern singer/songwriter material) as a source for part of their sound, and an inspiration for their own songwriting, into a group specializing in reinterpreting traditional English songs. There's only one original number here, the soaring "Come All Ye," the rest being adaptations of old English folk songs; at the time, however, very few groups were doing this with any success, or mixing acoustic and electric sounds quite as adeptly, with the result that *Liege and Lief* was practically a consciousness-raising album for a lot of listeners. "Farewell Farewell," "Matty Groves," "Reynardine," and "Tam-Lin" were highlights of an LP filled with gems in this style, ornamented with gorgeous harmonies and striking instrumental virtuosity. Sadly, this lineup was in the process of splitting up virtually as the record was being made—after Sandy Denny's and Ashley Hutchings' exits, it would be remembered with a tone of nostalgia that was somewhat unfair to the equally impressive lineup that followed. The CD edition of *Liege and Lief* is decent, although, as with almost any *A&M* CD release dating before the end of the 1990s, the album could use a 24-bit remastering one of these days. *—Bruce Eder*

Full House / Jul. 1970 / Hannibal ✦✦✦✦✦
Fairport Convention is a group that has always beaten the odds—that's why a version of the band is working in the 21st century. But even back when they had the ability to surprise everyone. By the time of this, the group's fifth album, key members Ashley Hutchings and Sandy Denny had exited the lineup, yet the group continued here without skipping a beat, for the first time without a female singer—and it turned out not to make a major difference. Richard Thompson and Dave Swarbrick took over as singers, and Dave Pegg (more recently of Jethro Tull) joined on bass, and the resulting album was actually more viscerally exciting than its predecessor, *Liege and Lief*, if not quite as important as that record, since it came first. Even vocally, this version of the group needed offer no apologies. Thompson, Swarbrick, Pegg, and Simon Nicol harmonize beautifully around strong lead vocals. Not only does the singing here retain the high standard of the earlier incarnation of the group (check out the harmony singing on "Sir Patrick Spens" and "Flowers of the Forest"), but the playing throughout has greater urgency and punch, from the rousing Thompson-Swarbrick opener "Walk Awhile" to the haunting, moody, dazzling nine-minute "Sloth," which remained part of the group's live set for years. An indispensable recording, and one that anybody who wants to truly know this band, or to take in some of the best work of Richard Thompson's career, must own (his playing on "Sloth" and "Doctor of Physick" makes it worthwhile). Swarbrick's fiddle and viola playing is also among the best of his career. Ironically, Thompson would make this his last full-time studio venture with Fairport, but what a way to go! *—Stephen Winnick & Bruce Eder*

Angel Delight / Jun. 1971 / Island ✦✦✦
Richard Thompson exits the Fairport line-up, leaving the band reduced to a quartet of Simon Nicol, Dave Swarbrick, Dave Pegg, and Dave Mattacks. The loss of big guns Thompson and Denny was felt, but amazingly, although it isn't nearly as well known as *Liege and Lief* or *Full House*, this record reached the highest chart position of any Fairport LP, making number eight in England. Swarbrick led the group in even more of a traditional British folk vein. By now everybody involved was singing (with Nicol and Swarbrick usually alternating on lead), and they managed to pull it off, mostly by virtue of the honesty of their voices and instrumental work almost as vital and animated as any in their history. From the beautifully sung and exciting opener "Lord Marlborough," the album should strike a responsive chord with any folk or folk-rock enthusiast—especially enjoyable are the singing on the buoyantly humorous title track, and the viola/violin duet between Swarbrick and Nicol on "Bridge Over The River Ash." *—Bruce Eder & William Ruhlmann*

Babbacombe Lee / Nov. 1971 / Island ✦✦✦
The group's only concept album (similar in some ways to the Pretty Things' *S.F. Sorrow*), built around the life story of John "Babbacombe" Lee, a Victorian-era condemned murderer. Lee's story, from his boyhood poverty to his time in the Royal Navy, his being invalided out and forced to work in the service of Miss Keyes, to her murder and his sentence of death, and the failure of the gallows three times, is told in song, and all but one of those songs are originals. The all-male Fairport seldom sang better, nor did the post-Thompson band ever play with more panache, and some of the songs are beautiful—but a few are lugubrious, and as with most other concept albums, the fit between the songs and the larger subject ultimately isn't entirely comfortable for the listener. All of the material was confusing because the group, for some reason, never put titles on the individual songs, instead stringing them together in longer sections. The critics loved it, but the listeners stayed away in droves for the first time since the band's debut album. *—Bruce Eder*

Rosie / Mar. 1973 / Island ✦✦✦

Nine / Oct. 1973 / A&M ✦✦

A Fairport Live Convention / Jul. 1974 / Island ✦✦✦

Rising for the Moon / Jun. 1975 / Island ✦✦✦
Although there's nothing here as overpowering as "Sailor's Life" or "Sloth," this record is still a choice release, as Sandy Denny's official return to Fairport. She wrote or co-wrote seven of its 11 songs, and dominates most of the others with her voice. This line-up (Denny, Dave Swarbrick, Dave Pegg, Jerry Donahue, Trevor Lucas, and Bruce Rowland, with Dave Mattacks—who quit partway through—drumming on some of the tracks) went for the gold with rock veteran Glyn Johns in the producer's spot. The result was the only Fairport album done after the departure of Richard Thompson that doesn't sound anemic in the electric guitar department. Some of the songs, especially the title track and "Restless," have the feel of compact, breezy pop/country-rock, reminiscent of the Eagles or Firefall, although it's hard to imagine either of those groups turning in anything with with ethereal beauty of Denny's performance "White Dress" or "Dawn." Those songs and "Stranger To Himself" could easily have been on one of her solo albums. Others, like Trevor Lucas's "Iron Lion," sound almost like Fairport's version of the Rolling Stones' "Dead Flowers." Only the Swarbrick/Pegg "Night-time Girl" resembles Fairport's established work from their earlier history. This was the last album and the last incarnation of Fairport Convention to present itself to the public as a contemporary rock group, and their last (apart from 1987's *In Real Time*) release on a major label. Beyond this point, they became part of the folk revival circuit, albeit with a huge audience. (British import) *—Bruce Eder*

Fairport Chronicles / 1976 / A&M ✦✦✦✦✦

Gottle O'Geer / May 1976 / Island ✦✦

Live at L. A. Troubadour / 1977 / Island ✦✦✦

Bonny Bunch of Roses / Feb. 1977 / Vertigo ✦✦

Tipplers Tales / May 1978 / Vertigo ✦✦✦

Farewell, Farewell / 1979 / Simon's ✦✦✦
Originally recorded as a memento of the group's "final" tour from May to August of 1979, *Farewell, Farewell* was intended as Fairport's last release. It hasn't worked out that way, luckily, as the re-formed version of the group has done some good work, but this was still a rarity, about 23,000 copies (distributed by the bandmembers) ever pressed on vinyl. It's not in league with *House Full*, but it is a worthwhile album, featuring the final version of Fairport Convention in its unbroken line from the original group—here including Simon Nicol, Dave Swarbrick, and Dave Pegg—in good form, covering a cross section of their history. Songs in-

clude a crunchy version of "Mr. Lacey"; faithful, emphatic renditions of "John Lee" and "Sir Patrick Spens"; a lustily sung "Walk Awhile"; and a warmly nostalgic "Meet on the Ledge"; with a finale of Mike Waterson's "Rubber Band." Reissued in 1997 with bonus tracks. *—Bruce Eder*

Moat on the Ledge / 1982 / Stony Plain ✦✦✦
Fairport Convention officially disbanded in 1979, only to become the hosts of a yearly folk festival/reunion concert every August in England. This album is taken from the 1981 show. It features original Fairport members Simon Nicol, Judy Dyble, and Richard Thompson, plus later members Dave Swarbrick, Dave Pegg, Dave Mattacks, and Bruce Rowland, and it's a good recapitulation of the band's style, with such numbers new to the repertoire as Bob Dylan's "Country Pie" and Thompson's "Woman or a Man." *—William Ruhlmann*

Gladys' Leap / 1985 / Varrick ✦✦✦

Expletive Delighted! / 1986 / Varrick ✦✦✦
The group's only all-instrumental album is alternately enjoyable and maddening. On the down side, there was no earthly reason why Dave Mattacks' drums had to be recorded as loud as they are on certain tracks. But "Portmeirion" and "Expletive Delighted" are as delicate and beautiful as any work that this version of the band has done. Richard Thompson and Jerry Donahue turn up on electric guitar for the rippling finale "Hanks For the Memories," a reconsideration of instrumentals ranging from "Apache" and "Pipeline" to "Peter Gunn." *—Bruce Eder*

House Full / 1986 / Hannibal ✦✦✦✦✦
Although its release date is 16 years later, this 1970 live recording is of a piece with *Full House* and should be discovered in tandem with the studio album. A revised version of *Live At The L.A. Troubadour* (originally released on vinyl in 1976), with different takes and/or songs, taken from a group of September 1970 concert performance by the Richard Thompson-led 1970 line-up of Fairport, one of its strongest incarnations. A 12-minute long version of "Sloth" dominates the proceedings, but even better is the fact that, at 48 minutes, this is one of Fairport's longer albums, so there is lots of room for other material, including a shattering Thompson-sung rendition of "Matty Groves," and a pair of numbers, "Staines Morris" and "Banks of the Sweet Primroses," scheduled for this group's never-realized second studio album (though the latter made it into the studio history of the four-man Fairport that followed). *—Bruce Eder & William Ruhlmann*

Heyday: BBC Radio Sessions, 1968-1969 / 1987 / Hannibal ✦✦✦✦✦
Fairport Convention has long been British folk-rock with the emphasis on British and folk, but listeners most familiar with their revved-up interpretation of traditional English ballads (and like-minded originals) often forget that the band started out as the U.K.'s response to Jefferson Airplane. *Heyday* collects 12 performances (ten of them covers) recorded for the BBC during the early period when Sandy Denny and Ian Matthews were both singing for the group (and a bus accident had not yet taken the life of original drummer Martin Lamble). While most of the songs were written by noted American folk-rockers of the day, the Fairports put a very individual stamp on every selection here; if you don't think you ever need to hear another version of Leonard Cohen's "Suzanne" or Bob Dylan's "Percy's Song," you might well change your mind after hearing Fairport work their magic with them, and their takes on Joni Mitchell's "I Don't Know Where I Stand" and Gene Clark's "Tried So Hard" actually improve on the very worthy originals. Fairport Convention approaches these songs with taste, skill, and subtle but potent fire, and Richard Thompson was already growing into one of the most remarkable guitarists in British rock (and if you're of the opinion that he doesn't know how to be funny, check out his goofy double entendre duet with Sandy, "If It Feels Good, You Know It Can't Be Wrong"). While Fairport Convention would create their most lasting work with *Liege and Leif* and *Full House, Heyday* offers delightful proof that this band's talents (and influences) took many different directions, and it captures one of the band's better lineups in superb form. *—Mark Deming*

In Real Time: Live '87 / 1987 / Island ✦✦

Five Seasons / Dec. 1990 / Rough Trade ✦✦✦

Jewel in the Crown / Jun. 6, 1995 / Green Linnet ✦✦✦

Old-New-Borrowed-Blue / Jul. 16, 1996 / Green Linnet ✦✦✦

● **Meet on the Ledge: The Classic Years (1967-1975)** / Jul. 27, 1999 / A&M ✦✦✦✦✦
Fairport Convention have had their fair share of anthologies, but the double-disc set *Meet on the Ledge: The Classic Years (1967-75)* is arguably the best yet, rivaling the classic *Fairport Chronicles*, which was released just as the classic lineup was splitting apart. *Meet on the Ledge* is more exhaustive than that collection, and it also boasts a number of rarities, including the previously unreleased "Bonny Bunch of Roses" and "Poor Will and the Jolly Hangman." Undoubtedly, those will be of interest to collectors, but the 32-track set is still primarily targeted at neophytes and casual fans. Happily, it fulfills its goal of offering a flawless introduction—not only does it provide a concise history of the band, but it's also tremendously entertaining. Which means that even if it satiates some appetites, it will whet others. But the best thing is that the compilation works well enough to remain entertaining, even if you know the albums inside out. *—Stephen Thomas Erlewine*

Faith No More

f. 1982, San Francisco, CA, **db.** Apr. 20, 1998
Group / Alternative Metal, Funk Metal, Heavy Metal, Alternative Pop/Rock
With their fusion of heavy metal, funk, hip-hop, and progressive rock, Faith No More earned a substantial cult following. By the time they recorded their first album in 1985, the band had already had a string of lead vocalists, including Courtney Love; their debut, *We Care a Lot*, featured Chuck Mosley's abrasive vocals but it was driven by Jim Martin's metallic guitar. Faith No More's next album, 1987's *Introduce Yourself*, was a more cohesive and impressive effort; for the first time, the rap and metal elements didn't sound like they were fighting each other. In 1988, the rest of the band fired Mosley; he was replaced by Bay Area vocalist Mike Patton during the recording of their next album, *The Real Thing*. Patton was a more accomplished vocalist, able to change effortlessly between rapping and singing, as well as adding a considerably more bizarre slant to the lyrics. Besides adding a new vocalist, the band had tightened their attack and the result was the genre-bending hit single, "Epic," which established them as a major hard-rock act. Following up the hit wasn't as easy, however. Faith No More followed their breakthrough success with 1992's *Angel Dust*, one of the more complex and simply confounding records ever released by a major label. Upon the conclusion of a tour in support of Album of the Year, Faith No More announced it was disbanding in April 1998. *—Stephen Thomas Erlewine*

We Care a Lot / 1985 / Mordam ✦✦✦
After listening to Faith No More's debut, *We Care A Lot*, it's hard to believe that this is the same band that we know today. They sound more like early Public Image Limited than the FNM that would eventually assault your senses with *Angel Dust* and *Album of the Year*. Obviously, one of the major reasons is because current singer Mike Patton is not on the album. Original frontman Chuck Mosley handles the vocal duties, and his singing style is the complete opposite of Patton's. While Patton is extremely talented and versatile (he can sing every style of music imaginable, including foreign music), Mosley's voice is often off-key, fairly monotonous, and colorless (but with lots of attitude). Musically, the group shows glimpses of the killer genre-bending band they would become in the near future. The original version of the title track is an anthem in typical twisted FNM style: it contains irresistible melodies and riffs, but challenges you lyrically (the words deal with the hypocritical situation surrounding the millionaire musicians who participated in 1985's Live Aid concert). The song is still featured at their concerts, as is the keyboard-laced "As the Worm Turns." Other highlights include the furious instrumental "Pills for Breakfast" and the near dance-track "Arabian Disco." Although most of FNM's important components are present—airy keyboards, tribal drumming, heavy metal guitar, and sturdy bass—the big picture is not as focused as it would eventually be. And it becomes more and more evident that the missing piece of the puzzle is Mike Patton. *—Greg Prato*

Introduce Yourself / 1987 / Slash/Rhino ✦✦✦✦
On Faith No More's major-label debut, *Introduce Yourself*, the Faith No More that you've grown to know and love finally rears it's ugly head (much more so than on their 1985 independent release *We Care a Lot*). All the ingredients are there, but like its predecessor there's one crucial item missing, super-vocalist Mike Patton. This would be original singer Chuck Mosley's last outing with the band, before he was ejected due to erratic and unpredictable behavior. Still, the album is consistent and interesting, with Mosley's out-of-tune vocals being an acquired taste to most. "The Crab Song" is one of their most underrated tracks, which packs quite a wallop when guitarist Jim Martin's heavily saturated guitar kicks in. The title track is an enjoyable and brief rant, and the loopy bass and irresistible melodicism of "Anne's Song" should have been a hit. There's also a slightly updated version of "We Care a Lot" included, and the resulting video gave the band their first taste of MTV success (but nothing compared to what they'd experience with their heavily rotated breakthrough "Epic"). A step in the right direction toward the deliciously twisted sound they'd achieve on later releases. *—Greg Prato*

● **The Real Thing** / Jun. 1989 / Slash ✦✦✦✦
Starting with the careening "From Out of Nowhere," driven by Bottum's doomy, energetic keyboards, Faith No More rebounded excellently on *The Real Thing* after Mosley's firing. Given that the band had nearly finished recording the music and Patton was a last minute recruit, he adjusts to the proceedings well. His insane, wide-ranging musical interests would have to wait for the next album for their proper integration, but the band already showed enough of that to make it an inspired combination. Bottum, in particular, remains the wild card, coloring Martin's nuclear-strength riffs and the Gould/Bordin rhythm slams with everything from quirky hooks to pristine synth sheen. It's not quite early Brian Eno joins Led Zeppelin and Funkadelic, but it's closer than might be thought, based on the nutty lounge vibes of "Edge of the World" and the Arabic melodies and feedback of "Woodpeckers From Mars." "Falling to Pieces," a fractured anthem with a delicious delivery from Patton, should have been a bigger single that it was, while "Surprise! You're Dead!" and the title track stuff riffs down the listener's throat. The best-known song remains the appropriately titled "Epic," which lives up to its name from the bombastic opening to the concluding piano and the crunching, stomping funk metal in between. The inclusion of a cover of Black Sabbath's "War Pigs" amusingly backfired on the band—at the time, Sabbath's hipness level was nonexistent, making it a great screw-you to the supposed cutting edge types. However, all the metalheads took the band to their hearts so much that, as a result, the quintet dropped it from their sets to play "Easy" by the Commodores instead! *—Ned Raggett*

Angel Dust / 1992 / Slash ✦✦✦✦✦
Warner Bros. figured that lightning could strike twice at a time when oodles of (most horribly bad) funk-metal acts were following in Faith No More and Red Hot Chili Peppers's footsteps. In response, the former recorded and released the bizarro masterpiece *Angel Dust*. Patton's work in Mr. Bungle proved just how strange and inspired he could get given the opportunity; now, in his more famous act, nothing was ignored. "Land of Sunshine" starts things off in a vein similar to *The Real Thing*, but Patton's vocal role-playing is smarter and more accomplished, with the lyrics trashing a smug bastard with pure inspired mockery. From there, *Angel Dust* mixes the meta-metal of earlier days with the expected puree of other influences, including a cinematic sense of atmosphere. The album ends with a cover of John Barry's "Midnight Cowboy" suits the mood perfectly, but the stretched-out, tense moments on "Caffeine" and the soaring charge of "Everything's Ruined" make for other good examples. Even a Kronos Quartet sample crops up on the frazzled sprawl of "Malpractice." Other sampling and studio treatments come to the fore throughout, adding quirks like the distorted voices on "Smaller and Smaller." The band's sense of humor crops up frequently—there's the hilarious portrayal of prepubescent angst on "Kindergarten," made all the more entertaining by the music's straightforward approach, or the beyond-stereotypical white trash cornpone narration of "RV," all while the music breezily swings along. Patton's voice is stronger and downright smooth at many points throughout, the musicians collectively still know their stuff, and the result is twisted entertainment at its finest. *—Ned Raggett*

King for a Day, Fool for a Lifetime / Mar. 28, 1995 / Slash/Reprise ✦✦

Album of the Year / Jun. 3, 1997 / Slash/Reprise ✦✦✦✦

Who Cares a Lot: Greatest Hits / Nov. 24, 1998 / Slash/Reprise ✦✦✦

Marianne Faithfull

b. Dec. 29, 1946, Hampstead, London, England
Vocals / Girl Group, British Invasion
Few stars of the 1960s have reinvented themselves as successfully as Marianne Faithfull. Coaxed into a singing career by Rolling Stones manager Andrew Loog Oldham in 1964, she had a big hit in both Britain and the U.S. with her debut single, the Jagger/Richards composition "As Tears Go By" (which prefaced the Stones' own version by a full year). Considerably more successful in her native land than the States, she had a series of hits in the mid-'60s that set her high, fragile voice against delicate orchestral pop arrangements—"Summer Night," "This Little Bird," Jackie De Shannon's "Come and Stay with Me." She offered a taste of things to come with her compelling 1969 single "Sister Morphine," which she co-wrote (and which the Stones released themselves on *Sticky Fingers* later). In the 1970s, Faithfull split up with Mick Jagger, developed a serious drug habit, and recorded rarely, with generally dismal results—until late 1979, when she pulled off an astonishing comeback with *Broken English.* Displaying a croaking, cutting voice that had lowered a good octave since the mid-'60s, Faithfull had also begun to write much of her own material, and addressed sex and despair with wrenching realism. After allowing herself to be framed as a demure chanteuse by songwriters and arrangers throughout most of her career, Marianne had found her own voice, and suddenly sounded more relevant and contemporary than most of the stars she had rubbed shoulders with in the '60s. *—Richie Unterberger*

Marianne Faithfull / May 1965 / Deram ✦✦✦
Her erratic, self-titled debut features lovely baroque arrangements by Mike Leander and decent tunes like "As Tears Go By," and Jackie DeShannon's "Come and Stay with Me" and "In My Time of Sorrow," and Bacharach-David's "If I Never Get to Love You," as well as fairly crummy covers of hits by the Beatles, Herman's Hermits, and Petula Clark. Look for the Japanese CD reissue: It adds six non-LP bonus tracks from mid-'60s singles, including a couple (the girl-groupish "The Sha La La Song," the melancholy "The Morning Sun") that rank among her best '60s recordings. *—Richie Unterberger*

Dreaming My Dreams / Jan. 1977 / Nems ✦✦✦
Marianne Faithfull's first new album in a decade revealed the weathered voice she later would put to good, if harrowing, use in a series of albums for Island Records starting with *Broken English* in 1979. Here, that voice was smoothed out and used for pop and country material including such songs as "I'll Be Your Baby Tonight," "I'm Not Lisa," and "It Wasn't God Who Made Honky Tonk Angels." Faithfull had loosened up considerably since the chaste schoolgirl days of "As Tears Go By," and *Dreaming My Dreams* suggested that her hard life could be analogous to that of a country music star. Faithfull didn't have the accent to match that assertion, but she did have the attitude. (Rereleased in slightly altered form as *Faithless* in March 1978.) *—William Ruhlmann*

Faithless / Mar. 1978 / Columbia ✦✦✦
Marianne Faithfull's first new album in a decade revealed the weathered voice she later would put to good, if harrowing, use in a series of albums for Island Records starting with *Broken English* in 1979. Here, that voice was smoothed out and used for pop and country material including such songs as "I'll Be Your Baby Tonight," "I'm Not Lisa," and "It Wasn't God Who Made Honky Tonk Angels." Faithfull had loosened up considerably since the chaste schoolgirl days of "As Tears Go By," and Faithless suggested that her hard life could be analogous to that of a country music star. Faithfull didn't have the accent to match that assertion, but she did have the attitude. (Faithless was a slightly altered version of the January 1977 album *Dreaming My Dreams.* It was reissued on CD in 1991 with four bonus tracks.) *—William Ruhlmann*

• **Broken English** / Nov. 1979 / Island ✦✦✦✦✦
After a lengthy absence, Faithfull resurfaced on this 1979 album, which took the edgy and brittle sound of punk rock and gave it a shot of studio-smooth dance rock. Faithfull's whiskey-worn vocals perfectly match the bitter and biting "Why'd Ya Do It" and revitalize John Lennon's "Working Class Hero." *—John Floyd*

Dangerous Acquaintances / Sep. 1981 / Island ✦✦✦
A rather lukewarm, disappointing follow-up to *Broken English,* on which Faithfull seemed to be retreating from that album's sonic and lyrical risks. Although *Broken English* had found most of its audience with the new wave/alternative crowd (songs like "Why'd Ya Do It," after all, were too shocking to get much commercial airplay), *Dangerous Acquaintances* seemed to be moving back to more mainstream rock territory, particularly in the arrangements. It's always a possible sign of trouble when there are over a dozen session musicians in the credits, and much of the record's music has a sort of anonymous feel. The songs, too, are less striking (and less angrily risque) than those of *Broken English,* although Faithfull was still carving her own identity with lyrics about romantic duplicity. The most commercially accessible track, "For Beauties Sake," was co-written by Faithfull and Steve Winwood. *—Richie Unterberger*

A Childs Adventure / Mar. 1983 / Island ✦✦

Marianne Faithfull's Greatest Hits / 1987 / ABKCO ✦✦✦✦✦
While missing a few fine album tracks, this is an excellent 16-song distillation of her '60s recordings. Includes all of her British and American hits—"As Tears Go By," "This Little Bird," "Summer Nights," and "Come and Stay with Me." Bonuses include "In My Time of Sorrow," an obscure mid-'60s folk-rocker co-written by Jackie DeShannon and Jimmy Page, and her 1969 single "Sister Morphine" (co-written with the Rolling Stones), predating the *Sticky Fingers* version; it's easily her most powerful performance of the decade. *—Richie Unterberger*

Strange Weather / Jul. 1987 / Island ✦✦✦✦✦
Faithfull's 1987 release recast her as a nicotine-stained chanteuse, approaching such standards as "Boulevard of Broken Dreams" and "Penthouse Serenade" with a ravaged, world-weary demeanor that recalls the latter-day recordings of Billie Holiday. She also tackles some blues and jazz material and turns "As Tears Go By" into the gut-wrenching torch ballad neither the Stones nor Faithfull could ever have done in the '60s. A dark, challenging masterpiece. *—John Floyd*

Blazing Away / Mar. 1990 / Island ✦✦✦✦

Faithfull: A Collection of Her Best Recordings / Aug. 23, 1994 / Island ✦✦✦
This best-of basically covers the years 1979 to 1994, though it reaches back to 1964 for Marianne Faithfull's first recording and first hit, "As Tears Go By," and includes "She," slated for the upcoming 1995 album *A Secret Life.* Five of the 11 songs are drawn from Faithfull's strongest album, 1979's *Broken English,* including the bitter title track and "Why'd Ya Do It." Otherwise, compiler Chris Blackwell makes little attempt to present a balance among Faithfull's recordings—there is nothing at all from *Dangerous Acquaintances* or *A Child's Adventure,* and only one track each from *Strange Weather* and *Blazing Away.* But there is a good newly recorded cover of Patti Smith's "Ghost Dance" co-produced by Keith Richards and featuring other members of the Rolling Stones, and Blackwell rescues Faithfull's rendition of the title theme for the movie *Trouble in Mind* from the soundtrack album. It adds up to an excellent compilation that highlights Faithfull's strengths as a singer. *—William Ruhlmann*

20th Century Blues / Jan. 14, 1997 / RCA ✦✦✦✦

The Seven Deadly Sins / Sep. 15, 1998 / RCA ✦✦✦✦

Perfect Stranger: The Island Anthology / Oct. 27, 1998 / Island ✦✦✦✦✦
Because more than half of the 35 songs on this two-disc retrospective of Marianne Faithfull's 1979-95 output come from her three great albums—*Broken English, Dangerous Acquaintances* and *Strange Weather*—or are previously unreleased outtakes or B-sides from them, *A Perfect Stranger: The Island Anthology* makes a fine primer to Faithfull's often challenging, always mesmerizing (or would that be always challenging, often mesmerizing—) music. "Ballad of the Soldier's Wife," her solid contribution to 1985's *Lost in the Stars: The Music of Kurt Weill,* is also included, giving Faithfull's hauntingly tragic voice the resonance and attention it demands. Weill and Faithfull seem made for each other, as the bulk of the second disc (comprised of songs from her 1990 live album and the underachieving *A Secret Life,* as well as the career-capping *Strange Weather*) makes clear. But there's also a strain to some of these tracks, as if Faithfull's aesthetic wandering eventually will bring her to that elusive cabaret of her dreams. On her best recordings, it indeed sounds like she's home. *—Michael Gallucci*

True / Sep. 26, 2000 / Music Club ✦✦✦

The Fall

f. 1977, Manchester, England
Group / College Rock, British Punk, Post-Punk, Alternative Pop/Rock, Punk
Out of all the late-'70s punk and post-punk bands, none were longer-lived or were more prolific than the Fall. Throughout their career, the band underwent a myriad of lineup changes, but at the center of it all was vocalist Mark E. Smith. With his snarling, nearly incomprehensible vocals and consuming bitter cynicism, Smith became a cult legend in indie and alternative rock. Over the course of their career, the Fall went through a number of shifts in musical style, yet the foundation of their sound was a near-cacophonic, amelodic jagged jumble of guitars, sing-speak vocals and keyboards. During the late '70s and early '80s, the band was at their most abrasive and atonal. In 1984, Smith's American wife Brix joined the band as a guitarist, bringing a stronger sense of pop melody to the group. By the mid-'80s, the band's British following was large enough to result in two U.K. Top 40 hits, but in essence, the group has always been a cult band—their music was always too abrasive and dense for the mainstream. Only hardcore fans can differentiate between the Fall's many albums, yet the Fall, like many cult bands, inspired a new generation of underground bands, ranging from waves of soundalike indie-rockers in the U.K. to acts in America and New Zealand, which is only one indication of the size and dedication of their small, devoted fan base. *—Stephen Thomas Erlewine*

Live at the Witch Trials / Jan. 1979 / Resurgent ✦✦✦✦✦
Perhaps of the early material, the best place to start is *Live at the Witch Trials.* Under the guidance of producer Bob Sargeant, this album harnesses the essence of the Fall's early sound: jagged, colliding guitars, stiff, repetitive percussion, and Mark E. Smith's nasal, singsong ranting. It's dissonant, but not so harsh as to be totally unapproachable. In fact, Sargeant (who later went on to produce records by far poppier bands like the English Beat) accents the rhythmic bottom, so that even when the music lurches like a drunken Frankenstein's monster, it does swing enough to be captivating. Of course, this is assuming that Smith's vocals haven't prevented you from enjoying this (and really, they shouldn't). Tunes like "Rebellious Jukebox" and "Music Scene" will win you over with their caustic appeal. *—John Dougan*

Grotesque (After the Gramme) / Nov. 1980 / Essential ✦✦✦

Early Years 1977-1979 / 1981 / Resurgent ✦✦✦
Like its predecessor, *Grotesque, Early Years 77-79* is more extreme than *Live at the Witch Trials.* Extreme in the sense that traditional song form is almost totally dispensed with for a din of cacophony built around thuddingly simple guitar riffs. It's not totally alienating, but it's not where potential Fall fans (unless you have a jones for barely structured rock noise) should start. Oddly, despite being anti-rock to the point of almost being anti-music, there are some great songs that emerge through the trebly crashing and bashing. *—John Dougan*

Hex Enduction Hour / Mar. 1982 / Resurgent ✦✦✦
The group's most rhythmic album, thanks in no small part to the presence of two drummers (Karl Burns and Paul Hanley), *Hex Enduction Hour* was recorded partially in Iceland with producer Richard Mazda. The percussion adds extra weight to the group's performance, but the songbook does not add much to the Fall's legacy, with the exception of "Deer Park" (which became a live favourite) and "Who Makes The Nazis?" *—Alex Ogg*

Perverted by Language / Dec. 1983 / Essential ♦♦♦♦♦
Closing the early Fall period is *Perverted By Language*, which also starts the (what I call) "Brix Period." It was during this time that Smith married American guitarist Brix Smith who brought a stronger pop sense to the band. Suddenly, Fall albums, although still essentially abrasive, were more tuneful, and loaded with fuzztone garage-raunch guitar playing. Brix's first effort as a full-time Fall member is a winner, with tracks like "I Feel Voxish" and the parody of the excessively health-conscious "Eat Y'self Fitter" pushing the Fall into a new terrain that would bring them (surprise!) chart success in England. A 1998 CD reissue by Essential/Castle added five tracks, including both sides of the singles "The Man Whose Head Expanded" and "Kicker Conspiracy." *—John Dougan*

Wonderful and Frightening World of the Fall / Sep. 1984 / Beggars Banquet ♦♦♦♦♦
The high point of the "Brix Period" may well have been the release of *Wonderful and Frightening World of the Fall.* Where before the music was tense, jumpy and anarchic, here it was focused, harder-hitting, and rocked more. To some, it signaled the end of the Fall, but that was an unfair assessment. Granted, the music changed slightly, but it didn't diminish the band's potency. And, for all the time that Mark Smith had dominated the band, it was becoming clear that Brix's talents as a writer and musician were formidable and deservedly taking some of the spotlight. *—John Dougan*

Hip Priests & Kamerads / Mar. 1985 / Atlantic ♦♦♦♦
A perfunctory but satisfying compilation of the group's recordings for Kamera, therefore including several superb early singles (beginning with "Lie Dream Of A Casino Soul"). In addition to this welcome archive, there's also an otherwise unobtainable live version of "Mere Pseud Mag Ed." And the taunting "I'm Into CB!", a sarcastic reflection on the communications craze that swept the western world in the early 80s, is worth the price of admission alone. *—Alex Ogg*

This Nation's Saving Grace / Sep. 1985 / Beggars Banquet ♦♦♦♦♦
"Feel the wrath of my Bombast!" exhorts Smith on this follow-up to their groundbreaking *Wonderful and Frightening World of... The Fall,* and this collection is ample proof of the pure confidence the group had at this time. Stompers like "Barmy," "What You Need," and the mighty "Gut of the Quantifier" are all led by Brix Smith's twanging lead hooks, filled by distorted guitars and bludgeoning drums, on top of which Smith rants with conviction. But it's the departures from this sound that mark the real interest here: The synth-driven "L.A." looks ahead to the Fall's experiments with electronica; "Paint Work" is an impressionist piece interrupted by Smith accidentally erasing over some of the track at home; and "I Am Damo Suzuki," a tribute to Can's lead singer, which borrows its arrangement from several of that group's songs. The Fall sound mysterious, down-to-earth, and hilarious all at the same time. The CD reissue adds the singles "Cruiser's Creek" and "Couldn't Get Ahead" as well as their B-sides making this an essential purchase. *—Ted Mills*

Bend Sinister / Oct. 1986 / Beggars Banquet ♦♦♦♦♦

The Frenz Experiment / Mar. 1988 / Beggars Banquet ♦♦♦

I Am Kurious Oranj / Oct. 1988 / Beggars Banquet ♦♦♦

Extricate / Feb. 1990 / Resurgent ♦♦♦♦♦
The Smiths had divorced around the time of *Extricate,* but Brix's presence could still be felt on Fall records. Some thought the mid-'80s signaled an end to the ragged, jagged Fall of old; the '90s must have made them apoplectic. Working with producers Rex Sergeant, Craig Leon, and Adrian Sherwood, the post-apocalyptic sound of the '70s had been smoothed to a sheen. There were still moments of anarchy and dissonance, but generally they were swaddled in synth-driven beats and high-tech production that smoothed out any remaining rough edges. Again, this was not a bad thing; after all, Mark E. Smith was still upfront and still ranting, but even he was singing more, and shocking as that was, it made for even better music. For this period, the place to start is *Extricate,* which proved beyond a doubt that the Fall were not too old to still be a part of this punk rock thang. Since this record follows on the heels of the Smiths' divorce, it's tempting to assume that Mark E. Smith's ranting has a more conspicuous target, but enigmatic as he tends to be, this is mere speculation. Still, "Sing! Harpy" and the title track will give you pause as to the source of Smith's considerable consternation. The band sounds great, especially longtime members Stephen Hanley and Craig Scanlon. Extra kudos to the solid backbeat provided by Simon Wolstencroft. *—John Dougan*

★ **458489 A-Sides** / Sep. 1990 / Beggars Banquet ♦♦♦♦♦
Bypassing their edgy, early singles and concentrating on their artier, more eclectic work of the mid- and late '80s, *458489 A-Sides* encapsulates nearly all of the Fall's many attributes. All of the singles on *A-Sides* are culled from the era when Brix Smith was in the band, arguably the band's most cohesive and rewarding years. Drawing from their strongest albums—*The Wonderful and Frightening World of the Fall, This Nation's Saving Grace, Bend Sinister, The Frenz Experiment—A Sides* offers an excellent introduction to the Fall. It is both a useful retrospective and a kind of road map, pointing out the differences between albums. For neophytes and the uninitiated, there is no better sampler, and for long-time fans, the collection reiterates what a fine singles band the Fall were in their heyday. *—Stephen Thomas Erlewine*

458489 B-Sides / Dec. 1990 / Beggars Banquet ♦♦♦♦♦
The title cleverly encapsulates the contents—the Fall's B-sides (45s) from 1984 to 1989. The Fall were a first-rate singles band, and the flip sides were often their equals. There is the odd dud here—there are a thousand Fall songs to hear and "Clear Off" and "Mark'll Sink Us" wouldn't be high on ones list of priorities. But there are also many genuinely great tracks: "Petty Thief Lout," "Australians in Europe," "No Bulbs." It should be noted that in the Fall's turbulent history, their six-year spell at Beggars Banquet was their most productive and artistically rewarding. There are actually 31 tracks on view here, including a handful of remixes—rich pickings (the album was never originally issued outside of Europe). *—Alex Ogg*

Code: Selfish / Mar. 1992 / Fontana ♦♦♦

The Infotainment Scan / May 18, 1993 / Matador ♦♦♦♦
Now financed by fellow mavericks Matador, the Fall returned to action following a period of (relative) inactivity with this convincing effort. It saw the guitars turned up loud again in preference to the keyboard domination of recent efforts (notably *Code: Selfish*). There's a degree of lightheartedness about the project which is as welcome as it is unfamiliar, notably on the ska-styled "Why Are People Grudgeful?" single—if the title doesn't indicate some degree of self-mockery from Smith, then he really is the most humorless old git in the universe. Best track: "A Past Gone Mad." Best title: "Paranoia Man in Cheap Sh*t Room." *—Alex Ogg*

Middle Class Revolt / May 1994 / Matador ♦♦♦♦♦
A mixture of lackluster performances and songs filled with vigor and fury, *Middle Class Revolt* is a puzzling proposition from the The Fall. After two opening tracks that seem ready to convince worried fans that Smith couldn't care less ("15 Ways" and "Reckoning") there follows the poppish "Behind the Counter" and their devilish cover of Henry Cow's "War," with Smith making up half the lyrics. Other highlights include the furious "Hey! Student" (a rewrite of a 1977 tune, "Hey! Fascist"), and yet another Monks cover: "Shut Up!" All find Smith in fine form, impassioned and deeply sarcastic. The band experiments with some techno, some tape manipulation, and sparse rock arrangements, though the vocals on this disc are the most layered of any Fall release. There's also some local (Manchester, that is) social criticism going on in tracks, such as "M5*1*" and "City Dweller," which takes on the aborted attempt to hold the Olympic games in Smith's city (the nerve!). *—Ted Mills*

Cerebral Caustic / May 18, 1995 / Permanent ♦♦♦♦
Credited with being the best Fall album of the 90s, *Cerebral Caustic* includes a cover of Frank Zappa's "I'm Not Satisfied" and a much-improved version of "Life Just Bounces" from the 1990 *Dredger* EP. Returning ex-wife Brix contributed to five of the songs, which surely attests for the return of a pop sensibility to the band. Though Smith's determinedly low-fi production argues against such peppy instincts, the compromise proves a happy one on tracks such as "Bonkers In Phoenix" (which also reveals Smith's interest in 60s garage psych bands) and, particularly, the Smith-Smith duo "Don't Call Me Darling." *—Alex Ogg*

The Light User Syndrome / 1996 / Jet ♦♦♦

Levitate / Sep. 1997 / Artful ♦♦♦♦

The Marshall Suite / Oct. 12, 1999 / Artful ♦♦♦♦

A Past Gone Mad: The Best of 1990-2000 / Sep. 5, 2000 / Artful ♦♦♦♦

Fatboy Slim (Norman Cook)

b. Jul. 13, 1963, Bromley, England
DJ, Producer / Big Beat, Funky Breaks, Electronica, Trip-Hop, Club/Dance
Norman "Jacker-Of-All-Genres" Cook, in addition to his former occupations as bassist for the Housemartins and one third of acid-house hitmakers Pizzaman, is also the man behind one of the most popular of the new flock of English "brit hop" producers, Fatboy Slim. Releasing his Fatboy material through club staple Skint, Cook's raucous blend of house, acid, funk, hip-hop, electro, and techno has added to his already formidable reputation as one of the foremost all-around producers on the U.K. club scene. In addition to his FBS work, Cook also recorded the *Skip to My Loops* sample CD, a popular studio tool sporting a melange of sample-ready drum loops, analog squelches, and assorted noises. In early 1998, his remix of Cornershop's "Brimful of Asha" spent several weeks at number one in the British charts. His eagerly anticipated second LP *You've Come a Long Way Baby* followed later that year, launching the breakthrough hits "Rockafeller Skank" and "Praise You." *—Sean Cooper*

Better Living Through Chemistry / 1996 / Astralwerks ♦♦♦♦
Fatboy Slim is one of DJ Norman Cook's many aliases, and has proven to be his most popular and successful yet. Although he consistently racks up dance hits in his native England (each under a different surname), he didn't achieve global success until the re-release of *Better Living Through Chemistry* in '97. On the insistence of his friends the Chemical Brothers, Cook released the track "Going Out of My Head" as the album's first single. Due to its popular video and instantly catchy sample from the Who classic "I Can't Explain," Cook earned his first U.S. hit. Another unlikely sample used to great effect was featured in the track "Michael Jackson," which used a snippet of Negativland's "Negativland." "The Weekend Starts Here" is similar to the Beastie Boys' funk instrumentals, featuring distant organ and lazy harmonica-blowing (which sounds an awful lot like the harmonica phrase at the beginning of Black Sabbath's "The Wizard"). Recommended to those who can't get enough of today's popular technoid-sampled-alternative-dance style. *—Greg Prato*

★ **You've Come a Long Way, Baby** / Oct. 12, 1998 / Skint ♦♦♦♦♦
Fatboy Slim's debut album, *Better Living Through Chemistry,* was one of the surprises of the big beat revolution of 1996—an eclectic blowout, all tracked to thunderous loops and masterminded by Norman Cook, a former member of the British pop band the Housemartins. It might not have been as startlingly fresh as the Chemical Brothers, but the hard-hitting beats and catchiness, not to mention consistency, of *Better Living* was a shock, and it raised expectations for Fatboy Slim's second album, *You've Come a Long Way, Baby.* And that record itself was something of a surprise, since it not only exceeded the expectations set by the debut, but came damn close to being the definitive big beat album, rivaling the Chemicals' second record, *Dig Your Own Hole.* The difference is, Cook is a record geek with extensive knowledge and eclectic tastes. His juxtapositions—the album swings from hip-hop to reggae to jangle pop, and then all combines into one sound—are wildly original, even if the music itself doesn't break through the confines of big beat. Then again, when a record is this forceful and catchy, it doesn't need to break new stylistic ground—the pleasure is in hearing a master work. And there's no question that Cook is a master of sorts—*You've Come a Long Way, Baby* is a seamless record, filled with great imagination, unexpected twists and turns, huge hooks, and great beats. It's the kind of record that gives big beat a good name. *—Stephen Thomas Erlewine*

Halfway Between the Gutter and the Stars / Nov. 7, 2000 / Astralwerks ♦♦♦♦
With his third LP, *Halfway Between the Gutter and the Stars,* Fatboy Slim's Norman Cook pulls away slightly from the notoriously fickle pop charts and crossover kids courted on his last record. Instead, he makes a conscious attempt to inject some real hedonism back into

the world of dance—he *is* a DJ, after all. After a short intro, Cook tears into an acid techno rampage named "Star 69," a track that takes few prisoners and sounds closer to Plastikman than Propellerheads. Despite the torrid pace set early on, there's still quite a bit of the used-bin scavenger left in Cook; the most patented big beat anthems here, "Ya Mama" and "Mad Flava," include all the expected displays of crowd-moving hip-hop calls, unhinged beatbox funk, continual drum breakdowns, and plenty of rawk riffs. The first single, "Sunset (Bird of Prey)," is another potential crossover move, featuring what is easily the album's most recognizable sample source—Jim Morrison from the Doors. Sniffy electronica purism aside, though, Cook remains, if not the best overall producer in the dance world, certainly in its top rank. Cook recruited collaborators for the first time—nu-soul diva Macy Gray, funk legend Bootsy Collins, fellow superstar DJ/producer Roger Sanchez—and the two tracks with Gray, "Love Life" and "Demons," are the highlights of the album. Cook's ample production talents are served best with a vocalist lending focus, and "Love Life" is a seven-minute ride veering from dirty, warped funk to noise-heavy hip-hop breakdowns while Gray scats, growls, and purrs with clearly audible glee. In all, *Halfway Between the Gutter and the Stars* is possibly Norman Cook's best possible statement after being—nearly simultaneously—picked up by a multitude of notoriously fickle pop consumers and thrown away by his previously rock-solid dance fanbase. *—John Bush*

Faust

f. 1971, Wumme, Germany

Group / Experimental Rock, Kraut Rock, Experimental, Prog-Rock/Art Rock

"There is no group more mythical than Faust," wrote Julian Cope in his book *Krautrocksampler,* which detailed the pivotal influence the German band exerted over the development of ambient and industrial textures. Issued on clear vinyl in a transparent sleeve, Faust's eponymously-titled debut LP surfaced in 1971; although sales were notoriously bad, the album—a noisy sound collage of cut-and-paste musical fragments—did earn the group a solid cult following. Another lavishly-packaged work, *Faust So Far,* followed in 1972, and earned the group a contract with Virgin, who issued 1973's *The Faust Tapes*—a fan-assembled collection of home recordings—for about the price of a single, a marketing ploy which earned considerable media interest. After *Outside the Dream Syndicate,* a collaboration with Tony Conrad, the band released 1973's *Faust IV,* a commercial failure which resulted in the loss of their contract with Virgin, who refused to release the planned *Faust 5.* They disbanded in 1975, and the members scattered throught Germany; however, after more than a decade of playing together in various incarnations, Faust officially reunited during the early 1990s. *—Jason Ankeny*

Faust / 1971 / Recommended ✦✦✦✦✦

Faust: So Far / 1972 / Recommended ✦✦✦✦✦

Faust's second album moves closer to actual song structure than their debut, but it still remains experimental. Songs progress and evolve instead of abruptly stopping or cutting into other tracks. The opening song "It's a Rainy Day, Sunshine Girl" begins as a repetitive 4/4 beat played on toms and piano with the title sung over the top. But for seven minutes the song adds instruments, including a lush analog synth line, and ends in a memorable sax riff. Faust's lyrical side appears on the acoustic "Picnic on a Frozen River" and "On the Way to Adamäe," whereas its abrasive side pops up on "Me Lack Space." "So Far," a jam shared by guitar, horns, and tweedy keyboard, rolls along with a funky hypnotic beat and wailing processed synths. And on "No Harm," the crazed delivery of such lines as "Daddy, take the banana, tomorrow Sunday" makes one want to believe something profound is going down. In terms of scope and the wealth of ideas, this is probably the most balanced of their first four albums. *—Ted Mills*

Faust IV / 1973 / Virgin ✦✦✦✦✦

Coming on the heels of the cut-and-paste sound-collage schizophrenia of *The Faust Tapes, Faust IV* seems relatively subdued and conventional, though it's still a far cry from what anyone outside the German avant-garde rock scene was doing. The album's disparate threads don't quite jell into something larger (as in the past), but there's still much to recommend it. The nearly 12-minute electro-acoustic opener "Krautrock" is sometimes viewed as a comment on Faust's droning, long-winded contemporaries, albeit one that would lose its point by following the same conventions. There are a couple of oddball pop numbers that capture the group's surreal sense of whimsy: one, "The Sad Skinhead," through its reggae-ish beat, and another, "It's a Bit of a Pain," by interrupting a pastoral acoustic guitar number with the most obnoxious synth noises the band can conjure. Aside from "Krautrock," there is a trend toward shorter track lengths and more vocals, but there are still some unpredictably sudden shifts in the instrumental pieces, even though it only occasionally feels like an idea is being interrupted at random (quite unlike *The Faust Tapes*). There are several beat-less, mostly electronic soundscapes full of fluttering, blooping synth effects, as well as plenty of the group's trademark Velvet Underground-inspired guitar primitivism, and even a Frank Zappa-esque jazz-rock passage. Overall, *Faust IV* comes off as more a series of not-always-related experiments, but there are more than enough intriguing moments to make it worthwhile. Unfortunately, it would be the last album the group recorded (at least in its first go-round). *—Steve Huey*

Faust Tapes / 1973 / Cuneiform ✦✦✦✦

This was the release that "broke" Faust to a British audience, mostly because of a marketing gimmick whereby the then-infant Virgin label sold it in shops for half a pound. Still, it's no mean feat to sell 50,000 copies of rock this avant-garde, no matter what the cost. A continuous 43-minute piece with about 26 discrete passages (which makes it hell to zero in on a specific bit on CD), it roams from crash'n'mash drums and fierce art rock jamming to rather pretty, if inscrutable, bits of folk-rock and spoken word, with odd shards of melody sticking out like glass in a tire. There are rough reference points to Zappa in the torrid editing and British Canterbury bands in the goofier, more rock-driven parts, but this is even less immediately accessible, taking a few plays to get a grip on, though most pop-oriented listeners won't get that far. *—Richie Unterberger*

Munich and Elsewhere / 1986 / Recommended ✦✦✦

Rien / Oct. 24, 1995 / Table of the Elements ✦✦✦

71 Minutes of Faust / 1996 / Cuneiform ✦✦✦✦✦

Basically an expanded version of *Munich and Elsewhere* (which was itself a compilation of unreleased material), with the addition of the unreleased LP *Faust Party Three* (parts of which had previously appeared only as limited-edition EPs and singles), as well as two previously unreleased tracks. Parts wed brutal drum patterns to insistently repetitive guitar riffing; there are prog rock keyboard passages that slightly recall Soft Machine; and "Don't Take Roots" sounds like an unintentional satire of the cheap California psychedelia that you might hear on a late-'60s youth culture exploitation flick. Sometimes it even sounds like a parody of early King Crimson-type pomp rock. It would be nice to have some liner notes explaining exactly what comes from where, but basically what you need to know is that it was all recorded in Germany from 1971 to 1975, and is on par with the quality of the albums they actually released during that time. *—Richie Unterberger*

You Know FaUSt / Feb. 25, 1997 / Recommended ✦✦✦

● **Faust/Faust So Far** / Oct. 3, 2000 / Collectors' Choice Music ✦✦✦✦✦

The Feelies

f. 1977, Hoboken, NJ, **db.** 1992

Group / College Rock, Jangle Pop, Alternative Pop/Rock

Of the countless bands to emerge from the New York City underground during the post-punk era, few if any were as unique and influential as the Feelies; nerdy, nervous and noisy, even decades later their droning, skittering avant-pop remains a key touchstone of the American indie music scene. Formed in suburban New Jersey in 1976, the group made its NYC debut and quickly created a buzz throughout the city's new wave circuit. In 1979, the Feelies cut their debut single "Fa Ce-La" for the British indie Rough Trade, though their refusal to work with outside producers jeopardized their immediate hopes for a major-label deal. Their brilliant 1980 LP *Crazy Rhythms* instead appeared on another UK indie, Stiff; although it made little impact outside of underground circles, many latter-day acts—R.E.M. chief among them—cited the album as a major influence. After Stiff pressured the Feelies for a hit single, the group was forced into a kind of suspended animation which saw them out of action for the better part of the early '80s. Frontmen Bill Million and Glenn Mercer reactivated the Feelies banner in 1983, and finally released their second album, *The Good Earth,* three years later. A&M released the follow-up *Only Life* in 1988, and *Time for a Witness* followed in 1991, but later that year the Feelies played their final show at the Hoboken club Maxwell's. Mercer and drummer Dave Weckerman later reteamed in two bands, Wake Ooloo and Sunburst. *—Jason Ankeny*

★ **Crazy Rhythms** / Apr. 1980 / A&M ✦✦✦✦✦

Even the cover is a winner, with a washed-out look that screams new wave via horn-rimmed glasses, even more so than contemporaneous pictures of either Elvis Costello or the Embarrassment. But if it was all look and no brain, *Crazy Rhythms* would long ago have been dismissed as an early-'80s relic. That's exactly what this album is not, right from the soft, haunting hints of percussion that preface the suddenly energetic jump of the appropriately titled "The Boy With the Perpetual Nervousness." From there the band delivers seven more originals plus a striking cover of the Beatles' "Everybody's Got Something to Hide" that rips along even more quickly than the original. The guitar team of Mercer and Million smokes throughout, whether it's soft, rhythmic chiming with a mysterious, distanced air or blasting, angular solos. But Fier is the band's secret weapon, able to play straight-up beats but aiming at a rumbling, strange punch that updates Velvet Underground/krautrock trance into giddier realms. Mercer's obvious Lou Reed vocal inflections make the VU roots even clearer, but even at this stage of the game there's something fresh about the work the quartet does, even 20 years on—a good blend of past and present, rave-up and reflection. When the group's later label, A&M, finally got around to reissuing the album for the first time stateside, a curious bonus was included: a version of the Rolling Stones' "Paint It, Black," recorded by the later lineup of the band in 1990. Mercer's voice is noticeably different from his decade-old self, but it's an enthusiastic rendition not too far out of place. *—Ned Raggett*

The Good Earth / 1986 / Twin/Tone ✦✦✦

After the various side projects and explorations the band got up to for most of the early '80s, not to mention switching some members around (with bassist Sauter and drummer Demeski now forming the rhythm section), the Feelies made a fine return with *The Good Earth.* With co-production from noted fan Peter Buck, the group exchanged some of the understated tense frazzle of *Crazy Rhythms* for a gentler propulsion without losing its trancy edge. Compared to the wispy jangle rock that passed for much of college radio at the time, the Feelies proposed a different path with the songs' steady pace and murkier feeling. Demeski's a more than fine replacement for Fier (his martial playing on "Tomorrow Today" is one of his many entertaining touches), Sauter's playing emphasizes controlled understatement, and the Million/Mercer guitar duo still nails it. The brisker jauntiness of songs like "The Last Roundup," which wears just enough of a country & western edge without seeming like a parody or half-assed, varies the calmer moods elsewhere very well. At the album's considerable best, such as the brief but really lovely acoustic/electric blend of "When Company Comes" or the title track, with an almost epic ending, Million and Mercer sound like they inhabit the same body playing two guitars, everything's that much in lovely sync. Their vocals ride low in the mix this time out, but thankfully the sometimes all-too-obvious hints of Lou Reed in Mercer's style have been replaced with a more unique, stronger edge—not that the connection still isn't there on a track like the building groove of "Slipping (Into Something)." Reed would also love its concluding guitar solo! Perhaps the only criticism is a slight sameness between a few songs, but there's more sly variety on display to offset this gentle treasure. *—Ned Raggett*

Only Life / 1988 / A&M ✦✦✦✦

With an unchanged lineup but more attention due to their A&M deal, the Feelies hit the jackpot with their third album, a warm, inviting collection that finally addresses the endless Lou Reed comparisons with a cover of his "What Goes On." With its clearer feeling and peppier overall delivery, it avoids simply cloning the original arrangement and performance. The rest of the album shows off the band's distinctive yet flexible sound, as much jangle as it is quietly moody. Mercer and Million's previously tense guitar power becomes attractive shadings, implying a louder approach without always delivering it, while the Demeski/Sauter rhythm team takes the lead throughout; his steady drums and her low, rolling performances giving the guitarists something to play around instead of dominate. The Feelies always make this tranced-out rock their own, but this time around it's as quietly thrilling, if not more so, than ever. "Higher Ground" is a great example, with Mercer and Million trading off not merely notes and passages but differing approaches, whether laden with distortion or chiming clearly. Though Weckerman's work, as earlier, isn't easily distinguished from Demeski's, from the sound of it everything fit in right when recording. Where appears more audibly, as on the start of "The Undertow," his percussion adds an intriguing wild card to the proceedings, aiming at the same goal with slightly different sonics. Mercer's ghost-of-you-know-who vocals still pop up at times, but here his own ability to actually sing and hold notes comes forward, giving him a technical edge that he uses to great effect on the brisk "Away." *—Ned Raggett*

Time for a Witness / Mar. 5, 1991 / A&M ✦✦✦

The 5th Dimension

f. 1966, Los Angeles, CA

Group / Sunshine Pop, Pop-Soul, Pop

They didn't sound anything like an R&B group, and their soaring, lighter-than-air harmonic blend frequently proved more palatable to pop audiences than to Black record buyers. But do not suggest, even for a second, that the 5th Dimension was in any way lacking in soul.

Formed as the Versatiles in 1965, the slick quintet changed its name at the request of Johnny Rivers, who had just signed them to his brand new label, Soul City. Up-and-coming songwriter Jimmy Webb supplied the group with their first pop smash "Up, Up and Away," in 1967, and the group's monumental rise mirrored the song's high-flying imagery. Another prolific composer, Laura Nyro, handed the 5th Dimension several megahits, notably "Stoned Soul Picnic" and "Wedding Bell Blues," but their biggest seller hailed from the groundbreaking musical *Hair*. The Grammy-winning "Aquarius/Let the Sunshine In" held down the number one slot on the pop lists for six weeks in 1969.

After several more hits, Marilyn McCoo and Billy Davis, Jr., who had married while part of the group, successfully branched off as a duo, while Lamonte McLemore, Ron Townson, and Florence LaRue kept the 5th Dimension on the soul charts, losing a head-to-head battle with Diana Ross for hit status on "Love Hangover" in 1976. *—Bill Dahl*

- **Greatest Hits on Earth** / Sep. 1972 / Arista ✦✦✦✦✦

Until Rhino issued its anthology, this was the best hits package for The 5th Dimension, a group that in its peak was among the best at doing light-hearted pop with a soulful foundation. Certainly, they weren't a hardcore R&B or earthy singing group, but they did put some punch into songs that were really kind of silly otherwise, like "Wedding Bell Blues." *—Ron Wynn*

Up Up & Away: The Definitive Collection / May 20, 1997 / Arista ✦✦✦✦✦

The subtitle on this anthology is correct: This is truly the definitive collection of the 5th Dimension's music, including all the hits and most of the album cuts that anyone could want. The 20-bit digital mastering provides a crisp, bright audio experience, and the joyous harmonies bring back the positive side of the late '60s/early '70s era in which the songs were recorded. The megahits are all here: Jimmy Webb's "Up Up and Away," Laura Nyro's "Stoned Soul Picnic" and "Wedding Bell Blues," the Bacharach-David opus "One Less Bell to Answer," the beautiful "(Last Night) I Didn't Get to Sleep at All" and the Grammy-winning number one smash from the spring of 1969, "Aquarius/Let the Sunshine In" from *Hair*. There are not-quite-Top-Ten hits like "Sweet Blindness," "Go Where You Wanna Go," "California Soul," "Workin' on a Groovy Thing," "Blowing Away," "Save the Country" and "Love's Lines, Angles and Rhymes." What a run this quintet had on the pop charts from 1967 to 1972. This two-disc set successfully makes the case for the 5th Dimension to be remembered among the finest purveyors of pop song vocal harmony in the rock era. Baby Boomers will delight at the memories this collection conjures up and will find surprises they may have forgotten or never known: "Paper Cup," "Carpet Man," "Puppet Man," "Light Sings" and the group's medley of "The Declaration/A Change Is Gonna Come/People Gotta Be Free." Listening to *Up Up and Away: The Definitive Collection* is a great antidote for the blues, lifting the listener up with a smile and reminding those who may have forgotten that there once was a time when it seemed that music really could bring us all together. *—Jim Newsom*

Fine Young Cannibals

f. 1984, Birmingham, England

Group / College Rock, Blue-Eyed Soul, Pop/Rock

When the English Beat splintered in two, bassist David Steele and guitarist Andy Cox formed the Fine Young Cannibals with Roland Gift. Although the band's fusion of rock, Motown-style R&B, pop, and modern dance is tight and loaded with hooks, the real attraction is Gift's soaring falsetto—he sounds like a classic soul singer. Their 1985 debut album was critically acclaimed, but it was the 1989 follow-up, *The Raw & the Cooked*—with the number one singles "She Drives Me Crazy" and "Good Thing"—that made the band major hit makers. Apart from a remix album in 1990 and Gift's occasional film role, the group has been quiet since their breakthrough success. *—Stephen Thomas Erlewine*

Fine Young Cannibals / Dec. 1985 / IRS ✦✦✦

Roland Gift's vocals are the find here, backed by the R&B/pop music provided by ex-Beat members Andy Cox and David Steele. *—William Ruhlmann*

- **The Raw & the Cooked** / Feb. 20, 1989 / IRS ✦✦✦✦✦

FYC rode to massive success on the tender-and-terrified singing of Roland Gift and the neo-Motown sheen of the *1 hits &"She Drives Me Crazy"* and "Good Thing." *—William Ruhlmann*

The Raw & the Remix / Dec. 1990 / IRS ✦✦

Finest / Nov. 26, 1996 / MCA ✦✦✦✦✦

Fine Young Cannibals only released two albums, so it's slightly unusual that they even have a greatest hits collection like *Fine Young Cannibals Finest*. After all, a dedicated fan will have both records, and casual fans will only want the singles on *The Raw and the Cooked*, thereby eliminating the audience for the collection. Despite these misgivings, *Finest* does its job well, featuring 12 of their biggest hits and best-known songs ("She Drives Me Crazy," "Johnny Come Home," "Good Thing," "Suspicious Minds," "Don't Look Back"), plus two unreleased cuts ("The Flame" and "Since You've Been Gone") to entice collectors. If you want the highlights, *Finest* is fine, but most fans will want to stick with the two original albums. *—Stephen Thomas Erlewine*

Finn Brothers

f. 1994

Group / Adult Alternative Pop/Rock, Pop/Rock

Brothers Tim and Neil Finn have been making music together since their childhood in Te Awamutu, New Zealand, continuing through to international success in Split Enz and Crowded House. However, it wasn't until late 1989 that they actually started writing together—a reunion that yielded more than a dozen songs for a proposed Finn Brothers side project. That album was scrapped and most of the material was absorbed by Crowded House's *Woodface* (1991) and *Together Alone* (1993), as well as Tim's 1993 solo album, *Before & After*. The brothers' project resumed in late 1994, and in four weeks, they completed an album called simply *Finn*. The album, released in the fall of 1995 (the summer of 1996 in the U.S.), showed a much more casual side of the Finns and was less pop-oriented than their previous musical collaborations—the brothers play nearly all of the instruments themselves, ranging from the primitive to the exotic. After initial pressings of *Finn*, the duo changed their name to the Finn Brothers to avoid confusion with a band going under a similar name. *—Chris Woodstra*

- **Finn** / Oct. 1995 / Discovery ✦✦✦✦✦

Finn is the long rumored and awaited collaboration between brothers Tim and Neil Finn. The first reports of the project in 1990 promised an album of "just acoustic guitars and lots of harmonies," and when that material was absorbed by Crowded House for *Woodface*, it was proven that the team was capable of making near-perfect pop. Those expecting *Woodface Part 2*, however, are in for a surprise—*Finn* is a moody, atmospheric album that shows a more spontaneous and experimental side with the brothers playing all of the instruments, including ukuleles, Chamberlain keyboards, mellotron, and tea chest bass. Though most projects of this nature get hung up on the "concept," this one succeeds because the Finns' pop songwriting sense allows the songs to come first. Despite the lack of polish and the odd setting, the material on this album is among the pair's finest, together or apart. *—Chris Woodstra*

Neil Finn

b. May 27, 1958, Te Awamutu, New Zealand

Vocals, Guitar / New Zealand Rock, Adult Alternative Pop/Rock, Singer/Songwriter

Neil Finn has consistently proven his knack for crafting high quality songs that combine irresistible melodies with meticulous lyrical detail, from his beginnings as the precocious junior member of Split Enz, through his leadership of Crowded House, earning commercial success, respect from his peers, praise from critics, and a devoted fan base.

Born Neil Mullane Finn, May 27, 1958, in Te Awamutu New Zealand, Finn cut his musical teeth as a child by performing for family friends, harmonizing with elder brother Tim. Finn took up piano, studying the songcraft of The Beatles, Elton John, and David Bowie, while watching his brother Tim's band, Split Enz, become a musical force in Australian. Following a few opening slots for Split Enz in 1976, he formed the After Hours. The group showed a great deal of promise, but came to a relatively quick end when Phil Judd left Split Enz and brother Tim offered the slot to Neil. Just before his 19th birthday, even though he'd never played electric guitar, Neil joined Split Enz as lead guitarist.

Neil stayed in the background for the first two albums of his membership—1977's *Dizrhythmia* and 1978's *Frenzy*—but emerged with the infectious "I Got You" for *True Colours*. The single was an immediate hit, saving the band from obscurity and, most likely, from imminent breakup. Split Enz enjoyed moderate international success for the next several years until disbanding in 1985. Neil followed with Crowded House, a combo that found both critical acclaim and massive commercial success internationally. In 1996, Neil decided to dissolve the band in favor of a solo career.

In 1998, he released his first solo album, the critically acclaimed *Try Whistling This*. That same year, he contributed a cover of "I Can See Clearly Now" to the animated feature *Antz* and, in mid-1999, he released the charity single, "Can You Hear Us?". In 2001 Finn prepared to release his second solo album, *One Nil*. *—Chris Woodstra*

- **Try Whistling This** / Jun. 16, 1998 / Work ✦✦✦✦✦

When Neil Finn closed the doors on Crowded House, all signs seemed to point to a more experimental direction for future solo releases; even the title of his first solo album, *Try Whistling This*, implies a reaction against his reputation for well-crafted, highly melodic songs. However, from the opening track, the light and breezy "Last One Standing," Finn puts all fears to rest. *Try Whistling This* does dabble in experimentation—most notably in the feedback and distorted vocals of the parnoid "Twisty Bass" and the mild trip-hop groove of "Sinner"—but thoughout, he shows restraint, tastefully incorporating more exotic effects while staying true to his high melodic standard and meticulous songcraft. Finn seems clearly freed from the restraints of being in a band, allowing him to try a lot of different ideas, from the sweeping "Souvenir" to the instant pop classic of "She Will Have Her Way" to more delicate atmospheric pieces like the title track, ultimately creating his most complex and diverse set to date. And though many of the songs take time to reveal their treasures, it's worth the effort. *Try Whistling This* features some of Finn's best work yet, and in a nearly flawless catalog like his, that's quite impressive. *— Chris Woodstra*

Tim Finn (Brian Timothy Finn)

b. Jun. 25, 1952, Te Awamutu, New Zealand
Vocals, Keyboards, Guitar / College Rock, Adult Alternative Pop/Rock, New Wave, Singer/Songwriter
Singer/songwriter keyboardist/guitarist Tim Finn was born in Te Awamutu, New Zealand. Influenced by not only British Invasion acts like the Beatles, the Move and the Kinks, but also his Catholic upbringing and the communal sing-alongs of the native Maori people, Finn founded the '70s art-rock turned New Wave band Split Enz leading the band through several albums to moderate international success. The success of the between-albums solo project, *Escapade,* led to his leaving the band in 1983. He followed with the more ambitious second album, *Big Canoe* (1985) which went virtually ignored (it was unreleased in the U.S. until the success of his brother's band, Crowded House, stirred up enough interest by 1988). Finn returned in 1989 with a self-titled album for Capitol Records. Despite good reviews, this too failed to make much impact. He joined his brother Neil Finn's band, Crowded House, for their *Woodface* album but left mid-tour and released his fourth solo album, *Before and After* in 1993. In 1995, he joined with Hothouse Flowers' Liam O Maonlai and Andy White, releasing an album under the group name ALT. A long-rumored collaboration between the Finn brothers was finally released in late 1995 under the name Finn Brothers (it was released in the spring of 1996 in the U.S.). Finn returned to his solo career by the fall of 1996. In 1999, Finn completed work on his fifth solo album, *Say It Is So,* which was released early the following year. *— Scott Bultman and Chris Woodstra*

Escapade / 1983 / A&M ♦♦♦
Following Split Enz's *Time & Tide,* Tim Finn took his first break from the band with *Escapade,* a collection of light pop songs, some of which dated back to the late '70s but never seemed to quite fit in the Enz format. A flawed though fun album, *Escapade* managed several hits in Australasia and Europe and revealed a considerably brighter, more mainstream aspect to Finn's writing. And while the album was successful and a satisfying diversion, it unquestionably served to derail the forward momentum of Split Enz and led to Finn's leaving the band the following year. *— Chris Woodstra*

Big Canoe / 1985 / Virgin ♦♦♦
Tim Finn teamed up with playwright Jeremy Brock for his second solo outing, *Big Canoe.* Although the collaboration is predictably ambitious—probably Finn's most ambitious since the early days of Split Enz—beneath all the overblown arrangements and slightly dated production lie some terrific songs. Material like "No Thunder No Fire No Rain," "Hyacynth," and "Carve You in Marble" deserves a better setting, but the album is still able to shine, and some minor flaws are forgivable, especially to diehard fans. *Big Canoe* also marks a welcome reunion between Finn and ex-Enz collaborator Phil Judd, who contributes sitar and rhythm guitar to a couple of tracks. *— Chris Woodstra*

● **Tim Finn** / 1989 / Capitol ♦♦♦♦♦
Perhaps in response to the failed big production of *Big Canoe* and the success of brother Neil's back-to-basics outfit, Crowded House, Finn simplified his approach for his self-titled album, joining forces with Crowded House producer Mitchell Froom. A touching and intensely personal album, Finn bares all, revealing self-doubts, regrets and a failed relationship with intricate detail. And despite the subject matter, the album has an optimistic, uplifting overall tone, with tasteful adult-pop arrangements perfectly complementing his strongest melodies and finest songwriting to date. Though the sound and sentiments could have (and should have) easily found an audience in the emerging "adult alternative pop" format, the album went virtually ignored. *— Chris Woodstra*

Before & After / Aug. 10, 1993 / Capitol ♦♦♦♦♦
On his fourth solo album, Finn dabbles in dance-pop, pseudo-reggae, and folky ballads, with a different set of producers on nearly every track. While this leads to a certain lack of consistency, Finn's songwriting has never been stronger. He has the most success on the self-produced, stripped-down tracks where his strong sense of melody and knack for catchy pop hooks are allowed to be in the forefront. "Persuasion," co-written by Richard Thompson and "In Love with It All," written with his brother Neil Finn (Crowded House) are highlights. *— Chris Woodstra*

Say It Is So / Feb. 29, 2000 / W.A.R.? ♦♦♦♦
Seven years separated Tim Finn's fourth album, 1993's *Before and After,* and his fifth, *Say It Is So,* by which time he was left without a label. With a backlog of songs and inspiration from American alt-country acts, Finn went to Nashville in late 1998 to record with producer and multi-instrumentalist Jay Joyce, lacking any clear idea where or when the record would be released. He eventually put it out himself, through Sonny's Pop Records, and it certainly sounds like his first full-fledged independent release. For the first time, Finn sounds entirely unconscious of the charts, which, coupled with his voice's new deep, gravelly texture, may be disarming at first. Although he hasn't concentrated on writing shiny pop songs, he also hasn't abandoned melody—it's just that this time, he writes melodies like singer/songwriters do, resulting in songs that take a little longer to take hold. They're coupled to production that is fairly stripped down, yet also atmospheric, with its blend of dry guitars, old keyboards, muted drums, and the occasional distorted meaning—an apt match for Finn's most shaded lyrics to date. All of these sonic textures and elliptical, yet vaguely rootsy songs are quite different from any of Finn's previous solo works. Consequently, *Say It Is So* may take some time before it reveals its rewards, but it eventually emerges as one of Finn's finest efforts. There may not be any initial standouts, but overall, there are no weak moments, and it's some of the sturdiest, most consistent songwriting he's ever done on one record. Some listeners may miss the pop sheen or Finn's good humor—this is a relatively sober affair, unlike much of his catalog—but *Say It Is So* feels like one of his strongest and most personal records. *— Stephen Thomas Erlewine*

Firefall

f. 1975, Boulder, CO, **db.** 1983
Group / Pop/Rock, Soft Rock, Country-Rock
The mellow, easy country-rock sounds of Firefall, coupled with the group's penchant for pop melodies and high-pitched harmonies, produced a series of successful LPs in the late '70s and a series of chart singles, including the Top Ten hit "You Are the Woman." The group was formed by former Flying Burrito Brother Rick Roberts, who handled vocals, guitar, and most of the songwriting duties; he was joined by fellow ex-Burrito and Byrd Michael Clarke on drums, ex-Spirit and Jo Jo Gunne bassist Mark Andes, guitarist/vocalist Jock Bartley, guitarist/vocalist/songwriter Larry Burnett, and keyboardist/woodwind player David Muse, who joined in 1977. The group recorded its self-titled debut in 1976; it and its follow-up, *Luna Sea,* both went gold, and their third album, *Elan,* went platinum. However, the group's commercial fortunes began to decline, and even though Muse experimented with adding different instruments to the overall sound, Firefall's relaxed, toned-down approach simply wore out its welcome as pop trends moved elsewhere. Jock Bartley reformed the group in 1994 for the album *Messenger. — Steve Huey*

● **Greatest Hits** / Sep. 1, 1992 / Rhino ♦♦♦♦♦
Sharing a light, lush airiness with bands like Poco, America, and Air Supply, Firefall sang fluffy love songs that were weak in lyrical nutrients but abundant with softened chords and harmonies. When radio was saturated with light rock in the mid to late seventies, they were right in the heart of it, reaching number nine on Billboard's Top 40 with the gentle "You Are The Woman," which remained on the charts for a startling fifteen weeks. Firefall's greatest hits collects all of their mellow rock favorites in one place, presenting some thin but not unlistenable soft rock tunes. Lead singer Rick Roberts pours his heart out but still manages to stir up a decent tempo with "Just Remember I Love You," their second biggest single. The blue of the Colorado skyline, the band's home state, is visioned on the soothing flow of "Break Of Dawn," and a slight attractiveness is felt throughout "Strange Way," another chart single in 1978. Roberts, who replaced Gram Parsons in The Flying Burrito Brothers and drummer Michael Clarke, a one time Byrds member, did give Firefall a talented history within it's lineup, but the music being produced contained ample amounts of schlock that soon faded as radio became tired of this shallow drivel. Sometimes harboring a country feel a la Michael Martin Murphy best heard in songs like "Someday Soon" and "It Doesn't Matter," it was evident that the band had only one direction, which was that of a folk-rock sound. Since their material never strayed from this subtle easiness, Firefall's greatest hits is their most worthwhile offering. *— Mike DeGagne*

fIREHOSE

f. 1985, **db.** 1994
Group / College Rock, Post-Punk, Alternative Pop/Rock
In 1985, after D. Boon's tragic death at age 28 signalled the end of the Minutemen, bassist Mike Watt and drummer George Hurley threw in their lot with then-22-year-old former Ohio State University student, guitar player and Minutemen fanatic Ed Crawford to form fIREHOSE. Taking their group name from a line in Bob Dylan's "Subterranean Homesick Blues," fIREHOSE continued in the Minutemen tradition of breathtaking musicianship combined with caustic lyrical fusillades inspired by the writing of the Beat Generation and the erect-middle-finger indignation of the Blank Generation. However, with Crawford's decidedly folkie bent insinuating itself into the mix, fIREHOSE's songs began to expand into more traditional verse-chorus-verse songwriting symmetry. And although fIREHOSE never equaled the Minutemen's output in terms of sheer audacity and emotional depth, Crawford, Watt and Hurley recorded rock that was muscular, dense and daring, along with being tremendously heartfelt. They never patronized audiences or comported themselves as "rock stars"; they were instead the quintessential post-punk "peoples' band." Although they achieved wider notoriety than did the Minutemen (eventually recording for a major label), fIREHOSE called it quits in early 1994 after a desultory, dispirited final LP (*Mr. Machinery Operator*). Still, nearly all of their recorded work stands as some of the best late-'80s/early-'90s indie rock. *— John Dougan*

Ragin', Full-On / 1986 / SST ♦♦♦

● **If'n** / 1987 / SST ♦♦♦♦♦
Whereas fIREHOSE's debut, 1986's *Ragin', Full On,* was issued quickly to get the new outfit off the ground (two of the three members were still reeling from the death of their previous band's frontman, the Minutemen's D. Boon), their sophomore effort, 1987's *If'n,* included more cohesive and focused songwriting. Touring together had obviously made Watt-Hurley-Crawford tighter as a unit, and several of their best all-time compositions reside here. Although the debut incorporated other musical forms besides punk and hard rock (funk, jazz, etc.), *If'n* was the first fIREHOSE release to feature folk-style originals—such as Crawford's "In Memory of Elizabeth Cotton." Standouts include the album opening highway anthem "Sometimes," the groovy '50s feel of "Honey, Please," the laid-back "Backroads," and the irate rockers "Anger" and "For the Singer of R.E.M." Also featured are several Mike Watt lead vocal spots—the perennial concert favorite "Making the Freeway" (included on the 1993 mini-album *Live Totem Pole EP*), the humorous "Me & You Remembering," "Operation Solitaire," and the closing epic "Thunder Child." *— Greg Prato*

Fromohio / 1989 / SST ♦♦♦♦♦
fIREHOSE's second release, 1987's *If'n,* was a major improvement over their 1986 debut, *Ragin', Full On.* And while their third album, 1988's *From Ohio,* was another solid set and contained its share of highlights, it seemed to be cut from the same musical cloth as its predecessor rather than a true progression. Again, the playing is inspired, and the new band had already established an original, identifiable sound. The best tracks prove to be Ed Crawford originals—"In My Mind" and "Time with You" (the latter was an MTV video), while "Whisperin' While Hollerin' " and "What Gets Heard" soon became concert staples. The band's appreciation of folk shines through with a reading of the traditional Black folk song "Vastopol" and the original "Liberty for Our Friend," and drummer George Hurley takes center stage on

a pair of short, unaccompanied drum solos—"Let the Drummer Have Some" and "'Nuf that Shit, George." Other highlights include the album opener "Riddle of the Eighties," the funky "Mas Cojones," the laid-back rock of "If'n" and "Understanding," plus the lethargic album closer, "The Softest Hammer." *—Greg Prato*

Flyin' the Flannel / Apr. 23, 1991 / Columbia ✦✦✦

Mr. Machinery Operator / Feb. 16, 1993 / Columbia ✦✦

The "5" Royales

f. 1952, Winston-Salem, NC, **db.** 1965

Group / R&B

The "5" Royales were a relatively unheralded, but significant, link between early R&B and early soul in their combination of doo wop, jump blues, and gospel styles. Their commercial success was relatively modest—they had seven Top Ten R&B hits in the 1950s. A few of their singles would prove extremely popular in cover versions by other artists, though—James Brown and Aretha Franklin tore it up with "Think," Ray Charles covered "Tell the Truth," and the Shirelles (and later the Mamas & the Papas) had pop success with "Dedicated to the One I Love." Almost all of their material was written by guitarist Lowman Pauling, who influenced Steve Cropper with his biting and bluesy guitar lines, which at their most ferocious almost sound like a precursor to blues rock. After forming as the Royal Sons Quintet, the group made their debut on the R&B charts in 1953 with a pair of number one singles for Apollo, "Baby Don't Do It" and "Help Me Somebody." After being lured away to King in 1954, they entered the R&B Top Ten only two more times, though they recorded for the label throughout the 1950s. After leaving King and recording some more sides in the early '60s, they finally broke up by 1965. *—Richie Unterberger*

Dedicated to You / 1957 / King ✦✦✦✦✦

This may be the great lost R&B record of the 1950s. The '5' Royales were a fine singing group long before this release, but on these sides recorded between 1955 and 1957, guitarist Lowman Pauling cuts loose with the most fiery guitar fills this side of Ike Turner. From the opening shout of "Think" to the closing notes of "Thirty Second Lover," Dedicated to You is a guitar tour-de-force. The album's crowning moment comes on "Say It," where Clarence Paul's pleading vocal is answered with Pauling's bluesy replies. Other highlights include Bill Doggett's gospel-tinged organ on "Someone Made You For Me," several fine sax solos ("Don't Be Ashamed," "Right Around the Corner") and the straightforward rocker "Messin' Up." An overlooked classic. *—J.P. Ollio*

★ **Monkey Hips and Rice: the "5" Royales Anthology** / Mar. 8, 1994 / Rhino ✦✦✦✦✦

The "5" Royales certainly did their share of forgettable period-piece tunes, but they also had transcendent songs like "Think," "Just as I Am" and "Dedicated to the One I Love." They enjoyed a lengthy run, creating many hits plus a few gems, which are all available on this sparkling two-disc set. The opening disc sets the stage, showing their gospel origins and also the rather routine cuts the band did in its formative period. They began to evolve into a more substantial unit in the mid-'50s, and by the late '50s were a sterling unit cutting emphatic, appealing numbers. Most of these appear on the second disc. By the early '60s, they had run their course, but their legacy and impact was secure. This offers the most complete picture of the "5" Royales and their superb music. *—Ron Wynn*

● **Apollo Sessions** / Sep. 1, 1995 / Collectables ✦✦✦✦✦

Although not the career-long survey of the Rhino anthology, this 23-song, 62-minute collection covers the Five Royals' very best years, spent with Apollo Records from 1951 until 1955, first as the Royals ("Give Me One More Chance") and then as a quintet under their more familiar name. Their sound here is vocally very smooth yet passionate, but the instrumental backings are exuberant and raunchy, the kind of combination that made acts like this such a threat to the established popular music of the era. The mix of jump blues with accomplished gospel-influenced harmony singing (best represented on the delightful "What's That" or "All Righty," or, most startling of all, "Baby Take All of Me," with its abandoned wailing in the background) helped make their music some of the most expressive and satisfying of the period. Their way with a chorus and a phrase made the Royals one of the top R&B acts of their era, although it wasn't until much later that they made the jump to pop stardom. Unfortunately, during the period represented here, they were one of those R&B acts whose radio play exceeded their record sales (at least, as reported by Apollo, one reason they jumped to King Records). From 1951 until 1955, they helped provide the soundtrack against which mainstream rock & roll was born and took root with the public. On that basis alone, this material is worth hearing and owning; it was the soil in which rock & roll sprouted, the stream in which other acts' commercial hits were spawned and nurtured. They later had their share of successes, but this is their real sound, raw, sweet and elegant all at the same time. *—Bruce Eder*

The Five Satins

f. 1956, New Haven, CT, **db.** 1961

Group / Doo Wop

The Five Satins are best-known for the doo wop classic "In the Still of the Night," a song that was popular enough to make the group one of the most famous doo wop outfits, although they never had another hit of the same magnitude. Led by Fred Parris, the group recorded for their first single "In the Still a Night," a song Parris had recently written, in the basement of a local church. Released in early 1956, it became a huge hit by the end of the year, peaking at number three on the R&B charts and number 25 on the pop charts. Though Parris spent more than a year in the Army just after the Five Satins' big success, Bill Baker temporarily took over lead vocals for another big hit, "To the Aisle." When Parris returned, he reorganized the group and had a minor hit in 1959 with "Shadows." During the remainder of the '60s and early '70s, Parris led various incarnations of the Five Satins through oldies revues in America and Europe; they also recorded occasionally during this time. After moderate success during the mid-'70s under the name Black Satin, the group reverted to the Five Satins and performed regularly at oldies shows in America and Europe. *—Stephen Thomas Erlewine*

● **In the Still of the Night** / 1990 / Relic ✦✦✦✦✦

Everything you need from this sumptuous and smoochy late-night doo wop quintet is here. The title cut is a work of art worth listening to over and over. *—John Floyd*

The Fixx

f. 1980

Group / Pop/Rock, New Wave

A London-based new wave group that managed to sustain a successful career in America for several years in the mid-'80s, the Fixx always flirted with mainstream pop with their catchy, keyboard-driven pop. They released their debut album, the Rupert Hine-produced *Shuttered Room,* in 1982. The record spawned two minor U.K. hits, "Stand or Fall" and "Red Skies," and spent a short time in the charts. In America, none of the singles were hits, yet the album stayed on the charts for nearly a year. *Reach the Beach,* released in 1983, established them as a hit-making force in the U.S. The terse, pulsating "One Thing Leads to Another" became a number four hit, sending the album into the Top Ten. *Reach the Beach* would go platinum by the end of the year, launching two more Top 40 singles—"Saved by Zero" and "Sign of Fire." Despite all of their American success, the Fixx failed to break back into the British charts with *Reach the Beach;* in fact, they never had another British hit in their career. The Fixx returned in 1984 with *Phantoms.* While it performed well—it peaked at number 19 and went gold—it didn't match the success of *Reach the Beach;* after it launched the number 15 single "Are We Ourselves?" the record fell off the charts. Although their audience was shrinking, the band kept their basic, synth-driven sound intact for 1986's *Walkabout,* which featured the hit "Secret Separation." *—Stephen Thomas Erlewine*

● **Ultimate Collection** / Nov. 9, 1999 / MCA ✦✦✦✦✦

At their very best, the Fixx were one of the great singles bands of the new wave era. They often don't get credit for it because they were a little out of step with the times. They certainly weren't as dark as the legions of critically acclaimed post-punk bands like the Cure and Gang of Four, nor were they as lightly quirky as many of the early-MTV one-hit wonders or as fashionable as the new romantics. Instead, the Fixx picked up the album-rock side of David Bowie, which meant that they were briefly in step with the times in the early '80s but then could carry on in the years immediately following new wave, since they were just slightly more traditional than their peers. In both their new wave and post-new wave incarnations, the Fixx turned out a handful of terrific singles—"Saved By Zero," "The Sign of Fire," "Are We Ourselves?" "Secret Separation," and "One Thing Leads to Another," which sounds as startlingly fresh years after its recording as it did at the time. All of these songs are on the aptly-titled *Ultimate Collection.* In addition to the hits, the 17-track compilation contains a number of lesser-known singles and album tracks, and while they're not quite as good as the classic singles, they're still solid songs in the same vein, and anyone that believes that the Fixx's five best singles are indeed classics should find plenty to enjoy here. *—Stephen Thomas Erlewine*

Roberta Flack

b. Feb. 10, 1939, Ashville, NC

Vocals, Piano / Smooth Soul, Quiet Storm, Soft Rock, Urban, Soul

Classy, urbane, reserved, smooth, and sophisticated—all of these terms have been used to describe the music of Roberta Flack, particularly her string of romantic, light-jazz ballad hits in the 1970s, which continue to enjoy popularity on MOR-oriented adult contemporary stations. Her first two albums were well-received but produced no hit singles; however, that all changed when a version of Ewan MacColl's "The First Time Ever I Saw Your Face," from her first LP, was included in the soundtrack of *Play Misty for Me.* The single zoomed to number one in 1972 and remained there for six weeks, becoming that year's biggest hit. Flack followed it with the first of several duets with Howard University classmate Donny Hathaway, "Where Is the Love." "Killing Me Softly with His Song" became Flack's second number one hit (five weeks) in 1973. She charted several more times over the next few years, but a major blow struck in 1979 when Hathaway committed suicide. Devastated, Flack was forced to find another partner and eventually did in Peabo Bryson, with whom she toured in 1980. The two recorded together in 1983, scoring a hit duet with "Tonight, I Celebrate My Love." *—Steve Huey*

First Take / 1969 / Atlantic ✦✦✦✦✦

The album that launched Roberta Flack's career. She had been doing background vocals and also recording with Les McCann, who helped her land at Atlantic. The single "The First Time Ever I Saw Your Face" zoomed into the pop stratosphere after it was included in Clint Eastwood's film *Play Misty For Me.* *—Ron Wynn*

Chapter Two / Aug. 1970 / Atlantic ✦✦✦✦✦

A great album and the release that made Roberta Flack a major soul and R&B artist in the early '70s. She had a soft, compelling, alluring voice, and was able to convincingly switch gears and also convey anger, regret, hurt, or despair. Those who thought Flack was a one-hit wonder, or didn't think she could make the transition from doing mostly jazz to other styles, were convinced otherwise. *—Ron Wynn*

Quiet Fire / Nov. 1971 / Atlantic ✦✦✦✦✦

Roberta Flack Featuring Donny Hathaway / Apr. 1972 / Atlantic ✦✦✦✦✦

A duet classic, and perhaps the most popular album Roberta Flack made. Their single "Where Is the Love" dominated urban contemporary radio for almost the entire year, while "You've Got a Friend" was just as influential and was later covered by numerous artists (of course they didn't write it, but a lot of folks thought they did). It did so well that Flack eventually did other duet material and also became very close to Hathaway. *—Ron Wynn*

Killing Me Softly / Aug. 1973 / Atlantic ✦✦✦✦✦
The title track was another smash for Roberta Flack, and the album continued in the same tradition as *Chapter Two* and *A Quiet Fire.* She made simmering ballads, declarative message songs, and better-than-average uptempo numbers, and at the time was among the top-selling female vocalists in any style. *—Ron Wynn*

Feel Like Makin' Love / Mar. 1975 / Atlantic ✦✦✦

Blue Lights in the Basement / Dec. 1977 / Atlantic ✦✦✦

● **Softly With These Songs: The Best of Roberta Flack** / Jun. 22, 1993 / Atlantic ✦✦✦✦✦
While it includes almost everything on *Best of Roberta Flack, Softly With These Songs* covers material after 1980, including the hits "Tonight, I Celebrate My Love" and "Making Love," which makes it the preferable compilation. *—Stephen Thomas Erlewine*

The Flamin' Groovies

f. 1965, San Francisco, CA, **db.** 1979
Group / Proto-Punk, Power Pop, Rock & Roll
One of America's greatest, most influential, and legendary cult bands, the Flamin' Groovies came out of the San Francisco area in 1965 playing greasy, bluesy, rock & roll dashed with a liberal sprinkling of British Invasion panache in an era soon to be dominated by hippie culture and hyperextended raga-rock freakouts. Caught in a double bind of playing the wrong kind of music at the wrong time (as well as not looking the part), the Groovies were almost completely forgotten as the Fillmore/Avalon Ballroom scenes, dominated by the Dead, the Jefferson Airplane, et al., rendered them anachronistic. The plain truth, however, was that despite not being in tune with the zeitgeist, the Groovies made great music, and managed to sustain a career that lasted for over two decades. *—John Dougan*

Supersnazz / 1968 / Sundazed ✦✦✦✦✦
For an unknown band, Epic sank a lot of money into this record, and wasn't happy when it didn't sell. But that's hardly the fault of the band, who sound great despite the intrusive overproduction of novice knob-twiddler Steve Goldman. Loney's yelping lead vocals are in fine form, and the rest of the band rocks with a reckless abandon and stunning succinctness that was totally out-of-step with the times. *—John Dougan*

Flamingo / 1970 / Kama Sutra ✦✦✦✦✦
While the Flamin Groovies' first album, *Supersnazz,* loaded their high-octane retro-rock down with a loving but overly intrusive production, their next long-player, *Flamingo,* went in exactly the opposite direction; for their second time at bat (and their second major label), the Groovies cranked up their amps and kicked up the tempos, while producer Richard Robinson stripped the band's sound to the bone. If *Flamingo* has a flaw, it's that the album is just a bit *too* basic; the recording sounds a bit flat and muddy, and it isn't very flattering to either Tim Lynch's guitar or Danny Mihm's drums (and who fell in love with the panning control while they were mixing?). But if *Flamingo* sometimes sounds more like a demo than a finished album, it's a demo of a great band firing on all cylinders; with "Gonna Rock Tonite," the album starts out in fifth gear and never stops, with even the less manic tunes (such as the bluesy "Childhood's End") sounding sharp and full of fire, and the many rave-ups raving mighty fine indeed (notable exception: the trippy "She's Falling Apart," which proves these guys didn't understand psychedelia and had no business playing it, which was a considerable virtue in the Bay Area during the late '60s and early '70s). If the engineering sometimes lets them down, *Flamingo* does a far, far better job of capturing what made the Groovies a great band than their debut and ranks alongside their very finest work. [Buddha Records' 1999 CD reissue tacks on six potent bonus tracks from a live-in-the-studio session which appeared in part on the 1976 compilation *Still Shakin'.*] *—Mark Deming*

Teenage Head / 1971 / Buddha ✦✦✦✦✦
Miriam Linna once opined that the Roy Loney-era line-up of The Flamin Grooves suggested what The Rolling Stones would have sounded like if they'd sworn their allegiance to the sound and style of Sun Records instead of Chess Records. If one wants to buy this theory (and it sounds reasonable to me), then *Teenage Head* was the Groovies' alternate-universe version of *Sticky Fingers,* an album that delivered their toughest rock and roll beside their most introspective blues workouts. (In his liner notes to Buddha's 1999 CD reissue of *Teenage Head,* Andy Kotowicz writes that Mick Jagger noticed the similarities between the two albums, and thought the Groovies did the better job.) While The Flamin Groovies didn't dip into the blues often, they always did right by 'em, and "City Lights" and "Yesterday's Numbers" find them embracing the mournful soul of the blues to superb effect, while their covers of "Doctor Boogie" and "32-20" honor the originals while adding a energy and attitude that was all their own. And the rockers are among the best stuff this band ever put to tape, especially "High Flying Baby", "Have You Seen My Baby?", and the brilliant title track. And unlike *Flamingo, Teenage Head* sounds just as good as it deserves to; Richard Robinson's production is clean, sharp, and gets the details onto tape with a clarity that never gets in the way of the band's sweaty raunch. While *Flamingo* rocks a bit harder, *Teenage Head* is ultimately the best album The Flamin Groovies would ever make, and after Roy Loney left the band within a few months of its release, they'd never sound like this again. *—Mark Deming*

☆ **Shake Some Action** / 1976 / Aim ✦✦✦✦✦
The Groovies disappeared into the wilds of Europe after *Teenage Head,* which barely earned them a cult following over here. They went through a few personnel changes, honed their sound to an even finer point, and developed a few more musical smarts. Then came *Shake Some Action,* the debut of the Flamin' Groovies' Mark II, where they rocked out British-style for most of it (while still acknowledging their American roots), only louder and more passionately than any British Invasion band had played since 1964. The sound was a complete anachronism in the mid-'70s, but it got them noticed and earned them a cult following. The guitar sound is straight 1964 Beatles (a la "Not a Second Time") alternating with Kinks material of the same era, the vocals are the plaintive wailing of lovesick young rock gods, and the effect is stunning even 20 years on. Maybe the greatest British Invasion album since 1964. Reissued by Australia's AIM Records on CD, and well worth tracking down as an import. *—Bruce Eder*

The Flamin' Groovies Now! / 1978 / Sire ✦✦✦✦✦
It looks like listeners are destined to rely on imports for most of the Groovies' Sire catalog. In 1978, the group was getting all kinds of great press, and even some radio play from their comeback *Shake Some Action* album on Sire, and embarked on a national tour playing clubs like *the Bottom Line* in New York in front of every rock V.I.P. who could wangle a ticket. And to accompany the tour, they put out *Flamin' Groovies Now!,* an album of more British Invasion tracks. The sound on this record, produced and engineered by Dave Edmunds, was a notable improvement over *Shake Some Action,* and the group had lost none of its flair for the period or the style, though there was also precious little new ground covered. The range of styles embraced on this record was astonishing—"Between the Lines" and "Take Me Back," and especially "Good Laugh Mun" were examples of Edmunds emulating Phil Spector, and had the Groovies sounding like the Beach Boys of "Don't Worry Baby" and recalled the way the early Kinks covered American music; "House of Blue Lights" gave nods to both Merrill Moore and Chuck Berry, as well as the Stones. The songs off of side two were harder, giving them more the kind of edge one associated with the Stones or the Rockin' Vickers. But their version of Gene Clark's "Feel a Whole Lot Better" was the crowning achievement on this record, the best contemporary cover of a Byrds track ever done, and one so good that some fans thought a re-formed Byrds should have done a cover of the Groovies' "Shake Some Action" in return. *—Bruce Eder*

Jumpin' in the Night / 1979 / Sire ✦✦✦

Flamin' Groovies Studio '68 / 1984 / Eva ✦✦✦

The Gold Star Tapes / 1984 / Skydog ✦✦✦

● **Groovies' Greatest Grooves** / Jul. 1989 / Sire ✦✦✦✦✦
During their early period with Roy Loney as lead singer, the Flamin' Groovies made one great album (*Teenage Head*), one very good one (*Flamingo*), and one that was flawed but enjoyable (*Supersnazz*). When Cyril Jordan took over as the band's unquestioned leader following Loney' s departure, the Groovies shifted gears from supercharged roots rock to neo-British Invasion pop, and while every record they released had more than a few brilliant moments, they seemed incapable of making an album that was solid from front to back. Thankfully, some bright penny at Sire Records got the idea of putting together a Flamin' Groovies compilation CD, and the result, *Groovies' Greatest Grooves,* makes a superb case for the inconsistent but undeniable brilliance of their post-Loney repertoire. *Groovies' Greatest Grooves* harvests pretty much every great track from the group's three albums for Sire (*Shake Some Action, Flamin' Groovies Now!,* and *Jumpin' in the Night*) and tosses in one superb cut with Loney (the masterful "Teenage Head"), two hard-to-find ravers with short-time vocalist Chris Wilson (including the much-covered "Slow Death"), and a rough but exciting demo of "River Deep, Mountain High" cut for a proposed collaboration with Phil Spector. While Jordan's edition of the Flamin' Groovies may not have rocked as hard as Loney's, that doesn't say that they couldn't rock hard when they wanted to, as "Jumpin' in the Night," "Tallahassee Lassie," and "Please Please Girl" easily prove, and "Shake Some Action," "You Tore Me Down," and "All I Wanted" are as transcendent as pop music gets. A satisfying 75 minutes of pure bliss, *Groovies' Greatest Grooves* is a one-stop shopping place for anyone wanting the cream of the Flamin' Groovies' faux-Brit era, and a fine introduction to one of the best American bands of the period. *—Mark Deming*

16 Tunes / 1995 / Munster ✦✦✦✦

Supersneakers / Nov. 19, 1996 / Sundazed ✦✦✦✦
A combination of the *Sneakers* indie ten-inch from 1968 and ten tracks from a 1968 gig at a San Francisco club. (The live material had previously been issued on the French import *Flamin Groovies '68* in the mid-'80s.) The studio tracks from *Sneakers* decidedly outshine the looser, more indulgent live takes, several of which duplicate *Sneakers* material. It's the definitive document of their pre-major label days, though, when they fused garage rock with blues, psychedelia, and the Lovin' Spoonful, complete with historical liner notes. *—Richie Unterberger*

In Person! / May 6, 1997 / Norton ✦✦✦

The Flaming Lips

f. 1983, Oklahoma City, OK
Group / Experimental Rock, Dream Pop, Neo-Psychedelia, Alternative Pop/Rock
Of the innumerable one-hit wonders littering the cultural landscape, few, if any, were so brave, so frequently brilliant and so deliciously weird as the Flaming Lips. To even classify the Lips as merely a one-hit wonder is to do the group a grave injustice: although their standing as a commercial entity proved little more than a blip on the radar screen, their moment of Top 40 success was simply another pit-stop on one of the more surreal and haphazard career trajectories in pop music—an acid-bubblegum band with as much affinity for sweet melodies as blistering noise assaults, their off-kilter sound, uncommon emotional depth and bizarre history (packed with tales of self-immolating fans and the like) firmly established them as one of the true originals of the post-punk era. Conventional wisdom dictates that artists lose their edge when they sign to a major label, but the Lips' tenure at Warner Bros. is irrefutable proof that some bands in fact reach new creative heights when allowed to romp around in the corporate sandbox. 1992's *Hit to the Death in the Future Head,* their Warner debut, bridged the gap between the monolithic noise of past efforts with a melodic beauty still in its embryonic stages—their first truly accessible effort to date, at the same time it somehow retains all of the idiosyncratic force of their prior white-noise freakouts. The hit "She Don't Use Jelly" aside, 1993's *Transmissions from the Satellite Heart* is even more strangely compelling—sonically dense, lyrically addled and melodically haywire, it's an idiot-savant classic. 1995's *Clouds Taste Metallic* is quite possibly a masterpiece, the *Lips'* very own *Pet Sounds* (complete with animal noises); it was followed by one of the most unique major label releases ever—1997's *Zaireeka,* a logistically-nightmarish set of four CDs designed to be played simultaneously. 1999's The Soft Bulletin might just be the best album of the decade, period. And somehow, in the

midst of it all the band even guest starred on *Beverly Hills 90210*—go figure. *—Jason Ankeny*

The Flaming Lips / 1985 / Restless ✦✦

Hear It Is / 1986 / Restless/Enigma ✦✦✦

Oh My Gawd!!! . . . The Flaming Lips / 1987 / Restless/Enigma ✦✦✦

Telepathic Surgery / 1989 / Restless/Enigma ✦✦✦

In a Priest Driven Ambulance / Sep. 1990 / Restless/Enigma ✦✦✦✦
In a Priest Driven Ambulance ranks as the first truly brilliant Flaming Lips album; the first effort to feature guitarist Jonathan "Dingus" Donahue, it's a loose concept record which brings Wayne Coyne's long-standing obsessions with religion bubbling to the surface. The thematic glue creates a structural framework unlike anything found on previous albums, resulting in a newfound sense of cohesion and depth: songs like "Rainin' Babies" and "Five-Stop Mother Superior Rain" offer unforeseen levels of poignancy, while guitar freak-outs such as "Unconsciously Screamin'" and "Mountain Side" slash and burn with remarkable potency. For the Lips, the future begins here. *—Jason Ankeny*

Hit to Death in the Future Head / Aug. 11, 1992 / Warner Brothers ✦✦✦
With *Hit to Death in the Future Head*, the Lips make the leap to major-label status as though it were the moment they've been waiting for all their lives. Though not as conceptually tight as *In a Priest Driven Ambulance*, the album is no less cohesive or imaginative, and in its way serves as the bridge between the band's noisier, more hallucinatory indie work and the acid-bubblegum aesthetic perfected on their later Warner Bros. albums. Nowhere are the band's pop smarts more evident than on "The Sun," which freely quotes Carole King's "So Far Away," or on the undeniably catchy "Gingerale Afternoon (The Astrology of a Saturday)" and "Frogs"; tracks like "Felt Good to Burn" and "Halloween on the Barbary Coast," meanwhile, indulge fully in the trademark weirdness that got the group this far. (And speaking of indulgence, check out the unlisted bonus track, which offers some 29 minutes of speaker-hopping static assault.) *—Jason Ankeny*

● **Transmissions from the Satellite Heart** / Jan. 1993 / Warner Brothers ✦✦✦✦✦
The addition of guitarist Ronald Jones and drummer Steven Drozd recharges the Lips' batteries for the superb *Transmissions from the Satellite Heart*, another prismatic delicacy which continues the group's drift toward pop nirvana. In typical fashion, the record's left-field hit, the freakshow sing-along "She Don't Use Jelly," bears little resemblance to the album as a whole; the remainder of *Transmissions* is much more sonically and structurally ambitious—the towering "Moth in the Incubator" keeps generating new layers of noise before erupting into an amphetamine waltz, "Pilot Can at the Queer of God" divebombs with kamikaze recklessness, and the slow-burning "Oh My Pregnant Head" is as mind-expanding as its title. *—Jason Ankeny*

Clouds Taste Metallic / Sep. 19, 1995 / Warner Brothers ✦✦✦✦✦
The same extraordinary madness which infected the best work of Brian Wilson rears its head on the shimmering and melodic *Clouds Taste Metallic*, a masterful collection which completes the Flaming Lips' odyssey into the pop stratosphere. The *Pet Sounds* comparisons are obvious—two of the highlights are titled "This Here Giraffe" and "Christmas at the Zoo"—yet not unfair; like Brian Wilson, Wayne Coyne has refined his unique vision into something both highly personal and powerfully universal. Similarly, while Coyne's lyrics remain as acid-damaged and inscrutable as ever, his densely-constructed songs convey emotional complexities far beyond the scope of their head-case titles ("Psychiatric Explorations of the Fetus with Needles," "Guy Who Got a Headache and Accidentally Saves the World"); galvanized by equal parts newfound maturity and childlike wonderment, *Clouds Like Metallic* is both the Flaming Lips' most intricate and most irresistible work. *—Jason Ankeny*

Zaireeka / Oct. 28, 1997 / Warner Brothers ✦✦✦✦
A combination of the words "Zaire" and "Eureka," *Zaireeka* is a term coined by Flaming Lips frontman Wayne Coyne symbolizing the fusion of anarchy and genius. It's a perfect title; *Zaireeka* is the culmination of the Lips' helter-skelter brilliance. Pushing the concept of interactive listening into new realms of possibility, the work extends Coyne's infamous "parking lot experiments" into not merely one album, but four separate discs that can be played separately or in groups of two, three, and four with multiple stereos. (Properly synchronized multi-disc playback requires more than one person—it's literally a party album.) Between combining the discs and toying with volume, balance, fidelity, etc., the options are truly limitless. No two multi-disc performances can be repeated, thanks to the space-time continuum and discrepancies from one CD player to another. Musically as well as conceptually, the Lips are defiantly experimental throughout *Zaireeka;* individually, each disc sounds more like free jazz than pop, although Coyne's diamond-sharp melodic sensibilities prevail even during the most chaotic moments. With each additional disc, the music's force and ingenuity reveals itself: "Riding to Work in the Year 2025 (Your Invisible Now)" is an epic orchestral noise suite, "Thirty-Five Thousand Feet of Despair" is a multi-narrative plane-crash drama remarkably evocative in its depiction of fear and chaos, and "How Will We Know? (Futuristic Crashendos)" features such extreme high and low frequencies that it can lead to disorientation, confusion, or nausea (the track is not recommended to be played while operating a motor vehicle or in the presence of infants). Logistical nightmares aside, *Zaireeka* is a dense, difficult work, recommended only for the hardiest Flaming Lips fetishists; however, they're in for the musical experience of a lifetime. *—Jason Ankeny*

A Collection of Songs Representing an Enthusiasm for Recording . . . By Amateurs / Sep. 29, 1998 / Restless ✦✦✦✦✦
With the exception of the superb *In a Priest Driven Ambulance*, the Flaming Lips' early albums for the Restless label are at best hit-or-miss affairs; *A Collection of Songs Representing an Enthusiasm for Recording . . . By Amateurs* sifts through the debris to rescue the most enduring material from those LPs, revealing a band still struggling to discover their voice but on occasion capable of flickers of startling brilliance. The best tracks here—"Unconsciously Screamin'," "Jesus Shootin' Heroin" and "One Million, Billionth of a Millisecond on a Sunday Morning"—rival anything in the group's catalog, while even the weaker selections still suggest a truly original musical vision in embryo. Complete with a batch of unreleased covers making the set as valuable to longtime fans as more recent converts, *A Collection of Songs* proves once and for all that the Lips didn't simply become a great band overnight—they always had it in them, with the best still yet to come. *—Jason Ankeny*

The Soft Bulletin / Jun. 22, 1999 / Warner Brothers ✦✦✦✦✦
So where does a band go after releasing the most defiantly experimental record of its career? If you're the Flaming Lips, you keep rushing headlong into the unknown—*The Soft Bulletin*, their follow-up to the four-disc gambit *Zaireeka*, is in many ways their most daring work yet, a plaintively emotional, lushly symphonic pop masterpiece eons removed from their past efforts' mind-warping noise of their past efforts. Though more conventional in concept and scope than *Zaireeka, The Soft Bulletin* clearly reflects its predecessor's expansive sonic palette. Its multi-dimensional sound is positively celestial, a shape-shifting pastiche of blissful melodies, heavenly harmonies and orchestral flourishes; but for all its headphone-friendly innovations, the music is still amazingly accessible, never sacrificing popcraft in the name of radical experimentation. (Its aims are so perversely commercial, in fact, that hit R&B remixer Peter Mokran tinkered with the cuts "Race for the Prize" and "Waitin' for a Superman" in the hopes of earning mainstream radio attention.) But what's most remarkable about *The Soft Bulletin* is its humanity—these are Wayne Coyne's most personal and deeply felt songs, as well as the warmest and most giving. No longer hiding behind surreal vignettes about Jesus, zoo animals and outer space, Coyne pours his heart and soul into each one of these tracks, poignantly exploring love, loss and the fate of all mankind; highlights like "The Spiderbite Song" and "Feeling Yourself Disintegrate" are so nakedly emotional and transcendently spiritual that it's impossible not to be moved by their beauty. There's no telling where the Lips will go from here, but it's almost beside the point—not just the best album of 1999, *The Soft Bulletin* might be the best record of the entire decade. *—Jason Ankeny*

The Flamingos

f. 1952, Chicago, IL
Group / Doo Wop
Both prolific and seminal in their influence and impact, the Flamingos may have been the greatest harmonizing vocal ensemble ever, and were certainly among the premier units of the doo wop/R&B era. Cousins Jake and Zeke Carey formed the group in Chicago, and added lead vocalist Sollie McElroy just before their recording debut for the Chance label, 1953's "If I Can't Have You." After McElroy left and was replaced by Nate Nelson, the Flamingos enjoyed their first chart success with Checker, scoring a Top Ten R&B hit with "I'll Be Home" in 1956. Signed to End in 1958, the following year's "I Only Have Eyes for You" became their biggest hit, peaking at number three R&B and number 11 pop. It was the start of a productive period that saw the Flamingos issue four albums for End and get two more R&B Top 30 singles, one the Sam Cooke composition "Nobody Loves Me Like You" in 1960. The group returned briefly to Checker in 1964 and later recorded for Phillips, Julman and Polydor, but couldn't regain their former standing. They remained among the genre's most beloved groups, and anthologies of their material on Chance and Checker have been reissued. In 1993, *The Flamingos Meet the Moonglows* was reissued by Vee-Jay. *—Ron Wynn*

★ **The Doo Bop She Bop: The Best of the Flamingos** / May 1990 / Rhino ✦✦✦✦✦
The Doo Bop She Bop: Best of the Flamingos is an 18-track collection that compiles all of the Flamingos' biggest hits and best songs. *The Doo Bop She Bop* ignores the group's latter-day soul hits and concentrates solely on their doo wop material, which makes for a stronger, more cohesive collection. "I Only Have Eyes for You" is the acknowledged classic, while "I'll Be Home" and "A Kiss from Your Lips" were hits in their own right, but the compilation proves that the Flamingos were one of the greatest doo-wop groups with its lesser-known numbers like "The Vow" and "The Ladder of Love." *—Stephen Thomas Erlewine*

Complete Chess Masters Plus / May 20, 1997 / Chess ✦✦✦✦✦
The Flamingos didn't have many hits while they were at Checker, but those two singles—"I'll Be Home" and "A Kiss from Your Lips"—were terrific, sketching out the lush sound they would later blossom on "I Only Have Eyes for You." *Complete Chess Masters Plus* contains all 18 songs, including two previously unreleased tracks, the group recorded for Checker and Chess. Although it's not a definitive career overview, it's an essential item for collectors of doo wop and vocal R&B, since it's lovingly packaged and contains numerous gems, including "The Vow" and "Dream of a Lifetime." *—Stephen Thomas Erlewine*

Fleetwood Mac

f. 1967, London, England
Group / Album Rock, British Blues, Pop/Rock, Soft Rock, Adult Contemporary, Blues-Rock
While most bands undergo a number of changes over the course of their career, few groups experienced such radical stylistic changes as Fleetwood Mac. Initially conceived as a hard-edged British blues combo in the late '60s, the band gradually evolved into a polished pop-rock act over the course of a decade. Throughout all of their incarnations, the only consistent members of Fleetwood Mac were drummer Mick Fleetwood and bassist John McVie—the rhythm section who provided the band with its name. Ironically, they had the least influence over the musical direction of the band. Originally, guitarists Peter Green and Jeremy Spencer provided the band with its gutsy, neo-psychedelic blues-rock sound, but as both guitarists descended into mental illness, the group began moving towards pop-rock with the songwriting of pianist Christine McVie. By the mid-'70s, Fleetwood Mac had relocated to California, where they added the soft-rock duo of Lindsey Buckingham and Stevie Nicks to their lineup. Obsessed with the meticulously arranged pop of the Beach Boys and the Beatles, Buckingham helped the band become one of the most popular groups of the late '70s. Combining soft-rock with the confessional introspection of singer-songwriters, Fleetwood Mac created a slick but emotional sound that helped 1977's *Rumours* become one of the biggest-selling albums of all-time. The band's retained their popularity through the early '80s, when Buck-

ingham, Nicks and Christine McVie all began pursuing solo careers. The band reunited for one album, 1987's *Tango in the Night*, before splintering in the late '80s. Buckingham left the group initially, but the band decided to soldier on, releasing one other album before Nicks and McVie left the band in the early '90s, hastening the group's commercial decline. — *Stephen Thomas Erlewine*

Peter Green's Fleetwood Mac / Feb. 1968 / Blue Horizon ✦✦✦✦✦
Fleetwood Mac's debut LP was a highlight of the late-'60s British blues boom. Green's always inspired playing, the capable (if erratic) songwriting, and the general panache of the band as a whole placed them leagues above the overcrowded field. Elmore James is a big influence on this set, particularly on the tunes fronted by Jeremy Spencer ("Shake Your Moneymaker," "Got to Move"). Spencer's bluster, however, was outshone by the budding singing and songwriting skills of Green. The guitarist balanced humor and vulnerability on cuts like "Looking for Somebody" and "Long Grey Mare," and with "If I Loved Another Woman," he offered a glimpse of the Latin-blues fusion that he would perfect with "Black Magic Woman." The album was an unexpected smash in the U.K., reaching number four on the British charts. — *Richie Unterberger*

Mr. Wonderful / Aug. 1968 / Castle ✦✦

English Rose / Jan. 1969 / Epic ✦✦✦✦✦
Under the direction of Peter Green, Fleetwood Mac is heard as a British blues group, although its most notable performances are on Green's original tunes "Black Magic Woman" and "Albatross," both British hits. — *William Ruhlmann*

● **Pious Bird of Good Omen** / Aug. 1969 / Columbia ✦✦✦✦✦
This is a compilation of Fleetwood Mac's early period, 1967-1968, featuring both sides of its debut single, "I Believe My Time Ain't Long"/"Rambling Pony" and many blues covers, as well as the hits "Albatross" and "Black Magic Woman." — *William Ruhlmann*

Then Play On / Oct. 1969 / Reprise ✦✦✦✦
This Peter Green-led edition of the Mac isn't just an important transition between their initial blues-based incarnation and the mega-pop band they became, it's also their most vital, exciting version. The addition of Danny Kirwan as second guitarist and songwriter foreshadows not only the soft-rock terrain of "Bare Trees" and "Kiln House" with Christine Perfect-McVie, but also predicts *Rumours*. That only pertains to roughly half of the also excellent material here, though; the rest is quintessential Green. The immortal "Oh Well," with its hard-edged, thickly layered guitars and chamber-like sections, is perhaps the band's most enduring progressive composition. "Rattlesnake Shake" is another familiar number, a down-and-dirty, even-paced funk, with clean, wall-of-sound guitars. Choogling drums and Green's fiery improvisations power "Searching for Madge," perhaps Mac's most inspired work save "Green Manalishi," and leads into an unlikely symphonic interlude and the similar, lighter boogie "Fighting for Madge." A hot Afro-Cuban rhythm with beautiful guitars from Kirwan and Green on "Coming Your Way" not only defines the Mac's sound, but the rock aesthetic of the day. Of the songs with Kirwan's stamp on them, "Closing My Eyes" is a mysterious waltz love song; haunting guitars approach surf music on the instrumental "My Dream"; while "Although the Sun Is Shining" is the ultimate pre-*Rumours* number someone should revisit. Blues roots still crop up on the spatial, loose, Hendrix-tinged "Underway," the folky blues tale of a lesbian affair on "Like Crying," and the final outcry of the ever-poignant "Show Biz Blues," with Green moaning "do you really give a damn for me?" *Then Play On* is a reminder of how pervasive and powerful Green's influence was on Mac's originality and individual stance beyond his involvement. Still highly recommended and a must-buy after all these years, it remains their magnum opus. — *Michael G. Nastos*

Kiln House / Sep. 1970 / Reprise ✦✦✦
Fleetwood Mac's first album after the departure of their nominal leader, Peter Green, finds the remaining members, Mick Fleetwood, John McVie, Jeremy Spencer, and Danny Kirwan (plus McVie's wife, Christine) trying to maintain the band's guitar-heavy, blues-rock approach, with the burden falling on Spencer and Kirwan. They don't embarrass themselves, but none of this is of the caliber of Green's work. — *William Ruhlmann*

Future Games / Nov. 1971 / Reprise ✦✦✦
By the time of this album's release, Jeremy Spencer had been replaced by Bob Welch and Christine McVie had begun to assert herself more as a singer and songwriter. The result is a distinct move toward folk-rock and pop; this album sounds almost nothing like Peter Green's Fleetwood Mac. Welch's eight-minute title track has one of his characteristic haunting melodies, and with pruning and better editing could have been a hit. Christine McVie's "Show Me a Smile" is one of her loveliest ballads. Initial popular reaction was mixed: the album didn't sell as well as *Kiln House*, but it sold better than any of the band's first three albums in the U.S. In the U.K., where the original lineup had been more successful, *Future Games* didn't chart at all, the same fate that would befall the rest of its albums until the Lindsey Buckingham-Stevie Nicks era. — *William Ruhlmann*

Bare Trees / Mar. 1972 / Reprise ✦✦✦✦✦

Penguin / Mar. 1973 / Reprise ✦✦
Fleetwood Mac's first album made after the departure of Danny Kirwan features the additions of guitarist Bob Weston and singer Dave Walker. By now Bob Welch and Christine McVie were the dominant forces in the band, and all traces of blues-rock were gone, replaced by Welch's hypnotic melodies and McVie's romantic sentiments married to uptempo pop tunes. This album gave Fleetwood Mac its best U.S. chart showing yet, but the wonder is that this phase in the band's career wasn't even more popular. — *William Ruhlmann*

Mystery to Me / Oct. 1973 / Reprise ✦✦✦
At this point, Fleetwood Mac is a mainstream rock band whose songs alternate between guitarist/singer Robert Welch and keyboard player/singer Christine McVie. — *William Ruhlmann*

Heroes Are Hard to Find / Sep. 1974 / Reprise ✦✦✦

Fleetwood Mac in Chicago / 1975 / Warner Brothers ✦✦

☆ **Fleetwood Mac** / Jul. 1975 / Reprise ✦✦✦✦✦
"Monday Morning," a sunny slice of folk-rock with Beach Boys harmonies, opens *Fleetwood Mac* and makes it clear that the band is no longer a blues-rock outfit. Lindsey Buckingham and Stevie Nicks were the catalyst for Fleetwood Mac's successful re-emergence as a mainstream pop/rock band. While Buckingham only contributed three songs, he helped the band develop a coherent vision, providing crystal-clear backings for Nicks' hippie anthems and Christine McVie's remarkably improved pop-soul. McVie dominates the album, contributing some of her finest songs, including the sighing "Over My Head" and the bouncy "Say You Love Me." Nicks' songs function as folky counterpoints to McVie's sweet pop, and she rarely ever wrote songs as memorably affecting as "Rhiannon" or "Landslide." Remarkably, *Fleetwood Mac* is a blockbuster album that isn't dominated by its hit singles, and its album tracks ("World Turning," "Sugar Daddy," "Crystal") demonstrate a depth of both songwriting and musicality that would blossom fully on *Rumours*. — *Stephen Thomas Erlewine*

Original Fleetwood Mac / 1977 / Sire ✦✦

★ **Rumours** / Feb. 4, 1977 / Reprise ✦✦✦✦✦
The new lineup that Fleetwood Mac successfully unveiled with their eponymous 1975 album became even more successful with the multi-platinum *Rumours*, which became the band's most celebrated album and one of the best-selling albums of all time. To be sure, this was a very different sounding Fleetwood Mac than the blues-rock outfit of the late '60s. This edition of the band generally wasn't well-received by rock critics (who tend to be critical of all things commercial). But as commercial and slick as *Rumours* is, the music has a lot of heart, and never comes across as insincere. From Christine McVie's optimistic "Don't Stop" (which President Bill Clinton used as his campaign theme song in 1992) to Lindsey Buckingham's remorseful "Go Your Own Way," *Rumours* is consistently memorable. And the folkish "Gold Dust Woman" (covered by Courtney Love and Hole in 1996) and the melancholy hit "Dreams" made it quite clear just how much depth and substance Stevie Nicks was capable of. — *Alex Henderson*

Tusk / Oct. 1979 / Reprise ✦✦✦✦✦
Where *Rumours* achieved greatness through turmoil, its double-album follow-up, *Tusk*, is the sound of a band imploding. Lindsey Buckingham began to assume control of Fleetwood Mac during the *Rumours* sessions, but he dominates *Tusk*, turning the album into a paranoid roller coaster ride where sweet soft rock is offset by feverish cocaine fantasies. Christine McVie and Stevie Nicks don't deviate from their established soft-rock and folk-rock templates, and all their songs are first-rate, whether it's McVie's "Over and Over" or Nicks' "Sara." Buckingham gives these mainstream-oriented songs off-kilter arrangements, so they can fit neatly with his nervy, insular, yet catchy songs. Alternating bracing pop-rockers like "The Ledge" and "What Makes You Think You're the One" with melancholic, Beach Boys-style ballads like "Save Me a Place" and "That's All for Everyone," Buckingham subverts pop/rock with weird arrangements and unpredictable melodies, which are nevertheless given accessible productions. Even the hit title track is a strange, menacing threat punctuated by a marching band. This is as strange as mainstream pop gets, even pushing on the borders of the avant-garde. Because of its ambitions, *Tusk* failed to replicate the success of its two predecessors (it still went double platinum, though), yet it earned a dedicated cult audience of fans of twisted, melodic pop. — *Stephen Thomas Erlewine*

Fleetwood Mac Live / Dec. 1980 / Reprise ✦✦✦

Mirage / Jun. 1982 / Reprise ✦✦✦
Fleetwood Mac retreated from the insular strangeness of *Tusk* and returned to straightforward pop songcraft for *Mirage*. Boasting a glossy, friendly production that makes even the lesser numbers pleasant and ingratiating, *Mirage* nonetheless suffers from a lack of substance. *Rumours* had raw emotion to give it a core, and *Tusk* had Lindsey Buckingham's runaway ambition. For its part, *Mirage* sounds as if its sole goal is to sustain Fleetwood Mac's popularity, and while there may be a handful of terrific songs—notably the hit singles "Gypsy," "Love in Store," and "Hold Me"—it simply isn't as compelling as the group's previous three albums. — *Stephen Thomas Erlewine*

Tango in the Night / 1987 / Reprise ✦✦✦
Artistically and commercially, the Stevie Nicks/Lindsey Buckingham/Mick Fleetwood/Christine and John McVie edition of Fleetwood Mac had been on a roll for over a decade when *Tango in the Night* was released in early 1987. This would, unfortunately, be Buckingham's last album with the pop/rock supergroup—and he definitely ended his association with the band on a creative high note. Serving as the album's main producer, Buckingham gives an edgy quality to everything from the haunting "Isn't It Midnight" to the poetic "Seven Wonders" to the dreamy "Everywhere." Though Buckingham doesn't over-produce, his thoughtful use of synthesizers is a major asset. Without question, "Family Man" and "Caroline" are among the best songs ever written by Buckingham, who consistently brings out the best in his colleagues on this superb album. — *Alex Henderson*

Greatest Hits / Nov. 1988 / Reprise ✦✦✦✦✦
Greatest Hits is a fine overview of Fleetwood Mac's hit-making years, containing the bulk of the group's Top 40 hits of the late '70s and '80s, including "Over My Head," "Rhiannon," "Say You Love Me," "Go Your Own Way," "Dreams," "Don't Stop," "Tusk," "Sara," "Hold Me," "Gypsy," and "Little Lies." Minor hits like "Think About Me," "Love in Store" and "Seven Wonders" are missing, making room for the new songs "As Long As You Follow" (which actually became a hit) and "No Questions Asked," but overall, *Greatest Hits* is an excellent choice for casual listeners. — *Stephen Thomas Erlewine*

Behind the Mask / Apr. 10, 1990 / Reprise ✦✦

25 Years: The Chain / Nov. 24, 1992 / Reprise ✦✦✦

Peter Green's Fleetwood Mac Live at the BBC / Oct. 1995 / Castle ✦✦

Time / Oct. 10, 1995 / Warner Brothers ✦✦

The Dance / Aug. 19, 1997 / Reprise ♦♦♦

The Complete Blue Horizon Sessions: 1967-1969 / Oct. 19, 1999 / Sire ♦♦♦

The Fleetwoods

f. 1958, Olympia, WA, **db.** 1963

Group / Doo Wop, Pop

Although the Fleetwoods' sound was smooth, without many of the rougher edges of doo wop groups, they were one of the few White vocal groups of the late '50s and early '60s to enjoy success not only on the pop charts, but also the R&B charts. The Fleetwoods' forte was ballads, beginning with their 1959 debut single "Come Softly to Me" and continuing through the next three years. The group broke up in 1963, but their songs became pop-rock classics of the pre-British Invasion era. A trio of Gretchen Christopher, Barbara Ellis and Gary Troxell, the group wrote "Come Softly to Me" quite early and released the single on Seattle's Dolphin (later Dolton) label. The song became an instant hit, climbing to number one on the American charts and the Top Ten in the UK. Later that year, "Mr. Blue" became their second chart-topper. After vocalist Troxell was drafted just at the height of their popularity though, the Fleetwoods hit the Top Ten just once more, with 1961's "Tragedy." Disbanded in 1963, the group reunited occasionally throughout the ensuing decades, including a 1973 recording session and a 1990 oldies tour following Rhino's release of *The Best of the Fleetwoods.* — *Stephen Thomas Erlewine*

● **The Best of the Fleetwoods** / May 1990 / Rhino ♦♦♦♦♦

Rhino's *Best of the Fleetwoods* contains all of their hits ("Come Softly to Me," "Mr. Blue," and sixteen other songs) on a smartly assembled collection. — *Stephen Thomas Erlewine*

A Flock of Seagulls

f. 1980, Liverpool, England

Group / New Romantic, New Wave, Synth Pop

As well-known for their bizarrely teased haircuts as their hit single "I Ran (So Far Away)," A Flock of Seagulls were one of the infamous one-hit wonders of the New Wave era. Growing out of the synth-heavy and ruthlessly stylish New Romantic movement, the band a little too robotic and arrived a little too late to be true New Romantics, but their sleek dance-pop was forever indebted to the short-lived movement. From their eponymous 1982 debut album, "I Ran (So Far Away)" was quickly picked up by MTV for its icily attractive video and made the American Top Ten. "Wishing (If I Had a Photograph of You)" hit the British Top Ten later that year, and reached the Top 40 in America. From the group's second album, 1983's *Listen,* the single "Wishing" was moderately successful though the band's fortunes crashed shortly after its release. After one more album, a splintered lineup bowed out with 1986's *Dream Come True.* In 1989, frontman Mike Score assembled a new lineup of A Flock of Seagulls, though the band failed to make an impact. They continued to tour worldwide, and in 1995 released a new album: *The Light at the End of the World.* — *Stephen Thomas Erlewine*

A Flock of Seagulls / 1982 / Jive ♦♦♦♦♦

The Liverpool quintet A Flock of Seagulls first gained attention in the dance clubs with "Telecommunication," included on this debut release. The band benefited from heavy play on MTV and quickly became known for their outrageous fashion and lead singer Mike Score's waterfall-like haircut. However, their self-titled debut is an enjoyable romp that was set apart from other synth-heavy acts of the time by Paul Reynolds' unique guitar style. The kinetic "I Ran (So Far Away)" became a video staple and a Top Ten radio hit. "A Space Age Love Song," with its synthesizer washes and echo-laden guitar, also managed to score at radio. The rest of the album consists of hyperactive melodies, synthesizer noodlings, and electronic drumming. The lyrics are forgettable. In fact, they rarely expand on the song titles, but its all great fun and a wonderful collection of new wave ear candy. — *Tom Demalon*

The Story of a Young Heart / Aug. 1984 / Jive/Arista ♦♦♦

Light at the End of the World / Jun. 25, 1996 / SAVA ♦♦

● **The Best of A Flock of Seagulls** / Jun. 30, 1998 / Music Club ♦♦♦♦

Eddie Floyd

b. Jun. 25, 1935, Montgomery, AL

Vocals / Soul

Eddie Floyd came aboard the good ship Stax at the behest of his friend Al Bell and immediately made himself useful as a composer for labelmates Carla Thomas, William Bell, Otis Redding (originally intended to be the recipient of "Knock on Wood"), and Atlantic's Wilson Pickett.

Floyd's own mid-'60s output included "Raise Your Hand," which utilized the same Booker T. & the MGs-powered thrust as "Knock on Wood," and "Big Bird," written partially in shocked response to the tragic death of Redding. Floyd remained loyal to Stax right up to its bitter demise, his engaging vocals resulting in major hits with the gentle "I've Never Found a Girl" and a lively remake of Sam Cooke's "Bring It on Home to Me."

Whenever Floyd re-teams with his old Stax pals—guitarist Steve Cropper, bassist Duck Dunn, and sometimes Booker T. Jones on organ—the long-ago Memphis magic instantly returns. With Floyd happily leading the throngs through "Raise Your Hand" and "Knock on Wood," it's 1966 all over again. — *Bill Dahl*

Knock on Wood / 1967 / Stax ♦♦♦♦

In contrast to the 1970s—when artists ranging from Curtis Mayfield to Parliament/Funkadelic were praised for their albums—singles defined soul music in the 1960s. It has often been pointed out that many Stax and Motown albums of the '60s had their share of filler—nonetheless, others were full of gems that should have been released as singles. Reissued on CD in 1991, *Knock On Wood* is one of Eddie Floyd's best albums. The soul shouter successfully embraced sleeker northern soul on other projects, but here, he sticks to the type of raw, hard-edged Memphis soul that Stax was first known for. From the unforgettable title song (a number one R&B hit) to covers of J.J. Jackson's "But It's Alright," Jerry Butler's "I Stand Accused" and Wilson Pickett's "634-5789," this CD beautifully illustrates the splendor of down-home Southern R&B. — *Alex Henderson*

● **Chronicle** / 1979 / Stax ♦♦♦♦♦

Singer/songwriter/producer Eddie Floyd, a former member of the Falcons, shines on originals such as "Soul Street" and "I've Got to Have Your Love" as well as covers such as Sam Cooke's "Bring It on Home to Me" and Smokey Robinson's "My Girl." This 1979 collection includes all of Floyd's singles between 1968 and 1974.

Rare Stamps / Mar. 21, 1993 / Stax ♦♦♦♦♦

A pair of remarkable soul hits, "Knock on Wood" and "I've Never Found a Girl," enabled Eddie Floyd to attain national success in 1968. But the longtime singer and composer, whose roots dated back to the Detroit group the Falcons in the late '50s, was a steady, if not spectacular, performer for many years before and after those two songs. Several of Floyd's finest pieces are compiled on the 25-track CD *Rare Stamps,* including a wonderful testimonial to Otis Redding, "Big Bird." There are also two super duets with Mavis Staples, "Never Let You Go" and "Ain't That Good," which rank with anything that the label issued. — *Ron Wynn*

The Flying Burrito Brothers

f. 1969, Nashville, TN

Group / Country-Rock

The Flying Burrito Brothers helped forge the connection between rock and country, and with their 1969 debut album, *The Gilded Palace of Sin,* they virtually invented the blueprint for country-rock. Though the band's glory days were brief, they left behind a small body of work that proved vastly influential both in rock and country.

Gram Parsons and Chris Hillman formed the Burrito Brothers after leaving the Byrds in 1968, adding pedal steel guitarist "Sneaky" Pete Kleinow and bassist Chris Ethridge to the lineup. *The Gilded Palace of Sin* was released in the spring of 1969. Although the album only sold 40,000 copies, the band developed a devoted following, including many prominent Los Angeles musicians, Bob Dylan and the Rolling Stones. Around this time, Parsons and Stones guitarist Keith Richards became good friends, which led to Parsons losing interest in the Burritos. Ethridge left the band before their second album; he was replaced by Bernie Leadon, and ex-Byrd Michael Clarkewas hired as their drummer.

Burrito Deluxe, the group's second album, was released in the spring of 1970. After its release, Parsons left the group and was replaced by Rick Roberts, a local Californian songwriter, who was featured on 1971's *The Flying Burrito Brothers.* After its release, Kleinow left the band and Leadon departed to join the Eagles. They were replaced by Al Perkins and Roger Bush, respectively, and guitarist Kenny Wertz and fiddler Byron Berline were added to the lineup. This new version of the group recorded the 1972 live album *The Last of the Red Hot Burritos.* Before its release, the band splintered apart. Berline, Bush, and Wertz all left to form Country Gazette, while Hillman and Perkins joined Manassas. After a European tour led by Roberts, the group disbanded. Throughout the remainder of the '70s, '80s and '90s, different incarnations of the Burrito Brothers, usually led by Kleinow, would form for recordings and tours, yet the band remains famous for their first tow records. — *Stephen Thomas Erlewine*

☆ **The Gilded Palace of Sin** / Feb. 1969 / Edsel ♦♦♦♦♦

By 1969, Gram Parsons had already built the foundation of the country rock movement through his work with The International Submarine Band and The Byrds, but his first album with The Flying Burrito Brothers, *The Gilded Palace of Sin,* was where he revealed the full extent of his talents, and it ranks among the finest and most influential albums the genre would ever produce. As a songwriter, Parsons delivered some of his finest work on this set; "Hot Burrito *1"* and "Hot Burrito *2"* both blend the hurt of classic country weepers with a contemporary sense of anger, jealousy, and confusion, and "Sin City" can either be seen as a parody or a sincere meditation on a city gone mad, and it hits home in both contexts. Parsons was rarely as strong as a vocalist as he was here, and his covers of "Dark End of the Street" and "Do Right Woman" prove just how much he had been learning from R&B as well as C&W. And Parsons was fortunate enough to be working with a band who truly added to his vision, rather than simply backing him up; the distorted swoops of Skeeky Pete Kleinow's fuzztone steel guitar provides a perfect bridge between country and psychedelic rock, and Chris Hillman's strong and supportive harmony vocals blend flawlessly with Parsons' (and he also proved to be a valuable songwriting partner, collaborating on a number of great tunes with Gram. While *The Gilded Palace of Sin* barely registered on the pop-culture radar in 1969, literally dozens of bands (The Eagles most notable among them) would find inspiration in this music and enjoy far greater success. But no one ever brought rock and country together quite like The Flying Burrito Brothers, and this album remains their greatest accomplishment. — *Mark Deming*

Burrito Deluxe / Apr. 1970 / Edsel ♦♦♦♦♦

Gram Parsons had a habit of taking over whatever band he happened to be working with, and on the first three albums on which he appeared—The International Submarine Band's *Safe at Home,* The Byrds' *Sweetheart of the Rodeo,* and The Flying Burrito Brothers' *The Gilded Palace of Sin*—he became the focal point, regardless of the talent of his compatriots. *Burrito Deluxe,* the Burritos' second album, is unique in Parsons' repertoire in that it's the only album where he seems to have deliberately stepped back to make more room for others; whether this was due to Gram's disinterest in a band he was soon to leave, or if he was simply in an unusually democratic frame of mind is a matter of debate. But while it is hardly a bad album, it's not nearly as striking as *The Gilded Palace of Sin.* Parsons didn't deliver many noteworthy originals for this set, with "Cody Cody" and "Older Guys" faring best but paling next to the highlights from the previous album (though he was able to wrangle the song "Wild Horses" away from his buddy Keith Richards and record it a year before The Rolling Stones' version would surface). And while the band sounds tight and they play with genuine enthusiasm, there's a certain lack of focus in these performances; the band's frontman sounds as if his thoughts are often elsewhere, and the other players can't quite compensate for him, though on tunes like "God's Own Singer" and a cover of Bob Dylan's "If You Gotta Go (Go Now)," they gamely give it the old college try. *Burrito Deluxe* is certainly a better than average country-rock album, but coming from the band who made the genre's most strongly defining music, it's something of a disappointment. *—Mark Deming*

The Flying Burrito Brothers / May 1971 / A&M ♦♦♦
On their first post-Parsons album, the Burritos (now led by Hillman and Rick Roberts, and with future Eagle Bernie Leadon replacing Ethridge) make an honest step forward in country-rock. Includes the Roberts song "Colorado." *— William Ruhlmann*

The Last of the Red Hot Burritos / Apr. 1972 / A&M ♦♦

★ **Farther Along: Best Of** / 1988 / A&M ♦♦♦♦♦
Farther Along: The Best of the Flying Burrito Brothers is a nearly flawless compilation, containing a full 21 tracks of the pioneering group's best material. All but two of the songs from *The Gilded Palace of Sin* are included on the collection, as are all of the highlights from *Burrito Deluxe* and a handful of rarities and outtakes. In short, it's a definitive collection containing all of the Burrito Brothers' finest moments. It's indespensible to any rock or country collection. *— Stephen Thomas Erlewine*

☆ **Hot Burritos! The Flying Burrito Brothers Anthology: 1969-1972** / Apr. 18, 2000 / A&M ♦♦♦♦♦
There's little question that the double-disc collection *Hot Burritos! The Flying Burrito Brothers Anthology: 1969-1972* is comprehensive, since it contains the entirety of the band's first three albums plus a bevy of rarities, including six songs from *Close Up the Hony-Tonks,* two cuts from *Sleepless Nights,* two tracks from *The Last of the Red Hot Burritos,* the non-LP single "The Train Song," and "Six Days on the Road," originally released on the 1988 collection, *Farther Along: The Best of the Flying Burrito Brothers.* That pretty much covers *everything* they cut during those four years. Since the Burritos were truly great while Gram Parsons was in the band—once he left, they were still solid, thanks to Chris Hillman—this may border on overkill for some listeners, especially since the Parsons years are covered expertly by *Farther Along,* which contained all but one song from *The Gilded Palace of Sin,* plus the best songs from *Deluxe* and rarities and highlights from posthumous releases. For neophytes, that's a better bet, yet the converted will find this quite nice. Apart from "The Train Song," which rarely shows up on collections, there aren't any revelations or even new songs, but there are nice liner notes, great outtakes from the photo shoot for *Gilded Palace,* and exquisite remastered sound. And, for Parsons fanatics, the Hillman-led *Flying Burrito Brothers* may seem like a new record, too, since they may have previously overlooked it. So, diehards get all the Parsons material in one place, while neophytes with a serious attention span will be introduced to one of the great bands of the last 25 years of the 20th century—and, yes, that means it qualifies as definitive. *— Stephen Thomas Erlewine*

Dan Fogelberg

b. Aug. 13, 1951, Peoria, IL
Vocals, Keyboards, Guitar / Soft Rock, Singer/Songwriter
Peoria, Illinois native Dan Fogelberg has built a devoted following over the years with his laid-back, folky singer/songwriter style. A pianist since 14, Fogelberg switched to guitar and played local coffeehouses while majoring in art at the University of Illinois, where he met ex-student and REO Speedwagon manager Irving Azoff. Fogelberg relocated to Los Angeles and played the folk circuit while doing session work, landing a tour spot with Van Morrison at one point. Fogelberg's 1972 debut, *Home Free,* didn't make much of an impact, and he was dropped from Columbia. However, Fogelberg's connection with Azoff led to a deal with Epic. Fogelberg's Epic debut, *Souvenirs,* became his first in a string of seven consecutive platinum albums. He increased his visibility by touring with the Eagles in 1975. Fogelberg's popularity peaked in 1980 with the release of *Phoenix,* which contained the number two hit single "Longer." His follow-up, *The Innocent Age,* was a double concept album, and four Top 20 singles were pulled from it. Following the release of a greatest hits package, Fogelberg's commercial appeal began to evaporate; none of his subsequent albums have gone platinum, but continue to sell well to a core of fans. 1993's *River of Souls* saw Fogelberg experimenting with worldbeat sounds as a backdrop for his lyrical musings. *No Resemblance Whatsoever,* a collaboration with Tim Weisberg, followed in 1995, and four years later Fogelberg returned with *First Christmas Morning. Live: Something Old New Borrowed and Some Blues* appeared in mid-2000. *— Steve Huey*

● **Greatest Hits** / 1982 / Full Moon/Epic ♦♦♦♦♦
Greatest Hits may ignore some of his better album tracks, but it does contain what the title says—Dan Fogelberg's biggest hits, prior to its release date of 1982. Really, that means only one big hit—"The Language of Love"—is missing, since his peak of popularity arrived in the early '80s, when "Longer," "Same Old Lang Syne," "Hard to Say" and "Leader of the Band" all made the Top Ten, and "Heart Hotels," "Run for the Roses," "Missing You" and "Make Love Stay" cracked the Top 40. All of those songs, along with his first hit "Part of the Plan," are here, on a collection that remains the best, most concise chronicle of his hitmaking years yet assembled. *— Stephen Thomas Erlewine*

Portrait: The Music of Dan Fogelberg From 1972-1997 / Jun. 3, 1997 / Full Moon/Epic ♦♦♦♦♦
Portrait: The Music of Dan Fogelberg 1972-1997 is an extensive, four-disc box set that covers the singer-songwriter's entire career in detail. In addition to all of the hits and favorite album tracks, the box also features the B-side "Hearts and Crafts" and four previously unreleased tracks, including the newly recorded "Don't Lose Heart." Those five songs aren't quite enough to entice hardcore Fogelberg collectors, who are the only listeners that will be interested in such a substantial box set, since casual fans will find the sheer length of this set intimidating and maybe even tedious. But for any devoted Fogelberg fan who doesn't already own his entire catalog, *Portrait* is a worthwhile purchase. *— Stephen Thomas Erlewine*

John Fogerty

b. May 28, 1945, Berkeley, CA
Vocals, Guitar / Heartland Rock, Roots Rock, Rock & Roll
John Cameron Fogerty achieved fame as the lead singer/songwriter and guitarist in Creedence Clearwater Revival and has since gone on to a chart-topping solo career. Born in Berkeley, CA, Fogerty and his brother Tom organized the group that would become Creedence as the Golliwogs in the late '50s. As Creedence, they released nine Top Ten singles, all written by Fogerty, between 1969 and 1971, starting with the standard "Proud Mary." They also scored eight gold albums between 1968 and 1972, all fueled by Fogerty's simple, driving rock songs and his burly baritone, intoning deceptively poetic ("Bad Moon Rising") and even political ("Fortunate Son") lyrics.

Creedence split up in 1972. Fogerty at first confused his considerable following by releasing an album of covers, on which he played all the instruments, under the name the Blue Ridge Rangers in 1973. This was followed by a formal solo album, *John Fogerty,* in 1975, and then silence for more than nine years while the artist worked out business problems with Creedence's old label. But Fogerty returned at the end of 1984 with a Top Ten single, "The Old Man Down the Road," and a No. 1 album, *Centerfield. Eye of the Zombie* was a less successful follow-up in 1986. Following the failure of *Eye of the Zombie,* Fogerty went into seclusion. For the next 11 years he remained quiet, finally resurfacing in 1997 with *Blue Moon Swamp;* the live *Premonition* appeared just a year later. *— William Ruhlmann*

Blue Ridge Rangers / 1973 / Fantasy ♦♦♦

John Fogerty / 1975 / Asylum ♦♦♦♦
This one-man extravaganza finds John Fogerty plowing the same ground he worked with Creedence Clearwater Revival. This mix of originals and rock & roll classics finds him in fine voice, with the familiar vocal scream and hot guitars augmented in places by saxophones reminiscent of CCR's "Travelin' Band." Several of these songs rank with the top tier of Fogerty's Creedence material, particularly "The Wall," "Almost Saturday Night," and the anthemic "Rockin' All Over the World." He also delivers satisfying versions of Jackie Wilson's "Lonely Teardrops" and Frankie Ford's "Sea Cruise" (written by Huey "Piano" Smith. The closer, "Flying Away," could have come off the Doobie Brothers' *Toulouse Street.* This underappreciated album is worth checking out. *—Jim Newsom*

● **Centerfield** / Jan. 1985 / Warner Brothers ♦♦♦♦♦
"Put me in coach, I'm ready to play." These are lines familiar to any baseball fan, for John Fogerty's "Centerfield" has become the unofficial song of our national pastime. Those lines also signaled Fogerty's return to the music business after a ten-year absence. The music is mighty familiar, as Fogerty works the same terrain he mined for gold with Creedence Clearwater Revival from 1968-1972. The riff of the opening track, "The Old Man Down the Road," sounds so much like the Creedence hit "Run Through the Jungle" that Fogerty was sued by his former record company for plagiarizing himself. (He won the suit, the court upholding a composer's right to sound like himself.) "Old Man" was a Top Ten single, and this album reached number one itself. "Big Train (From Memphis)" is a rockabilly salute to Elvis, while "I Saw It on TV" takes us on a trip through the '50s and '60s "from Hooter to Doodyville," via the boob tube. "Searchlight" recalls "Keep On Chooglin" and the other extended one-chord jams of the Creedence days. Fogerty also lashes out at his old nemesis Saul Zaentz, head of that former label, Fantasy Records, with whom he had battled (and lost) over rights to his own catalog of Creedence songs. On "Mr. Greed" and "Zanz Kant Danz" (renamed "Vanz Kant Danz" on later pressings due again to the threat of lawsuit), he vents his anger over these past legal battles and foretells the one to come over "Old Man."

Fans hoped *Centerfield* would indeed mark the return of John Fogerty to the playing field, but after releasing the bitter *Eye of the Zombie* the following year, he disappeared again, not to return until 1997's *Blue Moon Swamp. —Jim Newsom*

Eye of the Zombie / 1986 / Warner Brothers ♦♦

Blue Moon Swamp / May 20, 1997 / Warner Brothers ♦♦♦♦♦
Listening to the easy roots-rock shuffle of *Blue Moon Swamp,* it's hard to believe that it took John Fogerty a full decade to write and record the album. It's not just because the album isn't a great stylistic departure from his past work, it's because *Blue Moon Swamp* sounds so natural and unforced. Nothing on the album sounds fussy, nor does it sound like a meticulous reconstruction of the past. Instead, Fogerty's songs and performances are richly evocative of tradition, but they're vibrant and living for the present, which makes the rockabilly, blues, country and swampy rock & roll sound fresh. It's not as raw or as hooky as Creedence Clearwater Revival, nor as pop-oriented as *Centerfield,* but it's a warm, laidback and mature record of roots-rock at its very best. *— Stephen Thomas Erlewine*

Premonition / Jun. 9, 1998 / Warner Brothers ♦♦♦♦
Upon its release in the spring of 1997, John Fogerty's long-awaited comeback album *Blue Moon Swamp* was lavished with praise—it didn't become the crossover hit that *Centerfield* was, but it earned great reviews and a solid cult audience. Furthermore, his tour—his first ever to feature classic Creedence material—was, if anything, even better received than *Blue Moon Swamp,* so it made some sense that he quickly released *Premonition,* his first solo live album, in 1998. *Premonition* is frighteningly good—Fogerty doesn't sound like a veteran rocker, he sounds nearly as powerful as he did on old Creedence live shows. He also sounds more mature, bringing increased depth to his older songs as he energizes recent material from "The Old Man Down the Road" to "Walking in a Hurricane." *Premonition* is essentially the province of dedicated Fogerty fans—there's only one new song, and the differences in the live performances are things only the hardcore will spot—but they'll be delighted with the quality of the music. *— Stephen Thomas Erlewine*

Foghat

f. 1971, London, England, **db.** 1984

Group / Album Rock, Boogie Rock, Arena Rock, Heavy Metal, Hard Rock, Blues-Rock

Foghat specialized in a simple, hard-rocking blues-rock, releasing a series of best-selling albums in the mid-'70s. While the group never deviated from their basic boogie, they retained a large audience until 1978, selling out concerts across America and earning five gold albums, as well as two platinum. Once punk and disco came along, the band's audience dipped dramatically, yet the group continued performing until 1980.

With its straightahead, three-chord romps, the band's sound was American in origin, yet the members were all natives of England. Guitarist/vocalist "Lonesome" Dave Peverett, bassist Tony Stevens and drummer Roger Earl were members of the British blues band Savoy Brown, who left the group in the early '70s. Upon their departure, they formed Foghat with guitarist Rod Price. Foghat moved to the United States, signing a record contract with Bearsville Records, a new label run by Albert Grossman. Their first album, *Foghat,* was released in the summer of 1972 and it became a hit on album rock; a cover of Willie Dixon's "I Just Want to Make Love to You" even made it to the lower regions of the singles charts. For their next album, the group didn't change their formula at all—in fact, they didn't even change the *title* of the album. Like the first record, the second was called *Foghat;* it was distinguished by a picture of a rock and a roll on the front cover. Foghat's second album was their first gold record, and it established them as a popular arena rock act. Their next five albums—*Energized* (1974), *Rock and Roll Outlaws* (1974), *Fool for the City* (1975), *Night Shift* (1976), *Foghat Live* (1977), *Stone Blue* (1978)—all were best-sellers and all went at least gold. "Slow Ride," taken from *Fool for the City,* was their biggest single, peaking at number 20. *Foghat Live* was their biggest album, selling over two million copies. After 1975, the band went through a series of bass players; Price left the band in 1981 and was replaced by Erik Cartwright.

In the early '80s, Foghat's commercial fortunes declined rapidly, with their last album, 1983's *Zig-Zag Walk,* barely making the album charts. The group broke up shortly afterward, although they have reunited for various tours in the late '80s and early '90s, releasing *Road Cases* in 1998. Peverett died of cancer on February 7, 2000. *—Stephen Thomas Erlewine*

● **The Best of Foghat** / Oct. 1990 / Rhino ✦✦✦✦✦

Rhino's *Best of Foghat* is an excellent 16-track collection featuring every one of the hard-rocking boogie band's best-known songs, from "Slow Ride" and "I Just Want to Make Love to You" to "Fool for the City," "Drivin' Wheel" and "Ride, Ride, Ride." In short, it's all the Foghat most fans will ever need. *—Stephen Thomas Erlewine*

The Best of Foghat, Vol. 2 / Jan. 24, 1992 / Rhino ✦✦✦✦✦

If *Best of Foghat* made you hungry for more, *Best of Foghat, Vol. 2,* with no hit singles, only album tracks, and including two live cuts and an outtake, should satiate your desire. *—Stephen Thomas Erlewine*

Ben Folds

Vocals, Piano / Pop Underground, Adult Alternative Pop/Rock, Alternative Pop/Rock, Singer/Songwriter

Singer/pianist Ben Folds (born Sept. 12, 1966 in Winston-Salem, North Carolina) is best known as the leader of the power pop trio Ben Folds Five, but has also struck out on his own as a solo artist. Despite playing in bands in high school, his musical career didn't really get off the ground until the late-80's, as a bassist for Majsha. Proving his multi-instrumental talents, Folds also played drums in as a session musician in Nashville. Moving back to North Carolina, Folds formed Ben Folds Five in 1994. Whereas most alternative bands of the 90's specialized in distorted teen angst rock, the guitarless trio was a refreshing break from the norm. The band was signed to the independent Caroline Records shortly afterward, resulting in their self-titled debut one year later. Due to airings of their humorous anthem, "Underground" (which poked fun at the politics of the punk/alternative scene) on MTV's *120 Minutes* and constant touring, quite a buzz was stirring for the band by the time of their second album. Released in 1997, *Whatever And Ever Amen* was pure pop-perfection easily one of the year's best releases (and perhaps the best power pop release of the 90's). While 1998 didn't see a new studio album by the band, BF5's former label issued a 16-track rarities collection (*Naked Baby Photos*), as Folds released his first solo album, *Volume 1,* under the pseudonym Fear of Pop. Although the album went largely unnoticed, it included the song "In Love," which included overly-dramatic vocals from none other than Captain Kirk himself, Mr. William Shatner. Ben Folds Five regrouped with 1999' s *The Unauthorized Biography of Reinhold Messner,* which was a more mature work than its predecessors, although the energetic lead-off single, "Army," showed that Folds' humorous approach hadn't dulled at all. *—Greg Prato*

● **Ben Folds Five** / Aug. 8, 1995 / Passenger ✦✦✦✦

The debut album from piano-playing Ben Folds' smart-ass trio is a potent, and extremely fun, collection of post-modern rock ditties that comes off as a pleasantly workable combination of Tin Pan Alley showmanship, Todd Rundgren-style power pop and a myriad of alt-rock sensibilities. The gimmick here is that not a single guitar was used on the 12 songs; but the way that Folds and his bandmates unravel their instruments (piano, bass and drums make up this combo), even the most hardened noise enthusiasts will hardly miss it (it's the melodies that carry this album, and Folds has plenty of them up his sleeve). Some of it is a bit coy—Folds plays the joker as much as he does the musician—but with the dead-on "Underground," they manage to skewer, and pay loving tribute, to the oh-so-hip indie scene from which they came. *—Michael Gallucci*

Whatever and Ever Amen / Mar. 18, 1997 / 550 ✦✦✦✦

Expanding on the hook-laden songcraft of their eponymous debut, the Ben Folds Five turn in another glitzy array of Todd Rundgren-esque, piano-driven pop on their second album, *Whatever and Ever Amen.* Though it isn't as consistently tuneful and clever as their first record, *Whatever and Ever Amen* has a snazzy sense of popcraft—the hooks of "The Battle of Who Could Care Less," "Brick" and "Fair" sink in nearly as effortlessly as Billy Joel, Elton John or Joe Jackson—which makes the record enjoyable ear candy. Occasionally, Folds' smug humor—whether it's the alternative-rock skewering of "The Battle" or the borderline misogynist humor of "Song for the Dumped"—can undercut his melodic gifts, but *Whatever and Ever Amen* is confirmation that the showy pop pleasures of his first record were no fluke. *—Thom Owens*

Naked Baby Photos / Jan. 13, 1998 / Caroline ✦✦✦

As the title suggests, *Naked Baby Photos* opens the vaults to capture Ben Folds Five in their developmental stages, splitting its 16 tracks evenly between studio rarities and live performances; about half have never been available before in any recorded form. In addition to those previously unavailable tracks, Folds collectors will be enticed by the band's rare debut 7-inch, "Jackson Cannery," and the original demo of "Bad Idea," which the band considers superior to the version released on the *Truth About Cats and Dogs* soundtrack. *—Steve Huey*

Fear of Pop, Vol. 1 / Nov. 17, 1998 / 550 ✦✦✦

The Unauthorized Biography of Reinhold Messner / Apr. 27, 1999 / 550 ✦✦✦✦

Foo Fighters

f. 1995, Seattle, WA

Group / Grunge, Alternative Pop/Rock

While he was drumming with Nirvana, Dave Grohl was recording original songs at home that never received public release. Those tapes would become the foundation of the Foo Fighters, the band he formed in 1995. Like Nirvana, the Foo Fighters melded loud, heavy guitars with pretty melodies and mixed punk sensibilities with a sharp sense of pop songwriting. Following Kurt Cobain's suicide in 1994, the drummer kept quiet for several months, but then recorded the album that became the Foo Fighters' debut in a week. In no time, Dave Grohl's solo project became the object of a fierce record-company bidding war. Less than a year after its release, the album was certified platinum in the US. Throughout 1996, the Foo Fighters supported the album with an extensive tour, enjoying a crossover hit with "Big Me" that spring. *The Colour and the Shape,* the Foo Fighters' second album, was released in 1997. *—Stephen Thomas Erlewine*

● **Foo Fighters** / Jul. 4, 1995 / Roswell/Capitol ✦✦✦✦

Essentially a collection of solo home recordings by Dave Grohl, the Foo Fighters' eponymous debut is a modest triumph. Driven by big pop melodies and distorted guitars, Foo Fighters does strongly recall Nirvana, only with a decidedly lighter approach. If Kurt Cobain's writing occasionally recalled John Lennon, Dave Grohl's songs are reminiscent of Paul McCartney—they're driven by large, instantly memorable melodies, whether it's the joyous outburt of "This Is a Call" or the gentle pop of "Big Me." That doesn't mean Grohl shys away from noise; toward the end of the record, he piles on several thrashers that make more sense as pure aggressive sound than songs. Since he recorded the album by himself, they aren't as powerful as most band's primal sonic workouts, but the results are damn impressive for a solo musician. Nevertheless, they aren't as strong as his fully formed pop songs, and that's where the true heart of the album lies. *Foo Fighters* has a handful of punk-pop gems that show, given the right musicians and songwriters, the genre had not entirely become a cliche by the middle of the '90s. *—Stephen Thomas Erlewine*

The Colour and the Shape / May 20, 1997 / Capitol ✦✦✦✦

Since the first Foo Fighters album was a collection of Dave Grohl solo recordings, their second album *The Colour and the Shape* is in many ways their official debut, and it certainly does sound different than its predecessor. Producer Gil Norton has tightened up the sound considerably—his control was so tight that drummer William Goldsmith left the band during the recording, leaving Grohl to record the rhythm tracks for the bulk of the album. Certainly, Norton's big, shiny sound makes *The Colour and the Shape* sound more professional than the debut, but the presence of a full band makes a difference, too. The full Foo Fighters make Grohl's songs heavier, not punkier, which may be a little unsettling to fans of the debut's ragged, amateurish edge. It's also strange that the album has such a glossy, arena-ready sound, since Grohl's songs are introspective, quite different than the endearing punk-pop of its predecessor. They're also not quite as catchy as before, but the band compensates by delivering them with a brutal energy. Still, the lack of immediate hooks prevents *The Colour and the Shape* from truly catching fire. *—Stephen Thomas Erlewine*

There Is Nothing Left to Lose / Nov. 2, 1999 / RCA ✦✦✦✦

Foreigner

f. 1976, New York, NY

Group / Album Rock, Arena Rock, Pop/Rock, Hard Rock

Foreigner was formed in 1976 by Mick Jones (ex-Spooky Tooth) and Ian McDonald (ex-King Crimson). The band was an instant success with the release of their debut album in 1977, which showcased the talents of guitarist Jones and lead singer Lou Gramm. Jones and Gramm also wrote most of the band's material. The songs, mainly hard rock, boasted strong melodies and memorable guitar riffs. The band never strayed far from this formula but, to keep things fresh, added some interesting touches. For example, Junior Walker's sax on "Urgent" and the gospel vocals of Jennifer Holliday and the New Jersey Mass Choir on "I Want to Know What Love Is" helped elevate these songs above the ordinary. Gramm left the band in the late '80s for a solo career. Foreigner recruited a new lead singer but Gramm's writing and distinctive vocals are sorely missed. *—Kenneth M. Cassidy*

The Very Best . . . and Beyond / Sep. 22, 1992 / Atlantic ✦✦✦✦

Very Best . . . and Beyond not only collects all the major hits from Foreigner's early years ("Feels Like the First Time," "Head Games," "Hot Blooded"), but also features their hits from the late '80s ("I Want to Know What Love Is," "Say You Will"), making the set preferable to *Records.* *—Stephen Thomas Erlewine*

● **Jukebox Heroes: The Foreigner Anthology** / Aug. 15, 2000 / Rhino ✦✦✦✦✦

It's easy to say that Rhino's *Jukebox Heroes: The Foreigner Anthology* is the definitive Foreigner retrospective, simply because there's so much music here: 39 tracks over the course of two discs, including all the hits, the bulk of notable album tracks, solo cuts from Lou Gramm and Mick Jones, plus two tracks from Jones-era Spooky Tooth. Clearly, that does amount to a clearly comprehensive collection, but the question is, is this a clear-cut choice for most fans— Well, it all depends on a listener's needs. This will be too much Foreigner if you're just looking for nothing but hits, especially since the classic era (roughly defined as pre-*Agent Provocateur*) stops at the end of the first disc. But, anyone that truly enjoys Foreigner's big, glossy arena rock will find that this doesn't test their patience, even if it runs out of steam toward the end of the collection. *Anthology* keeps interest because of canny selection and sequencing. The addition of Gramm and Jones songs on the second disc works wonders, since it not only strengthens its value for consumers—it's terrific to be able to have all Foreigner and Foreigner-related songs in one place, especially since Gramm's peerless "Midnight Blue" is not just the best thing here, it's the last great single of the album-rock era—it accelerates the pace and keeps things interesting just as the band's output gets a little patchy. So, *Anthology* winds up more consistently entertaining than skeptics could have imagined. It still may not convert those skeptics, but it will prove to the listener with the curiosity to delve deeper than the hits that it's worth doing so. *—Stephen Thomas Erlewine*

The Four Seasons

f. 1961, Newark, NJ
Group / Pop

Although they were one of the very biggest rock & roll groups of the 1960s, the Four Seasons—unlike, say, the Beatles, Rolling Stones, or the Byrds—don't excite virtually automatic respect from listeners and critics. A big factor is their most distinguishing trademark, the shrill falsetto vocals of their lead singer, Frankie Valli. Many also find their material—gently moralistic, romantic tunes with tightly arranged group harmonies that updated doo wop ethos into the 1960s—too cornball and clean-cut. Whatever your feelings about the group, though, there's no denying their considerable importance. No other White American group of the time save the Beach Boys boasted such intricate harmonies, though the Four Seasons were much more firmly in the Italian-American doo wop tradition. Their uptown production values were contemporary and, in certain respects, innovative. The R&B influence in their music was large, and some of their early singles enjoyed success with the R&B audience; in fact, some listeners thought that the Four Seasons were Black when the group landed their first hits. And they were immensely successful, making the Top 10 thirteen times between 1962 and 1967 with hits like "Sherry," "Big Girls Don't Cry," "Dawn," "Rag Doll," and "Let's Hang On." *—Richie Unterberger*

25th Anniversary Collection / 1987 / Rhino ✦✦✦✦✦
This three-CD set is a reminder of just how rich and diverse the work of Frankie Valli and the Four Seasons was, beyond their ubiquitous chart hits. Those songs have been available from various labels over the years, but this collection is the best available look at the true range of their work, covering their history (and Valli's solo career) from 1962 through 1978 beyond the hits, including good B-sides and oft-overlooked album tracks. The group had a lot to offer on repertory beyond the Bob Gaudio-Bob Crewe originals through which they became famous. The 36 songs on disc one and two, covering the years 1962-1967, illustrate precisely how the quartet's sound evolved, and the complexity that it achieved. Moreover, the presence of these sides makes this collection far more interesting and exciting than just another compilation of hits by the group. The presence of cuts such as their parody of Bob Dylan's "Don't Think Twice, It's Alright" (credited to "The Wonder Who") and tracks off of the controversial *Genuine Imitation of Life Gazette* album makes this a truly ambitious effort. Valli's solo sides, including "The Sun Ain't Gonna Shine Anymore," are certain to add to the appeal of this disc. One comes away with far greater admiration for the group and, if anything, a desire to hear more of their work. Although this set was produced in the middle to late '80s, the production and engineering holds up surprisingly well, even in the wake of the huge advances in digital audio technology in the years since. This still may be more appropriate as a holiday gift than a casual purchase, but this set holds up remarkably well, and it will offer even the casual listener a range of delightful surprises. *—Bruce Eder*

★ **Anthology** / 1988 / Rhino ✦✦✦✦✦
Over the course of twenty tracks, *Anthology* covers all of The Four Seasons' essential hits, as well as Valli's solo "Can't Take My Eyes off You"; it's the definitive collection. *—Stephen Thomas Erlewine*

The Four Tops

f. 1956, Detroit, MI
Group / Pop-Soul, Motown, Soul

The Four Tops are the most stable, consistent, and dependable of the successful R&B/pop vocal acts to emerge from Motown Records in the 1960s. Unlike the Temptations, they have had no personnel changes; unlike the Supremes and the Miracles, their lead singer never felt the need to step out on his own. At the same time, the Four Tops personified the musical hybrid Motown sought—they had the grittiness of gospel and R&B, but they were smooth enough to appeal to pop audiences. Their first substantial hit came in 1964, one year after signing to Motown. "Baby, I Need Your Loving" set the pattern for a series of songs showcasing lead vocalist Levi Stubbs' emotive wail set against a solid harmony line. Need and longing would be the group's hallmarks on their biggest hits, the chart-toppers "I Can't Help Myself" and "Reach Out, I'll Be There." In 1967, the Four Tops' main songwriting and production team (Holland-Dozier-Holland) left Motown, though the group continued to pace the R&B charts with hits like "(It's the Way) Nature Planned It," before moving to Dunhill and later Casablanca for a steady series of moderate chart entries. The group recorded again for Motown during the mid-'80s, and remained a solid concert draw into the '90s. *—William Ruhlmann*

☆ **Anthology** / Jul. 1974 / Motown ✦✦✦✦✦
Until they get the deluxe box set CD treatment, this three-record/two-CD set qualifies as the ultimate Four Tops Motown statement. It includes all the landmark hits, plus good numbers from their final days at Motown in the 1970s (they did return in the mid-'80s), such as "Still Water" and "Just Seven Numbers." *—Ron Wynn*

The Best of the Four Tops (1972-1976) / Oct. 25, 1990 / MCA ✦✦✦✦✦
This collection covers their best Dunhill tracks from the 1970s, which did include two big hits in "Ain't No Woman (Like the One I Got)" and "Are You Man Enough." "Keeper of the Castle" was also a Top Ten R&B single, and it seemed as if the Four Tops were in stride again. The Dunhill period yielded two more Top Ten R&B smashes with "One Chain Don't Make No Prison" and "Midnight Flower," and is a much better period than some fans consider. *—Ron Wynn*

Until You Love Someone: More of the Best (1965-1970) / Feb. 16, 1993 / Rhino ✦✦✦✦
This compilation gathers 18 non-hit album tracks from eight LPs that the Four Tops cut for Motown between 1965 and 1970 (some of which appeared on B-sides). A major soul group they might have been, but the Tops' pinnacle was actually quite brief, and that's reflected in this collection. No less than two-thirds of the songs date from 1965 and 1966, six from 1965's *Second Album* alone. Not so coincidentally, all but one of those cuts were written by the legendary Holland/Dozier/Holland songwriting team. The production is faultless, the songs very characteristically HDH, and Levi Stubbs' lead vocals are unfailingly gritty and pleasurable. Yet none of these have the unforgettable hooks of their hit singles of the period like "Reach Out, I'll Be There" and "I Can't Help Myself." As enjoyable as the formula is, the uniformity of the sound limits this disc's appeal to serious Motown and soul collectors. Curiosities among the non-HDH cuts include little-known tunes by Smokey Robinson and Stevie Wonder, and a nonhit single from 1969, "What Is a Man." *—Richie Unterberger*

Keepers of the Castle: Their Best 1972-1978 / Jul. 29, 1997 / MCA ✦✦✦✦
When the Four Tops moved from Motown to Dunhill in the early '70s, they encountered the dilemma faced by most '60s soul giants, from Motown or elsewhere: how to update their sound while maintaining some degree of personality. Commercially at least, things got off to a smashing start with "Keeper of the Castle," "Ain't No Woman (Like the One I Got)," and "Are You Man Enough?" (all included here). Yet it was evident that the Four Tops, removed from the magic of '60s Motown, would be trend followers rather than pacesetters. Most of this 14-song compilation shows them as a competent but rather generic '70s soul vocal group, adding Philly soul and funk elements to their sound without asserting much of an identity. Even "Are You Man Enough?," as good as it is, is something of a son-of-"Back Stabbers"; "Ain't No Woman," similarly, could be easily mistaken for a Spinners cut by the unschooled. Save the occasional standout like "Love Music," not much else here measures up to the early Dunhill hits, though if you want one post-early-'70s Four Tops compilation, this is probably the best. *—Richie Unterberger*

★ **The Ultimate Collection** / Oct. 7, 1997 / Motown ✦✦✦✦✦
Featuring 25 tracks on a single disc, *The Ultimate Collection* nearly lives up to its billing, featuring all of the group's pop Top Ten hits for Motown, plus all but three of their Top Ten R&B hits. For most casual fans, this well-assembled compilation will be the definitive overview. *—Stephen Thomas Erlewine*

Lost and Found: Breaking Through / Sep. 28, 1999 / Uptown/Universal ✦✦✦
The Four Tops' early years as a jazz-vocal group are generally glossed over in capsule histories. Long before they signed to Motown—nearly a full decade as a matter of fact—they had been one of the popular Detroit jazz-vocal groups, earning the admiration of such luminaries as Smokey Robinson and Billy Eckstine, whom the group supported. After some persuasion, the group signed with Motown on the condition that they could record jazz. Over the course of a year, they cut nearly two albums' worth of material, which boiled down to one album, *Breaking Through*. Berry Gordy pulled the record at the last minute, believing that it would have been a commercial failure. Gordy's fears were not unfounded—indeed, had the album that comprises *Breaking Through (1963-1964)* been put out in 1964, it likely wouldn't have found much of an audience. Still, *Breaking Through* is a strong record, firmly within its tradition and working well on those terms. The Four Tops may not sound as distinctive singing jazz as they did with pop-soul, but they are convincing, as are the Motown house band. Neither of them take many chances, however. The songs are primarily standards, plus four new songs that feel like standards, all given good generic arrangements. This may sound like a dismissal, but it isn't; it's hard to do this kind of music right, but the group most certainly does. And it's not just one member that shines; everyone gets to take a lead, and the results are uniformly strong. Even so, *Breaking Through* appeals primarily to hardcore fans of the group, plus a handful of straight-ahead vocal-jazz aficionados. Reminiscent of a cross between Eckstine and the Four Freshmen, it's good stuff, but it's essentially a curiosity. *—Stephen Thomas Erlewine*

Peter Frampton

b. Apr. 22, 1950, Beckenham, Kent, England
Vocals, Guitar / Album Rock, Arena Rock, Pop/Rock

Before he shot to solo superstardom in the mid-'70s, guitarist Peter Frampton was a British teen idol in the late '60s thanks to his work with the Herd and looks worthy of being named "Face of 1968" in several British magazines. The following year, Frampton joined ex-Small Faces front man Steve Marriott in Humble Pie, remaining for two years before departing for a solo career. He recorded his solo debut *Wind of Change* in 1972; recorded at San Francisco's Winterland, 1976's double album *Frampton Comes Alive* was a staggering success, selling over six million copies and becoming the biggest-selling live rock album ever at that time. It showcased Frampton's mastery of the talk-box guitar effect and his penchant for in-concert theatrics, and produced three hit singles ("Show Me the Way," "Baby, I Love Your Way," and "Do You Feel Like We Do"). The follow-up LP, *I'm in You*, produced Frampton's biggest hit in the title track, but his career was temporarily put on hold by a near-fatal car crash in the Bahamas in 1978. Personal problems halted a full-scale comeback following Frampton's recovery; he recorded sporadically throughout the '80s, but none of these efforts caught fire with the public. *—Steve Huey*

Wind of Change / 1972 / A&M ✦✦✦✦✦
Peter Frampton's solo debut after leaving Humble Pie (as they stood on the brink of stardom) spotlights Frampton's well-crafted, though lyrically lightweight, songwriting and his fine guitar playing. The songs on *Wind of Change* are built primarily around acoustic guitar foundations, but "It's a Plain Shame" and "All I Want to Be (Is by Your Side)" sound like they could have been lifted off Humble Pie's *Rock On.* The sound is crisp, the melodies catchy, and Frampton's distinctive, elliptical Gibson Les Paul guitar leads soar throughout. A comparison between this album and Humble Pie's post-Frampton turn to generic boogie-rock shows why Frampton left that group. Although Humble Pie's *Smokin'* was much more successful, hitting the Top Ten in the spring of 1972, *Wind of Change* was far superior musically. With its mix of ballads and upbeat numbers with just enough of a rock edge, *Wind of Change* showed Frampton at his creative peak. The band here includes Ringo Starr, Billy Preston, and Klaus Voorman. *—Jim Newsom*

Frampton's Camel / 1973 / A&M ✦✦✦✦✦
Named after Frampton's touring band at the time, *Frampton's Camel* has a harder-rocking feel than its predecessor *Wind of Change,* with Mick Gallagher's percussive electric piano and organ taking a prominent position in the mix and Frampton getting a harder sound from his electric guitars (though his acoustic playing is so lush and lyrical that it dominates the album here and there in its quiet way). The sound on this recording lays out the formula that Frampton would take to mega-success three years later with the release of *Frampton Comes Alive.* The songs are all first-rate or close to it—included here is the original studio version of the group composition "Do You Feel Like We Do," a quicker-tempo, extended (albeit less majestic) version of which appeared on the latter album and became a staple of classic-rock radio, but the Frampton-composed "I Got My Eyes on You" and "Don't Fade Away" and the Frampton-Gallagher "All Night Long" are also compelling examples of '70s hard rock at its commercial best. This album also includes a nice cover of Stevie Wonder's "I Believe (When I Fall in Love With You It Will Be Forever)," the power ballad "Lines on My Face," the rollicking "White Sugar," and Frampton's gorgeously lyrical, all acoustic "Just the Time of the Year." As on *Wind of Change,* Frampton's use of dynamics and mix of acoustic and electric guitars keeps the music from becoming one-dimensional. The October 2000 CD reissue, remastered in state-of-the-art sound, adds an even more expansive feel to this album and enhances its melodic richness. *—Jim Newsom & Bruce Eder*

Frampton / 1974 / A&M ✦✦✦✦

Something's Happening / 1974 / A&M ✦✦✦

Frampton Comes Alive / 1976 / A&M ✦✦✦✦✦
In the 1980s and '90s, many artists (especially in R&B and urban contemporary) have been so reliant on technology that they their live shows pale in comparison to their studio recordings. But in the '70s, the opposite was sometimes true. Compared to *Frampton Comes Alive*—the best-selling live album ever—Peter Frampton's studio efforts sound downright tame. The Humble Pie graduate packed one hell of a punch onstage—where he was obviously the most comfortable—and in fact, the live versions of "Show Me the Way," "Do You Feel like I Do," "Something's Happening," "Shine On" and other album-rock staples are much more inspired, confident and hard-hitting than the studio versions. Commercially as well as artistically, this package (a two-LP set that later became a two-CD set) was undeniably Frampton's crowning achievement. Period. *—Alex Henderson*

I'm in You / 1977 / A&M ✦✦✦✦
It was almost inevitable that *I'm in You* would be thought of as a let down no matter now good it was. Following up to one of the biggest selling albums of the decade, Peter Frampton faced a virtually impossible task, made even more difficult by the fact that in the two years since he'd cut any new material, he had evolved musically away from some of the sounds on *Frampton Comes Alive.* The result was mostly a surprisingly laid-back album steeped in lyricism and craftsmanship, particularly in its use of multiple overdubs even on the harder rocking numbers. From the opening bars of "I'm in You," dominated by the sound of the piano (played by Frampton) and an ARP synthesizer-generated string section, rather than a guitar, it was clear that Frampton was exploring new sides of his music. Cuts like "Won't You Be My Friend," a piece of white funk that might've been better at six minutes running time, seemed to be dangerously close to self-indulgence at eight minutes long. The high points also include the title track, "Don't Have to Worry," and a killer cover of Stevie Wonder's "Signed, Sealed Delivered (I'm Yours)"; a couple of solid rock numbers, "Tried to Love" and the crunching "(I'm A) Roadrunner" also work their way in here to pump up the tension and excitement. *I'm in You* was successful on its own terms, and had Frampton recorded it before the live album, it would probably be very fondly looked back on. As it was, many listeners were not impressed. The spring 2000 reissue in 20-bit audio recreates the original album artwork and notes and is the best way to appreciate the multi-layered sound (and the crunchier rock moments) on this album. *—Bruce Eder*

Shine On: A Collection / Oct. 20, 1992 / A&M ✦✦✦✦✦

Peter Frampton / Jan. 25, 1994 / Sony Legacy ✦✦

● **Greatest Hits** / Jun. 18, 1996 / A&M ✦✦✦✦✦
By compiling all of Peter Frampton's biggest hits—in their hit versions, so "Show Me the Way" and "Baby, I Love Your Way" are from *Frampton Comes Alive,* not the studio albums—onto one disc, *Greatest Hits* functions as the definitive retrospective on the guitarist. It has a better selection than the single disc *Classics, Vol. 12,* and it is more concise and listenable than the double-disc box *Shine On: A Collection,* which means it's the only collection that provides an effective, manageable overview of Frampton. *—Stephen Thomas Erlewine*

Connie Francis

b. Dec. 12, 1938, Newark, NJ
Vocals / Brill Building Pop, Pop
Considered the leading pop female singer of her era, Connie Francis usually sang of her latest broken heart with a teardrop in her voice. The Newark, NJ, native started performing as a child, signing with MGM Records in 1955, but she suffered two years of bombs before the torch ballad "Who's Sorry Now" shot up the charts in 1958. Although she specialized in sobbing tales of woe, Francis proved she could rock with Neil Sedaka's "Stupid Cupid" in 1958 and "Lipstick on Your Collar" the next year. Francis scored two number one hits in 1960—the twangy "Everybody's Somebody's Fool" and "My Heart Has a Mind of Its Own," and she branched into acting with a starring role in *Where the Boys Are,* the archetypal spring-break movie. "Don't Break the Heart That Loves You" was Francis' last pop chart-topper in 1962, but she continued to rank high in the pop pantheon throughout the decade, with forays into ethnic and country idioms. *—Bill Dahl*

● **The Very Best of Connie Francis** / Oct. 1963 / Polydor ✦✦✦✦✦
Though many best-of's exist on the market, this one leans more heavily toward her earlier rock & roll hits. (Originally released in October 1963 as a 15-track LP by MGM Records, *The Very Best of Connie Francis* was reissued in 1986 on CD with six bonus tracks by Polydor Records.) *—Cub Koda*

White Sox, Pink Lipstick . . . & Stupid Cupid / Jul. 1993 / Bear Family ✦✦✦✦✦
Anyone who thinks they appreciate Connie Francis probably doesn't know half of what she could do as a singer—this five-CD box will set them straight. The revelation of Disc One lies in the fact that the three included demos and the other "failures" from her early career are all worthwhile, even inspired recordings. Francis had a superb voice, richly emotive and evocative, with an alluringly delicate enunciation when she wanted it. Listening to these sides today, one hears an extraordinary talent that was ignored until "Who's Sorry Now." After that, things really get going, because Francis was working under a contract that nobody—not even Frank Sinatra—had: the right to choose her own material. Disc Two picks up her career after the explosive success of "Who's Sorry Now"; these are more confident performances, and reveal Francis as not only a dazzlingly talented singer but an excellent judge of songs and arrangements. Disc Three showcases Francis's efforts in the long-player market, where she was really aiming her best work. The outstanding material here is the product of her Feb. 1959 New York sessions and the sessions a month later at Abbey Road in London; here she's starting to sound like a female analog to Sinatra, just when Sinatra was at his coolest and swinging-est. But at this point, it was the rock & roll singles that were moving, and she cut a whole album of standards in that genre, represented on Disc Four; also featured are her country sides. Disc Five is mostly made up of unissued tracks and various alternate takes. They're all first-rate, and a few should have been hits and could have redefined her career. The lavish booklet and the detailed notes and sessionography cap this reissue, which puts Polygram's efforts with Francis to shame. *—Bruce Eder*

Kissin', Twistin', Goin' Where the Boys Are / Apr. 16, 1996 / Bear Family ✦✦✦✦✦
Five more CDs of Connie Francis, picking up right where Bear Family's earlier *White Sox, Pink Lipstick* set left off, in 1960—although its 300+ minutes of music only cover the period of 1960 to 1962. By this time, Connie Francis was established as one of the top female vocal talents of her generation, and she was ready to experiment—we hear her successful move into country music, wonderful outtakes, and never-issued songs from her early-'60s sessions. Disc One has more highlights than most greatest-hits albums, notable among them a pair of unissued "Swinging Medley" tracks, and tracks from the most daring of all of her albums, *Songs to a Swinging Band.* Disc Two includes the rest of the *Swinging Band* album and also highlights her first Nashville folk-style sessions with the Jordanaires. Disc Three is devoted to the rest of Francis's Nashville sessions, including her outstanding covers of movie theme songs (one of her top-selling albums) and the folk-type songs with the Jordanaires. Disc Four is given over to her recordings of Irish songs and, more significantly, Francis's 1962 *Twist* album, including the first release of the risqué-sounding "Lovey Dovey Twist." Disc Five features more of her Irish songs, as well as a number of hit singles, but the highlight is the previously "lost" original recordings from Francis' April 1962 sessions in Rome, which were believed lost when the accompaniments from those sessions were wiped and replaced by new orchestrations. This set is a major investment of time and attention, but it is rewarding—Francis is one of those performers who seems hardly ever to have recorded anything second-rate. The booklet is lively, entertaining, and lavishly illustrated. *—Bruce Eder*

Frankie Goes to Hollywood

f. 1980, Liverpool, England, **db.** 1987
Group / Club/Dance, New Wave, Dance-Pop
Mixing slick dance-pop and a savvy publicity campaign, Liverpool's Frankie Goes To Hollywood dominated British music in 1984. Their music was a glossy version of hi-NRG, but the group's marketing—which included slogans, T-shirts, and homoerotic videos—created controversy in England and some buzz in the US. But their popularity was fleeting: the group's audience disappeared by the release of their second album.

Ex-Big in Japan vocalist Holly Johnson, vocalist Paul Rutherford, guitarist Nasher Nash, bassist Mark O'Toole, and drummer Peter Gill formed the band in 1980. Originally called Hollycaust, they switched to Frankie Goes to Hollywood—an old headline about Frank Sinatra's acting career—by the year's end. In 1982 they appeared on the British television program "The Tube" with a rough version of the video for "Relax"—a driving dance number with suggestive lyrics—which won them a deal with producer Trevor Horn's ZTT label. He also produced most of their material, including their 1983 debut single "Relax"/"Ferry Cross the Mersey."

Frankie's publicity director Paul Morley promoted the single with T-shirts that read "Relax" and "Frankie Says . . . ," and emphasized the band's stylish, homosexual imagery in their video for "Relax." British TV banned it and a new version was shot, but Radio 1 and the rest of BBC's radio and television networks banned the single; it shot to number one in early 1984, selling over a million copies. Frankie's double-album debut *Welcome to the Pleasuredome* and the singles "Two Tribes," and "The Power of Love" also topped the charts that year. Gradually, Frankie-mania reached the States: "Relax" hit number 67 and "Two Tribes" grazed the Top 40 in 1984; *Pleasuredome* reached number 33 in 1985 and "Relax" was re-released, making the American Top Ten.

1986's single "Rage Hard" peaked at number four in the UK and the second album *Liverpool* reached number five. The band began their final tour in early 1987 and broke up that spring. After legal battles with ZTT, Johnson pursued a solo career, as did Rutherford. Johnson retired from music after he was diagnosed with AIDS in the early '90s. *—Stephen Thomas Erlewine*

Welcome to the Pleasuredome / 1984 / ZTT/Island ♦♦♦♦♦
Upbeat British dance music with melodramatic vocals and lyrics that are sexually and politically provocative. The sound of Frankie Goes to Hollywood swept Britain in the years 1983-1985. Here is the wide-screen debut double album, containing the hits "Relax," "Two Tribes," "The Power of Love," and the title track. *—William Ruhlmann*

Liverpool / 1986 / ZTT/Island ♦♦♦

● **Bang! . . . The Greatest Hits of Frankie Goes to Hollywood** / Mar. 22, 1994 / Uptown/Universal ♦♦♦♦♦
Frankie Goes to Hollywood hyped their debut album *Welcome to the Pleasuredome* so much that when their second record, *Liverpool,* failed to live up to expectations, their career was effectively over. That didn't stop them from releasing greatest-hits albums, however, nor did it stop the inevitable wave of '80s nostalgia that surged forth in the '90s. To cash in on whatever meager Frankie nostalgia that may have existed, *Bang!. . . Greatest Hits of Frankie Goes to Hollywood* appeared in 1994 and was reissued in 1998, when the rights shifted to Universal Records. *Bang!* is as good a compilation of Frankie's material as could be assembled, featuring no less than eight songs from *Pleasuredome* (including, of course, "Relax," "Two Tribes," "The World is My Oyster," and "Bang") and five songs from *Liverpool.* There were a couple of good songs stranded on the second album ("Ferry Cross the Mersey," "Rage Hard") and certain casual fans may enjoy having those singles on the same disc with the hits, but the fact remains that Frankie can only truly be understood (and, to a certain extent, truly enjoyed) on *Pleasuredome.* That debut stood on its own, sounding unlike any other record of its time, and it contained all of the big hits in the first place. Consequently, many casual listeners will be satisfied with simply acquiring that record, even if the album versions were slightly different than the singles. If they feel otherwise, *Bang!* will serve as the definitive singles collection, satisfying both the hardcore and casual fan. *—Stephen Thomas Erlewine*

Aretha Franklin

b. Mar. 25, 1942, Memphis, TN
Vocals, Piano / Deep Soul, Southern Soul, Quiet Storm, Black Gospel, Urban, R&B, Soul
Aretha Franklin is one of the giants of soul music, and indeed of American pop as a whole. More than any other performer, she epitomized soul at its most gospel-charged. Her astonishing run of late-'60s hits with Atlantic Records—"Respect," "I Never Loved a Man," "Chain of Fools," "Baby I Love You," "I Say a Little Prayer," "Think," "The House That Jack Built," and several others—earned her the title "Lady Soul," which she has worn uncontested ever since. Yet as much of an international institution as she's become, much of her work—outside of her recordings for Atlantic in the late '60s and early '70s—is erratic and only fitfully inspired, making discretion a necessity when collecting her records. When Franklin left Columbia for Atlantic, producer Jerry Wexler was determined to bring out her most soulful, fiery traits. As part of that plan, he had her record her first single, "I Never Loved a Man (The Way I Love You)," at Muscle Shoals in Alabama with esteemed Southern R&B musicians. The combination was one of those magic instances of musical alchemy in pop: the backup musicians provided a much grittier, soulful, and R&B-based accompaniment for Aretha's voice, which soared with a passion and intensity suggesting a spirit that had been allowed to fly loose for the first time.

In the late '60s, Franklin became one of the biggest international recording stars in all of pop. Many also saw Franklin as a symbol of Black America itself, reflecting the increased confidence and pride of African-Americans in the decade of the civil rights movements and other triumphs for he Black community. Franklin was able to maintain creative momentum, in part, because of her eclectic choice of material. Franklin's commercial and artistic success was unabated in the early '70s, during which she landed more huge hits with "Spanish Harlem," "Bridge Over Troubled Water," and "Day Dreaming." Critically, as is the case with many '60s rock legends, there have been mixed responses to her later work. In the meantime, despite her lukewarm recent sales record, she's an institution, assured of the ability to draw live audiences and immense respect for the rest of her lifetime, regardless of whether there are any more triumphs on record in store. *—Richie Unterberger*

Aretha Arrives / 1967 / Rhino ♦♦♦
Recorded in 1967 after the first flush of back-to-back successes with "Respect" and "I Never Loved a Man," this captures Aretha Franklin in peak form. Lady Soul provides her own piano accompaniment on the majority of tracks here, and the core band is the same one that provided the fire on her previous album. The tunes are an eclectic batch, and while "Baby, I Love You" was the hit of the album, Franklin turns in strong versions of "Satisfaction," "You Are My Sunshine," "Night Life," "Ain't Nobody (Gonna Turn Me Around)," and a quirky cover of "96 Tears" for good measure. An essential addition to her discography. *—Cub Koda*

☆ **I Never Loved a Man (The Way I Love You)** / 1967 / Rhino ♦♦♦♦♦
While the inclusion of "Respect"—one of the truly seminal singles in pop history—is in and of itself sufficient to earn *I Never Loved a Man (The Way I Love You)* classic status, Aretha's Atlantic label debut is an indisputable masterpiece from start to finish. Much of the credit is due producer Jerry Wexler, who finally unleashed the soulful intensity so long kept under wraps during her Columbia tenure; assembling a crack Muscle Shoals backing band along with an abundance of impeccable material, Wexler creates the ideal setting to allow Aretha to ascend to the throne of Queen of Soul, and she responds with the strongest performances of her career. While the brilliant title track remains the album's other best-known song, each cut on *I Never Loved a Man* is touched by greatness; covers of Ray Charles' "Drown in My Own Tears" and Sam Cooke's "Good Times" and "A Change Is Gonna Come" are on par with the original recordings, while Aretha's own contributions—"Don't Let Me Lose This Dream," "Baby Baby Baby," "Save Me" and "Dr. Feelgood (Love Is a Serious Business)"—are perfectly at home in such lofty company. A soul landmark. *—Jason Ankeny*

Aretha in Paris / 1968 / Rhino ♦♦♦

Aretha Now / 1968 / Rhino ♦♦♦♦♦
Though a bit short on running time at ten songs, this still caught Franklin at the peak of her early form. "Think," "I Say a Little Prayer," "See Saw," and "I Can't See Myself Leaving You" were all big hits. Her choice of cover material included some of her most R&B-drenched early Atlantic cuts, like "Night Time Is the Right Time," "You Send Me," and "I Take What I Want." *—Richie Unterberger*

☆ **Lady Soul** / 1968 / Rhino ♦♦♦♦♦
Great personnel again—King Curtis, Bobby Womack, Frank Wess, and others, including a guest spot by Eric Clapton. Several classic songs, including the lesser-known "Ain't No Way" by Carolyn Franklin and the hits "Chain of Fools" and "Natural Woman." *—George Bedard*

Soul '69 / 1969 / Rhino ♦♦♦♦♦
One of her most overlooked '60s albums, on which she presented some of her jazziest material, despite the title. None of these cuts were significant hits, and none were Aretha originals; she displayed her characteristically eclectic taste in the choice of cover material, handling compositions by Percy Mayfield, Sam Cooke, Smokey Robinson, and, at the most pop-oriented end of her spectrum, John Hartford's "Gentle On My Mind" and Bob Lind's "Elusive Butterfly." Her vocals are consistently passionate and first-rate, though, as is the musicianship; besides contributions from The Muscle Shoals rhythm section, session players include respected jazzmen Kenny Burrell, Ron Carter, Grady Tate, David Newman, and Joe Zawinul. *—Richie Unterberger*

Spirit in the Dark / 1970 / Rhino ♦♦♦♦♦
Spirit in the Dark was one of Aretha Franklin's more overlooked albums from her Atlantic prime, despite the inclusion of a couple hit singles (the title track and "Don't Play That Song"). The disc includes five of her own compositions (the most she ever recorded for a single album) and her usual eclectic choice of cover material. On this record, the covers ranged from B.B. King and Dr. John to Jimmy Reed and Goffin/King's "Oh Not My Baby." The album also benefits from great backup players: Both the Muscle Shoals rhythm section and the Dixie Flyers contributed to the sessions, and Duane Allman lends his guitar to a couple of tracks. Though it doesn't rank with her very best Atlantic LPs, it's an exuberant and remarkably consistent effort. The 1993 CD reissue has detailed liner notes on the songs and sessions by David Nathan. *—Richie Unterberger*

This Girl's in Love with You / 1970 / Rhino ♦♦♦
The title song (a cover of Herb Alpert's "This Guy's In Love With You") might lead you to believe this is one of Aretha's more pop-oriented albums, but in fact, this is the only song of the sort on this solid and fairly earthy effort. Besides the hit singles "Call Me" and "Share Your Love With Me," it also includes her most well-known Beatle covers ("Eleanor Rigby" and "Let It Be"), and her interesting version of "The Weight," a Top 20 single featuring slide guitar by Duane Allman. *—Richie Unterberger*

Aretha Live at Fillmore West / 1971 / Rhino ♦♦♦

Young, Gifted & Black / 1971 / Rhino ♦♦♦♦♦

Amazing Grace / 1972 / Atlantic ♦♦♦♦♦
Aretha Franklin disproved the notion that once you leave the church, you can't go back. She returned in triumph on this 1972 double album, making what might be her greatest release ever in any style. Her voice was chilling, making it seem as if God and the angels were conducting a service alongside Franklin, Rev. James Cleveland, the Southern California Community Choir and everyone else in attendance. Her versions of "How I Got Over" and "You've Got a Friend" are legendary. *—Ron Wynn*

Hey Now Hey (The Other Side of the Sky) / 1973 / Rhino ♦♦♦

Let Me in Your Life / 1974 / Rhino ♦♦♦

With Everything I Feel in Me / 1974 / Atlantic ♦♦♦
This respectable but not earth-shattering release was part of the gradual decline of Franklin's artistic and commercial achievements at Atlantic. The lead-off track, "Without Love," was a Top Ten R&B hit, and the title track, written by Franklin, was Top 20 R&B. There were a couple of familiar but completely rearranged Burt Bacharach tunes and a contribution from Stevie Wonder. Franklin was in good voice, and the studio band was accomplished, but this was all a far cry from the standard Franklin had set in the late '60s. It was also a far cry from the sales she enjoyed then: This was her first new album since her 1967 breakthrough to peak below the Top 30. *—William Ruhlmann*

You / 1975 / Atlantic ♦♦

Sparkle / 1976 / Rhino ♦♦♦♦
Aretha Franklin's career was in a down period in the mid-'70s when she collaborated with Curtis Mayfield to sing his compositions for the film *Sparkle.* The film proved a non-event, but for Franklin it marked a return to glory. Once again she was the Queen of Soul, doing the chilling, spectacular leaps, cries, whoops and shouts that defined secularized gospel in the late '60s. The title cut was a sizable hit, while "Giving Him Something He Can Feel" became an anthem. Mayfield's lyrics and production shouldn't be overlooked; he added just the right amount of background trappings, and the Kitty Haywood Singers provided Franklin's best continuing backgrounds since the Sweet Inspirations. *—Ron Wynn*

Jump to It / 1982 / Arista ♦♦♦

Get It Right / 1983 / Arista ♦♦♦

Who's Zoomin' Who— / 1985 / Arista ♦♦♦

★ **30 Greatest Hits** / 1986 / Atlantic ♦♦♦♦♦
The double-disc set *30 Greatest Hits* contains all of Aretha Franklin's greatest hits from the '60s and early '70s, from 1967's "I've Never Loved a Man (The Way I Love You)" and "Respect"

to 1973's "Until You Come Back to Me (That's What I'm Gonna Do)." It's an essential, comprehensive collection—the ideal purchase for fans that want more than just the biggest hits, but don't want to invest in the box set. *—Stephen Thomas Erlewine*

Jazz to Soul / Jul. 14, 1992 / Columbia ✦✦✦
She's Billie Holiday. No, she's Ella Fitzgerald. No, wait, she's Dinah Washington. The conventional wisdom on Aretha Franklin's tenure at Columbia Records is that the label didn't know what to do with her, and that may be true, but you can't say they didn't try. On these 39 recordings, spread across two discs and cut between 1960 and 1965, Franklin and her producers look for ways to frame her obvious vocal talents, but always in terms of uptown jazz and non-rock-pop formats. Much of the result is appealing, and it's only in light of the transcendent soul music Franklin made from her first day at Atlantic Records in 1967 that this work comes across as merely exploratory. "Show me the way to get to Soulville," she demands in 1964. She finally found the way, and that was that. *—William Ruhlmann*

☆ **Queen of Soul: The Atlantic Recordings** / 1993 / Rhino ✦✦✦✦✦
The Queen of Soul: The Atlantic Recordings is an 86-track, four-disc box set that covers Aretha Franklin's Atlantic career, spanning from 1967's "I Never Loved A Man (The Way I Love You)" to 1976's "Something He Can Feel." Over the course of the set, all of Aretha's best-known songs, including all of her Top 10 pop and R&B singles, are included. For fans that only know the singles, the set is primarily notable for the wealth of album tracks and forgotten singles that are included, which nearly equal the hits in terms of quality. Stopping just short of her move to disco, *The Queen of Soul* just misses being a totally comprehensive collection, but it remains definitive—it may miss some of her later hits, but every one of her greatest tracks is on the box. *The Queen of Soul* is one the cornerstones of any soul collection. *—Stephen Thomas Erlewine*

Greatest Hits (1980-1994) / Feb. 22, 1994 / Arista ✦✦✦
Greatest Hits (1980-1994) rounds up the biggest hits from the latter part of Aretha Franklin's career, including "Jump to It," "Freeway of Love," "Who's Zoomin' Who," and "I Knew You Were Waiting (For Me)," a duet with George Michael. The album does a good job of selecting the highlights from a slightly uneven era for Aretha. *—Stephen Thomas Erlewine*

The Very Best of Aretha Franklin, Vol. 1 / Mar. 22, 1994 / Rhino ✦✦✦✦✦
30 Greatest Hits is still the preferred essential document for the Atlantic years, but this is certainly an excellent 16-track primer of her most popular late-'60s tracks. Most of them are also on *30 Greatest Hits.* But if you've got a particular yen for Aretha's early Atlantic period (which was also her very best), you'll find all the biggest smashes from that era here, including "Respect," "Chain of Fools," "Think," "The House That Jack Built," "Baby I Love You," "I Never Loved a Man," and so forth. *—Richie Unterberger*

The Very Best of Aretha Franklin, Vol. 2 / Mar. 22, 1994 / Rhino ✦✦✦✦✦
Covering 1970-76, this isn't quite as top-notch as *The Very Best of, Vol. 1.* And, like *Very Best of, Vol. 1,* much of this is also found on the more comprehensive *30 Greatest Hits* (although some of it is not). Still, it contains the prime stuff from the first half of the '70s, including "Spanish Harlem," "Don't Play That Song," "Bridge Over Troubled Water," and "Until You Come Back to Me," along with less-traveled items like "Oh Me Oh My" and "Brand New Me." *—Richie Unterberger*

The Delta Meets Detroit: Aretha's Blues / Jan. 13, 1998 / Rhino ✦✦✦
The Delta Meets Detroit: Aretha's Blues is one of the few non-hits compilations that makes sense. Selecting 16 tracks from her Atlantic recordings, the disc spotlights Aretha at her bluesiest—there are no hits here, but there's also no shortage of remarkable songs here, as "Today I Sing the Blues," "Night Life," "Night Time is the Right Time," "Good to Me As I Am to You," "Going Down Slow," "Drown in My Own Tears" and "Dr. Feelgood (Love Is a Serious Business)" rank among her grittiest performances. If you're only familiar with the hits, this is an excellent way to dig deeper into her catalog, and if you already have this material on their original albums, *The Delta Meets Detroit* actually offers some revelations you may not have expected. *—Stephen Thomas Erlewine*

A Rose Is Still a Rose / Mar. 10, 1998 / Arista ✦✦✦✦

Amazing Grace: The Complete Recordings / May 4, 1999 / Rhino ✦✦✦✦✦
Among Aretha aficionados, *Amazing Grace* has long been considered one of her high-watermarks, since it captured her glorious return to her gospel roots in front of a live audience. The original 1972 album contained just 14 tracks, culled from two live performances with the Southern California Community Choir, Ken Lupper, and the Rev. James Cleveland at the *New Temple Missionary Baptist Church* in Los Angeles. Fans have long wished for the release of the two complete concerts—which is exactly what Rhino's *Amazing Grace: The Complete Recordings* gives them. Over the course of two discs and 29 tracks, every performance Franklin gave that January, along with comments from Cleveland and solo tracks from Lupper and the Choir, is unfurled, and if anything, the music is even more impressive when heard complete and unedited. Of course, the nature of this set makes it of interest primarily to dedicated fans, but they'll likely be delighted by the entire package. *—Stephen Thomas Erlewine*

Free

f. 1968, London, England, **db.** 1973
Group / Album Rock, Hard Rock, Blues-Rock
Famed for their perennial "All Right Now," Free helped lay the foundations for the rise of hard rock, stripping the earthy sound of British blues down to its raw, minimalist core to pioneer a brand of proto-metal later popularized by 1970s superstars like Foreigner, Foghat and Bad Company. Although both of their first two albums fared poorly on the charts, 1970's *Fire and Water* became a tremendous hit on the strength of the primal "All Right Now," a Top Five smash powered by frontman Paul Rodgers' gritty, visceral vocals. After headlining 1970's Isle of Wight festival, the group appeared destined for superstardom, but the LP *Highway* did not fare nearly as well as anticipated, and after a grueling tour which yielded 1971's *Free Live,* the band dissolved amidst ego clashes and recriminations. The original lineup of Free re-formed to record 1972's *Free at Last,* which launched the hit "Little Bit of Love." However, drug problems nagged the group, and soon they disbanded again, this time for good; Rodgers and drummer Simon Kirke went on to found Bad Company. *—Jason Ankeny*

● **The Best of Free** / 1973 / A&M ✦✦✦✦✦
A solid compilation showcasing "All Right Now" and other semi-hits, this is a worthwhile sampler for the uninitiated. *—Dan Heilman*

● **Molten Gold: The Anthology** / Oct. 5, 1993 / A&M ✦✦✦✦✦
With their big riffs and bluesy melodies, Free virtually defined hard rock in the early '70s, and *Molten Gold: The Anthology* shows that this wasn't such a meager achievement. Throughout the two discs, it becomes clear that the key to Free's rock & roll was their rhythm section, which powered their riffs to perfection. This is the definitive Free, two discs of pure hard rock. *—Stephen Thomas Erlewine*

Fugazi

f. 1988, Washington, DC
Drums, Bass (Electric), Piano, Guitar / Emo, Indie Rock, Post-Punk, Hardcore Punk, Alternative Pop/Rock
If history is kind to Fugazi, their records won't be overshadowed by their reputation and methods of operation. Instead of being known for their community activism, five-dollar shows, ten-dollar CDs, resistance to mainstream outlets, and the laughably fictitious folklore surrounding their lifestyle, they will instead be identified as setting a high bar for artistic excellence that is frequently aimed for but seldom achieved with great frequency. During their existence, the four piece created some of the most intelligent, invigorating, and undeniably *musical* post-hardcore rock & roll. Along with their stridently underground ethics—which were more out of pragmatism and modesty than anything else—they gained an extremely loyal and numerous global following. More than anything, Fugazi inspired; they showed that art can prevail over commerce.

Drummer Brendan Canty, bassist Joe Lally, and guitarists/vocalists Ian MacKaye and Guy Picciotto formed the band in 1987, debuting on vinyl with two EPs recorded during 1988-89 (later coupled on CD as *13 Songs*). Their full-length debut, 1990's *Repeater,* was generally regarded as a classic, though it suffered slightly from lyrical shortcomings. Released in 1991, *Steady Diet of Nothing* branched out lyrically and limited the finger pointing, with more imaginative arrangements and less visceral qualities. Two years passed until *In on the Killtaker,* the band's most abrasively black-and-white record. As Fugazi's recordings and tours became more sporadic, *Red Medicine* was released another two years after *In on the Killtaker,* chipping away some of the latter's abrasion in favor of more jam-oriented experiments. The even wilder *End Hits* came in 1998, amidst rumors of the band being put to rest. One year later, the *Instrument* video and soundtrack hit the shelves. *—Andy Kellman*

★ **13 Songs** / Apr. 1990 / Dischord ✦✦✦✦✦
Disregarding all the wordiness and adjectives that can be heaped like a pile of horse dung at Disneyland upon great, timeless albums, the importance of this record can perhaps be more suitably measured by the number of people who remember the first time they heard it. *13 Songs* (a combination of the *Fugazi* and *Margin Walker* EPs) is usually amongst the first records that springs to mind when defining alternative rock. Furious, intelligent, artful, and entirely musical, it's a baker's dozen of cannon shots to the gut—not just a batch of emotionally visceral and defiant songs recorded by angry young men, but something greater. Nearly every song here reaches an anthemic level without falling prey to pomposity.

Most of these songs are anthems of the self rather than a rallying cry of accusation or unification, with "Waiting Room" and "Suggestion," serving at two examples. The attention-getting drop into silence that occurs at the 22-second mark of the former is instantly memorable. The relentless ska/reggae-inflected drive of the song is equally effective, as Ian MacKaye tells everyone listening to get off their behinds and do what they want. During the Meters-meets-Ruts thrust of "Suggestion," MacKaye switches genders for an entirely convincing rant on the objectification of women. Guy Picciotto takes on the persona of an addict on "Glue Man," whose blurred sense of reality is also conveyed in the warped, psychedelic guitars. Picciotto threatens to set himself on fire during "Margin Walker;" given the spirited play of the remaining members, it sounds like the same could be said for the rest of them. Foreshadowing the band's knack for introspective and mid-tempo concluding tracks, the disc ends with MacKaye's "Promises," examining the pitfalls of trust in relationships of any nature. A landmark record. *—Andy Kellman*

Repeater + 3 Songs / Apr. 1990 / Dischord ✦✦✦✦✦
With its righteous disdain for capitalism and the almighty dollar, *Repeater*'s themes update Gang of Four's *Solid Gold.* Lines/slogans like "When I need something, I reach out and grab it," and "You are not what you own," bear this out. *Repeater* honestly gets a little stifling in its unrelenting conviction and grandstanding. It's not too difficult to see why the band was allegedly lacking a sense of humor at this stage; they could have been yelling about filing their taxes, after all. The title makes sense, if only by mistake. But—and that's a *big* but—*Repeater* nearly matches the early EPs with its musical invention and skill, spitting out another serving of excellence, making the finger-pointing a little easier to digest. Few rhythm sections of the time had the great interplay of Joe Lally and Brendan Canty. Likewise, the guitar playing and interaction of Ian MacKaye and Guy Picciotto almost always get overlooked, thanks to all the other subjects brought up when the band is talked about. A guitar magazine even rated *Repeater* as one of the best guitar records of the '90s, and rightfully so. Anemic revs spiked by pig squeals (or is it a screeching train?) highlight the title track, one of the band's finest moments. As always, MacKaye and Picciotto's noise-terrorism-as-guitar-joust avoids flashiness, used as much as rhythm as punctuation device. Sharp, angular, jagged, and precise. Other gnarling highlights include the preachy "Styrofoam," the late-breaking "Sieve-Fisted Find," and the somewhat ironic "Merchandise," which skewers Mr. Business Owner by asking, "What could a businessman ever want more than to have us suck-

ing in his store?" Not everyone can do mail order, guys. [The CD version adds the *3 Songs 7"* as a bonus, titled *Repeater + 3 Songs*.] —*Andy Kellman*

Steady Diet of Nothing / Jul. 1, 1991 / Dischord ♦♦♦♦

In on the Kill Taker / Jun. 30, 1993 / Dischord ♦♦♦♦

In on the Kill Taker is like scrubbing your face with steel wool. It finds the band relying on rusty guitar shards that scrape, seethe, and hiss, further removing itself from the sound of *13 Songs* and *Repeater*. Harsh and grating, Fugazi surprisingly produces sheer noise at times, best witnessed in the lengthy closing of "23 Beats Off" and the unintentional *Gremlins* homage that opens "Walken's Syndrome." Joe Lally's bass and Brendan Canty's drums are relegated to acting as a guide; they're pushed—but not squashed—down in the mix, allowing for Ian MacKaye and Guy Picciotto's guitars to take control, corrosively so. It's probably Fugazi's least digestible record from front to back, but each track has its own attractive qualities, even if not immediately perceptible. "Facet Squared" and "Public Witness Program" open the record furiously, but the majority of the following "Return the Screw" is hardly audible, aside from occasional vocal tantrums. A good amount of time is spent alternating between low-key guitar noodling and intrusive bursts of aggression. They're smart with their sequencing, placing the gentle instrumental "Sweet and Low" (the only track where Lally plays a prominent role) after the exhaustive cacophony of "23 Beats Off," and generally piecing together a set of rather diverse tracks that flows well. Picciotto's anti-Hollywood rant on the properly titled "Cassavetes" is a classic Fugazi moment, as is his similarly name-dropping "Walken's Syndrome." Buried at the end of the record are two excellent lurchers, MacKaye's "Instrument" and Picciotto's "Last Chance for a Slow Dance." Not Fugazi's finest hour, but one of its most daring and rewarding. —*Andy Kellman*

Red Medicine / Jun. 1995 / Dischord ♦♦♦♦♦

Retreating from the skinned-knee production values of *In on the Kill Taker, Red Medicine* packs more rhythmic punch and shows more range. With more drive and playful goings-on, the arrangements sound much looser than on *Kill Taker*, while remaining just as gut-kicking and brainy. The experimentation, which adds liveliness, doesn't sound measured. Even Joe Lally is allowed to sing, and it just happens to be one of the best songs on the record. Running against the theory that Fugazi is a pack of killjoys, numerous instances pop up where the band's twisted sense of humor is apparent. The sinister ha-has that open "Birthday Pony," the android sample in the pleasant (!) instrumental "Combination Lock," and random piano plinks all manage to find a welcome place. But the most uncharacteristic track is the "*Blade Runner* in Kingston" slo-mo instrumental "Version," featuring clarinet skronks, dubwise rhythm, incidental zaps, and—get this—no guitars. Picciotto declares in the immediately following "Target" that he hates the sound of guitars. What gives? It's clearly a rumination against corporate America's capitalization/bastardization of "punk" aesthetics. If anyone had the right to comment, it was Fugazi. "Back to Base" and "Downed City" (another dubby intro here) return to more standard issue, hardcore roots Fugazi, full of the soaring guitars that the band is most known for. Closing out the nearly flawless second side is yet another contemplative exit track, "Long Distance Runner." Acting as a daily affirmation of sorts to combat lethargy, MacKaye opines, "If I stop to catch my breath/I might catch a piece of death." —*Andy Kellman*

End Hits / Apr. 28, 1998 / Dischord ♦♦♦

Instrument / Mar. 23, 1999 / Dischord ♦♦♦

The Fugs

f. 1964, **db.** 1970

Group / Comedy Rock, Proto-Punk, Folk-Rock, Psychedelic

Arguably the first "underground" rock group of all time, the Fugs formed at the Peace Eye bookstore in New York's East Village in late 1964. The nucleus of the band throughout its many personnel changes was Peace Eye owner Ed Sanders, and fellow poet Tuli Kupferberg. Sanders and Kupferberg had strong ties to the beat literary scene, but charged, in the manner of their friend Allen Ginsberg, full steam ahead into the maelstrom of '60s political involvement and psychedelia. Surrounded by an assortment of motley refugees from the New York folk and jugband scene, some of whom could barely play their instruments, the group nonetheless was determined to play rock & roll their way—which meant rife with political and social satire, as well as explicit profanity and sexual references, that were downright unheard of in 1965. Starting on the legendary avant-garde ESP label, the Fugs' debut was full of equal amounts of chaos and charm, but their songwriting and instrumental chops improved surprisingly quickly, resulting in a great second album that was undoubtedly the most shocking and satirical recording ever to grace the Top 100 when it was released. Moving on to Frank Sinatra's Reprise label, unleashing a few more albums of equally satirical material that was more instrumentally polished, but equally scathing lyrically. —*Richie Unterberger*

The Fugs' First Album / 1965 / Fantasy ♦♦♦

Engagingly sloppy, even raw performances on their debut, which draws on leftist politics, the poetry of William Blake, and the joys of sex. Some of this is wearily cacophonous, but "Slum Goddess," "Supergirl," "I Couldn't Get High," and "Nothing" are among their funniest songs. The CD reissue adds 11 bonus tracks: seven studio cuts from the same era (the sarcastic "CIA Man" is a highlight), three live songs from 1965, and an eight-minute spoken word piece. —*Richie Unterberger*

● **The Fugs** / 1966 / Fantasy ♦♦♦♦♦

At the time of its release, the Fugs' second (self-titled) album contained the most outrageous lyrics ever heard on a Top 100 rock & roll LP. The group, with roots in New York's underground folk and poetry scenes, flung themselves wholeheartedly into all-out rock & roll on this 1966 record, which addresses concerns like free love, the madness of war, and government repression. The CD reissue of this classic includes two previously unreleased live performances and three tracks from the unreleased album they recorded for Atlantic in 1967. —*Richie Unterberger*

Virgin Fugs / 1966 / ESP ♦♦♦♦♦

Tenderness Junction / 1967 / Reprise ♦♦♦

The band opted for a considerably more conventional rock sound more in keeping with the era's psychedelic tenor on their first major-label release. The material isn't as strong and the satirical humor not as biting as their earlier efforts, though it's characteristically witty stuff. Highlights include "Turn On/Tune In/Drop Out" and "War Song"; "Aphrodite Mass" is an ambitious if not terribly memorable five-part suite. —*Richie Unterberger*

It Crawled into My Hand, Honest / 1968 / Reprise ♦♦♦

Having attained a professional rock band sound on *Tenderness Junction*, the Fugs seemed determined to further expand their arrangements (aided, perhaps, by a major label budget) on *It Crawled Into My Hand, Honest*. Indeed, the album is ridiculously eclectic. There's stoned psychedelic folk-rock ("Crystal Liaison"); cry-in-your-beer country music with vehemently satirical or surrealistic lyrics ("Ramses II Is Dead My Love," "Johnny Pissoff Meets the Red Angel"); grand, sweeping classical orchestration ("Burial Waltz"); a Gregorian chant about "Marijuana"; down-home gospel with lyrics that no preacher would dare enunciate ("Wide Wide River," with the line "I've been swimming in this river of shit/more than twenty years and I'm getting tired of it"); and, almost buried along the way, the kind of tuneful, countercultural folk-rock Tuli Kupferberg contributed to earlier albums ("Life Is Strange"). Choral backup vocals abound, and the mere presence of a half dozen outside arrangers testifies to how much the group's attitude toward exploiting the studio had developed since the bare-bones ESP albums. Generally the songs (most written by the core trio of Sanders, Kupferberg, and Weaver) are more concerned with deft poetry and humor than political statements, although the customary social satire and calls for sexual freedom and drug use are present in diminishing degrees. Although side one is five discrete tracks, side two is a side-long cut-and-paste of tracks varying in length from three seconds to four minutes, the stylistic jump-cuts similar to those employed by the Mothers of Invention in the same era. It's an impressive and, usually, fun record, but it's also less lyrically cogent and powerful than their early albums. One senses that the Fugs' personality and individuality was ultimately somewhat muted by the more ambitious production values and frequent use of external musicians and arrangers. —*Richie Unterberger*

The Belle of Avenue A / 1969 / Reprise ♦♦

Golden Filth / 1969 / Reprise ♦♦♦

By the time of this recording on June 1, 1968 at *the Fillmore East*, the Fugs had evolved from their primitive beginnings into a pretty full and tight rock band. They'd also grown into a pretty large group, in fact, with ten musicians, including two drummers. However, most of the material was initially recorded between 1965 and 1966, ESP era. While some listeners might be disappointed by the absence of live versions of highlights from their Reprise records, this release actually has more value than the typical live album because it has notably different arrangements of well-known songs. On the Fugs' first recordings in particular, the sound and execution was pretty primitive, and it's good to have full, together rock versions of notable songs like "Slum Goddess," "Supergirl," "Nothing," "I Couldn't Get High," "Coca-Cola Douche," and "How Sweet I Roamed." The spoken intros haven't dated as well, with Sanders' monologues about lesbian dwarfs and zebra puke, and Kupferberg moaning at one point, "I want a titty"; what was once a shocking and taboo-breaking is now superfluous to the music. The reissue of this on Edsel in Britain may be easier to find now than the original LP. —*Richie Unterberger*

Live from the '60s / 1994 / Big Beat ♦♦♦♦♦

Bobby Fuller Four

f. Oct. 22, 1942, El Paso, TX, **db.** Jul. 18, 1966

Vocals / Rock & Roll

With his blatant reverence for Buddy Holly, fellow Texan Bobby Fuller was a bit of an anomaly in the mid-'60s. With his Stratocaster guitar and brash, full sound, at his best Fuller sounded like Holly might have had he survived into the '60s. Cracking the Top 30 in 1966 with a cover of Holly's "Love's Made a Fool of You," and then the Top Ten with "I Fought the Law," Fuller had just become a star when he died in mysterious circumstances in a parked car in Hollywood (the police thought it was a suicide, just about everyone who knew him disagreed). In the short time he recorded for Mustang in 1965 and 1966, he waxed quite a few fine tracks (most self-penned) besides his hits, including "Let Her Dance," "Another Sad and Lonely Night," "My True Love," "Never to Be Forgotten" and "The Magic Touch." Rocking, tuneful, and infectiously joyous, they showed Fuller to be a worthy inheritor of early rock & roll and rockabilly traditions without sounding self-consciously revivalist. A talented and prolific songwriter and a studio wiz who drew from Eddie Cochran and (though only slightly) the full guitar sound of the British Invasion as well as Buddy Holly, he recorded a great deal of unreleased studio and live material that was issued in the 1980s, when the depth of his loss began to be appreciated. —*Richie Unterberger*

● **The Best of Bobby Fuller Four** / 1981 / Rhino ♦♦♦♦♦

A great 18-track compilation of his best work that is truly all killer, no filler. While there's some other good Fuller to be found, this is definitely the prime stuff from his mid-'60s recordings for Mustang: "I Fought the Law," "Let Her Dance," "The Magic Touch," "Love's Made a Fool of You," "Fool of Love," "My True Love," and other equally fine if lesser-known sides. —*Richie Unterberger*

Never to Be Forgotten: The Mustang Years / 1998 / Del-Fi ♦♦♦♦♦

A three-CD box set that includes everything Fuller recorded for Mustang between 1964 and 1966: all the LP and 45 tracks, the previously import-only album recorded at PJ's on Sunset Strip, over a dozen cuts that were unreleased during Fuller's lifetime, and rarities. Although much of the music is excellent, it should be stressed that this is for the Bobby Fuller fanatic; most fans will be quite content with the all-killer no-filler distillation of his best mid-'60s cuts on Rhino's *Best Of* compilation. Fuller's albums were filled out with some unmemorable hot rod tunes and generic rockers that seemed to have been cranked out under pressure for product. The rare selections (some of which, despite being designated as unreleased, have shown up elsewhere) are largely alternates of songs that were already available, and although these are occasionally interesting, the variations are mostly on the slight side. A couple of cuts by the Randy Fuller Four (led by Bobby's brother and bassist) don't measure up to his sibling's output in the least, sounding jarring and clumsy by contrast. The *Live at PJ's* disc is disappointing: it consists mostly of covers of familiar rock standards, for one thing, and neither the sound quality nor performance match the excitement that Fuller routinely generated in the studio during this time. But make no mistake, this is a good thing for fans to have, and is superbly packaged, with a 64-page booklet of critical essays, speculation on his mysterious death, and an interview with Randy Fuller. *—Richie Unterberger*

I Fought the Law/KRLA King of the Wheels / Del-Fi ♦♦♦♦♦

Funkadelic

f. 1968, **db.** 1981

Group / Psychedelic, Hard Rock, Funk, Soul

Though it often took a back chair to its sister group Parliament, Funkadelic furthered the notions of black rock begun by Jimi Hendrix and Sly Stone, blending elements of '60s psychedelia and blues plus the deep groove of soul and funk. Led by sound architect George Clinton, the band pursued album statements of social/political commentary while Parliament stayed in the funk singles format, but Funkadelic nevertheless paralleled the more commercial artist's success, especially in the late '70s when the interplay between bands moved the Funkadelic sound closer to a unified P-Funk style. After debuting with an eponymous 1970 LP, the group hit its stride with acid-rock extravaganzas like the following year's *Maggot Brain*. By their mid-'70s major-label debut, 1975's *Hardcore Jollies*, the Funkadelic sound had gelled with cornerstones like bassist Bootsy Collins and keyboardist Bernie Worrell. The band's next studio LP, 1978's *One Nation Under a Groove*, became their biggest hit—the title track hit number one on the R&B charts (and the Top 40) while the album went platinum. In 1979, Funkadelic's "(Not Just) Knee Deep" hit number one as well, and its album (*Uncle Jam Wants You*) reached gold status. At just the point that Funkadelic appeared to be at the top of its powers, the band began to unravel. A splinter group also known as Funkadelic even hit the charts in 1981, and after George Clinton began a solo career the following year, Funkadelic effectively disbanded. *—John Bush*

Funkadelic / 1970 / Westbound ♦♦♦♦

Funkadelic's self-titled 1970 debut is one of the group's best early- to mid-'70s albums. Not only is it laden with great songs—"I'll Bet You" and "I Got a Thing..." are obvious highlights—but it retains perhaps a greater sense of classic '60s soul and R&B than any successive George Clinton-affiliated album. Recorded for the Detroit-based Westbound label, at the time Funkadelic were in the same boat as psychedeic soul groups such as the Temptations, who had just recorded their landmark *Cloud Nine* album across town at Motown, and other similar groups. Yet no group had managed to effectively balance big, gnarly rock guitars with crooning, heartfelt soul at this point in time. His songs are essentially conventional soul songs in the spirit of Motown or Stax—steady rhythms, dense arrangements, choruses of vocals—but also with a loud, overdriven, fuzzy guitar lurking high in the mix. And when Clinton's songs went into their chaotic moments of jamming, there was no mistaking the Hendrix influence. Furthermore, Clinton's half quirky, half trippy ad libs during "Mommy, What's a Funkadelic?" and "What Is Soul" can be mistaken for no one else—they're pure-cut P-funk. Successive albums found the group drifting further towards rock, funk, and eventually disco, especially once Bernie Worrell began playing a larger role in the group. Never again would they be this attuned to their '60s roots, making this a revealing and unique record that's certainly not short on quality songs. *—Jason Birchmeier*

Free Your Mind . . . And Your Ass Will Follow / 1970 / Westbound ♦♦♦

With its truly genius title and its equally brilliant cover art, *Free Your Mind... And Your Ass Will Follow* feels like a legendary album before you even hear a note of the music. Unfortunately, the album doesn't quite measure up with the standards most pre-*One Nation Under a Groove* Funkadelic albums will have you expecting. This album's primary flaws lie in its unsatisfying running time (six songs in a meager 30 minutes, with the near-instrumental title track monopolizing a third of that time). Granted, the majority of what's found here is of high quality, particularly "Funky Dollar Bill," "I Wanna Know If It's Good to You?," and the title track. There just aren't enough mind-blowing moments to rate this as one of the group's better albums, though. In fact, it's a near facsimile of *Maggot Brain*, the successive album that would take this album's style and improve upon it. So as alluring as the album title and cover art are, it's best to pick up the group's other, more satisfying albums first. If you're a diehard and already have a broad selection of P-funk albums, you'll want to pick this up sometime. It's undeniably worth hearing, particularly for the title track (not the best song on the album, but by far the most wowing initial listen). For any other group of the time, this would have been a perennial classic; for Funkadelic though, it's merely lackluster. *—Jason Birchmeier*

☆ **Maggot Brain** / 1971 / Westbound ♦♦♦♦♦

Perhaps the best early Funkadelic album, *Maggot Brain* showed guitarist Eddie Hazel's increased contribution to the band on the ten-minute title track, which epitomizes the P-Funk machine by working a Hendrix-fronting-the-Family Stone vibe. The album also increased the group's commercial status (with the number 27 R&B single "I Wanna Know If It's Good for You"), but its abstract thematical content discouraged less adventurous listeners. One exception to the abstractions was "You and Your Folks, Me and My Folks," which spoke of the beauty of an interracial romance. "Can You Get to That," the third single culled from the album, proved that Funkadelic remembered the sweet soul music on which most of its members had been reared. *—John Bush*

America Eats Its Young / 1972 / Westbound ♦♦♦

An ambitious double-LP, *America Eats Its Young* featured Funkadelic's first attempt at overt political criticism—the cover made the title explicit by depicting the Statue of Liberty gorging on infants. Besides the political commentary and the ecology bender of "If You Don't Like the Effects, Don't Produce the Cause," the band still manages to groove on several tracks, such as "Loose Booty" and "Biological Speculation." A bit bloated and definitely worthy of an editing job, *America Eats Its Young* still comes packed with great songs. *—John Bush*

Cosmic Slop / 1973 / Westbound ♦♦♦♦

Funkadelic's fifth LP backs away from the political commentary of *America Eats Its Young*, making it more of an inheritor to the unrestrained funk of *Maggot Brain* than anything else. Instead, the band is ready to get on the good foot, with classic tracks like "No Compute" and the title track, another long instrumental jam in the same league as the *Maggot Brain*'s title song. *—John Bush*

Standing on the Verge of Getting It On / 1974 / Westbound ♦♦♦

Let's Take It to the Stage / Apr. 1975 / Westbound ♦♦♦♦♦

Hardcore Jollies / 1976 / Priority ♦♦♦♦♦

In 1976, George Clinton enjoyed much greater commercial success than before and became more than a cult figure—only he didn't do it with Funkadelic. Parliament's 1976 albums *Mothership Connection* and *The Clones of Dr. Funkenstein* were what made him one of the most successful artists in soul and funk. Of course, Parliament and Funkadelic were essentially the same band, but while Parliament had an immediacy that appealed to singles-minded black radio, Funkadelic remained basically album oriented. Although more direct and less self-indulgent than early Funkadelic dates like *Maggot Brain* and *America Eats Its Young, Hardcore Jollies* was far from an album of hit singles. But it was definitely an album of irresistible funk grooves, and no Clinton devotee should be deprived of the joys of "Comin' Round the Mountain," the eerie "You Scared the Lovin' Out of Me," or an inspired remake of "Cosmic Slop." The guitar-crunching title song demonstrates how hard Clinton could rock, but in those days, album rock radio wouldn't touch Funkadelic no matter how much heavy guitar some of its songs employed. *—Alex Henderson*

Tales of Kidd Funkadelic / 1976 / Westbound ♦♦♦

★ **One Nation Under a Groove** / 1978 / Priority ♦♦♦♦♦

Early on *One Nation Under a Groove*, George Clinton asks the rhetorical question "Who Says a Funk Band Can't Play Rock?" Only a fool needs to ask for the answer, since the answer is the album itself. *One Nation Under a Groove* is the most fully-realized slice of P-Funk. Parliament put out albums as funky as this, but they got bogged down in their concepts, while Funkadelic always traded too heavily in psychedelic clichés and art rock trappings to really let loose. But that's not the case with *One Nation*. On this record, the concept is underplayed, letting the funk come to the forefront. Some died-in-the-wool Funkadelic fans might lament the lack of electric guitar freak-outs, but no matter—this is music of a supreme vision. Besides, the guitars are there, pushing along the funk in an effortless fashion, which helps draw attention to the vocals, which are alternately sexy and downright hilarious. Don't think of *One Nation Under a Groove* as a collection of songs. Think of it as one sustained funk symphony, and you'll be on the right track. Clinton never got this consistently funky again. *—Leo Stanley*

Uncle Jam Wants You / 1979 / Priority ♦♦♦♦♦

Fueled by the wildly addictive single "(Not Just) Knee Deep," *Uncle Jam Wants You* became one of Funkadelic's best-known albums. Nonetheless, this isn't all that commercial an effort. Like its predecessor, *One Nation Under a Groove, Uncle Jam* sold respectably thanks to a major hit, but only contained one truly visible single. For George Clinton, Funkadelic still functioned as Parliament's more esoteric, less radio-friendly alter ego. Pearls like "Foot Soldiers" (which incorporates bits of the World War I anthem "When Johnny Comes Marching Home," among other things), the goofy "Field Maneuvers," and the cute ballad "Holly Wants to Go to California" aren't the stuff that radio hits are made of, although the shadowy "Freak of the Week" could have been a major hit with the right promotion and exposure. Consistently entertaining, this is among the many Funkadelic albums that are truly essential. *—Alex Henderson*

The Electric Spanking of War Babies / 1981 / Priority ♦♦♦♦♦

With George Clinton, a humorous phrase could be nothing more than playful tomfoolery, or it could be a double entendre with a deep political meaning. The phrase "electric spanking of war babies" falls into the latter category—it referred to what the funk innovator saw as the U.S. government using the media to promote imperialistic wars. To Clinton, the American media functioned as a propaganda machine during wartime. But whether or not one cares to examine its hidden political messages, *Electric Spanking* is an above-average party album. *Spanking* falls short of the excellence of *One Nation Under a Groove* and *Uncle Jam Wants You* and didn't boast a major hit single, but amusing funk smokers like "Electro-Cuties" and "Funk Gets Stronger" aren't anything to sneeze at, nor is the reggae-influenced "Shockwaves." *Spanking* turned out to be the last album Clinton would produce under the name Funkadelic—when he hit the charts again in 1983, Mr. P-Funk was billing himself as a "solo artist." *—Alex Henderson*

★ **Music for Your Mother** / Mar. 31, 1993 / Westbound ♦♦♦♦♦

Music for Your Mother isn't the definitive collection you probably want it to be, no matter how comprehensive the track listing may look. It's missing "Maggot Brain," along with the group's other jams. In fact, it features nothing but the group's conventional material, though the large handful of B-sides certainly break away from that mold. Still, you're only getting one side of the story here. Since all the material on this collection was originally available on a 7" single, most of the songs clock under four minutes, so you're not only missing the epic psycedelic jams like "Free Your Mind And Your Ass Will Follow," you're also missing the full-length version of singles such as "Cosmic Slop." But if you look beyond these truths, it becomes evident how marvelous this double-disc collection is. Again, it isn't a one-stop answer to your Funkadelic needs, but it's probably the second best sampler available documenting the group's pre-Warner era (Ace's sweeping single-disc Finest is undeniably the most succinct). Furthermore, it features all the B-sides, something you can't get anywhere else. And the extensive liner notes are nearly as remarkable, documenting the days when the group was little more than a cult act. *—Jason Birchmeier*

Peter Gabriel

b. Feb. 13, 1950, London, England

Vocals, Keyboards, Percussion, Flute, Synthesizer, Producer / College Rock, Album Rock, Pop/Rock, Prog-Rock/Art Rock

As the leader of Genesis in the early '70s, Peter Gabriel helped move progressive rock to new levels of theatricality. In his solo career, Gabriel was no less ambitious, but he was more subtle in his methods. With his first eponymous solo album in 1977, he began exploring darker, more cerebral territory, incorporating avant-garde, electronic and worldbeat influences into his music. The record, as well as its two similarly titled successors, established Gabriel as a critically acclaimed cult artist, and with 1982's *Security,* he began to move into the mainstream; "Shock the Monkey" became his first Top 40 hit, paving the way for his multi-platinum breakthrough *So* in 1986. Accompanied by a series of groundbreaking videos and the number one single "Sledgehammer," *So* became a multi-platinum hit, and Gabriel became an international star. Instead of capitalizing on his sudden success, he began to explore other interests, including recording soundtracks and running his company Real World. By the time he returned to pop with 1992's *Us,* his mass audience had faded away, and he spent the remainder of the '90s working on multimedia projects for Real World. — Stephen Thomas Erlewine

Peter Gabriel [1] / 1977 / Atco ✦✦✦✦✦

Peter Gabriel tells why he left Genesis in "Solsbury Hill," the key track on his 1977 solo debut. Majestically opening with an acoustic guitar, the song finds Gabriel's talents gelling, as the words and music feed off each other, turning into true poetry. It stands out dramatically on this record, not because the music doesn't work, but because it brilliantly illustrates why Gabriel had to fly on his own. Though this is undeniably the work of the same man behind *The Lamb Lies Down on Broadway,* he's turned his artiness inward, making his music coiled, dense, vibrant. There is still some excess, naturally, yet it's the sound of a musician unleashed, finally able to bend the rules as he wishes. That means there are less atmospheric instrumental sections, as there were on his last few records with Genesis, but unhinged bizarreness in the arrangements, compositions, and productions, as the opener "Morbund the Burgermeister" vividly illustrates. He also has turned sleeker, sexier, capable of turning out a surging rocker of "Modern Love." If there is any problem with *Peter Gabriel,* it's that Gabriel is trying too hard to show the range of his talents, thereby stumbling occasionally with the doo wop-to-cabaret "Excuse Me" or the cocktail jazz of "Waiting for the Big One" (or, the lyric "you've got me cookin'/I'm a hard-boiled egg" on "Humdrum"). Still, much of the record teems with invigorating energy (as on "Slowburn," or the orchestral-disco pulse of "Down the Dolce Vita"), and the closer "Here Comes the Flood" burns with an anthemic intensity that would later become his signature in the '80s. Yes, it's an imperfect album, but that's a byproduct of Gabriel's welcome risk-taking—the very thing that makes the album work, overall. — *Stephen Thomas Erlewine*

Peter Gabriel [2] / 1978 / Atco ✦✦✦

The pairing sounds ideal—the former front man of Genesis, as produced by the leading light of King Crimson. Unfortunately, Peter Gabriel's second album (like his first, eponymous) fails to meet those grandiose expectations, even though it seems to at first. "On the Air" and "D.I.Y." are stunning slices of modern rock circa 1978, bubbling with synths, insistent rhythms, and polished processed guitars, all enclosed in a streamlined production that nevertheless sounds as large as a stadium. Then, things begin to drift, at first in a pleasant way ("A Wonderful Day in a One-Way World" is surprisingly nimble), but by the end, it all seems a little formless. It's not that the music is overly challenging—it's that the record is unfocused. There are great moments scattered throughout the record, yet it never captivates, either through intoxicating, messy creativity (as he did on his debut) or through cohesion (the way the third *Peter Gabriel* album, two years later, would). Certain songs work well on their own—not just the opening numbers, but the mini-epic "White Shadow," the tight "Animal Magic," the tense yet catchy "Perspective," the reflective closer "Home Sweet Home"—yet for all the tracks that work, they never work well together. Ironically, it holds together a bit better than its predecessor, yet it never reaches the brilliant heights of that record. In short, it's a transitional effort that's well worth the time of serious listeners, even it's still somewhat unsatisfying. — *Stephen Thomas Erlewine*

★ **Peter Gabriel [3]** / 1980 / Geffen ✦✦✦✦✦

Generally regarded as Peter Gabriel's finest record, his third eponymous album finds him coming into his own, crafting an album that's artier, stronger, more song oriented than before. Consider its ominous opener, the controlled menace of "Intruder." He's never found such a scary sound, yet it's a sexy scare, one that is undeniably alluring, and he keeps this going throughout the record. For an album so popular, it's remarkably bleak, chilly, and dark—even radio favorites like "I Don't Remember" and "Games Without Frontiers" are hardly cheerful, spiked with paranoia and suspicion, insulated in introspection. For the first time, Gabriel has found the sound to match his themes, plus the songs to articulate his themes. Each aspect of the album works, feeding off each other, creating a romantically gloomy, appealingly arty masterpiece. It's the kind of record where you remember the details in the production as much as the hooks or the songs, which isn't to say that it's all surface—it's just that the surface means as much as the songs, since it articulates the emotions as well as Gabriel's cubist lyrics and impassioned voice. He wound up having albums that sold more, or generated bigger hits, but this third *Peter Gabriel* album remains his masterpiece. — *Stephen Thomas Erlewine*

Security / 1982 / Geffen ✦✦✦

Security—which was titled *Peter Gabriel* everywhere outside of the U.S.—continues where the third Gabriel album left off, sharing some of the same dense production and sense of cohesion, yet lightening the atmosphere and expanding the sonic palette somewhat. The gloom that permeates the third album has been alleviated and while this is still decidedly somber and serious music, it has a brighter feel, partially derived from Gabriel's dabbling in African and Latin rhythms. These are generally used as tonal coloring, enhancing the synthesizers that form the basic musical bed of the record, since much of this is mood music (for want of a better word). *Security* flows easily and enticingly, with certain songs—the eerie "San Jacinto," "I Have the Touch," "Shock the Monkey"—arising from the wash of sound. That's not to say that the rest of the album is bland easy listening—it's designed this way, to have certain songs deliver greater impact than the rest. As such, it demands close attention to appreciate tone poems like "The Family and the Fishing Net," "Lay Your Hands on Me," and "Wallflower"—and not all of them reward such intensive listening. Even with its faults, *Security* remains a powerful listen, one of the better records in Gabriel's catalog, proving that he is becoming a master of tone, style, and substance, and how each part of the record enhances the other. — *Stephen Thomas Erlewine*

Plays Live / 1983 / Geffen ✦✦✦

Birdy / 1985 / Geffen ✦✦✦✦

So / 1986 / Geffen ✦✦✦✦

Peter Gabriel introduced his fifth studio album *So* with "Sledgehammer," an Otis Redding-inspired soul-pop raver that was easily his catchiest, happiest single to date. Needless to say, it was also his most accessible, and, in that sense it was a good introduction to *So,* the catchiest, happiest record he ever cut. "Sledgehammer" propelled the record toward blockbuster status, and Gabriel had enough songs with single potential to keep it there. There was "Big Time," another colorful dance number; "Don't Give Up," a moving duet with Kate Bush; "Red Rain," a stately anthem popular on album rock radio; and "In Your Eyes," Gabriel's greatest love song which achieved genuine classic status after being featured in Cameron Crowe's classic, *Say Anything.* These all illustrated the strengths of the album: Gabriel's increased melodicism and ability to blend soul, African music, jangly pop, and soul into his moody art rock. Apart from these singles, plus the urgent "That Voice Again," the rest of the record is as quiet as the album tracks of *Security.* The difference is, the singles on that record were part of the overall fabric; here, the singles *are* the fabric, which can make the album seem top-heavy (a fault of many blockbuster albums, particularly those of the mid-'80s). Even so, those songs are so strong, finding Gabriel in a newfound confidence and accessibility, that it's hard not to be won over by them, even if *So* doesn't develop the unity of its two predecessors. — *Stephen Thomas Erlewine*

Passion / Jun. 1989 / Geffen ✦✦✦✦✦

Passion is in actuality Peter Gabriel's soundtrack to the Martin Scorsese film *The Last Temptation of Christ,* retitled as a result of legal barriers; regardless of its name, however, there's no mistaking the record's stirring power. Like much of Gabriel's solo work, the album is a product of his continuing fascination with world music, which he employs here to create an exceptionally beautiful and atmospheric tapestry of sound perfectly evocative of the film's resonant spiritual drama; inspired by field recordings collected in areas as diverse as Turkey, Senegal and Egypt, *Passion* achieves a cumulative effect clearly Middle Eastern in origin, yet its brilliant fusion of ancient and modern musics ultimately transcends both geography and time. Remarkably dramatic, even visual, it is not only Gabriel's best film work but deserving of serious consideration as his finest music of any kind; equally worthwhile is *Passion: Sources,* which assembles the original native recordings which served as his creative launching pad. — *Jason Ankeny*

Shaking the Tree: Sixteen Golden Greats / Dec. 1990 / Geffen ✦✦✦✦

Greatest-hits albums are a traditional way of buying time for artists between albums. Peter Gabriel's, entitled *Shaking the Tree: Sixteen Golden Greats,* arrived in December of 1990, as he was toiling away at the follow-up to his smash *So,* which was four years old at that point. As greatest-hits albums go, it's pretty good, containing all the hits, plus an effective re-recording of "Here Comes the Flood" and a good new song in the form of the title track. While the sequencing may leave something to be desired—it is neither chronological, nor as supple as a good mix tape—it does contain nearly everything a casual fan could want (nothing from the second album, though; both "On the Air" or "D.I.Y." would have been nice additions), making it an effective sampler. — *Stephen Thomas Erlewine*

Us / Sep. 29, 1992 / Geffen ✦✦✦

Six years after earning his first blockbuster, Peter Gabriel finally delivered *Us,* his sequel to *So.* Clearly, that great span of time indicates that Gabriel was obsessive in crafting the album, and *Us* bears the sound of endless hours in the studio. It's not just that the production is pristine, clean, and immaculate, it's that the music is, with only a handful of exceptions (namely, the "Sledgehammer" rewrite "Steam" and the fellatio ode "Kiss That Frog"), remarkably subtle and shaded. It's also not a coincidence that *Us* is, as Gabriel says in his liner notes, "about relationships," since the exquisitely textured music lets him expose his soul, albeit in a typically obtuse way. Since the music is so muted, it's no surprise that the album failed to capture a mass audience the way *So* did, but it's foolish to expect anyone but serious fans to unravel an album this deliberate. Gabriel is as adventurous as ever, yet he is relentlessly sober about his experiments, burying exotic sounds and percussion underneath crawling tempos measured atmospherics—this is tastefully two-toned music, assembled by a consummate craftsman who became too immersed in detail to make anything but an insular, introspective work. Some gems are easier to unearth than others—"Digging in the Dirt" has an insistent pulse, "Blood of Eden" and "Come Talk to Me" are quite beautiful, "Secret World" is quietly anthemic—yet, given enough time, the record's understated approach and reflection becomes its most attractive element. But it takes a lot of spins and patience to get to that point, since this is an album he made for himself, and only those dedicated to the artist will wind with the patience to decode it. — *Stephen Thomas Erlewine*

Secret World Live / Sep. 13, 1994 / Geffen ✦✦

Serge Gainsbourg (Lucien Ginzburg)

b. Apr. 2, 1928, Paris, France, **d.** Mar. 2, 1991, Paris, France

Vocals, Piano, Guitar / French Rock, Baroque Pop, Foreign Language Rock, French Pop, Cabaret, Jazz-Pop

Serge Gainsbourg was the dirty old man of popular music; a French singer/songwriter and provocateur notorious for his voracious appetite for alcohol, cigarettes and women, his scandalous, taboo-shattering output made him a legend in Europe but only a cult figure in America. Gainsbourg initially wanted only to carve out a niche as a composer and producer, though he began recording in 1958 and followed with strong, jazz-inflected efforts like 1961's *L'Etonnant Serge Gainsbourg* and 1964's *Gainsbourg Confidentiel*. Still, his songwriting proved more successful than his performing until the late '60s, when he befriended the actress Brigitte Bardot. With Bardot as his muse, Gainsbourg's lushly-arranged music suddenly became erotic and delirious. His affair with Bardot was brief, but its effects were irrevocable: after he became involved with constant companion Jane Birkin, they recorded the 1969 duet "Je T'Aime... Moi Non Plus." Banned in many corners of the globe, it reached the top of the charts throughout Europe and grew in stature to become an underground classic. Gainsbourg returned in 1971 with *Histoire de Melody Nelson*, a dark, complex song cycle which signalled his increasing alienation from modern culture; his his work gradually grew more esoteric, inflammatory and outrageous with each passing release. He remained an imposing and controversial figure throughout Europe, where he was both vilified and celebrated for his shocking behavior. Along with his pop music oeuvre, Gainsbourg scored a number of films, and also directed and appeared in a handful of features. He died on March 2, 1991. *—Jason Ankeny*

Histoire de Melody Nelson / 1971 / Polydor ✦✦✦✦✦
You don't need to speak a word of French to understand *Histoire de Melody Nelson*—one need only to look at the front cover (with its nearly pornographic portrait of a half-naked nymphet clutching a rag doll) or hear the lechery virtually dripping from Serge Gainsbourg's sleazily seductive voice to realize that this is the record your mother always warned you about, a masterpiece of perversion and corruption. A concept record exploring the story of—and Gainsbourg's lust for—the titular teen heroine, *Histoire de Melody Nelson* is arguably his most coherent and perfectly realized studio album, with the lush arrangements which characterize the majority of his work often mixed here with funky rhythm lines which underscore the musky allure of the music; perhaps best described as a dirty old bastard's attempt to make his own R&B love-man's record along the lines of a *Let's Get It On* (itself still two years away from release), it's by turns fascinating and repellent, hilarious and grim, but never dull—which, in Gainsbourg's world, would be the ultimate (and quite possibly the only) sin. *—Jason Ankeny*

● **Comic Strip** / Feb. 11, 1997 / Polydor ✦✦✦✦✦
Serge Gainsbourg's remarkable pop hits are best represented on *Comic Strip*, an indispensable set collecting 20 tracks recorded between 1966 and 1969. In addition to the lushly erotic "Je T'Aime... Moi Non Plus"—Gainsbourg's best-known record—*Comic Strip* includes the title track and "Bonnie and Clyde," his collaborations with Brigitte Bardot, as well as "Initials B.B.," a sweeping paean to his duet partner, "the most beautiful woman on earth." Other highlights include "Chatterton" (a bouncy celebration of suicide), "Torrey Canyon" (a prescient warning against threats to the environment), and the self-explanatory "Soixante Neuf Annee Erotique" ("69 Erotic Year"). *—Jason Ankeny*

Couleur Cafe / Feb. 11, 1997 / Polydor ✦✦✦✦
A French craze for exotic rhythms and dances like the cha-cha and the mambo inspired Serge Gainsbourg to explore Latin and Caribbean rhythms at the outset of his career; *Couleur Cafe* collects 20 of these beat-driven recordings, which span from 1959 to work from as late as 1974. More than his jazz performances of the same period, the earliest songs on the set presage the direction taken on his pop records; in addition to the distinctly snotty attitude which pervades cuts like "Laissez-Moi Tranquille" and "L'Anthracite," the nine tracks taken from the 1964 recording *Gainsbourg Percussions* innovatively embrace African rhythms while focusing on the thematic concerns (specifically cigarettes, American culture and young girls) of his seminal later work. *—Jason Ankeny*

Du Jazz Dans Le Ravin / Feb. 11, 1997 / Polydor ✦✦✦✦
While Serge Gainsbourg rose to infamy as a pop star, he actually got his start playing jazz; the 20-track collection *Du Jazz Dans le Ravin* samples his early work from between 1958 and 1964, at which point he chose to "go commercial." While neither as imaginative nor as distinctive as his pop material, Gainsbourg's jazz sides clearly presage his future work; bright and colorful, cuts like "Requiem Pour un Twisteur" and "Ce Mortel Ennui" offer much of the same attitude and outlook which defined his later, more provocative music. *—Jason Ankeny*

Galaxie 500

f. 1986, Boston, MA, **db.** 1991
Group / College Rock, Indie Pop, Slowcore, Dream Pop, Indie Rock, Shoegazing, Alternative Pop/Rock
Though criminally overlooked in their own lifetime, Galaxie 500 later emerged as one of the pivotal underground groups of the post-punk era; dreamy and enigmatic, their minimalist dirges presaged the rise of both the shoegazer and slowcore movements of the 1990s. The group formed in Boston, Massachusetts in 1986 and comprised vocalist/guitarist Dean Wareham, bassist Naomi Yang and drummer Damon Krukowski. Named after a friend's car, Galaxie 500 began performing live throughout Boston and New York before recording a three-song demo tape which they sent to Shimmy Disc honcho Kramer, who agreed to become the trio's producer. After bowing in early 1988 with the singles "Tugboat" and "Oblivious," they issued their full-length debut, *Today*, which highlighted the group's distinct, evolving sound pitting Wareham's eerie, plaintive tenor, elliptical songs and slow-motion guitar textures against Yang's warm, fluid bass lines and Krukowski's lean drumming. After signing to the U.S. branch of Rough Trade, Galaxie 500 issued its defining moment, 1989's evocative *On Fire*, a remarkably assured and rich record including the superb singles "Blue Thunder" and "When Will You Come Home." The group returned in 1990 with *This Is Our Music;* following a subsequent tour, Galaxie 500 disbanded after Wareham phoned Yang and Krukowski to say he was quitting the group. A few months later,Wareham formed his new band, Luna, while Krukowski and Yang later recorded as Damon and Naomi. *—Jason Ankeny*

Today / 1987 / Rykodisc ✦✦✦✦
Galaxie 500's bow lacks the pea-soup atmosphere of the trio's later work; their early sound, though already unique and beautiful, is simply too skeletal to equal the all-enveloping intoxication of *On Fire*. The songs, however, are confident and assured, carefully balancing the gauzy torpor of Dean Wareham's guitar with the insistent rhythms of bassist Naomi Yang and drummer Damon Krukowski. An auspicious debut. *—Jason Ankeny*

● **On Fire** / 1989 / Rykodisc ✦✦✦✦✦
On Fire is Galaxie 500's crowning achievement; striking a perfect balance between the comparatively thin sound of *Today* and the overly-slick production of *This Is Our Music*, the album manufactures a thick, enveloping atmosphere all its own. Markedly more assured than *Today*, the interplay between Dean Wareham's gauzy guitar and Naomi Yang's warm, liquid bass immerses Wareham's minimalist songs in slow-motion waves of fragile noise; much of the appeal of such superb cuts as "Blue Thunder," "When Will You Come Home" and their cover of George Harrison's "Isn't It a Pity" derives from their seeming temporality—the songs threaten to evaporate at any given moment. *—Jason Ankeny*

This Is Our Music / 1990 / Rykodisc ✦✦✦✦
Having perfected their brand of atmospheric drone-pop with *On Fire*, Galaxie 500 smartly expand into more dynamic and structured ground with *This Is Our Music*, a brighter, more colorful collection which occasionally falls prey to uninspired songwriting; the lifeless melodies of "Hearing Voices" and "Summertime" pale in comparison to such standouts as the single "Fourth of July" (a shimmering example of the band's often-neglected sense of humor), "Way Up High," and an evocative cover of Yoko Ono's "Listen, the Snow Is Falling," sung by bassist Naomi Yang. *—Jason Ankeny*

Galaxie 500 / Sep. 24, 1996 / Rykodisc ✦✦✦✦✦
Rykodisc's *Galaxie 500* box set contains all three of the group's original albums—*Today*, *On Fire*, and *This Is Our Music*—plus an additional disc of rarities and singles, making it a definitive retrospective, designed with collectors in mind. The packaging is gorgeous and the sound is a considerable improvement from the original Rough Trade releases; the only drawback of the box set is the fact that it is the only place any Galaxie 500 albums are currently available, and it was issued in an extremely limited run. However, the box could not have been done any better. It's essential for all the band's fans. *—Stephen Thomas Erlewine*

Copenhagen / Apr. 29, 1997 / Rykodisc ✦✦✦
Released in 1997, seven years after Galaxie 500 disbanded, *Copenhagen* captures the group's final concert on their final European tour. The concert was recorded for Danish National Radio on December 1, 1990 and for listeners who always thought of Galaxie 500's music as so light that it would float away, the quiet force of the music will come as a revelation. *—Stephen Thomas Erlewine*

● **Portable Galaxie 500** / Sep. 29, 1998 / Rykodisc ✦✦✦✦✦

Game Theory

f. 1982, Sacramento, CA, **db.** 1990
Group / College Rock, Jangle Pop, Paisley Underground, Power Pop, Alternative Pop/Rock
Game Theory formed on the fringe of the Paisley Underground movement of the early-'80s and though they certainly had a retro-'60 sound with psychedelic leanings, the band owed its greatest debt to the proto-power pop of Big Star. Leader Scott Miller's song craft, distinctive voice (self-described as a "miserable whine") and intelligent lyrics (often obscure but rarely pretentious) carved a sound that, while firmly rooted in traditional pop, was truly original and defined an era of college rock. The band's first album, *Blaze of Glory*, was a pleasant amalgam of '60s pure pop and the quirkier elements of new wave, but only hinted at the band's potential. In 1985, with the help of producer Mitch Easter, they recorded their first proper album—*Real Nighttime*—for Enigma. With a radically different lineup spearheaded by Miller and Easter, 1985's *Big Shot Chronicles* showed great leaps in quality. Miller seemed to accept the destiny of the band (obscurity) when he created his most excessive, and ultimately most enjoyable album, 1987's *Lolita Nation*, a sprawling double album riddled with experimental sounds and song fragments. They took one more stab at the mainstream with the more accessible *Two Steps from the Middle Ages* in 1988, but its commercial failure led to several more personnel changes including the temporary exit of Miller himself. Miller finally dissolved the band in 1990 to form the similar-sounding, though more ecclectic, Loud Family. *—Chris Woodstra*

Blaze of Glory / 1982 / Alias ✦✦

Real Nighttime / 1985 / Alias ✦✦✦
While Game Theory had released three EPs between 1982 and 1984, their first full-length album, *Real Nighttime*, was where the band truly found their voice on vinyl. With Mitch Easter on board as producer, the band was finally working with a sympathetic craftsman who knew how to make the most of the band's sound, and Scott Miller was maturing into one of the finest and most distinctive pop songwriters in America. While Game Theory's most obvious influence was certainly Big Star (the album even features a cover of "You Can't Have Me" that sounds slightly more deranged than the original), *Real Nighttime*'s loose narrative suggested a mid-'80s smart-pop update of *Pet Sounds*, as it followed a young man from blissful innocence on "24" to crushing romantic defeat on "I Turned Her Away." Always tuneful, and by turns rollicking and heart-breaking, *Real Nighttime* was the album that announced Game Theory as one of the major talents to emerge from California's "Paisley Underground" scene. *—Mark Deming*

Big Shot Chronicles / 1986 / Alias ✦✦✦✦✦
Scott Miller broke in a new Game Theory lineup on *The Big Shot Chronicles* (a revolving-door cast of musicians was something he would get used to over the next decade or so), and if the album lacks the narrative cohesion of the group's first full-length effort, *Real Nighttime*, it's obvious from the album's first cut that the addition of Shelley LaFrenier on keyboards, Suzie Ziegler on bass, and Gil Ray on drums made Game Theory a stronger band in every respect. While Game Theory's attempts to rock out on *Real Nighttime* sometimes sounded a bit tentative, *The Big Shot Chronicles* reveals a band that's equally adept at flex-

ing their muscles ("I've Tried Subtlety" and "Make Any Vows") or easing into a song's subtleties ("Regenisraen" and "Like a Girl Jesus"). As a songwriter, Scott Miller continued to grow ("Erica's Word" and "Don't Look Too Closely" are both smart pop heaven on Earth), and while he's fond of referring to his voice as a "miserable whine," he sure knows how to make it communicate. Finally, Mitch Easter's production guides the record through moody neo-psychedelia and up-tempo hard pop with an equally sure hand; the record sounds just as good as the band plays. A superb set from one of the best (and most underappreciated) bands of the 1980s. *—Mark Deming*

Lolita Nation / 1987 / Enigma ✦✦✦✦✦
Game Theory leader Scott Miller has never made much of a secret of his fondness for Big Star, but while *Real Nighttime* favored the sound of *#1 Record* and *The Big Shot Chronicles* suggested the harder-edged tone of *Radio City, Lolita Nation* sounded like Game Theory's variation on the themes of Big Star's masterfully damaged swan song, *Third/Sister Lovers*. Certainly Game Theory's most ambitious album, *Lolita Nation* was a two-LP set that combined some of Miller's most user-friendly power pop with dark, moody ruminations on betrayal, failed love, and mortality, bursts of avant-garde noise, and fragments of unclassifiable studio doodling, all thrown into a sonic Cuisinart through Miller's aggressive use of aural montage. *Lolita Nation* is more than a bit disorienting on first listen, though it finds the band playing at the top of their form on challenging material (new guitarist Donnete Thayer makes an impressive debut), and there are more than a few flat-out brilliant tracks (such as "Chardonnay," "The Waist and the Knees," and "The Real Shelia") alongside such head-scratchers as "Turn Me on Dead Man," "Watch Who You're Calling Space Garbage Meteor Mouth," and the 22nd track (which stubbornly defies titling). Taken as a whole and given time to fully absorb, *Lolita Nation* is probably Game Theory's finest and most impressive album, though it's also the worst place for a beginner to start examining their work. *—Mark Deming*

Two Steps from the Middle Ages / 1988 / Enigma ✦✦

● **Tinker to Evers to Chance (Selected Highlights 1982-1989)** / Mar. 1990 / Enigma ✦✦✦✦✦
Scott Miller compiled and annotated this career-spanning retrospective of his band Game Theory, and anyone looking for a convenient introduction to the band's arch and intelligent power pop could hardly do better than to pick this up. *Tinker to Evers to Chance* boasts 22 songs that offer representative selections from the band's four studio albums and three EPs, including their relative "hits" (well, "Erica's Word" and "The Real Shelia" got some college radio airplay and made brief appearances on MTV in the middle of the night), as well as hard-to-find material from their early 12"s. For the completists, Miller also re-recorded two very early Game Theory tracks with the band's final lineup and even reworked "Beach State Rocking" by his pre-Game Theory combo Alternate Learning. A nice mix of obscurities and favorites for the fans, and a revelation for the uninitiated, *Tinker to Evers to Chance* is hardly the only Game Theory album worth owning, but it may well be the best way to go if you're only going to buy one. *—Mark Deming*

Distortion of Glory / 1994 / Alias ✦✦

Gang of Four

f. 1977, Leeds, England, **db.** 1984
Group / College Rock, Post-Punk, New Wave, Alternative Pop/Rock
Gang of Four produced some of the most exhilarating and lasting music of the early English post-punk era of 1978-1983. Fueled by the fury of punk rock and radical political theory, the group successfully welded the two in an inspired display of polemics and music that addressed the vagaries of life in the modern world (including love and romance) as matters of political inquiry. What made Gang of Four's polemical clang 'n' roll so compelling was that it worked as harsh, bracing, and ultimately liberating rock & roll. Andy Gill didn't play guitar as much as emit thick wads of semi-tuneful distortion, while vocalist Jon King "sang" in a dry, declamatory fashion similar to that of the Fall's Mark E. Smith. The group openly challenged the audience's preconceived notions about rock music, performance, the cult of celebrity and the nature of politics; in doing so, GOF conveyed rage, confusion and loss of identity as well as any band of its time. After three consecutive sensational albums, bassist Dave Allen left in 1982 to form the more danceable and less overtly political Shriekback, while the remaining trio recorded the misguided "radical soul/R&B" record *Hard*. After calling it quits in 1984, King and Gill put together a new Gang of Four in the early '90s for two albums, 1991's *Mall* and 1995's *Shrinkwrapped*. *—John Dougan*

★ **Entertainment!** / 1979 / Infinite Zero ✦✦✦✦✦
Entertainment! is one of those records where germs of influence can be traced through many genres and countless bands, both favorably and unfavorably. From groups whose awareness of genealogy spreads wide enough to openly acknowledge Gang of Four's influence (Fugazi, Rage Against the Machine), to those not in touch with their ancestry enough to realize it (rap/metal, some indie rock)—all have appropriated elements of their forefathers' trailblazing contribution. It's vaguely funky rhythmic twitch, its pungent, pointillistic guitar staccados, and its spoken/shouted vocals have all been picked up by many.

Lyrically, the album was apart from many of the day, and it still is. The band rants at revisionist history in "Not Great Men" ("No weak men in the books at home"), self-serving media and politicians in "I Found That Essence Rare" ("The last thing they'll ever do—/Act in your interest"), and sexual politics in "Damaged Goods" ("You said you're cheap but you're too much"). Though the brilliance of the record thrives on the faster material—especially the febrile first side—a true highlight amongst highlights is the closing "Anthrax," full of barely controlled feedback squalls and moans. It's nearly psychedelic, something post-punk and new wave were never known for. With a slight death rattle and plodding bass rumble, Jon King equates love with disease and admits to feeling "like a beetle on its back." In the background, Gill speaks in monotone of why Gang of Four doesn't do love songs. Subversive records of any ilk don't get any stronger, influential, or exciting than this. [In 1995, *Entertainment!* was reissued on Warner subsidiary Infinite Zero/American, with the *Yellow* EP appended.] *—Andy Kellman*

Solid Gold / May 1981 / Warner Brothers ✦✦✦✦✦
Gang of Four's existence had as much to do with Slave and Chic as it did the Sex Pistols and the Stooges, which is something *Solid Gold* demonstrates more than *Entertainment*. Any smartypants can point out the irony of a band on Warner Bros. railing against systematic tools of control disguised as entertainment media, but Gang of Four were more observational than condescending. True, Jon King and Andy Gill might have been hooting and hollering in a semiviolent and discordant fashion, but they were saying "think about it" more than "you lot are a bunch of mindless puppets." Abrasiveness was a means to grab the listener, and it worked. Reciting *Solid Gold*'s lyrics on a local neighborhood corner might get a couple interested souls to pay attention. It isn't poetry, and it's no fun; most within earshot would just continue power-walking or tune out while buffing the SUV.

Solid Gold has that unholy racket going on beneath the lyrics, an unlikely mutation of catchiness and atonality that made ears perk and (oddly) posteriors shake. With its slightly ironic title, *Solid Gold* is more rhythmically grounded than the fractured nature of *Entertainment!*, a politically charged, more teutonic take on funk. It's a form of release for paranoid accountants. Financial concerns form the basis of the subject matter; the hilarious but realistic "Cheeseburger" is a highlight with its thinly-veiled snipe at America: "No classes in the U.S.A./Improve yourself, the choice is yours/Work at your job and make good pay/Make friends, great/Buy them a beer!" This is a nickel less spectacular than the debut, but owning one and not the other would be criminal. [*Solid Gold* was reissued in 1995 on Warner subsidiary Infinite Zero/American, with *Another Day, Another Dollar* appended.] *—Andy Kellman*

Songs of the Free / 1982 / Warner Brothers ✦✦✦

Hard / 1983 / Warner Brothers ✦✦✦
The final studio LP released prior to the group's 1984 dissolution, *Hard* continues Gang of Four's long-standing tradition of ironic LP titles; this time, however, the joke's on them—produced by Ron and Howard Alpert, best known for their work with Crosby, Stills & Nash and Firefall, *Hard* is anything but. The taut, bracing energy of past glories has fallen by the wayside, replaced by morose, uninspired dirges; a strangely apolitical album, even Jon King's lyrics lack bite, and his vocals lack any sense of urgency. *—Jason Ankeny*

Peel Sessions / 1990 / Dutch East India ✦✦✦

● **A Brief History of the Twentieth Century** / Dec. 1990 / Warner Brothers ✦✦✦✦✦
Gang of Four emerged from the wreckage of punk rock in the early 1980s with a sound all their own. Characterized by blatantly political lyrics that were chanted, sung and yelled over spare, funky drumbeats and Andy Gill's scratch-and-kill guitar, the Gang's particular brand of angular dance punk was as refreshing as ice water in the face, and, as this collection shows, still holds up well almost twenty years later. Back when the members of Rage Against the Machine were still in grade school, Gang of Four's explicit politics were something of a curiosity; the desultory feminism of "It's Her Factory" and the pessimistic Marxist economic forecasting of "Capital (It Fails Us Now)" were not exactly common lyrical conceits in the immediate post-disco era. Those who know their Chinese history will recognize the band's name, though whether it was meant ironically or as a genuine tribute to the counterrevolutionist faction led by Lady Mao is unclear. This generous best-of recaps some of the Gang's finest moments, and will serve as a perfectly sufficient precis for all but completist fans. Half of the Gang's first full-length album (cheerfully titled *Entertainment!* as in "guerrilla war struggle is the new entertainment") is here, and so are some of the better tracks from their EPs. It also brings together some of the brighter moments from the band's protracted decline into synthesized dribble, such as the immortal "I Love a Man in a Uniform." There are occasional disappointments (the studio version of "To Hell with Poverty" was much better than the so-so live version included here), but overall this is an excellent collection. *—Rick Anderson*

Mall / May 7, 1991 / Polydor ✦✦

Shrinkwrapped / Sep. 19, 1995 / Castle ✦✦✦

A 100 Flowers Bloom / Nov. 3, 1998 / Rhino ✦✦✦✦
Two-CD, 40-song compilation that draws from all of their albums (including the ones from the 1990s) and a couple of early EPs, throwing in eight previously unreleased live performances, demos, and remixes (as well as the 7" single version of "To Hell With Poverty"). Although this is only two discs, it opens itself up to the usual box set criticisms. It's likely that anyone who has followed Gang of Four has already picked up the albums they want, and will thus need to shell out more money than they want for a bunch of not-too-essential rarities. For those who just want a compilation, the single-disc *Brief History of the Twentieth Century* is better and more economical, even though it has no '90s material. Most puzzling is the decision to present the tracks out of chronological sequence, meandering from 1979 to the 1990s and back again while visiting all points in between. All this taken into consideration, there's a lot of music here that Gang of Four fans will consider among the band's most essential, and the package is made more appealing with a 52-page booklet that has a lengthy band history by noted British punk historian Jon Savage. *—Richie Unterberger*

The Gap Band

f. 1967, Tulsa, OK
Group / Quiet Storm, Funk, Soul
A funk septet led by brothers Ronnie (vocals, trumpet, keyboards), Charles (lead vocals, keyboards), and Robert Wilson (vocals, bass), all cousins of Bootsy Collins, the Gap Band enjoyed a successful run on the R&B charts during the '80s with its Sly Stone-influenced boogie. The brothers met Leon Russell in 1974, who signed them to his Shelter label; this led to a recording session with A&M, a self-titled debut on Tattoo/RCA, and a deal with Mercury. A string of R&B Top Ten hits followed, including "I Don't Believe You Want to Get Up and Dance (Oops, Up Side Your Head)"; by the time of *Gap Band III*, the group was established as hitmakers, and the album and its follow-up went platinum on the strength of hits like "Burn Rubber (Why You Wanna Hurt Me)," "Early In the Morning," and "Outstanding." The Gap Band resumed recording after a six-year hiatus in 1995 with *Ain't Nothin' But a Party*, which

was followed in 1996 by *V Jammin. Funkin' 'Til 2000 Comz* followed in May of 1999. *—Steve Huey*

The Best of the Gap Band / 1995 / Mercury ✦✦✦✦
The Best of the Gap Band collects nearly every hit and key album track by the seminal funk group, making it the perfect introduction and arguably their only essential record. *—David Jehnzen*

The Best of the Gap Band, Vol. 2 / Sep. 22, 1998 / Simitar ✦✦✦
Volume 2 of Gap Band hits consists mainly of tunes designed for the *Soul Train* dancers and dancefloor demons that don't hold up well outside of that element. These are partying tunes with little music appreciation value. Two exceptions are the Tulsa, OK, band's sweet remake of the Friends of Distinction's "Going In Circles," where Charlie Wilson displays his vocal prowess and lyric sensitivity, and "I Found My Love," a mid-tempo groove. But booty shakers like "Beep a Freak," "Zibble, Zibble," "I'm Gonna Get You Sucka," and the rocksteady-ish "Big Fun" reign supreme. *—Andrew Hamilton*

Garbage

f. 1993, New York, NY
Group / Alternative Dance, Alternative Pop/Rock
Garbage built on the sonic landscapes of My Bloody Valentine, Curve, and Sonic Youth, adding a distinct sense of accessible pop songcraft. The brainchild of producers Butch Vig, Duke Erikson, and Steve Marker, the group began as an informal jam session between the three producers, of whom Vig was by far the most successful, having helmed breakout records by numerous American alternative superstars (Nirvana, Smashing Pumpkins, Sonic Youth). After recruiting vocalist Shirley Manson, Garbage released their eponymous first album in 1995 on Almo Sounds. After receiving support from radio and MTV, the album began to climb the charts toward the end of 1995, when the second single, "Queer," received heavy airplay. By the summer of 1996, *Garbage* had gone gold in the United States, and shortly afterward it achieved platinum status, as "Only Happy When It Rains" and "Stupid Girl" became radio hits. After a brief break, Garbage began work on their second album in the summer of 1997. The record, entitled *Version 2.0*, was released in May the following year, preceded by the single "Push It." *—Stephen Thomas Erlewine*

● **Garbage** / Aug. 15, 1995 / Almo Sounds ✦✦✦✦✦
Garbage's self-titled debut has all the trappings of alternative rock—off-kilter arrangements, occasional bursts of noise, a female singer with a thin, airy voice—but it comes off as pop, thanks to the glossy production courtesy of drummer Butch Vig. Not only is the sound of the record slick and professional, but all the songs are well-crafted pop songs. Unfortunately, only a handful of the songs are memorable, but those that are— "Vow" and "Queer," in particular—are small, trashy alternative pop gems. *—Stephen Thomas Erlewine*

Version 2.0 / May 12, 1998 / Almo Sounds ✦✦✦
Neither a flat-out retread nor a full-fledged progression, *Version 2.0* is almost too accurate a title for Garbage's second album. Everything that made *Garbage* a success is here—Shirley Manson's seductive strength, strong pop sensibility, a production that falls halfway between alternative rock and techno—presented in a slightly newer form. *Version 2.0* may be gilded with fresh drum loops and shiny, computerized production, but it lacks the thrilling immediacy of the debut. It isn't that Garbage's sound is no longer appealing—it's that high-tech production has a tendency to make the songs sound the same. That was a problem with the debut as well, but it's discouraging to find that those flaws are repeated, not solved. Still, when Garbage pulls it all together, the results are irresistible, and there are just enough moments on the album—including "Special," "Push It," "Temptation Waits," and "I Think I'm Paranoid"—to make it a successful follow-up, even if it isn't a brave step forward. *—Stephen Thomas Erlewine*

Gastr del Sol

f. 1991, Louisville, KY
Group / Math Rock, Experimental Rock, Indie Rock, Post-Rock/Experimental
Gastr del Sol was the most prominent vehicle of indie-rock stalwart David Grubbs, a former member of Squirrel Bait, Slint and Bastro. With Gastr del Sol, the Louisville, Kentucky-born vocalist/guitarist/pianist's evolution from conventional rock music into more intricate and sophisticated tone patterns became complete; debuting with the 1993 EP *The Serpentine Similar,* the group—a shifting aggregate of talents which initially inclued bassist Bundy K. Brown and drummer John McEntire—began exploring their new approach, taking off from often improvisational performances to embark on highly idiosyncratic sonic adventures. With the single "20 Songs Less," guitarist, composer, and tape manipulator Jim O'Rourke signed on, and following the departure of Brown, and with the decreased involvement of McEntire, Gastr del Sol became a kind of catch-all tag for Grubbs and O'Rourke's many eclectic projects; the acoustic *Crookt, Crackt or Fly* followed in 1994, as did the EP *Mirror Repair.* With 1995's *The Harp Factory on Lake Street,* Grubbs and O'Rourke composed a single 17-minute orchestral piece, while with 1996's *Upgrade and Afterlife* they returned to more more traditional dynamics to create their most beautiful and intriguing work to date. O'Rourke left Gastr del Sol in 1997, shortly after completing work on *Camoufleur,* which was released in Janurary 1998. *—Jason Ankeny*

The Serpentine Similar / 1993 / Drag City ✦✦✦✦

Crookt, Crackt, or Fly / 1994 / Drag City ✦✦✦✦✦
With the enigmatic *Crookt, Crackt, or Fly,* Gastr del Sol's focus shifted to the dual guitars of David Grubbs and Jim O'Rourke, translating into a strange but frequently sublime acoustic recording shaded by vague hints of tape manipulations and only the occasional touch of percussion. It's music of extremes—the songs are either very brief or very long, the lyrics are often inscrutable, and the music is wildly unpredictable, rejecting standard tonalities and compositional structures in favor of an elusive, baffling but nevertheless intoxicating otherness. *—Jason Ankeny*

Harp Factory on Lake Street / Aug. 1, 1995 / Table of the Elements ✦✦✦

Upgrade & Afterlife / Jun. 17, 1996 / Drag City ✦✦✦✦

● **Camoufleur** / Jan. 20, 1998 / Drag City ✦✦✦✦✦
Jim O'Rourke's last album with Gastr del Sol is a subdued, meditative affair, bringing together elements of folk, jazz, film music, and the avant-garde. "The Seasons Reverse" opens the album with a deceptive, gentle melody and strummed, hushed guitars. Its sound and leisurely pace set the tone, but not the style, for the rest of the album. Each track is intricate and layered, but the music isn't overly complex. Instead, *Camoufleur* is quiet and minimal, requiring attentive listening. Only "The Seasons Reverse" and the closer "Bauchredner," with its unexpected, catchy horn-driven coda, are straightforward. The remainder of the album demands concentration. Given some time, the album opens up, revealing layers of modest beauty. It's a nice way for O'Rourke to leave the fold, and it certainly suggests that David Grubbs is far from finished musically, whether he chooses to continue with Gastr del Sol or not. *—Stephen Thomas Erlewine*

Marvin Gaye (Marvin Pentz Gay, Jr.)

b. Apr. 2, 1939, Washington, D.C., **d.** Apr. 1, 1984, Los Angeles, CA
Vocals, Keyboards, Drums / Blaxploitation, Smooth Soul, Quiet Storm, Motown, Urban, R&B, Soul
One of the most gifted, visionary and enduring talents ever launched into orbit by the Motown hit machine, the career of Marvin Gaye blazed the trail for the continued evolution of popular black music: moving from lean, powerful R&B to stylish, sophisticated soul to finally arrive at an intensely political and personal form of artistic self-expression, his work not only redefined soul music as a creative force but also expanded its impact as an agent for social change. With 1963's "Pride and Joy," Gaye scored his first Top Ten smash, but often found his role as a hitmaker stifling—his desire to become a crooner of lush romantic ballads ran in direct opposition to Motown's all-important emphasis on chart success, and the ongoing battle between his artistic ambitions and the label's demands for commercial product continued throughout Gaye's long tenure with the company. After the chart-topping 1968 success of "I Heard It Through the Grapevine," his biggest hit and arguably the pinnacle of the Motown Sound, he increasingly found the material he recorded for the label to be increasingly irrelevant in the face of the tremendous social changes sweeping the nation; spending the majority of 1970 in seclusion, Gaye resurfaced early the next year with the self-produced *What's Going On,* a landmark effort heralding a dramatic shift in both content and style which forever altered the face of black music. A highly percussive album which incorporated jazz and classical elements to forge a remarkably sophisticated and fluid soul sound, *What's Going On* was a conceptual masterpiece which brought Gaye's deeply held spiritual beliefs to the fore to explore issues ranging from poverty and discrimination to the environment, drug abuse and political corruption; chief among the record's concerns was the conflict in Vietnam, as Gaye structured the songs around the point of view of his brother Frankie, himself a soldier recently returned from combat. The album's success guaranteed Gaye continued artistic control over his work and helped loosen the reins for other Motown artists, most notably Stevie Wonder, to also take command of their own destinies. *—Jason Ankeny*

☆ **What's Going On** / May 20, 1971 / Motown ✦✦✦✦✦
Shortly after Marvin Gaye turned 30, he became the first Motown artist with a measure of creative control. *What's Going On* was the result, surely Marvin's finest moment and, along with a number of Stevie Wonder's early-'70s releases, one of a handful of *great* Motown albums. A concept album, *What's Going On* chronicled a multitude of societal ills. Ironically, Motown owner Berry Gordy did not want to release it. He was convinced it held no commercial potential. Gordy couldn't have been more wrong: *What's Going On* catapulted Marvin Gaye into superstardom. Three number one singles were pulled from the album: the title song, "Mercy Mercy Me (The Ecology)," and "Inner City Blues (Make Me Wanna Holler)." This was the first album where Marvin overdubbed his voice multiple times, creating a one-man vocal group. The result was a level of timbral integration in the harmonies that became a Gaye trademark. *—Rob Bowman*

Trouble Man / Dec. 8, 1972 / Motown ✦✦✦
Marvin Gaye turned to soundtracks in the early '70s, and came out with one that ranked right alongside the epic scores done by Curtis Mayfield and Isaac Hayes. The film itself was a typical '70s "blaxploitation" effort, but Gaye's vocals, seamless production, and a nice mix of up-tempo funk, light ballads, and pseudo-macho camp were brilliant. *—Ron Wynn*

☆ **Let's Get It On** / Aug. 28, 1973 / Motown ✦✦✦✦✦
After brilliantly surveying the social, political and spiritual landscape with *What's Going On,* Marvin Gaye turned to more intimate matters with *Let's Get It On,* a record unparalleled in its sheer sensuality and carnal energy. Always a sexually-charged performer, Gaye's passions reach their boiling point on tracks like the magnificent title hit (a Number One smash) and "You Sure Love to Ball"; silky and shimmering, the music is seductive in the most literal sense, its fluid grooves so perfectly designed for romance as to border on parody. With each performance laced with innuendo, each lyric a come-on, and each rhythm throbbing with lust, perhaps no other record has ever achieved the kind of sheer erotic force of *Let's Get It On,* and it remains the blueprint for all of the slow jams to follow decades later—much copied, but never imitated. *—Jason Ankeny*

★ **Anthology [1974]** / 1974 / Motown ✦✦✦✦✦

Live [Motown] / Jun. 19, 1974 / Motown ✦✦✦

I Want You / Mar. 16, 1976 / Motown ✦✦✦✦
Together with Leon Ware, Gaye created 1976's *I Want You.* Some of these tracks were to go on Leon Ware's Motown debut, *Musical Massage* until Berry Gordy got a listen and decided that they'd be even better for Gaye, as the artist had not released a studio album since 1973's *Let's Get It On.* The title track to *I Want You* was the album's most successful effort, but certainly not the best. Like many of his albums, *I Want You* has Gaye's peaks not so much com-

ing from the singles but rather the album cuts and the totality of the effort itself. Not that all of the lyrics and intentions here are crystal clear, though. In fact, Gaye does sound somnolent in spots, and it gives credence to the rumors that he did some of the tracks lying on a couch. "Come Live With Me," produced by Ware and Hal Davis, is the most focused track here. The refined and atmospheric "Feel My Love Inside" has Gaye giving a commanding upper-register vocal and has some doo wop backing vocals thrown in for good measure. To most fans, *I Want You* probably sounds unlike anything Gaye recorded. They're not wrong. In fact, this has the feel of a Leon Ware album with a more persuasive voice on top. "Since I Had You" typifies that idea as Gaye skillfully maneuvers through Ware's compelling and complicated arrangement, and he puts an accent on notes that other singers wouldn't even think to. *I Want You* is one of Gaye's best albums, and the production set a standard that few have been able to match. *—Jason Elias*

Here, My Dear / Dec. 15, 1978 / Motown ✦✦✦✦✦
On one of the stranger releases in popular music, *Here, My Dear,* Gaye stands emotionally naked. Over the course of this two-album set, Marvin chronicles the dissolution of his marriage (to company president Berry Gordy's sister Anna). The level of detail is nearly painful as Marvin accuses Anna of keeping him from seeing his son, having a restraining order issued against him, and holding their separation up for ransom. Marvin also tells us of his cocaine habit and his obsession with prostitutes. In a trace of irony not lost on the singer, Anna received all royalties from the album as per their divorce agreement. Upon hearing it, she reportedly contemplated suing for invasion of privacy. *—Rob Bowman*

Midnight Love / Oct. 1982 / Columbia/Legacy ✦✦✦✦
Larkin Arnold, former CBS Records (Sony Music) senior executive VP, convinced Marvin Gaye to leave his flat in Belgium and sign with Columbia Records; the result would become the soul singer's last album before his untimely death. Of all his number one songs, this album's first release, "Sexual Healing," became his longest running number one single on the *Billboard* R&B charts (ten straight weeks). With the exception of the guitar, the Washington, D.C. native performed every instrument on this classic hit. Gaye concocted a pioneering percussive sound that was balladic in taste but stimulating in feel. As this project may not be an absolute erotic expression or a socially challenging plea from Gaye like on some of his previous albums, nonetheless, *Midnight Love* is a classic Marvin Gaye effort. In addition to this project thriving with Gaye's enthusiastic spirit, it has his harmonious background vocals, his stunning vocal arrangements and his creative penmanship, as he wrote all the selections. The 2000 CD reissue on Sony/Legacy adds historical liner notes by Gaye biographer David Ritz and a bonus track, an instrumental version of "Rockin' After Midnight" (which actually does feature a bit of vocalizing by Gaye). *—Craig Lytle*

The Marvin Gaye Collection / Sep. 1990 / Motown ✦✦✦

Seek & You Shall Find: More of the Best (1963-1981) / 1993 / Rhino ✦✦✦✦✦

Norman Whitfield Sessions / Aug. 23, 1994 / Motown ✦✦✦
All of Gaye's recordings with producer Norman Whitfield are collected on the appropriately titled *The Norman Whitfield Sessions.* The sessions proved beneficial to both Gaye and Whitfield, as they produced the classic "I Heard It Through the Grapevine." While nothing on the set matches that seminal single, most of the music is captivating. Nevertheless, the disc will appeal mainly to the devoted Marvin Gaye collector, since most of the material is either alternate takes or outtakes. *—Stephen Thomas Erlewine*

The Master 1961-1984 / Apr. 25, 1995 / Motown ✦✦✦✦✦
The average fan is better off with *Anthology,* which covers almost all of Gaye's true classics. But for those who want the hits and then some, and have the budget and interest to go further, this four-CD box set is an excellent retrospective of his career. The 89 tracks include all the chart hits (both on his own and with Mary Wells, Kim Weston, Tammi Terrell, and Diana Ross) and many interesting B-sides, album tracks, and misses. There are also over a dozen previously unreleased cuts, most dating from the early part of his career; they don't rank among his best work, but they're almost all good and interesting. With a long essay by his biographer, David Ritz, this is the best overview of Gaye's evolution and versatility, and a much-recommended alternative to the previous Gaye box, *The Marvin Gaye Collection.* *—Richie Unterberger*

★ **Anthology [1995]** / Aug. 22, 1995 / Motown ✦✦✦✦✦
The Marvin Gaye Anthology released in 1995 is an entirely different compilation from the three-LP *Anthology* originally released in 1974 and reissued as a double CD in 1986. The earlier version contained 40 tracks, starting with "Stubborn Kind of Fellow" and running through "Trouble Man." The new one, on two CDs or cassettes, contains 47 tracks, also starting with "Stubborn Kind of Fellow," but running through "Heavy Love Affair." As such, it is more comprehensive, containing such later hits as "Let's Get It On," "I Want You," and "Got to Give It Up, Pt. 1" that were not featured on the earlier edition (but not "Sexual Healing," which Gaye recorded after leaving Motown). Only a couple of Gaye's Top Ten R&B/Top 40 pop hits are missing, and there is a smattering of rarities. The 1995 *Anthology* falls neatly between the single-disc *Every Great Motown Hit* and the four-disc boxed set *The Master 1961-1984* as a thorough hits collection at a reasonable price. *—William Ruhlmann*

Lost and Found: Love Starved Heart [Expanded Edition] / Sep. 28, 1999 / Motown ✦✦✦✦
Originally issued as part of a 1994 box set and newly expanded here with nine additional performances, *Love Starved Heart* assembles 25 unreleased tracks recorded by Marvin Gaye between 1963 and 1971, Motown's golden era. That it took three decades for these songs to see the light of day speaks far more to the intensity of the label's assembly line production ethic than to the quality of the material itself—at their most pedestrian, these are fine performances simply lost in the shuffle, but at moments like "It's a Desperate Situation," "When I Feel the Need," and "This Love Starved Heart of Mine (It's Killing Me)," Gaye achieves the same peaks of his hits of the era, crafting performances of such sublime beauty and haunting poignance that their failure to reach the masses until now is nothing short of remarkable. Still, where classics like "I Heard It Through the Grapevine" and "Ain't That Peculiar" tend to suffer from years of oldies radio wear and tear, *Love Starved Heart* sounds positively refreshing—in their own way, these long-lost songs reaffirm the timelessness of Marvin Gaye's brilliance even more than the familiar hits on which his reputation rests. *—Jason Ankeny*

The Final Concert / May 23, 2000 / The Right Stuff ✦✦✦

J. Geils Band

f. 1967, Boston, MA, **db.** 1985
Group / Album Rock, Boogie Rock, Arena Rock, Pop/Rock, Hard Rock, Blues-Rock, Rock & Roll
The J. Geils Band were one of the most popular touring rock & roll bands in America during the '70s. Where their contemporaries were influenced by the heavy boogie of British blues-rock and the ear-splitting sonic adventures of psychedelia, the J. Geils Band were a bar band pure and simple, churning out greasy covers of obscure R&B, doo-wop and soul tunes, cutting them with healthy dose of Stonesy swagger. While their muscular sound and the hyper jive of frontman Peter Wolf packed arenas across America, it only rarely earned them hit singles. Seth Justman, the group's main songwriter, could turn out catchy R&B-based rockers like "Give It To Me" or "Must of Got Lost," but these hits never led to stardom, primarily because the group had trouble capturing the energy of their live sound in the studio. In the early '80s, the group tempered their driving rock with some pop, and the makeover paid off with the massive hit single "Centerfold," which stayed at number one for six weeks. By the time the band prepared to record a followup, tensions between Justman and Wolf had grown considerably, resulting in Wolf's departure, which quickly led to the band's demise. After working for years to reach to top of the charts, the J. Geils couldn't stay there once they finally achieved their goal. *—Stephen Thomas Erlewine*

The J. Geils Band / 1970 / Atlantic ✦✦✦✦✦
Their debut paid homage to the likes of Otis Rush, John Lee Hooker, and Motown through blistering covers, but originals such as "Wait" and "What's Your Hurry" more than hold their own. Magic Dick steals the show on this one. *—John Floyd*

The Morning After / 1971 / Atlantic ✦✦✦

Full House Live / 1972 / Atlantic ✦✦✦
Live is the way the J. Geils Band should be experienced; they put on a show like few others, and *Full House* is the proof. From start to finish, there is not one bad cut. From the opener, "First I Look at the Purse" right on through "Looking for a Love," these guys don't give up an inch. *—James Chrispell*

Bloodshot / 1973 / Atlantic ✦✦

Ladies Invited / 1973 / Atlantic ✦✦✦

Nightmares . . . and Other Tales from the Vinyl Jungle / 1974 / Atlantic ✦✦✦
After a brief sidestep, the J. Geils Band came roaring back with a very urban-jungle sort of album which percolates with beat and rocks with enthusiastic excitement. Here lies the reggae-ish "Give It To Me," as well as the concert staple "Detroit Breakdown." A fertile release from some of the hardest rockers of the seventies. *—James Chrispell*

Hotline / 1975 / Atlantic ✦✦

Blow Your Face Out / 1976 / Rhino ✦✦✦
If you're looking to put on a party record from the mid-seventies, grab a hold of *Blow Your Face Out* and crank up the volume. Always known as a great live band, J. Geils and Co. stomp through one of the most exciting live sets put on vinyl (and tape and CD). The title says it all. *—James Chrispell*

Monkey Island / 1977 / Atlantic ✦✦✦✦✦
One of the great lost albums, *Monkey Island* is where the Geils Band make the blues their own. It's an elaborately produced, adventurous set that analyzes their commerical failure and looks for answers to hard-to-ask questions. Unlike their 1972 live album *Full House, Monkey Island* refuses to pander to blues conservatists or boogie-rock hammerheads; the album is steeped in the kind of pathos and bitterness that infuse the Stones' *Sticky Fingers.* The album flopped, but it remains the group's most personal statement. *—John Floyd*

Sanctuary / 1978 / Razor & Tie ✦✦✦
Hot on the heels of the band's excellent but completely overlooked *Monkey Island,* the J. Geils Band severed ties with Atlantic and signed a fresh deal with EMI Records. The band's tenure with Atlantic only yielded a few successes, and on paper, teaming up with producer Joe Wissert, the man responsible for many of Earth, Wind & Fire's and Boz Scaggs' biggest hits, seemed like an odd choice. However, *Sanctuary* was a rebirth of sorts for the sextet: Wissert crystallized the band's attack, working off their leaner songwriting and simplifying their arrangements. Keeping their boogie-woogie bar band attack intact, Peter Wolf and Seth Justman delivered first-rate material, including the down and dirty opener "I Could Hurt You," the sublime title track and the lovely "One Last Kiss," which cracked the Top 40 in early 1978. The Stevie Wonder-ish "Take It Back," also a mild hit, predicted the commercial direction the band took on *Freeze Frame* three years later. The beautiful "Teresa," a heartbreaking ballad executed with help of a simple vocal/piano arrangement courtesy of the Wolf/Justman team, and "Wild Man," which sounds like a leftover from the Atlantic years, are also highlights. *Sanctuary*'s final song, the rollicking, Magic Dick-driven "Just Can't Stop Me," encapsulates everything magical (pun intended) and soulful about this band. With its effortless playing and a breakdown that'll have you on the edge of your seat, it served as the band's call into battle for the *Freeze Frame* tour. The Razor & Tie reissue features covers of "I Do" and "Land of a Thousand Dances" from the band's live record *Showtime,* recorded at the height of their *Freeze Frame* period. "Land of a Thousand Dances" in particular reminds you just how incredible these guys were live. *—John Franck*

● **The Best of the J. Geils Band** / 1979 / Atlantic ✦✦✦✦
Contractual obligations aside, *The Best of the J. Geils Band* is a worthy and yet somewhat disjointed collection of the band's more popular radio songs taken from their eight Atlantic records. Released just a year after J. Geils' EMI debut *Sanctuary,* one listen to these to two

works back to back can make an extraordinary argument for the band's growth. Or lack of it, depending on whom you ask. On their eight years with Atlantic, Peter Wolf and company released some of THE "best white R&B" records of all time. Some sold well, some sold moderately, and some just plain tanked. The one thing that remained a constant was the band's monolithically inspired live performances. Unfortunately for Atlantic, as soon as the band left the label, almost overnight, with a newly retooled, more compact sound, success would find the six-piece on 1980's *Love Stinks* and, of course, on the gigantic blockbuster *Freeze Frame*. If you want to find out just how powerful these guys were, this "best collection" is a decent starting point. Songs like joyous "Give It to Me" or the colossal "Detroit Breakdown" are just some of the highlights. For a brief overview, pick up this set, but if it's a college education that you're after, pick up the band's Rhino anthology, *Houseparty* (a much more worthy compilation replete with killer liner notes).

Love Stinks / 1980 / EMI America ✦✦✦

Freeze Frame / 1981 / EMI America ✦✦✦✦✦
Tempering their bar band R&B with a touch of new wave pop production, the J. Geils Band finally broke through into the big leagues with *Freeze Frame*. Fans of the hard-driving rock of the group's '70s albums will find the sleek sound of *Freeze Frame* slightly disorienting, but the production gives the album cohesion. Good-time rock & roll remains at the core of the group's music, but the sound of the record is glossier, shining with synthesizers and big pop hooks. With its singalong chorus, "Centerfold" exemplifies this trend, but it's merely the tip of the iceberg. "Freeze Frame" has a great stop-start chorus, "Flamethrower" and "Piss on the Wall" rush along on hard-boogie riffs, and "Angel in Blue" is terrific neo-doo wop. There are still a handful of throwaways, but even the filler has a stylized, synthesized flair that makes it enjoyable, and the keepers are among the band's best. *—Stephen Thomas Erlewine*

Showtime! / 1982 / BGO ✦✦

You're Gettin' Even While I'm Gettin' Odd / 1984 / EMI ✦✦

Flashback / 1988 / EMI America ✦✦✦

● **Houseparty: Anthology** / 1992 / Rhino ✦✦✦✦✦
The superb two-disc anthology *Houseparty* concentrates on the rousing, full-throttle blues-boogie of their heyday, including a full album's worth of live material (ten songs from their three live albums). The pop success of *Love Stinks* and *Freeze Frame* makes sense in the context of the set, but the songs that cut the deepest are the blues-rock numbers on the first disc and the live songs. Thankfully, the compilers (*Trouser Press* editor Ira Robbins and band members Peter Wolf and Seth Justman) end *Houseparty* with three songs from *Sanctuary*, helping secure the image of the J. Geils Band as one of America's top rock & roll groups. *—Stephen Thomas Erlewine*

Generation X

f. 1976, **db.** 1981
Group / British Punk, Punk
An early London punk band (1978-1981), Generation X featured Billy Idol and Tony James (later to form Sigue Sigue Sputnik). Often criticized as being too commercially minded, Gen X was definitely the smoothest and most pop-oriented of their rebellious crowd. Their first album is considered the best, with the U.S. version offering a slightly improved song set. Their third and last, *Kiss Me Deadly*, was more an Idol/James project than a band effort and was produced by Keith Forsey, who shaped Idol's solo sound. This album contained an early version of "Dancing with Myself," which was eventually Idol's first big solo pop success. As to whether they were a band of crass opportunists or true champions of the punk spirit, Billy Idol's career and Sigue Sigue Sputnik's dubious distinction of having the first advertisement on a pop record speak volumes. *—Scott Bultman*

Generation X / 1979 / JCI ✦✦✦✦✦
Generation X had punk attitude and subject matter on their debut album, which includes their answer song to the Who, "Your Generation," and the generic "One Hundred Punks." But the group's music already had more of a melodic mainstream rock sound than punk's raw assault, and frontman Billy Idol's snarl was straight out of Elvis Presley. *—William Ruhlmann*

Valley of the Dolls / 1979 / Chrysalis ✦✦

Kiss Me Deadly / 1981 / Chrysalis ✦✦✦
Idol and bassist Brian James rehearse for their post-Gen X careers, respectively as a solo artist and as the leader of Sigue Sigue Sputnik. This album contains the dance hit "Dancing with Myself." *—William Ruhlmann*

● **Perfect Hits 1975-1981** / 1985 / Chrysalis ✦✦✦✦

Genesis

f. 1966, Godalming, England
Group / Album Rock, Pop/Rock, Soft Rock, Prog-Rock/Art Rock, Adult Contemporary
One of the most successful rock acts of the 1970's, 1980's, and 1990's, Genesis enjoyed a longevity exceeded only by the likes of the Rolling Stones and the Kinks, in the process providing a launching pad for the superstardom of members Peter Gabriel and Phil Collins. The theatrical attributes of Gabriel's singing fit in well with the group's live performances, and he began to make ever more extensive use of masks, make-up, and props in concert, telling framing stories in order to set up their increasingly complicated songs. When presented amid the group's very strong playing, this aspect of Gabriel's work turned Genesis's performances into multi-media events. *Foxtrot*, issued in the fall of 1972, was the flashpoint in Genesis's history, and not just on commercial terms. The writing was as sophisticated as anything in progressive rock, and the lyrics were complex, serious and clever, a far cry from the usual overblown words attached to most prog-rock. The release of the ambitious double LP *The Lamb Lies Down on Broadway* in late 1974 marked the culmination of the group's early history; in 1975, Gabriel announced that he was leaving Genesis. Drummer Collins took over the role of lead singer, and the resulting *Trick of the Tail* made number three in England and number 31 in America, the best chart showing up to that time for a Genesis album. In 1978, Genesis released *And Then There Were Three*, which abandoned any efforts at progressive rock in favor of a softer, much more accessible and less ambitious pop sound. After a flurry of solo projects, the group reconvened for 1980's *Duke*, which became their first chart-topper in England while rising to number 11 in America. *Abacab*, released in late 1981, was another smash, and 1983's self-titled *Genesis* furthered the group's record of British chart-toppers and American top 10 hits, becoming their second million-selling U.S. album while also yielding their first American Top Ten single, "That's All." Two years later, the group outdid themselves with the release of their most commercially successful album to date, *Invisible Touch*. Their 1991 album *We Can't Dance* debuted at Number One in England and got to number four in America; it was Collins' last album with the group. *—Bruce Eder*

From Genesis to Revelation / Mar. 1969 / Decca ✦✦

Trespass / Oct. 1970 / MCA ✦✦
The group's first truly progressive album, and their first record for the Charisma label (although *Trespass* was released in America by ABC, which is how MCA comes to have it today), is important mostly as a formative effort. Peter Gabriel, Tony Banks, and Michael Rutherford are here, but the guitarist is Anthony Phillips, and the drummer is John Mayhew. Gabriel, Banks, Phillips, and Rutherford are responsible for the compositions, which are far more ambitious than the group's earlier efforts ("Silent Sun," etc.). Unfortunately, much of what is here is more interesting for what it points toward than what it actually *does*—the group reflects a peculiarly dramatic brand of progressive rock, very theatrical as music, but not very successful. The lyrics are complex enough, but lack the unity and clarity that would make Genesis' subsequent albums among the most interesting of prog-rock efforts to analyze. Gabriel's voice is very expressive but generally lacks power and confidence, while the conventional backup vocalizing by the others is wimpy, and Phillips' playing is muted. Tony Banks' keyboards are the dominant instruments, which isn't that bad, but it isn't the Genesis that everyone came to know. The soft, lyrical "Visions of Angels" and "Stagnation" are typical, gentle works by a band that later learned how to rock much harder. Only one of the songs here, "The Knife"—which rocks harder than anything else on *Trespass* and is easily the best track on the album—lasted in the group's concert repertory past the next album. The MCA CD sounds good enough, though it was not remastered at the time the Charisma/Atlantic output by the band was redone. *—Bruce Eder*

Nursery Cryme / Nov. 1971 / Atco ✦✦✦
The group's first fully realized, mature album is still somewhat uneven, but the stuff that does work well works so well that it carries the record. This includes "The Musical Box," which became a highlight of the group's live shows, presenting Gabriel's extraordinary abilities as a singer/actor as well as hinting at a level of lyrical sophistication that dazzled many fans and onlookers. "Return of the Giant Hogweed" was an even better showcase for the group's playing. The "Definitive Edition Remaster" version runs circles around the sound on all previous versions, although a certain weakness in the engineering (obviously in the original recording, and beyond repair) remains, especially where the presence of Collins' drums in relation to the rest of the band (particularly on the acoustic passages) is concerned. *—Bruce Eder*

☆ **Foxtrot** / Oct. 1972 / Atco ✦✦✦✦✦
This was the point where all of the talent simmering and occasionally boiling up out of Genesis blew the lid off the pot. There isn't a weak song here, and the two showpieces, "Watcher of the Skies" and "Supper's Ready," presented the group at its strongest in medium-length and extended-length songs. The lyrical complexities of the latter were not easily sorted out, but they were clever enough and inviting enough not to put off any potential fans, and as handled by Gabriel, they demanded attention. And not only is the band playing loud on a lot of this album, but the engineer captured them perfectly. The Definitive Remastered Edition released in 1995 supplants all prior versions of the compact disc. *—Bruce Eder*

Genesis: Live / Jun. 1973 / Atco ✦✦✦

★ **Selling England by the Pound** / Nov. 1973 / Atco ✦✦✦✦✦
By the Ezra Pound, no doubt—seriously, the influence of T.S. Eliot and other early 20th-century literary figures crops up throughout the opening and closing portions of this album, with the rest of the songs given over to more conventional subject matter. The original group's strongest single album and, for those not predisposed to enjoy the double-disc *Lamb Lies Down on Broadway*, the peak of their output. The production is note-perfect, and not an instrument is out of place. The Definitive Remastered Edition from 1996 is a significant improvement, in sound and packaging, over the earlier version from Atlantic. *—Bruce Eder*

★ **The Lamb Lies Down on Broadway** / Nov. 18, 1974 / Atco ✦✦✦✦✦
The group's only double studio album was the culmination of their early period, featuring Peter Gabriel in a bravura performance in the role of Rael, a New York street hustler, in this musical drama. The singing and playing are all strong, and the remastered edition from 1995 is the first CD edition that sounds as good as (or better than) the superb original Atco pressing from 1975. The piece's length makes it something of an acquired taste, but most serious fans regard this as the best record the group ever cut. *—Bruce Eder*

Trick of the Tail / Feb. 2, 1976 / Atco ✦✦✦✦✦
The quality of the group's first post-Peter Gabriel album astonished everyone, especially coming out after an 18-month gap following *The Lamb Lies Down on Broadway*. The opening number, "Dance on a Volcano," almost deliberately recalls "At the Cinema" from *Selling England by the Pound* in melody and structure, and Phil Collins sounds more like Peter Gabriel than Gabriel himself did. Tony Banks' and Steve Hackett's "Entangled" was the prettiest song the group had recorded up to that time, a gossamer-textured piece about sleep and dreaming in which a strummed acoustic guitar makes its most prominent appearance ever on a Genesis song, supported by the sweetest singing of Collins' career. Not all of the material is in league with these two songs, but all of it has some moments of tremendous beauty, and Tony Banks' "Robbery, Assault and Battery," with its bold, hard-rocking choruses and extended song structure, would have been worthy of inclusion on any of the group's earlier records. Even "Los Endos," an instrumental finale that ought to be considered a cop-out in the absence of a good song, provides the quartet with an opportunity to showcase its still con-

siderable collective skills to which few fans could object. The 1995 "Definitive Edition Remaster" is a vast improvement in sound and packaging over the earlier CD version, and is the one worth picking up. *—Bruce Eder*

Wind & Wuthering / Dec. 27, 1976 / Atco ✦✦✦✦
For many veteran fans, *Wind & Wuthering* was the last near-great Genesis album, as well as their last album to feature a progressive rock sound. The group's second (and last) album as a quartet, it features the requisite long-form songs, complete with slashing guitars, rippling synthesizers, sweeping Mellotron passages, and elegant piano parts, along with some beautifully complex and poetic lyrics. Songs like "Eleventh Earl of Mar," "One for the Vine," and "All in a Mouse's Night" are the equals of the better (but not the best) work from the band's Peter Gabriel era, but the most important song on this album was Michael Rutherford's "Your Own Special Way," an edited version of which became their first single to make the American charts (and only their second British chart hit). Although most of the songs are more complex and challenging, they also present a sense of marking time, while "Your Own Special Way" pointed the way toward the simpler, more accessible sound that the group was moving toward. The 1995 reissue, part of Atco's "Definitive Edition Remaster" series, from the original master tapes is considerably more impressive than the original late-'80s CD, and includes full lyrics and production credits as well. *—Bruce Eder*

Seconds Out / Nov. 1977 / Atlantic ✦✦

And Then There Were Three / Mar. 23, 1978 / Atlantic ✦✦✦
The birth of the modern Genesis, a pop-rock trio led by singer/drummer Phil Collins, playing tightly constructed, short, catchy songs. The best of the bunch here is "Follow You, Follow Me," a hit on both sides of the Atlantic. (The first Genesis gold album in the U.S.) *—William Ruhlmann*

Duke / Mar. 31, 1980 / Atlantic ✦✦✦
Released in April 1980, *Duke* found Genesis completely geared up as a maker of concise, appealing pop singles, and it was an immediate, across-the-board hit, topping the U.K. chart and almost making the U.S. Top 10, while the singles "Misunderstanding" and "Turn It On Again" became radio favorites on both sides of the Atlantic. *—William Ruhlmann*

● **Abacab** / Sep. 14, 1981 / Atlantic ✦✦✦✦✦
After gaining some limited commercial success with *Duke,* Genesis went for the jugular of American radio with the well-crafted pop of *Abacab.* While there are still some traces of their art rock past, the album is primarily filled with a new wave sound and concise songs. Phil Collins, who replaced Peter Gabriel years earlier as the lead vocalist, was finally comfortable with his role as the leader of the band, and his influence is more prominent. Although he's not a strong vocalist, Collins more than makes up for it with passionate performances. & "Man on the Corner," a modest hit, managed to make social commentary about the homeless without feeling preachy. *Abacab* rose to number seven on the charts, which is a tribute the band's ability to bring intellectual pop to the masses with catchy melodies. Genesis is no ordinary pop band—they use driving beats and unusual syncopation (by pop standards) on the title track and & "No Reply at All," a song that employs the horn section from Earth, Wind & Fire. This album is one of their most enjoyable, and it gave Genesis the success and recognition they deserved. *—Vik Iyengar*

Three Sides Live / Jun. 1982 / Atlantic ✦✦✦

Genesis / Oct. 1983 / Atlantic ✦✦✦✦
If Genesis still had one foot in the art rock world with *Abacab,* they jumped into pop with both feet on their eponymous release. Genesis used crisp, glossy production and mid-tempo arrangements designed for pop radio in the 1980s. After years of relative obscurity on this side of the Atlantic, one cannot blame the band, especially one so talented. There were many hits, the biggest of which were the slower easy listening songs such as "That's All" or "Taking It All Too Hard." While all the songs are unbelievable catchy, they often mask inane lyrics ("Illegal Alien") and the lack of musical innovation that fans had come to expect was a little disappointing. Although they had lost their edge, Genesis still had the ability to craft catchy songs. *Genesis* still represents the best pop radio of that era, and the album is still recommended for fans looking for 1980s nostalgia or fans of Phil Collins' solo work. *—Vik Iyengar*

Invisible Touch / Jun. 1986 / Atlantic ✦✦✦
The biggest Genesis hit to date, this multi-million-selling release features five Top Five hits, including the number one title track, "Throwing It All Away," "Land of Confusion," "Tonight, Tonight, Tonight," and "In Too Deep." *—William Ruhlmann*

We Can't Dance / Oct. 28, 1991 / Atlantic ✦✦✦
Genesis' first album in five years was another enormous hit, even if it failed to match the sales of 1986's *Invisible Touch.* In the U.K., it was the group's fifth straight studio album to hit number one; in the U.S., it was their fifth straight Top Ten and sold four million copies. "No Son of Mine" (something of an answer to "The Living Years," by Mike Rutherford's splinter group, Mike and the Mechanics) broke the group's string of Top Five singles by getting only to number 12, but it was followed by the number seven "I Can't Dance," as well as three more Top 25 hits: "Hold on My Heart," "Jesus He Knows Me" (a satire of evangelist preachers), and "Never a Time." *—William Ruhlmann*

Genesis Live: The Way We Walk, Vol. 1 (The Shorts) / Nov. 17, 1992 / Atlantic ✦✦

Genesis Live: The Way We Walk, Vol. 2 (The Longs) / Feb. 9, 1993 / Atlantic ✦✦

Genesis Archives, Vol. 1: 1967-1975—*The Gabriel Years* / *Jun. 16, 1998 / Atlantic* ✦✦✦✦
Prog-rock audiences have always been receptive to box sets, especially sets that include an abundance of rare material—witness the success of the numerous King Crimson sets. When it came time to assembling their own box sets, Genesis chose to follow the path of rarities instead of merely rehashing their old hits. That means, of course, that *Genesis Archives, Vol. 1: 1967-75—The Gabriel Years* is the province of hardcore fans and collectors, not casual listeners, since there is nothing but unreleased material on the four-disc set. The first two discs are devoted to a live performance of *The Lamb Lies Down on Broadway* at the Shrine Auditorium in Los Angeles on January 24, 1975; the third has a selection of live material from the London Rainbow Theatre on October 20, 1973, plus a handful of rare singles and a BBC session; the fourth has alternate mixes, BBC sessions and demos from 1967-1969. It's a virtual cornucopia of rare material, much of which will be necessary to dedicated fans. However, for some listeners, the set may be frustrating, and not because it contains rarities—it's because those rarities have been tampered with. Peter Gabriel recut some of his vocals for *The Lamb* in 1998, claiming that he didn't give his best possible performance because his elaborate costumes were constricting. Steve Hackett followed suit and "brushed up" some guitar lines. This may frustrate some fans who would prefer to have the original tapes preserved, but it may be a minor thing to collectors, who will likely delight in having all these rare recordings—many of which are quite terrific—in one place. *—Stephen Thomas Erlewine*

● **Turn It On Again: The Hits** / Oct. 26, 1999 / Atlantic ✦✦✦✦

Genesis Archives, Vol. 2: 1976-1992 / Nov. 7, 2000 / Atlantic ✦✦✦

The Germs

f. 1977, **db.** 1980
Group / American Punk, L.A. Punk, Hardcore Punk, Punk
Living fast and dying young is one of rock's great cliches, but no phrase better describes the reasons for the demise of L.A. punkers the Germs. Capable of creating a firestorm of noisy, confrontational music, they were ultimately undone by their perversely charismatic lead singer, madman Darby Crash, who died Sid Vicious-style out on the mainline at age 22. The Germs kicked up a hellacious racket that strayed from fast/loud punk into art-damage and garage grunge. On stage, their gigs bordered on performance art, with Crash in full Iggy frenzy, diving into the crowd, adorning himself with whatever foodstuffs the audience provided, wearing less and less clothing, all done with the band cranking out noisy spasms of simple, but effective, rock noise. Never capturing this mania on record (how could you—) the Germs' recording career is based on the sole record made during Crash's short life. *(GI)* was a fine hunk of early L.A. punk rock that was more literate and compelling that what was being offered by lesser local luminaries such as the Zeroes and the Weirdos. It may not be life-changing music, but the white-hot, adrenal rush is a little bit of heaven. *—John Dougan*

● **Germs (M.I.A.)—*The Complete Anthology* /** *Aug. 3, 1993 / Slash/Rhino* ✦✦✦✦✦
The essential Germs anthology contains all of *(GI)* as well as some of the best tracks from *What We Do Is Secret* and a handful of recordings made for the William Friedkin film, *Cruising.* (The filmmaker best known for *The Exorcist* reportedly saw the Germs live and was knocked out by their extreme performance.) Some of the early stuff, especially "Forming" and the live "Sex Boy," wander into avant-garde noise rock, all meandering atonality and screeching hysteria, still it's pretty good. But the material from *(GI)* still sounds great and proves conclusively that the Germs had, in spite of themselves, turned into a tight, explosive rock band. Generous at 30 tracks, this is seminal late-'70s L.A. punk that set the stage for a generation of hardcore bands to follow. *—John Dougan*

Gerry & the Pacemakers

f. 1959, Liverpool, England, **db.** 1990
Group / Merseybeat, British Invasion
As unfathomable as it seems from the distance of over 30 years, for a few months, Gerry & the Pacemakers were the Beatles' nearest competitors in Britain. Managed (like the Beatles) by Brian Epstein, Gerry Marsden and his band burst out of the gate with three consecutive number one U.K. hits in 1963, "How Do You Do It," "I Like It," and "You'll Never Walk Alone." If the Beatles defined Merseybeat at its best in early 1963, Gerry & the Pacemakers defined the form at its most innocuous, performing bouncy, catchy, and utterly lightweight tunes driven by rhythm guitar and Marsden's chipper vocals. Compared to the Beatles and other British Invasion heavies, they sound quaint indeed. That's not to say the group were trivial; their hits were certainly likable and energetic, and are fondly remembered today, even if the musicians lacked the acumen (or earthy image) to develop their style from its relentlessly upbeat and poppy base. *—Richie Unterberger*

● **The Best of Gerry & the Pacemakers: The Definitive Collection** / Oct. 15, 1991 / EMI America ✦✦✦✦✦

● **The Gerry Cross the Mersey: All the Hits of Gerry and the Pacemakers** / Oct. 1995 / Razor & Tie ✦✦✦✦✦
Sixteen-track best-of includes all of their British and American hits, as well as some of their best B-sides. The more extensive EMI America best-of has all of these songs and more, and so is still recommended as the first purchase. But for just about everybody, this has all the Gerry & the Pacemakers you need, and all but two of the songs are in stereo, if that's an important consideration. *—Richie Unterberger*

Gin Blossoms

f. 1987, **db.** Dec. 1997
Group / Adult Alternative Pop/Rock, Pop/Rock, Alternative Pop/Rock
Alternative power-popsters the Gin Blossoms were formed in 1987 in Tempe, Arizona by longtime friends Bill Leen (bass) and Doug Hopkins (guitar), with an initial lineup also featuring vocalist Jesse Valenzuela, guitarist Richard Taylor, and drummer Chris McCann. The following year saw several personnel shifts as the band struggled to solidify—McCann was replaced by Dan Henzerling and, shortly thereafter, Phillip Rhodes, while Taylor was fired and replaced by guitarist Robin Wilson. Wilson and Valenzuela subsequently switched roles, and the band recorded a self-released album, *Dusted,* in 1989. A&M signed them the following year. After an impressive 1991 debut EP, *Up and Crumbling,* the Gin Blossoms rocketed out of the college pop charts and into the mainstream with their 1993 hit single "Hey Jealousy." Combining the ringing guitar hooks of the Byrds and R.E.M. with a solid, rootsy drive, the band's breakthrough full-length album, *New Miserable Experience* (which had actually been released the previous year), was filled with songs equally as strong as "Hey Jealousy," including the second hit single, "Found Out About You." New Miserable Experience

and its singles dominated radio and MTV for the following year—"Hey Jealousy" and "Found Out About You," both penned by Hopkins, were in heavy radio rotation nearly a year after their initial release—pushing the sales of their debut album over a million copies. However, all was not well. Doug Hopkins' battle with alcoholism and depression had taken its toll on the band during the sessions for New Miserable Experience, and he was fired shortly after the record's release, with guitarist Scott Johnson taking his place. Speculation abounded as to whether the band would be able to maintain its success without Hopkins' melancholy songwriting voice. Tragically, on December 5, 1993, Hopkins shot and killed himself, even as the songs he had written were blanketing the airwaves.

In the summer of 1995, the Gin Blossoms contributed "Till I Hear It from You," a song they co-wrote with Marshall Crenshaw, to the soundtrack of Empire Records. "Till I Hear It from You" became a major radio hit, but it was never released as an official single until it was the B-side of "Follow You Down," the first single from the group's second album, *Congratulations... I'm Sorry.* Upon its release in February of 1996, Congratulations... I'm Sorry charted well, but within six months, it had disappeared from the charts. Following the supporting tour, the Gin Blossoms disbanded in 1997. *—Stephen Thomas Erlewine*

New Miserable Experience / Aug. 4, 1992 / A&M ✦✦✦✦

Congratulations I'm Sorry / Feb. 13, 1996 / A&M ✦✦✦

● **Outside Looking In: The Best of the Gin Blossoms** / Oct. 19, 1999 / Interscope ✦✦✦✦
In December 1997, the Gin Blossoms announced their breakup, and the lines of communication were severed so severely that the band didn't realize their former label was assembling a hits collection, *Outside Looking In: The Best Of.* The album may not have been compiled with the complete authorization of the band, but that doesn't mean it isn't good or useful. Aside from the live version of "Whitewash," a sap to collectors, this is a tight distillation of the band's two A&M albums, noteworthy for the first album appearance of "Til I Hear It From You." Some might think that a compilation of two albums is stretching the definition of compilation a little bit too much, but that's really just a reflection of the industry in the '90s—two albums and one non-LP single *was* the end result of a decade's worth of work. Ultimately, *Outside Looking In* is a good listen, from the hits to the album tracks, and it confirms that the Gin Blossoms were one of the first bands to really carve out the sound later known as adult alternative pop/rock. *—Stephen Thomas Erlewine*

Gary Glitter (Paul Gadd)

b. May 8, 1940, Banbury, Oxfordshire, England
Vocals / Glitter, Pop/Rock, Glam Rock, Hard Rock
After many years of trying to become a star, Paul Gadd finally hit the winning formula in 1972—the glam rock king, Gary Glitter. Complete with extravagant makeup, silver outfits, and high boots, Glitter looked as trashy as his music sounded. Glitter and producer Michael Leander created pop records that weren't intended to be serious music—infectious singles that sounded perfect for the three minutes that they were playing; after they were finished, they seemed slightly embarrassing. With its mammoth drum beat, growling guitar, dumb instrumental hook, and incessant chorus of "hey!," his debut single, "Rock and Roll, Part Two," was a huge hit in both the U.K. and the U.S. Although he never had another hit in America, Glitter was a superstar in Britain throughout the mid-'70s, scoring three number one singles. Surprisingly, Glitter's cheerfully idiotic, catchy glam rock became somewhat influential over the next decade; Joan Jett covered several of his songs, as did the Human League, Generation X, Planet Control, and Brownsville Station. *—Stephen Thomas Erlewine*

● **Rock 'n' Roll: The Best of Gary Glitter** / 1990 / Rhino ✦✦✦✦✦
Although he's best known for the knuckle-headed sports anthem "Rock & Roll Part Two," Glitter had plenty of other glam-rock delights that were equally as good, if not better. *Rock 'n' Roll—The Best of Gary Glitter* lovingly collects his best singles, from "Rock & Roll Part Two" to such unsung riff-rockers as "Do You Wanna Touch Me (Oh Yeah!)" and "I'm the Leader of the Gang (I Am!)." It's dumb, it's catchy, it's loud—everything good rock & roll should be. A nice guilty pleasure. *—Stephen Thomas Erlewine*

Rock & Roll: Gary Glitter's Greatest Hits / Jan. 13, 1998 / Rhino ✦✦✦✦✦
In 1998, Rhino Records reissued *Rock & Roll: Gary Glitter's Greatest Hits* with artwork that wasn't quite as silly as its original incarnation, with the intention of snagging sports fans who hold "Rock & Roll, Pt. 2" dear to their hearts. In either incarnation, *Rock & Roll* is the definitive Gary Glitter collection, containing all of his singles, including "Do You Wanna Touch Me (Oh Yeah!)," "I'm the Leader of the Gang" and "Hello! Hello! I'm Back Again." *—Stephen Thomas Erlewine*

The Go-Go's

f. 1978, Los Angeles, CA, **db.** May 1985
Group / Pop/Rock, New Wave
The Go-Go's were the most popular all-female band to emerge from the punk/new wave explosion of the late '70s and early '80s, becoming one of the first commercially successful female groups that wasn't controlled by male producers or managers. While their hit singles—"We Got the Beat," "Our Lips Are Sealed," "Vacation," "Head over Heels"—were bright, energetic new wave pop, the group was integral part of the Californian punk scene. And they did play punk rock, even if many of their rougher edges were ironed out by the time they recorded their first album, 1981's *Beauty and the Beat.* Even as they became America's darlings, the Go-Go's lived the wild life of rockers, swallowing as many pills and taking as much cocaine as possible, trashing hotel rooms and just generally being bad. More importantly, their earliest music—now collected on *Return to the Valley of the Go-Go's*—was raw and rocking; it may not have directly inspired the female alternative rockers and riot grrrls of the '90s, but it certainly foreshadowed it. *—Stephen Thomas Erlewine*

Beauty & the Beat / Jul. 1981 / IRS ✦✦✦✦✦
Although the relatively polished production belies the Go-Go's' punk roots, *Beauty & the Beat* remains one of the cornerstone albums of new wave, bristling with energy, revamped surf-rock and girl-group hooks, and an intoxicating sense of fun. The infectious, bouncy "We Got the Beat" and the pulsating "Our Lips Are Sealed," which Jane Wiedlin co-wrote with Terry Hall, sent *Beauty & the Beat* to unexepected hit status, but they only scratch the surface of the wonderful pop songs that comprise the record. Nearly every song on the record is a delight, propelled by big, catchy hooks and an exuberant sense of fun. "Lust to Love," "Skidmarks on My Heart," "Tonite" and "Fading Fast" could have been hits in their own right, but as it stands, they help make *Beauty & the Beat* into a terrifically exciting pop album. *—Stephen Thomas Erlewine*

Vacation / Aug. 1982 / IRS ✦✦✦
The surprise success of *Beauty & the Beat* meant that the Go-Go's were expected to remain hitmakers, so perhaps it shouldn't have come as a surprise that their second album, *Vacation,* was a considerably slicker affair than their debut. Sporting a glossy yet alluring finish, the album had an appealing, radio-ready sound, but it was at the expense of the giddy sense of fun that made *Beauty & the Beat* such a vibrant record. However, *Vacation* is far from a washout. Although half the album is padded with filler, the very best moments are terrific pop songs, highlighted by the bouncy "This Old Feeling" and the classic title track. *—Stephen Thomas Erlewine*

Talk Show / 1984 / IRS ✦✦✦
For their third album, the Go-Go's abandoned all pretense of being punk, or even new wave, and went for an unabashed mainstream pop masterpiece. They nearly achieved their goal with *Talk Show,* an album filled with great pop songs but undermined by its own ambition. *Talk Show* has a sharper sound than its predecessors, with bigger guitars and drums, which helps drive home the accomplished pop hooks of "Turn to You," "I'm the Only One," and "Yes or No." However, the record is cluttered with half-realized songs and an overly detailed production which occasionally prevents the songs from reaching their full potential. But when the production and song are teamed well, the results are incredible, such as the surging "Head Over Heels," another classic single. Unfortunately, those moments don't arrive frequently enough to make *Talk Show* the new wave classic that it wants to be. *—Stephen Thomas Erlewine*

Greatest / Oct. 1990 / IRS ✦✦✦✦

Return to the Valley of the Go-Go's / Oct. 18, 1994 / IRS ✦✦✦✦✦
Because it doesn't ignore the group's punk and new wave roots, the double-disc set *Return to the Valley of the Go-Go's* is far more entertaining than the single-disc collection *Greatest Hits.* All of the hits are included, as well as many rarities as good as anything they officially released. Not only is the music intoxicating, but the liner notes are filled with priceless photos and memorabilia, which makes the set the one definitive Go-Go's album. *—Stephen Thomas Erlewine*

● **VH-1 Behind the Music: Go-Go's Collection** / May 23, 2000 / Interscope ✦✦✦✦
Just in time for the debut of their episode of VH1's *Behind the Music* comes *VH1 Behind the Music: Go-Go's Collection,* which features 17 of the group's definitive tracks, including "We Got the Beat," "My Lips Are Sealed," "Head Over Heels," "Vacation," and "Turn to You." Not as exhaustive as the *Return to the Valley of the Go-Go's* but not as slight as the *Greatest* album, *Go-Go's Collection* strikes a nice balance between the group's early, punky days and their later work as new wave divas. *—Heather Phares*

The Go-Betweens

f. 1978, Brisbane, Australia, **db.** Dec. 31, 1989
Group / College Rock, Indie Pop, New Wave, Alternative Pop/Rock
The Go-Betweens were perhaps the quintessential cult band of the '80s: they came from an exotic locale (Brisbane, Australia), moved to a major recording center (in their case, London) in a sustained bid to make a career out of music, released album after album of music seemingly tailor-made for the radio in spite of their having little use for contemporary Top 40 musical/lyrical formulas and earned considerable critical praise and a small but fervent international fan base. Though they split up at the end of the decade, both songwriters have moved onto respectable solo careers, that, while rarely reaching the heights the Go-Betweens scaled, continue to uphold their legacy. Robert Forster and Grant McLennan began as a pair of teenagers obsessed with the earthy rock of Dylan, CCR and the Velvet Underground and encouraged by the Australian punk of the Saints. As collected on *The Able Label Singles,* their first two singles show a fondness for scruffy, British Invasion/New Wave-influenced pop rock. Picking up permanent drummer Lindy Morrisson, they recorded their debut LP, moved to England and signed a short-lived deal with Rough Trade. Going for a lush, tuneful sound crammed with nonstandard rock instrumentation, they went on to record five more excellent LPs. Though their pre-Beggars Banquet albums were traditionally hard to find in the States, that label finally reissued all six albums on CD in 1996. 2000 saw a reunion of the band with the production of a new album, *The Friends of Rachel Worth* which also featured all three members of Sleater-Kinney. *—Michael Ribas*

Send Me a Lullaby / 1981 / Beggars Banquet ✦✦✦

Before Hollywood / 1983 / Beggars Banquet ✦✦✦✦✦
Australia's Go-Betweens are a curious anomaly, an intellectual's pop band. The songs on this album show touches of R.E.M., the Cure, Television, and 1960s organ-dominated bands such as the Zombies—but these tunes are for the most part unlike those of any other group. Unusual chord progressions, frequent use of meter changes and uneven phrase lengths, inventive production touches, wide varieties of texture, and intelligent if sometimes obscure lyrics occur throughout this worthy album. Within their style, the band rocks in songs like "Ask" and "By Chance" or croons more sedately in selections such as "As Long as That" and "Dusty in Here." And "Two Steps Step Out" is a fine, memorable tune, perhaps the album's best. This release is highly recommended, especially for those who listen with their brains as well their feet. *—David Cleary*

Spring Hill Fair / 1984 / Beggars Banquet ✦✦✦✦✦
Their most overlooked album (probably because it never saw US release), the Go-Betweens'

third works best when it doesn't try to come on too clever. Thus, while the spoken-sung "River of Money" falls flat on its face, the poppier "Bachelor Kisses," "Draining the Pool for You," and "Man O'Sand to Girl O'Sea" are resounding successes, on par with the best music that the eighties had to offer. In all, one of their lushest, most affecting records. *—Michael Ribas*

Liberty Belle & the Black Diamond Express / 1986 / Beggars Banquet ✦✦✦✦✦
Here the Go-Bees (as their Japanese fans nicknamed them) continued the superb blend of ambitious lyrics and string- and horn-embellished rock music that they initiated in *Spring Hill Fair.* In a smart musical (and commercial) maneuver, they had Tracey Thorn of Everything but the Girl help sing on "Head Full of Steam," the album's highlight. That it also contains such gems as the graceful "Bow Down" and the rollicking "Spring Rain" makes it a strong contender for their best album. *—Michael Ribas*

Tallulah / 1987 / Beggars Banquet ✦✦✦✦✦
Though the they had moved from strength to strength up until this point, *Tallulah* sounds half-hearted. There are a few good songs but in general the music isn't as catchy as before and some of the lyrics are too self-conciously poetic to be enjoyable. However, the planets did align for the majestic "Bye Bye Pride," which is as close to an anthem as they ever came. *—Michael Ribas*

16 Lovers Lane / 1988 / Capitol ✦✦✦✦✦
Finally, after years of critical acclaim, a Go-Betweens album was released in the U.S. by a major label and given a reasonable promotional push. Though it's unusual for final albums by long-standing bands to be much good, *Sixteen Lovers Lane* was an improvement over *Tallulah.* The sound was more radio-friendly than ever (and the "big" single, "Streets of Your Town," even got a little airplay) but it was all for naught. *—Michael Ribas*

• **1978-1990** / Aug. 27, 1990 / Capitol ✦✦✦✦✦
A summation of the Go-Betweens' rewarding body of work. Frustratingly, several of their best numbers were left off in favor of some so-so ones. Even so, this collection is invaluable because besides a complete discography, personnel history, and liner notes courtesy of Forster and McLennan, it contains a few interesting unreleased tracks, two good early singles ("People Say" and "I Need Two Heads"), as well as some of the best of the Go-Betweens' frequently amazing B-sides, including the shimmering "Rock and Roll Friend." From that perspective, it's a worthy epitaph for a special band. [Collectors/world travelers: Look out for the double-CD/record Japanese/U.K. versions that include all the tracks mentioned above—the U.S. release is a single CD that eliminates six of the rarities.] *—Michael Ribas*

78-79: The Lost Album / Apr. 6, 1999 / Jetset ✦✦✦✦

• **Bellavista Terrace: Best of the Go-Betweens** / May 18, 1999 / Beggars Banquet ✦✦✦✦
Not quite as comprehensive or well-chosen as the earlier (and now out-of-print) *1978-1990* retrospective, *Bellavista Terrace* is nevertheless a fine introduction to the Go-Betweens' enduring brilliance. As Robert Forster's liner notes point out with painful accuracy, this 14-track compilation could scarcely be called a greatest-hits collection as none of the band's singles actually charted, a mystery which has only deepened with the passing years—that perfect pop confections like "Head Full of Steam," "Bye Bye Pride" and the sublime "Streets of Your Town" could fail to reach an audience is a crime. ("...Anyway, we were too good for the bloody charts," Forster continues—damn right.) There is consolation to be had in that these songs all sound as good today as when they first appeared—if the Go-Betweens' refusal to bow to current trends was a liability during their own era, that same timelessness is their music's greatest strength in the here-and-now. *—Jason Ankeny*

The Friends of Rachel Worth / Sep. 19, 2000 / Jetset ✦✦✦✦✦

Goo Goo Dolls

f. 1985
Group / Adult Alternative Pop/Rock, Post-Grunge, Alternative Pop/Rock, Hard Rock
Early in their career, Buffalo natives the Goo Goo Dolls were frequently dismissed by critics as mere imitators of the Replacements; however, the band refined and mainstreamed their sound enough to become of the most popular adult alternative rock bands of the latter half of the '90s, selling millions of records to audiences largely unfamiliar with their inspirations. That's no knock on the band, either—their music simply improved in craft and accessibility as the years progressed, and radio happened to be receptive to what a decade earlier would have been considered collegiate power-pop. Their early sound recalled the Replacements' origins as a bratty punk band (circa *Sorry, Ma, Forgot to Take Out the Trash*)—melodic and a little bit thrashy. That sound was the reason the band attracted the interest of the heavy metal label Metal Blade, which issued their debut album in 1987. A college-radio breakthrough came with their third album, 1990's *Hold Me Up,* a later-Replacements-ish power-pop record. 1993's *Superstar Car Wash* was the Goo Goo Dolls' artistic breakthrough; it was a finely crafted pop/rock record, and its lead single, "We Are the Normal," was co-written with Replacements leader Paul Westerberg himself. *Superstar Car Wash* wasn't the commercial force the band hoped it would be, but that all changed with 1995's *A Boy Named Goo,* which produced the Top Five acoustic-driven ballad "Name" and went platinum. The band next contributed the ballad "Iris" to the soundtrack of *City of Angels* in 1998; appearing that April, the song was a monster smash, spending nearly a year on *Billboard*'s airplay charts, including an astonishing 18 weeks at number one. The band's next album, *Dizzy Up the Girl,* was released in September and sold over three million copies. Its clean, polished sound completed the Goo Goo Dolls' transformation into mainstream pop-rockers who happened to have alternative roots. *—Steve Huey*

First Release / 1987 / Metal Blade ✦✦

Jed / 1989 / Metal Blade ✦✦

Hold Me Up / 1990 / Metal Blade ✦✦✦

• **Superstar Car Wash** / 1993 / Metal Blade ✦✦✦✦
The hard rock rawness of Buffalo's Goo Goo Dolls makes *Superstar Carwash* an album that is high on amicable guitar riffs and attractive hooks, with an edge that never goes away. All the choruses are sandwiched perfectly between the crunching throttle of electric guitar and pleasing rock rhythms, changing pace and style just a notch in each of the fourteen songs. Heavy but far from pretentious, songs like "Fallin' Down", "Cuz You're Gone" and "We Are The Normal", co-written by Paul Westerberg, combine pleasing elements of rough harmonies with infectious runs of six string grit. John Rzeznik's vocals resonate with a reckless, punk soaked ardor that lifts their music above and beyond the norm of power pop. The attitude that surrounds the album makes the Goo Goo Dolls out to be a rough and tumble outfit, outlining all the tunes with a rebellious tone. Quite different from their platinum *A Boy Named Goo* album, which sounded smoother and refined, *Superstar Carwash* has the band sounding loose and freewheeling, making the best of any musical misdirection. Before radio adopted their polished glimmer, they let loose and channeled their playful immaturity throughout the attractive impurity of this album. *—Mike DeGagne*

Boy Named Goo / 1995 / Metal Blade ✦✦✦✦
Following the relative success of *Superstar Car Wash, A Boy Named Goo* sees the Goo Goo Dolls turning up the volume and grunge on their guitars, kicking out a batch of messy rockers. They still echo the Replacements in both attitude and sound, yet their affection for the band is genuine, making the record both an affectionate tribute and an enjoyable, rocking record. *—Stephen Thomas Erlewine*

Dizzy up the Girl / Sep. 22, 1998 / Warner Brothers ✦✦✦✦
"Name" changed the game for the Goo Goo Dolls. Prior to that unexpected hit ballad, the Buffalo trio was pretty much content to turn out amiably sloppy rock & roll in the style of the Replacements. Like the latter-day 'Mats, they weren't adverse to cleaning up their sound a little bit, but once they had a hit, they were happy to jump head-first into the mainstream, cleaning up their rockers until they shone and embracing acoustic power ballads instead of shunning them. In fact, "Iris"—their contribution to the *City of Angels* soundtrack and lead single for their sixth album, *Dizzy Up the Girl*—is a virtual rewrite of "Name." The funny thing is, where most college-rock bands of the Bush era sounded awkward as mainstream rockers, the Goo Goo Dolls actually sound *better* as a mainstream band, partially because they were hardly underground in the first place. Like a less mannered and conflicted *Let Your Dim Light Shine*-era Soul Asylum, the trio balances hard rockers with ballads. The difference is, they enjoy the mainstreaming of their music, and respond with one of their catchiest sets of songs. There's nothing new on the record apart from their willingness to polish their music so it reaches the widest audience. That will alienate whatever hardcore followers they have left, but that attitude will likely please anyone brought aboard with "Name" and "Iris." *—Stephen Thomas Erlewine*

Lesley Gore

b. May 2, 1946, New York, NY
Vocals / Brill Building Pop, Girl Group, Pop
The most commercially successful solo singer to be identified with the girl group sound, Lesley Gore hit the number one spot with her very first release, "It's My Party," in 1963. She wasn't the most soulful girl group singer by a long shot, but she projected an archetype of female adolescent yearning. Her best songs survive as classics, particularly the irrestistibly melodic "Maybe I Know," "Look of Love" and "You Don't Own Me," an anthem of independence with a feminist theme that was considerably advanced for early 1964. The singles were also very well-produced, with orchestral arrangements (by Quincy Jones and later Claus Ogermann) that hewed closer to mainstream pop than Phil Spector's Wall of Sound. Gore appeared on the legendary *T.A.M.I. Show* alongside such heavyweights as the Rolling Stones, James Brown, and Smokey Robinson, but after 1964 her star plummeted rapidly. Mercury was still investing a lot of care in her sessions throughout the rest of the '60s, and her material and arrangements showed her capable of greater stylistic range than many acknowledged. "Sunshine, Lollipops and Rainbows" (1965) and "California Nights" (1967) would be her only Top 20 entries after 1964. She played the cabarets after her days as an active recording artist, and eventually had some success as a songwriter for other performers. *—Richie Unterberger*

It's My Party: The Mercury Anthology / Jun. 18, 1996 / Mercury ✦✦✦✦✦
Fifty-two-track double CD has all the hits and then some. It may seem excessive for those who *only* want the hits, and some of the selections (particularly from the late '60s) are weak. But Gore had more worthy B-sides, album cuts, and low-charting singles than most people assume, and there are a good number of those on this collection: "Wonder Boy" (a White Martha & the Vandellas cop), "Off and Running" (covered by the Mindbenders in the *To Sir with Love* film), "Look of Love" (one of Greenwich-Barry's greatest girl group-style songs), a cover of Laura Nyro's "Wedding Bell Blues" (which lost out on the charts to the Fifth Dimension's version), and interesting little-known compositions by Goffin-King, Paul Anka, Van McCoy, Marvin Hamlisch, and Lesley herself. Gore covered more territory than the teen self-pity anthems for which she's most remembered, and this anthology, while not enough to make you demand her election to the Rock and Roll Hall of Fame, is not nearly as relentlessly lightweight as her detractors would have you imagine. Includes some tracks that were previously unavailable on album, or previously unreleased in the U.S. *—Richie Unterberger*

• **Sunshine, Lollipops & Rainbows: The Best of Lesley Gore** / Jun. 16, 1998 / Rhino ✦✦✦✦✦
During the girl-group era of the early 1960s, no female singer broke down the barriers for women the way Lesley Gore did. She was battling it out in a totally dominated man's world, sending sentiments to the top of the charts that most women only whispered about at the time, years before it was hip, cool, politically correct and resolvable by the ACLU. This makes her music not only important from a historical standpoint, but a quick listen to this 20-track best-of will also reveal that it's some of the classiest music from that era as well. With Quincy Jones producing your sessions and the top songwriters money can buy (Ellie Greenwich, Carole King, and Marvin Hamlisch, just for openers), it's no small wonder that records like "It's My Party," "Maybe I Know," "You Don't Own Me," "I Don't Wanna Be a Loser," "Judy's Turn to Cry" and the title track shine so brightly. The transfers on this disc shine equally as bright, with heavy prominence given to Gore's incredibly tight and impeccable double-tracked vo-

cals. If you think of Lesley Gore as a one-hit wonder from a pre-feminist dark age of rock & roll, you *really* need to hear this collection. *— Cub Koda*

Grand Funk Railroad

f. 1968, Flint, MI, **db.** 1976

Group / Detroit Rock, Album Rock, Boogie Rock, Arena Rock, Hard Rock

One of the 1970s' most successful hard rock bands in spite of critical pans and somewhat reluctant radio airplay (at first), Grand Funk Railroad built a devoted fan base with constant touring, a loud, simple take on the blues-rock power trio sound, and strong working-class appeal. Formed by guitarist/songwriter Mark Farner and drummer Don Brewer with bassist Mel Schacher, the band gained a contract with Capitol. While radio shied away from Grand Funk Railroad, the group's strong work ethic and commitment to touring produced a series of big-selling albums over the next few years; five of their eight releases from 1969 to 1972 went platinum, and the others all went gold. The group finally scored a big hit single (number one, in fact) with the title track of the Todd Rundgren-produced *We're an American Band*. The follow-up, *Shinin' On*, contained another number one hit in a remake of Little Eva's "The Loco-Motion." However, following Grand Funk's next album, *All the Girls in the World Beware!!*, interest in the group began to wane. They remained together in 1976 solely to work with producer Frank Zappa on *Good Singin', Good Playin'*. Grand Funk Railroad re-formed in 1981 for two albums but disbanded once more. *— Steve Huey*

● **Capitol Collectors Series** / Feb. 26, 1991 / Capitol ✦✦✦✦

Grand Funk Railroad was, at best, a singles band, capable of turning a couple of crunching rockers and hooky singles out with each album. Though it may be missing a fan favorite or two—and that could mean something concise and catchy or meandering jams like "T.N.U.C." This does have the overwhelming majority of their best songs, including not just hits like "We're an American Band" and "Some Kind of Wonderful," but also album tracks. Some long-time fans, like Homer Simpson, may find favorites missing, but this remains a nearly ideal summary. *— Stephen Thomas Erlewine*

Thirty Years of Funk: 1969-1999 / Jun. 29, 1999 / Capitol ✦✦✦✦

The Grass Roots

f. 1964, Los Angeles, CA

Group / AM Pop, Sunshine Pop, Pop

The Grass Roots are one of the more enduring Top 40 acts from the late 1960's and early 1970's, with a series of major hits—most notably "Let's Live For Today," "Midnight Confessions," "Temptation Eyes" and "Two Divided By Love"—that help define the essence of the era's best AM radio in the minds of millions of listeners. Although the group's members weren't even close to being recognizable, and their in-house songwriting was next to irrelevant, the Grass Roots managed to make a mark on popular music about as important (though not as successful) as that of their Dunhill Records labelmates Three Dog Night, with 14 top 40 hits charted between 1966 and 1973, including seven gold singles and one platinum single during that period, and two hits collections that effortlessly went gold. Moreover, their influence can be found even in the work of such superstars of subsequent decades as Bruce Springsteen. *— Bruce Eder*

● **Anthology: 1965-1975** / Jul. 2, 1991 / Rhino ✦✦✦✦✦

It may be expensive, and two CDs of their work may seem like overkill, but this double-disc set is the one to get. Not only does it contain every hit and each single, and every B-side, from 1965's "Where Were You When I Needed You" through 1975's glorious "Mamacita," but the sound is extraordinary, far better than on any of the other hits compilations, and provides several revelations about the quality of their work. Highlights, in addition to the expected hits "Let's Live for Today," "Midnight Confessions," "Two Divided by Love" etc., include tracks like "Is It Any Wonder," with a chorus as radiant as anything the Mamas and the Papas ever recorded, and the seldom heard, vibrant "Mamacita." If you could never imagine listening to 120 minutes of Grass Roots material (this reviewer couldn't, either), this set will make you feel differently. *— Bruce Eder*

All Time Greatest Hits / Jul. 1996 / MCA ✦✦✦✦✦

This low-priced disc is far and away the best single-CD compilation ever issued of the Grass Roots' work, 16 chart singles covering every phase of their history, from 1966's "Where Were You When I Needed You" (in its actual hit version) thru "Let's Live for Today" and "Midnight Confessions" to their last hit, 1972's "The Runway." Listening to this 44-minute compilation, one not only encounters a superb array of catchy songs (and even some of the lesser hits, like the number 61-charting "Come On and Say It" and the number 34-charting "Glory Bound," are compelling pieces of soul-based pop/rock) but also virtuoso production and playing. The material has been remastered in state-of-the-art sound, giving one a chance to appreciate the production and engineering as well as the playing, which (regardless of whether it was provided by L.A.'s best session musicians or members of the actual band) is extraordinarily polished and quite powerful—the piano, drums, and bass on "Sooner or Later" sound like they're in the same room with the listener, and the singing seems even more up-close and personal. The annotation also explains the group's somewhat confusing formation, and their evolution from a folk-rock band to one of the most successful white pop-soul outfits of their era, closer in spirit to the Fifth Dimension than to Bob Dylan, Roger McGuinn, et al. *— Bruce Eder*

The Grateful Dead

f. 1965, San Francisco, CA, **db.** 1995

Group / Album Rock, Folk-Rock, Psychedelic, Country-Rock, Rock & Roll

Rock's longest, strangest trip, the Grateful Dead were the psychedelic era's most beloved musical ambassadors as well as its most enduring survivors, spreading their message of peace, love and mind-expansion across the globe throughout the better part of three decades. The object of adoration for popular music's most fervent and celebrated fan following—the Deadheads, their numbers and devotion legendary in their own right—they were the ultimate cult band, creating a self-styled universe all their own; for the better part of their career orbiting well outside of the mainstream, the Dead—originally singers/guitarists Jerry Garcia and Bob Weir, singer/keyboardist Ron "Pigpen" McKernan, bassist Phil Lesh and drummers Bill Kreutzmann and Mickey Hart—became superstars solely on their own terms, tie-dyed pied pipers whose epic, free-form live shows were rites of passage for an extended family of listeners which knew no cultural boundaries. *— Jason Ankeny*

The Grateful Dead [1967] / Mar. 17, 1967 / Warner Brothers ✦✦

The Grateful Dead's debut album finds them uncomfortable in the studio, rushing tempos and otherwise failing to reproduce the feel of their live shows. Nevertheless, the group covers much of its then-current repertoire, including such long-term favorites as "Beat It on Down the Line," "Cold Rain and Snow," and "New, New Minglewood Blues." *— William Ruhlmann*

Anthem of the Sun / Jul. 18, 1968 / Warner Brothers ✦✦✦✦

The Grateful Dead spent six months recording their second album in studios and at concerts. The result came closer to an accurate portrait of them, highlighted by the four-part, 12-minute "That's It for the Other One." Still, the extensive mixing and editing made the sound dense and uninviting, especially to those not yet converted to the group's approach. *— William Ruhlmann*

Aoxomoxoa / Jun. 20, 1969 / Warner Brothers ✦✦✦

The addition of poet Robert Hunter as lyricist marked the beginning of a consistent set of imagery in the Dead's words to match their musical interplay, especially on songs like "St. Stephen" and "China Cat Sunflower." But the aural experiments were still making for trying listening as the Dead continued to search for a way to capture their concert feel on disc. *— William Ruhlmann*

Live/Dead / Nov. 10, 1969 / Warner Brothers ✦✦✦✦✦

Long, trancelike songs with allusive lyrics (such as the classic "Dark Star") and R&B workouts featuring Pigpen's bluesy voice characterize this album, which is the basic document in the early Dead catalog—it's what most fans would like them to sound like every night. *— William Ruhlmann*

☆ **Workingman's Dead** / May 1970 / Warner Brothers ✦✦✦✦✦

The Grateful Dead were already established as paragons of the free-form, improvisational San Francisco psychedelic sound when they abruptly shifted gears for the acoustic *Workingman's Dead*, a lovely exploration of American roots music illuminating the group's country, blues and folk influences. The lilting "Uncle John's Band," their first radio hit, opens the record and perfectly summarizes its subtle, spare beauty; complete with a new focus on more concise songs and tighter arrangements, the approach works brilliantly. Despite its sharp contrast to the epic live space jams on which the group's legend primarily rests, *Workingman's Dead* nonetheless spotlights the Dead at their most engaging, stripped of all excess to reveal the true essence of their craft. *— Jason Ankeny*

★ **American Beauty** / Nov. 1970 / Warner Brothers ✦✦✦✦✦

A companion piece to the luminous *Workingman's Dead*, *American Beauty* is an even stronger document of the Grateful Dead's return to their musical roots. Sporting a more full-bodied and intricate sound than its predecessor thanks to the addition of subtle electric textures, the record is also more representative of the group as a collective unit, allowing for stunning contributions from Dave Torbert (the poignant opener "Box of Rain") and Bob Weir ("Sugar Magnolia"); at the top of his game as well is Jerry Garcia, who delivers the superb "Friend of the Devil," "Candyman" and "Ripple." Climaxing with the perennial "Truckin'," *American Beauty* remains the Dead's studio masterpiece—never again would they be so musically focused or so emotionally direct. *— Jason Ankeny*

The Grateful Dead [1971] / Oct. 1971 / Warner Brothers ✦✦✦

The Dead's second double live album (now on a single CD) introduces a couple of excellent Garcia/Hunter compositions, "Bertha" and "Wharf Rat," and allows Bob Weir to indulge his taste for what Deadheads would come to call "cowboy songs": Merle Haggard's "Mama Tried" and Kris Kristofferson's "Me & Bobby McGee." The album became the Dead's first gold record, probably on the momentum of *Workingman's Dead* and *American Beauty*. It also failed to match *Live/Dead* as a concert album, so that, coming off the band's recent peaks, it seemed less effective than it was. Now, it seems like one of the Dead's better, more coherent records. (Not to be confused with *The Grateful Dead*, the band's debut album. They resorted to *Grateful Dead* as a title when Warner wouldn't let them call the album *Skull Fuck*). *— William Ruhlmann*

Europe '72 / Nov. 1972 / Warner Brothers ✦✦✦✦✦

Released as a three-record set, *Europe '72* is now a double CD. But it's still a long album, notable for introducing more Garcia-Hunter songs, especially "Brown-Eyed Woman," and for incorporating onto one album the variety of musical styles to be heard at a Dead concert, as well as the sheer duration necessary to appreciate the experience. Which means that, while this may not be the place a new fan wants to start, it's a Deadhead favorite. *— William Ruhlmann*

History of the Grateful Dead, Vol. 1 (Bear's Choice) / Jul. 13, 1973 / Warner Brothers ✦✦✦

This is a contractual obligation album, a record given to Warner Brothers Records to complete the Dead's commitment to the label. It was recorded in February 1970 and is something of a tribute to the late keyboardist/vocalist Ron "Pigpen" McKernan, who is heard frequently. Pigpen highlights an 18-minute version of Howlin' Wolf's "Smokestack Lightnin'." But this is a nonessential Dead album. "Bear" is the band's friend/soundman/drug manufacturer Owsley Stanley. The album is misnamed: it does not provide a "history" and there was never any Volume 2. *— William Ruhlmann*

Wake of the Flood / Nov. 15, 1973 / Grateful Dead ✦✦✦✦✦

The Grateful Dead's first studio album in three years was also their first for their own record label. It's a strong collection, featuring such Garcia-Hunter songs as "Mississippi Half-Step Uptown Toodleoo," "Row Jimmy," and "Stella Blue," songs that would become concert staples, as well as Bob Weir's "Weather Report Suite." *— William Ruhlmann*

Skeletons from the Closet: The Best of the Grateful Dead / 1974 / Warner Brothers ✦✦✦
This is an 11-song compilation, five of whose songs come from *Workingman's Dead* or *American Beauty.* It presents a sampling of the Dead's 1967-1972 period, focusing on their more accessible material. In that sense, it is recommended to the uninitiated who want to get a feel for the group; not surprisingly, it is a perennial seller, turning up week after week on *Billboard* magazine's Top Pop Catalog chart. The initiated, however, despise it: In a survey of Deadheads conducted by *DeadBase,* it was rated above only *Dylan & the Dead* as the worst Grateful Dead album. *— William Ruhlmann*

The Grateful Dead From the Mars Hotel / Jun. 27, 1974 / Grateful Dead ✦✦✦

Blues for Allah / Sep. 1, 1975 / Grateful Dead ✦✦✦✦✦
Opening with the suite that has become a concert favorite, "Help on the Way"/"Slip Knot!"/"Franklin's Tower," and also containing the anthemic "The Music Never Stopped," *Blues for Allah* is another Grateful Dead album containing a few band classics and a lot of filler. Note, however, that some fans seem to like the filler. In its survey of Deadheads, *DeadBase* found *Blues for Allah* to be the band's most popular studio album after *Workingman's Dead* and *American Beauty. — William Ruhlmann*

Steal Your Face / Jun. 26, 1976 / Grateful Dead ✦✦

● **What a Long Strange Trip It's Been** / 1977 / Warner Brothers ✦✦✦✦✦
This is a two-disc compilation of the Grateful Dead covering its tenure at Warner Brothers Records, 1967-1972, and as such the most extensive sampler of their work in existence. Well-chosen, it contains many of their best songs from the period and is notable for giving album release to the studio-recorded single version of "Dark Star," the Dead's most requested song. Relative newcomers to the band (those who bought *Skeletons from the Closet* and liked it) can get a stronger dose here, and then perhaps go on to the individual albums. Of course, Deadheads hate this record. *— William Ruhlmann*

Terrapin Station / Jul. 27, 1977 / Arista ✦✦✦

Shakedown Street / Nov. 15, 1978 / Arista ✦✦

Go to Heaven / Apr. 28, 1980 / Arista ✦

Reckoning / Apr. 1, 1981 / Arista ✦✦✦
Having given up on studio work after the disaster of *Go to Heaven,* the Dead recorded a series of concerts in New York and San Francisco in October 1980 for two live albums. This is the first, a set of acoustic material that will remind many listeners of the rustic feel of the classic *Workingman's Dead* and *American Beauty* albums, although much of it consists of traditional and bluegrass material favored by Jerry Garcia. (The original two-LP set was fit onto one CD in 1987 by eliminating the Dead's cover of Elizabeth Cotten's "Oh Babe It Ain't No Lie.") *— William Ruhlmann*

Dead Set / Aug. 1981 / Arista ✦✦✦

In the Dark / Jul. 6, 1987 / Arista ✦✦✦✦✦
The comeback, with "Touch of Grey," "West L.A. Fadeaway," and "Black Muddy River." For anyone who wondered how these old hippies could have such a following 20 years after the hippies disappeared, here's the answer. *— William Ruhlmann*

Built to Last / Oct. 31, 1989 / Arista ✦✦

Without a Net / Sep. 1990 / Arista ✦✦✦

One from the Vault / Apr. 15, 1991 / Grateful Dead ✦✦✦
With this album, issued on the group's own merchandising label, The Grateful Dead began to address the needs of an audience that had long since taken to making their own tapes of every Dead performance. Such an audience, of course, would be interested in record releases containing vintage live shows, and The Dead began by issuing this 16-year-old concert, which occurred shortly after they completed their 1975 album *Blues for Allah* and while they were nominally retired from live work. It contains all the material featured on that album, plus such recent Dead songs as "U.S. Blues" and such favorites as "The Other One." It made for a modest beginning to The Dead's archival investigations, and only whetted fans' appetites for what might follow. *— William Ruhlmann*

Two from the Vault / 1992 / Grateful Dead ✦✦✦

Dick's Picks, Vol. 1 / Dec. 1993 / Grateful Dead ✦✦✦
This recording of a Grateful Dead concert performed in Tampa, FL, on December 19, 1973, inaugurates a new series of archival releases that differs from the band's already established *From the Vaults* series in that it is to feature somewhat lower-fidelity, "what you hear is what you get" tapes, as the liner notes put it, subject to editing problems, incompleteness, etc. Perhaps to make up for that, this double-CD album was not offered to retail, but distributed only through mail order, and it was sold at a discount price. For all that, this is a good, if laid-back, Dead set, led off by a 14-minute version of "Here Comes Sunshine." That song comes from *Wake of the Flood,* which was the band's current album release at the time, and much of that LP's other material turns up notably a complete, 16-minute "Weather Report Suite," along with favorites like "Truckin"' and "Playing in the Band" the latter at a running time of 21 minutes. As promised, the recording quality is noticeably unenhanced, but Deadheads won't mind, and casual fans won't bother. *— William Ruhlmann*

Dick's Picks, Vol. 2 / 1995 / Grateful Dead ✦✦✦

Hundred Year Hall / Sep. 26, 1995 / Grateful Dead ✦✦✦

Dick's Picks, Vol. 3 / Nov. 7, 1995 / Grateful Dead ✦✦✦

★ **Dick's Picks, Vol. 4** / Mar. 1, 1996 / Grateful Dead ✦✦✦✦✦
Though this is the third Grateful Dead album to be released since the death of bandleader Jerry Garcia and the group's subsequent decision to disband, it is the first one that wasn't in the pipeline already. Its release offers evidence that the Dead organization, which had begun releasing selected recordings of live shows as a courtesy to fans while raking in most of its revenues through roadwork, has changed its priorities. *Dick's Picks, Volume Four* isn't just another Grateful Dead concert recording, it's *the* recording: February 13-14, 1970, the Dead's debut at the Fillmore East, and a show consistently ranked by Deadheads as among the five best live tapes ever. This stand, some of which was released in 1973 on the *History Of The Grateful Dead, Vol. 1 (Bear's Choice)* (there is no overlap with this album) finds the Dead gearing up to record *Workingman's Dead,* and already songs like "Casey Jones" and "Dire Wolf" have crept into the set. But there is so much more: half-hour versions of "That's It for the Other One," "Turn on Your Lovelight" (a showcase for Pigpen), and, in a near-definitive performance, the Dead's signature song, "Dark Star." Much of the then recently released *Live/Dead* material is heard, not to mention a rare performance of "Mason's Children." But it isn't just the set list that makes this a legendary show, it's the playing, amazing interaction among the players on every song, with Garcia noodling his way to nirvana. While it would be an exaggeration to say that if you own this three-CD, three-hour-and-ten-minute album you have all you need of the Grateful Dead on disc, the overstatement is only slight. As Bob Weir says at the outset, "This ain't a show, it's a party." *— William Ruhlmann*

The Arista Years / Oct. 15, 1996 / Arista ✦✦✦✦✦
This well-chosen compilation makes the best of the eight albums (five studio LPs and three live collections) the Grateful Dead released on Arista Records between 1977 and 1990. The first three studio albums are not well regarded, but by focusing on the stronger compositions, such as "Estimated Prophet," "Terrapin Station," "Fire on the Mountain," "I Need a Miracle," and "Saint of Circumstance," the compilers have made them seem better than they did when they were released. It doesn't hurt that these are the songs that emerged as concert favorites, and if these performances often sound like distilled, sometimes stilted versions for those familiar with the live shows, they nevertheless serve as a kind of blueprint for the music the Dead played in the late '70s and '80s. A more confident band emerges in the later tracks, in part because the material is superior—not only the hit "Touch of Grey," but also "Black Muddy River" and "Foolish Heart," among others—but also because the performances are seasoned by frequent live playing of the songs. The album concludes with the group's 1990 live recording of "Eyes of the World" with Branford Marsalis sitting in from *Without a Net. The Arista Years* presents the sound of a band compromising with, but not capitulating to, the demands of the conventional record industry. Even the Dead themselves were never really able to capture lightning in a bottle, but, as one of their better songs here puts it, they managed to shine "Just a Little Light." *— William Ruhlmann*

Dozin' at the Knick / Oct. 29, 1996 / Arista ✦✦✦✦
Drawing upon the same spring 1990 East Coast tour that produced *Without a Net, Dozin' at the Knick* mixes performances from three successive shows performed at *Knickerbocker Arena* in Albany, NY, March 24-26. It contains most of the first set from March 26, all of the second set from March 24, and the second half of the second set from March 25. Deadheads might have preferred that the March 24 show be presented in its entirety instead, but at least the best feature of that show is included, namely a nearly eight-minute version of the rarely performed (and never before released on record) jam "Your Mind Has Left Your Body," here playfully renamed "Mud Love Buddy Jam." The Dead had reinvigorated their live shows in the fall of 1989, meanwhile reintroducing many of their older songs. By the spring of 1990, they were back to a more conventional repertoire (though this album contains such fairly unusual selections as "The Wheel" and the a cappella "And We Bid You Goodnight"), but their performance standard remained high, as demonstrated on this well-performed collection. — *William Ruhlmann*

So Many Roads (1965-1995) / Nov. 9, 1999 / Arista ✦✦✦✦✦
By the late '90s, box sets increasingly addressed the desires of ardent fans; since the uninitiated were satisfied with smaller compilations, a box set consisting mostly or entirely of unissued material often seemed more appropriate. Even within this paradigm, however, the Grateful Dead are an anomaly—most of their studio recordings are disdained by fans devoted to privately distributed tapes of their live performances. How, then, to approach a Dead box set— The compilers have scoured the group's extensive vault for a five-CD set which includes only a few tracks that have ever been released in any medium. Adopting a roughly chronological sequencing, they sought out rare songs and, especially, performance highlights spanning the Dead's 30-year career. The compilers are second-generation Deadheads, fans who came to the band in the '70s and '80s, responding to the marathon-length live instrumental improvisations. Time and again, the songs here begin in normal fashion and then take off into uncharted territory; as long as the soloing is interesting, it doesn't matter if lyrics are blown or the singing is off-key. In many cases, the compilers are so enamored of the group's interplay that they include excerpts without the songs that begin or conclude them. The rare songs include selections from the Dead's unreleased 1965 sessions for Autumn Records, outtakes from *Workingman's Dead* and *American Beauty,* and rehearsals and live performances of songs intended for a Dead album that was never formally recorded. In short, *So Many Roads (1965-1995)* was obviously made by Deadheads for Deadheads. The Dead have succeeded over the years by addressing the interests of a cult that welcomes neophytes but also revels in its exclusivity; it's no surprise that their version of a box-set retrospective holds true to that course. *— William Ruhlmann*

Macy Gray

Vocals / Contemporary R&B, Adult Alternative Pop/Rock, Urban
Alternative R&B singer Macy Gray was born and raised in Canton, OH, growing up on a steady diet of classic soul and early hip hop. A classically-trained pianist, she only began singing while studying screenwriting at the University of Southern California, recording a demo with a group of musician friends after the scheduled vocalist failed to show up at the studio. From there Gray sang with a local jazz band, also becoming a sought-after session vocalist; signing to Epic, she issued her debut album *On How Life Is* in mid-1999. What followed was critical praise and comparison, a string of live performances and awards. *—Jason Ankeny*

● **On How Life Is** / Jul. 27, 1999 / Epic ✦✦✦✦
Macy Gray is such an assured, original vocalist that it's hard to believe *On How Life Is* is her

debut album. She recalls a number of other vocalists, particularly jazz singers like Billie Holiday and Nina Simone, but she is unquestionably from the post-hip-hop generation, which is evident not just from the sound of the record, but the style of her songwriting, which is adventurous and unpredictable. Thankfully, she's worked with a producer (Andrew Slater, who pulled a similar trick with Fiona Apple's debut, *Tidal*), that lets her run wild and helps her find sounds that match her ideas. That's not to say that *On How Life Is* is a perfect album—at times, Gray attempts more than she can achieve—but it's always captivating, even during its stumbles. And when it works, it soars higher than most contemporary R&B. *—Stephen Thomas Erlewine*

Green Day

f. 1989, Berkeley, CA
Group / Punk-Pop, Post-Grunge, Punk Revival, Alternative Pop/Rock
Out of all the post-Nirvana American alternative bands to break into the pop mainstream, Green Day was second only to Pearl Jam in terms of influence. At their core, Green Day were simply punk revivalists, recharging the energy of speedy, catchy three-chord punk-pop songs. Though their music wasn't particularly innovative, they brought the sound of late-'70s punk to a new, younger generation with *Dookie*, their 1994 major-label debut. Green Day wasn't able to sustain their sucess—*Dookie* sold over eight million, while its follow-up *Insomniac* only sold a quarter of its predecessor—yet their influence was far-reaching, since they opened the doors for a flood of American neo-punk, punk metal, and third-wave ska-revivalists. Led by childhood friends Billie Jo Armstrong and Mike Dirnt, the band had cultivated a cult following since their album debut, 1989's *39/Smooth*. The underground success of 1992's *Kerplunk* led to a wave of interest from major record labels, and Green Day's subsequent Reprise debut *Dookie* became a major hit in 1994 (thanks to MTV support for the initial single "Longview") and eventually sold eight million copies in America. Green Day quickly followed up *Dookie* in 1995 with *Insomniac*, an album that performed comparatively poorly (it sold only two million copies). The band spent much of 1996 resting and writing new material, issuing *Nimrod* in 1997. *—Stephen Thomas Erlewine*

1039/Smoothed Out Slappy Hour / 1991 / Lookout ✦✦

Kerplunk / Jan. 17, 1992 / Lookout ✦✦✦

● **Dookie** / Feb. 1, 1994 / Reprise ✦✦✦✦✦
Green Day couldn't have had a blockbuster without Nirvana, but *Dookie* wound up being nearly as revolutionary as *Nevermind*, sending a wave of imitators up the charts and setting the tone for the mainstream \rock of the mid-'90s. Like *Nevermind*, this was accidental success, the sound of a promising underground group suddenly hitting its stride just as they got their first professional, big-budget, big-label production. Really, that's where the similarities end, since if Nirvana was indebted to the weirdness of \indie rock, Green Day was a straight-ahead \punk revivalist through and through. They were products of the underground \pop scene kept alive by such protagonists as All, yet what they really loved was the original \punk, particularly such British punkers as the Jam and Buzzcocks. On their first couple records, they showed promise, but with *Dookie*, they delivered a record that found Billie Joe Armstrong bursting into full flower as a songwriter, spitting out melodic ravers that could have comfortable sat alongside *Singles Going Steady*, but infused with an ironic self-loathing popularized by Nirvana, whose clean sound on *Nevermind* is also emulated here. Where Nirvana had weight, Green Day is deliberately adolescent here, treating nearly everything as joke and having as much fun as snotty punkers should. They demonstrate a bit of depth with "When I Come Around," but that just varies the pace slightly, since the key to this is their flippant, infectious attitude—something they maintain throughout the record, making *Dookie* a stellar piece of \modern punk that many tried to emulate but nobody bettered. *—Stephen Thomas Erlewine*

Insomniac / Oct. 10, 1995 / Reprise ✦✦✦✦
Dookie gave Green Day success, but it was never really clear whether they wanted it in the first place. However, given the incessantly catchy songwriting of Billie Joe, the success made sense. Green Day were traditionalists without realizing it, learning all of their tricks through secondhand records and second-generation California punk bands. They didn't change their sound in the slightest after signing to a major label, which meant that they couldn't revert back to a harsher, earlier sound as a way to shed their audience for *Dookie*'s follow-up, *Insomniac*. Instead, they kept their blueprint and made it a shade darker. Throughout *Insomniac*, there are vague references to the band's startling multi-platinum breakthrough, but the album is hardly a stark confessional on the level of Nirvana's *In Utero*. It's a collection of speedy, catchy songs in the spirit of the Buzzcocks, the Jam, the Clash, and the Undertones, but played with more minor chords and less melody and recorded with a bigger, hard rock-oriented production. While nothing on the album is as immediate as "Basket Case" or "Longview," the band has gained a powerful sonic punch, which goes straight for the gut but sacrifices the raw edge they so desperately want to keep and makes the record slightly tame. Billie Joe hasn't lost much of his talent for simple, tuneful hooks, but after a series of songs that all sound pretty much the same, it becomes clear that he needs to push himself a little bit more if Green Day ever wants to be something more than a good punk-pop band. As it is, they remain a good punk-pop band, and *Insomniac* is a good punk-pop record, but nothing more. *—Stephen Thomas Erlewine*

Nimrod / Oct. 14, 1997 / Reprise ✦✦✦
Following the cool reception to *Insomniac*, Green Day retreated from the spotlight for a year to rest and spend time with their families. During that extended break, they decided to not worry about their supposedly lost street credibility and make an album according to their instincts, which meant more experimentation and less of their trademark pop-punk. Of course, speedy, catchy punk is at the core of the group's sound, so there are plenty of familiar moments on the resultant album, *Nimrod*, but there are also new details that make the record an invigorating, if occasionally frustrating, listen. Although pop-punk is Green Day's forte, they sound the most alive on *Nimrod* when they're breaking away from their formula, whether it's the shuffling "Hitchin' a Ride," the bitchy, tongue-in-cheek humor of "The Grouch," the surging surf instrumental "Last Ride In," the punchy, horn-driven drag-queen saga "King for a Day," or acoustic, string-laced ballad "Good Riddance." It's only when the trio confines themselves to three chords that they sound tired, but Billie Joe has such a gift for hooky, instantly memorable melodies that even these moments are enjoyable, if unremarkable. Still, *Nimrod* suffers from being simply too much—although it clocks in at under 50 minutes, the 18 tracks whip by at such a breakneck speed that it leaves you somewhat dazed. With a little editing, Green Day's growth would have been put in sharper relief, and *Nimrod* would have been the triumphant leap forward it set out to be. As it stands, it's a muddled but intermittingly exciting record that is full of promise. *—Stephen Thomas Erlewine*

Warning / Oct. 3, 2000 / Adeline ✦✦✦✦✦
By 2000, Green Day had long been spurned as un-hip by the fourth-generation punks they popularized, and they didn't seem likely to replicate the MOR success of the fluke smash "Good Riddance (Time of Your Life)." Apparently, the success of that ballad freed the band from any classifications or stigmas, letting them feel like they could do anything they wanted on their fifth album, *Warning*. They responded by embracing their fondness for pop and making the best damn album they've ever made. There's a sense of fearlessness on *Warning*, as if the band didn't care if the album wasn't punk enough, or whether it produced a cross-platform hit. There are no ballads here, actually, and while there are a number of punchy, infectious rockers, the tempo is never recklessly breakneck. Instead, the focus is squarely on the songs, with the instrumentation and arrangements serving their needs. It's easy to say that Green Day has matured with this album, since they've never produced a better, more tuneful set of songs, or tried so many studio tricks and clever arrangements. However, that has the wrong connotation, since "mature" would indicate that *Warning* is a studious, carefully assembled album that's easier to admire than to love. That's not the case at all. This is gleeful, unabashed fun, even when Billie Joe Armstrong is getting a little cranky in his lyrics. It's fun to hear Green Day adopt a Beatlesque harmonica on "Hold On" or try out Kinks-ian musichall on "Misery," while still knocking out punk-pop gems and displaying melodic ingenuity and imaginative arrangements. *Warning* may not be an innovative record per se, but it's tremendously satisfying; it finds the band at a peak of songcraft and performance, doing it all without a trace of self-consciousness. It's the first great pure pop album of the new millennium. *—Stephen Thomas Erlewine*

Al Green

b. Apr. 13, 1946, Forrest City, AR
Vocals / Smooth Soul, Memphis Soul, Pop-Soul, Contemporary Gospel, Soul
Al Green was the first great soul singer of the '70s and arguably the last great Southern soul singer. With his seductive singles for Hi Records in the early '70s, Green bridged the gap between deep soul and smooth Philadelphia soul. He incorporated elements of gospel, interjecting his performances with wild moans and wails, but his records stylish, boasting immaculate productions that rolled along with a tight beat, sexy backing vocals, and lush strings. The distinctive Hi Records sound that the vocalist and producer Willie Mitchell developed made Al Green the most popular and influential soul singer of the early '70s, influencing not only his contemporaries, but also veterans like Marvin Gaye. Green was at the peak of his popularity when he suddenly decided to join the ministry in the mid-'70s. At first, he continued to record secular material, but by the '80s, he was concentrating solely on gospel. During the late '80s and '90s, he occasionally returned to R&B, but he remained primarily a religious performer for the rest of his career. Nevertheless, Green's classic early '70s recordings retained their power and influence throughout the decades, setting the standard for smooth soul. *—Stephen Thomas Erlewine*

Back Up Train / 1967 / Hot Line ✦✦✦

Green Is Blues / 1970 / The Right Stuff ✦✦✦
The first album linking the soul-singing greatness of Al Green with the production brilliance and expertise of Willie Mitchell. The results were mutually beneficial; Green got the great production, arrangements, and backing from the Hi Rhythm section that often turned good songs into classics, and he sang with the conviction and talent that provided the final component in an artistically and commercially satisfying union. *—Ron Wynn*

Gets Next to You / 1971 / The Right Stuff ✦✦✦✦✦
After the shaky start of *Green Is Blues*, Al Green and producer Willie Mitchell established their classic sound with Green's second album, *Gets Next to You*. The main difference is in the rhythm section. Abandoning the gritty syncopations of deep Southern soul, the Hi Rhythm Section plays it slow and seductive, working a sultry, steady pulse that Green exploits with his remarkable voice. Alternating between Sam Cooke's croon and Otis Redding's shout, Green develops his own distinctive style, and *Gets Next to You* only touches the surface of its depth. Although the album is filled with wonderful moments, few are as astonishing as Green and Mitchell's reinterpretation of the Temptations' "I Can't Get Next to You," which turns the original inside out. *—Stephen Thomas Erlewine*

☆ **Let's Stay Together** / Feb. 1972 / The Right Stuff ✦✦✦✦✦
Prior to this album, Al Green never had a number one song. The title track, "Let's Stay Together," achieved that status and held it for nine consecutive weeks. Green's ingenuity produced one of the all-time classics, which has the bounce of a dance cut and the passion of a ballad. The dynamic soul singer's whispers, animated cries, and riffing enhance his already stirring delivery. This album was sold on the strength of the title track as there were no other selections to grace the *Billboard* charts. However, this album includes the timeless gem "How Can You Mend a Broken Heart" and lesser-known beauties like the exulting "Judy," the cookin' testimonial "I Never Found a Girl," and the soothing blues effort "It Ain't No Fun to Me." The Arkansas native and his creative partner Willie Mitchell season these selections with lucid rhythm arrangements complemented by the faint strums of a guitar and brawn, unchiding horns. *—Craig Lytle*

☆ **I'm Still in Love with You** / Dec. 1972 / The Right Stuff ✦✦✦✦✦
I'm Still in Love with You shares many surface similarities to its predecessor, *Let's Stay Together*, from Al Green and Willie Mitchell's distinctive, sexy style to the pacing and song selection. Despite those shared traits, *I'm Still in Love with You* distinguishes itself with its suave, romantic tone and its subtly ambitious choice of material. Green began exploring country music with this album, performing a startling version of Kris Kristofferson's "For the Good Times," as well as a wonderful, slow reinterpretation of Roy Orbison's "Oh Pretty Woman." And the soul numbers are more complex than they would appear—listen to how the beat falls together at the beginning of "Love and Happiness," or the sly melody of the title track. There isn't a wasted track on *I'm Still in Love with You*, and in many ways it rivals its follow-up *Call Me* as Green's masterpiece. *—Stephen Thomas Erlewine*

☆ **Call Me** / Jul. 1973 / The Right Stuff ✦✦✦✦✦
Al Green reached his creative peak with the brilliant *Call Me*, the most inventive and assured album of his career. So silky and fluid as to sound almost effortless, Green's vocals revel in the lush strings and evocative horns of Willie Mitchell's superbly intimate production, barely rising above an angelic whisper for the gossamer "Have You Been Making Out O.K."; with barely perceptible changes in mood, *Call Me* covers remarkable ground, spanning from "Stand Up"—a call to arms delivered with characteristic understatement—to renditions of Hank Williams' "I'm So Lonesome I Could Cry" and Willie Nelson's "Funny How Time Slips Away," both of them exemplary fusions of country and soul. Equally compelling are the album's three Top Ten hits—"You Ought to Be With Me," "Here I Am (Come and Take Me)," and the shimmering title cut. A classic. *—Jason Ankeny*

Livin' for You / Dec. 1973 / The Right Stuff ✦✦✦

Al Green Explores Your Mind / 1974 / The Right Stuff ✦✦✦
Only one hit single this time out with "Sha-La-La (Make Me Happy)." *Explores Your Mind* also contains what may have become Green's best-known song, "Take Me to the River." *—Rob Bowman*

★ **Al Green's Greatest Hits** / Apr. 1975 / The Right Stuff ✦✦✦✦✦
Upon its original release in 1975, *Al Green's Greatest Hits* pretty much summed up everything about Green, containing his ten biggest hits up to that point. A few years later, it was followed by a second volume, which contained hit singles that charted since the release of the first collection. In 1995, the Right Stuff reissued *Al Green's Greatest Hits*, adding five of the highlights from the second volume of greatest hits as bonus tracks. The result was a definitive single-disc compilation, featuring 15 of Green's absolute best songs, including "Tired of Being Alone," "Let's Stay Together," "I'm Still in Love with You," "Call Me," "Here I Am," "Sha-La-La (Make Me Happy)," "L-O-V-E (Love)." The original version of *Greatest Hits* was great, but the revision made it nearly perfect. *—Stephen Thomas Erlewine*

Al Green Is Love / Oct. 1975 / The Right Stuff ✦✦✦✦

Full of Fire / Apr. 1976 / Hi ✦✦✦

Have a Good Time / Dec. 1976 / Hi ✦✦✦

The Belle Album / Dec. 1977 / The Right Stuff ✦✦✦✦
Al Green severed his ties with longtime producer Willie Mitchell in 1977, establishing his own backup band and seizing the production reins. But he hadn't yet made the final break with soul; this was the last secular work he would make for many years, and it was brilliant, even though it didn't come close to equaling his previous commercial heights. In retrospect, many just didn't understand where he was going, while others were turned off by the blurred lyrical focus of songs like "Belle." But "I Feel Good" had as much danceable energy and soulful fire as any Green uptempo tune, and "Lovin' You" and "Dream" were sorely underrated compositions. *—Ron Wynn*

Truth & Time / 1978 / Hi ✦✦✦

The Lord Will Make a Way / 1980 / Myrrh ✦✦✦✦✦
One of the best gospel albums by Rev. Green. The R&B and pop hits had stopped coming but the sacred peaks were the equal of any of his secular material. In 1992 Green was still performing the title song and "In the Holy Name of Jesus." *—Rob Bowman*

Tokyo Live / 1981 / The Right Stuff ✦✦✦✦
A wonderful live set that serves as both a retrospective and a defining release showing that Green sang the same way regardless of musical and lyrical content. He did many of his greatest soul hits, performing them with the relaxed, powerful grace that made him the '70s' finest soul vocalist and the '80s' best male gospel artist. *—Ron Wynn*

He Is the Light / 1985 / A&M ✦✦✦✦✦

Love Ritual / 1989 / MCA ✦✦✦

One in a Million / 1990 / Word ✦✦✦✦✦

Love Is Reality / 1992 / Word/Epic ✦✦✦
After years of refusing to sing anything but gospel, Green decided the time had finally come to fuse the godly and the secular elements of his soul. *Love Is Reality* made an overt play for the mainstream R&B market. Unfortunately, Christian dance-pop producer Tim Miner works from formulas, while Green runs on inspiration. Green sounded great, but the final result paled in comparison to the rest of his catalog. *—Brian Mansfield*

Your Heart's in Good Hands / Nov. 7, 1995 / MCA ✦✦✦

Anthology / Feb. 11, 1997 / Capitol ✦✦✦
Theoretically, an Al Green box set should be easy to assemble, given the overall excellence of his material, but the four-disc *Anthology* is a botch job. Instead of simply condensing the best of Green's prolific output, including all of the hits, the compilers were concerned with telling a story—literally. Three of the discs are spiked with lengthy interview segments; furthermore, most of the rarities are concert tracks, which means classics like "I Can't Get Next to You," "How Can You Mend a Broken Heart," "Love and Happiness" and "Sha-La-La (Make Me Happy)" are presented in inferior live versions. The live cuts, interviews and rarities cut severely into the set's pacing, and they don't make *Anthology* useful for the fan that wants one, definitive collection—their appeal is solely for collectors, who already have the material elsewhere. Consequently, *Anthology* isn't useful for either the casual or dedicated fan, both of whom would be better off with the original albums and the *Greatest Hits* collection, which does contain the essence of Al Green, and most of his hits, on one disc. *—Stephen Thomas Erlewine*

The Guess Who

f. 1963, Winnipeg, Manitoba, Canada, **db.** 1975
Group / Album Rock, Boogie Rock, Pop/Rock, Hard Rock
While the Guess Who did have several hits in America, they were superstars in their home country of Canada during the 1960s and early '70s. The band grew out of a Winnipeg-based group named the Expressions, formed by Chad Allan and Randy Bachman. After hitting the American Top 40 with 1965's "Shakin' All Over," the Expressions recorded an album that necessitated a name-change after the Quality label released it and listed their name as "Guess Who?" on the jacket, hoping to fool record buyers into thinking that it was a more famous group in disguise. Allan departed soon after and was replaced on lead vocals by Burton Cummings, though further American success eluded the Guess Who until the 1969 Top Ten hit "These Eyes." In 1970, the band released the cuttingly sarcastic riff-rocker "American Woman," which, given its anti-American putdowns, ironically became their only US chart-topper. Trouble was brewing on the horizon, though. Bachman left the group that year, and formed Brave Belt with Chad Allan, which later evolved into Bachman-Turner Overdrive. The Guess Who returned to the Top Ten at the end of the year with "Share the Land," and hit one last time in 1974 with "Clap for the Wolfman" before disbanding in 1975. The lineup from the Guess Who's glory years reunited in 1983, and a version of the group with constantly shifting musicians (occasionally original members) continued to tour into the '90s. *—Steve Huey*

Shakin' All Over / 1965 / Scepter ✦✦

Canned Wheat / 1969 / Buddha ✦✦✦✦✦

Share the Land / 1970 / Buddha ✦✦✦

American Woman / Jan. 1970 / Buddha ✦✦✦✦
The Guess Who's most successful LP, reaching number nine in America (and charting for more than a year), has held up well and was as close to a defining album-length statement as the original group ever made. It's easy to forget that until "American Woman," the Guess Who's hits had been confined to softer, ballad-style numbers—that song (which originated as a spontaneous on-stage jam) highlighted by Randy Bachman's highly articulated fuzz-tone guitar, a relentless beat, and Burton Cummings moving into Robert Plant territory on the lead vocal, transformed their image. As an album opener, it was a natural, but the slow acoustic blues intro by Bachman heralded a brace of surprises in store for the listener. The presence of the melodic but highly electric hit version of "No Time" (which the band had cut earlier in a more ragged rendition) made the first ten minutes a hard rock one-two punch, but the group then veers into progressive rock territory with "Talisman." Side two was where the original album was weakest, though it started well enough with "969 (The Oldest Man)." "When Friends Fall Out," a remake of an early Canadian release by the group, attempted a heavy sound that just isn't sustainable, and "8:15" was a similar space filler, but "Proper Stranger" falls into good hard rock groove. In August of 2000, Buddha Records issued a remastered version of this album with a bonus track from a subsequent session, "Got to Find Another Way." Ironically, *American Woman* was the final testament of the original Guess Who—guitarist/singer Randy Bachman quit soon after the tour behind this album; the group did endure and even thrive (as did Bachman), but *American Woman* represented something of an ending as well as a triumph. *—Bruce Eder*

The Best of Guess Who / 1971 / RCA ✦✦✦✦✦

The Guess Who Play Pure Guess Who / 1971 / Pickwick ✦✦

So Long, Bannatyne / 1971 / RCA ✦✦

Live at the Paramount / 1972 / Buddha ✦✦✦✦

Track Record: The Guess Who Collection / 1988 / RCA ✦✦✦✦✦
Even with the release of 1997's three-disc *The Ultimate Collection*, which is poorly sequenced and has few rarities, *Track Record* remains the definitive collection for the Guess Who. It hits all the band's commercial highs, and has two sets of song by song liner notes written by producer Jack Richardson and Burton Cummings. Flexible yet distinctive, everything they played was unmistakably the Guess Who: the aggressively melodic "Laughing," the quasi-jazz of "Undun," the defiant "Hand Me Down World." Though they were Canadian, they ruled the American pop charts; even "American Woman"'s vaguely anti-American sentiment couldn't slow its chart ascent. The lovely pop of "These Eyes" and the communal hymn "Share the Land" are faultless Top 40 pop/rock gems that capture the rage, idealism, and romanticism of late-'60s and early-'70s youth culture. The Guess Who had their fingers on the era's pulse, and an ominous foreboding bled its way into their melodies and performances. Cummings's voice ranged from an intense croon to a scratchy banshee yodel ("... it would have been nice to be both Robert Plant and Jim Morrison at once," he writes in his liners, and he came close), and Randy Bachman, Kurt Winter, and Greg Leskiw were all nervy guitarists who created tense, memorable guitar riffs. Though their later singles didn't match the early hits' commercial heights or cultural prescience, they were strong cuts. "Albert Flasher" is a wonderful honky tonk blues; "Rain Dance" is both poignant and vehement; and "Follow Your Daughter Home" is a Calypso-tinged jewel. Disc two is not as consistently listenable as the first, but includes the smash "Clap for the Wolfman" and B-sides and LP cuts like 1972's "Guns Guns Guns." But there is plenty of good Guess Who music not present on *Track Record*. *—Stanton Swihart*

● **Greatest Hits** / Feb. 23, 1999 / RCA ✦✦✦✦✦

Guided by Voices

f. 1985, Dayton, OH
Group / Indie Rock, Lo-Fi, Alternative Pop/Rock
Inspired equally by jangle-pop and arty post-punk, Guided By Voices created a series of trebly, hissy indie-rock records filled with infectiously brief pop songs that fell somewhere be-

tween the British Invasion and prog-rock. After recording six self-released albums between 1986 and 1992, the Dayton, Ohio-based band attracted a handful of fans within the American indie-rock underground. With the 1994 release of *Bee Thousand*, the group became an unexpected alternative rock sensation, winning positive reviews throughout the mainstream music press and signing a larger distribution deal with Matador Records. Despite all of the attention, the band never changed their aesthetic, continuing to record their albums on cheap four-tracks tape decks and thereby limiting their potential audience, yet that devotion to lo-fi indie-rock helped Guided By Voices maintain a sizable cult during the late '90s. *—Stephen Thomas Erlewine*

Propeller / 1992 / Scat ✦✦✦

Vampire on Titus / 1993 / Scat ✦✦✦✦✦

● **Bee Thousand** / Jun. 20, 1994 / Matador ✦✦✦✦✦
The cult of indie rock thrives on the unexpected discovery, and in 1994 Guided By Voices was just the sort of musical phenomenon no one figured was still out there—Thirtysomething rock obsessives cranking out fractured guitar-driven pop tunes in a laundry room. Robert Pollard and his stable of beer buddies/backing musicians had been churning out stuff like *Bee Thousand* for years, but the album's surprise critical success marked the first time the group found a significant audience outside their home town, and it made a clear case for Guided By Voices' virtues—as well as their flaws. From the moment "Hardcore UFOs" kicks in, it's obvious that Robert Pollard has an uncanny gift for a hook and a melody, and *Bee Thousand*'s twenty cuts are dotted with miniature masterpieces like "Echos Myron," "Smothered in Hugs," and "Queen of Cans and Jars." However, there are also more than a few duds that threaten to cancel out the good will the great songs generate, and Pollard is an acquired taste as a lyricist—his freakishly poetic verse has a real charm, but it's hard to figure out what he's on about. (GBV's other principle songwriter, Tobin Sprout, contributes less often, but manages a higher batting average.) The lo-tech rumble of the album's DIY production also wavers between being a help and a hindrance, depending on the songs, and as musicians Guided By Voices veer between sounding like inspired amateurs and ... well, just amateurs. On *Bee Thousand*, Guided By Voices sounds like a passionate and gloriously quirky garage band fronted by a thrillingly and maddeningly idiosyncratic songwriter; its many pearly moments make it a fascinating discovery for rock enthusiasts, but a few years would pass before this band was fully earning the new accolades showered upon it. *—Mark Deming*

Box / Feb. 28, 1995 / Scat ✦✦✦
Compiling all of Guided By Voices' '80s albums—*Devil Between My Toes, Sandbox, Self-Inflicted Aerial Nostalgia*, and *Same Place the Fly Got Smashed* (the vinyl version includes *Propeller*, which was on the *Vampire on Titus* CD)—and adding a collection of rarities called *King Shit and the Golden Boys*, *Box* is a bit of an intimidating listen for some devoted fans, let alone beginners. On each of their albums, Guided By Voices packs their records full of brief songs—if they reach the three-minute mark, it's an epic for the band. That can make such a massive collection of music rather daunting; it all seems to speed by without much distinction, if you're listening casually, but on closer inspection, it withstands repeated listens. The first records, *Devils* and *Sandbox*, are unpolished versions of R.E.M.'s *Murmur*. On the next two albums, the group's distinctive, British Invasion-inspired abbreviated pop begins to coalesce; their music sounds more like messages than songs, albeit messages that are driven by undeniable hooks. Retailing for under $50, *Box* is a worthwhile investment for dedicated fans. *—Stephen Thomas Erlewine*

Alien Lanes / Mar. 28, 1995 / Matador ✦✦✦

Under the Bushes Under the Stars / Mar. 26, 1996 / Matador ✦✦✦

Mag Earwhig! / May 20, 1997 / Matador ✦✦✦✦
After *Bee Thousand* gave Guided By Voices a wider audience, it became evident that Robert Pollard saw himself as more than just the band's songwriter and frontman, and as his career ambitions grew, he became increasingly frustrated with the limitations of his band. Matters came to a head prior to the recording of *Mag Earwhig!* as Pollard broke ties with longtime guitarist and fellow songwriter Tobin Sprout and fired the rest of the group. While Pollard and Sprout soon buried the hatchet, Sprout opted not to stay on as a full-time member of the group, and Pollard was now Guided By Voices' uncontested leader. He hired Cleveland-based blues/garage rockers Cobra Verde as his backing band for the next GBV album, and *Mag Earwhig!* sounded a good bit different as a result; while there were a few stray four-track experiments with Sprout scattered about, most of the album had a solid, professional sheen, and Cobra Verde rock harder and sound tighter than any of the lineups Pollard had worked with in the past. Unfortunately, his songwriting wasn't quite up to his usual standards, which the new clarity of this album makes all the more evident. Pollard is incapable of making an album without a few fine songs, and "Bulldog Skin," "Sad If I Lost It," "Not Behind the Fighter Jet," and "Portable Men's Society" certainly fill the bill, but it may well be significant that *Mag Earwhig!*'s most exciting song, the joyous "I Am a Tree," was written by Cobra Verde's Doug Gillard. While there's plenty to enjoy here, Robert Pollard's next experiment in hi-fi record making, *Do the Collapse*, would prove to be much more successful. *—Mark Deming*

Do the Collapse / Aug. 3, 1999 / TVT ✦✦

Guns N' Roses

f. 1985
Group / Album Rock, Heavy Metal, Hard Rock
At a time when pop was dominated by dance music and pop metal, Guns N' Roses brought raw, ugly rock & roll crashing back into the charts. They were not nice boys; nice boys don't play rock & roll. They were ugly, misogynist, violent; they were also funny, vulnerable, and occasionally sensitive, as their breakthrough hit "Sweet Child O' Mine" showed. While Slash and Izzy Stradlin ferociously spit out dueling guitar riffs worthy of Aerosmith or the Stones, Axl Rose screeched out his tales of sex, drugs, and apathy in the big city; bassist Duff McKagan and drummer Steven Adler were a limber rhythm section that kept the music loose and powerful. Guns N' Roses' music was basic and gritty, with a solid hard, bluesy base; they were dark, sleazy, dirty, and honest—everything that good hard rock and heavy metal should be. There was something refreshing about a band that could provoke everything from devotion to hatred, especially since both sides were equally right. There hadn't been a hard rock band this raw or talented in years, and they were given added weight by Axl Rose's primal rage, the sound of confused, frustrated white trash vying for his piece of the pie. As the '80s became the '90s, there simply wasn't a more interesting band around, but owing to intraband friction and the emergence of alternative rock, Rose's supporting cast gradually disintegrated, as he himself spent several years in seclusion. *—Stephen Thomas Erlewine*

★ **Appetite for Destruction** / 1987 / Geffen ✦✦✦✦✦
Guns N' Roses' debut *Appetite for Destruction* was a turning point for hard-rock in the late '80s—it was a dirty, dangerous and mean record in a time when heavy metal meant nothing but a good time. On the surface, Guns N' Roses may appear to celebrate the same things as their peers—namely, sex, liquor, drugs, and rock & roll—but there is a nasty edge to their songs, since Axl Rose doesn't see much fun in the urban sprawl of L.A. and its parade of heavy metal thugs, cheap women, booze and crime. The music is as nasty as the lyrics, wallowing in a bluesy, metallic hard-rock borrowed from Aerosmith, AC/DC and countless faceless hard-rock bands of the early '80s. It's a primal, sleazy sound that adds grit to already grim tales. It also makes Rose's misogyny, fear and anger hard to dismiss as merely an artistic statment—this is music that sounds lived-in. And that's exactly why *Appetite for Destruction* is such a powerful record—not only does Axl have fears, but he also is vulnerable, particularly on the power-ballad "Sweet Child o' Mine." He also has a talent for conveying the fears and horrors of the decaying inner city, whether it's on the charging "Welcome to the Jungle," the heroin ode "Mr. Brownstone," or "Paradise City," which simply wants out. But as good as Axl's lyrics and screeching voice are, they wouldn't be nearly as effective without the twin-guitar interplay of Slash and Izzy Stradlin, who spit out riffs and solos better than any band since the Rolling Stones, and that's what makes *Appetite for Destruction* the best metal record of the late '80s. *—Stephen Thomas Erlewine*

G N' R Lies / 1989 / Geffen ✦✦✦
Once *Appetite for Destruction* finally became a hit in 1988, Guns N' Roses bought some time by delivering the half-old/half-new LP *G N' R Lies* as a followup. Constructed as a double-EP, with the "indie" debut *Live ?!*@ Like A Suicide* coming first and four new acoustic-based songs following on the second side, *G N' R Lies* is where the band metamorphosized from genuine threat to joke. Neither recorded live nor released by an indie-label, *Live ?!*@ A Suicide* is competent bar-band boogie, without the energy or danger of *Appetite for Destruction*. The new songs are considerably more problematic. "Patience" is Guns N' Roses at their prettiest and their sappiest, the most direct song they have recorded to date. Its emotional directness makes the misogyny of "Used to Love Her (But I Had to Kill Her)" and the pitiful slanders of "One In A Million" sound genuine. Although the cover shrugs them off as a "joke," Axl's venom is frightening—there's little doubt that he truly does believe "faggots" come to America from another country, and that "niggers" should stay out of his way. Since he wasn't playing a character on the remainder of the album, there's little doubt that this is from the heart as well. And what makes it harder to dismiss is the musical skills of the band, who make the country-fried boogie of "Used to Love Her," the bluesy revamp of "You're Crazy" and the tough, paranoid fever-dream of "One In A Million" indelible. So, you either listen to the music and are satisfied, or listen to the lyrics and become disturbed not only by Axl's intentions, but the millions of record-buyers that identified with him. *—Stephen Thomas Erlewine*

Use Your Illusion I / Sep. 1991 / Geffen ✦✦✦✦✦
The "difficult second album" is one of the perennial rock & roll cliches, but few second albums ever were as difficult as *Use Your Illusion, Pts. I & II*. Not really conceived as a double album, but impossible to separate as individual works, *Use Your Illusion* is a shining example of a suddenly-successful band getting it all wrong and letting their ambitions run wild. Taking nearly three years to complete, the recording of the album was clearly difficult, and tensions between Slash, Izzy Stradlin and Axl Rose are evident from the start. The two guitarists, particularly Stradlin, are trying to keep the group closer to their hard-rock roots, but Axl has pretentions of being Queen and Elton John, which is particularly odd for a notoriously homophobic midwestern boy. Conceivably, the two aspirations could have been divided between the two records, but instead they are just thrown into the blender—it's just a coincidence that *I* is a harder-rocking record than *II*. Stradlin has a stronger presence on *I*, contributing three of the best songs—"Dust N' Bones," "You Ain't the First" and "Double Talkin' Jive"—which help keep the album in Stonesy Aerosmith territory. On the whole, the album is stronger than *II*, even though there's a fair amount of filler, including a song that takes its title from the Osmonds' biggest hit and a dippy psychedelic collaboration with Alice Cooper. But it also has two ambitious set-pieces, "Novermber Rain" and "Coma," which find Axl fulfilling his ambitions, as well as the ferocious metallic "Perfect Crime" and the original version of the power-ballad "Don't Cry." Still, it can be a chore to find the highlights on the record amid the over-blown production and endless amounts of filler. *—Stephen Thomas Erlewine*

Use Your Illusion II / Sep. 1991 / Geffen ✦✦✦✦✦
Use Your Illusion II is more serious and ambitious than *I*, but it's also considerably more pretentious. Featuring no less than four songs that run over six minutes, *II* is heavy on epics, whether it's the charging funk-metal of "Locomotive," the anti-war "Civil War," or the multi-part "Estranged." As if an attempt to balance the grandiose epics, the record is loaded with an extraordinary amount of filler. "14 Years" may have a lean, Stonesy rhythm, and Duff McKagan's Johnny Thunders homage "So Fine" may be entertaining, but there's no forgiving the ridiculous "Get in the Ring," where Axl threatens rock journalists *by name* because they gave him bad reviews; the misinterpretation of Dylan's "Knockin' On Heaven's Door"; *another* version of "Don't Cry"; and the bizarre closer "My World," which probably captures Axl's instabliity as effectively as the tortured poetry of his epics. That said, there are numerous strengths to *Use Your Illusion II;* a couple of songs have a nervy energy, and for all their

pretensions, the overblown epics are effective, though strangely enough, they reveal notorious homophobe Axl's aspirations of being a cross between Elton John and Freddie Mercury. But the pompous production and poor pacing make the album tiring for anyone who isn't a dedicated listener. *—Stephen Thomas Erlewine*

The Spaghetti Incident— / Nov. 23, 1993 / Geffen ✦✦

Live Era: '87-'93 / Nov. 23, 1999 / Geffen ✦✦✦

Sammy Hagar

b. Oct. 13, 1947, Monterey, CA

Vocals, Guitar / Arena Rock, Heavy Metal, Hard Rock

After spending several years as the lead vocalist and rhythm guitarist for the mid-'70s hard-rock band Montrose, Sammy Hagar began a solo career that produced several hits and made him an album rock favorite. Hagar became a true star once he joined Van Halen in 1985, but he was a popular hard rocker ever since his first album with Montrose. Former Edgar Winter guitarist Ronnie Montrose asked Hagar to join his band in 1973. Hagar recorded two albums with Montrose before going solo in 1976. Hagar's eponymous debut was his first chart entry, and his 1981 album *Standing Hampton* went platinum. His 1984 album *VOA* contained the hit single "I Can't Drive 55," which peaked at number 26. In 1985, Hagar replaced David Lee Roth in Van Halen; his first album with the group was 1986's *5150.* Hagar stayed with Van Halen through the remainder of the '80s and half of the '90s before tensions began to surface between Hagar and the rest of the band. In the summer of 1996, Hagar either quit Van Halen or was fired. The entire incident became a media sensation, ensuring that Hagar's 1997 solo album *Marching to Mars*—his first in 10 years—would be greeted with much media-generated fanfare. *Red Voodoo* followed two years later. *—Stephen Thomas Erlewine*

Rematch / 1982 / Capitol ✦✦✦✦

Standing Hampton / 1982 / Geffen ✦✦✦✦✦

Three Lock Box / 1983 / Geffen ✦✦✦✦✦

Continuing the sleek, driving pop-oriented sound of Hagar's breakthrough *Standing Hampton, Three Lock Box* equals its predecessor, featuring such highlights as the double entendres of the title track and the hit single "Your Love Is Driving Me Crazy." *—Stephen Thomas Erlewine*

VOA / 1983 / Geffen ✦✦✦✦

VOA was the last album Hagar recorded before he became the lead singer of Van Halen and the record shows why he was invited to join the band. With songs like "I Can't Drive 55" he adds a simple melody to the song which never distracts from the all-important hard-driving riff. On "Two Sides of Love," he shows that he has the ability to pull off a power ballad, wrenching every bit of feeling out of the song. Like Hagar himself, *VOA* is never subtle, but in hard rock, that's a positive attribute. *—Stephen Thomas Erlewine*

I Never Said Goodbye / 1987 / Geffen ✦✦

Sammy Hagar / 1987 / One Way ✦✦✦

The Best of Sammy Hagar / Nov. 16, 1992 / Capitol ✦✦✦✦✦

● **Unboxed** / Mar. 15, 1994 / Geffen ✦✦✦✦✦

In between his days with hard-rocking Montrose in the early '70s and his takeover of lead singing duties from David Lee Roth in Van Halen, Sammy Hagar had a moderately successful solo career. Many of his singles didn't receive the recognition they deserved, which were either staid guitar-driven party anthems or infectious AOR tunes with punchy choruses. *Unboxed* is a hits collection that takes Hagar's best work from *Standing Hampton, I Never Said Goodbye, VOA,* and *Three Lock Box,* plus two other fiery singles, and puts them all on one disc, which is both convenient and entertaining. Hagar did crack Billboard's Top 40 with three of the songs on this hits set, including the friendly six-string pounce of "Two Sides of Love," which hit number 38 in 1984. His most popular solo effort, the speed inducing raucous of "I Can't Drive 55," highlights the album, proving that the vocal abilities of Hagar are anything but limited. His semi-slower material is equally justified, especially the surprising sincerity found within "Give to Live," which broke the Top 30 in 1987. The thunderous chorus of "Heavy Metal," which is twice as fast as the rest of the song, spotlights Hagar at his most fervent and is outlined with raw chord-crunching power. Surprisingly, Sammy Hagar's highest-charting single up to the release of *Unboxed,* the radio-friendly "Your Love Is Driving Me Crazy," is missing from this collection. Nonetheless, this greatest hits presents Hagar in a light that many have either sidestepped or completely disregarded, but with all his best material in one place, his musicianship is better appreciated. *—Mike DeGagne*

Marching to Mars / May 20, 1997 / MCA ✦✦✦✦

Red Voodoo / Mar. 23, 1999 / MCA ✦✦✦

Bill Haley

b. Jul. 6, 1925, Highland Park, MI, **d.** Feb. 9, 1981, Harlingen, TX

Vocals, Guitar / Rockabilly, Western Swing, Rock & Roll

The Bill Haley and the Comets recording of "Rock Around the Clock," which topped the charts for eight weeks in 1955, is remembered as the beginning of the rock era. Though it also represented Haley's peak as a performer, his career had begun some time before and would continue for a long time after. Haley began leading Western swing bands under various names in the late '40s, slowly incorporating elements of R&B. Haley was among the first performers—perhaps he was even the very first—of any color to combine R&B and C&W in a way that can readily be identified by listeners of any era as bonafide rock & roll. His early-'50s sides rank among his most exciting, steering country and big band forms into uncharted regions. Haley also wrote much of his own material, and one of his compositions, "Crazy, Man, Crazy," became one of the first Top 20 rock & roll hits in 1953. In 1954, he moved to the major Decca label, where his sides became increasingly formulaic, though for a time very successful, after "Rock Around the Clock." Haley was largely eclipsed as the king of rock & roll by Elvis Presley and others who followed him from 1956 on. Nevertheless, he continued to perform overseas and in oldies shows in the United States. *—William Ruhlmann & Richie Unterberger*

★ **From the Original Master Tapes** / 1985 / MCA ✦✦✦✦✦

This is it—the Bill Haley record to own! Compiled by producer Steve Hoffman from the original session masters (you even get studio chatter ahead of "Rock Around the Clock"), this 20-song collection is the definitive Haley hits collection, with every song of consequence that he recorded for Decca Records during the years 1954-56. The sound is extraordinary—you haven't really heard Haley's music till you've heard this disc—and the sessionography adds a great deal to our knowledge of the players. From "Rock Around the Clock" and "Thirteen Women" to "Don't Knock the Rock," this is the best representation of Haley's peak years. *—Bruce Eder*

Rock the Joint! / Apr. 5, 1995 / Schoolkids ✦✦✦✦✦

A 22-track collection that collects sides from 1951-1953. Those who haven't heard this material before will be astonished to discover bona fide rock & roll dating from three to four years earlier than the era (1954-1955) more commonly associated with the music's birth. Haley's sound is similar to the country-boogie of the late '40s, retaining the steel guitar prominent in much of the era's country music, but it's clearly more driving and forward-looking. The songs owe a lot of jump R&B, but are transformed into the basic model of rock & roll with slapping bass, ricky-tick drums, and extended electric guitar riffing. Listen to his version of Jackie Brenston's "Rocket 88" (which has itself been pegged as one of the first rock & roll records) and you'll be astounded to note the basics of rockabilly already in place—in 1951. The low buzzing, distorted guitar on "Green Tree Boogie" (also from 1951) is also a revelation, as is the guitar solo on 1952's "Rock the Joint," which is almost identical to the much more famous one on "Rock Around the Clock" a couple of years later. The later sides introduce a honking sax, which would become such a prominent feature in 1950s rock & roll. Includes "Crazy Man Crazy," the first rock & roll song to make the Top 20. *—Richie Unterberger*

Half Japanese

f. 1977

Group / Experimental Rock, Indie Rock, Post-Punk, Alternative Pop/Rock

Depending on your point of view, Half Japanese is either a celebration of the pure, amateurish do-it-yourself rock & roll spirit or a pretentious, highly irritating example of noisy, self-conscious experimental rock at its most extreme. Formed by Jad and David Fair in 1977, the group started bashing out music in their parents' basement in Maryland, recording their debut EP by themselves. By the time the Fairs recorded their debut album, the three-record box set *1/2 Gentlemen/Not Beasts,* they had acquired a full-time drummer plus a saxophonist, yet their music was no less noisy and primitive; if anything, it was more atonal and difficult than before.

For the rest of their career, the band has proudly displayed nothing approaching instrumental virtuosity. David Fair left the band after their third record, rejoining briefly for 1988's *Charmed Life.* Throughout the years, the lineup has changed frequently—at times it has included Velvet Underground drummer Maureen Tucker and guitarist Don Fleming, as well as occasional contributions from Fred Frith and John Zorn—but Jad Fair has remained. That doesn't necessarily mean the music hasn't changed; their later records are slightly more musically varied and accessible, yet no less challenging. Fair has released a few solo albums that are stranger (believe it or not) than the typical Half Japanese release. *—Stephen Thomas Erlewine*

Half Gentlemen, Not Beasts / 1980 / Tec Tones ✦✦✦✦✦

As with any album that is three records long, *1/2 Gentlemen/Not Beasts* unwittingly shows Half Japanese's true roots. Over the three records, the band "covers" such minimalists as the Velvet Underground, the Stooges, and Jonathan Richman, as well as deconstructing such wordsmiths as Bruce Springsteen and Bob Dylan. Although they would have you believe that their untuned, almost unlistenable, instrumental clatter is the result of being so enthusiastic that they didn't bother to learn how to play their instruments, it's just the logical, inevitable intellectual extension of Richman's naivete and the Velvet Underground's stripped-down guitar. Half Japanese is consciously primitive and amateurish. *—Stephen Thomas Erlewine*

Music to Strip By / 1987 / 50 Skidillion Watts ✦✦✦

Produced by Kramer, *Music to Strip By* finds Jad Fair working without brother David for the group's most coherent and accessible outing to date. Scattered among the usual chaos ("My Sordid Past," "Stripping for Cash," "Sex at Your Parents' House," "Ouija Board Summons Satan") are telling covers of Fats Domino's "Blue Monday," Willie Dixon's "Hidden Charms" and "La Bamba." *—Jason Ankeny*

Charmed Life / 1988 / 50 Skidillion Watts ✦✦✦✦✦

The Band That Would Be King / 1989 / 50 Skidillion Watts ✦✦✦✦✦

● **Greatest Hits** / Mar. 13, 1995 / Safe House ✦✦✦✦✦

Half Japanese began their career with a three-LP box set, so it's little wonder that their *Greatest Hits* encompasses two CDs. Under the guidance of Jad Fair, the group has become more accessible over the years, but that's only a relative term. Fair has remained doggedly amateurish and noisy, letting the twisted pop structures peak out only every once in awhile. There's a lot of subtle differences between albums which only fans can tell, so *Greatest Hits* serves as a good introduction to Half Japanese as well as a kind of roadmap of their career. *—Stephen Thomas Erlewine*

Hall & Oates

f. 1972

Vocals / Blue-Eyed Soul, Pop/Rock, Folk-Rock, Soft Rock

With their savvy contemporary take on blue-eyed soul—spiked equally with pop skills, New Wave flourishes and rock production—Hall & Oates had a wave of chart-topping singles in the early '80s that broke records set by the Everly Brothers. Despite their success, they weren't critically respected at the time, although their catalog of songs, in retrospect, is one of the finest mainstream pop had to offer in their era.

Hall & Oates began their recording career with *Whole Oates*, an album that was closer to folk-rock. They wove soul into 1973's *Abandoned Luncheonette*, which resulted in their first moderate hit, "She's Gone." After the Todd Rundgren-produced *War Babies* stiffed, they left Atlantic Records for RCA. Their eponymous 1975 debut for the label was where they discovered their signature mix of rock, pop and soul, resulting in a Top 20 album and Top 10 single, "Sarah Smile." *Bigger Than the Both of Us* was even bigger, thanks to "Rich Girl," their first number one single. Hall & Oates couldn't sustain that success and their next three records failed to make as large an impact. With 1980's Voices they had their first blockbuster, as the record launched two Top five singles ("Kiss on My List," "You Make My Dreams"), staying on the charts for 100 weeks and making the duo stars. *Private Eyes* reached the Top Ten on the back of two number ones ("Private Eyes," "I Can't Go for That (No Can Do)"), and *H20* continued their winning streak in grand fashion, going double platinum and producing their biggest hit, "Maneater." Big Bam Boom (1984) went double platinum and featured a number one hit ("Out of Touch"), but it was their last album to enjoy this kind of success. Hall & Oates went on hiatus the following year. When they regrouped for 1988's *Ooh Yeah!*, their first record for Arista, they had another platinum album, but they'd lost their momentum. Following 1990's *Change of Season*, they quietly retreated from the spotlight. *—Stephen Thomas Erlewine*

Whole Oates / 1972 / Atlantic ✦✦✦
Hall & Oates' debut album was a tentative effort, with the two singers' hesitantly working their way around slick, but relatively undistinguished material that displayed their folk roots more than any other record they would later make. *—Stephen Thomas Erlewine*

Abandoned Luncheonette / 1973 / Atlantic ✦✦✦✦✦
Abandoned Luncheonette, Hall & Oates' second album, was the first indication of the duo's talent for sleek, soul-inflected pop/rock, featuring the single "She's Gone," which would become a big hit in 1975, when it was re-released following the success of "Sara Smile." *—Stephen Thomas Erlewine*

War Babies / 1974 / Atlantic ✦✦

Daryl Hall & John Oates / 1976 / Buddha ✦✦✦✦✦
Switching to RCA, Daryl Hall & John Oates recorded a self-titled album that fulfilled their early promise as pop-savvy blue-eyed soul craftsmen. A few of the tracks fall flat—including the reggae-tinged "Soldering" and the pompous "Ennui on the Mountain"—but much of the album is lush and catchy, featuring ballads and mid-tempo numbers that are nearly as engaging as their breakthrough single "Sara Smile." *—Stephen Thomas Erlewine*

Beauty on a Back Street / 1977 / RCA ✦✦✦
Beauty on a Back Street isn't quite as accomplished as its two predecessors, yet it is more ambitious and diverse, as Hall & Oates begin to add some arena-rock conventions to their sound, particularly distorted guitars and anthemic choruses. On *War Babies*, they had tried a similar attack, but on *Beauty on a Back Street*, the duo's songwriting was stronger, which meant that the instrumental approach didn't overwhelm the actual songs. *—Stephen Thomas Erlewine*

Bigger than the Both of Us / 1977 / RCA ✦✦

No Goodbyes / 1977 / Atlantic ✦✦

Along the Red Ledge / Sep. 1978 / RCA ✦✦✦
Continuing the more rock-oriented approach of *Beauty on a Back Street, Along the Red Ledge* is more successful than its predecessor, as the duo landed on a polished melodic pop/rock style that managed to retain their Philly soul influences without drowning their voices in distorted guitar flourishes. They would refine this sound two years later on *Voices*, the record that established them as pop/rock superstars. *—Stephen Thomas Erlewine*

X-Static / 1979 / Buddha ✦✦✦✦
After coming up with a sleek and soulful template on *Along the Red Ledge*, Hall & Oates took a temporary detour on *X-Static*, concentrating on disco rhythms. A few tracks were successful—in particular, "Wait for Me"—but the record sounds unfocused and misguided. *—Stephen Thomas Erlewine*

Voices / 1980 / RCA ✦✦✦✦✦
This is the album that took Hall & Oates from being a successful '70s pop duo to being one of the four biggest singles acts of the '80s (the others: Michael Jackson, Prince, and Madonna). The sound is a wonderful pop pastiche, from the Beatlesque "How Does It Feel to Be Back" to the neo-Philadelphia soul of the hits "Kiss on My List" and "You Make My Dreams." *—William Ruhlmann*

Private Eyes / 1981 / RCA ✦✦✦✦✦
Voices brought Hall & Oates into the new wave era, establishing their sleek fusion of synthesizers, Philly soul, mechanical beats and pop hooks, but they didn't quite perfect it until *Private Eyes*. Powered by no less than three Top Ten singles, the album is filled with effortlessly catchy hooks and a handful of great songs that don't stop at the hits. Sure, "Private Eyes," "I Can't Go for That (No Can Do)," and "Did It in a Minute" all have remarkably graceful melodies, but what's unexpected is how flat-out terrific the pounding soul of "Looking for a Good Sign" is, or how deftly the arena-rock hooks of "Head Above Water" are executed. There's still a bit of filler, highlighted by John Oates' supremely silly "Mano a Mano," but Hall & Oates never made a record quite as good as *Private Eyes* ever again. *—Stephen Thomas Erlewine*

H2O / 1982 / RCA ✦✦✦✦✦
From the Motown beat of "Maneater" to the lush ballad "One on One," Hall & Oates continue to make the top pop of the early '80s. Also contains "Family Man." *—William Ruhlmann*

☆ **Rock 'n' Soul Pt. 1: Greatest Hits** / 1983 / RCA ✦✦✦✦✦
Not a perfect hits collection but nonetheless an excellent compilation, *Rock 'n' Soul, Pt. 1: Greatest Hits* contains nine of Hall & Oates' biggest hits from 1974's "She's Gone" to 1983's "One on One," adding new songs—the wonderful "Say It Isn't So," plus "Adult Education"—plus a live take of "Wait for Me" for good measure. While several terrific singles are missing—particularly "Did It in a Minute" and "Family Man"—all the essential items are here, and they illustrate the duo's expertise in crafting soulful pop songs, making a convincing argument that Hall & Oates were the last great blue-eyed soul group. *—Stephen Thomas Erlewine*

Big Bam Boom / 1984 / RCA ✦✦✦
The last of the major Hall & Oates albums of the '80s features more of their patented soul-rock sound on the hits "Out of Touch" and "Method of Modern Love." *—William Ruhlmann*

Live at the Apollo / 1985 / RCA ✦✦

Ooh Yeah! / 1988 / Arista ✦✦

Change of Season / 1990 / Arista ✦✦

● **Atlantic Collection** / Jan. 23, 1996 / Rhino ✦✦✦✦✦
Drawing from Hall & Oates' four Atlantic albums and adding one previously unreleased song, *Atlantic Collection* is a definitive overview of the duo's early years. Although they only had one hit during this period—"She's Gone," which is included here in its full-length album version—their early recordings contained some of their richest, most diverse music. Much of the material is based in soul, particularly the smooth Phillie Soul of the early '70s, yet it also has strong folk overtones, as well as distinct pop/rock leanings. Within these 21 tracks, it is possible to hear the roots of their later hits, as well as directions they never wound up pursuing. For serious Hall & Oates fans, *The Atlantic Collection* can be a revelatory listen. *—Stephen Thomas Erlewine*

Marigold Sky / Sep. 30, 1997 / Push ✦✦✦

★ **The Very Best of Daryl Hall & John Oates** / Jan. 23, 2001 / RCA ✦✦✦✦✦
There's one thing wrong with *The Very Best of Daryl Hall & John Oates*, and it's minor—the promotional 12" mix of "Adult Education" is included in favor of the 7" version. This isn't a big deal and it doesn't mar what is the best overview of Hall & Oates' RCA years, the era when they became the biggest-selling duo in the history of rock. If the Atlantic years were more adventurous, dabbling in folk and\album rock, *The Very Best of* demonstrates the virtues of consistency, since these\blue-eyed soul songs rank among the very finest singles (and songs) of their time. And Hall & Oates weren't *un*adventurous, either, since they deftly blended elements of new wave, contemporary soul, and soft rock into their signature sound. Most impressively, smaller hits like "Wait for Me" and the splendid "Did It in a Minute" (easily one of the greatest songs they ever cut) more than hold their own alongside familiar items like "Sara Smile," "You Make My Dreams," "Private Eyes," and "Maneater." Hall & Oates may not have been hip, but they made addictive soul-pop that not only rocketed to the top of the charts, but has stood the test of time as some of the best pop made during the early '80s. *—Stephen Thomas Erlewine*

Happy Mondays

f. 1985, Manchester, England, **db.** 1992
Group / Madchester, Alternative Dance, Club/Dance, Alternative Pop/Rock, House
Along with the Stone Roses, the Happy Mondays were the leaders of the late '80s/early '90s dance club-influenced Manchester scene, experiencing a brief moment in the spotlight before collapsing in 1992. While the Stone Roses were based in '60s pop, adding only a slight hint of dance music, the Happy Mondays immersed themselves in the club and rave culture, eventually becoming the most recognizable band of that drug-fueled scene. The Mondays' music relied heavily on the sound and rhythm of house music, spiked with '70s soul licks, and swirling '60s psychedelia. It was bright, colorful music that had fractured melodies that never quite gelled into cohesive songs. Unwittingly or not, the Happy Mondays personified the ugly side of rave culture. Under the leadership of vocalist Shaun Ryder, the group sounded and acted like thugs. Ryder's lyrics were twisted and surrealistic, loaded with bizarre pop culture refrences, drug slang, and menacing sexuality. Appropriately, their music was as convoluted. The Happy Mondays were one of the first rock bands to integrate hip-hop techniques into their music. They didn't sample, but they borrowed melodies and lyrics and, in the process, committed rock blasphemy. For a band that celebrated their vulgarity and excessiveness, the Happy Mondays appropriately came undone by their addictions, but they left behind a surprisingly influential legacy, apparent in everyone from dance bands like the Chemical Brothers to rock & rollers like Oasis. *—Stephen Thomas Erlewine*

Squirrell & G Man Twenty-Four Hour Party People Plastic Face Carnt Smile / Apr. 1987 / Factory ✦✦

Bummed / Nov. 1988 / Elektra ✦✦✦✦
Happy Mondays first essayed their fusion of dance-club beats, hip-hop, funk, and rock & roll on *Bummed*. A considerable improvement from the unfocused *Squirrel and G-Man*, *Bummed* is slightly inconsistent, but the group's sound is beginning to gel. In particular, Shaun Ryder's incoherent bluster of non sequiturs, surreal imagery, and verbal threats is coming into its own, and it adds a sense of menace to dark grooves like "Lazy Itis," "Mad Cyril," and "Wrote for Luck." The latter was remixed by Vince Clarke after the album's release and the new version, which was included on later pressings, was the hardest dance the group had yet attempted, suggesting the direction they would follow on their next album. *—Stephen Thomas Erlewine*

★ **Pills 'n' Thrills & Bellyaches** / Apr. 1990 / Elektra ✦✦✦✦✦
A swirling, neo-psychedelic kaleidoscope of hallucinogenic drugs, trippy beats, borrowed hooks, and veiled threats, *Pills 'n' Thrills & Bellyaches* is Happy Mondays' masterpiece and the peak of the entire Madchester craze. Where the Stone Roses were pop classicists, Happy Mondays pushed pop into the ecstasy age. The Mondays' cut and paste rhythms and melodies are clearly influenced by hip-hop and electronic dance music, and their songs have the same sort of twisted internal logic, subverting conventional pop song structures while reinterpreting oldies, occasionally stealing entire songs and claiming them as their own (John Kongos' "He's Gonna Step on You Again" is transformed into "Step On," LaBelle's "Lady Marmalade"

provides the basis for "Kinky Afro"). Most of the musical collage is the creation of producers Paul Oakenfold and Steve Osborne, but the vision of *Pills 'n' Thrills & Bellyaches* belongs to Shaun Ryder, who reveals himself as a surreally gifted lyricist. Lifting melodies at will, Ryder paints a bizarre vision of modern urban life, fueled by sex, drugs, violence, and dead-end jobs—and instead of lamenting the state of affairs, he celebrates them in his hoarse, arrhythmic, tuneless holler. His thuggishly surreal sense of humor and appropriation of hooks became enormously influential on British rock & roll in the '90s, particularly on Oasis' sense of style. *—Stephen Thomas Erlewine*

Live / Nov. 19, 1991 / Elektra ✦✦

Yes, Please / Sep. 22, 1992 / Elektra ✦

Double Easy: The US Singles / Sep. 14, 1993 / Elektra ✦✦✦

Loads (& Loads More) / Oct. 30, 1995 / London ✦✦✦✦✦
With the exception of *Pills 'n' Thrills and Bellyaches*, the Happy Mondays had difficulty expanding their ideas into full albums, which makes the singles compilation *Loads* all the more useful. It contains all of the band's hit singles—"Step On," "Kinky Afro," "Hallelujah," "Lazyitis," "W.F.L.," "Tokoloshe Man," "Loose Fit," "Bob's Yer Uncle," "24 Hour Party People," "Mad Cyril"—plus several important album tracks, making it an excellent distillation of the band's career; as an album, only *Pills 'n' Thrills* provides better listening, and *Loads* is arguably just as good as an introduction, especially for casual fans. The first 10,000 copies of *Loads* included an extra disc, *Loads More*, a compilation of remixes making their debut appearance on CD, including Bernard Sumner's "Freaky Dancing," Mike Pickering's "Delightful," Martin Hannett's "Lazyitis," and Vince Clarke's "W.F.L."; all of the remaining mixes are by Paul Oakenfold. Since the remixes date from the height of Happy Mondays' career, they provide useful insight on the band's talents as a dance group. *—Stephen Thomas Erlewine*

Tim Hardin

b. Dec. 23, 1941, Eugene, OR, **d.** Dec. 29, 1980
Vocals, Keyboards, Guitar / Folk-Rock, Singer/Songwriter
A gentle, soulful singer who owed as much to blues and jazz as folk, Tim Hardin produced an impressive body of work in the late '60s without ever approaching either mass success or the artistic heights of the best singer/songwriters. By the time of his 1966 debut, he was writing confessional folk-rock songs of considerable grace and emotion. The first album's impact was slightly diluted by incompatible string overdubs (against Hardin's wishes), but by the time of his second and best LP, he'd achieved a satisfactory balance between acoustic guitar-based arrangements and subtle string accompaniment. It was the lot of Hardin's work to achieve greater recognition through covers from other singers, such as Rod Stewart (who did "Reason to Believe"), Nico (who covered "Eulogy to Lenny Bruce" on her first album), Scott Walker (who sang "Lady from Baltimore"), and most especially Bobby Darin, who took "If I Were a Carpenter" into the Top Ten in 1966. His end was not a pretty one: due to accumulated drug and health problems, as well as a scarcity of new material, he didn't complete any albums after 1973, dying of a drug overdose in 1980. *—Richie Unterberger*

Tim Hardin 1 / 1966 / Verve ✦✦✦✦✦
Although Tim Hardin would go on to make many other fine records, his debut album is a true pioneering folk-rock classic. It's a virtual template for the form, and also gives a fantastic overview of Hardin's awesome songwriting talents. "Don't Make Promises" and "Reason to Believe" were covered by dozens of artists following this album's release, and that should be reason enough to believe in this giant's talent. Aside from the excellent writing, the sound and feel of the record can easily be seen as a template for such groups as the Buffalo Springfield and others who followed. If you own just one Hardin album, make it this one. *—Matthew Greenwald*

This Is Tim Hardin / 1967 / Edsel ✦✦✦
Hardin's very earliest recordings from approximately 1964, not issued until the late '60s, when he had achieved some success with his albums for Verve. Accompanied by nothing besides his own guitar, Hardin's arrangements are far sparser and bluesier than his folk-rock work for Verve. Over half of the ten tracks are traditional blues numbers like "Hoochie Coochie Man" and "House of the Rising Sun," and even the four originals (one co-written by future Holy Modal Rounder Steve Weber) are in a very similar straight blues style. The material isn't nearly as distinctive as the best of Hardin's work, but the performances rank with Dave Van Ronk and Fred Neil as the best white blues/acoustic folk to emerge from the early-'60s Greenwich scene (indeed, Hardin covers Neil's "Blues on the Ceiling" here). The hollow, reverbed, one-man-sitting-alone-in-an-empty-room production gives this album a haunting, somber feel (though not to its detriment). While not as good as Fred Neil's similar material from this era, it's still well worth tracking down. *—Richie Unterberger*

Tim Hardin 2 / 1967 / Verve ✦✦✦
Probably his best single album, on which he eschewed blues nearly entirely and forged a distinctive, folk-rock voice, occasionally embellished by tasteful full arrangements. "Lady Came From Baltimore," "Red Balloon," and especially "If I Were A Carpenter" rank among his best and most famous songs. *—Richie Unterberger*

Live in Concert / 1968 / Polydor Chronicles ✦✦✦✦✦
Originally titled *Tim Hardin 3*, this set was recorded live in 1968 with a backing band comprised primarily of jazz musicians. The support crew is a bit tentative; it's evident that they hadn't played much with Hardin, and in places the tempo comes close to breaking down. It's still a good, effective performance; Hardin is in good voice (a condition which apparently couldn't be readily counted on, even in his early days), and on the songs that had already been released on his first two albums, the arrangements vary from the recorded versions in interesting fashions. *Live in Concert* includes renditions of most of his best early compositions ("If I Were a Carpenter," "Red Balloon," "Reason to Believe," "Misty Roses," "Lady Came From Baltimore," "Black Sheep Boy") and half a dozen Hardin originals that didn't make it onto his first pair of albums. The best of these is the Lenny Bruce tribute, "Lenny's Tune," which Nico covered on her first solo album (where it was retitled "Eulogy to Lenny Bruce"). The 1995 CD reissue of this album adds three previously unreleased bonus tracks from the same concert. *—Richie Unterberger*

● **Reason to Believe** / Oct. 25, 1990 / Polydor ✦✦✦✦✦
The great early work of this top-flight '60s singer/songwriter includes the title track, "If I Were a Carpenter," and "Misty Roses." *—Kenneth M. Cassidy & William Ruhlmann*

● **Hang On to a Dream: The Verve Recordings** / Feb. 22, 1994 / Polydor ✦✦✦✦✦
Double-CD set of 47 tracks that Hardin recorded for Verve between 1964 and 1966. His expressive, blues-inflected vocals and confessional songwriting are heard on covers and famous compositions like "If I Were A Carpenter," "Lady Came From Baltimore," and "Reason To Believe." The compilation includes every studio recording that Hardin released on the Verve label, as well as two alternate takes and 15 previously unreleased tracks. *—Richie Unterberger*

Simple Songs / Sep. 3, 1996 / Columbia/Legacy ✦✦✦✦✦
Hardin's Columbia period, lasting from the late '60s to the early '70s, was a troubled one that saw his songwriting muse wither and his personal life start to dissolve. Although his best work was behind him, he was still capable of recording good material. This 17-song collection is a good distillation of the highlights of his three Columbia LPs, which largely still found his voice in good shape. Original tunes were more of a problem: although the best of his compositions were on a rough par with his Verve work, by the time of 1972's *Painted Head*, he was devoting himself entirely to covers of songs by others. The *Painted Head* selections are the least impressive on this anthology, the spare folk-rock of the earlier Columbia sessions giving way to slicker arrangements that don't highlight his sad, wavering voice nearly as effectively. The remainder is pretty good, with the significant bonus of his sole chart single, a 1969 cover of Bobby Darin's "Simple Song of Freedom," and five decent (if sometimes unpolished) previously unreleased outtakes from late 1968. *Simple Songs of Freedom* is the one album of post-Verve Hardin music to own. *—Richie Unterberger*

John Wesley Harding

b. Oct. 22, 1965
Vocals, Guitar / College Rock, Alternative Folk, Contemporary Folk, Adult Alternative Pop/Rock, Alternative Pop/Rock, Singer/Songwriter, Urban Folk
John Wesley Harding may take his name from a Bob Dylan album and he's a modern day folk singer but with the biting, cynical observations in his songs, and sharp sense of humor combined with winning melodies, he shows his true forefathers are Elvis Costello and Nick Lowe with a hint of Billy Bragg. Far from being a follower or strict revivalist, however, Wes draws on a wide assortment of musical influences, pushing the boundaries of the all-too-often formulaic singer-songwriter tag to create something all his own. An opening slot for John Hiatt attracted the attention of Demon Records who signed him and released the live *It Happened One Night;* in 1990, he teamed up with producer Andey Paley and members of Elvis Costello's Attractions (the association would cause Costello comparisons that would continue to haunt him) to record *Here Comes the Groom* for Sire. While he received consistently good reviews, expanded on his cult following through constant touring, and finally shook (for the most part) the Elvis Costello comparisons, lack of a substantial push from Sire led to his leaving the label by the mid-90s. *—Chris Woodstra*

It Happened One Night / 1988 / Rhino ✦✦✦✦✦
This solo acoustic outing, recorded live in England in 1988, seems like an odd choice for a debut, but it comes off very well. Capturing both John Wesley Harding's folk roots and a wonderful sense of humor, *It Happened One Night* gives a very representative picture of the singer/songwriter. Included are early versions of songs appearing on the following two albums as well as unreleased gems such as his fun account of Live Aid ("July 13th 1985") and a cover of Prince's "Kiss." *—Chris Woodstra*

● **Here Comes the Groom** / 1989 / Sire ✦✦✦✦✦
His second album has him working in the studio with a band called the Good Liars, including Pete Thomas, and Bruce Thomas of the Attractions. Not surprisingly, *Here Comes the Groom* has a feel similar to classic Elvis Costello. Harding's articulate and biting vocal delivery, also reminiscent of Costello, retains a good dark sense of humor. *—Chris Woodstra*

The Name Above the Title / Feb. 19, 1991 / Sire ✦✦✦

Why We Fight / Mar. 1992 / Sire ✦✦✦
This 1992 release is more low-key and moody than any of his previous work. The subject matter is darker, though the melodies are still catchy and instantly memorable as always, this time with smoother production. Even a discussion about Hitler in the bizarre fantasy of "Hitler's Tears" is musically irresistible, placing him in the ranks of Nick Lowe and Elvis Costello. *—Chris Woodstra*

John Wesley Harding's New Deal / Feb. 13, 1996 / Rhino ✦✦✦
Four years passed since John Wesley Harding's previous long player and it seems he spent the time "growing up" a bit, shaking once-and-for-all the image of Elvis Costello's smart-ass kid brother. *John Wesley Harding's New Deal* (the title presumably refering to his parting of ways with Sire and his new signing to Forward Records) finds a gentler Harding doing some soul searching on his most introspective outing to date. Continuing in the trend set by 1992's *Why We Fight*, the album's warmer production—bare-boned arrangements consisting mainly of acoustic guitar with subtle use of violin, cello, hammond organ, and pedal steel—create the appropriate intimate setting for the subject matter. Thankfully the new John Wesley Harding's songs are still as clever as ever and, in a different way, just as catchy and memorable. *—Chris Woodstra*

Dynablob / Jun. 1996 / Mod Lang ✦✦✦
Dynablob is a collection of previously unreleased studio recordings from John Wesley Harding's first recording session in 1986 to 1994 with track-by-track commentary by Wes himself. This is obviously an essential purchase for fans, but it is also surprisingly consistent enough to offer a good listen and a good look at the artist in a more traditional singer/songwriter setting. Points should also be given for the detail of the Dylan-esque cover design. *—Chris Woodstra*

Awake / Mar. 10, 1998 / Zero Hour ♦♦♦♦♦
Billed as John Wesley Harding and the Gangsta Folk, *Dare* seems to be an attempt to recast the singer/songwriter in a different light, incorporating elements of electronica to earn more street cred. The Gangsta Folk are in truth not a band, but rather Harding handling multiple instruments (often of the more exotic variety like e-bow, moogs, and mellotron), along with a few guests like Scott McCaughey, Robert Lloyd, Kelly Hogan and pop purist Chris von Schneidern. And while the experimentation is implemented quite well—especially in the lighter-and-match-strike percussion loop of "Burn"—Harding's craft remains untouched. His acid-tongued, always-clever phrasing, folky leanings, and strong sense of melody show him to be one of the finest (and unfairly overlooked) songwriters of the nineties. *—Chris Woodstra*

Trad Arr Jones / Feb. 9, 1999 / Zero Hour ♦♦♦

Confessions of St. Ace / Aug. 29, 2000 / Mammoth ♦♦♦♦

Ben Harper

b. Oct. 28, 1969, Pomona, CA
Vocals, Guitar (Steel), Guitar / Jam Bands, Contemporary Blues, Adult Alternative Pop/Rock, Singer/Songwriter
Combining shuddering, groove-laden funky soul and folky, hand-crafted acoustics, singer/songwriter Ben Harper cultivated a cult following during the course of the '90s that gained full fruition toward the end of the decade. Harper combined elements of classic singer/songwriters, blues revivalists, Jimi Hendrix, and '90s jam bands like Blues Traveler, Hootie & the Blowfish, and Phish, which meant that he was embraced by critics and college kids alike.

A native of California, Harper grew up listening to blues, folk, soul, R&B, and reggae. After steady gigging in the Los Angeles area, Harper scored a deal with Virgin Records in 1992. He released his debut album, *Welcome to the Cruel World*, two years later to positive reviews.

Released in 1995, the politically-heavy *Fight For Your Mind* made for a strong sophomore effort, an obvious growth in musical experimentation and individual declamation. Harper's third album, 1998's *The Will to Live*, pushed his blues-oriented alternative folk into the middle mainstream, becoming a mainstay at college radio and making inroads at adult alternative radio. Recorded over two years of touring in support of *Fight for Your Mind*, *The Will to Live* introduced the Innocent Criminals, Harper's supporting band.

His most successful album thus far, 1999's *Burn to Shine* blended Harper's fondness of '20s jazz compositions and urban beatboxing, resulting in a clever and passionate collection of songs. "Steal My Kisses" and "Suzie Blue" were radio favorites, landing him two headlining world tours and an opening spot on the Dave Matthews Band's summer 2000 tour. *—MacKenzie Wilson*

Welcome to the Cruel World / Feb. 8, 1994 / Virgin ♦♦♦
The full range of Harper's influences would not come to bear until later albums, but this debut lays a strong foundation. "Like a King" and "Take That Attitude to Your Grave" burn with a political conviction rarely heard during the 1990s. "Forever" has a tenderness which demonstrates Harper's emotional range. Lackluster hippie jams that cultivated his early following may have served a purpose, but feel fluffy by comparison when compared to the meatier tracks. Ben closes the album with a song that frequently closes his concerts, "I'll Rise." This song, built around Maya Angelou's 1979 poem "And I Still Rise," reminds us of art's ability to pierce through society, self and the soul. *—Ryan Randall Goble*

● **Fight for Your Mind** / 1995 / Virgin ♦♦♦♦
Fight for Your Mind fully embraces Harper's influences (Dylan, Marley, Havens and Hendrix) into a complete sound while simultaneously broadening his thematic and musical palette. Oliver Charles' tactile drumming and Leon Mobley's percussion work give a sparkle to Harper's music that was absent on his debut. Songs like "Gold to Me" and "Excuse Me Mr." show Harper growing as a poet, approaching ideas via more subtle avenues. The single "Ground on Down" and epic jam "God Fearing Man" capture some of the explosive energy of his live performances. The latter makes allusions to "While My Guitar Gently Weeps," and that's exactly what Harper does—allow his trademark Weissenborn guitar to scream out to his audience. The only misstep on this album is his sophomoric weed anthem "Burn One Down," but one might argue that a little tarnish adds character. *—Ryan Randall Goble*

The Will to Live / Jun. 17, 1997 / Virgin ♦♦♦♦

Burn to Shine / Sep. 21, 1999 / Virgin ♦♦♦♦
Burn to Shine presents proof positive that you can always distill the essence of rock & roll down to a solitary man alone with his guitar and conscience. It sounds inventive yet firmly rooted in the blues-rock singer/songwriter/guitarist tradition of Taj Mahal and of Neil Young and Cat Stevens at their most confessional. Harper's guitar with falsetto vocal in "The Woman in You" even suggests a Curtis Mayfield tune in the hands of Prince. "Steal My Kisses" is one of those uncluttered, radio-friendly rock shuffles that simply makes you bob your head and feel better. Even Harper's detours—like the wobbling New Orleans shuffle with the Real Time Jazz Band, "Suzie Blue," and charred Black Sabbath metal in "Less"—prove worth exploring. Other cameos include guitarists David Lindley and former Bob Marley sideman Tyrone Downey. *Burn to Shine* is a minor masterpiece that may prove to be not so minor. *—Chris Slawecki*

George Harrison

b. Feb. 25, 1943, Liverpool, England
Slide Guitar, Vocals, Guitar (Electric), Guitar / Album Rock, Experimental Rock, Pop/Rock, Psychedelic, Singer/Songwriter
As lead guitarist for the Beatles, George Harrison provided the band with a lyrical style of playing in which every note mattered. The Beatlemania years, from 1963 through 1966, were a mixed blessing for Harrison, as his lead guitar was buried beneath the chiming chords of John Lennon's instrument. Additionally, he was thwarted as a songwriter by the presence of Lennon and McCartney—the quality and prolificacy of their output left very little room for songs by anyone else. In 1966, Harrison finally seemed to find his voice, with two of his songs on the *Revolver* album, "Taxman" and "Love You Too." In the wake of the group's decision to stop touring, Harrison's playing and songwriting grew exponentially. The period from 1968 onward was Harrison's richest with the Beatles. He displayed a smooth, elegant slide guitar technique that showed up on their last three albums, and contributed two classic songs, "While My Guitar Gently Weeps" and "Here Comes the Sun," along with "Something," which became the first Harrison song on the A-side of a Beatles single. For his first solo record following the group's 1970 break-up, *All Things Must Pass*, Harrison collaborated with producer Phil Spector, whose so-called "wall of sound" technique adapted well to Harrison's voice. *All Things Must Pass* and the accompanying single "My Sweet Lord" had the distinction of being the first solo recordings by any of the Beatles to top the charts following their breakup. Subsequent Harrison albums from the 1970s into the '80s always had an audience, but except for *Somewhere in England* (1981), released in the wake of the murder of John Lennon with the memorial song "All Those Years Ago," none seemed terribly well-crafted or executed. In 1987, Harrison made a return to the top of the charts with his album *Cloud Nine*, which featured his most inspired work in years. *—Bruce Eder*

Wonderwall Music / Dec. 2, 1968 / Capitol ♦♦

Electronic Sound / May 26, 1969 / Zapple ♦♦

★ **All Things Must Pass** / Nov. 27, 1970 / Capitol ♦♦♦♦♦
Without a doubt, Harrison's first solo recording, originally issued as a triple album, is his best. Drawing on his backlog of unused compositions from the late Beatle era, George crafted material that managed the rare feat of conveying spiritual mysticism without sacrificing his gifts for melody and grand, sweeping arrangements. Enhanced by Phil Spector's lush orchestral production and Harrison's own superb slide guitar, nearly every song is excellent: "Awaiting on You All," "Beware of Darkness," the Dylan collaboration "I'd Have You Anytime," "Isn't It a Pity," and the hit singles "My Sweet Lord" and "What Is Life" are just a few of the highlights. A very moving work, with a very significant flaw: the jams that comprise the final third of the album are entirely dispensable, and have probably only been played once or twice by most of the listeners that own this record. *—Richie Unterberger*

The Concert for Bangladesh / Dec. 20, 1971 / Capitol ♦♦♦♦♦
A unique live document showcasing Harrison near his best, with ex-Beatle Ringo Starr, Eric Clapton, and many other superstars. It has less-than-perfect sound but overall fine recreations of his best work, with work by Bob Dylan as an added bonus. *—Bruce Eder*

Living in the Material World / May 30, 1973 / Capitol ♦♦♦
How does an instant multi-million-selling album become underrated— George Harrison's follow-up to *All Things Must Pass* was necessarily a letdown for fans and critics, appearing after a two-and-a-half year interval without the earlier album's backlog of excellent songs to draw from. And it does seem like Harrison narrowed his sights and his vision for this record, which has neither the bold expansiveness nor the overwhelming confidence of its predecessor. And some of the most serious songs here, such as "The Light That Has Lighted the World," seem dirge-like. What *Living In the Material World* shows off far better than the earlier record, however, is Harrison's guitar work—he's the only axeman on *Material World*, and it does represent his solo playing and songwriting at something of a peak. Most notable are his blues stylings and slide playing, glimpsed on some of the later Beatles sessions but often overlooked by fans. "Don't Let Me Wait Too Long" is driven by a delectable acoustic rhythm guitar and has a great beat. The title track isn't great, but it does benefit from a tight, hard band sound; and "The Lord Loves the One (That Loves the Lord)," despite its title, is the high point of the record, a fast, rollicking, funky, bluesy jewel, with a priceless guitar break (maybe the best of Harrison's solo career) that should have been at the heart of any Harrison's concert set. Vocally, he isn't as self-consciously pretty or restrained here, but it is an honest performance, and his singing soars magnificently in his heartfelt performance on "The Day the World Gets Round." Perhaps a less serious titlewould have represented the album better, but nobody was looking for self-effacement from any ex-Beatle except Ringo (who's also here, natch) in those days. *—Bruce Eder*

Dark Horse / Dec. 9, 1974 / Capitol ♦♦

Extra Texture / Sep. 22, 1975 / Capitol ♦♦

The Best of George Harrison / Nov. 8, 1976 / Capitol ♦♦♦
The Harrison material is matched with some Beatles numbers in a good but routine collection. *—Bruce Eder*

33 & 1/3 / Nov. 24, 1976 / Dark Horse ♦♦♦♦♦
Having suffered the humiliation of being sued successfully over "My Sweet Lord," Harrison turned the ordeal into music, writing "This Song," a Top 25 hit. Even better was "Crackerbox Palace," which would have fit in nicely on any Beatles album. The rest was slight, although Harrison covering Cole Porter's "True Love" is an interesting idea. This was Harrison's first album on his Dark Horse custom label, formed after the completion of his contract with EMI/Capitol in June 1976 and initially distributed by A&M. *— William Ruhlmann*

George Harrison / Feb. 14, 1979 / Dark Horse ♦♦♦
Harrison's sixth solo studio album (released after a two-year hiatus) was another slight affair, boasting the Top 20 single "Blow Away," but otherwise unremarkable. "Not Guilty" was a Beatles-era song once short-listed for their *White Album*. "Here Comes the Moon" was a tepid sequel to "Here Comes the Sun." *— William Ruhlmann*

Somewhere in England / Jun. 1, 1981 / Dark Horse ♦♦

Gone Troppo / Oct. 27, 1982 / Dark Horse ♦♦

Cloud Nine / Nov. 2, 1987 / Dark Horse ♦♦♦♦♦
Teaming with legendary Beatles obsessive Jeff Lynne, George Harrison crafted a remarkably consistent and polished comeback effort with *Cloud Nine*. Lynne adds a glossy production, rem-

iniscent of ELO, but what is even more noticeable is that he's reined in Harrison's indulgences, keeping the focus on a set of 11 snappy pop-rock numbers. The consistency of the songs remains uneven, but the best moments—"Devil's Radio," "Cloud 9," "Just for Today," "Got My Mind Set On You," and the tongue-in-cheek Beatles pastiche "When We Was Fab"—make *Cloud 9* one of his very best albums. *—Stephen Thomas Erlewine*

The Best of Dark Horse (1976-1989) / Oct. 1989 / Dark Horse ♦♦♦♦♦
George Harrison's albums have been notoriously uneven, but despite the rough patches, his talent for songcraft never really left him, as the compilation *The Best of Dark Horse (1976-1989)* proves. A 15-song retrospective covering five albums, *The Best of Dark Horse* contains nearly every gem from *33 1/3, George Harrison, Somewhere in England, Gone Troppo,* and *Cloud Nine,* including "Crackerbox Palace," "All Those Years Ago," "Got My Mind Set on You," "Cloud 9," "When We Was Fab," and the lovely "Blow Away." For most casual fans, the record will be a welcome summation of a hit-and-miss era of Harrison's career. *—Stephen Thomas Erlewine*

Live in Japan / Jul. 1992 / Dark Horse ♦♦

PJ Harvey

b. Oct. 9, 1969, Yeovil, England
Vocals, Guitar / Adult Alternative Pop/Rock, Indie Rock, Alternative Pop/Rock, Singer/Songwriter
During the early-'90s alternative rock explosion, several female singer-songwriters rose to prominence, but few were as distinctive or as widely praised as Polly Jean Harvey. Over the course of three albums, Harvey established herself as one of the most individual and influential songwriters of the '90s, exploring themes of sex, love and religion with unnerving honesty, dark humor and a twisted theatricality. Her career began in 1991 with the formation of a trio named PJ Harvey, whose singles "Dress" and "Sheela-Na-Gig" received lavish praise in the UK music press. The band's debut album *Dry* earned American distribution through Island, and the group hired former Big Black frontman Steve Albini as the producer of their second album, *Rid of Me.* The album became a major critical success and expanded Harvey's cult greatly. At the end of the year, Harvey released *4-Track Demos,* a collection of her original versions of the songs on *Rid of Me.* Following the *Rid of Me* tour, Harvey became a solo act and recorded her third album *To Bring You My Love* with producer Flood; the album was hailed as a masterpiece by many critics and became a moderate commercial hit as well, entering the US charts at number 40. During 1996, she was relatively quiet, only appearing twice on record: once in a duet with Nick Cave on his *Murder Ballads* album and singing on John Parish's *Dance Hall at Louse Point. Is This Desire* followed in 1998. *—Stephen Thomas Erlewine*

Dry / Jun. 30, 1992 / Too Pure/Indigo ♦♦♦♦♦
Polly Jean Harvey arrives fully formed as a songwriter on PJ Harvey's debut album, *Dry.* Borrowing its primitive attack from post-punk guitar-rock and its form from the blues, *Dry* is a forceful collection of brutally emotional songs, highlighted by Harvey's deft lyricism and startling voice, as well as her trio's muscular sound. Her voice makes each song sound like it was an exposed nerve, but her lyrics aren't quite that simple. Shaded with metaphors and the occasional Biblical allusion, *Dry* is essentially an assault on feminine conventions and expectations, and while there are layers of dark humor, they aren't particularly evident, since Harvey's singing is shockingly raw. Her vocals are perfectly complemented by the trio's ferocious pounding, which makes even the slow ballads sound like exercises is controlled fury. And that's the key to *Dry:* the songs, which are often surprisingly catchy—"Dress" and "Sheela-Na-Gig" both have strong hooks—are as muscular and forceful as the band's delivery, making the album a vibrant and fully realized debut. *—Stephen Thomas Erlewine*

• **Rid of Me** / May 4, 1993 / Island ♦♦♦♦♦
Dry was shockingly frank in its subject and sound, as Polly Harvey delivered post-feminist manifestos with a punkish force. PJ Harvey's second album, *Rid of Me,* finds the trio, and Harvey in particular, pushing themselves to extremes. This is partially due to producer Steve Albini, who gives the album a bloodless, abrasive edge with his exacting production; each dynamic is pushed to the limit, leaving absolutely no subtleties in the music. Harvey's songs, in decided contrast to Albini's approach, are filled with gray areas and uncertainties, and are considerably more personal than those on *Dry.* Furthermore, they are lyrically and melodically superior to the songs on the debut, but their merits are obscured by Albini's black-and-white production, which is polarizing. It may be the aural embodiment of the tortured lyrics, and therefore a supremely effective piece of performance art, but it also makes *Rid of Me* a difficult record to meet halfway. But anyone willing to accept its sonic extremities will find *Rid of Me* to be a record of unusual power and purpose, one with few peers in its unsettling emotional honesty. *—Stephen Thomas Erlewine*

4-Track Demos / Oct. 19, 1993 / Island ♦♦♦♦

To Bring You My Love / Feb. 28, 1995 / Island ♦♦♦♦♦
Following the tour for *Rid of Me,* Polly Harvey parted ways with Robert Ellis and Stephen Vaughn, leaving her free to expand her music from the bluesy punk that dominated PJ Harvey's first two albums. It also left her free to experiment with her style of songwriting. Where *Dry* and *Rid of Me* seemed brutally honest, *To Bring You My Love* feels theatrical, with each song representing a grand gesture. Relying heavily on religious metaphors and imagery borrowed from the blues, Harvey has written a set of songs that are lyrically reminiscent of Nick Cave and Tom Waits' literary excursions into the gothic American heartland. Since she was a product of post-punk, she's nowhere as literally bluesy as Cave or Waits, preferring to embellish her songs with shards of avant-guitar, eerie keyboards and a dense, detailed production. It's a far cry from the primitive guitars of her first two albums, but Harvey pulls it off with style, since her songwriting is tighter and more melodic than before; the menacing "Down By the Water" has genuine hooks, as does the psycho-stomp of "Meet Ze Monsta," the wailing "Long Snake Moan" and the stately "C'Mon Billy." The clear production by Harvey, Flood and John Parish makes these growths evident, which in turn makes *To Bring You My Love* her most accessible album, even if the album lacks the indelible force of its predecessors. *—Stephen Thomas Erlewine*

Is This Desire— / Sep. 29, 1998 / Island ♦♦♦
Retreating from the limelight after the tour for *To Bring You My Love,* PJ Harvey returned to her small hometown of Yeovil and isolated herself from most pop trends, eventually writing the material that would come to comprise her fourth album, *Is This Desire?.* Released over 3Ω years after *To Bring You My Love, Is This Desire?* has all the hallmarks of a record written in isolation; subtle, cerebral, insular, difficult to assimilate, it's the album where Polly Harvey enters the ranks of craftsmen, sacrificing confession for fiction. It's an inevitable transition for any artist, especially one as lyrically gifted as Harvey, and though her words are more obtuse and not as brutal, painful or clever, she still draws some effective character sketches. Similarly, the music on *Is This Desire?* is hardly the immediate, blunt force that characterized her first albums, nor is it the grand theater of *To Bring You My Love*—it takes its time, slowly working its way into the subconsciousness. There are a few guitar explosions scattered throughout the record, but it's primarily a series of layered keyboards, electronic rhythms and acoustic guitars; it's so quiet that at times it barely rises above a murmur, and occasionally floats away without leaving a lasting impression. It seems to challenge the listener to accept it on its own grounds, but once you dig deeper, it winds up offering diminishing rewards. It is more concerned with texture than any of her previous records, but it doesn't push forward enough—it's either standard hard rockers or mournful ballads underpinned by lite electronica beats, which would have more impact if they were more pronounced. Since Harvey is an extraordinarily gifted songwriter, the album is hardly devoid of merit, but it's her least focused or successful record to date. *—Stephen Thomas Erlewine*

Stories From the City, Stories From the Sea / Oct. 24, 2000 / Island ♦♦♦♦
During her career, Polly Jean Harvey has had as many incarnations as she has albums. She's gone from the Yeovil art student of her debut *Dry,* to *Rid of Me's* punk poetess to *To Bring You My Love* and *Is This Desire?'s* postmodern siren; on *Stories From the City, Stories From the Sea*—inspired by her stay in New York City and life in the English countryside—she's changed again. The album cover's stylish, subtly sexy image suggests what its songs confirm: PJ Harvey has grown up. Direct, vulnerable lyrics replace the allegories and metaphors of her previous work, and the album's production polishes the songs instead of obscuring them in noise or studio tricks. On the album's best tracks, such as "Kamikaze" and "This Is Love," a sexy, shouty blues-punk number that features the memorable refrain "I can't believe life is so complex/When I just want to sit here and watch you undress," Harvey sounds sensual and revitalized. The New York influences surface on the glamorous punk rock of "Big Exit" and "Good Fortune," on which Harvey channels both Chrissie Hynde's sexy tough girl and Patti Smith's ferocious yelp. Ballads like the sweetly urgent, piano and marimba-driven "One Line and the Thom Yorke duet "This Mess We're In" avoid the painful depths of Harvey's darkest songs; "Horses in My Dreams" also reflects Harvey's new emotional balance: "I have pulled myself clear," she sighs, and we believe her. However, "We Float"'s glossy choruses veer close to *Lillith Fair* territory, and longtime fans can't help but miss the visceral impact of her early work, but *Stories From the City, Stories From the Sea* doesn't compromise her essential passion. Hopefully, this album's happier, more direct PJ Harvey is a persona she'll keep around for a while. *—Heather Phares*

Dale Hawkins

b. Aug. 30, 1938, Goldmine, LA
Vocals, Guitar / Rockabilly, Rock & Roll
This Louisiana guitarist's 1957 hit "Suzy Q," with its crackling bluesy guitar and insistent cowbell, was one of the most exciting early rockabilly singles. Recording for Chess (as one of its few White artists) between 1956 and 1961, Hawkins never quite duplicated its success, either commercially or artistically, but came close enough on a number of occasions to warrant respect as one of the better rockabilly singers. His drawling delivery, sense of humor, affinity for blues, and sharp guitar work (which was actually provided by such ace players as Roy Buchanan, Scotty Moore, and James Burton) are heard to good effect on his 1958 album and a number of nonhit singles. Hawkins went on to become a producer of some note in the 1960s, working with the Five Americans and Bruce Channel. *—Richie Unterberger*

My Babe / 1987 / Argo ♦♦♦
Rare singles and other interesting material that Hawkins cut, mostly for Chess, between 1958 and 1962. Includes his sole Top 40 hit besides "Suzie-Q" ("La-Do-Dada") and some fine rockabilly interpretations of blues hits. *—Richie Unterberger*

• **Oh Suzy Q** / Oct. 24, 1995 / Chess ♦♦♦♦♦
Eighteen tracks from Hawkins' Chess prime, all but one from the late '50s. Includes "Susie Q" and some obscure rockabilly cuts that are nearly as good, such as "Don't Treat Me This Way," "Liza Jane," and "Ain't That Lovin' You Babe." James Burton, Roy Buchanan, and Scotty Moore are the most prominent of the excellent guitarists to be heard on these sides. One could quibble over the absence of "Mrs. Mergitory's Daughter," "Yea Yea (Class Cutter)," and the post-Chess single "Stay at Home Lulu," but this is definitely the best Hawkins compilation ever assembled. *—Richie Unterberger*

Rock'n'Roll Tornado / Oct. 27, 1998 / Ace ♦♦♦♦♦
At first glance, this 30-track compilation of Hawkins' late-'50s and early-'60s Checker sides might seem like a preferable collection to MCA's briefer (18-song) best-of. Actually, however, this only repeats eleven of those 18 tracks, with the emphasis on some cuts that haven't been on CD before, as well as no less than eight previously unreleased songs. It's hard to figure if this was meant as a best-of compilation, or just a disc that mixes some of his biggest and best singles with obscure items; the omissions of "Ain't That Lovin' You Baby" (which is on the MCA collection) alone prevents this from being definitive. It does include a couple of songs that should be on any Dale Hawkins collection, *"Yea-Yea (Class Cutter)"* and "Mrs. Merguitory's Daughter," that do *not* appear on the MCA anthology. As for the more obscure material that's only on *Rock'n'Roll Tornado,* it's largely respectable, but not so essential that you would compare it to "Susie Q," "La-Do-Dada," tor other of Hawkins' best performances.

Sometimes it's heavily derivative — *"Boy Meets Girl"* sounds like it's trying very hard to imitate Jerry Lee Lewis, and "Someday, One Day" is quite Buddy Holly-like—and some of the unreleased cuts, like the cover of "Caldonia" and the country-soul ballad "Convicted," show him trying styles removed from rockabilly. In all, a good compilation that Hawkins fans should get even if they have the one on MCA. But if you just want one, it's a pretty tough call, each disc containing worthy selections not on the other, though each has his most essential recordings (i.e. "Susie Q," "Liza Jane," "La-Do-Dada"). *—Richie Unterberger*

Ronnie Hawkins

b. Jan. 10, 1935, Huntsville, AR
Vocals, Guitar / Rockabilly, Rock & Roll
Hawkins is a rockabilly singer who formed his original backing band, the Hawks, while attending the University of Arkansas. After auditioning unsuccessfully for Sun in 1957, he started working regularly in Canada the following year, eventually taking up permanent residence there. After one release on the Canadian Quality label, he signed with Roulette in New York in 1959, having hits with "Forty Days" and "Mary Lou." The live fervor of Hawkins (known as Mr. Dynamo) & the Hawks' show continued in Canada after all the original members except Levon Helm headed back to the US. Hawkins quickly hired Canadian players Robbie Robertson, Garth Hudson, Rick Danko, and Richard Manuel as the new Hawks. They stayed with him until 1963, but later became Bob Dylan's backing group and went on to a career of their own as the Band. Hawkins has remained a legend in Canada, recording unrepentant rockabilly sides and gigging constantly. He's still the original Mr. Dynamo, capable of shaking the walls down any old time he feels like it. *—Cub Koda*

● **The Best of Ronnie Hawkins & His Band** / Jun. 1990 / Rhino ✦✦✦✦✦
In the late 1950s and early 1960s, Ronnie Hawkins was one of the few rock & rollers committed to performing and recording unapologetic rockabilly while others were returning to their country roots or going the teen-idol route. This 18-song compilation focuses mostly on his initial burst of activity for Roulette in 1959 and 1960, with a few later odds and ends thrown in. While he deserves respect for keeping the torch of rock & roll's roots burning during some of its leaner years, he didn't match the greatness of rockabilly's kingpins. His voice and performance was energetic but not brilliant; his material was a bit pedestrian. The best of these tunes are "Mary Lou" (his sole Top 30 hit), "Forty Days" (an update of Chuck Berry's "Thirty Days"), and "One of These Days" (later covered by the Searchers). What he's really known for, of course, is giving a bunch of mostly Canadian kids their start as his backing band, the Hawks. A later edition of the Hawks eventually toured with Bob Dylan and evolved into the Band. Only two of these songs, though, feature that lineup (the 1963 single "Bo Diddley"/"Who Do You Love"). On "Who Do You Love" especially, Robbie Robertson lets rip with a roaring solo that's a good few years ahead of its time in its manic distorted intensity. It's by far the most exciting track on this compilation of a respectable but minor performer from rock's early days. *—Richie Unterberger*

The Roulette Years / 1995 / Sequel ✦✦✦✦✦
This 57-track double-CD set seems like a no-brainer—get almost all of Ronnie Hawkins' rock & roll recordings in one place. The packaging here is good, thoughtful, and legitimate, but could also be a little misleading to those who are buying this expecting to hear a lot of early work by the musicians who later became the Band—Levon Helm was aboard on drums from the Hawks' first official recordings, but the remainder didn't begin arriving on the scene until almost two years later; they're only on hand more than one or two at a time for less than half of what's here. Additionally, taken on its own terms, this is about as solid a rock & roll collection by a single white artist from this period as you're going to find—in 1959-60, as Elvis Presley, et al. were generally softening their sounds, Ronnie Hawkins was staying a true rock & roller. The alternate takes and demos featured here are about as worthwhile as any of Hawkins' hits, and the quality of everything about this set makes it practically scream to be purchased—the detailed notes, the complete sessionography, the bright, clean, yet raunchy sound on the masters. A straight, enjoyable (and probably revelatory to some) rock & roll document, Sequel deserves an award for this release—only Bear Family does it better, and this is a lot cheaper than one of their double CDs. *—Bruce Eder*

Screamin' Jay Hawkins

b. Jul. 18, 1929, Cleveland, OH, **d.** Feb. 12, 2000, Paris, France
Vocals, Vocals, Piano / Jump Blues, Rock & Roll, R&B
Screamin' Jay Hawkins was the most outrageous performer extant during rock's dawn. Prone to emerging out of coffins onstage, a flaming skull named Henry his constant companion, Screamin' Jay was an insanely theatrical figure long before it was even remotely acceptable. He debuted on wax for Gotham in 1952 with "Why Did You Waste My Time," backed by Grimes and his Rockin' Highlanders. Singles for Timely ("Baptize Me in Wine") and Mercury's Wing subsidiary (1955's otherworldly "[She Put The] Wamee [On Me]," a harbinger of things to come) preceded Hawkins' immortal 1956 rendering of "I Put a Spell on You" for Columbia's Okeh imprint. Hawkins originally envisioned the tune as a refined ballad. After he and his New York session aces (notably guitarist Mickey Baker and saxist Sam "The Man" Taylor) had imbibed to the point of no return, Hawkins screamed, grunted, and gurgled his way through the tune with utter drunken abandon. A resultant success despite the protests of uptight suits-in-power, "Spell" became Screamin' Jay's biggest seller. He cut several amazing 1957-58 follow-ups in the same crazed vein—"Hong Kong," a surreal "Yellow Coat," the Jerry Leiber/Mike Stoller-penned "Alligator Wine"—but none of them clicked the way "Spell" had. Hawkins' next truly inspired waxing came in 1969 when he was contracted to Philips Records (where he made two albums). His gross "Constipation Blues" wouldn't garner much airplay, but remains an integral part of his legacy to this day. *—Bill Dahl*

● **Voodoo Jive: The Best of Screamin' Jay Hawkins** / Feb. 1990 / Rhino ✦✦✦✦✦
Some maintain that Hawkins was a one-hit fluke and a one-dimensional performer with a limited singing voice and no other discernible skills. Others insist that Hawkins was a decent R&B and blues singer and an excellent entertainer and personality whose real talents were overshadowed by the success of "I Put a Spell on You." This anthology doesn't convincingly answer the argument, but it does collect 17 Hawkins singles from Okeh, Enrica and Phillips, including all of his major hits. The high (or low) point is perhaps 1969's "Constipation Blues." *—Ron Wynn*

Cow Fingers & Mosquito Pie / 1991 / Epic ✦✦✦✦✦
Magically weird 19-song collection of the bizarre shouter's mid-'50s OKeh/Epic output, when he was at the height of his strange and terrifying vocal powers. In addition to the prerequisite "I Put a Spell on You" and the surreal rockers "Yellow Coat," "Hong Kong," "Alligator Wine," and "Little Demon," there's the amusing "There's Something Wrong with You," a previously unissued "You Ain't Foolin' Me," and a deranged takeoff on the cowboy ditty "Take Me Back to My Boots and Saddle" (and what Jay does to the formerly stately "I Love Paris" and "Orange Colored Sky" is truly indescribable!). *—Bill Dahl*

Spellbound! 1955-74 / 1991 / Bear Family ✦✦✦
Bear Family's *Spellbound! 1955-74* is a double-disc set that captures highlights from Screamin' Jay Hawkins' recordings for Wing, Decca, Phillips and RCA. It's not quite the bargain it seems. Half of the 48 tracks were already issued on two Phillips albums, which were combined on one Edsel CD. Furthermore, most of these songs date from the '60s, with only a handful coming from Hawkins' '50s peak. Strangely, of those songs, not one of them is the original "I Put a Spell On You," which makes this hardly the definitive overview that it should be. Instead of focusing on the best of Screamin' Jay Hawkins' best material, it has the campy, silly stuff from the '60s, which will try the patience of anyone outside devoted fans—and those devoted fans will prefer more complete compilations than this strangely scattershot effort from Bear Family. There are some good moments here, but overall, it has to rank as a disappointment. *—Stephen Thomas Erlewine*

Isaac Hayes

b. Aug. 20, 1942, Covington, TN
Vocals, Saxophone, Keyboards, Piano, Arranger / Blaxploitation, Disco, Funk, Soul
Few figures exerted greater influence over the music of the 1960s and 1970s than Isaac Hayes; after laying the groundwork for the Memphis soul sound through his work with Stax-Volt Records, Hayes began a highly successful solo career which predated not only the disco movement but also the evolution of rap. In 1964, Hayes began playing sax with the Mar-Keys, which resulted in the beginning of his long association with Stax Records. After playing on several sessions for Otis Redding, Hayes was tapped to play keyboards in the Stax house band, and eventually established a partnership with songwriter David Porter. Under the name the Soul Children, the Hayes-Porter duo composed some 200 songs, reeling off a string of hits for Stax luminaries like Sam and Dave (the brilliant "When Something Is Wrong With My Baby," "Soul Man" and "Hold On, I'm Comin'"), Carla Thomas ("B-A-B-Y") and Johnnie Taylor ("I Got to Love Somebody's Baby," "I Had a Dream"). In 1967, he issued his debut solo LP *Presenting Isaac Hayes,* and with the release of 1969's landmark *Hot-Buttered Soul,* he made his commercial breakthrough, as the record's adventuresome structure (comprising four lengthy songs), ornate arrangements and sensual grooves—combined with the imposing figure cut by his shaven head, omnipresent sunglasses and fondness for gold jewelry—made Hayes one of the most distinct figures in music. He reached his commercial zenith in 1971 with the release of *Shaft,* the score from the Gordon Parks film of the same name. Not only did the album win Hayes an Academy Award for Best Score (the first African-American composer to garner such an honor), but the single "Theme from 'Shaft,'" a masterful blend of prime funk and pre-rap monologues, became a Number One hit. *—Jason Ankeny*

Presenting Isaac Hayes / 1968 / Stax ✦✦✦
Isaac Hayes' earliest single efforts, and he hadn't yet perfected his lengthy raps and symphonic soul formula. These were rather the same type of songs he and David Porter turned into classics for many other Stax artists. They were mostly short, gospel and country-tinged soul ballads, vamps, and uptempo numbers. Hayes sang them well, his domineering baritone revealing itself as a potent weapon. While none of them did that well, the album revealed the enormous potential Hayes would begin to fulfill with his next album. *—Ron Wynn*

☆ **Hot Buttered Soul** / 1969 / Stax ✦✦✦✦✦
Isaac Hayes had already co-written many immortal soul singles in the late '60s when he began forging a solo career. Hayes helped focus attention on the album as a creative source in soul and R&B. This seminal album went against the grain in several ways. There were only four cuts, three of them at least nine minutes. There were two with extensive monologues, and he used symphonic backing and elaborate production. The album went gold, cracked the Top 100 and helped usher soul and R&B into the concept album era. It also featured some superb vocals and fine keyboard work by Hayes. *—Ron Wynn*

Isaac Hayes Movement / 1970 / Stax ✦✦✦✦✦
His second huge hit album and a great follow-up to the superb *Hot Buttered Soul.* Those critics who thought there was no way Hayes could repeat that triumph got fooled. He included a brilliant remake of Jerry Butler's "I Stand Accused" and also did a 12-minute version of the Beatles' "Something," complete with a wailing violin solo from jazz-rocker John Blair. This album showed that Hayes was going to be around for a long time and perform just as consistently on his own as he did teaming with Porter. *—Ron Wynn*

To Be Continued / 1970 / Stax ✦✦✦

Black Moses / 1971 / Stax ✦✦✦
For many, this is Ike's finest overall effort, and despite the ego trippin' title—*Black Moses,* the music backs the brag. Hayes low register is mesmerizing on 14 refurbished R&B and Pop songs. Every track is carefully crafted, and well spaced "Ike Raps" enhances and bands them all together. The key is balance, while there's nothing as mournful as "By the Time I Get to Phoenix," soulful as "I Stand Accused," or bad as "Do Your Thing," every cut is a close second. "Going in Circles," "Man's Temptation," "Need to Belong to Someone," "Never Can Say Goodbye," and the rest are done with maturity and reverence by the self-acclaimed One. *—Andrew Hamilton*

Shaft / 1971 / Stax ✦✦✦✦✦
Of the many wonderful blaxpoitation soundtracks to emerge during the early '70s, *Shaft* certainly deserves mention as not only one of the most lasting but also one of the most successful. Isaac Hayes was undoubtedly one of the era's most accomplished soul artists, having helped elevate Stax to the esteemed status; therefore, his being chosen to score such a high-profile major-studio film shouldn't seem like a surprise. And with "Theme From Shaft," he delivered an anthem just as ambitious and revered as the film itself, a song that has only grown more treasured over the years, after having been an enormously popular hit at the time of its release. Besides this song, though, there aren't too many more radio-targeted moments here. "Soulsville" operates effectively as the sort of down-tempo ballad Hayes was most known for, just as the almost 20-minute "Do Your Thing" showcased just how impressive the Bar-Keys had become, stretching the song to unseen limits with their inventive, funky jamming. For the most part, though, this double-LP features nothing but cinematic moments of instrumentation, composed and produced by Hayes while being performed by the Bar-Kays—some down-tempo, others quite jazzy, nothing too funky, though. Even if it's not quite as enjoyable as Curtis Mayfield's *Superfly* due to its emphasis on instrumentals, *Shaft* still remains a powerful record; one of Hayes' pinnacle moments for sure. *—Jason Birchmeier*

Live at the Sahara Tahoe / 1973 / Stax ✦✦

Joy / Dec. 1973 / Stax ✦✦

Tough Guys / Mar. 1974 / Enterprise ✦✦

Truck Turner / Jul. 1974 / Enterprise ✦✦✦
This soundtrack was considerably lengthier and more varied than the one Hayes had released earlier in 1974 (*Tough Guys*), including Holiday Inn funk, a lugubrious vocal ("You're in My Arms Again"), and some jazz and blues riffs peppering the instrumental grooves. While the length ensured more variety, though, it also makes it a challenge to sit through the hour-plus program when you don't have images to fit the music. It's been combined with *Truck Turner* on the double-CD reissue *Double Feature*. *—Richie Unterberger*

Chocolate Chip / 1975 / Stax ✦✦✦

The Best of Isaac Hayes, Vol. 1 / 1986 / Stax ✦✦✦✦✦
A decent attempt to present some of Isaac Hayes' past hits on an anthology. But as one of R&B and soul's first concept and album artists, it's impossible to appreciate his contributions out of sequence. His early and mid-'70s albums helped change the course of contemporary black music production approaches, and that can't be understood by listening to condensed versions of hit singles, or even just by hearing the singles themselves removed from the album context. *—Ron Wynn*

The Best of Isaac Hayes, Vol. 2 / 1986 / Stax ✦✦✦✦✦
These two compilations dutifully boil down Isaac Hayes' sometimes long-winded albums to their essential parts—in other words, they're both singles collections, highlighted by '70s landmarks such as "Theme from *Shaft*" and "By the Time I Get to Phoenix." Fanatics may want to investigate *Hot Buttered Soul* and *Black Moses*. *—John Floyd*

• **Greatest Hit Singles** / Jun. 11, 1991 / Stax ✦✦✦✦✦
The place to start (and probably the place to end), with nearly an hour of music and 12 of his best-known singles, including "Theme From 'Shaft'," "By the Time I Get to Phoenix," "Walk on By," "Never Can Say Goodbye," "Do Your Thing," and "Joy (Part 1)." There's a separate two-volume series of Stax Hayes hits for those who want a little more, but this is the essential dose. *—Richie Unterberger*

Branded / May 23, 1995 / Pointblank ✦✦✦

Raw and Refined / May 23, 1995 / Pointblank ✦✦✦

Ultimate Collection / Apr. 11, 2000 / Hip-O ✦✦✦✦
Since the majority of Hayes' most memorable work was during the 70's, this collection nabs 13 of its 16 tracks from that decade. The two later cuts that close the disc—especially the meandering "Ike's Rap" from 1986—are disposable. More problematic though is the surreptitious editing of Hayes' longer material like "Never Can Say Goodbye," "Walk On By," and "Joy" (although interestingly not the nine minute "Hyperbol..") which are all severely shortened from their original versions. Unfortunately that essential information is nowhere to be found on the outside sleeve or liner notes. That said, the meat of those extended songs is still represented in the edits, and Hayes' trademarked slow-burn soul/funk permeates the bulk of this collection. The decision to eliminate most of his soundtrack work—save for two tracks from *Shaft*—was a smart one, and except for the cliché disco of "Don't Let Go," and the upbeat rubber band groove of "Out of the Ghetto," the album sticks primarily to Hayes' unhurried funk. Not as good as it could have been even with the single disc restrictions, the *Ultimate Isaac Hayes* is a reasonable place to start exploring, but falls short of providing a well-rounded look at the legendary musician. *—Hal Horowitz*

Roy Head

b. Jan. 9, 1943, Three Rivers, TX
Vocals / Pop-Soul, Blue-Eyed Soul, Traditional Country, Rock & Roll
Actually a country and rock vocalist rather than an R&B star, Roy Head nevertheless cut one of the great pieces of uptempo soul in the mid-'60s. "Treat Her Right" on Back Beat made it to number two on the R&B charts and number two pop, and the fact that Head was White was soft-pedaled in R&B circles while the song made its way up the charts. That performance alone was enough to qualify Head as one of the finest blue-eyed soul singers of the 1960s. But in fact, Roy was one of the most versatile stylists of the era, capable of hard R&B/rock tunes, mournful, soul-tinged country, and straight R&B and blues covers. The Texan singer is remembered as a one-shot artist, but he actually cut many records (some under the auspices of noted producer Huey Meaux) throughout the 1960s on a confusing variety of labels. A few of these were tiny hits in the wake of "Treat Her Right," only a couple ("Just a Little Bit" and "Apple of My Eye") sneaking into the Top 40. Quite a few of his records were dynamic, sleek hybrids (in varying degrees) of soul, rock, and country, all featuring Head's cocky, confident vocals. In the 1970s, after several years without success in the rock or R&B fields, Head returned to country, and landed quite a few chart hits in the arena between 1974 and 1985. *—Ron Wynn & Richie Unterberger*

• **Treat Her Right: The Best of Roy Head** / Aug. 29, 1995 / Varese ✦✦✦✦✦
A long overdue anthology of Head's best sides, mostly recorded for the Back Beat label in the mid-'60s. Besides "Treat Her Right," it has all five of his other singles that dented the charts at the time. These aren't necessarily the highlights of these 18 tracks; "Pain" is country-soul moan at its best (although it's a thinly veiled rewrite of Lonnie Mack's "Why"), "To Make a Big Man Cry" is his best foray into country-pop from the period, and "You're (Almost) Tuff" is one of his toughest rockers, with a sound that almost verges on Texas garage. This collection is the most solid evidence of Head's superb talents, which were never rewarded with the consistent material or national recognition he deserved. *—Richie Unterberger*

Heart

f. 1973, Seattle, WA
Group / Album Rock, Arena Rock, Pop/Rock, Hard Rock
Sisters Ann and Nancy Wilson were the creative spark behind Heart, a hard-rock group who initially found success in the mid-'70s, only to reach greater heights after engineering a major comeback a decade later. Based in Vancouver, Heart was actually formed as an all-male vocal group. After arriving in the group, both Ann and Nancy became romantically involved with other members of the band. One year later, the group's debut album *Dreamboat Annie* eventually sold platinum in the US. A legal battle after moving to the CBS affiliate Portrait delayed Heart's second album *Little Queen*, though it also went platinum.

After one more album, both of the band romances ended and precipitated a massive lineup change. The next two Heart albums failed miserably, and though the band moved to Capitol, it was largely written off by industry watchers. The band emerged In 1985 with a self-titled effort which ultimately sold more than five million copies on its way to launching four Top Ten hits (including the chart-topping "These Dreams"). The follow-ups, *Bad Animals* and *Brigade*, continued their comeback success. In the early '90s, the Wilson sisters took a brief hiatus from Heart to form the acoustic group the Lovemongers. Heart returned in 1993 with *Desire Walks On* and on 1995's *The Road Home*, enlisted onetime Led Zep bassist John Paul Jones to produce a live, acoustic set reprising several of their hits. *—Jason Ankeny*

Dreamboat Annie / Mar. 1976 / Capitol ✦✦✦✦✦
In the 1980s and '90s, numerous women recorded blistering rock, but things were quite different in 1976—when female singers tended to be pigeonholed as soft-rockers and singer-songwriters and were encouraged to take after Carly Simon, Melissa Manchester or Joni Mitchell rather than Led Zeppelin or Black Sabbath. Greatly influenced by Zep, Heart did its part to help open doors for ladies of loudness with the excellent *Dreamboat Annie* (reissued on a gold audiophile CD by DCC Compact Classics in 1995). Aggressive yet melodic rockers like "Sing Child," "White Lightning and White" and the rock radio staples "Magic Man" and "Crazy on You" led to the tag "the female Led Zeppelin." And in fact, Robert Plant did have a strong influence on Ann Wilson. But those numbers and caressing, folkish ballads like "How Deep It Goes" and the title song also make it clear that the Wilson sisters had their own identity and vision early on. *—Alex Henderson*

Little Queen / May 1977 / Portrait ✦✦✦✦✦
After acquiring a substantial following with *Dreamboat Annie*, Heart solidified its niche in the hard rock and arena rock worlds with the equally impressive *Little Queen*. Once again, loud-and-proud, Led Zeppelin-influenced hard rock was the thing that brought Heart the most attention. But while "Barracuda" and "Kick It Out" are the type of sweaty rockers one thought of first when Heart's name was mentioned, hard rock by no means dominates this album. In fact, much of *Little Queen* consists of such folk-influenced, acoustic-oriented fare as "Treat Me Well" and "Cry to Me." Anyone doubting just how much Heart's ballads have changed over the years need only play "Dream of the Archer" next to a high-volume power ballad like "Waiting for an Answer" from 1990's *Brigade*. *—Alex Henderson*

Magazine / Apr. 1978 / Cema Special Markets ✦✦

Dog & Butterfly / Sep. 1978 / Portrait ✦✦✦

Bebe Le Strange / Feb. 1980 / Epic ✦✦✦✦
Heart continued to pass their message over the airwaves with the release of *Bebe Le Strange* and spawned two smash hits, "Silver Wheels" and the rocking "Even It Up" in the process. Unfortunately, the rest of the disc was a bit of a letdown as Heart began to suffer from that same old same old tradition, but they still sold like hotcakes. *—James Chrispell*

Heart Greatest Hits: Live / Nov. 1980 / Epic ✦✦✦✦✦

Private Audition / May 1982 / Epic ✦✦

Heart / Jun. 1985 / Capitol ✦✦✦✦✦
Heart was pretty much considered washed up when they released *Heart* in 1985. They learned a few important things while they had taken a short sabbatical—they knew that hooks were important and they knew they could play up their looks for MTV. So, they delivered both with *Heart*, giving their audience anthemic hooks and tightly corseted bosoms, leading to the most popular album they ever had. This doesn't mean it's the best, since its calculated mainstream bent may disarm some long-term fans, but it is true that they do this better than many of their peers, not just because they have good polished material from professional songwriters, but because they can deliver this material professionally themselves. Yes, "These Dreams," "Never," and "What About Love" don't quite fit into the classic Heart mode, but they are good mid-'80s mainstream material, delivered as flawlessly as possible. There's still a lot of filler on this record, but the best moments are among the best mainstream AOR of its era. *—Stephen Thomas Erlewine*

Bad Animals / May 1987 / Capitol ✦✦✦

Brigade / Mar. 26, 1990 / Capitol ✦✦

Rock the House Live! / Sep. 1991 / Capitol ✦✦

The Road Home / Nov. 1995 / Capitol ✦✦✦

These Dreams: Heart's Greatest Hits / 1997 / Capitol ✦✦✦✦
Spanning 1975-1995, *These Dreams: Heart's Greatest Hits* isn't an ideal collection of Heart's best known songs, but it does a darn nice job trying to be. While this 1997 release boasts 17 of Heart's best known songs, it doesn't always contain the best known versions of those songs—because of licensing restrictions, Capitol didn't have access to all of Heart's material. Essential Capitol hits of the 1980s are provided, and that includes the power ballads ("Alone," "These Dreams," "What About Love,") as well as the rockers ("If Looks Could Kill," "Who Will You Run To," "Never"). But what about Heart's pre-Capitol hits— Thankfully, Capitol *did* have access to *Dreamboat Annie* and *Magazine;* so the definitive versions of "Magic Man," "Dreamboat Annie," "Crazy on You," and "Heartless" are included. But Capitol *didn't* have access to *Little Queen, Dog and Butterfly,* and other Epic/Portrait releases. So the company acknowledges Heart's Epic/Portrait years by offering a live version of "Barracuda" from 1990's *Rock The House: Live* and acoustic performances of "Dog and Butterfly" and "Straight On" from 1995's *The Road Home.* And while those aren't the most famous versions of those songs, they're very nice substitutes. Capitol, unfortunately, didn't have access to any versions of "Kick It Out" or "Little Queen," and the absence of any version of "How Can I Refuse" (which Heart performs on *Rock The House: Live*) is also regrettable. But all things considered, *These Dreams: Heart's Greatest Hits* provides a rewarding overview of the Wilson sisters' work in the '70s, '80s, and '90s. *—Alex Henderson*

● **Greatest Hits [1998]** / Aug. 25, 1998 / Epic/Legacy ✦✦✦✦✦
Heart had a pair of greatest hits collections to their credit by 1997, but both did not contain all the renown studio versions of their classic hits from the '70s (both 1980's *Greatest Hits/Live* on Epic and 1997's *Greatest Hits* on Capitol contained half studio and half live material). 1998's *Greatest Hits* on Epic/Legacy finally corrected this once and for all—collecting all of *Heart's* '70s studio hits on a single disc. Nearly all of the songs have become classic rock staples, the best known being the Zep-esque rockers "Crazy On You," "Barracuda" and "Magic Man," while the more subdued acoustic material ("Dreamboat Annie," "Love Alive," "Dog & Butterfly") showcases the immense talents of vocalist Ann Wilson. Other notables include "Kick It Out," "Heartless," "Bebe Le Strange," "Straight On" and "Even It Up," while an all new studio cut recorded in 1998 ("Strong, Strong Wind") and a live cover of Led Zeppelin's "Rock n' Roll" from 1980 are included as bonuses. While Heart may have enjoyed their biggest commercial success in the '80s with pop-oriented material, their more straight-ahead '70's work, showcased on *Greatest Hits* has stood the test of time incredibly well. *—Greg Prato*

● **Greatest Hits: 1985-1995** / Jun. 27, 2000 / Capitol ✦✦✦✦
Heart had a second run on the charts in 1985 when they signed to Capitol Records and refashioned themselves as a mainstream pop/rock band, heavy on melodies and power ballads. The move paid off immediately, as they scored four Top Ten hits from *Heart,* their first record for the label: "What About Love—," "Never," "These Dreams," and "Nothin' At All." Heart kept up their hot streak for several more years, reaching the Top Ten three other times with the number one hit "Alone," "Who Will You Run To," and "All I Wanna Do Is Make Love to You." All of those songs are on *Greatest Hits: 1985-1995,* along with 11 other tracks, including the semi-rarities of the Ann Wilson and Robin Zander duet "Surrender to Me" and the "studio version" of "You're the Voice." It may run a little long for the more casual fans, but overall, this is an excellent overview of the era, perfect for fans that don't need the full-length studio albums. *—Stephen Thomas Erlewine*

Richard Hell (Richard Myers)

b. Oct. 2, 1949, Lexington, KY
Vocals, Bass / American Punk, New York Punk, Proto-Punk, Punk
Some people will tell you Richard Hell was the main catalyst behind the birth of New York punk and its sensibilities. That's hardly true, but he's been around forever and did influence a number of budding punks (the Sex Pistols among them). In 1971 Hell and former high school buddy Tom Verlaine formed a group called the Neon Boys, who later became Television; he also cofounded the Heartbreakers with ex-New York Doll Johnny Thunders. In 1976 Hell formed the Voidoids, a caustic congregation that included guitarists Ivan Julian and Robert Quine and soon-to-be Ramones drummer Marc Bell. Hell's apocalyptic lyrics were steeped in alienated poetry, and his anguished howl of a voice set the pattern for scores of Bowery rockers. *—John Floyd*

● **Blank Generation** / 1977 / Sire ✦✦✦✦✦
Hell's debut isn't a masterpiece but it manages to re-create the intensity and exhilaration of the burgeoning days of American punk. "Love Comes in Spurts" defines Hell's romantic outlook, and the title cut is a classic piece of angst rock. *—John Floyd*

Destiny Street / 1982 / Razor & Tie ✦✦✦
It took five years for Hell to follow his debut, but *Destiny Street* is a moderately successful extension of *Blank Generation.* Some of the energy from the old days had disappeared, but Hell compensates with some fine ballads and another screwball classic, "The Kid with the Replaceable Head." *—John Floyd*

R.I.P.: The ROIR Sessions / 1984 / ROIR ✦✦✦✦✦
The Richard Hell compilation *R.I.P., ROIR Sessions* was originally released in 1984 as a cassette-only release, and has finally been re-released on CD (different cover, same track listing). *R.I.P.* collects a total of 14 tracks (most studio, some live), and serves as a solid anthology/greatest hits compilation. The selections span his career from 1975-1984, from one of his first bands (the legendary Heartbreakers with Johnny Thunders) up until a later-incarnation of the Voidoids. The sound quality is consistent for the most part, and the music is rough, raw, and rocking... in other words, classic Richard Hell. An early version of "Love Comes In Spurts" kicks off the album, and with a Heartbreakers' backup, is proof that Hell would have made a more-than-capable leader of the band (Thunders eventually gained control, effectively ending the original lineup). Also included is the depressed ballad "Betrayal Takes Two," the N.Y. new wave of "I'm Your Man," as well as the saxophone-laced "The Hunter Was Drowned." The only criticism of *R.I.P* is the omission of one of Hell's best-known tunes, "Blank Generation," but otherwise it's highly recommended. *—Greg Prato*

Jimi Hendrix

b. Nov. 27, 1942, Seattle, WA, **d.** Sep. 18, 1970, London, England
Vocals, Guitar (Electric), Guitar / Album Rock, Acid Rock, Psychedelic, Hard Rock, Blues-Rock
In his brief four-year reign as a superstar, Jimi Hendrix expanded the vocabulary of the electric rock guitar more than anyone before or since. Hendrix was a master at coaxing all manner of unforeseen sonics from his instrument, often with innovative amplification experiments that produced astral-quality feedback and roaring distortion. His frequent hurricane blasts of noise, and dazzling showmanship—he could and would play behind his back and with his teeth, and set his guitar on fire—has sometimes obscured his considerable gifts as a songwriter, singer, and master of a gamut of blues, R&B, and rock styles. *Are You Experienced?* was an astonishing debut, particularly from a young R&B veteran who had rarely sung, and apparently never written his own material, before the Experience formed. What caught most people's attention at first was his virtuosic guitar playing, which employed an arsenal of devices, including wah-wah pedals, buzzing feedback solos, crunching distorted riffs, and lightning, liquid runs up and down the scales. But Hendrix was also a first-rate songwriter, melding cosmic imagery with some surprisingly pop-savvy hooks and tender sentiments. He was also an excellent blues interpreter and passionate, engaging singer (although his gruff, throaty vocal pipes were not nearly as great assets as his instrumental skills). *Are You Experienced?* was psychedelia at its most eclectic, synthesizing mod pop, soul, R&B, Dylan, and the electric guitar innovations of British pioneers like Jeff Beck, Pete Townshend, and Eric Clapton. Amazingly, Hendrix would only record three fully conceived studio albums in his lifetime. *Axis: Bold as Love* and the double-LP *Electric Ladyland* were more diffuse and experimental than *Are You Experienced?* On *Electric Ladyland* in particular, Hendrix pioneered the use of the studio itself as a recording instrument, manipulating electronics and devising overdub techniques to plot uncharted sonic territory. *—Richie Unterberger*

★ **Are You Experienced—** / 1967 / MCA ✦✦✦✦✦
One of the most stunning debuts in rock history, and one of the definitive albums of the psychedelic era. On *Are You Experienced?,* Hendrix synthesized various elements of the cutting edge of 1967 rock into music that sounded both futuristic and rooted in the best traditions of rock, blues, pop, and soul. It was his mind-boggling guitar work, of course, that got most of the ink, building upon the experiments of British innovators like Jeff Beck and Pete Townshend to chart new sonic territories in feedback, distortion, and sheer volume. It wouldn't have meant much, however, without his excellent material, whether psychedelic frenzy ("Foxy Lady," "Manic Depression," "Purple Haze"), instrumental freakout jams ("Third Stone from the Sun"), blues ("Red House," "Hey Joe"), or tender, poetic compositions ("The Wind Cries Mary") that demonstrated the breadth of his songwriting talents. Not to be underestimated were the contributions of drummer Mitch Mitchell and bassist Noel Redding, who gave the music a rhythmic pulse that fused parts of rock and improvised jazz. Many of these songs are among Hendrix's very finest; it may be true that he would continue to develop at a rapid pace throughout the rest of his brief career, but he would never surpass his first album in terms of consistently high quality. The British and American versions of the album differed substantially when they were initially released in 1967; MCA's 17-song CD reissue does everyone a favor by gathering all of the material from the two records in one place, adding a few B-sides from early singles as well. *—Richie Unterberger*

☆ **Axis: Bold as Love** / 1967 / MCA ✦✦✦✦✦
When the Experience recorded their second album, they were in the process of solidfying their international stardom. That meant access to more studio time and more sophisticated technology, but not, alas, a great deal of time to write the material. That may be why *Axis* isn't quite as much of a tour de force as *Are You Exerienced?,* but it's nevertheless another major effort, showing Hendrix continue to grow, particularly in his increasing mastery of the studio and more sophisticated lyrics. Soul and R&B influences are more prominent here than on his debut, though psychedelic experimentalism ran rampant (to great effect) on "If 6 Was 9." "Spanish Castle Magic," "Up from the Skies," "You Got Me Floatin'," and "Castles Made of Sand" all had funky grooves that gave the spiraling guitars and crunchy rhythm section a much-needed buoyancy. The best song, though, might have been the mellowest: "Little Wing" was Hendrix at his most delicate, and perhaps his most personal. *—Richie Unterberger*

☆ **Electric Ladyland** / Oct. 1968 / MCA ✦✦✦✦✦
With *Electric Ladyland,* Hendrix took psychedelic experimentation as far as he could within the original Experience trio format. That meant pushing the barriers of late '60s studio technology as far as they could bend, particularly with regard to multitracking and effects that could only be achieved through certain treatments and manipulation of the tape itself. It also meant greater freedom and looseness in the playing and the songwriting, which could be both a plus and a drawback, as the compositions became both less constricted and less concise. Not all of the material here is top-of-the-line, but certainly much of this is Hendrix at his best: the dreamy wah-wah guitars of "Rainy Day, Dream Away" were only matched by the dreaminess of the lyrics, and "Have You Ever Been (To Electric Ladyland)" and "Gypsy Eyes" were also standouts. "1983... (A Merman I Should Turn to Be)" and "Voodoo Chile" were lengthy cuts dominated by jam-like instrumental passages; "Crosstown Traffic" and a cover of Dylan's "All Along the Watchtower," by contrast, were two of his catchiest and most pop-friendly tunes. "Voodoo Chile," "Voodoo Child (Slight Return)," and a cover of Earl King's "Come On" are three of his most determined forays into the blues, albeit the blues as fed through a nearly avant-garde filter. Originally released as a double album, the CD reissue fits the entire recording onto one 75-minute disc. *—Richie Unterberger*

Band of Gypsys / 1970 / Capitol ✦✦✦✦✦
Band of Gypsys was the only live recording authorized by Jimi Hendrix before his death. It was recorded and released in order to get Hendrix out from under a contractual obligation that had been hanging over his head for a couple years. Helping him out were longtime friends Billy Cox on bass and Buddy Miles on the drums because the Experience had broken up in June of 1969, following a show in Denver.

These new surroundings pushed Hendrix to new creative heights. Along with this new rhythm section, Hendrix took these shows as an opportunity to showcase much of the new material he had been working on. The music was a seamless melding of rock, funk, and R&B, and tunes like "Message to Love" and "Power to Love" showed a new lyrical direction as well. His absolute mastery of his guitar and effects is even more amazing considering that this was the first time he used the Fuzz Face, wah-wah pedal, Univibe *and* Octavia pedals on stage together. The guitar tones he gets on "Who Knows" and "Power to Love" are powerful and intense, but nowhere is his absolute control more evident than on "Machine Gun," where Hendrix conjures bombs, guns, and other sounds of war from his guitar, all within the context of a coherent musical statement. Two Buddy Miles compositions are also included, but the show belongs to Jimi all the way. *Band of Gypsys* is not only an important part of the Hendrix legacy, but one of the greatest live albums ever. *—Sean Westergaard*

Jimi Hendrix: Blues / Apr. 26, 1994 / MCA ✦✦✦✦
While Hendrix remains most famous for his hard rock and psychedelic innovations, more than a third of his recordings were blues-oriented. This CD contains eleven blues originals and covers, eight of which were previously unreleased. Recorded between 1966 and 1970, they feature the master guitarist stretching the boundaries of electric blues in both live and studio settings. Besides several Hendrix blues-based originals, it includes covers of Albert King and Muddy Waters classics, as well as a 1967 acoustic version of his composition "Hear My Train A-Comin'." *—Richie Unterberger*

First Rays of the New Rising Sun / Apr. 22, 1997 / MCA ✦✦✦✦
Because Hendrix's death in September 1970 occurred before his work on these tunes was completed, the questions still abound as to what Jimi's ultimate vision for this double album would have been. Minus the worthless—though well intentioned—overdubs and remix manipulation that occurred when this material was issued piecemeal over the years on *The Cry of Love, War Heroes, Rainbow Bridge* and the disappointing *Voodoo Soup*, this collection finally gets us back to the master tapes residing in the Electric Ladyland vaults. This gets the listener as close to what Hendrix had in mind as possible, as subject to change as these versions obviously were, and also places the tunes in their original context as an album. Because this collection utilizes mixes that Hendrix and engineer Eddie Kramer were working on at the time, the tracks perhaps lack the sonic wallop of the first three Experience albums, but have much more to offer than the stripped-away and redubbed versions that have been on the market until now. If one views *First Rays of the New Rising Sun* as an almost-completed work in progress, then it becomes obvious that Jimi was heading into a new direction and sound, one rife with funk and rhythm & blues as a bedrock foundation. The psychedelic workouts got more jamlike and experimental, and the ballads got prettier and even more dreamlike in their background soundscapes. What he would have eventually come up with and released as his next musical statement is anyone's guess, but this gets us as close to that answer—and that vision—as we're ever likely to get. *—Cub Koda*

South Saturn Delta / Oct. 7, 1997 / MCA ✦✦✦
Shortly after the Hendrix family reacquired the rights to Jimi's catalog, they signed a long-term deal with MCA Records and pulled many of the compilations of unreleased material and rarities off the shelves, with the intent of re-releasing the material in better collections. *First Rays of the New Rising Sun*, an attempt at assembling Hendrix's uncompleted last album, was the first release from Experience Hendrix, and it was followed months later by *South Saturn Delta*, a collection of rarities—all but one of the 15 tracks were never officially released in the U.S.—that spans his entire career. Its intent is to capture the full range of Hendrix's music through an alternate history, and it works pretty well. Among the highlights are tracks from the *War Heroes* and *Rainbow Bridge* albums ("Look Over Yonder," "Tax Free," "Midnight," "Pali Gap," "Bleeding Heart"), "Sweet Angel" (an early version of "Angel"), an instrumental "Little Wing," a solo take on "Midnight Lightning," and a studio version of "Message to the Universe (Message to Love)." There are also alternate mixes of "All Along the Watchtower," "Power of Soul," "Drifter's Escape," "South Saturn Delta" and "The Stars That Play with Laughing Sam's Dice." It's an intelligently sequenced, listenable collection of some of the very best outtakes and rarities from Hendrix, and is another sign that Experience Hendrix's restoration of Jimi's catalog will be smart, stylish and logical. *—Stephen Thomas Erlewine*

BBC Sessions / Jun. 2, 1998 / MCA ✦✦✦✦
These are the recordings that Jimi Hendrix made for BBC radio in the late 1960s. As such, they're loose, informal and off-the-top-of-his-head improvisational fun. These versions of the hits "Foxy Lady," "Fire," two versions of "Purple Haze," and "Hey Joe" stay surprisingly close to the studio versions, but the tone of Hendrix's guitar on these is positively blistering and worth the price of admission alone. There's also a lot of blues on this two-disc collection, and Hendrix's versions of "Hoochie Coochie Man" (with Alexis Korner on slide guitar), "Catfish Blues," "Killing Floor" and "Hear My Train A'Comin'" find him in excellent form. But perhaps the best example of how loosely conceived these sessions were are the oddball covers that Hendrix tackles, including Stevie Wonder's "I Was Made To Love Her" (featuring Wonder on drums), Dylan's "Can You Please Crawl Out Your Window—," the Beatles' "Day Tripper" and, in recognition of his immediate competition, Cream's "Sunshine of Your Love." No lo-fi bootleg tapes here (everything's from the original masters and gone over by Eddie Kramer), the music and sound are class A all the way, making a worthwhile addition to anyone's Hendrix collection. *—Cub Koda*

• **Experience Hendrix: The Best of Jimi Hendrix** / Nov. 3, 1998 / MCA ✦✦✦✦✦
Experience Hendrix: The Best of Jimi Hendrix is a terrific 20-track collection that features all of Hendrix's most essential material, from "Purple Haze" and "Hey Joe" to "All Along the Watchtower" and "Star Spangled Banner." There are a few fine moments missing, but everything a casual fan needs is here, making it a great introduction to the groundbreaking guitarist. *—Stephen Thomas Erlewine*

Live at the Fillmore East / Feb. 23, 1999 / MCA ✦✦✦✦
A series of performances from the *Band of Gypsys* concerts finally gets the deluxe treatment from MCA and Experience Hendrix, as tapes from both first and second shows are brought together, correctly identified (1986's *Band of Gypsys 2* actually featured three tracks that weren't by the band at all) in one deluxe two-disc set. This newly expanded edition contains the only live versions of "Earth Blues," "Auld Lang Syne," "Stepping Stone," and "Burning Desire"; Hendrix tunes specifically worked up for the performance that rarely surfaced again like "Izabella," "Power of Soul," and "Who Knows"; newly remastered versions of "Stop" and "Hear My Train A-Comin'" (both originally presented on *Band of Gypsys 2* in horrendous sound) and classic performances of "Stone Free," "Changes," "Voodoo Child (Slight Return)," and "Wild Thing." Equally as revelatory is one of the two alternate versions included of "Machine Gun," every bit as stunning as the better-known version. Though this new edition hardly makes all previous incarnations obsolete, it presents the man at his most challenged and brilliant. *—Cub Koda*

Live at Woodstock / Jul. 6, 1999 / MCA ✦✦✦

Don Henley

b. Jul. 22, 1947, Gilmer, TX
Vocals, Drums, Percussion / Pop/Rock, Soft Rock, Adult Contemporary, Singer/Songwriter
Out of all of the Eagles, Don Henley had the most successful solo career. After the group broke up in 1982, Henley released his first solo album, *I Can't Stand Still*. Although it wasn't as successful as an Eagles record, the album peformed respectably, launching the number three single "Dirty Laundry" and going gold. *Building the Perfect Beast* followed two years later and established Henley as a solo star in his own right. Featuring the Top 10 hits "Boys of Summer" and "All She Wants to Do Is Dance," the album sold over two million copies and stayed on the charts for over a year. Henley's third album, 1989's *The End of the Innocence*, was his most ambitious record yet, as well as his most commercially successful. The album sold over three million copies and stayed on the charts for nearly three years, launching the hit singles "The End of the Innocence," "Heart of the Matter," "New York Minute," "How Bad Do You Want It—," and "The Last Worthless Evening." Henley reunited with the Eagles in 1994, embarking on a worldwide tour. *—Stephen Thomas Erlewine*

I Can't Stand Still / 1982 / Asylum ✦✦✦
Don Henley's first solo album may still have had the ghost of the Eagles lingering in the corners, but for the most part it showcases his stalwart partnership with producer and songwriter Danny Kortchmar. Lyrically, Henley's songs are a tad weak, but for an inaugural album from a man who had spent most of his career surrounded by multi-talented musicians and writers, on the whole it fairs quite well. His material deals with the hardships of love, the fickleness of the media, and the declining state of education, all induced with a friendly pop sound. The title track, a trouble-in-paradise love song, has Henley pouring his heart out with sugary angst, but is helped along with some avid keyboard work. "Dirty Laundry" is Henley's attack on the shallowness of the network newsperson that peaked at number three on *Billboard*'s Top 40. Its bouncy chorus and contagious organ riffs proved that his role as a musician could conform to any style. His social commentary comes into fruition with "Johnny Can't Read," loosely based on the increasing amount of high-school dropouts at the time and helped bolster Henley's reputation as a musician with a concern for pressing issues. Numerous musicians help him out on this album as well, including former Eagles members Timothy B. Schmidt, Joe Walsh, and J.D. Souther; drummer Jeff Porcaro and guitarist Steve Lukather, both from Toto; and even Warren Zevon. Don Henley's adept combination of lyrical wit and thought-provoking staidness begins to materialize on *I Can't Stand Still*, paving the way for an extremely accomplished solo career. *—Mike DeGagne*

Building the Perfect Beast / 1984 / Geffen ✦✦✦✦✦
After experimenting with synthesizers and a pop sound on his solo debut, Don Henley hits the mark on his sophomore release, *Building the Perfect Beast*. This album established Henley as an artist in his own right after many successful years with the Eagles, as it spawned numerous hits. While the songs seem crafted for pop radio, it's hard to fault him for choosing arrangements that would get his messages to the masses. Unlike most pop in the 1980s, however, Henley had deep intellectual themes layered beneath the synthesizer sounds and crisp production. In the opening song "Boys of Summer," he talks about trying to recapture the past while knowing that things will never be the same. Henley has a gift for writing about the heart and soul of America, and mixing his love for the country and small-town life ("Sunset Grill") with cynicism about government ("All She Wants to Do Is Dance") and modernization (*"Month of Sundays"*). Although the politics and the sound of the album make the decade of release easy to place, Henley's earnest delivery and universal messages give many of the tracks a timeless feel, which is no small feat. This is Henley's most consistent album, and it is the place to start for those wanting to sample his solo work. *—Vik Iyengar*

The End of the Innocence / Jun. 1989 / Geffen ✦✦✦✦
Don Henley took some time before completing his highly anticipated third album, *The End of the Innocence*. Although he manages to duplicate much of the magic of his previous album, Henley has backed off of the synthesizers and expanded his musical palette. He uses background vocals to great effect, whether it's the tragic ballad "New York Minute" (with vocal group Take 6) or the angry rocker "I Will Not Go Quietly" (with Axl Rose of Guns N' Roses). His collaboration with Bruce Hornsby on the opening title track show a mature Henley singing about disillusionment over a beautiful piano riff that gives the song a timeless air of nostalgia. While he still tackles political issues and writes about small-town life in America, Henley also mixes in romantic ballads, including the closer "Heart of the Matter." In this epic song, Henley explores the emotional complexity of relationships and coming to terms with oneself during the aftermath. Throughout the album, he manages to balance being cynical yet hopeful, and his great melodies allow his poignant lyrics to penetrate. This al-

bum is highly recommended for those who like their pop music with a message. — *Vik Iyengar*

• **Actual Miles: Henley's Greatest Hits** / Nov. 21, 1995 / Geffen ♦♦♦♦♦
Although it is drawn from only three albums (with only one track, "Dirty Laundry," from *I Can't Stand Still*), *Actual Miles* was a well-chosen best-of from an artist who had had just enough hits to justify one. Five tracks each came from *Building the Perfect Beast* and *The End of the Innocence*, and they included all of Don Henley's Top 40 hits. The album was filled out with a cover of Leonard Cohen's "Everybody Knows" and two new tracks, among them the ambitious "The Garden of Allah," which seemed to be an attempt to create a new allegorical masterpiece along the lines of "Hotel California," but managed to be only pretentious. Still, the bulk of this album was the sound of AOR radio in the mid-1980s. That, of course, was the catch—this album should have come out about four years before it did, and probably would have if Henley hadn't been suing Geffen Records. Though destined to be a successful catalog item, in 1995 it was more a historical artifact than a major release. — *William Ruhlmann*

Inside Job / May 23, 2000 / Warner Brothers ♦♦♦
Don Henley essentially sat out his '90s recording contract, waiting until he could sign to another label that would allow him greater artistic freedom and royalties. He finally signed to Warner and released his fourth solo album, *Inside Job*, in the spring of 2000. Considering his long absence from recording, it shouldn't come as a total surprise that the album sounds as if it could have been cut in 1990 or even 1986 (check out the obnoxious synth solo on the opening track). That is not entirely a bad thing, however. It would have been rather embarrassing if Henley was trying to run with the young boys, and he sounds very comfortable settling into a role that is something less than an old master and something more than a crotchety old-timer. It falls somewhere between that, since his simmering anger—always apparent but raised to the surface on his solo records—still can be heard, which makes him seem a little cranky on occasion, when he gets carried away with his temper. For the most part, though, he sounds relaxed, comfortable, and reflective on *Inside Job*, more so than he ever has. The heart of the record is in the slower numbers, where he honestly lays out his feelings about his new love and marriage. Whenever he sticks to personal relationships, and thereby gentler music, *Inside Job* stays winning. It's brought down when he steps up to the podium to rail against the modern world, but this isn't quite enough to sink the record. *Inside Job* lacks the melodic craftsmanship that made *Building the Perfect Beast* a blockbuster, and it isn't as focused as *The End of the Innocence*, but it is a solid comeback record from an artist who spent a little too long out of the spotlight. — *Stephen Thomas Erlewine*

Clarence "Frogman" Henry

b. Mar. 19, 1937, Algiers, LA
Vocals, Trombone, Piano / New Orleans R&B, R&B
He could sing like a girl, and he could sing like a frog. That latter trademark croak, utilized to the max on his 1956 debut smash "Ain't Got No Home," earned good-natured Clarence Henry his nickname and jump-started a rewarding career that endures to this day around the Crescent City. Henry improvised the basic idea behind "Ain't Got No Home" on the bandstand one morning in the wee hours; when the crowd responded favorably, he honed it into something unique. Local deejay Poppa Stoppa laid the "Frogman" handle on the youngster when he spun the 45 (issued on the Chess subsidiary Argo), and it stuck. Despite some fine follow-ups—"It Won't Be Long," "I'm in Love," the inevitable sequel "I Found a Home"—Frog sank back into the marsh sales-wise until 1960, when Allen Toussaint's updated arrangement melded beautifully with a country-tinged Bobby Charles composition called "(I Don't Know Why) But I Do." Henry's rendition of the tune proved a huge pop smash in early 1961, as did a Domino-tinged "You Always Hurt the One You Love" later that year. Frogman continued to record a variety of New Orleans-styled old standards and catchy originals for Argo, but the hits dried up for good after 1961. — *Bill Dahl*

• **Ain't Got No Home: The Best of Clarence "Frogman" Henry** / 1994 / Chess/MCA ♦♦♦♦♦
The New Orleans R&B singer with the joyous frog's croak in his voice is served well by this 18-song collection of his 1956-1964 output for the Chess subsidiary Argo Records. Begins with his definitive "Ain't Got No Home," and follows with his vicious Crescent City rockers "Troubles, Troubles," "It Won't Be Long," and "I'm in Love," and visits his comeback hits "But I Do" and "You Always Hurt the One You Love." — *Bill Dahl*

But I Do / 1994 / Charly ♦♦♦♦♦
Twenty Argo waxings by the roly-poly pianist—much duplication with the easier-to-locate MCA disc as far as the hits go, though the inclusion of the sequel "I Found a Home" and the lesser-known rockers "Steady Date," "Oh Why," and "Live It Right" certainly make this one worth looking for. — *Bill Dahl*

Herman's Hermits

f. 1964, Manchester, England, **db.** 1970
Group / Merseybeat, British Invasion, Pop
Herman's Hermits began life in 1963 in Manchester, England; the group got its name when they were joined by 16-year-old TV actor Peter Noone, who was thought to resemble the Sherman character on the *Rocky & Bullwinkle* TV cartoon. Pop producer Mickie Most, induced to see the group by their managers, thought Noone looked like a young John Kennedy and agreed to sign them. Most chose the group's material, from revamped oldies and pub songs to tunes submitted by professional songwriters like Gerry Goffin and Carole King, and produced the recordings, generally using Noone as singer and a group of studio musicians. The result was two years of solid hits, starting with "I'm into Something Good," which topped the U.K. charts and broke the group in America. There were 11 Top Ten hits in the U.S. through 1967, among them the number one gold singles "Mrs. Brown You've Got a Lovely Daughter" and "I'm Henry VIII, I Am." Inevitably, the group's teenage heartthrob appeal waned, and they never became the kind of self-sustaining musical unit that could outlive that initial infatuation. — *William Ruhlmann*

• **Their Greatest Hits** / 1973 / ABKCO ♦♦♦♦♦
Basic hits package, but too brief and under par sound-wise. (Originally released as a 15-track LP in 1973, *Their Greatest Hits* was reissued as a 16-track CD in 1987.) — *Jeff Tamarkin*

John Hiatt

b. 1952, Indianapolis, IN
Slide Guitar, Vocals, Piano, Guitar / College Rock, Heartland Rock, Americana, New Wave, Roots Rock, Singer/Songwriter, Country-Rock
John Hiatt's sales have never quite matched his reputation. Hiatt's songs were covered successfully by everyone from Bonnie Raitt, Ronnie Milsap and Dr. Feelgood to Iggy Pop, Three Dog Night and the Neville Brothers, yet it took him 13 years to reach the charts himself. Of course, it nearly took him that long to find his own style. Hiatt began his solo career in 1974, and over the next decade, he ran through a number of different styles from rock & roll to new wave pop before he finally settled on a rootsy fusion of rock & roll, country, blues and folk with his 1987 album *Bring the Family*. Though the album didn't set the charts on fire, it became his first album to reach the charts, and several of the songs on the record became hits for other artists, including Raitt and Milsap. Following its success, Hiatt became a reliable hit songwriter for other artists, and he developed a strong cult following that continued to gain strength into the mid-'90s. — *Stephen Thomas Erlewine*

Hangin' Around the Observatory / 1974 / Epic ♦♦♦
John Hiatt mixed pop, folk, rock, R&B, country, and gospel on his debut album, immediately becoming an uncategorizable (and thus uncommercial) entity. Although this album was cut in Nashville, it owes more to Van Morrison than it does to Conway Twitty, and like the Belfast bluesman, Indianian Hiatt came to his influences somewhat secondhand, however sincerely he evoked them. What he really was, of course, was a singer/songwriter, albeit not in a style easily recognizable in 1974. The title indicates his position: Hiatt's songs show him an acute observer. But the performances require him to dig in, and although he does so with alacrity, the result is too diffuse. Nevertheless, Hiatt earned critical kudos for this album, and Three Dog Night (who knew good songwriting when they heard it) covered "Sure As I'm Sittin' Here," getting a Top 40 single out of it. — *William Ruhlmann*

Overcoats / 1975 / Epic ♦♦

Slug Line / 1979 / MCA ♦♦♦
Conventional wisdom at the time was that MCA Records had signed John Hiatt (who had languished without a record contract for four years) with the idea that he would be their Elvis Costello—a singer/songwriter in the fashionable punk/new wave style. Certainly, Hiatt has stripped down and roughed up from his Epic records here, fronting a straight ahead guitar rock band (that was capable, of course, of playing the obligatory reggae number), eschewing the stylistic diversity he reveled in before, and throwing out snappy, aphoristic lyrics in a highly processed voice. None of this quite turns him into Elvis Costello, although the mean streak he reveals would serve him well later. — *William Ruhlmann*

Two Bit Monsters / 1980 / MCA ♦♦♦

All of a Sudden / 1982 / Geffen ♦♦♦

Riding with the King / 1983 / Geffen ♦♦♦♦♦
One half of Hiatt's best Geffen album is played by him and Scott Matthews, while the other half features a band including Paul Carrack and Nick Lowe. But what matters is the songs: Hiatt's trenchant observations on life and love, especially the perceptive and painfully funny "She Loves the Jerk." — *William Ruhlmann*

Warming Up to the Ice Age / Jan. 1985 / Geffen ♦♦♦
Hiatt turned to veteran country producer Norbert Putnam here, but the result still rocked hard, with the occasional soul touch (notably those obnoxious thumb-struck bass lines that are so prevalent in '80s music). Highlights here are "The Usual," later covered by Bob Dylan, and "She Said the Same Things to Me." There is also an odd duet with Elvis Costello on the old Spinners hit "Living a Little, Laughing a Little" (try and tell them apart). Critics' darling or not, when this album went into the tank, Geffen became the third label to drop Hiatt. — *William Ruhlmann*

• **Bring the Family** / May 1987 / A&M ♦♦♦♦♦
Not only is the small-band playing impeccable, but this is Hiatt's best collection of songs, which is saying a lot for so talented a writer. "Memphis in the Meantime" is a knowledgeable look at the fame game, "Your Dad Did" perfectly skewers domestic life, and "Have a Little Faith in Me" is a touching evocation of persistent love. And that's just three of them. — *William Ruhlmann*

Slow Turning / 1988 / A&M ♦♦♦♦♦
Only a notch below *Bring the Family*, with such strong songs as "Drive South" and the wild criminals-on-the-loose song "Tennessee Plates." — *William Ruhlmann*

Y'All Caught— The Ones That Got Away 1979-1985 / Sep. 1989 / Geffen ♦♦♦♦♦
Though John Hiatt's three records for Geffen were all quite strong, none of them received much attention other than a handful of good reviews at the time of release. After *Bring the Family* brought Hiatt to a wider audience, Geffen compiled *Y'All Caught? The Ones That Got Away*, a collection of the highlights from his three Geffen records that attempted to win over his new fans. Though the new wave overtones of the production won't appeal to some of his roots rock fans, *Y'All Caught?* still features an abundance of first-rate songs, including "Radio Girl," "Riding with the King," "She Said the Same Things to Me," "It Hasn't Happened Yet," "Slug Line," and "She Loves the Jerk," making it an excellent sampler for fans of Hiatt's latter-day work. — *Stephen Thomas Erlewine*

Stolen Moments / Jun. 1990 / A&M ♦♦♦
John Hiatt's highest charting album yet is a step down from the dizzy heights of *Bring the Family* and *Slow Turning*, as he abandons his more acid commentaries and turns in a self-deprecating set full of promises of reformation and celebrations of marriage and family life.

But the observations remain acute, and Hiatt's singing (so much camouflaged in his early days) is becoming his secret weapon. *— William Ruhlmann*

Perfectly Good Guitar / Sep. 7, 1993 / A&M ✦✦

Hiatt Comes Alive at Budokan— / Nov. 22, 1994 / A&M ✦✦✦

Walk On / Oct. 24, 1995 / Capitol ✦✦✦

Living a Little, Laughing a Little / Jun. 4, 1996 / Raven ✦✦✦✦
Living a Little, Laughing a Little does a good job as an early-career summary, drawing material from each of his albums released from 1974 to 1985—*Hangin' Around the Observatory, Overcoats, Slug Line, Two Bit Monster, All of a Sudden, Riding With the King,* and *Warming Up to the Ice Ages.* For those who are only familiar with his critically acclaimed work from the late '80s on, this provides a introduction to the formative years and a facinating look at an man finding his voice—from an average '70s-style singer-songwriter to a rocker a la Elvis Costello to the first hints of his better known, later rootsy incarnation. A 1985 interview and a track Hiatt contributed to the *Cruisin'* soundtrack have been added as bonus to those who already have the albums. *— Chris Woodstra*

Little Head / Jul. 1, 1997 / Capitol ✦✦

The Best of John Hiatt / Aug. 25, 1998 / Capitol ✦✦✦✦
John Hiatt finally achieved some sort of fame in 1987, when his comeback album *Bring the Family* sparked a career renaissance. For the next decade, his albums sold well and his songs were continually covered by other artists, all of which earned him acclaim as one of the finest songwriters of his era. Despite its title, *The Best of John Hiatt 1973-1998* is a chronicle of those successful ten years. Only two songs—"Riding with the King" and "Take Off Your Uniform"—date from before 1987, which means that the collection effectively sidesteps Hiatt's years of searching for a style; it chooses to ride with him once he settled on roots-rock. Of course, that's where he did the bulk of his best work, and *The Best Of* does offer a good overview of his prime period. Since much of his best work was recorded for labels other than Capitol, the label releasing *The Best Of,* Hiatt entered the studio to record two new songs ("Love in Flames," "Don't Know Much About Love") and cut his first version of "Angel Eyes," the song he gave to Jeff Healey, who turned it into a hit in 1989. He also re-recorded "Have a Little Faith in Me" and "Drive South," two of his best songs from the late '80s. Although these new versions are OK, they don't compare with the originals and only hammer home the fact that this is merely an acceptable compilation, instead of the perfect one that it could have been. Nevertheless, it's a good sampler for the curious, and the hardcore fan will not be disappointed with the new material, even if they're frustrated that they have to purchase a whole new album to acquire it. *— Stephen Thomas Erlewine*

• **The Greatest Hits: The A&M Years '87-'94** / Oct. 27, 1998 / A&M ✦✦✦✦✦
Two months after Capitol's *The Best of John Hiatt* hit the stores, A&M released *Greatest Hits: The A&M Years '87-'94.* It's hard to surmise what weird licensing agreements led to this release pattern, since the similarities will cause confusion even among dedicated fans, but there are notable differences between the two discs. Since Hiatt's albums for A&M in the late '80s were his creative peak, it's not surprising that *Greatest Hits,* which concentrates his A&M work, is a more consistent album than *The Best of John Hiatt,* which balances classic A&M *cuts with two re-recorded songs, highlights from his two Capitol albums and two new songs. Aside from the inexplicable omission of &"Slow Turning,"* and one of his best rockers, *Greatest Hits* contains all the A&M songs that are on *The Best of John Hiatt* ("Thing Called Love," "Memphis in the Meantime," "Child of the Wild Blue Yonder," "Drive South," "Buffalo River Home," "Feels Like Rain," "Perfectly Good Guitar," "Tennessee Plates"), plus the original versions of "Drive South" and "Have a Little Faith in Me" (only available in butchered remakes on the Capitol disc), a live take of "Angel Eyes," and several fine numbers, such as "Thank You Girl," "Real Fine Love," "Paper Thin," "Lipstick Sunset" and "Through Your Hands." There are some excellent songs from *Bring the Family* and *Slow Turning* missing, but *Greatest Hits* remains the compilation to get for casual fans. *— Stephen Thomas Erlewine*

Crossing Muddy Waters / Sep. 26, 2000 / Vanguard ✦✦✦

The High Llamas

f. 1991, London, England
Group / Indie Pop, Chamber Pop, Post-Rock/Experimental, Alternative Pop/Rock
Although the High Llamas are nominally a group, they're pretty much the brainchild of singer and guitarist Sean O'Hagan. O'Hagan did some time in the London-by-way-of-Dublin band Microdisney, in which he was the songwriting partner of Cathal Coughlan. After Microdisney split in 1988 (Coughlan forming Fatima Mansions), O'Hagan released a couple of import-only solo albums before forming the High Llamas. The Llamas issued their debut, *Gideon Gaye,* in 1994 to high praise in the British press; it was released in the States a year later almost as an afterthought, with virtually no fanfare. Comparisons of the High Llamas/O'Hagan to Brian Wilson/the Beach Boys are unavoidable, and not just from arcane critics. Anyone with a large Beach Boys collection will detect the uncanny resemblance to 1966-70 Beach Boys, with the sophisticated melodies, the beautiful harmonies, and the elaborate production, with the emphasis on layered keyboards and orchestration. Echoes of *Pet Sounds, Smile, Wild Honey,* and *Surf's Up* predominate, though O'Hagan also claims Burt Bacharach as a major inspiration. At this point, however, the strong resemblance to Wilson's meisterwerks place O'Hagan closer to imitation than originality. Considering that he's been making records for about a decade, he might want to start aiming his sights higher. Subsequent efforts include 1996's *Hawaii,* 1997's *Cold and Bouncy* and 1999's *Snowbug. Buzzle Bee* arrived the following year, featuring a more stripped-down sound and guest vocals from Mary Hansen from Stereolab. *— Richie Unterberger*

• **Gideon Gaye** / 1994 / V2 ✦✦✦✦✦
Despite what Don Was, Van Dyke Parks, and others might be claiming, Brian Wilson is *not* going to return to the peak of his powers. In his absence, Sean O'Hagan might be the best available substitute. He's obviously done his homework, listening not only to all the albums between *Pet Sounds* and *Surf's Up,* but the widely circulated *Smile* bootlegs as well. Cheeky references to cuts like "Let's Get Away for a While" and "Surf's Up" pop up from time to time on this lush set, which takes its cues from both Wilson's most melodic and most eccentric qualities (though the ten-minute flute solo on "Track Goes By" does this to excess). It's an impressive outing that sounds like little else in the alternative rock world of the mid-'90s. But it only establishes O'Hagan and his various pals as charming emulators, rather than true innovators. *— Richie Unterberger*

Hawaii / 1996 / V2 ✦✦✦✦
Sean O'Hagan has a gift for orchestral pop, creating lush soundscapes that are awash with sonic detail. He clearly owes a lot to Brian Wilson, and *Hawaii,* the High Llamas' third album, falls somewhere between *Pet Sounds* and *Smile.* Sonically, the rich, orchestrated production is reminiscent of the former, but *Hawaii* is paced like *Smile,* with brief instrumentals and song fragments framing the full-fledged songs. Each is carefully arranged and recorded, offering an inviting tapestry of strings, guitars, keyboards, brass and percussion. For much of *Hawaii,* the sound of the record is intoxicating, but the album drags over the course of 77 minutes. Among the 29 tracks, there are some beautiful moments and gorgeous songs, but *Hawaii* winds up being too much of a good thing, lacking the focus of *Gideon Gaye.* [The American edition of *Hawaii* contains a 40-minute, six-track bonus disc, containing material previously unreleased in the U.S., including the B-sides for the *Nomads* single.] *— Stephen Thomas Erlewine*

Cold & Bouncy / Jan. 27, 1998 / V2 ✦✦✦✦
Cold and Bouncy is an accurate description of the High Llamas' music, in many ways. On the surface, it's light and airy, with sprightly or sighing melodies, sometimes quite detailed, but that very attention to detail keeps the music at an emotional distance—it's easy to admire Sean O'Hagan's skill, but a little more difficult to be moved by it. Still, there's a lot to be said for being evocative, which the High Llamas certainly are. Like its predecessor *Hawaii, Cold and Bouncy* floats between involved instrumentals and songs, relying on texture more than actual songwriting. O'Hagan is beginning to break away from his Brian Wilson obsessions, even if echoes of *Smile* and *Pet Sounds* are evident throughout the record. However, it sounds more than ever like original work, thanks to a subtle incorporation of retro-electronic textures, straight out of his work with Stereolab. Those keyboards open the sound up just enough to make *Cold and Bouncy* the group's most inviting release since *Gideon Gaye,* but it still suffers from O'Hagan's meandering tendencies. While its not the marathon of *Hawaii,* the album still runs way too long, lasting well over an hour. Instead of adding depth, the length makes O'Hagan's ideas difficult to assimilate, and by the end of the record, it sounds like he only has variations on a handful of themes. But when the album is consumed in small doses, however, O'Hagan's flair for arrangement and sonic detail burns brightly. *— Stephen Thomas Erlewine*

Snowbug / Oct. 26, 1999 / V2 ✦✦✦

His Name Is Alive

f. 1989, Livonia, MI
Group / Experimental Rock, Dream Pop, Indie Rock, Alternative Pop/Rock
Named after history class notes on Abraham Lincoln, the Livonia, MI-based sonic manipulators His Name Is Alive formed when multi-instrumentalist/producer Warren Defever (also of shockabilly group Elvis Hitler) was still in high school. Defever, former schoolmate Karin Oliver (vocals) and drummer Damian Lang released self-produced cassettes of their music, one of which made its way to Ivo Watts-Russell, founder of the pioneering art label 4AD. Intrigued with His Name Is Alive's blend of spectral vocals, poetic lyrics and textural guitars, Watts signed the band. The group recorded their first release for the label, *Livonia,* in Defever's home studio. The album features Oliver's shivery vocals along with tape loops, samples and guitar blasts, for a noise-damaged, ethereal collection of songs about ghosts, reincarnation and dreams. An epic 23 songs long, 1992's *Home is in Your Head* ranges from folky ballads to electrifying guitar maelstroms and tape collages. In 1993, His Name Is Alive released two albums: *King of Sweet,* a limited edition release that mixed tape effects, samples, demos and unreleased songs, and *Mouth By Mouth,* which added more pop structure into the group's inherently experimental and dreamy sound, resulting in their most accessible and diverse album to that date. Defever's diverse interests influenced His Name Is Alive's next release, 1996's *Stars on ESP.* Very little of the group's original ethereal sound remained, augmented instead with touches of dub, folk, gospel, and early to mid-'60s pop like the Beach Boys' *Pet Sounds.* The following year's *Nice Day* EP reached to garage rock and '60s R&B for its inspiration, and featured some of the gospel singers from *Stars on ESP,* including Lovetta Pippen, whose singing also gave His Name Is Alive's 1998 LP *Fort Lake* an earthy sensuality. *— Heather Phares*

Livonia / 1990 / 4AD ✦✦✦

Home Is in Your Head / Jul. 23, 1992 / Rykodisc ✦✦✦✦✦
Dark, disturbing, and beautiful, His Name Is Alive's *Home Is in Your Head* develops the deceptively simple, abstractly emotional music they introduced on *Livonia.* Held together by Warren Defever's artful production, its 23 songs range from jealous contemplation to spiritual concerns, from gentle folk to white noise guitar outbursts. Karin Oliver's supple voice lends itself to an array of musical and emotional settings: she's acidly sweet on "The Charmer"'s brittle taunt "Where is your head now—/I should nail it to her door/Where are your hands now—/I know what you'd use them for." On "Why People Disappear," she's pensive: "Maybe I know as much as I ever will/We've been forever." The numerous instrumentals and interludes add to the overall yearning, searching mood. "Her Eyes Were Huge Things" builds subtle strumming and Oliver's sighs into an evocative spell, while "Hope Called in Sick" crashes in with loud, wailing guitars. The group's sound collages also find more purpose here than on *Livonia;* the chanting children on "Put Your Finger in Your Eye" are downright unnerving, and "Spirit and Body" conjures a story of loss out of a ticking watch and just-audible snippets of conversation. With the oddly comforting finale, "Dreams Are of the Body," *Home is in Your Head* completes a seamless exploration of music and emotion. The Rykodisc reissue also includes the group's hard-to-find *The Dirt Eaters* EP. Named for Defever's rock-oriented side project, it features the spooky, subtly dissonant cover of Rainbow's "Man on the Silver Mountain," Ivo Watts-Russell's bleak

remix of "Are We Still Married—"and "The Dirt Eaters'" pastoral art folk. Added to *Home Is in Your Head,* it represents the band's best early work. *—Heather Phares*

• **Mouth by Mouth** / Apr. 13, 1993 / 4AD ✦✦✦✦✦
1993's *Mouth by Mouth* marks a high point in His Name Is Alive's career, consolidating the band's musical elements—sweet vocals, technicolor production, evocative guitar work and arty arrangements—into 16 songs that are as diverse as they are cohesive. Memories of Michigan summertimes, Theodore Roethke's poetry and sensuality collide, creating the fractured sugar-pop of "Baby Fish Mouth" and "Lip," which sit comfortably beside the stark, cello-driven "Cornfield." The band's sinister side pops up on "Ear," a deadpan retelling of Vincent VanGogh's self-amputation. *Mouth by Mouth* "rocks" more than any of the band's previous work, thanks to the continued involvement of the Dirt Eaters; they are credited with the album's louder songs, such as the fuzzed-out "Drink, Dress and Ink" and "The Torso." An electrified version of "The Dirt Eaters" rounds out *Mouth by Mouth,* hinting at the group's increasing pop tendencies. His Name Is Alive's spooky, ethereal side is here too, evident on songs like the spiritually inclined "Lord, Make Me a Channel of Your Peace" and the gamelan-pop of "Sort Of." "Can't Go Wrong Without You" manages to be creepy, catchy and beautiful all at once (surreal stop-motion filmmakers The Brothers Quay made a fittingly eerie video for this song). The blissed-out cover of Big Star's "Blue Moon" and the Roethke-inspired "Where Knock Is Open Wide" add a dreamy, folky feel to *Mouth by Mouth's* stylistic mix. A transitional work for a group whose very style is change, *Mouth by Mouth* begins His Name Is Alive's embrace of more traditional pop styles (for their own purposes, of course) and the departure from their overtly ethereal sound. It's a fresh, fascinating album that improves with repeated listening. *—Heather Phares*

Stars on ESP / Jul. 1996 / 4AD ✦✦✦✦
As usual, Michigan-based sonic envelope-pushers His Name Is Alive continue to boggle expectations with their beautiful, exciting music. On their fourth album for 4AD, *Stars on ESP,* the group mixes dub, dream pop, surf, country, and *Pet Sounds*-era Beach Boys into something altogether unique. The songs range from the deceptively simple, folky "Answer to Rainbow at Midnight" and "Famous Goodbye King" to bouncy pop like "Bad Luck Girl," "The Bees," and "Across the Street." Then there are the songs that defy easy description, like the beautiful, lilting "Dub Love Letter" and the "Good Vibrations" pastiche "Universal Frequencies." On the whole, *Stars on ESP* is their most acoustic-based since 1992's *Home Is in Your Head* and their brightest-sounding since *Mouth by Mouth.* However, the trademark strange, spacy noises that peppered the band's other releases can still be found on this album, particularly on "What Else Is New List" and "Wall of Speed." An eclectic, unique album—it even includes a gospel song—from an eclectic, unique band, *Stars on ESP* features His Name Is Alive at their most accessible and exciting. *—Heather Phares*

Ft. Lake / Aug. 25, 1998 / 4AD ✦✦✦✦

Always Stay Sweet / Feb. 23, 1999 / 4AD ✦✦✦✦✦

Robyn Hitchcock

b. Mar. 3, 1953, London, England
Vocals, Guitar, Bass / College Rock, Neo-Psychedelia, Jangle Pop, Folk-Rock, Alternative Pop/Rock, Singer/Songwriter
Robyn Hitchcock is one of England's most enduring contemporary singer-songwriters and live performers, although he's been branded with the tags eccentric and quirky during the course of his long career. Hitchcock started his recording career with the Soft Boys, a punk-era band specializing in melodic pop merged with comedic lyrics. His voice veers between John Lennon and Syd Barrett, helping to nurture his madman reputation, but his true influences lie more in English folk-rock; his guitar and vocal style and lyrical inanities recall Incredible String Band or Roy Harper. Hitchcock's solo debut, 1981's *Black Snake Diamond Role,* helped consolidate his reputation as an oddball, and was followed by the psychedelia of *Groovy Decay* in 1982 and the all-acoustic *I Often Dream of Trains* in 1984. By 1985, his penchant for zaniness and songsmithing coalesced with *Fegmania.* Three years later, Hitchcock landed his first major U.S. label contract with A&M Records and released *Globe of Frogs* in 1988 and *Queen Elvis* in 1989. He sustained and probably even grew his career; however, by this time, critical approval had fallen off for his work. It wasn't until the 1996 release of *Moss Elixir* that Hitchcock returned to form and fully embraced his folk roots. *Storefront Hitchcock,* the soundtrack to the Jonathan Demme-directed concert film, followed in 1998. *—Denise Sullivan*

Black Snake Diamond Role / 1981 / Rhino ✦✦✦
Robyn Hitchcock's first album after leaving the Soft Boys isn't that far removed from the edgy, warped guitar pop of his former band, which isn't surprising, considering the presence of former Soft Boys bassist Andy Metcalfe and drummer Morris Windsor. However, *Black Snake Diamond Role* removes much of the sharp, cutting guitars of *Underwater Moonlight* and replaces them with friendlier, ringing riffs. But that doesn't mean Hitchcock has gone soft—he's just refined his technique. And that doesn't mean his songwriting has improved. Cut by cut, *Black Snake Diamond Role* is weaker than *Underwater Moonlight,* but that's relative—the album contains pretty and twisted pseudo-psychedelic pop like "Brenda's Iron Sledge," "Acid Bird," "The Man Who Invented Himself," and "Do Policemen Sing?" which all rank among his finest songs. *—Stephen Thomas Erlewine*

Groovy Decay / 1982 / Combat ✦✦

I Often Dream of Trains / 1984 / Rhino ✦✦✦✦✦
Hitchcock was so shaken by the entire *Groovy Decay* disaster that he retired from recording for two years. When he returned in 1984 with *I Often Dream of Trains,* it was clear that the time off had affected his music. A collection of spare, acoustic-based pop-folk songs, *I Often Dream of Trains* is one of Hitchcock's most introspective and charming records. Instead of creating an impenetrably personal album, the stripped-down instrumentation actually opens up the songwriter's world, allowing the ballads ("Trams of Old London," "Cathedral," "Flavour of Night") to sit comfortably next to the jokes ("Uncorrected Personality Traits"). Alternating between acoustic guitars and solo piano, the music is never fragile, adding a strong support to Hitchcock's eccentric lyrics. *—Stephen Thomas Erlewine*

Fegmania! / Mar. 1985 / Rhino ✦✦✦✦✦
After the stripped-back collection *I Often Dream of Trains,* Hitchcock slowly formed a backing band called the Egyptians with ex-Soft Boys Andy Metcalfe and Morris Windsor and keyboardist Roger Jackson over the course of the next year. *Fegmania!,* the Egyptians' first album, was a distinct departure from both the Soft Boys and Hitchcock's previous solo work, featuring layered, intertwining guitars and keyboards that created lush and thick sonic textures. Even with the more detailed arrangements, the songs remained twitchy and off-kilter, with melodies that usually went in willfully unpredictable directions, yet remained catchy all the while. *Fegmania!* was Hitchcock's most consistent work to date, featuring such highlights as the Eastern-tinged "Egyptian Cream," and the creepy "My Wife & My Dead Wife," and the relatively straightforward "The Man with the Lightbulb Head." *—Stephen Thomas Erlewine*

• **Gotta Let This Hen Out** / Oct. 1985 / Rhino ✦✦✦✦✦
Recorded at the Marquee in London shortly after the release of *Fegmania!,* the live *Gotta Let This Hen Out!* is a tense and exciting record, finding the raw energy that usually goes untapped in Hitchcock's music. Although the album makes the Egyptians sound more like a rock & roll band than they actually were—they never played with such wreckless abandon before or since—the driving performances don't wreck the melodic and lyrical eccentricities of the songs; instead, the increased vigor gives the music a searing power, obliterating the notion that his songs are delicate and precious. The set list also accentuates Hitchcock's strengths, relying on his most accessible and melodic material, whether it's recent material like "Egyptian Cream," "Sometimes I Wish I Was a Pretty Girl," and "Acid Bird" or Soft Boys' tracks like "Kingdom of Love," "Only the Stones Remain," "The Face of Death," and "Leppo and the Jooves." *—Stephen Thomas Erlewine*

Element of Light / 1986 / Rhino ✦✦✦✦✦
Element of Light, Hitchcock's second studio album with the Egyptians, remains one of his finest moments and offers a convincing argument for his talents as a pop craftsman. Using John Lennon's work for *Revolver* and *The Beatles* as a template, Hitchcock wrote an elegant set of songs for *Element of Light,* songs that contained all of his cryptic lyrical sensibilities, yet featured more refined melodies and song structures. The Egyptians play with a subtle grace, moving between the stately "Winchester" and light psychedelia of "If You Were a Priest" to the bracing attack of "Tell Me About Your Drugs" with ease. While it sacrifices some of the edgy tension of Hitchcock's earlier work, *Element of Light* is his most melodic and eerily beautiful record. *—Stephen Thomas Erlewine*

Invisible Hitchcock / 1986 / Rhino ✦✦✦
As the reference to the Soft Boys' rarities collection, *Invisible Hits,* suggests, *Invisible Hitchcock* gathers together a selection of obscurities and nonalbum tracks Robyn Hitchcock recorded between 1980 and 1986. Granted, the material is a bit uneven, but the album holds together well, as it emphasizes Hitchcock's gift for warped wordplay and appealingly convoluted melodies. Upon its original release, the running order for *Invisible Hitchcock* was considerably different in Britain and America; Rhino's 1995 reissue standardized the album, including all the material from both versions of the album (with the exception of "Grooving on a Inner Plane," which appeared as a bonus track on the company's reissue of *Black Snake Diamond Role*), as well as adding two songs that never appeared on either version of the record. *—Stephen Thomas Erlewine*

• **Globe of Frogs** / 1988 / A&M ✦✦✦✦✦
Hitchcock's first foray into U.S. major-label territory disappointed some critics but helped expand his audience beyond the realm of college radio, thanks to the radio-friendly "Balloon Man." Aided by his band the Egyptians, it's the production that mars this record, along with half of the songs. "Sleeping With Your Devil Mask," "Chinese Bones," and "Flesh Number One (Beatle Dennis)," which features Peter Buck on guitar and Squeeze's Difford and Tilbrook on vocals, are the reasons to own this record. *—Denise Sullivan*

Queen Elvis / 1989 / A&M ✦✦✦
Hitchcock redeemed himself on this collection—song for song more vital than *Globe of Frogs.* "Madonna of the Wasps" is a timeless pop song, but the record is mired in modern-rock production and synthesizer sounds. "One Long Pair of Eyes" remains a Hitchcock standard, and the bizarre "Wax Doll" and "Veins of the Queen" kept Hitchcock at the fore of eccentric rock, making him the only appropriate heir to the English king-loony throne formerly occupied by Syd Barrett. *—Denise Sullivan*

Eye / 1990 / Rhino ✦✦✦✦✦
Robyn Hitchcock recorded *Eye,* his fourth proper solo album, after the disappointing *Queen Elvis. Eye* marked a return to the acoustic-oriented folk-pop of *I Often Dream of Trains,* featuring a collection of his most personal songs. Where *I Often Dream of Trains* was a kaleidoscopic journey through a colorfully twisted world, *Eye* sounds more confessional, although Hitchcock's exact lyrical sentiments can be difficult to sort out through his dense and willfully obscure imagery. Nevertheless, the immediacy of the music—which is delivered on acoustic guitars and piano—and the simple, delicate grace of Hitchcock's melodies make even the most cryptic lines sound direct and straightforward. *—Stephen Thomas Erlewine*

Perspex Island / Aug. 6, 1991 / A&M ✦✦

Respect / Feb. 23, 1993 / A&M ✦✦

Gravy Deco (The Complete Groovy Decay/Decoy Sessions) / Jan. 1995 / Rhino ✦✦

You & Oblivion / Mar. 1995 / Rhino ✦✦

Moss Elixir / Aug. 1996 / Warner Brothers ✦✦✦

Greatest Hits / Sep. 9, 1996 / A&M ✦✦✦✦✦
Covering Robyn Hitchcock & the Egyptians' four albums for A&M, *Greatest Hits* features many of Hitchcock's best-known songs, including "Balloon Man," "Madonna of the Wasps" and "So You Think You're In Love," as well as several rare B-sides and single mixes, designed to bait the dedicated collector. Even with the presence of these handful of rarities, *Greatest Hits* remains targeted to casual Hitchcock fans who just want to have his late-'80s and early-

'90s modern rock radio hits. Consequently, it functions as a streamlined introduction to some of Hitchcock's most memorable and melodic music. *—Stephen Thomas Erlewine*

Uncorrected Personality Traits: The Robyn Hitchcock Collection / Aug. 5, 1997 / Rhino ✦✦✦✦
Hitchcock is an album-oriented artist with an extensive oeuvre, so this 20-track anthology of '80s material is best valued as a summary of selected career highlights for those who don't want to collect all of his full-length efforts. As such, it does a decent job, offering college radio hits like "Egyptian Cream," "My Wife and My Dead Wife," "The Man with the Lightbulb Head," and "Heaven," along with less-heard cuts from early-'80s albums that some listeners may have missed. This has nothing from his A&M records of the late '80s and early '90s, and so couldn't properly be considered a career-spanning best-of (highlights of the A&M period are on A&M's *Greatest Hits*). It's well-packaged, though, with liner notes featuring detailed comments on the tracks by Hitchcock himself. *—Richie Unterberger*

Storefront Hitchcock: Music from Demme Picture / Oct. 27, 1998 / Warner Brothers ✦✦✦✦

Jewels for Sophia / Jul. 20, 1999 / Warner Brothers ✦✦✦

Hole

f. 1989, Los Angeles, CA
Group / Grunge, Alternative Pop/Rock
Throughout Hole's career, Courtney Love's notorious public image has overshadowed her band's music. In its original incarnation, Hole was one of the noisiest, most abrasive alternative bands performing in the early '90s. By the time of their second album, 1994's *Live Through This*, the band had smoothed out many of their rougher edges, as well as adding more melody and hooks to their songwriting. Through both versions of Hole, Love's combative, assaultive persona permeated both the group's music and lyrics, giving the band a tense, unpredictable edge even at their quietest moments. Hole's debut record, 1991's *Pretty on the Inside*, received numerous positive reviews, especially in the British weekly music press. One year later, Courtney Love married Kurt Cobain, the lead singer/songwriter of Nirvana. For a couple of months, the couple were the king and queen of the new rock world. Halfway through 1993, Love reassembled Hole and recorded the group's first major-label album, the more pop-oriented *Live Through This*. Four days before the album was released, Kurt Cobain's body was discovered in the couple's Seattle home; he died of a self-inflicted shotgun wound three days before. Two months after Cobain's death, Hole bassist Kristen M. Pfaff died of a heroin overdose. After *Live Through This* went gold in the summer of 1995, Hole toured with the fifth Lollapalooza tour. The often-delayed *Celebrity Skin* followed in 1998. *—Stephen Thomas Erlewine*

Pretty on the Inside / Jul. 1, 1991 / Caroline ✦✦✦

● **Live Through This** / Apr. 12, 1994 / DGC ✦✦✦✦
Courtney Love completely revamped Hole before recording their second album, keeping only Eric Erlandson in the lineup. That is one of the reasons why *Live Through This* sounds so shockingly different from *Pretty on the Inside*, but the real reason is Love's desire to compete in the same commercial alternative-rock arena as her husband, Kurt Cobain. In fact, many rumors have claimed that Cobain ghost-wrote a substantial chunk of the album, and while that's unlikely, there's no denying that his patented stop-start dynamics, bare chords and punk-pop melodies provide the blueprint for *Live Through This*. Love adds her signature rage and feminist rhetoric to the formula, but the lyrics that truly resonate are the ones that unintentionally predict Cobain's suicide. For all the raw pain of the lyrics, *Live Through This* rarely sounds raw, because of the shiny production and the carefully considered dynamics. Despite this flaw, the album retains its power because it was one of the few records patterned on *Nevermind* that gets the formula right, with a set of gripping hooks and melodies that retain their power even if they follow the predictable grunge pattern. *—Stephen Thomas Erlewine*

My Body, the Hand Grenade / Oct. 28, 1997 / City Slang ✦✦✦✦
As Hole were dragging their heels working on the followup to *Live Through This*, their British label City Slang released *My Body the Hand Grenade*, a collection of outtakes, live cuts and rare tracks. Most of this material dates from the days of *Pretty on the Inside*, when Courtney Love was tagged as a riot grrrl, since she screamed over sludgy, heavy guitars, but there are also cuts from their anticlimatic *MTV Unplugged* appearance in 1995. While the rarity value of this music certainly makes it interesting, the music itself is pretty average, with the dreck outweighing the good stuff (including a rewrite of the Nirvana rarity "Old Age," for which none of the members of Nirvana are credited) by a wide margin. *—Stephen Thomas Erlewine*

Celebrity Skin / Sep. 8, 1998 / Geffen ✦✦✦
From the moment the *Pyromania* guitars herald open the title track on *Celebrity Skin*, it's clear Hole no longer is tortured. Gone are the roaring guitars and noise, the pain and the anguish that informed *Pretty on the Inside* and *Live Through This*. Some angst remains, but it's buried under a glaze of shiny guitars and hazy melodies, all intended to evoke the heyday of Californian pop in the late '70s. Conceptually, it's a bold move for a band that's nearly synonymous with grunge, but the makeover doesn't quite work. Part of the reason is that Hole's music was always compelling as nakedly cathartic spectacle—and that's exactly what has been excised on *Celebrity Skin*. In the past, Courtney Love pushed her emotions to the forefront, and the sheer forcefulness of her personality disguised the anonymity of her bandmates. A toned-down Love still may not be able to carry a tune, but there's little grit to her performance on *Celebrity Skin*, so she effortlessly blends with the faceless musical support—which is strange, considering her overpowering public image. Walking the line between soft-rock and confessional grunge was a difficult task regardless, and to their credit, Hole—with the assistance of producer Michael Beinhorn and consultant Billy Corgan, who is credited with co-writing five songs and essentially pioneered the very sound of *Celebrity Skin* with his Smashing Pumpkins albums—have created an album that sounds like an arena-rock monster, but the hooks sink only halfway in, so it doesn't have much impact. It is a complete makeover, but instead of metamorphosing into a new band, Hole has unwittingly neutered itself. *—Stephen Thomas Erlewine*

The Hollies

f. 1962, Manchester, England
Group / Pop/Rock, Merseybeat, British Invasion, Pop
One of the best and most commercially successful pop/rock acts of the British Invasion, when the Hollies began recording in 1963, they relied heavily upon the R&B/early rock & roll covers that provided the staple diet for countless British bands of the time. They quickly developed a more distinctive style of three-part harmonies (heavily influenced by the Everly Brothers), ringing guitars, and hook-happy material. The best early Hollies records evoke an infectious, melodic cheer similar to that of the early Beatles, although the Hollies were neither in their class (not an insult: nobody else was) nor demonstrated a similar capacity for artistic growth. They tried, though, easing into somewhat more sophisticated folk-rock and mildly psychedelic sounds as the decade wore on, especially on their albums. Although their first singles were R&B covers, the Hollies were much more at home with pop/rock material that provided a sympathetic complement to their glittering harmonies. They ran off an awesome series of hits in the U.K. in the '60s, making the Top 20 almost 20 times. Some of their best mid-'60s singles, like "Here I Go Again," "We're Through," and the British number one "I'm Alive," passed virtually unnoticed in the United States, where they couldn't make the Top 40 until early 1966, when "Look Through Any Window" did the trick. The Hollies really didn't break in America in a big way until "Bus Stop" (1966), their first Stateside Top Tenner; "On a Carousel," "Carrie Ann," and "Stop Stop Stop" were also big hits. Here the Hollies were providing something of a satisfying option for pop-oriented listeners that found the increasingly experimental outings of groups like the Beatles and Kinks too difficult to follow. At the same time, the production and harmonies were sophisticated enough to maintain a broader audience than more teen- and bubblegum-oriented British Invasion acts like Herman's Hermits. *—Richie Unterberger*

In the Hollies Style / 1964 / BGO ✦✦✦✦✦
Released only ten months after their debut album, *Stay with the Hollies*, their second album was a huge leap forward in every respect. Their famous airtight harmonies were now in place, and the sloppiness of the instrumental attack gone. Most important, the group developed enormously as songwriters. Eight of the twelve tracks were Hollies originals, and quite skillful in their mastery of the British Invasion essentials of driving, catchy melodies and shining harmonies. A couple of the covers are duds, but the "Nitty Gritty/Something's Got a Hold of Me" medley is first-rate, and the version of "It's in His Kiss" (retitled "It's in Her Kiss") respectable. The Hollies weren't from Liverpool (though Manchester is fairly close), but this nonetheless ranks of one of the very best Merseybeat albums not released by The Beatles themselves. It doesn't include any British or American hits, but "Come On Home," "To You My Love," "Don't You Know," and "What Kind of Boy" (the last of which was written for them by one Big Dee Irwin) will appeal to any British Invasion fan. Surprisingly, none of the tracks were ever released in the United States, making the reissue all the more desirable an item for British Invasion collectors from U.S. shores, who most likely missed it entirely the first time around. *—Richie Unterberger*

Stay with the Hollies / 1964 / BGO ✦✦

The Hollies / 1965 / BGO ✦✦✦
The Hollies' third album saw a band in the throes of transition between the Merseybeat and rock & roll with which they established themselves, and the folk-rock and soul music that was blowing the strongest winds of change in 1965. They clean up their backlog of cover staples with versions of tunes by Lloyd Price, Buddy Holly, and Roy Orbison, and delve into soul by taking on The Miracles' "Mickey's Monkey" and Curtis Mayfield's "You Must Believe Me." Their attempt at "Fortune Teller" won't make you forget The Rolling Stones' version; nor, for that matter, are any of the other covers impressive. That leaves five reasonably good originals, the best of which are the gorgeous "So Lonely" and the excellent Merseybeat knockoff "When I Come Home to You." They also sound Beatlesque on "I've Been Wrong," but "Too Many People" and their cover of Peter, Paul & Mary's "Very Last Day" hearken to a folk-rock direction. The album was issued in the U.S. as *Hear! Here!*, replacing "Mickey's Monkey" with their number one British hit "I'm Alive." *—Richie Unterberger*

For Certain Because / 1966 / BGO ✦✦✦

Would You Believe— / Jun. 1966 / EMI ✦✦✦

Butterfly / 1967 / BGO ✦✦✦

Evolution / 1967 / Sundazed ✦✦

Words and Music by Bob Dylan / 1969 / Epic ✦✦✦
This is the most controversial album in the Hollies' entire output. Graham Nash claimed he quit over the decision to record it, and critics hated it. And on its face, this is all understandable—the Hollies' distinctive high harmony singing and British beat sound were not a natural fit with Bob Dylan's songs, with their mix of earthy sensibilities and raw musicality. With one possible exception, the songs here are not presented in their ideal forms, but that doesn't explain the hostility with which the album was greeted, until one remembers the reverence in which Dylan was held at the time and the Hollies' status as a pop/rock group; in many critics' eyes, the Hollies cutting an album of Dylan songs was only a step removed from Herman's Hermits recording one. The album has virtues, including Allan Clarke's powerful lead vocals and the soaring harmonies of Terry Sylvester and Tony Hicks, along with Hicks' lively and inventive guitar contributions to the album. The overblown, orchestrated version of "Blowin' in the Wind" may be the worst version of that song ever cut, though "Quit Your Low-down Ways" is well-sung and even better played, with some superb rockabilly-style acoustic guitar courtesy of Hicks. "All I Really Want to Do" has superb singing and a strange marimba accompaniment that somehow works. And then there is "My Back Pages," the best track on the album and the only one that sounds the way the Hollies of old would've done it, loose and flowing, with beautiful acoustic guitar at its center and a reed orchestra accompanying

the band. A 1993 CD reissue of this album included two live cuts with Graham Nash in the band, doing Dylan songs from his final days in the band. *—Bruce Eder*

Hollies Sing Hollies / Nov. 1969 / Polydor ♦♦♦

He Ain't Heavy, He's My Brother / Dec. 1969 / Epic ♦♦♦
After delving into more "serious" music with the Dylan album, the Hollies return to their pop roots with this fine effort. All 11 selections are self-penned, and as usual, there is inconsistency in the quality of songwriting. However, even the most inconsequential tunes boast a good melody and solid musicianship. Three songs stand out: "Why Didn't You Believe" is contemporary white gospel at its best, with an intensity that befits the subject matter (though lyrics could have stood improvement); "He Ain't Heavy, He's My Brother" became one of their biggest hits, with Allan Clarke giving a heartfelt reading of the lyrics; and "My Life Is Over with You" is one Hollies song where music, lyrics and arrangement all fit together nearly perfectly. The orchestration is tasteful and restrained, Bobby Elliot's drumming is particularly strong, and lyrically there is a depth that is fitting and welcome. Even the songs that seem most lightweight, such as "Please Sign Your Letters" and "You Love 'Cos You Like It," have a bouncy quality that make them quite tolerable. Though the Hollies never gained a reputation as serious album artists, this is a good effort that maintains a balance between lightweight and serious pop material. *—Michael Ofjord*

Moving Finger / 1970 / Sundazed ♦♦

Confessions of the Mind / Dec. 1970 / BGO ♦♦♦
The group's first album of original material after Nash's departure was a competent but unremarkable affair. The harmonies and concise execution were still intact, and the material still brightly pop-oriented, if increasingly serious in lyrical content and slightly more sophisticated in production. The Hollies were now becoming somewhat of an anachronism in a world of progressive album-oriented rock. Their considerable melodic strengths and professionalism ensured that their efforts were never embarrassing. But the hooks weren't as sharp as their vintage hits, and their content wasn't deep enough to establish them with an older rock audience. Most of the songs were originally issued in the U.S. on the Epic LP *Morning Finger,* which had a slightly different track lineup. *—Richie Unterberger*

Distant Light / Dec. 1971 / Epic ♦♦♦
The Hollies continued to tread water as the early '70s progressed. *Distant Light* offered nothing particularly new or unexpected, but the harmonies and songwriting remained at a high enough standard to refute any accusations of decline. Too pop for the album-oriented audience, and not light and frothy enough for the pop market, it would have been totally overlooked if not for the surprise success of the Creedence Clearwater Revival soundalike "Long Cool Woman in a Black Dress." Released in the States almost as an afterthought, it became (deservedly) their biggest American hit, reaching number two. Its success inspired the return of Allan Clarke to the fold, after he had left the group to briefly pursue a solo career. *—Richie Unterberger*

Romany / 1972 / Epic ♦♦♦

● **Epic Anthology** / Jun. 15, 1990 / Epic ♦♦♦♦♦
A 20-track compilation that picks up when the Hollies signed with Epic in 1967 and presents their biggest hits plus select album tracks and rarities through 1975. Includes "Carrie-Anne," "He Ain't Heavy, He's My Brother," "Long Cool Woman (In a Black Dress)," and "The Air That I Breathe." *—William Ruhlmann*

● **All Time Greatest Hits** / Sep. 1990 / Curb ♦♦♦♦♦
A 12 track all-singles compilation that includes the Hollies' biggest US hits on both Imperial ("Bus Stop," "Stop, Stop, Stop") and Epic Records from 1964 to 1975. *—William Ruhlmann*

Thirtieth Anniversary Collection 1963-1993 / 1993 / EMI America ♦♦♦♦♦
This three-CD, 57-track box set does a good if imperfect job of encapsulating the legacy of one of the British Invasion's better bands. This includes all of the Hollies' singles, A- and B-sides, from the '60s, as well as five previously unreleased tunes. The hits—"I'm Alive," "Bus Stop," "On a Carousel," and others—contain some of the finest beat harmonizing not done by the Beatles. The B-sides—many of them originals, some of them never before available in the United States—are often nearly equal in quality to the classic material. The compilation wisely touches upon only the essentials of their post-1970 singles ("Long Cool Woman" and "The Air That I Breathe"), and unwisely closes with three forgettable tracks from the early '90s. Don't be misled, however, that this box contains all of their best material—their early albums, though inconsistent, featured a fair number of strong original tunes which remain little known beyond collector circles. It's a good set, with an excellent booklet and thoroughly annotated discography, but not definitive. *—Richie Unterberger*

At Abbey Road, 1966-1970 / 1997 / EMI ♦♦♦♦
With a few exceptions, the song lineup on this 24-track CD sounds familiar, but that's a misconception. The remastering job has been done so well that precious little on this CD sounds familiar, and it's all good. This collection picks up right where its predecessor left off, presenting a string of Hollies hits, B-sides, and notable album tracks, newly remastered in state-of-the-art sound off of original session masters. The results are frequently startling; rather than just enhancing the hits, the producers have applied the same care to their B-sides, and those are a deceptively fine group of songs in their own right. It rips the envelope altogether by throwing in the group's previously unissued recording of Graham Gouldman's "Schoolgirl," maybe the best unreleased track to come out of an EMI group this side of the Beatles' pounding version of "Leave My Kitten Alone." The remastering also makes the standard material sound more spacious and less compressed than ever before, and opens up layers of sound on the guitars, percussion, and vocals that were previously obscured. Hollies fans may love this CD for a reason beyond the particular individual tracks or the dazzling sound textures; it's very much an affirmation of the peak that the band achieved in the late '60s, depicting their moves from British invasion-style rock & roll through psychedelia to pop/rock, all of it beautifully crafted and played. The notes by Bobby Elliott are highly entertaining as well as informative. *—Bruce Eder*

Buddy Holly (Charles Hardin Holley)

b. Sep. 7, 1936, Lubbock, TX, **d.** Feb. 3, 1959, Mason City, IA
Vocals, Guitar / Rockabilly, Rock & Roll
An enormously important and influential performer, Buddy Holly started in his native Texas doing country music, eventually adding R&B numbers to the set list after meeting Elvis Presley. He recorded early rockabilly sides in Nashville, resulting in the Decca singles "Blue Days, Black Nights" and "Modern Don Juan." But success didn't come until he formed the Crickets and recorded in Norman Petty's New Mexico studio, producing the number one hit "That'll Be the Day." Holly and Petty experimented in the studio, utilizing double-tracking ("Words of Love," different forms of echo ("Peggy Sue," a second gold-selling Top Ten hit), and close-miking techniques, now commonplace in the industry. With the Crickets, he had the further chart hits "Oh, Boy!" (October 1957) (another Top Ten), "Maybe Baby" (February 1958), and "Think It Over"/"Fool's Paradise" (May 1958), while "Rave On" (April 1958) was a Holly "solo" hit. He went solo for real during 1958, however, marrying and relocating to New York. He charted with "Early in the Morning" and "Heartbeat," and released "It Doesn't Matter Anymore"/"Raining in My Heart" before embarking on the Winter Dance Party package tour, during which, on February 3, he, the Big Bopper, and Ritchie Valens were killed in an airplane crash. In England, where "It Doesn't Matter Anymore" went to number one in the wake of his death, Holly continued to score posthumous hits through the mid-'60s, and he exerted tremendous influence on the developing beat groups both for his music and for his self-contained approach to his work—writing his own songs, playing them with his own group. *—Cub Koda & William Ruhlmann*

☆ **The Complete Buddy Holly** / 1979 / MCA ♦♦♦♦♦
In the wake of the number one British ranking for *20 Golden Greats* in 1978 and the release of the feature film *The Buddy Holly Story,* MCA U.K. assembled this six-LP box set (which finally was released in the U.S. in February 1981). It traces Buddy Holly's career from his country & western duo with Bob Montgomery in 1954/1955 to his 1956 Nashville sessions for Decca Records; the Clovis, NM, recordings with the Crickets and producer Norman Petty that launched his career in 1957; the New York sessions of 1958; the final 1958 demo recordings; the various posthumously overdubbed versions of the demos; and other assorted rarities. In other words, all the material that Decca/MCA previously had spread across seven LPs— *The "Chirping" Crickets, Buddy Holly, That'll Be the Day, Reminiscing, Showcase, Holly in the Hills,* and *Giant*—between 1957 and 1969 (not counting the many compilations) was here, plus more. The box also contained an extensive scrapbook, lots of liner notes, and a detailed discography. It was, thus, the state of the art in box sets just prior to the CD era, and given Holly's importance in the history of rock & roll, an essential album for any serious collector. With the passing of the LP era, it is out of print, and MCA claims to be gathering more unreleased material for some comparable box set, though years go by without its appearing. Meanwhile, if you needed one record album to demonstrate what the most popular music of the second half of the 20th century sounded like, this would be it. *—William Ruhlmann*

☆ **The Buddy Holly Collection** / Sep. 28, 1993 / MCA ♦♦♦♦♦
The first comprehensive, remastered CD retrospective of Holly's work, including early tracks recorded in the Holly family garage, the Owen Bradley-produced singles, all the rockin' hits, orchestrated ballads, and tracks overdubbed with instrumentation after Holly's tragic death. Two discs, solid liner notes. *—Roch Parisien*

★ **Greatest Hits** / Sep. 24, 1996 / MCA ♦♦♦♦♦
MCA re-mastered 18 of Buddy Holly's best-known songs for the 1996 gold-disc *Greatest Hits* album. While the sound is fine, it isn't markedly better than that on *From the Original Master Tapes,* which also boasted a more complete track selection. Nevertheless, the gold-disc *Greatest Hits* is one of the most thorough single-disc collection ever assembled on Holly, and for audiophiles, it may be worth the extra money. For most fans, *From the Original Master Tapes* remains the definitive single-disc set, with the double-disc *The Buddy Holly Collection* or the LP-only *The Complete Buddy Holly* providing better, more comprehensive overviews, which provide more value for your dollar than *Greatest Hits.* *—Stephen Thomas Erlewine*

Hootie & the Blowfish

f. 1989, Columbia, SC
Group / Jam Bands, American Trad Rock, Adult Alternative Pop/Rock
Hootie & the Blowfish's mainstream pop variation of blues-rock brought the band to the top of the charts in 1995. Formed at the University of South Carolina, the group features lead vocalist/guitarist Darius Rucker, Mark Bryan, Dean Felber, and Jim "Soni" Sonefeld; the name refers to two friends of the band, not Rucker and the group itself. *Cracked Rear View,* the group's first album was released in the fall of 1994 and a single, "Hold My Hand," worked its way into the Top Ten by the beginning of 1995. Its success propelled the album to number one, as well as launching a second hit, "Let Her Cry," which was quickly followed by "Only Wanna Be with You."

Cracked Rear View had become a massive success by the fall of 1995, going platinum several times over. By the time the group released their second album, *Fairweather Johnson,* in the spring of 1996, the debut had sold 13 million copies in the US alone. *Fairweather Johnson* initially didn't replicate that success. It entered the charts at number one and sold two million copies within its first four months of release, but it didn't produce any hit singles on the level of the debut's "Hold My Hand" or "Let Her Cry." *Musical*

Chairs followed in 1998. The album *Scattered, Smothered, and Covered* was issued two years later, featuring previously unreleased material, songs polled by the fans, and Hootie's own tribute to REM and The Smiths. *— Stephen Thomas Erlewine*

● **Cracked Rear View** / Jul. 5, 1994 / Atlantic ✦✦✦✦✦
Hootie and the Blowfish's debut album *Cracked Rear View* was *the* success story of 1994/1995, selling over 12 million copies. It's a startling large number, especially for a new band, but in some ways, the success of the record isn't that surprising. Although Hootie and the Blowfish aren't innovative, they deliver the goods, turning out an album of solid, rootsy folk-rock that have simple, powerful hooks. "Hold My Hand" has a sing-along chorus that epitomizes the band's good-times vibes. None of the tracks transcend their generic status, but they are strong songs for their genre, with crisp chords and bright melodies. Still, the songs wouldn't be convincing without the emotive vocals of Darius Rucker, whose gruff baritone has more grit than the actual songs. At their core, Hootie and the Blowfish is a bar band, but they managed to convince millions of listeners that they were the local bar band, and that's why *Cracked Rear View* was a major success. *— Stephen Thomas Erlewine*

Fairweather Johnson / Apr. 1996 / Atlantic ✦✦✦

Musical Chairs / Sep. 15, 1998 / Atlantic ✦✦✦✦
Although Hootie & the Blowfish delivered a fine second album, they had no hope of matching the phenomenal success of their debut, *Cracked Rear View,* so *Fairweather Johnson* was perceived as a flop, even though it moved over two million copies. In a way, that perception of failure was the best thing that could have happened to the band. With the spotlight being shone somewhere else (Alanis Morissette, to be exact), Hootie & the Blowfish could return to what they loved best—playing music and being in a band. *Musical Chairs,* the group's third album, illustrates what a blessing it was for the group. Despite a couple of production flourishes, such as the occasional horn section and strings, it's no breakthrough or stylistic departure—it's simply a well-made album, filled with catchy tunes. In other words, it's exactly like their first two records, but the performances are more kinetic and fun than on *Fairweather Johnson,* and the songs are arguably as consistent as those on *Cracked Rear View.* That's why *Musical Chairs* feels a bit like a comeback, but it really shouldn't be viewed that way—it's just a consolidation of their talents and further proof that Hootie & the Blowfish are a fine mainstream pop-rock band. *— Stephen Thomas Erlewine*

Scattered, Smothered and Covered / Oct. 24, 2000 / Atlantic ✦✦✦

Bruce Hornsby

b. Nov. 23, 1954, Williamsburg, VA
Vocals, Accordion, Piano / Heartland Rock, Adult Alternative Pop/Rock, Pop/Rock, Adult Contemporary
Bruce Hornsby and his band the Range signed to RCA in 1985. Their debut album, *The Way It Is,* eventually produced three Top 20 hits, the biggest of which was the socially conscious "The Way It Is," which featured Hornsby's characteristically melodic right-hand piano runs. The album stayed in the charts almost a year and a half, and sold two million copies. Hornsby and the Range won the Best New Artist Grammy Award for 1986. Their second album, *Scenes from the Southside,* was not as successful as the debut, though it sold a million copies, and produced the Top Ten single "The Valley Road." Hornsby also began to make his mark as a songwriter for others: Huey Lewis had a hit with his "Jacob's Ladder," as did Don Henley with "The End of the Innocence." Hornsby's third album, *A Night on the Town* (1990), found him trying to break out of his signature sound into other areas. It was less successful than its predecessors but, along with the pianist's extensive session work, it signaled his determination to tackle new musical challenges. Hornsby worked extensively as a producer and sideman in the early '90s, notably doing temporary duty in the Grateful Dead after their keyboardist, Brent Mydland, died in July 1990. *— William Ruhlmann*

● **The Way It Is** / Aug. 1986 / RCA ✦✦✦✦✦
One of the best collections of new songs released in the 1980s, performed to perfection by a versatile band led by a seasoned (if new to the listener) artist. The songs provide an American panorama, in terms both of landscape and social mores. This is smart, compassionate music for thinking adults... and you can dance to it, too. Includes "The Way It Is" and "Mandolin Rain." *— William Ruhlmann*

Scenes From the Southside / 1988 / RCA ✦✦✦✦✦
Although many bands feel pressure to record the follow-up to a successful debut, Bruce Hornsby is a seasoned musician who is comfortable in his own skin. For the most part, he and his band stick to the same formula that brought them success with *The Way It Is.* In other words, *Scenes From the Southside* is another strong set of piano-based pop with catchy melodies. While the other musicians are able, they just fill out the sound—this is Hornsby's gig. One of his greatest strengths is that, despite being an accomplished musician, he never shows off his chops at the expense of the song. The lyrics offer a slice of Americana; co-written with his brother, John Hornsby, the songs conjure up feelings of national pride ("Defenders of the Flag") as well as small-town nostalgia ("The Road Not Taken"). However the highlights of the album are the minor hits "Look out Any Window" and "The Valley Road," with their sprawling, grandiose arrangements that rank among his finest work. While not quite as consistent as their debut, *Scenes From the Southside* is one of Hornsby's best efforts and a must-own for fans. *— Vik Iyengar*

A Night on the Town / Jul. 1990 / RCA ✦✦✦✦

Harbor Lights / Apr. 6, 1993 / RCA ✦✦✦

Hot House / Jul. 18, 1995 / RCA ✦✦✦

Spirit Trail / Oct. 13, 1998 / RCA ✦✦✦

Here Come the Noise Makers / Oct. 24, 2000 / RCA ✦✦✦✦

The Housemartins

f. 1984, Hull, England, **db.** Jun. 1988
Group / College Rock, Jangle Pop, Alternative Pop/Rock
One of Britain's more popular indie guitar-pop groups of the late '80s, the Housemartins' post-Smiths guitar jangle and subtle updating of catchy, melodic British beat groups earned the Hull-based quartet a substantial critical and popular following within the UK. Though the group never gained much more than a cult following in America, their balance of simple, memorable melodies and cutting sarcasm helped them rise into the British Top Ten, as well as earn consistently strong reviews. The Housemartins broke up in 1988, just before they fully broke into the mainstream. The group's lead songwriter, Paul Heaton, formed the Beautiful South the following year, and his new band capitalized on the success of the Housemartins to become one of the more popular U.K. groups of the early '90s.

Paul Heaton (vocals, guitar) formed the Housemartins with Ted Key (guitar), Stan Cullimore (bass) and Hugh Whitaker (drums) in 1984. From the outset, the group cultivated a distinctly English image, blending a cynical sense of humor with leftist political leanings and low-key, commonplace appearance. "Happy Hour," the Housemartins' third single, became the group's first hit in the summer of 1986, climbing all the way to number three. *Hull 4, London 0,* their debut album, followed shortly afterward. At the end of the year, the a capella "Caravan of Love" became a number one hit. *The People Who Grinned Themselves to Death* followed in 1987, spawning the hit singles "Five Get Over Excited" and "Me and the Farmer." Though the Housemartins were developing into one of the most popular bands within Britain, they broke up in the summer of 1988. With drummer Hemmingway, Heaton formed the Beautiful South, which carried on the aesthetic of the Housemartins, but added more complex melodies and arrangements. Toward the end of 1988, a compilation of Housemartins singles and rarities called *Now That's What I Call Quite Good!* was released. *— Stephen Thomas Erlewine*

● **London 0 Hull 4** / 1986 / Go! Discs ✦✦✦✦✦
The Housemartins had a bouncy pop-rock sound that was reminiscent of the British beat groups of the mid-'60s. This album is full of catchy tunes, although the lyrics are sometimes more serious than the music might suggest. *— William Ruhlmann*

The People Who Grinned Themselves to Death / 1987 / Go! Discs ✦✦✦✦
It may lack the punch of their debut, but the Housemartins' sophomore release was no slump. Drummer tk is replaced by Dave Hemingway with little loss of vocal or band power. Heaton's lyrics still assault yuppies and Thatcher's Britain, and reveal a Christian slant on socialist ideas ("The World's on Fire" and their number one "Caravan of Love," an Isley Brothers spiritual not included on the album but released at the time). A few songs simply repeat the beat group sound of "Happy Hour" to little effect ("Me and the Farmer" and "Five Get Over Excited"), but the title track, "I Can't Put My Finger on It," and the sentimental "Build" are excellent songs in their own right. Heaton's vocals show influences from Curtis Mayfield to Morrissey. After this album, the band split and Heaton and Hemingway went on to form the Beautiful South. *— Ted Mills*

Now That's What I Call Quite Good! / 1988 / Go! Discs ✦✦✦✦✦
Gathering singles, B-sides, BBC sessions and key album cuts from all chapters of the Housemartins' brief but brilliant career, the posthumous *Now That's What I Call Quite Good!* is both a glowing greatest hits package and an odds-and-ends clearinghouse—a fitting epitaph for a band which thrived on contradictions in consistently pitting the personal versus the political and the secular versus the spiritual. Despite the uniform excellence of their two studio LPs, this release confirms once and for all that the Housemartins were first and foremost a singles band—even removed from their album context, highlights including "Bow Down," "Build," and "The Light Is Always Green" boast all the immediacy and infectiousness of classic pop radio fodder, even if their actual mainstream appeal was minimal at best. The previously uncollected material, meanwhile, reveals a warmth and intimacy often missing from Paul Heaton's most trenchant social commentaries—in particular, the "garage gospel" approach which distinguishes remarkable readings of Luther Ingram's "I'll Be Your Shelter" and the Isley Brothers' "Caravan of Love" (the latter the Housemartins' lone UK chart-topper) radiate an intensely humanistic empathy which underlines the utter conviction at the heart of all the group's work. *— Jason Ankeny*

Whitney Houston

b. Aug. 9, 1963, Newark, NJ
Vocals / Club/Dance, Adult Contemporary, Urban, Dance-Pop
With pure pop music melded to stunning beauty, Whitney Houston's star shines bright whether she is singing ballads, uptempo dance material, the national anthem, or cola commercials. Coming from a solid musical background, this daughter of soul singer Cissy Houston and cousin of Dionne Warwick debuted in 1985. Her first album, *Whitney Houston,* was the first in *Billboard* chart history by a woman to enter at number one, and with sales of 14 million copies, was the best-selling debut album until Alanis Morrisette's *Jagged Little Pill.* She scored heavily on MTV with classy videos, helping to break the "color barrier" originally knocked down by Michael Jackson. Her second album, *Whitney,* was just as popular, scoring seven consecutive number ones in the U.S., shattering the previous record held by the Beatles.

After the disappointing performance of her third album, *I'm Your Baby Tonight,* Houston rocketed back to the top of the charts in late 1992 with the soundtrack from her first movie, *The Bodyguard.* The love theme from the movie, a version of Dolly Parton's "I Will Always Love You," broke all previous sales and airplay records, becoming the biggest single in pop music history; it also won her an almost innumerable amount of awards, including several Grammies.

Her work on the soundtracks to *Waiting to Exhale* and her second film *The Preachers Wife* tided fans over until she returned with a new album of her own, *My Love Is Your Love,* in 1998. *— Cub Koda & Stephen Thomas Erlewine*

● **Whitney Houston** / 1985 / Arista ✦✦✦✦✦
The legend of Whitney Houston began with this self-titled album. It marked her shift away

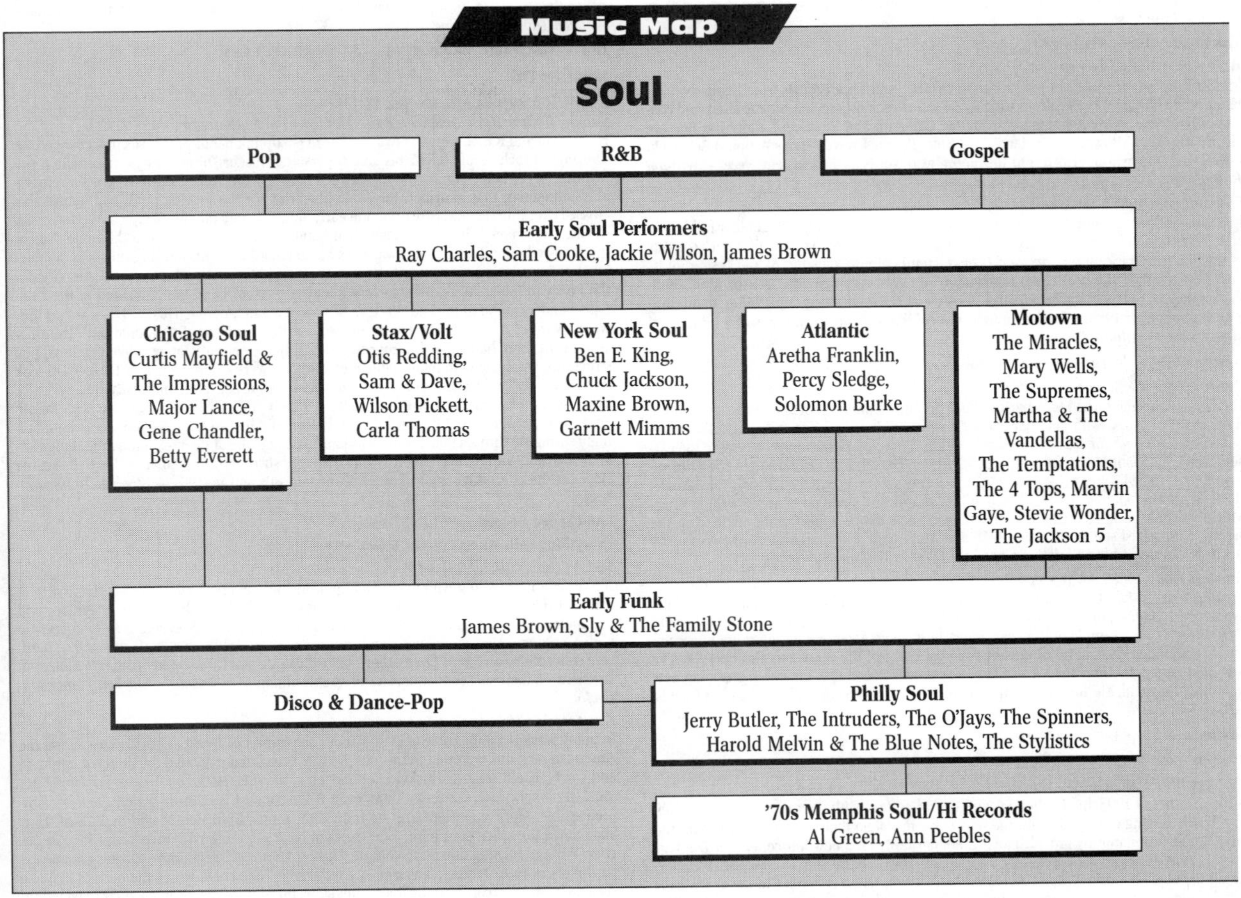

from the experimental songs she did with the group Material and a move into heavily produced, very slick urban contemporary and adult pop. Although Houston had learned her craft working in New York nightclubs and singing in a Baptist church in Newark, she was steered into radio-friendly ballads that emphasized style over substance. The album did yield an unprecedented string of number one hits, but "Saving All My Love for You" and "How Will I Know" created an impression of an incredibly talented vocalist using only a minimum of her skills. It also contained one of her few legitimate soul workouts in "The Greatest Love of All." *—Ron Wynn*

Whitney / 1987 / Arista ✦✦✦✦
Whitney Houston became an international star with this album. It sold more than ten million copies around the world, yielded a string of number hit singles across the board like "I Wanna Dance with Somebody (Who Loves Me)," "Didn't We Almost Have It All" and "Love Will Save the Day," and established Houston as the era's top female star. She later went on to more than solidify that status, with other hit albums and a budding film career. While this is a far cry from soul, it's the ultimate in polished, super-produced urban contemporary material. *—Ron Wynn*

I'm Your Baby Tonight / 1990 / Arista ✦✦

My Love Is Your Love / Nov. 17, 1998 / Arista ✦✦✦✦

The Greatest Hits / Apr. 18, 2000 / Arista ✦✦✦✦
Although *Whitney Houston's Greatest Hits* is a double-disc package, only the first disc actually contains original versions of Houston's hit singles; the second disc, *The Greatest Remixes*, collects remixes new and old for hardcore fans. Of course, it would be impossible to fit all of Houston's 20-plus chart singles onto one disc, but that format still could have produced a fantastic and near-definitive collection. That is, if Arista hadn't made the ridiculous choice not to include four number one hits: "How Will I Know," "So Emotional," "I Wanna Dance With Somebody (Who Loves Me)," and "I'm Your Baby Tonight." Granted, those songs are all present on *The Greatest Remixes*, but anyone wanting the original versions will have to purchase the *three* different albums they appeared on. That said, the compilation does do fans a few favors; there are three new tracks, including one duet apiece with Deborah Cox and Enrique Iglesias, and two hits make their first appearance on a Houston album: "One Moment in Time" (the 1988 Olympic theme) and "If You Say My Eyes Are Beautiful," a 1986 duet with Jermaine Jackson. Houston's Top 20 hit recording of "The Star-Spangled Banner," performed at Super Bowl XXV during the Gulf War, is tacked onto the remix disc as well. The *Greatest Hits* disc amply reinforces what a fine singles artist Houston has been for the entirety of her career. Overall, though, it's a frustrating package marred by record company greed—not only because of the glaring and intentional omissions, but also because casual fans won't appreciate paying double the money for a remix disc they probably aren't interested in owning. *—Steve Huey*

Human League

f. 1977, Sheffield, Yorkshire, England
Group / New Romantic, New Wave, Synth Pop, Dance-Pop
Synth-pop's first international superstars, the Human League were among the earliest and most innovative bands to break into the pop mainstream on a wave of synthesizers and electronic rhythms, their marriage of infectious melodies and state-of-the-art technology proving enormously influential on countless acts following in their wake. Formed by synth players Martyn Ware and Ian Marsh with vocalist Philip Oakey and Adrian Wright, Human League released two albums before internal tensions forced Ware and Marsh to leave in 1980, at which time they formed the British Electric Foundation (and later Heaven 17). Oakey and Wright recruited a bassist and schoolgirls Susanne Sulley and Joanne Catherall to handle additional vocal duties, which paved the way for their breakthrough "Don't You Want Me," from the album *Dare!*; both topped their respective charts in England, and went on to become major hits in the U.S. as well. The much-anticipated follow-up *Hysteria* finally surfaced in 1984, but failed to match the massive success of *Dare!*. To the surprise of many, the Human League resurfaced in 1986 with *Crash*, produced by the duo of Jam and Lewis; the plaintive lead single "Human" soon topped the U.S. charts, but the group failed to capitalize on its comeback success, disappearing from the charts for the remainder of the decade. The group's two 1990s albums, *Romantic*— and *Octopus*, both went largely unnoticed both at home and overseas. *—Jason Ankeny*

Reproduction / 1979 / Virgin ✦✦✦
Pop fans a bit put off by Human League's dispassionate vocals on their breakout hit "Don't You Want Me" would have been shocked by the degree of emotionlessness heard two years earlier on the band's 1979 debut. The trio of Marsh, Ware, and Oakey all handled vocals and synthesizers to create a set of grim, rigid tracks that revealed a greater lack of humanity than even Kraftwerk. It's a surprise that Human League hit the British charts at all (with the single

"Empire State Human"), since this could well be the most detached synth-pop record ever released. *—John Bush*

Travelogue / 1980 / Virgin ✦✦✦

☆ **Dare** / 1981 / A&M ✦✦✦✦✦
Martin Rushent's fresh, clean production keeps the synthesized music from being too cluttered, while Philip Oakey's voice is used for its self-consciously melodramatic effect and contrasted with the untrained singing of Joanne Catherall and Susanne Sulley. The hits are "Don't You Want Me" and (in England) "The Sound of the Crowd," "Love Action (I Believe in Love)," and "Open Your Heart," but the album also works as a consistent piece. *—William Ruhlmann*

Fascination! / 1983 / A&M ✦✦✦
Instead of following *Dare*, its internationally successful third album, with another full-length effort, the Human League re-emerged with this under-27-minute, six-track EP, which consists of the one new track on its *Love and Dancing* remix album, plus the A- and B-sides of its post-*Dare* singles "(Keep Feeling) Fascination" (in two versions) and "Mirror Man." Both those songs were hits in the pop-synthesizer style of *Dare*, but the group's failure to produce a new album after 19 months was an indication of the instability it would suffer for the rest of its career. *—William Ruhlmann*

Hysteria / 1984 / Virgin ✦✦✦

Crash / 1986 / A&M ✦✦✦
The Human League turned to American R&B producers Jimmy Jam and Terry Lewis in the wake of their success with Janet Jackson's *Control*, and the combination brought the group its second *1 hit with the $Jam*-Lewis composition "Human," awhich harked back to the earlier "Don't You Want Me," albeit with a gentler tone. The album's second single, the *Control*-soundalike "I Need Your Loving," was also a Jam-Lewis song (as was the UK-only third single, "Love Is All That Matters"), but the bulk of the album was made up of group-written songs with appealing backing tracks that maintained their dance appeal while eschewing the overtly synthesized sound of previous albums. That made *Crash* an improvement over the lackluster *Hysteria*, but still not on a par with *Dare*. *—William Ruhlmann*

Greatest Hits / 1988 / A&M ✦✦✦✦✦
Greatest Hits reminds that popular tracks like "Don't You Want Me" successfully bridged the gap between dance, pop, and rock audiences. With "Being Boiled," the 16-strong collection even offers a token sample of the League's earliest, more experimental machine music approach—although their atmospherically funereal cover of the Righteous Brothers' "You've Lost That Loving Feeling" should also have made the cut. Includes the rather engaging new recording "Stay with Me Tonight" from the currently active version of Phil Oakey and friends. *—Roch Parisien*

Romantic— / Sep. 1990 / A&M ✦✦

Octopus / Jan. 27, 1995 / East West ✦✦✦

● **The Very Best of the Human League** / Jul. 14, 1998 / Ark 21 ✦✦✦✦✦
In the summer of 1998, the Human League set out on tour with the reunited Culture Club, both bands hoping to capitalize on the new wave nostalgia that was slowly sweeping the country. The tour naturally provided an ideal opportunity for a new hits collection, *The Very Best of the Human League*. Essentially, it's a slightly reworked version of *Greatest Hits*, sharing all the obvious tracks ("Don't You Want Me," "Love Action (I Believe in Love)," "Mirror Man," "Fascination (Keep Feeling)," "Human," "Being Boiled," "The Lebanon") and subsituting earlier cuts like "The Sound of the Crowd" and "Open Your Heart" for middle-of-the-road '90s singles "Tell Me When," "Stay With Me Tonight," "Heart Like a Wheel," and "One Man in My Heart." Clearly, this collection is for fans who prefer *Crash* to *Dare*, and they'll likely be satisfied, since it's fairly consistent. That said, *Dare* fans should note that this album features a genuine rarity in "Together in Electric Dreams," Philip Oakey's collaboration with Giorgio Moroder for the 1984 film *Electric Dreams*. It doesn't pop up all that often on either Human League releases or various-artists collections, which means this is all the more valuable for collectors, who may also enjoy the "Audio Liner Notes" which feature the group retelling their history. The Snap remix of "Don't You Want Me," however, will be of little interest to either camp. *—Stephen Thomas Erlewine*

Humble Pie

f. 1968, Essex, England, **db.** 1975
Group / Album Rock, Boogie Rock, British Blues, Arena Rock, Hard Rock, Blues-Rock
A showcase for former Small Faces frontman Steve Marriott and onetime Herd guitar virtuoso Peter Frampton, the hard rock outfit Humble Pie formed in 1969. Signed to the Immediate label, Humble Pie soon issued their debut single "Natural Born Boogie," which hit the British Top Ten and paved the way for the group's premiere LP, *As Safe as Yesterday Is*. As Marriott directed the group towards a harder-edged, grittier sound far removed from the acoustic melodies favored by Frampton, his raw blues shouting began to dominate subsequent LPs like 1970's eponymous effort and 1971's *Rock On;* Frampton's role in the band he cofounded gradually diminished, and finally, after a highly charged U.S. tour which yielded 1971's commercial breakthrough *Performance—Rockin' the Fillmore*, the guitarist exited Humble Pie to embark on a solo career. The band grew even heavier for 1972's *Smokin'*, their most successful album to date. However, while 1973's ambitious double studio/live set *Eat It* fell just shy of the Top Ten, its 1974 follow-up *Thunderbox* failed to crack the Top 40. After 1975's *Street Rats* reached only number 100 before disappearing from the charts, Humble Pie disbanded, reforming in 1980. *—Jason Ankeny*

● **Classics, Vol. 14** / 1987 / A&M ✦✦✦✦✦
Released in 1987, during the thick of the *Classics* series, this compilation winds up being one of the most successful of its brethren, containing almost all of Humble Pie's greatest hits, including "I Don't Need No Doctor," "Hot N Nasty," "Shine On," "30 Days in the Hole," and "C'Mon Everybody." This isn't a strict hits compilation, yet it summarizes the band's strengths better than most of its ilk and winds up being an effective introduction to the band. *—Stephen Thomas Erlewine*

Hot N' Nasty—the Anthology / Jun. 7, 1994 / A&M ✦✦✦✦

Hüsker Dü

f. 1979, Minneapolis, MN, **db.** Dec. 17, 1987
Group / College Rock, American Punk, Hardcore Punk, Alternative Pop/Rock
Hüsker Dü and R.E.M. were the two American post-punk bands of the '80s that changed the direction of rock & roll. R.E.M. became superstars; Hüsker Dü never was more than a cult favorite. Nevertheless, their albums between between 1981 and 1987 have proven remarkably influential; they provided the sonic blueprint for the roaring punk-pop hybrid that crossed over into the mainstream in the early '90s. Not only did they shape the sound of the music, they shaped the way independent bands made the transition to the major labels; they showed other bands that it was possible to record uncompromising music on a major label without losing any integrity or creative control. From the Replacements to Nirvana, the Pixies to Superchunk, nearly every major and minor band that appeared in the alternative underground in the late '80s and '90s owed a major debt to Hüsker Dü, whether they were aware of it or not. The band's two songwriters, guitarist Bob Mould and drummer Grant Hart, both had a knack for writing songs that essentially followed conventional pop structures, complete with memorable melodies, but were still punk songs. Hüsker Dü took the Buzzcocks' pioneering punk pop and made it harder, both musically and lyrically. Throughout their career, Hüsker Dü never lost their edge, never turned down their amplifiers, never compromised their music. While Hart and bassist Greg Norton were an unflailingly strong rhythm section, Mould would prove to be one of the most influential guitarists of the decade. With his slashing rhythms, distorted strumming, and blazing leads, he set the stage for the alternative guitar heroes of the late '80s and the '90s. *—Stephen Thomas Erlewine*

Land Speed Record / 1981 / SST ✦✦

Everything Falls Apart / 1982 / Reflex ✦✦✦

Metal Circus / 1983 / SST ✦✦✦
A five-song EP bristling with energy and pummeling guitars, *Metal Circus* is the first indication of Hüsker Dü's greatness. With these five songs, the band shows more invention, skill and melody than they did over the course of a full album with *Everything Falls Apart*, and both Mould and Hart emerge as significant songwriters. While they both stay within hardcore conventions on *Metal Circus*, their songs illustrate that they would break free of its constrictions on their subsequent, masterful double album, *Zen Arcade*. *—Stephen Thomas Erlewine*

☆ **Zen Arcade** / 1984 / SST ✦✦✦✦✦
In many ways, it's impossible to overestimate the impact of Husker Du's *Zen Arcade* on the American rock underground in the '80s. It's the record that exploded the limits of hardcore and what it could achieve. Hüsker Dü broke all of the rules with *Zen Arcade*. First and foremost, it's a sprawling concept album, even if the concept isn't immediately clear or comprehensible. More important are the individual songs. Both Bob Mould and Grant Hart abandoned the strict "fast, hard, loud" rules of hardcore punk with their songs for *Zen Arcade*. Without turning down the volume, Hüsker Dü tries everything—pop songs, tape experiments, acoustic songs, pianos, noisy psychedelia. Hüsker Dü willed themselves to make such a sprawling record—as the liner notes state, the album was recorded and mixed within 85 hours and consists almost entirely of first takes. That reckless, ridiculously single-minded approach does result in some weak moments—the sound is thin and the instrumentals drag on a bit too long—but it's also the key to the success of *Zen Arcade*. Hüsker Dü sounds phenomenally strong and possessed, as if they could do anything. The sonic experimentation is bolstered by Mould and Hart's increased sense of songcraft. Neither writer is afraid to let their pop influences show on *Zen Arcade*, which gives the songs—from the unrestrained rage of "Something I Learned Today" and the bitter, acoustic "Never Talking to You Again" to the eerie "Pink Turns to Blue" and anthemic "Turn On the News"—their weight. It's music that is informed by hardcore punk and indie-rock ideals without being limited by it. *—Stephen Thomas Erlewine*

☆ **Flip Your Wig** / 1985 / SST ✦✦✦✦✦
Spot—*SST's* house producer who manned the boards for *Zen Arcade* and *New Day Rising*—didn't produce *Flip Your Wig*, Hüsker Dü's second album of 1985, and the difference is immediately noticeable. Everything on *Flip Your Wig* is cleaner and brighter than on its two immediate predecessors, which is appropriate, considering that Bob Mould and Grant Hart have only increased their debt to '60s pop. The hooks and melodies are on the surface, right from the kick-start call-and-response of the title track. On paper, it might sound as if Hüsker Dü have watered down their hardcore ideals, but it doesn't play that way. *Flip Your Wig* is pop played as punk, as if this is the only time these songs could ever be heard. Which means Hart's love song "Green Eyes" and Mould's pure pop single "Makes No Sense at All" are delivered with the same rage and passion as Mould's blistering "Divide and Conquer" and Hart's "Keep Hanging On," or the pair of surging, neo-psychedelic and noise-wracked instrumentals that close the album. *Flip Your Wig* would be a remarkable record on its own terms, but the fact that it followed *New Day Rising* by a matter of months and *Zen Arcade* by just over a year is simply astonishing. *—Stephen Thomas Erlewine*

★ **New Day Rising** / 1985 / SST ✦✦✦✦✦
For *New Day Rising*, the followup to their breakthrough double-album *Zen Arcade*, Hüsker Dü replaced concept with conciseness, concentrating on individual songs delivered as scalding post-hardcore pop. *New Day Rising* is not only a more vicious and relentless record than *Zen Arcade*, it's more melodic. Bob Mould and Grant Hart have written tightly crafted, melodic pop songs that don't compromise Hüsker's volcanic, unchecked power. Mould and Hart's songs owe a great deal to '60s pop, as the verses and choruses ebb and flow with immediately catchy hooks. Occasionally, the razor-thin production and waves of noise mean that it takes a little bit of effort to pick out the melodies, but more often the furious noise and

melodies fuse together to create an overwhelming sonic force. It's possible to hear the rivalry between Mould and Hart on the album itself—each song is like a game of oneupmanship, as Mould responds to "The Girl Who Lives on Heaven Hill" with "Celebrated Summer." Neither songwriter slips—both turn in songs that are catchy, clever and alternately wracked with pain or teeming with humor. *New Day Rising* is a positively cathartic record and ranks as Hüsker Dü's most sustained moment of pure power. *—Stephen Thomas Erlewine*

Candy Apple Grey / 1986 / Warner Brothers ✦✦✦
Moving to a major label doesn't affect Hüsker Dü's sound greatly—although the production is more full-bodied than Spot's razor-thin work, the Hüskers don't change their blazing attack at all. Much of *Candy Apple Grey* charges along on the same frenzied beat that propelled *New Day Rising* and *Flip Your Wig,* and both Mould and Hart are in fine form, spinning out fine punk-pop with "Sorry Somehow" and "Don't Want to Know If You Are Lonely." However, the sound is beginning to seem a bit tired, which is what makes Mould's two acoustic numbers, "Too Far Down" and "Hardly Getting Over It," so welcome. Demonstrating that punks can mature without losing their edge, Mould inverts the rules of conventional confessional singer-songwriter songs with these two haunting numbers, and in doing so, he illustrates the faults with the relatively staid post-hardcore punk that dominates the remainder of the record. *—Stephen Thomas Erlewine*

☆ **Warehouse: Songs & Stories** / 1987 / Warner Brothers ✦✦✦✦✦
It's cleaner and more produced than any of their records, which is one reason why many Hüsker Dü fans have never fully embraced their second double-album, *Warehouse: Songs and Stories.* Granted, *Warehouse* boasts a fuller production—complete with multitracked guitars and vocal, various percussion techniques and endless studio effects—that would have seemed out of place a mere two years before its release. However, *Flip Your Wig* and *Candy Apple Grey* both *suggested* this full-fledged pop production and its to Hüsker Dü's credit that they never sound like they are selling out with *Warehouse.* What they do sound like is breaking up. Although there was a schism apparent between Bob Mould and Grant Hart on *Candy Apple Grey,* they don't even sound like they are writing for the same band on *Warehouse.* But the individual songs on the album are powerhouses in their own right, as both songwriters exhibit a continuing sense of experimentation—Hart writes a sea shanty with "She Floated Away" and uses bubbling percussion on "Charity, Chastity, Prudence and Hope," while Mould nearly arrives at power-pop with "Could You Be the One?" and touches on the singer/songwriter-styled folk rock with "No Reservations." *Warehouse* doesn't have the single-minded sense of purpose or eccentric sprawl of *Zen Arcade,* but as a collection of songs, it is of the first-order. Furthermore, its stylish production—which makes pop concessions without abandoning a punk ethos—pointed the way to the kind of "alternative" rock that dominated the mainstream in the early '90s. In all, it was a fine way for one of the most important bands of the '80s to call it a day. *—Stephen Thomas Erlewine*

Everything Falls Apart and More / 1993 / Rhino ✦✦✦
Rhino's reissue of Hüsker Dü's shattering first studio album includes a couple of rare singles, making it a must-have for the band's fans, as well as anyone interested in hardcore punk rock. Anyone unfamiliar with Hüsker Dü's early work should brace themselves for a breakneck force like no other. Not for the faint of heart. *—Stephen Thomas Erlewine*

The Living End / Oct. 1994 / Warner Brothers ✦✦✦
Recorded on their final tour, *The Living End* is an invigorating document of Hüsker Dü's blistering live power, highlighted by a couple unreleased songs and a manic cover of "Sheena Is a Punk Rocker." *—Stephen Thomas Erlewine*

Billy Idol (William Broad)

b. Nov. 30, 1955, Middlesex, England
Vocals / Album Rock, Pop/Rock, New Wave, Hard Rock
Billy Idol represents the bridge between punk rock and hard rock/metal, a logical enough connection that somehow seemed unlikely until he made the transition. Idol left Sussex University in 1976 to join the punk movement, specifically the group of rabid Sex Pistols fans called the Bromley Contingent. Many of the members formed their own bands, and Idol began Generation X with Tony James. Generation X became a moderate success during the punk heyday of the late '70s, especially in England, with Idol on snarling lead vocals.

When the band split in 1981, Idol went to New York and hooked up with manager Bill Aucoin (who had handled Kiss, among others). This resulted in Idol's grooming as more of a mainstream rock figure. His debut album, *Billy Idol,* came out in 1982 and spent two years on the charts as the result of such video hits as "White Wedding" and "Hot in the City." But it was Idol's second album, *Rebel Yell,* that was his big breakthrough, selling two million copies and spawning hits in the raucous title track and the ballad "Eyes without a Face." Idol followed it up with *Whiplash Smile* in 1986 and *Charmed Life* in 1990.

Idol's first commercial failure came in 1993, with *Cyberpunk,* his stab at techno-influenced rock. *—William Ruhlmann*

Billy Idol / Jul. 1982 / Chrysalis ✦✦✦✦
Billy Idol's self-titled debut album was a snarling take on hard rock, injected with the spite and attitude of punk and new wave. While the record is spotty, Idol pulls it all together on the classic single "White Wedding." *—Stephen Thomas Erlewine*

Rebel Yell / 1983 / Chrysalis ✦✦✦✦
A slick, carefully crafted follow-up to his debut, *Rebel Yell* was Billy Idol's catchiest, most consistent fusion of synth-driven new wave pop and hard rock guitar pyrotechnics (courtesy of Steve Stevens). The eerie ballad "Eyes Without a Face" gave Idol his first U.S. Top Ten hit, while "Flesh for Fantasy" and the title track became MTV staples. Like much of Idol's solo output, it's all calculated for maximum appeal, but *Rebel Yell* also works too well not to be an infectiously guilty pleasure. *—Steve Huey*

Vital Idol / 1986 / Chrysalis ✦✦

Whiplash Smile / 1986 / Chrysalis ✦✦✦
While *Whiplash Smile* is Idol's most ambitious album, it only comes to life on hard-rocking pseudo-rockabilly like *To Be A Lover."* Unfortunately, there aren't many songs that are as good as that single on this album. *—Stephen Thomas Erlewine*

● **Idol Songs: The Best of Billy Idol** / 1988 / Chrysalis ✦✦✦✦

Charmed Life / 1990 / Chrysalis ✦✦✦✦
Like any Billy Idol album, *Charmed Life* is wildly inconsistent, but it has enough strong songs—like the gloriously tongue-in-cheek hard rock of "Cradle of Love"—to make most of the filler on the record forgivable. *—Stephen Thomas Erlewine*

Cyberpunk / Jun. 29, 1993 / Chrysalis ✦

The Impressions

f. 1958, Chicago, IL, **db.** 1983
Group / Chicago Soul, Uptown Soul, Pop-Soul, Northern Soul, Soul
The first Impressions hit, "For Your Precious Love," was an anachronism when released in 1958. Jerry Butler's robust, yearning vocal was a throwback to deep-South gospel, and Curtis Mayfield's arrangement was decidedly barebones. But this song also precipitated the changes coming in R&B; you can hear the groundwork for soul music being laid, from the melisma of Butler's phrasing to Mayfield's skeletal guitar. The song literally flew in the face of then-popular doo wop formulas. Butler left the group in 1960, but the pared-down trio, led by Mayfield, cut a path that altered the R&B map. Mayfield's high falsetto and the trade-off vocals of Fred Cash and Sam Gooden framed a new kind of R&B: smooth and graceful, at times lilting, soaked in the history of gospel, and, thanks to Mayfield's lyrical examinations of racism and urban decay, the catalyst for the wave of socially aware Black hits recorded in the '70s. The group's hits varied from supple statements of affirmation ("It's All Right," "People Get Ready") and romantic declarations ("Talking About My Baby," "I'm So Proud") to songs that were sociopolitical ("Choice of Colors," "This Is My Country") or mystical ("Gypsy Woman"). Their chart run ended by the late '60s, as did Mayfield's Midas touch; after recording the brilliant *Superfly* in 1972, his talents ran dry. Nonetheless, Mayfield's reputation as one of soul's supreme innovators cannot be exaggerated. *—John Floyd*

The Complete Vee-Jay Recordings / Nov. 22, 1993 / Vee-Jay ✦✦✦✦✦
The Impressions' early music has taken a back seat to what they did after Jerry Butler departed and Mayfield began doing the lead vocals, writing, producing, and arranging. This excellent 18-track disc helps put the early years into focus, with Butler showcased on seven cuts and Mayfield on eight. The Impressions weren't a bad five-member harmony unit; they just were not a great one in an era when you had to be fantastic simply to break out of the pack. These are mostly nice love songs, and they aren't lyrically different from thousands of similar tracks, but they did deserve a better fate than to be dropped from the Vee-Jay label in 1959. *—Ron Wynn*

Keep on Pushing/People Get Ready / Mar. 19, 1996 / Kent ✦✦✦✦✦
Two good Impressions albums from the mid-'60s, combined onto one CD, making them handier to collect in this fashion than hunting down good-quality copies of the rare original vinyl editions. As usual, the singles ("Keep On Pushing," "People Get Ready," "Amen," "I've Been Trying," "Woman's Got Soul," "You Must Believe Me") overshadow the LP-only cuts. But the Impressions made a higher standard of albums than most '60s soul groups, investing a lot of care in the songwriting and production, making this a decent pickup for those who want to go beyond the greatest-hits anthologies. *—Richie Unterberger*

This Is My Country/The Young Mods' Forgotten Story / Apr. 24, 1996 / Sequel ✦✦✦✦✦
Two fine late-'60s albums, combined onto one CD, including some hits and a wealth of good overlooked Mayfield compositions that touched on sensitive racial issues as well as romance. Offering excellent value, the CD is a recommended alternative to tracking down the hard-to-find original vinyl editions. *—Richie Unterberger*

Check out Your Mind!/Times Have Changed / Dec. 17, 1996 / Sequel ✦✦✦
Sequel's *Check Out Your Mind/Times Have Changed* combines two albums the Impressions recorded for Curtom Records in 1970 and 1972, respectively. These albums have their moments, and are quite attractive to fans of the smooth, funky sound of Philly soul in the early '70s, but they're too uneven to be recommended unconditionally. *—Stephen Thomas Erlewine*

● **The Very Best of the Impressions** / Feb. 4, 1997 / Rhino ✦✦✦✦✦
A good 16-track anthology for the moderate Impressions fans, sticking to their most famous smashes—"Gypsy Woman," "It's All Right," "Keep on Pushing," "Amen," "People Get Ready," "We're a Winner," "Choice of Colors," "Check Out Your Mind," and so forth. Most of it's from the '60s, but it does end with three hits from the mid-'70s, after Mayfield's departure from the group. *—Richie Unterberger*

One by One/Ridin' High / Jun. 23, 1998 / Kent ✦✦✦
A two-for-one combination of two mid-1960s LPs on one compact disc. *One by One* is a misstep that was not uncommon among soul stars in the '60s: the record is dedicated almost entirely to standards such as "Twilight Time," "I Wanna Be Around," "Nature Boy," and "Mona Lisa." The strategy was to widen their appeal to a more adult pop audience, but supperclub ballads are not what you turn to the Impressions (or for that matter, any soul stars) for, and the album sounds mediocre decades later, with the expected syrupy big-band orchestration. Sam Gooden and Fred Cash take leads on one unmemorable song each; the three Curtis Mayfield-penned numbers, in bold contrast, are more soulful and understated, particularly the dramatically arranged "Just One Kiss from You." *Ridin' High* is a much more palatable kettle of fish, as Mayfield wrote almost all of the tunes and the production was back-to-business, straightahead Chicago soul. It's a bit of a treadmill affair as some of the songs had been previously recorded by Billy Butler, Major Lance, and Jerry Butler, but it's still quality ebullient music with fine leads and harmonies, exemplified by the small hit "I Need You." "Gotta Get Away," previously done by Billy Butler, and the sassy "Too Slow" are other highlights of a pretty solid album. *—Richie Unterberger*

Fabulous Impressions/We're a Winner / Sep. 29, 1998 / Kent ✦✦✦✦✦
A reissue that combines 1967's *The Fabulous Impressions* and 1968's *We're a Winner* onto one CD. Although *The Fabulous Impressions* was a solid enough soul record on its own mer-

its, it's not one of the more notable entries in the Impressions' catalog. There aren't any big hits, although a couple cuts, "You Always Hurt Me" and "I Can't Stay Away from You," were modest R&B charters. At times it seemed that Mayfield was trying to follow in Motown's footsteps, as on "You Always Hurt Me" and "You Ought to Be in Heaven." "It's All Over" is the Impressions' version of a song that had already been a hit for Walter Jackson, and the cover of Gene McDaniels' "One Hundred Pounds of Clay" (the only selection not written by Mayfield) is filler. The above comments might lead you to believe this album is worse than it actually is; it's dependable, enjoyable, quality soul, with "Isle of Sirens" recalling earlier efforts like "Gypsy Woman," and "She Don't Love Me" offering a chunkier and tougher approach than their typical heartfelt optimism. While the title track of *We're a Winner* was one of Mayfield's classic civil rights-conscious anthems, most of this album was actually dedicated to standard romantic themes. Almost every cut was a quality Mayfield original, and the harmonies and vocal interplay among the group were outstanding. "Nothing Can Stop Me," which had been a hit in 1965 for Gene Chandler, was an uptempo highlight, and "Little Brown Boy" showed more of the African-American pride that had been explored in "We're a Winner," albeit in a more tender ballad mode. The closing cover of "Up Up and Away" is misplaced, but overall this is one of the better Impressions albums to pick up if you want more than what's found on the greatest-hits collections. *—Richie Unterberger*

Check Out . . . / Jan. 18, 1999 / Music Club ✦✦✦

The ABC Rarities / Jun. 8, 1999 / Kent ✦✦✦
Twenty-six song compilation of non-LP singles, rarities that only showed up on obscure reissues and various-artists collections, and material (both released and unreleased) from their sessions for their late-'60s *The Versatile Impressions* album. As a listen it's a little uneven, due in large part to the over-preponderance of standards from *Versatile*. None of this is on level with the best '60s recordings by Mayfield and the Impressions. Much of it, though, is the fairly solid sort of stuff that fans who care enough about the act to go beyond greatest-hits compilations will like to have. Actually, some of these were not terribly obscure; "Never Could You Be" was a small R&B hit in the mid-'60s, and "We're Rolling On (Pts. 1 & 2)" was a small pop entry in 1968, as was the 1968 antiwar ballad "Don't Cry My Love" (written by Mayfield with jazz singer Oscar Brown Jr.). Oddities from the *Versatile* LP include the two lushly orchestrated songs they did for the *East of Java* soundtrack. However, much of the *Versatile* period is unsuitably pop in both material and production for the Impressions, although "Sermonette" and the previously unreleased "Devil in Your Soul" eschew that approach for some pretty gutsy, bluesy soul. *—Richie Unterberger*

● **Indelible Impressions** / Jun. 20, 2000 / Sequel ✦✦✦✦✦

Indigo Girls

f. 1985, Decatur, GA
Group / College Rock, Adult Alternative Pop/Rock, Singer/Songwriter
While they came into prominence as part of the late-'80s folky-singer/songwriter revival, the Indigo Girls have had staying power where other artists from the same era quickly faded. Their two-women-with-guitars formula may not seem very revolutionary on paper, but the combination of two distinct personalities and songwriting styles provides a tension and an interesting balance—Emily Saliers, hailing from the more traditional Joni Mitchell school, has the gentler sound, is more complex musically, and often leans toward the abstract and spiritual while Amy Ray draws heavily from the singer/songwriter aspects of punk rock for her more abrasive and direct approach. In more than a decade of recording, they have managed respectable mainstream success as well as keeping their rabid core following. Their eponymous national debut, released in 1989, gave them initial college radio credibility and the single "Closer to Fine" became a hit—the album eventually broke the Top 30 and earned a Grammy for Best Folk Recording that year. Though the follow-up, 1990's *Nomads Indians Saints*, didn't fare quite as well, the Indigo Girls made a comeback with 1992's *Rites of Passage*, which debuted at number 22 and went platinum by year's end. Almost exactly two years later, *Swamp Ophelia* was released and entered the charts at number nine. *—Chris Woodstra*

Strange Fire / 1987 / Epic/Legacy ✦✦✦

● **Indigo Girls** / 1989 / Epic/Legacy ✦✦✦✦✦
With their first major label release, the Indigo Girls come on strong with an outstanding batch of tunes, watertight harmonies, impeccable musicianship, and flawless production. And entering the folk-rock music scene on the successful heels of R.E.M., Tracy Chapman, and 10,000 Maniacs pushed their sales over the million mark and earned the duo a Grammy for Best Folk Recording. The eponymous release kicks off with the upbeat jangle bounce of "Closer to Fine," a modest hit, all-time fan favorite written by Emily Saliers, and a tune the Girls still play at every concert. A particularly fascinating point is that the Indigo Girls never write songs together, but they compliment each other perfectly. The difference in styles becomes immediately apparent when the more dark and brooding Amy Ray steps up. Her remarkable contributions include "Secure Yourself," "Kid Fears," and "Blood and Fire," spiritual ruminations of life, love, pain, and faith which bury themselves deep inside your core whether invited or not. Weighting the opposite scales, Saliers offers a tender balance to Ray with two beautiful ballads, "Love's Recovery" and "History of Us." (Ray's "Land of Canaan" was once a ballad, but then she heard The Replacements and it became a bit of a rocker.) Chiming in with musical support are Hothouse Flowers, Luka Bloom, and fellow Georgians R.E.M. This self-titled release captures the passion of their youth with voices that are a little cloudy, untamed, and raw, but the power that surges through them suggests a maturity far beyond their years. The same can be said of the songwriting—sheer poetry. To attempt examinations of these songs would not do them justice, for the layers of meaning and emotion unfold best upon repeated listening. *—Kelly McCartney*

Nomads Indians Saints / Sep. 1990 / Epic ✦✦✦✦✦
Following the success of their 1989 debut and the reissue of the previously independent *Strange Fire*, the Indigo Girls answered with another Grammy-nominated offering. *Nomads Indians Saints* shows Emily Saliers and Amy Ray in fine form, delving a little deeper into the themes of love and faith that run through all of their work. Now that they've had the chance to travel around, see the world, and hear people's stories, their poetic vision has expanded somewhat to include a more global perspective, but without losing the intimacy that makes their songs so potent. The title of the record is lifted from "World Falls"—"I wish I was a nomad, an Indian, or a saint./Give me walking shoes, feathered arms, and a key to Heaven's gate"—Ray's exploration of the world's captivating beauty and her options in hopes of avoiding departure—aka the moment of death. Beguiling stuff this is. The catchy melodies allow you to sing along without thinking too much, but should you choose to dive in further they give you plenty to work with. The powerful metaphors of our individual and societal conditions Ray sets forth in "Pushing the Needle Too Far" should certainly not go unnoticed, nor should any of the songs on *Nomads Indians Saints*, including Saliers' "You and Me of the 10,000 Wars," a heart-wrenching examination of the pain and comfort of a relationship. One without the other is all but impossible to achieve and would feel almost hollow without its reflection. That's the way it is with the Indigo Girls—perfect harmony between the elements. *—Kelly McCartney*

Live: Back on the Bus Y'all / Jun. 4, 1991 / Epic ✦✦

Rites of Passage / Feb. 1992 / Epic ✦✦✦✦
Though not what you'd call polished or slick, *Rites of Passage* introduces a sound and structure that are a touch more refined than previous albums by Indigo Girls. Thanks to producer Peter Collins and a slew of amazing guests, including Jackson Browne, David Crosby, the Roches, and Lisa Germano, the added harmonies and diverse instrumentation put on a whole other spin. Heck, they even tossed in strings arranged and conducted by Michael Kamen. But lest you think otherwise, the songs themselves are pure Indigo Girls. One of the threads that runs through tunes by both Amy Ray and Emily Saliers seems to center around what it takes to be a good, kind person in this world, to do the right thing even in the face of danger or at all costs. Both women also express humility and reverence for a power greater than themselves, be it a cause, a god, a love, a fear, or a poet. Vocally, their harmonies have never been cleaner and clearer than on songs like Saliers' "Love Will Come to You" and "Virginia Woolf." And, naturally, Ray's fiery passion rears its head on "Jonas and Ezekial," "Joking," and "Chickenman." The Girls continue to be two of the most literate, engaging, and important songwriters in the folk-rock scene as they tackle issues ranging from Native American awareness to governmental misdoing. No misfires here, just a steady shot echoing forth. *—Kelly McCartney*

Swamp Ophelia / May 10, 1994 / Epic ✦✦✦

1200 Curfews / Oct. 24, 1995 / Epic ✦✦✦✦

● **Retrospective** / Oct. 3, 2000 / Epic/Legacy ✦✦✦✦✦
The Indigo Girls' 1999 album *Come on Now Social* was their first commercial failure after six consecutive gold or platinum albums. The appearance of the duo's first domestic compilation a year later is an unavoidably ominous sign, as their label takes its profits while it can. But that's no reason not to celebrate Amy Ray and Emily Saliers' remarkable run of high-quality recordings dating back to 1987's *Strange Fire*. Most of the songs with which they are most readily identified are included, among them the two chart singles "Closer to Fine" and "Galileo." (The only missing title that earned significant airplay is "Hammer and a Nail.") Feminist author Susan Faludi properly contextualizes the Indigo Girls in her liner notes as a group that created an assertive, independent female response to the Reagan-Bush era. But that aspect of their work was always framed by the music itself, dominated by their interweaving acoustic guitars and voices, and the commitment with which they sang. That combination of substance and fervor characterized the Indigo Girls' work, even when their songwriting flagged occasionally or their sound became repetitive. *Retrospective* captures the highlights of their work from 1987 to 1999, but proceeding chronologically, it also traces the changes that may have hurt the duo commercially by the end. Gradually, their politics became more explicit, which always tends to splinter an audience (though, of course, their views were not secret to their many fervent fans). And in their search for different sounds, they sometimes subverted their basic two-voices, two-acoustic-guitars identity. It remains possible that Indigo Girls will continue to score good, consistent sales, and the two new songs suggest that there's still creative fuel for this group to burn. But if they have crested, *Retrospective* confirms their status as one of the most accomplished recording units of their time. *—William Ruhlmann*

INXS

f. 1977, Sydney, Australia
Group / College Rock, Album Rock, Alternative Dance, Post-Punk, Pop/Rock, New Wave
INXS hailed from the pubs of Australia, which is part of the reason they never comfortably fit in with new wave. Even when the band branched out into synth-pop on its early recordings, they were underpinned by a hard, Stonesy beat and lead singer Michael Hutchence's Jaggeresque strut. Ultimately, these were the very things that made INXS into international superstars in the late '80s. By that time, the group had harnessed their hard rock, dance and new wave influences into a sleek, stylish groove that made their 1987 album *Kick* into a multi-million-selling hit. While that sound was their key to stardom, it also proved to be their undoing; the group became boxed in by their Stonesy pop-funk in the early '90s, when their audience became entranced by harder-edged alternative rock. In spite of declining sales, INXS soldiered on, continuing to tour and record for a dedicated fan base into the late '90s, until Hutchence's tragic 1997 suicide cast the group's future in serious doubt. *—Stephen Thomas Erlewine*

INXS / 1980 / Atco ✦✦

Underneath the Colours / 1981 / Atco ✦✦✦

Shabooh Shoobah / 1982 / Atco ✦✦✦
On *Shabooh Shoobah*, INXS finally hit upon a smooth, stylish fusion of new wave synth-pop and rock & roll that drew equally from the Stones' dirty R&B-inspired rhythms and AC/DC's loud crunch. However, the group hits their stride only on a handful of tracks. The droning synth riff of "Don't Change" masks a hard, funky groove and "The One Thing" is an infectious, catchy pop single, yet most of the album lacks memorable songwriting. *—Stephen Thomas Erlewine*

Dekadance / 1983 / Atco ✦✦

The Swing / 1984 / Atco ✦✦✦
Consolidating the strengths of *Shabooh Shoobah, The Swing* is the first consistently impressive INXS album. With the Nile Rodgers-produced "Original Sin" acting as the centerpiece, *The Swing* retains the new wave pop sense and rock attack of their earlier albums, while adding a stronger emphasis on dance rhythms. At the same time, the group's songwriting had improved, with more than half of the album featuring memorable hooks. —*Stephen Thomas Erlewine*

Listen like Thieves / 1985 / Atlantic ✦✦✦✦
INXS completes its transition into an excellent rock & roll singles band with this album. Unfortunately, the new configuration only works for three songs: "What You Need," "Listen like Thieves," and "Kiss the Dirt (Falling Down the Mountain)." But these three songs are so strong that the album cannot be dismissed completely. The album is worth its price just for "What You Need," a strong Stonesy groove with Michael Hutchence singing more warmly than he ever has. —*Stephen Thomas Erlewine*

Kick / 1987 / Atlantic ✦✦✦✦✦
"What You Need" had taken INXS from college radio into the American Top Five, but there was little indication that the group would follow it with a multi-platinum blockbuster like *Kick*. Where the follow-ups to "What You Need" made barely a ripple on the pop charts, *Kick* spun off four Top Ten singles, including the band's only American number one, "Need You Tonight." *Kick* crystallized all of the band's influences—Stones-y rock & roll, pop, funk, contemporary dance-pop—into a cool, stylish dance/rock hybrid. It was perfectly suited to lead singer Michael Hutchence's feline sexuality, which certainly didn't hurt the band's already inventive videos. But it wasn't just image that provided their breakthrough. For the first (and really only) time, INXS made a consistently solid album that had no weak moments from top to bottom. More than that, really, *Kick* is an impeccably crafted pop *tour de force*, the band succeeding at everything they try. Every track has at least a subtly different feel from what came before it; INXS freely incorporates tense guitar riffs, rock & roll anthems, swing-tinged pop/rock, string-laden balladry, danceable pop-funk, horn-driven '60s soul, '80s R&B, and even a bit of the new wave-ish sound they'd started out with. More to the point, every song is catchy and memorable, branded with indelible hooks. Even without the band's sense of style, the flawless songcraft is intoxicating, and it's what makes *Kick* one of the best mainstream pop albums of the '80s. —*Steve Huey*

X / Sep. 1990 / Atlantic ✦✦✦
The seventh album from Australia's INXS basically sticks to the formula set up on *Kick*, mixing solid remixable dancefloor beats with slightly quirky production tricks, Michael Hutchence's rough-edged, bluesy vocals, and some good solid song hooks. The most immediate numbers are, of course, the two singles, "Suicide Blonde" and "Disappear," but other tracks stand out as potential hit material as well, including the anthemic "The Stairs." The biggest problems with the album are a tendency to play it safe, sticking to the tried and true—echoing a line in the thumping "Who Pays the Price," when Hutchence sings "it's all been felt before"—and the fact that there's very little in the way of subtlety on the entire album. All of the songs are designed for immediate radio contact—they don't really give you a chance to grow into them, they just grab you by the throat and start shaking. "Know the Difference," as an example, threatens to be sneaky but immediately switches to an obvious assault instead. In the finish, the overwhelming lack of subtlety and sense of sameness overcomes the album as a whole. It's not that's it's a bad album. It's just nowhere near as good as it could—and should—have been. —*Steven McDonald*

Live Baby Live / 1991 / Atlantic ✦

Welcome to Wherever You Are / Aug. 4, 1992 / Atlantic ✦✦✦✦
Although INXS needed to experiment badly, their attempt at self-reinvention, *Welcome to Wherever You Are*, didn't even come close to gaining commercial or critical acceptance. From the start of the album, it's clear that INXS is out to confuse the standard perceptions of the band; the first instrument on the album is an Eastern-flavored horn. Special recording effects and exotic rhythms and sounds are abundant on the album. Evidently, the pop audience didn't care about INXS anymore, since nobody bought the album. And that is a shame, since it is one of their strongest. —*Stephen Thomas Erlewine*

Full Moon, Dirty Hearts / Nov. 2, 1993 / Atlantic ✦

● **The Greatest Hits** / 1994 / Atlantic ✦✦✦✦✦
While INXS have made a few consistent albums, singles are the best format for the group's stylish dance-rock. Throughout the '80s and early '90s, the group racked up nine Top 40 hits and seven of those singles hit the Top Ten. *Greatest Hits* collects all of those hits—including "Need You Tonight," "What You Need," "Devil Inside," "New Sensation," "Disappear," "Suicide Blonde," and "Never Tears Us Apart"—adding minor hits like "Original Sin" and "Listen like Thieves," but curiously bypassing the pivotal "Don't Change" and excellent "Bitter Tears," which was a bigger hit than several songs on the record. Nevertheless, *Greatest Hits* lives up to its title and provides a fine introduction to the band. —*Stephen Thomas Erlewine*

Elegantly Wasted / Apr. 15, 1997 / Mercury ✦✦

Iron Butterfly

f. 1966, San Diego, CA, **db.** 1971
Group / Acid Rock, Heavy Metal, Psychedelic, Hard Rock
The heavy, psychedelic acid rock of Iron Butterfly may seem dated to some today, but the group was one of the first hard-rock bands to receive extensive radio airplay, and their best-known song, the 17-minute epic "In A Gadda Da Vida," established that more extended compositions were viable entries in the radio marketplace, paving the way for progressive AOR. *In A Gadda Da Vida* sold four million copies, spent over a year in the Top Ten, and was the first album to receive platinum certification after the RIAA instituted the award. (The title has been translated as "in the garden of Eden" or "in the garden of life.") A shortened version of the title track, which contained extended instrumental passages with loud guitars and classical/Eastern-influenced organ, plus a two-and-a-half-minute drum solo, reached number 30 on the singles charts. The follow-up, *Ball*, showed greater musical variety and went gold, but it also marked the beginning of the band's decline. Iron Butterfly broke up in 1971, reforming in the mid-'70s without success. —*Steve Huey*

● **In-A-Gadda-Da-Vida [Atco]** / 1968 / Atco ✦✦✦✦✦
With its endless, droning minor-key riff and mumbled vocals, "In-a-Gadda-Da-Vida" is arguably the most notorious song of the acid-rock era. According to legend, the group was so stoned when they recorded the track that they could neither pronounce the title "In the Garden of Eden" or end the track, so it rambles on for a full 17 minutes, which to some listeners sounds like eternity. But that's the essence of its appeal—it's the epitome of heavy psychedelic excess, encapsulating the most indulgent tendencies of the era. Iron Butterfly never matched the warped excesses of "In a Gadda Da Vida," either on their debut album of the same name or the rest of their catalog, yet they occasionally made some enjoyable fuzz-guitar-driven psychedelia that works as a period piece. The five tracks that share space with their magnum opus on *In-a-Gadda-Da-Vida* qualify as good artifacts, and the entire record still stands as the group's definitive album, especially since this is the only place the full-length title track is available. —*Stephen Thomas Erlewine*

Light and Heavy: The Best of Iron Butterfly / Jan. 19, 1993 / Rhino ✦✦✦✦
Although the compilation is quite generous, featuring 21 tracks on CD, *Light and Heavy: The Best of Iron Butterfly* isn't all that entertaining, due to Iron Butterfly's difficulties with producing compelling material. All of the group's highlights from 1968-1970 are included, although the career-making, 17-minute "In A Gadda Da Vida" is presented in its three-minute single edit. Since that is the only Iron Butterfly song most listeners know, the lack of the full-length version could potentially sink the album, but the fact of the matter is, "In A Gadda Da Vida" gets quite repetitive over the course of nearly 20 minutes. While the quality of the rest of *Light and Heavy* is spotty—ranging from heavy psychedelic rock to light psychedelic pop—it is a more intriguing listen than *In A Gadda Da Vida*, even if it doesn't have the period-piece charm of the original hit record. —*Stephen Thomas Erlewine*

Iron Maiden

f. 1976, London, England
Group / New Wave of British Heavy Metal, British Metal, Heavy Metal
Known for such powerful hits as "Two Minutes to Midnight" and "The Trooper," Iron Maiden was and is one of the most influential bands of the heavy metal genre. The often-imitated band has existed for over twenty years, pumping out wild rock similar to Judas Priest. Iron Maiden has always been an underground attraction; although failing to ever obtain any real media attention in the U.S. (critics claimed them to be Satanists due to their dark musical themes and their use of grim mascot "Eddie"), they still became well-known throughout the world and have remained consistently popular throughout their career. Iron Maiden was one of the first groups to be classified as "British Metal," and, along with Black Sabbath, Led Zeppelin and a host of other bands, set the style for the rock scene of the '80s. —*Barry Weber*

Iron Maiden / 1980 / Capitol ✦✦✦✦
Iron Maiden's 1980 self-titled album is certainly one of heavy metal's all-time best debuts. Surfacing from the underground along with a host of other New Wave of British Heavy Metal bands (e.g., Def Leppard, Motorhead), Maiden's debut proved to be incredibly influential for future metal bands—it was one of the first to merge heavy metal's power with punk's riffing and attitude, forging a blueprint for such genres as thrash, speed, death and hardcore metal. While the band would branch out musically on future releases, *Iron Maiden* contains some of their most straight-ahead compositions, such as "Prowler," "Sanctuary," "Charlotte the Harlot" and the title track. The group's more-progressive direction is signaled by the 7 1/2 minute epic "Phantom of the Opera," as well as by the breakneck instrumental "Transylvania." Also featured was Maiden's first Top 40 U.K. single, the anthemic "Running Free," plus several calmer compositions like "Remember Tomorrow" and "Strange World," which showed that there was more to this young band than just bashing away. Bassist/leader Steve Harris proved to be the band's main songwriter/wordsmith early on, with lyrics that often proved thought-provoking—a sharp detour from the expected topic of sex, drugs and rock & roll that most metal bands relied on, while vocalist Paul Di'Anno's oft-rough vocals were also a main ingredient. Add to it inspired performances by the other members (including second guitarist Dennis Stratton's sole album appearance with Maiden), and you have a promising, ultimately classic debut. [As with all of Iron Maiden's 1998 re-issues on Raw Power, a multimedia section is featured on the CD, which includes videos, band biographies, tour date history and photo galleries.] —*Greg Prato*

Killers / 1981 / Capitol ✦✦✦✦
Iron Maiden's sophomore effort, 1981's *Killers*, proved to be a more focused and developed affair than its predecessor. Contributing factors included the first appearance by new guitarist Adrian Smith, who helped develop Maiden's signature twin-guitar harmonies with original member Dave Murray, plus respected metal producer Martin "Deep Purple" Birch manning the controls for the first time (his first of ten albums with the band). *Killers* contains a much livelier sound than the debut, while bassist Steve Harris again played a prominent role in the songwriting, penning ten of the album's 11 tracks, while co-writing another. Chock full of classics, *Killers* is one consistent highlight—the homicidal tales of "Murders in the Rue Morgue" and the title track, the crushing instrumental "Genghis Khan," as well as such forgotten first-rate rockers as "Innocent Exile," "Purgatory," "Twilight Zone" and "Drifter." Inexplicably, the album's two best tracks—the shout-along anthem "Wrathchild" and the melodic "Prodigal Son"—were never issued as singles. Another hit album back home in England, *Killers* also gave the quintet their first taste of U.S. chart success, spurred on by their first stateside tour. *Killers* is another bona-fide Maiden classic, but would also prove to be vocalist Paul Di'Anno's last with the group. [As with all of Iron Maiden's 1998 re-issues on Raw Power, a multimedia section is featured on the CD, which includes videos, band biographies, tour date history and photo galleries.] —*Greg Prato*

The Number of the Beast / 1982 / Capitol ✦✦✦✦✦
Even though Iron Maiden was on the brink of worldwide superstardom after their break-

through sophomore effort, *Killers*, vocalist Paul Di'Anno left the band at the conclusion of their 1981 world tour. Many fans wondered if this would signal the end to one of metal's most promising new bands, but their worries were soon erased after hearing the 1982 masterpiece *The Number of the Beast*. Ex-Samson singer Bruce Dickinson replaced Di'Anno, and his strong, operatic vocals proved to be one of Maiden's most distinctive trademarks. And while the music on their first albums contained elements of punk, *Beast* was a 100 percent true heavy metal album, as Maiden's songwriting and sound continued to solidify. Topping the charts in the U.K., and becoming their first U.S. Top 40 record, *Number of the Beast* spawned a pair of all-time classic metal anthems—"Run to the Hills" (which dealt with the plight of the American Indian) and the demonic title track (which caused controversy among religious groups, who wrongfully labeled the band Satan worshippers). But, like its predecessor, not a single weak track is included—"Invaders," "The Prisoner," "22 Acacia Avenue" (a follow-up to 1980's "Charlotte the Harlot"), and "Gangland" were all rocking highlights; the quieter "Children of the Damned" and "Hallowed Be Thy Name" were also featured. *The Number of the Beast* is quite simply one of the best heavy metal albums ever released. *—Greg Prato*

Piece of Mind / 1983 / Capitol ♦♦♦♦

Powerslave / 1984 / Capitol ♦♦♦

Live After Death (The World Slavery Tour) / 1985 / Capitol ♦♦♦♦♦

Somewhere in Time / 1986 / Capitol ♦♦

Seventh Son of a Seventh Son / 1988 / Capitol ♦♦♦♦♦

In 1988, harsh thrash metal and radio-friendly glam rock were the two chief heavy metal genres. Instead of aligning themselves to either camp, Iron Maiden stuck to their guns and issued a concept album, *Seventh Son of a Seventh Son*. Concept albums had spelled disaster for other metal bands in the past, but this proved not to be the case with Maiden, resulting in what many fans consider their last true classic album (and the last with guitarist Adrian Smith, until their late-'90s reunion). Although the songs are all lyrically tied together by the story of a prophet who tries (unsuccessfully) to warn a village of an impending holocaust, they don't have to be listened to in succession to be enjoyed—one of the main reasons the album worked so well. A total of four singles were issued in the U.K. (all Top Tens)—"Can I Play With Madness?," "The Evil That Men Do," "The Clairvoyant," and "Infinite Dreams"—which all prove to be the album's best cuts. But like earlier Maiden albums, this is a complete album—while "Moonchild," "The Prophecy," "Only the Good Die Young," and the epic title track are not as well-known as the singles, they are just as noteworthy. *Seventh Son of a Seventh Son* marked the end of a golden era for one of metal's all-time best bands. [Note: As with all of Iron Maiden's 1998 reissues on Raw Power, a multimedia section is featured on the CD, which includes videos, band biographies, tour date history, and photo galleries.] *—Greg Prato*

No Prayer for the Dying / 1990 / Epic ♦♦

● **The Best of the Beast** / Sep. 24, 1996 / Raw Power ♦♦♦♦♦

Chris Isaak

b. Jun. 26, 1956, Stockton, CA

Vocals, Guitar / College Rock, Pop/Rock, Roots Rock

Chris Isaak clearly loves the reverb-laden rockabilly and country of Sun Studios. In particular, he transfers the sweeping melancholy of Roy Orbison's sweeping, classic melancholy Monument singles ("Crying," "Oh, Pretty Woman," "In Dreams") to the more stripped-down, rootsy sound of Sun. His stylized take on '50s and '60s rock & roll eventually made him into a star in the early '90s, thanks to the hit single "Wicked Game." Isaak released his first album, *Silvertone*, on Warner Brothers in 1985. It was crtically well-received, yet it didn't sell. Two years later, he released *Chris Isaak* which managed to scrape into the Top 200 album charts. After its release, the singer began an acting career with a bit part in Jonathan Demme's 1988 film, *Married to the Mob;* he would later have parts in *Wild at Heart* and *The Silence of the Lambs*. Released in 1989, *Heart Shaped World* didn't manage to break big until late 1990, when "Wicked Game" was featured in David Lynch's *Wild at Heart*. Soon, the single became a Top Ten hit; the album also made it into the Top Ten and sold over a million copies. Both 1993's *San Francisco Days* and 1995's *Forever Blue* mine essentially the same vein as *Heart Shaped World*, yet both went gold and spawned a handful of hits. *—Stephen Thomas Erlewine*

Silvertone / 1985 / Warner Brothers ♦♦♦♦♦

Chris Isaak's debut album, *Silvertone*, named after his three-piece backup group, sets the pattern for his subsequent albums in its meticulously constructed retro sound. Isaak enters a time machine and emerges around 1960, when Roy Orbison is ruling the charts with his melodramatic ballads and Elvis Presley has just returned from the Army. Of course, what passed for a style 25 years before is in Isaak's hands stylization, and when he wails in an Orbison falsetto of romantic desperation, then does a flat, Presley-like recitation in the album-closing "Western Skies," it all seems over the top. But he is just about sincere enough to pull it off, and James Calvin Wilsey is a strong enough guitarist to keep the arrangements on track. So, to the extent that you can resist the "Is this guy kidding?" impression, the music is appealing. *—William Ruhlmann*

Chris Isaak / Dec. 1986 / Warner Brothers ♦♦♦

● **Heart Shaped World** / Jun. 1989 / Reprise ♦♦♦♦♦

When filmmaker David Lynch backed a disquieting scene in *Blue Velvet* with Roy Orbison's "In Dreams," he demonstrated the eerie atmosphere behind its pre-'60s innocence. Orbison disciple Chris Isaak played those qualities to the hilt in his shimmering, spare "Wicked Game," so it was no surprise when Lynch included the ballad in *Wild at Heart*. What was surprising, given the fact that it sounded like nothing else on pop radio in 1990, was that "Wicked Game" became a breakout Top Ten hit, pushing Isaak's accompanying album *Heart Shaped World* to platinum status. Of course, there's more than that one moody masterpiece of a single to recommend *Heart Shaped World*. Isaak faithfully recreates his influences with production that's infinitely cleaner than Sun rock & roll, drawing more on its form than its attitude, but he's particularly suited to the sort of Orbison/Presley-style balladry that brought him a mass audience. His rich, sobbing croon is simply a gorgeous instrument, whether he's in a sonorous baritone or quavering falsetto. And he uses that instrument to tremendous effect here, coming across as a brooding romantic with a broken heart and swoon-inducing style. Of itself, *Heart Shaped World* is a pretty effective mood piece, showcasing Isaak doing a whole lot of what he does best. He does attempt a couple of rockers, but they never really *rock*—much like Orbison, it's clear that ballads are his true forte, and given the spirit Isaak wants to channel, the numbers feel much too tame. But aside from that flaw, the rest of *Heart Shaped World* is a supremely elegant late-night soundtrack, equally suited to steamy romance or solitary heartache. *—Steve Huey*

San Francisco Days / Apr. 13, 1993 / Reprise ♦♦♦♦

Forever Blue / May 23, 1995 / Reprise ♦♦♦

Baja Sessions / Oct. 8, 1996 / Reprise ♦♦♦

Wicked Ways: Anthology / Jun. 30, 1998 / Reprise ♦♦♦♦♦

Speak of the Devil / Sep. 22, 1998 / Reprise ♦♦♦♦

Speak of the Devil explores the same moody terrain as Isaak's previous records, though the songs are fleshed out with more contemporary touches. The leadoff track "Please" is unusually hard-hitting, with its acoustic/electric/soft/crash structure, mellotron and soundbite lyrics. "I'm Not Sleepy," is a roots-rock rave-up (wherein Isaak lyrically quotes Lennon's "Oh Yoko": "In the middle of the night I cry your name"); the title cut is an eerie celebration of love lost and found; "Talkin' 'Bout a Home" is the album's tour de force. Yet, some of the loungey vocal touches in "Flying" and the final instrumental track, "Super Magic 2000," would be right at home on an indie-rock record. And of course there's plenty of that thing Isaak does best: quintessential love's-gone-wrong 'n' let's-make-it-right songs, as on the loping, country-tinged "This Time" and the teary "Walk Slow." *—Denise Sullivan*

The Isley Brothers

f. 1954, Cincinnati, OH

Group / Frat Rock, Quiet Storm, Urban, R&B, Funk, Soul

First formed in the early '50s, the Isley Brothers enjoyed one of the longest, most influential and most diverse careers in the pantheon of popular music. In 1957, the siblings debuted with a string of failed doo-wop singles. Their first effort for RCA, the call-and-response classic "Shout," failed to reach the pop Top 40 on its initial release, although it eventually became a frequently-covered favorite. Still, success eluded the Isleys, and only after they left RCA in 1962 did they again have another hit, this time with their seminal cover of the Topnotes' "Twist and Shout." Like so many of the brothers' early R&B records, "Twist and Shout" earned greater commercial success when later rendered by a white group—in this case, the Beatles; other acts who notched hits by closely following the Isleys' blueprint were the Yardbirds ("Respectable," also covered by the Outsiders) and the Human Beinz ("Nobody But Me"). The Isleys signed to the Motown subsidiary Tamla in 1965, where they joined forces with the famed Holland-Dozier-Holland writing and production team. Their first single, the shimmering "This Old Heart of Mine," was their finest moment yet, and barely missed the pop Top Ten. The record was their only hit on Motown, however. The muscular and funky "It's Your Thing" hit Number Two on the U.S. charts in 1969, and became their most successful record. Spearheaded by Ernie Isley's hard-edged guitar leads, the group began incorporating more and more rock material into its repertoire as the 1970s dawned, and scored hits with covers of Stephen Stills' "Love the One You're With," Eric Burdon & War's "Spill the Wine" and Bob Dylan's "Lay Lady Lay." In 1973, the Isleys scored a massive hit with their rock-funk fusion cover of their own earlier single "Who's That Lady," retitled "That Lady (Part I)"; as the decade wore on, the group again altered its sound to fit into the booming disco market, and while their success on pop radio ran dry, they frequently topped the R&B charts. *—Jason Ankeny*

Twist & Shout! / 1962 / Sundazed ♦♦♦

The Brothers: Isley / 1969 / T Neck ♦♦♦♦

A marvelous reissue by Sony Records, originally released by the Isley Brothers on T-neck Records in 1969. The late '60s and early '70s remain a favorite period in the Isley Brothers evolution. Ronald sung hard, and brothers O'Kelly & Rudolph supplied church-inspired backing whoops to his lead. The tunes had catchy titles and creative, rhyming lyrics. This recording is loaded with that rocking, "It's Your Thing" style. "The Blacker the Berry the Sweeter Juice" isn't about fruit but speaks of the desirability of dark-complexioned women. "I Turned You On" has a grinding, churning rhythm; "sock it to me" was a catch phrase at the time and the Isleys included the popular phrase prominently in the song. "Feels Like the World" is a slow morbid statement about one's condition, while "Was It Good to You" is fast, fluid and asks the universal lover's question. A good period for the trio, Ron sung close to his natural register, which will please those who dislike the softer falsetto voice he fell in love with later. *—Andrew Hamilton*

Get into Something / 1970 / T Neck ♦♦♦

Another T-Neck release to receive reissue through Sony's Legacy division in the late '90s, *Get Into Something* boasts six Top 30 R&B chart hits. The first side serves up horn-inflected party jams, including the rousing title track and "Freedom," the latter of which sums up the record's overall uplifting theme of independence. The record isn't without its missteps—the sexist lyrics of "Take Inventory" are highly questionable: "Don't be so loyal and don't be so true/ 'cause if you are boy, they'll run over you." "Bless" is an obvious re-write of "It's Your Thing"; the Isleys would have been better off leaving that classic alone. A trio of ballads are offered up on the flip, including "I Got to Find Me One." A song of devotion, it pleads for "one girl who believes in me and wants to marry me." Call me crazy, but wouldn't marriage render the taking of inventory an impossibility— Though not revolutionary or trailblazing, *Get Into Something* is every bit an excellent and vibrant funk/soul record. *—Andy Kellman*

Givin' It Back / 1971 / T Neck ♦♦♦

Containing two Stephen Stills selections, as well as CSNY's "Ohio", on the outside this album comes across like a tribute to the roots-rockers who once dubbed themselves the "Frozen Noses". Yet, the Isleys being the Isleys, they do a wonderful job reinterpreting the hit songs of CSNY and others, as their searing version of "Ohio," almost sensualizing violence in its crawling tempo, demonstrates. Also included is a great version of "Spill the Wine," as well as Bill Withers' "Cold Bologna." By no means a top priority for R&B fans, or even fans of the Isley Brothers, *Givin' It Back* is, nevertheless, an interesting album to hear if you can find it. *—Steve Kurutz*

Brother, Brother, Brother / 1972 / T Neck ♦♦♦♦
With 1972's *Brother, Brother, Brother,* younger brothers Ernie and Marvin, along with in-law relative Chris Jasper, began to play major roles in the groups' sound. This also marked their first attempt to Isleyize classics made famous by others. Their rendition of Carole King's "It's Too Late" rivals the original, Ron Isley sings the tender ballad in a softer voice then he used on previous recordings. An update of Jackie Shannon's "Put a Little Love in Your Heart" is an uplifter. They didn't completely alienate fans of their harsher sound, the rocking, humorous "Pop That Thang" and "Lay Away" are fine examples of R&B/Rock. "Pop That Thang" has a sloopy beat and biting lyrics, while "Lay Away" takes off on the popular buying option before the advent of the credit card. The Isleys were big Carole King fans, in addition to "It's Too Late," they perform two other King songs, "Brother, Brother" and "Keep On Walkin'." The latter is coupled with "Sweet Season." Their own "Work To Do" is a stone rocker that has been recorded by many, including the Average White Band, who scored big with the cooker thirty years after its release, it remains one of the Isley Brothers' most requested songs. *—Andrew Hamilton*

The Isleys Live / 1972 / Rhino ♦♦♦♦♦
The 1973 Isley Brothers album *Isleys Live* received the makeover treatment in 1996 by Rhino Records, who remastered the whole disc, and lengthened it with several extra selections not included on the original. The end result is one of the finest funk/soul live albums ever recorded. The first eight tracks come from club gigs in 1971 and '72, while the last three are from a 1969 show at *Yankee Stadium.* The group's biggest and most identifiable hit, "It's Your Thing," and is featured twice, each version extremely inspired. But the most interesting thing about *The Isleys Live* is the inclusion of several cover songs, such as Carole King's "It's Too Late," Neil Young's "Ohio," Bob Dylan's "Lay Lady Lay," and Stephen Stills' "Love the One You're With." The covers aren't straight-ahead rock readings, either; the Isleys inject their own funk 'n' soul into them, making the songs their own. The album is also a showcase for the talents of the woefully underrated guitarist Ernie Isley, who simply wails on a cover of Jimi Hendrix's "Machine Gun," and plays fantastically throughout. *—Greg Prato*

☆ **3 + 3** / 1973 / T Neck ♦♦♦♦♦
Recorded in 1973, *3 + 3* was a major turning point for the Isley Brothers. With this album, the Isleys moved their T-Neck label from Buddah to Epic/CBS (which became Epic/Sony in the early '90s), and it was at Epic that they unveiled their new lineup. Lead singer Ronald Isley and his siblings O'Kelly and Rudolph remained, but the Isleys became a sextet instead of a trio when cousin Chris Jasper and younger brothers Ernie and Marvin were added. This new lineup was called 3 + 3, and the addition of Jasper on keyboards, Ernie on guitar, and Marvin on bass added exciting new elements to the Isleys' sound. One of finest R&B bassists of the 1970s, the ever-so-funky Marvin is in a class with heavyweights like Larry Graham and Louis Johnson—and Ernie is a stunning guitarist who is heavily influenced by Jimi Hendrix but has a distinctive style of his own. The Isleys had always been lovers of rock, but with the addition of Ernie, their sound became even more overtly rock-influenced. Nonetheless, the rock and pop elements didn't alienate R&B audiences, which ate this album up. The single "That Lady" (which is based on an Impressions-like gem they had recorded in 1964) was a major hit, and the Isleys are equally captivating on soul interpretations of Seals & Crofts' "Summer Breeze," James Taylor's "Don't Let Me Be Lonely Tonight," and the Doobie Brothers' "Listen to the Music." With this superb album, the Isley Brothers sounded better than ever—and they gained a lot of new fans without sacrificing the old ones. *—Alex Henderson*

The Heat Is On / 1975 / T Neck ♦♦♦♦♦
1975's *The Heat Is On* was the third album that the Isley Brothers recorded with their 3 + 3 lineup, and by that time, the lineup had really perfected its attractive soul/rock sound. The Isleys were providing great R&B long before keyboardist Chris Jasper, bassist Marvin Isley, and the distinctive guitarist Ernie Isley came on board in 1973; nonetheless, the newcomers added a lot to the group and helped it provide some of its best recordings. Marvin's bass lines are as funky as it gets, and the Jimi Hendrix-influenced Ernie is a killer guitarist; he would have been perfect for Deep Purple, Blue Oyster Cult, or Judas Priest if the Isley Brothers hadn't kept him busy in the 1970s. One of the 3 + 3 gems that no Isleys fans should be without is *The Heat Is On,* which is best known for the sweaty funk classic "Fight the Power" and the sexy quiet storm slow jam "For the Love of You." Lead vocalist Ronald Isley is as convincing on the funk scorchers as he is on caressing ballads like "Make Me Say It Again Girl" and "Sensuality." Meanwhile, "Hope You Feel Better Love" is brilliant because it contrasts those two sides of the *3 + 3* lineup—the verses are sweetly melodic, but the chorus is forceful and explosive. Superb from start to finish, *The Heat Is On* is among the Isleys' most essential albums. *—Alex Henderson*

Live It Up / Jan. 1975 / T Neck ♦♦♦♦
One of the many classic albums the Ohio natives recorded. This set features two up-tempo numbers: the title track "Live It Up" and "Midnight Sky." The former is a soulful funk track paced by a humpin' bass line, robust background vocals, and Ernie Isley's electrifying guitar solos. It checked in at number four on the *Billboard* R&B charts. The latter is a smoother dance number in which Ronald Isley's vocals go from a cool, calm delivery to a resolute clamor. It peaked at number eight. Both have lengthy vamps, ideal for parties. As for the romance, "Hello It's Me" and "Brown Eyed Girl" are two gems. "Hello It's Me" is the classic ballad. Ronald Isley's melodic intro is mesmerizing as he finesses the lyric "Hello," which sets the tone for this beautiful number. His artistic interpretation of the lyric is demonstrated without blemish. This song was formerly recorded by Todd Rundgren who also wrote it. "Brown Eyed Girl" is a mid-tempo number that's seasoned with a folk-like guitar and the rich vocals of Ronald Isley. Neither single was ever a release, but today both are radio regulars. *—Craig Lytle*

Go for Your Guns / 1977 / T Neck ♦♦♦♦

Showdown / 1978 / T Neck ♦♦♦♦

The Complete UA Sessions / Mar. 26, 1991 / EMI America ♦♦♦

Shout: the RCA Sessions / Jul. 1996 / RCA ♦♦♦♦♦

● **It's Your Thing: The Story of the Isley Brothers** / Aug. 24, 1999 / Epic/Legacy ♦♦♦♦♦
Divided into two volumes and spanning three discs, Rhino's 1991 compilation *The Isley Brothers Story* was the definitive retrospective of the ground-breaking R&B outfit, containing all of the hits plus key album tracks. Epic/Legacy's similarly-titled *It's Your Thing: The Story of the Isley Brothers* attempts to best that record by offering a three-disc box set, filled with all the hits, plus an abundance of rarities. As a matter of fact, in order to differentiate this box from the previous retrospective, the compilers leaned a little too heavily on rarities, putting on alternate takes, live cuts, and outtakes with abandon, sequencing them between the hits and album tracks (at times, this even results in songs repeated-back to back, as when "Shout" is followed by a live performance of the same song). All this is worthy material and will certainly be of interest to collectors. On the other hand, they weigh down the collection somewhat for less dedicated listeners. They hardly ruin the set, which is quite useful for anyone that wants a comprehensive hits and highlights collection, but compared to the earlier Rhino set, it isn't as engaging or exciting a listen. Ironically, by trying to outdo *The Isley Brothers Story* as a historical piece, it undercuts the band slightly—on the Rhino set, the Isleys always seem as if they're bursting vitality. That same music still sounds extraordinary here, but the context is somewhat a little too studied to replicate that same sense of dynamism. It's still a worthy set, but *It's Your Thing* nevertheless remains in the shadow of *The Isley Brothers Story. —Stephen Thomas Erlewine*

Shake It Up, Baby: Shout, Twist and Shout / Mar. 21, 2000 / Varese ♦♦♦♦
If you've been collecting Isley Brothers compilations over the years, you might not be enthused at the prospect of getting "Shout," "Twist and Shout," "Nobody but Me," "Respectable," and "Twistin' With Linda" for the second or third time. Indeed, 12 of these 16 cuts show up on Sundazed's reissue of the *Twist & Shout* album. That consideration aside, this is a good compilation of their early years, spanning the late 1950s to the early 1960s, and focusing mostly on the sides they cut for Wand. In fact, it's all from Wand, except for the key early RCA sides "Shout" and "Respectable"; there's nothing from their UA or T-Neck sessions. Overall, this collection represents the Isleys at their most untamed and gospel-R&B-informed, though it's definitely rock & roll, with a pop appeal added by New York production and outside songwriters like Bert Berns. As for the sides you might not have yet on CD if you're an Isley Brothers fan, the two to look out for are their nice cover of "Make It Easy on Yourself" (which wasn't released until it showed up on an Ace import in 1990) and the upbeat, so-so 1964 single "I'm Laughing to Keep From Crying." *—Richie Unterberger*

● **The Ultimate Isley Brothers** / Oct. 17, 2000 / Epic/Legacy ♦♦♦♦♦
The Isley Brothers have had such a long and varied career that trying to sum up their highlights in a best-of package is bound to fall short of the mark. That hasn't, of course, kept people from trying to do so, in both single-disc and multi-disc sets. Every song on this 17-song, single-disc anthology was a hit. Yet it's so chronologically unbalanced, and so debatably chosen, as to be nothing more than a trek though some of their most commercially successful releases, entirely omitting many of their finest songs and severely short-changing their vital (and extensive) pre-1970 output. The pre-"It's Your Thing" era is represented by just two tracks, "Twist and Shout" and "Shout," omitting not just bona fide hits like "This Old Heart of Mine," but great cuts like "Nobody But Me" and "Testify." As a survey of their 1970s and early-1980s hits this does a more reasonable job. But still, few would agree that their cover of Seals & Crofts' "Summer Breeze," for instance, is among their best 17 songs, even if it did make number ten on the R&B listings in 1973. One good thing this collection *does* manage to do is include their cool 1971 cover of "Spill the Wine," which somehow did not make it onto the three-CD 1999 box set, *It's Your Thing: The Story of the Isley Brothers.* Other than "Spill the Wine," every song here appears on that box set, which is a recommended alternative if you can cough up a little more dough. Or better yet, try to find Rhino's two-volume, three-CD *Story* series, which not only has better selection and packaging than the Epic/Legacy collections, but sensibly divides the pre-"It's Your Thing" era and the post-"It's Your Thing" era into separate installments. *—Richie Unterberger*

The Jackson 5

f. 1966, Gary, IN
Group / Pop-Soul, Philly Soul, Motown, Soul
The Jackson 5 was Motown's last great pop group and among the most successful singles acts of the '70s. The group consisted of five brothers—Jackie (b. May 4, 1951), Tito (b. Oct. 15, 1953), Jermaine (b. Dec. 11, 1954), Marlon (b. Mar. 12, 1957), and Michael Jackson (b. Aug. 29, 1958). They grew up in Gary, IN, and were first organized as a group by their father, Joe Jackson, in 1966. In essence, the group was a vocal ensemble centered on Michael, who, though the youngest, was clearly the most talented. The group came to the attention of Motown and was signed in 1969. Their first four singles, "I Want You Back," "ABC," "The Love You Save," and "I'll Be There," all hit number one in 1970; "Mama's Pearl" and "Never Can Say Goodbye" did almost as well in 1971.

In 1972, Motown launched both Michael Jackson and Jermaine Jackson as solo acts, and the group's efforts were gradually less successful in the following years, though "Dance Machine" was a big hit in 1974. In 1975, Jackie, Tito, Marlon, and Michael signed to Epic Records, adding brother Randy (b. Oct. 29, 1961) and became the Jacksons (the name the Jackson 5 was owned by Motown). (Although Jermaine stayed at Motown, he rejoined the group in 1984.) *—William Ruhlmann*

Diana Ross Presents the Jackson 5 / 1969 / Motown ♦♦♦♦♦
This Gary, Indiana family ensemble exploded onto the national scene with immediate and

long-lasting impact in 1970. This album's combination of youthful exuberance and innocence, coupled with Motown production magic, yielded quick results, as "I Want You Back" topped both R&B and pop charts. Michael Jackson, the nine-year-old lead singer, became a national darling. Once they hit the big time, there was controversy over whether Diana Ross actually discovered them, but there was no question that Motown had unveiled another superstar act. *—Ron Wynn*

ABC / Apr. 1970 / Motown ✦✦✦✦✦
A fabulous album, arguably their best on Motown. While the debut album established the group's sound, this one cemented it and also made it clear that Michael was going to be a huge star for a long time. His blend of gentility, soul, and innocence sparkled on the title cut and throughout the album, while the songs, production, arrangement, and musical support were superb. *—Ron Wynn*

Third Album / Aug. 1970 / Motown ✦✦✦
The Jackson 5 solidified the audience they enjoyed with their first two albums by turning in a consistently produced and occasionally exciting third record. It included the fine ballad "I'll Be There" and another hit in "Mama's Pearl"; the group hadn't yet become hardened by Motown manipulation or troubled by internal dissension. Michael Jackson was still widely beloved and seen as the 1970s' Frankie Lymon, and this LP became their third Top Ten album in a row. *—Ron Wynn*

The Jacksons / 1976 / Epic ✦✦✦

Goin' Places / 1977 / Epic ✦✦✦
The Jacksons' move to Epic regenerated their enthusiasm and spirit for several years. The Gamble/Huff team brought them fresh material and new production ideas, as well as better tracks and arrangements than they'd gotten in quite a while on Motown. This album got them R&B and pop hits and kept the family act in the spotlight for a little while longer. *—Ron Wynn*

Destiny / 1978 / Epic ✦✦✦✦✦
The Jacksons are finally turned loose to write and produce themselves, and the result is their best (non-hits collection) ever. The dance tracks still sound fresh; "Blame It on the Boogie," "Shake Your Body (Down to the Ground)"; and the ballads are heartfelt and smooth. This album is a dry run for Michael Jackson's adult solo career. *—William Ruhlmann*

Triumph / 1980 / Epic ✦✦✦✦✦
An excellent follow-up, featuring the hits "Can You Feel It" and "Heartbreak Hotel." *—William Ruhlmann*

Victory / 1984 / Epic ✦✦✦
Victory has the distinctions of being the only Jacksons album to feature all six brothers and the last Jacksons album to feature Michael Jackson. In the four years that had passed since the last Jacksons studio album, *Triumph,* Michael had become the biggest pop star in the world because of 1982's *Thriller.* He had little excuse other than family ties to work with his brothers again, but he agreed to a final album and tour. So, here one has the ludicrous situation of an album in which Marlon Jackson has as prominent a role as Michael Jackson. That's how it sounded to listeners in 1984, anyway, and they weren't fooled—"State of Shock," on which Michael shared vocals with Mick Jagger, was a gold Top Ten hit, and "Torture," which teamed Michael with Jermaine, made the Top 40, while the album went platinum. But the tracks by other group members went virtually ignored. In retrospect, *Victory* is a competent album of slick contemporary R&B, occasionally goosed toward greatness by the appearance of one of pop music's most identifiable voices. Which is the same thing you can say about nearly the entire Jackson 5/Jacksons catalog. *—William Ruhlmann*

Soulsation! / Jun. 27, 1995 / Motown ✦✦✦✦✦
Nineteen years after the release of *Anthology,* Motown finally tops that 33-track, three-LP compilation with this 82-track, four-and-a-half-hour, four-CD/cassette box set. The Jackson 5 were long overdue for box set treatment, and this one is well done. All the hits by the group as well as those by Michael and Jermaine Jackson are here (that is, from 1969-1975, the J5's tenure at Motown), along with a representative sampling of album cuts. The J5's albums were afterthoughts to their singles, but some of these songs are nevertheless interesting, whether the group is covering Sly and the Family Stone or Jackson Browne. An entire disc is given over to previously unreleased or rare tracks from the Motown vaults. Taken together, it may be more than all but the most die-hard fan wants to hear, which may be why Motown rushed out yet another single-disc hits collection, *The Ultimate Collection,* a couple of months later. But if you want the Jackson 5 on Motown, a big chunk of it is here. *—William Ruhlmann*

★ **The Ultimate Collection** / Aug. 15, 1995 / Motown ✦✦✦✦✦
Not quite as extensive as the 33-song *Anthology,* this 21-song single disc does include the group's biggest Motown hits, as well as early solo hits by Michael Jackson and Jermaine Jackson. *Anthology* is still the best way to go for those whose interest isn't deep enough to spring for the *Soulsation!* box. However, if you're on a budget, this does nail down most or all of the key cuts that most listeners want or need. *—Richie Unterberger*

Pre-History: The Lost Steeltown Recordings / Jun. 4, 1996 / Brunswick ✦✦✦

Anthology [2000] / Oct. 24, 2000 / Motown ✦✦✦✦✦
Newly remastered and recompiled for 2000, this version of the Jackson 5's *Anthology* takes the place of the original double-CD set, which was first issued on LP back in 1976. The main difference is that where the first *Anthology* featured some of Michael and Jermaine's earliest solo hits, this one is devoted exclusively to Jackson 5 material, with a little more detail added to the pictures of their early pop-soul years and their later, disco-influenced work. All of the group's charting singles are here, as well as important B-sides and album tracks, including several songs that have never previously appeared on CD. Later hits like "Dancing Machine" and "Hum Along and Dance" are also presented in their full-length LP versions. *—Steve Huey*

Chuck Jackson

b. Jun. 22, 1937, Latta, SC
Vocals / Uptown Soul, Pop-Soul, R&B, Soul
He's relatively forgotten today, and his brand of "uptown" soul is dismissed by the relatively vocal clique of critics who prefer their soul deep and down-home. But Chuck Jackson was a regular visitor to the R&B charts (and an occasional one to the pop listings) in the early '60s with such early pop-soul concoctions as "I Don't Want to Cry," "Any Day Now," and "Tell Him I'm Not Home." His records were very much of a piece with New York pop-rock-soul production, with cheeky brass, sweeping strings, and female backup vocalists. Spotted by Scepter Records while performing with Jackie Wilson's Revue, he started recording for the label in 1961. As was the case with labelmates Dionne Warwick and the Shirelles, Jackson's early-'60s arrangements blended pop, R&B, and New York session professionalism. Like Warwick, Jackson was one of the first singers to successfully record Bacharach-David material. Chuck had some success with some duets with Maxine Brown in the mid-'60s, but he left Wand in 1967 for Motown, at the urging of Smokey Robinson. Jackson was (perhaps understandably) lost in the shuffle during his four years at Motown, and he's barely been heard from since, although he remains a favorite on England's "Northern soul" scene. *—Richie Unterberger*

The Great Recordings: The Best of Chuck Jackson / 1995 / Tomato ✦✦✦✦✦
This 46-song, double-CD compilation of Wand-era recordings is the most extensive Jackson retrospective, though it doesn't include every last worthwhile track. It does contain his most important songs, as well as a few of his duets with Maxine Brown, but the programming leaves something to be desired, inserting some half-baked instrumentals, live cuts, and Elvis Presley covers among the prime stuff. *—Richie Unterberger*

Something You Got / Jun. 1996 / Soul Classics/Ichiban ✦✦✦✦✦
All 20 of the duet tracks that Jackson recorded with Maxine Brown for the Wand label between 1965 and 1967, comprising the entirety of their two albums for the company. It's reasonable pop/soul, but not nearly as memorable as the best male-female soul duets of the era (like the ones by Marvin Gaye and various Motown partners, or by Otis Redding and Carla Thomas). Highlights are the early compositions by the Jo Armstead-Nick Ashford-Valerie Simpson team, including a version of "Let's Go Get Stoned" that was recorded (though not released) before Ray Charles' more famous hit rendition. *—Richie Unterberger*

★ **The Very Best of Chuck Jackson 1961-1967** / Jun. 17, 1997 / Varese ✦✦✦✦✦
Varese's *The Very Best of Chuck Jackson* is a 16-track retrospective of his classic Wand recordings, featuring all of his biggest hits ("I Don't Want to Cry," "I Wake Up Crying," "Any Day Now," "Tell Him I'm Not Home," and the Maxine Brown duet "Something You Got") and several fine, lesser-known singles. Jackson's work was remarkably consistent, and there are many fine songs that didn't make the cut, but *The Very Best of Chuck Jackson* is the best single-disc overview of his greatest music yet assembled. *—Stephen Thomas Erlewine*

Smooth, Smooth Jackson / Jan. 27, 1998 / Sequel ✦✦✦✦
An import compilation of Chuck Jackson's All Platinum sides recorded in the '70s. Many are unaware Jackson recorded on the label that spawned the Moments, the Whatnauts, Sylvia, and Shirley Goodman before transforming into rap city with Sugar Hill Records. He only mustered two tiny hits: "Needing You, Wanting You" and "I've Got the Need," both written by Al Goodman, Harry Ray, and Walter Morris. The former features the Moments crooning delicately behind Jackson's smooth baritone; the latter is a duet with Sylvia Robinson that sounds like Al Goodman singing and not Jackson. The good stuff here includes "Cover up or Get Ready," which is about as risqué as Jackson gets; he tells his lady "I've had a hard day but if you keep lying there like that you're gonna pay." "True Believer" and "Keep Ringing My Bell" are solid, as are Jacksons' updates of his own "I Don't Want to Cry" and "Any Day Now." He transforms chart busters—"And I Am Telling You," "It's Not Unusual," and "After the Loving"—into his personal toys. A worthy collection by an R&B legend. *—Andrew Hamilton*

Janet Jackson

b. May 16, 1966, Gary, IN
Vocals / Club/Dance, Adult Contemporary, Urban, Dance-Pop
Janet Jackson is the ninth and last child in the musically talented Jackson family that includes the Jackson 5, Michael Jackson, and Jermaine Jackson. Janet Jackson performed on stage with her brothers at the age of seven. At ten, she acted in the TV series *Good Times* and was later seen in *Diff'rent Strokes* and *Fame.* She released her first album, *Janet Jackson,* in 1982 and her second, *Dream Street,* in 1984, but neither of these records was notably successful. Then, in 1985, Jackson turned to the production team of Jimmy Jam and Terry Lewis (formerly of the Time) for the album *Control,* which, ironically, emphasized the artist's new maturity and independence, even though most of the songs were co-compositions of the three. *Control* was a massive hit: it topped the charts, selling more than four million copies, and spawned five Top Ten hits, including the #1 "When I Think of You." The follow-up, *Rhythm Nation 1814,* did even better, spawning seven Top Ten hits, among them the number ones "Miss You Much," "Escapade," and "Black Cat." In 1991, Jackson signed a new recording contract with Virgin Records for a reported $32 million.

1993's *janet.* proved to be as successful as her previous two releases, featuring a series of Top Ten singles including "If" and "That's the Way Love Goes." *—William Ruhlmann*

Janet Jackson / 1982 / A&M ✦✦

Dream Street / 1984 / A&M ✦✦

Control / 1986 / A&M ✦✦✦✦✦
Jam and Lewis tailor their contemporary dance-pop to the emerging personality of Jackson, who is attempting to take "Control" of her life on this record. In the course of that attempt, she comes across as an aggressive, independent woman, notably on "What Have You Done for Me Lately." But the album is primarily a production showcase; it may be tailored to Jackson's persona, but the real artists are Jam and Lewis. *—William Ruhlmann*

Rhythm Nation 1814 / 1989 / A&M ✦✦✦✦✦
After shocking the R&B world with 1986's *Control*—a gutsy, risk-taking triumph that was a radical departure from her first two albums—Michael and Jermaine Jackson's younger sister reached an even higher artistic plateau with the conceptual *Rhythm Nation 1814*. Once again, she enlists the help of Time graduates Jimmy Jam & Terry Lewis (one of the more soulful production/songwriting teams of 1980s and '90s R&B) with wildly successful results. In 1989, protest songs were common in rap, but rare in R&B—Jackson, following rap's lead, dares to address social and political topics on "The Knowledge," the disturbing "State of the World" and the poignant ballad "Living in a World" (which decries the reality of children being exposed to violence). Jackson's voice is wafer-thin, and she doesn't have much of a range—but she definitely has lots of soul and spirit, and uses it to maximum advantage on those gems as well as non-political pieces ranging from the Prince-influenced funk/pop of "Miss You Much" and "Alright" to the caressing, silky ballads "Someday Is Tonight," "Alone" and "Come Back to Me" to the pop/rock smoker "Black Cat." For those purchasing their first Janet Jackson release, *Rhythm Nation* would be an even wiser investment than *Control*—and that's saying a lot. *—Alex Henderson*

Janet / May 18, 1993 / Virgin ✦✦✦
After *Control* and *Rhythm Nation 1814*, Janet Jackson had quite a lot to live up to. Anyone who expected Jackson to top *Rhythm Nation*—her crowning achievement and an incredibly tough act to follow—was being unrealistic. But with *janet.*, she delivered a respectable offering that, although not as strong as either *Control* or *Nation*, has many strong points. As before, Jackson is joined by the prolific Jimmy Jam/Terry Lewis team, and their input is valuable on everything from the angry "This Time" and the hypnotic "That's the Way Love Goes" to the '60s-flavored "What'll I Do" and the sociopolitical "The New Agenda" (which features Public Enemy leader Chuck D). But perhaps the CD's most exciting track is "Funky Big Band," which samples jazz legend Lionel Hampton's 1938 big band classic "I'm In the Mood for Swing" with thrilling results. There are a few throwaways (including the lightweight ballad "Again"), but despite its shortcomings, *janet.* is a welcome addition to her catalog. *—Alex Henderson*

★ **Design of a Decade: 1986-1996** / Oct. 10, 1995 / A&M ✦✦✦✦✦
Design of a Decade: 1986/1996 is a misleading title. The bulk of Janet Jackson's greatest hits collection concentrates on *Control* and *Rhythm Nation 1814*, simply by contractual necessity. That is far from a fatal flaw. The hits from those two albums were state-of-the-art dance-pop productions at the time of their release, filled with bottomless beats and memorable, catchy hooks. None of the songs have lost any of their impact, from the funk of "Miss You Much" and "What Have You Done for Me Lately" to the ballads "Let's Wait Awhile" and "Come Back to Me." In addition to all 13 Top 40 hits from *Control* and *Rhythm Nation*—all but one went into the Top Five—*Design of a Decade* includes the biggest and best hit from *janet.*, the sultry "That's the Way Love Goes," and two new songs, "Runaway" and "Twenty Foreplay." It's a credit to Janet Jackson that the two new numbers feel like genuine hits, not tacked-on filler, and help make the album a compulsively listenable greatest hits collection. *—Stephen Thomas Erlewine*

The Velvet Rope / Oct. 7, 1997 / Virgin ✦✦✦
Where *janet.*, Ms. Jackson's third blockbuster album, implied sexuality with its teasing cover and seductive grooves, its sequel, *The Velvet Rope*, is sexually explicit, offering tales of bondage, body piercing and bisexuality. Not that you'd necessarily know that from listening to *The Velvet Rope*, since the album sags with endless interludes, murmured vocals and subdued urban grooves. Working with her mainstays Jimmy Jam and Terry Lewis, Jackson essentially reworks the hushed atmosphere of *janet.*, neglecting to put a new sonic spin on the material—for an album that wants to push the limits, it sounds surprisingly tame. Similarly, Jackson's attempts to broaden her sexual horizons frequently sound forced, whether it's the references to piercing or her recasting of Rod Stewart's "Tonight's the Night" as a lesbian anthem. Furthermore, the album is simply too long, which means the best moments sink into the murk. And that's unfortunate, because there are good moments on *The Velvet Rope*, but at its running time of 70+ minutes and 22 tracks, it's hard to work up the patience to find them. *—Stephen Thomas Erlewine*

Joe Jackson

b. Aug. 11, 1955, Burton-upon-Trent, England
Vocals, Keyboards, Piano / College Rock, Pop/Rock, New Wave, Singer/Songwriter
Of the three angry young men that emerged in the British new wave movement of the early '80s, Joe Jackson was perhaps the most idiosyncratic. Not content with being a pop songwriter, Jackson went to considerable lengths to prove himself as a composer—often, he even seemed to have contempt for pop music itself. Appearing a few years after Elvis Costello and Graham Parker, Joe Jackson was doomed to always live their shadow. Jackson was considerably more ambitious than Parker, rivaling Costello in his stylistic detours. After establishing himself as a gifted songwriter with a pair of edgy new wave pop records, he quickly set out to prove his eclecticism, recording album-length tributes to reggae, jump blues, traditional pop and jazz. While such diversity earned him critical praise and a cult following, it didn't result in widespread acclaim until 1982's *Night and Day*, which launched the jazzy hits "Steppin' Out" and "Always Something Breaking Us In Two." Once he had a taste of success, Jackson didn't become more accessible—he became weirder, crafting a number of self-consciously difficult records intended to push the boundaries of pop. Following his 1987 classical album *Will Power*, Jackson's audience began to decline, and by the early '90s, his cult was a fraction of its size a decade earlier. Despite his shrinking audience, Jackson was even less compromising in the '90s than he was in the '80s, eventually abandoning pop altogether. *—Stephen Thomas Erlewine*

★ **Look Sharp!** / Apr. 1979 / A&M ✦✦✦✦✦
A brilliant, accomplished debut, *Look Sharp!* established Joe Jackson as part of that camp of angry, intelligent young new wavers (i.e., Elvis Costello, Graham Parker) who approached pop music with the sardonic attitude and tense, aggressive energy of punk. Not as indebted to pub-rock as Parker and Costello, and much more lyrically straightforward than the latter, Jackson delivers a set of bristling, insanely catchy pop songs that seethe with energy and frustration. Several deal with the lack of thoughtful reflection in everyday life ("Sunday Papers," "Got the Time"), but many more concern the injuries and follies of romance. In the caustic yet charming witticisms of songs like the hit "Is She Really Going Out With Him?," "Happy Loving Couples," "Fools In Love," and "Pretty Girls," Jackson presents himself on the one hand as a man of integrity seeking genuine depth in love (and elsewhere), but leavens his stance with a wry, self-effacing humor, revealing his own vulnerability to loneliness and to purely physical attraction. *Look Sharp!* is the sound of a young man searching for substance in a superficial world—and it also happens to rock like hell. *—Steve Huey*

I'm the Man / Oct. 1979 / A&M ✦✦✦✦✦
Nearly a rewrite of *Look Sharp*, and capturing all of its brilliance, *I'm the Man* is pure power-pop—hook filled, concise, and fun. Includes the wonderful "It's Different for Girls", a marginal hit in both the U.S. and U.K. *—Chris Woodstra*

Beat Crazy / 1980 / A&M ✦✦✦✦✦
Credited to the Joe Jackson Band, *Beat Crazy* completes Jackson's power-pop period. Jackson begins to stretch a bit stylistically, flirting with reggae and more experimental styles while in the confines of the three-minute form he would later dismiss. Every bit as charming as the first two. *—Chris Woodstra*

Jumpin' Jive / 1981 / A&M ✦✦✦✦✦
A delightful trip back to '40s and '50s jump blues and big-band swing. With faithful covers of Louis Jordan and Cab Calloway, Jackson appears to be having fun, while helping a new generation discover these classics. *—Chris Woodstra*

Night and Day / 1982 / A&M ✦✦✦✦✦
Since Jackson has already demonstrated his broad musical tastes by turning from rock to "jumpin' jive" on his last album, that he was able to incorporate Latin, dance, and sophisticated ballad styles into his music wasn't so surprising. But that he could do it all so well was delightful. Includes "Steppin' Out" and "Breaking Us in Two." *—William Ruhlmann*

Body & Soul / 1984 / A&M ✦✦✦
Continuing in his move away from pop music that began with *Night and Day*, Jackson shows his love of '50s jazz with detail best represented by the cover photo (nearly identical to the Sonny Rollins album of the same name). Features his last U.S. hit, "You Can't Get What You Want" and the beautiful "Be My Number Two." *—Chris Woodstra*

Big World / 1986 / A&M ✦✦✦
A brilliant collection of songs, running over an hour, finds Jackson as biting as ever as he surveys the world, but also tenderly reflective on "Home Town." *—William Ruhlmann*

Will Power / 1987 / A&M ✦✦

Live . . . 1980-1986 / 1988 / A&M ✦✦✦
A double-disc live collection, *Live . . . 1980-1986* manages to effectively trace the development of Joe Jackson's diverse career. Drawing from four different periods in the songwriter's career—with each period featuring a new backing band—*Live* captures Jackson with his original new wave trio, a 1983 quintet that was dominated by keyboards, a horn-driven group from 1984, and a 1986 quartet that specialized in straightahead rock & roll. The resulting album highlights his musical diversity, not his songwriting, which means the record is more intriguing as a historical document than as casual listening *—Stephen Thomas Erlewine*

Blaze of Glory / 1989 / A&M ✦✦✦
A loose concept album about a second-generation rock & roller struggling to come to terms with maturity, *Blaze of Glory* holds together fairly well, as the story takes a backseat to individual songs. While that does mean that the concept is never fleshed out, the approach results in a handful of brisk, stylish pop songs—including "Nineteen Forever" and "Down to London"—that are more compelling than the story itself. *—Stephen Thomas Erlewine*

Laughter & Lust / Apr. 30, 1991 / Virgin ✦✦✦

Greatest Hits / May 7, 1996 / A&M ✦✦✦✦✦

This Is It! The A&M Years / Feb. 1997 / A&M ✦✦✦✦✦
This Is It! The A&M Years is a double-disc, 37-track collection covering Joe Jackson's commercial and creative heyday. Over the course of two discs, *This Is It!* runs through all of his biggest hits—"Is She Really Going Out With Him?," "It's Different for Girls," "Steppin' Out," "Breaking Us in Two," "You Can't Get What Want (Till You Know What You Want)"—plus a number of significant album tracks and lesser-known singles, making it a comprehensive retrospective of Jackson's pop-oriented work. While it's unfortunate that the compilation stops just short of his last pop album, 1991's *Laughter & Lust*, because it was released on Virgin Records, the great majority of his best work is here, making it a perfect choice for fans who want something more—and better assembled—than *Greatest Hits*, and those who don't want to dig as deep as the actual albums. *—Stephen Thomas Erlewine*

Heaven & Hell / Sep. 2, 1997 / Sony Classical ✦✦

Symphony 1 / Oct. 19, 1999 / Sony Classical ✦✦✦

Summer In The City: Live In New York / May 6, 2000 / Sony Classical ✦✦✦✦✦

Night and Day II / Oct. 24, 2000 / Sony Classical ✦✦✦

Michael Jackson

b. Aug. 29, 1958, Gary, IN
Vocals / New Jack Swing, Club/Dance, Pop/Rock, Motown, Urban, Funk, Dance-Pop, Soul
As part of the Jackson 5, a group made up of his brothers, Michael Jackson was among the most popular singing stars of the '70s. On his own, he was the biggest pop star of the '80s. Jackson was always the visual and vocal focus of the Jackson 5, who broke through to national success on the Motown label in 1970, when he was 11, with the first of four straight number one hits, "I Want You Back." Jackson was also promoted as a solo artist, and he scored

his first hit, "Got to Be There," in 1971. The Jackson 5's fortunes declined somewhat after the early '70s, and the group moved to Epic at mid-decade, with Michael temporarily abandoning his solo career and subsuming his group leadership to other members of what was now called the Jacksons. The group gradually built back its popularity by writing its own material. Jackson returned to solo work in 1979 with *Off the Wall*, a mature combination of driving dance songs ("Don't Stop 'til You Get Enough") and feelingly sung ballads ("She's Out of My Life") that outsold any previous group or solo effort, and spawned four Top Ten hits. Jackson again recorded and toured with the Jacksons, but his next album, *Thriller* (1982), became a musical phenomenon. It was the biggest-selling album of all time, moving 20 million copies in the U.S. alone and including seven Top Ten hits. His follow-up album, *Bad* (1987), accompanied by a solo world tour, sold six million copies domestically. Only six of its seven singles hit the Top Ten, but five in a row hit number one. In late 1991, Jackson returned with *Dangerous*, which, by mid-1992, had sold four million copies and spawned the hits "Black and White," "Remember the Time," "In the Closet," and "Jam." *— William Ruhlmann*

☆ **Off the Wall** / 1979 / Epic ✦✦✦✦✦
This album is viewed by many as Michael Jackson's best. That notion can easily be supported by the album's excellent songwriting and polished production. Jackson wasted no time seizing the top spot on the *Billboard* R&B and pop charts with the dazzling number "Don't Stop 'Til You Get Enough." The suspenseful intro is enticing enough, but Jackson's lyrical cry is the magnet that locks the attention of all ears. From there, the force of the rhythm takes over. The rhythm is solidified by strings, guitar licks, and Jackson's impassioned delivery. "Rock With You," the second single, has a sensuous flow where Jackson injects a mesmerizing tone that is as captivating as the song's melody; it was a number one song on both charts as well.

With its gothic intro, the title track settles into a blazing dance number enhanced by Jackson's chilling background vocals sung in unison. While Jackson wrote the initial release, former Heatwave member Rod Temperton penned the second and third. "Off the Wall" sealed the Top Five on the *Billboard* R&B charts and was number ten on the pop. The ballad "She's out of My Life" was the fourth and final release. With a mournful melody, Jackson's intense delivery conveys the pain and hurt of the lyric. It peaked at a mere 43 on the R&B charts while closing out the Top Ten on the pop. There were no other releases, and that's unfortunate because there is much here to savor. For instance, "I Can't Help It," co-written by Stevie Wonder, has aerial flow. Jackson swerves and curves his way through this splendid number. Needless to say, this is great album and would be a great addition to every collection. [*Off the Wall* is also available in a limited-edition import release.] *— Craig Lytle*

The Best of Michael Jackson / 1981 / Motown ✦✦✦
Michael Jackson's greatest hits, 1971-1975, emphasize his waiflike charm and youth (he was 13 when the first of these songs appeared) in ballads such as "Got to Be There," "Ben" (even if it is a love song to a rat), and "I Wanna Be Where You Are." The upbeat cover of "Rockin' Robin" is equally appealing. *— William Ruhlmann*

★ **Thriller** / 1982 / Epic ✦✦✦✦✦
What impresses after a decade is Jackson's range of musical expression, one that touches the schmaltzy pop of Paul McCartney (his duet partner on "The Girl Is Mine") on one side and the hard rock of Van Halen (whose guitarist, Eddie Van Halen, is heard on "Beat It") on the other, with plenty of mainstream rock/pop and dance music in between. It's no accident that the record found a home in so many record collections—there's good music here for everyone. And of course, by summing up the state of pop music, Jackson also redefined it—this was a high-water mark for pop music never equaled since, even in his subsequent music. *— William Ruhlmann*

Anthology / 1986 / Motown ✦✦✦✦✦
When a teenage Michael Jackson was known primarily for his membership in the Jackson 5, rock critics tended to dismiss him as bubblegum. But even at his most waifish, the pre-*Thriller*, pre-Quincy Jones Jackson could be soulful. Spanning 1971-1975, this two-CD set shows how inviting some of Jackson's early solo recordings were. Major hits like "Ben" (his oddly poignant ode to a rat), "I Wanna Be Where You Are," and "Got to Be There" are included, along with noteworthy album tracks like Bill Withers' "Ain't No Sunshine" and the standard "All the Things You Are." Anyone who doubted that he was a serious R&B/pop singer should have examined Jackson's moving version of the Philly soul classic "People Make the World Go Round" (which is heard with different lyrics than on the Stylistics' much better-known version). The package also contains a handful of Jackson 5 hits, including "Never Can Say Goodbye" and the infectious "Dancing Machine." To be sure, Jackson's solo albums of the early to mid-'70s had their share of filler, something this package isn't devoid of either. But thankfully, *Anthology* has a lot more pluses than minuses. For an introductory overview of Jackson's early accomplishments on his own, *Anthology* is the most logical choice. *— Alex Henderson*

Bad / 1987 / Epic ✦✦✦✦✦
A partially successful attempt to remake *Thriller*. Interestingly, Jackson did not turn to a softer, more broadly commercial approach but instead upped the dance-rock ante. Songs such as "Dirty Diana" and "Smooth Criminal" found him striding forward in terms of rhythm and beat. And with seven hit singles out of ten tracks (five at #1), this, like *Thriller*, is in effect a Michael Jackson greatest-hits record, covering 1987-1989. *— William Ruhlmann*

Dangerous / 1992 / Epic ✦✦✦
Wisely, Jackson altered his creative process here, jettisoning producer Quincy Jones in favor of Teddy Riley and bringing in several songwriting collaborators. The result is an updated dance-floor success (the drums are way up in the mix), though the songwriting sometimes seem schematic. When Jackson is left more or less to himself, he is less R&B-oriented, notably on the pop ballad "Heal the World" and the guitar-driven pop/rock song "Black or White" (a Stones riff, though taken at a tempo the Stones never attempted). Rather than resting on his laurels, Jackson continues to work hard to maintain and further the quality of his work. *— William Ruhlmann*

History: Past, Present and Future, Book 1 / Jun. 20, 1995 / Epic ✦✦✦
Michael Jackson's double-disc *HIStory: Past, Present, and Future, Book I* is a monumental achievement of ego. Titled *HIStory Begins*, the first disc is a collection of his post-Motown hits, featuring some of the greatest music in pop history including "Billie Jean," "Don't Stop Til Ya Get Enough," "Beat It," and "Rock with You." It leaves some hits out—including the number ones "Say Say Say" and "Dirty Diana"—yet it's filled with enough prime material to be thoroughly intoxicating. That can't be said for the second disc, called *HIStory Continues* and consisting entirely of new material—which also happen to be the first songs he released since being accused of child molestation. *HIStory Continues* is easily the most personal album Jackson has recorded. References to the scandal permeate almost every song, creating a thick atmosphere of paranoia. If Jackson's music had been the equal of *Thriller* or *Bad*, the nervous, vindicative lyrics wouldn't have been quite as overbearing. However, *HIStory Continues* reiterates musical ideas Jackson has been exploring since *Bad*. Jackson certainly tries to stay contemporary, yet he has a tendency to smooth out all of his rougher musical edges with show-biz schmaltz. Occasionally, Jackson produces some well-crafted pop that ranks with his best material: R. Kelly's "You Are Not Alone" is seductive, "Scream" improves on the slamming beats of his earlier single "Jam," and "Stranger in Moscow" is one of his most haunting ballads. Nevertheless, *HIStory Continues* stands as his weakest album since the mid-'70s. *— Stephen Thomas Erlewine*

Blood on the Dance Floor: History in the Mix / May 20, 1997 / Epic ✦✦

Wanda Jackson

b. Oct. 20, 1937, Maud, OK
Vocals / Country Gospel, Rockabilly, Traditional Country
Wanda Jackson was only halfway through high school when, in 1954, country singer Hank Thompson heard her on an Oklahoma City radio show and asked her to record with his band, the Brazos Valley Boys. By the end of the decade, Jackson had become one of America's first major female country and rockabilly singers. She had wanted to sign with Capitol, Thompson's label, but was turned down so she signed with Decca instead. Her mother made and helped design Wanda's stage outfits. "I was the first one to put some glamour in the country music—fringe dresses, high heels, long earrings," Jackson says of these outfits. When she first toured in 1955 and 1956, she was placed on a bill with none other than Elvis Presley, who encouraged her to sing rockabilly. In 1956, Jackson finally signed with Capitol, a relationship that lasted until the early '70s. Her recording career bounced back and forth between country and rockabilly; she did this by often putting one song in each style on either side of a single. Jackson cut the rockabilly hit "Fujiyama Mama" in 1958, which became a major success in Japan. Her version of "Let's Have a Party," which Elvis had cut earlier, was a U.S. Top 40 pop hit for her in 1960, after which she began calling her band the Party Timers. A year later, she was back in the country Top Ten with "Right or Wrong" and "In the Middle of a Heartache." In 1965, she topped the German charts with "Santa Domingo," sung in Dutch. In 1966, she hit the U.S. Top 20 with "The Box It Came In" and "Tears Will Be the Chaser for the Wine." Jackson's popularity continued through the end of the decade. *— Kurt Wolff*

There's a Party Goin' on / 1959 / Capitol ✦✦✦
While this doesn't have most of Wanda's best rockabilly sides (check the compilation *Rockin' With Wanda* for those), it's a pretty solid and energetic set. About half of it is taken up with retreads of the "Let's Have a Party" theme and covers of early rock hits like "Tweedlee Dee" and "Kansas City" which are, admittedly, well done. "Fallin'" and, especially, "Hard Headed Woman" are really fine cuts that rank among her best rock & roll performances. The real surprise of this album is the lightning-speed rockabilly riffing by Roy Clark; his playing on "Hard Headed Woman" is downright savage, almost enough to redeem all those horrible *Hee-Haw* programs. *— Richie Unterberger*

Rockin' with Wanda / 1960 / Capitol ✦✦✦✦✦
Absolutely the best collection of her rockabilly recordings, including her key 1956-60 singles—"Fujiyama Mama," "Mean Mean Man," "Hot Dog! That Made Him Mad," and others. A leading candidate for the best female rock & roll album of the 1950s. The British reissue adds four worthwhile bonus cuts, including the essential "Let's Have A Party." *— Richie Unterberger*

Rockin' in the Country: The Best of Wanda Jackson / Jun. 1990 / Rhino ✦✦✦✦✦
Perhaps the greatest of the rockabilly women, Wanda Jackson later turned to pure country. Rhino's *Best of Wanda Jackson—Rockin' in the Country* presents the best of both eras here on this 18-track collection. *— Jeff Tamarkin*

Right or Wrong / 1993 / Bear Family ✦✦✦✦
This four-CD set is like a photo album of Wanda Jackson growing up, from innocent adolescent to rockabilly star and the dominant female country singer of the early 1960s. Her complete recordings from the first Decca session in March 1954 until her Capitol session of November 2, 1962 constitute the part of her career that rock & roll and rockabilly fans most care about. Disc One covers those early years, the 15 songs she cut for Decca Records through 1955, when she was still treading a fine line in country music, seemingly trying to be the next Kitty Wells at least part of the time. The singing is glorious and the playing solid, although Jackson, working in this idiom, was like a racing thoroughbred being asked to canter around a track. Then comes "Baby Loves Him," a Jackson original that redefined her for the next few years as a rockabilly star. Disc Two features Jackson treading that fine line between straight country and rock & roll, interspersed with slower, more traditional numbers. As late as 1961, Disc Three reveals, Jackson was still courting the rock & roll audience, although the main thrust of her career was moving back toward pure country, with forays into pop and country-pop. The country material on Disc Four had a serious edge to it by now, and the rock & roll was almost superfluous. By late 1962 and early 1963, however, her sides show the kind of opulent overproduction, complete with choruses and string sections, that would help give country-pop a bad name; her voice is as good as ever, but the material is a stretch after the hot rockin' sides. The booklet is more thorough than most from Bear Family. *— Bruce Eder*

Vintage Collections Series / Jan. 23, 1996 / Capitol ✦✦✦✦✦
This 20-track anthology of Jackson's early work is roughly equal to Rhino's *Rockin' in the*

Country in value. *Rockin' in the Country* offers a considerably wider range, chronologically speaking. *Vintage Collections*, on the other hand, focuses on 1956-61 recordings, affording greater depth for what is acknowledged as her most fertile period. Although it's issued on Capitol Nashville, it mixes rockabilly and straight country, including her biggest hits in each style ("Let's Have a Party," "Fujiyama Mama," "Right or Wrong") and some worthy obscurities. Those with an appetite for both rock & roll and country will find this the best compilation of her work; those who want just the rock & roll should look for the harder-to-find *Rockin' with Wanda* instead. *—Richie Unterberger*

● **Queen of Rockabilly** / Oct. 17, 2000 / Ace ✦✦✦✦✦

The Jam

f. 1975, Woking, Surrey, England, **db.** 1982

Group / British Punk, Mod Revival, New Wave, Punk

The Jam were the most popular band to emerge from the initial wave of British punk rock in 1977; along with The Sex Pistols, the Clash, and the Buzzcocks, the Jam had the most impact on pop music. While they could barely get noticed in America, the trio became genuine superstars in Britain, with an impressive string of Top Ten singles in the late '70s and early '80s. The Jam could never have a hit in America because they were thoroughly and defiantly British. Under the direction of guitarist/vocalist/songwriter Paul Weller, the trio spearheaded a revival of mid-'60s mod groups, in the style of the Who and the Small Faces. Like the mod bands, the group dressed stylishly, worshipped American R&B, and played it loud and rough. By the time of the group's third album, Weller's songwriting had grown substantially, as he was beginning to write social commentaries and pop songs in the vein of the Kinks. Both his political songs and his romantic songs were steeped in British culture, filled with references and slang in the lyrics, as well as musical allusions. Furthermore, as the Jam grew more popular and musically accessible, Weller became more insistent and stubborn about his beliefs, supporting leftist causes and adhering to the pop aesthetics of '60s British rock without ever succumbing to hippie values. Paradoxically, that meant even when their music became more pop than punk, they never abandoned the punk values—if anything, Weller stuck to the strident independent ethics of 1977 more than any other punk band just by simply refusing to change. *—Stephen Thomas Erlewine*

In the City / May 20, 1977 / Polydor ✦✦✦✦✦

On their debut, the Jam offered a good balance between the forward-looking, "destroy everything" aggression of punk with a certain reverence for '60s beat and R&B. In an era that preached attitude over musicianship, the Jam bettered the competition with good pop sense, strong melodies and plenty of hooks that compromised none of punk's ideals or energy, plus youth culture themes and an abrasive, ferocious attack. Even though the band would improve exponentially over the next couple of years, *In the City* is a remarkable debut and stands as one of the landmark punk albums. *—Chris Woodstra*

This Is the Modern World / Nov. 18, 1977 / Polydor ✦✦✦

As is so often the case for overnight successes, the Jam rush-recorded their sophomore effort during a hurried schedule to capitalize on the debut. This, combined with Weller's various personal distractions and temporary lack of interest, led to less than satisfying results, especially in comparison to *In the City*. *This Is the Modern World* can be faulted for borrowed Who licks, pale rewrites of the debut, somewhat cliched sloganeering, and unfinished ideas, but there were still some moments of inspiration, especially in more introspective Weller songs like "Life From a Window" and "I Need You (For Someone)"—both songs feature personal sentiments that the debut was clearly missing. *This Is the Modern World* is a flawed album by Jam standards, but it would certainly have received praise had it been released by another band. [The U.S. edition added the single "All Around the World" with a different track order.] *—Chris Woodstra*

☆ **All Mod Cons** / Nov. 3, 1978 / Polydor ✦✦✦✦✦

The band regrouped and re-focused for *All Mod Cons*, an album that marked a great leap in songwriting maturity and sense of purpose. For the first time, Weller built, rather than fell back, upon his influences, carving a distinct voice all his own; he employed a story-style narrative with invented characters and vivid British imagery *a la* Ray Davies to make incisive social commentary—all in a musically irresistible package. The youthful perspective and impassioned delivery on *All Mod Cons* first earned Weller the "voice of a generation" tag, and it certainly captures a moment in time, but really, the feelings and sentiments expressed on the album just as easily speak to any future generation of young people. Terms like "classic" are often bandied about, but in the case of *All Mod Cons*, it is certainly deserved. *—Chris Woodstra*

☆ **Setting Sons** / Nov. 16, 1979 / Polydor ✦✦✦✦✦

Setting Sons was originally planned as a concept album about three childhood friends who, upon meeting after some time apart, discover the different directions in which they've grown apart. Only about half of the songs ended up following the concept due to a rushed recording schedule, but where they do, Weller vividly depicts British life, male relationships, and coming to terms with entry into adulthood. Weller's observations of society are more pointed and pessimistic than ever, but at the same time, he's employed stronger melodies with a slicker production and comparatively fuller arrangements, even using heavy orchestration for a reworked version of Foxton's "Smithers-Jones." *Setting Sons* often reaches brilliance and stands among their best albums, but the inclusion of a number of throwaways and knock-offs (especially the out-of-place cover of "Heat Wave" which closes the album) mars an otherwise perfect album. *—Chris Woodstra*

☆ **Sound Affects** / Nov. 28, 1980 / Polydor ✦✦✦✦✦

Unhappy with the slicker approach of *Setting Sons*, the Jam got back to basics, using the direct, economic playing of *All Mod Cons* and "Going Underground," the simply brilliant single which preceded *Sound Affects* by a few months. Thematically, though, Weller explored a more indirect path, leaving behind (for the most part) the story-song narratives in favor of more abstract dealings in spirituality and perception—the approach stemming from his recent readings of Blake and Shelley (who was quoted on the sleeve), but more specifically Geoffrey Ash, whose *Camelot and the Vision of Albion* made a strong impression. Musically, Weller drew upon *Revolver*-era Beatles as a primary source (the bass line on "Start," which comes directly from "Taxman," being the most obvious occurrence), incorporating the occasional odd sound and echoed vocal, which implied psychedelia without succumbing to its excesses. From beginning to end, the songs are pure, clever, infectious pop—probably their catchiest—with "That's Entertainment and the should-have-been-a-single "Man in the Corner Shop" standing out. *—Chris Woodstra*

The Gift / Mar. 12, 1982 / Polydor ✦✦✦

As good mods, the Jam always had a healthy respect for R&B and soul—even the first album featured the revved-up Northern soul of "Non-Stop Dancing." With *The Gift*, however, Weller seems to have become completely absorbed in it, and more specifically, in Stax-style soul with more than a hint of psychedelia *a la* "Psychedelic Shack." An uneven album marked by overindulgences like the instrumental "Circus" and unnecessarily long songs, *The Gift* still has no shortage of terrific songs, like the simply sublime "Ghost," "Town Called Malice" (the hit), and the funk workout of "Precious." Weller can obviously do "soulful"—his voice has never sounded better—but unfortunately, *The Gift*, with its excesses and marginal tracks, doesn't show his talents in the proper light. Points for ambition, but ultimately, this is their least consistent effort since *This Is the Modern World*. *—Chris Woodstra*

Dig the New Breed / Dec. 10, 1982 / Polydor ✦✦✦

★ **Snap!** / Oct. 14, 1983 / Polydor ✦✦✦✦✦

Snap! collects all of the Jam's singles, from "In the City" to "Beat Surrender," including several B-sides ("'A' Bomb in Wardour Street," "Dreams of Children") and a handful of rarities, like a demo of "That's Entertainment" and the rock version of "Smithers-Jones." For its compact disc release, several songs were trimmed, but *Snap!* remains a brilliant summation of why the Jam were one of the most important and beloved British bands of their era. The latter-day collection *Greatest Hits* covers much the same ground as *Snap!*, but the earlier compilation remains preferable because of sequencing and its inclusion of essential items like "'A' Bomb in Wardour Street" and "Dreams of Children." *—Stephen Thomas Erlewine*

Greatest Hits / Jul. 1, 1991 / Polydor ✦✦✦✦✦

Greatest Hits covers nearly the same ground as *Snap!*, with all the tracks but "Just Who Is the Five O'Clock Hero" included on the previous compilation. Granted, "That's Entertainment" is presented in the album version and "Funeral Pyre" in its original mix, but the album isn't quite as strong as *Snap!*. Nevertheless, it has all of their hit singles, making it a thoroughly entertaining record, as well as an effective introduction to the group. *—Stephen Thomas Erlewine*

Extras: A Collection of Rarities / Apr. 6, 1992 / Polygram ✦✦✦✦✦

Extras offers 26 B-sides, rarities and unreleased tracks that, while far from complete (the wonderful "See Saw" is absent, for instance), is a fan's dream come true. This is a fans' album, to be sure, but for fans, the never-before-heard demos (like "Burning Sky" and "Thick as Thieves") have a certain spine-tingling effect, and the covers (like "So Sad About Us," "And Your Bird Can Sing," and "Disguises") are undeniably fun—often more so than the covers they chose to include on the proper albums. *Extras* is not a good introduction, to be sure, but for the converted, this is essential. *—Chris Woodstra*

Live Jam / Oct. 25, 1993 / Polydor ✦✦

☆ **Direction Reaction Creation** / May 26, 1997 / Polydor ✦✦✦✦✦

Direction Reaction Creation is the ultimate Jam package, offering 117 tracks over five discs—essentially the band's complete studio recordings. With a strict adherence to chronological order, the box presents each single followed by its B-side(s) (six of which appear on CD for the first time, including the brilliant "See Saw"), followed by the proper album tracks—oddly, though, the album versions of the singles are chosen in most places. Unfortunately, this approach sometimes disrupts the flow of the albums, especially in the case of *All Mod Cons*, which loses three tracks to the treatment, and *Setting Sons*, which loses "Eton Rifles" to a separate disc. This is a small point for purists to debate—the difference is really unnoticeable in light of the truly great music found on the discs. In addition to the regular studio tracks, Disc Five offers over an hour of studio demos—22 previously unreleased tracks of considerably different takes of better-known material, a few never-before-heard Weller and Foxton originals, and some interesting covers like "Rain," "Dead End Street," and "Every Little Bit Hurts." A lavish 88-page booklet accompanies the set with great liner notes, an extensive band chronology and discography, and the band's complete gig list, along with plenty of rare photos and memorabilia. The Jam, simply put, were one the finest bands in rock & roll history, and *Direction Reaction Creation* offers the proof, showing both their remarkably rapid growth and their incredible consistency. *—Chris Woodstra*

James Gang

f. 1966, Cleveland, OH, **db.** 1976

Group / Album Rock, Arena Rock, Hard Rock, Blues-Rock

For a brief period in the early '70s, the James Gang was one of the top hard-rock acts in America, thanks to the songwriting and inventive instrumental work of singer/guitarist Joe Walsh. The band was founded in Cleveland by drummer Jim Fox; its first lineup was fleshed out by bassist Tom Kriss and guitarist Glen Schwartz. The group toured the Midwest and built a name for itself, but Schwartz left the band in 1969. Walsh stepped in admirably, and word of the new guitar phenom spread quickly; the James Gang recorded its debut, *Yer Album*, later that year. The follow-up, *The James Gang Rides Again*, proved to be arguably the group's strongest and contained their best-known song, "Funk 49" (they never had a hit single). The album went gold, as did their next two, and hit the Top 20. James Gang fan Pete Townshend invited the group to open for the Who on a European tour in 1971; shortly thereafter, Walsh left the group, feeling constrained by the power-trio formula. He first formed Barnstorm; later, he recorded several solo albums and joined the Eagles for *Hotel California* and *The Long Run*. Dominic Troiano served as guitarist until 1973, when he joined the Guess Who; Tommy Bolin played on the *Bang* and *Miami* albums, but when he left to join Deep Purple, it essentially spelled the end of the James Gang, whose sales declined steadily following Walsh's departure. The James Gang finally broke up for good in 1976. *—Steve Huey*

Yer' Album / 1969 / One Way ♦♦♦♦
The James Gang's debut LP, *Yer' Album*, was very much a first record and very much a record of its time. The heavy rock scene of the period was given to extensive jamming, and four tracks ran more than six minutes each. The group had written some material, but they were still something of a cover band, and the disc included their extended workouts on Buffalo Springfield's "Bluebird" and the Yardbirds' "Lost Woman," the latter a nine-minute version complete with lengthy guitar, bass, and drum solos. But in addition to the blues rock there were also touches of pop and progressive rock, mostly from Walsh who displayed a nascent sense of melody, not to mention some of the taste for being a cutup that he would display in his solo career. Walsh's "Take a Look Around" must have made an impression on Pete Townshend during the period before the album's release when the James Gang was opening for the Who since Townshend borrowed it for the music he was writing for the abortive *Lifehouse* follow-up to *Tommy*. If "Wrapcity (i.e., Rhapsody) in English," a minute-long piano and strings interlude, seems incongruous in retrospect, recall that this was an eclectic era. But the otherwise promising "Fred," which followed, broke down into a pedestrian jazz routine, suggesting that the band was trying to cram too many influences onto one record and sometimes into one song. Nevertheless, they were talented improvisers, as the open-ended album closer, Jerry Ragavoy and Mort Shuman's "Stop," made clear. After ten minutes, Szymczyk faded the track out, but Walsh was still going strong. *Yer' Album* contained much to suggest that the James Gang, in particular its guitarist, had a great future, even if it was more an album of performances than compositions. *—William Ruhlmann*

Rides Again / 1970 / MCA ♦♦♦♦♦
With their second album *The James Gang Rides Again*, the James Gang came into their own. Under the direction of guitarist Joe Walsh, the group—now featuring bassist Dale Peters—began incorporating keyboards into their hard rock, which helped open up their musical horizons. For much of the first side of *Rides Again*, the group tears through a bunch of boogie numbers, most notably the heavy groove of "Funk *49*." On the second side, the James Gang departs from their trademark sound, adding keyboard flourishes and elements of country-rock to their hard rock. Walsh's songwriting had improved, giving the band solid support for their stylistic experiments. What ties the two sides of the record together is the strength of the band's musicianship, which burns brightly and powerfully on the hardest rockers, as well as on the sensitive ballads. *—Stephen Thomas Erlewine*

Live in Concert / 1971 / One Way ♦♦♦

Thirds / 1971 / MCA ♦♦♦♦
The James Gang Rides Again sett the stage for the group's third album to propel them to Top Ten, headliner status, but that didn't happen. The band was on its last legs, rent by dissension as Walsh became the focus of attention, and the appropriately titled *Thirds* reflected the conflict. Among the nine original songs, four were contributed by Walsh, two each by bass player Dale Peters and drummer Jim Fox, and one was a group composition. But it was Walsh's songs that stood out. His "Walk Away," was the first single, and it climbed into the Top 40 in at least one national chart, the group's only 45 to do that well. "Midnight Man," the follow-up single, was another Walsh tune, and it also made the charts. The Fox and Peters compositions were a step down in quality, particularly Peters'. But the problem wasn't just material, it was also musical approach. *James Gang Rides Again* had emphasized the band's hard rock sound, which was its strong suit. But they had never given up the idea of themselves as an eclectic unit, and *Thirds* was their most diverse effort yet, with pedal steel guitar, horn and string charts, and backup vocals by the Sweet Inspirations turning up on one track or another. At a time when Walsh was being hailed as a guitar hero to rank with the best rock had to offer, he was not only submerging himself in a group with inferiors, but also not playing much of the kind of lead guitar his supporters were raving about. As a result, though *Thirds* quickly earned a respectable chart position and eventually went gold, it was not the commercial breakthrough that might have been expected. *—William Ruhlmann*

Passin' Thru / 1972 / One Way ♦♦

Straight Shooter / 1972 / One Way ♦♦

Bang / 1973 / Atco ♦♦♦

Miami / 1974 / Atco ♦♦♦
Like *Bang* before it, *Miami* was a success solely because of the presence of guitarist Tommy Bolin. Bolin's energetic, muscular playing reinvigorated the James Gang, sparking the rest of the band into giving lively performances. Again, there was a noticeable lack of memorable songs, but *Miami* is worthwhile for guitar aficionados. *—Stephen Thomas Erlewine*

● **Greatest Hits** / May 2, 2000 / MCA ♦♦♦♦♦
Designed to supersede the previous MCA compilation *15 Greatest Hits*, this *Greatest Hits* features 16 James Gang tracks remastered for CD, plus detailed notes and commentary. The last two songs—"You're Gonna Need Me," and "The Ashes, the Rain, and I"—were recorded live, and there are also two tracks from the film *Zachariah* ("Laguna Salada" and "Country Fever") making their first appearances on a James Gang compilation. Another first timer is the complete version of "The Bomber," an extended medley featuring an oft-edited bolero section that appears in full here. Thanks to the better sound and packaging, this one gets the nod over *15 Greatest Hits*—unless you're looking for specific songs on that one that don't appear here, or unless you're a more devoted fan, in which case you might prefer the double-disc Repertoire compilation *The Best of the James Gang*. *—Steve Huey*

James

f. 1982
Group / College Rock, Madchester, Adult Alternative Pop/Rock, Alternative Pop/Rock
As one of the first groups to be dubbed "the next Smiths," James became an institution on the British alternative music scene of the '80s and '90s with their pleasant folk-pop. Early in their career, James was blessed by praise from their idol Morrissey, which turned out to be both a blessing and a curse. The group was pegged as second-rate Smiths, yet continued to tour and record, eventually gaining a sizable following. In the late '80s, the group, like many of their British peers, became involved in the acid-house-inspired "baggy" scene and recorded the baggy-inspired "Sit Down," which became their breakthrough hit. Shortly after "Sit Down," James became more experimental, culminating in a collaboration with Brian Eno that resulted in their biggest American album, *Laid*, in 1993. James took four years to follow *Laid*, by which time their audience had returned to a cult following. *—Stephen Thomas Erlewine*

Stutter / 1986 / Blanco y Negro/Sire ♦♦♦

Strip-Mine / 1988 / Blanco y Negro/Sire ♦♦♦
Boasting a more detailed production than its predecessor, *Strip-Mine* accentuates James' more anthemic tendencies, but it's generally a stronger album than the first, featuring such charming folk-pop gems as "Stripmining." *—Stephen Thomas Erlewine*

One Man Clapping / 1989 / One Man/Rough Trade ♦♦♦

Gold Mother / Aug. 1990 / Fontana ♦♦♦♦
James completely revamped their lineup for *Gold Mother*, adding a violinist, a keyboardist and a trumpeter to the band and attempting to write grand, ambitious arena-rock that recalled U2 and the Waterboys. Although a few of the tracks captured the sprawling, epic splendor that James wished to achieve, they have difficulty writing convincing material, and they aren't nearly as interesting as they were when they concentrated on jangling folk-pop. [*Gold Mother* was reissued in 1991 after a re-recorded version of "Sit Down" became a hit. "Sit Down" and "Lose Control" replaced "Crescendo" and "Hang On," but the baggy beats of the new songs sat uncomfortably with the sprawling, anthemic rock of *Gold Mother*.] *—Stephen Thomas Erlewine*

Seven / Mar. 17, 1992 / Fontana/Mercury ♦♦♦♦♦
Instead of following the Madchester leanings of "Sit Down," James carried on with the anthemic rock of *Gold Mother* on its follow-up, *Seven*. While *Seven* may indulge in the same arena-rock excesses as its predecessor, the group's writing and playing is controlled and textured, making a captivating exercise in grand, sprawling rock & roll. *—Stephen Thomas Erlewine*

Laid / Oct. 5, 1993 / Mercury ♦♦♦♦♦
Teaming up with producer Brian Eno had a considerable effect on James. Instead of pursuing the grandiose inclinations of *Gold Mother* and *Seven*, the group reduced their scale, choosing to explore texture in a dark, atmospheric and intimate setting. As a result, *Laid* is by far the most subdued album the band has ever made, and it benefits as a result—rarely have Tim Booth's vocal theatrics and poetics sounded so affecting. But what really makes *Laid* resonate is James' subtle, textured playing, which gives the record a quiet, graceful power. *—Stephen Thomas Erlewine*

Wah Wah / Oct. 1994 / Mercury ♦♦♦

Whiplash / Feb. 25, 1997 / Mercury ♦♦♦

● **The Best of James** / Jun. 30, 1998 / Fontana/Mercury ♦♦♦♦
An imperfect collection of a frustratingly uneven band, *The Best of James* is a tantalizing missed opportunity. James was always full of ambition and big ideas, from their early days as Smiths-like folk-rockers through their flirtation with baggy to their experimental dabbling with Brian Eno. Throughout it all, they hit as often as they missed, landing a handful of British hits and creating several more worthy album tracks. As album artists, however, they only occasionally were successful, as on 1993's terrific *Laid*. That's the reason why they are the perfect candidates for an 18-track retrospective like *The Best of*. Too bad the compilers botched this disc. It's not that the collection overlooks their first two albums for Sire—those had their moments, but they're not especially missed—it's that they gather most of the best Fontana material (plus "Hymn from a Village," one of their early singles for Factory, and two new tracks), then throw it all in the air, not caring where each song lands. Since James changed drastically from album to album, this really is a block-headed move; it's difficult to listen to these songs out of chronological order and the sequencing makes their achievements seem less impressive. That said, *The Best of* is nevertheless recommended as a starting point because no other James album accurately conveys their eclectism or their musical strengths; it's also nice to get all of these songs on one disc. Just be prepared to dig a little deeper—or at least learn how to program the CD player—if the collection sparks your interest. *—Stephen Thomas Erlewine*

Millionaires / Oct. 13, 1999 / Mercury ♦♦♦♦♦

Rick James (James Johnson)

b. Feb. 1, 1952, Buffalo, NY
Vocals, Keyboards, Guitar, Bass / Quiet Storm, Urban, Funk
In the late '70s, when the fortunes of Motown Records seemed to be flagging, Rick James came along and rescued the company, providing funky hits that updated the label's style and saw it through into the mid-'80s. James had a journeyman's career playing bass in various groups before signing to Motown in 1978 as an artist, songwriter, and producer. His first two singles, "You and I" and "Mary Jane," did well on both the R&B and pop charts. James broke big with "Give It to Me Baby" and "Super Freak," two hits from his second album *Street Songs*. He turned his production attention to resuscitating the career of the Temptations, and also worked with Teena Marie and the Mary Jane Girls during the early '80s. He recorded a few more hits for Motown, including "Dance wit' Me" and "Sweet and Sexy Thing," before signing to Reprise. He charted briefly during the late '80s and gained attention in 1990 when MC Hammer scored a massive hit with a track containing significant portions of "Super Freak." Still, James has been plagued by drug and legal problems that have found him more frequently in court and in jail than in the recording studio. *—William Ruhlmann*

Bustin' Out: The Very Best of Rick James / May 17, 1994 / Motown ♦♦♦♦♦
In the late 1970s and early '80s, Rick James did more than anyone to challenge George Clin-

ton's place on the funk throne. Eventually, his music would turn into a very tired cliche, but at his creative peak, James was among the most exciting and vital artists funk had to offer. Summarizing his Motown output from 1978-1986 and offering four new tracks from 1994 as well, this two-CD anthology reminds us just how great he once was, but provides evidence of his artistic decline as well. Though some of the songs are mediocre, most are outstanding. Even the most casual funk fans owe it to themselves to savor such rowdy classics as "Super Freak," "You and I," "Love Gun," "Give It To Me, Baby" and "Ghetto Life." James was equally superb when it came to soul ballads—and anyone who thinks otherwise should give a serious listen to "Fire and Desire" (a stunning duet with Teena Marie), "Dream Maker" and "Ebony Eyes" (which features Smokey Robinson). Sadly, "Cold Blooded" and "17" illustrate how formulaic James' funk often sounded by the mid-1980s. Meanwhile, some of the new material (including an enjoyable remake of Norman Connors' "You Are My Starship") indicated that he had the potential make a comeback with the right guidance. Boasting many more pluses than minuses, this set is the best place for novices to start. *—Alex Henderson*

● **Ultimate Collection** / Mar. 25, 1997 / Motown ♦♦♦♦♦
This excellent overview of Rick James' Motown hits features seven Top Ten hits, including the seminal "Super Freak" as well as "Cold Blooded," "Give It to Me Baby," "You and I," "Mary Jane," "Dance Wit' Me" and "Bustin' Out." *—Jason Ankeny*

Tommy James & The Shondells

f. 1960, Dayton, OH, **db.** 1970
Group / Brill Building Pop, Bubblegum, Pop/Rock, Soft Rock, Pop, Rock & Roll
Tommy James & the Shondells—the very mention of their name evokes images of dances and the fun that rock & roll represented, before it redefined itself on more serious terms. And between 1966 and 1969, the group enjoyed 14 Top 40 hits, most of which remain among the most eminently listenable examples of pop/rock. Because they weren't completely self-contained (they wrote some, but not all, of their hits) and weren't as rooted in rock & roll, it took decades for writers and pop historians to look with favor upon them. In 1960, with his family living in Niles, MI, 13-year-old Tommy James and a group of friends got together to play dances and parties. Their second release on the local Snap label, "Hanky Panky," became enormously popular in the area in 1963. The original Shondells broke up over the next two years, but suddenly, "Hanky Panky" broke out in Pittsburgh after a promoter found it in a used record bin. James recruited a new group of Shondells in the Raconteurs, a local Pittsburgh quintet, and the nationally re-released single topped the charts in 1966. Tommy James & the Shondells spent the next three and a half years trying to keep up with their own success. They were lucky enough to be making pop-oriented rock & roll while most of the rock world was trying to make more serious records. The group did grab a piece of the prevailing style in late 1968 with the number one hit "Crimson and Clover," which utilized some creative sound distortion techniques. The end came simply from their desire to take a break in 1970—James was getting involved in other projects, including his own solo career, which saw some limited success. Though long regarded as a bubblegum act, the Shondells' music revealed its staying power during the '80s in fresh recordings by Joan Jett, Billy Idol, and Tiffany. *—Bruce Eder*

Tighter, Tighter / Apr. 4, 2000 / Varese ♦♦♦♦♦
Varese Sarabande's *Tighter, Tighter* chronicles Tommy James' work for Fantasy Records in the mid- to late '70s, plus a couple of MCA singles from the mid-'70s. During this time James had *no* hits whatsoever and he was even trying to cash in on the success *Alive & Kicking* had with "Tighter, Tighter" in 1971. James may have been shooting for big success, but also was taking advantage of the artistic freedom Fantasy allowed him. As he says in Kenneth Pobo's liner notes, he "loved it out at Fantasy (because) they gave me run of the place." Consequently, the music compiled on *Tighter, Tighter* has to be seen as some of James' most personal work and the results are pretty magnificent. Yes, everything here is firmly within the '70s soft-rock tradition—whether its ballads or surprisingly numerous covers of Gary Glitter glam-rock (let's face it, anything more than one qualifies as "numerous")—but it's all exceptionally well-crafted and some cuts, like "Bobby Don't Leave Me Alone" the seven-minute tribute to James' friend Bobby Bloom, have a real emotional undercurrent. The rest of the compilation, which culls from the albums *In Touch* and *Midnight Rider,* may not have that pull, but it's still fantastically well-crafted soft-rock. The genre was rarely as well-made and subtle as the 16 tracks on this compilation, both in terms of songcraft and production and, at least to these ears, it lends itself to repeat plays better than James' '60s work, which is, of course, just a matter of taste. But, if you're a big fan of the 1980 hit "Three Times in Love" or the softer side of James, this is the album you need to own. *—Stephen Thomas Erlewine*

● **Anthology** / 1990 / Rhino ♦♦♦♦♦
James and his band had a remarkable string of hits from the mid-'60s to the early '70s, largely because of an uncanny ability to keep current with fast-changing pop trends, from their first garage-band hit, "Hanky Panky," to their psychedelicized songs like "Crimson and Clover." Even more remarkable, the music holds up entertainingly today, and this well-annotated, 27-track compilation contains all the hits and more. *—William Ruhlmann*

Crimson & Clover/Cellophane Symphony / Aug. 27, 1991 / Rhino ♦♦♦

The Very Best of Tommy James / Apr. 20, 1993 / Rhino ♦♦♦♦
A condensed version of Rhino's two Tommy James compilations combines solo tracks like "Draggin' the Line" with hits from the Shondells like "I Think We're Alone Now." Given its budget price, the selection is rather skimpy and leaves out several tracks. Most listeners will want the more comprehensive Shondells and solo James collections, but there is nothing wrong with the music here. *—AMG*

Hanky Panky/Mony Mony / Jan. 9, 1996 / Sequel ♦♦♦♦

Jan & Dean

f. 1958, **db.** Apr. 1966
Group / Folk-Rock, Doo Wop, Surf, Pop, Rock & Roll
Besides the Beach Boys, no other vocal group captured the sound of California surf music with as much success—both commercial and artistic—as Jan & Dean. When the Beach Boys began their climb to superstardom, Jan & Dean followed suit with a series of surf and hot rod hits that featured falsetto harmonies, chugging guitars, and Jan Berry's clean production. Brian Wilson himself sang backup vocals on their biggest hit (which he co-wrote with Jan), "Surf City," in 1963. While they lacked the Beach Boys' depth and capacity for artistic growth, Jan & Dean's hits from 1963 and 1964—which also included "The Little Old Lady (From Pasadena)," "Drag City," "Honolulu Lulu," and the mini-soap opera "Dead Man's Curve"—are in the same class as the Beach Boys' early work in their infectious, energetic invocation of good times and California sunshine, adding an irresistibly reckless humor to the genre. The duo's success, already on the wane a bit, was tragically cut short by Jan Berry's near-fatal auto accident in April 1966, which had been eerily foreshadowed by the lyrics of "Dead Man's Curve." *—Richie Unterberger*

● **Surf City: The Best of Jan & Dean** / 1990 / EMI America ♦♦♦♦♦
Remembered mostly for their surfing hits, Jan & Dean had a bit more range than they're generally given credit for. Their roots were in doo wop, and after scoring surf and hot rod hits, they also cut some decent straight pop/rock songs and zany singles that verged on pop satire. *Surf City* includes just about all the material you'd want from the duo. The 22 songs include the big hits "Surf City," "Dead Man's Curve," and "The Little Old Lady (From Pasadena)," of course, but also feature nifty smaller successes like "Honolulu Lulu," "The New Girl in School," and "Ride the Wild Surf." The pair was second only to the Beach Boys in blending high, soaring harmonies with driving vocal surf and hot rod sounds. Of course, they weren't nearly as talented as Brian Wilson's group, but even their minor material has an irrepressible sense of fun and sparking L.A. pop/rock production and melodies. Other highlights include their rearrangement of the old standard "Linda" and the 1965 Top 40 hit "I Found a Girl," written by P.F. Sloan and Steve Barri. Sloan-Barri also penned their infectious theme for the classic rock film *The T.A.M.I. Show,* "(Here They Come) From All Over the World," which deserved to be a bigger hit than it was. The only major omissions of this well-packaged set are their early, heavily doo wop-influenced hits "Jennie Lee," "Baby Talk," and "Heart and Soul," which weren't recorded for EMI. *—Richie Unterberger*

● **All the Hits: From Surf City to Drag City** / Nov. 12, 1996 / EMI ♦♦♦♦♦
Two discs, each running over 70 minutes, of the duo's most celebrated performances from the late '50s through the mid-'60s. If you're stacking this up against the *Legendary Masters Series* compilation, the advantage of getting this one is that it adds their doo wop-influenced, pre-Liberty hits ("Baby Talk," "Heart and Soul," "A Sunday Kind of Love"), as well as the pre-Jan & Dean smash by Jan & Arnie ("Jennie Lee"). It also has a few good tunes not on the previous anthology, like "My Mighty G.T.O." and the original version of "Bucket 'T'" (covered by the Who in 1966). And it's stuffed with alternate takes of some of their most famous tunes, which could be viewed as either a boon or an irrelevance. Some of their flop singles were really cringe worthy: "The Universal Coward" is a stupid parody of "Universal Soldier," and "A Beginning From an End," a melodrama in which the singer's wife dies in childbirth (!) against a typically sunny Top 40 arrangement, is downright tasteless fare. Collectors will appreciate these bonuses mightily, but less intense fans, if they're not determined to have "Baby Talk" and "Jennie Lee," will probably be better off with the more focused and consistent *Legendary Master Series* disc. *—Richie Unterberger*

Jane's Addiction

f. 1984, Los Angeles, CA, **db.** 1991
Group / College Rock, Alternative Metal, Alternative Pop/Rock
Jane's Addiction were one of the most hotly pursued rock bands when they gained notice in Los Angeles in the mid-'80s, with record companies at their feet. Flamboyant frontman Perry Farrell, formerly of the band Psi Com, has an undeniable charisma and an interest in provocative art (he designed the band's album covers) and Jane's Addiction plays a hybrid of rock music—metal with strains of punk, folk, jazz, or you-name-it. Warner Brothers won the bidding war and released *Nothing Shocking* in 1988. The band's abrasive sound and aggressive attitude (typified by the nude sculpture on the cover) led to some resistance, but Jane's Addiction began to break through to an audience: the album spent 35 weeks in the charts. *Ritual de lo Habitual* followed in 1990 and was the band's commercial breakthrough, reaching the Top 20 and going gold. Farrell designed the travelling rock festival Lollapalooza as a farewell tour for Jane's Addiction—after the tour was completed at the end of the summer of 1991, the group split. *—William Ruhlmann*

Jane's Addiction / 1987 / Triple X ♦♦♦
When this live date was recorded at Hollywood's famous Sunset Strip club the Roxy in 1987, Jane's Addiction hadn't yet become the darlings of alternative-rock culture. The L.A. band's unorthodox fusion of Led Zeppelin-influenced hard rock, dark Velvet Underground-ish imagery and stream-of-consciousness art rock wasn't as focused or confident as it would be on the commanding *Ritual de Lo Habitual.* But even so, the band showed considerable potential. As erratic and self-indulgent as this set gets, many of the songs are quite memorable. Lead singer/composer Perry Farrell was always fascinated with the dark side of the human psyche, and that fascination serves him well on "Pigs in Zen," the twisted "Whores" and the alternative-rock favorite "Jane Says." And things get enjoyably trashy on covers of the Velvet Underground's "Rock N' Roll" and the Rolling Stones' "Sympathy for the Devil." But while this CD will interest completists, more casual listeners should stick to *Ritual de Lo Habitual.* *—Alex Henderson*

Nothing's Shocking / 1988 / Warner Brothers ♦♦♦♦♦
Although Jane's Addiction's 1987 self-titled debut was an intriguing release (few alternative bands at the time had the courage to mix modern rock, prog rock, and heavy metal together), it paled in comparison to their now classic major-label release one year later, *Nothing's Shocking.* Produced by Dave Jerden and J.A.'s vocalist Perry Farrell, the album was more focused and packed more of a sonic wallop than it's predecessor; the fiery performances often create an amazing sense that it could all fall apart at any second, creating a fantastic musical tension. Such tracks as "Up the Beach," "Ocean Size," and one of alt-rock's greatest anthems, "Mountain Song," contain the spaciousness created by the band's two biggest influ-

ences, Led Zeppelin and the Cure. Elsewhere, "Ted, Just Admit It" (about serial killer Ted Bundy) and the haunting yet gorgeous "Summertime Rolls" stretched to epic proportions, making great use of changing moods and dynamics (something most alt-rock bands of the time were oblivious to). An incredibly consistent and challenging album, other highlights included the rockers "Had a Dad" and "Pigs in Zen," the horn-driven "Idiots Rule," the jazz instrumental "Thank You Boys," and the up-tempo "Standing in the Shower... Thinking." Like most great bands, it was not a single member whose contribution was greater: Perry Farrell's unique voice and lyrics, Dave Navarro's guitar riffs and wailing leads, Eric Avery's sturdy bass lines, and one of rock's greatest and most powerful drummers, Stephen Perkins. *Nothing's Shocking* is a must-have for lovers of cutting-edge, influential, and timeless hard rock. *—Greg Prato*

★ **Ritual de lo Habitual** / Aug. 1990 / Warner Brothers ✦✦✦✦✦
1990's *Ritual de lo Habitual* served as Jane's Addiction's breakthrough to the mainstream (going gold and reaching the Top 20), and remains one of rock's all-time sprawling masterpieces. While it's predecessor, 1988's *Nothing's Shocking*, served as a fine introduction to the group, *Ritual de lo Habitual* proved to be even more daring; few (if any) alt-rock bands have composed a pair of epics that totaled nearly 20 minutes, let alone put them back to back for full dramatic effect. While the cheerful ditty "Been Caught Stealing" is the album's best known track, the opening "Stop!" is one of the band's best hard rock numbers, propelled by guitarist Dave Navarro's repetitive trashy funk riff, while "Ain't No Right" remains explosive in its defiant and vicious nature. Jane's Addiction always had a knack for penning beautiful ballads with a ghostly edge, again proven by the album closer, "Classic Girl." But it's the aforementioned epics that are the album's cornerstone: "Three Days" and "Then She Did...." Although Perry Farrell has never truly admitted what the two songs are about lyrically, it appears to be about an autobiographical romantic tryst between three lovers, as each composition twists and turns musically through every imaginable mood. And while the tracks "No One's Leaving," "Obvious," and "Of Course" may not be as renowned as other selections, they prove integral in the makeup of the album. Surprisingly, the band decided to call it a day just as *Ritual de lo Habitual* hit big, headlining the inaugural *Lollapalooza* tour (the brainchild of Farrell) in the summer of 1991 as their final road jaunt. Years later, it remains one of alt-rock's finest moments. *—Greg Prato*

Live and Rare / 1991 / Warner Brothers ✦✦

Kettle Whistle / Nov. 4, 1997 / Warner Brothers ✦✦✦
According to alterna-rock legend, Jane's Addiction was the band responsible for laying the groundwork of the alternative rock explosion in the early '90s, but like most legends, that's half true and half lie. Jane's was instrumental in making alternative rock accessible to the metal audience, mainly because they were essentially a metal band with neo-psychedelic, neo-prog pretensions—two genres that have always appealed to metal and hard rock audiences. Nothing confirms that fact like *Kettle Whistle*, an odds-and-ends collection of live tracks, demos, alternate takes and new tracks recorded by a "relapsed" Jane's featuring all the original members minus Eric Avery, who is replaced by Flea. Unfortunately, *Kettle Whistle* isn't the best place to hear their achievements, whether you're a diehard or a curious fan. Simply put, nothing here needed to be released, and there are no revelations. If anything, cuts like the embarassing "My Cat's Name Is Maceo" detract from the Jane's myth, and the reunited cuts sound like standard-issue Porno for Pyros. The demos and alternate takes are all unnecessary, sounding like minature, emasculated versions of the finished product, with the exception of the swinging "Been Caught Stealing." The live tracks are another matter, capturing both the power and the transcendence of Jane's Addiction's live performances. That's still not enough to make *Kettle Whistle* a worthy release, because there is no sense or logic to its sequencing, and only a few tracks capture the power of Jane's (and even those will be familiar to diehards through bootlegs). It's not a terrible record, but it isn't a very good one, and it's hard to picture *Kettle Whistle* as anything other than an attempt to cash in on their legend. *—Stephen Thomas Erlewine*

Jayhawks

f. 1985, Minneapolis, MN
Group / Americana, Alternative Country-Rock
Led by the gifted songwriting, impeccable playing and honeyed harmonies of vocalists/guitarists Mark Olson and Gary Louris, the Jayhawks' shimmering blend of country, folk and bar-band rock made them one of the most widely-acclaimed artists to emerge from the alternative country scene. The group sprung up in 1985 out of the fertile Minneapolis musical community, and drew on influences like Gram Parsons, the Louvin Brothers, Tim Hardin and *Nashville Skyline*-era Bob Dylan for their eponymous debut in 1986. The Minneapolis independent label Twin/Tone issued an album of group demos titled *The Blue Earth*, and the exposure gained the Jayhawks a contract with the major label American Records. With the help of producer George Drakoulias, the band recorded their breakthrough album *Hollywood Town Hall* in 1991. The fourth Jayhawks album, 1995's *Tomorrow the Green Grass*, was the group's finest, a beautiful collection of songs led off by the elegiac single "Blue," the recepient of significant airplay. Though Olson announced he was quitting the band, the Jayhawks released *Sound of Lies* in 1997. *—Jason Ankeny*

The Jayhawks / 1986 / Bunkhouse ✦✦✦

Blue Earth / 1989 / Twin/Tone ✦✦✦
The songs which make up *Blue Earth* originated as demos, and save for some minor studio tinkering, are presented here in their original embryonic state. As a consequence, the record lacks punch; spare and economical, the songs are simply too primitive to come to life in this setting. Nonetheless, the growth of the band's songwriting skills over their debut is substantial; while many of the themes—drifting, drinking, and lost love—remain the same, they're handled with greater insight and clarity than before, with a keen eye for detail and nuance. *—Jason Ankeny*

● **Hollywood Town Hall** / Sep. 15, 1992 / American ✦✦✦✦✦
Hollywood Town Hall is the Jayhawks' breakthrough record, a uniformly strong collection heralding a dramatic leap in maturity and depth over the band's earlier work. Benefitting greatly from the increased production values afforded by their newfound major label status, the group's songs—a handful of them redone from the earlier *Blue Earth*—shimmer like never before; the guitars crackle with energy, and Mark Olson and Gary Louris' harmonies lock together so organically that at times it's impossible to distinguish where one voice ends and the other begins. *—Jason Ankeny*

Tomorrow the Green Grass / Feb. 14, 1995 / American ✦✦✦✦
The Jayhawks' final record with singer/songwriter Mark Olson, *Tomorrow the Green Grass* is also the group's finest. While the band's earlier efforts perfected a more traditional brand of country-rock, their fourth record is marvelously eclectic, both musically and emotionally; never before had they rocked as hard as on "Real Light," adug as painfully deep as on "Two Hearts," or hit quite the same peaks of exuberance as on "Miss Williams' Guitar," a tribute to Olson's new wife, neo-folkie Victoria Williams. The addition of keyboardist Karen Grotberg brings rich new layers to the Jayhawks' sound, as does the inclusion of a string section on cuts like "Blue" and "I'd Run Away," a soaring pop song that's quite possibly the best thing the group ever recorded. A fitting legacy, indeed. *—Jason Ankeny*

Sound of Lies / Apr. 22, 1997 / American ✦✦✦
Following Mark Olson's amicable departure, the remaining Jayhawks reconvened under the direction of Gary Louris to record *Sound of Lies*, the band's most ambitious album to date. Like Wilco's *Being There*, *Sound of Lies* uses country-rock as a foundation and wanders off into a variety of different sonic territories, including surf-rock and Beatlesque pop, bringing the music closer to the sound of adult-alternative pop/rock. Although the surface of the album is pleasant and melodic, Louris has written a uniformly harrowing set of songs, inspired both by the dissolution of his partnership with Olson and a recent divorce. The lyrics have a naked, emotional honesty which would have been more affecting if the music echoed its sentiment, yet the record still has a subtle grace and power, proving that the Jayhawks remain a distinctive band without Olson. *—Thom Owens*

Smile / May 9, 2000 / American ✦✦✦

Jefferson Airplane

f. 1965, San Francisco, CA, **db.** 1973
Group / Album Rock, Folk-Rock, Psychedelic, Hard Rock
Jefferson Airplane was the first of the San Francisco psychedelic rock groups of the 1960s to achieve national recognition, and in its later configurations, billed as Jefferson Starship or simply Starship, it remained a significant popular recording act well into the 1980s. The band was organized in the summer of 1965 by singer/songwriter Marty Balin (b. Jan. 30, 1943, Cincinnati), who recruited a band to play at the Matrix, a club he was planning to launch in San Francisco. RCA signed the Airplane and released their debut album, *Jefferson Airplane Takes Off* in 1966 to little commercial response. The group then invited in the lead singer of a rival group, Grace Slick of the Great Society. The new lineup released 1967's *Surrealistic Pillow*, a gold-selling Top Ten hit that spawned the Top Ten singles "Somebody to Love" and "White Rabbit." This success made Jefferson Airplane the top San Francisco group during the 1967 Summer of Love and helped touch off the national craze for psychedelic music, the hippie lifestyle, and youthful drug-taking. *After Bathing at Baxter's* was a more experimental effort that was less successful. But *Crown of Creation* was another gold-selling Top Ten hit, despite the lack of a successful single. *Bless Its Pointed Little Head* (Feb. 1969) was a live album, followed by *Volunteers* (Nov. 1969), another gold studio album. After a series of lineup changes, in 1974 the group name was changed to Jefferson Starship. *—William Ruhlmann*

Takes Off / Sep. 1966 / RCA ✦✦✦
The debut Jefferson Airplane album was dominated by singer Marty Balin, who wrote or co-wrote all the original material and sang most of the lead vocals in his heart-breaking tenor with Paul Kantner and Signe Anderson providing harmonies and backup. (Anderson's lead vocal on "Chauffeur Blues" indicated she was at least the equal of her successor, Grace Slick, as a belter.) The music consisted mostly of folk-rock love songs, the most memorable of which were "It's No Secret" and "Come Up the Years." (There was also a striking version of Dino Valenti's "Get Together" recorded years before the Youngbloods' hit version.) Jorma Kaukonen already displayed a talent for mixing country, folk, and blues riffs in a rock context and Jack Casady already had a distinctive bass sound. But the Airplane of Balin-Kantner-Kaukonen- Anderson-Casady-Spence is to be distinguished from the Balin-Kantner-Kaukonen Casady-Slick-Dryden version of the band that would emerge on record five months later chiefly by Balin's dominance. Later, Grace Slick would become the group's vocal and visual focal point. On *Takes Off*, the Airplane was Balin's group. (*Jefferson Airplane Takes Off* was released as RCA 3584 in September 1966. It was reissued as RCA 66797 on January 30, 1996, as a CD that contained both the stereo and mono versions and that added back the track "Runnin' 'Round This World," which had been deleted from all but initial copies due to the sexual and perceived drug references of the line "The nights I've spent with you have been fantastic trips." But the included version still eliminated the word "trips.") *—William Ruhlmann*

★ **Surrealistic Pillow** / Feb. 1967 / RCA ✦✦✦✦✦
Their groundbreaking folk-based psychedelic album hit like a shot heard round the world. From "White Rabbit" and "Somebody to Love" to the sublime "3/5 of a Mile in 10 Seconds," the sensibilities are fierce, the material is melodic, and the performances, sparked by new member Grace Slick on most of the lead vocals, are magnificent and inspired. The long-awaited remastered reissue (look for the 1996 release date on back of the CD jewel box) is a real treasure, featuring both the stereo and mono mixes of each song, which differed significantly in texture and focus. But the real beauty is the remastered sound, which captures the majesty of this album about as well as any '60s reissue yet heard—the 1996 reissue is the first CD version to sound better than original pressings of the LP, and it makes the album even more compelling. Every song is perfect, and the pity is that RCA didn't record any of the group's shows from this era for official release, apart from the all-too-brief set at Monterey the following summer, when this material made up the bulk of their repertory; and

Grace Slick and Marty Balin (who never had a prettier song than "Today" from this album) shared the vocals and songwriting, and before politics and excessive experimentation, musical and chemical, began affecting the band's ability to do a straightforward song. The group never made a better album, and few artists from the era ever did. *—Bruce Eder*

After Bathing at Baxter's / Dec. 1967 / RCA ✦✦✦
Jefferson Airplane's third album was both a further exploration of the more unusual aspects of their second album, *Surrealistic Pillow*, and a reaction against that album's more conventional aspects and its commercial success. *After Bathing at Baxter's* was dominated by rhythm guitarist/singer Paul Kantner, who wrote or co-wrote six of the 11 selections, including the two singles "The Ballad of You & Me & Pooneil" and "Watch Her Ride." While Grace Slick wrote and sang the bizarre "rejoyce" (based on James Joyce's writings) and "Two Heads" (songs well to the left of the already-daring "White Rabbit"), the album also marked the emergence of the bass/guitar team of Jack Casady and Jorma Kaukonen, whose nine-minute instrumental "Spare Chaynge" foreshadowed their spinoff group Hot Tuna. *After Bathing at Baxter's* was the album on which the Airplane, touted as the leaders of the San Francisco acid-rock scene, actually tried to catch up to the movement. Unlike other psychedelic exponents, they had been primarily song-based rather than performance-based; despite the studio gimmicks and self-indulgence, they remained so. *— William Ruhlmann*

Crown of Creation / Sep. 1968 / RCA ✦✦✦
An impressive but meandering journey through the drugged-out sensibilities of 1967. The science-fiction content gives it some cohesiveness, but not enough. *—Bruce Eder*

Bless Its Pointed Little Head / Feb. 1969 / RCA ✦✦✦
Jefferson Airplane's first live album demonstrated the group's development as concert performers, taking a number of songs that had been performed in concise, pop-oriented versions on their early albums—"3/5's of a Mile in 10 Seconds," "Somebody to Love," "It's No Secret," "Plastic Fantastic Lover"—and rendering them in arrangements that were longer, harder rocking, and more densely textured, especially in terms of the guitar and bass lines constructed by Jorma Kaukonen and Jack Casady. The group's three-part vocal harmonizing and dueling was on display during such songs as a nearly seven-minute version of Fred Neil's folk-blues standard "The Other Side of This Life," here transformed into a swirling rocker. The album emphasized the talents of Kaukonen and singer Marty Balin over the team of Paul Kantner and Grace Slick, who had tended to dominate recent records: the blues song "Rock Me Baby" was a dry run for Hot Tuna, the band Kaukonen and Casady would form in two years, and Balin turned in powerful vocal performances on several of his own compositions, notably "It's No Secret." Jefferson Airplane was still at its best in concise, driving numbers, rather than in the jams on Donovan's "Fat Angel" (running 7:35) or the group improv "Bear Melt" (11:21); they were just too intense to stretch out comfortably. But *Bless Its Pointed Little Head* served an important function in the group's discography, demonstrating that their live work had a distinctly different focus and flavor from their studio recordings. *— William Ruhlmann*

Volunteers / Nov. 1969 / RCA ✦✦✦✦
Controversial at the time, delayed because of fights with the record company over lyrical content and the original title (*Volunteers of America*), *Volunteers* was a powerful release that neatly closed out and wrapped up the '60s. Here, the Jefferson Airplane presents itself in full revolutionary rhetoric, issuing a call to "tear down the walls" and "get it on together." "We Can Be Together" and "Volunteers" bookend the album, offering musical variations on the same chord progression and lyrical variations on the same theme. Between these politically charged rock anthems, the band offers a mix of words and music that reflect the competing ideals of simplicity and getting "back to the earth," and overthrowing greed and exploitation through political activism, adding a healthy dollop of psychedelic sci-fi for texture. Guitarist Jorma Kaukonen's beautiful arrangement of the traditional "Good Shepherd" is a standout here, and Jerry Garcia's pedal steel guitar gives "The Farm" an appropriately rural feel. The band's version of "Wooden Ships" is much more eerie than that released earlier in the year by Crosby, Stills & Nash. Oblique psychedelia is offered here via Grace Slick's "Hey Frederick" and ecologically tinged "Eskimo Blue Day." Drummer Spencer Dryden gives an inside look at the state of the band in the country singalong "A Song for All Seasons."

The musical arrangements here are quite potent. Nicky Hopkins' distinctive piano highlights a number of tracks, and Kaukonen's razor-toned lead guitar is the recording's unifying force, blazing through the mix, giving the album its distinctive sound. Although the political bent of the lyrics may seem dated to some, listening to *Volunteers* is like opening a time capsule on the end of an era, a time when young people still believed music had the power to change the world. *—Jim Newsom*

The Worst of Jefferson Airplane / Nov. 1970 / RCA ✦✦✦

Bark / Sep. 1971 / RCA ✦✦✦
By the time of *Bark*, personnel changes had gutted much of the original vision of the group, especially with the departure of Marty Balin. Paul Kantner and Grace Slick remained, but their compositions were growing increasingly ill-focused, and Jorma Kaukonen and new drummer Joey Covington were ill-equipped to pick up the songwriting slack. The result was an album that bore hallmarks of the classic Airplane sound, but lacked any classic Airplane songs. That said, the record isn't as bad as many reviewers have made it out to be. It's just mediocre, with little that sticks in the memory, despite occasional nice moments in cuts like Covington's "Pretty as You Feel" and Kantner's delicate "Third Week in the Chelsea." *—Richie Unterberger*

Long John Silver / Jul. 1972 / RCA ✦✦

Thirty Seconds Over Winterland / Apr. 1973 / RCA ✦✦

The Best of Jefferson Airplane / 1980 / RCA ✦✦✦✦
The Best of Jefferson Airplane is an imperfect but serviceable collection, featuring ten of the Airplane's best-known songs: "White Rabbit," "Somebody to Love," "Wild Tyme," "Won't You Try Saturday Afternoon," "Wooden Ships," "Third Week in the Chelsea Hotel" and "Long John Silver." This basic collection will be of use to a listener just looking for the hits, but more serious listeners will be better serviced by the more thorough compilations available, or the band's original albums. *—Stephen Thomas Erlewine*

2400 Fulton Street: An Anthology / Mar. 1987 / RCA ✦✦✦✦
This was the first serious effort to assemble the best and most interesting of the Jefferson Airplane's work from beginning to end. At the time, the group's catalog on CD was in a woeful state of disrepair, hastily mastered from LP production sources and sounding worse than original vinyl copies of many of the titles, and there was no comprehensive anthology, just the *Worst of Jefferson Airplane* compilation from 1970. *2400 Fulton Street* isn't ideal, jumping around a little too much, but provides a look for the uninitiated into the evolution of the group's sound from a mixed electric-acoustic folk rock ensemble, not too different from the Mugwumps et al., into a high-energy rock band and, for a time, one of the more daring psychedelic outfits. Additionally, even longtime fans will appreciate most of the jumps that are made, for all of the essentials are here—most of *Surrealistic Pillow*, along with highlights from the surrounding albums up through the end of the group's history (with a Levi's radio commercial featuring the band thrown in for good measure) and a few odd singles and B-sides that otherwise usually get overlooked. Moreover, the sound was a major improvement at the time (though it has since been outdone on the re-releases of the individual albums), and the notes contained what was, at the time, perhaps the best easily available account of the group's history. *—Bruce Eder*

Jefferson Airplane / Sep. 1989 / Epic ✦

Jefferson Airplane Loves You / Oct. 1992 / RCA ✦✦✦
A three-disc box set loaded with rarities, *Jefferson Airplane Loves You* is necessary for hardcore fans, but the double-disc *2400 Fulton Street* offers a better portrait of the band and is the essential purchase for casual fans. *—Stephen Thomas Erlewine*

● **Hits** / Sep. 29, 1998 / RCA ✦✦✦✦✦
There has been no dearth of greatest-hits and best-of albums devoted to Jefferson Airplane, Jefferson Starship, and Starship, but this is the first one combining tracks from all three editions of the group that started in San Francisco in the mid-'60s and ended its run in the early '90s with entirely different personnel. The band continued to maintain the same basic elements for most of its run, the constants being a soaring male tenor (either Marty Balin or Mickey Thomas) and a stinging lead guitar (either Jorma Kaukonen or Craig Chaquico), even if its best-remembered sound was the icy, stentorian contralto of on-again, off-again member Grace Slick. To say that the elements held constant is not to say that the band continued to sound the same, but if you listen to the chronologically sequenced album through, you can hear the transition clearly. True to its title, the 35-track *Hits* contains all of the band's most successful singles, omitting only two of its Top 40 entries. All the big hits are here, from "Somebody to Love" through "Miracles" to "We Built This City," accounting for 18 of the tracks. The rest of the album is filled out with less-successful singles and album tracks that became band standards. As this list indicates, compiler Paul Williams is more interested in Jefferson Airplane than Jefferson Starship and Starship, which are represented exclusively by singles, and a more balanced portrait of the later ensembles might have been provided by including illuminating album tracks. But this is the best two-disc summary of a group that, despite dizzying personnel changes, maintained its commercial acumen for over 20 years. *— William Ruhlmann*

Jefferson Starship

f. 1974, **db.** 1984
Group / Album Rock, Arena Rock, Pop/Rock, Hard Rock
With their 1974 metamorphosis into the Jefferson Starship, the group once known as the Jefferson Airplane underwent a radical facelift which resulted not only in a change of name but also a new line-up and a new musical identity. Formerly torch-bearers of the Haight-Ashbury counterculture, famed for psychedelic-era landmarks including *Surrealistic Pillow* and *Volunteers*, as the Starship the group reached even greater heights of success, forging a more mainstream sound and attitude which established them as one of the predominant hard rock units of their era. 1975's *Red Octopus*, became the Starship's most successful effort, topping the charts off and on throughout the year on the strength of the Top Three ballad "Miracles." Despite singer Grace Slick's protests that the music was growing too commercial, the band continued to hone a more mainstream identity on 1976's *Spitfire*, their first platinum-selling release, while 1978's *Earth* spawned the Top Ten hit "Count on Me." However, in the wake of the record's release Slick's long-standing drinking problem spun out of control, and she left the group during a European tour. Vocalist Marty Balin exited later in 1978, leaving the Starship without a lead singer; finally, in 1979 the remaining members recruited vocalist Mickey Thomas. Slick rejoined the group for 1982's *Winds of Change*. As simply Starship, they later scored the hits "We Built This City," "Sara" and "Nothing's Gonna Stop Us Now." *—Jason Ankeny*

Dragon Fly / 1974 / RCA ✦✦✦
Credited to "Grace Slick/Paul Kantner/Jefferson Starship," *Dragon Fly* was the transitional album between the various shifting aggregations Slick and Kantner had been recording with as Jefferson Airplane dissolved in the early 1970s and the new Jefferson Starship (which essentially was the Airplane with a new guitarist and bassist—Craig Chaquico and Pete Sears). But where such preceding efforts as *Sunfighter*, *Manhole*, and *Baron Von Tollbooth and the Chrome Nun* had suffered from indulgence and a lack of focus, *Dragon Fly*, from the first note of its rocking leadoff track, "Ride the Tiger" (a chart single), was a unified effort. Like much of the Airplane catalog and all of the Starship albums to follow, the album suffered from the band's communal approach to song selection (the eight tracks credited 12 writers, half of them band members), leading to an unevenness in the material. But unlike the recent Kantner/Slick/etc. albums, it sounded like the work of a seasoned band. (It didn't hurt that the album was cut just after a tour, instead of before one.) Especially notable was Chaquico, who on such tracks as "All Fly Away" and "Hyperdrive" demonstrated that he was a distinctive lead guitarist able to define the Starship sound just as the very different Jorma Kaukonen had the Airplane. But what turned *Dragon Fly* into an artistic and commercial triumph

(it was the most popular album any of these people had been involved with in five years) was the return, for one song, of former Airplane singer Marty Balin, since that one song was the epic power ballad "Caroline," which became a radio favorite and remains one of the best songs the Airplane/Starship ever did. *—William Ruhlmann*

● **Red Octopus** / 1975 / RCA ✦✦✦✦✦
Technically speaking, *Red Octopus* was the first album credited to Jefferson Starship, though practically the same lineup made *Dragon Fly*, credited to Grace Slick/Paul Kantner/Jefferson Starship. The difference, however, was crucial: Marty Balin was once again a fully integrated band member, writing or co-writing five of the ten tracks. And there can be little doubt that it was Balin's irresistible ballad "Miracles," the biggest hit single in the Jefferson Whatever catalog, that propelled *Red Octopus* to the top of the charts, the only Jefferson album to chart that high and the best-selling album in their collective lives. This must have been sweet vindication for Balin, who founded Jefferson Airplane, but then drifted away from the group as it veered away from his musical vision. Now, the collective was incorporating his taste without quite integrating it—"Miracles," with its strings and sax solo by non-band member Irv Cox, was hardly a characteristic Airplane/Starship track. But then, neither exactly was Papa John Creach's showcase, "Git Fiddler," or bassist Pete Sears' instrumental "Sandalphon," which sounded like something from an early Procol Harum album. Slick has three strong songs, among them the second single "Play on Love." Like *Dragon Fly, Red Octopus* reflected a multiplicity of musical tastes; there were ten credited songwriters, seven of whom were in the band. If there is any consistency in this material, it is in subject matter (love songs). The album is more ballad-heavy and melodic than the Airplane albums, which made it more accessible to the broader audience it reached, though "Sweeter Than Honey" is as tough a rocker as the band ever played. *—William Ruhlmann*

Spitfire / 1976 / RCA ✦✦✦
Trying to follow-up the overwhelming success of their last record proved too much for the Starship. Nothing here can compare with the hit sound they had forged previously although they did get chart action with the song "With Your Love." Otherwise, a bad bump in the road for Jefferson Starship. *—James Chrispell*

Earth / 1978 / RCA ✦✦

Freedom at Point Zero / 1979 / RCA ✦✦✦

Gold / 1979 / RCA ✦✦✦✦✦

Modern Times / 1981 / RCA ✦✦✦
Slick comes back for one song, and "Find Your Way Back" becomes a hit. Also included is "Stairway to Cleveland," as gutsy a statement of purpose as any in rock. *—William Ruhlmann*

Winds of Change / 1982 / Grunt ✦✦

Nuclear Furniture / 1984 / RCA ✦✦

At Their Best / 1993 / RCA ✦✦✦✦
At Their Best is a ten-track, budget-priced collection that contains some of the Jefferson Starship's biggest hits—"Miracles," "Ride the Tiger," "Count On Me," "Jane," "Find Your Way Back"—plus five album tracks. As budget-line collections go, *At Their Best* isn't bad, especially since it contains the original versions of five hits, but better collections with better song selections are available for not much more money, which means this disc is unnecessary. *—Stephen Thomas Erlewine*

The Jesus & Mary Chain

f. 1984, Glasgow, **db.** 1998
Group / College Rock, Noise Pop, Post-Punk, Alternative Pop/Rock
Like the Velvet Underground, their most obvious influence, the chart success of the Jesus and Mary Chain was virtually non-existent, but their artistic impact was incalculable; quite simply, the British group made the world safe for white noise, orchestrating a sound dense in squalling feedback which served as an inspiration to everyone from My Bloody Valentine to Dinosaur Jr. Though the supporting players drifted in and out of focus, the heart of the Mary Chain remained vocalists and guitarists William and Jim Reid, Scottish-born brothers heavily influenced not only by underground legends like the Velvets and the Stooges but also by the sonic grandeur and pop savvy of Phil Spector and Brian Wilson. In the Jesus and Mary Chain, these two polarized aesthetics converged; equal parts bubblegum and formless guitar distortion, their sound both celebrated pop conventions and thoroughly subverted them. In late 1984, the band issued its seminal debut single, "Upside Down," a remarkable blast of livewire feedback anchored by a caveman-like drumbeat; the record made the Mary Chain an overnight sensation in the U.K., as did their nascent live shows, 20-minute sets of confrontational noise (performed with the band's members backs to the audience) which frequently ended in rioting. The follow-up, "You Trip Me Up," further perfected the formula, and led to their 1985 debut LP Psychocandy, which gift-wrapped sweet, simple pop songs in ribbons of droning guitar fuzz. After a two-year layoff, the Jesus and Mary Chain returned with *Darklands*, a dramatic shift in approach which stripped away the feedback to expose the skeletal guitar-pop at the music's core. *—Jason Ankeny*

★ **Psychocandy** / Nov. 1985 / Blanco y Negro/Warner Brothers ✦✦✦✦✦
The album that launched a thousand shoegazer bands, the visceral power of *Psychocandy* has diminished not one whit in the years since it made its bow. Still far and away the Mary Chain's defining moment, standout cuts like "Just Like Honey," "The Hardest Walk" and "You Trip Me Up" represent the purest fusion of the Jeckyl-and-Hyde mindset that dominates the group—in subsequent years, they've been a noise band at times, while at others they've been a pop band, but here, they're both, and it's glorious. *—Jason Ankeny*

Darklands / Sep. 1987 / Blanco y Negro/Warner Brothers ✦✦✦✦✦
It's completely emblematic of the Mary Chain's perversity that they followed up the dissonant squalor of *Psychocandy* with the minimal, almost gentle guitar-pop of *Darklands*. Here, the melodies which the previous album's squalls of feedback threatened to rip open are left to their own devices; the results are quite stunning, with songs like "Deep One Perfect Morning," "Cherry Came Too" and the title track revealing unforseen layers of beauty. *—Jason Ankeny*

Barbed Wire Kisses / Apr. 1988 / Blanco y Negro/Warner Brothers ✦✦✦
Despite the overall inconsistency of *Barbed Wire Kisses*, a collection of singles, B-sides and other rarities, the record does contain more than enough superior moments to make it an essential purchase for all serious Mary Chain aficionados. Chief among them is "Upside Down," athe group's feedback-mad debut single and the purest distillation of their aesthetic they ever recorded. Other highlights include the menacing "Kill Surf City," a brutal deconstruction of "Surfin' U.S.A." and the sleek single "Sidewalking." *—Jason Ankeny*

Automatic / Oct. 1989 / Blanco y Negro/Warner Brothers ✦✦✦
Too much of *Automatic* is just that—formulaic, uninspired and essentially rote music recorded with the aid of a drum machine. Splitting the difference between the feedback pyrotechnics of *Psychocandy* and the gentle pop of *Darklands*, the record sports a metallic, glossy guitar sheen which complements the synthetic beats all too well: robotic and processed, much of *Automatic* is simply lifeless. Even at their most lackluster, however, the Reid brothers can still spit out some terrific songs—both the menacing "Blues From a Gun" and "Head On" (later covered by the Pixies) are twisted, infectious gems. *—Jason Ankeny*

Honey's Dead / Mar. 1992 / Blanco y Negro/Def American ✦✦✦✦✦
A vast improvement over the preceding *Automatic, Honey's Dead* teams the Mary Chain with engineer/mixer Alan Moulder, who layers the album with a more organic and aggressive guitar sound than the Reid brothers have enjoyed in some time. The opening "Reverence"—a live-wire feedback fever-dream stretched across a loping dance rhythm—quickly establishes the tone: *Honey's Dead* brings the noise, but it also emphasizes the group's unerring pop instincts, as further evidenced by such gems as "Far Gone and Out," "Rollercoaster" and "Sugar Ray." *—Jason Ankeny*

Stoned & Dethroned / Aug. 23, 1994 / Blanco y Negro/American ✦✦✦

The Jesus & Mary Chain Hate Rock N' Roll / Sep. 26, 1995 / Blanco y Negro/American ✦✦

Munki / Jun. 9, 1998 / Sub Pop ✦✦✦
As befits an album bookended by tracks titled "I Love Rock N Roll" and "I Hate Rock N Roll," the Jesus and Mary Chain's Sub Pop label debut *Munki* is schizophrenic and impassioned, a record which both summarizes the band's career to date and cleans the slate for their future. Virtually each of the 17 tracks here echoes a prior moment in the Chain's existence, moving at breakneck pace from the volcanic noise of their earliest material to the bleak grace of *Darklands*, through to the sleek, supercharged pop of *Automatic*—even Mazzy Star's Hope Sandoval makes a cameo, as she did on *Stoned and Dethroned*. In a sense, it's an ideal primer to the Reid brothers' mercurial world, flirting with both brilliance and mediocrity; even after well over a decade, the Jesus and Mary Chain continue to thrill, irritate and confound—they're a true love/hate obsession. *—Jason Ankeny*

Jethro Tull

f. 1967, Blackpool, England, **db.** 1982
Group / Album Rock, Arena Rock, Prog-Rock/Art Rock, Hard Rock
Jethro Tull was a unique phenomenon in popular music history. Their mix of hard rock, folk melodies, blues licks, surreal, impossibly dense lyrics, and overall profundity defied easy analysis, but that didn't dissuade fans from giving them 11 gold and five platinum albums. At the same time, critics rarely took them seriously, and they were off the cutting edge of popular music since the end of the 1970's. But no record store in the country would want to be without multiple copies of each of their most popular albums (*Benefit, Aqualung, Thick as a Brick, Living in the Past*), or their various "best of" compilations, and few would knowingly ignore their newest releases. Of their contemporaries, only Yes could claim a similar degree of success, and Yes endured several major shifts in sound and membership in reaching the 1990s, while Tull remained remarkably stable over the same period. As co-founded and led by wildman-flautist-guitarist-singer-songwriter Ian Anderson, the group carved a place all its own in popular music. *—Bruce Eder*

This Was / 1968 / Chrysalis ✦✦✦

Stand Up / Sep. 1969 / Chrysalis ✦✦✦

Benefit / Apr. 1970 / Chrysalis ✦✦✦
Benefit was the album on which the Tull sound solidified around folk music, abandoning blues as a major source. Beginning with the opening number, "With You There to Help Me," Anderson adopts his now-familiar slightly mournful folksinger/sage persona—his acoustic guitar carried the melody, joined by Martin Barre's electric instrument for the crescendos. This would be the model for much of the material on *Aqualung* and, especially, *Thick As a Brick*, although the acoustic/electric pairing would be executed more effectively on those albums. Most of the songs here display pleasant, delectably folk-like melodies, with Barre's guitar adding enough wattage to keep the rock listeners interested. "To Cry You a Song," "Son," and "For Michael Collins, Jeffrey and Me" all defined Tull's future sound: Barre's amp cranked up to ten (especially on "Son"), coming in above Anderson's acoustic strumming, a few unexpected changes in tempo, and Anderson spouting lyrics filled with dense, seemingly profound imagery and statements. As on *Stand Up*, the group was still officially a quartet, with future member John Evan appearing as a guest on keyboards. *—Bruce Eder*

● **Aqualung** / Apr. 1971 / Chrysalis ✦✦✦✦✦
Released at a time when a lot of bands were embracing pop-Christianity (*a la Jesus Christ, Superstar*), *Aqualung* was a bold statement for a rock group, a pro-God anti-church tract that probably got lots of teenagers wrestling with these ideas for the first time in their lives. This was the album that made Jethro Tull a fixture on FM radio, with riff-heavy songs like "My God," "Hymn 43," "Locomotive Breath," "Cross-Eyed Mary," "Wind Up," and the title track. And from there, they became a major arena act, and a fixture at the top of the record charts for most of the 1970's. Mixing hard-rock and folk melodies with Ian Anderson's dour musings on faith and religion (mostly how organized religion had restricted man's relationship

with God), the record was extremely profound for a No. 7 chart hit, one of the most cerebral albums ever to reach millions of rock listeners. Indeed, from this point on, Anderson and company were compelled to stretch the lyrical envelope right to the breaking point. As a compact disc, *Aqualung* has gone through numerous editions, mostly owing to problems finding an original master tape when the CD boom began. When the album was issued by Chrysalis through Columbia Records in the mid-1980's, the source tape was an LP production master, and the first release was criticized for thin, tinny sound; Columbia remastered it sometime around 1987 or 1988, in a version with better sound. Chrysalis later switched distribution to Capitol-EMI, and they released a decent sounding CD that is currently available. Chrysalis also issued a 25th anniversary edition in 1996. *—Bruce Eder*

Thick as a Brick / Apr. 1972 / Chrysalis ✦✦✦✦✦
Jethro Tull's first LP-length epic is a masterpiece in the annals of progressive rock, and one of the few works of its kind that still holds up 25 years later. Mixing hard rock and English folk music with classical influences, set to stream-of-consciousness lyrics so dense with the imagery that one might spend weeks pondering their meaning—assuming one feels the need to do so—the group created a dazzling tour-de-force, at once playful, profound, and challenging, without overwhelming the listener. The original LP was the best sounding, best engineered record Tull had ever released, easily capturing the shifting dynamics between the soft all-acoustic passages and the electric rock crescendos surrounding them. The sound on the original Columbia Records CD (not identified as such, but recognizable by a "VK" prefix in its catalog number) was harsh and thin, and left a lot to be desired in terms of richness—the current Chrysalis disc is an improvement as well. *—Bruce Eder*

Living in the Past / Oct. 1972 / Chrysalis ✦✦✦✦✦
Listen to this 20-song collection, put together to capitalize on the explosive growth in the group's audience after *Aqualung,* and it is easy to understand just how fine a group Jethro Tull was in the early '70s. Most of the songs, apart from a few heavily played album tracks ("Song for Jeffrey" etc.) and a pair of live tracks from a 1970 Carnegie Hall show, came off of singles and EPs that, apart from the title song, were scarcely known in America, and it's all so solid that it needs no apology or explanation. Not only was Ian Anderson writing solid songs every time out, but the group's rhythm section was about the best in progressive rock's pop division. Along with any of the group's first five albums, this collection is seminal and essential to any Tull collection, and the only compilation by the group that is a must-own disc. *—Bruce Eder*

A Passion Play / Jul. 1973 / Chrysalis ✦✦✦✦
Jethro Tull's second album-length composition, *A Passion Play* is very different from—and not quite as successful as—*Thick as a Brick.* Ian Anderson utilizes reams of biblical (and biblical-sounding) references, interwoven with modern language, as a sort of rock equivalent to T.S. Eliot's *The Wasteland.* As with most progressive rock, the words seem important and profound, but their meaning is anyone's guess ("The ice-cream lady wet her drawers, to see you in the Passion Play..."), with Anderson as a dour but engaging singer/sage (who, at least at one point, seems to take on the role of a fallen angel). It helps to be aware of the framing story, about a newly deceased man called to review his life at the portals of heaven, who realizes that life on Earth is preferable to eternity in paradise. But the music puts it over successfully, a dazzling mix of old English folk and classical material, reshaped in electric rock terms. The band is at its peak form, sustaining the tension and anticipation of this album-length piece across 45 minutes, although the music runs out of inspiration about five minutes before it actually ends. The sound on the CD is significantly brighter than the LP, bringing out the full impact of the electric instruments once the piece takes off, but also imparting more presence to the acoustic instruments (such as Anderson's guitar over the line "God of ages/Lord of time" and the sax part that follows). The only serious complaint about the compact disc is that it isn't indexed to separate the two halves of *A Passion Play* from the A.A. Milne-style interlude "The Story of the Hare That Lost His Spectacles," instead being treated as one long track. *—Bruce Eder*

War Child / Oct. 1974 / Chrysalis ✦✦✦

Minstrel in the Gallery / Sep. 1975 / Chrysalis ✦✦✦✦

M.U.: The Best of Jethro Tull / Jan. 1976 / Chrysalis ✦✦✦✦
M.U. falls into the classic example of a compilation that is bound to irritate the dedicated yet will satisfy the needs of less devoted listeners. Since Jethro Tull is a prog-rock band that made cohesive concept albums, there will always be an audience that will believe it is impossible to assemble a coherent anthology, but the fact of the matter is, the group had a lot of songs that were staples on album-rock radio and *M.U.* simply compiles those tracks for listeners that don't want to invest in a series of concept records. Besides, the resulting compilation is an entertaining listen, thanks to such genre classics as "Aqualung," "Thick as a Brick," "Bungle in the Jungle," "Locomotive Breath," "Living in the Past" and "A Passion Play." These are the songs that define Tull for both hardcore and casual fans, and that's the reason why *M.U.* remains a popular and useful compilation, even if it isn't definitive. *—Stephen Thomas Erlewine*

Heavy Horses / Apr. 1978 / Chrysalis ✦✦✦✦

Stormwatch / Sep. 1979 / Chrysalis ✦✦

A / Sep. 1980 / Chrysalis ✦✦✦

Nightcap: The Unreleased Masters 1973-1991 / 1994 / Capitol ✦✦✦

The Ultimate Set / Apr. 8, 1997 / Valley ✦✦

● **The Best of Jethro Tull** / Oct. 5, 1999 / Capitol ✦✦✦✦✦
Not only are there an awful lot of Jethro Tull compilations, there is a ton of comprehensive multi-disc collections in their catalog, so it's very easy to confuse the individual albums. For instance, the 1999 double-disc set *The Best of Jethro Tull* is billed as a digitally remastered album, which gives the impression that it is a remastered version of an older set, when it is actually a new collection culled from remastered tapes. Basically, this set is unnecessary for collectors, who will certainly have everything here, and any casual fan that already has a collection—whether it's the original *M.U.* or any of the many box sets—won't need this. But casual fans looking for a comprehensive yet fairly concise anthology should choose this *Best of* since it does have all the hits and key album tracks among its 36 songs, all presented in good remastered sound. It's not worth replacing an existing compilation in your collection, but if you need a Tull set, this is a good choice. *—Stephen Thomas Erlewine*

Joan Jett (Joan Larkin)

b. Sep. 22, 1960, Philadelphia, PA
Vocals, Guitar / Album Rock, Arena Rock, Hard Rock
By playing pure and simple rock & roll without making an explicit issue of her gender, Joan Jett became a figurehead for several generations of female rockers. Jett's brand of rock & roll is loud and stripped down, yet with overpowering hooks—a combination of the Stones' tough, sinewy image and beat, AC/DC chords and glam-rock hooks. As the numerous covers she has recorded show, she adheres both to rock tradition and breaks with it—she plays classic three-chord rock & roll, yet she also loves the trashy elements (in particular, Gary Glitter) of it as well, and she plays with a defiant sneer. From her first band, the Runaways, through her hit-making days in the '80s with the Blackhearts right until her unexpected revival in the '90s, she hasn't changed her music, yet she's kept her quality control high, making one classic single ("I Love Rock-n-Roll") along the way. *—Stephen Thomas Erlewine*

Bad Reputation / 1981 / Blackheart ✦✦✦✦
Jett's debut album is an infectious romp through her influences, ranging from classic '50s and '60s rock & roll through glam-rock, three-chord loud'n'fast Ramones punk, and poppier new wave guitar-rock. Half the songs on the original album (not counting bonus tracks on the remastered reissue) are covers, but whether it's Lesley Gore's feminist girl-group anthem "You Don't Own Me" (featuring the Sex Pistols' Steve Jones and Paul Cook) or a roaring version of Gary Glitter's "Do You Wanna Touch Me (Oh Yeah)," Jett makes them all work. The production can be a little weak in spots, but Jett's exuberance and tough-girl attitude overcome most deficiencies. Plus, the title track is a classic. *—Steve Huey*

I Love Rock & Roll / 1981 / Blackheart ✦✦✦✦
I Love Rock & Roll, Joan Jett's first record with the Blackhearts, was a tougher, louder album than *Bad Reputation,* primarily because her new backing band gave her a more coherent sound. That dynamic, hard-rock crunch is what made the title track into an international hit, but it also gives the album dimension—not only can Jett and the Blackhearts tear up heavy glam-rockers, but they also pull off the mock psychedelia of Tommy James & the Shondells' "Crimson and Clover" with aplomb. On the whole, *I Love Rock & Roll* doesn't have as many strong songs as its predecessor, but the band's muscular, gritty sound makes the album just as good as *Bad Reputation. —Stephen Thomas Erlewine*

Album / 1983 / Blackheart ✦✦✦✦✦
Album is arguably Joan Jett's strongest non-compilation release, featuring a consistent, free-wheelingly wide range of material (which the Blackhearts really tear into) and punchier, more detailed production. Once again, Jett delivers strong, enthusiastic performances, but this time, the quality of the material lends her equal support. The singles "Fake Friends" and "Everyday People" (the Sly and the Family Stone song) scraped the bottom of the Top 40 charts; other highlights include Jett's original "French Song," which details a ménage à trois. *—Steve Huey*

Glorious Results of a Misspent Youth / 1984 / Blackheart ✦✦✦✦
From her days with the all-girl band the Runaways through her work with her own band, Joan Jett has been a pioneer, if not an innovator. She has always paid loving tribute to the riffy rock music that she loves. On album number six, *Glorious Results of a Misspent Youth,* Jett, backed by her Blackhearts, churned out more of the same, but with some of the most satisfying and strongest material of her career. The album is an engaging collection that ranges from a glam-inflected update of the Runaways' classic "Cherry Bomb" to the swagger of the Gary Glitter hit "I Love You Love Me Love." Other songs include Jett's versions of "I Need Someone" and "New Orleans" and standout originals like the rocking "Frustrated," the full-tilt boogie of "Long Time," and a ballad, "Hold Me," that would sound mawkish coming from anyone else. Infectious choruses, crunchy melodies, and Jett's growling vocals make this album an excuse to turn the stereo up just a bit more. *—Tom Demalon*

Good Music / 1986 / Epic ✦✦✦
On *Good Music,* Joan Jett's hot streak showed signs of subsiding, with the production tending to weigh down some of the numbers and an overall weaker selection of material than her then-recent efforts. Still, the album did contain some fine moments, especially in the title track and the anthemic "Black Leather." *—Steve Huey*

Up Your Alley / 1988 / Epic ✦✦

The Hit List / 1990 / Epic ✦✦

Notorious / Aug. 20, 1991 / Epic ✦✦✦

Flashback / 1994 / Blackheart ✦✦✦✦✦
While it includes a healthy share of rarities, nothing on Joan Jett's career overview, *Flashback,* is second rate. Even though she vacillated between punky hard rock and smoothed-out arena-rock for much of the '80s, the disc accentuates her rebellious nature, making *Flashback* an effective introduction to her career. Besides, it rocks like hell. *—Stephen Thomas Erlewine*

Pure and Simple / Jun. 14, 1994 / Warner Brothers ✦✦✦

● **Fit to Be Tied: Great Hits by Joan Jett** / Nov. 18, 1997 / Mercury/Blackheart ✦✦✦✦✦
While it isn't a perfect collection, *Fit to Be Tied: Great Hits by Joan Jett & the Blackhearts* is a strong overview of Jett's career, featuring 15 of her biggest hits and best moments. Nearly all of her charting singles—"I Love Rock 'n Roll," "Crimson and Clover," "Do You Wanna Touch Me (Oh Yeah)," "Fake Friends," "Everyday People," "The Light of Day," "I Hate Myself for Loving You," "Little Liar"—are included, along with the Runaways staple "Cherry Bomb," several storming album cuts (including "Bad Reputation"), her cult cover of the *Mary Tyler*

Moore theme "Love Is All Around" and the previously unreleased "World of Denial." Jett certainly made good albums, but the high points were almost always the singles, which is why *Fit to Be Tied* is such a successful, listenable collection. It should have been sequenced in chronological order, but it remains a first-rate summary of the peak of her career, as well as an excellent introduction to her straight-ahead style. *—Stephen Thomas Erlewine*

Fetish / Jun. 8, 1999 / Blackheart ✦✦✦

Jewel

b. May 23, 1974

Guitar, Vocals / Adult Alternative Pop/Rock, Singer/Songwriter

A contemporary folkie renowned for her expressive, crystalline voice, singer/songwriter Jewel was among the most successful of the many new female performers who dominated the pop charts throughout the 1990s. Raised in remote Homer, AK, she began her music career at the age of six, regularly performing alongside her singer/songwriter parents in local Eskimo villages and tourist attractions. While attending Michigan's Interlochen Fine Arts Academy, Jewel began writing her first songs; upon graduating, she moved into her van and began focusing on a career in music. After signing to Atlantic, in early 1995 Jewel issued her debut LP, *Pieces of You;* the record was a slow starter, not even breaking into the *Billboard* pop charts until some 14 months after its release, but eventually the single "Who Will Save Your Soul" became a major hit, and soon the album was a best-seller as well. Two other hits, "You Were Meant for Me" and "Foolish Games," followed. In 1998 Jewel returned with *Night Without Armor,* a collection of her spoken-word poetry; her hotly-anticipated second album *Spirit* followed later that year. *—Jason Ankeny*

• **Pieces of You** / Feb. 28, 1995 / East West ✦✦✦✦

Pieces of You is a charming debut that is somewhat undone by its own naiveté. Jewel has a rich voice and an innocent, beguiling charm that makes "Who Will Save Your Soul?," "I'm Sensitive" and "You Were Meant for Me"—songs with slight, simple lyrics and catchy, sweet melodies—quite endearing; they sound like a high school diary brought to life. Songs this simple and sweet need clean, direct arrangements, but *Pieces of You* was largely recorded live, which means it often sounds ragged and rough. "Who Will Save Your Soul?," "You Were Meant for Me" and "Foolish Game" were all re-recorded before they became hit singles, and all three are superior in their single versions, since these live album cuts sound hurried. It's an unfortunate situation, since the slapdash production emphasizes the awkwardness of the lesser songs. Still, *Pieces of You* has enough charm to make it an ingratiating debut, even if the album doesn't quite fulfill Jewel's potential. *—Stephen Thomas Erlewine*

Spirit / Nov. 17, 1998 / Atlantic ✦✦✦✦

Billy Joel

b. May 9, 1949, Hicksville, Long Island, NY

Vocals, Keyboards, Piano, Harmonica, Synthesizer, Organ / Album Rock, Pop/Rock, Soft Rock, Singer/Songwriter

Although Billy Joel never was a critic's favorite, the pianist emerged as one of the most popular singer/songwriters of the latter half of the '70s. Joel's music consistently demonstrates an affection for Beatlesque hooks and a flair for Tin Pan Alley and Broadway melodies. His fusion of two distinct eras made him a superstar in the late-'70s and '80s, as he racked an impressive string of multi-platinum albums and hit singles.

As a teenager, Joel worked his way into the music industry by playing piano on several recordings produced by George "Shadow" Morton. He joined the Hassles in 1967, and the soul-inflected rock & roll band recorded two albums for United Artists that went nowhere. After the Hassles disbanded, Joel and the group's drummer formed the short-lived heavy metal organ-drum duo, Atilla. Joel struck out on a solo career in 1971, fashioning himself as a sensitive singer/songwriter with his debut album *Cold Spring Harbor.* The record went nowhere, so Joel hightailed it out to California, playing piano bars. The experience led to "Piano Man," the song that gave him his first hit in 1973. Two albums followed, neither of which were particularly successful, then Joel hooked up with producer Phil Ramone for his fifth album, *The Stranger.* Sleek, well-crafted and unabashedly melodic, the record became a blockbuster, establishing Joel as a star. Throughout the late '70s and early '80s, Billy Joel was among the most popular rock & rollers, turning out a series of albums that sold millions of copies, spun off Top 10 singles and won Grammys. His pace slowed in the second half of the '80s, as he retreated into the superstar pace of the '80s, releasing only two studio albums between 1985 and 1990 (both were huge successes). This was only the start of a slow-down—during the '90s, he released only one album, not counting compilations and live affairs. Despite the lack of new material, he remained a star, selling out stadiums on his concert tours.

Cold Spring Harbor / 1971 / Columbia ✦✦✦

A few short months after abandoning the heavy organ-and-drums duo Attila—partially because their sole record flopped, partially because he stole the drummer's wife—Billy Joel reinvented himself as a sensitive singer-songwriter. He had shown signs of McCartneyesque songcraft on *Hour of the Wolf,* the last Hassles album, but his debut album *Cold Spring Harbor* is where these talents blossomed. The record was uneven but very charming, boasting two of his finest songs—the lovely "She's Got a Way" and the bitterly cynical "Everybody Loves You Now"—and a score of flawed but nicely-crafted songs that illustrated Joel's gift for melody, as well as his pretensions (the mock-gospel in "Tomorrow is Today," a classical stab entitled "Nocturne"). In its own way, *Cold Spring Harbor* was a minor gem of the sensitive singer-songwriter era; Joel may have been in his formative stages as a craftsman, but his talents are apparent, and he never made an album as intimate and vulnerable ever again. Ironically, it didn't sound upon its original release. Through a bizarre mastering error, the tapes were sped up—legend has it that upon hearing the completed album, he ripped it off the turntable, ran out of the house and threw it down the street. It wasn't until 1983 that Columbia released a corrected reissue. The speed wasn't the only thing changed—some songs were edited drastically ("You Can Make Me Free," one of the standouts, was chopped by nearly five minutes) and instruments and backing vocals were stripped away from numerous tracks. It may be a bastardization of the original release, but it's an acceptable one, since these changes only accentuate the intimacy and vulnerability of the recording. *—Stephen Thomas Erlewine*

Piano Man / Nov. 1973 / Columbia ✦✦✦✦

Embittered by legal disputes with his label and an endless tour to support a debut that was dead in the water, Billy Joel hunkered down in his adopted hometown of Los Angeles, spending six months as a lounge singer at a club. He didn't abandon his dreams—he continued to write songs, including "Piano Man," a fictionalized account of his weeks as a lounge singer. Through a combination of touring and constant hustling, he landed a contract with Columbia and recorded his second album in 1973. Clearly inspired by Elton John's *Tumbleweed Connection,* not only musically but lyrically, as well as James Taylor, Joel expands the vision and sound of *Cold Spring Harbor,* abandoning introspective numbers (apart from "You're My Home," a love letter to his wife) for character sketches and epics. Even the title track, a breakthrough hit based on his weeks as a saloon singer, focuses on the colorful patrons, not the singer. If his narratives are occasionally awkward or incomplete, he compensates with music that gives the songs a sweeping sense of purpose—they *feel* complete, thanks to his indelible melodies and savvy stylistic re-purposing. He may have borrowed his basic blueprint from *Tumbleweed Connection,* particularly with its Western imagery and bluesy gospel flourishes, but he makes it his own, largely due to his melodic flair, which is in greater evidence than on *Cold Spring Harbor. Piano Man* is where he suggests his potential as a musical craftsman. He may have weaknesses as a lyricist—such mishaps as the "instant pleasuredome" line in "You're My Home" illustrate that he doesn't have an ear for words—but *Piano Man* makes it clear that his skills as a melodicist can dazzle. *—Stephen Thomas Erlewine*

Streetlife Serenade / Oct. 1974 / Columbia ✦✦✦

Turnstiles / May 1976 / Columbia ✦✦✦✦✦

There's a reason *Turnstiles* begins with the Spectoresque epic "Say Goodbye to Hollywood." Shortly after *Streetlife Serenade,* Joel ditched California—and, by implication, sensitive Californian soft-rock from sensitive singer-songwriters—for his hometown of New York. "Say Goodbye to Hollywood" was a celebration of his move, a repudiation of his past, a fanfare for a new beginning, which is exactly what *Turnstiles* was. He still was a singer-songwriter—indeed, "Summer, Highland Falls" was his best ballad to date, possibly his best ever—but he decided to run with his musical talents, turning the record into a whirlwind tour of pop styles, from Sinatra to Springsteen. There's little question that the cinematic sprawl of *Born to Run* had an effect on *Turnstiles,* since it has a similar wide-screen feel, even if it clocks in at only eight songs. The key to the record's success is variety, the way the album whips from the bouncy, McCartneyesque "All You Wanna Do is Dance" to the saloon song "New York State of Mind;" the way the bitterly cynical "Angry Young Man" gives way to the beautiful "I've Loved These Days" and the surrealistic apocalyptic fantasy "Miami 2017 (Seen the Lights Go Out On Broadway)." No matter how much stylistic ground Joel covers, he's kept on track by his backing group. He fought to have his touring band support him on *Turnstiles,* going to the lengths of firing his original producer, and it was clearly the right move, since they lend the album a cohesive feel. It may not have been a hit, but it remains one of his most accomplished and satisfying records, clearly paving the way to his twin peaks of the late '70s, *The Stranger* and *52nd Street. —Stephen Thomas Erlewine*

The Stranger / Sep. 1977 / Columbia ✦✦✦✦✦

Billy Joel teamed with Phil Ramone, a famed engineer who had just scored his first producing hits with Art Garfunkel's *Breakaway* and Paul Simon's *Still Crazy After All These Years* for *The Stranger,* his follow-up to *Turnstiles.* Joel still favored big, sweeping melodies but Ramone convinced him to streamline his arrangements and clean up the production. The results aren't necessarily revelatory, since he covered so much ground on *Turnstiles,* but the commercialism of *The Stranger* is a bit of a surprise. None of his ballads have been as sweet or slick as "Just the Way You Are"; he never had created a rocker as bouncy or infectious as "Only the Good Die Young"; and the glossy production of "She's Always a Woman" disguises its latent misogynist streak. Joel balanced such radio-ready material with a series of New York vignettes, seemingly inspired by Springsteen's working-class fables and clearly intended to be the artistic centerpieces of the album. They do provide *The Stranger* with the feel of a concept album, yet there is no true thematic connection between the pieces, and his lyrics are often vague or mean-spirited. His lyrical shortcomings are overshadowed by his musical strengths. Even if his melodies sound more Broadway than Beatles—the epic suite "Scenes from an Italian Restaurant" feels like a show-stopping closer—there's no denying that the melodies of each song on *The Stranger* are memorable, so much so that they strengthen the weaker portions of the album. Joel rarely wrote a set of songs better than those on *The Stranger,* nor did he often deliver an album as consistently listenable. *—Stephen Thomas Erlewine*

52nd Street / Oct. 1978 / Columbia ✦✦✦✦

Once *The Stranger* became a hit, Joel quickly re-entered the studio with producer Phil Ramone to record the follow-up, *52nd Street.* Instead of breaking from the sound of *The Stranger,* Joel chose to expand it, making it more sophisticated and somewhat jazzy. Often, his moves sounded as if they were responses to Steely Dan—indeed, his phrasing and melody for "Zanzibar" is a direct homage to Donald Fagen circa *The Royal Scam,* and it also boasts a solo from jazz great Freddie Hubbard, *a la* Steely Dan—but since Joel is a working-class populist, not an elitist college boy, he never shies away from big gestures and melodies. Consequently, *52nd Street* unintentionally embellishes the Broadway overtones of its predecessor, not only on a centerpiece like "Stiletto," but when he's rocking out on "Big Shot." That isn't necessarily bad, since Joel's strong suit turns out to be showmanship—he dazzles with his melodic skills and his enthusiastic performances. He also knows how to make a record. Song for song, *52nd Street* might not be as strong as *The Stranger,* but there are no weak songs—indeed, "Honesty," "My Life," "Until the Night" and the three mentioned above are among his best—and they all flow together smoothly, thanks to Ramone's seamless production and Joel's melodic craftsmanship. It's remarkable to think that in a matter of three records, Joel had hit upon a workable, marketable formula—one that not only made him one of the biggest-selling artists of his era, but one of the most enjoyable mainstream hit-makers. *52nd Street* is a testament to that achievement. *—Stephen Thomas Erlewine*

Glass Houses / Mar. 1980 / Columbia ✦✦✦✦✦
The back-to-back success of *The Stranger* and *52nd Street* may have brought Billy Joel fame and fortune, even a certain amount of self-satisfaction, but it didn't bring him critical respect, and it didn't dull his anger. If anything, being classified as a mainstream rocker—a soft-rocker—infuriated him, especially since a generation of punks and New Wave kids were getting the praise that eluded him. He didn't take this lying down—he recorded *Glass Houses*. Comparatively a harder-rocking album than either of its predecessors, with a distinctly bitter edge, *Glass Houses* still displays the hallmarks of Billy Joel the pop craftsman and Phil Ramone the world-class hitmaker. Even its hardest songs—the terrifically paranoid "Sometimes a Fantasy," "Sleepin' with the Television On," "Close to the Borderline," the hit "You May Be Right"—have bold, direct melodies and clean arrangements, ideal for radio play. Instead of turning out to be a fiery rebuttal to his detractors, the album is a remarkable catalog of contemporary pop styles, from McCartneyesque whimsy ("Don't Ask Me Why") and arena-rock ("All for Leyna") to soft-rock ("C'etait Toi (You Were the One)") and stylish New Wave pop ("It's Still Rock and Roll to Me," which ironically is closer to New Wave pop than rock). That's not a detriment; that's the album's strength. *The Stranger* and *52nd Street* were fine albums in their own right, but it's nice to hear Joel scale back his showman tendencies and deliver a solid pop-rock record. It may not be punk—then again, it may be his concept of punk—but *Glass Houses* is the closest Joel ever got to a pure rock album. *—Stephen Thomas Erlewine*

Songs in the Attic / Sep. 1981 / Columbia ✦✦✦✦
Having scored three multi-platinum hits in a row, Billy Joel took a breather, releasing his first live album, *Songs in the Attic*, as he worked on his ambitious follow-up to *Glass Houses*. Joel wisely decided to use the live album as an opportunity to draw attention to songs from his first four albums. Apart from "Piano Man," none of those songs had been heard by the large audience he had won with *The Stranger*. Furthermore, he now had a seasoned backing band that helped give his music a specific identity—in short, it was an opportunity to reclaim these songs, now that he had a signature sound. And Joel didn't botch the opportunity—*Songs in the Attic* is an excellent album, ranking among his very best work. With the possible exception of the *Turnstiles* material, every song is given a fuller, better arrangement that makes them all spring to life. "Los Angelenos" and "Everybody Loves You Now" hit harder in the live setting, while ballads like "She's Got a Way," "Summer, Highland Falls" and "I've Loved These Days" are richer and warmer in these versions. A few personal favorites from these albums may be missing, but what is here is impeccable, proving that even if Joel wasn't a celebrity in the early '70s, his best songs of the era rivaled his biggest hits. *—Stephen Thomas Erlewine*

The Nylon Curtain / Sep. 1982 / Columbia ✦✦✦
Billy Joel hit back as hard as he could with *Glass Houses*, his bid to prove that he could rock as hard as any of those New Wave punks. He might not have proven himself a punk—for all of his claims of being a hard rocker, his work inevitably is pop because of his fondness for melody—but he proved to himself that he could still rock, even if the critics didn't give him any credit for it. It was now time to mature, to move pop-rock into the middle age and, in the process, earn critical respect. In short, *The Nylon Curtain* is where Billy Joel went serious, consciously crafting a song cycle about Baby Boomers in the Reagan era. Since this was an album about Baby Boomers, he chose to base his music almost entirely on the Beatles, the pivotal rock band for his generation. Joel is naturally inclined to write big melodies like McCartney, but he idolizes Lennon, which makes *The Nylon Curtain* a fascinating cross between ear candy and social commentary. His desire to record a grand concept album is admirable, but his ever-present lyrical shortcomings mean that the songs paint a picture without arriving at any insights. He occasionally gets lost in his own ambition, as on the waterlogged second side, but the first half of the song suite—"Allentown," "Laura," "Pressure," "Goodnight Saigon," "She's Right on Time"—are layered, successful, mature pop songs that bring Joel tantalizingly close to his ultimate goal of sophisticated pop-rock for mature audiences. *—Stephen Thomas Erlewine*

An Innocent Man / Aug. 1983 / Columbia ✦✦✦✦
Recording *The Nylon Curtain* exhausted Billy Joel, and even though it had a pair of major hits, it didn't rival its predecessors in terms of sales. Since he labored so hard at the record, he decided it was time for a break—it was time to record an album just for fun. And that's how his homage to pre-Beatles pop, *An Innocent Man*, was conceived: it was designed as a breezy romp through the music of his childhood. Joel's grasp on history isn't remarkably astute—the opener "Easy Money" is a slice of Stax/Volt pop-soul, via the Blues Brothers (quite possibly the inspiration for the album), and the label didn't break the pop charts until well after the British Invasion—but he's in top form as a craftsman throughout the record. Only once does he stumble on his own ambition ("This Night," which appropriates its chorus from Beethoven). For the rest of the record, he's effortlessly spinning out infectious, memorable melodies in a variety of styles, from the Four Seasons sendup "Uptown Girl" and the soulful "Tell Her About It" to a pair of doo-wop tributes, "The Longest Time" and "Careless Talk." Joel has rarely sounded so carefree either in performance or writing, possibly due to "Christie Lee" Brinkley, a supermodel who became his new love prior to *An Innocent Man*. He can't stop writing about her throughout the album—only three songs, including the haunted title track, *aren't* about her in some form or fashion. That giddiness is infectious, helping make *An Innocent Man* an innocent delight that unwittingly closes Joel's classic period. *—Stephen Thomas Erlewine*

● **Greatest Hits, Vols. 1 & 2 (1973-1985)** / 1985 / Columbia ✦✦✦✦✦
Although it's missing a few important (not to mention big) hits, *Greatest Hits, Vols. 1 & 2* is an excellent retrospective of the first half of Billy Joel's career. Beginning with "Piano Man," and the first disc runs through a number of early songs before arriving at the hit-making days of the late '70s; some of these songs, including "Captain Jack" and "New York State of Mind," weren't strictly hits, but were popular numbers within his stage show and became radio hits. Once the songs from *The Stranger* arrive half-way through the first disc, there's no stopping the hits (although "Scenes from an Italian Restaurant," an album track from *The Stranger*, manages its way onto the collection). In fact, over the next disc and a half, there's so many hits, it's inevitable that some are left off—to be specific, "Honesty," "Sometimes a Fantasy," "An Innocent Man," "Leave a Tender Moment," and "Keeping the Faith" aren't included. But all the other hits—including "Just the Way You Are," "Only the Good Die Young," "My Life," "You May Be Right," "It's Still Rock and Roll to Me," "Don't Ask Me Why," "Allentown," "Tell Her About It" and "Uptown Girl," among many others—*are* present and accounted for, as are two new songs ("You're Only Human (Second Wind)," "The Night Is Still Young") that became hits as well. In short, *Greatest Hits, Vols. 1 & 2* does its job perfectly, encapsulating exactly why Billy Joel was one of the most popular singer/songwriters of the late '70s and early '80s. *—Stephen Thomas Erlewine*

The Bridge / Jul. 1986 / Columbia ✦✦✦

Kohuept (Live in Leningrad) / Oct. 1987 / Columbia ✦✦

Storm Front / Oct. 1989 / Columbia ✦✦

River of Dreams / Aug. 10, 1993 / Columbia ✦✦

Greatest Hits, Vol. 3 / Aug. 19, 1997 / Columbia ✦✦✦

2000 Years: The Millennium Concert / May 2, 2000 / Columbia ✦✦✦

Elton John (Reginald Dwight)

b. Mar. 25, 1947, Pinner, Middlesex, England
Vocals, Keyboards, Piano / Album Rock, Pop/Rock, Soft Rock, Adult Contemporary, Singer/Songwriter, Rock & Roll
In terms of sales and lasting popularity, Elton John was the biggest pop superstar of the early '70s. Initially marketed as a singer/songwriter, John soon revealed he could craft Beatlesque pop and pound out rockers with equal aplomb. He could dip into soul, disco and country, as well as classic pop balladry and even progressive rock. His versatility, combined with his effortless melodic skills, dynamic charisma and flamboyant stage shows made him the most popular recording artist of the '70s. Unlike many pop stars, John was able to sustain his popularity, charting a Top 40 single every single year from 1970 to 1996. During that time, he had temporary slumps in creativity and sales, as he fell out of favor with critics, had fights with his lyricist Bernie Taupin, and battled various addictions and public scandals. But through it all, John remained a remarkably popular artist and many of his songs—including "Your Song," "Rocket Man," "Goodbye Yellow Brick Road," and "Don't Let the Sun Go Down On Me"—became contemporary pop standards. *—Stephen Thomas Erlewine*

Empty Sky / 1969 / Rocket/Island ✦✦
Although he had made a number of re-recordings of popular songs for a budget record label in the late '60s, *Empty Sky* was the first true solo album John recorded after leaving Bluesology; it also marked the beginning of his long and fruitful collaboration with lyricist Bernie Taupin. *Empty Sky* is quite indicative of the post-*Sgt. Pepper* era. With its ambitious arrangements and lyrics, it's clear that John and Taupin intended the album to be a major statement. Though it shows some signs of John's R&B roots, most of the album alternates between vaguely psychedelic rock and burgeoning pop songcraft, capped off by a bizarre reprise of brief moments of *all* of the songs on the record. There aren't any forgotten gems on *Empty Sky*, but it does suggest John's potential. (The CD reissue includes the bonus tracks "Lady Samantha," "All Across the Havens," "It's Me That You Need," and "Just Like Strange Rain.") *—Stephen Thomas Erlewine*

Elton John / Aug. 1970 / Rocket/Island ✦✦✦✦✦
Empty Sky was followed by *Elton John*, a more focused and realized record that deservedly became his first hit. John and Taupin's songwriting had become more immediate and successful; in particular, John's music had become sharper and more diverse, rescuing Taupin's frequently nebulous lyrics. "Take Me to the Pilot" might not make much sense lyrically, but John had the good sense to ground its willfully cryptic words with a catchy blues-based melody. Next to the increased sense of songcraft, the most noticeable change on *Elton John* is the addition of Paul Buckmaster's grandiose string arrangements. Buckmaster's orchestrations are never subtle, but they never overwhelm the vocalist, nor do they make the songs schmaltzy. Instead, they fit the ambitions of John and Taupin, as the instant standard "Your Song" illustrates. Even with the strings and choirs that dominate the sound of the album, John manages to rock out on a fair share of the record. Though there are a couple of underdeveloped songs, *Elton John* remains one of his best records. (The CD reissue includes the bonus tracks "Bad Side of the Moon," "Grey Seal," and "Rock 'n' Roll Madonna.") *—Stephen Thomas Erlewine*

☆ **Tumbleweed Connection** / Jan. 1971 / Rocket/Island ✦✦✦✦✦
Instead of repeating the formula that made *Elton John* a success, John and Taupin attempted their most ambitious record to date for the follow-up to their breakthrough. A loose concept album about the American West, *Tumbleweed Connection* emphasized the pretentions that always lay beneath their songcraft. Half of the songs don't follow conventional pop song structures; instead, they flow between verses and vague choruses. These experiments are remarkably successful, primarily because Taupin's lyrics are evocative and John's melodic sense is at its best. As should be expected for a concept album about the Wild West, the music draws from country and blues in equal measures, ranging from the bluesy choruses of "Ballad of a Well-Known Gun" and the modified country of "Country Comfort" to the gospel-inflected "Burn Down the Mission" and the rolling, soulful "Amoreena." Paul Buckmaster manages to write dramatic but appropriate string arrangements that accentuate the cinematic feel of the album. (The CD reissue includes the bonus tracks "Into the Old Man's Shoes" and the original, stringless version of "Madman Across the Water.") *—Stephen Thomas Erlewine*

11-17-70 / Mar. 1971 / Rocket/Island ✦✦✦

Madman Across the Water / Nov. 1971 / Rocket/Island ♦♦♦♦♦
Trading the cinematic aspirations of *Tumbleweed Connection* for a tentative stab at prog-rock, Elton John and Bernie Taupin delivered another excellent collection of songs with *Madman Across the Water.* Like its two predecessors, *Madman Across the Water* is driven by the sweeping string arrangements of Paul Buckmaster, who gives the songs here a richly dark and haunting edge. And these are songs that benefit from grandiose treatments. With most songs clocking in around five minutes, the record feels like a major work, and in many ways it is. While it's not as adventurous as *Tumbleweed Connection,* the overall quality of the record is very high, particularly on character sketches "Levon" and "Razor Face," as well as the melodramatic "Tiny Dancer" and the paranoid title track. *Madman Across the Water* begins to fall apart toward the end, but the record remains an ambitious and rewarding work, and John never attained its darkly introspective atmosphere again. *—Stephen Thomas Erlewine*

☆ **Honky Chateau** / May 1972 / Rocket/Island ♦♦♦♦♦
Considerably lighter than *Madman Across the Water, Honky Chateau* is a rollicking collection of ballads, rockers, blues, country-rock and soul songs. On paper, it reads like an eclectic mess, but it plays as the most focused and accomplished set of songs Elton John and Bernie Taupin ever wrote. The skittering boogie of "Honky Cat" and the light psychedelic pop of "Rocket Man" helped send *Honky Chateau* to the top of the charts, but what is truly impressive about the album is the depth of its material. From the surprisingly cynical and nasty "I Think I'm Gonna Kill Myself" to the moving ballad "Mona Lisas and Mad Hatters," John is at the top of his form, crafting immaculate pop songs with memorable melodies and powerful hooks. While Taupin's lyrics aren't much more comprehensible than before, John delivers them with skill and passion, making them feel more substantial than they are. But what makes *Honky Chateau* a classic is the songcraft, and the way John ties disparate strands of roots music into distinctive and idiosyncratic pop—it's one of the finest collections of mainstream singer-songwriter pop of the early '70s. *—Stephen Thomas Erlewine*

Don't Shoot Me I'm Only the Piano Player / Jan. 1973 / Rocket/Island ♦♦♦♦
Elton John became a true superstar with 1972's *Honky Chateau.* He followed that album with *Don't Shoot Me I'm Only the Piano Player,* his most direct, pop-oriented album to date. Designed as a pastiche of classic and contemporary pop styles, the album almost sounds like an attempt to demonstrate the diversity of the John/Taupin team. Though the hits are remarkable—"Daniel" is a moving ballad and "Crocodile Rock" is a sly take on '50s rock & roll—the album is slightly uneven. Several of the album tracks, particularly the knowing "I'm Gonna Be a Teenage Idol" and the rocking "Elderberry Wine," are as strong as anything John had recorded but there are too many melodies that simply don't catch hold. Nevertheless, the singles were strong enough to keep the album at the top of the charts and at its best, it is a very enjoyable piece of well-crafted pop/rock. (The CD reissue includes the bonus tracks "Screw You (Young Man's Blues)," "Jack Rabbit," "Whenever You're Ready (We'll Go Steady Again)," and the piano version of "Skyline Pigeon.") *—Stephen Thomas Erlewine*

Goodbye Yellow Brick Road / Oct. 1973 / Rocket/Island ♦♦♦♦♦
Goodbye Yellow Brick Road was where Elton John's personality began to gather more attention than his music, as it topped the American charts for eight straight weeks. In many ways, the double album was a recap of all the styles and sounds that made John a star. *Goodbye Yellow Brick Road* is all over the map, beginning with the prog-rock epic "Funeral for a Friend (Love Lies Bleeding)" and immediately careening into the balladry of "Candle in the Wind." For the rest of the album, John leaps between pop-craft ("Bennie and the Jets"), ballads ("Goodbye Yellow Brick Road"), hard rock ("Saturday Night's Alright for Fighting"), novelties ("Jamaica Jerk-Off"), Taupin's literary pretensions ("The Ballad of Danny Bailey") and everything in between. Though its diversity is impressive, the album doesn't hold together very well. Even so, its individual moments are spectacular and the glitzy, crowd-pleasing showmanship that fuels the album pretty much defines what made Elton John a superstar in the early '70s. *—Stephen Thomas Erlewine*

Caribou / Jun. 1974 / Rocket/Island ♦♦♦
Glitzy showmanship is what fuels *Caribou,* the least successful collection to be reissued in this batch of albums. Though the shiny surface of the album is alluring, only a few tracks on the record rank among John's best work. "The Bitch Is Back" is one of his best hard-rock cuts and "Don't Let the Sun Go Down On Me" is one of his classic ballads, but the album tracks tend to be ridiculous filler on the order of "Solar Prestige a Gammon" or competent genre exercises like "You're So Static." There are a couple of exceptions—"Pinky" is a fine ballad and "Dixie Lily" is an endearing stab at country—but on the whole, *Caribou* is a disappointment. (The CD reissue includes the bonus tracks "Pinball Wizard," "Sick City," "Cold Highway," and "Step into Christmas.") *—Stephen Thomas Erlewine*

★ **Greatest Hits** / Nov. 1974 / Polydor ♦♦♦♦♦
Rarely has a greatest hits collection been as effective as Elton John's first compilation of *Greatest Hits.* Released at the end of 1974, after *Goodbye Yellow Brick Road* and *Caribou* had effectively established him as a superstar, *Greatest Hits* is exactly what it says it is—it features every one of his Top 10 singles ("Your Song," "Rocket Man," "Honky Cat," "Crocodile Rock," "Daniel," "Goodbye Yellow Brick Road," "Bennie and the Jets," "Don't Let the Sun Go Down on Me"), plus the number 12 "Saturday Night's Alright for Fighting" and radio and concert favorites "Border Song" and "Candle in the Wind." Despite the exclusion of a couple of lesser hits from this era, most notably "Levon" and "Tiny Dancer," *Greatest Hits* is a nearly flawless collection, offering a perfect introduction to Elton John and providing casual fans with almost all the hits they need. *—Stephen Thomas Erlewine*

☆ **Captain Fantastic & the Brown Dirt Cowboy** / May 1975 / Rocket/Island ♦♦♦♦♦
Sitting atop the charts in 1975, Elton John and Bernie Taupin recalled their rise to power in *Captain Fantastic & the Brown Dirt Cowboy,* their first explicitly conceptual effort since *Tumbleweed Connection.* It's no coincidence that it's their best album since then, showcasing each at the peak of their powers, as John crafts supple, elastic, versatile pop and Taupin's inscrutable wordplay is evocative, even moving. What's best about the record is that it works best of a piece—although it entered the charts at number one, this only had one huge hit in "Someone Saved My Life Tonight," which sounds even better here, since it tidily fits into the musical and lyrical themes. And although the musical skill on display here is dazzling, as it bounces between country and hard rock within the same song, this is certainly a grower. The album needs time to reveal its treasures, but once it does, it rivals *Tumbleweed* in terms of sheer consistency and eclipses it in scope, capturing John and Taupin at a pinnacle. They collapsed in hubris and excess not long afterward—*Rock of the Westies,* which followed just months later is as scattered as this is focused—but this remains one a testament to the strengths of their creative partnership. *—Stephen Thomas Erlewine*

Rock of the Westies / Oct. 1975 / Rocket/Island ♦♦

Here & There / May 1976 / Rocket/Island ♦♦♦

Blue Moves / Oct. 1976 / MCA ♦♦
An unprecedented year in the making, the two-record *Blue Moves* was Elton John's opening farewell, a dreary song cycle full of self-pity and recycled melodies by an artist who had finally run out of gas. The inevitable hit was "Sorry Seems to Be the Hardest Word," although "Tonight," the album's other memorable song, was just as indicative of the low emotional ebb of the John-Taupin team. As the Mamas and the Papas once said in an album title, "Farewell to the first golden era." *—William Ruhlmann*

A Single Man / Oct. 1978 / Polydor ♦♦♦
An unusually well-crafted album, and the beginning of John's comeback. "Part-Time Love" was the hit, but "Madness" and the instrumental "Song for Guy" were musical highlights. *—William Ruhlmann*

Victim of Love / 1979 / MCA ♦

21 at 33 / May 1980 / MCA ♦♦♦

The Fox / 1981 / MCA ♦♦

Jump Up! / Apr. 1982 / MCA ♦♦♦
John began finding his greatest successes with ballads in the 1980s, and this album still finds him mixing collaborators, including Tim Rice (with whom he would write the 1994 soundtrack to *The Lion King*), this time to good effect: Gary Osborne contributes "Blue Eyes," while Bernie Taupin effectively eulogizes John Lennon in "Empty Garden." Originally on Geffen, this album has since been acquired by MCA. *—William Ruhlmann*

Too Low for Zero / May 1983 / MCA ♦♦♦♦♦
With Taupin (and his old band) on board full-time, John turned out one of his best '80s albums—one full of remorse ("Cold as Christmas") and fierce reaffirmation ("I'm Still Standing"), not to mention such irresistible tunes as "Kiss the Bride" and "I Guess That's Why They Call It the Blues." *—William Ruhlmann*

Breaking Hearts / Jul. 1984 / MCA ♦♦♦
This album was paced by its number five big ballad hit, "Sad Songs (Say So Much)," one of Elton John's most memorable latter day tunes. There were also two more Top 40 entries in "Who Wears These Shoes?" and "In Neon," but in retrospect, this is one of John's slighter albums of the '80s. *—William Ruhlmann*

Ice on Fire / Nov. 1985 / MCA ♦♦♦

Leather Jackets / 1986 / MCA ♦♦

☆ **Greatest Hits, Vol. 2** / Apr. 28, 1986 / Polydor ♦♦♦♦♦
Greatest Hits, Vol. 2 rounds up the handful of singles that weren't included on Elton John's first *Greatest Hits* collection ("Levon," "Tiny Dancer") and adds the highlights from *Caribou, Captain Fantastic and the Brown Dirt Cowboy,* and *Rock of the Westies* ("The Bitch is Back," "Someone Saved My Life Tonight," "Island Girl," "Grow Some Funk of Your Own," "I Feel Like a Bullet (In the Gun of Robert Ford)"), plus two non-LP hit singles, ("Lucy in the Sky with Diamonds," "Philadelphia Freedom") and John's version of "Pinball Wizard," taken from the soundtrack to *Tommy.* In short, it's an excellent continuation of the first collection and taken together, they function as an ideal singles retrospective of the most successful singles artist of the early '70s. *—Stephen Thomas Erlewine*

Elton John Live in Australia (With the Melbourne Symphony Orchestra) / Jun. 1987 / MCA ♦♦

Reg Strikes Back / Jun. 1988 / MCA ♦♦

The Complete Thom Bell Sessions / 1989 / MCA ♦♦♦
Elton John released a three-song EP from his abortive 1977 sessions with Philadelphia International producer Thom Bell in 1979. Ten years later, he issued a six-song EP containing the initial three tracks and three more that are unremarkable. The things an artist will do for record collectors . . . *—William Ruhlmann*

Sleeping with the Past / Aug. 1989 / MCA ♦♦

To Be Continued . . . / 1990 / MCA ♦♦♦♦♦
The inevitable Elton John box set is a four-disc, 68-track affair covering 25 years of the biggest pop star since the Beatles. Hit after hit is heard, plus good album tracks and rarities. There's a big booklet with commentary by John and his lyricist, Bernie Taupin. In a pinch, you can get by with the two MCA and one Geffen greatest hits collections, but for a complete overview of Elton John's career, this is the place to come. *—William Ruhlmann*

The One / Jun. 23, 1992 / MCA ♦♦

Rare Masters / Oct. 20, 1992 / Polydor Chronicles ♦♦♦♦
A two-disc collection of rarities from the early '70s, it includes B-sides and the entire *Friends* soundtrack, which has previously been unavailable on CD. *Rare Masters* is essential for any hardcore Elton John fan. *—AMG*

Greatest Hits, 1976-1986 / Nov. 10, 1992 / MCA ♦♦♦♦♦
When Elton John left Geffen for MCA, *Greatest Hits, 1976-1986* replaced *Greatest Hits, Vol. 3 (1979-1987).* The newer collection is a better collection than its predecessor, since it trims the failed single "Heartache All Over the World," which was added as an incentive for hardcore collectors, and "Too Low for Zero," replacing them with "Sorry Seems to Be the Hardest

Word," "Don't Go Breaking My Heart" and "Who Wears These Shoes?" Those three cuts are added to 10 songs that illustrate that John could still craft a killer pop single during the '80s. *— Stephen Thomas Erlewine*

Duets / Nov. 23, 1993 / MCA ✦✦

Chartbusters Go Pop! 20 Legendary Covers from 1969/70 as Sung by Elton John / 1994 / Cleopatra ✦✦

Made in England / Mar. 21, 1995 / Rocket/Island ✦✦✦

Big Picture / Sep. 23, 1997 / Mercury ✦✦✦

Aida / Mar. 23, 1999 / Rocket/Island ✦✦✦

One Night Only / Nov. 21, 2000 / Uptown/Universal ✦✦✦

Freedy Johnston

b. Kinsley, KS

Vocals, Guitar / Americana, Adult Alternative Pop/Rock, Singer/Songwriter

Pitting acute, evocative portraits of outsiders and beautiful losers against fragile, shimmering country-pop melodies, the acclaimed work of Freedy Johnston earned him a reputation as one of the brightest singer/songwriters to emerge in the 1990s. His debut LP, 1990's *The Trouble Tree*, attracted a cult following domestically while becoming a sizable hit abroad, especially in the Netherlands, where he became a star. However, Johnston remained a struggling musician at home, and in order to complete his 1992 sophomore effort *Can You Fly?*, he was forced to sell the family farm, which he had inherited from his grandfather. The resulting recording, however, was a critical smash that ended up on a number of prominent year-end lists, and after another EP, *Unlucky*, he was signed to Elektra Records. His 1994 major-label debut, the Butch Vig-produced *This Perfect World*, proved to be Johnston's most satisfying release to date; its first single, "Bad Reputation," even earned him significant airplay on alternative radio formats. *Never Home* surfaced in early 1997. *—Jason Ankeny*

Trouble Tree / 1990 / Bar/None ✦✦✦✦

Johnston's debut, though not without its rough edges, firmly established him as a talent to be reckoned with—even his earliest songs are marked by great maturity and insight. *—Jason Ankeny*

Can You Fly / Apr. 14, 1992 / Bar/None ✦✦✦✦✦

"Well I sold the dirt to feed the band" goes the opening line of Johnston's sophomore effort, a reference to the sale of his family farm, a measure necessary to pay for the record's completion. The move was a risky one, but *Can You Fly* was worth it; this is a uniformly excellent collection of songs, highlighted by the lilting "Tearing Down This Place" and "Down in Love," a beautiful duet with Syd Straw. *—Jason Ankeny*

Unlucky / 1993 / Bar/None ✦✦✦

The six-song EP *Unlucky* features *Can You Fly*'s tale of Las Vegas woe, "The Lucky One," in both its completed and demo forms. In addition to three new Johnston originals, it also contains a terrific cover of Jimmy Webb's "Wichita Lineman." *—Jason Ankeny*

● **This Perfect World** / Jun. 28, 1994 / Elektra ✦✦✦✦✦

The songwriting gifts of Freedy Johnston grow in depth and resonance with each effort, and with *This Perfect World*, he makes his biggest leap yet. Richly produced by Butch Vig, the record is a collection of poignant character studies, finely-etched portraits of alienation, loneliness and rejection. *—Jason Ankeny*

Never Home / Feb. 25, 1997 / Elektra ✦✦✦✦✦

From the propulsive opener "On the Way Out" to the lilting closer "Something's Out There" (about, of all things, a UFO abduction), the sparkling *Never Home* is Johnston's most musically and emotionally expansive outing to date. Finding a sympathetic ear in producer and guitarist Danny Kortchmar, Johnston's songs transcend their dark themes to reveal unexpected and heretofore unseen moments of warmth and sentimentality; even edgy, Randy Newman-like character studies such as "He Wasn't Murdered" and "Gone to See the Fire" offer moments of tenderness which their subjects (suicide and arson, respectively) can't suppress. *—Jason Ankeny*

Blue Days Black Nights / Jul. 20, 1999 / Elektra ✦✦✦✦

The darkest, most understated Freedy Johnston record to date, *Blue Days Black Nights* is also the singer's most intimate effort, largely rejecting the quirky character studies of prior outings in favor of more plainly personal narratives, and revealing new shades of depth and honesty in the process. Co-producers T-Bone Burnett and Roger Moutenot cloak Johnston's songs in dusky atmospherics which underscore the music's spare beauty—far removed from the crackling pop flavor of the preceding *Never Home* or even the shimmering folk of *This Perfect World*, *Blue Days Black Nights* possesses a hushed gravity which insinuates itself only over repeated listens. At times the results are overly ponderous, but a handful of tracks—the opening "Underwater Life" and "Moving on a Holiday" included—rank among Johnston's finest. *—Jason Ankeny*

Howard Jones (John Howard Jones)

b. Feb. 23, 1955, Southampton, Hants, England

Vocals, Keyboards / Pop/Rock, New Wave, Synth Pop

One of the defining figures of mid-'80s synth-pop, Howard Jones merged the technology-intensive sound of new wave with the cheery optimism of hippies and late-'60s pop. After playing with jazz and funk bands after college, Jones began performing as a solo artist with only synthesizers and drum machines. By 1983, he had recorded his first single, the number three hit "New Song." "What Is Love" performed even better, prompting his debut album *Humans Lib* to top the charts in England. Jones' second album *Dream into Action* went platinum in the US, and spawned hit singles like "Things Can Only Get Better," "Like to Get to Know You Well" and "Life in One Day." A new version of the album track "No One Is to Blame" became Jones' biggest US hit, peaking at number four. In 1989, his "Everlasting Love" single became a Top 20 hit in America, though the album *Cross That Line* stalled on the charts. Jones returned three years later with the acoustic set titled *In the Running*, that failed to make the charts at all. Elektra dropped him in 1993, prompting Jones to hit the road, performing acoustic shows. He released *Working in the Backroom* on his own Dtox label, and followed in 1996 with *Live Acoustic America*. *People* followed two years later. *—Stephen Thomas Erlewine*

Human's Lib / 1984 / Elektra ✦✦✦✦✦

His debut album is almost entirely performed on synthesizers. The material on *Human's Lib*, like all of the following albums, is very inconsistent; Jones either writes hits or flops, with very little in between. Contains two of Jones' best songs, "New Song" and "What Is Love?" *—Iotis Erlewine*

Dream into Action / 1985 / Elektra ✦✦✦✦

This album shows the synthesizer pop idol at the height of his creativity—*Dream Into Action* is definitely the most interesting of Jones' albums. It contains some of his best songs—"Things Can Only Get Better," "Life in One Day," and "No One Is to Blame." The CD includes two bonus tracks, "Bounce Right Back" and "Like to Get to Know You Well," both of which are worthwhile additions. *—Iotis Erlewine*

Action Replay / 1986 / Elektra ✦✦

One to One / 1986 / Elektra ✦✦

Cross That Line / 1989 / Elektra ✦✦✦

In the Running / Apr. 14, 1992 / Elektra ✦✦

● **The Best of Howard Jones** / Jun. 29, 1993 / Elektra ✦✦✦✦✦

The Best of Howard Jones compiles all the necessary material ever put forth by this pop synthesizer master and is overabundant with a hearty 18 tracks. Jones had a remarkable eight Top 40 singles throughout the course of the mid-1980s, churning out keyboard laden dance/pop songs that were bright and lively. His debut album, *Human's Lib*, was a blend of new wave shine and friendly pop, which harbored the uppity "New Song" and the Duran Duran sound-alike ballad "What Is Love?" Worthy of its number four mark on *Billboard* is the beautiful "No One Is to Blame," which was one of the prettiest songs from the era. His flair for catchy melodies comes alive on both "Things Can Only Get Better" and the synth spicy "Life In One Day." Other highlights include the rich textured "Everlasting Love" from 1989 and the vibrant elevated chorus of "Lift Me Up," illuminating Jones' surprising vocal range. Sounding similar to the British trio the Thompson Twins, who were popular at the same time, Howard Jones' music reflected the synth driven sound of the decade. This compilation gathers all of his hits and then some, making for a perfect one stop album. *—Mike DeGagne*

Live Acoustic America / Feb. 13, 1996 / Plump ✦✦✦

Angels & Lovers / Aug. 1997 / Pony Canyon International ✦✦✦

People / Jul. 14, 1998 / Ark 21 ✦✦✦

Rickie Lee Jones

b. Nov. 8, 1954, Chicago, IL

Vocals, Keyboards, Guitar / Folk-Rock, Singer/Songwriter

Once touted as the natural successor to Joni Mitchell, singer/songwriter Rickie Lee Jones proved no less idiosyncratic or mercurial; like Mitchell, Jones experienced significant commercial success at the outset of her career, but a restless creative spirit—combined with a stubborn refusal to fit comfortably into any one musical niche—sealed her ultimate destiny as that of a highly-regarded cult heroine. She began performing around Los Angeles in the mid-'70s, honing her unique, Beat-influenced spoken-word monologues. Her first measure of success was as a songwriter, though she gained her own contract from Warner Brothers for her self-titled 1979 debut LP. Spurred by the success of the jazz-flavored hit single "Chuck E's in Love," *Rickie Lee Jones* became a smash both commercially and critically, earning praise for Jones' elastic vocals, vivid wordplay and unique fusion of folk, jazz and R&B. With 1981's follow-up *Pirates*, she began employing longer and more complex song structures. *The Magazine*, released in 1984, was her most slick, synth-driven outing to date. She was silent for most of the decade, finally resurfacing with 1989's sterling *Flying Cowboys*. For 1991's *Pop Pop*, Jones covered ballads ranging in origin from Tin Pan Alley to the Haight-Ashbury. After 1993's *Traffic From Paradise*, she embarked on an acoustic tour; *Naked Songs*, a document of those unplugged shows, followed in 1995. *—Jason Ankeny*

★ **Rickie Lee Jones** / Mar. 1979 / Warner Brothers ✦✦✦✦✦

One of the most impressive debuts for a singer/songwriter ever, this infectious mixture of styles not only features a strong collection of original songs (the hits are "Chuck E's in Love" and "Young Blood," but "Danny's All-Star Joint" and "Coolsville" are just as good) but also a singer with a savvy, distinctive voice that can be streetwise, childlike, and sophisticated, sometimes all in the same song. *— William Ruhlmann*

Pirates / Jul. 1981 / Warner Brothers ✦✦✦✦

After the critical (and commercial) success of her debut two years earlier, Rickie Lee Jones had a lot riding on her sophomore album, *Pirates*. From the opening track, "We Belong Together," Jones served notice that she was willing to challenge herself and experiment with more unusual, complex song structures. Her unique phrasing and style reflect her interest in beat poets and the Bohemian lifestyle, and on this album she relies on more obscure imagery than the direct, detailed observations on comrades used on her first album. There are a wide range of musical influences represented (rock, jazz, soul), but the acoustic arrangements are more piano-based than most of her other albums. While there is an undercurrent of reflection on failed romances, Jones also reveals her playful side with songs like "Woody and Dutch." The musical and lyrical variety on the album is best represented in the album's centerpiece, "Pirates (So Long Lonely Avenue)," where she moves through mood and tempo changes with ease. Although the songs may not immediately grab the listener, the lyrical and musical complexities ultimately make this album more rewarding with every listen. *— Vik Iyengar*

The Magazine / Sep. 1984 / Warner Brothers ✦✦

Flying Cowboys / Sep. 1989 / Geffen ✦✦✦✦✦
Five years after the disappointing *The Magazine*, Rickie Lee Jones returned to form with *Flying Cowboys*, which shared much of the playful, childlike charm of her debut, *Rickie Lee Jones*, and some of the musically diffuse, lyrically ambitious form of its follow-up, *Pirates*. From the opening track, "The Horses," twhich suggested a mother's delight with her child as much as a lover's devotion, Jones reintroduced the joyous tone of her early work as well as establishing the Western theme that would run through the album—cowboys, rodeos, horses, deserts—without adding up to an actual story line. The easy rhythms and lazy, flexible singing on the first few songs were reminiscent of Laura Nyro's work with Labelle on their *Gonna Take a Miracle* album, after which Jones branched out into reggae and folk-blues, coming up with an affectionate bluesman voice on "Ghost Train." "Satellites," the college radio hit, used the sprung rhythms and surprising choral parts familiar from her popular early songs. If Jones could be obscure and unfocused as a writer, that weakness was also her strength, since it was an expression of the imagination that also produced her most striking musical effects. Producer Walter Becker may have helped keep things from getting as grandiose as they had on *The Magazine*, but it was really the artist herself who managed to rein in from that album's self-importance. If what resulted was not as accomplished as *Pirates*, it was the most accessible and enjoyable music Jones had made since her debut. *—William Ruhlmann*

Pop Pop / Aug. 1991 / Geffen ✦✦✦

Traffic from Paradise / Sep. 14, 1993 / Geffen ✦✦

Naked Songs / Sep. 19, 1995 / Reprise ✦✦✦✦✦
Rickie Lee Jones "unplugged"—in fact, solo with an acoustic guitar or piano on all but a couple of tunes—*Naked Songs* is otherwise a retrospective concert album on which Jones cherrypicks songs from her five studio albums, including the hits "Chuck E.'s in Love" and "Young Blood," and others from her breakthrough debut record. The studio album arrangements always tried to support and augment Jones' idiosyncratic writing and playing style, which sounds less unusual when she is simply accompanying herself, and in many ways more effective. "Altar Boy," a previously unreleased song, strays into Leonard Cohen territory, mixing religion with eroticism. *—William Ruhlmann*

Ghostyhead / Jun. 17, 1997 / Warner Brothers ✦✦✦
Ghostyhead finds Rickie Lee Jones in the odd position of following a younger generation, as its languid trip-hop beats suggest that she has been listening to Portishead, Tricky, and Beth Orton. It is certainly a precarious situation, since she could seem out of touch and old-fashioned, but it is a makeover she pulls off surprisingly well. Jones tends to follow the trippy, free-form structures of trip-hop, which means the melodies occasionally meander and the lyrics are more impressionistic than usual, concentrating on the overall effect instead of the details. There are still more solidly constructed songs than atmospheric instrumentals, which gives the album an anchor, making the electronic echoes and rolling beats all the more effective. Although the songs aren't among Jones' best, the musical adventurousness of *Ghostyhead*—which manages to be contemporary without sacrificing her style—makes the album a revitalization of sorts. *—Stephen Thomas Erlewine*

It's Like This / Sep. 12, 2000 / Artemis ✦✦✦

Tom Jones (Thomas Jones Woodward)

b. Jun. 7, 1940, Pontypridd, South Wales
Vocals / Club/Dance, Vocal Pop, Pop, Country-Pop
Tom Jones became one of the most popular vocalists to emerge from the British Invasion. Since the mid-'60s, Jones has applied his full-throated, robust baritone to nearly every form of popular music, from pop, rock, and show tunes to country, dance, and techno. While performing, Jones always radiated a raw sexuality, which earned him a large following of devoted female fans who frequently threw underwear on stage. Jones' following never diminished over the decades; he was able to exploit trends, earning new fans while retaining his core following.

Born Thomas Jones Woodward, Tom Jones began singing professionally in 1963, and recorded his first single for Decca, "Chills and Fever," in late 1964. "Chills and Fever" didn't chart but "It's Not Unusual," released in early 1965, became a number one hit in the U.K. and a Top Ten hit in the U.S. A series of hits followed but Jones' popularity began to slip somewhat by the middle of 1966, causing Mills to redesign the singer's image into a more respectable, mature tuxedoed crooner. For the remainder of the '60s, he scored a consistent string of hits in both Britain and America. At the end of the decade, Jones relocated to America, where he hosted the television variety program, "This Is Tom Jones." Lucrative performances took up his time and he would not record again until the early '80s when he released a series of slick Nashville-styled country-pop albums that earned him a handful of hits.

Jones' next image makeover came in 1988, when he sang Prince's "Kiss" with the electronic dance outfit, the Art of Noise. In 1994, he was on the comeback trail again, releasing the alternative-dance-pop album *The Lead and How to Swing It;* the record was a moderate hit, gaining some play in dance clubs. *—Stephen Thomas Erlewine*

• **The Best of Tom Jones** / Jun. 2, 1998 / Polygram ✦✦✦✦✦
The Best of Tom Jones is a comprehensive collection of his greatest hits that supplants *The Complete Tom Jones* as being the definitive CD-era hits collection. Running 22 tracks where *The Complete* only featured 20, the disc contains everyone of Jones' classic singles, from "It's Not Unusual," "What's New Pussycat," "Thunderball," "Deliah" and "She's a Lady" to "Kiss." Even though this features the cream of the crop, there are a few weak moments here and there—Tom Jones wasn't exactly a consistent artist—but there's no denying that this is the pick for casual fans. *—Stephen Thomas Erlewine*

Janis Joplin

b. Jan. 19, 1943, Port Arthur, TX, **d.** Oct. 4, 1970, Los Angeles, CA
Vocals / Album Rock, Hard Rock, Blues-Rock
The greatest White female rock singer of the 1960s, Janis Joplin was also a great blues singer, making her material her own with her wailing, raspy, supercharged emotional delivery. First rising to stardom as the frontwoman for San Francisco psychedelic band Big Brother & the Holding Company, she left the group in the late '60s for a brief and uneven (though commercially successful) career as a solo artist. Although she wasn't always supplied with the best material or most sympathetic musicians, her best recordings, with both Big Brother and on her own, are some of the most exciting performances of her era. She also did much to redefine the role of women in rock with her assertive, sexually forthright persona and raunchy, electrifying onstage presence. Joplin was sometimes criticized for screeching at the expense of subtlety, but her final album *Pearl* was solid evidence of her growth as a mature, diverse stylist who could handle blues, soul, and folk-rock. "Mercedes Benz," "Get It While You Can," and Kris Kristofferson's "Me and Bobby McGee" are some of her very best tracks. Tragically, she died before the album's release, overdosing on heroin in a Hollywood hotel in October 1970. "Me and Bobby McGee" became a posthumous #1 single in 1971, and thus the song with which she is most frequently identified. *—Richie Unterberger*

I Got Dem Ol' Kozmic Blues Again Mama / 1969 / Columbia ✦✦✦
Joplin's solo debut was a letdown at the time of release, suffering in comparison with Big Brother's *Cheap Thrills* from the previous year, and shifting her style towards soul-rock in a way that disappointed some fans. Removed from that context, it sounds better today, though it's still flawed. Fronting the short-lived Kozmic Blues Band, the arrangements are horn heavy and the material soulful and bluesy. The band sounds a little stiff, though, and although Joplin's singing is good, she would sound more electrifying on various live versions of some of the songs that have come out over the years. The shortage of quality original compositions—indeed, there are only eight tracks total on the album—didn't help either, and the cover selections were erratic, particularly the Bee Gees' "To Love Somebody." On the other hand, "Try" is one of her best soul outings, and the reading of Rodgers-Hart's "Little Girl Blue" is inspired. The 1999 CD reissue adds three bonus tracks: a cover of Bob Dylan's "Dear Landlord" from the *Kozmic Blues* sessions that was first heard on the *Janis* box set and previously unreleased versions of "Summertime" and "Piece of My Heart" from *the Woodstock Festival*. "Summertime" is okay, but this "Piece of My Heart" really pales next to the Big Brother interpretation. *—Richie Unterberger*

☆ **Pearl** / Feb. 1971 / Columbia/Legacy ✦✦✦✦✦
Joplin's second masterpiece (after *Cheap Thrills*), *Pearl* was designed as a showcase for her powerhouse vocals, stripping down the arrangements that had often previously cluttered her music or threatened to drown her out. Thanks also to a more consistent set of songs, the results are magnificent—given room to breathe, Joplin's trademark rasp conveys an aching, desperate passion on funked-up, bluesy rockers, ballads both dramatic and tender, and her signature song, the posthumous number one hit "Me and Bobby McGee." The unfinished "Buried Alive In the Blues" features no Joplin vocals—she was scheduled to record them on the day after she was found dead. Its incompleteness mirrors Joplin's career; *Pearl*'s power leaves the listener to wonder what else Joplin could have accomplished, but few artists could ask for a better final statement. The 1999 CD reissue adds four previously unreleased live July 1970 recordings: "Tell Mama," "Little Girl Blue," "Try," and "Cry Baby." *—Steve Huey*

In Concert / May 1972 / Columbia ✦✦✦
About half of this two-record set features Janis Joplin with Big Brother and the Holding Company in 1968, performing songs like "Down on Me" and "Piece of My Heart." The rest, recorded in 1970, finds her with her backup group, Full Tilt Boogie, mostly performing songs from *I Got Dem Ol' Kozmic Blues Again Mama!* Joplin puts herself out on stage, both in terms of singing until her voice is raw and describing her life to her audiences. Parts of this album are moving, parts are heartbreaking, and the rest is just great rock & roll. *—William Ruhlmann*

• **Janis Joplin's Greatest Hits** / Jul. 1973 / Columbia/Legacy ✦✦✦✦✦
A solid, if skimpy, ten-track best-of that gathers the most important songs from Joplin's solo career, as well as her stint with Big Brother & the Holding Company. The compilation *18 Essential Songs* offers a wider selection, but does not include the original version of "Me and Bobby McGee," which makes *Greatest Hits* the better purchase for those who only want one Janis Joplin disc, even if it isn't definitive. The 1999 CD reissue adds two bonus tracks, "Maybe" and "Mercedes Benz." *—Steve Huey*

Farewell Song / 1983 / Columbia ✦✦✦
A ragtag collection of odds and ends, live and studio, from both the Big Brother and solo era. The best cuts are on the *Janis* box in different versions, but serious fans will find some interesting items here, especially the *Cheap Thrills*-era outtakes and live performances; "Misery 'N'," "Farewell Song," and "Catch Me Daddy" were easily good enough to have qualified for inclusion on that album. *—Richie Unterberger*

Janis / Nov. 23, 1993 / Columbia/Legacy ✦✦✦✦✦
This 3-CD box set is the most thorough and valuable retrospective of Janis Joplin's career. Besides including all of her most essential recordings with and without Big Brother and the Holding Company, this 49-song package features quite a few enticing rarities; 18 of the tracks were previously unissued. These include a 1962 home recording of the Joplin original "What Good Can Drinkin' Do," which marked the first time her singing was captured on tape; a pair of acoustic blues tunes from 1965 with backup guitar by future Jefferson Airplane star Jorma Kaukonen, an acoustic demo of "Me and Bobby McGee," a 1970 birthday song for John Lennon, and live performances from her appearance on "The Ed Sullivan Show" in 1969. The real showstopper is the previously unissued, eight-minute version of "Ball and Chain" from Big Brother's first set at the 1967 Monterey Pop Festival (the cut on the *Monterey Pop* box set is from their second set). The more forgettable tracks from her solo albums are wisely excised, as are the Big Brother songs which did not feature her vocals. This is the rare multidisc set of a major artist which manages to cover all the official milestones and present a bounty of worthwhile rarities at the same time. *—Richie Unterberger*

18 Essential Songs / Jan. 24, 1995 / Columbia/Legacy ✦✦✦✦✦
18 Essential Songs is a one-disc distillation of the triple-disc *Janis* box set. Running 70 minutes, it is a more extensive best-of than the ten-track 1973 *Janis Joplin's Greatest Hits* album.

But it is denied "first pick" status because, unlike that album, it does not contain the hit version of Joplin's only number one single, "Me and Bobby McGee." (It does, however, contain an alternate demo version of that song.) *— William Ruhlmann*

Journey

f. 1973, San Francisco, CA

Group / Album Rock, Arena Rock, Pop/Rock, Soft Rock, Hard Rock

During its 14-year existence (1973-1987), Journey altered its musical approach and its personnel extensively while becoming a top touring and recording band. The only constant factor was guitarist Neal Schon, a music prodigy who had been a member of Santana in 1971-1972. The earliest lineup recorded *Journey* (1974), the first of three moderate-selling jazz-rock albums given over largely to instrumentals. By 1977, however, the group decided it needed a strong vocalist/frontman and hired Steve Perry. The results were immediately felt on the fourth album, *Infinity* (1978), which had sold a million copies by the end of the year. *Evolution* (1979) was similarly successful, as was *Departure*. After a live album, *Captured* (1981), Journey released *Escape*, which broke them through to the top ranks of pop groups by scoring three Top Ten hit singles, all ballads featuring Perry's smooth tenor: "Who's Crying Now," "Don't Stop Believin'," and "Open Arms." *Frontiers* (1983), featuring the hit "Separate Ways," was another big success, after which Perry released a successful solo album, *Street Talk* (1984). Following the *Raised on Radio* tour, Journey disbanded. *— William Ruhlmann*

Journey / Apr. 1975 / Columbia ✦✦

Look into the Future / Jan. 1976 / Columbia ✦✦

Next / Feb. 1977 / Columbia ✦✦

Infinity / May 1978 / Columbia ✦✦✦

Evolution / Apr. 1979 / Columbia ✦✦✦✦✦

Departure / Mar. 1980 / Columbia ✦✦✦

Featuring the driving "Any Way You Want It" and the Top 40 hit "Walks like a Lady," *Departure* didn't mark a departure from Journey's successful pop/rock formula, but overall the record was a little weaker than their previous two albums. *— Stephen Thomas Erlewine*

Captured / Feb. 1981 / Columbia ✦✦✦

Escape / Aug. 1981 / Columbia ✦✦✦✦✦

Escape was a groundbreaking album for San Francisco's Journey, charting three singles inside *Billboard*'s Top Ten, with "Don't Stop Believing" reaching number nine, "Who's Crying Now" at number four, and "Open Arms" peaking at number two and holding there for six weeks. *Escape* flung Journey steadfastly into the AOR arena, combining Neil Schon's grand yet palatable guitar playing with Jonathan Cain's blatant keyboards. All this was topped off by the passionate, wide-ranged vocals of Steve Perry, who is the true lifeblood of this album, and this band. The songs on *Escape* deemed more rock flavored, with more hooks and a harder cadence compared to their former sound. "Who's Crying Now" spotlights the sweeping fervor of Perry's voice, whose theme about the ups and downs of a relationship was plentiful in Journey's repertoire. With "Don't Stop Believing," the whisper of Perry's ardor is crept up to with Schon's searing electric guitar work, making for a perfect rock song. One of rock's most beautiful ballads, "Open Arms" gleams with an honesty and feel only Steve Perry could muster. Outside of the singles, there is a certain electricity that circulates through the rest of the album. The songs are timeless, and as a whole, they have a way of rekindling the innocence of youthful romance and the rebelliousness of growing up, built from heartfelt songwriting and sturdy musicianship. *— Mike DeGagne*

Frontiers / Feb. 1983 / Columbia ✦✦✦✦

Frontiers managed to give Journey four Top 40 hits, with "After the Fall" and "Send Her My Love" both reaching number 23, "Faithfully" at number 12, and "Separate Ways" peaking at number eight—the same amount that 1981's *Escape* brandished. While they tried to use the same musical recipe as *Escape*, *Frontiers* comes up a little short, mainly because the keyboards seem to overtake both Schon's guitar playing and Steve Perry's strong singing. An overabundance of Jonathan Cain's synth work cloaks the quicker tunes and seeps into the ballads, slightly widening the strong partnership of Perry and Schon. "Faithfully" tried to match the powerful beauty of "Open Arms," and while it is a gorgeous ballad, it just comes inches away from conjuring up the same soft magic. "Separate Ways" grabs attention right off the bat with stinging synthesizer and a catchy guitar riff, and "Send Her My Love" emphasizes Perry's keen ability to pour his heart out. The rest of the songs on the album lack the warmth that Journey is famous for, especially in their mix of fervor and intimacy shown on this album's predecessor. *— Mike DeGagne*

Raised on Radio / May 1986 / Columbia ✦✦✦

Journey's ninth and last new studio album found the group reduced to a trio of guitarist Neal Schon, singer Steve Perry, and keyboard player Jonathan Cain. But even without their regular rhythm section, the group was able to re-create the accessible pop/rock sound perfected on earlier albums such as *Escape* and *Frontiers*. Schon's guitar still cut through the fat keyboard chords, and Perry's fluid tenor still gave the songs an airy, melodic appeal. All of that was good for sales of two million copies and five chart singles, four of which made the Top 40 and one of which, "Be Good to Yourself," reached the Top Ten. That didn't match the seven-million-selling number one *Escape*, but it confirmed that Journey's music had a large audience right to the end of its career. *— William Ruhlmann*

● **Greatest Hits** / Nov. 15, 1988 / Columbia ✦✦✦✦✦

Greatest Hits is an excellent, thorough 14-track collection containing all of Journey's big hits, from 1978's "Wheel in the Sky" to 1986's "I'll Be Alright Without You." Although the songs aren't presented in chronological order and a handful of minor hits ("Suzanne," "Walks Like a Lady") aren't included, it doesn't matter, since every essential Journey single—"Only the Young," "Don't Stop Believin'," "Any Way You Want It," "Separate Ways," "Lovin', Touchin' Squeezin'," "Open Arms," "Send Her My Love"—is here, which means that it's all most casual fans will ever need. *— Stephen Thomas Erlewine*

Time 3 / Dec. 1, 1992 / Columbia ✦✦✦✦

Journey has given radio some of AOR's finest three-minute gems, both in hard rock and ballad form. *Time 3* strings together all their best songs, most of them popular and some not so well known, but all extremely enjoyable and laid out over the course of three discs. Set up chronologically, the first disc unleashes their raw sound, with the first eight songs being pre-Steve Perry. With tracks from *Infinity*, *Evolution*, and *Departure* rounding out disc one, a young Perry sets a musical precedent with his soaring voice. Even so, "Any Way You Want It" steals the show amidst all of their early material. Disc two is where this set truly shines, containing their biggest hits and covering the most entertaining and fruitful part of Journey's career. Seven of the songs here are from 1981's *Escape* album, including of course "Open Arms," "Don't Stop Believing," and "Who's Crying Now." The first half of the disc finishes off hits from the *Departure* album, and smoothly rolls into songs from the live *Captured*. The third disc starts off with the B-side "La Raza Del Sol," and follows with "Only Solutions" from the movie *Tron*. The best songs from *Frontiers* and *Raised on Radio* make up the next ten tracks, and finishes with wonderful live performances of "Girl Can't Help It" and "I'll Be Alright Without You." *Time 3*, which comes with a colorful booklet and informative liner notes about each song (released in this style when the set first hit shelves), is an extremely comprehensive overview. There is an overabundance of material here, but all of it is incredibly pleasing. *— Mike DeGagne*

Trial by Fire / Oct. 22, 1996 / Columbia ✦✦

Joy Division

f. 1977, **db.** May 18, 1980

Group / Post-Punk

Formed in the wake of the punk explosion in England, Joy Division became the first band in the post-punk movement by later emphasizing not anger and energy but mood and expression, pointing ahead to the rise of melancholy alternative music in the '80s. Though the group's raw initial sides fit the bill for any punk band, Joy Division later incorporated synthesizers (taboo in the low-tech world of '70s punk) and more haunting melodies, emphasized by the isolated, tortured lyrics of its lead vocalist, Ian Curtis. While the British punk movement shocked the world during the late '70s, Joy Division's quiet storm of musical restraint and emotive power proved to be just as important to independent music in the 1980s. Founded in 1977, the group signed to Manchester's Factory label and released *Unknown Pleasures* in 1979. The album enjoyed immense critical acclaim and a long stay on the UK's independent charts. During late 1979, Joy Division's manic live show gained many converts, partly due to rumors of Curtis' ill health. An epilepsy sufferer, he was prone to breakdowns and seizures while on stage—it soon grew difficult to distinguish the fits from his usual onstage jerkiness and manic behavior. Just before their first US tour, Curtis hung himself and the group quickly disbanded. Ironically, their final studio work, the single "Love Will Tear Us Apart" and the LP *Closer*, became big British hits. Early in 1981, the remaining trio formed New Order. *— John Bush*

☆ **Unknown Pleasures** / 1979 / Qwest ✦✦✦✦✦

Raw and vital, Joy Division's full-length debut juxtaposes the taut, visceral energy of the group's evolving sound with the ghostly presence of vocalist Ian Curtis, whose grasp on the corporeal world seems to diminish with each passing song. While as claustrophobic and remote as any of the band's records, *Unknown Pleasures* is informed by a sense of punk-influenced aggression absent from Joy Division's later work; the album's tangible tension derives from the efforts of the primal rhythm battery of Peter Hook and Stephen Morris to breathe life into the music at the same time that the vortex of Curtis' soul threatens to suck it all out. Remarkable. *— Jason Ankeny*

☆ **Closer** / 1980 / Qwest ✦✦✦✦✦

Released in the wake of Ian Curtis' suicide, *Closer* travels through the looking glass into a cold, hopeless world of menace and loss. The opener "Atrocity Exhibition" sets both the sonic and emotional tone of the record: brutal and distant, the music is stripped bare of its humanity, finding its foothold instead in metallic rhythms, damaged synth patterns and jagged guitars. Looming over the proceedings are Curtis' disembodied vocals, which grip the songs from seemingly beyond the physical plane; while the singer dominates *Closer*, his presence is remote and ephemeral—while he can be felt at every moment, in truth he was already gone. *— Jason Ankeny*

Still / 1981 / Qwest ✦✦✦

Still collects outtakes and rarities along with a live set recorded on May 2, 1980, just over two weeks prior to Ian Curtis' death. In addition to the atmospheric "Glass" and the haunting funeral march "Dead Souls," the studio sides include four leftover tracks from the sessions for *Unknown Pleasures*, while the concert set includes performances of seminal tracks such as "Transmission," "Isolation" and "A Means to an End." Although neither as cogent nor as indispensible as the band's two studio records or the *Substance* compilation, *Still* is nonetheless a valuable chronicle of Joy Division's remarkable evolution, a growth charted by the inclusion of an early live cover of the Velvet Underground's "Sister Ray" to the only recorded version of the hypnotic "Ceremony," the ultimate Ian Curtis composition which later resurfaced as the first single from New Order. *— Jason Ankeny*

★ **Substance** / 1988 / Qwest ✦✦✦✦✦

Despite recording two of the greatest albums of the post-punk era (*Unknown Pleasures* and *Closer*, respectively), Joy Division was primarily a singles band, a legacy borne out by the stunning *Substance*. Beginning with the raw power of "Warsaw" and concluding with the classic "Love Will Tear Us Apart," the set collects the majority of the group's non-LP material, chronologically charting their monumental growth from visceral guitar noise to music of remarkable texture and emotional density; tracks like the oppressive "Digital," the hypnotic "Transmission" and the self-explanatory "Atmosphere" (rescued from an obscure French flexi-disc) are simply stunning, unparalleled in their obsessive and haunting power. *— Jason Ankeny*

Warsaw / 1994 / Intermusic ✦✦✦✦

What was planned to be Joy Division's first LP (unreleased until 1994, except in bootleg form) sounds like an album from the punk era—raw and edgy, undisciplined but tuneful, unlike the group's proper debut, *Unknown Pleasures.* All of the tracks were later seen in different form, but *Warsaw* still manages to captivate through its pure energy. In addition to the twelve tracks from the bootleg recordings, the album also includes five tracks from July 1977, the most punk-inspired songs in the group's discography. *—John Bush*

Permanent / Aug. 15, 1995 / Warner Brothers ✦✦✦
Featuring selected highlights from *Unknown Pleasures* and *Closer, Permanent* contains some of Joy Division's best songs, but the compilation isn't as useful as *Substance,* which featured early demos and B-sides, nor is it as mesmerizing as the band's two original studio albums. Consequently, *Permanent* is not only useless for dedicated fans, it's an incomplete and misleading introduction for casual fans, even though it contains a wealth of brilliant music. *—Stephen Thomas Erlewine*

Heart & Soul / 1998 / London ✦✦✦✦✦
For serious fans, the four-disc box set *Heart and Soul* is the ultimate Joy Division collection, containing almost everything the quartet recorded, from the Warsaw demos to *Closer,* as well as a full disc of live material. Even if this lovingly assembled set (compiled by Jon Savage, with the assistence of Bernard Sumner and Peter Hook) does contain the bulk of everything the band recorded, it might be a little disconcerting to longtime fans to hear *Unknown Pleasures* and *Closer* surrounded by the EP tracks and B-sides, but the pleasures of this set outweigh that problem. Any Joy Division collector will have much of the previously unreleased material in some bootleg form, but they won't have it in such good fidelity. There are also several rarities, such as flexi-disc versions and alternate takes, that have been hard to find, and the live recordings, while not revelatory, are very strong. The end result is the rare box set that is actually succeeds as a full career retrospective that's equally appealing to dedicated fans and neophytes. *—Stephen Thomas Erlewine*

Judas Priest

f. 1970, Birmingham, England, **db.** 1996
Group / New Wave of British Heavy Metal, Album Rock, British Metal, Heavy Metal, Hard Rock
Judas Priest was one of the most influential heavy metal bands of the '70s, spearheading the "new wave of British heavy metal" late in the decade. Decked out in leather and chains, the band fused the gothic doom of Black Sabbath with the riffs and speed of Led Zeppelin, adding a vicious two-lead guitar attack (by K.K. Downing and Glenn Tipton) to Rob Halford's dramatic vocals; in doing so, they set the pace for much popular heavy metal from 1975 until 1985, as well as laying the groundwork for the speed- and thrash-metal of the '80s. Judas Priest was formed in Birmingham, England in 1970, and recorded their debut, *Rocka Rolla,* for the independent U.K. label Gull in 1974. The follow-up, 1976's *Sad Wings of Destiny,* earned positive reviews and led to an international contract with CBS Records. *Sin After Sin* (1977) also received positive reviews, but 1978's *Stained Class* was the record that established them as an international force in metal. Along with 1979's *Hell Bent for Leather* (*Killing Machine* in the U.K.), *Stained Class* began the "new wave of British heavy metal" movement. A significant number of bands adapted Priest's leather-clad image and driving sound, making their music harder, faster and louder. 1980's more mainstream *British Steel* entered the British charts at number three, and launched the hit singles "Breaking the Law" and "Living After Midnight"; *Point of Entry,* released the following year, was nearly as successful. Featuring the hit "You've Got Another Thing Comin'," *Screaming for Vengeance* (1982) marked the height of their popularity, peaking at number 17 in America and selling over a million copies. However, metal tastes were changing, and Judas Priest began to seem out of touch; as a result, their sales slipped in the latter half of the '80s. Following the creative return to form of 1990's *Painkiller,* Halford left to form his own thrash band, Fight. Judas Priest rebounded with singer Tim "Ripper" Owens and the album *Jugulator,* released in late 1997 to mostly poor reviews. *—Stephen Thomas Erlewine*

Rocka Rolla / 1974 / Koch International ✦✦✦

Sad Wings of Destiny / 1976 / Koch International ✦✦✦✦

Sin After Sin / 1977 / Columbia ✦✦✦✦

Stained Class / Apr. 1978 / Columbia ✦✦✦✦✦
An indisputable metal masterpiece, *Stained Class* is the apex of '70s Judas Priest, a sinister, muscular collection that ties the disparate strands of their style together while jacking the adrenaline rush up to previously undreamed-of levels. Even the lone slow-tempo track, "Beyond the Realms of Death," has an exciting, visceral intensity, and the whole band is at the absolute peak of its powers in terms of technical execution. Lyrically, *Stained Class* is probably the darkest moment in a career filled with them; the whole second half of the record is positively obsessed with death, although the ridiculous 1989-90 court case alleging that the album provoked two Nevada teenagers' suicides was instead centered around the Gary Wright/Spooky Tooth cover "Better By You, Better Than Me," in which Rob Halford allegedly embedded the subliminal, backwards-recorded message, "Do it." At any rate, the air of malevolence about *Stained Class,* and the sheer power of its jackhammer guitar riffs, was unrivaled in heavy metal upon its release (even in Priest's own catalog), stamping the album an instant classic and solidifying Judas Priest's status as arguably the most original and musical metal band of its time. More than any other Priest album, the style of *Stained Class* also laid the groundwork for the thrash and speed metal that would rise to dominance in the mid to late '80s, making it a defining moment for the New Wave of British Heavy Metal movement and one of the genre's all-time landmarks. *—Steve Huey*

Hell Bent for Leather / Mar. 1979 / Columbia ✦✦✦✦✦
In 1979, Judas Priest was growing more and more influential. And as the 1980s progressed, it would become crystal clear that the British headbangers—who influenced everyone from Iron Maiden to Metallica to King Diamond—had every bit as great an impact as fellow British headbangers Black Sabbath. One of the Priest's strongest albums, *Hell Bent for Leather* cannot be described in anything less than glowing terms. Although gothic themes are present on such treasures as "The Green Manalishi (With the Two-Pronged Crown)"—originally recorded by Fleetwood Mac—"Evil Fantasies" and "Before the Dawn," the album generally isn't as dark or morbid as *Stained Class* or *Sin After Sin.* But musically, the band is as aggressive and brutally intense as ever. The two-guitar attack of Glenn Tipton and KK Downing is characteristically blistering, and lead singer Rob Halford never sounded more inspired. For those with even a casual interest in metal, *Hell Bent for Leather* is essential listening. *—Alex Henderson*

Unleashed in the East (Live in Japan) / Oct. 1979 / Columbia ✦✦✦✦

● **British Steel** / 1980 / Columbia ✦✦✦✦✦
With *Hell Bent for Leather,* Judas Priest had begun the task of developing their image for increased mainstream attention, reveling in leather-and-motorcycle trappings while beginning to simplify and streamline their sound. *British Steel* brings that process full circle, offering the band's catchiest, most accessible set of tunes yet, while retaining the precision guitar assault and quasi-operatic vocals that had come to define their sound. It was the simplest music Priest had yet attempted, but thanks to the (mostly) top-notch songwriting and AC/DC-like willingness to allow the songs' grooves room to breathe, the record is a smashing success overall, with maybe one or two subpar tracks. There are a couple of trends beginning here that would take their toll later on—the lyrics are a bit more juvenile, and the music seems to prize commercialism over complexity—but in this context, neither really matters, as Priest display a real penchant for stadium-ready anthems. "Breaking the Law" and "Living After Midnight" became genuine hit singles in the U.K., and deservedly so, while the album became their first to reach the U.S. Top 40, going platinum in the process. *—Steve Huey*

Point of Entry / 1981 / Columbia ✦✦✦
Having reinvented themselves as an arena-metal act with the hugely successful *British Steel,* Judas Priest naturally opted to stay the course with *Point of Entry,* keeping things simple while adding a bluesy boogie in places, a sound they hadn't really attempted in quite some time. However, where *British Steel*'s simplicity was an effective reworking of the band's sound, *Point of Entry*'s songs aren't always up to par, making its less well crafted tracks sound like lunkheaded, low-effort filler. When *Point of Entry* works, it works well—"Heading Out to the Highway," "Solar Angels," and "Desert Plains," for example, are great, driving hard-rock songs, but British rock-anthem hits "Don't Go" and "Hot Rockin'" seem oddly generic, given Priest's reputation for inventiveness. Even if *Point of Entry* is somewhat disappointing overall, though, it's partly because of the album's genre-transforming predecessors; it does have enough good moments to make it worthwhile to diehards and fans of the group's more commercial '80s output. *—Steve Huey*

Screaming for Vengeance / 1982 / Columbia ✦✦✦✦
Following the under-written, erratic *Point of Entry, Screaming for Vengeance* returned Judas Priest to the top of the metal heap, boasting a much more consistent set of songs, highlighted by the monumental "You've Got Another Thing Comin'." Some of the bluesier elements of *Point of Entry* are still here, but the heavier moments tend to dominate the album's flavor (particularly the title track); plus, there are arena-ready headbanging anthems like "Electric Eye," "Bloodstone," and, of course, "You've Got Another Thing Comin'," the latter two proof that the band really knew how to work a midtempo rock groove. Although the sound is commercial, *Screaming for Vengeance* doesn't feel like it's pandering, as *Point of Entry* sometimes did; it's a catchy, accessible metal record in the best sense of the description, and it rivals *British Steel* as Priest's best album of the '80s. *—Steve Huey*

Defenders of the Faith / 1984 / Columbia ✦✦✦
Having recaptured their heavyweight status with *Screaming for Vengeance,* Judas Priest stuck with their successful formula for the follow-up, *Defenders of the Faith.* Overall, it's a solidly constructed, unapologetically commercial metal record, and it doesn't feel underdeveloped as *Point of Entry* sometimes did. It isn't quite up to the level of *British Steel* or *Screaming for Vengeance,* partly because (unlike those two) it lacks a truly standout single, and partly because of a few lowest-common-denominator moments. Still, it's far from a bad entry in Priest's '80s arena-metal period, and it remains a favorite among many fans who prefer those recordings to the band's '70s work. *—Steve Huey*

Turbo / 1986 / Columbia ✦✦✦

Ram It Down / 1988 / Columbia ✦✦

● **Metal Works '73-'93** / May 18, 1993 / Columbia ✦✦✦✦✦
Although the double-disc *Metal Works '73-'93* is an intoxicating listen, it isn't quite the definitive Judas Priest retrospective it could have been. Six of the band's eleven U.K. chart singles aren't here, and while "Johnny B. Goode" probably won't be missed, *Hell Bent for Leather*'s "Take On the World" and "Evening Star," *British Steel*'s "United," and *Point of Entry*'s "Don't Go" and "Hot Rockin'" ought to have been included, especially since they were released during the band's influential prime. One could also argue for more material from the *Stained Class* era and less from the weaker mid- to late-'80s albums. Plus, the songs aren't arranged in chronological order, which makes it difficult to piece together the band's evolution and (sometimes trend-following) stylistic shifts. But quibbles aside, the collection makes a strong case for Judas Priest's versatility, drawing from nearly all of their albums material that encompasses dark, driving riff-rockers, melodic heavy metal, radio-ready commercial hard rock, the occasional ballad, and lyrics ranging from street-tough aggression and party anthems to sci-fi/fantasy themes and hints at Satanic posturing. The band's musicianship shines throughout; Priest's tightly controlled style was played with a sense of groove that allowed the music to breathe and kept it from sounding too tight-assed. In between the lesser-known tracks, which are often impressive, comes one metal classic after another—"Victim of Changes," "Living After Midnight," "Breaking the Law," "Hell Bent for Leather," "You've Got Another Thing Comin'," "Screaming for Vengeance," and more. Even if it isn't quite a definitive portrait of the band, it is an enjoyable one; many necessary items are here, and it rocks hard from start to finish. *—Steve Huey*

Jules & The Polar Bears

f. 1978, **db.** 1980
Group / New Wave
After the demise of the Funky Kings, singer/songwriter Jules Shear formed his own band consisting of Stephen Hague (keyboards and, later, a noted producer), Richard Bredice (guitar), David White (bass), and David Beebe (drums). They were signed to Columbia Records in 1978 solely on the basis of Shear's demos—at the time, the band had never played live together. They recorded their first LP, *Got No Breeding*, in 1978, which quickly found critical acclaim, drawing favorable comparisons to Jackson Browne, the Kinks, Bob Dylan, and Bruce Springsteen. Unfortunately, it failed to sell when Columbia tried to lump the band in with its new wave promotion. 1979's *Fenetiks*, another fine effort, went virtually unnoticed as well. A third LP, *Bad for Business*, was recorded, but Columbia decided to pass on it and the band folded. Shear moved on to a distinguished, though commercially unsuccessful, solo career, and Hague focused on production. The albums, especially *Got No Breeding*, remain cult favorites. *Bad for Business* was finally released in late '96 by Columbia/Legacy. *—Chris Woodstra*

Bad for Business / Sep. 3, 1996 / Columbia/Legacy ✦✦✦
Deemed not commercially viable and a bit on the weird side by the powers that be at Columbia Records in 1980, *Bad for Business*, the third album from Jules and the Polar Bears, remained in the Columbia vaults for 16 years before being issued in 1996. *Bad for Business* still seems somewhat quirky after all these years, although not really much more than its predecessor *Fenetiks*, with which it shares a similar sound thanks to Stephen Hague's keyboards.

The real treat in Columbia's decision to release the record is its batch of hook-laden tunes and the frenetic spurts of lyrics from Jules Shear. Songs such as the driving pop of "In Love with the Ballet" and the sweet but edgy "Only a Motion" show Shear to be in fine form on *Bad for Business*. This is a chance to further discover a terrific songwriter and one of the criminally overlooked bands of the late '70s. *—Brett Hartenbach*

● **Got No Breeding** / 1978 / Columbia/Legacy ✦✦✦✦✦
Though it is packed with memorable hooks and Jules Shear's subtle twist-of-phrase, *Got No Breeding* was virtually ignored upon release, due in part to Columbia Records mismarketing the band as part of the new wave. The Polar Bears were, in reality, just a good, hard-working rock band jamming with a sometimes overenthusiastic Shear. The songs are among Shear's finest and the album is one of his most consistently enjoyable. *—Chris Woodstra*

Phonetics/Fenetiks / 1979 / Columbia ✦✦✦
The second Polar Bears album follows much of the same formula as *Got No Breeding*, with less memorable results. The band still rocks in places but the overall production is slicker and a little more synthesizer heavy. Shear's songwriting is top-notch ranging from the pure pop of "Good Reason" to the beautiful ballad "Real Enough to Love." His delivery seems more restrained this time around. *—Chris Woodstra*

Kansas

f. 1970, Topeka, KS
Group / Album Rock, Arena Rock, Prog-Rock/Art Rock
Fusing the complexity of British prog-rock with an American heartland sound representative of their name, Kansas was among the most popular bands of the late 1970s; though typically dismissed by critics, many of the group's hits remain staples of AOR radio playlists to this day. Formed in Topeka in 1970, the founding members of the group—guitarist Kerry Livgren, bassist Dave Hope and drummer Phil Ehart—first played together while in high school; with the 1971 addition of violinist Robby Steinhardt, they changed their name to White Clover, reverting back to the Kansas moniker for good upon the 1972 arrivals of vocalist/keyboardist Steve Walsh and guitarist Richard Williams.

Kansas' self-titled debut LP appeared in 1974; their fan base grew to the point that their third effort, 1975's *Masque*, sold a quarter of a million copies. In 1977, *Leftoverture* truly catapulted Kansas to stardom. On the strength of the smash hit "Carry on Wayward Son," the album reached the Top Five and sold over three million copies. 1977's *Point of Know Return* was even more successful, spawning the monster hit "Dust in the Wind." *Monolith*, the band's first self-produced effort, also reached the Top Ten.

In the wake of 1980's *Audio-Visions*, Kansas began to splinter; Walsh soon quit to form a new band, Streets; the remaining members forged on without him, tapping vocalist John Elefante as his replacement. The group disbanded after only two albums, 1982's *Vinyl Confessions* and 1983's Drastic Measures. In 1986, however, Kansas re-formed around Ehart, Williams and Walsh; adding guitarist Steve Morse as well as bassist Billy Greer, the refurbished band debuted with the album *Power*.When the follow-up, 1988's *In the Spirit of the Things*, failed to hit, seven years passed before the release of their next effort, *Freaks of Nature*. *Always Never the Same* followed in 1998. Seeing the return of founder singer/songwriter Kerry Livgren, Somewhere to Elsewhere was released in 2000. *—Jason Ankeny*

Box Set / Jul. 12, 1994 / Epic/Legacy ✦✦✦✦
The Kansas Boxed Set is a double-disc, 26-track that contains all of the group's most popular songs—"Carry On Wayward Son," "Dust In the Wind," "Point of Know Return," "Hold On"—plus three previously unreleased live tracks, one demo and the newly recorded "Wheels." Collectors will certainly want those tracks, but they'll probably be frustrated by the album-rock staples that dominate the album. Conversely, most casual Kansas fans will be satisfied by the single-disc *Greatest Hits*, which contains all of the songs they know. The songs that they don't know—that is, the songs that form the bulk of this collection—may be among the best of the album tracks, but they still are weighed down by pomp and circumstance and are primarily of interest to hardcore fans, who will already have the original records. *—Stephen Thomas Erlewine*

● **The Best of Kansas** / Feb. 23, 1999 / Epic/Legacy ✦✦✦✦
Although it isn't perfect, *The Best of Kansas* is a solid 12-track collection that contains the bulk of the prog-rock group's greatest hits, including "Carry on Wayward Son," "Point of Know Return," "Dust in the Wind," "Hold On," "Play the Game Tonight" and "Fight Fire with Fire." A few fan favorites may be missing, but casual listeners will find that the best-known cuts are here. [The 1999 CD reissue adds three bonus tracks: "The Pinnacle," "The Devil Game," and "Closet Chronicles."] *—Stephen Thomas Erlewine*

K.C. & The Sunshine Band

f. 1973, Miami, FL
Group / Disco
In the early '70s, two white men, Harry "KC" Casey (b. Jan. 31, 1951) and Richard Finch (b. Jan. 25, 1954), created a racially integrated disco band that based its music on various soul styles. They became one of the most commercially successful groups of the early disco era. KC & the Sunshine Band's disco was funky enough to be a staple in the clubs, while remaining melodic and sweet enough to be huge pop hits. The group continued to have hits until the early '80s; their last hit single, "Give It Up," was credited to KC in the U.S. *—Bil Carpenter*

● **The Best of KC & the Sunshine Band** / Jun. 1990 / Rhino ✦✦✦✦✦
A percussive mix of steel drums, whistle flutes, and funky group harmonies, this most soulful disco set includes all of their hits—"Get Down Tonight," "Please Don't Go," "That's the Way (I Like It)," "I'm Your Boogie Man," "(Shake, Shake, Shake) Shake Your Booty," and KC's solo hit, "Give It Up." *—Bil Carpenter*

R. Kelly

Vocals, Keyboards, Producer / New Jack Swing, Urban
Urban R&B producer/vocalist/multi-instrumentalist/songwriter R. Kelly and his supporting band Public Announcement began recording in 1992 at the tailend of the New Jack Swing era, yet he was able to keep much of its sound alive while remaining commercially successful. While he's created a smooth, professional mixture of hip-hop beats, soul-man crooning, and funk, the most distinctive element of Kelly's music is its explicit carnality. Over the course of two albums, the singer has been able to make songs like "Sex Me," "Bump n' Grind," and "Your Body's Callin'" into hits because his production has been seductive enough to sell such blatant come-ons. *—Stephen Thomas Erlewine*

Born into the 90's / Jan. 14, 1992 / Jive ✦✦✦
One of the last popular New Jack groups, this East Coast unit had some smash singles in 1992 doing both conventional R&B/soul and hip-hop/New Jack tracks. They did both originals and covers, had an enthusiastic attitude, were well produced, and stayed on the urban contemporary outlets throughout the year. *—Ron Wynn*

● **12 Play** / Nov. 9, 1993 / Jive ✦✦✦✦✦
New jack swing may have been on its way out as a primary R&B sound, but R. Kelly didn't lose any points by employing it here. Kelly skillfully mixes '70s-style funk beats, '90s hip-hop production and his own raps, as well as those of Deandre Boykins and Carey Kelly. Sometimes things come perilously close to sounding corny and dated, but he manages to bring things off successfully. Kelly is a competent vocalist, but a master at striking and maintaining a heated mood, keeping a light touch no matter how explicit the language gets and giving this album distinction even as it mines territory that's essentially played out. *—Ron Wynn*

R. Kelly / Nov. 14, 1995 / Jive ✦✦✦✦✦
With the salacious *12 Play*, R. Kelly established himself as one of the top R&B hitmakers of the mid-'90s, rivalled only by Babyface and Dr. Dre for overall consistency. *12 Play* was marred by occasionally slight tunes which were obscured by the explicit sexuality of the lyrics. *R. Kelly* isn't hampered by those flaws, although it isn't a perfect record by any means. Throughout the album, Kelly relies on melody and grooves instead of overtly carnal imagery. But that doesn't mean he has cleaned up—Kelly remains a sly, seductive crooner, and his sexiness is more effective when it is suggestive. Nevertheless, his lyrics and music are never subtle—even on the ballads which dominate this album—which can make *R. Kelly* tiresome if taken as a whole. Taken as individual songs, the album works better than anything he has recorded to date. *—Stephen Thomas Erlewine*

R / Sep. 29, 1998 / Jive ✦✦✦

TP-2.Com / Nov. 7, 2000 / Jive ✦✦✦✦

Kid Rock (Robert James Ritchie)

b. Jan. 17, 1971, Romeo, MI
Vocals / Rap-Rock, Rap-Metal, Alternative Metal, Heavy Metal, Hard Rock
One of the unlikeliest success stories in rock at the turn of the millennium, Detroit rap-rocker Kid Rock shot to superstardom with his fourth full-length album, 1998's *Devil Without a Cause*. What made it so shocking was that Rock had recorded his first demo a full decade before, been booted off major label Jive following his Beastie Boys-ish 1990 debut *Grits Sandwiches for Breakfast*, and toiled for most of the decade in obscurity, releasing albums to a small, mostly local fan base while earning his fair share of ridicule around his home state. Nevertheless, Rock persevered, and by the time rap-metal had begun to attract a substantial audience, he had perfected the outlandish, over-the-top white-trash persona that made *Devil Without a Cause* such an infectious party record. Rock briefly became notorious in 1990 when a New York college radio station aired *Grits Sandwiches*' profanity-laced ode to oral sex, "Yodelin' in the Valley," and was fined over $20,000 (a judgment later rescinded). After being dropped from Jive, Rock recorded two small-label albums on a shoestring budget; he also set about forming a backing band, dubbed Twisted Brown Trucker. Rapper Joe C. (b. Joseph Calleja) was one of the first to join, catching Rock's eye in 1994 because of his diminutive stature (due to a digestive condition known as celiac disease). As rap-metal acts began to dominate the hard rock landscape, Atlantic Records decided to take a chance on signing Rock. *Devil Without a Cause* didn't do much upon its initial release in August 1998, but a big promotional push helped make the second single and video, "Bawitdaba," a nationwide smash. The follow-up, "Cowboy," achieved similar success, and suddenly, after a decade of

trying, Kid Rock was a superstar with a Top Five, seven-times-platinum album and a gig at Woodstock '99. Rock acquired the rights to his indie-label recordings and remixed or re-recorded the best material for 2000's *The History of Rock*. Sadly, a year after being forced to take a break from touring by his medical difficulties, Joe C. passed away in his sleep on November 16, 2000. *—Steve Huey*

● **Devil Without a Cause** / Aug. 18, 1998 / Lava/Atlantic ✦✦✦✦✦
I don't suspect that even Kid Rock believed he had an album as good as *Devil Without a Cause* in him. Nobody else believed it, that's for sure. But he didn't just find the perfect extention of his Beastie and Diamond Dave infatuations here, he came up with the great hard rock album of the late '90s—a fearlessly funny, bone-crunching record that manages to sustain its strength, not just until the end of its long running time, but through repeated plays. The key to its sucesss is that it's never trying to be a hip-hop record. It's simply a monster rock album, as Twisted Brown Trucker turns out thunderous, funky noise—and that's funky not just in the classic sense, but also in a Southern-fried, white trash sense, as he gives this as much foundation in country as he does hip-hop. But what really reigns supreme on *Devil Without a Cause* is a love of piledriving, classic hard rock, not just that of hometown hero Bob Seger, but Lynyrd Skynyrd, Van Halen, and faceless arena rock ballads. The Kid makes it all shine with rhymes so clever and irresistible that it's impossible not to quote them. For all its modernity—Rock's rapping, the titanic metallic guitars, Joe C's sideshow sidekick, the plea to "get in the pit and try to love someone"—this is firmly in the tradition of classic hard rock, and it's the best good-time hard rock album in years (certainly the best of the last three years of the '90s). *—Stephen Thomas Erlewine*

The History of Rock / May 30, 2000 / Lava/Atlantic ✦✦✦✦
Devil Without a Cause was so good it caused everybody to re-evaluate Kid Rock, including Rock himself. As he prepped a follow-up, he unleashed *The History of Rock*, a hodgepodge of new songs, unreleased tunes, demos, old cuts, and re-recordings. This not only bought the Kid time, it gave him a chance to revamp a past that was bordering on the seriously lame. According to *The History*, Rock always knew what he was doing. Anyone that's heard *The Polyfuze Method* knows that's not the case, but that's the beauty of *The History*, since the early stuff now sounds of piece with *Devil*. It isn't nearly as good, but it has some of the same thrills since his band hits harder and funkier than any of its rap-rock peers and Rock now has a fully cultivated persona. Still, the songs just aren't here. Apart from the "Get out of Denver" rewrite "Born 2 B a Hick," "Early Mornin' Stoned Pimp," "3 Sheets to the Wind" and maybe the Skynyrd-aping "Prodigal Son", the older recordings are still clumsy, something the new song "American Bad Ass" is not. A shameless slab of self-mythology where the former Bob Ritchie calls out tag-lines from *Devil* and places himself in the company of Seger, the Beasties, and No-Show Jones, all to a sample of Metallica's "Sad But True," it's cool, more or less, but not as monumental as "Bawitdaba," which had true wit, original riffs, and a sense of purpose. But, once you've worn out *Devil* and you need a new fix, you're not going to find it on the older Kid Rock albums—you're going to find it here. It's not a great listen, but its swagger and white-trash style make it the second-best record in his catalog. *—Stephen Thomas Erlewine*

King Crimson

f. 1969, England
Group / Album Rock, Prog-Rock/Art Rock
If there is one group that embodies progressive rock, it is King Crimson. Led by guitar/Mellotron virtuoso Robert Fripp, during its first five years of existence the band stretched both the language and structure of rock into realms of jazz and classical music, all the while avoiding pop and psychedelic sensibilities. The absence of mainstream compromises and the lack of an overt sense of humor ultimately doomed the group to nothing more than a large cult following, but made their albums among the most enduring and respectable of the prog-rock era. Crimson's 1969 debut *In the Court of the Crimson King* was one of the most challenging albums of the entire fledgling progressive rock movement, but somehow it caught the public's collective ear at the right moment, becoming a hit in England and America. At the peak of the LP's success, the original band broke up; Fripp recorded albums with several other lineups through 1972, none of them stable. Later that year, however, Fripp put together a skilled new band; their debut album, *Larks' Tongues in Aspic*, made it all the way to the Top 20 in England in 1973. 1974's *Starless and Bible Black* made this the first lineup to remain intact for more than one American tour and more than one album. But, alas, even it had begun to splinter. One more album, *Red*, was completed that summer; Fripp disbanded the group on September 25, 1974, seemingly for the last time, and moved on to other projects. In 1981, Fripp formed a new group called Discipline; by the time their album was released that year, the group's name had been changed to King Crimson (the album was still titled *Discipline*, however). This band had a herky-jerky sound completely different from any of the other lineups to use that name; they splintered after two more albums, 1982's *Beat* and 1984's *Three of a Perfect Pair*. King Crimson remained silent until 1994, when Fripp reunited with an augmented version of the *Discipline*-era lineup, re-establishing Crimson as a viable touring and recording concern. *—Bruce Eder*

★ **In the Court of the Crimson King** / 1969 / EG ✦✦✦✦✦
The group's definitive album, and one of the most daring debut albums ever recorded by anybody. At the time, it blew all of the progressive/psychedelic competition (the Moody Blues, the Nice etc.) out of the running, although it was almost too good for the band's own good—it took them nearly four years to come up with a record as strong or concise. Ian McDonald's Mellotron is the dominant instrument, along with his saxes and Fripp's guitar, making this a somewhat different-sounding record from everything else they ever did. And even though that Mellotron sound is muted and toned down compared to their concert work of the era (see *Epitaph*, below), it is still fierce and overpowering—coupled with some strong songwriting, most of it filled with dark and doom-laden visions, the strongest singing of Greg Lake's entire career, and Fripp's guitar playing (a strange mix of elegant classic, Hendrix-like rock explosions, and jazz noodling), the mix was overpowering. Fripp would be the only survivor on their subsequent records. Note: Be sure the CD you buy indicates it was made or distributed by Caroline Records—earlier versions sounded awful. *—Bruce Eder*

In the Wake of Poseidon / 1970 / EG ✦✦✦✦✦
King Crimson opened 1970 scarcely in existence as a band, having lost two key members (Ian McDonald and Michael Giles), with a third (Greg Lake) about to leave. Their second album—largely composed of Robert Fripp's songwriting and material salvaged from their stage repertory ("Pictures of a City" and "The Devil's Triangle")—is actually better produced and better sounding than their first. Surprisingly, Fripp's guitar is not the dominant instrument here: The Mellotron, taken over by Fripp after McDonald's departure—and played even better than before—still remains the band's signature. The record doesn't tread enough new ground to precisely rival *In the Court of the Crimson King*. Fripp, however, has made an impressive show of transmuting material that worked on stage ("Mars" aka "The Devil's Triangle") into viable studio creations, and "Cadence and Cascade" may be the prettiest song the group ever cut. "The Devil's Triangle", which is essentially an unauthorized adaptation of "Mars, Bringer of War" from Gustav Holst's *The Planets*, was later used in an eerie Bermuda Triangle documentary of the same name. In March of 2000, Caroline and Virgin released a 24-bit digitally remastered job that puts the two Mellotrons, Michael Giles' drums, Peter Giles' bass, and even Fripp's acoustic guitar and Keith Tippett's acoustic piano practically in the lap of the listener. *—Bruce Eder*

Lizard / 1970 / EG ✦✦✦
Lizard is very consciously jazz-oriented—the influence of Miles Davis (particularly *Sketches of Spain*) being especially prominent—and very progressive, even compared with the two preceding albums. The pieces are longer and have extensive developmental sections, reminiscent of classical music, and the lyrics are more ornate, while the subject matter is more exotic and rarified—epic, Ragnarok-like battles between good and evil that run cyclically. The doom-laden mood of the first two albums is just as strong, except that the music is prettier; the only thing missing is a sense of humor. Jon Anderson of Yes guests on one key number, "Prince Rupert Awakes" (which vocalist/bassist Gordon Haskell never completed), and the album is stronger for his presence. At the time of its release, some critics praised *Lizard* for finally breaking with the formula and structure that shaped the two preceding albums, but overall it's an acquired taste. *—Bruce Eder*

Islands / 1971 / EG ✦✦✦

Larks' Tongues in Aspic / 1973 / EG ✦✦✦✦✦
King Crimson reborn yet again—the newly configured band makes its debut with a violin (courtesy of David Cross) sharing center stage with Robert Fripp's guitars and his Mellotron, which is pushed into the background. The music is the most experimental of Fripp's career up to this time—though some of it actually dated (in embryonic form) back to the tail end of the Boz Burrell-Ian Wallace-Mel Collins lineup. And John Wetton was the group's strongest singer/bassist since Greg Lake's departure three years earlier. What's more, this lineup quickly established itself as a powerful performing unit working in a more purely experimental, less jazz-oriented vein than its immediate predecessor. "*Outer Limits* music" was how one reviewer referred to it, mixing Cross' demonic fiddling with shrieking electronics, Bill Bruford's astounding dexterity at the drum kit, Jamie Muir's melodic and usually understated percussion, Wetton's thundering (yet melodic) bass, and Fripp's guitar, which generated sounds ranging from traditional classical and soft pop-jazz licks to hair-curling electric flourishes. The remastered edition, which appeared in the summer of 2000 in Europe and slightly later in America, features beautifully remastered sound—among other advantages, it moves the finger cymbals opening the first section of the title track into sharp focus, with minimal hiss or noise to obscure them, exposes the multiple percussion instruments used on the opening of "Easy Money," and gives far more clarity to "The Talking Drum." This version is superior to any prior CD release of *Larks' Tongues in Aspic*, and contains a booklet reprinting period press clippings, session information, and production background on the album. *—Bruce Eder*

Starless and Bible Black / Mar. 1974 / EG ✦✦✦✦✦
Starless and Bible Black is even more powerful and daring than its predecessor, *Larks' Tongues in Aspic*, with jarring tempo shifts, explosive guitar riffs, and soaring, elegant, and delicate violin and Mellotron parts scattered throughout its 41 minutes, often all in the same songs. The album was on the outer fringes of accessible progressive rock, with enough musical ideas explored to make *Starless and Bible Black* more than background for tripping the way Emerson, Lake & Palmer's albums were used. "The Night Watch," a song about a Rembrandt painting, was, incredibly, a single release, although it was much more representative of the sound that Crimson was abandoning than where it was going in 1973-1974. More to that point were the contents of side two of the original LP, a pair of instrumentals that threw the group's hardest sounds right in the face of the listener, and gained some converts in the process. This album was remastered again for CD in the summer of 2000, in significantly improved sound that brought out the details (and surprising lyricism) of much of the material in far greater detail. The booklet included with the remastered version is not as impressive as some of the rest of the series entries in terms of information, but has great photos. *—Bruce Eder*

Red / Nov. 1974 / EG ✦✦✦✦
King Crimson falls apart once more, seemingly for the last time, as David Cross walks away during the making of this album. It became Robert Fripp's last thoughts on this version of the band, a bit noiser overall but with some surprising sounds featured, mostly out of the group's past—Mel Collins' and Ian McDonald's saxes, Marc Charig's cornet, and Robin Miller's oboe, thus providing a glimpse of what the 1972-era King Crimson might've sounded like handling the later group's repertory (which nearly happened). Indeed, Charig's cornet gets just about the best showcase it ever had on a King Crimson album, and the truth is that few intact groups could have gotten an album as good as *Red* together. The fact that it was put together by a band in its death throes makes it all the more impressive an achievement. Indeed, *Red* does improve in some respects on certain aspects of the previous album—including "Starless," a cousin to the prior album's title track—and only the lower quality of the

vocal compositions keeps this from being as strongly recommended as its two predecessors. *Red* was reissued on CD in the summer of 2000 in a remastered edition that features killer sound and an excellent booklet, containing a good account of the circumstances surrounding the recording of this album. *—Bruce Eder*

Discipline / 1981 / EG ✦✦✦✦✦
When King Crimson leader Robert Fripp decided to assemble a new version of the band in the early '80s, prog-rock fans rejoiced, and most new wave fans frowned. But after hearing this new unit's first release, 1981's *Discipline*, all the elements that made other arty new wave rockers successful (i.e., Talking Heads, Pere Ubu, the Police, etc.) were evident. Combining the futuristic guitar of Adrian Belew with the textured guitar of Fripp doesn't sound like it would work on paper, but the pairing of these two originals worked out magically. Rounding out the quartet was bass wizard Tony Levin and ex-Yes drummer Bill Bruford. Belew's vocals fit the music perfectly, sounding like David Byrne at his most paranoid at times (the funk track "Thela Hun Ginjeet"). Some other highlights include Tony Levin's "stick"- (a strange bass-like instrument) driven opener "Elephant Talk," the atmospheric "The Sheltering Sky" and the heavy rocker "Indiscipline." Many Crimson fans consider this album one of their best, right up there with *In the Court of the Crimson King*. It's easy to understand why after you hear the inspired performances by this hungry new version of the band. *—Greg Prato*

Beat / 1982 / EG ✦✦✦✦✦
Beat is not as good as its predecessor (1981's *Discipline*), but it's not too shabby, either. The '80s version of Crimson (Robert Fripp—guitar, Adrian Belew—vocals/guitar, Tony Levin—bass, and Bill Bruford—drums) retains the then-modern day new wave sound introduced on *Discipline*. The band's performances are still inspired, but the songwriting isn't as catchy or strong. The moody love song "Heartbeat" has become a concert favorite for the band, and contains a Jimi Hendrix-like backwards guitar solo. Other worthwhile tracks include "Waiting Man," which features world music sounds (thanks to some stunning bass/percussion interplay), and "Neurotica" does an excellent job of painting an unwavering picture of a large U.S. city, with its jerky rhythms and tense vocals. With lots of different guitar textures, bass explorations, and uncommon drum rhythms present, King Crimson's *Beat* will automatically appeal to other musicians. But since they're fantastic songwriters as well, you don't have to be a virtuoso to feel the passion of their music. *—Greg Prato*

Frame by Frame / 1991 / Caroline ✦✦✦✦✦
With its varying short-lived phases, King Crimson is well suited to the box set treatment, and overall, *Frame by Frame: The Essential King Crimson* doesn't disappoint. At four discs, it's perhaps a little hefty to serve as a comprehensive introduction for newcomers, even though it could work very well in that context; in the end, the box is more of a close-to-definitive package for fans who fall somewhere in between the realms of casual and devoted. The first three discs do an excellent job of summarizing King Crimson's extremely distinct prime-period lineups: the first disc concentrates on the often jazzy symphonic rock of 1969-1971 (including *almost* the entirety of *In the Court of the Crimson King*), the second covers the heavy, experimental soundscapes of 1973-1974, and the third features the off-kilter, new wave-influenced prog pop of 1981-1984. The fourth disc is a career-spanning sampler of live Crimson, and although the varying sound quality and musical styles make it a less cohesive listen than the other discs, it does give an excellent idea of the various lineups' extraordinary performing range. Bandleader/compiler Robert Fripp's selections are sometimes skewed toward particular albums, and devotees may cringe at the fact that some of the longer songs have been edited for time, but, in fact, all of this makes for a better, tighter listen; it's difficult to argue with what is here, and the edits often chop out less interesting sections of the pieces. Additionally, the remastering job and the liner notes are both excellent. So, in spite of its minor flaws, *Frame by Frame* is really everything one could want from a basic King Crimson box set. *—Steve Huey*

The Great Deceiver (Live 1973-1974) / Oct. 30, 1992 / Caroline ✦✦✦✦✦

VROOOM / 1994 / Discipline ✦✦

Thrak / Apr. 1995 / Virgin ✦✦✦

King Curtis (Curtis Ousley)

b. Feb. 7, 1934, Fort Worth, TX, **d.** Aug. 14, 1971, New York, NY
Sax (Tenor) / Southern Soul, East Coast Blues, Soul-Jazz, Instrumental Rock, R&B
King Curtis was the last of the great R&B tenor sax giants. He came to prominence in the mid-'50s as a session musician in New York, recording, at one time or another, for most East Coast R&B labels. A long association with Atlantic/Atco began in 1958, especially on recordings by the Coasters. He recorded singles for many small labels in the '50s—his own Atco sessions (1958-1959), then Prestige/New Jazz and Prestige/TruSound for jazz and R&B albums (1960-1961). Curtis also had a number one R&B single with "Soul Twist" on Enjoy Records (1962). He was signed by Capitol (1963-1964), where he cut mostly singles, including "Soul Serenade." Returning to Atlantic in 1965, he remained there for the rest of his life. He had solid R&B single success with "Memphis Soul Stew" and "Ode to Billie Joe" (1967). Beginning in 1967, Curtis started to take a more active studio role at Atlantic—leading and contracting sessions for other artists, producing with Jerry Wexler and later on his own. He also became the leader of Aretha Franklin's backing unit, the Kingpins. He compiled several albums of singles during this period. All aspects of his career were in full swing at the time he was murdered in 1971. *—Bob Porter*

Soul Meeting / Apr. 21, 1960-Sep. 18, 1960 / Prestige ✦✦✦✦✦
King Curtis, an influential and greatly in-demand R&B tenorman, made relatively few jazz dates in his career. This CD has two of the best, complete albums originally called *The New Scene of King Curtis* and *Soul Meeting;* the former is also available as a separate CD but should be skipped in favor of this one. Curtis teams up with the passionate cornetist Nat Adderley, pianist Wynton Kelly, either Paul Chambers or Sam Jones on bass and Oliver Jackson or Belton Evans on drums. The music is blues-based bop, with seven basic Curtis originals and four standards. Highly recommended, this set serves as proof that King Curtis could have been a viable jazz player. *—Scott Yanow*

● **Instant Soul: The Legendary King Curtis** / Oct. 19, 1994 / Razor & Tie ✦✦✦✦✦
Nice overview of Curtis' solo career, beginning with breakthrough success of "Soul Twist" and "Soul Serenade" and moving through his later recordings for Atlantic. It's interesting to hear Curtis in both the Memphis and Muscle Shoals settings and how he adapts his horn to different grooves along the way. A solid collection of this artist's best, although points get shaved off for the inclusion of a later recut version of "Wiggle Wobble," rather than the original by Les Cooper that Curtis blew so magnificently on. *—Cub Koda*

Ben E. King (Benjamin Earl Nelson)

b. Sep. 23, 1938, Henderson, NC
Vocals / Pop-Soul, Brill Building Pop, Soul
Swirling strings, subtly shaded orchestrations, and Ben E. King's assured baritone were a blueprint for uptown soul success during the early '60s. King and his vocal group, the Five Crowns, were in the right place at the right time when, in 1959, the manager of the Drifters decided to sack his entire group and solicit replacements. As new lead singer for the Drifters, King crooned the soulful smashes "There Goes My Baby," "Save the Last Dance for Me," and "I Count the Tears" before heading out on his own in 1960. The vocalist's own Atco singles mirrored the sumptuous production of his Drifter sides, and "Spanish Harlem," "Don't Play That Song (You Lied)," and the R&B chart-topping "Stand by Me" were all huge successes. King remained with Atco through 1969, then triumphantly returned to Atlantic in 1975 with another number one soul hit, "Supernatural Thing (Part 1)." With the re-release of "Stand by Me" as the theme to the 1986 film of the same title, King was in demand all over again, the stirring song improbably scaling the charts for a second time, despite being a quarter-century old. *—Bill Dahl*

Anthology / Apr. 20, 1993 / Rhino ✦✦✦✦✦
This two-disc, 50-song box set thoroughly documents the recordings that Ben E. King cut for Atlantic. Starting as the lead voice of the Drifters on such hits as "There Goes My Baby" and "Save the Last Dance for Me," King went on to a successful solo career with a string of singles that matched his smooth, sexy baritone with tastefully arranged string sections and Latin rhythms. All of those early hits—"Stand by Me" and "Spanish Harlem" were the biggest—are included here, along with non-hit 45s by the likes of Leiber/Stoller, Doc Pomus, Mort Shuman, Phil Spector, and Goffin/King that were nearly equal in worth. As the '60s progressed, King moved toward a more mainstream, heavier soul sound and less distinctive material, culminating in his parting from Atlantic in 1969. He returned to the label in the mid-'70s for a string of mainstream R&B successes. This compilation includes 16 non-LP singles from the '60s, which together with the hits constitute the definitive overview of this influential soul singer's work. *—Richie Unterberger*

● **Very Best of Ben E King** / Feb. 3, 1998 / Rhino ✦✦✦✦✦
The Very Best of Ben E. King is an excellent 16-track collection that features his biggest hits from 1959-1975, including hits he had with the Drifters in addition to his solo smashes. Among the featured songs are "There Goes My Baby," "Dance With Me," "This Magic Moment," "Save the Last Dance for Me," "Spanish Harlem," "Stand By Me," "Amor," "Don't Play That Song (You Lied)," "How Can I Forget," "I (Who Have Nothing)" and "Supernatural Thing, Pt. 1." All of his best-known songs are available on this concise, affordable disc, which makes for an ideal introduction to this legendary R&B/soul vocalist. *—Stephen Thomas Erlewine*

Carole King

b. Feb. 9, 1942, Brooklyn, NY
Vocals, Keyboards, Piano, Guitar, Synthesizer / Brill Building Pop, Pop/Rock, Soft Rock, Pop, Adult Contemporary, Singer/Songwriter
While the landmark album *Tapestry* earned her superstar status, singer/songwriter Carole King had already firmly established herself as one of pop music's most gifted and successful composers, with work recorded by everyone from the Beatles to Aretha Franklin. With partner Gerry Goffin, whom she eventually married, King began writing under publishers Don Kirshner and Al Nevins in the famed pop songwriting house the Brill Building. In 1961, Goffin and King scored their first hit with the Shirelles' chart-topping "Will You Love Me Tomorrow;" their next effort, Bobby Vee's "Take Good Care of My Baby," also hit Number One, as did "The Locomotion," recorded by their baby-sitter, Little Eva. Together, the couple wrote over 100 chart hits in a vast range of styles, including the Chiffons' "One Fine Day," the Monkees' "Pleasant Valley Sunday," the Drifters' "Up on the Roof," the Cookies' "Chains" (later covered by the Beatles) and Aretha Franklin's "(You Make Me Feel) Like a Natural Woman." King also continued her attempts to mount a solo career, but scored only one hit, 1962's superb "It Might as Well Rain Until September." In 1971, however, she released *Tapestry*, which stayed on the charts for over six years and was the best-selling album of the era. A quiet, reflective work which proved seminal in the development of the singer/songwriter genre, *Tapestry* also scored a pair of hit singles, "So Far Away" and the chart-topping "It's Too Late," whose flip-side, "I Feel the Earth Move," garnered major airplay as well. 1971's *Music* also hit Number One, and generated the hit "Sweet Seasons;" 1972's *Rhymes and Reasons* reached Number Two on the charts, and 1974's *Wrap Around Joy*, which featured the hit "Jazzman," hit the Number One spot. *—Jason Ankeny*

Writer / 1970 / Epic/Legacy ✦✦✦
Writer, Carole King's solo debut, finds the legendary melodist searching for her voice. Stylistically, she dabbles with pop ("No Easy Way Down"), country ("To Love") and rock ("I Can't Hear You No More") with mixed results. While the political message of "Eventually" hasn't held up, neither have throwaways like "Raspberry Jam" and "Spaceship Races." Only on the yearning "Goin' Back" and a remake of "Up on the Roof" (backed by James Taylor's guitar and harmonies) does she settle into the living room intimacy that led to the landmark *Tapestry* album. *—J.P. Ollio*

★ **Tapestry** / Mar. 1971 / Epic/Legacy ✦✦✦✦✦
Carole King brought the fledgling singer/songwriter phenomenon to the masses with *Tapestry*, one of the most successful albums in pop music history. A remarkably expressive and intimate record, it's a work of consummate craftsmanship. Always a superior pop composer, King reaches even greater heights as a performer; new songs like the hits "It's Too Late" and "I Feel the Earth Move" rank solidly with past glories, while chestnuts like "You've Got a Friend," "Will You Still Love Me Tomorrow," and "(You Make Me Feel Like) A Natural Woman" take on added resonance when delivered in her own warm, compelling voice. With its reliance on pianos and gentle drumming, *Tapestry* is a light and airy work on its surface, occasionally skirting the boundaries of jazz, but it's also an intensely emotional record, the songs confessional and direct; in its time it connected with listeners like few records before it, and it remains an illuminating experience decades later. The 1999 CD reissue on Sony adds two bonus tracks: the previously unreleased outtake "Out in the Cold" and a previously unreleased live 1973 version (on solo piano) of "Smackwater Jack." *—Jason Ankeny*

Music / Dec. 1971 / Epic ✦✦✦✦
After years as one of the most prolific and successful songwriters in pop music, Carole King emerged in the '70s with *Tapestry*, an album that catapulted her to the forefront of the singer/songwriter movement. While she had mined her back catalog for that album, she relied more heavily on songs written with new collaborator Toni Stern for *Music*. Coming out on the heels of the classic *Tapestry*, it's hard not to feel like this album was a bit of a letdown. However, time has shown this album to be one of her finest. While these songs lyrically lack the simplistic beauty of Gerry Goffin-penned tunes, the melodies are very strong and Carole King adds some nice texture to her piano-based tunes with the tasteful percussion of Bobbye Hall. When King goes for grand statements, however, it doesn't always work. Her call for peace and brotherhood works on songs like the opening track, "Brother, Brother," but her voice is not strong enough and does not convey enough emotion to prevent uplifting tunes like "Carry Your Load" from sounding a bit hollow and preachy. But her songwriting is still in peak form, and there are many highlights including "It's Gonna Take Some Time" (also made into a hit by the Carpenters) and "Song of Long Ago" (with backing vocals by James Taylor). *—Vik Iyengar*

Rhymes & Reasons / Nov. 1972 / Epic/Legacy ✦✦✦
On her second follow-up to *Tapestry* and third new album in less than two years, King turned entirely to new compositions; most of them co-written with Toni Stern; rather than relying partly on songs from her back catalog. The result was a thinner collection than *Tapestry* or *Music*, although the album still went to number two and featured the Top 25 hit "Been to Canaan," as well as the warm love song "The First Day in August." *—William Ruhlmann*

Fantasy / Jun. 1973 / Epic ✦✦✦

Really Rosie / 1975 / Epic/Legacy ✦✦✦✦✦
The soundtrack to a television special originating from the pen of author Maurice Sendak, *Really Rosie* is that rare children's album with the wit and intelligence to capture the imaginations of adult listeners as well. Sendak's sharp, clever lyrics tell the story of young Brooklynite Rosie and a cast of vividly etched supporting characters including the apathetic Pierre and a boy named Chicken Soup; Carole King's melodies serve the material remarkably well, transforming even the most deliberately silly songs into catchy, piano-driven pop confections. In fact, it's in many ways her most fully realized record since *Tapestry*, with a sparkling charm and heartfelt sincerity that interim releases lacked. *—Jason Ankeny*

Thoroughbred / Jan. 1976 / Epic/Legacy ✦✦✦

Simple Things / Jul. 1977 / Capitol ✦✦

Welcome Home / 1978 / Capitol ✦✦

Her Greatest Hits: Songs Of Long Ago / Mar. 1978 / Epic/Legacy ✦✦✦✦✦
This album was always sort of a joke among King's serious fans, containing 12 songs drawn from six albums, and liner notes that fail even to acknowledge the existence of *Writer*, her one pre-*Tapestry* solo LP. *A Natural Woman* supplanted it a few years ago, and the addition of two live cuts, "Eventually" and "(You Make Me Feel Like) A Natural Woman" from the *Carnegie Hall* concert on the 1999 reissue (Ode/Epic/Legacy 65846) doesn't extended the range or depth of the selection sufficiently. On the other hand, the 1999 remastering does improve the listening pleasure inherent in what is here—the material off of *Tapestry, Music, Rhymes & Reasons* and others is now very robust, with vivid instrumentation and a close, rich profile of King's voice. The selection of King's work is still only an inch deep, but it's a more rewarding inch. *—Bruce Eder*

A Natural Woman: The Ode Collection (1968-1976) / Sep. 13, 1994 / Epic/Legacy ✦✦✦✦✦
Carole King had already written an enormous amount of pop classics by the time she began her solo career in earnest in the late '60s. With her second album, *Tapestry*, King became one of the most popular and artistically successful singer-songwriters of the early '70s. King never matched the consistent brilliance of *Tapestry*, yet managed to record many fine songs during the rest of the decade. *A Natural Woman* collects all of her finest moments over the course of two discs. *Tapestry* is included in its entirety, along with the highlights from her other albums, making *A Natural Woman* the one essential King album—apart from *Tapestry* itself, of course. *—Stephen Thomas Erlewine*

Carnegie Hall Concert: June 18 1971 / Oct. 29, 1996 / Epic/Legacy ✦✦✦✦✦

The Kingsmen

f. 1957, Portland, OR, **db.** 1968
Group / Frat Rock, Garage Rock, Rock & Roll
A rock & roll band from Portland, Oregon, the Kingsmen's one big hit "Louie, Louie" defined the garage-band style and became one of the all-time classics. After singer/guitarist Jack Ely had "incorrectly" taught the rest of the band the Wailers' version of Richard Berry's "Louie Louie" (thus altering the basic rhythm into the now famous duh-duh-duh, duh-duh, duh-duh-duh, duh-duh riff that has become the only way anyone has played it since), they recorded it for fifty dollars at a primitive local recording studio with only three mikes, Ely hollering the lyrics into an overhead boom mike suspended ten feet in the air. Released on a local label, the record went nowhere after Paul Revere & the Raiders quickly covered it in the Northwest market, although it had quickly become a standard for all teen bands in that area. In 1964, the record started to break nationally; though the song itself has been covered repeatedly, the version by Ely and the original lineup remains definitive. *—Cub Koda*

● **The Best of the Kingsmen** / 1989 / Rhino ✦✦✦✦✦
Although the Kingsmen's original albums are enjoyable as artifacts, they're unnecessary for anyone but hardcore collectors. For most listeners, Rhino's *The Best of the Kingsmen* will be all the Kingsmen they'll ever need to hear. Over the course of 18 tracks, all of the garage-rock band's greatest hits—not just "Louie Louie," but trashy gems like "Little Latin Lupe Lu," "Death of an Angel," "The Jolly Green Giant," "Annie Fanny," "Killer Joe" and "The Climb"—are featured, along with several fine album tracks which make this the definitive compilation. *—Stephen Thomas Erlewine*

The Very Best of the Kingsmen / Jun. 2, 1998 / Varese ✦✦✦✦✦
Far from being a "one hit wonder" group, the Kingsmen had more than their share of hit records and charting albums to go with it. This 18-track collection brings together all the tunes that enhance and extend their reputation as one of the all time great party bands. Of course, "Louie Louie" is here, but so is its demonic flip, "Haunted Castle" along with "Jolly Green Giant," "Money," "Long Green," "Little Latin Lupe Lu" and "The Climb," chart entries all. Also along for the ride are album tracks like "Shake a Tail Feather," "Do You Love Me?," "Shout," "Twist and Shout" and "Killer Joe," making a strong case for the group as the ultimate in early to mid-'60s dance floor mania. Though other greatest hit packages exist on the band (and the original albums as well), this one does the best job of giving the full picture of what they really did and the transfers sound absolutely wonderful. Start your collection with this one. *—AMG*

The Kinks

f. 1963, London, England
Group / Album Rock, Pop/Rock, British Invasion, Hard Rock, Rock & Roll
The Kinks were one of the most influential bands of the British Invasion. Like most groups of their era, they began as an R&B/blues outfit. Despite lead singer Ray Davies' fey, foppish manner, they were rocked harder than their peers, thanks to the pulverizing guitar riffs of his brother, Dave. The Kinks' early singles ("You Really Got Me," "All Day and All of the Night") were brutal, three-chord ravers, popular in both the UK and US; they also paved the way toward punk and metal, while inspiring their peers (the Who's early singles aped the Kinks). Toward the mid-'60s, Davies came into his own as a songwriter, developing a wry wit and eye for social commentary and the Kinks' music changed subtly, becoming more subtle and melodic, culminating in *Face to Face* and *Something Else*. Just as every rock band embraced psychedelia, the Kinks retreated from turbulent changes in rock. Banned from touring America, due to a mishap with a musicians' union, Ray Davies turned inward and nostalgic, creating the defiantly quaint and English *Village Green Preservation Society*. The album flopped upon its 1968 release, yet it earned a devoted cult, proving quite influential over the years. Davies continued to pursue conceptual works with *Arthur* and *Lola*, the latter giving them their first genuine hit in five years. During the early '70s, the Kinks lost their audience in the UK while remaining a cult act in America, due to Davies' increasingly impenetrable concept albums. The Kinks refashioned themselves as hard-rock stadium act in the late '70s, which increased their American popularity, culminating in the Top 10 1979 hit, *Low Budget*. The Kinks remained a popular concert attraction in the early '80s and they were MTV favorites as well, resulting in their late Top 10 hit, "Come Dancing." Their commercial fortunes declined in the second half of the '80s and by the time of 1993's *Phobia*, Ray and Dave were the only original members left. Following a live acoustic album in the mid-'90s, the Kinks faded away, as both brothers pursued solo projects. *—Stephen Thomas Erlewine*

Kinks / Oct. 1964 / Castle ✦✦✦
Although the best of the Kinks' early work is among the best British Invasion music, their initial pair of albums was far less consistent than those of the Beatles, Stones, and Who. Aside from the great "You Really Got Me," and this was a scrabby, disappointing set with surprisingly thin production. As R&B cover artists, the Kinks weren't nearly as adept as the Stones and Yardbirds; Ray Davies' original tunes were, "You Really Got Me" aside, perfunctory Merseyish pastiches; and a couple of tunes that producer Shel Talmy penned for the group, "Bald Headed Woman" and "I've Been Driving On Bald Mountain," were simply abominable. The rave-up treatments of the R&B standards "Got Love If You Want It" and "Cadillac" were good, and the simple "Stop Your Sobbing" would eventually be covered by the Pretenders, but overall this is real patchy. The CD reissue, however, is a great improvement, adding a wealth of bonus tracks from early singles and their first EP, some excellent. The ferocious "All Day and All of the Night" was a classic hit whose razor-riffing outdid even "You Really Got Me," and the B-sides "It's Alright" and "I Gotta Move" are tremendous frenetic lost gems. There are also a couple of previously unissued cuts: an alternative take of "Too Much Monkey Business" and an early, Beatleish original, "I Don't Need You Any More." *—Richie Unterberger*

The Kink Kontroversy / 1965 / Castle ✦✦✦✦✦
The Kinks came into their own as album artists—and Ray Davies fully matured as a songwriter—with *Kontroversy*, which bridged their raw early British Invasion sound with more sophisticated lyrics and thoughtful production. There are still powerful ravers like the hit "Till the End of the Day" (utilizing yet another "You Really Got Me"-type riff) and the abrasive, Dave Davies-sung cover of "Milk Cow Blues," but tracks like the calypso pastiche "I'm On an Island," where Ray sings of isolation with a forlorn yet merry bite, were far more indicative of their future direction. Other great songs on this underrated album include the uneasy nostalgia of "Where Have All the Good Times Gone?," the plaintive, almost fatalistic ballads "Ring the Bells" and "The World Keeps Going Round," and the Dave Davies-sung declaration of independence, "I Am Free." Some mediocre filler detracts from the disc's overall punch, though the CD reissue adds the great swinging London satire hit "Dedicated Follower

of Fashion," as previously unissued alternate takes of "When I See That Girl of Mine" and "Dedicated Follower of Fashion." *—Richie Unterberger*

Kinda Kinks / Feb. 1965 / Castle ♦♦♦
The Kinks' second album (which, like their debut, now has a running order and track selection restored to the original British version) found the band relying more on original material, but had similarly threadbare production and songwriting for the most part. This sounded like a rush job in both composition and performance, largely devoted to unexceptional, even generic, British Invasion pop-rock. Aside from the great hit "Tired of Waiting for You" and its driving B-side "Come On Now," in fact, nothing here stood out, with the exception of the lovely ballad "Something Better Beginning." On the CD reissue, however, a fine clutch of bonus tracks help save the day. "Set Me Free" is a great cut with a minor melody reminiscent of the Zombies; "Everybody's Gonna Be Happy" is a peppy if unremarkable single; "See My Friends" is a super-cool excursion into Indian-influenced folk-rock, also showing Ray Davies start to flower into a lyricist of touching vulnerability and ambiguity; and "Well Respected Man" was his first blow of savage social satire. There's also a previously unissued, piano-dominated ballad, "I Go to Sleep," although this has been recorded by several artists, including the Pretenders. *—Richie Unterberger*

☆ **Face to Face** / Oct. 28, 1966 / Castle ♦♦♦♦♦
The Kink Kontroversy was a considerable leap forward in terms of quality, but it pales next to *Face to Face,* one of the finest collections of pop songs released during the '60s. Conceived as a loose concept album, *Face to Face* sees Ray Davies' fascination with English class and social structures flourish, as he creates a number of vivid character portraits. Davies' growth as a lyricist has coincided with the Kinks' musical growth. *Face to Face* is filled with wonderful moments, whether it's the mocking Hawaiian guitars of the rocker "Holiday in Waikiki," the droning Eastern touches of "Fancy," the music-hall shuffle of "Dandy" or the lazily rolling "Sunny Afternoon." And that only scratches of the surface of the riches of *Face to Face,* which offers other classics like "Rosy Won't You Please Come Home," "Party Line," "Too Much on My Mind," "Rainy Day in June" and "Most Exclusive Residence for Sale," making the record one of the most distinctive and accomplished albums of its time. [Castle Communication's 1998 CD reissue of *Face to Face* included six bonus tracks: the singles and B-sides "I'm Not Like Everybody Else," "Dead End Street," "Big Black Smoke," "Mister Pleasant" and "This Is Where I Belong," plus the previously unreleased "Mr. Reporter" and backing track "Little Women."] *—Stephen Thomas Erlewine*

☆ **Something Else by the Kinks** / 1967 / Castle ♦♦♦♦♦
Face to Face was a remarkable record, but its follow-up *Something Else* expands its accomplishments, offering 13 classic British pop songs. As Ray Davies' songwriting becomes more refined, he becomes more nostalgic and sentimental, retreating from the psychedelic and mod posturings that had dominated the rock world. Indeed, *Something Else* sounds like nothing else from 1967. The Kinks never rock very hard on the album, preferring acoustic ballads, music-hall numbers and tempered R&B to full-out guitar attacks. Part of the album's power lies in its calm music, since it provides an elegant support for Davies' character portraits and vignettes. From the martial stomp of "David Watts" to the lovely, shimmering "Waterloo Sunset," there's not a weak song on the record, and several—such as the allegorical "Two Sisters," the Noel Coward-esque "End of the Season," the rolling "Lazy Old Sun" and the wry "Situation Vacant"—are stunners. And just as impressive is the emergence of Dave Davies as a songwriter. His Dylanesque "Death of a Clown" and bluesy rocker "Love Me Til the Sun Shines" hold their own against Ray's masterpieces, and help make *Something Else* the endlessly fascinating album that it is. [Castle's 1998 CD reissue of *Something Else* contained eight bonus tracks: several A and B-sides from non-LP singles, from both the Kinks and Dave Davies as a solo act—"Act Nice and Gentle," "Autumn Almanac," "Susannah's Still Alive," "Wonderboy," "Polly," "Lincoln County," "There's No Life Without Love"—plus an alternate take of "Lazy Old Sun."] *—Stephen Thomas Erlewine*

Live at Kelvin Hall / Jan. 12, 1968 / Castle ♦♦♦

☆ **The Village Green Preservation Society** / Nov. 22, 1968 / Castle ♦♦♦♦♦
Ray Davies' sentimental, nostalgic streak emerged on *Something Else,* but it developed into a manifesto on *The Village Green Preservation Society,* a concept album lamenting the passing of old-fashioned English traditions. As the opening title song says, the Kinks—meaning Ray himself, in this case—were for preserving "draft beer and virginity," and throughout the rest of the album, he creates a series of stories, sketches and characters about a picturesque England that never really was. It's a lovely, gentle album, evoking a small British country town, and drawing the listener into its lazy rhythms and sensibilities. Although there is an undercurrent of regret running throughout the album, Davies' fondness for the past is warm, making the album feel like a sweet, hazy dream. And considering the subdued performances and the detailed instrumentations, it's not surprising that the record feels more like a Ray Davies solo project than a Kinks album. The bluesy shuffle of "Last of the Steam-Powered Trains" is the closest the album comes to rock & roll, and Dave's cameo on the menacing "Wicked Annabella" comes as surprise, since the album is so calm. But calm doesn't mean tame or bland—there are endless layers of musical and lyrical innovation on *The Village Green Preservation Society,* and its defiantly British sensibilities became the foundation of generations of British guitar-pop. [Castle's 1998 CD reissue of *Village Green Preservation* contained both the original 15-track mono version of the album, plus the 12-track stereo album that was initially planned for release in September 1968, but scrapped. The stereo album contains a slightly different running order and features two songs—"Days" and "Mr. Songbird"—that didn't make the final album. The CD also includes the mono single version of "Days" as a bonus track.]*—Stephen Thomas Erlewine*

☆ **Arthur or the Decline and Fall of the British Empire** / Oct. 10, 1969 / Castle ♦♦♦♦♦
Arthur (Or the Decline and Fall of the British Empire) extends the British-oriented themes of *Village Green Preservation Society,* telling the story of a London man's decision to move to Australia during the aftermath of World War II. It's a detailed and loving song cycle, capturing the minutiae of suburban life, the numbing effect of bureaucracy and the horrors of war. On paper, *Arthur* sounds like a pretentious mess, but Ray Davies' lyrics and insights have rarely been so graceful or deftly executed, and the music is remarkable. An edgier and harder-rocking affair than *Village Green, Arthur* is as multi-layered musically as it is lyrically. "Shangri-La" evolves from English folk to hard rock, "Drivin'" has a lazy grace, "Young and Innocent Days" is a lovely, wistful ballad, "Some Mother's Son" is one of the most uncompromising anti-war songs ever recorded, while "Victoria" and "Arthur" rock with simple glee. The music makes the words cut deeper, and the songs never stray too far from the album's subject, making *Arthur* one of the most effective concept albums in rock history, as well as one of the best and most influential British pop records of its era. [Castle's 1998 CD reissue of *Arthur* contained 10 bonus tracks, including mono and stereo versions of the non-LP singles "Plastic Man," "Mindless Child of Motherhood" and "This Man He Weeps Tonight," mono versions of "Drivin'" and "She's Bought a Hat Like Princess Marina," the B-side "King Kong" and the previously unreleased "Mr. Shoemakers Daugher."] *—Stephen Thomas Erlewine*

Lola vs. the Powerman & the Money-Go-Round, Part One / Nov. 27, 1970 / Castle ♦♦♦♦♦
"Lola" gave the Kinks an unexpected hit and its crisp, muscular sound, pitched halfway between acoustic folk and hard-rock, provided a new style for the band. However, the song only hinted at what its accompanying album *Lola versus the Powerman and the Moneygoround, Pt. One* was all about. It didn't matter that Davies just had his first hit in years—he had suffered greatly at the hands of the music industry and he wanted to tell the story in song. Hence, *Lola*—a loose concept album about Ray Davies' own psychosis and bitter feelings toward the music industry. Davies never really delivers a cohesive story, but the record holds together because it's one of his strongest set of songs. Dave contributes the lovely "Strangers" and the appropriately paranoid "Rats" but this is truly Ray's show, as he lashes out at ex-managers (the boisterous vaudevillian "The Moneygoround"), publishers ("Denmark Street"), TV and music journalists (the hard-hitting "Top of the Pops"), label executives ("Powerman") and, hell, just society in general ("Apeman," "Got to Be Free"). If his wit wasn't sharp, the entire project would be insufferable, but the album is as funny as it is angry. Furthermore, he balances his bile with three of his best melancholy ballads: "This Time Tomorrow," "A Long Way from Home" and the anti-welfare and union "Get Back in Line," which captures working-class angst better than any other rock song. These songs provide the spine for a wildly unfocused but nonetheless dazzling tour-de-force that reveals Davies' artistic strengths and endearing character flaws in equal measure. *—Stephen Thomas Erlewine*

Percy [Original Soundtrack] / Mar. 26, 1971 / Castle ♦♦

Muswell Hillbillies / Nov. 24, 1971 / Velvel ♦♦♦♦♦
How did the Kinks respond to the fresh start afforded by *Lola*? By delivering a skewed, distinctly British, cabaret take on Americana, all pinned down by Davies' loose autobiography and intense yearning to be anywhere else but here—or, as he says on the opening track, "I'm a 20th Century Man, but I don't want to be here." Unlike its predecessors, *Muswell Hillbillies* doesn't overtly seem like a concept album—there are no stories, as there are on *Lola*—but each song undoubtedly shares a similar theme, namely the lives of the working class. Cleverly, the music is a blend of American and British roots music, veering from rowdy blues to boozy vaudeville. There's as much good humor in the performances as there are in Davies' songs, which are among his savviest and funniest. They're also quite affectionate, a fact underpinned by the heartbreaking "Oklahoma USA," one of the starkest numbers Davies ever penned, seeming all the sadder surrounded by the careening country-rock and musichall. That's the key to *Muswell Hillbillies*—it mirrors the messy flow of life itself, rolling from love letters and laments to jokes and family reunions. Throughout it all, Davies' songwriting is at a peak, as are the Kinks themselves. There are a lot of subtle shifts in mood and genre on the album, and the band pulls it off effortlessly and joyously—but it's hard not to hear Dave Davies' backing vocals and have it not sound joyous. Regardless of its commercial fate, *Muswell Hillbillies* stands as one of the Kinks' best albums. *—Stephen Thomas Erlewine*

★ **The Kink Kronikles** / 1972 / Reprise ♦♦♦♦♦
Strictly speaking, the double-album compilation *The Kink Kronikles* isn't a greatest hits collection. Covering the years 1966 through 1970, *The Kink Kronikles* may not be packed with hits—out of the album's 28 tracks, only nine were hits in the UK or the US—yet it's a definitive overview of this era, which was one of Ray Davies' most productive (and influential) periods. Apart from the hits—the lazy, sardonic "Sunny Afternoon," and the gorgeous "Waterloo Sunset," and the 1970 comeback hits "Lola" and "Apeman"—there is a wealth of music that ranks among their very best material that isn't available on any other album. First off, non-LP British hit singles like the music-hall raver "Dead End Street" and the wry "Autumn Almanac" are included, as are Dave Davies' two solo hits, "Death of a Clown" and "Suzannah's Still Alive." Then there are the wealth of non-LP singles and B-sides that *didn't* make the British charts, plus worthy unreleased songs, obscurities like "This is Where I Belong" and "She's Got Everything," and album tracks that demonstrate another side of the Kinks' musical versatility and Davies' abilities. The key to the success of *The Kink Kronikles* is how the singles and rarities compliment each other and, taken together, present a full portrait. It's the rare compilation that is equally valuable to the collector and to the neophyte fan. *—Stephen Thomas Erlewine*

Everybody's in Show-Biz / Aug. 1972 / Velvel ♦♦♦
Everybody's in Showbiz is a double album with one record devoted to stories from the road and another devoted to songs from the road. It could be labeled "the drunkest album ever made," without a trace of hyperbole, since this is a charmingly loose, rowdy, silly record. It comes through strongest on the live record, of course, as it's filled with Ray's notoriously campy vaudevellian routine (dig the impromptu "Banana Boat Song" that leads into "Skin & Bone," or the rollicking "Baby Face"). Still, the live record is just a bonus, no matter how fun it is, since the travelogue of the first record is where the heart of *Everybody's in Showbiz* lies. Davies views the road as monotony—an endless stream of identical hotels, drunken sleep, anonymous towns, and really, really bad meals (at least three songs are about food, or have food metaphors). There's no sex on the album, at all, not even on Dave's contribution, "You Don't Know My Name." Some of this is quite funny—not just Ray's trademark wit, but musical jokes like the woozy beginning of "Unreal Reality" or the unbearably tongue-in-

cheek "Look a Little on the Sunnyside"—but there's a real sense of melancholy running throughout the record, most notably on the album's one unqualified masterpiece, "Celluloid Heroes." By the time it gets there, anyone that's not a hardcore fan may have turned it off. Why? Because this album is where Ray Davies begins indulging his eccentricities, a move that only solidified their status as a cult act. There are enough quirks to alienate even fans of their late '60s masterpieces, but those very things make *Everybody's in Showbiz* an easy album for those cultists to hold dear to their hearts. *—Stephen Thomas Erlewine*

The Great Lost Kinks Album / 1973 / Reprise ✦✦✦✦✦
An aptly titled collection; out of print for many years, there are even some Kinks cultists who have never been able to hear this ragtag but worthy collection of late-'60s and early-'70s outtakes and rarities. Most of these were recorded around the same time as the 1968 LP *Village Green Preservation Society;* these low-key, wry, bouncy tunes would have fit in well with that record. Lyrically, they're on the whole slighter than much of their late-'60s work, perhaps accounting for why the group did not deign to release them at the time. Still, songs like "Rosemary Rose," "Misty Water," and "Mr. Songbird" would have hardly embarrassed the group, and rank as the highlights of this anthology. Besides 1969-era outtakes, it includes the single "Plastic Man," a couple of okay, way-obscure B-sides featuring Dave Davies, and some songs penned for long-forgotten film and television productions. It also has the dynamite 1966 B-side "I'm Not Like Everybody Else," though that's easily available on reissue these days. That's not the case for most of the rest of this album; Kinks fans will find it quite worthwhile, and should be on the lookout for it in the used bins. *—Richie Unterberger*

Preservation: Act 1 / 1973 / Velvel ✦✦✦
Preservation is Ray Davies' most ambitious project—a musical that used the quaint, small-town nostalgia of *Village Green* as a template to draw the entirety of society and how it works. Or, at least that's what the concept seems to be, since the storyline was so convoluted, it necessitated three separated LPs, spread over two albums, and it still didn't really make sense because the first album, *Preservation, Act 1,* acted more like an introduction to the characters, and all the story was condensed into the second album. Davies intended all of *Preservation* to stand as one double-album set, but he scrapped the first sessions for the album, which led to record company pressure to deliver an album before the end of 1973—hence, the appearance of *Preservation, Act 1* in mid-November. Stripped of much of the narrative, *Preservation* winds up playing like an explicitly theatrical *Village Green,* this time with specific characters—a bit like a novella instead of short stories. There are moments where everything clicks on *Preservation* and they're the ones that are closest to typical Davies—the stately "Daylight," the endearingly lazy "Sitting in the Midday Sun," the fairly rocking "Here Comes Flash," "Where Are They Now?," and the absolutely gorgeous "Sweet Lady Genevieve," a real candidate for Davies' forgotten masterpiece. Then, there's the rest of the record: unfocused attempts at story, showtunes, and characterizations, some of which is interesting, but the whole of it is rather tedious. *Preservation, Act 1* winds up as listenable due to the strength of those five songs, which form the core not only of this record, but the musical drama as a whole. The rest plays as artistic hubris, which is exactly what swallows *Preservation, Act 2* alive. *—Stephen Thomas Erlewine*

Preservation: Act 2 / 1974 / Velvel ✦✦

The Kinks Present a Soap Opera / 1975 / Velvel ✦✦

The Kinks Present Schoolboys in Disgrace / 1975 / Velvel ✦✦

Sleepwalker / 1977 / Velvel ✦✦✦
Arista had made it clear they would not accept any concept albums from the Kinks, and *Sleepwalker,* their first effort for the label, makes good on the band's promise. Comprised entirely of glossy arena-rockers and power ballads, the album is more of a stylistic exercise than a collection of first-rate songs. Davies contributed a handful of fairly strong songs, highlighted by the exceptional "Juke Box Music," which sees Ray in a shockingly resigned frame of mind, claiming that rock & roll is just rock & roll, and nothing more. Unfortunately, he chose to illustrate that fact by loading the rest of *Sleepwalker* with competent but undistinguished mainstream rock. While that might have made the album a hit at the time, its processed sound and weak songs sound dated today, especially compared to the lively arena rock the Kinks later released. *—Stephen Thomas Erlewine*

Misfits / 1978 / Velvel ✦✦✦✦✦
The Kinks became arena rockers with *Sleepwalker,* and its follow-up, *Misfits,* follows in the same vein, but it's a considerable improvement on its predecessor. Ray Davies has learned how to write within the confines of the arena rock formula, and *Misfits* is one of rock & roll's great mid-life crisis albums, finding Davies considering whether he should even go on performing. "Misfits," a classic outsider rallying cry, and "Rock and Roll Fantasy" provide the two touchstones for the album—Davies admits that he and the Kinks will never be embraced by the rock & roll mainstream, but after Elvis' death, he's not even sure if rock & roll is something for mature adults to do. Over the course of *Misfits,* he finds answers to the question, both in his lyrics and through the band's muscular music. Eventually, he discovers that it is worth his time, but the search itself is superbly affecting—even songs like the musichall shuffle "Hay Fever," which appear as filler at first, have an idiosyncratic quirk that make them cut deeper. Although Ray would return to camp on their next album, *Misfits* is a moving record that manages to convey deep emotions while rocking hard. The Kinks hadn't made a record this good since *Muswell Hillbillies.* *—Stephen Thomas Erlewine*

Low Budget / 1979 / Velvel ✦✦✦✦
Low Budget doesn't have a narrative like *Preservation* or *Soap Opera,* but Ray Davies cleverly designed the album as a sly satire of the recession and oil crisis that gripped America in the late '70s—thereby satisfying his need to be a wry social commentator while giving American audiences a hook to identify with. It was a clever move that worked; not only did *Low Budget* become their highest-charting American album (not counting the 1966 *Greatest Hits* compilation), but it was also a fine set of arena-rock, one of the better mainstream hard rock albums of its time. And it certainly was of its time—so much so, that many of the concerns and production techniques have dated quite a bit in the decades since its initial release. Nevertheless, that gives the album a certain charm, since it now plays like a time capsule, a snapshot of what hard rock sounded like at the close of the '70s. Perhaps not so coincidentally, Davies' songwriting fluctuates throughout the album, since it's dictated as much by commercial as artistic concerns, but the moments when he manages to balance the two impulses—as on the disco-fueled "(Wish I Could Fly Like) Superman," the vaudevillian "Low Budget," "A Gallon of Gas," the roaring "Attitude" (possibly their best hard rocker of the era, by the way) and "Catch Me Now I'm Falling," where Ray takes on the persona of America itself—are irresistible. *Low Budget* may not have the depth of, say, *Arthur* or *Village Green,* but it's a terrifically entertaining testament to their skills as a professional rock band and Davies' savviness as a commercial songwriter. *—Stephen Thomas Erlewine*

One for the Road / 1980 / Velvel ✦✦

Give the People What They Want / 1981 / Velvel ✦✦✦
Riding high on the success of *Low Budget,* the Kinks turned out another collection of hard-driving, arena-ready rock & roll with *Give the People What They Want*—in short, they delivered exactly what the title suggests. Throughout the record, the band kicks up a storm, rocking out with a surprising amount of precision, and although Ray Davies' writing isn't as strong as it was on the group's two previous albums, he has contributed a set of professional hard rock that is distinguished by solid hooks and a clever sense of humor. After all, there's a certain charm in hearing him rework "All Day and All of the Night" into the paranoid "Destroyer," or his pure cynicism on the title track. But the minor masterpiece of the album is "Better Things," a sweet piece of charming sentimentalism which is the only time Davies lets his guard down during the entire album. *—Stephen Thomas Erlewine*

State of Confusion / 1983 / Velvel ✦✦✦

Word of Mouth / 1984 / Velvel ✦✦

Think Visual / Dec. 1986 / MCA ✦✦

★ **Greatest Hits, Vol. 1** / 1989 / Rhino ✦✦✦✦✦
Featuring a total of 18 highlights from the Kinks' early career, Rhino's *Greatest Hits* is the definitive compilation of the group's hit singles from the mid-'60s. Beginning with "You Really Got Me" and ending with "Sunny Afternoon," all of the Kinks' essential garage-rockers and British Invasion singles are here—"All Day and All of the Night," "Till the End of the Day," "Tired of Waiting for You," "A Well Respected Man," "Stop Your Sobbing," "Dedicated Follower of Fashion," "I'm Not Like Everybody Else," "Where Have All the Good Times Gone." Only the ambitious, Indian-tinged British hit "See My Friends" is missing, but it isn't a major oversight, especially since the disc distills the group's uneven early albums into manageable form for many fans. While *Kinkdom, Kontroversy* and *Face to Face* have many excellent album tracks in their own right, *Greatest Hits* remains a terrific summation of the group's earliest, hardest-rocking work. *—Stephen Thomas Erlewine*

UK Jive / Sep. 1989 / MCA ✦✦

Kinks Live: the Road / 1990 / MCA ✦✦

Lost & Found (1986-89) / Aug. 27, 1991 / MCA ✦✦

Phobia / Apr. 13, 1993 / Columbia ✦✦

To the Bone / 1996 / Guardian ✦✦✦

Come Dancing With the Kinks: The Best of the Kinks 1977-1986 [2000] / 2000 / Velvel ✦✦✦
Although it closely resembles the 1986 Arista collection (and even boasts the same cover and title), this is not quite that album—it's a reinterpretation of that collection, spearheaded by Ray Davies. It restores "Catch Me Now I'm Falling," "Misfits," and "Sleepwalker" (the three songs dropped from the CD version of Arista's *Come Dancing*) and eliminates the excellent "Long Distance" along with "Heart of Gold" and the masterpiece "Juke Box Music," while adding "A Gallon of Gas," "Full Moon," and "Good Day," and shuffling the track order. Do all these monkeyshines result in a better album? No. It's close, but the subtle differences do make a difference, and the original still does reign supreme, since the running order on the original was simply superior. This new incarnation is still enjoyable—the substitutions are good, even if they don't match the originals—and it even remains an accurate introduction to this era. But anyone who can find the Arista issue of *Come Dancing* will find a better compilation than this Koch/Konk reworking. *—Stephen Thomas Erlewine*

Kiss

f. 1973, New York, NY
Group / Album Rock, Arena Rock, Heavy Metal, Hard Rock
Rooted in the campy theatrics of Alice Cooper and the sleazy glam of the New York Dolls, Kiss became a favorite of American teenagers in the '70s. Decked out in outrageously flamboyant costumes and makeup, the band fashioned a captivating stage show featuring dry ice, smoke bombs, elaborate lighting, blood spitting and fire breathing. But Kiss' music shouldn't be dismissed—it was a commercially potent mix of anthemic, fist-pounding hard rock and ballads powered by loud guitars, cloying melodies and sweeping strings. Their sound laid the groundwork for both arena rock and the pop-metal that dominated rock in the late '80s. Kiss was the brainchild of Gene Simmons (bass, vocals) and Paul Stanley (rhythm guitar, vocals), who found drummer Peter Criss and guitarist Ace Frehley through ads. By April of 1975, the group had released three albums in just over a year, and built up a sizable fan base through constant touring. Culled from those numerous concerts, *Alive!* (released in the fall of 1975) made the band rock & roll superstars. The follow-up, *Destroyer,* became the group's first platinum album; it also featured their first Top Ten single, Peter Criss' power ballad "Beth." By 1977, Kiss was the most popular band in America; thousands of pieces of merchandise flooded the marketplace. Heralding a commercial slump, Criss left in 1980, as did Frehley in 1982. Sensing it was time for a change, Kiss dispensed with their makeup for the first time for 1983's *Lick It Up;* the publicity helped the album recapture their niche. For the next decade, Kiss turned out a series of best-selling albums with guitarist Bruce Kulick, culminating in the 1990 hit ballad "Forever," their biggest single since "Beth." In November

1991, drummer Eric Carr died at the age of 41 after a bout with cancer. In 1996, the original lineup of Kiss reunited to perform an international tour, complete with their notorious makeup and special effects. The tour was one of the most successful of 1996, and in 1998 the reunited group issued *Psycho Circus.* *—Stephen Thomas Erlewine*

Kiss / Apr. 1974 / Casablanca ✦✦✦✦
Kiss' 1974 self-titled debut is one of hard rock's all-time classic studio recordings. *Kiss* is chock full of their best and most renowned compositions, containing elements of Rolling Stones/New York Dolls party-hearty rock & roll, Beatles tunefulness, and Sabbath/Zep heavy metal, and wisely recorded primal and raw by producers Richie Wise and Kenny Kerner (of Gladys Knight fame). Main songwriters Stanley and Simmons each had a knack for coming up with killer melodies and riffs, as evidenced by "Nothin' to Lose" and "Deuce" (by Simmons), "Firehouse" and "Black Diamond" (by Stanley), as well as "Strutter" and "100, 000 Years" (a collaboration by the two). Also included is the Ace Frehley alcohol anthem "Cold Gin," "Let Me Know" (a song that Stanley played for Simmons upon their very first meeting, then titled "Sunday Driver"), and one of Kiss' few instrumentals: the groovy "Love Theme From Kiss" (penned by the entire band). The only weak track is a tacky cover of the 1959 Bobby Rydell hit "Kissin' Time," which was added to subsequent pressings of the album to tie in with a "Kissing Contest" promotion the band was involved in at the time. Along with 1976's *Destroyer,* Kiss' self-titled debut is their finest studio album, and has only improved over the years. *—Greg Prato*

Hotter Than Hell / Nov. 1974 / Casablanca ✦✦✦✦✦
Although Kiss' self-titled debut performed respectably on the charts, it was not the blockbuster they had hoped for. With the album fading on the charts in the summer of 1974, Kiss was summoned back into the studio to work on a follow-up. Producers Richie Wise and Kenny Kerner were on board again, and even though the sonics are muddier (and more filler is present composition-wise), *Hotter Than Hell* is another quintessential Kiss release. Many of the songs have been forgotten over the years (few are featured in concert anymore), but there are still more than a few gems to be found. It's unclear if the members of Kiss were having problems with their personal relationships at the time, but it's a common thread that runs through the songs. The plodding "Got to Choose" and the rapid-fire "Parasite" deal with love gone bad; the title track is about unobtainable love, while "Goin' Blind" is a disturbing tale of a 93-year-old having an affair with a 16-year-old. Also included are the early favorites "Let Me Go Rock n' Roll" and "Watchin' You," as well as the original electric version of "Comin' Home" (an acoustic version was the opener of 1996's *Unplugged*) and "Strange Ways," which contains one of Ace Frehley's best guitar solos. Even though *Hotter Than Hell* actually fared worse on the charts than the debut, it has become a revered album among Kiss fans over the years—and rightfully so. *—Greg Prato*

Dressed to Kill / Apr. 1975 / Casablanca ✦✦✦✦✦
By the release of their third album, 1975's *Dressed To Kill,* Kiss was fast becoming America's top rock concert attraction, yet their record sales up to this point did not reflect their ticket sales. Casablanca label head Neil Bogart decided to take matters into his own hands, and produced the new record along with the band. The result is more vibrant-sounding than its predecessor, 1974's sludgefest *Hotter Than Hell,* and the songs have more of an obvious pop edge to them. The best-known song on the album by far is the party anthem "Rock and Roll All Nite," but it was the track "C'Mon and Love Me" that became a regional hit in the Detroit area, giving the band their first taste of radio success. Since the band was on the road for a year straight, songs such as "Room Service" and "Ladies In Waiting" deal with life on the road (i.e. groupies), and a pair of songs were reworked from Kiss' precursor band, Wicked Lester ("Love Her All I Can" and "She"). With *Dressed to Kill*'s Top 40 showing on the *Billboard* charts, the stage was now set for Kiss' big commercial breakthrough with their next release. *—Greg Prato*

● **Alive!** / Oct. 1975 / Casablanca ✦✦✦✦✦
Alive! was the album that catapulted Kiss from cult attraction to mega-superstars. It was their first Top Ten album, remaining on the charts for 110 weeks and eventually going quadruple platinum. Culled from shows in Detroit, New Jersey, Iowa, and Cleveland on the *Dressed to Kill* tour, producer Eddie Kramer did a masterful job of capturing the band's live performance on record. The band's youthful energy is contagious, and with positively electric versions of their best early material, it's no mystery why *Alive!* is widely regarded as one of the greatest live hard rock recordings of all time. "Rock and Roll All Nite" became a Top 20 smash and was the main reason for the album's success, but there are many other tracks that are just as strong—"Deuce," "Strutter," "Firehouse," "Parasite," "She," "100, 000 Years," "Black Diamond," and "Cold Gin" all shine in a live setting. Although there's been some speculation of extensive overdubbing to correct mistakes, *Alive!* remains Kiss' greatest album ever. An essential addition to any rock collection. *—Greg Prato*

Destroyer / 1976 / Casablanca ✦✦✦✦✦
The pressure was on Kiss for their fifth release, and the band knew it. Their breakthrough, *Alive!,* was going to be hard to top, so instead of trying to recreate a concert setting in the studio, they went the opposite route. *Destroyer* is one of Kiss' most experimental studio albums, but also one of their strongest and most interesting. Alice Cooper/Pink Floyd producer Bob Ezrin was on hand, and he strongly encouraged the band to experiment—there's extensive use of sound effects (the album's untitled closing track), the appearance of a boy's choir ("Great Expectations"), and an orchestra-laden, heartfelt ballad ("Beth"). But there's plenty of Kiss' heavy thunder-rock to go around, such as the demonic "God of Thunder" and the sing-along anthems "Flaming Youth," "Shout It Out Loud," "King of the Night Time World," and "Detroit Rock City" (the latter a tale of a doomed concert-goer, complete with violent car crash sound effects). But it was the aforementioned Peter Criss ballad "Beth" that made *Destroyer* such a success; the song was a surprise Top Ten hit (it was originally released as a B-side to "Detroit Rock City"). Also included is a song that Nirvana would later cover ("Do You Love Me?"), as well as an ode to the pleasures of S&M, "Sweet Pain." *Destroyer* also marked the first time that a comic book illustration of the band appeared on the cover, confirming that the band was transforming from hard rockers to superheroes. *—Greg Prato*

Rock and Roll Over / 1976 / Casablanca ✦✦✦✦

Love Gun / Jul. 1977 / Casablanca ✦✦✦✦✦
Love Gun was Kiss' fifth studio album in three years (and seventh release overall, peaking at number four on Billboard), and proved to be the last release that the original line-up played on. By 1977, Kiss merchandising was flooding the marketplace (lunchboxes, makeup kits, comic books, etc.), and it would ultimately lead to a Kiss backlash in the '80s. But the band was still focused on their music for *Love Gun,* similar in sound and approach to their previous straight-ahead rock release, *Rock And Roll Over.* It included Ace Frehley's first lead vocal spot (the eventual concert staple "Shock Me"), as well as one of Kiss' best and most renowned hard rockers in the thunderous title track. The album's opener, "I Stole Your Love," also served as the opening number on Kiss' ensuing tour, while "Christine Sixteen" is one of the few Kiss tracks to contain piano prominently. "Almost Human" is an underrated rocker, and features a great Jimi Hendrix-esque guitar solo from Frehley (no doubt due to ex-Hendrix producer Eddie Kramer manning the boards again), while "Plaster Caster" is a tribute to the famous groupies of the same name. The only weak spots on an otherwise stellar album are an obvious "Rock And Roll All Nite" ripoff titled "Tomorrow and Tonight," and a pointless remake of the Phil Spector-penned classic "Then He Kissed Me" (reworked as "Then She Kissed Me"). *—Greg Prato*

Alive II / Nov. 1977 / Casablanca ✦✦✦✦

Double Platinum / 1978 / Casablanca ✦✦✦✦✦
Double Platinum (Greatest Hits) is a double-album, 20-track collection that gathers all of Kiss' biggest hits ("Rock and Roll All Nite," "Beth," "Detroit Rock City," "Calling Dr. Love," "Love Gun"), but what makes it an essential retrospective and introduction is that it doesn't overlook key album tracks and concert favorites like "Cold Gin," "Deuce," "Black Diamond" and "She." If "Strutter" was represented by the original version, instead of a pointless 1978 remake—which was recorded only to entice collectors into buying an album of music they already owned—*Double Platinum* would have been a definitive collection, but as it stands, it's simply a very, very good overview. *—Stephen Thomas Erlewine*

Dynasty / 1979 / Casablanca ✦✦✦

Kiss Unmasked / Jun. 1980 / Casablanca ✦✦

Music from 'The Elder' / 1981 / Casablanca ✦✦

Creatures of the Night / Oct. 10, 1982 / Casablanca ✦✦✦✦

Lick It Up / Sep. 18, 1983 / Mercury ✦✦✦✦

Animalize / Sep. 13, 1984 / Mercury ✦✦

Asylum / Sep. 16, 1985 / Mercury ✦

Crazy Nights / Sep. 18, 1987 / Mercury ✦

Smashes, Thrashes & Hits / 1988 / Mercury ✦✦✦✦
Smashes, Thrashes & Hits is a compilation of Kiss's greatest hits from their '80s career. Since there weren't enough chart-toppers from that period to fill an entire album, however, '70s classics from their more theatrical days are also included, such as "Love Gun," "Shout It Out Loud" and "Rock and Roll All Nite." (Peter Criss's power ballad, "Beth," is also featured on the album, but is a re-recorded version with then-drummer Eric Carr on vocals.) This combination of classic power rock and pop-metal is what makes the record entertaining, and the album's two new tracks, "Let's Put the X In Sex" and "(You Make Me) Rock Hard," continue to display Kiss' interesting melodies. Although necessary only to the avid Kiss fan, *Smashes, Thrashes & Hits* is an acceptable compilation and is another good introduction to the band. *—Barry Weber*

Hot in the Shade / Oct. 17, 1989 / Mercury ✦✦

Revenge / 1992 / Mercury ✦✦✦

Alive III / May 18, 1993 / Mercury ✦✦

Psycho Circus / Sep. 22, 1998 / Mercury ✦✦

The KLF

f. 1987, Liverpool, England, **db.** May 5, 1992
Group / Ambient House, Rave, Club/Dance, Newbeat, Acid House, House
More than any pop band in history, the KLF ripped off the music industry for a bucketful of loot and got away with it—as illustrated in their own guidebook to creating number one singles, *The Manual.* Bill Drummond and Jimi Cauty applied the tactics of punk shock-terrorism to late-'80s acid-house and became one of Britain's best-selling artists (recording also as the JAMS and the Timelords) just before their retirement in 1992. The duo then deleted their entire back catalogue—a potential loss in the millions of pounds—and declared they wouldn't release another record until peace was declared throughout the world. Debuting with a 1987 LP of rampant sonic piracy, the duo tempered the sampling only slightly for their big breakthrough, the arena anthem "Doctorin' the Tardis" by the Timelords. Even while the single was hitting number one on the charts though, the duo were playing a major part in the development of the '90s boom in ambient music, recording the classic *Chill Out* LP. The following year, Cauty and Drummond moved back to acid-house and earned the greatest success of their career with three Top Ten singles (including the chart-topper "3 A.M. Eternal") from the number one album *The White Room.* The popularity even carried over to American charts, though Cauty and Drummond retired in mid-1992 and refused to release any more material. They partially re-emerged in 1997 with the single "***k the Milennium," recorded as 2K. *—John Bush*

The History of the JAMS a.k.a. The Timelords / 1988 / TVT ✦✦✦✦
Interesting more for its sample-and-scatter philosophy than the thick Scottish brogue with which Drummond tries to emulate Run-D.M.C., *The History of the JAMs a.k.a. The Timelords* takes no prisoners: Dave Brubeck's familiar saxophone riff from "Take Five" is looped onto the James Brown-style jam "Don't Take Five (Take What You Want)," Whitney Houston "guests" on the hilarious "Whitney Joins the JAMs" (a dry run for the later, actually *live,* appearance of

Tammy Wynette), and assorted other stars of the past also make appearances (including the Beatles, MC5, Jimi Hendrix, and Petula Clark). Aside from the novelty tracks—which wear as thin as their production values—this is the only available KLF full-length containing "Doctorin' the Tardis," perhaps the most popular sports anthem ever recorded . *—John Bush*

- **Chill Out** / Jan. 1990 / Wax Trax! ✦✦✦✦✦

One of the initial works in the ambient house canon, *Chill Out* is the practically beatless soundtrack to a late-night journey along the Gulf Coast, and the track titles tell much of the story: "Six Hours to Louisiana, Black Coffee Going Cold," "3AM Somewhere Out of Beaumont," "Elvis on the Radio, Steel Guitar in My Soul." Recorded live by Drummond and Cauty (with much unintended help from sample victims Elvis Presley, Fleetwood Mac, and the throat singers of Tüva), *Chill Out* consists largely of fragmented, heavily reverbed steel guitar, environmental sounds (birds, trains), occasional synth, and an angelic vocal chorus repeating the KLF's own "Justified and Ancient" theme. Throughout, Drummond and Cauty display an instinctive talent for wallpaper music that's truly diverting, making *Chill Out* one of the essential ambient albums. *—John Bush*

The White Room / Mar. 1991 / Arista ✦✦✦✦✦

After the incredible success of their "Doctorin' the Tardis" single in 1988 (better known as that theme from *Dr. Who*), Drummond and Cauty had plenty of money to hire talented musicians (instead of merely sampling them, as on their early recordings). *The White Room* is the result, an album bursting with hit singles that nevertheless flows as well as any concept album. Often overlooked as a classic from the acid house era (mostly because of the KLF's retirement one year later), *The White Room* represents the commercial and artistic peak of late-'80s acid-house. *—John Bush*

The Knack

f. 1978, Los Angeles, CA, **db.** 1981

Group / Power Pop, New Wave

Forming in Los Angeles in the late '70s, the Knack were neither punk nor rock, but pure simple pop, standing out amongst the musical dross that littered the Sunset Strip. Signing with Capitol after a feeding frenzy of label offers, they released their debut, *Get the Knack*, in 1979. With its leadoff single "My Sharona," the Knack climbed both the album and singles charts (eventually selling millions of copies around the globe), gained wide commercial acceptance, and regenerated the power-pop scene that had laid dormant for half a decade. The Knack's image, or lack thereof, was often unfavorably compared to the Beatles, but their music relied on the rough punchiness of the Kinks and the Who rather than the Fab Four. Their refusal to do interviews turned critics against them, and by the time they released their second album, *...But the Little Girls Understand*, less than a year after the debut, the backlash had already begun. *—Steven "Spaz" Schnee*

- **Get the Knack** / 1979 / Capitol ✦✦✦✦✦

The band attempted to update the Beatles sound for the new wave era on their debut. A good idea that was well executed, but critics cried "foul" when millions sold after Capitol's prerelease hype (it went gold in 13 days and eventually sold five million copies, making it one of the most successful debuts in history). *Get the Knack* is at once sleazy, sexist, hook-filled and endlessly catchy—above all, it's a guilty pleasure and an exercise in simple fun. When is power-pop *legitimate* anyway— Includes the unforgettable hits "My Sharona" and "Good Girls Don't." *—Chris Woodstra*

... But the Little Girls Understand / Dec. 1979 / Razor & Tie ✦✦✦

Mike Chapman summed it up best in the liner notes—"The songs are an assortment of feelings and emotions expressed redundantly as only the Knack can... This record is very dear to me and my bank manager." The self-deprecating title (which quotes Willie Dixon's "Back Door Man") isn't really an attempt to apologize but rather to let everyone know that they were in on the joke all along—and they're laughing all the way to the bank. This is essentially a rewrite of the debut, especially evident on the lead-off single "Baby Talks Dirty." It's not as good as *Get the Knack* and didn't sell nearly as well, but it *is* a good time for those who don't take rock & roll too seriously. *—Chris Woodstra*

Serious Fun / Jan. 16, 1991 / Charisma ✦✦

The Retrospective: The Best of the Knack / Nov. 16, 1992 / Capitol ✦✦✦✦✦

Very Best of the Knack / May 19, 1998 / Rhino ✦✦✦✦

Released to coincide with the group's 1998 reunion, Rhino's *The Very Best of the Knack* is designed to replace the 1992 compilation *Retrospective: The Best of the Knack*, and in many ways it does. Twelve of the 16 tracks are greatest hits, all but two of which were featured on *Retrospective*. Granted, "Rocket O' Love" appeared as a demo on the earlier compilation, and "Can't Put a Price on Love" is included here as a single edit, but it still contains all of the essentials—"My Sharona," "Baby Talks Dirty," "Good Girls Don't"—plus one strong song apiece from each of their first two albums ("That's What the Little Girls Do," "How Can Love Hurt So Much"), both of which probably should have been on the original compilation. Then again, *Retrospective* stretched to 17 songs, covering *Round Trip* and *Serious Fun* with some concentration, and *Retrospective* contains no less than four new songs: the solid original "She Says," a winning take on the infectious mock-Merseybeat "That Thing You Do!," and strong readings of two Nick Lowe tunes, "Teacher Teacher" and "I Knew the Bride (When She Used to Rock & Roll)." They're good songs and good performances, but they make the album feel less like a compilation, for better and for worse. *The Very Best of the Knack* remains a good choice for most casual fans, but listeners who want a compilation that concentrates on the body of the band's career might want to seek out *Retrospective*. *—Stephen Thomas Erlewine*

Zoom / Jul. 14, 1998 / Rhino ✦✦✦

Gladys Knight

b. May 28, 1944, Atlanta, GA

Vocals / Smooth Soul, Pop-Soul, Quiet Storm, Motown, Soul

One of the great soul singers, Gladys Knight didn't hit her commercial stride until she moved to Motown in 1966. Steeped in the gospel tradition, like so many soul singers, Knight and backing group the Pips developed into one of Motown's most dependable acts, although they never quite scaled the commercial or artistic heights of fellow stars on the label like the Supremes, Marvin Gaye, and the Temptations. With Norman Whitfield providing the production and much of the songwriting, the Pips fit into the mainstream of Motown's machine well, scoring big hits with some rabble-rousers (like "Friendship Train" and the original version of "I Heard It Through the Grapevine"), mainstream mid-tempo soul ("It Should Have Been Me" and "The End of Our Road,") and smooth ballads like "If I Were Your Woman." In 1973, Knight had her biggest Motown hit with "Neither One of Us," which made number two; shortly afterwards, she and the Pips left Motown for Buddah. The group were briefly superstars in 1973-74, reeling off the smashes "Midnight Train to Georgia" (their only number one), "I've Got to Use My Imagination," and "Best Thing That Ever Happened to Me." This ranked as some of their best material, but Knight soon moved toward an easy listening, adult contemporary direction, one that she's maintained to this day. *—Richie Unterberger*

Anthology / 1974 / Motown ✦✦✦✦✦

Atlanta family-group Gladys Knight & the Pips had performed together for 14 years before signing with Motown in 1966. Earlier recordings for Huntom (the master recordings were later sold to Vee-Jay), Fury, and Maxx had generated five chart hits, including the Top Ten R&B smashes "Every Beat of My Heart" and "Letter Full of Tears," but it was on the Motown subsidiary Soul that Gladys Knight and company hit their stride. This compilation more than adequately covers this period of the Pips' career. Working primarily with producer Norman Whitfield from 1967 through 1969, the group created such Motor City classics as "Everybody Needs Love," "I Heard It Through the Grapevine," "The End of Our Road," and "Friendship Train." From 1970 through 1973 the Pips worked with a variety of Motown producers, concentrating on ballads. Although they were perhaps a little less consistent, there was no shortage of hits, the most notable being 1970's "If I Were Your Woman" and 1973's "Neither One of Us (Wants to Be the First to Say Goodbye)." The updated double-CD version of *Anthology*, featuring digitally remastered sound, replaces about a dozen songs with different ones, though this 40-track collection still contains all of the essential hits and adds lengthy liner notes. Be aware that the three early-'60s hits that lead off the volume (on both versions of *Anthology*) are Motown re-recordings, not the originals. *—Rob Bowman*

Every Beat of My Heart / 1989 / Prime Cuts ✦✦✦

The best collection of Knight's pre-Motown sides, including both of their big early-'60s hits (the title track and "Letter Full of Tears"), but concentrating more heavily on their mid-'60s sessions. These were overseen by Van McCoy, who supplied the group with several of his own compositions as well. McCoy was one of the most melodically ambitious pop/soul composers of the era, and his songs on this compilation—"Either Way I Lose," "Why Don't You Love Me," "Lovers Always Forgive"—are achingly beautiful and rife with unexpected key changes. His "Stop and Get a Hold of Myself," on the other hand, is a more conventional (but equally first-rate) uptempo soul stomper. If there's any criticism of these sides, it's that Knight and the group don't establish a strong identity, handling doo wop-like ballads, girl-group-tinged pop, McCoy's idiosyncratic songs, and more modern pop-soul with chameleon-like skill. In the end, that doesn't detract from the strength of this CD, which is a collection of fine early to mid-'60s pop/soul. The major flaw is the inexplicable omission of the McCoy composition "Giving Up," a Top 40 hit for the group in 1964. *—Richie Unterberger*

Soul Survivors: The Best of Gladys Knight & the Pips 1973-1988 / Oct. 1990 / Rhino ✦✦✦✦✦

Soul Survivors—The Best of Gladys Knight & the Pips picks up where the Motown anthology left off, containing the most important singles that Gladys Knight And The Pips recorded for Buddah, Columbia, and MCA from the early '70s until the late '80s. The Buddah tracks, highlighted by the Jim Weatherly-written "Midnight Train in Georgia" and "Best Thing That Ever Happened to Me," contain some of Knight's most impassioned vocal performances. *—Rob Bowman*

Blue Lights in the Basement / Apr. 1996 / RCA ✦✦✦

The Ultimate Collection / Oct. 7, 1997 / Motown ✦✦✦✦✦

The Ultimate Collection nearly lives up to its billing, featuring 22 tracks on a single disc. Among the featured cuts are all of Gladys Knight & the Pips' Top Ten pop hits for Soul Records, including "Everybody Needs Love," "I Heard It Through the Grapevine," "The End of Our Road," "It Should Have Been Me," "The Nitty Gritty," "Friendship Train," "I Don't Want to Do Wrong," "If I Were Your Woman," and "Neither One of Us (Wants to Be the First to Say Goodbye)." For most casual fans, those who just want the hits, this will be the definitive collection of Knight's early career. *—Stephen Thomas Erlewine*

Best of Gladys Knight & the Pips / Jan. 27, 1998 / The Right Stuff ✦✦✦✦

The Right Stuff's *The Best of Gladys Knight & the Pips* is a nice, brief ten-track summary of the group's first four albums with Buddah, showcasing such hit singles as "Where Peaceful Waters Flow," "Midnight Train to Georgia," "I've Got to Use My Imagination," "Best Thing That Ever Happened to Me," "On and On," "I Feel a Song (In My Heart)" and "The Way We Were / Try to Remember," plus the album tracks "Make Yours a Happy Home," "The Going Ups and the Coming Downs" and "I Can See Clearly Now." Although it's missing a couple of minor hits, it's a solid, concise collection that's ideal for fans of Knight's smooth mid-'70s soul, even though it isn't as complete or thorough as Rhino's *Soul Survivors*. *—Stephen Thomas Erlewine*

- **Essential Collection** / Sep. 28, 1999 / Hip-O ✦✦✦✦✦

There have been many Gladys Knight & the Pips collections over the years, yet few have drawn from all periods of their career. Hip-O's 1999 compilation *Essential Collection* does, beginning with their first hit for Vee-Jay, "Every Beat of My Heart," and ending with their last R&B number one, 1987's "Love Overboard." It doesn't feature every hit they ever had, but it does provide a good chronology of their career by featuring their biggest hits: "I Heard It Through the Grapevine," "If I Were Your Woman," "Neither One of Us (Wants to Be the First to Say Goodbye)," "Daddy Could Swear, I Declare," "Midnight Train to Georgia," "I've Got to Use My Imagination," "The Best Thing That Ever Happened to Me," "On and On,"

"Save the Overtime (For Me)," "Hero (Wind Beneath My Wings)." Anyone looking for a single disc covering the entire career of Gladys Knight & the Pips should turn here. — *Stephen Thomas Erlewine*

Cub Koda

b. Oct. 1, 1948, Detroit, MI, **d.** Jul. 1, 2000

Vocals, Harmonica, Guitar, Liner Notes / Detroit Rock, Retro-Rock, Rockabilly, Blues-Rock, Electric Chicago Blues, Rock & Roll

Best known as the leader of Brownsville Station and composer of their hit, "Smokin' in the Boys Room," Cub Koda has proven that his roots went far deeper, both before the band's formation, during its days in the sun, and long after its demise. His high school band, the Del-Tinos, was dipping into blues and rockabilly as far back as 1963—not only pre-Butterfield, but pre-Beatles. Similarly, he recorded legendary home tapes during his off hours from Brownsville, before the rockabilly revival had uttered its first hiccup, and later teamed with Hound Dog Taylor's former rhythm section, the Houserockers, to play the blues in the '80s. Along the way he cranked out a monthly column ("The Vinyl Junkie") and recorded a series of albums that kept roots music of all kinds alive without ever treating it like a museum piece. After a couple of bands in the late '60s that largely went unrecorded, Koda formed Brownsville Station in early 1969. The band debuted one year later, but it wasn't until 1973's number three hit "Smokin' in the Boys Room" that Brownsville gained a genuine hit. When Brownsville disbanded in 1979, Cub established himself as an expert record collector and critic through columns for *Goldmine* and *DISCoveries*. In 1980, Koda began working with Hound Dog Taylor's backing band, the Houserockers, and the trio ended up together for 15 years. Throughout the '80s and '90s, Koda has continued to divide his time equally between touring, recording, and writing. —*Stephen Thomas Erlewine*

Cub Koda & the Points / 1980 / Fan Club ✦✦✦✦
Koda's first solo album after Brownsville Station. Highlights include "Jail Bait" and "Welcome to My Job." —*Stephen Thomas Erlewine*

It's the Blues / 1981 / Fan Club ✦✦✦
The addition of bass and special guests Left Hand Frank and Lefty Dizz only distract from the chemistry between Cub and the Houserockers (even more obvious on their belated live follow-up), but this is a strong session, with the ex-stadium boogie boy sounding totally at home with these blues veterans. His vocal duet with Brewer Phillips on J.B. Lenoir's "Talk to Your Daughter" is a joy, and thankfully not every note is perfectly in place—or in the case of Brewer's guitar, in tune. Added treats: Koda's big-toned harp on "Rockin' This Joint Tonight" and humorous dialog with Frank on "Dirty Duck Blues." —*Dan Forte*

Cub Digs Chuck / 1989 / Garageland ✦✦✦
Koda's tribute album to Chuck Berry, featuring blistering versions of "Johnny B. Goode," "Maybellene," and others. —*Stephen Thomas Erlewine*

Cub Digs Bo / 1991 / Garageland ✦✦✦✦
Koda's tribute album to Bo Diddley, including powerhouse renditions of "Mumblin' Guitar," "Roadrunner," and "Background to a Music." —*Stephen Thomas Erlewine*

Live at B.L.U.E.S. 1982 / 1991 / Wolf ✦✦✦✦✦
What's wrong with this picture? The sawed-off bespectacled singer/guitarist from Brownville Station fronting the late Hound Dog Taylor's ex-rhythm section, the Houserockers—blasphemy, you say? Get a life. Koda smokes like he's: 1) out to dispel any doubts about his legitimacy, and 2) having the time of his life. Opening with Howlin' Wolf's "Highway 49" (a rather tall order), the Cubmaster grabs the Chicago crowd by its collective neck and shakes it into submission. His guitar trade-offs with Brewer Phillips (no bass in this band) are a delight, and by "You Can't Sit Down" drummer Ted Harvey is blowing his police whistle—signalling that things be rockin'! Eddie Clearwater sits in on one tune, and Koda tips his hat to the guitarist with a stellar rendition of Eddie's "Hillbilly Blues." This is worthy of wider release, not to mention an encore. —*Dan Forte*

● **Welcome to My Job: The Cub Koda Collection 1963-93** / 1993 / Blue Wave ✦✦✦✦✦
Covering everything from his pre-Brownsville Station days to two brand-new songs, *Welcome to My Job* is the definitive collection of Cub Koda's versatile solo career. —*Stephen Thomas Erlewine*

Abba Dabba Dabba: A Bananza of Hits / Jul. 19, 1994 / Schoolkids ✦✦✦✦✦
Cub Koda's first album for Schoolkids' Records is his wildest, funniest, and simply best album in years. —*Stephen Thomas Erlewine*

The Joint Was Rockin' / 1996 / Deluge ✦✦✦✦
The Joint Was Rockin' is a raw, rowdy and deliriously fun record capturing Cub Koda live with the Houserockers in the early '80s. The Houserockers bash away like they were supporting Hound Dog Taylor and Cub proves that he can play the blues with true passion and feeling. More than anything, however, *The Joint Was Rockin'* is a bracing jolt of energy and fun that's just as good as *Live at B.L.U.E.S. 1982*, his previous live set with the Houserockers. —*Stephen Thomas Erlewine*

Box Lunch / 1997 / J-Bird ✦✦✦✦
Cub Koda has tried a lot of different things in his long career, but he has never made anything close to *Box Lunch*. It's not just that the album consists of nothing but acoustic material; he has never been this open with his emotions. There are a few rockers—"Double Barrel Hell" is menacing and "Gimme Trash" is a tongue-in-cheek kitsch celebration—but the heart of the record is in the ballads, whether it's the nostalgic "We Were Crazy Back Then," the yearning "Runaway Heart," or the lovely "How Could Life Turn Out This Way," which evokes the spirit of Hank Williams. Cub has rarely been this naked with his feelings and the results are frequently moving. And, to cap it all off, he throws out "Susan Hayward's Diary," a charming finger-picked instrumental. Moments like this make you hope that it's not the last acoustic album Cub will make—*Box Lunch* is so good, you wish there were seconds. —*Stephen Thomas Erlewine*

Noise Monkeys / Mar. 2000 / J-Bird ✦✦✦✦
Arriving on the heels of the introspective, acoustic *Box Lunch, Noise Monkeys*—Cub Koda's reunion album with the Points, his first band after the demise of Brownsville Station—may come as a bit of a surprise. Make no mistake about it, the title of the record tells you what this album is all about: this is loud, dumb, fun, hard-driving rock & roll, the kind that sounds like it was cut by a bunch of noise monkeys. Some fans may have forgotten that Koda can rock hard when he wants to, and that's what he does with the Points on *Noise Monkeys*. The bulk of the album was recorded live in the studio in one day in June 1999; the final two songs were recorded live in concert, the following day. Not surprisingly, the album is a bracing, immediate, and above all, loud record, filled with guitars, guitars, and guitars. He hasn't rocked this hard or this intensely since the first Points album. But this record is a better one on many levels, due to the fact that the band members have matured as musicians. They can now knock off these songs in one take and sound totally convincing and energetic. But don't think that this is sophisticated music—this is dumb rock & roll, and proudly so—and it's all the better for it. Koda and the Points pound away, sounding stronger and better at the turn of the millennium than they did at the turn of the '70s. Sure, some of the songs are silly, but that's the point. The end result is a satisfying hard rock album with humor and character—something like that doesn't come along every day. —*Stephen Thomas Erlewine*

Kool & The Gang

f. 1964, Jersey City, NJ

Group / Urban, Funk, Soul

Formed as a jazz ensemble in the mid-'60s, Kool & the Gang became one of the most inspired and influential funk units during the '70s, and one of the most popular R&B groups of the '80s after their breakout hit "Celebration" in 1979. Just as funky as James Brown or Parliament (and sampled almost as frequently), Kool & the Gang relied on their jazz backgrounds and long friendship to form a tightly knit group with the interplay and improvisation of a jazz outfit, plus the energy and spark of a band with equal ties to soul, R&B and funk. Kool & the Gang became a quick success on the R&B charts, and with their sixth LP, *Wild and Peaceful*, they hit the big time. "Funky Stuff" became their first Top 40 hit at the end of 1973. Then both "Jungle Boogie" and "Hollywood Swinging" reached the pop Top Ten. In 1979, the group added two new vocalists, Earl Toon, Jr. and, more importantly, James "J.T." Taylor, a former Jersey nightclub singer. Kool & the Gang also began working with jazz fusion arranger Eumir Deodato, who produced their records from 1979 to 1982. The first such album, *Ladies Night*, was their biggest hit yet, the first of three consecutive platinum albums, with the Top Ten singles "Too Hot" and the title track. *Celebrate!*, released in 1980, spawned Kool & the Gang's only number one hit, "Celebration," an anthem favored by innumerable wedding receptions since. With Deodato, the group produced several more hits, including the singles "Take My Heart (You Can Have It If You Want It)," "Get Down on It" and "Big Fun," and the albums *Something Special* in 1981 and *As One* a year later. After Deodato left the fold in late 1982, Kool & the Gang proved their success wasn't solely due to him; they had two immense hits during 1984-85 ("Joanna" and "Cherish"), as well as two more Top Tens, "Misled" and "Fresh." —*John Bush*

● **The Very Best of Kool & the Gang** / Mar. 30, 1999 / Mercury ✦✦✦✦✦
The Very Best of Kool & the Gang describes this collection aptly: their early, funky beginnings are represented with songs like "Jungle Boogie," "Funky Stuff," and "Celebration," as well the smooth urban stylings the band developed later on "Fresh" and "Cherish." Over 21 tracks, *The Very Best of Kool & the Gang* delivers exactly what the title promises. —*Heather Phares*

Korn

f. 1992, Bakersfield, CA

Group / Alternative Metal

Korn's cathartic alternative funk-metal sound positioned the group among the most popular and provocative to emerge during the post-grunge era. Korn began its existence as the Bakersfield, California-based metal band LAPD, which included guitarists James "Munky" Shaffer and Brian "Head" Welch, bassist Reginald "Fieldy Snuts" Arvizu, and drummer David Silveria. After issuing an LP, the members of LAPD in 1993 crossed paths with Jonathan Davis, a mortuary science student moonlighting as the lead vocalist for the local group Sexart; they soon asked Davis to join the band, and upon his arrival, the quintet rechristened themselves Korn. After signing to Epic's Immortal imprint, they issued their debut album in late 1994; thanks to a relentless tour schedule that included stints opening for Ozzy Osbourne, Megadeth, Marilyn Manson and 311, the record slowly but steadily rose the charts, eventually going gold. Its 1996 follow-up, *Life Is Peachy*, was a more immediate smash, reaching the number three spot on the pop album charts. The following summer, they headlined Lollapalooza, but were forced to drop off the tour when Shaffer was diagnosed with viral meningitis. While recording their best-selling 1998 LP *Follow the Leader*, Korn made national headlines when a student in Zeeland, Michigan was suspended for wearing a T-shirt emblazoned with the group's logo; the school's principal later declared their music "indecent, vulgar and obscene," prompting the band to issue a cease-and-desist order. *Issues* followed in 1999. —*Jason Ankeny*

● **Korn** / Oct. 11, 1994 / Immortal/Epic ✦✦✦✦✦
With little publicity, radio play or MTV exposure, Korn took their eponymous 1995 debut to platinum status. Like all unexpected successes, it's easier to understand its popularity in retrospect. Although they disdain the "metal" label, there's no question that Korn is among the vanguard of post-grunge alt-metal outfits. Borrowing from Jane's Addiction, Rage Against The Machine, Pantera, Helmet, Faith No More, Anthrax, Public Enemy and N.W.A, Korn developed a testosterone-fueled, ultra-aggressive metal-rap hybrid. They're relentless, both in their musical attack and in lead singer Jonathan Davis' bleak, violent lyrics. Tales of abuse and alienation run rampant throughout the record. It's often disturbing and, to some ears, even offensive, but their music can have a cathartic effect that makes up for their vulgarity and questionable laspes in taste. It's a powerful sound and one that actually builds on the

funk-metal innovations of the late '80s/early '90s instead of merely replicating them. —*Stephen Thomas Erlewine*

Life Is Peachy / Oct. 15, 1996 / Immortal/Epic ✦✦✦

Follow the Leader / Aug. 18, 1998 / Immortal/Epic ✦✦✦✦
More than anything, Korn is about sound. They write songs, but those wind up not being nearly as memorable as their lurching metallic hip-hop grind. They have yet to exhaust that sound, and that's why their third album *Follow the Leader* is an effective follow-up to their first two alt-metal landmarks. Not that it offers anything new—it's the same sound, offered in a more focused forum than *Life is Peachy,* but not sounding as fresh as *Korn.* In fact, it begins to wear a little thing toward the end fo the album, but guitarists Head Welch and Munky Shaffer find enough tonal variations over the course of the album to keep it interesting, and vocalist Jonathan Davis nearly matches them with his cavalcade of voices. If the songs themselves don't leave much of an impression, it's because they're not supposed to—they're simply vehicles for the metallic grind, which provides all the visceral rush any Korn fan needs. —*Stephen Thomas Erlewine*

Issues / Nov. 16, 1999 / Immortal/Epic ✦✦✦✦
Released in the fall of 1999, when Korn was in danger of being overshadowed by such protégés as Limp Bizkit, *Issues* reaffirm the group's status as alt-metal leaders, illustrating that the true difference between Korn and their imitators is their mastery of sound. Korn is about nothing if not sound. Sure, Jonathan Davis doesn't merely toss off lyrics but in the end, it doesn't matter since voice and the various words that float to the surface simply enhance the mood. Similarly, the band doesn't really have any distinguished riffs or hooks—everything each member contributes adds to the overall sound—so, casual listeners can be forgiven if they think the songs sound the same, since not only do the tracks bleed into one other, the individual songs have no discernable high points. Each cut rises from the same dark sonic murk, occasionally surging forward with volume, power and aggression. It's mood music—songs don't matter, but the foreboding feeling and gloomy sounds do. To a certain extent, this has always been true of Korn albums, but it's particularly striking on *Issues* because they pull off a nifty trick of stripping their sound back to its bare essentials and expanding and rebuilding from that. They've decided to leave rap-metal to the likes of Limp Bizkit, since there is very little rapping or appropriation of hip-hop culture anywhere on *Issues.* By doing this, they have re-emphasized their skill as a band, and how they can find endless, often intriguing, variations on their core sound. *Issues* may not be the cathartic blast of anger their debut was, nor is it as adventurous as *Follow the Leader,* but it better showcases the sheer raw power of the band than either. —*Stephen Thomas Erlewine*

Kraftwerk

f. 1970, Düsseldorf, Germany
Group / Experimental Rock, Proto-Punk, Kraut Rock, Club/Dance, Electronic
During the mid-'70s, Germany's Kraftwerk established the sonic blueprint followed by an extraordinary number of artists in the decades to come. From the British New Romantic movement to hip-hop to techno, the group's self-described "robot pop"—hypnotically minimal, obliquely rhythmic music performed solely via electronic means—resonates in virtually every new development to impact the contemporary pop scene of the late 20th century, and as pioneers of the electronic music form, their enduring influence cannot be overstated. Primary members Florian Schneider and Ralf Hütter first met as classical music students at the Düsseldorf Conservatory, and recorded one LP as Organisation before rechristening themselves Kraftwerk (German for "power station"). Immersing their music in the fledgling world of minimalist electronics, the pair made a surprising breakthrough into the pop market with their fourth album, 1974's *Autobahn;* an edited single version of the epic title track was a major hit at home and abroad. Subsequent albums *Radio-Activity, Trans-Europe Express* and *The Man Machine* explored futuristic technology concepts and increased the movement towards seeming musical mechaninization. By this time, the members of Kraftwerk even publicly portrayed themselves as automatons, an image solidified by tracks like "We Are the Robots." The group disappeared from view during much of the '80s, releasing albums in 1981 (with the British chart-topping "Computer Love") and 1986. Except for a 1991 remixed best-of collection titled *The Mix* and an occasional live tour, they remained silent in the years to follow. —*Jason Ankeny*

Kraftwerk 1 / 1971 / Philips ✦✦✦✦

Kraftwerk 2 / 1972 / Philips ✦✦✦

Ralf & Florian / 1973 / Warner Brothers ✦✦✦

★ **Autobahn** / 1974 / Philips ✦✦✦✦✦
Although Kraftwerk's first three albums were groundbreaking in their own right, *Autobahn* is where the group's hypnotic electro-pulse genuinely came into its own. The main difference between *Autobahn* and its predecessors is how it develops an insistent, propulsive pulse which makes the repeated rhythms and riffs of the shimmering electronic keyboards and trance-like guitars all the more hypnotizing. The 22-minute title track, in a severely edited form, became an international hit single and remains the peak of the band's achievements—it encapsulates the band and why they are important within one track—but the rest of the album provides soundscapes equally as intriguing. Within *Autobahn,* the roots of electro-funk, ambient, and synth-pop are all evident—it's a pioneering album, even if its electronic trances might not capture the attention of all listeners. —*Stephen Thomas Erlewine*

Radio-Activity / 1975 / Capitol ✦✦✦

☆ **Trans-Europe Express** / 1977 / Capitol ✦✦✦✦✦
Although *Autobahn* was a left-field masterpiece, *Trans-Europe Express* is often cited as perhaps the archetypal (and most accessible) Kraftwerk album. Melodic themes are repeated often and occasionally interwoven over deliberate, chugging beats, sometimes with manipulated vocals; the effect is mechanical yet hypnotic. Thematically, the record feels like parts of two different concept albums: one a meditation on the disparities between reality and image ("Hall of Mirrors" and "Showroom Dummies" share recurring images of glass, reflection, illusion and confused identities, as well as whimsical melodies), and the other the glorification of Europe. There is an impressive composition paying homage to "Franz Schubert," but the real meat of this approach is contained in the opening love letter, "Europe Endless," and the epic title track which shares themes and lyrics with the following track, "Metal on Metal." The song "Trans-Europe Express" is similar in concept to "Autobahn," as it mimics the swaying motion and insistent drive of a cross-continent train trip. What ultimately holds the album together, though, is the music, which is more consistently memorable even than that on *Autobahn.* Overall, *Trans-Europe Express* offers the best blend of minimalism, mechanized rhythms, and crafted, catchy melodies in the group's catalog; henceforth, their music would take on more danceable qualities only hinted at here (although the title cut provided the basis for Afrika Bambaataa's enormously important dancefloor smash "Planet Rock"). —*Steve Huey*

The Man Machine / 1978 / Capitol ✦✦✦✦✦
The Man-Machine is closer to the sound and style that would define early new wave electro-pop—less minimalistic in its arrangements and more complex and danceable in its underlying rhythms. Like its predecessor, *Trans-Europe Express,* there is the feel of a divided concept album, with some songs devoted to science fiction-esque links between humans and technology, often with electronically processed vocals ("The Robots," "Spacelab," and the title track); others take the glamour of urbanization as their subject ("Neon Lights" and "Metropolis"). Plus, there's "The Model," a character sketch which falls under the latter category but takes a more cynical view of the title character's glamorous lifestyle. More pop-oriented than any of their previous work, the sound of *The Man-Machine*—in particular among Kraftwerk's oeuvre—had a tremendous impact on the cold, robotic synth-pop of artists like Gary Numan, as well as Britain's later New Romantic movement. —*Steve Huey*

Computer World / 1981 / Warner Brothers ✦✦✦✦✦
The first of Kraftwerk's many extended periods of silence was broken with the release of *Computer World,* a record exploring the ramifications of living in a society dominated by technology. A tightly honed, starkly minimalist effort, its implementation of recent technological advances yields a brighter and sharper sound than ever before; the single "Pocket Calculator" typifies the group at their most playful, while "Home Computer" eerily presages the emergence of techno and house music later in the decade. —*Jason Ankeny*

Electric Cafe / 1986 / Elektra ✦✦✦
Five long years after *Computer World,* Kraftwerk finally resurfaced with another LP, *Electric Cafe;* the rest of the pop music industry having finally caught up with the group's vision, they no longer seem so innovative and inspired—indeed, the record's brief running time (under 36 minutes) seems indicative of a lack of ideas and new directions, with the spartan opening tracks "Technopop" and "Musique Non-Stop" virtually interchangeable and the remaining cuts surprisingly mainstream in both form and content. —*Jason Ankeny*

The Mix / Jun. 11, 1991 / Elektra ✦✦✦

Lenny Kravitz

b. May 26, 1964, New York, NY
Vocals, Drums, Guitar, Bass / Album Rock, American Trad Rock, Neo-Psychedelia, Pop/Rock
As a musician and a producer, Lenny Kravitz is unquestionably gifted. He can successfully recreate the sound and feeling of countless groups from the past; his music recalls everyone from Lennon, Hendrix, and Bowie to the Velvet Underground, Curtis Mayfield and Prince. What Kravitz can't do is synthesize these influences into a distinctive style—every song on each of his albums sounds like it was recorded by a different artist. However, that's not entirely a bad thing, because Kravitz *can* reproduce the sound of his favorite artists exactly; "It Ain't Over 'Til It's Over" sounds like it was recorded in 1972, "Are You Gonna Go My Way" sounds like a forgotten track from 1968. His music might not be original, but it is quite enjoyable. Since his 1989 debut, *Let Love Rule,* Kravitz's songwriting and production skills have been consistently improving. His second album, *Mama Said,* gave him a number two hit with "It Ain't Over 'Til It's Over." *Are You Gonna Go My Way,* Kravitz's third album, was released in 1993; it was a stronger album than anything he had released in the past and is was his most commercially successful record yet. 1995's *Circus,* however, was something of a letdown, and he did not resurface with his fifth effort—titled, appropriately enough, *5*—until mid-1998. —*Stephen Thomas Erlewine*

Let Love Rule / Sep. 1989 / Virgin ✦✦✦✦✦
In many ways, Lenny Kravitz's *Let Love Rule* is a thoroughly impressive debut. Like Prince, he plays nearly every instrument on the record, yet makes it sound organic and alive. Musically, it's a startlingly accurate replication of late-'60s psychedelia, crossed with a Princely groove and a heavy John Lennon fixation. Kravitz has no desire to move forward, he only wants to recreate classic rock, and as a result, *Let Love Rule* is an enormous, guilty pleasure. His songcraft may be derivative, but it's catchy—the title track has a lean groove and a colorful chorus, "Sittin' on Top of the World" and "Does Anybody Out There Even Care" have strong hooks, and while the stately psychedelia of "I Build This Garden for Us" can sound like a parody, it is quite effective. Kravitz stumbles when he gets preachy (the awkward "Mr. Cab Driver") or flowery ("Flower Child"), but that doesn't diminish the pleasures of *Let Love Rule.* —*Stephen Thomas Erlewine*

Mama Said / Apr. 2, 1991 / Virgin ✦✦✦
Moving forward a couple years from the psychedelic fixations of his debut, *Mama Said* finds Lenny Kravitz in the early '70s, trying to graft Curtis Mayfield and Jimi Hendrix influences to his Prince and Lennon obsessions. This time around, he synthesizes his influences better; it's essentially a seamless record, with all of its classic rock homages so carefully produced that it sounds as if it could have been released in 1972. Kravitz's songcraft has gotten better as well, with the swirling Philly soul of "It Ain't Over Till It's Over" and the rampaging Sly Stone-meets-Hendrix "Always on the Run" standing out as instantly addictive singles. Still, some of the joy that informed *Let Love Rule* has worn off, largely because it's more polished and studied than its predecessor. That, however, doesn't prevent *Mama Said* from being another thoroughly enjoyable guilty pleasure—its sweet soul and fuzzy hard rock are slyly se-

ductive. Ironically for such an inviting record, *Mama Said* is Kravitz's divorce album, yet it never quite conveys any true pain or emotion, since he puts sound over substance. Essentially, the lyrics are afterthoughts, but with a record as immaculately produced and sonically pleasurable as *Mama Said*, it doesn't really matter that it's talking loud and saying nothing, because it sounds good while it's talking. *—Stephen Thomas Erlewine*

• **Are You Gonna Go My Way—** / Nov. 22, 1993 / Virgin ✦✦✦✦✦
The cover indicates that *Are You Gonna Go My Way?* is Lenny Kravitz's bid for rock stardom. Designed in the style of an early-'70s record, it features Kravitz in hippie clothing, apparently exposing himself to a photographer—in other words, he's a dangerously sexy counterculture rebel. That may have been true in 1970, but in 1993, he simply sounds like a weird sideshow exhibit, the man who never lived past 1973. Of course, it's easy to make such potshots, but Kravitz opens himself up to such attacks. No other artist, especially a successful one, has been quite so devoted to the past and ignorant of the present. Since he has considerable talent for songcraft and production, Kravitz isn't nearly as bad as could be, and *Are You Gonna Go My Way* is just as enjoyable and more accomplished than its predecessors. This time around, Hendrix is his chief influence, as evidenced by the roaring title track, and he does expand that with his traditional Lennon, Curtis Mayfield and Prince obsessions. Song for song, it's his most consistent album, although by the end of the record, his painstaking reproduction of classic rock sounds begins to appear a bit too studied, suggesting that Kravitz may have hit a creative wall. Nevertheless, that does nothing to diminish the enjoyment of this record. *—Stephen Thomas Erlewine*

Circus / Sep. 12, 1995 / Virgin ✦✦

5 / May 12, 1998 / Virgin ✦✦✦
Lenny Kravitz must have realized he bottomed out with the turgid *Circus*, so he decided to shake things up a bit on its follow-up, *5*. Like any veteran in the late '90s, he dabbled in electronica, adding a few trip-hop loops and analog synths to his bedrock rock n' soul. It's enough to make *5* sound relatively fresh, at least compared to the retro dead-end of *Circus*, yet it sounds like Kravitz *read* about the idea of electronica without actually listening to any music. Anemic synths and stilted drum loops (sampled from Kravitz's playing, not old records) are scattered throughout the record, along with vaguely distorted vocals. It's not enough to make Kravitz sound *hip*, especially since he still loves endless funk jams and electric sitars, but it does revitalize his sound. At least for a little while. By the end of the album, his songwriting sounds as tired and unmemorable as on *Circus*. Without hooks, melodies, and style, Kravitz's Sly, Mayfield, Hendrix, Lennon, and Prince pastiches are a bore. *5* has a few passable cuts, yet it falls short of the quirky hero worship and melodic smarts that made his first three records so enjoyable. *—Stephen Thomas Erlewine*

Greatest Hits / Oct. 24, 2000 / Virgin ✦✦✦✦✦

L7

f. 1985, Los Angeles, CA
Group / Riot Grrrl, Alternative Metal, Grunge, Alternative Pop/Rock
L7's heavy, punk-inflected, riff-oriented guitar grind—a mix of the Ramones, Motorhead, and Joan Jett—was what earned them a dedicated following of fans in the early '90s, not the fact that they were female. While the band is strongly feminist, they never let their rhetoric stand in the way of their roaring guitars. L7 always relies on the sheer sonic aggression of rock, not its lyrical power. When the group was on Sub Pop early in the '90s, the band sounded punkier and more abrasive; signing to a major label didn't cause them to lose that aggression—they just had a better production, courtesy of Butch Vig (Nirvana, Smashing Pumpkins, Sonic Youth). Featuring "Pretend We're Dead," 1992's *Bricks Are Heavy* was a major alternative hit; their second major-label album, the coarse *Hungry for Stink*, was released right before L7 toured with 1994's Lollapalooza. The acclaimed *Beauty Process: Triple Platinum* followed in 1997, and a year later the group issued *Live—Omaha to Osaka*. 1999 saw the release of the L7 film documentary *The Beauty Process*, directed by former Nirvana bassist Krist Novoselic; a new studio LP, *Slap-Happy*, appeared later that same year. *—Stephen Thomas Erlewine*

L7 / 1990 / Epitaph ✦✦✦

Smell the Magic / Jul. 12, 1991 / Sub Pop ✦✦✦✦
On 1991's *Smell the Magic*, L7 begins to find the sense of melody to complement its distorted punk guitar assault. The band deserves ultimate praise for writing from a completely female perspective at all times, and the fabulous "Fast and Frightening" just might be the ultimate "riot grrrrl" anthem. "Shove" pleads the case for mosh pit etiquette, while "Just Like Me" demands equal rights (and vices) for male and female rock stars. The self-mocking "Broomstick" celebrates any "rock & roll hags" accusations with a sense of humor. "'Til the Wheels Fall Off" is another standout, thanks to it's relentless descending riff, and points the way toward the band's breakthrough album, *Bricks Are Heavy*. *—Ed Rivadavia*

• **Bricks Are Heavy** / Apr. 14, 1992 / Slash ✦✦✦✦✦
Though they hailed from sunny L.A., L7 became the poster girls for grunge, and more specifically the "riot grrrl" movement in 1992, with the meteoric success of their third album, *Bricks are Heavy*. While their previous efforts had sounded sloppy and uneven, *Nevermind* producer Butch Vig helped the girls obtain a tight, compact sound on *Bricks*, pushing them to focus on their songwriting to boot. After all, great albums need great songs, and that's exactly what you have here. Mosh-pit anthem "Everglade" (sung by bassist Jennifer Finch) will simply knock you on your ass, and big single "Pretend We're Dead" is so good that its tough swagger harks back to seminal bad girl anthems like Joan Jett's "I Love Rock'n'Roll," Pat Benatar's "Hit Me With Your Best Shot," and even the Go-Go's—well, maybe not the Go-Go's. The sardonic "Diet Pill" tackles female compulsions with clever irony, and even when they let their mega-riffing take over on such full-throttle stomps as "Wargasm," "Mr. Integrity," and "Shitlist," L7 still manage to imbue their lyrics with humor and substance. Inevitably, a few songs (especially "Slide") tend to push the Nirvana envelope just a tad, but Vig's involvement aside, these four ladies had been doing this kind of thing for as long as the Seattle trio. L7's crowning achievement, *Bricks Are Heavy* sadly proved to be an impossible act to follow, and the band gradually faded into obscurity thereafter. *—Ed Rivadavia*

Hungry for Stink / Jul. 12, 1994 / Slash/Reprise ✦✦

The Beauty Process: Triple Platinum / Feb. 25, 1997 / Slash/Reprise ✦✦✦

Live: Omaha to Osaka / Dec. 15, 1998 / Man's Ruin ✦✦✦

Slap-Happy / Aug. 24, 1999 / Bong Load ✦✦✦

Best of L7: The Slash Years / May 2, 2000 / EMI ✦✦✦✦
L7 had the sound, style, and tough-grrrl attitude to hit it big in the aftermath of grunge's mainstream breakthrough, but unfortunately, the band was too often hampered by uneven songwriting. *The Best of L7: The Slash Years* collects four songs apiece from *Bricks Are Heavy*, *Hungry for Stink*, and *The Beauty Process: Triple Platinum* (although, as the title suggests, there's nothing from the fine Sub Pop album *Smell the Magic*). It's a pretty good distillation of the cream of those records, even if there are still a few tunes on *Bricks Are Heavy* that could have made the cut on a less mathematically selected best-of. In fact, as L7's most pop-oriented record, *Bricks Are Heavy* is still a slightly more accessible introduction, since following that album, the band tended to rely more on sheer power than melody. Nevertheless, *The Best of L7: The Slash Years* does encapsulate what the group was all about, and it's a great way to dig deeper into their catalog without having to buy all the individual albums. *—Steve Huey*

The La's

f. 1986
Group / College Rock, Britpop, Alternative Pop/Rock
When the La's released their debut album in 1990, it made immediate waves in the British pop scene, as well as American college radio. Drawing from the hook-laden, ringing guitars of mid-'60s British pop as well as the post-punk pop of the Smiths, the La's self-titled first album—heralded by the hit single "There She Goes"—had a timeless, classic feel. It seemed like effortless music, yet that was not the case. From their inception in 1986 to the present day, lead singer/guitarist/songwriter Lee Mavers has been a perfectionist with a nearly obsessive eye for detail. Consequently, the La's were never able to totally fulfill their promise. *—Stephen Thomas Erlewine*

The La's / 1990 / Go! Discs/London ✦✦✦✦✦
The La's were one of the few English alternative groups to keep traditional British guitar-pop alive during the late '80s and early '90s. Drawing heavily from the punchy British Invasion sound of early Beatles, the Hollies, the Searchers and Small Faces, the group's eponymous debut is a swirling array of ringing guitar hooks and strong, undeniable pop melodies. Throughout the record, chief songwriter Lee Mavers turns out small, well-crafted gems, highlighted by the hit single "There She Goes," whose jangling hooks and sighing melodies simply scratch the surface of the abundance of pleasures on the record. While Mavers claimed at the time that the label forced him to release *The La's*, it's hard to imagine the record being any more infectious. As it stands, *The La's* was a refreshing slice of classicist guitar-pop at the time of its release, and its charms have not faded over the years. *—Stephen Thomas Erlewine*

Labelle

f. 1970, **db.** 1977
Group / Disco, Funk, Soul
A girl-group from Philadelphia, they formed in 1962. Initially known as the Blue Belles, and then Patti LaBelle and the Bluebelles, the group's personnel consisted of Patti LaBelle, Cindy Birdsong, Sarah Dash, and Nona Hendryx. The quartet scored six R&B hits from 1962 through 1967 before Birdsong departed to join Diana Ross and the Supremes. Continuing as a trio, for the next seven years the group languished in obscurity. British manager Vicki Wickham remade their image in the early '70s and shortened the name to Labelle. Decked out in ersatz futuristic garb, the threesome appeared as whirling dervishes delivering an explosive gospel/funk hybrid. Between late 1974 and late 1976, Labelle enjoyed five R&B hits, the first, "Lady Marmalade," reaching the number one spot on the R&B and pop charts. Labelle split up in early 1977. *—Rob Bowman*

• **Lady Marmalade: The Best of Patti and Labelle** / Feb. 28, 1995 / Epic/Legacy ✦✦✦✦
Lady Marmalade: The Best of Labelle features eight of the group's best tracks—including their two hits, "Lady Marmalade" and "What Can I Do for You?"—as well as eight of Patti LaBelle's R&B hits from the late '70s, which were among the funkiest tracks she ever recorded. *—Stephen Thomas Erlewine*

Patti Labelle (Patricia Holt)

b. May 24, 1944, Philadelphia, PA
Vocals / Quiet Storm, Urban, Soul
Soul diva Patti LaBelle enjoyed one of the longest-lived careers in contemporary music, notching hits in a variety of sounds ranging from girl-group pop to space-age funk to lush ballads. Her first musical success came with the Blue Belles, who hit the Top 20 in 1962 with "I Sold My Heart to the Junkman." By the time they signed to Atlantic three years later, the quartet was known as Patti LaBelle and the Blue Belles. The group earned only one minor hit until a change of direction in 1970—including a new name (Labelle) and a more rock-oriented, funky sound—produced a hit, the chart-topping "Lady Marmalade." The group disbanded in the mid-'70s and its namesake mounted a solo career, issuing her eponymous debut in 1977. Upon signing with Philadelphia International, LaBelle scored a number one R&B hit with "If You Only Knew," from 1983's *I'm in Love Again*. Two years later, she reached the pop Top 20 with her *Beverly Hills Cop* soundtrack contribution "New Attitude." Her subsequent MCA debut, 1986's *The Winner in You*, went platinum on the strength of the Burt Bacharach-penned "On My Own," a duet with Michael McDonald. 1991's *Burnin'* earned a Grammy for Best Female R&B Performance. LaBelle recorded less and less frequently in the years to follow, however. *—Jason Ankeny*

• **Something Silver** / Feb. 11, 1997 / Warner Brothers ✦✦✦✦✦
Most of the past LaBelle CD-era compilations have been poorly assembled, but this one is

an exception. Whereas those other sets usually consist of a measly ten songs and some of their weaker commercial ventures, this set features their only major mainstream commercial hit, "Lady Marmalade," and fourteen underappreciated, stellar songs. Most of these songs were culled from the trio's two acclaimed Warner Brothers albums and a single RCA set in the 1971-73 period. Some of the selections demonstrate Nona Hendryx's flare for poignantly creative lyrics and intricate melodies on such confessionals as "Can I Speak To You Before You Go To Hollywood?" and "Sunday's News." However, the set also features their rock/funk-edged high-voltage covers of Aretha Franklin's "Runnin' Out of Fools," Cat Stevens' "Moon Shadow" and the Rolling Stones' "Wild Horses," among others. This set more than any other honestly reveals what we lost when the group disbanded in 1976. *—Bill Carpenter*

The Best of Patti Labelle / 1986 / Epic ♦♦♦♦♦
This anthology includes the biggest pop hit that the trio Labelle scored, the classic "Lady Marmalade," plus other staples from Patti LaBelle's solo phase, including "You Are My Friend," "Joy to Have Your Love" and "I Don't Go Shopping." LaBelle didn't make her best or most successful records while on Epic, so these aren't the tunes currently associated with her. They were decently produced and often well performed, but lack the depth of her best MCA cuts. *—Ron Wynn*

The Best of the Bluebelles / Apr. 14, 1994 / Relic ♦♦♦♦♦
This anthology collects the early, often charming and sometimes overly cute singles from Patti LaBelle and the Bluebelles. Besides the classic "I Sold My Heart to the Junkman" (which was really LaBelle backed by the Starlets), there are lesser-known numbers like "Down the Aisle (The Wedding Song)" and "I'm Still Waiting." Overall, this is competent period-piece material, but it's clear that LaBelle and company preferred more aggressive and assertive material and were never quite comfortable with most of these songs. *—Ron Wynn*

Over the Rainbow: The Atlantic Years / Aug. 23, 1994 / Ichiban Soul Classics ♦♦♦♦♦
The Bluebelles' stint with Atlantic in the '60s was not a great commercial success, yielding only a couple minor R&B hits ("I'm Still Waiting" and "Take Me for a Little While," both included here), but that wasn't due to any shortcomings on the records themselves, either in performance or material. Patti and the group recorded fine sides in pop-soul, Motown, Aretha Franklin, and early Philly soul styles, making full use of their powerful gospel-derived lead vocals and harmonies. This 22-track anthology features most of the singles (many previously non-LP) and some key album tracks that they recorded for Atlantic between 1965 and 1969, using top-notch writers like Carole Bayer, Pam Sawyer, Lori Burton, Bert Berns, Jeff Barry, Bacharach-David, Lorraine Ellison, Spooner Oldham, Dan Penn, and Curtis Mayfield (who produced some of the later sides), as well as the Bluebelles' own Nona Hendryx and Sarah Dash. Highlights include the original version of "Groovy Kind of Love" (a big hit for the Mindbenders), the Supremes-like "Tender Words," the dramatic "All or Nothing," and the moody Oldham-Penn ballad "Dreamer." *—Richie Unterberger*

• **Greatest Hits** / 1996 / MCA ♦♦♦♦♦
The first Patti LaBelle compilation to span her work from the '60s to the '90s. It's weighted heavily toward her pop-R&B material from the '80s and '90s, with hits like "New Attitude," "On My Own," and "Feels Like Another One." It does lead off with the version of "Over the Rainbow" that she recorded with the Bluebelles in '60s, and also has four LaBelle cuts, including the chart-topping "Lady Marmalade." *—Richie Unterberger*

Major Lance

b. Apr. 4, 1941, Chicago, IL, **d.** Sep. 3, 1994, Decatur, GA
Vocals / Chicago Soul, Uptown Soul, Pop-Soul, Northern Soul, Soul
Blessed with a warm, sweet voice, Major Lance was one of the leading figures of Chicago soul during the '60s and the top-selling artist for OKeh Records during the decade. Lance not only had a lovely voice, but his material was excellent. During the height of his success, the majority of his songs were written by Curtis Mayfield and produced by Carl Davis, and the pair developed a smooth, Latin-flavored sound that was punctuated by brass and layered with vocal harmonies, usually from the Impressions. It was urban, uptown soul and while it was considerably less gritty than its Southern counterpart, its breezy rhythms and joyous melodies made songs like "The Monkey Time" and "Um, Um, Um, Um, Um, Um" some of the most popular good-time R&B of its era. Major Lance's career declined significantly after he parted ways with Mayfield and Davis in the late '60s, but his classic OKeh recordings remain some of the best-loved soul music of the decade. *—Stephen Thomas Erlewine*

• **Everybody Loves a Good Time!: The Best of Major Lance** / Feb. 28, 1995 / Epic/Legacy ♦♦♦♦♦
Delightful 40-song, double-CD compilation of Lance's best work for OKeh between 1962 and 1967, including all of the chart singles, quite a few misses and B-sides, five previously unreleased cuts, and some Curtis Mayfield songs from his debut LP. The later tracks, recorded after producer Carl Davis and songwriter Mayfield had moved on to other projects, suffer in comparison with Lance's 1963-65 output, as he tried to keep abreast of contemporary soul trends, especially Motown. For many listeners, a briefer best-of Lance compilation will suffice. But for soul fans, this is prime stuff, dominated by the classic Latin-influenced Chicago soul sound of the Davis-produced tracks. *—Richie Unterberger*

The Very Best of Major Lance / Sep. 5, 2000 / Epic/Legacy ♦♦♦♦♦
This 16-song, single-disc compilation concentrates on Lance's most well-known hits, including all of his highest-charting 45's: "Um, Um, Um, Um, Um, Um," "Hey Little Girl," "The Monkey Time," "Rhythm," and "The Matador." It's excellent Chicago '60s soul, but all of the cuts are also found on Epic/Legacy's 40-song, two-CD anthology *Everybody Loves a Good Time! The Best of Major Lance.* That compilation has a good number of decent non-hit tracks from the era (such as "Sweet Music") and remains the preferred alternative unless you're on a strict budget, or the type of listener who finds it hard to hear more than a single-disc's worth of an artist that you like but don't love. That's not to say the selection for this best-of isn't good, with 11 of the 16 songs coming from the pen of Curtis Mayfield. *—Richie Unterberger*

Cyndi Lauper

b. Jun. 20, 1953, Queens, NY
Vocals, Guitar / Pop/Rock, New Wave
Cyndi Lauper was one of the biggest stars of the early MTV era, selling five million copies of her debut album, *She's So Unusual,* as well as scoring a string of four Top Ten hits from the record, including the major hits "Girls Just Want to Have Fun" and "Time After Time." Lauper's thin, girlish voice and gleefully rag-tag appearance became one of the most distinctive images of the early '80s, which helped lead her not only to the top of the charts, but also to stardom. Throughout America, there were numbers of teenage girls dressing like Lauper and using "Girls Just Want to Have Fun" as an athem, a call to arms for self-expression. At first, her music was a bright, colorful new wave fusion of a number of styles, including new wave, post-punk, reggae, pop, and funk. Both her music and her appearance helped popularize—and just importantly, sanitize —- the image of punk and new wave for America, making it an acceptable part of the pop landscape. Lauper didn't follow through on the success of *She's So Unusual,* choosing to turn toward middle-of-the-road balladry and mainstream pop, but her first album remains a benchmark of the early '80s. *—Stephen Thomas Erlewine*

• **She's So Unusual** / 1984 / Epic/Legacy ♦♦♦♦♦
One of the great new wave/early MTV records, *She's So Unusual* is a giddy mix of self-confidence, effervescent popcraft, unabashed sentimentality, subversiveness, and clever humor. In short, it's a multifaceted portrait of a multifaceted talent, an artist that's far more clever than her thin, deliberately girly voice would indicate. Then again, Lauper's voice suits her musical persona, since its chirpiness adds depth, or reconfigures the songs, whether it's the call to arms of "Girls Just Want to Have Fun" or the tearjerking "Time After Time." Lauper is at her very best on the first side, all of which were singles or received airplay, and this collection of songs—"Money Changes Everything," "Girls," "When You Were Mine," "Time," "She Bop," "All Through the Night"—is astonishing in its consistency, so strong that it makes the remaining tracks—all enjoyable, but rather pedestrian—charming by their association with songs so brilliantly alive. If Lauper couldn't maintain this level of consistency, it's because this captured her persona better than anyone could imagine—when a debut captures a personality so well, let alone a personality so tied to its time, the successive work can't help but pale in comparison. Still, when it's captured as brightly and brilliantly as it is here, it does result in a debut that retains its potency, long after its production seems a little dated. [The 2000 reissue contains three live bonus tracks, all enjoyable, all not really necessary.] *—Stephen Thomas Erlewine*

True Colors / 1986 / Portrait ♦♦♦

A Night to Remember / 1989 / Epic ♦♦

A Hat Full of Stars / 1992 / Epic ♦♦

12 Deadly Cyns / Jul. 18, 1995 / Epic ♦♦♦♦
Regrettably bypassing the Top Ten hit "The Goonies 'R' Good Enough," *12 Deady Cyns* features almost all of Cyndi Lauper's Top 40 hits, tacking on a handful of new tracks at the end, including "Hey Now (Girls Still Wanna Have Fun)," an updated version of her breakthrough hit single, "Girls Just Wanna Have Fun." As hits collections go, the album is fine, but with the exception of the ballad "True Colors" and the pop confection "Change of Heart," all of her finest songs and biggest hits were on *She's So Unusual,* which is a more consistent and entertaining album. *—Stephen Thomas Erlewine*

Sisters of Avalon / Apr. 1, 1997 / Epic ♦♦♦
Cyndi Lauper made a valient effort to jump-start her career with the varied and eclectic *Sisters of Avalon.* Working with producer Mark Saunders, Lauper attempts to work worldbeat, adult alternative and even trip-hop influences into her trademark adult-contemporary pop, and while the results aren't always successful, the record is the most intriguing and rewarding album she has made since *True Colors. —Stephen Thomas Erlewine*

The Leaves

f. 1965, San Fernando Valley, CA, **db.** 1967
Group / Folk-Rock, Garage Rock
One of the first L.A. folk-rock groups to spring up in the wake of the Byrds in the mid-'60s, the Leaves are most remembered for recording the first—and one of the most successful—rock versions of "Hey Joe," which reached the Top 40 (and was a huge Californian hit) in 1966. None of their other releases approached this success (although "Too Many People" was a local hit), but the group recorded a fair number of strong covers and original songs during their brief existence. More explicitly Stones and Beatles-influenced than the Byrds, they didn't project as strong an identity as competitors like the Byrds or Love, despite displaying considerable talent for harmony rockers in both the folk-rock and British Invasion styles. After cutting some singles and a decent album for the tiny Mira label, they moved to Capitol, and disbanded after a disappointing follow-up (*All the Good That's Happening,* 1967) that offered less distinguished material and a more diluted sound. Leaves bassist Jim Pons went on to join the Turtles for a while in the late '60s. *—Richie Unterberger*

• **Leaves Are Happening!** / 2000 / Sundazed ♦♦♦♦
At last, a legitimate and well-distributed reissue of everything the Leaves released on Mira between 1965 and 1966: the entire *Hey Joe* album, all of the non-LP songs from their singles, the single version of "Too Many People," and *three* versions of "Hey Joe" (from the hit single and two previous 45s which used slightly different arrangements). This is not the complete work of the Leaves, as it doesn't include anything from their 1967 Capitol LP *All the Good That's Happening,* but this is no loss, as that album was pretty lousy. (Two covers of unspecified origin from the compilation *1966* are also missing.) Although the Leaves were erratic, at their best they were a fine band who drew from the Byrds' folk-rock, the Beatles' melodicism, and the hard rock of the Rolling Stones, as best heard on "Hey Joe" and the less celebrated "Too Many People," "Be With You," "Just a Memory," "Dr. Stone," "Funny Little World," and "Words." The reissue is enhanced by the detailed history in the accompanying 16-page booklet. *—Richie Unterberger*

Led Zeppelin

f. Jul. 1968, England, **db.** Dec. 1980, London, England

Group / Album Rock, British Blues, British Metal, Arena Rock, Heavy Metal, Hard Rock, Blues-Rock

Led Zeppelin was the definitive heavy metal band. It wasn't just their crushingly loud blues-rock, it was how they built upon that foundation, incorporated mythology, mysticism, and a variety of other genres (most notably world music and British folk).

Zeppelin refused to release popular songs from their albums as singles, thereby helping album-oriented rock grow in popularity during the '70s. As important as their music was their mystique. Led Zeppelin never granted interviews, letting legends arise around the band. Zeppelin had power and mystery, retaining both qualities after their 1980 disbandment.

Led Zeppelin had phenomenal success from the outset, as their 1969 debut was a surprise Top 10 hit in the UK and US. *Led Zeppelin II* also reached number one, spending more time on the charts; musically, its brutal blend of Chess blues and Sun rock & roll became the template for heavy metal. On its third album, Zeppelin laced English folk into its hard rock and while it wasn't as popular as its predecessors, it pointed toward 1971's untitled fourth album in 1971. *IV* was their highwater mark, selling millions of copies and remaining a hard rock perennial thanks to "Stairway to Heaven," "Black Dog" and "Rock & Roll." After this record, Led Zeppelin were the biggest band in the world and, since they gave almost no interviews, all sorts of myths surrounded the band, particularly rumors of occultism—rumors they played up with their next album, 1973's *Houses of the Holy.* That album, along with its double-album sequel *Physical Graffiti* (1975) and 1976's *Presence* were also blockbusters. Zeppelin's pace slowed in the second half of the '70s, as they dealt with a number of personal problems. They returned in 1979 with *In Through the Out Door,* which was an immediate massive success. As the group prepared for a world tour, drummer John Bonham died in an alcohol-related accident. Instead of continuing, Led Zeppelin disbanded, releasing the rarities and outtakes collection *Coda* in 1982. Although they were gone, Zeppelin's popularity didn't wane, and they continued to earn new generations of listeners over the next two decades. *—Stephen Thomas Erlewine*

☆ **Led Zeppelin [I]** / Jan. 12, 1969 / Atlantic ✦✦✦✦✦

Led Zeppelin had a fully formed, distinctive sound from the outset, as their eponymous debut illustrates. Taking the heavy, distorted electric blues of Jimi Hendrix, Jeff Beck, and Cream to an extreme, Zeppelin created a majestic, powerful brand of guitar rock constructed around simple, memorable riffs and lumbering rhythms. But the key to the group's attack was subtlety: It wasn't just an onslaught of guitar noise, it was shaded and textured, filled with alternating dynamics and tempos. As *Led Zeppelin* proves, the group was capable of such multi-layered music from the start. Although the extended psychedelic blues of "Dazed and Confused," "You Shook Me," and "I Can't Quit You Baby" often gather the most attention, the remainder of the album is a better indication of what would come later. "Babe I'm Gonna Leave You" shifts from folky verses to pummeling choruses; "Good Times Bad Times" and "How Many More Times" have groovy, bluesy shuffles; "Your Time Is Gonna Come" is an anthemic hard rocker; "Black Mountain Side" is pure English folk; and "Communication Breakdown" is a frenzied rocker with a nearly punkish attack. Although the album isn't as varied as some of their later efforts, it nevertheless marked a significant turning point in the evolution of hard rock and heavy metal. *—Stephen Thomas Erlewine*

☆ **Led Zeppelin II** / Oct. 22, 1969 / Atlantic ✦✦✦✦✦

Recorded quickly during Led Zeppelin's first American tours, *Led Zeppelin II* provided the blueprint for all the heavy metal bands that followed it. Since the group could only enter the studio for brief amounts of time, most of the songs that compose *II* are reworked blues and rock & roll standards that the band were performing onstage at the time. Not only did the short amount of time result in a lack of original material, it made the sound more direct. Jimmy Page still provided layers of guitar overdubs, but the overall sound of the album is heavy and hard, brutal and direct. "Whole Lotta Love," "The Lemon Song," and "Bring It on Home" are all based on classic blues songs—only, the riffs are simpler and louder and each song has an extended section for instrumental solos. Of the remaining six songs, two sport light acoustic touches ("Thank You," "Ramble On"), but the other four are straight-ahead heavy rock that follow the formula of the revamped blues songs. While *Led Zeppelin II* doesn't have the eclecticism of the group's debut, it's arguably more influential. After all, nearly every one of the hundreds of Zeppelin imitators used this record, with its lack of dynamics and its pummeling riffs, as a blueprint. *—Stephen Thomas Erlewine*

☆ **Led Zeppelin III** / Oct. 5, 1970 / Atlantic ✦✦✦✦✦

On their first two albums, Led Zeppelin unleashed a relentless barrage of heavy blues and rockabilly riffs, but *Led Zeppelin III* provided the band with the necessary room to grow musically. While there are still a handful of metallic rockers, *III* is built on a folky, acoustic foundation which gives the music extra depth. And even the rockers aren't as straightforward as before: The galloping "Immigrant Song" is powered by Plant's banshee wail, "Celebration Day" turns blues-rock inside out with a warped slide guitar riff, and "Out on the Tiles" lumbers along with a tricky, multi-part riff. Nevertheless, the heart of the album lies on the second side, when the band delve deeply into English folk. "Gallows Pole" updates a traditional tune with a menacing flair, and "Bron-Y-Aur Stomp" is an infectious acoustic romp, while "That's the Way" and "Tangerine" are shimmering songs with graceful country flourishes. The band haven't left the blues behind, but the twisted bottleneck blues of "Hats Off To (Roy) Harper" actually outstrips the epic "Since I've Been Loving You," which is the only time Zeppelin sound a bit set in their ways. *—Stephen Thomas Erlewine*

★ **Led Zeppelin IV** / Nov. 8, 1971 / Atlantic ✦✦✦✦✦

Encompassing heavy metal, folk, pure rock & roll, and blues, Led Zeppelin's untitled fourth album is a monolithic record, defining not only Led Zeppelin but the sound and style of '70s hard rock. Expanding on the breakthroughs of *III,* Zeppelin fuse their majestic hard rock with a mystical, rural English folk that gives the record an epic scope. Even at its most basic—the muscular, traditionalist "Rock & Roll"—the album has a grand sense of drama, which is only deepened by Plant's burgeoning obsession with mythology, religion, and the occult. Plant's mysticism comes to a head on the eerie folk ballad "The Ballad of Evermore," a mandolin-driven song with haunting vocals from Sandy Denny, and on the epic "Stairway to Heaven." Of all of Zeppelin's songs, "Stairway to Heaven" is the most famous, and not unjustly. Building from a simple fingerpicked acoustic guitar to a storming torrent of guitar riffs and solos, it encapsulates the entire album in one song. Which, of course, isn't discounting the rest of the album. "Going to California" is the group's best folk song, and the rockers are endlessly inventive, whether it's the complex, multi-layered "Black Dog," the pounding hippie satire "Misty Mountain Hop," or the funky riffs of "Four Sticks." But the closer, "When the Levee Breaks," is the one song truly equal to "Stairway," helping give *IV* the feeling of an epic. An apocalyptic slice of urban blues, "When the Levee Breaks" is as forceful and frightening as Zeppelin ever got, and its seismic rhythms and layered dynamics illustrate why none of their imitators could ever equal them. *—Stephen Thomas Erlewine*

☆ **Houses of the Holy** / Mar. 28, 1973 / Atlantic ✦✦✦✦✦

Houses of the Holy follows the same basic pattern as *Led Zeppelin IV,* but the approach is looser and more relaxed. Jimmy Page's riffs rely on ringing, folky hooks as much as they do on thundering blues-rock, giving the album a lighter, more open atmosphere. While the pseudo-reggae of "D'Yer Mak'er" and the affectionate James Brown send-up "The Crunge" suggest that the band were searching for material, they actually contribute to the musical diversity of the album. "The Rain Song" is one of Zep's finest moments, featuring a soaring string arrangement and a gentle, aching melody. "The Ocean" is just as good, starting with a heavy, funky guitar groove before slamming into an a cappella section and ending with a swinging, doo-wop-flavored rave-up. With the exception of the rampaging opening number, "The Song Remains the Same," the rest of *Houses of the Holy* is fairly straightforward, ranging from the foreboding "No Quarter" and the strutting hard rock of "Dancing Days" to the epic folk/metal fusion "Over the Hills and Far Away." Throughout the record, the band's playing is excellent, making the eclecticism of Page and Plant's songwriting sound coherent and natural. *—Stephen Thomas Erlewine*

☆ **Physical Graffiti** / Feb. 24, 1975 / Swan Song ✦✦✦✦✦

Led Zeppelin returned from a nearly two year hiatus in 1975 with *Physical Graffiti,* a sprawling, ambitious double album. Zeppelin treat many of the songs on *Physical Graffiti* as forays into individual styles, only occasionally synthesizing sounds, notably on the tense, Eastern-influenced "Kashmir." With John Paul Jones' galloping keyboard, "Trampled Underfoot" ranks as their funkiest metallic grind, while "House of the Holy" is as effervescent as pre-Beatles pop and "Down By the Seaside" is the closest they've come to country. Even the heavier blues—the 11-minute "In My Time of Dying," the tightly-wound "Custard Pie," and the monsterous epic "The Rover"—are subtly shaded, even if they're thunderously loud. Most of these heavy rockers are isolated on the first album, with the second half of *Physical Graffiti* sound a little like a scrap-heap of experiments, jams, acoustic workouts and neo-covers. This may not be as consistent as the first platter, but its quirks are entirely welcome, not just because they encompass the mean, decadent "Sick Again," but the heart-breaking "Ten Years Gone" and the utterly charming acoustic rock & roll of "Boogie with Stu" and "Black Country Woman." Yes, some of this could be labeled as filler, but like any great double-album, it's appeal lies in its great sprawl, since it captures elements of the band's personality rarely showcased elsewhere—and even at its worst, *Physical Graffiti* towers above its hard-rock peers of the mid-'70s. *—Stephen Thomas Erlewine*

Presence / 1976 / Swan Song ✦✦✦

Presence scales back the size of *Physical Graffiti* to a single album, but it retains the grandiose scope of that double record. If anything, *Presence* has more majestic epics than its predecessor, opening with the surging, ten-minute "Achilles Last Stand" and closing with the meandering, nearly ten-minute "Tea for One." In between, Zeppelin add the lumbering blues workout "Nobody's Fault but Mine" and the terse, menacing "For Your Life," which is the best song on the album. These four tracks take up the bulk of the album, leaving three light-hearted throwaways to alleviate the foreboding atmosphere—and pretensions—of the epics. If all of the throwaways were as focused and funny as those on *Physical Graffiti* or *Houses of the Holy,* Zeppelin would have had another classic on their hands. However, the Crescent City love letter of "Royal Orleans" sags in the middle, and the ersatz rockabilly of "Candy Store Rock" doesn't muster up the loose, funky swagger of "Hots on for Nowhere," which it *should* in order to work. The three throwaways are also scattered haphazardly throughout the album, making it seem more ponderous than it actually is, and the result is the weakest album Zeppelin had yet recorded. *—Stephen Thomas Erlewine*

The Song Remains the Same / 1976 / Swan Song ✦✦

In Through the Out Door / 1979 / Swan Song ✦✦✦

Somewhere between *Presence* and *In Through the Out Door,* disco, punk, and new wave had overtaken rock & roll, and Led Zeppelin chose to tentatively embrace these pop revolutions, adding synthesizers to the mix and emphasizing John Bonham's inherent way with a groove. The album's opening number, "In the Evening," with its stomping rhythms and heavy, staggered riffs, suggests that the band haven't deviated from their course, but by the time the rolling shuffle of "South Bound Suarez" kicks into gear, it's apparent that they've regained their sense of humor. After "South Bound Suarez," the group try a variety of styles, whether it's an overdriven homage to Bakersfield County called "Hot Dog," the layered, Latin-tinged percussion and pianos of "Fool in the Rain," or the slickly seductive ballad "All My Love." "Carouselambra," a lurching, self-consciously ambitious synth-driven number, and the slow blues "I'm Gonna Crawl" aren't quite as impressive as the rest of the album, but the record was a graceful way to close to their career, even if it wasn't intended as the final chapter. *—Stephen Thomas Erlewine*

Coda / 1982 / Swan Song ✦✦✦

An odds-and-sods collection assembled after John Bonham's death, *Coda* is predictably a hit-or-miss affair. The best material comes from later in their career, including the ringing folk stomp of "Poor Tom," the jacked-up '50s rock & roll of "Ozone Baby," and their response to punk rock, the savage "Wearing and Tearing." The rest of the album—sadly including the Bonham showcase "Bonzo's Montreux"—is average, despite the presence of some stellar

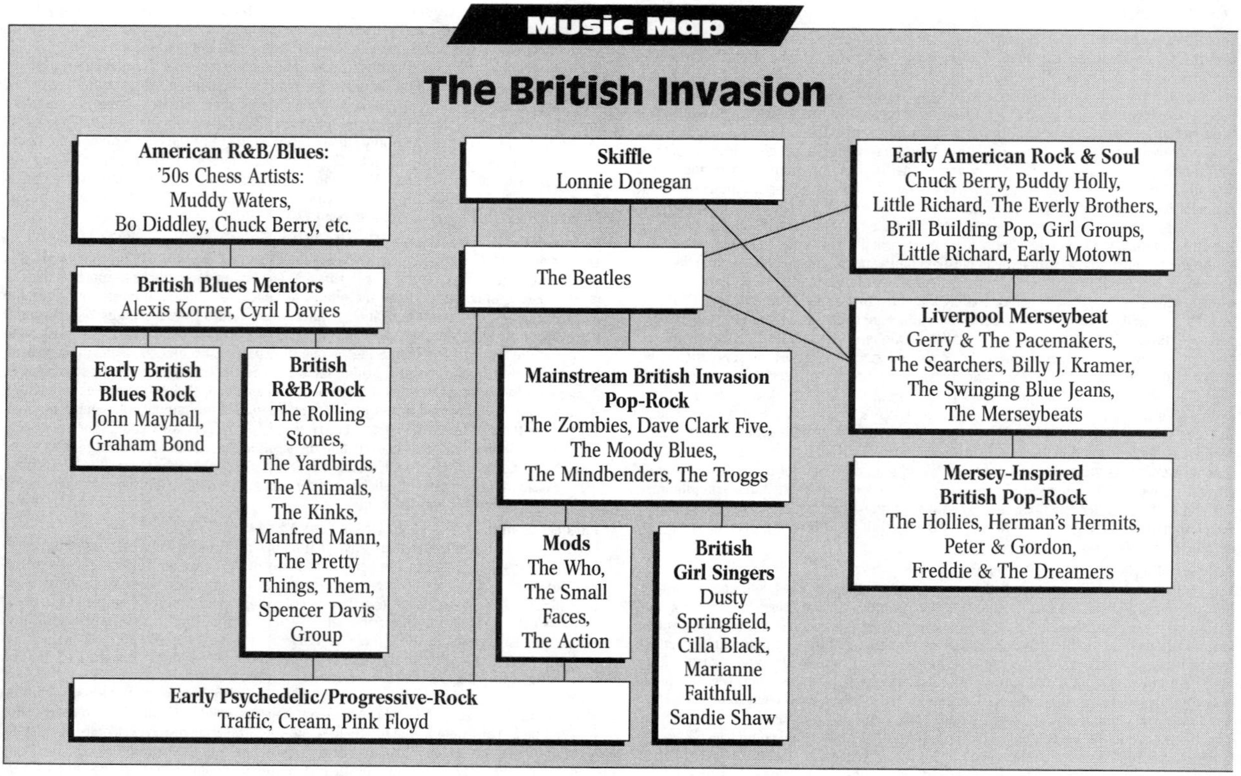

playing, especially on the early blues-rock blitzkrieg "I Can't Quit You Baby" and "We're Gonna Groove." *—Stephen Thomas Erlewine*

Led Zeppelin [Box Set] / Sep. 1990 / Swan Song ♦♦♦
Led Zeppelin's primary method of artistic expression was their albums. Although they had a handful of hit singles and selected album tracks were played endlessly on the radio, the true range of their music is only evident on the original albums, which were carefully sequenced and assembled. Consequently, the notion of a Led Zeppelin anthology is a bit strange—their records worked as individual pieces. Nevertheless, the four-disc box set *Led Zeppelin* includes most of their best and most famous material. Jimmy Page determined the set's running order, taking the songs out of their familiar contexts and placing them in a new, occasionally jarring, sequence, providing new insights to the band's music that dedicated fans will appreciate. *Led Zeppelin* is the only album in their catalog to include the classic B-side "Hey Hey What Can I Do," as well as their unreleased version of Robert Johnson's "Travelling Riverside Blues" and a live medley of Page's "White Summer/Black Mountain Side." Most fans will find these three tracks essential, but will balk at the price, especially since all of Zeppelin's albums have been re-mastered since the original release of the box set. While the box contains a wealth of brilliant music, all of it is better-heard in its original incarnation. *—Stephen Thomas Erlewine*

Led Zeppelin [Box Set 2] / Mar. 19, 1993 / Swan Song ♦♦♦
Rounding up all of the studio tracks that didn't appear on the first box (as well as the pleasant, but unremarkable, "Baby Come on Home"), *Boxed Set 2* is the perfect way to complete a Led Zeppelin library begun with the first box set. *—Stephen Thomas Erlewine*

BBC Sessions / Nov. 11, 1997 / Atlantic ♦♦♦♦♦
Led Zeppelin's BBC sessions were among the most popular bootleg items of the rock & roll era, appearing on a myriad of illegal records and CDs. They were all the more popular because of the lack of official Led Zeppelin live albums, especially since *The Song Remains the Same* failed to capture the essence of the band. For anyone that hadn't heard the recordings, the mystique of Zeppelin's BBC Sessions was somewhat mystifying, but the official 1997 release of the double-disc *BBC Sessions* offered revelations for any fan who hadn't yet heard this music. While some collectors will be dismayed by the slight trimming on the "Whole Lotta Love Medley," almost all of the group's sessions are included here, and they prove why live Zeppelin was the stuff of legend. The 1969 sessions, recorded shortly after the release of the first album, are fiery and dynamic, outstripping the studio record for sheer power. Early versions of "You Shook Me," "Communication Breakdown," "What Is & What Should Never Be" and "Whole Lotta Love" hit harder than their recorded counterparts, while covers of Sleepy John Estes' "The Girl I Love She Got Long Black Wavy Hair," Robert Johnson's "Travelling Riverside Blues" and Eddie Cochran's "Something Else" are welcome additions to the Zeppelin catalog, confirming their folk, blues and rockabilly roots as well as their sense of vision. Zeppelin's grand vision comes into sharper relief on the second disc, which is comprised of their 1971 sessions. They still have their primal energy, but they're more adventurous, branching out into folk, twisted psychedelia, and weird blues-funk. Certainly, *BBC Sessions* is the kind of album that will only appeal to fans, but anyone who's ever doubted Zeppelin's power or vision will be set straight with this record. *—Stephen Thomas Erlewine*

Early Days: The Best of Led Zeppelin, Vol. 1 / Nov. 23, 1999 / Atlantic ♦♦♦♦

Latter Days: The Best of Led Zeppelin, Vol. 2 / Mar. 21, 2000 / Atlantic ♦♦♦♦

The Left Banke

f. 1965, New York, NY, **db.** 1969
Group / Sunshine Pop, Psychedelic Pop, Baroque Pop, Pop
This New York group pioneered "Baroque'n'Roll" in the '60s with their mix of pop/rock and grand, quasi-classical arrangements and melodies. Featuring teenage prodigy Michael Brown as keyboardist and chief songwriter, the group scored two quick hits with "Walk Away Renee" and "Pretty Ballerina." Chamber-like string arrangements, Steve Martin's soaring, near-falsetto lead vocals, and tight harmonies that borrowed from British Invasion bands like the Beatles and the Zombies were also key elements of the Left Banke sound. Unfortunately the group, which early on showed tremendous promise, was quickly torn asunder by dissension. Due to the nature of their music (which often employed session musicians), the Left Banke's sound was difficult to reproduce on the road, and one could sympathize with Brown's wishes to become a Brian Wilson-like figure, concentrating on writing and recording while the rest of the musicians took to the road. Most of the group's second and final album, *The Left Banke Too,* was recorded without Brown, who left in late 1967. While it still sported baroque arrangements and contained some fine moments, Brown's presence was sorely missed, and the record pales in comparison to their debut. Brown went onto form a Left Banke-styled group, Montage, which released a fine and underappreciated album in the late '60s. The original group, minus its key visionary Michael Brown, made an album's worth of ill-advised reunion recordings in 1978. *—Richie Unterberger*

● **There's Gonna Be a Storm: The Complete Recordings 1966-69** / 1992 / Mercury ♦♦♦♦♦
Though it's missing a few rarities—namely the Steve Martin single for Buddha that reunited him with Michael Brown—this is the most definitive Left Banke compilation. It features the entirety of their two late-'60s albums, as well as a couple of singles that didn't make it onto LPs at the time (though they later appeared on Rhino's *History*) and a previously unissued cut, "Men Are Building Sand." Their debut 1967 LP, *Walk Away Renee/Pretty Ballerina,* is an underrated classic of the time, matching smart harmonies and pop hooks to baroque orchestration. Its brilliance casts a bit of a shadow over the rest of this collection. The group's 1968 album *Too* suffered from bloated production and, more importantly, the absence of chief songwriter/arranger Michael Brown. In turn, the 1967 single Brown cut under the Left Banke moniker with singer Bert Sommer suffers from the absence of lead vocalist Steve Martin. By the time Brown and Martin tenuously reunited for a late-1969 single, some of the

spark had gone. All of the aforementioned highs and lows of this prodigiously talented but strife-ridden group are on this disc. *—Richie Unterberger*

The Lemonheads

f. 1984, Boston, MA

Group / College Rock, Punk-Pop, Adult Alternative Pop/Rock, Hardcore Punk, Alternative Pop/Rock

The Lemonheads' evolution from post-Hüsker Dü hardcore punk rockers to teenage heartthrobs is one of the strangest sagas in alternative music. Initially, the group was punk-pop trio formed by three teenage Boston suburbanites, but over the years, the band became a vehicle for Evan Dando. Blessed with good looks and a warm, sweet voice, Dando became a teen-idol in the early '90s, when Nirvana's success made alternative bands commercially viable. While his simple, catchy songs were instantly accessible, they tended to hide the more subversive nature of his lyrics, as well as his gift for offbeat covers and devotion to country-rock father Gram Parsons. After developing his signature blend of pop, punk and country-rock on several independent records in the late '80s, Dando moved the Lemonheads to Atlantic Records in 1990. Two years later, *It's A Shame About Ray* made the group into media sensations, as Dando's face appeared on music and teen magazines across America and Britain. Though the Lemonheads were poised to become superstars, the band never quite found the right breakthrough single, and their popularity peaked in the early '90s. Around the same time, Dando descended into severe drug abuse that he curbed by the 1996 release of *Car Button Cloth.* However, he had missed his chance at stardom—though the group retained their cult, much of their audience had already slipped away. *—Stephen Thomas Erlewine*

Create Your Friends / 1989 / Taang! ♦♦♦

Lick / 1989 / Taang! ♦♦♦♦

Although it's fairly incoherent, bouncing back and forth between punk-pop and folky pop, *Lick* is a thoroughly engaging record. The tensions between Evan Dando and Ben Deily are fairly evident throughout the album, especially since Dando's songs, with their immediate hooks and melodies, outshine his bandmates, but that unevenness makes the record endearingly messy. Also, the mess makes the group's best songs, including an inspired electric cover of Suzanne Vega's "Luka," shine all the more brightly. *—Stephen Thomas Erlewine*

Lovey / 1990 / Atlantic ♦♦♦

Moving to a major label didn't affect the Lemonheads' sound as much as the departure of Ben Deily; without him, Evan Dando was free to let his sensitive side run wild, which is exactly what he does on *Lovey.* Dando never completely abandons punk-pop on *Lovey,* but he does balance it with excursions into jangle-pop and country-rock, many of which contain his best songwriting to date. By now, he has begun to develop a signature voice, a distinctly suburban and middle-class voice that embraces the mundane details of everyday life. That gives songs like "Stove" and "Lil' Seed" an off-kilter sensibility, which is made all the more appealing by his gift for simple hooks. Even though Dando has made significant strides forward, the most affecting moment on the record remains his stark and very pretty cover of Gram Parsons' "Brass Buttons." *—Stephen Thomas Erlewine*

● **It's a Shame About Ray** / Jun. 2, 1992 / Atlantic ♦♦♦♦♦

If *Lovey* captured Evan Dando as he found his signature blend of punk-pop, jangle-pop and folk-rock, *It's a Shame About Ray* is where he perfected that style. Breezing by in under half an hour, the album is a simple collection of sunny melodies and hooks, delivered with typical nonchalance by Dando. None of the songs are about anything major, nor do they have astonishingly original melodies, but that's part of their charm—they're immediately accessible and thoroughly catchy. Dando's laidback observations of middle-class outcasts are minor gems. The heartbroken title track or "Confetti," the crushes of "Bit Part in Your Life," the love letter to substances "My Drug Buddy" or the wonderful "Alison's Starting to Happen," where a girl finds herself as she discovers punk rock, capture the laconic rhythms of suburbia, and his warm, friendly voice, which is offset by Juliana Hatfield's girlish harmonies, gives the songs an emotional resonance. [*It's a Shame About Ray* was later re-released with a competent punk-pop remake of Simon & Garfunkel's "Mrs. Robinson" added as a bonus track. As Dando approached stardom, the album was re-pressed again with the title of "My Drug Buddy" truncated to "Buddy." It was later restored to its original title.] *—Stephen Thomas Erlewine*

Come on Feel the Lemonheads / Oct. 12, 1993 / Atlantic ♦♦♦♦

Come on Feel the Lemonheads should have been the album that propelled the trio and Evan Dando to stardom, but instead of delivering a concise pop record in the vein of *It's a Shame About Ray,* they made a messy album that never quite found its focus. That's not to say that *Come On Feel* is without merit, because that's hardly the case. In many ways, it's the most interesting record that the Lemonheads have released, because it finds Dando confused about everything, particularly love, both for girls and drugs, and his burgeoning fame. There are moments of self-indulgence, whether it's the aimless piano instrumental "The Jello Fund" or two versions of the drug-obsessed "Style," yet they are as essential to the album's desperate tone as the heartbreaking acoustic ballad of "Favorite T." Between those two extremes are some of the finest power-pop and country-rock Dando has ever written. He still has a tendency to be too cutesy, as on the otherwise winning country-rock of "Being Around" and "Big Gay Heart," but the hooky rush of "The Great Big No," the bright "I'll Do It Anyway" and the lovely simplicity of "Into Your Arms" are irresistible. *Come On Feel* may not be as consistent or immediate as *It's a Shame About Ray,* but finding its pleasures is quite rewarding. *—Stephen Thomas Erlewine*

Car Button Cloth / Oct. 15, 1996 / Atlantic ♦♦♦

If *Come on Feel the Lemonheads* was a bit confused, *Car Button Cloth* is positively a mess, filled with perfect pop, stoned rock and rambling country-rock, which is alternately ingratiating and infuriating. Evan Dando may have (relatively) sobered up between the two records, but the sound of *Car Button Cloth* is even wearier than before—his voice is beginning to show signs of abuse, while the tempos often sag and lurch, occasionally becoming burdened with lead guitars that steal directly from J. Mascis. The turgid grunge that wears at the fringes of the record actually makes the gems all the more endearing. "If I Could Talk I'd Tell You" is one of Dando's finest three-chord sing-a-longs; the self-depricating "The Outdoor Type" is excellent country-rock; the stop-start verses of "It's All True" are fleshed out by Dando's weary croak and the grunge interpretation of "Knoxville Girl" is actually very affecting. However, only dedicated fans will be willing to sort through the hubris to actually find these songs, which is unfortunate, because at its best, *Car Button Cloth* is as good as anything Dando has yet recorded. *—Stephen Thomas Erlewine*

The Best of the Lemonheads: The Atlantic Years / Jul. 14, 1998 / Atlantic ♦♦♦♦

Evan Dando—for all intents and purposes, he *is* the Lemonheads—is a sporadically brilliant songwriter. Every one of his albums contains as many flops as masterpieces, sometimes more. Hardcore fans have learned to live with this and even cherish his dopey detours, but there are many others who would prefer to have all the best bits on one disc. Which means, of course, that *The Best of the Lemonheads: The Atlantic Years* offered the perfect opportunity to achieve that goal. Unfortunately, it was bungled, at least in America (it was released in Europe and Japan with more tracks). With the exception of "Mrs. Robinson" (never a favorite of hardcore fans, but included for those nostalgic Gen-Xers), it's hard to argue with what's here, but it feels criminally brief at 12 tracks, especially since the songs are rarely over three minutes long. It's entertaining, to be sure, and it makes a convincing argument that Dando is a clever pop craftsman, but it leaves you wanting more—which isn't really what best-of albums should do. *—Stephen Thomas Erlewine*

John Lennon

b. Oct. 9, 1940, Liverpool, England, **d.** Dec. 8, 1980, New York, NY

Vocals, Keyboards, Guitar / Album Rock, Pop/Rock, Singer/Songwriter, Rock & Roll

Out of all the Beatles, John Lennon had the most interesting—and frustrating—solo career. Lennon was capable of inspired, brutally honest confessional songwriting and melodic songcraft; he also had a tendency to rest on his laurels, churning out straight-ahead rock & roll without much care. But the extremes, both in his music and his life, were what made him fascinating. Where Paul McCartney was content to be a rock star, Lennon dabbled in everything from revolutionary politics to the television talk-show circuit during the early '70s. After releasing a pair of acclaimed albums, *John Lennon/Plastic Ono Band* and *Imagine,* in the early '70s, Lennon sunk into an infamous "lost weekend" where his musical output was decidedly uneven and his public behavior was often embarassing. Halfway through the decade, he sobered up and retired from performing to become a house-husband and father. In 1980, he launched a comeback with his wife Yoko Ono, releasing the duet album *Double Fantasy* that fall. Just as his career was on an upswing, Lennon was tragically assassinated outside of his New York apartement building in December of 1980. He left behind an enormous legacy, not only as a musician, but as a writer, actor and activist. *—Stephen Thomas Erlewine*

Unfinished Music, No. 1: Two Virgins / Nov. 11, 1968 / Rykodisc ♦♦

Life with the Lions: Unfinished Music #2 / May 26, 1969 / Rykodisc ♦♦

Wedding Album / Oct. 20, 1969 / Rykodisc ♦♦

Live Peace in Toronto 1969 / Dec. 12, 1969 / Capitol ♦♦♦

☆ **John Lennon/Plastic Ono Band** / Dec. 11, 1970 / Capitol ♦♦♦♦♦

The cliché about singer-songwriters is that they sing confessionals direct from their heart, but John Lennon exploded the myth behind that cliché, as well as many others, on his first official solo record, *John Lennon/Plastic Ono Band.* Inspired by his primal scream therapy with Dr. Walter Janov, Lennon created a harrowing set of unflinchingly personal songs, laying out all of his fears and angers for everyone to hear. It was a revolutionary record—never before had a record been so explicitly introspective, and very few records made absolutely no concession to the audience's expectations, daring the listeners to meet all the artist's demands. Which isn't to say that the record is unlistenable. Lennon's songs range from tough rock & rollers to piano-based ballads and spare folk songs, and his melodies remain strong and memorable, which actually intensifies the pain and rage of the songs. Not much about *Plastic Ono Band* is hidden. Lennon presents everything on the surface, and the song titles—"Mother," "I Found Out," "Working Class Hero," "Isolation," "God," "My Mummy's Dead"—illustrate what each song is about, and charts his loss of faith in his parents, country, friends, fans and idols. It's an unflinching document of bare-bones despair and pain, but for all its nihlism, it is ultimately life-affiriming; it is unique not only in Lennon's catalog, but in all of popular music. Few albums are ever as harrowing, difficult, and rewarding as *John Lennon/Plastic Ono Band. —Stephen Thomas Erlewine*

☆ **Imagine** / Sep. 9, 1971 / Capitol ♦♦♦♦♦

After the harrowing *Plastic Ono Band,* Lennon returned to calmer, more conventional territory with *Imagine.* While the album had a softer surface, it was only marginally less confessional than its predecessor. Underneath the sweet strings of "Jealous Guy" lies a broken and scared man, the jaunty "Crippled Inside" is a mocking assault at an acquaintance, and "Imagine" is a paean for peace in world with no Gods, possessions or classes, where everyone is equal. And Lennon doesn't shy away from the hard rockers—"How Do You Sleep" is a scathing attack on Paul McCartney, "I Don't Want to Be a Soldier" is a hypnotic anti-war song, and "Give Me Some Truth" is bitter hard rock. If *Imagine* doesn't have the thematic sweep of *Plastic Ono Band,* it is nevertheless a remarkable collection of songs that Lennon would never be able to better again. *—Stephen Thomas Erlewine*

Sometime in New York City/Live Jam / Jun. 12, 1972 / Capitol ♦♦

Mind Games / Nov. 2, 1973 / Capitol ♦♦♦♦

After the hostile reaction to the politically charged *Sometime in New York City,* John Lennon moved away from explicit protest songs and returned to introspective songwriting with *Mind Games.* Lennon didn't leave politics behind—he just tempered his opinions with humor on songs like "Bring on the Lucie (Freda People)," which happened to undercut the intention of the song. It also indicated the confusion that lays at the heart of the album. Lennon doesn't know which way to go, so he tries everything. There are lovely ballads like "Out of the Blue" and "One Day (At A Time)," forced ham-fisted rockers like "Meat City" and "Tight As," sweeping Spectoresque pop on "Mind Games" and many midtempo, indistinguishable pop-rockers. While the best numbers are among Lennon's finest, there's only a handful of them, and the remainder of the record is simply pleasant. But compared to *Sometime in New York City*, as well as the subsequent *Walls and Bridges*, *Mind Games* sounded like a return to form. *—Stephen Thomas Erlewine*

Walls and Bridges / Sep. 26, 1974 / Capitol ♦♦♦
Walls and Bridges was recorded during John Lennon's infamous "lost weekend," as he exiled himself in California during a separation from Yoko Ono. Lennon's personal life was scattered, so it isn't surprising that *Walls and Bridges* is a mess itself, containing equal amounts of brilliance and nonsense. Falling between the two extremes was the bouncy Elton John duet "Whatever Gets You Thru the Night," which was Lennon's first solo number one hit. Its bright, sunny surface was replicated throughout the record, particularly on middling rockers like "What You Got" but also on enjoyable pop songs like "Old Dirt Road." However, the best moments on *Walls and Bridges* come when Lennon is more open with his emotions, like on "Going Down on Love," "Steel and Glass" and the beautiful, soaring "#9 Dream." Even with such fine mometns, the album is decidedly uneven, containing too much mediocre material like "Beef Jerky" and "Ya Ya," which are weighed down by weak melodies and heavy overproduction. It wasn't a particularly graceful way to enter retirement. *—Stephen Thomas Erlewine*

Rock 'n' Roll / Feb. 17, 1975 / Capitol ♦♦♦
It was a common practice in the early 1970s for artists to satisfy record companies' demands for frequent album releases by recording albums of cover songs (see the Band's *Moondog Matinee* and David Bowie's *Pinups* for other examples). The story of John Lennon's covers album is a little more complicated, but the result is the same, with the artist tackling songs from the '50s by many of his favorites, from Gene Vincent to Lloyd Price. Of course, these are the kinds of songs that turned up on early Beatles albums, and while Lennon doesn't reinvent them as strikingly as his old group did, he gives them an affectionate, knowing treatment. *—William Ruhlmann*

Shaved Fish / Oct. 24, 1975 / Capitol ♦♦♦♦
At the time of its release, *Shaved Fish* didn't attract as much attention as any compilation of John Lennon's work would have either a few years before or a few years after. Lennon had just issued the somewhat disappointing genre album, *Rock 'n' Roll*, and was only a year from *Walls and Bridges*, not one of his strongest albums, and had also grown somewhat stale as a public figure. Drawing on his singles up to that point in his career, it shows a punkier, more defiant vision of Lennon's work than subsequent compilations, which would dwell on a broader cross section of his output. "Happy Christmas" and "Imagine" are moments of peace in the company of artifacts from his political/agitprop ("Power to the People") and primal scream ("Mother") periods, and his attempts at topical songwriting ("Woman Is the Nigger of the World"), and "Whatever Gets You Through the Night," which was unique to this LP, was a better piece of mainstream rock & roll than any of the late-'50s numbers that he ground out for *Rock 'n' Roll*. This collection, which was the last LP release to come from Lennon in any form until *Double Fantasy* five years later, was the only compilation of his work released in Lennon's own lifetime, and has since been supplanted by various posthumous assemblies of his music. *—Bruce Eder*

Double Fantasy / Nov. 17, 1980 / Capitol ♦♦♦♦
The most distinctive thing about *Double Fantasy*, the last album John Lennon released during his lifetime, is the very thing that keeps it from being a graceful return to form from the singer/songwriter, returning to active duty after five years of self-imposed exile. As legend has it, Lennon spent those years in domestic bliss, being a husband, raising a baby, and, of course, baking bread. *Double Fantasy* was designed as a window into that bliss and, to that extent, he decided to make it a joint album with Yoko Ono, to illustrate how complete their union was. For her part, Ono decided to take a stab at pop and while these are relatively tuneful for her, they nevertheless disrupt the feel and flow of Lennon's material, which has a consistent tone and theme. He's surprisingly sentimental, not just when he's expressing love for his wife ("Dear Yoko," "Woman") and child ("Beautiful Boy (Darling Boy)"), but when he's coming to terms with his quiet years ("Watching the Years," "Cleanup Time") and his return to creative life. These are really nice tunes, and what's special about them is their niceness—it's a sweet acceptance of middle age, which, of course, makes his assassination all the sadder. For that alone, *Double Fantasy* is noteworthy, yet it's hard not to think that it's a bit of a missed opportunity—primarily because its themes would be stronger without the Ono songs, but also because the production is just a little bit too slick and constrained, sounding very much of its time. Ultimately, these complaints fall by the wayside because Lennon's best songs here cement the last part of his legend, capturing him at peace and in love. According to some reports, that perception was a bit of a fantasy, but sometimes the fantasy means more than the reality, and that's certainly the case here. *—Stephen Thomas Erlewine*

● **The John Lennon Collection** / Nov. 10, 1982 / Capitol ♦♦♦♦♦
This 15-song collection (expanded to 19 in 1989 for the CD), released just short of two years after Lennon's death, provided a very generous overview of his solo career on a single LP, drawing on most of the major singles and also on songs that were widely covered, and from all periods of his career, from his late-Beatles-era solo political explorations up to the release of *Double Fantasy*. The producers, obviously working in collaboration with his widow and seeking to put the very best face on his career, and showcase his strongest and most memorable songs, pass right over *Sometime in New York* and much of the partly successful works that followed, which is sort of a shame—"Woman Is the Nigger of the World" may not quite rate alongside the stuff that is here, but it was a song that he did care about and played live more than once (significant in a career that included barely any scheduled concerts), and "John Sinclair" showed him playing blues with a ferocious passion. One also misses "Cold Turkey," which is as powerful a song as he wrote in his early solo career, but at the time of its release this was the broadest overview of Lennon's career to be found, and even included (on its CD version) the otherwise unanthologized B-side "Move Over Ms. L." *—Bruce Eder*

Milk & Honey / Jan. 27, 1984 / Polydor ♦♦♦

Live in New York City / Feb. 10, 1986 / Capitol ♦♦♦

Menlove Ave. / Nov. 3, 1986 / Capitol ♦♦♦

Lennon / 1990 / Capitol ♦♦♦♦♦
Two years after the first great Lennon revival—arriving in 1988, as an attempt to deflate Albert Goldman's trash-talking biography—Capitol released *Lennon*, a four-disc box set summary of his solo career. It does a remarkably good job, providing a thorough overview containing all the hits plus expertly chosen album tracks from his decidedly uneven records. The question is, is *Lennon* the one collection everybody needs? Not really. This may contain almost every great song Lennon recorded as a solo artist, yet the packaging is a little shoddy, and it could have been sequenced a little bit better. Still, as a summary, it's first-rate, rounding up the non-LP singles and condensing the records to their essence and thereby conveying the scope of Lennon's solo career very well. If you have the albums, plus a good singles collection, this isn't really necessary since it doesn't have anything too rare, but if you want one simple, albeit exhaustive, collection with everything you need, this fits the bill. *—Stephen Thomas Erlewine*

Anthology / Nov. 3, 1998 / Capitol ♦♦♦
During the great Lennon revival of the late '80s, Yoko Ono licensed to have the Westwood One Radio Network air scores of unreleased home recordings and demos as the Lost Lennon Tapes radio show. At the time, there was endless speculation about when highlights would be released, likely as a box set. The proposed set never materialized, yet most of the material was heavily bootlegged, as the producers and Ono must have suspected. Despite the bootlegs, Ono didn't agree to an official collection of unreleased Lennon material until 1998, after the Beatles' *Anthology* series proved a critical and commercial success. Hence, the birth of Lennon's *Anthology*—a four-disc box set, comprised entirely of unreleased home recordings, demos and outtakes, many of which have never been previously bootlegged. As it's constructed, it's more of an aural biography than a music album. All the dialogue snippets, half-finished songs, throwaways and parodies ensure that it's never casual listening, yet that very approach creates an intriguing portrait of Lennon—a portrait of the man, not the artist. As such, there aren't really any forgotten treasures buried on the collection, even if many of these songs and takes are either completely unheard of or legendary among collecting circles. For every small pleasure, such as the Cheap Trick-backed version of "I'm Losing You," there is a small disappointment, such as how the Dylan diatribe, "Serve Yourself," doesn't quite live up to its legend. Ultimately, it doesn't matter if there are no major works or revelations, just a few good alternate tracks, because *Anthology* goes a long way toward capturing Lennon with all of his strengths and weaknesses. *—Stephen Thomas Erlewine*

Wonsaponatime / Nov. 3, 1998 / Capitol ♦♦♦
Released simultaneously with *Anthology*, *Wonsaponatime* condenses a four-disc box set to into a digestable single-disc that feels more revelatory than its parent. That's because the compilers did an excellent job of selecting the highlights from the long-winded box, spotlighting the best alternate takes and unreleased songs. *Wonsaponatime* has a similar feel to *Anthology*, since it is culled from the same rough takes and studio rambling, but it's simply more accessible, letting less dedicated fans appreciate everything from the Cheap Trick-backed "I'm Losing You" and "God Save Oz," to alternates of "Working Class Hero," "God," "I Found Out" and "How Do You Sleep?" Again, these outtakes are not revelatory in the manner of Dylan's *Bootleg Series*, or even the Beatles' own *Anthology*, but they humanize Lennon, who has often been viewed as something of a saint in the years since his assisination. For that alone, *Wonsaponatime* is as welcome addition to his catalog as the exhaustive *Anthology*. *—Stephen Thomas Erlewine*

Annie Lennox

b. Dec. 25, 1954, Aberdeen, Scotland
Vocals, Keyboards / Adult Alternative Pop/Rock, Club/Dance, Pop/Rock, Adult Contemporary
Following the disbandment of the Eurythmics in 1991, vocalist Annie Lennox began a solo career that rivaled her former group in terms of crossover popularity. During the early '80s, the sleek synth-pop of the Eurythmics became one of the most popular sounds of new wave, racking up a number of hits in both the U.S. and U.K., including "Sweet Dreams (Are Made of This)," "Love Is A Stranger," "Who's That Girl," and "Here Comes The Rain Again." *Diva*, Lennox's solo debut, arrived in 1992 and it showcased a calmer, more mature vocalist designed to crossover into the adult contemporary audience. On the strength of the singles "Walking on Broken Glass" and "Why," *Diva* sold over two million copies in the U.S. alone. Lennox delivered her second solo album, a covers collection entitled *Medusa*, in 1995. *—Stephen Thomas Erlewine*

● **Diva** / Apr. 28, 1992 / Arista ♦♦♦♦♦
Those expecting Annie Lennox to come out full guns blazing for her solo debut with the high energy Euro-electro-pop-meets-American-R&B of her Eurythmics work may have to wind their pacemakers down a notch. The enigmatic vocalist who made a career toying with different notions of gender now plays on the concept of fame—Lennox dressing up in the persona of a solitary *Diva* trapped by counterfeit glory. The framework offers an effective stage for Lennox's husky voice, showcasing her as much more of a chanteuse than in the past. But the music is strangely muted and understated. In fact, the album almost works best as one integrated mood-piece rather than a collection of individual songs. While Lennox succeeds in carving out a personality distinct from her Eurythmics days with *Diva*, one can't help but crave a shot of former partner Dave Stewart's musical muscle. *—Roch Parisien*

Medusa / Mar. 14, 1995 / Arista ♦♦

Let's Active

f. 1981, Chapel Hill, NC, **db.** 1988
Group / College Rock, Jangle Pop, Power Pop
Mitch Easter carved his place in music history as a hip producer in the '80s, most notably for the early R.E.M. albums *Murmur* and *Reckoning;* unfortunately, these achievements often overshadowed and distracted him from giving his full commitment to his own record-

ing career with Let's Active, a band that, between 1983 and 1988, released some of the finest Southern power-pop/jangle-pop of the decade. Easter set up his legendary Drive-In Studios in 1981 and formed Let's Active with bassist Faye Hunter and drummer Sara Romweber. The trio released a six-song EP, 1983's *Afoot*, on IRS Records. In 1984, the band released the more experimental *Cypress*. While the EP and album sold modestly, they found a strong following in the emerging alternative/"college rock" audience. Hunter and Romweber left shortly after the release, leaving Let's Active as essentially a solo project for Easter. 1986's *Big Plans For Everybody* was another critically praised yet commercially undervalued album. The harder-edged *Every Dog Has His Day* was released in 1988. Following a small-scale promotional tour of college campuses, the band hung in limbo—no subsequent albums were recorded. Easter has continued producing into the '90s while infrequently playing with other bands, including Velvet Crush and Vinyl Devotion. *—Chris Woodstra*

Afoot / 1983 / IRS ✦✦✦✦
Afoot, their six-song debut EP, features Mitch Easter's own brand of Southern power-pop. With infectious, hook-filled songs, Easter proves to be a master of the three-minute form especially on the classic "Every Word Means No." *—Chris Woodstra*

Cypress / 1984 / IRS ✦✦✦✦✦
The band stretch out a bit on their first proper LP. While it is still every bit a jangly guitar-pop effort, Easter seems to be enjoying the powers of his studio, experimenting in different electronic sounds and neo-psychedelic textures. "Waters Part," the failed single from the album, is still one of his finest moments as a songwriter. *—Chris Woodstra*

Big Plans for Everybody / 1986 / IRS ✦✦✦
Essentially a Mitch Easter solo project, *Big Plans for Everybody* moves into darker territory than the previous album. Though Easter's trademark bright production and quirky songwriting still stand out, the mood is decidedly melancholy. *—Chris Woodstra*

Every Dog Has His Day / Aug. 22, 1988 / IRS ✦✦✦
Every Dog Has His Day features some of Easter's strongest songs in a harder-edged setting. Almost completely ignored, this was the band's last effort before disbanding indefinitely. *—Chris Woodstra*

● **Cypress/Afoot** / Jun. 1989 / IRS ✦✦✦✦✦
This CD combines their first EP, *Afoot*, and their first album, *Cypress*. Featuring highly memorable songs like "Every Word Means No" and "Waters Part," this perfect Southern power-pop is worth seeking out. *—Chris Woodstra*

Barbara Lewis

b. Feb. 9, 1943, South Lyon, MI
Vocals / Uptown Soul, Pop-Soul, Soul
Pop-soul doesn't get much better than Barbara Lewis, whose seductive, emotive croon took "Hello Stranger" to number three in 1963. Lewis wrote all of the songs on her debut LP (including "Hello Stranger"), and confidently handled harmony soul numbers (some with backing by the Dells) and more pop-savvy tunes, some of which, like "Hello Stranger," were driven by an organ and a bossa nova-like beat. Follow-ups to "Hello Stranger" didn't sell nearly as well, and in the mid-'60s, she began doing some recordings in New York City, with assistance from producers like Bert Berns and Jerry Wexler, that employed more orchestral arrangements and pop-conscious material. The approach clicked, both commercially and artistically: "Baby I'm Yours" and "Make Me Your Baby" were both big hits, and both among the best mid-'60s girl-group style productions. Lewis cut an album in the late '60s for Stax (on the Enterprise subsidiary) that, as one would expect, gave her sound a grittier approach, without compromising the smooth and poppy elements integral to the singer's appeal. *—Richie Unterberger*

Many Grooves of Barbara Lewis / 1969 / Stax ✦✦✦
Although this late-'60s album isn't nearly as well known as her poppier mid-'60s hits, this is excellent sweet soul that avoids slickness. Still working with producer Ollie McLaughlin, Lewis recorded this set of strong soul-pop in Chicago. The slightly updated, gutsier tone of the arrangements did nothing to obscure her characteristically smooth and assured delivery. The CD reissue adds three bonus tracks from singles. *—Richie Unterberger*

★ **Hello Stranger: The Best of Barbara Lewis** / Jul. 19, 1994 / Rhino ✦✦✦✦✦
At last! Twenty great Barbara Lewis songs in glorious remastered digital sound. In fact, the sound is so good it's like hearing these classic sides for the first time. The only significant omission is the song "On Bended Knee," but then again, I would have liked a two-disc compilation. Thank you Rhino! *—Michael Erlewine*

Gary Lewis (Gary Levitch)

b. Jun. 31, 1946, Manhatten, New York
Vocals, Drums, Guitar / Pop
The son of comedian Jerry Lewis formed this American rock group in 1964. After landing a gig at Disneyland, they were immediately signed to Liberty Records and handed over to pop production genius Snuff Garrett. Utilizing the best songwriters and studio players available, Garrett fashioned five Top Five hits in a matter of 18 months (15 in the Hot 100 by 1969) around Lewis's meager abilities, sometimes augmenting his voice in the studio with backup singers doubling his part. Lewis pretty well held his own against the British invasion, but the combination of his draft call in late 1966 and the rising tide of psychedelia put his days on the charts to an end. Still active on the oldies circuit, he fronts various backup bands under the name the Playboys. *—Cub Koda*

● **Legendary Masters Series** / 1990 / Capitol ✦✦✦✦✦
One of the most engaging pop acts of the mid-'60s, The Playboys benefited from strong songwriting (Al Kooper cowrote "This Diamond Ring") and studio personnel (courtesy of Leon Russell). It's still light, catchy pop with the enjoyable, unaffected vocals of Gary Lewis on top, and still fun. *—William Ruhlmann*

Huey Lewis (Hugh Anthony Cregg III)

b. Jul. 5, 1950, New York, NY
Vocals, Harmonica / Bar Band, Album Rock, Pop/Rock
With their straight-forward rock & roll, the San Francisco-based Huey Lewis & the News became one of America's most popular pop-rock bands of the mid-'80s. Inspired equally by British pub-rock (their previous incarnation, Clover, backed Elvis Costello on his debut album) and '60s R&B and rock & roll, the News had a driving, party-hearty spirit. At their core, the group were a working band, and they knew how to target their audience, writing odes to 9-to-5 jobs and sports. That much was clear on their first album, a simple bar-band record that earned some fans, but not widespread recognition. They had their first real taste of success with their second album, 1982's *Picture This*, thanks to a slicker production and a heavy dose of pop, evident on their first hit single, "Do You Believe in Love." This set the stage for *Sports*, one of the biggest blockbusters of the mid-'80s. Featuring the hits "I Want a New Drug," "Heart and Soul," "If this is It" and "The Heart of Rock & Roll," its driving rock & roll appealed to bluecollar audiences, while their celebration of good times appealed to yuppies—the combination made the group stars. After reaching number one with "The Power of Love" from the soundtrack to *Back to the Future*, Lewis & the News returned in 1986 with *Fore!*, an album that emphasized their new-found slickness and mainstream appeal; as the single said, they now celebrated that it was "Hip to Be Square." *Fore!* was another smash success, but its sequel, 1988's *Small World*, found the group's popularity slipping as they experimented with roots music. They returned to basics with 1991's *Hard At Play*, but by that point, Huey Lewis & the News were off the pop mainstream radar. For the remainder of the '90s, the group worked sporadically, recording the occasional album and doing the occasional tour, where they remained a popular attraction. *—Stephen Thomas Erlewine*

Huey Lewis & the News / 1980 / Chrysalis ✦✦✦✦
On their eponymous debut, Huey Lewis & the News essentially act as a pub-rock band, turning out hard-driving covers and originals in a workmanlike fashion. While that usually makes for great club gigs, it only occasionally makes for great records, and the debut suffers from an uneven selection of material and a somewhat stiff prouction, mainly because the group can't quite reproduce their sound in the studio. Even with such flaws, the album shows signs of promise, particularly in the charging "Some of My Lies are True (Sooner or Later)." *—Stephen Thomas Erlewine*

Picture This / 1982 / Chrysalis ✦✦✦✦
Huey Lewis & the News sound considerably more focused on their second album, *Picture This*. By incorporating stronger elements of R&B and doo wop (their cover of "Buzz Buzz Buzz" is first-rate) and embracing pop to a much greater extent, the News find their own distinctive sound—clean-cut, steady middle-class rock & roll. They still suffer from uneven material, but "Do You Believe In Love?" is a stunner, a tight set of polished, anthemic hooks that is one of the best mainstream pop singles of the early '80s. *—Stephen Thomas Erlewine*

● **Sports** / 1983 / Chrysalis ✦✦✦✦✦
Picture This found Huey Lewis & the News developing a signature sound, but they truly came into their own on their third album, *Sports*. It's true that the record holds together better than its predecessors because it has a clear, professional production, but the real key is the songs. Where their previous albums were cluttered with generic filler, nearly every song on *Sports* has a huge hook. And even if the News aren't bothered by breaking new ground, there's no denying that the craftmanship on *Sports* is pretty infectious. There's a reason why well over half of the album ("Heart of Rock & Roll," "Heart and Soul," "I Want a New Drug," "Walking on a Thin Line," "If This Is It") were huge American hit singles—they have instantly memorable hooks, driven home with economical precision by a tight bar band, who are given just enough polish to make them sound like superstars. And that's just what *Sports* made them. *—Stephen Thomas Erlewine*

Fore! / 1986 / Chrysalis ✦✦✦

Small World / 1988 / Chrysalis ✦✦

Hard at Play / Jan. 1991 / EMI America ✦✦✦

The Heart of Rock & Roll: The Best of Huey Lewis & the News / Nov. 18, 1992 / Chrysalis ✦✦✦✦✦
For four years, the U.K. compilation *The Heart of Rock & Roll: The Best of Huey Lewis & the News* was the only hits collection available on the San Franciscan bar band, and in some ways it's a better overview than the American retrospective, *Time Flies*. Although it does include a live version of "Workin' for a Livin'" and overlooks "Doing it All for My Baby" and "I Know What I Like," it contains several key tracks that aren't on *Time Flies*: "Hip to Be Square," "Back in Time" (which is only available on the *Back to the Future* soundtrack), "Jacob's Ladder," "Perfect World," the *We Are the World* track "Trouble in Paradise" and the terrific LP cut "Some of My Lies Are True." These tracks are added to the familiar hits to make *The Heart of Rock & Roll* a more thorough retrospective, and, in many ways, a better introduction than *Time Flies*. *—Stephen Thomas Erlewine*

Four Chords & Several Years Ago / Nov. 1, 1994 / Elektra ✦✦

The Time Flies: The Best of Huey Lewis & the News / Oct. 29, 1996 / Elektra ✦✦✦✦
Theoretically, it should be easy to assemble a greatest-hits collection from Huey Lewis & the News, since they spent most of the '80s in the Top Ten. *Time Flies... The Best of Huey Lewis & the News* proves that assumption false. Although many of the band's biggest hits are here—"Do You Believe in Love," "Workin' for a Livin'," "Heart and Soul," "I Want a New Drug," "The Heart of Rock & Roll," "If This Is It," "The Power of Love," "Stuck with You" and "Doing It All for My Baby"—the selection is remarkably uneven, bypassing many major hits from *Fore!* ("Hip to be Square," "Jacob's Ladder," "I Know What I Like") and neglecting the latter-day hit singles "Perfect World" and "Couple Days Off" completely, both of which were the only things worth salvaging from their respective albums. In their place are four new songs, which are pleasant but unremarkable. Even though it is flawed, *Time Flies* remains a useful compilation, since it gathers all of the very best singles, particularly the ones from *Sports* and

Picture This, in one place. However, the group could use an even better retrospective in the future. *— Stephen Thomas Erlewine*

Jerry Lee Lewis

b. Sep. 29, 1935, Ferriday, LA

Vocals, Piano / Honky Tonk, Rockabilly, Traditional Country, Rock & Roll

Is there an early rock & roller that has a crazier reputation than the Killer, Jerry Lee Lewis— His exploits as a piano-thumping egocentric wild man with an unquenchable thirst for living have become the fodder for numerous biographies, film documentaries, and a full-length Hollywood movie. Certainly few other artists came to the party with more ego and talent than he and lived to tell the tale. And certainly even fewer could successfully channel that energy into their music and prosper doing it as well as Jerry Lee. When he broke on the national scene in 1957 with his classic "Whole Lotta Shakin' Goin' On," he was every parents' worst nightmare perfectly realized: a long, blonde-haired Southerner who played the piano and sang with uncontrolled fury and abandon, while simultaneously reveling in his own sexuality. He was rock & roll's first great wild man and also rock & roll's first great eclectic. Ignoring all manner of musical boundaries is something that has not only allowed his music to have wide variety, but to survive the fads and fashions as well. Whether singing a melancholy country ballad, a lowdown blues or a blazing rocker, Lewis' wholesale commitment to the moment brings forth performances that are totally grounded in his personality and all singularly of one piece. Like the recordings of Hank Williams, Louis Armstrong and few others, Jerry Lee's early recorded work is one of the most amazing collections of American music in existence. *— Cub Koda*

The Greatest Live Show on Earth / 1964 / Bear Family ✦✦✦✦✦

Combining two live albums originally issued in the '60s, Lewis proves that the onslaught of the British Invasion hadn't lowered his rocking quotient one single bit. Blazing performances. *— Cub Koda*

☆ **Live at the Star Club** / 1980 / Bear Family ✦✦✦✦✦

The rock & roll landscape changed dramatically between the mid-1950s and 1964, when this five-star performance was recorded in Hamburg, Germany. The British Invasion was in full swing, and '50s icons like Chuck Berry, Little Richard, Elvis Presley and Bill Haley were no longer considered cutting-edge. Be that as it may, Lewis would continue to make live audiences sweat for decades to come. Amazingly, *Live at the Star Club* was only released in West Germany in the '60s and didn't come out in the U.S. until 1992. At 29, the Killer spares no passion whatsoever on frenzied versions of "Great Balls of Fire," "Whole Lotta Shakin' Goin' On," "Hound Dog" and other '50s classics. Though Lewis would record more and more country in the '60s, the only honky tonk treasure embraced here is Hank Williams' "Your Cheatin' Heart." For both hardcore Lewis devotees and more casual listeners, this stunning CD is essential. *— Alex Henderson*

★ **18 Original Sun Greatest Hits** / 1984 / Rhino ✦✦✦✦✦

This 18-song CD contains Jerry Lee Lewis' best rock & roll sides from the 240 or so tracks that he recorded for Sun Records. If that sounds like the very tiny tip of a very large iceberg—it is. But this 1984 compilation remains 40 of rock & roll's hottest minutes, revealing as much about Jerry Lee Lewis as it's possible to learn from watching the movie *Great Balls of Fire*! The hit singles and best B-sides are assembled around the core of his 1957 Sun album—a great, and instructive, musical decision. Lewis' rocking version of "Jambalaya" and his ivory-based rendition of "Matchbox," "Big Blon' Baby," "Big Legged Woman," and "It'll Be Me", are all prime examples of his fiercely sexual personality, pounding away on those keys and whooping and hollering like a white version of Piano Red. Equally important, "Crazy Arms" held what would prove to be the key to his professional salvation: a distinct way with a country song that didn't blow the song right apart and also didn't lose the rock 'n roll audience. A big hunk of this stuff is available on the Sun debut album, which should be heard at least once (assuming one can't afford the Bear Family label's *Classic* box with his whole Sun output), but this is the place to start. The mid-'80s digital transfer is still sounds good; its quality proves that Rhino always gave good value to its customers. The guitars on "Put Me Down" and "Wild One"—yes, there is guitar on a lot of these sides—are nice and crunchy, even though they're buried under the piano. If there's a flaw here, it's the absence of any liner notes (not that much needs to be said about music like this). *— Bruce Eder*

Classic / 1989 / Bear Family ✦✦✦✦✦

Eight-disc boxed set of Lewis' complete output for Sun Records. Along with Muddy Waters' Chess recordings, Louis Armstrong's *Hot Fives & Sevens*, and Hank Williams's undubbed MGM sides, this box comprises one of the finest bodies of American music ever recorded. *— Cub Koda*

★ **All Killer, No Filler: The Anthology** / May 18, 1993 / Rhino ✦✦✦✦✦

Out of all of the Jerry Lee Lewis compilations available on the market, only *All Killer, No Filler* contains material from all of the different labels he recorded for. Although there are twelve Sun tracks (including all of the major hits), the set doesn't draw enough from those early years; but then again, that's the intent. *All Killer, No Filler* is out to prove to an audience only familiar with his Sun singles that his country material is as brilliant as his rock & roll, and it succeeds. Stick with the *18 Original Sun Greatest Hits* if you only want rock & roll. If you want an idea of the scope of Lewis' talents and how consistently rich his music was throughout his career, you can't go wrong here. *— Stephen Thomas Erlewine*

Locust Years . . . And the Return to the Promised Land / Nov. 29, 1994 / Bear Family ✦✦✦✦✦

Picking up where the eight-CD set *Classic* left off, the eight-CD box *The Locust Years . . . and the Return to the Promised Land* rivals its predecessor in musical quality. Tracing Jerry Lee Lewis' '60s career at Smash Records, the first two discs find the pianist trying to replicate his rock & roll success; while the performances were good, it was clear he was out of touch with the times. During the third disc, he begins to concentrate on country music. The fourth, fifth, and sixth discs match his Sun recordings for consistently brilliant performances; several of the songs became big hits on the country charts, establishing him as a country star. The seventh disc chronicles an exciting unreleased show, while the eighth disc is an unexceptional interview. For dedicated Jerry Lee Lewis fans, *The Locust Years* is every bit as essential as *Classic*. *— Stephen Thomas Erlewine*

● **Killer Country** / 1995 / Mercury ✦✦✦✦✦

Killer Country is a well-chosen selection of Jerry Lee Lewis' biggest and best country hits between 1963 and 1977, which feature some of his finest performances, including "Another Place, Another Time," "What's Made Milwaukee Famous," "She Still Comes Around (To Love What's Left of Me)," "She Even Woke Me Up to Say Goodbye." *— Stephen Thomas Erlewine*

25 All-Time Greatest Sun Recordings / Jun. 6, 2000 / Varese ✦✦✦✦✦

Just one of many Jerry Lee's Sun best-ofs, this one largely sticks to the original single releases with a few strays like "Drinkin' Wine Spo-Dee-O-Dee" throw in to fill things out. The transfers are as clean as it gets and although this doesn't replace Rhino's version of essentially the same material, it does offer a few stray tracks ("Love on Broadway," "Waitin' for a Train," "I Can't Seem fo Say Goodbye," "One Minute Past Eternity," "Invitation to Your Party") you might want or need if you don't feel like popping for Bear Family's exhaustive eight disc box set. *— Cub Koda*

Mercury Smashes & Rockin' Sessions / Dec. 13, 2000 / Bear Family ✦✦✦✦✦

Smiley Lewis

b. Jul. 5, 1913, DeQuincey, LA, **d.** Oct. 7, 1966, New Orleans, LA

Vocals, Piano, Guitar / New Orleans R&B, New Orleans Blues, Piano Blues, R&B

Dave Bartholomew has often been quoted to the effect that Smiley Lewis was a "bad luck singer," because he never sold more than 100,000 copies of his Imperial singles. In retrospect, Lewis was a lucky man in many respects—he enjoyed stellar support from New Orleans' ace sessioneers at Cosimo's, benefited from top-flight material and production (by Bartholomew), and left behind a legacy of marvelous Crescent City R&B. He began recording in 1947 and signed with Imperial three years later. As the New Orleans R&B sound developed rapidly during the early '50s, so did Lewis, rocking ever harder on "Lillie Mae," "Ain't Gonna Do It," and "Big Mamou." He scored his first national hit in 1952 with "The Bells Are Ringing," but enjoyed his biggest sales in 1955 with the exultant "I Hear You Knocking." (Pop chanteuse Gale Storm swiped his thunder for any pop crossover possibilities with her ludicrous whitewashed cover.) His blistering "Shame, Shame, Shame" found its way onto the soundtrack of the steamy Hollywood potboiler *Baby Doll* in 1957 but failed to find entry to the R&B charts. Lewis recorded one single each for OKeh, Dot and Loma in the '60s before dying in 1966, all but forgotten outside his New Orleans homebase. *— Bill Dahl*

★ **The Best of Smiley Lewis** / Nov. 3, 1992 / Capitol ✦✦✦✦✦

Smiley Lewis made several fabulous singles, had a booming, terrific voice, and received the same great backing and support that defined the city's R&B sound. But Lewis' records seldom made it outside New Orleans, even though they were frequently brilliant. This great 24-track anthology contains the four that did make it to the charts, among them the signature song "I Hear You Knocking." It shows Lewis doing first-rate novelty tracks, ballads, weepers, up-tempo wailers, and blues, and making wonderful recordings. The set also includes a thorough discography and good notes and is superbly mastered. It's magnificent, exuberant R&B, and deserved a much better national fate than it enjoyed. *— Ron Wynn*

Shame, Shame, Shame / 1993 / Bear Family ✦✦✦✦✦

Exhaustive, multi-disc set comprising everything recorded on this New Orleans singer. With the songwriting talents of Dave Bartholomew aboard, utilizing the sound of the legendary J&M Studios, and the best Crescent City musicians available, this is truly New Orleans music at its very best. *— Cub Koda*

Little Anthony & the Imperials

f. 1958, Brooklyn, NY, **db.** 1975

Vocals / Doo Wop, R&B

Featuring the high-pitched vocals of Anthony Gourdine and a brace of solid material, Little Anthony & the Imperials had a much longer chart run than the majority of doo wop from the '50s. When the dust finally settled, the group clocked in with a total of ten entries in the Hot 100 between 1958 to 1974, including "Tears on My Pillow," "Two People in the World," "Wishful Thinking," "Oh Yeah," "So Much," "Shimmy Shimmy Ko Ko Bop" (not to be confused with the similarly titled "Shimmy Shimmy Ko Ko Wop" by the El Capris), "When You Wish Upon a Star," "Going Out of My Head," "Better Use Your Head," and "Hurt So Bad." The group was originally called the Chesters, but had their name changed to the Imperials by popular New York disc jockey Alan Freed. Gourdine's vocal similarities to the popular Frankie Lymon-inspired "kiddie group" sound, coupled with a tendency to chop up syllables and overstress lyrics, made theirs a style deceptively simple yet enduring. After revamping the group in 1964 down to a quartet, the sound changed from doo wop to a harder, more uptown R&B sound, best exemplified on hits like "I'm on the Outside Looking In." For many lovers of the genre, Little Anthony & the Imperials are simply New York styled doo wop at its smoothest and finest. *— Cub Koda*

We Are the Imperials (Featuring Little Anthony) / 1959 / Collectables ✦✦✦

This is a straight-up reissue (no bonus tracks) of this '50s group's debut album on the End label. As such, it contains their first couple of big hits, "Two People in the World" and "Tears on My Pillow," along with album filler such as "Cha Cha Henry" and "Oh Yeah," as well as old standards like "When You Wish Upon a Star" and "Over the Rainbow." Almost worth having for the cover alone, this is one of the classics of '50s vocal-group harmony. *— Cub Koda*

● **The Best of Little Anthony & the Imperials [Rhino]** / Oct. 1989 / Rhino ✦✦✦✦✦

"Little" Anthony Gourdine's angst-ridden leads were ideal for tearjerkers and heartache ballads. Although this Brooklyn group began in the doo wop era, they were much more effective on soul songs, where group harmonies were low-key and Gourdine's voice was the major focus. This anthology includes "Hurt So Bad," "I'm on the Outside Looking In" and "Take

Me Back," arguably their three finest hits, plus several others with equally theatrical vocals, but dissimilar chart performances. *—Ron Wynn*

The Best of Little Anthony & the Imperials [EMI] / May 28, 1996 / EMI ♦♦♦
Unlike the collection of the same name on Rhino, this focuses solely on their mid-to-late-'60s recordings for Veep and United Artists. That means you don't get any doo wop, but slickly arranged pop/soul that sometimes borders on easy listening, featuring string charts and Little Anthony's choked vocals (which could bring to mind an effeminate Johnny Mathis). The best and biggest of these cuts are also on the Rhino comp ("I'm on the Outside Looking In," "Goin' Out of My Head," "Hurt So Bad"), which gets the edge for its wider chronology. This is a satisfactory alternative, though, for those who prefer the Imperials' later phase, or want a more extensive sampler of their '60s stuff. *—Richie Unterberger*

We Are the Imperials/Shades of the 40's / Jun. 9, 1998 / West Side ♦♦♦♦

Little Eva

b. Jun. 29, 1943, Bellhaven, NC
Vocals / Brill Building Pop, Girl Group
Little Eva Narcissus Boyd was a babysitter for Carole King and Gerry Goffin when the songwriting team was inspired to write "Locomotion," a song based on a dance that Eva would do around the house. Eva also got to sing on their demo, which impressed Don Kirshner enough to release it as it was. One of the greatest girl-group hits, "Locomotion," hit number one in 1962; the follow-up, "Keep Your Hands Off My Baby," was also written by Goffin-King. Almost as good as her debut, it reached the Top 20, and was even covered by the Beatles on stage in their early days (though they never recorded it in the studio). Unfortunately, Eva was then pigeonholed as a dance-craze singer and given inferior material. She never again reached the soulful heights of her first two singles; "Let's Turkey Trot" (1963) was her only other Top 20 hit. *—Richie Unterberger*

● **The Best of Little Eva** / 1988 / Collectables ♦♦♦♦♦
Fifteen songs, most cut for the Dimension label between 1962 and 1964. Includes all the hits and some pleasant girl-group flops in a more lightweight style than "Locomotion." *—Richie Unterberger*

The Loco-Motion / Feb. 27, 1996 / Rhino ♦♦♦
Some collectors will be glad to have some Little Eva available on CD domestically. At only ten cuts (and no liner notes), however, it's on the skimpy side, and "Let's Turkey Trot" is unexpectedly missing. The 15-song best-of on Murray Hill is considerably more extensive and well annotated (albeit getting harder to find). On the other hand, this Rhino comp does have seven songs not on the Murray Hill LP (including some obscure Goffin/King compositions), although some of these are covers of popular early '60s hits. *—Richie Unterberger*

Little Feat

f. 1969, Los Angeles, CA
Group / Album Rock, Boogie Rock, Southern Rock, Hard Rock, Blues-Rock, Rock & Roll
Though they had all the trappings of a Southern-fried blues band, Little Feat were hardly conventional. Led by songwriter/guitarist Lowell George, Little Feat was a wildly eclectic band, bringing together strains of blues, R&B, country and rock & roll. The group was exceptionally gifted technically and their polished professionalism sat well with the slick sounds coming out of Southern California during the '70s. However, Little Feat were hardly slick—they had a surreal sensibility, as evidenced by George's idiosyncratic songwriting, which helped the band earn a cult following among critics and musicians. Though the band earned some success on album-oriented radio, the group was derailed after George's death in 1979. Little Feat re-formed in the late '80s, and while they were playing as well as ever, they lacked the skewed sensibility that made them cult favorites. Nevertheless, their albums and tours were successful, especially among American blues-rock fans. *—Stephen Thomas Erlewine*

☆ **Little Feat** / 1971 / Warner Brothers ♦♦♦♦♦
It sold poorly (around 11,000 copies) and the band never cut anything like it again, but Little Feat's eponymous debut isn't just one of their finest records, it's one of the great lost rock & roll albums. Even dedicated fans tend to overlook the album, largely because it's the polar opposite of the subtly intricate, funky rhythm & roll that made their reputation during the mid-'70s. *Little Feat* is a raw, hard-driving, funny and affectionate celebration of American weirdness, equal parts garage rock, roadhouse blues, post-Zappa bizarreness, post-Parsons country rock and slightly bent folk storytelling. Since it's grounded in roots rock, it feels familiar enough, but the vision of chief songwriter/guitarist/vocalist Lowell George is wholly unique and slightly off-center. He sees everything with a gently surreal sense of humor that remains affectionate, whether it's on an ode to a "Truck Stop Girl," the weary trucker's anthem "Willin'," or the goofy character sketch of the crusty old salt "Crazy Captain Gunboat Willie." That affection is balanced by gutsy slices of Americana like the careening travelogue "Strawberry Flats," the darkly humorous "Hamburger Midnight" and a jaw-dropping Howlin' Wolf medley guest-starring Ry Cooder, plus keyboardist Bill Payne's terrific opener "Snakes on Everything." The songwriting itself is remarkable enough, but the band is its equal—they're as loose, vibrant and alive as the Stones at their best. In most respects, this album has more in common with George's earlier band the Factory than the rest of the Little Feat catalog, but there's a deftness in the writing and performance that distinguishes it from either band's work, which makes it all the more remarkable. It's a pity that more people haven't heard the record, but that just means that anyone who owns it feels like they're in on a secret only they and a handful of others know. *—Stephen Thomas Erlewine*

☆ **Sailin' Shoes** / 1972 / Warner Brothers ♦♦♦♦♦
Little Feat's debut may have been a great album but it sold so poorly, they had to either broaden their audience or, in all likelihood, they'd be dropped from Warner. So, *Sailin' Shoes* is a consciously different record from its predecessor—less raw and bluesy, blessed with a varied production and catchier songs. That still doesn't make it a pop record, since Little Feat, particularly in its first incarnation, was simply too idiosyncratic, earthy and strange for that. It is, however, an utterly thrilling, individual blend of pop, rock, blues and country, due in no small part to a stellar set of songs from Lowell George. If anything, his quirks are all the more apparent here than they were on the debut, since Ted Templeman's production lends each song its own character, plus his pen was getting sharper. George truly finds his voice on this record, with each of his contributions sparkling with off-kilter humor, friendly surreal imagery and humanity, and he demonstrates he can authoritatively write anything from full-throttle rock & roll ("Teenage Nervous Breakdown"), sweet ballads ("Trouble," a sublimely reworked "Willin'"), skewered folk ("Sailin' Shoes"), paranoid rock ("Cold, Cold, Cold") and blues ("A Apolitical Blues") and, yes, even hooky mainstream rock ("Easy to Slip," which should have been the hit the band intended it to be). That's not to discount the contributions of the other members, particularly Bill Payne and Richie Hayward's "Tripe Face Boogie," which is justifiably one of the band's standards, but the thing that truly stuns on *Sailin' Shoes* is George's songwriting and how the band brings it to a full, colorful life. Nobody could master the twists and turns within George's songs better than Little Feat, and both the songwriter and his band are in prime form here. *—Stephen Thomas Erlewine*

★ **Dixie Chicken** / 1973 / Warner Brothers ♦♦♦♦♦
Following Roy Estrada's departure during the supporting tour for *Sailin' Shoes*, Lowell George became infatuated with New Orleans R&B and mellow jamming, all of which came to a head on their third album, 1973's *Dixie Chicken*. Although George is firmly in charge—he dominates the record, writing or co-writing seven of the 10 songs—this is the point where Little Feat found its signature sound as a band, and no album they would cut from this point on was too different from this seductive, laid-back, funky record. But no album would be quite as good, either, since *Dixie Chicken* still had much of the charming lyrical eccentricities or the first two albums, plus what is arguably George's best-ever set of songs. Partially due to the New Orleans infatuation, the album holds together better than *Sailin' Shoes* and George takes full advantage of the band's increased musical palette, writing songs that sound easy but are quite sophisticated, such as the rolling "Two Trains," the gorgeous, shimmering "Juliette," the deeply soulful and funny "Fat Man in the Bathtub" and the country-funk of the title track, which was covered nearly as frequently as "Willin'." In addition to "Walkin' All Night," a loose bluesy jam by Barrere and Bill Payne, the band also hauls out two covers which fit George's vibe perfectly: Allan Toussaint's slow burner "On Your Way Down" and "Fool Yourself," which was written by Fred Tackett, who later joined a reunited Feat in the '80s. It all adds up to a nearly irresistible record, filled with great songwriting, sultry groove and virtuosic performances that never are flashy. Little Feat, along with many jam bands that followed, tried to top this album, but they never managed to make a record this understated, appealing and fine. *—Stephen Thomas Erlewine*

Feats Don't Fail Me Now / 1974 / Warner Brothers ♦♦♦♦
If *Dixie Chicken* represented a pinnacle of Lowell George as a songwriter and band leader, its sequel *Feats Don't Fail Me Now* is the pinnacle of Little Feat as a group, showcasing each member at their finest. Not coincidentally, it's the moment where George begins to recede from the spotlight, leaving the band as a true democracy. These observations are only clear in hindsight, since if *Feats Don't Fail Me Now* is just taken as a record, it's nothing more than a damn good rock & roll record. That's not meant as a dismissal, either, since it's hard to make a rock & roll record as seemingly effortless and infectious as this. Though it effectively builds on the Southern-fried funkiness of *Dixie Chicken*, it's hardly as mellow as that record—there's a lot of grit, tougher rhythms, lots of guitar and organ. It's as supple as *Chicken*, though, which means that it's the sound of a touring band at their peak. As it happens, the band is each on the top of their writing game, as well, with Bill Payne contributing the rollicking "Oh Atlanta" and Paul Barrere turns in one of his best songs, the jazzy funk of "Skin it Back." Each has a co-writing credit with George—Payne on the unreleased *Little Feat*-era nugget "The Fan" and Barrere (plus Fred Martin) on the infectious title track—who also has a couple of classics with "Rock and Roll Doctor" and the great "Spanish Moon." *Feats* peters out toward the end, as the group delves into a 10-minute medley of two *Sailin' Shoes* songs, but that doesn't hurt one of the best albums Little Feat ever cut. It's so good, the group used it as the template for the rest of their career. *—Stephen Thomas Erlewine*

The Last Record Album / 1975 / Warner Brothers ♦♦♦
The title of *The Last Record Album* isn't literally accurate, but it cuts a lot closer than the band intended, for this is really is the last album of the group's classic era. Starting with this album, leader Lowell George fades into the woodwork, and while the remainder of the group tries valiantly to keep the band afloat, the timing of friction was wrong and the amount of tension was too great. Musically, the group attempts to make *Feats Don't Fail Me Now, Pt. 2*, but the production from George is curiously flat, and, truth be told, the group just isn't inspired enough to make a satisfying album. For a very short album—only eight songs—too many of the cuts fall flat. Those that succeed, however, are quite good, particularly Paul Barrere and Bill Payne's gently propulsive "All That You Dream," Lowell George's beautiful "Long Distance Love," and the sublime "Mercenary Territory." Even these songs don't have the spark or character they would have had on the more organic *Feats*, due to George's exceedingly mellow So-Cal production, which is pleasant but doesn't provide Little Feat with enough room to breathe. There are enough signs of Little Feat's true character on *The Last Record Album*—the three previously mentioned songs are essential for any Feat fan—to make it fairly enjoyable, but it's clear that the band is beginning to run out of steam. [The CD reissue of *The Last Record Album* includes two bonus tracks, "Don't Bogart That Joint" and "A Apolitical Blues," that were originally included on the 1978 live album *Waiting for Columbus*. They were pulled from the CD reissue of that album due to time restrictions, and appeared here instead.] *—Stephen Thomas Erlewine*

Time Loves a Hero / 1977 / Warner Brothers ♦♦♦
When Little Feat headed into the studio to record *Time Loves a Hero*, tensions between the band members—more specifically, Lowell George and the rest of the band—were at a peak. George had not only succumbed to various addictions, but he was growing restless with the group's fondness for extending their jams into territory strikingly reminiscent of jazz fusion. The rest of the group brought in Ted Templeman, who previously worked on their debut and

produced *Sailin' Shoes*, to mediate the sessions. George wasn't thrilled with that, but that's probably not the only reason why his presence isn't large on this release—all signs point to his frustration with the band, and he wasn't in great health, so he just didn't contribute to the record. He wrote one song, the pleasant but comparatively faceless "Rocket in My Pocket," and collaborated with Paul Barrere on "Keepin' Up With the Joneses." Barrere was responsible for the only bright moments on the album, the ingratiatingly silly "Old Folks' Boogie" and, along with Bill Payne and Ken Gradney, the funky singalong title track. Elsewhere, Barrere and Payne come up dry, turning out generic pieces that are well-played but not as memorable as comparable Doobie Brothers' cuts from the same time. Then there's "Day at the Dog Races," a lengthy fusion jam that Templeman and everyone in the band loved—except for George, who, according to Bud Scoppa's liner notes in *Hotcakes & Outtakes*, disparagingly compared it to Weather Report. He was right—no matter how well Feat play on this track, it comes across as self-serving indulgence, and the clearest sign on this muddled album that they had indeed lost the plot. *—Stephen Thomas Erlewine*

Waiting for Columbus / 1978 / Warner Brothers ✦✦✦✦✦
Little Feat was one of the legendary live bands of the '70s, showered with praise by not only their small, fiercely dedicated cult of fans, but such fellow musicians like Bonnie Raitt, Robert Palmer and Jimmy Page. Given all that acclaim, it only made sense for the group to cut a live album. Unfortunately, they waited until 1977, when the group had entered in its decline, but as the double-album *Waiting for Columbus* proves, Little Feat in its decline was still pretty great. Certainly, the group is far more inspired on stage than they were in the studio after 1975—just compare "All That You Dream," "Oh Atlanta," "Old Folks' Boogie," "Time Loves a Hero," and "Mercenary Territory" here to the cuts on *The Last Record Album* and *Time Loves a Hero*. The versions on *Waiting* are full-bodied and fully-realized, putting the studio cuts to shame. Early classics like "Fat Man in the Bathtub" and "Tripe Face Boogie" aren't as revelatory, but it's still a pleasure to hear a great band run through their best songs, stretching them out and finding new quirks within them. If there are any flaws with *Waiting for Columbus*, it's that the Feat do a little bit too much stretching, veering toward excessive jamming on occasion—and that mildly fuzzy focus is really the only way you'd be able to tell that this is a great live band recorded slightly after their prime. Even so, there's much to savor on *Waiting for Columbus*, one of the great live albums of its era, thanks to rich performances that prove Little Feat were one of the great live bands of their time. *—Stephen Thomas Erlewine*

Down on the Farm / 1979 / Warner Brothers ✦✦

Hoy-Hoy / 1981 / Warner Brothers ✦✦✦✦✦
Perhaps realizing that *Down on the Farm* wasn't the proper swan song for Little Feat, the group persuaded Warner Brothers to release a compilation of rarities and overlooked tracks as a swan song and farewell to fans. Filled with live performances, obscurities, album tracks, and a new song apiece from Bill Payne and Paul Barrere, *Hoy Hoy* is a bit scattered, a bit incoherent, a little bewildering, and wholly delightful—a perfect summation of a group filled with quirks, character, and funk, traits which were as much a blessing as they were a curse. *Hoy Hoy* is one of those rare albums that may be designed for diehards—who else really needs radio performances, early recordings from before the band was signed, and outtakes, especially if they're surrounding by early album tracks—but still is a great introduction for novices. That doesn't mean it's as good as such masterpieces as *Sailin' Shoes*, *Dixie Chicken*, or *Waiting for Columbus*, but it does capture the group's careening, freewheeling spirit, humor, and musical versatility, arguably better than any single album. That's one of the nice things compilations like this can do—they can summarize what a band was all about in a way a straight studio album couldn't. So, that's why it may be a good gateway into the band for novices, even though it's missing such essentials as "Willin'" and "Fat Man in the Bathtub," but it's truly for the dedicated, who will not only love the rarities (and these live cuts are hotter, on whole, than *Columbus*) but will savor the context. *—Stephen Thomas Erlewine*

Let It Roll / Jul. 1988 / Warner Brothers ✦✦✦
When Little Feat reunited in 1988, they were embraced by some dedicated fans, but were spurned by nearly an equal number of cultists. That's because to certain diehards, Little Feat belonged to Lowell George and, without him, the group doesn't exist. While it is true that George was the main songwriter and visionary during the early years of the group, he had pulled away from the group in the last half of the '70s and only had a marginal impact on their final three albums of the '70s. Also, throughout their career, the band contributed significantly, co-writing songs with George, writing their own tunes and, of course, shaping the band's sound with their musicianship. Although George was gone, they still had the desire to perform, so it was understandable that they wanted to reunite, with Craig Fuller taking George's place. What's surprising about *Let It Roll* is not just that it works, but that works smashingly. It sounds as if the group picked up after *The Last Record Album*, deciding to return to the sound of *Feats Don't Fail Me Now*. True, the songwriting might not have the idiosyncratic genius of George, but it's strong, catchy and memorable, from the fine singles "Hate to Lose Your Lovin'" and "Let it Roll" to album tracks. More importantly, the band sounds lively and playful—Little Feat hasn't sounded this good in the studio since *Feats*, so it's easy to see why the members wanted to regroup. Yes, George is missed—it's hard not to miss such a gifted songwriter and musician—but *Let It Roll* isn't disrespectful of his memory, it keeps his music alive, which is the greatest compliment it can be paid. *—Stephen Thomas Erlewine*

Representing the Mambo / 1989 / Warner Brothers ✦✦

Shake Me Up / Sep. 24, 1991 / Morgan Creek ✦✦

● **The Best of Little Feat: As Time Goes By** / Feb. 10, 1994 / Warner Brothers ✦✦✦✦✦
As Time Goes By: The Best of Little Feat is an extraordinary collection that contains almost every essential Little Feat song from their '70s heyday with Lowell George, plus the two hits ("Let It Roll," "Hate to Lose Your Lovin'") from their late-'80s comeback. Most of the band's albums are worth hearing, but this is a great introduction for the curious and—since it features "Dixie Chicken," "Willin'," "Two Trains," "Fat Man in the Bathtub," "Sailin' Shoes," "Oh Atlanta" and "All That You Dream" in one place—it's a great summation of the group's achievements, and George's songwriting talent in particular. Unfortunately, *As Time Goes By* has only been released by the British division of Warner Brothers, but it's worth tracking down. *—Stephen Thomas Erlewine*

Ain't Had Enough Fun / Apr. 25, 1995 / Zoo ✦✦✦

Live from Neon Park / Jun. 18, 1996 / Zoo ✦✦✦

Under the Radar / Jun. 16, 1998 / CMC International ✦✦✦

Chinese Work Songs / Jun. 20, 2000 / CMC International ✦✦✦

Hotcakes and Outtakes: 30 Years of Little Feat / Sep. 19, 2000 / Rhino/Warner Archives ✦✦✦✦✦
Rhino's four-disc box set *Hotcakes & Outtakes* treats all of Little Feat's incarnations with equal respect. This even-handed approach has advantages, even if Lowell George dominates the proceedings. How could he not— He was a musician of immense talents, shaping the band's core sound while building an impressive body of songs. This set reveals that the rest of the band, while not writers of George's ilk, still wrote their share of great songs and, best of all, their fusion of funk, blues, country, rock and jazz still sounded lively, even when they reunited a decade after his death. Yes, it was missing his unique brilliance and vision, yet the reunited Feat still carried the torch well, which this set proves. Still, the best thing about they box is the fourth disc, devoted to "Studio Artifacts," all dating from George's heyday with the band. Actually, it goes a little further than that, beginning with cuts from George and Roy Estrada's mid-'60s band the Factory and pre-Warner Bros recordings, plus a generous selection of outtakes and demos, including selections from George's solo album, *Thanks I'll Eat It Here*. It's a treasure trove for any Little Feat fan, filled with amazing cuts like the barn-storming "Rat Faced Dog"—tracks so good, it's hard to believe they haven't been released before. This fourth disc is reason for any devoted fan to pick up this set, but is this worthwhile for the curious— Well, yes, since this offers a great summary of their fascinating career, even if it duplicates some songs at the expense of album tracks like "A Apolitical Blues" which really should be here. Even with that flaw, *Hotcakes & Outtakes* performs its job well, proving that Little Feat is an American rock & roll band like no other. *—Stephen Thomas Erlewine*

Little Richard (Richard Wayne Penniman)

b. Dec. 5, 1935, Macon, GA
Vocals, Piano / New Orleans R&B, Rock & Roll, R&B
One of the original rock'n'roll greats, Little Richard merged the fire of gospel with New Orleans R&B, pounding the piano and wailing with gleeful abandon. While numerous other R&B greats of the early 1950s had been moving in a similar direction, none of them matched the sheer electricity of Richard's vocals. With his bullet-speed deliveries, ecstatic trills, and the overjoyed force of personality in his singing, he was crucial in upping the voltage from high-powered R&B into the similar, yet different, guise of rock'n'roll. Although he was only a hitmaker for a couple of years or so, his influence upon both the soul and British Invasion stars of the 1960s was vast, and his early hits remain core classics of the rock repertoire. In 1955, at Lloyd Price's suggestion, Richard sent a demo tape to Specialty Records, who were impressed enough to sign him and arrange a session for him in New Orleans. That session, however, didn't get off the ground until Richard began fooling around with a slightly obscene ditty during a break. With slightly cleaned-up lyrics, "Tutti Frutti" was the record that gave birth to Little Richard as we know him—the gleeful "woo!"s, the furious piano playing, the sax-driven, pedal-to-the-metal rhythm section. In 1956 and 1957, Richard reeled off a string of classic hits—"Long Tall Sally," "Slippin' and Slidin'," "Jenny, Jenny," "Keep a Knockin'," "Good Golly, Miss Molly," "The Girl Can't Help It"—that remain the foundation of his fame. Little Richard was at the height of his commercial and artistic powers when he suddenly quit the business during an Australian tour in late 1957, enrolling in a bible college in Alabama shortly after returning to the States. By 1962, though, Richard had returned to rock'n'roll. At this point it's safe to assume that he never will get that much-hungered-for comeback hit, but he remains one of rock'n'roll's most colorful icons, still capable of turning on the charm and charisma in his infrequent appearances in the limelight. *—Richie Unterberger*

☆ **18 Greatest Hits** / 1985 / Rhino ✦✦✦✦✦
18 Greatest Hits is the definitive single-disc collection of Little Richard's Specialty singles, especially for listeners who only want the hits. Every one of Richard's biggest hits—"Tutti Frutti," "Long Tall Sally," "Slippin' and Slidin'," "Rip It Up," "Ready Teddy," "The Girl Can't Help It," "Lucille," "Send Me Some Lovin'," "Keep A-Knockin'," "Good Golly Miss Molly"—are here, plus singles like "Heeby-Jeebies," "She's Got It," "Ooh! My Soul," "Miss Ann," "Kansas City/Hey Hey Hey," and "Bama Lama Bama Loo" that were bigger hits on the R&B charts than the pop charts. All of the singles are presented in chronological order, and the disc simply rips it up from beginning to end. It's a definitive collection. *—Stephen Thomas Erlewine*

The Specialty Box Set / 1989 / Specialty ✦✦✦✦✦
Dig it—a collection of all 73 songs that Little Richard cut for Specialty Records from 1955 through 1959, including early working versions of hits including "Long Tall Sally" and "Slippin' and Slidin'," may seem like overkill to the casual listener, but if you're thinking of buying this three-CD box, chances are you're not a casual listener. And if you're not thinking about it, then you should be. This set covers only four years in Little Richard's career, but manages to sum up virtually everything you need to know about him (his earlier sides, available on Bear Family, are an interesting appendix, but of his later stuff, only the early- and mid-'60s material, with Jimi Hendrix on guitar, hold any significance, mostly as a curiosity). Not only does the music make you want to get up and dance, but the notes—spread out on a lavishly illustrated booklet and the individual jewel boxes—tell the whole story of Specialty Records and the people behind it, including Art Rupe, Bumps Blackwell, Dave Bartholomew, and, of course, Richard Penniman himself. The session information alone could keep owners busy for a week. The sound is nothing less than breathtaking, loud and raunchy but razor sharp, and the price of this set—about $42 retail—makes it competitive

with other Little Richard single-disc sets as well as more attractive than the price of boxes devoted to Elvis Presley and Chuck Berry. The only complaint—why couldn't the producers list the songs on the individual jewel boxes— *—Bruce Eder*

The Formative Years 1951-53 / Jul. 1989 / Bear Family ♦♦♦♦

★ **The Georgia Peach** / Aug. 5, 1991 / Specialty ♦♦♦♦♦
Perhaps the greatest of Little Richard's greatest hits compilations, the 25-track *Georgia Peach* features all of his biggest hits in chronological order, as well as terrific singles that never were as big as "Tutti Frutti" and "Good Golly Miss Molly." On top of the sublime song selection and sound, the liner notes by compiler Billy Vera are splendid and insightful. *—Stephen Thomas Erlewine*

Shag on Down by the Union Hall / Feb. 13, 1996 / Specialty ♦♦♦♦♦
For those who want more classic Little Richard than a greatest-hits collection but aren't devoted enough to spring for the expensive box sets, this is an excellent anthology of 24 of his best lesser-known tracks. Most of it dates from his classic era at Specialty (1955-57), with alternate takes of a lot of his hits and some decent B-sides; there are also a few songs that he cut for the label during his 1964 comeback, including the minor hit "Bama Lama Bama Loo." *—Richie Unterberger*

Little River Band

f. Mar. 1975, Melbourne, Australia
Group / Pop/Rock, Soft Rock, Adult Contemporary
One of Australia's most prominent musical exports of the 1970s, the Little River Band shot to fame on the strength of their glowing harmonies and mellow country-pop sound. After signing to Capitol, they issued their self-titled 1975 debut, scoring a Top 30 U.S. hit with the single "It's a Long Way There." In the States, the next Little River Band release—titled *Diamantina Cocktail*—compiled material from their first two Australian LPs; it proved to be their commercial breakthrough, launching the single "Help Is On Its Way" into the Top 20. Over the next two years, the band scored four Top Ten hits—"Reminiscing," "Lady," "Lonesome Loser" and "Cool Change"—and earned platinum status with their fifth album, *First Under the Wire*. The legendary George Martin produced the Little River Band's next studio effort, 1981's *Time Exposure*, scoring another pair of Top Ten smashes with "Take It Easy on Me" and "Night Owls." Another single, "Man on Your Mind," was also a success. 1983's *The Net*, which failed to match the popularity of the albums which preceded it, however, although the group continued recording into the 1990s. *—Jason Ankeny*

Reminiscing: The 20th Anniversary Collection / 1995 / Rhino ♦♦♦♦

● **Greatest Hits [Expanded Edition]** / Jan. 25, 2000 / Capitol ♦♦♦♦♦
A group like Little River Band is the epitome of a fine singles act. They had two gold and two platinum album in its late-'70s, early-'80s prime, but it's no surprise that its biggest seller is 1982's double-platinum *Greatest Hits*. In 2000, a 24-bit digitally remastered expanded edition was released and it's simply excellent. It adds six songs to the original's dozen, and these include the rest of LRB's charted singles. The 2000 version polishes the Australian band's smooth, irresistibly catchy brand of pop/rock. The sound quality is crisp and clean. All the instruments jump out. LRB—which featured an unusual-for-pop three-guitar lineup—was kind of faceless, so its many personnel changes didn't necessarily alienate fans. Glenn Shorrock sang most of the signature hits like "Lonesome Loser," "Reminiscing," "Cool Change," "Help Is on Its Way," "Take It Easy on Me," "Man on Your Mind," and "Happy Anniversary." Bassist Wayne Nelson sang "The Night Owls," one of LRB's most rock-oriented numbers. All the previously mentioned songs are included, of course, but the newly added ones help provide a clearer picture of the band's career. The most notable were LRB's last two Top 40 hits, "We Two" and the funky, horns-based "Youre Driving Me Out of My Mind," both sung by Shorrock's replacement, John Farnham. Another Farnham track, "Playing to Win," is a surprising burst of hard rock with hyperactive synthesizer. The Shorrock-era extras are "I'll Always Call Your Name" and "It's Not a Wonder." The latter in particular is a welcome addition. 2000's *Greatest Hits*, which features a bare-bones essay by Simon Glickman, unquestionably supersedes its predecessor. It's a mid-line-priced gem for casual fans. Collectors should note that early copies of *Greatest Hits* mistakenly included alternate versions of some hits. *—Bret Adams*

Little Willie John (William Edgar John)

b. Nov. 15, 1937, Cullendale, AK, **d.** May 26, 1968, Walla Walla, WA
Vocals / R&B, Soul
He's never received the accolades given to the likes of Sam Cooke, Clyde McPhatter, and James Brown, but Little Willie John ranks as one of R&B's most influential performers. His muscular high timbre and enormous technical and emotional range belied his early age (his first hit came when he was 18), but his mid-'50s work for Syd Nathan's King label would play a great part in the way soul music would sound. Everyone from Cooke, McPhatter, and Brown to Jackie Wilson, B.B. King, and Al Green has acknowledged his debt to this most overlooked of rock and soul pioneers. His debut recording, a smoking version of Titus Turner's "All around the World" from 1955, set the pattern for a remarkable string of hits: "Need Your Love So Bad," "Suffering with the Blues," "Fever," "Let Them Talk," and his last, "Sleep," from 1961. His version of "Fever" was copied note for note by Peggy Lee and Elvis Presley, both of whom had bigger hits with it; John's version, however, remains definitive. His second hit, "Need Your Love So Bad," contains one of the most intimate, tear-jerking vocals ever caught on tape. *—John Floyd*

● **Fever: The Best of Little Willie John** / Nov. 16, 1993 / Rhino ♦♦♦♦♦
Little Willie John had a commanding delivery, remarkable projection and a charismatic sound that was both instantly recognizable and unforgettable. His magical singles are all contained on this superb 20-track anthology, arguably the best single-disc set of John material available. It includes his best-known song, "Fever" (Peggy Lee's cover version became a huge smash), plus such marvelous numbers such as "Home at Last," "Heartbreak (It's Hurtin' Me)" and "You Hurt Me." While John was a dynamic heartache wailer, he could also do excellent dance/novelty and double-entendre tunes such as "Let's Rock While the Rockin's Good" and "Leave My Kitten Alone." This anthology demonstrates why he's still held in such high regard throughout the world of R&B and soul. *—Ron Wynn*

Live

f. 1988, York, PA
Group / Post-Grunge, Alternative Pop/Rock
Live rose to chart success on the strength of its anthemic music and idealistic, overtly spiritual songwriting, two hallmarks which earned the group frequent comparisons to U2. The fledgling group played under a series of names before settling on Public Affection. After earning a rabid local following, in 1989 Public Affection released a cassette, *The Death of a Dictionary*, on their own Action Front label. Before drawing their new name out of a hat, Live recruited Talking Head Jerry Harrison to produce their 1991 debut, *Mental Jewelry*. A collection of songs based on the writings of Indian philosopher Jiddu Krishnamurti, the record made Live one of the key players in the post-Nirvana alternative music scene thanks to singles like "Operation Spirit (The Tyranny of Tradition)" and "Pain Lies on the Riverside." Three years later, Live returned with the muscular *Throwing Copper*, which lingered a number of months on the charts before pushing the group into the rock mainstream; after a series of popular singles like "Selling the Drama" and "I Alone," the album's slow build climaxed with the funereal "Lightning Crashes," which propelled the album to the top of the charts and paved the way for the hits "White, Discussion" and "All Over You." *—Jason Ankeny*

Mental Jewelry / Dec. 31, 1991 / Radioactive ♦♦♦♦
Live's debut album was an impressive set of righteous, hard-driving alternative rock; *Mental Jewelry* was in the vein of such college-radio favorites as U2, but was more vulnerable and less sanctimonious. *—Stephen Thomas Erlewine*

● **Throwing Copper** / Apr. 19, 1994 / Radioactive ♦♦♦♦
Not only did Live's songwriting improve on their second album, *Throwing Copper*, but their sound was much stronger; their hooks were powerful and memorable, and their melodies were carefully crafted and catchy. The result was a major crossover hit, thanks to the singles "Selling the Drama," "I Alone," and "Lightning Crashes." *—Stephen Thomas Erlewine*

Secret Samadhi / Feb. 18, 1997 / Radioactive ♦♦♦

The Distance to Here / Oct. 5, 1999 / Radioactive ♦♦♦

The Lively Ones

f. 1963
Group / Surf
One of the best of the many instrumental surf bands working the Southern Californian region in 1963, the Lively Ones' recordings were built around storming, reverb-drenched Fender guitars, embellished by occasional raunchy sax breaks. Originality was not the Lively Ones' forte: over a period of about 12 months, they ground out about five albums, filled out with many covers or retitled numbers based on other rock and R&B compositions. They had a couple of hits in the L.A. area in 1963 ("Surf Rider" and "Rik-A-Tik"), but their best moment was probably "Goofy Foot," whose staccato gunfire of riffs deservedly propelled the track onto several modern best-of-surf anthologies. They ranged far and wide for source material, giving the surf treatment to "Telstar," "Exodus," "Rawhide," and Cole Porter's "Night and Day." Even the overdone standards are arranged and executed with panache. One best-of compilation is all you need, but anyone who likes Dick Dale will dig the Lively Ones' similar sleek arrangements and prototypically twangy, classy surf guitar leads. *—Richie Unterberger*

● **Hang Five!!! The Best of the Livelys** / Jan. 17, 1995 / Del-Fi ♦♦♦♦♦
A well-chosen 24-song retrospective, with six pages of informative liner notes by surf authority Domenic Priore. Includes "Goofy Foot," "Surf Rider," "Rik-A-Tik," and lots of other highlights from their Del-Fi releases, as well as a rare single they did for Smash. *—Richie Unterberger*

Loggins & Messina

f. 1970, California, **db.** Jul. 1976
Group / Pop/Rock, Folk-Rock, Soft Rock
Kenny Loggins and Jim Messina were the most successful pop/rock duo of the first half of the '70s. Loggins was a staff songwriter who had recently enjoyed success with a group of songs recorded by the Nitty Gritty Dirt Band when he came to the attention of Messina, a record producer and former member of Buffalo Springfield and Poco. Messina agreed to produce Loggins' first album, but somewhere along the way it became a duo effort that was released in 1972 under the title *Kenny Loggins with Jim Messina Sittin' In*. The album was a gold-seller that stayed in the charts more than two years.

In the next four years, Loggins & Messina released a series of gold or platinum albums, most of which hit the Top Ten. They were all played in a buoyant country-rock style with an accomplished band. *Loggins & Messina* (1972) featured the retro-rock hit "Your Mama Don't Dance." *Full Sail* (1973), *On Stage* (a double live album, 1974), and *Mother Lode* (1974) all hit the Top Ten. *So Fine* was an album of '50s cover songs. The pair's last new studio album, *Native Sons*, came out at the start of 1976.

Loggins & Messina split for two solo careers by the end of that year, their catalog completed by a greatest-hits album, *Best of Friends*, and a live record, *Finale*. *—William Ruhlmann*

Sittin' In / Jan. 1972 / Columbia ♦♦♦♦♦
This debut album was credited to "Kenny Loggins with Jim Messina" because the project had begun as a solo record by Loggins being produced by Messina. By the time it was finished, however, Messina had written or co-written six of the 11 songs, contributed "first guitar," and shared lead vocals on many tracks. Messina's "Nobody but You" and "Vahevala," co-written by Loggins' brother Dave, were the singles chart entries, but today everybody remembers the album for Loggins' "House at Pooh Corner," which had earned Loggins his record con-

tract, and "Danny's Song," which Anne Murray took into the Top Ten the following year. The only thing wrong with this record is that it was too perfect—with their infectious blend of country, folk, rock and Caribbean music, L&M started out at the top of their game, and although they were able to match some of the material and performances on later records, the team never got any better than this. *— William Ruhlmann*

Loggins & Messina / Oct. 1972 / Columbia ✦✦✦✦✦
The first full-fledged L&M album found the duo in good form as songwriters, with Messina turning in the sparkling "Thinking Of You" and the two collaborating on the hit single "Your Mama Don't Dance" and "Angry Eyes." Their backup band was anchored by multi-instrumentalist Al Garth and also featured keyboardist Michael Omartian and Poco steel guitarist Rusty Young. *— William Ruhlmann*

Full Sail / Oct. 1973 / Columbia ✦✦✦
This is every inch a followup to *Loggins And Messina*, including a '50s rock & roll pastiche in the style of "Your Mama Don't Dance" called "My Music" that hit number 16 as a single. Other notable material included Messina's island-rock anthem "Lahaina" and one of Loggins' sensitive-but-generic ballads, typically called "A Love Song." But then, the charm of L&M was that they could get away with something this sappy. Balance is the key to L&M albums, and it's the chief talent (among many) that producer Messina brings to them. Here, as on *L&M's* first two albums, he achieves a musical flow that's exhilarating, and the record is only denied a "finest" rating because the quality of the songwriting doesn't quite match those LPs. *— William Ruhlmann*

On Stage / Apr. 1974 / Columbia/Legacy ✦✦✦

Mother Lode / Oct. 1974 / Columbia ✦✦✦

Native Sons / Jan. 1976 / Columbia ✦✦✦

● **The Best of Friends** / Nov. 1976 / Columbia ✦✦✦✦✦

Finale / 1977 / Columbia ✦

Kenny Loggins

b. Jan. 7, 1948, Everette, WA
Vocals, Keyboards, Guitar / Pop/Rock, Soft Rock
Singer, songwriter, and guitarist Kenny Loggins was born in Everett, WA, and moved to Los Angeles in his teens. He got a job as a staff writer and wrote four songs used on a Nitty Gritty Dirt Band album in 1970, among them the hit "House at Pooh Corner." This brought him to the attention of former Poco member Jim Messina, now a staff producer at CBS, who intended to produce Loggins' debut album. The two ended up in a duo, however, and Loggins & Messina made a series of successful albums during the '70s.

Loggins & Messina broke up in 1976, and Loggins went on to solo stardom with such million-selling albums as *Celebrate Me Home, Nightwatch* (which included the hit "Whenever I Call You Friend"), and *Keep the Fire*, all in the cheerful, sensitive style he had displayed in Loggins & Messina. Loggins also became known as the king of the movie soundtrack song, scoring Top Ten hits with "I'm Alright" (from *Caddyshack*), "Footloose" (from *Footloose*), "Danger Zone" (from *Top Gun*), and "Nobody's Fool" (from *Caddyshack II*). His own albums sold less well (and came less frequently) throughout the '80s, with later efforts like 1991's *Leap of Faith*, 1997's *The Unimaginable Life* and 1998's *December* finding favor primarily in adult contemporary circles; in 1994, he also issued a children's album, *Return to Pooh Corner*, releasing its sequel *More Songs from Pooh Corner* in early 2000. *— William Ruhlmann*

● **Yesterday, Today, Tomorrow: The Greatest Hits** / Mar. 25, 1997 / Columbia ✦✦✦✦✦
Yesterday Today Tomorrow compiles Loggins' biggest solo hits, including the chart-topping "Footloose" theme, "Danger Zone" (from *Top Gun*) and "I'm Alright" (from the classic *Caddyshack*), along with the newly recorded single "For the First Time." *—Jason Ankeny*

The Long Ryders

f. 1981, **db.** 1987
Group / College Rock, Jangle Pop, Paisley Underground, Roots Rock
Although they played the same clubs as most of Los Angeles' "paisley underground" bands (i.e., Dream Syndicate, Rain Parade) and even featured Dream Syndicate leader Steve Wynn in an early lineup, the Long Ryders were actually more a roots-rock group strongly influenced by Gram Parsons. The group was founded by Kentucky native Sid Griffin, a Parsons devotee who moved to Los Angeles after hearing about that city's punk scene, with guitarist Stephen McCarthy, the only two members to remain throughout the group's tenure. The group's first rhythm section featured bassist Barry Shank and drummer Matt Roberts; they, along with Griffin, had previously been members of the Unclaimed. The band's 1983 debut EP, *10-5-60*, was a blend of punk attitude,'60s rock, and traditional country (Griffin played steel guitar, autoharp, and mandolin). Their first full-length album, the following year's *Native Sons*, was also arguably their best, and featured guest vocals from former Byrd Gene Clark. Subsequent albums failed to find an audience, and unhappy with their label's promotional efforts but unable to secure a release from their contract, the Long Ryders called it quits in 1987. McCarthy formed Gutterball and, along with Griffin, contributed to the 1993 Gram Parsons tribute album *Commemorativo*. Griffin, meanwhile, moved to London and formed the Coal Porters; today he works as a music critic and writer, foreshadowed by his definitive 1985 biography of (who else—) Gram Parsons. *— Steve Huey*

Native Sons / 1984 / Frontier ✦✦✦✦✦
Native Sons was the first full-length album by the Long Ryders and the one that established their eclectic mixture of Byrds/Clash/Flying Burrito Brothers' influences. The band wore those influences on their sleeve, literally, going so far as to recreate the cover of an unreleased Buffalo Springfield album, *Stampede*, for *Native Sons* and using the producer of the first two Flying Burrito Brothers albums, Henry Lewy. *Native Sons* lovingly captures the band's musical obsessions, while turning in an original sound that became the banner for both the paisley underground and cow punk styles in the mid-'80s. Highlights include several forays into country on "Final Wild Son," the Mel Tillis composition "Sweet Mental Revenge," "Fair Game," and the humorous "Never Got to Meet the Mom," complete with a raging down-home banjo break. "Ivory Tower," featuring the late ex-Byrd Gene Clark on vocals, remains the greatest song the Byrds never wrote and one of the most sincere tributes to that band's sound. The album's final track, "I Had a Dream," reveals the punk sensibility, cranking the jangling Rickenbackers up to ten, closing with cacophonous feedback. On *Native Sons*, the Long Ryders pioneered a musical design that future alternative roots rockers would use as a manual. *Native Sons* has been reissued on CD with the Long Ryders' initial EP, *10-5-60*. *— Al Campbell*

The State of Our Union / 1985 / Prima ✦✦✦✦

Two Fisted Tales / 1987 / Prima ✦✦✦

● **Looking for Lewis & Clark: Anthology** / Jul. 21, 1998 / Polygram ✦✦✦✦
The Long Ryders were one of the greatest bands to come out of L.A. during the 1980s. The band combined rootsy influences such as Gram Parsons and Buffalo Springfield with an unlikely punk sensibility. They were refreshing, they cared about the songwriting, and they could rock. Coming from the long-lamented Paisley Underground scene, which included such bands as The Dream Syndicate, the Bangles and Rain Parade, the Ryders were easily the tightest, and well-deserving of their major record label deal with Island Records, following their brilliant debut for Frontier in 1984. Polygram Chronicles has neatly compiled all the above material, plus the early *10-5-60* EP, and loads of rare and unreleased tracks on *The Long Ryders Anthology*. It's an excellent collection from one of the most honest and genuinely gifted bands of the period. Tracks such as Ryders founder Sid Griffin's "Final Wild Son" and bassist Tom Stephens' "Years Long Ago" capture the essence of the band, which can almost be compared to a meeting of The Flying Burrito Brothers, Neil Young, and The Sex Pistols. Lead guitarist Stephen McCarthy's material has probably aged the best, with such polished tracks as "I Had a Dream" (one of the band's finest) and "Mason-Dixon Line" leaving you to wonder why we haven't heard a solo album from him. Individual praise, however, is not what The Long Ryders were about. They were a great *band*, and should be remembered as such. *The Long Ryders Anthology* accomplishes just that. *— Matt Greenwald*

Los Lobos

f. 1973, East Los Angeles, CA
Group / College Rock, Heartland Rock, American Trad Rock, Americana, Adult Alternative Pop/Rock, Roots Rock, Tex-Mex
Los Lobos were one of America's most distinctive and original bands of the '80s. They may have had a hit with "La Bamba" in 1987, yet that cover barely scratches the surface of their talents. Los Lobos are eclectic in the best sense of the word. While they draw equally from rock, Tex-Mex, country, folk, R&B, blues, and traditional Spanish and Mexican music, their music never sounds forced or self-consicious. Instead, all of their influences became one graceful, gritty sound. From their very first recordings their rich musicality was apparent; on nearly every subsequent record they have found ways to redefine and expand their sound, without ever straying from the musical traditions that form the heart and soul of the band. *— Stephen Thomas Erlewine*

. . . And a Time to Dance / 1983 / Slash ✦✦✦
Only seven songs but they're a perfect summation of what the band does and why it's important. This perfectly seamless fusion of Tex-Mex, R&B, and rock & roll has powerhouse covers of the Ritchie Valens hit "Come on, Let's Go" and the norteño classic "A Te Dejo en San Antonio" thrown in for good measure. *— Kit Kiefer*

How Will the Wolf Survive— / 1984 / Slash/Warner Brothers ✦✦✦✦✦
A broader spectrum of music without a measure of the all-out joy of *. . . And a Time to Dance, How Will the Wolf Survive?* features at least two raveup rockers ("Don't Worry Baby" and "I Got Loaded"), an irresistible shuffle ("Evangeline"), two traditional Mexican numbers ("Seranata Norteña" and "Corrida #1") and a stirring title tune. The album is well rounded and fully realized. *— Kit Kiefer*

By the Light of the Moon / 1987 / Slash/Warner Brothers ✦✦✦✦

La Bamba [Original Soundtrack] / Jun. 1987 / Slash/Warner Brothers ✦✦✦

La Pistola y El Corazon / Sep. 1988 / Slash/Warner Brothers ✦✦✦
Los Lobos used the commercial breakthrough represented by *La Bamba* to turn to its first love, Mexican folk music, and recorded this excellent collection of norteño songs. If this is a band that seems to do too many things well, in a sense they are at their best when they narrow their focus, and they are certainly masters of their style here. *— William Ruhlmann*

The Neighborhood / Aug. 1990 / Slash/Warner Brothers ✦✦✦✦
Recharged by their set of Mexican music, Los Lobos return with arguably their finest straight rock & roll record. *The Neighborhood* effortlessly combines rock, R&B, blues, and country into a singular, powerful sound that manages to be as darkly funky as "I Walk Alone" and "Georgia Slop" and as gently moving as "Emily." *— Stephen Thomas Erlewine*

Kiko / May 1992 / Slash/Warner Brothers ✦✦✦✦
With its highly textured layers of sound, *Kiko* sounds like nothing else Los Lobos has done. Although their sound is still based in roots music of all kinds (rock, folk, Mexican, country), the band has shaped it into a dense, impressionistic wall of sound that intensifies the emotions behind such carefully constructed and moving songs as "Two Janes," "Angels with Dirty Faces," and "Kiko and the Lavender Moon." It's certainly their most ambitious album, and it's arguably their best. *— Stephen Thomas Erlewine*

● **Just Another Band from East L.A.: A Collection** / Aug. 31, 1993 / Warner Brothers ✦✦✦✦✦
Just Another Band from East L.A.: A Collection is a splendid double-disc collection that draws an accurate picture of Los Lobos, one of the most musically versatile bands of the 1980s. Featuring all of the band's hits and best-known songs, as well as several rare and previously unreleased tracks, there isn't a weak spot among the compilation's forty-one songs. *— Stephen Thomas Erlewine*

Colossal Head / Mar. 19, 1996 / Warner Brothers ✦✦✦

This Time / Jul. 20, 1999 / Hollywood ✦✦✦

Del Este de Los Angeles / Sep. 12, 2000 / Hollywood ✦✦✦

El Cancionero: Mas y Mas / Nov. 7, 2000 / Rhino/Warner Archives ✦✦✦✦✦
A multi-disc, authoritative box set usually arrives toward the end of an artist's career, which is what made the appearance of Los Lobos' four-disc retrospective *El Cancionero: Mas Y Mas* in 2000 a little surprising. They weren't selling as many records, nor were they quite as hip as they were ten years earlier, yet they retained a devoted cult and critical following—they were still in the prime of their career, not ready to be enshrined. Fortunately, the band and Rhino went ahead and assembled a box, which winds up capturing a band at the height of its powers. The set smartly spends a lot of time on side projects, including the Latin Playboys, Los Super Seven, Houndog, and selections from Cesar Rosas' solo album, plus a healthy number of live songs, B-sides, tribute album tracks, and 11 previously unreleased tracks. These tracks deepen the already rich musical tapestry Los Lobos weaves, and the end result is pretty impressive. As the set winds from the authentic Mexican folk music of 1977 through the gutsy roots rock of 1987 and the dreamy soundscapes of 1992 to the daring music of the mid-'90s and then the consolidation of their strengths on 1999's *This Time*, it's hard not to be astonished not just by the band's range, but the fact that they do it all really well. This is the definitive portrait of Los Lobos, highlighting everything that they can do and containing almost all of their greatest songs; this is one of the rare times that a four-disc box set summarizes all of an artist's strengths, while telling a great musical story, as well. *—Stephen Thomas Erlewine*

Love

f. 1965, Los Angeles, CA, **db.** 1974
Group / Baroque Pop, Folk-Rock, Garage Rock, Psychedelic
One of the best West Coast folk-rock/psychedelic bands, Love may have also been the first widely acclaimed cult/underground group. During their brief heyday—lasting all of three albums—they drew from Byrdsish folk-rock, Stonesish hard rock, blues, jazz, flamenco, and even light orchestral pop to create a heady stew of their own. They were also one of the first integrated rock groups, led by genius singer/songwriter Arthur Lee, one of the most idiosyncratic and enigmatic talents of the 1960s. Stars in their native Los Angeles, and an early inspiration to the Doors, they perversely refused to tour until well past their peak. This ensured their failure to land a hit single or album, though in truth the band's vision may have been too elusive to attract mass success anyway. Their self-titled debut album (1966) introduced their marriage of the Byrds and the Stones on a set of mostly original material, and contained a small hit, their punkish adaptation of Bacharach-David's "My Little Red Book." 1967's *Da Capo* included their only Top 40 hit, the corkscrew-tempoed "7 and 7 Is." The first side was psychedelia at its best, with an eclectic palette encompassing furious jazz structures, gentle Spanish guitar interludes, and beautiful baroque pop with dream-like images ("She Comes in Colors"). It was also psychedelia at its most reckless, with the whole of side two taken up by a meandering 19-minute jam. One of the finest rock albums of all time, *Forever Changes* was an exceptionally strong set of material graced by captivating lyrics and glistening, unobtrusive horn and string arrangements; it was not a commercial hit in the U.S. (though it did pretty well in Britain), but remains an all-time favorite of many critics. *—Richie Unterberger*

Love / 1966 / Elektra ✦✦✦✦✦
Their debut is both their hardest-rocking early album, and their most Byrds-influenced. Lee's songwriting muse hadn't fully developed at this stage, and in comparison with their second and third efforts, this is the least striking of the LPs featuring their classic lineup, with some similar-sounding folk-rock compositions and stock riffs. A few of the tracks are great, though: their punky rendition of Bacharach/David's "My Little Red Book" was a minor hit, "Signed D.C." and "Mushroom Clouds" were superbly moody ballads, and Bryan Maclean's "Softly to Me" served notice that Lee wasn't the only songwriter of note in the band. *—Richie Unterberger*

☆ **Da Capo** / 1967 / Elektra ✦✦✦✦✦
Love broadened their scope into psychedelia on their sophomore effort, Lee's achingly melodic songwriting gifts reaching full flower. The six songs that comprised the first side of this album when it was first issued are a truly classic body of work, highlighted by the atomic blast of pre-punk rock "7 and 7 Is" (their only hit single), the manic jazz tempos of "Stephanie Knows Who," and the enchanting "She Comes in Colors," perhaps Lee's best composition (and reportedly the inspiration for the Rolling Stones' "She's a Rainbow"). It's only half a great album, though; the seventh and final track, "Revelation," is a tedious 19-minute jam which keeps *Da Capo* from attaining truly classic status. *—Richie Unterberger*

★ **Forever Changes** / 1967 / Elektra ✦✦✦✦✦
It wasn't a hit, but *Forever Changes* continues to regularly appear on critics' lists of the top ten rock albums of all time, and it had an enormously far-reaching and durable influence that went way beyond chart listings. The best fusion of folk-rock and psychedelia, it features Lee's trembling vocals, beautiful melodies, haunting orchestral arrangements, and inscrutable but poetic lyrics, all of which sound nearly as fresh and intriguing upon repeated plays. One of rock's most organic, flowing masterpieces, every song has a lingering, shimmering beauty, including the two penned by the band's other talented songwriter/guitarist/singer, Bryan MacLean. [A 2001 expanded CD reissue on Rhino/Elektra adds lengthy historical liner notes and seven bonus tracks: the 1968 single "Your Mind and We Belong Together"/"Laughing Stock," the genuine *Forever Changes* outtake "Wonder People (I Do Wonder)," the demo "Hummingbirds" (essentially an instrumental version of "The Good Humor Man He Sees Everything Like This"), and alternate mixes of "Alone Again Or" and "You Set the Scene."] *—Richie Unterberger*

Four Sail / 1969 / Elektra ✦✦✦

Out Here / 1969 / One Way ✦✦

False Start / 1970 / One Way ✦✦

★ **Love Story 1966-1972** / 1995 / Rhino/Elektra Traditions ✦✦✦✦✦
Double-CD box contains most of their classic first three albums (including the entirety of *Forever Changes*), all three non-LP tracks from their 1966-68 prime, and highlights of the post-Bryan Maclean albums from the late '60s and early '70s. Great booklet of liner notes and photos, but considering that all of those first three albums remain easy to find, and that the post-*Forever Changes* material is much inferior to the early recordings, it's not an essential purchase. The absence of "Revelation" from *Da Capo* is no big deal, but a few tracks from the debut are missing, including one of the better ones, "Mushroom Clouds." *—Richie Unterberger*

Love and Rockets

f. 1984, **db.** Apr. 29, 1999
Group / College Rock, Goth Rock, Alternative Pop/Rock
Love & Rockets comprised guitarist/vocalist Daniel Ash, bassist/vocalist David J, and drummer Kevin Haskins, all former members of the pioneering goth band Bauhaus. However, the group didn't sound very similar to their first group. Instead, Love & Rockets emphasized the strains of psychedelia and glam rock that appeared underneath Bauhaus' gloomy drone, adding elements of pop songcraft, folk and R&B, as well as cryptic, self-important lyrics. For most of the late '80s, the group had a devoted cult following, resulting in a surprise Top Ten hit single, "So Alive," in 1989. During the early '90s, the group's audience steadily declined, although they still retained a number of loyal fans. *—Stephen Thomas Erlewine*

Seventh Dream of Teenage Heaven / 1985 / Beggars Banquet/RCA ✦✦✦
From behind the black shrouds and smoky din of Bauhaus—very much in contrast to their dark, gothic angst, very much like a nighttime liftoff—arises Love and Rockets. Their debut *Seventh Dream of Teenage Heaven*, a vast divergence from the Bauhaus sound, is marked by an ethereal quality, as much by the transcendental lyrics as the richly layered depth of the production: the atmosphere is one of reflection, yet all the while remaining enlightened, without the somber negativity often induced by such a journey into the mind. The title track sounds like a hot night under blue neon, and is totally addicting, as are many of the tracks; perhaps the most distinctive is the instrumental "Saudade," remarkable in its almost pastoral beauty. Another track, "Haunted When the Minutes Drag," starts deep in a funk, with overwhelming vocals pulling you into the song, yet shifts subtly to a feel of self-affirmation. Symbolizing the band's transition from gothic negativity to fields of thought and light, this is truly an album to attach memories to. *—Bob Sakomano*

● **Earth, Sun, Moon** / 1987 / Beggars Banquet/Big Time ✦✦✦✦✦
Earth, Sun, Moon reins in the rampant excesses of *Express* while remaining psychedelic; the near-white-out of the cover gives a clue to the music, as many of the songs emerge from a soup of white-noise guitar distortion. Much of the record addresses, in their nebulous fashion, hope and disappointment; the title track and "Youth" are two of their most simple, yet most affecting, songs. Not a "normal" pop record by any means, it is more straight-ahead than their previous work and includes the upbeat single "No New Tale to Tell," a college radio hit which set the stage for their popular breakthrough a year later. *—Jonathan Ball*

Love and Rockets / Apr. 1989 / Beggars Banquet/RCA ✦✦✦
As the band's breakthrough record in the U.S., riding high on the left-field success of the slinky T. Rex homage "So Alive," this album still divides the band's fans to the present. Charges of sell-out are incredibly curious, because aside from "So Alive," absolutely nothing here sounds like it would have gotten anywhere on the airwaves. While Ash and David J were clearly dividing their songwriting efforts, resulting in a rather schizophrenic album, what they were writing and performing were some of the best songs of their collected careers. David J gets to indulge rock & roll and blues traditionalism on a number of his tracks, beginning with the opening "**** (Jungle Law)," a radical reworking of the old "Signifying Monkey" standard with compressed production and an almost industrial beat from Haskins. Another redone oldie is "Bound for Hell," a tale of the Devil driving a train to down below; David J runs his vocals through crackly distortion, playing harmonica while Ash plays a huge, thrashy guitar line. Perhaps his best number is his most atypical: "Rock and Roll Babylon," a barbed study of fame with Ash's sax and a string quartet fleshing out the sound beautifully. Ash's songs do some roots revisiting as well, in their own ways. "No Big Deal" and especially "Motorcycle" show that the man's been listening to some Jesus and Mary Chain, but his wonderful vocal purr marks them as his own songs. An unexpected addition to everything is "The Purest Blue," a radical reworking of *Earth Sun Moon*'s "Waiting for the Flood" which leaves almost nothing of the original. *—Ned Raggett*

Hot Trip to Heaven / Sep. 27, 1994 / American ✦✦

Sweet F.A. / Mar. 19, 1996 / American ✦✦

Lift / Oct. 13, 1998 / Red Ant ✦✦✦

Loverboy

f. 1978, Vancouver, British Columbia, Canada
Group / Album Rock, Arena Rock, Pop/Rock, Hard Rock
With a string of three multi-platinum albums, Loverboy was one of the most successful mainstream hard rock groups of the early '80s. The band formed in Toronto, Canada, in 1980 and immediately signed with CBS Records. Later that year, their Bruce Fairbairn-produced debut album appeared. Featuring the slick, hard-rocking singles "Turn Me Loose" and "The Kid Is Hot Tonite," the album went platinum in both Canada and America. Loverboy recorded the follow-up, *Get Lucky*, in 1981. Driven by the anthemic "Working for the Weekend," the Fairbairn-produced record was a major success in the U.S. and Canada, yet it failed to gain an audience anywhere in Europe. Nevertheless, the band was a staple on AOR stations across North America, as well as a popular concert attraction. The band's good fortunes continued with the 1983 album *Keep It Up*. Again, Loverboy worked with Fairbairn, who kept their melodic yet tough sound intact; the album featured the hit single "Hot Girls In Love." Loverboy's fortunes began to slip with 1985's *Lovin' Every Minute of It*—producer Tom Allom gave the band a harder edge which didn't prove as commercially successful as their past records. *—Stephen Thomas Erlewine*

Big Ones / Oct. 1989 / Columbia ✦✦✦✦
Released the year that Loverboy decided to go their separate ways, *Big Ones* is about as thor-

ough a hits compilation as one could expect from the group. There are a few singles missing—like "Queen of the Broken Hearts," "Dangerous" and "Lead a Double Life," as well as Mike Reno's duet with Ann Wilson, "Almost Paradise"—but the core hits are all here: "Turn Me Loose," "The Kid Is Hot Tonite," "Working for the Weekend," "When It's Over," "Hot Girls in Love," "Lovin' Every Minute of It," "This Could Be the Night," "Heaven in Your Eyes," "Notorious." Even though the subsequent *Loverboy Classics* covered more ground, *Big Ones* is a good, basic collection, ideal for any fan of the group. *—Stephen Thomas Erlewine*

● **Loverboy Classics: Their Greatest Hits** / Oct. 11, 1994 / Columbia ✦✦✦✦✦

Lyle Lovett

b. Nov. 1, 1957, Klein, TX

Vocals, Guitar / Alternative Country, Singer/Songwriter

Lyle Lovett was one of the most distincitve and original singer/songwriters to emerge during the '80s. Though he was initially labeled as a country singer, the tag never quite fit him. Lovett had more in common with '70s singer/songwriters like Guy Clark, Jesse Winchester, Randy Newman and Townes Van Zandt, combining a talent for incisive, witty lyrical detail with an eclectic array of music, ranging from country and folk to big-band swing and traditional pop. Lovett's literate, multi-layered songs stood out among the formulaic Nashville hit singles of the late '80s, as well as the new traditionatlists that were beginning to take over country music. Drawing from alternative country and rock fans, Lovett quickly built up a cult following which began to spill over into the mainstream with his second album, 1988's *Pontiac*. Following *Pontiac*, his country audience declined but his reputation as a songwriter and musician continued to grow, and he sustained a dedicated cult following well into the '90s. *—Stephen Thomas Erlewine*

Lyle Lovett / 1986 / Curb ✦✦✦✦✦

With his eponymously-titled debut LP, Lyle Lovett quickly established himself as the quirkiest, most gifted songwriter to emerge from Nashville in ages; like Steve Earle and Dwight Yoakam, who also issued debuts the same year, his music reflects a remarkably personal and unique vision—a breath of fresh air after so many years of cookie-cutter country-pop. Even from the outset, Lovett owes more to the likes of storytellers like Randy Newman and Tom Waits than to any of his country contemporaries; his songs are too wryly subversive and iconoclastic to fit within the Nashville straitjacket, whether acutely mocking stereotypes on "Cowboy Man," subverting cliches on "God Will" or delivering painterly narratives like "This Old Porch." More than simply a gifted lyricist, he's also a melodic, inventive and highly adaptable composer: "Closing Time" is a stately piano ballad, "You Can't Resist It" approaches anthemic rock territory, and the deliciously morbid "An Acceptable Level of Ecstasy (The Wedding Song)" introduces the rich, bluesy sound he would continue to explore in greater depth on subsequent outings. An outstanding debut. *—Jason Ankeny*

★ **Pontiac** / 1987 / Curb ✦✦✦✦✦

Greatly expanding upon the seemingly unlimited promise of his self-titled debut, Lyle Lovett returns with the exemplary *Pontiac*, which finds him sharpening his renowned songwriting skills while moving further away from traditional country without a single misstep. Opening with the arch "If I Had a Boat," Lovett proceeds to subvert the Nashville formula at every turn, next delivering "Give Back My Heart," a not-so-subtle dig at country's key demographic, and "L.A. County," awhich twists the classic revenge song to its ultimate extreme; in between he delivers a pair of stunning love songs, "I Loved You Yesterday" and the elegaic "Walk Through the Bottomland," athe latter adorned by haunting vocal support from Emmylou Harris. Still, it's the second half of *Pontiac* where Lovett really spreads his wings, rejecting Nashville conventions to move headlong into jazz and blues territory: tipping his hand with the wonderfully snarky "She's No Lady," ahe quickly asserts himself as a jack of all musical trades, capable of mastering big band workouts like the slinky "Black and Blue" as well as beautifully mournful ballads like "Simple Song," *Pontiac*'s centerpiece and arguably Lovett's finest moment to date. *—Jason Ankeny*

Lyle Lovett & His Large Band / 1989 / Curb ✦✦✦✦✦

Lyle Lovett's excellent third album is his kiss-off to Nashville; here, for the last time, he compartmentalizes his music according to genre—country and non-country, essentially, although the lines are occasionally as blurred as the cover photo. Where on the previous *Pontiac* Lovett stuck all of his non-country material on the record's second half, here—clearly bristling from Nashville pigeonholing—he opens with a horn-powered instrumental, "The Blues Walk," before sliding into the absurdist narrative deadpan of "Here I Am;" as indicated by the title, big-band jazz is a crucial element of his ever-developing sound, as is his vocal interplay with the soulful Francine Reed, culminating in the wonderfully sassy duet "What Do You Do/The Glory of Love." Even when *Lyle Lovett and His Large Band* does turn its focus to country, the results are anything but ordinary, including a straightforward, albeit transgender, cover of the perennial "Stand by Your Man" as well as the haunting "Nobody Loves Me," one of the most deceptively simple and devastating cheating songs ever written. *—Jason Ankeny*

Joshua Judges Ruth / Mar. 31, 1992 / Curb ✦✦✦

Lyle Lovett goes folk-gospel. To be fair, the country tag was never a comfortable fit for Lovett's eclectic musings. *Joshua Judges Ruth* distances him from the category without firmly boxing him into any new ones. There is a southern-fried gospel feel throughout much of the album, even if it's sometimes irreverent. "Church" best displays Lovett's surreal, dry wit, recounting a hunger-driven church rebellion complete with full gospel backing vocals. "She's Leaving Me," featuring guest vocals from Emmylou Harris, is the one sop offered to traditional country. Overall, though, the mood is somber bordering on bleak. Like the album cover and insert photos, *Joshua* deals in shades of gray and themes of loneliness and death. What one misses the most on this release is the infrequent surfacing of Lovett's weird, playful sense of humor. *—Roch Parisien*

I Love Everybody / Sep. 27, 1994 / Curb ✦✦✦✦

A collection of odds and ends that Lyle Lovett has written over the years (some of the tunes date back to the late '70s), *I Love Everybody* doesn't have the self-conscious artistic importance of *Joshua Judges Ruth*, and it's all the better for it. Instead, Lovett offers a set of relaxed, casual songs, accentuating his infamous, off-kilter sense of humor ("Skinny Legs," "Penguins"). At the same time, the songs offer hints of Lovett's sly, subtle sense of menace, particularly "Creeps Like Me." *—Stephen Thomas Erlewine*

Road to Ensenada / Jun. 18, 1996 / Curb ✦✦✦✦✦

Since *Pontiac*, Lyle Lovett has been experimenting with different sounds, whether it was the big band posturing of *His Large Band*, the gospel overtones of *Joshua Judges Ruth*, or the '70s singer/songwriter flourishes of *I Love Everybody*. With *The Road to Ensenada*, he hunkers down and produces his most straight forward album since *Pontiac*. As it happens, it is also his best record since that breakthrough album. Lovett strips the sound of the album down to the bare country essentials, allowing it to drift into western swing, country-rock, folk and honky tonk when necessary. He also decides to balance his weightier material ("Private Conversation," "Who Loves You Better," "It Ought to Be Easier," "I Can't Love You Anymore," "Christmas Morning") with fun, light-hearted numbers like "Don't Touch My Hat," "Fiona," and "That's Right (You're Not from Texas)," which are funny without being silly. In fact, *The Road to Ensenada* is the lightest album Lyle Lovett has ever made—the darkness that hung around the fringes of *Pontiac*, *Joshua Judges Ruth*, and *I Love Everybody* has drifted away, leaving his wry sense of humor and a newly found empathetic sentimentality. The combination of straight forward instrumentation and lean, catchy and incisive songwriting results in one of the best albums of his career—he's just as eclectic and off-handedly brilliant as he always been, but on *The Road to Ensenada* he's more focused and less flashy about his own talent than he's ever been. *—Stephen Thomas Erlewine*

Step Inside This House / Sep. 22, 1998 / MCA ✦✦✦

Live in Texas / Jun. 29, 1999 / MCA ✦✦✦✦

The Lovin' Spoonful

f. 1965, New York, NY, **db.** 1968

Group / Folk-Rock, Pop

Right on the tails of the Beau Brummels and the Byrds, the Lovin' Spoonful were among the first American groups to challenge the domination of the British Invasion bands in the mid-'60s. Between mid-1965 and the end of 1967, the group was astonishingly successful, issuing one classic hit single after another, including "Do You Believe in Magic?," "You Didn't Have to Be So Nice," "Daydream" and "Summer in the City." Like most of the folk-rockers, the Lovin' Spoonful were more pop and rock than folk, which didn't detract from their music at all. Much more than the Byrds, and even more than the Mamas & the Papas, the group exhibited a brand of unabashedly melodic, cheery, and good-time music, though their best single, "Summer in the City," was uncharacteristically riff-driven and hard-driving. More influenced by blues and jug bands than other folk-rock acts, their albums were spotty and their covers at times downright weak. As glorious as their singles were, the group lacked the depth and innovation of the Byrds, their chief competitors for the crown of best folk-rock band, and their legacy hasn't been canonized with nearly as much reverence as their West Coast counterparts. *—Richie Unterberger*

☆ **Anthology** / Jan. 1990 / Rhino ✦✦✦✦✦

Unquestionably the finest collection of a major band that did much to launch American folk-rock in the mid-'60s. *Anthology* jams 26 cuts onto a single CD, including all of their hits and some of their strongest album tracks, drawing mostly from their 1965-66 prime. As for the more interesting non-smashes, these include the original version of John Sebastian's "Younger Girl," awhich was a hit in a more commercial version by the Critters; the minor 1967 hit "She Is Still a Mystery," a dreamily psychedelic number that holds its own with their other standards, but has somehow been forgotten by oldies radio; and "Good Time Music," recorded early in 1965 for an obscure Elektra sampler (and a small hit in a cover version by the Beau Brummels). The most overlooked find here is the instrumental "Lonely (Amy's Theme)," afrom the early Francis Ford Coppola film *You're a Big Boy Now*, a lushly orchestrated, melancholy tune featuring Sebastian's wistful harmonica. There are also little-known Sebastian originals, with vocals, from *You're a Big Boy Now* and Woody Allen's early screen venture *What's Up, Tiger Lily?* The accompanying booklet features comments from Sebastian himself about some of the group's most famous songs. *—Richie Unterberger*

Do You Believe in Magic/Hums / 1995 / Kama Sutra ✦✦✦✦✦

What's Up, Tiger Lily—/You're a Big Boy Now / Jul. 14, 1998 / Razor & Tie ✦✦✦

★ **Greatest Hits** / Feb. 22, 2000 / Buddha ✦✦✦✦✦

Although it sports the same amount of tracks (26) as Rhino's 1993 *Anthology*, up to now the last word in comprehensive Spoonful compilations, the 2000 issue of the umpteenth collection from this short-lived '60s band gets the nod over all others. Taken from the original first-generation masters, apparently for the first time, the sound quality—with a crispness and definition previously unheard—and even track selection, is the finest yet. "On the Road Again," "Wild About My Lovin'," and "Darlin' Companion," all excellent tunes representative of the Spoonful's good-time folksy/jugband style that were omitted from the Rhino set, are included, further reinforcing this as the last word in single-disc anthologies from this legendary band. What's startling is how many great songs the group recorded in such a short time span. The majority of the tracks were released within a two-year period from 1965-1967, almost all springing from the pen of John Sebastian who also took lead vocals on all the hits. The band was a textbook example of compressed quality, with only three tracks here breaking the three-minute barrier, and many clocking in at just under two. Which means there still could be an even more definitive compilation created by adding five more songs and extending the running time to the 77-minute CD maximum. Until then, this is the Lovin' Spoonful disc to own. *—Hal Horowitz*

Nick Lowe

b. Mar. 25, 1949, Woodchurch, Suffolk, England

Vocals, Bass, Producer / Pub Rock, Pop/Rock, Power Pop, New Wave, Roots Rock, Country-Rock, Rock & Roll

As the leader of the seminal pub rockers Brinsley Schwarz, a producer and a solo artist, Nick Lowe held considerable influence over the development of punk rock. With the Brinsleys, Lowe began a back-to-basics movement that flowered into punk rock in the late '70s. As the house producer for Stiff, he recorded many seminal records by the likes of the Damned, Elvis Costello and the Pretenders. His rough, ragged production style earned him the nickname "Basher," and also established the amateurish, D.I.Y. aesthetics of punk. Despite his massive influence on punk rock, Lowe never really was a punk rocker. Lowe was concerned with bringing back the tradition of three-minute pop singles and hard-driving rock & roll, but he subverted his melodic songcraft with a nasty sense of humor. His early solo singles and albums *Jesus of Cool* and *Labour of Lust* overflowed with hooks, bizzare jokes and an infectious energy that made them some of the most acclaimed pop records of the New Wave era. As New Wave began to fade away in the early '80s, Lowe began to explore roots-rock, eventually becoming a full-fledged country-rocker in the '90s. While he never had another hit after 1980's "Cruel to Be Kind," his records found a devoted cult audience, and often were critically-praised. *—Stephen Thomas Erlewine*

★ **Jesus of Cool** / 1978 / Demon ✦✦✦✦✦

For his first solo album, *Pure Pop for Now People*, Nick Lowe completely abandoned the rootsy underpinnings of his work with Brinsley Schwarz and refashioned himself as a pop craftsman—or, as the original British title put it, the *Jesus of Cool*. Lowe tries anything and everything on the record, from the sweet pop of "Tonight" to the blinding rock of "Heart of the City." It's a veritable tour de force of his songwriting talent, as well as his wit. Not only does he turn in a set of wildly eclectic pop songs, he writes lyrics that slyly and gleefully subvert and pervert rock & roll tradition. *Pure Pop for Now People* sounds like '60s pop from an alternate universe, where hit singles are about actresses who are eaten by their pet dogs, castrating Castro, and grown men who write odes to teen idols. He also writes about the sleaziness of the music business itself with unrestrained joy. If Lowe's sense of humor wasn't so sharp and his melodies weren't so catchy, the amalgam of pop music and pop culture wouldn't have been so successful. However, he not only can write pop songs, he knows how to record them—each song sounds like an individual single, and the cheap production means that the album sounds like it's coming out of tinny radio speakers. And that also means that it doesn't matter what sequence these songs are put in—the album is like a jukebox, where different musical styles can follow each other and all make perfect sense. *—Stephen Thomas Erlewine*

☆ **Labour of Lust** / 1979 / Demon ✦✦✦✦✦

Jesus of Cool was a jukebox, spinning out a series of perfectly crafted—and decidedly quirky and subversive—pop singles. In contrast, Nick Lowe's second album *Labour of Lust* is the work of a bar band, in this case Rockpile, playing the hell out of the same type of songs. Naturally, the result is a more coherent sound that may be a little less freewheelingly eclectic, but it is no less brilliant. Recorded simultaneously with Dave Edmunds' *Repeat When Necessary*, *Labour of Lust* benefits from the muscular support of Rockpile, who make Lowe's songs crackle with vitality. Working primarily in the roots-rock vein of Brinsley Schwarz, but energizing his traditionalist tendencies with strong pop melodies, a sense of humor and an edgy new wave sensibility, Lowe comes up with one of his best sets of songs. Not only is his only hit, the propulsively hook-laden "Cruel to Be Kind," and here, but so are the rampaging outsider anthem "Born Fighter," the tongue-in-cheek, Chuck Berry-style "Love So Fine," the wonderful pure pop of "Dose of You," the haunting "Endless Grey Ribbon," the druggy "Big Kick, Plain Scrap!," and the terrific "Cracking Up," as well as his definitive version of Mickey Jupp's "Switchboard Susan." It's an exceptional collection of inventive pop songs, delivered with vigor and energy, making it one of the great records of the new wave. *—Stephen Thomas Erlewine*

Nick the Knife / 1982 / Demon ✦✦✦

Following the dissolution of Rockpile, Nick Lowe recorded *Nick the Knife* with the group's guitarist Billy Bremner and drummer Terry Williams, accentuating the real reason behind the band's split—the difference between Dave Edmunds' rigid roots-rock and Lowe's carefree, funny revisionism. *Nick the Knife* may work in the conventions of classic rock & roll and pop, but it never sounds enslaved to his roots—any record with a song as infectiously ridiculous as "Ba Doom" can't take itself too seriously, and that's the charm of the album. While the songs aren't as consistently strong as those on *Labour of Lust*, Lowe contributes a handful of classics, including "Heart," "Stick It Where the Sun Don't Shine," "Too Many Teardrops," "Burning," "Queen of Sheba," "Couldn't Love You (Any More Than I Do)" and the silly "Zulu Kiss." And even in its weakest moments, *Nick the Knife* has a sunny, relaxed charm that makes the album a thoroughly enjoyable listen. *—Stephen Thomas Erlewine*

The Abominable Showman / 1983 / Demon ✦✦

Nick Lowe & His Cowboy Outfit / 1984 / Demon ✦✦✦

The title isn't entirely in jest—*Nick Lowe & His Cowboy Outfit* does represent Lowe's reinvention as a roots-rocker, as he delves into Tex-Mex, country-rock, garage rock and, of course, pop. After the muddled *The Abominable Showman*, *Cowboy Outfit* sounds positvely vibrant, thanks in no small part to Lowe's backing band, comprised largely of veteran pub-rockers. The songs are also more consistently memorable, from the Farfisa-driven "Half a Boy and Half a Man" to the sublime covers of Mickey Jupp's "You'll Never Get Me Up In One of Those" and Sandie Shaw's "Breakaway." The rest of the album's pleasures, however, are subtle. "Maureen" and "God's Gift to Women" are charming yet slight, and the songs become increasingly lightweight as the album approaches its close. Even with the uneven songs, the Cowboy Outfit make the material appealing, and Lowe certainly sounds more appealing—and comfortable—as a roots-rocker than as an aging new wave popster. *—Stephen Thomas Erlewine*

The Rose of England / 1985 / Demon ✦✦✦✦✦

Following through on the roots-rock leanings of *Cowboy Outfit*, Nick Lowe delivered the delightful *The Rose of England*. While some of the material is still rather lightweight—"Lucky Dog" and "Bo Bo Skediddle" are defiant and thoroughly entertaining throwaways—much of the record is clever and charming, delivered with laidback confidence from the Cowboy Outfit. "Darlin' Angel Eyes" and "The Rose of England" are minor classics in the Lowe canon, while his cover of John Hiatt's "She Don't Love Nobody" and the revival of the rockabilly standard "7 Nights to Rock" keep the album moving. Still, it's his stark take on Elvis Costello's lovely "Indoor Fireworks" that gives the album an anchor, and it's a performance so affecting that it makes the neutered reworking of "I Knew the Bride" completely forgivable. *—Stephen Thomas Erlewine*

Pinker and Prouder Than Previous / 1988 / Demon ✦✦✦

● **Basher: The Best of Nick Lowe** / Sep. 1989 / Columbia ✦✦✦✦✦

Containing no less than 25 tracks, *Basher: The Best of Nick Lowe* is an excellent overview of Lowe's solo career, detailing how he evolved from a quirky, innovative new wave pop craftsman a fine roots-rocker. All of Lowe's absolutely essential songs—from "So It Goes" and "Heart of the City" through "Cracking Up," "Born Fighter," and "Cruel to Be Kind" to "American Squirm," "The Rose of England" "Half a Boy and Half a Man" and "Raging Eyes"—are here, and while *Jesus of Cool* and *Labour of Lust* are essential in their own right, *Basher* is a terrific introduction to his body of work. *—Stephen Thomas Erlewine*

Party of One / 1990 / Upstart ✦✦

The Wilderness Years / 1991 / Demon ✦✦✦✦✦

Between the disbanding of Brinsley Schwarz in 1974 and the formation of Rockpile in 1977, Nick Lowe recorded a lot, attempting to settle on a sound. Simultaneously, he became the house producer at Stiff Records, where he became notorious for his raw, quickly produced records. That attitude shines through on *The Wilderness Years*, a compilation of singles, outtakes, covers, rarities and demos Lowe recorded during this year. With the exception of *Pure Pop/Jesus of Cool*, no other record captures Lowe's sense of humor or love of pop music quite as well. Divided equally between gems and glorious throwaways, *The Wilderness Years* is all over the place, but that's its charm. It has the notorious songs Lowe wrote to break his contract with United Artists ("Bay City Rollers We Love You," "Let's Go to the Disco," "Rollers Show"), both sides of his first Stiff single ("So It Goes," "Heart of the City"), his "erstwhile Stiff advertising jingle" "I Love My Label," terrific covers of "Halfway to Paradise" and Sandy Posey's "Born a Woman," plus forgotten gems like the demo for "Endless Sleep" and "Heart," "Fool Too Long" (which was written for Dr. Feelgood), and "I Got a Job," a song Nick claims he doesn't remember writing or recording. In fact, Nick doesn't think much of any of this material, but an artist isn't always the best judge of his own work—he rarely got any better than he did here. *—Stephen Thomas Erlewine*

The Impossible Bird / Nov. 29, 1994 / Upstart ✦✦✦✦✦

Nick Lowe's best records have always been full of clever lyrics and undeniable pop craftsmanship; the exception is *The Impossible Bird*. For most of the 1980s, Lowe had been appropriating country and R&B influences, but *The Impossible Bird* is where he fully incorporates those styles into his songwriting. Lowe doesn't abandon his gift for melody; "Soulful Wind" and "12-Step Program (To Quit You Babe)" are as catchy as anything he's ever written. The difference is haunting songs like "The Beast in Me" and "Withered on the Vine," two rich, sad, introspective numbers that Lowe would never have put on previous albums. And that's what makes *The Impossible Bird* his best album since *Labour of Lust*—it's the most focused, mature, personal music of his career, without a single throwaway. *—Stephen Thomas Erlewine*

Dig My Mood / Jan. 26, 1998 / Upstart ✦✦✦✦

The Impossible Bird revitalized Nick Lowe's career, finding him in a rare moment of reflection and focus, resulting in one of the very best records of his career. Its follow-up, *Dig My Mood*, doesn't reach the same peaks, but it matches the same high standard, offering 12 songs with no filler or novelties. The dark, torchy opener "Faithless Lover" may come as a bit of a surprise, especially since it's followed a song later by "You Inspire Me," another torch number, this time in the vein of k.d. lang. These two songs actually are a good indicator of the tone of *Dig My Mood*, since the country-rock that dominated *The Impossible Bird* actually fades into the background over the course of the album, popping up most directly on the funny Johnny Cash homage "Man That I've Become" and "I Must Be Getting Over You." The rest of the record is a skillful, laidback hybrid of torchy pop, R&B and country that is subtle in its execution. Lowe's voice is in the forefront, but it's gentle and unassuming, blending perfectly with the guitars, pianos and accordions. His songs are quietly ambitious, exploring new territory lyrically and musically, without leaving his signature style. As always, his taste in covers is impeccable, finding Henry McCullough's little-known "Failed Christian" and the wonderful, overlooked Ivory Joe Hunter gem "The Cold Grey Light of Dawn." They are the final, irresistible grace notes to an album that finds Lowe at his best. *—Stephen Thomas Erlewine*

The Doings / Jul. 27, 1999 / Demon ✦✦✦✦

The subtitle of the four-disc box set *The Doings* is *The Solo Years*, and the 86-track compilation never once strays from that edict. Disc one kicks off with Nick Lowe's seminal single "So It Goes," bypassing his early work with Brinsley Schwarz. By the end of that first disc, the compilation is already at *Nick the Knife*, his first album after the disbandment of Rockpile, and none of that group's official recordings are here. As it stands, *The Doings* falls just below the definitive mark, mainly because of those omissions. It's still a worthwhile set, though, playing much like an expanded version of *Basher*. It could be argued that it moves a little too quickly through Lowe's '70s and '80s material, especially since the third disc contains almost all of his '90s albums *Impossible Bird* and *Dig My Mood*. Then again, those two records really are among the best music he's ever made, so they deserve such an elevated position. Still, such decisions help point out what's missing from *The Doings*, and there are some great songs not included, but that's nit-picking. What's here is excellent, tracing a good history of

Nick's solo career, perfect for casual fans wanting a comprehensive anthology. But *The Doings* is really for obsessive fans, and they'll be pleased by the rarities. Not only is the original fast version of "Cruel to Be Kind" here, but there's a full disc of live recordings, demos, and home recordings, all of high quality. Not only does *The Doings* do a good job of collecting obscurities, it does an even better job of drawing a portrait of Lowe's solo recordings. Ultimately, that's what makes *The Doings* a success. *—Stephen Thomas Erlewine*

Lulu (Marie MacDonald McLaughlin Lawrie)

b. Nov. 3, 1948, Lennox Castle, Glasgow
Vocals / Girl Group, British Invasion, Pop
Most Americans first heard of Lulu when she soared to the top of the charts with the pop ballad "To Sir with Love," the theme to the film of the same name, in 1967. Actually, the Scottish singer—born Marie McDonald McLaughlin Lawrie—had been a star in Britain since 1964, when she hit the Top Ten with a raucous version of "Shout." Lulu's mid-'60s recordings (which included a version of "Here Comes the Night" that preceded Them's hit rendition) were often surprisingly rowdy and R&B-influenced. Although she didn't match Dusty Springfield, her Brenda Lee-like rasp could be quite gutsy and soulful. Her career was headed in a determinedly middle-of-the-road direction by the late '60s, which saw her hosting a British variety show and marrying Bee Gee Maurice Gibb (they have since divorced). Recording intermittently ever since, she raised a few eyebrows by traveling to Muscle Shoals studios to record her 1970 album *New Routes,* and releasing a single of David Bowie tunes (which Bowie also played on and co-produced) in 1973. *—Richie Unterberger*

• **From Crayons to Perfume: The Best of Lulu** / Nov. 15, 1994 / Rhino ♦♦♦♦♦
By far the most wide-ranging retrospective of a singer who never found the consistently good material that her considerable talents deserved. Starting with her 1964 British hit cover of "Shout," ait also includes the number one single "To Sir with Love" and a few of her other British Top Ten hits from the '60s, including the nice '65 soul ballad "Leave a Little Love" and the chirpy 1967 Neil Diamond tune "The Boat That I Row" (the flipside of "To Sir with Love," which wasn't a hit at all in the U.K.). Unfortunately, it gives short shift to the raunchy R&B she recorded in the mid-'60s, but it does include the sadly neglected, moody "Dreary Nights and Rows" (penned by "To Sir with Love" author Mark London) and the Top 40 orchestrated ballad "Best of Both Worlds," co-arranged by future Led Zepper John Paul Jones. You also get nifty covers of Tim Rose's "Morning Dew" and Nilsson's "Without Him," along with a few songs she recorded with Atlantic (some with the Dixie Flyers) that gave her more sympathetic soul material than she was accustomed to, including the hit "Oh Me Oh My." There's also her semi-legendary 1974 single "Watch That Man"/"The Man Who Sold the World," a double-sided 45 of David Bowie covers produced by Bowie himself, and the theme song to the James Bond film *The Man with the Golden Gun.* This 20-song compilation doesn't gather together all her fine material by any means, but it's the only one to cover most of her career. *—Richie Unterberger*

Lush

f. Oct. 1988, London, England, **db.** Feb. 23, 1998
Group / Dream Pop, Britpop, Shoegazing, Alternative Pop/Rock
Meshing dreamy, feedback-drenched guitars with airy, catchy melodies, Lush were one of the most prominent shoegazing bands of the early '90s. Led by guitarists Miki Berenyi and Emma Anderson, the British band earned a cult following within the British and American undergrounds with their first EPs, yet they never quite attained the critical respect given to their peers My Bloody Valentine and Ride. Even so, the group lasted longer than any other their contemporaries (with the exception of the Boo Radleys), developing sharp pop skills as their career progressed. By the time of their final album, 1996's *Lovelife,* the band had converted themselves into a power-pop band with dream-pop overtones, which resulted in the greatest chart success of their career. Their success was dealt a blow when drummer Chris Acland committed suicide in the fall of 1996, effectively bringing the band to an end. *—Stephen Thomas Erlewine*

Gala / Dec. 1990 / 4AD/Reprise ♦♦♦♦
Serving as an introduction to the U.S. market, *Gala* compiles the band's first three EPs and adds a couple outtakes. One thing that went overlooked about Lush was their ability to veer from violent and edgy noise breaks to pop effervescence. They were *always* capable of spewing out Saturday morning glow and Sunday evening doom from song to song. Their early reliance on sheets of distortion, buried vocals, and production issues didn't help this situation. As a result, their out-the-gate raw talent went rather unnoticed, evidenced on their earliest works. *Scar* demonstrated their under-appreciated diversity immediately. "Thoughtforms" is an example of their heavenly pop greatness, with the vocals sweeter and lighter than angel food cake. The haunting, atmospheric vocals and jittery tempos on the doomy "Second Sight" would end up laying the foundation for Chapterhouse's early material. Not a bad start. Guthrie and his beard hopped on board for the *Mad Love* EP, immediately chucking the guitars through the Guthrie-izer(tm). Most criticism of the EP pointed at the Cocteau Twin himself, who was accused of heavy-handedness. The guitars do sound a bit like Guthrie's own, but in a more assaultive, jabbing manner. A bad thing— No. All four tracks are goodies, from the cascading and shimmering walls of "De-Luxe" to the darker and heavier middle tracks. Production was an issue again on the *Sweetness and Light* EP. Tim Friese-Greene kind of polarizes the band's extreme ends, separating the noise and pop just a little too much. Despite a patched-on noise break during the title track, it's still one of the band's career highlights. "Sunbathing" is left in the sun too long, muffling the guitars and shrinking the sparse percussion. "Breeze" wafts by gracefully. *—Andy Kellman*

Spooky / Jan. 1992 / 4AD/Reprise ♦♦♦

• **Split** / Jun. 1994 / 4AD/Reprise ♦♦♦♦♦
Entire albums spent exploring the depths of the various nasty things surrounding romantic relationships were nothing new by the mid-'90s, but the vaguely cinematic and slightly conceptual *Split* is something more. Perhaps it's the manner in which each distinctive song manages to melt into the next. Or maybe it's the across-the-board improvements over *Spooky.* Most knew they were capable of more after the decent but flawed record, but it's doubtful many could have predicted something this thoroughly wonderful and varied. Throughout, Lush sounds confident and downright muscular, as opposed to the feathery wisps of earlier material that could be knocked down with the slightest of breezes. Miki Berenyi's high-heaven vocals have increased range, power, and presence. Chris Acland's drums propel the proceedings more than before, perhaps pushed into better realms by new bassist Phil King. Producer Mike Hedges knows just what to do with the band's elements, adding grace and balance that no other could previously achieve. Kudos as well to a bang-up job by mixmaster Alan Moulder.

It's an ardent roller coaster ride, centered around the lengthy mourners "Desire Lines" (oddly a single) and "Never-Never," which clock in at eight minutes apiece. Berenyi effectively conveys the resigned and soul-deadened nature of the lyrics. "Blackout" and "Hypocrite" prove the band's ability to be more assaultive, laying the foundation for their sound on *Lovelife.* Through breezy pop ("Lit Up"), brief shards of electrocuting dread ("Invisible Man"), and tales of obsessive voyeurism ("Starlust"), *Split* touches on most forms of emotional turbulence. Not necessarily a comeback but certainly a legitimizing stunner, the record prevented the band from being lost amidst the bunker of form-over-function dream pop bands. *Split* shattered every negative aspect of those failed acts with flying colors. A fantastic record within any realm. *—Andy Kellman*

Lovelife / Mar. 5, 1996 / 4AD/Reprise ♦♦♦♦♦
Lovelife represents a major shift in style for Lush. Nearly abandoning the trancy melodies and droning guitars that were their trademark, the band has crafted an album full of sharp hooks and melodies, one that owes a great deal to the Britpop mania of 1995. From the circular melody of the opening "Ladykillers," ait's clear that Lush had been influenced by the direct, jagged pop of Elastica, but they also have reached back into '60s pop. All of the ballads on *Lovelife* are rooted in the hazy dream-pop of the early '90s, but they are given stylish, mod arrangements complete with muted brass. Even more startling is the Nancy Sinatra/Lee Hazlewood pastiche of "Ciao!," an irresistible duet between Miki Berenyi and Pulp's Jarvis Cocker. *Lovelife* would have simply been an embarrassing attempt to seem fashionable if Lush hadn't succeeded in updating their sound. However, they have been able to recreate themselves as a pop band and the result is their most direct—and arguably their most rewarding—album. *—Stephen Thomas Erlewine*

Frankie Lymon

b. Sep. 30, 1942, Harlem, NY, **d.** Feb. 28, 1968, Harlem, New York City, NY
Vocals / Doo Wop, R&B
Frankie Lymon (1942-1968) & the Teenagers were a New York doo-wop group consisting of Joe Negroni, Herman Santiago, Jimmy Merchant, and Sherman Garnes but centered around the extraordinary talents of their lead singer, thirteen-year-old Frankie Lymon. Lymon was credited with their first big hit, "Why Do Fools Fall in Love" (In the early-90s, a federal judge ruled after a lengthy trial that Lymon hadn't written "Why Do Folls Fall in Love"—another member of the Teenagers had). His wise-beyond-his-years vocal and performing abilities not only made the Teenagers a group several notches above the competition but made Lymon the first Black teenage pop star. Though only together for a brief 18-month period, Lymon & the Teenagers exerted an enormous influence, spawning several "kid" vocal groups and providing initial inspiration to Berry Gordy to model his entire Motown production approach around Lymon's original vocal style. Inexplicably, the group split into two factions at the height of their success, and neither had a hit again. Lymon died from a drug overdose at age 26. Diana Ross, Smokey Robinson, Len Barry, and his principal protégé, Michael Jackson (whose early recordings with the Jackson 5 are virtual re-creations of the early Lymon sound, merely updated) all show the influence of Frankie Lymon & the Teenagers's groundbreaking work. *—Cub Koda*

★ **The Very Best of Frankie Lymon & the Teenagers** / Oct. 6, 1998 / Rhino ♦♦♦♦♦
Although finally getting their due in the last few years of the 20th century, Frankie Lymon & The Teenagers have nonetheless been the subjects of several best-of packages, even including multi-album and CD box sets on Bear Family and Murray Hill. This 16-track very-best-of comes almost ten years after Rhino's release of an excellent 20-track best-of, and like that single-disc collection, all the big hits are here: "Why Do Fools Fall In Love," "ABC's of Love," "I Want You to Be My Girl," "I Promise to Remember," "I'm Not a Juvenile Delinquent," and later sides like "Goody Goody" and his last solo hit, "Little Bitty Pretty One." In fact, this new reissue appropriates most of Bob Hyde's excellent notes from the 1989 package, trackwise only differing in the leaving off of later tracks like "Thumb Thumb," "Portable On My Shoulder," "Creation of Love" and the Teenagers' rocking "Love Is a Clown." The perfect entry-level compilation for digging this groundbreaking vocal group. *—Cub Koda*

The Complete Recordings / Bear Family ♦♦♦
This five-CD set contains more Frankie Lymon & the Teenagers than any casual fan has likely ever thought of listening to, much less owning. Only one of its five CDs is less than satisfying, yet only a portion of this collection contains music that is actually important to the history of rock & roll. The first disc contains everything that Lymon and the Teenagers recorded together for official release. By the second disc, we're already into the Teenagers' recordings without Lymon, as well as live performances by Lymon and the Teenagers from *The Ed Sullivan Show* and various Alan Freed concert events. The final three discs are made up entirely of Lymon's solo sides from 1957 through 1968. From the 20 or so familiar early songs, one hears them "progress" to the later numbers, where their vocalizing became more sophisticated and subtle, but less cohesive. Disc Three opens the Frankie Lymon solo material, and with all due respect to his memory, it's a disaster. His early solo sides, from 1957 through early 1958, tried to appeal strictly to pop listeners, with results that had no beat or any other serious appeal. Disc Four finds him back on track, featuring 30 entertaining and engaging rock & roll songs that show Lymon in extraordinarily good voice. Disc Five continues with Lymon's recordings for Columbia in 1964 to his final records in 1968. The sad and surprising part is that a lot of it isn't bad at all. Lymon's voice matured into a fairly non-

descript instrument, but he could still put a good song over, as many of these later tracks show. *—Bruce Eder*

Lynyrd Skynyrd

f. 1965, Jacksonville, FL

Group / Album Rock, Boogie Rock, Arena Rock, Southern Rock, Hard Rock, Blues-Rock

Lynyrd Skynyrd was the definitive Southern Rock band, fusing the overdriven power of blues-rock with a rebellious, Southern image and a hard-rock swagger. Skynyrd never relied on the jazzy improvisations of the Allman Brothers. Instead, they were a hard-living, hard-driving rock & roll band—they may have jammed endlessly on stage, but their music remained firmly entrenched in blues, rock and country. For many, Lynyrd Skynyrd's redneck image tended to obscure the songwriting skills of its leader, Ronnie Van Zant. Throughout the band's early records, Van Zant demonstrated a knack for lyrical detail and a down-to-earth honesty that had more in common with country than rock & roll. During the height of Skynyrd's popularity in the mid-'70s, however, Van Zant's talents were overshadowed by the group's gritty, greasy blues-rock. Sadly, it wasn't until he was killed in a tragic plane crash in 1977 along with two other band members that many listeners began to realize his talents. Skynyrd split up after the plane crash, but they reunited a decade later, becoming a popular concert act during the early '90s. *—Stephen Thomas Erlewine*

☆ **Pronounced Leh-Nerd Skin-Nerd** / Sep. 1973 / MCA ✦✦✦✦✦

The Allman Brothers came first, but Lynyrd Skynyrd epitomized Southern rock. The Allmans were exceptionally gifted musicians, as much bluesmen as rockers. Skynyrd was nothing but rockers, and they were Southern rockers to the bone. This didn't just mean that they were rednecks, but that they brought it all together—the blues, country, garage rock, Southern poetry—in a way that sounded more like the South than even the Allmans. And a large portion of that derives from their hard, lean edge, which was nowhere more apparent than on their debut album, *Pronounced Leh-Nerd Skin-Nerd*. Produced by Al Kooper, there are few records that sound this raw and uncompromising, especially records by debut bands. Then again, few bands sound this confident and fully formed with their first record. Perhaps the record is stronger because it's only eight songs, so there isn't a wasted moment, but that doesn't discount the sheer strength of each song. Consider the opening juxtaposition of the rollicking "I Ain't the One" with the heartbreaking "Tuesday's Gone." Two songs couldn't be more opposed, yet Skynyrd sounds equally convincing on both. If that's all the record did, it would still be fondly regarded, but it wouldn't have been influential. The genius of Skynyrd is that it unself-consciously blended album-oriented hard rock, blues, country, and garage rock, turning it all into a distinctive sound that sounds familiar but thoroughly unique. On top of that, there's the highly individual voice of Ronnie VanZant, a songwriter that isn't afraid to be nakedly sentimental, spin tales of the South, or to twist macho conventions with humor. And, lest we forget, while he does this, the band rocks like a motherfucker. It's the birth of a great band who birthed an entire genre with this album. *—Stephen Thomas Erlewine*

☆ **Second Helping** / Apr. 1974 / MCA ✦✦✦✦✦

Lynyrd Skynyrd wrote the book on Southern rock with their first album, so it only made sense that they followed it for their second album, aptly titled *Second Helping*. Sticking with producer Al Kooper (who, after all, discovered them), the group turned out a record that replicated all the strengths of the original, but was a little tighter and a little more professional. But it also revealed that the band, under the direction of songwriter Ronnie VanZant, was developing a truly original voice. Of course, the band had already developed their own musical voice, but it was enhanced considerably by VanZant's writing, which was at turns plainly poetic, surprisingly clever, and always revealing. Though *Second Helping* isn't as hard a rock record as *Pronounced*, it are the songs that make the record. "Sweet Home Alabama" became ubiquitous, yet it's rivaled by such terrific songs as the snide, punkish "Workin' for MCA," the Southern groove "Don't Ask Me No Questions," the affecting "The Ballad of Curtis Loew," and "The Needle and the Spoon," a drug tale as affecting as their rival Neil Young's "Needle and the Damage Done," but much harder rocking. This is the part of Skynyrd that most people forget—they were a great band, but they were indelible because that was married to great writing. And nowhere was that more evident than on *Second Helping*. *—Stephen Thomas Erlewine*

Fancy / Mar. 1975 / MCA ✦✦✦

Second Helping brought Lynyrd Skynyrd mass success and for the follow-up they offered *Nuthin' Fancy*. It was a self-deprecating title for a record that may have offered more of the same, at least on the surface, but was still nearly peerless as a Southern rock record. The biggest difference with this record is that the band, through touring, has become heavier and harder, fitting right in with the heavy album rock bands of the mid-'70s. The second notable difference is that Ronnie VanZant may have been pressed for material, since there are several songs here that are just good generic rockers. But, he and Skynyrd prove that what makes a great band great is how they treat generic material, and Skynyrd makes the whole of *Nothin' Fancy* feel every bit as convincing as their first two records. For one, the record has a rawer edge than *Second Helping*, which helps make the slight preponderance of predictable (but not bad) material easy to accept, since it all sounds so good. Then, there's the fact that many of these eight songs still showcase VanZant at the top of his game, whether it's the storming opener "Saturday Night Special," "Railroad Song," "On the Hunt," or the rollicking "Whiskey Rock-A-Roller." Yes, this does pale in comparison with its predecessors, but most hard rock bands would give their left arm for a record that swaggers and hits as hard as *Nuthin' Fancy*. *—Stephen Thomas Erlewine*

Gimme Back My Bullets / Feb. 1976 / MCA ✦✦✦

Lynyrd Skynyrd begins to show signs of wear on their third album, *Gimme Back My Bullets*. The band had switched producers, hiring Tom Dowd, the producer that served Atlantic's roster so well during the label's heyday. Unfortunately, he wasn't perfectly suited for Skynyrd, at least at this point in their history. The group had toured regularly since the release of their debut and it showed, not just in their performance, but in the songwriting of Ronnie VanZant, who had been so consistent through their first three albums. Not to say that he was spent—the title track was defiant as "All I Can Do Is Write About It" was affecting, while "Searching" was a good ballad and "Double Trouble" was a good rocker. These songs, however, were surrounded by songs that leaned to the dull side of generic (unlike those on *Nuthin' Fancy*) and Dowd's production didn't inject energy into the group's performances. This doesn't mean *Gimme Back My Bullets* is a bad record, since the group was still in fairly good shape and they had some fine songs, but coming after three dynamite albums, it was undoubtedly a disappointment—so much so that it still sounds like a disappointment years later, even though it's one of only a handful of records by the original band. *—Stephen Thomas Erlewine*

One More From the Road / Sep. 1976 / MCA ✦✦✦

Double live albums were commonplace during the '70s, even for bands that weren't particularly good in concert. As a travelin' band, Lynyrd Skynyrd made their fame and fortune by being good in concert, so it made sense that they released a double-live, entitled *One More From the Road*, in 1976, months after the release of their fourth album, *Gimme Back My Bullets*. That might have been rather quick for a live album—only three years separated this record from the group's debut—but it was enthusiastically embraced, entering the Top Ten (it would become one of their best-selling albums, as well). It's easy to see why it was welcomed since this album demonstrates what a phenomenal catalog of songs they accumulated. *Street Survivors*, which appeared the following year, added "That Smell" and "You Got That Right" to the canon, but this pretty much has everything else, sometimes extended into jams as long as the Allmans on this record, but always much rawer, nearly dangerous. That catalog, as much as the strong performances, makes *One More From the Road* worth hearing. Heard here, on one record, the consistency of Skynyrd's work falls into relief, and they not only clearly tower above their peers based on what's here, the cover of "T for Texas" illustrates that they're carrying on the Southern tradition, not starting a new one. Like most live albums, this is not necessarily essential, but if you're a fan, it's damn hard to take this album off after it starts. *—Stephen Thomas Erlewine*

Street Survivors / Oct. 1977 / MCA ✦✦✦✦✦

Street Survivors appeared in stores just days before Lynyrd Skynyrd's touring plane crashed, tragically killing many members of the band, including lead singer and songwriter Ronnie Van Zant. Consequently, it's hard to see *Street Survivors* outside of the tragedy, especially since the best-known song here, "That Smell," reeks of death and foreboding. If the band had lived, however, *Street Survivors* would have been seen as an unqualified triumph, a record that firmly re-established Skynyrd's status as the great Southern rock band. As it stands, it's a triumph tinged with a hint of sadness, sadness that's projected onto it from listeners aware of what happened to the band after recording. Viewed as merely a record, it's a hell of an album. The band springs back to life with the addition of guitarist Steve Gaines, and Van Zant used the time off the road to write a strong set of songs, highlighted by "That Smell," "You Got That Right," and the relentless boogie "I Know a Little." It's tighter than any record since *Second Helping* and as raw as *Nuthin' Fancy*. If the original band was fated to leave after this record, at least they left with a record that serves as a testament to Skynyrd's unique greatness. *—Stephen Thomas Erlewine*

Skynyrd's First and . . . Last / Sep. 1978 / MCA ✦✦✦

★ **Gold & Platinum** / Dec. 1979 / MCA ✦✦✦✦✦

Gold and Platinum was compiled by Gary Rossington and Allen Collins, the two surviving members of Lynyrd Skynyrd, after the band's tragic plane crash of 1977. Though many years have elapsed since its 1980 release, the double-record set remains the best, most concise compilation of the ground-breaking southern rock band. Over the course of two albums, all of Skynyrd's hits—"Sweet Home Alabama," "Free Bird," "Saturday Night Special," "What's Your Name," "You Got That Right"—are featured, as well as essential album tracks like "That Smell," "Down South Jukin'," "Gimme Three Steps," "I Know A Little," and "Tuesday's Gone." Some great songs like "Working for MCA" are missing, and the four-disc box set may be more comprehensive, but it's hard to imagine a better, more concise greatest hits collection than *Gold and Platinum*. *—Stephen Thomas Erlewine*

Lynyrd Skynyrd 1991 / Jun. 11, 1991 / Atlantic ✦✦

Lynyrd Skynyrd / Nov. 12, 1991 / MCA ✦✦✦✦✦

It was only fitting that the ultimate Southern rock institution Lynyrd Skynyrd—certainly one of the more tragic stories in rock & roll history—should be one of the first bands to benefit from a comprehensive box set. Following the format of the highly successful Led Zeppelin box set, this three-disc, 47-song anthology provides a near-perfect career retrospective, complete with a carefully researched booklet with meticulous historical essays and rare photos for the new and rabid fan alike. The latter will probably be most interested in Disc One, which features a number of early demos dating back as early as 1970 and not featured in prior collections, as well as an embryonic demo of "Freebird" minus its extended-jam coda. The nine-minute version from the band's milestone debut, *Pronounced...* is also featured here, of course, as is most of the material from the group's next album, *Second Helping*, generally regarded as their career peak. Disc Two alone could serve as a greatest-hits set, as classic after classic is rattled off in mind-blowing succession. And even when the creative fires finally begin to wane somewhat as the set approaches the *Nuthin' Fancy* and *Gimme Back My Bullets* material (recorded at a time when the band was plagued by over-work and escalating drug abuse), the set wisely offers alternate versions and live renditions to keep things interesting. The first half of Disc Three alternates never-before-heard concert performances with other, equally inspired live versions. Its second half is dominated by the unintentional swan song *Street Survivors*. Released only three days before the fateful plane crash, the album saw a re-energized Skynyrd achieving a new level of maturity, power, and purpose. Although most box sets tend to be a bit too much for the casual fan to swallow, this one feels just right. *—Ed Rivadavia*

Solo Flytes / Oct. 12, 1999 / MCA ✦✦✦

All Time Greatest Hits / Mar. 14, 2000 / MCA ✦✦✦✦

Skynyrd Collectybles / Nov. 21, 2000 / MCA ✦✦✦✦

Kirsty MacColl

b. Oct. 10, 1959, **d.** Dec. 19, 2000
Vocals, Guitar / College Rock, Adult Alternative Pop/Rock, Folk-Rock, Singer/Songwriter
Kirsty MacColl, daughter of folk singer/songwriter Ewan MacColl, began her own musical career while still in her teens, singing in a band called the Addix, and eventually signed to the legendary Stiff Records. Her first single, the modern girl-group gem, "They Don't Know," was released in 1979. Though it failed in the charts, it was later a major hit for Tracey Ullman. She switched to Polydor in the '80s and landed a U.K. Top 20 hit with the novelty song "There's a Guy Works Down the Chip Shop (Swears He's Elvis)." She followed the single with her first LP, *Desperate Character*, in 1981. In 1984, she married producer Steve Lillywhite and put her solo career on hold, raising their two children and working as a backup singer. MacColl returned in 1989 with a more mature effort, *Kite*, which reached the U.K. Top 20. Two more albums, *Electric Landlady* (1991) and *Titanic Days* (1993), displayed great talent and diversity and, above all, good pop sensibilities; after a lengthy hiatus, MacColl resurfaced in 2000 with *Tropical Brainstorm*. Shortly after, on December 18, 2000, MacColl was killed by a speedboat while swimming off of the coast of Mexico. *—Chris Woodstra*

Desperate Character / 1981 / Polydor ✦✦✦

Kite / 1989 / Capitol ✦✦✦
After nearly a decade's absence as solo performer, MacColl released the low-key *Kite*, a decidedly more mature effort. Her literate and sharp vocals are perfectly matched with lush, textured folk-pop arrangements. Johnny Marr contributes his distinctive guitar playing on several tracks. *—Chris Woodstra*

Electric Landlady / Jun. 25, 1991 / Capitol ✦✦✦✦✦
MacColl is in peak form on the more experimental *Electric Landlady*. Playing with a different band on nearly every track, she effortlessly moves from the hip-hop of "Walking Down Madison," to the Latin-tinged "My Affair," to the Smiths' sound-alike "Children of the Revolution" (co-written by Smiths guitarist Johnny Marr). Overall, she builds on the folk-pop of her previous effort with much stronger material. Her lyrics have become more personal, mainly focusing on her relationship with and the recent death of her father. *—Chris Woodstra*

The Essential Collection / 1993 / Stiff ✦✦✦✦✦
A fine collection of Kirsty MacColl's early singles for Stiff Records in the late '70s. She wrote effortlessly melodic three-minute pop singles that managed to recast the classic girl-group sound of the '60s into a style that was contemporary and timeless, much like how Rockpile energetically recast '50s and '60s rock & roll. Not only were these singles some of the best she's ever written, the singles were among the best pop songs of the era, including the original version of Tracey Ullman's hit "They Don't Know" and the infectious "There's a Guy Works Down the Chip Shop (Swears He's Elvis)." *—Chris Woodstra*

Titanic Days / Oct. 5, 1993 / IRS ✦✦✦
MacColl delivers another brilliant album with 1993's *Titanic Days*. The arrangements have become more ambitious, as evident in the jazzy "Bad" and the heavily orchestrated "Soho Square." The lyrics are still sharp with biting commentary, this time backed by a more dance-oriented pop. *—Chris Woodstra*

● **Galore** / Jan. 24, 1995 / Virgin ✦✦✦✦✦
Eighteen-track compilation. The strength of these collected forces may just be sufficient to overcome Kirsty MacColl's two fatal commercial "flaws": she spreads herself all over the musical map, and writes intelligent, often drily humorous lyrics about life and relationships that never pander to chart sentimentality. MacColl oozes a pure, fresh-scrubbed, girl-next-door quality that belies the sophistication of her songwriting without ever resorting to vacant innocence. *—Roch Parisien*

What Do Pretty Girls Do— / Jun. 16, 1998 / Hux ✦✦✦✦✦
What Do Pretty Girls Do? is a collection of four performances Kirsty MacColl did for BBC radio from 1989 to 1995—fifteen tracks in all. Aside from the obvious album tracks from each period (this was for promotion afterall), MacColl pulls out some old favorites from the early days—a country take on "There's a Guy Works Down the Chip Shop Swears He's Elvis," "A New England" (a duet with the song's writer, Billy Bragg), and "He's on the Beach"—as well as a couple of well-chosen covers like "Walk Right Back" and the charming "Darling, Let's Have Another Baby" (also a duet with Billy Bragg). BBC sets are always fun for fans, but for an artist like MacColl, who has always shyed away from live performance and whose albums have always been so meticulously produced, with multi-layered vocals and carefully conceived arrangements, this one is particularly revealing. She sounds relaxed—there's no doubt that she's genuinely having a good time—and, the sheer quality of the songs (and her voice) is made even more apparent in this straightforward, no-frills setting. *—Chris Woodstra*

Tropical Brainstorm / Apr. 25, 2000 / V2 International ✦✦✦✦

Madness

f. 1978, Camden, London, England, **db.** 1986
Group / Pop/Rock, Ska Revival, New Wave
Along with the Specials, Madness were one of the leading bands of the ska-revival of the late '70s and early '80s. As their career progressed, Madness expanded their trademark "nutty sound," incorporating elements of Motown, soul and British pop. They were one of the most beloved bands Britain produced during the '80s, yet they influenced bands on both sides of the Atlantic.

Taking their name from a Prince Buster song, Madness' first single was "The Prince." Released on Two-Tone in 1978, it was a surprise success. After it reached the Top 20, Madness signed with Stiff, quickly releasing "One Step Beyond," their first Top 10 hit, which was followed by an album of the same name. Over the next three years, Madness had a virtually uninterrupted run of 13 Top Ten singles, making them one of the most popular bands in the UK, rivaling only the Jam in widespread popularity. Where the Jam appealed to teenagers and young adults, Madness had a broad fan base, reaching from children to the elderly. Despite their phenomenal success in the UK, they made little headway in the US. Madness began to expand their sound with their 1982 album, *The Rise and Fall*, a pop-oriented, Kinksian album. This record featured "Our House," the single that gave them their first American hit, but just as the group had broken into the US, lead songwriter Mike Barson left the group. Their popularity immediately started to slide. They managed to stay in the British Top 10 with 1984's *Keep Moving*, but their next album didn't capture a sizable audience. The group disbanded in 1986, only to return two years later as *the* Madness, in a comeback bid that didn't go anywhere. Their days as hitmakers may have been over, but in the '90s, Madness had successful reunion tours. Lead singer Suggs released a solo album in 1995, yet he returned for more reunion shows during the late '90s. *—Stephen Thomas Erlewine*

One Step Beyond / 1979 / Sire ✦✦✦✦✦
Madness made a name for themselves early on with a silly image and irresistible novelty-dance numbers like "One Step Beyond" and the similar-sounding "Night Boat to Cairo." They did that extremely well on their debut—certainly these singles are among the finest of the era—but what made *One Step Beyond* such a remarkable record was not only the fun-time music they created, but also the diversity they displayed. Combining ska with distinctly British flavors of music-hall and '60s pop along with soul and even a hint of punk, Madness created a unique sound that, while very much a part of the 2-Tone ska-revival, also managed to transcend it. *One Step Beyond* is a charming album packed with some terrific songs, and it arguably stands as the high point of their distinguished career. *—Chris Woodstra*

Absolutely / Oct. 1980 / Sire ✦✦✦
For their second album, Madness continued the bright and bouncy fun of their debut. *Absolutely* placed slightly more emphasis on their novelty aspect, creating something of a fun-house atmosphere with stray sounds, exaggerated accents, faster tempos, and often unintelligible lyrics rattled off by Suggs at breakneck speed. Although the album shows a dip in quality control and much less diversity than *One Step Beyond*, it is nevertheless a charming romp with its share of inspired moments, like the classic singles "Baggy Trousers" and "Embarrasment." *—Chris Woodstra*

Seven / Sep. 1981 / Stiff ✦✦✦
Their "nutty sound" seems to fall to the background somewhat on this move toward more mature songwriting. Expanding beyond the limited scope of ska, this is a fine pop effort at times dabbling in more experimental sounds such as sitars and Arabic rhythms. Includes the splendid single "It Must Be Love." *—Chris Woodstra*

☆ **Complete Madness** / 1982 / Stiff ✦✦✦✦✦
The 16-track compilation *The Complete Madness* compiles all of the group's early singles—from "The Prince" to "House of Fun"—and adds a handful of classic album tracks and concert favorites like "In the City," "Bed and Breakfast Man," and "Madness." It's thorough and a thoroughly entertaining collection, encapsulating exactly why Madness were significant and, more importantly, how much fun their "nutty sound" was. Furthermore, *The Complete Madness* isn't just an introduction—since it contains a wealth of non-LP singles like "Cardiac Arrest" and "House of Fun," it's essential for any Madness collectors. The compilation is definitive proof that Madness were one of the great singles acts of their era. *—Stephen Thomas Erlewine*

Rise and Fall / 1982 / Stiff ✦✦✦✦✦
Madness Present the Rise and Fall marks the band's most mature effort and artistic statement. Completely devoid of their early ska influence, they paint a picture of British life in the spirit of the Kinks' *Village Green Preservation Society*. Though it was never released in the U.S., several tracks were later placed on the compilation *Madness*, including "Our House," their biggest Stateside hit. *—Chris Woodstra*

Madness / 1983 / Geffen ✦✦✦✦✦
Madness is a U.S. compilation released to capitalize on the success of "Our House." Aside from handful of earlier singles like "Night Boat to Cairo," "It Must Be Love," "Cardiac Arrest" and "House of Fun," the collection's real focus is on material from the previous year's *Madness Present the Rise and Fall*, which wasn't released in America. The collection suffers from a mixture of two distinct periods in the band's career and some glaring omissions, but there is no shortage of great material, making for a pretty good, though far from perfect, introduction. *—Chris Woodstra*

Keep Moving / 1984 / Geffen ✦✦

Mad Not Mad / 1985 / Geffen ✦✦✦

The Business / 1992 / Virgin ✦✦✦
The Business is not the comprehensive, one-stop shopping solution for Madness that it appears to be based on the track listing. The three-disc box does contain all of the singles and B-sides, but the inclusion of spoken bits between and overlapping into the songs makes for an awkward listen. Certainly the goal of this package was to tell the story of the band, but both the band and listener would be better served by letting the music speak for itself. *—Chris Woodstra*

Total Madness: The Very Best of Madness / Sep. 9, 1997 / Geffen ✦✦✦

Wonderful / Dec. 14, 1999 / EMI ✦✦✦✦

★ **Ultimate Collection** / Nov. 14, 2000 / Hip-O ✦✦✦✦✦
The Madness volume of Hip-O's *Ultimate Collection* series is one of the few entries that actually lives up to its title. The 19-track disc is about the most complete single-disc collection of Madness' British and American hits yet, containing everything from "One Step Beyond" and "My Girl" to "Michael Caine" and "Wings of a Dove." The quality of the music does drop off a bit in the post-*Rise and Fall* years, but it's hard not to listen to this collection and not be impressed by the depth and strength of Madness as a single act. And there's no better place to be seduced by Madness' infectious, nutty sound than this single-disc set. *—Stephen Thomas Erlewine*

Madonna (Madonna Louise Veronica Ciccone)

b. Aug. 16, 1958, Rochester, MI
Vocals / Club/Dance, Pop/Rock, Adult Contemporary, Dance-Pop
Madonna's celebrity tends to overshadow her music, and in some ways, her mastery of image and marketing seems greater than her recordings. Nevertheless, she wouldn't have been able to sustain superstardom for two decades if she didn't also deliver musically, and her albums have usually been fascinating, creative affairs that brought underground dance-club trends into the mainstream.

Madonna first made an impression with her 1982 with club hit, "Everybody." She released her debut album the following year; thanks to the Top 40 "Holiday," it became a hit. Madonna's star rose during 1984, as "Borderline" and "Lucky Star" reached the Top 10. Her second album *Like a Virgin* arrived late that year, with her first film *Desperately Seeking Susan* following that next summer. With these two projects, Madonna rocketed to international superstardom. "Like a Virgin" and "Material Girl" were defining anthems, teenage girls started dressing like her and she became a favorite of tabloids, thanks in no small part to her own past—nude photos from 1977 were published in both Playboy and Penthouse, yet this simply added to her mystique. *True Blue* (1986) was more complex than her previous work, earning critical acclaim as well as hits in "Papa Don't Preach" and "Open Your Heart." After two film flops, (*Shanghai Surprise, Who's That Girl*), she returned with *Like a Prayer* in 1989; it was her most ambitious and acclaimed album to date, sparking both hits and controversy. Soon, that controversy began to overwhelm the music, as her video for "Justify My Love" was banned by MTV. Following her tour documentary *Truth or Dare*, Madonna released a softcore photo book called *Sex* in 1992. Her new album, the well-reviewed *Erotica*, was released simultaneously, but *Sex* was a disaster, hurting the album's sales. *Bedtime Stories*, released two years later, was a more subdued affair than *Erotica*, and it spawned her biggest hit, "Take a Bow." Following her starring role in the 1995 film adaptation of Andrew Lloyd Webber's *Evita*, Madonna returned in 1998 with the electronica-inspired *Ray of Light*, which restored her critical and popular cache as a trailblazer. She followed through on its success with 2000's *Music*, a glitzy dance album. *—Stephen Thomas Erlewine*

Madonna / 1983 / Sire ✦✦✦✦✦
Madonna's self-titled debut was one of the strongest dance records of the early '80s, featuring a state-of-the-art production and a handful of great songs. Although her voice was still quite thin at this point, Madonna projected a powerful charisma, bringing slight material like "Everybody," "Physical Attraction," and "Burning Up" to life. However, it was on well-constructed pop songs like "Borderline," "Lucky Star," and "Holiday" that the record became truly impressive, as the material matched Madonna's performance. All three of the songs became hits and wrote the blueprint for dance-pop divas that dominated much of the remaining decade. *—Stephen Thomas Erlewine*

Like a Virgin / 1984 / Sire ✦✦✦✦✦
Armed with the talents of producer Nile Rodgers, Madonna surpassed the excellence of her self-titled debut album with its superb, hit-laden follow-up *Like a Virgin*—arguably, the album that really made Miss Ciccone a superstar. While Rodgers' early projects outside of Chic (including Sister Sledge and Diana Ross) sounded very much like that seminal disco group, that was no longer the case in the mid-'80s (when he was working with everyone from David Bowie to Duran Duran). *Virgin* never sounds like anything but a Madonna album, although Rodgers' gift for sleek, seductive dance music (Chic's specialty) is evident on such gems as "Dress You Up," "Angel" and the Motownish title song. Though R&B and dance music are dominant, Madonna obviously wasn't content to focus on the urban-contemporary market exclusively, and she embraces quirky, new wave-ish pop with likeable results on "Over and Over" and the infectious "Material Girl." Everything on *Virgin* is well worth hearing, including non-hits like Madonna's pleasant ballad "Shoo Be Doo" and her remake of Rose Royce's "Love Don't Live Here Anymore." All too many dance-floor divas are never heard outside the clubs—a fate that Madonna, like Donna Summer before her, guarded against. With *Virgin*, Madonna became one of the 1980s' best-selling pop icons without losing her sizeable club following. *—Alex Henderson*

True Blue / 1986 / Sire ✦✦✦✦✦
A staggering album from an artist known for hot singles, the hits include "Papa Don't Preach," "Open Your Heart," and "True Blue." "Live to Tell," her best, is also to be found here. *—John Floyd*

You Can Dance / 1987 / Sire ✦✦✦

Who's That Girl / Jul. 21, 1987 / Sire ✦✦

☆ **Like a Prayer** / 1989 / Sire ✦✦✦✦✦
Out of all of Madonna's albums, *Like a Prayer* is her most explicit attempt at a major artistic statement. Even though it is apparent that she is trying to make a "serious" album, the kaleidoscopic variety of pop styles on *Like a Prayer* is quite dazzling. Ranging from the deep funk of "Express Yourself" and "Keep It Together," to the haunting "Oh Father" and "Like a Prayer," Madonna displays a commanding sense of songcraft, making this her best and most consistent album. *—Stephen Thomas Erlewine*

★ **The Immaculate Collection** / 1990 / Sire ✦✦✦✦✦
On the surface, the single-disc hits compilation *The Immaculate Collection* appears to be a definitive retrospective of Madonna's heyday in the '80s. After all, it features 17 of Madonna's greatest hits, from "Holiday" and "Like a Virgin" to "Like a Prayer" and "Vogue." However, looks can be deceiving. It's true that *The Immaculate Collection* contains the bulk of Madonna's hits, but there are several big hits that aren't present, including "Angel," "Dress You Up," "True Blue," "Who's That Girl," and "Causing a Commotion." The songs that are included are frequently altered. Everything on the collection is remastered in Q-sound, which gives an exaggerated sense of stereo separation that often distorts the original intent of the recordings. Furthermore, several songs are faster than their original versions and some are faded out earlier than either their single or album versions, while others are segued together. In other words, while all the hits are present, they're simply not in their correct versions. Nevertheless, *The Immaculate Collection* remains a necessary purchase, because it captures everything Madonna is about and it proves that she was one of the finest singles artists of the '80s. Until the original single versions are compiled on another album, *The Immaculate Collection* is the closest thing to a definitive retrospective. *—Stephen Thomas Erlewine*

Dick Tracy: "I'm Breathless" (Music from & Inspired by the Film) / May 1990 / Sire ✦✦

Erotica / Oct. 20, 1992 / Maverick ✦✦✦

Bedtime Stories / Oct. 25, 1994 / Maverick ✦✦✦✦
Perhaps Madonna correctly guessed that the public overdosed on the raw carnality of her book *Sex*. Perhaps she wanted to offer a more optimistic take on sex than the distant *Erotica*. Either way, *Bedtime Stories* is a warm album, with deep, gently pulsating grooves; the album's title isn't totally tongue-in-cheek. The best songs on the album ("Secret," "Inside of Me," "Sanctuary," "Bedtime Story," "Take a Bow") slowly work their melodies into the subconscious as the bass pulses. In that sense, it does offer an antidote to *Erotica*, which was filled with deep but cold grooves. The entire production of *Bedtime Stories* suggests that she wants listeners to acknowledge that her music isn't one-dimensional. She has succeeded with that goal, since *Bedtime Stories* offers her most humane and open music; it's even seductive. *—Stephen Thomas Erlewine*

Something to Remember / Nov. 7, 1995 / Maverick ✦✦✦✦✦
Something to Remember is Madonna's second greatest hits collection, compiling a selection of the singer's ballads. Several of her biggest hits are included, including the number ones "Crazy for You," "Live to Tell," "This Used to Be My Playground," and "Take a Bow," as well as a handful of first-rate album tracks (a remixed "Love Don't Live Here Anymore," "Something to Remember," "Oh Father"), and three new tracks, most notably a version of Marvin Gaye's "I Want You" recorded with the British trip-hop group Massive Attack. Only two tracks on the album overlap with *The Immaculate Collection*, and the disc also marks the first appearance of "This Used to Be My Playground" and "I'll Remember" on one of Madonna's albums. Throughout the album, Madonna proves that she's a terrific singer whose voice has improved over the years. Not one of the tracks is second-rate, and the best songs on *Something to Remember* rank among the best pop music of the '80s and '90s. *—Stephen Thomas Erlewine*

Selections from Evita / Jul. 29, 1997 / Warner Brothers ✦✦✦

Ray of Light / Mar. 3, 1998 / Maverick ✦✦✦✦
Returning to pop after a four-year hiatus, Madonna enlisted respected techno producer William Orbit as her collaborator for *Ray of Light*, a self-conscious effort to stay abreast of contemporary trends. Unlike other veteran artists who attempted to come to terms with electronica, Madonna was always a dance artist, so it's no real shock to hear her sing over breakbeats, pulsating electronics, and blunted trip-hop beats. Still, it's mildly surprising that it works as well as it does, largely due to Madonna and Orbit's subtle attack. They've reigned in the beats, tamed electronica's eccentricities, and retained her flair for pop melodies, creating the first mainstream pop album that successfully embraces techno. Sonically, it's the most adventurous record she has made, but it's far from inaccessible, since the textures are alluring and the songs have a strong melodic foundation, whether it's the swirling title track, the meditative opener, "Substitute for Love," or the ballad "Frozen." For all of its attributes, there's a certain distance to *Ray of Light*, born of the carefully constructed productions and Madonna's newly mannered, technically precise singing. It all results in her most mature and restrained album, which is an easy achievement to admire, yet not necessarily an easy one to love. *—Stephen Thomas Erlewine*

Music / Sep. 19, 2000 / Maverick ✦✦✦✦
Filled with vocoders, stylish neo-electro beats, dalliances with trip-hop, and, occasionally, eerie synthesized atmospherics, *Music* blows by in a kaleidoscopic rush of color, technique, style, and substance. It has so many layers that it's easily as self-aware and earnest as *Ray of Light*, where her studiousness complimented a record heavy on spirituality and reflection. Here, she mines that territory occasionally, especially as the record winds toward its conclusion, but she applies her new tricks toward celebrations of music itself. That's not only true of the full-throttle dance numbers but also for ballads like "I Deserve It" and "Nobody's Perfect," where the sentiments are couched in electronic effects and lolling, rolling beats. Ultimately, that results in the least introspective or revealing record Madonna has made since *Like a Prayer*, yet that doesn't mean she doesn't invest herself in the record. Working with a stable of producers, she has created an album that is her most explicitly musical and restlessly creative since, well, *Like a Prayer*. She may have sacrificed some cohesion for that willful creativity but it's hard to begrudge her that, since so much of the album works. If, apart from the haunting closer "Gone," the Orbit collaborations fail to equal *Ray of Light* or "Beautiful Stranger," they're still sleekly admirable, and they're offset by the terrific Guy Sigsworth/Mark "Spike" Stent mid-tempo cut "What It Feels Like for a Girl" and Madonna's thriving partnership with Mirwais. This team is responsible for the heart of the record, with such stunners as the intricate, sensual, folk-psych "Don't Tell Me," the eerily seductive "Paradise (Not for Me)," and the thumping title track, which sounds funkier, denser, sexier with each spin. Whenever she works with Mirwais, *Music* truly comes alive with the spark and style. *—Stephen Thomas Erlewine*

Magazine

f. 1977, **db.** 1981
Group / Post-Punk
After leaving the Buzzcocks in 1977, vocalist Howard Devoto formed Magazine; one of the first post-punk bands, they kept the edgy, nervous energy of punk, adding elements of art-rock, particularly with their theatrical live shows and shards of keyboards. Devoto's lyrics were combinations of social commentary and poetic fragments, while the band alternated between cold, jagged chords and gloomy, atmospheric sonic landscapes. Magazine's first single, "Shot by Both Sides," appeared in early 1978, gathering good reviews on both sides of the Atlantic and charting in the U.K. at number 41. *Real Life*, released later in 1978, con-

tinued the confrontational, arty pop-punk of "Shot by Both Sides." *Secondhand Daylight* was somewhat of a departure from the debut, featuring more keyboards, smoother rhythms, and streamlined lyrics from Devoto. Despite its ambitiousness, the record was poorly received by the press. In the summer of 1980, Magazine released "Sweetheart Contract," which became their second and last British chart hit, peaking at number 54. *Magic, Murder and the Weather* was released in the spring of 1981; it proved to be Magazine's last album. Devoto left the group in May of 1981 to pursue a solo career and the band broke up shortly afterward. —*Stephen Thomas Erlewine*

Real Life / Apr. 1978 / Blue Plate ✦✦✦✦✦

Secondhand Daylight / 1979 / Blue Plate ✦✦✦✦

The Correct Use of Soap / 1980 / Blue Plate ✦✦✦✦✦

Play. / 1980 / EMI ✦✦

Magic Murder & the Weather / Sep. 1981 / EMI ✦✦✦

Maybe It's Right to Be Nervous Now / Sep. 25, 2000 / Virgin ✦✦✦✦
Magazine's three-disc box set is a mess. Breaking the group's history down to two eras spread across the first two thirds of the box and adding a fantastic and well-needed third disc dedicated solely to Peel Sessions, it's yet another multi-disc package that half-pleases both fan and neophyte. Only *four* of the 45 tracks come directly from the band's four studio LPs. Oddly enough, seven tenths of the decent live album *Play* is strewn across the first two discs. Why include the majority of a live album that caters to diehards, therefore leaving out the better studio versions— Eight B-sides are scattered throughout, most of which were previously available on *Scree*. Four "alternative mixes" add further frustration, including a sub-standard (demo?) "Shot by Both Sides." That could be the biggest gripe. Not including the definitive version of "Shot by Both Sides," which is to post-punk what "Anarchy in the U.K." is to punk, would be similar to leaving "Love Is the Drug" off of a Roxy Music collection. So aside from the Peel Sessions, a fan is getting hardly anything new. The neophyte would be better off picking up the single-disc *Where the Power Is*, which draws from this and obviously costs less. The Peel Sessions disc is the real meat. Four sessions yield 15 thoroughly exciting songs. Everything is delivered with excellence, although Howard Devoto might have wanted impair keyboardist Dave Formula's busy hands. Some versions might be preferable to their album counterparts, including the furious take on the Devoto/Pete Shelley-penned "Boredom." Despite the numerous complications with this box, the high rating is deserved. Many would argue that it could have been done better, but the material is undoubtedly strong. The package itself is a treat, containing the results of Devoto's personal archive ransacking. —*Andy Kellman*

● **Where the Power Is** / Sep. 25, 2000 / Virgin ✦✦✦✦✦
An accurate title, *Where the Power Is* successfully trots out the bouncier, assaultive side of Magazine. They were one of the best in the early era of post-punk, rarely doing anything mediocre. Released simultaneously with the triple-disc *Maybe It's Right to Be Nervous Now*, it oddly duplicates much of 1987's *Rays and Hail* compilation. So why not keep *Rays and Hail* in print and just reissue it with additional liner notes or something? Well, the answer's commerce. A new title means new sales, and even completists will apprehensively shell out again for the same batch of songs. Literally—there's only a handful of songs here that aren't on *Rays and Hail*. Though some of the versions may differ (album version versus single version), only compulsive completists give a toss about such things. Confusingly, *Rays and Hail did remain in print* when this was issued, even getting a re-pressing! Did someone in Virgin's catalog department fall asleep— Fine as an isolated release for the newbie, *Where the Power Is* just makes things quite confusing for the rest, basically a baffler amongst the rest of Magazine's discography. Not a great deal can be debated as far as it being representative is concerned, so in that manner it succeeds. —*Andy Kellman*

Magnetic Fields

f. 1990, Boston, MA
Group / Indie Pop, Indie Rock, Lo-Fi
The Magnetic Fields are a bonafide band, but in most essential respects they are the project of studio wunderkind Stephin Merritt, who writes, produces, and (lately) sings all of their material, as well as plays many of the instruments, concocting a sort of indie-pop synth-rock. While the Magnetic Fields may draw upon the electronic textures of vintage acts like ABBA, Kraftwerk, Roxy Music with Eno, Joy Division, and Gary Numan, Merritt's vision is far more pointed toward the alternative rock underground. His songs are also far warmer and more pure pop-oriented than the above reference points might lead you to believe, sounding at times like late-20th century equivalents to Phil Spector or Brian Wilson, with an emphasis on pop hooks and eccentric, romantically reflective lyrics rather than the bedrock synthetic rhythms and textures. In addition to his work with Magnetic Fields, Merritt has involved himself in several side projects, the most notable being the 6ths' all-star *Wasps Nests* album. —*Richie Unterberger*

Distant Plastic Trees / 1990 / Red Flame ✦✦✦

The Wayward Bus / 1991 / Feel Good All Over ✦✦✦✦
The last of the two Magnetic Fields albums to feature Susan Amway as lead singer, this has Merritt's most gorgeous melodies and most pop-friendly production, strongly recalling Phil Spector in particular (more than one of the songs quotes the opening "Be My Baby" rhythms). Merge has combined this album and its predecessor, *Distant Plastic Trees*, onto one disc with its CD reissue. —*Richie Unterberger*

The Charm of the Highway Strip / 1994 / Merge ✦✦✦✦
Merritt took more of a narrative approach than usual on this album, which was in part inspired (as the title indicates) by on-the-road experiences, and exhibited a (very slight) country influence. Not as good as *Holiday*, although it has characteristically agile songwriting and production. —*Richie Unterberger*

Holiday / 1994 / Merge ✦✦✦✦
Starting with this album Merritt, who had never sung on previous Magnetic Fields discs, took over the vocal chores with the departure of Susan Amway. His low and somewhat sober tones are less accessible, and the music began to move in a more percolating electro-pop direction as well. This is probably the most enjoyable of their Merritt-sung efforts, though, with a couple of real standouts in "The Trouble I've Been Looking For" and "In My Car." —*Richie Unterberger*

The Wayward Bus/Distant Plastic Trees / Jan. 23, 1995 / Merge ✦✦✦✦
Both of the group's debut album are combined onto one CD for this reissue, which effectively summarizes the period in which all of the Magnetic Fields' material was sung by Susan Amway, rather than Stephin Merritt. There are reservations attached to recommending this as the first purchase, since the subsequent albums, on which Merritt handles all of the vocals, are obviously a more accurate reflection of his auteurist vision. The fact is, however, that the Amway-sung albums are more immediately attractive to most listeners, especially *The Wayward Bus*. —*Richie Unterberger*

Get Lost / Oct. 24, 1995 / Merge ✦✦✦

● **69 Love Songs** / Sep. 7, 1999 / Merge ✦✦✦✦✦
As the sprawling magnitude of its cheeky title suggests, *69 Love Songs* is Stephin Merritt's most ambitious as well as fully realized work to date, a three-disc epic of classically chiseled pop songs that explore both the promise and pitfalls of modern romance through the jaundiced eye of an irredeemable misanthrope. A true A-to-Z catalog of touchingly bittersweet love songs that runs the gamut from tender ballads to pithy folk tunes to bluesy vamps, the sheer scope of the record allows all of Merritt's musical personas to converge: the regular use of guest vocalists recalls his work as the 6ths, the romantic fatalism suggests the Gothic Archies project, and the stately melodies evoke the Future Bible Heroes. The whole is much greater than the sum of its parts, however; for all of Merritt's scathing wit and icy detachment, there's a depth and sensitivity to these songs largely absent from his past work, and each one of these 69 tracks approaches *l'amour* from refreshing angles, galvanizing the love song form with rare sophistication and elegance. Naturally, given a project of this size there's the occasional bit of filler, but all in all, *69 Love Songs* maintains a remarkable consistency throughout, and the highlights ("I Don't Believe in the Sun," "All My Little Words," "Asleep and Dreaming," "Busby Berkeley Dreams," and "Acoustic Guitar," to name just a few) are jaw-droppingly superb. Also available as three individual releases, *69 Love Songs* was nevertheless conceived as a whole and is best absorbed as such, with all of its twists and turns taken in stride; despite its three-hour length, the music boasts the craftsmanship and economy that remain the hallmarks of classic American pop songwriting, a tradition Merritt upholds even as he subverts the formula in new and brilliant ways. —*Jason Ankeny*

The Mamas & the Papas

f. 1964, New York, NY, **db.** 1972
Group / Sunshine Pop, Folk-Rock, Pop
The leading California-based vocal group of the '60s, the Mamas & the Papas epitomized the ethos of mid- to late-'60s pop culture: live free, play free, and love free. Their music, built around radiant harmonies and a solid electric-folk foundation, was gorgeous on its own terms, but a major part of its appeal lay in the easygoing Southern California lifestyle it endorsed.

Founder and leader John Phillips came out of early rock roots and a partly successful folk career, as did Cass Elliott and Denny Doherty, while Phillips' wife Michelle was an ex-model who also sang. They got together out of several failed folk groups just as the music was going electric, pulled up stakes in New York and headed west, where they signed with Lou Adler and wowed the world with a song called "California Dreamin."

Phillips was a pop poet with a commercial edge, and a good arranger. The group had enviable chart success, lived well, and indulged themselves lavishly yet retained credibility with the counterculture. But it all came apart in a couple of years, as the quartet's intertwining romantic entanglements, coupled with their chemical excesses (detailed in separate books by John and Michelle Phillips), strangled their ability to work. By 1971 they were a fond memory, although a reconstituted version of the quartet has done well on the oldies circuit in the late '80s and early '90s. —*Bruce Eder*

Creeque Alley / Mar. 12, 1991 / MCA ✦✦✦✦✦
They weren't the most important folk-rock group of the mid-'60s; the Byrds and others produced more enduring music. Yet the Mamas & the Papas were undoubtedly the most commercially successful folk-rock group of their time, racking up an astonishing nine Top 30 hits in little more than a year and a half. This 43-song double CD is by far the most comprehensive document of their legacy. It draws most heavily from their two 1966 albums (nine songs originate from their debut album *If You Can Believe Your Eyes and Ears* alone), when John Phillips' songwriting talent had yet to exhaust itself. Beyond the hits, the material is variable. Quite a few album tracks—especially "Got a Feelin'," "Straight Shooter," "Go Where You Wanna Go," "Once Was a Time I Thought," and their cover of Lennon/McCartney's "I Call Your Name"—were strong enough to have been hits under their own steam. Their slowed-down, California-ized versions of rock oldies were more problematic. And there's no doubt that their later material is less spirited and memorable than their initial burst of glory. The set includes various late-'60s and '70s solo recordings by each of the group's members (including small hit singles by John Phillips and Cass Elliott). Perhaps the most intriguing rarities are from the members' pre-Mamas days. These include commercial folk by the Big Three (featuring Cass Elliott) and primitive pop-folk-rock by the Mugwumps (including Elliott, Denny Doherty, and future Lovin' Spoonful member Zal Yanovsky). —*Richie Unterberger*

● **Greatest Hits** / Mar. 10, 1998 / MCA ✦✦✦✦✦
Not to be confused with earlier hits compilations, the catalog number on this 20-song collection is MCAD-11740. This is the single-CD successor to *Creeque Alley*, the double-disc career retrospective issued in the early 1990s. All of the hits from "California Dreamin'" to "Dream a Little Dream of Me" are here, along with their more celebrated album tracks, and the notes by Joseph Laredo provide a decent overview of the group's formation and history.

The stuff has been remastered yet again, although the level of improvement over *Creeque Alley* seems modest (*Creeque Alley* sounded really good) compared with that double disc's improvement over the earlier, wholly inadequate masters from the 1980s. For someone who doesn't have a lot of money to spend on the band, this is the place to start, superseding all other single-disc hits collections. *—Bruce Eder*

Manic Street Preachers

f. 1991

Group / Britpop, Alternative Pop/Rock

Dressed in glam clothing, wearing heavy eyeliner and shouting political rhetoric, the Manic Street Preachers emerged from their hometown of Blackwood, Wales in 1991 as self-styled "Generation Terrorists." Fashioning themselves after the Clash and the Sex Pistols, the Manics were on a mission, intending to restore revolution to rock & roll at a time when Britain was dominated by trancy shoegazers and faceless, trippy acid-house. Their self-consciously dangerous image, leftist leanings, crunching hard rock and outsider status made them favorites of the British music press and helped them build a rabidly dedicated following. For much of the band's early career, it was impossible to separate the rhetoric from the music and even from the members themselves—the group's image was forever associated with lyricist/guitarist Richey James carving the words "4 Real" into his arm during an early interview. As the British pop music climate shifted toward Brit-pop in the wake of Suede, the Manics didn't achieve fame, but they had notoriety. Legions of followers emerged, including many bands that formed the core of the short-lived New Wave of New Wave movement. But as the group climbed toward stardom, the story didn't get simpler—it got weirder. James' behavior became increasingly bizarre, culminating on the group's harrowing 1994 album, *The Holy Bible*. Early in 1995, James disappeared, leaving no trace of his whereabouts. The remaining trio carried on with 1996's *Everything Must Go*, the album that established them as superstars in England, yet that came at the expense of the arrogant, renegade gender-bending and revolutionary rhetoric that earned them their initial fan base. *—Stephen Thomas Erlewine*

Generation Terrorists / Feb. 1992 / Columbia ✦✦✦✦

Debut albums rarely come as ambitious as the Manic Street Preachers' *Generation Terrorists*. Released in England as a double album (it was trimmed to the length of a single record in America), the album teemed with slogans, political rhetoric, and scarily inarticulate angst. Since the Manics deliver these charged lyrics as heavy guitar-rockers, the music doesn't always hit quite as forcefully as intended. The relatively polished production and big guitar sound occasionally sell the music short, especially the lesser songs, yet the Manics' passion is undeniable, even on the weaker cuts. While the album is loaded with a little bit too much unrealized material in retrospect, its best moments—the fiery "Slash N' Burn," "Little Baby Nothing," the incendiary "Stay Beautiful," the sardonic "You Love Us," and the haunting "Motorcycle Emptiness"—capture the Manics in all their raging glory. *—Stephen Thomas Erlewine*

Gold Against the Soul / Jun. 1993 / Columbia ✦✦✦

The Holy Bible / Aug. 1994 / Epic ✦✦✦✦✦

It's difficult not to look at *The Holy Bible* as Richey James' last will and testament, yet that only makes the record all the more powerful. A remarkable step forward from the Manic Street Preachers' first two records, *The Holy Bible* is a tense, harrowing collection of tortured, cryptic declarations of depression—the diary of anorexia "4st 7lb" is one of the most chilling songs in rock & roll. James' lyrics, which are punctuated by Nicky Wire's political tirades, are unflinching in their bleakness. Every song has a passage frightening in its imagery. Although the music itself isn't as scarily intense, its tight, terse hard rock and glam hooks accentuate the paranoia behind the songs, making the lyrics cut deeper. *—Stephen Thomas Erlewine*

● **Everything Must Go** / May 1996 / Epic ✦✦✦✦✦

Months after the release of the harrowing *The Holy Bible*, Manic Street Preachers guitarist Richey James disappeared, leaving no trace of his whereabouts or his well-being. Ultimately, the remaining trio decided to carry on, releasing their fourth album *Everything Must Go* in 1996. Considering the tragic circumstances that surrounded it, *Everything Must Go* is the strongest, most focused, and certainly the most optimistic album the Manics ever released. Five of the songs feature lyrics Richey left behind before his disappearance, and while offering no motivation for his actions, they do hint at the depths of his despair. Nicky Wire wrote the remaining lyrics, and his songs give the record its weight and balance, confronting the issue of Richey's disappearance in a roundabout way, never explicitly mentioning the topic but offering a gritty dose of realistic optimism offering the hope that things *will* get better; after the nihilism of *The Holy Bible*, the outlook is all the more inspiring. Furthermore, the Manics' musical attack has become leaner; their music still rages, but it's channeled into concise, anthemic rock songs that soar on their own belief. Above all, *Everything Must Go* is a cathartic experience—it is genuinely moving to hear the Manics offering hope without sinking to mawkish sentimentality or collapsing under the weight of their situation. *—Stephen Thomas Erlewine*

This Is My Truth Tell Me Yours / Aug. 25, 1998 / Virgin ✦✦✦✦

If *Everything Must Go* found the Manic Street Preachers coping with Richey James' sudden, unexplained disappearance, its follow-up *This Is My Truth, Tell Me Yours* finds them putting the tragedy behind them and flourishing as a trio. Wisely, the group builds on the grand sound of *Everything Must Go*, creating a strangely effective fusion of string-drenched, sweeping arena rock and impassioned, brutally honest punk. Since the band never writes about anything less than major issues, whether it be political or personal, it's appropriate that their music sounds as majestic and overpowering as their pretensions. Given that the first single was title "If You Tolerate This, Then Your Children Will Be Next," calling the Manics pretentious is fair game, but they make their pretensions work through a blend of intelligence, passion and sheer musicality. *This Is My Truth* sports more musical variety than its predecessors, which means it can meander a bit, particularly toward the end. Nevertheless, these misgivings disappear with repeated listens, as each song logically flows into the next. If the album ultimately isn't as raw or shattering as *The Holy Bible* or emotionally wrenching as *Everything Must Go*, it's because the ghost of Richey has been put behind them. That doesn't mean that *This Is My Truth* is light, easygoing listening—the portentous, murky closer "SYMM" guarantees that—but it's not as torturous as its immediate predecessors. But what it shares with them is a searing passion and intelligence that is unmatched among their peers on either side of the ocean—and, in doing so, it emphasizes the Manics' uniqueness as one of the few bands of the '90s that can deliver albums as bracing intellectually as they are sonically. *—Stephen Thomas Erlewine*

Barry Manilow (Barry Alan Pincus)

b. Jun. 17, 1946, Brooklyn, NY

Vocals, Piano / Soft Rock, Adult Contemporary

Although he has never earned the respect of critics or much of the public, Barry Manilow was one of the most successful recording artists of the '70s. Manilow began his pop music career by writing advertising jingles in the '60s; during this time, the Juilliard-trained musician honed his pop instincts, as evidenced by the sheer number of successful advertisements he wrote. In 1971, he began accompanying Bette Midler on piano as she performed in New York City's gay bathhouses. Manilow arranged her first two albums, which helped him earn a record contract with Bell. His self-titled first album was a flop, yet his second featured the number one ballad "Mandy."

"Mandy" began a decade's worth of polished MOR hits for Manilow, which included the number one singles "I Write the Songs" and "Looks Like We Made It," as well as Top Tens "Could It Be Magic," "Copacabana (At the Copa)" and "I Made It Through the Rain." Manilow also became a popular live act during this time. By the mid-'80s, he decided to broaden his musical horizons by making records of jazz and pop standards. At the end of the decade, the widow of Johnny Mercer invited him to set music to a number of the great songwriter's unpublished lyrics. Manilow continued in a similar vein on the records *Singin' with the Big Bands* (1994) and *Another Life* (1995), before he made the nostalgia-drenched *Summer of '78* in 1996. *Sings Sinatra* followed two years later. *—Stephen Thomas Erlewine*

● **Greatest Hits, Vol. 1** / Nov. 1978 / Arista ✦✦✦✦✦

The first half of the 1978 two-record set *Greatest Hits*, the CD issue of *Greatest Hits, Vol. 1* contains ten tracks from Manilow's '70s prime; however, since it's incomplete without the material on *Vol. 2*, those looking for a more or less definitive overview will need both volumes. For those who want more, the rest of this period's worthwhile songs not on these two volumes can be found on *Live*. *—Steve Huey*

Greatest Hits, Vol. 2 / Nov. 1983 / Arista ✦✦✦✦✦

The second half of the 1978 two-record set *Greatest Hits*, the CD issue of *Greatest Hits, Vol. 2* contains nine tracks from Manilow's '70s prime; however, since it's incomplete without the material on *Vol. 1*, those looking for a more or less definitive overview will need both volumes. For those who want more, the rest of this period's worthwhile songs not found on these two volumes can be heard on *Live*. *—Steve Huey*

Greatest Hits, Vol. 3 / 1989 / Arista ✦✦✦✦✦

Manilow's third volume of *Greatest Hits* is less essential than the first two, covering mostly selections from his less successful post-'70s career (*One Voice* onward). This isn't his most popular or memorable material, but it is a handy overview of his more uneven early-'80s career for fans who want to dig a little deeper but don't want to search out those albums. *—Steve Huey*

Aimee Mann

b. Aug. 9, 1960

Vocals, Guitar, Bass / Pop Underground, Adult Alternative Pop/Rock, Singer/Songwriter

During the '80s, Aimee Man led the post-new wave pop group, Til Tuesday. After releasing three albums with the group, Mann broke up the band and embarked on a solo career. Her first solo album, *Whatever*, was a more introspective, folk-tinged effort than Til Tuesday's albums and received uniformly positive reviews upon its release in the summer of 1993. Early in 1995, Mann had a modest hit with "That's Just What You Are," a song included on the soundtrack to the television series, *Melrose Place*. After her long dispute with former label Imago was finally settled, she signed with DGC Records. Mann's second album, *I'm with Stupid*, was released in England in the late fall of 1995 and in January of 1996 in America. Again, it was greeted to positive reviews, but weak sales. *—Stephen Thomas Erlewine*

Whatever / May 11, 1993 / Geffen ✦✦✦✦✦

On her solo debut *Whatever*, the former vocalist for Til Tuesday cements her position as a center-stage artist and top-notch songwriter, and Aimee Mann's blend of wit, smarts, cynicism, and downright humability make for a wonderfully pleasing collection of catchy songs. Musically, the jangle-pop feel of *Whatever* harkens back to the Beatles and the Byrds but without forsaking its contemporary origin. Lyrically, it is often hard to know whether Mann is spilling her guts out over a love or a deal gone bad. In fact, it is often a combination. But the seamless ease with which she tells the tales, moving from her head to her heart and back again, exposes her mighty talent. Teaming with some of her former bandmates, including longtime collaborator Jon Brion, gives Mann a comfort and a sure footing from which to climb and stretch, which she does with certainty. "I Should've Known," "Could've Been Anyone," and "Say Anything" get the heads bobbing, while the more somber "4th of July" and "Stupid Thing" will beckon forth even the loneliest of hankies. And how many artists pay tribute to Charles Dickens? (Witness "Jacob Marley's Chain.") Talk about literate songwriters and you have to speak of Aimee Mann. The dismissive tone of the title belies the time that was put into this album, for even after its recording, it took Mann quite a long while to find a home. Initially released on Imago Records, *Whatever* was later reissued by Geffen Records. *—Kelly McCartney*

I'm with Stupid / Nov. 1995 / Geffen ✦✦✦

From the opening of "Long Shot," twith its rolling hip-hop-derived beat and its nonchalant profanity, it's clear that Aimee Mann is trying to appeal to a wider audience with her second solo album, *I'm with Stupid*. Taking her cues from Liz Phair and Beck, she adds alternative rock flourishes to her music but she never abandons her love of the basic, three-minute pop single. Mann builds from the more pop-oriented songs on *Whatever,* incorporating her confessional singer/songwriter instincts into the pop songs while working with a more adventerous production and instrumentation. Occasionally, the fusion is a bit awkward, but the best moments on *I'm with Stupid*—the sighing "Choice in the Matter," the nearly perfect "That's Just What You Are," featuring backing vocals by Glenn Tilbrook, and the Bernard Butler collaboration "Sugarcoated"—surpass even the best moments on *Whatever.* However, *I'm With Stupid* falls short of matching Mann's debut for consistent song quality—there are several tracks that are pleasant, but simply don't lead anywhere. Nevertheless, the album confirms that she is a distinctive, talented songwriter. At her best, she is as capable of melding melody with intelligent lyrics as her idols Elvis Costello, Difford/Tilbrook, and Ray Davies. *—Stephen Thomas Erlewine*

● **Bachelor No. 2** / May 2, 2000 / Superego ✦✦✦✦✦
It's no shock that *Bachelor No. 2, or the last remains of the dodo* sounds identical to her songs for Paul Thomas Anderson's *Magnolia,* since it was written and recorded at roughly the same time (the two records share four songs). Yet *Bachelor No. 2* is hardly a retread, having its own identity and flow; it's more intimate, a little more fragile, a little more craftsmanslike—more like an Aimee Mann record, really. That, of course, is not a bad thing, especially since Mann has never sounded as assured as she does here, nor has she ever had a better set of songs. Surprisingly, this cohesive album was produced by a handful of different producers and Mann collaborated with three songwriters (Jon Brion being the most noteworthy of both categories). It sounds like the work of one writer and one production team, which is testament to the fact that Mann has finally found the ideal sound to match her literate, mildly self-deprecating, clever, melancholy, melodic style. *Bachelor No. 2* is crisp, clear, and direct, but deceptive. It's hardly a guitar-and-voice record, there are layers of details in the arrangements, particularly in how the various guitars and keyboards weave seamlessly together. There has never been a better sound for her songs, and she's never been more consistently compelling as a writer either. To call *Bachelor No. 2* a masterpiece may be overstating the matter somewhat, since an album this unassuming (but not unconfident) is too intimate to be labeled as such, yet it isn't hyperbole to call it the finest record Mann has made to date. *—Stephen Thomas Erlewine*

Ultimate Collection / Sep. 12, 2000 / Hip-O ✦✦✦✦✦
Unable to get an album released between 1995 and 1999, Aimee Mann suddenly had three on the market within 12 months, including this September 2000 compilation. There is, of course, a certain irony that the current configuration of a record company that gave her so much trouble (demanding changes to her third album, refusing to release it, dropping her, and then forcing her to buy back the album's master tapes) is now attempting to cash in on the exposure she received due to her 1999 Academy Award nomination for "Save Me" from *Magnolia.* Mann's music is catchy, guitar-based pop/rock, which *sounds* like it should be at the top of the charts. But since Mann has reached the Top 40 only twice in 15 years, she has largely been subject to standard operating procedure in the major-label record business. Journalists have howled largely on critical grounds, and *Ultimate Collection* should give them more ammunition despite its limits. One of her two hits, "What About Love," is not included, and only three tracks have been licensed from her most popular period. Two regular albums doesn't seem like much material to choose from for a best-of, so to make up for the limited choice of material, compilation producer Rhonda Shields has pulled a variety of stray tracks, turning this into a virtual rarities album. Several songs were contributed to movie soundtracks, and five tracks are drawn from the non-LP B-sides of singles. Thus, even those who have copies of *Whatever* and *I'm With Stupid* will need this album, and they will find that the rarities are some of her better performances. Aimee Mann is unquestionably one of the most impressive singer/songwriters of her time, but her lyrics of bitter romantic complaint may destine her to a limited audience. *—William Ruhlmann*

Manfred Mann (Manfred Lubowitz)

b. Oct. 21, 1940, Johannesburg, South Africa
Vocals, Keyboards / Jazz-Rock, Pop/Rock, British Invasion, Prog-Rock/Art Rock
The scion of a wealthy South African family, Manfred Lubowitz recognized while still a teenager that his real interests lay far from Johannesburg and its white-dominated culture—rather, he wanted to play jazz and blues. To do this, he ultimately had to leave South Africa for England, where he picked up a new stage name, Manfred Manne (the last name borrowed from Shelly Manne), later Manfred Mann. He also found a friend and collaborator in one Mike Hugg, a drummer with whom he formed a band that—against his wishes—was ultimately christened Manfred Mann. The various incarnations of Manfred Mann, playing jazz and r&b-based rock and later pop-rock and progressive rock, lasted until 1971, when the man took back his name. Future group names, mostly designated Manfred Mann's Earth Band, would have an apostrophe attached to his name, as Mann also embarked on a career as a producer and songwriter. He has also released recordings designated as solo projects, usually under the title "Manfred Mann's Plain Music." *—Bruce Eder*

The Manfred Mann Album / 1964 / Ascot ✦✦✦
Manfred Mann's debut full-length U.S. platter was probably their strongest, and indeed one of the stronger British Invasion albums of the very competitive year of 1964. Besides the smash "Do Wah Diddy Diddy," ait contained a number of fine soul and R&B covers. Standouts were the versions of "Untie Me" and Ike & Tina Turner's "It's Gonna Work Out Fine," as well as the strong pounding Paul Jones original, "Without You." *—Richie Unterberger*

☆ **The Five Faces of Manfred Mann** / Sep. 11, 1964 / EMI ✦✦✦✦✦
The debut album by Manfred Mann holds up even better 40 years on than it did in 1964. It's also one of the longest LPs of its era, clocking in at 39 minutes, and there's not a wasted note or a song extended too far among its 14 tracks. The Manfreds never had the reputation that the Rolling Stones enjoyed, which is a shame, because *The Five Faces of Manfred Mann* is one of the great blues-based British invasion albums; it's a hot, rocking record that benefits from some virtuoso playing as well, and some of the best singing of its era, courtesy of Paul Jones, who blew most of his rivals out of the competition with his magnificently impassioned, soulful performance on "Untie Me," and his simmering, lusty renditions of "Smokestack Lightning" and "Bring It to Jerome." The stereo mix of the album, which never surfaced officially in England until this 1997 EMI anniversary reissue (remastered in 24-bit digital sound), holds up very nicely, with sharp separation between the channels yet—apart from a few moments on "Untie Me"—few moments of artificiality. *—Bruce Eder*

Mann Made / 1965 / HMV ✦✦✦✦✦
The group's second British album, released just as the original lineup was entering a state of collapse with the impending departure of two key members, shows some of the changes that can happen in a year, as they move away from Chess Records' brand of blues as their baseline. Instead, they produce a sound that slightly smoother and a lot more soulful. A handful of originals, mostly by Mike Vickers and Mike Hugg with one Paul Jones-authored number thrown in, are scattered amid covers of songs originated by the Temptations, the Skyliners, and T-Bone Walker. If it isn't as fierce, bold, or daringly ambitious as the Manfreds' debut long-player, *Mann Made* is just as much a virtuoso effort, and a surprisingly cohesive one considering that it was released immediately after Mike Vickers and Paul Jones announced their respective departures from the band. The 1997 EMI 100th Anniversary series edition features 24-bit digital EMI CD remastering that is as sharp and clean as one could possibly hope for. *—Bruce Eder*

My Little Red Book of Winners / 1965 / Ascot ✦✦✦✦

Soul of Mann / 1967 / See For Miles ✦✦✦

Chapter Three, Vol. 1 / 1969 / Polydor ✦✦✦✦

The Roaring Silence / 1976 / Warner Brothers ✦✦✦✦✦
A later edition of Mann's band, which had a '70s hit with Bruce Springsteen's "Blinded by the Light" (on this album). *—William Ruhlmann*

● **The Best of Manfred Mann: The Definitive Collection** / Jun. 2, 1992 / EMI America ✦✦✦✦✦
This is one of nearly a dozen anthologies of Manfred Mann's music that cover their EMI period, and the 25 songs here make it the biggest of them. Additionally, there is an 11-minute interview with the band here, dating from December of 1964, that has never before appeared on record in the United States. The hits are all here, sometimes in more than one version, along with a cross-section of album tracks and B-sides, and it all sounds very good, though EMI's recent 24-bit remasterings of the band's original British LPs are much more impressive. But this CD misses being "definitive" because it leaves out some key B-sides to their early singles and overlooks the contents of several top-selling British EPs. The truth be told, no single CD, even one 73 minutes long, would be adequate to the task of defining this group's history or sound, even just covering the years 1963-66. As it is, the presence here of numbers like "She" and "The One in the Middle" (both written by Paul Jones) and their version of "My Little Red Book" (not a favorite of the band members, incidentally), makes this an essential part of any collection of the band's work, but one should also own *The Singles Plus* to get access to numbers like "Groovin'" and "Brother Jack," and the individual U.K. albums have enough merit to make them every bit as essential. In fairness, *The Definitive Collection* is the most thoroughly annotated compilation of the group's work to surface as of the year 2000, and the group interview, though superficial and awkward, makes it unique. *—Bruce Eder*

Chapter Two: The Best of the Fontana Years / Oct. 11, 1994 / Fontana ✦✦✦
The departure of Paul Jones for a solo career in 1966 spelled major reorganization for Manfred and his troops, who recruited lead vocalist Mike D'Abo and bassist (and Beatle chum) Klaus Voormann. To the surprise of many, the new lineup rattled off seven Top Ten British hits in the next three years in a far less R&B-oriented style. Emphasizing harmonies and Manfred Mann's inventiveness as arranger and keyboardist (often employing the then-futuristic Mellotron), this represented the group's most commercial phase, with an upbeat approach that bordered on downright chipper. These 20 tracks include all the key singles from this time, as well as a few LP cuts. Frankly, this rather lightweight, prototypically cheery late-'60s British pop—sounding rather like a more commercial version of the *Odessey & Oracle*-era Zombies—hasn't aged nearly as well as their far gutsier Paul Jones-era recordings. Only one of these songs was a hit in the U.S., but it was a big one—their great 1968 arrangement of the then-unreleased Bob Dylan song "The Mighty Quinn." *—Richie Unterberger*

The Best of Manfred Mann's Earth Band / 1996 / Warner Archives ✦✦✦

Groovin' with the Manfreds (The Manfred Mann R&B Album) / 1996 / EMI ✦✦✦✦

● **The Best of the EMI Years** / Jan. 23, 1996 / Griffin ✦✦✦✦✦
This double-CD replaces EMI's *Best Of* anthology (1992) as the collection of choice for their British Invasion years due to its slightly more extensive length (34 tracks), including most of the tracks on the previous compilation. It has all of the British and American hits, as well as some standout B-sides and album tracks, some of which have been quite hard to come by on reissues. Classic British Invasion music by one of the most versatile bands of the era, comfortable with both straight pop/rock and jazz-tinged R&B. *—Richie Unterberger*

Manfred Mann Album/Five Faces of Manfred Mann / Feb. 20, 1996 / EMI ✦✦✦✦✦

BBC Sessions / Nov. 3, 1998 / EMI ✦✦✦

The Mar-Keys

f. 1958, Memphis, TN
Group / Southern Soul, Instrumental Rock, Soul
Despite scoring only one national hit, the 1961 instrumental smash "Last Night," the Mar-Keys remain one of the most important groups ever to emerge from the Memphis music scene. As the first house band for the legendary Stax label, they appeared on some of the greatest records in soul history, with their ranks also producing such renowned musicians as guitarist Steve Cropper and bassist Donald "Duck" Dunn. The Mar-Keys formed in 1958 and included drummer Terry Johnson, pianist Jerry Lee "Smoochie" Smith, saxophonists Don Nix and Charles Axton, and trumpeter Wayne Jackson in addition to Cropper and Dunn. Origi-

nally dubbed the Royal Spades, in 1960 the group joined the staff at Axton's mother Estelle's Satellite label, backing artists that included Rufus Thomas and his daughter Carla. A year later, the Mar-Keys headlined the Chips Moman-penned "Last Night," which reached the number three spot in the summer of 1961. When Satellite changed its name to Stax, the Mar-Keys remained on board, laying the foundation for the classic Memphis soul sound through with their funky, sophisticated grooves; concurrently they recorded a series of singles including "Pop-Eye Stroll," "The Morning After," and "Philly Dog," although none repeated the commercial success of "Last Night." In 1962 Cropper and Dunn left the lineup to co-found the famed Booker T. and the MG's. Other personnel changes followed, although the Mar-Keys continued on for several more years before the name was eventually dropped. Jackson then formed another top-notch session group, the Memphis Horns, while Axton led the Packers, scoring a 1965 hit with "Hole in the Wall". Nix, meanwhile, mounted a solo career, also producing records for artists including Freddie King, Jeff Beck, and Furry Lewis. *—Jason Ankeny*

Back to Back / 1967 / Atlantic ✦✦✦✦✦
Recorded live at Paris in 1967, when the Stax-Volt Revue was touring Europe. This is just about exactly what you'd expect: solid, straight-ahead live versions of the instrumental group's best-known tunes, in good sound. Booker T. & the MG's take seven of album's ten tracks, including their hits "Green Onions" and "Hip Hug-Her"; the Mar-Keys do "Last Night" and a couple of other numbers. *—Richie Unterberger*

● **Damifiknow!/Memphis Experience** / May 20, 1994 / Stax ✦✦✦✦
A two-for-one disc combining a couple strange releases, neither of which were truly the Mar-Keys. *Damnifiknow!* was played by Booker T. & the MG's, supplemented by a horn section that would become the Memphis Horns; *Memphis Experience* combined Bar-Kays outtakes with instrumentals by Memphis musicians with no connection to prior Mar-Keys lineups. It's a convenient way for major Stax/soul collectors to pick up two of the group's odder records, but it's not a representative reflection of the Mar-Keys. Nor is the music especially noteworthy: *Damifiknow!* is easygoing, rather humdrum soul instrumentals that don't pack nearly the punch of the MG's at their best, while *Memphis Experience* is average wordless early '70s soul-funk with occasional psychedelic/hard rock tinges. *—Richie Unterberger*

Marilyn Manson

f. 1989
Group / Industrial Metal, Alternative Metal
Love him or hate him, the self-proclaimed "Antichrist Superstar" Marilyn Manson was indisputably among the most notorious and controversial entertainers of the 1990s. Celebrated by supporters as a crusader for free speech and denounced by detractors as little more than a poor man's Alice Cooper, he was the latest in a long line of shock rockers. Widely dismissed by critics, Manson was a major draw with the youth market as a mainstream anti-hero, much to the chagrin of conservative politicians and concerned parents. Born Brian Warner, he formed the band in the late '80s with guitarist Scott Mitchell; by 1992 their Gothic stage show made them a popular act in the South Florida area. In 1993, Nine Inch Nails' Trent Reznor came calling and the group's debut LP, *Portrait of an American Family,* was released in 1994 on Reznor's Nothing label. Manson's notoriety began to soar—he ripped apart a copy of the Book of Mormon while onstage in Salt Lake City, and was bestowed the title of "Reverend" by the Church of Satan's founder Anton LaVey. His cult following—comprised almost entirely of disaffected white suburban teens—continued to swell, and 1996's *Antichrist Superstar* debuted at number three on the album charts. As Manson's popularity grew, so did the furor surrounding him—his performances and albums were the subject of widespread attacks from the right-wing and religious fronts. The glam-inspired *Mechanical Animals* followed in 1998. *—Jason Ankeny*

Portrait of an American Family / Jul. 12, 1994 / Nothing/Interscope ✦✦✦
Coming up screaming from the depths of Florida—there being no scarier state in the union—Marilyn Manson cannily positioned themselves as a goth-industrial hybrid on their debut album, *Portrait of an American Family.* At this stage in their evolution, Marilyn Manson was clearly a band, not just the project of Brian Warner a.k.a. Mr. Manson, who would later simply adopt his band's name as his own. Also, horror-show schlock was a bigger factor than it would be later on, when he wanted to be the Antichrist Superstar for the world at large. In other words, it's Manson at his silliest, singing about "My Monkey" and "Snake Eyes and Sissies." Beneath all the camp shock, there are signs of Warner's unerring eye for genuine outrage and musical talent, particularly on the trio of "Cake and Sodomy," "Lunch Box" and "Dope Hat." But even a few years on from its 1994 release, *Portrait of an American Family* has begun to sound a little dated, especially since its Nine Inch Nails-meets-WASP-meets-Alice Cooper formula was fully realized on Manson's follow-up album, *Antichrist Superstar.* Here, it's in sketch form, and by the end of the album it's clear that Warner, Manson, whatever you want to call him, needs a full canvas to truly wreak havoc. *—Stephen Thomas Erlewine*

Smells Like Children / Oct. 24, 1995 / Nothing/Interscope ✦✦✦

● **Antichrist Superstar** / Sep. 8, 1996 / Nothing/Interscope ✦✦✦✦✦
Boasting a fuller sound and a more focused sense of purpose, *Antichrist Superstar* is a substantial improvement on Marilyn Manson's debut album, *Portrait of an American Family.* The band draws equally from schlock-metal, progressive metal, new wave, goth-rock and industrial rock, and with the help of producers Trent Reznor and Dave Ogilvie, the group creates a boiling, mockingly satanic mess of guitars, synthesizers and ridiculously "scary" vocals. Though the sonic details make *Anitchrist Superstar* an intriguing listen, it's not as extreme as it could have been—in particular, the guitars are surprisingly anemic, sounding like buzzing vacuums instead of unweildly chainsaws. Even with that considered, *Antichrist Superstar* is an unexpectedly cohesive album from a silly shock-metal band and will stand as Marilyn Manson's definitive statement. *—Stephen Thomas Erlewine*

Mechanical Animals / Sep. 15, 1998 / Nothing/Interscope ✦✦✦✦
Antichrist Superstar performed its intended purpose—it made Marilyn Manson internationally famous, a living realization of his fictional "antichrist superstar." He had gained the attention of not only rock fans, but the public at large; however, many critics bestowed their praise not on the former Brian Warner, but on Trent Reznor, Manson's mentor and producer. Surely angered by the attention being focused elsewhere, he decided to break from Reznor and industrial metal with his third album, *Mechanical Animals.* Taking his image and musical cues from Bowie, Warner reworked Marilyn Manson into a sleek, androgynous space alien named Omega, *a la* Ziggy Stardust, and constructed a glammy variation of his trademark goth-metal. With pal Billy Corgan as an unofficial consultant and Soundgarden producer Michael Beinhorn manning the boards, Manson turns *Mechanical Animals* into a big, clean rock record—the kind that stands in direct opposition to the dark, twisted industrial nightmares he painted with his first two albums. It can make for a welcome change of pace, since his glammed-up goth is more tuneful than his clattering industrial cacophony, but it lacks the cartoonish menace and that distinguished his prior music. And without that, Marilyn Manson seems a little ordinary, believe it or not—more like a '90s version of Alice Cooper than ever before. True, *Mechanical Animals* is the group's most accessible effort, but Manson should have remembered one thing—demons are never that scary in the light. *—Stephen Thomas Erlewine*

The Last Tour on Earth / Nov. 16, 1999 / Nothing/Interscope ✦✦✦

Holy Wood (In the Shadow of the Valley of Death) / Nov. 14, 2000 / Nothing/Interscope ✦✦✦✦✦
In 2000, he not only was recovering from his fans' rejection of *Mechanical Animals,* he was scarred from Columbine and, worst of all, he was no longer America's demon dog. What was Brian Warner to do, standing on such uneasy ground— As a smart man and savvy marketer, he knew that it was time to consolidate his strengths, blend Omega with the Anti-Christ Superstar, and return with a harsh, controversial, operatic epic: a vulgar concept album to seduce his core audiences of alienated teens and cultural cops. The resulting album, *Holy Wood (In the Shadow of the Valley of Death),* is intended as the third part of the trilogy beginning with *Anti Christ Superstar,* and its convoluted story line is fairly autobiographical, but the amazing isn't the story—it's that he figured out to meld the hooks and subtle sonic shading of *Mechanical Animals* with the ugly, neo-industrial metallicisms of *Anti-Christ.* Consequently, it's easy to see this as the definitive Marilyn Manson album, since it's tuneful *and* abrasive. Then again, much of its charm lies in Manson trying so hard, perfecting details in the concept, lyrics, themes, production, sequencing, the tarot card parodies in the liner notes, the self-theft, the self-consciously blasphemous cover art. There's so much effort, *Holy Wood* winds up stronger and more consistent album than any of his other work. If there's any problem, it's that Manson's shock rock seems a little quaint in 2000. Eminem's vibrant, surrealistic white-trash fantasias were the sound of 2000, while Marilyn Manson's rock operas, religious baiting, and goth gear are from an era passed. It's to Warner's credit as, yes, an artist that *Holy Wood* works anyway. *—Stephen Thomas Erlewine*

Martha & the Vandellas

f. 1963, Detroit, MI, **db.** 1972
Group / Pop-Soul, Girl Group, Motown, Soul
Along with the Supremes, Martha & the Vandellas defined the distaff side of the Motown Sound in the 1960s; their biggest hits, including "Heat Wave," "Dancing in the Street" and "Nowhere to Run," remain among the most potent and enduring dance records of the era. The Top 30 success of the 1963 ballad "Come and Get These Memories" first brought the group the attention of Motown's hit-making production team Holland-Dozier-Holland, who crafted their next smash, the galvanizing Top 5 classic "Heat Wave," which perfected the mix of impassioned call-and-response vocals, pulsing rhythms and full-bodied horns that became the trio's trademark. After singer Kim Weston turned down the Marvin Gaye/Ivy Jo Hunter/Mickey Stevenson composition "Dancing in the Street," the song was shuttled to Martha & the Vandellas; refashioned by Holland-Dozier-Holland to fit the group's formula, the anthem became their biggest hit and definitive statement, reaching Number Two in the summer of 1964. A year later, they returned with another smash, the savage "Nowhere to Run," followed by "I'm Ready for Love." 1967's "Jimmy Mack" and "Honey Chile" were the last records overseen by the Holland-Dozier-Holland team before their defection from Motown, and were also the final significant Vandellas hits; the trio continued unsuccessfully for a few more years before breaking up in the wake of a December, 1972 farewell performance at Detroit's Cobo Hall. *—Jason Ankeny*

☆ **Live Wire! The Singles (1962-1972)** / Sep. 7, 1993 / Motown ✦✦✦✦✦
This two-CD box set includes all of the top singles and many of their flipsides that Martha Reeves & the Vandellas cut for Motown. All the hits are here, of course; the collector will be especially interested in the B-sides and non-hit singles, many of which employed the songwriting talents of Motown regulars like Holland-Dozier-Holland and Mickey Stevenson. There's also the rare single (featuring Gloria Williamson on lead vocals) cut by the Vells in 1962, before Reeves took top billing and the group changed their name. Eight of these cuts have never been released on album before. Among the non-hits, there isn't anything to match "Heat Wave" or "Dancing in the Street," but Reeves' astonishingly powerful voice never falters. She was arguably Motown's most talented female singer, but the label's investment in her seemed to flag as the decade progressed. The later material lacks the distinction of her classic period, though the 1970 album track "I Should Be Proud" is a little-known (if somewhat heavy-handed) protest against the Vietnam War. *—Richie Unterberger*

★ **The Ultimate Collection** / Feb. 10, 1998 / Motown ✦✦✦✦✦
Motown is notorious for recycling their catalog as endless hit collections, but *The Ultimate Collection* is one of the finest series of greatest-hits CDs they have ever assembled. Each disc contains all of the major hits from an artist, plus important B-sides, album tracks and minor hits. Martha & the Vandellas' entry in the series is no exception to the rule, boasting all their Top Ten pop and R&B hits—"Come and Get These Memories," "Heat Wave," "Quicksand," "Dancing in the Street," "Nowhere to Run," "My Baby Loves Me," "I'm Ready for Love," "Jimmy Mack"—plus smaller hits and B-sides, resulting in a total of 25 tracks. For anyone who wants a definitive hits collection but is hesitant to invest in the double-disc *Live Wire!, The Ultimate Collection* is an ideal choice. *—Stephen Thomas Erlewine*

The Marvelettes

f. 1960, Inkster, MI

Group / Pop-Soul, Girl Group, Motown, Soul

Probably the most pop-oriented of Motown's major female acts, the Marvelettes didn't project as strong an identity as the Supremes, Mary Wells, or Martha Reeves, but recorded quite a few hits, including Motown's first number one single, "Please Mr. Postman" (1961). "Postman," as well as other chirpy early '60s hits like "Playboy," "Twistin' Postman," and "Beechwood 4-5789," were the label's purest girl group efforts. After a few years, they moved from girl group sounds to uptempo and midtempo numbers that were more characteristic of Motown's production line. They received no small help from Smokey Robinson, who produced and wrote many of their singles; Holland-Dozier-Holland, Berry Gordy, Mickey Stevenson, Marvin Gaye, and Ashford-Simpson also got involved with the songwriting and production at various points. While the Marvelettes didn't cut as many monster smashes as most of their Motown peers after the early '60s, they did periodically surface with classic hits like "Too Many Fish in the Sea," "Don't Mess with Bill," and "The Hunter Gets Captured by the Game." There were also plenty of fine minor hits and misses, like 1965's "I'll Keep Holding On," which is just as memorable as the well-known Motown chart-toppers of the era. *—Richie Unterberger*

Deliver: The Singles (1961-1971) / Sep. 7, 1993 / Motown ✦✦✦✦✦

Forty-one songs, featuring most of both the A-sides and B-sides, nine of which had never been issued on album before. The ace Motown songwriting and production stable was involved in virtually every one of these tracks, making for a surprisingly strong and consistent collection. Includes all the chart hits, as well as rarities like the Phil Spector-style single they released in 1963 as the Darnells. *—Richie Unterberger*

● **The Ultimate Collection** / Feb. 10, 1998 / Motown ✦✦✦✦✦

Motown is notorious for recycling their catalog as endless hit collections, but *The Ultimate Collection* is one of the finest series of greatest-hits CDs they have ever assembled. Each disc contains all of the major hits from an artist, plus important B-sides, album tracks and minor hits. The Marvelettes' entry in the series is no exception to the rule, boasting all their Top Ten pop and R&B hits, not only from their early-'60s heyday but also their late-'60s comeback: "Please Mr. Postman," "Playboy," "Beechwood 4-5789," "Someday, Someway," "Strange I Know," "Don't Mess with Bill," "My Baby Must Be a Magician," "The Hunter Gets Captured By the Game," "When You're Young and In Love." The disc also features a number of smaller hits and B-sides, resulting in a total of 25 tracks. For anyone who wants a definitive hits collection but is hesitant to invest in the double-disc *Deliver, The Ultimate Collection* is an ideal choice. *—Stephen Thomas Erlewine*

Massive Attack

f. 1987, Bristol, England

Group / Electronica, Alternative Dance, Trip-Hop, Club/Dance, Alternative Pop/Rock

The pioneering force behind the rise of trip-hop, Massive Attack was among the most innovative and influential groups of their generation; their hypnotic sound—a darkly sensual and cinematic fusion of hip-hop rhythms, soulful melodies, dub grooves and choice samples—set the pace for much of the dance music to emerge throughout the 1990s, paving the way for such acclaimed artists as Portishead, Sneaker Pimps, Beth Orton and Tricky, himself a Massive Attack alumnus. The group was formed by Mushroom and Daddy G., two members of a successful Bristol soundsystem named the Wild Bunch, plus grafitti artists 3D. Two other Wild Bunch alums, Nellee Hooper and Tricky, also spent time in the new group. After several classic singles, including "Unfinished Sympathy" and "Safe from Harm," Massive Attack issued their LP debut *Blue Lines* in 1991. While by no means a huge commercial success, the record was met with major critical praise, and was dubbed an instant classic in many quarters. Shara Nelson, featured on many of the album's most memorable tracks, left for a solo career soon after, and a three-year layoff preceded their second album, *Protection,* another commercial and critical hit. Soon after its release, both Hooper and Tricky made formal exits to work as independent producers. The third full-length Massive Attack effort, *Mezzanine,* appeared in 1998. *—Jason Ankeny*

★ **Blue Lines** / Aug. 6, 1991 / Virgin ✦✦✦✦✦

The first masterpiece of what was only termed trip-hop much later, *Blue Lines* filtered American hip-hop through the lens of British club culture, a stylish, nocturnal sense of scene that encompassed music from rare groove to dub to dance. The album balances dark, diva-led club jams along the lines of Soul II Soul with some of the best British rap (vocals and production) heard up to that point, occasionally on the same track. The opener "Safe From Harm" is the best example, with diva vocalist Shara Nelson trading off lines with the group's own monotone (yet effective) rapping. Even more than hip-hop or dance, however, dub is the big touchstone on *Blue Lines.* Most of the productions aren't quite as earthy as you'd expect, but the influence is palpable in the atmospherics of the songs, like the faraway electric piano on "One Love" (with beautiful vocals from the near-legendary Horace Andy). One track, "Five Man Army," makes the dub inspiration explicit, with a clattering percussion line, moderate reverb on the guitar and drums, and Andy's exquisite falsetto flitting over the chorus. *Blue Lines* isn't all darkness, either—"Be Thankful for What You've Got" is quite close to the smooth soul tune conjured by its title, and "Unfinished Sympathy"—the group's first classic production—is a tremendously moving fusion of up-tempo hip-hop and dancefloor jam with slow-moving, syrupy strings. Flaunting both their range and their tremendously evocative productions, Massive Attack recorded one of the best dance albums of all time. *—John Bush*

Protection / 1994 / Virgin ✦✦✦✦

Massive Attack's sophomore effort could never be as stunning as *Blue Lines,* and a slight drop in production and songwriting quality made the comparisons easy. Still, from the first two songs *Protection* sounds worthy of their debut. The opening title track is pure excellence, with melancholy keyboards, throbbing acid lines, and fragmented beats perfectly complementing the transcendent vocals of Tracey Thorn (an inspired choice to replace the departed Shara Nelson as their muse). Tricky, another soon-to-be-solo performer, makes his breakout on this record, with blunted performances on "Karmacoma," another highlight, as well as "Eurochild." But even though the production is just as intriguing as on *Blue Lines,* there's a bit lacking here—Massive Attack don't summon quite the emotional power they did previously. Guest Craig Armstrong's piano work on the aimless tracks "Weather Storm" and "Heat Miser" leans uncomfortably close to Muzak, and his arrangement and conducting for "Sly" isn't much better (vocals by Nicolette save the track somewhat). Though it's still miles ahead of the growing raft of trip-hop making the rounds in the mid-'90s, *Protection* is rather a disappointment. *—John Bush*

No Protection: Massive Attack Vs. Mad Professor / 1995 / Gyroscope ✦✦✦✦

☆ **Mezzanine** / Apr. 27, 1998 / Virgin ✦✦✦✦✦

Increasingly ignored amidst the exploding trip-hop scene, Massive Attack finally returned in 1998 with *Mezzanine,* a record immediately announcing not only that the group was back, but that they'd recorded a set of songs just as singular and revelatory as on their debut, almost a decade back. It all begins with a stunning one-two-three-four punch: "Angel," "Risingson," "Teardrop," and "Inertia Creeps." Augmenting their samples and keyboards with a studio band, Massive Attack open with "Angel," a stark production featuring pointed beats and a distorted bass line that frames the vocal (by group regular Horace Andy) and a two-minute flame-out with raging guitars. "Risingson" is a dense, dark feature for Massive Attack themselves (on production as well as vocals), with a kitchen sink's worth of dubby effects and reverb. "Teardrop" introduces another genius collaboration—with Elizabeth Fraser from Cocteau Twins—from a production unit with a knack for recruiting gifted performers. The blend of earthy with ethereal shouldn't work at all, but Massive Attack pull it off in fine fashion. "Inertia Creeps" could well be the highlight, another feature for just the core threesome. With eerie atmospherics, fuzz-tone guitars, and a wealth of effects, the song could well be the best production from the best team of producers the electronic world had ever seen.

Obviously, the rest of the album can't compete, but there's certainly no sign of the side-two slump (heard on *Protection*), as both Andy and Fraser return for excellent, mid-tempo tracks ("Man Next Door" and "Black Milk," respectively). *—John Bush*

matchbox twenty

f. 1996

Group / American Trad Rock, Adult Alternative Pop/Rock, Post-Grunge, Pop/Rock

Upon the release of their debut album *Yourself or Someone Like You* in the fall of 1996, Matchbox 20 was pigeonholed as one of the legions of post-grunge guitar-bands that roamed the American pop scene in the middle of the '90s. As their breakthrough single, "Push," climbed the charts, it was widely assumed that they were a one-hit wonder, but *Yourself or Someone Like You* continued to spin off singles well into 1998. By then, the Orlando based group made up of Rob Thomas, Brian Yale, Paul Doucette, Adam Gaynor and Kyle Cook had managed to make their mix of '70s arena rock and early '90s American alterna-rock the sound of mainstream American rock.

Matchbox 20 reserved 1999 as the year to record their eagerly-anticipated second album, but they didn't disappear from the spotlight, due to the unexpected success of "Smooth," a Santana song co-written and sung by Rob Thomas. Throughout the second half of 1999, "Smooth" was inescapable, as it and *Supernatural* sat on the top of the pop charts. Its success brought more attention to Matchbox 20, and sales of *Yourself or Someone Like You* rocketed to over 10 million copies.

All of this success happened as Matchbox 20 was recording its second album. The success raised expectations for the new album, entitled *Mad Season,* which was released in May, 2000. The album, while as polished and radio-friendly as their debut release, nevertheless failed to make the outstanding commercial impact that *Yourself of Someone Like You* had achieved. *—Stephen Thomas Erlewine*

● **Yourself or Someone Like You** / Oct. 1, 1996 / Atlantic ✦✦✦

Yourself or Someone Like You turned out to be the standard-bearer for post-alternative rock because it has a '90s sheen in its production, but, for all the world, its core sounds like classic rock. Lead singer/songwriter Rob Thomas adopted some of Eddie Vedder's vocal mannerisms, but they were smoothed out, lacking the angst and pain that were Vedder's hallmark. matchbox twenty functioned much the same way, picking up at Pearl Jam's fascination for album rock, but deciding to stick to the classic blueprint instead of personalizing it. All of this resulted in a record that is much more straightforward than most alt-rock albums, even if it follows the pattern of a classic '90s album—not just in its production dynamics, but down to the acoustic-based slow number that closes the record. It blends the most familiar elements of the two golden eras of album-oriented rock, finding a balance that is comfortable for mainstream fans of either side. Other bands with similar sounds that could have done the same thing, yet matchbox twenty distanced themselves from the pack with sturdy songs and fairly strong hooks, all delivered forcefully with Thomas' distinctive bravado. Their music is not flashy, nor is it as ingratiating as Third Eye Blind's pop instincts. It is, however, solid, American rock, reminiscent of a blend of Petty and Pearl Jam. So, it shouldn't have been surprising when the album found a wide audience. For many observers, it was still unexpected, because the sound seemed a little plain. What they didn't realize was that *Yourself or Someone Like You* wound up being the point where mainstream American rock stopped being willfully eccentric and returned to being unassuming and kind of ordinary. *—Stephen Thomas Erlewine*

Mad Season / May 23, 2000 / Atlantic ✦✦✦✦

On *Yourself or Someone Like You,* Matchbox Twenty's ability to craft sturdy, mainstream rock was overshadowed by their reliance on loud guitars, colorless production, and bombastic vocalizing. They trade that sound for a varied, accomplished, smooth production on their second album, *Mad Season.* Throughout this record, Matchbox Twenty seem unashamed that they sound their best when they're simply a mainstream rock band. They exploit this strength by expanding the production, adding horns and layers of keyboards to their sound, opening up the mix, and emphasizing their melodies. That shift in direction may disarm some fans of the debut, which was pretty much just guitars, but the band winds up with a big, bright, shiny album that's livelier than its predecessor. That alone makes *Mad Season* more engaging than the debut, but the real surprise is the group's growth as craftsmen and Rob Thomas' progression as a songwriter and singer. Prior to this album, Thomas had a tendency to oversell his songs, not just in the delivery but in the writing, and the band followed him along. Here, they tone down their performances and while the end result is heavily produced, the overall feel is more relaxed and welcoming than the debut. Of course, it also helps that they have a solid set of songs—a set that eclipses their previous effort, even if there are a few dull moments here and there. Even with those occasional missteps, the end result is a strong, unabashedly mainstream record that finds the band coming into their own. *—Stephen Thomas Erlewine*

Dave Matthews

Vocals, Guitar / Jam Bands, American Trad Rock, Adult Alternative Pop/Rock

The South-African vocalist/guitarist Dave Matthews formed his namesake band in Virginia in the early '90s. The group's music presents a more pop-oriented version of The Grateful Dead, crossed with the worldbeat explorations of Paul Simon and Sting. The band built up a strong word-of-mouth following in the early '90s by touring the country constantly, concentrating on college campuses. In addition to amassing a sizable following, their self-released album *Remember Two Things* sold well for an independent release; soon, they were attracting the attention of majors. Signing with RCA, the Dave Matthews Band released their major-label debut, *Under the Table and Dreaming,* in the fall of 1994. By spring of 1995, the record had launched the hit single "What Would You Say" and sold over a million copies. A year and a half after its release, the record had sold over four million copies in the US alone. In April of 1996, the Dave Matthews Band released *Crash,* which entered the charts at number two and quickly went platinum. *—Stephen Thomas Erlewine*

Remember Two Things / 1993 / RCA ✦✦✦

● **Under the Table & Dreaming** / Apr. 1994 / RCA ✦✦✦✦✦

On their major-label debut, *Under the Table & Dreaming,* the Dave Matthews Band is helped by the lean production of Steve Lillywhite, who manages to rein in the group's tendency to meander. The result is a set of eclectic pop/rock is accentuated by bursts of instrumental virtuosity instead of being ruled by it. That also means that the Dave Matthews Band is capable of turning out pop songs, and as the hit single "What Would You Say" and "Ants Marching" illustrate, they have a flair for catchy hooks. *—Stephen Thomas Erlewine*

Crash / Apr. 1996 / RCA ✦✦✦

Under the Table & Dreaming, the Dave Matthews Band's first major label album, was their popular breakthrough, bringing their mildly eclectic sound to a mass audience. Although the group appeals to the same audience as Blues Traveler, Hootie & the Blowfish, and the Spin Doctors, the Dave Matthews Band has more influences than their peers. Fusing together folk-rock, worldbeat, jazz, and pop, the band is arguably the most musically adept of all their contemporaries. However, they have trouble coming up with engaging hooks, as their third album, *Crash,* proves. Although the band continues to get better—their musical cross-breeding is effortless and seamless—they often don't have an attractive frame for their skills. Strangely, the lack of memorable melodies doesn't particularly hurt the album—it actually emphasizes the band's instrumental talents. Nevertheless, since there's a lack of strong pop hooks, *Crash* is an album that will please fans, but not novices. *—Stephen Thomas Erlewine*

Live at Red Rocks 8-15-95 / Oct. 28, 1997 / Bama Rags/RCA ✦✦✦✦

Before These Crowded Streets / Apr. 28, 1998 / RCA ✦✦✦✦

The Dave Matthews Band made their reputation through touring, spending endless nights on the road improvising. Often, their records hinted at the eclecticism and adventure inherent in those improvisation, but *Before These Crowded Streets* is the first album to fully capture that adventurous spirit. Not coincidentally, it's their least accessible record, even if it's more of a consolidation than it is a step forward. Early Dave Matthews albums were devoted to the worldbeat fusions of *Graceland* and Sting, but his RCA efforts incorporated these influences into a smoother, pop-oriented style. Here, everything hangs out. Old trademarks, like jittery acoustic grooves and jazzy chords, are here, augmented by complex polyrhythms, Mideastern dirges and, on two tracks, the slashing strings of the Kronos Quartet. Some fans may find the new, darker textures a little disarming at first, but they're a logical extension of the group's work, and in many ways, this sonic daring results in the most rewarding album they've yet recorded. The Dave Matthews Band hasn't completely vanquished their demons, however—songwriting remains a problem, especially since relying on grooves, improvisation and texture allows them to skimp on melody, and Matthews' lyrics can be awkward and embarrassing, especially if he's writing about sex. Still, these are minor flaws on an album that relies on tone and improvisation, both of which are in ample supply on *Before These Crowded Streets. —Stephen Thomas Erlewine*

Live at Luther College / Jan. 19, 1999 / RCA ✦✦✦✦

Listener Supported / Nov. 23, 1999 / RCA ✦✦✦

John Mayall

b. Nov. 29, 1933, Macclesfield, Cheshire, England

Vocals, Ukulele, Tambourine, Keyboards, Harpsichord, Harmonium, Piano, Harmonica, Guitar, Organ / Blues Revival, British Blues, Electric Harmonica Blues, Blues-Rock

The elder statesman of British blues, it is John Mayall's lot to be more renowned as a bandleader and mentor than as a performer in his own right. Throughout the '60s, his band, the Bluesbreakers, acted as a finishing school for the leading British blues-rock musicians of the era. Guitarists Eric Clapton, Peter Green, and Mick Taylor joined his band in a remarkable succession in the mid-'60s, honing their chops with Mayall before going on to join Cream, Fleetwood Mac, and the Rolling Stones, respectively. John McVie and Mick Fleetwood, Jack Bruce, Aynsley Dunbar, Dick Heckstall-Smith, Andy Fraser (of Free), John Almond, and Jon Mark also played and recorded with Mayall for varying lengths of times in the '60s. Mayall's personnel has tended to overshadow his own considerable abilities. Only an adequate singer, the multi-instrumentalist was adept in bringing out the best in his younger charges (Mayall himself was in his thirties by the time the Bluesbreakers began to make a name for themselves). Doing his best to provide a context in which they could play Chicago-style electric blues, Mayall was never complacent, writing most of his own material (which ranged from good to humdrum), revamping his lineup with unnerving regularity, and constantly experimenting within his basic blues format. Some of these experiments (with jazz-rock and an album on which he played all the instruments except drums) were forgettable; others, like his foray into acoustic music in the late '60s, were quite successful. Mayall's output has caught some flak from critics for paling next to the real African-American deal, but much of his vintage work—if weeded out selectively—is quite strong, especially his legendary 1966 LP with Eric Clapton, which both launched Clapton into stardom and kick-started the blues boom into full gear in England. *—Richie Unterberger*

John Mayall Plays John Mayall / Mar. 26, 1965 / Decca ✦✦✦

Recorded live at the British club Klooks Kleek in late 1964 before Clapton joined (Roger Dean plays lead guitar), this is a fine set of early British R&B with a more pronounced rock feel (akin to the Rolling Stones) than Mayall's other '60s work. Mayall wrote all but one of the songs on this overlooked but driving, highly enjoyable LP that is recommended to connisseurs of early British blues-rock. *—Richie Unterberger*

★ **Bluesbreakers With Eric Clapton** / Jul. 1966 / Deram ✦✦✦✦✦

Bluesbreakers With Eric Clapton was Eric Clapton's first fully realized album as a blues guitarist—more than that, it was a seminal blues album of the 1960s, perhaps the best British blues album ever cut, and the best LP ever recorded by John Mayall's Bluesbreakers. Standing midway between Clapton's stint with the Yardbirds and the formation of Cream, this album featured the new guitar hero on a series of stripped-down blues standards, Mayall pieces, and one Mayall/Clapton composition, all of which had him stretching out in the idiom for the first time in the studio. This album was the culmination of a very successful year of playing with John Mayall, a fully realized blues creation, featuring sounds very close to the group's stage performances, and with no compromises. Credit has to go to producer Mike Vernon for the purity and simplicity of the record; most British producers of that era wouldn't have been able to get it recorded this way, much less released. One can hear the very direct influence of Buddy Guy and a handful of other American bluesmen in the playing. And lest anyone forget the rest of the quartet: future pop-rock superstar John McVie and drummer Hughie Flint provide a rock-hard rhythm section, and Mayall's organ playing, vocalizing, and second guitar are all of a piece with Clapton's work. His guitar naturally dominates most of this record, and he can also be heard taking his first lead vocal, but McVie and Flint are just as intense and give the tracks an extra level of steel-strung tension and power, none of which have diminished across four decades. In 1998, Polygram Records issued a remastered version of this album on CD, featuring both the stereo and mono mixes of the original tracks and new notes. *—Bruce Eder*

Raw Blues / Jan. 1967 / Deram ✦✦

A Hard Road / Feb. 17, 1967 / Deram ✦✦✦✦

Eric Clapton is usually thought of as Mayall's most important righthand man, but the case could also be made for his successor, Peter Green. The future Fleetwood Mac founder leaves a strong stamp on his only album with the Bluesbreakers, singing a few tracks and writing a couple, including the devastating instrumental "Supernatural." Green's use of thick sustain on this track clearly pointed the way to his use of this feature on Fleetwood Mac's hits "Albatross" and "Black Magic Woman," as well as providing a blueprint for Carlos Santana's style. Mayall acquits himself fairly well on this mostly original set (with occasional guest horns), though some of the material is fairly mundane. Highlights include the uncharacteristically rambunctious "Leaping Christine" and the cover of Freddie King's "Someday After a While (You'll Be Sorry)." *—Richie Unterberger*

Crusade / Sep. 1, 1967 / London ✦✦✦✦✦

The personnel changes in John Mayall's Bluesbreakers continued on his fourth album, and although Mayall had vowed not to, he had added two permanent horn players. Perhaps because he was putting out his second album within a year, Mayall wasn't able to fill up the record with his own compositions and turned to blues standards, which certainly didn't hurt the record overall. Mayall's heroes included Buddy Guy, Otis Rush, Freddie King, and Sonny Boy Williamson, and he did them proud. The album became his third straight U.K. Top Ten and, following the Bluesbreakers' first U.S. tour in the summer of 1967, his first charting album in America. *—William Ruhlmann*

The Blues Alone / Nov. 1967 / Deram ✦✦✦

Bare Wires / Jun. 21, 1968 / Deram ✦✦✦

Looking Back / Aug. 1969 / Deram ✦✦✦

The Turning Point / 1969 / Deram ✦✦✦✦✦

Recorded just after Mick Taylor departed for the Stones, Mayall eliminated drums entirely on this live recording. With mostly acoustic guitars and John Almond on flutes and sax, Mayall and his band, as his typically overblown liner notes state, "explore seldom-used areas within the framework of low volume music." But it does work. The all-original material is flowing and melodic, with long jazzy grooves that don't lose sight of their bluesy underpinnings. Lyrically, Mayall stretches out a bit into social comment on "The Laws Must Change" on this fine, meditative mood album. *—Richie Unterberger*

Thru the Years / 1971 / Deram ✦✦✦✦✦

A grab bag of rare tracks from the '60s, some of which stand among Mayall's finest. His debut 1964 single "Crawling up a Hill" is one of his best originals; this comp also includes a couple of 1964-65 flipsides that were never otherwise issued in the U.S. The eight songs featuring Peter Green include some top-notch material that outpaces much of the only album recorded by the Green lineup (*A Hard Road*), particularly the Green originals "Missing You" and "Out of Reach," a great B-side with devastating, icy guitar lines and downbeat lyrics that ranks as one of the great lost blues-rock cuts of the '60s. The set is filled out with a few songs from the Mick Taylor era, the highlight being the vicious instrumental "Knockers Step Forward." Look for the CD reissue and not the early-'70s double U.S. album of the same name, which includes a lot of superfluous material and omits the three 1964-65 songs from British 45s. *—Richie Unterberger*

A Sense of Place / Mar. 1990 / Island ✦✦✦

London Blues (1964-1969) / Oct. 20, 1992 / Deram ✦✦✦✦✦
Featuring forty tracks over two discs, *London Blues* is an excellent collection of most of the best moments from Mayall and the Bluesbreakers' early recordings, a time when Eric Clapton, Peter Green, and Mick Taylor all passed through the band. *—Stephen Thomas Erlewine*

Room to Move (1969-1974) / Oct. 20, 1992 / Polydor ✦✦✦✦✦
The majority of Mayall and the Bluesbreakers' best material from the early '70s is collected on this 29-track, double-disc set. Although Clapton appears on a couple of songs, the playing on *Room to Move* isn't as universally breathtaking as it is on *London Blues*, but the collection is thoroughly listenable, and it does feature many fine musicians. *—Stephen Thomas Erlewine*

As It All Began: The Best of John Mayall & the Bluesbreakers 1964-1969 / Jan. 27, 1998 / Polydor ✦✦✦✦✦
As It All Began: The Best of John Mayall & the Bluesbreakers 1964-1968 is an excellent 20-track retrospective, capturing Mayall's band at their peak. The Bluesbreakers went through several different lineups during those four years, with musicians the caliber of Eric Clapton, Mick Taylor, Paul Butterfield, Mick Fleetwood, John McVie and Peter Green floating through the group. Hardcore fans of any of those musicians, or of British blues, will naturally want to familiarize themselves with the original albums, but *As It All Began* is a fine sampler for the casual fan, featuring such staples as "Lonely Years," "Bernard Jenkins," "All Your Love," "Parchman Farm," "Double Trouble," "The Death of J.B. Lenoir" and "Miss James." Even at 20 tracks, there are a number of fine moments missing from this collection, but *As It All Began* remains the best available single-disc overview of the Bluesbreakers' prime period. *—Stephen Thomas Erlewine*

Drivin' On: The ABC Years (1975-1982) / Sep. 22, 1998 / MCA ✦✦✦✦
This two-disc, 32-track compilation brings together highlights from Mayall's output for ABC Records in the 1970s. Pulled from the albums *New Year, New Band, New Company, Notice to Appear, Lots of People, A Banquet of Blues, A Hard Core Package* and *Last of the British Blues*, these cherry-picked tracks also do a nice job of highlighting Mayall's estimable writing skills as well. Highlights include "Seven Days Too Long," "Old Time Blues," "You Can't Put Me Down," "Sitting On the Outside," "My Train Time" and the title track. As a special bonus, there's the second disc inclusion of four live tracks from a 1982 Bluesbreaker reunion gig featuring John McVie back at his original post on bass and Mick Taylor on lead guitar providing the fireworks. *—Cub Koda*

Curtis Mayfield

b. Jun. 3, 1942, Chicago, IL, **d.** Dec. 26, 1999
Vocals, Guitar (Electric), Guitar / Blaxploitation, Chicago Soul, Uptown Soul, Quiet Storm, R&B, Funk, Soul

Perhaps because he didn't cross over to the pop audience as heavily as Motown's stars, it may be that the scope of Curtis Mayfield's talents and contributions have yet to be fully recognized. Judged merely by his records alone, the man's legacy is enormous. As the leader of the Impressions, he recorded some of the finest soul vocal group music of the 1960s. As a solo artist in the 1970s, he helped pioneer funk, and helped introduce hard-hitting urban commentary into soul music. "Gypsy Woman," "It's All Right," "People Get Ready," "Freddie's Dead," and "Superfly" are merely the most famous of his many hit records. But Curtis Mayfield isn't just a singer. He wrote most of his material, at a time when that was not the norm for soul performers. He was among the first—if not the very first—to speak openly about African-American pride and community struggle in his compositions. As a songwriter and a producer, he was a key architect of Chicago soul, penning material and working on sessions by notable Windy City soulsters like Gene Chandler, Jerry Butler, Major Lance, and Billy Butler. In this sense, he can be compared to Smokey Robinson, who also managed to find time to write and produce many classics for other soul stars. Mayfield was also an excellent guitarist, and his rolling, Latin-influenced lines were highlights of the Impressions' recordings in the '60s. During the next decade, he would toughen up his guitar work and production, incorporating some of the best features of psychedelic rock and funk. *—Richie Unterberger*

☆ **Curtis** / Sep. 1970 / Rhino ✦✦✦✦✦
The first solo album by the former leader of the Impressions, *Curtis* represented a musical apotheosis for Curtis Mayfield—indeed, it was practically the "*Sgt. Pepper's*" album of '70s soul, helping with its content and its success to open the whole genre to much bigger, richer musical canvases than artists had previously worked with. All of Mayfield's years of experience of life, music, and people were pulled together into a rich, powerful, topical musical statement that reflected not only the most up-to-date soul sounds of its period, finely produced by Mayfield himself, and the immediacy of the times and their political and social concerns, but also embraced the most elegant R&B sounds out of the past. As a producer, Mayfield embraced the most progressive soul sounds of the era, stretching them out compellingly on numbers like "Move on Up," but also drew on orchestral sounds (especially harps), to achieve some striking musical timbres (check out "Wild and Free"), and wove all of these influences, plus the topical nature of the songs, into a neat, amazingly lean whole. There was only one hit single off of this record, "(Don't Worry) If There's a Hell Down Below We're All Going to Go," which made number three, but the album as a whole was a single entity, and really had to be heard that way. In the fall of 2000, Rhino Records reissued *Curtis* with upgraded sound and nine bonus tracks that extended its running time to over 70 minutes. All but one are demos, including "Miss Black America" and "The Making of You," but mostly consist of tracks that he completed for subsequent albums; they're fascinating to hear, representing very different, much more jagged and stripped-down sounds. The upgraded CD concludes with the single version of "(Don't Worry) If There's a Hell Below We're All Going to Go." *—Bruce Eder*

Curtis/Live! / 1971 / Rhino ✦✦✦✦
Recorded and released at one of the high points of Curtis Mayfield's career, this live album provides several reasons why the late Mayfield is regarded as the black Bob Dylan. The performances contained herein represent the high-water mark of social consciousness. Newer numbers such as "Stone Junkie" and "Superfly" (from the soundtrack of the same name), along with classics like "People Get Ready," are enough to give credence to Mayfield's stature. Awesome. *—Matthew Greenwald*

Roots / 1971 / Rhino ✦✦✦✦✦
Curtis Mayfield's visionary album, a landmark creation every bit as compelling and as far-reaching in its musical and extra-musical goals as Marvin Gaye's contemporary *What's Goin' On*. Opening on the hit "Get Down," the album soars on some of the sweetest and most eloquent—yet driving—soul sounds heard up to that time. Mayfield's growing musical ambitions, first manifested on the *Curtis* album, and his more sophisticated political sensibilities, presented with a lot of raw power on *Curtis Live!*, are pulled together here in a new, richer studio language, embodied in extended song structures ("Underground"), idealistic yet lyrically dazzling anthems ("We Got to Have Peace," "Keep On Keeping On," and, best of all, the soaring "Beautiful Brother of Mine"), and impassioned blues ("Now You're Gone"). The music is even bolder than the material on the *Curtis* album, with Mayfield expanding his instrumental range to the level of a veritable soul orchestra; and the recording is better realized, as Mayfield, with that album and a tour behind him, shows a degree of confidence that only a handful of soul artists of this era could have mustered. Charly Records had this album out on CD in the 1980s, but Rhino's acquisition of the Curtom catalog in 1996 led to a remastered and expanded reissue in 1999 with superior sound, detailed annotation, and the addition of four bonus tracks. Apart from a slow, funky, stripped-down but eminently listenable demo of "Underground" (which reveals just how sophisticated Mayfield's conceptions—forget the finished versions—of his songs were), the latter consist of the single edits of "Get Down," "We Got to Have Peace," and "Beautiful Brother of Mine." They seem redundant after the album versions, though they don't detract at all from the extraordinary value of this mid-priced CD. *—Bruce Eder*

☆ **Superfly** / Jul. 1972 / Curtom ✦✦✦✦✦
A post-Impressions Curtis Mayfield recorded one dynamic solo project after another in the 1970s, but if a listener could own only one of them, *Superfly* would be the ideal choice. The sleek yet earthy soundtrack to one of the '70s' most celebrated blaxploitation films, *Superfly* is full of riveting, sometimes chilling sociopolitical commentary reflecting on the drugs, violence and crime plaguing the inner city. Unlike so many soundtracks, this outstanding CD can be fully appreciated whether or not one has seen the film. From the infectious title song to "Freddie's Dead" (a reflection on a junkie's tragic life as troubling as it is poignant) to the hard-hitting "Pusherman" (brilliantly interpreted by rapper Ice-T in 1988), *Superfly* is clearly Mayfield's finest hour. *—Alex Henderson*

Curtis in Chicago / 1973 / Curtom ✦✦✦✦✦

Back to the World / May 1973 / Curtom ✦✦✦✦✦
Another stirring album by Curtis Mayfield, now in a groove on his own label. Mayfield's works issued challenges across the board, urging everyone to examine his or her prejudices and then seek a solution. While he always included one or two wonderful love songs for balance, these albums were largely examinations of American issues in the 1970s. He scored three R&B chart hits, with "Future Shock" just missing the Top 10, but that was icing on the cake. Mayfield's music had far more importance than simply getting hits. *—Ron Wynn*

Got to Find a Way / 1974 / Curtom ✦✦✦
Curtis Mayfield continued his run of excellent albums in the '70s with this followup to the huge hit *Superfly* soundtrack. This album had more love songs than some of his earlier material, although he didn't tone down his searing attacks on American injustice and hyprocisy. His vocals continued to be alternately poignant, urgent, and accusatory, while his lyrics, production, and arrangements were once again magnificent. *—Ron Wynn*

Move On Up / 1974 / Buddah ✦✦✦

Sweet Exorcist / 1974 / Curtom ✦✦✦
Curtis Mayfield hit a stride during the '70s that was unparalleled among R&B/soul performers from an album standpoint. He was writing, producing, arranging, and performing on great album after great album, then distributing them on his own label as well. This one included the big hit "Kung Fu," plus the title song, and once more perfectly blended rigorous message tracks and steamy love songs. Sadly, it hasn't been reissued on CD and isn't on the list to be at this time. *—Ron Wynn*

There's No Place Like America Today / 1975 / Curtom ✦✦✦✦✦
Curtis Mayfield continued his string of powerful, assertive message albums with this mid-'70s release, but, as luck would have it, the only hit the album scored came with a love tune, "Only You, Babe." Still, the title tune, "Hard Times," "When Seasons Change" and "Blue Monday People" were unrelenting, unapologetic statements of frustration and anger. Mayfield also included "So In Love" and "Love to the People" to balance the menu, but the finest cuts addressed the inequities and injustices he saw being ignored. *—Ron Wynn*

Give Get Take Have / 1976 / Ichiban ✦✦✦

Never Say You Can't Survive / 1977 / Ichiban ✦✦

Do It All Night / 1978 / Curtom ✦✦✦

★ **The Anthology 1961-1977** / Dec. 8, 1992 / MCA ✦✦✦✦✦
MCA's double-disc *The Anthology 1961-1977* is the definitive overview of Curtis Mayfield's career, as the only compilation to draw from both his solo work and the best of his output with the Impressions. In fact, even discounting the four Curtom tracks that spill over onto disc two, the first disc's 26 selections constitute far and away the most extensive Impressions best-of on the market. Toss in ten of the most essential Mayfield solo tracks, and the result is breathtaking in its progression from romantic soul, often informed by doo wop and gospel, to expansive, ambitiously arranged funk jams. It's also fascinating to hear Mayfield's social

conscience emerging as the '60s progress, since he was among the very first R&B artists to explore political issues in his music, paving the way for countless others to do so during the '70s. If you're only interested in Mayfield's funkier solo work, Rhino's *The Very Best of Curtis Mayfield* features all but one of the solo tracks included here, plus several more. But in order to fully grasp Mayfield's impact on R&B and his talent as a singer, songwriter, musician, and producer, *The Anthology 1961-1977* is absolutely essential. *—Steve Huey*

People Get Ready: The Curtis Mayfield Story / Feb. 27, 1996 / Rhino ✦✦✦✦✦
Like most large box sets, this three-CD, 51-song production is too extensive for the casual fan, and sacrifices consistency in an attempt to span an entire career. The focus is on Mayfield's solo work; much of the first disc is devoted to his most popular work with the Impressions, but the remainder of the compilation surveys his solo output, from 1970 to 1990. The Impressions tracks are uniformly excellent, but the Mayfield-only cuts are more problematic. The best of these—the *Superfly* highlights, of course, and early '70s singles like "(Don't Worry) If There's a Hell Below We're All Going to Go" and "Beautiful Brother of Mine"—are as good as everything he ever did. But even in the early '70s, he was erratic, and after *Superfly* (his career summit), nothing he did smacked of brilliance. Some of the post-*Superfly* stuff is okay, but considering that this period takes up half of disc two and all of disc three, it means you're in for a pretty swift downhill slide over the last half of the box. Mayfield never lost his vocal abilities, or his production skills, but after the late '70s his material was simply unimpressive, getting into pedestrian dance music and romantic urban contemporary. For a Mayfield retrospective, you're much better off with MCA's two-disc *Anthology*, which goes into the Impressions period with much greater depth, and includes the cream of his '70s solo recordings. *—Richie Unterberger*

The Very Best of Curtis Mayfield / Mar. 10, 1996 / Rhino ✦✦✦✦✦
Rhino's *The Very Best of Curtis Mayfield* is devoted to material the legendary soul man recorded after leaving The Impressions, focusing particularly on his classic songs from the early '70s. There are more comprehensive compilations on the market, namely the sublime double-disc *Anthology* and the flawed but worthwhile box *People Get Ready*, but this is the best bet for anyone wanting a concise sampler of Mayfield's groundbreaking funk-soul, since it contains all of the bare-bone essentials: "(Don't Worry) If There's a Hell Below, We're All Going to Go"; "Move on Up"; "We Got to Have Peace"; "Freddie's Dead"; "Superfly"; "Pusherman"; "Future Shock"; and "Kung Fu." Yes, Mayfield also made cohesive, frequently stunning albums during this era and his work with The Impressions was just as influential, but this disc benefits from its narrow focus, since the end result is a collection ideal for the curious and the novice, while also providing a great listen for anyone who already knows the records. *—Stephen Thomas Erlewine*

New World Order / Oct. 1, 1996 / Warner Brothers ✦✦✦

Gospel / Jan. 19, 1999 / Rhino ✦✦✦

MC5

f. 1964, Lincoln Park, MI, **db.** 1972
Group / Detroit Rock, Proto-Punk, Hard Rock
Alongside their Detroit-area brethren the Stooges, the MC5 essentially laid the foundations for the emergence of punk—deafeningly loud and uncompromisingly intense, the group's politics were ultimately as crucial as their music, their revolutionary sloganeering and anti-establishment outrage crystallizing the counterculture movement at its most volatile and threatening. The MC5 celebrated the holy trinity of sex, drugs and rock'n'roll, their incendiary live sets offering a defiantly bacchanalian counterpoint to the peace-and-love reveries of their hippie contemporaries. Although corporate censorship, label interference and legal hassles combined to cripple the band's hopes of mainstream notoriety, both their sound and their sensibility remain seminal influences on successive generations of artists.

The Motor City Five was formed in 1964 by vocalist Rob Tyner plus guitarists Fred "Sonic" Smith and Wayne Kramer, later adding bassist Michael Davis and drummer Dennis Thompson. In 1966, the MC5 landed a regular gig at the famed Detroit venue *the Grande Ballroom*, building a fanatical local fanbase on the strength of their increasingly anarchic live appearances. Their debut album, the classic *Kick Out the Jams*, reached the national Top 30, though retailers refused to carry copies due to its inclusion of Tyner's trademark battle cry of "Kick out the jams, motherfuckers!" Dropped by Elektra, they signed to Atlantic and released 1970's *Back in the USA*. The political stance and feedback-driven fury were gone, however, dividing fans and critics. When the 1971 follow-up *High Time* failed to even reach the charts Atlantic released the MC5 from their contract. In 1972, both Tyner and Thompson announced their retirement from active touring.

As the years went by, however, the MC5's influence expanded—punk, hard rock and power pop all clearly reflected the band's impact. Following the band's demise its members pursued new projects: Tyner released several solo records before suffering a fatal heart attack in 1991. Smith, meanwhile, formed Sonic's Rendezvous, and in 1980 he wed Patti Smith, dying of heart failure in 1994. Kramer resurfaced in 1995 with a blistering solo album, *The Hard Stuff*, the first of several new efforts for punk label Epitaph. *—Jason Ankeny*

☆ **Kick out the Jams** / 1969 / Elektra ✦✦✦✦✦
Rather than try to capture their legendary onstage energy in a studio, MC5 opted to record their first album during a live concert at their home base, Detroit's *Grande Ballroom*, and while some folks who were there have quibbled that *Kick out the Jams* isn't the most accurate representation of the band's sound, it's certainly the best of the band's three original albums, and easily beats the many semi-authorized live recordings of MC5 that have emerged in recent years, if only for the clarity of Bruce Botnick's recording. From Brother J.C. Crawford's rabble-rousing introduction to the final wash on feedback on "Starship," *Kick out the Jams* is one of the most powerfully energetic live albums ever made; Wayne Kramer and Fred "Sonic" Smith were a lethal combination on tightly interlocked guitars, bassist Michael Smith and drummer Dennis Thompson were as strong a rhythm section as Detroit ever produced, and Rob Tyner's vocals could actually match the soulful firepower of the musicians, no small accomplishment. Even on the relatively subdued numbers (such as the blues workout "Motor City Is Burning"), the band sounds like they're locked in tight and cooking with gas, while the full-blown rockers (pretty much all of side one) are as gloriously thunderous as anything ever committed to tape; this is an album that refuses to be played quietly. For many years, Detroit was considered the High Energy Rock & Roll Capital of the World, and *Kick out the Jams* provided all the evidence anyone might need for the city to hold on to the title. *—Mark Deming*

Back in the U.S.A. / 1970 / Rhino ✦✦✦✦✦
While lacking the monumental impact of *Kick Out the Jams*, the MC5's second album is in many regards their best and most influential, its lean, edgy sound anticipating the emergence of both the punk and power-pop movements to follow later in the decade. Bookended by a pair of telling covers—Little Richard's "Tutti Frutti" and Chuck Berry's "Back in the USA"—the disc is as much a look back at rock & roll's origins as it is a push forward into the music's future; given the Five's vaunted revolutionary leanings, for instance, it's both surprising and refreshing to discover the record's emotional centerpiece is a doo-wop-inspired ballad, "Let Me Try," that's the most lovely and gentle song in their catalog. The recurring theme which drives *Back in the USA* is adolescence, its reminiscences alternately fond and embittered—while cuts like "Tonight," "Teenage Lust," "High School" and "Shakin' Street" celebrate youth in all its rebellious glory, others like "The American Ruse" and "The Human Being Lawnmower" condemn a system which eats its young, filling their heads with lies before sending them off to war. Equally gripping is the record's singular sound—produced by Jon Landau with an almost complete disregard for the bottom end, *Back in the USA* captures a live-wire intensity 180 degrees removed from the group's live sound yet perfectly suited to the material at hand, resulting in music which not only salutes the power of rock & roll but also reaffirms it. *—Jason Ankeny*

High Time / 1971 / Rhino ✦✦✦✦
MC5 was nearing the end of their long and bumpy trail when they cut *High Time* in 1971, and it was widely ignored upon initial release. While it lacks the flame-thrower energy and "Off the man!" politics of *Kick out the Jams* or the frantic pace and "AM Radio of the People" sound of *Back in the USA*, heard in 2000, *High Time* sounds like MC5's relative equivalent to the Velvet Underground's *Loaded*, their last and most accessible album, but still highly idiosyncratic and full of well-written, solidly played tunes. Fred Smith's "Sister Anne" and "Skunk (Sonically Speaking)" bookend the album with a pair of smart, solidly performed hard rockers (bolstered by fine horn charts), and Wayne Kramer's "Poison" ranks with the best songs he brought to the band (he later revived it for his solo album *The Hard Stuff*). For a group that was apparently on the verge of collapse, MC5 approaches this material with no small amount of skill and enthusiasm, and Geoffrey Haslam's production gives the band a big, punchy sound that suits them better than the lean, trebly tone of *Back in the USA*. It's interesting to imagine what MC5's history might have been like if *High Time* had been their first or second album rather than their last; while less stridently political than their other work, musically it's as uncompromising as anything they ever put to wax and would have given them much greater opportunities to subvert America's youth if the kids had ever had the chance to hear it. *—Mark Deming*

American Ruse / 1994 / Total Energy ✦✦

★ **The Big Bang: The Best of the MC5** / Feb. 15, 2000 / Rhino ✦✦✦✦✦
A best-of for a group who only made three albums might be considered an inessential addition to their discography, particularly as all three of those albums remain available on CD. However, if you only want one MC5 album, this compilation makes more sense than if might appear at first. It draws judiciously from each of the three records; adds three somewhat rare tracks from pre-*Kick out the Jams* singles; and finishes with a live 1972 cut, "Thunder Express," recorded for French TV and previously available on a Skydog CD. In somewhat of a surprise, it leans most heavily on *Back in the USA* (with eight tracks), and not so much on the album that most would view as their most significant effort, *Kick out the Jams* (only four tracks). That decision works out better than you might think. The three tracks from 1967-68 singles are fairly similar to the *Kick out the Jams* vibe anyway, and if you don't own *Kick out the Jams* already, you may well be ready for something a little cleaner-sounding and less assaultive by the time seven songs have gone by. It's unfortunate, nonetheless, that the two remaining pre-*Kick out the Jams* tracks from non-LP 45s, "One of the Guys" and a different version of *Kick out the Jams*' "Borderline," were not included. *Kick out the Jams* itself would get most people's nod as the first and most essential MC5 purchase, but this is a close second, its value enhanced by detailed historical liner notes. *—Richie Unterberger*

Paul McCartney

b. Jun. 18, 1942, Liverpool, England
Vocals, Keyboards, Guitar (Electric), Piano, Guitar, Bass, Guitar (Acoustic) / Album Rock, Pop/Rock, Soft Rock, Adult Contemporary, Rock & Roll
Out of all the former Beatles, Paul McCartney by far had the most successful solo career, maintaining a constant presence in the British and American charts during the '70s and '80s. In America alone, he had nine number one singles and seven number one albums during the first 12 years of his solo career. Although he sold records, McCartney never attained much critical respect, especially when compared to his former partner John Lennon. Then again, he pursued a different path than Lennon, deciding early on that he wanted to be in a rock band. Within a year after the Beatles' break-up, McCartney had formed Wings with his wife Linda, and the group remained active for the next 10 years, racking up a string of hit albums, singles and tours in the meantime. By the late '70s, many critics were taking pot-shots at McCartney's effortlessly melodic songcraft, but that didn't stop the public from buying his records. His sales didn't slow considerably until the late '80s, and he retaliated with his first full-scale tour since the '70s, which was a considerable success. During the '90s, McCartney recorded less frequently, concentrating on projects like his first classical recording, a techno album and the Beatles' *Anthology*.*—Stephen Thomas Erlewine*

McCartney / Apr. 20, 1970 / Capitol ✦✦✦✦
Paul McCartney retreated from the spotlight of the Beatles by recording his first solo album

at his home studio, performing nearly all of the instruments himself. Appropriately, *McCartney* has an endearingly ragged, homemade quality that makes even its filler—and there is quite a bit of filler—rather ingratiating. Only a handful of songs rank as full-fledged McCartney classics, but those songs—the light folk-pop of "That Would Be Something," the sweet, gentle "Every Night," the ramshackle Beatles leftover "Teddy Boy" and the staggering "Maybe I'm Amazed" (not coincidentally the only rocker on the album)—are full of all the easy melodic charm that is McCartney's trademark. The rest of the album is charmingly slight, especially if it is read as a way to bring Paul back to earth after the heights of the Beatles. At the time the throwaway nature of much of the material was a shock, but it has become charming in retrospect. Unfortunately, in retrospect it also appears as a harbinger of the nagging mediocrity that would plague McCartney's entire solo career. *—Stephen Thomas Erlewine*

☆ **Ram** / May 17, 1971 / Capitol ✦✦✦✦✦
Compared to *McCartney*, Paul McCartney's second solo album *Ram*—which was credited as a collaboration with his wife Linda—is a more substantial and produced effort, yet it has much of the same homemade charm as its predecessor. Divided between simple pop-rockers and cleverly constructed mini-suites like "Uncle Albert/Admiral Halsey" and "Back Seat of My Car," *Ram* doesn't gel into any major statement, but it has many pleasurable detours. McCartney layers the ramshackle rhythm tracks with odd sound effects and off-kilter arrangements. While the production might not always work, it does make for pleasant ear candy, not only on lovely songs like "Heart of the Country," but also on throwaway numbers like the hard-rocking "Smile Away" and "Monkberry Moon Delight." Unfortunately, most of *Ram* is comprised of filler, and while it's *enjoyable* filler, it prevents the record from being much more than pleasurable diversion. *—Stephen Thomas Erlewine*

Wild Life / Dec. 7, 1971 / Capitol ✦✦✦
The irony of the first Wings album is that it seems more domesticated than *Ram*, feeling more like a Paul 'n' Linda effort than that record. Perhaps it's because this album is filled with music that's defiantly lightweight—not just the cloying cover of "Love Is Strange" but two versions *apiece* of songs called "Mumbo" and "Bip Bop." If this is a great musician bringing his band up to speed, so be it, but it never seems that way—it feels like one step removed from coasting, which is wanking. It's easy to get irritated by the upfront cutesiness, since it's married to music that's featherweight at best. Then again, that's what makes this record bizarrely fascinating—it's hard to imagine a record with less substance, especially from an artist who's not just among the most influential of the 20th century, but from one known for precise song and studiocraft. Here, he's thrown it all to the wind, trying to make a record that sounds as pastoral and relaxed as the album's cover photo. He makes something that sounds easy—easy enough that you and a couple of neighbors who you don't know very well could knock it out in your garage on a lazy Saturday afternoon—and that's what's frustrating and amazing about it. Yeah, it's possible to call this a terrible record, but it's so strange in its domestic bent and feigned ordinariness that it winds up being a pop album like no other. *—Stephen Thomas Erlewine*

Red Rose Speedway / Apr. 30, 1973 / Capitol ✦✦✦✦
All right, he's made a record with his wife and a record with his pickup band where democracy is allegedly the conceit even if it never sounds that way, so he returns to a solo effort, making the most disjointed album he ever cut. There's a certain fascination to its fragmented nature, not just because it's decidedly on the softer side of things, but because his desire for homegrown eccentricity has been fused with his inclination for bombastic art rock à la *Abbey Road*. Consequently, *Red Rose Speedway* winds up being a really strange record, one that veers toward the schmaltzy AOR MOR (especially on the hit single "My Love"), yet is thoroughly twisted in its own desire toward domestic art. As a result, this is every bit as insular as the lo-fi records of the early '90s, but considerably more artful, since it was, after all, designed by one of the great pop composers of the century. Yes, the greatest songs here are slight—"Big Barn Bed," "One More Kiss," and "When the Night"—but this is a deliberately slight record (slight in the way a snapshot album is important to a family yet glazes the eyes of any outside observer). Work your way into the inner circle, and McCartney's little flourishes are intoxicating—not just the melodies, but the facile production and offhand invention. If these are miniscule step forwards, consider this: if Brian Wilson can be praised for his half-assed ideas and execution, then why not McCartney, who has more character here than the Beach Boys did on their Brother records— Truthfully. *—Stephen Thomas Erlewine*

Band on the Run / Dec. 5, 1973 / Capitol ✦✦✦✦✦
Neither the dippy, rustic *Wild Life* nor the slick AOR flourishes of *Red Rose Speedway* earned McCartney much respect, so he made the self-consciously ambitious *Band on the Run* to rebuke his critics. On the surface, *Band on the Run* appears to be constructed as a song cycle in the vein of *Abbey Road*, but subsequent listens reveal that the only similarities the two albums share are simply superficial. McCartney's talent for songcraft and nuanced arrangements is in ample display throughout the record, which makes many of the songs—including the nonsensical title track—sound more substantial than they actually are. While a handful of the songs are excellent—the surging, inspired surrealism of "Jet" is by far one of his best solo recordings, "Bluebird" is sunny acoustic pop and "Helen Wheels" captures McCartney rocking with abandon—most of the songs are more style than substance. Yet McCartney's melodies are more consistent than any of his previous solo records, and there are no throwaways; the songs just happen to be not very good. Still, the record is enjoyable, whether it's the minor-key "Mrs. Vanderbilt" or "Let Me Roll It," a silly response to John Lennon's "How Do You Sleep," which does make *Band on the Run* one of McCartney's finest solo efforts. However, there's little of real substance on the record. No matter how elaborate the production is, or how cleverly his mini-suites are constructed, *Band on the Run* is nothing more than a triumph of showmanship. *—Stephen Thomas Erlewine*

Venus & Mars / May 27, 1975 / Capitol ✦✦✦
Band on the Run was a commercial success, but even if it was billed as a Wings effort, it was primarily recorded by Paul, Linda, and Denny Laine. So, it was time to once again turn Wings into a genuine band, adding Joe English and Jimmy McCulloch to the lineup and even letting the latter contribute a song. This faux-democracy isn't what signals that this is a band effort—it's the attitude, construction, and pacing, which McCartney acknowledges as much, opening with an acoustic title track that's a salute to arena rock, leading to a genuine arena rock anthem, "Rock Show." From that, it's pretty much rocking pop tunes, paced with a couple of ballads and a little whimsy, all graced with a little of the production flair that distinguished *Band on the Run*. But where that record was clearly a studio creation and consciously elaborate, this is a straightforward affair where the sonic details are simply window dressing. McCartney doesn't really try anything new, but the songs are a little more varied than the uniform, glossy production would suggest; he dips into soft-shoe music hall shuffle on "You Gave Me the Answer," gets a little psychedelic with "Spirits of Ancient Egypt," kicks out a '50s rock & roll groove with "Magento and Titanium Man," and unveils a typically sweet and lovely melody on "Listen to What the Man Said." These are a slight shifts on an album that certainly feels like the overture for the arena rock tour that it was, which makes it one of McCartney's more consistent listens, even though it's possible to scan the song listing after several listens and not recognize any song outside of "Listen to What the Man Said" and the opening medley by title. *—Stephen Thomas Erlewine*

Wings at the Speed of Sound / Mar. 25, 1976 / Capitol ✦✦
If *Venus and Mars* had the façade of being an album by a band, *At the Speed of Sound* really is a full-band effort, where everybody gets a chance to sing, even contribute a song. This, ironically, winds up as considerably less cohesive than its predecessor despite these efforts for community, not because Wings was not a band in the proper sense, but because nobody else in the band pulsed as much weight as McCartney, who was resting on his laurels here. Consider this: The two hits "Let 'Em In" and "Silly Love Songs" are so lightweight that their lack of substance seems nearly defiant. They have sweet, nice melodies and are well-crafted, but as songs they're nonexistent, working primarily as effervescent popcraft of their time. And that's the case for most of *At the Speed of Sound*, as tracks like "She's My Baby" play like the hits, only without memorable hooks. There is a bit of charm to the record, arriving in Linda's awkwardly sung "Cook of the House," the mellow "Must Do Something About It," and especially "Beware My Love," the best-written song here that effortlessly moves from sun-drenched harmonies to hard rock. Apart from the latter, these are modest pleasures buried on an album that may have been a chart-topping blockbuster, but now seems like one of McCartney's most transient works. [The CD reissue contains three bonus tracks, including the trad jazz instrumental "Walking in the Park with Eloise," which his father wrote, and the charming laid-back country "Sally G," which is better than most of the songs on *Speed*.] *—Stephen Thomas Erlewine*

Wings Over America / Dec. 11, 1976 / Capitol ✦✦✦

London Town / Mar. 31, 1978 / Capitol ✦✦✦✦
Reduced to the core trio of McCartney, McCartney, and Laine after the successful *Speed of Sound* tour, *London Town* finds Wings dropping the band façade slightly, turning in their most song-oriented effort since *Band on the Run*—which, not coincidentally, was recorded with this very trio. And although its high points don't shine as brightly as those on its two immediate predecessors, it's certainly stronger than *Speed* and, in its own way, as satisfying as *Venus and Mars*. What *London Town* has in its favor is Wings' (or, more likely, McCartney's) decision to settle into slick soft rock, relying on glossy, synth-heavy productions as he ratchets up the melodic quotient. This gives the album a distinctly European flavor, a feeling that intensifies when the lyrics are taken into the equation, and this gives *London Town* a different flavor than almost any other record in his catalog. And if its best moments aren't as strong as McCartney at his best they, along with the album tracks, find him skillfully crafting engagingly light, tuneful songs that charm with their offhanded craft, domesticity, and unapologetic sweetness. McCartney's humor is in evidence here, too, with the terrific "Famous Groupies," which means there's a little of everything he does here, outside of flat-out rocking. It's a laid-back, almost effortless collection of professional pop and, as such, it's one of his strongest albums. *—Stephen Thomas Erlewine*

Wings Greatest / Nov. 22, 1978 / Capitol ✦✦✦✦✦

Back to the Egg / May 24, 1979 / Capitol ✦✦

McCartney II / May 21, 1980 / Capitol ✦✦✦

Tug of War / Apr. 26, 1982 / Capitol ✦✦✦✦✦
Reuniting with producer George Martin was a bit of a masterstroke on the part of Paul McCartney, since it guaranteed that *Tug of War* would receive a large, attentive audience. Martin does help McCartney focus, but it's hard to give all the credit to *Tug of War*, since McCartney was showing signs of creative rebirth on *McCartney II*, a homemade collection of synth-based tunes. This lush, ambitious, sprawling album couldn't be further from that record. That was deliberately experimental and intimate, while this is nothing less than a grand gesture, playing as McCartney's attempt to summarize everything he can do on one record. There's majestic balladry, folky guitars, unabashed whimsy, unashamed sentimentality, clever jokes, silliness, hints of reggae, a rockabilly duet with Carl Perkins, two collaborations with Stevie Wonder, and, of course, lots of great tunes. If anything, McCartney's trying a bit too hard here, and there are times that the music sags with its own ambition (or slightly dated production, as on the smash single "Ebony and Ivory"). But, at its best—the surging title track, the giddy "Take It Away," the vaudevillian stomp "Ballroom Dancing," the Lennon tribute "Here Today," the wonderful "Wanderlust"—it's as good as McCartney gets. *—Stephen Thomas Erlewine*

Pipes of Peace / Nov. 1983 / Capitol ✦✦✦

Give My Regards to Broad Street / Oct. 1984 / Capitol ✦✦

Press to Play / Sep. 19, 1986 / Capitol ✦✦✦

● **All the Best** / 1987 / Capitol ✦✦✦✦✦
Technically, *All the Best* was the first compilation of McCartney's solo material, since *Wings Greatest* covered songs released under the Wings aegis. Well, there is considerable overlap between the two records—no less than *ten* of that album's 12 songs are here, yet only the hard-rocking "Hi Hi Hi" is truly missed—although the seven new songs do give

this album a different character, for better or worse. With the U.S. version of *All the Best,* which has four different songs than its British counterpart, the balance shifts toward the positive, since it simply boasts a better selection of songs. Yes, "Once Upon a Long Ago," the single offered as bait on the British *All the Best,* isn't here, but it's not missed since two of the four songs exclusive to the American version are among McCartney's best solo singles ("Junior's Farm," "Uncle Albert/Admiral Halsey") and the other two are good adult contemporary easy listening (the previously non-LP "Goodnight Tonight," "With a Little Luck"). These songs add to the retrospective, although it's still not perfect—such highlights as "Maybe I'm Amazed" and "Take It Away" really should have been included. However, as a cross section of McCartney's solo singles, this is very, very good. It may be a little heavy on the schmaltz at times, yet this is still mainstream pop craft of the highest order. —*Stephen Thomas Erlewine*

Flowers in the Dirt / May 1989 / Capitol ✦✦✦

McCartney must not only have been conscious of his slipping commercial fortunes, he must have realized that his records hadn't been treated seriously for years, so he decided to make a full-fledged comeback effort with *Flowers in the Dirt.* His most significant move was to write a series of songs with Elvis Costello, some of which appeared on Costello's own *Spike* and many of which surfaced here. These may not be epochal songs, the way many wished them to be, but McCartney and Costello turn out to be successful collaborators, spurring each other toward interesting work. And, in McCartney's case, that carried over to the album as a whole, as he aimed for more ambitious lyrics, themes, sounds, and productions for *Flowers in the Dirt.* This didn't necessarily result in a more successful album than its predecessors, but it had more heart, ambition, and nerve, which was certainly welcome. And the moments that did work were pretty terrific. Many of these were McCartney/McManus collaborations, from the moderate hit "My Brave Face" to the duet "You Want Her Too" and "That Day Is Done," but McCartney also demonstrates considerable muscle on his own, from the domestic journal "We Got Married" to the lovely "This One." This increased ambition also means McCartney meanders a bit, writing songs that are more notable for what they try to achieve than what they do, and at times the production is too fussy and inextricably tied to its time, but as a self-styled comeback affair, *Flowers in the Dirt* works very well. —*Stephen Thomas Erlewine*

Tripping the Live Fantastic / Oct. 1990 / Capitol ✦✦

Liverpool Oratorio / 1991 / Angel ✦✦

Unplugged (The Official Bootleg) / May 1991 / Capitol ✦✦✦✦

Released after the studied, meticulous *Flowers in the Dirt,* the live acoustic concert album *Unplugged* was a breath of fresh air, and it remains one of the most enjoyable records in McCartney's catalog. Running through a selection of oldies—not only his own, but Beatles and rock & roll chestnuts—McCartney is carefree and charming, making songs like "Be-Bop-a-Lula" and "Blue Moon of Kentucky" (which finds Paul melding Bill Monroe with Elvis) sound fresh. But the real revelations of the record are the songs McCartney hauls out from his debut—"That Would Be Something," "Every Night," and "Junk"—which sound lovely and timeless, restoring them to their proper place in his canon. They help make *Unplugged* into a thoroughly enjoyable minor gem. —*Stephen Thomas Erlewine*

Choba B CCCP / Oct. 28, 1991 / Capitol ✦✦

Off the Ground / Feb. 1993 / Capitol ✦✦

Paul Is Live / Nov. 16, 1993 / Capitol ✦✦

Flaming Pie / May 27, 1997 / Capitol ✦✦✦✦✦

According to McCartney, working on the Beatles *Anthology* project inspired him to record an album that was stripped-back, immediate and fun, one less studied and produced than most of his recent work. In many ways, *Flaming Pie* fulfills those goals. A largely acoustic collection of simple songs, *Flaming Pie* is direct and unassuming, and at its best, it recalls the homely charm of *McCartney* and *Ram.* McCartney still has a tendency to wallow in trite sentiment, and his more ambitious numbers, like the string-drenched epic "Beautiful Night" or the silly Beatlesque psychedelia of "Flaming Pie," end to fall flat. But when he works on a small scale, as on the waltzing "The Song We Were Singing," "Calico Skies," "Great Day" and "Little Willow," the's gently affecting, and the moderately rocking pop of "The World Tonight" and "Young Boy" is more ingratiating than the pair of aimless bluesy jams with Steve Miller. Even with the filler, which should be expected on any McCartney album, *Flaming Pie* is one of his most successful latter-day efforts, mainly because McCartney is at his best when he doesn't try so hard and lets his effortless melodic gifts rise to the surface. —*Stephen Thomas Erlewine*

Standing Stone / Sep. 23, 1997 / Angel ✦✦✦

Run Devil Run / Oct. 5, 1999 / EMI ✦✦✦✦

When Paul McCartney returned to the studio a year after his wife Linda's death, he wanted to cut loose and have a good time. He gathered a bunch of friends, most notably guitarist David Gilmour, with the intention of cutting a collection of rock & roll oldies with minimal rehearsal and a handful of takes. On the surface, that makes *Run Devil Run* like *Choba B CCCP,* but there are subtle differences that make *Devil* a far superior effort. This time around, there's a real freshness to the performances. Gilmour, in particular, amazes, turning in some of his finest playing in years. Similarly, McCartney is invigorated, leaving behind his vocal schtick, laying back and rocking out with a set of fairly unfamiliar oldies. Only three songs—"All Shook Up," "Lonesome Town," and "Brown Eyed Handsome Man"—are radio staples; and while "I Got Stung," "Blue Jean Bop," "She Said Yeah," "Honey Hush," and "Movie Magg" are known by aficionados, they're not ubiquitous standards. This leaves room for a few more obscure numbers, such as Little Richard's "Shake a Hand," the Vipers' "No Other Baby," and the Fats Domino B-side "Coquette," plus three terrific new songs from McCartney: "Run Devil Run", a fantastic Chuck Berry-styled narrative; "Try Not to Cry", a strong bluesy pop number; and "What It Is", a catchy uptempo shuffle. Best of all, McCartney and co-producer Chris Thomas create an appealingly out of time production—heavily compressed sound, yes, but cleaner than '50s recordings and livelier, grittier than most '90s albums. It all adds up to a dynamic, loose, carefree, and utterly infectious record, one of his best solo albums. —*Stephen Thomas Erlewine*

Liverpool Sound Collage / Sep. 5, 2000 / Capitol ✦✦✦

Michael McDonald

b. 1952, St. Louis, MO

Vocals, Keyboards / Blue-Eyed Soul, Pop/Rock, Soft Rock, Adult Contemporary

With his husky, soulful baritone, Michael McDonald became one of the most distinctive and popular vocalists—both as a lead singer, and as a harmony singer for the likes of Steely Dan, Kenny Loggins, Toto, Christopher Cross and Robbie Dupree—to emerge from the laidback California pop/rock scene of the late '70s. McDonald found the middle ground between blue-eyed soul and smooth soft-rock, a sound which made him a star. He initially essayed his signature style with the Doobie Brothers, ushering in the group's most popular period with hits like "What A Fool Believes" and "Taking It To the Streets." McDonald disbanded the group in 1982 to pursue a solo career. Initially, his solo career was quite successful, as his first album generated the Top 10 hit "I Keep Forgettin' (Every Time You're Near)," which also reached the R&B Top Ten, plus the James Ingram duet "Yah Mo B There." He lost some momentum with his second album, 1985's *No Lookin' Back,* but that was followed by a chart-topping duet with Patti LaBelle, "On My Own," plus the Top 10 hit, "Sweet Freedom." By the end of the decade, his popularity had faded away, since he was reluctant to work regularly and hesitant to update his sound to suit shifting popular tastes. In the '90s, he reunited with the Doobies on occasion and he was featured on Donald Fagen's 1994 New York Rock and Soul Revue. His recording career was hampered by conflicts with his label, Reprise, which delayed his 1997 album by three years—it finally appeared in 2000 on an independent label. —*Stephen Thomas Erlewine*

● **Sweet Freedom: The Best of Michael McDonald** / 1986 / Warner Brothers ✦✦✦✦✦

A solid collection that features all of McDonald's greatest hits from the early '80s. —*Stephen Thomas Erlewine*

Sarah McLachlan

b. Jan. 28, 1968, Halifax, Nova Scotia, Canada

Vocals, Piano, Guitar / Adult Alternative Pop/Rock, Alternative Pop/Rock, Singer/Songwriter

Sincer her debut in 1988, Sarah McLachlan's atmospheric folk-pop has gained a devoted following of fans not only in Canada, where she has established star status, but also in the U.S. and U.K. Each album has shown her growing both as a musician and songwriter, continually redefining herself and emerging as a major voice in the growing Adult Alternative Pop format. On the strength of her debut, 1988's *Touch,* she was signed to Arista for international distribution. The album eventually reached gold status in Canada and was reissued worldwide in 1989. In 1991, she followed up with *Solace,* an impressive collection that showed a great leap in songcraft and built a strong cult following in the U.S. *Fumbling Toward Ecstasy,* her strongest and most personal effort to date, was released in late 1993. The album peaked in the U.S. charts at number 50 and by the end of 1994, it reached platinum status after 62 weeks on the chart. "Possession," the single from the album, broke the Top 100 and received considerable airplay, especially on modern rock radio, where it reached number 14. "Good Enough" also found a home in that format, reaching number 16. In 1997, McLachlan began work on her fourth album, the enormously successful *Surfacing,* which debuted at number two on the pop albums chart. In addition to her own albums, she organized the successful Lilith tour, a package tour focusing on emerging women singer/songwriters. —*Chris Woodstra*

Touch / 1989 / Arista ✦✦✦

Solace / Sep. 10, 1991 / Arista ✦✦✦✦✦

Solace is at once comforting, mysterious, expansive, timeless, and familiar. The sophomore jinx was certainly eluded here, as McLachlan sets forth a superior collection of songs and performances with the help of longtime producer Pierre Marchand. The opening track, "Drawn to the Rhythm," serves its title well and does the job of luring you in. Intelligent, intriguing lyrics and lilting melodies abound, whether amidst the pulsing rhythms of "Into the Fire" and "Back Door Man" or the quietly profound stories of "Home" and "Shelter." Although pretty much all of the tunes will grab you at one point or another, "The Path of Thorns (Terms)" and "I Will Not Forget You" are especially memorable, the latter not to be confused with McLachlan's "I Will Remember You," which appears on the 1995 soundtrack for *The Brothers McMullen. Solace* is a wonderful record that offers a glimpse of the astounding talent of a young Sarah McLachlan. —*Kelly McCartney*

● **Fumbling Towards Ecstasy** / Feb. 1, 1994 / Arista ✦✦✦✦✦

Fumbling Towards Ecstasy finds Sarah McLachlan racing towards success as she re-teams with producer Pierre Marchand on her breakthrough release and finest offering to date. Stretching her lyrical wings and experimenting a bit more instrumentally, the radiance of her work has somehow solidified here. Ecstasy is certainly attained, though not by fumbling, for McLachlan has far too much finesse to be so awkward as that. "Possession," the track that caught people's attention and began her pop-chart ascension, is a twisted tale of love as told through the mind and heart of a stalker, although as voiced by McLachlan, many would wish to have such a problem. Two versions of "Possession" are included: the first is a fully produced, upbeat, drum-looped groove that comes off as all but happy; the second is a minimalist hidden track with just McLachlan and her piano sketching the story in a much more haunting, almost eerie fashion. From the light-hearted comparisons of love's sweetness in "Ice Cream" to the more somber experience of the impending death of a loved one in "Hold On," McLachlan never flinches, never takes the easy route of cliché and formula. This care and attention given to her art allows each song to stand strong individually, making the whole an extraordinary collection. —*Kelly McCartney*

The Freedom Sessions / Mar. 28, 1995 / Arista ✦✦✦

Rarities, B-Sides, and Other Stuff / 1996 / Nettwerk ✦✦✦

Surfacing / Jul. 15, 1997 / Arista ♦♦♦
Surfacing was released as the first Lilith Fair tour hit the road, and Sarah McLachlan benefited enormously from the timing. As the organizer of Lilith Fair, McLachlan was on the cover of magazines across America and Canada, which helped *Surfacing* debut at number two on the U.S. charts—a particularly remarkable feat, since its predecessor, *Fumbling Towards Ecstasy,* peaked at number 50. All the commercial success and media hype disguised the fact that *Surfacing* not only didn't offer anything new from McLachlan, but it wasn't a particularly strong consolidation of her talents. That it isn't to say it's a bad record, because it certainly isn't—there are several fine songs on the album, including the single "Building a Mystery"—but it doesn't offer anything new, and the songs aren't as consistently captivating as they were on *Fumbling Towards Ecstasy.* And that suggests that even though McLachlan is at the height of her popularity, she may beginning to run out of ideas. *—Stephen Thomas Erlewine*

Mirrorball / Jun. 15, 1999 / Arista ♦♦♦

Don McLean

b. Oct. 2, 1945, New Rochelle, NY
Vocals, Guitar / Folk-Rock, Soft Rock, Singer/Songwriter

Famed for—and ultimately defined by—his perennial "American Pie," singer-songwriter Don McLean was born October 2, 1945 in New Rochelle, New York. After getting his start in the folk clubs of New York City during the mid-'60s, McLean built a small following through his work with Pete Seeger on the Clearwater, a sloop which sailed up and down the eastern seaboard to promote environmental causes.

Still, McLean was primarily singing in elementary schools and the like when in 1970 he issued his debut album, *Tapestry.* The album fared poorly, but he returned in 1971 with *American Pie;* the title track, an elegiac eight-and-a-half-minute folk-pop epic inspired by the tragic death of Buddy Holly, became a number one hit, and the LP soon reached the top of the charts as well.

Subsequent records like 1972's self-titled effort and 1974's *Playin' Favorites* deliberately avoided any attempts to recreate the "American Pie" flavor; not surprisingly, his sales plummeted. After 1974's *Homeless Brother* and 1976's *Solo,* United Artists dropped McLean from his contract; he resurfaced on Arista the next year with *Prime Time,* but when it too fared poorly, he spent the next several years without a label.

McLean enjoyed a renaissance of sorts with 1980's *Chain Lightning;* his first Top 30 LP in close to a decade. However, 1981's *Believers* failed to sustain the comeback, and after 1983's *Dominion* he was again left without benefit of label support. McLean spent the remainder of his career primarily on the road, grudglingly restoring "American Pie" to his set list and drawing inspiration from the country market; he also returned to the studio for projects like 1990's *For the Memories* and 1995's *River of Love. —Jason Ankeny*

American Pie / Oct. 1971 / BGO ♦♦♦♦♦
The album that made McLean famous. The title track is the only real rocker, but the rest is intelligently produced and at times quite haunting, if a little angst-ridden. *—Bruce Eder*

● **Greatest Hits Then & Now** / 1987 / EMI America ♦♦♦♦♦
For most fans, the single-disc *Greatest Hits Then & Now* will be all the Don McLean they need, since it compiles all of his hits and best-known songs on one concise disc. *—Stephen Thomas Erlewine*

Clyde McPhatter

b. Nov. 15, 1932, Durham, NC, **d.** Jun. 13, 1972, Teaneck, NJ
Vocals / R&B

As the lead singer for Billy Ward & His Dominoes and the Drifters, Clyde McPhatter was one of the most important R&B vocalists of the '50s. His high, passionate vocals were charged with gospel inflections, as well as blues—his fusion of the sacred and the secular was crucial in the develpoment of R&B and soul. While his recordings with Ward and the Drifters were his most influential, McPhatter's solo records were equally excellent, as well as popular—his first nine solo singles were all Top 10 R&B hits, and three of those—"Treasure of Love," "Long Lonely Nights," "A Lover's Question"—were number one. However, his career began to slide in the '60s as he became increasingly depedent on alcohol. His abuse eventually led to his early death in 1972, yet Clyde McPhatter's legacy could be heard throughout the soul and R&B of the '60s and '70s, particularly in the seductive smooth soul of Al Green and the Spinners.*—Stephen Thomas Erlewine*

★ **Deep Sea Ball: The Best of Clyde McPhatter** / Oct. 1, 1991 / Atlantic ♦♦♦♦♦
This is about as perfect a summary of Clyde McPhatter's solo years with Atlantic as there is to buy, in the absence of a box of his complete output for the label or a Sequel Records reissue of his Atlantic LPs. Those who are most familiar with McPhatter's singing from his days with the Drifters will be pleased by all 19 songs here, which represent a more mature voice, and embody musical ambitions that carried McPhatter toward the same kind of expansive, pop-oriented R&B that Sam Cooke also started working toward (and would hit bigger with) a couple of years later. He could still rock out, as on the title track, but he also had a sense of the dramatic in his singing and used it to powerful effect on songs like "Without Love." "Treasure of Love" and "A Lover's Question" may be McPhatter's best remembered solo hits, but even the non-chart sides here, like "I Can't Stand Up Alone" (which harkens back to McPhatter's roots as a gospel singer) and the big-band R&B of "I'm Lonely Tonight," are gorgeous pieces of music that demand to be heard. The only drawback is that the material isn't in chronological order, which wouldn't be a problem at all if the recording dates had been listed next to the tracks in the notes. But it sounds fine and the music is so compelling that it holds up regardless of the programming decisions. *—Bruce Eder*

★ **Forgotten Angel** / Sep. 29, 1998 / 32 Jazz ♦♦♦♦♦
Finally, a definitive compilation of Clyde McPhatter! This two-disc collection chronicles McPhatter's hits (and some tunes that should have been hits) from the early '50s through the early '60s. It begins with over a dozen selections of Drifters material from mid-1953 to late 1954, including "Lucille" and "Money Honey." After these come classics from McPhatter's solo career (the recordings here pick up in 1955), including "Without Love (There Is Nothing)," "Lover Please," "Thirty Days," "Lovey Dovey," "I Can't Stand Up Alone," and the oldies-radio regular "A Lover's Question." With this collection, which has relatively excellent sound quality (except the few live cuts), the 32 label has done fans of early R&B vocals a great service, for McPhatter is one of the undisputed greats (Smokey Robinson and Jackie Wilson were *his* fans). *The Forgotten Angel* will stand up to a lifetime of listening. *—Joslyn Layne*

A Shot of Rhythm and Blues / Jul. 18, 2000 / Sundazed ♦♦♦
McPhatter was dropping out of sight commercially when he recorded for Amy from 1965 to 1967. This compilation of both sides of his five 1965-1967 Amy singles (augmented by four previously unreleased alternate takes) demonstrates that although his voice was still in decent shape, there was really no compelling reason to think that he should have had been worthy of attention during this period. It's middling mid-'60s soul, and although McPhatter was able to record material by some name players—such as Joe Tex, Rick Hall, Billy Sherrill, and Van McCoy—he wasn't coming across great songs. And the truth was, McPhatter's voice wasn't as well-suited to 1960s soul with full-bodied production as it was to doo wop and 1950s R&B. There's nothing that objectionable about these tracks, yet nothing too memorable, either, with McPhatter and his producers trying various settings, usually slick uptown soul ones. It hasn't been too easy to hear this stuff, and this reissue thus does have its value to big McPhatter fans, with Sundazed's typical thorough liner notes and documentation. *—Richie Unterberger*

Meat Loaf (Marvin Lee Aday)

b. Jan. 22, 1946, Dallas, TX
Vocals / Album Rock, Arena Rock, Pop/Rock, Hard Rock

Marvin Lee Aday was a singer and occasional actor who, for reasons never definitively answered, recorded under the name Meat Loaf. In all likelihood a childhood nickname, the tag stuck, and many puns followed as the performer—who tipped the scales at well over 300 pounds—became one of the biggest chart acts of the 1970s before enjoying a commercial renaissance two decades later. A member of several touring musicals and off-Broadway productions, Meat Loaf gained the help of classically trained pianist/composer Jim Steinman and producer Todd Rundgren to record 1977's *Bat Out of Hell,* a teen rock opera which spawned three Top 40 singles—"Two Out of Three Ain't Bad," "Paradise by the Dashboard Light" and "You Took the Words Right out of My Mouth"—on its way to becoming one of the best-selling albums of the decade. After Meat Loaf and Steinman had a falling out, solo records like 1984's *Bad Attitude* and 1986's *Blind Before I Stop* bombed. Several years were spent in relative obscurity, though the pair reunited in 1993 for *Bat Out of Hell II: Back into Hell,* which continued the original's storyline, duplicated its thunderous sound and proved almost as successful, selling over five million copies. Without Steinman, Meat Loaf returned in 1995 with *Welcome to the Neighborhood. —Jason Ankeny*

● **Bat out of Hell** / 1978 / Epic/Legacy ♦♦♦♦♦
There is no other album like *Bat out of Hell,* unless you want to count the sequel. This is grand guginol pop—epic, gothic, operatic, and silly, and it's appealing because of all of this. Jim Steinman was a composer without peer, simply because nobody else wanted to make mini-epics like this. And there never could have been a singer more suited for his compositions than Meat Loaf, a singer partial to bombast, albeit shaded bombast. The compositions are staggeringly ridiculous, yet Meat Loaf finds the emotional core in each song, bringing true heartbreak to "Two Out of Three Ain't Bad" and sly humor to "Paradise By the Dashboard Light." There's no discounting the production of Todd Rundgren, either, who gives Steinman's self-styled grandiosity a production that's staggeringly big, but never overwhelming and always alluring. While the sentiments are deliberately adolescent and filled with jokes and exaggerated clichés, there's real (albeit silly) wit behind these compositions, not just in the lyrics but in the music, which is a savvy blend of oldies pastiche, show tunes, prog rock, Springsteen-esque narratives, and blistering hard rock (thereby sounding a bit like an extension of Rocky Horror Picture Show, which brought Meat Loaf to the national stage). It may be easy to dismiss this as ridiculous, but there's real style and craft here and its kitsch is intentional. It may elevate adolescent passion to operatic dimensions, and that's certainly silly, but it's hard not to marvel at the skill behind this grandly silly, irresistible album. *—Stephen Thomas Erlewine*

Meatloaf (Featuring Stoney) / 1979 / Prodigal ♦♦

Dead Ringer / 1981 / Epic ♦♦♦
Although it took Meat Loaf and composer Jim Steinman another 12 years to come up with the marketing gimmick of positioning an album as a deliberate follow-up to the multi-platinum *Bat out of Hell, Dead Ringer* was the real *Bat II.* Once again, Steinman wrote extended, operatic songs with hyperbolic lyrics ("I'll Kill You If You Don't Come Back" was one title) and organized a backup band anchored by E Street Band members Max Weinberg (drums) and Roy Bittan (keyboards), while Meat Loaf sang with a passion all the more compelling for its hint of the ridiculous. In the U.S., with four years separating *Bat* and *Dead Ringer,* nobody cared much. But in the U.K., where *Bat* was still going strong, *Dead Ringer* topped the charts, and the title track, featuring a perfectly cast Cher as duet singer, went Top Ten. In retrospect, the missing ingredient in the album is Todd Rundgren's pop sensibility as producer; he was the one who knew how long the compositions could go for maximum dramatic impact without becoming exhausting. It was Rundgren who made *Bat out of Hell* a fiery listening experience—producing himself, Meat Loaf often sounded only warmed over. *—William Ruhlmann*

Midnight at the Lost & Found / 1983 / Epic ♦♦

Bad Attitude / 1984 / RCA ♦♦♦
Meat Loaf collects a couple of Jim Steinman songs and he, Paul Jacobs, and Mack work at recreating the Todd Rundgren production sound for an album of high-voltage rock. (Originally released on Arista Records in the U.K. in October 1984, *Bad Attitude* was released in the U.S. on RCA Records in April 1985.) *—William Ruhlmann*

Hits Out of Hell / 1984 / Epic ✦✦✦

Blind Before I Stop / 1986 / Atlantic ✦✦

Bat out of Hell II: Back into Hell / 1993 / MCA ✦✦✦✦✦
Although Meat Loaf has made several albums since *Bat out of Hell* (most of them never released in the U.S.), *Bat out of Hell II: Back into Hell* is an explicit sequel to that milestone of '70s pop culture. Reprising the formula of the original nearly to the letter, *Back into Hell* is bombastic and has too much detail, thanks to the pseudo-operatic splendor of Jim Steinman's grandly cinematic songs. From the arrangements to the length of the tracks, everything on the album is overstated; even the album version of the hit single, "I Would Do Anything for Love (But I Won't Do That)," is twelve minutes long. Yet that's precisely the point of this album, and is also why it works so well. No other rock & roller besides Meat Loaf could pull off the humor and theatricality of *Back into Hell* and make it seem real. In that sense, it's a worthy successor to the original. *—Stephen Thomas Erlewine*

Welcome to the Neighbourhood / Nov. 14, 1995 / Virgin ✦✦✦

The Very Best of Meatloaf / Nov. 10, 1998 / Epic ✦✦✦✦
Unlike previous collections Epic has assembled, the double-disc *The Very Best of Meat Loaf* draws not only from his recordings for the label, but it also licenses his '90s comeback recordings for MCA. Which means, of course, that the 20-track collection is indeed the "very best" of Meat Loaf. Not all of his charting hits are here—"What You See Is What You Get," his 1971 single with Stoney, is absent, as is "I'm Gonna Love Her for the Both of Us," the only hit he had between the two *Bat Out of Hell* albums—but all of the key album tracks from the two blockbusters are here, along with highlights from the sequels to the sequel, which means everything that anyone but a diehard Meat Loaf fan could want is on this collection ("Paradise by the Dashboard Light," "Two Out of Three Ain't Bad," "You Took the Words Right Out of My Mouth," "Bat out of Hell," "I'd Do Anything for Love (But I Won't Do That)," "Rock 'N' Roll Dreams Come True," "Objects in the Rear View Mirror May Appear Closer Than They Are," a remix of "Life is a Lemon and I Want My Money Back"). That said, it is true that either *Bat Out of Hell* is a more cohesive listen than this set, simply because they were designed as complete albums. Consquently, casual fans may be just as happy to purchase those two discs, which will set them back about as much as *The Very Best of Meat Loaf*, but anyone who wants all the hits on one set should pick this up. *—Stephen Thomas Erlewine*

Meat Puppets

f. 1980
Group / College Rock, American Punk, Cowpunk, Hardcore Punk, Alternative Pop/Rock
Out of all of the bands that made SST Records a towering force in the American underground during the mid-'80s, the Meat Puppets lasted the longest, surviving where other bands fell apart. The Meat Puppets never had the dedicated following of Hüsker Dü or the Minutemen—two fellow SST bands that played the same circuit as the Puppets—but they were able to carve out a long career where other hardcore bands could not because they always drew from conventional hard rock as well as punk. Not only did they play hard, loud, and fast, but they also had elements of the blues-rock of ZZ Top, the ambling folk-rock of the Grateful Dead, and Neil Young's country-rock and hard rock. As they grew older, the band matured musically, developing an accomplished instrumental technique and moving closer to the traditional hard rock that was always underneath their punk; but they never quite abandoned their punk roots, even when they briefly broke into the mainstream in the early '90s. *—Stephen Thomas Erlewine*

Meat Puppets / 1982 / Rykodisc ✦✦✦
Although the Meat Puppets would later become best known for their intriguing blend of country, punk, rock, folk, psychedelia, and whatever else they could toss in their musical blender, the trio's 1982 self-titled full-length debut was a furious hardcore album. Totally ferocious and red hot, the album rarely lets up on its full-throttle attack—Curt Kirkwood's vocals bear little resemblance to the wasted, off-key country-rock warbling on such seminal releases as *Meat Puppets II* and *Up on the Sun;* instead, the singing style consists of larynx-shredding screaming that renders the lyrics incomprehensible. Still, there's something special about such slop-rockers as "Love Offering," "Blue-Green God," "Saturday Morning," and "Our Friends." And as a sign of things to come, for a few brief fleeting moments, the band attempts to conquer country (on covers of "Walking Boss" and "Tumblin' Tumbleweeds"). The 1999 Rykodisc reissue more than doubled the original album's track listing, including their early *In a Car* EP and a total of 12 outtakes/demos, the best of the bunch being covers of the Stooges' "I Got a Right," Neil Young's "I Am a Child," and the Grateful Dead's "Franklin's Tower." *—Greg Prato*

★ **Meat Puppets II** / 1983 / Rykodisc ✦✦✦✦✦
The Meat Puppets' second album, 1984's appropriately titled *Meat Puppets II*, has since gone down in the rock history books as an all-time classic, and rightfully so. The Puppets were one of the first punk acts to inject different musical styles into their sound, something that was an absolute no-no at the time—especially the sparkling sounds of country. The trio resembles a more conventional band than on their white-noise self-titled debut; the songwriting had improved dramatically, and you could even clearly decipher the playing and singing this time around. As many '90s alt-rock fans know, *Meat Puppets II* reached a whole new generation of fans when Nirvana covered the album's three best tracks on their *MTV Unplugged* special from 1994—"Plateau," "Lake of Fire," and "Oh, Me." But this was an incredibly consistent recording from beginning to end; other highlights included the instrumentals "Magic Toy Missing," "Aurora Borealis" and "I'm a Mindless Idiot," the rockers "Split Myself In Two" and "New Gods," plus such mellower fare as "Lost," "We're Here," "Climbing," and "The Whistling Song." The 1999 Rykodisc reissue contained seven additional tracks, including the contrasting two-part epic "Teenager(s)," as well as "What to Do" and "100% of Nothing." An essential recording that sounds as fresh and inviting as the day it was released. *—Greg Prato*

Up on the Sun / 1985 / Rykodisc ✦✦✦✦✦
What does a band do when they're trying to follow up a masterpiece— Release another masterpiece, of course. That's exactly what the Meat Puppets did with 1985's *Up on the Sun*. Issued one year after *Meat Puppets II*, the songwriting had become more focused, the performances were tighter, and Curt Kirkwood's vocals had progressed from a high-pitched warbling to a soothing monotone. *Up on the Sun* catches the Arizona trio in a relaxed mood, for the most part; the tunes aren't wound up as tightly as its predecessor, with the album-opening title track, the instrumental "Seal Whales," and "Hot Pink" being fine examples. Other highlights include "Maiden's Milk," which contains some great instrumental interplay between the band members, as well as the upbeat "Away," the funky "Buckethead," the psychedelic "Two Rivers," and the furious "Enchanted Porkfist." As with the other 1999 Meat Puppets reissues on Rykodisc, rarities and demos are included as bonus tracks, including a haunting demo of the album's title track. *—Greg Prato*

Out My Way / 1986 / Rykodisc ✦✦✦✦

Huevos / 1987 / Rykodisc ✦✦✦✦
Recorded and released just a few months after the experimental *Mirage*, 1987's *Huevos* was a return to the Meat Puppets' earlier, more straight-ahead direction. The band (guitarist/singer Curt Kirkwood in particular) had always voiced their admiration of ZZ Top, and *Huevos* contained Billy Gibbons & Co.'s influence more than any other Puppets release. But don't be misled—it wasn't a ripoff, the trio simply incorporated ZZ's sound into their energetic, unpredictable rock. It also didn't hurt that *Huevos* contained the band's best set of songs since 85's classic *Up on the Sun*, comprised almost entirely of heavy rockers ("Paradise," "Look at the Rain," "Crazy," "Fruit," "Automatic Mojo," "Dry Rain," etc.). Another major improvement of *Huevos* over *Mirage* was that Derrick Bostrom's drums no longer sounded metronome-perfect and robotic, giving the performances a much livelier edge. The bonus tracks included on the '99 Ryko reissue included several demos of *Huevos* tunes, including a lengthier and much more laid-back version of "Sexy Music," as well as a medley of "I Can't Be Counted On" and Jimmy Reed's "Baby What You Want Me to Do." *—Greg Prato*

Mirage / 1987 / Rykodisc ✦✦✦
As many Meat Puppets fans had realized by 1987's *Mirage*, the trio would change gears and broaden their sound with each successive album. This was never more apparent than on their fourth full-length release. Synthesizers were used to add textures to the tunes, while the drums sounded metronome-perfect, almost as if a drum machine was supplying the patterns. Strangely, although *Mirage* was the trio's most experimental album, it also turned out to be one of their most psychedelia-based works. The groovy little ditty "Get on Down" turned out to be one of the band's first videos aired on MTV, while the title track, the melodic "Leaves," the country rocker "Confusion Fog," the unrelenting "Beauty," and the album-closing punk freak-out "Liquified" are all standouts. Several previously unreleased demos were included on the 1999 Rykodisc reissue, as well as a solo Curt Kirkwood original, "Grand Intro." *—Greg Prato*

Monsters / 1989 / Rykodisc ✦✦✦

Forbidden Places / Jul. 9, 1991 / London ✦✦✦

Too High to Die / Jan. 25, 1994 / London ✦✦✦✦
Although the Meat Puppets' previous album, 1991's *Forbidden Places*, was one of the Arizona trio's finest, the band wasn't completely happy with the album's sound, courtesy of longtime Dwight Yoakam producer Pete Anderson. So on their second album for London Records, 1994's *Too High To Die*, the trio hooked up with Butthole Surfer Paul Leary to put them back on track. Not only did they succeed, but they scored a big radio hit with the melodic rocker "Backwater," and the release became their first to be certified gold. The electrified album opener "Violet Eyes" kicks things off, and immediately thereafter, the trio takes you on a wild musical rollercoaster ride. Hard rock ("We Don't Exist," "Station," an unlisted remake of "Lake of Fire"), blues rock ("Roof With a Hole"), ballads ("Shine," "Why?"), country ("Comin' Down"), and demented pop rock ("Never To Be Found," "Severed Goddess Hand," "Flaming Heart," "Things") help make up perhaps the band's most musically varied album. *—Greg Prato*

No Joke! / Oct. 3, 1995 / London ✦✦

Live in Montana / Feb. 23, 1999 / Rykodisc ✦✦✦

Golden Lies / Sep. 26, 2000 / Atlantic ✦✦✦

Joe Meek

b. 1929, Glouster, England, **d.** Feb. 3, 1967
Producer / Early British Pop/Rock, Pop, Instrumental Rock
Not an artist in the traditional sense of the term—he couldn't play or sing at all—producer Joe Meek has nonetheless been belatedly recognized as an important, even inimitable, figure of early British rock & roll. Like Phil Spector, Meek developed idiosyncratic production techniques that, much more than the artists he worked with, stamped a vision of mad genius on his recordings. In Meek's case, this usually amounted to super-compressed sound, wavering sped-up vocals, ghostly backing violins and choruses, spooky echo and reverb, ticky-tack varispeed piano, and all manners of Halloween and outer-space sound effects. The recordings were all the more remarkable for being produced not in a state-of-the-art studio, but in Meek's own bedroom-sized facility, located over a shop within the flat he rented. Meek couldn't rightly be compared to Phil Spector—he favored gawky, dippy teen-idol fare for gawky, dippy teen idols, not the gutsy soul and R&B-infused Wall of Sound. But he was a trailblazer in his own right—even before Spector, he set up shop as rock & roll's very first independent producer of note, making recordings on his own terms and leasing them to labels for distribution. *—Richie Unterberger*

★ **It's Hard to Believe: The Amazing World of Joe Meek** / Oct. 1995 / Razor & Tie ✦✦✦✦✦
Twenty of Meek's most notable hit singles and misses from 1960 to 1966. Includes his biggest hit productions (the Tornados' "Telstar," the Honeycombs' "Have I the Right," Heinz' "Just like Eddie," Mike Berry's "Tribute to Buddy Holly," John Leyton's "Johnny Remember Me"). Just as intriguing, though, are the more obscure items, some of which are hard or impossible to find on other compilations. Among these are the wild horror-rock of Screaming Lord Sutch's

"'Til the Following Night," the super-creepy Moontrekkers instrumental "Night of the Vampire," the soul-pop of the Riot Squad (with Mitch Mitchell on drums), brassy femme pop by Glenda Collins, and a couple of excerpts from *I Hear a New World*, his bizarre outer-space opus. There are many other interesting Meek discs out there for those who want to go further, but this is an excellent introduction. *—Richie Unterberger*

Megadeth

f. 1983, Los Angeles, CA

Group / Speed Metal, Heavy Metal, Thrash

After he left Metallica in 1983, guitarist/vocalist Dave Mustaine formed the thrash metal quartet Megadeth. Though Megadeth followed the basic blueprint of Metallica's relentless attack, Mustaine's group distinguished themselves from his earlier band by lessening the progressive-rock influences, adding an emphasis on instrumental skills, speeding the tempo up slightly and making the instrumental attack harsher. By streamlining the classic thrash-metal approach and making the music more threatening, as well as making the lyrics more nihilistic, Megadeth became one of the leading bands of the genre during the mid- to late '80s. Each album they released went at least gold, and they continually sold out arenas across America, in addition to developing a strong following overseas. By the early '90s, they had toned their music down slightly, yet that simply increased their following—all of their proper '90s albums debuted in the Top Ten. *—Stephen Thomas Erlewine*

Killing Is My Business . . . And Business Is Good! / 1985 / Combat ✦✦✦

After his exit from Metallica, Dave Mustaine regrouped with his own band on this debut album, accentuating his own chaotic, driving rhythm guitar work and careening, lightning-fast solos. The music here is as raw as Megadeth gets, and that can be both good and bad—Megadeth's later precise, complex riffing and composition aren't completely developed, but the music is performed with a great deal of energy, while Mustaine's vocals (never his strong point) are amateurish at best. Highlights include a retooled version of Nancy Sinatra's "Boots" and "Mechanix," a Mustaine composition written with Metallica which turned into the latter's "The Four Horsemen." *—Steve Huey*

● **Peace Sells . . . But Who's Buying—** / 1986 / Capitol ✦✦✦✦✦

Arguably Megadeth's strongest effort and a classic of early thrash, *Peace Sells* combines a punkish political awareness with a dark, threatening, typically heavy-metal worldview, preoccupied with evil, the occult, and the like. The anthemic title track and "Wake Up Dead" are the two major standouts, and there is also a cover of Willie Dixon's "I Ain't Superstitious," which takes on an air of supernaturally induced paranoia in the album's context. The lines between hell and earth are blurred throughout the album, and the crashing, complex music backs up Mustaine's apocalyptic vision of life as damnation—his limited vocal style is used to great effect, growling and snarling in a barely intelligible fashion under all the complicated guitar work. Vital, necessary thrash. *—Steve Huey*

So Far, So Good . . . So What! / 1988 / Capitol ✦✦✦

Rust in Peace / Sep. 24, 1990 / Capitol ✦✦✦✦✦

A sobered-up Mustaine returns with yet another lineup, this one featuring ex-Cacophony guitar virtuoso Marty Friedman and drummer Nick Menza, for what is easily Megadeth's strongest musical effort. As Metallica was then doing, Mustaine accentuates the progressive tendencies of his compositions, producing rhythmically complex, technically challenging thrash suites that he and Friedman burn through with impeccable execution and jaw-dropping skill. Thanks to Mustaine's focus on the music rather than his sometimes clumsy lyrics, *Rust In Peace* arguably holds up better than any other Megadeth release, even for listeners who think they've outgrown heavy metal. While the whole album is consistently impressive, the obvious highlight is the epic, Eastern-tinged "Hangar 18." *—Steve Huey*

Countdown to Extinction / Jul. 14, 1992 / Capitol ✦✦✦✦

Megadeth guns for arena-thrash success and gets it on *Countdown to Extinction*. Following the lead of 1991's *Metallica*, Megadeth trades in their lengthy, progressive compositions for streamlined, tightly written and played songs more conducive to radio and MTV airplay. Cries of "sellout" seem pointless when the results are artistically (as well as commercially) successful; songs like the mega-hit "Symphony of Destruction," "Skin O' My Teeth," "Foreclosure of a Dream," and "Sweating Bullets" are among the band's best. *—Steve Huey*

Youthanasia / Nov. 1, 1994 / Capitol ✦✦✦

Hidden Treasures / Jul. 18, 1995 / Capitol ✦✦

Cryptic Writings / Jun. 17, 1997 / Capitol ✦✦✦

Risk / Aug. 31, 1999 / Capitol ✦✦✦

Capitol Punishment: The Megadeth Years / Oct. 24, 2000 / Capitol ✦✦✦✦

A 14-track career retrospective featuring two new songs, *Capitol Punishment: The Megadeth Years* attempts to distill the output of a primarily album-oriented band into a set of their best-known (among audiences in 2000) work. Most immediately obvious to fans of old-school Megadeth is that there's hardly anything from the thrash years: one track apiece from *Peace Sells . . . But Who's Buying?* and *So Far, So Good . . . So What!* and two from *Rust in Peace*. Instead, *Capitol Punishment* concentrates on their more recent, radio-oriented sound—about two-thirds of its tracks date from *Countdown to Extinction* on. And it doesn't even cover that territory very well; two of the four singles from *Countdown* ("Skin O' My Teeth" and "Foreclosure of a Dream") are missing, as are the movie-soundtrack contributions collected on *Hidden Treasures* ("Go to Hell," "99 Ways to Die," "Angry Again") that helped build their popular audience in between albums. It's hard to fault what *was* chosen, because the tracks here do represent some of Megadeth's most memorable recordings. It's also arranged in reverse chronological order, which, to the collection's credit, allows listeners only familiar with the band's recent albums to trace their development back to its roots. That's only to a certain extent, though, since those roots are portrayed so sketchily here. A best-of compilation for any group with as large a discography as Megadeth's is bound to omit at least a couple fan favorites, but *Capitol Punishment* is far too incomplete to qualify as an essential retrospective and too scattershot to make for a cohesive listen; instead, it's more of a sampler for casual fans who simply want one disc with some of the group's most popular songs. *—Steve Huey*

The Mekons

f. 1976, Leeds, England

Group / College Rock, Post-Punk, Alternative Pop/Rock

More than any band that came out of late-'70s England, the Mekons have perhaps the most devoted fans of any band even remotely connected to punk rock. And why not— After over two decades together, this band, with an ever-shifting lineup (only Jon Langford and Tom Greenhaigh remain from the original lineup), has produced some of the best rock & roll on the planet, from amateurish rock-noise to cool synth-driven pop to guitar rave-ups to post-modern country. The group's early singles were exceedingly low-fi, fun, challenging and anarchic—principles to which the band has clung, musical genre notwithstanding, since their inception. With their debut album, the Mekons turned into a slightly more accomplished post-punk band who wielded trebly guitars and shouted vocals over semi-funky rhythms tracks. In 1985, they released the startling *Fear and Whiskey*, a ragged country album influenced by the ghosts of Hank Williams and Gram Parsons. Thus began the second coming of the Mekons, who finally began to reach an underground/alternative rock audience that had missed them the first time around. Since the mid-'80s, the group has continually reinvented itself: sodden country band, wiseass folk-rock band, cranked-up guitar band, troublemaking punk band; whatever the scenario, what has remained consistent throughout the Mekons' existence has been great, great music. *—John Dougan*

The Quality of Mercy Is Not Strnen / 1979 / Caroline ✦✦✦

Here's where it all began. Not the best Mekons album available, but *Quality*, along with their second album, *Devils, Rats and Piggies*, and a *A Special Message from Godzilla* (Red Rhino, 1980, now out of print) shows off the Mekons' noisy, avant-garde side. It's abrasive and not as user-friendly as their later records, but this was an exciting time for British punk-rock, and this music, as dense and difficult as it may be, reflects punk's seemingly limitless possibilities. Issued by Blue Plate on CD in 1990. *—John Dougan*

Fear and Whiskey / 1985 / Sin ✦✦✦✦✦

A startling, unexpected record that sounds as wonderful now as it did when it was released. *Fear and Whiskey* uses American country music as its foundation, and the Mekons (ever the playful band) screw around with the genre, alternating between an honest-to-God reverence and flat-out parody. Don't expect sharply executed singing and playing; that's never been the Mekons' style. Instead, plan on a rambling, sodden opus of cowpunk with Hank Williams' ghost lurking in the shadows. In 1989, *Fear and Whiskey* was issued on CD by the Minneapolis-based indie label Twin/Tone with extra material and retitled *Original Sin*. *—John Dougan*

Edge of the World / 1986 / Sin ✦✦✦✦✦

Hot on the heels of *Fear* came this terrific follow-up that mined the same cowpunk terrain as its predecessor. The new members (Timms, et al) sound fully integrated into the lineup, and the manic intensity doesn't let up for an instant. It's a party, but a very weird one indeed. *—John Dougan*

Honky Tonkin' / 1987 / Twin/Tone ✦✦✦✦

Finally, nearly a decade after the first Mekons release and after years of purchasing high-priced English imports, one of America's coolest indie labels manages to unleash the mighty Mekons domestically. The wonderful *Honky Tonkin'* marks the Mekons' last overt country/cowpunk record as they slowly shifted into more guitar-oriented rock. Its title taken from the classic Hank Williams song, this is slightly less essential than *Fear* or *Edge*, but with songs as great as "If They Hang You" and the goofy "Sympathy for the Mekons," you most certainly need it as you build your Mekons collection. *—John Dougan*

New York / 1987 / Combat ✦✦✦✦✦

So Good It Hurts / 1988 / Twin/Tone ✦✦✦

The second release for Twin/Tone showed The Mekons putting a bit of reggae and Latin rhythms into the more-folk-than-country mix. *So Good* sounds a tad subdued in comparison to earlier records, but that does not indicate a lackadaisical attitude or a softening of the band after nearly a decade of recorded work. In fact, its best moments ("Sometime I Feel Like Fletcher Christian") live up to the album's title. *—John Dougan*

● **The Mekons Rock 'n' Roll** / Sep. 1989 / A&M ✦✦✦✦✦

Asking a Mekons fan to select a favorite Mekons record is crazy—there isn't one; there are many. But, if the situation were such that a choice had to be made, this might be the record. Loud, unruly guitars, pissed-off vocals—the Mekons have made an unregenerate, unapologetic punk rock record. This is a dark record, one that comfortably negotiates the dark recesses of rock & roll. They rip the messianic aspirations of U2's Bono ("Blow Your Tuneless Trumpet"), sing a tale of substance abuse that is both cautionary and parodic ("Cocaine Lil"), all the while cranking up a sonic tar pit of guitar noise. Bands this far on in a career, generally speaking, don't make records this good. But *The Mekons Rock 'n' Roll* is one of those cathartic records that only righteously indignant, justifiably pissed-off, grizzled veterans could make. Sadly, and perhaps unsurprisingly, it sold next to nothing and precipitated the band's departure from A&M, who didn't want to release another record like this one. *—John Dougan*

Curse of the Mekons / 1991 / Blast First ✦✦✦✦✦

It's amazing that as down and out as the Mekons were at this point, they could manage to summon up the emotional wherewithal to make a record as excellent as *Curse*, but they did. The title most definitely reflects the band's mindset at this time, but this is not the music of self-pity and despair ("We're right in all we distrust," yelps Greenhaigh on the title track); in fact, if it weren't for *The Mekons Rock 'n' Roll*, this might be the Mekons' finest moment. Politically charged songs despairing about communism and capitalism, a return to C&W (Sally Timms' passionate reading of John Anderson's "Wild and Blue"), and a dig at America's status as the world's only post-Cold War superpower ("100% Song"). Heady stuff, and not all happy, but remarkably assured and very rewarding. *—John Dougan*

It Falleth like Gentle Rain from Heaven: The Mekons Story / 1993 / CNT ✦✦

I Love Mekons / Oct. 18, 1993 / Quarterstick ✦✦✦✦✦
A series of rancorous disagreements with the high and mighty at Warner Bros. subsidiary Loud forced the Mekons into an unanticipated two years of silence that nearly scuttled this record and ended the band's career. Eventually, Warner relented (they had maintained the record was not good enough to release), and the increasingly restless Mekons fans were able to judge for themselves that this was another terrific Mekons record. More traditionally rock-oriented and less prone to stylistic leaps than before, *I Love Mekons* is a strong, confident record that should have placed the Mekons at the forefront of the growing alternative rock market. It didn't, but often there's no accounting for taste. *—John Dougan*

Retreat From Memphis / May 2, 1994 / Quarterstick ✦✦✦

Me / May 19, 1998 / Quarterstick ✦✦✦

I Have Been to Heaven and Back . . . , Vol. 1 / Apr. 20, 1999 / Quarterstick ✦✦✦✦

Where Were You?: Hens Teeth and Other Lost Fragments of Popular Culture, Vol. 2 / Sep. 7, 1999 / Quarterstick ✦✦✦✦✦

Journey to the End of the Night / Mar. 7, 2000 / Quarterstick ✦✦✦✦✦

John Cougar Mellencamp

b. Oct. 7, 1951, Seymour, IN
Vocals, Guitar / Bar Band, Heartland Rock, Pop/Rock, Roots Rock, Hard Rock
Throughout his career, John Mellencamp has had to fight, whether it was for the right to record under his own name or for respect as an artist. Of course, he never made it easily on himself. Mellencamp began his career in the late '70s as a Bruce Springsteen clone called Johnny Cougar. As his career progressed, his music became more distinctive, developing into a Stonesy blend of hard-rock and folk-rock. His musical development coincided with his growth in popularity—by the time "Hurts So Good" and "Jack and Diane" became hits in 1982, Mellencamp had created his own variation of the heartland rock of Springsteen, Tom Petty and Bob Seger. While he had the record sales, it took several years before rock critics took him seriously. For some artists, this would be easy to ignore, but Mellencamp had the desire to be a serious social commentator, chronicling the times and trials of Midwestern baby boomers. *Scarecrow,* released in 1985, fulfilled his wish of being taken serious, and every record he released after it was greeted warmly by critics. Furthermore, he sustained his popularity into the late '90s, only occasionally experiencing dips in record sales. *—Stephen Thomas Erlewine*

Chestnut Street Incident / 1976 / Original Masters ✦

The Kid Inside / 1977 / Original Masters ✦

John Cougar / 1979 / Riva ✦

Nothin' Matters & What If It Did / 1980 / Riva ✦✦

American Fool / 1982 / Mercury ✦✦✦
John Cougar's first albums were so bereft of strong material that the lean swagger of *American Fool* came as a shock. The difference is evident from the opening song "Hurts So Good," a hard, Stonesy rocker with an irresistibly sleazy hook. Cougar never wrote anything as catchy as this before, nor had his romantic vision of small-town America resonated like it did on "Jack & Diane," a minor and remarkably affecting sketch of dead-end romance. These two songs are the only true keepers on *American Fool,* but the rest of the record works better than his previous material because his band is tighter than ever before, making his weaker moments convincing. Besides, songs like "Hand to Hold On to" and "China Girl," for all their faults, do indicate that his sense of craft is improving considerably. *—Stephen Thomas Erlewine*

Uh-Huh / 1983 / Mercury ✦✦✦✦✦
Since *American Fool* illustrated that John Cougar was becoming an actual songwriter, it's only proper that he reclaimed his actual last name, Mellencamp, for the follow-up, *Uh-Huh.* After all, now that he had success, he wanted to be taken seriously, and *Uh-Huh* reflects that in its portraits of broken-hearted life in the Midwest and its rumbling undercurrent of despair. Although his lyrics still had the tendency to be a little too vague, they were more effective than ever before, as was his music; he might not have changed his style at all—it was still a fusion of the Stones and Springsteen—except that he now knew how to make it his own. *Uh-Huh* runs out of steam toward the end, but the first half—with the dynamic rocker "Crumblin' Down," this best protest song, "Pink Houses," the punky "Authority Song," the melancholy "Warmer Place to Sleep" and the garage-rocker "Play Guitar"—makes the record his first terrific album. *—Stephen Thomas Erlewine*

● **Scarecrow** / 1985 / Mercury ✦✦✦✦✦
Uh-Huh found John Mellencamp coming into his own, but he perfected his Heartland rock with *Scarecrow.* A loose concept album about lost innocence and the crumbling of small-town America, *Scarecrow* says as much with its tough rock and gentle folk-rock as it does with its lyrics, which remain a weak point for Mellencamp. Nevertheless, his writing has never been more powerful: "Rain on the Scarecrow" and "Small Town" capture the hopes and fears of middle America, while "Lonely Ol' Night" and "Rumbleseat" effortlessly convey the desperate loneliness of being stuck in a dead-end life. Those four songs form the core of the album, and while the rest of the album isn't quite as strong, that's only a relative term, since it's filled with lean hooks and powerful, economical playing that make *Scarecrow* one of the definitive blue-collar rock albums of the mid-'80s. *—Stephen Thomas Erlewine*

The Lonesome Jubilee / 1987 / Mercury ✦✦✦✦✦
John Mellencamp's fascination with the American heartland came into full flower on *Scarecrow,* but with its follow-up *The Lonesome Jubilee,* he began exploring American folk musics, adding fiddle, accordions and acoustic guitars to his band, which allowed him to explore folk and country. The expansion of his band coincided with his continuing growth as a songwriter. Song for song, *The Lonesome Jubilee* is Mellencamp's strongest album, the record where he captured his romantic, if decidedly melancholy, vision of working-class America. He may recycle the same lyrical ideas as before, but he captures them better than ever, and his music is richer, which gives the album resonance. Again, there are a few moments where Mellencamp's reach exceeds his grasp, but "Paper in Fire," "Check It Out," "Cherry Bomb," "Empty Hands" and "Hard Times for an Honest Man" make the record his best. *—Stephen Thomas Erlewine*

Big Daddy / May 1989 / Mercury ✦✦✦
Continuing with the folk inclinations of *The Lonesome Jubilee,* John Mellencamp recorded his most ambitious and serious-minded album with *Big Daddy.* Mellencamp produced the record himself, giving the album a concise and stripped-down sound, which help give his songs the appearance of being gritty statements of truth. Unfortunately, Mellencamp isn't saying nearly as much as he believes he is, since his lyrics tend to be cliched and half-baked, making much of the album feel pompous and self-serving. This is only reinforced by the lack of rockers on *Big Daddy,* since he saves the most carefree moment—a ripping cover of the Hombres' "Let It Out (Let It All Hang Out)"—for an unlisted bonus track. Still, when he does hit his target, like on the gentle "Jackie Brown," the stuttering, fiddle-driven "Sometimes a Great Notion" and even the self-pitying "Pop Singer," Mellencamp proves that his talents haven't abandoned him. *—Stephen Thomas Erlewine*

Whenever We Wanted / Oct. 8, 1991 / Mercury ✦✦✦
Mellencamp took his signature blend of Stonesy rock and folk as far as it could go on *Big Daddy,* so he wisely returned to straight-ahead rock & roll with *Whenever We Wanted. Uh-Huh* was the last record he made that rocked as hard and consistently as this, and his songwriting had improved considerably in the years since that breakthrough release. Which means, of course, that *Whenever We Wanted* is more consistent than the earlier record, but it never reaches the highs of *Uh-Huh.* Even its best moments ("Love and Happiness," "Get a Leg Up," "Whenever We Wanted," "Again Tonight") shine because of their craftmenship, failing to achieve the kinetic energy of his earlier work. *Whenever We Wanted* remains a solid record, but it's one that feels like a holding pattern. *—Stephen Thomas Erlewine*

Human Wheels / Sep. 7, 1993 / Mercury ✦✦✦✦

Dance Naked / Jun. 21, 1994 / Mercury ✦✦✦

Mr. Happy Go Lucky / Sep. 10, 1996 / Mercury ✦✦✦

● **The Best That I Could Do (1978-1988)** / Nov. 18, 1997 / Mercury ✦✦✦✦✦
The Best That I Could Do is an appropriately self-deprecating title for John Mellencamp's greatest-hits collection, considering that the heartland rocker never seemed too convinced of his own worth. Of course, he had to struggle to get any respect after he was saddled with the stage name Johnny Cougar early in his career, but this 14-track collection proves that he was one of the best unabashed, straight-ahead rockers of the '80s. Fourteen tracks actually turns out to be a little too short to contain all of his great singles—songs like "Rain on the Scarecrow," "Rumbleseat," "Pop Singer," "Again Tonight" and "What If I Came Knocking" are left off the collection (there's nothing from 1988's *Big Daddy* at all)—but it's hard to argue with what's here. Over the course of 14 tracks, such classic rock hits as "I Need a Lover," "Hurts So Good," "Jack and Diane," "Crumblin' Down," "Pink Houses," "Lonely Ol' Night," "Small Town," "Paper in Fire," "Cherry Bomb," "Check It Out," "Get a Leg Up" and "Wild Night" are chronicled, with a new cover of Terry Reid's "Without Expression" added for good measure. It may fall short of being definitive, but only by a small margin, and it remains an excellent overview and introduction to Mellencamp's remarkably consistent body of work. *—Stephen Thomas Erlewine*

John Mellencamp / Oct. 6, 1998 / Columbia ✦✦✦

Rough Harvest / Aug. 17, 1999 / Mercury ✦✦✦

Harold Melvin

b. Jun. 25, 1939, Philadelphia, PA, **d.** Mar. 24, 1997, Philadelphia, PA
Vocals / Philly Soul, Doo Wop, Soul
Starting out in 1954 in Philadelphia as a doo-wop group with Harold Melvin as lead singer, the Blue Notes first recorded for the New York-based Josie label two years later. They debuted on the R&B charts in 1960 on the Value label with "My Hero," but it was not until 1972, when drummer Teddy Pendergrass took over lead vocal chores and the group came under the wing of producers Kenny Gamble and Leon Huff and their Philadelphia International label, that Harold Melvin & the Blue Notes became consistent chart-makers. Pendergrass' vocals smoldered with sensuality. Combined with the smooth group harmonies that had always been a Blue Note trademark, Gamble and Huff's superior writing, and lush productions, the superb TSOP house band records, such as "I Miss You," "If You Don't Know Me by Now," and "The Love I Lost" were staples on both Black and White radio from 1972 to 1975. Pendergrass went solo in 1975 and the Blue Notes' glory days came to an end. *—Rob Bowman*

Wake Up Everybody / 1975 / Philadelphia International ✦✦✦✦

★ **Collector's Item** / 1976 / Philadelphia International ✦✦✦✦✦
It rounds up such hits as "Wake Up Everybody," "Bad Luck," "If You Don't Know Me by Now," and "The Love I Lost," all benchmarks of an era. *—John Floyd*

☆ **If You Don't Know Me by Now: The Best of Harold Melvin & the Blue Notes** / Feb. 28, 1995 / Epic/Legacy ✦✦✦✦✦
Although the ten-track disc is criminally brief, *The Best of Harold Melvin & the Bluenotes* contains most of their biggest hits and offers a good portrait of one of the finest soul groups of the '70s. *—Stephen Thomas Erlewine*

Men at Work

f. 1979, Melbourne, Australia, **db.** 1985
Group / Pop/Rock, New Wave
One of the New Wave era's more surprising success stories, Men at Work rocketed out of Melbourne, Australia in 1982, becoming the year's most successful group. Transplanted Scot Colin Hay (lead vocals, guitar) formed the group as an acoustic duo with Ron Strykert (gui-

tar, vocals) in 1979, but they soon expanded, adding John Rees (bass), Greg Ham (saxophone, flute, keyboards) and Jerry Speiser (drums). Favorites on Australia's pub circuit, they became the country's highest-paid unsigned band; by 1981, they landed a contract with Australian Columbia and released "Who Can It Be Now?" It became a huge hit, as did their 1982 debut album, *Business as Usual;* its Police-styled rhythms, catchy guitar hooks, wailing saxophones and off-kilter sense of humor made it an international blockbuster, topping the Australian charts for 10 weeks and America's for 15. Funny, irreverent videos for "Who Can It Be Now" and "Down Under" helped send both singles to number one. After winning a Grammy for 1982's Best New Artist, the band's momentum continued with 1983's *Cargo,* which reached number three in the US and generated the Top 10 singles "Overkill" and "It's a Mistake." But soon, the bottom fell out of the band's popularity. After an extensive tour that included dates with the Clash and the Stray Cats, the band took an extended break; after releasing 1985's *Two Hearts,* which failed to generate one Top 40 single, they broke up. Hay pursued a solo career, but neither of his two American solo albums—1987's *Looking for Jack* and 1990's *Wayfaring Sons* (1990)—were successes. In the '90s, Hay continued to release albums in Australia and began an acting career. He and Ham reformed Men at Work in 1998, issuing the live hits collection *Brazil.* —*Stephen Thomas Erlewine*

Business as Usual / 1981 / CBS ✦✦✦✦✦
Business as Usual became a surprise international hit on the basis "Who Can It Be Now?" and "Down Under," two excellent singles that merged straightahead pop-rock hooks with a quirky New Wave production and an off-beat sense of humor. Colin Hay's keening vocals uncannily recall Sting, and the band's rhythmic pulse and phased guitars also bring to mind a bar-band version of the Police. And that helps make the remainder of *Business as Usual* enjoyable. There's a fair amount of filler on the record, but "Be Good Johnny," "I Can See It In Your Eyes" and "Down By the Sea" are all fine New Wave pop songs, making *Business as Usual* one of the more enjoyable mainstream-oriented efforts of the era. —*Stephen Thomas Erlewine*

Cargo / 1983 / CBS ✦✦✦✦✦
Cargo was bashed out fairly quickly, but it its release was delayed because of the success of Men at Work's debut, *Business as Usual.* Though it was recorded on the road, *Cargo* is considerably more diverse—but not necessarily more ambitious—than its predecessor. Again, the album is anchored by two extraordinary singles. Fortunately, the soaring ballad "Overkill" and the satiric, anti-nuclear "It's a Mistake" aren't rewrites of "Who Can It Be Now?" and "Down Under," demonstrating more depth than anything on the debut. Despite this growth, the remainder of *Cargo* is weighed down by filler. "Doctor Heckyll and Mr. Jive" might be goofy fun and "High Wire" and "Blue for You" are tight pop songs, but the rest are simply pleasant, ocassionally embarassing ("I Like To," "Settle Down My Boy"), New Wave pop. —*Stephen Thomas Erlewine*

Two Hearts / 1985 / CBS ✦✦

● **Contraband: The Best of Men at Work** / Mar. 26, 1996 / Columbia/Legacy ✦✦✦✦
Men at Work's records were always somewhat uneven affairs. Certainly, the singles were the highlights, but they had a handful of first-rate album tracks that made the records necessary for dedicated fans, even if the overall album was inconsistent. *Contraband: The Best of Men at Work* does a terrific job of consolidating all of their highlights onto one disc. From hits like "Who Can It Be Now?," "Down Under," "Overkill," and "It's a Mistake" to slightly neglected album tracks like "Be Good Johnny," *Contraband* has every great track from the Australian new wave band. For most fans, it will be the only disc they need. —*Stephen Thomas Erlewine*

Men Without Hats

f. 1980, Montreal, Quebec, Canada, **db.** 1991
Group / New Wave, Synth Pop
The new wave synth-pop collective Men Without Hats was formed in 1980 by brothers Ivan and Stefan Doroschuk. The group independently released their debut EP, *Folk of the 80's,* in 1980; it was reissued the following year by Stiff in Britain. Taken from their 1982 debut *Rhythm of Youth,,* the single "The Safety Dance" became a major hit, peaking on the American charts at number three in 1983. Driven by an insistent three-chord synthesizer riff, the song was one of the biggest synth-pop hits of the new wave era. The group wasn't able to exploit its success, however. *Folk of the '80s (Part III)* stalled at number 127 on the charts in America and made even less of an impact in other parts of the world. Thanks to the minor hit title track, 1987's *Pop Goes the World* was a bigger success, yet it didn't recapture the audience their first album had gained. Released two years later, *The Adventures of Women & Men Without Hats in the 21st Century* failed to chart, as did its follow-up, 1991's *Sideways.* The two albums' lack of success effectively put an end to Men Without Hats' career. —*Stephen Thomas Erlewine*

Rhythm of Youth / 1982 / MCA ✦✦✦✦✦

Folk of the '80s, Pt. / 1984 / MCA ✦✦✦

Pop Goes the World / 1987 / Mercury ✦✦✦✦

● **Collection** / Feb. 20, 1996 / Oglio ✦✦✦✦✦
Men Without Hats were never an album-oriented band, so *Collection* does the casual fan a favor by compiling all of their hits—namely "The Safety Dance" (included in its original single mix) and "Pop Goes the World"—onto one disc. While many of the songs aren't as strong as those two singles, they are enjoyable New Wave artifacts, making the compilation a fun nostalgia trip. Still, some casual fans will be disappointed that there aren't any lost classics on *Collection,* but less-discerning listeners will be pleased. —*Stephen Thomas Erlewine*

Mercury Rev

f. Buffalo, NY
Group / Noise Pop, Dream Pop, Neo-Psychedelia, Indie Rock, Alternative Pop/Rock
Not so much a band as a long, strange trip, the chaotic avant-pop pranksters Mercury Rev formed in Buffalo, New York in the late '80s. Always rife with personality conflicts, group members interacted with one another infrequently, and their first recordings evolved simply as a means of creating soundtracks for their experimental student films. Encouraged to further their music by academic mentor Tony Conrad, the loosely-connected aggregate dubbed Mercury Rev (a name whose inspiration was variously attributed to an imaginary Russian ballet dancer, a sharp rise in temperature or a revved-up auto) began to emerge, and eventually the group recorded a demo onto a reel of 35mm magnetic film. The demo tape somehow made its way to the British offices of the Rough Trade label, which contacted singer David Baker about signing the group. Soon, the band convened to record their debut *Yerself Is Steam,* a brilliantly melodic and free-form set highlighted by distorted art-pop epics like "Chasing a Bee," "Coney Island Cyclone" and "Frittering," *Yerself Is Steam* was issued to widespread acclaim in 1991; however, within weeks of the LP's release Rough Trade's American branch declared bankruptcy, aborting any hopes of proper distribution or promotion. Mercury Rev then set up studio space in a barn to craft their second album, *Boces;* after completing the principle recording sessions, the group collected samples from sites as far ranging as Times Square and NASA's Cape Canaveral to flesh out the music's dense, prismatic sound. After relations soured to the point where Baker was travelling to gigs apart from his bandmates, he was dismissed from Mercury Rev's ranks; 1995's shimmering *See You on the Other Side* found the group—newly freed of Baker's darker impulses—exploring increasingly diverse stylistic territory with newfound emotional depth. The lovely *Deserter's Songs* followed in the fall of 1998. —*Jason Ankeny*

Yerself Is Steam / 1991 / Columbia ✦✦✦✦✦
Music dictated not by logic but by intuition, *Yerself Is Steam* is an album at war with itself, split by its desire to achieve both melodic pop bliss and white-noise transcendence within the same space; it succeeds brilliantly, avant-bubblegum fuel injected by fits and flourishes of prismatic chaos. From the comic malevolence of David Baker's mad-scientist creations to Jonathan Donahue's opiate lullabies, *Yerself Is Steam* is vividly cinematic—between the roller coaster feedback of "Coney Island Cyclone" and the narcoleptic ebb and flow of the climactic "Very Sleepy Rivers," the songs perfectly evoke their titular aspirations; likewise, from the album title (say it out loud) onward, the lyrics revel in the quirks and idiosyncrasies of language, buoyed by a homophonous prankishness and dada rhyme schemes, which, in their own odd way, suggest a kind of poetry. A near-perfect debut from a band that would only get better from here on out. [The American edition appends the superb single "Car Wash Hair," while some foreign releases include the bonus disc *Lego My Ego,* a crazy quilt knitted together from unlikely covers (Sly Stone's "If You Want Me to Stay," Miles Davis' "Shhh"), *Peel Sessions* highlights, and wonderfully loopy studio chatter.] —*Jason Ankeny*

● **Boces** / Jun. 1, 1993 / Columbia ✦✦✦✦✦
Boces, Mercury Rev's second album, is an even stronger affair than their first, showcasing the possibilities of their truly mind-bending neo-psychedelic guitar rock. All of their flights into the netherworld are fascinating; even the eleven-minute songs seem too short. —*Stephen Thomas Erlewine*

See You on the Other Side / Sep. 19, 1995 / Work ✦✦✦✦
Without David Baker, Mercury Rev opens up, relying on the bright psychedelia of Jonathan Donahue's songwriting. While that means the band has a greater tendency to indulge themselves in noisy, free-form jams that don't lead anywhere, it also means that the music is more accessible, since Baker's dark hallucinations no longer dominate the group's experimental instrumental section. However, the music on *See You on the Other Side* isn't quite as compelling without the tension between Donahue's colorful pop and Baker's haunting voice and lyrics—which means that although they've progressed musically, they've lost an essential element of what made their first two records distinctive. —*Stephen Thomas Erlewine*

Deserter's Songs / Sep. 29, 1998 / V2 ✦✦✦✦✦
Four albums in and Mercury Rev remains as surprising and daring as ever—exchanging the volcanic noise and twisted sensibilities of earlier releases for ornate arrangements and ethereal strings, *Deserter's Songs* unlocks the beauty always hidden just below the band's surface, its lush harmonics and soothing textures bathing in an almost unearthly light. Standouts including the exquisitely waltz-like "Tonite It Shows" and the celestial "Endlessly" are like lullabies, their music-box melodies gentle and narcotic; even the most pop-oriented moments like "Opus 40" and "Hudson Line" share a symphonic, candy-colored majesty far removed from conventional rock idioms. Complete with its fractured instrumental interludes and odd effects, *Deserter's Songs* sounds like no other album—for that matter, it doesn't even sound like Mercury Rev, yet there's no mistaking the record's brilliance for anyone else. —*Jason Ankeny*

Metallica

f. 1981, Los Angeles, CA
Group / Speed Metal, Heavy Metal, Thrash, Hard Rock
Metallica was easily the best, most influential heavy metal band of the '80s, responsible for bringing the music back to earth. Instead of playing the usual rock star games of metal stars of the early '80s, the band looked and talked like they were from the street. Metallica expanded the limits of thrash, using speed and volume not for their own sake, but to enhance their intricately structured compositions. The release of 1983's *Kill 'Em All* marked the beginning of the legitimization of heavy metal's underground, bringing new complexity and depth to thrash metal. With each album, the band's playing and writing improved; James Hetfield developed a signature rhythm playing that matched his growl, while lead guitarist Kirk Hammett became one of the most copied guitarists in metal. Lars Ulrich's thunderous, yet complex, drumming clicked in perfectly with Cliff Burton's innovative bass playing. After releasing their masterpiece *Master of Puppets* in 1986, tragedy struck the band when their tour bus crashed while traveling in Sweden, killing Burton. Jason Newsted was his replacement. Two years later, the band released the conceptually ambitious *...And Justice for All,* which hit the Top Ten without any radio play and very little support from MTV. But Metallica completely crossed over into the mainstream with 1991's *Metallica,* which found the band trading in their long compositions for more concise song structures; it resulted in a Number One album that sold over seven million copies in the U.S. alone. By the '90s, Metallica had changed the rules for all heavy metal bands; they were the leaders of the genre, respected not only by headbangers, but by mainstream record buyers and critics. No other heavy metal band has ever been able to pull off such a trick. —*Stephen Thomas Erlewine*

☆ **Kill 'Em All** / 1983 / Elektra ✦✦✦✦✦
The true birth of thrash. On *Kill 'Em All,* Metallica fuses the intricate riffing of N.W.O.B.H.M. bands like Judas Priest, Iron Maiden, and Diamond Head with the velocity of Motorhead and hardcore punk. James Hetfield's highly technical rhythm guitar style drives most of the album, setting new standards of power, precision, and stamina. But really, the rest of the band is just as dexterous, playing with tightly controlled fury even at the most ridiculously fast tempos. There are already several extended, multi-sectioned compositions foreshadowing the band's later progressive epics, though these are driven by adrenaline, not texture. A few tributes to heavy metal itself are a bit dated lyrically. Like Diamond Head, the band's biggest influence, *Kill 'Em All*'s most effective tone is one of supernatural malevolence—as pure sound, the record is already straight from the pits of hell. Ex-member Dave Mustaine cowrote four of the original ten tracks, but the material all sounds of a piece. And actually, anyone who worked backwards through the band's catalog might not fully appreciate the impact of *Kill 'Em All* when it first appeared, unlike later releases, there simply wasn't much musical variation (apart from a lyrical bass solo from Cliff Burton). The band's musical ambition also grew rapidly, so today, *Kill 'Em All* sounds more like the foundation for greater things to come. But that doesn't take anything away from how fresh it sounded upon first release, and time hasn't dulled the giddy rush of excitement in these performances. Frightening, awe-inspiring, and absolutely relentless, *Kill 'Em All* is pure destructive power, executed with jaw-dropping levels of scientific precision. An Elektra reissue added the cover songs "Blitzkrieg" and "Am I Evil?" from the European *Creeping Death* EP, which were deleted and later included on *Garage, Inc.* —*Steve Huey*

Ride the Lightning / 1984 / Elektra ✦✦✦✦✦
Kill 'Em All may have revitalized heavy metal's underground, but *Ride the Lightning* was even more stunning, exhibiting staggering musical growth and boldly charting new directions that would affect heavy metal for years to come. Incredibly ambitious for a one-year-later sophomore effort, *Ride the Lightning* finds Metallica aggressively expanding their compositional technique and range of expression. Every track tries something new, and every musical experiment succeeds mightily. The lyrics push into new territory as well—more personal, more socially conscious, less metal posturing. But the true heart of *Ride the Lightning* lies in its rich musical imagination. There are extended, progressive epics; tight, concise groove-rockers; thrashers that blow anything on *Kill 'Em All* out of the water, both in their urgency and the barest hints of melody that have been added to the choruses. Some innovations are flourishes that add important bits of color, like the lilting, pseudo-classical intro to the furious "Fight Fire With Fire," or the harmonized leads that pop up on several tracks. Others are major reinventions of Metallica's sound, like the nine-minute, album-closing instrumental "The Call of Ktulu," or the haunting suicide lament "Fade to Black." The latter is an all-time metal classic; it begins as an acoustic-driven, minor-key ballad, then gets slashed open by electric guitars playing a wordless chorus, and ends in a wrenching guitar solo over a thrashy yet lyrical rhythm figure. Basically, in a nutshell, Metallica sounded like it could do anything. Heavy metal hadn't seen this kind of ambition since Judas Priest's late-'70s classics, and *Ride the Lightning* effectively rewrote the rule book for a generation of thrashers. If *Kill 'Em All* was the manifesto, *Ride the Lightning* was the revolution itself. —*Steve Huey*

★ **Master of Puppets** / 1986 / Elektra ✦✦✦✦✦
Even though *Master of Puppets* didn't take as gigantic a leap forward as *Ride the Lightning,* it was the band's greatest achievement, hailed as a masterpiece by critics far outside heavy metal's core audience. It was also a substantial hit, reaching the Top 30 and selling three million copies despite absolutely nonexistent airplay. Instead of a radical reinvention, *Master of Puppets* is a refinement of past innovations. In fact, it's possible to compare *Ride the Lightning* and *Master of Puppets* song for song, and note striking similarities between corresponding track positions on each record (although *Lightning*'s closing instrumental has been bumped up to next-to-last in *Master*'s running order). That hint of conservatism is really the only conceivable flaw here. Though it isn't as startling as *Ride the Lightning, Master of Puppets* feels more unified, both thematically and musically. Everything about it feels blown up to epic proportions (indeed, the songs are much longer on average), and the band feels more in control of its direction. You'd never know it by the lyrics, though—in one way or another, nearly every song on *Master of Puppets* deals with the fear of powerlessness. Sometimes they're about hypocritical authority (military and religious leaders), sometimes primal, uncontrollable human urges (drugs, insanity, rage), and, in true H.P. Lovecraft fashion, sometimes monsters. Yet by bookending the album with two slices of thrash mayhem ("Battery" and "Damage, Inc."), the band reigns triumphant through sheer force—of sound, of will, of malice. The arrangements are thick and muscular, and the material varies enough in texture and tempo to hold interest through all its twists and turns. Some critics have called *Master of Puppets* the best heavy metal album ever recorded; if it isn't, it certainly comes close. —*Steve Huey*

Garage Days Re-Revisited / 1987 / Elektra ✦✦✦
Following Cliff Burton's death, Metallica took some time off and initiated new bassist Jason Newsted with a raw, unpolished EP of covers originally recorded by Diamond Head, Holocaust, Killing Joke, Budgie, and the Misfits. Most fit the band's style quite well; only "Last Caress" sounds out of place, as the original seemed looser and more dangerous. As a showcase for some strong metal riffs and material by mostly underground bands, the EP works quite well. —*Steve Huey*

. . . And Justice for All / 1988 / Elektra ✦✦✦✦✦
The most immediately noticeable aspect of *. . . And Justice for All* isn't Metallica's still-growing compositional sophistication, or the apocalyptic lyrical portrait of a society in decay. It's the weird, bone-dry production. The guitars buzz thinly, the drums click more than pound, and Jason Newsted's bass is nearly inaudible. It's a shame that the cold, flat sound obscures some of the sonic details, because *. . . And Justice for All* is Metallica's most complex, ambitious work; every song is an expanded suite, with only two of the nine tracks clocking in at under six minutes. It takes a while to sink in, but given time, *. . . And Justice for All* reveals some of Metallica's best material. It also reveals the band's determination to pull out all the compositional stops, throwing in extra sections, odd-numbered time signatures, and dense webs of guitar arpeggios and harmonized leads. At times, it seems like they're doing it simply because they can; parts of the album lack direction, and probably should have been trimmed for momentum's sake. Pacing-wise, the album again loosely follows the blueprint of *Ride the Lightning,* though not as closely as *Master of Puppets.* This time around, the fourth song—once again a ballad with a thrashy chorus and outro—gave the band one of the unlikeliest Top 40 singles in history "One" was an instant metal classic, based on Dalton Trumbo's anti-war novel *Johnny Got His Gun* and climaxing with a pulverizing machine-gun imitation. As a whole, opinions on *. . . And Justice for All* remain somewhat divided: some think it's a slightly flawed masterpiece and the pinnacle of Metallica's progressive years; others see it as bloated and overambitious. Either interpretation can be readily supported, but the band had clearly taken this direction as far as it could. The difficulty of reproducing these songs in concert eventually convinced Metallica that it was time for an overhaul. —*Steve Huey*

Metallica / Aug. 1991 / Elektra ✦✦✦✦✦
After the muddled production and ultra-complicated song structures of *. . . And Justice For All,* Metallica decided that they had taken the progressive elements of their music as far as they could, and that a simplification and streamlining of their sound was in order. While the assessment made sense from a musical standpoint, it also presented an opportunity to commercialize their music, and *Metallica* accomplishes both goals. The best songs are more melodic and immediate, the crushing, stripped-down grooves of "Enter Sandman," "Sad But True," and "Wherever I May Roam" sticking to traditional structures and using the same main riffs throughout; the crisp, professional production by Bob Rock adds to their accessibility. "The Unforgiven" and "Nothing Else Matters" avoid the slash-and-burn guitar riffs that had always punctuated the band's ballads; the latter is a full-fledged love song complete with string section, which works much better than might be imagined. The song- and riff-writing slips here and there, a rare occurrence for Metallica, which some longtime fans interpreted as filler next to a batch of singles calculated for commercial success. The objections were often more to the idea that Metallica was doing *anything* explicitly commercial, but millions more disagreed. In fact, the band's popularity exploded so much that most of their back catalog found mainstream acceptance in its own right, while other progressively inclined speed-metal bands copied the move toward simplification. In retrospect, *Metallica* is a good, but not quite great, album, one whose best moments deservedly captured the heavy metal crown, but whose approach also foreshadowed a creative decline. —*Steve Huey*

Live Shit: Binge and Purge / Nov. 23, 1993 / Elektra ✦✦✦

Load / Jun. 4, 1996 / Elektra ✦✦✦

Reload / Nov. 18, 1997 / Elektra ✦✦✦

Garage, Inc. / Nov. 24, 1998 / Polygram International ✦✦✦✦
For many years, Metallica's 1987 EP *Garage Days Re-Revisited* was the most sought-after item their catalog; it was constantly bootlegged in the '90s, and often supplemented by a host of covers Metallica had released on singles and compilations throughout the years. By 1998, the band had understandably grown frustrated with this situation and decided to confront the problem head-on by reissuing all these rarities. Savvy businessmen that they are, they also realized they needed to give hardcore fans who already owned all the covers a reason to purchase the new set—hence, the expansion of the *Garage Days* EP to the double-disc blowout *Garage Inc.* The second disc's rarities are balanced by the first disc's new covers, the bulk of which were recorded following the *Re-Load* tour. It shouldn't come as a surprise that these covers recall the blooze-'n'-boogie heavy rock of the *Load*s, but what is a surprise is that Metallica seems to have found their footing in this style through other people's songs. Whether it's Bob Seger, Blue Oyster Cult, Thin Lizzy, Nick Cave, or the all-star jam on Lynyrd Skynyrd's "Tuesday's Gone," the band effortlessly makes the songs seem like their own, through a bizarre mix of respect and ballsy irreverence. Sure, it may not be nearly as raw as early Metallica, but it is a better listen than either of the *Load* records. And if raw is what you want, the equally diverse Disc Two provides all the thrills you could hope for. At one time, it might have seemed a little odd that Metallica would cover Budgie, Diamond Head, the Misfits, and Queen, but if *Garage Inc.* proves anything, it's that the group's musical instincts, risks, and sense of humor have made them the greatest metal band of the '80s and '90s. —*Stephen Thomas Erlewine*

S&M / Nov. 23, 1999 / Elektra ✦✦✦

The Meters

f. 1966, New Orleans, LA, **db.** 1977
Instrumental / New Orleans R&B, R&B, Funk, Soul
The Meters defined New Orleans funk, not only on their own recordings, but also as the backing band for numerous artists, including many produced by Allen Toussaint. Where the funk of Sly Stone and James Brown was wild, careening and determinedly urban, the Meters were down-home and earthy. Nearly all of their own recordings were instrumentals, putting the emphasis on the organic and complex rhythms. The syncopated, layered percussion intertwined with the gritty grooves of the guitar and organ, creating a distinctive sound that earned a small, devoted cult during the '70s, including musicians like Paul McCartney and Robert Palmer, both of whom used the group as a backing band for recording. Despite their reputation as an extraordinary live band, the Meters never broke into the mainstream, but their sound provided the basis for much of the funk and hip-hop of the '80s and '90s. —*Stephen Thomas Erlewine*

The Meters / 1969 / Sundazed ✦✦✦
This seminal New Orleans funk group's debut album features the semi-hit "Cissy Strut" and its follow-up, "Sophisticated Sissy." This 1999 reissue also offers two previously unreleased bonus tracks, "The Look of Love" and "Soul Machine." Other highlights include "Here Comes the Meter Man," "Live Wire," and "Sehorn's Farm." —*Cub Koda*

Struttin' / 1970 / Sundazed ✦✦✦

Look-Ka Py Py / Jan. 1970 / Sundazed ✦✦✦✦
The second album by Art Neville's band continues the sound that made them New Orleans

legends. In addition to the title track, there's plenty of funk aboard in songs like like "Pungee," "9 'Til 5," "Rigor Mortis," "Funky Miracle," and "Yeah, You're Right." This 1999 reissue also features two previously unreleased bonus tracks, "Grass" and "Borro." *—Cub Koda*

Cabbage Alley / 1972 / Sundazed ✦✦✦✦✦

Cissy Strut / 1974 / Island ✦✦✦✦✦
The Meters made their anthemic funk cuts on Josie in the late '60s. The New Orleans crew backed Fats Domino, Lee Dorsey, and Aaron Neville before they started jamming on their own in the late '60s. Island issued this anthology of Josie material in the mid-'70s. It came out in the U.S. too. Rounder has since reissued some of this material. *—Ron Wynn*

Rejuvenation / 1974 / Sundazed ✦✦✦
A nice, but not as definitive, mid-'70s Meters session. Their Reprise albums were never as transcendent, energetic, or freewheeling as the Josie tracks, but were better produced and engineered. This was one of the better sessions, and sometimes The Meters seemed to recapture that old New Orleans funk energy. But Reprise's attempts to bring them crossover success inevitably disrupted their chemistry, as they tried to blend a formulaic rock sensibility with the group's close-knit funk. *—Ron Wynn*

Fire on the Bayou / 1975 / Sundazed ✦✦✦

Trick Bag / 1976 / Sundazed ✦✦

New Directions / 1977 / Sundazed ✦✦

Uptown Rulers: The Meters Live on the Queen Mary / 1992 / Rhino ✦✦✦✦✦

The Meters Jam / Mar. 1, 1992 / Rounder ✦✦

☆ **Funkify Your Life** / Feb. 28, 1995 / Rhino ✦✦✦✦✦
Two discs of the Meters is a lot to ask of most casual fans, yet for the devoted few, *Funkify Your Life* is essential. Featuring tracks from both their Josie and Warner years, the double-disc set captures some of the rawest New Orleans funk recorded in the Crescent City. *—Stephen Thomas Erlewine*

★ **The Very Best of the Meters** / Jun. 10, 1997 / Rhino ✦✦✦✦✦
In keeping with the drift of Rhino's *Very Best of* volumes, this 16-track disc provides a more concise, budget-minded retrospective for listeners who might not want a set that offers twice as much or more (in this case, Rhino's own two-disc *Funkify Your Life* anthology). That's not necessarily a criticism—funk grooves can get tiring over the course of two hours if you're not a rhythm fiend. Should you want to keep your Meters to the one-sitting level, this smartly chosen, well-annotated set is fine, including all of the cuts ("Cissy Strut," "Sophisticated Cissy," "Look-Ka Py Py," "Hey Pocky A-Way," "Fire on the Bayou") you'd expect to find on a greatest-hits set. *—Richie Unterberger*

George Michael

b. Jun. 25, 1963, Bushey, England
Vocals, Guitar / Pop/Rock, Adult Contemporary, Urban, Dance-Pop
Yorgos Kyriatou Panayioutou (George Michael) achieved fame in the duo Wham! in his native U.K. in 1982. Through 1986, he and his partner, Andrew Ridgeley, scored hit after hit in a variety of styles from rap to up-tempo pop to slow ballads. As songwriter and lead singer, Michael gradually overshadowed the group, and by the time they split, he was ready for a massively successful solo career. This began with the 1987 album *Faith,* which featured a series of chart-topping hit singles and sold more than seven million copies. That Michael had not achieved a similar critical success was evident from the title of his follow-up album, *Listen Without Prejudice—Vol. 1,* which, though it sold a million copies, included two Top Ten hits, and hit #2, must be considered a major commercial disappointment. After the failure of *Listen Without Prejudice,* Michael engaged in a bitter legal battle with his record company, eventually buying his way out his Columbia contract and signing with Dreamworks. In 1996, he released *Older,* its sales clearly hampered by his long hiatus away from performing. In 1998, Michael made tabloid headlines when he was arrested for lewd conduct in a men's public restroom at a park near his Beverly Hills home; following the incident, he appeared on CNN and publicly revealed his homosexuality. *—William Ruhlmann*

★ **Faith** / 1987 / Columbia ✦✦✦✦✦
A superbly crafted mainstream pop/rock masterpiece, *Faith* made George Michael an international solo star, selling over ten million copies in the U.S. alone as of 2000. Perhaps even more impressively, it also made him the first white solo artist to hit number one on the R&B album charts. Michael had already proven the soulful power of his pipes by singing a duet with Aretha Franklin on the 1987 smash "I Knew You Were Waiting (For Me)," but he went even farther when it came to crafting his own material, using sophisticated '70s soul as an indispensable part of his foundation. Of course, it's only a part. *Faith*'s ingenuity lies in the way it straddles pop, adult contemporary, R&B, and dance music as though there were no distinctions between them. In addition to his basic repertoire of funky dance-pop and airy, shimmering ballads, Michael appropriates the Bo Diddley beat for the rockabilly-tinged title track, and proves himself a better-than-decent torch singer on the cocktail jazz of "Kissing a Fool." Michael arranged and produced the album himself, and the familiarity of many of these songs can obscure his skills in those departments—close listening reveals his knack for shifting elements in and out of the mix, and adding subtle embellishments when a little emphasis or variety is needed. Though *Faith* couldn't completely shake Michael's bubblegum image in some quarters, the album's themes were decidedly adult. "I Want Your Sex" was the most notorious example, of course, but even the love songs were strikingly personal and mature, grappling with complex adult desires and scarred by past heartbreak. All of it adds up to one of the finest pop albums of the '80s, setting a high-water mark that Michael has only been able to reach in isolated moments since. *—Steve Huey*

Listen Without Prejudice, Vol. 1 / Aug. 1990 / Columbia ✦✦✦✦
Michael's follow-up to the massive success of *Faith* found him turning inward, trying to gain critical acclaim as well as sales. *Listen Without Prejudice* is not an entirely successful effort; Michael cut back on the effortless hooks and melodies that crammed not only *Faith* but also his singles with Wham!, and his socially conscious lyrics tend to be heavy-handed. But the highlights—the light, Beatlesque harmonies of "Heal the Pain," and the plodding #1 "Praying for Time," "Waiting for That Day," and the Top Ten "Freedom '90"—make a case for his talents as a pop craftsman. *—Stephen Thomas Erlewine*

Older / Apr. 1996 / DreamWorks ✦✦✦

Ladies & Gentlemen: The Best of George Michael / Nov. 10, 1998 / Columbia ✦✦✦✦✦
When George Michael was riding high on the charts, only a handful of critics acknowledged that he was a brilliant mainstream pop singer/songwriter who, at his best, rivaled his idol Elton John in crafting state-of-the-art pop songs and productions. For nearly a full decade, he was a superstar in his native U.K. and the U.S., and even when *Older* failed to win an American audience, he retained his stranglehold on the British and European charts. As a solo male hitmaker, virtually nobody could touch him between 1984 and 1994, and even when his grasp began to slip, he still made compelling music. All of this is proven by his first hits compilation, *Ladies & Gentlemen: The Best of George Michael.* Spanning two discs, 28 songs and two distinctive halves—one "For the Heart" (ballads), one "For the Feet" (dance tunes)—the collection is a monster, as impressive for its size as it is for its achievements. To some casual listeners, the sheer scope of the collection may seem overwhelming, since it doesn't just have the hits, but also rarities, compilation tracks, lesser-known singles and duets. Of course, that's precisely what makes it worthwhile for anyone who owns all the albums. (They'll also be interested that many of the mixes sound slightly different—as if the masters were run through the antiquated "Q Sound" process that marred Madonna's similar *Immaculate Collection.*) And some skeptics may be swayed after listening to the individual discs, which are surprisingly consistent works that reveal forgotten gems, and thereby the true depth of his talent. It is true that listening to both discs in a row is a little exhausting, but there's little question that *Ladies & Gentlemen* comes close to being definitive. *—Stephen Thomas Erlewine*

Songs From the Last Century / Dec. 14, 1999 / Virgin ✦✦✦

Mickey & Sylvia

f. 1956, **db.** 1965
Group / Rock & Roll, R&B
Although this duo is primarily remembered as a one-hit act—for "Love Is Strange," which reached number eleven in 1957—they actually recorded quite a few exciting hybrids of R&B and rock & roll in the mid- and late '50s. Playing on countless '50s sessions for various labels (especially Atlantic and OKeh), Mickey Baker was one of the greatest guitar players of early rock & roll. With his partner (and former guitar student) Sylvia Robinson, he got to stretch out a bit from his usual role, with some trailblazing piercing, lean and bluesy leads. Vocally, Mickey & Sylvia had an engagingly playful, occasionally sly 'n' sassy repartee that makes up in charm what it might lack in smoke and firepower. Their recordings were inconsistent, but at their best they offered a fetching blend of blues, Bo Diddley, calypso, and doo wop.

After "Love Is Strange," whose devastating licks inspired countless guitarists, the duo notched a couple more substantial R&B hits. But although they recorded as late as 1965, they never approached the Top 20 again. Mickey Baker recorded as a solo artist and enjoyed a fairly successful career as an expatriate sessionman in France. Sylvia Robinson unexpectedly re-emerged with the number three pre-disco hit "Pillow Talk" in 1973, and cofounded the pioneering rap label Sugar Hill in the late '70s. *—Richie Unterberger*

Love Is Strange [Bear Family] / 1990 / Bear Family ✦✦✦
This two-CD, 60-song (!) set includes many alternate takes and a fair amount of previously unreleased material, spanning 1955 to 1964. A lot of the obscurities are in the close harmony, doo wop vein, and are disappointingly short on verbal sparring and scorching Baker guitar. Lovingly packaged, but everyone except hardcore specialists should stick with the RCA compilation. *—Richie Unterberger*

● **"Love Is Strange" & Other Hits** / Mar. 1990 / RCA ✦✦✦✦✦
Unless you're a major R&B collector, it's likely you've never heard anything by this duo besides "Love Is Strange," their only major hit (and a great one). With 20 cuts from 1956–1960, this disc reissues the bulk of their most interesting work. "Love Is Strange" will remain their most memorable tune after you've heard this, but on the whole, this is way-above-average '50s R&B/rock. If you're hungering for more great solos like the ones in "Love Is Strange," you'll find some here, especially in "There Oughta Be a Law" and the instrumental "Shake It Up," although Baker's virtuosity doesn't dominate most of the songs. Some of these tunes are routine doo wop, but a little over half the material is pretty strong, ranging from the calypso-rock they're best remembered for to ballads to straight-ahead R&B shouters, with King Curtis on sax. *—Richie Unterberger*

The Willow Sessions / 1995 / Sequel ✦✦✦
Mickey & Sylvia are properly thought of as '50s rock & rollers, but they actually did a good deal of recording in the '60s, though without much notable commercial success. Most of this 19-track CD was recorded in the early '60s for their own label, Willow; only one song, "Baby You're So Fine," was a hit, making the R&B Top 30. The album doesn't have the fire of their best sides for RCA in the '50s, but it's not bad, usually purveying a groove similar to their early work, though tamer. Occasionally Mickey brandishes blues-rock chops to show that he can still cut deep with his axe, especially on "Darling (I Miss You So)" and the previously unissued instrumentals "Sylvia's Blues" and "Mickey's Blues." There are also a few curious (but fairly respectable) cuts dating from the late '60s that Sylvia recorded for the All Platinum label in a much more contemporary soul vein. *—Richie Unterberger*

Midnight Oil

f. 1975, Sydney, Australia
Group / College Rock, Aussie Rock, Album Rock, Alternative Pop/Rock
Australia's Midnight Oil brought a new sense of political and social immediacy to pop music: not only did incendiary hits like "Beds Are Burning" and "Blue Sky Mine" bring global

attention to the plight of, respectively, aboriginal settlers and impoverished workers, but the group also put its money where its mouth was—in addition to mounting benefit performances for groups like Greenpeace and Save the Whales, frontman Peter Garrett even ran for the Australian Senate on the Nuclear Disarmament Party ticket. Christened Midnight Oil just after Garrett joined in 1975, the group formed the label Powderworks to issue their self-titled debut—a taut, impassioned collection of guitar rock which quickly established the group's sound—in 1978. With their 1979 sophomore effort *Head Injuries*, the band scored their first hit single, "Cold Cold Change." Their third album *Place Without a Postcard* achieved platinum status on the strength of the smash "Armistice Day," which won the group an American deal with Columbia Records. Their follow-up, 1982's *10, 9, 8, 7, 6, 5, 4, 3, 2, 1*, spent over two years in the Australian Top 40. The Australian aborigines' plight came to the fore on 1987's *Diesel and Dust*, the Oils' breakthrough record: Sparked by the hit single "Beds Are Burning," the album reached the U.S. Top 20, and made the band a household commodity. *—Jason Ankeny*

Midnight Oil / 1978 / Columbia ✦✦

Head Injuries / 1979 / Columbia ✦✦✦✦✦
Fortunately the same was not true on their second release, *Head Injuries* (great title). From start to finish this is a stoked and smokin' piece of punk-inspired hard rock with Garrett wailing away as though his life depended on it. Furious, relentless, chocked to the brim with solid songs and fierce playing, *Head Injuries* is hands-down the best of the Oil's early output. *— John Dougan*

Bird Noises / 1980 / Columbia ✦✦✦

Place Without a Postcard / 1981 / Columbia ✦✦✦
Place Without a Postcard, produced by the usually reliable Glyn Johns, is so-so, but a real letdown after the intensity of *Head Injuries*. The songs are very good and at its best, it hints at the consistency that was to mark the rest of their recorded work, but it never coalesces into a whole. Even after repeated plays, *Place Without a Postcard* is too much of a mess to recommend unequivocally. *—John Dougan*

10, 9, 8, 7, 6, 5, 4, 3, 2, 1 / 1983 / Columbia ✦✦✦✦✦
Midnight Oil's first album to have a full-scale production, this album effectively brings out the band's driving rock sound, Peter Garrett's impassioned vocals, and the band's forthright political standpoint. *— William Ruhlmann*

Red Sails in the Sunset / 1984 / Columbia ✦✦✦✦✦
Midnight Oil's second international release found them ambitiously taking on a variety of lyrical causes in a variety of musical styles. Their basic approach, with its martial rhythms, chanted vocals, and guitar textures, served as a jumping-off place, but they always sounded more assured when they stuck to that, rather than trying other things. And the unrelentingly judgmental tone of the lyrics, sung with dead seriousness by Peter Garrett, tended to douse the album's potential enjoyment, too. It's hard to dance when you're being lectured to. It wasn't much of a surprise when Garrett decided to run for the Australian Senate shortly after this album's release. (Originally released on CBS Records Australia in 1984, *Red Sails in the Sunset* was released on Columbia Records in the U.S. in July 1985.) *— William Ruhlmann*

Species Deceases / 1985 / Columbia ✦✦✦

● **Diesel and Dust** / Aug. 1987 / Columbia ✦✦✦✦✦
A thematic album dealing with the plight of Aborigines in Australia, *Diesel and Dust* contains Midnight Oil's most focused and compelling music. Its single most impressive song, "The Dead Heart," works powerfully, both as agit-pop and as moving rock music. Also included is the anthemic hit single "Beds Are Burning." (Originally released by CBS Records Australia in August 1987, *Diesel and Dust* was released on Columbia Records in the U.S. in January 1988.) *— William Ruhlmann*

Blue Sky Mining / Feb. 1990 / Columbia ✦✦✦✦
Success hadn't changed Midnight Oil with its 1990 album *Blue Sky Mining*. The Australian band had finally broken through with its previous record, *Diesel and Dust*, but chart accomplishments didn't temper the group. *Blue Sky Mining* found lead singer Peter Garrett and the boys singing about familiar themes with their usual passion. The songs aren't quite on par with those from *Diesel and Dust*, but there's still enough here to make it a worthy follow-up. The lead track, "Blue Sky Mine," dealt with the oppression of the lower working class within the context of a mining company. The immediately catchy cut managed to find mid-chart success. Other notable tracks are the driving "Forgotten Years," which also managed a bit of airplay, and the menacing "Mountains of Burma." The band stumbles only once, on the clumsy love song "Shakers and Movers." *— Tom Demalon*

Scream in Blue Live / May 5, 1992 / Columbia ✦✦

Earth and Sun and Moon / Apr. 1993 / Columbia ✦✦✦✦✦
If *Earth and Sun and Moon* isn't Midnight Oil's best effort, it's certainly close. The band still sticks to themes that are close to its heart—the environment, native peoples, and other social causes—but rarely has it managed to fashion an albumful of songs that are as musically intoxicating as on this 1993 release. "My Country" is full of jangling guitars and keyboards; the punchy title track has an infectious singalong harmony; and "Bushfire" adds some mean wah-wah guitar. The Oils managed to score some radio play on AOR and modern rock stations with the bracing "Truganini," the dramatic, piano-tinged rocker "Drums of Heaven," and the grinding shuffle of "Outbreak of Love." A satisfying release for longtime fans and new converts alike. *— Tom Demalon*

Breathe / Oct. 15, 1996 / Columbia ✦✦✦

20,000 Watt R.S.L.: Greatest Hits / Nov. 4, 1997 / Columbia ✦✦✦
As Midnight Oil's first compilation, *20, 000 Watt R.S.L.: Greatest Hits* isn't all it could have been. Most of the group's late '80s/early '90s hits are here—"Beds Are Burning," "The Dead Heart," "Dreamworld," "Blue Sky Mine," "Forgotten Years," "King of the Mountain," "Truganini"—and many highlights from the group's early albums ("Power and the Passion," "Koscluszko," "US Forces," "Best of Both Worlds," "Back on the Borderline," "Don't Wanna Be the One") are also present. However, the music is not sequenced chronologically—it flips between the two periods of the group's career with no rhyme or reason, adding two new tracks ("What Goes On," "White Skin Black Heart") from the group's forthcoming 1998 album, *Redneck Wonderland*. The result is a jumble that doesn't give a good sense of Midnight Oil's career, but provides enough of their highlights to make it worthwhile for casual fans. However, anyone wanting a true sense of the band's progression will have to wait for another compilation. *— Stephen Thomas Erlewine*

Redneck Wonderland / Nov. 3, 1998 / Columbia ✦✦✦

The Real Thing / Jul. 17, 2000 / Columbia ✦✦✦✦

The Mighty Mighty Bosstones

f. 1985
Group / Ska-Punk, Third Wave Ska Revival, Alternative Pop/Rock
A great deal of the groundwork for the mid- to late-'90s explosion of ska and ska-metal was laid by the Mighty Mighty Bosstones, who were one of the first bands to cross high-energy ska with hardcore punk and heavy metal, and also helped shift its tone towards testosterone-filled party music. The Bosstones built up a devoted cult following throughout their career, but even in spite of their 1997 radio smash "The Impression That I Get," their level of commercial success has not yet matched that of more pop-oriented third-wave ska bands, like No Doubt and Sublime, who followed in their wake. After a few mis-starts, the Bosstones recorded their debut album, *Devil's Night Out*, in 1989. The follow-up, 1992's *More Noise and Other Disturbances*, earned the group a major-label deal with Mercury for *Don't Know How to Party*. One year after 1994's *Question the Answers* (one of their finest efforts), the Mighty Mighty Bosstones appeared in the film *Clueless*, performing "Where'd You Go" and "Someday I Suppose," two of their most popular numbers. They also landed a main-stage slot on that summer's Lollapalooza tour. In 1997, thanks to the breakthrough of ska-pop bands like No Doubt and Sublime, *Let's Face It* became the band's biggest-selling album yet, buoyed by the modern-rock radio smash "The Impression That I Get." *Live from the Middle East* followed in 1998. *— Steve Huey*

Devils Night Out / 1990 / Taang! ✦✦✦✦

More Noise & Other Disturbances / 1992 / Taang! ✦✦✦

Don't Know How to Party / Mar. 1993 / Mercury ✦✦✦

Question the Answers / Oct. 4, 1994 / Mercury ✦✦✦✦✦
A skanking return to form for the Bosstones, sporting probably the band's best songwriting since its debut album. Their ska, funk, punk, and metal influences blend together in seamless, exciting ways, using the horn section in unexpected places, and the melodies are undeniably strong. Highlights include "Pictures to Prove It," "Bronzing the Garbage," "Toxic Toast," and "Hell of a Hat." *— Steve Huey*

● **Let's Face It** / Mar. 11, 1997 / Mercury ✦✦✦✦✦
With No Doubt and Sublime having dominated the pop airwaves in 1996, it wasn't too much of a stretch for the Mighty Mighty Bosstones to hope for similar success, even if their sound was louder and heavier overall—after all, they had been arguably the best-known ska band in the American underground for some time and had laid much of the groundwork for the style's commercial success. So the Bosstones took their time with *Let's Face It*, crafting a catchy, solidly written record with accessible mainstream production courtesy of longtime collaborator Paul Q. Kolderie and Sean Slade. The results paid immediate dividends, with "The Impression That I Get" becoming a runaway smash on modern-rock radio and pushing the album into the Top 30 (it eventually went platinum). Some longtime fans complained that the band had toned down their manic metal tendencies too much in their push for mainstream acceptance, but really, *Let's Face It* simply draws more upon other influences the band had had all along. It's the Bosstones album most inspired by the British Two-Tone movement of the early '80s, when pop melodies and pleas for tolerance and equality were often as important as the grooves—and that's certainly the case here, as the band turns in probably their most substantive set of lyrics to date. There are a few punky hard rock numbers, too, and even if they don't quite have the hard-partying energy of past efforts in that vein, they are well-constructed songs that keep the album's momentum flowing. Even if the production is a tiny bit slick, and the playing time is rather short (a little over half an hour), it's still difficult to view *Let's Face It* as anything but a rousing success and easily one of the band's best albums. *— Steve Huey*

Pay Attention / May 2, 2000 / Island Def Jam ✦✦✦✦

Steve Miller

b. Oct. 5, 1943, Milwaukee, WI
Vocals, Keyboards, Guitar / Album Rock, Arena Rock, Pop/Rock, Psychedelic, Blues-Rock
Steve Miller's career has encompassed two distinct stages: one of the top San Francisco blues-rockers during the late '60s and early '70s, and one of the top-selling pop/rock acts of the mid-to-late '70s and early '80s. Miller moved to Chicago in 1964 to get involved in the local blues scene, teaming with Barry Goldberg for two years. He then moved to San Francisco and formed the first incarnation of the Steve Miller Blues Band. Capitol signed the group following the Monterey Pop Festival, and they flew to London to record *Children of the Future*, which was praised by critics and received some airplay on FM radio. It established Miller's early style as a blues-rocker influenced but not overpowered by psychedelia. The follow-up, *Sailor*, has been hailed as perhaps Miller's best early effort. A series of high-quality albums followed; while Miller remained a popular artist, pop radio failed to pick up on any of his material at this time, even though tracks like "Space Cowboy" and "Brave New World" had become FM rock staples. Things looked bad for Miller when he broke his neck in a car accident and subsequently developed hepatitis, which put him out of commission for most of 1972 and early 1973. He spent his recuperation time reinventing himself as a blues-influenced pop-rocker, writing compact, melodic, catchy songs. This approach was introduced on his 1973 LP *The Joker* and was an instant success, with the album going platinum

and the title track hitting number one on the pop charts. *Fly Like an Eagle* was released in 1976 and eclipsed its predecessor in terms of quality and sales. The title track from 1982's *Abracadbra* gave him his third number one single and proved to be his last major commercial success. *—Steve Huey*

Children of the Future / 1968 / Capitol ✦✦✦✦
Steve Miller Band's debut *Children of the Future* is certainly an album of its time, awash in studio effects and lyrical conceits. The odd thing is, it's a record that's part English and part San Franciscan, draping its blues-rock in spacey sound effects usually heard on U.K. psych. This results in a bit of a dichotomy, but a pleasant one, since the group has a lazy, relaxed way with a groove, an ingratiating singer in Miller, and a very good singer/songwriter in Boz Scaggs, whose "Baby's Callin' Me Home" and "Steppin' Stone" are certainly highlights. Still, this is a record that's about surface as much as it is about substance, and essays a fairly intriguing space blues that, like many hippie records, meanders a bit too long for its own good. Still, *Children of the Future* is a fairly satisfying psych-blues relic, and a promising start for SMB. *—Stephen Thomas Erlewine*

Sailor / 1968 / Capitol ✦✦✦✦✦
Sailor, the second album from the Steve Miller Band, follows the same pattern as its predecessor, yet improves on it considerably, thanks to a better selection of material, sharper production, and less meandering. The band hasn't lost its identity as space blues merchants, but it has married it to focused performances and tight, catchy songs, highlighted by "Living in the USA," the lovely "Quicksilver Girl," and Boz Scaggs' "Overdrive" and "Dime-A-Dance Romance," plus a fine cover choice in "Gangster of Love." Sonically, this still may be a little bit too dated for some listeners, evoking 1968 just a bit too strongly, but it is a welcome step forward for the SMB. *—Stephen Thomas Erlewine*

Your Saving Grace / 1969 / Capitol ✦✦✦

Brave New World / 1969 / Capitol ✦✦✦✦✦
Blasting out of stereo speakers in the summer of 1969, *Brave New World* was more fully realized, and rocked harder, than the Steve Miller Band's first two albums. From the opening storm of the uplifting title track to the final scorcher, "My Dark Hour," featuring Paul McCartney (credited as "Paul Ramon"), this recording was the strongest project before Miller's *Fly Like an Eagle* days. "Celebration Song" has a sliding bassline, while "LT's Midnight Dream" features Miller's slide guitar. "Can't You Hear Your Daddy's Heartbeat" sounds like it was lifted right off of Jimi Hendrix's *Are You Experienced,* and "Got Love 'Cause You Need It" also has a Hendrix-ian feel. "Kow Kow" is a wonderfully oblique song featuring Nicky Hopkins' distinctive piano style. Hopkins' piano coda on that song alone is worth the price of this album. "Space Cowboy," one of several songs co-written with Ben Sidran, defined one of Miller's many personas. "Seasons," another Sidran collaboration, is a beautifully atmospheric, slow-tempoed piece. Steve Miller's guitar playing is the star of this album, blazing across the whole affair more prominently than on any other release in his lengthy career; many of the songs have a power-trio feel. In addition to the fine guitar work, Miller's vocals are stronger here, and during this era in general, than they would be in his hit-making days in the mid-'70s, when he was much more laid-back and overdubbed. Ever the borrower, adapter, and integrator, Steve Miller shapes the blues, psychedelia, sound effects, sweet multi-tracked vocal harmonies, and guitar-driven hard rock into one cohesive musical statement with this release. *—Jim Newsom*

Number Five / 1970 / Capitol ✦✦✦✦

Anthology / 1972 / Capitol ✦✦✦✦✦
Released in 1972, *Anthology* provides a 16-track summary of the Steve Miller Band's first five albums, distilling their uneven space blues into a tight, effective collection of highlights. These songs are hardly as tuneful or effortlessly catchy as the songs on 1978's *Greatest Hits*—apart from "Living in the USA," "Space Cowboy," and "Going to Mexico," there's nothing particularly immediate here—but they're first-rate period pieces, capturing Miller's space blues at its most effectively spacey. *—Stephen Thomas Erlewine*

The Joker / 1973 / Capitol ✦✦✦

Fly Like an Eagle / 1976 / Capitol ✦✦✦✦✦
Steve Miller had started to essay his classic sound with *The Joker,* but 1976's *Fly Like an Eagle* is where he took flight, creating his definitive slice of space blues. The key is focus, even on an album as stylishly, self-consciously trippy as this, since the focus brings about his strongest set of songs (both originals and covers), plus a detailed atmospheric production where everything fits. It still can sound fairly dated—those whooshing keyboards and cavernous echoes are certainly of their time—but its essence hasn't aged, as "Fly Like an Eagle" drifts like a cool breeze, while "Take the Money and Run" and "Rock'n Me" are fiendishly hooky, friendly rockers. The rest of the album may not be quite up to those standards, but there aren't any duds either, as "Wild Mountain Honey" and "Mercury Blues" give this a comfortable backdrop, thanks to Miller's offhand, lazy charm. Though it may not quite transcend its time, it certainly is an album rock landmark of the mid-'70s and its best moments (namely, the aforementioned singles) are classics of the idiom. *—Stephen Thomas Erlewine*

Book of Dreams / 1977 / Capitol ✦✦✦✦✦

● **Greatest Hits 1974-1978** / 1978 / Capitol ✦✦✦✦✦
Greatest Hits 1974-1978 collects the majority of Steve Miller's biggest hits—"The Joker," "Take the Money and Run," "Rock'n Me," "Fly Like an Eagle," "Jet Airliner," "Jungle Love," "Swingtown"—and seven album tracks that received a fair amount of airplay on album rock radio. The collection only covers a total of three albums—*The Joker, Fly Like an Eagle, Book of Dreams*—with the latter two providing the bulk of the material. Because of this, "Living in the USA," one of Miller's biggest hits of the late '60s/early '70s, isn't included but it isn't missed, since all of his other hits of the '70s are included. The thoroughness of *Greatest Hits 1974-1978* makes it an excellent introduction to Miller and for many casual fans, it also means that they can contain their Steve Miller collection to one disc. *—Stephen Thomas Erlewine*

Circle of Love / 1981 / Capitol ✦✦✦

Abracadabra / 1982 / Capitol ✦✦✦
Steve Miller was always catchy and tuneful, but he never turned out an unabashed pop album until 1982's *Abracadabra.* This isn't just pop in construction, it's pop in attitude, filled with effervescent melodies and deeply silly lyrics, perhaps none more noteworthy than the immortal couplet "Abra-Abracadabra/I wanna reach out and grab ya." Those words graced the title track, which turned out to be one of his biggest hits, and if nothing else is quite as irresistibly goofy as that song, there still is a surplus of engagingly tuneful material, all dressed up in psuedo-new wave production so favored by AOR veterans in the early '80s. All of that may not make this one of Miller's definitive albums, especially in the view of hardcore space blues heads, but it's pretty damn irresistible for listeners who find "Abracadabra" one of the highlights of faux-new wave AOR. *—Stephen Thomas Erlewine*

Living in the 20th Century / Dec. 15, 1987 / Capitol ✦✦

Born 2B Blue / 1988 / Capitol ✦✦✦

The Best of Steve Miller (1968-1973) / 1990 / Capitol ✦✦✦✦✦
The Best of 1968-1973 is a solid collection that features many of the highlights from Steve Miller's first five years of recording, including "The Joker," "Living in the U.S.A.," "Space Cowboy," and "Gangster of Love." This compilation isn't as consistently thrilling as *Greatest Hits 1974-1978,* which also features "The Joker," and it's not as sharply assembled as 1972's *Anthology,* but it remains an adequate overview of Miller's early records, especially for fans only familiar with *Greatest Hits. —Stephen Thomas Erlewine*

Wide River / Jun. 8, 1993 / Polydor ✦✦

Steve Miller Band / Jul. 26, 1994 / Capitol ✦✦✦✦✦
Close to definitive is the best way to describe the three-disc box *Steve Miller Band.* That, or missed opportunity. The set is divided pretty well, with the first disc being devoted to the early years, the second to the hitmaking era, and the third to the blues. Now, this isn't a hard-and-fast breakdown, since there's no one on God's green earth who would call "Abracadabra" blues, but it's a pretty good template for a box. The problem is the execution, particularly as the box gets off the ground. The historical childhood recordings that kick off the first disc are interesting, but they're alienating for anyone outside of hardcore fans. Then, much of the early work is present in oddly edited versions, which aren't particularly welcome. Still, this does round up nearly all of the highlights from Miller's career, which does make it valuable for fans who want a pretty exhaustive, but not definitive, compilation. Nevertheless, *Anthology* and *Greatest Hits,* especially, remain the best way to hear Miller at his peak. *—Stephen Thomas Erlewine*

Ministry

f. 1981, Chicago, IL
Group / Industrial Dance, Industrial Metal, Alternative Metal, Alternative Pop/Rock, Industrial
Until Nine Inch Nails crossed over to the mainstream, Ministry did more than any other band to popularize industrial music, injecting large doses of punky, over-the-top aggression and roaring heavy metal guitar riffs that helped their music find favor with metal and alternative audiences outside of industrial's cult fan base. That's not to say Ministry had a commercial or generally accessible sound: They were unremittingly intense, abrasive, pounding, and repetitive, and not always guitar-oriented (samples, synthesizers, and tape effects were a primary focus just as often as guitars and distorted vocals). However, both live and in the studio, they achieved a huge, crushing sound that put most of their contemporaries in aggressive musical genres to shame. Plus, founder and frontman Al Jourgensen gave the group a greater aura of style and theater than other industrial bands, who seemed rather faceless when compared with Jourgensen's leather-clad cowboy/biker look and the edgy shock tactics of such videos as "N.W.O." and "Just One Fix." Jourgensen formed Ministry in 1981 as a synth-pop group, eventually giving the band a complete overhaul in 1987 with the addition of bassist/co-producer Paul Barker and a loose aggregation of supporting musicians. 1988's *The Land of Rape and Honey* proved to be Ministry's stylistic breakthrough, a taut, explosive fusion of heavy metal, industrial dance beats and samples, and punk aggression. After 1989's *The Mind Is a Terrible Thing to Taste* built on its predecessor's artistic success, Jourgensen embarked on a flurry of side projects, the most prominent being Revolting Cocks. The 1991 single "Jesus Built My Hotrod" and its accompanying album *Psalm 69* (issued in 1992) represented the peak of Ministry's popularity, helping earn them a spot on the inaugural Lollapalooza tour. However, their recorded output subsequently dwindled, partially because of the myriad side projects and partially due to heroin abuse within the band. Ministry did resurface periodically during the '90s, but their albums didn't match prior critical or commercial success. *—Steve Huey*

With Sympathy / 1983 / Arista ✦✦✦

Twelve Inch Singles (1981-1984) / 1985 / Wax Trax! ✦✦✦

Twitch / 1986 / Sire ✦✦✦
The name Ministry brings to mind images of big, dumb guitars and arena rock sensibility. But before they created their influential third album, *The Land of Rape and Honey,* there was *Twitch.* And this album probably owes more to Front 242 than anything. The only thing remotely resembling their later music is the use of psychotic sampling that Al Jourgensen and Paul Barker will always be known for. A good example being "Like You," the first track on the album. Other differences include Patty Jourgensen singing on the song "The Angel" and Al Jourgensen actually trying to sound unaggravated at times. It's interesting though repetitive at times ("Crash and Burn"), and if you care to listen to Mr. Jourgensen's rants, he really does have something to say. "Isle of Man" tells the story of the arrival of Columbus and how the persecution of the Indians will be revisited on the offenders in time. Make no mistake: This sounds nothing like any of Ministry's other albums; listeners may hear how they became what they did. *—Alan Esher*

● **The Land of Rape and Honey** / 1988 / Sire ✦✦✦✦✦
The Land of Rape and Honey represented Ministry's stylistic breakthrough, combining as-

saultive percussion, samples, synths, and (sometimes) crunching guitars with distorted, barking vocals. For all the emphasis on the group's metal/industrial fusion, it's really only the first three (and best) tracks on *Rape and Honey*—"Stigmata," "The Missing," and "Deity"—that employ guitars extensively. The remainder of the album merely suggests heavy metal aggression through its electronic and sampled elements; it is far more industrial in feel, even though it's just as dark. Ministry was the industrial band that, more than any other, appealed to metal fans, and it was *The Land of Rape and Honey* that began to lay claim to that status. *—Steve Huey*

The Mind Is a Terrible Thing to Taste / Nov. 1989 / Sire ✦✦✦✦✦
In what many consider to be Ministry's peak, the band creates another wonderful album to follow *The Land of Rape and Honey.* Fusing thrash guitars with excellent synth and percussion work, Ministry lay the foundation for even more followers of the band's music. But what makes the album even more commendable is the unique flair and the avoidance of cliché elements that have brought down the guitar-heavy industrial-rock genre. Purists might argue that Ministry has given up these roots; but it's plain to see that the roots remain, and are only revamped by the necessary progression of a band that has been around for so many years. The sound is Ministry's, most definitely. *—Marc van der Pol*

In Case You Didn't Feel Like Showing Up (Live) / Sep. 4, 1990 / Sire ✦✦✦✦

Psalm 69: The Way to Succeed & The Way to Suck Eggs / Jul. 14, 1992 / Sire ✦✦✦✦
Although this is Ministry's most accessible album, it is not a sellout. Al Jourgensen and company never let the intensity up, with the machine-like grind of the rhythm section constantly driving the same sixteenth-note rhythms again and again. "Just One Fix" is the best track on a remarkable, intense album, which also includes the single "Jesus Built My Hotrod." *—Stephen Thomas Erlewine*

Filth Pig / 1995 / Sire ✦✦

The Dark Side of the Spoon / Jun. 8, 1999 / Warner Brothers ✦✦✦

Minor Threat

f. 1980, Washington, DC, **db.** 1983
Group / Straight-Edge, American Punk, Hardcore Punk
Minor Threat was the definitive Washington, D.C. hardcore punk band, setting the style for the straight-edge punk movement of the early '80s. Led by vocalist Ian MacKaye, the band was staunchly independent and fiercely sober. Through their songs, the group rejected drugs and alcohol, espoused anti-establishment politics and led a call for self-awareness. Every song was fast, sharp, and lethal, often clocking in at just around a minute. Their speed and fury often hid their fairly catchy melodies, but the band's main function was to vent rage. Over the course of three years, Minor Threat released two EPs, one album and several singles, all of which were quite popular in the American punk underground. Their records and concerts helped spawn straight-edge, an American punk lifestyle based on the group's intense, clean-living ideology.

The origins of Minor Threat lie in the Teen Idles, Ian MacKaye's first band. MacKaye formed the Teen Idles while still in high school, and founded the Dischord label to put out his group's records. Shortly after graduation, the Teen Idles broke up and MacKaye formed Minor Threat with former Idles drummer Jeff Nelson, bassist Brian Baker, and guitarist Lyle Preslar. During 1980-81, Minor Threat released several singles and EPs and played many concerts along the East Coast. In 1982, bassist Baker left and was replaced by Steve Hansen. With Hansen on board, the group recorded their only full-length album, *Out of Step.* Upon its 1983 release, the album became popular within the underground and Minor Threat was becoming alternative stars, which didn't sit well with MacKaye. By the end of the year, he broke up the band. MacKaye and Nelson continued to run Dischord, which thrived well into the '90s. MacKaye later played in Egg Hunt (with Nelson), Embrace, Skewbald, and Pailhead before forming Fugazi, who carried on the aesthetic, if not the sound, of Minor Threat. *—Stephen Thomas Erlewine*

★ **Complete Discography** / 1988 / Dischord ✦✦✦✦✦
Complete Discography compiles Minor Threat's entire body of recordings on a single compact disc. Hardcore, as a rule, wasn't particularly musically diverse, but Minor Threat was one of the genre's groundbreaking acts and their music has held up better than most of their contemporaries. As the de-facto leaders of the Washington, D.C. hardcore scene, the band pioneered the straight-edge mentality by emphasizing impossibly fast tempos, brief songs, political lyrics, and a drug and alcohol-free lifestyle. Besides setting the precedent for several generations of punk rockers with their music and ideals, Minor Threat was simply a better band than most hardcore groups. They had a tight, distinctive sound that wasn't as heavy as their Californian counterparts and, therefore, was often more bracing and effective. Although some of the music on *Complete Discography,* like much of hardcore in general, hasn't aged particularly well—with its cheap production, rigid song structures and political concerns, it is very much a piece of the early '80s—the sound remains invigorating; the band possessed a visceral energy matched by only a handful of their peers. *Complete Discography,* in fact, is not only one of the cornerstones of any hardcore collection, it's not a bad way to become acquainted with hardcore. *—Stephen Thomas Erlewine*

Minutemen

f. 1980, San Pedro, CA, **db.** 1986
Group / College Rock, Post-Punk, Hardcore Punk, Alternative Pop/Rock
More than any other hardcore band, the Minutemen epitomized the free-thinking independent ideals that formed the core of punk/alternative music. Wildy eclectic and politically revolutionary, the Minutemen never stayed in one place too long—they moved from punk to free jazz to funk to folk at a blinding speed. And they toured and recorded at blinding speed—during the early '80s, they were constantly on the road, turning out records whenever they had a chance. Like their peers Black Flag, Hüsker Dü, R.E.M., Sonic Youth, and the Meat Puppets, the Minutemen built a large, dedicated cult following throughout the U.S. through their relentless touring. Like their fellow American indie bands, the trio was poised to break into the world of major labels in 1986, and they would have if it wasn't for the tragic death of guitarist/vocalist D. Boon in December of 1985. Even though bassist Mike Watt and drummer George Hurley carried on with fIREHOSE in the late '80s, the legacy of the Minutemen overshadowed the new band in the late '80s and early '90s, as the San Pedro trio influenced several generations of musicians. *—Stephen Thomas Erlewine*

Paranoid Time / 1980 / SST ✦✦✦

The Punch Line / 1981 / SST ✦✦✦

Buzz or Howl Under the Influence of Heat / 1983 / SST ✦✦✦✦✦

What Makes a Man Start Fires— / 1983 / SST ✦✦✦✦✦
The Minutemen had already come up with a sound as distinctive as anything to come out of the American punk underground—lean, fractured, and urgent—with their debut album, 1981's *The Punch Line.* But on their second (relatively) long-player, *What Makes a Man Start Fires?,* the three dudes from Pedro opted to slow down their tempos a bit, and something remarkable happened—the Minutemen revealed that they were writing really great songs, with a remarkable degree of stylistic diversity. If you were looking for three-chord blast, the Minutemen were capable of delivering, as the opening cut proved (the hyper-anthemic "Bob Dylan Wrote Propaganda Songs"), but there was just as much churning, minimalistic funk as punk bile in their sound (bassist Mike Watt and drummer George Hurley were already a strikingly powerful and imaginative rhythm section), and D. Boon's guitar solos were the work of a man who could say a lot musically in a very short space of time. Leaping with confidence and agility between loud rants ("Split Red"), troubled meditations ("Plight"), and plainspoken addresses on the state of the world ("Mutiny in Jonestown"), the Minutemen were showing a maturity of vision that far outstripped most of their contemporaries, and a musical intelligence that blended a startling sophistication with a street kid's passion for fast-and-loud. It says a lot about the Minutemen's growth that *The Punch Line* sounded like a great punk album, but a year later *What Makes a Man Start Fires?* sounded like a great album—period. *—Mark Deming*

★ **Double Nickels on the Dime** / 1984 / SST ✦✦✦✦✦
If *What Makes a Man Start Fires?* was a remarkable step forward from the Minutemen's promising debut album, *The Punch Line,* then *Double Nickels on the Dime* was a quantum leap into greatness, a sprawling 44-song set that was as impressive as it was ambitious. While punk rock was obviously the starting point for the Minutemen's musical journey (which they celebrated on the funny and moving "History Lesson Part II"), by this point the group seemed up for almost anything—D. Boon's guitar work suggested the adventurous melodic sense of jazz tempered with the bite and concision of punk rock, while Mike Watt's full-bodied bass was the perfect foil for Boon's leads and drummer George Hurley possessed a snap and swing that would be the envy of nearly any band. In the course of *Double Nickels on the Dime's* four sides, the band tackles leftist punk ("Political Song for Michael Jackson to Sing"), Spanish guitar workouts ("Cohesion"), neo-Nortena polka ("Corona"), blues-based laments ("Jesus and Tequila"), avant-garde exercises ("Mr. Robot's Holy Orders"), and even a stripped-to-the-frame Van Halen cover ("Ain't Talkin' 'Bout Love"). From start to finish, the Minutemen play and sing with an estimable intelligence and unshakable conviction, and the album is full of striking moments that cohere into a truly remarkable whole; all three members write with smarts, good humor, and an eye for the adventurous, and they hit pay dirt with startling frequency. And if Ethan James' production is a bit Spartan, it's also efficient, cleaner than their work with Spot, and captures the performances with clarity (and without intruding upon the band's ideas). Simply put, *Double Nickels on the Dime* was the finest album of the Minutemen's career, and one of the very best American rock albums of the 1980s. *—Mark Deming*

The Politics of Time / 1984 / SST ✦✦✦

My First Bells / 1985 / SST ✦✦✦✦✦
A superb collection of all Minutemen recordings from their first EP (*Paranoid Time*) up to and including *What Makes a Man Start Fires.* Rather than going crazy looking for those hard-to-find bits of vinyl, here's the whole shootin' match from 1980-83 in one spot. Cheap at twice the price. *—John Dougan*

Project Mersh / 1985 / SST ✦✦✦✦✦

3-Way Tie for Last / Oct. 1985 / SST ✦✦✦✦✦
D. Boon's death in December 1985 was one of rock's most tragic occurrences. And, a decade later, I find that it still affects the way I listen to this, the "final" Minutemen record. Boon was hitting his stride here; the songs were emphatic, smart and marked by his increasing sociopolitical awareness. Boon did not suffer fools gladly, and this record (as does the best of the Minutemen) retains a strong sense of moral indignation (listen to "The Price of Paradise" and "The Big Stick"). One fact that shouldn't be lost in eulogizing over Boon was the significant role Mike Watt was playing in the band. This hadn't happened overnight, but with each successive record Watt's confidence as a bass player and songwriter was growing, and by the time of *3-Way Tie,* his skills were in full flower—so much so that one side of the record is called Side D., the other Side Mike. Dense and driving, this is a bittersweet moment closing an excellent band's career. *—John Dougan*

Ballot Result / 1987 / SST ✦✦✦✦
Before they had even released *3-Way Tie for Last* in the fall of 1985, the Minutemen had blocked out plans for their next album, which was to be a sprawling three-LP set featuring three sides of studio material and three sides of live recordings. Initial pressings of *3-Way Tie* included a ballot so fans could vote for the songs to be included on the live half of the upcoming album; the tragic death of D. Boon meant the Minutemen would never make another studio album, but Mike Watt and George Hurley compiled the ballots sent in by fans and used the results as the basis for this album, which uses radio broadcasts, studio outtakes, rehearsal tapes, and audience recordings to assemble a final tribute to their fallen comrade. As you might expect, the quality of the sound varies quite a bit from track to track (though there's nothing as awful as the stuff on side two of *The Politics of Time*), and there are a few items here that were outtakes for a good reason (like the overlong version of "Mr. Robot's

Holy Orders," or the spontaneous soundtrack improvisation "Hell"). But for the most part, *Ballot Result* is a fitting memorial that makes clear the Minutemen were just as strong onstage as they were in the studio, and that their songs were smart, provocative, adventurous, and stand up well to the test of time. The fiery first side of material from the WREK-FM broadcast previously bootlegged on *Just a Minute, Men* alone makes this album well worth owning, and there are plenty of other gems scattered through the rest of the set. *Ballot Result* is hardly the ideal Minutemen live album, but it offers tangible evidence that they were one of the greatest American bands of their time, and that's not an accomplishment to be sneezed at. *—Mark Deming*

Post-Mersh, Vol. 1 / 1987 / SST ✦✦✦✦✦
The Minutemen's *Post-Mersh* is a valuable series, collecting all of the group's official discography, with the exception of *Double Nickels on the Dime, 3-Way Tie For Last*, and *Ballot Result*, over the course of three discs. *Post-Mersh, Vol. 1* starts at the beginning, combining the trio's first two albums, *The Punch Line* (1981) and *What Makes A Man Start Fires?* (1983) on one disc. *—Stephen Thomas Erlewine*

Post-Mersh, Vol. 2 / 1987 / SST ✦✦✦✦✦
Picking up where the first volume left off, *Post-Mersh, Vol. 2* contains the Minutemen's 1983 *Buzz or Howl Under the Influence of Heat* LP and the 1985 *Project Mersh* EP. *—Stephen Thomas Erlewine*

Post-Mersh, Vol. 3 / 1989 / SST ✦✦✦✦✦
The third and final volume of *Post-Mersh* crams an extraordinary amount of music on one-disc, compiling the EPs *Paranoid Time* (1980), *Bean-Spill* (1982), and *Tour-Spiel* (1985), the 1981 "Joy" single, and the 1984 rarities and outtakes collection *The Politics of Time*. *—Stephen Thomas Erlewine*

The Misfits

f. 1977, **db.** 1983
Group / Hardcore Punk
Genuinely shocking or tasteless, campy fun— It was sometimes hard to tell which way the Misfits wanted to be taken, and the immense cult following that has grown up in the years after their actual existence (1977-1983) seems divided in its own assessment. It certainly wasn't the Misfits' musicianship—which was as crude as the recording quality of most of their oeuvre—that endeared them to so many, although Glenn Danzig possessed one of the most distinctive and tuneful bellows in hardcore punk. Rather, it was Danzig's penchant for catchy, anthemic melodies, often delivered at warp speed, and his lyrical obsession with grade-B horror films and splatter imagery that helped the Misfits build a rabid posthumous following. Namedrops and covers by metal bands like Metallica and Guns N' Roses kept the Misfits' songs circulating during the mid- to late '80s, when their tangled discography remained only sporadically in print—reissues were maddeningly incomplete, and much of the band's prime material was confined to rare singles and EPs. The mid-'90s saw a spate of CD reissues that, while not quite presenting all of the Misfits' songs in the most concise, collectible format, at least succeeded in getting them all back into print, allowing those who missed the band the first time around to hear why they've enjoyed such enduring cult popularity. *—Steve Huey*

Walk Among Us / 1982 / Slash/Rhino ✦✦✦✦✦
With imagery lifted from sci-fi flicks and gory horror films, Glenn Danzig and Co. sound all revved up and ready to go on their debut record. With Ramones-influenced punk that occasionally veers into speedy, unintelligible hardcore, this is a ferocious, relentless record that makes no apologies for its capacity to alienate listeners. Ugly, unrepentantly nasty, and essential. Issued on CD in 1988. *—John Dougan*

Earth A.D./Wolfsblood / 1983 / Plan 9/Caroline ✦✦✦✦✦
With their second album, the incredibly short *Earth A.D./Wolfsblood*, the Misfits speed up the tempo even more, which combines with their amateurish musicianship to produce a wall of thrashy sonic murk. Additionally, *Earth A.D.* doesn't have the same catchy melodies that made previous Misfits records so exciting; however, the CD reissue appends the "Die Die My Darling" single, which injects a burst of melodicism that makes the set more listenable. Dedicated fans will certainly want this album; others might be more inclined to hear it broken up over the two CD compilations, which contain all of its tracks. *—Steve Huey*

Legacy of Brutality / 1985 / Plan 9/Caroline ✦✦✦

• **Misfits** / 1986 / Plan 9/Caroline ✦✦✦✦✦
Purists may disagree, but for the benighted, this is the best place to start—a 20-track anthology that gives you the most Misfits for your money. Everything that made the Misfits great is here, including the odd remix, alternate take, and re-edited version. The band is loud and defiant, as is Danzig, whose considerable vocal chops are well displayed here. The perfect music for an evening of headbanging or watching gore films. Collectors who don't want to invest in the box set should note that this is also the only place to get "London Dungeon" and "Ghouls' Night Out," the B-sides of the "Night of the Living Dead" single. *—John Dougan*

Die Die My Darling / 1987 / Plan 9/Caroline ✦✦✦

Collection II / 1995 / Caroline ✦✦✦✦
Collection II picks up where the *Misfits* collection left off, making widely available for the first time many of the band's legendary early tracks, including "Attitude," "Last Caress," "We Are 138," and several other non-LP singles. There are also a selection of tracks from *Walk Among Us* not covered by the first compilation, as well as the remainder of the *Earth A.D.* album. If you began your Misfits collection with the first compilation, *Collection II* makes an excellent supplement, and the two put together are close to being definitive. *—Steve Huey*

Static Age / Oct. 31, 1995 / Caroline ✦✦✦

Box Set / Feb. 27, 1996 / Caroline ✦✦✦✦✦

American Psycho / May 13, 1997 / Geffen ✦✦✦

Famous Monsters / Oct. 5, 1999 / Roadrunner ✦✦

Mission of Burma

f. 1980, Boston, MA, **db.** 1983
Group / American Punk, Post-Punk, Punk
Of all the punk-inspired bands that came out of Boston in the early '80s, none were better than Mission of Burma. Arty without being too pretentious, capable of writing gripping songs and playing with ferocious intensity, the group galvanized Boston's alternative rock scene, and despite a too-short existence, set a standard for excellence that has rarely been equalled. Burma's music is vintage early-'80s post-punk: jittery rhythms, odd shifts in time, declamatory vocals; an aural assault similarly employed by bands such as the Gang of Four, Mekons, and Pere Ubu. Also, conspicuously present in the mix was the proto-punk of the Stooges and Velvet Underground, bands that inspired Burma's darker songwriting impulses and tendencies toward longish, repetitive jams capable of boring holes into your skull. What Burma added was a sonic texture through the use of extreme volume. After debuting with the explosive single "Academy Fight Song," Burma released the full-length *Vs.* Unbeknownst to fans, this was the beginning of the end. After a bittersweet farewell tour in 1983, the shows were released as a live LP entitled *The Horrible Truth About Burma*, an occasionally thrilling example of their considerable stage prowess. Frontman Roger Miller went on to a career as a solo artist and with his non-touring band Birdsongs of the Mesozoic. *—John Dougan*

Vs. / 1982 / Rykodisc ✦✦✦✦✦
The EP *Signals, Calls and Marches* suggested that Mission of Burma had the talent and vision to become one of America's great rock bands; the subsequent album *Vs.* proved beyond a doubt that the group had arrived, and was fully realizing its potential. MOB's blend of punk rock fury and post-collegiate musical had been honed to a razor-sharp point by the time *Vs.* was recorded, and they had fully worked through the British influences that occasionally surfaced on *Signals, Calls and Marches*, maturing into a band whose sound was as distinctive as anyone of its generation. Roger Miller's guitar work had gained greater depth and confidence in the year since *Signals*, the rhythm section of Clint Conley and Peter Prescott epitomized both strength and intelligence, and MOB was exploring trickier structures and more dramatic use of dynamics this time out. The subtle tension of "Trem Two" and the powerful mid-tempo angst of "Einstein's Day" were a genuine step forward in the group's development, while "The Ballad of Johnny Burma," "Fun World," and "That's How I Escaped My Certain Fate" made it clear that the band had lost none of its rib-cracking impact along the way. It's daunting to imagine just how far Mission of Burma could have taken its music had Roger Miller's hearing problems not caused the band to break up the following year, but regardless of lost potential, very few American bands from the 1980s released an album as ambitious or as powerful as *Vs.*, and it still sounds like a classic. Rykodisc's remastered 1997 reissue sounds terrific, and adds four solid bonus tracks. *—Mark Deming*

The Horrible Truth About Burma / 1985 / Rykodisc ✦✦✦

Forget / 1987 / Taang! ✦✦✦

• **Mission of Burma** / 1988 / Rykodisc ✦✦✦✦✦
The essential collection of Burma's artful punk rock on one disc. Revised for greater clarity, this thing burns from start to finish, with Roger Miller wielding his guitar like a lethal weapon. *—John Dougan*

Let There Be Burma / 1990 / Taang! ✦✦✦
With so little material available, it's common for outtakes and assorted ephemera to be released to a ravenous horde of uncritical fans. These are interesting, but non-essential releases. The Rykodisc release serves as the most exhaustive and authoritative document. Caveat Emptor: *Let There Be Burma* is a re-release of *Mission of Burma* (not to be confused with the Rykodisc release) and *Forget* on one disc. *—John Dougan*

Joni Mitchell

b. Nov. 7, 1943, Fort McLeod, Alberta, Canada
Vocals, Keyboards, Piano, Guitar / Album Rock, Vocal Jazz, Jazz-Rock, Folk-Rock, Singer/Songwriter
When the dust settles, Joni Mitchell may stand as the most important and influential female recording artist of the late 20th century. Uncompromising and iconoclastic, Mitchell confounded expectations at every turn; restlessly innovative, her music evolved from deeply-personal folk stylings into pop, jazz, avant-garde and even world music, presaging the multicultural experimentation of the 1980s and 1990s by over a decade. Fiercely independent, her work steadfastly resisted the whims of both mainstream audiences and the male-dominated recording industry—while Mitchell's records never sold in the same numbers enjoyed by contemporaries like Carole King, Janis Joplin, or Aretha Franklin, none experimented so recklessly with their artistic identities or so bravely explored territory outside of the accepted confines of pop music. The commercial and critical approval awarded her landmark 1971 record *Blue* was unprecedented: a luminous, starkly confessional set, it firmly established Mitchell as one of pop music's most remarkable and insightful talents. Predictably, she turned away from *Blue*'s incandescent folk with 1972's *For the Roses*, the first of the many major stylistic turns she would take over the course of her daring career. Backed by rock-jazz performer Tom Scott, Mitchell's music began moving into more pop-oriented territory, a change typified by the single "You Turn Me On (I'm a Radio)," her first significant hit. The follow-up, 1974's classic *Court and Spark*, was her most commercially-successful outing: a sparkling, jazz-accented set, it reached the Number Two spot on the U.S. album charts and launched three hit singles— "Help Me," "Free Man in Paris" and "Raised on Robbery." 1975's *The Hissing of Summer Lawns* was a bold, almost avant-garde record which housed her increasingly complex songs in experimental, jazz-inspired settings; "The Jungle Line" introduced the rhythms of African Burundi drums, placing her far ahead of the pop world's mid-1980s fascination with world music. *—Jason Ankeny*

Joni Mitchell (aka Song to a Seagull) / Mar. 1968 / Reprise ✦✦✦
Joni Mitchell's debut release is a concept album. Side one, subtitled "I Came to the City," and

generally exhibits songs about urban subjects that are often dour or repressed in some way. "Out of the City and Down to the Seaside," by contrast, is a celebration of nature and countryside, mostly containing selections of a charming, positive, or more outgoing nature. What sets this release apart from those of other confession-style singer/songwriters of the time is the craft, subtlety, and evocative power of Mitchell's lyrics and harmonic style. Numbers such as "Marcie," "Michael from Mountains," "The Dawntreader," and "The Pirate of Penance" effectively utilize sophisticated chord progressions rarely found in this genre. Verses are substantive and highly charged, exhibiting careful workmanship. "Song to a Seagull" has graceful and vivid lyrics about the joys of freedom set to a haunting, wide-ranging vocal line. Conversely, "Cactus Tree" explores the downside of a no-strings-attached approach to life, the fear of committing to a relationship (ironically wedding these words to a hopeful melody and pulsating guitar texture). "Marcie" utilizes poignant, twisting music to set desolately lonely lyrics about a jilted woman; the recurrent use of red and green imagery in the verses is especially clever. Character studies such as "I Had a King" and "Nathan La Franeer" are painfully bleak in contrast to the lithe domestic scene of "Sisotowbell Lane" and the winsomely reserved love song "Michael From Mountains." Unusual in her oeuvre are the overlapping dialogue prose manner of "The Pirate of Penance" and the jaunty honky-tonk stylings of "Night in the City." Mitchell sings in a light, gossamer, at times diffident manner; vocal harmony is sparingly employed here. David Crosby's production is simple and effective. This excellent debut is well worth hearing. *—David Cleary*

Clouds / May 1969 / Reprise ✦✦✦
Clouds is a stark stunner, a great leap forward for Joni Mitchell. Vocals here are more forthright and assured than on her debut and exhibit a remarkable level of subtle expressiveness. Guitar alone is used in accompaniment, and the variety of playing approaches and sounds gotten here is most impressive. "The Fiddle and the Drum," a protest song that imaginatively compares the Vietnam-era warmongering U.S. government to a bitter friend, dispenses with instrumental accompaniment altogether. The sketches presented of lovers by turns depressive ("Tin Angel"), roguish ("That Song About the Midway"), and faithless ("The Gallery") are vividly memorable. Forthright lyrics about the unsureness of new love ("I Don't Know Where I Stand"), misuse of the occult ("Roses Blue"), and mental illness ("I Think I Understand") are very striking. Mitchell's classic singer/songwriter standards "Chelsea Morning" and "Both Sides, Now" respectively receive energetically vibrant and warmly thoughtful performances. Imaginatively unusual and subtle harmonies abound here, never more so in her body of work than on the remarkable "Songs to Aging Children Come," which sets floridly impressionistic lyrics to a lovely tune that is supported by perhaps the most remarkably sophisticated chord sequence in all of pop music. Mitchell's riveting self-portrait on the album's cover is a further asset. This essential release is a must-listen. *—David Cleary*

Ladies of the Canyon / Apr. 1970 / Reprise ✦✦✦✦✦
This wonderfully varied release shows a number of new tendencies in Joni Mitchell's work, some of which would come to fuller fruition on subsequent albums. "The Arrangement," "Rainy Night House," and "Woodstock" contain lengthy instrumental sections, presaging the extensive non-vocal stretches in later selections such as "Down to You" from *Court and Spark*. Jazz elements are noticeable in the wind solos of "For Free" and "Conversation," exhibiting an important influence that would extend as late as *Mingus*. The unusually poignant desolation of "The Arrangement" would surface more strongly in *Blue*. A number of the selections here ("Willy" and "Blue Boy,") use piano rather than guitar accompaniment; arrangements here are often more colorful and complex than before, utilizing cello, clarinet, flute, saxophone, and percussion. Mitchell sings more clearly and expressively than on prior albums, most strikingly so on "Woodstock," her celebration of the pivotal 1960s New York rock festival. This number, given a haunting electric piano accompaniment, is sung in a gutsy, raw, soulful manner; the selection proves amply that pop music anthems don't all have to be loud production numbers. Songs here take many moods, ranging from the sunny, easygoing "Morning Morgantown" (a charming small-town portrait) to the nervously energetic "Conversation" (about a love triangle in the making) to the cryptically spooky "The Priest" (presenting the speaker's love for a spartan man) to the sweetly sentimental classic "The Circle Game" (denoting the passage of time in touching terms) to the bouncy and vibrant single "Big Yellow Taxi" (with humorous lyrics on ecological matters) to the plummy, sumptuous title track (a celebration of creativity in all its manifestations). This album is yet another essential listen in Mitchell's recorded canon. *—David Cleary*

☆ **Blue** / Jun. 1971 / Reprise ✦✦✦✦✦
Sad, spare and beautiful, *Blue* is the quintessential confessional singer/songwriter album. Forthright and poetic, Mitchell's songs are raw nerves, tales of love and loss (two words with relative meaning here) etched with stunning complexity; even tracks like "All I Want," "My Old Man," and "Carey"—the brightest, most hopeful moments on the record—are darkened by bittersweet moments of sorrow and loneliness. At the same time that songs like "Little Green" (about a child given up for adoption) and the title cut (a hymn to salvation supposedly penned for James Taylor) raise the stakes of confessional folk-pop to new levels of honesty and openness, Mitchell's music moves beyond the constraints of acoustic folk into more intricate and diverse territory, setting the stage for the experimentation of her later work. Unrivaled in its intensity and insight, *Blue* remains a watershed. *—Jason Ankeny*

For the Roses / Nov. 1972 / Asylum ✦✦✦✦✦
On *For the Roses*, Joni Mitchell began to explore jazz and other influences in earnest. As one might expect from a transitional album, there is a lot of stylistic ground explored, including straight folk selections using guitar ("For the Roses") and piano ("Banquet," "See You Sometime," "Lesson in Survival"), overtly jazzy numbers ("Barangrill," "Cold Blue Steel and Sweet Fire"), and hybrids that cross the two ("Let the Wind Carry Me," "Electricity," "Woman of Heart and Mind," "Judgment of the Moon and Stars"). "Blonde in the Bleachers" grafts a rock & roll band coda onto a piano-based singer/songwriter main body. The hit single "You Turn Me On I'm a Radio" is an unusual essay into country-tinged pop, sporting a Dylanesque harmonica solo played by Graham Nash and lush backing vocals. Arrangements here build solidly upon the tentative expansion of scoring first seen in *Ladies of the Canyon*. "Judgment of the Moon and Stars" and "Let the Wind Carry Me" present lengthy instrumental interludes. Lyrics here are among Mitchell's best, continuing in the vein of gripping honesty and heartfelt depth exhibited on *Blue*. As always, there are selections about relationship problems, such as "Lesson in Survival," "See You Sometime," and perhaps the best of all her songs in this genre, "Woman of Heart and Mind." "Cold Blue Steel and Sweet Fire" presents a gritty inner-city survival scene, while "Barangrill" winsomely extols the uncomplicated virtues of a roadside truckstop. More than a bridge between great albums, this excellent disc is a top-notch listen in its own right. *—David Cleary*

★ **Court & Spark** / Jan. 1974 / Asylum ✦✦✦✦✦
Mitchell reached her commercial high point with *Court and Spark*, a remarkably deft fusion of folk, pop, and jazz which stands as her best-selling work to date. While as unified and insightful as *Blue*, the album—a concept record exploring the roles of honesty and trust in relationships, romantic and otherwise—moves away from confessional songwriting into evocative character studies: the hit "Free Man in Paris," written about David Geffen, is a not-so-subtle dig at the machinations of the music industry, while "Raised on Robbery" offers an acutely funny look at the predatory environment of the singles bar scene. Much of *Court and Spark* is devoted to wary love songs: Both the title cut and "Help Me," the record's most successful single, carefully measure the risks of romance, while "People's Parties" and "The Same Situation" are fraught with worry and self-doubt (standing in direct opposition to the music, which is smart, smooth and assured from the first note to the last). *—Jason Ankeny*

Miles of Aisles / Nov. 1974 / Asylum ✦✦✦
Like most live albums, this two-record set was a profit-taking release on which the artist represented many of her old songs for a new acceptance now that she had a larger pop audience. Backed by the pop-jazz ensemble the L.A. Express Mitchell reprised the best from her first five albums, pointedly ignoring *Court and Spark*, and including two new cuts, "Love or Money" and "Jericho." *— William Ruhlmann*

The Hissing of Summer Lawns / Nov. 1975 / Asylum ✦✦✦✦✦
Mitchell evolved from the smooth jazz-pop of *Court and Spark* to the radical *The Hissing of Summer Lawns*, an adventurous work which remains among her most difficult records. After opening with the graceful "In France They Kiss on Main Street," the album veers sharply into "The Jungle Line," an odd, Moog-driven piece backed by the rhythms of the warrior drums of Burundi—a move into multiculturalism which beat the likes of Paul Simon, Peter Gabriel, and Sting to the punch by a decade. While not as prescient, songs like "Edith and the Kingpin" and "Harry's House—Centerpiece" are no less complex or idiosyncratic, employing minor-key melodies and richly detailed lyrics to arrive at a strange and beautiful fusion of jazz and shimmering avant-pop. *—Jason Ankeny*

Hejira / Nov. 1976 / Asylum ✦✦✦
Joni Mitchell's *Hejira* would be the last in an astonishingly long run of top-notch studio albums dating back to her debut. Some vestiges of her old style remain here; "Song for Sharon" utilizes the static, pithy vocal harmonies from *Ladies of the Canyon*'s "Woodstock," "Refuge of the Roads" features woodwind touches reminiscent of those in "Barangrill" from *For the Roses*, and "Coyote" is a fast guitar-strummed number that has precedents as far back as *Clouds*' "Chelsea Morning." But by and large, this release is the most overtly jazz-oriented of her career up to this point—hip and cool, but never smug or icy. "Blue Motel Room" in particular is a prototypic slow jazz-club combo number, appropriately smooth, smoky, and languorous. "Coyote," "Black Crow," and the title track are by contrast energetically restless fast-tempo selections. The rest of the songs here cleverly explore variants on mid- to slow-tempo approaches. None of these cuts are traditionally tuneful in the manner of Mitchell's older folk efforts; the effect here is one of subtle rolls and ridges on a green meadow rather than the outgoing beauty of a flower garden. Mitchell's verses, many concerned with character portraits, are among the most polished of her career; the most striking of these studies are that of the decrepit Delta crooner of "Furry Sings the Blues" and the ambivalent speaker of "Song to Sharon," who has difficulty choosing between commitment and freedom. Arrangements are sparse, yet surprisingly varied, the most striking of which is the kaleidoscopically pointillistic one used on "Amelia." Performances are excellent, with special kudos reserved for Jaco Pastorius' melodic bass playing on "Refuge of the Roads" and the title cut. This excellent album is a rewarding listen. *—David Cleary*

Don Juan's Reckless Daughter / Dec. 1977 / Asylum ✦✦
A big chunk of the pop audience Mitchell had earned with *Court and Spark* in 1974 deserted her in 1975 and 1976 when the follow-ups, *The Hissing of Summer Lawns* and *Hejira*, proved more difficult works. With this pretentious double album, Mitchell lost many of the loyal fans who'd stuck with her from the beginning but who now, as she spread her obscure poetic observations and thin melodies across whole sides of the album, found her disengaged from the close, personal observations that filled her best songs. This was Mitchell's last album to go gold. *— William Ruhlmann*

Mingus / Jun. 1979 / Asylum ✦✦✦

Shadows and Light / Sep. 1980 / Asylum ✦✦✦

Wild Things Run Fast / Oct. 1982 / Geffen ✦✦✦

Dog Eat Dog / Oct. 1985 / Geffen ✦✦

Chalk Mark in a Rain Storm / Mar. 1988 / Geffen ✦✦✦

Night Ride Home / Feb. 19, 1991 / Geffen ✦✦✦

Turbulent Indigo / Oct. 25, 1994 / Reprise ✦✦✦

Hits / Oct. 29, 1996 / Reprise ✦✦✦✦✦
The album is a long overdue anthology of one of Canada's most celebrated ex-pats, Joni Mitchell. She sanctioned the release only on the condition that she be allowed to compile companion album *Misses*. While the 15-strong *Hits* focuses on the her earlier folk-pop crossover successes, many made famous initially by others ("Both Sides Now," "Woodstock," "The Circle Game"), *Misses* is a personal crosssection of her more challenging early material and more recent recordings—the riveting "The Wolf That Lives in Lindsey" from *Mingus* es-

pecially enlightening. One should not pick up one disc without the other. With the flood of box sets released in recent years for far less deserving artists, it's odd that Reprise didn't go all out and make this a more elaborate tribute. *—Roch Parisien*

Misses / Oct. 29, 1996 / Reprise ✦✦✦
Misses intends to round up the best of Joni Mitchell's failed singles and forgotten album tracks, which is a daunting task, to be sure. In a career as acclaimed, idiosyncratic and prolific as Mitchell's, it's problematic to boil all the forgotten favorites down to one disc, but the task is made all the more difficult by the fact that the songwriter herself compiled the collection and she has an agenda. Mitchell is out to prove that her neglected Geffen recordings during the '80s were as consistent as her classic '70s albums for Reprise. Although she is correct in her assessment that the albums should be given more respect, her execution could have been better. The bulk of *Misses* is comprised of the Geffen recordings, which were frequently difficult to appreciate, and in this presentation, they aren't any easier to digest. "A Case of You," which probably should have been on *Hits*, is added as bait, but casual fans of that song won't find the rest of *Misses* as illuminating as *Blue*. In fact, only the converted will be willing to make an effort with the bulk of *Misses*, and they'll probably find the individual albums more rewarding. So, the record doesn't appeal to its intended audience, leaving it without one *—Stephen Thomas Erlewine*

Taming the Tiger / Sep. 29, 1998 / Reprise ✦✦✦

Both Sides Now / Feb. 8, 2000 / Reprise ✦✦✦

Moby (Richard Melville Hall)

b. Sep. 11, 1965, Darien, CT
Vocals, Mixing, DJ, Producer / Electronica, Ambient-Techno, Ambient-Dub, Trip-Hop, Trance, Club/Dance, Techno, Alternative Pop/Rock, House
Moby was one of the most controversial figures in techno music, alternately praised for bringing a face to the notoriously anonymous electronic genre, as well as being scorned by hordes of techno artists and fans for diluting and trivalizing the form. In either case, Moby was one of the most important dance music figures of the early '90s, helping bring the music to a mainstream audience both in England and in America. Moby fused rapid disco beats with heavy distorted guitars, punk rhythms, and detailed productions that drew equally from pop, dance, and movie soundtracks. Not only did his music differ from both the cool surface textures of ambient music and the hedonistic world of house music, but so did his lifestyle—Moby was infamous for his devout, radical Christian beliefs, as well as his environmental and vegan activism. "Go" became a British Top Ten hit in 1991, establishing him as one of the premier techno producers. By the time he came to the attention of American record critics with 1995's *Everything Is Wrong*, his following from the early '90s had begun to erode, particularly in Britain. Nevertheless, he remained one of the most recognizable figures within techno, even after he abandoned the music for guitar-rock with 1996's *Animal Rights*. He returned to a heavy electronic base with 1997's *I Like to Score* and 1999's *Play*. *—Stephen Thomas Erlewine*

Moby / 1992 / Instinct ✦✦✦✦✦
After recording a string of dance classics culminating with the pop hit "Go," Moby released his full-length debut balancing those songs with a few decidedly inventive album tracks. Moby's melodic sense developed much quicker than other early techno producers; despite the criticisms leveled at his later direction (or lack thereof), his first album is a masterpiece of challenging, unrepetitive, beautifully programmed rave-techno. Though the familiar tracks "Drop a Beat," "Next Is the E," and "Go" are the highlights here, the final two tracks, "Slight Return" and "Stream," are fine examples of early chill-out techno. *—John Bush*

Early Underground / Apr. 28, 1993 / Instinct ✦✦✦✦
A fifteen-track compilation of Moby's early career, collected from seven releases, this album fails to show the diversity that makes his self-titled LP such a joy. The tracks here are acceptable early rave-techno, but they won't appeal to those who think repetition is a sign of artistic deficiency. Most of the vocal samples are typical fare for the early '90s, but "Go (Original)" is more than worthy. *—John Bush*

Ambient / Aug. 17, 1993 / Instinct ✦✦✦
Hoping to cash in on the ambient-house craze in 1993, Instinct Records released a collection of Moby's softer tracks (which, to his credit, had been recorded long before). Tracks like "My Beautiful Blue Sky," "Piano and Strings," and "Myopia" showcase his talent for majestic orchestral sounds and melodic synth layered over slower beats and percussion. *—John Bush*

Everything Is Wrong / Mar. 14, 1995 / Elektra ✦✦✦✦✦
For his first major-label album, Moby pulled out all the stops, trying to fit as many different styles as possible into 50 minutes. From fast breakbeats to pseudo-industrial thrash, ambient-trance to dance-pop, Moby tries it all. It's not quite a statement of genius—for all the bluster, there really isn't that much difference between his songs, which are nearly all standard three-chord progressions; it's all in the production. What ties everything together is Moby's understanding of the beat. The pulse holds steady throughout the record, making it sound like a very good night at a club. *—Stephen Thomas Erlewine*

Animal Rights / Feb. 11, 1996 / Elektra ✦✦

Rare: Collected B-Sides / Aug. 1996 / Instinct ✦✦✦

I Like to Score / Aug. 26, 1997 / Mute ✦✦✦

● **Play** / Jun. 1, 1999 / Mute ✦✦✦✦✦
Following a notorious flirtation with alternative rock, Moby returned to the electronic dance mainstream on the 1997 album *I Like to Score*. With 1999's *Play*, he made yet another leap back toward the electronica base that had passed him by during the mid-'90s. The first two tracks, "Honey" and "Find My Baby," weave short blues or gospel vocal samples around rather disinterested breakbeat techno. This version of blues-meets-electronica is undoubtedly intriguing to the all-important NPR crowd, but it is more than just a bit gimmicky to any techno fans who know their Carl Craig from Carl Cox. Fortunately, Moby redeems himself in a big way over the rest of the album with a spate of tracks that return him to the evocative, melancholy techno that's been a specialty since his early days. The tinkly piano line and warped string samples on "Porcelain" frame a meaningful, devastatingly understated vocal from the man himself, while "South Side" is just another pop song by someone who shouldn't be singing—that is, until the transcendent chorus redeems everything. Surprisingly, many of Moby's vocal tracks are highlights; he has an unerring sense of how to frame his fragile vocals with sympathetic productions. Occasionally, the similarities to contemporary dance superstars like Fatboy Slim and Chemical Brothers are just a bit too close for comfort, as on the stale big-beat anthem "Bodyrock." Still, Moby shows himself back in the groove after a long hiatus, balancing his sublime early sound with the breakbeat techno evolution of the '90s. *—John Bush*

Moby Grape

f. Sep. ??, 1966, San Francisco, CA
Group / Folk-Rock, Psychedelic, Country-Rock
One of the best '60s San Francisco bands, Moby Grape was also one of the most versatile. Although they are most often identified with the psychedelic scene, their specialty was combining all sorts of roots music—folk, blues, country, and classic rock & roll—with some Summer of Love vibes and multilayered, triple-guitar arrangements. All of those elements only truly coalesced, however, for their 1967 debut LP. Although subsequent albums had more good moments than many listeners are aware of, a combination of personal problems and bad management effectively killed off the group by the end of the 1960s. Matthew Katz, who managed the Jefferson Airplane in their early days, helped put together Moby Grape around Skip Spence. Spence, a legendarily colorful Canadian native who played drums in the Airplane's first lineup. Their 1967 self-titled debut remains their signature statement, though the folk-rock and country-rock worked better than the boogies; "Omaha," "Sittin' by the Window," "Changes," and "Lazy Me" are some of their best songs. Moby Grape's follow-up, the double LP *Wow*, was one of the most disappointing records of the '60s, in light of the high expectations fostered by the debut. The studio half of the package had much more erratic songwriting than the first recording, and the group members didn't blend their instrumental and vocal skills nearly as well. *—Richie Unterberger*

● **Moby Grape** / Jun. 1967 / San Francisco Sound ✦✦✦✦✦
Some consider this 1967 debut to be the most impressive of the San Francisco rock revolution. Not a wasted moment, and the Grape do jam. *—Jeff Tamarkin*

Grape Jam / 1968 / Columbia ✦✦

Wow / 1968 / Columbia ✦✦

Truly Fine Citizen / 1969 / Columbia ✦✦

Moby Grape '69 / Jan. 30, 1969 / Columbia ✦✦✦

● **Vintage: The Very Best of Moby Grape** / May 11, 1993 / Columbia/Legacy ✦✦✦✦✦
It's hard to imagine a better-produced package of Moby Grape's work than this two-disc, 48-track condensation of their best late-'60s recordings. The first disc of this set centers around their entire 1967 self-titled debut LP (included in its entirety), which mixed blues, country, and folk influences with hard-charging psychedelic rock & roll. The result was one of the Summer of Love's more enduring works. The second disc boils their wildly inconsistent 1968-69 material down to a fairly strong and coherent selection. While it doesn't match the peak of the group's initial burst, it features some strong folk and country-rock originals that wear much better in the absence of the bloated jams and half-baked hard rock that could make their albums a chore to sit through. Each disc includes interesting demos, outtakes, and live performances that round out the legacy of this prodigiously talented but ill-fated band, which was overcome by internal strife and label/management difficulties after their promising debut. *—Richie Unterberger*

Eddie Money

b. Mar. 2, 1949, Brooklyn, NY
Vocals, Saxophone, Keyboards / Album Rock, Arena Rock, Pop/Rock
Arriving at the height of album-rock's popularity in the late '70s, Eddie Money didn't have a remarkable voice, but he did have a knack for catchy, blue-collar rock & roll, which he delivered with a surprising amount of polished, radio-friendly finesse. The son of a Brooklyn cop, Eddie Mahoney initially followed in his father's footsteps and attended the New York Police Academy during the early '70s, but at night, he sang in rock bands under the name Eddie Money. He decided to pursue music full-time: quitting the Academy, he moved to Berkeley, California and became a regular at Bay Area clubs. Thanks to legendary promoter Bill Graham' Money signed a contract with Columbia Records, and released his eponymous debut in 1977. During the late '70s, he had a handful of album rock and Top 40 "Baby Hold On" and "Maybe I'm a Fool." He survived the early MTV era with clever videos for songs like "Shakin'" and "Think I'm In Love," but he couldn't resist the temptations of a rock & roll lifestyle: His popularity dipped as he struggled with various addictions in the mid-'80s. A few years later, Money was sober again and made a remarkable comeback with Top Ten singles like 1986's "Take Me Home Tonight" and 1988's "Walk on Water." 1990's "Peace In Our Time," which reached #11, was last big hit—during the early '90s, his popularity faded and he retired to the oldies circuit. He returned with a new album, *Ready Eddie*, in 1999. *—Stephen Thomas Erlewine*

● **Greatest Hits: The Sound of Money** / Oct. 1989 / Columbia ✦✦✦✦✦
Eddie Money was always reliable for turning out a hit single or radio anthem on each of his records. Often, it felt like all of his energy went into a couple of songs per album, since the remainder of each record, while frequently enjoyable, was cluttered with filler. Which is a roundabout way of saying what a welcome addition *Greatest Hits: The Sound of Money* is to Money's catalog: Not only is it a fine collection of his hits, it's the most consistent record he's assembled. Not that it's perfect. Some of his smaller hits are missing and there's a bit of filler even on this hits disc, but the truly essential items—"Baby Hold On," "Two Tickets to Paradise," "I Wanna Go Back," "Walk on Water," "Shakin'," "Take Me Home Tonight," "Think I'm

in Love," even "Peace in Our Time"—are here, and the best of them really do define what album rock was all about at the turn of the '70s and early '80s. *—Stephen Thomas Erlewine*

The Monkees

f. 1965, Los Angeles, CA, **db.** 1969

Group / Sunshine Pop, Psychedelic Pop, Bubblegum, Pop/Rock, Pop

Formed primarily for the purpose of starring in a television series, the Monkees were on one hand a cynically manufactured group, devised to cash in on the early Beatles' success by applying the most superficial aspects of the British Invasion formula to capture a preteen audience. On the other hand, they weren't devoid of musical talent, and at their best managed to craft some enduring pop/rock hits. "I'm a Believer," "Last Train to Clarksville," "A Little Bit Me, a Little Bit You," "Pleasant Valley Sunday," "Stepping Stone," "Take a Giant Step," "Valleri," "Words"—all were pleasantly jangling, harmony rock numbers with hooks big enough for a meat locker, and all were huge hits in 1966-68. Scorned at their peak by hipsters for not playing on many of their own records, the group gained some belated critical respect for their catchy, good-time brand of pop. It would be foolish to pretend, however, that they were a band of serious significance, despite the occasional genuinely serious artistic aspirations of the members. From the outset, it was made clear that the Monkees were hired to be television actors first, and musicians a distant second. There would be original material generated for them to sing in the series, mostly by professional songwriters like Tommy Boyce, Bobby Hart, Carole King, Gerry Goffin, and Neil Diamond. There would be records, as well—had to be, with that kind of weekly exposure, to promote the tunes—but the group wouldn't do much more than sing, although the series would give the impression that they played their own instruments. *—Richie Unterberger*

The Monkees / Oct. 1966 / Rhino ✦✦✦✦
The Monkees did virtually nothing besides sing lead vocals on their full-length debut; poor Peter Tork didn't even get to do that, his contribution being limited to one of the six guitar parts on "Papa Gene's Blues." Given that it wasn't a project of high integrity, it wasn't bad—in fact, much of this is reasonably gutsy pop/rock, including their TV theme song, the hits "Last Train to Clarksville" and "Take a Giant Step," and various decent songs by top Brill Building tunesmiths like Goffin/King, Boyce/Hart, and David Gates. Nesmith was allowed one composition ("Papa Gene's Blues") that indicated his country-rock direction. The CD reissue includes unremarkable bonus tracks of alternate versions of the Monkees theme and a couple of songs that would turn up on subsequent LPs. *—Richie Unterberger*

More of the Monkees / Jan. 10, 1967 / Rhino ✦✦✦✦
Second album, same as the first, virtually: a huge single ("I'm a Believer"/"Steppin' Stone"), a couple of token Mike Nesmith songs (including "Mary, Mary," previously recorded by the Paul Butterfield Blues Band and a rap hit for Run-D.M.C. in 1988), tunes by Boyce/Hart, Goffin/King, Neil Diamond, Jeff Barry, Neil Sedaka, and Carole Bayer; no participation from the group other than lead vocals. The band was quite upset at their lack of input at the time, but it's relatively decent (if quite harmless) pop/rock, featuring one of their best album tracks, "She." Like all of the Rhino CD reissues, it adds marginally interesting bonus tracks of unreleased alternate versions, including an early take of "I'm a Believer." *—Richie Unterberger*

Headquarters / May 22, 1967 / Rhino ✦✦✦✦✦
For their third album, the Monkees were determined to wrest control of the creative process, and with producer Chip Douglas functioning as frequent bassist and auxiliary member, they were indeed able to play most of the instruments and write much of the material. It would be nice to report that the result far exceeded previous efforts and established the group as visionary artists, but in fact this was, again, pleasantly inoffensive pop/rock. There was more of a country flavor and a sense of personal involvement, though the group still tapped songwriting pros like Boyce/Hart and Mann/Weil for about half the songs. Standouts included Nesmith's "You Just May Be the One," one of his best Monkee tunes, and Tork's "For Pete's Sake," which became the show's closing theme. The CD reissue includes six unreleased tracks and alternate takes, a couple of which (Nilsson's "All of Your Toys" and Nesmith's "The Girl I Knew Somewhere") rank among their finest. *—Richie Unterberger*

Pisces, Aquarius, Capricorn & Jones Ltd. / Nov. 14, 1967 / Rhino ✦✦✦✦✦
One of their better efforts, featuring the double-sided hit "Pleasant Valley Sunday"/"Words," and some of their best album tracks, like "She Hangs Out," "Star Collector," and "Cuddly Toy," the last of which was one of the first Nilsson songs to be covered by a major artist. As usual, some of the country-rockers and half-baked psychedelic tunes are tedious, though a couple of tracks are notable for featuring some of the first uses of a Moog synthesizer on a rock record. The CD reissue adds some previously unissued alternate mixes, as well as the killer soulful B-side "Goin' Down," which ranks as one of their very best tracks despite its obscurity. *—Richie Unterberger*

The Birds, the Bees & the Monkees / Apr. 22, 1968 / Rhino ✦✦✦
Not one of their better efforts, dominated almost wholly by session musicians (with the occasional songwriting and instrumental contribution by Mike Nesmith) and containing too many sickly sweet Davy Jones-sung numbers. It does have the hits "Daydream Believer" and "Valleri," as well as Nesmith's "Tapioca Tundra," which just inched into the Top 40, but overall the material is pretty weak. The CD adds some previously unissued songs and alternate takes, the only one of interest being Peter Tork's "Lady's Baby," which sounds like a Buffalo Springfield outtake with its laidback country/folk/rock flavor. *—Richie Unterberger*

Head / Dec. 1, 1968 / Rhino ✦✦✦
Like the film from which it came, the soundtrack to *Head* was far from a masterpiece, but had some inspired moments. These include the spacy "Porpoise Song," written by Gerry Goffin and Carole King; the tough-rocking "Circle Sky," probably the best song Mike Nesmith wrote for the group; "Can You Dig It," one of Peter Tork's best contributions; and "As We Go Along" and "Daddy's Song," little-known songs by Carole King and Nilsson, respectively. As a listening experience, it's made more difficult by the juxtaposition of music and dialogue from the film. The CD reissue adds bonus unissued jingles and alternate takes, highlighted by a live version of "Circle Sky." *—Richie Unterberger*

Instant Replay / Feb. 15, 1969 / Rhino ✦✦✦

The Monkees Present / Oct. 1969 / Rhino ✦✦✦

Changes / Jun. 1970 / Rhino ✦✦

Missing Links / 1987 / Rhino ✦✦✦

Missing Links, Vol. 2 / 1990 / Rhino ✦✦✦

Listen to the Band / Sep. 24, 1991 / Rhino ✦✦✦✦✦

★ **Greatest Hits** / Nov. 1995 / Rhino ✦✦✦✦✦
Twenty-song collection includes all of their big chart hits, as well as key album tracks like "(Theme From) the Monkees" and "Mary, Mary," and the ace B-side "Goin' Down." The slightly more extensive Arista anthology still has the edge, due to the inclusion of two good cuts ("Take a Giant Step" and "She") that are somehow omitted from this Rhino compilation. On the other hand, if you're still in the market for just one Monkees album, this will do just fine. Good, extensive liner notes, though the last two songs (from 1987 singles that only featured Dolenz and Tork) are a waste. *—Richie Unterberger*

Missing Links, Vol. 3 / Mar. 26, 1996 / Rhino ✦✦✦

Justus / Oct. 15, 1996 / Rhino ✦✦✦

Anthology / Apr. 21, 1998 / Rhino ✦✦✦✦
Rhino's *Listen to the Band* box set was for the collectors, and their terrific 20-song *Greatest Hits* was for the casual fans. Their third attempt at a Monkees compilation, the double-disc *Anthology*, falls somewhere in between. Over the course of an exhausting 56 tracks, all of the group's hits are hauled out again, with such fine album tracks as "She," "Take a Giant Step," "Your Auntie Grizelda," "You Just May Be the One" and "What Am I Doing Hangin' Round" added for good measure. On the surface of things, this seems like a good thing, but the set is padded out with lesser album cuts and latter-day tracks from their three reunion albums that makes *Anthology* more of a chore than a pleasure. Since there are no genuine rarities here, it won't quite appeal to collectors, and since *Greatest Hits* suits the purposes of the average fans, it remains a mystery just who this set is for, even if it is loaded with good music. *—Stephen Thomas Erlewine*

Headquarters Sessions / Sep. 21, 2000 / Rhino Handmade ✦✦✦✦

The Monks

f. 1964, **db.** 1967

Group / Garage Rock, Rock & Roll

One of the strangest stories in rock history, the Monks were formed in the early '60s by American G.I.'s stationed in Germany. After their discharge, the group stayed on in Germany as the Torquays, a fairly standard "beat" band. After changing their name to the Monks in the mid-'60s, they also changed their music, attitude, and appearance radically. Gone were standard oldie covers, replaced by furious, minimalistic original material that anticipated the blunt, harsh commentary of the punk era. Their insistent rhythms recalled martial beats and polkas as much as garage rock, and the weirdness quotient was heightened by electric banjo, berserk organ runs, and occasional bursts of feedback guitar. To prove that they meant business, the Monks shaved the top of their heads and performed their songs—crude diatribes about the Vietnam war, dehumanized society, and love/hate affairs with girls—in actual monks' clothing. This was pretty strong stuff for 1966 Germany, and their shocking repertoire and attire were received with more confusion than hostility or warm praise. They disbanded in confusion around 1967, but their sole album—one of the most oddball constructions in all of rock—gained a hardcore cult following among collectors, and has ironically made them much more popular and influential on an international level than they were during their lifetime. *—Richie Unterberger*

● **Black Monk Time** / 1966 / Infinite Zero/American ✦✦✦✦✦
The Monks' only album is packed with angst anthems on the order of "Shut Up," "I Hate You," "Complication," and "Drunken Maria." One of the strangest recordings of all time, it's now finally available in the U.S. as a 1997 CD reissue on Infinite Zero. The repackage is made all the more appealing with the inclusion of their two later non-LP singles, the live 1966 "Monk Chant," and a couple of 1965 demos, making it the definitive document of the Monks' recorded legacy. *—Richie Unterberger*

The Moody Blues

f. 1964, Birmingham, England

Group / British Psychedelia, Album Rock, Pop/Rock, British Invasion, Prog- Rock/Art Rock

Although they're best known today for their lush, lyrically and musically profound (some would say bombastic) psychedelic-era albums and singles, the Moody Blues started out as one of the better R&B based combos of the British Invasion. The group's first single, 1964 "Steal Your Heart Away," didn't touch the British charts, but the follow-up "Go Now" fulfilled every expectation and more, reaching number one in England. Despite their fledgling songwriting efforts and the access they had to American demos, this version of the group never came up with another single success, and in late 1966, after the addition of vocalist Justin Hayward, the reconstituted Moody Blues scored their big break when Deram Records decided that it needed a long-playing record to promote its new "Deramic Stereo." The Moody Blues were picked for the proposed project, a rock version of Dvorak's *New World Symphony*, and immediately convinced the staff producer and the engineer to abandon the source material and permit the group to use a series of its own compositions that depicted an archetypal "day," from morning to night. Using the tracks laid down by the band, and orchestrated by conductor Peter Knight, the resulting album *Days of Future Passed* became a landmark in the band's history. The mix of rock and classical sounds was new, and at first puzzled the record company, but eventually the record was issued. This album, and its singles "Nights in White Satin" and "Tuesday Afternoon," hooked directly into the musical sides of the Summer of Love and its aftermath. *In Search of the Lost Chord* (1968) abandoned the orchestra in favor of the Mellotron, which quickly became a part of their signature sound. Beginning with *A Question of Balance* (1970), the group made the decision to record albums that they could play in concert, reducing their reliance on overdubbing and toughening up their sound. *—Bruce Eder*

Go Now/Moody Blues #1 / 1965 / London ✦✦✦

The Magnificent Moodies / 1965 / Repertoire ✦✦✦

Days of Future Passed / 1967 / Polydor ✦✦✦✦✦
The 1997 remastered reissue (check the catalog number) of the reconstituted Moody Blues' first album, complete with significantly improved sound and new notes, featuring interview material with the band members about the songs, the album, and its evolution. New members Justin Hayward and John Lodge established themselves on guitar, bass, and vocals, and the band begins its venture into progressive rock territory with the London Festival Orchestra. The material, highlighted by the presence of Hayward's "Tuesday Afternoon" and "Nights In White Satin," has an air of pretentiousness, but it really rocks fairly hard, especially as heard here, and the orchestral interludes, courtesy of the late Peter Knight, have an epic sweep that is enhanced on the 1997 reissues. In 1967, a lot of people hungry for something to put on the turntable after *Sgt. Pepper* turned to this, and made it into an international hit. *—Bruce Eder*

In Search of the Lost Chord / 1968 / Polydor ✦✦✦
This 1997 remastered edition of the group's second progressive album was long overdue (the original release from the '80s had an audible crack in the sound on one song). The sound is significantly better than the old PolyGram version, so close that you can actually hear the action on many of the instruments, and even displays somewhat better resolution than the Mobile Fidelity gold-plated audiophile disc. The original credits and interior gatefold art are gone, but in their place are new notes by the band members, which provide some insights into the making of the album, on which the Moody Blues discovered drugs and mysticism as a basis for songwriting, and came up with a compelling psychedelic creation, filled with songs about Timothy Leary and the astral plane, and other psychedelic-era concerns. They dumped the orchestra this time out in favor of Mike Pinder's Mellotron, which was a more than adequate substitute, and the rest of the band joined in with flutes, sitar, tablas, and cellos, the playing of which was mostly learned on the spot. The whole album was one big experiment to see how far the group could go with any instruments they could find, thus making this album a rather close cousin to the Beatles' records of the same era. It is all beautiful and elegant, and "Legend of a Mind's" chorus about "Timothy Leary's dead/Oh, no—he's outside, looking in" ended up anticipating reality; upon his death in 1996, Leary was cremated and launched into space on a privately owned satellite, with the remains of *Star Trek* creator Gene Roddenberry (another '60s pop-culture icon) and other well-heeled clients. *—Bruce Eder*

On the Threshold of a Dream / 1969 / Polydor ✦✦✦✦✦
The 1997 remastered edition of this album can be considered definitive, superior in sonic detail to either the original PolyGram CD or the Mobile Fidelity audiophile disc, though the latter has some appeal, recreating the original LP's elaborate libretto. The new notes reveal something of the creative process that the band used in devising its albums and preparing its songs. The group abandoned the Oriental and Indian influences from the prior album in favor of more traditional Western melody, as well as science fiction and religious imagery. Similarly, the sitars and tablas disappear, replaced by much heavier use of the Mellotron and the grand piano, among other Western instruments. Both keyboards come to the fore in the album's centerpiece, "Have You Heard/The Voyage," a Mike Pinder tour de force and a wonderful piece of progressive psychedelia. The songs also rock much harder in spots than their previous records—"To Share Our Love" has a much harder sound than ever before, capturing the master's true sound better than any prior release, CD or vinyl. *—Bruce Eder*

To Our Children's Children's Children / 1969 / Polydor ✦✦✦

Question of Balance / 1970 / Polydor ✦✦✦

• **Every Good Boy Deserves Favour** / 1971 / Polydor ✦✦✦✦✦
The best realized of the group's classic albums finally comes into its own in this beautifully remastered edition from 1997. The lush melodies and the sound of Michael Pinder's Mellotron was never richer, and the guitar pyrotechnics on pieces like "The Story In Your Eyes" were never more vivid. "Emily's Song," "Nice To Be Here," and "My Song" are among the best work the group has ever done, and "The Story In Your Eyes" is the best rock number they ever cut, with a bracing beat and the kind of lyrical complexity one more expected out of George Harrison at the time—the sound here is so crisp that the sustain on the feedback over the opening is now clearly audible well into the number. *—Bruce Eder*

Seventh Sojourn / 1972 / Polydor ✦✦✦

This Is the Moody Blues / 1974 / Polydor ✦✦✦✦✦

Caught Live + 5 / 1977 / Polydor ✦✦✦✦

Octave / 1978 / Polydor ✦✦✦

Long Distance Voyager / 1981 / Polydor ✦✦✦
The group's biggest-selling album of the '80s also marked a turning point in their fortunes, where they began losing even the mainstream critics. The music has drive, and is extremely well played and produced (this was the only album the band ever got to do at their own, custom-designed Threshold Studios), but also seemed very dated in its time, with a '60s sensibility that was out of place. *—Bruce Eder*

The Present / 1983 / Polydor ✦✦

The Other Side of Life / 1986 / Polydor ✦✦✦
The group's best album in several years benefitted mostly from the presence of the Top Ten single "Your Wildest Dreams," which managed to turn their status as dinosaurs from the '60s psychedelic era into a plus, with a great beat to boot and a very entertaining video featuring young British psychedelic rockers the Mood Six playing the young Moody Blues. The rest was fairly routine, alas, but the single was strong enough on its own terms to revive interest in the group one more time out. *—Bruce Eder*

Prelude / 1987 / Polydor ✦✦✦

Time Traveller / Sep. 27, 1994 / Polydor ✦✦✦✦✦
When the Moody Blues were due for the box set treatment, it would have been uncharacteristic for the production to be lacking in overstated grandiosity. On that count, this four-CD retrospective does not disappoint, including the bulk of their most famous work (from their 1967-72 albums), lots from their later records and side projects, and a few rarities. There's not a great deal of reason for anyone but fanatics to fork out for this package; the albums (which were specifically programmed to work as separate entities) remain readily available, there's too much late stuff and Hayward/Blue Jays tracks, and there's nothing from the Denny Laine era. The three non-LP 1967 cuts that open the set are available on the double import LP *A Dream*, an album that also has the additional 1967 B-side "Really Haven't Got the Time," which somehow doesn't make it onto *Time Traveller*. As consolation, the liner notes are pretty good and extensive, and the first printings of the box include a bonus disc of a 1992 concert with the Colorado Symphony Orchestra. *—Richie Unterberger*

• **The Best of the Moody Blues** / Jan. 28, 1997 / Polydor ✦✦✦✦✦
The 17-track *The Best of the Moody Blues* contains all of the group's biggest hits, from 1964's "Go Now" to 1988's "I Know You're Out There Somewhere." Between those two songs, all of the Moodies' best-known songs are featured, including "Nights in White Satin," "Tuesday Afternoon," "Ride My See-Saw," "Story in Your Eyes," and "Your Wildest Dreams," making the compilation an excellent choice for casual fans. *—Stephen Thomas Erlewine*

Strange Times / Aug. 1999 / Uptown/Universal ✦✦✦

The Moonglows

f. 1951, Louisville, KY
Group / Doo Wop, R&B
Among the most seminal R&B and doo wop groups of all time, the Moonglows' lineup featured some of the genre's greatest pure singers. The original lineup from Louisville included Bobby Lester, Harvey Fuqua, Alexander Graves, and Prentiss Barnes, with guitarist Billy Johnson. They were originally called the Crazy Sounds, but were renamed by disc jockey Alan Freed as the Moonglows. The group also cut some recordings as the Moonlighters. Their first major hit was the number one R&B gem "Sincerely" for Chess in 1954, which reached number 20 on the pop charts. They enjoyed five more Top Ten R&B hits on Chess from 1955 to 1958, among them "Most of All," "We Go Together," "See Saw," and "Please Send Me Someone to Love," as well as "Ten Commandments of Love." Fuqua, the nephew of Charlie Fuqua of the Ink Spots, left in 1958. He recorded "Ten Commandments of Love" as Harvey & the Moonglows with Marvin Gaye, Reese Palmner, James Knowland, and Chester Simmons before founding his own label, Tri-Phi. Fuqua created and produced the Spinners in 1961 and wrote and produced for Motown until the early '70s. The Moonglows disbanded in the '60s, then reunited in 1972 with Fuqua, Lester, Graves, Doc Williams, and Chuck Lewis. They recorded for RCA and a reworked version of "Sincerely" eventually charted, but wasn't a major hit. *—Ron Wynn*

Blue Velvet: The Ultimate Collection / Dec. 7, 1993 / Chess ✦✦✦✦✦
Few rivaled the Moonglows in musical sophistication, inventiveness or flair. They could sing gorgeous heartache ballads, rollicking uptempo rhythm tunes, creditable period-piece novelty numbers, wonderful pop covers or shattering originals. This two-disc set contains 44 outstanding numbers, with every major Moonglows anthem and several others that weren't big hits but deserved to be, such as "Penny Arcade" and "Love Is a River." This collection updates and expands the *Greatest Sides* single LP release briefly available when Sugar Hill had the Chess catalog in the 1970s. It wisely restricts material to the era when they were at their best, the 1950s, and includes an excellent booklet. *—Ron Wynn*

• **Their Greatest Hits** / May 20, 1997 / MCA ✦✦✦✦✦
At 16 tracks, *Their Greatest Hits* isn't nearly as comprehensive as the two-CD *Blue Velvet*, which has 44 songs. But for someone who wants just the highlights, as opposed to just about everything, *Their Greatest Hits* is the better buy, including their most celebrated tunes ("Ten Commandments of Love," "Sincerely," "Blue Velvet"). The only selection not on *Blue Velvet* is a different take of "Over and Over Again," presented in its "fast version." It does not, however, include "Mama Loocie," which featured Marvin Gaye's first recorded lead vocal. *—Richie Unterberger*

Alanis Morissette

b. Jun. 1, 1974, Ottawa, Ontario, Canada
Vocals / Adult Alternative Pop/Rock, Post-Grunge, Pop/Rock, Alternative Pop/Rock, Singer/Songwriter
Alanis Morissette was one of the most unlikely stars of the mid-'90s. A former child actress turned dance-pop diva, Morissette transformed herself into a confessional alternative singer/songwriter, in the vein of Liz Phair and Tori Amos. However, she added enough pop sensibility, slight hip-hop flourishes and marketing savvy to that formula to become a superstar with her third album, *Jagged Little Pill*. A former cast member of *You Can't Do That on Television*, a children's television program, in 1991 she released her debut album, *Alanis*, a collection of pop-oriented dance numbers and ballads that was successful in Canada, selling over 100,000 copies. Following the release of 1992's *Now Is the Time*, Morissette relocated to Los Angeles, where she met writer/producer Glen Ballard in early 1994. Despite the duo's mainstream pop pedigree, they decided to pursue an edgier, alternative rock-oriented direction. The result was *Jagged Little Pill*, which on the strength of the single "You Oughta Know" rocketed into the Top Ten and multi-platinum status. The second and third singles from *Jagged Little Pill*, "Hand in My Pocket" and "All I Really Want," kept the album in the Top Ten. Her fourth single, "Ironic," proved to be her biggest crossover success. Morissette won several Grammy awards in 1996, including Album of the Year and Song of the Year. Her

much-anticipated follow-up, *Supposed Former Infatuation Junkie,* was released in the autumn of 1998.— *Stephen Thomas Erlewine*

● **Jagged Little Pill** / Jun. 13, 1995 / Maverick/Reprise ♦♦♦♦♦
It's remarkable that Alanis Morissette's *Jagged Little Pill* struck a sympathetic chord with millions of listeners, because it's so doggedly, determinedly insular. This, after all, plays like an emotional purging, prompted by a bitter relationship—and, according to all the lyrical hints, that's likely a record executive who took advantage of a young Alanis. She never disguises her outright rage and disgust, whether it's the vengeful wrath of "You Oughta Know" or asking him "you scan the credits for your name and wonder what it's not there." This is such insider information that it's hard to believe that millions of listeners not just bought it, but embraced it, turning Alanis Morisette into a mid-'90s phenomenon. Perhaps it was the individuality that made it appealing, since its specificity lent it genuineness—and, even if this is clearly an attempt to embrace the "women in rock" movement in alterna-rock, Morissette's intentions are genuine. Often, it seems like Glenn Ballard's pop inclinations fight against Alanis' exorcisms, as her bitter diary entries are given a pop gloss that gives them entry to the pop charts. What's all the more remarkable is that Alanis isn't a particularly good singer, stretching the limits of pitch and credibility with her octave-skipping caterwauling. At its core, this is the work of an ambitious but sophomoric 19-year-old, once burned by love, but still willing to open her heart a second time. All of this adds up to a record that's surprisingly effective, an utterly fascinating exploration of a young woman's psyche. As slick as the music is, the lyrics are unvarnished and Morissette unflinchingly explores emotions so common, most people would be ashamed to articulate them. This doesn't make *Jagged Little Pill* great, but it does make it a fascinating record, a phenomenon that's intensely personal. — *Stephen Thomas Erlewine*

Supposed Former Infatuation Junkie / Nov. 3, 1998 / Maverick ♦♦♦♦
While it's not a repudiation of her blockbuster, *Supposed Former Infatuation Junkie* is a clear step forward, teeming with ambition and filled with new musical ideas and different sonic textures. Morissette's voice still sears, but she has more control over her singing, rarely reaching the piercing heights that occasionally made *Pill* jarring. Also, she has clearly spent some time crafting her lyrics; not only do they never sound like straight diary entries, she no longer is trying to fit too many syllables into a phrase. These two differences are subtle—the brooding, Eastern-styled music that dominates *Supposed* is not. There are numerous extensions of the vague hip-hop and pop fusions that made "Hand in Pocket" and "All I Really Want" huge hits ("Front Row," "UR," "Thank U," "So Pure"), but much of the album is devoted to moody ballads and mid-tempo pop, where the textured production functions as a backdrop for Morissette's crypticly introspective lyrics. Far from being alienating, this approach works surprisingly well—not only do the pop tunes sound catchier, but the ballads, with their winding melodies and dark colors, sound strong and brave. If anything, the record is more coherent album than its predecessor and even if it isn't as accessible or as compulsively listenable, it's a richer record. That said, it won't win any new fans—for all of her success, Morissette is a weird acquired taste, due to her idiosyncratic vocals and doggedly convoluted confessionals—but it certainly confirms that she doesn't quite sound like anyone else, either. — *Stephen Thomas Erlewine*

Alanis Unplugged / Nov. 9, 1999 / Maverick ♦♦♦

Van Morrison

b. Aug. 31, 1945, Belfast, Northern Ireland
Vocals, Saxophone, Keyboards, Harmonica, Guitar / Celtic Rock, Album Rock, Jazz-Rock, Blue-Eyed Soul, Pop/Rock, Folk-Rock, Soft Rock, Adult Contemporary, Singer/Songwriter
Equal parts blue-eyed soul shouter and wild-eyed poet-sorcerer, Van Morrison was among popular music's true innovators, a restless seeker whose alchemical fusion of R&B, jazz, blues, and Celtic folk produced perhaps the most spiritually transcendent body of work in the rock & roll canon. Morrison enjoyed a massive cult following which grew exponentially throughout the course of his lengthy and prolific career; his recordings cover extraordinary stylistic ground yet retain a consistency and purity virtually unmatched among his contemporaries.

George Ivan Morrison was born in Belfast, Northern Ireland on August 31, 1948. At 15 he quit school to join the local R&B band the Monarchs, touring military bases throughout Europe before returning home to form his own group, Them. The band enjoyed modest success after their debut in 1964; Morrison left the band following a 1966 tour of the U.S.

Morrison's first solo sessions produced arguably his most familiar hit, the jubilant "Brown-Eyed Girl". 1968's *Astral Weeks* remains not only Morrison's masterpiece, but one of the greatest records ever made—a haunting, deeply personal collection of impressionistic folk-styled epics. The follow-up, 1970's *Moondance,* was every bit as brilliant—buoyant and optimistic where *Astral Weeks* was dark and anguished, it cracked the Top 40, generating the perennials "Caravan" and "Into the Mystic."

The first half of the 1970s was the most fertile creative period of Morrison's career—after *His Band and the Street Choir* yielded his biggest chart hit, "Domino," Morrison released 1971's *Tupelo Honey* and 1974's stunning *Veedon Fleece.*

Into the Music, released in 1979, was first in a series of albums which dealt with spiritual themes. 1989's *Avalon Sunset* heralded a commercial rebirth of sorts—"Whenever God Shines His Light," a duet with Cliff Richard, became Morrison's first U.K. Top 20 hit in over two decades.

1991's ambitious double set *Hymns to the Silence,* was widely hailed as his most impressive outing in years. Throughout the '90s, and into the new century, Morrison continued alternating between new studio albums and collections of rare and live material, including the surprising *The Skiffle Sessions: Live in Belfast* which was released in 2000. —*Jason Ankeny*

Blowin' Your Mind! / 1967 / Epic/Legacy ♦♦♦
Although his first solo album is remembered for containing the immortal pop hit "Brown Eyed Girl," *Blowin' Your Mind!* is actually a dry run for Van Morrison's masterpiece, *Astral Weeks.* Songs like "Who Drove The Red Sports Car" look to that song cycle, even as "Midnight Special" nods to Morrison's R&B past. But it is the agonizing "T.B. Sheets"—all nine-and-three-quarters minutes of it—that dominates this record and belies its trendy title and pop association. "T.B. Sheets" takes the blues and reinvents it as noble tragedy and humiliating mortality. It is where Van Morrison emerges as an artist. (*Blowin' Your Mind!* was superseded by *Bang Masters,* which contains all of its tracks except "He Ain't Give You None," presented in an alternate take, plus Morrison's other recordings for Bang, in 1991.) — *William Ruhlmann*

☆ **Astral Weeks** / Nov. 1968 / Warner Brothers ♦♦♦♦♦
Astral Weeks is generally considered one of the best albums in pop music history. For all that renown, *Astral Weeks* is anything but an archetypal rock & roll album: In fact, it isn't a rock & roll album at all. Employing a mixture of folk, blues, jazz, and classical music, Van Morrison spins out a series of extended ruminations on his Belfast upbringing, including the remarkable character "Madame George" and the climactic epiphany experienced on "Cyprus Avenue." Accompanying himself on acoustic guitar, Morrison sings in his elastic, bluesy voice, accompanied by a jazz rhythm section (Jay Berliner, guitar, Richard Davis, bass, Connie Kay, drums), plus reeds (John Payne) and vibes (Warren Smith, Jr.), with a string quartet overdubbed. An emotional outpouring cast in delicate musical structures, *Astral Weeks* has a unique musical power. Unlike any record before or since, it nevertheless encompasses the passion and tenderness that have always mixed in the best postwar popular music, easily justifying the critics' raves. — *William Ruhlmann*

☆ **Moondance** / Feb. 1970 / Warner Brothers ♦♦♦♦♦
The yang to *Astral Weeks'* yin, the brilliant *Moondance* is every bit as much a classic as its predecessor; Morrison's first commercially successful solo effort, it retains the previous album's deeply spiritual thrust but transcends its bleak, cathartic intensity to instead explore themes of renewal and redemption. Light, soulful and jazzy, *Moondance* opens with the sweetly nostalgic "And It Stoned Me," the song's pastoral imagery establishing the dominant lyrical motif recurring throughout the album—virtually every track exults in natural wonder, whether it's the nocturnal magic celebrated by the title cut or the unlimited promise offered in "Brand New Day." At the heart of the record is "Caravan," an incantatory ode to the power of radio; equally stirring is the majestic "Into the Mystic," a song of such elemental beauty and grace as to stand as arguably the quintessential Morrison moment. —*Jason Ankeny*

His Band & Street Choir / Oct. 1970 / Warner Brothers ♦♦♦♦♦
After the brilliant one-two punch of *Astral Weeks* and *Moondance, His Band and Street Choir* brings Morrison back down to earth, both literally and figuratively. While neither as innovative nor as edgy as its predecessors, *His Band and Street Choir* also lacks their overt mysticism; at heart, the album is simply Morrison's valentine to the rhythm and blues that inspired him, resulting in the muscular and joyous tribute "Domino" as well as the bouncy "Blue Money" and "Call Me Up in Dreamland." —*Jason Ankeny*

Tupelo Honey / Oct. 1971 / Mercury ♦♦♦♦♦
Tupelo Honey is typical of Morrison's early-1970s work in both sound and structure; after dispensing with the requisite hit—here, the buoyant, R&B-inflected "Wild Night"—he truly gets down to business, settling into a luminously pastoral drift typified by the nostalgic "Old Old Woodstock." At the heart of the record are a pair of stunning love songs, "You're My Woman" and the hymn-like title cut, one of Morrison's most enduring and transcendent compositions. —*Jason Ankeny*

Saint Dominic's Preview / 1972 / Mercury ♦♦♦♦♦
While less thematically and sonically cohesive than Morrison's prior albums, *Saint Dominic's Preview* nonetheless hangs together on the strength of its songs, an intriguingly diverse collection which draws together the disparate threads of the singer's recent work into one sterling package. The opener, "Jackie Wilson Said (I'm in Heaven When You Smile)" is pure R&B jubilation, while the title cut, although essentially a rewrite of "Tupelo Honey," is stunning gospel-pop; both "Listen to the Lion" and "Almost Independence Day," meanwhile, mark a return to the epic mystical explorations of Morrison's earlier work, and offer a pair of his most primal performances. —*Jason Ankeny*

Hard Nose the Highway / Aug. 1973 / Mercury ♦♦♦
Although it marks a decline from the astonishing run of five great albums Van Morrison had made from 1968 through 1972, *Hard Nose the Highway* is still a respectable, if uneven, effort, notably containing "Snow in San Anselmo" (which features the Oakland Symphony Chamber Chorus) and "Warm Love." Nevertheless, it marked the end of Morrison's greatest period of creativity and accomplishment. — *William Ruhlmann*

It's Too Late to Stop Now / Jan. 1974 / Mercury ♦♦♦♦♦
While Morrison is, to be kind, an erratic and temperamental live performer, he's in stellar form throughout the double album *It's Too Late to Stop Now,* a superb concert set which neatly summarizes his career from his days with Them (represented by scorching renditions of "Gloria" and "Here Comes the Night") through 1973's *Hard Nose the Highway* ("Warm Love," "Wild Children"). In addition to the hits, including "Caravan," "Domino," and "Into the Mystic" (the final line of which gives the album its title), Morrison even pulls out a handful of R&B chestnuts ("Bring It on Home to Me," "Ain't Nothin' You Can Do") before capping off the collection with a show-stopping rendition of *Astral Weeks'* "Cyprus Avenue." An engaging, warm portrait of the Man at the peak of his powers. —*Jason Ankeny*

Veedon Fleece / Feb. 1974 / Mercury ♦♦♦♦♦
The final album of Morrison's remarkably prolific and innovative 1968-1974 period (followed by three years of silence), *Veedon Fleece* brings the singer full circle, returning him to the introspection and poignancy of *Astral Weeks.* Composed following his sudden divorce from wife Janet Planet and subsequent retreat from the U.S., the songs are subtle and spartan, the performances deeply felt; though less tortured and cathartic than *Astral Weeks,* it's a record fraught with emotional upheaval, as evidenced by such superior moments as "Linden Arden Stole the Highlights," "Who Was That Masked Man," and "You Don't Pull No Punches, But You Don't Push the River." —*Jason Ankeny*

A Period of Transition / 1977 / Mercury ♦♦♦

Wavelength / 1978 / Mercury ♦♦♦♦
Wavelength essentially picks up where *A Period of Transition* left off, offering a focused, full-bodied alternative to that record's warmly fuzzy lack of direction. Like that album, it's hardly a major entry in his catalog, but there are signs that Morrison is finding his footing for his latter-day voice. Again, the primary appeal of this record is its atmosphere, a charmingly relaxed outing, high on mildly swinging mid-tempo numbers and round, welcoming ballads. Surely, an album of subtle pleasures like this is primarily for the converted, but once you're there, it's hard not to resist *Wavelength*. *—Stephen Thomas Erlewine*

Into the Music / 1979 / Warner Brothers ♦♦♦♦♦
Into the Music may not seem like a great Van Morrison record upon first listen, especially if you're trying to compare it to such masterpieces as *Astral Weeks* and *Moondance*, or even *Tupelo Honey*. Yet this is certainly one of his best records, one that is quietly winning and thoroughly ingratiating, sounding stronger, even irresistible, with each new spin. In a sense, this is the definitive post-classic era Morrison, since it summarizes all of his attributes while showcasing each at a peak. Musically, this is a little harder and rootsier than its two predecessors, but only a little; this is still remarkably relaxed music, where the charm is in its ease of delivery and compositions. The difference, there's more grit in the performances, more substance in the songs, letting Van the craftsman shine through along with his spirituality and grace. There may be no masterworks on the level of his early-'70s records, but these are deft, subtle songs that are full-bodied songs, unlike their counterparts on this album's immediate predecessors or successors. There's little question that this is not a knock-out record, and some could even be excused if they find its charms elusive—but once you've entered Van's sizeable cult, few records sound as much like Morrison as this, a record that served as culmination of where he was coming from and served as blueprint for where he was going. *—Stephen Thomas Erlewine*

Common One / 1980 / Warner Brothers ♦♦♦

Beautiful Vision / 1982 / Warner Brothers ♦♦♦

The Inarticulate Speech of the Heart / Mar. 1983 / Warner Brothers ♦♦♦

Live at the Grand Opera House Belfast / 1985 / Mercury ♦♦♦

A Sense of Wonder / 1985 / Mercury ♦♦♦
Van Morrison's U.S. label debut with PolyGram (which had issued his *Live at the Opera House Belfast* album in England earlier) is a strong effort, mixing some of his familiar influences—R&B, poetry, mysticism—on such characteristic tracks as "Tore Down A La Rimbaud." It might be fair to say that, by now, Morrison's fans had heard what he had to say and the rest was just repetition, but he continued to write and perform at a high level at this mature stage in his career. *—William Ruhlmann*

No Guru, No Method, No Teacher / Jul. 1986 / Mercury ♦♦♦

Poetic Champions Compose / 1987 / Mercury ♦♦♦♦
If the title didn't tip you off, the opening five-minute jazz instrumental "Spanish Steps" certainly reveals that *Poetic Champions Compose* is an art record. Of course, Morrison has been making art records since at least *The Inarticulate Speech of the Heart*, perhaps *Common One*, so that shouldn't come as a surprise. What is a bit of a shock is that Morrison begins to shake off his self-conscious straitjacket here, letting a little more grit into the music, even if the record still is firmly ensconced in mid-tempos and ballads, with only Van's voice (soulful, yet not histrionic), to pull you in. Much of this tends to float by, with only the occasional song ("I Forgot That Love Existed," "Did Ye Get Healed?") distinguishing themselves. The overly mellow atmosphere and Van's arch artiness may not make it universally appealing, yet this record is warmer, stronger than many of its predecessors, one of his highlights from the '80s. *—Stephen Thomas Erlewine*

Irish Heartbeat / 1988 / Mercury ♦♦♦♦♦
Although still purposeful, Van Morrison's '80s albums were becoming repetitive when he took a break for this collaboration with the Chieftains on traditional Irish songs. The result takes him back to his earliest days and finds him singing with renewed conviction. This album should appeal to all fans of Irish music as well as Morrison lovers. *—William Ruhlmann*

Avalon Sunset / Jun. 1989 / Mercury ♦♦♦♦♦
Van Morrison scored one of his biggest commercial successes with *Avalon Sunset*, a record highlighted by the gorgeous "Have I Told You Lately," one of his most heartfelt love songs and a major radio hit which helped introduce his music to a new generation of listeners. Not a consistently strong LP, *Avalon Sunset* is nevertheless the work of a master craftsman, its lush orchestration and atmospheric production casting an irresistibly elegant spell; a deeply spiritual record, it also includes the standout opener "Whenever God Shines His Light," a collaboration with Cliff Richard. *—Jason Ankeny*

★ **The Best of Van Morrison** / Jan. 1990 / Mercury ♦♦♦♦♦
For an artist that's doggedly album-oriented, plus a songwriter who revels in subtlety, Van Morrison doesn't seem like a logical candidate for a successful greatest-hits compilation. Nevertheless, *The Best of Van Morrison* is a cracker-jack compilation, tracing Van the Man from his days with Them, through his best-known tunes ("Brown-Eyed Girl," "Moondance," "Blue Money," "Wild Night"), to highlights from the '70s and '80s cult efforts, topped off by "Wonderful Remark," a song first heard on the *King of Comedy* soundtrack. This collection makes Morrison's work seem a little more immediate and accessible than it usually is, but that's a blessing, since it provides a great summary of his hits and a nice introduction for the curious. Yes, it could have dug deeper into the catalog, but as a sampler, it can't be faulted. *—Stephen Thomas Erlewine*

Enlightenment / Feb. 1990 / Mercury ♦♦♦

The Bang Masters / Feb. 26, 1991 / Epic ♦♦♦♦♦
During the period between his departure from Them and his masterpiece *Astral Weeks*, Van Morrison tenured with Bert Berns' Bang label, notching his biggest solo hit with the classic single "Brown Eyed Girl" and laying the groundwork for the transcendent material to follow. *The Bang Masters* compiles the best of his recordings for the label, and although a good part of it is negligible in comparison to Morrison's greatest work, it's still necessary listening for fans. The remarkable "T.B. Sheets" captures Morrison at his most emotionally shattering, while early attempts at "Beside You" and "Madame George" hint at the genius just around the corner. *—Jason Ankeny*

Hymns to the Silence / Sep. 24, 1991 / Mercury ♦♦♦

The Best of Van Morrison, Vol. 2 / Mar. 9, 1993 / Mercury ♦♦♦♦♦
No big hit singles are here, or even familiar songs for that matter. Van Morrison compiled *The Best Of, Volume 2* himself, leaning heavily toward his recent work. As an anthology, it doesn't completely work, since it's uneven and lacking a sense of scope; what makes the album fascinating is to see how Morrison views himself. Although there are many good (even great) songs here, *The Best Of, Volume 2* only works as an introduction to Morrison's idiosyncratic recent work instead of his entire career. *—Stephen Thomas Erlewine*

Too Long in Exile / Jun. 8, 1993 / Mercury ♦♦

A Night in San Francisco / May 17, 1994 / Mercury ♦♦♦

Days Like This / Jun. 20, 1995 / Mercury ♦♦

How Long Has This Been Going On / Feb. 1996 / Verve ♦♦

Tell Me Something: The Songs of Mose Allison / Oct. 8, 1996 / Verve ♦♦♦

The Healing Game / Mar. 4, 1997 / Mercury ♦♦♦

The Philosopher's Stone / Jun. 16, 1998 / Polydor ♦♦♦
Van Morrison has always been a prolific artist, releasing nearly an album a year for 30 years. All the while, he had a stockpile of unreleased material in the vaults, many of which became legendary among collectors. A selection of this material was planned for inclusion on a box set, but when he realized the sheer amount of worthy material, he decided to separate the unreleased cuts and release them as the double-disc set *The Philosopher's Stone*. Certainly, the collection is for fans, but not just hardcore fans—there are a number of great songs here, from "Madame Joy" and "Naked in the Jungle" to "Crazy Jane on Gold" and "The Street Only Knew Your Name." A full 26 of the 30 tracks on the album have never been released in any form, while the remaining four—"Wonderful Remark," "Real Real Gone," "Flamingoes Fly," "Bright Side of the Road"—are present in alternate takes. In all, *The Philosopher's Stone* is a welcome addition to Van Morrison's official catalog—some of these songs are so good, it would have been a shame if they had stayed locked in the vaults. *—Stephen Thomas Erlewine*

The Skiffle Sessions: Live In Belfast 1998 / Jan. 18, 2000 / Pointblank ♦♦♦♦

You Win Again / Oct. 3, 2000 / Virgin ♦♦♦

Morrissey

b. May 22, 1959, Manchester, England
Vocals / College Rock, Alternative Pop/Rock
With the Smiths, singer/songwriter Morrissey established himself as a post-punk hero, becoming the spokesman for millions of disaffected teenagers and young adults with his literate, biting, and sensitive lyrics and dramatic vocals. After the band broke up in 1987, he pursued a solo career, releasing his first album the following year. While he released several excellent singles in the late '80s, he ultimately began to sink into his persona without producing enough quality songs. After 1991's self-absorbed *Kill Uncle*, many critics considered him as a has-been, with his best work in the past. Thanks to the explosive, Mick Ronson-produced *Your Arsenal*, Morrissey regained his credibility; it was almost universally acclaimed as one of the best albums of the year and many said it was his best work since the Smiths' masterpiece *The Queen Is Dead*. His fan base continued to grow, both in size and devotion. With 1994's *Vauxhall and I*, he even had a hit single ("The More You Ignore Me, the Closer I Get") scrape the Top 50 singles chart in America, which would have been unthinkable when "Hand in Glove" was released a decade earlier. However, 1997's *Maladjusted* was a commerical failure; the compilation *My Early Burglary Years* followed a year later. *—Stephen Thomas Erlewine*

Viva Hate / Mar. 22, 1988 / Sire ♦♦♦♦♦
Following the breakup of the Smiths, Morrissey needed to prove that he was a viable artist without Johnny Marr, and *Viva Hate* fulfilled that goal with grace. Working with producer Stephen Street and guitarist Vini Reilly (of the Durutti Column), Morrissey doesn't drastically depart from the sound of *Strangeways, Here We Come*, offering a selection of 12 jangling guitar-pop sounds. One major concession is the presence of synthesizers—which is ironic, considering the Smiths' adamant opposition to keyboards—but neither the sound, nor Morrissey's wit, is diluted. And while the music is occasionally pedestrian, Morrissey compensates with a superb batch of lyrics, ranging from his conventional despair ("Little Man, What Now—," "I Don't Mind If You Forget Me") to the savage political tirade of "Margaret on a Guillotine." Nevertheless, the two master strokes on the album—the gorgeous "Everyday is Like Sunday" and the infectious "Suedehead"—were previously singles, and both are on the compilation, *Bona Drag*. *—Stephen Thomas Erlewine*

Bona Drag / Oct. 8, 1990 / Sire ♦♦♦♦♦
As he was toiling on *Kill Uncle*, Morrissey released *Bona Drag*, a compilation of singles and B-sides, including "Everyday is Like Sunday" and "Suedehead" from *Viva Hate*. While the record conveniently overlooks some rarities, the selections on *Bona Drag* are uniformly first-rate and many of the songs—"Picadilly Palare," "Interesting Drug," "November Spawned a Monster," "The Last of the Famous International Playboys," "Lucky Lisp," "Disappointed," "He Knows I'd Love to See Him," and "Ouija Board, Ouija Board"—are Morrissey classics, arguably making *Bona Drag* a more consistent and entertaining record than *Viva Hate*. *—Stephen Thomas Erlewine*

Kill Uncle / Mar. 5, 1991 / Sire ♦♦
With *Kill Uncle*, Morrissey descended into the ranks of self-parody, churning out a series of

pleasant but tired alternative jangle pop songs that had neither melody nor much wit to distinguish them. Part of the problem lies with his choice of collaborators. Producers Clive Langer and Alan Winstanley don't provide the appropriately sympathetic backdrop for Morrissey's sly humor, while guitarist Mark E. Nevin is incapable of developing hooks. A few cuts, such as "(I'm) The End of the Family Line" and "There's a Place in Hell for Me and My Friends," stand out, but *Kill Uncle* is Morrissey's least distinguished record. *—Stephen Thomas Erlewine*

● **Your Arsenal** / Jul. 28, 1992 / Sire ✦✦✦✦✦
Morrissey bounced back from the lackluster *Kill Uncle* with the terrific *Your Arsenal*. A dynamic, invigorating fusion of glam-rock and rockabilly, *Your Arsenal* rocks harder than any other record Morrissey ever made. Guitarist Alan Whyte's riffs swagger with a self-absorbed arrogance, and producer Mick Ronson gives the music a tough, stylish sheen—it may be a break from Morrissey's jangle pop, but the music is sharper than it has been since the Smiths, and so is Morrissey's pen. Running through his trademark litany of emotional, social, and personal observations, Morrissey is viciously clever and occasionally moving. And the songs—whether it's the rush of "You're Gonna Need Someone on Your Side," the menacing "We'll Let You Know," the spare rockabilly bop of "Certain People I Know," the gospel-tinged "I Know It's Gonna Happen Someday" or "Tomorrow"—are uniformly excellent, forming the core of Morrissey's finest solo record and his best work since *The Queen Is Dead*. *—Stephen Thomas Erlewine*

Vauxhall and I / Mar. 22, 1994 / Sire ✦✦✦✦✦
While it isn't a gutsy rock & roll record like *Your Arsenal*, *Vauxhall and I* is equally impressive. Filled with carefully constructed guitar pop gems, the album contains some of Morrissey's best material since the Smiths. Out of all of his solo albums, *Vauxhall and I* sounds the most like his former band, yet the textured, ringing guitar on this record is an extension of his past, not a replication of it. In fact, with songs like "Now My Heart Is Full" and "Hold on to Your Friends," Morrissey sounds more comfortable and peaceful than he ever has. And "The More You Ignore Me, The Closer I Get," "Speedway," and "Spring-Heeled Jim" prove that he hasn't lost his vicious wit. *—Stephen Thomas Erlewine*

World of Morrissey / Feb. 21, 1995 / Sire ✦✦✦

Southpaw Grammar / Aug. 28, 1995 / Reprise ✦✦
If *Vauxhall and I* represented a more mature Morrissey, *Southpaw Grammar* superficially presents a more rough & tumble version of the singer. As his previous single, "Boxers," indicated, Morrissey's fascination with boxing and violence has reached full fruition. The music appropriately reflects this, with growling, distorted guitars and martial rhythms. But *Southpaw Grammar* doesn't rock as hard or with as much style as the rockabilly-inflected *Your Arsenal*—instead, it's his art-rock album, complete with strings, drum solos, and two ten-minute songs. Of these, the winding, menacing "The Teachers Are Afraid of the Pupils" works the best, and it represents a significant change in Morrissey's outlook; instead of the children being outsiders, the teachers are. Throughout *Southpaw Grammar*, the privileged are oppressed by their fortunes, while working-class toughs are celebrated for their violence. However, there is no cohesive glue to the record. "The Teachers" uses its 11 minutes effectively, but "Southpaw" is merely ponderous. "Reader Meet Author" and "Dangenham Dave" are classic three-minute pop songs, but "Do Your Best and Don't Worry" is strictly by the books. Nevertheless, there is plently of enjoyable music on the record, even if the concept is flawed. *—Stephen Thomas Erlewine*

Maladjusted / Aug. 12, 1997 / Mercury ✦✦✦

● **Suedehead: The Best of Morrissey** / Sep. 8, 1997 / EMI ✦✦✦✦✦
Morrissey has always favored compilations, releasing such hodgepodges of singles, B-sides and album tracks as *Bona Drag* and *World of Morrissey*, but the 19-track *Suedehead: The Best of Morrissey* is the first official "hits" collection he has released in his solo career. Spanning his years at EMI—from 1988's *Viva Hate* to 1994's *Vauxhall and I*, with the 1995 single "Sunny" added as a bonus—*Suedehead* is an imperfect collection, especially since it's sequenced out of chronological order, but it's pretty great all the same, featuring a basic selection of singles such as "Suedehead," "Everyday Is Like Sunday," "Tomorrow," "Interesting Drug," "Our Frank," "Piccadilly Palare," "We Hate It When Our Friends Become Successful," "The Last of the Famous International Playboys," "Boxers" and "The More You Ignore Me, The Closer I Get." There's also a handful of rarities, such as the extended version of "Interlude" and his cover of the Jam's "That's Entertainment," but at its core, this disc is a solid collection that may convince skeptics that Morrissey's solo records did indeed have a lot to offer. *—Stephen Thomas Erlewine*

My Early Burglary Years / Sep. 15, 1998 / Reprise ✦✦✦

Mötley Crüe

f. 1981
Group / Pop-Metal, Album Rock, Hair Metal, Heavy Metal, Hard Rock
Known for having more "sex, drugs, and rock & roll" than any other band in rock history, Mötley Crüe's infamous reputation left them a force to be reckoned with in the '80s, and that reputation evolved into the '90s as the band continued to retain massive record sales. Some know them best for their controversial approaches to metal; others might remember them as the performers of such songs as "Wild Side" and "Dr. Feelgood," but no one knows the Crüe better than the bands they have influenced, from Lita Ford to Ratt to Guns N' Roses to Marilyn Manson. These four high school dropouts who seemed rejected by the rest of the world—singer Vince Neil, guitarist Mick Mars, bassist Nikki Sixx and drummer Tommy Lee—eventually became one of the biggest metal bands of all time, but their road to success was anything but easy. *—Barry Weber*

Too Fast for Love / 1981 / Beyond ✦✦✦

Shout at the Devil / 1983 / Beyond ✦✦✦✦✦

Theater of Pain / 1985 / Beyond ✦✦✦✦
Backing away from the mild pseudo-Satanic posturing on parts of *Shout at the Devil* in favor of a more glammed-up image, Mötley Crüe really began to hit their commercial stride with *Theatre of Pain*, which broke them on MTV with the power ballad "Home Sweet Home" and a remake of Brownsville Station's "Smokin' in the Boys Room"; the latter also landed them on the Top 40 singles chart for the first time. Overall, the guitar riffing sounds less *heavy* metal and more pop-metal; similarly, the sound of the record is slicker and more arranged, polished for mainstream acceptance and airplay. A higher percentage of dull filler has crept into the songwriting, but there are still enough high points to rescue the album's momentum. [In 1999, the Crüe remastered and reissued *Theatre of Pain* on their own Motley/Beyond label with five bonus tracks: demos of "Home Sweet Home," "Keep Your Eye on the Money," and "City Boy Blues," plus rough mixes of "Smokin' in the Boys Room" and "Home Sweet Home" (the latter an instrumental).] *—Steve Huey*

Girls, Girls, Girls / 1987 / Beyond ✦✦✦✦
Girls, Girls, Girls continued Mötley Crüe's commercial hot streak, eventually going quadruple-platinum as its predecessor *Theatre of Pain* had; meanwhile, the title track brought them their second Top 20 single, and "Wild Side" became a popular MTV item. In general, the Crüe really plays up the sleaze factor on this album, trying to recapture some of the street-tough grittiness that fueled *Too Fast for Love*—even appearing on the cover astride motorcycles and wearing leather; this time around, the influence of Aerosmith is felt to a much greater degree. The production is too polished to really give the record a raw, dirty feel, but the raunchiness comes through all the same. Again, there's a bit of filler, as though the band knew they didn't have to make a *completely* consistent record to maintain their popularity, but there are enough high points along the way to make *Girls, Girls, Girls* an entertaining party-metal platter. (In 1999, the Crüe remastered and reissued *Girls, Girls, Girls* on their own Motley/Beyond label with four bonus tracks: instrumental mixes of three selections, plus the previously unreleased song "Rodeo.") *—Steve Huey*

Dr. Feelgood / Sep. 1989 / Beyond ✦✦✦✦✦
Mötley Crüe's albums were a lot like episodes of *Married with Children* in the sense that they may not be great works of art, but can be darn entertaining. With Bob Rock serving as producer, the L.A. headbangers savor the joys of trashy, unapologetically decadent fun on *Dr. Feelgood*—an album that makes no pretense at being anything else. While nothing here is quite as commanding as "Shout at the Devil," "Wild Side," or "Live Wire," such hook-oriented MTV smashes as "Kickstart My Heart," the amusing "Don't Go Away Mad (Just Go Away)" and the title song are infectious and hard to resist, and helped make this the best-selling Mötley Crüe album ever, as well as providing their first Top Ten singles. Unfortunately, the album would be lead singer Vince Neil's last album with the band. Neil's departure—and pop-metal's decline in popularity in the mid-'90s—proved to be severe blows to Mötley Crüe. [In 1999, the Crüe remastered and reissued *Dr. Feelgood* on their own Motley/Beyond label with bonus tracks.] *—Alex Henderson*

Decade of Decadence / 1991 / Elektra ✦✦✦✦✦

Mötley Crüe / Mar. 15, 1994 / Beyond ✦✦

Generation Swine / Jun. 24, 1997 / Beyond ✦✦

● **Greatest Hits** / Oct. 27, 1998 / Motley/Beyond/BMG ✦✦✦✦✦
Motley Crue parted ways with Elektra in the spring of 1998, releasing their second compilation, *Greatest Hits*, on their own label that fall. Weighing in at 17 tracks, including two pedestrian new songs, *Greatest Hits* duplicates much of *Decade of Decadence* featuring no less than eight songs—"Looks That Kill," "Home Sweet Home" (original, not the *Decade* version), "Smokin' in the Boys' Room," "Girls, Girls, Girls," "Wild Side," "Dr. Feelgood," "Kickstart My Heart" (original, not the live version that was on *Decade*), "Primal Scream"—that were on the previous collection. Considering all that overlap, you can be forgiven for thinking that the two compilations are interchangeable, but *Greatest Hits* actually has the edge, not just because it doesn't feature the silly "Anarchy in the U.K." cover, but because it features a greater selection of hits from their masterpiece, *Dr. Feelgood*, including "Without You," "Don't Go Away Mad (Just Go Away)," and "Same Ol' Situation (S.O.S.)," all of which weren't on *Decade*. It has its flaws, to be sure—the sequencing is illogical, the newer songs are lame and the original "Shout at the Devil" should have been featured instead of the atrocious *Generation Swine* re-recording—but it's still the best overview yet assembled. *—Stephen Thomas Erlewine*

Supersonic and Demonic Relics / Jun. 29, 1999 / Beyond ✦✦

New Tattoo / Jun. 20, 2000 / Beyond ✦✦✦

Motörhead

f. 1975, London, England, **db.** 1982
Group / New Wave of British Heavy Metal, British Metal, Speed Metal, Heavy Metal, Thrash, Hard Rock
Motörhead's overwhelmingly loud and fast style of heavy metal was one of the most groundbreaking styles the genre had to offer in the late '70s. Though the group's leader Lemmy Kilminster had his roots in the hard-rocking space-rock band Hawkwind, Motörhead didn't bother with his old group's progressive tendencies, choosing to amplify the heavy biker-rock elements of Hawkwind with the speed of punk rock. Motörhead wasn't punk rock—they formed before the Sex Pistols and they loved the hell-for-leather imagery of bikers too much to conform with the safety-pinned, ripped T-shirts of punk—but they were the first metal band to harness that energy and, in the process, they created speed metal and thrash metal. Unlike many of their contemporaries, Motörhead continued performing well into the '90s. Although the band changed its lineup many, many times—Lemmy was its only consistent member—they never changed their raging sound. *—Stephen Thomas Erlewine*

Motörhead / 1977 / Roadrunner ✦✦✦

Bomber / 1979 / Castle ✦✦✦✦
Sensing that the commercial tides were changing for them by mid-1979 (thanks to the surprise chart success of *Overkill*), the mighty Motörhead returned to studio to issue their second release of the year, *Bomber*. Again behind the boards was longtime Rolling Stones producer Jimmy Miller, and while it was another solid outing, with hindsight it was a shade less exceptional than its predecessor was or its successor (1980's *Ace of Spades*) would be. Still, the trio of Lemmy, "Fast" Eddie Clarke, and "Philthy Animal" Taylor are in fine form, crank-

ing out another slab of prime metallic punk. "Stone Dead Forever" and the album-closing title track proved to be the best-known selections, while other standouts include "Dead Men Tell No Tales," "Stone Dead Forever," and "Poison." *Bomber* proved that its predecessor's success was no fluke, becoming the band's first to crack the U.K. Top 20, and reaching #12 on the album chart. Included on the 1999 Castle reissue was the B-side "Over the Top," as well as the four-track live EP *The Golden Years*. *—Greg Prato*

Overkill / 1979 / Castle Music America ✦✦✦✦✦
While Motörhead's self-titled debut had performed respectfully on the British charts, it was their second release, 1979's *Overkill*, that went Top 30, selling 100,000 units in Europe (all the while without proper distribution in the U.S.). Produced by ex-Rolling Stones main man Jimmy Miller (*Sticky Fingers, Exile on Main Street*), *Overkill* can be pinpointed as the album that finally focused the Motorhead sound—part metal, part punk, and part good old rock & roll. While several tracks would become cornerstones for their superb 1981 live album *No Sleep 'Til Hammersmith* (such as the title track, "Stay Clean," "Capricorn," "No Class," and "Metropolis"), other lesser-known tracks are just as exceptional—"(I Won't) Pay Your Price," "Damage Case," "Limb From Limb," etc. Included on the 1999 Castle reissue were five bonus tracks, including such B-sides as "Too Late, Too Late" and "Like a Nightmare," as well as a fun cover of the party standard "Louie Louie." *—Greg Prato*

Ace of Spades / 1980 / Castle Music America ✦✦✦✦✦
1980's *Ace of Spades* was the album that put Motörhead on the top of the heavy metal heap, albeit for a brief length of time. The band's raw sound was still in place, but the anthemic title track broke the band through to a broader audience; the single reached the British Top 20, while the album peaked at number four on the charts. The trio couldn't have picked a better time to issue their best studio album yet, as England was in the midst of a massive heavy metal movement—bands such as Australia's AC/DC and Judas Priest had released big albums, while newcomers such as Iron Maiden and Def Leppard were making a big splash as well. As with 1979's *Overkill*, Lemmy & Co. had issued another extremely consistent album—while tracks such as "(We Are) The Road Crew" and "The Hammer" would become instant concert standards, such lesser-known titles as "Shoot You In the Back," "Jailbait," and the brief "Bite the Bullet" are all standouts as well. Unfortunately, *Ace of Spades* would prove to be the original lineup's last classic studio album; Lemmy would be the only original member remaining by 1984. The 1999 Castle reissue included three bonus tracks, including the B-side "Dirty Love" and a Top Five collaboration with the U.K. all-female metal band Girlschool, "Please Don't Touch." *—Greg Prato*

No Sleep Til Hammersmith / 1981 / Castle Music America ✦✦✦✦✦
If you had to pinpoint an album that gave birth to thrash metal, many metalheads would agree it was Motörhead's classic 1981 live album *No Sleep 'Til Hammersmith*. The original lineup of Motörhead was sheer electricity and excitement in concert, and the live set captures the trio at their peak. Nearly all of the best tracks from their first four studio albums are featured here (1977's self-titled debut, 1979's *Overkill* and *Bomber*, and 1980's *Ace of Spades*), but the live versions often prove to be even better than the originals. Such all-time metal anthems as "Ace of Spades," "Stay Clean," "(We Are) The Road Crew," "Overkill," "Bomber," and "Motörhead" are featured in all their eardrum-shattering glory, as is the mini-epic "Metropolis," "Iron Horse," and "No Class." Originally released on Bronze, the 1999 Castle reissue included excellent remastered sound, as well as three bonus tracks not on the original release—"Over the Top," "Capricorn (Alternative Version)," and a cover of the Yardbirds' blues-rock classic "Train Kept A-Rollin." If you could only own a single Motörhead disc, *No Sleep 'Til Hammersmith* might be your best bet. *—Greg Prato*

Iron Fist / 1982 / Castle Music America ✦✦✦✦
Five years after its self-titled debut album, Motörhead wasn't compromising or softening its approach one iota. *Iron Fist* is state-of-the-art Mötorhead—bombastic, abrasive, and thoroughly captivating. Having done more than its part to define the emerging thrash metal genre, Motörhead was known for taking no prisoners. And songs like "Speedfreak" (which could be considered a Motörhead manifesto), "Go To Hell," and the title song made it clear that it wasn't about to stop. The last album by the Lemmy/Fast Eddie Clarke/Philthy Animal Taylor edition of the band, *Fist* was reissued on CD in 1990 with the obscure "Remember Me, I'm Gone" added. *—Alex Henderson*

★ **No Remorse** / 1984 / Castle Music America ✦✦✦✦✦
1984's *No Remorse* is an awesome double-disc anthology of nothing but Motörhead's very best tracks. The 1999 reissue on Castle expanded the track listing to a meaty 29 selections, five of which weren't included on the original. While it doesn't come with a leather cover as the original limited-edition vinyl version did, the music still holds up as some of the most lethal, high-voltage heavy metal ever. Easily one of the most important and influential bands to come out of the late-'70s/early-'80s New Wave of British Heavy Metal movement (just listen to Metallica and Megadeth), *No Remorse* is the ultimate purchase for the newcomer just discovering this great outfit. Mixing studio with live material, highlights include the album-opening "Ace of Spades," "Stay Clean," "Iron Fist," "Overkill," and "(We Are) The Road Crew," as well as a few interesting collaborations with Girlschool ("Please Don't Touch") and Wendy O. Williams ("No Class" and "Stand By Your Man"). There is no better Motörhead collection than *No Remorse*. *—Greg Prato*

Orgasmatron / 1986 / Castle Music America ✦✦✦

Rock 'N' Roll / 1987 / Castle Music America ✦✦✦

1916 / Feb. 26, 1991 / WTG ✦✦✦✦✦

March or Die / Jul. 14, 1992 / WTG ✦✦

Mott the Hoople

f. 1969, **db.** 1976
Group / Album Rock, Proto-Punk, Glam Rock, Hard Rock, Rock & Roll
Mott the Hoople are one of the great also-rans in the history of rock & roll. Though the band scored a number of album rock hits in the early '70s, they never quite broke through into the mainstream. Nevertheless, their nasty fusion of heavy metal, glam rock and Bob Dylan's sneering hipster cynicism provided the groundwork for many British punk bands, most notably the Clash. At the center of Mott the Hoople was lead vocalist/pianist Ian Hunter, a late addition to the band who developed into its focal point as his songwriting grew. Hunter was able to subvert rock & roll conventions with his lyrics and the band, led by guitarist Mick Ralphs, had a tough, muscular sound that kept the band firmly in hard rock territory, even when they flirted with homosexual imagery and glammy makeup. However, the group's lack of success meant that they inevitably splintered apart in the '70s, with Ralphs forming Bad Company and Hunter launching a cult solo career. *—Stephen Thomas Erlewine*

Mott the Hoople / 1969 / Atlantic ✦✦✦✦
Enough works on Mott the Hoople's eponymous debut album, and enough is so imaginatively freewheeling, that it's easier to think of the record as a bit more successful than it actually is. After all, their combination of Stonesy swagger, Kinksian crunch, and Dylanesque cynicism is one of the great blueprints for hard rock, and its potential is apparent the moment their monumental instrumental "You Really Got Me" kicks off the record. This is followed by two covers, Doug Sahm's "At the Crossroads" and Sonny Bono's "Laugh at Me," that demonstrate their musicality more than their depth, since all three of these songs sound like they derive from the same vantage point. Then, to cap it off, Ian Hunter turns in "Backsliding Fearlessly" and Mick Ralphs gives Mott their first anthem with the pile-driving "Rock and Roll Queen." Up to this point, the album is wildly imaginative and invigorating, and that's enough to make this a fine debut, even if it falls off the tracks during the second side. The first side and those two originals reveal a band whose rowdy power is matched by sly humor, clever twists, and fierce intelligence—all qualities they built a career on, and this blueprint still stands the test of time. *—Stephen Thomas Erlewine*

Mad Shadows / 1970 / Atlantic ✦✦

Wildlife / 1971 / Atlantic ✦✦✦

Brain Capers / 1971 / Atlantic ✦✦✦✦✦
Re-teaming with producer Guy Stevens, Mott the Hoople delivered the great forgotten British hard rock album with their fourth album, *Brain Capers*. Stevens was a legendary rock & roll wild man and he kept Mott careening through their performances; they sound harder than ever, even dangerous at times. This fortunately coincided with Ian Hunter's emergence as a fantastic songwriter, as tuneful and clever as any of his peers. All these changes are evident from the moment *Brain Capers* kicks in with the monumental "Death May Be Your Santa Claus," a phenomenally pile-driving number that just seems *inevitable*. As it gives way to a cover of Dion's "Your Own Backyard," it becomes clear that Mott has pulled off the trick of being sensitive while still rocking. And that's not the end of it—they ride an epic wave on the nine-minute "The Journey," pull off a love song on "Sweet Angeline," and generally rock like hell throughout the record. The most amazing thing about the album is that none of the songs really change character—it's all straightforward hard rock, graced with Dylanesque organ—but there are all sorts of variations on that basic sound, proving how versatile they are. It's a fantastic album, the culmination of their early years. When a record this confident and tremendous is stiffed, it's little wonder they thought about chucking it all in; and it isn't a surprise that, when they decided to continue, it was with a change in sound. They couldn't have topped this if they tried. *—Stephen Thomas Erlewine*

☆ **All the Young Dudes** / 1972 / Columbia ✦✦✦✦✦
Just at the moment they were calling it a day, David Bowie swooped in and convinced them to stick around. Bowie spearheaded an image makeover, urging them to glam themselves up. He gave them a surefire hit with "All the Young Dudes," had them cover his idol's "Sweet Jane," and produced *All the Young Dudes*, the album that was designed to make them stars. Lo and behold, it did, which is as much a testament to Bowie's popularity as it is to his studio skill. Not to discount his assistance, since his production results in one of the most satisfying glam records and the title track is one of the all-time great rock songs, but the album wouldn't have worked if Mott hadn't already found its voice on *Brain Capers*. True, *Dudes* isn't nearly as wild as its predecessor, but the band's swagger is unmistakable underneath the flair and Hunter remains on a songwriting roll, with "Momma's Little Jewel," "Sucker," and "One of the Boys" standing among his best. Take a close look at the credits, though—these were all co-written by his bandmates, and the other highlight, "Ready for Love/After Lights," is penned entirely by Mick Ralphs who would later revive the first section with Bad Company. The entire band was on a roll here, turning out great performances, and writing with vigor. They may not be as sexy as either Bowie or Bolan, but they make up for it with knowing humor, huge riffs, and terrific tunes, dressed up with style by Ziggy himself. No wonder it's not just a great Mott record—it's one of the defining glam platters. *—Stephen Thomas Erlewine*

☆ **Mott** / 1973 / Columbia ✦✦✦✦✦
All the Young Dudes actually brought Mott the Hoople success, but you wouldn't know that from its sequel, *Mott*. Ian Hunter's songs are a set of road tales fraught with exhaustion, disillusionment, and dashed dreams, all told with a wry sense of humor so evident on Mott's earlier work. So, this is no ordinary road album, where a band whines about the perils of traveling—it's more of a wry commentary on rock & roll itself, which, as Hunter notes, is a "loser's game." *Mott* doesn't sound that way, though—it's as winning and infectious as rock & roll gets. Even with the undercurrents of ironic despair and restrained hostility, this is a fun record (partially *because* of that despair and hostility, of course). This sounds better, looser, than *All the Young Dudes*, as the band jives through "All the Way From Memphis" and "Honaloochie Boogie," beats the living hell outta "Violence," swaggers on "Whizz Kid," and simply drives it home on "Drivin' Sister." Apart from the New York Dolls (who, after all, were in a league of their own), glam never sounds as *rock* as it does here. To top it all off, Hunter writes the best lament for rock ever with "Ballad of Mott the Hoople," a song that conveys just how heartbreaking rock & roll is for the average band. If that wasn't enough, he *trumps* that song with the closer "I Wish I Was Your Mother," a peerless breakup song that still surprises, even after it's familiar. It's a graceful, unexpected way to close a record that stands as one of the best of its era. *—Stephen Thomas Erlewine*

The Hoople / 1974 / Columbia ✦✦✦✦✦
Mott was so good that the sequel, appropriately named *The Hoople*, has been unfairly dismissed as not living up to the group's promise. Yes, it doesn't compare to its predecessor, but most records don't. The bigger problem is that Mick Ralphs chose to leave during the supporting tour for *Mott*, leaving Ian Hunter as the undisputed leader of the group and subtly changing the character of the band's sound. Even with Hunter as the band's main songwriter, Ralphs helped shape their musical direction, so without a collaborator in hand, Hunter was left without a center. So, it isn't surprising that the record seems a little uneven, both in terms of songwriting and sound, but it's hardly without merit. "Roll Away the Stone," a leftover from *Mott*, is first-rate; "Crash Street Kidds" rocks viciously; "The Golden Age of Rock & Roll" is a pleasant spin on Bowie-esque nostalgia (think "Drive-In Saturday"); and Overend Watts follows through on that theme with "Born Late '58," a perfectly credible rocker. This all makes *The Hoople* an entertaining listen, even if it doesn't compare to Mott's earlier masterpieces. *—Stephen Thomas Erlewine*

Drive On / 1975 / Columbia ✦

Shouting and Pointing / 1976 / Columbia ✦

★ **The Ballad of Mott: A Retrospective** / Jun. 15, 1993 / Columbia/Legacy ✦✦✦✦✦
Mott the Hoople were punks without realizing it. Combining a heavy-metal roar with the sneering hipster stance of 1965 Bob Dylan, Mott the Hoople made some of the best, most original rock & roll of the early '70s. This two-disc set chronicles their Columbia recordings, with four tracks from their early Atlantic albums thrown in for good measure. Because of David Bowie's production of *All the Young Dudes* and their stage costumes, Mott was tossed into the glam rock scene, but their music was often wittier and meaner than other glam rock bands. This made the group an enormous element in the punk/new wave movement. Although it isn't definitive because it doesn't contain enough material from *Mott the Hoople* or *Brain Capers, The Ballad of Mott* is all the Mott most people will need. Nearly all of the songs from their two classic Columbia albums, *All the Young Dudes* and *Mott*, are included, as is a generous selection of tracks from *The Hoople* and a number of B-sides and unreleased tracks. While the band didn't receive much attention at the time, their music still sounds vital over 20 years later. *—Stephen Thomas Erlewine*

Backsliding Fearlessly: The Early Years / Apr. 19, 1994 / Rhino ✦✦✦✦✦
A compilation of 16 songs from their first four albums, covering their strongest material from the records pre-dating their *All the Young Dudes* breakthrough. This shows the band casting about, sometimes wildly, for an identity. The earliest tunes (including a cover of Sonny Bono's "Laugh at Me") are perhaps the most blatant imitations of Dylan's *Blonde on Blonde* period ever attempted. Subsequent efforts found them getting into boogie and hard rock, with a few Stones riffs copped here and there. The gut-stomping "Death May Be Your Santa Claus" is a highlight, and Ian Hunter's piano-based ballad "When My Mind's Gone" hints at the more complex psychological territory he'd explore during Mott's prime. This isn't bad and is often interesting, but it is neither very similar to Mott's best work, nor nearly as good as Mott's best stuff. Weirdest cut: a cover of Melanie's "Lay Down." But where is their instrumental version of "You Really Got Me"— *Richie Unterberger*

Bob Mould

b. 1961, Malone, NY
Vocals, Guitar / College Rock, Indie Rock, Alternative Pop/Rock, Singer/Songwriter
Guitarist/singer/songwriter Bob Mould was initially a member of Hüsker Dü, one of the most influential American bands of the '80s. Hüsker Dü was a post-hardcore punk band that helped define the sound and ideals of alternative rock. After Hüsker Dü broke up, Bob Mould signed a solo contract with Virgin in 1988 and released his first solo album, *Workbook*, one year later. A major shift in sonic direction, the album was an introspective collection, featuring keyboards, acoustic guitars, and even strings. Mould returned to loud, guitar-driven rock on his second solo album, 1990's *Black Sheets of Rain*. In 1992, he formed a new group named Sugar. Their debut album, *Copper Blue*, became Mould's most successful project to date. The second Sugar album, 1994's *File Under: Easy Listening*, received good reviews but didn't match the performance of *Copper Blue*. By 1995, Mould had broken up the band and begun to work on a third album entirely by himself. Mould played all of the instruments on his self-titled third album, which was released in the spring of 1996. *The Last Dog and Pony Show* followed in 1998. *—Stephen Thomas Erlewine*

● **Workbook** / Apr. 1989 / Virgin ✦✦✦✦✦
Arriving after years of sonic bombast in Hüsker Dü, the reflective, acoustic nature of Bob Mould's first solo album, *Workbook*, was a bold statement of renewal. Like all of Mould's work, it's an intensely introspective record, finding him purging demons left over from the dissolution of Hüsker Dü. Instead of relying on raging guitars, Mould explores a wide variety of styles, from pure pop ("See a Little Light") to reflective folk laced with cellos. It's an astonishing array of styles, and the songs are among Mould's finest. For many observers, the record established him as a major songwriter, but it also established a way for underground post-punk artists to mature—echoes of *Workbook* could be heard throughout the '90s, from R.E.M.'s elegiac *Automatic for the People* to Nirvana's use of cellos on *In Utero* and *Unplugged*. But *Workbook* remains a stunning work of individuality, marrying a distinctive body of songs with an original musical vision. Occasionally, the production is a little too pristine, but the power of the songs can not be diminished. *—Stephen Thomas Erlewine*

Black Sheets of Rain / May 1990 / Virgin ✦✦✦

Poison Years / Jul. 26, 1994 / Virgin ✦✦✦

Bob Mould / Apr. 30, 1996 / Rykodisc ✦✦✦✦✦
As he was promoting the last Sugar album, *File Under: Easy Listening*, Bob Mould hinted that he was tired of working with a band and was fascinated by the simple, four-track recordings of Sebadoh and Guided By Voices. So, it didn't come as a complete surprise when he disbanded Sugar a year after the release of *FU:EL* and began working on a record by himself. *Bob Mould*, his third solo album, was recorded entirely by Mould, but it doesn't sound like a lo-fi project—it doesn't have the professional production of Sugar's records, but it has all their sonic detail. What has changed is the details themselves. *Bob Mould* may not surge on waves of loud guitars like Hüsker Dü or Sugar, but Mould is reaching into new territory, using distortion as a coloring device and exploring trancier melodies. And Mould sounds revitalized throughout the album—although it is clear that this isn't a collection of first-takes, his obsession with making the album entirely on his own makes the music fierce and alive. Mould may be heading further into singer/songwriter territory with each album he releases, but he keeps his music away from stodginess by continually changing his approach and delving new sonic territories. It also doesn't hurt that his increasingly bitter lyrics are gut-wrenchingly provocative and his melodies are consistently engaging. *—Stephen Thomas Erlewine*

The Last Dog & Pony Show / Aug. 25, 1998 / Rykodisc ✦✦✦✦
Just before *The Last Dog and Pony Show* hit the streets, Bob Mould announced that his supporting tour would be the last time he hit the road with a full electric band. From this point on, he would be challenging himself, finding different musical avenues to explore and leaving his trademark tower of guitars behind. Presumably, this also meant that *The Last Dog and Pony Show* would be the recorded farewell to this sound, and it is indeed an excellent consolidation of all of his musical quirks and signatures. *The Last Dog and Pony Show* is the work of a craftsman, not a nakedly emotional confessional like *Workbook* or *Bob Mould*. That's not to say the album is lightweight, since seriousness is one of Mould's signatures, but there is a sense of humor that hasn't been heard since Sugar, and he, overall, sounds more relaxed than he has in years. He's so relaxed, in fact, that he lets down his guard on the cheerfully ridiculous pseudo-rap "Megamanic," the only track on *Show* that offers a musical departure from Mould's past. The rest of the record is clearly a Mould album, from the rushing rockers to the impassioned acoustic ballads, but the craft in both the songwriting and the production guarantees that the music never sounds like a retread, even if it does sound familiar. And that's not a bad way to draw to a close the first part of his career, if Mould does indeed turn his back on his signature sound. *—Stephen Thomas Erlewine*

The Move

f. 1966, **db.** 1972
Group / British Psychedelia, Psychedelic Pop, Psychedelic, British Invasion, Prog Rock/Art Rock, Rock & Roll
The Move were the best and most important British group of the late '60s that never made a significant dent in the American market. Through the band's several phases (which were sometimes dictated more by image than musical direction), their chief asset was guitarist and songwriter Roy Wood, who combined a knack for Beatlesque pop with a peculiarly British, and occasionally morbid, sense of humor. On their final albums (with considerable input from Jeff Lynne), the band became artier and more ambitious, hinting at the orchestral rock that Wood and Lynne would devise for the Electric Light Orchestra. The Move, however, always placed more emphasis on the pop than the art, and never lost sight of their hardcore rock & roll roots.

Formed from several established Birmingham groups, the band moved to London and crafted an explosive live act with early singles heavily influenced by mod pop in their chunky chords and oddball character sketches. With Wood handling all of the writing, the group's first four singles ("Night of Fear," "I Can Hear the Grass Grow," "Flowers in the Rain," and "Fire Brigade") all made the British Top Ten in 1967-68. They topped the British charts for the only time in 1969 with one of their best songs, "Blackberry Way," a kind of black-humored flipside to "Penny Lane." The group's second album, *Shazam* (1970), was one of their best, allowing them to stretch out in more progressive and experimental directions than they could within the format of hit singles. A rapid succession of personnel changes made the Move, if anything, a more interesting group in the early '70s. This was due primarily to the addition of Jeff Lynne, whose cheerier pop inclinations would effectively counterpoint Wood's darker and more ironic compositions for the later albums *Looking On* (1971) and *Message from the Country* (1972). As a result of their increasing fascination with orchestral rock, Wood and Lynne discontinued the Move in the early '70s to form the Electric Light Orchestra. Wood left ELO in 1972 to pursue a career as a leader of Wizzard and as a solo artist. *—Richie Unterberger*

The Move / 1968 / Repertoire ✦✦✦✦
The Move's debut album was a solid effort of mod-pop-psychedelia, boasting a number of fine Roy Wood compositions: the British hits "Flowers in the Rain" and "Flower Brigade," the original version of "Cherry Blossom Clinic," and the lesser-known but equally worthy "Yellow Rainbow" and "Walk Upon the Water." The three routine covers (of Eddie Cochran, the Coasters, and Moby Grape) that pad the album dilute it only slightly. The German CD reissue adds seven bonus tracks from late-'60s singles, but if you can live with vinyl, you should still seek out the A&M double-LP compilation *The Best of the Move*, which has the entire debut album and even more of their late-'60s and early-'70s 45s. *—Richie Unterberger*

Something Else from the Move / 1968 / Regal Zonophone ✦✦✦
When the Move were reaching the peak of their popularity after a burst of fine psychedelic-tinged power pop singles, they issued this rather odd live five-song 12" EP consisting entirely of covers. If nothing else, it proves the Move were a dynamic live act with an eclectic range, to say the least, as they cover tunes by the Byrds, Love, Eddie Cochran, Jerry Lee Lewis, and Spooky Tooth on this set. They really burn it up, in fact, on the Byrds' "So You Want to Be a Rock and Roll Star" and Love's "Stephanie Knows Who," with spinning and frenetic guitar work. The rest of the set is more routine, coming off more as a tribute to some of their idiosyncratic favorites. *—Richie Unterberger*

☆ **Shazam** / 1970 / Repertoire ✦✦✦✦✦
The single most accomplished album to be recorded by any of the Birmingham rock bands (which include the Moody Blues), *Shazam* is sort of *Sgt. Pepper* with an attitude, a mixture of expansive progressive rock worthy of the Beatles and high energy music honed by years of playing loud on stage. The rendition of Tom Paxton's "The Last Thing on My Mind" pushes these guys simultaneously into Byrds and Jimi Hendrix territory, while "Beautiful Daughter"

is one of the most unabashedly pretty records of this era, and "Cherry Blossom Clinic Revisited" is defiantly strange. The album only exists as an import from Japan, paired up on one CD with the earlier *Flowers in the Rain* album (all songs in print domestically or a better German version filled out with five live tracks from London's Marquee Club, off of the super-rare *Something Else* EP). *—Bruce Eder*

Looking On / 1971 / Repertoire ✦✦✦
Probably their weakest album, finding the group trying to blend progressive elements with lumpy hard rock boogie on obscure, extended tracks. The songs do look forward to the Electric Light Orchestra, for good or ill, in the helium-like high harmonies and the wide palette of instruments. Most of the multi-instrumentation is provided by Roy Wood, who picks up oboe, sitar, slide guitar, cello, and saxophone in addition to his usual guitar chores. Includes the British Top Ten single "Brontosaurus." *—Richie Unterberger*

Message from the Country / 1971 / BGO ✦✦✦✦✦

BBC Sessions / 1994 / Band of Joy ✦✦✦

★ **Great Move! The Best of the Move** / Jun. 15, 1994 / EMI America ✦✦✦✦✦
The title is really a misnomer; it includes much of the best of the Move, but can hardly stake a claim as a definitive collection, as it only covers their final years in the early '70s. Which isn't to say it isn't good. This is basically a spruced-up version of their final album, *Message From the Country* (1971), with the addition of five bonus tracks from early-'70s singles. *Message From the Country* itself was an erratic affair, alternating between lumbering forays into hard rock, revivalist roots rock, and country, and some of Roy Wood and Jeff Lynne's most inspired Beatlesque progressive compositions. The singles, most of which were previously issued on the *Split Ends* compilation, include some of their most memorable moments. "Tonight" (a British hit) is Roy Wood at his most tuneful, wistful, and folk-rockish; "Chinatown," though not quite as good (and not quite as big a British hit), is in much the same vein; and "Do Ya," redone with much more success by ELO, is one of their catchiest all-out rockers. Wood also gets into heavy sounds on the Top Ten British hit "California Man." Includes informative liner notes by respected rock critic Ira Robbins. *—Richie Unterberger*

Movements / 1997 / West Side ✦✦✦✦✦
This may be more Move than the casual fan wants, but it's not just another rehashed collection. From the remastered sound to the presence of various outtakes (including lost live tracks), the 30th anniversary triple-disc *Movements* is as definitive a set as we'll ever have on this band, containing everything except for the *Message from the Country* album. Disc One consists of the group's early singles plus *The Move* album and one outtake ("Disturbance"), all sounding really clear and tough, the loudest pop-psychedelic music you'll ever hear out of England. Disc Two contains the complete *Shazam* album, as well as alternate stereo or undubbed mixes of such songs as "Cherry Blossom Clinic," "(Here We Go Round) The Lemon Tree," and "Fire Brigade," and an Italian-sung version of "Something." The sound is okay, with brilliant delineation on the guitars and basses, but not quite the revelation that one would hope (20-bit remastering would have been a real treat on *Shazam*). "Wild Tiger Woman Blues" is worth the price of this disc by itself, and the early version of "Curly" is lots of fun, while the undubbed "Fire Brigade" is raw and punkish. Disc Three starts off with the complete *Looking On* album, which still lacks some presence, but is the best version yet heard. The real deal here, however, is the first-ever CD version of the live *Something Else* EP remastered from the original live tapes. The notes by John Platt are pretty cool, too, and coupled with the remastered *Message from the Country*, this set pretty well closes the books on the Move, as far as reissues of fully authorized stuff goes. *—Bruce Eder*

★ **Omnibus: The 60's Singles A's & B's** / Aug. 24, 1999 / Edsel ✦✦✦✦✦
Subtitled "The 60s Singles As and Bs," here's almost all the Move you'll ever need. If you're a fan of '60s British pop with alternating heavy dashes of psychedelia and '50s retro-rock thrown in, the Move were the perfect embodiment of that odd blend. For newcomers, this is the group that Jeff Lynne later joined which permutated into the Electric Light Orchestra after scoring one last hit as the Move with the two-sided killer "Do Ya" b/w "California Man," both outside the timeline of this package, thus making it sadly incomplete. But the 20 tracks aboard are the original group with Carl Wayne and deliver all the other hits, B-sides, and even include two bonus tracks, an Italian version of "Something" and the withdrawn B-side "Vote for Me." Fans of the early Who will go bonkers for this one, solid Brit pop all the way. *—Cub Koda*

Mudhoney

f. 1988, Seattle, WA
Group / Garage Punk, Grunge, Alternative Pop/Rock
With their fuzzed-out guitars and Mark Arm's straining vocals, Mudhoney defined '80s and '90s grunge rock. In fact, their 1988 debut single "Touch Me, I'm Sick" is the definitive grunge song—an obnoxious, dirty song driven by massively distorted guitars and a screaming vocal. It was a terrific, invigorating song that the band rewrote on each album that followed, but that's alright because Mudhoney only has one other song—a slow, sludgy Stooges grind. But their limitations are ultimately endearing; The band is a punk band, not like a '70s or '80s group, but like a '60s garage band, kicking out the same three chords with an unbridled enthusiasm. Leave the serious themes to Nirvana, Pearl Jam, Soundgarden, and Alice in Chains—Mudhoney takes the same themes but makes them sleazy and trashy, like the Russ Meyer film they named themselves after. Their records are inconsistent but when they are good, they are great. *—Stephen Thomas Erlewine*

Superfuzz Bigmuff (& Early Singles) / 1988 / Sub Pop ✦✦✦✦✦
Named after the band's favorite distortion pedal, *Superfuzz Bigmuff* was actually Mudhoney's first EP; the *Superfuzz Bigmuff (Plus Early Singles)* package collects that recording, as well as the A- and B-sides of their first two 45s and two covers (of the Dicks and Sonic Youth), all released in 1988-89. Taken as a whole, this output makes a case for Mudhoney as the first true grunge band; due to the time constraints of the forms in which this material was originally released, it also makes for their best, most consistent album, as the band largely refrains from the sort of aimless, grinding Stooges updates that slow the momentum of most of their records. Instead, *Superfuzz Bigmuff* has all the best attributes of Mudhoney's Stooges fixation—whether slow or fast, this music is grimy, raucous, and violently enthusiastic, with a stronger melodic sensibility than Iggy's band possessed. Mudhoney's dominant traits are simple chord progressions and a filthy-sounding, ultra-distorted guitar racket, punctuated by Mark Arm's snarling, demonic howls. It isn't the most original approach to rock & roll, but when it all comes into focus—as on their (and Sub Pop's) debut single, the ultimate grunge anthem "Touch Me I'm Sick"—Mudhoney's power is absolutely throttling. "Touch Me I'm Sick" would be essential listening for anyone even remotely interested in the genesis of the Seattle scene, but the album is full of menacing, vital rock & roll, plus sharp songwriting that elevates several other songs to classic status. Mudhoney's musical range may be quite limited, but as *Superfuzz Bigmuff* proves, they can be amazing at what they can do. This is the birth of grunge, and a reminder of exactly why the music was christened with a word meaning "dirt." *—Steve Huey*

Mudhoney / Jul. 1989 / Sub Pop ✦✦✦

Every Good Boy Deserves Fudge / Jul. 26, 1991 / Sub Pop ✦✦✦✦

Piece of Cake / Oct. 1992 / Reprise ✦✦✦

Five Dollar Bob's Mock Cooter Stew / Oct. 26, 1993 / Reprise ✦✦✦

My Brother the Cow / Mar. 28, 1995 / Reprise ✦✦✦✦
Mudhoney didn't invent grunge, but they were one of the first bands to truly define the style, and thanks to the bizarro-world logic that has defined their career, they seemed to loose interest in the stuff once you could actually make serious money playing it, ensuring that they wouldn't have to deal with the mainstream adulation that made followers like Nirvana, Pearl Jam, and Soundgarden into multi-platinum cash cows. By 1995, grunge's brief fling on the charts was pretty much over–just in time for Mudhoney to decide they liked the stuff again, and make the finest album of their career, *My Brother the Cow*. On *My Brother the Cow*, Mudhoney finally found a noisy middle ground where their fondness for Billy Childish and Blue Cheer could peacefully co-exist, and the songs are less sludgy and more driving than their early classics, but with enough cheap stomp-box thunder to remind you of who's playing. A few years on the road had made Mudhoney a much stronger and tighter band, able to fully grasp the hard rock guitar figures they dearly loved to mock, but without falling into big rock pomp. And they came up with a dozen tunes that gave them plenty of room to sneer brilliantly (one of their greatest gifts), especially "Generation Spokesmodel," "F.D.K. (Fearless Doctor Killers)," and "Into Yer Shtik" (in which some nameless rock scene figure is advised to "blow your brains out too"). And as icing on the cake, the CD has the greatest hidden bonus track of all time. For better or worse, Mudhoney always played their game their own way, and they never played it better than on *My Brother the Cow*. *—Mark Deming*

Tomorrow Hit Today / Sep. 22, 1998 / Reprise ✦✦✦✦

● **March to Fuzz** / Jan. 18, 2000 / Sub Pop ✦✦✦✦✦
Mudhoney was most convincing when the 7" recording format limited their more indulgent tendencies. In general (especially early on), their albums were always peppered with great songs—usually variations on the band's trademark scuzzy sound and sneering attitude—but rarely sustained momentum all the way through, thanks in part to the band's weakness for ponderous jams. The sorely needed, two-disc best-of *March to Fuzz* attempts to have it both ways: The first disc is a generous, 22-track overview of their recordings from 1988-1998, while the second compiles 30 rarities for the devotees. It's a tactic that's been used before, and it's usually maddening, giving both casual and die-hard fans an entire disc they don't want. But *March to Fuzz* actually works very well. For one, it's not priced as a double-disc set, and for another, both discs are actually very strong. Mudhoney's sound didn't change very much over the course of their career, which means that even though disc one isn't arranged chronologically, everything is pretty much of a piece. It's also very well-chosen, even if the surprisingly strong latter-day albums *My Brother the Cow* and *Tomorrow Hit Today* aren't heavily represented. But the disc makes a convincing case that Mudhoney never stopped making bruising, vital rock & roll, or writing great (albeit samey) songs. The rarities disc is surprisingly entertaining, featuring plenty of cover versions, cranky goofs, and songs that were certainly better than some of their album tracks, but were relegated to B-sides or indie compilations. Their '60s garage and surf roots are actually summed up very effectively here, as well as their love of early-'80s hardcore. *March to Fuzz* might be a little hard to handle all in one sitting, but it's hard to imagine a better overview of Mudhoney's career. *—Steve Huey*

The Music Machine

Group / Garage Rock, Psychedelic
Most famous for "Talk Talk," a Top 20 single from 1966 that was one of the most manic '60s garage-punk hits, the Music Machine had much more depth and songwriting talent than the typical one-hit wonders of the day. Lead singer and songwriter Sean Bonniwell's strangled lyrics and dark, verbose vision paced the group's wiry psychedelic guitar lines and ominous, minor-key Farfisa organ. Only one album was released with the original lineup, and the group's ferocious energy was diluted on subsequent recordings. Despite chalking up only one more minor hit single ("The People in Me"), the Music Machine recorded quite a few excellent, imaginatively produced singles and album tracks that found them exploring the darker side of psychedelia with compelling intensity and imagination. *—Richie Unterberger*

(Turn On) The Music Machine / 1966 / Original Sound ✦✦✦

Bonniwell's Music Machine / 1967 / Warner Brothers ✦✦✦

● **The Best of the Music Machine** / 1984 / Rhino ✦✦✦✦✦
Besides "Talk Talk" and "The People in Me," this features the best cuts from their first LP, some fine non-LP singles that rank among the best obscure gems of the psychedelic era, and some decent previously unissued cuts. The package is enhanced by detailed liner notes by Sean Bonniwell. *—Richie Unterberger*

Turn On: The Best of the Music Machine / Mar. 23, 1999 / Collectables ✦✦✦✦✦
This album contains all 12 tracks from the Music Machine's 1966 debut album, *(Turn On) The*

Music Machine (Original Sound 5015), including their two chart singles, "Talk Talk" and "The People in Me," plus both sides of both of their third and fourth singles, "Double Yellow Line"/"Absolutely Positive" and "I've Loved You"/"The Eagle Never Hunts the Fly." This is the group's entire output for Original Sound Records; they switched to Warner Bros. in 1967 and changed their personnel and their name, to Bonniwell's Music Machine. Singer/guitarist/songwriter Sean Bonniwell dominates the proceedings with his sonorous voice, whether the band is playing originals like the unforgettable garage rock classic "Talk Talk" or such covers as the Beatles' "Taxman" and fellow garage dwellers ? and the Mysterians' "96 Tears." The playing is rudimentary, but more disciplined than that of many of the rock bands that came into existence in the mid-'60s, and Bonniwell's songwriting is so sufficiently varied that it is regrettable the group didn't get much of a chance beyond its initial hit. *—William Ruhlmann*

Ignition / Jun. 27, 2000 / Sundazed ✦✦✦
As this has a mixture of rare singles and unreleased tracks from 1965-1969, it's primarily for converted Music Machine fans, not for those who want just one album by the group or a place to start investigation. That said, it's a pretty interesting assortment of odds and ends, a few of which are among the band's best efforts. Foremost among them is the explosive (and quite innovative for its time) 1966 number "Point of No Return" with its unusual mixture of folk-rock and pre-acid guitar work, as well as a magnificent anguished, subtly anti-war vocal by singer and songwriter Sean Bonniwell. The moody, building-from-a-smolder-to-a-roar "Dark White," a 1969 outtake, was already heard on the out-of-print Rhino best-of LP. It's also one of Bonniwell's better creations, as well as one of the best lyrical meditations upon the ambiguous tension of sexual desire that you're likely to hear. "Advise and Consent" is a decent obscure flop single, though not one of the group's greatest. As for the previously unveiled outings, the 1965 demos by the Ragamuffins (the trio of future Music Machine members Bonniwell, drummer Ron Edgar, and bassist Keith Olsen) are especially interesting, catching them in their tentative transition from folk-pop to garage psychedelia. "Citizen Fear," one of the latest tracks (from 1969), has the careering sonics and intriguing sociometaphysical (if that's a word) words typical of Bonniwell's better songs. Much of the rest, though, is simply not up to the caliber of the band's best stuff. Still, it's a worthy complement to the *(Turn On) The Music Machine* album and Sundazed's previous collection of lesser-known material, *Beyond the Garage*. *—Richie Unterberger*

My Bloody Valentine

f. 1984, Dublin, Ireland
Group / Dream Pop, Shoegazing, Alternative Pop/Rock
Like the Velvet Underground, Sonic Youth, and the Jesus & Mary Chain before them, My Bloody Valentine redefined what noise meant within the context of pop songwriting. Led by guitarist Kevin Shields, the group released several EPs in the mid-'80s before recording the era-defining *Isn't Anything* in 1988, a record that merged lilting, ethereal melodies of the Cocteau Twins with crushingly loud, shimmering distortion. Though My Bloody Valentine rejected rock & roll conventions, it didn't subscribe to the precious tendencies of anti-rock art-pop bands. Instead, it rode crashing waves of white noise to unpredictable conclusions, particularly since their noise wasn't paralyzing like the typical avant-garde noise rock band: It was translucent, glimmering, and beautiful. Shields was a perfectionist, especially when it came to recording, as much of My Bloody Valentine's sound was conceived within the studio itself. Nevertheless, the band was known as a formidible live act, even though they rarely moved, or even looked at the audience, while they were on stage. Their notorious lack of movement was branded "shoegazing" by the British music press, and soon there were legions of other shoegazers—Ride, Lush, the Boo Radleys, Chapterhouse, Slowdive—that, along with the rolling dance-influenced Madchester scene, dominated British indie rock of the late '80s and early '90s. As shoegazing reached its peak in 1991, My Bloody Valentine released *Loveless*, which broke new sonic ground and was hailed as a masterpiece. Though the band was poised for a popular breakthrough, they disappeared into the studio and didn't emerge over the next five years, leaving behind a legacy that proved profoundly influential in the direction of '90s alternative rock. *—Stephen Thomas Erlewine*

Isn't Anything / 1988 / Creation/Sire ✦✦✦✦✦
Though it's often seen as just a precursor to their magnum opus *Loveless*, in its own way, My Bloody Valentine's *Isn't Anything* is nearly as groundbreaking as their 1991 masterpiece. Not only was it the most lucid, expansive articulation yet of the group's sound, it virtually created the shoegazing scene and spawned legions of followers. The album's tightly structured songs still bore traces of My Bloody Valentine's previous incarnation as jangly indie popsters, but Kevin Shields and company crafted wide-ranging experiments within those confines. "Feed Me With Your Kiss"'s mix of bruising guitars, drums, and sensual boy-girl vocals define My Bloody Valentine's signature sound, while "All I Need"'s weightless guitars and vocal melodies melt into a heady haze. Shields' unique tunings, tremolo, and micing techniques stand out on "You Never Should" and "Nothing Much to Lose," but Deb Googe's surprisingly funky bass line on "Soft As Snow (But Warm Inside)" reaffirms that all of the Valentines contributed to their innovative sound. Indeed, many of *Isn't Anything*'s disturbingly beautiful highlights come from Blinda Butcher. On the wrenching "No More Sorry," she sings abstractly pained lyrics like "Your septic heart and deadly hand/Loved me black and blue," barely audible over a swarm of fragile yet menacing guitars, while on "Several Girls Galore," she's sexy, yet dazed and distant; it sounds like she's whispering in your ear outside of a blaring nightclub. The Valentines' dark side is especially prominent on the album, particularly on "Sueisfine," where the chorus slyly morphs from "Sue is fine" to "Suicide." *Isn't Anything* captures My Bloody Valentine's revolutionary style in its infancy and points the way to *Loveless*, but it's far more than just a dress rehearsal for the band's moment of greatness. *—Heather Phares*

Ecstasy & Wine / 1989 / Lazy ✦✦✦✦

Glider [EP] / 1989 / Sire ✦✦✦✦

★ **Loveless** / Nov. 5, 1991 / Sire ✦✦✦✦✦
Isn't Anything was good enough to inspire an entire scene of My Bloody Valentine soundalikes, but *Loveless*' greatness proved that the band was inimitable. After two painstaking years in the studio and nearly bankrupting their label Creation in the process, the group emerged with their masterpiece, which fulfilled all of the promise of their previous albums. If *Isn't Anything* was the Valentines' sonic blueprint, then *Loveless* saw those plans fleshed out, in the most literal sense: "Loomer," "What You Want," and "To Here Knows When"'s arrangements are so lush, they're practically tangible. With its voluptuous yet ethereal melodies and arrangements, *Loveless* intimates sensuality and sexuality instead of stating them explicitly; Kevin Shields and Blinda Butcher's vocals meld perfectly with the trippy sonics around them, suggesting druggy sex or sexy drugs. From the commanding "Only Shallow" and "Come in Alone" to breathy reflections like "Sometimes" and "Blown a Wish," the album balances complexity and immediately memorable pop melodies with remarkable self-assurance, given its difficult creation. But *Loveless* doesn't just perfect the group's approach, it also hints at their continuing growth: "Soon" fuses the Valentines' roaring guitars with a dance-inspired beat, while the symphonic interlude "Touched" suggests an updated take on Fripp and Eno's pioneering guitar/electronics experiments. These glimpses into the band's evolution make Shields' difficulty in delivering a follow-up to *Loveless* even more frustrating, but completely understandable—the album's perfection sounded shoegazing's death-knell and raised expectations for the next My Bloody Valentine album to unreasonably high levels. Though Shields' collaborations with Yo La Tengo, Primal Scream, J. Mascis, and others were often rewarding, they were no match for *Loveless*. However, as My Bloody Valentine fans—and, apparently, Shields himself—will attest, nothing is. *—Heather Phares*

'N Sync

Group / Teen Pop, Euro-Dance, Adult Contemporary, Dance-Pop
Like the Backstreet Boys before them, the teenage male vocal group 'N Sync emerged from Orlando, Florida; though formed in 1996, their roots trace back much earlier to singers JC Chasez and Justin Timberlake, who together previously co-starred on the Disney Channel's *The Mickey Mouse Club* before later relocating to Nashville, where they worked on solo projects with the same vocal coach and songwriters. Timberlake soon returned to Orlando, where he befriended Chris Kirkpatrick and Joey Fatone; with Chasez, the four agreed to form a band, and with the addition of bass James Lance Bass, 'N Sync was complete. Hooking up with a series of producers including Denniz Pop, the group recorded their self-titled debut LP, initially released on BMG Ariola Munich; 'N Sync soon became an overnight success throughout much of Europe, with the singles "I Want You Back" and "Tearing Up My Heart" both becoming major hits. The album was released in the U.S. in the spring of 1998, and—accompanied by a tour of the nation's roller rinks—it became an American hit as well; *Home for Christmas* followed later that same year, and in the spring of 2000, the group broke sales records with *No Strings Attached*, which sold close to 2.5 million copies in its first week of release. *—Jason Ankeny*

'N Sync / Mar. 24, 1998 / RCA ✦✦✦
Riding the wave of post-Spice Girls dance-pop groups and sounding suspiciously like a low-rent, American Take That, the Orlando, Florida-based'N Sync came bursting out of roller rinks across the U.S. in the spring of 1998 with their eponymous debut. The group hired a number of producers, including the Backstreet Boys' Kristian Lundin and Denniz Pop & Max Martin, the team behind Robyn and Ace of Base, who help turn the album into a pleasing piece of ear candy. They don't have the charisma or tunes of the Spice Girls or All Saints, nor do they have a visionary like Gary Barlow or a sex symbol like Robbie Williams in the group. The only thing the five boys of 'N Sync have is good looks, good producers, and a couple of catchy singles, like "I Want You Back." That's enough for a hit, and not quite enough for an album. Even so, the filler is well-made and competently performed, which means their teen fans will enjoy the album while it's hot. Whether they return to it again—either out of affection or kitsch—is another matter entirely. *—Stephen Thomas Erlewine*

● **No Strings Attached** / Mar. 21, 2000 / Jive ✦✦✦✦
Prior to the release of their second album, 'N Sync split from their manager in a bitter dispute and signed with Jive, the kings of teen-pop. For 'N Sync, the move provided them with an opportunity to, in the immortal words of George W. Bush, "define themselves," to prove that they were an independent unit—hence the title *No Strings Attached*. To cynical critics, they very well might sound the same as ever, yet this really blows away their previous record. That much is clear from the storming lead single "Bye Bye Bye," a pile-driving dance number with the catchiest chorus they've ever sang. However, the album isn't really just singles-n-filler, it actually is well-sequenced and fairly balanced, much like the Backstreet Boys' *Millennium* or Christina Aguilera's album. Like those records, *No Strings Attached* pulls away from the standard dance-pop formula, strengthening it with harder street beats, electronica flourishes, ballads with some grit, and well-crafted pop tunes. Nobody is going to mistake this for Fatboy Slim, Beck, or TLC—it's still lightweight teen pop. Yet, it's very good teen pop, managing to not only work well within its limitations, but to push it slightly while retaining its breezy, hooky identity. 'N Sync still can seem a little ordinary, lacking a truly charismatic punch ála Britney or Christina, yet they do deserve credit for shaking things up a little bit, since it's resulted in an effervescent, ingratiatingly cheerful album that's a vast improvement on the debut. *—Stephen Thomas Erlewine*

The Nazz

f. 1967, Philadelphia, PA, **db.** 1969
Group / Power Pop, Psychedelic
Inspired by a variety of British Invasion groups, from the omnipresent Beatles to the cult favorites the Move, Todd Rundgren and his Woody's Truck Stop colleague Carson Van Osten formed the Nazz in 1967. Taking their name from an obscure Yardbirds song, the Nazz were arguably the first Anglophiles in rock history. There had been many groups that drew inspiration from the Beatles and the Stones, but none had been so self-consciously reverent as the Nazz. One of their first singles, "Open My Eyes," twisted the riff from the Who's "I Can't Explain," and much of their music felt like homages to Brit-rock from the Kinks to Cream, thereby setting a precedent that was followed by scores of North American guitar-pop bands from the Raspberries to Sloan. *—Stephen Thomas Erlewine*

● **Nazz** / 1968 / Rhino ✦✦✦✦
Though many of their American peers interpreted the sounds of the British Invasion in different ways, the Nazz's take on jangly guitar pop and nascent heavy psychedelia turned into a blueprint for the American Anglophile power-pop guitar bands that followed in the '70s. Which is why the Nazz's eponymous debut album is still a fascinating listen, even if portions of the record haven't dated particularly well. Ironically, one of the songs that hasn't aged well is "Hello, It's Me," a ballad that Todd Rundgren later turned into a contemporary standard. It fails here because its dirgey arrangement meanders—something that can't be said for the rest of *Nazz*. That's not to say that the band knows exactly where they're going, since it often seems like they don't; they just like to try a lot of different styles, cross-breeding their favorite bands in a blatant act of fanboy worship. At their best, the results of this approach are flat-out stunning, as on the lead cut "Open My Eyes," which twists the Who's "I Can't Explain" around until it winds up in Roy Wood territory. While that may be the only undisputed classic on the record, almost everything else on the album will be interesting to listeners that are as obsessive about '60s Brit-rock as the Nazz themselves. It's great to hear Rundgren and lead vocalist Stewkey approximate the high-pitched harmonies of Cream on "Back of Your Mind," or hearing them swing through London on "See What You Can Be." It's possible that some pure pop fans will hear too much Cream and Hendrix on the record, but they're exceptional showpieces for Rundgren's fine guitar. And that's what shines through on *Nazz*—even when the record gets muddled, it's possible to hear the first flowering of Rundgren's talents. —*Stephen Thomas Erlewine*

Nazz Nazz / 1969 / Rhino ✦✦✦✦
Originally intended as a double album titled *Fungo Bat*, *Nazz Nazz* is at once as equally diverse and more cohesive than the Nazz's eponymous debut. It's a weird trick, but the group pulls it off, largely due to the rapidly maturing talents of Rundgren, their main songwriter and producer. Thorughout the Nazz's first record, he proved that he was a gifted mimic and a savvy melodicist, yet he never quite landed upon a signature style, outside of their debut single "Hello It's Me"/"Open My Eyes." Not coincidentally, these were the two songs on the record that the Nazz produced themselves, and they followed that lead on *Nazz Nazz*, fusing their sundry influences into a distinctive psych-pop sound. Sonically, it's certainly more ambitious than it's predecessor and, apart from the odd forays into soul and blues (filtered through Cream, naturally) on "Featherbedding Lover" and "Kiddie Boy," it's more consistent. In many ways, that makes *Nazz Nazz* a better listen than its predecessor, even if it doesn't have a knockout punch like "Open My Eyes." That's because Rundgren's songs exhibit a stronger sense of identity, as ballads like "Letters Don't Count" and snarky pop-rockers like "Hang on Paul" point the way toward his solo career. There are a few embarassing detours, such as the hippie-dippy "Meridian Leeward," but the second Nazz record rivals the first because it offers a progression. It shows that the band, or at least Rundgren, have figured out how to blend their influences into something original. The Nazz may never have delivered a follow-up to this—*Nazz III* consists of the remaining sessions from the abandoned double album—but this is certainly ground zero for Rundgren's fascinating solo career. —*Stephen Thomas Erlewine*

Nazz III / 1970 / Rhino ✦✦✦
Fungo Bat was scrapped for a variety of reasons, among them Todd Rundgren's insistence on singing lead vocals on his newer songs. *Nazz Nazz* was released instead, leaving the second half of the proposed LP temporarily in the vaults. Rundgren left the group before it was released. Taking hold of uncontested leadership of the group, lead vocalist Robert "Stewkey" Antoni erased Rundgren's lead vocals, replacing them with his own, releasing the entire project as *Nazz III*. This is, at the very least, sour grapes, but the situation is made all the more peculiar since much of the material finds Rundgren's songwriting moving toward the signature pop style that dominated his first solo records. Stewkey has publicly stated his distaste for Rundgren's Laura Nyro infatuation, so it's a little odd to hear him sing such finely crafted songs as "Only One Winner" and "Some People." That aside, *Nazz III* is an impressive effort that, if taken in conjunction, would have resulted in a very good double record. Sure, there's some clutter, but such detours as "Loosen Up," a po-faced parody of Archie Bell & the Drells' "Tighten Up," reveal the snotty side of Rundgren's humor. More importantly, the bulk of the record indicates how rapidly he was developing as a songwriter and a producer. Where he proved himself as a gifted mimick on *Nazz*, the group's second two albums found him assimilating those influences and developing a signature style. If anything, *Nazz III* demonstrates that better than its predecessor, which often seemed a little disjointed. There still isn't anything as immediate and indelible as "Open My Eyes," yet the best moments easily provide the road map for Rundgren's solo career. Even if he doesn't sing on it. —*Stephen Thomas Erlewine*

Rick Nelson (Eric Hilliard Nelson)

b. May 8, 1940, Teaneck, NJ, **d.** Dec. 31, 1985, DeKalb, TX
Vocals, Guitar / Teen Idol, Rockabilly, Country-Rock, Rock & Roll
Rick Nelson was one of the very biggest of the '50s teen idols, so it took a while for him to attain the same level of critical respectability as other early rock greats. Yet now the consensus is that he made some of the finest pop/rock recordings of his era. Sure, he had more promotional push than any other rock musician of the '50s; no, he wasn't the greatest singer; and yes, others rocked harder. But Nelson was extraordinarily consistent during the first five years of his recording career, crafting pleasant pop-rockabilly hybrids with ace session players, and projecting an archetype of the sensitive, reticent young adult with his accomplished vocals. He also played a somewhat underestimated role in rock & roll's absorption into mainstream America—how bad could rock be if it was featured on one of America's favorite family situation comedies on a weekly basis— Ricky could rock pretty hard when he wanted to, as on "Be-Bop Baby" and "Stood Up," though in a polished fashion that wasn't quite as wild and threatening as rockabilly's Southern originators. Nelson really hit his stride, though, with mid-tempo numbers and ballads that provided a more secure niche for his calm vocals and narrow range. From 1957 to 1962, he was about the highest-selling singer in the U.S. except for Elvis, making the Top 40 about 30 times. "Poor Little Fool" and "Lonesome Town" (1958) were early indications of his ballad style; in the early '60s, "Travelin' Man," "Young World," "Teen Age Idol," and other hits pointed to a more countrified, mature style as he honed in on his 21st birthday (by which time he would shorten his billing from "Ricky" to "Rick"). Nelson had a strong country feel to much of his material from the beginning, and by the late '60s it was becoming dominant. He formed one of the earliest country-rock groups, the Stone Canyon Band, and though a cover of Bob Dylan's "She Belongs to Me" made the Top 40 in 1970, his country-rock outings attracted more critical acclaim than commercial success, until 1972's "Garden Party." A rare self-composed number, based around the frosty reception granted his contemporary material at a rock & roll oldies show, it became his last Top Ten hit. —*Richie Unterberger*

★ **Legendary Masters** / 1990 / EMI America ✦✦✦✦✦
Legendary Masters compiles all of the hits Ricky Nelson released for Imperial Records in the late '50s, including "Be-Bop Baby," "Stood Up," "Lonesome Town," "It's Late," "Poor Little Fool," "Sweeter Than You," "Just a Little Too Much," "Never Be Anyone Else but You," and "Believe What You Say." A few essential items are missing—such as the Verve sides "A Teenager's Romance" and "I'm Walking"—and it would have been nice if the disc had extended into the early '60s, so songs like "Travelin' Man" and "Mary Lou" could have been included, but *Legendary Masters* remains a vital collection from one of the most undervalued early rock & rollers. —*Stephen Thomas Erlewine*

The Best of Rick Nelson, Vol. 2 / Mar. 18, 1991 / EMI America ✦✦✦✦✦
Focusing primarily on Rick's early-'60s material for Imperial, this 27-cut disc is not quite as rocking as *Volume One*, but still offers plenty of worthy moments. It includes all of his massive, mid-tempo teen idol ballad hits of the era: "Young World," "A Wonder Like You," "Teenage Idol," "It's Up to You," and the number one hit "Travelin' Man." Teen ballads they might have been, but James Burton's masterful guitar licks and Nelson's assured, committed delivery placed them leagues above other teen-idol hits of the period. Of more interest to serious fans are the inclusion of several minor hit singles and covers of R&B tunes. And of course, there's the first-class rockabilly hit "Hello Mary Lou" (penned by Gene Pitney), perhaps his best recording of the decade. His surprisingly raucous cover of "Summertime" features, amazingly, the same bass line used as a hook on the Blues Magoos' psych-pop-garage hit "We Ain't Got Anything Yet" years later. The pleasures of this CD are modest but consistent. —*Richie Unterberger*

Stay Young: The Epic Recordings / Aug. 31, 1993 / Epic ✦✦✦✦

Ricky Nelson & Stone Canyon Band / Apr. 25, 1995 / Edsel ✦✦✦✦✦

Rockin' with Ricky / 1996 / Ace ✦✦✦✦✦
Originally released as an LP in 1984, the CD version of this collection of Nelson's hardest-rocking early material doubles in length to include a whopping 32 tracks (on one disc) from the late '50s and early '60s. This has most of his up-tempo smashes, a la "Be-Bop Baby," "Waitin' in School," and "Believe What You Say," with a host of LP tracks, many of them covers of songs made famous by Elvis, Carl Perkins, Roy Orbison, and the like. The two volumes of greatest hits on EMI are more well-rounded, and on the whole better, retrospectives of his classic era. This is pretty good proof that he could rock respectably, though, with some good cuts that are hard to find on reissues, like "You're So Fine" and "Poor Loser." —*Richie Unterberger*

The Best of the Later Years (1963-1975) / 1997 / Ace ✦✦✦
On the surface, this would appear to have the advantage over its American counterpart (MCA's *Best of 1963-75* compilation). It's got far more material, for one thing: 26 songs, which is eleven more than the domestic retrospective. There are a couple of significant omissions of tracks that appear on the U.S. set, though, most notably the moody Billy Vera-penned "Mean Old World." Its absence from this anthology is inexcusable, as it was his best mid-'60s recording. Judgment calls aside, this does have the hits Nelson managed to squeeze in on Decca before the rise of the Beatles ("For You" and the great "Fools Rush In"), along with some rocking obscurities like "I Got a Woman" and "Gypsy Woman"; the ballads "The Very Thought of You," "I Wonder," and "There's Nothing I Can Say" are also quite good. After 1964 he slid into early country-rock, which veered from decent to dispensable. "Garden Party" is here, of course, but the additional late-'60s and early-'70s cuts not present on MCA's disc really don't add much. —*Richie Unterberger*

For Your Sweet Love/Sings for You / 1997 / Ace ✦✦✦

Very Thought of You/Spotlight on Rick / Dec. 9, 1997 / Ace ✦✦✦

Best Always/Love and Kisses / Mar. 10, 1998 / Ace ✦✦✦

Bright Lights & Country Music/Country Fever / Jun. 23, 1998 / Ace ✦✦✦
This is a reissue of the two albums—1966's *Bright Lights & Country Music*, and 1967's *Country Fever*—on which Nelson plunged for the first time into country music whole hog. On *Bright Lights* he still used his regular band, but augmented them with Glen Campbell and future Byrd Clarence White, and regular guitarist James Burton played dobro. It wasn't country-rock, but straight country without any Nashville gloss in the production, emphasizing covers of songs by Willie Nelson, Merle Travis, Bill Anderson, and Doug Kershaw. Nelson sounded more engaged with the material than he had in years and the album was a decent effort, but as it relied so heavily on songs that had already been made famous by others, it wasn't going to make him stand out as an innovator. Nelson acquitted himself well with his one original, "You Just Can't Quit," and Campbell contributed "Here I Am," yet the best cut was the fastest: "Night Train to Memphis." *Country Fever* was similarly weighted toward interpretations of country classics. Hank Williams, Jimmie Rodgers, and Acuff-Rose all get covered, and his sensitive reading of Willie Nelson's "Funny How Time Slips Away" was a standout. There's no denying, though, that the best cut is the one that gets closest to rockabilly (a cover of "Mystery Train"). Nelson's two original compositions weren't much, but on the other hand there was an obscure Bob Dylan tune that the composer had not released ("Walkin' Down the Line"), and "Things You Gave Me," with its steady beat and harmonies, sounded more like a foreshadowing of late-'60s California country-rock than anything else Nelson had recorded up to this point. —*Richie Unterberger*

Another Side of Rick/Perspective / Sep. 29, 1998 / Ace ✦✦✦

Legacy / Nov. 21, 2000 / Capitol ✦✦✦✦✦
As a four-CD set spanning Rick Nelson's entire career, this will likely stand as the most thorough overview of the singer's music ever issued. This doesn't mean, though, that it's the best anthology of his work, unless you subscribe to the viewpoint that his post-mid-'60s records were about as good as his pre-mid-'60s ones, since a full two discs (or half) of this package is devoted to that post-mid-'60s output. Basically, it illustrates his trajectory in phases: disc one, as a good-to-great pop-rockabilly singer; disc two, as a still-good but not quite as vital teen idol in the late '50s and early '60s; disc three, as a fair but not great country-rocker; and disc four, as a has-been playing out the string with uninspired adult contemporary and revival tracks during his final years. The album is an impressive feat of cross-licensing, though, starting with three songs from his first singles (for Verve, and never easy to find on reissues), drawing a lot from his creative peak at Imperial, and then from his spottier efforts for Decca and other labels. All of his Top Forty hits are here, along with a dozen or so previously unreleased tracks, none too remarkable, as well as the 45-single versions of a few early hits. The song selection is very good, but not infallible: The absence of the moody "Mean Old World," which was about the best thing he did in the mid-'60s, is inexplicable. If you are a big fan and do like Nelson's country-rock phase, this is a reasonable investment, but if you don't, you should stick to those collections that focus on his 1957-1965 recordings. *—Richie Unterberger*

Michael Nesmith

b. Dec. 30, 1942, Houston, TX
Vocals, Guitar / Folk-Rock, Singer/Songwriter, Country-Rock
The comparatively level-headed member of '60s teen sensation the Monkees, Michael Nesmith was the most proficient instrumentalist in the group and wrote their best in-house songs, rootsy pop numbers like "Papa Gene's Blues," "You Told Me," "You Just May Be the One," and "Tapioca Tundra." In fact, he had written many songs before even joining the group, and one of his compositions, "Different Drum," was a hit for Linda Ronstadt and the Stone Poneys in 1968. After he left the Monkees one year later, it wasn't a surprise that he became the only one of his bandmates to sustain a solo career; in fact, his dozen (or so) '70s LPs were among the most groundbreaking country-rock recordings of the era. Throughout the 1970s and into the '80s, Nesmith continued to record sporadically, though his communications company, Pacific Arts, began taking up more of his time by the early '80s. Pacific Arts proved to be an important pioneer in the development of music video, the concept he had furthered in the rough-and-tumble pace of the Monkees' TV show. *—John Bush*

Wichita Train Whistle Songs / 1968 / Dot ✦✦✦

Loose Salute / Nov. 1970 / Pacific Arts ✦✦✦
With this record, Nesmith's momentum builds as this album is even better than the first. While the single from this album didn't do as well as his previous hit, it was a better song and kicks off the album nicely. Also, steel player extraordinaire, "Red" Rhodes, is beginning to take a more dominant role in the sound of the band. Of special interest are Nesmith's third go at recording "Listen to the Band," a fine cover of Patsy Cline's "I Fall to Pieces," and his renewed interest in Latin rhythms. *—Jim Worbois*

Magnetic South / Jul. 1970 / Pacific Arts ✦✦✦✦✦

Nevada Fighter / 1971 / Pacific Arts ✦✦✦

And the Hits Just Keep on Comin' / 1972 / Pacific Arts ✦✦✦✦✦
If you don't own this record, there is a huge hole in your collection. Nesmith's own version of "Different Drum" (a song which introduced Linda Ronstadt to many back in 1968 and which most had only heard Nesmith do as a sped up, mumbled "audition" on an old Monkees episode) may be the key to lure you in, but every song is a gem. This is easily some of Nesmith's finest work as both a songwriter and an artist. Also, between Nesmith and Red Rhodes, the sound is so full that it's easy to forget that a full band wasn't used in creating this record. *—Jim Worbois*

Tantamount to Treason / 1972 / Pacific Arts ✦✦✦
Tantamount to Treason has a lazy feel to it, perhaps inspired by the beer recipe Papa Nes includes in the album's liner notes. That laziness is the reason the album is not as listenable as the previous three records, since you almost need to be "in the mood" to put this one on. That said, it's still quite a nice album and is worth tracking down. *—Jim Worbois*

Pretty Much Your Standard Ranch Stash / 1973 / Pacific Arts ✦✦✦✦✦
Despite the comment inside the cover that "after two or three months this album may lose potency although some of the aroma may linger," this record holds up years later as one of Nesmith's finest. He continues to mix originals and a nice selection of covers as before but somehow this record feels more "comfortable" than his previous efforts. This seems to be, in part, due to the strong musical bond between Nesmith and steel player Red Rhodes. If the "Buy This Record" inducement on the front cover doesn't make this a must for your collection, one listen to the music inside will! *—Jim Worbois*

The Prison / 1974 / Pacific Arts ✦✦

From a Radio Engine to the Photon Wing / 1977 / Pacific Arts ✦✦

Live at Palais / 1978 / Pacific Arts ✦✦✦✦

Infinite Rider on the Big Dogma / 1979 / Pacific Arts ✦✦✦
This is easily Nesmith's most interesting record from the '70s Pacific Arts material, and the one that most often calls for repeated listenings. By this time, he was getting heavily into video, so a number of these tracks were also turned into music videos (check out the Grammy-winning *Elephant Parts*). While not a must, it's still a record worth searching out. *—Jim Worbois*

Newer Stuff / 1989 / Rhino ✦✦✦

The Older Stuff: Best of Michael Nesmith (1970-1973) / 1991 / Rhino ✦✦✦✦✦

Tropical Campfires / Oct. 27, 1992 / Pacific Arts ✦✦✦✦
Along with Lindsay Buckingham's *Out of the Cradle* this album may be one of the finest and most underrated albums of the 1990s. Nesmith and his crack band run through 12 of the most delicious slices of Americana to be put on record in ages. The mood of the album is a cross between Bahamian, Tropical, Country, and other forms, all forging a unique synthesis of pop that might be very hard to match. Nesmith's songs and vocals are wholly original and personal, and tunes such as "I Am Not That" and "Laugh Kills Lonesome" bear the indefinable Nesmith stamp of humor with a compact and irresistible force. In addition to the excellent originals, Nesmith and his band cover two classic Cole Porter songs with excellent results, and both ("In the Still of The Night" and Begin the Beguine") fit the menu perfectly. Absolutely delectable. *—Matthew Greenwald*

● **Complete** / Sep. 28, 1993 / Pacific Arts ✦✦✦✦✦
All of Michael Nesmith and the First National Band's three albums are collected on this superb two-disc set, proving what a surprisingly inventive musician the former Monkee is. *—Stephen Thomas Erlewine*

16 Original Classics / Sep. 28, 1999 / Collectables ✦✦✦
16 Original Classics is actually the 1970 Mike Nesmith album *Magnetic South* with five extra bonus tracks tacked on. This was one of the highlights from any of the post Monkee recording careers, confirming Nesmith as a pioneer of the country-rock genre with an incredible vocal range, proven talent as a songwriter, and the ability to arrange a group of top notch country pickers. The First National Band featured longtime Nesmith cohorts, petal steel guitarist Red Rhodes, bassist John London, and drummer John Ware. The moderate success of the single "Joanne" (included on this package) made Nesmith the first ex-Monkee to put a solo record on the charts. *—Al Campbell*

Neu!

f. 1971, Düsseldorf, Germany, **db.** 1975
Group / Proto-Punk, Kraut Rock, Prog Rock/Art Rock, Electronic
While little-known and relatively unheralded during their brief existence, the Krautrock duo Neu! cast a large shadow over later generations of musicians, and served as a major influence on artists as diverse as David Bowie, Sonic Youth, Pere Ubu, Julian Cope, and Stereolab.

Neu! formed in Düsseldorf, Germany in 1971 after multi-instrumentalists Michael Rother and Klaus Dinger both split from Kraftwerk. Recorded in the space of four days with Can producer Conrad Plank, the duo's self-titled debut appeared early in 1972, and quickly established their affection for minimalist melodies and lock-groove rhythms. While virtually ignored throughout the rest of the world, the album sold extremely well in West Germany, resulting in a tour with support from Guru Guru's Uli Trepte and Eberhard Krahnemann.

Rother and Dinger returned to the studio in 1973 for *Neu! 2*, where a shortfall of cash allowed the duo to complete only two songs, "Super" and "Neueschnee," which they subsequently remixed at varying and disorienting speeds in order to flesh out a full-length album. After the record's release, Rother joined Dieter Moebius and Joachim Roedelius of Cluster to form Harmonia, but Neu! officially reunited in 1975 to record *Neu! 75*. After its release, they again disbanded; Rother continued on as a solo performer, while Dinger and drummer Hans Lampe formed La Dusseldorf. In the mid-'80s, Rother and Dinger reformed yet again, although the recording sessions, titled *Neu! 4*, did not officially surface until 1996. *—Jason Ankeny*

● **Neu!** / 1972 / Billingsgate ✦✦✦✦✦
Neu!'s visionary debut is an intensely visceral record which reinvents rock in its own visage: a shifting soundscape of drones, feedback, proto-ambient textures, processed effects, and industrial rhythms hung upon minimalist melodies, the album has few precedents, and the fingerprints of its influence are still smeared across experimental music decades later. *—Jason Ankeny*

Neu! 2 / 1973 / United Artists ✦✦✦✦✦
A perverse effort, *Neu! 2* mocks the very concept of recorded music: after a lack of cash forced the group to curtail their studio sessions after finishing only a handful of songs, they simply remixed the singles "Super" and "Neueschnee" at various speeds—complete with scratches and pops—to ensure enough material for a full-length LP. Other tracks consist simply of music being played back in the studio, ending when the needle is pulled off the turntable; another concludes with the sound of a cassette being eaten by a tape machine. Confrontational, subversive, and brilliant. *—Jason Ankeny*

Neu! 75 / 1975 / United Artists ✦✦✦
A work of polar extremes, *Neu! 75* is essentially a group record in name only; anticipating the duo's imminent breakup, the album splits evenly between the diametrically opposed work of Klaus Dinger and Michael Rother, resulting in a jarring juxtaposition of Rother's ambient minimalism and Dinger's proto-punk abrasion. *—Jason Ankeny*

Neu! 4 / 1996 / Captain Trip ✦✦✦
Recorded sometime in the mid-'80s but not released until over a decade later, *Neu! 4* picks up where the duo left off in 1975, exploring the extremes of both white noise and ambient beauty. Like *Neu! 2*, the album fills out with remixes of the basic tracks, but where the earlier effort simply varied playback speeds, the material on *Neu! 4* undergoes radical, even alien transformations. Much of the record predates 1990s electronic music with remarkable foresight: "Fly Dutch II" is a spacy techno loop which stakes out territory later claimed by Mouse on Mars, "Danzing" is a brutal electro experiment, and "86 Commercial Trash" is constructed around samples from German television advertisements. *—Jason Ankeny*

The Neville Brothers

f. 1977, New Orleans, LA
Group / New Orleans R&B, R&B, Funk, Soul
Throughout their long careers as both solo performers and as members of the group which bore their family name, the Neville Brothers proudly carried the torch of their native New Orleans' rich R&B legacy. Although the four siblings—Arthur, Charles, Aaron and Cyril—did not officially unite under the Neville Brothers aegis until 1977, all had crossed musical

paths in the past, while also enjoying success with other unrelated projects: eldest brother Art was the first to tackle a recording career, when in 1954 his high school band, the Hawketts, cut "Mardi Gras Mambo," a song which later became the annual carnival's unofficial anthem. In 1960, Aaron scored his first solo hit, "Over You"; in 1966, he notched a pop smash with the classic "Tell It Like It Is," a lush ballad showcasing his gossamer vocals. In 1977 the siblings offically banded together as the Neville Brothers. Despite their gift for intricate four-part harmonies, their self-titled 1978 debut unsuccessfully cast the vocal quartet as a disco band, and following a dismal response they were dropped by their label, Capitol. The Nevilles spent the following three years without a contract, but after signing with A&M, fan Bette Midler helped secure the services of producer Joel Dorn for 1981's superior *Fiyo on the Bayou.* Despite widespread critical acclaim, the album sold poorly, and again the Nevilles were cut loose from their contract. In 1989, they re-signed to A&M and recruited the services of famed New Orleans producer Daniel Lanois; the atmospheric *Yellow Moon,* the group's finest hour, finally earned them success on the charts, thanks in part to the anthemic single "Sister Rosa." 1990's *Brother's Keeper* fared even better, no doubt spurred by Aaron's concurrent success with Linda Ronstadt on the smash duet "Don't Know Much." *—Jason Ankeny*

★ **Treacherous: A History of the Neville Brothers** / 1986 / Rhino ♦♦♦♦♦
The music of the Neville Brothers was more a matter of rumor than documentation to most record buyers outside the New Orleans area until 1986, when Rhino Records finally gathered together their various solo and group records dating back 30 years and presented their story coherently on this two-disc set. Suddenly, it all makes sense, and the Nevilles' mixture of styles emerges as a singular American genre unto itself. This record is a revelation. *—William Ruhlmann*

● **The Very Best of the Neville Brothers** / Jan. 14, 1997 / Rhino ♦♦♦♦♦
Sixteen-track compilation focusing almost exclusively on the period spanning the late '70s to the late '80s. A couple of Aaron Neville's big '60s hits ("Tell It like It Is" and "Over You") are thrown in as well, as are a couple of cuts from the Wild Tchoupitoulas' 1976 album. Some may argue that the Nevilles' sprawling output is too difficult to condense into a single disc. On the other hand, given how often they're criticized for underachieving on record, this is a pretty suitable purchase for someone whose interest only runs deep enough for one anthology. *—Richie Unterberger*

Uptown Rulin': The Best Of / Aug. 24, 1999 / Interscope ♦♦♦♦
The Neville Brothers had always been critic's favorites, but never more so than during their tenure at A&M *Records* during the late '80s and early '90s. They released their first album, *Yellow Moon,* for the label in 1989, a few years after the acclaimed Rhino compilation *Treacherous: A History of the Neville Brothers* appeared on the shelves. *Treacherous* contained selections from all the Neville Brothers—not just group recordings but side-projects and solo cuts—and helped cement their reputation among record collectors and critics, which in turn set the stage for the enthusiastic reception of *Yellow Moon.* That enthusiasm failed to wane over the next few years, as each subsequent album was greeted by critics with open arms. The problem was, each record was pretty much the same. With producer Daniel Lanois, the Nevilles attempted to create grand, mythical albums, heavy with import and meaning. Lanois didn't abandon his trademark hazy, murkily mysterious production—a style that wasn't necessarily suited for the organic Nevilles, even if it did result in some evocative sonic hybrids. Consequently, each of the A&M albums functioned best as a series of moments, even if they were designed to work as individual albums (the prototype, *Yellow Moon,* unsurprisingly standing as the lone exception to the rule). That's why *Uptown Rulin': The Best Of* is a solid addition to their catalog. By collecting highlights from the A&M albums, it offers fans a good summary of these intriguing but mixed years. It isn't on the same level as *Treacherous* or its sequel, but it's a nice addendum to fans of that groundbreaking compilation. *—Stephen Thomas Erlewine*

Aaron Neville

b. Jan. 24, 1941, New Orleans, LA
Vocals / Pop-Soul, New Orleans R&B, Adult Contemporary, R&B, Soul
Although Neville is often compared to singer Sam Cooke in terms of sheer vocal refinement, he has a voice and style uniquely his own. Today he is well known as part of the New Orleans sound of the Neville Brothers. Yet, aside from the 1967 number one R&B hit "Tell It Like It Is," few have heard his incredible early solo recordings. Many of the first recordings of Aaron Neville, in the early and mid-'60s, were arranged, produced, and often written by the brilliant Allen Toussaint—another talent only now being really appreciated. Most of these sides were cut for the Minit (and later) Parlo labels. Songs like "She Took You for a Ride" and "You Think You're So Smart" on Parlo are masterpieces. While his more recent work, including that with Linda Ronstadt, makes for pleasant listening, it lacks the sheer persuasion of his early songs. Aaron has re-recorded his early work often, and it is important to hear the originals. The early sides of Aaron Neville are just waiting to be heard. *—Michael Erlewine and Ron Wynn*

Greatest Hits / 1957 / Curb ♦♦♦
Early New Orleans soul from velvet-voiced Aaron Neville, including the smooth, aching "Tell It Like It Is" and the gutsy, declarative "Over You," a shuffling R&B number. The eight other selections, especially "Jail House," "Hard Nut to Crack," and "Since You're Gone," offers an insightful overview of the golden tenor whose vocal abilities get more amazing with time. *—Andrew Hamilton*

● **Tell It Like It Is: Golden Classics** / 1989 / Collectables ♦♦♦♦♦
One of many collections covering Aaron Neville's superb early R&B and soul classics. The burly Neville, whose delicate, feathery voice stands in vivid contrast to his muscular body, made great heartache ballads, up-tempo wailers, and brilliantly sung originals for tiny New Orleans labels, often not even getting widespread soul airplay. Now that's he's hot property, the domestic anthologies are coming out left and right. This one is as good as any other, although for my money the import labels have still done a better job on early Neville than the American companies. *—Ron Wynn*

The Very Best of Aaron Neville / Jan. 11, 2000 / A&M ♦♦♦♦
In some ways, *The Very Best of Aaron Neville* is a very welcome addition to his catalog, since it's the first collection to touch on all areas of Neville's long career. However, it winds up being a bit unsatisfying, not just because it only has one cut from the Neville Brothers, but because his New Orleans R&B and down-home soul just don't fit that well with his smooth, cleanly produced latter-day work. Then again, the compilers didn't spend too much time with the early recordings, since the collection contains only a handful of R&B nuggets (including, of course, "Tell It Like It Is," plus "Over You") before settling into the '80s and '90s albums. It's not a bad summary of those albums, actually, containing such hits as "Don't Know Much" and "Everybody Plays the Fool," plus a good cross-section of album tracks and lesser-known cuts, such as his version of "Stardust" with Rob Wasserman. As such, *The Very Best of Aaron Neville* is recommended primarily to fans of his later recordings. Listeners who prefer the early R&B work or the Neville Brothers should look to compilations of that material, since they won't be satiated by this disc. *—Stephen Thomas Erlewine*

New Edition

f. 1982, Boston, MA
Group / Teen Pop, New Jack Swing, Urban, Hip-Hop
When Maurice Starr assembled New Edition in the early '80s, he never could have guessed that the group would produce some of the biggest, most influential urban R&B stars of the following decade. At the time of their first record, Bobby Brown, Ralph Tresvant, Ricky Bell, Mike Bivins, and Ronald Davoe were barely in their teens, yet they had impressive voices and a natural charisma that sent them to the charts with their first single, "Candy Girl." Their second album was even bigger, featuring the number two single "Cool It Now." New Edition's songs were either light funk or sweet ballads, yet they followed their formula well, even if much of it seems quaint now, especially compared to their groundbreaking solo work.

Brown left the band after their third album, being replaced by Johnny Gill. The band released two more albums before splitting. After the group was finished, they each became successful as solo artists in the late '80s. New Edition reunited in 1996, releasing a new album title *Home Again* in the fall of that year. The *Lost in Love: The Best of Slow Jams* collection appeared in 1998. *—Stephen Thomas Erlewine*

New Edition Solo Hits / Dec. 3, 1996 / MCA ♦♦♦
A 12-track compilation of four tracks each by spinoff acts of New Edition seems like a strange way to pick up their work, to say the least. Still, if you want some hits by Bobby Brown, Bell Biv DeVoe, and Ralph Tresvant, and are for some reason uninterested in scoping out their albums or waiting for their one-artist-only greatest-hits collections, this is a succinct mini-primer of one of the most successful clans in urban contemporary music. *—Richie Unterberger*

● **Greatest Hits, Vol. 1** / Oct. 1, 1991 / MCA ♦♦♦♦♦
For anyone who missed New Edition in either its Jackson 5 imitation phase or final days as a funkier, more aggressive urban contemporary vocal group with a slight dance influence, this collection contains examples of both incarnations. Kiddie-pop hits such as "Candy Girl," "Cool It Now," and "Mr. Telephone Man" are included, along with their final hits "If It Isn't Love," "Can You Stand the Rain," and the appropriately titled "Is This the End." This anthology shows how dominant New Edition was during the '80s and early '90s. *—Ron Wynn*

All the Number Ones / May 9, 2000 / Hip-O ♦♦♦♦♦
An excellent idea that might be slightly disappointing in the execution, *All the Number Ones* collects 18 singles that topped Billboard magazine's R&B charts, all performed either by New Edition or its members in their various outside projects. That results in a terrific, endlessly playable collection of urban pop-soul and new jack swing, but it also means that several of the collective's best-known songs are left off simply because they didn't top the R&B charts. Missing in action are Bobby Brown's "Roni" and "Rock Wit'cha," Bell Biv DeVoe's "Do Me!," Johnny Gill's "Fairweather Friend," and Ralph Tresvant's "Stone Cold Gentleman" and "Do What I Gotta Do," plus a bevy of New Edition hits. In fact, it might have been an even better idea to gather the biggest hits by the various New Edition spin-offs and leave the parent group's output alone; such an approach would have erased the contrast between the early New Edition bubblegum singles that lead off this collection and the grittier, funkier new jack hits that follow. Still, at least these omissions are due to the compilation's stated intent (collecting *All the Number Ones* and nothing else), rather than a record company marketing tactic. Even casual fans will undoubtedly miss at least a couple of the aforementioned hits, but really, what *is* here makes for a great listen and a fine introduction to one of the most influential R&B family trees of the '80s and early '90s. *—Steve Huey*

New Kids on the Block

f. 1984, Boston, MA
Group / Teen Pop, Urban, Dance-Pop
After his success with New Edition, producer Maurice Starr decided to replicate the group, subsituting the young Black teenagers for suburban White kids. The result was New Kids on the Block, which quickly eclipsed the popularity of Starr's previous group. Comprising Boston area singers Donnie Wahlberg, Jordan Knight, Jon Knight, Danny Wood, and Joe McIntyre, the New Kids were awkward and enthusiastic on their 1986 debut, which wasn't surprising considering that the oldest members were barely 16 years old. With their next album, 1988's *Hangin' Tough,* the group's image had toughened up and they had the material to support it. From the saccharine ballad "I'll Be Loving You Forever" to the title track's stab at funk, the band had a seemingly endless streak of hits in 1988 and 1989; their Christmas album even went double platinum. New Kid mania continued with 1990's *Step By Step,* but that was the end of the road for their short time in the sun. *—Stephen Thomas Erlewine*

● **Greatest Hits** / Feb. 16, 1999 / Columbia ♦♦♦♦

New Order

f. 1980, Manchester, England

Group / College Rock, Alternative Dance, Club/Dance, Post-Punk, New Wave, Alternative Pop/Rock, Synth Pop, House

Rising from the ashes of the legendary British post-punk unit Joy Division, the enigmatic New Order triumphed over tragedy to emerge as one of the most influential and acclaimed bands of the 1980s. Embracing the electronic textures and disco rhythms of the underground club culture many years in advance of their contemporaries, the group's pioneering fusion of new wave aesthetics and dance music successfully bridged the gap between the two worlds, creating a distinctively thoughtful and oblique brand of synth-pop appealing equally to the mind, body, and soul. After completing sessions for Joy Division's sophomore effort, *Closer*, frontman Ian Curtis hanged himself on May 18, 1980; devastated, the remaining trio re-formed a few months later as New Order. With the single "Everything's Gone Green," the group first began adorning their sound with synthesizers and sequencers, inspired by the music of Kraftwerk as well as the electro beats coming up from the New York underground; 1982's "Temptation" continued the trend, and like its predecessor was a major favorite among clubgoers. After a year-long hiatus, New Order resurfaced in 1983 with their breakthrough hit "Blue Monday"; packaged in a provocative sleeve designed to recall a computer disk, with virtually no information about the band itself—a hallmark of their mysterious, distant image—it perfectly married singer Bernard Sumner's plaintive yet cold vocals and abstract lyrics with cutting-edge drum-machine rhythms ideal for club consumption. "Blue Monday" went on to become the best-selling 12" release of all time, moving over three million copies worldwide. In 1987 they issued *Substance*, a much-needed collection of singles and remixes; it was New Order's American breakthrough, cracking the Top 40 on the strength of the newly recorded single "True Faith," which itself reached number 32 on the U.S. pop charts. *—Jason Ankeny*

Movement / 1981 / Qwest ✦✦✦

New Order's debut album *Movement* bridges the gap between the synthesizer-heavy music the group would later develop and Joy Division's languid, morbid drone. *Movement* pointed the way toward New Order's future by featuring more synthesizers than any of Joy Division's records, as well as more accessible hooks and melodies. *—Stephen Thomas Erlewine*

Power, Corruption & Lies / 1983 / Qwest ✦✦✦✦✦

New Order's second album was their giant step out of the looming shadow of Joy Division, clearly establishing their own unique and innovative musical identity. Seamlessly incorporating Gillian Gilbert's lush synth patterns into the mix, *Power, Corruption and Lies* springs from the propulsive, almost liquid bass of Peter Hook and the increasingly strong compositional skills of Bernard Sumner to firmly install the group as a cutting-edge electronic dance unit, one with unsurpassed reserves of humanity and depth—tracks like "Age of Consent" and the shimmering "Your Silent Face" speak to the mind and the body in equal measure. The U.S. release also appended their breakthrough club hit "Blue Monday," a masterpiece of the genre. *—Jason Ankeny*

Low-life / 1985 / Qwest ✦✦✦✦✦

New Order's evolution from post-punk survivors to state-of-the-art electronic unit became complete with the superb *Low-life*, the first of their albums to receive a proper American release. Tracks like "Sub-Culture" and "The Perfect Kiss" represent dance-pop at its very finest—propulsive, smart, and edgy, they combine lush synth patterns and programmed beats with a level of emotional investment seemingly at odds with its environs, creating a tension which keeps the music fresh and involving where other club hits from the era now seem dated and vacuous. In spite of their new technological mastery, the group remains as eccentric and unpredictable as ever—"Elegia" is a delicate instrumental piece, while the opening "Love Vigilantes" is quite nearly a folk song, complete with a squawking harmonica intro, and is utterly unlike anything else in the New Order catalog; still, it succeeds brilliantly, the work of a band at the very top of its game. *—Jason Ankeny*

Brotherhood / 1986 / Qwest ✦✦✦✦

One of the least-synthesized albums in New Order's discography, *Brotherhood* offers the simultaneous peak of the group's hook-filled songwriting (not just on the single "Bizarre Love Triangle") and Peter Hook's trademark bass work, which takes a plaintive, upper-register lead on highlights like "Weirdo" and "Broken Promise." As usual, the lines dividing organic and electronic are quite fuzzy, resulting in stark drum-machine lines for the tender ballad "All Day Long." Sumner's fondness for bizarre, enigmatic lyrics continues apace with songs like the closer ("Every second counts, when I am with you/I think you are a pig, you should be in a zoo"). *—John Bush*

☆ **Substance** / 1987 / Qwest ✦✦✦✦✦

Substance is a double-disc set collecting New Order's singles, including several songs that were never available on the group's albums, at least in these versions. While there are a couple of re-recordings of earlier singles, most of *Substance* consists of 12" single mixes designed for danceclub play. Arguably, these 12" mixes represent New Order's most groundbreaking and successful work, since they expanded the notion of what a rock & roll band, particularly an indie rock band, could do. *Substance* collects the best of their remixes, and in the process it showcases not only the group's musical innovations, but also their songwriting prowess—"Temptation," "Blue Monday," "Bizarre Love Triangle," and "True Faith" are some of the finest pop songs of the '80s. Although it is a double-disc set, *Substance* isn't overly long. Instead it offers a perfect introduction to New Order, while providing collectors with an invaluable collection of singles. *—Stephen Thomas Erlewine*

Technique / 1989 / Qwest ✦✦✦✦✦

The first post-acid house masterpiece of British pop, *Technique* presents New Order doing what they'd done best for close to a decade—writing brilliant left field pop songs and consistently blurring the line between electronic dance and alternative pop. From the driving singles "Fine Time," "Run," and "Round & Round," it would appear that *Technique* was the band's most dance-slanted record yet, though rockier album tracks like "Love Less" and "All the Way" reveal the band having it both ways. "Mr. Disco" proves that the group's baffling sense of humor is still intact. *—John Bush*

Republic / May 11, 1993 / Qwest ✦✦✦✦

Pulling back slightly from the raw, dance-oriented *Technique*, New Order took a break for four years and then crafted another slice of prime guitar pop. In keeping with previous work, *Republic* simply borrows elements of contemporary innovations in club music to frame a set of effortlessly enjoyable alternative pop songs. As on *Technique*, the singles ("World," "Spooky") are the most danceable on the record, while lyrical concerns are among the most direct of the group's career, including "Ruined in a Day" and "Times Change," sure signs of the demise of Factory Records. *—John Bush*

The Rest of New Order / 1995 / London ✦✦✦

★ **The Best of New Order** / Mar. 14, 1995 / Qwest ✦✦✦✦✦

Instead of presenting New Order as a progressive dance band as *Substance* did, *The Best of New Order* showcases New Order the pop band, condensing most of their hit singles onto one disc. A couple of remixes are thrown in (Shep Pettibone takes over "Blue Monday"), and several classics, including "Temptation" and "Ceremony" are missing, but it is still a concise explanation of why the group was one of the most important dance groups of the '80s. *—Stephen Thomas Erlewine*

The New York Dolls

f. 1971, New York, NY, **db.** 1977

Group / New York Punk, Album Rock, Proto-Punk, Glam Rock, Hard Rock

The New York Dolls created punk rock before there was a term for it. Building on the Rolling Stones' dirty rock & roll, Mick Jagger's androgyny, girl group pop, the glam rock of David Bowie and T. Rex, and the Stooges' anarchic noise, the New York Dolls created a new form of hard rock that presaged both punk rock and heavy metal. Their drug-fueled, shambolic performances influenced a generation of musicians in New York and London, who all went on to form punk bands. And although they self-destructed quickly, the band's two albums remained two of the most popular cult records in rock & roll history.

After generating considerable buzz in New York and England, the New York Dolls signed with Mercury Records in late 1972. Their eponymous 1973 debut, produced by Todd Rundgren, received overwhelmingly positive reviews, but it didn't stir the interest of the general public, stalling at 116 on the U.S. charts. The band's follow-up, 1974's *Too Much Too Soon*, was produced by the legendary girl group producer George "Shadow" Morton. Although the sound of the record was relatively streamlined, the album was another commercial failure. Mercury dropped the band soon afterward, and the group hooked up with manager Malcolm McLaren, who used the Dolls as a test ground for the provocative promotions that would later bring the Sex Pistols notoriety. Every strategy he tried with the Dolls backfired, chief amongst those his idea to give the group a communist chic makeover, dressing them in red leather and perform in front of the U.S.S.R.'s flag. This tactic didn't stir interest and soon the group began to splinter, with guitarist Johnny Thunders leaving in 1975. Vocalist David Johansen and guitarist Syl Sylvain fired McLaren and worked with a variety of lineups before disbanding in 1977. *—Stephen Thomas Erlewine*

★ **New York Dolls** / 1973 / Mercury ✦✦✦✦✦

There are hints of girl group pop and more than a hint of the Rolling Stones, but *The New York Dolls* doesn't really sound like anything that came before it. It's hard rock with a self-conscious wit, a celebration of camp and kitsch that retains a menacing, malevolent edge. The New York Dolls play as if they can barely keep the music from falling apart and David Johansen sings and screams like a man possessed. *The New York Dolls* is a noisy, reckless album that rocks and rolls with a vengance. The Dolls rework old Chuck Berry and Stones riffs, playing them with a sloppy, violent glee. "Personality Crisis," "Looking for a Kiss," and "Trash" strut with confidence, while "Vietnamese Baby" and "Frankenstein" sound otherworldly, working the same frightening drone over and over again. *The New York Dolls* was the definitive proto-punk album, even more than anything the Stooges released. It plunders history while celebrating it, creating a sleazy urban mythology along the way. *—Stephen Thomas Erlewine*

☆ **Too Much, Too Soon** / 1974 / Mercury ✦✦✦✦✦

After the clatter of their first album failed to bring them a wide audience, the New York Dolls hired producer Shadow Morton to work on the follow-up, *Too Much, Too Soon*. The differences are apparent right from the start of the ferocious opener, "Babylon." Not only are the guitars cleaner, but the mix is dominated by waves of studio sound effects and female backing vocals. Ironically, instead of making the Dolls sound safer, all the added frills emphasize their gleeful sleaziness and reckless sound. The Dolls sound on the verge of falling apart throughout the album, as Johnny Thunders and Syl Sylvain relentlessly trade buzz-saw riffs while David Johansen sings, shouts and sashays on top of the racket. Band originals—including the bluesy raver "It's Too Late," the noisy girl-group pop of "Puss N' Boots," and the Thunders showcase "Chatterbox"—are rounded out by obscure R&B and rock & roll covers tailor-made for the group. Johansen vamps throughout Leiber & Stoller's "Bad Detective," Archie Bell's "(There's Gonna Be A) Showdown," the Cadets "Stranded in the Jungle," and Sonny Boy Williamson's "Don't Start Me Talkin'," yet it's with grit and affection—he really means it, man! The whole record collapses with the scathing "Human Being," on which a bunch of cross-dressing misfits defiantly declare that it's OK that they want too many things, 'cause they're human beings, just like you and me. Three years later, the Sex Pistols failed to come up with anything as musically visceral and dangerous. Perhaps that's why the Dolls never found their audience in the early '70s: Not only were they punk rock before punk rock was cool, but they remained weirder and more idiosyncratic than any of the bands that followed. And they rocked harder, too. *—Stephen Thomas Erlewine*

Rock & Roll / Oct. 18, 1994 / Mercury ✦✦✦✦✦

Rock & Roll contains all of the original material from the Dolls' two classic albums and adds a couple of outtakes and rarities. So why isn't it as much fun as *New York Dolls* or *Too Much Too Soon*? For starters, the Dolls' versions of "Pills," "Stranded in the Jungle," "Don't Start Me Talkin'," and "(There's Gonna Be A) Showdown" weren't filler, they were essential to the overall feeling of the albums. And that brings us to the main problem of *Rock & Roll*—it isn't sequenced in an inviting manner. Instead of showcasing the New York Dolls in all of their trashy glory, the disc manages to make them sound rather tedious, which is something their proper albums certainly aren't. Nevertheless, there's plenty of fine music here, and hardcore fans will want the rarities. But the original albums remain the best way to hear the Dolls. —*Stephen Thomas Erlewine*

Hard Night's Day / Aug. 15, 2000 / Norton ♦♦♦
This collection of 1973 studio demos includes just about everything in the Dolls' repertoire at the time (21 songs) and was recorded just prior to their entering the studio with producer Todd Rundgren to lay down their first album. While the takes aren't drastically different, they are rawer. Rundgren added a sheen to the album that just isn't here (which makes David Johansen's off-key singing and Johnny Thunders' missed guitar notes all the more obvious). A fine fan souvenir, but no replacement for the official studio work. —*Michael Gallucci*

Randy Newman

b. Nov. 28, 1943, New Orleans, LA
Vocals, Piano, Conductor, Composer, Arranger / Album Rock, Original Score, Film Music, Soundtracks, Brill Building Pop, Pop/Rock, Pop, Singer/Songwriter
Randy Newman was an anomaly among early '70s singer/songwriters. Though he was slightly influenced by Bob Dylan, his music owed more to New Orleans R&B and traditional pop than folk. Newman developed an idiosyncratic style that alternated between sweeping, cinematic pop and rolling R&B, which were tied together by his nasty sense of humor. Where his peers concentrated on confessional songwriting, Newman drew characters, creating a world filled with misfits, outcasts, charlatans, and con-men. Though he occasionally showed sympathy for his characters, he became well-known for his biting sense of satire, highlighted by his fluke 1978 hit "Short People" and his parody of '80s yuppies, "I Love L.A." While Newman's records consistently received strongly positive reviews, he made his money through composing film scores for films like *Ragtime* and *The Natural.* His albums may never have sold in large amounts, but his work influenced several generations of songwriters, including Lyle Lovett and Mark Knopfler. —*Stephen Thomas Erlewine*

Randy Newman / 1968 / Reprise ♦♦♦♦♦
"Randy Newman creates something new under the sun," read the banner on the back of Newman's debut album, but it wasn't so much that as that, in keeping with the intended irony of the statement, Newman was intent upon taking clichés and using them to satirize social conventions, a popular parlor game in the late '60s. Thus, we have "Love Story" (predating the sappy book/movie of the same title), in which the lovers retire to Florida and pass away, "So Long Dad," in which a son squares things with his old man, and "Davy the Fat Boy," in which an affectionate friend exploits the title character. But there were also songs like "Living Without You" and "I Think It's Gonna Rain Today," which were so painfully lonely you wished they weren't so sincere. Taken together, this was an audacious first album by a major, if extremely quirky, talent. —*William Ruhlmann*

★ **12 Songs** / 1970 / Reprise ♦♦♦♦♦
On his debut album, Randy Newman sounded as if he was still getting used to the notion of performing his own songs in the studio (despite years of cutting songwriting demos), but apparently he was a pretty quick study, and his second long player, *12 Songs,* was a striking step forward for Newman as a recording artist. While much of *Randy Newman* was heavily orchestrated, *12 Songs* was cut with a small combo (Ry Cooder and Clarence White take turns on guitar), leaving a lot more room for Newman's Fats Domino-gone-cynical piano and the bluesier side of his vocal style, and Randy sounds far more confident and comfortable in this context. And Newman's second batch of songs were even stronger than his first (no small accomplishment), rocking more and grooving harder but losing none of their intelligence and careful craft in the process. "Have You Seen My Baby?" and "Mama Told Me Not to Come" are a pair of sly, updated New Orleans-style rockers (both of which would be much-covered in the coming years); "Let's Burn Down the Cornfield" and "Suzanne" are subtly ominous tales of love and sex; "Yellow Man" was an early meditation on one of Newman's favorite themes, the absurdity of racial prejudice (which he would also glance at in his straight-but-twisted cover of "Underneath the Harlem Moon"); and "My Old Kentucky Home" is a hilarious and quite uncharitable look at life in the deep South (another theme that would pop up in his later work). Newman's humor started getting more acidic with *12 Songs,* but here even his most mordant character studies boast a recognizable humanity, which often make his subjects both pitiable and all the more loathsome. Superb material brilliantly executed, *12 Songs* was Randy Newman's first great album, and is still one of his finest moments on record. —*Mark Deming*

Randy Newman Live / 1971 / Reprise ♦♦♦

☆ **Sail Away** / 1972 / Reprise ♦♦♦♦♦
On his third studio album, Randy Newman found a middle ground between the heavily orchestrated pop of his debut and the more stripped-down, rock-oriented approach of *12 Songs,* and managed to bring new strength to both sides of his musical personality in the process. The title track, which Newman has described as a sort of commercial jingle written for slave traders looking to recruit naïve Africans, and "Old Man," in which an elderly man is rejected with feigned compassion by his son, were set to Newman's most evocative arrangements to date, and rank with the most intelligent and effective use of a large ensemble by anyone in pop music. On the other end of the scale, "Last Night I Had a Dream" and "You Can Leave Your Hat On" are lean, potent mid-tempo rock tunes, the former featuring some slashing and ominous slide guitar from Ry Cooder, and the latter a witty and willfully perverse bit of erotic absurdity that later became a hit for Joe Cocker (who sounded as if he took the joke at face value). Elsewhere, Newman cynically ponders the perils of a stardom he would never achieve ("Lonely at the Top," originally written for Frank Sinatra), offers a broad and amusing bit of political satire ("Political Science"), and concludes with one of the most bitter rants against religion that anyone committed to vinyl prior to the punk era ("God's Song (That's Why I Love Mankind)"). Whether he's writing for three pieces or 30, Newman makes superb use of the sounds available to him, and his vocals are the model of making the most of a limited instrument. Overall, *Sail Away* is one of Newman's finest works, musically adventurous and displaying a lyrical subtlety that would begin to fade in his subsequent works. —*Mark Deming*

☆ **Good Old Boys** / 1974 / Reprise ♦♦♦♦♦
Randy Newman's songwriting often walks a narrow line between intelligent satire and willful cruelty, and that line was never finer than on the album *Good Old Boys.* Newman had long displayed a fascination with the American South, and *Good Old Boys* was a song cycle where he gave free reign to his most imaginative (and venomous) thoughts on the subject. The album's scabrous opening cut, "Rednecks," is guaranteed to offend practically anyone with it's tale of a slow-witted, willfully (and proudly) ignorant Southerner obsessed with "keeping the n—?-s down." "A Wedding in Cherokee County" is more polite but hardly less mean-spirited, in which an impotent hick marries a circus freak; if the song's melody and arrangement weren't so skillful, it would be hard to imagine anyone bothering with this musical geek show. But elsewhere, *Good Old Boys* displays a very real compassion for the blighted history of the South, leavened with a knowing wit. "Birmingham" is a funny but humane tale of working class Alabamians, "Louisiana 1927" and "Kingfish" are intelligent and powerfully evocative tales of the deep South in the depths of the Great Depression, and "Rollin'" is cheerful on the surface and troubling to anyone willing to look beneath it. Musically, Newman dives deep into his influences in Southern soul, and also adds potent country accents (with the help of Al Perkins pedal-steel guitar) while dressing up his songs in typically expert string and horn arrangements. And Newman assumes each character, either brave or foolish, with the skill of a gifted actor, giving even his most loathsome characters enough depth that they're human beings, despite their flaws. *Good Old Boys* is one of Newman's finest albums; it's also one of his most provocative and infuriating, and that's probably just the way he wanted it. —*Mark Deming*

Little Criminals / 1977 / Reprise ♦♦♦
After *Good Old Boys,* one of the most ambitious and thematically unified albums of his career, Randy Newman seemed to beat a willful retreat for his next project, 1977's *Little Criminals.* For the most part abandoning the carefully structured orchestral arrangements that dominated *Good Old Boys* and *Sail Away,* Newman cut *Little Criminals* with a handful of pop-friendly session musicians and L.A. Mellow Mafia regulars (including most of the Eagles), and his arch, cutting satire gave way to a lighter but less thoughtful tone, with the humor becoming less mean-spirited (though becoming much *more* venomous than "Rednecks" might have been difficult). Newman even revisited one of his favorite themes, the pointlessness of racial prejudice, with a metaphor so silly no one could fail to understand it. Or at least that's what he thought when he wrote "Short People"; the song unexpectedly took off as a novelty hit, and the vertically challenged across the country began attacking Newman for what they saw as an affront to their dignity and well-being. As a result, *Little Criminals* became Newman's first (and only) gold album in the United States, but this set wasn't an especially good way to introduce the average record buyer to his work. *Little Criminals* lacks the scope of Newman's best work, the music is skillful but bland, and several of the songs sound like padding (especially "You Can't Fool the Fat Man" and "Jolly Coppers on Parade"). While the title tune, "Rider in the Rain," "In Germany Before the War," and "Sigmund Freud's Impersonation of Albert Einstein in America" (which was written for the movie *Ragtime* but not used) are fine songs, much of *Little Criminals* sounds like Newman was treading water; it's not his worst album, but it sounds like the work of a man figuring out what his next move should be. —*Mark Deming*

Born Again / 1979 / Reprise ♦♦♦

Trouble in Paradise / 1983 / Reprise ♦♦♦♦♦
Randy Newman began the slow process of transforming himself into a polished L.A. songcrafter on the album *Little Criminals,* and with *Trouble in Paradise* the metamorphosis was complete; by this time, Newman could make a record just as ear-pleasing as anything Paul Simon, Don Henley, or Lindsey Buckingham could come up with, and proved it by persuading all three to appear on the sessions. But no matter how polished the arrangements and smooth the production, Newman's songs don't sound like they're ready for radio, and he's too bright not to understand that songs about apartheid, self-pitying white bluesmen, and arrogant yuppies are poor prospects for the pop charts. *Trouble in Paradise* marked the high point of Newman's struggle between pop sheen and his satiric impulses, and the album is a significant improvement over *Little Criminals* and *Born Again.* The targets of Newman's satirical gaze are easy to skewer, and his pen is hardly subtle, but the overall tone is more respectful than on *Born Again,* and the results are stronger. The bitter Afrikaner in "Christmas in Capetown" and the egocentric blowhard in "My Life Is Good" have at least *earned* Newman's disgust, and while many of the character studies ("Mikey," "I'm Different") and vignettes ("Miami," "Take Me Back") take a less than charitable view of their protagonists, like the losers and half-wits that populate *Good Old Boys,* they're human beings whose flaws reveal a hint of tragedy. And the closing number, "Song for the Dead," is a stunner in which a soldier explains to the bodies he's burying the purpose behind the war that took their lives. While too slick for Newman's core audience, *Trouble in Paradise* was his most intelligent and best realized work since *Good Old Boys,* and his finest album of the '80s. —*Mark Deming*

Land of Dreams / 1989 / Reprise ♦♦♦♦
Unlike his contemporaries in the singer/songwriter community, Randy Newman has displayed little interest in writing about himself, with nearly every song in his repertoire set in the voice of some imagined character. So 1988's *Land of Dreams* was startling because its first three songs formed a triptych about Newman's childhood; for the first time on one of his albums, Newman was clearly writing about his own life, and the results were extraordinary. "Dixie Flyer" tells how Newman and his mother came to move from Los Angeles to New Orleans during World War II; "New Orleans Wins the War," introduces young Newman to the issues of race in the Deep South as he ponders the odd realities of life in The City That Care Forgot; and in "Four Eyes," cross-eyed Newman is forced to confront responsibility (and cruelty) for the first time on his first day in school. But while *Land of Dreams* begins as an unusually strong and compelling concept album, Newman apparently lost interest in writing

about himself, and from track four onward, *Land of Dreams* is content to pick up where *Trouble in Paradise* left off. Themes of race and class in America dominate the second half of the album, most potently on "Roll With the Punches" and "I Want You to Hurt Like I Do," two "responses" to the grandstanding compassion of "We Are the World." *Land of Dreams* is a strong piece of work from Randy Newman, but if he'd had the courage to follow what he'd started with the first three songs, he might have had a masterpiece. *—Mark Deming*

Faust / Sep. 19, 1995 / Warner Brothers ✦✦

Guilty: 30 Years of Randy Newman / Nov. 3, 1998 / Rhino ✦✦✦✦
There was no Randy Newman compilation available in America until Rhino released the four-disc box set *Guilty: 30 Years of Randy Newman* in the fall of 1998. Boasting two discs of album highlights, a disc of rarities, and a disc devoted to "Film Music," *Guilty* attempts to be a definitive artistic portrait, yet it winds up a little frustrating. Dedicated fans don't have much need for the first two discs; even if they provide an excellent summary, they're designed for casual listeners, who won't have much interest in the other two discs. "Odds & Ends," the third disc, is the jewel in this crown for longtime fans, since it contains a wealth of rarities, including the excellent "Gone Dead Train" from *Performance*, a weird Pat Boone-produced single from 1961 ("Golden Gridiron Boy"), a selection of 1968 songwriting demos, a host of working tracks for films, and a revelatory "Masterman and Baby J," which contains no rapping. "Film Music," the fourth disc, is another welcome addition to his catalog. Newman is a sensitive, accomplished film composer in the classic Hollywood style, and not only are his scores rewarding on their own merits (as are the excerpts here), he's written a handful of great songs, such as "I Love to See You Smile" (*Parenthood*) and "You've Got a Friend In Me" (*Toy Story*), which have not appeared on a Newman album until now. These final discs are valuable for serious fans, yet they may not want to purchase the entire box in order to acquire the rarities. And that's the problem with *Guilty*—the package is lovely and the execution first-rate, but both casual and dedicated fans would have been better served if the set had been divided into two different compilations. *—Stephen Thomas Erlewine*

Bad Love / Jun. 1, 1999 / DreamWorks ✦✦✦

Olivia Newton-John

b. Sep. 26, 1948, Cambridge, England
Vocals / Soft Rock, Adult Contemporary, Country-Pop
Olivia Newton-John skillfully made the transition from popular country-pop singer to popular mainstream soft rock singer, becoming one of the most successful vocalists of the '70s in the process. The transition itself wasn't much of a stretch—her early '70s hits "I Honestly Love You" and "Have You Never Been Mellow" were country only in the loosest sense—yet the extent of her success in both fields was remarkable. As a country singer, her first five charting singles all went Top 10 in the U.S.; as a pop singer, she had no less than 15 Top 10 hits, including five number one singles, highlighted by "Physical," which spent 10 weeks at number one in 1981-82. Newton-John's sweet voice suited both country-pop and soft rock perfectly, which is what kept her at the top of the charts until the mid-'80s. After 1984, she was no longer able to reach the Top 40, partially because of shifting musical tastes and partially because she was unable to successfully record sexy dance-pop, no matter how hard she tried. Nevertheless, her '70s and '80s hits remained soft rock and adult contemporary staples into the '90s, when she was no longer recording frequently. *—Stephen Thomas Erlewine*

● **Back to Basics** / Jun. 9, 1992 / Geffen ✦✦✦✦✦
An artist well-defined by her hit singles, Olivia Newton-John has had a stylistically varied career, as is illustrated on *Back to Basics: The Essential Collection 1971-1992*, a set that ranges from her teary ballad "I Honestly Love You" to that bouncy paean to getting horizontal, "Physical." Fans may quibble that such hits as "Let Me Be There" and "Make a Move on Me" are not included, but Newton-John's two greatest-hits albums are out of print, and this is the only collection to combine both her good-girl and bad-girl personae. *—William Ruhlmann*

Stevie Nicks

b. May 26, 1948, Phoenix, AZ
Vocals / Album Rock, Pop/Rock, Soft Rock
Famed for her mystical chanteuse image, singer/songwriter Stevie Nicks enjoyed phenomenal success not only as a solo artist but also as a key member of Fleetwood Mac. During high school, Nicks met fellow student Lindsey Buckingham, with whom she formed the band Fritz. Even after the group disbanded, Buckingham remained her partner and soon became her lover as well. After moving to Los Angeles, the duo recorded their 1973 debut LP, *Buckingham-Nicks*. Though the album flopped, it caught the attention of the members of Fleetwood Mac, who invited Buckingham and Nicks to join their ranks in 1974. In quick time, the revitalized group achieved unparalled success with 1975's *Fleetwood Mac* and 1977's *Rumours*. Major hit singles like "Dreams" and "Rhiannon" made Nicks a focal point of Fleetwood Mac, and in 1981 she took time off from the group to record her solo debut, *Bella Donna*, which hit number one. In 1983, Nicks released her second solo effort, *The Wild Heart*, highlighted by the Top Five smash "Stand Back." *Rock a Little* appeared in 1985, and was followed by *The Other Side of the Mirror* in 1989. She left Fleetwood Mac in 1993, and issued *Street Angel* a year later. In 1997, she rejoined Fleetwood Mac for the tour album, *The Dance*. A Nicks solo box set, *Enchanted*, followed in 1998. *—Jason Ankeny*

Bella Donna / 1981 / Modern ✦✦✦✦✦
Stevie Nicks' solo career was off to an impressive, if overdue, start with *Bella Donna*, which left no doubt that she could function quite well without the input of her colleagues in Fleetwood Mac (a band she would remain a member of until 1993). The album yielded a number of hits that seemed omnipresent in the '80s, including the moving "Leather and Lace" (which unites Nicks with Don Henley), the poetic "Edge of Seventeen," and her rootsy duet with Tom Petty, "Stop Draggin' My Heart Around." But equally engaging are less exposed tracks like the haunting "After the Glitter Fades." Hit producer Jimmy Iovine wisely avoids overproducing, and keeps things sounding organic on this striking debut. *—Alex Henderson*

The Wild Heart / 1983 / Modern ✦✦✦
Stevie Nicks was following both her debut solo album, *Bella Donna* (1981), which had topped the charts, sold over a million copies (now over four million), and spawned four Top 40 hits, and Fleetwood Mac's *Mirage* (1982), which had topped the charts, sold over a million copies (now over two million), and spawned three Top 40 hits (including her "Gypsy"), when she released her second solo album, *The Wild Heart*. She was the most successful American female pop singer of the time. Not surprisingly, she played it safe: *The Wild Heart* contained nothing that would disturb fans of her previous work and much that echoed it. As on *Bella Donna*, producer Jimmy Iovine took a simpler, more conventional pop/rock approach to the arrangements than Fleetwood Mac's inventive Lindsey Buckingham did on Nicks' songs, which meant the music was more straightforward than her typically elliptical lyrics. Iovine did get a Mac-like sound on "Nightbird," in which Nicks repeated her invocation to "the white winged dove" from *Bella Donna*'s "Edge of Seventeen," and on "Sable on Blond," a "Gypsy" soundalike. His most daring effort was the album's lead-off single, "Stand Back," which boasted a disco tempo. Elsewhere, the songs were largely interchangeable with those on *Bella Donna*, even down to the obligatory duet with Tom Petty. Nicks seemed to know what she was up to—one song was called, "Nothing Ever Changes." As a result, *The Wild Heart* sold to the faithful—it made the Top Ten, sold over a million copies, and spawned three Top 40 hits ("Stand Back," "Nightbird," and "If Anyone Falls"). And that was appropriate: If you loved *Bella Donna*, you would like *The Wild Heart* very much. *—William Ruhlmann*

Rock a Little / 1985 / Modern ✦✦✦✦✦

The Other Side of the Mirror / May 1989 / Modern ✦✦✦

● **Timespace: The Best of Stevie Nicks** / Sep. 3, 1991 / Modern ✦✦✦✦✦
With material produced by names such as Jon Bon Jovi, Danny Kortchmar, and Jimmy Iovine, Stevie Nicks' solo work singled her out as a prominent artist outside of her glory days with Fleetwood Mac. With a remarkable 11 Top 40 singles that spawned from only four solo albums, not including 1994's *Street Angel*, Nicks proved that her sometimes fragile, sometimes pleasingly sharp voice could stand up well without the backing of Lindsay Buckingham's revered guitar work. *Timespace* groups together her biggest songs and makes for a favorable compilation of her material. Only a few of her charted singles are left off *Timespace*, like 1982's "After the Glitter Fades" and "Needles and Pins," the other duet with Tom Petty. The beautiful "Leather and Lace," sung with Don Henley from her first album *Bella Donna*, is an obvious inclusion here, as is her highest charting single "Stop Draggin' My Heart Around," taken from the same debut release. Nicks' surging vocal range thunders through "Stand Back," and even more so alongside the guitar thrust of "Edge of Seventeen," her most rock-induced single. *Timespace* captures the softer side of Nicks as well, best heard within the lushness of "Beauty and the Beast" and the wholehearted approach put forth on "Has Anyone Ever Written Anything for You." Capped off with her last big hit of the '80s in "Rooms on Fire" from the otherwise substandard *The Other Side of the Mirror*, this compilation is a splendid representation of her lone material. *—Mike DeGagne*

Street Angel / Sep. 21, 1993 / Modern ✦✦

Enchanted: The Works of Stevie Nicks / Apr. 7, 1998 / Atlantic ✦✦✦
Stevie Nicks certainly was a major star in the '70s and early '80s, both as a key member of Fleetwood Mac and as a solo artist. She had a long string of hit singles with the group and alone, enough to justify a double-disc set, but the three-disc box set *Enchanted* is a case of overkill for anyone but hardcore fans. *Enchanted* is devoted entirely to Nicks' solo career, contianing no Mac hits whatsoever. All of her hits—"Bella Donna," "Stop Draggin' My Heart Around," "Edge of Seventeen," "Leather and Lace," "Stand Back," "Talk to Me," and "I Can't Wait"—are here, as are minor singles and album cuts, plus non-LP B-sides, soundtrack cuts, unreleased items, demos, and live tracks. All of those rarities are interesting only to hardcore collectors, and tend to weigh down the listenability of the set. Still, there are enough rarities (and enough good rarities) to make this box necessary for collectors. It's just that less dedicated fans—and that includes fans who are only familiar with her Fleetwood Mac work—should probably stick to the greatest-hits collection or *Bella Donna*. *—Stephen Thomas Erlewine*

Nico (Christa Paffgen)

b. Oct. 16, 1938, Cologne, Germany, **d.** Jul. 18, 1988
Vocals / Proto-Punk, Euro-Dance, Experimental, Prog Rock/Art Rock
One of the most fascinating figures of rock's fringes, Nico hobnobbed, worked, and was romantically linked with an incredible assortment of the most legendary entertainers of the 1960s. The paradox of her career was that she herself never attained the fame of her peers, pursuing a distinctly individualistic and uncompromising musical career that was uncommercial, but wholly admirable and influential. Nico first rose to fame as a European supermodel before moving to New York, where Andy Warhol installed her as a vestigial presence and occasional lead singer for the Velvet Underground. After contributing unforgettable deadpan vocals to three of the songs on their classic 1967 debut album, Nico embarked on a solo career, recording folk-rock flavored songs for her debut *Chelsea Girl* album with assistance from Jackson Browne, Lou Reed, and John Cale. Her 1969 follow-up, *The Marble Index*, was a dramatic departure that unveiled her doom-laden, gothic persona, produced by Cale and prominently featuring her deep vocals, impenetrable lyrics, and ghostly harmonium. Her career fell into disarray during the rest of the '70s and the '80s, as she struggled with a massive drug habit and tangled personal life. The original goth-rocker, Nico's albums are demanding and bleak, but map a unique and starkly powerful vision that has become more influential with age. *—Richie Unterberger*

● **Chelsea Girl** / 1967 / Polydor ✦✦✦✦✦
Nico's distanced, German-accented voice is presented over austere strings and, in one case, electric guitar on a series of songs reminiscent of her work with the Velvet Underground and written by Velvets John Cale and Lou Reed. Other songs (some unrecorded elsewhere) were written by a young Jackson Browne. *—William Ruhlmann*

The Marble Index / 1969 / Elektra ✦✦✦
The quirky, orchestrated folk-rock of Nico's 1968 debut album *Chelsea Girl* in no way prepared listeners for the stark, almost avant-garde flavor of her 1969 follow-up, *The Marble Index.* Produced by former Velvet Underground partner John Cale, the chanteuse presented an uncompromisingly bleak, gothic soundscape on her second album. Dominated by spare harmonium and Nico's deep, brooding vocals, this album unveiled her singularly morose songwriting (her first record featured none of her compositions). Owing more to European classical and folk music than rock, it found little favor with 1969 audiences. But like the work of the Velvet Underground, it proved to be quite influential in the long run on a future generation of black-clad goth-rockers. The 1991 reissue of this recording adds two previously unreleased songs, "Roses in the Snow" and "Nibelungen." *—Richie Unterberger*

Desert Shore / 1971 / Reprise ✦✦✦✦✦
John Cale produces, arranges, and plays almost all the instruments on this atmospheric collection of songs well suited to Nico's droning delivery. *—William Ruhlmann*

The End / 1974 / Island ✦✦✦
The most remote and Teutonic of Nico's studio albums features Roxy Music guitarist Phil Manzanera, Brian Eno on synthesizer, and John Cale (who also produced) on a dozen instruments. After five Nico originals, it concludes with chilling readings of the Doors' "The End" and "Das Lied Der Deutschen." *—Richie Unterberger*

The Classic Years / Sep. 15, 1998 / Island ✦✦✦✦
The Classic Years is an excellent, portable introduction to the challenging and singular work of Nico. It's questionable as to why Chronicles opted to include her three vocal contributions to *The Velvet Underground and Nico,* however. What are the odds of someone *not* owning that record prior to checking out the ice queen's solo material— nonetheless, the tracks certainly don't sound out of place. A handful of songs are taken from each of her first four (and best) albums, including her debut single for Immediate from 1965. *—Andy Kellman*

Harry Nilsson

b. Jun. 15, 1941, Brooklyn, NY, **d.** Jan. 15, 1994, Agoura Hills, CA
Vocals, Piano / Album Rock, Psychedelic Pop, Baroque Pop, Brill Building Pop, Pop/Rock, Soft Rock, Pop, Singer/Songwriter

Although he synthesized disparate elements of both rock and pop traditions, singer/songwriter Harry Nilsson was at heart a maverick whose allegiance belonged to neither. His initial series of albums in the late '60s made him a personal favorite of the Beatles, who found a natural affinity with his knack for catchy melodies, witty lyrics, and extraordinary vocal range. Thought of as a songwriter first and a performer second, he became a pop star himself in the late '60s and early '70s with "Everybody's Talking" and "Without You."

Nilsson had been struggling to make inroads into the music business for over five years before his critically acclaimed 1967 album, *Pandemonium Shadow Show.* Three Dog Night took Harry's "One" into the Top Ten in 1969, and Nilsson's second LP, *Aerial Ballet,* continued the ambitious pop/rock direction of his debut. When one of its songs, "Everybody's Talkin'," was used as the theme for the *Midnight Cowboy* film, Nilsson had his first Top Ten hit. The irony was that, although Nilsson was primarily identified as a singer/songwriter, the song was a cover of a composition by folk-rocker Fred Neil.

Nilsson would never be content to be pigeonholed into definite categories, as demonstrated by his two 1970 albums. One was devoted entirely to covers of songs by Randy Newman; another was his soundtrack to an animated children's special, *The Point.* And it was another cover (of a Badfinger album track) that gave him his biggest single, the number smash "Without You." Yet Nilsson didn't cash in on his stardom in a conventional manner; he never performed in concert (there were occasional television appearances), preferring to craft his artistry in the studio.

During the first half of the '70s, he broadened his range from the well-crafted, peppy, sensitive tunes that had dotted his early releases, cutting some tougher, more sour work. Much of Nilsson's notoriety stems from a period in the mid-'70s when he was a drinking buddy of John Lennon in Los Angeles. Lennon produced Nilsson's *Pussycats,* his last album to make the Top 100. After a few rather unsuccessful late '70s album, Nilsson withdrew from the studio into family life. In failing health in the 1990s, diagnosed with diabetes and suffering a massive heart attack, he died in early 1994, just after finishing the vocal tracks for a new album. *—Richie Unterberger*

Pandemonium Shadow Show / 1967 / RCA ✦✦✦✦✦
Harry Nilsson's debut album *Pandemonium Shadow Show* was notoriously loved by the Beatles, and it's easy to see why. This is the only record of its time that feels akin to *Sgt. Pepper* and, in some ways, it's every bit as impressive. Nilsson works on a much smaller scale, leaning heavily on whimsy yet cutting it with sardonic humor and embellishing it with remarkable song and studiocraft–it's as if McCartney and Lennon were fused into the same body. *Pandemonium* can't help but feel like a cheeky show of strength by a remarkably gifted imp, spinning out psychedelic fantasias and jokes and trumping his idols by turning out a cover of "She's Leaving Home" (recorded ten days after *Sgt. Pepper*'s release) that rivals the original. Beneath all the light playful melodies ("There Will Never Be" is swinging London, LA style) or glorious laments (he rarely equaled "Sleep Late, My Lady Friend"). There are serious strains: the lyrics of "Cuddly Toy" are as unsettling as the melody catchy, the circus-stomp "Ten Little Indians" is a darkly addictive retelling of the Ten Commandments, and "1941" is quietly heartbreaking beneath its jaunty cabaret. Throughout it all, Nilsson impresses with his humor, cleverness and, above all, how his songwriting blossoms under his shockingly inventive studiocraft. Psychedelic-pop albums rarely came better than this, and it remains a thorough delight. *—Stephen Thomas Erlewine*

Aerial Ballet / 1968 / RCA ✦✦✦✦✦
As "Daddy's Song" opens *Aerial Ballet* with a cheeky saunter, it's clear that Harry Nilsson decided to pick up where he left off with his debut, offering another round of effervescent, devilishly clever pop, equal parts lite psychedelia, pretty ballads, and music hall cabaret. It's not a carbon copy, however. In one sense, he entrenches himself a little bit, emphasizing his lighter edges and humor, writing songs so cheerfully lightweight—a love song about his mom and dad, an ode to his favorite desk, an address or two to a "Little Cowboy"—that it may be a little too cloying for some tastes, even for fans of *Pandemonium Shadow Show.* Those are balanced by a couple major steps forward, namely "Everybody's Talkin'" and "One." The former finds Nilsson adopting a rolling folk-pop backing for a Fred Neil song, making it into an instant, Grammy-winning classic. The latter was the greatest song he had written to date, a haunting tale of loneliness reminiscent of McCartney, yet with its own voice. These are the songs anchoring an album that may be a little lightweight, but it's engagingly, deliberately lightweight. If it's a bit dated, it wears its old charms well. *—Stephen Thomas Erlewine*

Nilsson Sings Newman / Feb. 1970 / Buddha ✦✦✦✦✦
Named *Stereo Review*'s album of the year (and, really, can you ask for a better endorsement than that?) upon its release and generally regarded as the album that introduced Randy Newman the songwriter to a wide audience, *Nilsson Sings Newman* has gained a reputation of being a minor masterwork. This, in a way, is misguiding, since this isn't an obvious record, where the songs are delivered simply and directly. It's deliberately an album of subtle pleasures, crafted, as the liner notes state, line-by-line in the studio. As such, the preponderance of quiet piano-and-voice tracks (featuring Newman himself on piano, Nilsson on vocals) means the record can slip away upon the first few listens, especially for anyone expecting an undeniable masterpiece. Yet, a masterpiece is what this is, albeit a subtle, graceful masterpiece where the pleasure is in the grace notes, small gestures, and in-jokes. Not to say that this is devoid of emotion, it's just that the emotion is subdued, whether it's on a straightforward love song ("Caroline") or a tongue-in-cheek tale like "Love Story." For an album that introduced a songwriter as idiosyncratic as Newman, it's only appropriate that Nilsson's interpretations are every bit as original as the songs. His clear intonation and sweet, high voice are more palatable than Randy's slurred, bluesy growl, but the wild thing is, these versions demand that the listeners surrender to Nilsson's own terms. He's created gentle, intricate arrangements of tuneful yet clever songs and, as such, the album may be as much an acquired taste as Newman. Once you've acquired that taste, this is as sweet as honey. *—Stephen Thomas Erlewine*

Aerial Pandemonium Ballet / 1971 / Buddha ✦✦✦✦
What is hubris— It is *Aerial Pandemonium Ballet,* a folly Harry Nilsson crafted after winning a Grammy for "Everybody's Talkin'." Riding upon the good will generated by the award, he decided to compress and edit his first two (quite brilliant) albums into one record. He remixed tracks, erased old vocals, over-sang some new ones, edited sections out of certain songs, and slowed others down. Apart from the intros and outros, there are no brand-new items, just old tunes presented in slightly new, slightly off-putting ways. If you're not familiar with the debut, this will be pretty enchanting since the two records weren't that far apart stylistically and, let's face it, he was working with pretty terrific source material. Still, it's no substitute for the originals, and if you have a chance (and you do, with Britain's RCA Camden reissue), pick up the originals. *—Stephen Thomas Erlewine*

Nilsson Schmilsson / Nov. 1971 / RCA ✦✦✦✦✦
Nilsson had a hit, a Grammy, and critical success, yet he still didn't have a genuine blockbuster to his name when it came time to finally deliver a full-fledged follow-up to *Nilsson Sings Newman,* so he decided it was time to make that unabashed, mainstream pop/rock album. Hiring Streisand's producer Richard Perry as a collaborator, Nilsson made a streamlined, slightly domesticated, unashamed set of mature pop/rock, with a slight twist. This is an album, after all, that begins by pining for the reckless days of youth, then segues into a snapshot of suburban disconnectedness before winding through a salute to and covers of old R&B tunes ("Early in the Morning" and "Let the Good Times Roll," respectively), druggie humor ("Coconut"), and surging hard rock ("Jump Into the Fire"). There are certainly hints of the Nilsson of old, particularly in his fondness for Tin Pan Alley and McCartney melodicism—as well as his impish wit—yet he hadn't made a record as cohesive as this since his first time out, nor had he ever made something as shiny and appealing as this. It may be more accessible than before, yet it's anchored by his mischievous humor and wonderful idiosyncracies. Chances are that those lured in by the grandly melodramatic "Without You" will not be prepared for either the subtle charms of "The Moonbeam Song" or the off-kilter sensibility that makes even his breeziest pop slightly strange. In short, it's a near-perfect summary of everything Nilsson could do; he could be craftier and stranger, but never did he achieve the perfect balance as he did here. *—Stephen Thomas Erlewine*

Son of Schmilsson / Jul. 1972 / RCA ✦✦✦✦✦
Emboldened by a huge hit and hanging with Lennon and Ringo, Harry Nilsson was ready to let it all go when it came time to record a follow-up to *Nilsson Schmilsson.* The very title of *Son of Schmilsson* implies that it's a de facto sequel to its smash predecessor but, as always with Nilsson, don't take everything at face value. Yes, he's back with producer Richard Perry and he's working from the same gleefully melodic, polished pop/rock territory as before, but this is an incredibly schizoid record, an album by an enormously gifted musician deciding that, since he's already going unhinged, he might as well *indulge* himself while he's at it. And, wow, are the results ever worth it. Opening with a song to a groupie—he sang his balls off, baby, he nearly broke the microphone—and ending with an ode to "The Most Beautiful World in the World," this record careens all over the place, bouncing from one idea to another, punctuated with B-horror movie sound effects, bizarre humor, profanity, and belches. There are song parodies, seemingly straight piano ballads, vulgar hard rock, lovely love songs, and a cheerful singalong with retirees at an old folks home who all proclaim, "I'd rather be dead than wet my bed." The sheer perversity of it all would be fascinating, yet if that's all it had to offer, it'd merely be a curiosity, the way his post-*Pussy Cats* records are. Instead, this is all married to a fantastic set of songs that illustrate what a skilled, versatile songsmith Nilsson was. No, it may not be the easiest album to warm to—and it's just about the weirdest record to reach number 12 and go gold—but if you appreciate Nilsson's musicality and weirdo humor, he never got any better. *—Stephen Thomas Erlewine*

A Little Touch of Schmilsson in the Night / 1973 / RCA ✦✦

Pussy Cats / Aug. 19, 1974 / Buddha ✦✦✦
The relationship between Nilsson and Lennon is legendary. They were notorious booze-hounds and carousers, getting kicked out of clubs for misbehavior and generally terrorizing L.A. during Lennon's "Lost Weekend" of 1974. They wanted to make an album together—hell, anyone working at such a peak *would*—and the result was *Pussy Cats*, a Nilsson album produced by Lennon. Almost immediately, Nilsson got sick, resulting in a ruptured vocal cord. Not wanting Lennon to stop the sessions, Nilsson never told his friend, stubbornly working his way through the sessions until he lost his voice entirely. These are the sessions that make up *Pussy Cats*, an utterly bewildering record that's more baffling than entertaining. Like many superstar projects of its time, this is studded with contributions from friends and studio musicians, all intent on having a good time in the studio—which usually means hammering out rock & roll oldies. In this case, it meant both Dylan's "Subterranean Homesick Blues" and the childrens song "Loop De Loop," which gives a good idea where Nilsson was at. Through its messiness, *Pussy Cats* winds up showing how he and Lennon violently careened between hedonism and self-loathing. Of the new songs, the inadvertently revealing "All My Life" is the strongest, followed by the sweet "Don't Forget Me," yet this is more about tone than substance. It's about hearing Nilsson's voice getting progressively harsher, as the backing remains appealingly professional and slick. It doesn't quite jibe, and it's certainly incoherent, but that's it's charm. It may not be as wild as the Lost Weekend itself, but it couldn't have been recorded at any other time and remains a fascinating aural snapshot of the early days of 1974. *—Stephen Thomas Erlewine*

Duit on Mon Dei / 1975 / RCA ✦✦✦

Sandman / 1975 / RCA ✦✦✦

That's the Way It Is / 1976 / RCA ✦✦

Knnillssonn / 1977 / RCA ✦✦✦

● **All-Time Greatest Hits** / 1978 / RCA ✦✦✦✦✦
Nilsson's albums tended to hang together well, but that didn't keep him from throwing off singles, at least in the late '60s and early '70s. This collection contains all ten of his chart singles (including "Everybody's Talkin'"), plus his version of his song "One," which was a hit for Three Dog Night. *—William Ruhlmann*

Personal Best: The Harry Nilsson Anthology / Feb. 28, 1995 / RCA ✦✦✦✦✦

Skidoo/The Point / Sep. 12, 2000 / RCA/Camden ✦✦✦
Nilsson's two late-'60s/early-'70s soundtrack albums, *Skidoo* and *The Point!*, were released as a single-disc two-fer as part of RCA Camden's Nilsson reissue campaign. Of the two, *The Point!* holds up a bit better, since it was designed to stand on its own more than *Skidoo*, yet the two are an ideal pairing, showing Nilsson's silly humor, studio inventiveness, and pop songcraft if not at a peak, then at least in a highly distinctive, amusing setting. There are three bonus tracks: an alternate mix of "I Will Take You There" from *Skidoo*, "Girlfriend," and "Down to the Valley." *—Stephen Thomas Erlewine*

Nine Inch Nails

f. 1989, Cleveland, OH
Group / Industrial Metal, Alternative Metal, Alternative Pop/Rock, Industrial
Nine Inch Nails, the one-man band of Trent Reznor, brought industrial music to the masses with 1989's *Pretty Hate Machine*. With its electronic rush, incessant beats, and distorted guitars, the album appeared to be like much industrial music on the surface, yet Reznor wrote pop songs, not the soundtrack to a personal horror movie. NIN's scarred, harsh soundscapes were bleak enough, yet Reznor's lyrics raise the despair and self-loathing to new heights; at times, his relentless darkness can veer dangerously close to self-parody. *Pretty Hate Machine* wasn't a hit when it was released, but by the time Reznor assembled a band for the first Lollapalooza tour in 1991, the group had a sizable following that only grew with NIN's ferocious performances on the tour. Legal troubles with his record company delayed the release of a second album. In 1992, he released a stop-gap EP, *Broken*, that was harder and more abrasive than the debut, yet still conformed to conventional song structures; it debuted in the *Billboard* Top Ten. With their second full-length album, Reznor showed his true roots—'70s progressive rock. *The Downward Spiral* was promoted as a concept album, a cohesive piece of work; it also featured ex-King Crimson guitarist Adrian Belew. Still, NIN is able to straddle two seemingly opposing genres easily, gaining alternative and mainstream hard rock fans alike; whether he likes it or not, Trent Reznor is the man that made industrial palatable for pop fans. *—Stephen Thomas Erlewine*

★ **Pretty Hate Machine** / Nov. 1989 / TVT ✦✦✦✦✦
Virtually ignored upon its 1989 release, *Pretty Hate Machine* gradually became a word-of-mouth cult favorite; despite frequent critical bashings, its stature and historical importance only grew in hindsight. In addition to its stealthy rise to prominence, part of the album's legend was that budding auteur Trent Reznor took advantage of his low-level job at a Cleveland studio to begin recording it. Reznor had a background in synth-pop, and the vast majority of *Pretty Hate Machine* was electronic. Synths voiced all the main riffs, driven by pounding drum machines; distorted guitars were an important textural element, but not the primary focus. *Pretty Hate Machine* was something unique in industrial music—certainly no one else was attempting the balladry of "Something I Can Never Have," but the crucial difference was even simpler. Instead of numbing the listener with mechanical repetition, *Pretty Hate Machine*'s bleak electronics were subordinate to catchy riffs and verse-chorus song structures, which was why it built such a rabid following with so little publicity. That innovation was the most important step in bringing industrial music to a wide audience, as proven by the frequency with which late-'90s alternative metal bands copied NIN's interwoven guitar/synth textures. It was a new soundtrack for adolescent angst—noisily aggressive and coldly detached, tied together by a dominant personality. Reznor's tortured confusion and self-obsession gave industrial music a human voice, a point of connection. His lyrics were filled with betrayal, whether by lovers, society, or God; it was essentially the sound of childhood illusions shattering, and Reznor was not taking it lying down. Plus, the absolute dichotomies in his world—there was either purity and perfection, *or* depravity and worthlessness—made for smashing melodrama. Perhaps the greatest achievement of *Pretty Hate Machine* was that it brought emotional extravagance to a genre whose main theme had nearly always been dehumanization. *—Steve Huey*

Broken / Sep. 22, 1992 / Nothing/Interscope ✦✦✦✦✦
During the time that *Pretty Hate Machine* was becoming an underground sensation, Trent Reznor became embroiled in legal difficulties with his label that prevented the release of any new Nine Inch Nails material. But the three-year wait actually helped—most of NIN's fans were relatively recent converts, and they eagerly snapped up 1992's *Broken*, which afforded the already angst-ridden Reznor the opportunity to vent his ample frustration over the imbroglio. Where *Pretty Hate Machine* had a few moments of reflection and sardonic humor, *Broken* is a concentrated blast of caustic, naked rage. Given how draining it is, a full-length album in its style would unquestionably have been wearisome, even self-parodic. So, *Broken* is the rare EP that's conceptually focused and complete unto itself. Production-wise, it's also a step up from *Pretty Hate Machine*, and a showcase for Reznor's flowering studio acumen. While *Pretty Hate Machine* was primarily electronic, *Broken* is loaded with heavy, jagged guitars, processed through a veritable meat grinder of effects into a massive wall of distortion. Each song one-ups the viciousness of its predecessor; even the two relatively subdued instrumental interludes are full of abrasive textures. There are two hidden bonus cuts at the end of the CD (early pressings had them on a separate disc); they're neither as produced nor as intense, and thus separated conceptually as well as physically. The cover of Adam Ant's "(You're So) Physical" was something of a revelation—not just demonstrating Reznor's fondness for new wave, but serving as a touchstone for his self-conscious, glammed-up sense of style. That—and his skills as a producer and arranger—would reach their fullest realization on *The Downward Spiral*, but *Broken*'s tight focus and frothing intensity make it a major work in its own right. *—Steve Huey*

The Downward Spiral / Mar. 8, 1994 / Nothing/Interscope ✦✦✦✦
The Downward Spiral positioned Trent Reznor as industrial's own Phil Spector, painting detailed, layered soundscapes from a wide tonal palette. Not only did he fully integrate the crashing metal guitars of *Broken*, but several newfound elements—expanded song structures, odd time signatures, shifting arrangements filled with novel sounds, tremendous textural variety—can be traced to the influence of progressive rock. So can the painstaking attention devoted to pacing and contrast—*The Downward Spiral* is full of striking sonic juxtapositions and sudden about-faces in tone, which make for a fascinating listen. More important than craft in turning Reznor into a full-fledged rock star, however, was his brooding persona. Grunge had the mainstream salivating over melodramatic angst, which had always been Reznor's stock in trade. The left field hit "Closer" made him a post-modern shaman for the '90s, obsessed with exposing the dark side he saw behind even the most innocuous façades. In fact, his theatrics on *The Downward Spiral*—all the preening self-absorption and serpentine sexuality—seemed directly descended from Jim Morrison. Yet Reznor's nihilism often seemed like a reaction against some repressively extreme standard of purity, so the depravity he wallowed in didn't necessarily seem that depraved. That's part of the reason why, in spite of its many virtues, *The Downward Spiral* falls just short of being the masterpiece it wants to be. For one thing, fascination with texture occasionally dissolves the hooky songwriting that fueled *Pretty Hate Machine*. But more than that, Reznor's unflinching bleakness was beginning to seem like a carefully calibrated posture; his increasing musical sophistication points up the lyrical holding pattern. Having said that, the album ends on an affecting emotional peak—"Hurt" mingles drama and introspection in a way Reznor had never quite managed before. It's evidence of depth behind the charisma that deservedly made him a star. *—Steve Huey*

The Fragile / Sep. 21, 1999 / Nothing/Interscope ✦✦✦
As the double-disc *The Fragile* unfurls, all of Nine Inch Nails' trademarks—gargantuan, processed guitars, ominous electro rhythms, near-ambient keyboards, Trent Reznor's shredded vocals and tortured words—are unveiled, all sounding pretty much how they did on *The Downward Spiral*. Upon closer inspection, there are new frills, yet these aren't apparent without digging—and what's on the surface isn't necessarily inviting, either. There is nothing as rhythmic or catchy as "Closer," nothing as jarring as the piano chorus of "March of the Pigs," no ballad as naked as "Hurt." When Reznor does try for something immediate and visceral, he sounds recycled. Fortunately, *The Fragile* lives up to its title once the first disc is over. There are some detours into noisy bluster (some, like the Marilyn Manson disc "Starfuckers, Inc.," work quite well) but they're surrounded by long, evocative instrumental sections that highlight Reznor's gifts for arrangement. Whenever Reznor crafts delicate, alternately haunting and pretty soundscapes or interesting sonic juxtapositions, *The Fragile* is compelling. Since they provide a change of pace, the bursts of industrial noise assist the flow of the album, which never feels indulgent, even though it runs over 100 minutes. Still, *The Fragile* is ultimately a let-down. There's no denying that it's often gripping, offering odd and interesting variations on NIN themes, but that's the problem—they're just variations, not progressions. Considering that it arrives five years after *Spiral*, that is a disappointment. It's easy to tell where the time went—Reznor's music is immaculately crafted and arranged, with every note and nuance gliding into the next—but he spent more time constructing surfaces than songs. Those surfaces can be enticing but since it's just surface, *The Fragile* winds up being vaguely unsatisfying. *—Stephen Thomas Erlewine*

Nirvana

f. 1987, Aberdeen, WA, **db.** 1994
Group / Grunge, Alternative Pop/Rock
Prior to Nirvana, alternative music was consigned to specialty sections of record stores and major labels considered it to be, at the very most, a tax write-off. After the band's second album, 1991's *Nevermind*, nothing was ever quite the same, for better and for worse. Nirvana popularized punk, post-punk, and indie rock, unintentionally bringing it into the American mainstream like no other band before it. While its sound was equal parts Black Sabbath (as learned by fellow Washington underground rockers, the Melvins) and Cheap Trick, Nirvana's

aesthetics were strictly indie rock. They covered Vaselines songs, they revived New Wave cuts by Devo, and leader Kurt Cobain relentlessly pushed his favorite bands—whether it was the art-punk of the Raincoats or the country-fried hardcore of the Meat Puppets—as if his favorite records were always more important than his own music. While Nirvana's ideology was indie rock and their melodies were pop, the sonic rush of their records and live shows merged the post-industrial white noise with heavy metal grind. And that's what made the group an unprecedented multi-platinum sensation. Jane's Addiction and Soundgarden may have proven to the vast American heavy metal audience that alternative could rock, and the Pixies may have merged pop sensibilities with indie rock white noise, but Nirvana pulled it all together, creating a sound that was both fiery and melodic. Since Nirvana was rooted in the indie aesthetic, but loved pop music, they fought their stardom while courting it, becoming some of the most notorious anti-rock stars in history. The result was a conscious attempt to shed their audience with the abrasive *In Utero,* which only partially fulfilled the band's goal. But by that point, the fate of the band and Kurt Cobain had been sealed. Suffering from drug addiction and manic depression, Cobain had become destructive and suicidal, though his management and label were able to hide the extent of his problems from the public until April 8, 1994, when he was found dead of a self-inflicted shotgun wound. Cobain may not have been able to weather Nirvana's success, but the band's legacy stands as one of the most influential in rock & roll history. *—Stephen Thomas Erlewine*

Bleach / 1989 / Sub Pop ♦♦♦
This is one case where the legend really precedes the record itself. Cut for about 600 dollars in Jack Endino's studio over just a matter of days, this captures Nirvana at a formative stage, still indebted to the murk that became known as grunge, yet not quite finding their voice as songwriters. Which isn't to say that they were devoid of original material, since even at this stage Kurt Cobain illustrated signs of his considerable songcraft, particularly on the minor-key ballad "About a Girl" and the dense churn of "Blew." A few songs come close to that level, but that's more a triumph of sound than structure, as "Negative Creep" and "School" get by on attitude and churn, while the cover of "Love Buzz" winds up being one of the highlights because this gives a true menace to their sound, thanks to its menacing melody. The rest of it sinks into the sludge, as the group itself winds up succumbing to grinding sub-metallic riffing that has little power, due to lack of riffs and lack of a good drummer. *Bleach* is more than a historical curiosity since it does have its share of great songs, but it isn't a lost classic—it's a debut from a band that shows potential but haven't yet achieved it. *—Stephen Thomas Erlewine*

★ **Nevermind** / Sep. 24, 1991 / DGC ♦♦♦♦♦
Nevermind was never meant to change the world, but you can never predict when the zeitgeist will hit, and Nirvana's second album turned out to be the place where alternative rock crashed into the mainstream. This wasn't entirely an accident, either, since Nirvana did sign with a major label, and they did release a record with a shiny surface, no matter how humongous the guitars sounded. And, yes, *Nevermind* is probably a little shinier than it should be, positively glistening with echo and fuzz-box distortion, especially when compared with the black-and-white murk of *Bleach.* This doesn't discount the record, since it's not only much harder than any mainstream rock of 1991, its character isn't on the surface, it's in the exhilaratingly raw music and haunting songs. Kurt Cobain's personal problems and subsequent suicide naturally deepens the dark undercurrents, but no matter how much anguish there is on *Nevermind,* it's bracing because he exorcises those demons through his evocative wordplay and mangled screams—and because the band has a tremendous, unbridled power that transcends the pain, turning into pure catharsis. And, that's as key to the record's success as Cobain's songwriting, since Krist Novoselic and Dave Grohl help turn this music that is gripping, powerful, and even fun (and, really, there's no other way to characterize "Territorial Pissings" or the surging "Breed"). In retrospect, *Nevermind* may seem a little too unassuming for its mythic status—it's simply a great modern punk record—but even though it may no longer seem life-changing, it is certainly life-affirming, which may just be better. *—Stephen Thomas Erlewine*

Incesticide / Dec. 1992 / DGC ♦♦♦♦♦
Buying time and thwarting bootleggers, Nirvana and DGC released the rarities compilation *Incesticide* toward the end of 1992. Like any odds 'n' sods collection, this is uneven, but that's its charm since this captures Nirvana's character better than any official album. After all, this was a band that was born equally from '70s sludge metal, bubblegum pop, post-punk artiness, and indie rock inclusiveness, each of which are apparent on this collection. There are some non-entities here, particularly on the second side, but the plodding sub-metallic grind was part of their identity, one part of their multi-faceted character. Nirvana meant everything to everyone, from the jangle pop veterans to the garage rock ravers that worshipped the Stooges to stoner metal fetishes and indie rock bed-sits that adopted Sebadoh just as they outgrew Morrissey—everybody LOVED Nirvana, and there's something for every kind fan here, thanks to murky sludge, Devo and Vaseline covers, BBC sessions, instrumentals, and limited-edition singles, plus sub-Melvins goop, everything visceral where *Bleach* was tame. *Nevermind* doesn't capture this freewheeling indie spirit but *Incesticide* does, piling on some essentials in the meantime—the pummeling "Dive," the childhood snapshot "Sliver," the terrific forgotten indie pop tune "Been a Son," and "Aneurysm," perhaps the greatest single song the group ever recorded. Yeah, there's some filler here, but *this* is the sound of what Nirvana were actually like. *—Stephen Thomas Erlewine*

☆ **In Utero** / Sep. 21, 1993 / DGC ♦♦♦♦♦
Nirvana probably hired Steve Albini to produce *In Utero* with the hopes of creating their own *Surfer Rosa,* or at least shoring up their indie cred after becoming a pop phenomenon with a glossy punk record. *In Utero,* of course, turned out to be their last record and it's hard not to hear it as Kurt Cobain's suicide note, since Albini's stark, uncompromising sound provides the perfect setting for Cobain's bleak, even nihlistic, lyrics. Even if the album wasn't a literal suicide note, it was certainly a conscious attempt to shed their audience—an attempt that worked, by the way, since the record had lost its momentum when Cobain died in the spring of 1994. Even though the band tempered some of Albini's extreme tactics in a remix, the record remains a deliberately alienating experience, front-loaded with many of its strongest songs, then descending into a series of brief, dissonant squalls before concluding with "All Apologies," which only gets sadder with each passing year. Throughout it all, Cobain's songwriting is typically haunting, and its best moments rank among his finest work, but the overamped dynamicism of the recording seems like a way to camoflauge his dispiritedness—as does the fact that he consigned such great songs as "Verse Chorus Verse" and "I Hate Myself and Want to Die" to compilations, when they would have fit, even illuminated the themes of *In Utero.* Even without those songs, *In Utero* remains a shattering listen, whether it's viewed as Cobain's farewell letter or self-styled audience alienation. Few other records are as willfully difficult as this. *—Stephen Thomas Erlewine*

☆ **MTV Unplugged in New York** / Nov. 1, 1994 / DGC ♦♦♦♦♦
If *In Utero* is a suicide note, *MTV Unplugged in New York* is a message from beyond the grave, a summation of Kurt Cobain's talents and pain so fascinating, it's hard to listen to repeatedly. Is it the choice of material or the spare surroundings that make it so effective? Well, it's certainly a combination of both, how the version of the Vaselines' "Jesus Doesn't Want Me for a Sunbeam" or the three covers of *Meat Puppets II* songs mean as much as "All Apologies" or "Something in the Way." This, in many senses, isn't just an abnormal Nirvana record, capturing them in their sincerest desire to be R.E.M. circa *Automatic for the People,* it's the Nirvana record that nobody, especially Kurt, wanted revealed. It's a nakedly emotional record, unintentionally so, as the subtext means more than the main themes of how Nirvana wanted to prove its worth and diversity, showcasing the depth of their songwriting. As it turns out, it accomplishes its goals rather too well; this is a band, and songwriter, on the verge of discovering a new sound and style. Then, there's the subtexts, as Kurt's hurt and suicidal impulses bubble to the surface, even as he's trying to suppress them. Few records are as unblinkingly bare and naked as this, especially albums recorded by their peers. No other band could have offered covers of David Bowie's "The Man Who Sold the World" and the folk standard "Where Did You Sleep Last Night" on the same record, turning in chilling performances of both—performances that reveal as much as their original songs. *—Stephen Thomas Erlewine*

From the Muddy Banks of the Wishkah / Oct. 1, 1996 / Geffen ♦♦♦♦

No Doubt

f. 1987
Group / Ska-Punk, Adult Alternative Pop/Rock, Third Wave Ska Revival, Post-Grunge, Alternative Pop/Rock
With the return of the punks in the mid-'90s came a resurgence of their slightly more commercial rivals, new wave bands. No Doubt found a niche as a new wave/ska band, on the strength of vocalist Gwen Stefani's persona—alternately an embrace of little-girl-lost innocence and riot grrl feminism—exemplified on the band's breakout single, "Just a Girl." When No Doubt's live act began to attract regional interest, Interscope Records signed them in 1991. The band's debut a year later, an odd fusion of '80s pop and ska, sank without a trace in the wake of the grunge movement. As a result, Interscope refused to support No Doubt's tour or further recordings. The band responded by recording on their own during 1993-94; the result was the self-released *The Beacon Street Collection,* much rawer and more punk-inspired than the debut. By late 1994, Interscope allowed recordings to resume, and *Tragic Kingdom* was released in October 1995. The album served as a document of the breakup of Stefani and bassist Tony Kanal, whose relationship had lasted seven years. Thanks to constant touring and the appearance of "Just a Girl" and "Spiderwebs" on MTV's Buzz Bin, the album hit the Top Ten in 1996. By the end of the year, *Tragic Kingdom* hit number one on the album charts, almost a year after its first release. *—John Bush*

No Doubt / Mar. 17, 1992 / Interscope ♦♦♦

Beacon Street Collection / Mar. 1995 / Beacon Street/Interscope ♦♦♦♦
When No Doubt's debut album proved a disappointment to Interscope executives, the label withdrew support from the band and refused to release them from their contract. The group's self-produced reply, recorded during several sessions from 1993 to early 1995, is their finest album. The synth and new wave influences of the debut are pushed to the background and replaced by a raw sound inspired more by punk. *—John Bush*

● **Tragic Kingdom** / Oct. 10, 1995 / Trauma/Interscope ♦♦♦♦
Led by the infectious, pseudo-new wave single "Just A Girl," No Doubt's major-label debut *Tragic Kingdom* straddles the line between '90s punk, third-wave ska, and pop sensibility. The record was produced by Matthew Wilder, the auteur behind "Break My Stride"—a clever mainstream co-opting of new wave quirkiness, and, as such, an ideal pairing. Wilder kept his production lean and accessible, accentuating No Doubt's appealing mix of new wave melodicism, post-grunge rock, and West Coast sunshine. Even though the band isn't always able to fuse their edgy energy with pop melodies, the combination worked far better than anyone could have hoped. When everything does click, the record is pure fun, even if some of the album makes you wish they could sustain that energy throughout the record. *Tragic Kingdom* might not have made much of an impact upon its initial release in late 1995, but throughout 1996 "Just a Girl" and "Spiderwebs" positively ruled the airwaves, both alternative and mainstream, and in 1997 they cemented their cross-generational appeal with the ballad hit "Don't Speak." *—Stephen Thomas Erlewine*

Return of Saturn / Apr. 11, 2000 / Interscope ♦♦♦♦♦
Return to Saturn is an almost defiantly mature record about two things: Stefani's exploration of a troubled romance and her own romantic ideals, plus a serious attempt by the group to not only keep new wave alive, but to make that adolescent music relevant to an older audience. It's a high concept, but *Return to Saturn* is filled with satisfying contradictions. It's melodic, but deceptively complex; it can seem frothy, but it's never frivolous. No Doubt's desire to expand the emotional template of new wave is the perfect match for Stefani's themes—she may be writing about love, but she's not writing adolescent love songs. Fragments of her teenaged romantic fantasies remain, but she's writing as a woman in her late 20s. She's tired of being another "ex-girlfriend"—she wants to fall in love, get married, and

have a family. It's a subject that's surprisingly uncommon in pop music, which would alone make *Return to Saturn* an interesting album. What makes it a successful one is that the band delivers an aural equivalent of Stefani's lyrical themes. They also begin with their adolescent musical ideals, adding depth and detail to their pop-ska foundation. They've balance their non-ironic love of new wave with contemporary production and a sensibility borrowed from classic rock: that albums are greater than the sum of their parts. Surprisingly, they pull it off—it's a far stronger record than *Tragic Kingdom*, even if the catchiest numbers don't have the same swagger and punch as their previous hit singles. So be it. With *Return to Saturn*, No Doubt have made a terrific, layered record that exceeds any expectations set by *Tragic Kingdom*. Not only have they found their voice, they know what to do with it. *—Stephen Thomas Erlewine*

NRBQ

f. 1967, Miami, FL

Group / Bar Band, Roots Rock, Rock & Roll, Novelty

NRBQ (the New Rhythm and Blues Quartet) have amassed a fanatical cult following over more than two decades of recording and touring with their incredibly versatile eclecticism; their music might veer from country to rockabilly to pop to bar-band R&B to blues to free jazz, all in the same album. The group's wacky, sometimes corny sense of humor and in-concert unpredictability (sometimes vowing to play whatever song audience members request) have endeared them to fans, even if some find them a bit precious. Formed in 1967, NRBQ attracted immediate attention with their wide-ranging musicianship and were signed to Columbia. On their 1969 self-titled debut, the band covered rockabilly and Sun Ra on one record and pulled it off; not surprisingly, rave reviews followed. NRBQ followed it with *Boppin' the Blues*, a collaboration with rockabilly singer Carl Perkins; it too received critical praise, but Columbia was unhappy with the group's sales and dropped it. After a series of short-lived label stays, in 1989 the band got another one-album major-label deal with Virgin, which resulted in *Wild Weekend*, their first album to make the charts since the debut record. *—Steve Huey*

NRBQ [1969] / 1969 / Columbia ✦✦✦

The Q's debut is as succinct a summation of what this band was about than perhaps anything they've released since. After opening the record with a storming version of Eddie Cochran's "C'mon Everybody," they take a breath and leap headlong into a raucous version of Sun Ra's "Number 9." Add to that a songwriting collaboration between Terry Adams and jazz composer Carla Bley, and the great guitar playing of Steve Ferguson (really great on "Stomp"), and you've got the makings of a tremendously important record by a furiously eclectic and always wonderful band. *—John Dougan*

Scraps / 1972 / Rounder ✦✦✦✦

Workshop / 1973 / Kama Sutra ✦✦✦

All Hopped Up / 1977 / Rounder ✦✦✦

NRBQ at Yankee Stadium / 1978 / Mercury ✦✦✦✦✦

More than just NRBQ's best record, but one of the great records of the '70s (maybe ever!). This album contains the strongest batch of new Q songs on one record, many of them the best and most memorable songs in the band's long and storied career. Starting with Terry Adams' herky-jerky "Green Lights" to the rollicking "I Want You Bad," the band has rarely sounded better. The record's gem, however, is an Al Anderson song left over from their previous record (*All Hopped Up on Red Rooster*), "Ridin' in My Car." A song about lost love and blown chances, it has Anderson's characteristic wry sensibility and (non-fatal) heartache, all wrapped up in a ebullient pop package driven by Terry Adams' melodic keyboard riffing and Tom Ardolino's amazingly assertive drumming. *Yankee Stadium* should have been a huge album, but Mercury booted it and never capitalized on the band's fanatical support base. Caveat emptor: When this record was issued by Mercury on CD just a couple of years back, they inexplicably left off "Ridin' in My Car." *—John Dougan*

Kick Me Hard / 1979 / Rounder ✦✦✦✦✦

Tiddlywinks / 1980 / Rounder ✦✦✦✦✦

After being unceremoniously dumped by Mercury after *Yankee Stadium*, NRBQ returned to the warm embrace of Rounder and recorded a string of fine records that started with *Kick Me Hard*. This lineup was to remain intact for nearly 20 years, but here, fairly early on, the synchronicity among the quartet was apparent; it was if they'd been playing together forever, and the music excelled as a result. The songwriting was getting better too: Al, Terry, and Joey were dividing the chores but never losing the group's cohesiveness. At times, Terry's songs would be a little too goofy, and Joey's heartfelt pop might dip into saccharine sweetness now and again, but never so much that it became a huge problem. Of these two excellent records, *Kick Me Hard* lives up to its title, especially during the bluesy organ workout "Don't You Know" and the riff-happy "All Night Long" (great solo by Al). *Tiddlywinks* is carried by "Me and the Boys" (later to be recorded by Bonnie Raitt) and Anderson's beautiful "Never Take the Place of You." *—John Dougan*

Grooves in Orbit / 1983 / Bearsville/Rhino ✦✦✦

Back to a major label, NRBQ came up with a solid record that, again, didn't significantly increase their audience, even though many musicians (Elvis Costello, Bonnie Raitt) were singing their praises. Although very good, *Grooves* is not significantly better (actually it's not any better) than *Kick Me Hard* or *Tiddlywinks*. Both sides end with a whimper rather than a bang, and it seems that the band was developing an overreliance on recycling material (their cover of Johnny Cash's "Get Rhythm" shows up on *Yankee Stadium*). Still, the crucial stuff ("Rain at the Drive-In" and "Smackeroo") fit the bill. *—John Dougan*

Tap Dancin' Bats / 1983 / Rounder ✦✦✦

While the Q's were recording *Grooves* for Bearsville, Rounder released this bizarre chunk of odds and sods that featured the band's experimental side. Ask anyone who's ever gone to an NRBQ gig and they'll tell you that the Q's are as likely to play Sun Ra as they are Carl Perkins, or sometimes fuse the two. *Tap Dancin' Bats* has such supremely strange moments: their paean to wrestler/actor Lou Albano, "Captain Lou," a crazy novelty song from the '50s, "Rats in My Room," some straightahead (but slightly skewed) rock & roll, and the title track, a dissonant jazz blurt that sounds like Ornette Coleman. Truly inspiring stuff. *—John Dougan*

She Sings, They Play / 1985 / Rounder ✦✦✦

During the mid-'80s, bassist Joey Spampinato married country music legend Skeeter Davis, and what better way to celebrate than with a record that featured Skeeter's great voice with the Q backing her up. To those who have little patience for classic country performers, and who simply want to hear NRBQ rock, this is probably a minor work. But, for the rest of us, it's an unfettered joy. *—John Dougan*

God Bless Us All / 1987 / Rounder ✦✦✦

Wild Weekend / Sep. 1989 / Virgin ✦✦

● **Peek-A-Boo: The Best of NRBQ (1969-1989)** / Oct. 1990 / Rhino ✦✦✦✦✦

A two-CD set that does a great job of hitting the band's high spots, without sacrificing any of the freewheeling stylistic leaps or engaging lunacy that has made NRBQ one of America's longest-lived bands. If you're interested in a career overview and little more, this is the ideal release. However, it is my considered opinion that anyone who loves this stuff (and to emphatically use a double negative, there's nothing not to love) will have their appetite whetted for more. Not a slow spot, ill-chosen track, or bad decision among the 35 songs, this is as great a statement for NRBQ as one of the best rock bands America has ever produced. Few bands, genre notwithstanding, have been able to effortlessly recombine styles, be so defiantly off-the-wall, and rock like all get-out for so long and still sound so good. God bless them all. *—John Dougan*

Stay with We: The Best of NRBQ / May 11, 1993 / Columbia/Legacy ✦✦✦

Message for the Mess Age / Feb. 22, 1994 / Forward/Rhino ✦✦✦

You're Nice People You Are / Jul. 8, 1997 / Rounder ✦✦✦

Riding in My Car / Apr. 6, 1999 / Rounder ✦✦✦

NRBQ [1999] / Sep. 14, 1999 / Rounder ✦✦✦

Ted Nugent

b. Dec. 13, 1948, Detroit, MI

Vocals, Percussion, Guitar, Bass / Detroit Rock, Album Rock, Arena Rock, Heavy Metal, Hard Rock

Nugent started in a local Detroit teen band, the Lourds, and formed the Amboy Dukes in late '65 or early '66. He scored his first hit with "Journey to the Center of Your Mind" in 1968. Several albums using the Amboy Dukes tag followed, with the personnel changing with almost every album. Nugent went solo in 1975, marking his greatest success to date with one album after another in the charts; he put his solo career on hold to become a member of the group Damn Yankees in 1990. He resumed his solo career in 1995 with *Spirit of the Wild*. A powerful, high-decibel guitarist, Nugent's energy more than makes up for whatever subtleties he lacks. *—Cub Koda*

Free-for-All / 1976 / Epic ✦✦✦✦✦

While Ted Nugent's second solo album, 1976's *Free-for-All*, was another raging slab of rock & roll, it wasn't quite as consistent as his self-titled debut. The main reason was due to singer/rhythm guitarist Derek St. Holmes' departure from the band just as recording of the album began (due to constant grappling with the Nuge about certain musical issues). To solve the problem, producer Tom Werman convinced a then unknown singer by the name of Meat Loaf to handle the vocal chores on the songs Derek was going to sing. While it seems like a mismatch in theory, the results were not catastrophic—such rockers as "Writing on the Wall" (a virtual rewrite of "Stranglehold"), "Street Rats," and "Hammerdown" are classic Nuge stompers. But they would have been stronger with St. Holmes' contributions, as evidenced by a bonus outtake of "Street Rats" with St. Holmes on vocals and the turbo-charged "Turn It Up." But still, the title track is one of Ted's all-time best (featuring a downright vicious groove), as is the rocking tale about the 1967 Detroit riots, "Dog Eat Dog." Despite St. Holmes' absence (he would return in time for the album's subsequent tour), *Free-for-All* solidified Ted's commercial success, reaching the Top 25. [Note: As with Nugent's other 1999 re-issues, an insightful essay on this Ted era by journalist Gary Graff is included, plus bonus tracks.] *—Greg Prato*

Cat Scratch Fever / 1977 / Epic ✦✦✦✦✦

Despite becoming one of the rock's biggest concert attractions, Ted Nugent needed that one album and single that would break through in a big way, and the 1977 album and single of the same name, *Cat Scratch Fever*, did the trick. *Cat Scratch Fever* matched the focused ferocity of Nugent's excellent 1975 debut (due to singer Derek St. Holmes' re-entry into the band), featuring another first-rate set of brash hard rockers. While the title track is a certified classic anthem (the only solo-Nugent single to crack the Top 30), other tracks are just as delightful, such as the oh so subtle "Wang Dang Sweet Poontang." Further standouts include such underrated compositions as "Live It Up," "Workin' Hard, Playin' Hard," and "Out of Control," plus the exquisitely melodic instrumental "Home Bound," which the Beastie Boys would sample on their 1992 mega-hit album *Check Your Head* (the track "The Biz vs. the Nuge"). A Top 20 release, *Cat Scratch Fever* was the last Nugent release to feature his original solo band, (St. Holmes, along with bassist Rob Grange, left for good in 1978). And while he enjoyed further chart success with such titles as *Weekend Warriors* and *Double Live Gonzo*, many consider *Cat Scratch Fever* to be Ted Nugent's finest hour. [Note: As with Nugent's other 1999 re-issues, an insightful essay on this Nugent era by journalist Gary Graff is included, plus bonus tracks.] *—Greg Prato*

Double Live Gonzo / 1978 / Epic ✦✦✦✦✦

As exciting as they were, Ted Nugent's first three albums lacked the sonic punch in the gut of his outrageous live performances, something readily proved by 1978's classic *Double Live Gonzo!* Both Nugent and his band are in top form, yielding a fierce performance of their numerous mid-'70s classics. Mega hit "Cat Scratch Fever" makes an obligatory appearance, but it's the songs from Nugent's self-titled debut which truly stand out. "Just What the Doctor Ordered" is damn near perfect and the band really clicks on extended jams through "Motor City Madhouse" and the fantastic "Stranglehold." A consummate showman, Nugent also unleashes a number of hilarious, motormouth stage raps on "Baby Please Don't Go" and "Wang Dang Sweet Poontang" before offering the definitive version of his early classic "Great White Buffalo." In the year of the live album (1978), this one's about as good as they come. *—Ed Rivadavia*

Weekend Warriors / 1978 / Epic ✦✦✦

• **Great Gonzos!: The Best of Ted Nugent** / 1981 / Epic/Legacy ✦✦✦✦✦
When originally released in 1981, the ten-track *Great Gonzos!: The Best of Ted Nugent* was an expertly selected collection of Ted Nugent's best-known material. But with the advent of the CD, the length of albums can now be stretched out, such is the case with the 1999 reissue of *Great Gonzos!* All of the previous ten tracks are remastered and featured in all of their ferocious glory, as well as three extra tracks not included on the original: the exceptional instrumental from 1977, "Home Bound," plus the explosive rockers "Yank Me, Crank Me" and "Give Me Just a Little." While the Nuge is known primarily for his shorter compositions that are still classic rock radio favorites ("Cat Scratch Fever," "Just What the Doctor Ordered," "Free-For-All," "Dog Eat Dog"), his longer tracks are just as gripping ("Stranglehold," "Wango Tango," "Wang Dang Sweet Poontang"). The selections are taken mostly from Nugent's first three albums (his best work), but *Great Gonzos!* still neglects several standouts, such as "Hey Baby," "Live It Up," and "Out of Control." Still, *Great Gonzos!: The Best of Ted Nugent* remains an essential purchase for admirers of fine '70s-era hard rock/heavy metal. *—Greg Prato*

Out of Control / Jun. 22, 1993 / Epic/Legacy ✦✦✦✦✦
Out of Control is a comprehensive double-disc set that contains 34 songs from all stages of Nugent's career, tracing his rise from the Amboy Dukes to the arena-rock "madman" of the '70s. Along the way, all of his most popular songs are heard: "Journey to the Center of Your Mind," "Call of the Wild," "Great White Buffalo," "Stranglehold," "Cat Scratch Fever," "Wango Tango." There are a couple of unreleased songs and alternate takes to entice collectors, but for most listeners, this—or *Double Live Gonzo*—will be all the Nuge they need. *—Stephen Thomas Erlewine*

Spirit of the Wild / May 2, 1995 / Atlantic ✦✦✦✦✦

Loaded for Bear: The Best of Ted Nugent & Amboy Dukes / Jun. 22, 1999 / Epic/Legacy ✦✦✦✦

Gary Numan (Gary Anthony James Webb)

b. Mar. 8, 1958, Hammersmith, London, England
Vocals, Keyboards, Synthesizer / New Romantic, New Wave, Electronic, Synth Pop
Gary Numan managed to incorporate the electronic innovations of Kraftwerk, Brian Eno, and David Bowie into pop music, creating some of the first synth-pop hits of the new wave era. Numan originally performed under the name Tubeway Army, which had a chart-topping British single with "Are 'Friends' Electric?" The first record he released under his own name, 1979's *Pleasure Principle,* featured the international hit "Cars"; the single hit number one in the U.K. and reached the U.S. Top Ten. Throughout the early '80s, Numan was one of the most popular artists in the U.K., amassing several Top Ten hits and two number one albums. Around 1983, his career began to slip, as each record became indistinguishable from the other. Even as he fell out of the Top Ten, Numan held on to his diehard fans. He continued to record into the '90s, releasing *Fury* in 1998 and *Dramatis Project* and *Pure* in 2000. Early 2001 saw the release of *Live at Labatt's Hammersmith Apollo. —Stephen Thomas Erlewine*

Tubeway Army / Nov. 1978 / Beggars Banquet ✦✦✦✦
The classic, long out of print self-titled debut by Gary Numan's Tubeway Army was finally reissued by Beggars Banquet, who have done a masterful job remastering the tracks and adding a live set from 1978 as a bonus. In the past, many have felt that Numan's debut disc didn't measure up to his later triumphs (1979's *Replicas,* 1980's *Telekon,* etc.), but listening to it today, you discover that it's the most underrated of all his early albums. Numan & the Tubeway Army were one of the first new wave/punk bands (along with Kraftwerk and Devo) to successfully fuse robotic synthesizers with rock & roll. Gary Numan's guitar riffing is more prominent here than on any other of his albums, which gives the tunes a splendid *Ziggy Stardust* feel at times. Kicking things off with several strong compositions—"Listen to the Sirens," "The Life Machine," and "Friends"—the album sags momentarily in the middle ("My Love Is Liquid"), but soon returns to its high standards with "Are You Real?" and "Jo the Waiter." The reissue of *Tubeway Army* wraps up with the 13-track *Living Ornaments '78: Live at the Roxy* set, which was previously released only as a bootleg. Although lo-fi, it's an audience recording containing songs that didn't make it to the debut. [Note: In addition to bonus tracks, all of the Gary Numan/Begggars Banquet re-releases contain classic photographs and informative liner notes by Numan biographer Steve Malins.] *—Greg Prato*

Replicas / 1979 / Beggars Banquet ✦✦✦✦
By the release of their second album, *Replicas,* Gary Numan was the undisputed focal point and leader of icy electro-punkers Tubeway Army. And the move proved to be massively successful back home in the U.K., where both the album and the single "Are 'Friends' Electric?" topped the charts. The band had made a conscious effort to streamline the sound heard on their 1978 self-titled debut—the distorted guitar riffs were played on Moog synthesizers instead, and Numan had perfected his faux-space-age persona. And the paranoia that is very evident in the lyrics and vocals on Numan's next release, *The Pleasure Principle,* can be detected on *Replicas.* Another near-perfect album by the band, highlights are many—"Me! I Disconnect From You," "The Machman," "You Are in My Vision," and one of the most underrated new wave/synth-driven compositions of the whole era, the chilling ballad "Down in the Park." And out of all the Gary Numan/Beggars Banquet reissues, *Replicas* contains the strongest bonus tracks, such as never heard outtakes from the recording sessions, including "The Crazies," "Only a Downstat," and the B-side to the original "Are 'Friends' Electric?" single, "We Are So Fragile." [Note: In addition to bonus tracks, all of the Gary Numan/Begggars Banquet re-releases contain classic photographs and informative liner notes by Numan biographer Steve Malins.] *—Greg Prato*

The Pleasure Principle / Sep. 1979 / Beggars Banquet ✦✦✦✦✦
The most popular of all the Gary Numan albums is undeniably 1979's *The Pleasure Principle.* The reasons are simple—there is not a single weak moment on the disc, it contains his sole U.S. (number one worldwide) hit, "Cars," and new drummer Cedric Sharpley adds a whole new dimension with his powerful percussion work. *The Pleasure Principle* is also one of the first Gary Numan albums to feature true ensemble playing, especially heard within the airtight, killer groove of "Metal" (one of Numan's all-time best tracks). Starting things off with the atmospheric instrumental "Airlane," the quality of the songs get stronger and stronger as the album progresses—"Films," "M.E.," "Observer," "Conversation," the aforementioned "Cars," and the U.K. Top Ten hit "Complex" all show Numan in top form. The 1998 reissue contains three unreleased instrumentals (one the B-side to the "Cars" single, "Asylum"), as well as four live tracks. If you had to own just one Gary Numan album, *The Pleasure Principle* would be it. [Note: In addition to bonus tracks, all of the Gary Numan/Begggars Banquet re-releases contain classic photographs and informative liner notes by Numan biographer Steve Malins.] *—Greg Prato*

Telekon / 1980 / Beggars Banquet ✦✦✦

I, Assassin / 1982 / Arista ✦✦✦

• **Premier Hits** / Mar. 25, 1997 / Beggars Banquet ✦✦✦✦✦
In the U.S., Gary Numan is remembered as a one-hit-wonder, while back home in his native England, he continued to crank out hit after hit and became a superstar in the process. His icy space-age persona and sound may be forever associated with early-80's British new wave (Flock of Seagulls, early-Duran Duran, etc.), but he was the originator, and today seems pretty darned original. Numan was a scholar of the David Bowie *Ziggy Stardust*-era, and used Bowie's space alien approach as a starting point. While retaining his futuristic lyrics, Gary stripped *Ziggy's* sound free of the distorted guitar riffing and posturing, and replaced it with clinical synthesizers and a standoffish stage persona. His music also gives off a paranoid vibe at times, as evidenced on the hits "I Die: You Die" and "Are 'Friends' Electric?" But Numan's songs can also sedate you ("Down in the Park"), while other times sneak up on you (the unexpected punk rocker "Bombers"). And of course there's his sole U.S. hit, "Cars," which sounds like a not so distant ancestor to fellow futuristic weirdos Devo. *—Greg Prato*

Remodulate: The Numa Chronicles / Aug. 4, 1998 / Cleopatra ✦✦✦✦
Remodulate: The Numa Chronicles is a two-CD retrospective covering Gary Numan's output for his own Numa label from 1984-1995; however, fans looking for a concise overview of that period should be warned that the second CD consists of live material from throughout Numan's career. Also, some fans will appreciate the fact that some singles on the first disc are included in their extended versions, while others might find that they detract from the overall playability. [Note: the vinyl release of *Remodulate* contains two bonus tracks.] *—Steve Huey*

Laura Nyro

b. Oct. 18, 1947, New York, NY [The Bronx], **d.** Apr. 9, 1997
Vocals, Piano, Guitar / Pop, Singer/Songwriter
Laura Nyro was one of pop music's true originals: a brilliant and innovative composer, her songs found greater commercial success in the hands of other performers, but her own records—intricate, haunting works highlighting her singularly powerful vocal phrasing, evocative lyrics and alchemical fusion of gospel, soul, folk and jazz structures—remain her definitive artistic legacy. Her first LP, 1966's *More Than a New Discovery,* was commercially unsuccessful though it proved a treasure trove of material for artists like the Fifth Dimension, Barbra Streisand, and Blood, Sweat & Tears. After an appearance at 1967's Monterey Pop Festival, Nyro gained a fan in David Geffen, who became her manager. He also won Nyro a contract with Columbia, and in 1968 she returned with the extraordinary *Eli and the Thirteenth Confession,* which earned vast critical acclaim. At the age of 24 however, Nyro announced her retirement; she married and severed her industry connections. However, the marriage ended in divorce, and in 1975 she resurfaced with *Smile.* However, the long layoff derailed whatever chart momentum her music had accrued, and after the dismal sales of 1978's *Nested,* she again retreated from the music business. When Nyro finally returned from her self-imposed exile in 1984 with *Mother's Spiritual,* her music had grown more reserved and introspective. *Walk the Dog and Light the Light,* her first collection of new material in nearly a decade, followed in 1993. Nyro died of ovarian cancer in 1997. *—Jason Ankeny*

• **Eli and the 13th Confession** / 1968 / Columbia ✦✦✦✦✦
The hits (for others) keep coming—"Sweet Blindness," "Eli's Comin'," and "Stoned Soul Picnic" are all here, sung by their author—but Nyro not only proves herself a powerful singer in her own right, comfortable in styles from jazz to gospel/R&B to stark balladry, she also begins to turn to a more introspective, personal writing and singing which no one will be able to replicate. *—William Ruhlmann*

New York Tendaberry / 1969 / Columbia ✦✦✦✦✦
A stunning musical journey through love, loss, religion, and eroticism, by turns passionate, inspired, and suicidal, this is Nyro's most accomplished, most idiosyncratic record, and one of the greatest singer/songwriter works ever made. Using a wide vocal range and her often delicate piano work with deftly added instrumental touches, Nyro creates an aural landscape that spans the extremes of human emotion. It's not listed as her "pick" album only because it's not the place to start; rather, it's the logical conclusion of her musical development. *—William Ruhlmann*

Gonna Take a Miracle / 1971 / Columbia ✦✦✦✦✦
A joyous change of pace, this album presents inspired readings of pop/R&B hits of the '60s, songs like "Jimmy Mack" and "Nowhere to Run," produced by creamy-smooth soul producers Gamble & Huff and sung rapturously by Nyro, with gorgeous backing by Patti LaBelle, Sarah Dash, and Nona Hendryx. *—William Ruhlmann*

The First Songs / 1973 / Columbia ✦✦✦
Columbia Records acquired Laura Nyro's 1967 debut album from Verve Forecast and reissued it in 1973, by which time such songs as "Wedding Bell Blues," "Stoney End," and "And When I Die" had become enormously successful copyrights for Nyro. *—William Ruhlmann*

Smile / 1976 / Columbia ✦✦✦
This warm comeback album is Laura Nyro's *Double Fantasy,* a return to action by a mature artist, who retains her emotional power but has worked through her problems and beaten back her demons to emerge as a "Sexy Mama." *—William Ruhlmann*

Season of Lights . . . Laura Nyro in Concert / 1977 / Columbia ✦✦

Nested / 1978 / Columbia ✦✦✦✦

Mother's Spiritual / 1984 / Columbia ✦✦

Live at the Bottom Line / 1990 / A&M ✦✦✦

Walk the Dog & Light the Light (Run the Dog Darling Light Delight) / Aug. 17, 1993 / Columbia ✦✦✦

Stoned Soul Picnic: The Best of Laura Nyro / Feb. 18, 1997 / Columbia/Legacy ✦✦✦✦✦
A double-CD, career-spanning retrospective that offers little in the way of surprises: it's a tastefully selected overview of her career highlights, heaviest (and justifiably so) on her late '60s albums. There's the inevitable feeling of letdown as disc two progresses; her post-early '70s material is far less interesting than her earliest work, even if it's inoffensive. All of the first five albums (through 1971's *Gonna Take a Miracle*) are now on CD, so this is most suitable for the fan who isn't passionate enough to be a completist. Includes a couple of previously unreleased live tracks from the '90s; the version of "Sweet Blindness," unfortunately, is not the original late '60s recording, but from a late '70s live album. *—Richie Unterberger*

● **Time and Love: The Essential Masters** / Oct. 10, 2000 / Columbia/Legacy ✦✦✦✦✦
As a 16-song, single-disc best-of, this does the job very nicely for those who want Nyro's best and most famous songs in one place. Only nine tracks into the CD you've already heard "Sweet Blindness," "Wedding Bell Blues," "And When I Die," "Blowin' Away," "Eli's Comin'," "Stoney End," and "Stoned Soul Picnic," which should be enough to convince anyone that Nyro was a major singer/songwriter. An argument could be made that, as an album-oriented performer whose career spanned about three decades, this is too brief a sampling of her discography, and too lopsided, as just one of the songs was recorded after 1970 (at which point she had yet to reach her 25th birthday). Still, the hard facts are that Nyro's best recordings and compositions were those from the beginning of her career. If you want greater breadth, there's the two-CD *Stoned Soul Picnic: The Best of Laura Nyro* compilation. But if a best-of's all you want, you don't lose much by springing for *Time and Love* instead, as disc two of *Stoned Soul Picnic* really isn't that good. Another good reason to consider this the first choice: *Time and Love* uses the original 1968 studio version of "Sweet Blindness" (a 1976 live rendition was used on *Stoned Soul Picnic*). *—Richie Unterberger*

Oasis

f. 1993, Manchester, England
Group / British Trad Rock, Britpop, Pop/Rock, Alternative Pop/Rock, Hard Rock
Oasis shot from obscurity to stardom in 1994, becoming one of Britain's most popular and critically acclaimed bands of the decade; along with Blur and Suede, they are responsible for returning British guitar-pop to the top of the charts. Led by guitarist/songwriter Noel Gallagher and his vocalist brother Liam, the Manchester quintet adopts the rough, thuggish image of the Stones and the Who, crosses it with Beatlesque melodies and hooks, distinctly British lyrical themes and song structures like the Jam and the Kinks, and ties it all together with a massive, loud guitar roar, as well as a defiant sneer that draws equally from the Sex Pistols' rebelliousness and the Stone Roses' cocksure arrogance. Gallagher's songs frequently rework previous hits from T. Rex ("Cigarettes and Alcohol" borrows the riff from "Bang a Gong") to Wham! ("Fade Away" takes the melody from "Freedom"), yet the group always puts the hooks in different settings, updating past hits for a new era. *—Stephen Thomas Erlewine*

● **Definitely Maybe** / Aug. 1994 / Epic ✦✦✦✦✦
Definitely Maybe manages to encapsulate much of the best of British rock & roll—from the Beatles to the Stone Roses—in the space of 11 songs. Their sound is louder and more guitar-oriented than any British band since the Sex Pistols, and the band is blessed with the excellent songwriting of Noel Gallagher. Gallagher writes perfect pop songs, offering a platform for his brother Liam's brash, snarling vocals. Not only does the band have melodies, but they have the capability to work a groove with more dexterity than most post-punk groups. But what makes *Definitely Maybe* so intoxicating is that it already resembles a greatest hits album. From the swirling rush of "Rock 'n' Roll Star," through the sinewy "Shakermaker," to the heartbreaking "Live Forever," each song sounds like an instant classic. *—Stephen Thomas Erlewine*

(What's the Story) Morning Glory? / Oct. 3, 1995 / Epic ✦✦✦✦✦
If *Definitely Maybe* was an unintentional concept album about wanting to be a rock & roll star, *(What's the Story) Morning Glory?* is what happens after the dreams come true. Oasis turns in a relatively introspective second record, filled with big, gorgeous ballads instead of ripping rockers. Unlike *Definitely Maybe,* the production on *Morning Glory* is varied enough to handle the range in emotions; instead of drowning everything with amplifiers turned up to 12, there are strings, keyboards, and harmonicas. This expanded production helps give Noel Gallagher's sweeping melodies an emotional resonance that he occasionally can't convey lyrically. However, that is far from a fatal flaw; Gallagher's lyrics work best in fragments, where the images catch in your mind and grow, thanks to the music. Gallagher may be guilty of some borrowing, or even plagiarism but he uses the familiar riffs as building blocks. This is where Gallagher's genius lies: He's a thief and doesn't have many original thoughts, but as a pop/rock melodicist he's pretty much without peer. Likewise, as musicians, Oasis are hardly innovators, yet they have a majestic grandeur in their sound that makes ballads like "Wonderwall" or rockers like "Some Might Say" positively transcendent. Alan White does add authority to the rhythm section, but the most noticeable change is in Liam Gallagher. His voice sneered throughout *Definitely Maybe,* but on *Morning Glory* his singing has become more textured and skillful. He gives the lyric in the raging title track a hint of regret, is sympathetic on "Wonderwall," defiant on "Some Might Say," and humorous on "She's Electric," a bawdy rewrite of "Digsy's Diner." It might not have the immediate impact of *Definitely Maybe,* but *Morning Glory* is just as exciting and compulsively listenable. *—Stephen Thomas Erlewine*

Be Here Now / Aug. 26, 1997 / Epic ✦✦✦✦
Arriving with the force of a hurricane, Oasis' third album, *Be Here Now,* is a bright, bold, colorful tour de force that simply steamrolls over any criticism. The key to Oasis' sound is its inevitability—they are unwavering in their confidence, which means that even the hardest rockers are slow, steady, and heavy, not fast. And that self-possessed confidence, that belief in their greatness, makes *Be Here Now* intensely enjoyable, even though it offers no real songwriting breakthroughs. Noel Gallagher remains a remarkably talented synthesist, bringing together disparate strands—"D'You Know What I Mean" has an N.W.A. drum loop, a Zeppelinesque wall of guitars, electronica gurgles, and lyrical allusions to the Beatles and Dylan—to create impossibly catchy songs that sound fresh, no matter how many older songs he references. He may be working familiar territory throughout *Be Here Now,* but it doesn't matter because the craftsmanship is good. "The Girl In the Dirty Shirt" is irresistible pop, and epics like "Magic Pie" and "All Around the World" simply soar, while the rockers "My Big Mouth," "It's Getting Better (Man!!!)," and "Be Here Now" attack with a bone-crunching force. Noel is smart enough to balance his classicist tendencies with spacious, open production, filling the album with found sounds, layers of guitars, keyboards, and strings, giving the record its humungous, immediate feel. The sprawling sound and huge melodic hooks would be enough to make *Be Here Now* a winner, but Liam Gallagher's vocals give the album emotional resonance. Singing better than ever, Liam injects venom into the rockers, but he also delivers the nakedly emotional lyrics of "Don't Go Away" with affecting vulnerability. That combination of violence and sensitivity gives Oasis an emotional core, and makes *Be Here Now* a triumphant album. *—Stephen Thomas Erlewine*

The Masterplan / Nov. 3, 1998 / Epic ✦✦✦✦✦

Standing on the Shoulder of Giants / Feb. 29, 2000 / Epic ✦✦✦✦
Since Noel Gallagher plays most of the parts on the album, *Standing on the Shoulder of Giants* isn't really the debut of the new, post-Guigsy/Bonehead lineup, but it is clearly the beginning of Oasis, Mark II. Such a grandiose statement may imply that it's a clear break from Oasis' past, yet that's hardly the case, since many signatures are still in place—strummed acoustic guitars, big hooks, undeveloped lyrics, familiar rhymes, and a gigantic wall of sound. The arrangements are every bit as detailed as *Be Here Now,* but they're clearer and better focused, since Oasis' brains weren't clouded with excess and hubris. Ironically, this is also their most overtly druggy, psychedelic release to date—Gallagher and Mark "Spike" Stent spent endless hours adding mellotrons, swirling guitars, and vague dancefloor ideas borrowed from the Chemical Brothers and the Charlatans [U.K.], while Noel's melodies invariably follow the minor-key patterns typical of '60s psychedelic pop. Yet for all of its heavy psychedelic influence, *Standing on the Shoulder of Giants* is really a self-consciously mature departure from the group's usual ebullience, a deliberately mellow, mid-tempo album spiked with hints of big beat and electronica to prove that he's with it. This may result in the most cohesive Oasis record since *Definitely Maybe,* but that cohesion has come at a price. Few songs are as bracing as Noel's best work from the first three albums; not even the rockers have the giddy rush or alluring sparkle of classic Oasis. Yes, this flows well, but it's the work of a self-consciously older band and it's hard not to miss the hard rock, pure attitude, and gigantic hooks that made the group's reputation in the first place. *—Stephen Thomas Erlewine*

Familiar to Millions / Nov. 21, 2000 / Epic ✦✦✦

Ocean Colour Scene

f. 1990
Group / British Trad Rock, Britpop, Alternative Pop/Rock
Falling between the energetic pop/rock of mod revival and the psychedelic experimentations of Traffic, Ocean Colour Scene came to be one of the leading bands of the traditionalist, post-Oasis British rock of the mid-'90s. Although they had formed in the late '80s and had several hits during the height of "Madchester" in the early '90s, the band didn't earn a large following until 1996, when their second album *Mosley Shoals* became a multi-platinum success story in the U.K. Their ascent was greatly aided by Paul Weller and Oasis' Noel Gallagher, who both publicly praised Ocean Colour Scene for keeping the flame of real rock & roll burning during the '90s. And, according to one specific definition, they were right, since Ocean Colour Scene was nothing if not rock & roll traditionalists, drawing heavily from British Invasion pop, psychedelia, soul, R&B, and blues-rock to create a reverential homage to classic rock. Their devotion to trad rock may have earned them decidedly mixed reviews, but that was the very thing that earned them a sizable following. *—Stephen Thomas Erlewine*

Ocean Colour Scene / Sep. 8, 1992 / Fontana ✦✦✦

● **Moseley Shoals** / Apr. 1996 / MCA ✦✦✦✦✦
By the time the Ocean Colour Scene released their debut album in 1992, they were already considered has-beens. The band had formed during the height of Madchester, but they never released their first album until the scene was already dead, which left them without a following. But between their debut and their second album, 1996's *Moseley Shoals,* a strange thing happened—the band was taken under the wings of two of Britain's biggest pop stars, Paul Weller and Noel Gallagher. The band suddenly catapulted back into the spotlight because of their superstar connections, but the music actually deserved the attention. The Ocean Colour Scene had spent the time between their two albums improving their sound. On *Moseley Shoals,* they are looser, funkier and have strong, organic R&B vibe that was inherited from the Small Faces and Weller's solo recordings. They sprinkle Beatlesque and

Stonesy flourishes throughout the album, as well as the odd prog rock flair, adding an even more eclectic flavor to their traditionalist pop/rock. The Ocean Colour Scene is still developing their songwriting skills—the sound is more impressive than the songs throughout *Moseley Shoals*—but their second album is an unexpectedly enjoyable record. *—Stephen Thomas Erlewine*

B-Sides: Seasides & Freerides / Mar. 1997 / MCA ✦✦✦✦
Rounding up all the B-sides, demos, and rarities Ocean Colour Scene released over the course of 1996, when the band was riding the crest of their popularity, *B-Sides: Seasides & Freerides*, for all its inconsistency, illustrates the depth of their ambition, as well as their flaws. Primarily comprised of acoustic material, including a demo of "The Circle" and a fine, stripped-down version of "The Day We Caught the Train," the 16 tracks on *B-Sides* can tend to sound a little samey, but when the group branches out to the neo-prog rock of the very English "Huckleberry Grove" or to the funky instrumental "Chicken Bones and Stones," they sound better than ever, and a couple of early songs by the pre-Ocean Colour Scene band the Fanatics are interesting. Still, about half of the songs suggest that OCS may be a little too reverent in their appreciation for late-'60s rock, since they come across as only stylistic exercise, not full songs. And their live cover of "Day Tripper," featuring Noel Gallagher on guitar and Liam Gallagher on vocals, is an embarassment, simply because Liam's restrained vocals slay Simon Fowler's bellowing. But this is an isolated moment on *B-Sides: Seasides & Freerides*, since it contains enough first-rate material to make it necessary for dedicated fans. *—Stephen Thomas Erlewine*

Marchin' Already / Sep. 1997 / MCA ✦✦✦✦✦
Ocean Colour Scene reinvented themselves as trad rock journeymen with their second album, *Moseley Shoals*, a record indebted to late-'60s blues-rock, mod pop, psychedelia, and prog rock. Surprisingly, the album became a blockbuster in the U.K., so it isn't entirely surprising that its successor, *Marchin' Already*, is essentially Moseley Shoals, Pt. 2 with a bigger budget. Despite a few production flourishes—heavily panned, distorted psychedelic guitars, trombone solos, and two P.P. Arnold backing vocals—Ocean Colour Scene doesn't sound at all different on *Marchin' Already*, and their songwriting shows no noticeable improvement. But the album isn't a retreat; it's a continuation of everything that made *Moseley Shoals* such an entertaining record, and it's nearly as good as its predecessor. *Marchin' Already* is equally balanced between soulful stompers ("Travellers Tune"), rockers ("Hundred Mile High City"), and prog-inflected ballads ("Better Day," "Besides Yourself"), all delivered with almost too much passion. But the key to Ocean Colour Scene is that they are fervently committed to trad rock, which means they pour themselves into predictable songs that turn out to be quite satisfying, even if they are guilty pleasures. And if that's the case, *Marchin' Already* is a great guilty pleasure. *—Stephen Thomas Erlewine*

One From the Modern / Sep. 13, 1999 / Island ✦✦✦✦

Sinéad O'Connor

b. Dec. 8, 1966, Dublin, Ireland
Vocals, Keyboards, Guitar / College Rock, Adult Alternative Pop/Rock, Alternative Pop/Rock, Singer/Songwriter
Sinead O'Connor ranked among the most distinctive and controversial pop music stars of the 1990s, the first and in many ways the most influential of the numerous female performers whose music dominated airwaves throughout the decade. Brash and outspoken, with her shaven head, angry visage, and shapeless wardrobe a direct challenge to the popular culture's long-prevailing notions of femininity and sexuality, O'Connor irrevocably altered the image of women in rock. Railing against long-standing stereotypes simply by asserting herself not as a sex object but as a serious artist, she kick-started a revolt which led the way for performers ranging from Liz Phair to Courtney Love to Alanis Morissette. *The Lion and the Cobra* was one of the most acclaimed debut records of 1987, with a pair of alternative radio hits in the singles "Mandinka" and "Troy." However, O'Connor remained a cult figure prior to the release of 1990's chart-topping *I Do Not Want What I Haven't Got*, a harrowing masterpiece sparked by the recent dissolution of her marriage to drummer John Reynolds. Boosted by the single and video "Nothing Compares 2 U," the album established her as a major star, but controversy dogged her—she refused to perform in New Jersey if "The Star Spangled Banner" was played prior to her appearance, a move which brought public criticism from no less than Frank Sinatra, who threatened to "kick her ass." Guesting on *Saturday Night Live* in 1992, O'Connor ended her performance by ripping up a photo of Pope John Paul II, resulting in a wave of condmemnation unlike any she'd previously encountered. Two weeks after the *SNL* performance, she appeared at a Bob Dylan tribute concert at Madison Square Garden, and was promptly booed off the stage. Now a virtual pariah, O'Connor kept a low profile for the next several years; 1994's *Universal Mother*, despite good reviews, failed to relaunch her to superstar status. *—Jason Ankeny*

The Lion and the Cobra / 1987 / Ensign/Chrysalis ✦✦✦✦✦
Sinéad O'Connor's debut *The Lion and the Cobra* was a sensation upon its 1987 release, and it remains a distinctive record, finding a major talent striving to achieve her own voice. Like many debuts, it's entirely possible to hear her influences, from Peter Gabriel to Prince and contemporary rap, but what's striking about the record is how she synthesizes these into her own sound—an eerie, expansive sound heavy on atmosphere and tortured passion. If the album occasionally sinks into its own atmospheric murk a little too often, she pulls everything back into focus with songs as bracing as the hard-rocking "Mandinka" or the sexy hip-hop of "I Want Your (Hands on Me)." Still, those ethereal soundscapes are every bit as enticing as the direct material, since "Troy," "Jackie," and "Jerusalem" are compelling because of their hushed, quiet intensity. It's not a perfect album, since it can succumb to uneven pacing, but it's a thoroughly impressive debut—and it's all the more impressive when you realize she only topped it with its immediate successor, before losing all focus. *—Stephen Thomas Erlewine*

• **I Do Not Want What I Haven't Got** / Mar. 1990 / Ensign/Chrysalis ✦✦✦✦✦
I Do Not Want What I Haven't Got became Sinéad O'Connor's popular breakthrough on the strength of the stunning Prince cover "Nothing Compares 2 U," which topped the pop charts for a month. But even its remarkable intimacy wasn't adequate preparation for the harrowing confessionals that composed the majority of the album. Informed by her stormy relationship with drummer John Reynolds, who fathered O'Connor's first child before the couple broke up, *I Do Not Want What I Haven't Got* lays the singer's psyche startlingly and sometimes uncomfortably bare. The songs mostly address relationships with parents, children, and (especially) lovers, through which O'Connor weaves a stubborn refusal to be defined by anyone but herself. In fact, the album is almost *too* personal and cathartic to draw the listener in close, since O'Connor projects such turmoil and offers such specific detail. Her confrontational openness makes it easy to overlook O'Connor's musical versatility. Granted, not all of the music is as brilliantly audacious as "I Am Stretched on Your Grave," which marries a Frank O'Connor poem to eerie Celtic melodies and a James Brown "Funky Drummer" sample. But the album plays like a *tour de force* in its demonstration of everything O'Connor can do: dramatic orchestral ballads, intimate confessionals, catchy pop/rock, driving guitar rock, and protest folk, not to mention the nearly six-minute a cappella title track. What's consistent throughout is the frighteningly strong emotion O'Connor brings to bear on the material, while remaining sensitive to each piece's individual demands. Aside from being a brilliant album in its own right, *I Do Not Want What I Haven't Got* foreshadowed the rise of deeply introspective female singer/songwriters like Tori Amos and Sarah McLachlan, who were more traditionally feminine and connected with a wider audience. Which takes nothing away from anyone; if anything, it's evidence that, when on top of her game, O'Connor was a singular talent. *—Steve Huey*

Am I Not Your Girl— / Sep. 22, 1992 / Ensign/Chrysalis ✦✦

Universal Mother / Sep. 13, 1994 / Ensign/Chrysalis ✦✦✦

So Far . . . The Best of Sinead O'Connor / Nov. 18, 1997 / Chrysalis ✦✦✦
So Far . . . The Best of Sinead O'Connor is a missed opportunity, failing to deliver a comprehensive overview of the first part of O'Connor's career, or an adequate hits collection. Part of the problem is the fact that O'Connor is an album artist that happens to deliver great singles as well, which means there will be essential tracks missing from a collection, even if it relies solely on the singles. *So Far* decides to circumvent this problem by combining album tracks with singles, but that doesn't work, since it gives the patchy *Universal Mother* preference over the excellent *The Lion and the Cobra* and omits such singles as "Three Babies." Things are further muddled by the inclusion of the non-LP rarities "Heroine," "You Made Me the Thief of Your Heart," and "Empire." All three songs are worthy, but they would make more sense on a rarities collection, which could also feature B-sides and non-LP singles like "Silent Night" and "My Special Child," which have never appeared on an album. Their inclusion was designed to convince hardcore fans into buying this album, but they make the collection less appealing to casual fans. In a way, that's not a bad thing, since *So Far* doesn't provide a good introduction to O'Connor, even if it does contain such essential songs as "Mandinka," "Troy," "Nothing Compares 2 U," "I Want Your (Hands on Me)," "I Am Stretched on Your Grave," and "The Emperor's New Clothes." However, those moments of brilliance sound awkward when put in a collection as poorly conceived as this. Only extremely casual fans, those that just want the hits on one disc, need this, since most listeners with a passing interest in O'Connor are much better served by the original albums. *—Stephen Thomas Erlewine*

Faith and Courage / Jun. 13, 2000 / Atlantic ✦✦✦

Offspring

f. 1985, Garden Grove, CA
Group / Punk-Pop, Post-Grunge, Punk Revival, Alternative Pop/Rock
Offspring's metal-inflected punk became a popular sensation in 1994, selling over four million copies on an independent record label. While the group's credentials and approach follows the indie rock tradition of the '80s, sonically they sound more like an edgy, hard-driving heavy metal band, with their precise, pulsing power chords and Dexter Holland's flat vocals. The Offspring released their first album, *Ignition*, in 1993. It was an underground hit, setting the stage for the across-the-board success of 1994's *Smash*. The Nirvana-soundalike "Come out and Play," the first single from the album, became a hit in the summer of 1994 as the band was played on both alternative and album rock stations, confirming their broad-based appeal. "Self Esteem," the second single, followed the same soft verse/loud chorus fomula and stayed on the charts nearly twice as long as "Come out and Play." Following a prolonged bidding war and much soul-searching, the Offspring decided to leave Epitaph Records in 1996 for Columbia Records. The move was particularly controversial within the punk community. After much delay, the Offspring finally released their Columbia debut, *Ixnay on the Hombre*, in February of 1997. Expectation for the record was high and it did receive good reviews, but failed to become a crossover hit on the level of *Smash*, and the group also lost a significant portion of their hardcore punk audience due to the album's major-label status. *Americana* followed in 1998, scoring the hit "Pretty Fly (For a White Guy)." *—Stephen Thomas Erlewine*

Offspring / 1989 / Epitaph ✦✦✦

Ignition / Mar. 8, 1993 / Epitaph ✦✦✦✦

• **Smash** / Aug. 23, 1994 / Epitaph ✦✦✦✦✦
The Offspring's second album for Epitaph did the impossible: it landed in the Top Five, unheard of for independent records. The Offspring crossed over due to the raucous, Eastern-tinged single "Come out and Play (Keep 'Em Separated)," which stopped and started just like Nirvana, only without the Seattle trio's recklessness. The record stayed in the charts because The Offspring sounded relentlessly heavy, no matter how much the band claimed to be punk. Their tempos are slower than traditional hardcore, and their attack is as heavy as Metallica. But they acted like they were punk, with odes to no "Self Esteem" and singing about fighting in school. Nothing on the album matches the incessant catchiness of the singles, but *Smash* is a solid record, filled with enough heavy riffs to keep most teenagers happy. *—Stephen Thomas Erlewine*

Ixnay on the Hombre / Feb. 4, 1997 / Columbia ♦♦♦

Americana / Nov. 10, 1998 / Columbia ♦♦♦
With integrity intact and a hearty combination of poppy punk and wit throughout, the Offspring's fifth album is a raucous ride through America as seen through the eyes of a weary, but still optimistic, young kid. Riffs on political correctness, '70s radio fodder, and suburban disquiet are spread thick on *Americana*. If the band's targets seem a bit simple and predictable, its music rarely is. The SoCal roots aren't played to a fault, the blend of salsa and alterna-rock sounds natural, and the Offspring pretty much laugh at their culture, as well as themselves, the entire time. Best track is "Pretty Fly (For a White Guy)," which manages to bridge Def Leppard and Latin hip-hop (and the musical timeline they represent), and, in the process, disrobes Middle America's average white teen's quick fascination with and instant disposability of a once-regional heritage. With *Americana*, the Offspring are merely contributing their part. *—Michael Gallucci*

Conspiracy of One / Nov. 14, 2000 / Columbia ♦♦♦

The Ohio Players

f. 1959, Dayton, OH
Group / Funk, Soul
With their slinky, horn-powered grooves, impeccable musicianship, and eye-popping album covers, the Ohio Players were among the top funk bands of the mid-'70s. Emerging from the musical hotbed of Dayton in 1959, their debut "Trespassin'" hit the R&B charts in early 1968. Although the Players' trademark bottom-heavy, horn-driven sound was already blossoming, their follow-up, "It's a Cryin' Shame" flopped; increasingly influenced by the groundbreaking funk of Sly and the Family Stone, their single "Pain" reached the R&B Top 40 in late 1971. A year later, *Pleasure* launched the absurdist smash "Funky Worm." At Mercury, the Ohio Players enjoyed their greateat success; not only did their sound coalesce, but they became notorious for their sexually provocative LP covers, a tradition begun during their Westbound tenure. Their 1974 Mercury debut *Skin Tight* was their first unequivocal classic, launching the hit title track as well as "Jive Turkey." Its follow-up, *Fire*, remains the Players' masterpiece, topping the pop charts on the strength of its bone-rattling title cut, itself a number one hit; "I Want to Be Free," one of the band's few attempts at social commentary, was also highly successful. 1975's *Honey*—which featured perhaps the Players' most controversial and erotic cover to date—was another monster, generating the chart-topping masterpiece "Love Rollercoaster" in addition to the hits "Sweet Sticky Thing" and "Fopp."

The insistent "Who'd She Coo—," from 1976's *Contradiction*, was the Players' last number one R&B hit, and as the '70s drew to a close, the band's fortunes continued to decline. —*Jason Ankeny*

Pain / 1972 / Westbound ♦♦♦♦

Ecstacy / 1973 / Westbound ♦♦♦

Pleasure / 1973 / Westbound ♦♦♦♦

Climax / 1974 / Westbound ♦♦♦

Skin Tight / 1974 / Mercury ♦♦♦♦♦

Fire / 1975 / Mercury ♦♦♦♦♦

Honey / 1975 / Mercury ♦♦♦♦♦
Honey may have had the most controversial LP cover of 1975. Its erotic cover, which depicted a nude model covered in honey, was protested by feminists when it was alleged that the model had become stuck to the floor during the photo shoot. Some retailers, in fact, refused to carry it. All the controversy certainly didn't hurt the album commercially. In 1975, the Ohio Players were once of R&B's most successful acts, and were inescapable for anyone who listened to Black radio at the time. The album kept the band's commercial momentum going thanks to such hard-driving funk as "Love Rollercoaster" (a song that was sampled to death by rappers in the '80s and '90s and covered by the Red Hot Chili Peppers in 1996), "Fopp," and the playfully jazz-influenced hit "Sweet Sticky Thing." While the Players' outstanding contributions to funk would continue to have an enormous impact long after the band's popularity faded, it's important to stress that only about half of *Honey* falls into the funk category. In fact, lead singer Sugarfoot's moving performance on the remorseful "Alone" makes one wish that the Players' ballads were discussed more often. *—Alex Henderson*

Rattlesnake / 1975 / Westbound ♦♦♦

★ **Ohio Players Gold** / 1976 / Mercury ♦♦♦♦♦
When it get right down to it, the Ohio Players' albums were as memorable for their risque album covers as they were for their music. Sure, there were some seriously funky individual tracks, but the Players couldn't keep the momentum up throughout the course of an entire album. And that's why *Ohio Players Gold* is such a useful collection, even in light of more comprehensive latter-day collections. *Ohio Players Gold* has the good stuff and absolutely no filler. From the scorching "Fire" and the wild "Love Rollercoaster" to the sly "Jive Turkey" and "Who'd She Coo—," nearly every one of the group's finest songs are present and accounted for on *Gold*. Naturally, there are some omissions—"Funky Worm" really should have been on the collection, especially since it was their first number one R&B hit—but this album should satisfy most listeners that just want the hits. If you want to dig a little deeper into their catalog without sampling their albums, try *Funk on Fire: The Mercury Anthology* but otherwise, stick with the *Gold* and you'll reap its rewards. *—Leo Stanley*

Angel / 1977 / Mercury ♦♦♦

Funk on Fire: The Mercury Anthology / Jun. 6, 1995 / Mercury Funk Essentials ♦♦♦♦♦
One hour, 54 minutes and 12 seconds of innovative funk on two discs is nothing to sneeze at, particularly when the tracks are prime Ohio Players cuts. Mercury adroitly chronicles their chart-blazing career with full-length, unedited versions of winners and album treats. From the bluesy, strutting "Jive Turkey" to "More Than Love," the group displays their superb musicianship and ingenuity on 28 slabs of funk and soul. The guys proved they can slow-jam with anyone on "Together" and the super-lush "Honey." The Ohio Players were affectionally known as Sugarfoot, Billy, Pee Wee, Merv, Diamond, Jones, and Satch, all of whom contributed collectively in the writing and production of all the songs. Everyone is familiar with the hits, and most of their fans already have them; it's unsung pearls like "Good Luck Charm," and the convenience of having these smokin' grooves in one sweet package, makes *Funk on Fire* a must. *—Andrew Hamilton*

Orgasm: The Very Best of the Ohio Players / Jun. 30, 1998 / Southbound ♦♦♦♦♦
The majority of music fans are familiar with the legendary Ohio Players through such mid- to late-'70s pop-funk hits as "Love Rollercoaster," "Fire," and "Fopp." What many don't realize is that the band had been around since the '60s, and released a trilogy of hard funk records from 1972-1973 on the Westbound label—*Pain, Pleasure*, and *Ecstasy*—that were easily comparable to the early-'70s classics by their rival Westbound labelmates, Funkadelic. And since the albums have been out-of-print for some time, the European import *Orgasm: The Very Best of the Westbound Years* is a solid collection of tracks from this era. Included is the 1972 novelty hit "Funky Worm," as well as all the sizzling title tracks from the three albums. A pair of songs from outside the trilogy are added, "Climax" (one of the collection's best tracks) and a cover of Marvin Gaye's "What's Going On," both from 1974. A previously unissued track, "Ain't That Lovin' You (For More Reasons Than One)," is tacked on the end, making *Orgasm* an excellent anthology of the Ohio Players' early years, before they achieved mass mainstream success. *—Greg Prato*

The O'Jays

f. 1958, Canton, OH
Group / Pop-Soul, Quiet Storm, Philly Soul, Urban, Soul
Perhaps the reigning vocal group of the '70s and '80s, the O'Jays began in Canton as the Triumphs in 1958. The original lineup was Eddie Levert, Walter Williams, William Powell, Bobby Massey, and Bill Isles. They recorded as the Mascots for King in 1961 and were renamed by Cleveland disc jockey Eddie O'Jay. Isles departed in 1965 and Massey left in 1971 to become a producer, making the group a trio. They got their first chart single in 1963 for Imperial, for whom they recorded until 1967. The O'Jays' first major hit was "I'll Be Sweeter Tomorrow (Than I Was Today)" for Bell in 1967, which reached number eight on the R&B charts. They continued on Bell and Neptune until they attained stardom in 1972 on Philadelphia International. "Back Stabbers" was the first of eight number one R&B hits they would get on the label from 1972-1987. Others included "Love Train," "Give the People What They Want," "I Love Music," "Livin' for the Weekend," "Message to Our Music," "Use Ta Be My Girl," "Darlin' Darlin' Baby (Sweet, Tender, Love)," and "Lovin' You." They also had eight other Top Ten R&B hits and four other Top Ten pop smashes, while "Love Train" also topped the pop charts in 1973. They moved to EMI in 1987 and continued recording. *—Ron Wynn*

The O'Jays in Philadelphia / 1969 / Epic/Legacy ♦♦♦♦♦

☆ **Back Stabbers** / 1972 / Epic/Legacy ♦♦♦♦♦
Although you could lean toward *Ship Ahoy*, it would be hard to argue with the general assessment that *Back Stabbers* is the O'Jays' greatest album. Certainly, no other single in 1973 was as transcendent and definitive as "Love Train," without question their greatest track. "Back Stabbers" isn't far behind it; the message, harmonies, Eddie Levert's lead, and the group's refrains are all testimonies to soul's glory, and Gamble and Huff were in peak form. There were other good songs on the record, like "Listen to the Clock on the Wall" and "Shiftless, Shady, Jealous Kind of People," and three other hit singles, "992 Arguments," "Time to Get Down," and "Sunshine," but they were completely blown away by "Love Train" and "Back Stabbers." (Originally released in August 1972 as Philadelphia International 31712, *Back Stabbers* was reissued on March 12, 1996, as Epic Associated/Legacy 661Jl3, as part of Legacy's *Rhythm & Soul* Series, with liner notes by David Ritz.) *—Ron Wynn & William Ruhlmann*

Ship Ahoy / 1973 / Philadelphia International ♦♦♦♦♦
The "other" O'Jays album masterpiece, *Ship Ahoy* combined shattering message tracks and stunning love songs in a fashion matched only by Curtis Mayfield's finest material. From the album cover showing a slave ship to the memorable title song and incredible "For the Love of Money," Gamble and Huff addressed every social ill from envy to racism and greed. Eddie Levert's leads were consistently magnificent, as were the harmonies, production, and arrangements. "Put Your Hands Together" and "You Got Your Hooks In Me" would be good album cuts, but on *Ship Ahoy* they were merely icing on the cake. *—Ron Wynn*

Family Reunion / 1975 / Philadelphia International ♦♦♦

Survival / 1975 / Epic Associated/Legacy ♦♦♦♦♦

Message in Our Music / 1976 / The Right Stuff ♦♦♦

★ **Collector's Item** / 1977 / Philadelphia International ♦♦♦♦♦
After enjoying an impressive string of gold and platinum albums, The O'Jays had this collection of their biggest hits on Philadelphia International released in 1978. There was no way to lose with such songs as "Back Stabbers," "Love Train," "For the Love of Money," and "I Love Music." Unfortunately, Philadelphia International haphazardly sequenced the collection, ignoring chronological and stylistic considerations and just sticking tracks on the two sides without any attention to pacing. That gaffe aside, it's a worthy anthology for the casual listener, although the hardcore fan should look elsewhere. *—Ron Wynn*

So Full of Love / 1978 / The Right Stuff ♦♦♦

Love Train: The Best of the O'Jays / Aug. 9, 1994 / Epic/Legacy ♦♦♦♦♦
All of the band's monster 1972-76 Philadelphia International hits are here, as well as a couple of small ones. The essay by Robert Palmer is good, but at a mere ten tracks, the selection is unaccountably skimpy. *—Richie Unterberger*

Let Me Make Love to You / Jan. 24, 1995 / Epic/Legacy ♦♦♦

The Ultimate Collection / 1999 / Marginal ♦♦♦♦♦
This collection contains most of the O'Jays' Imperial/Minit Records sides, one, "I'll Be Sweeter Tomorrow" from their Bell Records stint, and "Miracles," an early recording on

Dayco Records. Collectors go crazy over these highly sought after pre-Philadelphia International tracks. The biggest pop record was "Lipstick Traces" led by Walter Williams. The others were awesome in Northeast Ohio, including "How Does It Feel," "Lonely Drifter," "Crack Up Laughing," and "Stand in for Love." Two falsetto-led chillers by William Powell ("Oh How You Hurt Me," and "Working on Your Case,") along with the occasional lead from Williams add diversity to Eddie Levert's frequent leads. While this is not definitive—that would take another CD—it is essential. *—Andrew Hamilton*

The Best of the O'Jays: 1976-1991 / Feb. 9, 1999 / The Right Stuff ✦✦✦✦✦

Olivia Tremor Control

f. 1992

Group / Experimental Rock, Neo-Psychedelia, Indie Rock, Lo-Fi

As much a concept as a band, the Olivia Tremor Control was one of the most visible and innovative members of the Elephant 6 Recording Company collective, a coterie of like-minded, lo-fi indie groups—including the Apples (in stereo), Neutral Milk Hotel, and Secret Square—who shared musicians, ideas, and sensibilities. In 1995, the OTC debuted with the EP *California Demise,* the first chapter in an ongoing series of high-concept recordings built around the surreal plot of an imaginary film conceived by singers/songwriters/multi-instrumentalists William Cullen Hart and Bill Doss. The follow-up 7", "The Giant Day," led directly into the group's 1996 debut double-LP, *Music from the Unrealized Film Script 'Dusk at Cubist Castle',* a sprawling collection of Beatlesque psychedelia, popcraft and tape loops culled from some 200 unrecorded songs. The first few thousand copies of the album also included a bonus disc of ambient "dream sequences." *Black Foliage: Animation Music By The Olivia Tremor Control* followed in 1999. *—Jason Ankeny*

● **Dusk at Cubist Castle** / Aug. 1996 / Flydaddy ✦✦✦✦✦

Not the Beatles, but an incredible facsimile: on their sprawling 27-song debut opus *Music From the Unrealized Film Script 'Dusk at Cubist Castle',* the Olivia Tremor Control manage to summon not only the sound of the *White Album*-era Fab Four, but also the unfettered creativity. The soundtrack to an as-yet unmade film about a pair of women named Olivia and Jacqueline and a massive earthquake dubbed the California Demise, the album incorporates a slew of influences and textures (including Beach Boys-flavored pop, psychedelia, Krautrock, noise, and folk-rock) and synthesizes them into a distinct homebrew of shimmering harmonies, guitar drones, backwards tape loops, and inventive effects. As an added bonus, the first few thousand copies come with a bonus CD of ambient "dream sequences"—titled *Explanation II*—which, when played simultaneously with the first disc, realizes true quadraphonic sound. Amazing. *—Jason Ankeny*

Black Foliage: Animation Music / 1999 / Flydaddy ✦✦✦✦

If the preceding *Dusk at Cubist Castle* was the Olivia Tremor Control's very own *White Album,* then the labyrinthine *Black Foliage* is their *Smile*—it's an imploding masterpiece, a work teetering on the cliff's edge between genius and madness. Torn at the seams between pop transcendence and noise radicalism, the group attempts to have it both ways, meaning teenage symphonies to God like "A New Day" rest uneasily alongside musique concrete-styled tape pastiches such as "Combinations" (which, along with the similarly styled, multipart title track, is one of the many sonic motifs snaking its way throughout the record); there are at least enough ideas for five albums here, which is both *Black Foliage's* strength and its weakness—it's impossible not to get lost inside of the OTC's swirling schizophrenia, and too often snatches of brilliance flash by too quickly to savor the moment. Moreover, with songs like "California Demise 3" continuing the oblique narrative running through previous OTC records, the artistic statement the record is making (and there undoubtedly is one) is impenetrable at best; still, with each of the band's successive releases seeming like just part of a much bigger picture only now beginning to come into focus, maybe that's the point—ultimately, *Black Foliage* just might be an end-of-the-millennium appeal which speaks directly and solely to the unconscious. *—Jason Ankeny*

Singles and Beyond / Aug. 8, 2000 / Emperor Norton ✦✦✦

Singles and Beyond, as the title suggests, collects most of the material Olivia Tremor Control released before their first full-length, *Dusk at Cubist Castle.* Although the "band sound" is still coalescing, apparently all the ingredients were in place even from the start. Sure, there's plenty of solid guitar pop/psych in store, but many of the more experimental aspects of the band (that are often released under other names like Black Swan Network or Frosted Ambassador) are also in place. Also in place is a vague "concept," of sorts, that not only links these tunes to their later, full-length recordings but provides a sense of cohesion that often lacks in singles compilations. These guys are true masters of home recording; most of these tracks were recorded at their various abodes, on four-track machines. Whether it's the tastefully bizarre production touches at the end of "Fireplace" or the Burroughs-ian cut up technique of "Christmas With William S.," The Olivia Tremor Control not only knows what they want, but they know how to achieve it as well; no small feat for home recorders. Since Elephant 6 bands tend to release material on a variety of labels with a variety of formats, *Singles and Beyond* is a welcome addition for folks who missed out the first time around. *—Sean Westergaard*

The Only Ones

f. 1977, **db.** 1981

Group / Power Pop, New Wave, Punk

Led by the raffish and slightly scuzzy romance-obsessed Peter Perrett, the Only Ones were one of the punk era's most underrated bands. Not as confrontational as the Sex Pistols, as politically indulgent as the Clash, or as stripped-down as the Ramones, the Only Ones played not-so-fast guitar rock that sounded deeply indebted to the New York Dolls and other mid-'70s proto-punks. Singing his intelligently crafted pop songs in a semi-tuneful whine of a voice and backed by a band that effectively combined youthful exuberance with gracefully aging veterans, Perrett was an astute chronicler of the vagaries of modern, dysfunctional love. Despite a career that lasted from 1978-1981 and one certifiable "hit" song to their credit (the brilliant "Another Girl, Another Planet") the Only Ones became the archetypal contenders that never broke big, despite assurances from fans and critics that they couldn't miss. *—John Dougan*

The Only Ones / Apr. 1978 / Columbia ✦✦✦✦✦

"Another Girl, Another Planet" is here, but then again, it surfaces on a number of Only Ones records. The best of their studio releases, this record is a tuneful anomaly of mid-'70s rock that stands in stark contrast to the prevailing punk zeitgeist. Still, the band (even the old guys) play with an infectious enthusiasm, and Perrett, despite his tendency toward adenoidal Dylanesque vocals, is particularly winning. *—John Dougan*

● **Special View** / 1979 / Epic ✦✦✦✦✦

In America, Epic couldn't decide whether or not to release any Only Ones recordings, so they came up with this half-way measure: a sampler. *Special View* took the strongest tracks from their debut, added tracks from their so-so second album, *Even Serpents Shine,* and the result was (surprise) a great record. All these years later, *Special View* is as good a sampler of early Only Ones as anyone could have hoped for and should be considered an important purchase, although I think it's no longer in print. *—John Dougan*

Live / 1989 / Edsel ✦✦

Peel Sessions / 1989 / Strange Fruit ✦✦✦✦✦

Frankly, one could argue an eloquent case either way as to why *Special View* or the *Peel Sessions* are the most important Only Ones recordings. I tend to recommend the *Peel Sessions,* because it's rougher, a little meaner, and The Only Ones were in the midst of their 15 minutes of fame as a rock band; plus, there's a swagger here that's missing on other recordings. *—John Dougan*

The Orb

f. 1989, London, England

Group / Ambient House, Electronica, Ambient Techno, Ambient Dub

The Orb virtually invented the electronic genre known as ambient-house, resurrecting slower, more soulful rhythms and providing a soundtrack for early-morning ravers once the clubs closed their doors. The group popularized the genre as well, by appearing on the British chart show *Top of the Pops* and hitting number one in the U.K. with the 1992 album *U.F.Orb.* Frontman Dr. Alex Paterson's formula was quite simple: he slowed down the rhythms of classic Chicago house and added synthwork and effects inspired by '70s ambient pioneers Brian Eno and Tangerine Dream. The Orb's breakout singles, 1989's "A Huge Ever Growing Pulsating Brain That Rules from the Centre of the Ultraworld" and 1990's "Little Fluffy Clouds," hit the U.K. charts upon release and sparked their debut album, 1991's *The Orb's Adventures Beyond the Ultraworld.* Second album *U.F.Orb* reached number one in Britain during 1992, thanks to the Top Ten single "Blue Room." Contract troubles delayed for three years their third studio LP, *Orbus Terrarum,* and the distance resulted in a collection of dense rhythms far removed from previous material. The Orb returned to the great beyond with the spacey sounds of 1997's *Orblivion.* *—John Bush*

★ **The Orb's Adventures Beyond the Ultraworld** / Aug. 1991 / Big Life/Island Red ✦✦✦✦✦

Much like the early Orb-related project recorded as Space, *Adventures Beyond the Ultraworld* simulates a journey through the outer realms—progressing from the soaring ambient-pop of "Little Fluffy Clouds" and the stoned "Back Side of the Moon" (a veiled Pink Floyd reference) to "Into the Fourth Dimension" and ending (after more than two hours) with the glorious live mix of "A Huge Ever Growing Pulsating Brain." A varied cast of samples (*Flash Gordon,* space broadcasts, foreign-language whispers) and warm synthesizer tones provide a convincing bed for the mid-tempo house beats and occasionally dub-inflected ambience. With a clever balance of BBC Radiophonics Workshop soundtracks, '70s ambient meisterworks by Eno, Hillage, and Floyd, plus the steady influence of Larry Heard's sublime Chicago house, *Adventures Beyond the Ultraworld* is the album that defined the ambient-house movement. *—John Bush*

☆ **U.F.Orb** / Mar. 1992 / Big Life/Island Red ✦✦✦✦✦

The commercial and artistic peak of the ambient-house movement, *U.F.Orb* strides past the debut with more periods of free-form ambience and less reliance on a standard 4/4 beat. From the opener "O.O.B.E." through the bass-heavy gait of "Blue Room" and "Towers of Dub," the flow is more natural and ranges farther than most would have expected. The bevy of contributors (including Steve Hillage, Jah Wobble, Youth, Thomas Fehlmann, and Slam) never threaten to overload the proceedings, though the minimalist sampling of *Ultraworld* is replaced by a production focus much more dense and busy, especially on the rain-forest-on-Saturn ethno-ambience of "Close Encounters." Elsewhere, Paterson maintains his fascination with the earthy dub bass lines of Mad Professor and Lee Perry, even while he's indulging in flights of fancy indebted to Sun Ra. *—John Bush*

Live 93 / Nov. 22, 1993 / Island Red ✦✦✦✦

Pomme Fritz / Jun. 13, 1994 / Island Red ✦✦✦

Orbus Terrarum / Apr. 4, 1995 / Island ✦✦✦✦

The perfect response to a music-scene swamped by what Paterson himself called "lame ambient noodling for seventy minutes," *Orbus Terrarum* brings the mothership back to earth for a collision with some surprisingly harsh percussion and noisy synth. The melodies and dub lines of previous Orb recordings are still in the mix, and the esoteric bent of *Pomme Fritz* is muted somewhat. *Orbus Terrarum* is definitely not the place to start, but it's still a worthy successor to *U.F.Orb.* The final track "Slug Dub" is an ambient epic with vocal samples taken from a children's story. *—John Bush*

Orblivion / Feb. 24, 1997 / Island ✦✦✦✦✦

If the Orb's 1995 release *Orbvs Terrarvm* was an extended meditation on the earthbound, the band's follow-up in *Orblivion* rises from the muck of primordial ectoplasm for a guided tour of late-20th century Western culture's more paranoid face. From the Cold War (the album kicks off with Kennedy's intoning of the immortal invective "Are you now, or have you ever been . . .") to the pre-millenial ranting of David Thewlis' warped, apocalyptic monologue from

Mike Leigh's *Naked* ("The bar code! The ubiquitous bar code!"), *Orblivion* does for post-industrial, turn-of-the-century mania what earlier albums such as *The Orb's Adventures Beyond the Ultraworld* and *U.F.Orb* did for aliens and flying saucers. Like the previous record—an effusive mix of sprawling environmental textures; clanging, treated percussion; and humorous, trainspottery samples—*Orblivion* brings with it another adjustment in mood, combining elements of downbeat, electro, and drum'n'bass with dense, soupy amalgams of treated electronics and shimmering rhythms. *Orblivion* also evidences a renewed interest in the more immediately engaging, upbeat pop of "Perpetual Dawn"- and "Little Fluffy Clouds"-era Orb, with a deeper, more embellished sound marked, in all likelihood, by the first full-time contributions from former engineer Andy Hughes (who replaced Kris Weston after the latter's departure in 1994). Dub is still the organizing principle of the Orb's music, however, and whatever one's opinion of the actual album (reactions are likely to range from "genius" to "aimless") the production is undeniably amazing. *—Sean Cooper*

U.F. Off: The Best of Orb / Oct. 5, 1998 / Island ♦♦♦♦
A brief, twelve-track trip through the Orb' singles archive, *U.F.Off* includes mixes of just about every single from "A Huge Evergrowing Pulsating Brain" through "Toxygene" (though not in strictly chronological order). Singles compilations for electronic artists hardly ever fit the bill for long-time listeners or neophytes, yet this one is put together well and remains a solid addition to any collection. The double-disc version inludes additional remixes plus a few unreleased tracks ("Mickey Mars," "Pi"). *—Keith Farley*

Roy Orbison

b. Apr. 23, 1936, Vernon, TX, **d.** Dec. 6, 1988, Madison, TN
Vocals, Guitar / Pop/Rock, Pop, Rockabilly, Rock & Roll
Although he shared the same rockabilly roots as Carl Perkins, Johnny Cash, and Elvis Presley, Roy Orbison went on to pioneer an entirely different brand of country/pop-based rock & roll in the early '60s. What he lacked in charisma and photogenic looks, Orbison made up for in spades with his quavering operatic voice and melodramatic narratives of unrequited love and yearning. In the process, he established rock & roll archetypes of the underdog and the hopelessly romantic loser. Orbison made his first widely distributed recordings for Sun Records in 1956. Roy was a capable rockabilly singer, and had a small national hit with his first Sun single, "Ooby Dooby." But even then, he was far more comfortable as a ballad singer than as a hepped-up rockabilly jive cat. He finally found his voice with Monument Records, scoring a number two hit in 1960 with "Only the Lonely." This established the Roy Orbison persona for good: a brooding rockaballad of failed love with a sweet, haunting melody, enhanced by his Caruso-like vocal trills at the song's emotional climax. These and his subsequent Monument hits also boasted innovative, quasi-symphonic production, with Roy's voice and guitar backed by surging strings, ominous drum rolls, and heavenly choirs of backup vocalists. Between 1960 and 1965, Orbison would have 15 Top 40 hits for Monument, including such nail-biting mini-dramas as "Running Scared," "Crying," "In Dreams," and "It's Over." Not just a singer of tear-jerking ballads, he was also capable of effecting a tough, bluesy swagger on "Dream Baby," "Candy Man," and "Mean Woman Blues." In fact, his biggest and best hit was also his hardest-rocking: "Oh, Pretty Woman" soared to number one in late 1964, at the peak of the British Invasion. *—Richie Unterberger*

There Is Only One / 1965 / MGM ♦♦

The All-Time Greatest Hits of Roy Orbison / 1976 / Monument ♦♦♦♦♦

★ **For the Lonely: 18 Greatest Hits** / 1988 / Rhino ♦♦♦♦♦
Appearing as it did just a few months before Roy Orbison's death, this single CD best-of was incredibly fortuitous for Rhino Records. It was the first compilation to include both Orbison's early successes on Sun Records along with his early-'60s hits for Monument Records and, thus, was as definitive as most casual fans needed it to be. The sound is impeccable, as is the choice of material (which was not difficult to assemble). One gets only a somewhat sketchy overview of Orbison's developing talent, ignoring the years between his Sun and Monument recordings, but that's usually the purpose of a greatest hits collection anyway. For those who want more, *The Legendary Roy Orbison* gives a better overall acoount, but as a four-CD set is a lot more expensive; *All-Time Greatest Hits* gives a somewhat fuller account of the Monument years (and all of his Monument albums were available individually as well); and the out-of-print MGM best-of covers the music from the years following his departure from Monument. (The best of the latter doesn't sound that different from the Monument material—Orbison's post-Monument songs just never caught the public's ear or managed to become hit records.) But *For the Lonely* is the best account of the music that everyone already recognizes and knows. *—Bruce Eder*

The Legendary Roy Orbison / 1988 / Columbia ♦♦♦♦♦
Tracing Roy Orbison's career from its beginnings at Sun through his big hits at Monument to his largely forgotten late-'60s recordings for MGM, the four-disc set is an exhaustive, definitive history of Orbison's peak years. Yes, his late-'80s comeback is missing (this was released a year before *Mystery Girl*, after all), but this is still as exhaustive as most serious listeners will likely need, since it contains nearly every crucial track, plus such rarities as non-LP soundtrack contributions (including the title song to the Orbison-starrer *Fastest Guitar Alive*). It does lose momentum toward the end, since Orbison's material starts to dip in quality, but there still are some hidden gems to be discovered. Hardcore fans will probably be better off with Bear Family's exhaustive *Orbison*, which has all the Sun and Monument recordings, and wait for the inevitable MGM sequel. Those that want a comprehensive, but not complete, overview will be more than satisfied with this set. *—Stephen Thomas Erlewine*

The Classic Roy Orbison (1965-1968) / 1989 / Rhino ♦♦♦
The hits dried up when Orbison left the Monument label for MGM in 1965. The 14 recordings here, taken from singles and LP tracks, feature arrangements and production not far removed from his classic Monument era. The singing is wonderful, but stacked up against his classic hits, a lot is missing. Lacking the ace songwriting of his best work, there's lots of midtempo, melodramatic rock balladry here, but somehow nothing nearly as gripping as his best compositions. *—Richie Unterberger*

Mystery Girl / 1989 / Virgin ♦♦♦♦
Although it had been years since his last recording, Roy Orbison was inducted into the Rock and Roll Hall of Fame in 1987. Perhaps as a result of the newfound interest in his music, he was invited to record with the supergroup the Traveling Wilburys. Roy Orbison had a renewed sense of purpose, and also began recording material for a new solo album. Collaborating with Jeff Lynne and Tom Petty, Roy Orbison recreates the feel of his old recordings while sounding modern. His voice sounds as strong as ever, and he is still able to hit the high notes that convey a sad, lonely ache. The highlight of the album is "She's a Mystery to Me," a haunting ballad penned by U2's Bono and the Edge that perfectly plays to all of Orbison's strengths as a singer. Released in the months after his death, *Mystery Girl* was the highest-charting album of his career and spawned the hit "You Got It"—it is a shame that Orbison was not around to experience his success. This comeback album represents Roy Orbison at his best. *—Vik Iyengar*

The Sun Years 1956-58 / Apr. 1989 / Bear Family ♦♦♦♦♦
Roy Orbison wasn't among the great rockabilly cats, as his voice was a little too rich and his performances a little too mannered to truly rock with abandon. Nevertheless, he did cut a pair of terrific rockabilly singles for Sun with "Ooby Dooby" and "Domino." He never quite reached those heights again while on Sun, as Bear Family's single-disc collection *The Sun Years 1956-58* illustrates. Containing every track he recorded for the label, including alternate takes and undubbed mixes, the collection suffers from too much similar-sounding material. Apart from the previously mentioned singles, Orbison only made a handful of songs that really rocked, and they tend lose their impact when mixed in among the mediocre songs and minutely different alternate takes. For hardcore Orbison and rockabilly collectors, the very comprehensiveness of *The Sun Years 1956-58* makes the disc necessary, but most fans—especially those enamored with his grandiose, theatrical ballads—will find that this collection is overkill. *—Stephen Thomas Erlewine*

Singles Collection / Oct. 1990 / Polygram ♦♦♦
Overlooked at the time of its issue, as it was almost simultaneously released with Rhino's *The Classic Roy Orbison (1965-1968)*, this offers a more comprehensive look at his post-Monument recordings. That doesn't mean that it's better. Most of the 1965-1968 cuts on this album are also on the Rhino one, though "She" and "Heartache," which are only on *Singles Collection*, are a couple of his better late-'60s songs. The post-1968 tracks that take up the rest of the anthology are a waste, an embarrassment at worst, as Orbison failed to either successfully incorporate contemporary influences or offer quality variations on his tested formula. Stick with the cheaper, more succinct, and easier to find *The Classic Roy Orbison* for an overview of this era. *—Richie Unterberger*

16 Biggest Hits / Feb. 2, 1999 / Monument/Legacy ♦♦♦♦♦
Roy Orbison scored 20 consecutive Top 40 hits between 1960 and 1965, all but the last of them on the Monument Records label. This compilation presents 16 of the first 17 of those hits (missing is the 1963 Christmas song "Pretty Paper"), from the 1960 gold-seller "Only the Lonely" to the 1964 chart-topper "Oh, Pretty Woman," with Orbison's seven other Top Ten hits of the era in between. Technically, a few of Orbison's singles of 1965 and 1966 did a little better in the charts than a few of the ones here, and, of course, he scored a final, posthumous Top Ten hit with "You Got It" on Virgin Records in 1989. But this collection presents the music from the hottest part of his career in chronological order, with standards like "Crying" sharing space with lesser, but still worthy songs like "I'm Hurtin'." Aficionados know Orbison's Sun works, and his later recordings earned him a new audience, but the Monument hit singles of the early '60s are what he is best remembered for, and they're all here. *—William Ruhlmann*

Orbital

f. 1987, Sevenoaks, Kent, England
Group / Electronica, Ambient Techno, Techno
Orbital became one of the biggest names in techno during the mid-'90s by solving the irreconcilable differences previously inherent in the genre: to stay true to the dance underground and, at the same time, force entry into the rock arena, where an album functions as an artistic statement—not a collection of singles—and a band's prowess is demonstrated by the actual performance of live music. Though Phil and Paul Hartnoll first charted with a single, they later became known for critically praised albums that sold well with a surprising amount of rock fans as well as electronic listeners. The duo's first single, 1989's "Chime," was an unusually sublime rave anthem that hit the British Top 20 and gained the duo a full-length release, a self-titled 1991 album. Orbital's second LP, also untitled but nicknamed the "brown" album, unified the disjointed feel of its predecessor. An American tour plus appearances at *Woodstock 2* and *the Glastonbury Festival* confirmed the duo's status as one of the premier live acts in electronic music. Following in 1994, *Snivilization* became Orbital's biggest hit, reaching number four in the British album charts. The Hartnolls' fifth album, 1996's *In Sides*, became their most acclaimed album, with many excellent reviews in publications that had never covered electronic music. Still, it was over three years before the release of Orbital's next album, 1999's *Middle of Nowhere*. *—John Bush*

Orbital / Oct. 1991 / ffrr ♦♦♦♦
The U.S. version of Orbital's debut album serves as a good primer to the group's early history, including standard versions of the early singles "Chime," "Omen," "Satan" and "Midnight," in addition to two B-sides which showed Phil and Paul's first stab at varying their Kraftwerk-inspired sound. "Belfast" (from the "Satan" single) is a warm, mid-tempo synth track inspired by Depeche Mode; "Choice," at the other extreme, is an aggro-house piece with vocal samples (i.e. "Wake Up!") that recall socially conscious punks like Crass. *—John Bush*

● **Orbital 2** / 1992 / ffrr ♦♦♦♦♦
Opening with a looped *Star Trek* sample, Orbital's second album progresses through eight tracks of warm, unrepetitive techno in what sounds more like a DJ mix album than an LP, with no bows to mainstream sensibilities. Here, the duo's acknowledged inspiration from Kraftwerk, present before but always in the background, came to the fore. The brilliant man-

ner in which the Hartnolls weave several synth lines, samples, sung vocals, and percussion—mathematically precise but still beautifully orchestrated—updated Kraftwerk's mastery of minimalist electronic music. One of the highlight of the '90s techno movement, the "brown" album is still Orbital's most exciting work. *—John Bush*

Snivilisation / Aug. 23, 1994 / ffrr ✦✦✦✦
The political commentary inherent in 1994's *Snivilization* extended even to the Top 30 single "Are We Here?," whose criminal justice bill mix voiced Phil and Paul's concern over what the bill might lead to—silence. Musically, the album delivers on the diverse promises of early B-sides "Choice" and "Belfast," with more harbingers to their thrash background—especially on "Quality Seconds"—and the addition of a third member, vocalist Alison Goldfrapp, on two songs. The shuffling, quasi-Eastern jungle rhythms of "Are We Here—," a beautiful piano run to begin "Kein Trink Wasser," and the glorious ambient climax "Attached" also reflect the fact that *Snivilization* is Orbital's most varied LP. *—John Bush*

In Sides / Mar. 1996 / ffrr/London ✦✦✦✦✦
In Sides isn't Orbital's best album, or the most accomplished, but it is the most definitive. It pulses with the energy of the debut, the lush flow of the second, and the conceptual theme of *Snivilisation*. The focus this time, though, is ecology. "The Girl with the Sun in Her Head" was recorded on a Greenpeace bus using only solar power, and "Dwr Budr" (Welsh for 'dirty water') also criticizes the misuse of natural resources. Phil and Paul's respect for the jungle/drum'n'bass movement showed in the moderate breakbeat rhythms on several tracks. *—John Bush*

Middle of Nowhere / Jun. 8, 1999 / Sire ✦✦✦✦
Electronica routinely covers more ground, more quickly, than any style of music on the planet; the hottest new sound in January is old hat by March and downright foolish to even mention in June. Orbital, however, is the great constant in the world of techno. Every few years, the brothers Hartnoll manage to turn in excellent albums that occasionally reference the latest sound but rarely vary from the chord-heavy melodics of their debut single, "Chime." Though it took a bit longer to release, *Middle of Nowhere* is another typically excellent Orbital album. Experiments with breakbeats and other styles of music made interesting mixers of their previous two albums, *Snivilisation* and *In Sides*, and this fifth album includes nods to big beat-techno ("I Don't Know You People") and soundtrack composers. The latter is hardly a surprise, considering the Hartnolls' sideline gig as score composers (*Event Horizon, The Saint*). The opener, "Way Out," adds trumpet solos and a symphonic grandeur—reminiscent of John Barry's scores for the *James Bond* films—to the quintessential Orbital sound. Even considering the lack of real progression in sound, *Middle of Nowhere* reflects the pair once again making all the right moves and not slowing down a bit. *—John Bush*

The Orioles

f. 1948, Baltimore, MD, **db.** 1954
Group / Doo Wop, R&B
Led by Sonny Til, the Orioles were the first Black vocal group to sing music directly for a Black audience. Through their early recordings—which were made in the late '40s and early '50s—the band laid the groundwork for R&B vocal groups and doo wop. The Orioles fused traditional pop songs with gospel sensibilities and arranged blues and gospel material with smooth harmonies, designed to appeal to the broadest audience possible. In 1948, their debut "It's Too Soon to Know" became a number one R&B hit and crossed over to number 13 on the pop charts. At the time of its release, no Black group had managed to cross over to the pop charts with what was then-known as a "race" record. The Orioles immediately followed the success of their debut single with the seasonal "(It's Gonna Be A) Lonely Christmas," which reached the R&B Top Ten at the end of 1948. "Tell Me So" became the Orioles' second number one R&B hit in the spring of 1949, beginning a streak of hit R&B singles that year. In addition to "Tell Me So," the group charted with "A Kiss and a Rose," "I Challenge Your Kiss" and "Forgive and Forget." Following their peak year of 1949, the group ran into tragedy in 1950 when guitarist Tommy Gaither was killed in an automobile accident that also injured two other members. The Orioles scored their next hit in 1952, when "Baby Please Don't Go" reached number eight on the R&B charts. The following year, the group had their biggest hit with "Crying in the Chapel," which spent five weeks on the R&B charts and reached number 11 on the pop charts, eventually going gold; Elvis Presley had a hit with the song 12 years later. Toward the end of the year, the group had another Top Ten R&B hit with "In the Mission of St. Augustine." The single would turn out to be their last hit. *—Stephen Thomas Erlewine*

★ **Sing Their Greatest Hits** / Nov. 25, 1991 / Collectables ✦✦✦✦✦
This Orioles hit package is about equal to any other that's available, but pales next to the Bear Family boxed set. The now defunct Murray Hill also had a great Orioles box several years ago. Save your money and grab the Bear Family if you really want the real story on The Orioles. *—Ron Wynn*

Jubilee Sides / 1993 / Bear Family ✦✦✦✦✦

Jim O'Rourke

b. 1969, Chicago, IL
Multi Instruments, Guitar, Producer / Experimental Rock, Indie Rock, Post-Rock/Experimental
American post-classical composer Jim O'Rourke has been a key component in the increasing overlap of of the American and European experimental music avant-garde, working in everything from jazz and rock to ambient and electro-acoustic and building many a bridge in between. A Chicago native, his work has found equal truck with experimental jazz and noise fanatics, chill room denizens, and bedroom experimentalists, and has had the resultant effect of cross-polinating many otherwise isolated compositional communities. Dealing most often with prepared guitar in improvisational group settings, O'Rourke has also released a fair bit of material as a soloist, althought more often in the electro-acoustic/musique concrete vein. He's collaborated with such contemporary improv heroes as Derek Bailey, Henry Kaiser, Eddie Prevost and Keith Rowe (of English improv group AMM), KK Null, David Jackman (Organum), and early Krautrock experimentalists Faust. O'Rourke was also engaged in an ongoing exploration of experimental rock as a member of Gastr Del Sol, who released albums through the Teen Beat and Table of the Elements labels. *—Sean Cooper*

Terminal Pharmacy / 1995 / Tzadik ✦✦✦✦

Bad Timing / Aug. 25, 1997 / Drag City ✦✦✦✦✦
With *Bad Timing*, O'Rourke attempts a return to the organic atmosphere of acoustic guitar from his explorations in electronica. The album consists of four songs clocking in at roughly ten minutes each, and is characterized by O'Rourke's ambient acoustic exploration. Three of the tracks enlist various instruments from cello to trumpet and even drums. The songs are highly textured and require patience, as they slowly evolve from abstract riffs into clear melodies. The album encompasses a rich dynamic range despite the seeming limitations that acoustic guitar could impose. There is a fair amount of splicing and mixing, which attests to the fact that O'Rourke has not completely dispensed with his passion for electronic music, but these interludes often provide a unique perspective. The highlight of the album is the final track, "Happy Trails," which begins with distorted acoustic noise, followed by an upbeat country rhythm provided by Tortoise's John McEntire. In sum, *Bad Timing* is a consistent effort and well worth a listen, especially during the mellow early morning hours. *—Marc Gilman*

● **Eureka** / Feb. 16, 1999 / Drag City ✦✦✦✦✦
It's a good bet to expect the unexpected with Jim O'Rourke—no matter which hat he's wearing (solo artist, bandmate, producer, remixer, etc.), each of the endlessly prolific projects that bears his name takes on a shape and identity all its own while retaining the originality and ingenuity that have become the hallmarks of his singular body of work. *Eureka* is perhaps his most stunning and surprising detour yet, a full-blown excursion into lush, melodic pop; granted, there's something inherently perverse about the very notion of O'Rourke and Chicago underground cronies like trombonist Jeb Bishop and cornetist Rob Mazurek tackling such classicist stuff, but instead the album is short on irony and long on affection—in fact, its most subversive dimension is its very real mainstream appeal. What's most fascinating about *Eureka* is that its big, bright pop is actually the perfect showcase for O'Rourke's mastery of sound—highlights like the epic opener "Women of the World" and a joyously schmaltzy cover of the Bacharach/David chestnut "Something Big" are crafted with remarkable care and depth, the former in particular building and blooming in truly majestic fashion. On a conceptual level, of course, it's easy to view *Eureka* as another in a long line of deconstructionist experiments, a reading more overtly avant songs like "Movie on the Way Down" and "Through the Night Softly" certainly bears out; on a deeper level, however, it's a true labor of love, and its sheer exuberance and creativity go further in re-shaping the pop aesthetic than any pure intellectual exercise ever could. *—Jason Ankeny*

Halfway to a Threeway [EP] / Jan. 20, 2000 / Drag City ✦✦✦✦

Beth Orton

b. Dec. 1970, Norwich, England
Vocals, Guitar / Alternative Folk, Adult Alternative Pop/Rock, Trip-Hop, Singer/Songwriter
Singer/songwriter Beth Orton combined the passionate beauty of the acoustic folk tradition with the electronic beats of trip-hop to create a fresh, distinct fusion of roots and rhythm. Born in Norwich, England in December 1970, Orton debuted as one half of the duo Spill, a one-off project with William Orbit which released a cover of John Martyn's "Don't Wanna Know About Evil." She continued working with Orbit on his 1993 LP *Strange Cargo 3*, co-writing and singing the track "Water from a Vine Leaf" before appearing with the group Red Snapper on their first singles "Snapper" and "In Deep." In 1995 Orton teamed with the Chemical Brothers for "Alive: Alone," the ultimate track on their *Exit Planet Dust* LP. After assembling a backing band comprised of double bassist Ali Friend, guitarist Ted Barnes, keyboardist Lee Spencer and drummer Wildcat Will, she finally issued her 1996 debut EP *She Cries Your Name;* her stunning full-length bow *Trailer Park*, produced in part by Andrew Weatherall, followed later in the year. In 1997, Orton released the superb *Best Bit* EP, a move towards a more organic, soulful sound highlighted by a pair of duets with folk-jazz legend Terry Callier; the full-length *Central Reservation* followed in 1999. *—Jason Ankeny*

Trailer Park / 1996 / Dedicated ✦✦✦✦✦
A folkie for the electronica age, Beth Orton brilliantly bridges the gap between acoustic songcraft and digital dance beats with her extraordinary debut album, *Trailer Park*. Fusing the plaintive emotional power of the singer/songwriter tradition with the distanced cool of trip-hop rhythms, Orton creates a fresh, distinct, and surprisingly organic sound without obvious precedent; blessed with a warm, ethereal voice capable of adapting comfortably to Spartan folk ("Whenever," a touching cover of the Spector/Greenwich/Barry-penned "I Wish I Never Saw the Sunshine"), buoyant pop ("Live As We Dream," "How Far"), and spacey, densely layered electronica ("Tangent," "Touch Me With Your Love"), she shifts gears with remarkable ease, the depth and clarity of her unique perspective connecting even the most disparate tracks together into a unified whole. Simply put, *Trailer Park* is one of the most promising and innovative debuts of its era. *—Jason Ankeny*

● **Central Reservation** / Mar. 9, 1999 / Arista ✦✦✦✦✦
On her stunning sophomore album, *Central Reservation*, Beth Orton slips free of the electronic textures that colored her acclaimed 1996 debut, *Trailer Park*, stripping her music down to its raw essentials to produce a work of stark simplicity and rare poignancy. With the exception of a pair of Ben Watt-produced tracks ("Stars All Seem to Weep" and a remix of the title cut), *Central Reservation* rejects synthetic sounds and beats altogether in favor of an organic atmosphere somewhere between folk, jazz, and the blues; the focal point is instead Orton's evocatively soulful voice, which invests songs like "Sweetest Decline" and "Feel to Believe" with remarkable warmth and honesty. It's a risky move creatively as well as commercially—after all, the club culture was the first to champion Orton's talents—but it pays off handsomely; for all its brilliance, elements of *Trailer Park* already feel dated, but the new material possesses a timelessness that recalls the best of Nick Drake or Sandy Denny,

with a haunting beauty to match. And while much has been made of the melancholy that pervades her music, ultimately *Central Reservation* is first and foremost a record about hope and survival; its emotional centerpiece, the seven-minute "Pass in Time" (a spine-tingling duet with legendary folk-jazz mystic Terry Callier), grapples with the death of Orton's mother, but its underlying message of healing and perseverance is powerfully life-affirming—her music hasn't merely discovered the light at the end of the tunnel, it's now bathing in it. *—Jason Ankeny*

Ozzy Osbourne (John Osbourne)

b. Dec. 3, 1948, Birmingham, England

Vocals / Album Rock, British Metal, Heavy Metal, Hard Rock

Though many bands have succeeded in earning the hatred of parents and media worldwide throughout the past few decades, arguably only such acts as Alice Cooper, Judas Priest and Marilyn Manson have tied the controversial record of Ozzy Osbourne. The former Black Sabbath frontman has been ridiculed over his career, mostly due to rumors denouncing him as a psychopath and Satanist. Despite his outlandish reputation, however, one cannot deny that Osbourne has had an immeasurable effect on heavy metal. While he doesn't possess a great voice (it's thin and doesn't have much range), he makes up for it with his good ear and dramatic flair. As a showman, his instincts are nearly as impeccable; his live shows have been overwrought spectacles of gore and glitz that have endeared him to adolescents around the world. Indeed, Osbourne has managed to establish himself as an international superstar, capable of selling millions of records with each album and packing arenas across the globe, capturing new fans with each record. *—Barry Weber*

Blizzard of Ozz / 1980 / Jet ✦✦✦✦✦

Ozzy Osbourne's 1981 solo debut *Blizzard of Ozz* was a masterpiece of neo-classical metal that, along with Van Halen's first album, became a cornerstone of '80s metal guitar. Upon its release, there was considerable doubt that Ozzy could become a viable solo attraction. *Blizzard of Ozz* demonstrated not only his ear for melody, but also an unfailing instinct for assembling top-notch backing bands. Onetime Quiet Riot guitarist Randy Rhoads was a startling discovery, arriving here as a unique, fully formed talent. Rhoads was just as responsible as Osbourne—perhaps even moreso—for the album's musical direction, and his application of classical-guitar techniques and scales rewrote the rulebook just as radically as Eddie Van Halen had. Rhoads could hold his own as a flashy soloist, but his detailed, ambitious compositions and arrangements revealed his true depth, as well as creating a sense of doomy, sinister elegance built on Ritchie Blackmore's minor-key innovations. All of this may seem to downplay the importance of Ozzy himself, which shouldn't be the case at all. The music is a thoroughly convincing match for his lyrical obsession with the dark side (which was never an embrace, as many conservative watchdogs assumed); so, despite its collaborative nature, it's unequivocally stamped with Ozzy's personality. What's more, the band is far more versatile and subtle than Sabbath, freeing Ozzy from his habit of singing in unison with the guitar (and proving that he had an excellent grasp of how to frame his limited voice). Nothing short of revelatory, *Blizzard of Ozz* deservedly made Ozzy a star, and it set new standards for musical virtuosity in the realm of heavy metal. *—Steve Huey*

Diary of a Madman / 1981 / Jet ✦✦✦✦✦

The follow-up to the masterful *Blizzard of Ozz, Diary of a Madman* was rushed into existence by a band desperate to finish its next album before an upcoming tour. As a result, it doesn't feel quite as fully realized—a couple of the ballads are overly long and slow the momentum, and Randy Rhoads' guide solo on "Little Dolls" was never replaced with a version intended for the public. Yet despite the fact that some songs could have used a longer gestation period, there are numerous moments of brilliance on *Diary of a Madman*—at least half of it stands up to anything on *Blizzard*, and the title track is a jaw-droppingly intricate epic that represents the most classically influenced work of Rhoads' all-too-brief career. But even if parts of the album don't quite live up to the band's previous (and incredibly high) standards, they're by no means bad; moreover, the production is fuller, and the instruments better recorded this time around. It's not uncommon to find fans who prefer *Diary* to *Blizzard*, since it sets an even more mystical, eerie mood, and since Rhoads' playing is progressing to an even higher level. One can only wonder what the Osbourne/Rhoads collaboration might have produced in the future, had Rhoads not been killed in a bizarre and sadly avoidable plane crash. *—Steve Huey*

Speak of the Devil / 1982 / Jet ✦✦✦

Bark at the Moon / 1983 / Epic ✦✦✦

Osbourne finds a permanent replacement for Rhoads in Jake E. Lee, a more standard metal guitarist without Rhoads' neo-classical compositional ability or stylistic flair. Still, Osbourne and his band turn in a competent, workmanlike set of heavy metal featuring the crunching title track, whose video (featuring Osbourne dressed as a werewolf) became popular on MTV. Unfortunately, substance abuse problems would help prevent Osbourne from releasing another record up to the standards of *Bark at the Moon* for nearly the rest of the decade. *—Steve Huey*

Tribute / 1987 / Epic ✦✦✦✦✦

This live double album, released five years after Randy Rhoads's death, showcases a hard rock guitarist whose all-around ability was arguably second only to Eddie Van Halen. Osbourne leads his best band lineup through the entire *Blizzard* repertoire, plus a few *Diary* and Sabbath numbers. Of special note are Rhoads's unaccompanied solos, leaving no doubts about his virtuosity, and the studio outtakes of his short solo piece, "Dee." Rhoads's entire output is absolutely essential for guitar freaks, but he sounds even better live than in the studio. *—Steve Huey*

No Rest for the Wicked / 1989 / Epic ✦✦✦

Just Say Ozzy / Jan. 1990 / Epic ✦✦

No More Tears / Sep. 17, 1991 / Epic ✦✦✦✦

Live & Loud / Jun. 15, 1993 / Epic ✦✦✦

Ozzmosis / Oct. 24, 1995 / Epic ✦✦

● **The Ozzman Cometh: Greatest Hits [US]** / Nov. 11, 1997 / Epic ✦✦✦✦✦

Theoretically, a greatest-hits collection should be an easy job for someone like Ozzy Osbourne, whose career always thrived on singles. However, this is not the case, as *Ozzman Cometh* proves. While the compilation does boast some of his biggest hits, including "Crazy Train," "Goodbye to Romance" and "Shot In the Dark," some of his most memorable songs, such as "I Don't Know," "Flying High Again," and "Miracle Man," are surprisingly missing. Instead of extra tracks from his 15-year career, listeners aren't even given definitive Ozzy—the album is unfortunately overshadowed with Black Sabbath basement tapes, including "Fairies Wear Boots" and "War Pigs." Although Osbourne never failed to put Sabbath hits into his live shows and albums, the idea that re-recorded material from his former band replaces some of his best songs is a little depressing. The album also includes one new track, "Back on Earth," which continues the musical setting similar to *Ozzmosis* (where Osbourne counts on synthesizers instead of guitars). Despite its flaws, however, *Ozzman Cometh* certainly delivers a good collection of hits, making it and *Tribute* the only necessary Ozzy albums for casual fans. *—Barry Weber*

Palace

f. 1992

Vocals, Guitar / Alternative Country, Alternative Country-Rock, Indie Rock, Singer/Songwriter

Will Oldham, the brains and brawn behind releases as Palace Brothers, Palace Songs, Palace Music and just plain Palace, is loosely grouped with the '90s anti-folk movement that also includes Bill Callahan of Smog, a label-mate of Oldham's on Chicago's Drag City Records. Often mistaken for an old man due to his cracking vocals, sparse guitar pickings and biblical dialect, Oldham has recorded since 1992 with a variety of sidemen—basically, any friends or acquaintances that can play an instrument. He debuted with the single "Ohio River Boat Song" on Drag City Records. Though he's credited as Palace Songs on the single, Oldham's debut album the following year was filed under Palace Brothers—in part to denote the work of Todd Brashear. *There Is No-One What Will Take Care of You* introduced several of Oldham's continuing themes: drunkenness, sin in general, and the varied results of each. His second album—self-titled but also listed as *Days in the Wake*—was issued by Drag City in 1994. Oldham mixed things up for late-1995's *Viva Last Blues* (as Palace Music), recruiting a band with guitarist Bryan Rich, organist Liam Hayes and bassist Jason Loewenstein (from Sebadoh). The following year's *Arise, Therefore* found Oldham back in a largely solitary setting; he dropped the Palace banner soon after. *—John Bush*

There Is No-One What Will Take Care of You / Jun. 14, 1993 / Drag City ✦✦✦

Will Oldham's first album under the Palace rubric, *There Is No-One What Will Take Care of You,* seemed to emerge from under a cloud of mystery on its first release in 1993. The first edition had no credits save a list of names under the heading "Impossible Without," leading to all manner of speculation in the indie community about who was responsible; the album sounded as if some ancient songsters who had somehow escaped Harry Smith's attention years before had recorded a session in their living room, which somehow found its way to the offices of Drag City. On *There Is No-One What Will Take Care of You,* Oldham sounds like a lost-lost cousin of the Louvin Brothers who, after ending up on skid row, is equally convinced that Satan is real, since he smells his foul breath every waking moment of his life. Oldham's stark, intimate tales of sin, lust, alcohol, and hopelessness are fascinating, horribly compelling stuff, and while it would be easy for this material to sound ironic or condescending, it isn't—Oldham makes his characters' shame, confusion, and desperate search for grace real and genuinely moving. *There Is No-One What Will Take Care of You* may not be the best Palace album, but it is the work where Will Oldham's obsession with sin and redemption shines forth with the most painful and absorbing clarity. *—Mark Deming*

Days in the Wake / Aug. 29, 1994 / Drag City ✦✦✦✦✦

The second album from Palace Brothers would seem to barely qualify on either count—at a shade over 27 minutes, *Days in the Wake* seems a bit skimpy in the era of the 80-minute CD, and only one song, "Come a Little Dog," clearly features any musicians besides Will Oldham and his rickety acoustic guitar. But the stark simplicity and *audio vérité* ambience of *Days in the Wake* builds on the already dramatic emotional power of *There Is No-One What Will Take Care of You,* and if Will Oldham's obsession with sin and retribution is less forcefully stated in these songs, that's not to say it isn't clearly present on most of these songs, especially the cautionary tale "You Will Miss Me When I Burn," the mournful but fiercely proud "No More Workhorse Blues," and & "Pushkin," which begins with the declaration "God is the answer/God lies within," without making it sound like a concept in which Oldham can take much comfort. Oldham's lyrics would become increasingly cryptic from this point on, but while the literal meaning of songs like "Wither Thou Goest" and "I Am a Cinematographer" is elusive, the emotional power of these performances is as eloquent as anyone could hope for. *Days in the Wake* is the simplest work in the Palace canon, and among the very best. (*Days in the Wake* was originally released simply as *Palace Brothers.*) *—Mark Deming*

Viva Last Blues / Aug. 21, 1995 / Drag City ✦✦✦

Arise, Therefore / Apr. 1996z / Drag City ✦✦✦✦

Once again Will Oldham emerges out of the murky, Midwestern haze with another helping of lovely, low-key musings on his fourth full-length album, *Arise Therefore,* this time recorded under the name Palace Music (previously Palace Brothers, Palace Songs, or just plain Palace). Much quieter than last year's *Viva Last Blues,* and less Appalachian in its folk-spirit than Palace's earlier music, the songs on *Arise Therefore* shift and moan with breathy cracks and shivers, Oldham's meandering, poet-speak vocals and guitar accompanied by his brother Ned's bass, David Grubbs's piano, and (surprise!) a Maya Tone drum machine. The lyrics (included for the first time) are beautiful in their stark, pale honesty as often as they are indecipherable. "I watch things painted on public walls, now but I see other things as well, behind but right fuck in front of my spirit is how the real road's laid out in a line" he sings on "Kid of Harith." Don't ask for an interpretation: It will come with time, or it won't. *—Kurt Wolff*

• **Lost Blues & Other Songs** / Mar. 24, 1997 / Drag City ♦♦♦♦♦
Lost Blues and Other Songs collects various singles and rarities Will Oldham released under his various Palace incarnations during the early '90s. Nearly all of the material is haunting, spare acoustic-based material, drawing from traditional folk and country, but undercut by Oldham's detached postmodern sensibilities. Occasionally, his removed, affected vocals can make Palace's music seem emotionally distant, but it often works, and *Lost Blues and Other Songs* finds him at his very best. *—Stephen Thomas Erlewine*

Robert Palmer

b. Jan. 19, 1949, Batley, England
Vocals, Guitar / Album Rock, Blue-Eyed Soul, Pop/Rock, Adult Contemporary
The career of blue-eyed soul singer Robert Palmer was a study in style versus substance. While the performer's earliest work won praise for its skillful assimilation of rock, R&B and reggae sounds, his records typically sold poorly, and he achieved his greatest notoriety as an impeccably-dressed lounge lizard. By the mid-'80s, however, Palmer became a star, although his popularity owed less to the strength of his material than to his infamous music videos: taking their cue from the singer's suave presence, Palmer's clips established him as a dapper, suit-and-tied ladies' man who performed his songs backed by a band comprised of leggy models, much to the delight of viewers who made him one of MTV's biggest success stories. He first mounted a solo career in 1974, after several years with the Stax-influenced soul group Vinegar Joe. An avowed stylistic experimenter, Palmer recorded albums indebted to reggae and synth-pop as well as more rock-oriented material during the late '70s and early '80s. After teaming with the Duran Duran side project Power Station for the hit singles "Some Like It Hot" and "Get It On," his next solo album (1985's *Riptide*) included the number one hit "Addicted to Love," the first in a string of videos which offered him in front of a bevy of beautiful women. Two follow-ups, "I Didn't Mean to Turn You On" and "Simply Irresistible," both hit number two. By 1990's *Don't Explain* though, Palmer had returned to the eclecticism of his earliest material and his sales plummeted. *—Jason Ankeny*

Sneakin' Sally Through the Alley / 1974 / Island ♦♦♦♦
Before becoming a slick, sharp-dressed pop star in the 1980s, Robert Palmer was a soul singer deeply rooted in R&B and funk. Those influences are on full display on his debut album *Sneakin' Sally Through the Alley.* With a backing band including members of Little Feat and the Meters, the music has a laid-back groove whether Palmer's covering New Orleans legend Allen Toussaint (the title track) or singing originals ("Hey Julia," "Get Outside"). While the music is tight and solid, it is Robert Palmer's voice that is revelatory—he sounds supremely confident among these talented musicians, and they seem to feed off his vocal intensity. Fans of the Meters or people who want to discover the funky side of Robert Palmer should check this one out. *—Vik Iyengar*

Pressure Drop / 1976 / Island ♦♦♦♦♦
Palmer's own songs (especially the silky "Give Me an Inch" and "Work to Make It Work") and the backing of Little Feat help make this a worthy followup to *Sally.* *—William Ruhlmann*

Some People Can Do What They Like / 1976 / Island ♦♦♦♦♦
Palmer's "Keep in Touch," "Man Smart, Woman Smarter," and "Spanish Moon" (the latter by Little Feat's Lowell George) pace *Some People Can Do What They Like,* another terrific collection. *—William Ruhlmann*

Double Fun / 1978 / Island ♦♦♦
Palmer produces and writes more songs than usual, resulting in the hit "Every Kinda People" and a somewhat lighter, more pop approach. *—William Ruhlmann*

Secrets / 1979 / Island ♦♦♦♦♦
Palmer scores his biggest hit single of the '70s with the uptempo rocker "Bad Case of Loving You (Doctor, Doctor)" on an album that also includes a wonderful version of Todd Rundgren's ballad "Can We Still Be Friends." *—William Ruhlmann*

Clues / 1980 / Island ♦♦♦
A move toward fast-paced electronic dance-rock. It's successful about half the time, especially on Palmer's UK hits "Looking for Clues" and "Johnny and Mary." (Rod Stewart Xeroxed "Johnny and Mary" for his hit "Young Turks" the following year.) *—William Ruhlmann*

Maybe It's Live / 1982 / Island ♦♦

Pride / 1983 / Island ♦♦

Riptide / Nov. 1985 / Island ♦♦♦♦♦
Palmer's commercial breakthrough, much of it in the hard rock style of his one-shot band Power Station, and featuring the hits "Discipline of Love," "Addicted to Love" (a number one hit), "Hyperactive," and "I Didn't Mean to Turn You On." *—William Ruhlmann*

Heavy Nova / Jun. 1988 / EMI America ♦♦

• **Addictions, Vol. 1** / Oct. 1989 / Island ♦♦♦♦♦
Thirteen-track compilation containing Palmer's biggest hits, not only the ones on Island but also The Power Station singles and "Simply Irresistible," from Palmer's first EMI album. *—William Ruhlmann*

Addictions, Vol. 2 / May 5, 1992 / Island ♦♦♦
Apart from "I Didn't Mean to Turn You On," there are no big hits, only album tracks and failed singles, all of which are quite good. Unfortunately, the majority of the material has been remixed, remade, or has new vocal tracks; the album may sound great, but it isn't an accurate retrospective. *—Stephen Thomas Erlewine*

The Very Best of Robert Palmer / Jan. 28, 1997 / Capitol ♦♦♦
Despite my (yet rationalized) fondness for his 1980 electro-pop hit "Johnny and Mary" (included here), the 16-track collection *The Very Best of Robert Palmer* mostly leaves me cold. Palmer has the tools, but the mechanicals lack potency and soul. Still, if combining mid-'80s hits like "Addicted to Love" and "Simply Irresistible" with a whiff of earlier material, several more recent constructions, and a pair from side project the Power Station sounds like your kind of fun, this disc does the job... efficiently. Includes a new cover of the Staple Singers' "Respect Yourself." *—Roch Parisien*

Pantera

f. 1982
Group / Alternative Metal, Speed Metal, Heavy Metal, Thrash
Pantera's massively brutal, aggressive, jagged heavy metal earned them a large cult following in the early '90s. During the early '80s, the band explored several different styles of hard rock; sometimes they sounded like Kiss and Aerosmith, others Def Leppard. After several years of struggling the band changed their tune in 1988, becoming rougher and harder, much like Metallica. Guitarist Diamond Darrell (aka "Dimebag") rejected an offer to join Megadeth, concentrating on Pantera's new direction. The change in style proved successful; 1992's *A Vulgar Display of Power* became an underground metal hit, eventually scaling *Billboard*'s Top 50. When their new album, *Far Beyond Driven,* was released in 1994, the band debuted at number one. Some chart-watchers were surprised, but anyone that followed their rise from obscurity to *A Vulgar Display of Power* knew that Pantera was one of the most popular metal bands of the early '90s. *Great Southern Trendkill* was released in May 1996, and a year later the group issued *Official Live: 101 Proof; Reinventing the Steel* followed in the spring of 2000. *—Stephen Thomas Erlewine*

Metal Magic / 1983 / Metal Magic ♦♦♦

Cowboys from Hell / Jul. 1990 / East West ♦♦♦♦♦
Pantera's breakthrough album, *Cowboys From Hell,* is largely driven by the band's powerful rhythm section and guitarist Diamond Darrell's (as he was then known) unbelievably forceful riffing, which skittered around the downbeats to produce unexpected rhythmic phrases and accents, as well as his inventive soloing. Phil Anselmo displayed a vocal range that could switch from a growling shout to a high falsetto—listen to him match Darrell's harmonic squeals at the end of "Cemetery Gates." The album gradually becomes more same-sounding as it goes on, but the first half, featuring such brutal slices of thrash as "Psycho Holiday," "Primal Concrete Sledge" and the title track, pretty much carries its momentum all the way through. *—Steve Huey*

• **Vulgar Display of Power** / Feb. 25, 1992 / East West ♦♦♦♦♦
One of the most influential heavy metal albums of the 1990s, *Vulgar Display of Power* is just what is says: a raw, pulverizing, insanely intense depiction of naked rage and hostility that drains its listeners and pounds them into submission. Even the "ballads," "This Love" and "Hollow," have thunderingly loud, aggressive chorus sections. Preaching power through strength and integrity, Phil Anselmo discards any further attempts at singing in favor of a militaristic bark and an unhinged roar, while the crystal-clear production sets Darrell's pummeling riffs against a rhythmic backdrop so thunderously supportive that Darrell often solos without underlying rhythm guitar parts. The album again follows *Cowboys From Hell*'s strategy of stacking the best songs at the beginning and letting their momentum carry the listener through the rest, but the riffs and sonic textures are more consistently interesting this time around. Pantera's thick-sounding, post-hardcore power-metal and outraged, testosterone-drenched intensity would help pave the way for alternative-metal acts like Korn and Tool; *Vulgar Display of Power* is the best distillation of those virtues. *—Steve Huey*

Far Beyond Driven / Mar. 15, 1994 / East West ♦♦♦♦
Far Beyond Driven finds Pantera in a bit of a holding pattern. Although the riffs are still lethally fast, the band shows no signs of musical development, and the songs aren't any better than those on *Vulgar Display of Power.* Nevertheless, there's enough primal metal here to satisfy most of their fans. *—Stephen Thomas Erlewine*

Great Southern Trendkill / May 1996 / Elektra/Asylum ♦♦♦

Reinventing the Steel / Mar. 14, 2000 / Elektra ♦♦♦

Graham Parker

b. Nov. 15, 1950, East London, England
Vocals, Guitar / Album Rock, Pub Rock, New Wave, Singer/Songwriter
Stereotyped early in his career as the quintessential angry young man, Graham Parker was one of the most successful singer-songwriters to emerge from England's pub-rock scene of the early '70s. Drawing heavily from Van Morrison and the Rolling Stones, Parker developed a sinewy fusion of driving rock & roll and confessional folk-rock, highlighted by his indignant passion, biting sarcasm and bristling anger. At the outset of his career, his albums crackled with pub-rock energy, snide witticisms and gentle insights, earning him a devoted following of fans and critics, who lavished praise on his debut, *Howlin' Wind.* Despite all of the positive word-of-mouth, Parker never managed to become a star, and he was soon overshadowed by the emergence of Elvis Costello, a singer-songwriter who shared similar roots. After delivering *Squeezing Out Sparks* in 1979, Parker attempted to make a few crossover albums before settling into a cult following in the late '80s, continuing to garner critical acclaim. *—Stephen Thomas Erlewine*

☆ **Howlin Wind** / Jul. 1976 / Mercury ♦♦♦♦♦
For most intents and purposes, Graham Parker emerged fully formed on his debut album, *Howlin' Wind.* Sounding like the bastard offspring of Mick Jagger and Van Morrison, Parker sneers his way through a set of stunningly literate pub-rockers. Instead of blindly sticking to the traditions of rock & roll, Parker invigorates them with cynicism and anger, turning his songs into distinctively original works. "Back to Schooldays" may be reconstituted rockabilly, "White Honey" may recall Morrison's white R&B bounce, and "Howlin' Wind" is a cross of Van's more mystical moments and the Band, but the songs themselves are original and terrific. Similarly, producer Nick Lowe gives the album a tough, spare feeling, which makes Parker and the Rumour sound like one of the best bar bands you've ever heard. *Howlin' Wind* remains a thoroughly invigorating fusion of rock tradition, singer-songwriter skill, and punk spirit, making it one of the classic debuts of all time. *—Stephen Thomas Erlewine*

Heat Treatment / Oct. 1976 / Mercury ✦✦✦✦✦
On his second album *Heat Treatment*, Graham Parker essentially offered more of the same thing that made *Howlin' Wind* such a bracing listen. However, his songwriting wasn't as consistent, with only a handful of songs—like "Pourin' It All Out" and the title track—making much of an impression. Unfortunately, the record was also tamed by the production of Mutt Lange, who polishes the record just enough to make the Rumour sound restrained. Which means, of course, the sheer musicality of the band can't save the lesser material. *Heat Treatment* remains an enjoyable listen—at this stage of the game, Parker hadn't soured into a curmudgeon, and his weaker songs were still endearing—but it's a disappointment in light of its predecessor. *—Stephen Thomas Erlewine*

Stick to Me / Oct. 1977 / Mercury ✦✦✦✦✦
Graham Parker and the Rumour's third new studio album to be released in 18 months finds the bandleader running short of top-flight material; "Thunder And Rain" and "Watch The Moon Come Down" are up to his usual standards, but songs like "The Heat In Harlem" find him dangerously out of his depth. As a result, although fiercely played, this star-crossed release (it had to be re-recorded when the first version suffered technical problems) is a cut below Parker's first two albums. *—William Ruhlmann*

The Parkerilla/Live / 1978 / Mercury ✦✦

☆ **Squeezing out Sparks** / Mar. 1979 / Arista ✦✦✦✦✦
Generally regarded as Graham Parker's finest album, *Squeezing Out Sparks* is a masterful fusion of pub rock classicism, new wave pop, and pure vitriol that makes even his most conventional singer/songwriter numbers bristle with energy. Not only does Parker deliver his best, most consistent set of songs, but he offers more succinct hooks than before—"Local Girls" and "Discovering Japan" are powered by quirky hooks that make them new wave classics. But Parker's new pop inclinations are tempered by his anger, which seethes throughout the hard rockers and even his quieter numbers. Throughout *Squeezing Out Sparks*, Graham spits out a litany of offenses which make him feel like an outsider, but he's not a liberal, he's a conservative. The record's two centerpieces—"Passion Is No Ordinary Word" and the anti-abortion "You Can't Be Too Strong"—indicate that his traditionalist musical tendencies are symptomatic of a larger conservative trend. But no one ever said conservatives made poor rock & rollers, and Parker's ruminations over a lost past give him the anger that fuels *Squeezing Out Sparks*, one of the great rock records of the post-punk era. *—Stephen Thomas Erlewine*

The Up Escalator / May 1980 / Razor & Tie ✦✦✦✦✦
On his last album with The Rumour, Parker goes for mainstream rock success, employing the widescreen production style of Jimmy Iovine and such guests as Bruce Springsteen. It didn't sell, but it was a great try. *—William Ruhlmann*

Another Grey Area / Mar. 1982 / Razor & Tie ✦✦✦✦✦
Parker begins to make his peace with human imperfection (though he can still be sharp-tongued) and starts to look for love ("It's All Worth Nothing Alone"), backed by a smooth session band and a clean Jack Douglas production, which cool his usual fire without putting it out. *—William Ruhlmann*

The Real Macaw / Jul. 1983 / Razor & Tie ✦✦✦
Parker finds love, and manages to write about it without losing his usual wit ("Last Couple on the Dance Floor"). He also re-employs Rumour guitarist Brinsley Schwartz and goes back to the uptempo pub rock of his 70s albums. *—William Ruhlmann*

Steady Nerves / Mar. 1985 / Elektra ✦✦✦
Graham Parker moves to his third record label (following stints at Mercury and Arista), forms a backup band called the Shot (again led by guitarist Brinsley Schwarz) and continues alternately arguing with existence ("Break Them Down") and praising his romantic life ("Wake Up [Next To You]"). *—William Ruhlmann*

The Mona Lisa's Sister / Apr. 1988 / Buddha ✦✦

Live! Alone in America / Jul. 1989 / RCA ✦✦✦
Graham Parker's second commercially released live album is a solo affair that finds him connecting with his audience and singing a lot of his 1970s favorites. *—William Ruhlmann*

Human Soul / Jan. 1990 / Diablo ✦✦

Struck by Lightning / Feb. 1991 / Diablo ✦✦✦
Struck By Lightning was the culmination of Graham Parker's previous two records, where he increasingly began to chronicle domestic tasks and affairs of the married heart. For such an intimate subject, Parker wisely decided to scale back the musical ambition of *Human Soul* on *Struck By Lightning*, recording a lean, stripped-down album that relies heavily on acoustic guitars. Appropriately, his lyrics were some of the most concise he has written in years, breathing life into tales like "The Kid With the Butterfly Net" and "Wrapping Paper." Parker's music is similarly simple and tuneful, making *Struck By Lightning* his best effort since the early '80s. *—Stephen Thomas Erlewine*

Burning Questions / Jul. 20, 1992 / Diablo ✦✦

Live Alone! Discovering Japan / 1993 / Gadfly ✦✦

● **Passion Is No Ordinary Word: the Graham Parker Anthology 1976-1991** / Sep. 21, 1993 / Rhino ✦✦✦✦✦
With its smart song selection and entertaining liner notes, *Passion is No Ordinary Word* is an excellent 2-CD anthology covering Parker's entire career, complete with such rarities as "Mercury Poisoning" and "I Want You Back (Alive)" among such signature songs as "White Honey" and "You Can't Be Too Strong." A terrific introduction to Parker's career. *—Stephen Thomas Erlewine*

12 Haunted Episodes / Mar. 14, 1995 / Razor & Tie ✦✦✦

Acid Bubblegum / Sep. 24, 1996 / Razor & Tie ✦✦✦

☆ **Squeezing Out Sparks - Live Sparks** / Oct. 1, 1996 / Arista ✦✦✦✦✦

The Last Rock N Roll Tour / Apr. 22, 1997 / Razor & Tie ✦✦✦

Not If It Pleases Me: BBC Live 76-77 / May 1998 / Hux ✦✦✦

Loose Monkeys, Spare Tracks and Lost Demos / Jan. 20, 1999 / Razor & Tie ✦✦

Van Dyke Parks

b. Jan. 3, 1941
Vocals, Keyboards, Accordion, Piano, Synthesizer, Producer, Arranger / Baroque Pop, Experimental Rock, Experimental, Singer/Songwriter
Composer, arranger, producer, and musician Van Dyke Parks has had a varied career in popular music without ever getting near the popular mainstream. Parks worked as a songwriter in the early '60s and became a producer, handling such mid-'60s acts as Harper's Bizarre. He was enlisted by Beach Boy Brian Wilson to write lyrics for what turned out to be an abortive album project called *Smile* (now one of the legendary lost albums of the '60s), resulting in such songs as the hit "Heroes and Villains." Parks released his own album, the eclectic *Song Cycle*, to critical acclaim and minimal sales in 1968. He then did session work with a variety of artists, not releasing his second album, *Discover America*, which revealed his immersion in Trinidadian music, until 1972. *Clang of the Yankee Reaper*, another eclectic collection, followed in 1975. But Parks maintained his "day job"—film work on scores by Ry Cooder and others, writing and arranging for Shelley Duvall's children's TV series, and other pursuits. Finally, in 1984, came the brilliant *Jump!*, a concept album based on the Uncle Remus tales of Joel Chandler Harris. It was followed in 1989 by *Tokyo Rose*, which concerned the state of American-Japanese relations. *—William Ruhlmann*

● **Song Cycle** / 1968 / Warner Brothers ✦✦✦✦✦
Van Dyke Parks moved on from the Beach Boys' abortive *Smile* sessions to record his own solo debut, *Song Cycle*, an audacious and occasionally brilliant attempt to mount a fully orchestrated, classically minded work within the context of contemporary pop. As indicated by its title, *Song Cycle* is a thematically coherent work, one which attempts to embrace the breadth of American popular music; bluegrass, ragtime, showtunes—nothing escapes Parks' radar, and the sheer eclecticism and individualism of his work is remarkable. Opening with "Vine Street," authored by Randy Newman (another pop composer with serious classical aspirations), the album is both forward-thinking and backwards-minded, a collision of bygone musical styles with the progressive sensibilities of the late 1960s; while occasionally overambitious and at times insufferably coy, it's nevertheless a one-of-a-kind record, the product of true inspiration. *—Jason Ankeny*

Discover America / 1972 / Warner Brothers ✦✦✦✦✦
Parks turns to the music of Trinidad here, especially as it was heard in the 40s, which means tributes to "Bing Crosby" and "The Four Mills Bros.," not to mention "G-Man Hoover" and "FDR in Trinidad," played on steel drums and other indigenous instruments. A charming, idiosyncratic genre exercise. *—William Ruhlmann*

The Clang of the Yankee Reaper / May 1976 / Warner Brothers ✦✦✦
Expanding from the Caribbean approach he took with *Discover America*, Van Dyke Parks explores more arcane Americana on an album that ranges from New Orleans to the islands to the classics. Only the title track bears a co-composing credit for the artist, but Parks' exuberant, eclectic musical personality is the unifying force in an collection of music that varies from the Sandpipers' "Another Dream" to Pachelbel's "Canon in D." *—William Ruhlmann*

Jump! / Feb. 1984 / Warner Brothers ✦✦✦✦✦
An exhilarating song cycle based on the Uncle Remus tales. It incorporates the styles of Stephen Foster, ragtime, 30s movie-soundtrack music, you name it, all in the service of playful, touching lyrics that correspond to the source material, without actually aping it. A delight from start to finish. *—William Ruhlmann*

Tokyo Rose / Jul. 1989 / Warner Brothers ✦✦✦
One can hear "America" as played on a Japanese koto on this history of relations between East and West, which covers everything from the "Trade War" to baseball with Parks's typically eclectic and broad musical imagination. A charming album. *—William Ruhlmann*

Moonlighting: Live at the Ash Grove / Feb. 10, 1998 / Warner Brothers ✦✦✦✦

Parliament

f. 1970, Detroit, MI, **db.** 1980
Group / R&B, Funk, Soul
Inspired by Motown's assembly-line of sound, George Clinton gradually assembled a collective of over 50 musicians and recorded the ensemble during the '70s both as Parliament and Funkadelic. While Funkadelic pursued band-format psychedelic rock, Parliament engaged in a funk free-for-all, blending influences from the godfathers (James Brown and Sly Stone) with freaky costumes and themes inspired by '60s acid culture and science fiction. From its 1970 inception until Clinton's dissolving of Parliament in 1980, the band hit the R&B Top Ten several times but truly excelled in two other areas: large-selling, effective album statements and the most dazzling, extravagant live show in the business. In an era when Philly soul continued the slick sounds of establishment-approved R&B, Parliament scared off more white listeners than it courted. *—John Bush*

Osmium / 1970 / Invictus ✦✦

Up for the Down Stroke / 1974 / Casablanca ✦✦✦✦
Forget for a moment that George Clinton had released an earlier 1970 album as Parliament. In the four years leading up to the release of *Up for the Down Stroke* many things changed for Clinton, most notably his music. The Parliament found on this album is a very different Parliament than the one found on Osmium; wilder, quirkier, weirder, funkier, and more rock-oriented, this album's lineup—led by Bernie Worrell, Bootsy Collins, and Clinton—inaugurated the mid- to late-'70s P-Funk era with arguably the group's strongest roster ever. The album's opening track, "Up for the Down Stroke," stands as a perfect summation of what this band was capable of. The song had enough up-tempo funk to set a dancefloor on fire, enough vocal hook to make it a popular concert singalong, enough meandering to make it an epic jam, and enough allure to make it a successful R&B hit despite its lack of conventional at-

tributes. After getting past this monster opening track, the album opens up a bit, exploring various strains of R&B without ever venturing too far into rock, disco, or synth-driven vamping as later albums would. In fact, it's a rather straightforward R&B album if you break it down, with the benefit of having Bootsy's worming bass guitar as its foundation, of course, something that instantly makes it out of the ordinary. Most similar to *Chocolate City, Up for the Down Stroke* also lacks the thematic tendencies of later albums such as *Mothership Connection*, but its almost straightforward R&B tendencies and its Bootsy-heavy sound make it worth hearing. Even if it's not one of their best, it's a unique moment in the P-Funk library that alluded to what was to come. *—Jason Birchmeier*

Chocolate City / 1975 / Casablanca ✦✦✦✦
"Chocolate City" stands out as a trademark P-Funk moment, with it's languid meandering, rich synth washes, and spoken-word vocals—a perfect way to jump start the album. From there, the album kicks into high gear, moving from one up-tempo R&B song to the next, every song driven by Bootsy's slippery bass riffs and most showered with harmonious vocal choruses. Every song has its quirks, with "Let Me Be" being the only song that gets too unconventional for its own good, featuring only synth, piano, and vocals. Most of the other songs are fairly equal, none being lackluster and none being too noteworthy, with the exception of "Together"; this song's soulful chorus drifts momentarily away from the funk for a moment, offering one of the album's most beautiful moments. For the most part, though, this isn't a beautiful album—it's fairly grimy with its funk-infused R&B thumping and worming relentlessly, never taking too much time to worry about catchy hooks. Yet for as understated as this stubborn focus is, never venturing too far into rock, disco, or jamming territory, it's an effective focus, making Chocolate City a slight improvement from Up for the Down Stroke. There's something rewarding about how consistent and focused this album is, probably because of its amazing lineup featuring Bootsy Collins, Bernie Worrel, and Eddie Hazel. As such, Chocolate City won't disappoint those looking for the R&B side of the P-funk library. *—Jason Birchmeier*

Clones of Dr. Funkenstein / 1976 / Casablanca ✦✦✦✦✦
Few will argue that *Mothership Connection* wasn't the turning point for Clinton's funk mob, bringing them commercial success as well as opening the door for more ambitious songwriting. Part of that ambition was the introduction of more conceptual albums, something that Clinton returned to on *Clones of Dr. Funkenstein*. Unfortunately, despite the inventive sci-fi themes, this follow-up didn't quite live up to the brilliance of its predecessor; every song here is great, but the album lacks any truly divine moments and regresses a bit away from disco-funk aesthetics, looking back to conventional R&B songwriting. One moment Parliament is playing traditional horn-laden dance songs like "Do That Stuff," while at another the band is getting all cosmic with trippy synth like on "Dr. Funkenstein." The balance between horns and synth that made *Mothership Connection* such a cohesive album is clearly divided here, even if Bootsy never fails to deliver ass-wiggling bass lines. Other songs more directly hark back to the band's R&B-oriented days, as if they were leftovers from the *Chocolate City* album; the crooning ache of "I've Been Watching You (Move Your Sexy Body)" is an example. In the end, this album doesn't have any obvious weak moments, even if some songs—such as "Do That Stuff" and "Children of Production"—stand above the rest, and even if it's an unbalanced album. Its worth often depends on whether you value or mourn the album's stylistic diversity; however, not even an appreciation for diversity can compensate for the album's lack of cohesion. Either way, time has somewhat banished this album into oblivion alongside *Chocolate City*, mainly because there aren't any perennial anthems here, and also because this album's R&B rather than disco or rock feel made it less of an influence on contemporary music. *—Jason Birchmeier*

★ **Mothership Connection** / 1976 / Casablanca ✦✦✦✦✦
The addition of ex-JB's Fred Wesley and Maceo Parker to the Parliament roster on *Mothership Connection* elevated an already mind-blowing band into the best funk band of the '70s, arguably the best funk band ever. With these two funk veterans supplying the horns, Clinton had everything he could ask for in his already stellar group. The opening song, "P-Funk (Wants to Get Funked Up)," harkened back to the opening title track from Parliament's previous album, *Chocolate City*, laying down a languid synth aura for a spoken-word intro. When "P-Funk (Wants to Get Funked Up)" steps into second gear though, bringing in Bootsy's bass, Wesley's horn, Worrell's piano, and a chorus of vocalists, it's fairly evident just how large a step forward *Mothership Connection* is from the conventional R&B roots of *Chocolate City* and *Up for the Down Stroke*. The second song, "Mothership Connection (Star Child)," makes the differentiation glaringly evident, most noticeably when the song enters the cosmic, proto-hip-hop "swing down sweet chariot" bridge with its accompanying melody from beyond. The funk doesn't stop there though, with the remaining five songs keeping the tempo laden with dense interweaving rhythms, peaking on "Give Up the Funk (Tear the Roof Off the Sucker)." In the end, there's no questioning this album's impact, one that is still being felt via rap-induced aftershocks. In addition to its contemporary impact and continued longevity, the album was a massive success for Clinton and company upon its release in 1975, elevating the P-Funk collective to unparalleled heights in terms of audience. Some Parliament albums may be flawless, and others may be innovative, but this is the P-Funk zenith in more ways than one, perfect as well as perennial. *—Jason Birchmeier*

☆ **Funkentelechy Vs. The Placebo Syndrome** / 1977 / Casablanca ✦✦✦✦✦
Coming on the heels of the monumental *Mothership Connection* album and ever-expanding concert extravaganzas, Parliament's *Funkentelechy Vs. the Placebo Syndrome* gave George Clinton's Parliament/Funkadelic collective its first number one R&B hit, "Flashlight." Chart concerns aside, this somewhat overlooked release is easily the equal of top Parliament discs like *Mothership* and *Chocolate City*. And as for the songs themselves— Well, in addition to the unstoppable, zigzagging bass synthesizer line defining "Flashlight," plenty of delicacies are to be had: there's the cool jubilation and space-age doo wop of "Wizard of Finance" (recalling Clinton's original Parliaments vocal group from the late '50s), "Placebo Syndrome"'s casual bit of pop-funk brilliance, and the comically surreal social critique on "Funkentelechy." Finally, evoking the homemade, 12" mix aesthetic that is Parliament/Funkadelic's ongoing party, there are fine extended jams like "Bop Gun (Endangered Species)" and "Sir Nose d'Voidoffunk (Pay Attention—B3M)." Clinton, of course, orchestrates the incredible collage of vocal harmonies, horn lines, and in-the-pocket ensemble playing heard throughout: a veritable three-ring circus on wax. Special mention should also be made of the top contributions by arranger, composer, and keyboard wiz Bernie Worrell, bassist Bootsy Collins, the Horny Horns, and the lovely and talented Brides of Funkenstein vocal quartet. One of a handful of essential Parliament/Funkadelic records. *—Stephen Cook*

Live: P-Funk Earth Tour / 1977 / Casablanca ✦✦✦✦

Motor Booty Affair / 1978 / Casablanca ✦✦✦✦✦

Gloryhallastoopid / 1979 / Casablanca ✦✦✦

Trombipulation / 1980 / Casablanca ✦✦

Greatest Hits (The Bomb) / 1984 / Casablanca ✦✦✦✦✦

☆ **Tear the Roof Off, 1974-1980** / May 18, 1993 / Casablanca ✦✦✦✦✦
The Best of Parliament: Give Up the Funk may capture the band's bare essentials, but given the band's penchant for stretching out on extended jams (which included some of their best songs), it's hard to get anything beyond the most basic overview of their work on just one disc. Unless you're a very casual fan, a much better bet is the double-disc *Tear the Roof Off 1974-1980*, whose 25 tracks add plenty of much-needed detail behind the best-known and most-sampled hits. Slightly more party-oriented than Funkadelic, Parliament created the wildest atmosphere of all the projects in the George Clinton oeuvre, full of loopy humor and way-out sci-fi concepts. Parliament was also more of a singles act than the frequently album-oriented Funkadelic, and while Parliament produced its share of classic albums, their material doesn't lose any of its potency when boiled down into compilation form. What's more, *Tear the Roof Off* contains several full-length 12" mixes that were never previously available on CD. These are some of the most unstoppable, widely imitated grooves of all time, and they still carry the same impact today, making *Tear the Roof Off* an obvious necessity. *—Steve Huey*

Dope Dogs / 1995 / Hot Hands ✦✦✦

★ **The Best of Parliament: Give Up the Funk** / Jun. 6, 1995 / Mercury Funk Essentials ✦✦✦✦✦
To some, boiling Parliament's legacy down to a single-disc collection is the equivalent of heresy, since most fans treat each album as an individual work of art. Still, there is no denying that Parliament was an untouchable singles act, recording some of the greatest soul/funk singles of the '70s. For those listeners that just want an introduction, or only need the hits, *The Best of Parliament: Give Up the Funk* is the ideal choice. A more complete and logical collection than the previous *Greatest Hits (The Bomb), The Best of Parliament* supplies all of the great group's greatest hits, from "Up for the Down Stroke" and "Tear the Roof off the Sucker" to "Flash Light" and "Aqua Boogie." For those that can only handle the funk in moderation, there is no better collection. *—Leo Stanley*

Alan Parsons

Keyboards, Engineer, Producer / Album Rock, Pop/Rock, Prog-Rock/Art Rock
As indicated by its name, the Alan Parsons Project was not a band so much as a concept overseen by the titular Parsons, a successful producer and engineer who first garnered significant industry exposure via his work on the Beatles' 1969 masterpiece *Abbey Road* before solidifying his reputation by working on Pink Floyd's *Dark Side of the Moon*. Influenced by his work on Al Stewart's concept album *Time Passages*, Parsons decided to begin creating his own thematic records; along with songwriter Eric Woolfson, he soon founded the Alan Parsons Project. Although Parsons played keyboards and infrequently sang on his records, the Project was designed primarily as a forum for a revolving collection of vocalists and session players to interpret and perform Parsons and Woolfson's conceptually-linked, lushly-synthesized music. The Project debuted in 1975 with *Tales of Mystery and Imagination*, and with 1980's *The Turn of a Friendly Card*, a meditation on gambling, Parsons scored a Top 20 hit, "Games People Play;" 1982's *Eye in the Sky*, was their most successful effort, and notched a Top Three hit with its title track. *—Jason Ankeny*

● **I Robot** / Jun. 1977 / Arista ✦✦✦✦✦
With its title originating from an Isaac Asimov novel, *I Robot*'s main concept is one that deals heavily in the field of science fiction. The album's idea is based around Parsons' concern with the onslaught of machinery and its inevitable takeover of man, both in a physical sense and a spiritual one. As one of the Alan Parsons Project's strongest efforts, its wise blend of keyboard-dominated instrumentals partnered with the warmth of the vocals during the lyrical songs emblazons the man-vs.-machine idea. The mechanical-sounding title track is the opening song, setting the tone for the album's futuristic motif. Man's regret for his mechanical creations sweeps through "I Wouldn't Want to Be Like You," with a passionate Lenny Zakatek singing lead. The human being's rebellious nature is the theme behind "Breakdown," sung by ex-Hollies member Allan Clarke, while the strength of the human will is the focal point of "Don't Let It Show," a heartening ballad performed by Dave Townsend. Ending with the instrumental "Genesis Ch. 1 V. 32," the promising tempo and air of this song invoke hope for all mankind. As a final product, *I Robot* leaves the listener with much to contemplate, which is its purpose, but also presents a collage of well-crafted songs that aren't easily forgotten. This album still remains one this band's most accomplished pieces. *—Mike DeGagne*

Pyramid / Jun. 1978 / Arista ✦✦✦

Eve / Sep. 1979 / Arista ✦✦

The Turn of a Friendly Card / Nov. 1980 / Arista ✦✦✦✦✦

Eye in the Sky / Jun. 1982 / Arista ✦✦✦✦✦

The Best of the Alan Parsons Project / 1983 / Arista ✦✦✦✦✦

Ammonia Avenue / Feb. 1984 / Arista ✦✦✦

Vulture Culture / Mar. 1985 / Arista ✦✦

Stereotomy / Nov. 1985 / Arista ✦✦

Gaudi / 1987 / Arista ✦✦

The Best of the Alan Parsons Project, Vol. 2 / 1988 / Arista ✦✦✦✦✦

The Instrumental Works / 1988 / Arista ✦✦

The Definitive Collection / Jul. 15, 1997 / Arista ✦✦✦✦✦

● **Master Hits: Alan Parsons Project** / Jul. 27, 1999 / Arista ✦✦✦✦✦
Arista celebrated its 30th anniversary by releasing *The Heritage Series,* spotlighting the most popular artists on the label. The Alan Parsons Project installment in *The Heritage Series* is pretty much a straight hits collection, featuring highlights from their stint at the label. While the Parsons Project was at Arista, they achieved the peak of their popularity with such radio hits as "I Robot," "I Wouldn't Want to Be Like You," "Games People Play," "Time," "Ammonia Avenue" and the crossover single "Eye in the Sky." All those songs are here, along with some highlights from their albums, providing a nice retrospective of their time with Arista, which just happened to be the peak of their career. *— Stephen Thomas Erlewine*

The Time Machine / Sep. 28, 1999 / Miramar ✦✦✦✦

Tales of Mystery and Imagination / 1975 / Mercury ✦✦✦✦✦

Gram Parsons (Cecil Ingram Connor)

b. Nov. 5, 1946, Winter Haven, FL, **d.** Sep. 19, 1973, Joshua Tree, CA
Vocals, Guitar / Country-Rock
With the International Submarine Band, the Byrds and the Flying Burrito Brothers, Gram Parsons pioneered the concept of a rock band playing country music, and as a solo artist he blended country and rock to the point that they became indistinguishable from each other. While he was alive, Parsons never sold many records, yet he influenced many of his peers. In the years since his death, numerous rock and country artists build on his body of work.

Parsons' first band, the International Submarine Band released their debut *Safe at Home,* in early 1968. By the time it hit the stores, Parsons had already joined the Byrds, pushing the group toward the country-rock unveiled on their 1968 record, *Sweetheart of the Rodeo.* He and Chris Hillman left the Byrds shortly after the album's completion, forming the Flying Burrito Brothers, debuting with *The Gilded Palace of Sin,* in 1969. Though it wasn't a hit, it earned a cult, including Keith Richards, who became fast friends with Parsons. Due to his friendship with Richards and its resulting excess, Parsons didn't have much interest in the Brothers anymore, leaving the group after finishing their second album, *Burrito Deluxe.* For the next few years, he was more rock star than musician, partying and hanging with the Stones. He finally returned to music in 1972, recording a solo album, *GP,* that year. Though it received good reviews, including praise for his backing vocalist Emmylou Harris, it didn't sell. Following a brief tour with his backing band, the Fallen Angels, he entered the studio to record his second album, *Grievous Angel.* A few weeks after the sessions, Parsons went on a vacation near the Joshua Tree National Monument in California. On September 19, 1973, he died from an overdose of morphine and tequila. After his death, Parsons' legacy continued to grow, as both country and rock musicians built on the music; if anything, he was more popular 20 years after his death than he was when he was alive. *— Stephen Thomas Erlewine*

★ **G.P./Grievous Angel** / 1973 / Reprise ✦✦✦✦✦
In the year before his death in the fall of 1973, Gram Parsons recorded two superb solo albums, and Warner Brothers has conveniently reissued them in their entirety on a single compact disc. Since many of the same musicians played on both *G.P.* (released in January of 1973) and *Grievous Angel* (which appeared in stores almost exactly a year later), the two albums flow together quite well as a single set. And while no bonus tracks were added, the booklet features well-written essays on Parsons from John M. Delgatto and Marley Brant, the complete liner notes from both albums, and lyrics for all the songs on the disc (which weren't included in the original vinyl issues). While the material and performances on *G.P.* are a shade stronger than on *Grievous Angel,* both albums have more than their share of pearly moments, and this disc is a treat from start to finish; James Burton's guitar leads are chicken-pickin' at its smartest and most tasteful, Al Perkins' pedal steel is the definitive sound of country & western heartache, fiddler Byron Berline effortlessly reveals how he became one of Nashville's leading session musicians, and Parsons' duets with the young Emmylou Harris are nothing less than sublime. And would anyone who loves either country or rock really want to be without a CD that includes songs like "A Song for You," "The New Soft Shoe," "Big Mouth Blues," & "$1,000 Wedding," or "In My Hour of Darkness"— While the definitive Gram Parsons collection has yet to be compiled, *G.P./Grievous Angel* gives you everything you really need from his solo career, and these 20 performances are among the most influential and satisfying music the genre of country-rock would ever produce. *— Mark Deming*

Sleepless Nights / Apr. 1976 / A&M ✦✦✦
Three years after Gram Parsons' untimely death, his frequent duet partner Emmylou Harris helped arrange for the release of this collection of outtakes—three songs he cut with Harris for his final solo album *Grievous Angel* in 1973, and nine others recorded live in the studio with The Flying Burrito Brothers in 1970. Anyone hoping to find the great lost Gram Parsons song is out of luck here; all 12 tunes are covers of vintage country classics, except for "Honky Tonk Women" (which at least *sounds* like a C&W classic in this arrangement) and The Louvin Brothers' "The Angels Rejoiced Last Night," which is as spiritually uplifting as ever with Harris' pure, clear voice helping to bring it home. The three tracks with his duet partner fare best, while most of the cuts with the Burritos sound like demos, and though a few are inspired (particularly the deeply felt versions of "Sing Me Back Home" and & "Green, Green Grass of Home," a lot of the time both Parsons and the band sound like a solid bar band in the middle of a Wednesday night set—more than competent, but less than inspired. *Sleepless Nights* was certainly a labor of love and it's a worthy purchase for committed fans, but neophytes are better off giving a listen to The Flying Burrito Brothers' masterpiece *The Gilded Palace of Sin,* or either solo album, *G.P.* or *Grievous Angel.* *— Mark Deming*

Warm Evenings, Pale Mornings, Bottled Blues / 1992 / Raven ✦✦✦✦✦
Although all of Parsons' albums are essential, this import-only collection provides an excellent sampling of his entire career, including his stints with the Shilos, the International Submarine Band, the Byrds (complete with Parsons' vocals restored), the Flying Burrito Brothers, and the solo years. *— Chris Woodstra*

Live 1973 / Mar. 4, 1997 / Rhino ✦✦✦✦

Another Side of This Life: The Lost Recordings of Gram Parsons, 1965-1966 / Dec. 19, 2000 / Sundazed ✦✦

Pavement

f. 1989, Stockton, CA
Group / Indie Rock, Lo-Fi, Alternative Pop/Rock
With their fractured songs, unexpected blasts of feedback, laconic vocals, cryptic literate lyrics, and defiant low-fidelity, Pavement is one of the most influential and distinctive bands to emerge from the American underground in the '90s. Pavement, along with Sebadoh, were the leaders of the low-fi movement which dominated US indie-rock in the early '90s. Initially conceived as a studio project between guitarists/vocalists Stephen Malkmus and Scott Kannberg in the '80s, Pavement gradually became a band during the early '90s. Along the way, their initial EPs and debut album, 1992's *Slanted and Enchanted,* earned a devoted following of musicians, indie fans and critics. Before long, the group's aesthetics—a combination of elliptic, cryptic underground American rock, unrepentant Anglophilia, a fondness for white noise, off-kilter arrangements and winding melodies, songs that frequently had shifting titles, and literate, clever lyrics—were imitated by underground bands through America and Britian. By that point, Pavement had become an actual band, one with a notorious acid-fried, ex-hippie drummer called Gary Young. Young left the band in 1993, as the band made the move to clean up their sound, if not their sensibility, on 1994's *Crooked Rain, Crooked Rain.* Their revampment resulted in a near-hit with "Cut Your Hair," but the mainstream decided Pavement was too strange for their tastes, and the band decided they preferred the underground, leaving the band as one of the most popular—and the most influential—*American indie-rock band of the '90s.* —Stephen Thomas Erlewine

★ **Slanted & Enchanted** / May 1992 / Matador ✦✦✦✦✦
Slanted & Enchanted is a left-field classic, a record that came out of nowhere to help establish a new subgenre of rock & roll. Pavement had already sketched out their sound, as well as their amateurish lo-fi aesthetic, on a series of indie singles before recording their debut, but *Slanted & Enchanted* is where they pulled all of their disparate sounds together into a distinctive style. At first, the primitive sound of the record is the most gripping thing about *Slanted,* but soon the true innovations of the record appear through the songs themselves. Stephen Malkmus and Spiral Stairs subvert conventional pop structures, turning melodies inside out, reinterpreting and reworking older songs, and bending genres together. It's a complex, enthralling record, filled with fractured riffs, strong melodies, and cryptic melodies, and with all the hiss and static, *Slanted & Enchanted* sounds like listening to a distant college radio station—melodies and hooks keep floating in and out of the mix, with individual lines instead of full lyrics surfacing through the murk. This unique song structure as much as the sound of the album itself makes *Slanted & Enchanted* an individual, signature work and one of the most influential records of the '90s. *— Stephen Thomas Erlewine*

Watery, Domestic / Nov. 1992 / Matador ✦✦✦

Westing (By Musket and Sextant) / Mar. 30, 1993 / Drag City ✦✦✦✦
A collection of all of Pavement's low-fidelity early singles and EPs, which feature considerably less melody than *Slanted and Enchanted.* It's nice to have this rare material on one CD, although the music is defiantly anti-CD. Those who boarded the train with the acclaimed *Slanted and Enchanted* should catch up on what they've missed. *— Stephen Thomas Erlewine*

☆ **Crooked Rain, Crooked Rain** / Feb. 1994 / Matador ✦✦✦✦✦
Although it's much calmer than the critically acclaimed *Slanted and Enchanted, Crooked Rain, Crooked Rain* shares the same spirit of the band's debut—it's a messy, impossibly catchy catalog of pop music and culture. On their second full-length album, Pavement have abandoned much of the low-fi squalor of their earlier work, opting for a laidback, subdued sound that borders on country-rock and jazz-rock at times, and pure pop and rock & roll at others. In other words, it's more accessible than *Slanted and Enchanted* but just as distinctive and original. Ultimately, *Crooked Rain, Crooked Rain* revamps rock history and reinvents it for the slacker generation. *— Stephen Thomas Erlewine*

Wowee Zowee / Apr. 1995 / Matador ✦✦✦✦✦
With its vast array of musical styles, *Wowee Zowee* isn't as accessible as *Crooked Rain, Crooked Rain* or as immediate as the bracing, noisy pop of *Slanted & Enchanted.* Pavement never abandon their warped pop aesthetic, they simply expand it, incorporating elements of folk-rock, English music-hall, soul, jazz, country, as well as adding asides to such contemporaries as Suede ("We Dance"), Ween ("Brinx Job") and Stereolab ("Half a Canyon"). Alternating between majestic epics like "Grounded" and ragged narratives like "Rattled by the Rush" and "Father to a Sister of Thought," to song fragments like "Brinx Job" and the punkish "Serpentine Pad," the record might seem disjointed at first. After repeated listens, the songs play off each other, creating a dense collage of '90s rock & roll that recasts the past and present into one rich, kalidescopic and blissfully cryptic world view. *— Stephen Thomas Erlewine*

Brighten the Corners / Feb. 11, 1997 / Matador/Capitol ✦✦✦✦
There's a difference between accessibility and focus, which Pavement illustrate with their fourth album, *Brighten the Corners.* Arriving on the heels of the glorious mess of *Wowee Zowee,* the cohesive sound and laid-back sarcasm of *Brighten the Corners* can give the record the illusion of being accessible, or at the very least a retreat toward the songcraft of *Crooked Rain, Crooked Rain.* And the record is calm, with none of the full-out blasts of noise that marked all of their previous releases. It would be easy to dismiss the absence of noise as mere maturity, or a move toward more accessible songcraft, but neither statement is entirely true. *Brighten the Corners* is mature but wise-assed, melodic but complex—it's a record that reveals its gifts gradually, giving you enough information the first time to make you want come

back for more. At first, the dissonant sing-song verse of "Stereo" seems awkward, but it's all pulled into perspective with the gleeful, addictive outburst of the chorus, and that is a microcosm of the album's appeal. The first time around, the winding melody of "Shady Lane," the psycho jangle-pop of "Date With Ikea," the epic grace of "Type Slowly" and the speedy rush of "Embassy Row" make an impression, but repeated listens reveal sonic and lyrical details that make them indelible. Similarly, Malkmus' hip-hop inflections on "Blue Hawaiian" and the quiet beauty of "Transport is Arranged" unfold over time. While the preponderance of slow songs and laid-back production make the album more focused than *Wowee Zowee*, it doesn't have the rich diversity of its predecessor—"Type Slowly" comes closest to the grand, melancholic beauty of "Grounded"—but it remains a thoroughly compelling listen. —*Stephen Thomas Erlewine*

Terror Twilight / Jun. 8, 1999 / Matador ✦✦✦✦
Since Pavement switched course with each record—*Crooked Rain, Crooked Rain* was nothing like *Slanted & Enchanted*, and *Brighten the Corners* was decidedly different from the brilliant, warped *Wowee Zowee*—it's a little disarming to realize that *Terror Twilight* merely deepens the sound of its predecessor. Guitars burst to the forefront every so often—most notably on the dense jam "Platform Blues" and the shouted choruses of "Billie"—yet they're usually used as texture. Nothing rocks hard and "The Hexx," which was heard on the *Brighten* tour as a metallic epic, has been transformed into a surrealistic dream, reminiscent of the Velvet Underground's "Ocean." That's typical of *Terror Twilight*—it's reflective, with the occasional flight of fancy that fits neatly into the laid-back flow. It's also the tightest record Pavement ever made, largely due to producer Nigel Godrich, who helped reign in excessive tendencies in Radiohead and Beck and does the same here. The band still sounds like Pavement—their loping interplay is unmistakable—and Stephen Malkmus' songs are typically dense and literate, yet they're easier to digest. That, along with the lack of Spiral Stairs songs, gives *Terror Twilight* a cohesion missing even on earlier Pavement albums, no matter how great they were. All the focus makes the album feel a little less like Pavement—after all, this is a band whose imperfections were among their most endearing qualities—and a bit more like Malkmus' first solo album, which it essentially is. Though its hard not to miss the gloriously messy sprawl of Pavement at their peak, this carefully-crafted, languid recasting of their signature sound is effective and winds up as a fitting, bittersweet farewell for the best band of the '90s. —*Stephen Thomas Erlewine*

Pearl Jam

f. 1990
Group / Grunge, Alternative Pop/Rock, Hard Rock
Pearl Jam rose from the ashes of Mother Love Bone to become the most popular American rock & roll band of the '90s. After vocalist Andrew Wood overdosed on heroin, guitarist Stone Gossard and bassist Jeff Ament assembled a new band, bringing in Mike McCready on lead guitar, Dave Krusen on drums, and vocalist Eddie Vedder. Naming themselves Pearl Jam, the band recorded their debut album, *Ten*, in the beginning of 1991. *Ten* didn't begin selling in significant numbers until early 1992, after Nirvana made mainstream rock radio receptive to alternative rock acts. Soon, Pearl Jam outsold Nirvana, which wasn't surprising. Pearl Jam fused the riff-heavy stadium rock of the '70s with the grit and anger of '80s post-punk, without ever neglecting hooks and choruses; "Jeremy," "Evenflow," and "Alive" fit perfectly into album rock radio stations that were looking for new blood. Pearl Jam's audience continued to grow during 1992, thanks to a series of radio and MTV hits, as well as a successful appearance on the second Lollapalooza tour. Despite their status as rock & roll superstars, the band refused to succumb to the accepted conventions of the music industry, refusing to release any videos or singles from their second album, 1993's *Vs*. Nevertheless, it was another multi-platinum success, debuting at number one and selling nearly a million copies in its first week of release. *Vitalogy*, the band's third album, appeared at the end of 1994, and in early 1995, they recorded *Mirror Ball*, an album with Neil Young. In late summer of 1996, Pearl Jam released their fourth album, *No Code*. Although the album was greeted with fairly positive reviews and debuted at number one, its weird amaglam of rock, worldbeat and experimentalism dissatisfied a large portion of their fan base, and it quickly fell down the charts. By the end of the year, Pearl Jam had completed a new, harder-rocking record entitled *Yield*. —*Stephen Thomas Erlewine*

★ **Ten** / Aug. 27, 1991 / Epic Associated ✦✦✦✦✦
Nirvana's *Nevermind* may have been the album that broke grunge and alternative rock into the mainstream, but there's no underestimating the role that Pearl Jam's *Ten* played in keeping them there. Nirvana's appeal may have been huge, but it wasn't universal; rock radio still viewed them as too raw and punky, and some hard rock fans dismissed them as weird misfits. In retrospect, it's easy to see why Pearl Jam clicked with a mass audience—they weren't as metallic as Alice in Chains or Soundgarden, and of Seattle's Big Four, their sound owed the greatest debt to classic rock. With its intricately arranged guitar textures and expansive harmonic vocabulary, *Ten* especially recalled Jimi Hendrix and Led Zeppelin. But those touchstones might not have been immediately apparent, since—aside from Mike McCready's Clapton/Hendrix-style leads—every trace of blues influence has been completely stripped from the band's sound. Though they rock hard, Pearl Jam is too anti-star to swagger, too self-aware to puncture the album's air of gravity. Pearl Jam tackles weighty topics—abortion, homelessness, childhood traumas, gun violence, rigorous introspection—with an earnest zeal unmatched since mid-'80s U2, whose anthemic sound they frequently strive for. Similarly, Eddie Vedder's impressionistic lyrics often make their greatest impact through the passionate commitment of his delivery rather than concrete meaning. His voice had a highly distinctive timbre that perfectly fit the album's warm, rich sound, and that's part of the key—no matter how cathartic *Ten*'s tersely titled songs got, they were never abrasive enough to affect the album's accessibility. *Ten* also benefited from a long gestation period, during which the band honed the material into this tightly focused form; the result is a flawlessly crafted hard rock masterpiece. —*Steve Huey*

Vs. / Oct. 19, 1993 / Epic Associated ✦✦✦✦
Pearl Jam took to superstardom like deer in headlights. Unsure of how to maintain their rigorous standards of integrity in the face of massive commercial success, the band took refuge in willful obscurity—the title of their second album, *Vs.*, did not appear *anywhere* in the packaging, and they refused to release any singles or videos. (Ironically, many fans then paid steep prices for import CD singles, a situation the band eventually rectified.) The eccentricities underline Pearl Jam's almost paranoid aversion to charges of hypocrisy or egotism—but it also made sense to use the spotlight for progress. You could see that reasoning in their ensuing battle with Ticketmaster, and you could hear it in the record itself. *Vs.* is often Eddie Vedder at his most strident, both lyrically and vocally. It's less oblique than *Ten* in its topicality, and sometimes downright dogmatic; having the world's ear renders Vedder unable to resist a few simplistic potshots at favorite white-liberal targets. Yet a little self-righteousness is an acceptable price to pay for the passionate immediacy that permeates *Vs.* It's a much rawer, looser record than *Ten*, feeling like a live performance; Vedder practically screams himself hoarse on a few songs. The band consciously strives for spontaneity, admirably pushing themselves into new territory—some numbers are decidedly punky, and there are also a couple of acoustic-driven ballads, which are well suited to Vedder's sonorous low register. Sometimes, that spontaneity comes at the expense of *Ten*'s marvelous craft—a few songs here are just plain underdeveloped, with supporting frameworks that don't feel very sturdy. But, of everything that does work, the rockers are often frightening in their intensity, and the more reflective songs are mesmerizing. *Vs.* may not reach the majestic heights of *Ten*, but at least half the record stands with Pearl Jam's best work. —*Steve Huey*

Vitalogy / Dec. 6, 1994 / Epic Associated ✦✦✦✦✦
Thanks to its stripped-down, lean production, *Vitalogy* stands as Pearl Jam's most original and uncompromising album. While it isn't a concept album, *Vitalogy* sounds like one. Death and despair shroud the album, rendering even the explosive celebration of vinyl "Spin the Black Circle" somewhat muted. But that black cloud works to Pearl Jam's advantage, injecting a nervous tension to brittle rockers like "Last Exit" and "Not For You," and especially introspective ballads like "Corduroy" and "Better Man." In between the straight rock numbers and the searching slow songs, Pearl Jam contributes their strangest music—the mantra-funk of "Aye Davanita," the sub-Tom Waits accordion romp of "Bugs" and the chilling sonic collage "Hey Foxymophandlemama, That's Me." Pearl Jam are at their best when they're fighting, whether it's TicketMaster, fame, or their own personal demons. —*Stephen Thomas Erlewine*

No Code / Aug. 27, 1996 / Epic ✦✦✦✦
A strange phenomenon with anthemic hard rock bands is that when they begin to mature and branch out into new musical genres, they nearly always choose to embrace both the music and spirituality of the East and India, and Pearl Jam is no exception. Throughout *No Code*, Eddie Vedder expounds on his moral and spiritual dilemmas: where on previous albums his rage was virtually all-consuming, it is clear on *No Code* that he has embraced an unspecified religion as a way to ease his troubles. Fortunately, that has coincided with an expansion of the group's musical palette. From the subtle, winding opener "Sometimes" and the near-prayer of the single "Who You Are," the band reaches into new territory, working with droning, mantra-like riffs and vocals, layered exotic percussion and a newfound subtlety. Of course, they haven't left behind hard rock, but, like any Pearl Jam record, the heart of *No Code* doesn't lie in the harder songs, it lies in the slower numbers and the ballads, which give Vedder the best platform for his soul-searching: "Present Tense," "Off He Goes," "In My Tree" and "Around the Bend" equal the group's earlier masterpieces. While a bit too incoherent, *No Code* is Pearl Jam's richest and most rewarding album, as well as its most human. They might be maturing in a fairly conventional method, but they still find new ways to state old truths. —*Stephen Thomas Erlewine*

Yield / Feb. 3, 1998 / Epic ✦✦✦

Live on Two Legs / Nov. 24, 1998 / Epic ✦✦✦

Binaural / May 16, 2000 / Epic ✦✦✦✦
If anything, Pearl Jam was even more in the wilderness—at least as far as the mainstream was concerned—at the beginning of 2000 than they were in the second half of the '90s. Even with "Last Kiss," their first big hit single since *Ten*, under their belts, they were an anomaly on the pop and rock scenes. They were the only one of their old grunge colleagues still standing intact, and they were genuinely alone. No peers, and too sincere to even considering fitting into a pop scene dominated by 'N Sync on one side and Limp Bizkit on the other. Not surprisingly, they chose to persevere, ignoring trends, completely in favor of being a classicist rock band. This should come as no surprise, since that's what they've done since *No Code* and, perhaps, *Vitalogy*, but the real surprise about their sixth studio album *Binaural* is that it finds the group roaring back to life without dramatically changing the direction they followed on *No Code* and *Yield*. Maybe the addition of a new drummer, former Soundgarden member Matt Cameron, has kicked the band to life, but that unfairly dismisses Jack Irons' worthy contributions. Instead, the difference is focus—though Pearl Jam is trying a lot of different styles, certainly more so than on *Yield*, they pull it all off better. The songs are sharper, the production is layered, and the performances are as compassionate as ever, resulting in their finest album since *Vitalogy*. —*Stephen Thomas Erlewine*

Ann Peebles

b. Apr. 27, 1947, St. Louis, MO
Vocals / Memphis Soul, Soul
Ann Peebles was the queen of Willie Mitchell's Memphis-based Hi Records roster during the '70s, when Al Green was its undisputed king. Sung in a voice as bittersweet as it is riveting, her always-dramatic recordings include one undisputed masterpiece, "I Can't Stand the Rain," cited as a favorite by John Lennon and most recently covered by Tina Turner. Other covers abound—Robert Palmer took "I'm Gonna Tear Your Playhouse Down," and Bette Midler claimed "Breakin' Up Somebody's Home." Backed by the brilliant Hi rhythm section and flawlessly produced by Mitchell, Peebles sang and wrote (often in partnership with husband Don Bryant) of the feminine perspective on the darker side of love—sometimes untrusting love, but love, for better or worse. Her work represents, with elegance and grit, some of the best of Memphis soul.

After a long absence from recording, Ann Peebles returned to the wars with the CD *Full*

Time Love in 1992 for Bullseye/Rounder. While it didn't get much exposure or recognition in urban circles, it was a wonderfully sung and well-produced attempt at giving Peebles some contemporary tweaking without losing her gritty qualities. *—Christine Ohlman and Ron Wynn*

Part Time Love / 1971 / The Right Stuff ✦✦✦✦✦
The title track was a masterpiece, and everything else on this dynamic early '70s soul session is a jewel. Ann Peebles may have been the most overlooked great soul singer, male or female, who emerged in the '70s. Hi couldn't strike crossover gold twice, and Al Green was becoming a superstar. But Peebles deserved a better fate than obscurity, as this collection of soul wailers and weepers proves. *—Ron Wynn*

I Can't Stand the Rain / 1974 / Hi ✦✦✦
The title song was an instant classic, and its lyrics are among the most moving and gripping in soul annals. This was Ann Peebles' finest album for Hi Records, and it should have been a massive success. Instead, while it's celebrated in Europe and now considered an anthem, it floundered and barely scraped the pop charts, although the single was her biggest R&B hit. It's sad and ridiculous that the only Ann Peebles session presently available on CD is the one she did for Bullseye Blues in '92. *—Ron Wynn*

St. Louis Woman / 1996 / Hi ✦✦✦✦
St. Louis Woman is a terrific four-disc, 63-track box set covering Ann Peebles' entire career, concentrating (rightly so) on her seminal early-'70s recordings for Hi Records. All of her hits are here, of course, along with underappreciated album tracks, lost singles, B-sides, rarities and a handful of unreleased cuts. Certainly, this isn't the choice for the casual fan—there's simply too much music here—but for the dedicated fan and collector, this is a treasure. *—Stephen Thomas Erlewine*

● **The Best of Ann Peebles: The Hi Records Years** / Jul. 23, 1996 / Capitol ✦✦✦✦✦
The Best of the Hi Records Years collects all the highlights from Ann Peebles' creative and commercial heyday, featuring the majority of her hits for the label, including "I Can't Stand the Rain" and "Part Time Love," as well as several terrific lesser-known singles and album tracks. *—Stephen Thomas Erlewine*

This Is Ann Peebles/The Handwriting Is on the Wall / Mar. 4, 1997 / Hi ✦✦✦✦

Teddy Pendergrass

b. Mar. 26, 1950, Philadelphia, PA
Vocals, Drums / Quiet Storm, Club/Dance, Urban, Soul
Teddy Pendergrass' tender ballads and slow, sensual singing style helped make him a favorite among women. By his late teens, he was a drummer for the Cadillacs. In the late 60s, the Cadillacs merged with another more-established group, Harold Melvin and The Blue Notes. Melvin soon became aware of Pendergrass' vocal prowess asked him to take the lead singer spot. Beginning with & Miss You",a steady stream of hit singles flowed from the band.

Around 1976, Pendergrass left Melvin's Blue Notes and formed his own Blue Notes, featuring Teddy Pendergrass. Soon, however, Pendergrass disbanded his group in favor of a solo career. He burst back on the scene with his self-titled platinum solo debut. Around this time, Pendergrass began to institute his infamous "Ladies Only" concerts. His next three albums went gold or platinum. The singer received several Grammy nominations during 1977 and 1978, Billboard's 1977 Pop Album New Artist Award, an American Music Award for best R&B performer of 1978 and awards from Ebony Magazine and the NAACP. The seventies ended, but Pendergrass kept racking up the hits. *TP*, his fifth solo album went platinum the summer of 1980. *It's Time For Love* gave Pendergrass another gold album in summer 1981. A 1982 car accident left Pendergrass paralyzed from the waist down. After almost a year of physical therapy and counseling, Pendergrass returned to the recording scene in 1983. His ninth solo album, *Love Language* went gold the spring of 1984. Pendergrass continued to record sporadically throughout the '80s and '90s, but failed to top his previous work. *—Ed Hogan*

● **The Best of Teddy Pendergrass** / Mar. 31, 1998 / The Right Stuff ✦✦✦✦✦
The Right Stuff's *The Best of Teddy Pendergrass* is a definitive 18-track collection, containing all of his big hits from 1977's "I Don't Love You Anymore" to 1991's "It Should've Been You." In between those two songs, such romantic smooth soul classics as "Can't We Try," "You're My Latest, My Greatest Inspiration," "Close the Door," "Turn off the Lights," "Love TKO" and "Joy" are heard. Some Top Ten R&B hits, like "Love 4/2" and "I Can't Live Without Your Love," are missing, but the disc remains a near-perfect summary of Pendergrass at the peak of his powers. *—Stephen Thomas Erlewine*

The Penguins

f. 1954, Los Angeles, CA, **db.** 1959
Group / Brown Eyed Soul, Doo Wop
Best known for their hit single "Earth Angel," the doo wop quartet the Penguins were never able to replicate the success of their only Top 40 hit, but the song became a rock & roll classic. Although he wasn't the lead singer, Curtis Williams was the leader of the group. He learned "Earth Angel" from vocalist Jesse Belvin—some sources claim that Williams wrote the song alone, others say he co-wrote the song with Belvin, while others claim Gaynel Hodge, a member of the doo wop group the Turks, wrote the song with the duo (in fact, Hodge won a lawsuit filed in 1956 that gave him a co-writing credit)—and had the Penguins sing the song.

Around 1954, the Penguins signed with the local Los Angeles independent label Dootone Records. The group's first single was going to be the uptempo "Hey Sinorita" and the ballad "Earth Angel" was going to be the B-side. Upon the release of the single in the latter half of 1954, Los Angeles radio stations were receiving more requests for "Earth Angel" than "Hey Sinorita," and by the beginning of 1955, the single had scaled the national charts, spending three weeks at the top of the R&B charts and peaking at number eight on the pop charts. After cutting some sides for Mercury, the Penguins moved to Atlantic, where they had their second and final hit, "Pledge of Love," which climbed to number 15 on the R&B charts in the summer of 1957. *—Stephen Thomas Erlewine*

● **Authentic Golden Hits** / 1993 / Juke Box Treasures ✦✦✦✦✦
At long last, a well-thought-out compilation that gathers up all of the group's best sides for Dooto Records, including the original versions of the classics "Earth Angel" and "Hey, Senorita" in their original, unedited form. *—Cub Koda*

Michael Penn

b. Aug. 1, 1958
Vocals, Guitar / Pop Underground, College Rock, Adult Alternative Pop/Rock, Pop/Rock, Singer/Songwriter
One of the most acclaimed singer/songwriters to emerge during the late 1980s, Michael Penn was seemingly destined for a career in show business—the oldest son of director Leo Penn and actress Eileen Ryan, his younger siblings included Sean (later recognized among the finest actors of his generation) and Chris (a noted character actor acclaimed for his work in features like *Reservoir Dogs*). While his brothers focused on acting, Michael turned to music, and in the early 1980s he formed the group Doll Congress, which garnered a fervent local following but never expanded their fan base outside of Southern California. In 1987, he reunited with ex-Doll Congress keyboardist Patrick Warren to begin composing the songs which comprised his 1989 debut, *March*. Upon its release, the album became a significant critical favorite, earning acclaim for its sparkling Beatlesque folk-pop and clever, Elvis Costello-like wordplay; the lead single, "No Myth," even became a surprise hit and helped launch the LP into the Top 40. In the wake of his initial success, Penn went on a lengthy hiatus; when he returned in 1992 with his sophomore effort, *Free For All*, he met much greater commercial resistance than he faced with *March*, and after only a few weeks, the album fell off the charts. He then spent five years pondering his next move, finally resurfacing in 1997 with *Resigned*. *—Jason Ankeny*

● **March** / Sep. 1989 / RCA ✦✦✦✦✦
Michael Penn's debut album, *March*, released in late 1989, served notice there was another talented Penn brother, in additon to actors Sean and Chris. The album kicks off with one of the top singles of the winter of 1989-1090, "No Myth," and proceeds through an engrossing myriad of folk-tinged ballads and up-tempo rockers. Despite several literary allusions and the ponderous title and lyrics of "Cupid's Got a Brand New Gun," on the whole, Penn doesn't take himself too seriously. "Brave New World" is an absurd Dylan-esque hodgepodge of rhyme, and "Big House" is devoted to the childhood prank of ringing doorbells, then running. The coda is "Evenfall," maybe the best '60s "frat-rock" song since the '60s, with a horn section that makes you want to dance until the campus police close down the party. *—Mark Morgenstein*

Free-for-All / Sep. 15, 1992 / RCA ✦✦✦
Free For All, Michael Penn's second album, isn't as immediately accessible as *March*, but his cryptic lyrics and twisting melodies will work their way into your memory if given some time. *—Stephen Thomas Erlewine*

Resigned / Jun. 3, 1997 / 57 Records/Epic ✦✦✦✦
Backing away from the introspective inclinations of *Free-for-All*, Michael Penn delivers a concise and thoroughly infectious guitar-pop album with *Resigned*. Like most of Penn's music, the album relies heavily on *Revolver*-era Beatles, but his melodies are uniformly tighter and catchier than before, and producer Brendan O'Brien gives the record a crisp, attractive sound. None of the tracks initially stand out like "No Myth" or "Long Way Down," yet each song is well constructed and filled with hooks, making *Resigned* a terrific third album from Penn. *—Stephen Thomas Erlewine*

MP4: Days Since a Lost Time Accident / Feb. 1, 2000 / Epic ✦✦✦✦
When Michael Penn released *MP4: Days Since a Lost Time Accident*, the strict playlist of adult-alternative radio made it pretty clear that it'd be difficult for him to have a hit, so Penn doesn't even try—he just creates a record for himself and his cult. Brendan O'Brien, the producer of *Resigned*, mans the boards on the opening cut "Lucky One.". It's not just the only song on *MP4* not produced by Penn, it's the only song that sounds like a blatant attempt at a radio-ready single. That it succeeds gloriously—it's the first sure-fire follow-up to "No Myth"—speaks of Penn's prodigious abilities as a craftsman. The rest of the album is equally well crafted, but more subtle in construction and production, without hooks that leap out of the speaker. They're there, but they're delivered subtly, letting each song to slowly work its way into a listener's memory. Penn knows that whoever puts on *MP4* is willing to delve deeply into the record, willing to spend time with it to find its rewards. It's to his considerable credit that he delivers. *MP4* doesn't have a knockout punch, but it is an expert pop album—tightly sequenced and written, filled with small gems. It's the kind of album that's ideal for cult audiences, since it's familiar yet doesn't stand still (the production takes some risks, albeit minor ones). It may not win Michael Penn any new fans, but it'll certainly satisfy the devoted. *—Stephen Thomas Erlewine*

Pere Ubu

f. Aug. 1975, Cleveland, OH
Group / American Punk, Experimental Rock, Post-Punk, Alternative Pop/Rock
Emerging from the urban wasteland of '70s Cleveland, Pere Ubu shaped the American underground. Through their long, convoluted career—which was marked by constant lineup shifts and several hiatuses—Ubu's art-punk focused on hulking frontman David Thomas's rapturously demented voice and lyrics and the group's volatile melodies and rhythms. While their early work captured the era's chaos with apocalyptic fervor and surprising humanity, their sound evolved into clever, elliptical pop on their later releases. Named for Alfred Jarry's surrealist play Ubu Roi, Pere Ubu formed in 1975 from the ashes of Rocket from the Tombs, which featured Thomas and guitarist Peter Laughner. Ubu's original lineup also included guitarist Tom Herman, bassist Tim Wright, keyboardist Allen Ravenstine and drummer Scott Krauss. The group's early singles, such as "30 Seconds Over Tokyo" and "The Final Solution, sent shock waves through the underground rock scene. After Laughner's and Wright's departures, Pere Ubu continued as a quintet with bassist Tony Maimone. In 1977, Mercury *AR*

exec Cliff Burnstein convinced the label to form a new imprint in order to sign Pere Ubu; Blank Records released their 1978 debut LP The Modern Dance, which sold little but influenced countless post-punk acts with its dark, manic intensity. Dub Housing pushed the band to further extremes, but they disbanded upon completing 1979's New Picnic Time (working title: "Goodbye"). They quickly reformed, releasing 1980's The Art of Walking, their most accessible work yet. They disbanded again after 1982's *Song of the Bailing Man,* and Thomas pursued a solo career. His 1987 album *Blame* the Messenger featured Ravenstine and Maimone; when Krauss sat in on a hometown date, they revived Pere Ubu, and 1988's The Tenement Year and 1989's *Cloudland* were their poppiest albums to date. 1995's *Ray Gun Suitcase* was planned as their swan song, but the box set Datapanik in the Year Zero revived interest in the band. Thomas reunited with Tom Herman to record 1998's Pennsylvania; the live *Apocalypse Now* followed a year later. *—Jason Ankeny*

The Modern Dance / 1978 / Geffen ✦✦✦✦✦
There isn't an Ubu recording I can imagine living without, but even so, the *Modern Dance* remains the essential Ubu purchase (as does the follow-up *Dub Housing*). I'm sure Mercury had no idea what they had on their hands when the released this as part of their punk rock offshoot label Blank, but it remains a classic slice of art-punk. It announces itself quite boldly: the first sound you hear is a painfully high-pitched whine of feedback, but then Tom Herman's postmodern Chuck Berry riffing kicks off the brilliant "Non-Alignment Pact," and you soon realize that this is punk rock unlike anything you've ever heard. David Thomas' caterwauling is funny and moving, Scott Krauss (drums) and Tony Maimone (bass) are one of the great unheralded rhythms sections in all of rock, and the "difficult" tracks like "Street Waves," "Chinese Radiation," and the terrifying "Humor Me" are revelatory, and way ahead of their time. Now 20 years old and available on CD for the first time, *The Modern Dance* is the signature sound of the avant-garage: art-rock, punk-rock and garage-rock mixing together joyously and fearlessly. *—John Dougan*

Dub Housing / 1979 / Rough Trade ✦✦✦✦✦
Though Pere Ubu's tenure on Mercury lasted one record, their departure for their unlikely home of Chrysalis (at the time the label of Jethro Tull) resulted in *Dub Housing,* widely considered their masterpiece. Darker and more difficult than *The Modern Dance* (indicated by the cover's darkened apartment complex and stormy Cleveland skyline) with plenty of bleak soundscapes (e.g., "Codex"), *Dub Housing* also includes "Navvy"'s bouncy burble (featuring Thomas yelping "I have desires!"), and "(Pa) Ubu Dance Party"'s surreal big beat. Make no mistake, as much as Ubu indulged in arty dissonance and mucked about with song structure, this is very much a rock & roll record, albeit one made by a band interested in pushing the envelope when it came to sound, song construction, and performance. As much as this is a band effort, the guitar of Tom Herman and the synthesizer of Allen Ravenstine frequently stand out. Herman's strong, polished playing veers from assertive riffing to assaultive noise; Ravenstine, who may be one of the all-time great synth players (especially compared to complete wankers as Rick Wakeman) colors the sound with ominous whooshes of distortions, blips and blurbs that sound like a sped-up Pong game. But, as is often the case with Ubu, it's David Thomas' singing (here at its most engagingly unrestrained) that is front and center. Part comic foil, part raging madman, Thomas utilizes all of his limited range in a wacked expressiveness built around hiccups, yodels, screeches, and, sometimes, singing. *Dub Housing* sold next to nothing and signaled the beginning of the end of Ubu's relationship with Chrysalis, but it remains an important and influential American rock record. *—John Dougan*

New Picnic Time / 1979 / Rough Trade ✦✦✦✦✦
It was not surprising that after *Dub Housing,* Ubu couldn't get a record released in the U.S. *New Picnic Time* originally surfaced on Chrysalis as a British import, but when Rough Trade made it available domestically, U.S. fans could take solace in that the band had finally hooked up with a label more sympathetic to their decidedly unique approach to music. *New Picnic Time* was also the last Ubu record with guitarist Tom Herman, and for many Ubu fans (myself included) this signals the end of Pere Ubu phase one (or phase two, depending on one's feelings for the *Datapanik*-era band). *New Picnic Time* also finds David Thomas' lyrical explorations reflecting his religious involvement with the Jehovah's Witnesses, pieties that are stated quite emphatically on the record's closing track "Jehovah's Kingdom Comes." *—John Dougan*

The Art of Walking / 1980 / Rough Trade ✦✦✦

390° Degrees of Simulated Stereo (Live) / 1981 / Rough Trade ✦✦

Song of the Bailing Man / 1982 / Rough Trade ✦✦✦
Continuing in the spirit of *The Art of Walking,* this record marks the departure of drummer Scott Krauss (replaced by ex-Feelies Anton Fier), a fact significant in that when combined with the earlier departure of guitarist Tom Herman, means that at this juncture Ubu was more art and less rock. Personally, I never understood why people were so knocked out by Fier; I think he lacks aggressiveness, plays behind the beat, and generally speaking, doesn't push the band as hard as a drummer ought to. That said, *Bailing Man* is a fine, occasionally wonderful record that, at its slackest moments, sounds strained and forced, as if it were no fun to make, and it's this seriousness (instead of the usual Ubu silly seriousness) that prevents this record from being great. It's no surprise that the band went on a hiatus for six years after the release of this record, returning with 1988's *The Tenement Year.* *—John Dougan*

★ **Terminal Tower** / 1985 / Twin/Tone ✦✦✦✦✦
At the outset of their career, Pere Ubu released some of the very first independent-label American punk singles on their own Hearthan (later Hearpen) label, which constitute some of their most celebrated and legendary work. *Terminal Tower: An Archival Collection* gathers eleven tracks, mostly from the crucial Hearthan/Hearpen period (including the entire *Datapanik in the Year Zero* EP), plus a couple of later U.K. singles. This music's historical importance is undeniable—not only because of the band's pioneeringly independent status in an area not as celebrated for its punk scene, but also because Pere Ubu was one of the first bands to push their art-punk sound into territory later classified as "alternative," a testament to their forward-looking approach. None of that wouldn't matter if *Terminal Tower* didn't hold up so well as a listening experience, but Pere Ubu still sounds utterly original. David Thomas' unearthly voice mumbles and sobs the angular melodies over a backdrop of garagey guitars, startling sound effects (from both guitar and synth), and odd dissonances. Moments of jarring, apocalyptic terror ("Heart of Darkness," the creeping, crawling "30 Seconds Over Tokyo") sit next to oddly beautiful introspection, sometimes on the same song (the aching angst and evocative guitar solo of "Final Solution"). Meanwhile, poppier tracks incorporate those avant-garde textures into a gleeful dada bounce. The two tracks unavailable anywhere else, "Not Happy" and "Lonesome Cowboy Dave," are slices of poppy dementia that may make the collection worthwhile for devotees who already own the box, especially since this is such a strong, coherent listen. *Terminal Tower* stands as the best introduction to the band not only because of its stellar material and relative accessibility, but also because it largely lacks the arty indulgences that popped up even on the group's most consistent albums. Now that it's back in print, it's essential, groundbreaking listening. *—Steve Huey*

The Tenement Year / 1988 / Enigma ✦✦✦✦✦
Since the re-formed version of Pere Ubu reins in (slightly) the group's more extreme tendencies, this album, which nevertheless presents David Thomas's unique vision and the band's somewhat off-kilter approach to rock more or less intact, may be the place for neophytes to get their feet wet with a highly unusual group. This one should give you the idea—then you're on your own. *—William Ruhlmann*

One Man Drives While the Other Man Screams / 1989 / Rough Trade ✦✦

Cloudland / May 1989 / Fontana ✦✦✦✦✦
It's funny, this might be the most controversial recording Ubu ever made. After years of brilliant chunks of avant-garde garage rock tomfoolery, they release a pop record, one with smooth corners, and production help from Stephen Hague (Pet Shop Boys). It's not as if Ubu is unrecognizable; the familiar idiosyncracies are here and in full effect. It's more that the songs themselves—love songs—are very different from their usual dramas from the urban landscape. But David Thomas' pastoral mumblings and utopian visions remain central to the record's lyrical heart. Hardcore fans, a boring group who want everything to sound like *Dub Housing,* felt betrayed by this record, seeing it as the band's egregious attempt at selling out. But nothing could have been further from the truth. *Cloudland* is an amazing record that allows room for growth and change without sacrificing panache and attitude. *—John Dougan*

Worlds in Collision / May 21, 1991 / Fontana ✦✦✦✦

Story of My Life / Apr. 6, 1993 / Imago ✦✦✦

Ray Gun Suitcase / Aug. 22, 1995 / Tim Kerr ✦✦✦

Datapanik in the Year Zero / Aug. 27, 1996 / Geffen ✦✦✦✦✦
Pere Ubu's troubles with record companies are legendary within certain underground rock circles. In perhaps the most bizarre turn of events, the group's collected works of 1978-1982—after being out of print for nearly a decade—were reissued by Geffen as five-disc box set, *Datapanik in the Year Zero.* Named after the group's 1978 EP, the set is arranged chronologically and occasionally substitutes live versions for studio tracks, but that hardly matters—nearly every song the band recorded during the five-year time span is included. In addition to the official Pere Ubu material, the box incluedes a disc of rare singles from early incarnations of Ubu and other Cleveland-area punk rockers like Rocket from the Tombs, 15-60-75, and Mirrors, which were released on David Thomas' independent record label. With this much material, it's safe to say that the set is a definitive retrospective and its worth is increased because most of this material hasn't been widely available on compact disc, so collectors won't feel like they've paid a lot of money for a handful of rarities. However, if you're simply interested in Pere Ubu, consider the set carefully before investing. Pere Ubu was indeed one of the most innovative and challenging bands of their era, which means that their music is an acquired taste. However, for those willing to invest in the box will find a wealth of inventive, hard-edged avant-rock & roll. *—Stephen Thomas Erlewine*

Pennsylvania / Mar. 17, 1998 / Tim Kerr ✦✦✦✦

Apocalypse Now / Aug. 24, 1999 / Thirsty Ear ✦✦✦✦

Carl Perkins

b. Apr. 9, 1932, Tiptonville, TN, **d.** Jan. 19, 1998
Vocals, Guitar / Rockabilly, Traditional Country, Rock & Roll
While some ill-informed revisionist writers of rock history would like to dismiss Carl Perkins as a rockabilly artist who became a one hit wonder at the dawn of rock & roll's early years, a deeper look at his music and career reveals much more. A quick look at his songwriting portfolio shows that he has composed "Daddy Sang Bass" for Johnny Cash, "I Was So Wrong" for Patsy Cline, and "Let Me Tell You About Love" for the Judds, big hits and classics all. His influence as the quintessential rockabilly artist has played a big part in the development of every generation of rocker to come down the pike since, from the Beatles' George Harrison to the Stray Cats' Brian Setzer to a myriad of others in the country field as well. His guitar style is the other twin peak—along with that of Elvis' lead man Scotty Moore—of rockabilly's instrumental center, so pervasive that modern day players automatically gravitate toward it when called upon to deliver the style, not even realizing that they're playing Carl Perkins licks, sometimes note for note. As a singer, his interpretation of country ballads is every bit as fine as his better known rockers. And within the framework of the best of his music is a strong sense of family and roots, all of which trace straight back to Carl's humble beginnings. *—Cub Koda*

★ **Original Sun Greatest Hits** / 1986 / Rhino ✦✦✦✦✦
Original Sun Greatest Hits is exactly what it says it is—16 tracks of Carl Perkins' best sides for Sun, including all of the hits ("Blue Suede Shoes," "Boppin' the Blues," "Your True Love") and all of his most legendary songs ("Honey, Don't," "Everybody's Trying to Be My Baby," "Movie Magg," "All Mam's Children," "Matchbox," "Dixie Fried," "Lend Me Your Comb," "Glad All Over"). It's the essential compilation, providing everything you need to know about Carl Perkins and offering no filler. *—Stephen Thomas Erlewine*

The Classic / Feb. 1990 / Bear Family ✦✦✦✦✦
This is a Bear Family release that even casual listeners can sort of agree with. The five CDs

contain close to 150 tracks, most notably Perkins' complete Sun Records output in close, glittering sound, plus all of his Columbia sides from 1958 through 1962, and his oft-overlooked early-'60s recordings for both American and English Decca. The Sun material is the best part of this box, and while it has been available as a triple CD from Charly, the latter is now out of print and had nothing like the crisp, clean sound you get here. The Sun outtakes may make the casual listener hesitate, but it's in the multiple takes that rock & roll as we know it was born, and all of the stuff is different enough between the takes to make hearing it worthwhile even for the non-scholar, to show that classics like that don't just "happen." Moreover, these differences aren't the little arrangement polishes and little tempo changes that one finds in most outtakes, but represent the evolution of a style—musically, they're at least as interesting as any of Elvis' Sun session outtakes. Beyond the rock & roll history, however, the reality is also that anyone buying it should have as much love of good honky-tonk style country music as they do for rock & roll. The Columbia sides are available separately, but they just aren't as interesting. The Decca stuff, which is unique to this set, represents Perkins' serious attempts at a comeback in the face of his huge concert success in England in the wake of the Beatles' recording of his music. The booklet is good, though not quite as comprehensive as one would have liked. *—Bruce Eder*

Jive After Five: The Best of Carl Perkins (1958-1978) / Sep. 1990 / Rhino ♦♦♦♦
A nice single-disc set that examines the best of Perkins' recordings after his tenure at Sun Records. The earlier Columbia sides continue the rockabilly mold that launched him, although tracks like "Pink Pedal Pushers" and "Jive After Five" are literally swimming in tape echo and reverb, unlike the sparseness of the Sun sides. The later tracks on Decca, Mercury, and others find him moving from rockabilly into a more mature country style, closing with a solo instrumental, "Just Coastin'," which shows his deep playing debt to both Chet Atkins and Merle Travis. A nice and important companion to the Sun sides. *—Cub Koda*

The Complete Sun Singles / Jun. 6, 2000 / Varese ♦♦♦♦♦
As part of their Sun series, this brings together all 18 of Perkins' original singles for the Flip and Sun labels. In addition to the 16 sides, there's also the inclusion of "Tennessee" and "Sure to Fall," the single by the Perkins Brothers band that features both Carl and Jay. Although there's much duplication with Rhino's *All-Time Greatest Sun Recordings* collection here, there are still enough new wrinkles aboard this one to make a nice stand alone set. *—Cub Koda*

Back on Top / Jul. 12, 2000 / Bear Family ♦♦♦♦
Back on Top, Bear Family's four-disc retrospective of Carl Perkins' late-'60s and early-'70s work, collects everything he recorded during his second tenure with Columbia, his tribute to Elvis ("E.P. Express"), and his complete recordings with NRBQ. Over the course of 99 tracks, the set also covers his two-year stint with Mercury, the complete *My Kind of Country* sessions, and a full disc's worth of previously unreleased demos. As with all of Bear Family's releases, *Back on Top* also features impressive supplemental material, including liner notes by Grammy winner Colin Escott, a complete discography, and previously unpublished photos. A Perkins completist's dream come true, *Back on Top* paints an expansive portrait of his comeback years. *—Heather Phares*

The Persuaders

f. 1969, New York, NY
Group / Smooth Soul, Soul
This group made a pair of marvelous heartache ballads in 1971, but have the unfortunate legacy of having their finest cuts turned into pop hits via covers. Lead singer Douglas Scott, whose nickname appropriately was "Smokey," Willie Holland, James Barnes, and Charles Stodghill formed in New York in 1969. They signed with Atlantic in the early '70s, and had their lone R&B chart topper in 1971, the shattering classic "Thin Line Between Love & Hate." It was also their only gold single. The follow-up was nearly as strong; "Love's Gonna Pack Up (And Walk Out)" reached number eight on the R&B charts, but had no crossover appeal. They continued on Win & Lose until 1973, then moved to Atco, where "Some Guys Have All the Luck" was a number seven R&B single in 1973. It was their final hit, though they kept recording until the late '70s, doing their last session for Calla. Besides the Pretenders re-doing "Thin Line Between Love & Hate," Rod Stewart had a Top Ten pop hit with his version of "Some Guys Have All the Luck" in 1984. *—Ron Wynn*

● **Thin Line Between Love & Hate** / 1974 / Collectables ♦♦♦♦♦
A gritty soul unit, adept at tragic encounter tunes. The title song is a soul anthem. *—Ron Wynn*

Pet Shop Boys

f. Aug. 1981, London, England
Group / Alternative Dance, Club/Dance, House, Dance-Pop
Postmodern ironists cloaked behind a veil of buoyantly melodic and lushly romantic synth-pop confections, the Pet Shop Boys' cheeky, smart and utterly danceable music established them among the most commercially and critically successful groups of their era. Always remaining one step ahead of their contemporaries, the British duo navigated the constantly shifting landscape of modern dance-pop with rare grace and intelligence, moving easily from disco to house to techno with their own distinctive image remaining completely intact; satiric and irreverent—yet somehow strangely affecting—the Pet Shop Boys transcended the seeming disposability of their craft, offering wry and thoughtful cultural commentary communicated by the Morse code of *au courant* synth washes and drum-machine rhythms. When 1985's "West End Girls" became an international chart-topper, its massive success propelled the Pet Shop Boys' 1986 debut LP *Please* into the Top Ten. In 1987 the duo resurfaced with the superb *actually.,* which launched three more Top Ten smashes—"It's a Sin," a lovely cover of the perennial "Always on My Mind," and "What Have I Done to Deserve This—," a duet between singer Neil Tennant and the great Dusty Springfield. A year later, the Pet Shop Boys issued their third studio LP, the eclectic *Introspective;* the single "Domino Dancing" was their final Top 40 hit in the U.S. *—Jason Ankeny*

Please / 1986 / EMI America ♦♦♦
A collection of immaculately crafted and seamlessly produced synthesized dance-pop, the Pet Shop Boys' debut album, *Please,* sketches out the basic elements of the duo's sound. At first listen, most of the songs come off as mere excuses for the dancefloor, driven by cold, melodic keyboard riffs and pulsing drum machines. However, the songcraft that the beats support is surprisingly strong, featuring catchy melodies that appear slight because of Neil Tennant's thin voice. Tennant's lyrics were still in their formative stages, with half of the record failing to transcend the formulaic constraints of dance-pop. The songs that do break free—the crass "Opportunities (Let's Make Lots of Money)," the lulling "Suburbia," and the hypnotic "West End Girls"—are not only classic dance singles, they're classic pop singles. *—Stephen Thomas Erlewine*

Disco / Oct. 1986 / EMI America ♦♦

Actually / Jun. 1987 / EMI America ♦♦♦♦♦
With their second album, *Actually,* the Pet Shop Boys perfected their melodic, detached dance-pop. Where most of *Please* was dominated by the beats, the rhythms on *Actually* are part of a series of intricate arrangements that create a glamorous but disposable backdrop for Neil Tennant's tales of isolation, boredom, money, and loneliness. Not only are the arrangements more accomplished, but the songs themselves are more striking, incorporating a strong sense of melody, as evidenced by "What Have I Done to Deserve This?," a duet with Dusty Springfield. Tennant's lyrics are clever and direct, chronicling the lives and times of urban, lonely, and bored yuppies of the late '80s. And the fact that dance-pop is considered a disposable medium by most mainstream critics and listeners only increases the reserved emotional undercurrent of *Actually,* as well as its irony. *—Stephen Thomas Erlewine*

Introspective / Apr. 1988 / EMI America ♦♦♦
Featuring a mere six tracks, most of them well over six minutes in length, *Introspective* was a move back to the clubs for the Pet Shop Boys. Over the course of the album, they incorporated various dance techniques that were currently in vogue, including Latin rhythms and house textures. The title isn't entirely an arch joke, however. Like *Actually, Introspective* was an exploration of distant, disaffected yuppies, which naturally resulted in a good deal of self-analyzation. Melodically, the essential song structures were as strong and multi-layered as the previous album, yet that was hard to hear beneath the varying rhythmic textures that composed the bulk of each track. Nevertheless, the mixes are more compelling than the remixes on *Disco,* and the songs include several of their best numbers, including "Left to My Own Devices" and "Domino Dancing," as well as the reconstruction of "Always on My Mind" and a cover of Blaze's club classic, "It's Alright." *—Stephen Thomas Erlewine*

Behavior / Oct. 1990 / EMI America ♦♦♦♦♦
Behavior was a retreat from the deep dance textures of *Introspective,* as it picked up on the carefully constructed pop of *Actually.* In fact, *Behavior* functions as the Pet Shop Boys' bid for mainstream credibility, as much of the album relies more on popcraft than rhythmic variations. Although its a subtle maneuver, it would have been rather disastrous if the results weren't so captivating. Tennant takes this approach seriously, singing the lyrics instead of speaking them. That doesn't necessarily give the album added emotional baggage—all of the distance and detachment in the duo's music is not a hindrance, it's part of the concept—but it does result in an ambitious and breathtaking pop album, which manages to include everything from the spiteful "How Can You Expect to Be Taken Seriously?" to the wistful "Being Boring." *—Stephen Thomas Erlewine*

★ **Discography: The Complete Singles Collection** / Nov. 5, 1991 / EMI America ♦♦♦♦♦
Most of the Pet Shop Boys' albums are well-crafted and thoroughly intriguing in their own right, but dance-pop is a medium that is driven by hit singles. *Discography* collects all the duo's numerous hit singles, including a handful of non-albums tracks, in their original 7" single mix, which occasionally varies from the album version, particularly in the case of the *Introspective* material. Presented chronologically, the singles not only demonstrate the band's increasing musical sophistication, they illustrate what fine songwriters Tennant and Lowe are. These 19 songs form one of the most consistent and innovative bodies of work of its era. Some of the production techniques have dated slightly, but the music has remained impressive. *—Stephen Thomas Erlewine*

Very / Oct. 5, 1993 / Capitol ♦♦♦♦♦
Because they work in a field that isn't usually taken seriously, the Pet Shop Boys are often ignored in the rock world. But make no mistake—they are one of the most talented pop outfits working today, witty and melodic with a fine sense of flair. *Very* is one of their very best records, expertly weaving between the tongue-in-cheek humor of "I Wouldn't Normally Do This Kind of Thing," the quietly shocking "Can You Forgive Her—," and the bizarrely moving cover of the Village People's "Go West." Alternately happy and melancholy, *Very* is the Pet Shop Boys at their finest. *—Stephen Thomas Erlewine*

Disco 2 / Sep. 20, 1994 / Capitol ♦♦

Alternative / Aug. 29, 1995 / Capitol ♦♦♦♦♦

Bilingual / Sep. 1996 / Atlantic ♦♦♦
As a title, *Bilingual* is a double-edged sword. Disregard it's sexual connotations and concentrate on its musical implications—*Bilingual* is a rich, diverse album that delves deeply into Latin rhythms. It's not a crass, simplistic fusion, where the polyphonic rhythms are simply grafted over synthesizers and a disco pulse. Instead, *Bilingual* is an enormously subtle album, with shifting rhythms and graceful, understated melodies. The music isn't the only thing subtle about the album—Neil Tennant's voice and lyrics are nuanced, suggesting more than they actually say. Furthermore, *Bilingual* consists of the most optimistic, happy set of songs the Pet Shop Boys have ever recorded. Whether it's the smooth disco of "Before" or the insistent rhythms of "Se a Vida E," Bilingual is filled with joyous, if subdued, sounds. If anything, it's further proof that even if the Pet Shop Boys aren't gracing the top of the charts as frequently as they did during the late '80s, they are crafting albums that are more adventurous and successful than they did when they were one of the top singles acts in pop music. *—Stephen Thomas Erlewine*

Nightlife / Nov. 2, 1999 / Sire ♦♦♦

Peter & Gordon

f. 1963, London, England, **db.** 1968

Group / Merseybeat, British Invasion, Pop

In June 1964, Peter & Gordon became the very first British Invasion act after the Beatles to take the number one spot on the American charts with "A World Without Love." That hit, and their subsequent successes, were due as much or more to their important connections as to their talent. Peter Asher was the older brother of Jane Asher, Paul McCartney's girlfriend for much of the 1960s. This no doubt gave Asher and Gordon Waller access to Lennon-McCartney compositions that were unrecorded by the Beatles, such as "A World Without Love" and three of their other biggest hits, "Nobody I Know," "I Don't Want to See You Again," and "Woman." But Peter & Gordon were significant talents in their own right, a sort of Everly Brothers-styled duo for the British Invasion that faintly prefigured the folk-rock of the mid-'60s. They duo continued to hit the charts for a couple of years, with updates of Buddy Holly's "True Love Ways" and Del Shannon's "I Go to Pieces." The overtly cute British novelty "Lady Godiva," though, became their last big hit in late 1966. After Peter & Gordon broke up in 1968, Asher became an enormously successful producer. Relocating to Los Angeles, in the 1970s he was one of the principal architects of mellow Californian rock, producing James Taylor and Linda Ronstadt. *—Richie Unterberger*

The Best of Peter & Gordon / Aug. 27, 1991 / Rhino ✦✦✦✦✦

● **EP Collection** / Sep. 5, 1995 / See For Miles ✦✦✦✦✦

Although this 29-track compilation is ostensibly a roundup of songs that appeared on foreign EPs, it actually serves as a greatest-hits collection of sorts. The sequencing is unfortunately haphazard, jumping all over the place chronologically, but it does include all ten of their U.S. Top 40 singles. In fact, it's a substantially better deal than the domestic best-of that appeared on Rhino a few years before this; it has more songs, presents some pretty good B-sides and non-45 tracks, and puts a greater weight on their original compositions. The inclusion of four French songs from a rare EP will please collectors, although for general listeners' purposes it would have been wiser to feature the English versions. *—Richie Unterberger*

Tom Petty

b. Oct. 20, 1950, Gainesville, FL

Vocals, Guitar / Bar Band, Heartland Rock, Album Rock, Hard Rock, Rock & Roll

Upon the release of their first album in the late '70s, Tom Petty & the Heartbreakers were shoehorned into the punk/new wave movement by some observers, who picked up on the tough, vibrant energy of the group's blend of Byrds riffs and Stonesy swagger. In a way, the categorization made sense. Compared to the heavy metal and art-rock that dominated mid-'70s guitar-rock, the Heartbreakers' bracing return to roots was nearly as unexpected as the crashing chords of the Clash. As time progressed, it became clear that the band didn't break from tradition like their punk contemporaries. Instead, they celebrated it, culling the best parts of the British Invasion, American garage rock, and Dylanesque singer/songwriters to create a distinctively American hybrid that recalled the past without being indebted to it. The Heartbreakers were a tight, muscular and versatile backing band that provided the proper support for Petty's songs, which cataloged a series of middle-class losers and dreamers. While his slurred, nasal voice may have recalled Dylan and Roger McGuinn, Petty's songwriting was lean and direct, recalling the simple, unadorned style of Neil Young. Throughout his career, Petty & the Heartbreakers never departed from their signature rootsy sound, but they were able to expand it, bringing in psychedelic, southern rock and New Wave influences; they were also one of the few of the traditionalist rock & rollers who embraced music videos, filming some of the most inventive and popular videos in MTV history. His willingness to experiment with the boundaries of classic rock & roll helped Petty sustain his popularity well into the '90s. *—Stephen Thomas Erlewine*

Tom Petty & the Heartbreakers / 1976 / Gone Gator ✦✦✦✦✦

At the time Tom Petty & the Heartbreakers' debut was released in 1976, they were fresh enough to almost be considered punk. They weren't as reckless or visionary as the Ramones, but they shared a similar love for pure '60s rock and, for the Heartbreakers, that meant embracing the Byrds as much as the Stones. And that's pretty much what this album is—tuneful jangle balanced by a tough garage swagger. At times, the attitude and the sound overrides the songwriting, but that's alright, since the slight songs ("Anything That's Rock & Roll," to pick a random example) are still infused with spirit and an appealing surface. Petty and the Heartbreakers feel underground on this album, at least to the extent that power pop was underground in 1976; with Dwight Twilley providing backing vocals for "Strangered in the Night," the similarities between the two bands (adherence to pop hooks and melodies, love of guitars) become apparent. Petty wound up eclipsing Twilley because he rocked harder, something that's evident throughout this record. Take the closer "American Girl"—it's a Byrds song by any other name, but he pushed the Heartbreakers to treat it as a rock & roll song, not as something delicate. There are times where the album starts to drift, especially on the second side, but the highlights—"Rockin' Around (With You)," "Hometown Blues," "The Wild One, Forever," the AOR staples "Breakdown" and "American Girl"—still illustrate how refreshing Petty & the Heartbreakers sounded in 1976. *—Stephen Thomas Erlewine*

You're Gonna Get It! / May 1978 / Gone Gator ✦✦✦

☆ **Damn the Torpedoes** / Nov. 1979 / MCA ✦✦✦✦✦

Not long after *You're Gonna Get It,* Tom Petty & the Heartbreakers' label, Shelter, was sold to MCA Records. Petty struggled to free himself from the major label, eventually sending himself into bankruptcy. He settled with MCA and set to work on his third album, digging out some old Mudcrutch numbers and quickly writing new songs. Amazingly, through all the frustration and anguish, Petty & the Heartbreakers delivered their breakthrough and arguably their masterpiece with *Damn the Torpedoes.* Musically, it follows through on the promise of their first two albums, offering a tough, streamlined fusion of the Stones and Byrds that, thanks to Jimmy Iovine's clean production, sounded utterly modern yet timeless. It helped that the Heartbreakers had turned into a tighter, muscular outfit, reminiscent of, well, the Stones in their prime—all of the parts combine into a powerful, distinctive sound capable of all sorts of subtle variations. Their musical suppleness helps bring out the soul in Petty's impressive set of songs. He had written a few classics before—"American Girl," "Listen to Her Heart"—but here his songwriting truly blossoms. Most of the songs have a deep melancholy undercurrent—the tough "Here Comes My Girl" and "Even the Losers" have tender hearts; the infectious "Don't Do Me Like That" masks a painful relationship; "Refugee" is a scornful, blistering rocker; "Louisiana Rain" is a tear-jerking ballad. Yet there's purpose and passion behind the performances that makes *Damn the Torpedoes* an invigorating listen all the same. Few mainstream rock albums of the late '70s and early '80s were quite as strong as this, and it still stands as one of the great records of the album-rock era. *—Stephen Thomas Erlewine*

Hard Promises / May 1981 / MCA ✦✦✦✦✦

Damn the Torpedoes wasn't simply a culmination of Tom Petty's art; it happened to be a huge success, enabling him to call the shots on its successor, *Hard Promises.* Infamously, he used his first album as a star to challenge the record industry's practice of charging more for A-list artists, demanding that *Hard Promises* should be listed for less than most records by an artist of his stature, but if that was the only thing notable about the album, it would have disappeared like *Long After Dark.* Instead, it offered a reaffirmation that *Damn the Torpedoes* wasn't a fluke. There's not much new on the surface, since it continues the sound of its predecessor, but it's filled with great songwriting, something that's as difficult to achieve as a distinctive sound. As the opener, "The Waiting" became the best-known song on the record, but there's no discounting "A Woman in Love (It's Not Me)," "Nightwatchman," "Kings Road," "Insider," and "The Criminal Kind," album tracks that would become fan favorites. If *Hard Promises* doesn't have the sweep of *Damn the Torpedoes,* that's because its predecessor was blessed with good timing and an unusually strong set of songs. *Hard Promises* isn't quite so epochal, yet it has a tremendous set of songs and a unified songs that makes it one of Petty's finest records. *—Stephen Thomas Erlewine*

Long After Dark / Nov. 1982 / MCA ✦✦✦

Southern Accents / Apr. 1985 / MCA ✦✦✦

Pack up the Plantation: Live! / Jan. 1986 / MCA ✦✦✦

Let Me Up (I've Had Enough) / Apr. 1987 / MCA ✦✦✦

Full Moon Fever / Apr. 29, 1989 / MCA ✦✦✦✦✦

Although *Let Me Up (I've Had Enough)* found the Heartbreakers regaining their strength as a band and discovering a newfound ease at songcraft, it just didn't sell that well. Perhaps that factor, along with road fatigue, led Tom Petty to record his first solo album, *Full Moon Fever.* Nevertheless, the distinction between "solo" and "Heartbreakers" is a fuzzy one, because *Full Moon Fever* is essentially in the same style as the Heartbreakers albums; Mike Campbell co-wrote two songs and co-produced the record, and he, along with Benmont Tench and Howie Epstein, all play on the album. However, the album sounds different from any Heartbreakers record due to the presence of former Electric Light Orchestra leader Jeff Lynne. Petty co-wrote the lion's share of the album with Lynne, who also is the record's main producer. In his hands, Petty's roots-rock becomes clean and glossy, layered with shimmering vocal harmonies, keyboards and acoustic guitars. It was a friendly, radio-ready sound, and if it has dated somewhat over the years, the craft is still admirable and appealing. But the real reason *Full Moon Fever* became Petty's biggest hit is that it boasted a selection of songs that rivaled *Damn the Torpedoes. Full Moon Fever* didn't have a weak track; even if a few weren't quite as strong as others, the album was filled with highlights—"I Won't Back Down," the wistful "A Face in the Crowd," the rockabilly throwaways "Yer So Bad" and "A Mind with a Heart of Its Own," the Byrds cover "Feel a Whole Lot Better," the charging "Runnin' Down a Dream" and "Free Fallin'," a coming-of-age ballad that could be Petty's best song. *Full Moon Fever* might have been meant an off-the-cuff detour, but it turned into a minor masterpiece. *—Stephen Thomas Erlewine*

Into the Great Wide Open / Jul. 2, 1991 / MCA ✦✦✦

★ **Greatest Hits** / Nov. 16, 1993 / MCA ✦✦✦✦✦

All of Petty's biggest hits collected, along with two new tracks—the excellent "Mary Jane's Last Dance" and a cover of Thunderclap Newman's "Something In the Air"—on one essential disc. Everything from "American Girl" to "Free Fallin'" is included, with sixteen tracks proving that Petty is one of the best rockers of the past fifteen years. *—Stephen Thomas Erlewine*

Wildflowers / Nov. 1, 1994 / Warner Brothers ✦✦✦✦✦

Under the guidance of producer Rick Rubin, Tom Petty turns in a stripped-down, subtle record with *Wildflowers.* Coming after two albums of Jeff Lynne-directed bombast, the very sound of the record is refreshing; Petty sounds relaxed and confident. Most of the songs are small gems, but a few are a little too laidback, almost reaching the point of carelessness. Nevertheless, the finest songs here ("Wildflowers," "You Don't Know How It Feels," "It's Good to Be King," and several others) match the quality of his best material, making *Wildflowers* one of Petty's most distinctive and best albums. *—Stephen Thomas Erlewine*

Playback / Nov. 20, 1995 / MCA ✦✦✦✦✦

The consequence of Tom Petty and the Heartbreakers' enduring affection for the music of the mid-'60s was that, in essence, they were a singles band, a fact driven home on the first three CDs of the six-disc set *Playback;* even when abbreviating each of their first nine studio albums to four to six cuts, the songs break down into the hits and the also-rans. To be fair, there are quite a few of the former, and some of the latter are could-have-beens; and since Petty is more a song maker (or, more precisely, a track cutter) than an album artist, his work is more amenable to compilation. Still, three discs are more than enough, and then come *three more discs* of rarities and outtakes. The first of these contains non-LP B-sides, most of which are pleasant throwaways (although "Trailer" suggests that the failed concept album *Southern Accents* could have been a more of a success if it had been included). The last two discs present early and alternate histories of Petty, as his pre-Heartbreakers group, Mudcrutch, searches for a sound; later, he tries out different approaches that never made it onto his regular albums. Some of this material will be of interest to hardcore fans, but to justify the length and price of the box, there would have to be real lost treasures here. Not surprisingly, then, *Playback* is a box set that would have been twice as good at half the size. *—William Ruhlmann*

Songs and Music from "She's the One" / Aug. 1996 / Warner Brothers ✦✦✦

Echo / Apr. 13, 1999 / Warner Brothers ✦✦✦✦

Anthology: Through the Years / Oct. 31, 2000 / MCA ✦✦✦✦✦

Liz Phair

b. Apr. 17, 1967, New Haven, CT

Vocals, Guitar / Adult Alternative Pop/Rock, Indie Rock, Lo-Fi, Alternative Pop/Rock, Singer/Songwriter

A product of the American underground of the late '80s, Liz Phair fused lo-fi, indie-rock production with the sensibility and structure of classic singer/songwriters. *Exile in Guyville*, Phair's debut album, was enthusiastically praised upon its 1993 release and it spawned a rash of imitators, over the following years. Phair first made an impact with her home-made tapes, released under the name Girlysound, which provided an entry point to the Chicago alternative music scene; in particular, she became friends with Urge Overkill and drummer Brad Wood. The Girlysound made their way to Gerard Cosley, the head of record label, Matador. By the summer of 1992, Matador had signed Phair.Her debut *Exile in Guyville* was released to strong reviews in the summer of 1993. The record slowly built a dedicated following in America among critics and alternative rock fans; it topped many Best-of-the-Year critics polls, including *The Village Voice* and *Spin*. Early in 1994, she launched her first tour, around the same time MTV began airing "Never Said," leading toward *Exile*'s brief appearance on the charts in February. By the spring of 1994, it had sold over 200,000 copies—a remarkable number for an independent release. Phair's second album, *Whip-Smart* was released in fall of 1994 to a whirlwind of media attention—including Phair, dressed only in negligee, on the cover of *Rolling Stone*—that eclipsed her actual celebrity. Though *Whip-Smart* debuted at number 27 it received mediocre reviews and never became a crossover hit. Phair quietly retreated from the spotlight during 1995, getting married and releasing the *Juvenelia* EP, which had the first official release of Girlysound material. After having a child, finally released her third album *whitechocolatespaceegg* in mid-1998; it received generally positive reviews and moderately strong sales. *—Stephen Thomas Erlewine*

★ **Exile in Guyville** / Jun. 22, 1993 / Matador ✦✦✦✦✦

If *Exile in Guyville* is shockingly assured and fully formed for a debut album, there are a number of reasons why. Most prominent of these is that many of the songs were initially essayed on Liz Phair's homemade cassette *Girlysound*, which means that the songs are essentially cream of the crop from an exceptionally talented songwriter. Second, there's its structure, infamously patterned after the Stones' *Exile on Main Street*, but not the song-by-song response Phair promoted it as. (Just try to match the albums up: Is the "blow-job queen" fantasy of "Flower" *really* the answer to the painful elegy "Let it Loose—") Then, most notably, there's Phair and producer Brad Wood's deft studio skills, bringing a variety of textures and moods to a basic, lo-fi production. There is as much hard rock as there are eerie solo piano pieces, and there's everything in between from unadulterated power pop, winking art rock, folk songs, and classic indie rock. Then, there are Phair's songs themselves. At the time, her gleefully profane, clever lyrics received endless attention (there's nothing that rock critics love more than a girl who plays into their geek fantasies, even—or maybe especially—if she's mocking them), but years later, what still astounds is the depth of the writing, how her music matches her clear-eyed, vivid words, whether it's on the self-loathing "Fuck and Run," the evocative mood piece "Stratford-on-Guy," or the swaggering breakup anthem "6' 1"," or how she nails the dissolution of a long-term relationship on "The Divorce Song." Each of these 18 songs maintains this high level of quality, showcasing a singer/songwriter of immense imagination, musically and lyrically. If she never equaled this record, well, few could. *—Stephen Thomas Erlewine*

Whip-Smart / Sep. 20, 1994 / Matador ✦✦✦

Expectations ran extremely high for Phair's follow-up to *Exile In Guyville*, one of the most critically acclaimed debut albums of all time. If there are flaws in this generally first-rate followup, they mostly arise in comparison with *Guyville*, a record of such unexpected impact that most anything Phair could have done may have been found lacking. She continues to explore sex and relationships with exhilarating frankness and celebration, employing her much-touted profanity to a conversational rather than a sensational effect. The sound is somewhat more produced, though still pretty basic, and the compositions are by and large tuneful and lyrically intriguing. It's not, after all is said and done, quite as striking as *Guyville;* like many sophomore efforts, it mines similar territory without making huge strides forward. Several songs are reprised from her widely circulated *Girly Sound* demo tapes, and in some instances the more heavily produced, self-consciously ingenious arrangements here suffer in comparison to their blueprints. The title track, one of the highlights of those tapes, comes off as particularly gimmicky in its new incarnation, with the addition of all manner of superfluous animal noises. There's no question that Phair is a major songwriter and artist, but this album is more a solidification of her talents than a breakthough statement. *—Richie Unterberger*

Juvenilia / Aug. 2, 1995 / Matador ✦✦✦

Whitechocolatespaceegg / Aug. 11, 1998 / Matador/Capitol ✦✦✦

Phish

f. 1983

Group / Jam Bands, American Trad Rock, Alternative Pop/Rock

During the early '90s, Phish emerged as the heirs to the Grateful Dead's throne. Although their music is somewhat similar to the Dead's—it's an eclectic, free-form rock & roll encompassing folk, jazz, country, bluegrass, and pop—the group adheres more to jazz-derived improvisation than folk tradition, and they have a looser, goofier attitude. After all, their drummer regularly plays a vacuum during their concerts. Phish's main claim as the inheritors to the Dead's legacy is their approach to their musical career. The band didn't concentrate on albums, they dedicated themselves to live improvisation. Within a few years of their 1988 debut album, Phish had become an institution in certain sections of America, particularly college campuses. And their in-concert popularity didn't necessarily translate to huge record sales—their biggest-selling albums usually halted at gold status. Phish were the de facto leaders of the neo-hippie jam band movement until deciding to go on hiatus in 2000. *—Stephen Thomas Erlewine*

Junta / 1988 / Elektra ✦✦✦✦

Elektra finally got around to reissuing Phish's first album as part of their WEA-based catalog, tucking two discs into a slimline two-CD case. To Elektra's credit, three additional tracks have been added, recorded in 1988 at Nectar's (the club that gave Phish their start with a regular gig). The live tracks are somewhat dubious in sonic terms, but they're excellent for revealing the improvisational side of the band—the 25:31 "Union Federal" totters to a start and has a couple of wobbly moments, but it's actually fun to listen to. The original album is even better, of course, with great sound and better playing, not to mention the typical wild and woolly Phish humor spilling out all over the lengthy tracks. Highly recommended whether you're starting to discover Phish or are backing up to the beginning. *—Steven McDonald*

Lawn Boy / 1991 / Elektra ✦✦

● **A Picture of Nectar** / Aug. 1991 / Elektra ✦✦✦✦✦

Phish's second major-label release is still in many ways their best and most accomplished album. Expanding on the musical explorations that dominated *Lawn Boy, Nectar* incorporates a remarkable mixture of styles, from country, jazz, and calypso to straight-up rock & roll. Lyrically, the band's trademark goofiness is intact, but the playing is more muscular and Trey Anastasio's arrangements have increased intensity and focus. In fact, it's a surprisingly tight record for a band that built their reputation on endless concert jams, although "Guelah Papyrus" and "Tweezer" should satisfy those who enjoy that facet of their personality. The album also boasts the classic "Chalk Dust Torture" and most of Phish's finest moments, which are hard to resist for even the most apprehensive listeners. *—Jim Smith*

Rift / Feb. 2, 1993 / Elektra ✦✦✦

Hoist / Mar. 29, 1994 / Elektra ✦✦✦

A Live One / Jun. 27, 1995 / Elektra ✦✦✦✦✦

Billy Breathes / Oct. 15, 1996 / Elektra ✦✦✦✦✦

Thanks to producer Steve Lillywhite, Phish finally delivered a concise pop album with *Billy Breathes*. Lillywhite had the band cut away their jams and accentuate their songwriting, resulting in a series of tightly-written, melodic folk-rock and psychedelic pop songs. Phish still delve into the deeper waters with sweeping songs like "Theme from the Bottom," but what truly impresses about *Billy Breathes* is the group's seamless eclecticism and how they master all varieties of roots-rock and psychedelic styles. With the shorter songs, their musical depth and breadth is all the more apparent and impressive, making *Billy Breathes* the definitive Phish album the band has always strived to deliver. *—Stephen Thomas Erlewine*

Slip, Stitch & Pass / Oct. 28, 1997 / Elektra ✦✦✦✦✦

Released a mere two years after Phish's first live album, *Slip, Stitch & Pass*, the group's second live record, in many ways surpasses its predecessor, drawing a more complete picture of the Phish concert experience. Spanning two discs, *A Live One* had the scope of a Phish concert but there's actually more adventure and surprise on *Slip, Stitch & Pass*, whether its in the group's improvisations or the inventive cover of Talking Heads' "Cities." It's not the kind of record that will convert the sceptical—there's simply too many long, involved instrumental passages that many doubters will label "indulgent"—but it's the closest Phish has come to capturing their live spirit on record. *—Stephen Thomas Erlewine*

The Story of the Ghost / Oct. 27, 1998 / Elektra/Asylum ✦✦✦

Hampton Comes Alive / Nov. 23, 1999 / Elektra ✦✦✦✦✦

Like the Grateful Dead, the line on Phish runs a little like this—they make sense in concert, but never quite gel on record. However, the Dead's true character revealed itself because they thrived on improvisations; it wasn't quite the same with Phish, because the live experience revealed the band's humor, taste, eclecticism, and (foremost) skill, not just their character. Thing is, a lot of this, particularly skill, is evident on the band's studio albums. So, what does two full evenings of Phish—four sets to be exact—on the six-disc box set *Hampton Comes Alive* offer. Well, not any revelations or anything unexpected—just the fullest representation of the band yet available. Everything evident on *Hampton Comes Alive*, a live album consisting of four sets recorded on two dates in late November 1998, is present on one or another of Phish's studio albums, but never in one place at the same time, as it is here. Furthermore, the group's eclecticism, stretched to a full-length running time, becomes stunning, since it all seems seamless. Their covers don't seem cutesy or condescending when they're placed among the band's original freewheeling genre-hopping, and that's not a minor point. Phish prides itself on its taste, not only in covers but in its own writing, and here they prove that they're right, because they not only deliver everything with conviction, but put a slight spin on it to make it their own. Even if this isn't your thing, you'd be hard pressed to listen to *Hampton Comes Alive* and not agree that this is a band of exceptional talent. This is the kind of record that converts doubters—it's just too bad that its hefty price tag makes it a reasonable purchase only for the dedicated. *—Stephen Thomas Erlewine*

Farmhouse / May 16, 2000 / Elektra ✦✦✦✦✦

The party line on Phish is that the band's live shows are so extraordinary, their studio records are almost superfluous by comparison; frankly, it's a ridiculous contention—apples and oranges, really—and moreover, each successive Phish album reveals new layers of intricacy and melodic invention otherwise lost in the epic explosiveness of their concert sets. Their rootsiest and most organic effort to date, *Farmhouse* is also their most fully developed—these are complete, concise songs and not simply outlines for extended jams, boasting a beauty and intimacy which expands the group's scope even as it serves notice of a newfound pop accessibility. It's a brave record, much less an exhibition of the band's vaunted instrumental prowess than it is a showcase for Trey Anastasio's increasingly skilled and far-reaching songwriting. The opening title cut, a gorgeously rustic country-pop ballad, immediately establishes *Farmhouse's* muted, relaxed tone, and despite the occasional detour like the sunny funk workout "Gotta Jibboo" or the closing instrumental jam "First Tube," by and large the set opts against kitchen-sink eclecticism in favor of an evocatively pastoral uniformity. In short, *Farmhouse* is everything Phish's die-hard legions no doubt hoped it wouldn't be, but as a radical reassessment of their music's purpose and approach, in many ways it's closer to the band's true spirit of innovation than any record they've made. *—Jason Ankeny*

Wilson Pickett

b. Mar. 18, 1941, Prattville, AL

Vocals / Deep Soul, Southern Soul, Soul

Of the major '60s soul stars, Wilson Pickett was one of the roughest and sweatiest, working up some of the decade's hottest dancefloor grooves. Although he tends to be held in somewhat lower esteem than more versatile talents like Otis Redding and Aretha Franklin, he is often a preferred alternative of fans who like their soul on the rawer side. He also did a good deal to establish the sound of Southern Soul with his early hits, often recorded with the cream of the session musicians in Memphis and Muscle Shoals. One of his first singles as a solo act, "In the Midnight Hour," was recorded at Stax in Memphis. The single's chugging horn line, loping funky beats, and impassioned vocals made it a substantial pop hit and thousands of bands covered it onstage and on record. Pickett had a flurry of other galvanizing soul hits over the next few years, including "634-5789," "Mustang Sally," and "Funky Broadway," all of which were also frequently adapted by other bands as a dance-ready number. He also cut tracks in Muscle Shoals and in Philadelphia (with the Gamble-Huff production team). Though his chart activity slowed down in the '70s, he continued to be active on the tour circuit. *—Richie Unterberger*

In the Midnight Hour / 1965 / Rhino ✦✦✦

The Exciting Wilson Pickett / 1966 / Rhino ✦✦✦✦✦

Less of a hodgepodge than his debut *In The Midnight Hour* album, Pickett's second album established—if there had been any doubt—his stature as a major '60s soul man. The 12 tracks include his monster hits "634-5789," "Ninety-Nine And A Half (Won't Do)," "In The Midnight Hour," and "Land Of 1000 Dances" (the last of which was his first Top Ten pop hit). Collectors will be more interested in the non-hit cuts, which are of nearly an equal level. These include covers of the R&B standards "Something You Got," "Mercy Mercy," and "Barefootin'"; several original tunes written in collaboration with Memphis soul greats Steve Cropper, Eddie Floyd, and David Porter; and Bobby Womack's "She's So Good To Me." It all adds up to one of the most consistent 1960s soul albums. The CD reissue of this 1966 record features detailed liner notes and session documentation. *—Richie Unterberger*

The Wicked Pickett / 1966 / Atlantic ✦✦✦✦✦

A fabulous album, done when Pickett was in the midst of his best period at Atlantic. It had everything—great songs, wonderful production and arrangements, and a hungry, galvanizing Wilson Pickett hollering, screaming, shouting, and soaring on anything he covered, from ballads to uptempo dance and midtempo wailers. It also has been deleted at present. *—Ron Wynn*

The Sound of Wilson Pickett / 1967 / Atlantic ✦✦✦✦✦

A masterpiece, perhaps his finest '60s album. This wasn't a hits collection, but a batch of great singles. His version of "Funky Broadway" may still be the best; it was certainly the most swaggering and posturing, punctuated by his screams and jubilant cries. Pickett was all over the R&B charts in 1967, and this was one of three albums Atlantic issued on him that year. Each one was a classic. *—Ron Wynn*

I'm in Love / 1968 / Rhino ✦✦✦

A Man and a Half: The Best of Wilson Pickett / Apr. 21, 1992 / Rhino ✦✦✦✦✦

A Man and a Half—The Best of Wilson Pickett is a double-disc set that collects the absolute cream of Pickett's early sides with The Falcons and all the highlights of his successful alliance with the Atlantic label. With "Mustang Sally," "In the Midnight Hour," "Ninety Nine & a Half," "Hey Jude," "Land of a 1000 Dances," "You're So Fine," and "634-5789" all included, this excellent compilation should be one of the cornerstones of anybody's soul collection. *—Cub Koda*

★ **The Very Best of Wilson Pickett** / 1993 / Rhino/Atlantic ✦✦✦✦✦

Although the double-disc set *A Man and A Half* is necessary for serious soul fans, *The Very Best of Wilson Pickett* should satiate the needs of any casual fan. Featuring 16 of his biggest Atlantic hits—including "In the Midnight Hour," "634-5789 (Soulsville, U.S.A.)," "Land of 1000 Dances," "Mustang Sally," "Funky Broadway," "She's Looking Good," and "I'm A Midnight Mover"—*The Very Best of Wilson Pickett* contains all of his truly essential items, making it both an excellent introduction and the closet thing possible to definitive single-disc retrospective. *—Stephen Thomas Erlewine*

Pink Floyd

f. 1965, London, England

Group / Multimedia, British Psychedelia, Album Rock, Psychedelic, British Invasion, Prog-Rock/Art Rock, Hard Rock

Pink Floyd are the premier space-rock band. Since the mid-'60s, their music has relentlessly tinkered with electronics and all manner of special effects to push pop formats to their outer limits. At the same time they have wrestled with lyrical themes and concepts of such massive scale that their music has taken on almost classical, operatic quality, in both sound and words. While Pink Floyd are mostly known for their grandiose concept albums of the 1970s, they started as a very different sort of psychedelic band. Soon after they first began playing together in the mid-'60s, they fell firmly under the leadership of lead guitarist Syd Barrett, the gifted genius who would write and sing most of their early material. The Cambridge native shared the stage with Roger Waters (bass), Rick Wright (keyboards), and Nick Mason (drums). Pink Floyd quickly began to experiment, stretching out songs with wild instrumental freak-out passages incorporating feedback, electronic screeches, and unusual, eerie sounds created by loud amplification, reverb, and such tricks as sliding ball bearings up and down guitar strings; Syd Barrett began to compose pop-psychedelic gems that combined unusual psychedelic arrangements (particularly in the haunting guitar and celestial organ licks) with catchy melodies and incisive lyrics that viewed the world with a sense of poetic, childlike wonder. Around mid-1967, though, the prodigy began showing increasingly alarm signs of mental instability. Dependent upon Barrett for most of their vision and material, the rest of the group were nevertheless finding him impossible to work with, live or in the studio. Around the beginning of 1968, guitarist Dave Gilmour, a friend of the band who was also from Cambridge, was brought in as a fifth member; within a few months, however, Barrett was out of the group. Such calamities would have proven insurmountable for 99 out of 100 bands in similar predicaments. Incredibly, Pink Floyd would regroup and not only maintain their popularity, but eventually become even more successful. *—Richie Unterberger*

★ **The Piper at the Gates of Dawn** / Aug. 5, 1967 / Capitol ✦✦✦✦✦

The title of Pink Floyd's debut album is taken from a chapter in Syd Barrett's favorite children's book, *The Wind in the Willows*, and the lyrical imagery of *The Piper at the Gates of Dawn* is indeed full of colorful, childlike, distinctly British whimsy, albeit filtered through the perceptive lens of LSD. Barrett's catchy, melodic acid pop songs are balanced with longer, more experimental pieces showcasing the group's instrumental freak-outs, often using themes of space travel as metaphors for hallucinogenic experiences—"Astronomy Domine" is a poppier number in this vein, but tracks like "Interstellar Overdrive" are some of the earliest forays into what has been tagged space rock. But even though Barrett's lyrics and melodies are mostly playful and humorous, the band's music doesn't always bear out those sentiments—in addition to Rick Wright's eerie organ work, dissonance, chromaticism, weird noises, and vocal sound effects are all employed at various instances, giving the impression of chaos and confusion lurking beneath the bright surface. *The Piper at the Gates of Dawn* successfully captures both sides of psychedelic experimentation—the pleasures of expanding one's mind and perception, and an underlying threat of mental disorder and even lunacy; this duality makes *Piper* all the more compelling in light of Barrett's subsequent breakdown, and ranks it as one of the best psychedelic albums of all time. *—Steve Huey*

Tonite Lets All Make Love in London [Original Soundtrack] / 1968 / Columbia ✦✦✦

A Saucerful of Secrets / Jun. 29, 1968 / Capitol ✦✦✦

A transitional album on which the band moved from Barrett's relatively concise and vivid songs to spacy, ethereal material with lengthy instrumental passages. Barrett's influence is still felt (he actually did manage to contribute one track, the jovial "Jugband Blues"), and much of the material retains a gentle, fairy-tale ambience. "Remember a Day" and "See Saw" are highlights; on "Set The Controls for the Heart of the Sun," "Let There Be More Light," and the lengthy instrumental title track, the band begin to map out the dark and repetitive pulses that would characterize their next few records. *—Richie Unterberger*

More / Jul. 27, 1969 / Capitol ✦✦

Ummagumma / Oct. 25, 1969 / Capitol ✦✦✦

For many years, this double LP/CD was one of the most popular albums in Pink Floyd's pre-*Dark Side of the Moon* output, containing a live disc and a studio disc all for the price of one (in the LP version). The live set, recorded in Birmingham and Manchester in June 1969, is limited to four numbers, all drawn from the group's first two LPs or their then recent singles. Featuring the band's second line-up (i.e. no Syd Barrett), the set shows off a very potent group, their sound held together on stage by Nick Mason's assertive drumming and Roger Waters' powerful bass work, which keeps the proceedings moving no matter how spaced out the music gets; they also sound like they've got the amplifiers to make their music count, which is more than the early band had. "Astronomy Domine," "Careful With That Axe Eugene," "Set the Controls for the Heart of the Sun," and "A Saucerful of Secrets" are all superior here to their studio originals, done longer, louder, and harder, with a real edge to the playing. The studio disc was more experimental, each member getting a certain amount of space on the record to make their own music—Richard Wright's "Sysyphus" was a pure keyboard work, featuring various synthesizers, organs, and pianos; David Gilmour's "The Narrow Way" was a three-part instrumental for acoustic and electric guitars and electronic keyboards; and Nick Mason's "The Grand Vizier's Garden Party" made use of a vast range of acoustic and electric percussion devices. Roger Waters' "Grantchester Meadows was a lyrical folk-like number unlike almost anything else the group ever did. In 1994 the album was remastered and reissued in a green slipcase, in a version a lot louder and sharper (and cheaper) than the original CD release. *—Bruce Eder*

Atom Heart Mother / Oct. 5, 1970 / Capitol ✦✦✦

Appearing after the sprawling, unfocused double-album set *Ummagumma, Atom Heart* may boast more focus, even a concept, yet that doesn't mean it's more accessible. If anything, this is the most impenetrable album they released while on Harvest, which also makes it one of the most interesting of the era. Still, it may be an acquired taste even for fans, especially since it kicks off with a side-long, 23-minute extended orchestral piece that may not seem to head anywhere, but is often intriguing, more in what it suggests than what it achieves. Then, on the second side, Roger Waters, David Gilmour, and Rick Wright have a song a piece, winding up with the group composition "Alan's Psychedelic Breakfast" wrapping it up. Of these, Waters begins developing the voice that made him the group's lead songwriter during their classic era with "If," while Wright has an appealingly mannered, very English psychedelic fantasia on "Summer 68," while Gilmour's "Fat Old Sun" meanders quietly before ending with a guitar workout that leaves no impression. "Alan's Psychedelic Breakfast," the 12-minute opus that ends the album, does the same thing, floating for several minutes before ending on a drawn-out jam that finally gets the piece moving. So, there are interesting moments scattered throughout the record, and the work that initially seems so impenetrable winds up being *Atom Heart Mother's* strongest moment. That it lasts an entire side illustrates that Pink Floyd was getting better with the larger picture instead of the details, since the second side just winds up falling off the tracks, no matter how many good moments there are. This lack of focus means *Atom Heart Mother* will largely be for cultists, but its unevenness means there's also a lot to cherish here. *—Stephen Thomas Erlewine*

Relics / May 1971 / Capitol ✦✦✦✦✦
A singles collection from the Syd Barrett era, containing the British hits "Arnold Layne" and "See Emily Play," among other psychedelic nuggets. *—William Ruhlmann*

Meddle / Nov. 11, 1971 / Capitol ✦✦✦✦✦
Atom Heart Mother, for all its glories, was an acquired taste, and Pink Floyd wisely decided to trim back its orchestral excesses for its follow-up, *Meddle*. Opening with a deliberately surging "One of These Days," *Meddle* spends most of its time with sonic textures and elongated compositions, most notably on its epic closer "Echoes." If there aren't pop songs in the classic sense (even on the level of the group's contributions to *Ummagumma*), there is a uniform tone, ranging from the pastoral "A Pillow of Winds" to "Fearless," with its insistent refrain hinting at latter-day Floyd. Pink Floyd were nothing if not masters of texture, and *Meddle* is one of their greatest excursions into little details, pointing the way to the measured brilliance of *Dark Side of the Moon* and the entire Roger Waters era. Here, David Gilmour exerts a slightly larger influence, at least based on lead vocals, but it's not all sweetness and light—even if its lilting rhythms are welcome, "San Tropez" feels out of place with the rest of *Meddle*. Still, the album is one of the Floyd's most consistent explorations of mood, especially from their time at Harvest, and it stands as the strongest record they released between Syd's departure and *Dark Side*. *—Stephen Thomas Erlewine*

Obscured by Clouds / Jun. 3, 1972 / Capitol ✦✦

★ **Dark Side of the Moon** / Mar. 24, 1973 / Capitol ✦✦✦✦✦
By condensing the sonic explorations of *Meddle* to actual songs and adding a lush, immaculate production to their trippiest instrumental sections, Pink Floyd inadvertently designed their commercial breakthrough with *Dark Side of the Moon*. The primary revelation of *Dark Side of the Moon* is what a little focus does for the band. Roger Waters wrote a series of songs about mundane, everyday details which aren't that impressive by themselves, but when given the sonic backdrop of Floyd's slow, atmospheric soundscapes and carefully placed sound effects, they achieve an emotional resonance. But what gives the album true power is the subtly textured music, which evolves from ponderous, neo-psychedelic art rock to jazz fusion and blues-rock before turning back to psychedelia. It's dense with detail, but leisurely paced, creating its own dark, haunting world. Pink Floyd may have better albums than *Dark Side of the Moon*, but no other record defines them quite as well as this one. *—Stephen Thomas Erlewine*

☆ **Wish You Were Here** / Sep. 15, 1975 / Capitol ✦✦✦✦✦
Pink Floyd followed the commercial breakthrough of *Dark Side of the Moon* with *Wish You Were Here*, a loose concept album about and dedicated to their founding member Syd Barrett. The record unfolds gradually, as the jazzy textures of "Shine On You Crazy Diamond" reveal its melodic motif, and in its leisurely pace, the album shows itself to be a warmer record than its predecessor. Musically, it's arguably even more impressive, showcasing the group's interplay and David Gilmour's solos in particular. And while it's short on actual songs, the long, winding soundscapes are constantly enthralling. *—Stephen Thomas Erlewine*

Animals / Jan. 23, 1977 / Capitol ✦✦✦✦
Of all of the classic-era Pink Floyd albums, *Animals* is the strangest and darkest, a record that's hard to initially embrace yet winds up yielding as many rewards as its equally nihilistic successor, *The Wall*. It isn't that Roger Waters dismisses the human race as either pigs, dogs, or sheep, it's that he's constructed an album who's music is as bleak and bitter as that worldview. Arriving after the warm-spirited (albeit melancholy) *Wish You Were Here*, the shift in tone comes as a bit of a surprise, and there are even less proper songs here than on either *Wish* or *Dark Side*. *Animals* is all extended pieces, yet it never drifts—it slowly, ominously works its way toward its destination. For an album that so clearly is Waters', David Gilmour's guitar dominates thoroughly, with Richard Wright's keyboards rarely rising above a mood-setting background (such as on the intro to "Sheep"). This gives the music, on occasion, immediacy and actually heightens the dark mood by giving it muscle. It also makes *Animals* as accessible as it possibly could be, since it surges with bold blues-rock guitar lines and hypnotic space rock textures. Through it all, though, the utter blackness of Waters' spirit holds true and since there are no vocal hooks or melodies, everything rests on the mood, the near-nihilistic lyrics, and Gilmour's guitar. These are the kind of things that satisfy cultists, and it will reward their attention—there's just no way in for casual listeners. *—Stephen Thomas Erlewine*

The Wall / Nov. 30, 1979 / Capitol ✦✦✦✦✦
Roger Waters constructed *The Wall*, a narcissistic, double-album rock opera about an emotionally crippled rock star who spits on an audience member daring to cheer during an acoustic song. Given its origins, it's little wonder that *The Wall* paints such an unsympathetic portrait of the rock star, cleverly named "Pink," who blames everyone—particularly women—for his neuroses. Such lyrical and thematic shortcomings may have been forgivable if the album had a killer batch of songs, but Waters took his operatic inclinations to heart, constructing the album as a series of fragments that are held together by larger numbers like "Comfortably Numb" and "Hey You." Generally, the fully developed songs are among the finest of Pink Floyd's later work, but *The Wall* is primarily a triumph of production: Its seamless surface, blending melodic fragments and sound effects, makes the musical shortcomings and questionable lyrics easy to ignore. But if *The Wall* is examined in depth, it falls apart, since it doesn't offer enough great songs to support its ambition, and its self-serving message and shiny production seem like relics of the late-'70s Me Generation. *—Stephen Thomas Erlewine*

A Collection of Great Dance Songs / Nov. 1981 / Capitol ✦✦

Works / 1983 / Capitol ✦✦

The Final Cut / Mar. 21, 1983 / Columbia ✦✦✦
The Final Cut extends the autobiography of *The Wall*, concentrating on Roger Waters' pain when his father died in World War II. Waters spins this off into a treatise on the futility of war, concentrating on the Falkland Islands, setting his blistering condemnations and scathing anger to an impossibly subdued music that demands full attention. This is more like a novel than a record, requiring total concentration since shifts in dynamics, orchestration, and instrumentation are used as effect. This means that while this has the texture of classic Floyd, somewhere between the brooding sections of *The Wall* and the monolithic menace of *Animals*, there are no songs or hooks to make these radio favorites. The even bent of the arrangements, where the music is used as texture, not music, means that *The Final Cut* purposely alienates all but the dedicated listener. Several of those listeners maintain that this is among Pink Floyd's finest efforts, and it certainly is an achievement of some kind—there's not only no other Floyd album quite like it, it has no close comparisons to anybody's else work (apart from Waters' own *The Pros and Cons of Hitch-Hiking*, yet that had a stronger musical core). That doesn't make this easier to embrace, of course, and it's damn near impenetrable in many respects, but with its anger, emphasis on lyrics, and sonic textures, it's clear that it's the album that Waters intended it to be. And it's equally clear that Pink Floyd couldn't have continued in this direction—Waters had no interest in a group setting anymore, as this record, which is hardly a Floyd album in many respects, illustrates. Distinctive, to be sure, but not easy to love and, depending on your view, not even that easy to admire. *—Stephen Thomas Erlewine*

A Momentary Lapse of Reason / Sep. 8, 1987 / Columbia ✦✦

Delicate Sound of Thunder / Nov. 22, 1988 / Columbia ✦✦✦

The Division Bell / Mar. 30, 1994 / Columbia ✦✦
The second post-Roger Waters Pink Floyd album is less forced and more of a group effort than *A Momentary Lapse of Reason*—keyboard player Rick Wright is back to full band-member status and has co-writing credits on five of the 11 songs, even getting lead vocals on "Wearing the Inside Out." Some of David Gilmour's lyrics (co-written by Polly Samson and Nick Laird-Clowes of the Dream Academy) might be directed at Waters, notably "Lost for Words" and "A Great Day for Freedom," with its references to "the wall" coming down, although the more specific subject is the Berlin Wall and the fall of Communism. In any case, there is a vindictive, accusatory tone to songs such as "What Do You Want from Me" and "Poles Apart," and the overarching theme, from the album title to the graphics to the "I-you" pronouns in most of the lyrics, has to do with dichotomies and distinctions, with "I" always having the upper hand. Musically, Gilmour, Nick Mason, and Wright have largely turned the clock back to the pre-*Dark Side of the Moon* Floyd, with slow tempos, sustained keyboard chords, and guitar solos with a lot of echo. *—William Ruhlmann*

Pulse / Jun. 1995 / Columbia ✦✦

Is There Anybody out There— The Wall: Live 1980-1981 / Apr. 18, 2000 / Columbia ✦✦✦

Gene Pitney

b. Feb. 17, 1941, Hartford, CT
Vocals / Brill Building Pop, Teen Idol, Pop
One of the most interesting and difficult-to-categorize singers in '60s pop, Gene Pitney had a long run of hits distinguished by his pained, one-of-a-kind melodramatic wail. Pitney is sometimes characterized (or dismissed) as a shallow teen idol-type prone to operatic ballads. It's true that some of his biggest hits—"Town Without Pity," "Only Love Can Break a Heart," "I'm Gonna Be Strong," "It Hurts to Be in Love," and "Twenty Four Hours from Tulsa"—are archetypes of adolescent or just-post-adolescent agony, characterized by longing and not a little self-pity. But Pitney was not just an archetype of his style—he was one of the best at his style, and indeed one of the few (along with Roy Orbison) that could pull it off convincingly. Also (like Orbison), he had more range than he's generally given credit for, making forays into tough pop/rock, country, and even borderline rockabilly. Other than Dionne Warwick, he was the best interpreter of Bacharach-David's early compositions. Although he didn't pen much of his material, he was a composer of note, writing "He's a Rebel" for the Crystals, and "Hello Mary Lou" for Rick Nelson. He was also something of a closet hipster—he was the first American artist to cover a Jagger-Richards song ("That Girl Belongs to Yesterday," which was a British hit before the Rolling Stones had ever entered the U.S. Top 100), contributed to an actual Rolling Stones session in early 1964 (during which they recorded "Not Fade Away"), had a brief fling with a teenage Marianne Faithfull, and recorded songs by Randy Newman and Al Kooper long before those musicians became famous. *—Richie Unterberger*

● **Anthology 1961-1968** / 1986 / Rhino ✦✦✦✦✦
This CD, dating from the mid-'80s, is, ironically enough, a perfect companion in design and layout to Rhino's out of print Dionne Warwick *Anthology* collection. The 16 songs here represent the basis of Pitney's renown as a vocalist—rock's Caruso, critic Jeff Tamarkin called him—and is the handiest single CD collection to be found on him in the United States, covering the highlights of his primary years of success. The music is steeped in romantic angst and heartbreak, reminiscent of Roy Orbison's work from the same era, and displaying a stunning vocal range—"24 Hours From Tulsa" and "True Love Never Runs Smooth," along with much of the rest, sound like their romantic screenplays in embryonic form, and "Town Without Pity" was, indeed, from a movie. Those desiring a somewhat broader picture of Pitney's music should look to Sequel Records low-priced two-CD import *Looking Through: The Ultimate Collection*, containing 50 songs. *—Bruce Eder*

More Greatest Hits / Apr. 11, 1995 / Varese Sarabande ✦✦✦✦✦
A very worthy supplement to *Anthology;* in fact, it's almost as good. Has a lot of minor hits, some of which ("I Must Be Seeing Things," "Backstage") rank among his best; "Nobody Needs Your Love," an early Randy Newman composition that was a number two hit in England in 1966; Pitney's own versions of his compositions "Hello Mary Lou" and "Today's Teardrops," much better known via their interpretations by Rick Nelson and Roy Orbison, respectively; and interesting album tracks and flop singles. All cuts are from the '60s, except the 1989 version of "Something's Gotten Hold Of My Heart," aperformed as a duet with Marc Almond. *—Richie Unterberger*

Pixies

f. 1986, Boston, MA, **db.** 1993
Group / College Rock, Alternative Pop/Rock
Combining jagged, roaring guitars and stop-start dynamics with melodic pop hooks, intertwining male-female harmonies and evocative, cryptic lyrics, the Pixies were one of the most

influential American alternative rock bands of the late '80s. The Pixies weren't accomplished musicians—Black Francis wailed and bashed out chords while Joey Santiago's lead guitar squealed out spirals of noise. But the band were inventive, rabid rock fans that turned conventions inside out, melding punk and indie guitar rock, classic pop, surf rock, and stadium-sized riffs with singer/guitarist Black Francis' bizarre, fragmented lyrics about space, religion, sex, mutilation, and pop culture; while the meaning of his lyrics may have been impenetrable, the music was direct and forceful. The Pixies' busy, brief songs, extreme dynamics and subversion of pop song structures proved one of the touchstones of '90s alternative rock. From grunge to Brit-pop, the Pixies shadow loomed large—it's hard to imagine Nirvana without the Pixies' signature stop-start dynamics and lurching, noisey guitar solos. While the Pixies were touted as the band to bring indie-rock into the mainstream, they simply laid the ground-work for the alternative explosion of the early '90s. MTV was reluctant to play their videos, while even modern rock radio didn't put their singles into regular rotation. Furthermore, tensions between leader Black Francis and bassist/vocalist Kim Deal, who wanted to incorporate her songs into the band's repertoire, crippled the band's prorgress. By the time Nirvana broke the doors down for alternative rock in 1992, the Pixies were effectively broken-up. *—Stephen Thomas Erlewine*

Come on Pilgrim [EP] / 1987 / 4AD/Elektra ✦✦✦✦✦
Amazingly, Pixies' 1987 debut EP *Come on Pilgrim* was compiled from the quickly, inexpensively made demo tape—paid for by Black Francis' dad—the band made at Boston's legendary *Fort Apache* studio soon after they formed. 4AD was so taken with the tape that they released eight of the songs as this mini-album. It's easy to see why they were so impressed: The Pixies' essential sound—Francis' unearthly shriek of a voice, David Lovering's propulsive drumming, Joey Santiago's insistent, prickly guitar playing, and Kim Deal's sugar-and-sandpaper vocals and steady bass lines—arrives fully formed on songs like the bouncy, yet twisted, surfer-girl ode "Ed Is Dead." Influences like '80s college-rock peers the Violent Femmes, the Stooges, Lou Reed and hardcore punk crop up on songs like ("I've Been Tired," the group's surreal take on sexual frustration and "Isla de Encanta." Most importantly, the EP introduces the spooky, theatrical vision the group brought to their simple guitar-bass-drums lineup. Francis' lyrical fetishes for sex, death, and religion and his twisted sense of humor crop up on every track, from the eerie opener "Caribou," which urges listeners to "Reeeeep-ent!" to the final song "Levitate Me," which borrows Christian folk singer Larry Norman's catchphrase "Come on pilgrim, you know he loves you!" "The Holiday Song" and "Nimrod's Son" provide voyeuristic, back-to-back glimpses at incest, as well as the priceless lyric "My sister held me close and whispered to my bleeding head/You are the son of a motherfucker" (from "Nimrod's Son"). Gary Smith's less-is-more production allows the full, primal impact of the band's combustive sound to blast through, offering what may be the purest version of their perverse punk-pop. An electrifying debut, *Come on Pilgrim* remains as raw, vibrant, and engaging as the day it was recorded. *—Heather Phares*

☆ **Surfer Rosa** / 1988 / 4AD/Elektra ✦✦✦✦✦
One of the most compulsively listenable college rock albums of the '80s, the Pixies' 1988 full-length debut *Surfer Rosa* fulfilled the promise of *Come on Pilgrim* and, thanks to Steve Albini's production, added a muscular edge that made their harshest moments seem even more menacing and perverse. On songs like "Something Against You," Black Francis' cryptic shrieks and non sequiturs are backed by David Lovering and Kim Deal's punchy rhythms, which are so visceral that they'd overwhelm any guitarist except Joey Santiago, who takes the spotlight on the epic "Vamos." Albini's high-contrast dynamics suit *Surfer Rosa* well, especially on the explosive opener "Bone Machine" and the kinky, T-Rex-inspired "Cactus." But, like the black-and-white photo of a flamenco dancer on its cover, *Surfer Rosa* is the Pixies' most polarized work. For each blazing piece of punk, there are softer, poppier moments such as "Where Is My Mind?," Francis' strangely poignant song inspired by scuba diving in the Caribbean, and the Kim Deal-penned "Gigantic," which almost outshines the rest of the album. But even *Surfer Rosa*'s less iconic songs reflect how important the album was in the group's development. The "song about a superhero named Tony" ("Tony's Theme") was the most lighthearted song the Pixies had recorded, pointing the way to their more overtly playful, whimsical work on *Doolittle*. Francis' warped sense of humor is evident in lyrics like "Bone Machine"'s "He bought me a soda and tried to molest me in the parking lot/Yep yep yep!" In a year that included landmark albums from contemporaries like Throwing Muses, Sonic Youth, and My Bloody Valentine, the Pixies managed to turn in one of 1988's most striking, distinctive records. *Surfer Rosa* may not be the group's most accessible work, but it is one of their most compelling. *—Heather Phares*

★ **Doolittle** / 1989 / 4AD/Elektra ✦✦✦✦✦
After 1988's brilliant but abrasive *Surfer Rosa*, the Pixies' sound couldn't get much more extreme. Their Elektra debut *Doolittle*, reigns in the noise in favor of pop songcraft and accessibility. Producer Gil Norton's sonic sheen adds some polish, but Black Francis' tighter songwriting focuses the group's attack. *Doolittle*'s most ferocious moments, like "Dead," a visceral retelling of David and Bathsheba's affair—are more stylized than the group's past outbursts. Meanwhile, their poppy side surfaces on the irresistible single "Here Comes Your Man" and the sweetly surreal love song "La La Love You." The Pixies' arty, noisy weirdness mix with just enough hooks to produce gleefully demented singles like "Debaser,"—inspired by Bunuel's classic surrealist short *Un Chien Andalou*—and "Wave of Mutilation," their surfy ode to driving a car into the sea. Though *Doolittle*'s sound is cleaner and smoother than the Pixies' earlier albums, there are still plenty of weird, abrasive vignettes: the blankly psychotic "There Goes My Gun," "Crackity Jones," a song about a crazy roommate Francis had in Puerto Rico, and the nihilistic finale "Gouge Away." Meanwhile, "Tame," and "I Bleed" continue the Pixies' penchant for cryptic kink. But the album doesn't just refine the Pixies' sound; they also expand their range on the brooding, wannabe spaghetti western theme "Silver" and the strangely theatrical "Mr. Grieves." "Hey" and "Monkey Gone to Heaven," on the other hand, stretch Francis' lyrical horizons: "Monkey"'s elliptical environmentalism and "Hey"'s twisted longing are the Pixies' versions of message songs and romantic ballads. Their most accessible album, *Doolittle*'s wide-ranging moods and sounds make it one of their most eclectic and ambitious. A fun, freaky alternative to most other late-'80s college rock, it's easy to see why the album made the Pixies into underground rock stars. *—Heather Phares*

Bossanova / Aug. 1990 / 4AD/Elektra ✦✦✦✦✦
When *Bossanova* arrived in 1990, it reflected the exhaustion the Pixies felt after *Doolittle*'s enormous success: For the first time, the band seems to be running out of ideas. Tellingly, Kim Deal contributes no songs, having formed the Breeders to give her work an outlet; that summer, their debut *Pod* won a warmer response than *Bossanova* received. Arguably the Pixies' weakest album—though Francis has said it's his favorite—most of it finds the band in fine form. Gil Norton's spacious, reverb-heavy production makes the Pixies sound like a Martian bar band, which fits the cover of the Surftones' "Cecilia Ann" and the glorious, shimmering closer "Havalina" perfectly. On the theremin-driven "Velouria," science fiction imagery displaces Francis' penchant for fetishistic lyrics; next to the token kinky song "Down to the Well"'s tired sound, it's a refreshing change. The similarly cryptic "All Over the World" and alien abduction tale "The Happening" add to the sci-fi feel. Quirky pop songs like "Allison," a tribute to jazz cool-cat Mose Allison, and "Dig for Fire," Francis' self-professed Talking Heads homage, heighten *Bossanova*'s playful, slightly off-kilter vibe, but rockers like "Hang Wire" and "Blown Away," fall flat. However, "Rock Music" is one of the group's most fiery outbursts, and "Is She Weird"'s chugging grind and sexy, funny lyrics make it a classic Pixies song. The band was so consistently amazing on their previous albums that when they released a slightly weaker one, critics and fans alike judged them too harshly. But on *Bossanova*'s strongest moments, the Pixies explored their softer side and found different uses for their extreme dynamics. Like a straight-A student who suddenly receives a B+, *Bossanova* might have been a disappointment initially, but its (small) failings emphasize the strengths of the rest of the Pixies' work. *—Heather Phares*

Trompe le Monde / Oct. 8, 1991 / 4AD/Elektra ✦✦✦✦
The title might be French for "fool the world," but with *Trompe Le Monde*, the Pixies weren't fooling anyone: this was essentially Black Francis' solo debut. It focuses on Francis' sci-fi fascination and lacks any Kim Deal songs; even her backing vocals are far and few between. Yet the band sounds revitalized on *Trompe Le Monde*, as if it was planned as their last hurrah. The raucous "Distance Equals Rate Times Time" and the explosive cover of the Jesus & Mary Chain's "Head On" are fairly straightforward, but the lyrics remain quirky on "Planet Of Sound," a song about a Martian who lands on Earth, and "Palace of the Brine," a tribute to sea monkeys and Utah's Salt Lake. He even disses hipsters and pretentious students—basically, the Pixies' fanbase—with nasty little digs like "Subbacultcha"'s "I was wearing eyeliner / She was wearing eyeliner" and "U-Mass"' "It's eduuucaaationaal!" Musically, "Trompe Le Monde"'s psychedelic sheen and "Alec Eiffel"'s atmospheric keyboards prove that the Pixies' sound wasn't defined by Steve Albini-style rawness. There's also more emotional depth: "The Sad Punk" features the strangely poignant bridge "And evolving from the sea / would not be too much time for me / to walk beside you in the sun," and "Letter to Memphis" is a heartfelt, if cryptic, love song. Though *Trompe Le Monde* doesn't sound quite like the Pixies' other work, *Come On Pilgrim*'s spooky beginnings, *Surfer Rosa*'s abrasive assault, *Doolittle*'s deceptively accessible punk-pop and *Bossanova*'s spacy sonics helped make *Trompe Le Monde* a rousing swan song and a precursor to alternative rock's imminent success. Whether that means their music remained pure or they missed their chance to cash in is debatable; either way, the Pixies are one of America's greatest, most influential bands. *—Heather Phares*

Death to the Pixies: 1987-1991 / Oct. 7, 1997 / 4AD/Elektra ✦✦✦✦

Pixies at the BBC / Jul. 14, 1998 / 4AD/Elektra ✦✦✦

Robert Plant

b. Aug. 20, 1948, Birmingham, England
Vocals, Harmonica / Album Rock, Hard Rock
British hard rock/heavy metal singer Robert Plant had released a couple of singles and worked with a number of bands before he hooked up with Jimmy Page's New Yardbirds, subsequently renamed Led Zeppelin, around the time of his 20th birthday in 1968. For the next 12 years, Plant was one of the biggest rock stars on the planet. He gradually developed as a singer, branching out into other styles within Zeppelin's hard rock framework, and he blossomed as a songwriter as well.

Plant launched a solo career in 1982 with the album *Pictures at Eleven*, a gold-selling hit. He did even better the following year with *The Principle of Moments*. It sold a million copies, included the Top 20 hit "Big Log," and led to his first post-Zeppelin concert tour. Surprisingly, Plant then organized a one-off mini-album, *The Honeydrippers—Vol. One*, recording some rock oldies with a superstar pickup band. He faced greater consumer resistance with his third solo album, *Shaken 'n' Stirred*, perhaps because joint appearances with Page led an audience to desire for a Zeppelin reunion. To an extent, Plant fed that desire with *Now and Zen*, which sampled Zeppelin tracks and featured Page. It was another million-seller. Plant's 1990 follow-up, *Manic Nirvana*, went gold. *—William Ruhlmann*

Pictures at Eleven / 1982 / Swan Song ✦✦✦✦
The directions in which Plant seemed to be heading in the later Zeppelin records—toward lighter, more melodic music, tempered with sometimes odd rhythms—are continued on his first solo album, which finds him singing more and screaming less. It wasn't Led Zeppelin, but then, that was the whole point. *—William Ruhlmann*

Principle of Moments / 1983 / Es Paranza ✦✦✦✦
Plant reinvents rock and pop oldies in much the way Led Zeppelin did old blues songs. "Other Arms" recasts "Lay Down Your Arms," as Plant declares, "I'm not a prisoner of the big parade," while "In the Mood" retools an old pop theme. The playing is propulsive (thanks to guest drummer Phil Collins) and Plant's singing unusually supple. *—William Ruhlmann*

Shaken 'N' Stirred / 1985 / Es Paranza ✦✦✦
Robert Plant continued to expand the horizons of his music with his third album, *Shaken 'N' Stirred*, adding elements of worldbeat to his increasingly atmospheric and synth-driven pop-rock. Although the experimentation is admirable, and occasionally successful, the most suc-

cessful tracks on the album are straightforward numbers like "Little By Little." — *Stephen Thomas Erlewine*

● **Now & Zen** / 1988 / Es Paranza ✦✦✦✦
After years of trying to separate himself from his legendary status as Led Zeppelin's frontman, Robert Plant finally reconciles with his past on *Now & Zen.* He borrows a few Zeppelin riffs, and even enlists Jimmy Page to play guitar on his hit "Tall Cool One." This album is also notable in that it marks his first collaboration with keyboardist Phil Johnstone, who would continue to play and write with Plant on subsequent albums. Musically, the album relies on standard rock arrangements except that the vocals and drums are at the forefront and keyboards instead of guitars are used to fill out the sound. Although most of album is comprised of mid-tempo songs aimed at rock radio, Plant includes the lovely ballad "Ship of Fools," which demonstrates that he is more than capable of vocal subtlety. Plant, who often uses mysterious (and mystical) lyrics, writes some of his most direct songs, and the way in which the lyrics complement the melodic arrangements are partially responsible for the commercial success of *Now & Zen.* This is Robert Plant's best solo album, and a must-own for fans of Led Zeppelin. — *Vik Iyengar*

Manic Nirvana / Mar. 1990 / Es Paranza ✦✦

Fate of Nations / May 27, 1993 / Es Paranza ✦✦✦

The Platters

f. 1953, Los Angeles, CA
Group / Vocal Pop, Doo Wop, R&B
The Platters started out as a Los Angeles based Black doo wop group with little identity of their own to make them stand out from the pack. What changed their fortunes can be reduced down to one very important name: their mentor, manager, producer, songwriter and vocal coach, Buck Ram. Ram took what many would say was a run of the mill R&B doo wop vocal group and turned them into stars and one of the most enduring and lucrative groups of all time. After getting the Platters out of a Federal Records contract, Ram placed them with the burgeoning national independent label Mercury, automatically getting them into pop markets through the label's distribution contacts alone. He then put the lead vocal status squarely on the shoulders of lead tenor Tony Williams, whose emoting power was turned up full blast. With Ram's pop songwriting classics as its musical palette, the group quickly became a pop and R&B success, eventually earning the distinction of being the first Black act of the era to top the pop charts. Considered the most romantic of all the doo wop groups, hit after hit came tumbling forth in a seemingly effortless manner: "Only You," "The Great Pretender," "My Prayer," "Twilight Time," "Smoke Gets in Your Eyes," "Harbor Lights," all of them establishing the Platters as the classiest of all. — *Cub Koda*

☆ **The Magic Touch: An Anthology** / Oct. 22, 1991 / Mercury ✦✦✦✦✦
Double-disc set of all their best sides, including "The Great Pretender," "Smoke Gets in Your Eyes," "Only You," "Harbor Lights," and the title track. Great annotation and impeccable sound. All compilations should be done this well. — *Cub Koda*

The Very Best of the Platters / Oct. 22, 1991 / Mercury ✦✦✦✦
The Platters' twelve biggest hits are featured on this brief, but solid, collection; it's fine for those who don't want to spend the money on the double-disc set. — *Stephen Thomas Erlewine*

The Very Best of the Platters 1966-1969 / Jun. 17, 1997 / Varese ✦✦✦
After Tony Williams left the Platters in 1959, a new replacement was found in Charles "Sonny" Turner. But the group's label (Mercury) brought Turner in for album sessions only and kept releasing old tracks with Williams' voice on them as singles, even keeping his name off the liner notes to their new album. It wasn't until their contract was up with Mercury and the group moved on to Musicor Records in 1966 that Turner was allowed to sing on a record by the Platters in his true voice, five to six years after he came on board. This 14-track compilation covers the group's stay at the label between 1966 and 1969, a period of time that saw the Platters recast themselves as a beach music group ("Washed Ashore [On a Lonely Island In the Sea]") while swimming against the tide of the burgeoning soul music movement. The hits didn't dry up, and "I Love You 1,000 Times," "Devri," "With This Ring," "Sweet Sweet Lovin'" and "I'll Be Home" showed that the group was breaking new ground while still making the charts. This collection chronicles the last stage of the Platters as a recording group of any significance and also features two previously unissued tracks, "Keep On Loving Me" and "Atlanta." Nothing here will ever take the place of the original hits on Mercury (which didn't sound anything like their early recordings for King), but those who want to get the big picture will do well to add this one to the collection. — *Cub Koda*

★ **Enchanted: The Best of the Platters** / Jun. 16, 1998 / Rhino ✦✦✦✦✦
For too many years, there was no single-disc collection of the Platters' greatest hits. Mercury's *Magic Touch* offered two discs' worth of prime material, but it was really too much for anyone outside of serious listeners; it also stopped short of their uneven but occasionally worthwhile Musicor recordings. Rhino's *Enchanted: The Best of the Platters* is the first compilation of the CD era to feature all of their biggest Mercury and Musicor hits on one disc, and it's a stunner. All of their Top Ten pop hits, from "Only You" to "Harbor Lights," are here, along with 18 other charting hits, all in their original hit versions. For any fan, both casual and dedicated, it's essential, since no other compilation features as many hits on one disc and no other compilation is quite so consistently entertaining. — *Stephen Thomas Erlewine*

Poco

f. 1968, Los Angeles, CA, **db.** 1984
Group / Pop/Rock, Soft Rock, Country-Rock
Founded by Jim Messina and Richie Furay during the dying days of Buffalo Springfield, with Randy Meisner (who dropped out shortly before the recording of their first album), Rusty Young, and George Grantham, Poco built a solid reputation in Los Angeles as an innovative country-rock ensemble. Their first album, *Pickin' Up the Pieces,* was one of the strongest debut records of its era, a blend of country and western influences, Beatlesque harmonies, and mainstream rock, all within one cover. They began developing a major national reputation with the release of their second album, *Poco,* at the same time that the group's membership entered what proved to be a virtually constant state of flux. By the mid-'70s, the band had become an established fixture in the middle reaches of the national charts but Messina and Furay were long gone. The band continued recording well into the late '70s on MCA after leaving Epic, and their following was strong enough to justify a posthumous live album from Epic at the same time. The original quintet, which never did get to record, finally went into the studio under the auspices of RCA in the late '80s. — *Bruce Eder*

Pickin' Up the Pieces / 1969 / Epic/Legacy ✦✦✦✦✦
The group went into the studio with a sudden loss of one member (Randy Meisner), an engineer who didn't quite get what they were trying for, and a lot of pressure for a first album—and came up with this startlingly great record, as accomplished as any of the Buffalo Springfield, and also reminiscent of the Beatles and the Byrds. *Pickin' Up the Pieces* is all the more amazing when one considers that Messina and Grantham were both covering for the departed Meisner in hastily learned capacities on bass and vocals, respectively. The title track is practically an anthem for the virtues of country-rock, with the kind of sweet harmonizing and tight interplay between the guitars that the Byrds, the Burritos, *et al* had to work a while to achieve. The mix of good-time songs ("Consequently So Long," "Calico Lady"), fast-paced instrumentals ("Grand Junction") and overall good feelings makes this a great introduction to the band, as well as a landmark in country-rock only slightly less important (and more enjoyable than) *Sweetheart of the Rodeo.* — *Bruce Eder*

Poco / May 6, 1970 / Epic ✦✦✦✦

From the Inside / 1971 / Epic ✦✦

Deliverin' / Jan. 13, 1971 / Epic ✦✦✦✦✦
Poco had originally made their name as a live act, and they'd always been at their best and most easygoing onstage. The result is this live album of all new material, featuring Jim Messina's swan song with the band and some of the tightest playing and best singing in their recorded history. Jewels include "C'mon," "Hear That Music," "Kind Woman," and "You'd Better Think Twice." About as perfect an album as they ever made and, not coincidentally, by far the biggest seller the early group ever had. — *Bruce Eder*

A Good Feelin' to Know / Oct. 25, 1972 / Epic ✦✦✦

Crazy Eyes / 1973 / Epic/Legacy ✦✦✦✦✦
The third biggest-selling album in the group's history, *Crazy Eyes* is also the group's most lively and bracing work, and contains some of their most soulful music. In short, it is the fruition of everything they'd been working toward for four years. Curiously, it is also one of a handful of examples of their use of outside help, including Chris Hillman on mandolin. The resulting sound is richer than anything found on any other Poco album, and the only tragedy is that the band reportedly cut enough tracks for two whole albums—one longs to hear the material that remained in the can. As it is, there's not a weak song, or even a wasted note anywhere on this album, and most bands would kill for a closing track as perfect as "Let's Dance Tonight." The sound is excellent on this CD reissue, and only some historical notes would have improved it. — *Bruce Eder*

Seven / 1974 / Epic/Legacy ✦✦✦

Cantamos / Dec. 1974 / Epic ✦✦✦

Head over Heels / Jul. 1975 / MCA ✦✦✦✦

The Very Best of Poco / Sep. 1975 / Epic ✦✦✦✦✦
Originally a two-LP set, *The Very Best of Poco* was a decent compilation in its time, assembling the group's best-known songs from singles and album cuts in a straightforward order with no particular surprises. It was reissued with upgraded sound in 1999, and for the very casual fan with a budget to consider the latter is adequate, showing their evolution as a band from the first flourish of their birth, as an offshoot of the Buffalo Springfield, with the same sort of vast potential displayed by the latter group (similarly unrealized by constant membership changes) into one of the premiere country-rock outfits of the 1970s. Anyone serious about a deep enjoyment of the group, however, will opt for the more extensive and revelatory *The Forgotten Trail* instead, which contains numerous outtakes and—no pun—forgotten tracks. — *Bruce Eder*

Crazy Loving: The Best of Poco 1975-1982 / Oct. 1989 / MCA ✦✦✦✦

The Forgotten Trail (1969-1974) / Oct. 1990 / Epic ✦✦✦✦✦
This excellent two-disc collection captures Poco's finest moments from the days when they were laying down the template for all the country-rock music that was to follow. It's hard to remember now, but when the Eagles first hit the scene, they were thought by many to be a Poco-wannabe band. Listen to this set and you'll hear why. *The Forgotten Trail* culls tracks from Poco's first eight albums, as well as unreleased cuts and singles. From the classic anthem "Pickin' Up the Pieces," which kicks things off, through "You Better Think Twice," "C'mon," "Kind Woman," "From the Inside," "A Good Feelin' to Know," "Crazy Eyes," and on and on . . . this is wonderful music, ahead of its time in many ways. If Poco had arrived on the scene in the early 1990s, they would have been kings of the country charts. Of course, without Poco, country music wouldn't have taken on the rock trappings that it did in the '80s and '90s. As it was, the band was considered too country for the Top 40 rock format of the time, and too rock & roll for country radio. This set is the place to start for an appreciation of the original Poco, when the group was considered to be Richie Furay's band. All the ingredients are here that made their music so delightful: the trademark high vocal harmonies, Rusty Young's pedal steel guitar wizardry, Furay's patented juxtapositions of sad lyrics against bouncy, harmony-filled tunes, their spirit of optimism and good feelings even in the face of hard luck and bad weather. The 36-page booklet does a fine job of telling the story in print, and the 38 songs speak volumes about the band's place and influence. Thanks to this compilation, Poco's trailblazing days need be forgotten no longer. — *Jim Newsom*

• **Ultimate Collection** / Nov. 17, 1998 / Hip-O ♦♦♦♦♦
There has been no lack of Poco compilations, but this is the first one to span the four record labels the band recorded for between 1969 and 1989. Ten of the group's 13 chart singles are included, among them its biggest hits, "Crazy Love," "Call It Love," and "Heart of the Night." Also included are some of its best songs, such as "Pickin' Up the Pieces" and "A Good Feelin' to Know." The country-rock hybrid Poco achieved during its lengthy, commercially under-rewarded recording career is on display in songs written by Richie Furay, Jim Messina, Paul Cotton, Timothy B. Schmit, and Rusty Young. Anyone looking for the missing link between Buffalo Springfield and the Eagles will find it here. *—William Ruhlmann*

The Pogues

f. 1982, Kings Cross, London, England, **db.** 1996
Group / College Rock, Celtic Rock, British Folk, Alternative Pop/Rock
By demonstrating that the spirit of punk could live in traditional Irish folk music, the Pogues were one of the most radical bands of the mid-'80s. Led by Shane MacGowan, whose slurred, incomprehensible voice often disguised the sheer poetry of his songs, the Pogues were undeniably political—not only were many of their songs explicitly in favor of working-class liberalism, but the wild, careening sound of their punk-injected folk was implicitly radical. While the band was clearly radical, they also had a wickedly warped sense of humor, which was abundantly clear on their biggest hit, the fractured Christmas carol "Fairy Tale of New York." The group's first three albums—*Red Roses for Me, Run Sodomy and the Lash, If I Should Fall From Grace From God*—were widely praised in both Britain and America, and by 1988 they had earned substantial cult followings in both countries. Yet MacGowan's darkly romantic, wasted lifestyle, which was so key to their spirit and success, ultimately proved to be their downfall. By the end of the decade, he had fallen deep into alcoholism and drug addiction, forcing the band to fire him if they wanted to survive. The Pogues carried on without him in the early '90s, playing to a slowly shrinking audience, before finally disbanding in 1995. *—Stephen Thomas Erlewine*

Red Roses for Me / 1984 / WEA International ♦♦♦
What set the Pogues apart from any number of other energetic Irish traditional bands was the sheer physical force of their performances, the punky swagger of their personalities, and Shane MacGowan's considerable gifts as a songwriter. Unfortunately, none of these qualities come through very clearly on their first album, *Red Roses for Me.* While the Pogues are in good form here, the production (by Stan Brennan) is thin and lacks the body or nuance to capture the finer details of the performances, robbing this recording of the fire the group would display on their later albums. And it's clear that Shane MacGowan had not yet fully matured as a songwriter; there are a handful of superb songs here, such as "Transmetropolitan," "Streams of Whiskey", and "Down in the Ground Where the Dead Men Go," but some of the others suggest MacGowan was still learning how to fit all his ideas into his songs. *Red Roses for Me* is good and rowdy fun, but on *Run, Sodomy & the Lash* and *If I Should Fall From Grace With God,* the Pogues would prove they were capable of a lot more than that. *—Mark Deming*

Rum Sodomy & the Lash / 1985 / WEA International ♦♦♦♦♦
"I saw my task ... was to capture them in their dilapidated glory before some more professional producer f—ked them up," Elvis Costello wrote of his role behind the controls for the Pogues' second album, *Rum Sodomy & the Lash.* One spin of the album proves that Costello accomplished his mission; this album captures all the sweat, fire, and angry joy that was lost in the thin, disembodied recording of the band's debut, and the Pogues sound stronger and tighter without losing a bit of their edge in the process. *Rum Sodomy & the Lash* also found Shane MacGowan growing steadily as a songwriter; while the debut had its moments, the blazing and bitter roar of the opening track, "The Sick Bed Of Cuchulainn," made it clear MacGowan had fused the intelligent anger of punk and the sly storytelling of Irish folk as no one had before, and the rent boys' serenade of "The Old Main Drag" and the dazzling, drunken character sketch of "A Pair of Brown Eyes" proved there were plenty of directions where he could take his gifts. And like any good folk group, the Pogues also had a great ear for other people's songs. Bassist Cait O'Riordan's haunting performance of "I'm a Man You Don't Meet Every Day" is simply superb (it must have especially impressed Costello, who would later marry her), and while Shane MacGowan may not have written "Dirty Old Town" or "And the Band Played Waltzing Matilda," his wrought, emotionally compelling vocals made them his from then on. *Rum Sodomy & the Lash* falls just a bit short of being the Pogues best album, but was the first one to prove that they were a great band, and not just a great idea for a band. *—Mark Deming*

• **If I Should Fall From Grace With God** / 1987 / Island ♦♦♦♦♦
If *Rum Sodomy & the Lash* captured the Pogues on plastic in all their rough-and-tumble glory, *If I Should Fall From Grace With God* proved they could learn the rudiments of proper record making and still come up with an album that captured all the sharp edges of their musical personality. Producer Steve Lillywhite imposed a more disciplined approach in the studio than Elvis Costello, but he had the good sense not to squeeze the life out of the band in the process; as a result, the Pogues sound tighter and more precise than ever, while still summoning up the glorious howling fury that made *Rum Sodomy & the Lash* so powerful. And Shane MacGowan continued to grow as a songwriter, as his lyrics and melodies captured with brilliant detail his obsession with the finer points of Anglo-Irish culture. "Fairytale of New York," a glorious sweet-and-sour duet with Kristy MacColl, and "The Broad Majestic Shannon" were subtle in a way many of his previous work was not, "Birmingham Six" found him addressing political issues for the first time (and with all the expected venom), and "Fiesta" and "Turkish Song of the Damned" found him adding (respectively) faux-Spanish and Middle Eastern flavors into the Pogues' heady mix. And if you want to hear the Pogues blaze through some fast ones, "Bottle of Smoke" and the title song find them doing just what they've always done best. Brilliantly mixing passion, street smarts, and musical ambition, *If I Should Fall From Grace With God* is the best album the Pogues would ever make. *—Mark Deming*

Peace and Love / Jul. 1989 / Island ♦♦♦♦

Hell's Ditch / 1990 / Island ♦♦♦
From the beginning, the Clash had been one of the Pogues' primary influences. So it's most appropriate that Joe Strummer produced *Hell's Ditch.* The former Clash guitarist wisely and insightfully avoids smoothing out too many of the date's rough edges, and seems to encourage rawness and go-for-broke passion (which generally serve the band well). This time, elements of Middle Eastern and Latin music are added to the Pogues' intriguing rock/Irish folk mix. It's hard to miss the effect that drugs and alcohol were having on the self-destructive Shane MacGowan, whose vocals are even more garbled than they were on *Peace And Love.* In fact, he sounds like he's in a drunken stupor most of the time. Nonetheless, his songwriting is often superb and brilliant on this risk-taking, if uneven, project. *—Alex Henderson*

Yeah Yeah Yeah Yeah Yeah / Sep. 1990 / Island ♦♦

The Essential Pogues / Nov. 19, 1991 / Island ♦♦♦♦♦
Essential Pogues doesn't cover *Red Roses for Me* or *Rum Sodomy and the Lash,* so it isn't a definitive collection. However, it does capture the majority of the highlights from their Island albums and functions as a good introduction to the band. One complaint: the tedious extended remix of "Yeah, Yeah, Yeah, Yeah, Yeah" was included instead of the punchy, energetic original single. *—Stephen Thomas Erlewine*

Waiting for Herb / Oct. 19, 1993 / Chameleon ♦♦

The Pointer Sisters

f. 1971, East Oakland, CA
Group / Adult Contemporary, Urban, Dance-Pop, Soul
Versatile Ruth, Anita, June, and Bonnie Pointer regularly scored pop and soul hits throughout the '70s and '80s in a chameleonic variety of styles. Formed in Oakland, with their first successes for Blue Thumb Records blending funky rhythms with a novel nostalgic attitude (beginning with their 1973 revival of Allen Toussaint's "Yes We Can Can"), leading up to their first #1 R&B item in 1975, "How Long (Betcha' Got a Chick on the Side)."

Bonnie signed with Motown in 1978 and kicked off her own string of R&B hits with "Free Me from My Freedom/Tie Me to a Tree (Handcuff Me)." (June and Anita also tried the solo route during the '80s, without leaving the fold.)

By 1979, when the remaining trio covered Bruce Springsteen's "Fire," The Pointers were headed in a more contemporary direction on the Planet label, and "He's So Shy" (1980), "Slow Hand" (1981), "Automatic," and the anthemic "Jump (For My Love)" (the last two both 1984) were savvy ditties that blazed trails across the R&B and pop charts. However, the group's success declined during the late '80s, as their records began to sound more formulaic. The Pointer Sisters lost their major-label record contract in the early '90s, and the group began performing on oldies circuits occasionally. In 1995, the trio made a tenative return to the spotlight when they joined a revival performance of the Fats Waller musical *Ain't Misbehavin',* yet the accompanying soundtrack album failed to gain much attention. *—Bill Dahl*

• **Yes We Can: The Best of the Blue Thumb Recordings** / Jul. 15, 1997 / Hip-O ♦♦♦♦♦
Next to LaBelle, the Pointer Sisters were the most unorthodox and adventurous R&B "girl group" of the mid-1970s R&B scene. (Of course, they'd still be having hits long after LaBelle's 1977 breakup). Beautifully illustrating the siblings' eclectic nature, this CD focuses on their early material for Blue Thumb Records from 1973-77. Sweaty, passionate hits like "Yes We Can Can," "How Long (Betcha Got a Chick on the Side)," "Going Down Slowly" and "You Gotta Believe" show that they were a first-class soul group, but that's not all they were. The collection also reminds us that they could be equally exciting when it came to blues (Willie Dixon's "Wang Dang Doodle"), jazz ("Cloudburst," "Black Coffee" and Dizzy Gillespie's "Salt Peanuts") and even country ("Fairytale"). One of the most fun tracks is the delightfully silly "Steam Heat," which finds them going on about how rough the winters were in Oakland, CA. One thing the Sisters never lost was their sense of fun, which continued to serve them well on their slicker and much more pop-minded (though equally engaging) hits of the 1980s. But never were they more risk-taking than when they recorded for Blue Thumb. Pop fans who know the Sisters primarily for "Jump" or "Neutron Dance" but might be unaware of their Blue Thumb output owe it to themselves to hear this magnificent collection. *—Alex Henderson*

• **Best of the Pointer Sisters** / Feb. 22, 2000 / RCA ♦♦♦♦♦
RCA's *The Best of the Pointer Sisters* picks up where Hip-O's *Yes We Can: The Best of the Blue Thumb Recordings* leaves off, presenting 18 of the trio's hits for Planet and RCA Records. The collection begins with 1979's "Fire" and ends with "Goldmine," which peaked on the charts in 1987. In between those two songs are such massive hits as "He's So Shy," "Slow Hand," "Automatic," "Jump (For My Love)," "I'm So Excited," and "Neutron Dance." As these hits prove, the Pointer Sisters got a lot smoother once they left Blue Thumb, choosing to record seductive quiet-storm ballads and sprightly dance-pop. Fans of the Blue Thumb years may find this a little distasteful, but as this fine collection illustrates, the Pointer Sisters excelled in this area, just as they did with the funkier material for Blue Thumb. Anyone who is a fan of the group's late-'70s and early-'80s hits will not be disappointed by this disc, since it offers a definitive portrait of the Pointer Sisters at Planet and RCA. *—Stephen Thomas Erlewine*

Poison

f. 1983, Harrisburg, PA, **db.** 1993
Group / Pop-Metal, Hair Metal
In a decade fueled by party anthems and power ballads, Poison found massive popularity in the late 1980s, with only such related bands as Bon Jovi and Def Leppard outselling them. While the group had a long string of hits, they soon became just as renowned for their stage show, and continued to be a major attraction over the course of their first three albums. Poison was signed to Enigma Records in 1987, where they released their first album, *Look What the Cat Dragged In.* The record, spawning the Top Ten hits "I Want Action," "Talk Dirty to Me" and "I Won't Forget You," was a surprise success, selling two million copies within a year following its release. While the band was already quite popular by the end of 1987, 1988's *Open Up and Say ... Ahhh!* was their commercial breakthrough, due to the massive hits

"Fallen Angel," "Nothin' But a Good Time" and "Every Rose Has Its Thorn." Poison returned to the studio to record *Flesh and Blood* in 1990. The album, which included the upbeat "Unskinny Bop" and the sentimental "Something to Believe In," was another major success. 1993's *Native Tongue* album, despite some strong reviews and a hit single, "Stand," was a commercial disappointment. *—Barry Weber*

Look What the Cat Dragged In / 1986 / EMI-Capitol Special Markets ✦✦✦
Poison's debut album took its cues from the big, anthemic pop hooks of Def Leppard and the rebellious street-tough posturing of Motley Crue, as well as a raunchy, adolescent obsession with sex. But Poison really carved out its niche as the ultimate glam-metal band, using tight-assed boogie and over-the-top visual extravagance—costumes, makeup, teased hair, etc.—to an even greater extent than most of their contemporaries. It was derivative and formulaic, to be sure, but Poison wholeheartedly embraced that formula from the beginning with a conviction often missing in their peers, and it's that ridiculous, good-time excess that keeps *Look What the Cat Dragged In*'s catchiest songs, especially the party anthems "Talk Dirty to Me" and "I Want Action," just as much fun today, if not moreso. *—Steve Huey*

Open Up & Say . . . Ahh! / 1988 / Capitol ✦✦✦✦
Poison's best album still has a bit of filler that fails to deliver the big hooks and catchy riffs of their best material; when that happens, Bret Michaels' affected "rawk & rowl" singing accent begins to grate. But thankfully, that doesn't happen very often on *Open Up and Say . . . Ahh!*, which solidified the group's status as hair-metal's top party band. The ballad "Every Rose Has Its Thorn," Poison's only number one hit, and the Top Ten "Nothin' But a Good Time" became their most widely recognized signature songs; a cover of Loggins & Messina's "Your Mama Don't Dance" also hit the Top Ten, and the sometimes-overlooked "Fallen Angel," one of their best songs, got plenty of MTV airplay. But the agreeable raunch of album tracks like "Love on the Rocks," "Good Love," and "Look But You Can't Touch" helps make *Open Up and Say . . . Ahh!* Poison's best overall album. *—Steve Huey*

Flesh and Blood / Jun. 21, 1990 / Capitol ✦✦✦✦

Native Tongue / Feb. 8, 1993 / Capitol ✦✦

● **Poison's Greatest Hits: 1986-1996** / Nov. 26, 1996 / Capitol ✦✦✦✦
Greatest Hits 1986-96 is as definitive as a Poison compilation could hope to be. Featuring a full 18 tracks, including all of their Top 50 hits ("Talk Dirty to Me," "I Want Action," "Nothin' But a Good Time," "Fallen Angel," "Every Rose Has Its Thorn," "Your Mama Don't Dance," "Unskinny Bop," "Something to Belive In," "Stand," among others) plus two unreleased cuts ("Sexual Thing," "Lay Your Body Down"), the album boasts every worthwhile song the group ever recorded, augmented by Brett Michaels' track-by-track commentary. Though the album isn't sequenced in chronological order, it plays like an excellent mix tape, which actually makes the album more listenable. Even on a compilation, Poison wears a little thin—there are still dull moments among these 18 songs, mainly in the form of lesser-known album tracks and singles—but still, *Greatest Hits 1986-96* is the most enteraining album the band ever released. *—Stephen Thomas Erlewine*

The Police

f. 1977, London, England, **db.** 1985
Group / Album Rock, Pop/Rock, New Wave
Nominally, the Police were punk rock, but that's only in the loosest sense of the term. The trio's nervous, reggae-injected pop-rock was punky, but it wasn't necessarily punk. All three members were considerably more technically proficient than the average punk or New Wave band. Andy Summers had a precise guitar attack that created dense, interlocking waves of sounds and effects. Stewart Copeland could play polyrhythms effortlessly. And Sting, with his high, keening voice, was capable of constructing infectiously catchy pop songs. While they weren't punk, the Police certainly demonstrated that the punk spirit could have a future in pop music. As their career progressed, the Police grew considerably more adventurous, experimenting with jazz and various world musics. All the while, the band's tight delivery and mastery of the pop single kept their audience increasing and by 1983, they were the most popular rock & roll band in the world. Though they were at the height of their fame, internal tensions caused the band to splinter apart in 1984, with Sting picking up the majority of the band's audience to become an international superstar. *—Stephen Thomas Erlewine*

Outlandos d'Amour / Nov. 1978 / A&M ✦✦✦✦✦
While their subsequent chart-topping albums would contain far more ambitious songwriting and musicianship, the Police's 1978 debut, *Outlandos D'Amour* (translation: *Outlaws of Love*) is by far their most direct and straightforward release. Although Sting, Andy Summers, and Stewart Copeland were all superb instrumentalists with jazz backgrounds, it was much easier to get a record contract in late-'70s England if you were a punk/new wave artist, so the band decided to mask their instrumental prowess with a set of strong, adrenaline-charged rock, albeit with a reggae tinge. Some of it may have been simplistic ("Be My Girl-Sally," "Born in the '50s"), but Sting was already an ace songwriter, as evidenced by all-time classics like the good-girl-gone-bad tale of "Roxanne," and a pair of brokenhearted reggae-rock ditties, "Can't Stand Losing You" and "So Lonely." But like all other Police albums, the lesser-known album cuts are often highlights themselves—the frenzied rockers "Next to You," "Peanuts" and "Truth Hits Everybody," as well as more exotic fare like the groovy album closer "Masoko Tanga" and the lonesome "Hole in My Life." *Outlandos D'Amour* is unquestionably one of the finest debuts to come out of the '70s punk/new wave movement. *—Greg Prato*

Reggatta de Blanc / Oct. 1979 / A&M ✦✦✦
By 1979's *Reggatta De Blanc* (translation: *White Reggae*), non-stop touring had sharpened the Police's original blend of reggae-rock to perfection, resulting in breakthrough success. Containing a pair of massive hit singles—the inspirational anthem "Message in a Bottle" and the spacious "Walking on the Moon"—the album also signaled a change in the band's sound. Whereas their debut got its point across with raw, energetic performances, *Reggatta De Blanc* was much more polished production-wise, and fully developed from a songwriting standpoint. While vigorous rockers did crop up from time to time ("It's Alright for You," "Deathwish," "No Time This Time," and the Grammy-winning instrumental title track), the material was overall much more sedate than the debut—"Bring On the Night," "The Bed's Too Big Without You," and "Does Everyone Stare." Also included was Stewart Copeland's one and only lead vocal appearance on a Police album, the witty "On Any Other Day," as well as one of the band's most eerie tracks, "Contact." With *Reggatta De Blanc*, many picked Sting and Co. to be the superstar band of the '80s, and the Police would prove them correct on their next release. *—Greg Prato*

☆ **Zenyatta Mondatta** / Oct. 1980 / A&M ✦✦✦✦✦
The stage was set for the Police to become one of the '80s' biggest acts, and the band delivered with their 1980 classic *Zenyatta Mondatta*. The album proved to be the trio's second straight number one album in the U.K., while peaking at number three in the U.S. Arguably the best Police album (perhaps second only to *Synchronicity*), *Zenyatta* contains perhaps the quintessential new wave anthem, the haunting "Don't Stand So Close to Me," the story of an older teacher lusting after one of his students. While other tracks follow in the same spooky path (their second Grammy-winning instrumental "Behind My Camel," "Shadows in the Rain"), most of the material is upbeat, such as the carefree U.S./U.K. Top Ten "De Do Do Do, De Da Da Da," "Canary in a Coalmine," and "Man in a Suitcase." Sting includes his first set of politically charged lyrics in "Driven to Tears," "When the World Is Running Down, You Make the Best of What's Still Around," and "Bombs Away," which all observe the declining state of the world. While Sting would later criticize the album as not all it could have been (the band was rushed to complete the album in order to begin another tour), *Zenyatta Mondatta* remains one of the finest rock albums of all time. *—Greg Prato*

Ghost in the Machine / Oct. 1981 / A&M ✦✦✦
For their fourth album, 1981's *Ghost in the Machine*, the Police had streamlined their sound to focus more on their pop side, and less on their trademark reggae-rock. Their jazz influence had become more prominent, as evidenced by the appearance of saxophones on several tracks. The production has more of a contemporary '80s sound to it (courtesy of Hugh Padgham, who took over for Nigel Gray), and Sting proved once and for all to be a master of the pop-songwriting format. The album spawned several hits, such as the energetic "Spirits in the Material World" (notice how the central rhythms are played by synthesizer instead of guitar to mask the reggae connection) and a tribute to those living amid the turmoil and violence in Northern Ireland circa the early '80s, "Invisible Sun." But the best and most renowned of the bunch is undoubtedly the blissful "Every Little Thing She Does Is Magic," which topped the U.K. singles chart and nearly did the same in the U.S. (3). Unlike the other Police releases, not all of the tracks are stellar ("Hungry for You," "Omegaman"), but the vicious jazz rocker "Demolition Man," the barely containable "Rehumanize Yourself," and a pair of album-closing ballads ("Secret Journey," "Darkness") proved otherwise. While it was not a pop masterpiece, *Ghost in the Machine* did serve as an important stepping stone between their more direct early work and their more ambitious latter direction, resulting in the trio's exceptional blockbuster final album, 1983's *Synchronicity*. *—Greg Prato*

Synchronicity / Jun. 1983 / A&M ✦✦✦
Although The Police's 5th release, 1983's *Synchronicity*, would be their most commercially successful and lead to a sold-out tour of enormodomes (including New York's *Shea Stadium*), it would turn out to be the trio's final album and tour. Like all Police recordings, *Synchronicity* contains some obvious 'filler' (such as the silly dinosaur tale of "Walking in your Footsteps" and the almost unlistenable "Mother"), but for the most part, it's exceptional. One of 1983's biggest singles, the haunting "Every Breath You Take," is an obvious highlight, as well as other hits—the cacophonic rocker "Synchronicity II," plus the far more temperate "Wrapped Around Your Finger" and "King of Pain." Also included are the oft-overlooked tracks "O My God," "Synchronicity I" (used as a concert opener on the ensuing tour), "Tea in the Sahara," "Murder By Numbers," and the Stewart Copeland original "Miss Gradenko." Few other albums from 1983 merged tasteful pop, sophistication, and expert songwriting as well as *Synchronicity* did, resulting in yet another all-time classic. *—Greg Prato*

Message in a Box: The Complete Recordings / Sep. 28, 1993 / A&M ✦✦✦✦✦
Despite their legendary status, the Police only released five albums during their brief reign from 1978-1983. In addition, the trio had amassed a healthy amount of both studio and live B-sides, plus songs that only appeared on soundtracks. For the 1993 four-CD box set *Message in a Box: The Complete Recordings*, every single song the Police ever recorded is included. All the tracks were digitally remastered for the project, sounding superior to the original CD versions of the single albums. Also included is a 68-page booklet that includes an interesting (and often humorous) biography, a timeline and notes from all three band members regarding the rarities that appear for the first time on compact disc here. But of course, the real charm of the box set is the music—album tracks ("Hole in My Life," "It's Alright for You," "Driven to Tears"), hits ("Message in a Bottle," "Can't Stand Losing You," "Spirits in the Material World"), and rarities ("Fallout," a live version of "Next to You") are all timeless classics. While the set is highly recommended to newcomers just discovering the wonders of the Police, long-time fans should consider replacing their tinny-sounding single CDs with the definitive *Message in a Box*. After all, it contains a total of 24 tracks unavailable (for the most part) anywhere else. *—Greg Prato*

Live / Jun. 13, 1995 / A&M ✦✦✦

★ **Every Breath You Take: The Classics** / Sep. 12, 1995 / A&M ✦✦✦✦✦
By deleting the 1986 hits collection *Every Breath You Take: The Singles* and replacing it nearly ten years later with *Every Breath You Take: The Classics*, A&M improved the original set . . . but only slightly. Instead of finally adding the missing hits that were mysteriously absent the first time around ("Synchronicity II," "Demolition Man," "So Lonely," etc.), there are only two additional tracks—the original version of "Don't Stand So Close to Me" and a "New Classic Rock Mix" of "Message in a Bottle." Again, the included hits speak for themselves—"Roxanne," "Walking on the Moon," "Every Little Thing She Does Is Magic," "Wrapped Around Your Finger,"—but ultimately, *The Classics* misses the mark. Why would a Police fan who already owns *The Singles* want to replace it with a modestly different repackaging—A&M should have added some of the missing classics instead of just rehashing what many fans already own. *—Greg Prato*

Iggy Pop (James Newell Osterberg)

b. Apr. 21, 1947, Ypsilanti, MI

Vocals / Detroit Rock, Album Rock, Proto-Punk, Hard Rock

After the disbandment of the proto-punk group the Stooges, vocalist Iggy Pop (born James Osterberg) embarked on a solo career that flirted with the mainstream while keeping his fiery punk spirit alive. Pop laid low for a couple of years following the breakup of the Stooges, resurfacing in 1977 with two David Bowie-produced albums, *The Idiot* and *Lust for Life.* These records expanded his trademark full-throttle rock & roll, incorporating a more pop-oriented approach that increased his audience; *The Idiot* remains his highest-charting album, peaking at number 72 in America. Released in 1982, the Chris Stein-produced *Zombie Birdhouse* (which appeared on Stein's label, Animal) was the most varied collection Pop had created since *Lust for Life.* After the release of *Zombie Birdhouse,* Pop took some time off, reappearing four years later with the Bowie-produced *Blah-Blah-Blah;* the record became his highest-charting album since *The Idiot.* He followed it in 1989 with *Instinct,* another return to basic hard rock. Released the following year on Virgin Records, the Don Was-produced *Brick By Brick* was his most accessible and commercially successful album, producing his first Top 40 hit, "Candy." *—Stephen Thomas Erlewine*

☆ **The Idiot** / 1977 / Virgin ✦✦✦✦✦

In 1976, the Stooges had been gone for two years, and Iggy Pop had developed a notorious reputation as one of rock & roll's most spectacular waste cases. After a self-imposed stay in a mental hospital, a significantly more functional Iggy was desperate to prove he could hold down a career in music, and he was given another chance by his longtime ally, David Bowie. Bowie co-wrote a batch of new songs with Iggy, put together a band, and produced *The Idiot,* which took Iggy in a new direction decidedly different from the guitar-fueled proto-punk of the Stooges. Musically, *The Idiot* is of a piece with the impressionistic music of Bowie's "Berlin Period" (such as *Heroes* and *Low*), with it's fragmented guitar figures, ominous bass lines, and discordant, high-relief keyboard parts. Iggy's new music was cerebral and inward-looking, where his early work had been a glorious call to the id, and Iggy was in more subdued form than with the Stooges, with his voice sinking into a world-weary baritone that was a decided contrast to the harsh, defiant cry heard on "Search and Destroy". Iggy was exploring new territory as a lyricist, and his songs on *The Idiot* are self-referential and poetic in a way that his work had rarely been in the past; for the most part the results are impressive, especially "Dum Dum Boys," a paean to the glory days of his former band, and "Nightclubbing," a call to the joys of decadence. *The Idiot* introduced the world to a very different Iggy Pop, and if the results surprised anyone expecting a replay of the assault of *Raw Power,* it also made it clear that Iggy was older, wiser, and still had plenty to say; it's a flawed but powerful and emotionally absorbing work. *—Mark Deming*

☆ **Lust for Life** / 1977 / Virgin ✦✦✦✦✦

On *The Idiot,* Iggy Pop looked deep inside himself, trying to figure out how his life and his art had gone wrong in the past. But on *Lust for Life,* released less than a year later, Iggy decided it was time to kick up his heels, as he traded in the mid-tempo introspection of his first album and began rocking hard again. Musically, *Lust for Life* is a more aggressive set than *The Idiot,* largely thanks to drummer Hunt Sales and his bassist brother Tony Sales. The Sales' proved they were a world class rhythm section, laying out power and spirit on the rollicking title cut, the tough groove of "Tonight," and the lean neo-punk assault of "Neighborhood Threat," and with guitarists Ricky Gardner and Carlos Alomar at their side, they made for a tough, wiry rock & roll band—a far cry from the primal stomp of the Stooges, but capable of kicking Iggy back into high gear. (David Bowie played piano and produced, as he had on *The Idiot,* but his presence is less clearly felt on this album.) As a lyricist and vocalist, Iggy Pop rose to the challenge of the material; if he was still obsessed with drugs ("Tonight"), decadence ("The Passenger"), and bad decisions ("Some Weird Sin"), the title cut suggested he could avoid a few of the temptations that crossed his path, and songs like "Success" displayed a cocky joy that confirmed Iggy's was back at full strength. On *Lust for Life,* Iggy Pop managed to channel the aggressive power of his work with the Stooges with the intelligence and perception of *The Idiot,* and the result was the best of both world; smart, funny, edgy, and hard-rocking, *Lust for Life* is the best album of Iggy Pop's solo career. *—Mark Deming*

TV Eye / 1978 / RCA ✦

New Values / 1979 / Buddha ✦✦✦✦

From the time the Stooges first broke onto the music scene in 1967, Iggy Pop was rock's most remarkable one-man freak show, but by the mid-'70s, after the Stooges' messy collapse, Iggy found himself in need of a stable career. The rise of punk rock finally created a context in which Iggy's crash-and-burn theatrics seemed like inspired performance rather than some sort of cry for help, and in 1979, with everyone who was anyone name-checking Iggy as punk's Founding Father, he scored a deal with Arista Records, and *New Values* became his first recording since the new rock gained a foothold. These days, *New Values* sounds like Iggy Pop's new wave album; while former Stooges associates James Williamson and Scott Thurston worked on the album, the arrangements were dotted with synthesizer patches and electronic percussion accents that have not stood the test of time well at all, and the mix speaks of a more polite approach than the raw, raging rock of Iggy's best work. But the growth as a songwriter that David Bowie encouraged in Iggy on *The Idiot* and *Lust for Life* is very much in evidence here; "Tell Me a Story," "Billy Is a Runaway," and "How Do Ya Fix a Broken Part" are tough, unblinking meditations on Iggy's war with the persona he created for himself, and "I'm Bored" and & "Five Foot One" proved rock's first great minimalist still had some worthy metaphors up his sleeve. If *New Values* wasn't a great Iggy Pop album, it was a very good one, and proved that he had a future without David Bowie's guidance, something that didn't seem so certain at the time. *—Mark Deming*

Soldier / 1980 / Buddha ✦✦✦

Party / 1981 / Buddha ✦✦

Zombie Birdhouse / 1982 / IRS ✦✦

Blah Blah Blah / 1986 / A&M ✦✦✦

Instinct / 1988 / A&M ✦✦

Brick by Brick / Jun. 1990 / Virgin ✦✦✦✦✦

While Don Was is best known for his work with mutant funkateers Was (Not Was), he was also a Motor City boy with fond memories of the Stooges' glory days, and when he was hired to produce an album for Iggy Pop Was said, "The guy is incredibly intelligent, writes great lyrics, is a great singer, and I just wanted to get that across." And he did: *Brick by Brick* refined Iggy's gifts without watering them down, adding a polish that focused his talents rather than blurring them. Working with a mixture of L.A. session heavyweights (Waddy Wachtel, David Lindley) and rock stars paying their respects (Slash and Duff McKagan from Guns n' Roses, Kate Pierson from the B-52's), *Brick by Brick* leans to tough, guitar-based hard rock, leavened with a few more pop-oriented tunes that still speak of a hard-nosed lyrical approach. But the triumph here is Iggy's; he's rarely sang better on record, finding a middle ground between precision and abandon that honors both and surrenders to neither, and as a lyricist he reached a new level of maturity that proved he could expand his boundaries without loosing touch with his roots. On *Brick by Brick,* Iggy's dominant theme is the cultural and moral decay of modern America, and finding the strength to rise above it and reach a place in the world. That might sound a bit grand for Iggy, but as a man who sent himself to Hell and back (and learned a few things in the process), he expresses his ideas with plenty of piss, vinegar, and hard-bitten wit. Smart, tough, and impressive on all counts, *Brick by Brick* was Iggy Pop's strongest work since *Lust for Life,* and marked a new high point in his career as a songwriter. *—Mark Deming*

American Caesar / 1993 / Virgin ✦✦✦✦

Boasting a big-name producer and appearances from several actual rock stars, *Brick by Brick* was a remarkably successful attempt to create an "event album" around Iggy Pop, so the follow-up came as a surprise—*American Caesar* was cut fast and loose in a New Orleans studio, with Iggy's road band backing him up. But the real shock was that *American Caesar* ranks with Iggy's very best solo work; dark, loud, and atmospheric, it's a far riskier album than *Brick by Brick,* lyrically following that disc's themes of America teetering on the edge of collapse with the same degree of hard-won maturity, but adding a wacked-out passion and force that recalls the heady days of *Raw Power.* While Iggy's group doesn't play with the subtlety of the studio cats on *Brick by Brick,* they also sound tight and forceful, like a real band with muscle and experience. Eric Schermerhorn's guitar meshes with Iggy's vocals as well as anyone he's worked with since Ron Asheton, and Malcolm Burn's production is clear and detailed but adds subtle textures that season the formula just right. The rockers are full-bodied ("Wild America," "Plastic and Concrete"), the calmer tunes still bristle with tension and menace ("Mixing the Colors," "Jealousy"), the manic remake of "Louie Louie" tops the version on *Metallic K.O.,* and the title cut is a bizarre bit of performance art that's as strange as the entirety of *Zombie Birdhouse,* and a rousing success where that album was a brave failure. In a note printed on the CD itself, Iggy says "I tried to make this album as good as I could, with no imitations of other people and no formula shit." Iggy succeeded beyond anyone's expectations, and *American Caesar* is an overlooked masterpiece. *—Mark Deming*

Naughty Little Doggie / Mar. 5, 1996 / Virgin ✦✦✦

● **Nude & Rude: The Best of Iggy Pop** / Oct. 29, 1996 / Virgin ✦✦✦✦✦

Nude & Rude: The Best of Iggy Pop is an excellent 17-track overview of Pop's career, from the Stooges into the '90s. With the exception of *The Idiot, Lust for Life* and *Brick by Brick,* Iggy's solo career has been decidedly uneven and many of his albums have been flat-out dull. *Nude & Rude* does a terrific job of selecting the best moments from these records, as well as many of the best Stooges tracks, therby providing a nearly flawless introduction to Iggy's music. With "I Wanna Be Your Dog," "No Fun," "Search & Destroy," "Gimme Danger," "I'm Sick of You" and "Kill City," representing the Stooges, a few of the band's essential items are missing, but all the essential solo tracks are here, including "Funtime," "Nightclubbing," "China Girl," "Lust for Life," "Real Wild Child," "Cold Metal," "Candy," and "Home." *—Stephen Thomas Erlewine*

Avenue B / Sep. 14, 1999 / Virgin ✦✦

Portishead

f. 1991, Bristol, England

Group / Electronica, Adult Alternative Pop/Rock, Trip-Hop, Alternative Pop/Rock

Portishead may not have invented trip-hop, but they were among the first to popularize it, particularly in America. Taking their cue from the slow, elastic beats that dominated Massive Attack's *Blue Lines* and adding elements of cool jazz, acid house, and soundtrack music, Portishead created an atmospheric, alluringly dark sound. The group wasn't as avant-garde as Tricky, nor as tied to dance traditions as Massive Attack; Instead, the band wrote evocative psuedo-cabaret pop songs that subverted their conventional structures with experimental productions and rhythms of trip-hop. As a result, Portishead appealed to a broad audience—not just electronic dance and alternative rock fans, but thirtysomethings who found techno, trip-hop and dance as exotic as worldbeat. Before Portishead released their debut album *Dummy* in 1994, trip-hop's broad appeal wasn't apparent, but the record became an unexpected success in Britain, topping most year-end critics polls and earning the prestigious Mercury Music Prize; in America, it also became an underground hit, selling over 150,000 copies before the group toured the US. Following the success of *Dummy,* legions of imitators appeared over the next two years, but Portishead remained quiet, finally issuing their eponymous second album in 1997. *—Stephen Thomas Erlewine*

★ **Dummy** / Oct. 1994 / Go! Discs ✦✦✦✦✦

Portishead's album debut is a brilliant, surprisingly natural synthesis of claustrophobic spy soundtracks, dark breakbeats inspired by frontman Geoff Barrow's love of hip-hop, and a vocalist (Beth Gibbons) in the classic confessional singer/songwriter mold. Beginning with the otherworldly theremin and martial beats of "Mysterons," *Dummy* hits an early high with "Sour Times," a post-modern torch song driven by a Lalo Schifrin sample. The chilling atmospheres conjured by Adrian Utley's excellent guitar work and Barrow's turntables and keyboards prove the perfect foil for Gibbons, who balances sultriness and melancholia in equal measure. Occasionally reminiscent of a torchier version of Sade, Gibbons provides a clear focus for these songs, with Barrow and company behind her laying down one of the best full-length productions ever heard in the dance world. Where previous acts like Massive Attack had attracted dance heads in the main, Portishead crossed over to an American, alternative audience, connecting with the legion of angst-ridden indie fans as well. Better than any album before it, *Dummy* merged the pinpoint-precise productions of the dance world with pop hallmarks like great songwriting and excellent vocal performances. *—John Bush*

Portishead / Sep. 30, 1997 / Go! Discs/London ✦✦✦✦✦
Portishead's debut album, *Dummy,* popularized trip-hop, making its slow, narcotic rhythms, hypnotic samples, and film-noir production commonplace among sophisticated, self-consciously "mature" pop fans. The group recoiled from such widespread acclaim and influence, taking three years to deliver their eponymous second album. On the surface, *Portishead* isn't all that dissimilar from *Dummy,* but its haunting, foreboding sonic textures make it clear that the group isn't interested in the crossover success of such fellow travelers as Sneaker Pimps. Upon repeated plays, the subtle differences between the two albums become clear. Geoff Barrow and Adrian Utley recorded original music that they later sampled for the backing tracks on the album, giving the record a hazy, dreamlike quality that shares many of the same signatures of *Dummy,* but is darker and more adventurous. Beth Gibbons has taken the opportunity to play up her tortured diva role to the hilt, emoting wildly over the tracks. Her voice is electronically phased on most of the tracks, adding layers to the claustrophobic menace of the music. The sonics on *Portishead* would make it an impressive follow-up, but what seals its success is the remarkable songwriting. Throughout the album, the group crafts impeccable modern-day torch songs, from the frightening, repetitive "Cowboys" to the horn-punctuated "All Mine," which justify the detailed, engrossing production. The end result is an album that reveals more with each listen and becomes more captivating and haunting each time it's played. *—Stephen Thomas Erlewine*

PNYC / Nov. 10, 1998 / Go! Discs ✦✦✦

Elvis Presley (Elvis Aron Presley)

b. Jan. 8, 1935, Tupelo, MS, **d.** Aug. 16, 1977, Memphis, TN
Vocals, Guitar / Pop/Rock, Pop, Rockabilly, Rock & Roll
Elvis Presley may be the single most important figure in American 20th-century popular music. Not necessarily the *best,* and certainly not the most consistent. But no one could argue that he was not the musician most responsible for popularizing rock & roll on an international level. Viewed in cold sales figures, his impact was phenomenal. Dozens upon dozens of international smashes from the mid-'50s to the mid-'70s, as well as the steady sales of his catalog and reissues since his death in 1977, may make him the single highest-selling performer in history. More important from a music lover's perspective, however, are his remarkable artistic achievements. Presley was not the very first White man to sing rhythm and blues; Bill Haley predated him in that regard, and there may have been others as well. Elvis was certainly the first, however, to assertively fuse country and blues music into the style known as rockabilly. While rockabilly arrangements were the foundations of his first (and possibly best) recordings, Presley could not have become a mainstream superstar without a much more varied palette that also incorporated pop, gospel, and even some bits of bluegrass and operatic schmaltz here and there. His 1950s recordings established the basic language of rock and roll; his explosive and sexual stage presence set standards for the music's visual image; his vocals were incredibly powerful and versatile. Unfortunately, to much of the public, Elvis is more icon than artist. Innumerable bad Hollywood movies, increasingly caricatured records and mannerisms, and a personal life that became steadily more sheltered from real-world concerns (and steadily more bizarre) gave his story a somewhat mythic status. By the time of his death, he'd become more a symbol of gross Americana than of cultural innovation. The continued speculation about his incredible career has sustained interest in his life, and supported a large tourist/entertainment industry, that may last indefinitely, even if the fascination is fueled more by his celebrity than his music. *—Richie Unterberger*

★ **Elvis Presley** / Mar. 1956 / RCA ✦✦✦✦✦
Today it all seems so easy—RCA signs up the kid from Memphis, television gets interested at around the same time, and the rest is history. The circumstances surrounding this album were neither simple nor promising, however, nor was there anything in the history of popular music up to that time to hint that Elvis Presley was going to be anything other than "Steve Sholes' folly," which was what rival executives were already whispering. So a lot was unsettled and untried at the first of two groups of sessions that produced the *Elvis Presley* album—it wasn't even certain that there was any reason for a rock & roll artist to cut an album, because teenagers bought 45s, not LPs. The first of Elvis's RCA sides yielded one song, "Heartbreak Hotel," that seemed a potential single, but which no one thought would sell, and a few tracks that would be good enough for an album, if there were one. But no one involved knew anything for sure about this music. Seventeen days later, "Heartbreak Hotel" was released, and for about a month it did nothing—then it began to move, and then Elvis appeared on television, and had a number one pop single. The album Sholes wanted out of Elvis came from two groups of sessions in January and February, augmented by five previously unissued songs from the Sun library. This was as startling a debut record as any ever made, representing every side of Elvis's musical influences except gospel—rockabilly, blues, R&B, country, and pop were all here in an explosive and seductive combination. *Elvis Presley* became the first rock & roll album to reach the number one spot on the national charts, and RCA's first million dollar-earning pop album. *—Bruce Eder*

☆ **Elvis** / Oct. 1956 / RCA ✦✦✦✦✦
If *Elvis* isn't quite as important historically as the *Elvis Presley* album that preceded it, that's only because it came second—musically, it's a more confident and bolder work than his debut, and in any other artist's output it would have been considered a crowning achievement. At the sessions for his first album, the singer and all concerned were treading into unmapped territory and not sure what they were doing or if they were ready for it—by September of 1956, when the three days of sessions behind the *Elvis* album took place, he was on top, a national phenomenon of a kind that hadn't been seen in music since Frank Sinatra a dozen years earlier, and he had some more experience recording. And with that confidence came better singing. The songs here were, for the most part, material that he knew well, with one new submission by Otis Blackwell. He slides through them seemingly effortlessly, transforming the 1940s country number "When My Blue Moon Turns to Gold Again" into a smooth rocker; roaring through the Little Richard numbers "Long Tall Sally," "Ready Teddy," and "Rip It Up"; returns to his blues roots with a killer rendition of Arthur Crudup's "I'm So Glad You're Mine" (a leftover, amazingly enough, from his first RCA session); and shows how refined his voice was becoming on the ballad "First in Line" and the sentimental favorite "Old Shep." The *Elvis* album was reissued in 1999 with vastly improved sound and eight bonus tracks from the same and chronologically adjoining recording sessions, including the singles "Hound Dog," "Don't Be Cruel," and "Anyway You Want Me," and that is the version to own on CD. *—Bruce Eder*

Elvis' Golden Records / Apr. 1958 / RCA ✦✦✦✦✦
This was rock & roll's first greatest hits album, and it set the standard for all others to follow. As originally conceived, it was a 14-song collection of most of the King's biggest hits up to that time, released on the eve of his start of military service—a dearth of material being in the offing, it seemed only logical to assemble these hits. Each of the 14 songs had earned a gold record award for a million sales, a record unequaled at that time by anyone else in rock & roll. The album wasn't intended as a history lesson, so "Hound Dog" and "Loving You" precede "Heartbreak Hotel"—the 1997 remastering also tampers with the concept a bit, adding six bonus tracks. Elvis' singing never sounded richer or more expressive, and one can fully appreciate in vivid detail the delicate nuances of his phrasing on songs like "Too Much." On the down side, the remastering has made the sound so clean on some of the harder songs that some of the raw, "dirty" ambience that characterized this stuff on the radio and the original 45s is lacking. Still, Scotty Moore's groundbreaking lead guitar part on "Hound Dog" and the Jordanaires' backup singing never came through more sharply or cleanly, and the all-important rhythm section is almost up front in the mix. Those who own the first Elvis box from RCA, covering the '50s masters, may hesitate to pick up this or the other parts of this latest remastered series, but the sound has been upgraded one more level, and *Golden Hits* does give a bite-sized glimpse of where Elvis had come from and where he was going (for better or worse) musically on the eve of heading into the Army. *—Bruce Eder*

50,000,000 Elvis Fans Can't Be Wrong: Elvis' Golden Records, Vol. 2 / Dec. 1959 / RCA ✦✦✦✦✦
The release of this album, seen in its proper historical context, is an indicator of just how bright Elvis Presley's star shone in the late '50s. His first hits collection was issued in March 1958, on the eve of his going into the Army; his second was the first "volume two" greatest-hits album ever issued on a rock & roll star, appearing weeks ahead of his leaving the Army in March 1960. Anyone who buys the notion that Elvis was "tamed" during his first years at RCA will find revelation in "A Big Hunk of Love," "I Need Your Love Tonight" and "I Got Stung," some of the greatest pieces of hard rock & roll that the King ever cut—and all were recorded in the midst of Elvis' stay in the Army, in a hastily arranged session in Nashville during June 1958. The 1997 remastering works better on this material than it did on the earlier *Golden Hits;* the more expansive sound doesn't detract a bit from the power of the music, and the quality of Elvis' singing, coupled with his choice of material, was reaching its peak. By this time, his voice was becoming one of the finest instruments in rock & roll, his idolization of Dean Martin and other popular singers paying off with a degree of control and articulation that his rivals could only envy, and it's all laid out here on what are still some pretty hard-rocking sides. The remastered edition not only improves the sound significantly, but adds eight songs to the original ten. The notes are thorough, although they reveal the stretching that the producers were engaged in by citing British releases as the justification for inclusion. But the quality of the music is undeniable. *—Bruce Eder*

Elvis Is Back! / Apr. 1960 / RCA ✦✦✦✦✦
The 1999 remastering of this classic album features the complete contents of the March 20, 1960, RCA Hollywood session plus the dawn-to-dusk April 2 Nashville session that rounded out the album, for a total of 18 songs, including the three singles and their B-sides from those sessions. Although they have common recording origins, two of the three singles, "It's Now or Never" and "Are You Lonesome Tonight," were very quirky by the standards of Elvis songs at the time—the former inspired by Elvis's admiration for Tony Martin's 1949 hit "There's No Tomorrow," while the latter was recorded at the request of Col. Parker as a favor to his wife. They add to the diversity of sounds on this record, which shows a mature Elvis Presley. "Dirty, Dirty Feeling" and "It Feels So Right" showed he could still rock out and challenge authority and propriety, while "Reconsider Baby" and "Like a Baby" offer some of his best blues performances; but "The Thrill of Your Love" (a very gospel-tinged number), "Soldier Boy," "Girl of My Best Friend," and "Girl Next Door Went a' Walking," also displayed the rich, deep vocalizing that would challenge critics' expectations of Elvis Presley playing rhythm guitar throughout. He also comes off, better than on any of his other albums since arriving at RCA, as a musician as much as a "star" (he'd always had a lot more to say about running his sessions than the critics who loathed his RCA years indicated). The sound on the 1999 remastering is extraordinarily close yet natural, giving the listener full value for the presence of Scotty Moore, Hank Garland (who also plays bass on a few tracks), D.J. Fontana, Boots Randolph, and Floyd Cramer. *—Bruce Eder*

Something for Everybody / Jun. 1961 / RCA ✦✦✦

Elvis' Golden Records, Vol. 3 / Sep. 1964 / RCA ✦✦✦✦✦
The original *Elvis' Golden Records Vol. 3* was, like its predecessors, an unprecedented release—no one in rock & roll up to that point, other than Elvis, had ever legitimately earned a second greatest-hits volume, much less a third. This is also the place where the legitimately softer, more mature Presley replaces the angry young Elvis represented on the first two volumes. On a sexual level, songs like "Stuck on You," "It's Now or Never," "Fame and Fortune,"

"I Gotta Know" and "Surrender" offer seduction rather than diverting violation. He might no longer have been a rebel, but as represented on the original ten songs of this album, he was still making the Top Five and even the top of the charts regularly with work that was legitimately fine early-'60s rock & roll and pop-rock. "His Latest Flame" or "Good Luck Charm" might not have been groundbreaking musical statements of the caliber of "Heartbreak Hotel" or "Blue Suede Shoes," but in Elvis' hands they were worth hearing over and over. The original 12 songs have been augmented by six more, including "Can't Help Falling In Love" (which should have been on this disc to begin with) and the hauntingly beautiful "Girl of My Best Friend," which was a number two hit in England (and may be the prettiest song Elvis ever cut), plus "Wild in the Country" and "Wooden Heart" (a hit in Europe) from *G.I. Blues*. The producers have stuck with the most tasteful and intriguing numbers from the films, within the time frame of the original release, the annotation is thorough, and the 1997 remastered sound runs circles around all prior editions. *—Bruce Eder*

Elvis' Gold Records, Vol. 4 / Feb. 1968 / RCA ✦✦✦✦✦
The fourth volume of *Elvis' Gold Records* was the first of his hits compilations to be issued at a point when Elvis Presley wasn't considered a very important rock & roll star anymore (a few months later he would embark on his network television "comeback"). Indeed, it appeared at a point when it seemed, as Neal Umphred pointed out, "Elvis's gold was drained up and he was reduced to filling up the fourth volume with B-sides." Covering the early '60s through the end of 1967, the original collection had the bad fortune to appear at a point when politics, international affairs and a generational change in the listening public all combined to render Elvis Presley seemingly irrelevant. A great deal of social and musical change had taken place while Elvis withdrew from concerts and television appearances, made his movies, and scarcely attempted the recording of any non-soundtrack albums. So at the time, the album's arrival and even its title might have seemed like a joke to a lot of observers. That having been said, there is some extraordinary music on *Gold Records Vol. 4,* especially in its remastered 18-song version. "Wooden Heart" and "Can't Help Falling in Love" have been moved from *Volume 4* to *Volume 3* in reconfiguring the *Elvis' Gold Records* series. The additional songs have been chosen with care and even some inspiration, and the remastered sound is most impressive, and the notes are reasonably thorough. Pop-culture mavens may want to note the presence of the indirect Ed Wood connection here—"Rock-A-Hula" was co-written by Dolores Fuller, Wood's companion and collaborator during the period of *Glen or Glenda*. *—Bruce Eder*

Elvis TV Special / Dec. 1968 / RCA ✦✦✦✦✦
After years of making abysmal movies, Presley appeared before a live audience, scared to death. That he more than rose to the challenge is evidenced here, a masterly performance highlighted by the jam-session segment with DJ Fontana and Scotty Moore, where Presley plays electric guitar and knocks out drop-dead versions of "Baby, What You Want Me to Do" and "Tiger Man." *—Cub Koda*

☆ **From Elvis in Memphis** / May 1969 / RCA ✦✦✦✦✦
After a 14-year absence from Memphis, Elvis Presley returned to cut what was certainly his greatest album (or, at least, a tie effort with his RCA debut LP from early 1956). The fact that *From Elvis in Memphis* came out as well as it did is something of a surprise, in retrospect—Presley had a backlog of songs he genuinely liked that he wanted to record and had heard some newer soul material that also attracted him, and none of it resembled the material that he'd been cutting since his last non-soundtrack album, six years earlier. And he'd just come off of the NBC television special which, although a lot of work, had led him to the realization that he could be as exciting and vital a performer in 1969 as he'd been a dozen years before. And for what was practically the last time, the singer cut his manager, Tom Parker, out of the equation, turning himself over to producer Chips Moman. The result was one of the greatest white soul albums (and one of the greatest soul albums) ever cut, with brief but considerable forays into country, pop, and blues as well. Presley sounds rejuvenated artistically throughout the dozen cuts off the original album, and he's supported by the best playing and back-up singing of his entire recording history. The spring 2000 remastered edition matches the sound quality on the two-CD set *Suspicious Minds*, but restores the original album's classic cover and song order, with six bonus tracks cut at the same sessions but only released as singles at the time. This disc proves that he not only came back—he was *better* than he'd ever been as a singer or stylist—and is an essential part of any music collection. *—Bruce Eder*

Elvis in Person (At the International Hotel, Las Vegas, NV) / Apr. 1970 / RCA ✦✦✦✦✦

On Stage: February 1970 / Jun. 1970 / RCA ✦✦✦✦

That's the Way It Is / Dec. 1970 / RCA ✦✦✦✦✦

☆ **Elvis Country (I'm 10,000 Years Old)** / Jan. 1971 / RCA ✦✦✦✦✦
Western swing, blues, countrypolitan, traditional country, gospel—if it was music that even brushed the airwaves of a Southern state, Elvis Presley at his best could make it his own, and Elvis was at his peak when he cut *Elvis Country.* Actually, Elvis Presley was positively on a roll at the time. A decade after the end of what were thought to be his prime years, he was singing an ever-widening repertory of songs with more passion and involvement than he'd shown since the end of the 1950s. What's more, his voice had achieved a peak of perfection as an instrument, acquiring a depth and richness, a beauty to go with its power at which even his best work of the early years had only hinted. And it all came together on *Elvis Country,* which has lots of country music on it but also a lot else. His greatest long-player of the 1970s, and one of his three or four best albums ever, *Elvis Country* was a record that he threw himself into with every bit of the passion displayed on the better known, soul-oriented *From Elvis in Memphis,* and it was even more personal; he was cutting songs that he was either very impressed with at the moment or had loved for a lot of years, but they were all songs he cared about, which gives him a commanding and charismatic vocal presence. He doesn't necessarily supplant the originals, but he gives you more than enough reason to listen, again and again, to everything here. Producer Felton Jarvis and a cadre of Nashville sidemen (augmented by James Burton) provided backup as good as Presley ever got. *—Bruce Eder*

Aloha from Hawaii Via Satellite / Feb. 1973 / RCA ✦✦✦

Promised Land / Jan. 1975 / RCA ✦✦✦✦

Moody Blue / Jul. 1977 / RCA ✦✦✦

The Number One Hits / 1987 / RCA ✦✦✦✦✦
Number One Hits contains 18 #1 records from the charts of *Billboard,* who somehow didn't rank "Crying in the Chapel," "In the Ghetto," "Burning Love," and "Way Down" as chart-toppers, although other national surveys did. In fact, according to RCA, every copy of "Way Down" was sold out within days after Presley's death, not just here but all over the planet, and somehow, amazingly, it didn't even make the magazine's Top Ten! *—Neal Umphred*

★ **Top Ten Hits** / 1987 / RCA ✦✦✦✦✦
The Top Ten Hits is exactly what it says it is—every Top Ten hit that Elvis Presley ever had during the course of his career, from "Heartbreak Hotel" in 1956 to "Burning Love" in 1972. Even though this double-disc set covers a lot of ground, there's a huge amount of terrific material that *isn't* included on the compilation. There's none of his Sun recordings, none of his gritty blues, none of his gospel, precious little of his country recordings, and many great singles for RCA aren't included. Still, the 38 songs on *The Top Ten Hits* are absolutely first-rate—there's no arguing with "I Want You, I Need You, I Love You," "Don't Be Cruel," "Hound Dog," "Love Me Tender," "Love Me," "All Shook Up," "Jailhouse Rock," "One Night," "A Fool Such As I," "(Marie's the Name) His Latest Flame," "Can't Help Falling In Love," "Little Sister," "Return to Sender," "Suspicious Minds," and many, many others. It's the perfect way to start an Elvis collection and, for many casual fans, the only set to own. *—Stephen Thomas Erlewine*

☆ **The Million Dollar Quartet** / Feb. 1990 / RCA ✦✦✦✦✦
For years available only as a poor-fidelity bootleg, this is Elvis jamming in the Sun studios with Carl Perkins, Jerry Lee Lewis, and others on a set of primarily gospel and hillbilly material. Loose as a goose, with a true jam-session spirit to it, it offers a fascinating glimpse of one of the few times Presley let his true musical soul come up for air with somebody (Sam Phillips) there to record it. *—Cub Koda*

☆ **The King of Rock 'n' Roll: The Complete 50's Masters** / Jun. 23, 1992 / RCA ✦✦✦✦✦
A casual Elvis fan wanting to assemble a decent overview of the King's '50s sides could probably sweat it down to the *Sun Sessions* CD and Volume 1 of the *Top Ten Hits* compilation. But for those of you who take your '50s Presley seriously, *The King of Rock 'n' Roll—The Complete 50's Masters* is absolutely essential. For the hardcore Elvis fan, the booklet and CD graphics for this five-disc set provide incentive enough to justify its purchase. The liner notes by Presley expert Peter Guralnick are passionate, contagious in their enthusiasm, and filled with a real sense of history, time, and place. The treasure-trove of unpublished photos, session information and Elvis memorabilia accompanying the booklet text is no less inspiring. But it's the music (140 tracks in all) that's the real meat and potatoes of this set. Every studio track cut during the '50s—the seminal Sun sides, the early RCA hits, movie soundtracks, alternates, live performances, rarities (including both sides of the long-lost acetate he cut for his mother back in 1953)—it's all here in one gorgeous package. Soundwise, this box makes any of the previous issues of this material pale by comparison, the proper (non-reverbed) inclusion of the Sun masters being a particular treat. This is no mere rehash of what's been around a dozen times before—there's a lot of thought and care behind this package, and no serious fan of American rock & roll should consider a collection complete without it. *—Cub Koda*

☆ **From Nashville to Memphis: The Essential 60's Masters** / Sep. 28, 1993 / RCA ✦✦✦✦✦
Continues the tradition of first-quality sound remastering and packaging. Much of Elvis' '60s work is arguably not as essential as the '50s stuff, but this meticulous five-disc/130-track set makes an impressive case for the defense. A thick booklet contains riveting liner notes, full-color photos, complete discography and session listings; a sheet of RCA album cover stamps tops off the set. *—Roch Parisien*

Amazing Grace: His Greatest Sacred Songs / Oct. 25, 1994 / RCA ✦✦✦✦

Command Performances: The Essential 60's Masters II / Jul. 18, 1995 / RCA ✦✦✦
Elvis Presley's 1960s film soundtracks are renowned as the repository of his most frivolous (many would say ridiculous) material. This 62-song, double CD draws from no less than 26 of those screen vehicles to present the "best" of these performances; the idea is to complement the first volume of *Essential 60's Masters,* which focused on his non-soundtrack recordings from the decade, and doesn't include any of the cuts from this collection. The goal of this package may have been to boil away the dross (as big as this is, there's a LOT of stuff they left off). But if anything, it perhaps inadvertently demonstrates just how lousy most of those recordings were; even this selective, chronologically programmed set feels way too long, and could have probably been cut in length to a single CD without too much loss. That's not to say that what's here is entirely negligible. There are some classic singles ("Return to Sender," "Can't Help Falling in Love"), fair rockers ("What'd I Say," "Little Egypt"), and more than a few cuts that are transcendentally great/awful in their mindless silliness ("Rock-A-Hula Baby," "Viva Las Vegas," "Do the Clam"), songs which are archetypes, for better or worse, of the kitschiest facet of Presley's myth. But much of the rest is just unremarkable, or even bad: stupid novelties ("Poison Ivy League"), drab ballads, and many mediocre rock tunes. This doesn't include such legendarily idiotic tunes as "No Room to Rhumba in a Sports Car," "Yoga Is as Yoga Does," and "Fort Lauderdale Chamber of Commerce"; you can find those on the original soundtracks, or a famous bootleg, the aptly-titled *Elvis' Greatest Shit.* *—Richie Unterberger*

☆ **Walk a Mile in My Shoes: The Essential 70's Masters** / Oct. 10, 1995 / RCA ✦✦✦✦✦
In most conventional rock criticism, Elvis Presley's '70s records are considered his weakest, as they were recorded while he was falling deeper into drug addiction. However, as Dave Marsh argues in the liner notes of *Walk a Mile in My Shoes—The Essential 70's Masters,* the music on the five-CD box set is among the most personal and adventurous of Elvis's career, even if the individual albums don't always reflect that diversity. By cutting away all of the dross that accumulated over the decade and sequencing the songs in a logical, entertaining manner, *Walk a Mile in My Shoes* supports the argument. On the first two discs, all of the

singles Presley released during the '70s are presented, and while there are a couple of weak numbers, the music stands as an impressive continuation of his artistic rebirth of the late '60s. *— Stephen Thomas Erlewine*

Elvis '56 / Mar. 5, 1996 / RCA ✦✦✦✦✦

★ **Sunrise** / Feb. 9, 1999 / RCA ✦✦✦✦✦
Elvis Presley's legendary recordings for Sun Records had been reissued many times before *Sunrise* appeared in early 1999, most notably in the 1987 collection *The Complete Sun Recordings*. Despite its title, *The Complete Sun Recordings* was missing a few odds and ends, plus its sequencing on CD was a little didactic, resulting in a repetitive listen. Those flaws are corrected on the exceptional *Sunrise*, a generous 38-song double-disc set that contains all of Elvis' Sun recordings, including alternate takes and several previously unreleased live performances. The compilers wisely decided to devote the first disc to the original takes, dedicating the second to alternate takes: six live cuts from 1955 and four private demos from 1953 and 1954. This sequencing emphasizes the brilliance of this music. Not only is listening to all 19 masters in a row quite breathtaking, but the second disc winds up as a revelatory experience, since it offers a kind of alternate history by following Elvis' pre-professional recordings from his Sun sessions to early live performances. As such, *Sunrise* is essential for the curious and the collector alike. *— Stephen Thomas Erlewine*

☆ **Suspicious Minds** / Apr. 13, 1999 / RCA ✦✦✦✦✦
Elvis Presley's comeback recordings from the late '60s are generally regarded as some of the finest music he ever made, not only because they proved he could still be exciting, but because they're musically diverse and emotionally rich. That was evident on *From Elvis in Memphis*, the first record released from his landmark sessions of 1968 and 1969, and latter-day compilations like *The Memphis Record* made clear how deep those recordings were. Twelve years after *The Memphis Record*, the double-disc set *Suspicious Minds* was released, and it stands as the definitive overview of these sessions. All of the familiar hits are here, of course, but for collectors, what makes this essential is that it not only contains all the master takes, but it provides nine alternate takes of classics such as "True Love Travels on a Gravel Road," "Kentucky Rain," "Suspicious Minds," "In the Ghetto" and "I'm Movin' On." None of these are particularly revelatory, but they are interesting enough to be the icing on the cake on an exceptional collection. Since they're more concise, *The Memphis Record* or *From Elvis in Memphis* remain better bets for some listeners, but any true aficionado or rock historian will need to add *Suspicious Minds* to their collection. *— Stephen Thomas Erlewine*

☆ **Artist of the Century** / Jul. 13, 1999 / RCA ✦✦✦✦✦

Can't Help Falling in Love: The Hollywood Hits / Sep. 14, 1999 / RCA ✦✦✦
Can't Help Falling in Love: The Hollywood Hits compiles 22 hit singles that were originally featured on soundtracks for films starring Elvis Presley. Where the double-disc set *Command Performances: The Essential 60's Masters II* concentrated on the '60s, specifically the cream of what was not on the five-disc box *From Nashville to Memphis*, this compilation draws from a random selection of movies Elvis made between 1956 and 1972. That's not necessarily a bad thing, even if the sequencing is also at random, since these featured songs are usually either quite good ("Jailhouse Rock," "Loving You," "King Creole," "Return to Sender," "Viva Las Vegas") or are embarrassing guilty pleasures ("Bossa Nova Baby," "Rock-a-Hula Baby," etc.). So, this isn't a definitive collection of movie hits, nor does it have all the movie hits that a casual may want. It's simply a reasonably enjoyable Elvis collection, one among many others of the same stripe in his catalog. *— Stephen Thomas Erlewine*

Peace in the Valley: The Complete Gospel Recordings / Sep. 12, 2000 / RCA ✦✦✦
An expanded three-disc collection that attempts to trump a 1994 double-disc set (*Amazing Grace: His Greatest Sacred Songs*) by offering virtually every single Elvis recording of a sacred song, *Peace in the Valley: The Complete Gospel Recordings* accomplishes the mission in its title, but at a hefty price that won't appeal to any but the most obsessive-compulsive fan. Obviously, it includes each track from his three gospel LPs—1960's *His Hand in Mine*, 1967's *How Great Thou Art*, and 1972's *He Touched Me*—plus scattered alternate takes that are previously unreleased. The third disc is padded out with an array of Elvis' sacred recordings that are easily available elsewhere, like the 13 gospel tracks on the raw *Million Dollar Quartet* session recorded at Sun in 1956, the "Gospel Medley" from his 1968 TV Special, and a version of "(There'll Be) Peace in the Valley" originally aired on Ed Sullivan's television show. Though there's no doubt that *Peace in the Valley: The Complete Gospel Recordings* is a complete set, most Elvis fans will gain little from owning it. *—John Bush*

Billy Preston

b. Sep. 9, 1946, Houston, TX
Vocals, Keyboards, Piano, Organ / Pop-Soul, Soul
It's advantageous to get an early start on your chosen career, but Billy Preston took the concept to extremes. By age ten, he was playing keyboards with gospel diva Mahalia Jackson, and two years later, in 1958, he was featured in Hollywood's film bio of W. C. Handy, *St. Louis Blues*, as young Handy himself. Preston was a prodigy on organ and piano, recording during the early '60s for Vee-Jay and touring with Little Richard. He was a loose-limbed regular on the mid-'60s ABC-TV *Shindig* series, proving his talent as both vocalist and pianist, and he built an enviable reputation as a session musician, even backing The Beatles on their *Let It Be* album. That impressive Beatles connection led to Preston's big break as a solo artist with his own Apple album, but it was his early-'70s soul smashes "Outa-Space" and the high-flying vocal "Will It Go Round in Circles" for A&M that put Preston on the permanent musical map. Sporting a humongous Afro and an omnipresent gap-toothed grin, Preston showed that his enduring gospel roots were never far removed from his joyous approach, less so now than ever. *— Bill Dahl*

● **Ultimate Collection** / Mar. 21, 2000 / Hip-O ✦✦✦✦
Hip-O's *Ultimate Collection* may not have the original hit recording of "That's the Way God Planned It," due to licensing restrictions (it was recorded for the Beatles ill-fated label, Apple), but that's about the only thing missing from this near-definitive single-disc set. Over the course of 20 tracks, the collection chronicles every one of Preston's hits, from the funky "Outa-Space," "Slaughter," and "Will It Go Round in Circles" to the smooth, quiet storm soul of his duets with Syreeta ("With You I'm Born Again," "Go for It," "One More Time for Love"). Since it's quite a transition between the two extremes, fans of either side of the spectrum may not enjoy everything here, but it's nevertheless a nearly flawless collection, providing an accurate portrait of Preston's career. It is true that the lesser-known hits aren't as compelling as the smash singles, but this is still an entertaining collection, regardless. *— Stephen Thomas Erlewine*

The Pretenders

f. 1978, London, England
Group / Album Rock, Pop/Rock, New Wave, Hard Rock
Over the years, the Pretenders have become a vehicle for guitarist/vocalist Chrissie Hynde's songwriting, yet it was a full-fledged band when it was formed in the late '70s. With their initial records, the group crossed the bridge between punk/new wave and Top 40 pop more than any other band, recording a series of hard, spiky singles that were also melodic and immediately accessible. Hynde was an invigorating, sexy singer that bended the traditional male roles of rock & roll to her own liking, while guitarist James Honeyman-Scott created a sonic palate filled with suspended chords, effects pedals, and syncopated rhythms that proved remarkably influential over the next two decades. After Honeyman-Scott's death, The Pretenders became a more straightforward rock band, yet Hynde's semi-autobiographical songwriting and bracing determination meant that the group never became just another rock band, even when their music became smoother and more pop-oriented. *— Stephen Thomas Erlewine*

★ **Pretenders** / Jan. 19, 1980 / Sire ✦✦✦✦✦
Few rock & roll records rock as hard or with as much originality as the Pretenders' eponymous debut album. A sleek, stylish fusion of Stonesy rock & roll, new wave pop, and pure punk aggression, *Pretenders* is teeming with sharp hooks and a viciously cool attitude. Although Chrissie Hynde establishes herself as a forceful and distinctively feminine songwriter, the record isn't a singer/songwriter's tour de force—it's a rock & roll album, powered by a unique and aggressive band. Guitarist James Honeyman-Scott never plays conventional riffs or leads, and his phased, treated guitar gives new dimension to the pounding rhythms of "Precious," "Tattooed Love Boys," "Up the Neck," and "The Wait," as well as the more measured pop of "Kid," "Brass in Pocket," and "Mystery Achievement." He provides the perfect backing for Hynde and her tough, sexy swagger. Hynde doesn't fit into any conventional female rock stereotype, and neither do her songs, alternately displaying a steely exterior or a disarming emotional vulnerability. It's a deep, rewarding record, whose primary virtue is its sheer energy. *Pretenders* moves faster and harder than most rock records, delivering an endless series of melodies, hooks, and infectious rhythms in its 12 songs. Few albums, let alone debuts, are ever this astonishingly addictive. *— Stephen Thomas Erlewine*

Pretenders II / Aug. 15, 1981 / Sire ✦✦✦✦
The Pretenders' debut album was such a powerful, monumental record that its sequel was bound to be a bit of a disappointment, and *Pretenders II* is. Essentially, this album is an unabashed sequel, offering more of the same sound, attitude, and swagger, including titles that seem like rips on its predecessors and another Ray Davies cover. This gives the record a bit too much of a pat feeling, especially since the band seems to have a lost a bit of momentum—they don't rock as hard, Chrissie Hynde's songwriting isn't as consistent, James Honeyman Scott isn't as inventive or clever. These all are disappointments, yet this first incarnation of the Pretenders was a tremendous band, and even if they offer diminished returns, it's still diminished returns on good material, and much of *Pretenders II* is quite enjoyable. Yes, it's a little slicker and more stylized than its predecessor, and, yes, there's a little bit of filler, yet any album where rockers as tough as "Message of Love" and "The Adultress" are balanced by a pop tune as lovely as "Talk of the Town" is hard to resist. And when you realize that this fantastic band only recorded two albums, you take that second album, warts and all, because the teaming of Hynde and Honeyman Scott was one of the great pairs, and it's utterly thrilling to hear them together, even when the material isn't quite up to the high standards they set the first time around. *— Stephen Thomas Erlewine*

☆ **Learning to Crawl** / Jan. 21, 1984 / Sire ✦✦✦✦✦
Chrissie Hynde and drummer Martin Chambers reassembled the Pretenders in 1982, following the death of James Honeyman-Scott and the departure of bassist Pete Farndon. *Learning to Crawl*, appropriately, is the sound of a band coming to grips with loss and the responsibilities that come with maturity. Even though the subject matter is undeniably serious, the Pretenders rock with a vigorous energy that was missing on *Pretenders II*. It helps that Hynde's songs are among her best, of course. "Middle of the Road" encapsulates the contradictions in the album's main themes; "Back on the Chain Gang" is a moving tribute to Scott; "My City Was Gone" is a vicious attack on Reagan-era economic devastation; and the beautiful, ringing "2000 Miles" is one of the few rock & roll songs about Christmas to actually work. And while "Watching the Clothes" is a bit embarrassing, it isn't enough to stop *Learning to Crawl* from being one of the best rock & roll records of the early '80s. *— Stephen Thomas Erlewine*

Get Close / Nov. 1, 1986 / Sire ✦✦✦
By now, Hynde is writing songs to her child and taking on social issues. But the chiming guitars are gorgeous, and Hynde's caught-in-the-throat voice has never been more expressive. *— William Ruhlmann*

☆ **The Singles** / Nov. 17, 1987 / Sire ✦✦✦✦✦
The Pretenders burst on the scene in the early '80s with one of the most compelling presentations of rock & roll ever seen. This collection, which highlights their A and B sides up until the mid-'80s, shows that Chrissie Hynde and co-conspirators were true masters of the rock single. Tracks such as "Brass in Pocket," "Middle of the Road," and the highly underrated "Message of Love" are spectacularly performed, written, and produced. The early band, especially with James Honeyman-Scott's hook-laden guitar playing, was capable of miracles, and you'll find examples of that on virtually every cut. *— Matthew Greenwald*

Packed! / May 22, 1990 / Sire ✦✦

Last of the Independents / May 10, 1994 / Sire ✦✦✦

The Isle of View / Oct. 24, 1995 / Warner Brothers ✦✦✦

Viva el Amor / Jun. 22, 1999 / Warner Brothers ✦✦✦✦

The Pretty Things

f. 1963, Kent, England, **db.** 1980

Group / Freakbeat, British Psychedelia, Album Rock, Psychedelic, British Invasion, Prog-Rock/Art Rock, Hard Rock, Rock & Roll

Of all the original British Invasion groups, perhaps none is as underappreciated in the United States as the Pretty Things. Featuring the hoarse vocals of Mick Jagger-lookalike Phil May and the stinging leads of guitarist Dick Taylor (who actually played in early versions of the Rolling Stones with Jagger and Keith Richards), the Pretties recorded a clutch of raunchy R&B rockers in the mid-'60s that offer a punkier, rawer version of the early Stones' sound. Their first two albums, as well as a brace of fine major and minor British hits (of which "Don't Bring Me Down" and "Honey I Need" were the biggest), feature first-rate original material and covers, and remain the group's most exciting and influential recordings. Unfortunately, they remained virtually unknown to American audiences. After their initial run of success, the group took a sharp left turn into psychedelia with the orchestrated album *Emotions* (1967), impressive singles that owed more to Pink Floyd than Bo Diddley, and, most significantly, *S.F. Sorrow* (1968). The first rock opera, *S.F. Sorrow* was a major influence upon Pete Townshend, who released his much more successful opera, *Tommy,* with the Who the following year. *—Richie Unterberger*

The Pretty Things / 1965 / Original Masters ✦✦✦✦✦

The Pretty Things' debut was one of the prime cuts of early British R&B, featuring such definitively raunchy exponents of the genre as "Roadrunner," "Big City," "Mama, Keep Your Big Mouth Shut," "Pretty Thing," and "Honey I Need." A couple of weak jams prevent the album from ranking as a true classic. The British version differed slightly from the U.S. version of the record, which took off four tracks and substituted four others. The 1998 CD reissue on Snapper, however (issued in both the U.S. and U.K.), is the definitive edition of the album, as it includes all of the tracks from the American and British versions of the LP, as well as "Big Boss Man" (the B-side of their first single) and the outtake "Get Yourself Home," which was not released in the 1960s. Several tracks that originally only appeared on the 1965 U.S. version of the album ("Don't Bring Me Down," "Rosalyn," "I Can Never Say") are particularly essential to rounding out the picture of the band as they sounded at their outset. Half of the songs from this CD are on the *Get a Buzz* compilation. *—Richie Unterberger*

Get the Picture— / Dec. 1965 / Original Masters ✦✦✦✦✦

The band's second album (released Dec. 1965) has not only been remastered from original session tapes, so the group sound like their amps are practically right in your lap, but it's also been expanded to 18 songs with the addition of tracks cut for singles and EP releases from the same sessions. That's enough to recommend it even to casual fans—this is now a record that's just a few notches short of Rolling Stones level in the charisma department and pretty tough any way you want to look at it. On "Rainin' in My Heart," they sound exactly like the Stones from the same era, missing only the little harmonica flourish that might have been added on the break. The notes go into the history of the group during this period in delightful detail, and the histories of various songs, most particularly "L.S.D.," which, amazingly, was cut as a demo and never re-done for release, just put out that way. In their good moment here, the Pretty Things approach Rolling Stones territory, and even in their off moments they're flying at the same level as the Kinks' album tracks. The real enhancement, alas, only concerns those fans with CD-Rom drives (PC Windows 3.1 or later, minimum 486 66Mhz or Mac 68040 or better, running system 7.1 or later)—they get to see the Pretty Things playing the 100 club in London from 1965, looking wilder and scruffier than the Stones or almost any other benchmark band. *—Bruce Eder*

Emotions / 1967 / Original Masters ✦✦✦✦

In accordance with their label's (and not the band's) wishes, the Pretties were teamed with a middle-aged orchestra directed by Reg Tilsley on this album, which saw the Phil May-Dick Taylor songwriting team making an effort to move beyond R&B knockoffs into more sophisticated territory. Sometimes the arrangements (dubbed onto tracks without much involvement from the group) worked; more often, they were an unnecessary hindrance. An interesting failure, it contained some genuinely top-rank originals that saw the group expanding their vision into social observation and tentative psychedelia, including "My Time," "The Sun," and especially the moody, folk-rock-ish "Death of a Socialite." The CD reissue on Snapper adds the 1966 singles "House in the Country" (a Kinks cover) and "Progress," neither of which were that great, and five tracks from *Emotions* that are stripped of their infamous brass and string overdubs. Note that these versions are not identical to the ones which appear on the *Pure and Pretty* bootleg, which has a couple of overdub-less *Emotions* cuts ("Out in the Night" and "Bright Lights of the City") that do not appear on the expanded *Emotions* CD in overdub-less versions. *—Richie Unterberger*

S.F. Sorrow / 1968 / Original Masters ✦✦✦✦

No amount of scrutiny can disguise the fact that this rock opera—built around a short story by Phil May—is ultimately a bit of a confusing effort. Although it may have helped inspire *Tommy,* it is, simply, not nearly as good. That said, it was first, and has quite a few nifty ideas and production touches. The CD reissue on Snapper adds four valuable songs from their 1967-68 singles ("Defecting Grey," "Mr. Evasion," "Talkin' About the Good Times" and "Walking Through My Dreams"). This version of "Defecting Grey" is the original, long, uncut five-minute rendition, and not of trivial importance; it's superior to the shorter one used on the official single. *—Richie Unterberger*

Parachute / 1970 / Demon ✦✦✦

The last Pretty Things album to explore interesting territory, this progressive rock is grounded by some solid harmonies and riffs, but is ultimately not nearly as compelling as its *Rolling Stone* Album of the Year award would suggest. The CD reissue on Snapper adds seven tracks from 1970-71 singles that show the group sliding from the psychedelia of the late 1960s into more standard progressive rock and hard rock approaches. *—Richie Unterberger*

Silk Torpedo / 1974 / Swan Song ✦✦✦

Savage Eye / 1975 / Swan Song ✦✦

● **Get a Buzz: The Best of the Fontana Years** / 1992 / Fontana ✦✦✦✦✦

It's missing a few good tracks, but this is a good retrospective of their British Invasion-era work, running through the 1967 *Emotions* LP. Includes all their major singles—"Rosalyn," "Don't Bring Me Down," "Honey I Need," "Midnight to Six Man," "Come See Me." *—Richie Unterberger*

On Air / 1992 / Dutch East India ✦✦

Lloyd Price

b. Mar. 9, 1933, Kenner, LA

Vocals / New Orleans R&B, Rock & Roll, R&B

Not entirely content with being a 1950s R&B star on the strength of his immortal New Orleans classic "Lawdy Miss Clawdy," singer Lloyd Price yearned for massive pop acceptance. He found it, too, with a storming rock & roll reading of the ancient blues "Stagger Lee" and the unabashedly pop-slanted "Personality" and "I'm Gonna Get Married" (the latter pair sounding far removed indeed from his Crescent City beginnings). At his very first Specialty label date in 1952, Price sang his classic eight-bar blues "Lawdy Miss Clawdy" (its rolling piano intro courtesy of a moonlighting Fats Domino). It topped the R&B charts for an extended period, making Price a legitimate star before he was old enough to vote. Four more Specialty smashes followed—"Oooh, Oooh, Oooh," "Restless Heart," "Tell Me Pretty Baby," "Ain't It a Shame"—before Price was drafted into the Army and deposited most unhappily in Korea. "Stagger Lee," Price's adaptation of the old Crescent City lament "Stack-A-Lee," topped both the R&B and pop lists in 1958. By now, his sound was taking on more of a cosmopolitan bent, with massive horn sections and prominent pop background singers. Dick Clark insisted on toning down the violence inherent to the song's storyline for the squeaky-clean *American Bandstand* audience, accounting for the two different versions of the song you're likely to encounter on various reissues. After Price hit with another solid rocker, "Where Were You (On Our Wedding Day)—," in 1959, the heavy brass-and-choir sound became his trademark at ABC-Paramount. "Personality," "I'm Gonna Get Married," and "Come Into My Heart" all shot up the pop and R&B lists in 1959, and "Lady Luck" and "Question" followed suit in 1960. *—Bill Dahl*

★ **Lawdy!** / Aug. 5, 1991 / Specialty ✦✦✦✦✦

Twenty-five stellar 1952-1956 examples of why Lloyd Price ranks with the greatest R&B performers ever to emerge from the Crescent City. Beginning with his debut smash "Lawdy Miss Clawdy," Price wails the rocking "Mailman Blues," "Where You At—," "Rock 'N' Roll Dance," and "Baby Please Come Home" in front of fat sax cushions, rolling pianos, and steamy rhythm sections. *—Bill Dahl*

Heavy Dreams, Vol. 2 / 1993 / Specialty ✦✦✦✦✦

No discernible artistic dropoff on Specialty's encore Price retrospective, distinguished by his classics "Oooh-Oooh-Oooh," "Tell Me Pretty Baby," "Ain't It a Shame?" (not Fats Domino's hit), "Country Boy Rock," and "Why" (he's later recut the latter for ABC-Paramount). *—Bill Dahl*

★ **Greatest Hits: The Original ABC-Paramount Recordings** / 1994 / MCA ✦✦✦✦✦

Chronicling Lloyd Price's tenure at ABC Paramount Records, the 18 tracks here include many of his best recordings. A choral group backs him, along with a large orchestra featuring a boisterous sax that goes berserk quite often. "Personality," "Lawdy Miss Clawdy," "I'm Gonna Get Married," and "Just Because" are everlasting. His most noted recording is "Stagger Lee"; the violent song about two gamblers comes in two versions: the unedited and the *Bandstand* version, as Dick Clark made Price clean up the lyrics. The song glorifies Stagger Lee, a cheat spot gambler who shoots and ultimately murders a guy named Billy over a dice game dispute—and people complain about gangsta rap! Price's energized, strident tenor is infectious; he loved recording and throws down on every track. *—Andrew Hamilton*

Primal Scream

f. 1984, Glasgow, Scotland

Group / C-86, Electronica, Alternative Dance, Club/Dance, Acid House, Alternative Pop/Rock, House

Primal Scream's career could in many ways be read as a microcosm of British indie rock in the '80s and '90s. Bobby Gillespie formed the band in the mid-'80s while drumming for goth-tinged noise-rockers the Jesus & Mary Chain, who were the exact opposite of Primal Scream—the latter specialized in infectious, jangly pop on its early records. After a brief detour to punky hard rock, the group reinvented themselves as a dance band in the early '90s, following through on the pop and acid-house fusions of the Stone Roses and Happy Mondays. With the assistance of producers Andrew Weatherall and Hugo Nicholson, Primal Scream created the ultimate indie-pop and dance fusion album, *Screamadelica,* in 1991. *Screamadelica* broke down boundaries and changed the face of British pop music in the '90s, helping to make dance and techno acceptable to the rock mainstream. Instead of following through on the promise of the album, Primal Scream retreated to Stonesy boogie for their 1994 follow-up *Give Out But Don't Give Up.* When that record was greeted with indifference, they returned to dance-rock fusions with 1997's *Vanishing Point,* which re-established the group as a major force in British rock. *—Stephen Thomas Erlewine*

Sonic Flower Groove / Sep. 1987 / Elevation ✦✦✦

Primal Scream / Sep. 1989 / Mercenary ✦✦

★ **Screamadelica** / Oct. 8, 1991 / Sire ✦✦✦✦✦

There's no underestimating the importance of *Screamadelica,* the record that brought acid house, techno, rave culture crashing into the British mainstream—an impact that rivaled that of Nirvana's *Nevermind*, the other 1991 release that changed rock. Prior to *Screamadelica*, Primal Scream were Stonesy classic rock revivalists with a penchant for Detroit rock. They retained those fascinations on *Screamadelica*—one listen to the Jimmy Miller-produced, Stephen Stills-rip "Movin' on Up" proves that—but they burst everything wide open here, turning rock inside out by marrying it to a gleeful rainbow of modern dance textures. This is such a brilliant, gutsy innovative record, so unlike anything the Scream did before, that it's little wonder that there's been much debate behind who is actually responsible for its grooves, especially since Andrew Weatherall is credited with production with eight of the tracks, and its clearly in line with his work. Even if Primal Scream took credit for Weatherall's endeavors, that doesn't erase the fact that they shepherded this album, providing the ideas and impetus for this dubtastic, elastic, psychedelic exercise in deep house and neo-psychedelic. Like any dance music, this is tied to its era to a certain extent, but it transcends it due to its fierce imagination and how it doubles back on rock history, making the past present and vice versa. It was such a monumental step forward that Primal Scream stumbled before regaining their footing, but by that point, the innovations of *Screamadelica* had been absorbed by everyone from the underground to mainstream. There's little chance that this record will be as revolutionary to first-time listeners, but after its initial spin, the genius in its construction will become apparent—and it's that attention to detail that makes *Screamadelica* an album that transcends its time and influence. *—Stephen Thomas Erlewine*

Give Out But Don't Give Up / Mar. 1994 / Sire ✦✦✦

Vanishing Point / Jul. 7, 1997 / Sire/Reprise ✦✦✦✦
Primal Scream found themselves in danger of losing their hip audience in the wake of their misconceived trad-rock record, *Give Out but Don't Give Up*. As a reaction, they returned to the genre-bending, electronic dance-rock of the seminal *Screamadelica* for *Give Out*'s follow-up, *Vanishing Point*. Instead of recycling the dazzlingly bright neo-psychedelia of *Screamadelica*, Primal Scream reaches deep into cavernous dub and '60s pop. *Vanishing Point* is a dark, trippy album, filled with mind-bending rhythms and cinematic flourishes. The addition of former Stone Roses bassist Mani to the Scream gives their music an organically funky foundation that had been lacking. Over those rhythms are samples, reverbed guitars, and synthesizers that echo spy movies, Southern soul, and the Stones. Above anything else, *Vanishing Point* is about sound and groove. Words remain a weak point for Bobby Gillespie, who only manages cohesive lyrics on the swirling "Burning Wheel" and "Star," but that is a secondary concern, since Primal Scream is at its best when working the rhythms. Songs like "Kowaliski" and, in particular, the extended instrumentals of "Get Duffy" and "Trainspotting" illustrate that the group is still capable of creating exotic, thoroughly entrancing sounds, which is what makes *Vanshing Point* a remarkable comeback. *—Stephen Thomas Erlewine*

Echo Dek / Oct. 27, 1997 / Creation ✦✦✦✦

XTRMNTR / May 2, 2000 / Astralwerks ✦✦✦✦✦
Whenever indie music seems hopelessly self-righteous, unchallenging and inoffensive, Primal Scream rides in to try and save it all. *Screamadelica* tried to encapsulate the importance of ecstasy culture; *Vanishing Point* tried to exorcise their own insanity. *XTRMNTR* is a nasty, fierce realization of an entire world that has lost the plot. The album starts with a gloriously vindictive sample of a kid commanding "Kill All Hippies"; this roughly states the album's modus operandi. There are songs shouting with furious, feedback-splayed anger ("Blood Money," "Exterminator"), songs of club-based revolt (both house-influenced versions of "Swastika Eyes"), and songs of utterly manic desperation ("Accelerator"). But when lead singer Bobby Gillespie's weedy vocals can't keep up with the music, *XTRMNTR* falters, especially on the meandering "Insect Royalty" and the half-realized hip-hop "Pills"; Gillespie diminishes its power on every verse—it only saves itself when it delivers the album's central theme: "Sick fuck fuck sick fuck fuck sick fuck...". Thankfully, *XTRMNTR*'s highs, such the gentle "Keep Your Dreams" (sounding like a sibling of 1991's "I'm Coming Down" or 1997's "Star"), and the monstrous, apocalyptic "MBV Arkestra (If They Move, Kill 'Em)," shower down with purely visceral poise. It's not the flawless statement against complacency the band intended, but it succeeds at tearing heads off, shooting fascists, and asking questions later with unbelievable fury. These aren't the aggro-simpleton maneuvers of Rage Against the Machine or Korn; the implosive production and sheer political belief prove that ingenuity must go hand in hand with "statement" if an idea is to come across effectively. *XTRMNTR* is simply a protest—sonically as well as lyrically—and maybe this would be a fine time to once again rally behind something worthwhile. *—Dean Carlson*

Primus

f. 1986
Group / Alternative Metal, Funk Metal, Heavy Metal, Alternative Pop/Rock
Primus is all about Les Claypool; there isn't a moment on any of their other records where his bass isn't the main focal point of the music, with his vocals acting as a bizarre side show. Which isn't to deny guitarist Larry LaLonde or drummer Tim "Herb" Alexander any credit—no drummer could weave in and around Claypool's convoluted patterns as effortlessly as Alexander and few guitarists would as willingly push the spotlight away like LaLonde, so he can produce a never-ending spiral of avant-noise. All of this means that they are miles away from being another punk-funk combo like the Red Hot Chili Peppers; Claypool may slap and pop his bass, but there is little funk in the rhythm he and Alexander lay down. Instead, they're a post-punk Rush spiked with the sensibility and humor of Frank Zappa. Primus doesn't want to make you dance, they want to play music; songs are secondary to showcasing their instrumental prowess. Primus' music is willfully weird and experimental, yet it's not alienating; the band was able to turn their goofy weirdness into pop stardom. *—Stephen Thomas Erlewine*

Suck on This / Jan. 1990 / Caroline ✦✦✦
Originally released on their own Prawn Song label (a parody of Led Zeppelin's Swan Song Records), this is their debut, recorded live in a small club and featuring all of the greatness this trio has. It's hard, thrashy funk and punk with a sense of humor. The reissue on Caroline sounds a little muddy. Find the original vinyl pressing on Prawn, which sounds more like a CD than the CD. *—John Book*

Frizzle Fry / Feb. 1990 / Caroline ✦✦✦✦
Primus' eccentric, dissonant blend of avant-rock, funk, punk and thrash has inspired comparisons to everyone from Frank Zappa to Devo to the Red Hot Chili Peppers. But whatever comparison is made, the fact is that this trio has created strikingly original music. *Frizzle Fry* is sometimes a bit too self-indulgent for its own good, but in general, Les Claypool's willingness to experiment and his risk-taking nature come through the most. "Too Many Puppies," "To Defy The Laws Of Tradition" and "Mr. Knowitall" are among the nutty, weird treasures that helped establish Primus as alternative rock heroes and make *Frizzle Fry* the classic that it is. *—Alex Henderson*

● **Sailing the Seas of Cheese** / May 14, 1991 / Interscope ✦✦✦✦✦
The first Primus album to achieve much widespread airplay (thanks to its release on a major), and the one that broke them on MTV, *Sailing the Seas of Cheese* completely redefined the possibilities of the electric bass in rock music for those who'd never heard the group before. Slapping like a funk player, but strumming power chords and finger-tapping like a metal guitar hero, Les Claypool coaxed sounds from his instrument that had rarely if ever been made the focus of a rock band. Claypool's riffs were so full and dominant that they hardly needed to be doubled by guitarist Larry LaLonde (and wouldn't have had the same effect anyway), which freed him up on most songs to launch into dissonant, atonal solos that essentially functioned as texture, complementing Claypool's oddly whimsical sense of melody. The combination results in a weird atmosphere that could be transformed into something dark or eerie, but Claypool's thin, nasal voice and demented blue-collar persona place the record firmly in the realm of the cheerfully bizarre. The compositions are mostly riff-driven, fleshing out their heavy metal roots with prog rock tricks from Rush and Frank Zappa, as well as the novelty side of Zappa's sense of humor. The willful goofiness may alienate some listeners, but it can also obscure some genuinely dark humor, and it never detracts from the band's frequently stunning musicianship. Somewhat analogous to jazz trumpeter Dizzy Gillespie, Claypool hasn't inspired many direct imitators because of his tremendous feats of dexterity. But his stature as a virtuoso able to take his instrument into previously undreamed-of realms is without question. Though *Sailing the Seas of Cheese* tones down Primus' penchant for jamming, it's the tightest, most song-oriented representation of their jaw-dropping, one-of-a-kind style. *—Steve Huey*

Miscellaneous Debris / Mar. 12, 1992 / Interscope ✦✦✦✦

Pork Soda / Apr. 20, 1993 / Interscope ✦✦✦✦✦
Once audiences got a chance to hear Primus' instantly recognizable sound, driven by Les Claypool's bizarrely virtuosic bass riffs, their audience grew by leaps and bounds. It was enough to make their second major-label album, *Pork Soda*, one of the strangest records ever to debut in the Top Ten. Stylistically, it isn't much different from *Sailing the Seas of Cheese*, though the band does stretch out and jam more often. This can result in some overly repetitive sections, since Claypool's riffs are the basis for most of the compositions, but it also showcases the band's ever-increasing level of musicianship. Their ensemble interplay continues to grow in complexity and musicality, and that's really what fans want from a Primus record anyway. The material isn't quite as consistent as *Seas of Cheese*, though there are numerous high points; among them are "My Name Is Mud," on which Claypool plays his instrument like percussion, and "Mr. Krinkle," where he switches to a bowed upright bass. There are hints of lyrical darkness stripped of the band's usual goofiness (especially in the suicide lament "Bob"), but for the most part, the humor is again split between eccentric character sketches, cheery paranoia, and annoying novelties (with a slightly higher percentage of the latter than before). Still, despite occasional flaws, what makes *Pork Soda* a success is that the band keeps finding novel variations on their signature sound, even if they never step out of it. *—Steve Huey*

Tales from the Punch Bowl / May 23, 1995 / Interscope ✦✦✦

The Brown Album / Jul. 8, 1997 / Interscope ✦✦✦✦

Rhinoplasty / Jul. 28, 1998 / Interscope ✦✦✦

Antipop / Oct. 19, 1999 / Interscope ✦✦✦✦

Prince (Prince Rogers Nelson)

b. Jun. 7, 1958, Minneapolis, MN
Vocals, Keyboards, Guitar (Electric), Drums, Guitar, Bass / College Rock, Album Rock, Neo-Psychedelia, Club/Dance, Pop/Rock, Hard Rock, Urban, Funk, Dance-Pop, Soul
Prince is one of the singular talents of the rock era. Not only did he release a series of groundbreaking albums, he toured frequently, produced albums and wrote songs for other artists, he recorded hundreds of songs that remain unreleased. Occasionally, his music is maddeningly inconsistent, but none of his peers were as dazzlingly diverse and musically rich.

After releasing two albums of solid funk-pop in the late '70s, Prince came into his own with 1980's *Dirty Mind*, a one-man *tour de force*, bursting with hard funk, catchy Beatlesque melodies, sweet soul ballads, and rocking guitar-pop. *1999* launched Prince into the mainstream in 1982, thanks to singles like "Little Red Corvette," setting the stage for 1984's *Purple Rain*. Recorded with The Revolution, the record made Prince a superstar, spending 24 weeks at number one and selling over ten million copies. With 1985's *Around the World in a Day*, he veered off into bizarre psycho-psychedelia and the next year, he released the even stranger *Parade;* for all their quirks, both were Top 10 hits. Prince delivered a sprawling masterpiece with 1987's double-album *Sign O' the Times*, then entered a period of uncertainty. He scrapped plans to release the hard funk *The Black Album* late in 1987, releasing the confused *Lovesexy* instead in 1988; it was his first flop. His soundtrack to 1989's *Batman* went to number one, but it owed its success to the Tim Burton blockbuster. Prince reasserted his mastery of contemporary R&B with 1991's *Diamonds and Pearls*, resulting in his biggest hit since 1985. His twelfth album was titled with a cryptic symbol; in 1993, Prince changed his name to that symbol in an effort to free himself from his Warner contract. Throughout the mid-'90s, his battle with Warner received more attention than his music. He finally freed himself from Warner in 1996, releasing the triple-album set *Emancipation* at the end of the year. Though it received considerable media attention, it didn't sell well, nor did its successors. He signed a one-album deal with Arista in 1999, releasing a self-styled comeback effort, *Rave Un2 the Joy Fantastic*, which failed to capture its desired mass audience. *— Stephen Thomas Erlewine*

For You / Oct. 1978 / Warner Brothers ✦✦

Prince / Oct. 1979 / Warner Brothers ✦✦✦

☆ **Dirty Mind** / Oct. 1980 / Warner Brothers ✦✦✦✦✦
Neither *For You* or *Prince* was adequate preparation for the full-blown masterpiece of Prince's third album, *Dirty Mind*. Recorded in his home studio, with Prince playing nearly every instrument, *Dirty Mind* is a stunning, audacious amalgam of funk, new wave pop, urban R&B, and pop, fueled by grinningly salacious sex and the desire to shock. Where other pop musicians suggested sex in lewd double entendres, Prince left nothing to hide—before its release, no other rock or funk record was ever quite as explicit as *Dirty Mind*, with its gleeful tales of oral sex, threesomes, and even incest. Certainly, it opened the doors for countless sexually explicit albums, but to reduce its impact to mere profanity is too reductive—the music of *Dirty Mind* is as shocking as its graphic language, bending styles and breaking rules with little regard for fixed genres. Basing the album on a harder, rock-oriented beat than before, Prince tries everything—there's pure new wave pop ("When You Were Mine"), soulful crooning ("Gotta Broken Heart Again"), robotic funk ("Dirty Mind"), rock & roll ("Sister"), sultry funk ("Head," "Do It All Night"), and relentless dance jams ("Uptown," "Partyup"), all in the space of half an hour. It's a breathtaking, visionary album, and its fusion of synthesizers, rock rhythms, and funk set the style for much of the urban soul and funk of the early '80s. *— Stephen Thomas Erlewine*

Controversy / Nov. 1981 / Warner Brothers ✦✦✦
Controversy continues in the same vein of new wave-tinged funk on *Dirty Mind*, emphasizing Prince's fascination with synthesizers and synthesizing disparate pop music genres. It is also more ambitious than its predecessor, attempting to tackle social protest ("Controversy," "Ronnie, Talk to Russia," "Annie Christian") along with sex songs ("Jack U Off," "Sexuality"), and it tries hard to bring funk to a rock audience and vice versa. Even with all of Prince's ambitions, the music on *Controversy* doesn't represent a significant breakthrough from *Dirty Mind*, and it is often considerably less catchy and memorable. Nevertheless, Prince's talents as musician make the record enjoyable, even if it isn't as compelling as most of his catalog. *— Stephen Thomas Erlewine*

☆ **1999** / Feb. 1983 / Warner Brothers ✦✦✦✦✦
With *Dirty Mind*, Prince had established a wild fusion of funk, rock, new wave, and soul that signaled he was an original, maverick talent, but it failed to win him a large audience. After delivering the sound-alike album *Controversy*, Prince revamped his sound and delivered the double-album *1999*. Where his earlier albums had been a fusion of organic and electronic sounds, *1999* was constructed almost entirely on synthesizers by Prince himself. Naturally, the effect was slightly more mechanical and robotic than his previous work and strongly recalled the electro-funk experiments of several underground funk and hip-hop artists at the time. Prince had also constructed an album dominated by computer funk, but he didn't simply rely on the extended instrumental grooves to carry the album—he didn't have to when his songwriting was improving by leaps and bounds. The first side of the record contained all of the hit singles, and, unsurprisingly, they were the ones that contained the least amount of electronics. "1999" parties to the apocalypse with a P-funk groove much tighter than anything George Clinton ever did, "Little Red Corvette" is pure pop, and "Delirious" takes rockabilly riffs into the computer age. After that opening salvo, all the rules go out the window—"Let's Pretend We're Married" is a salacious extended lust letter, "Free" is a elegiac anthem, "All the Critics Love U in New York" is a vicious attack at hipsters, and "Lady Cab Driver," with its notorious bridge, is the culmination of all of his sexual fantasies. Sure, Prince stretches out a bit too much over the course of *1999*, but the result is a stunning display of raw talent, not wallowing indulgence. *— Stephen Thomas Erlewine*

★ **Purple Rain** / Aug. 6, 1984 / Warner Brothers ✦✦✦✦✦
Prince designed *Purple Rain* as the project that would make him a superstar, and, surprisingly, that is exactly what happened. Simultaneously more focused and ambitious than any of his previous records, *Purple Rain* finds Prince consolidating his funk and R&B roots while moving boldly into pop, rock, and heavy metal with nine superbly crafted songs. Even its best-known songs don't tread conventional territory: the bass-less "When Doves Cry" is an eerie, spare neo-psychedelic masterpiece; "Let's Go Crazy" is a furious blend of metallic guitars, Stonesy riffs, and a hard funk backbeat; the anthemic title track is a majestic ballad filled with brilliant guitar flourishes. Although Prince's songwriting is at a peak, the presence of the Revolution pulls the music into sharper focus, giving it a tougher, more aggressive edge. And, with the guidance of Wendy and Lisa, Prince pushed heavily into psychedelia, adding swirling strings to the dreamy "Take Me With U" and the hard rock of "Baby I'm a Star." Even with all of his new, but uncompromising, forays into pop, Prince hasn't abandoned funk, and the robotic jam of "Computer Blue" and the menacing grind of "Darling Nikki" are among his finest songs. Taken together, all of the stylistic experiments add up to a stunning statement of purpose that remains one of the most exciting rock & roll albums ever recorded. *— Stephen Thomas Erlewine*

Around the World in a Day / 1985 / Paisley Park ✦✦✦
Purple Rain made Prince sound like he could do anything, but it still didn't prepare even his most fervent fans for the insular psychedelia of *Around the World in a Day*. Prince had made his interior world sound fascinating and utopian on *Purple Rain*, but *Around the World in a Day* is filled with cryptic religious imagery, bizarre mysticism, and confounding metaphors, which were drenched in heavily processed guitars, shimmering keyboards, grandiose strings, and layers of vocals. As an album, the record is a bit impenetrable, requiring great demands of the listener, but individual songs do shine through: "Raspberry Beret" is a brilliant piece of neo-psychedelia with an indelible chorus, "Pop Life" is snide swipe at stardom that emphasizes Prince's outsider status, "Condition of the Heart" is a fine ballad, "America" is a good funk jam, "Paisley Park" is heavy and slightly frightening guitar psychedelia, while the title track is a sunny, kaleidoscopic pastiche of *Magical Mystery Tour*. The problem is, only a handful of the songs have much substance outside of their detailed production and intoxicating performances, and the album has a creepy sense of paranoia that is eventually its undoing. *— Stephen Thomas Erlewine*

Parade (Music from the Motion Picture "Under the Cherry Moon") / May 19, 1986 / Paisley Park ✦✦✦✦✦
Undaunted by the criticism *Around the World in a Day* received, Prince continued to pursue his psychedelic inclinations on *Parade*, which also functioned as the soundtrack to his second film, *Under the Cherry Moon*. Originally conceived as a double album, *Parade* has the sprawling feel of a double record, even if it clocks in around 45 minutes. Prince and the Revolution shift musical moods and textures from song to song—witness how the fluttering psychedelia of "Christopher Tracy's Parade" gives way to the spare, jazzy funk of "New Position," which morphs into the druggy "I Wonder U"—and they're determined not to play it safe, even on the hard funk of "Girls and Boys" and "Mountains," as well as the stunning "Kiss," which hits hard with just a dry guitar, keyboard, drum machine, and layered vocals. All of the group's musical adventures, even the cabaret-pop of "Venus de Milo" and "Do U Lie—," do nothing to undercut the melodicism of the record, and the amount of ground they cover in 12 songs is truly remarkable. Even with all of its attributes, *Parade* is a little off-balance, stopping too quickly to give the haunting closer, "Sometimes It Snows in April," the resonance it needs. For some tastes, it may also be a bit too lyrically cryptic, but Prince's weird religious and sexual metaphors develop into a motif that actually gives the album weight. If it had been expanded to a double album, *Parade* would have equaled the subsequent *Sign O' the Times*, but as it stands, it's an astonishingly rewarding near-miss. *— Stephen Thomas Erlewine*

The Black Album / 1987 / Paisley Park ✦✦✦
Originally scheduled for release in November of 1987—following the double-album *Sign O' the Times* by a matter of months—Prince pulled *The Black Album* weeks before its release, guaranteeing it near-mythic status. Urban legends spread like wildfire: Prince believed it was too bleak to release; Warner Brothers balked at its explicit lyrics; no CDs were ever pressed, and all the LPs were destroyed. That final rumor was certainly untrue, since bootlegs immediately appeared, and when it finally received official release in the fall of 1994, nearly every die-hard fan already had the record. That limited-edition release of *The Black Album* turned out to be a bit anti-climatic, since the album itself isn't a lost masterwork—it's fun, but not much more. If anything, it's a little labored, as Prince works hard to win back the black audience he willfully abandoned after *Purple Rain*. So, he serves up "When 2 R in Love," an urban ballad every bit as nondescript as the genre, and offers "Dead on It," trying to one-up rappers with a mocking attack that winds up as one of the lamest things he ever waxed. The rest of the eight-song album is brilliant pure funk, ranging from the unrelenting "Le Grind," a deliriously lustful plea to supermodel Cindy Crawford, the hyper-tense James Brown workout "2 Nigs United 4 West Compton" to "Bob George," a perverse tale of a macho lunk-head (Prince, electronically affecting a deep, idiotic drawl) who discovers his lady just slept with Prince—or "that skinny motherfucker with a high voice," as Bob calls him. All this may not add up to a lost classic, but it is a terrific little record that still delights, even after its mystique has faded. *— Stephen Thomas Erlewine*

☆ **Sign O' the Times** / Mar. 31, 1987 / Paisley Park ✦✦✦✦✦
Fearless, eclectic, and defiantly messy, Prince's *Sign O' the Times* falls into the tradition of tremendous, chaotic double albums like *The Beatles*, *Exile on Main St.*, and *London Calling*—albums that are fantastic because of their over-reach, their great sprawl. Prince shows nearly all of his cards here, from bare-bones electro-funk and smooth soul to pseudo-psychedelic pop and crunching hard rock, touching on gospel, blues, and folk along the way. This was the first album Prince recorded without the Revolution since 1982's *1999* (the band does appear on the in-concert rave-up, "It's Gonna Be a Beautiful Night"), and he sounds liberating, diving into territory merely suggested on *Around the World in a Day* and *Parade*. While the music overflows with generous spirit, these are among the most cryptic, insular songs he's ever written. Many songs are leftover from the aborted triple album *Crystal Ball* and the abandoned Camille project, a Prince alter-ego personified by scarily sped-up tapes on "If I Was Your Girlfriend," the most disarming and bleak psycho-sexual song Prince ever wrote, as well as the equally chilling "Strange Relationship." These fraying relationships echo in the social chaos Prince writes about throughout the album. Apocalyptic imagery of drugs, bombs, empty sex, abandoned babies and mothers, and AIDS pop up again and again, yet he balances the despair with hope, whether it's God, love, or just having a good time. In its own roundabout way, *Sign O' the Times* is the sound of the late '80s—it's the sound of the good times collapsing and how all that doubt and fear can be ignored if you just dance those problems away. *— Stephen Thomas Erlewine*

Lovesexy / Feb. 1988 / Paisley Park ✦✦✦
It's nearly impossible to judge *Lovesexy* as anything but a hastily assembled substitute for the withdrawn *Black Album*, which does the record a disservice. An exactingly sequenced song cycle—the compact disc didn't have index markings to separate the individual tracks—*Lovesexy* is quite a different record than not only *The Black Album*, but anything else Prince had recorded. Where *Dirty Mind* was single-minded in its lust, *Lovesexy* connects the carnal with spiritual, and the calmness of the music reflects this outlook. Even when the record dips into hard funk, such as on the title track or the single "Alphabet Street," there's a relaxed, casual quality to the music that is shocking after the dense paranoia of *Parade*, *Sign O' the Times*, and *Black Album*. Prince intends to enter a new phase of maturity with such considered music and ambitious lyrical themes, but neither his music nor his lyrics are consistently well-stated over the course of the album. A handful of tracks are worthwhile—the sappy ballad "When 2 R in Love," the moving "I Wish U Heaven," the weird psychedelia of "Anna Stesia" and "Glam Slam," as well as the wonderful "Alphabet Street"—but it is his weakest album since *Controversy*. *— Stephen Thomas Erlewine*

Batman / Jun. 1989 / Paisley Park ♦♦♦

Graffiti Bridge / Aug. 21, 1990 / Paisley Park ♦♦♦

Diamonds and Pearls / Oct. 1991 / Paisley Park ♦♦♦
Prince spent the latter half of the '80s courting the pop audience, and by the time of *Graffiti Bridge,* he had lost much of his R&B fan base. As a response, he formed the New Power Generation and recorded *Diamonds and Pearls,* his first record to reconnect with the urban audience since *1999,* as well as his first to acknowledge the hip-hop revolution. Although he still has a problem with rap—"Jughead" is simply embarassing—he manages to skillfully reinvent himself as an urban soulman without sacrificing his musical innovation. The New Power Generation is a more skilled band than the Revolution, and they are able to make Prince's funk jazzier, particluarly on "Willing and Able," the breezy "Strollin'" and "Walk Don't Walk." It's clear that these subtly textured songs are where his heart is at, but the songs designed to win back his audience—the slamming dance-floor rallying cry "Gett Off," the sexy T. Rex groove "Cream," the extraordinary Philly soul of the neglected masterpiece "Money Don't Matter 2 Night" and the drippy mainstream ballad "Diamonds and Pearls"—are all terrific pop singles. However, much of the rest of *Diamonds and Pearls* is comprised of middling funk and R&B that sounds less like inspired workouts than stylistic exercises. Even with such weak moments, *Diamonds and Pearls* is a fine record, even though it's only marginally better than *Lovesexy* and *Graffiti Bridge.* —*Stephen Thomas Erlewine*

The Love Symbol Album / Oct. 13, 1992 / Paisley Park ♦♦♦♦♦
The New Power Generation is the most talented and versatile band Prince has ever fronted, and they fulfill their potential on *Symbol.* Although the NPG factored heavily on *Diamonds and Pearls,* it still sounded like a solo Prince album. *Symbol* sounds like a band performing together, working off of each other's strengths and weaknesses. Opening with the dance smash "My Name Is Prince" and the deep funk of "Sexy M.F.," *Symbol* has Prince's best dance tracks since the *Black Album.* But Prince wasn't content; he decided to run the gamut of modern pop/R&B/dance, and the music is uniformly accomplished and excellent. Unfortunately, he also decided to make a "rock soap opera," so the music is saddled with ridiculous lyrics and annoying sound bridges by Kirstie Alley. However, *Symbol* has some of the finest, most inventive music of Prince's career. —*Stephen Thomas Erlewine*

☆ **The Hits 1** / Sep. 14, 1993 / Paisley Park ♦♦♦♦♦
The primary fault with Prince's two-part *Hits* collection is that both volumes are missing some important singles and are sequenced incoherently, thereby failing to give an accurate impression of his astonishing musical growth. However, they do contain enough necessary items to illustrate why he was one of the most influential and gifted musicians of the '80s, as well as providing a reasonable introduction and compilation for casual fans. *Hits 1* contains a good cross-section of his biggest hits—"When Doves Cry" (presented in an edited version), "When You Were Mine," "Let's Go Crazy," "1999," "Sign O' the Times," "Alphabet Street," "Diamonds and Pearls," "7"—plus new items like "Pink Cashmere" and "Nothing Compares 2 U" (a Prince song that Sinead O'Connor took to number one) which are nearly as good as the familiar tracks. However, it provides an incomplete portrait, making *Hits 2* a necessary purchase. —*Stephen Thomas Erlewine*

☆ **The Hits 2** / Sep. 14, 1993 / Paisley Park ♦♦♦♦♦
Like *Hits 1, Hits 2* presents an illogically sequenced cross-section of some of Prince's biggest hits and most notorious songs, including "Dirty Mind," "I Wanna Be Your Lover," "Head," "Delirious," "Little Red Corvette," "I Would Die 4 U," "Raspberry Beret," "Kiss," "U Got the Look," "Cream," and "Purple Rain." Two new tracks, "Peach" and "The Pope," are included among the 18 cuts and while they don't match the rest of the songs (or the new cuts on *Hits 1*), they are nevertheless enjoyable. On the whole, *Hits 2* is a slightly stronger collection than its predecessor, but it still gives a rather incomplete portrait—if you buy *Hits 2,* you need to buy *Hits 1.* —*Stephen Thomas Erlewine*

The Hits/The B-Sides / Sep. 14, 1993 / Paisley Park ♦♦♦♦♦

Come / Aug. 16, 1994 / Paisley Park ♦♦

Gold Experience / Oct. 1995 / Warner Brothers/NPG ♦♦♦♦

Chaos & Disorder / Jul. 1996 / Warner Brothers ♦♦♦

Emancipation / Nov. 19, 1996 / NPG/EMI ♦♦♦♦

Crystal Ball / Mar. 3, 1998 / NPG ♦♦♦

New Power Soul / Jun. 30, 1998 / New Power Generation ♦♦

The Vault: Old Friends 4 Sale / Aug. 24, 1999 / Warner Brothers ♦♦♦

Rave Un2 the Joy Fantastic / Nov. 2, 1999 / NPG/Arista ♦♦♦

John Prine

b. Oct. 10, 1946, Maywood, IL
Vocals, Guitar / Progressive Folk, Contemporary Folk, Singer/Songwriter
An acclaimed singer/songwriter whose literate work flirted with everything from acoustic folk to rockabilly to straight-ahead country, John Prine became a fixture on the Chicago folk music scene in the late 1960s before his compositions caught the ear of Kris Kristofferson, who was instrumental in helping him win a recording contract. In 1971, he released his eponymously-titled debut album; though not a commercial success, songs like "Sam Stone," the harsh tale of a drug-addled Vietnam veteran, won critical approval. Neither 1972's *Diamonds in the Rough* nor 1973's *Sweet Revenge* fared any better on the charts, but Prine's work won great renown among his fellow performers, with covers from the Everly Brothers, Bette Midler and Joan Baez. For 1975's *Common Sense,* Prine turned to producer Steve Cropper, the highly-influential house guitarist for the Stax label; while the album's sound shocked the folk community with its reliance on husky vocals and booming drums, it served notice that Prine was not an artist whose work could be pigeonholed, and was his only LP to reach the U.S. Top 100. Under his own Oh Boy imprint, Prine's music thrived, as 1986's country-flavored *German Afternoons* earned a Grammy nomination; 1991's Grammy-winning *The Missing Years* was his most successful outing to date, featuring guest appearances from Bruce Springsteen, Bonnie Raitt and Tom Petty. —*Jason Ankeny*

☆ **John Prine** / 1971 / Atlantic ♦♦♦♦♦
A revelation upon its release, this album is now a collection of standards: "Illegal Smile," "Hello in There," "Sam Stone," "Donald and Lydia," and, of course, "Angel from Montgomery." Prine's music, a mixture of folk, rock, and country, is deceptively simple, like his pointed lyrics, and his easy vocal style adds a humorous edge that makes otherwise funny jokes downright hilarious. —*William Ruhlmann*

Diamonds in the Rough / 1972 / Atlantic ♦♦♦
John Prine's second album was a cut below his first, only because the debut was a classic and the followup was merely terrific. "Sour Grapes" showed Prine's cracked sense of humor and "Souvenirs" his sentiment. Even if it was the second rank of his writing, *Diamonds In The Rough* demonstrated that Prine had an enduring talent that wasn't exhausted by one great album. —*William Ruhlmann*

Sweet Revenge / 1973 / Atlantic ♦♦♦♦♦
A bold and brilliant stab at (almost) straight country, it tempers Prine's cynical streak with the tone of a jaded humorist and social commentator. —*John Floyd*

Common Sense / 1975 / Atlantic ♦♦♦
A brash album, it's full of aggressive rock rhythms and morose tunes. Even the Chuck Berry cover, "You Never Can Tell," is shot full of melancholy. —*John Floyd*

Prime Prine / 1976 / Atlantic ♦♦♦♦♦
Atlantic Records' compilation of John Prine's first four albums was good for its time (and became his only gold record) but has been superseded by Rhino's *Great Days* anthology. —*William Ruhlmann*

Bruised Orange / 1978 / Asylum ♦♦♦♦♦
Despite some brilliant songs, Prine's followup albums to his stunning debut were uneven until this, his fifth, produced by his friend Steve Goodman. Here, Prine's always finely-tuned sense of absurdity once again collides with his ability to depict pain sympathetically for a whole album, typified by "That's the Way That the World Goes 'Round," a neat statement of his philosophy, and "Sabu Visits the Twin Cities Alone," perhaps the best depiction ever written of life on the road in the entertainment business. —*William Ruhlmann*

Pink Cadillac / 1979 / Oh Boy ♦♦♦
John Prine went to Sam Phillips's studio in Memphis to make his sixth album, *Pink Cadillac,* and got some of the Sun Records sound of 1950s rockabilly on a record produced by Phillips's sons Knox and Jerry. (Sam produced two of the tracks himself.) Slap-back bass here, a Bo Diddley beat there, and an overall loose feel characterized music that may have been more fun to make than it is to listen to, even though it's quite entertaining. Prine wrote only five of the ten songs, however, and even though the covers were of high caliber—notably Roly Salley's "Killing the Blues" and Arthur Gunter's "Baby Let's Play House," a song Elvis Presley did at Sun—*Pink Cadillac* was a good idea that went slightly awry in the execution. If Prine had had the songs as well as the studio, it would have been among his best. —*William Ruhlmann*

Storm Windows / 1980 / Oh Boy ♦♦♦
A relaxed effort, it's defined by straightforward love songs and subdued vocals. Modest but quite nice. —*John Floyd*

Aimless Love / 1984 / Oh Boy ♦♦♦

German Afternoons / 1986 / Oh Boy ♦♦♦

Live / 1988 / Oh Boy ♦♦♦♦
With years of experience playing club dates, John Prine has evolved into a very entertaining live performer, and this album, originally a double-LP and now a single CD, presents him at his intimate best, telling funny stories and performing his most impressive material in unadorned arrangements. —*William Ruhlmann*

The Missing Years / Sep. 1991 / Oh Boy ♦♦♦♦♦
Prine took five years between his ninth studio album and this, his tenth—enough time to gather his strongest body of material in more than a decade. From the caustic "All the Best" to the cliche compilation "It's a Big Old Goofy World," Prine's gifts for emotional revelation and off-the-wall humor are on display in abundance, and he's aided by excellent production (courtesy of Heartbreaker Howie Epstein) and strong backup musicians. *The Missing Years* won the 1991 Grammy Award for Best Contemporary Folk Album. —*William Ruhlmann*

★ **The Great Days: John Prine Anthology** / Aug. 17, 1993 / Rhino ♦♦♦♦♦
Prine's career has been rich but scattered, and *Great Days* gathers together almost all of his finest moments, providing a comprehensive introduction to one of the best songwriters of the past twenty years. —*Stephen Thomas Erlewine*

John Prine Christmas / 1994 / Oh Boy ♦♦♦

Lost Dogs and Mixed Blessings / Apr. 4, 1995 / Oh Boy ♦♦♦
John Prine's followup to his comeback album, *The Missing Years,* is more of the same in terms of freeing up Prine's idiosyncratic muse and marrying the result to Howie Epstein's top-flight production sound. Fans of the early Prine may find that sound overproduced, but the songs never get lost, and with Prine's typically humorous, off-center view of the world (song titles include "Humidity Built the Snowman" and "He Forgot That It Was Sunday"), it's the songs that count. Actually, this is not quite as strong a collection of material as *The Missing Years,* but it has its moments, and Prine and Epstein show it off in its best possible light. —*William Ruhlmann*

Live on Tour / Apr. 8, 1997 / Oh Boy ♦♦♦

Lucky 13 / Nov. 10, 1998 / Oh Boy ♦♦♦

In Spite of Ourselves / Sep. 14, 1999 / Oh Boy ♦♦♦♦♦

Souvenirs / Oct. 31, 2000 / Oh Boy ♦♦♦

Procol Harum

f. 1967, London, England
Group / British Psychedelia, Psychedelic, Prog-Rock/Art Rock
Procol Harum is arguably the most successful "accidental" group creation—that is, a band originally assembled to take advantage of the success of a record created in the studio—in the history of progressive rock. With "A Whiter Shade of Pale" a monster hit right out of the box, the band evolved from a studio ensemble into a successful live act, their music built around an eclectic mix of blues-based rock riffs and grand classical themes. With singer/pianist Gary Brooker and lyricist Keith Reid providing the band's entire repertory, their music evolved in decidedly linear fashion, the only major surprises coming from the periodic line-up changes that added a new instrumental voice to the proceedings. At their most accessible, as on "Whiter Shade of Pale" and "Conquistador," they were one of the most popular of progressive rock bands, their singles outselling all rivals, and their most ambitious album tracks still have a strong following. *—Bruce Eder*

Procul Harum / 1967 / Deram ✦✦✦✦✦

Shine on Brightly / 1968 / Repertoire ✦✦✦✦
After the multi-million selling "A Whiter Shade Of Pale", Procol Harum coalesced around a new line-up and cut a debut album in two days, the sales of which (because the hit song wasn't on it originally) were only fair, and a couple of new singles also failed to sell. Then they did *Shine On Brightly,* which initially drew on recordings going back to late 1967—in the course of preparing their first proper LP, the band junked an entire side of blues-based numbers in favor of the 18 minute suite "In Held 'Twas I", which rivaled anything yet heard from such established progressive rock outfits as the Nice or the Moody Blues in length and surpassed them in audacity, with an extensive spoken part surrounded by virtuoso classical and psychedelic passages (and even a featured spot for Dave Knights' bass). It all proved that they were more than a one-hit wonder and, released in late 1968, the album extended the definition of progressive rock, even as it kept much of the music rooted in established rock genres. "Skip Softly", for all of its grand piano pyrotechnics, was also a showcase for Robin Trower's bluesy, high-energy guitar attack, and "Wish Me Well" was an even better vehicle for his instrument, while "Magdalene (My Regal Zonophone)" was an interesting exercise in nostalgia highlighted by Matthew Fisher's organ. *—Bruce Eder*

A Salty Dog / Mar. 1969 / A&M ✦✦✦✦✦
This album, the group's third, was where they showed just how far their talents extended across the musical landscape, from blues to R&B to classical-rock. In contrast to their hastily recorded debut, or its successor, done to stretch their performance and composition range, *A Salty Dog* was recorded in a reasonable amount of time, giving the band a chance to fully develop their ideas. The title track is one of the finest songs ever to come from Procol Harum and one of the best pieces of progressive rock ever heard, and a very succinct example at that at under five minutes' running time—the lyric and the music combine to form a perfect mood piece, and the performance is bold and subtle at once, in the playing and the singing, respectively. The range of sounds on the rest includes "Juicy John Pink," a superb piece of pre-World War II-style country blues, while "Crucifiction Lane" is a killer Otis Redding-style soul piece, and "Pilgrim's Progress" is a virtuoso keyboard workout. *A Salty Dog* was reissued by Repertoire Records in 1997 with enhanced sound and the lost B-side "Long Gone Geek," a Robin Trower guitar workout par excellence. *—Bruce Eder*

Home / 1970 / Repertoire ✦✦✦✦

The Best of Procol Harum / 1973 / A&M ✦✦✦✦✦

Exotic Birds & Fruit / 1974 / Essential ✦✦✦

● **Greatest Hits** / May 7, 1996 / A&M ✦✦✦✦✦
Procul Harum's 1996 collection *Greatest Hits* features the same songs and sequencing as 1987's *Classics, Vol. 17,* except the music has been remastered. For most ears, the remastering isn't particularly noticeable, so if you already own *Classics, Greatest Hits* is completely unnecessary, yet the collection remains an adequate introduction for casual fans. *—Stephen Thomas Erlewine*

30th Anniversary Anthology / Nov. 17, 1997 / Westside ✦✦✦✦✦
The best collection yet devoted to Procol Harum's classic early period ties together the many facets of their sound and their early history, including numerous outtakes and all of the music on four albums from 1967 through 1970. The clarity of the sound makes the first album—which was roundly criticized, especially in England, for having been cut in mono in late 1967—seem a lot more muscular and progressive here than it did in its original release form. The producers have tampered with the song order on *A Salty Dog,* moving that record's title track in amongst Disc Three's single sides for time considerations while still leaving "Whiter Shade of Pale" and "Homburg" off of the first CD (the original commercial flaw with the debut album in England was the absence of either of those songs, and the seven-month-plus delay in getting it out). From the psychedelic/progressive blues stylings of *Shine On Brightly* to the self-consciously leaner, harder *Home,* this is the optimum way to hear the band. The collection also documents the change from somewhat light, optimistic psychedelia in 1967/68 to the darker, edgier psychedelia of 1970 and beyond. The best part for collectors will be Disc Three, which, in addition to the group's hit singles and surprisingly fascinating B-sides from 1967-70, also includes outtakes from unfinished early album sessions and alternate takes (with different personnel) of "Whiter Shade of Pale," "Homburg," etc., some in stereo. The notes are reasonably thorough, although they skimp a little in telling the story of the recording of "Whiter Shade of Pale" and the subsequent assembling of the permanent band. *—Bruce Eder*

The Prodigy

f. 1990, Braintree, Essex, England
Group / Big Beat, Electronica, Rave, Club/Dance, Techno
Prodigy navigated the high-wire balancing artistic merit and mainstream visibility with more flair than any electronica act of the 1990s. Ably defeating the image-unconscious attitude of most electronic artists in favor of a focus on nominal frontman Keith Flint, the group crossed over to the mainstream of pop music with an incendiary live experience that approximated the original atmosphere of the British rave scene even while leaning uncomfortably close to arena-rock showmanship and punk theatrics. True, Flint's spiky hairstyle and numerous piercings often made for better advertising, but it was producer Liam Howlett whose studio wizardry launched Prodigy to the top of the charts, spinning a web of hard-hitting breakbeat techno with king-sized hooks and unmissable samples. Despite electronic music's diversity and quick progression during the 1990s—from rave/hardcore to ambient/downtempo and back again, thanks to the breakbeat/drum'n'bass movement—Howlett modified Prodigy's sound only sparingly; swapping the rave-whistle effects and ragga samples for metal chords and chanted vocals proved the only major difference in the band's evolution from their 1991 debut to their worldwide breakthrough with third album *The Fat of the Land.* Even before the band took its place as the premiere dance act for the alternative masses, Prodigy had proved a consistent entry in the British charts, with over a dozen consecutive singles in the Top 20. *—John Bush*

☆ **Experience** / Oct. 20, 1992 / Elektra ✦✦✦✦✦
One of the few non-compilation rave albums of any worth, *Experience* balances a supply of top-this siren whistles and chipmunk divas with Howlett's surprising flair at constructing track after track of intense breakbeat techno. Almost every song sounds like a potential chart-topper (circa 1992, of course) while the true singles "Your Love," "Charly," "Music Reach 1/2/3/4" and "Out of Space" add that extra bit of energy to the fray. More than just a relic of the rave experience, *Experience* shows the Prodigy near the peak of their game from the get-go. *—John Bush*

Music for the Jilted Generation / Feb. 28, 1995 / Mute ✦✦✦✦✦
The Prodigy's response to the sweeping legislation and crackdown on raves contained in 1994's Criminal Justice Bill is an effective statement of intent. Pure sonic terrorism, *Music for the Jilted Generation* employs the same rave energy that charged their debut *Experience* up the charts in Britain, but yokes it to a cause other than massive drug intake. Compared to their previous work, the sound is grubbier and less reliant on samples; the effect moved Prodigy away from the American-influenced rave and acid-house of the past and toward a uniquely British vision of breakbeat techno that was increasingly allied to the limey invention, drum'n'bass. As on *Experience,* there are so many great songs here that first-time listeners would be forgiven for thinking of a greatest-hits compilation instead of a proper studio album. After a short intro, the shattering of panes of glass on "Break & Enter" catapults the album ahead with a propulsive flair. Each of the four singles—"Voodoo People," "Poison," "No Good (Start the Dance)," and "One Love"—are excellent, though album tracks like "Speedway" and "Their Law" (with help from Pop Will Eat Itself) don't slip up either. If *Experience* seemed like an excellent fluke, *Music for the Jilted Generation* was the album that announced Prodigy was on the charts to stay. *—John Bush*

● **The Fat of the Land** / Jul. 1, 1997 / XL Mute/Maverick/Warner Bros. ✦✦✦✦✦
Few albums were as eagerly anticipated as *The Fat of the Land,* the Prodigy's long-awaited follow-up to *Music for the Jilted Generation.* By the time of its release, the group had two number one British singles with "Firestarter" and "Breathe," and had begun to make inroads in America. *The Fat of the Land* was touted as the album that would bring electronica/techno to a wide American audience; in Britain, the group already had a staggeringly large following that was breathlessly awaiting the album. *The Fat of the Land* falls short of masterpiece status, but that isn't because it doesn't deliver. Instead, it delivers exactly what anyone would expect: intense hip-hop-derived rhythms, imaginatively reconstructed samples, and meaningless shouted lyrics from Keith Flint and Maxim. Half of the album does sound quite similar to "Firestarter," especially when Flint is singing. Still, Howlett is an inventive producer, and he can make empty songs like "Smack My Bitch Up" and "Serial Thrilla" kick with a visceral power, but he is at his best on the funky hip-hop of "Diesel Power" (which is driven by an excellent Kool Keith rap) and "Funky Shit," as well as the mind-bending neo-psychedelia of "Narayan" (featuring guest vocals by Crispian Mills of Kula Shaker) and the blood-curdling cover of L7's "Fuel My Fire," which features vocals by Republica's Saffron. All those guest vocalists mean something—Howlett is at his best when he's writing for himself or others, not his group's own vocalists. "Firestarter" and all of its rewrites capture the fire of the Prodigy at its peak, and the remaining songs have imagination that give the album weight. *The Fat of the Land* doesn't have quite enough depth or variety to qualify as a flat-out masterpiece, but what it does have to offer is damn good. *—Stephen Thomas Erlewine*

The Dirtchamber Sessions, Vol. 1 / Apr. 6, 1999 / XL/Beggars Banquet ✦✦✦✦

The Psychedelic Furs

f. 1977, London, England, **db.** 1991
Group / College Rock, Post-Punk, New Wave, Alternative Pop/Rock
The Psychedelic Furs, whose name belies their punk-influenced music, were formed in England in 1977 by brothers Richard Butler (vocals) and Tim Butler (bass), along with saxophone player Duncan Kilburn and guitarist Roger Morris. Their self-titled 1980 debut album, featuring Butler's hoarse voice (the tone of which suggested John Lydon without the sneer) was a bigger hit in England, where it reached the Top 20, than in the U.S. *Talk Talk Talk* (1981) did better, reaching the U.S. Top 100 and producing two British singles-chart entries, one of which was "Pretty in Pink," later also a hit in the U.S. when a new version was used as the title song of a film. Turning to producer Todd Rundgren, the Furs scored a U.S. Top 50 hit with "Love My Way." *Mirror Moves* (1984) was the biggest Psychedelic Furs hit yet, and the film *Pretty in Pink* helped spread their name further before the release of their next album, *Midnight to Midnight* (1986), which consequently got to #12 in the U.K. and the Top 30 in the US and included the Top 30 U.S. hit "Heartbreak Beat." After *World Outside* (1991) failed to find an audience, the Psychedelic Furs folded up shop, and Richard Butler launched a new group, Love Spit Love. *—William Ruhlmann*

The Psychedelic Furs / 1980 / Columbia ✦✦✦✦✦
Emerging from the incipient post-punk London scene with a healthy fascination for late-'70s Bowie (and in turn, for his own attraction to Krautrock), the then-sextet kicked up a slightly monochromatic but still attractive storm on their debut. Richard Butler's Thin-White-Duke-after-smoking vocal rasp has a surprising appeal, serving up a wry, slightly detached series of lyrics on life. The core band, meanwhile, had clearly honed their chops well on stage; Ashton's lead guitar work avoids both wankery and simplicity in favor of a balanced, artistic power. Production mainly comes from Steve Lillywhite, who smartly steers away from the soon-to-be-clichéd touches he would bring to U2's early work. "India" is a good example; it has a brooding, quiet beginning with strange telegraphic signals and turns into a brawling rocker without sounding like the Edge or Larry Mullins going off. The record comes off as serious without being self-consciously deep, occasional toe-dipping into humor aside ("We Love You" has Butler idly listing off things he loves, sometimes with appropriate if sarcastically delivered song quotes: "I'm in love with Frank Sinatra... fly me to the moon..."). "Imitation of Christ" is the most frazzled, with lyrics detailing someone else metaphorically nailing himself up over a light but still strange guitar line. "Wedding Song" is amusingly prescient as one of the first "white rockers go hip-hop" numbers of its kind, along with Blondie's "Rapture," though its inspiration could equally be dub. Ely lays down a pounding funk beat while Butler breaks into a mid-song rap no better or worse than most such efforts of the time. *—Ned Raggett*

Talk Talk Talk / Jun. 1981 / Columbia ✦✦✦✦✦
This time working solely with Steve Lillywhite, the Furs introduce a brighter, poppier side to their underground rock edge, with smashing results throughout. The group produces some powerful songs, even more rough-edged than before. Especially striking is "Dumb Waiters," with its queasy, slow-paced arrangement that allows both Kilburn's sax and Ashton's guitar to go wild. However, the six still create some undeniable pop classics. Most well-known is the lead track, "Pretty in Pink," inspiration for the iconic John Hughes film years later and re-recorded as a result. The original is still where to go though, with Butler's catchy description of a romantically unsure woman matched by a killer band performance. Similarly lighter numbers on the record call to mind a rockier version of Roxy Music's output in later years: elegant, romantic angst given a slightly rougher edge in both music and vocals. "She Is Mine" is especially fine as a gently swinging number with some of Butler's best, quietly ruminative lyrics. Straight-up anthems abound as well, the best being the amazing "Into You Like a Train," which mixes the blunt desire of the title with a sparkling Ashton guitar line and a fast rhythm punch. *Talk Talk Talk* ends on another high with "All of This and Nothing." A soft, acoustic guitar-sax-rhythm combination introduces the song, then fades away for the main section to begin; Butler details bits and pieces from a lost relationship over a sharp full-band performance, and a final drum smash leads into a reprise of the start—a fine way to end a fine record. *—Ned Raggett*

Forever Now / 1982 / Columbia ✦✦✦

Mirror Moves / 1984 / Columbia ✦✦✦

Midnight to Midnight / 1987 / Columbia ✦✦✦

● **All of This and Nothing** / 1988 / Columbia ✦✦✦✦✦
Not a perfect Furs compilation, but this 12-track look back does contain the notable tracks from the albums *Mirror Moves* and *Midnight to Midnight*, plus some of the necessary ones from the albums listed above and a good new song, "All That Money Wants." *—William Ruhlmann*

Book of Days / Oct. 1989 / Columbia ✦✦

World Outside / Jul. 30, 1991 / Columbia ✦✦✦

B-Sides & Lost Grooves / Oct. 25, 1994 / Columbia/Legacy ✦✦✦

Should God Forget: A Retrospective / Oct. 21, 1997 / Columbia/Legacy ✦✦✦
The double-disc set *Should God Forget: A Retrospective* may be a little bit too much for casual fans who only want the hit singles—after all, this is filled with B-sides, live tracks, rarities and a handful of outtakes—but for hardcore fans, this is a definitive collection, containing the majority of the group's best work. It also may convince skeptics that the group found one of the best fusions of the Sex Pistols, Roxy Music and David Bowie, inventing a stylish but menacing post-punk style that sounded like nothing else in the new wave era. *—Stephen Thomas Erlewine*

Greatest Hits / Jan. 30, 2001 / Columbia/Legacy ✦✦✦✦

Public Image Ltd.

f. 1978, London, England, **db.** 1993
Group / College Rock, Noise-Rock, Alternative Dance, Post-Punk, Alternative Pop/Rock
Public Image Ltd. (PiL) originally was a quartet led by singer John Lydon (formerly Johnny Rotten) and guitarist Keith Levene, who had been a member of the Clash in one of its early lineups. It was formed in the wake of the 1978 breakup of Lydon's former group, the Sex Pistols. For the most part, it devoted itself to droning, slow-tempo, bass-heavy noise rock, overlaid by Lydon's distinctive, vituperative rant. The group's debut single, "Public Image," was more of an uptempo pop/rock song, however, and it hit the U.K. Top Ten upon its release in October 1978. *Metal Box*, the band's second U.K. album, came in the form of three 12-inch, 45 RPM discs in a film cannister. It was released in the U.S. in 1980 as the double album *Second Edition*. In 1983, PiL scored its biggest U.K. hit, when "This Is Not a Love Song" reached number five. By this time, however, Levene had left, and the name from here on would be, more than anything else, a vehicle for John Lydon. *This Is What You Want... This Is What You Get* marked the start of Lydon's move toward a more accessible dance-rock style, a direction that would be pursued further in *Album* (1986) (also called *Cassette* or *Compact Disc*, depending on the format), notably on the hit "Rise." After completing his memoirs in late 1993, Lydon decided to put an end to PiL and pursue a solo career. *—William Ruhlmann*

Public Image/First Issue / Dec. 1978 / Warner Brothers ✦✦✦✦

★ **Second Edition** / Jul. 1980 / Warner Brothers ✦✦✦✦✦
PiL managed to avoid boundaries for the first four years of their existence, and *Metal Box* is undoubtedly the apex. It's a hallmark of uncompromising, challenging post-punk, hardly sounding like anything of the past, present, or future. Sure, there were touchstones that got their imaginations running—the bizarreness of Captain Beefheart, the open and rhythmic spaces of Can, and the dense pulses of Lee Perry's productions fueled their creative fires—but what they achieved with their second record is a completely unique hour of avant garde noise.

Originally packaged in a film canister as a trio of 12" records played at 45 RPMs, the bass and treble are pegged at 11 throughout, with nary a tinge of mid-range to be found. It's all scrapes and throbs (dubscrapes—), supplanted by John Lydon's caterwauling about such subjects as his dying mother, resentment and murder. Guitarist Keith Levene splatters silvery, violent, percussive shards of metallic scrapes onto the canvas, much like a one-armed Jackson Pollock. Jah Wobble and Martin Atkins lay down a molasses-thick rhythmic foundation throughout that's just as funky as Can's Czukay/Leibezeit and Chic's Edwards/Thompson. It's alien dance music.

Metal Box might not be recognized as a ground-breaking record with the same reverence as *Never Mind the Bollocks*, and you certainly can't trace numerous waves of bands who wouldn't have existed without it like the Sex Pistols record. But like a virus, it's tones have sent miasmic reverberations through a much broader scope of artists and genres.

[*Metal Box* was issued in the States in 1980 with different artwork and cheaper packaging under the title *Second Edition;* the track sequence differs as well. The UK reissue of *Metal Box* on CD boasts better sound quality than the *Second Edition* CD.] *—Andy Kellman*

The Flowers of Romance / 1981 / Warner Brothers ✦✦✦✦
As opposed to the axis of throbbing bass and guitar slashings of *Metal Box, The Flowers of Romance* is centralized on razor-sharp drums and typically haranguing vocals. No dubwise grooves here—bassist Jah Wobble was kicked out prior to the recording for ripping off PiL backing tracks for his solo material. And growing more disenchanted with the guitar, Keith Levene's infatuation with synthesizers was reaching a boiling point. His scythe-like guitar is truly brought out for only one song. Stark and minimal are taken to daring lengths, so it's no surprise that Virgin initially balked at issuing the heavily percussive record.

"Four Enclosed Walls" opens with something of a mechanical death rattle and John Lydon's quavering warble, framed by backwards piano and Martin Atkins' spartan, dry-as-a-bone drumming. His rapier-like drums seem to serve a similar purpose to Levene's guitar on *Metal Box*. An unsteady drum pattern and fragile, wind chime-like guitar from Levene shape "Track 8," a bleak look at sexual relationships. Lydon adds color with pleasant imagery of Butterball turkeys and elephant graves. "Under the House" and "Francis Massacre" are the most violent tracks due to Atkins' machine gun firing and Levene's chilling atmosperics. Lydon lashes out at zealous fans on the only bottom-heavy tune, "Banging the Door": "The walls are so thin/ The neighbors listen in/ Keep the noise down."

Perhaps the band's most challenging work (in the avant garde sense), it's just as "love it or hate it" as *Metal Box;* it'll either go down a treat or like a five pound block of liverwurst. [The UK version adds three bonus tracks: an instrumental version of "The Flowers of Romance," "Another," (essentially "Graveyard" with vocals) and "Home Is Where the Heart Is." The latter two can be found on *Plastic Box*.] *—Andy Kellman*

This Is What You Want ... This Is What You Get / 1984 / Virgin ✦✦

Album/Compact Disc/Cassette / 1986 / Elektra ✦✦✦
After the release of *This Is What You Want,* Lydon assembled yet another touring band. Martin Atkins stayed on, with Jebin Bruni and Mark Schulz joining the band's ranks. While gigging, Bruni and Schulz assisted in writing the material that wound up on *Album*. Atkins left to spend more time on his own projects after touring, and Lydon again scrapped his associates prior to recording. Anyone's first thousand guesses as to who Lydon would work with next couldn't possibly come close, as the unlisted credits for *Album* read as a motley crew of established musicians who literally have no business being anywhere near Lydon, let alone in a studio with him or with one another. Well, maybe that made perfect sense, given Lydon's ability to baffle. Bill Laswell produced and played bass, which isn't too much of a stretch. But Steve Vai, Ryuichi Sakamoto and Ginger Baker— Baker's involvement is especially odd since PiL played an April Fools' joke on the press by announcing his membership in the early '80s.

"Rise" successfully marries rock with Celtic folk (a heavier Dexy's Midnight Runners—); Lydon's chorus is his most hospitable yet. Opener "FFF" and "Home" are other strong points, driving and defiant.. The former is as good as hard rock got in 1985. But *Album* can be found lacking in its reliance on outright professionalism and polish, emphasizing skill over craft. Vai's scorched shredding likely repelled Lydon's fans more than any of PiL's earlier attempts to alienate and frustrate. The 90-second wailing over closer "Ease" is anything but; at most points, Vai's playing just doesn't fit. Unfortunately, Yellow Magic Orchestra member Sakamoto pops up only a couple times. His talent is pretty much wasted here. On the whole, *Album* is just as generic as its title. *—Andy Kellman*

Happy— / 1987 / Virgin ✦✦✦

9 / 1989 / Virgin ✦✦✦

● **The Greatest Hits, So Far** / 1990 / Virgin ✦✦✦✦
The Greatest Hits, So Far mines the singles PiL released through 1990. Ten years after its release, it was doubtful that a second volume would surface (the '90s saw one lone studio release, not to mention a John Lydon "solo" record), so thankfully Lydon didn't embarrass himself by titling it "The Greatest Hits, Volume One." That said, not many outfits under the guise of one name can boast a collection of singles so diverse and ranging in quality. And really, the title should be "The Singles, So Far." By attempting to hit upon all the studio releases, bright moments like "Bad Baby," "Banging the Door," and "The Order of Death" get left behind. The distance between 1979's "Death Disco" and 1990's "Don't Ask Me" would be impossible to traverse with the trustiest of vehicles. The back cover of the disc depicts Stonehenge and an earthbound spacecraft, with a howling dog in the middle. That's accurate. With peers mutating from the Pop Group ("Careering") to Information Society ("Warrior"), PiL

couldn't possibly expect to concoct a compilation that would appeal to all ears. In that regard, *GHSF* is more of a Denny's sampler than a thematic banquet spread. (To clarify: "Rules and Regulations" is a cheese stick, not tasty bean pâté.) Whether or not this is a proper first place to go for PiL is up for debate, as it takes a *very* eclectic head to thrill to both their early discordance and later chart-targeted tunefulness. It's not going to provide a solid idea of where they stood at any point in their existence, but it's just enough to pique further investigation. *—Andy Kellman*

That What Is Not / 1992 / Virgin ✦✦

Plastic Box / Jun. 8, 1999 / Virgin ✦✦✦✦
Most who own *Plastic Box* probably use the second half as coasters. Those who don't probably get headaches when listening to the first two, and a select few find much to love about the whole thing. As if conceding to the consensus that PiL's early years were their best, the first half is devoted to the band's first three studio LPs cut over four years, while the second half covers the remainder. Listeners get the entirety of *Public Image/First Edition sans* "Fodderstompf." The majority of *Metal Box* (issued as *Second Edition* in the U.S.) is included, with three of the original versions sacrificed for Peel Session counterparts that really take the cake. "Careering" is especially wonderful and harrowing, arguably the collective's finest recorded moment. Keith Levene goes bonkers with the keyboards, perhaps fostering the increased intensity amongst the remaining members. The 12" mix of "Swan Lake" ("Death Disco") gets the box set upgrade too, as well as a couple other worthwhile *Metal Box* outtakes. Closing out the second disc is the entirety of *The Flowers of Romance*, sequentially shuffled with an additional non-album track. The second half of *Plastic Box* hits upon each of the remaining studio LPs, with the odd rarity, single mix and Peel Session thrown in for completist bait. For those who want improved sound over their early CD issues, the money spent is a smart investment. A quick comparison of the first 20 seconds of "Annalisa" to the version found on an old copy of *Public Image* should be evidence enough; the bass line of "Chant" makes the gut feel as if it's being endlessly pummelled by a bouncing battering ram. Though vast and relatively pricey, *Plastic Box* is an excellent introduction, if only for the adventurous. *—Andy Kellman*

Pulp

f. 1978, Sheffield, Yorkshire, England
Group / Britpop, Post-Punk, Alternative Pop/Rock
Most bands hit the big time immediately and fade away, or they build a dedicated following and slowly climb their way to the top. Pulp didn't follow either route. For the first 12 years of their existence, Pulp languished in near total obscurity, releasing a handful of albums and singles in the '80s to barely any attention. At the turn of the decade, the group began to gain an audience, sparking a remarkable turn of events that made the band one of the most popular British groups of the '90s. By the time Pulp became famous, the band had gone through numerous different incarnations and changes in style, covering nearly every indie-rock touchstone from post-punk to dance. Pulp's signature sound is a fusion of David Bowie and Roxy Music's glam rock, disco, new wave, acid-house, Euro-pop, and British indie-rock. The group's cheap synthesizers and sweeping melodies reflect the lyrical obsessions of lead vocalist Jarvis Cocker, who alternates between sex and sharp, funny portraits of working class misfits. Out of second-hand pop, Pulp fashioned a distinctive, stylish sound that made camp into something grand and glamourous that retained a palpable sense of gritty reality. *—Stephen Thomas Erlewine*

It / 1983 / Velvel ✦✦

Freaks / 1986 / Velvel ✦✦

Separations / 1992 / Razor & Tie ✦✦✦

Pulpintro—*The Gift Recordings* */ 1993 / Island* ✦✦✦✦✦
All of the singles Pulp recorded for Gift Records, including both the A- and B-sides, are collected on *Pulpintro—The Gift Recordings*. From the opening track, "Space," it's clear that Pulp's confidence and talents have grown considerably, even from the relatively accomplished *Separations*. Now, the band has created a signature sound that relies heavily on cheap, synthesized sounds as well as tight pop melodies and a theatrical attack that approximates the art rock of Roxy Music and David Bowie. However, Pulp is too concerned with earthly pleasures to really recall Roxy or Bowie. Furthermore, the band's knack for creating terrific pop singles prevents them from being too pretentious, as the singles "O.U.," "Razzamatazz," and, particularly, "Babies" illustrate. And even though it's just a collection of singles, *Pulpintro* holds together as well as *Separations*, if not better. *—Stephen Thomas Erlewine*

Masters of the Universe / 1994 / Velvel ✦✦

His 'n' Hers / Jun. 21, 1994 / Island ✦✦✦✦✦
Jarvis Cocker's update on Bryan Ferry's lounge lizard persona works because recognizes the sleaziness beneath the style. Instead of chronicling the lives and times of jet-setting club-hoppers, Cocker sneaks into the closet of his girlfriend to watch her sister have sex, reveals a fetish for pink gloves among other things, and remembers the first time. Pulp's fake, synthetic backdrop sound like they were constructed on bargain Casio keyboards, adding an extra layer of seaminess to Cocker's songs. That sense of cheap, faux-glamor is essential to the success of *His N' Hers*, Pulp's commerical and artistic breakthrough. It's the sound of a poor man giving up everything he has so he can act out his expensive, elegant fantasies. He may never get there, but the approximation of glamor is more appealing and compelling than the reality, which is what gives *His N' Hers* a grand tragic romanticism. *—Stephen Thomas Erlewine*

● **Different Class** / Oct. 30, 1995 / Island ✦✦✦✦✦
After years of obscurity, Pulp shot to stardom in Britain with 1994's *His N' Hers*. By the time *Different Class* was released at the end of October 1995, the band, particularly lead singer Jarvis Cocker, were genuine British superstars, with two number two singles and a triumphant last-minute performance at Glastonbury under their belts, as well as one tabloid scandal. On the heels of such excitement, anticipation for *Different Class* ran high, and not only does it deliver, it blows away all their previous albums, including the fine *His N' Hers*. Pulp doesn't stray from their signature formula at all—it's still grandly theatrical, synth-spiked pop with new wave and disco flourishes, but they have mastered it here. Not only are the melodies and hooks significantly catchier and more immediate, the music explores more territory. From the faux-showtune romp of the anthemic opener "Mis-Shapes" and the glitzy, gaudy stomp of "Disco 2000" (complete with a nicked riff from Laura Branigan's "Gloria") to the aching ballad "Underwear" and the startling sexual menace of "I Spy," Pulp construct a diverse, appealing album around the same basic sound. Similarly, Jarvis Cocker's lyrics take two themes, sex and social class, and explore a number of different avenues in bitingly clever ways. As well as perfectly capturing the behavior of his characters, Cocker grasps the nuances of language, creating a dense portrait of suburban and working-class life. All of his sex songs are compassionate, while the subtle satire of "Sorted for E's & Wizz" is affectionate, but the best moment on the album is the hit single "Common People," about a rich girl who gets off by slumming with the lower class. Coming from Cocker, who made secondhand clothes and music glamourous, the song is undeniably affecting and exciting, much like *Different Class* itself. *—Stephen Thomas Erlewine*

Countdown 1992-1983 / Mar. 1996 / Velvel ✦✦✦✦
A double-disc collection released to cash in on Pulp's massive success with *Different Class*, *Countdown* might be a rip-off compilation, but it does offer an effective introduction to Pulp's '80s catalog. Since their recordings on Fire were decidedly uneven, *Countdown* does distill all the highlights a casual fan could want to hear. Beginning with the latest track, the 1990 single "Countdown," and working its way backwards, the compilation's sequencing eases newer fans into both the band's more experimental and folkier work. Even though all of Pulp's best material from this era is included, they lacked the pop sense that they developed in the early '90s, which could make this rough sailing for some recent fans. For those that want to dig deeper, there is plenty of fascinating material here. *—Stephen Thomas Erlewine*

This Is Hardcore / Mar. 31, 1998 / Island ✦✦✦✦
"This is the sound of someone losing the plot/you're gonna like it, but not a lot." So says Jarvis Cocker on "The Fear," the opening track on *This Is Hardcore*, the ambitious follow-up to Pulp's breakthrough *Different Class*, thereby providing his own review for the album. Cocker doesn't quite lose the plot on *This Is Hardcore*, but the ominous, claustrophobic "The Fear" makes it clear that this is a different band, one that no longer has anthems like "Common People" in mind. The shift in direction shouldn't come as a surprise—Pulp was always an arty band—but even the catchiest numbers are shrouded in darkness. *This Is Hardcore* is haunted by disappointments and fear—by the realization that what you dreamed of may not be what you really wanted. Nowhere is this better heard than on "This Is Hardcore," where drum loops, lounge piano, cinematic strings, and a sharp lyric create a frightening monument to weary decadence. It's the centerpiece of the album, and the best moments follow its tone. Some, like "The Fear," "Seductive Barry," and "Help the Aged," wear their fear on their sleeves, some cloak it in Bowie-esque dance grooves ("Party Hard") or in hushed, resigned tones ("Dishes"). A few others, such as the scathing "I'm a Man" or "A Little Soul," have a similar vibe without being explicitly dark. Instead of delivering an entirely bleak album, Pulp raises the curtain somewhat on the last three songs, but the attempts at redemption—"Sylvia," "Glory Days," "The Day After the Revolution"—don't feel as natural as everything that precede it. It's enough to keep the album from a masterpiece, but it's hardly enough to prevent it from being an artistic triumph. *—Stephen Thomas Erlewine*

On Fire / Dec. 1, 1999 / Recall ✦✦

Pure Prairie League

f. 1971, Cincinnati, OH, **db.** 1983
Group / Soft Rock, Country-Rock
For a short time, Pure Prairie League were one of America's best country-rock bands, but personnel shifts ultimately destroyed its early promise. The group was formed in 1971 by vocalists/guitarists Craig Lee Fuller (the band's main songwriter) and George Powell, steel guitarist John Call, bassist Jim Lanham, and drummer Jim Caughlin, and recorded their self-titled debut album just a year later. Its fusion of laid-back singer-songwriter-styled rock and country earned critical praise, but much of the group departed, leaving only Fuller, Powell, and several session musicians. Even so, *Bustin' Out* proved to be an unqualified success, featuring the innovative addition of string arrangements by David Bowie guitarist Mick Ronson. Unfortunately, Fuller left in 1975, leaving the group without a strong songwriter or leader. Powell carried on with guitarist Larry Goshorn, bassist Mike Reilly, and pianist Michael Connor for several albums, none of which were as commercially or artistically successful as *Bustin' Out*. The group did enjoy a brief resurgence in 1980 with the Top Ten single "Let Me Love You Tonight," featuring future country star Vince Gill on lead vocals, but finally called it quits in 1983. Fuller has since joined Little Feat. *—Steve Huey*

Bustin' Out / 1972 / RCA ✦✦✦✦✦

Pure Prairie League / 1972 / RCA ✦✦✦✦✦
For all those who think The Eagles are the be all and end all of country-rock, you owe it to yourself to search out this album. Any track here (or on the followup, *Bustin' Out*) holds up as well, if not better than, anything by The Eagles. This album also proves that Craig Fuller is a grossly underrated songwriter. A country-rock must! *—Jim Worbois*

Two Lane Highway / 1975 / RCA ✦✦✦

Amie & Other Hits / 1981 / RCA ✦✦✦✦
At eight tracks, this is really skimpy, but *Amie & Other Hits* nevertheless does offer a nice sampler of Pure Prairie League's RCA recordings. This does mean that their biggest hit, "Let Me Love You Tonight," is missing, along with anything else from their time at Casablanca, but this does give a basic overview of their earliest material, when they were led by the fine singer/songwriter Craig Fuller. *—Stephen Thomas Erlewine*

The Best of Pure Prairie League / Aug. 8, 1995 / Mercury Nashville ✦✦✦✦

● **Greatest Hits** / Sep. 28, 1999 / RCA ✦✦✦✦✦
RCA's 1999 compilation *Greatest Hits* is the definitive portrait of Pure Prairie League at their peak. Although it contains none of their Casablanca recordings, and therefore it's missing their biggest hit, "Let Me Love You Tonight," it does have a comprehensive chronicle of the group's first four albums, including their breakthrough hit "Aime," the non-LP "She Darked the Sun," and nearly all of their best album, *Bustin' Out*, albeit not in sequence. It would have been nice to have "Let Me Love You Tonight" added to this collection, but it's hard to argue with what's here, since it is the best of the best years of the Pure Prairie League. *—Stephen Thomas Erlewine*

Suzi Quatro

b. Jun. 3, 1950, Detroit, MI
Vocals, Bass / Glitter, Pop/Rock, Glam Rock, Hard Rock
It's pretty far-fetched, as some revisionists are now claiming, to view Suzi Quatro as a precursor to the "riot grrrls" of the '90s. Her brand of mid-'70s glam-pop was far more innocuous and, in any case, often supplied by professional songwriters. What she did prove was that it was possible for a petite woman to play bass, sing, and wear leather with a reasonable degree of raunch and pride. That, with enough musical hooks to draw in the teenage pop crowd, was enough to reel off a series of big British hit singles just before the advent of punk, although she remained virtually unknown in her native US. While playing in an all-girl Detroit band named Cradle, Quatro was spotted by British producer Mickie Most and encouraged to begin recording in London. Her second single "Can the Can" went to number one in the UK in 1973. In the US though, she could barely get into the Top 100, though she did somehow get on the cover of *Rolling Stone* during a slow month. Her American fortunes changed in the late '70s, when she had a short-lived semi-regular stint on the sitcom *Happy Days* as the guitar-playing, sassy Leather Tuscadero. In 1979, she made the American Top Five with "Stumblin' In," although this was a duet with Chris Norman. She's kept a low profile in the '80s and '90s, although she's done some television and theatrical work in Britain. *—Richie Unterberger*

● **The Wild One: Classic Quatro** / Apr. 1996 / Razor & Tie ✦✦✦✦✦
The definitive compilation—20 tracks, mostly from her mid-'70s prime, including all of her British and American hits and a few album tracks. *—Richie Unterberger*

Queen

f. 1971, London, England, **db.** 1995
Group / Album Rock, British Metal, Arena Rock, Pop/Rock, Glam Rock, Prog-Rock/Art Rock, Hard Rock
Few bands embodied the pure excess of the '70s like Queen. Embracing the exaggerated pomp of prog-rock and heavy metal, as well as vaudevellian music-hall, the British quartet delved deeply into camp and bombast, creating a huge, mock-operatic sound with layered guitars and overdubbed vocals. Queen's music was a bizarre yet highly accessible fusion of the macho and the fey. For years, their albums boasted the motto "no synthesizers were used on this record," signaling their allegiance with the legions of post-Led Zeppelin hard rock bands. But vocalist Freddie Mercury brought an extravagant sense of camp to the band, pushing them towards kitschy humor and pseudo-classical arrangements, as epitomized on their best-known song, "Bohemian Rhapsody." Mercury, it must be said, was a flamboyant homosexual, who managed to keep his sexuality in the closet until his death from AIDS in 1992. Nevertheless, his sexuality was apparent throughout Queen's music, from their very name to their veiled lyrics—it was truly bizarre to hear gay anthems like "We Are the Champions" turn into celebrations of sports victories. That would have been impossible without Mercury, one of the most dynamic and charismatic frontmen in rock history. Through his legendary theatrical performances, Queen became one of the most popular bands in the world in the mid-'70s; in England, they remained second only to the Beatles in popularity and collectibility in the '90s. Despite their enormous popularity, Queen were never taken seriously by rock critics—an infamous *Rolling Stone* review labeled their 1979 album *Jazz* as "fascist." In spite of such harsh criticism, the band's popularity rarely waned; even in the late '80s, the group retained a fanatical following except America. In the States, their popularity peaked in the early '80s, just as they finished nearly a decade's worth of extraordinarily popular records. And while those records were never praised, they sold in enormous numbers, and traces of Queen's music could be heard in several generations of hard rock and metal bands in the next two decades, from Metallica to Smashing Pumpkins. *—Stephen Thomas Erlewine*

Queen / Sep. 4, 1973 / Hollywood ✦✦✦
Although it may not be up to par with such future classics as *A Night at the Opera* and *The Game*, Queen's 1973 self-titled debut is one of the most underrated hard rock debuts of all time. Chances are that many will only be familiar with one song (the classic rock radio staple "Keep Yourself Alive"), but it is a very consistent and solid album; even the more uncommon compositions are impressive and memorable. Unlike other notable hard rock debuts of the '60s/'70s (Led Zeppelin, Van Halen, Kiss, etc.), Queen's first album was not recorded quickly, but over the course of a year or two, since the band had to record during the studio's off-hours to minimize costs. Even so, the album does retain continuity, a perfect balance of anthems (the aforementioned "Keep Yourself Alive"), gorgeous ballads ("The Night Comes Down," "Doing All Right"), and raging heavy metal ("Liar," "Great King Rat," "Son & Daughter"). All of the band's future musical trademarks can be detected here as well—Brian May's sweeping guitar orchestras (several different guitars overdubbed to create harmonies), Freddie Mercury's vocal acrobatics, and the solid rhythm section of drummer Roger Taylor and bassist John Deacon (listed as Deacon John in the credits here). At the time, many critics dismissed the band and the debut (unfairly classifying Queen as "disposable glam"), but in hindsight, Queen laid down the groundwork for this legendary band's future triumphs. *—Greg Prato*

Queen II / Apr. 9, 1974 / Hollywood ✦✦✦
Queen's second album, 1974's *Queen II*, is their heaviest and also darkest release. Upset by the lashing the critics bestowed upon their underrated self-titled debut a year earlier (and its underachieving chart performance), the band were determined to hit the big time with their second try. And succeed they did—the album reached number five on the U.K. charts, while its breakthrough single, "Seven Seas of Rhye," reached number ten. The band also created a buzz stateside by opening a tour for Mott the Hoople, and in return received FM radio support. The first side of the record was titled the "white" side, while the second was the "black" side; still, both include an equal amount of rockers and ballads. Opening with the lush guitar orchestration of Brian May's "Procession," the album kicks into high gear with one of Queen's most underrated tracks, the haunting "Father to Son." Like the debut, the album switches from style to style throughout ballads ("White Queen," "Nevermore"), pop ("Some Day One Day"), heavy metal ("Ogre Battle," "Seven Seas of Rhye"), and mutated prog-rock ("The March of the Black Queen," "The Fairy Feller's Master-Stroke"). A stellar release that has only improved over the years, *Queen II* also proved to be an influential album for future musicians—*Smashing Pumpkins' Billy Corgan considers it an all-time personal favorite.* —Greg Prato

Sheer Heart Attack / Nov. 12, 1974 / Hollywood ✦✦✦✦✦
Queen's second album of 1974 (and third overall), *Sheer Heart Attack*, helped bridge the gap between the mystical heavy metal of their early years and the hard rock/pop perfection of future releases. The main reason why Queen issued another album so soon after *Queen II* (only eight months apart) was due to guitarist Brian May's hepatitis, which had forced the band off their touring schedule. Instead of waiting, Freddie Mercury and Co. used their time wisely and worked diligently on their third record. The result was what many fans consider Queen's first true classic, featuring their U.S. breakthrough single "Killer Queen" (which almost reached the top of the charts in England), and the radio/concert favorite "Now I'm Here." Also included is a song that Metallica would later cover (and win a Grammy Award for), "Stone Cold Crazy," as well as the impressive opening guitar showcase, "Brighton Rock." Besides including the expected ballads ("Dear Friends," "Lily of the Valley") and hard rock ("Flick of the Wrist," "Tenement Funster"), Queen takes on musical styles previously unexplored by hard rock bands—uplifting sounds from the Caribbean ("Misfire") and a ragtime ditty ("Bring Back That Leroy Brown"). Closing with the epic composition "In the Lap of the Gods... Revisited" (the set-closer on the ensuing tour), *Sheer Heart Attack* captured Queen's first true U.S. success. But their next album would make them a worldwide phenomenon. [Note: There has been some confusion over the years concerning the album *Sheer Heart Attack* and the song of the same name. The album was released in 1974, while the song appeared on 1977's *News of the World*.] *—Greg Prato*

★ **A Night at the Opera** / Dec. 2, 1975 / Hollywood ✦✦✦✦✦
Queen was straining at the boundaries of hard rock and heavy metal on *Sheer Heart Attack*, but they broke down all the barricades on *A Night at the Opera*, a self-consciously ridiculous and overblown hard rock masterpiece. Using the multi-layered guitars of its predecessor as a foundation, *A Night at the Opera* encompasses metal ("Death on Two Legs," "Sweet Lady"), pop (the lovely, shimmering "You're My Best Friend"), campy British music-hall ("Lazing on a Sunday Afternoon," "Seaside Rendezvous") and mystical prog-rock ("'39," "The Prophet's Song"), eventually bringing it all together on the pseudo-operatic "Bohemian Rhapsody." In short, it's a lot like Queen's own version of *Led Zeppelin IV*, but where Zep finds dark menace in their bombast, Queen celebrates its own pomposity. No one in the band takes anything too seriously, otherwise the arrangements wouldn't be as ludicrously exaggerated as they are. But the appeal—and the influence—of *A Night at the Opera* is in its detailed, meticulous productions. It's prog-rock with a sense of humor as well as dynamics, and Queen never bettered their approach anywhere else. *—Stephen Thomas Erlewine*

A Day at the Races / Dec. 18, 1976 / Hollywood ✦✦✦
There was no way that Queen could top their 1975 masterpiece *A Night at the Opera* and its epic single "Bohemian Rhapsody," so they did the next best thing—they recorded a companion album, 1976's *A Day at the Races*. Although not as meticulously detailed or all-encompassing as its brilliant predecessor, *A Day at the Races* showed that the band was shedding their five-minute-plus epics in favor of more succinct songs, and becoming one of the world's top rock bands in the process. The album's centerpiece is undoubtedly the hit single "Somebody to Love"—whereas "Bohemian Rhapsody" had its roots in opera, "Somebody" was centered in gospel sounds (and features a surprisingly authentic-sounding gospel choir, using only the band members' voices!). Queen also tackled their first serious political statement with "White Man" (which details the plight of the American Indian), but also showed their fun side with such tracks as "The Millionaire Waltz," "Good Old Fashioned Lover Boy," and the rocking concert standard "Tie Your Mother Down." Also included is the album closer "Teo Torriatte," a hauntingly beautiful ballad that includes both English and Japanese lyrics. *A Day at the Races* proved to Queen's detractors that they hadn't run out of steam with the colossal *A Night at the Opera*. *—Greg Prato*

News of the World / Nov. 1, 1977 / Hollywood ✦✦✦
By 1977, Queen had perfected and succeeded at several different musical styles—heavy metal, glam, progressive, pop, ballads, and forays into genres not usually associated with hard rock (opera and gospel). By their next release, the band had progressed toward arena rock, and *News of the World* contained two of rock's best and most renowned all-time anthems, "We Will Rock You" and "We Are the Champions" (worldwide Top Ten hits). Punk rock was in full force by 1977, and Queen was among the elite bands being criticized by the punks. Instead of ignoring it, the band issued their answer to punk with the amphetamine-fueled "Sheer Heart Attack." *News of the World* bears some resemblance to 1974's *Queen II* due to their darkness—the tracks "All Dead, All Dead," "Spread Your Wings," and "My Melancholy Blues" smack the listener with cold, hard reality. But not all of the tracks are so serious, such as the fun salsa sounds of "Who Needs You," the epic Zep-rock of "It's Late," the groovy blues jam "Sleeping On the Sidewalk," the tasty funk of "Fight From the Inside," and the robotic, overtly sexual "Get Down, Make Love" (later covered by Nine Inch Nails). Their third blockbuster release in a row, *News of the World*, solidified Queen's status as global stadium headliners. *—Greg Prato*

Jazz / Nov. 14, 1978 / Hollywood ✦✦✦✦
Jazz has been unfairly slagged in some quarters as an inconsistent and unfocused record;

granted, there's a bit of filler cluttering the second half, but as for the latter criticism, it's not like *A Night at the Opera* wasn't all over the map. The fact that it didn't produce any huge hit singles in the U.S. probably hasn't helped its reputation, but given half a chance, *Jazz* emerges as one of Queen's most playful, manically entertaining records. There are a few Freddie Mercury piano ballads and unusually hopped-up metallic rockers, but about half of *Jazz* is given over to quirky lyrics and/or stylistic detours (which, oddly enough, don't include any jazz, unless you count the music hall swing of "Dreamers Ball"). Kicking off with the pseudo-Middle Eastern kitsch of "Mustapha," *Jazz's* first half is its strongest, highlighted by the double-A-sided single "Fat Bottomed Girls"/"Bicycle Race"; the former is a hilariously macho boogie that finds Mercury posing as Sir Mix-A-Lot's spiritual forebear, and the latter's childlike enthusiasm masks a subtle double entendre and an indirect reference to the all-female nude bicycle race the band staged as a promotional stunt (a poster of which was included). The second half climaxes with the, er, flamboyant U.K. Top Ten hit "Don't Stop Me Now," a Broadway showstopper at heart; it's preceded by the disco-rock of "Fun It" and the almost pastoral ballad "Leaving Home Ain't Easy," among others. It's difficult to discuss *Jazz* without referring to individual tracks one by one, since it can come off as a collection of moments, but its anything-goes diversity actually helps tie it together. Plus, there's a giddy sense of fun through most of the album, which helps make it Queen's strongest since *A Night at the Opera*. *—Steve Huey*

The Game / Jun. 30, 1980 / Hollywood ✦✦✦✦✦

Along with 1975's *A Night At the Opera*, Queen's 1980 chart-topper *The Game* is one of their best and most commercially successful records. But *The Game* was the polar opposite of *Opera*, composition-wise. Whereas their 1975 classic was completely over-the-top and bombastic (it included "Bohemian Rhapsody," after all), *The Game* was full of succinct songs that included their trademark hard rock and ballads, as well as styles previously unexplored by the band—funk, disco, rockabilly, and new wave. The album's success is obviously linked to its pair of worldwide number one singles, the Elvis Presley tribute "Crazy Little Thing Called Love" and the contagious disco anthem "Another One Bites the Dust." Other highlights included the British hits "Play the Game" and "Save Me" (the latter being one of Queen's best ballads), the funk-rocker "Dragon Attack," the tuneful "Need Your Love Tonight" and "Sail Away Sweet Sister," plus the modern sounds of "Don't Try Suicide" and "Coming Soon." Although Queen would remain superstars throughout the rest of the world, *The Game* proved to be the band's last true hit studio album in the U.S. *—Greg Prato*

Flash Gordon / Jan. 27, 1981 / Hollywood ✦✦

Hot Space / May 25, 1982 / Hollywood ✦✦✦

By taking the better part of 1981 off to work on the follow-up to their big 1980 hit *The Game*, Queen fans were confident that the band's next release would follow in their winning tradition of classic albums. Unfortunately, this would not be the case. Unlike its predecessor, *Hot Space* was an inconsistent effort, marred by unfocused songwriting and material that was simply not as strong as their earlier work. Since they had just previously enjoyed a massive hit with the discofied "Another One Bites the Dust," Queen decided to dedicate the entire first side of the album to dance music, something that alienated their longtime rock fans. And while the single "Body Language" nearly cracked the U.S. Top Ten, the rest of the dance material was easily forgettable—"Back Chat," "Staying Power," "Action This Day," etc. However, the album was not a total washout. The more rock-oriented second side did contain some great tracks, such as "Put Out the Fire," "Calling All Girls," "Las Palabras De Amor," and the David Bowie collaboration "Under Pressure." But it was not enough to save *Hot Space* from a cruel critical and commercial fate, as its ensuing world tour marked the last time Queen would perform in the U.S. *—Greg Prato*

The Works / Feb. 28, 1984 / Hollywood ✦✦

Live Magic / 1986 / Hollywood ✦✦✦

A Kind of Magic / Jun. 3, 1986 / Hollywood ✦✦

The Miracle / Jun. 6, 1989 / Hollywood ✦✦

Innuendo / Feb. 5, 1991 / Hollywood ✦✦✦

Classic Queen / Mar. 10, 1992 / Hollywood ✦✦✦✦✦

Essentially, this 17-track album is a second-volume Queen's *Greatest Hits*, picking up the story from that album's 1981 release and taking it to the end of Queen's career. But the album also contains a few tracks—"Bohemian Rhapsody," "Keep Yourself Alive," and "Under Pressure"—that appeared on that first set, as well as a couple—"Stone Cold Crazy" and "Tie Your Mother Down"—from the same era. The remaining 12 tracks, culled from *The Works*, *A Kind of Magic*, *The Miracle*, and *Innuendo*, represent songs that were not big hits in the U.S. Nevertheless, with a resurgence of interest in Queen and the second coming of "Bohemian Rhapsody," courtesy of *Wayne's World*, this album returned Queen to platinum status and the U.S. Top 5 for the first time since the early '80s. *—William Ruhlmann*

★ **Greatest Hits** / Sep. 15, 1992 / Hollywood ✦✦✦✦✦

This is going to take a little explaining. In 1981, when it was contracted to Elektra Records in the U.S., Queen released an album called *Greatest Hits* (Elektra 564), which contained 14 songs that chronicled singles from 1973 to 1981. In 1990, Hollywood Records acquired CD rights to Queen's catalog, by which time the Elektra *Greatest Hits* had gone out of print on vinyl. Hollywood released *Classic Queen*, a compilation that covered Queen's hits from 1982 to its demise in 1991, with a few older songs thrown in. Then it released this album, its version of *Greatest Hits*, which is a 17-track album that deletes the songs from the first *Greatest Hits* that appeared on *Classic Queen* (among them Queen's biggest hit, "Bohemian Rhapsody") and adds a few tracks from the 1973-1982 era that did not appear on the original release. The Elektra *Greatest Hits* LP had a superior selection, but it's gone now, so you're stuck with this. (New fans don't seem to have minded, as this new *Greatest Hits* sold better than the first one.) *—William Ruhlmann*

Greatest Hits, Vols. 1-2 / 1995 / Hollywood ✦✦✦✦✦

Queen's greatest hits collections have contained different tracklistings throughout the world. In the band's native England they scored more hits than anywhere else, hence their compilations are usually more extensive. When Hollywood Records purchased the U.S. Queen catalogue in the early '90s, they reissued the long-out-of-print *Greatest Hits* album (basing the tracklisting on the 1981 British album of the same name but with a few changes), and released a companion album entitled *Classic Queen*. The rest of the world received *Greatest Hits II* in 1991, which contained their U.K. hits from 1981-1991(*Classic Queen* contained tracks by the band from all eras). Sensing that Queen completists in the U.S. would want both British-only releases for their collection, Hollywood released the 2-CD *Greatest Hits I & II* in 1995. Most of the tracks are available on the U.S. versions, but *Greatest Hits II* is the only compilation that includes such tracks as "Innuendo," "Breakthru," "It's a Hard Life," "The Invisible Man," and "Friends Will Be Friends." The set also comes with a special 40-page booklet. *—Greg Prato*

At the BBC / Mar. 7, 1995 / Hollywood ✦✦✦

Made in Heaven / Nov. 7, 1995 / Hollywood ✦✦

Greatest Hits, Vol. 3 / Nov. 9, 1999 / Hollywood ✦✦✦

Queensryche

f. 1981, Bellevue, WA

Group / Album Rock, Progressive Metal, Heavy Metal

Although they were initially grouped in with the legions of pop/metal bands that dominated the American heavy metal scene of the '80s, Queensryche were one of the most distinctive bands of the era. Where their contemporaries built on the legacy of Van Halen, Aerosmith and Kiss, Queensryche constructed a progressive form of heavy metal that drew equally from the guitar pyrotechnics of post-Van Halen metal and '70s art-rock, most notably Pink Floyd and Queen. After releasing a handful of ignored albums, the band began to break into the mainstream with the acclaimed 1988 album, *Operation: Mindcrime*. Its follow-up, *Empire*, was the group's biggest success, selling over two million copies due to the hit single, "Silent Lucidity." Queensryche never sustained that wide-spread popularity—like most late-'80s metal bands, their audience disappeared after the emergence of grunge. Nevetheless, they retained a large cult following well into the '90s. *—Stephen Thomas Erlewine*

Queensryche / 1983 / EMI America ✦✦✦

The Warning / Sep. 7, 1984 / EMI America ✦✦✦

Rage for Order / Jul. 1986 / EMI America ✦✦

Operation: Mindcrime / Apr. 27, 1988 / EMI America ✦✦✦✦✦

Queensrÿche scored their breakthrough success with the ambitious concept album *Operation: Mindcrime*, which tells the story of a fortune hunter whose disillusionment with Reagan-era American society leads him to join a shadowy plot to assassinate corrupt leaders. For such a detailed storyline (there is also a tragic romance thrown in), the band keeps its focus remarkably well, and the music is just as ambitious, featuring a ten-minute track with orchestrations by Michael Kamen. Those experiments don't tend to work as well as the tighter, more melodic prog-metal songs, which are frequently gems, especially the singles "Eyes of a Stranger" and "I Don't Believe In Love." Granted, the lyrics and political observations can sometimes be too serious and intellectual for their own good (few bands, metal or otherwise, can make lines like "There's no *raison d'être*" work). But despite the occasional flaws, it's surprising how well *Operation: Mindcrime does* work, and it's a testament to Queensrÿche's creativity and talent that they can pull off a project of this magnitude. *—Steve Huey*

● **Empire** / Aug. 1990 / EMI America ✦✦✦✦✦

One of the most praised metal albums of the late 1980s, *Operation: Mindcrime* was an extremely tough act to follow. But while *Empire* isn't quite on a par with that gem, it is certainly one of the most absorbing headbanger efforts of 1990. Highly conceptual and anything but redundant, *Empire* demonstrates beautifully just how imaginative Queensryche can be. If anyone has bridged the gap between the bombast of Iron Maiden and the artsiness of Pink Floyd, it is Queensryche. But as much as one may be reminded of Floyd's *The Wall* on pieces like "Anybody Listening—," "Silent Lucidity" and "Resistance," *Empire* leaves no doubt that Queensryche has a rich personality all its own. *—Alex Henderson*

Promised Land / Oct. 18, 1994 / EMI America ✦✦✦

Hear in the Now Frontier / Mar. 25, 1997 / Capitol ✦✦✦

Q2k / Sep. 14, 1999 / Atlantic ✦✦✦

Greatest Hits / Jun. 27, 2000 / Virgin ✦✦✦✦✦

? & the Mysterians

f. 1962

Group / Detroit Rock, Frat Rock, Garage Rock

Originally formed in Flint, MI, in 1962, this group took its name from the obscure science-fiction movie *The Mysterians*. They recorded the anthemic "96 Tears" for the local Spanish music label Pa-Go-Go in 1966. It was immediately picked up for national consumption by Cameo-Parkway, going on to be one of the most covered garage band classics of the '60s. Lead singer Question Mark (real name listed as both Rudy Martinez and Reeto Rodriguez) continues to front a version of the band on oldies package shows across the U.S. *—Cub Koda*

● **96 Tears** / 1966 / Cameo ✦✦✦✦✦

● **Original Recordings** / 1995 / Campark ✦✦✦✦✦

This is probably an unauthorized compilation, with 30 of the group's original '60s recordings, including, of course, "96 Tears." Since the owners of the original tracks have obstinately refused to officially reissue the Mysterians' '60s catalog on CD in the U.S., they really have no cause to complain if frustrated collectors turn to this anthology as the only reasonable option. The sound quality is good, although the brief liner notes unfortunately do not detail the specific origin of each cut. Even with so much vintage work in one place, it is still striking how much better"96 Tears" was than anything else they did. Garageheads might be disappointed with how many of the cuts sound like lesser, similar "96 Tears" derivations, all heavy on the cheap organ sound and Rudy Martinez's quasi-studly vocals. For "Do You Feel It," they rip off someone other than themselves, as it's a retitled cover of the Rolling Stones' instrumental, "2120 South Michigan Avenue." At least they wrote most of their own material, and there are occasional cuts that hold their own weight. *—Richie Unterberger*

Do You Feel It Baby— / Apr. 28, 1998 / Norton ✦✦✦✦
Recorded live at Cavestomp '97 at the Coney Island High School in New York City, this capturea the original version of Question Mark & the Mysterians (accept no substitutes) shaking the joint down to the last brick. Amazingly, they sound *exactly* like they did some 30-odd years ago, fortified with some vintage equipment (no synthesizers here) and an enthusiastic crowd to goad them on. Kicking off with a Stones-like "2120 South Michigan Avenue" riff that gets turned into the title track, the band gets into fourth gear right from the start and pretty much stays there. Running through a 19-song set list that combines old favorites from their Cameo and Capitol recordings along with new songs that sound exactly like they were written 30 years ago (and who's to say they weren't—), this is one of the very, very few modern-day "reunion" albums that really works and makes you wish you were there. *—Cub Koda*

Quicksilver Messenger Service

f. 1965, San Francisco, CA, **db.** 1973
Group / Acid Rock, Psychedelic
The band that became Quicksilver Messenger Service originally was conceived as a rock vehicle for folk singer/songwriter Dino Valenti, author of "Get Together." As the band was being put together, however, Valenti was imprisoned on a drug charge and he didn't rejoin Quicksilver until later. They debuted at the end of 1965 and played around the Bay Area and then the West Coast for the next two years, building up a large following but resisting offers to record that had been taken up by such San Francisco acid-rock colleagues as Jefferson Airplane and the Grateful Dead. Quicksilver finally signed to Capitol toward the end of 1967 and recorded their self-titled debut album in 1968. *Happy Trails,* the 1969 follow-up, was recorded live. *— William Ruhlmann*

Quicksilver Messenger Service / May 1968 / Capitol ✦✦✦✦✦
The band's debut effort was a little more restrained and folky than some listeners had expected, given their reputation for stretching out in concert. While some prefer the mostly live *Happy Trails,* this is inarguably their strongest set of studio material, with the accent on melodic folk-rockers. Highlights include their cover of folksinger Hamilton Camp's "Pride of Man," probably their best studio track; "Light Your Windows," probably the group's best original composition; and founding member Dino Valenti's "Dino's Song" (Valenti himself was in jail when the album was recorded). "Gold and Silver" is their best instrumental jam, and the 12-minute "The Fool" reflects some of the best and worst traits of the psychedelic era. *— Richie Unterberger*

Happy Trails / Mar. 1969 / Capitol ✦✦✦✦✦
Quicksilver was heard at its best on this partially live album, which contained a 25-minute version of Bo Diddley's "Who Do You Love." *— William Ruhlmann*

Shady Grove / Dec. 1969 / Edsel ✦✦✦✦✦

Just for Love / Aug. 1970 / BGO ✦✦✦

What About Me / Dec. 1970 / One Way ✦✦✦
Recorded in part at the same 1970 sessions that produced *Just for Love, What About Me* was a similar effort, again dominated by Dino Valenti's songwriting and singing. It was also the swan song of the band, with guitarist John Cipollina, pianist Nicky Hopkins, and bassist David Freiberg dropping out after its completion. *— William Ruhlmann*

Quicksilver / Nov. 1971 / One Way ✦✦✦✦

Comin' Thru / Apr. 1972 / One Way ✦✦✦

Anthology / Mar. 1973 / EMI-Capitol Special Markets ✦✦✦✦✦

Solid Silver / Oct. 1975 / Edsel ✦✦

Maiden of the Cancer Moon / 1983 / Psycho ✦✦✦
A double album of live material from 1968, this duplicates a lot of the material on *Happy Trails* and adds considerably more. This erratic collection reflects Quicksilver's best and worst qualities: The hard-driving blend of raga/folk/psychedelic rock is fine, while the blues jams are fairly awful. Besides "Who Do You Love?" and "Mona" (two versions), this LP has covers of "Back Door Man," "Smokestack Lightning," Buffy St. Marie's "Codine," and versions of most of the songs from the first Quicksilver LP. The rendition of "The Fool" here eclipses the studio take, and the performance of "Gold and Silver" is fine except for the "Toad"-like drum solo. John Cippolina's slithery leads are consistently fine, and Quicksilver fans will find this worth the search. *—Richie Unterberger*

Peace by Piece / Jul. 1986 / Capitol ✦

● **Sons of Mercury (1968-75)** / Jul. 2, 1991 / Rhino ✦✦✦✦✦
This thorough two-disc best-of contains Quicksilver's most familiar material from its various lineups, plus some rarities. The only thing keeping this from being essential is the exclusion of the complete live version of "Who Do You Love," over a single edited version. *— William Ruhlmann*

Quiet Riot

f. 1975, **db.** 1988
Group / Heavy Metal, Hard Rock
In the early '80s, Quiet Riot became one of the first metal bands to hit the top of the pop charts with their remake of Slade's "Cum On Feel the Noize." By that time, Quiet Riot had been recording for a number of years, experiencing several changes. During the late '70s, the band was a straightahead metal group, distinguished only by the talented young guitarist Randy Rhoads; he left in 1979 to join Ozzy Osbourne's band, causing Quiet Riot to change their sound slightly, adding more pop elements to their hard rock. It paid off with 1983's *Metal Health,* which hit number one. However, their following albums didn't have the same crossover appeal and started to slip down the charts. Throughout the '80s, the band was a solid concert attraction even if their albums didn't sell particularly well. In 1988, the band broke up; vocalist Kevin DuBrow assembled a new version of Quiet Riot in 1993 for a tour and an album. *Alive & Well (Latest & Greatest)* followed in 1999. *—Stephen Thomas Erlewine*

Metal Health / 1983 / Pasha ✦✦✦✦

The Randy Rhoads Years / Oct. 26, 1993 / Rhino ✦✦✦✦
A fine collection of Quiet Riot's earliest records, *The Randy Rhoads Years* captures the influential guitarist in his formative years. That alone would have made the disc essential for his fans, but it also includes some prime unreleased material, making it all the more desirable. *—Stephen Thomas Erlewine*

● **The Greatest Hits** / Feb. 20, 1996 / Columbia ✦✦✦✦
For those interested in the genre, *The Best of Quiet Riot* contains all of Quiet Riot's biggest hits, from "Cum On Feel The Noize" to a live version of "Metal Health." While some favorites such as "Winners Take All" are missing, the most enjoyable pop-metal songs produced by Quiet Riot through 1988 all made it to this compilation. *—Barry Weber*

Radiohead

f. 1989, Oxford, England
Group / Britpop, Alternative Pop/Rock
Radiohead was one of the few alternative bands of the early '90s to draw heavily from the grandiose arena-rock that characterized U2's early albums. But the band internalized that epic sweep, turning it inside out to tell tortured, twisted tales of angst and alienation. Vocalist Thom Yorke's pained lyrics were brought to life by the group's three-guitar attack, which relied on texture—borrowing as much from My Bloody Valentine and Pink Floyd as R.E.M. and the Pixies—instead of virtuosity. It took Radiohead a while to formulate their signature sound. Their 1993 debut, *Pablo Honey,* only suggested their potential, and one of its songs, "Creep," became an unexpected international hit, its angst-ridden lyrics making it an alternative rock anthem. Many observers pigeonholed Radiohead as a one-hit wonder, but the group's second album, *The Bends,* was released to terrific reviews in the band's native Britain in early 1995, helping build a more stable fan base. Having demonstrated unexpected staying power, as well as increasing ambition, Radiohead next released *OK Computer,* a progressive, electronic-tinged masterpiece that became one of the most acclaimed albums of the '90s. *—Stephen Thomas Erlewine*

Pablo Honey / Apr. 20, 1993 / Capitol ✦✦✦
Radiohead's debut album *Pablo Honey* is a promising collection that blends U2's anthemic rock with long, atmospheric instrumental passages and an enthralling triple-guitar attack that is alternately gentle and bracingly noisy. The group has difficulty writing a set of songs that are as compelling as their sound, but when they do hit the mark—such as on "Anyone Can Play Guitar," "Blow Out," and the self-loathing breakthrough single "Creep"—the band achieves a rare power that is both visceral and intelligent. *—Stephen Thomas Erlewine*

The Bends / Apr. 4, 1995 / Capitol ✦✦✦✦✦
Pablo Honey in no way was adequate preparation for its epic, sprawling follow-up, *The Bends.* Building from the sweeping, three-guitar attack that punctuated the best moments of *Pablo Honey,* Radiohead create a grand and forceful sound that nevertheless resonates with anguish and despair—it's cerebral anthemic rock. Occasionally, the album displays its influences, whether it's U2, Pink Floyd, R.E.M. or the Pixies, but Radiohead turn clichés inside out, making each song sound bracingly fresh. Thom Yorke's tortured lyrics give the album a melancholy undercurrent, as does the surging, textured music. But what makes *The Bends* so remarkable is that it marries such ambitious, and often challenging, instrumental soundscapes to songs that are at their cores hauntingly melodic and accessible. It makes the record compelling upon first listen, but it reveals new details with each listen, and soon it becomes apparent that with *The Bends,* Radiohead have reinvented anthemic rock. *—Stephen Thomas Erlewine*

★ **OK Computer** / Jul. 1, 1997 / Capitol ✦✦✦✦✦
Using the textured soundscapes of *The Bends* as a launching pad, Radiohead delivered another startlingly accomplished set of modern guitar rock with *OK Computer.* The anthemic guitar heroics present on *Pablo Honey* and even *The Bends* are nowhere to be heard here. Radiohead have stripped away many of the obvious elements of guitar rock, creating music that is subtle and textured, yet still has the feeling of rock & roll. Even at its most adventurous—such as the complex, multi-segmented "Paranoid Android"—the band is tight, melodic, and muscular, and Thom Yorke's voice effortlessly shifts from a sweet falsetto to vicious snarls. It's a thoroughly astonishing demonstration of musical virtuosity, and becomes even impressive with repeated listens, which reveal subtleties like electronica rhythms, eerie keyboards, odd time signatures, and complex syncopations. Yet all of this would simply be showmanship if the songs weren't strong in themselves, and *OK Computer* is filled with moody masterpieces, from the shimmering "Subterranean Homesick Alien" and the sighing "Karma Police" to the gothic crawl of "Exit Music (For a Film)." *OK Computer* is the album that establishes Radiohead as one of the most inventive and rewarding guitar-rock bands of the '90s. *—Stephen Thomas Erlewine*

Kid A / Oct. 3, 2000 / Capitol ✦✦✦✦
Instead of simply adding club beats or sonic collage techniques, Radiohead strives to incorporate the unsettling "intelligent techno" sound of Autechre and Aphex Twin, characterized by its skittering beats and stylishly dark sonic surfaces, for *Kid A.* To their immense credit, Radiohead don't sound like carpetbaggers, because they share the same post-post-modern vantage point as their inspirations. As a result, *Kid A* is easily the most successful electronica album from a rock band—it doesn't even sound like a rock band, even if it does sound like Radiohead. So, *Kid A* is an unqualified success— Well, not quite. Despite its admirable

ambition, *Kid A* is never as visionary or stunning as *OK Computer*, nor does it really repay the time it demands. *OK Computer* required many plays before revealing the intricacies of its densely layered mix; here, multiple plays are necessary to discern the music's form, to get a handle on quiet, drifting, minimally arranged songs with no hooks. Of course, the natural reaction of any serious record geek is that if the music demands so much work, it must be worth it—and at times, that supposition is true. But *Kid A*'s challenge doesn't always live up to its end of the bargain. It's self-consciously alienating and difficult, and while that can be intriguing, it seems deeper on than it actually is. Repeated plays dissipate the mystique and reveal a number of rather drab songs (primarily during the second half), where there isn't enough under the surface to make Radiohead's relentless experimentation satisfying. But mixed results are still results, and about half of the songs positively shimmer with genius. *—Stephen Thomas Erlewine*

Rage Against the Machine

f. 1991
Group / Rap-Metal, Alternative Metal, Alternative Pop/Rock
Rage Against the Machine earned acclaim from disenfranchised fans (and not insignificant derision from critics) for their bombastic, fiercely polemical music, which brewed sloganeering leftist rants against corporate America, cultural imperialism and government oppression into a Molotov cocktail of punk, hip hop and thrash. Rage debuted in 1992 with a self-released, self-titled 12-song cassette featuring the song "Bullet in the Head," which became a hit when re-issued as a single later in the year. The tape won the band a deal with Epic, and their leap to the majors did not go unnoticed by detractors, who questioned the revolutionary integrity of Rage Against the Machine's decision to align itself with the label's parent company, media behemoth Sony. Undeterred, the quartet emerged in late 1992 with another eponymous release, which scored the hits "Killing in the Name" and "Bombtrack." After touring with Lollapalooza and declaring their support of groups like FAIR (Fairness and Accuracy in Reporting), Rock for Choice and Refuse & Resist, Rage spent a reportedly tumultous four years working on their follow-up; despite rumors of a break-up, they returned in 1996 with *Evil Empire*, which entered the U.S. album charts at Number One and scored a hit single with "Bulls on Parade." *—Jason Ankeny*

● **Rage Against the Machine** / Nov. 3, 1992 / Epic ✦✦✦✦✦
The first album to successfully merge the amazingly disparate sounds of rap and heavy metal, Rage Against the Machine's self-titled debut was groundbreaking enough when it was released, and many would argue that its importance and influence remains unchallenged and unsurpassed to this day. The living embodiment of this culture clash, guitar wizard Tom Morello fuses his roots in '80s metal-style shredding with an unprecedented array of six-string acrobatics and rhythmic special effects, most of which no one has even tried to imitate. And from vocalist Zack de la Rocha, the group receives the meaningful rhymes and emotionally charged delivery that white-boy metal could never hope to achieve. Still, despite the unique elements upon which they are built, songs like "Bombtrack," "Take the Power Back," and "Know Your Enemy" are immediately memorable, surprisingly straightforward slabs of hard rock. And one need not look further than the main riff of the venomous "Wake Up"—lifted straight out of Zeppelin's "Kashmir"—for conclusive proof of Morello's influences. Even more impressive is the group's talent for injecting slowly mounting tension into such highlights as "Settle for Nothing" and "Bullet in the Head," both of which finally explode with awesome power and rage. In contrast, the band manages to convey their message with even more urgency through stubborn repetition, as seen on "Freedom" and their signature track, "Killing in the Name." With its relentlessly rebellious mantra of "Fuck you, I won't do what you tell me," the song is a rallying cry of frightening proportions and the unequivocal climax of their vision. A stunning debut that remains absolutely essential. *—Ed Rivadavia*

Evil Empire / Apr. 1996 / Epic ✦✦✦✦
Rage Against the Machine spent four years making their second album, *Evil Empire*. As the title suggests, their rage and contempt for the "fascist" capitalist system in America hasn't declined in the nearly half-decade they were away. Their musical approach didn't change, either. Lead vocalist Zach De La Rocha is caught halfway between the militant raps of Chuck D and the fanatical ravings of a street preacher, shouting out his simplistic, libertarian slogans over the sonically dense assault of the band. Since the band did not perform together much after 1993, there isn't a collective advance in their musicianship. Nevertheless, guitarist Tom Morello demonstrates an impressive palette of sound, creating new textures in heavy metal, which is quite difficult. Even with Morello's studied virtuosity, the band sounds leaden, lacking the dexterity to fully execute their metal/hip-hop fusion—they don't get into a groove, they simply pound. But that happens to fit the hysterical ravings of De La Rocha. Though his dedication to decidedly left-wing politics is admirable, his arhythmic phrasing and grating shouting cancel out any message he is trying to make. And that means *Evil Empire* succeeds only on the level of a sonic assault. *—Stephen Thomas Erlewine*

The Battle of Los Angeles / Nov. 2, 1999 / Epic ✦✦✦✦
Rage Against the Machine isn't really the only metal band that matters, but their aggressive social and political activism is refreshing, especially in an age of blind (or usually self-directed) rage due to groups like Limp Bizkit, Bush, or Nine Inch Nails. Recorded in less than a month, *The Battle of Los Angeles* is the most focused album of the band's career, exploding from the gate and rarely letting go the whole way through. Like a few other famous revolution-in-the-head bands (most notably Minor Threat), Rage Against the Machine has always been blessed by the fact that the band is spewing just as much vitriol as its frontman. Any potential problems created here by Zack de la Rocha's one-note delivery and extremist polemics are smoothed over by songs and grooves that make it sound like the revolution really *is* here, from the single "Guerrilla Radio" to album highlights like "Mic Check," "Calm Like a Bomb," and "Born of a Broken Man." As on the previous two Rage Against the Machine albums, Tom Morello's roster of guitar effects and vicious riffs are nigh-overpowering, and are as contagious as the band has ever been since their debut. De la Rocha is best when he has specific targets (like the government or the case against *Mumia Abu Jamal*), but when he attempts to cover more general societal problems, he falters. If anything less than one of the most talented and fiery bands in the music world were backing him, *The Battle of Los Angeles* wouldn't be nearly as high-rated as it is. *—John Bush*

Renegades / Dec. 5, 2000 / Epic ✦✦✦✦

Raincoats

f. 1978, London, England, **db.** 1984
Group / Post-Punk
The Raincoats were one of the most experimental bands that immediately followed the initial burst of punk rock in the late '70s. With their minimalistic approach to guitar-driven folk-rock, the band developed a distinctive, jagged sound, punctuated by a shrill violin. The Raincoats were also one of the first all-female post-punk bands, which wasn't common in the late '70s and early '80s. When they were recording, the band gained a small cult following in their native England and an even smaller audience in America; they broke up in 1984. Nearly ten years later, the band became a hip name in alternative rock, thanks to Kurt Cobain's mention of the group in the liner notes to a Nirvana album. Geffen picked up the rights to the Raincoats' catalog and reissued their albums in late 1993 and 1994. The band reunited and toured with Nirvana in the U.K. before heading out on their own tour of the U.S. in 1994. Two years later, the Raincoats released *Looking in the Shadows*, which was produced by Sonic Youth's Steve Shelley. *—Stephen Thomas Erlewine*

● **The Raincoats** / 1980 / DGC ✦✦✦✦✦
Picking the "best" Raincoats is more an intellectual exercise than it is a work of thoughtful criticism. So, to make it easy for the benighted, all three studio releases are absolutely essential. Their live cassette is wonderful, but I wouldn't start there. Better yet, start with their debut, a soaring, daring, avant-garde-influenced folk-punk record. Don't let the words "avant-garde" scare you off; the Raincoats are not harsh or unapproachable. In fact, this music, even at its most dissonant, is stunning and captivating. There's a great cover of the Kinks' "Lola" that's so skewed and obtuse, I'm sure Ray Davies never dreamed it could sound this way. Reissued by Geffen on CD with extra tracks in 1995. *—John Dougan*

Odyshape / 1981 / DGC ✦✦✦✦✦
It was the late Kurt Cobain (with some help from labelmates Sonic Youth) that initiated Geffen's reissue of the Raincoats' catalog. And listening to *Odyshape*, it's easy to see why Cobain loved them so. There's an emotional directness about these songs that hooks you from the start. Mostly you hear about emotions and situations, sometimes indirectly, almost as if you are eavesdropping on a conversation. Then it hits you: it's almost like you're talking to old friends. That's the way the Raincoats' music worked: it's deceptively simple, but extremely complicated. Also, as on this record, it makes demands of the listener. But songs like "Red Shoes" and "Dancing in My Head" say this far more eloquently. Reissued by Geffen with extra tracks in 1995. *—John Dougan*

Kitchen Tapes / 1983 / ROIR ✦✦✦✦
Rough, loose-limbed, warm, exciting and everything you'd expect from the Raincoats onstage. Bolstered by the heavy percussion of Richard Dudanski and Derek Godard, this recording pulsates, while the band dances around the beat tossing in shards of guitar, vocals and violin. Excellent liner essay by Greil Marcus. *—John Dougan*

Bonnie Raitt

b. Nov. 8, 1949, Burbank, CA
Slide Guitar, Vocals, Guitar / Slide Guitar Blues, Album Rock, Pop/Rock, Adult Contemporary, Singer/Songwriter, Blues-Rock
Long a critic's darling, singer/guitarist Bonnie Raitt did not begin to win the comparable commercial success due her until the release of the aptly titled 1989 blockbuster *Nick of Time;* her tenth album, it rocketed her into the mainstream consciousness nearly two decades after she first committed her unique blend of blues, rock and R&B to vinyl. Debuting in 1971 with an eponymously titled effort, Raitt immediately emerged as a critical favorite. Throughout the middle of the decade she released an LP annually, and scored her first significant pop airplay with a hit cover of the Del Shannon classic "Runaway." She remained a committed activist, playing hundreds of benefit concerts and working tirelessly on behalf of the Rhythm and Blues Foundation. By the early '80s, however, her own career was in trouble—1982's *Green Light*, while greeted with the usual good reviews, again failed to break her to a wide audience and led to Warners dropping her. Many had written Raitt off when she recorded *Nick of Time* though, seemingly out of the blue, the LP won a handful of Grammys (including Album of the Year) and overnight she was a superstar. The follow-up, 1991's *Luck of the Draw*, was also a smash. *—Jason Ankeny*

Bonnie Raitt / 1971 / Warner Brothers ✦✦✦

Give It Up / Sep. 1972 / Warner Brothers ✦✦✦✦✦
Bonnie Raitt may have switched producers for her second album *Give It Up*, hiring Michael Cuscuna, but she hasn't switched her style, sticking with the thoroughly engaging blend of folk, blues, R&B, and Californian soft rock. If anything, she's strengthened her formula here, making the divisions between the genres nearly indistinguishable. Take the title track, for instance. It opens with a bluesy acoustic guitar before kicking into a New Orleans brass band about halfway through—and the great thing about it is that Raitt makes the switch sound natural, even inevitable, never forced. And that's just the tip of the iceberg here, since *Give It Up* is filled with great songs, delivered in familiar, yet always surprising, ways by Raitt and her skilled band. For those that want to pigeonhole her as a white blues singer, she delivers the lovely "Nothing Seems to Matter," a gentle mid-tempo number that's as mellow as Linda Ronstadt and far more seductive. That's the key to *Give It Up:* Yes, Raitt can be earthy and sexy, but she balances it with an inviting sensuality that makes the record glow. It's all delivered in a fantastic set of originals and covers performed so naturally it's hard to tell them apart and roots music so thoroughly fused that it all sounds original, even when it's possible to spot the individual elements or influences. Raitt would go on to greater chart successes, but she not only had trouble topping this record, generations of singers, from Sheryl Crow

to Shelby Lynne, have used this as a touchstone. One of the great Southern California records. *—Stephen Thomas Erlewine*

Takin' My Time / 1973 / Warner Brothers ♦♦♦♦
This album is an overlooked gem in the catalog of Bonnie Raitt. On *Takin' My Time*, she wears her influences proudly in an eclectic musical mix containing blues, jazz, folk, New Orleans R&B, and calypso. Although she did not write her own material for this album, she demonstrates an excellent ear for songs and chooses material from some of the best songwriters of the day. She is a great interpreter, and her renditions of Jackson Browne's "I Thought I Was a Child" and Randy Newman's "Guilty" from this album are the definitive versions of these songs. The highlights of this album are the romantic ballads "I Gave My Love a Candle" and "Cry Like a Rainstorm," where Raitt adds an emotional depth to the performance unusual for such a young woman. (Perhaps that's a result of her spending time with elder statesmen of the blues community such as Mississippi Fred McDowell and Sippie Wallace.) Although the faster-paced songs like the calypso "Wah She Go Do" seem a little out of place, the playful tune is welcome among an album filled with the heartache of the slower tunes. Despite being a relative newcomer, Raitt had already earned the respect of her mentors and her peers, as evidenced by the musical contributions of Taj Mahal, and Little Feat members Lowell George and Bill Payne on the album. This is the last consistent album she would make until her comeback in the mid-'80s. *—Vik Iyengar*

Streetlights / 1974 / Warner Brothers ♦♦♦

Homeplate / 1975 / Warner Brothers ♦♦♦

Sweet Forgiveness / Apr. 1977 / Warner Brothers ♦♦

The Glow / 1979 / Warner Brothers ♦♦♦

Green Light / 1982 / Warner Brothers ♦♦♦♦♦

Nine Lives / 1986 / Warner Brothers ♦♦♦

● **Nick of Time** / Mar. 1989 / Capitol ♦♦♦♦♦
Prior to *Nick of Time*, Bonnie Raitt had been a reliable cult artist, delivering a string of solid records that were moderate successes and usually musically satisfying. From her 1971 debut through 1982's *Green Light*, she had a solid streak, but 1986's *Nine Lives* snapped it, falling far short of her usual potential. Therefore, it shouldn't have been a surprise when Raitt decided to craft its follow-up as a major comeback, collaborating with producer Don Was on *Nick of Time*. At the time, the pairing seemed a little odd, since he was primarily known for the weird hipster funk of Was (Not Was) and the B-52's quirky eponymous debut, but the match turned out to be inspired. Was used Raitt's classic early '70s records as a blueprint, choosing to update the sound with a smooth, professional production and a batch of excellent contemporary songs. In this context, Raitt flourishes; she never rocks too hard, but there is grit to her singing and playing, even when the surfaces are clean and inviting. And while she only has two original songs here, *Nick of Time* plays like autobiography, which is a testament to the power of the songs, performances and productions. It was a great comeback album that made for a great story, but the record never would have been a blockbuster success if it wasn't for the music, which is among the finest Raitt ever made. She must have realized this, since *Nick of Time* served as the blueprint for the majority of her '90s albums. *—Stephen Thomas Erlewine*

The Bonnie Raitt Collection / Jun. 28, 1990 / Warner Brothers ♦♦♦♦♦

Luck of the Draw / Jun. 1991 / Capitol ♦♦♦♦♦
Nick of Time not only was an artistic comeback for Bonnie Raitt, it brought her largest audience yet, so there was no reason to mess with success for its sequel, *Luck of the Draw*. And sequel is the appropriate word, since *Luck of the Draw* is nothing if it isn't "Nick of Time, Part 2." True, there's a heavier reliance on original material this time around, but the sound and feel of the record is identical to its predecessor. There is one slight difference—several of the songs appear tailor-made for crossover success, where *Nick of Time* felt organic. Nevertheless, *Luck of the Draw* is an unqualified success, filled with strong songs—including the hits "Something to Talk About" and "I Can't Make You Love Me," plus the Delbert McClinton duet "Good Man, Good Woman"—appealing productions and just enough dirt to make old-school fans feel at home. *—Stephen Thomas Erlewine*

Longing in Their Hearts / Mar. 14, 1994 / Capitol ♦♦♦♦♦

Road Tested / Nov. 7, 1995 / Digital Sound ♦♦♦♦♦

Fundamental / Apr. 7, 1998 / Capitol ♦♦♦

The Ramones

f. 1974, New York, NY, **db.** 1996
Group / College Rock, American Punk, New York Punk, Punk
The Ramones are the first punk rock band. There were other bands, such as the Stooges and the New York Dolls, that came before them and set the stage and aesthetic for punk and bands that immediately followed, such as the Sex Pistols, that made the latent violence of the music more explicit, but the Ramones crystallized the musical ideals of the genre. By cutting rock & roll down to its bare essentials—four chords, a simple, catchy melody, and irresistably inane lyrics—speeding up the tempo considerably, the Ramones created something that was rooted in early '60s, pre-Beatles rock & roll and pop but sounded revolutionary. Since their breakthrough was theoretical as well as musical, they comfortably became the leaders of the emerging New York punk rock scene. While their peers such as Patti Smith, Television, Talking Heads and Richard Hell all were more intellectual and self-consciously artistic than the Ramones, they nevertheless appealed to the same mentality because of how they turned rock conventions inside out and celebrated kitschy pop culture with stylized stupidity. The band's first four albums set the blueprint for punk, especially American punk and hardcore, for the next two decades. And the Ramones themselves were major figures for the next two decades, playing essentially the same music without changing their style much at all. Although some punk diehards—including several of their peers—would have claimed the band's long career wound up undercutting the ideals the band originally stood for, the Ramones always celebrated not just the punk aesthetic, but the music itself. *—Stephen Thomas Erlewine*

☆ **Ramones** / May 1976 / Sire ♦♦♦♦♦
With the three-chord assault of "Blitzkrieg Bop," *The Ramones* begins at a blinding speed and never once over the course of its 14 songs does it let up. *The Ramones* is all about speed, hooks, stupidity and simplicity. The songs are imaginative reductions of early rock & roll, girl group pop, and surf-rock. Not only is the music only boiled down to its essentials, but the Ramones offer a twisted, comical take on pop culture with their lyrics, whether it's the horror schlock of "I Don't Wanna Go Down to the Basement," the drug deals of "53rd and 3rd," the gleeful violence of "Beat on the Brat" or the maniacal stupidity of "Now I Wanna Sniff Some Glue." And the cover of Chris Montez's "Let's Dance" isn't a throwaway—with its single-minded beat and lyrics, it encapsulates everything the group loves about pre-Beatles rock & roll. They don't alter the structure, or the intent, of the song, they simply make it louder and faster. And that's the key to all of the Ramones' music—it's simple rock & roll, played simply, loud, and very, very fast. None of the songs clock in at any longer than two and half minutes and most are considerably shorter. In comparison to some of the music the album inspired, *The Ramones* sounds a little tame—it's a little too clean and compared to their insanely fast live albums, it even sounds a little slow—but there's no denying that it still sounds brilliantly fresh and intoxicatingly fun. *—Stephen Thomas Erlewine*

The Ramones Leave Home / Feb. 1977 / Sire ♦♦♦♦♦
Of course the Ramones' second album *Leave Home* is simply more of the same—14 songs, including one oldie ("California Sun"), delivered at breakneck speed and concluding in under a half hour. The Ramones have gotten slightly poppier, occasionally delivering songs like "I Remember You" that are cloaked neither in irony nor seedy rock & roll chic. Still, the biggest impressions are made by the cuts that strongly recall the debut, whether it's the ersatz Beach Boys of "Sheena Is a Punk Rocker," the sing-along of "Pinhead" or the warped anthems "Gimme Gimme Shock Treatment" and "Commando." Song for song, it's slightly weaker than its predecessor, but the handful of mediocre cuts speed by so fast that you don't really notice its weaknesses until after it's all over. *—Stephen Thomas Erlewine*

☆ **Rocket to Russia** / Nov. 1977 / Sire ♦♦♦♦♦
The Ramones provided the blueprint and *Leave Home* duplicated it with lesser results, but the Ramones' third album, *Rocket to Russia*, perfected it. *Rocket to Russia* boasts a cleaner production than its predecessors, which only gives the Ramones' music more force. It helps that the group wrote its finest set of songs for the album. From the mindless, bopping opening of "Cretin Hop" and "Rockaway Beach" to the urban surf-rock of "Sheena Is a Punk Rocker" and ridiculous anthem "Teenage Lobotomy," the songs are teeming with irresistibly catchy hooks; even their choice of covers, "Do You Want to Dance?" and "Surfin' Bird," provide more hooks than usual. The Ramones also branch out slightly, adding ballads to the mix. Even with these (relatively) slower songs, the speed of the album never decreases. However, the abundance of hooks and slight variety in tempos makes *Rocket to Russia* the Ramones' most listenable and enjoyable album—it doesn't have the revolutionary impact of *The Ramones*, but it's a better album and one of the finest records of the late '70s. *—Stephen Thomas Erlewine*

Road to Ruin / Jun. 1978 / Sire ♦♦♦♦♦
The loud-and-fast, campy-and-catchy formula began to wear a little thin by the time of the Ramones' fourth album, *Road to Ruin*. Following the exact same blueprint as its three predecessors, *Road to Ruin* simply doesn't yield the same results as the other records. In part, it's because the band sounds a little forced on the harder numbers, but the main problem lies with the undistinguished material. "I Wanna Be Sedated" is a classic, and "Questioningly" proves that the Ramones are just as effective when they slow the tempo down, yet much of the record sounds like the Ramones trying to give the people what they want. Since they were still in their prime, such nondescript material sounds good, but the record has neither the exuberant energy or abundant hooks of *Ramones* and *Rocket to Russia*, and it's the first suggestion that the Ramones may have painted themselves into a corner. *—Stephen Thomas Erlewine*

It's Alive / May 1979 / Sire ♦♦♦♦
One of the greatest live albums of all time, *It's Alive* captures the Ramones at their absolute peak. Recorded at London's *Rainbow Theater* on New Year's Eve 1977, the album contains 28 songs (every one a classic) from the band's landmark first three albums: *Ramones, Ramones Leave Home*, and *Rocket to Russia* performed at breakneck speed in under an hour. In fact, the band only pauses long enough for bassist Dee Dee to count off the next tune—"one-two-three-four!"—and for singer Joey to complain about some bad chicken vindaloo. It has often been said that the Ramones helped save rock & roll by making it fun again—*It's Alive* is the perfect case in point. Long live the Ramones! *—Ed Rivadavia*

End of the Century / Jan. 1980 / Sire ♦♦♦♦
Road to Ruin found the Ramones stretching their signature sound to its limits; even though there were several fine moments, nearly all of them arrived when the group broke free from the suddenly restrictive loud-fast-hard formula of their first records. Considering that the Ramones did desire mainstream success and that they had a deep love for early-'60s pop/rock, it's not surprising that they decided to shake loose the constrictions of their style by making an unabashed pop album, yet it was odd that Phil Spector produced *End of the Century* because his painstaking working methods seemingly clashed with the Ramones' instinctual approach. However, the Ramones were always more clever than they appeared, so the matching actually worked better than it could have. Spector's detailed production helped bring "Rock 'N' Roll High School" and "Do You Remember Rock & Roll Radio?" to life, yet it also kept some of the punkier numbers in check. Even so, *End of the Century* is more enjoyable than its predecessor, since the record has stronger material, and in retrospect, it's one their better records of the '80s. *—Stephen Thomas Erlewine*

Pleasant Dreams / Jul. 1981 / Sire ♦♦♦

Subterranean Jungle / May 1983 / Sire ♦♦♦

Too Tough to Die / Jan. 1985 / Warner Brothers ✦✦✦✦✦
With the Ramones' original drummer Tommy Erdelyi producing, the group returns to simple, scathing punk rock on *Too Tough to Die.* The group takes the big guitar riffs of *Subterranean Jungle* and makes them shorter and heavier. The Ramones rhythms are back up to jackhammer speed and the songs are down to short, terse statements. The results read like a reaction to hardcore punk, but the Ramones are more melodic than any hardcore band, as well as smarter than most. Apart from the occasional foray into pop, such as the surprisingly effective Dave Stewart-produced "Howling at the Moon," the album is a sterling set of lethal punk, the best the Ramones had made since the end of the '70s. It was also the last great record they would ever make. *—Stephen Thomas Erlewine*

Animal Boy / May 1986 / Sire ✦✦✦

Halfway to Sanity / Sep. 15, 1987 / Sire ✦✦

Ramones Mania / May 31, 1988 / Sire ✦✦✦✦✦
Ramonesmania is a relentless collection of 30 tracks from the Ramones' first ten albums, ranging from the classic *Ramones* to the less-than-classic *Halfway to Sanity.* Although not all of great '70s songs are included, it boils down the highlights from the inconsistent '80s albums quite effectively, making it a useful summation of their peak period, even if the sequencing is not chronological. *—Stephen Thomas Erlewine*

Brain Drain / May 23, 1989 / Sire ✦✦

☆ **All the Stuff & More, Vol. 2** / 1990 / Sire ✦✦✦✦✦
The second volume of *All the Stuff & More* compiles the Ramones' third and fourth albums—*Rocket to Russia* and *Road to Ruin*—onto one compact disc, adding several live cuts, demos and B-sides as bonus tracks. Like its predecessor, *All the Stuff & More, Vol. 2* suffers slightly from its length, which happens to contradict the loud-fast nature of the band's songs and albums, yet the music isn't hurt by its presentation. *Rocket to Russia* is one of the classic rock & roll albums, and while *Road to Ruin* isn't as consistent, it does have its moments, making *All the Stuff & More, Vol. 2* a good bargain. *—Stephen Thomas Erlewine*

★ **All the Stuff & More, Vol. 1** / May 1990 / Sire ✦✦✦✦✦
All the Stuff & More, Vol. 1 compiles the Ramones first two albums—*Ramones* and *Leave Home*—onto one compact disc, adding a handful of B-sides, demos and live songs as bonus tracks as well. While the music on the disc is terrific and timeless, having both albums on one disc actually dilutes some of its impact, since the records were designed as a relentless rush of brief, speedy songs; in this form, the assault becomes a little tiring, and the distinctions between the two albums—and they are there—are lost. Still, these are minor flaws, especially considering that the music on *All the Stuff & More, Vol. 1* is essential for any rock & roll library. *—Stephen Thomas Erlewine*

Loco Live / Oct. 1991 / Sire ✦✦

Mondo Bizarro / Sep. 1992 / Radioactive ✦✦

Acid Eaters / Dec. 1993 / Radioactive ✦✦

Adios Amigos / Jul. 18, 1995 / Radioactive ✦✦✦

Greatest Hits Live / Jun. 18, 1996 / Radioactive ✦✦✦

● **Hey! Ho! Let's Go: The Anthology** / Jul. 20, 1999 / Rhino ✦✦✦✦✦
In a way, the Ramones are an ideal band to anthologize. No matter how cohesive their records were (or not), their albums always played like collections of singles and since singles are easy to anthologize, it stands to reason that the best of the Ramones' songs will sound good in nearly any context; hell, the haphazard *Ramones Mania* proved that. However, Rhino's double-disc *Hey! Ho! Let's Go: The Anthology* has much greater goals than being just being another collection—it strives to be the final word on the Ramones. Weighing in at nearly 60 songs, with a hardcover book that includes an excellent history by David Fricke, it has to be said that the set has the heft of history, which is both a blessing and a curse. It's a blessing because *Anthology* does its job perfectly—apart from "We're a Happy Family," no major songs are missing and it tells its history succinctly, even at its length. The problem is that the Ramones did drop in quality sometime after *End of the Century.* They never bottomed out, but their music became less exciting, which is evident in this anthology, as the second disc is simply not as compelling as the first. That's not to say it isn't good—with "The KKK Took My Baby Away" and "My Brain Is Hanging Upside Down (Bonzo Goes to Bitburg)," it can be great—but it isn't timeless like the entire first disc is. Yet, this is nitpicking, since *Anthology* does a flawless job in summarizing the band's career. True, most listeners will wear out the first disc while rarely reaching for the second, but this is still essential. *—Stephen Thomas Erlewine*

Willis Alan Ramsey

Vocals, Guitar / Folk-Rock, Soft Rock, Singer/Songwriter
Willis Alan Ramsey was one of the bright lights of Austin's singer/songwriter movement of the '70s, and his laidback folky airs and sweet melodies impressed many contemporaries. Indeed, his 1972 self-titled debut album featured songs later covered by Jimmy Buffett, America, Waylon Jennings and Captain & Tennille, who took "Muskrat Love" to the Popular Top Five in 1976. His star shines less bright if only for the fact that he practically disappeared in the mid-'70s. A small cult of fans remained true, however, and their adoration was somewhat rewarded when Ramsey re-surfaced, working with Lyle Lovett, who has also covered Ramsey in concert. *—John Bush*

Willis Alan Ramsey / 1972 / Koch ✦✦✦✦✦
One of the great (and sadly overlooked) albums of the '70s, Willis Alan Ramsey's self-titled debut had great impact among Austin's progressive country-folk songwriters. Although best known as the writer of "Muskrat Love," which Captain & Tennille took to the Top Ten, Ramsey's muse was rooted much deeper in American lore and folk music. Influences from Robert Johnson to Jimmie Rodgers to Woody Guthrie can be felt if not actually heard on these eleven highly original tracks. Unfortunately, Ramsey, a unique talent with a clear and idiosyncratic artistic vision, hasn't been heard from since. *—Tom Graves*

Rancid

f. 1991, Berkeley, CA
Group / Ska-Punk, Punk-Pop, Third Wave Ska Revival, Punk Revival, Alternative Pop/Rock
Drawing an enormous influence from the Clash, the Bay Area quartet Rancid followed the lead of fellow latter-day punks Green Day and the Offspring to mainstream success. The group was led by singer/guitarist Tim Armstrong, a lifelong hardcore fan who first found underground success teamed with childhood friend and bassist Matt Freeman in the late-'80s ska-punk band Operation Ivy. Unable to deal with their growing popularity, Op Ivy disbanded in 1989, and Armstrong and Freeman founded Rancid in 1991 with Brett Reed on drums. The trio issued their five-song debut in 1992, followed in 1993 by a self-titled full-length release on the prominent indie label Epitaph. After the addition of second guitarist Lars Frederiksen, formerly a member of the UK Subs, Rancid recorded its 1994 breakthrough album *Let's Go,* which sold close to a million copies on the strength of the single and video "Salvation." A major bidding war followed, but the band remained with Epitaph for 1995's *...And Out Come the Wolves,* which featured the hits "Time Bomb" and "Ruby Soho." *Life Won't Wait* followed in 1998. *—Jason Ankeny*

Rancid [1993] / May 10, 1993 / Epitaph ✦✦✦✦

Let's Go / Jun. 14, 1994 / Epitaph ✦✦✦✦✦
Whatever Rancid lacks in innovation, it makes up with sheer energy. The group rushes through *Let's Go* with an invigorating wrecklessness, sounding like a less-serious, party-ready version of the Clash. It's almost impossible to understand what vocalist Tim Armstrong sings at any given moment, yet there is no great meaning in what Rancid says—the message is in the buzzing guitars and speeding rhythms. It doesn't hurt that the band can throw out the occasional memorable hook or melody, like the single "Salvation," as well. *—Stephen Thomas Erlewine*

● **And Out Come the Wolves** / Oct. 1995 / Epitaph ✦✦✦✦✦
In the wake of the Offspring's success, Rancid became a hot band, earning a dedicated cult and sparking a major-label bidding war. After flirting with a handful of major labels, the band decided to stick with Epitaph and returned with *And Out Come the Wolves.* While the title is a veiled reference to the attention the band gained, the album doesn't mark an isolationist retreat into didactic, defiantly underground punk rock. Instead, Rancid develop their own identity on the record, which ironically makes them more accessible. Although they continue to draw heavily from the Clash and the Specials—and their roots in the ska-punk band Operation Ivy are quite clear throughout the record—the band plays with such energy and conviction, it's easy to forgive their derivativeness. On the whole, *And Out Come the Wolves* is a little too long to make a major impact, but individual tracks are classic moments of revivalist punk, including the skittering 2-Tone tribute "Time Bomb." *—Stephen Thomas Erlewine*

Life Won't Wait / Jun. 30, 1998 / Epitaph ✦✦✦✦

Rancid [2000] / Aug. 1, 2000 / Epitaph ✦✦✦✦✦

The Rascals

f. 1964, New York, NY, **db.** 1972
Group / AM Pop, Blue-Eyed Soul, Pop
The Rascals, along with the Righteous Brothers, Mitch Ryder, and precious few others, were the pinnacle of '60s blue-eyed soul. The Rascals' talents, however, would have to rate above their rivals, if for nothing else than the simple fact that they, unlike many other blue-eyed soulsters, penned much of their own material. They also proved more adept at changing with the fast-moving times, drawing much of their inspiration from British Invasion bands, psychedelic rock, gospel, and even a bit of jazz and Latin music. They were at their best on classic singles like "Good Lovin'," "How Can I Be Sure," "Groovin'," and "People Got to Be Free." When they tried to stretch their talents beyond the impositions of the three-minute 45, they couldn't pull it off, a failure which—along with crucial personnel losses—effectively finished the band as a major force by the 1970s. *—Richie Unterberger*

The Young Rascals / 1966 / Atlantic ✦✦✦✦✦
The history of '60s rock is littered with stories of great rock classics—the Savages' album, the Thirteenth Floor Elevators' first two albums, the first two Chocolate Watch Band albums—that should have been better known than they were. *The Young Rascals* is that rare example of a genuinely great album that got heard and played, and sold and sold. Apart from the presence of a hit ("Good Lovin'") to drive sales, every kid (and his girlfriend) in any aspiring white rock band on the East Coast in 1966 seemingly owned a copy. And it's easy to see why—the Rascals' debut couples a raw garage band sound with compelling white soul more successfully than just about any record since the Beatles' *Please Please Me.* The band had three powerful singers in Felix Cavaliere, Eddie Brigati, and Gene Cornish, and an attack honed in hundreds of hours of playing dance clubs on Long Island and New York City. The result is a record without a weak moment or a false note anywhere in its 35 minutes: "Do You Feel It" shows them crossing swords stylistically with Smokey Robinson & the Miracles; "Just a Little" and "Like a Rolling Stone" show off their folk-rock chops; and "Slow Down," "Good Lovin'," "Mustang Sally," and "In the Midnight Hour" are all '60s rock & roll classics in these versions. "Like a Rolling Stone," in particular, today seems all the more compelling, pointing the way toward a future that included Hendrix's version of "All Along the Watchtower." The CD is one of Warner Special Products' better sounding reissues, having been remastered by Rhino's Bill Inglot. The original album was on Atlantic, and was one of the label's best-sellers of the mid-'60s. *—Bruce Eder*

Collections / Jan. 1967 / Atlantic ✦✦✦✦✦
The garage-band feel has been banished almost entirely from the group's second album, whose release followed a pair of disappointing singles ("What Is the Reason," "Come On Up"). It also includes their first misjudgment on an album, Gene Cornish's too-quiet, too-introspective, and way-too-languid "No Love to Give," amid an otherwise wonderfully soulful body of music that picks up right where "In the Midnight Hour" from the prior album left

off. Most of this record is among the most danceable White rock music of its period—even the Eddie Brigatti-sung cover of the then-current pop standard "More" has a certain rocking credibility. Their attempt at bluesy rock & roll, Cornish's "Nineteen Fifty-Six," a bit of a "Kansas City" ripoff, with a pair of crunchy guitar parts and Cornish singing lead, also comes off extremely well. They're even better with the more soulful tracks, however. "Land of 1000 Dances" was the best track on which to end this album, but it was Cavaliere and Brigatti's "Love Is a Beautiful Thing" that pointed to the future, showing the group moving toward the mix of sounds and sentiments behind "People Got to Be Free." The CD reissue of this album (originally on Atlantic) has no notes but very good sound. *—Bruce Eder*

Groovin' / Jul. 1967 / Warner Brothers ✦✦✦✦✦
The Rascals move into the era of psychedelia with a vengeance on this album—their best of their entire history—which also retains a soulful core and adds a bit of a Latin beat. The original album on Atlantic was a monster seller thanks to the title track, practically the group's signature tune (number one on the pop charts, number three on R&B), but "Groovin'" was only one small strong point on the album of the same name. "Find Somebody" marked a return to the group's garage band sound with a psychedelic twist, including phased fuzztone guitars and some catchy lyrics and choruses. "How Can I Be Sure" is the second best known song off of this album, but it has a fully successful companion piece, "I'm So Happy Now," which applies similar instrumentation to very different (but pleasing) effect. Gene Cornish's "I Don't Love You Anymore" could be the finest pop song in the band's repertory apart from "How Can I Be Sure," with a delectable guitar part, scrumptious melody, and delicious chorus. "You Better Run" was more than a year old when it turned up on this album, and its garage-band sensibilities are a bit more primitive than those of "Find Somebody," but it's a great piece of rock & roll. The band turns in one superb Motown cover, "A Place in the Sun," done in a surprisingly subdued fashion. And for a finale, Cavaliere and Brigati turn in an exultant period piece, "It's Love," whose soaring lyrics are matched by guest artist Hubert Laws' flute—alas, his presence would point the way toward less effective, more disjointed work in the group's future, as they moved more deeply into psychedelia. *—Bruce Eder*

Once Upon a Dream / 1968 / Rhino ✦✦✦

Freedom Suite / 1969 / Rhino ✦✦✦

See / Dec. 1969 / Atlantic ✦✦✦

Peaceful World / 1971 / Sundazed ✦✦✦✦

Anthology (1965-1972) / Jul. 14, 1992 / Rhino ✦✦✦✦✦
Boasting all of the Rascals' essential hits as well as many enjoyable album tracks, this two-CD set does a fine job of summarizing the New Yorkers' accomplishments. Whether the Rascals are tearing into rockers like "You Better Run" (covered by Pat Benatar in 1980) and the Olympics' "Good Lovin'" (a frat-rock staple) or expressing their love of soul music (both Northern and Southern) on "Groovin'," "A Beautiful Morning" and "I've Been Lonely Too Long," the package shows us just how dynamic they could be. The Rascals' cover of Wilson Pickett's "In the Midnight Hour" is hard to resist, and it should be noted that their version of Sir Mac Rice's "Mustang Silly" was recorded before the song became a major hit for Pickett. Sadly, things broke down for the Rascals commercially in the early 1970s, but the socially aware soul-pop songs "Love Me," "Saga of New York" and "Brother Tree" show that they still had some creative life left in them. And they indicate that with the right guidance and input (working with someone like Curtis Mayfield, maybe—), the band could have made a comeback and become an important part of the '70s soul-pop scene. From obvious choices to surprises, *Anthology: 1965-72* is a package that both rock and soul aficionados should savor. *—Alex Henderson*

● **The Very Best of the Rascals** / 1994 / Rhino ✦✦✦✦✦
Although Rhino issued a deluxe two-CD set covering the Rascals a few years ago, this single disc set contains enough essential songs for you to get the point. The Rascals, along with the Righteous Brothers, defined blue-eyed soul singing, making records that were as churchy, earthy, and convincing as anything that came out of the South or Motown in the '60s, backed by tight, anthemic arrangements and excellent combo playing. The 16 cuts include their first hit, "I Ain't Gonna Eat Out My Heart Anymore," and continues on into their flirtation with psychedelia in 1970. The only quibble is their failure to include "Look Around," a sociopolitical cut from the *Freedom Suite* album that's just a cut below "People Got to Be Free" or "A Ray of Hope." *—Ron Wynn*

The Raspberries

f. 1970, Mentor, OH, **db.** 1975
Group / Pop/Rock, Power Pop
The Raspberries cut through the epic pretensions and pomposity of '70s-era rock to proudly reclaim the spirit and simplicity of classic pop, recalling the heyday of the British Invasion with their exquisitely crafted melodies and achingly gorgeous harmonies, not to mention their short hair and matching suits. The group was formed in Cleveland in early 1970 by singer/songwriter Eric Carmen and drummer Jim Bonfanti; guitarist Wally Bryson and bassist John Aleksic completed the original lineup; Aleksic left in March 1971, and with the addition of rhythm guitarist Dave Smalley, Carmen assumed bass duties. In the wake of a major label bidding war, the band signed to Capitol, issuing their self-titled debut LP in the spring of 1972. The second single, "Go All the Way," sold over a million copies on its way to cracking the Top Five. 1972's *Fresh* generated two more hits, "I Wanna Be With You" and the beautiful "Let's Pretend," and solidified the band's stature as critical favorites. Nevertheless, tensions within the ranks—sparked largely by Carmen's creative primacy and the shadow it cast over the songwriting contributions of Bryson and Smalley—were beginning to boil over, and accordingly 1973's *Side 3* boasted a more aggressive sound than its predecessors. *Side 3* failed even to crack the Top 100, however, and both Smalley and Bonfanti exited the Raspberries to form their own band. 1974's acclaimed *Starting Over* continued the harder-edged approach of *Side 3*, yielding the band's final chart smash, the superb "Overnight Sensation (Hit Record)." A nasty post-gig confrontation between Carmen and Bryson soon resulted in the latter's departure, and the Raspberries disbanded in 1975. Carmen mounted a sometimes-successful solo career; Bryson, meanwhile, joined the power pop group Fotomaker for three albums during the late '70s. *—Jason Ankeny*

Raspberries / 1972 / Capitol ✦✦✦✦
An excellent first effort, highlighted by "Go All the Way," "Don't Want to Say Goodbye," "I Saw the Light," and "Come Around and See Me." At the time, audiences thought they heard echoes of Paul McCartney's work with the Beatles, and they weren't far wrong, in terms of what the group was capable of. *—Bruce Eder*

Fresh / Dec. 1972 / Capitol ✦✦✦✦✦
The second best of the four albums issued by the band, with "I Wanna Be with You," "If You Change Your Mind," and "Drivin' Around" as highlights amid some overall incredibly superb rock craftsmanship. The band's sound overall is more confident, and more powerful. *—Bruce Eder*

Side Three / 1973 / Capitol ✦✦✦
One of the group's most accomplished album, almost Beatles-like in its richness, romanticism, cleverness, and even its packaging, which is one of the few "novelty" jacket designs (it's shaped like a basket of… you guessed it) that works. The band was at its peak and it showed in "Ecstacy" and "Last Dance," among numerous others. *—Bruce Eder*

Starting Over / 1974 / Capitol ✦✦✦
The band's last album is something of a disappointment, much louder and punchier than their previous work but lacking the elegance that characterized their overall sound. None of the songs is bad, and some are quite good, but they sound like they're going through the motions at this point, and they did break up soon after. *—Bruce Eder*

★ **Capitol Collectors Series** / Feb. 26, 1991 / Capitol ✦✦✦✦✦
Intermixing singles with the band's best accompanying album tracks, this 20-song retrospective gives a good overall impression of the Raspberries' strengths across their two years of recording, as well as hints of some weaknesses in the way they were represented on record. As expected, Eric Carmen is the dominant songwriter, but Wally Bryson and David Smalley also show up with "Last Dance" and "Hard to Get Over a Heartbreak," respectively, along with Scott McCarl ("Rose Coloured Glasses"), to give a hint of the range of composing talent in the band in its different phases. It's astonishing how many of their LP cuts would have made superb singles in their own right. It's clear listening to this collection that, between the record company's apparent inability to market their material to its fullest potential and the group's fear of sounding too English, that some killer tracks, like "Nobody Knows" with appealing hooks, a great beat, and overflowing with melodic teen angst, and "Hard to Get Over a Heartbreak," were overlooked as potential singles. Of course, the disputes over songwriting and the matter of who was represented on their singles (and where, the A- or B-side) were among the factors that helped kill the Raspberries after only a couple of years. This collection delineates a lot of the problems in the course of presenting the group's triumphs. An unusual amount of care has been taken in assembling the songs—they all sound better than the original records, and the hotter single mix of "Overnight Sensation" graces this disc. A serious fan may well want to own CDs of the group's complete albums (available on RPM Records on two CDs), but this is one time that Capitol Records did right by one of its own acts. *—Bruce Eder*

Greatest Hits / Aug. 1, 1995 / Capitol ✦✦✦✦✦
Although it isn't as comprehensive as *Capitol Collectors Series, Greatest Hits* is a terrific overview of the Raspberries' best songs, containing all of their hits—"Go All the Way," "I Wanna Be With You," "Let's Pretend," "Tonight," "Overnight Sensation (Hit Record)"—plus selected album tracks and lesser-known singles. Even though it does have fewer songs than its predecessor, it contains everything a casual fan will need. *—Stephen Thomas Erlewine*

Power Pop, Vol. 1 / 1996 / RPM ✦✦✦✦✦
Featuring the hit singles "Go All the Way," "Don't Want to Say Goodbye," "I Wanna Be with You," and "Let's Pretend," *Power Pop, Vol. 1* combines the Raspberries' first two albums—*Raspberries* and *Fresh Raspberries*—onto one compact disc. *—Stephen Thomas Erlewine*

Power Pop, Vol. 2 / 1996 / RPM ✦✦✦✦✦
Featuring the hit singles "Tonight," "I'm a Rocker" and "Overnight Sensation (Hit Record)," *Power Pop, Vol. 2* combines the Raspberries' last two albums—*Side Three* and *Starting Over*—on one compact disc. *—Stephen Thomas Erlewine*

Ratt

f. 1983, **db.** 1992
Group / Album Rock, Hair Metal, Heavy Metal, Hard Rock
Ratt's brash, melodic heavy metal made the Los Angeles quintet one of the most popular rock acts of the mid-'80s. The group had its origins in the '70s group Mickey Ratt, which had evolved into Ratt by 1983; at that time the band featured vocalist Stephen Pearcy, guitarist Robbin Crosby, guitarist Warren D. Martini, bassist Juan Croucier, and drummer Bobby Blotzer. The band released their self-titled first album independently in 1983, which led to a major label contract with Atlantic Records. Their first album under this deal, 1984's *Out of the Cellar,* was a major success, reaching the American Top Ten and selling over three million copies. "Round and Round," the first single drawn from the album, hit number 12, proving the band had pop crossover potential. While their second album, 1985's *Invasion of Your Privacy,* didn't match the multi-platinum figures of *Out of the Cellar,* it also reached the Top Ten and sold over a million copies. By that time, the band could sell out concerts across the country and were a staple on MTV and AOR radio. Both *Dancin' Undercover* (1986) and *Reach for the Sky* (1988) continued the band's platinum streak and their audience, had only slipped slightly by the time of their final album, 1990's *Detonator.* In 1992, Pearcy left Ratt to form his own band; his departure effectively put an end to the group for the better part of the decade before reuniting for 1997's *Collage* and a self-titled 1999 LP. *—Stephen Thomas Erlewine*

● **Ratt & Roll 8191** / Sep. 1991 / Atlantic ✦✦✦✦✦
A terrific and comprehensive overview of Ratt's entire career, *Ratt & Roll 81-91* contains 19

tracks, including all of the group's hits ("Round and Round," "Wanted Man," "Lay It Down," "You're in Love," "Dance," "Way Cool Jr."), as well as all the best album tracks from their frequently uneven records. In other words, it's a definitive package, containing everything that anyone but hardcore fans could ever need. *—Stephen Thomas Erlewine*

Lou Rawls (Louis Allen Rawls)

b. Dec. 1, 1935, Chicago, IL
Vocals / Vocal Jazz, Philly Soul, R&B, Soul
When Chicago-born Lou Rawls croons a soulful love song, his deep-hued pipes rumble with simmering passion. Rawls did the usual gospel apprenticeship before breaking out on a landmark jazz album with pianist Les McCann's trio for Capitol that launched his secular career. But it took Rawls a while to establish himself as a soul artist—perhaps he was perceived as a little too sophisticated and jazzy (although his uncredited responses on Sam Cooke's "Bring It on Home to Me" certainly proved he could wail). "Love Is a Hurtin' Thing" instantly changed that notion when it topped the R&B charts in 1966, and the unyielding "Dead End Street" and "Your Good Thing (Is About to End)" perpetuated his success.

After memorably delivering Bobby Hebb's powerful "A Natural Man" in 1971, Rawls joined forces with Philadelphia producers Kenny Gamble and Leon Huff in 1976, emerging with the silky "You'll Never Find Another Love Like Mine," another gigantic R&B and pop smash tailor-made for nattily sweeping across the classiest disco dance floors. The disco era's long gone now, but Rawls maintains elegantly. He's still as cool as cool can be. *—Bill Dahl*

Spotlight on Lou Rawls / Feb. 5, 1962 Jan. 2, -196 / Capitol ✦✦✦
This 18-track compilation isolates his most pop-oriented output for Capitol in the '60s, consisting largely of standards on the order of "St. James Infirmary," "Stormy Weather," and "Willow Weep for Me," often with orchestration. Includes one previously unreleased cut, "When It's Sleepy Time Down South." *—Richie Unterberger*

Stormy Monday / Feb. 5, 1962 - Feb. 12, 1962 / Blue Note ✦✦✦✦✦

Love Is a Hurtin' Thing: The Silk & Soul of Lou Rawls / Jun. 3, 1997 / Capitol ✦✦✦✦✦

● **The Best of Lou Rawls: Classic Philadelphia Recordings** / Nov. 24, 1998 / Music Club ✦✦✦✦✦

● **Anthology** / Jun. 6, 2000 / Capitol ✦✦✦✦✦
True, this two-CD compilation of 1962-1970 tracks isn't the most balanced Lou Rawls retrospective, as it favors his early soul output and has nothing from his commercial peak in the late '70s with Philadelphia International. It's also true that if you favor Rawls at his earthiest, you'll likely find this the best Rawls compilation available. Not that Rawls ever got too down 'n' dirty, but these are the songs on which his bluesiest leanings came most to the fore, leavened by various degrees of jazz and pop. His three big Capitol hits ("Love Is a Hurtin' Thing," "Dead End Street," and "Your Good Thing (Is About to End)") are all here, but the 33-song program includes a good many other satisfying outings that most listeners will have never heard. There's the previously unreleased 1962 cover of Sam Cooke's "What Makes the Ending"; the odd soul-jazz reading of "It Was a Very Good Year"; and the first-rate soul of 1967's "You Can Bring Me All Your Heartaches." The somewhat weird "Down Here on the Ground" is soul-pop tinged by disoriented psychedelic allusions in the lyrics about wanting to fly, and a bad-trip swirl of strings; co-written by Lalo Schifrin and folk-pop one-hit wonder Gale Garnett, it was used in the *Cool Hand Luke* movie. It's not all soul; indeed, there are a few smoothies like "Willow Weep for Me" and straight jazz interpretations that are among the less interesting selections. On the other hand, cuts like "Dead End Street" and "Blues Is a Woman" show Rawls to be one of the more talented songwriters of hard-luck blues-soul-jazz tunes, though he penned just a handful of the cuts on this anthology. *—Richie Unterberger*

The Red Hot Chili Peppers

f. 1983
Group / College Rock, Rap-Rock, Funk Metal, Alternative Pop/Rock
A quartet with varying personnel, anchored by lead singer Anthony Kiedis and bassist Flea (born Michael Balzary), the Red Hot Chili Peppers play a hybrid rock, incorporating punk, funk, rap, and metal. Though the mixture was ahead of its time when the group was first organized in the early '80s in Los Angeles, the music industry has since caught up to it, which earns the group the right to call itself the forerunner of an approach now adopted by such acts as Living Colour and Faith No More, and also means the Peppers themselves have finally hit the big time. They scored a commercial breakthrough with *Mother's Milk*, which went gold after its release in 1989. They ascended to real star status with the release of *Blood Sugar Sex Magik*, which sold two million copies and included the Top Ten hit "Under the Bridge." Although it went platinum and spent nearly a year on the charts, 1995's *One Hot Minute* was ultimately a disappointment, failing to live up to the expectations set by *Blood Sugar Sex Magik*. *—William Ruhlmann*

Red Hot Chili Peppers / 1984 / EMI America ✦✦✦✦✦

Freaky Styley / 1985 / EMI America ✦✦✦✦✦

The Uplift Mofo Party Plan / 1987 / EMI America ✦✦✦

Mother's Milk / Aug. 1989 / EMI America ✦✦✦
The Chili Peppers' playing on *Mother's Milk* is more metallic than ever, thanks to newcomers Chad Smith (drums) and especially John Frusciante (guitar). Thanks to their presence, Kiedis and Flea sound reinvigorated in their performances, but the material is inconsistent, with too much of the second half in particular seeming like undeveloped, loud-fast-manic schtick. Still, there are more than enough quality tracks to make the filler worth sorting through, most obviously the heavy reworking of Stevie Wonder's "Higher Ground" and the cautionary, heartfelt "Knock Me Down," as well as several others scattered over the album. *—Steve Huey*

Blood Sugar Sex Magik / Sep. 1991 / Warner Brothers ✦✦✦✦✦
The Chili Peppers' best album, *Blood Sugar Sex Magik* benefits immensely from Rick Rubin's production—Frusciante's guitar is less overpoweringly noisy, leaving room for differing textures and clearer lines, while the band overall is more focused and less indulgent, even if some of the grooves drag on too long. Lyrically, Kiedis is as preoccupied with sex as ever, whether invoking it as his muse, begging for it, or boasting in great detail about his prowess, best showcased on the infectiously funky singles "Give It Away" and "Suck My Kiss." However, he tempers his testosterone with a more sensitive side, writing about the emotional side of failed relationships ("Breaking the Girl," "I Could Have Lied"), his drug addictions ("Under the Bridge" and an elegy for Hillel Slovak, "My Lovely Man"), and some hippie-ish calls for a peaceful utopia. Three of those last four songs (excluding "My Lovely Man") mark the band's first consistent embrace of lilting acoustic balladry, and while it's not what Kiedis does best as a vocalist, these are some of the album's finest moments, varying and expanding the group's musical and emotional range. Frusciante departed after the supporting tour, leaving *Blood Sugar Sex Magik* as probably the best album the Chili Peppers will ever make. *—Steve Huey*

● **What Hits!—** / Sep. 29, 1992 / EMI America ✦✦✦✦✦
After the Red Hot Chili Peppers left EMI for Warner Bros. and hit the big time with "Under the Bridge," their former label gathered most of the best tracks from the group's first four albums for the compilation *What Hits!*. Since *Blood Sugar Sex Magik*, the Peppers' most popular album, was recorded for Warner, none of its songs are present—with the exception of "Under the Bridge," which was somehow licensed for use. *What Hits!* does a pretty good job of sifting through the Peppers' uneven discography and picking out the best moments, making it a very useful sampler; it also contains "Show Me Your Soul," the band's contribution to the *Pretty Woman* soundtrack. *—Steve Huey*

One Hot Minute / Sep. 12, 1995 / Warner Brothers ✦✦✦

Californication / Jun. 8, 1999 / Warner Brothers ✦✦✦✦
Many figured that the Chili Peppers' days of undisputed alternative kings were numbered after their lackluster 1995 release *One Hot Minute*, but like the great phoenix rising from the ashes, this legendary and influential outfit returned back to greatness with 1999's *Californication*. An obvious reason for their rebirth is the reappearance of guitarist John Frusciante (replacing Dave Navarro), who left the Peppers in 1992 and disappeared into a haze of hard drugs before cleaning up and returning to the fold in 1998. Frusciante was a main reason for such past band classics as 1989's *Mother's Milk* and 1991's *Blood/Sugar/Sex/Magik*, and proves once and for all to be the quintessential RHCP guitarist. Anthony Kiedis' vocals have improved dramatically as well, while the rhythm section of bassist Flea and drummer Chad Smith remains one of rock's best. The quartet's trademark punk-funk can be sampled on such tracks as "Around the World," "I Like Dirt" and "Parallel Universe," but the more pop-oriented material proves to be a pleasant surprise—"Scar Tissue," "Otherside," "Easily" and "Purple Stain" all contain strong melodies and instantly memorable choruses. And like their 1992 introspective hit "Under the Bridge," there are a even a few mellow moments—"Porcelain," "Road Trippin'" and the title track. With the instrumentalists' interplay at an all time telepathic high and Kiedis peaking as a vocalist, *Californication* is a bonafide Chili Peppers classic. It would be a crime for this stellar, definitive lineup to not remain intact the second time around. *—Greg Prato*

Red House Painters

f. 1989, San Francisco, CA
Group / Sadcore, Dream Pop, Indie Rock, Alternative Pop/Rock, Singer/Songwriter
Red House Painters was primarily the vehicle of singer/songwriter Mark Kozelek, an evocative, compelling performer of rare emotional intensity. Like Mark Eitzel of American Music Club, to whose work the Painters were invariably compared and to whom their early success owed a tremendous debt, Kozelek laid his soul bare on record, conjuring harrowingly acute tales of pain, despair and loss; unlike Eitzel, Nick Drake and other poets of decay, Kozelek's autobiographical songs walked their tightrope without a net—forsaking the safety offered by metaphor and allegory, he faced his demons in the first person, creating a singularly haunting body of work unparalleled in its vulnerability and honesty. While performing on the Bay Area club circuit, the quartet came to the attention of American Music Club's Eitzel, who often named Red House Painters his favorite band. Through Eitzel, a demo tape of recordings cut in 1989 and 1990 made their way to the London offices of 4AD Records, which signed the group and in 1992 issued the unvarnished demos—a superb collection of spartan, atmospheric melodies lurking behind Kozelek's ghostly vocals—as the LP *Down Colorful Hill*. In 1993, Red House Painters emerged from the studio with over two dozen new recordings, which they issued on back-to-back eponymously-titled albums. Taken in tandem, the LPs established Kozelek as a unique songwriter capable of conveying stunning emotional depths; compositions like "Grace Cathedral Park," "Katy Song," "Strawberry Hill," "Evil" and "Uncle Joe" expanded greatly upon the emotional palette evidenced on the first record, unflinchingly detailing Kozelek's erratic, abusive nature and troubled background. *—Jason Ankeny*

Down Colorful Hill / Sep. 15, 1992 / 4AD ✦✦✦✦✦

Red House Painters [I] / May 25, 1993 / 4AD ✦✦✦✦✦
The first of the group's two eponymously titled 1993 efforts is a sprawling, remarkable set distinguished by Mark Kozelek's continuing maturation as a songwriter; far removed from the uniform darkness of *Down Colorful Hill*, *Red House Painters* offers an expansion of both emotional and musical possibilities. Working outward from the cutting "Mistress"—included as both a Spartan piano ballad and as a gauzy rock number—the record moves through a shifting, impressionistic backdrop of textures and sounds; from the luminous folk-pop of "Grace Cathedral Park" to the epic dissonance of the gut-wrenching "Strawberry Hill," the songs resonate with depth and poignancy, and rank as Kozelek's most fully realized collection of compositions. *—Jason Ankeny*

Red House Painters [II] / Sep. 1993 / 4AD ✦✦✦

● **Ocean Beach** / Mar. 28, 1995 / 4AD ✦✦✦✦✦
Red House Painters has always been Mark Kozelek's project, but *Ocean Beach* represents the first record that is almost entirely a solo project. Not that that distinction has made a great

change in the music—*Ocean Beach* is a spare, gentle, nearly painfully introspective folk-rock album that draws more from Simon & Garfunkel than Bob Dylan. Kozelek reigns in the droning, experimental tendencies of the group's first full-length album, yet he is more generous with his melodies and arrangements than the band's second untitled record. While Red House Painters remains very arty and self-conscious, *Ocean Beach* shows the singer/songwriter breaking out of his shell ever so slightly, bringing more fully developed songs and melodies with him. *—Stephen Thomas Erlewine*

Songs for a Blue Guitar / Jul. 23, 1996 / Supreme ♦♦♦

Retrospective / May 18, 1999 / 4AD ♦♦♦♦
Retrospective collects some of the finest moments from the Red House Painters' albums for 4AD as well as some previously unreleased work. Compiled by Mark Kozelek and Ivo Watts-Russell, this two CD set features one disc spanning Kozelek's four-album output for the label. Kozelek's cover of Kiss' "Shock Me," which was previously available only on a UK single, opens the first disc; tracks like "Katy Song," "Medicine Bottle," "San Geronimo," "New Jersey," "Mistress," and "Drop" are also included. Demos, outtakes, and live recordings are included on the second disc, including two songs, "Waterkill" and "Instrumental" that were previously unreleased. Alternate versions of Painters favorites like "Japanese to English," "Funhouse," "Dragonflies," and "Brockwell Park" also appear on the second disc, making *Retrospective* an affordable starting point for newcomers, and a welcome addition for collectors. *—Heather Phares*

Otis Redding

b. Sep. 9, 1941, Dawson, GA, **d.** Dec. 10, 1967, Madison, WI
Vocals / Deep Soul, Southern Soul, Soul
One of the most influential soul singers of the 1960s, Otis Redding exemplified to many listeners the power of Southern "Deep Soul"—hoarse, gritty vocals, brassy arrangements, and an emotional way with both party tunes and aching ballads. He was also the most consistent exponent of the Stax sound, cutting his records at the Memphis label/studios that did much to update rhythm and blues into modern soul. After Redding's 1962 ballad "These Arms of Mine" became an R&B hit, his solo career was truly on its way, though the hits didn't really start to fly until 1965 and 1966, when "Mr. Pitiful," "I've Been Loving You Too Long," "I Can't Turn You Loose," a cover of the Rolling Stones' "Satisfaction," and "Respect" were all big sellers on the R&B charts. In 1967, he began to show signs of making major inroads into the White audience, particularly with a well-received performance at the Monterey Pop Festival. Redding's biggest triumph, however, came just days before his death, when he recorded the wistful "(Sittin' on) The Dock of the Bay," which represented a significant leap as far as examination of more intensely personal emotions. Also highlighted by crisp Cropper guitar leads and dignified horns, it rose to the top of the pop charts in early 1968. Otis Redding, however, had perished in a plane crash in December 1967. *—Richie Unterberger*

Pain in My Heart / Jan. 1964 / Rhino ♦♦♦♦♦
Redding's blistering debut set the tone for all his later releases and brought the rough, emotional delivery of gospel into R&B in what would soon be called soul. Listen and try to tell yourself Redding was only 22 when he recorded this; there's a lifetime of love and broken hearts in his delivery already. The 12 songs here pay tribute to his favorite singers, mainly Sam Cooke ("You Send Me"), Ben E. King ("Stand By Me"), and the most influential rock & roll shouter Little Richard ("Lucille"). Redding and band play it safe in these initial covers; there's nothing yet as daring as the bizarre twisting of Cooke's "Chain Gang" of three years later. Redding's originals, apart from the rather derivative "Hey Hey Baby," are fabulous: "Pain in My Heart," the slow, burning ballad of "These Arms of Mine," and "That's What My Heart Needs," all singles taken from the album. *—Ted Mills*

The Great Otis Redding Sings Soul Ballads / Mar. 1965 / Rhino ♦♦♦♦♦

☆ **Otis Blue: Otis Redding Sings Soul** / 1966 / Atco ♦♦♦♦♦
Otis Redding's third album, and his first fully realized album, presents his talent unfettered, his direction clear, and his confidence emboldened, with fully half the songs representing a reach that extended his musical grasp. More than a quarter of this album is given over to Redding's versions of songs by Sam Cooke, his idol, who had died the previous December, and all three are worth owning and hearing. Two of them, "A Change Is Gonna Come" and "Shake," are every bit as essential as any soul recordings ever made, and while they (and much of this album) have reappeared on several anthologies, it's useful to hear the songs from those sessions juxtaposed with each other, and with "Wonderful World," which is seldom compiled elsewhere.

Also featured are Redding's spellbinding renditions of "Satisfaction" (a song epitomizing the fully formed Stax/Volt sound and which Mick Jagger and Keith Richards originally wrote in tribute to and imitation of Redding's style), "My Girl," and "You Don't Miss Your Water." "Respect" and "I've Been Loving You Too Long," two originals that were to loom large in his career, are here as well; the former became vastly popular in the hands of Aretha Franklin and the latter was an instant soul classic. Among the seldom-cited jewels here is a rendition of B.B. King's "Rock Me Baby" that has the singer sharing the spotlight with Steve Cropper, his playing alternately elegant and fiery, with Wayne Jackson and Gene "Bowlegs" Miller's trumpets and Andrew Love's and Floyd Newman's saxes providing the backing. Redding's powerful, remarkable singing throughout makes *Otis Blue* gritty, rich, and achingly alive, and an essential listening experience. *—Bruce Eder*

The Soul Album / Apr. 1966 / Rhino ♦♦♦♦

☆ **The Complete & Unbelievable: The Otis Redding Dictionary of Soul** / Oct. 1966 / Rhino ♦♦♦♦♦
Otis Redding's fourth album delivers a dozen towering performances on material fully worthy of his talents, ranging from originals like "Fa-Fa-Fa-Fa-Fa (Sad Song)" to covers of the Beatles' "Day Tripper" and the country standard "Tennessee Waltz," with the classics "My Lover's Prayer" and "Try a Little Tenderness" sandwiched in there. What separates this album from its immediate predecessor is the intensity of his performance and the range of repertory—most of the highlights have been anthologized many times over, but this album is still worth hearing all in one, capturing the moment when the singer was approaching his peak. He was only to complete one more solo studio album (*Otis Blue*) before his untimely death, and this and it are indispensable additions to any serious soul collection. *—Bruce Eder*

King & Queen / Mar. 1967 / Atco ♦♦♦♦♦
Otis Redding never recorded a lighter, more purely entertaining record than *King and Queen*, a collection of duets with Stax labelmate Carla Thomas. In all likelihood inspired by a series of popular duets recorded by Marvin Gaye—indeed, "It Takes Two," and Gaye's sublime collaboration with Kim Weston, is covered here—the record serves no greater purpose than to allow Redding the chance to run through some of the era's biggest soul hits, including *"Knock on Wood,"* "Tell It Like It Is" and "When Something Is Wrong with My Baby," and while clearly not a personal triumph on a par with either *Otis Blue* or *The Dictionary of Soul*, the set is still hugely succcessful on its own terms. Redding and Thomas enjoy an undeniable chemistry, and they play off each other wonderfully; while sparks fly furiously throughout *King and Queen*, the album's highlight is the classic *"Tramp,"* where their battle of the sexes reaches its fever pitch in supremely witty fashion. *—Jason Ankeny*

Live in Europe / Jul. 1967 / Rhino ♦♦♦

☆ **The Dock of the Bay** / Feb. 1968 / Atco ♦♦♦♦♦
It was never supposed to be like this: "(Sittin' on the Dock of the Bay" was supposed to mark a beginning of a new phase in Otis Redding's career, not an ending. Producer/guitarist Steve Cropper had a difficult task to perform in pulling together this album, the first of several posthumous releases issued by Stax/Volt in the wake of Otis Redding's death. What could have been a cash-in effort or a grim memorial album instead became a vivid, exciting presentation of some key aspects of the talent that was lost when Redding died. *Dock of the Bay* is, indeed, a mixed bag of singles and B-sides going back to July of 1965, one hit duet with Carla Thomas, and a pair of previously unissued tracks from 1966 and 1967, respectively. There's little cohesion, stylistic or otherwise, in the songs, especially when the title track is taken into consideration—nothing else here resembles it, for the obvious reason that Redding never had a chance to follow it up. Despite the mix-and-match nature of the album, however, this is an impossible record not to love. Cropper chose his tracks well, selecting some of the strongest and most unusual among the late singer's orphaned songs: "I Love You More Than Words Can Say" is one of Redding's most passionate performances; "Let Me Come on Home" presents an ebullient Otis Redding accompanied by some sharp playing; and "Don't Mess With Cupid" begins with a gorgeous guitar flourish and blooms into an intense, pounding, soaring showcase for singer and band alike. No one could complain about the album then, and it still holds more than three decades later. Reissued on CD by the Atco label through Rhino Records in excellent sound. *—Bruce Eder*

The Immortal Otis Redding / Jun. 1968 / Rhino ♦♦♦

☆ **In Person at the Whisky a Go Go** / Oct. 1968 / Rhino ♦♦♦♦♦
This album, released posthumously, captured Otis Redding's show at the Whisky A Go Go from April of 1966 in Los Angeles. What is essential here was that it captured Otis Redding's sound in a small club with his own touring band, as opposed to his work on stage with Booker T. & The MG's—an ideal band, to be sure, which is why they were sent over to Europe with him and why they were at Monterey with him a year later, but not the group that Redding normally worked on stage with. This album is closer to how Otis Redding sounded in the years coming up and working his way to the top, and the way that his original audience on the chitlin' circuit heard him. The singer and his band (including a pair of tenor saxes, a trombone, and four trumpets, with James Young, Ralph Stewart, and Elbert Woodson pounding out the rhythm on guitar, bass, and drums, respectively, go through roaring versions of "Respect", "I Can't Turn You Loose", "These Arms of Mine", "Pain in My Heart", "Satisfaction" and "Papa's Got a Brand New Bag" and four more, in Redding's only full-length recording in a small-scale setting. They may not have the musical elegance of Booker T. and company, but they create this intense, hypnotic sound that is spellbinding. The set itself lasts less than 40 minutes but the singer and his band are so energetic, that it doesn't feel short or lacking. This album was, in more ways than one, Redding's equivalent to Sam Cooke's *Live At The Harlem Square Club*, and just as essential. Reissued in 1992 on the Atco label through Rhino Records. *—Bruce Eder*

Love Man / Jun. 1969 / Rhino ♦♦♦

Tell the Truth / Jul. 1970 / Rhino ♦♦♦

Remember Me / 1992 / Stax ♦♦♦

★ **The Very Best of Otis Redding** / 1993 / Rhino ♦♦♦♦♦
The Very Best of Otis Redding wasn't the first Otis Redding compilation but it is the best of the the single-disc collections, distilling the high points across his career (up thru the posthumous hits "(Sitting' On) The Dock of the Bay" and the heartbreaking "I've Got Dreams to Remember") in 16 tracks, every one a musical milestone and a soul music high-point of one kind or another. Although aimed at the casual listener and the neophyte fan, there are some astonishing realizations to be had in listening to this disc and looking at the chart placements of the early sides, and realizing just how uniform his musical influence is—"These Arms of Mine" and, especially, "Pain In My Heart", from 1962 and 1963, respectively, sold only a fraction of what his later singles did, yet they've been covered by so many artists since, that they're as familiar as any of the other, bigger hits on this disc. The collection is hardly comprehensive, but all of the major bases are touched, right down to his 1967 hit duet "Tramp" with Carla Thomas. The other advantage, especially for those on a budget, is that this was the first Otis Redding compilation to avail itself of the improved master tape research and analog-to-digital technology of the early '90s. *—Bruce Eder*

Good to Me: Live at the Whiskey A Go Go, Vol. 2 / Jan. 25, 1993 / Stax ♦♦♦

☆ **Otis! The Definitive Otis Redding** / Nov. 9, 1993 / Rhino ♦♦♦♦♦
Anyone who wants to understand the different phases of Otis Redding's career, and the reason for his having made a major impact across the 1960s and beyond, can have no better place to start than *Otis! The Definitive Otis Redding.* There are 73 studio cuts here and the

producers have reached back beyond the Atlantic and Stax vaults: They've include numbers like "She's All Right," cut by the Shooters featuring Otis Redding in the summer of 1960 for the Transworld label; "Gettin' Hip," which was done for the Alshire label in 1960; and "Shout Bamalama" by Otis Redding & the Pinetoppers, recorded for Confederate, all prior to Redding's signing with Stax. The selection of studio cuts suggests that the makers thought long and hard about each and every track on this disc—the first three CDs are a mix of single A- and B-sides, coupled with important album tracks, all culminating with "(Sittin' On) The Dock of the Bay." Little or nothing that's essential is missing along the way (though one could argue very persuasively that anything on the albums that Redding released in his lifetime was essential in some respect). The fourth disc is the real killer, however; 23 live songs drawn from the complete range of his concert tapes in the Atlantic (and Stax) vaults, from the *Apollo Theater* in New York in November of 1963 to his final tour of Europe and the *Monterey International Pop Festival* in the spring of 1967, including individual tracks that were unheard until the 1980s. An extensive booklet is also included. *—Bruce Eder*

☆ **The Very Best of Otis Redding, Vol. 2** / Apr. 25, 1995 / Rhino ✦✦✦✦✦

Dreams to Remember: The Otis Redding Anthology / Aug. 18, 1998 / Rhino ✦✦✦✦✦
Dreams to Remember: The Otis Redding Anthology presents an interesting dilemma. Certainly, the music on the double-disc set is superb—all of his hits are here, along with a wealth of great album tracks and five live cuts from the Monterey International Pop Festival. The question is, was the collection *necessary*? Casual listeners who just want the hits will be satisfied with the excellent *Very Best of Otis Redding*, while those who want to dig deeper will find the four-disc box *Otis! The Definitive Otis Redding* essential, or will opt for the actual albums. *Dreams to Remember* falls somewhere between the two extremes, containing too much music for the casual listener and not being extensive enough for serious listeners. Perhaps realizing this, Rhino added several tracks here that weren't featured on the box set, but any true collector will have these songs on the original albums. So, *Dreams to Remember* is in limbo—a fine collection that isn't really necessary. It's not a bad choice, to be sure, but *The Very Best of Otis Redding* and *Otis!* are better choices, depending on your tastes. *—Stephen Thomas Erlewine*

Lou Reed

b. Mar. 2, 1942, Freeport, Long Island, NY
Vocals, Keyboards, Guitar (Electric), Guitar / New York Punk, Album Rock, Proto-Punk, Glam Rock, Hard Rock, Singer/Songwriter
The career of Lou Reed defies capsule summarization. Like David Bowie (whom Reed directly inspired in many ways), he has made over his image many times, mutating from theatrical glam-rocker to scary-looking junkie to avant-garde noiseman to straight rock & roller to yer average guy. A firmer grasp of rock's earthier qualities has ensured a more consistent career path than Bowie's, particularly in his latter years. Yet his catalog is extremely inconsistent, in both quality and stylistic orientation. Liking one Lou Reed LP, or several, or all of the ones he did in a particular era, is no guarantee that you'll like all of them, or even most of them.

Few would deny Reed's immense importance and considerable achievements, however. As has often been written, he expanded the vocabulary of rock & roll lyrics into the previously forbidden territory of kinky sex, drug use (and abuse), decadence, transvestites, homosexuality, and suicidal depression. As has been pointed out less often, he remained (and remains) committed to using rock & roll as a forum for literary, mature expression well into middle age, without growing lyrically soft or musically complacent. By and large, he's taken on these challenging duties with uncompromising honesty and a high degree of realism. For these reasons, he's often cited as punk's most important ancestor. It's often overlooked, though, that he's equally skilled at celebrating romantic joy, and rock & roll itself, as he is at depicting harrowing urban realities. Most would have to concede that with the exception of Neil Young, no other star that rose to fame in the 1960s has continued to push himself so diligently into creating work that is meaningful and contemporary. If that means he relies on stock musical and lyrical ideas at times (as Young does), it also means he's proved that rock can remain relevant to listeners other than hormone-crazed teenagers. *—Richie Unterberger*

Lou Reed / 1972 / RCA ✦✦✦

Transformer / 1972 / RCA ✦✦✦✦✦
David Bowie has never been shy about acknowledging his influences, and since the boho decadence and sexual ambiguity of the Velvet Underground's music had a major impact on Bowie's work, it was only fitting that as *Ziggy Stardust*-mania was reaching its peak, Bowie would offer Lou Reed some much needed help with his career, which was stuck in neutral after his first solo album came and went. Musically, Reed's work didn't have too much in common with the sonic bombast of the glam scene, but at least it was a place where his eccentricities could find a comfortable home, and on *Transformer* Bowie and his right-hand man, Mick Ronson, crafted a new sound for Reed that was better fitting (and more commercially astute) than the ambivalent tone of his first solo album. Ronson adds some guitar raunch to "Vicious" and "Hangin' Round" that's a lot flashier than what Reed cranked out with the Velvets, but still honors Lou's strengths in guitar-driven hard rock, while the imaginative arrangements Ronson cooked up for "Perfect Day," "Walk on the Wild Side," and "Goodnight Ladies" blend pop polish with musical thinking just as distinctive as Reed's lyrical conceits. And while Reed occasionally overplays his hand in writing stuff he figured the glam kids wanted ("Make Up" and "I'm So Free" being the most obvious examples), "Perfect Day," "Walk on the Wild Side," and "New York Telephone Conversation" proved he could still write about the demimonde with both perception and respect. The sound and style of *Transformer* would in many ways define Lou Reed's career in the 1970s, and while it led him into a style that proved to be a dead end, you can't deny that Bowie and Ronson gave their hero a new lease on life—and a solid album in the bargain. *—Mark Deming*

Berlin / 1973 / RCA ✦✦✦
Transformer and "Walk on the Wild Side" were both major hits in 1972, to the surprise of both Lou Reed and the music industry, and with Reed suddenly a hot commodity, he used his newly won clout to make the most ambitious album of his career, *Berlin*. *Berlin* was the musical equivalent of a drug-addled kid set loose in a candy store; the album's songs, which form a loose storyline about a doomed romance between two chemically fueled bohemians, were fleshed out with a huge, boomy production (Bob Ezrin at his most grandiose) and arrangements overloaded with guitars, keyboards, horns, strings, and any other kitchen sink that was handy (the session band included Jack Bruce, Steve Winwood, Aynsley Dunbar, and Tony Levin). And while Reed had often been accused of focusing on the dark side of life, he and Ezrin approached *Berlin* as their opportunity to make The Most Depressing Album of All Time, and they hardly missed a trick. This all seemed a bit much for an artist who made such superb use of the two-guitars/bass/drums lineup with the Velvet Underground, especially since Reed doesn't even play electric guitar on the album; the sheer size of *Berlin* ultimately overpowers both Reed and his material. But if *Berlin* is largely a failure of ambition, that sets it apart from the vast majority of Reed's lesser works; Lou's vocals are both precise and impassioned, and though a few of the songs are little more than sketches, the best—"How Do You Think It Feels," "Oh Jim," "The Kids," and "Sad Song"—are powerful, bitter stuff. It's hard not to be impressed by *Berlin*, given the sheer scope of the project, but while it earns an A for Effort, the actual execution merits more of a B-. *—Mark Deming*

Rock & Roll Animal / 1974 / RCA ✦✦✦✦
In 1974, after the commercial disaster of his album *Berlin*, Lou Reed needed a hit, and *Rock & Roll Animal* was a rare display of commercial acumen on his part, just the right album at just the right time. Recorded in concert with Reed's crack road band at the peak of their form, *Rock & Roll Animal* offered a set of his most anthemic songs (most dating from his days with the Velvet Underground) in arrangements that presented his lean, effective melodies and street-level lyrics in their most user-friendly form (or at least as user friendly as an album with a song called "Heroin" can get). Early '70s arena-rock bombast is often the order of the day, but guitarists Dick Wagner and Steve Hunter use their six-string muscle to lift these songs up, not weigh them down, and with Reed's passionate but controlled vocals riding over the top, "Sweet Jane," "White Light/White Heat," and "Rock 'n' Roll" finally sound like the radio hits they always should have been. Reed would rarely sound this commercial again, but *Rock & Roll Animal* proves he could please a crowd when he had to. The revised CD reissue of *Rock & Roll Animal* released in 2000 offers markedly better sound than the album's initial release, along with two bonus cut that give a better idea of how this band approached the material from *Berlin* on stage, as well as an amusing moment of Reed verbally sparring with a heckler. *—Mark Deming*

Sally Can't Dance / 1974 / Buddha ✦✦

Lou Reed Live / 1975 / RCA ✦✦✦

Metal Machine Music / 1975 / Buddha ✦
One would be hard-pressed to name a major artist who ever released an album as thoroughly alienating at Lou Reed's *Metal Machine Music;* at a time when noise rock and punk had yet to make their presence known, Reed released this 64-minute aural assault that offered up a densely layered soundscape constructed from feedback, distortion, and atonal guitar runs sped-up or slowed-down until they were all but unrecognizable. *Metal Machine Music* seems a bit less startling today, now that bands like Sonic Youth and the Boredoms have created some sort of context for it, but it hasn't gotten any more user friendly with time—while Thurston Moore may go nuts on his guitar like this for three or four minutes at a stretch, *Metal Machine Music* goes on and on and on for over an hour, pausing only for side breaks with no rhythms, melodies, or formal structures to buffer the onslaught. If you're brave enough to listen to the whole thing, it's hard not to marvel at the scope of Reed's obsession; it's obvious he spent a lot of time on these layered sheets of noise, and enthusiasts of the violent guitar freakout may find it pleasing in short bursts. But confronting *Metal Machine Music* from front to back in one sitting is an experience that's both brutal and numbing. It's hard to say what Lou Reed had in mind when he made *Metal Machine Music*, and Reed has done little to clarify the issue over the years, though he summed it up quite pointedly in an interview in which he said, "Well, anyone who gets to side four is dumber than I am." For the record, I did get to side four. But I got paid for it. *—Mark Deming*

Coney Island Baby / Feb. 1976 / RCA ✦✦✦✦✦
From 1972's *Transformer* onward, Lou Reed spent most of the '70s playing the druggy decadence card for all it was worth, with increasingly mixed results. But on *Coney Island Baby*, Reed's songwriting began to move into warmer, more compassionate territory, and the result was his most approachable album since *Loaded*. On most of the tracks, Reed stripped his band back down to guitar, bass, and drums, and the results were both leaner and a lot more comfortable than the leaden over-production of *Sally Can't Dance* or *Berlin*. "Crazy Feeling," "She's My Best Friend," and "Coney Island Baby" found Reed actually writing recognizable love songs for a change, and while Reed pursued his traditional interest in the underside of the hipster's life on "Charlie's Girl" and "Nobody's Business," he did so with a breezy, free-wheeling air that was truly a relief after the lethargic tone of *Sally Can't Dance*. "Kicks" used an audio-tape collage to generate atmospheric tension that gave its tale of drugs and death a chilling quality that was far more effective than his usual blasé take on the subject, and "Coney Island Baby" was the polar opposite, a song about love and regret that was as sincere and heart-tugging as anything the man has ever recorded. *Coney Island Baby* sounds casual on the surface, but emotionally it's as compelling as anything Reed released in the 1970s, and proved Reed could write about real people with recognizable emotions as well as anyone in rock music—something you might not have guessed from most of the solo albums that preceded it. *—Mark Deming*

Rock & Roll Heart / Nov. 1976 / Buddha ✦✦

Walk on the Wild Side: The Best of Lou Reed / 1977 / RCA ✦✦✦✦✦

Live: Take No Prisoners / 1978 / Buddha ✦✦✦

Street Hassle / 1978 / Arista ✦✦✦✦
The rise of the punk/new wave movement in the late '70s proved just how pervasive Lou

Reed's influence had through the past decade, but it also gave him some stiff competition, as suddenly Reed was no longer the only poet of the New York streets. 1978's *Street Hassle* was Reed's first album after punk had gained public currency, and Reed appeared to have taken the minimal approach of punk to heart. With the exception of *Metal Machine Music, Street Hassle* was Reed's rawest set of the 1970s; partly recorded live, with arrangements stripped to the bone, *Street Hassle* was dark, deep, and ominous, a 180-degree turn from the polished neo-glam of *Transformer.* Lyrically, *Street Hassle* found Reed looking deep into himself, and not liking what he saw. Opening with an uncharitable parody of "Sweet Jane," *Street Hassle* found Reed acknowledging just how much a self-parody he'd become in the 1970's, and just how much he hated himself for it, on songs like "Dirt" and "Shooting Star." *Street Hassle* was Reed's most creatively ambitious album since *Berlin,* and it sounded revelatory on first release in 1978. Sadly, time has magnified its flaws; the Lenny Bruce-inspired "I Wanna Be Black" sounds like a bad idea today, and the murk of the album's binaural mix isn't especially flattering to anyone. But the album's best moments are genuinely exciting, and the title cut, a three-movement poetic tone poem about life on the New York streets, is one of the most audacious and deeply moving moments of Reed's solo career. Raw, wounded, and unapologetically difficult, *Street Hassle* isn't the masterpiece Reed was shooting for, but it's still among the most powerful and compelling albums he released during the 1970s, and too personal and affecting to ignore. *—Mark Deming*

The Bells / 1979 / Buddha ♦♦♦♦
After the harrowing triumph of *Street Hassle,* Lou Reed's *The Bells* sounded like a bit of a step back; it returned Reed to the more listener-friendly, keyboard-dominated sound of *Rock & Roll Heart,* the lyrics lacked the caustic self-loathing of songs like "Dirt" or "I Wanna Be Black," and it even featured a four-and-a-half funk workout called "Disco Mystic" (hey, this WAS 1979). But lyrically, *The Bells* found Reed moving away from the boho decadence of most of his 1970s work and towards a more compassionate perspective on his characters; "Families" and "All Through the Night" display an empathy and emotional depth Reed didn't often allow himself as a solo artist, and "Stupid Man" and & "Looking for Love" rocked hard while making the loneliness of their protagonists felt. And the title cut, with Reed experimenting with a guitar synthesizer and free jazz hero Don Cherry inviting the spirit on trumpet, is both a brave exploration of musical space and a lyrically touching sketch of loss and salvation. An album that's worn well over time, *The Bells* gains depth with each playing and now sounds like one of Reed's finest solo efforts of the 1970s. *—Mark Deming*

Growing Up in Public / 1980 / Buddha ♦♦♦

The Blue Mask / 1982 / RCA ♦♦♦♦♦
In 1982, 12 years after he left the Velvet Underground, Lou Reed released *The Blue Mask,* the first album where he lived up to the potential he displayed in the most groundbreaking of all American rock bands. *The Blue Mask* was Reed's first album after he overcame a long-standing addiction to alcohol and drugs, and it reveals a renewed focus and dedication to craft—for the first time in years, Reed had written an entire album's worth of moving, compelling songs, and was performing them with keen skill and genuine emotional commitment. Reed was also playing electric guitar again, and with the edgy genius he summoned up on *White Light/White Heat.* Just as importantly, he brought Robert Quine on board as his second guitarist, giving Reed a worthy foil who at once brought great musical ideas to the table, and encouraged the bandleader to make the most of his own guitar work. (Reed also got superb support from his rhythm section, bassist extrordinaire Fernando Saunders and ace drummer Doane Perry). As Reed stripped his band back to a muscular two-guitars/bass/drums format, he also shed the faux-decadent "Rock 'n' Roll Animal" persona that had dominated his solo work and wrote clearly and fearlessly of his life, his thoughts, and his fears, performing the songs with supreme authority whether he was playing with quiet subtlety (such as the lovely "My House" or the unnerving "The Gun") or cranked-to-ten fury (the paranoid "Waves of Fear" and the emotionally devastating title cut). Intelligent, passionate, literate, mature, and thoroughly heartfelt, *The Blue Mask* was everything Lou Reed's fans had been looking for in his work for years, and it's vivid proof that for some rockers, life can begin on the far side of 35. *—Mark Deming*

Legendary Hearts / 1983 / RCA ♦♦♦♦

Live in Italy / 1984 / RCA ♦♦♦♦♦
Robert Quine has said that the personal and musical differences which led to the end of his working relationship with Lou Reed had put a wall between them well before he finally gave Reed his notice. While Quine never failed to deliver on stage, the tension became audible in their music, and *Live in Italy* captures the best band of Lou Reed's solo career about a year past their peak, not long before they fell apart for the first time (Lou would reassemble the group for the world tour that followed *New Sensations*—a job Quine said he took solely for the money). Consequently, this isn't the ideal document of this band—but it also makes clear that even on a lesser night, Lou Reed, Robert Quine, Fernando Saunders, and Fred Maher were a force to be reckoned with. While Quine's performance isn't flattered by this album's mix, his edgy lines blend superbly with Reed's, and both are in fine fettle, while Fernando Saunders shines on bass and Fred Maher's rock-solid drumming holds everything firmly in place. Reed is on fire on most of these songs, and while this plays for the most part like a "Best of Lou Reed" set, he pulls out sharp, impassioned performances on every cut, doing lean-and-mean justice to Velvet Underground classics like "White Light/White Heat" and "Sister Ray," and rescuing the unnerving "Kill Your Sons" from the oblivion of *Sally Can't Dance.* Are there bootlegs or live videos that capture this band on better nights— Yes. Does that change the fact this is Reed's strongest live album— Not a bit. *—Mark Deming*

New Sensations / 1984 / RCA ♦♦♦♦♦
Lou Reed never struck anyone as one of the happiest guys in rock & roll, so some fans were taken aback when his 1984 album, *New Sensations,* kicked off with "I Love You, Suzanne," a catchy up-tempo rocker that was sounded a lot like a pop tune. After reaffirming his status as one of rock's greatest poets with *The Blue Mask* and *Legendary Hearts,* what was Lou Reed doing here— Lou was having a great time, and his pleasure was infectious—*New Sensations* is a set of straight-ahead rock & roll that ranks with the most purely enjoyable albums of Lou's career. Reed opted not to work with guitarist Robert Quine this time out, instead overdubbing rhythm lines over his own leads, and if the guitars don't cut quite as deep, they're still wiry and in the pocket throughout, and the rhythm section of Fernando Saunders and Fred Maher rocks hard with a tough, sinewy groove. And while much of *New Sensations* finds Reed in a surprisingly optimistic mood, this isn't "Don' t Worry, Be Happy" by any stretch of the imagination. On "Endlessly Jealous," "My Friend George," and "Fly Into the Sun," Reed makes it clear that happiness can be a hard-won commodity, and when Reed embraces life's pleasures on "Turn To Me" and "New Sensations," he does so with a fierce joy that's realistic, unblinking, and deeply felt, like a man whose signed on for the full ride and is going to enjoy the good times while they last. Like *Coney Island Baby, New Sensations* showed that Reed had a lot more warmth and humanity than he was given credit for, and made clear that he could "write happy" when he felt like, with all the impact of his "serious" material. *—Mark Deming*

Mistrial / 1986 / RCA ♦♦♦

New York / 1989 / Sire ♦♦♦♦♦
New York City figured so prominently in Lou Reed's music for so long that it's surprising it took him until 1989 to make an album simply called *New York,* a set of 14 scenes and sketches that represents the strongest, best-realized set of songs of Reed's solo career. While Reed's 1982 comeback, *The Blue Mask,* sometimes found him reaching for effects, *New York*'s accumulated details and deft caricatures hit bull's-eye after bull's-eye for 57 minutes, and does so with an easy stride and striking lyrical facility. *New York* also found Reed writing about the larger world rather than personal concerns for a change, and in the beautiful, decaying heart of New York City, he found plenty to talk about—the devastating impact of AIDS "Halloween Parade," the vicious circle of child abuse "Endless Cycle," the plight of the homeless "Xmas in February"—and even on the songs where he pointedly mounts a soapbox, Reed does so with an intelligence and smart-assed wit that makes him sound opinionated rather than preachy—like a New Yorker. And when Reed does look into his own life, it's with humor and perception; "Beginning of a Great Adventure" is a hilarious meditation on the possibilities of parenthood, and "Dime Store Mystery" is a moving elegy to his former patron Andy Warhol. Reed also unveiled a new band on this set, and while guitarist Mike Rathke didn't challenge Reed the way Robert Quine did, Reed wasn't needing much prodding to play at the peak of his form, and Ron Wasserman proved Reed's superb taste in bass players had not failed him. Produced with subtle intelligence and a minimum of flash, *New York* is a masterpiece of literate, adult rock & roll, and the finest album of Lou Reed's solo career. *—Mark Deming*

Songs for Drella / Jul. 1990 / Sire ♦♦♦♦♦

Magic and Loss / Jan. 14, 1992 / Sire ♦♦♦

Between Thought and Expression: The Lou Reed Anthology / Apr. 14, 1992 / RCA ♦♦♦

Set the Twilight Reeling / Feb. 20, 1996 / Warner Brothers ♦♦♦

● **Different Times: Lou Reed in the '70s** / May 1996 / RCA ♦♦♦♦♦
Reed is very much an album-oriented artist, and those who think they may develop a serious interest in his work are better advised to seek individual titles than compilations. If you just want some of his best songs around the house, though, this is a well-chosen, economic 17-track survey of his best material from his best period as a solo act (the early to mid-'70s). Drawing most heavily from the *Transformer* and *Berlin* albums, this has his most famous/notorious early solo works ("Walk on the Wild Side," "Vicious," "Satellite of Love," "Caroline Says"); some inferior but notably different remakes of songs he recorded with the Velvet Underground ("Lisa Says," "I Can't Stand It," "Sweet Jane"); and other high points like "Kill Your Sons" and "Coney Island Baby." *—Richie Unterberger*

Perfect Night: Live in London / Apr. 21, 1998 / Warner Brothers ♦♦♦

R.E.M.

f. 1980, Athens, GA
Group / College Rock, Jangle Pop, Alternative Pop/Rock
R.E.M. mark the point when post-punk turned into alternative rock. When their first single, "Radio Free Europe," was released in 1981 it sparked a back-to-the-garage movement in the American underground. While there were a number of hardcore and punk bands in the US during the early '80s, R.E.M.—singer Michael Stipe, guitarist Peter Buck, bassist Mike Mills and drummer Bill Berry—brought guitar-pop back into the underground lexicon. Combining ringing guitar hooks with mumbled, cryptic lyrics and an D.I.Y. aesthetic borrowed from post-punk, the band simultaneously sounded traditional and modern. Though there were no overt innovations in their music. R.E.M. had an identity and sense of purpose that transformed the American underground. Throughout the '80s, they worked relentlessly, releasing records every year and touring constantly, playing both theaters and backwoods dives. Along the way, they inspired countless of bands, from the legions of jangle-pop groups in the mid-'80s to scores of alternative-pop groups in the '90s, who admired their slow climb to stardom. By the late '80s, the group's fanbase had grown large enough to guarantee strong sales, but the Top 10 success in 1987 of *Document* and "The One I Love" was unexpected, especially since R.E.M. had only altered its sound slightly. Following *Document,* R.E.M. slowly became one of the world's most popular bands. After an exhaustive international tour supporting 1988's *Green,* the band retired from touring for six years and retreated into the studio to produce their most popular records, *Out of Time* (1991) and *Automatic for the People* (1992). By the time they returned to performing with the *Monster* tour in 1995, the band had been acknowledged by critics and musicians as one of the forefathers of the thriving alternative rock movement, and they were rewarded with the most lucrative tour of their career. Toward the late '90s, R.E.M. was an institution, as its influence was felt in new generations of bands. *—Stephen Thomas Erlewine*

Chronic Town / 1982 / IRS ♦♦♦

☆ **Murmur** / 1983 / IRS ♦♦♦♦♦
Leaving behind the garagey jangle-pop of their first recordings, R.E.M. developed a strangely subdued variation of its trademark sound for its full-length debut album, *Murmur.* Height-

ening the enigmatic tendencies of *Chronic Town* by de-emphasizing the backbeat and accentuating the ambience of the ringing guitar, R.E.M. created a distinctive sound for the album—one that sounds eerily timeless. Even though it is firmly in the tradition of American folk-rock, post-punk and garage-rock, *Murmur* sounds as if it appeared out of nowhere, without any ties to the past, present or future. Part of the distinctiveness lies in the atmospheric production, which exudes a detached sense of mystery, but it also comes from the remarkably accomplished songwriting. The songs on *Murmur* sound if they've existed forever, yet they subvert folk and pop conventions by taking unpredictable twists and turns into melodic, evocative territory, whether it's the measured riffs of "Pilgrimage," the melancholic "Talk About the Passion" or the winding guitars and pianos of "Perfect Circle." R.E.M. may have made albums as good as *Murmur* in the years following its release, but they never again made anything that sounded quite like it. *—Stephen Thomas Erlewine*

☆ **Reckoning** / 1984 / IRS ♦♦♦♦♦
R.E.M. abandoned the enigmatic post-punk experiments of *Murmur* for their second album *Reckoning,* returning to their garage-pop origins instead. Opening with the ringing "Harborcoat," and *Reckoning* runs through a set of ten jangle-pop songs that are different not only in sound but in style from the debut. Where *Murmur* was enigmatic in its sound, *Reckoning* is clear, which doesn't necessarily mean that the songs themselves are straightforward. Stipe continues to sing powerful melodies without enunciating, but the band has a propulsive kick that makes the music vital and alive. And, if anything, the songwriting is more direct and memorable than before—the interweaving melodies of "Pretty Persuasion" and the country-rocker "(Don't Go Back to) Rockville" are as affecting as the melancholic dirges of "Camera" and "Time After Time," while the ringing minor-key arpeggios of "So. Central Rain," the pulsating riffs of "7 Chinese Bros.," and the hard-rocking rhythms of "Little America" make the songs into classics. On the surface, *Reckoning* may not be as distinctive as *Murmur,* but the record's influence on underground American rock in the '80s is just as strong. *—Stephen Thomas Erlewine*

Fables of the Reconstruction / 1985 / IRS ♦♦♦♦
For their third album, R.E.M. made a conscious effort to break from the traditions *Murmur* and *Reckoning* established, electing to record in England with legendary folk-rock producer Joe Boyd. For a variety of reasons, the sessions were difficult, and that tension is apparent throughout *Fables of the Reconstruction.* A dark, moody rumination on American folk—not only the music, but its myths—*Fables* is creepy, rustic psychedelic folk, filled with eerie sonic textures. Some light breaks through occasionally, such as the ridiculous collegiate blue-eyed soul of "Can't Get There From Here," but the group's trademark ringing guitars and cryptic lyrics have grown sinister, giving even sing-alongs like "Driver 8" an ominous edge. *Fables* is more inconsistent than its two predecessors, but the group does demonstrate considerable musical growth, particularly in how perfectly it evokes the strange rural legends of the South. And many of the songs on the record—including "Feeling Gravitys Pull," "Maps and Legends," "Green Grow the Rushes," "Auctioneer (Another Engine)" and the previously mentioned pair—rank among the group's best. *—Stephen Thomas Erlewine*

Life's Rich Pageant / 1986 / IRS ♦♦♦♦♦
Fables of the Reconstruction was intentionally murky, and *Life's Rich Pageant* was constructed as its polar opposite. Teaming with producer Don Gehman, who previously worked with John Mellencamp, R.E.M. developed their most forceful record to date. Where previous records kept the rhythm section in the background, *Pageant* emphasizes the beat, and the band turns in its hardest rockers to date, including the anthemic "Begin the Begin" and the punky "Just a Touch." But the cleaner production also benefits the ballads and the midtempo janglers, particularly since it helps reveal Stipe's growing political obsessions, especially on the environmental anthems "Fall on Me" and "Cuyahoga." The group hasn't entirely left myths behind—witness the Civil War ballad "Swan Swan H"—but the band sounds more contemporary both musically and lyrically than they did on either *Fables* or *Murmur,* which helps gives the record an extra kick. And even with excellent songs like "I Believe," "Flowers of Guatemala," "These Days" and "What If We Give It Away," it's ironic that the most memorable moment comes from the garage rock obscurity "Superman," which is sung with glee by Mike Mills. *—Stephen Thomas Erlewine*

Dead Letter Office / 1987 / IRS ♦♦♦
Arriving mere months before *Document* took the group into the Top Ten, the B-sides and rarities collection *Dead Letter Office* sums up all of the quirks and idiosyncracies that made R.E.M. the leading underground guitar-pop band of the '80s. While only a handful of songs on *Dead Letter Office* rank among the group's best, the record is extremely entertaining, even for casual fans, particularly because it captures the wild spirit of R.E.M. that was evident at their concerts, but not always on their records. Among the gems scattered throughout the collection are the cheerily ridiculous "Band Wagon," "Voice of Harold" (which features Stipe singing the liner notes to a gospel album over the backing of "7 Chinese Brothers)," covers of the Velvet Underground, Pylon and Aerosmith, the ringing pop of "Burning Down" (which is later reworked as "Ages of You"), and "Walter's Theme," a drunken attempt at a commercial for a local restaurant that segues into a clueless cover of "King of the Road." The material may be slight, but it's fun—and R.E.M.'s albums aren't always fun. [The CD version of *Dead Letter Office* contains the group's debut EP, *Chronic Town.*] *—Stephen Thomas Erlewine*

☆ **Document** / 1987 / IRS ♦♦♦♦♦
R.E.M. began to move toward mainstream record production on *Lifes Rich Pageant,* but they didn't have a commercial breakthrough until the following year's *Document.* Ironically, *Document* is a stranger, more varied album than its predecessor, but co-producer Scott Litt—who would go on to produce every R.E.M. album in the following decade—is a better conduit for the band than Don Gehman, giving the group a clean sound without sacrificing their enigmatic tendencies. "Finest Worksong," the stream-of-conscious rant "It's the End of the World As We Know It (And I Feel Fine)" and the surprise Top Ten single "The One I Love" all crackle with muscular rhythms and guitar riffs, but the real surprise is how political the midtempo jangle-pop of "Welcome to the Occupation," "Disturbance At the Heron House" and "King of Birds" is. Where *Lifes Rich Pageant* sounded a bit like a party record, *Document* is a fiery statement, and its memorable melodies and riffs are made all the more indelible by its righteous anger. In other words, it's not only a commercial breakthrough, but a creative breakthrough as well, offering evidence of R.E.M.'s growing depth and maturity, and helping usher in the P.C. era in the process. *—Stephen Thomas Erlewine*

● **Eponymous** / 1988 / IRS ♦♦♦♦♦
Basically a singles collection from R.E.M.'s first five albums, *Eponymous* gives the listener a sense of R.E.M.'s change from a folk-rock band to a rock band. The songs are intelligently selected, distilling most of the best moments from their first five albums for I.R.S. Included is the original single of "Radio Free Europe," and different mixes of "Gardening at Night" (where it's actually possible to hear the vocal) and "Finest Worksong," and the previously unreleased (and unspectacular) "Romance." (Note: An import collection, *The Best of R.E.M.,* doesn't have the rarities, but has 16 songs, including the remainder of *Eponymous,* plus many other important songs from their I.R.S. years. Worth the couple of extra dollars for the beginner.) *—Stephen Thomas Erlewine*

Green / 1988 / Warner Brothers ♦♦♦
As major-label debuts by underground bands go, *Green* is fairly uncompromising. While it displays a more powerful guitar sound on "Get Up," "Turn You Inside Out" and "Orange Crush," it also takes more detours than *Document,* whether it's the bizarrely affecting contemporary folk of "The Wrong Child" and "You Are the Everything," the bubblegum of "Stand" and "Pop Song 89" or the introspection of the lovely "Hairshirt" and "World Leader Pretend." But instead of presenting a portrait of a band with a rich, eclectic vision, *Green* is incoherent. While its best moments are flat-out great, the band has bitten off more than it can chew; many of the songs sound like failed experiments, and its arena-ready production now sounds slightly dated. Nevertheless, half of the record is brilliant, and it certainly indicates that R.E.M. is continuing to diversify its sound. *—Stephen Thomas Erlewine*

Out of Time / Mar. 12, 1991 / Warner Brothers ♦♦♦
The supporting tour for *Green* exhausted R.E.M., and they spent nearly a year recuperating before reconvening for *Out of Time.* Where previous R.E.M. records captured a stripped-down, live sound, *Out of Time* was lush with sonic detail, featuring string sections, keyboards, mandolins, and cameos from everyone from rapper KRS-1 to the B-52's' Kate Pierson. The scope of R.E.M.'s ambitions is impressive, and the record sounds impeccable, its sunny array of pop and folk songs as refreshing as Michael Stipe's decision to abandon explicitly political lyrics for the personal. Several R.E.M. classics—including Mike Mills' Byrdsy "Near Wild Heaven," and the haunting "Country Feedback," and the masterpiece "Losing My Religion"—are present, but the album is more notable for its production than its songwriting. Most of the songs are slight but pleasant, or are awkward experiments like "Radio Song"'s stab at funk, and while this sounds fine as the record is playing, there's not much substantive material to make the record worth returning to. *—Stephen Thomas Erlewine*

☆ **Automatic for the People** / Jul. 1992 / Warner Brothers ♦♦♦♦♦
Turning away from the sweet pop of *Out of Time,* R.E.M. created a haunting, melancholy masterpiece with *Automatic for the People.* At its core, the album is a collection of folk songs about aging, death and loss, but the music has a grand, epic sweep provided by layers of lush strings, interweaving acoustic instruments and shimmering keyboards. *Automatic for the People* captures the group at a crossroads, as they moved from cult heroes to elder statesmen, and the album is a graceful transition into their new status. It is a reflective album, with frank discussions on mortality, but it is not a despairing record—"Nightswimming," "Everybody Hurts" and "Sweetness Follows" have a comforting melancholy, while "Find the River" provides a positive sense of closure. R.E.M. have never been as emotionally direct as they are on *Automatic for the People,* nor have they ever created music quite as rich and timeless, and while the record is not an easy listen, it is the most rewarding record in their oeuvre. *—Stephen Thomas Erlewine*

Monster / Sep. 27, 1994 / Warner Brothers ♦♦

New Adventures in Hi-Fi / Sep. 10, 1996 / Warner Brothers ♦♦♦

In the Attic: Alternative Recordings 1985-1989 / Oct. 7, 1997 / Capitol ♦♦♦

Up / Oct. 27, 1998 / Warner Brothers ♦♦♦

Renaissance

f. 1969, Surrey, England
Group / Prog-Rock/Art Rock
The history of Renaissance is essentially the history of two separate groups—the original group was founded in 1969 by ex-Yardbirds members Keith Relf and Jim McCarty as a sort of progressive folk-rock band, who recorded two albums but never quite made it, despite some success on England's campus circuit. The band went through several membership changes, with Relf and his sister Jane exiting and McCarty all but gone after 1971. The new line-up formed around the core of bassist Jon Camp, keyboard player John Tout, and Terry Sullivan on drums, with Annie Haslam, an aspiring singer with operatic training and a three-octave range. Their first album in this incarnation, *Prologue,* released in 1972, was considerably more ambitious than the original band's work, with extended instrumental passages and soaring vocals. Their breakthrough came with their next record, 1973's *Ashes Are Burning. Turn of the Cards* had a much more ornate songwriting style and was awash in lyrics that alternated between the topical and the mystical. The group's ambitions, by now, were growing faster than its audience—*Scheherazade* (1975) was built around a 20-minute extended suite for rock group and orchestra that dazzled the fans but made no new converts. As the 1970s closed out, the group was running headlong into the punk and new wave booms that made them seem increasingly anachronistic and doomed to cult status. *—Bruce Eder*

Renaissance / 1969 / Renaissance ♦♦♦
The original group's debut album was a then-groundbreaking meld of progressive rock with classical and jazz influences. The album is a little clunky by today's standards, and far druggier than the later group in its ambience (cofounders Keith Relf and Jim McCarty were the

heavily psychedelic half of the final lineup of the Yardbirds, which made them anathema to Jimmy Page), but vocalist Jane Relf had a striking individual style and the classical influence was unique for its time. *—Bruce Eder*

Illusion (UK, 1976) / 1971 / Island ✦✦✦
The group's second album is more polished in its sound, but the record never found an audience because it has never remained in print for very long or been very easy to find. The classical influence is more pronounced, and Jane Relf stretches out further in her vocalizing, as the original group evolved somewhat in the direction of Renaissance, mark II. *—Bruce Eder*

Prologue / 1972 / One Way ✦✦✦✦✦
The debut of Renaissance, mark II, featuring Annie Haslam on lead vocals and John Tout on keyboards, is a solid meld of classical and rock, most of the material built around long, highly developed instrumental lines and Haslam's soaring three-octave range. Nineteenth-century European classical influences (especially Chopin) abound, in a mix of electric and acoustic rock. Reissued on CD by One Way Records in the '90s. *—Bruce Eder*

Ashes Are Burning / 1973 / One Way ✦✦✦

Turn of the Cards / 1974 / Repertoire ✦✦✦✦✦
The third album by this incarnation of Renaissance was a match for their previous success, *Ashes Are Burning,* with equally impressive performances and songwriting and a few new musical twists added. The songs here fit more easily into a rock vein, and the prior album's folk influences are gone. *Turn of the Cards* rocks a bit harder, albeit always in a progressive rock manner, and Jon Camp's bass and Terence Sullivan's drums are both harder and heavier here, the bass (the group's only amplified instrument) in particular much more forward in the mix. This change works in giving the band a harder sound that leaves room for Jimmy Horowitz's orchestral accompaniments, which are somewhat more prominent than those of Richard Hewson on the prior album, with the horns and strings, in particular, more exposed. Annie Haslam is in excellent voice throughout, and finds ideal accompaniment in Michael Dunford's acoustic guitar and John Tout's piano. The writing team of Dunford and Betty Thatcher also adds some new wrinkles to the group's range—in addition to progressive rock ballads like "I Think of You," they delivered "Black Flame," a great dramatic canvas for Haslam and Tout, in particular; and "Mother Russia" is a surprising (and effective) move into topical songwriting, dealing with the plight of Alexander Solzhenitsyn and other victims of Soviet repression (you had to be there in the '70s to realize what a burning issue this was). And then there were the soaring, pounding group virtuoso numbers like "Things I Don't Understand," which managed to hold audience interest across nine or ten minutes of running time. *—Bruce Eder*

Scheherazade & Other Stories / 1975 / Repertoire ✦✦✦✦
This album was the group's magnum opus in the perception of many on-lookers and fans, and it still plays well, though its flaws are more evident now than they were at the time. The "Song of Scheherazade," really a suite for the group supported by the London Symphony Orchestra and a chorus, started with guitarist-composer Mick Dunford, who had a personal fascination with the medieval literary work *Tales of 1,001 Arabian Nights,* and was realized by Dunford and his composing partner Betty Thatcher, with bassist Jon Camp and pianist John Tout. The piece, really nine sections assembled together, was one of the more ambitious works to come out of the progressive rock boom—it fits together nicely and does have some gorgeous passages and many lyrical, powerful sections, although it also seems slightly repetitive, overstaying its welcome somewhat; additionally, it never uses the orchestra quite as effectively as one senses it might have, for anything except embellishment. Less ambitious and more completely successful are "Ocean Gypsy," "The Vultures Fly High," and "Trip to the Fair" on side one, all relatively unpretentious pieces which feature extraordinary singing by Annie Haslam. There's no domestic CD release, though there is an import that does improve on the original vinyl, which suffered from a fair amount of noise in its pressings and somewhat compressed sound. *—Bruce Eder*

Live at Carnegie Hall / 1976 / Repertoire ✦✦

Novella / 1977 / Sire ✦✦

In the Beginning / 1978 / Capitol ✦✦✦
This compilation of the *Prologue* and *Ashes Are Burning* albums should be great, but it isn't. The sound is flat and two major songs from *Ashes* were cut mercilessly. Good for a glimpse at the band. *—Bruce Eder*

A Song for All Seasons / 1978 / Sire ✦✦

● **Tales of 1001 Nights, Vol. 1** / 1990 / Sire ✦✦✦✦
This 75-minute compilation and its companion volume are just about the only acknowledgments on the part of Sire Records that it ever had a progressive rock catalog, somewhere in between signing the Ramones and Madonna. The song lineup on this first volume heavily favors the group's early repertory, including songs originally done for the Sovereign label, represented here in concert recordings from *Renaissance Live at Carnegie Hall.* How attractive that is depends upon how one feels about those performances, versus the original studio renditions (available from One Way Records domestically and, in superior versions, from HTD Records in England). They were never too impressive on vinyl, although the digital remastering and re-equalization of the material seems to have solved much of that problem. The original Sire studio material, including "Running Hard" and "Black Flame," sound better here than they did on their original vinyl releases, which had fairly noisy pressings and were somewhat top-heavy on the bass. The accompaniments all sound crisper on the CD, the nuances and fine balances between the band and the orchestra much easier to appreciate, and the only major flaw—and it is a big one—is the absence of "Song of Scheherazade," their biggest orchestral-accompanied piece ever. Only a four-minute excerpt is included; admittedly, the work as a whole is somewhat overblown, taking up a little more time than it is worth, but it was the centerpiece of two separate albums, which should have told the programmers something about how much it registered to fans. *—Bruce Eder*

REO Speedwagon

f. 1967, Champaign, IL
Group / Arena Rock, Pop/Rock, Soft Rock, Adult Contemporary
REO Speedwagon may not have been the most talented arena-rock band of the '70s, but they were almost certainly worked harder than any other group on the same circuit. In 1971, they released their first album of competent hard rock, but they didn't chart until 1974 with *Ridin' the Storm Out.* That album was recorded with temporary vocalist Michael Murphey, who would later have some solo success of his own; regular vocalist/rhythm guitarist Kevin Cronin rejoined the band in 1975. The first album released after Cronin rejoined REO was only moderately successful, but 1977's *REO Speedwagon Live/You Get What You Play For* began a string of gold and platinum albums, culminating with the 1980 album *Hi-Infidelity,* which sold over seven million copies in America. Although their style had shifted to a slick, mainstream AOR rock and they were known for power ballads, their hits didn't stop coming until 1990, when the band's support dropped off sharply; their 1991 album didn't even chart. However, the band remains a solid touring attraction, and they continue to release albums into the '90s. *—Stephen Thomas Erlewine*

R E O Speedwagon / Dec. 1971 / Epic ✦✦✦

R.E.O. 2 / Dec. 1972 / Epic ✦✦✦✦

Ridin' the Storm Out / Jan. 1974 / Epic ✦✦✦✦
REO Speedwagon began to come into its own with its third album, *Ridin' the Storm Out.* Over the years, the record became a platinum-seller, but it originally charted at number 171, due to the strength of their series of opening shows for more successful rock acts. While the group still had elements of their bar-bad boogie, they began to streamline their approach on this album. Although it only resulted in one minor hit, with the title track scraping the bottom of the singles charts, the record was one of their most consistent efforts. *—Stephen Thomas Erlewine*

R.E.O. / Jun. 1976 / Epic ✦✦

You Can Tune a Piano, But You Can't Tuna Fish / Apr. 1978 / Epic/Legacy ✦✦✦✦
You Can Tune a Piano, But You Can't Tuna Fish was REO Speedwagon's biggest hit of the '70s, featuring the singles "Roll with the Changes" and "Time for Me to Fly." *—AMG*

Decade of Rock & Roll '70-'80 / 1980 / Epic ✦✦✦✦
This is a well-chosen recap of REO's dues-paying years. *—Dan Heilman*

Hi-Infidelity / Dec. 1980 / Epic/Legacy ✦✦✦✦✦
The band's breakthrough album with the masses. Heavy on the syrupy ballad formula that brought them success. *—Cub Koda*

Wheels Are Turnin' / Nov. 1984 / Epic ✦✦✦
Wheels Are Turnin' was REO Speedwagon's most popular post-*Hi-Infidelity* album, selling over two million copies and featuring the number one single "Can't Fight This Feeling," as well as "I Do'wanna Know" and "One Lonely Night." *—AMG*

Live: You Get What You Play For / 1985 / Epic ✦✦✦

● **The Hits** / 1988 / Epic ✦✦✦✦✦
Over the course of the 1980s, REO Speedwagon became one of the decade's leading power balladeers. However, these singles sapped the band's reputation as a rock & roll band. Although it may focus more on ballads such as "Time for Me to Fly," "Keep on Loving You," and "Can't Fight This Feeling," *Hits* does not completely overlook the band's rock anthems, taking care to also include such underrated rockers as "I Don't Want to Lose You," "Don't Let Him Go," and a live version of "Ridin the Storm Out," the band's first and best rock single from the 1970s. Though there is a rather large quantity of REO compilations, *Hits* remains the wisest investment for most listeners. *—Barry Weber*

Second Decade of Rock & Roll / Sep. 24, 1991 / Epic ✦✦✦
Second Decade of Rock & Roll isn't as strong a compilation as *The Hits,* lacking the focused concentration of the previous compilation, but it does contain a fair amount of highlights from REO Speedwagon's '80s albums. *—AMG*

The Replacements

f. 1979, Minneapolis, MN, **db.** 1991
Group / College Rock, Jangle Pop, Alternative Pop/Rock, Hard Rock
The Replacements were one of the most beloved bands of the American underground in the '80s, due to their raucous live performances and Paul Westerberg's heartbreaking songs. Though they tried to break into the mainstream, they never succeeded, spending their career as a cult act. Like many great cult acts, they inspired many fans to start bands of their own, and their records remain highlights of the '80s.

After a fairly nondescript debut, the Replacements developed their voice with 1982's *Hootenanny.* Here, the group started playing around with other genres, sometimes ironically. *Hootenanny* was a dry run for 1984's *Let It Be,* the band's critical and artistic breakthrough which proved that Westerberg had developed into a first-rate songwriter. Critics and fellow musicians were quick to praise the band, and they developed a large underground following, leading to a contract with Sire.

Their major-label debut *Tim* garnered rave reviews upon its 1985 release, yet the band couldn't quite leap into the mainstream. Frequently, the band was barely able to play, let alone stand up, during their concerts. The Replacements also refused to make accessible videos—the video for "Bastards of Young" featured nothing but a stereo system, playing the song—thereby cutting themselves off from MTV mass exposure.

After *Tim,* founding member Bob Stinson was fired from the band, allegedly for substance addictions. The Replacements' next album, the relatively streamlined *Pleased to Meet Me,* received another round of terrific reviews upon its spring 1987 release, but the band couldn't expand their cult. *Don't Tell a Soul* was their slickest to date, yet it earned mixed reviews, even if they cracked the charts with the single "I'll Be You."

Defeated by *Don't Tell a Soul*'s lackluster performance, Paul Westerberg planned on recording a solo album, but Sire rejected the idea. Consequently, the next Replacements album, the stripped-down *All Shook Down*, was a solo Westerberg record in all but name. Following a supporting tour for the album, the Replacements quietly disbanded in the summer of 1991. *—Stephen Thomas Erlewine*

Sorry Ma, Forgot to Take Out the Trash / 1981 / Twin/Tone ♦♦

The Stink / 1982 / Twin/Tone ♦♦♦

Hootenanny / 1983 / Twin/Tone ♦♦♦
The Replacements came into their own with *Hootenanny*, a careening, drunken stumble through punk, rock & roll, country, blues and folk. The eclecticism of the album separated the Replacements from the post-punk hardcore pack, but it's also what makes the record a mess. Half of the record is devoted to ironic jokes, whether it's the Beatles pastiche of "Mr. Whirly," and the tongue-in cheek title track or the silly closer "Treatment Bound." Not so coincidentally, those are songs where Westerberg branches out into other styles, and he found it easier to experiment under the guise of a joke. He does let his guard down on the extraordinary "Within Your Reach," a disarmingly open plea for love that he recorded entirely himself. It's the only truly vulnerable moment on the record, but the snide "Color Me Impressed" also comes close to true emotion. And it's fun to hear Westerberg act tough on "Take Me Down to the Hospital," "Run It," and "You Lose," especially considering how the group has improved. They're still sloppy, to be sure, but Bob Stinson's guitar stings and the rhythm section of Tommy Stinson and Chris Mars rocks with a loose abandon that makes even the filler—and there's a lot of filler—enjoyable garage-punk. *—Stephen Thomas Erlewine*

☆ **Let It Be** / 1984 / Twin/Tone ♦♦♦♦♦
The Replacements half-heartedly tried to expand their reach on *Hootenanny*, and they followed through on that album's promise on *Let It Be*. Kicking off with the country-rock shuffle of "I Will Dare," the record explodes into a series of psuedo-hardcore ravers before hitting Paul Westerberg's piano-driven rumination, "Androgynous," one of four major ballads that cuts to the core of Midwestern suburban alienation. "Sixteen Blue" is one of the definitive teenage anthems of the '80s, while "Unsatisfied" rages in despair and Westerberg rarely was more affecting than the solo performance of "Answering Machine." All four, along with "I Will Dare," tform the core of Westerberg and the Replacements' canon, and are enough to make *Let It Be* a cornerstone post-punk album, even if the rest of the record pales next to the songs. All the remaining songs are convincing garage-rockers, even if they reveal the Replacements' former punk stance to be a bit of a pose—a cover of Kiss' "Black Diamond" comes off as a tribute, as does the co-opting of Ted Nugent's "Cat Scratch Fever" for "Gary's Got a Boner." Furthermore, the original numbers lean toward the Faces, leaving the Ramones behind and while everything except "Seen Your Video," which now sounds as dated as a "Disco Sucks" rant, are bracing rockers, they're a bit inconsequential and point the way toward the band's deadly fascination with classic rock. *—Stephen Thomas Erlewine*

★ **Tim** / 1985 / Sire ♦♦♦♦♦
Let it Be made the Replacements into college-radio and critical favorites, leading the group to a major-label contract with Sire. The band's major-label debut *Tim* does represent a bit of a compromise of the group's garage-punk sound. Producer Tommy Erdelyi (formerly of the Ramones) helped clean up the band's sound, primarily by harnassing the rhythm section to a click track—no longer does the band thrash all over the place, they keep a steady rocking beat. Similarly, Bob Stinson is kept in check, and his wildfire guitar bubbles the surface only on two cuts, "Dose of Thunder" and "Lay it Down Clown," which are both filler. Some of the rockers, even the anthemic "Bastards of Young," are gutted by the by the cleaner sound, but the overall effect of the record isn't hurt because Paul Westerberg turns in his finest overall set of songs, ranging from the charming love song "Kiss Me On the Bus" and the college-radio anthem "Left of the Dial" to the detailed chronicles of loneliness like "Here Comes a Regular," "Hold My Life" and "Swingin' Party." Westerberg's melodies and observations are sharper than ever, giving *Tim* an eloquent but edgy power that can't be diluted by the tame production. *—Stephen Thomas Erlewine*

Pleased to Meet Me / 1987 / Sire ♦♦♦♦♦
Bob Stinson was kicked out of the band after *Tim*, allegedly because he was unwilling to make the musical leap forward necessary for *Pleased to Meet Me*. With Stinson left the Replacements' hardcore roots, leaving behind the conflicting desires of Westerberg's wish to be a serious singer/songwriter and for the group to become either the Faces or Big Star. That conflict is played out throughout *Pleased to Meet Me*, and it isn't helped by the stultifyingly clean and detailed production by Jim Dickinson. Chris Mars and Tommy Stinson are reigned in tighter than ever before, giving most the songs a strangled, distanced feel which isn't helped by Dickinson's canned guitar sounds and the odd production flourishes, including the occasional sax and keyboard. The full-blown production works on the horn and string-drenched "Can't Hardly Wait," but it makes mindlessly rocking filler like "Shooting Dirty Pool" and "Red Red Wine" irritating. For the most part, Westerberg's songs make the clean sound tolerable, particularly on Stonesy "I.O.U.," the suicide sketch of "The Ledge," the power-pop of "Never Mind" and "Valentine," and the lovely acoustic "Skyway." But the fan love-letter "Alex Chilton" reveals more than necessary—even though Westerberg is shooting for stardom, he has more affinity for the self-styled loser, which means he never wants to make the full leap to the mainstream. And that can only hurt a record like *Pleased to Meet Me*, which has stardom in its sights. *—Stephen Thomas Erlewine*

Don't Tell a Soul / 1989 / Sire ♦♦♦
All of the slick production of *Pleased to Meet Me* couldn't prepare listeners for the glossy sound of *Don't Tell A Soul*, the Replacements' last-ditch attempt at mainstream success. Bathed with washes of synthesizers, shining guitars, backing vocals and a shimmering, AOR-oriented production, *Don't Tell a Soul* puts an end to the Replacements and begins Paul Westerberg's solo career. The bulk of the songs are self-consciously mature, as Westerberg looks back on his career (the autobiographical "Talent Show") and is haunted by the past ("Rock N Roll Ghost," "Darlin' One"), as he attempts to refashion himself as a craftsman. A few of these attempts work, particularly the country-rock ballad "Achin' to Be" and the arena-rock stab "I'll Be You," but the lite-funk workout "Asking Me Lies" and the stuttering "I Won't" are flat-out embarassing. And the rest of the album suffers from Westerberg's determination to be adult. The songs are too self-consciously mature and the band is functions as a supporting act for the lyrics, which lack the unpretentious poetry of his best work. Ironically, Westerberg's desire to be an "adult" is the reason why radio ignored *Don't Tell a Soul*, because it meant that the record lacked both rockers or power-ballads which would have given them air-time. And most old fans found the production too heavy to make sorting through the album worthwhile. *—Stephen Thomas Erlewine*

All Shook Down / 1990 / Sire ♦♦♦♦♦
Although *Don't Tell A Soul* sounded like a Replacements record, it felt like a Paul Westerberg album. *All Shook Down* continues that trend—it's a Replacements record only in name. Recorded with a variety of session musicians and sporting no individual credits, *All Shook Down* emphasizes the songs, not the band, and it's a weary, beaten set of songs. Despite a handful of forced rockers—especially the down-right embarrassing Johnette Napolitano duet "My Little Problem"—the album is low-key and primarily acoustic set, finding Westerberg knowing that the band is over and wondering where it all went wrong. While *All Shook Down* doesn't have any nakedly emotional stunners like "Answering Machine" or "Skyway," it has a unified atmosphere and an off-the-cuff, unpretentious feel which comes as a relief after the weighty ambitions of *Don't Tell a Soul*. It also has a number of excellently crafted songs, ranging from the wistful "Sadly Beautiful" and the druggy "All Shook Down" to snappy pop-rockers like "Merry Go Round," "When It Began" and "Happy Town." As the loungey closer suggests, the record is meant to be "The Last, "and few bands ended their career in such a knowing, worn-out fashion. *—Stephen Thomas Erlewine*

All For Nothing/Nothing for All / Oct. 28, 1997 / Sire ♦♦♦

Paul Revere & the Raiders

f. 1960, Portland, OR

Group / Frat Rock, Pop/Rock, Garage Rock, Pop, Rock & Roll

With their Revolutionary War costumes and upbeat attitude, Paul Revere & the Raiders were one of the more entertaining rock & roll bands of the mid-'60s. They began in the late '50s as a more hard-edged outfit, and after the mid-'70s, they evolved into a musical-comedy lounge act. It wasn't until the summer of 1965, when they were chosen as the house band on the afternoon TV show "Where the Action Is," that Paul Revere & the Raiders really took off, with singer Mark Lindsay becoming a teenage heartthrob. In 1966 and 1967, they enjoyed four Top Ten hits—"Kicks," "Hungry," "Good Thing," and "Him or Me—What's It Gonna Be?"—and four Top Ten, gold-selling albums—*Just Like Us!, Midnight Ride, The Spirit of '67*, and *Greatest Hits*. Their good-time style became less fashionable in the late '60s, though they continued to reach the Top 40. After a temporary name change to simply "Raiders," they scored their sole number one hit with the gold single "Indian Reservation (The Lament of the Cherokee Reservation Indian)" in 1971. *—William Ruhlmann*

● **The Essential Ride '63-'67** / Jun. 6, 1995 / Columbia/Legacy ♦♦♦♦♦
A much more sensible buy than the double-CD *Legend of Paul Revere*, this 20-track compilation focuses on their toughest (and therefore best) early material. Has all the big early hits, and about half the songs weren't on *Legend*, most notably their fine pre-Monkees version of "Steppin' Stone." Note that the version of "Hungry" here is an alternate take, good or bad news depending on whether you have the original hit rendition already. *—Richie Unterberger*

Just Like Us! [Sundazed] / 1998 / Sundazed ♦♦♦♦♦
This is Paul Revere & the Raiders the way garage-band fanatics want to remember them. The Sundazed version of this album is twice the record that the original LP was, with louder, sharper, denser sound that captures the punk edge that this band had on its best days, which were frequent during this part of their history. Released in May of 1965, *Just Like Us* was the group's first full studio album for Columbia, recorded just a few weeks earlier, and the first record on which they were allowed to stretch out in the studio, utilizing multiple overdubs to fulfill their potential. Despite this luxury, the band still had their edge, mixing dance-rock with R&B on numbers like "Steppin' Out" and "Just Like Me," amid covers of contemporary hits like Marvin Gaye's "I'll Be Doggone," Them's (and Big Joe Williams') "Baby Please Don't Go," and "Night Train," as well as white rock (and folk-rock) hits such as "Satisfaction" (featuring lots of organ), "I'm Cryin'," and "Catch the Wind," not to mention the Tommy Boyce co-authored "Action," from *Where the Action Is*. The Raiders do okay with "I'm Cryin'," but the group's covers of the R&B classics come off rather better than their work with stuff originated by the Stones and Donovan. CD producer Bob Irwin went back about as far into the master tapes as anyone ever will, and the sound is amazing; the guitars, organ, saxes, and everything else are real close, but the density of the original mixes remains (and the volume is very, very loud). The notes by Mark Lindsay are almost as engaging as the music, and the original notes have been reproduced as well. *—Bruce Eder*

● **Greatest Hits [Bonus Tracks]** / Feb. 8, 2000 / Columbia/Legacy ♦♦♦♦♦
Paul Revere and the Raiders scored seven chart hits between the fall of 1965 and the winter of 1967, and all of them—"Steppin' Out," "Just Like Me," "Kicks," "Hungry," "The Great Airplane Strike," "Good Thing," and "Ups and Downs"—were included among the 11 tracks on the group's first hits collection. Also included were "Louie, Louie," the Raiders' first Columbia single, and its follow-up, "Louie, Go Home," a B-side instrumental, plus the newly penned "Legend of Paul Revere," which told the band's story. Thus, the album traced the band from its beginnings as a Northwest club band to its reign as an L.A. pop/rock success. There would be more hits, but this brief compilation (it originally ran under 30 minutes) contained the essence of the Raiders' most successful period and indeed marked the end of the band's lineup, as the rhythm section split to form another group, leaving Revere and lead singer Mark Lindsay to recruit a new edition of the Raiders. The 2000 CD reissue on Columbia/Legacy adds four bonus tracks: "Him or Me—What's It Gonna Be?" (their biggest post-1966 hit of the 1960s), "I'm Not Your Steppin' Stone" (which predated the Monkees' version), "Action," and "Peace of Mind." *—William Ruhlmann*

Emitt Rhodes

b. Feb. 25, 1950, Hawthorne, CA

Vocals, Keyboards / Baroque Pop, Pop, Singer/Songwriter

Hawthorne, California, native Emitt Rhodes made his first mark in the music world in 1967 as the leader of the baroque-pop band the Merry-Go-Round. The band achieved some marginal success with the Rhodes-penned "Live," and "You're a Very Lovely Woman," recording one album of *Magical Mystery Tour*-inspired pop. When the band broke up in 1969, Rhodes set up a home studio in his parents' garage and began his solo career, engineering and playing all instruments himself. The strength of his initial demos, now showing a strong Paul McCartney influence, helped him get signed to ABC/Dunhill. His critically acclaimed, self-titled debut managed to break into the Top 40 in 1971, but pressure from his record company forced him to rush-release a follow-up, *Mirror,* the same year. *Mirror* was predictably a lesser effort, barely charting. By the time of the third album, 1973's *Farewell to Paradise,* Rhodes was running into legal problems with ABC, since he was unable to fulfill his contract, which demanded he deliver a new album every six months. Disillusioned, he retired from the performing side of the business, working instead as an engineer and studio operator for Elektra/Asylum. Though he hasn't released an album since *Farewell to Paradise,* he continues to write and demo new songs. *—Chris Woodstra*

Emitt Rhodes / 1970 / One Way ✦✦✦✦✦

Although this probably wasn't meant to be, this album is Emitt Rhodes' definitive statement. Soon after disbanding the Merry Go Round (of "Live" fame) Rhodes scored a solo deal with Dunhill. Rather than recording with a band or using studio musicians (which he did with his first "solo" album *American Dream*), the multi-instrumentalist decided to build a small, primitive home studio and record the entire affair there, 'At Home.' The results are, in a word, staggering. Tracks such as "With My Face on the Floor," "Someone Made For Me," and the entire album as a whole showcase Rhodes' genius, and in the end, the songs are probably what most Beatles-maniacs wanted to hear from Paul McCartney's debut album. Rhodes' individuality shines through despite this; the album is a true classic of the period. *—Matthew Greenwald*

The American Dream / 1971 / A&M ✦✦✦✦

Although this album may have been a contractual obligation, there is no doubt that Emmit Rhodes did not take the task of recording *American Dream* lightly. After disbanding his first group, Merry Go Round, Rhodes still owed A&M *Records* another album. Several new sessions were held, and along with a few old tracks such as the remarkable "You're a Very Lovely Woman," they make up the body of this fine, if fragmented album. "Mother Earth" is without a doubt one of Rhodes' McCartney-influenced masterpieces, led by a strident 12-string acoustic guitar and a masterful lead vocal. For the first (and possibly only) time in his career, Rhodes utilized session musicians, but he used the very best. Awesome playing from Hal Blaine, Larry Knechtel, Drake Levin, Joel Larson, and others lift this track and others to a level of greatness. This album may be seen as a sort of a warm-up for Rhodes' brilliant, self-recorded Dunhill albums. *—Matthew Greenwald*

Mirror / 1972 / Dunhill ✦✦✦✦

Following the critical success of his debut *solo* album, Emitt Rhodes, the one man Beatles, entered his home studio for the follow-up, and he did not disappoint. Although not as cohesive as his last record, *Mirror* is home to some of his finest material. "Birthday Lady" and "Really Wanted You" are almost Stones-like in their attack, aggression, and feel, and Rhodes pulls them off with fantastic results. "Golden Child of God" is also one of his finest compositions—it also would have easily been at home on Paul McCartney's *Ram.* All in all, this album is not a disappointment, coming off his self-titled debut *Emitt Rhodes,* which can easily be described as one of the classics of the period. *—Matthew Greenwald*

● **Listen, Listen: The Best of Emitt Rhodes** / Aug. 29, 1995 / Varese Sarabande ✦✦✦✦✦

For someone who could almost out-Beatle the Beatles, either in a group situation or as a solo artist, it's hard to match Emmit Rhodes. From his earliest recordings with the long-lamented Merry Go Round, to his critically-acclaimed Dunhill albums, Rhodes always seemed to have a flair for effervescent, McCartney-styled songs and audacious studio performances. This fine collection covers most of the bases, and even includes an excellent, previously unreleased studio track from 1980, "Isn't It So," which, had it been released, would have easily fit in the milieu of Top-40 radio of the time. Aside from some strange omissions (1970's "Somebody Made for Me" comes to mind), this is an excellent overall sampler. *—Matthew Greenwald*

Cliff Richard (Harry Webb)

b. Oct. 14, 1940, Lucknow, India

Vocals / Early British Pop/Rock, Teen Idol, Pop/Rock, Pop, Rock & Roll

Britain's answer to Elvis Presley, Cliff Richard dominated the pre-Beatles British pop scene in the late '50s and early '60s. An accomplished singer with a genuine feel for the music, Richard's artistic legacy is nonetheless meager, as he was quickly steered toward a middle-of-the-road pop direction. Several of his late '50s recordings, however, were genuinely exciting Presley-esque rockers—especially his first hit, "Move It" (1958)—and gave British teenagers their first taste of genuine homegrown rock & roll talent. Backed by the Shadows—clean-cut instrumental virtuosos who became legends of their own—Richard embarked on a truly awesome string of hit singles in Britain, scoring no less than 43 Top 20 hits between 1958 and 1969. In his homeland, Richard's popularity was diminished only slightly by the rise of the Beatles, but in his prime, he had a much rougher time in the U.S., hitting the Top 40 only twice (with "Living Doll" in 1959 and "It's All in the Game" in 1963). He remains an institution in Britain, where he is one of the nation's most popular all-around entertainers of all time. *—Richie Unterberger*

● **20 Rock N'Roll Hits** / 1979 / EMI-Columbia ✦✦✦✦✦

Concentrating mostly on his 1958-59 material, this has Richard's most untamed recordings (bearing in mind that they're still pretty polished compared to most U.S. rockabilly). Includes his first brace of hits—"Move It," "High Class Baby," "Mean Streak," and "Never Mind"—along with the megasmash "Livin' Doll," which pointed the way toward the pop-ballad path he would follow in the '60s. *—Richie Unterberger*

Collection 1976-1994 / 1994 / Razor & Tie ✦✦✦✦

Collection 1976-94 is a 20-track collection that covers the latter half of Cliff Richard's career, which is when had his first taste of American success as an adult contemporary crooner. Of course, his hitmaking career continued in England as well, but that American success is the reason Razor & Tie assembled *Collection* for U.S. release. Either way, the disc is a terrific overview of his latter-day American and British hits, featuring such singles as "Devil Woman," "We Don't Talk Anymore," "A Little in Love," "Carrie," "Dreamin'," "Wired for Sound," "Daddy's Home," "The Only Way Out," "True Love Ways," "My Pretty One," "Mistletoe and Wine" and his duet with Olivia Newton-John, "Suddenly." It leaves out only a handful of big U.K. hits and has all his U.S. Top 40 hits, making it a definitive portrait of the last half of Richard's career. *—Stephen Thomas Erlewine*

The Rock 'n Roll Years 1958-1963 / 1997 / EMI ✦✦✦✦✦

This four-CD set, issued for EMI's 100th anniversary, is *almost* perfect, and, but for the absence of one track, as good as pre-Beatles British rock & roll ever got. Cliff Richard isn't widely recognized as a rock & roller due to his switch to a softer sound in 1959 and his subsequent shift toward more mainstream pop-style music. For six years, Richard cut a steady if narrowing stream of solid guitar-based rock & roll, backed by his band the Shadows. This material was among the most energetic, high-grade rock & roll to be heard in England at the time, and it was competitive with the American product—a bit smoother and cleaner, but bracing. It's not quite all here—his first hit, the number two-charting "Move It," isn't present in its original hit studio version. But the set does contain the stereo mix of the rock & roll tracks off of Richard's first album, a live concert performance at EMI's studios. The set also contains songs excerpted from unreleased live shows recorded circa 1962, lost demos and rehearsals, promotional recordings from the early '60s, radio performances, and faster alternate takes of various released songs. If all of this sounds like overkill, it isn't—into the early '60s, Richard could sing rock & roll about as well as anyone signed to a record label in England, and the Shadows were a great guitar band. On most of what's here, there's no apology needed, nor any explanation—it could pass for the real American article, and a good example of it. The accompanying booklet, lavishly illustrated, also includes good historical information, interview transcripts and commentary, and a very thorough sessionography and discography. *—Bruce Eder*

Keith Richards

b. Dec. 18, 1943, Dartford, Kent, England

Vocals, Keyboards, Guitar (Electric), Guitar / Album Rock, Hard Rock, Rock & Roll

One of the few White guitarists with strong blues roots who has been able to take the form to new places, Richards' contribution to the vocabulary of rock guitar cannot be overestimated. His heavy reliance on Delta blues open tunings (mostly played on guitars with only five strings) has provided licks that are part and parcel for any player who wants to get the joint rocking and the dance floor packed. Though much has been made of his lifestyle, and time has reduced his voice to a sore-throated husk, it is as a guitarist and songwriter that Richards has ultimately established his reputation. *—Cub Koda*

● **Talk Is Cheap** / 1988 / Virgin ✦✦✦✦✦

Richards' first solo album includes "Take It So Hard," "Struggle," "I Could Have Stood You Up," and "Make No Mistake," with a classic Hi Rhythm Section groove and featuring great guest vocals by Sarah Dash. *—Cub Koda*

Live at the Hollywood Palladium (Dec. 15, 1988) / Dec. 1991 / Virgin ✦✦✦

A nicely ragged live album that captures Richards and the Winos at the top of their form. *—Stephen Thomas Erlewine*

Main Offender / Oct. 20, 1992 / Virgin ✦✦✦

Richards' second solo album is even more delightfully focused than his first. Highlights include "Wicked as It Seems," "Eileen," and the searing "999." New Rolling Stones albums should rock this hard. *—Cub Koda*

Lionel Richie

b. Jun. 20, 1949, Tuskegee, AL

Vocals, Keyboards / Quiet Storm, Soft Rock, Adult Contemporary, Urban

After he left the Commodores in 1981, Lionel Richie became one of the most successful solo artists of the early '80s, earning a string of thirteen Top Ten hits between 1981 and 1987, including five number one singles ("Endless Love," "Truly," "All Night Long (All Night)," "Hello," "Say You, Say Me"). Between 1986 and 1992 he didn't release any new material, but in 1996 he re-emerged with a new album that sold well, although not up to the standards he set a decade earlier. *Time* followed in 1998. A ninth solo effort, *Renaissance,* was issued in early 2001 and showcased production by Brian Rawling, Mark Taylor, Rodney Jerkins and Grammy winning producer Walter Afanasieff. *—Stephen Thomas Erlewine*

Lionel Richie / 1982 / Motown ✦✦✦✦✦

Can't Slow Down / 1983 / Motown ✦✦✦✦✦

Dancing on the Ceiling / 1986 / Motown ✦✦✦✦✦

● **Back to Front** / May 5, 1992 / Motown ✦✦✦✦

On his own and as part of the Commodores, by 1992 Lionel Richie amassed more than enough singles for a greatest-hits collection. Unfortunately, this is one of those compilations that, good intentions aside, falls so flat there's not much point in buying it. By trying to cover his solo material, while touching base with his Commodores fans, and adding some new cuts, no part of his career is well represented. It's easy to figure out what record companies are thinking when they release greatest-hits compilations without all the hits—they can release another collection a few years down the road with the "missing" singles in order to get you to spend more money. For the record, *Back to Front* lacks "Oh No," "Lady You Bring Me Up," "Ballerina Girl," "You Are," "My Love," "Stuck on You," "Love Will Conquer All," "Se La," and "Dancing on the Ceiling," all Top 40 hits. If Motown had concentrated solely on solo Richie, with another collection of Commodores hits, this could have been a solid, career-topping CD.

As it is, it's strong, but hearing such gems as "Still," "Truly," "Say You, Say Me," and "Running With the Night" makes you long to hear the cuts that aren't here. Of the three new songs, "Do It to Me" and "My Destiny" are classic, smooth Richie, but "Love, Oh Love" is so schmaltzy, you're almost embarrassed for him; kids singing about peace on earth is just too cheesy, no matter how middle-of-the-road you are. If you're a casual Lionel Richie fan, this might suffice, but for anyone who truly enjoys pop music, this collection is not worth your money. *—Bryan Buss*

Louder Than Words / Apr. 1996 / Mercury ✦✦✦

Time / Jun. 23, 1998 / Mercury ✦✦✦

Jonathan Richman

b. May 15, 1951, Boston, MA
Vocals, Guitar / College Rock, Proto-Punk, Alternative Pop/Rock
Jonathan Richman was one of rock's most eccentric and unpredictable cult figures, a performer whose eternally childlike public persona and seeming naivete tended to obscure the dexterity and craft of his music, which skirted from garage rock to country to Latin stylings and back. In 1970, he formed the first incarnation of the influential proto-punk band the Modern Lovers, though it was most of two years before the group recorded the demos which comprised their seminal self-titled debut, featuring long-standing Richman favorites like "Roadrunner," "Pablo Picasso" and "Hospital." Problems with their label, however, blocked the songs' release until 1976. Eventually, he formed a new, acoustic version of the group that debuted on record with 1977's *Jonathan Richman and the Modern Lovers.* That same year, he scored a major European hit with the instrumental "Egyptian Reggae." In 1979, Richman issued his first solo album, *Back in Your Life.* After a period of self-imposed exile, he resurfaced in the mid-'80s with a series of strong pop records. In 1990, he released the self-explanatory *Jonathan Goes Country;* later, he made another left turn with 1993's *Jonathan, Te Vas a Emocionar!,* a collection of Latin-influenced songs performed entirely in Spanish. No matter what path his music took, however, Richman's cult following remained fiercely loyal, and saw its ranks expand courtesy of a prominent appearance in the 1998 hit film comedy *There's Something About Mary. I'm So Confused* appeared later that year. *—Jason Ankeny*

☆ **Modern Lovers** / 1976 / Rhino ✦✦✦✦✦
Compiled of demos the band recorded with John Cale in 1971, *The Modern Lovers* is one of the great proto-punk albums of all-time, capturing an angst-ridden adolescent geekiness which is married to a stripped-down, minimalistic rock & roll derived from the art-punk of the Velvet Underground. While the sound is in debt to the primal three-chord pounding of early Velvet Underground, the attitude of Jonathan Richman and the Modern Lovers is a million miles away from Lou Reed's jaded urban nightmares. As he says in the classic two-chord anthem "Roadrunner," Richman is in love with the modern world and rock & roll. He's still a teenager at heart, which means he's not only in love with girls he can't have, but also radios, suburbs, and fast food, and it also means he'll crack jokes like "Pablo Picasso was never called an asshole... not like you." "Pablo Picasso" is the classic sneer, but "She Cracked" and "I'm Straight" are just as nasty, made all the more edgy by the Modern Lovers' amateurish, minimalist drive. But beneath his adolscent posturing, Richman is also nakedly emotional, pleaing for a lover on "Someone I Care About" and "Girl Friend," or romanticizing the future on "Dignified and Old." That combination of musical simplicity, driving rock & roll and gawky emotional confessions makes *The Modern Lovers* one of the most startling proto-punk records—it strips rock & roll to its core and establishes the rock tradition of the geeky, awkward social-outcast venting his frustrations. More importantly, the music is just as a raw as exciting now as when it was recorded in 1971, or when it was belatedly released in 1977. *—Stephen Thomas Erlewine*

Jonathan Richman & the Modern Lovers / Jan. 1977 / Beserkley ✦✦✦✦✦
Richman's second collection of Modern Lovers, over which he was billed (eventually, the group name would be dropped) had a lighter rock & roll sound than the first. In fact, as often as not, Richman played acoustic guitar. And his lyrical concerns had similarly lightened up, to the point of childlike whimsy on such songs as "Hey There Little Insect" and "Here Come the Martian Martians." But the focus was still Richman's unabashed vocalizing (the word "sings" is put in quotes on the back cover), giving the whole album an amateurish charm. *—William Ruhlmann*

Rock 'N' Roll with the Modern Lovers / Feb. 1977 / Beserkley ✦✦✦✦✦
Rock 'N' Roll with the Modern Lovers. Richman branches out to Japanese music, a "South American Folk Song," and even "Egyptian Reggae" (the last earning him a UK Top 5 hit), but the real highlight on *Rock 'N' Roll with the Modern Lovers* is that ode to a totaled car, "Dodge Veg-O-Matic." *—William Ruhlmann*

The Original Modern Lovers / 1981 / Bomp! ✦✦✦

Rockin' & Romance / 1985 / Twin/Tone ✦✦✦✦✦
While it is generally true that many of Richman's post-1980 albums are all but interchangeable, with their earnest naive cheerfulness, this stands as one of the best, if you like his schtick and need to make a choice. The production is sparse, accentuating the acoustic guitar and the doo wop harmonies (both male and female), with light but purposeful drums. Jonathan covers his usual terrain here: juvenilia ("My Jeans," "The U.F.O. Man," "Chewing Gum Wrapper"), cultural heroes ("Vincent Van Gogh," "Walter Johnson"), and optimistic paeans to the simple pleasures of life ("The Beach"). Heart-warming and melodic stuff that might well sound insipid in the hands of others. *—Richie Unterberger*

● **Beserkley Years** / 1987 / Rhino ✦✦✦✦✦
After the first Modern Lovers album, Richman's records were enjoyable but fairly spotty. Thankfully, *The Beserkley Years* collects the best moments from his '70s records, when his cutesiness was endearing, not irritating. With "Roadrunner," "Pablo Picasso," "Here Come the Martian Martians," "Important In Your Life," "Ice Cream Man," and "Dodge Veg-O-Matic" forming its core, this collection is a definitive portrait of his goofy, catchy minimalist pop and rock. *—Stephen Thomas Erlewine*

Modern Lovers 88 / 1988 / Rounder ✦✦✦
One of his better '80s efforts, and certainly one of the most basic, performed in an acoustic trio format. It's nonetheless quite rocking, with heavy debts to doo wop and Bo Diddley rhythms, and a jolly (though not sappy) summertime campfire feel. Some of his best up-tempo tunes are here, including "I Love Hot Nights," "California Desert Party," and "Gail Loves Me." *—Richie Unterberger*

Jonathan Goes Country / 1990 / Rounder ✦✦✦

Having a Party with Jonathan Richman / 1991 / Rounder ✦✦✦

I, Jonathan / Sep. 16, 1992 / Rounder ✦✦✦✦✦

Jonathan, Te Vas a Emocionar! / Feb. 28, 1994 / Rounder ✦✦✦

Precise Modern Lovers Order / Aug. 2, 1994 / Rounder ✦✦✦
Of the major pre-punk bands of the late '60s and early '70s (such as the Velvet Underground, the MC5, the Stooges, and the New York Dolls), the Modern Lovers probably seemed the most eccentric—while the aforementioned groups each took a very individual approach to rock & roll, they were still rock bands who worked hard to deliver on stage for an audience. Jonathan Richman, on the other hand, was just as likely to let his bruised and bleeding heart hang on his sleeve for five long, slow minutes of "Hospital" or "Dance With Me" as he was to rip it up on a tune like "Roadrunner" or "Someone I Care About." *Precise Modern Lovers Order* combines a ten-song set the Modern Lovers played in Berkley, CA, during a 1972 West Coast tour with a half-dozen tracks recorded at student mixers at Harvard University between 1971 and 1973, and the audiences seem uniformly befuddled throughout this disc—there aren't any audible catcalls of disapproval, but no one seems to know how to react to Richman's vivid tales of teenage angst. And the Modern Lovers sound a good bit more stark and extreme in these performances than they did on their few studio recordings (hard to imagine, but that first album sounds slick by comparison), though Jonathan Richman's vocals are strikingly impassioned, and the band supports him with a clean, sympathetic simplicity (Jerry Harrison and David Robinson, later to play with Talking Heads and the Cars, respectively, were still members of the Modern Lovers at this point, and future Real Kids leader John Felice is on the Harvard-recorded tracks). *Precise Modern Lovers Order* captures a great and groundbreaking band blazing trails the hard way on stage; it's worth owning as psychodrama, living history, and great music. *—Mark Deming*

You Must Ask the Heart / Apr. 25, 1995 / Rounder ✦✦✦✦✦

Surrender to Jonathan / Sep. 10, 1996 / Vapor ✦✦✦

I'm So Confused / Oct. 20, 1998 / Vapor ✦✦✦

Ride

f. 1988, Oxford, England, **db.** Jan. 1996
Group / British Trad Rock, Dream Pop, Shoegazing, Alternative Pop/Rock
With their first records, Ride created a unique wall of sound that relied on massive, trembling distortion in the vein of My Bloody Valentine but with a simpler, more direct melodic approach. The shatteringly loud, droning neo-psychedelia the band performed was dubbed "shoegazing" by the British press, because they stared at the stage while they performed. Along with their initial influence, My Bloody Valentine, Ride stood apart from the shoegazing pack, primarily because of their keen sense of songcraft and dynamics. Signed to Creation in 1989 by virtue of their blisteringly loud, intense live shows, the band recorded two successful EPs and quickly became darlings of the UK press. *Nowhere,* Ride's first album, became a significant hit in England during 1990, peaking at number 14. The group's second album, 1992's *Going Blank Again,* earned a Top Ten hit in "Leave Them All Behind." Tensions between frontmen Mark Gardner and Andy Bell forced an extended break though, and it was two years before Ride re-emerged with their third album, *Carnival of Light.* The album represented a major shift toward conventional psychedelic rock and turned out to be a commercial misstep. Tensions between Bell and Gardner escalated throughout the recording sessions for 1995's *Tarantula.* Both left Ride even before the album's release, and the group announced its disbandment in early 1996. *—Stephen Thomas Erlewine*

Smile / Jul. 1990 / Sire ✦✦✦✦
A compilation of Ride's first two EPs for Creation, *Smile* is a batch of eight muddy, shambling wrecks that run dangerously close to obscuring great pop songs. In fact, much of *Smile* makes My Bloody Valentine's blurry *Isn't Anything* sound as polished as a *Steely Dan* record. What makes the tunes remarkable is the spirit of the band, along with a good mix. The band probably knew exactly what they were doing, but wanted to sound clueless. It's the sound of four art students losing themselves in their record collections, wanting to naive and fresh but well-studied.

Mark Gardener sounds like he couldn't sing himself out of a paper bag on the original "Chelsea Girl," but it's no matter. The relentless rush of Loz Colbert's drums and distorted guitars of Gardener and Andy Bell carry the song, topped off by a nifty wah wah climax. Though the mid-tempo, chugging "Drive Blind" couldn't be taken literally, it could double as a metaphor for throwing oneself headlong into a relationship—closing your eyes and not caring if a brick wall or cliff is up a mile ahead. The remainder is filled out with sticky riffs and melodies which avoid sounding like the standard pop fair. It sounds a bit amateurish, and Gardener and Bell hadn't quite found their footing vocally. Nonetheless, *Smile* brought something new to the table, and the U.K. audience and more adventurous U.S. fans clutched onto the sound for dear life. Rightfully so. [Oddly, *Smile's* mastering comes from the vinyl versions of the EPs. If you can track down the CD versions of the EPs separately, you'll notice a difference in quality.] *—Andy Kellman*

● **Nowhere** / Oct. 15, 1990 / Sire ✦✦✦✦✦
1990 was a banner year for Ride, capped off by this fantastic full-length, which seems to hold consensus as the second best record of the shoegaze era (My Bloody Valentine's *Loveless* being number one). All of the common words, phrases, and adjectives commonly used with the short lived sub-genre fit properly here, and they're all positive—depending on your taste. Whir, whoosh, hazy, fuzzy, swirly, ad nauseum. But it all boils down to quality *songs,* which *Nowhere* delivers.

Ride's catalog is a bit shoddy in the lyrics department, but *Nowhere* boasts Andy Bell's best pen work. Musically it's undeniably their zenith—dense, tight, and hypnotic. "Seagull" serves as a dynamic opener; after a couple seconds of light feedback, bassist Steve Queralt kicks in with a rubbery, elliptical line, which is soon followed by Bell and Gardener's guitar twists and Loz Colbert's alternately gentle and punishing drum patterns. After the upbeat "Kaleidoscope," the record falls into a tempo lull that initially seems impenetrable and meandering. However, patience reveals a five song suite of sorts, full of lovely instrumental passages that are punctuated with violent jabs of manic guitars. Don't miss the endlessly escalating "Polar Bear," with expertly placed tom rolls from Colbert. Only for the last track does the pace significantly pick up. The wistful "Vapour Trail" is likely Ride's signature song, with Gardener and Bell's chiming background guitars throughout and mournful strings to close the record out.

The U.S. version of *Nowhere* was bolstered significantly with the addition of the *Fall* EP, which was released just a month prior to the LP in the U.K. "Taste" is one of their better pure pop numbers. The moody "Here and Now" matches the best of *Nowhere*, and the five minute "Nowhere" is a decent distortion freakout. *—Andy Kellman*

Going Blank Again / Oct. 1991 / Sire ✦✦✦✦
From the sounds of cloistered, chaotic opener "Leave Them All Behind," *Going Blank Again* sounds like it could be headed down the same *Nowhere* path. Guitars as far as the ear can hear—not far removed from the effect gained after riding a sit-and-spin for eight straight minutes—dizzy you just as "Seagull" did on the debut. But rather than sink into a thick underbelly of melancholy, *Going Blank Again* offers sunshine and streamlined production. All the band's elements are more pliable, and overall it's pretty cheery. In fact, some of the album could be loosely classified as power pop. Bouncy tunes like "Twisterella," "Not Fazed," "Mouse Trap," and "Time of Her Time" each share more than a thing or two in common with the likes of Teenage Fanclub but with more layered vocals and less-cutting guitars. Though Ride's guitars don't bite as much, there are loads of them; the band doesn't completely sacrifice their love of reverberating noise, but it's more done in the name of pop than to merely cause a racket.

As with much of Ride's catalog, the lyrics aren't so hot. Though reading as overtly simple or obtuse, Mark Gardener and Andy Bell's voices are too pretty to let this shortcoming mar things. They create enough of a mood with their proper instruments, and their sighing and random vocal intonations are undeniably lovely. No longer do they hide shortcomings with sheets of distortion, and there's a lot more focus and confidence on display throughout. Don't let a Ride fan tell you otherwise; *Going Blank Again* is anything but empty. *—Andy Kellman*

Carnival of Light / Jun. 28, 1994 / Sire ✦✦✦

Tarantula / Mar. 12, 1996 / Sire ✦✦

The Righteous Brothers

f. 1962, California
Group / Blue-Eyed Soul, Brill Building Pop, Pop
They weren't brothers, but Bill Medley and Bobby Hatfield were most definitely righteous, defining (and perhaps even inspiring) the term "blue-eyed soul" in the mid-'60s. They initially recorded quite a few energetic R&B tunes on the Moonglow label that bore similarity to the gospel/soul/rock style of Ray Charles, copping their greatest success with "Little Latin Lupe Lu," which became a garage band favorite covered by Mitch Ryder, the Kingsmen, and others. The duo wouldn't break out nationally until they put themselves at the services of Phil Spector, who gave the wall-of-sound treatment to the grandiose ballad "You've Lost That Lovin' Feelin'." At nearly four minutes, the song was pushing the limits of what could be played on radio in the mid-'60s, and some listeners thought they were hearing a 45 single played at 33 rpm due to Medley's low, blurry lead vocal. No matter; the song had a power that couldn't be denied, and went all the way to number one. The Righteous Brothers had three more big hits in 1965 on Spector's Philles label ("Just Once in My Life," "Unchained Melody," and "Ebb Tide"), all employing similar dense orchestral arrangements and swelling vocal crescendos. Yet by 1966 the Righteous Brothers had left Philles for a lucrative deal with Verve, where the duo had another number one hit with "(You're My) Soul and Inspiration." It's a bit of a mystery as to why the Righteous Brothers never came close to duplicating that success during the rest of their tenure at Verve. *—Richie Unterberger*

★ **Anthology 1962-1974** / Jul. 1989 / Rhino ✦✦✦✦✦
For some listeners, a double-disc of the Righteous Brothers might seem like overkill, but *Anthology 1962-1974* should silence most skeptics. Over the course of the two discs, it becomes clear that the duo were the finest blue-eyed soul singers of their era. Not only do the hits ("Little Latin Lupe Lu," "You've Lost That Lovin' Feeling," "Unchained Melody," "Ebb Tide," "(You're My) Soul and Inspiration," "Rock and Roll Heaven") retain their power, there are numerous forgotten gems, like the harder-rocking "Justine" and an excellent version of "This Little Girl of Mine." For listeners who want to dig a little deeper into the Righteous Brothers' music than the hits, they'll be generously rewarded by *Anthology. —Stephen Thomas Erlewine*

● **The Unchained Melody: The Very Best of the Righteous Brothers** / 1990 / Polydor ✦✦✦✦✦

Minnie Riperton

b. Nov. 8, 1947, Chicago, IL, **d.** Jul. 12, 1979, Los Angeles, CA
Vocals / Smooth Soul, Chicago Soul, Uptown Soul, Pop-Soul, Soul
One of soul music's most unique and unforgettable voices, Minnie Riperton was blessed with an angelic five-octave vocal range and scored her greatest commercial success with the chart-topping pop ballad "Lovin' You." As a youth, she studied music, drama and dance at the city's Lincoln Center, and later contemplated a career in opera. Her pop career began in 1961 when she joined the local girl group called the Gems. After graduating high school, she worked as a receptionist at the famed Chess label and in 1968, was installed as the lead vocalist of the psychedelic soul band the Rotary Connection, which debuted that year with a self-titled LP. While still a member of the Connection, Riperton mounted a solo career, issuing her brilliant debut *Come to My Garden* in 1970. After the Rotary Connection dissolved in the wake of 1971's *Hey Love*, she toured as a member of Stevie Wonder's backing unit.

Wonder agreed to co-produce Riperton's 1974 album *Perfect Angel*, which contained the international blockbuster "Lovin' You"; the record made her a household name, although subsequent LPs like 1975's *Adventures in Paradise* and 1977's *Stay in Love* failed to repeat its success. By this time, however, commercial woes were the least of Riperton's concerns—diagnosed with breast cancer, she underwent a mastectomy in 1976, later becoming a spokesperson for the American Cancer Society. Riperton continued performing despite her declining condition, with 1979's *Minnie* the final record completed during her lifetime. Unreleased vocal tracks with new instrumental backing comprised 1980's posthumous collection *Love Lives Forever. —Jason Ankeny*

Petals: The Minnie Riperton Collection / Feb. 13, 2001 / The Right Stuff ✦✦✦✦

● **Capitol Gold: The Best of Minnie Riperton** / Jun. 21, 1993 / Capitol ✦✦✦✦✦

Her Chess Years (50th Anniversary Collection) / Nov. 4, 1997 / Chess ✦✦✦✦
While this compilation is credited to Minnie Riperton, none of the 16 tracks was actually released under her name. Indeed, a more apt title might have been *Best of Minnie Riperton and the Rotary Connection*, as 13 of the songs are Rotary Connection cuts on which she sang lead. The other three date from before the Rotary Connection days, with a couple of tracks by the Gems (a mid-'60s girl group) that bear Riperton's lead vocals, as well as the 1966 single "Lonely Girl," which is actually Riperton solo, but was released under the pseudonym Andrea Davis. The pre-Rotary Connection numbers are fair but unremarkable pop-soul, with Minnie unveiling her stratospheric operatic vocals on "Lonely Girl." The Rotary Connection material is taken from five albums recorded by the group in the late '60s and early '70s; there's nothing from their most famous LP, the self-titled 1967 debut, as Riperton sang no leads on that record (it's been reissued on its own by Chess anyway). This stuff is a very mixed bag, including dubious Cream and Hendrix covers, as well as a ghoulish mauling of "Respect." On the other hand, "Magical World" shows their odd psychedelic-soul-as-MGM-musical production style at its best, and "A-Muse" is a surprisingly pretty, acoustic singer-songwriter type ballad, delivered with sensitivity by Riperton. As a whole, this music isn't so much notable for Riperton's vocals (as wide-ranging as they are) as its eccentric genre-mashing, from a rare period in which mainstream pop and soul tried to be self-consciously avant-garde and eclectic without getting too far out. *—Richie Unterberger*

Johnny Rivers (John Ramistella)

b. Nov. 7, 1942, New York, NY
Vocals, Guitar / Pop/Rock, Pop
Among the most successful yet underrated solo acts of the 1960s, Johnny Rivers reeled off a lengthy series of rock favorites which together sold over 30 million copies. Distinguished throughout by his reedy vocals and soulful guitar leads, Rivers' body of work is characterized by a rare consistency and versatility which stretches from his earnest yet rousing covers of R&B classics to his later, self-penned hits. Strongly influenced by the swamp-blues sound of his hometown of Baton Rouge, LA, Rivers—born John Ramistella in New York City on November 7, 1942—picked up the guitar as a child and played with local groups throughout his school years. After stints in New York (where he met disc jockey Alan Freed, who suggested he change his name to Rivers and Nashville, he settled in Los Angeles. He headlined at the newly opened *Whisky-a-Go-Go*, which became one of the area's hottest nightspots and earned its star attraction a rabid following among Tinseltown clubgoers. His 1964 debut *Johnny Rivers Live at the Whisky-a-Go-Go* featured hits like the Chuck Berry covers "Memphis" and "Maybelline". Over the years, Rivers returned to the club to record his albums and most of his early hits were covers, including his smash 1965 rendition of Willie Dixon's "Seventh Son," and the traditional "Midnight Special." Over the next two years, Rivers charted with hits like the theme to the television spy thriller *Secret Agent Man*, the elegiac "Poor Side of Town" (which he co-wrote with Lou Adler) and a pair of Motown covers, "Baby I Need Your Lovin'" and "The Tracks of My Tears." But after the subsequent "Summer Rain," he disappeared from the Top 40 for the rest of the decade. For the rest of his career, he returned to his roots. During the '70s, he charted with his renditions of Huey "Piano" Smith's "Rockin' Pneumonia and the Boogie Woogie Flu," Carl Perkins' "Blue Suede Shoes" and the Beach Boys' "Help Me Rhonda." His recording career wound down in the '80s, but he continued touring into the '90s, increasingly returning to the blues that inspired him initially. In 1998, Rivers reactivated his Soul City imprint and released *Last Train to Memphis*, his first new studio album in 15 years. *—Jason Ankeny*

Realization / 1968 / Soul City ✦✦✦
Not a concept album, but a song cycle depicting life in Southern California in the late '60s, *Realization* is a fine cycle to catch a ride on. From the opening "Hey Joe" right through to the rather delicate reading of "Positively Fourth Street" at the close, Rivers succeeds in evoking so many thoughts and emotions. Including the hits "Look to Your Soul" and "Summer Rain," this record captures a certain place and time with great accuracy. *Realization* is a must for any fan. *—James Chrispell*

● **Anthology, 1964-1977** / Mar. 1991 / Rhino ✦✦✦✦✦
The 36 songs here, spread over two CDs, don't cover Johnny Rivers' early, pre-Liberty Records career, but they do represent the broadest cross section of his hits for that label and beyond, B-sides, and superior album tracks assembled to date in one place. As revealed here, Rivers is a very versatile, somewhat underrated talent whose range extends far beyond Top 40 rock, "Secret Agent Man" or any other single hit, into folk, soul, and blues, all of which he plays with an unpretentious honesty. He remained remarkably consistent through the psychedelic era and into the 1970s, even amid the twin onslaughts of disco and punk, and there are no real weak points on this set. Additionally, the notes give a reasonably detailed picture of Rivers' life and career, which started far earlier (1957) than most listeners realize, and the sound is up to Rhino Records' usual standard, in terms of quality and the selection of masters. *—Bruce Eder*

The Rivieras

f. South Bend, IN, **db.** 1966

Group / Frat Rock, Garage Rock, Rock & Roll

A South Bend, IN, rock & roll band, the Rivieras' one big hit was one of the last great gasps of pure American rock & roll before the British Invasion took over the charts. Original members Otto Nuss (organ), Doug Gean (bass), Marty "Bo" Fortson (vocals and guitar), Joe Pennell (guitar), and Paul Dennert (drums) were local teen ballroom heroes. They recorded a supercharged version of the Joe Jones R&B semi-hit "California Sun" featuring a powerful drum intro and the now-famous signature guitar and organ riff. The song became a hit in the midst of the first flush of Beatlemania, only nudged out of the 1 spot on the national charts by "I Want to Hold Your Hand." Although several equally fine 45s and two albums followed, the band's relatively young ages, coupled with numerous personnel changes caused by the draft and the changing musical climate, caused the band to break up by 1966. Nuss, Gean, and Fortson reunited the Rivieras in the mid '80s, recording and doing local shows, sounding as great as ever. Though their time in the spotlight was brief, their one big hit continues to define for future generations everything that's pulsatingly great about American teen-band rock & roll. *—Cub Koda*

- **The Best of the Rivieras: California Sun** / Apr. 4, 2000 / Norton ✦✦✦✦✦

At long last, 'Nthe pride of South Bend, IN, finally get a legally sanctioned best-of that serves their legacy well. This brings together all of their original singles, the best cuts from their two albums, and the first-time reissue of "Played On," the original B-side of "California Sun." The band storm through these tracks with an energy that's palpable, and the result is '60s garage band rock & roll at its absolute finest. Highly, highly recommended. *—Cub Koda*

The Rivingtons

f. 1962, Los Angeles, CA

Group / Doo Wop, R&B

Though they are best known for their string of early-'60s novelties, the Rivingtons in reality had a rich tradition of doo wop in their background, going back to their original recordings for Federal as the Lamplighters in 1953. They did extensive backup group work throughout the '50s between their own stray releases under a number of different names; the Sharps (singing on the original "Little Bitty Pretty One" and "Over and Over" by Thurston Harris), the Rebels (they do all the backups on the Duane Eddy hits), the Four After Fives—they even sang backup on Paul Anka's first record, credited as the Jacks! In 1962 they became the Rivingtons and hit pay dirt with their first record, the self-penned "Pa Pa Ooh Mow Mow," one of the truly great rock & roll songs to make a virtue of sheer gibberish. They hit the charts again a year later with "The Bird's the Word," capitalizing on a current West Coast dance fad that teenagers were doing to "Pa Pa Ooh Mow Mow." A landlocked surf-teen combo from Minnesota called the Trashmen combined the two songs, revved up the beat to warp factor nine, and scored a massive hit with "Surfin' Bird." Despite no further chart success, their place in rock & roll history is assured. *—Cub Koda*

- **The Liberty Years** / Jun. 1991 / EMI America ✦✦✦✦✦

An excellent 23-track CD with detailed notes and great sound, featuring both sides of all their original-issue 45s (including the insane follow-up "Mama Ooh Mow Mow") plus all the tracks from their lone Liberty album, *Doin' the Bird*. *—Cub Koda*

Robbie Robertson (Jaime Robbie Robertson)

b. Jul. 5, 1943, Toronto, Ontario, Canada

Vocals, Keyboards, Guitar / Album Rock, Ethnic Fusion, Singer/Songwriter

One of the premier songwriters of the rock era, Robbie Robertson hooked up with rockabilly star Ronnie Hawkins' backing band the Hawks in 1958. After remaining with Hawkins through 1963, the Hawks began working on their own; they soon came to the attention of Bob Dylan, and became the support unit on the singer's now-legendary 1965-1966 world tour. Continuing their affiliation with Dylan, the group, renamed simply the Band, went on to become one of rock's seminal acts; propelled by Robertson's acute, evocative examinations of American mythology and lore, they made a series of seminal LPs, including 1968's *Music From Big Pink* and the following year's self-titled masterpiece. The Band dissolved on Thanksgiving Day, 1976 following an all-star concert filmed by director Martin Scorsese and later released as *The Last Waltz*. The project marked the beginning of Robertson's long affiliation with Scorsese, and in 1980 he composed the score to the director's brilliant *Raging Bull;* they later teamed for the acerbic 1983 satire *The King of Comedy* and 1986's *The Color of Money*. Finally, in 1987 Robertson released his self-titled solo debut to much acclaim. *Storyville*, a conceptual piece steeped in the sounds and imagery of a famed area of New Orleans, followed in 1990. In 1994, Robertson teamed with the Native American group the Red Road Ensemble for *Music for 'The Native Americans,'* a collection of songs composed for a television documentary series. *Contact From the Underworld of Redboy* appeared in 1998. *—Jason Ankeny*

- **\ Robertson** / 1987 / Geffen ✦✦✦✦✦

Robbie Robertson's first solo album, released 11 years after the Band called it quits at *The Last Waltz*, found the singer/guitarist mining radically new territory. Hiring Daniel Lanois as co-producer, Robertson crafted an album that owed very little to the Band's roots-Americana sound. Instead, Robertson opted for a quirky, enigmatic modern approach, using drum programs, the stick, and guest musicians such as U2, Peter Gabriel, and Bill Dillon. If the album had a weakness, it was in the vocal department. Robertson had only sung lead on a couple of songs with the Band. His reedy ghost of a voice can be quite effective but wears a bit thin over the course of a whole album. Ultimately that is a minor complaint, as the songwriting, arrangements, playing, and sound-painting are superb. Highlights: "Broken Arrow" and "Somewhere Down the Crazy River." *—Rob Bowman*

Storyville / Sep. 1991 / Geffen ✦✦✦

Robertson's second album was four years in the making. Once again he set out to explore an approach and sound markedly different from any of his previous work. The album is conceptual, roughing out a story over ten songs set in New Orleans' legendary turn-of-the-century Storyville red-light district. Co-produced by Robertson, Stephen Hague, and Gary Gersh, the record was recorded in New Orleans with members of the Neville Brothers, Mardi Gras Indians, the Meters, and the Zion Harmonizers. Legendary New Orleans arranger Wardell Quezergue contributed stunning horn charts. More aggressive than Robertson's first solo release, *Storyville* is perhaps a little less mysterious and enigmatic. *—Rob Bowman*

Music for the Native Americans / Oct. 4, 1994 / Capitol ✦✦✦

Contact from the Underworld of Red Boy / Mar. 10, 1998 / Capitol ✦✦✦

Smokey Robinson (William Robinson)

b. Feb. 19, 1940, Detroit, MI

Vocals, Producer / Quiet Storm, Motown, Urban, R&B, Soul

If you're looking for the all-time number one purveyor of mainstream romantic soul, Smokey Robinson may well be the man, in the face of some towering competition. With the Miracles in the 1960s, he paced dozens of tuneful Motown hits with his beautiful high tenor. As a solo performer from the 1970s onwards, he's been one of the staples of urban contemporary music. But his singing gifts, as notable as they are, comprise only one of his hats: he's also one of pop's best and most prolific songwriters. As a songwriter and producer, he was the most important musical component to Motown's early success, not only on the hits by the Miracles, but for numerous other acts as well (especially Mary Wells and the Temptations). Robinson first crossed paths with Motown founder Berry Gordy, Jr. in the late 1950s in Detroit. In retrospect, this may have been the most important meeting in both men's lives. There was no national action for the Miracles until "Shop Around" in late 1960; it made number two, doing much not only to establish the Miracles, but to establish the Motown label itself. The song also heralded many of the important elements of the Motown sound, with its gospelish interplay between lead and backup vocals, its rhythmic groove, and its blend of R&B and pop. While Smokey Robinson is most often thought of as a romantic balladeer, the Miracles were also capable of grinding out some excellent uptempo party tunes, particularly in their early days. The 1962 Top Ten hit "You've Really Got a Hold on Me," however, was the key cut in forming Robinson's romantic persona, with its pleading, soaring vocals, exquisite melody, and carefully crafted lyrics. Bob Dylan was impressed enough by Robinson's facility for imaginative wordplay to dub him "America's greatest living poet" (a phrase which has possibly become the most quoted example of one rock giant praising another). *—Richie Unterberger*

Hi, We're the Miracles / Jun. 1961 / Motown ✦✦✦✦✦

The Miracles' first album is a magnificent debut, filled with impeccable vocal performances, inventive and occasionally brilliant songwriting, and an aching romantic aura. "Shop Around" was the big hit on the record, but another highlight is the group's recut version (also available on the old Miracles' *Anthology* double-disc set) of their single "Way Over There" in a lusher, more beguiling arrangement, which anticipated Phil Spector's "pop symphony" productions with the Crystals, Darlene Love, the Ronettes, and Tina Turner. Smokey Robinson authored or co-authored (with Berry Gordy or fellow Miracle Ronnie White) all but one track here—all are winners, and songs like the ethereal Robinson-White "Heart Like Mine" are worth the price of the disc. They'd do classier, more elaborate work later on, but the youthful verve of Robinson, Claudette Rogers Robinson, Ronnie White, Bobby Rogers, Pete Moore, and Marv Tarplin on these tracks makes this an indispensable record, even for casual fans. *—Bruce Eder*

I'll Try Something New / Jul. 1962 / Motown ✦✦✦✦

Cookin' with the Miracles / Nov. 1962 / Motown ✦✦✦

The Fabulous Miracles / Feb. 1963 / Motown ✦✦✦

A Quiet Storm / Mar. 26, 1975 / Motown ✦✦✦✦✦

The genius of William "Smokey" Robinson is immeasurable. As many of his prior songs had shaped R&B and pop music, this album would have a similar effect. The title track became the namesake for a music format. The album itself had three singles hit the charts. Arranged in an intermittent rhythm, "Baby That's Backatcha" ran up the *Billboard* R&B charts to number one inside 16 weeks. It was Robinson's first number one single since leaving the Miracles. The lyric of the ballad "The Agony and the Ecstasy" hit the Top Ten at number seven, and it was followed by the masterpiece "A Quiet Storm." Although it only managed to seal the Top 25, it has since made a greater impact on the music charts and music industry. Briefly, radio mogul Cathy Hughes, owner of Radio One, was the general manager at Howard University radio WHUR during the early '70s when she created the format "the quiet storm." She used Smokey Robinson's composition as the theme song. Before long, it caught on around the country and evolved into a new market. This album also features the "Wedding Song" which was written for Hazel and Jermaine Jackson's wedding and the "Happy" theme from the movie *Lady Sings the Blues*. *—Craig Lytle*

Where There's Smoke . . . / May 22, 1979 / Motown ✦✦✦

Being with You / Feb. 17, 1981 / Motown ✦✦✦

One Heartbeat / Feb. 24, 1987 / Motown ✦✦✦

Whatever Makes You Happy: More of the Best . . . / Feb. 16, 1993 / Rhino ✦✦✦✦✦

Solid compilation of 18 of the most interesting non-hits from Smokey's (and Motown's) golden era. Culled from 11 albums, this is an intelligent and consistent overview of Robinson's relatively unknown tunes. These cuts show the stylistic evolution of Motown as surely as any greatest hits collection, moving from bluesy, raucous R&B to assembly-line soul to songs reflecting the lyrical and instrumental innovations of the psychedelic era. Robinson's peerless soul songwriting and the Miracles' smooth harmonies remained constant no matter what the era, making this a much more fluid set than you might expect. Ultimately, the songs don't boast hooks quite as memorable as their classic hit singles, despite their similarities in structure and production. The early-'60s tracks are perhaps the record's most interesting, displaying a gritty, almost salacious approach that had yet to be toned down by slicker production values. Dominated by Robinson originals, this collection also includes scattered covers of "Money" and hits by the Temptations and Supremes, as well as the original version of "From Head to Toe," later covered by Elvis Costello. *—Richie Unterberger*

☆ **The 35th Anniversary Box** / Feb. 22, 1994 / Motown ✦✦✦✦✦
This four-CD boxed set covers every essential track that Smokey Robinson and the Miracles ever recorded, and then some—at least a dozen never previously anthologized tracks are included here, among them the original single versions of "Way Over There" (unavailable elsewhere) and "Shop Around" (which had already been released locally in Detriot when Berry Gordy decided one night to get a session together, punch up the rhythm, and lay down a new version, which became the hit). Even better is the remastering, which runs circles around any previous edition of the Miracles' work, and the annotation—including an essay by Claudette Robinson—that gives credit to all of the participants, including the backup musicians who were seldom if ever mentioned during Motown's heyday. The Smokey Robinson & the Miracles *Anthology* is a fine collection, but this set is the definitive history, and irreplaceable for anyone who genuinely loves the group. *—Bruce Eder*

★ **Anthology** / 1995 / Motown ✦✦✦✦✦
Detroit vocal group the Miracles were a fixture at Motown from day one. Driven by Robinson's superior writing and smooth, silky falsetto, the Miracles placed a stunning 48 singles on the Billboard charts, 39 of those with Smokey in tow. Virtually all of them are included on this collection. Songs such as "Ooh Baby Baby," "The Tracks of My Tears," and "The Tears of a Clown" define much that was good about the '60s. The 1995 double-CD reissue is digitally remastered and includes virtually the same tracks, adding a couple previously unreleased songs and extensive liner notes. *—Rob Bowman*

★ **The Ultimate Collection [1998]** / Feb. 10, 1998 / Motown ✦✦✦✦✦
Motown is notorious for recycling their catalog as endless hit collections, but *The Ultimate Collection* is one of the finest series of greatest-hits CDs they have ever assembled. Each disc contains all of the major hits from an artist, plus important B-sides, album tracks and minor hits. Smokey Robinson & the Miracles' entry in the series is no exception to the rule, boasting all their Top Ten pop and R&B hits between 1960 and 1969—"Shop Around," "You've Really Got a Hold on Me," "Mickey's Monkey," "Ooo Baby Baby," "The Tracks of My Tears," "My Girl Has Gone," "Going to a Go-Go," "(Come 'Round Here) I'm the One You Need," "The Love I Saw in You Was Just a Mirage," "More Love," "I Second That Emotion," "If You Can Want," "Yester Love," "Special Occasion," "Baby, Baby Don't Cry"—plus the 1970 number one "The Tears of a Clown" and important B-sides like "Choosey Beggar" and "Who's Lovin' You," resulting in a total of 25 tracks. For anyone who wants a definitive hits collection but is hesitant to invest in the four-disc *35th Anniversary Box, The Ultimate Collection* is an ideal choice. *—Stephen Thomas Erlewine*

Lost and Found: Along Came Love (1958-1964) / Sep. 28, 1999 / Motown ✦✦✦✦
As part of Motown's *Lost and Found* series, this brings together 20 previously unreleased tracks and rarities of prime Smokey and the Miracles from various early time frames in the Motown catalog. Some of the earliest, like "My Mama Told Me," echo Motor City role models Nolan Strong and the Diablos right down to the guitar riffs behind Smokey's uncharacteristically bluesy vocals, while others, like "Please Say You Love Me," splendidly wear their doo-wop roots on their sleeves. Here we find the group taking on Broadway show tunes in modern jazz harmonies and *nailing* it on "If I Were a Bell" and "Easy Street." The title track is one of Smokey's patented slow burners. In the rarities department, there's the lost Ron and Bill B-side, "Don't Say Bye Bye," only outdone by "Mr. Misery," a rare lead vocal by Claudette Robinson in the grand girl group style, and a live version of "Shop Around" that's as raw as anything Smokey ever committed to wax. In the final analysis, however, most of the tracks here just make you wonder how material this great could have languished in unreleased forms for so long. Smokey's worst session is still better than most superstars' best work; here's a whole CD that makes even his leftovers a tantalizing prospect. *—Cub Koda*

The Ultimate Collection [1997] / Mar. 25, 1997 / Motown ✦✦✦✦✦
While Robinson's solo work pales in comparison to his hits with the Miracles, this 17-track collection of Motown singles uncovers such gems as "Baby Come Close," "I Am I Am," "Cruisin'," "Let Me Be," "The Clock," "Tell Me Tomorrow," "I've Made Love to You a Thousand Times," "One Heartbeat," "Just to See Her," "Everything You Touch," "Baby That's Backatcha," "The Agony and the Ecstacy" and "Open." *—Jason Ankeny*

Tom Robinson

b. Jun. 1, 1950
Vocals, Bass / British Punk, Pub Rock, New Wave, Hard Rock, Punk
Although his career had pretty much flamed out by the start of the '80s, there were few punk-era major label performers as intensely controversial as Tom Robinson. Cutting his teeth with folk-rockers Cafe Society, he roared into the spotlight in 1978 with a great single ("2-4-6-8 Motorway") and a much-ballyhooed contract with EMI. What was remarkable about this was that Robinson was the kind of politically conscious, confrontational performer that major labels generally ignored: he was openly gay and sang about it ("Glad to be Gay"), vociferous in his hatred for then-British Prime Minister Margaret Thatcher, helped form Rock Against Racism, and generally spoke in favor of any leftist political tract that would embarrass the ruling ultraconservative Tory government. His debut album, 1978's *Power in the Darkness,* was an occasionally stunning piece of punk/hard rock agit-prop that, along with being ferociously direct, was politicized rock that focused more on songs than slogans. However, by the release of the second album, the Todd Rundgren-produced *TRB Two,* the songs were getting weaker and Robinson began sounding like a boring idealogue. *—John Dougan*

Power in the Darkness / 1978 / Razor & Tie ✦✦✦✦✦

TRB Two / 1979 / Razor & Tie ✦✦✦

● **Rising Free: the Very Best of Tom Robinson Band** / 1997 / EMI ✦✦✦✦✦
The Tom Robinson Band straddled the border between pub rock and punk, turning out hard-driving rock anthems that were filled with attitude, if not venom. They were a stripped-down rock & roll band, delivering charging, catchy three-chord rockers at their best. Occasionally, as on the notorious anthem "Glad to Be Gay," Robinson dipped into social commentary, yet he was best at just rocking out, like on the lost classic "2-4-6-8 Motorway," one of the very best driving songs of all time. "2-4-6-8 Motorway" is the highlight on *Rising Free—The Very Best of the Tom Robinson Band,* which proves that the group was a good band, but not great. Few songs on *Rising Free* have the intoxicating hook of "2-4-6-8 Motorway," and few are as acidic as "Glad to Be Gay." By and large, it's simply competent pub rock that's harder than average. As the years progressed, TRB's edge softened, and they began experimenting with disco. All of these progressions, and all of the group's best moments, are found on *Rising Free,* and while it doesn't reveal many hidden gems, there are enough good songs to make it worthwhile for pub and punk fanatics. *—Stephen Thomas Erlewine*

Rockpile

f. 1976, **db.** 1981
Group / Pub Rock, Pop/Rock, New Wave, Rock & Roll
During the late '70s, Rockpile was the touring band for both Dave Edmunds and Nick Lowe. Like Edmunds, the band was passionate about traditional rock & roll. Like Lowe, the band played with a reckless, trashy abandon. Driven by the powerful rhythm section of drummer Terry Williams and Lowe's bass, guitarists Billy Bremner and Edmunds were free to spit out crushing rock, blues, rockabilly, and country licks. With their fierce live energy and unpretentious rock & roll, the band fit easily into the post-punk new wave at the end of the decade.

Although they only released one album as a group—1980's *Seconds of Pleasure*—the band provided support for most of the albums Lowe and Edmunds recorded in the late '70s. After the rushed release of *Seconds of Pleasure,* the band toured one last time before splitting apart, largely due to mismanagement. All of the members continued to occasionally collaborate with each other throughout the '80s. *—Stephen Thomas Erlewine*

Seconds of Pleasure / 1980 / Columbia ✦✦✦✦✦
If *Seconds of Pleasure,* the only album Rockpile issued under their name, doesn't quite capture the intensity of their ferocious live performances, attribute it to the confines of a studio setting, plus the fact that most of their set list derived from Nick Lowe's *Labour of Lust* and Dave Edmunds' *Repeat When Necessary* (both of which featured Rockpile as backing band). So, much of their great songs had already been cut elsewhere, leaving *Seconds* to be split equally between covers and originals. Since Edmunds was never a songwriter, this gave Lowe the upper-hand, not only because Dave sings Nick's "*Fool too Long,*" but because he's in tremendous form. He unearths the Gene Chandler "*Teacher Teacher,*" gives the irrepressible Billy Bremner the joyous "*Heart,*" offers the jangling Buddy Holly-esque "*Now and Always*" where the sweetness masks the suicidal undertones, sleazes it up with "*Pet and Hold You*" and then delves into tongue-in-cheek autobiography with "*When I Write a Book,*" one of his very finest and funniest songs. These give Dave's covers, which are barroom ravers of the highest order, whether it's Joe Tex's "*If Sugar Was as Sweet as You*" or Difford & Tilbrook's "*Wrong Again (Let's Face It).*" Yes, the production has the gloss of new wave, which actually gives them some freshness. Not that they needed it. Although Rockpile are unabashedly rock revivalists, they make it sound fresh—they have so much joy, it's hard not to get wrapped up in its momentum. Maybe not a flat-out classic, but rock & roll rarely gets as flat-out fun as this. [The CD reissue is even better, since it contains the bonus seven-inch of four Everly covers, sung by Nick and Dave, alone with acoustics, at a radio station.] *—Stephen Thomas Erlewine*

The Rolling Stones

f. Jan. 1963, London, England
Group / British Psychedelia, Album Rock, British Blues, Pop/Rock, Psychedelic, British Invasion, Hard Rock, Blues-Rock, Rock & Roll
By the time the Rolling Stones began calling themselves the World's Greatest Rock & Roll Band in the late '60s, they had already staked out an impressive claim on the title. As the self-consciously dangerous alternative to the bouncy Merseybeat of the Beatles in the British Invasion, the Stones had pioneered the gritty, hard-driving blues-based rock & roll that came to define hard rock. With his preening machismo and latent maliciousness, Mick Jagger became the prototypical rock frontman, tempering his macho showmanship with a detached, campy irony, while Keith Richards and Brian Jones wrote the blueprint for sinewy, interlocking rhythm guitars. Backed by the strong, yet subtly swinging rhythm section of bassist Bill Wyman and drummer Charlie Watts, the Stones became the breakout band of the British blues scene, eclipsing such contemporaries as the Animals and Them. Over the course of their career, the Stones never really abandoned blues, but as soon as they reached popularity in the U.K., they began experimenting musically, incorporating the British pop of contemporaries like the Beatles, Kinks and Who into their sound. After a brief dalliance with psychedelia, the Stones re-emerged in the late '60s as a jaded, blues-soaked hard rock quintet. They always flirted with the seedy side of rock & roll, but as the hippie dream began to break apart, they exposed and reveled in the new rock culture. It wasn't without difficulty, of course. Shortly after he was fired from the group, Jones was found dead in a swimming pool, while at a 1969 free concert at Altamont, a concertgoer was brutally murdered during the Stones' show. But the Stones never stopped going. For the next thirty years, they continued to record and perform, and while their records weren't always blockbusters, they were never less than the most visible band of their era—certainly, none of their British peers continued to be as popular or productive as the Stones. And no band since has proven to have such a broad fan base or far-reaching popularity, and it is impossible to hear any of the groups that followed them without detecting some sort of influence, whether it was musical or aesthetic. *—Stephen Thomas Erlewine*

The Rolling Stones (England's Newest Hitmakers) / May 30, 1964 / ABKCO ✦✦✦✦✦
The group's debut album was the most uncompromisingly blues/R&B-oriented full-length recording they would ever release. Mostly occupied with covers, this was as hard-core as British R&B ever got; it's raw and ready. But the Stones succeeded in establishing themselves as creative interpreters, putting '50s and early '60s blues, rock, and soul classics (some quite

obscure to White audiences) through a younger, more guitar-oriented filter. The record's highlighted by blistering versions of "Route 66," "Carol," the hyper-tempoed "I Just Want to Make Love to You," "I'm a King Bee," and "Walking the Dog." Their Bo Diddleyized version of Buddy Holly's "Not Fade Away" gave them their first British Top Ten hit (and their first small American one). The acoustic ballad "Tell Me" was Jagger-Richards' first good original tune, but the other group-penned originals were little more than rehashed jams of blues cliches, keeping this album from reaching truly classic status. *—Richie Unterberger*

☆ **12 ×5** / Oct. 17, 1964 / ABKCO ♦♦♦♦♦
The evolution from blues to rock accelerated with the Stones' second American LP. They turned soul into guitar rock for the hits "It's All Over Now" and "Time Is on My Side" (the latter of which was their first American Top Ten single). "2120 South Michigan Avenue" is a great instrumental blues-rock jam; "Around and Around" is one of their best Chuck Berry covers; and "If You Need Me" reflects an increasing contemporary soul influence. On the other hand, the group originals (except for the propulsive "Empty Heart") are weak and derivative, indicating that the band still had a way to go before they could truly challenge the Beatles' throne. *—Richie Unterberger*

☆ **The Rolling Stones Now!** / Apr. 1965 / ABKCO ♦♦♦♦♦
Although their third American album was patched together (in the usual British Invasion tradition) from a variety of sources, it's their best early R&B-oriented effort. Most of the Stones' early albums suffer from three or four very weak cuts; *Now!* is almost uniformly strong start-to-finish, the emphasis on some of their Blackest material. The covers of "Down Home Girl," and Bo Diddley's vibrating "Mona," Otis Redding's "Pain in My Heart," and Barbara Lynn's "Oh Baby" are all among the group's best R&B interpretations. The best gem is "Little Red Rooster," a pure blues with wonderful slide guitar from Brian Jones (and a number one single in Britain, although it was only an album track in the U.S.). As songwriters, Jagger and Richards are still struggling, but they come up with one of their first winners (and an American Top 20 hit) with the yearning, soulful "Heart of Stone." *—Richie Unterberger*

Out of Our Heads / Aug. 1965 / ABKCO ♦♦♦♦♦
In 1965, the Stones finally proved themselves capable of writing classic rock singles that mined their R&B/blues roots, but updated them into a more guitar-based, thoroughly contemporary context. The first enduring Jagger-Richards classics are here—"The Last Time," and its menacing, folky B-side "Play with Fire," and the riff-driven "Satisfaction," which made them superstars in the States and defined their sound and rebellious attitude better than any other single song. On the rest of the album, they largely opted for mid-'60s soul covers, Marvin Gaye's "Hitch Hike," Otis Redding's "Cry to Me," and Sam Cooke's "Good Times" being particular standouts. "I'm All Right" (based on a Bo Diddley sound) showed their '65 sound at its rawest, and there are a couple of fun, though derivative, bluesy originals in "The Spider and the Fly" and "The Under Assistant West Coast Promotion Man." *—Richie Unterberger*

December's Children / Dec. 1965 / ABKCO ♦♦♦♦♦
The last Stones album in which cover material accounted for 50% of the content was thrown together from a variety of singles, British LP tracks, outtakes, and a cut from an early '64 U.K. EP. Haphazard assembly aside, much of it's great, including the huge hit "Get Off of My Cloud" and the controversial, string-laden acoustic ballad "As Tears Go By" (a Top Ten item in America). Raiding the R&B closet for the last time, they also offered a breathless run-through of Larry Williams' "She Said Yeah," a sultry Chuck Berry cover ("Talkin' About You"), and exciting live versions of "Route 66" and Hank Snow's "I'm Moving On." More importantly, Jagger-Richards' songwriting partnership had now developed to the extent that several non-A-side tracks were reasonably strong in their own right, such as "I'm Free" and "The Singer Not the Song." And the version of "You Better Move On" (which had featured on a British EP at the beginning of 1964) was one of their best and most tender soul covers. *—Richie Unterberger*

Big Hits: High Tide and Green Grass / Mar. 1966 / ABKCO ♦♦♦♦♦

☆ **Aftermath** / Jun. 1966 / ABKCO ♦♦♦♦♦
The Rolling Stones finally delivered a set of all-original material with this LP, which also did much to define the group as the bad boys of rock 'n' roll with their sneering attitude toward the world in general and the female sex in particular. The borderline misogyny could get a bit juvenile in tunes like "Stupid Girl." But on the other hand the group began incorporating the influences of psychedelia and Dylan into their material with classics like "Paint It Black," an eerily insistent number one hit graced by some of the best use of sitar (played by Brian Jones) on a rock record. Other classics included "Mother's Little Helper" (whose lyrics had extremely blatant and controversial drug references); Jones also added exotic accents with his vibes (on the jazzy "Under My Thumb") and dulcimer (the delicate Elizabethan ballad "Lady Jane"). Some of the material is fairly ho-hum, to be honest, as Jagger and Richards were still prone to inconsistent songwriting; "Goin' Home," a 11-minute blues jam, was remarkable more for its barrier-crashing length than its content. Look out for an obscure gem, however, in the brooding, meditative "I Am Waiting." *—Richie Unterberger*

Got Live If You Want It / Nov. 4, 1966 / ABKCO ♦♦

☆ **Between the Buttons** / Jan. 1967 / ABKCO ♦♦♦♦♦
The Rolling Stones' 1967 recordings are a matter of some controversy; many critics felt that they were compromising their raw, rootsy power with trendy emulations of the Beatles, Kinks, Dylan, and psychedelic music. Approach this album with an open mind, though, and you'll find it to be one of their strongest, most eclectic LPs, with many fine songs that remain unknown to all but Stones devotees. The lyrics are getting better (if more savage), and the arrangements more creative, on brooding near-classics like "All Sold Out," "My Obsession," and "Yesterday's Papers." "She Smiled Sweetly" shows their hidden romantic side at its best, while "Connection" is one of the record's few slabs of conventionally driving rock. But the best tracks were the two songs that gave the group a double-sided number one in early 1967: the lustful "Let's Spend the Night Together" and the beautiful, melancholy "Ruby Tuesday," which is as melodic as anything Jagger and Richards would ever write. *—Richie Unterberger*

Flowers / Jun. 1967 / ABKCO ♦♦♦♦♦
Dismissed as a ripoff of sorts by some critics, as it took the patchwork bastardization of British releases for the American audience to extremes, gathering stray tracks from the U.K. versions of *Aftermath* and *Between the Buttons*, 1966-67 singles (some of which had already been used on the U.S. editions of *Aftermath* and *Between the Buttons*), and a few outtakes. Judged solely by the music, though, it's rather great. "Lady Jane," "Ruby Tuesday," and "Let's Spend the Night Together" are all classics (although they had all been on LP before); the 1966 single "Mother's Little Helper," a 1966 Top Ten hit, is also terrific; and "Have You Seen Your Mother, Baby, Standing in the Shadow" making its first album appearance, is the early Stones at their most surrealistic and angst-ridden. A lot of the rest of the cuts rate among their most outstanding 1966-67 work. "Out of Time" is hit-worthy in its own right (and in fact topped the British charts in an inferior cover by Chris Farlowe); "Back Street Girl," with its European waltz flavor, is one of *the* great underrated Stones songs. The same goes for the psychedelic Bo Diddley of "Please Go Home," and the acoustic, pensively sardonic "Sittin' on a Fence," with its strong Appalachian flavor. Almost every track is strong, so if you're serious about your Stones, don't pass this by just because a bunch of people slag it as an exploitative marketing trick (which it is). There's some outstanding material you can't get anywhere else, and the album as a whole plays very well from end-to-end. *—Richie Unterberger*

Their Satanic Majesties Request / Nov. 1967 / ABKCO ♦♦♦♦
Without a doubt, no Rolling Stones album—and, indeed, very few rock albums from any era—split critical opinion as much as the Rolling Stones' psychedelic outing. Many dismiss the record as sub-*Sgt. Pepper* posturing; others confess, if only in private, to a fascination with the album's inventive arrangements, which incorporated some African rhythms, mellotrons, and full orchestration. Never before or since did the Stones take so many chances in the studio. This writer, at least, feels that the record has been unfairly undervalued, partly because purists expect the Stones to constantly champion a blues 'n' raunch worldview. About half the material is very strong, particularly the glorious "She's a Rainbow," with its beautiful harmonies, piano, and strings; the riff-driven "Citadel"; the hazy, dream-like "In Another Land," Bill Wyman's debut writing (and singing) credit on a Stones release; and the majestically dark and doomy cosmic rocker "2000 Light Years from Home," with some of the creepiest synthesizer effects (devised by Brian Jones) ever to grace a rock record. The downfall of the album was caused by some weak songwriting on the lesser tracks, particularly the interminable psychedelic jam "Sing This All Together (See What Happens)." It's a much better record than most people give it credit for being, though, with a strong current of creeping uneasiness that undercuts the gaudy psychedelic flourishes. In 1968, the Stones would go back to the basics, and never wander down these paths again, making this all the more of a fascinating anomaly in the group's discography. *—Richie Unterberger*

☆ **Beggars Banquet** / Nov. 1968 / ABKCO ♦♦♦♦♦
The Stones forsook psychedelic experimentation to return to their blues roots on this celebrated album, which was immediately acclaimed as one of their landmark achievements. A strong acoustic Delta blues flavor colors much of the material, particularly "Salt of the Earth" and "No Expectations," which features some beautiful slide guitar work. Basic rock & roll was not forgotten, however: "Street Fighting Man," a reflection of the political turbulence of 1968, was one of their most innovative singles, and "Sympathy for the Devil," with its fire-dancing guitar licks, leering Jagger vocals, African rhythms, and explicitly satanic lyrics, was an image-defining epic. On "Stray Cat Blues," Jagger and crew began to explore the kind of decadent sexual sleaze that they would take to the point of self-parody by the mid-'70s. At the time, though, the approach was still fresh, and the lyrical bite of most of the material ensured *Beggars Banquet*'s place as one of the top blues-based rock records of all time. *—Richie Unterberger*

☆ **Let It Bleed** / Nov. 28, 1969 / ABKCO ♦♦♦♦♦
Mostly recorded without Brian Jones—who died several months before its release (although he does play on two tracks) and was replaced by Mick Taylor (who also plays on just two songs)—this extends the rock & blues feel of *Beggar's Banquet* into slightly harder-rocking, more demonically sexual territory. The Stones were never as consistent on album as their main rivals, the Beatles, and *Let It Bleed* suffers from some rather perfunctory tracks, like "Monkey Man" and a countrified remake of the classic "Honky Tonk Woman" (here titled "Country Honk"). Yet some of the songs are among their very best, especially "Gimme Shelter," with its shimmering guitar lines and apocalyptic lyrics; the harmonica-driven "Midnight Rambler"; the druggy party ambience of the title track; and the stunning "You Can't Always Get What You Want," which was the Stones' "Hey Jude" of sorts, with its epic structure, horns, philosophical lyrics, and swelling choral vocals. "You Got the Silver" (Keith Richards' first lead vocal) and Robert Johnson's "Love in Vain," by contrast, were as close to the roots of acoustic down-home blues as the Stones ever got. *—Richie Unterberger*

Get Yer Ya-Ya's Out / Sep. 4, 1970 / ABKCO ♦♦♦♦♦
Recorded during their American tour in late 1969, and centered around live versions of material from the *Beggars Banquet-Let It Bleed* era. Often acclaimed as one of the top live rock albums of all time, its appeal has dimmed a little today. The live versions are reasonably different from the studio ones, but ultimately not as good, a notable exception being the long workout of "Midnight Rambler," with extended harmonica solos and the unforgettable section where the pace slows to a bump-and-grind crawl. Some Stones aficionados, in fact, prefer a bootleg from the same tour (*Liver Than You'll Ever Be*, to which this album was unleashed in response), or their amazing the-show-must-go-on performance in the jaws of hell at Altamont (preserved in the *Gimme Shelter*... film). Fans that are unconcerned with picky comparisons such as these will still find *Ya Ya's*... an outstanding album, and it's certainly the Stones' best official live recording. *—Richie Unterberger*

☆ **Sticky Fingers** / Apr. 23, 1971 / Virgin ♦♦♦♦♦
Pieced together from outtakes and much-labored-over songs, *Sticky Fingers* manages to have a loose, ramshackle ambience that belies both its origins and the dark undercurrents of the songs. It's a weary, drug-laden album—well over half the songs explicitly mention drug use, while the others merely allude to it—that never fades away, but it barely keeps afloat. Apart

from the classic opener, "Brown Sugar" (a gleeful tune about slavery, interracial sex, and lost virginity, not necessarily in that order), the long workout "Can't You Hear Me Knocking" and the mean-spirited "Bitch," *Sticky Fingers* is a slow, bluesy affair, with a few country touches thrown in for good measure. The laid-back tone of the album gives ample room for new lead guitarist Mick Taylor to stretch out, particularly on the extended coda of "Can't You Hear Me Knocking." But the key to the album isn't the instrumental interplay—although that is terrific—it's the utter weariness of the songs. "Wild Horses" is their first non-ironic stab at a country song, and it is a beautiful, heart-tugging masterpiece. Similarly, "I Got the Blues" is a ravished, late-night classic that ranks among their very best blues. "Sister Morphine" is a horrifying overdose tale, and "Moonlight Mile," with Paul Buckmaster's grandiose strings, is a perfect closure: sad, yearning, drug-addled, and beautiful. With its offhand mixture of decadence, roots music, and outright malevolence, *Sticky Fingers* set the tone for the rest of the decade for the Stones. *—Stephen Thomas Erlewine*

● **Hot Rocks, 1964-1971** / Jan. 1972 / ABKCO ✦✦✦✦✦
This two-LP/two-CD set is both a lot more and a bit less than what it seems. It is seven years worth of mostly very high-charting, and all influential and important, songs, leaving out some singles in favor of well-known album tracks and, in the process, giving an overview not just of the Rolling Stones' hits but of their evolving image. One hears them change from loud R&B-inspired rockers covering others' songs ("Time Is on My Side") into originators in their own right ("Satisfaction"); then into taste-makers and style-setters with a particularly decadent air ("Get off of My Cloud," "19th Nervous Breakdown"); and finally into self-actualized rebel-poets ("Jumping Jack Flash," "Midnight Rambler") and Shaman-like symbols of chaos. On its initial release, *Hot Rocks* sold well, not only as a unique compilation but also as a panorama of the 1960s. The only flaw was that it didn't give a good look at the Stones' full musical history, ignoring their early blues period and the psychedelic era. There are also some anomalies in *Hot Rocks'* history for the collector—the very first pressings included an outtake of "Brown Sugar" featuring Eric Clapton that was promptly replaced; and the original European CD version, issued as two separate discs on the Decca label, was also different from its American counterpart, featuring a version of "Satisfaction" mastered in stereo and putting the guitars on separate channels for the first time. Those musicologist concerns aside, this is still an exciting assembly of material. *—Bruce Eder*

☆ **Exile on Main Street** / May 12, 1972 / Virgin ✦✦✦✦✦
Greeted with decidedly mixed reviews upon its original release, *Exile on Main Street* has become generally regarded as the Rolling Stones' finest album. Part of the reason why the record was initially greeted with hesitant reviews is that it takes a while to assimilate. A sprawling, weary double album encompassing rock & roll, blues, soul, and country, *Exile* doesn't try anything new on the surface, but the substance is new. Taking the bleakness that underpinned *Let It Bleed* and *Sticky Fingers* to an extreme, *Exile* is a weary record, and not just lyrically. Jagger's vocals are buried in the mix, and the music is a series of dark, dense jams, with Keith Richards and Mick Taylor spinning off incredible riffs and solos. And the songs continue the breakthroughs of their three previous albums. No longer does their country sound forced or kitschy—it's lived-in and complex, just like the group's forays into soul and gospel. While the songs, including the masterpieces "Rocks Off," "Tumbling Dice," "Torn and Frayed," "Happy," "Let It Loose," and "Shine a Light," are all terrific, they blend together, with only certain lyrics and guitar lines emerging from the murk. It's the kind of record that's gripping on the very first listen, but each subsequent listen reveals something new. Few other albums, let alone double albums, have been so rich and masterful as *Exile on Main Street,* and it stands not only as one of the Stones' best records, but sets a remarkably high standard for all of hard rock. *—Stephen Thomas Erlewine*

● **More Hot Rocks (Big Hits and Fazed Cookies)** / Nov. 1972 / ABKCO ✦✦✦✦✦
Hot Rocks covers most of the monster hits from the Stones' first decade that remain in radio rotation in the 1990s. *More Hot Rocks* goes for the somewhat smaller hits, some of the better album tracks, and a whole LP side worth of rarities that hadn't yet been available in the United States when this compilation was released in 1972. The material isn't as famous as what's on *Hot Rocks,* but the music is almost as excellent, including such vital cuts as "Not Fade Away," "It's All Over Now," "The Last Time," "Lady Jane," the psychedelic "Dandelion," "She's a Rainbow," "Have You Seen Your Mother, Baby, Standing in the Shadow—," "Out of Time," "Tell Me," and "We Love You." The eight rarities are pretty good as well, including their 1963 debut single "Come On," early R&B covers of "Fortune Teller" and "Bye Bye Johnnie," great slide guitar on Muddy Waters' "I Can't Be Satisfied," and the soulful 1966 U.K. B-side, "Long Long While." *—Richie Unterberger*

Goats Head Soup / Aug. 31, 1973 / Virgin ✦✦✦
Sliding out of perhaps the greatest winning streak in rock history, the Stones slipped into decadence and rock star excess with *Goats Head Soup,* their sequel to *Exile on Main St.* This is where the Stones image began to eclipse their accomplishments, as Mick ascended to jet-setting celebrity and Keith slowly sunk deeper into addiction, and it's possible hearing them moving in both directions on *Goats Head Soup,* at times in the same song. As Jagger plays the devil (or, dances with Mr. D, as he likes to say), the sex and sleaze quotient is increased, all of it underpinned by some genuinely affecting heartbreak, highlighted by "Angie." This may not be as downright funky, freaky, and fantastic as *Exile,* yet the extra layer of gloss brings out the enunciated lyrics, added strings, wah-wah guitars, explicit sex, and violence, making it all seem trippily decadent. If it doesn't seem like there's a surplus of classics here, all the songs work well, illustrating just how far they've traveled in their songcraft, as well as their exceptional talent as a band—they make this all sound really easy and darkly alluring, even when the sex'n'satanism seems a little silly. To top it all of, they cap off this utterly excessive album with "Star Star," a nasty Chuck Berry rip that grooves on its own mean vulgarity—it's real title is "Starfucker," if you need any clarification, and even though they got nastier (the entirety of *Undercover,* for instance), they never again made something this dirty or nasty. And, it never feels more at home than it does at the end of this excessive record. *—Stephen Thomas Erlewine*

It's Only Rock and Roll / Oct. 18, 1974 / Virgin ✦✦✦
It's uneven, but at times *It's Only Rock and Roll* catches fire. The songs and performances are stronger than those on *Goats Head Soup;* the tossed-off numbers sound effortless, not careless. Throughout, the Stones wear their title as the "World's Greatest Rock & Roll Band" with a defiant smirk, which makes the bitter cynicism of "If You Can't Rock Me" and the title track all the more striking, and the reggae experimentation of "Luxury," the aching beauty of "Time Waits for No One," and the agreeable filler of "Dance Little Sister" and "Short and Curlies" all the more enjoyable. *—Stephen Thomas Erlewine*

Metamorphosis / Jun. 1975 / ABKCO ✦✦

Black & Blue / Apr. 20, 1976 / Virgin ✦✦✦

Love You Live / Sep. 23, 1977 / Rolling Stones ✦✦

☆ **Some Girls** / Jun. 9, 1978 / Virgin ✦✦✦✦✦
During the mid-'70s, the Rolling Stones remained massively popular, but their records suffered from Jagger's fascination with celebrity and Keith's worsening drug habit. By 1978, both punk and disco had swept the group off the front pages, and *Some Girls* was their fiery response to the younger generation. Opening with the disco-blues thump of "Miss You," *Some Girls* is a tough, focused, and exciting record, full of more hooks and energy than any Stones record since *Exile on Main Street.* Even though the Stones make disco their own, they never quite take punk on their own ground. Instead, their rockers sound harder and nastier than they have in years. Using "Star Star" as a template, the Stones run through the seedy homosexual imagery of "When the Whip Comes Down," the bizarre, borderline-misogynistic vitriol of the title track, Keith's ultimate outlaw anthem, "Before They Make Me Run," and the decadent closer, "Shattered." In between, they deconstruct the Temptations' "(Just My) Imagination," unleash the devastatingly snide country parody "Far Away Eyes," and contribute "Beast of Burden," one of their very best ballads. *Some Girls* may not have the backstreet aggression of their '60s records, or the majestic, drugged-out murk of their early-'70s work, but its brand of glitzy, decadent hard rock still makes it a definitive Stones album. *—Stephen Thomas Erlewine*

Emotional Rescue / Jun. 23, 1980 / Virgin ✦✦✦

Tattoo You / Aug. 30, 1981 / Virgin ✦✦✦✦✦
Like *Emotional Rescue* before it, *Tattoo You* was comprised primarily of leftovers, but unlike its predecessor, it never sounds that way. Instead, *Tattoo You* captures the Stones at their best as a professional stadium-rock band. Divided into a rock & roll side and a ballad side, the album delivers its share of thrills on the tight, dynamic first side. "Start Me Up" became the record's definitive Stonesy rocker, but the frenzied doo wop of "Hang Fire," the reggae jam of "Slave," the sleazy Chuck Berry rockers "Little TA" and "Neighbours," and the hard blues of "Black Limousine" are all terrific. The ballad side suffers in comparison, especially since "Heaven" and "No Use in Crying" are faceless. But "Worried About You" and "Tops" are effortless, excellent ballads, and "Waiting on a Friend," with its Sonny Rollins sax solo, is an absolute masterpiece, with a moving lyric that captures Jagger in a shockingly reflective and affecting state of mind. "Waiting on a Friend" and the vigorous rock & roll of the first side make *Tattoo You* an essential latter-day Stones album, ranking just a few notches below *Some Girls.* *—Stephen Thomas Erlewine*

Still Life / Jun. 1, 1982 / Rolling Stones ✦

Undercover / Nov. 7, 1983 / Virgin ✦✦✦

Dirty Work / 1986 / Virgin ✦✦✦

☆ **Singles Collection: The London Years** / 1989 / ABKCO ✦✦✦✦✦
The three-disc box set *Singles Collection: The London Years* contains every single the Rolling Stones released during the '60s, including both the A and B-sides. It is the first Stones compilation that tries to be comprehensive and logical—for all their attributes, the two *Hot Rocks* sets and the two *Big Hits* collections didn't present the singles in chronological order. In essence, the previous compilations were excellent samplers, where *Singles Collection* tells most of the story (certain albums, like *Aftermath, Beggars Banquet* and *Let It Bleed,* fill in the gaps left by the singles). The Rolling Stones made genuine albums—even their early R&B/blues albums were impeccably paced—but their singles had a power all their own, which is quite clearly illustrated by the *Singles Collection.* By presenting the singles in chronological order, the set takes on a relentless, exhilerating pace with each hit and neglected B-side piling on top of each other, adding a new dimension to the group; it has a power it wouldn't have had if it tried to sample from the albums. Although it cheats near the end, adding singles from the *Metamorphosis* outtakes collection and two singles from *Sticky Fingers,* this captures the essence of the '60s Stones as well as any compilation could. Casual fans might want to stick with the *Hot Rocks* sets, since they just have the hits, but for those that want a little bit more, the *Singles Collection* is absolutely essential. *—Stephen Thomas Erlewine*

Steel Wheels / Aug. 1989 / Virgin ✦✦✦

Flashpoint / Apr. 1991 / Virgin ✦✦

Voodoo Lounge / Jul. 19, 1994 / Virgin ✦✦✦
Funny that the much-touted "reunion/comeback" album *Steel Wheels* followed *Dirty Work* by just three years, while it took the Stones five years to turn out its sequel, *Voodoo Lounge*—a time frame that seems much more appropriate for a "comeback." To pile on the irony, *Voodoo Lounge* feels more like a return to form than its predecessor, even if it's every bit as calculated and Bill Wyman has flown the coup. With Don Was, a neo-classic rock producer that always attempts to reclaim his artist's original claim to greatness, helming the boards with the Glimmer Twins, the Stones strip their sound back to its spare, hard rocking basics. The Stones act in kind, turning out a set of songs that are pretty traditionalist. There are no new twists or turns in either the rockers or ballads (apart maybe from the quiet menace of "Thru and Thru," later used to great effect on *The Sopranos*), even if they revive some of the English folk and acoustic country-blues, that was on *Beggars Banquet.* Still, this approach works, because they are turning out songs that may not be classics, but are first-rate examples of the value of craft. If this was released 10 years, even five years earlier, this would be a near-triumph of classicist rock, but since *Voodoo Lounge* came out in the CD age, it's padded out to 15 tracks, five of which could have been chopped to make the album much stronger. Instead, it runs on for nearly an hour, an ironically bloated length for an album

whose greatest strengths are its lean, concentrated classic sound and songcraft. Still, it makes for a stronger record than its predecessor. *—Stephen Thomas Erlewine*

Stripped / Nov. 14, 1995 / Virgin ♦♦♦

Rolling Stones Rock and Roll Circus / Oct. 15, 1996 / ABKCO ♦♦♦

Bridges to Babylon / Sep. 23, 1997 / Caroline ♦♦♦

No Security / Nov. 3, 1998 / Caroline ♦♦♦

The Romantics

f. 1977, Detroit, MI

Group / Pop/Rock, Power Pop

In the early '80s, the Romantics were a terrific rock band, joyously tearing through loose, infectious power pop gems like the classic "What I Like About You." After two albums of energetic pop-rock, the band shifted its direction to a slicker, more radio-friendly pop; the change of style worked, resulting in the hit singles "Talking in Your Sleep" and "One in a Million" in 1983. Surprisingly, their drummer Jimmy Marinos left after their success; the band recorded one more album in 1985 before breaking up. In the early '90s, "What I Like About You" began appearing in television commercials, leading the band to reunite. They have recorded one EP and have toured several times since re-forming. *—Stephen Thomas Erlewine*

The Romantics / Feb. 1980 / Nemperor/Epic ♦♦♦♦♦

The cover, featuring the four members decked out in identical red leather outfits with the de rigeur skinny ties, leaves no doubt as to the album's content. This is your basic artifact of the era—lusty, girl-crazed, teen anthems sung to hard-driving, punchy power-pop. "What I Like About You" was the hit, but any of these songs could have been hits. It's easy to dismiss this band, but few albums provide this much guilty pleaure. *—Chris Woodstra*

National Breakout / Dec. 1980 / Nemperor/Epic ♦♦♦

Their sophomore effort follows much of the same formula of the debut. Unfortunately, none of the songs had the instantly endearing catchiness of "What I Like About You" and the album failed to live up to the optimistic title's promise. *—Chris Woodstra*

Strictly Personal / Oct. 1981 / Nemperor/Epic ♦♦♦

Rhythm Romance / 1985 / Nemperor/Epic ♦♦

● **What I Like About You (& Other Romantic Hits)** / Dec. 1990 / Nemperor/Epic ♦♦♦♦♦

What I Like About You (& Other Romantic Hits) is a ten-track best-of including the classic "What I Like About You," as well as some other fondly remembered hits like "Talking In Your Sleep" and "One in a Million." While this is a good distillation of the band's best moments (especially from the later albums), nothing matches the debut for consistent quality and power-packed catchiness. *—Chris Woodstra*

The Ronettes

f. 1959, New York, NY, **db.** 1966

Group / Girl Group

Before Phil Spector took them under his wing in the early '60s, the Ronettes had already recorded several singles and were regionally successful. But the Spector-produced records are what everyone remembers and for a good reason—they featured some of his biggest, best productions along with equally impressive songs. Beneath his monumental wall of sound, lead vocalist Ronnie Bennett, who would later marry Spector, sang songs of teenage love in a plain, girlish voice; "Be My Baby," the group's first and biggest hit, was the pinnacle of the group's talent, as well as being one of the producer's finest moments. None of their following singles (including "Baby, I Love You," "(The Best Part of) Breaking Up," and "Walking in the Rain") were quite as successful commercially, although they were nearly as strong artistically. While Spector was inactive in the mid-'60s, the Ronettes were also inactive; together they re-emerged in 1969, to a small commercial reception. After Ronnie divorced Spector in 1973, she formed a new version of the Ronettes that lasted for three years; after the group disbanded, she launched a solo career. *—Stephen Thomas Erlewine*

The Ronettes: The Early Years / 1965 / Rhino ♦♦♦♦♦

The early Ronettes songs weren't as immaculately produced or as evocative as Phil Spector's productions. Their sound was more generic and resembled other girl groups like The Shirelles or Chiffons. They recorded for Colpix and Dimension during 1961 and 1962, with Ronnie Bennett doing most of the leads, while her sister Estelle and cousin Nedra added soothing harmonies and backgrounds. At times, as on "My Guiding Angel" or "You Bet I Would," they came close to the appealing mix of innocence and earnestness that characterized their later (and greatest) tracks. But despite getting material from such songwriters as Jackie DeShannon and Carole King, many of these cuts were more serviceable than classic. Still, this is the foundation for the sound that exploded in the mid-'60s. *—Ron Wynn*

★ **The Best of the Ronettes** / Sep. 22, 1992 / ABKCO ♦♦♦♦♦

For a couple of years, the Ronettes made music that was as moving and unforgettable as any made during the rock era. Their voices merged sensuality, longing, anguish, and sentimentality, with Ronnie Spector's angelic leads framed by Phil Spector's sweeping production, and the lyrics of Ellie Greenwich, Jeff Barry, Barry Mann, Cynthia Weil, Spector, and others. While such songs as "Walking in the Rain," "Be My Baby," "Baby, I Love You," and "(The Best Part of) Breaking Up" may seem hopelessly naive and possibly sexist in today's cynical world, they're still classic love poems. Ronnie Spector's voice retains its allure and appeal, and the 18 tracks on this CD will never become dated. *—Ron Wynn*

Linda Ronstadt

b. Jul. 15, 1946, Tucson, AZ

Vocals / Traditional Pop, Pop/Rock, Folk-Rock, Soft Rock, Adult Contemporary, Country-Pop, Country-Rock

With roots in the Los Angeles country and folk-rock scenes, Linda Ronstadt was one of the most popular interpretive singers of the '70s, earning a string of platinum-selling albums and Top 40 singles. Ronstadt began her professional career with the Los Angeles folk-rock group the Stone Poneys. Shortly after their first hit "Different Drum," the group disbanded and Ronstadt went solo. She found her voice with her 1971 eponymous third album. Featuring a group of session musicians that would later form the Eagles, the album was laidback country-rock, built around songs by singer/songwriters like Jackson Browne and Eric Anderson. *Don't Cry Now* (1973) followed the same formula to greater success, yet she perfected it with 1974's *Heart Like a Wheel*. Thanks to hit covers of "You're No Good," "When Will I Be Loved," and "It Doesn't Matter Anymore," the record made her a star. *Prisoner in Disguise* (1975) and *Hasten Down the Wind* (1976) were nearly as successful, while she rocked a little harder on 1977's *Simple Dreams*. She tentatively experimented with New Wave on *Living in the U.S.A* (1978) and *Mad Love* (1980). Ronstadt's popularity declined in the early '80s, as 1982's *Get Closer* failing to go platinum. Afterward, she starred in Broadway and movie productions of Gilbert & Sullivan's *Pirates of Penzance*, which led to a collaboration with Nelson Riddle, who arranged and conducted her 1983 collection of pop standards, *What's New*. While it received lukewarm reviews, it was a hit, leading to two more albums with Riddle. Ronstadt returned to contemporary pop in 1986, having a number two single with "Somewhere Out There," a duet with James Ingram, followed by the 1987 *Trio* album with Dolly Parton and Emmylou Harris. That same year, Ronstadt recorded *Canciones de mi Padre*, a set of traditional Mexican songs. Two years later, she recorded *Cry Like a Rainstorm—Howl Like the Wind*—her first contemporary pop album since 1982's *Get Closer*.Throughout the '90s, she alternated between adult contemporary and Mexican albums, with the latter earning greater acclaim than the former. *—Stephen Thomas Erlewine*

Hand Sown Home Grown / 1969 / Capitol ♦♦

Silk Purse / 1970 / Capitol ♦♦♦

Linda Ronstadt / 1971 / Capitol ♦♦♦

Linda Ronstadt's self-titled third album captured the singer moving away from the rootsier charms of her first two albums, toward a more polished take on country rock. Supported by the Eagles throughout the record, Ronstadt turns in a strong performance, aided by a fine selection of material, including "Rock Me on the Water," "Crazy Arms," "I Still Miss Someone," and "I Fall to Pieces." *—Stephen Thomas Erlewine*

Don't Cry Now / 1973 / Asylum ♦♦♦

Different Drum / 1974 / Capitol ♦♦♦♦♦

Different Drum collects the highlights of Linda Ronstadt's first three solo albums, adding five Stone Poneys tracks, including the hit "Different Drum," for good measure. It misses some fine tracks from her solo records, but the album remains a fine introduction to her early years. *—Stephen Thomas Erlewine*

☆ **Heart Like a Wheel** / 1974 / Capitol ♦♦♦♦♦

Following the same formula as her early records, *Heart Like a Wheel* doesn't appear to be a great breakthrough on the surface. However, Ronstadt comes into her own on this mix of oldies and contemporary classics. Backed by a fleet of Los Angeles musicians, Ronstadt sings with vigor and passion, helping bring the music alive. But what really makes *Heart Like a Wheel* a breakthrough is the inventive arrangements that producer Peter Asher, Ronstadt, and the studio musicians have developed. Finding the right note for each song—whether it's the soulful reworking of "When Will I Be Loved," the hit "You're No Good," or the laid-back folk-rock of "Willing"—the musicians help turn *Heart Like a Wheel* into a veritable catalog of Californian soft rock, and it stands as a landmark of '70s mainstream pop/rock. *—Stephen Thomas Erlewine*

Prisoner in Disguise / 1975 / Asylum ♦♦♦♦♦

Linda Ronstadt followed the commercial and critical breakthrough success of *Heart Like a Wheel* with *Prisoner in Disguise*, a record that essentially repeated the formula of its predecessor. While it lacked the consistency of *Heart Like a Wheel*, it was thoroughly enjoyable, highlighted by sturdy remakes of the Motown classics "Tracks of My Tears" and "Heat Wave." *—Stephen Thomas Erlewine*

Hasten Down the Wind / 1976 / Asylum ♦♦♦

Simple Dreams / 1977 / Asylum ♦♦♦♦♦

Featuring a broader array of styles than any previous Linda Ronstadt record, *Simple Dreams* reconfirms her substantial talents as an interpretive singer. Ronstadt sings Dolly Parton ("I Never Will Marry") with the same conviction as the Rolling Stones ("Tumbling Dice"), and she manages to update Roy Orbison ("Blue Bayou") and direct attention to the caustic, fledgling singer/songwriter Warren Zevon ("Poor Poor Pitiful Me" and "Carmelita"). The consistently adventurous material and Ronstadt's powerful performance makes the record rival *Heart Like a Wheel* in sheer overall quality. *—Stephen Thomas Erlewine*

Living in the U.S.A. / 1978 / Asylum ♦♦♦

Greatest Hits, Vol. 2 / 1980 / Asylum ♦♦♦♦♦

Picking up where the first volume left off, *Greatest Hits, Vol. 2* contains Linda Ronstadt's biggest hits from the late '70s, including such songs as "It's So Easy," "Hurt So Bad," "Blue Bayou," "Back in the USA," "Poor Poor Pitiful Me," "Ooh Baby Baby," "How Do I Make You" and "Tumbling Dice." Since Ronstadt's late-'70s albums tended to be a little spotty, this is a very useful summation of their highlights. *—Stephen Thomas Erlewine*

Mad Love / 1980 / Asylum ♦♦

Get Closer / 1982 / Asylum ♦♦

What's New / 1983 / Asylum ♦♦♦

Lush Life / 1984 / Asylum ♦♦

For Sentimental Reasons / Feb. 1986 / Asylum ♦♦

Round Midnight with Nelson Riddle and his Orchestra / 1986 / Asylum ♦♦♦

Round Midnight is a triple-disc box set that compiles all three of the traditional pop albums Linda Ronstadt recorded with Nelson Riddle (*What's New*, *Lush Life*, and *For Sentimental*

Reasons). Only dedicated fans will need to own all three of the albums, and, for those listeners, this is a classy way to purchase them. —*Stephen Thomas Erlewine*

Canciones de Mi Padre / 1987 / Asylum ✦✦✦
Linda Ronstadt abandoned the pop audience in 1983, turning toward traditional pop music. She recorded three albums with Nelson Riddle before changing direction yet again, this time recording a set of traditional Mexican songs titled *Canciones de Mi Padre*. As the title suggests, the record is a fairly sentimental collection, since these are songs from her childhood and her heritage. Occasionally, Ronstadt oversells the songs but overall, the album is charming, affectionate, entertaining and more successful than her stilted Nelson Riddle collaborations. —*Stephen Thomas Erlewine*

Cry Like a Rainstorm—*Howl Like the Wind* / *Sep. 1989 / Asylum* ✦✦✦

Mas Canciones / 1990 / Asylum ✦✦✦

Frenesi / Aug. 25, 1992 / Asylum ✦✦

Winter Light / 1994 / Asylum ✦✦✦

Feels Like Home / Mar. 14, 1995 / Asylum ✦✦

Dedicated to the One I Love / Jun. 1996 / Elektra/Asylum ✦✦✦

● **Greatest Hits, Vol. 1** / Jan. 13, 1998 / Asylum ✦✦✦✦✦
Greatest Hits, Vol. 1 is good 12-track collection of Linda Ronstadt's biggest hits from the early '70s, beginning with the Stone Poneys' "Different Drum" and running through "Tracks of My Tears," from 1975's *Prisoner in Disguise*. In between, all of her best-known songs—"You're No Good," "When Will I Be Loved," "Heat Wave"—are included, plus selected minor hits, making it an excellent overview of her peak years. —*Stephen Thomas Erlewine*

We Ran / Jun. 23, 1998 / Elektra ✦✦✦

Western Wall: The Tucson Sessions / Aug. 24, 1999 / Elektra ✦✦✦✦✦

The Linda Ronstadt Box Set / Nov. 16, 1999 / Elektra ✦✦✦✦

Diana Ross (Diane Earle)

b. Mar. 26, 1944, Detroit, MI
Vocals / Pop-Soul, Motown, Urban, Disco, Soul
As a solo artist, Diana Ross is one of the most successful female singers of the rock era. If you factor in her work as the lead singer of the Supremes in the 1960s, she may be *the* most successful. The Supremes scored 12 number one pop hits during the '60s, though by the end of the decade Ross had launched a solo career. Motown initially paired her with writer/producers Ashford & Simpson, who gave her four quick pop hits, including the number one "Ain't No Mountain High Enough." Ross branched out into acting in 1972, starring in a film biography of Billie Holiday (*Lady Sings the Blues*) that earned her an Academy Award nomination (as well as a number one soundtrack). She returned to record-making with the number one hit "Touch Me in the Morning," earned several hits from a duet album with Marvin Gaye, and followed with two more chart-topping singles in 1976 ("Do You Know Where You're Going To" and the disco-oriented "Love Hangover"). After two more number one singles, 1980's "Upside Down" and the following year's "Endless Love," she decamped for RCA and was rewarded immediately with the million-selling album *Why Do Fools Fall in Love*. After a few more hits, Ross began to have trouble selling records in the late '80s. By 1989, she had returned to Motown, and by 1993 had turned more to pop standards. —*William Ruhlmann*

Lady Sings the Blues / Dec. 1971 / Motown ✦✦✦

Mahogany / Oct. 1975 / Motown ✦✦

Diana Ross / 1976 / Motown ✦✦✦✦

Diana / May 1980 / Motown ✦✦✦

● **All the Great Hits** / Oct. 1981 / Motown ✦✦✦✦✦
Yet another Motown anthology/greatest hits package. The songs are fine and the mastering is good. It's really a question of choice and need. If you want everything, get either the new Ross boxed set or the original anthology. If you only want a few hits, then either this or any other package will suffice. —*Ron Wynn*

Forever Diana: Musical Memoirs / Oct. 5, 1993 / Motown ✦✦✦
Plagued by inferior sound and a weak track selection, *Forever Diana* is a major disappointment for fans. Only one disc is devoted to the Supremes, with Ross's spotty solo career occupying the other three discs, featuring decidedly poorer sound than previous Motown releases. Besides poor audio, the liner notes are skimpy and incomplete. Ultimately, *Forever Diana* is a wasted opportunity. —*Stephen Thomas Erlewine*

One Woman: The Ultimate Collection / Oct. 18, 1994 / Motown ✦✦✦✦✦
This compilation attempts to condense Diana Ross's most successful recordings into one 20-song, 71+-minute disc. Well, there's good news and bad news. The good news is that Ross (who produced the album, which is to say picked the tracks) has included six of her Supremes recordings from the 1960s (one of them, "Someday We'll Be Together," in a new disco mix) and licensed a few songs from her stay at RCA in the 1980s, making this the most wide-ranging of her compilations. The bad news is that she has jettisoned many possible hits (only ten of her 18 chart-toppers are included) in the name of featuring four tracks from the 1990s that do not rank with her best, either aesthetically or in terms of popularity. In other words, Ross has constructed the album as she might a concert—a sprinkling of early Supremes hits, all her biggest solo hits, and what she considers the highlights of her current work. The result is a less than perfect, or "ultimate" portrait, since the selection implies erroneously that a forgettable piece of tripe like the 1991 Top 40 hit "When You Tell Me That You Love Me" is as much a milestone in the Ross catalog as "You Can't Hurry Love" or "Upside Down" (and that Ross remained as significant an artist in 1994 as she was in 1964 and 1974). But the album still makes a good sampler of Ross's entire 30+-year career for beginners. —*William Ruhlmann*

Anthology / Sep. 28, 1995 / Motown ✦✦✦✦✦
The double-disc set *Anthology* contains all of Diana Ross' solo hits for Motown Records, from "Ain't No Mountain High Enough" to "Endless Love." It's a comprehensive collection, featuring all of her biggest hits plus many important album tracks and smaller hit singles. Since it doesn't delve too deeply into obscurities and contains all of Ross' most popular songs, *Anthology* is the definitive career compilation for fans who want more than just the standard cuts but are unwilling to explore the original albums or invest in the box set. —*Stephen Thomas Erlewine*

Greatest Hits: The RCA Years / Mar. 25, 1997 / RCA ✦✦✦✦
Diana Ross' glossy 1981-1987 tenure on RCA is the subject of this 18-track collection, which includes her hit tribute to the late Marvin Gaye, "Missing You." Other highlights include her cover of Frankie Lymon and the Teenagers' "Wht Do Fools Fall in Love," "Mirror, Mirror," "Swept Away" and a solo version of the chart-topping "Endless Love." —*Jason Ankeny*

David Lee Roth

b. Oct. 10, 1955, Bloomington, IN
Vocals / Pop-Metal, Album Rock, Pop/Rock, Hard Rock
With Van Halen, vocalist David Lee Roth raised the role of a heavy metal frontman to a performance art. After the band's commercial breakthrough with the *1984* album, Roth released *Crazy from the Heat*, a 1985 EP that displayed his blatant pop roots, covering everything from the Beach Boys to Louis Prima. With two hit singles, *Crazy from the Heat* confirmed Roth's solo commercial potential, prompting his decision to leave Van Halen in June of 1985.

For his first full-length album, 1986's *Eat 'em and Smile*, Roth hired guitarist Steve Vai and bassist Billy Sheehan for a grossly exaggerated take on heavy arena rock. It was a mammoth hit, as was the more pop-oriented follow-up, *Skyscaper*. After *Skyscraper*, Vai and Sheehan left to form their own bands (the Steve Vai Band and Mr. Big, respectively). Roth put together a new band for 1991's *A Little Ain't Enough*, which was his first album not to go platinum. Sensing that it was time for a change, he tried to refashion himself as a slick hard rock singer/songwriter with 1994's *Your Filthy Little Mouth*, but it resulted in his least successful album yet. *DLR Band* followed in 1998. —*Stephen Thomas Erlewine*

Crazy from the Heat / 1985 / Warner Brothers ✦✦✦✦

Eat 'Em & Smile / 1986 / Warner Brothers ✦✦✦✦✦

Skyscraper / 1988 / Warner Brothers ✦✦✦

A Little Ain't Enough / Apr. 1991 / Warner Brothers ✦✦

Your Filthy Little Mouth / Mar. 8, 1994 / Warner Brothers ✦✦

● **Best of David Lee Roth** / Oct. 28, 1997 / Rhino ✦✦✦✦✦
Considering that David Lee Roth's solo career crashed after two albums and an EP, it should have been easy to assemble a 20-track greatest-hits compilation. Rhino's *The Best* proves that isn't so. Most of Roth's best-known songs are here, including "California Girls, "Just a Gigolo/I Ain't Got Nobody," "Yankee Rose," "Ladies Night in Buffalo—," "Goin' Crazy," "Skyscraper," "Just Like Paradise," and "Stand Up." However, the collection contains too many mediocrities from the flat albums *A Lil' Ain't Enough* and *Your Filthy Little Mouth* while overlooking radio and MTV staples like "Damn Good" and "That's Life." Furthermore, the collection isn't assembled in chronological order, which makes it a bit of a difficult listen. Even with these faults, there's no arguing that *The Best* does distill Roth's best solo recordings to one disc, making it a useful compilation for most casual fans. Nevertheless, after listening to all of *The Best*, many listeners will probably think a lil' is enough and 20 tracks might be a bit too much. —*Stephen Thomas Erlewine*

DLR Band / Jun. 9, 1998 / Wawazat ✦✦✦

Roxy Music

f. 1971, **db.** 1983
Group / Album Rock, Proto-Punk, Pop/Rock, Glam Rock, Prog-Rock/Art Rock
Evolving from the late-'60s art-rock movement, Roxy Music had a fascination with fashion, glamour, cinema, pop art, and the avant-garde, which separated the band from their contemporaries. Dressed in bizarre, stylish costumes, the group played a defiantly experimental variation of art-rock which vascillated between avant-rock and sleek pop hooks. During the early '70s, the group was driven by the creative tension between Bryan Ferry and Brian Eno, who each pulled the band in separate directions: Ferry had a fondness for American soul and Beatlesque art-pop, while Eno was intrigued by deconstructing rock with amateurish experimentalism inspired by the Velvet Underground. This incarnation of Roxy Music may have only recorded two albums, but it inspired a legion of imitators—not only the glam-rockers of the early '70s, but art-rockers and new wave pop groups of the late '70s. Following Eno's departure, Roxy Music continued with its arty inclinations for a few albums before gradually working in elements of disco and soul. Within a few years, the group had developed a sophisticated, seductive soul-pop that relied on Ferry's stylish crooning. By the early '80s, the group had developed into a vehicle for Ferry, so it was no surprise that he disbanded the group at the height of its commercial success in the early '80s to pursue a solo career. —*Stephen Thomas Erlewine*

Roxy Music / 1972 / Virgin ✦✦✦
Falling halfway between musical primitivism and art-rock ambition, Roxy Music's eponymous debut remains a startling redefinition of rock's boundaries. Simultaneously embracing kitschy glamour and avant-pop, *Roxy Music* shimmers with seductive style and pulsates with disturbing synthetic textures. Although no musician demonstrates much technical skill at this point, they are driven by boundless imagination—Brian Eno's synthesized "treatments" exploit electronic instruments as electronics, instead of trying to shoehorn them into conventional acoustic patterns. Similarly, Bryan Ferry finds that his vampiric croon is at its most effective when it twists conventional melodies, Phil Manzanera's guitar is terse and unpredictable, while Andy Mackay's saxophone subverts rock & roll cliches by alternating R&B

honking with atonal flourishes. But what makes *Roxy Music* such a confident, astonishing debut is how these primitive avant-garde tendencies are married to full-fledged songs, whether it's the free-form, structure-bending "Remake/Remodel" or the sleek glam of "Virginia Plain," the debut single added to later editions of the album. That was the trick that elevated Roxy Music from an art-school project to the most adventurous rock band of the early '70s. *—Stephen Thomas Erlewine*

☆ **For Your Pleasure** / 1973 / Virgin ♦♦♦♦♦
On Roxy Music's debut, the tensions between Brian Eno and Bryan Ferry propelled their music to great, unexpected heights, and for most of the group's second album, *For Your Pleasure,* the band equals, if not surpasses, those expectations. However, there are a handful of moments where those tensions become unbearable, as when Eno wants to move toward texture and Ferry wants to stay in more conventional rock territory; the nine-minute "The Bogus Man" captures such creative tensions perfectly, and it's easy to see why Eno left the group after the album was completed. Still, those differences result in yet another extraordinary record from Roxy Music, one that demonstrates even more clearly than the debut how avant-garde ideas can flourish in a pop setting. This is especially evident in the driving singles "Do the Strand" and "Editions of You," which pulsate with raw energy and jarring melodic structures. Roxy also illuminates the slower numbers, such as the eerie "In Every Dream Home a Heartache," with atonal, shimmering synthesizers, textures that were unexpected and innovative at the time of its release. Similarly, all of *For Your Pleasure* walks the tightrope between the experimental and the accessible, creating a new vocabulary for rock bands, and one that was exploited heavily in the ensuing decade. *—Stephen Thomas Erlewine*

Stranded / 1973 / Virgin ♦♦♦♦♦
Without Brian Eno, Roxy Music immediately becomes less experimental, yet it remains adventurous, as *Stranded* illustrates. Under the direction of Bryan Ferry, Roxy moves toward relatively straightforward territory, adding greater layers of piano and heavy guitars. Even without the washes of Eno's synthesizers, Roxy's music remains unsettling on occasion, yet in this new incarnation, they favor more measured material, whether it's the reflective "A Song for Europe" or the shifting textures of "Psalm." Even the rockers, such as the surging "Street Life" and the segmented "Mother of Pearl," are distinguished by subtle songwriting that emphasizes both Ferry's tortured glamour and Roxy's increasingly impressive grasp of sonic detail. *—Stephen Thomas Erlewine*

★ **Country Life** / 1974 / Virgin ♦♦♦♦♦
Continuing with the stylistic developments of *Stranded, Country Life* finds Roxy Music at the peak of its powers, alternating between majestic, unsettling art-rock and glamorous, elegant pop-rock. At their best, Roxy combines these two extremes, like on the exhilarating opener "The Thrill of it All," but *Country Life* benefits considerably from the ebb and flow of the group's two extremes, since it showcases the group's deft instrumental execution and their textured, enthralling songwriting. And, in many ways, *Country Life* offers the greatest and most consistent set of Roxy Music songs, illustrating their startling depth. From the sleek rock of "All I Want is You" and "Prairie Rose" to the elegant, string-laced pop of "A Really Good Time," *Country Life* is filled with thrilling songs, and Roxy Music rarely sounded as invigorating as they do here. *—Stephen Thomas Erlewine*

☆ **Siren** / 1975 / Virgin ♦♦♦♦♦
Abandoning the intoxicating blend of art-rock and glam-pop that distinguished *Stranded* and *Country Life,* Roxy Music concentrates on Bryan Ferry's suave, charming crooner persona for the elegantly modern *Siren.* As the discofied opener "Love is the Drug" makes clear, Roxy embraces dance and unabashed pop on *Siren,* weaving them into their sleek, arty sound. It does come at the expense of their artier inclinations, which is part of what distinguished Roxy, but the end result is captivating. Lacking the consistently amazing songs of its predecessor, *Siren* has a thematic consistency that works in its favor, and helps elevate its best songs—"Sentimental Fool," "Both Ends Burning," "Just Another High"—as well as the album itself into the realm of classics. *—Stephen Thomas Erlewine*

Viva! / 1976 / Virgin ♦♦

Manifesto / 1979 / Virgin ♦♦♦

Flesh + Blood / 1980 / Virgin ♦♦

☆ **Avalon** / 1982 / Virgin ♦♦♦♦♦
Flesh & Blood suggested that Roxy Music was at the end of the line, but they regrouped and recorded the lovely *Avalon,* one of their finest albums. Certainly, the lush, elegant soundscapes of *Avalon* are far removed from the edgy avant-pop of their early records, yet it represents another landmark in their career. With its stylish, romantic washes of synthesizers and Ferry's elegant, seductive croon, *Avalon* simultaneously functioned as sophisticated make-out music for yuppies and as the maturation of synth-pop. Ferry was never this romantic or seductive, either with Roxy or as a solo artist, and *Avalon* shimmers with elegance in both its music and its lyrics. "More Than This," "Take a Chance With Me," "While My Heart is Still Beating" and the title track are immaculately crafted and subtle songs, where the shifting synthesizers and murmured vocals gradually reveal the melodies. It's a rich, textured album and a graceful way to end the band's career. *—Stephen Thomas Erlewine*

Atlantic Years (1973-1980) / 1983 / Atco ♦♦♦♦♦

Street Life: 20 Greatest Hits / 1986 / Reprise ♦♦♦♦♦
While the packaging and song selection leave something to be desired, *Street Life: 20 Greatest Hits* is a strong collection of Roxy Music and Bryan Ferry's crossover hits. Ignoring Roxy's art-rock inclinations, the collection concentrates on latter-day hits like "More Than This," "Over You," "Love Is the Drug," and "Jealous Guy," adding early singles like "Virginia Plain," "Do the Strand" and "Pyjamarama" for good measure. But a large portion of the record is devoted to Ferry's solo material, not only mid-'80s hits like "Slave to Love" but also '70s covers like "A Hard Rain's A-Gonna Fall," "These Foolish Things" and "Let's Stick Together." Consequently, *Street Life* is rather uneven, but it is an adequate collection for anyone who wants all the hits on one disc. *—Stephen Thomas Erlewine*

Heart Still Beating / Oct. 30, 1990 / Virgin ♦♦

Thrill of It All / Nov. 20, 1995 / Virgin ♦♦♦♦♦
Album-rock artists like Roxy Music always make a difficult subject for comprehensive, multi-disc box sets. Frequently, their albums were designed as a cohesive whole and the idea of individual singles never really entered the picture at all. Roxy Music was slightly different than the average art/prog-rock band—not only did they make albums, they also made singles. And that is one of the reasons why the four-disc set *The Thrill of It All* is successful. Roxy's songs stand as individual works, and they make sense outside of their original context, even if they make more sense *within* their original context. Thankfully, the majority of each of their major albums are reproduced on the first three discs of this collection, leaving the fourth disc for non-LP singles, remixes, and B-sides. Most of this material has not been available on CD before, making *The Thril of it All* essential for collectors. Nevertheless, it's a helpful guide to Roxy's career for casual fans—it contains all of the essential songs and shows why the group was one of the seminal bands of the '70s. *—Stephen Thomas Erlewine*

Royal Trux

f. 1985, Chicago, IL, **db.** 2001
Group / Noise-Rock, Indie Rock, Alternative Pop/Rock
From the noisy demise of underground kingpins Pussy Galore came two interesting bands. The first was Jon Spencer's blues deconstruction unit the Jon Spencer Blues Explosion; the second was Neil Hagerty and Jennifer Herrema's dissonant junkie nightmare known as Royal Trux. Interestingly, both bands started out as avant-noise combos playing little that resembled traditional rock & roll. After a protracted period of making harsh, nearly inaccessible records, both bands, by the mid-'90s, were making records that sounded like '70s rock, only with gobs more attitude and noise. Early Royal Trux (two self-titled records and *Twin Infinitives*) are, to say the least, extreme. Herrema and Hagerty played mostly beat-to-shit, thrift-store guitars, howled over the noise, and let a crappy little drum machine keep a beat. By 1993's *Cats and Dogs,* the duo began making music that sounded grimy and raunchy, the way the Stones did in the mid-'70s. After exhibiting a little stability, Royal Trux was signed by Virgin and cut 1995's *Thank You,* a great, greasy glob of lo-fi rock fueled by cigarettes and junk food. *Sweet Sixteen* followed in 1997, after which Virgin dropped the group and released tapes of 1998's *Accelerator* to the duo's previous label, Drag City. *—John Dougan*

Royal Trux [#1] / 1988 / Drag City ♦♦♦

Twin Infinitives / 1990 / Drag City ♦♦♦

Royal Trux [#2] / Oct. 5, 1992 / Drag City ♦♦♦

Cats & Dogs / Jun. 14, 1993 / Drag City ♦♦♦♦♦

Thank You / Apr. 1995 / Virgin ♦♦♦♦♦
I realize that this runs contrary to the beliefs of longtime Royal Trux fans, but the more Royal Trux resembles a standard rock band, the better they sound. If you want a little guitar skronk with your sci-fi surrealism (as in Herrema's lyrics), but like a little funky backbeat now and again, this is Royal Trux at their scuzzy best. It's still not for the weak, nor for those who like pretty melodies or great musicianship. But for the rest of us who like the occasional run through the jungle, songs like "The Sewers of Mars" and "You're Gonna Lose" are prime chunks of non-commercial alternative rock. It's a safe bet to assume that more '90s bands will continue to appropriate '70s rock stylings, but few will do it with the panache of Royal Trux. *—John Dougan*

Sweet Sixteen / Feb. 11, 1997 / Virgin ♦♦♦

Singles Live Unreleased / Nov. 4, 1997 / Drag City ♦♦♦♦
Royal Trux celebrated their freedom from Virgin and return to Drag City by releasing *Singles Live Unreleased,* a sprawling double-disc set filled with rarities and obscurities. Sure, it seems like this falls into the "fans-only" category, but this mess has a certain charm. Also, in its own way, it captures what Royal Trux is all about, containing equal amounts of pretension, noise, blues-rock, attitude and menace. Neil Hagerty and Jennifer Herrema were the perfect fusion of the Rolling Stones and Sonic Youth, a concept which didn't always yield listenable or great results—how could it?—but when it worked, it was among the greatest indie-rock of their era. And while this is by definition arcane music, it also frequently captures the group at its best and, even better, captures the group the way they really are. *—Stephen Thomas Erlewine*

● **Accelerator** / Apr. 21, 1998 / Drag City ♦♦♦♦♦
Not long after they received *Sweet Sixteen,* complete with its notorious cover of an excrement- and vomit-filled toilet, Virgin Records realized Royal Trux may not be a crossover act. They were willing to let the band go, giving them severance pay and the master tapes to their recently completed album, *Accelerator,* which was then released on their old home, Drag City. Listening to the album, it's hard to believe that a major label funded such an exhilaratingly noisy record. Ostensibly the third installment in their ongoing salute to particular decades in rock history—i.e., *Thank You* took on the '60s, *Sweet Sixteen* saluted the '70s—Royal Trux deconstructs '80s rock on *Accelerator,* running all the instruments through some sort of electronic distortion, taking away the bass, trying to make it sound processed. Since this is Royal Trux, the result still is indebted to the Stones and astoundingly messy, but that's why *Accelerator* rocks like a demon, running over everything in sight. The album sounds chaotic, but there are some great songs hidden under the cacophony, like the explosive "I'm Ready," the soul vamp "Juicy, Juicy, Juice" and the soul-tinged closer "Stevie." Royal Trux have rarely had both their songwriting and noise under control like they do here, and the result is pure dynamite—possibly their best album to date. *—Stephen Thomas Erlewine*

Veterans of Disorder / Sep. 7, 1999 / Drag City ♦♦♦♦♦
With 1998's excellent *Accelerator,* Royal Trux completed their rock history trilogy and returned to Drag City. On *Veterans of Disorder*—the title of which title attests to the band's mix of classic rock and noisy experimentation, and to their status as survivors of their own chaotic excesses—the Trux move forward and look back at the same time. Splitting the difference between their increasingly focused yet subversive rock and their early, sludgy experimen-

talism, *Veterans of Disorder* begins with seven (relatively) radio-friendly versions of the Trux aesthetic. "Waterpark," is an almost-straightforward rawk charge led by Neil Hagerty's driving guitars and Jennifer Herrema's sultry, snarling vocals; the sexy "Second Skin" follows suit, and the duo shares vocal duties on "The Exception" and "Yo Se!"'s the Glimmer Twins-style funk. Latin percussion adds a twist to "Lunch Money," while "Witch's Tit" and "Stop" show off Royal Trux's softer side. None of these songs last longer than 3Ω minutes, but the group crams as many big guitars and weird ideas as they can into these "singles." The album's second half returns to *Twin Infinitives*-era noise jams for inspiration, especially on the shambolic "Sickazz Dog." Herrema's wonderfully sneery vocals on "Coming Out Party" serve sharp-tongued lyrics like "He's going to be a playboy in his mind/He's trying to pretend he's making friends," while "Blue Is the Frequency" mixes jazz, cock rock and a bit of slide guitar into a nearly nine-minute workout. Though the album sounds cleaner and more focused than anything Royal Trux released on Virgin, it's the duo's closest tie to their trashy underground roots. One of their most accomplished works, *Veterans of Disorder* could only be made by artists as creatively and financially independent as Royal Trux. *—Heather Phares*

Pound for Pound / Jun. 6, 2000 / Drag City ♦♦♦♦
On *Pound for Pound*, Royal Trux's second album within a year, the increasingly prolific group revisits the laid-back, scuzzy sound of albums like *Thank You* and *Sweet Sixteen*—albeit with a warmer, cleaner production, not unlike the sound they gave the Make Up's *In Mass Mind*. Touted by their label as a "party record," *Pound for Pound* comes pretty close to living up to that description, alternating between summery, boogie rock-inspired numbers like "Fire Hill" and "Dr. Gone" and more aggressive rockers like "Accelerator (The Original)" and "Teenage Murder Mystery." The Trux also find room for the almost-wistful summer love song "Sunshine," as well as the witchy blues-rock of "Deep Country Sorcerer" and "Small Thief," and despite the sound-effects weirdness on "Platinum Tips" and the trippy flutes on "Blind Navigator," this is their most straightforward collection of songs since their Virgin label output. Weighing in at a short and sweet ten tracks, *Pound for Pound* may not be as combustive or inventive as their recent output, but it reaffirms that there is plenty of room for just plain enjoyment in Royal Trux's subversive agenda. *—Heather Phares*

Rufus

f. 1970, Chicago, IL, **db.** 1983
Group / Quiet Storm, Funk, Soul
Rufus was one of the most commercially successful funk bands of the mid-'70s, primarily because lead vocalist Chaka Khan was a dynamic singer, capable of making even the band's pedestrian material seem interesting. Their self-titled debut album suffered from a lack of strong single material, but the follow-up featured Stevie Wonder's "Tell Me Something Good," which he wrote specifically for the band after hearing Khan sing; it became a number three hit single. After that song, the hits kept coming until the end of the '70s. Chaka Khan began a solo career that eventually eclipsed Rufus' success in 1978, continuing to record with the band until 1983; the group fell apart shortly after her departure. *—Stephen Thomas Erlewine*

● **The Very Best of Rufus Featuring Chaka Khan** / Nov. 19, 1996 / MCA ♦♦♦♦♦
The Very Best of Rufus & Chaka Khan contains all of the group's biggest hits, including the number one R&B hits "You Got the Love," "Sweet Thing," "At Midnight (My Love Will Lift You Up)," "Do You Love What You Feel" and "Ain't Nobody," plus the Top 10 hits "Tell Me Something Good," "Stay," "Hollywood," "Sharing the Love" and "Dance Wit Me." *—Stephen Thomas Erlewine*

The Runaways

f. 1975, Los Angeles, CA, **db.** 1979
Group / Heavy Metal, Hard Rock
This rock & roll band featured vocalist Cherie Currie and guitarists Joan Jett and Lita Ford. Organized by producer Kim Fowley in 1976, their raw, punkish style became a cult item in Japan and Europe, but unfortunately never connected with any kind of mainstream success stateside until Jett and Ford each went solo. *—Cub Koda*

The Runaways / 1976 / Touchwood ♦♦♦♦♦
When the Runaways debuted in 1976 with this self-titled LP, aggressive female rockers were the exception instead of the rule. Women had no problem becoming folk-rockers, singer-songwriters or Top 40 icons, but female artists who had more in common with Led Zeppelin and Aerosmith than Joni Mitchell were hardly the norm. With this album, the Runaways made it crystal clear that women (or specifically, adolescent girls) were more than capable of playing intense, forceful hard rock that went directly for the jugular. Lusty classics like "Cherry Bomb" and "You Drive Me Wild" made no attempt to conceal the fact that teenage girls could be every bit as sexual as the guys—a message that both men and women found intimidating. And on "Is It Day or Night," Cherie Currie sings about life in the fast lane with every bit as much conviction as Axl Rose would eleven years later. Currie and Joan Jett are equally riveting, and a 17-year-old Lita Ford was already an impressive guitarist. This LP was far from a commercial hit in the U.S., where timid rock radio programmers simply didn't know what to make of the Runaways. But interestingly, it did earn the band a strong following in the major rock market of Japan. *—Alex Henderson*

Queens of Noise / 1977 / Touchwood ♦♦♦♦♦
The Runaways didn't compromise a bit on their outstanding sophomore effort, *Queens of Noise*. Melodic yet tough and aggressive, this is hard rock that pulls no punches either musically or lyrically. Classics like "Neon Angels (On the Road to Ruin)," "Take It or Leave It" and "I Love Playing With Fire" wouldn't have been shocking coming from Aerosmith or Kiss, but suburban adolescent girls singing openly and honestly about casual sex, intoxication, and wild, all-night parties was certainly radical for 1977. Joan Jett and Cherie Currie articulated the thoughts and feelings of the "bad girls" Kiss and countless others were describing, and they didn't hesitate to say that yes, women fantasized about sex. "Johnny Guitar" is a fine vehicle for guitarist/singer Lita Ford, who had solid chops before she was old enough to vote. *Queens of Noise* would be Currie's last album with the groundbreaking band. *—Alex Henderson*

Waitin' for the Night / 1977 / Mercury ♦♦♦

● **The Best of the Runaways** / 1987 / Mercury ♦♦♦♦♦
A good collection of the Runaways' finest moments, *Best of the Runaways* is the only consistently enjoyable disc from these trashy hard-rockers. *—Stephen Thomas Erlewine*

Todd Rundgren

b. Jun. 22, 1948, Upper Darby, PA
Saxophone, Keyboards, Drums, Piano, Guitar, Bass, Synthesizer / Album Rock, Comedy Rock, Blue-Eyed Soul, Proto-Punk, Pop/Rock, Power Pop, Soft Rock, Prog Rock/Art Rock, Hard Rock
Todd Rundgren's best-known songs—the Carole King pastiche "I Saw the Light," the ballads "Hello, It's Me" and "Can We Still Be Friends," and the goofy novelty "Bang on the Drum All Day"—suggest that he is a talented pop craftsman, but nothing more than that. On one level, that perception is true, since he is undoubtedly a gifted pop songwriter, but at his core Rundgren is a rock & roll maverick. Once he had a taste of success with his 1972 masterwork *Something/Anything*—, Rundgren chose to abandon stardom and, with it, conventional pop music. He began a course through uncharted musical territory, becoming a pioneer not only in electronic music and prog rock, but in music video, computer software, and Internet music delivery. As his career wound into its third decade, Rundgren concentrated on behind-the-scenes innovations, but during the '70s and '80s he maintained a relentless work schedule, releasing up to two albums a year, either as a solo artist or with his band Utopia, while producing acclaimed, successful records for artists as diverse as Badfinger, Meat Loaf, Grand Funk Railroad, the New York Dolls, and XTC. Given such an extensive catalog, it's not surprising that there's a vast variety of styles within Rundgren's music—which is either rewarding or frustrating, depending on the album. Also, more often than not, the singles from each record do not offer an accurate indication of what the remainder of the album sounds like. Such an approach severely curtailed his mass appeal, but it helped him cultivate a ferociously dedicated cult audience. *—Stephen Thomas Erlewine*

Runt / Sep. 1970 / Bearsville/Rhino ♦♦♦♦♦
Reluctant to start a full-fledged solo career after leaving the Nazz, Todd Rundgren formed Runt, a band that was a front for what was in effect a solo project. Such isolationism lends *Runt* its unique atmosphere—it is the insular work of a fiercely talented artist finally given the opportunity to pursue his off-kilter musical vision. From the moment the slow, bluesy psychedelic grind of "Broke Down and Busted" starts the album, it's apparent that Rundgren could never have made *Runt* with the Nazz—and that's before the introspective ballads or the willfully strange stuff kicks in. Throughout the record, Rundgren reveals himself as a gifted synthesist, blending all manners of musical styles and quirks into a distinctive signature sound. He's as interested in sound as he is in song and while he would later pursue these tendencies to extremes, *Runt* finds him learning how to create an effective sound with the studio, which may be the reason why the album runs the gamut from hard rockers like "Who's That Man?" to ballads like "Once Burned." Although these songs are instantly appealing, the album really gets interesting when he reaches between those two extremes, whether it's in the classic pop medley "Baby Let's Swing," the bizarrely tongue-in-cheek "I'm in the Clique," or the equally impish "We Gotta Get You a Woman," which gave Rundgren his first hit. All the details buried within these songs—not only in the deceptively direct productions, but within the writing itself—confirm Rundgren's exceptional skill at songcraft. He occasionally slips on *Runt*, delivering tracks that rely on production instead of a blend of studiocraft and songcraft, but it remains a thoroughly impressive debut and one of his finest pop records. *—Stephen Thomas Erlewine*

☆ **Runt: The Ballad of Todd Rundgren** / Jun. 1971 / Ampex ♦♦♦♦♦
Upon its release, *Rolling Stone* called *The Ballad of Todd Rundgren* "the best album Paul McCartney" never made, and even if the album doesn't sound particularly McCartney-esque, it does share the homespun, melodic charm of the best of his early albums. Arguably, it's better than Paul's solo work, since it is focused and subtle, never drawing attention to Rundgren's considerable skills as a writer and producer. He tones down the hard rock and his impish wit, lending the album a sense of direction missing on *Runt*. That's not to say he abandoned his sense of humor—as if the cover shot of Rundgren sitting at a piano with a noose around his neck left any doubt. This time around, it takes some careful listening to hear the jokes, such as the opening Floyd Cramer piano lick on "Range War." On such clever in-jokes as "Chain Letter," as well as ballads like "Hope I'm Around," the artist reveals himself as an exceptional craftsman and songsmith. In fact, *Ballad* is considerably more song-oriented than its predecessor, with very little of the jams and instrumental sections that occasionally bogged down *Runt*. Here, even propulsive pop tunes as "Bleeding" and "Long Flowing Robe," along with the hard rocker "Parole," are as much about the song as the performance, which is probably appropriate for an album called *The Ballad of Todd Rundgren*. Another thing about that title—it may be a joke, but the album inarguably offers a glimpse into Rundgren's inner world through a combination of introspective ballads, off-hand jokes, musical virtuosity, outright weirdness, and unabashed showmanship. And that's the charm of *The Ballad*—it's the slyly sardonic masterwork of a loner who may be sensitive, but is certainly not shy. *—Stephen Thomas Erlewine*

★ **Something/Anything?**/ Feb. 1972 / Bearsville/Rhino ♦♦♦♦♦
Others had recorded one-man albums before Todd Rundgren, most notably Stevie Wonder and Paul McCartney, but with *Something/Anything?* he captured the homemade ambience of *McCartney* with the visionary feel of *Music of My Mind*, adding an encyclopedic knowledge of pop music from Gilbert & Sullivan through Jimi Hendrix, plus the crazed zeal of a pioneer. Listening to *Something/Anything?* is a mind-altering trip in itself, no matter how many shamelessly accessible pop songs are scattered throughout the album, since each side of the double-record is a concept onto itself. The first is "a bouquet of ear-catching melodies"; side two is "the cerebral side"; on side three "the kid gets heavy"; side four is his mock pop

operetta, recorded with a full band including the Sales Brothers. It gallops through everything—Carole King tributes ("I Saw the Light"), classic ballads ("Hello It's Me," "It Wouldn't Have Made Any Difference"), Motown ("Wolfman Jack"), blinding power pop ("Couldn't I Just Tell You"), psychedelic hard rock ("Black Maria"), pure weirdness ("I Went to the Mirror"), blue-eyed soul ("Dust in the Wind"), and scores of brilliant songs that don't fall into any particular style ("Cold Morning Light," "It Takes Two to Tango"). It's an amazing journey that's remarkably unpretentious. Rundgren peppers his writing with self-aware, self-deprecating asides, indulging his bizarre sense of humor with gross-outs ("Piss Aaron") and sheer quirkiness, such as an aural tour of the studio at the beginning of side two. There are a ton of loose ends throughout *Something/Anything?*, plenty of studio tricks, slight songs (but no filler), snippets of dialogue, and purposely botched beginnings, but all these throwaways simply add context—they're what makes the album into a kaleidoscopic odyssey through the mind of an insanely gifted pop music obsessive. *—Stephen Thomas Erlewine*

☆ **A Wizard, A True Star** / Mar. 1973 / Bearsville/Rhino ✦✦✦✦✦
Something/Anything? proved that Todd Rundgren could write a pop classic as gracefully as any of his peers, but buried beneath the surface were signs that he would never be satisfied as merely a pop singer-songwriter. A close listen to the album reveals the eccentricities and restless spirit that surges to the forefront on its follow-up, *A Wizard, A True Star*. Anyone expecting the third record of *Something/Anything?*, filled with variations on "I Saw the Light" and "Hello It's Me," will be shocked by *A Wizard*. As much a mindfuck as an album, *A Wizard, A True Star* rarely breaks down to full-fledged songs, especially on the first side, where songs and melodies float in and out of a hazy post-psychedelic mist. Stylistically, there may not be much new—he touched on so many different bases on *Something/Anything?* that it's hard to expand to new territory—but it's all synthesized and assembled in fresh, strange ways. Often, it's a jarring, disturbing listen, especially since Rundgren's humor has turned bizarre and insular. It truly takes a concerted effort on the part of the listener to unravel the record, since Rundgren makes no concessions—not only does the soul medley jerk in unpredictable ways, but the anthemic closer, "Just One Victory," is layered with so many overdubs that it's hard to hear its moving melody unless you pay attention. And that's the key to understanding *A Wizard, A True Star*—it's one of those rare rock albums that demands full attention and, depending on your own vantage, it may even reward such close listening. *—Stephen Thomas Erlewine*

Todd / Feb. 1974 / Bearsville/Rhino ✦✦✦
Maybe some listeners thought that the sonic trip *A Wizard, A True Star* was a necessary exercise in indulgence and that he would return to the sweet pop of *Something/Anything?* for its follow-up. Not a chance. As it turned out *A Wizard* was the launch pad for futher dementia—and, depending on your point of view, indulgence. Its follow-up was *Todd*, an impenetrable double album filled with detours, side roads, collisions, and the occasional pop tune. That those pop tunes are among his best may come as little consolation to the lightweight fan who has stumbled upon *Todd*. Conceptually, *A Wizard, A True Star* may be the wilder record, but *Todd* is a more difficult listen, thanks to the layers of guitar solos and blind synth prog tunes, such as "In and Out the Chakras We Go." Large stretches of the album are purely instrumental, foreshadowing the years of synth experiments with Utopia that were just around the corner. The murk subsides every so often, revealing either exquisite ballads ("A Dream Goes on Forever"), blistering rock ("Heavy Metal Kids"), or, more murk and dementia (particularly with how Gilbert & Sullivan rear their heads not only on the requisite novelty "An Elpee's Worth of Tunes," but an honest-to-goodness cover of "Lord Chancellor's Nightmare Song"). These are some major additions to his catalog, but the experiments and the excesses are too tedious to make *Todd* a necessary listen for anyone but the devoted. But for those listeners, the gems make the rough riding worthwhile. *—Stephen Thomas Erlewine*

Initiation / May 1975 / Bearsville/Rhino ✦✦

Faithful / Apr. 1976 / Bearsville/Rhino ✦✦✦
Todd Rundgren considered 1976 the beginning of his professional musical career, largely because the Nazz formed around that time. As a celebration, he recorded *Faithful*. Presumably, *Faithful* celebrates the past and the future by juxtaposing a side of original pop material with a side of covers. Actually, "covers" isn't accurate—the six oldies that comprise the entirety of side one are re-creations, with Rundgren "faithfully" replicating the sound and feel of the Yardbirds ("Happenings Ten Years Time Ago"), Bob Dylan ("Most Likely You Go Your Way and I'll Go Mine"), Jimi Hendrix ("If Six Was Nine"), the Beach Boys ("Good Vibrations") and the Beatles ("Rain," "Strawberry Fields Forever"). All of this is entertaining, to a certain extent, especially since it's remarkable how close Rundgren comes to duplicating the very feel of the originals. Still, it's hard to see it as much more than a flamboyant throwaway, especially when compared with the glorious second side. For the first time since *Something/Anything?*, Rundgren allows himself to write and—more importantly—record straight-ahead pop songs. Certainly, *A Wizard*, *Todd* and *Initiation* had their share of great songs, but they weren't delivered as pop songs; they were telegraphed as art. Here, Rundgren delivers pop and rock songs with ease, letting the melodies glide to the forefront. There are embellishments, of course, but the end result is a lushness that's apparent even on the hard rockers. If Rundgren had made all of *Faithful* originals, it would have been a pure pop masterpiece. As it stands, it's essential for the faithful—not only for hardcore Toddheads, but for devoted pop fans as well. *—Stephen Thomas Erlewine*

Hermit of Mink Hollow / Apr. 1978 / Bearsville/Rhino ✦✦✦✦✦
Over the course of 1977, Todd Rundgren moved Utopia toward a more pop-oriented direction, winding up with the slick mainstream arena rock of *Oops! Wrong Planet*. With that in mind, it makes sense that *The Hermit of Mink Hollow*—his first full-fledged solo album since *Initiation*, if you discount the half-cover/half-original *Faithful*—finds Rundgren in his pop craftsman persona. The difference is, he's heartbroken. His relationship with Bebe Buell collapsed during 1977 and it's clear that the separation has pained him, since pain and melancholy underpin the album, whether it's on ballads ("Can We Still Be Friends") or on apparently joyous revelries, like "All the Children Sing." That said, this is a Rundgren solo album and he has not abandoned his trademarks, which means that the lush ballads are paired with novelties ("Onomatopoeia," which sounds exactly how you hope it does), ersatz soul ("You Cried Wolf") and pure pop ("Hurting for You"). *Hermit* is also the first record Rundgren recorded completely alone since *Something/Anything?*. Where that record sounded like the inner workings of a madman, with each song providng no indication what the next would sound like, *Hermit* is more cohesive. It also feels less brilliant, even if it is, in many ways, nearly as excellent as Rundgren's masterwork, mainly because it doesn't have such a wide scope. Still, the reason *The Hermit of Mink Hollow* is such a milestone in Rundgren's career is because it's a small album, filled with details, and easily the most emotional record he made. *—Stephen Thomas Erlewine*

Back to the Bars / Dec. 1978 / Bearsville/Rhino ✦✦✦

Healing / Feb. 1981 / Rhino ✦✦✦
Healing is a subdued, reflective effort unlike anything else in Todd Rundgren's catalog. Certainly, there are some familiar elements throughout *Healing*, particularly on majestic ballads like "Compassion," but there are more new variations on his style than any album since *Initiation*. Not coincidentally, that record had hints of the spirituality that surges to the forefront on *Healing*, but it was nowhere near as musically focused as the latter record. Apart from "Compassion," there is a true lack of singles, which doesn't mean that there aren't standouts—since "Golden Goose" has a weird, jerky hook and the opener "Healer" is a terrific pop single—that stand on their own merit. Instead, the record works as a whole, flowing as seamlessly as *Something/Anything?* or *Hermit*. Unfortunately, it's not as strong as either of those records, largely because it's about texture and spirit, not individual songs. In a case like that, the music and ambience are as important as the actual songs, and while they're often very provocative, they tend to meander as well, particularly on the three-part "Healing" suite that comprises the last side of the record. On CD, its calming effect is dissipated because the bonus seven-inch single "Time Heals"/"Tiny Demons" is added at the end. Their presence makes it clear that *Healing* was intended as an album unto itself, without much in the way of singles, because each song—the former being excellent new wave pop, the other a fine ballad—could have been a single unto itself. In this context, they may deflate the lasting spiritual impression of the album, but they add musical weight, helping make the disc a fine effort. *—Stephen Thomas Erlewine*

The Ever Popular Tortured Artist Effect / Jan. 1983 / Rhino ✦✦✦✦
As the early '80s continued to unfold, Todd Rundgren grew increasingly disenchanted with Bearsville, especially since the label wasn't supporting Utopia. He wrangled the band free in 1982, but he still had to deliver solo records to Bearsville. Not entirely pleased with the situation, Rundgren hammered out a collection of pop songs on his own, cyncially titling the effort *The Ever Popular Tortured Artist Effect*. In later years, Rundgren disavowed the album, but it stands as one of his better collections of pop songs, even if it lacks a theme or a unifying sound. There are a fair share of throwaways, not only coming in the expected form of covers (a fine but pointless remake of the Small Faces' "Tin Soldier") and Gilbert & Sullivan parodies ("Emperor of the Highway"), but also in the monumentally silly "Bang the Drum All Day," which not only became a hit, but a hit that refused to die, lasting as a radio staple into the late '90s. These three songs are anomalies on *Tortured Artist*, which for the most part is pure pop and pop-soul, delivered with little fuss or pretention. There's also little deep meaning to the songs themselves, which is quite unusual for Rundgren, yet the best tunes—"Hideaway," "Influenza," "There Goes Your Baybay," "Drive," "Chant"—are indelible, irresistible pop confections that prove Rundgren can be quite involving, even when he's not trying his hardest. *—Stephen Thomas Erlewine*

A Cappella / Sep. 1985 / Rhino ✦✦✦

Anthology (1968-1985) / May 1989 / Rhino ✦✦✦✦
The flagship of Rhino's Todd Rundgren reissue series was *Anthology (1968-1985)*, a double-disc set that traced the rock & roll maverick's career from the Nazz through his decade and a half with Bearsville Records. Designed as the definitive statement of Rundgren's solo work (his work with Utopia received its own *Anthology*), *Anthology* comes very close to fulfilling its goal. Since it covers so much ground, it's inevitable that a few essential items and fan favorites are missing, especially since Rundgren was incredibly prolific during these 17 years. And it is true that early masterpieces like "I'm in the Clique," "Once Burned," "Chain Letter," "The Range War," and "Long Flowing Robe" are missing, as are several highlights from *Something/Anything?*, but in their place are stronger tracks from less consistent albums, which makes it a nice retrospective for converted fans who want a comprehensive compilation to supplement the acknowledged classics. That said, the curious or casual listener may find *Anthology* a bit too sprawling for their tastes, even it does provide an excellent summary of Rundgren's heyday as a cult recording artist. In that case, Rhino's *The Very Best of Todd Rundgren* is a good choice, since it is a more concise collection that contains all the hits and rock-bottom essentials, plus several Utopia cuts and "The Want of a Nail." *—Stephen Thomas Erlewine*

Nearly Human / May 1989 / Warner Brothers ✦✦✦✦
As the '80s drew to a close, Todd Rundgren turned over a new leaf with his first album recorded specifically for Warner Bros. Not long after the release of *A Cappella*, he separated from Bearsville and disbanded Utopia, choosing to embark on a few years as a producer and session man. He finally returned with *Nearly Human*, his first album of new material in four years, in the summer of 1989. During his hiatus as a recording artist, Rundgren became fascinated with recording live music, deciding to record *Nearly Human* live in the studio—not nearly as flamboyant as *A Cappella*, but a gimmick nonetheless. If anything, the live-in-the-studio gimmick works better than the all-vocal track, not only because it's easier to execute, but because the production style complements the soul-inflected songs. Song for song, *Nearly Human* is his best record since *The Hermit of Mink Hollow*, because not only is the bulk of the album filled with charging blue-eyed soul like "The Want of a Nail" or sweet ballads like "Parallel Lines," but because there are no novelties and the cover choice (Elvis Costello's "Two Little Hitlers") is fresh and surprising. At times, his eccentricities get the best of him, as he overstuffs his arrangements or lyrics with unnecessary details, but these are minor points—*Nearly Human* finds Rundgren at the top of his game as a performer, producer, and song-

writer, sustaining his momentum in a way he hadn't for nearly a full decade. *—Stephen Thomas Erlewine*

Second Wind / Jan. 1991 / Warner Brothers ✦✦✦

No World Order / Jul. 6, 1993 / Forward/Rhino ✦✦

The Individualist / 1995 / Digital ✦✦✦

● **The Very Best of Todd Rundgren** / Jul. 22, 1997 / Rhino ✦✦✦✦✦
The Very Best of Todd Rundgren distills the Runt's career to just the hit singles, which is surprsisingly effective. Most casual Todd fans will only want the hits—"We Gotta Get You A Woman," "I Saw the Light," "Hello, It's Me," "Bang on the Drum"—and not invest in the double-disc set *Anthology (1968-1985)*, which simply contains too much music for most listeners. With *The Very Best of*, all of the good stuff (including "The Want of a Nail," which is not on *Anthology*) is here, satisfying the needs of the casual and curious. *—Stephen Thomas Erlewine*

With a Twist / Sep. 23, 1997 / Guardian ✦✦

One Long Year / Jun. 20, 2000 / Artemis ✦✦✦

Rush

f. 1968, Toronto, Ontario, Canada
Group / Album Rock, Arena Rock, Prog Rock/Art Rock, Hard Rock
Over the course of their decades-spanning career, the Canadian power trio Rush emerged as one of hard rock's most highly-regarded bands; although typically brushed aside by critics and rare recipients of mainstream pop radio airplay, the group nonetheless won an impressive and devoted fan following, while their virtuoso performance skills solidified their standing as musicians' musicians. Just after a 1974 self-titled LP, the group's lineup gelled around guitarist Alex Lifeson, vocalist/bassist Geddy Lee, and drummer Neil Peart. Peart assumed the role of the band's primary songwriter, composing the cerebral lyrics (influenced by works of science fiction and fantasy) which gradually became a hallmark of the group's aesthetic. Rush's fourth album, 1976's *2112*, proved to be their breakthrough release, fusing the elements of the trio's sound—Lee's high-pitched vocals, Peart's epic-length compositions and Lifeson's complex guitar work—into a unified whole. The album established a formula from which the band rarely deviated throughout the duration of their career. The band achieved even greater popularity with 1980's *Permanent Waves*, a record marked by Peart's dramatic shift into shorter, less sprawling compositions. Thanks to heavy exposure on album-oriented radio, 1981's "Tom Sawyer" became perhaps their best-known song. As the 1980s drew to a close, the trio cut back on its touring schedule, while hardcore followers complained of a sameness afflicting slicker, synth-driven efforts. After Rush returned to the heavier sound of their early records, both 1991's Roll the Bones and 1993's Counterparts reached the Top Three on the U.S. album charts. *—Jason Ankeny*

Rush / 1974 / Mercury ✦✦

Caress of Steel / 1975 / Mercury ✦✦

Fly by Night / 1975 / Mercury ✦✦

2112 / 1976 / Mercury ✦✦✦✦✦
Whereas Rush's first two releases, their self-titled debut and *Fly By Night*, helped create a buzz among hard rock fans worldwide, the more progressive third release, *Caress of Steel*, confused many of their supporters. The band knew it was now or never with their fourth release, and they delivered just in time—1976's *2112* proved to be their much sought-after commercial breakthrough and remains one of their most popular albums. Instead of choosing between prog rock or heavy rock, both styles are merged together to create an interesting and original approach. The whole entire first side is comprised of the classic title track, which paints a chilling picture of a future world where technology is in control (Peart's lyrics for the piece being influenced by Ayn Rand). Comprised of seven "sections," the track proved that the trio was fast becoming rock's most accomplished instrumentalists. The second side contains shorter selections, such as the Middle Eastern-flavored "A Passage to Bangkok" and the album-closing rocker "Something for Nothing." *2112* is widely considered by Rush fans as their first true "classic" album, the first in a string of similarly high-quality albums. *—Greg Prato*

All the World's a Stage / 1976 / Mercury ✦✦✦

A Farewell to Kings / 1977 / Mercury ✦✦✦

Hemispheres / 1978 / Mercury ✦✦✦
While such albums as 1980's *Permanent Waves* and 1981's *Moving Pictures* are usually considered Rush's masterpieces (and with good reason), 1978's *Hemispheres* is just as deserving. Maybe the fact that the album consists of only four compositions (half are lengthy pieces) was a bit too intimidating for some, but the near 20-minute long "Cygnus X-1 Book II—Hemispheres" is arguably the band's finest extended track. While the storyline isn't as comprehendible as "2112" was, it's much more consistent musically, twisting and turning through five different sections which contrast heavy rock sections against more sedate pieces. Neil Peart had become one of rock's most accomplished lyricists by this point, as evidenced by "The Trees," which deals with racism and inequality in a unique way (set in a forest!). And as always, the trio proves to be experts at their instruments, this time on the complex instrumental, "La Villa Strangiato." Geddy Lee's shrieking vocals on the otherwise solid "Circumstances" may border on the irritating, but Hemispheres remains one of Rush's greatest releases. *—Greg Prato*

Permanent Waves / 1980 / Mercury ✦✦✦✦✦
Since Neil Peart joined the band in time for 1974's *Fly By Night*, Rush had been experimenting and growing musically with each successive release. By 1980's *Permanent Waves*, the modern sounds of new wave (the Police, Peter Gabriel, etc.) began to creep into Rush's sound, but the trio still kept their hard rock roots intact. The new approach paid off—two of their most popular songs, the "make a difference" anthem. "Freewill," and a tribute to the Toronto radio station, CFNY, "The Spirit of Radio" (the latter a U.K. Top 15 hit) are spectacular highlights. Also included were two "epics," the stormy "Jacob's Ladder" and the album closing, "Natural Science," which contains a middle section that contains elements of reggae. Geddy Lee also began singing in a slightly lower register around this time, which made their music more accessible to fans outside of the heavy prog-rock circle. The album proved to be the final breakthrough Rush needed to become an arena headliner throughout the world, beginning a string of albums that would reach inside the Top Five of the U.S. Billboard album charts. *Permanent Waves* is an undisputed hard rock classic, but Rush would outdo themselves with their next release. *—Greg Prato*

Exit... Stage Left / 1981 / Mercury ✦✦✦✦✦
Rush was planning on releasing a live album after the *Permanent Waves* tour, but manager Cliff Burnstein convinced the group that they were peaking musically, and should go straight back into the recording studio—resulting in their finest album, 1981's *Moving Pictures*. So after the tour wound down, their postponed live album was finally assembled, released as *Exit... Stage Left* the same year. The album turned out to be the polar opposite of its predecessor, 1976's raw and direct *All the World's a Stage*, in fact, the performances often sound identical to the recently released studio versions. The contagious energy that helped make *All the World's a Stage* such a success is muted, replaced by workmanlike renditions that border on the uninspired. There's no denying the high quality of the songs selected—"Spirit of Radio," "Tom Sawyer," "Xanadu," "The Trees," "Closer to the Heart," "Jacob's Ladder," etc.—it's just that the performances rarely catch fire. Compared to Rush's three other concert albums (the aforementioned *All the World's a Stage*, 1988's *A Show of Hands* and 1998's *Different Stages*), *Exit... Stage Left* is probably the weakest. *—Greg Prato*

● **Moving Pictures** / 1981 / Mercury ✦✦✦✦✦
Not only is 1981's *Moving Pictures* Rush's best album, it is undeniably one of the greatest hard rock albums of all time. The new wave meets hard rock approach of *Permanent Waves* is honed to perfection—all seven of the tracks are classics (four are still featured regularly in concert and on classic rock radio). While other hard rock bands at the time experimented unsuccessfully with other musical styles, Rush was one of the few to successfully cross over. The whole entire first side is perfect—their most renowned song, "Tom Sawyer," kicks things off, and is soon followed by the racing "Red Barchetta," the instrumental "YYZ," and a song that examines the pros and cons of stardom, "Limelight." And while the second side isn't as instantly striking as the first, it is ultimately rewarding. The long and winding "The Camera Eye" begins with a synth-driven piece before transforming into one of the band's more straight-ahead epics, while "Witch Hunt" and "Vital Signs" remain two of the trio's more underrated rock compositions. Rush proved with *Moving Pictures* that there was still uncharted territory to explore within the hard rock format, and was rewarded with their most enduring and popular album. *—Greg Prato*

Signals / 1982 / Mercury ✦✦✦✦✦
Instead of playing it safe and writing Moving Pictures Part II, Rush replaced their heavy rock of yesteryear with even more modern sounds for 1982's *Signals*. Synthesizers were now an integral part of the band's sound, and replaced electric guitars as the driving force for almost all the tracks. And more current and easier to grasp topics (teen peer pressure, repression, etc.) replaced their trusty old sci-fi inspired lyrics. While other rock bands suddenly added keyboards to their sound to widen their appeal, Rush gradually merged electronics into their music over the years, so such tracks as the popular MTV video, "Subdivisions," did not come as a shock to longtime fans. And Rush didn't forget how to rock out—"The Analog Kid" and "Digital Man" were some of their most up-tempo compositions in years. The surprise hit, "New World Man" and "Chemistry" combined reggae and rock (begun on 1980's *Permanent Waves*), "The Weapon" bordered on new wave, the placid "Losing It" was one of the band's few guitarless tracks, while the epic closer "Countdown" painted a vivid picture of a space shuttle launch. *Signals* proved that Rush was successfully adapting to the musical climate of the early 80's. *—Greg Prato*

Grace Under Pressure / 1984 / Mercury ✦✦

Power Windows / 1985 / Mercury ✦✦✦

Hold Your Fire / 1987 / Mercury ✦✦✦

A Show of Hands / Jan. 2, 1988 / Mercury ✦✦✦

Presto / Nov. 1989 / Atlantic ✦✦✦✦✦

Chronicles / Jul. 1, 1991 / Mercury ✦✦✦✦✦

Roll the Bones / Jul. 1, 1991 / Atlantic ✦✦✦

Counterparts / Oct. 19, 1993 / Atlantic ✦✦

Test for Echo / Sep. 9, 1996 / Atlantic ✦✦✦

● **Retrospective, Vol. 1 (1974-1980)** / May 5, 1997 / Mercury ✦✦✦✦✦
Retrospective, Vol. 1 (1974-80) was designed to replace the double-disc set *Chronicles*, and it is, in fact, a better compilation than its predecessor. By concentrating on Rush's earliest albums—from 1974's *Rush* to 1980's *Permanent Waves*—the album draws an excellent portrait of the group's artiest work, leaving their hard-rock radio-rock hits for *Retrospective, Vol. 2* Meanwhile, *Vol. 1* contains nearly all of the highlights from their '70s albums, including "Closer to the Heart" and "Fly By Night," making it a near-flawless encapsulation of their early career. *—Stephen Thomas Erlewine*

Retrospective, Vol. 2 (1981-1987) / Jun. 3, 1997 / Mercury ✦✦✦✦✦
Retrospective, Vol. 2 (1981-1987) picks up where *Retrospective, Vol. 1* left off, the time period when Rush became an arena-rock sensation with each of their albums reaching the Top Ten. The set begins with several selections from their most popular album, 1981's *Moving Pictures*, and ends with 1987's *Hold Your Fire*. In between, many of the trio's most familiar songs—"Tom Sawyer," "New World Man," "Limelight," "Distant Early Warning," "Time Stand Still"—are featured, making this an excellent overview of the group's hard-rock heyday. *—Stephen Thomas Erlewine*

Different Stages / Nov. 10, 1998 / Atlantic ✦✦✦

Leon Russell (Claude Russell Bridges)

b. Apr. 2, 1941, Lawton, OK

Vocals, Keyboards, Piano, Guitar, Bass / Album Rock, Pop/Rock, Singer/Songwriter, Country-Rock

The ultimate rock & roll session man, Leon Russell's long and storied career includes collaborations with a virtual who's who of music icons spanning from Jerry Lee Lewis to Phil Spector to the Rolling Stones. A similar eclecticism and scope also surfaced in his solo work, which couched his charmingly gravelly voice in a rustic yet rich swamp-pop fusion of country, blues, and gospel. As a member of Spector's renowned studio group, Russell played on many of the finest pop singles of the '60s, also arranging classics like Ike and Tina Turner's monumental "River Deep, Mountain High." He scored his first songwriting hit with Joe Cocker's reading of "Delta Lady," and in 1970, he also organized Cocker's legendary Mad Dogs and Englishmen tour. After the subsequent tour film earned Russell his first real mainstream notoriety, he issued a self-titled solo LP. Russell reached the number two spot with 1972's *Carny* and scored his first pop hit with the single "Tight Rope." While the success of 1973's three-LP set *Leon Live* further established his reputation as a top concert draw, response to the country-inspired studio effort *Hank Wilson's Back* was considerably more lukewarm. 1975's *Will O' the Wisp,* however, restored his commercial luster. In June 1975, Russell married singer Mary McCreary; the following year the couple collaborated on *The Wedding Album,* issued through his newly formed Paradise Records label. Among other subsequent projects, Russell teamed with Willie Nelson for 1979's *Willie and Leon,* and spent the next two years touring with his bluegrass band the New Grass Revival, issuing a live LP in 1981. After two albums in 1984, Russell spent the remainder of the decade largely outside of music, and did not resurface until 1992's Bruce Hornsby-produced *Anything Can Happen.* Another long period of relative inactivity followed prior to a 1998-1999 recording comeback. *—Jason Ankeny*

Leon Russell / 1970 / The Right Stuff ✦✦✦✦✦

Leon Russell never quite hit all the right notes the way he did on his eponymous debut. He never again seemed as convincing in his grasp of Americana music and themes, never again seemed as individual, and never again did his limited, slurred bluesy voice seem as ingratiating. He never again topped his triptych of "A Song for You," "Hummingbird," and "Delta Lady," nor did his albums contain such fine tracks as "Dixie Lullaby." Throughout it all, what comes across is Russell's idiosyncratic vision, not only in his approach but in his very construction—none of the songs quite play out as expected, turning country, blues, and rock inside out, not only musically but lyrically. Yes, his voice is a bit of an acquired taste, but it's only appropriate for a songwriter with enough chutzpah to write songs of his own called "I Put a Spell on You" and "Give Peace a Chance." And if there ever was a place to acquire a taste for Russell, it's here. *—Stephen Thomas Erlewine*

And the Shelter People / 1971 / The Right Stuff ✦✦✦✦✦

Asylum Choir II / 1971 / The Right Stuff ✦✦

Carney / 1972 / The Right Stuff ✦✦✦✦

"Tight Rope" leads off *Carney,* and it's not just his biggest hit, it offers an excellent introduction to an off-kilter, confused, fascinating album. In a sense, it consolidates his two extremes, offering a side of fairly straightforward roots rock before delving headfirst into twisted psychedelia on the second side. On the whole, the second side deflates the first side, since it's just too fuzzy—it's intriguing, at least in parts, but it never adds up to anything. Besides, the first side is already odd enough, but in a meaningful way; here, his fascination with Americana sideshows is married to songs that work, instead of just being vehicles for tripping in the studio. Of course, part of what makes *Carney* interesting is that it contains a bit of both, but interesting doesn't equal compelling, as the whole of *Carney* bears out. *—Stephen Thomas Erlewine*

Hank Wilson's Back / 1973 / The Right Stuff ✦✦✦✦

A skewed but interesting Hank Williams tribute album, with capable country backing. *—Cub Koda*

Leon Live / 1973 / The Right Stuff ✦✦✦

A solid concert offering that showcases Russell's strengths (and weaknesses) as a live performer, with A-1 support throughout. *—Cub Koda*

• **Gimme Shelter: The Best of Leon Russell** / Nov. 12, 1996 / EMI ✦✦✦✦✦

It's a little problematic to put together a compilation of such an album-oriented artist. But unless you're very deeply into the Russell catalog, this two-CD, 40-track best-of will serve as a retrospective of all that you need, largely covering his work from the first half of the '70s (a couple of songs from his 1992 Virgin album are also included), and featuring his best-known hits, big and small. It's a well-done tour through his blend of swamp rock, gospel, and bits of blues and country, with material from eight of his Shelter LPs, including the one he recorded in 1969 as part of the Asylum Choir. Interesting rarities include a 1974 single of "Wild Horses," a 1970 cover of Dylan's "She Belongs to Me" that only showed up on a compilation, and a folk-rockish 1965 single for Dot. *—Richie Unterberger*

• **Retrospective** / Oct. 21, 1997 / The Right Stuff/Shelter ✦✦✦✦

Retrospective is an 18-track collection that features the bulk of Leon Russell's greatest hits ("Tight Rope," "Roll in My Sweet Baby's Arms," "Lady Blue," "Back to the Island"), plus many key album tracks. Since Russell was primarily an album artist, this approach doesn't necessarily do him justice, but for listeners who only want the hits, this will do. However, the double-disc *Gimme Shelter: The Best of Leon Russell* is a better, more thorough overview and is the one serious fans should acquire. *—Stephen Thomas Erlewine*

Mitch Ryder (William Levise, Jr.)

b. Feb. 26, 1945, Hamtramck, MI

Vocals / Detroit Rock, Frat Rock, Album Rock, Blue-Eyed Soul, Hard Rock, Rock & Roll

The unsung heart and soul of the Motor City rock & roll scene, Mitch Ryder and the Detroit Wheels' blue-eyed R&B attack boasted a gritty passion and incendiary energy matched by few artists of any color. Born William Levise, Jr. in Hamtramck, MI on February 26, 1945, the teenage Ryder sang with the local black quartet the Peps but suffered so much racial harassment that he left to form his own combo, Billy Lee and the Rivieras. While opening for the Dave Clark Five in 1965, they were noticed by producer Bob Crewe, who immediately signed them and, according to legend, rechristened the singer Mitch Ryder after randomly selecting the name from a phone book. Backed by the peerless Detroit Wheels—guitarists James McCarty and Joseph Cubert, bassist Earl Elliot, and drummer Johnny "Bee" Badanjek—Ryder reached the Top Ten in early '66 with the breathless, intense "Jenny Take a Ride", a frenzied combination of Little Richard's "Jenny Jenny" and Chuck Willis' "C.C. Rider." Ryder and the Detroit Wheels returned to the charts "Little Latin Lupe Lu," "Sock It to Me Baby!" and the Top Five smash "Devil with a Blue Dress On/Good Golly Miss Molly." At Crewe's insistence, Ryder split from the rest of the band to mount a solo career; outside of the Top 30 entry "What Now My Love," the hits dried up. In 1970, he reunited with Badanjek in the seven-piece band Detroit, who scored a major FM radio hit with their cover of Lou Reed's "Rock and Roll." Ryder's throat problems, forced him to retire until the late '70s, when he released several albums on his own Seeds and Stems label. He made his major label comeback with 1983's John Cougar Mellencamp-produced *Never Kick A Sleeping Dog.* The album's minor hit, the Prince cover "When You Were Mine," didn't return the singer to mainstream success in the U.S., but in Europe he retained a large fan following. He remained active for the rest of the '80s and '90s, working on his biography and continuing to tour and release albums. *—Jason Ankeny*

Breakout . . . !!! / 1966 / Sundazed ✦✦✦✦✦

Ryder & the Wheels' second album, featuring the classic "Devil with a Blue Dress On /Good Golly, Miss Molly" workout, continues the pattern of their debut; strong renditions of R&B classics, chopped and channeled and revved up to maximum torque. With the use of the original two-track master, the sound of it fairly sparkles. *—Cub Koda*

Take a Ride / 1966 / Sundazed ✦✦✦✦✦

The debut album of Ryder and the Wheels, fresh from the teenage ballroom circuit in Detroit, where they held court in earlier days as Billy Lee & the Rivieras. One of the defining moments in the history of Motor City music, *Take a Ride* is the sound of poor White kids claiming the music as theirs, too, while infusing it with the manic energy of the color-blind dreams of anybody who ever wanted to be somebody. Built entirely around their stage act, this album captures a band in full cry at the peak of their powers. This is what they mean when they say the words "high-energy Motor City rock & roll." *—Cub Koda*

All Mitch Ryder Hits! / 1967 / Sundazed ✦✦✦✦✦

Greatest-hits packages sometimes can rob an artist of their wider focus, only zeroing in on the hits and not giving the true big picture. But this is one time when the hits and the subsequent singles fills the bill in an absolutely perfect way. Although many of these songs turn up on other Mitch Ryder albums, many of the versions included here differ greatly, the most noticeable being the kickoff track, "Devil With a Blue Dress/Good Golly Miss Molly." The reason is simple enough: These are the single mixes, the ones edited and compacted to fit on one side of a 45-rpm vinyl record. As a result, they aurally exude a brighter, more shimmering presence, and although not much else is done in the way of audio chicanery here (no sped-up tracks, etc.), this one *does* have the sound. If you truly want to experience what a great kick-ass band the Detroit Wheels were in their prime and what a skunk-hot singer Mitch Ryder was in his young man days, this is the one you want to stick in the CD player and play over and over again. *—Cub Koda*

Sock It to Me / 1967 / Sundazed ✦✦✦✦

Ryder's last album with the Detroit Wheels before going solo finds the material reverting to producer Bob Crewe's readymades, no match for the authentic R&B found on the first two albums, but still strutted out with typical Detroit-like flair. Three bonus tracks and the use of the original stereo masters makes this a must have for serious Mitch Ryder collectors. *—Cub Koda*

• **Rev-Up: The Best of Mitch Ryder & the Detroit Wheels** / 1990 / Rhino ✦✦✦✦✦

Perhaps the most raucous White soul band of the '60s, Ryder and the Detroit Wheels scored a series of hits, 1966-1968, by souping up rock and R&B ravers to fever pitch. This is hard party music. *—William Ruhlmann*

Sade (Helen Folsade Adu)

b. Jan. 16, 1959, Ibadan, Nigeria

Vocals / Sophisti-Pop, Quiet Storm, Adult Contemporary, Urban

When Sade first came on the recording scene in the '80s, her record company, Epic, made a point of printing "pronounced shar-day" after her name on the record labels of her releases. Soon enough the world would have no problem in correctly pronouncing her name. Born Helen Folasade Adu in a village 50 miles from Lagos, the capital of Nigeria, she grew up on the North End of London.

Around 1980, she started singing harmony with a Latin funk group called Arriva. One of the more popular numbers that the group would perform was "Smooth Operator," which would later become her first stateside hit. The following year she joined an eight-piece funk band, Pride, as a background singer. The group played live frequently, helping Sade obtain a recording contract with the U.K. division of Epic Records. Her debut album, *Diamond Life* went Top Ten in the U.K. in late 1984. Her third album, *Promise* (November 1985), featured "Never As Good As the First Time" and arguably her signature song, "The Sweetest Taboo," which stayed on the U.S. pop charts for six months. Sade was so popular that some radio stations reinstated the '70s practice of playing album tracks, adding "Is It a Crime" and "Tar Baby" to their play lists. In 1986, Sade won a Grammy for Best New Artist. Sade's third album was 1988's *Stronger Than Pride* and had her first number one soul single "Paradise." 1992's *Love Deluxe* continued the unbroken streak of multi-platinum Sade albums, spinning off the hits "No Ordinary Love," "Feel No Pain," and "Pearls." but after its release, the singer kept a low profile, performing only occasionally. *—Ed Hogan*

Diamond Life / 1984 / Epic ✦✦✦✦

Former model Sade made an immediate and huge impact with her 1984 debut album. Her sound and approach were deliberately icy, her delivery and voice aloof, deadpan, and cold, and yet she became an instant sensation through such songs as "Smooth Operator" and "Your Love Is King," where the slick production and quasi-jazz backing seemed to register with audiences thinking they were hearing a jazz vocalist. Sade won the Best New Grammy Award for 1984, and *Diamond Life* sold more than two million copies. *—Ron Wynn*

Promise / 1985 / Epic ✦✦✦
Sade's second album improved on the performance of her debut, as "Sweetest Taboo" was a huge hit and "Never as Good as the First Time" landed in both the R&B and pop Top 20. She was once again the personification of cool, laidback singing, seldom extending or embellishing lyrics, registering emotion or projecting her voice. This demeanor made her more desirable in the minds of many fans and was perhaps the ultimate misapplication of the notion of sophistication. But this album topped the pop album charts and eventually went triple platinum. *—Ron Wynn*

Stronger Than Pride / 1988 / Epic ✦✦✦
After two LPs with little or no energy, Sade demonstrated some intensity and fire on her third release. Whether that was just an attempt to change the pace a bit or a genuine new direction, she had more animation in her delivery on such songs as "Haunt Me," "Give It Up," and the hit "Paradise." Not that she was suddenly singing in a soulful or bluesy manner; rather, Sade's dry and introspective tone now had a little more edge, and the lyrics were ironic as well as reflective. This was her third consecutive multi-platinum album, and it matched the two-million-plus sales level of her debut. *—Ron Wynn*

Love Deluxe / Oct. 20, 1992 / Epic ✦✦✦✦✦
Sade's fourth album included the hit "No Ordinary Love" and marked a return to the detached, cool jazz backing and even icier vocals that made her debut album a sensation. Although Sade's style is more suggestive than hypnotic, and her production and arrangements are in an urbane mode rather than a jazz one, she's maintained her popularity among the fusion and urban-contemporary audiences. This release also included "Mermaid," "Pearls," and "Feel No Pain." *—Ron Wynn*

● **The Best of Sade** / 1994 / Epic ✦✦✦✦✦
It's easy to dismiss Sade as makeout music for Calvin Klein Obsession models, but she created an impressive body of work over the course of a decade, a series of moody singles with cool jazz passion and the kick of good R&B. All the hits are here, of course, from "Smooth Operator" to "No Ordinary Love." *—Eddie Huffman*

Lovers Rock / Nov. 14, 2000 / Epic ✦✦✦✦✦
Lovers Rock, the title of Sade's first album of the 21st century, could be taken on many levels. Never before has the singer infused more mainstream rock elements (prominent strummed guitars) into her music as evidenced by the first single, "By Your Side." That's not to say that she has eschewed her own tried-and-true brand of smoky, dusky ballads. The singer/songwriter is reunited with co-producer Mike Pela and musician/songwriters Andrew Hale, Stuart Matthewman, and Paul S. Denman; and *Lovers Rock* finds them all in fine form. "Somebody Already Broke My Heart," "Every Word," and "Lovers Rock" are vintage Sade. *—Ed Hogan*

Doug Sahm

b. Nov. 6, 1941, San Antonio, TX, **d.** Nov. 18, 1999, Taos, NM
Vocals, Violin, Guitar / Americana, Roots Rock, Tex-Mex, Country-Rock, Progressive Country, Blues-Rock, Rock & Roll
Guitarist, composer, arranger, and songwriter Doug Sahm was a knowledgeable music historian and veteran performer equally comfortable in a range of styles, including Texas blues, country, rock & roll, Western swing and Cajun. Beginning in 1955, the San Antonio-born Sahm recorded a series of singles for a procession of Texas-based record companies. After being prompted in 1965 to assemble a group by producer Huey Meaux, Sahm recruited some friends who became the Sir Douglas Quintet. The group had some success on the radio with "The Rains Came," but later broke up, and Sahm moved to California. There he reformed the Quintet and recorded a now-classic single, "Mendocino." The resulting album of the same name was a groundbreaking record in the then-emerging country-rock scene. The Sir Douglas Quintet followed *Mendocino* with *Together After Five*, another album that led them to a larger fan base. Atlantic Records producer Jerry Wexler realized that country-rock sounds were coming into vogue (and that there was no place in Nashville for people like Sahm), and signed both Sahm and Willie Nelson. One of Sahm's greatest albums, 1973's *Doug Sahm and Band*, was recorded in New York City with Bob Dylan, Dr. John, and accordionist Flaco Jiminez. The Sir Douglas Quintet later got back together again to record two more albums, *Wanted Very Much Alive* and *Back to the 'Dillo*. Among Sahm's most essential blues records are 1980's *Hell of a Spell* and his Grammy-nominated studio album for Antone's, *The Last Real Texas Blues Band*. For his other material, there are several good compilations, including *The Best of Doug Sahm* (Rhino). Sahm died on November 18, 1999. *—Richard Skelly*

● **The Best of Doug Sahm (1968-1975) [Rhino]** / 1991 / Rhino ✦✦✦✦✦
This is not as thorough as *Sir Doug's Recording Trip*, but it's easier to find and gives you 22 essential tracks in sterling digital fidelity. *—John Floyd*

The Best of Doug Sahm (1968-1975) [Sequel] / 1995 / Sequel ✦✦✦✦

She's About a Mover: The Best of Crazy Cajun Recording / Oct. 26, 1999 / Edsel ✦✦✦✦
This differs from Music Club's package in that this set also includes tracks issued as Doug Sahm solo sides, giving us a time frame between 1964 and 1977 to hear Sahm's art unfold. Of course, the early SDQ sides are the big ticket here. Rough and raw, they include the two big hits "She's About a Mover" and "The Rains Came." Yet the solo sides that fill up the cracks here are every bit as raw, sometimes disconcertingly so, like the bass and drums that lose track of each other in the middle of "Seguin," or the maracas that never quite catch up to the band track on "You've Got Your Good Thing Down." If you wondered what Huey Meaux had in the vault on Sahm, here's your chance to find out. *—Cub Koda*

San Antonio Rock: The Harlem Recordings 1957-1961 / Apr. 4, 2000 / Norton ✦✦✦✦
If you think Doug Sahm's career began with the Sir Douglas Quintet, guess again. This 18-track collection rounds up all of Sahm's early 45s and demos, as well as rarities with Doug playing sideman in various Texas combos, the majority of it issued on the Harlem label out of Fort Worth. It's raw Texas music, soaked in R&B and rock & roll, and Sahm goes through no less than seven different backing units on this set, not to mention his sideman work with Spot Barnett, Jimmy Dee, and Red Hilburn. Lots of alternate takes, great booklet with loads of information, all putting into historical perspective the missing chapter in the history of this modern Texas troubadour. *—Cub Koda*

In the Beginning / Aug. 29, 2000 / Aim ✦✦✦
In the Beginning chronicles the earliest singles released by the late Texas renegade Doug Sahm. Recorded between 1958 and 1962, these 14 songs encompass Tex-Mex, R&B, doon wop, polka, and early rock & roll from Sahm's pre-Sir Douglas Quintet days on the Harlem, Cobra, and Renner labels. Rare regional singles "Crazy Daisy," "Why, Why, Why," "Slow Down," "Baby Tell Me," and "Just a Moment" are a few of the gems collected. *—Al Campbell*

St. Etienne

f. 1988, Croydon, Surrey, England
Group / Indie Pop, Alternative Dance, Brit-pop, Club/Dance, Alternative Pop/Rock
Like most bands formed by former music journalists, St. Etienne was a highly conceptual group. The trio's concept was to fuse the British pop sounds of '60s London with the dance club rhythms and productions that defined the post-acid house England of the early '90s. Led by songwriters Bob Stanley and Pete Wiggs, and fronted by vocalist Sarah Cracknell, the group managed to carry out their concept, and, in the process, they helped make indie dance a viable genre within the U.K. Throughout the early '90s, St. Etienne racked up a string of indie hit singles that were driven by deep club beats—encompassing anything from house and techno to hip-hop and disco—and layered with light melodies, detailed productions, clever lyrics, and Cracknell's breathy vocals. They revived the sounds of swinging London, as well as the concept of the three-minute pop single being a catchy, ephemeral piece of ear candy, in post-acid house Britan, thereby setting the stage for Brit-pop. Though most Brit-pop bands rejected the dance inclinations of St. Etienne, they nevertheless adopted the trio's aesthetic, which celebrated the sound and style of classic '60s pop. *—Stephen Thomas Erlewine*

Foxbase Alpha / Jan. 14, 1992 / Warner Brothers ✦✦✦

So Tough / Mar. 9, 1993 / Warner Brothers ✦✦✦✦✦
St. Etienne's second album, *So Tough*, is a remarkable step forward from *Fox Base Alpha*, boasting a stronger set of songs and a sharper focus. Not only are the pop melodies catchier than before, the group's mastery of swinging '60s arrangements and Eurodisco rhythms is positively infectious, and Sarah Cracknell's light, airy vocals are alluringly dreamy, giving the record a wonderful, floating quality. The cool club beats, occasional samples, and synthesized textures provide an inviting sonic backdrop for Bob Stanley and Pete Wiggs' infectious pop songs, and while the singles "You're in a Bad Way" and "Hobart Paving" stand out, there are several other tracks here that are nearly as good, making *So Tough* an irresistible set of danceable, well-constructed pop. *—Stephen Thomas Erlewine*

Tiger Bay / Jun. 28, 1994 / Warner Brothers ✦✦✦✦
Tiger Bay abandons the unassuming charm of *So Tough* for a grander sound. St. Etienne fills *Tiger Bay* with sonic details, from sampled bits of dialogue to musical references that give the record some depth, but occasionally those very sounds make the album feel over-labored. Still, the group frequently fulfills their ambitions, particularly on "Hug My Soul," "Like a Motorway," and the delightfully exuberant "I Was Born on Christmas Day," which features guest vocals by the Charlatans' Tim Burgess. Moments like these, plus St. Etienne's widening sonic palette, make *Tiger Bay* a thoroughly enjoyable affair, despite its handful of faults. *—Stephen Thomas Erlewine*

● **Too Young to Die** / Nov. 1995 / Heavenly ✦✦✦✦✦
Although their albums were considerably more consistent than most dance-pop acts, Saint Etienne's high points were always their singles. Released prior to a quiet, lengthy hiatus, *Too Young to Die* collects all of their singles, from their debut disco cover of Neil Young's "Only Love Can Break Your Heart" to their last, "He's on the Phone," providing a thoroughly entertaining chronicle of the group's career. Much of the music sounds somewhat dated—which is always a problem with dance music—but Saint Etienne was essentially a very good Europop band, reveling in kitsch and style in equal measure. At their best—"Only Love Can Break Your Heart," "You're in a Bad Way," "Join Our Club," "Who Do You Think You Are," among others—they found the heart in nightclubbing. The quality of the music dips slightly in the latter half of the album, but there is prime pop throughout the disc. [Initial pressings came with a bonus disc of remixes, all of which are worthwhile for dedicated fans.] *—Stephen Thomas Erlewine*

Casino Classics / Oct. 7, 1996 / Heavenly ✦✦✦

Good Humor / Sep. 1998 / Sub Pop ✦✦✦✦

Places to Visit / May 4, 1999 / Sub Pop ✦✦✦

Sound of Water / Jun. 22, 2000 / Sub Pop ✦✦✦✦

The Saints

f. 1977, Brisbane, Australia
Group / College Rock, Aussie Rock, Post-Punk, Alternative Pop/Rock, Punk
Roaring out of Brisbane, Australia in 1977 with the punk-era classic "(I'm) Stranded," the Saints, despite going through numerous incarnations, have been a part of rock & roll for over 20 years, thanks mainly to their indefatigable leader (and founder) Chris Bailey. Saints fans fall into two distinct camps: the punk-era fans (up to about 1980) and the mature pop fans, which for American audiences begins with the release of *All Fools Day* in 1987; for many, the feral assault of their first three records (when co-founder Ed Kuepper was in the band) is more interesting and exciting. After the LP *(I'm) Stranded* became a modest hit in England in 1977, the follow-up record, *Eternally Yours*, showed some changes (more varied tempos, acoustic guitars) that would set the stage for their third record, *Prehistoric Sounds*, which

combined horn arrangements into a punkish sort of R&B. Kuepper left in 1979 to form the arty Laughing Clowns and eventually made a number of records as a solo act. Bailey, however, got to keep the name the Saints and soldiered on, taking time here and there to record his own solo records; the twists and turns he took the band through (horns, folk-blues arrangements, etc.) produced some good music, but it was mostly scattershot and too difficult to wade through the mediocre material. By the time *All Fools Day* was released in 1987, there were many who thought the Saints were a brand new band—and they were right. Gone were the rapid-fire guitar sound and bellowing vocals, replaced by sophisticated pop arrangements and more technically accomplished singing. The music was strong, intelligent pop that was better than much late-'80s new wave. The next LP, *Prodigal Son,* wasn't as good, but did nothing to hurt the reputation of the "new" Saints. Despite extended dormant periods, the Saints have never officially broken up, and Bailey always seems to have another version of the band ready. *—John Dougan*

● **(I'm) Stranded** / 1977 / Captain Oi! ♦♦♦♦♦
Around the time Sire was scooping up every band under the sun that played like the Ramones, they had the smarts to sign the Saints, who were creating great punk rock. Along with the title track, there are rough and ready bits of speed-burn, like "Erotic Neurotic," and very unpunk-like tracks in terms of song length, six minutes of "Messin' With the Kid" (not the Junior Wells song). Toss in a piss-take of Elvis' "Kissin' Cousins," and you've got the makings of a fine slice of history. This is their best record, for a lot of reasons, but primarily for its energy, high spirits, and smarts. *—John Dougan*

Eternally Yours / 1978 / Captain Oi! ♦♦♦♦♦

The Monkey Puzzle / 1981 / New Rose ♦♦♦♦♦

All Fools Day / 1987 / TVT ♦♦♦♦♦
Call this the second coming of the Saints, but the only thing this record has in common with previous Saints recordings is Chris Bailey. Still, it's a sharp, tuneful, and (ahem) mature work that shows Bailey's increasing confidence as a singer and songwriter. One listen to songs as grabbing as "Celtic Ballad" or the great "Just like Fire Would" (which is kind of a neat pun) will convince you that despite the differences, the new Saints were a good band for completely different reasons than the old Saints. *—John Dougan*

Everybody Knows the Monkey / Oct. 27, 1998 / Amsterdamned ♦♦♦

● **Wild About You (1976-1978)** / 2000 / Raven ♦♦♦♦♦
The Australian compilation *Wild About You (1976-1978)* is the first place to go for the Saints in more ways than one. The thorough, double-disc anthology exhaustively includes the Australian band's first three records (1977's *(I'm) Stranded* and 1978's *Prehistoric Sounds* and *Eternally Yours*), as well as every stray EP and single track recorded by the Ed Kuepper/Chris Bailey era of the Saints—the period that spawned the band's best material. To lure the rabid fans, four previously unissued recordings are included. The results of the vault looting aren't anywhere near the levels of "(I'm) Stranded" or "Brisbane (Security City)," but they weren't unearthed just to take advantage of the consumer, either.

Additionally, the package is dolled up with scads of photos and extensive liner notes provided by numerous sources. It's odd that such a collection would surface in close proximity to the individual U.K. re-issues of *(I'm) Stranded* and *Eternally Yours,* but this is the kind of package that appeals to beginners and longtime fans. At two discs, the price isn't much of a financial risk for the newbie, and the scope of the material is too grand to be ignored by the familiar. As far as punk and post-punk are considered, this is a rather essential document. *—Andy Kellman*

Sam & Dave

f. 1961, Miami, FL
Group / Deep Soul, Southern Soul, Soul
Perhaps no act epitomized soul music as the secularization of gospel more than Sam & Dave. The original pairing of Sam Moore and Dave Prater met in Florida in 1961, and they recorded unsuccessfully for several years before being signed to Atlantic Records in 1965. Atlantic persuaded their Memphis affiliate Stax Records to produce them, and in December that year the writing and production team of Isaac Hayes and David Porter delivered the crisply soulful "You Don't Know Like I Know." Hayes and Porter became the "eminences grises" behind Sam & Dave, much as Holland-Dozier-Holland pulled the strings behind the Supremes. They wrote, they produced—and the result was a string of hits, including "Soul Man," "Hold on I'm Comin', and "I Thank You," songs that survive as the very epitome of Southern soul. Certainly, Sam & Dave's hits are among the most soulful ever to crack the Hot 100. Their albums often bore the hallmarks of hasty execution, though. The dissolution of the partnership between Stax and Atlantic virtually sealed the fate of Sam & Dave; there were a few more hits (and, later, a revival of interest thanks to the Blues Brothers), but the glory days were over. *—Colin Escott & Stephen Thomas Erlewine*

☆ **Sweat 'n' Soul** / Jul. 20, 1993 / Rhino/Atlantic ♦♦♦♦♦
Sam Moore and Dave Prather were the ultimate soul duo; one a high-voiced wailer, the other a low-toned blaster. They came together in the mid-'60s to form a superb duo, singing tunes penned by soul's finest writing tandem, Isaac Hayes and David Porter. They made a host of great singles before ego battles broke them apart. This 50-cut, two-disc anthology not only has every song of significance, but plenty of obscure worthwhile items, like a "Stay in School" promo, some overlooked material done with the Dixie Flyers, and a couple of numbers cut by Moore as a solo act in the early '70s. The sound quality, annotation, and song sequencing are as outstanding as the songs themselves. *—Ron Wynn*

★ **The Very Best of Sam & Dave** / Feb. 28, 1995 / Rhino ♦♦♦♦♦
The Very Best of Sam & Dave contains all of Sam & Dave's Top 40 hits, including "You Don't Know Like I Know," "Hold On! I'm Comin'," "Said I Wasn't Gonna Tell Nobody," "You Got Me Hummin'," "When Something Is Wrong with My Baby," "Soothe Me," "Soul Man," and "I Thank You," plus a handful of essential album tracks and B-sides like "I Can't Stand Up for Falling Down." It's an expertly compiled, concise collection that contains everything you need to know. If you need to dig deeper, the double-disc *Sweat 'n' Soul* is essential, but most casual fans will be completely satisfied by *The Very Best of Sam & Dave. —Stephen Thomas Erlewine*

Santana

f. 1966, San Francisco, CA
Guitar / Latin Rock, Album Rock, Pop/Rock, Psychedelic, Fusion, Hard Rock, Blues-Rock
Santana is the name of a band that has successfully married elements of blues, rock, and Latin music and enjoyed international acclaim for more than two decades. It is also the name of the guitarist, Carlos Santana, who has led that band and made other recordings over the same period of time. In its original manifestation, the Santana Blues Band was a group of equals, with Carlos named as leader only because of a musicians-union requirement that such a designation be made. The group was formed in San Francisco in the mid-'60s and first gained recognition in the same dance halls that hosted the psychedelic rock groups of the era, although, with its Latin and African roots, Santana never quite fit in with the psychedelic sound. The group came under the direction of promoter Bill Graham and had already scored a contract with Columbia when it appeared at the Woodstock Festival in August 1969. *Santana,* the debut album, was a massive success, including the #4 hit "Evil Ways." *Abraxas* (1970) did even better, topping the charts for six weeks and featuring the hits "Black Magic Woman" and "Oye Como Va." In subsequent years, "Santana" for the most part referred to Carlos and a band of hired musicians playing in the established Santana style, while the leader also made occasional solo albums that varied the style somewhat. *—William Ruhlmann*

Santana / Aug. 1969 / Columbia/Legacy ♦♦♦♦♦

★ **Abraxas** / Sep. 1970 / Columbia/Legacy ♦♦♦♦♦
The San Francisco Bay Area rock scene of the late '60s was one that encouraged radical experimentation and discouraged the type of mindless conformity that's often plagued corporate rock. When one considers just how different Santana, Jefferson Airplane, Moby Grape, and the Grateful Dead sounded, it becomes obvious just how much it was encouraged. In the mid-'90s, an album as eclectic as *Abraxas* would be considered a marketing exec's worst nightmare. But at the dawn of the 1970s, this unorthodox mix of rock, jazz, salsa, and blues proved quite successful. Whether adding rock elements to salsa king Tito Puente's "Oye Como Va," tembracing instrumental jazz-rock on "Incident at Neshabur" and "Samba Pa Ti," or tackling moody blues-rock on Fleetwood Mac's "Black Magic Woman," the band keeps things unpredictable yet cohesive. Many of the Santana albums that came out in the '70s are worth acquiring, but for novices, *Abraxas* is an excellent place to start. [Columbia/Legacy's 1998 reissue of *Abraxas* featured three previously unreleased tracks—"Se A Cabo," "Toussaint L'Overture," "Black Magic Woman/Gypsy Queen"—which were all recorded live at the Royal Albert Hall on April 18, 1970.] *—Alex Henderson*

Santana III / Sep. 1971 / Columbia/Legacy ♦♦♦♦♦

Love, Devotion and Surrender / 1972 / Columbia ♦♦♦♦♦

Carlos Santana & Buddy Miles! Live! / Jun. 1972 / Columbia ♦♦♦♦
From December 1971 to April 1972, Carlos Santana and several other members of Santana toured with drummer/vocalist Buddy Miles, a former member of the Electric Flag and Jimi Hendrix's Band of Gypsys. The resulting live album contained both Santana hits ("Evil Ways") and Buddy Miles hits ("Changes"), plus a 25-minute, side-long jam. It was not, perhaps, the live album Santana fans had been waiting for, but at this point in its career, the band could do no wrong. The album went into the Top Ten and sold a million copies. (Reissued on CD on September 6, 1994.) *—William Ruhlmann*

Caravanserai / Oct. 1972 / Columbia ♦♦♦♦♦
Drawing on rock, salsa, and jazz, Santana recorded one imaginative, unpredictable gem after another in the 1970s. But *Caravanserai* is daring even by Santana's high standards. Carlos Santana was obviously very hip to jazz fusion—something the innovative guitarist provides a generous dose of on the largely instrumental *Caravanserai.* Whether its approach is jazz-rock or simply rock, this album is consistently inspired and quite adventurous. Full of heartfelt, introspective guitar solos, it lacks the immediacy of *Santana* or *Abraxas.* Like the type of jazz that influenced it, this pearl (which marked the beginning of keyboardist/composer Tom Coster's highly benefical membership in the band) requires a number of listenings in order to be absorbed and fully appreciated. But make no mistake: this is one of Santana's finest accomplishments. *—Alex Henderson*

Welcome / Nov. 1973 / Columbia ♦♦♦

Lotus / May 1974 / Columbia ♦♦♦♦♦
Recorded in Japan in July 1973, this massive live album, originally on three LPs and now on two compact discs, was available outside the United States in 1974, but held back from domestic release until long into the CD age. It features the same "New Santana Band" that recorded *Welcome* and combines that group's jazz and spiritual influences with performances of earlier Latin rock favorites like "Oye Como Va." *—William Ruhlmann*

Greatest Hits / Jul. 1974 / Columbia ♦♦♦♦♦
This ten-song sampler presents the best of Santana, 1969-71, the period of its greatest popularity. The hits include "Black Magic Woman," "Evil Ways," "Everybody's Everything," and "Oye Como Va." But note that this is a bare minimum of prime Santana. Not only does the sampler choose from only Santana's first three albums, but it leaves out such seminal numbers as "Nobody to Depend On" and "Soul Sacrifice." Those looking for a more extensive overview should consider *Viva Santana! — William Ruhlmann*

Illuminations / Sep. 1974 / Columbia ♦♦

Borboletta / Oct. 1974 / Columbia ♦♦♦

Amigos / Mar. 1976 / Columbia ♦♦♦♦♦
By the release of *Amigos,* the Santana band's seventh album, only Carlos Santana and David Brown remained from the band that conquered Woodstock, and only Carlos had been in the

band continuously since. Meanwhile, the group had made some effort to arrest its commercial slide, hiring an outside producer, David Rubinson, and taking a tighter, more uptempo, and more vocal approach to its music. The overt jazz influences were replaced by strains of R&B/funk and Mexican folk music. The result was an album more dynamic than any since *Santana III* in 1971. "Let It Shine" *(77)*, an R&B-tinged tune, became the group's first chart single in four years, and the album returned Santana to Top Ten status. *—William Ruhlmann*

Festival / Jan. 1977 / Columbia ✦✦✦

Moonflower / Oct. 1977 / Columbia ✦✦✦

Inner Secrets / Oct. 1978 / Columbia ✦✦

Oneness: Silver Dreams Golden Realities / Mar. 1979 / Columbia ✦✦✦
This is the first Carlos Santana solo album. It features members of the Santana band as backup, however, so the difference between a group effort and a solo work seems to be primarily in the musical approach, which is more esoteric and more varied than on a regular band album. The record is mostly instrumental and given over largely to contemplative ballads, although there is also, for example, in the song "Silver Dreams Golden Smiles," a traditional pop ballad sung by Saunders King. *—William Ruhlmann*

Marathon / Sep. 1979 / Columbia ✦✦

The Swing of Delight / Aug. 1980 / Columbia ✦✦

Zebop! / Apr. 1981 / Columbia ✦✦

Shango / Aug. 1982 / Columbia ✦✦

Havana Moon / Apr. 1983 / Columbia ✦✦✦

Beyond Appearances / Feb. 1985 / Columbia ✦✦

Freedom / Feb. 1987 / Columbia ✦✦✦

Blues for Salvador / Oct. 1987 / Columbia ✦✦✦✦✦

Viva Santana! / Aug. 1988 / Columbia ✦✦✦✦✦
Released in 1988, *Viva Santana!* is a generous 30-track overview of Santana's first 20 years of recording. Appropriately, it concentrates on the band's glory years of the late '60s and early '70s, when both Carlos Santana and his supporting musicians were on fire. There are several unreleased cuts, including live tracks included for hardcore fans, but *Viva Santana!* is most useful as a thorough overview for curious listeners. *—Stephen Thomas Erlewine*

Spirits Dancing in the Flesh / Jun. 1990 / Columbia ✦✦✦

Milagro / May 5, 1992 / Polydor ✦✦✦

Dance of the Rainbow Serpent / Aug. 8, 1995 / Columbia/Legacy ✦✦✦

Live at the Fillmore 1968 / Mar. 11, 1997 / Columbia/Legacy ✦✦✦✦
Live at the Fillmore 1968 is a two-CD package drawn from performances at the Fillmore West in December 1968, with an early lineup including Bob Livingston on drums and Marcus Malone on congas (both of whom would be gone by the time the group recorded their official debut in 1969). The band sound only a bit more tentative here than they would in their Woodstock-era incarnation, running through several of the highlights of their first album ("Jingo," "Persuasion," "Soul Sacrifice," and "Treat"). More interesting to collectors will be the five songs that have not previously appeared on any Santana recording, including covers of songs by jazzmen Chico Hamilton and Willie Bobo, and a half-hour original jam that concludes the set, "Freeway." The sound is excellent, and the arrangements a bit more improv-oriented than what ended up on the early studio records. Its appeal isn't solely limited to committed fans; on its own terms it's a fine release, highlighted by some burning organ-guitar interplay in particular. *—Richie Unterberger*

● **The Best of Santana** / Mar. 31, 1998 / Columbia/Legacy ✦✦✦✦✦
The Best of Santana is a 16-track collection that greatly expands the scope of Santana's previous hits compilation, *Greatest Hits*. Drawing from the band's entire 30-year career, the disc contains such familiar items as "Evil Ways," "Jingo," "Black Magic Woman/Gypsy Queen," and "Oye Como Va," but it also has a number of longtime favorites of the band and fans. Furthermore, all the songs have been subjected to Super Bit remastering, resulting in the best sound ever. For some casual fans, *Greatest Hits* remains definitive, since it's a portrait of the band at its peak, but anyone wanting a career-spanning single-disc compilation will find that *The Best of Santana* suits their needs. *—Stephen Thomas Erlewine*

Supernatural / Jun. 15, 1999 / Arista ✦✦✦✦
Santana was still a respected rock veteran in 1999, but it had been years since he had a hit, even if he continued to fare well on the concert circuits. Clive Davis, the man who had signed Santana to Columbia in 1968, offered him the opportunity to set up shop at his label, Arista. In the tradition of comebacks and label debuts by veteran artists in the '90s, *Supernatural*, Santana's first effort for Arista, is designed as a star-studded event. At first listen, there doesn't seem to be a track that doesn't have a guest star, which brings up the primary problem with the album—despite several interesting or excellent moments, it never develops a consistent voice that holds the album together. The fault doesn't lay with the guest stars or even with Santana, who continues to turn in fine performances. There's just a general directionless feeling to the record, enhanced by several songs that seem like excuses for jams, which, truth be told, isn't all that foreign on latter-day Santana records. Then again, the grooves often play better than the ploys for radio play, but that's not always the case, since Lauryn Hill's "Do You Like the Way" and the Dust Brothers-produced, Eagle-Eye Cherry-sung "Wishing It Was" are as captivating as the Eric Clapton duet, "The Calling." But that just confirms that *Supernatural* just doesn't have much of a direction, flipping between traditional Santana numbers and polished contemporary collaborations, with both extremes being equally likely to hit or miss. That doesn't quite constitute a triumph, but the peak moments of *Supernatural* are some of Santana's best music of the '90s, which does make it a successful comeback. *—Stephen Thomas Erlewine*

The Best of Santana, Vol. 2 / Nov. 21, 2000 / Columbia/Legacy ✦✦✦✦
These 14 tracks lean heavily on the earliest phase of Santana. Nine of them, in fact, were recorded prior to 1972, and just one postdates 1978. As 1969-71 was Santana's most vital period, however, that's no cause for complaint, and indeed the later cuts really pale in comparison. For someone who wants a little more than a greatest hits collection, but wants to stop after two volumes, this is good enough, with first-rate items like "Persuasion," "Se Acabo," and "Guajira." Nothing here is rare, and note that the versions of "Black Magic Woman" and "Europa" are live ones. *—Richie Unterberger*

Boz Scaggs (William Royce Scaggs)

b. Jun. 8, 1944, Ohio
Slide Guitar, Vocals, Guitar / Album Rock, Pop/Rock, Soft Rock, Blues-Rock
After first finding acclaim as a member of the Steve Miller Band, singer/songwriter Boz Scaggs went on to enjoy considerable solo success in the 1970s. Joining former schoolmate Miller in his fledgling group in 1967, Scaggs exited after recording two acclaimed albums with the unit, *Children of the Future* and *Sailor*. With the aid of *Rolling Stone* magazine publisher Jann Wenner, Scaggs secured a solo contract with Atlantic; his soulful self-titled debut failed to find an audience despite winning critical favor, and the track "Loan Me a Dime" later became the subject of a court battle when bluesman Fenton Robinson successfully sued for composer credit. After signing to Columbia, Scaggs teamed with producer Glyn Johns to record 1971's *Moments*, a skillful blend of rock and R&B which, like its predecessor, failed to make much of an impression on the charts. Scaggs remained a critics' darling over the course of LPs like 1972's *My Time* and 1974's *Slow Dancer*, but he did not achieve a commercial breakthrough until 1976's *Silk Degrees*, which reached number two on the album charts while spawning the Top Three single "Lowdown," as well as the smash "Lido Shuffle." 1977's *Down Two Then Left* was also a success, and 1980's *Middle Man* reached the Top Ten on the strength of the singles "Breakdown Dead Ahead" and "Jo Jo." *—Jason Ankeny*

Boz Scaggs / 1969 / Atlantic ✦✦✦✦✦
Produced by Jann Wenner and featuring crack accompaniment by the Muscle Shoals house band, Scaggs' solo debut is a near-masterwork, mingling the pathos and heartbreak of vintage honky tonk with the celebration and release of Southern soul. The highlights of the album also flaunt its diversity: "Loan Me a Dime," an extended blues dirge, which features some of Duane Allman's finest work, and "Waiting on a Train," Scaggs's marvelous revamping of Jimmie Rodgers' classic hobo song. *—John Floyd*

Moments / 1971 / Columbia ✦✦✦

Boz Scaggs & His Band / Dec. 1971 / Columbia ✦✦✦✦✦

My Time / 1972 / Columbia ✦✦✦✦✦

Slow Dancer / 1974 / Columbia ✦✦✦

Silk Degrees / Feb. 1976 / Columbia ✦✦✦✦✦
Both artistically and commercially, Boz Scaggs had his greatest success with *Silk Degrees*. The laidback singer hit the R&B charts in a big way with the addictive, sly "Lowdown" (which has been sampled by more than a few rappers, and remains a favorite among baby-boomer soul fans) and expressed his love of smooth soul music almost as well on the appealing "What Can I Say." But Scaggs was essentially a pop/rocker, and in that area, he has a considerable amount of fun on "Lido Shuffle" (another major hit single), "What Do You Want the Girl to Do," and "Jump Street." Meanwhile, "We're All Alone" and "Harbor Lights" became staples on adult contemporary radio. Though not remarkable, the ballads have more heart than most of the bland material dominating that format. *—Alex Henderson*

Down Two Then Left / Nov. 1977 / Columbia ✦✦✦

Middle Man / Apr. 1980 / Columbia ✦✦

● **Hits!** / Nov. 1980 / Columbia ✦✦✦✦✦
In spite of the inclusion of "Dinah Flo," *Hits!* primarily focuses on Scaggs' '80s pop hits like "Lowdown," "Jojo," "Break Down Dead Ahead," and "Look What You've Done to Me." *—Bil Carpenter*

Other Roads / 1988 / Columbia ✦✦

Some Change / Apr. 5, 1994 / Virgin ✦✦✦✦✦

Come on Home / Apr. 8, 1997 / Virgin ✦✦✦✦

My Time: The Anthology (1969-1997) / Oct. 7, 1997 / Columbia/Legacy ✦✦✦✦
My Time: Anthology (1969-1997) is an excellent double-disc retrospective of Boz Scaggs' entire career, containing all of his hits, several key album tracks, and a handful of rarities designed to entice the hardcore collector. For any serious fan who wants a comprehensive overview of Scaggs' career, *My Time* is an ideal purchase. *—Thom Owens*

Scorpions

f. 1969, Hannover, Germany
Group / Album Rock, Heavy Metal, Hard Rock
German hard rockers the Scorpions have sold over 22 million records, making them one of the most successful rock bands to ever come out of continental Europe. The band was originally formed in 1969 by Rudolf Schenker, whose younger brother Michael joined in 1971 to play lead guitar; good friend Klaus Meine became the vocalist that year as well. Michael's guitar playing was noticed by the band UFO, who hired him as their lead guitarist in 1973; Uli Jon Roth replaced him, and under his guidance the group released four albums on RCA from 1974-77. Roth subsequently left the band; in 1979, Michael Schenker was kicked out of UFO for alcohol abuse and came back to play with the Scorpions, who had recently signed with Mercury Records. The group released *Lovedrive* that same year and played their first American tour. Still coping with addiction, Michael missed tour dates repeatedly, and guitarist Matthias Jabs was hired to fill in; Michael eventually would leave the band a second time. The band released *Animal Magnetism* in 1980, which surprisingly went gold in the United States. 1982's *Blackout* contained the cult hit "No One Like You" and was a major success worldwide, selling over one million copies in the U.S. alone. But it was the powerful follow-up, *Love at First Sting*, that succeeded in making them superstars. Released in 1984,

the album boasted the MTV hit "Rock You Like a Hurricane" and achieved double-platinum status. In 1990, the album *Crazy World* became the Scorpions' biggest-selling record to date, drawing on the strength of the hit ballad "Wind of Change." However, *Crazy World* was the last successful Scorpions release in the U.S.; many fans lost interest due to the alternative explosion of the early '90s. Still, they continued to record for a core audience, and in 1997, Mercury assembled a double album of the band's greatest hits, *Deadly Sting: The Mercury Years*. *—Barry Weber*

The Best of Rockers 'n' Ballads / Oct. 1989 / Mercury ♦♦♦♦♦

• **Deadly Sting: The Mercury Years** / Jul. 15, 1997 / Mercury ♦♦♦♦♦
Presently, it is quite difficult to find a young person who knows about the Scorpions. Even when their careers were peaking in the '80s, they were never widely recognized, existing always as more of an underground band. The lack of hit singles produced by the group is by no means a judgment of their talent, however, as *Deadly Sting: The Mercury Years* proves. Some may find the fact that Mercury made the compilation a double-disc set surprising—again due to the band's small following—but the album is far better than the single-disc collection *Best of Rockers 'n Ballads*. Following chronologically from 1979 to 1993 (thus covering the years in which the band enjoyed their most success), *Deadly Sting* rips through the favorites "Loving You Sunday Morning," "The Zoo," "Blackout," "No One Like You," "Big City Nights," "Still Loving You," "Rock You Like a Hurricane," "Rhythm of Love," "Wind of Change," and "Don't Believe Her," finally concluding with two unreleased recordings from 1995. Though these tracks are far cries from the songs which proceeded them, that doesn't stop *Deadly Sting: The Mercury Years* from being the most essential album from one of the most underrated hair bands of all time. *—Barry Weber*

Gil Scott-Heron

b. Apr. 1, 1949, Chicago, IL
Vocals, Piano, Guitar / Folk-Jazz, Fusion
One of the most influential progenitors of rap music, Gil Scott-Heron's aggressive, no-nonsense street poetry inspired a legion of intelligent rappers while his engaging songwriting skills placed him square in the R&B charts later in his career, backed by increasingly contemporary production courtesy of Malcolm Cecil and Nile Rodgers (of Chic). Born in Chicago but transplanted to Tennessee for his early years, Scott-Heron spent most of his high-school years in the Bronx, where he learned first-hand many of the experiences which later made up his songwriting material. He had begun writing before reaching his teenage years, however, and completed his first volume of poetry at the age of 13. Though he attended college in Pennsylvania, he dropped out after one year to concentrate on his writing career, and earned plaudits for his novel, *The Vulture*. Encouraged at the end of the '60s to begin recording by legendary jazz producer Bob Thiele—who had worked with every major jazz great, from Louis Armstrong to John Coltrane—Scott-Heron released his 1970 debut, *Small Talk at 125th & Lennox*, inspired by a volume of poetry of the same name. With Thiele's Flying Dutchman Records until the mid-'70s, he signed to Arista soon after and found success on the R&B charts. Though his jazz-based work of the early '70s was tempered by a slicker disco-inspired production, Scott-Heron's message was as clear as ever on the Top 30 single "Johannesburg" and the number 15 hit "Angel Dust." Silent for almost a decade, after the release of his 1984 single "Re-Ron," the proto-rapper returned to recording in the mid-'90s with a message for the gangsta rappers who had come in his wake; Scott-Heron's 1994 album *Spirits* began with "Message to the Messengers," pointed squarely at the rappers whose influence—positive or negative—meant much to the children of the 1990s. *—John Bush*

Winter in America / Sep. 4, 1973–Oct. 11, 1973 / Strata East ♦♦♦
Gil Scott-Heron was at his most righteous and provocative on this album. The title cut was a moving, angry summation of the social injustices Scott-Heron felt had led the nation to a particularly dangerous period, while "The Bottle" was a great treatise on the dangers of alcohol abuse. He also offered his thoughts on Nixon's legacy with "The H2O Gate Blues," a classic oral narrative. Brian Jackson's capable keyboard, acoustic piano, and arranging talents helped make this a first-rate release, one of several the duo issued during the 1970s. *—Ron Wynn*

From South Africa to South Carolina / Jan. 1976 / TVT ♦♦♦♦
The Gil Scott-Heron/Brian Jackson collaboration was now a formal one, as they were issuing albums as a team. This was their second duo project to make the pop charts, and it included antinuclear and antiapartheid themes, plus less political, more autobiographical/reflective material like "Summer of '42," "Beginnings (The First Minute Of A New Day)," and "Fell Together." Scott-Heron was now a campus and movement hero, and Brian Jackson's production and arranging savvy helped make his albums as arresting musically as they were lyrically. *—Ron Wynn*

• **The Revolution Will Not Be Televised** / 1988 / Bluebird/RCA ♦♦♦♦♦
Spanning 1970-1972, this superb collection takes us back to Gil Scott-Heron's early years, when he was working with jazz producer Bob Thiele—a man who had been in the studio with everyone from John Coltrane and Pharoah Sanders to Coleman Hawkins. But *The Revolution Will Not Be Televised* isn't a jazz collection per se; it's a collection of innovative R&B and spoken poetry that contains jazz influences and finds Scott-Heron employing such jazz musicians as flutist Hubert Laws and bassist Ron Carter. Like the Last Poets, Scott-Heron has been described as "one of the first rappers"—and while he was hardly the first person to speak in rhyme to music, there are definitely parallels between angry sociopolitical poems like "Whitey on the Moon," "No Knock," and "Brother" and hip-hop commentary from the 1980s. Poetry, however, doesn't dominate this album—most of the selections illustrate Scott-Heron's excellence as a singer, including "Home Is Where the Hatred Is," "Did You Hear What They Said?" and the poignant "Save the Children." One of the collection's less political tracks is "Lady Day and John Coltrane," an R&B classic that articulates how easily jazz can lift a person's spirits. *The Revolution Will Not Be Televised* isn't the last word on Scott-Heron's artistry—he recorded many more treasures after leaving Flying Dutchman for Arista in 1975. But it's one of the collections to acquire if you're exploring his artistry for the first time. *—Alex Henderson*

Evolution & Flashback: The Very Best of Gil Scott-Heron / Feb. 9, 1999 / RCA ♦♦♦♦

Seal (Sealhenry Samuel)

b. Feb. 19, 1963, Paddington, London, England
Vocals / Club/Dance, Pop/Rock, Adult Contemporary, Urban, House, Dance-Pop
Seal emerged from England's house music scene in the early '90s to become the most popular British soul vocalist of the decade. Although his earliest material still showed signs of the acid-house, by the mid-'90s he had created a distinctive fusion of soul, folk, pop, dance, and rock that brought him success on both sides of the Atlantic. The son of Nigerian and Brazilian parents, Seal was raised in England and got early experience with the funk band Push. After providing the lyrics and vocals to the number one hit "Killer" by acid-house producer Adamski, he signed his own contract and began recording with Trevor Horn. Seal's eponymous debut gained a Top 20 British hit with the first single "Crazy," which reached number seven in America in 1991. The album eventually sold over three million copies around the world. Seal took three years to complete his second album, also titled *Seal*. Preceded by the American Top 40 hit "Prayer for the Dying," the album did well upon release but didn't really take off until nearly a year had passed, after the single "Kiss from a Rose" was featured on the soundtrack to *Batman Forever*. It hit number one in America and spent a total of 12 weeks at the top of the adult contemporary charts, sending its parent album into multi-platinum status. *Human Being* followed in 1998. *—Stephen Thomas Erlewine*

Seal [1991] / Jun. 11, 1991 / Sire ♦♦♦♦♦
London singer/songwriter Seal certainly made a name for himself with his eponymous debut despite the comparison to fellow London mate, the raspy-soul singer Terence Trent D'Arby. But Seal is more relaxed, and his craftsmanship is delicate and well-defined. Lyrical depictions are light, songwriting is personal, and production credits are most impressive. With star-studded work from both Trevor Horn (Tina Turner, Art of Noise, Rod Stewart) and Trevor Rabin (Yes, John Miles), *Seal* is surely a critical hit. Becoming a mainstream radio mainstay for the summer of 1991, the single "Crazy" carried heavy notoriety for Seal and instantly made him a household name. His collaborative effort with Adamski for "Killer" was a massive club hit thanks to its Hi-NRG strength, but house elements showcased other album tracks such as "The Beginning." Seal is not necessarily a dance innovator so to speak, but he makes for a select crossover artist with impeccable talent worthy of heavy acclamation and critical recognition. The general mood captured on his debut album is refreshing for the early-'90s mediocrity of post-hair metal and manufactured synth bands.

His music was a major force throughout the decade and well into the new millennium. With Trevor Horn at his side, it's undeniable. Together they go for exactly what Seal is looking for: the beauty, desire, and simplicity in creating a new sound. Seal is the face and Horn is the face behind it all. *—MacKenzie Wilson*

• **Seal [1994]** / 1994 / Sire ♦♦♦♦♦
Fresh from his 1991 self-titled debut, Seal follows up with his again self-titled second release. It's another stunning and moving piece of work, and a musical maturation has obviously taken place. Produced by ex-Buggles frontman Trevor Horn (Pet Shop Boys, ABC, Yes, Tina Turner, Rod Stewart, Frankie Goes to Hollywood), *Seal* is far more enchanting than on his preceding debut with his more than minimal emotion and heartfelt depictions. The warmth is there, sultry and attractive.

But *Seal* is a bit too relaxed at times, making for stripped lyrical stories. Aside from that brief cut, *Seal* is lush in harmonies and over-the-top melodies. "Don't Cry" flows with luxuriant vibes of hushing vocals and bellowing string arrangements. Showcasing more talent comes "If I Could," the duet between Seal and Canadian folky Joni Mitchell. The elegance of the contemporary "Prayer for the Dying" finally established Seal as a household name after the song became a mainstream radio and television mainstay. The soul is there, hauntingly similar to singer Terence Trent D'arby. But what's so unique about Seal is his gift of transforming free-flowing songs into quick dancefloor tracks into a transcending step into musical magic. His voice has spell a like that. His second album picks up on such skills. *—MacKenzie Wilson*

Human Being / Nov. 17, 1998 / Warner Brothers ♦♦♦

Seals & Crofts

f. 1969, Los Angeles, CA, **db.** 1980
Group / Pop/Rock, Soft Rock, Singer/Songwriter
One of the 1970s' most successful soft-rock acts, the duo of Jim Seals and Dash Crofts met while playing with singer Dean Beard in 1958. That year, Beard was invited to join the Champs (of "Tequila" fame), and Seals and Crofts tagged along, remaining with the group until 1965. After striking out on their own as a duo, from 1972 to 1976 they had a string of five gold albums for Warner Brothers; their hit singles from this period include "Summer Breeze," "Diamond Girl," "We May Never Pass This Way (Again)," and "Get Closer." The group became embroiled in controversy in 1974 due to the title track of their *Unborn Child* album, an antiabortion song written from the fetus's point of view; the album was a critical failure, while the single flopped and outraged abortion advocates, who held demonstrations at many of the group's shows. By 1976, Seals & Crofts' appeal began to decline; their albums failed to sell as well, and they scored their last Top 40 hit in 1978 with "You're the Love." *—Steve Huey*

Summer Breeze / 1972 / Warner Archives ♦♦♦♦♦
The title cut and "Hummingbird" are perfect for listening to on a summer's day. Breezy melodies and words that sound great even today help make *Summer Breeze* a worthy addition to anyone's music collection. And for a little melodrama, check out the cut "The Boy Down the Road." All around, this is a solid effort. *—James Chrispell*

Year of Sunday / 1972 / Warner Brothers ♦♦♦

Diamond Girl / 1973 / Warner Brothers ♦♦♦♦♦

• **Greatest Hits** / 1975 / Warner Brothers ♦♦♦♦♦

The Searchers

f. 1957, Liverpool, England

Group / Pop/Rock, Folk-Rock, Merseybeat, Power Pop, British Invasion

Founded in 1957 by John McNally (guitar/vocals), the Searchers were originally one of thousands of skiffle groups formed in the wake of Lonnie Donegan's success with "Rock Island Line." One of the top acts on the Liverpool band scene, playing textured renditions of American R&B, rock & roll, country, soul, and rockabilly, the group was signed to Pye Records in mid-1963, and their first single, a cover of the Drifters' "Sweets for My Sweet," hit number one on the British charts. While the Beatles quickly outdistanced all comers, the Searchers did, indeed, go to the top of the charts with two of their next three singles, "Needles and Pins" and "Don't Throw Your Love Away." Another record, "Sugar and Spice," stalled at the number two spot. Over the next nine months, the band staked out a sound that was one of the most distinctive in a rock scene crawling with hundreds of bands. Their music was built around the sound of a crisply played 12-string guitar, coupled with strong lead vocals and carefully, sometimes exquisitely arranged harmonies, so that they could credibly cover American R&B standards like "Love Potion No. 9" or Phil Spector-based girl-group pop like "Be My Baby." The Searchers' 1964 singles included a venture into folk-rock before the genre had been "invented" in the press. The turning point for the band came in 1965, as the British and international fascination with the Liverpool sound faded away; by the beginning of 1966, the group's string of chart hits seemed to have run out. *—Bruce Eder*

Meet the Searchers / 1963 / Castle ✦✦

Sugar & Spice / 1963 / Castle ✦✦✦
The Searchers' 1963 debut LP was typical of most early British Invasion albums, built around one hit ("Sugar and Spice," a number one hit in the U.K.) and 11 covers of American rock & roll standards. This wasn't destined to be remembered as an artistic statement along the lines of *With the Beatles*, but it's better than the average period artifact, due to the group's always enjoyable harmonies and arrangements. Actually, nearly half of the tracks are first-rate. Their energetic rave-up of the Coasters' "Ain't That Just Like Me" was actually a minor U.S. hit; "All My Sorrows" was an excellent arrangement of a Glenn Yarborough song that foreshadowed folk-rock; and "Hungry for Love" has the irresistibly saccharine appeal of Gerry & the Pacemakers' early hits. *—Richie Unterberger*

It's the Searchers / 1964 / Castle ✦✦✦✦✦
Perhaps the best studio album by a band that is really best represented by greatest-hit collections. This 1964 LP includes the classic hits "Needles and Pins" and "Don't Throw Your Love Away." It also features some of their best LP cuts, on which they applied their famed harmonies to American material that was both strong and obscure. The best of these covers are Bacharach/David's "This Empty Space" (originally by Dionne Warwick), the Jackie DeShannon-penned "Can't Help Forgiving You," the Drifters' "I Count the Tears," the folkish "Sea of Heartbreak," and "Where Have You Been" (which was also part of the Beatles' repertoire during their Hamburg days). The harder-rocking songs don't lend themselves as well to the group's talents, which always (with some notable exceptions) lay more in the folk-rock and Merseybeat direction than R&B/rockabilly. *—Richie Unterberger*

Love Melodies / 1981 / Sire ✦✦✦✦✦
These two albums (*The Searchers* and *Loves Melodies*) represent the Searchers at their peak as a recording outfit, having maintained their original mid-'60s emphasis on excellent harmonies and crisply played guitars but also absorbed lessons from such '70s pub rockers as Brinsley Schwarz and roots-rock expert Dave Edmunds. The material is some of the most beautiful recorded anywhere in this era, and anyone lucky enough to spot a copy of either of these records—neither of which has yet shown up on compact disc—should grab them. *—Bruce Eder*

● **Greatest Hits** / 1985 / Rhino ✦✦✦✦✦
The best American best-of on the band, and the most desirable for those on a budget, with superior sound to the *Silver Searchers* collection. *—Bruce Eder*

30th Anniversary Collection / 1992 / Collectables ✦✦✦✦✦
Although it's missing one or two fairly strong tracks, this three-CD, 84-song set is a pretty definitive collection of the group's best '60s material, for those who want to go beyond the greatest hits. Aside from all of their key A- and B-sides, it has an entire disc of their best '60s album tracks. The rarities disc includes foreign-language versions, outtakes, mid-'60s BBC performances, and solo discs by Tony Jackson and Chris Curtis. Highlights here include an alternate take of "Someday We're Gonna Love Again," a BBC version of "Blowin' in the Wind," and the previously unreleased "Once Upon a Time" (recorded by Dusty Springfield). The package includes liner notes, discography, and a family tree. *—Richie Unterberger*

Sire Sessions: The Rockfield Recordings / Jun. 10, 1997 / Raven ✦✦✦✦✦
The 23 songs here comprise the band's 1979-1980 recordings for Seymour Stein's Sire label, originally spread among two LPs that appeared in different versions in England and America. The original tapes have been remastered using Sony's Super Bit Mapping system, which has resulted in crisp and detailed resolution—the fact that the CD producers weren't afraid to pump up the volume has helped also, giving these songs more of a punch than the original LPs (at least, in America) ever had. Some of the songs haven't withstood the test of time—the Pender/McNally/Allen original "This Kind of Love Affair" is a little too repetitive—while others, like Dave Edmunds bassist John David's beautiful "You Are the New Day," have taken on a life of their own (it was later covered by the King's Singers). "Love's Melody," "Hearts In Her Eyes," "Switchboard Susan," "It's Too Late," "Lost In Your Eyes," and "You Are the New Day" rate among the group's all-time best tracks. Additionally, this is overall the best-sounding of all the group's CDs, far more impressive than any of the Pye/PRT recordings from the early '60s, as well as the most sophisticated music in their history. (Beware of identically packaged sets with sound in only one channel.) *—Bruce Eder*

The Greatest Hits Collection / 1998 / Castle Select ✦✦✦✦✦
This British compilation contains within its 20 tracks all of the Searchers' U.K. and U.S. Top 40 hits—"Sweets for My Sweet," "Sugar and Spice," "Needles and Pins," "Don't Throw Your Love Away," "Someday We're Gonna Love Again," "When You Walk in the Room," "Love Potion Number Nine," "What Have They Done to the Rain," "Goodbye My Love," "Bumble Bee," "He's Got No Love," "When I Get Home," "Take Me for What I'm Worth," and "Take It or Leave It"—all released between 1963 and 1966. Actually, the Searchers' peak period of popularity lasted less than two years, from the summer of 1963 to the spring of 1965, corresponding to and complementing the era of Beatlemania. Also hailing from Liverpool, they pursued a similar Merseybeat sound to the Beatles', complete with sweet harmonies and chiming guitars. Bedeviled by personnel changes and unable to develop the capacity for hit songwriting, they fell by the wayside after the first wave of the British Invasion, but their singles remain charming artifacts of the time. *—William Ruhlmann*

The Second Take: The Complete RCA/UK Recordings / Jun. 15, 1999 / Taragon ✦✦✦✦
This 25-song collection covers the least-known era of recordings by the Searchers, the two years (1971-73) they spent with RCA's British division. A single, "Desdemona," scraped into the lower reaches of the American Hot 100, and an album, *Second Take* (later retitled *Needles & Pins*), made up of the single plus re-recordings of the group's classic mid-'60s hits, appeared briefly in England. This disc offers much more than the mere filling of a major gap in a particular band's history—there's an astonishing amount of good music here. The Searchers weren't crazy about recutting their old sides, because they never did become an "oldies" act; they were still a working band, and were doing a good portion of this repertory nightly to clubgoers in England and Germany. So they recorded these songs with a degree of passion, and a few fresh flourishes and embellishments, that may surprise some listeners. "Desdemona" is more soulful than almost anything the band cut in its classic years, and will prove a major surprise to most listeners—the attack on their axes by John McNally and Michael Pender, as well as the largely successful attempt at a white group soul sound, highlight a great collection of material. Their voices had aged beautifully, allowing them to sing in a far more mature and passionate manner than their '60s sides ever showed possible; many songs here show the Searchers off as a surprisingly dexterous unit, equally capable of covering their own British Invasion-era hits in fresh fashion, or delving into sophisticated modern pop. Colin Escott's notes provide a vivid overview of the sessions and the joys and frustrations attending the release of this material (almost all of which will be new to 99% of the group's fans). *—Bruce Eder*

Sebadoh

f. 1989, Amherst, MA

Group / Indie Rock, Lo-Fi, Alternative Pop/Rock

As much a musician's collective as a band, Sebadoh was the quintessential lo-fi band of the '90s. Formed by singer/songwriter Lou Barlow while he was the bassist for Dinosaur Jr. in the late '80s, Sebadoh's music was a virtual catalog of '80s alternative rock and '90s indie-rock, featuring everything from jangle-pop to noise-rock experimentalism. Upon being kicked out of Dinosaur in 1989, Barlow turned his attention toward Sebadoh, a home-recording project that he and drummer/songwriter Eric Gaffney began in 1987. Sebadoh soon developed into a backing band for both Barlow and Gaffney, as each submitted home-recorded tapes for release and toured behind the albums. Eventually adding drummer/songwriter Jason Loewenstein, the trio became an indie-rock sensation, as well-known for the size and inconsistency of its output as the music itself. Often, Sebadoh sounded schizophrenic, flipping between Barlow's sensitive folk-rock and Gaffney's noise experiments without warning. This very diversity became the band's calling card, and by 1992, the band had earned a devoted following. As the media focused on Barlow—who also released a number of solo records under the name Sentridoh—Gaffney grew frustrated. Gaffney left in 1994, and with new drummer Bob Fay, Sebadoh produced its most accessible albums—*Bakesale* and *Harmacy*—which expanded its cult somewhat. Despite the group's flirtation with (relatively) polished production and the fluke success of Barlow's side-project Folk Implosion, Sebadoh remained a cult band, and became one the largest touchstones of '90s indie-rock. *—Stephen Thomas Erlewine*

Freed Weed / 1990 / Homestead ✦✦✦

Weed Forestin / 1990 / Homestead ✦✦

● **III** / 1991 / Homestead ✦✦✦✦✦
Far removed from the primitivism of the band's early work, *III* marks a pivotal moment in Sebadoh's creative evolution. The first full-length record to feature Jason Loewenstein, it's a radically diverse affair, offering vastly improved production and a newly-discovered dedication to focused, controlled songcraft; though no two cuts sound even remotely similar, taken as a whole the album is a surprisingly cohesive affair. Among the highlights—and with 23 songs, there are many—are "The Freed Pig" (Lou Barlow's vicious swipe at former Dinosaur Jr. bandmate J Mascis), Eric Gaffney's ominously jaunty "Violet Execution," and Barlow's tongue-in-cheek ode to sexual confusion, "Hassle." *—Jason Ankeny*

Smash Your Head on the Punk Rock / Nov. 6, 1992 / Sub Pop ✦✦✦
Sebadoh made its Sub Pop debut with *Smash Your Head on the Punk Rock*, which collects the highlights of the import compilations *Rockin' the Forest* and *Sebadoh vs. Helmet*. Lou Barlow's contributions are the gems here, especially the transcendent "Brand New Love," which first appeared in acoustic form on *Weed Forestin* (and was later punked up by Superchunk); almost as good are "Vampire" and "Good Things," while an apt and poignant cover of David Crosby's "Everybody's Been Burned" underscores the emotional frailty which binds all of Barlow's work. *—Jason Ankeny*

Bubble & Scrape / Apr. 26, 1993 / Sub Pop ✦✦✦✦
Bubble and Scrape is the last Sebadoh record to feature Eric Gaffney, and accordingly, his contributions are not so much songs as tantrums; blistering rants like "Telecosmic Alchemy" and "Elixir Is Zog" offer much in the way of dissonant noise, but little in the way of substance. Still, the album has much to recommend it—not only does Jason Loewenstein emerge here as an increasingly adept songwriter, but Lou Barlow truly hits his stride: both "Soul and Fire" and "Think (Let Tomorrow Bee)" are sterling additions to one of the most impressive catalogues of love songs on the planet, while "Cliche" stings with bitter intensity. *—Jason Ankeny*

Bakesale / Sep. 1994 / Sub Pop ✦✦✦✦✦
With *Bakesale*, Sebadoh has trimmed down to Lou Barlow, Jason Loewenstein, and Bob Fay, with Barlow and Loewenstein taking on the lion's share of the songwriting. Maybe the change in personnel was needed, because *Bakesale* is their most accessible, concise work to date. Without the noise that usually envelops their records, the solid, unconventional pop songwriting of Barlow and Loewenstein shines through brightly. *—Stephen Thomas Erlewine*

Harmacy / Aug. 20, 1996 / Sub Pop ✦✦✦✦✦
Part of Sebadoh's charm is that their records are always rather inconsistent, flipping wildly between sonic extremes as well as musical genres. In a sense, *Harmacy* is no different than its predecessors, but there are some crucial differences that makes it their most accessible effort. Previously, that title was held by 1994's *Bakesale*, but in between that record and *Harmacy*, Lou Barlow had a genuine Top 40 hit with the Folk Implosion's "Natural One." Although nothing on *Harmacy* sounds much like the hip-hop hybrid of "Natural One," its success did have an effect on Barlow, leading him toward more straightforward song structures and cleaner productions—"Willing to Wait" even features strings. Instead of diluting the impact of Sebadoh's music, the clearer production actually strengthens it. Barlow's sighing melodies and jangling indie rock become more resonant and affecting, and his batch of songs are among his best ever. Jason Loewenstein, Sebadoh's other main songwriter, suffers somewhat at the hands of cleaner production. Loewenstein tends to stick closer to the band's hardcore punk roots than Barlow, so his songs usually could use the extra layer of hiss and murk that cheap productions lend recordings. It also doesn't help that he tends to sink into rather faceless indie-noise rock. When Loewenstein takes a stab at pop melodies, such as "Can't Give Up," his songs are memorable, but on the whole, his songs are uneven and occasionally tedious. If it weren't for Loewenstein's erratic songwriting, *Harmacy* might rank as Sebadoh's masterpiece, but as it stands it's just another very fine and sometimes frustrating record from a band that produces nothing but very fine and sometimes frustrating records. *—Stephen Thomas Erlewine*

The Sebadoh / Feb. 23, 1999 / Sire ✦✦✦

Neil Sedaka

b. Mar. 13, 1939, Brooklyn, NY
Vocals, Piano / Brill Building Pop, Soft Rock, Pop
If Neil Sedaka had been born a bit earlier, he probably would have felt quite at home as a straight Tin Pan Alley tunesmith. Rock & roll had taken over by 1960, though, so he made a niche for himself as one of the Brill Building's most pop-oriented writers. Unlike most of the Brill Building heavyweights, he sang most of his hit records (which were composed in association with Howard Greenfield). And he had a lot of them in the late '50s and early '60s: "Oh Carol," "The Diary," "Stairway to Heaven," "Calendar Girl," "Next Door to an Angel," and "Happy Birthday, Sweet Sixteen." "Breaking Up Is Hard to Do," a number one hit in 1962, was probably his best-known tune. Sedaka's hits were well-crafted, but were probably the most innocuous, saccharine smashes to come out of the early Brill Building crowd. His rather thin, high vocals were boosted by multi-tracking, which was still a novel technique at the time. He made an unexpectedly successful comeback in England in the early '70s, where three of his albums were co-produced by Graham Gouldman of 10cc. By the mid-'70s he was recording for Elton John's Rocket label, and got a number one hit with the ballad "Laughter in the Rain" in 1974. That and "Love Will Keep Us Together," which he and Greenfield wrote for the Captain and Tennille, did much to get MOR pop off the ground. Sedaka got another number one hit, "Bad Blood," in 1975, with Elton John helping out on background vocals. Although he would never enter the Top 40 after 1980, he was assured of a successful career as a perennial on the MOR circuit. *—Richie Unterberger*

• **All-Time Greatest Hits** / 1975 / RCA ✦✦✦✦✦
Includes "Calendar Girl," "Happy Birthday, Sweet Sixteen," "Breaking Up Is Hard to Do," and other sprightly pop numbers. *—Dan Heilman*

• **Laughter in the Rain: The Best of Neil Sedaka, 1974-1980** / Sep. 27, 1994 / Varese Sarabande ✦✦✦✦✦
His biggest and best work for MCA and Elektra are represented in this set, with "Laughter in the Rain," "Bad Blood," "Love in the Shadows," and his reconstruction of "Breaking Up is Hard to Do" being the highlights. *—John Lowe*

Sings the Hits / Oct. 26, 1999 / RCA ✦✦✦✦✦
The double-disc collection *Neil Sedaka Sings the Hits* is a comprehensive chronicle of Sedaka's hit-making stint at RCA, from his first hit in 1958 ("The Diary") to his last recordings for the label in the late '60s. That means it's not quite definitive, since it bypasses his '70s comeback on Rocket Records, but this is about as exhaustive as an RCA compilation can get, containing all of his hits (including the big ones "Oh! Carol," "Stairway to Heaven," "Calendar Girl," "Happy Birthday, Sweet Sixteen," "Breaking Up Is Hard to Do," and "Next Door to an Angel") plus a bunch of lesser-known singles and album tracks. It may be too much for casual listeners—34 tracks on two discs is a whole lotta Sedaka—but it's well done and entertaining, and easily the best compilation yet assembled on this era. *—Stephen Thomas Erlewine*

The Seeds

f. 1965, Los Angeles, CA, **db.** 1970
Group / Acid Rock, Garage Rock, Psychedelic
Best-known for rock & roll standard "Pushin' Too Hard," the Seeds combined the raw, Stonesy appeal of garage rock with a fondness for ragged, trashy psychedelia. And though they never quite matched the commercial peak of their early singles, the band continued to record for the remainder of the '60s, eventually delving deep into post-*Sgt. Pepper* psychedelia and art rock. None of their new musical directions resulted in another hit single, and the group disbanded at the turn of the decade. Singer Sky Saxon and guitarist Jan Savage formed the Seeds in Los Angles in 1965. By the end of 1966, they had secured a contract with GNP Crescendo, releasing "Pushin' Too Hard" as their first single. The song climbed into the Top 40 early in 1967, and the group immediately released two soundalike singles, "Mr. Farmer" and "Can't Seem To Make You Mine," in an attempt to replicate their success; the latter came the closest to being a hit, just missing the Top 40. While their singles were garage-punk, the Seeds attempted to branch out into improvisation blues-rock and psychedelia on their first two albums, *The Seeds* (1966) and *Web of Sound* (1966). With their third album, *Future* (1967), the band attempted a psychedelic concept album in the vein of *Sgt. Pepper*. *—Stephen Thomas Erlewine*

The Seeds / 1966 / GNP Crescendo ✦✦✦✦✦

Web of Sound / 1966 / GNP Crescendo ✦✦✦

• **Evil Hoodoo** / 1988 / Drop-out ✦✦✦✦✦
The only serious attempt at a best-of Seeds retrospective features 16 songs culled from their half-dozen or so '60s albums. Besides "Pushin' Too Hard," it features their sole other hit single of any magnitude ("Can't Seem to Make You Mine"), as well as other fairly well-remembered cuts like "The Wind Blows Your Hair," "Tripmaker," "Falling off the Edge of My Mind," "Mr. Farmer," and "Up in Her Room." Non-converts to the Sky Saxon legend may be excused for wondering what all the fuss is about: Even distilled to 16 cuts, the melodies and arrangements are almost interminably monotonous. Comes with an extensive group history by rock archivist Brian Hogg. *—Richie Unterberger*

Flower Punk / Nov. 19, 1996 / Demon ✦✦✦✦
The Seeds did write two garage rock classics with "Pushin' Too Hard" and "Can't Seem To Make You Mine," but that didn't mean their remaining records were as interesting as that pair of raw, vital rockers. *Flower Punk* acts otherwise, compiling all of the group's albums onto a triple-disc, book-bound collection. It's a beautifully packaged set and no song is overlooked, yet *Flower Punk* is only for serious garage rock and Seeds fetishists, since the band rarely ever hit the heights of "Pushin' Too Hard" and "Can't Seem To Make You Mine" again. Indeed, for many listeners, a simple greatest hits collection can sound samey, but over the course of three CDs, it becomes apparent that the Seeds and Sky Saxon were only capable of a few sounds, and you already have to be indoctornated to find more than a handful of cuts on *Flower Punk* interesting. *—Stephen Thomas Erlewine*

The Seekers

f. 1963, Australia, **db.** 1968
Group / Folk-Rock, Pop
Although it's difficult for those who weren't there to believe, for a short time during late 1965 and early 1966, the popularity of this singing quartet from Australia was sufficient to rival the Beatles and the Rolling Stones. The Seekers were at the head of the British Invasion's acoustic folk-rock division, right there with Peter & Gordon and Chad & Jeremy but without the personal Beatles connection of the former and more successful than either—they scored a string of number one hits in England and Top Ten successes in America that lasted into 1967, two years later than most of the rest of the British exports to this country. They played acoustic instruments (even the upright bass), and they were closer in image and inspiration to the likes of the Rooftop Singers ("Walk Right In"), the New Christy Minstrels ("Green Green," etc.), or Peter, Paul & Mary, than to the Beatles or even the Searchers, yet they managed to hang onto young listeners, as well as older teenagers and their parents, with songs like "I'll Never Find Another You," "A World of Our Own," "Come the Day," or "Georgy Girl." *—Bruce Eder*

• **Capitol Collectors Series** / Jul. 28, 1992 / Capitol ✦✦✦✦✦

The Very Best of the Seekers / Apr. 7, 1998 / Collectables ✦✦✦✦✦
This is a nicely comprehensive Seekers collection; a bit expensive, but affordable next to the multi-disc imports that EMI has been issuing overseas in the late '90s. Essentially a successor and redesigned version of the old Capitol Collectors Series compilation, this disc features some highly ambiguous credits, listing Ron Furmanek as producer and compiler with Steve Kolanjian, but also stating that Bob Hyde—a major figure in the field of oldies restoration—has "newly remastered" the contents of this disc; the notes from 1992 are slightly outdated, given the quartet's reunion activities; and a typesetting error credits Bruce Woodley rather than Paul Simon as the author of "Cloudy." Whatever the particulars, the sound is rich, loud, and sharp, and the choice of the 23 songs is ideal, alternating between major hits, minor singles, and worthy B-sides and album tracks, reaching out to the occasional notable Simon song and oddities like the original World Record Club version of "Morningtown Ride" (released by mistake in America). There is one strange Kim Fowley "authored" piece, "Emerald City," which uses the Beethoven "Symphony No. 9's 'Ode to Joy'" (a la "Nutrocker") as its jumping off point—the producers might better have included the group's version of "The Last Thing on My Mind." It's a sensible collection, however, balanced to suit the serious fan and the casual listener. *—Bruce Eder*

Bob Seger

b. May 6, 1945, Dearborn, MI
Vocals, Piano, Guitar / Detroit Rock, Heartland Rock, Album Rock, Garage Rock, Hard Rock, Singer/Songwriter, Rock & Roll
A hard-driving Michigan garage-rocker in the vein of the Rationals, Bob Seger developed into one of the most popular heartland rockers over the course of the '70s. While he never attained the critical respect of Bruce Springsteen, Seger did develop a dedicated following through constant touring with his Silver Bullet Band. Seger's first taste of national success came with the Bob Seger System whose 1968 debut album, *Ramblin' Gamblin' Man* had a Top 20 hit in its title track. Their followup, *Noah*, stiffed, and Seger decided to quit the music business. Seger returned in late 1969 with a new band, releasing *Mongrel*, the last album credited to the System. The singer/songwriter effort *Brand New Morning* followed in 1971. Although regionally successful, 1972's covers album *Smokin' O.P.'s* didn't dent the American mainstream, nor did *Back in '72* (1973) or *Seven* (1974). For the recording of 1975's *Beautiful Loser*, Seger formed the Silver Bullet Band, who joined him on an extensive tour after the album's release.

Live Bullet (1976) became a smash, spending over three years on the U.S. charts, setting the stage for *Night Moves*, which went into the Top Ten early in 1977. *Stranger in Town* was just as successful, cementing his status as one of America's most popular rockers. *Against the Wind* (1980) became his first number one album, while 1981's live *Nine Tonight* continued his multi-platinum success. *The Distance* (1982) was Seger's first album since *Seven* to be recorded with additional session musicians, and over the next decade, the membership of the Silver Bullet Band shifted constantly. *The Distance* featured "Shame on the Moon," his biggest hit single to date, yet its sales plateaued at a million copies. Following its release, Seger drastically cut back his recording and touring—1986's *Like A Rock* was the only other record he released during the '80s. Four years later, he returned with *The Fire Inside*. Although the album went platinum and reached the Top Ten, it only appealed to Seger's devoted following, as did 1995's *It's A Mystery*, which became his first album since *Live Bullet* to fail to go platinum. He spent the rest of the '90s quiet. *—Stephen Thomas Erlewine*

Ramblin' Gamblin' Man / 1968 / Capitol ✦✦✦✦
The Bob Seger System throw everything into *Rambin' Gamblin' Man*, dabbling in folk, blues-rock, psychedelia, and piledriving rock & roll synonymous with Detroit. Typical of such a wide-ranging debut, not everything works. The System stumbles when they take psychedelic San Franciscan bands on their own turf. Trippy soundscapes like "Gone" drift into the ether, and the longer jams, "White Wall" and "Black Eyed Girl," meander. But the things that do work are absolute monsters, highlighted by the title track, a thunderous bit of self-mythology driven by a relentless rhythm, wailing organ riff, and gospel chorus. It's a stunningly great record, and while nothing here quite equals it, the songs that come close (with the exception of "Train Man," the first inkling of Seger's knack for reflective, intimate ballads) are sterling examples of spare, bluesy, angry Michigan rock & roll. "Tales of Lucy Blue" has a spooky, menacing edge, "Ivory" a great Motown-styled raver, and "Down Home" rides a manic riff and a simple blues harp to be one of the best rockers on the record. Then there's "2+2≠?", a ferocious anti-war song in the vein of Creedence Clearwater Revival's "Fortunate Son," but here Seger can't imagine why the nice guy in high school is now buried in the mud. It's a frightening, visceral song that stands among the best anti-Vietnam protests. Finally, the album closes with "The Last Song (Love Needs to Be Loved)," an unabashed peace, love 'n' understanding anthem styled in the manner of West Coast hippie pop, particularly Love. It's atypical of anything on the album or anything Seger would ever do again, but in many ways, it's the perfect way to close an exciting, flawed debut that winds up being a symbol of its times by its very diversity. *—Stephen Thomas Erlewine*

Noah / Sep. 1969 / Capitol ✦✦

Mongrel / Aug. 1970 / Capitol ✦✦✦✦✦
Most artists that deliver a second record as shaky as *Noah* fold on their third album. Not Bob Seger. He reasserted control of the System, consigning Tom Neme to a fanboy's footnote, and returning the group to the piledriving rock that was his trademark. All of this was evident with his third album, the superb *Mongrel*. Never before, and never since, has Seger rocked as recklessly and viciously as he did here—after a spell in the wilderness, he's found his voice. He's so assured, he elevates his *Ramblin' Gamblin' Man* characters Lucy Blue and Chicago Green to mythic status in the pulverizing "Lucifer," perhaps the greatest song on this lean, muscular record. That assurance carries over not just through the ferocious rockers that dominate the album—"Evil Edna," "Highway Child," "Leaning on My Dream," and "Song to Rufus" all hit harder than latter-day MC5—but to quieter moments like "Big River," where he first hits upon the wistful, passionate ballad style later popularized with "Night Moves." The fact that the System connects on both illustrates that Seger is not just fronting an excellent band, but that he's developing into a first-class songwriter. Put it this way—the only time the System sounds ill at ease is when they tackle "River Deep—Mountain High," and that's not because they're ill-suited to the epic—it's because they find the lie in the song's artificial pretensions and deliver a performance that eclipses the song itself. That two-fisted punch of terrific performances and songs is unexpected, especially after an album as conflicted as *Noah*, but the truly remarkable thing is that *Mongrel* showcases a band so powerful and a songwriter so distinctive, that it still sounds white-hot decades after its release. *—Stephen Thomas Erlewine*

Brand New Morning / Oct. 1971 / Capitol ✦✦✦

Smokin' O.P.'s / 1972 / Capitol ✦✦✦

Back in '72 / 1973 / Reprise ✦✦✦✦✦
Returning to independent status, Bob Seger recorded *Back in '72*, not only the finest of his early-'70s albums, but one of the great lost hard rock albums of its era. Seger didn't limit himself to self-penned songs on this excursion; borrowing an idea from *Smokin' O.P.'s*, he covers quite a few tunes, providing a balance to his own tunes. He makes "Midnight Rider" sound as if it were a Motor City raver instead of a sultry, late-afternoon Southern rocker, while casually tossing off "Rosalie," an irresistible ode to a local DJ that turned into a hard rock anthem when Thin Lizzy decided to record it later in the decade. That's the brilliance of *Back in '72*—there's no separation between the original and cover, it's all united in a celebration of rock & roll. That's why "Turn the Page," perhaps the weariest travelogue ever written, never feels self-pitying—that's just the facts, according to a first-rate Midwestern band that never got a break. All the same, *Back in '72* is a testament to great rock & roll, thanks to Seger's phenomenal songwriting and impassioned songwriting. *—Stephen Thomas Erlewine*

☆ **Seven** / Mar. 1974 / Capitol ✦✦✦✦✦
With his seventh album, appropriately titled *Seven*, Bob Seger delivered one of his strongest, hardest-hitting rock records—the toughest since the days of the Bob Seger System. Not to say that he ever abandoned rock & roll, since *Back in '72* was filled with fantastic rockers, but it was tempered with reflective singer/songwriter material. Not here. Even the slowest song, "20 Years From Now," is a steady mid-tempo ballad that showcases the band. Still, that's a rare moment of reflection on a record that opens with "Get Out of Denver," the greatest Chuck Berry knock-off ever written, and never loses momentum. Great, raucous rockers pile up one after the other, as Seger spins out barroom anthems ("Seen a Lot of Floors"), anti-establishment tirades ("Long Song Comin'," "Cross of Gold"), jokes ("U.M.C. (Upper Middle Class)"), bluesy rock ("All Your Love"), and simple garage rockers ("Need Ya," "School Teacher"). Only nine songs, lasting just over a half hour, but it's one of the most infectious sets Seger ever cut, proving that he wasn't just a dynamite rocker, but he had the songs to match. And, again, it didn't have any success—it didn't even chart, actually. That doesn't change the fact that this is one of his very best albums. *—Stephen Thomas Erlewine*

Beautiful Loser / Apr. 1975 / Capitol ✦✦✦✦✦
Beautiful Loser winds up sounding more like *Back in '72* than its immediate predecessor, *Seven*, largely because Bob Seger threaded reflective ballads and mid-tempo laments back into his hard-driving rock. He doesn't shy away from it, either, opening with the lovely title track. And why shouldn't he? These ballads were as much a part of his success as his storming rockers, since his sentimental streak seemed all the more genuine when contrasted with the rockers. If anything, *Beautiful Loser* might err a little bit in favor of reflection, with much of the album devoted to introspective, confessional mid-tempo cuts. There are a couple of exceptions to the rule, of course—"Katmandu" roars with humor, and his cover of "Nutbush City Limits" shames Tina Turner's original—but they are the only full-throttle rockers here, with "Black Night" coming in as a funky, swaggering cousin. It's the exact opposite of *Seven*, in other words, and in its own way, it's just as satisfying. Occasionally, it might be a little too sentimental for some tastes, but it's all heartfelt and he's written some terrific songs here, most notably "Jody Girl" and "Travelin' Man." Seger has started turning inward, searching his soul in a way he hadn't since the since disowned *Brand New Morning*, and, in doing so, he was setting the stage for his first genuine blockbuster. *—Stephen Thomas Erlewine*

★ **Live Bullet** / Apr. 1976 / Capitol ✦✦✦✦✦
Live Bullet introduced Bob Seger to a wide audience, revealing a rocker of unbridled passion and a songwriter of considerable talent. Prior to its release, Seger had been toiling away, releasing seven albums and touring constantly ever since his debut scraped the national consciousness in 1968. The psychedelicized days of *Ramblin' Gamblin' Man* are long gone on *Live Bullet*, leaving behind a rocker who loved the Stones for their toughness, Dylan for his honesty, and Chuck Berry for his narrative—and one who found his own sound when the Silver Bullet Band came into their own through countless tours. *Live Bullet* was recorded live at Detroit's Cobo Hall, in front of a passionate, loving hometown audience spurring him into a great performance. The song selection relies heavily on *Beautiful Loser*, yet it dips into the previous albums enough to prove that Seger had been delivering consistently as a songwriter for years. But what really sold *Live Bullet* is how these terrific songs are delivered with a ferocious, committed intensity. This might not be much more than a simple rock & roll album, but it's one of the best of its kind, establishing Seger, in the eyes of skeptics, as a first-rate performer and writer. Here, "Heavy Music," "Get Out of Denver," "Turn the Page," and "Ramblin' Gamblin' Man" all become hard rock classics, as does the band itself. It's a rare occasion when a double live album captures an artist at an absolute peak, while summarizing his talents, and that's exactly what *Live Bullet* does. *—Stephen Thomas Erlewine*

★ **Night Moves** / Oct. 1976 / Capitol ✦✦✦✦✦
Seger recorded the bulk of *Night Moves* before *Live Bullet* brought him his first genuine success, so it shouldn't come as a surprise that it's similar in spirit to the introspective *Beautiful Loser*, even if it rocks harder and longer. Throughout much of the album, he's coming to grips with being on the other side of 30 and still rocking. He floats back in time, turning in high school memories, remembering when wandering down "Mainstreet" was the highlight of an evening, covering a rockabilly favorite in "Mary Lou." Stylistically, there's not much change since *Beautiful Loser*, but the difference is that Seger and his Silver Bullet Band—who turn in their first studio album here—sound intense and ferocious, and the songs are subtly varied. Yes, this is all hard rock, but the acoustic ballads reveal the influence of Dylan and Van Morrison, filtered through a Midwestern sensibility, and the rockers reveal more of Seger's personality than ever. Seger may have been this consistent before (on *Seven*, for example), but the mood had never been as successfully varied, nor had his songwriting been as consistent, intimate, and personal. Thankfully, this was delivered to a mass audience eager for Seger, and it not only became a hit, but one of the universally acknowledged high points of late-'70s rock & roll. And, because of his passion and craft, it remains a thoroughly terrific record years later. *—Stephen Thomas Erlewine*

Stranger in Town / May 1978 / Capitol ✦✦✦✦✦
Night Moves was in the pipeline when *Live Bullet* hit and that album wound up eclipsing the double-live set anyway, so *Stranger in Town* is really the record where Bob Seger started grasping the changes that happened when he became a star. It happened when he was old enough to have already formed his character. Even as celebrity creeps in, as on "Hollywood Nights," Seger remains a middle-class, Midwestern rocker, celebrating "Old Time Rock & Roll," realizing old flames are still the same and still feeling like a number. Musically, it's as lively as *Night Moves*, rocking even harder in some places and being equally as introspective in the acoustic numbers. If it doesn't feel as revelatory as that record, in many ways it does feel like a stronger set of songs. Yes, musically, it doesn't offer any revelations, but it still feels impassioned, both in its performances and songs, and it's still one of the great rock records of its era. *—Stephen Thomas Erlewine*

Against the Wind / Feb. 1980 / Capitol ✦✦✦✦
Though there are still some traces of the confessionals that underpinned *Beautiful Loser* through *Stranger in Town*, *Against the Wind* finds Bob Seger turning toward craft. Perhaps he had to, since *Against the Wind* arrived after three blockbuster albums and never-ending tours. Even so, this record winds up not feeling as immediate or as soulful as its predecessors, especially since it begins with a tossed-off rocker called "The Horizontal Bop," possibly his most careless tune since "Noah." It's fun, but once it's done, the record really starts to kick into high gear with "You'll Accomp'ny Me," a ballad the equal of anything on its two predecessors. Throughout *Against the Wind*, Seger winds up performing better on the ballads than the rockers, which, while good, tend to sound a little formulaic. Still, Seger's formula is good and if "Her Strut" and "Betty Lou's Gettin' Out Tonight" would have been second stringers on *Stranger in Town*, they offer a nice balance here, and the rest of the record alternates be-

tween similarly well-constructed rockers and introspective ballads like "Against the Wind" and "Fire Lake." Compared to its predecessors, this does feel a little weak, but compared with its peers, it's a strong, varied heartland rock album that finds Seger at a near peak. *—Stephen Thomas Erlewine*

Nine Tonight / Sep. 1981 / Capitol ♦♦♦

The Distance / Dec. 1982 / Capitol ♦♦♦♦

Like a Rock / Apr. 1986 / Capitol ♦♦♦

The Fire Inside / Aug. 19, 1991 / Capitol ♦♦♦

Greatest Hits / 1994 / Capitol ♦♦♦♦♦
For over 20 years, Bob Seger has been one of the best mainstream rock & rollers in America, developing a distinctive body of honest, hard-rocking songs. More songs that can be put on this single-disc set, unfortunately. While many of Seger's trademarks are here— "Turn the Page," "Old Time Rock N' Roll," "Night Moves"—there is no "Rock and Roll Never Forgets," "Katmandu," "Shame on the Moon," or any of his pulverizing early records, when he was as tough as fellow Michigan rockers the MC5 and the Stooges; this is one time when a double-disc set would have held enough quality material. Nevertheless, what is here is fine and contains enough first-rate material to satisfy most fans. *—Stephen Thomas Erlewine*

It's a Mystery / Oct. 24, 1995 / Capitol ♦♦♦

Brian Setzer

b. Apr. 10, 1959, Long Island, NY
Vocals, Guitar / Retro-Rock, Retro-Swing, Rockabilly Revival, Roots Rock
Former Stray Cat Brian Setzer began having dreams of leading a big band with horns as a teen, but got sidetracked by punk. Initially, as a guitarist and songwriter, he took his inspiration from blues-rock bands like Led Zeppelin, although as a teen he'd take the train into New York to hang around the jazz clubs, sneaking into places like the Village Vanguard and the Village Gate. After seeing the Mel Lewis Orchestra, he had the idea of leading his own big band, but in the early '80s, Setzer instead formed the Stray Cats, a rockabilly band that took England by storm and then came back home to convert audiences in the U.S. The Stray Cats' U.S. breakthrough album was *Built for Speed*, which spurred three separate Top Ten hits, including "Stray Cat Strut," "Rumble in Brighton," and "Rock This Town." Finally, after the group's demise and a largely unsuccessful turn as a solo roots-rocker, Setzer formed a 17-piece big band in Los Angeles for a series of club dates. 1996's *Guitar Slinger* blended jump blues and swing Texas blues. *Dirty Boogie* followed in 1998, launching the hit "Jump Jive an' Wail." *—Richard Skelly*

The Knife Feels Like Justice / 1986 / Razor & Tie ♦♦♦♦
Upon disbanding the Stray Cats, Brian Setzer reinvented himself as a heartland rocker much in the vein of John Mellencamp or Bruce Springsteen; his solo debut, *The Knife Feels Like Justice*, possessed a maturity and depth largely lacking from his previous retro-rockabilly efforts, and although he was still too quick to succumb to rock clichés—there's actually a song here called "Boulevard of Broken Dreams"—moments like the hit title track and "Barbwire Fence" offered solid proof that behind all of his wildman posturing, there existed genuine talent as well. *—Jason Ankeny*

Live Nude Guitars / Feb. 1988 / EMI America ♦♦♦

The Brian Setzer Orchestra / 1994 / Hollywood ♦♦♦♦

Guitar Slinger / Apr. 1996 / Interscope ♦♦♦

● **The Dirty Boogie** / Jun. 23, 1998 / Interscope ♦♦♦♦
Evidently, Brian Setzer doesn't take the jump blues and swing of the Brian Setzer Orchestra as a joke. *Dirty Boogie* is his third album with his large band, and instead of sounding tired, the record is the group's best effort yet. Setzer rocks the band hard, tearing through blues and rock & roll covers with vigor, and delivering made-to-order originals that are surprisingly well-crafted and memorable. Much attention will be paid to "You're the Boss," a cover of the Elvis Presley/Ann Margaret staple from *Viva Las Vegas*, performed as a duet with No Doubt's Gwen Stefani, but that's hardly the only highlight here—it's a swinging, rocking record that suggests Setzer's skills are only improving with time. *—Stephen Thomas Erlewine*

Brian Setzer Collection: 1981-1988 / Nov. 16, 1999 / Capitol ♦♦♦

Vavoom! / Jun. 23, 2000 / Interscope ♦♦♦

The Sex Pistols

f. 1975, **db.** 1978
Group / British Punk, Punk
The Sex Pistols may have only been together for two years in the late '70s, but they changed the face of popular music, giving birth to the massive independent music underground in England and America. Through their raw, nihilistic singles and violent performances, the band revolutionized the idea of what rock & roll could be. In England, the group was considered dangerous to the very fabric of society and were banned across the country; in America, they didn't have the same impact, but countless bands in both countries were inspired by the sheer sonic force of their music, while countless others were inspired by their independent, do-it-yourself ethics. While the band—guitarist Steve Jones, drummer Paul Cook, and bassist Glen Matlock—played simple rock & roll loudly and abrasively, vocalist Johnny Rotten (b. John Lydon) arrogantly sang of anarchy, abortion, violence, fascism, and apathy; without Rotten, the band wouldn't have been threatening to England's government—he provided the band's conceptual direction, calculated to be as confrontational and threatening as possible. The publicity caused by their caustic first single "Anarchy in the U.K." caused the band to be dropped by their record label, EMI. Matlock was fired before their next single "God Save the Queen," which was released on Virgin; it was banned by the BBC. Matlock's replacement was Sid Vicious, a street tough kid who, unlike the rest of the band, couldn't play his instrument. After releasing one album—*Never Mind the Bollocks, Here's the Sex Pistols*—in 1977, the band headed to the U.S. for a tour in January 1978; it lasted just 14 days before the band imploded. Subsequently, an endless stream of outtakes, demos, repackagings, and live shows were released on a variety of labels. In 1996, the Sex Pistols reunited for an international tour, with original bassist Matlock taking the place of the deceased Sid Vicious; the *Filthy Lucre Live* album was released that summer. *—Stephen Thomas Erlewine*

★ **Never Mind the Bollocks, Here's the Sex Pistols** / Oct. 1977 / Warner Brothers ♦♦♦♦♦
While mostly accurate, dismissing *Never Mind the Bollocks* as merely a series of loud, ragged midtempo rockers with a harsh, grating vocalist and not much melody would be a terrible error. Already anthemic songs are rendered positively transcendent by Johnny Rotten's rabid, foaming delivery. His bitterly sarcastic attacks on pretentious affectation and the very foundations of British society were all carried out in the most confrontational, impolite manner possible. Most imitators of the Pistols' angry nihilism missed the point: Underneath the shock tactics and theatrical negativity were social critiques carefully designed for maximum impact. *Never Mind the Bollocks* perfectly articulated the frustration, rage, and dissatisfaction of the British working class with the establishment, a spirit quick to translate itself to strictly rock & roll terms. The Pistols paved the way for countless other bands to make similarly rebellious statements, but arguably none were as daring or effective. It's easy to see how the band's roaring energy, overwhelmingly snotty attitude, and Rotten's furious ranting sparked a musical revolution, and those qualities haven't diminished one bit over time. *Never Mind the Bollocks* is simply one of the greatest, most inspiring rock records of all time. *—Steve Huey*

The Great Rock & Roll Swindle / 1979 / Warner Brothers ♦♦♦♦♦
A wildly inconsistent but often entertaining collection, the soundtrack to the Pistols' pseudo-documentary contains great music, wacked-out novelties, and flat-out tripe in approximately equal proportions. Some formative recordings are included—mostly covers like "(I'm Not Your) Stepping Stone," plus a demo of "Anarchy in the U.K." that somehow manages to top the version on *Never Mind the Bollocks* in terms of raw rage and sheer power. "I Wanna Be Me" and a veiled chronicle of the band's breakup, "Silly Thing," are also necessary items. Devoted fans will enjoy the Black Arabs' disco medley of Pistols hits, a French version of "Anarchy in the U.K." complete with accordion, two tracks sung by loony Edward Tudor-Pole (later of Tenpole Tudor), and Sid Vicious's awful but strangely appropriate reading of Frank Sinatra's "My Way." *—Steve Huey*

Flogging a Dead Horse / 1980 / Virgin ♦♦♦♦
Flogging a Dead Horse collects the A- and B-sides of the Sex Pistols' seven British singles. It's not really the best way to hear those singles, though—there was a sharp decline in the quality and relevance of the Pistols' material when Johnny Rotten left the band, and some of the later goofiness dilutes the impact of early songs like "God Save the Queen" and "Anarchy in the U.K." It is a useful compilation in that two songs—"Did You No Wrong" and "No Fun"—are unavailable on both *Never Mind the Bollocks* and *The Great Rock & Roll Swindle*, and it is perfect for fans who don't want to sift through the latter and will be content with a brief overview. Still, *Dead Horse* doesn't match *Never Mind the Bollocks* (still the necessary purchase) for start-to-finish venom, and as inconsistent as *Swindle* is, it can be quite entertaining. So, *Flogging a Dead Horse* is not the best compilation, but it will do in some cases. *—Steve Huey*

We've Cum for Your Children / 1988 / Skyclad ♦♦♦

Filthy Lucre Live / Jul. 1996 / Caroline ♦♦♦

Ron Sexsmith

b. 1964
Vocals, Guitar (Acoustic) / Adult Alternative Pop/Rock, Singer/Songwriter
The earnest work of boyish Canadian singer/songwriter Ron Sexsmith won acclaim not from only critics but from fellow performers like Paul McCartney, Elvis Costello, and John Hiatt—some of the same artists, ironically enough, who initially inspired Sexsmith himself to become a musician. Born in 1964 and raised in the Niagara Falls area, he started his first band at the age of 14, and within a few years earned his first regular gig at an area club. Influenced by Pete Seeger, he began making the rounds on the folk circuit, but soon decided to focus his attentions on becoming a songwriter.

After moving to the Toronto area, Sexsmith formed the Uncool and began issuing his own material in 1985 with the cassette *Out of the Duff*, followed a year later by *There's a Way*. He continued performing while maintaining a day job as a courier, but did not release anything more until 1991's *Grand Opera Lane*, recorded by Blue Rodeo's Bob Wiseman. The collection of songs helped earn Sexsmith a songwriting contract, and eventually a recording deal, with Interscope Records; teamed with producer Mitchell Froom, he released his self-titled debut in 1995. A follow-up, *Other Songs*, appeared two years later. In 1999, Sexsmith returned with *Whereabouts*, again produced by Froom. *—Jason Ankeny*

● **Ron Sexsmith** / May 16, 1995 / Interscope ♦♦♦♦♦
Ron Sexsmith is so anti-cool that this may actually be one the coolest albums you hear. The Toronto singer-songwriter's appearance matches his music perfectly—hair falling in tousled bangs over doe eyes and baby face, one of those guys who always got beat up in high school and couldn't string two words together in front of a real live girl without stammering. A wide-eyed innocent, Sexsmith's eponymous release marries the wonder of Jonathan Richman with the darker atmosphere of a Daniel Lanois. Superficially, the songs are so sparsely childlike that you're tempted to wonder if Sexsmith is either a master of affectation or some kind of idiot savant. *—Roch Parisien*

Other Songs / Jun. 17, 1997 / Interscope ♦♦♦♦
Ron Sexsmith opens *Other Songs*, the follow-up to his 1995 self-titled debut, with the line "Thinking out loud is all I'm doing...", and his seemingly simple ruminations come across so pure and unadulterated that it actually seems at times as if you are eavesdropping on someone's thoughts. Some may, at first listen, want to dismiss Sexsmith's innocent lyrics as simply naive musings, but his beautiful melodies help reveal his subtle, lyrical charm. Like the child on the bus in his "Pretty Little Cemetery," who innocently tells the old man, "This

is where you go to when you die, my papa told me so," there's an underlying sweetness and sense of wonder in his songs, yet with a touch of darkness. Both the songs and the performances, with the help of Mitchell Froom and Tchad Blake's understated, sympathetic production, make their point without melodrama or histrionics. *Other Songs* is as strong and delightful a second effort as you could hope. *—Brett Hartenbach*

Whereabouts / May 18, 1999 / Interscope ♦♦♦♦
Ron Sexsmith's third album continues the singer/songwriter's talent—and perhaps his need—for revealing his delicate and contemplative reflections on life and himself. On *Whereabouts,* Sexsmith sounds vulnerable yet a bit more worldly than on his previous two albums, and his clear, plaintive vocals sound best on the most introspective tracks like "Riverbed," "The Idiot Boy" and "Doomed." The only minor flaw is the production—somewhat cold and soulless, it detracts from Sexsmith's intimacy instead of complementing it. *—Gina Boldman*

Phil Seymour

b. May 15, 1952, Tulsa, OK, **d.** Aug. 17, 1993, Tarzana, California
Vocals, Drums / Power Pop, New Wave
Phil Seymour is best remembered as one half of the creative force behind the Dwight Twilley Band, co-writing, with Dwight Twilley, some of the finest pop songs of the era, including the classic "I'm On Fire." After two albums (1976's *Sincerely* and 1978's *Twilley Don't Mind*), Seymour left to pursue a solo career. While waiting for a recording deal, he began recording solo sessions, as well as contributing session work for Tom Petty, 20/20, and Moon Martin. In 1980, he signed to Boardwalk Records after selling the label on a batch of demos recorded with fellow Tulsa natives 20/20. His self-titled debut was well received at the time (the single "Precious to Me" made it to number 22 on the pop charts) and has become highly revered in power-pop circles as one of the landmark albums of the era. He followed in 1982 with *Phil Seymour 2,* a less satisfying album both creatively and commercially. Seymour was left without a label when Boardwalk president Neil Bogart died shortly after the record's release. In 1984, he joined Carla Olsen's Textones, drumming and singing on their *Midnight Mission* album for A&M. While supporting the album, Seymour was diagnosed with lymphoma. He returned to Tulsa, carrying on at a diminished pace and recording infrequently, until the disease took his life in August of 1993 while he was preparing a new album. *—Chris Woodstra*

Phil Seymour / 1980 / Boardwalk ♦♦♦♦♦

2 / 1982 / Boardwalk ♦♦♦

● **Precious to Me** / Jun. 25, 1996 / The Right Stuff ♦♦♦♦♦
Precious to Me attempts to collect the many phases of Phil Seymour's all-too-brief career. The disc's 15 tracks cover his period as Dwight Twilley's partner, his solo work, a song he did with the Textones and a handful of rarities and stray tracks. And while it is certainly a welcome compilation of his long-out-of-print work on to compact disc, this collection could have been better. Considering Seymour's small cult of obsessive fans, the Twilley tracks are redundant—anyone who buys this collection undoubtedly has the Dwight Twilley discs already—and the absence of any songs from Seymour's second solo album is simply a disservice. Any of Seymour's recordings are pure pop fun so *Precious to Me* is good listen and for the uninitiated, this is a good enough starting point if only because so much of his work is unavailable. *—Chris Woodstra*

Shadows of Knight

f. 1964, Chicago, IL, **db.** 1969
Group / Garage Rock
"The Stones, Animals and Yardbirds took the Chicago Blues and gave it an English interpretation. We've taken the English version of the Blues and re-added a Chicago touch." The Shadows of Knight's self-description was fairly accurate. Although this mid-'60s garage band from the Windy City did not match the excellence of either their British or African-American idols, the teen energy of their recordings remains enjoyable, if not overwhelmingly original. The group took a tamer version of Them's classic "Gloria" into the American Top Ten in 1966, and also took a Yardbirdized version of Bo Diddley's "Oh Yeah" into the Top 40 the same year. Their patchy albums contained a few exciting R&B covers in the Yardbirds/Stones style and a few decent originals in the same vein. The group's original lineup splintered quickly, and the Shadows faded in the late '60s after briefly pursuing a more commercial pop sound. *—Richie Unterberger*

Gloria / 1966 / Sundazed ♦♦♦♦♦
Although revisionist historians will claim that any Shadows of Knight best-of that includes "Gloria" will cover just about everything you'll ever need on this Chicago punk band (and usually acting as if Van Morrison's and Them's original was the actual hit—Wrong!!), true believers have long championed their two original albums for the Dunwich label, especially their debut long player named after their big hit. Why? Simply because it positively rocks with a raw energy of a band straight out of the teen clubs, playing with a total abandon and an energy level that seems to explode out of the speakers. Equal parts Rolling Stones, Yardbirds, Who, and snotty little Chicago-suburb bad boys, the Shadows of Knight could easily put the torch to Chess blues classics, which make up the majority of the songs included here. Their wild takes on "I Just Want to Make Love to You," "Oh Yeah," and "I Got My Mojo Working" rank right up there with any British Invasion band's version from the same time period. Original material was never plentiful on either SOK long player, but worth checking out are "Light Bulb Blues," the blues ballad "Dark Side" and the why-me? rocker, "It Always Happens That Way." Completing the package is the inclusion of three bonus tracks, the single-only "Someone Like Me" and an alternate version, and "I Got My Mojo Working," which is vastly superior to the take on the original album. A not-too-vastly-different alternate mix of "Oh Yeah" completes the bonus tracks, although the original album version is curiously missing from this otherwise excellent package. Nonetheless, a reissue well worth adding to the collection. If you're only going to own one Shadows of Knight package, you could, and should, start right here. *—Cub Koda*

Back Door Men / 1967 / Sundazed ♦♦♦♦♦
The original LP version of this album, the second by the legendary white Chicago garage punk/blues outfit, was one of the most sought-after artifacts of mid-'60s punk rock. *Back Door Men* was a loud, feedback-laden, sneering piece of rock & roll defiance, mixing raunchy anthems to teenage lust ("Gospel Zone," "Bad Little Woman"), covers of Chicago blues classics (Willie Dixon's "Spoonful," Jimmy Reed's "Peepin' and Hidin'"), raga rock ("The Behemoth"), folk-rock ("Hey Joe," "Three for Love," "I'll Make You Sorry"), and a blues-punk grab off of commercial Top 40 ("Tomorrow's Gonna Be Another Day") all on one 12" platter. What makes the record even more startling is that every one of these tracks, however far afield they go from one another, works. The band strides across the music spectrum with a reach and boldness that most listeners usually only associate with the likes of the Beatles or the Rolling Stones, and a grasp that, for a moment here, may have exceeded either of those groups, as they slide from electric guitar into extended Chess-style blues instrumentals ("New York Bullseye"). *—Bruce Eder*

Gee-El-O-Are-I-Ay / 1985 / Edsel ♦♦♦♦♦

Raw 'N Alive at the Cellar, Chicago 1966! / 1992 / Sundazed ♦♦♦

● **Dark Sides: The Best of the Shadows of Knight** / Aug. 16, 1994 / Rhino ♦♦♦♦♦
More easily available to North Americans than the British Edsel best-of, but not necessarily an improvement. Adds some tracks from both the original lineup and their unimpressive, more pop-oriented singles from the late '60s, and has more comprehensive liner notes, but also omits a few decent covers that are on the U.K. compilation, particularly their smoking, over-the-top version of "I Just Want to Make Love to You." *—Richie Unterberger*

The Shaggs

f. 1969, **db.** 1975
Group / Obscuro, Alternative Pop/Rock, Novelty
One of the great stories of rock & roll is that of the three Wiggins sisters (Dot, Helen, and Betty), better known as the Shaggs. Growing up dirt poor in New Hampshire, the three girls were turned onto forming a band by their father, Austin Wiggins, buying their instruments and paying for lessons. Despite their lack of musical expertise, Austin drove the girls down to a studio in Massachusetts, determined to get them on tape "while they were still hot." Striking a deal with a local, fly by night record company called Third World, the Shaggs recorded their debut album, *Philosophy of the World,* in one day, recording a dozen tunes all written by Dot. One thousand copies were pressed and all but 100 of them quickly dispappeared, along with the president of the company. When Austin Wiggins passed away in 1975, the group disbanded and never played together again. But over the intervening years, their lone misguided attempt at recording started gaining cult status. In a *Playboy* magazine interview, Frank Zappa called *Philosophy of the World* his third all time favorite album and by the time NRBQ had reissued it in 1980, its legendary status was already confirmed, keeping the music of the Shaggs (which one can view as either guileless primitive art or just a garage band that *really* can't play or sing) alive. *—Cub Koda*

● **Philosophy of the World** / 1969 / RCA ♦♦♦♦♦
Supplanting the Rounder single disc that combined the group's original album with later sides, this brings the package back to its original form. It features the original mixes (the Rounder reissue used remixes), sequencing, cover and liner notes along with updated historical notes from producer Irwin Chusid. While a 12-song reissue that replaces a fuller and longer collection would seem like a beat for the money, this puts the Wiggins sisters' primitive attempt to make original rock & roll in its proper context. The guilelessness that permeates these performances is simply amazing, making a virtue out of artlessness. There's an innocence to these songs and their performances that's both charming and unsettling. Hacked-at drumbeats, whacked-around chords, songs that seem to have little or no meter to them ("My Pal Foot Foot," "Who Are Parents," "That Little Sports Car," "I'm So Happy When You're Near" are must-hears) being played on out-of-tune, pawn-shop-quality guitars all converge, creating dissonance and beauty, chaos and tranquility, causing any listener coming to this music to rearrange any pre-existing notions about the relationships between talent, originality, and ability. There is no album you might own that sounds *remotely* like this one. *—Cub Koda*

The Shangri-Las

f. 1963, Queens, NY, **db.** 1969
Group / Brill Building Pop, Girl Group, Rock & Roll
Along with the Shirelles and the Ronettes, the Shangri-Las were the greatest girl group; if judged solely on the basis of attitude, they were the greatest of them all. They combined an innocent adolescent charm with more than a hint of darkness, singing about dead bikers, teenage runaways, and doomed love affairs as well as ebullient high-school crushes. These could be delivered with either infectious, hand-clapping harmonies or melodramatic, almost operatic recitatives that were contrived but utterly effective. Tying it all together in the studio was Shadow Morton, a mad genius of a producer that may have been second in eccentric imagination only to Phil Spector in the mid-'60s. The quality of Morton's work with the Shangri-Las on Red Bird (with assistance from Jeff Barry and Artie Butler) was remarkable considering that he had virtually no prior experience in the music business. The group's material, so over-the-top emotionally that it sometimes bordered on camp, was lightened by the first-class production, which embroidered the tracks with punchy brass, weeping strings, and plenty of imaginative sound effects. Nowhere was this more apparent than on "Leader of the Pack," with its periodic motorcycle roars and crescendo of crashing glass. The death-rock classic became the Shangri-Las' signature tune, reaching number one. *—Richie Unterberger*

Remember the Shangri-Las at Their Best / Mar. 6, 1990 / Collectables ♦♦♦

● **Myrmidons of Melodrama** / 1994 / RPM ♦♦♦♦♦
Until the release of this import, there had never been a truly satisfactory Shangri-Las anthology; in fact, the group had been subject to worse piecemeal mangling than almost any other significant act of the '60s. This 33-track production finally sets the record straight, in-

cluding all of the significant A-sides, B-sides, and album tracks they recorded for Red Bird between 1964 and 1966, as well as an earlier single for a different label, and four radio commercials. It includes every one of their hits, but anyone who likes those will be enchanted by quite a few of their more obscure numbers here: "Dressed in Black," "Paradise," "It's Easier to Cry," "Never Again," and "Heaven Knows" are all first-class (if sometimes mordant). Not everything is up to that level, but enough is to make a case for them as one of the very best girl groups, and the good sound and thorough liner notes are significant bonuses. It may be more extensive and expensive than some fans wish, but don't settle for the numerous skimpy/rip-off domestic compilations, all of which manage to leave off some key tunes; this is the definitive document. *—Richie Unterberger*

● **The Best of the Shangri-Las** / Jun. 18, 1996 / Mercury/Chronicles ✦✦✦✦✦
This 25-song best-of actually covers most of their discography, containing all of the chart singles, and notable misses and B-sides like "Paradise" and "Dressed in Black." An excellent package, but the British *Myrmidons of Melodrama* (on RPM) is just a bit better, assembling a few more of their Red Bird tracks, including a couple of pretty notable ones ("It's Easier to Cry" and "The Boy") that this domestic anthology omits. The Mercury CD does have their rare (but unexceptional) final two singles, which don't appear on *Myrmidons of Melodrama.* *—Richie Unterberger*

Del Shannon (Charles Westover)

b. Dec. 30, 1934, Coopersville, MI, **d.** Feb. 8, 1990, Santa Clarita, CA
Vocals, Guitar / Teen Idol, Pop/Rock, Pop, Rock & Roll
One of the best and most original rockers of the early '60s, Del Shannon was also one of the least typical. Although classified at times as a teen idol, he favored brooding themes of abandonment, loss, and rejection. In some respects he looked forward to the British Invasion with his frequent use of minor chords and his ability to write most of his own material. His 1961 debut single "Runaway" was one of the greatest hits of the early '60s; with its unforgettable riffs, Shannon's amazing vocal range (which often glided off into a powerful falsetto), and the creepy, futuristic organ solo in the middle, it made number one on the pop charts. He became even more successful in England; he played some shows with the Beatles, and with 1963's "From Me to You," became the first American artist to cover a Beatles song.

A switch to a bigger label (Liberty), however, didn't bring the expected commercial results. He continued to evolve, developing a more baroque, orchestrated pop/rock sound on sessions with Rolling Stones producer Andrew Loog Oldham, though much to Shannon's frustration, Liberty decided not to release the material. Shannon began devoting his energy to production and became popular on the oldies circuit. An early-'80s album produced by Tom Petty got him into the Top 40 again with a cover of "Sea of Love," and he was working on another comeback album with Jeff Lynne when he unexpectedly killed himself in 1990, while on anti-depressant drugs. *—Richie Unterberger*

Little Town Flirt / 1963 / Rhino ✦✦✦

The Vintage Years / 1975 / Sire ✦✦✦✦✦
A very strong 28-track compilation of his best '60s work. Most fans will want to stick with *Greatest Hits,* but this more extensive (though out-of-print) overview goes deeper without much filler. Major advantages are its inclusion of material from both the earlier and later part of the decade (with emphasis on pre-1966 sides), and extensive liner notes by Greg Shaw. *—Richie Unterberger*

★ **Greatest Hits** / 1990 / Rhino ✦✦✦✦✦
Greatest Hits features 20 tracks from Del Shannon's early '60s heyday, including all of the big hits—"Runaway," "Hats off to Larry," "Little Town Flirt," "Handy Man," "Keep Searchin' (We'll Follow the Sun)," "Stranger in Town"—plus a generous selection of lesser-known but equally fine singles and album tracks. Completists should fill in the gaps with his neglected gem *I Go To Pieces,* but *Greatest Hits* remains a definitive retrospective from one of the finest pre-Beatles rockers of the '60s. *—Stephen Thomas Erlewine*

I Go to Pieces / 1990 / Edsel ✦✦✦✦✦
At the time this 16-song collection was put together at the end of the 1980s, it was intended to fill some major gaps in Del Shannon's CD and LP catalog, and Shannon himself appreciated the effort. He has since passed on, and, ironically, the major part of his catalog is now available on CD. Some of the songs on this collection, including the title track, are now available elsewhere, but some of the best, such as "You Never Talked About Me" (a catchy, dramatic love song that he sang in the movie *It's Trad, Dad*) and the gorgeous "Ginny in the Mirror" and "Don't Gild the Lily, Lily," are unique to *I Go to Pieces.* *—Bruce Eder*

The Liberty Years / Apr. 23, 1991 / EMI America ✦✦✦✦

1961-1990: A Complete Career Anthology / Jan. 27, 1998 / Raven ✦✦✦
To most casual listeners, Del Shannon was a one-hit (or, at best, two-hit) wonder. This two-CD anthology goes a long way toward correcting that inaccurate perception, covering virtually every high point in a career that, admittedly with some ups and downs, yielded some great and popular music across nearly 30 years. Every phase of the late singer-composer-guitarist's career is represented, and though "Runaway" is usually the only song associated with Shannon, this collection reveals many other sides to his work and sound, from the romantic Shannon original "Jody" to the defiant Pomus-Shuman song "Ginny in the Mirror."

The really good part about this set is that a lot of the songs appear here in their rare stereo mixes. With most classic rock & roll, that would not necessarily be a virtue, stereo being superfluous as well as harmful to its impact, but in Shannon's case it is—his records usually featured very busy, complex instrumental parts (an attribute that he shared in common with the Beatles and a lot of other British invasion acts) that can be discerned much more easily in the stereo versions. All of the bases are covered right up through his work in the late '60s with Andrew "Loog" Oldham and into the '70s and 1980s obscurities. His version of the Zombies' hit "Tell Her No" (cut for Island Records in the mid-'70s) and the Dave Edmunds-produced "And the Music Plays On" are represented, along with the results of his collaboration with Tom Petty and his comeback with the early-'80s NBC television series *Crime Story* (which returned "Runaway," used as the show's title theme, to the charts). As is usual with Raven Records, the annotation is extremely thorough and the mastering is impeccable. *—Bruce Eder*

Sandie Shaw (Sandra Goodrich)

b. Feb. 26, 1947, Dagenham, Essex, England
Vocals / Girl Group, British Invasion, Pop
British singer Sandie Shaw had a string of girl group-styled singles in the mid-'60s before she retired in the early '70s. Shaw was discovered by pop singer Adam Faith in 1963, who led her to his manager, Eve Taylor; she released her debut single, "As Long as You're Happy," the following year. It didn't hit the charts, yet her next record, "(There's) Always Something There to Remind Me," hit number one in the U.K. For the next three years, she had a string of hits—most of them written by her producer Chris Andrews—that kept her at the top of the charts. In 1967, Taylor began to move Shaw into cabaret territory; the approach proved a success when the song "Puppet on a String" hit number one. However, none of her further work with Andrews resulted in hit singles. Released in early 1969 her English version of the French "Monsieur Dupont" managed to crack the Top 20; it would turn out to be her last hit. Shaw returned to recording in the early '80s when BEF, a Heaven 17 side-project, prompted her to record "Anyone Who Had a Heart," an old Cilla Black hit. The Smiths' lead singer Morrissey began championing her in interviews, as well, which led her to record a version of the band's "Hand in Glove" supported by the Smiths themselves; the single briefly appeared on the U.K. charts. *—Stephen Thomas Erlewine*

Collection / 1990 / Castle ✦✦✦✦✦
Collection is an effective overview of Sandie Shaw's entire career, from her early hits to her '80s collaborations with the Smiths. It covers more ground than the double-disc *Complete,* but it doesn't have quite as much prime material. *—Stephen Thomas Erlewine*

● **64-67 Complete Sandie Shaw Set** / 1994 / Sequel ✦✦✦✦✦
A double-disc set that features all of her big hits as well as all of her minor ones, this provides the definitive portrait of the British girl group vocalist. *—Stephen Thomas Erlewine*

Nothing Less Than Brilliant: The Best of Sandie Shaw / 1995 / Virgin ✦✦✦✦✦
Most of Sandie Shaw's biggest hits are included on *Nothing Less than Brilliant,* but the collection tries to balance her '60s hits with her '80s comeback, which makes the disc somewhat inconsistent. Nevertheless, it is a good career portrait, featuring many of her finest moments. *—Stephen Thomas Erlewine*

Princess of Britpop / Aug. 10, 1999 / Castle Music America ✦✦✦✦

Jules Shear

b. Mar. 7, 1952, Pittsburgh, PA
Vocals, Guitar / College Rock, Adult Alternative Pop/Rock, Pop/Rock, Singer/Songwriter
Though he's never been able to record a hit of his own, singer/songwriter Jules Shear has recorded several albums of highly accessible, hit-worthy material, and as a testament to his abilities, he's penned hits for others including "All Through the Night" for Cyndi Lauper and "If She Knew What She Wants" for the Bangles. He relocated to Los Angeles in the mid-'70s, joining his first band, a typically laidback combo called the Funky Kings. The band released one album for Arista in 1976. Shear left the following year to form his own group, Jules & the Polar Bears, who released two critically acclaimed, though commercially overlooked, albums for Columbia. When a third album was rejected by the label, Shear forged on as a solo artist. Signing on to EMI-America, he released two solo albums, 1983's *Watch Dog* and 1985's *Eternal Return;* both received critical praise but few sales. Shear then formed the Reckless Sleepers with the Cars' Elliot Easton. In 1988, without Easton, the Reckless Sleepers released their sole album for IRS, *Big Boss Sounds;* it failed to make much impact though "If We Never Meet Again" from the album was later covered by Roger McGuinn. Shear teamed up with the Church's Marty Willson-Piper for an all acoustic, Dylanesque album, *The Third Party* in 1989. The album ultimately led to a spot on MTV, hosting the first 13 episodes of *Unplugged*—he left when the show switched to the single-artist format. *—Chris Woodstra*

Watch Dog / 1983 / EMI ✦✦✦✦✦
His first solo album following the breakup of the Polar Bears, *Watch Dog,* features a newfound maturity in songwriting with an eclectic mix of styles from ultra-smooth pop to R&B-inflected rockers. Shear sounds much more comfortable on his own, even under Todd Rundgren's heavy-handed production. Highlights include "All Through the Night" (a hit for Cyndi Lauper), "Whispering Your Name," and the the more experimental, Brian Wilson-inspired "Longest Drink." Another unjustified commercial sleeper. *—Chris Woodstra*

Eternal Return / 1985 / EMI America ✦✦✦
Seemingly unfazed by *Watch Dogs* failure, Shear again produces a slick, pop delight in *Eternal Return.* Shear explores a more soulful side in songs like "Steady" and the yearning "You're Not Around" while perfecting his hook-laden melodies. Despite being perfectly in line with the mid-'80s sound, this one also slipped through the cracks. The Bangles would later find a hit in the lead-off track, "If She Knew What She Wants." *—Chris Woodstra*

Demo-Itis / 1987 / Enigma ✦✦

The Third Party / 1989 / IRS ✦✦✦
Jules Shear joined up with the Church's Marty Willson-Piper in Sweden for *Third Party,* a stark, bare-bones acoustic album. Stripped of all of the excessive production that sometimes marred earlier work, Shear's songs are allowed to come to the forefront, as they should. Shear's voice, phrasing, and the minimalistic, often folky arrangements led to Dylan comparisons, but the album really features Shear's own clever craftsmanship; the back-to-basics approach is certainly a welcome one (as are the guitar chords included in the booklet). Shear had proven long before his strong melodic sense, but with *Third Party,* his clever wordplay and interesting turns of phrase were allowed the proper platform. Though the album failed commercially, the approach undoubtedly led to Shear's hosting the first several *MTV Unplugged* episodes, which gave him more exposure than ever before. *—Chris Woodstra*

The Great Puzzle / Jan. 28, 1992 / Polydor ✦✦✦✦✦
Jules Shear left behind several albums' worth of terrific music, from his earliest days with the Funky Kings to his work with Jules & the Polar Bears and on to a distinguished solo career. Even with tough competition, *The Great Puzzle* stands as Shear's high point, combining his never-failing gift of melody with tasteful, organic arrangements, highly personal yet universal lyrics, and probably his most consistent batch of songs to date. [Initial pressings of *The Great Puzzle* were packaged with a bonus disc, *Unplug This*, which had Shear reprise his best-known songs along with a couple from *The Great Puzzle* in a solo acoustic setting.] *—Chris Woodstra*

● **Horse of a Different Color (1976-1989)** / 1994 / Razor & Tie ✦✦✦✦✦
Horse of a Different Color collects tracks from all of the early phases of the sadly overlooked songwriter's career from 1976 to 1989, including "Nothing Was Exchanged" (a song that still stands as one of his finest moments) from the sole Funky Kings album, a couple of tracks each from the two released Jules & the Polar Bears albums, a handful from each of his proper solo albums up to 1989's *Third Party*, and the two high points from the short-lived Reckless Sleepers project. Since so much of his early output is long out of print, this collection is a welcome addition, and as a career summary, it's invaluable. Liner notes outlining Shear's ever-changing career would have been nice, but the sheer quality and consistency of music like this really speaks for itself. *—Chris Woodstra*

Healing Bones / Aug. 23, 1994 / Island ✦✦✦
While Shear's albums are always packed with craftsmanlike songwriting, the production and arrangements often end up dating them. What sets *The Healing Bones* apart from most of his back catalog is a certain timelessness of the sound. The songs are definitely among his finest. Includes a cover of the Walker Brothers' classic "The Sun Ain't Gonna Shine Anymore." *—Chris Woodstra*

Between Us / Feb. 24, 1998 / High Street ✦✦✦✦✦
Between Us is a duets album teaming Shear with a veritable who's who of singer/songwriters, from veterans like Carole King and Rosanne Cash to new-breed performers like Paula Cole, Freedy Johnston, Ron Sexsmith, and Amy Rigby. Shear, who has never received proper credit for his distinctive vocal style, is in particularly good voice, blending perfectly with his partner on each song. In a low-key, "unplugged" setting, Shear and company sing tales of heartache and troubled relationships, with Shear's acute eye for detail and evocative lyrics capturing the wide range of feelings with odd turns of phrase that manage to express a certain universality while avoiding obvious clichés. And despite the sparse, tasteful arrangements, the songs once again reveal Shear to be a rare master of melody—these are some of his finest yet, and despite the subject matter, they're extremely catchy. *—Chris Woodstra*

Allow Me / Apr. 25, 2000 / Rounder/Zoe ✦✦✦
Master pop craftsman Jules Shear is also one of the genre's great humanists: His clear-eyed takes on love, regret, and failure can be tenderhearted or scathing, but are never less than compassionate. *Allow Me*, his first recording for Rounder Records, finds Shear back in solo mode after 1998's collection of duets, *Between Us*. Like that record, *Allow Me* is a collection of love songs, but the mood here is comparatively optimistic. Shear's melodies are as catchy and his lyrics as sharp as ever, especially on "Nothing Is New" and the opener, "Hard Enough," one of Shear's patented wake-up calls to a troubled friend; he's also in fine, relaxed vocal form. But *Allow Me* is not Shear's strongest overall effort: "Deep" and "Love With You" are unexceptional bar-band rockers, and the latter features flashy backing vocals that are singularly at odds with his down-to-earth persona. The album is also less cohesive than some of his other works, and some songs are obscured by clunky arrangements. Still, even lesser Jules Shear is a gift to fans of intelligent pop. *—Kristi Coulter*

The Shirelles

f. 1958, Passaic, NJ, **db.** 1982
Group / Brill Building Pop, Girl Group
The Shirelles were instrumental in defining the girl-group sound, and were one of the style's most successful acts between 1960 and 1963, when they placed six singles in the Top Ten. Bridging doo wop and uptown New York pop-soul, the group projected a beguiling mixture of tenderness and innocence that was grounded in R&B as much as pop/rock. Forming as high school classmates in New Jersey, the Shirelles came under the wing of manager Florence Greenberg, who also ran the Scepter label. Many of their classic early sides featured innovative, occasionally string-laden production by Luther Dixon, who also penned several of their greatest songs. Top Brill Building songwriters like Goffin-King, Bacharach-David, and Van McCoy also supplied the group with material. "Will You Love Me Tomorrow," "Baby It's You," "Foolish Little Girl," "Soldier Boy," "Dedicated to the One I Love," and "Mama Said" were their biggest hits, but they also cut a number of delightful less famous sides, including "Boys," which (like "Baby It's You") was covered by the Beatles on their first LP. After mid-1963, the Shirelles were unable to dent the Top 40, although they recorded some excellent songs, including the original version of "Sha La La" (covered for a hit by Manfred Mann). The group recorded well into the '70s, updating their sound into a more soul-oriented mode that was lacking in comparison. *—Richie Unterberger*

Baby It's You / 1962 / Sundazed ✦✦✦
The best songs on here—the title track, "Big John," "A Thing of the Past," "Make the Night a Little Longer," "Soldier Boy," and "Putty in Your Hands"—are available on the Rhino best-of double album. Still, it's a pretty solid effort for its day, featuring state-of-the-art orchestral early-'60s New York girl group production and decent songwriting. *—Richie Unterberger*

A Shirelles & King Curtis Give a Twist Party / 1962 / Sundazed ✦✦✦
A rather strange concept for an early-'60s album, pairing the Shirelles, then at the peak of their success, with R&B/soul sax great King Curtis. It's not so much a collaboration as an alternation; Curtis gets three instrumentals to himself, and sings "I Got a Woman" and another cut. Curtis does duet with the girls on "I Still Want You," and the Shirelles handle the rest of the material, mostly written by their chief producer/songwriter Luther Dixon, in a much more up-tempo vein than their famous singles. No hits on this record, which is respectable but not terribly exciting, and a bit schizo in concept. *—Richie Unterberger*

Anthology (1959-1964) / 1986 / Rhino ✦✦✦✦✦
In the course of eight years, Rhino came out with two separate but very similar Shirelles anthologies. The first was 1986's *Anthology: 1959-1964*, followed by *The Very Best of the Shirelles* in 1994. Both are 16-song CDs, and many of the essential hits that were included on *Very Best* were also found on this CD, including "Tonight's The Night," "Dedicated to the One I Love," "Mama Said," and "Will You Love Me Tomorrow" (as well as "Boys," "A Thing of the Past," "Soldier Boy," and "Big John"). The main reason *Very Best Of* has a slight edge over this disc is because of its inclusion of the 1958 doo wop classic "I Met Him on a Sunday (Ronde-Ronde)," which is missing from *Anthology*. Both CDs, however, are full of gems that would greatly influence countless girl groups. These songs were undeniably seminal, and the late-1950s/early-1960s harmonies of the Shirelles would directly or indirectly influence everyone from The Supremes, The Marvelettes, The Shangri-Las and Martha & the Vandellas in the 1960s to LaBelle, First Choice, the Three Degrees and The Pointer Sisters in the 1970s. How many groups who influenced The Go-Gos and Blondie also had an impact on En Vogue— The importance of the Shirelles hits found on this CD cannot be overstated. *—Alex Henderson*

Lost & Found / Dec. 1, 1995 / Ace ✦✦

★ **25 All-Time Greatest Hits** / Jul. 27, 1999 / Varese ✦✦✦✦✦
An excellent 26-song single-disc collection that has all of the significant hits, and several very fine low-charting 45s and B-sides. Some good tracks are missing, however, notably "Putty" (which the Yardbirds covered) and Goffin-King's "Make the Night a Little Longer." Rhino's *Anthology* double LP still has a tiny edge in song selection if you can find it, but if you're not real picky this is certainly a quality summary of their career highlights. There are also a few items that don't show up on all the best-ofs, like the 1961 B-side "The Things I Want to Hear" and the small 1964 hit "Thank You, Baby." *—Richie Unterberger*

Shirley & Lee

f. 1951, New Orleans, LA, **db.** 1963
Group / New Orleans R&B, R&B
Shirley Goodman and Leonard Lee, born just ten days apart in 1936, scored three massive R&B hits before either one of them were both twenty years old: "Feel So Good," "Let The Good Times Roll" and "I Feel Good" were all written by the talented young couple.

They had one trait common among their recordings; this New Orleans-based duo almost never sang in harmony, let alone together at all. Their contrasting male-female duet style was later influential on early ska and reggae productions from Jamaica.Shirley & Lee recorded extensively for Eddie Messner and Leo Messner's L.A.-based Aladdin label. The Messners—along with former NBC radio exec Lew Chudd's Imperial Records and Art Rupe's Specialty—seemed to have a knack for signing talent straight out of the Crescent City.

Shirley & Lee's debut single, "I'm Gone" was written and produced by Dave Bartholomew, Imperial's writer/arranger/producer/A&R man and a major contributor to New Orleans-style R&B acts. (It was Bartholomew's production work with Fats Domino, which utilized that talents of a great house band—pianist Allen Toussaint, bassist Frank Fields, drummer Earl Palmer, and saxophonists Lee Allen, Red Tyler and Herb Hardesty —that elevated nearly everything he worked on to 'legendary' status). With their backing "I'm Gone" went on to become a major R&B hit in the fall of 1952.

Early in their careers, Shirley & Lee became known as "The Sweethearts of the Blues," a nickname given not for their personal relationship, but for their romantic sagas of their songs, which often bordered on telling a fictitional soap opera storyline about two lovers. Their fans would buy the singles simply to keep up with the continuing story of the two sweethearts. The story continued with the very next single, "Shirley Come Back To Me," a heartbreaker released in early 1953, followed by "Shirley's Back" later that year. This happy theme continued through the happy-ending for the next single, "The Proposal" b/w "Two Happy People."

By the end of the year, Aladdin were reveling in success of the story of Shirley & Lee. Of course, the couple in the songs had already been apart and were now back together, so they had to shake things up with the next release, called "Lee Goofed," and followed that with "Confessin'," but by now, the audience seemed to be tiring of the soap opera so Shirley & Lee moved on to new lyrical subject matter.

Messner decided to try something new for the duo in May of 1955, issuing a medium tempo rocker, called "Feel So Good." The song featured full vocal group backup (reportedly by the Spiders), and did well, but it was the bluesy b-side, "You'd Be Thinking Of Me" that put the duo back on the R&B hit charts. "Lee's Dream" also charted. In early 1956, Aladdin released the duo's slow blues ballad, "A Little Word," which received good airplay but sales weren't spectacular. Trying to get back on track, Aladdin finally opted to issue a full-length album, *Let The Good Times Roll*, in December. It was re-issued two years later on Score, Aladdin's budget label.

By the middle of 1957, Shirley & Lee were back on top, this time with the biggest hit in their careers. Goodman and Lee borrowed one of N' Orleans' most familiar refrains and built a rocking tune around it called "Let The Good Times Roll." The recording was an instant smash and received substantial airplay, climbing up the charts in the process. It sold well over one million copies, and for more than forty years, has been a staple of oldies playlists. To date, there are over a hundred cover versions of the song, but most still prefer the original.

The pair stayed on Aladdin into 1959 before moving to Warwick, where they ended up re-recording "Let The Good Times Roll." Other tunes followed—"I Feel Good" and "The Flirt" among them—but like many acts, Shirley & Lee were never able to recapture the nationwide success of their biggest hit. After a few final singles in 1962-1963, this time for Imperial—Aladdin and Imperial continued their rivalry and tried to one-up each other until Aladdin was acquired by Imperial outright—the "Sweethearts of the Blues" decided to call it a day.

In 1974, Shirley Goodman reappeared on the R&B scene, this time paired with studio musicians— they called themselves Shirley and Company—for "Shame, Shame, Shame" released on the Vibration label. (The song also featured Jesus Alvarez supplying lead vocals). The disco-fied hit topped the R&B charts at number one that summer and peaked at #12 on the Pop charts. It was written by producer Sylvia Robinson, who had also been part of a successful '50s duo, Mickey & Sylvia, with Mickey Baker. Robinson also penned Goodman's less successful follow-up "Cry, Cry, Cry." They issued one more single on Vibration, then dropped out of sight.

Leonard Lee passed away on October 23, 1976. *—Bryan Thomas*

Legendary Masters Series, Vol. 1 / Mar. 16, 1990 / EMI America ♦♦♦♦♦

● **Let the Good Times Roll** / May 2, 2000 / Ace ♦♦♦♦♦
The track listing of this 30-song disc is based on the 1973 double-LP Shirley & Lee compilation in United Artists' *Legendary Masters* series, with "I Feel Good" substituted for "Do You Mean to Hurt Me So." Spanning their 1952-59 work for Aladdin, it's comprehensive enough to serve as a best-of, particularly as it included the four songs that are by far their most famous cuts: "Let the Good Times Roll," "I'm Gone," "I Feel Good," and "Feel So Good." As the American best-of CD compilation *Legendary Masters* (issued first on EMI America, then on Collectables) has only 20 numbers, one might presume that this 30-track anthology has the edge. It doesn't make the *Legendary Masters* CD redundant, though, as *Legendary Masters* has seven songs that don't appear here. At any rate, *Let the Good Times Roll* will almost certainly be a sufficient overview of the duo's prime output for those who haven't picked up a Shirley & Lee greatest hits anthology yet. Truth to tell, for most listeners 30 Shirley & Lee songs is more than enough, as the accomplished, good-timey New Orleans R&B/rock groove gets pretty similar-sounding over the course of an hour-plus. One thing you could note is how the contrasting male-female duet style of Shirley & Lee was influential on early ska and reggae productions from Jamaica; listen to "Marry Me" for one instance in which Shirley & Lee themselves played calypso/Caribbean rhythms. It's also interesting to note that almost all of the material on this disc was self-penned, an impressive feat for teenage R&B singers of the '50s. *—Richie Unterberger*

Michelle Shocked

b. Feb. 24, 1962, Dallas, TX
Vocals, Guitar/College Rock, Alternative Folk, Anti-Folk, Alternative Pop/Rock, Singer/Songwriter, Urban Folk
According to her own, undoubtedly semi-fictional account, Michelle Shocked was born Michelle Johnston in Dallas, TX, in 1962, where she spent her early childhood travelling around army bases. After being introduced to country bluesmen Big Bill Broonzy and Leadbelly and contemporary songwriters Guy Clark and Randy Newman, she spent the next several years exploring the folk underground, spending the early '80s in Austin, where she began honing her own songwriting skills. The next few years were chaotic—she spent time in San Francisco, Amsterdam, New York, and was briefly committed to a mental hospital by her mother.

In 1986, Shocked attended the Kerrville Folk Festival, where English producer Pete Lawrence was impressed by her campfire-side playing and recorded her on his Sony Walkman. The recordings surfaced in the fall of that year as *The Texas Campfire Tapes* and became a surprise hit in England, eventually topping the independent charts. The success led to her signing with Mercury Records in 1988. *Short Sharp Shocked*, displayed even more talent, combining the informal, tradition-rooted folkiness of *The Texas Campfire Tapes* with a strong post-modern feminist perspective and punk attitude. In an unexpected move, Shocked returned in 1989 with *Captain Swing*, a '40s-style big-band swing outing that shocked her fans initially but had no shortage of strong material. In 1992, she took something of a step back with *Arkansas Traveller*, a rootsy collection that covered all forms of early American, homegrown music. In 1993, Mercury finally became fed up with her confusing style jumping and refused to release her proposed gospel album. She then left on a solo tour, selling her newly recorded, independently produced, *Kind Hearted Woman*. Late in 1995, Shocked began legal action against Mercury Records to break her contract.

By 1996, Shocked was released from Mercury and another independent release, *Artists Make Lousy Slaves*, was sold at her shows. *Kind Hearted Woman* was picked up for release by Private Music in 1996. *—Chris Woodstra*

The Texas Campfire Tapes / 1986 / Mercury ♦♦♦

★ **Short Sharp Shocked** / 1988 / Mercury ♦♦♦♦♦
Michelle Shocked is asked in the song "Anchorage," "What's it like to be a [New York City] skateboard punk rocker?" Perhaps it takes a flashback like *Short Sharp Shocked* to fully answer the more interesting question, "How did you get there?" The album finds Shocked taking a semi-fond trip back to an East Texas childhood, and all of the defined roles, limited expectations, claustrophobia, and ultimate rebellion coming from that environment. Musically, she tackles the spectrum of rootsy folk in a warm way that shows not only a love for, but also a great deal of knowledge of the forms (producer Pete Anderson added a Nashville gloss to the recordings that shouldn't go unnoticed). The songs have a very personal, almost diary feel, but at the same time, they speak a universal language—none so poignant as the album's centerpiece, "Anchorage," a touching letter from an old friend. The cover photo, which shows Shocked restrained by police officers during a protest, indicates little about the music found within (save for the uncredited album closer, the hardcore punk work-up of "Fog Town" featuring MDC), but the music certainly reveals much about the protestor. *—Chris Woodstra*

Captain Swing / Oct. 1989 / Mercury ♦♦♦
Shocked made a big jump from *The Texas Campfire Tapes* to *Short Sharp Shocked*, but no one expected the direction she would take for *Captain Swing*. Rather than continuing as a folky singer-songwriter, she opted instead to take on '40s swing and big-band music, complete with horn-heavy arrangements and bright orchestration. And although the cartoon image of her on the cover gives a smirk and a sly wink, the album is surprising devoid of irony. She treats the genre with affection, and she's obviously having a good time swinging. *Captain Swing* may have confused fans of *Short Sharp Shocked* (and the material isn't nearly as consistently strong either), but the album has several great moments, and most of all, it offers a good time. *—Chris Woodstra*

Arkansas Traveler / Oct. 1991 / Mercury ♦♦♦♦
Part three of the trilogy that began with *Short Sharp Shocked*, *Arkansas Traveler* focuses this time on American roots music of the South, mainly rural-blues and country; according to her theory in the album's liner notes, all of these songs are based on the legacy of blackface minstrels. Recorded with a mobile studio at various non-conventional locations around the country, it features an amazing array of guest musicians including Pops Staples, Doc Watson, and Gatemouth Brown. Those who were put off by the unexpected direction of *Captain Swing* will certainly welcome this return to form—her best since *Short Sharp Shocked*. *—Chris Woodstra*

Kind Hearted Woman / 1994 / Private Music ♦♦♦
Shocked released *Kind Hearted Woman* on her own, selling it exclusively at live shows, when she ran into troubles with Mercury Records. Accompanied by only her own Stratocaster playing, she has produced her most touching, personal document to date even though the subject matter is decidedly dark and bleak. Private Music reissued the album in 1996. *—Chris Woodstra*

Artists Make Lousy Slaves / 1996 / Independent ♦♦♦

Mercury Poise: 1988-1995 / Nov. 5, 1996 / Mercury ♦♦♦♦♦
With a title that plays on Graham Parker's corporate-venomous song and EP *Mercury Poisoning*, the disc skims a dozen layers of feminist-folk-punk cream from three eclectic albums (folk-rock, swing-jazz, and Southern roots music) recorded for the label between 1988 and 1991, plus tracks previously only available on soundtracks, compilations, and 1994 indie release *Kind Hearted Woman*. *—Roch Parisien*

Shoes

f. 1975, Zion, IL
Group / Power Pop, New Wave
It may not have been the hip thing to do at the time, but Shoes carried on the pure pop traditions of the Beatles and the Raspberries during the late '70s and early '80s with a charming innocence and execution unmatched by the more derivative bands lumped into the category "power pop." After one self-made and extremely limited album (only 300 were pressed), 1975's *Un Dans Versalles*, and the unreleased *Bazooka* (1976), they recorded their true debut for national consumption, *Black Vinyl Shoes* and released it on their own label, Black Vinyl Records. Though it was barely distributed, enough critics and key people heard the record to start a word-of-mouth buzz. Eventually, Greg Shaw, the head of Bomp! Records, heard the record and arranged for the band to release one single, the brilliant "Tommorrow Night"/"Okay," on his label. A contract with Elektra Records soon followed. Elektra released the group's next three, textbook power-pop albums: *Present Tense* (1979), *Tongue Twister* (1981), and *Boomerang* (1982). Despite the instantly accessible, catchy quality of the songs, they were unable to achieve mainstream success—among specialists, however, these albums, along with the debut, stand as the high points of the era. *—Chris Woodstra*

Black Vinyl Shoes / 1977 / Black Vinyl ♦♦♦♦♦
A homemade demo that became their first national release, this is a dazzling collection of pop songs driven by thick sheets of guitar and warm, emotive singing. *—John Dougan*

Present Tense / 1979 / Elektra ♦♦♦♦♦
Their major-label debut suffers from a bit of overwhelming post-production, but there isn't enough interference to ruin this great collection of tunes. The CD version is a two-fer which combines *Present Tense* with *Tongue Twister*. *—John Dougan*

Tongue Twister / 1981 / Elektra ♦♦♦

Boomerang/Shoes on Ice / May 1982 / Black Vinyl ♦♦♦♦♦

Silhouette / 1984 / Black Vinyl ♦♦♦
Now reduced to a three-piece (John Murphy, Jeff Murphy, and Gary Klebe), the band recorded their fifth album independently in their home studio in Illinois. A pleasant, though unexceptional album, *Silhouette* is a softer, more keyboard-dominated effort. Without an American outlet (they left Elektra prior to recording), this album was only available in Europe until the band's own label, Black Vinyl Records, reissued it in the late '80s. *—Chris Woodstra*

● **Shoes' Best** / 1987 / Black Vinyl ♦♦♦♦♦
A 22-song compilation, this is a wonderfully comprehensive overview of this wonderful band. Good liner notes by former *Trouser Press* head honcho Ira Robbins. *—John Dougan*

Stolen Wishes / 1989 / Black Vinyl ♦♦

Propeller / 1994 / Black Vinyl ♦♦

Fret Buzz / May 2, 1995 / Black Vinyl ♦♦♦

As Is / 1996 / Black Vinyl ♦♦♦♦
The limited edition, two disc *As Is* is simply a delight for die-hard Shoes fans. Boasting a disc of 27 demos and unreleased tracks as well as the ultra-rare *Bazooka* and *One in Versailles* albums in their entirety—both released before their official debut, *Black Vinyl Shoes*—and a detailed booklet, this collection works well not only as a rarities collection but also as a testament to the band's power-pop legacy. *—Chris Woodstra*

The Showmen

f. 1960, **db.** 1968
Group / Pop-Soul, Northern Soul, New Orleans R&B, Soul
The Showmen were one of the R&B groups to bridge the gap between doo-wop and soul in the early '60s, creating a buoyant, energetic fusion of harmonies and propulsive R&B beats. Released in the fall of 1961, their debut "It Will Stand" was a hit, particularly on the East Coast and in the New Orleans era, but it only peaked at number 61 on the pop charts. Nevertheless, the song's popularity never decreased, and it became a hit three years later, when re-released on the Imperial label. On its second release, the single peaked at number 80 on both the R&B and pop charts. Between the two chart appearances of "It Will Stand," the Showmen kept recording and performing. During this time, they had no national hits, but

"39-21-46" became a significant regional hit. In 1965, the group signed with Swan Records, but none of the ensuing singles became hits. In 1968, lead singer General Johnson left the band and moved to Detroit, where he formed the Chairmen of the Board. *—Stephen Thomas Erlewine*

• **It Will Stand** / Apr. 24, 1990 / Collectables ✦✦✦✦✦
A nice collection featuring the stuttering, sputtering vocals of General Norman Johnson and company, otherwise known as the Showmen. The title track was one of the great pieces of rock and R&B testimony. They never quite equaled it, although they produced some fine ballads and good uptempo tunes. "It Will Stand" wasn't a hit the first time out of the box; it didn't make it onto the R&B charts until 1964, three years after it had peaked at number 61 on the pop charts, and then it only reached number 80. *—Ron Wynn*

Silver Apples

f. 1967, New York, NY
Group / Obscuro, Experimental Rock, Proto-Punk, Psychedelic, Electronic
Decades after their brief yet influential career first ground to a sudden and mysterious halt, the Silver Apples remain one of pop music's true enigmas: a surreal, almost unprecedented duo, their music explored interstellar drones and hums, pulsing rhythms and electronically-generated melodies years before similar ideas were adopted in the work of acolytes ranging from Suicide to Spacemen 3 to Laika. The Silver Apples formed in New York in 1967 and comprised percussionist Danny Taylor and lead vocalist Simeon, a bizarre figure who played an instrument also dubbed the Simeon, which (according to notes on the duo's self-titled 1968 debut LP) consisted of "nine audio oscillators and eighty-six manual manual controls.... The lead and rhythm oscillators are played with the hands, elbows and knees and the bass oscillators are played with the feet." Although the utterly uncommercial record—an ingenious cacophony of beeps, buzzes, and beats—sold poorly, the Silver Apples resurfaced a year later with their sophomore effort, *Contact*, another far-flung outing which fared no better than its predecessor. After the record's release, the duo seemingly vanished into thin air, perhaps returning to the alien world from whence they purportedly came; however, in 1996 the Silver Apples mysteriously resurfaced, as Simeon and new partner Xian Hawkins released the single "Fractal Flow." American and European tours followed, and a year later a new LP, *Beacon*, was released to wide acclaim. The follow-up *Decatur* appeared in 1998, and was soon joined by *A Lake of Teardrops* (a collaboration with avowed fans Spectrum) as well as *The Garden*, the long-unreleased third and final effort from the original Simeon/Taylor partnership. However, on November 1, 1998, the Silver Apples' van crashed while returning from a New York gig; the accident left Simeon with a broken neck and spinal injuries, casting his continued musical career in grave doubt. *—Jason Ankeny*

• **Silver Apples** / 1997 / MCA ✦✦✦✦✦
The group's two '60s albums (*Silver Apples* and *Contact*) were previously combined as a two-fer a few years before this identical release, but as this is on a major label, it will find wider distribution. It also benefits from the addition of newly penned historical liner notes from Simeon, and vintage photos of the band, along with a diagram of the Simeon (the instrument) and Taylor's drum setup. *—Richie Unterberger*

The Silver Jews

f. 1992, VA
Group / Indie Rock, Alternative Pop/Rock, Singer/Songwriter
Writer/musician David Berman formed the Silver Jews in 1989 with his friends, guitarist/singer Stephen Malkmus and drummer Bob Nastanovich. They played noisy, often improvised songs, mostly for the sheer enjoyment they got out of playing together after a hard day's work, often recording songs into people's answering machines; this basic idea of friends playing together in a spontaneous way became the Silver Jews' trademark style. Malkmus then founded Pavement with his childhood friend Scott Kannberg. As Pavement's acclaim and visibility grew, the notion arose that the Silver Jews were a "Pavement side-project," despite the fact Berman's writing, singing, and guitar playing led the band's music. However, the Jews' sometimes frustrating "Pavement connection" did bring some important attention to the band: Dan Koretsky, founder of the Chicago-based indie label Drag City, met Berman at a Pavement show; when he heard of the Jews' tapes, Koretsky offered to release them. On their first EPs for the label, 1990's *Dime Map of the Reef* and 1992's *The Arizona Record*, the band held to their ultra low-fi aesthetic and recorded both mostly on a walkman. Berman recorded the Jews' third album *The Natural Bridge* in the summer of 1996 with members of New Radiant Storm King and Drag City artist/producer Rian Murphy. 1998's *American Water* featured a kind of reunion of the original lineup, with Malkmus returning to the fold. *—Heather Phares*

The Arizona Record [EP] / 1993 / Drag City ✦✦✦

• **Starlite Walker** / Oct. 24, 1994 / Drag City ✦✦✦✦✦
Starlite Walker is a first for the Silver Jews on many levels. Not only is it the group's first full-length album, it's also the first recorded in a full-fledged studio—Memphis' 24-track Easley Recordings—as well as the first collection of songs penned almost entirely by Berman. The album's lyrical and musical richness comes partly from Berman's retreat to the woods of Oxford, MS in preparation for the record, and partly from the understated, intimate production. As a result, *Starlite Walker* collects some of the Jews' most diverse and affecting songs. Wry lyrics like "I just got back from a dream attack" from "Trains Across the Sea" and "On the last day of your life/Don't forget to die" from "Advice to the Graduate" let Berman's easygoing charm come to the front, while jangly and crunchy guitars, Malkmus' backing vocals, and Nastanovich's steady drumming punctuate his observations.

Though *Starlite Walker* is a more low-key, reflective affair than the Silver Jews' EPs, the album benefits from it, combining the laid-back experimentalism of the Jews' early work with more sophisticated and expressive songwriting. "Advice to the Graduate" and "New Orleans" turn from humorous to poignant with a simple chord change; "Rebel Jew" draws on the group's affection for country music; and instrumentals like "The Moon is Number 18" and "The Silver Pageant" add to the relaxed, homespun feel of the album. Repeated listening just enhances *Starlite Walker's* warm, off-the-cuff appeal. *—Heather Phares*

The Natural Bridge / Oct. 1, 1996 / Drag City ✦✦✦✦
The Silver Jews' 1996 recording, *The Natural Bridge* continues the band's shift from their early, sprawling racket into a smooth foil for David Berman's laid-back vocals and evocative lyrics. When sessions with original Jews Stephen Malkmus and Bob Nastanovich and with members of the Scud Mountain Boys didn't work out the way Berman hoped, they were scrapped; the final version of *The Natural Bridge* was recorded in the summer of 1996 at Hartford, Connecticut's Studio .45, which was originally a gun factory.

New Radiant Storm King's Peyton Pinkerton and Matt Hunter, Drag City producer/session man Rian Murphy, and keyboardist Michael Deming joined Berman in this version of the Jews' lineup, resulting in a more spacious sound than on any of the group's previous recordings. *The Natural Bridge* is also darker than the band's previous work, with lyrics like "I think we may be losing now/Please guard my bed" from "Pet Politics" and "Burnout tramp/Waits by the ramp/For one more car" from "Ballad of Reverend War Character." However, this darkness blends and contrasts with the wry, wistful "Dallas" and "Pretty Eyes." "The Frontier Index" combines jokes and a beautiful, descending guitar line for a really nice mix of ideas and emotion. Though *The Natural Bridge* lacks some of the immediacy of the Jews' earlier work, and Berman's voice slips into a monotone occasionally, this album offers some of the Silver Jews' finest moments. *—Heather Phares*

American Water / Oct. 20, 1998 / Drag City ✦✦✦✦✦
American Water, the Silver Jews' third full-length release, reunites David Berman and Stephen Malkmus and adds new members Mike Fellows, Tim Barnes, and Chris Stroffolino. Named after a poster Berman saw at his veterinarian's office for American Water Spaniels, the album boasts some of the Jews' best arrangements and playing, from the flute and brass-tinged "Random Rules" to the driven but eloquent guitars on "Night Society" to the wah-wah friendly, '70s-style pop of "People."

American Water also varies in tempo and mood more than any Silver Jews album since *Starlite Walker*. "Send in the Clouds" and "Smith & Jones Forever" gallop along, while "We Are Real" and "The Wild Kindness" stroll. Though most of the album's lyrics aren't as personal as those on *The Natural Bridge*, they still feature Berman's detailed wit, like this couplet from "People": "The drums march along at the clip of an IV drip/Like sparks from a muffler dragged down the strip." The tight, sunny-sounding production sparkles on songs like "Honk If You're Lonely Tonight," and Berman and Malkmus' twin vocals brighten songs like "Blue Arrangements" and "Federal Dust." As with all of the Jews' best work, *American Water* sounds like it was made for the band's own enjoyment, and the listener is just eavesdropping on their fun. *—Heather Phares*

Simon & Garfunkel

f. 1964, New York, NY, **db.** 1970
Group / Folk-Rock, Pop
The most successful folk-rock duo of the 1960s, Paul Simon and Art Garfunkel crafted a series of memorable hit albums and singles featuring their choirboy harmonies, ringing acoustic and electric guitars, and Simon's acute, finely wrought songwriting. Simon & Garfunkel's early albums were erratic, but they steadily improved as Simon sharpened his songwriting, and as the duo became more comfortable and adventurous in the studio. Their execution was so clean and tasteful that it cost them some hipness points during the psychedelic era, which was a bit silly. They were far from the raunchiest thing going, but managed to pull off the nifty feat of appealing to varying segments of the pop and rock audience—and various age groups, not just limited to adolescents—without compromising their music. *Parsley, Sage, Rosemary and Thyme* (late 1966) was their first really consistent album; *Bookends* (1968), which actually blended previously released singles with some new material, reflected their growing maturity. One of its songs, "Mrs. Robinson," became one of the biggest singles of the late '60s after it was prominently featured in one of the best films of the period, *The Graduate* (which also had other Simon & Garfunkel songs on the soundtrack). Their final studio album, *Bridge Over Troubled Waters*, was an enormous hit, topping the charts for ten weeks, and containing four hit singles (the title track, "The Boxer," "Cecilia," and "El Condor Pasa"). It was certainly their most musically ambitious, with "Bridge Over Troubled Waters" and "The Boxer" employing thundering drums and tasteful orchestration, and "Cecilia" marking one of Simon's first forays into South American rhythms. It also caught the confused, reflective tenor of the times better than almost any other popular release of 1970. *—Richie Unterberger*

Wednesday Morning, 3 A.M. / Oct. 1964 / Columbia ✦✦
This is something of a folk sampler, circa 1964. Only five of the 12 songs were written by Paul Simon, and they include the mournful "He Was My Brother," which Garfunkel, in his liner notes, accurately says is "cast in the Bob Dylan mold" and has "no subtlety." But "The Sounds Of Silence," here in its original acoustic version, is the first Paul Simon song in the mature sense. And the album also contains such early '60s folk standards as Ed McCurdy's "Last Night I Had The Strangest Dream" and Bob Gibson and Hamilton Camp's "You Can Tell The World," sung in Simon & Garfunkel's trademark tenor harmonies. A promising beginning. *—William Ruhlmann*

The Sounds of Silence / Jan. 1966 / Columbia ✦✦✦
The sudden, if belated, success of the folk-rock version of "The Sounds of Silence" as a single called for an immediate accompanying album, so Simon & Garfunkel, who had more or less disbanded after the commercial failure of *Wednesday Morning, 3 A.M.*, quickly reformed and recut many of the songs Simon had recorded in England for his *Paul Simon Songbook* solo album (issued only in the U.K. at the time). The album did not contain the followup hit to "The Sound of Silence," "Homeward Bound," but it did contain the followup to that, "I Am A Rock," as well as Simon's musical rewrite of Edward Arlington Robinson's poem "Richard

Cory" and other songs that aspired to poetry with an earnestness that made up for their preciousness. Still, this was a rushed album (Simon & Garfunkel would never rush again), and it shows. *— William Ruhlmann*

Parsley, Sage, Rosemary & Thyme / Sep. 1966 / Columbia ✦✦✦✦✦
A far more considered album than the rushed *Sounds Of Silence*, *Parsley, Sage, Rosemary & Thyme* features "Homeward Bound" and Simon & Garfunkel's fourth hit single, "The Dangling Conversation" (their first not to be a big hit), plus a slew of memorable album tracks: "Scarborough Fair/Canticle," which became a single in the wake of its appearance in the film *The Graduate;* "The 59th Street Bridge Song (Feelin' Groovy)," which became a hit for Harpers Bizarre; and "For Emily, Whenever I May Find Her," a showcase for Garfunkel's heavenly voice, among other songs. *— William Ruhlmann*

Bookends / Mar. 1968 / Columbia ✦✦✦✦✦
A conceptual album about friendship and old age, *Bookends* was one of the best and most ambitious records of the 1960s. Album tracks like "America" and "Old Friends" have become Simon & Garfunkel's standards, and the collection also contains four hit singles: "Mrs. Robinson," "A Hazy Shade of Winter," "Fakin' It," and "At the Zoo" (the last two redone from their single versions). *— William Ruhlmann*

☆ **Bridge Over Troubled Water** / Feb. 1970 / Columbia ✦✦✦✦✦
The massive commercial success of *Bridge Over Troubled Water*—it topped the charts for 10 weeks, won the Grammy Award for Album of the Year, included four hit singles, and has sold more than five million copies in the U.S.—tends to exaggerate its significance in the Simon & Garfunkel catalog. Actually, it's a step down from the masterpiece of *Bookends*, containing some filler, such as the comic if slight "Baby Driver" and the pleasant if inessential live cover of the Everly Brothers' "Bye Bye Love"; it also lacks the previous album's musical and thematic unity. Still, one is admittedly splitting hairs when talking about an album that contains such classics as the title song and "The Boxer," as well as such notable tunes as "Cecilia," "El Condor Pasa," and "So Long, Frank Lloyd Wright." This is Simon & Garfunkel's most popular album because it legitimately spoke to its audience, and much of it continues to set standards in thoughtful pop music decades later. *— William Ruhlmann*

Greatest Hits / Jun. 1972 / Columbia ✦✦✦✦✦
Although it's hardly a definitive retrospective, Simon & Garfunkel's *Greatest Hits* is a useful compilation of the group's biggest hits, featuring all of their most familiar items— "Mrs. Robinson," "The 59th Street Bridge Song," "Sound of Silence," "Scarborough Fair," "Homeward Bound," "Bridge Over Troubled Water," "Cecilia" and "The Boxer," among many others. *— Stephen Thomas Erlewine*

Concert in Central Park / Feb. 1982 / Warner Brothers ✦✦✦✦✦
Simon & Garfunkel reunited on September 19, 1981, to perform a free concert in Central Park, New York City. This two-record set presents some of the duo's biggest hits in a live context and also allows listeners a chance to hear what many Simon solo numbers could sound like in Simon & Garfunkel mode. *— William Ruhlmann*

Old Friends / Oct. 28, 1997 / Columbia ✦✦✦
The Collected Works was a triple-disc box set that included all of the duo's albums, but no rarities. For the average fan—even the fairly dedicated fan—that set contained most everything they would need, even if the sound quality was a little below average. *Old Friends* is a three-disc box set that was designed to replace *The Collected Works*, but it fails to achieve its goals, despite its improved remastered sound. Part of the reason is the contents itself—all five albums plus the rarities on this set could have fit on three discs, offering a real complete recorded studio works, but the compilers decided to truncate the albums and toss on a handful of rarities. The result certainly isn't bad—after all, it features all of the hits, most of the major album tracks, the 1975 reunion "My Little Town," and a couple of good rarities, like "Blues Run the Game"—but it isn't all it could have been. If you already own *The Collected Works, Old Friends* serves little purpose unless you're a collector or audiophile, and if you're a neophyte, you're better off obtaining the original albums, not this well-intentioned and enjoyable but ultimately unsuccessful compilation. *— Stephen Thomas Erlewine*

★ **The Best of Simon & Garfunkel** / Nov. 9, 1999 / Columbia/Legacy ✦✦✦✦✦
This supersedes *Greatest Hits* as the best Simon & Garfunkel compilation, with more tracks (20 compared to *Greatest Hits*' 14). Among the new additions are some notable hits: "Hazy Shade of Winter," "At the Zoo," "Fakin' It" (in its "mono single version," for what that's worth), "The Dangling Conversation," and the 1975 reunion "My Home Town." Includes the A-sides of all 16 Simon & Garfunkel singles to make the *Billboard* charts, as well as three B-sides and one album cut. The only number lost from the *Greatest Hits* set is "Kathy's Song." *— Richie Unterberger*

Carly Simon

b. Jun. 25, 1945, New York, NY

Vocals, Keyboards, Piano, Guitar/Pop/Rock, Soft Rock, Adult Contemporary, Singer/Songwriter

Carly Simon was one of the most popular of the confessional singer/songwriters who emerged in the early '70s. She got her start in music as part of the Simon Sisters, a duo with her sister Lucy that had a charting single in 1964. Her eponymous solo debut album appeared in 1971, and she found a Top 40 hit with the title track from her second album, *Anticipation*. Her third album *No Secrets* was a gold number one, and included her best-known hit "You're So Vain." During 1977-78, two singles ("Nobody Does It Better" from the James Bond film *The Spy Who Loved Me*, and "You Belong to Me") became Top Ten hits.

Though Simon curtailed her concert appearances after collapsing of exhaustion onstage in 1980, she scored a Top Ten U.K. hit two years later with "Why." Her U.S. career was in decline, however, as two mid-'80s albums were poor sellers. Her movie-related hits, including "Coming Around Again" (from *Heartburn*) and "Let the River Run" (from *Working Girl*), defined the mid- to-late '80s. In 1990, Simon released both *My Romance*, her second album of pop covers, and *Have You Seen Me Lately?*, an album of original songs. In 1993, her "family opera" *Romulus Hunt* premiered and was released on record, and one year later she released a new album, *Letters Never Sent*. *— William Ruhlmann*

Carly Simon / Feb. 1971 / Elektra ✦✦✦
"That's the Way I've Always Heard It Should Be," the lead-off track of Carly Simon's first album and a Top Ten hit, in which the singer expresses reservations about getting married, benefitted from a sense of role reversal—it's such a guy sentiment, but sung by a woman in 1971, came across as a feminist statement, consistent with the overall disillusionment so prevalent then. Nothing on the rest of the album was quite as pointed, though the other songs maintained the same ambivalence toward romance. The one other standout track, "Dan, My Fling," in which the singer tries to rekindle a relationship with a man she has discarded, was, like the single, co-written by Jacob Brackman (in this case, with Fred Gardner, not Simon), suggesting that the real creative talent here was him and not her (especially since the writing credits also featured another four names). And since Simon, with her plaintive, proper, and relatively inexpressive voice, was such an unremarkable performer, her debut seemed less auspicious than the attention it attracted might have implied. *— William Ruhlmann*

Anticipation / Nov. 1971 / Elektra ✦✦✦
Carly Simon's second album found her extending the gutsy persona she had established on her debut album, notably on the title track, "Legend In Your Own Time" (both of them hit singles), and "I've Got To Have You." The last especially suggested a frankly passionate person whose vulnerability was a source of strength, not weakness, a valuable feminist trait and one Simon would pursue in her later work. *— William Ruhlmann*

No Secrets / Nov. 1972 / Elektra ✦✦✦✦✦
Carly Simon's best album was also her commercial breakthrough, topping the charts and going gold, along with its lead-off single, "You're So Vain." That song set the album's saucy tone, with its air of sexually frank autobiography ("You had me several years ago / When I was still quite naive") and its reflections on the jet set lifestyle. But Simon's honesty meant that her lyrical knife was double-edged; now that she felt she had found true love ("The Right Thing To Do," another Top Ten hit, was her celebration of her relationship with James Taylor), she was as willing to acknowledge her own mistakes and regrets as she was to point fingers. But it wasn't only Simon's forthrightness that made the album work, it was also Richard Perry's simple, elegant pop/rock production, which gave Simon's music a buoyancy it previously lacked. And Perry paid particular attention to Simon's vocals in a way that made her more engaging (or at least less grating) to listen to. *— William Ruhlmann*

Hotcakes / Jan. 1974 / Elektra ✦✦

Playing Possum / Apr. 1975 / Elektra ✦✦✦
Though it reached the Top Ten on career momentum, Carly Simon's fifth album, *Playing Possum*, marked a creative downturn. The burst of autobiographical songwriting that had taken her from her early twenties into married life seemed to have run out, as she sang generic love songs, while Richard Perry's production gave everything an anonymous pop veneer. "Attitude Dancing" made the Top 40, and "Waterfall" and "More and More" charted, but *Playing Possum* was the album of an artist treading water, unsure of her next step. *— William Ruhlmann*

● **The Best of Carly Simon** / Nov. 1975 / Elektra ✦✦✦✦✦
Carly Simon was among the pop royalty of the singer/songwriter era of the early 1970s. This album collects her most popular songs of the first five years of her solo career. Opening with the powerful "That's the Way I've Always Heard It Should Be," and for which Simon received the 1971 Best New Artist Grammy Award, it includes three tunes from the classic *No Secrets* album, including the number one hit "You're So Vain." Simon's duet with then-husband James Taylor on "Mockingbird" was also a Top Ten hit. "Anticipation," with its classic "I rehearsed those words just late last night," and the repetitive coda "these are the good old days," though merely a ketchup commercial to a later generation, still retains its power here in the original version. Simon's insightful lyrics and evocative voice remain fresh years later. This album is a good starting point for those interested in discovering why. *— Jim Newsom*

Another Passenger / Jun. 1976 / Elektra ✦✦✦
Carly Simon tried for a fresh start on her sixth new studio album, *Another Passenger*, changing to producer Ted Templeton and employing his clients the Doobie Brothers as backup musicians, along with Little Feat and other notable West Coast session players. The result was an album full of tasty licks that sometimes didn't sound much like Carly Simon. Had Elektra released "Fairweather Father" (a sufficiently cutting song that Simon felt compelled to write a sleeve note saying it didn't refer to her husband, James Taylor) or "Dishonest Modesty," a finger-pointing song in the tradition of "You're So Vain," as singles, they might have better represented the album than they did by instead releasing Michael McDonald's "It Keeps You Runnin'," which had already appeared on the Doobie Brothers' *Takin' It To the Streets*, though it had not yet become a hit for the group. For Simon, it made the singles chart but didn't ignite her usual audience or round up a new one, and her commercial appeal continued to decline. *— William Ruhlmann*

Boys in the Trees / Apr. 1978 / Elektra ✦✦✦

Spy / Jun. 1979 / Elektra ✦✦✦

Come Upstairs / Jun. 1980 / Warner Brothers ✦✦✦

Torch / 1981 / Warner Brothers ✦✦✦

Hello Big Man / Sep. 1983 / Warner Brothers ✦✦✦

Spoiled Girl / 1985 / Epic ✦✦

Coming Around Again / Mar. 1987 / Arista ✦✦✦

My Romance / Mar. 1990 / Arista ✦✦✦

This Is My Life / Apr. 14, 1992 / Qwest ✦✦

Letters Never Sent / Nov. 1, 1994 / Arista ✦✦✦

Clouds in My Coffee 1966-1996 / Nov. 7, 1995 / Arista ♦♦♦
Rather than focusing on hits and other material most beloved by fans, retrospectives compiled by the artists themselves tend to reflect personal favorites, overbalanced with more recent material. By organizing this three-disc set into three different, non-chronological collections, Carly Simon partially defeats those tendencies. The first disc, "The Hits," performs the valuable function of bringing together most of her biggest singles, previously spread across many records on many labels. The second disc, "Miscellaneous & Unreleased," seems aimed at the collector. And the third, "Cry Yourself to Sleep," is the best-intentioned one of all—though perceived as a singles artist, Simon has written some of her best and most personal music on isolated album tracks. However, her choices frequently are not the best songs in her catalog; what is included is good stuff—it's just that a box set can offer the opportunity to provide an alternate view of an artist who may have been misjudged, as Carly Simon has, and that opportunity has been missed. *—William Ruhlmann*

The Very Best of Carly Simon: Nobody Does It Better / Dec. 15, 1998 / Global/Warner ♦♦♦♦

Bedroom Tapes / May 16, 2000 / Arista ♦♦♦

Joe Simon

b. Sep. 2, 1943, Simmesport, LA
Vocals / Deep Soul, Southern Soul, Pop-Soul, Disco, Soul
His plaintive baritone equally conversant with R&B and country phrasing, Joe Simon married the two genres with startling success during the late '60s, adapting Nashville material to the soul sound and repeatedly coming up a winner. Simon began recording in the Bay Area, but a switch in recording sites (first to Muscle Shoals for Vee-Jay and then to Nashville, upon signing with deejay John Richbourg's Sound Stage 7 label in 1966) heightened his national appeal. With easy access to prime country-oriented material, Simon soon found his true calling, scoring major hits with "Nine Pound Steel," "(You Keep Me) Hangin' On," and the number one R&B smash "The Chokin' Kind," penned by Music Row tunesmith Harlan Howard. Still dabbling in country covers after switching to the Spring imprint in 1970, Simon was even more successful when assigned to Philadelphia wizards Kenny Gamble and Leon Huff, who produced the moody "Drowning in the Sea of Love" the next year. Simon tried his hand at disco in 1975 with the sizzling "Get Down, Get Down (Get on the Floor)" and "Music in My Bones," two of the most palatable artifacts of the era. Simon eventually retired from active performing to devote his life to the church. *—Bill Dahl*

Greatest Hits: The Spring Years, 1970-1977 / 1997 / Ace ♦♦♦♦♦
Of all the soul singers who got their first hits during the 1960s, Joe Simon proved to be one of the most adaptable to the sweeter and slicker sounds of the 1970s. This 23-track compilation, covering his output at the Spring label, is not necessarily the best Simon anthology, omitting as it does his less elaborately produced work of the 1960s, which some find preferable to his Philly soul outings. It does, however, feature all his major pop hits of the era—"Drowning in the Sea of Love," "Power of Love," "Your Time to Cry," "Get Down, Get Down," and "Theme From Cleopatra Jones"—as well as a number of singles that only made a strong impression on R&B audiences, like his cover of Kris Kristofferson's "Help Me Make It Through the Night." As usual with this sort of overview, the music gets more tedious the further you get into the disco era, but it's certainly a good pickup for those who like their soul with a bow tie on it. *—Richie Unterberger*

● **Music in My Bones: The Best of Joe Simon** / Nov. 11, 1997 / Rhino ♦♦♦♦♦
Music in My Bones: The Best of Joe Simon is a superb 20-track collection that contains the best of the soul singer's recordings between 1966 and 1976. During those ten years, he recorded for Sound Stage 7, Spring and Warner and had 13 Top 10 R&B hits, all of which are included on this collection. Simon was one of the best country-soul and smooth soul singers, as evidenced by such hits as "The Chokin' Kind," "Your Time to Cry," "Drowning in the Sea of Love," "Power of Love," "Step By Step," "Theme from Cleopatra Jones," "Get Down, Get Down (Get on the Floor)" and "Music in My Bones," and there is no better place to listen to his music than on this excellent collection. *—Stephen Thomas Erlewine*

Paul Simon

b. Oct. 13, 1941, Newark, NJ
Vocals, Guitar / Album Rock, Pop/Rock, Folk-Rock, Soft Rock, Worldbeat, Adult Contemporary, Singer/Songwriter
In a career dating back to the '50s, Paul Simon has established himself among the best and most popular songwriters of the rock era. A charting artist with Art Garfunkel since the age of 16 (under the name Tom and Jerry), Simon spent five years as half of one of the most successful acts in pop music. Simon wrote the songs, and harmonized with Garfunkel on a series of hit singles and albums between 1965 and 1970. After two solo albums that both sold a million copies, he released 1975's *Still Crazy After All These Years* which topped the charts, won the Grammy for Album of the Year, and included the number one hit "50 Ways to Leave Your Lover." Simon took his time following this success, writing songs for the soundtrack to the 1980 film *One Trick Pony* and releasing another proper album, *Hearts and Bones,* in 1983. After experimenting with songwriting styles and becoming interested in South African music, Simon released 1986's *Graceland,* which became his biggest selling solo album and won him another Album of the Year Grammy. Four years later, he delivered *The Rhythm of the Saints* (October 1990), which did for Brazilian music what *Graceland* had done for South African music and was another multi-platinum seller. In 1993, he undertook a tour that featured Garfunkel on their old hits, as well as covering other aspects of his career. *—William Ruhlmann*

☆ **Paul Simon** / Jan. 1972 / Warner Brothers ♦♦♦♦♦
If any musical justification were needed for the breakup of Simon & Garfunkel, it could be found on this striking collection, Paul Simon's post-split debut. From the opening cut, "Mother and Child Reunion" (a Top Ten hit), Simon, who had snuck several subtle musical explorations into the generally conservative Simon & Garfunkel sound, broke free, heralding the rise of reggae with an exuberant track recorded in Jamaica for a song about death. From there, it was off to Paris for a track in South American style and a rambling story of a fisherman's son, "Duncan" (which made the singles chart). But most of the album had a low-key feel, with Simon on acoustic guitar backed by only a few trusted associates (among them Joe Osborn, Larry Knechtel, David Spinoza, Mike Manieri, Ron Carter, and Hal Blaine, along with such guests as Stefan Grossman, Airto Moreira, and Stephane Grappelli), singing a group of informal, intimate, funny, and closely observed songs (among them the lively Top 40 hit "Me and Julio Down by the Schoolyard"). It was miles removed from the big, stately ballad style of *Bridge Over Troubled Water* and signalled that Simon was a versatile songwriter as well as an expressive singer with a much broader range of musical interests than he had previously demonstrated. You didn't miss Art Garfunkel on *Paul Simon,* not only because Simon didn't write Garfunkel-like showcases for himself, but because the songs he did write showed off his own, more varied musical strengths. *—William Ruhlmann*

There Goes Rhymin' Simon / May 1973 / Warner Brothers ♦♦♦♦♦
Retaining the buoyant musical feel of *Paul Simon,* but employing a more produced sound, *There Goes Rhymin' Simon* found Paul Simon writing and performing with assurance and venturing into soulful and R&B-oriented music. Simon returned to the kind of vocal pyrotechnics heard on the Simon & Garfunkel records by using gospel singers. On "Love Me Like a Rock" and "Tenderness" (which sounded as though it could have been written to Art Garfunkel), the Dixie Hummingbirds sang prominent backup vocals, and on "Take Me to the Mardi Gras," the Reverend Claude Jeter contributed a falsetto part that Garfunkel could have handled, though not as warmly. For several tracks, Simon traveled to the Muscle Shoals Sound Studios to play with its house band, getting a variety of styles, from the gospel of "Love Me Like a Rock" to the Dixieland of "Mardi Gras." Simon was so confident that he even included a major ballad statement of the kind he used to give Garfunkel to sing: "American Tune" was his musical State of the Union, circa 1973, but this time Simon was up to making his big statements in his own voice. Though that song spoke of "the age's most uncertain hour," *Rhymin' Simon* was a collection of largely positive, optimistic songs of faith, romance, and commitment, concluding, appropriately, with a lullaby ("St. Judy's Comet") and a declaration of maternal love ("Loves Me Like a Rock")—in other words, another mother and child reunion that made *Paul Simon* and *There Goes Rhymin' Simon* bookend masterpieces Simon would not improve upon (despite some valiant attempts) until *Graceland* in 1986. *—William Ruhlmann*

Live Rhymin' / Feb. 1974 / Warner Brothers ♦♦♦

Still Crazy After All These Years / Oct. 1975 / Warner Brothers ♦♦♦♦♦
Replacing the guitar with the piano as the primary instrument, Simon produced a quiet, introspective Grammy-winning album centering around lost love. Simon reunites with Garfunkel on "My Little Town," a track that sounds nothing like old Simon & Garfunkel songs. *Still Crazy* doesn't really resemble Simon's two previous albums; it is a serious, somber album with none of the light touches present on *Paul Simon* and *Rhymin' Simon.* *—Stephen Thomas Erlewine*

One Trick Pony [Original Soundtrack] / Aug. 1980 / Warner Brothers ♦♦♦

Hearts and Bones / Oct. 1983 / Warner Brothers ♦♦♦♦♦
Hearts and Bones was a commercial disaster, the lowest-charting new studio album of Paul Simon's career. It is also his most personal collection of songs, one of his most ambitious, and one of his best. It retains a personal vision, one largely devoted to the challenges of middle-aged life, among them a renewed commitment to love; the title song was a notable testament to new romance, while "Train in the Distance" reflected on romantic discord. Elsewhere, "The Late Great Johnny Ace" was his meditation on John Lennon's murder and how it related to the mythology of pop music. Musically, Simon moved forward and backward simultaneously, taking off from the jazz fusion style of his last two albums into his old loves of doo wop and rock & roll while also incorporating current sounds with such new collaborators as dance music producer Nile Rodgers and minimalist composer Philip Glass. The result was Simon's most impressive collection in a decade, and the most underrated album in Paul Simon's catalog. *—William Ruhlmann*

☆ **Graceland** / Aug. 1986 / Warner Brothers ♦♦♦♦♦
With *Graceland,* Paul Simon hit on the idea of combining his always perceptive songwriting with the little-heard mbaqanga music of South Africa, creating a fascinating hybrid that reenchanted his old audience and earned him a new one. It is true that the South African angle (including its controversial aspect during the apartheid days) was a powerful marketing tool and that the catchy music succeeded in presenting listeners with that magical combination: something they'd never heard before that nevertheless sounded familiar. As eclectic as any record Simon had made, it also delved into zydeco and conjunto-flavored rock & roll while marking a surprising new lyrical approach (presaged on some songs on *Hearts and Bones*); for the most part, Simon abandoned a linear, narrative approach to his words, instead drawing highly poetic ("Diamonds on the Soles of Her Shoes"), abstract ("The Boy in the Bubble"), and satiric ("I Know What I Know") portraits of modern life, often charged by striking images and turns of phrase torn from the headlines or overheard in contemporary speech. An enormously successful record, *Graceland* became the standard against which subsequent musical experiments by major artists were measured. *—William Ruhlmann*

● **Negotiations and Love Songs 1971-1986** / Oct. 1988 / Warner Brothers ♦♦♦♦♦
Paul Simon replaced his earlier compilation, *Greatest Hits, Etc.* (1977), with this new one, allowing *Hits* to go out of print. Fans may well wish that he had simply put together a *Greatest Hits, Etc., Volume II* instead, however, since this is a case of a 16-track album covering 15 years replacing a 14-track album covering five years while containing nine of the same songs. All the major hits have been retained (though "Mother and Child Reunion" and "Loves Me Like a Rock" each have been shortened by 15 seconds), along with some of Simon's odd album track choices, such as "Have A Good Time." From the post-1977 period, we have the 1980 Top Ten hit "Late in the Evening," three selections from the underrated *Hearts and Bones,* and two from *Graceland.* (The original double-LP version of *Negotiations and Love Songs* contained a third, the Grammy Record of the Year-winning title song, but the in-print

CD and cassette versions do not.) The result is more sampler than compilation. An artist of Simon's calibre is difficult to condense, and most of the tracks here are worthy, but as a single-album career retrospective, this could have been better. *—William Ruhlmann*

Rhythm of the Saints / Oct. 1990 / Warner Brothers ✦✦✦✦

Paul Simon's Concert in the Park, August 15, 1991 / Nov. 1991 / Warner Brothers ✦✦✦✦✦

1964-1993 / Sep. 28, 1993 / Warner Brothers ✦✦✦
Artist-designed box-set retrospectives tend to be idiosyncratic, and this one is no exception. Take the title, which describes a 52-track, 200-plus minute, three-disc set, the earliest recording from which actually was released in 1957 (that's Tom and Jerry's chart single, "Hey, Schoolgirl") and which contains no recordings from 1964 or from later than 1991. While Simon has included all of his biggest solo hits and most of those by Simon & Garfunkel (excepting "Homeward Bound" and "I Am a Rock"), and has grouped the songs into three roughly chronological sections (1957-1973, 1973-1983, and 1986-1991), he has made song choices and sequencing decisions within each section more reflective of his own taste than any historical or audience-based consideration. The music is so good it almost doesn't matter, but with only one previously unreleased song (a 1991 outtake from *The Rhythm of the Saints*), *Paul Simon 1964-1993* is little more than an abridged reshuffling of Simon's existing catalog, and one hopes for more from box sets than that. (Note also that Simon's tendency to edit his songs for use on compilations continues: "Loves Me Like a Rock" is 13 seconds shorter than the version on *There Goes Rhymin' Simon*, while "50 Ways to Leave Your Lover" has lost 29 seconds from the *Still Crazy After All These Years* version.) *—William Ruhlmann*

Songs from the Capeman / Nov. 18, 1997 / Warner Brothers ✦✦

You're the One / Oct. 3, 2000 / Warner Brothers ✦✦✦

Nancy Sinatra

b. Jun. 4, 1940, Jersey City, NJ
Vocals / Sunshine Pop, Psychedelic Pop, Baroque Pop, Pop
Frank Sinatra's daughter Nancy enjoyed a brief run of superstardom between 1966 and 1968. Not nearly the vocalist her father is, the family name didn't hurt her advances in the business, nor did the fact that she recorded for Frank's label, Reprise. Her first few singles met with little success, and Nancy was on the verge of being dropped when she hooked up with producer Lee Hazlewood and arranger Billy Strange. They urged her to lower her voice and toughen her delivery, and crafted material emphasizing growling bass lines and "go-go" tempos. One of their first efforts, the 1966 single "These Boots Are Made for Walkin'," topped the charts, inaugurating a series of hits over the next couple years, the biggest of which were "Sugar Town," "Lightning's Girl," "Love Eyes," and her number one hit duet with her father, "Somethin' Stupid." Nancy's singles were as notable for their distinctive arrangements and the odd, brooding compositions of Hazlewood, who wrote most of her hits, as her own sex-kitten vocals. Specializing in oddly disquieting songs with a sort of modern Western theme, Hazlewood teamed up with Sinatra for a few duets which presented the chalk'n'cheese combination of Nancy's thin voice with Lee's gravelly, almost spoken delivery, which recalled an off-kilter Johnny Cash. The team actually managed a few hits, some of which, especially "Some Velvet Morning," rank as some of the most bizarre MOR Top 40 pop hits of all time. *—Richie Unterberger*

• **The Hit Years** / 1986 / Rhino ✦✦✦✦✦
Contains all the essential tracks: every hit, including those with her father and with Hazlewood, and a bunch of interesting misses, such as the theme song to the James Bond film *You Only Live Twice*. It focuses mostly on material penned by Hazlewood, and has comprehensive liner notes. An Australian best-of on the Raven label, *Lightning's Girl*, has a few more songs, but this less expensive 18-track domestic compilation covers all the key bases. *—Richie Unterberger*

Fairy Tales & Fantasies: The Best of Nancy Sinatra and Lee Hazelwood / 1989 / Rhino ✦✦✦
Basically a reissue of the 1968 album *Nancy and Lee*, with some bonus tracks. This has all of the duo's hits ("Summer Wine," "Jackson," "Sand," "Lady Bird," and "Some Velvet Morning"), which easily outclass the filler material. And those hits are about as inspired as middle-of-the-road pop gets, especially the eerie "Some Velvet Morning," one of the strangest songs ever to crack the Top 40. *—Richie Unterberger*

Siouxsie & the Banshees

f. 1976, London, England, **db.** 1996
Group / College Rock, British Punk, Post-Punk, Goth Rock, Alternative Pop/Rock, Punk
Siouxsie & the Banshees were among the longest-lived and most successful acts to emerge from the London punk community; over the course of a career which lasted two decades, they evolved from an abrasive, primitive art-punk band into a stylish, sophisticated unit which even notched a left-field Top 40 hit. Throughout their numerous line-up changes and textural shifts, the group remained under the leadership of vocalist Siouxsie Sioux, born Susan Dallion; she and the Banshees' initial line-up emerged from the Bromley Contingent, a notorious group of rabid Sex Pistols fans. In addition to bassist Steve Severin and guitarist Marco Perroni, the band included drummer John Simon Ritchie, who assumed the name Sid Vicious. Soon after, Vicious joined the Sex Pistols, while Perroni went on to join Adam and the Ants. The core duo of Sioux and Severin reached the U.K. Top Ten with their 1978 debut single, "Hong Kong Garden;" their grim, dissonant first LP, *The Scream*, followed later in the year. During a 1979 tour, drummer Budgie became a permanent member of the group, and remained with the Banshees' throughout the duration of their career. The band returned to the studio for 1980's *Kaleidoscope*, a more subtle and melodic effort than their prior records; on the strength of the U.K. Top 20 smash "Happy House," the album reached the Top Five. With 1986's *Tinderbox*, Siouxsie and the Banshees finally reached the U.S. Top 100 album charts, largely on the strength of the excellent single "Cities in Dust." 1988's *Peep Show*, a techno-inspired outing, gave the group their first U.S. chart single with "Peek-a-Boo." 1991's *Superstition* was their most commercially successful effort, spawning their lone U.S. Top 40 hit "Kiss Them for Me." *—Jason Ankeny*

Join Hands / 1979 / Geffen ✦✦

Kaleidoscope / 1980 / Geffen ✦✦✦✦✦
After *Join Hands*, guitarist John McKay and drummer Kenny Morris departed the Banshees, leaving the band at a crossroads. Siouxsie Sioux and Steven Severin elected to soldier on with ex-Slits drummer Budgie and two guitarists, ex-Sex Pistol Steve Jones and John McGeoch of Magazine as guest Banshees. Despite the personnel upheaval, the result is a surprisingly strong record. While a number of the songs here are still dark-hued and feature bleak lyrics, they are made very palatable by extraordinarily imaginative production values featuring intricate synthesizer-flecked arrangements; psychedelic touches in "Christine," and spaceship synthesizer swoops in "Tenant," and rhythmic camera clicks in "Red Light" all enliven their respective songs. Sound quality here is lighter and much clearer than on previous releases. Sioux's singing shows noticeable improvement here, still tuneless at times but also exhibiting more range and subtlety than previously. The song "Hybrid," a Joy Division-style number, shows her vocals running the gamut from primitive to inspired. Other highlights include the galloping, vibrant uptempo number "Skin," the spooky and atmospheric "Lunar Camel," the medium tempo rocker "Trophy," and the punky vocalise "Clockface." This was a make-or-break album for the band, and happily they came through strongly. *—David Cleary*

• **Once Upon a Time: The Singles** / 1981 / Geffen ✦✦✦✦✦
Once Upon a Time: The Singles collects all ten of Siouxsie & the Banshees' A-sides spanning the years 1978-1981, with four songs otherwise unavailable on LP. It's a neat and accessible encapsulation of the group's early guitar-driven sound—a frosty, dissonant art-punk that had a tremendous impact on the emerging goth-rock scene. Unlike similarly forbidding work by such proto-goth contemporaries as Joy Division or the Cure, the early Banshees were tense and visceral; the darkness of the *Once Upon a Time* singles doesn't come from a sense of downcast gloom so much as it does from a jittery angst. Yet as challenging as the music is, it's also accessible enough for eight of these singles to have charted in the British Top 50. The melodies are angular and almost alien, yes, but oddly memorable once the listener has assimilated them. Starting shortly after the period covered by this collection, Siouxsie Sioux's icy detachment would be fused with an elegant romanticism and lusher, smoother arrangements. Which means that *Once Upon a Time* isn't the one, definitive Banshees compilation, but it is a cohesive and essential overview of the band's edgy, influential peak. *—Steve Huey*

Juju / Aug. 1981 / Geffen ✦✦✦✦
They're shifting gradually toward a more straightforward rock sound, but the Banshees also add Middle Eastern touches here. Contains the British hits "Spellbound" and "Arabian Knights." *—William Ruhlmann*

Kiss in the Dream House / 1982 / Geffen ✦✦✦

Nocturne / 1983 / Geffen ✦✦✦

Hyaena / 1984 / Geffen ✦✦✦

Tinderbox / 1986 / Geffen ✦✦✦✦✦
This is the most musically uptempo of all the Banshees' albums and the most stylistically consistent one since *The Scream* and *Join Hands*. Most of the selections here feature urgently rocking drumming, drivingly aggressive yet fully textured guitar playing, and masterful, gutsy singing. The songs here are intense and unfold slowly, some starting off less vigorously but becoming hard rockers further along. There is of course a fine line between consistency and lack of contrast, but this album stays firmly on the side of the former; in fact, there's a certain satisfying feel to the musically uniform wall of sound here. The arrangements are less complex than in immediately preceding albums, but there are still plenty of subtle, effective production touches to be found throughout, most notably in the song "Cannons." "Cities in the Dust," a dance-pop number with a bell-like synthesizer opening section stretches the above-mentioned boundaries the most, though typically bleak lyrics keep this selection from any sense of vacuity. This excellent release is well worth purchasing. *—David Cleary*

Through the Looking Glass / 1987 / Geffen ✦✦✦

Peep Show / 1988 / Geffen ✦✦✦
As good as it is in places, this is the sound of a once-terrific band treading water. Some of the songs are fine, but they're too layered in self-referential mystique to actually win over listeners. The single ("Peek-a-Boo") is one exception—a seductive glimpse of the sleek lines and pouty truculence of old. But other songs, including two singles—"Killing Jar" and "Last Beat of My Heart"—fail to convince. The obituary writers had started sharpening their pencils. *—Alex Ogg*

Superstition / 1991 / Geffen ✦✦✦

• **Twice Upon a Time: The Singles** / Oct. 13, 1992 / Geffen ✦✦✦✦✦
Siouxsie Sioux has always maintained that it was not her intention to create the goth-rock movement. While that lofty statement may be a little self-serving, it's partly right. The Banshees' post-1982 singles (documented in entirety on *Twice Upon a Time*) have a lush and expansive sound that directly influenced the goth sound. From the opening of "Fireworks" it is immediately apparent that Siouxsie and the Banshees were growing up. By the time of "Peek-a-Boo," the band had learned how to incorporate their early dissonance with their majestic, late-'80s sound. The *Twice Upon a Time* collection is one great step after another, with the only drawback being a poor remix of 1991's "Fear of the Unknown." A solid introduction for the unknowing. *—Chris True*

Rapture / Feb. 1995 / Geffen ✦✦

The Sir Douglas Quintet

f. 1964, San Antonio, TX, **db.** 1972
Group / Tex-Mex, Rock & Roll
Texas had always had its own brand of rock & roll—a little bit o' country, a little bit o' blues, with a heapin' helpin' o' hot sauce poured over the top. Doug Sahm was no stranger to the

studio when he formed the Sir Douglas Quintet in 1964; he'd been at it since the age of six, and already possessed an encyclopedic knowledge and innate understanding of those local flavors when the band cut its first big hit, "She's About a Mover."

The ingredient that set the Quintet apart was Tex-Mex, that curious, joyous, irresistible, danceable, festive feast that married the jumpy Mexican *conjunto* to good ol' rock & roll. With Augie Meyers on the organ and a rhythm section that couldn't stop cookin', Sir Doug Sahm let it be known that good-time music was alive and kickin' in San Antone.

After the Quintet itself dissolved, Sahm cut numerous solo albums and collaborations, spreading the Tex-Mex influence. In the late '80s he and Meyers teamed up with two of their mentors, Freddy Fender and Flaco Jimenez, to form the Texas Tornados, keeping that high and happy sound alive. *—Jeff Tamarkin*

Live Texas Tornado / Aug. 11, 1998 / Takoma ✦✦✦✦

• **Prime of Sir Douglas Quintet** / Oct. 19, 1999 / Music Club ✦✦✦✦✦
It is unfortunate that no one can seem to muster a definitive collection of Sir Douglas Quintet's early (pre-*Smash*) recordings. This 15-song disc is a pretty good try, and has very good music, but doesn't quite take the cigar. No original recording or release dates are given, and the liner notes are vague about the sources for the material. About half of the tracks did show up on Tribe singles (and their sole Tribe LP) in the mid-'60s. The rest are of more mysterious origin, some sounding like casual demos, and some sounding as if they may date from a later period. The important thing to note is that this *does* have the original versions of their mid-'60s hits "She's About a Mover" and the equally worthy, though lesser known, "The Rains Came." "In Time" is an awkward but appealing attempt to incorporate British Invasion influences; "Beginning of the End" has that special lazy Texas doo wop/pop feel typical of Meaux's early-'60s productions; "Please Just Say So" is top-drawer Tex-Mex rock; and "Bacon Fat" is an engagingly sloppy cover of the Andre Williams R&B dance tune. The more obscure selections have less of a "band" sound and more of a country/folk/blues orientation that puts Sahm's great roots vocals at the fore. On some of the slow country tunes, he sounds uncannily like Elvis Costello *wants* to sound when doing country music. "Blue Pass Me By" sounds like a Tribe-era outtake with its smoky barroom feel, while Sahm's "I Don't Want to Go Home" and the cover of Dylan's "One Too Many Mornings" have a more mature folk-rock feel. Sahm's singing is cool throughout, and almost everything is a good listen; it's just that a significant group such as Sir Douglas deserves a more thorough, and more thoroughly documented, compilation. *—Richie Unterberger*

• **Best of the Sir Douglas Quintet** / Mar. 20, 2000 / Beat Rocket ✦✦✦✦✦
A more or less straight-up reissue of the group's Tribe album. When producer Huey Meaux released this disc in 1966, he probably though it was the end of the group, as they had hadn't hit the Top 40 in almost a year and a drug bust decimated their ranks. Cobbled together from their 1965 sessions, this brings together "She's About a Mover," "The Rains Came," and strong versions of "Bacon Fat," "Quarter to Three," and "It's a Man Down There." If you're going to slim the collection down to just one Sir Doug collection, this is the one to grab. *—Cub Koda*

Sir Douglas Quintet Is Back! / Mar. 20, 2000 / Beat Rocket ✦✦✦✦
This and Beat Rocket's companion reissue of the 1966 *The Best of Sir Douglas Quintet* album seem to gather most or all of what the group recorded for Tribe in the mid-'60s. Seems simple enough, but it's cause for rejoicing among '60s collectors, considering that this back catalog had somehow eluded the marketplace for more than 30 years prior to these two sets. If you're looking to choose one over the other, *The Best of* would get the nod for its inclusion of their only two Tribe hits: ("She's About a Mover" and "The Rains Came"). However, the various flop singles and outtakes comprising *The Sir Douglas Quintet Is Back!* are about equal in quality to the sister volume, with the same invigorating, erratic combination of British Invasion, Cajun, blues, soul, country, and even folk-rock. Certainly "In Time," a minor-key Sahm original with echoes of the Animals and the Zombies, and "Blues Pass Me By," a grand illustration of Sahm's stature as one of the finest white soul-rock vocalists ever, rate among their finer moments. Another Sahm original, "She Digs My Love," has astonishing fluttering blues-rock guitar licks that sound a hell of a lot like Jimi Hendrix—although Hendrix had yet to release records under his own name when it came out. According to the liner notes, their debut 1964 single "Sugar Bee" preceded the Beatles' "She's a Woman" by several months, boasting a *very* similar riff and rhythm. It does make you wonder whether some of rock's giants somehow managed to borrow some ideas from Sir Douglas Quintet singles that very few people heard. At times the material on this disc can be perfunctory, but the mix of so many elements in one band (and sometimes in one song) are seldom less than interesting. *—Richie Unterberger*

Sister Sledge

f. 1971, North Philadelphia, PA
Group / Smooth Soul, Quiet Storm, Urban, Disco, Soul
Best known for their work with Chic in the late 1970s, siblings Debbie, Kim, Joni, and Kathy Sledge—collectively Sister Sledge—reached the height of their popularity during the Disco Era but had been recording since the early 1970s and were still active in the late 1990s. The group was formed in Philadelphia in 1971, when the sisters' ages ranged from 12 to 16 and they recorded their first single, "Time Will Tell," for the Philly-based Money Back label. At first, the group called itself *Sisters* Sledge, but after a few years, decided to change Sisters to Sister. In 1972, Sister Sledge signed with Atco and recorded its second single, "Weatherman," which was followed by the Jackson 5-like "Mama Never Told Me" in 1973. Sister Sledge's first national hit came in 1974, when "Love, Don't You Go Through No Changes on Me" reached number 31 on the R&B charts and the Philadelphians recorded their debut album, *Circle of Love.* Their second album, *Together,* was released in 1977 and contained the number 61 R&B hit "Blockbuster Boy." It wasn't until 1979, when Chic leaders Nile Rodgers and Bernard Edwards produced *We Are Family,* that Sister Sledge really exploded commercially. "He's the Greatest Dancer" and *We Are Family*'s title song both soared to number 1 on the R&B charts, and the latter (a number 2 pop smash) was adopted as a theme by the Pittsburgh Pirates. Sister Sledge's next album, *Love Somebody Today,* (1980) was also produced by the Rodgers/Edwards team, and the single "Got to Love Somebody" became a number 6 R&B hit. In 1981, Sister Sledge switched producers and worked with Narada Michael Walden, who produced 1981's excellent *All American Girls.* The title song was a number 3 R&B hit, and in 1982, Sister Sledge had a number 14 R&B hit with a cover of Mary Wells' "My Guy" that appeared on *The Sisters.* But after that, the foursome's popularity faded, and it never had another Top 20 hit in the U.S.—although 1985's "Frankie" (a number 32 R&B hit in the States) became a pop number 1 hit in England. Sister Sledge left Atlantic for good in 1985, but its members kept busy in the 1990s. Epic released Kathy Sledge's debut solo album, *Heart,* in 1992, and 1997 found the sisters recording their risk-taking Farenheit date *African Eyes*—arguably one of the finest albums they ever recorded. *—Alex Henderson*

We Are Family / 1979 / Rhino ✦✦✦✦✦
Before 1979's *We Are Family,* Sister Sledge wasn't a huge name in the R&B/disco world. The group had enjoyed a small following and scored a few minor hits, including "Love, Don't You Go Through No Changes on Me" in 1974 and "Blockbuster Boy" in 1977. But it wasn't until *We Are Family* that the Philadelphia siblings finally exploded commercially, and the people they have to thank for their commercial success are Chic leaders Nile Rodgers and Bernard Edwards. The Rodgers/Edwards team handles all of the writing, producing, and arranging on this album; so not surprisingly, almost everything on *We Are Family* is very Chic-sounding. That is true of the sexy "He's the Greatest Dancer" and the anthemic, uplifting title song (both of which soared to number 1 on the R&B charts), as well as excellent album tracks like the lush "Easier to Love," the perky "One More Time," and the addictive "Thinking of You." The least Chic-sounding tune on the album is the ballad "Somebody Loves Me," which favors a classic sweet soul approach and is the type of song one would have expected from Thom Bell, Gamble & Huff, or Holland-Dozier-Holland rather than Rodgers/Edwards. Meanwhile, the intoxicating "Lost in Music" (a number 35 R&B hit) is about as Chic-sounding as it gets. When Rhino reissued *We Are Family* on CD in 1995, it added four bonus tracks, all of which are remixes of either the title song or "Lost in Music." These remixes are intriguing; it's interesting to hear late '70s classics turned into high-tech 1990s dance-pop. But they are less than essential, and the original versions are by far the best—how can you improve on perfection? Both creatively and commercially, *We Are Family* is Sister Sledge's crowning achievement. *—Alex Henderson*

• **The Best of Sister Sledge (1973-1985)** / Sep. 1, 1992 / Rhino ✦✦✦✦✦
Sister Sledge evolved quite a bit during the 12 years documented on this 1992 collection, which traces the Philadelphians' evolution from bubblegum soulsters to sexy but wholesome disco-era darlings to struggling urban-contemporary act. After early numbers like "Mama Never Told Me" and "Love Don't You Go Through No Changes on Me" (both recorded at a time when the sisters were still in their teens and came across as sort of a female Jackson 5), they dive head first into disco/soul with "Cream of the Crop" (an underrated, Philly-sounding pearl) and finally hit the big time with the Chic-produced megahits "We Are Family" and "He's the Greatest Dancer." One hears Sledge entering the '80s on a high note with "Got to Love Somebody" but by the middle of the decade sounding less inspired on the singles "Frankie" and "Dancing on the Jagged Edge." One of the collection's most disappointing tracks is the reggae remix of "He's Just a Runaway." While it's true that this is the version that became a medium-size hit, the more rock-ish version found on *All American Girls* packs a much greater punch. But despite a few weak spots here and there, this is a gem-laden CD that paints a generally impressive picture of the group. *—Alex Henderson*

Sisters of Mercy

f. 1980, Leeds, England, **db.** 1990
Group / College Rock, Goth Rock, Alternative Pop/Rock
One of England's leading "goth" bands of the 1980s, the Sisters of Mercy play a slow, gloomy, ponderous hybrid of metal and psychedelia, often incorporating dance beats; the one constant in the band's career has been deep-voiced singer Andrew Eldritch. (There is some disagreement as to whether the group took its name from an order of Catholic nuns or from the Leonard Cohen song of the same name.) Eldritch originally formed the band in 1980 with guitarist Gary Marx and recorded its first single with a drum machine dubbed Doktor Avalanche. Guitarist Ben Gunn and bassist Craig Adams were added to make live gigs feasible, and the Sisters built a reputation through several singles and EPs. Gunn left the band in 1983 and was replaced by Wayne Hussey. The Sisters of Mercy recorded their first full-length album, *First and Last and Always,* in 1985, but two years later, internal dissent had split them apart. Marx left to form Ghost Dance, and Adams and Hussey departed shortly thereafter. A legal dispute ensued over the rights to the name Sisters of Mercy; Adams and Hussey attempted to use the name Sisterhood, but Eldritch released an EP under the name to prevent its usage, and the two finally settled on the Mission. Eldritch chiefly utilized a corps of temporary sidemen from this point on (although former Gun Club bassist Patricia Morrison was an official member of the group for a short time) and rebounded with his two biggest-selling American LPs, *Floodland* and *Vision Thing.* He is currently the group's only member. *—Steve Huey*

First and Last and Always / 1985 / Elektra ✦✦✦

Floodland / 1987 / Elektra ✦✦✦✦✦
While the goth scene in England was picking up commercial steam in the mid-1980s, the Sisters of Mercy may have seemed quiet, but they roared back with 1987's *Floodland.* Opening with the driving two part hymn "Dominion/Mother Russia," Sisters leader Andrew Eldtrich (along with bassist Patricia Morrison) creates a black soundscape that is majestic and vast. While the earlier Sisters releases were noisy, sometimes harsh affairs, *Floodland* is filled with lush production (thanks to Meatloaf writer/producer Jim Stienman and the New York Choral Society) and lyric imagery that is both scary and glorious. The slower tracks, like "Flood" and "1959," are some of the best ethereal sounds goth has to offer, and the downright regal "This Corrosion" is one of the best songs of the genre. A definite milestone. *—Chris True*

Vision Thing / Nov. 1990 / Elektra ✦✦✦✦✦

• **Some Girls Wander by Mistake** / Oct. 20, 1992 / Elektra ✦✦✦✦✦
Collecting a number of their better singles, *Some Girls Wander by Mistake* offers a good introduction to the Sisters of Mercy. *—AMG*

A Slight Case of Overbombing: Greatest Hits, Vol. 1 / 1993 / Elektra ✦✦✦✦
A Slight Case of Overbombing gathered together material from goth merchants the Sisters of Mercy's three major label releases. That fact immediately sets the stage for complaints from long-time fans desiring their indie music. However, for the listener more familiar with the band's mid- to late-'80s college radio tracks, this is a very good collection. The lyrics are rather pointless and Andrew Eldritch's vocals lack dynamics, but his singing has personality that overcomes his limitations. It's the edgy, hard, gothic rock of the music that is their strength. There's an undeniable pull to songs like the galloping "This Corrosion" or the epic "More" (both produced by Jim Steinman). There's also a mix of "Temple of Love," featuring Ofra Haza, and an unreleased track, "Under the Gun." Not essential, but a good record for the casual fan (although more extensive liner notes would have been nice). *—Tom Demalon*

Skinny Puppy

f. 1982, Vancouver, British Columbia, Canada, **db.** 1996
Group / Industrial Dance, Alternative Pop/Rock, Industrial
Drawing from the pioneering work of artists like Throbbing Gristle, Cabaret Voltaire, and Suicide, the dark avant-industrial group Skinny Puppy formed in 1982 around vocalist cEVIN Key and Nivek Ogre. Subsequent releases like 1986's *Mind: The Perpetual Intercourse*, 1987's *Cleanse, Fold and Manipulate*, and 1988's *VIVIsectVI* further honed the trio's style, as well as introducing the outspoken lyrical agenda that remained a thematic constant throughout much of the group's work. In 1989, Ministry's Al Jourgensen added vocals, guitars, and production work to *Rabies*. In 1993, Skinny Puppy signed to American Recordings and relocated to Los Angeles to begin production work. The subsequent album, titled *The Process*, wasn't released until 1996 amidst problems with producers and the death of keyboardist Dwayne Goettel. A multi-media history of the band, *Brap: Back and Forth, Series 3&4*, followed a few months later, while Key returned to his new project, Download. Released in 1998, *ReMix Dys Temper* featured Skinny Puppy reworkings by Autechre, Neotropic, and Adrian Sherwood in addition to industrial groups like KMFDM and God Lives Underwater. *—Jason Ankeny*

Bites / 1985 / Nettwerk ✦✦✦✦

Mind: The Perpetual Intercourse / 1986 / Nettwerk ✦✦

Cleanse, Fold and Manipulate / 1987 / Nettwerk ✦✦✦

VIVISect VI / Jul. 1988 / Nettwerk ✦✦✦

Rabies / 1989 / Nettwerk ✦✦✦✦

Too Dark Park / 1990 / Nettwerk ✦✦✦✦

12" Anthology / Jun. 1990 / Nettwerk ✦✦✦✦✦

The Process / Feb. 27, 1996 / American ✦✦

B-Sides Collect / Nov. 16, 1999 / Nettwerk ✦✦✦✦
Skinny Puppy was indeed one of the most collectable industrial bands, issuing many singles that contained surprisingly strong tracks. In 1999, Nettwerk compiled some of the best for the companion to *The Singles Collect*. These tracks aren't the rarest in the Skinny Puppy catalog, considering most are B-sides from later singles like "Testure," "Worlock," "Censor," "Tormentor," and "Spasmolytic." Still, the group's quality control was practically undisputed among industrial bands, and for fans who may have missed out on a single or two the first time, it's the perfect acquisition. Highlights include remixes of "Addiction" and "Shore Lined Poison," plus notable tracks like "Brak's Talk," "Bark," "Punk in Park Zoo's," and "Yes He Ran." *—John Bush*

• **The Singles Collect** / Nov. 16, 1999 / Nettwerk ✦✦✦✦✦
It's not a compilation of across-the-board greatest songs, but the Skinny Puppy singles collection does the old *12" Anthology* one better by including tracks from the group's three Nettwerk albums of the 1990s (*Rabies, Too Dark Park*, and *Last Rights*). For fans, it's long been a dream to have the full fruits of the industrial kingpins' long career all on one disc—"Dig It," one of Skinny Puppy's first and best singles, appears right beside "Worlock," from 1989's *Rabies*. Also aboard are a baker's dozen of well-selected career highlights, including "Assimilate," "Tormentor," "Deep Down Trauma Hounds," "Stairs and Flowers," "Testure," "Tin Omen," "Inquisition," and "Killing Game." Though a chronologically ordered compilation would have been a better idea, *The Singles Collect* sounds excellent all the way through and proves that Skinny Puppy was, hands down, the best and most adventurous band of the industrial era. *—John Bush*

The Skyliners

f. 1959, Pittsburgh, PA
Group / Doo Wop
This Pittsburgh vocal group made a magnificent heartache ballad in 1959, "Since I Don't Have You." It remains among R&B's ultimate agonizing triumphs, and Chuck Jackson later did an equally gripping version. Jimmy Beaumont was the lead vocalist, with Janet Vogel, Wally Lester, Joe VerScharen, and Jackie Taylor. Beaumont, Taylor, and Lester had been in the Crescents, while Vogel and VerScharen were alumni of the El Rios. Their follow-up, "This I Swear," was a creditable effort that peaked at number 20 on the R&B charts, but few remember it. Oddly, "Since I Don't Have You" only reached number three on the R&B side and number 12 on the pop charts. But it's certainly one song for whom the numbers really don't come close to telling the story. The Skyliners had two chart singles on Callico and then had one other song reach the R&B Top 40 in 1965, "The Loser," for Jubilee. *—Ron Wynn*

• **The Skyliners' Greatest Hits** / 1986 / Original Sound ✦✦✦✦✦

Slade

f. 1966
Group / Glam Rock, Hard Rock
One of the most successful British bands of the early '70s, Slade made it to the top of the charts after several years on the road. The band formed in 1966 in Wolverhapton as the N'-Betweens. After taking on former Animals bassist Chas Chandler as their manager, they changed their name to Ambrose Slade, then shortened it to Slade.

Many of their records were a variations of upfront lead vocals, fat, loud, distorted guitar chords, a basic foot-stomping beat, and anthemic choruses. The simplicity of it all was played up even further by the deliberate misspelling of words in the song titles. At the turn of the '70s, "Get Down and Get with It" cracked the U.K. Top 20 and there was no turning back. Their next dozen singles were U.K. Top Five hits, six of them reaching number one. Their success wasn't limited to the singles charts, either; three of their albums also topped the charts during the same period. Their holiday song, "Merry Xmas Everybody," has entered the U.K. charts seven times, as well.

Despite their British success Slade barely cracked the U.S. Hot 100. Even in England, the big hits stopped coming during the punk revolution in the late '70s. They enjoyed a brief revival in the early '80s when Quiet Riot covered "Cum on Feel the Noize" and took it to the top of the charts around the world. This revival even enabled Slade to chart in the American Top 40 with "Run Runaway" and "My Oh My." Slade recently celebrated its 25th anniversary and shows no sign of stopping. *—Jim Powers*

• **Feel the Noize: The Very Best of Slade** / 1997 / Polydor ✦✦✦✦✦
The finest collection ever assembled on Slade's hit-making heyday, *Feel the Noize: The Very Best of Slade*, contains all of the group's hit singles from the early '70s, from 1971's "Get Down and Get With It" to 1975's "Thanks for the Memory (Wham Bam Thank You Mam)." In between those two songs, all of the group's big, dumb, irresistible, and misspelled hits—"Cuz I Luv You," "Take Me Bak 'Ome," "Mama Weer All Crazee Now," "Gudbuy T'Jane," "Cum on Feel the Noize," "Skweeze Me Pleeze Me"—are featured. Though it is missing latter-day hits like "My Oh My," Slade never got better than they did at their stomping glitter-rock peak, and *Feel the Noize* captures the essence of that era. *—Stephen Thomas Erlewine*

Slayer

f. 1982, Huntington Beach, CA
Group / Speed Metal, Heavy Metal, Thrash
Slayer was one of the most distinctive, influential, and extreme thrash-metal bands of the 1980s. Their graphic lyrics deal with everything from death and dismemberment to war and the horrors of hell. Their full-throttle velocity, wildly chaotic guitar solos, and powerful musical chops paint an effectively chilling sonic background for their obsessive chronicling of the dark side; this correspondence has helped Slayer's music hold up arguably better than the remaining Big Three '80s thrash outfits (Metallica, Megadeth, Anthrax). Naturally, Slayer has stirred up quite a bit of controversy over the years, with rumors flying about Satanism and Nazism that have only added to their mystique. Over the years, Slayer has put out some high-quality albums, one undisputed classic (*Reign in Blood*), and seen the numbers of naysayers and detractors shrinking as their impact on the growing death-metal movement was gradually and respectfully acknowledged. Slayer has survived into the 1990s with arguably the most vitality and the least compromise of any pre-Nirvana metal band, and their intensity still inspires similar responses from their devoted fans. *—Steve Huey*

Show No Mercy / 1983 / Metal Blade ✦✦

Hell Awaits / 1985 / Metal Blade ✦✦✦

★ **Reign in Blood** / 1986 / American ✦✦✦✦✦
Widely considered the pinnacle of speed metal, *Reign in Blood* is Slayer's undisputed masterpiece, a brief (under half an hour) but relentless onslaught that instantly obliterates anything in its path and clears out just as quickly. Producer Rick Rubin gives the band a clear, punchy sound for the first time in its career, and they largely discard the extended pieces of *Hell Awaits* in favor of lean assaults somewhat reminiscent of hardcore punk (though distinctly metallic and much more technically demanding). *Reign in Blood* opens and closes with slightly longer tracks (the classics "Angel of Death" and "Raining Blood") whose slower riffs offer most of the album's few hints of melody. Sandwiched in between are eight short (all under three minutes), lightning-fast bursts of aggression that change tempo or feel without warning, producing a disjointed, barely controlled effect. The album is actually more precise than it sounds, and not without a sense of groove, but even in the brief slowdowns, the intensity never lets up. There may not be much variation, but it's a unified vision, and a horrific one at that. The riffs are built on atonal chromaticism that sounds as sickening as the graphic violence depicted in many of the lyrics, and Kerry King and Jeff Hanneman's demented soloing often mimics the screams of the songs' victims. It's monstrously, terrifyingly evocative, in a way that transcends *Reign in Blood*'s metal origins. The album almost single-handedly inspired the entire death metal genre (at least on the American side of the Atlantic), and unlike many of its imitators, it never crosses the line into self-parodic overkill. *Reign in Blood* was a stone-cold classic upon its release, and it hasn't lost an ounce of its power today. *—Steve Huey*

South of Heaven / 1988 / American ✦✦✦✦
When it comes to death metal, no band is more convincing than Slayer. For other bands, focusing on death, satanism, the supernatural and the occult became a cliche; but Slayer's controversial reflections on evil always came across as honest and heartfelt. The group's sincerity is the thing that makes *South of Heaven* so disturbing and powerful—when the influential thrashers rip into such morbid fare as "Spill the Blood," "Mandatory Suicide," and "Ghosts of War," they are frighteningly convincing. With its fourth album, Slayer began to slow its tempos without sacrificing an iota of heaviness or incorporating any pop elements. *South of Heaven* would be Slayer's last album for Def Jam. When Rick Rubin and Russell Simmons (brother of Joseph "Run" Simmons of Run-D.M.C.) parted company, Slayer went to Rubin's new company Def American, while LL Cool J, Slick Rick and other rappers recorded for Simmons at Def Jam. *—Alex Henderson*

Seasons in the Abyss / 1990 / American ✦✦✦✦✦
After staking out new territory with the underrated *South of Heaven*, Slayer brought back some of the pounding speed of *Reign in Blood* for its third major-label album, *Seasons in the Abyss*. Essentially, *Seasons* fuses its two predecessors, periodically kicking up the midtempo grooves of *South of Heaven* with manic bursts of aggession. "War Ensemble" and the title track each represented opposite sides of the coin, and they both earned Slayer their heaviest MTV airplay to date. In fact, *Seasons in the Abyss* is probably their most accessible album, displaying the full range of their abilities all in one place, with sharp, clean production. Since the band is refining rather than progressing or experimenting, *Seasons* doesn't have quite the freshness of its predecessors, but aside from that drawback, it's strong almost all the way from top to bottom (with perhaps one or two exceptions). Lyrically, the band rarely turns to demonic visions of the afterlife anymore, preferring instead to find tangible horror in real life—war, murder, human weakness. There's even full-fledged social criticism, which should convince any doubters that Slayer isn't trying to promote the subjects they sing about. Like Metallica's *Master of Puppets* or Megadeth's *Peace Sells... But Who's Buying*, *Seasons in the Abyss* paints Reagan-era America as a cesspool of corruption and cruelty, and the music is as devilishly effective as ever. *—Steve Huey*

Decade of Aggression: Live / Oct. 22, 1991 / American ✦✦✦

Divine Intervention / Sep. 27, 1994 / American ✦✦✦

Undisputed Attitude / Jun. 1996 / American ✦✦✦

Diabolus in Musica / Jun. 9, 1998 / American/Columbia ✦✦✦

Sleater-Kinney

f. 1994, Olympia, WA
Group / Riot Grrrl, Indie Rock, Alternative Pop/Rock
The anthemic Olympia, Washington-based punk trio Sleater-Kinney formed from the ashes of Heavens to Betsy and Excuse 17, a pair of groups which rode the first wave of the riot-grrrl movement. Singers/guitarists Corin Tucker and Carrie Brownstein first met in 1992, when Tucker was one half of the duo Heavens to Betsy; Brownstein, a classically-trained pianist, was so inspired by Tucker and other grrrl musicians like Bikini Kill and Bratmobile (not coincidentally Tucker's own influences) that she formed her own band, Excuse 17, a year later. Sleater-Kinney, which earned its name from a local freeway off-ramp, initially began as Tucker and Brownstein's side project. In late 1994, Australia-born Lora Macfarlane signed on as the group's first permanent drummer, and over the course of the following two weeks the trio recorded their self-titled 1995 debut for Team Dresch, bassist Donna Dresch's Chainsaw label. Upon its release, the album earned widespread acclaim for its visceral intensity as well as the group's provocative, politically-charged lyrics, passionate vocals, and intricate melodies. With 1996's brilliant *Call the Doctor*, Sleater-Kinney garnered even greater media exposure and critical applause on the strength of their incisive rants against gender inequity, consumerism and indie rock's male-dominated hierarchy. Their Kill Rock Stars label debut *Dig Me Out*, recorded with new drummer Janet Weiss, followed in 1997, and was again among the most acclaimed releases of its season; *The Hot Rock* appeared two years later, and in the spring of 2000 Sleater-Kinney resurfaced with *All Hands on the Bad One*. *—Jason Ankeny*

Sleater-Kinney / 1995 / Chainsaw ✦✦✦

● **Call the Doctor** / Mar. 25, 1996 / Chainsaw ✦✦✦✦✦
Sleater-Kinney's masterful sophomore effort *Call the Doctor* fulfills all the promise of the group's debut and more, forging taut melodicism and jaw-dropping sonic complexity out of barbed-wire emotional potency. The emergence of Carrie Brownstein as an equal shareholder in Corin Tucker's vision is the key—her four contributions (particularly "Stay Where You Are" and "I Wanna Be Your Joey Ramone") are stellar, while her harmonies complete Tucker's equally superb lead turns by reading between the lines to verbalize the naked aggression at the core of the songs' polemic power. Forget the riot grrrl implications inherent in the trio's music—*Call the Doctor* is pure, undiluted punk, and it's brilliant. *—Jason Ankeny*

Dig Me Out / Apr. 8, 1997 / Kill Rock Stars ✦✦✦✦✦
Having reinvented the girl-punk wheel with *Call the Doctor*, Sleater-Kinney continues to expand the boundaries of the form with the stunning *Dig Me Out*. Leaner and more intricate than its predecessor, the record is remarkably confident and mature; instead of succumbing to the pressures of "next big thing" status, the trio finds vindication in all of their critical adulation—the vocals are even more ferocious, the melodies are even more infectious and the ideals are even more passionate. *—Jason Ankeny*

Hot Rock / Feb. 23, 1999 / Kill Rock Stars ✦✦✦✦

All Hands on the Bad One / May 2, 2000 / Kill Rock Stars ✦✦✦✦✦

Percy Sledge

b. Nov. 25, 1941, Leighton, AL
Vocals / Deep Soul, Southern Soul, Soul
Percy Sledge will forever be associated with "When a Man Loves a Woman," a pleading, soulful ballad he sang with wrenching, convincing anguish and passion. Sledge sang all of his songs that way, delivering them in a powerful rush where he quickly changed from soulful belting to quavering, tearful pleas. It was a voice that made him one of the key figures of deep Southern Soul during the late '60s, based around the Muscle Shoals studio in Alabama. Formerly the vocalist for a Southern vocal group, Percy Sledge went solo in 1966, and recorded "When a Man Loves a Woman" as his first single. Released on Atlantic, it became a huge hit that summer and topped both pop and R&B charts. It was quickly followed that year by two Top Ten R&B hits, "Warm and Tender Love" and "It Tears Me Up," which were both in the vein of his first hit. Sledge's sales declined considerably during the early '70s, and after one surprise return to the R&B charts with 1974's "I'll Be Your Everything," he recorded little but toured often. After a revival of his major hit (used in numerous soundtracks and television ads) during the late '80s, Sledge's concerts became even more successful and he released the album *Blue Night* in 1994. *—Stephen Thomas Erlewine*

★ **It Tears Me Up** / Apr. 21, 1992 / Rhino/Atlantic ✦✦✦✦✦
This stunning compilation from the vaults of Atlantic Records spotlights the voice that gave us the original version of "When a Man Loves a Woman." Lesser-known hits like "It Tears Me Up," "Take Time to Know Her," and "Warm and Tender Love" are equally wonderful, and all are included in this must-have package. Great liner notes by Dave Marsh. Soul music just doesn't get any more heart-wrenching than this. Absolutely essential! *—Christine Ohlman*

Slint

f. 1987, Louisville, KY, **db.** 1991
Group / Math Rock, Experimental Rock, Indie Rock, Post-Rock/Experimental, Alternative Pop/Rock, Instrumental Rock
Though largely overlooked during their brief lifespan, Slint grew to become one of the most influential and far-reaching bands to emerge from the American underground rock community of the 1980s; innovative and iconoclastic, the group's deft, extremist manipulations of volume, tempo, and structure cast them as clear progenitors of the post-rock movement which blossomed during the following decade. Slint grew out of Louisville, KY's legendary Squirrel Bait, another seminal band which languished in relative obscurity during its own lifetime but ultimately spawned the likes of Gastr del Sol, Bitch Magnet, and Bastro as well. With producer Steve Albini, the quartet recorded 1989's *Tweez*, issued on their own Jennifer Hartman label; a collection of odd stylistic approaches, fractured rhythms, and strange lyrical fragments, the album owed debts to few (if any) historical precedents and steadfastly defied easy classification. 1991's *Spiderland* was an even more sophisticated and adventurous set, but (with the exception of a posthumous 1994 EP originally recorded between the two full-length albums) was Slint's swan song, although individual members remained key figures in the independent scene in acts including Tortoise, the Breeders, King Kong, Palace, and the For Carnation. *—Jason Ankeny*

Tweez / 1989 / Touch & Go ✦✦✦

● **Spiderland** / 1991 / Touch & Go ✦✦✦✦✦
More known for its frequent name-checks than its actual music, *Spiderland* remains one of the most essential and chilling releases in the mumbling post-rock arena. Even casual listeners will be able to witness an experimental power-base that the American underground has come to treasure. Indeed, the lumbering quiet-loud motif has been lifted by everybody from Lou Barlow to Mogwai, the album's emotional gelidity has done more to move away from prog-rock mistakes than almost any of the band's subsequent disciples, and it's easy to hear how the term "Slint dynamics" has become an indie categorization of its own. Most interestingly, however, is how even a seething angularity to songs like "Nosferatu Man" (disquieting, vampirish stop-starts) or "Good Morning, Captain" (a murmuring nod to *The Rime of the Ancient Mariner*) certainly signaled the beginning of the end for the band. Recording was intense, traumatic, and one more piece of evidence supporting the theory that band members had to be periodically institutionalized during the completion of the album. *Spiderland* remains, though, not quite the insurmountable masterpiece its reputation may suggest. Brian McMahan softly speaks/screams his way through the asphyxiated music and too often evokes strangled pity instead of outright empathy. Which probably speaks more about the potential dangers of pretentious post-rock than the frigid musical climate of the album itself. Surely, years later, *Spiderland* is still a strong, slightly overrated, compelling piece of investigational despair that is a worthy asset to most any experimentalist's record collection. *—Dean Carlson*

Slint / Aug. 29, 1994 / Touch & Go ✦✦✦✦✦

The Slits

f. 1976, **db.** 1981
Group / Post-Punk, Punk
Along with the Raincoats and Liliput, the Slits are one of the most significant female punk-rock bands of the late '70s. Not only did they bravely (or foolishly, you be the judge) leap into the fray with little, if any, musical ability, but through sheer emotion and desire created some great music, especially when they began working with veteran reggae producer Dennis Bovell, setting the stage for a future generation of riot grrrls. Formed by barely teenaged Ari Upp and Palmolive, the group made some crude recordings, though it wasn't until they nabbed the opening spot on the Clash's "White Riot" tour of England in 1977 that the Slits became a part of the punk pantheon. In 1979, the Slits made their first proper record *Cut* with reggae vet Dennis Bovell, who replaced the raging guitars with subtle reggae riddims. Palmolive was later replaced by new drummer Budgie (soon to join Siouxsie & the Banshees), and it was two years before a second record was released (*Return of the Giant Slits*), which was denser, darker and full of surprises. By the close of 1981, Arri Up was singing in Adrian Sherwood's dub/funk aggregation the New Age Steppers, and the Slits had become both legendary and somewhat notorious. Though much derided in their short existence, what the Slits achieved and what they meant to succeeding generations of young female rockers cannot be underestimated. *—John Dougan*

● **Cut** / 1979 / Island ✦✦✦✦✦
Its amateurish musicianship, less-than-honed singing, and thick, dubwise rhythms might not be for everyone, but there's little denying the crucial nature of the Slits' first record. Along with more recognized post-punk records like Public Image Limited's *Metal Box*, the Pop Group's *Y*, and less recognized fare like Ruts DC and Mad Professor's *Rhythm Collision Dub*, *Cut* displayed a love affair with the style of reggae that honed in on deep throbs, pulses, and disorienting effects, providing little focus on anything other than that and periodic scrapes from guitarist Viv Albertine. But more importantly, *Cut* placed the Slits along with the Raincoats and Liliput as major figureheads of unbridled female expression in the post-punk era. You could call some of these songs a reaction to the more knuckledragging *Nuggets* bands, or the '60s garage acts that would find as many ways possible to say "women bad." Songs

like "Instant Hit" (about PiL guitarist Keith Levene), "So Tough" (about Sid Vicious and Johnny Rotten), "Ping Pong Affair," and "Love Und Romance" point out the shortcomings of the opposite sex and romantic involvements with more precision and sass than the men were ever able to. "Spend Spend Spend" and "Shoplifting" target consumerism with an equal sense of humor ("We pay fuck all!"). Despite the less-than-polished nature and street tough ruggedness, *Cut* is entirely fun and catchy; it's filled with memorable hooks, whether they're courtesy of the piano lick that carries "Typical Girls" or Ari Up's exuberant vocals. (One listen to Up will demonstrate that Björk might not be as original as you've been led to believe.) Island's 2000 reissue blows away the earlier issue in sound and presentation, adding to the essential nature of this wildly influential record. *—Andy Kellman*

Y3LP / 1980 / Rough Trade ♦♦♦

Return of the Giant Slits / 1981 / CBS ♦♦♦

The Peel Sessions / 1989 / Strange Fruit ♦♦♦♦♦

P.F. Sloan

b. 1944

Vocals, Harmonica, Guitar / Folk-Rock, Pop, Singer/Songwriter

He was there at the dawn of surf music, he was crowned king of the West Coast protest folkies, and he created some of the great American pop records of the '60s, yet today, the name P.F. Sloan is scarcely remembered outside of a circle of collectors and other period enthusiasts. Teamed early with Steve Barri, Sloan had a lasting partner. The duo cashed in on the surf craze as the Fantastic Baggies, and Sloan has claimed to be involved with countless more surf productions. Sloan and Barri wrote and produced hits for the likes of the Turtles and Johnny Rivers, and may best be remembered for Barry McGuire's "Eve of Destruction." Sloan's own albums for Dunhill were based on the kind of material he had given McGuire, and despite being dismissed by the "serious" protest-folk community of the day, they stand as excellent on their own merits.

Sloan's attempt to shift away from the West Coast folk-rock he largely created was reflected with the R&B-tinged album *Measure for Pleasure*, and following another album in the early '70s, he was gone. In spite of the occasional live gig and rumors of a comeback, it appears that P.F. Sloan will remain forever connected with his '60s work, his behind-the-scenes efforts overshadowing the fine music under his own name. *—Steve Aldrich*

The Best of P.F. Sloan (1965-1966) / 1986 / Rhino ♦♦♦♦♦

While One Way's *Anthology* has a wider range, it may be that many listeners will prefer this 14-song collection, as it focuses exclusively on tracks from Sloan's first two LPs. This means you get nothing but sub-Dylanesque folk-rock, but after all, that's what many people value most by Sloan. The tracks are universally strong, including his most famous tunes ("Eve of Destruction," "The Sins of a Family," "Take Me for What I'm Worth") and lesser-known, equally worthy ones like "Lollipop Train," "From a Distance," "Here's Where You Belong," and "I Get out of Breath." *—Richie Unterberger*

P.F. Sloan/The Grass Roots / 1988 / Big Beat ♦♦♦

While this isn't as solid as the other P.F. Sloan collections, the concept is interesting, combining some of his most famous solo performances with five songs that were credited to the Grass Roots in the mid-'60s, but were for most intents and purposes Sloan performances. You can avoid this confusing approach by getting the Grass Roots' *Where Were You When I Needed You?* CD and Sloan's first two LPs. But those original Sloan albums are pretty hard to come by these days, meaning that our choices are largely limited to relatively pathwork compilations such as these. *—Richie Unterberger*

● **Anthology** / Jul. 18, 1993 / One Way ♦♦♦♦♦

A well-compiled 18-track anthology featuring Sloan's overlooked recording career. This is essential folk-rock in the singer/songwriter tradition. Included is his wonderful version of "Eve of Destruction," which was written by Sloan and popularized by Barry McGuire. *—Chris Woodstra*

Sly & the Family Stone

f. 1967, San Francisco, CA, **db.** 1970

Group / Pop/Rock, Funk, Soul

Sly & the Family Stone harnessed all of the disparate musical and social trends of the late '60s, creating a wild, brilliant fusion of soul, rock, R&B, psychedelia, and funk that broke boundaries down without a second thought. Led by Sly Stone, the Family Stone was comprised of men and women, and Blacks and Whites, making the band the first fully integrated group in rock's history. That integration shone through the music, as well as the group's message. Before Stone, very few soul and R&B groups delved into political and social commentary; after him, it became a tradition in soul, funk, and hip-hop. And, along with James Brown, Stone brought hard funk into the mainstream. The Family Stone's arrangements were ingenious, filled with unexpected group vocals, syncopated rhythms, punchy horns, and pop melodies. Their music was joyous, but as the '60s ended, so did the good times. Stone became disillusioned with the ideals he had been preaching in his music, becoming addicted to a variety of drugs in the process. His music gradually grew slower and darker, culminating in 1971's *There's a Riot Going On,* which set the pace for '70s funk with its elastic bass, slurred vocals, and militant Black power stance. Stone was able to turn out one more modern funk classic, 1973's *Fresh,* before slowly succumbing to his addictions, which gradually sapped him of his once prodigious talents. Nevertheless, his music continued to provide the basic template for urban soul, funk, and even hip-hop well into the '90s. *—Stephen Thomas Erlewine*

Whole New Thing / 1967 / Epic/Legacy ♦♦♦

Dance to the Music / Apr. 27, 1968 / Epic/Legacy ♦♦♦

Sly & the Family Stone came into their own with their second album, *Dance to the Music.* This is exuberant music, bursting with joy and invention. If there's a surfeit of classic material, with only the title track being a genuine classic, that winds up being nearly incidental, since it's so easy to get sucked into the freewheeling spirit and cavalier virtuosity of the group. Consider this—prior to this record no one, not even the Family Stone, treated soul as a psychedelic sun-splash, filled with bright melodies, kaleidoscopic arrangements, inextricably intertwined interplay, and deft, fast rhythms. Yes, they wound up turning "Higher" into the better "I Want to Take You Higher," and they recycle the title track in the long jam "Dance to the Medley." But there's such imagination to this jam that the similarities fade as they play. And, if these are just vamps, well, so are James Brown's records, and those didn't have the vitality or friendliness of this. Not a perfect record, but a fine one all the same. *—Stephen Thomas Erlewine*

Life / 1968 / Epic/Legacy ♦♦♦♦♦

Just a matter of months after *Dance to the Music,* Sly & the Family Stone turned around and delivered *Life,* a record that leapfrogged over its predecessor in terms of accomplishment and achievement. The most noteworthy difference is the heavier reliance on psychedelics and fuzz guitars, plus a sharpening of songcraft that extends to even throwaways like "Chicken." As it turns out, *Life* didn't have any hits—the double A-sided single "Life"/"M'Lady" barely cracked the Top 100—yet this feels considerably more song-oriented than its predecessor, as each track is a concise slice of tightly wound dance-funk. All the more impressive is that the group is able to strut their stuff within this context, trading off vocals and blending into an unstoppable force where it's impossible to separate the instruments, even as they solo. The songwriting might still be perfunctory or derivative in spots—listen to how they appropriate "Eleanor Rigby" on "Plastic Jim"—but what's impressive is how even the borrowed or recycled moments sound fresh in context. And then there's the cuts that work on their own, whether it's the aforementioned double-sided single, "Fun," "Dynamite!," or several other cuts here—these are brilliant, intoxicating slices of funk-pop that get by as much on sound as song, and they're hard not to resist. *—Stephen Thomas Erlewine*

☆ **Stand!** / May 3, 1969 / Epic ♦♦♦♦♦

Stand! is the pinnacle of Sly & the Family Stone's early work, a record that represents a culmination of the group's musical vision and accomplishment. *Life* hinted at this record's boundless enthusiasm and blurred stylistic boundaries, yet everything simply gels here, resulting in no separation between the astounding funk, effervescent irresistible melodies, psychedelicized guitars, and deep rhythms. Add to this a sharpened sense of pop songcraft, elastic band interplay, and a flowering of Sly's social conscious, and the result is utterly stunning. Yes, the jams ("Don't Call Me Nigger, Whitey," "Sex Machine") wind up meandering ever so slightly, but they're surrounded by utter brilliance, from the rousing call to arms of "Stand" to the unification anthem "Everyday People" to the unstoppable "I Want to Take You Higher." All of it sounds like the Family Stone, thanks not just to the communal lead vocals but to the brilliant interplay, but each track is distinct, emphasizing a different side of their musical personality. As a result, *Stand!* winds up infectious and informative, invigorating and thought-provoking—stimulating in every sense of the word. Few records of its time touched it, and Sly topped it only by offering its opposite the next time out. *—Stephen Thomas Erlewine*

★ **Greatest Hits** / Nov. 21, 1970 / Epic ♦♦♦♦♦

Released in 1970, during the stopgap between *Stand!* and *There's a Riot Goin' On, Greatest Hits* inadvertently arrived at precisely the right moment, summarizing Sly & the Family Stone's joyous hit-making run on the pop and R&B charts. Technically, only four songs here reached the Top Ten, with only two others hitting the Top 40, but judging this solely on charts is misleading, since this is simply a peerless singles collection. This summarizes their first four albums perfectly (almost all of *Stand!* outside of the two jams and "Somebody's Watching You," is here), adding the non-LP singles "Hot Fun in the Summertime," "Thank You (Falettinme Be Mice Elf Agin)," and "Everybody Is a Star," possibly the loveliest thing they ever recorded. But, this isn't merely a summary (and, if it was just that, *Anthology,* the early-'80s comp that covers *Riot* and *Fresh* would be stronger than this), it's one of the greatest party records of all time. Music is rarely as vivacious, vigorous, and vibrant as this, and captured on one album, the spirit, sound, and songs of Sly & the Family Stone are all the more stunning. Greatest hits don't come better than this—in fact, music rarely does. *—Stephen Thomas Erlewine*

☆ **There's a Riot Goin' On** / Nov. 20, 1971 / Epic ♦♦♦♦♦

It's easy to write off *There's a Riot Goin' On* as one of two things—Sly Stone's disgusted social commentary or the beginning of his slow descent into addiction. It's both of these things, of course, but pigeonholing it as either winds up dismissing the album as a whole, since it is so bloody hard to categorize. What's certain is that *Riot* is unlike any of Sly & the Family Stone's other albums, stripped of the effervescence that flowed through even such politically aware records as *Stand!* This is idealism soured, as hope is slowly replaced by cynicism, joy by skepticism, enthusiasm by weariness, sex by pornography, thrills by narcotics. Joy isn't entirely gone—it creeps through the cracks every once and awhile and, more disturbing, Sly revels in his stoned decadence. What makes *Riot* so remarkable is that it's hard not to get drawn in with him, as you're seduced by the narcotic grooves, seductive vocals slurs, leering electric pianos, and crawling guitars. As the themes surface, it's hard not to nod in agreement, but it's a junkie nod, induced by the comforting coma of the music. And damn if this music isn't funk at its deepest and most impenetrable—this is dense music, nearly impenetrable, but not from its deep grooves, but its utter weariness. Sly's songwriting remains remarkably sharp, but only when he wants to write—the foreboding opener "Luv 'n' Haight," the scarily resigned "Family Affair," the cracked cynical blues "Time" and "(You Caught Me) Smilin'." Ultimately, the music is the message and while it's dark music, it's not alienating—it's seductive despair, and that's the scariest thing about it. *—Stephen Thomas Erlewine*

☆ **Fresh** / Jun. 30, 1973 / Epic ♦♦♦♦♦

Fresh expands and brightens the slow grooves of *There's a Riot Goin' On,* turning them, for the most part, into friendly, welcoming rhythms. There are still traces of the narcotic haze of *Riot,* particularly on the brilliant, crawling inversion of "Que Sera Sera," yet this never feels like an invitation into a junkie's lair. Still, this isn't necessarily lighter than *Riot*—in fact, his social commentary is more explicit, and while the music doesn't telegraph his resignation the way *Riot* did, in comes from the same source. So, *Fresh* winds up more varied, musically and lyrically, which may not make it as unified, but it does result in more traditional funk that certainly is appealing in its own right. Besides, this isn't conventional funk—it's eccentric, where even concise catchy tunes like "If You Want Me to Stay" seem as elastic as the opener, "In Time." That's the album's ultimate charm—it finds Sly precisely on the point where he's balancing funk and pop, about to fall into the brink, but creating an utterly individual album that wound up being his last masterwork and one of the great funk albums of its era. *—Stephen Thomas Erlewine*

Small Talk / 1974 / Epic ♦♦♦

★ **Anthology** / 1981 / Epic ♦♦♦♦♦
Anthology essentially replicates the previous collection *Greatest Hits* and adds singles from *There's a Riot Goin' On* and *Fresh* to the end of the album. Where *Greatest Hits* didn't follow chronological order, *Anthology* presents every single in the order they were released—and, with the exception of the latter-day singles and the inclusion of "Don't Call Me Nigger, Whitey," that is the major difference between the two collections. *Anthology* goes for a sweeping, definitive overview, while *Greatest Hits* is a brief blast of 12 of the finest singles of the rock & roll era. Either compilation functions as an excellent introduction, but *Anthology* is more comprehensive, giving it the edge as a first purchase. *—Stephen Thomas Erlewine*

The Small Faces

f. 1965
Group / British Psychedelia, Mod, Psychedelic, British Invasion
The Small Faces were the best English band never to hit it big in America. On this side of the Atlantic, all anybody remembers them only for is their sole stateside hit, "Itchycoo Park"—but in England, the Small Faces were one of the most extraordinary and successful bands of the mid-'60s; their music remains some of the most valuable and enjoyable of the era. Lead singer/guitarist Steve Marriott's formal background was on the stage, though he was earning his living at a music shop when he met bassist Ronnie Lane and drummer Kenney Jones, members of the Pioneers. The band—with Marriott installed permanently—cast its lot with a faction of British youth known as the Mods, stylish posers who, among their other attributes, affected a dandified look and a fanatical love of American R&B. Now christened the Small Faces ("face" being a piece of Mod slang for a fashion leader), the band recorded two singles ("Sha-La-La-La-Lee" and "Hey Girl") which hit the Top Ten in 1966, heralded with their first album, *Small Faces*. "All or Nothing" marked their first chart-topping entry, and its follow-up, "My Mind's Eye," followed it nearly as high.

After moving to the Immediate label, the Small Faces released their second album, also entitled *Small Faces* (but known in the USA as *There Are but Four Small Faces*). The band had bigger aspirations than doing more hit singles, and set to work across five months during 1968 recording what proved to be their magnum opus, *Ogden's Nut Gone Flake*. Though recorded as a joke, the single "Lazy Sunday" rose to number two on the British charts. The group began showing serious signs of strain, however, and the end came when Marriott suddenly left the stage during a concert; he later called Peter Frampton and the two eventually formed Humble Pie. The Small Faces did carry on into 1969, replacing Marriott with Rod Stewart and Ron Wood and carrying on for one album before going on to greater glory as the Faces. During the mid-'70s, the band reunited (without Ronnie Lane) for two albums, *Playmates* and *78 in the Shade*. *—Bruce Eder*

The Small Faces / 1966 / Deram ♦♦♦♦♦
This CD and the accompanying 1996 reissue of *From the Beginning* makes collecting the Small Faces' Decca sides complicated, containing as it does many tracks that are not on the anthology double-disc. The new remastering has turned this into a must-own disc for anyone who enjoys the early Rolling Stones or, especially, the early Who, and wants to hear a British Invasion band as good as they were that never quite made it in the U.S., and which could have crossed swords with any garage band you care to name and carried the day. In those days, Steve Marriott had an even more soulful voice than Mick Jagger or Roger Daltrey; the main influences on the group were Sam Cooke and Marvin Gaye, and he was pretty formidable on guitar as well. The songs all have that really cool crunchy sound on the early Who records, except the sound is a little fuller and the tempos are better conceived, and there's even a pretty impressive bit of feedback throughout. The French EP tracks that comprise this disc's bonus songs are all distinctly different from the standard cuts, generally much more raw—like *real* American-style garage band stuff—including a feedback-laden opening to a completely different take of "What'cha Gonna Do About It" and totally different versions of "Shake" and "E to D." The sound on these cuts isn't quite up to the original album's 12 established tracks, as master tapes were impossible to find, but they—and the improved sound of the rest—make this a must-own CD, even more than *The Decca Anthology*. *—Bruce Eder*

From the Beginning / 1967 / Deram ♦♦♦♦♦
Another remastering of a classic piece of mid-'60s British rock & soul, and as important and enjoyable a record as, say, the Beatles' *Rubber Soul* or the Stones' *Aftermath*, even if the album itself was slapped together by Decca in an effort to undercut the band's first new release for rival Immediate Records in 1967. Steve Marriott's honest, agonized cover of the Del Shannon classic "Runaway" almost makes up for the fact that neither Otis Redding nor Marvin Gaye ever got around to applying their respective talents to this jewel of a song. That's just the opening number, and there's some stuff even better than that here. There are some songs that overlap with the Immediate stuff, including some really spaced-out psychedelia ("Yesterday, Today, and Tomorrow"), cool dance numbers ("Have You Ever Seen Me"), some repeated tracks ("What'cha Gonna Do About It," "Sha-La-La-La-Lee") from the Decca *Small Faces* album) killer Motown paeans ("You've Really Got a Hold on Me"—picture the early Who on a really, really good day covering this), and one original ("All or Nothing") that should be required listening for anyone who thinks they know the best music of the British Invasion. And then there are the five bonus tracks, four from French-issued EPs that are completely different (and better) takes of "Baby Don't You Do It", and a live BBC-recorded version of "What'cha Gonna Do About It." Marriott's playing on the latter is so loud and powerful, it could have melted the instruments of any American garage band this side of the Litter. At $11.99 list, this disc and its companion *Small Faces* reissue are the biggest British Invasion bargains going. *—Bruce Eder*

☆ **There Are But Four Small Faces** / 1968 / Columbia ♦♦♦♦♦
The band's first album for Andrew "Loog" Oldham's Immediate label originally appeared in two different forms in England (where it was known as *Small Faces*) and America, and the two song lineups have been combined on an early-'90s American Sony Music reissue. The music here is much more fully developed and experimental than their preceding album, still largely R&B-based (apart from the delightfully trippy "Itchycoo Park," the band's sole American hit) but with lots of unusual sounds and recording techniques being attempted. *—Bruce Eder*

☆ **Ogden's Nut Gone Flake** / 1968 / Castle ♦♦♦♦♦
The best album the Small Faces ever released, and one of the great records of the late '60s, a kind of cockney *Sgt. Pepper*, with tough, grinding rock numbers, blues shouts, and psychedelia all mixing together into one brilliant whole. A vital addition to any record or CD collection, and also a controversial one at the time—a promotional ad taken out in the British music trades at the time managed to blaspheme several religions at once. Alas, Steve Marriott decided to call it quits with the group less than six months after this record was released. *—Bruce Eder*

Autumn Stone / 1969 / Castle ♦♦♦♦
An excellent collection of most of the band's most important songs from both their later Decca and their entire Immediate history, rounded out with their final single, "The Universal," and five live tracks taken from a 1968 concert. A decent set of liner notes would have been nice, though. *—Bruce Eder*

Playmates / 1977 / Atlantic ♦

78 in the Shade / 1978 / Atlantic ♦♦

★ **25 Greatest Hits** / 1992 / Repertoire ♦♦♦♦♦
Featuring all of their big British hits from "What'cha Gonna Do About It" to "The Universal," as well as worthy obscurities like "Donkey Rides a Penny a Glass," *25 Greatest Hits* is the best Small Faces compilation available, even if the tracks aren't presented in chronological order. *—Stephen Thomas Erlewine*

All or Nothing / Jun. 30, 1992 / Columbia ♦♦♦♦♦
The best collection to date of odd outtakes, obscure B-sides, and other rarities, remastered for superior sound and reconfigured so that, among other advantages, the live tracks from *The Autumn Stone* are assembled together in sequence. Also contains lots of alternate takes, instrumental backing tracks etc. *—Bruce Eder*

The Immediate Years / Jan. 1996 / Charly ♦♦♦♦♦

The Definitive Anthology of the Small Faces / Feb. 1996 / Repertoire ♦♦♦♦♦

BBC Sessions: 1965-1968 / Feb. 29, 2000 / Varese ♦♦♦

★ **The Darlings of Wapping Wharf Launderette** / May 16, 2000 / Immediate/Sequel ♦♦♦♦♦
Here's the question for Small Faces fans: Is it better to own the original Immediate albums or to invest in the splendid double-disc set, *The Darlings of Wapping Wharf Launderette: The Immediate Anthology*? The question is a tricky one, since *Darlings* contains all of their Immediate recordings, meaning all of *Autumn Stone* (or *There Are but Four Small Faces*, as its known in its American incarnation), plus all of the landmark *Ogden's Nut Gone Flake*. Granted, *Ogden's* is divided cleanly in half, with the first side appearing on disc one and the second on disc two, which may irritate listeners who like to hear the concept album uninterrupted. Nevertheless, it's hard not to view *Darlings* as a real bargain, since it gathers all the singles, albums, B-sides, plus some outtakes and alternate mixes and versions from the group's most creative period. And, hearing them in this setting, it's hard not to be stunned by the depth of the group's songwriting and restless musicality, which holds its own with peers like the Kinks and the Who. So, the question may indeed be an easy one, after all—if you want to be stunned by the Small Faces' peak, there's no better place to turn. *—Stephen Thomas Erlewine*

Smash Mouth

f. San Jose, CA
Group / Ska-Punk, Post-Grunge, Alternative Pop/Rock
A novelty rock band in the same vein as Presidents of the United States of America, but with surf and garage influences instead of the Presidents' punk/thrash background, Smash Mouth found a hit in 1997 with the '50s-influenced "Walkin' on the Sun." The group was formed in 1994 in San Jose, California by vocalist Steve Harwell, a former rapper with the group F.O.S. After that group disintegrated, he began jamming with an old friend, drummer Kevin Coleman. Harwell's former manager introduced him to guitarist Greg Camp (fresh from the local band Lackadaddy) and bassist Paul De Lisle. The quartet recorded two demos, and got the songs into rotation on a local radio station. After playing a summer festival with No Doubt and Beck, Smash Mouth decided to record an album. After finishing *Fush Yu Mang*, the group were signed by Interscope, which released "Walkin' on the Sun" as the first single. It became a number one modern rock hit, and pushed the album into the Top 40. The follow-up album, *Astro Lounge*, was released in 1999, generating the hit "All Star"; a collection of early material, *East Bay Sessions*, also appeared that same year. *—John Bush*

● **Fush Yu Mang** / Jul. 8, 1997 / Interscope ♦♦♦♦
The groovy, '60s soul-funk of "Walking on the Sun" disguised the fact that Smash Mouth wasn't much more than a run-of-the-mill ska-punk band, and their debut, *Fush Yu Mang*, wasn't much more than an average modern-rock album. With its organ riff and breezy melody, "Walking on the Sun" was a great one-shot single, yet Smash Mouth never came close to replicating its easy charm anywhere on *Fush Yu Mang*. They sound clumsy when they rock, and their uptempo numbers never quite catch fire. There are some moments that'll satisfy third-wave ska-revival fans, but anyone hooked in by the single will find the album disappointing. *—Stephen Thomas Erlewine*

Astro Lounge / Jun. 8, 1999 / Interscope ♦♦♦♦
Based on their infectious summer single "Walking on the Sun," it was easy to dismiss Smash Mouth as a one-hit wonder, since it was hard to believe that they'd be able to top that sun-kissed delight which was easily the highlight of their debut, *Fush Yu Mang.* Perhaps that's why their second record, *Astro Lounge,* feels like such a surprise, since it carries through on the promise of "Walking on the Sun." Like Sugar Ray—a fellow veteran of the ska-punk underworld who delivered a follow-up which owed more to melodic pop and new wave than its hit predecessor—Smash Mouth has created an album that is unabashedly fun, catchy, and lightweight; the ideal music for a car radio or a day at the beach. It's true that nothing on *Astro Lounge* is as immediately grabbing as "Walking on the Sun," but every song shares the same party-ready mentality and irresistible, trashy AM-radio vibe. No, nothing on *Astro Lounge* is particularly deep, but it's all good fun and it never disappoints—which is quite a remarkable feat, since one-hit wonders rarely deliver a second album that betters their first. *—Stephen Thomas Erlewine*

The Smashing Pumpkins

f. 1988, Chicago, IL, **db.** Dec. 2, 2000
Group / Alternative Pop/Rock
Of all the major alternative rock bands of the early '90s, Smashing Pumpkins were the group least influenced by traditional underground rock. Lead guitarist/songwriter Billy Corgan fashioned an amalgam of progressive rock, heavy metal, goth rock, psychedelia and dream pop, creating a layered, powerful sound driven by swirling, distorted guitars. Corgan was wise enough to exploit his angst-ridden lyrics, yet he never shied away from rock-star posturing, even if he did cloak it in allegedly ironic gestures. In fact, the Smashing Pumpkins became the model for alternative rock success—Nirvana was too destructive, Pearl Jam shunned success. The Pumpkins, on the other hand, knew how to play the game—signing to a major-subsidized indie for underground credibility, moving to the major in time to make the group a multi-platinum act. And when the group did achieve mass success with 1993's *Siamese Dream,* they went a long way to legitimize heavy metal and orchestrated prog rock, helping move alternative rock even closer to '70s AOR rock, especially in the eyes of radio programmers and mainstream audiences. And, unlike many of their contemporaries, the Pumpkins were able to withstand many internal problems and keep selling records, emerging as the longest-lasting and most successful alternative band of the early '90s. *—Stephen Thomas Erlewine*

Gish / May 1991 / Virgin ♦♦♦♦♦
Arriving several months before Nirvana's *Nevermind,* the Smashing Pumpkins' debut album *Gish,* which was also produced by Butch Vig, was the first shot of the alternative revolution that transformed the rock & roll landscape of the '90s. While Nirvana was a punk band, the Smashing Pumpkins and guitarist/vocalist Billy Corgan are arena-rockers, co-opting their metallic riffs and epic art-rock song structures with self-absorbed lyrical confessions. Though Corgan's lyrics fall apart upon close analysis, there's no denying his gift for arrangements. Like Brian May and Jimmy Page, he knows how to layer guitars for maximum effect, whether it's on the pounding, sub-Sabbath rush of "I Am One" or the shimmering, psychedelic dream-pop surfaces of "Rhinoceros." Such musical moments like these, as well as the rushing "Siva" and the folky "Daydream," which features D'Arcy on lead vocals, demonstrate the Smashing Pumpkins' potential, but the rest of *Gish* falls prey to undistinguished songwriting and showy instrumentation. *—Stephen Thomas Erlewine*

Lull / 1992 / Caroline ♦♦♦

● **Siamese Dream** / Jul. 27, 1993 / Virgin ♦♦♦♦♦
While *Gish* had placed Smashing Pumpkins on the "most promising artist" list for many, troubles were threatening to break the band apart. Singer/guitarist/leader Billy Corgan was battling a severe case of writer's block and was in a deep state of depression brought on by a relationship in turmoil; drummer Jimmy Chamberlin was addicted to hard drugs; and bassist D'Arcy and guitarist James Iha severed their romantic relationship. The sessions for their sophomore effort, *Siamese Dream,* were wrought with friction—Corgan eventually played almost all the instruments himself (except for percussion). Some say strife and tension produces the best music, and it certainly helped make *Siamese Dream* one of the finest alt-rock albums of all time. Instead of following Nirvana's punk rock route, *Siamese Dream* went in the opposite direction—guitar solos galore, layered walls of sound courtesy of the album's producers (Butch Vig and Corgan), extended compositions that bordered on prog rock, plus often reflective and heartfelt lyrics. The four tracks that were selected as singles became alternative radio standards—the anthems "Cherub Rock," "Today," and "Rocket," plus the symphonic ballad "Disarm"—but as a whole, *Siamese Dream* proved to be an incredibly consistent album. Such underrated compositions as the red-hot rockers "Quiet" and "Geek U.S.A." were standouts, as were the epics "Hummer," "Soma," and "Silverfuck," plus the soothing sounds of "Mayonaise," "Spaceboy," and "Luna." After the difficult recording sessions, Corgan stated publicly that if *Siamese Dream* didn't achieve breakthrough success, he would end the band. He didn't have to worry for long—the album debuted in the *Billboard* Top Ten, and had sold more than four million copies in three years. *Siamese Dream* stands alongside *Nevermind* and *Superunknown* as one of the decade's finest (and most influential) rock albums. *—Greg Prato*

Pisces Iscariot / Oct. 4, 1994 / Virgin ♦♦♦
Although Smashing Pumpkins had only released two studio albums by 1994 (1991's *Gish* and 1993's *Siamese Dream*), they had an overflow of songs that were either relegated to B-sides on European singles or remained unreleased. Billy Corgan proved to be one of rock's most prolific songwriters of the 1990s' alt-rock movement—as the quality of these early leftovers were often just as strong as the songs that were officially released. Since nearly all of these songs were never issued domestically, the B-side/rarity collection *Pisces Iscariot* was issued alongside their first long-form home video, *Vieuphoria.* The collection proved to be a feast for fans—it's inexplicable why such exceptional rockers ("Plume," "Hello Kitty Kat," "Frail and Bedazzled," "Blue") and ballads ("Obscured," "La Dolly Vita") weren't featured on albums. Also included is the long and winding, 11-minute epic jam fest "Starla," which proves that Corgan was one of the finest (and most underrated) rock guitarists of the '90s, as well as a pair of unlikely covers—Fleetwood Mac's gentle "Landslide" and the Animals' psychedelic "Girl Named Sandoz." Also included are insightful liner notes (strewn with typos) from Corgan. While it's not the definitive B-sides collection of pre-*Mellon Collie* Pumpkins (such tracks as "Bullet Train to Osaka," "Purr Snickety," "Apathy's Last Kiss," "My Dahlia," "Jackie Blue," "Glynis," and others are nowhere to be found), *Pisces Iscariot* contains some of Corgan and company's finest moments. Hopefully a second collection will eventually see the light of day. *—Greg Prato*

Mellon Collie and the Infinite Sadness / Oct. 24, 1995 / Virgin ♦♦♦♦♦
Smashing Pumpkins didn't shy away from making the follow-up to the grand, intricate *Siamese Dream.* With *Mellon Collie and the Infinite Sadness,* the band turns in one of the most ambitious and indulgent albums in rock history. Lasting over two hours and featuring 28 songs, the album is certainly a challenging listen. To Billy Corgan's credit, it's a rewarding and compelling one as well. Although the artistic scope of the album is immense, the Smashing Pumpkins flourish in such an overblown setting. Corgan's songwriting has never been limited by conventional notions of what a rock band can do, even if it is clear that he draws inspiration from scores of '70s heavy metal and art-rock bands. Instead of copying the sounds of his favorite records, he expands on their ideas, making the gentle piano of the title track and the sighing "1979" sit comfortably against the volcanic rush of "Jellybelly" and "Zero." In between those two extremes lay an array of musical styles, drawing from rock, pop, folk, and classical. Some of the songs don't work as well as others, but *Mellon Collie* never seems to drag. Occasionally they fall flat on their face, but over the entire album, the Smashing Pumpkins prove that they are one of the more creative and consistent bands of the '90s. *—Stephen Thomas Erlewine*

The Aeroplane Flies High / Nov. 26, 1996 / Virgin ♦♦♦

Adore / Jun. 2, 1998 / Caroline ♦♦♦

MACHINA/The Machines of God / Feb. 29, 2000 / Caroline ♦♦♦

Huey "Piano" Smith

b. Jan. 26, 1934, New Orleans, LA
Piano / New Orleans R&B, R&B
At one time a madcap vocalist and underrated pianist, Huey "Piano" Smith was a star in New Orleans during the '50s. He sang with Earl King in the early '50s, then recorded with Guitar Slim from 1951 to 1954. He did several sessions and also led the Clowns, whose roster at one point included Bobby Marchan. Smith's biggest hit wasn't the song he's best known for, "Rocking Pneumonia and the Boogie Woogie Flu," but "Don't You Just Know It," which was his only Top Ten pop and R&B hit. It reached number four R&B and number nine pop in 1958, a year after "Rocking Pneumonia" peaked at number five R&B. Smith kept going until he became a Jehovah's Witness and left the music business. *—Ron Wynn*

● **This Is Huey Piano Smith** / Apr. 21, 1998 / Music Club ♦♦♦♦♦
For years, Huey "Piano" Smith lacked a comprehensive overview of his recording career, and no compilation ever appeared on CD in the United States. The budget-line label Music Club rectified that situation in 1998 with the release of *This Is Huey Piano Smith,* an 18-track collection that features all of his hit singles for Ace plus several failed singles and New Orleans staples. Smith's hits and standards—"Rockin' Pneumonia and the Boogie-Woogie Flu," "Don't You Just Know It," "High Blood Pressure," "Pop-Eye," the original version of "Sea Cruise," with his vocals instead of Frankie Ford's—are so good that it's an inevitable disappointment to find many of the songs here are blatant attempts to get back on the charts ("Tu-Ber-Cu-Lucas and the Sinus Blues," "Would You Believe It (I Have a Cold)"). These fall flat, as do a couple of the other cuts, but unfortunately, that's an accurate portrait of Smith's career—he had a handful of wonderful, essential songs and was a hell of a performer, but he wasn't a consistent hitmaker. Nevertheless, the strong stuff is so good—even essential—that this is still highly recommended for New Orleans R&B fans and R&B fans in general.*—Stephen Thomas Erlewine*

Patti Smith

b. Dec. 30, 1946, Chicago, IL
Vocals / New York Punk, Album Rock, Proto-Punk, Hard Rock
Patti Smith is a poet and rock singer who first gained notice when reading her poetry at gatherings in New York City in the early '70s. By 1974 Smith had edged toward music by reading with the backup of electric guitarist and rock critic Lenny Kaye, notably on her independent-label single, "Piss Factory." By 1975 Smith had organized a band that was playing in such clubs as the punk birthplace in New York, CBGB's, and she earned a contract with Arista Records. This resulted in the release of *Horses,* a critically acclaimed album that featured her songs, sometimes melded to dramatic readings, and such rock oldies as "Land of 1,000 Dances." *Radio Ethiopia* was both mainstream-rock-oriented and more experimental, depending on which track you played. With 1978's *Easter,* Smith was definitely moving in a more commercial direction, especially by pairing with Bruce Springsteen for the hit single "Because the Night." That marked the high point of Smith's rock career. *Wave* (1979) found her waving goodbye; she married ex-MC5 guitarist Fred "Sonic" Smith and retired from the music business. Her return came with the promising 1988 album *Dream of Life,* but she was not back to full-time duty. Smith's husband died suddenly at the end of 1994. In 1995, she began making concert appearances again while preparing a new album due in 1996. In June 1996, Smith released *Gone Again; Peace and Noise* appeared a year later, and in the spring of 2000 she returned with *Gung Ho. —William Ruhlmann*

★ **Horses** / Nov. 1975 / Arista ♦♦♦♦♦
It isn't hard to make the case for Patti Smith as a punk rock progenitor based on her debut album, which anticipated the new wave by a year or so: the simple, crudely played rock & roll, featuring Lenny Kaye's rudimentary guitar work, the anarchic spirit of Smith's vocals, and the emotional and imaginative nature of her lyrics, all prefigure the coming movement

as it evolved on both sides of the Atlantic. Smith is a rock critic's dream, a poet as steeped in '60s garage rock as she is in French Symbolism; "Land" carries on from the Doors' "The End," marking her as a successor to Jim Morrison, while the borrowed choruses of "Gloria" and "Land of 1,000 Dances" are more in tune with the era of sampling than they were in the '70s. Producer John Cale respected Smith's primitivism in a way that later producers did not, and the loose, improvisatory song structures worked with her free verse to create something like a new spoken word/musical art form: *Horses* was a hybrid, the sound of a post-Beat poet, as she put it, "dancing around to the simple rock & roll song." *— William Ruhlmann*

Radio Ethiopia / Oct. 1976 / Arista ♦♦♦
After the success of *Horses,* Patti Smith had something to prove to reviewers and to the industry, and *Radio Ethiopia* aimed at both. Producer Jack Douglas gave "the Patti Smith Group," as it was now billed, a hard rock sound, notably on the side-opening "Ask the Angels" and "Pumping (My Heart)," songs that seemed aimed at album-oriented rock radio. But the title track was a ten-minute guitar extravaganza that pushed the group's deliberate primitivism closer to amateurish thrashing. Elsewhere, Smith repeated the reggae excursions and vocal overlaying that had paced *Horses* on "Ain't It Strange" and "Poppies," but these efforts were less effective than they had been the first time around, perhaps because they were less inspired, perhaps because they were more familiar. A schizophrenic album in which the many elements that had worked so well together on *Horses* now seemed jarringly incompatible, with *Radio Ethiopia* Smith and her band encountered the same development problem the punks would—as they learned their craft, and competence set in, they lost some of the unself-consciousness that had made their music so appealing. *— William Ruhlmann*

Easter / Mar. 1978 / Arista ♦♦♦♦♦
Patti Smith came back from the year-and-a-half break caused by her fall from a stage in January 1977 without having resolved the arts vs. commerce argument that had marred her second album, *Radio Ethiopia.* In fact, that argument was in some ways the theme of her third. *Easter,* produced by Bruce Springsteen associate Jimmy Iovine, was Smith's most commercial-sounding effort yet and, due to the inclusion of Springsteen's "Because the Night" (with Smith's revised lyrics), a Top Ten hit, it became her biggest seller, staying in the charts more than five months and getting into the Top 20 LPs. But Smith hadn't so much sold out as she had learned to use her poetic gifts within an album-rock context. Certainly, a song that proclaimed, "Love is an angel disguised as lust / Here in our bed until the morning comes," was pushing the limits of pop radio, and on "Babelogue," Smith returned to her days of declaiming poetry on New York's Lower East Side. That rant (significantly ending, "I have not sold my soul to God") led into the provocative "Rock N Roll Nigger," a charged rocker with a chorus that went, "Outside of society / Is where I want to be." Smith made the theme from the '60s British rock movie *Privilege* her own and even got into the U.K. charts with it. And on songs like "25th Floor," Iovine, Smith, and her group were able to accommodate both the urge to rock out and the need to expound. So, *Easter* turned out to be the best compromise Smith achieved between her artistic and commercial aspirations. *— William Ruhlmann*

Wave / May 1979 / Arista ♦♦♦
The Patti Smith Group's most conventional album, *Wave* was given a bright pop/rock sound by producer Todd Rundgren. It was the last album Smith made before marrying and retiring from record-making for nine years, and it can be heard as a farewell to the music business, from "Frederick," the love song to her husband-to-be, Fred "Sonic" Smith, that leads it off, to the version of "So You Want to Be (A Rock 'n' Roll Star)," among the most bitter accounts of fame on record. But Smith also achieves a sense of charm and sincerity on *Wave* that she hadn't even attempted on her earlier albums, even to the point of her imagined small-talk encounter with the late Pope John Paul I on the title track. Still, the overall mediocre quality of the material makes this the slightest of Smith's efforts. *— William Ruhlmann*

Dream of Life / Jun. 1988 / Arista ♦♦♦

Gone Again / Jun. 18, 1996 / Arista ♦♦♦

Peace and Noise / Sep. 30, 1997 / Arista ♦♦♦

Gung Ho / Mar. 21, 2000 / Arista ♦♦♦

Warren Smith

b. Feb. 7, 1933, **d.** Jan. 31, 1980
Vocals, Guitar / Rockabilly, Traditional Country
For sheer, heartfelt vocalizing abilities, of all the folks who stood in front of the microphone at Sun studio, Warren Smith may have been the most talented. Equally adept at storming rockabilly and the most gut-wrenching of country ballads, Smith always sang it from the heart, without giving in to phony rasping or histrionics. Though typecast as strictly a rocker, Smith left Sun and achieved minor success in the '60s as a country singer, his first love. *— Cub Koda*

Call of the Wild / 1990 / Bear Family ♦♦♦♦♦

● **The Classic Recordings 1956-59** / 1992 / Bear Family ♦♦♦♦♦
This is Smith's entire output (31 tracks in all) for Sun Records. It includes the rockabilly classics "Rock & Roll Ruby," "Ubangi Stomp," and "Miss Froggie," as well as heartfelt country performances on "The Darkest Cloud," "I'd Rather Be Safe than Sorry," and "Goodbye Mr. Love." No Sun collection can really be considered complete without adding this one to the list. *— Cub Koda*

Uranium Rock: The Best of Warren Smith / May 23, 1995 / AVI ♦♦♦♦♦
Uranium Rock: The Best Of Warren Smith is a wonderful 24-track collection containing all of the essential Sun recordings, from "Rock 'n' Roll Ruby" and "Ubangi Stomp" to "Black Jack David," "Red Cadillac and a Black Moustache," and "Uranium Rock." It's a more concise and more effective compilation than Bear Family's *The Classic Recordings,* and therefore, it's arguably the definitive overview. *— Stephen Thomas Erlewine*

The Smithereens

f. 1980, Carteret, New Jersey
Group / College Rock, Bar Band, Power Pop, Hard Rock
Dressed in leather, brandishing heavy guitars, and sporting an unabashed fetish for British Invasion pop, the Smithereens were an anomaly in the American college rock scene of the mid-'80s. Lead singer/songwriter Pat DiNizio stood out because his catchy hooks were haunting, not punchy, and his lyrics morose. As time wore on, the group became more straightforward, attacking pop songs with the weight of AC/DC. A few hits followed, but once alt-rock burst into the mainstream in the early '90s, the Smithereens' classicist pop seemed out of date (even if, ironically, DiNizio's lyrics were equally as angst-ridden), and they quietly faded into a cult working band.

Of course, the Smithereens essentially started out as a working band. Pat DiNizio (vocals, guitar) joined New Jersey high school students Dennis Diken (drums), Jim Babjak (guitar), and Mike Mesaros (bass), who had all played together in school, toward the end of the '70s. By the end of 1980, they had independently released the EP *Girls About Town.* The group played New Jersey and New York for the next three years, not releasing another record until 1983's EP *Beauty and Sadness,* which received college radio airplay and a positive review in *Rolling Stone.* Their Don Dixon-produced debut album *Especially for You* appeared in 1986 to enthusiastic reviews. The album became a sizable indie hit, leading to a major-label contract with Capitol. *Green Thoughts,* appeared early in 1988, and its first single, "Only a Memory" crossed over to album-rock stations. Producer Ed Stasium brought a heavier guitar sound to 1989's *11,* which made "A Girl Like You" a Top 40 hit, sending the album to gold status. "Too Much Passion," the first single from their fourth album *Blow Up,* became a Top 40 hit, yet the album didn't replicate its predecessor's success. After 1994's reunion with producer Don Dixon, *A Date With the Smithereens,* the band released a pair of compilations in 1985. Four years later, they returned with *God Save the Smithereens,* released on the independent label, Koch. *— Stephen Thomas Erlewine*

Beauty & Sadness / 1983 / Enigma ♦♦♦

Especially for You / 1986 / Enigma ♦♦♦♦♦
The Smithereens' superb full-length debut *Especially for You* marries an unapologetically nostalgic affection for the melodic crunch of the British Invasion era with an equally unapologetic helping of postmodern melancholia. In tandem with Don Dixon's moodily atmospheric production, Pat DiNizio's lovelorn lyrics and world-weary vocals reveal the dark underbelly of his otherwise crisply infectious songs, lending standout tracks like "Strangers When We Meet," "Behind the Wall of Sleep," and the minor hit "Blood and Roses," both a unique flavor and an immediate familiarity. *—Jason Ankeny*

Green Thoughts / 1988 / Capitol ♦♦♦♦♦
The Smithereens' excellent sophomore effort picks up where their debut, *Especially for You,* left off, with Pat DiNizio delivering another impressive batch of superbly constructed pop gems; tracks like "Only a Memory," "House We Used to Live In," and "Drown in My Own Tears" are immediately ingratiating—instantly familiar, yet performed with more than enough energy and flair to sound new and exciting. Equally compelling are *Green Thoughts'* curveballs, like the countryish "Something New," the lovely ballad "Especially for You," and the dark, atmospheric "Deep Black," all of which deliver intriguing variations on the Smithereens' basic power pop formula. Another winner. *—Jason Ankeny*

11 / 1990 / Capitol ♦♦♦
The third full-length album from The Smithereens, *11* (a title which presumably referred to Spinal Tap's fabled guitar amps, which could be cranked past 10) was something of a letdown after the solid, tough-pop perfection of their first two albums, *Especially for You* and *Green Thoughts.* While their previous sets boasted strong material from front to back, *11* is dotted with filler. And while "A Girl Like You", "Blue Period," and "William Wilson" are all great songs, many of the others sound like by-the-numbers pop tunes cranked out to pad the set to full length. Producer Don Dixon made the most of the dark and mysterious undercurrents of Pat DiNizio's songs and Jim Babjak's guitar, here Ed Stasium gives the band a solid, professional sound that is sadly lacking in personality; there's nothing wrong with the way the album sounds, but there isn't anything terribly engaging about it, either. As a band, the Smithereens still sound rock solid here, but as an album it was sadly indicative of the creative ups and downs that would mark their recording career from this point forward. *— Mark Deming*

Blow Up / Sep. 10, 1991 / Capitol ♦♦♦

Date with the Smithereens / Apr. 26, 1994 / RCA ♦♦

● **Blown to Smithereens: The Best of the Smithereens** / Apr. 4, 1995 / Capitol ♦♦♦♦♦
With their British Invasion style of rock, New Jersey's the Smithereens weren't exactly in step with the musical landscape of the mid- to late '80s. It didn't stop the quartet from being critical darlings and perennial candidates to break through to a wider audience. *Blown to Smithereens* gathers together ample evidence that the attention was more than merited. There's nary a weak moment on this collection, which includes all of the band's best-known songs and radio hits. Sequenced chronologically, *Blown to Smithereens* leads off with the Beatlesque "Beauty & Sadness" and proceeds with gems like the moody "Blood & Roses," "In a Lonely Place" (with its Bacharach vibe), the driving "House We Used to Live In," the sweet, melodic "Blue Period," and closes with a cover of "Time Won't Let Me." Pat DiNizio's often bittersweet, romantic lyrics compliment the polished, yet gritty, power pop resulting in timeless songs like "Behind the Wall of Sleep," "Only a Memory," and "A Girl Like You." For the uninitiated, *Blown to Smithereens* is a perfect introduction. For fans, it isn't necessarily essential, but rather a wonderful opportunity to revisit one of the more underappreciated bands of the past two decades. *— Tom Demalon*

Attack of the Smithereens / Nov. 21, 1995 / Capitol ♦♦♦♦
At first glance, a Smithereens rarities compilation might seem like an odd release. After all, the band never had more than one gold album and none of their singles cracked the Top 30. That doesn't mean the band didn't have fans, however, nor does it mean that their music was

undistinctive, as *Attack of the Smithereens* proves. Filled with B-sides, demos, rare singles, and live tracks, the collection has a loose charm and freewheeling energy their proper albums occasionally lacked. Much of this material is as good as anything the group released, making it a necessary purchase for most fans. Even casual fans will find something to cherish on *Attack of the Smithereens*. *—Stephen Thomas Erlewine*

God Save the Smithereens / Oct. 19, 1999 / Koch ✦✦✦

The Smiths

f. 1982, Manchester, England, **db.** Aug. 1987

Group / College Rock, Indie Pop, Alternative Pop/Rock

The Smiths were the definitive British indie-rock band of the '80s, marking the end of synth-driven New Wave and the beginning of the guitar rock that dominated English rock into the '90s. Sonically, the group was indebted to the British Invasion, crafting ringing, melodic three-minute pop singles, even for their album tracks. But their scope was far broader than that of a revivalist band. The group's core members, vocalist Morrissey and guitarist Johnny Marr, were obsessive rock fans inspired by the D.I.Y. ethics of punk, but they also had a fondness for girl groups, pop, and rockabilly. Morrissey and Marr also represented one of the strangest teams of collaborators in rock history. Marr was the rock traditionalist, looking like an elegant version of Keith Richards during the Smiths' heyday, and meticulously layering his guitar tracks in the studio. Morrissey, on the other hand, broke from rock tradition by singing in a keening, self-absorbed croon, embracing the forlorn, romantic poetry of Oscar Wilde, publicly declaring his celibacy, performing with a pocketful of gladiolas and a hearing aid, and making no secret of his disgust for most of his peers. While it eventually led to the Smiths' early demise, the friction between Morrissey and Marr resulted in a flurry of singles and albums over the course of three years that provided the blueprint for British guitar rock in the following decade. *—Stephen Thomas Erlewine*

☆ **The Smiths** / 1984 / Sire ✦✦✦✦✦

Arriving in an era dominated by synth-pop and gloomy post-punk, the Smiths' eponymous debut was the bracing beginning of a new era. On the surface, the Smiths' sound wasn't radically different from traditional British guitar pop—Johnny Marr's ringing layered guitars were catchy and melodic—but it was actually an astonishing subversion of the form, turning the structure inside out. Very few of the songs followed conventional verse-chorus structure, yet they were quite melodic within their own right. Marr's inventive songwriting was made all the more original and innovative by Morrissey's crooning and lyrics. Writing about unconventional topics, from homosexuality ("Hand in Glove") to child molestation and murder, Morrissey had a distinctively ironic, witty, and literate viewpoint whose strangeness was accentuated by his off-kilter voice, which would move from a croon to a yelp in a matter of seconds. While the production of *The Smiths* is a little pristine, the songs are vital and alive, developing a new, unique voice within pop music. Though the Smiths continued to improve over the course of their career, their debut remains startling and exciting. *—Stephen Thomas Erlewine*

☆ **Hatful of Hollow** / 1984 / Sire ✦✦✦✦✦

Several months after releasing their first album, the Smiths issued the singles and rarities collection *Hatful of Hollow,* establishing a tradition of repackaging their material as many times and as quickly as possible. While several cuts on *Hatful of Hollow* are BBC versions of songs from *The Smiths,* the versions on the compilation are nervy and raw—and they're also not the selling point of the record. The Smiths treated singles as individual entities, not just ways to promote an album, and many of their finest songs were never issued on their studio albums. *Hatful of Hollow* contains many of these classics, including the sweet rush of "William, It Was Really Nothing," and the sardonic "Heaven Knows I'm Miserable Now," the tongue-in-cheek lament of "Please, Please, Please Let Me Get What I Want," the wistful "Back to the Old House," "Girl Afraid," and the pulsating, tremolo-laced masterpiece "How Soon Is Now?" With such strong material forming the core of the album, it's little wonder that *Hatful of Hollow* is as consistent as *The Smiths,* and arguably captures the excitement surrounding the band even better. *—Stephen Thomas Erlewine*

Meat Is Murder / 1985 / Sire ✦✦✦

With their second proper album *Meat Is Murder,* the Smiths begin to branch out and diversify, while refining the jangling guitar pop of their debut. In other words, it catches the group at a crossroads, unsure quite how to proceed. Taking the epic, layered "How Soon Is Now?" as a starting point (the single, which is darker and more dance-oriented than the remainder of the album, was haphazardly inserted into the middle of the album for its American release), the group crafts more sweeping, mid-tempo numbers, whether it's the melancholy "That Joke Isn't Funny Anymore" or the failed, self-absorbed protest of the title track. While the production is more detailed than before, the Smiths are at their best when they stick to their strengths—"The Headmaster Ritual" and "I Want the One I Can't Have" are fine elaborations of the formula they laid out on the debut, while "Rusholme Ruffians" is an infectious stab at rockabilly. However, the rest of *Meat Is Murder* is muddled, repeating lyrical and musical ideas of before without significantly expanding them or offering enough hooks or melodies to make it the equal of *The Smiths* or *Hatful of Hollow.* *—Stephen Thomas Erlewine*

★ **The Queen Is Dead** / 1986 / Sire ✦✦✦✦✦

Meat Is Murder may have been a holding pattern, but *The Queen Is Dead* is the Smiths' great leap forward, taking the band to new musical and lyrical heights. Opening with the storming title track, *The Queen Is Dead* is a harder-rocking record than anything the Smiths had attempted before, but that's only on a relative scale—although the backbeat is more pronounced, the group certainly doesn't rock in a conventional sense. Instead, Johnny Marr has created a dense web of guitars, alternating from the minor-key rush of "Bigmouth Strikes Again" and the faux-rockabilly of "Vicar in a Tutu" to the bouncy acoustic pop of "Cemetry Gates" and "The Boy With the Thorn in His Side," as well as the lovely melancholy of "I Know It's Over" and "There Is a Light That Never Goes Out." And the rich musical bed provides Morrissey with the support for his finest set of lyrics. Shattering the myth that he is a self-pitying sap, Morrissey delivers a devastating set of clever, witty satires of British social mores, intellectualism, class, and even himself. He also crafts some of his finest, most affecting songs, particularly in the wistful "The Boy With the Thorn in His Side" and the epic "There Is a Light That Never Goes Out," two masterpieces that provide the foundation for a remarkable album. *—Stephen Thomas Erlewine*

Louder Than Bombs / 1987 / Sire ✦✦✦✦✦

A compilation of singles, B-sides, album tracks, and BBC sessions assembled for the American market, *Louder Than Bombs* is an overlong and unfocused collection that nevertheless boasts a wealth of brilliant material. Since *Hatful of Hollow* was unavailable in the U.S. at the time of the release of *Louder Than Bombs,* the record contains large chunks of that album, as well as several cuts from *The Smiths,* which makes the record a little redundant for most Smiths fans. Also, the album contains some of the worst material the group ever recorded, including the bland instrumental "Oscillate Wildly" and a cover of Twinkle's "Golden Light." Excluding all of this material, the remainder of the record is brilliant. The singles "Shakespeare's Sister," "Panic," "Ask," "Shoplifters of the World Unite," and "Sheila Take a Bow" are all definitive, as are the elegiac "Unloveable," "Asleep," "Stretch Out and Wait," and "Half a Person," which are all unavailable anywhere else (excluding the British counterpart to *Louder Than Bombs, The World Won't Listen*). Furthermore, the sneering, bouncing pop of "You Just Haven't Earned It Yet, Baby" and the bizarre travelogue of "Is It Really So Strange?" are two other essential songs not available anywhere else. Though *The World Won't Listen* is a more concise collection, *Louder Than Bombs* is a necessary purchase for any Smiths fan. *—Stephen Thomas Erlewine*

Strangeways, Here We Come / 1987 / Sire ✦✦✦✦

Recorded as the relationship between Morrissey and Marr was beginning to splinter, *Strangeways, Here We Come* is the most carefully considered and elaborately produced album in the group's catalog. Though it aspires greatly to better *The Queen Is Dead,* it falls just short of its goals. With producer Stephen Street, the Smiths created a subtly shaded and skilled album, one boasting a fuller production than before. Morrissey and Marr also labored hard over the songs, working to expand the Smiths' sound within their very real boundaries. For the most part, they succeed. "I Started Something I Couldn't Finish," "Girlfriend in a Coma," "Stop Me if You Think You've Heard This One Before," and "I Won't Share You" are classics, while "A Rush and a Push and the Land is Ours," "Death of a Disco Dancer," and "Last Night I Dreamt That Somebody Loved Me" aren't far behind. However, the songs also have a tendency to be glib and forced, particularly on "Unhappy Birthday" and the anti-record company "Paint a Vulgar Picture," which has grown increasingly ironic in the wake of the Smiths' and Morrissey's love of repackaging the same material in new compilations. Still, *Strangeways* is a graceful way to bow out. While it doesn't match *The Queen Is Dead* or *The Smiths,* it is far from embarrassing and offers a summation of the group's considerable strengths. *—Stephen Thomas Erlewine*

Rank / 1988 / Sire ✦✦

The Best, Vol. 1 / 1992 / Sire ✦✦

The Best, Vol. 2 / Dec. 8, 1992 / Sire ✦✦

★ **Singles** / May 23, 1995 / Reprise ✦✦✦✦✦

The *Best of the Smiths* collections didn't work because they didn't have a sense of history and distorted the underlying sense of urgency that helped make the Smiths important. *Singles* simply collects all of the singles from one of the greatest singles bands since the Beatles. It's essential and influential guitar pop, presented in a way that makes sense and is endlessly listenable *—Stephen Thomas Erlewine*

Smog

Group / Sadcore, Indie Rock, Lo-Fi, Singer/Songwriter

An underrecognized pioneer of the lo-fi revolution, Smog was essentially the alias of one Bill Callahan, an enigmatic singer/songwriter whose odd, fractured music neatly epitomized the tenets and excesses of the home-recording boom. Melancholy, poignant, and self-obsessed, Callahan's four-track output offered a peepshow view into an insular world of alienation and inner turmoil, his painfully intimate songs ping-ponging wildly through a scrapbook of childhood recollections, failed relationships, bizarre fetishes, and dashed hopes. Smog debuted in 1988 with the spare, primitive *Macrame Gunplay,* a cassette-only release issued on Callahan's own Disaster label. With 1991's *Floating* EP, Smog signed to the Chicago-based indie label Drag City, and with the move began an advancement toward more traditional songcraft; the subsequent full-length *Forgotten Foundation* was his most well-rounded effort yet, employing a stronger sense of melody while remaining true to the trademark bare-bones atmosphere. 1993's superb *Julius Caesar* raised the stakes considerably, expanding the Smog palette to include touches of cello, violin, and even banjo. 1995's *Wild Love* continued this approach toward relative sonic grandeur. *—Jason Ankeny*

Forgotten Foundation / 1992 / Drag City ✦✦

Julius Caesar / 1993 / Drag City ✦✦✦✦

Smog's third album, 1993's *Julius Caesar,* features increasingly creative songwriting and arrangements that celebrate the lo-fi recording process. Like grainy snapshots taken in an instant-photo booth, *Julius Caesar*'s 13 songs have a fuzzy, distinctive character, heightened by their low-budget surroundings. Darker songs like "Your Wedding" and "What Kind of Angel" sound even blacker because of the muddy, distorted sound quality. "What Kind of Angel" in particular exploits lo-fi's fuzziness, blurring Bill Callahan's vocals and slide guitars into a rage of noise. Poignant moments like the cello-based instrumental "One Less Star" and ballads such as "Golden" and "Chosen One" have a naive, bittersweet feel thanks to the bedroom-quality production. Other tracks use the lo-fi aesthetic as their musical focus: "I Am Star Wars!" uses a cheap drum machine and tape loops of the Rolling Stones' "Start Me Up" and "Honky Tonk Women" for an unusual, funny foray into sampling on the cheap, while the drums on "Parade" sound suspiciously like tin cans. *Julius Caesar*'s wide emotional and sonic palette is contrasted by Callahan's consistently honest, often blunt lyrics. Whether they're self-mocking ("I feel like Travis Bickle, listening to 'Highway to Hell'/It's a shitty little tape I taped off the radio," from "37 Push Ups") or nonsensically logical ("I am Star Wars today/I am no longer English Grey," from "I Am Star Wars!") or wistful ("Chosen One's" lament, "Maybe it's best for you to ride into the sun"), Callahan's sentiments are anything but sentimental. An immensely creative album, *Julius Caesar*'s artistic, arranged approach to lo-fi displays Callahan's willingness to grow and experiment as a musician and storyteller. —*Heather Phares*

Burning Kingdom / Sep. 20, 1994 / Drag City ✦✦✦

Wild Love / Mar. 27, 1995 / Drag City ✦✦✦✦✦
Building on *Julius Caesar*'s artful songcraft, *Wild Love* expands Bill Callahan's lyrical and musical horizons, balancing roughness and polish in just the right amounts. Recorded in a proper studio with Drag City's favorite producer, Rian Murphy, the album benefits from a wider musical palette; instead of *Julius Caesar*'s lo-fi patchwork, the sound is focused into a hypnotic blend of chamber music and indie rock. Keyboards, chamberlin, and cello add a theatrical flair to *Wild Love*'s dark, witty portraits of domestic frustration, especially the opening and closing songs, "Bathysphere" and "Goldfish Bowl." The arrangements are key; sometimes they reflect the moody, detailed lyrics. On the frail, flickering ballad "The Candle," Callahan sings "I'm gathering these splinters to make a raft someday," accompanied by delicate, feeble guitars and keyboards, while "Be Hit"'s awkward drumming and out of tune strumming mirror its ugly lyrics: "Every girl I've ever loved has wanted to be hit/and every girl I've ever loved has left me because I wouldn't do it." At other times, the dense orchestrations are ironic; "Sleepy Joe" and "Prince Alone in the Studio" are emotionally detached. As usual, the lyrics are sad, funny, and often cut to the quick. Couplets like "The Candle"'s "I was on her body/he was on her mind./I caressed her/he possessed her," provoke a reaction somewhere between a wince and a grin. On a purely musical level, the album is of Smog's most remarkable achievements, combining studio effects and low-budget innovation. The snare drums and chamberlins on "The Emperor" sound like fireworks over a parade, while the chiming guitars on "It's Rough" add a touch of empathy. A finely wrought, magnetic work, *Wild Love*'s music and lyrics are too artful to be just the outpourings of a completely miserable soul. —*Heather Phares*

Sewn to the Sky / Nov. 29, 1995 / Drag City ✦✦✦

Kicking a Couple Around [EP] / Apr. 1996 / Drag City ✦✦✦✦

Doctor Came at Dawn / Sep. 10, 1996 / Drag City ✦✦✦✦
The Doctor Came at Dawn documents romantic decay and deception with Bill Callahan's typical unflinching honesty. Over the album's ten songs, he recounts every painful detail of falling in and out of love. "You Moved In" recalls an affair's desperate, obsessive beginnings with grim humor: "You could have done better, but oh well." The song's eerie, foreboding strings and piano arrangement, as well as Callahan's deadpan vocals, give fair warning that *The Doctor Came at Dawn*'s intimate sound hits close to home. The deadly aim of "Lize," a duet between Callahan and his sometime creative and romantic partner Cindy Dall, spares no one. "You don't make lies like you used to," they sing in near-unison, creating the tense, charged atmosphere of a stifled argument. As always, Smog walks the fine line between self-deprecation and self-parody; "Somewhere in the Night"'s handclaps and acoustic strumming make it sound like a rousing, inspirational folk song—except for the sneer embedded in Callahan's voice as he urges his beloved to devote herself to someone else. But *The Doctor Came at Dawn* is at its best when Callahan's sense of empathy emerges on the remarkable "All Your Women Things." Initially, it seems like a fetishistic ballad about keeping an ex-lover's things, but with deeper listening, it reveals itself as a very sincere (albeit unnerving) love song, praising the beloved's different aspects: "How could I ignore your hardness, your softness, and your mercy?" Lyrically and emotionally complex, the song exemplifies the depth of Smog's songwriting. The album is also musically deep, with understated guitar, piano, and string arrangements that give the rich vocals and lyrics added impact. It's Smog's darkest collection of songs, but it's also among the most mature and rewarding. —*Heather Phares*

● **Red Apple Falls** / May 20, 1997 / Drag City ✦✦✦✦✦
Over the course of his previous albums, Bill Callahan explored every nuance of humor and despair; with 1997's *Red Apple Falls*, he adds hope and possibility to Smog's scope. Musically, the album concentrates on spacious, acoustic-based music rather than Callahan's prior lo-fi experiments. With flourishes of piano, horns, drum machines, and pedal steel, *Red Apple Falls* appropriates the best of folk, rock, and country, defying easy classification. "Blood Red Bird" and "Red Apples" focus on Callahan's voice and mournful pianos, while epics like "Red Apple Falls" and "Inspirational" use weepy steel guitars for maximum emotional impact. Lyrically, the album's intensity and clarity is equally strong: motifs of apples, horses, and widows thread through the album, evoking rustic, traditional songs as they tell the story of a star-crossed love affair. "Most of my fantasies are to be of use/like a spindle, like a candle," Callahan sings on "To Be of Use," blending pain, pleasure, selfishness, and selflessness in a typically Smog manner. But the best songs here combine the album's musical expansiveness and lyrical intensity. On "I Was a Stranger" Callahan sings, "Why do you women in this town let me look at you so bold?/You should have seen what I was in the last town/or in the last town/I was worse than a stranger/I was well known," backed by more sighing steel guitars. "Ex Con" blends synth washes, horns, and a stiff, mechanical beat in a unique country/new wave hybrid, emphasizing the bleak wit of lyrics like "Out on the streets/I feel like a robot by the river/looking for a drink." *Red Apple Falls*' subtle mix of contrasting sounds and emotions makes it a high point in Bill Callahan's distinguished, distinctive musical career. —*Heather Phares*

Knock Knock / Jan. 12, 1999 / Drag City ✦✦✦✦✦
Smog's seventh full-length album *Knock Knock* proves to be singer/songwriter Bill Callahan's subtlest collection of songs yet. Indeed, one of the album's greatest accomplishments is its gently optimistic tone; if his other albums made a deadpan joke out of misery, on this album Callahan delivers the punchlines with traces of a grin. It's a moving album on many levels; not only do the songs have Smog's usual emotional intimacy, their subjects move away from difficult, claustrophobic situations toward maturity and acceptance. "Let's Move to the Country" and "I Could Drive Forever" are all about escape, whether it's from the rat race or bad relationships—"I feel light and strong," Callahan sings on "I Could Drive Forever," summing up *Knock Knock*'s lyrical tenor. But moving also implies distance. As the album travels the emotional spaces between people, Callahan himself seems more removed from these songs; more than ever, his songs read more like short stories than diary entries, particularly on "River Guard," about a warden watching prisoners swim, and the enigmatic "Sweet Treat." "Cold Blooded Old Times" and "Teenage Spaceship" capture the awkwardness of youth, while "Left Only With Love" accepts a lover's departure in stride. Musically, *Knock Knock* builds on *Red Apple Falls*' folky, flowing sound, but throws in twists like drum loops, electric guitars, and, surprisingly, a children's choir. "Hit the Ground Running" combines all three elements, driven by rolling guitars and accented with strings, with the children's choir urging Callahan on his way. "Held"'s drum, guitar, and feedback loops take a collage approach to a classic rock sound; along with "Cold Blooded Old Times" and "No Dancing," it's one of Callahan's most up-tempo songs since 1995's "Wild Love." Over time, *Knock Knock* reveals itself as one of Smog's finest moments. —*Heather Phares*

Dongs of Sevotion / Apr. 4, 2000 / Drag City ✦✦✦✦

The Soft Boys

f. 1976, Cambridge, England, **db.** 1981
Group / College Rock, British Punk, Jangle Pop, Post-Punk, New Wave
The Soft Boys have turned out to be one of the most influential bands in shaping contemporary alternative music, though few are completely familiar with the quirky band's legacy. Formed in Cambridge, England in 1976 on the heels of the punk revolution, the Soft Boys eschewed the three-chord nihilism of punk and opted for a crude version of psychedelic/folk-rock that was well on its way out of fashion, but oddly, just on the cusp of a resurgence. Led by singer/songwriter Robyn Hitchcock, the band released a single, "(I Want to Be an) Anglepoise Lamp," followed by the *Can of Bees* album in 1979. *Underwater Moonlight* found the band trading psychedelic jams for a more straight-ahead jangle-guitar-rock sound. The LP has become extremely influential in the guitar rock canon—the Replacements, R.E.M., and the L.A. Paisley Underground scene all claimed it as a prime influence. The album launched a thousand bands, but it turned out to be the Soft Boys' swan song. Hitchcock has had a prolific post-Soft Boys recording career, sticking to the unusual style he's forged and finessed since 1976, with a series of albums to his credit. —*Denise Sullivan*

A Can of Bees / 1979 / Rykodisc ✦✦✦✦✦
One of the band's earliest recordings, featuring their signature tune "Give It to the Soft Boys," *A Can of Bees* includes a lot of the zaniness principal member Robyn Hitchcock would become known for in his later work, but the band had not yet jelled and found them still in search of their ultimate sound, an amalgam of new wave and psychedelia. However, the record is essential to any Soft Boys collection, as it demonstrates the band flying in the face of what was happening musically at the time and creating their own unique style. —*Denise Sullivan*

★ **Underwater Moonlight** / 1980 / Rykodisc ✦✦✦✦✦
A watershed guitar rock album—the one that launched a thousand bands, including the Replacements and R.E.M., and a quintessential cult favorite. Beautiful harmonies and Byrdsian guitar dominate this set of songs, the standouts being the punk-pop of "I Wanna Destroy You," "Positive Vibrations," and the chiming "Queen of Eyes." Robyn Hitchcock found his voice on this record, singing his mostly nonsensical lyrics with unusual conviction, and guitarist Kimberley Rew played with a tidiness rarely heard on most underground recordings from the era. —*Denise Sullivan*

Invisible Hits / 1983 / Rykodisc ✦✦✦✦
A collection of lost recordings and previously unreleased tracks, a number of this album's cuts remain Soft Boys classics, like "Rock 'n' Roll Toilet," "Wey Wey Hep Uh Hole," "Have a Heart Betty (I'm Not Fireproof)," and "He's a Reptile." Most of the songs were recorded in 1978-79 during the sessions prior to *A Can of Bees* and *Underwater Moonlight*, and though it isn't as strong as the latter, it is essential to the Soft Boys collector—their recorded output is so spare that every last detail is crucial. —*Denise Sullivan*

1976-1981 / Aug. 10, 1993 / Rykodisc ✦✦✦✦
This double-CD set compiles unreleased material, select cuts from *Give It to the Soft Boys*, *A Can of Bees*, *Invisible Hits*, and *Underwater Moonlight*, as well as two tracks from the live bootleg *At the Portland Arms* and "Only the Stones Remain" from the *Two Halves for the Price of One* EP. Alhough it may appear to be a good introduction to the Soft Boys oeuvre, the inclusion of rarities and alternate takes makes it ideal for diehard Soft Boys fans and inappropriate for the novice. —*Denise Sullivan*

Soft Cell

f. 1980, Leeds, England, **db.** 1984
Group / New Romantic, Post-Punk, New Wave, Synth-Pop
A synth-pop duo famed for its uniquely sleazy electronic sound, art students Marc Almond and David Ball formed Soft Cell in Leeds, England in 1980. A self-financed EP titled *Mutant Moments* brought the duo to the attention of Some Bizzare label head Stevo, who enlisted Daniel Miller to produce their underground hit single "Memorabilia" the following year. It was the next Soft Cell effort, 1981's "Tainted Love," that brought the duo to international prominence; already a cult favorite thanks to Gloria Jones' soulful reading, the song was reinvented as a hypnotic electronic dirge which became the year's best-selling British single, as well as a major hit abroad. The group's debut LP, *Non-Stop Erotic Cabaret*, was also enormously successful, and while 1983's *The Art of Falling Apart* proved as popular as its predecessor, the LP's title broadly hinted at the internal problems plaguing the duo; prior to the release of 1984's *This Last Night in Sodom*, Soft Cell had already broken up. —*Jason Ankeny*

Non-Stop Ecstatic Dancing / 1982 / Sire ✦✦✦✦
The version of "Memorabilia" included here is notable for its energy, but the only other thing on the U.S. edition that really catches the attention is "What." The U.K. edition of the mini-album included "Insecure... Me?," the B-side to the single version of "What," improving the odds a little. *—Steven McDonald*

Non-Stop Erotic Cabaret / 1982 / Sire ✦✦✦✦✦
Reissued with a staggering number of B-sides, this Soft Cell album should not be missed, though the point is not the over-referenced "Tainted Love." More interesting are the astoundingly sleazy "Sex Dwarf," the grim trash of "Bedsitter," the dual punches of "Seedy Films" and "Secret Life," and the melancholy "Say Hello, Wave Goodbye." The hard black heart that beat under the skin of Soft Cell was located squarely in the middle of London's Soho district, red lights, strip clubs, alleyway hookers, and all; if ever a city district had a soundtrack, this was it. *—Steven McDonald*

The Art of Falling Apart / 1983 / Sire ✦✦✦
While it has some mediocre moments, this tense, quirky release also has some magnificent outings, including the epic "Martin" (based on the obscure George Romero psycho/vampire movie), a cut that was originally included on a bonus 12", and the relentless title cut. Not as cheap or sleazy in its sound as *Non-Stop Erotic Cabaret,* the album was still prone to melodramatic writing and performance. By all means, miss the "Hendrix Medley," another bonus cut. *—Steven McDonald*

The Singles 1981-1985 / 1986 / Some Bizarre ✦✦✦✦

● **Memorabilia: Singles** / Oct. 8, 1991 / Mercury ✦✦✦✦✦
Although it doesn't contain a couple of key tracks, including the 12-inch version of "Tainted Love/Where Did Our Love Go," *Memorabilia* is the best Soft Cell collection available. *—Stephen Thomas Erlewine*

Soft Machine

f. 1966, **db.** 1976
Group / Canterbury Scene, British Psychedelia, Jazz-Rock, Experimental, Psychedelic, Prog Rock/Art Rock
The Soft Machine were never a commercial enterprise, and indeed still remain unknown even to many listeners that came of age during the late '60s, when the group was at their peak. In their own way, however, they were one of the more influential bands of their era, and certainly one of the *most* influential underground ones. One of the original British psychedelic groups, they were also instrumental in the birth of both progressive rock and jazz-rock. They were also the central foundation of the family tree of the "Canterbury school" of British progressive-rock acts, a movement that also included Caravan, Gong, Matching Mole, and National Health, not to mention the distinguished solo careers of founding members Robert Wyatt and Kevin Ayers. The group was among the very first underground psychedelic bands in Britain, and quickly became well-loved in the burgeoning London psychedelic underground, although the considerable melodic elements and vocal harmonies of their early material soon gave way to more challenging, artier postures that sought—sometimes successfully, sometimes not—to meld the energy of psychedelic rock with the improvisational pulse of jazz. Their second album, *Vol. 2* (1969), further submerged the band's pop elements in favor of extended jazzy compositions, with an increasingly lesser reliance on lyrics and vocals. For their third album, they went even further in these directions, expanding to a seven-piece by adding a horn section. This record virtually dispensed with vocals and conventional rock songs entirely, and is considered a landmark by both progressive-rock and jazz-rock aficionados, though it was too oblique for many rock listeners. *—Richie Unterberger*

Volume One / Dec. 1968 / One Way ✦✦✦✦✦

Volume Two / Apr. 1969 / One Way ✦✦✦✦✦

Third / Jun. 1970 / Columbia ✦✦✦✦
This album marks the beginning of their penchant for long, jazz-influenced pieces, and the end of the youthful, madcap era. *—Myles Boisen*

Fourth / Feb. 1971 / One Way ✦✦✦

● **Vols. 1 & 2** / Sep. 1989 / Big Beat ✦✦✦✦✦
A combination of their first two studio albums onto one CD. Their first (originally titled *The Soft Machine,* from 1968), recorded with the trio of Wyatt, Ratledge, and Ayers, combines goofy humor, psychedelia, and some free jazz into an erratic but invigorating brew that was comparable to little else in the late-'60s rock world. Ayers had left to be replaced by Hugh Hopper for 1969's *Volume Two,* which took a definite spin toward jazz and increasingly surrealistic material, stringing together whimsical bits and pieces for side-long suites. Not as pop-oriented as their initial 1967 recordings or as jazz-oriented as their final albums with Wyatt, the material compiled here is perhaps the best representation of the Soft Machine's accomplishments. *—Richie Unterberger*

Peel Sessions / 1990 / Dutch East India ✦✦✦✦

Jet-Propelled Photographs / Charly ✦✦✦✦✦
The latest available CD version of a title which has been repackaged and retitled several times over the last 20 years. Recorded in London in April 1967 and produced by the legendary Giorgio Gomelsky, these nine demos feature the original Soft Machine lineup of Robert Wyatt, Kevin Ayers, Mike Ratledge, and Daevid Allen. Although not intended for release, these rough but accomplished performances show the band at their most pop- and song-oriented. Not far removed from Syd Barrett-era Pink Floyd, the jazzy chord changes, unpredictable bursts of scat singing, glib free-association lyrics, ominous buzzing organ, and Robert Wyatt's soulful rasp convey the freewheeling abandon and giddy high spirits that characterized the best early British psychedelia. For similar but more elaborately produced relics from the Daevid Allen lineup, check for the three tracks on the hard-to-find triple LP *Triple Echo.* *—Richie Unterberger*

Sonic Youth

f. 1981, New York, NY
Group / College Rock, Experimental Rock, Noise Rock, Indie Rock, Alternative Pop/Rock
Sonic Youth was one of the most unlikely success stories of underground American rock in the '80s. Where contemporaries R.E.M. and Husker Du were fairly conventional in terms of song-structure and melody, Sonic Youth began their career by abandoning any pretense of traditional rock & roll conventions. Borrowing heavily from the free-form noise experimentalism of the Velvet Underground and the Stooges, and melding it with a performance-art aesthetic borrowed from the New York post-punk avant garde, Sonic Youth redefined what noise meant within rock & roll. Sonic Youth rarely rocked, though they were inspired directly by hardcore punk, post-punk, and no wave. Instead, their dissonance, feed-back, and alternate tunings created a new sonic landscape, one that redefined what rock guitar could do. Their trio of independent late '80s records—*EVOL, Sister, Daydream Nation*—became touchstones for a generation of indie rockers, who either replicated the noise or reinterpreted it a more palatable setting. As their career progressed, Sonic Youth grew more palatable, as well, as their more free-form songs began to feel like compositions and their shorter works began to rock harder. During the '90s, most American indie bands, and many British underground bands, displayed a heavy debt to Sonic Youth, and the band themselves had become a popular cult band, with each of their albums charting in the Top 100. *—Stephen Thomas Erlewine*

Confusion Is Sex / Feb. 1983 / SST ✦✦

Sonic Death: Early Sonic 1981-1983 / 1984 / SST ✦✦

Bad Moon Rising / 1985 / DGC ✦✦

EVOL / 1986 / DGC ✦✦✦✦✦
Sonic Youth made its first moves toward rock with *EVOL,* a stunningly fluent mixture of avant-garde instrumentation and subversions of rock & roll. The band benefits greatly from the addition of structure, which gives their aural experiments a firm grounding, but the addition of drummer Steve Shelley is essential to the group's new, dangerous edge. With the added propulsion, the fearless rush of "Expressway to Yr Skull" (a.k.a. "Madonna, Sean and Me") and the near-pop of "Green Light" are undeniably powerful, as are the eerie textures of "Shadow of a Doubt." *—Stephen Thomas Erlewine*

Made in USA / 1986 / Rhino ✦✦

☆ **Sister** / 1987 / DGC ✦✦✦✦✦
EVOL was a major leap forward for Sonic Youth, but *Sister* is a masterpiece, demonstrating the group's rapidly evolving musicality. More than ever before, Sonic Youth's songs sound like actual songs, and their collages of noise, distortion, and alternate tunings are now used to provide texture and depth to the music, which is original, complex, and rewarding. Not only is there the full-throttle roar of "Tuff Gnarl," but there are shimmering layers of ambient harmonics and dissonance which are as haunting and challenging as any of their barrages of feedback. Furthermore, *Sister* has a warm sound, which lures the listeners into music that's defiantly arty but never indulgent. It's one of the singular art-rock records of the '80s, surpassed only by Sonic Youth's next album, *Daydream Nation.* *—Stephen Thomas Erlewine*

★ **Daydream Nation** / 1988 / DGC ✦✦✦✦✦
By refining the song-oriented breakthroughs of *Sister* and developing their fascination with noise and alternate tunings, Sonic Youth created a masterpiece of post-punk art rock with the double album *Daydream Nation.* Though the self-conscious sprawl of the album might appear self-indulgent on the surface, *Daydream Nation* is powered by a sustained vision, one that encapsulates all of the group's quirks and strengths. Alternating between tense, hypnotic instrumental passages and furious noise explosions, the music demonstrates a range of emotions and textures, and in many ways, it's hard not to listen to the record as one long piece of shifting dynamics. But the songs themselves are remarkable, from the anti-anthem of "Teen Age Riot" and the punky "Silver Rocket" to the hazy drug dreams of "Providence" and the rolling waves of "Eric's Trip." *Daydream Nation* demonstrates the extent to which noise and self-conscious avant-art can be incorporated into rock, and the results are nothing short of stunning. *—Stephen Thomas Erlewine*

Goo / Jun. 1990 / DGC ✦✦✦
Any doubts as to the continuing relevance of Sonic Youth upon their jump to major label status were quickly laid to rest by *Goo,* their follow-up to the monumental *Daydream Nation.* While paling in the shadow of its predecessor, the record is nevertheless a defiant call to arms against mainstream musical values; the Geffen logo adorning the disc is a moot point—*Goo* is, if anything, a portrait of Sonic Youth at their most self-indulgently noisy and contentious, covering topics ranging from Karen Carpenter ("Tunic") to U.F.O.'s ("Disappearer") to dating Jesus' mom ("Mary-Christ"). Even Public Enemy's Chuck D. joins the fracas on the single "Kool Thing," which teeters on the brink of a cultural breakthrough but which falls just shy of the mark; the same could be said of *Goo* itself—by no means a sellout, it nevertheless lacks the coherence and force of the group's finest work, and the opportunity to violently rattle the mainstream cage slips by. *—Jason Ankeny*

Dirty / Jul. 21, 1992 / DGC ✦✦✦✦
Sonic Youth could never sell out, no matter how hard they tried. Their sound—a jarring barrage of distorted guitars and feedback—is entirely too singular and avant-garde to ever completely cross over. However, *Dirty* is the closest Sonic Youth has ever come to the mainstream, and it is their most accessible album to date. "100%" is nearly a pop single, complete with hooks and an identifiable song structure. But Sonic Youth hasn't lost their edge, as Kim Gordon's tracks in particular prove. *—Stephen Thomas Erlewine*

Experimental Jet Set, Trash & No Star / May 3, 1994 / DGC ✦✦

Screaming Fields of Sonic Love / Apr. 25, 1995 / DGC ✦✦✦

Washing Machine / Oct. 1995 / DGC ✦✦✦✦
After the regressive, low-key *Experimental Jet Set, Trash and No Star,* Sonic Youth appeared

to be floundering somewhat, but *Washing Machine* erased any notion that the band had run out of things to say. Easily their most adventurous, challenging, and best record since *Daydream Nation,* the album finds Sonic Youth returning to the fearless exploration of their SST records, but the group has found a way to work that into tighter song structures. Not only are the songs more immediate than most of the material on their earlier records, the sound here is warm and open, making *Washing Machine* their most mature and welcoming record to date. It's not a commercial record, nor is it a pop record, but *Washing Machine* encompasses everything that made Sonic Youth innovators and shows that they can continue to grow, finding new paths inside their signature sound. *—Stephen Thomas Erlewine*

SYR 1 / Jun. 10, 1997 / SYR ✦✦✦✦

SYR 2 / Sep. 2, 1997 / SYR ✦✦✦

SYR 3 / Feb. 24, 1998 / SYR ✦✦✦✦

A Thousand Leaves / May 12, 1998 / DGC ✦✦✦✦
Truth be told, the grunge era never quite fit Sonic Youth. They may have been at the peak of their popularity, but they had traded their experimentalism for sheer, bracing noise. It may have sounded good, but ultimately *Dirty* didn't have the cerebral impact of *Sister,* largely because it was tied to an admittedly effective backbeat. Beginning with *Washing Machine,* Sonic Youth returned to more adventurous territory, and in 1997, they released a series of EPs that illustrated their bond with such post-rock groups as Tortoise and Gastr Del Sol. Those EPs, as well as the epic *Washing Machine* closer "The Diamond Sea," provide the foundation for *A Thousand Leaves,* the band's most challenging and satisfying record in years. The blasts of dissonance that characterized their SST masterworks have been replaced, by and large, by winding, intricate improvisations. There's a surprising warmth to the subdued guitars of Thurston Moore, Lee Ranaldo, and Kim Gordon, which keeps the lengthy songs captivating. Both Moore and Ranaldo concentrate on quiet material, which almost makes Gordon's noisy politicized rants sound a little out of place, but her best moments ("French Tickler," "Heather Angel") have unsettling, unpredictable twists and turns that greatly contribute to the success of *A Thousand Leaves.* It may be their most cerebral album in ages, but that only makes it all the more engaging. *—Stephen Thomas Erlewine*

Silver Session for Jason Knuth / Jul. 14, 1998 / SYR ✦✦✦

Goodbye 20th Century / Nov. 16, 1999 / SYR ✦✦

NYC Ghosts & Flowers / May 16, 2000 / Geffen ✦✦✦

The Sonics

f. Tacoma, WA
Group / Garage Rock, Rock & Roll
A rock & roll band from Tacoma, Washington, the Sonics' original members were Gerry Roslie (lead singer and piano/organ), Andy Parypa (guitar), Larry Parypa (bass), Bob Bennett (drums), and Rob Lind (saxophone). Forming in the wake of the early-'60s success of local favorites the Kingsmen and the Wailers (whose Etiquette label they recorded for), the Sonics combined the classic Northwest-area teen-band raunch with early English band grit (particularly influenced by the Kinks), relentless rhythmic drive, and unabashed '50s-style blues-shouting for a combination that still makes their brand of rock & roll perhaps the raunchiest ever captured on wax. Lead singer Gerry Roslie was no less than a White Little Richard, whose harrowing soul-screams were startling even to the Northwest teen audience, who liked their music powerful and driving with little regard to commercial subtleties. With hit after hit on the local charts (and influencing every local band that ever took the stage), the band inexplicably was never able to break out nationally, leaving their sound largely undiluted for mass consumption. Breaking up in the late '60s (after one ill-fated album attempt to water down their style for national attention), the Sonics continue today to be revered by '60s collectors the world over for their unique brand of rock & roll raunch. *—Cub Koda*

Here Are the Sonics!!! / 1965 / Norton ✦✦✦
The Sonics that Wailers bassist Buck Ormsby took into a small studio and unleashed on the world shows a live band at the peak of their powers, ready to mow down the competition without even blinking twice. Their debut long player (originally issued on the Etiquette imprint) is reprised here with new liner notes by Norton prexy Miriam Linna in the original mono. Their flame-throwing hits of "The Witch," "Psycho," "Boss Hoss," and "Strychnine" are aboard, along with versions of "Do You Love Me," "Dirty Robber," "Have Love-Will Travel," and "Walkin' the Dog" that are no less potent. This long-play vinyl reissue also boasts the addition of four bonus tracks: "Keep A-Knockin'" (the original B-side of "The Witch") and three selections from an Etiquette Christmas album, "Don't Believe In Christmas," "The Village Idiot," and "Santa Claus." Another important chunk of Seattle rock & roll history. *—Cub Koda*

Introducing the Sonics / 1966 / Beat Rocket ✦✦✦
This is a limited-edition, 180-gram premium vinyl audiophile pressing of the group's final album for Jerry Dennon's Jerden label. In addition to the band's two original hits (recorded and originally issued on the Etiquette label), there are 13 sides that were cut at the band's last session in 1966. All of the material on here is the same as on Jerden's compact disc version of the same material (issued as *Maintaining My Cool*), save for the exclusion of a lame version of "Hanky Panky," mercifully replaced here with Gerry Roslie's original "Love Lights." This makes a more than interesting comparison for audiophiles when compared to Jerden's CD version of this, minus the track swap. This also features the original album cover art of the band captured in a blue duo-tone in their matching gaucho outfits. Hardcore fans of the band and completists will want both versions of this. *—Cub Koda*

The Sonics Boom / 1966 / Norton ✦✦✦
The Sonics' second album is every bit as explosive and influential as their debut outing, loaded with gritty Northwest rock & soul. This 1998 vinyl reissue bonus tracks out with an alternate take of "The Witch" plus hot 1972 live reunion tapes of the band doing "Psycho" and "The Witch." Sandwiched in between the abrasive classics of "Cinderella," "Don't Be Afraid of the Dark" (with the Wailers on backing vocals), the funk sass of "The Hustler" and "Shot Down," the demonic "He's Waitin,'" and the sledgehammer, inside-out version of "Louie Louie" (only three chords to play and they don't even *play 'em*) are the band's straight ahead takes on old R&B chestnuts like "Skinny Minnie," "Let the Good Times Roll," "Don't You Just Know It," "Since I Fell for You," "Hitch Hike," and a nice barn-burning version of "Jenny Jenny." Where the Wailers cut down the trees and paved the highway, the Sonics were the first group from their neck of the woods to take that music somewhere wilder than their original inspirations. The second chapter of Northwest rock & roll after you absorb the Wailers' Golden Crest sides. *—Cub Koda*

● **Here Are the Ultimate Sonics** / 1991 / Etiquette ✦✦✦✦✦
Combining all the tracks from their first two Etiquette albums, three tracks from the label's Christmas album, live tracks, and an alternate take of "The Witch," this compilation more than lives up to its title. The definitive overview. *—Cub Koda*

Sonny & Cher

f. 1964, **db.** 1974
Group / Pop/Rock, Folk-Rock, Pop
Sonny & Cher proved to be one of the magical musical combinations of the mid '60s and one of the better rock-influenced MOR acts of the early '70s, their wisecracking repartee providing counterpoint to a series of adoring hit duets. They were a strange duet in the sense that neither had a great voice and, indeed, their voices were so similar that Atlantic Records president Ahmet Ertegun was convinced that Sonny had come close to breaking a contract by turning up singing with her on her solo hit "All I Really Want to Do." Their biggest success was as a duet on Atco, with "I Got You Babe" and "The Beat Goes On." For a time, from 1965 until 1967, they were rock & roll's hottest couple, so much so that in some conservative communities they were considered almost morally subversive; parents locked up their kids when Sonny & Cher were passing through for a concert appearance. And then nothing—the hits stopped coming, and the couple made some daringly creative but unsuccessful commercial missteps. Soon they were playing supper clubs and Las Vegas nightclubs; their stage act—which had evolved into a kind of "with it" domestic comedy routine nearly as prominent as the music, with the tall, wry-witted Cher cutting up on the seemingly dim-witted Sonny—was spotted by Fred Silverman, who was then the head of programming for CBS. They ended up with a summer replacement try-out show that did so well that Sonny & Cher were given a regular spot in the CBS lineup in 1972 with a comedy-variety series.The couple's recording career was revived initially by a live album cut in one night at Las Vegas, featuring new versions of their early hits as well as parts of their current repertory; the album went gold. The first couple of singles by Cher and Sonny & Cher failed, but then producer Snuff Garrett was brought in, and the result was "Gypsies, Tramps and Thieves," a career-reviving number one hit. After that, "The Way of Love," "All I Ever Need Is You" (which became the theme for their TV show), "A Cowboy's Work Is Never Done," "Half Breed," and "Dark Lady" kept either Cher or the couple in the Top Ten at various times through 1974. By then, however, their marriage had fallen apart, and with it, the success of their TV show. *—Bruce Eder*

● **The Beat Goes On: The Best of Sonny & Cher** / 1975 / Rhino/Atco ✦✦✦✦✦
Weighing in at a generous 21 tracks, Atco's *The Beat Goes On: The Best of Sonny & Cher* is the definitive portrait of Sonny and Cher in their glory years. The duo left Atco in the late '60s, staging a comeback on Kapp/MCA records in the early '70s, which means latter-day hits such as "All I Ever Need Is You" and "A Cowboy's Work Is Never Done" aren't here, but chances are most listeners won't even notice, since all the big songs are here: "I Got You Babe," "Laugh at Me," "Baby Don't Go," "Just You," "But You're Mine," "What Now, My Love?" "The Revolution Kind," "Little Man," and "The Beat Goes On." True, the collection may run a little long for some tastes, but there's no denying that it has all that a casual or dedicated fan could ever want from a Sonny & Cher compilation. *—Stephen Thomas Erlewine*

All I Ever Need: The Kapp/MCA Anthology / Jan. 1996 / MCA ✦✦✦✦✦
A single CD of the dozen or so key tracks from Sonny & Cher's second era of success (1971-74) on Kapp Records will probably be preferable to all but the biggest fans. What's more, even this set, which starts with the first failed Kapp singles ("Classified 1A," etc.) is missing five cuts available on the Cher greatest hits package, as well as three Sonny Bono solo tracks, and the long version of "Mama Was a Rock 'n' Roll Singer." Still, it's difficult to complain about the contents, 38 songs drawn from four years on the label, nicely remastered and assembled in impeccably logical fashion. The duo's (and Cher's solo) studio cuts make up the first disc, while the second is comprised of songs from the duo's two live recordings done two years apart in Las Vegas. It does show off the various facets of their appeal, even if what they were doing was more mainstream music than anything near the cutting edge of even pop music—no more Dylan songs, or any songs by would-be Dylan successors carried to the top of the charts, but lots of sales, and the live albums' sections not only includes covers of the most obvious of the duo's early songs ("The Beat Goes On," "I Got You Babe," etc.) but also titles like "You Better Sit Down Kids," as well as their humor and marital sparring. *—Bruce Eder*

Cher and Sonny & Cher Greatest Hits / 1998 / MCA ✦✦✦✦✦

Soul Asylum

f. 1983, Minneapolis, MN
Group / College Rock, Americana, Adult Alternative Pop/Rock, Alternative Pop/Rock, Hard Rock
Soul Asylum is the quintessential little band that could; it only took ten years to turn them from a teenage garage band into multiplatinum-selling rock stars. After several albums recorded for the local Minneapolis label Twin Tone, the band signed to A&M Records in 1989 as part of a distribution pact between Twin Tone and A&M for the harder rock-sounding *Hang Time,* produced by Lenny Kaye. The record garnered some college radio attention, but by 1990's *And the Horse They Rode in On,* Soul Asylum had fallen out of favor with the indie-rock set and were left languishing in limbo, having almost entirely forsaken their post-punk indie roots. Signed to Columbia for 1992's *Grave Dancers Union,* Soul Asylum eventually earned a multiplatinum record after a slow start. The magical third single, "Runaway Train" helped push the single to number five and the album to number 11 and turned the

band into a household name. Though 1995's *Let Your Dim Light Shine* charted at number six and a single, "Misery," hit the Top 20, the band never reached the dizzying heights nor masses they touched with "Runaway Train." Still, the band returned in 1998 with *Candy from a Stranger.* Needless to say, the little band's fame ultimately eclipsed those other guys from Minneapolis. *—Denise Sullivan*

Say What You Will / 1984 / Twin/Tone ♦♦♦

Made to Be Broken / 1986 / Twin/Tone ♦♦

While You Were Out / 1986 / Twin/Tone ♦♦♦

Hang Time / Feb. 1988 / A&M ♦♦♦♦
More riff-heavy than usual, with considerable help from producer Lenny Kaye, *Hang Time* turned out to be the best of Soul Asylum's early records. The guitars of Pirner and Dan Murphy synchronize into a sonic wad of incredible power, while the songs (especially "Cartoon," "Some Time to Return," and "Beggars and Choosers") showed that Pirner had become a first-rate songwriter. Clever without being glib, and heartfelt without resorting to clichés, Pirner was doing something that eluded many of his peers: dealing with the transition from youth to adulthood and all the inherent conflicts that arise during this time. They would become superstars later, but this record should have done the trick. *—John Dougan*

And the Horse They Rode in On / 1990 / A&M ♦♦♦
The band had already begun to trade in the loud and fast sound for something a little more roots-based, as found on "We 3," while other songs dabbled in heavy metal ("All the King's Friends"). On alternate tracks, the experiment didn't really work, and it left old fans confused and cold while arriving a little too early to cash in on the alt-rock explosion. Consequently, this otherwise fine record was left unheralded. It stands as one of the last pre-grunge alternative rock records, but had it not been perceived to fail so miserably, the band's success with its following album wouldn't have been nearly as sweet. *—Denise Sullivan*

Grave Dancer's Union / May 1992 / Columbia ♦♦♦♦
The band's breakthrough, million-selling album yielded the mega-hit "Runaway Train" and put Soul Asylum in a whole new league; longtime fans were predictably disappointed with the slick results. This is a solid alternative rock record with singer/songwriter/vocalist Dave Pirner up front, a role he was built for but always seemed to resist until the clear do-or-die moment for the band. They did; however, they've never matched the success or consistency of this album. Tracks like "Home Sick" and "New World" bear the roots of the country-rock revival later forged by Son Volt and Wilco, while the angst-ridden "Somebody to Shove" is pure joy Soul Asylum style. *—Denise Sullivan*

Let Your Dim Light Shine / Jun. 6, 1995 / Columbia ♦♦

Candy from a Stranger / May 12, 1998 / Columbia ♦♦♦

● **Black Gold: The Best of Soul Asylum** / Sep. 26, 2000 / Columbia/Legacy ♦♦♦♦
Unusually, for a best-of by a band that started indie and didn't become stars into hooking up with a major, *Black Gold: The Best of Soul Asylum* spans their entire pre-2000 career, starting with a 1985 track from their second LP. Naturally, their output on the major label that issued this compilation, Columbia, is emphasized; there are just four songs from the Twin/Tone era, and nothing at all from their 1984 debut, *Say What You Will Clarence... Karl Sold the Truck.* So it's mostly Soul Asylum the 1990s stars you hear here. Its appeal to collectors, and simultaneous aggravation to completists who have most of this but need everything, is guaranteed by the inclusion of a few rarities. There are previously unreleased live versions of "Stranger" (from *MTV Unplugged*) and "Closer to the Stars" and the *Candy From a Stranger* outtake "Lonely for You." There's also the song that's actually titled "Candy From a Stranger," although, oddly, this didn't make it onto the actual *Candy From a Stranger* album; before this compilation, it was only released on a commercially unavailable promo CD. And, finally, there's "Summer of Drugs" from the benefit album *Sweet Relief: A Benefit for Victoria Williams.* In addition, Lenny Kaye, who produced the band's *Hang Time* LP, contributes liner notes. *—Richie Unterberger*

Soul II Soul

f. 1989, London, England
Group / Club/Dance, Acid House, Urban, House, Dance-Pop
Led by producer/vocalist/songwriter DJ Jazzie B, Soul II Soul was one of the most innovative dance/R&B outfits of the late '80s, creating a seductive, deep R&B that borrowed from Philly soul, disco, reggae, and '80s hip-hop. Featuring the vocals of Caron Wheeler, Soul II Soul's third single, "Keep on Movin'," reached the U.K. Top Five in March of 1989. Released in the summer of 1989, "Back to Life" also featured Wheeler and became another Top Ten hit. Soul II Soul released their debut album, *Club Classics Volume One* (known as *Keep on Movin'* in the U.S.), shortly afterward. Wheeler left the group before the recording of the group's second album, *Vol. II: 1990—A New Decade.* The album debuted at number one in the U.K., yet it caught the group in a holding pattern. Producer/arranger Hooper soon left the collective, leaving Jazzie B. to soldier on alone. Hooper went on to work with several of the most influential and popular acts of the early '90s, including Massive Attack (*Blue Lines*), Bjork (*Debut* and *Post*), Madonna (*Bedtime Stories*), and U2 ("Hold Me, Thrill Me, Kiss Me, Kill Me"). *—Stephen Thomas Erlewine*

● **Keep on Movin'** / Jun. 1989 / Virgin ♦♦♦♦♦
When American urban-contemporary radio was bombarding its listeners with one Guy clone after another in the late '80s and early '90s, British neo-soulsters like Soul II Soul, Lisa Stansfield, and the Chimes offered highly creative and gutsy alternatives. With influences ranging from Chic to hip-hop to African music, Soul II Soul's debut album, *Keep on Movin'* (titled *Club Classics, Vol. 1* in its original British incarnation), was among the most rewarding R&B releases of 1989. Soul II Soul leader/producer/composer Jazzie B takes one risk after another—all of which pay off. The group enjoyed major hits with the Chic-influenced gems "Keep on Movin'" and "Back to Life" (both of which feature the gifted Caron Wheeler), and equally superb are the African-influenced reflections of "Dance" and "Holdin' On," the soulful grit and intensity of "Feel Free," and the hypnotic house music of "Happiness." Though Wheeler was Soul II Soul's best known singer and went on to enjoy a career as a solo artist, Rose Windross and Do'Reen (both expressive soul divas) also do their part to make *Keep on Movin'* the artistic triumph that it is. *—Alex Henderson*

Vol. II: 1990, A New Decade / May 21, 1990 / Virgin ♦♦♦♦
A better album but a deceptive one: even the best songs here don't intoxicate as thoroughly as "Keep On Movin'," but within the context of the album, each plays a vital part. In other words, this is a genuine *album,* and not a pastiche of singles. *—John Floyd*

Vol. III: Just Right / Apr. 13, 1992 / Virgin ♦♦

Vol. IV: The Classic Singles 1988-1993 / Dec. 6, 1993 / Virgin ♦♦♦♦♦

Vol. V: Believe / Aug. 11, 1995 / Virgin ♦♦♦

Soundgarden

f. 1984, Seattle, WA, **db.** Apr. 9, 1997
Group / Alternative Metal, Grunge, Alternative Pop/Rock
Soundgarden made a place for heavy metal in alternative rock. Their fellow Seattle rockers Green River may have spearheaded the grunge sound, but they relied on noise rock in the vein of the Stooges. Similarly, Jane's Addiction was too fascinated with prog rock and performance art to appeal to a wide array of metal fans. Soundgarden, however, developed directly out of the grandiose blues-rock of Led Zeppelin and the sludgy, slow riffs of Black Sabbath. Which isn't to say they were a straightahead metal band. Soundgarden borrowed the D.I.Y. aesthetics of punk, melding their guitar-driven sound with an intelligence and ironic sense of humor that was indebted to the American underground of the mid-'80s. Furthermore, the band rarely limited themselves to simple, pounding riffs, often making detours into psychedelia. But the group's key sonic signatures—the gutsy wail of vocalist Chris Cornell and the winding riffs of guitarist Kim Thayil—were what brought the band out of the underground. Not only were they one of the first groups to record for the legendary Seattle indie Sub Pop, but they were the first grunge band to sign to a major label. In fact, most critics expected Soundgarden to be the band that broke down the doors for alternative rock, not Nirvana. However, the group didn't experience an across-the-boards success until 1994, when *Superunknown* became a number one hit. *—Stephen Thomas Erlewine*

Ultramega OK / 1988 / SST ♦♦♦♦
The best expression of Soundgarden's early, Stooges/MC5-meets-Zeppelin/Sabbath sound, *Ultramega OK* is a dark, murky, buzzing record that simultaneously subverts and pays tribute to heavy metal. At times, the band and its recasting of over-the-top '70s hard rock seem smirky (Hiro Yamamoto's ridiculous vocal on "Circle of Power"; a "cover" of John Lennon's "One Minute of Silence"); a few, like the cover of "Smokestack Lightning," really do sink into turgid metal silliness. But the best moments are startling fusions of classic metal, punk rock, and psychedelia of the fuzz-guitar variety, plus the local flavor of Green River and the Melvins. The difference was, Soundgarden was made up of better songwriters, and their feel for memorable riffs and hooks lends greater power to both the rockers and the creepy, dirge-like slow numbers. It's a shame the album as a whole isn't more fully realized, because when separated out from the filler, the numerous highlights show why Soundgarden had such an enormous impact on the development of grunge. It may not be quite as complex or consistent as some of Soundgarden's later albums, but *Ultramega OK* is easily the best document of grunge's early, pre-Nirvana days. *—Steve Huey*

Louder Than Love / 1990 / A&M ♦♦♦
Signing to a major label, Soundgarden takes a step toward the metal mainstream with *Louder Than Love,* a slow, grinding, detuned mountain of Sabbath/Zeppelin riffs and Chris Cornell wailing. The production is even murkier than usual—this time too much so, as the rest of the band tries to poke its way through Kim Thayil's guitar squall; additionally, too much of the album drifts along without focus or variety. But there are some essential Soundgarden items mixed in, among them the haunting "Hands All Over," the punky "Full on Kevin's Mom," and the stereotypically macho metal stupidity of "Big Dumb Sex," whose ironic intent is often misconstrued. Unfortunately, that irony is missing from the plodding, overblown filler that constitutes about half of the album. It's worthwhile to sift through *Louder Than Love,* but don't expect consistency. *—Steve Huey*

Screaming Life/Fopp / Jun. 1990 / Sub Pop ♦♦♦

Badmotorfinger / 1991 / A&M ♦♦♦♦♦
Bidding for a popular breakthrough with their second major-label album, Soundgarden suddenly developed a sense of craft, with the result that *Badmotorfinger* became far and away their most fully realized album to that point. Pretty much everything about *Badmotorfinger* is a step up from its predecessors—the production is sharper and the music more ambitious, while the songwriting takes a quantum leap in focus and consistency. In so doing, the band abolishes the murky meandering that had often plagued them in the past, turning in a lean, muscular set that signaled their arrival in rock's big leagues. Conventional wisdom has it that despite platinum sales, *Badmotorfinger* got lost amidst the blockbuster success of *Nevermind* and *Ten* (all were released around the same time). But the fact is that, though they're all great records, *Badmotorfinger* is much less accessible by comparison. Not that it isn't melodic, but it also sounds twisted and gnarled, full of dissonant riffing, impossible time signatures, howling textural solos, and weird, droning tonalities. It's surprisingly cerebral and arty music for a band courting mainstream metal audiences, but it attacks with scientific precision. Part of that is due to the presence of new bassist Ben Shepherd, who gives the band its thickest rhythmic foundation yet—and, moreover, immediately shoulders the departed Hiro Yamamoto's share of songwriting duties. But it's apparent that the whole band has greatly expanded the scope of their ambitions. And *Badmotorfinger* fulfills them, pulling all the different threads of the band's sound together into a mature, confident, well-written record. This is heavy, challenging hard rock full of intellectual sensibility and complex band interplay. And with their next album, Soundgarden would learn how to make it fully accessible to mainstream audiences as well. *—Steve Huey*

- **Superunknown** / Mar. 8, 1994 / A&M ✦✦✦✦✦
Soundgarden's finest hour, *Superunknown* is a sprawling, 70-minute magnum opus that pushes beyond any previous boundaries. Soundgarden had always loved replicating Led Zeppelin and Black Sabbath riffs, but *Superunknown*'s debt is more to mid-period Zep's layered arrangements and sweeping epics. Their earlier punk influences are rarely detectable, replaced by surprisingly effective appropriations of pop and psychedelia. *Badmotorfinger* boasted more than its fair share of indelible riffs, but here the main hooks reside mostly in Cornell's vocals; accordingly, he's mixed right up front, floating over the band instead of cutting through it. The rest of the production is just as crisp, with the band achieving a huge, robust sound that makes even the heaviest songs sound deceptively bright. But the most important reasons *Superunknown* is such a rich listen are twofold: the band's embrace of psychedelia, and their rapidly progressing mastery of songcraft. Soundgarden had always been a little mind-bending, but the full-on experiments with psychedelia give them a much wider sonic palette, paving the way for less metallic sounds and instruments, more detailed arrangements, and a bridge into pop (which made the eerie ballad "Black Hole Sun" an inescapable hit). That blossoming melodic skill is apparent on most of the record, not just the poppier songs and Chris Cornell-penned hits; though a couple of drummer Matt Cameron's contributions are pretty undistinguished, they're easy to overlook, given the overall consistency. The focused songwriting allows the band to stretch material out for grander effect, without sinking into the pointlessly drawn-out muck that cluttered their early records. The dissonance and odd time signatures are still in force, though not as jarring or immediately obvious, which means that the album reveals more subtleties with each listen. It's obvious that *Superunknown* was consciously styled as a masterwork, and it fulfills every ambition. *—Steve Huey*

Down on the Upside / May 21, 1996 / A&M ✦✦✦

- **A-Sides** / Nov. 4, 1997 / A&M ✦✦✦✦✦
For an act that was one of the definitive album artists of the late '80s and '90s, Soundgarden was a surprisingly effective singles band. Their singles effectively conveyed all of their best ideas, from their sludgy early Sub Pop recordings to the elaborate, post-metal psychedelia of their last two albums, *Superunknown* and *Down on the Upside*. That's the reason why the 17-track compilation *A-Sides* is such a successful overview of the band's too-brief career. Most of their peers wouldn't be well represented by a compilation that concentrated solely on singles, but Soundgarden is, because their singles *do* capture what they're all about. There are many great songs left off *A-Sides*, from "Big Dumb Sex" to "My Wave," but it's hard to argue with what's here. Each single from every album—from the 1987 debut EP *Screaming Life* through SST's *Ultramega OK*, to their four records for A&M—is here, with the *Down on the Upside* outtake "Bleed Together" added as an enticement for collectors. Almost every one of the group's best-known songs are here, including "Hands All Over," "Loud Love," "Jesus Christ Pose," "Outshined," "Rusty Cage," "Black Hole Sun," "The Day I Tried to Live," "Spoonman," "Fell on Black Days," "Pretty Noose," "Burden in My Hand," and "Blow Up the Outside the World," resulting in a near-definitive summary of one of the most important and influential bands of the '90s. *—Stephen Thomas Erlewine*

Spacemen 3

f. 1982, Rugby, Midlands, England, **db.** 1991
Group / College Rock, Space Rock, Neo-Psychedelia, Post-Punk, Alternative Pop/Rock
Spacemen 3 was psychedelic in the loosest sense of the word; their guitar explorations were colorfully mind-alterating, but not in the sense of the acid rock of the '60s. Instead, the band developed its own minimalistic psychedelia, relying on heavily distorted guitars to clash and produce their own harmonic overtones; frequently, they would lead up to walls of distortion with over-amplified acoustic guitars and synths. Often the band would jam on one chord or play a series of songs, all in the same tempo and key. Though this approach was challenging, often bordering on the avant garde, Spacemen 3 nevertheless gained a dedicated cult following. At first the band sounded a bit like a punked-up garage rock band, but their music quickly evolved into their signature trance-like neo-psychedelia. Spacemen 3's second album, 1987's *The Perfect Prescription*, was the first to capture the group's distinctive style. By the time of the release of *Recurring*, singer/guitarist Jason Pierce was performing in a new band called Spiritualized, while fellow singer/guitarist Scott "Sonic Boom" Kember formed Spectrum. *—Stephen Thomas Erlewine*

Sound of Confusion / 1986 / Taang ✦✦✦

Perfect Prescription / 1987 / Taang ✦✦✦✦✦
A record mirroring the evolution of drug-induced euphoria from its inception (the blistering "Take Me to the Other Side") to its peak ("Feel So Good") to, finally, the inevitable crash ("Call the Doctor"), Spacemen 3's brilliant sophomore effort greatly expands the parameters of the narcotic drone-rock of *Sound of Confusion* to forge a rapturous and intensely visceral sonic experience. Recorded with a minimal use of percussion and a maximum use of spatial atmosphere, tracks like "Walkin' With Jesus" and a glistening symphonic cover of the Red Crayola's "Transparent Radiation" are masterpieces of texture, evocative and darkly beautiful; a representation of the band's unique vision at its most unified, *The Perfect Prescription* travels beyond the corporeal into new realms of consciousness and bliss. *—Jason Ankeny*

Performance / 1988 / Rough Trade ✦✦✦✦

Playing with Fire / 1989 / Taang ✦✦✦✦✦
A transitional effort bridging the dark, droning riffs of *The Perfect Prescription* with the ethereal atmospherics of *Recurring*, *Playing With Fire* ties together the disparate threads of the Spacemen 3 sound into an integrated whole. Apart from the incendiary single "Revolution" and the throbbing tribute "Suicide," the record is delicate and spare, a carefully modulated and expressive collection of elliptical melodies and pulsing backdrops tempered by an increasing fascination with minimalism and repetition. Although cohesive and organic, the album underscores the growing dichotomy separating Jason Pierce and Sonic Boom—while the former's songs are yearning and spiritual, the latter's are obsessive and ominous; not surprisingly, the follow-up, *Recurring*, was to be a Spacemen 3 album in name only. *—Jason Ankeny*

Taking Drugs to Make Music to Take Drugs To / 1990 / Bomp ✦✦✦

- **Recurring** / Mar. 1991 / Dedicated ✦✦✦✦✦
In essence, *Recurring* is as much the final Spacemen 3 studio effort as it is the joint debut of Spectrum and Spiritualized, the two pivotal groups to emerge from the band's ashes. Split evenly between solo music from Pete "Sonic Boom" Kember and Jason Pierce, the record diverges from the shared mindset of earlier releases to paint a portrait of a band at the breaking point: While Pierce's tracks—recorded with the same battery of musicians with whom he formed Spiritualized—are minimalist symphonies, Sonic's are more pop-oriented, even employing sequencers on the ten-minute opener, "Big City (Everybody I Know Can Be Found Here)." Still, the record is surprisingly cohesive; even when moving in opposite directions, Sonic and Pierce retain the same point of departure and the same objectives—throughout, *Recurring* is beautiful and transcendent, a fitting farewell. *—Jason Ankeny*

Singles / Jun. 17, 1994 / Taang ✦✦✦✦

For All the Fucked-Up Children of This World, We Give You Spacemen 3 / Apr. 28, 1995 / Sympathy for the Record Industry ✦✦✦
For All the Fucked-Up Children of This World, We Give You Spacemen 3 contains the group's first-ever recordings; never again were their garage-punk influences clearly as evident as on these embryonic stabs at "Walkin' With Jesus" and "Things Will Never Be the Same." *—Jason Ankeny*

Spandau Ballet

f. Nov. 1979, **db.** 1990
Group / New Romantic, Pop/Rock, New Wave
As one of the leading New Romantic bands, Spandau Ballet racked up a number of British hits—as well as one Top Ten American hit, "True"—during the early '80s, becoming one of the most successful groups to emerge during new wave. The only other new romantic band to enjoy greater commercial success was Duran Duran, yet Spandau Ballet was there first, scoring three Top Ten hit singles during 1981 with their synthesized dance-pop. By 1983, the London-based quintet had shed its Roxy Music-inspired robotic art-disco and picked up on Bryan Ferry's latter-day crooner persona, revamping themselves as a slick, stylish white soul act. It was in this incarnation that Spandau Ballet experienced its greatest success, as "True" reached number one in Britain and number four in America. However, their time in the spotlight was shortlived. Though they had a few more hits in Britain, none of them were particularly big, and in America they disappeared at the end of 1984. By the end of the decade, the group had split, with their core members, brothers Gary and Martin Kemp, launching acting careers with the 1990 film, *The Krays*. *—Stephen Thomas Erlewine*

- **The Singles Collection** / 1985 / Chrysalis ✦✦✦✦✦
Traces the group's development from the melodramatic, New Romantic dance-pop style of "To Cut a Long Story Short" to the lush ballad "True." Spandau Ballet always went in for big effects, but they became more subtle as they went along. *—William Ruhlmann*

Sparks

f. 1970, Los Angeles, CA
Group / Proto-Punk, Club/Dance, Pop/Rock, New Wave
Sparks was a vehicle for the skewed pop smarts and wiseguy wordplay of brothers Ron and Russell Mael. While attending UCLA in 1970, the Maels formed their first group, Halfnelson. Todd Rundgren helped land the group a contract and produced their self-titled 1971 debut. Their quirky, tongue-in-cheek art-pop failed to find an audience, however, and their manager convinced the Maels to change the group's name to Sparks. They almost reached the charts with "Wonder Girl," and 1972's sublimely bizarre *A Woofer in Tweeter's Clothing* cemented the band's cult status with another near-hit, "Girl from Germany."

Warmly received by the British music press, the Mael brothers ultimately relocated to London to record 1974's glam-bubblegum opus *Kimono My House*—it spawned two major British hits, "This Town Ain't Big Enough for the Both of Us" and "Amateur Hour." Sparks returned later in 1974 with *Propaganda*, another smash which scored with the hits "Never Turn Your Back on Mother Earth" and "Something for the Girl With Everything." The Maels eventually returned to the U.S., however, treading water for two albums before enlisting disco producer Giorgio Moroder to helm 1979's synth-powered dance-pop confection *No. 1 in Heaven*. The album spurred the group to renewed success in England on the strength of the hit singles "The Number One Song in Heaven," "Beat the Clock," and "Tryouts for the Human Race." Sparks left disco in the dust with 1981's *Whomp That Sucker* and the following year's *Angst in My Pants*. The wonderful single "Cool Places", a duet with the Go-Go's Jane Wiedlin, nearly reached the Top 40, and was the band's biggest American hit. After three lackluster LPs during the '80s, Sparks remained silent until *Gratuitous Sax and Senseless Violins*, released in 1994. *Plagiarism* followed four years later. *—Jason Ankeny*

Sparks / 1971 / Bearsville ✦✦✦

A Woofer in Tweeter's Clothing / 1972 / Bearsville ✦✦✦

Kimono My House / 1974 / Island ✦✦✦✦✦
Sparks specializes in keyboard-based pop songs with clever, ironic lyrics (by Ron Mael), sung in a near-falsetto by Russell Mael. Examples include "Here in Heaven" (in which a disappointed, dead Romeo sings to a still-living Juliet who "broke our little pact"), "Thank God It's Not Christmas," and the U.K. hits "This Town Ain't Big Enough for the Both of Us" and "Amateur Hour." *—William Ruhlmann*

Propaganda / 1974 / Island ✦✦✦✦✦
More of Ron's wit ("Don't Leave Me Alone with Her," "Who Don't Like Kids") and Russell's operatic singing with catchy rock backings, though it's hard to get the jokes without the lyric sheet. *—William Ruhlmann*

Indiscreet / 1975 / Island ✦✦✦✦✦
On their third terrific album in as many years, producer Tony Visconti provides the Mael brothers the best production and arrangements of their careers; they responded with some of their catchiest, cleverest material. Ron Mael's lyrics explore some of the same themes as Ray Davies: the regrets of an aging drunk ("T*ts"), the loss of gentility and innocence ("It Ain't 1918"), and other observations about decorum and courtship. And relationships ranging from the wholesome to the depraved to the baffling. A classic of quirky pop, one that surely influenced bands like They Might Be Giants and Barenaked Ladies. *—James A. Gardner*

Big Beat / 1976 / Island ✦✦✦✦

No. 1 in Heaven / 1979 / Virgin ✦✦✦✦
It may not have been the most natural match in music history, but the marriage of Sparks' focus on oddball pop songs to the driving disco-trance of Giorgio Moroder produced the duo's best album in years. From the chart hits "Number One Song in Heaven" and "Beat the Clock" to solid album tracks like "La Dolce Vita," *No. 1 in Heaven* surprises by succeeding on an artistic and commercial level despite the fact that neither the Mael brothers nor Moroder tempered their respective idiosyncrasies for the project. Moroder's production is just as dizzying, chunky, and completely rhythm-driven as on his best work with Donna Summer, and the Mael brothers prove on "Tryouts for the Human Race" and "Academy Award Performance" that their bizarre songwriting wasn't compromised. *—John Bush*

Terminal Jive / 1979 / Oglio ✦✦✦✦
The second Giorgio Moroder collaboration of Sparks' career doesn't have quite the emphasis on Moroder trademarks compared to its predecessor; he has only two songwriting credits here, while the Mael brothers take most of them alone. Still, the breakout single "When I'm With You" and "Just Because You Love Me" have an ineffable disco stomp and the requisite cymbal slaps on the off-beat, while "Noisy Boys" and "Stereo" have an experimental, laddish feel that looks past disco into '80s synth-pop and New Romantic. Though disco fans can feel safe with *No. 1 in Heaven*, those more interested in new wave would be well served to pick up *Terminal Jive* first. *—John Bush*

The History of Sparks / 1981 / Underdog ✦✦✦✦

Whomp That Sucker / 1981 / Oglio ✦✦

Angst in My Pants / 1982 / Oglio ✦✦✦

Pulling Rabbits out of a Hat / 1984 / Oglio ✦✦

Mael Intuition: The Best of Sparks 1974-1976 / 1990 / Island ✦✦✦✦
A well-chosen, 20-track compilation derived from the group's three best albums (*Kimono My House, Propaganda,* and *Indiscreet*), released during their brief, productive tenure with Island Records. Producers Muff Winwood (for the first two, harder-rocking albums) and Tony Visconti (the more varied and elaborately arranged *Indiscreet*) both provide the Mael brothers with solid, sympathetic settings for their witty, rapid-fire lyrics and manic delivery. Songs range from the aggressive riff of "At Home, at Work, at Play" (a precursor to the heavier sound of the 1976 album, *Big Beat*) to the uncanny Andrews Sisters evocation "Looks, Looks, Looks." Russell Mael's quavery falsetto is an acquired taste, and his vocal affectations can try the listener's nerves on prolonged exposure. Also, their tendency to deliver a few hundred lyrics in as many seconds makes interpretation a challenge, but their perverse humor rewards the effort. This is probably all the Sparks the casual fan needs. *—James A. Gardner*

● **Profile: The Ultimate Sparks Collection** / Apr. 1991 / Rhino ✦✦✦✦✦
Unfortunately, Sparks never enjoyed more than a small, though devoted, cult following. But it certainly wasn't for a lack of effective hooks and clever, insanely funny lyrics. While a few of the L.A. pop/rockers' albums were disappointing, many others were exceptional. For those seeking an introductory overview of Sparks' legacy, this two-CD set is highly recommended. From "Achoo" to "Tips for Teens" to "This Town Ain't Big Enough for the Both of Us," *Profile* makes it clear just how delightfully goofy Sparks could be. Often willing to experiment, the group embraces everything from hard rock on "Big Boy" to Euro-disco on Giorgio Moroder-produced songs like "The Number One Song in Heaven" and "Beat the Clock." Despite the inclusion of a few throwaways—such as the disappointing *Music You Can Dance To*'s title song—*Profile* paints an impressive picture of a wrongly neglected band. *—Alex Henderson*

Plagiarism / 1997 / Oglio ✦✦✦

Balls / Aug. 22, 2000 / Oglio ✦✦✦

Britney Spears

b. Dec. 2, 1981, Kentwood, LA
Vocals / Teen Pop, Adult Contemporary, Dance-Pop
Dance-pop singer Britney Spears was born in Kentwood, LA on December 2, 1981. After honing her chops in local dance showcases and church choirs, at age eight she auditioned for a role on the Disney Channel's *Mickey Mouse Club* show, and although the series' producers deemed her too young for the job, they were sufficiently impressed with the girl's talent to assist her in gaining entry to New York's Off-Broadway Dance Center and the Professional Performing Arts School. After a series of television commercials and stage appearances, at 11 Spears finally joined *The Mickey Mouse Club,* where she remained for two seasons; continuing on as a solo artist, she signed to Jive Records and in early 1999 issued her first LP ... *Baby One More Time.* The record was a massive hit, debuting atop the pop charts and reeling off a series of radio smashes including the title track, "(You Drive Me) Crazy," and "From the Bottom of My Broken Heart" on its way to becoming the best-selling album ever released by a teenage girl. Spears' success also spawned legions of imitators, most notable among them Christina Aguilera and Jessica Simpson. Her sophomore effort, *Oops!... I Did It Again,* followed in the spring of 2000. *—Jason Ankeny*

● **... Baby One More Time** / Jan. 12, 1999 / Jive ✦✦✦✦
At the beginning of the '90s, teen currency shifted from bubblegum'n'*Tiger Beat* to grunge'n'*Maximum Rock & Roll.* Although it may have been pushed from the spotlight, teen pop hadn't died—it, in a way, went underground, spending time on the fringes of pop culture. One of the leading lights of the exiled teen brigade was *The New Mickey Mouse Club.* For several years, it toiled away on the Disney Network, earning a small fan base—but, more importantly, providing a launchpad for several careers, including that of Britney Spears. Like her fellow *NMMC* alumni 'N Sync, Spears shot to stardom in the late '90s, just as she was on the verge of late adolescence. By that time, everything old was new again. Albums like her debut, *... Baby One More Time,* were topping the charts as if they were *Hangin' Tough,* which is only appropriate since it sounded as if it could have been cut in 1989, not 1999. ... *Baby One More Time* has the same blend of infectious, rap-inflected dance-pop, and smooth balladry that propelled the New Kids and Debbie Gibson, due to the Backstreet Boys' producer, Max Martin, who is also the mastermind behind Spears' debut. He has a knack for catchy hooks, endearing melodies, and engaging Euro-dance rhythms, all of which are best heard on the hits: the ingenious title track, "Sometimes," "(You Drive Me) Crazy," and the utterly delightful, bubblegum-ragga album track "Soda Pop." Like many teen pop albums, ... *Baby One More Time* has its share of well-crafted filler, but the singles, combined with Britney's burgeoning charisma, make this a pretty great piece of fluff. *—Stephen Thomas Erlewine*

Oops!... I Did It Again / May 16, 2000 / Jive ✦✦✦✦
Given the phenomenal success of Britney Spears' debut, *... Baby One More Time,* it should come as no surprise that its sequel offers more of the same. After all, she gives away the plot with the ingenious title of her second album *Oops!... I Did It Again,* essentially admitting that the record is more of the same. It has the same combination of sweetly sentimental ballads and endearingly gaudy dance-pop that made *One More Time.* Fortunately, she and her production team not only have a stronger overall set of songs this time, but they also occasionally get carried away with the same bewildering magpie aesthetic that made the first album's "Sodapop"—a combination of bubblegum, urban soul, and raga—a gonzo teen-pop classic. It doesn't happen all that often—the clenched-funk revision of the Stones' deathless "Satisfaction" is the most obvious example—but it helps give the album character apart from the well-crafted dance-pop and ballads that serve as its heart. In the end, it's what makes this an entertaining, satisfying listen. *—Stephen Thomas Erlewine*

The Specials

f. 1977, Coventry, England, **db.** 1985
Group / Ska Revival, New Wave
True innovators of the punk era, the Specials began the British ska-revival craze, combining the highly danceable ska and rocksteady beat with punk's energy and attitude, and taking on a more focused and informed political and social stance than their predecessors and peers. Despite early interest from major labels, frontman Jerry Dammers opted to start his own 2-Tone label, named for its multiracial agenda and after the two-tone tonic suits favored by the like-minded mods of the '60s. The band debuted with the single "Gangsters" which reached the U.K. Top Ten. Soon after, hordes of bands and fans followed in the same tradition and the movement was in full swing with hits by similar-sounding 2 Tone bands, such as Madness, the (English) Beat, and the Selecter. Late in 1979, the Specials released their landmark self-titled debut album. The title track of a subsequent EP, *Too Much Too Young,* reached the number one spot. At this time, the band switched musical directions, releasing album number two, *More Specials,* with a new neo-lounge persona. The 1981 single "Ghost Town" also jumped to number one, but the band began falling apart soon after. A splinter trio left to form Fun Boy Three, while Dammers held on and returned with one final album, 1984's *In the Studio.* In 1996, a Dammers-less version of the band reappeared with a shameful cash-in album, *Today's Specials.* *—Chris Woodstra*

★ **The Specials** / Nov. 1979 / 2 Tone/Chrysalis ✦✦✦✦✦
The Specials' self-titled debut sparked the Two-Tone movement in the late '70s. With well-chosen ska classics and Prince Buster-inspired originals, the band mixed political and social activism and blended punk's intensity with an infectious dance beat. *The Specials* is a landmark recording that, while very much a product of its time, hasn't really dated at all. Produced by Elvis Costello. *—Chris Woodstra*

More Specials / Oct. 1980 / 2 Tone/Chrysalis ✦✦✦✦✦
Branching away from their ska roots, the band moves somewhat directionlessly into a neo-lounge act. Still in full force is the biting social commentary only in a slightly skewed environment. While this can be seen as a slight disappointment after the brilliant debut, with time *More Specials* can be nearly as rewarding—many of the songs are just as strong. *—Chris Woodstra*

In the Studio / 1984 / 2 Tone/Chrysalis ✦✦✦
When Hall, Staples, and Golding left to become Fun Boy Three, Jerry Dammers decided to continue with the addition of vocalist Stan Campbell. Nearly three years in the making, *In the Studio* lacks any hint of ska and Campbell's vocals, while good, lack the tension needed for the overtly political direction of the band. The highpoints "Racist Friend" and the anthem "Free Nelson Mandela" can be found on the *Singles Collection* so only completists need to bother. *—Chris Woodstra*

☆ **The Singles Collection** / Sep. 1991 / 2 Tone/Chrysalis ✦✦✦✦✦
All of the essential singles from their three albums are present on this 15-track collection. Not only the perfect starting point for the curious, the inclusion of B-sides and rarities, like an inspired cover of Dylan's "Maggie's Farm," makes this essential for fans. *—Chris Woodstra*

Coventry Automatics Aka the Specials: Dawning of a New Era / Mar. 1994 / Receiver ✦✦

Today's Specials / May 1996 / Virgin ✦

Phil Spector (Harvey Phillip Spector)

b. Dec. 26, 1940, New York, NY [The Bronx]
Vocals, Producer / Baroque Pop, Brill Building Pop, Girl Group, Pop, Rock & Roll
Though he very rarely released records under his name, as a producer Phil Spector has influenced the course of rock & roll more than all but a handful of performers. The "Wall of

Sound" that he perfected in the early '60s opened unlimited possibilities for arrangements and sound construction in rock and pop, and his brilliant talents imprinted the discs that he produced with an artistic vision that was much more attributable to him than the talented performers with whom he worked.

To an extent that had never been imagined in rock & roll, Spector pumped his records full of orchestration—strings, horns, rattling percussion—that coalesced into teenage symphonies, never overwhelming the material or the passionate vocals. Though he enjoyed a lot of success with blue-eyed soul duo the Righteous Brothers, in the mid-'60s, Spector's teen operas quickly became out of fashion. After the failure of Ike & Tina Turner's 1966 single "River Deep, Mountain High"—which he always considered among his greatest achievements—he retired to his L.A. mansion, marrying Ronnie Spector, lead singer of the Ronettes.

Spector re-emerged in the late '60s to do post-production on the Beatles' controversial *Let It Be* album, and he also produced George Harrison and John Lennon's first solo albums. For the past couple of decades, he's been active only sporadically, producing isolated albums by Dion, Leonard Cohen, and the Ramones. Today he's one of rock's most legendary recluses, rarely appearing in public, but his accomplishments cast a shadow over all performers and producers who aspire to create works of art in the studio. *—Richie Unterberger*

☆ **A Christmas Gift for You from Phil Spector** / 1963 / ABKCO ✦✦✦✦✦
Featuring Phil Spector's "Wall of Sound" in its prime and his early stable of artists, the Ronettes, Crystals, Darlene Love, and Bob B. Soxx & the Blue Jeans, this stands as inarguably the greatest Christmas record of all time. Spector believed he could produce a record for the holidays that would capture not only the essence of the Christmas spirit, but also be a pop masterpiece that would stand against any work these artists had already done. He succeeded on every level, with all four groups/singers recording some of their most memorable performances. This is the Christmas album by which all later holiday releases had to be judged, and it has inspired a host of imitators. (Note: This CD is available separately and as part of the highly recommended four-CD box set, *Phil Spector: Back to Mono [1958-1969].*) *—Dennis MacDonald*

Early Productions 1958-1961 / 1983 / Rhino ✦✦✦✦
A sampling of Spector's earliest work, generally more pop-oriented, sappy, and far less distinguished than his early and mid-'60s classics. The Teddy Bears' "To Know Him Is to Love Him," Gene Pitney's "Every Breath I Take," the Paris Sisters' "I Love How You Love Me," and Curtis Lee's "Pretty Little Angel Eyes" are fine hits that reveal much of the talent that would fully blossom on his Philles singles. The other tracks, including rarities by the Ducanes, Kell Osborne, and Spector's Three, suffer from weak songwriting, and would be downright dispensable if not for their historical significance. *—Richie Unterberger*

★ **Back to Mono (1958-1969)** / Nov. 12, 1991 / ABKCO ✦✦✦✦✦
If you look hard enough, you can find decent one-album samplers of Phil Spector's greatest recordings, but this four-disc boxed set (three sets of singles and the entire *A Christmas Gift for You* on the fourth) is the jewel of Spector's legacy. Aside from his sporadic '70s productions, *Back to Mono* contains everything you'd ever want by rock's supreme romantic: early productions with Curtis Lee, Ben E. King, and Gene Pitney; the girl group effervescence of the Ronettes, the Crystals, and Darlene Love; the soul innovations of the Righteous Brothers and the Checkmates; and his notorious sessions with Ike & Tina Turner. Throughout the set, Spector's artistic vision (which has influenced dozens of producers and hundreds of performers) shines like the smile on a lover's lips. This is one of the greatest and most fully realized boxed sets ever issued. *—John Floyd*

Jon Spencer Blues Explosion

f. 1990, New York, NY
Vocals, Guitar / Indie Rock, Alternative Pop/Rock
After a long and semi-successful tenure as leader of scuzz-rock heroes Pussy Galore, Jon Spencer took his anti-rock vision and hooked up with guitarist Judah Bauer and drummer Russell Simins to create the scuzz-blues trio the Jon Spencer Blues Explosion. Postmodern to the core, little of what this band plays resembles standard blues. There is, however, a blues feel to what they play, meaning that in many instances they appropriate aspects of the blues (very often cliches) and incorporate them into their anarchic, noisy sound. Not part of alternarock's commercial establishment, Spencer has also managed to sharply divide critics who tend to see him as either inspired showman or mendacious con man (frankly, he's both). As with Royal Trux, the other band to emerge after the breakup of Pussy Galore, the Blues Explosion's earliest recordings are virtually incomprehensible (and impossible to find). The Blues Explosion's "breakthrough" came (as it did for Royal Trux) when they began to sound like a '70s rock band, with the release of 1993's *Extra Width. Orange* netted the band even more fans upon its release in 1994; 1996's *Now I Got Worry* and 1998's *Acme* were also successful. Still, there is a compelling argument to be made that despite his hip credentials, Spencer is more style than substance. Love him or loathe him (and it's easy to do both), he's a force to reckoned with. *—John Dougan*

Jon Spencer Blues Explosion / Apr. 24, 1992 / Caroline ✦✦✦

Extra Width / Nov. 1, 1993 / Matador ✦✦✦✦✦
Much more accessible than the aforementioned record, but in no way does its accessibility detract from the record's adventurousness. *Extra Width* is a crankin' piece of bluesoid ranting, with Spencer working up one hysterical performance after another. "Afro" is as funky as all get-out and sounds like an old Curtis Mayfield track. Similarly, "Soul Letter" is a hefty chunk of riff-muck, as is the noisy bliss of "Soul Typecast." The playing is energetic and unhinged, and Spencer drives the engine with his whoopin' and hollerin'. Plenty of noticeably '70s production techniques add to the atmosphere, contributing significantly to what may be Spencer's best record. *—John Dougan*

Orange / Oct. 1994 / Matador ✦✦✦✦
By this juncture, you either love Spencer enough to listen to every record, or you've heard plenty and are decidedly uninterested. Still, *Orange* mines the same territory as *Extra Width*, and that may not be enough. At times, even during *Orange*'s best tracks ("Bell Bottoms"), the thin, retro-'70s worshipping sounds phoned-in and lacking in real emotional commitment. But, as with a lot of junk-rock, sometimes it can be appreciated for simply being junk, and that's fine. But I'm willing to bet that Spencer's core fans like the idea of the blues more than the reality. In other words, they don't mind the pose, nor do they mind the facade. In Jon Spencer's world, image is everything. *—John Dougan*

Mo Width / Jan. 1, 1995 / Au-Go-Go ✦✦✦

● **Now I Got Worry** / Oct. 15, 1996 / Matador/Capitol ✦✦✦✦✦
Where *Orange* had some awkward attempts at funk, *Now I Got Worry* is a raw bluesy workout, full of harsh guitars and barked vocals. The sound of the Blues Explosion is so fiery and alive that it overshadows Spencer's habit for campy posturing, and that's what keeps *Now I Got Worry* afloat. Once it's finished, it becomes hard not to second-guess Spencer's intentions, but the album is the closest the Blues Explosion has come to capturing their wild, intense live show on record. *—Stephen Thomas Erlewine*

Acme / Oct. 20, 1998 / Matador/Capitol ✦✦✦

Spice Girls

f. 1993
Group / Teen Pop, Club/Dance, Euro-Dance, Europop, Adult Contemporary, Dance-Pop
The Spice Girls were the first major British pop music phenomenon of the mid-'90s to not have a debt to independent pop/rock. Instead, the all-female quintet derived from the dance-pop tradition that made Take That the most popular British group of the early '90s, but there was one crucial difference. The Spice Girls used dance-pop as a musical base, but they infused the music with a fiercely independent, feminist stance that was equal parts Madonna, post-riot-grrrl alternative-rock feminism, and a co-opting of the good-times-all-the-time stance of England's new lad culture. Their proud, all-girl image and catchy dance-pop appealed to younger listeners, while their colorful, sexy personalities and sense of humor appealed to older music fans, making the Spice Girls a cross-generational success. The group also became chart-toppers throughout Europe in 1996, before concentrating in America in early 1997. *—Stephen Thomas Erlewine*

● **Spice** / 1996 / Virgin ✦✦✦✦✦
Spice doesn't need to be original to be entertaining, nor do the Spice Girls need to be good singers. It just has to be executed well, and the innocuous dance-pop of *Spice* is infectious. None of the Spice Girls have great voices, but they do exude personality and charisma, which is what drives bouncy dance-pop like "Wannabe," with its ridiculous "zig-a-zig-ahhh" hook, into pure pop guilty pleasure. What is surprising is how the sultry soul of "Say You'll Be There" is more than just a guilty pleasure, and how ballads like "2 Become 1" are perfect adult contemporary confections. The rest of the album isn't quite as catchy as those first three singles, but it is still an irresistible, immaculately crafted pop that gets by on the skills of the producer and the charisma of the five Spices. Sure, the last half of the album is forgettable, but it sounds good while it's on, which is the key to a good dance-pop record. *—Stephen Thomas Erlewine*

Spiceworld / Nov. 4, 1997 / Virgin ✦✦✦✦✦
The Spice Girls, as well as their managers and songwriters, are nothing if not clever, and *Spiceworld*, the group's second album, illustrates exactly how sharp they are. Conventional wisdom dictates that *Spiceworld* should be a weak fascimile of *Spice*, which itself featured a handful of great singles surrounded by filler. Conventional wisdom, in this case, is wrong—*Spiceworld* is a better record than its predecessor, boasting a more consistent (and catchier) set of songs and an intoxicating sense of fun. Instead of merely re-writing *Spice*, *Spiceworld* consolidates and expands the group's style, adding Latin flourishes ("Spice Up Your Life"), kitschy blues ("The Lady Is a Vamp"), and stomping, neo-Motown blue-eyed soul in the vein of Culture Club ("Stop"). The girls—Mel C. in particular—are actually turning into good vocalists, and each song plays to their strengths, giving each Spice a chance to shine. Best of all, each song has a strong melody and a strong, solid beat, whether it's a ballad or a dance number. It's a pure, unadulterated guilty pleasure and some of the best manufactured mainstream dance-pop of the late '90s. *—Stephen Thomas Erlewine*

Forever / Nov. 7, 2000 / Virgin ✦✦

Spin Doctors

f. 1988, New York, NY
Group / Jam Bands, American Trad Rock, Pop/Rock
There were many pseudo-hippie, jam-oriented blues rockers in New York during the early '90s, but only the Spin Doctors made it big. And they made it big because not only could they immerse themselves in a groove, but they also had concise pop skills. "Little Miss Can't Be Wrong" and "Two Princes" were cleverly written singles, full of clean, blues-inflected licks, and ingratiating pop melodies. *Pocket Full of Kryptonite* had been around for nearly a year when MTV and radio began playing "Little Miss Can't Be Wrong," but once they started playing it, they couldn't stop. The Spin Doctors became an overnight sensation, selling millions of albums around the world.

Their second album, 1994's *Turn It Upside Down*, didn't sell very well when it was released, largely because the first single, "Cleopatra's Cat," was a failed experiment in funk. But the second single, "You Let Your Heart Go Too Fast," was in the vein of "Two Princes," and the album began to sell after the song was released. In the summer of 1996 the Spin Doctors released *You've Got to Believe in Something*. After the album failed to make an impression on the charts, the Spin Doctors were dropped from Epic in the fall of the year. After a couple of years, the group found a new label; their first record for Uptown/Universal, *Here Comes the Bride*, appeared in the summer of 1999. *—Stephen Thomas Erlewine*

● **Just Go Ahead Now: A Retrospective** / Oct. 24, 2000 / Epic/Legacy ✦✦✦✦✦

The Spinners

f. 1961, Detroit, MI

Group / Smooth Soul, Quiet Storm, Philly Soul, Soul

The Spinners were the greatest soul group of the early '70s, creating a body of work that defined the lush, seductive sound of Philly Soul. Ironically, the band's roots lay in Detroit, where they formed as a doo-wop group during the late '50s. Throughout the '60s, the Spinners tried to land a hit by adapting to the shifting fashions of R&B and pop. By the mid-'60s, they had signed with Motown Records, but the level never gave the group much consideration. "It's a Shame" became a hit in 1970, but the label continued to ignore the group, and dropped the band two years later. Unsigned and featuring new lead singer Phillippe Wynne, the Spinners seemed destined to never break into the big-leagues, but they managed to sign with Atlantic Records, where they began working with producer Thom Bell. With his assistence, the Spinners developed a distinctive sound, one that relied on Wynne's breathtaking falsetto and the group's intricate vocal harmonies. Bell provided the group with an appropriately detailed production, creating a detailed web of horns, strings, backing vocals, and lightly funky rhythms. Between 1972 and 1977, the Spinners and Thom Bell recorded a number of soul classics, including "I'll Be Around," "Could It Be I'm Fallin in Love," "Mighty Love," "Ghetto Child," "Then Came You," "Games People Play," and "The Rubberband Man." Wynne left in 1977 and the Spinners had hits for a few years after his departure, but the group will always be remembered for its classic mid-'70s work. *—Stephen Thomas Erlewine*

Spinners / 1972 / Rhino ✦✦✦✦✦

A superb album, arguably their finest, though not their biggest, crossover work. The Spinners teamed with Thom Bell and made Motown look stupid with this album of glorious anthems. "I'll Be Around" and "Could It Be I'm Falling In Love" ended any discussions, mentions, or even thoughts of their former lead singer G.C. Cameron, as Phillippe Wynne was emerging as the king of immaculate, sophisticated soul. They had three R&B chart toppers from this album and were now dominating the Motown acts they once idolized. *—Ron Wynn*

Mighty Love / Jan. 1974 / Rhino ✦✦✦✦✦

Phillippe Wynne's twisting, soulful, frequently captivating voice was at its finest on this 1974 album. The title track was a smash in edited single form, and the extended album version contains marvelous Wynne ad-libs and exchanges nicely contrasted by the group's harmonizing. The album contains many other fine songs, like "Ain't No Price on Happiness" and "I'm Coming Home," and was their second Atlantic release. It equaled the gold-selling pace of its predecessor and cemented the Spinners' status as R&B stars. *—Ron Wynn*

New and Improved / Feb. 1974 / Rhino ✦✦✦✦

The Spinners were on a roll; after years of neglect at the hands of Motown, their ship just kept coming in, and in, and in with Atlantic Records. *New and Improved* is an absolute classic, yet it gets less run than some of their other LPs. Everything from the romanticism of "Smile We Have Each Other," a real tearjerker, to the self-assured, driven "I've Got to Make It on My Own" is on board, and it all works. "Sadie," a song about the death of a mother, became a signature song for the Spinners; it was revived in the '90s by R. Kelly, who introduced it to new fans, many of whom thought he created the touching tribute. Dionne Warwick struts her soul on "Then Came You," accompanied by Bobby Smith; it's a mover from the first note. A strong effort from Thom Bell and the Spinners. *—Andrew Hamilton*

Pick of the Litter / 1975 / Rhino ✦✦✦✦✦

The Spinners were rolling in the 1970s, and this proved to be their biggest album ever. It peaked in the pop Top Ten at number eight, and they racked up four consecutive R&B Top Ten singles, including the chart topper "They Just Can't Stop It (The Games People Play)." Phillippe Wynne sang with an amazing mix of class and fire, sophistication and earthiness, that hadn't been heard in soul circles for years. Of course, this is now out of print. *—Ron Wynn*

☆ **One of a Kind Love Affair** / Nov. 5, 1991 / Rhino ✦✦✦✦✦

Spanning from their first single, 1961's "That's What Girls Are Made For," to their last charting single more than 20 years later, *One of a Kind Love Affair—The Anthology* is the definitive Spinners collection. The bulk of the 2-CD compilation is the group's work with Thom Bell during the mid-'70s, easily the best work they ever recorded and arguably the finest Philly soul singles. All of the Spinners' major hits are here, as are excellent, informative liner notes (including complete personnel and discography). *—Stephen Thomas Erlewine*

★ **The Very Best of the Spinners** / Apr. 20, 1993 / Rhino ✦✦✦✦✦

The Very Best of the Spinners contains all of the group's essential hits, from "It's a Shame" and "I'll Be Around" to "The Rubberband Man" and "Working My Way Back to You/Forgive Me, Girl." A few hits are missing, but the serious fan can find those on the double disc set *One of A Kind Love Affair*. For the casual fan, who only wants the biggest hits, *The Very Best of the Spinners* is a necessary purchase. In a concise 16 tracks, it makes a convincing case that the group was the greatest soul vocal group of the '70s. *—Stephen Thomas Erlewine*

The Very Best of the Spinners, Vol. 2 / May 27, 1997 / Rhino ✦✦✦✦

The Very Best of the Spinners, Vol. 2 rounds up the lesser-known hits that didn't make the first volume, plus selected album tracks, including "Heaven on Earth," "You're Throwing a Good Love Away," "Love or Leave," "Wake Up Susan," and "Easy Come, Easy Go." *—Stephen Thomas Erlewine*

Spiritualized

f. 1989, Rugby, Midlands, England

Group / Noise Pop, Ambient Pop, Dream Pop, Space Rock, Neo-Psychedelia, Alternative Pop/Rock

Formed from the ashes of the trance-rockers Spacemen 3, singer/guitarist Jason Pierce's group Spiritualized did not break away from his prior band's trademark hypnotic minimalism; instead, they perfected it. Drawing on the continued influence of the Velvet Underground, LaMonte Young, and Steve Reich, Spiritualized staked out a common ground between minimalism and lush symphonics—while powered by simple, repetitious motifs, their songs simultaneously blossomed into rich, shimmering sonic panoramas inspired by the majestic studio wizardry of Phil Spector and Brian Wilson. Such seeming contradictions were essential to the group's alchemy: while the infamous Spacemen 3 tag of "taking drugs to make music to take drugs to" remained a cornerstone of their craft, at the same time Spiritualized's very name acknowledged the existence of other forces, further reflected in their heavy debt to gospel and soul music as well as an affinity for mantras and devotional hymns. *—Jason Ankeny*

Lazer Guided Melodies / 1992 / Dedicated ✦✦✦✦✦

The group's seminal debut album is aptly titled: The melodies shimmer and drone and hum like otherworldly pop tunes, and Radley and Pierce's vocals hover gently in the mix. One of the premier dream-pop albums, *Lazer-Guided Melodies* is both beautiful and innovative. *—Heather Phares*

Pure Phase / Mar. 28, 1995 / Dedicated ✦✦✦

Spiritualized's eagerly-awaited second album continues the group's ethereal tradition, this time with a loopier, more symphonic sound. Many of the songs swell past the six-minute mark, ebbing and flowing majestically. "Medication," "Electric Phase," "Lay Back in the Sun," and "Spread Your Wings" typify the dreamy grandeur of most of the album. *—Heather Phares*

● **Ladies and Gentlemen We Are Floating in Space** / Jul. 1, 1997 / Arista ✦✦✦✦✦

Spiritualized's third collection of hypnotic headphone symphonies is their most brilliant and accessible to date. Largely forsaking the drones and minimalistic, repetitive riffs which have characterized his work since the halcyon days of Spacemen 3, Jason Pierce re-focuses here and spins off into myriad new directions; in a sense, *Ladies and Gentlemen We Are Floating in Space*, with its majestic, Spector-like glow, is his classic rock album. "Come Together" and the blistering "Electricity" are his most edgy, straightforward rockers in eons, while the stunning "I Think I'm in Love" settles into a divided-psyche call-and-response R&B groove, and the closing "Cop Shoot Cop" (with guest Dr. John) locks into a voodoo blues trance. Lyrically, Pierce is at his most open and honest: The record is a heartfelt confessional of love and loss, with redemption found only in the form of drugs—designed, no less, to look like a prescription pharmaceutical package, *Ladies and Gentlemen* is pointedly explicit in its description of drug use as a means of killing the pain on track after track. Conversely, never before have the literal implications of the name "Spiritualized" been explored in such earnest detail—the London Community Gospel Choir appears prominently on a number of songs, while another bears the title "No God, Only Religion," pushing the music even further toward the kind of cosmic gospel transcendence it craves. A masterpiece. *—Jason Ankeny*

Royal Albert Hall October 10 1997 / Nov. 10, 1998 / Arista ✦✦✦✦

Split Enz

f. 1972, Auckland, New Zealand, **db.** 1985

Group / New Zealand Rock, Pop/Rock, New Wave

Best-known for their early '80s new wave pop hits, particularly "I Got You," Split Enz—after surviving a dizzying array of image, style, and personnel changes—became the first New Zealand band to achieve worldwide success. Although they never reached superstar status outside of Australia and New Zealand, the band developed a strong international cult following which continued to thrive over a decade after their breakup. Split Enz's output always seemed slightly outside of the times and often frustratingly obscure, but in the end, they left behind an impressively diverse body of work. Though no two of their albums were the same, their history can roughly be broken down into two periods—their highly theatrical, wildly original first period and the more mainstream new wave period of the early-80s.

The group was founded in 1972 around songwriters Tim Finn and Phil Judd as an acoustic combo called Split Ends. The team proved to be an interesting combination—Judd drew his inspiration from a wild variety of often non-musical sources while Finn's tastes leaned toward the British pop of the Beatles, the Kinks, and the Move. They expanded into a progressive rock band with complex, neo-classical structures and arrangements, blending an eclectic mix of styles. They became Split Enz in1974, building a strong following in Australia through theatrical shows and outrageous hair styles and cosumes. 1975 saw the impressive debut of *Mental Notes* (a re-recorded version was released the following year as *Second Thoughts*). When Phil Judd left in 1977, they replaced Judd with Tim's younger brother Neil and added a new rhythm section, essentially creating a new band.

Tim Finn assumed leadership of the new Split Enz, shifting away from their early artiness with *Dizrhythmia* (1977) and *Frenzy* (1978), but they made their big breakthrough with 1979's *True Colours*, showcasing Neil Finn's emerging songwriting talents, especially on the irresistible new wave classic "I Got You." The band's early practice of making conceptual videos for their songs made them favorites of the new MTV. *Corroborree* followed in 1981 with memorable hits such as "History Never Repeats" and "One Step Ahead", and in 1982 they hit a creative peak with the introspective *Time & Tide*. Tim Finn left the band in 1984 following *Conflicting Emotions* to pursue a solo career. The remaining members carried on for 1984's *See Ya Round* but disbanded following a farewell tour of Australia and New Zealand. The band members continued to record in a variety of projects with Neil Finn's Crowded House being the highest profile. *—Chris Woodstra*

Mental Notes / 1975 / Mushroom ✦✦✦✦✦

The first proper Enz album features the band at its eccentric best. *Mental Notes* is completely non-commercial art rock filled with ambitious arrangements and slightly disturbing themes courtesy of the Phil Judd and Tim Finn songwriting partnership. Finn's bittersweet crooning perfectly compliments Judd's madman persona on tracks like "Stranger Than Fiction." Although the album would be repackaged, renamed, and re-recorded in years to come, the band would never again produce anything like it. *—Chris Woodstra*

Second Thoughts / 1976 / Mushroom ✦✦✦✦

After *Mental Notes* failed commercially, the band left for England to rework the tracks with Roxy Music's Phil Manzanera producing. *Second Thoughts* is an eccentric album filled with the theatrics that gained the band its early notoriety. Mainly new versions of old songs, the album adds some new tracks such as the brilliant "Late Last Night" and "Woman Who Loves You." Released in America and the U.K. as *Mental Notes* with a modified cover. *—Chris Woodstra*

Dizrhythmia / Oct. 1977 / Mushroom ✦✦✦✦
Dizrhythmia marks a change not only in personnel (half of the band had been replaced) but also musically and lyrically. With Tim Finn taking over the band, gone almost entirely are the neo-classical arrangements and abstract imagery in favor of a more direct approach that draws heavily from British Invasion era pop as well as incorporating British music hall and straight-ahead rock & roll. And though the band is still hiding behind hair, colorful costumes, and the occasional swirl of carnival sounds, beneath it all Finn makes his most personal statements to date, showing his optimism and determination for the band's future while also revealing his uncertainty and fears. Most of the songs deal with relationships and, more specifically, his parting of ways with former collaborator and close friend, Phil Judd. *—Chris Woodstra*

Frenzy / 1978 / Mushroom ✦✦✦✦
Although often thought of as a transitional album, *Frenzy* shows the band in top form. Produced in England on a diminished budget, the album showcases pure pop with a hungry edge. "I See Red," added after the initial pressing, became a moderate hit in Australia and New Zealand, allowing the band the financial freedom to follow up with the blockbuster *True Colours* in 1980. Stripped down of the earlier excesses, the album hints at the direction the band would take in the '80s while capturing a rare, rougher side to their music. [The album was reissued in the U.S. in 1981, dropping half of the tracks and adding songs from the legendary "Rootin' Tootin' Luton Tapes" recorded in 1978.] *—Chris Woodstra*

Beginning of the Ends / 1979 / Mushroom ✦✦✦✦✦
A compilation of demos from 1972-1975. This Australian-only release shows the band in its eccentric formative years before a recording contract. Light acoustic arrangements of songs appearing on later albums coupled with long forgotten gems make this a favorite among die-hard fans. Not the most representative picture of the band, but an interesting one. *—Chris Woodstra*

True Colours / 1979 / Mushroom ✦✦✦✦
Split Enz found their place in new wave with *True Colours*, shedding the eccentricities and excesses of their past in favor of bright, highly memorable, Beatlesque pop. The album also marked Neil Finn's emergence as a great songcraftsman—his infectious "I Got You" helped to push the album and the band to international success. Both the single and the album stand as highpoints of the new wave era. As part of its marketing, the album was released in several different colored covers with laser-etched vinyl. *—Chris Woodstra*

Waiata (Corroboree) / May 1981 / Mushroom ✦✦✦
Because of the hurried schedule of newfound international success, the follow-up to *True Colours* suffered. *Waiata* follows much of the same formula of its predecessor, though in a slightly darker form that often lacks the punch that made *True Colours* great. Despite a couple of classic singles—"One Step Ahead" and "History Never Repeats"—and a handful of other inspired tracks, the album marks the band's first lateral move. Waiata is the Maori word for party (the album was given the Aboriginal party title, *Corroboree* in Australia). Following in the trend of *True Colours*, A&M issued three different colored covers for the worldwide release. *—Chris Woodstra*

Time & Tide / 1982 / Mushroom ✦✦✦✦✦
Time & Tide stands as the band's creative peak and most fully realized effort. On previous albums, Split Enz remained distant and removed, only revealing what little they did between the lines; for *Time & Tide*, Tim and Neil Finn, while still clearly standing as outsiders, opened up, giving a rare glimpse at their feelings and thought processes. Tim exorcised demons and fears in the funky workout of "Dirty Creature," experienced a joyful communion with nature in "Never Ceases to Amaze Me," outlined a global view in "Small World," and explored ancient folk music with "Six Months in a Leaky Boat" and "Haul Away," an autobiographical sea shanty. Neil, on the other hand, gave darkly evocative yet slightly more abstract accounts in "Giant Heartbeat," "Take a Walk," and the claustrophobic "Log Cabin Fever" while still producing an infectious rocker in "Hello Sandy Allen." In addition to the peaks in songwriting, the Enz never sounded tighter as a band, with lean, tasteful arrangements. The result is a timeless, thoroughly consistent album and the high point of the Enz catalog. *—Chris Woodstra*

Conflicting Emotions / 1983 / Mushroom ✦✦✦
The distraction of a Tim Finn solo project (1983's *Escapade*) may have robbed Split Enz of the creative momentum produced by *Time & Tide;* Tim obviously spent much of his energy on that project, leaving him with a minority of songwriting credits for the first time since taking leadership of the band. So, despite a strong batch of songs from Neil—which includes the achingly beautiful love song "Message to My Girl" and the contemplative "Our Day," which intimates the thoughts of the soon-to-be father—the album suffers from a general lack of focus. A misguided overreliance on drum machines and generally heavy-handed production are the real downfall, though, ultimately dating a solid though unexceptional album. The telling title track, as well as the album closer, "Bon Voyage," hinted at Tim Finn's imminent departure from the band. [Initial pressings of the album in New Zealand included a bonus 12" of "Kia Kaha" and "Parasite"—songs unavailable elsewhere until the release of the box sets.] *—Chris Woodstra*

Enz of an Era / 1983 / Mushroom ✦✦✦✦✦
A solid collection of the singles from *Second Thoughts* (1976) to *Time & Tide* (1982). Although not all of the singles are present, all of the hits from that period are covered. *Enz of an Era* was originally most notable for inclusion of the rare "Another Great Divide," but it has been superseded by more current (and more easily found) collections. *—Chris Woodstra*

See Ya Round / 1984 / Mushroom ✦✦
With Tim Finn departing for a solo career, Neil Finn takes charge of the aging band for their final studio album. While not living up to the band's previous brilliance, songs such as "Years Go By," "One Mouth Is Fed," and an early version of "I Walk Away" are delightful Finn compositions. Side two features songs written by each of the remaining members. Released only in Australia, New Zealand, and Canada. *—Chris Woodstra*

Living Enz / 1985 / Mushroom ✦✦✦
A double live album with tracks from the farewell *Enz with a Bang* tour and a few from the 1982 *Time & Tide* tour. Rather than just focusing on the hit singles, the album revives old album favorites with new live arrangements. Mainly a gift for the fans, this album is a showcase for the band at its crowd-pleasing best. *—Chris Woodstra*

● **History Never Repeats: The Best of Split Enz** / 1987 / A&M ✦✦✦✦✦
Split Enz are probably best remembered in the U.S. for their new wave-era singles; *History Never Repeats: The Best of Split Enz* collects all of the major singles from the band's A&M albums in a single disc package. For the casual fan, there is no better starting point. The Australian issue is far superior as a career overview however, as it covers their pre-hit period beginning in the mid-'70s and adds a rare mix of "Late Last Night." *—Chris Woodstra*

1973-1979: Oddz & Enz / 1993 / Mushroom ✦✦✦✦✦
This Australian-only box set covers the band's more experimental beginnings (1973-1979). From the light acoustic demos of *Beginning of the Enz* and the art rock of *Mental Notes*, to the edgy-pop of *Frenzy*, the listener gets a strong sense of the band's pre-popularity evolution. With over an hour of non-LP tracks on the bonus disc and improved sound quality, this is essential for fans. *—Chris Woodstra*

1980-1984: Rear Enz / 1993 / Mushroom ✦✦✦✦✦
This Australian-only box set covers the period of the band's peak in popularity (1980-1984). Beginning with *True Colours* and ending with their swansong, *See Ya Round*, it shows the band in perfect pop form. While this is too ambitious for the casual fan, the devoted will find this essential for considerably improved sound and the bonus disc of previously unreleased tracks. *—Chris Woodstra*

Anniversary / 1994 / Fuel 2000 ✦✦

● **The Best of Split Enz** / Jun. 28, 1994 / Chrysalis ✦✦✦✦
Chrysalis Records handled the band's non-Australia/New Zealand releases from 1976-1977—an extremely low point in terms of sales. Not surprisingly, *Best of Split Enz* focuses a little too heavily on this early period to truly give the casual listener a representative collection of the band's better-known period. The big A&M new-wave era hits ("I Got You," "One Step Ahead") are covered adequately, but this was clearly an attempt to cash in on Crowded House's success in Europe the year before. *—Chris Woodstra*

● **Spellbound** / 1997 / Mushroom ✦✦✦✦✦
Spellbound is an Australian-only two-disc collection which offers 39 of the band's biggest hits and best-known favorites. There is no shortage of Enz collections on the market, and this is the best to date. All of the tracks have been remastered, and as an incentive to collectors, the rare Luton version of "Semi-Detached" and a drastically remixed version of "Stuff and Nonsense" have been added. The one major flaw is the non-chronological sequencing, which, for a band with two distinct phases and a clear career arc, misses the opportunity to tell the band's story completely. Minor complaints aside, *Spellbound* is a good starting point for those who want more than any of the single-disc collections have to offer. [In typical Enz fashion, *Spellbound* was released in several different-colored covers.] *—Chris Woodstra*

Dusty Springfield (Mary Isabel Catherine Bernadette O'Brien)

b. Apr. 16, 1939, Hampstead, London, England, **d.** Mar. 2, 1999
Vocals / Smooth Soul, Pop-Soul, Blue-Eyed Soul, Girl Group, British Invasion, Soul
Britain's greatest pop diva, Dusty Springfield was also the finest white soul singer of her era, embracing everything from lushly-orchestrated pop to gritty R&B to disco with unparalleled sophistication and depth. She was born Mary O'Brien on April 16, 1939 ; after completing her schooling she joined the Lana Sisters, a pop vocal trio which issued a few singles on Fontana before dissolving. In 1960, upon teaming with her brother Dion and his friend Tim Field in the folk trio the Springfields, O'Brien adopted the stage name Dusty Springfield; thanks to a series of hits the group was soon the U.K.'s best-selling act.

In 1963 she left the Springfields at the peak of their fame to pursue a solo career. Her first single, "I Only Want to Be with You," quickly reached the British Top Five. Propelled by hits like "Wishin' & Hopin'," by the end of 1964 Springfield was arguably the biggest solo act in British pop. In1966, she scored her biggest international hit with the devastating ballad "You Don't Have to Say You Love Me". In 1968, she traveled to Memphis to record *Dusty in Memphis*, which remains her masterpiece, a perfect marriage of pop and soul stunning in its emotional complexity and earthy beauty. The album and its fine 1970 follow-up, *A Brand New Me*, unfortunately were commercial failures, as was another critical success, 1973's *Cameo.*

Springfield spent the mid-1970s mostly outside of music while battling substance abuse problems. A comeback was orchestrated in 1987 when she collaborated with techno-pop innovators the Pet Shop Boys on a duet titled "What Have I Done to Deserve This?" The single was a global blockbuster, peaking at number two in both the U.S. and the U.K. Neil Tennant and Chris Lowe also agreed to produce a handful of tracks for 1990's *Reputation*, which became Springfield's best-selling new album since her '60s-era peak. Breast cancer detected during sessions for 1995's *A Very Fine Love* eventually took her life on March 2, 1999; just ten days later, she was inducted into the *Rock and Roll Hall of Fame. —Jason Ankeny*

Dusty / 1964 / Mercury ✦✦✦
Although not quite as good as her first American LP, *Dusty* is a good mix of soul/R&B covers and orchestrated pop/rock in the manner of early Dionne Warwick. Standouts include the cover of Bacharach-David's "I Just Don't Know What to Do With Myself" (a British hit), "All Cried Out," and the epic ballad "Summer Is Over," which foreshadows the style she'd use on her later hit "You Don't Have to Say You Love Me." The 1999 Mercury CD reissue adds three rare bonus tracks: the Stax soul tune "Every Ounce of Strength" (a 1966 U.K. B-side), the 1966 B-side "I'm Gonna Leave You," and an unreleased cover of Gloria Jones' soul stormer "Heartbeat." *—Richie Unterberger*

Stay Awhile/I Only Want to Be with You / 1964 / Mercury ♦♦♦♦♦

Ev'rything's Coming Up Dusty / 1965 / BGO ♦♦♦♦♦

Ooooooweeee!!! / 1965 / Mercury ♦♦♦♦

You Don't Have to Say You Love Me / 1966 / Mercury ♦♦♦♦♦

The Look of Love / 1967 / Mercury ♦♦♦

Where Am I Going / 1967 / Philips ♦♦♦

★ **Dusty in Memphis** / Mar. 1969 / Mercury ♦♦♦♦♦
Sometimes memories distort or inflate the quality of recordings deemed legendary, but in the case of *Dusty in Memphis*, the years have only strengthened its reputation. The idea of taking England's reigning female soul queen to the home of the music she had mastered was an inspired one. The Jerry Wexler/Tom Dowd/Arif Mardin production and engineering team picked mostly perfect songs, and those that weren't so great were salvaged by Springfield's marvelous delivery and technique. This set has definitive numbers in "So Much Love," "Son of a Preacher Man," "Breakfast in Bed," "Just One Smile," "I Don't Want to Hear About It Anymore," and "Just a Little Lovin'" and offers exquisite mastering, informative notes, and an unreleased version of "What Do You Do When Love Dies." It's truly a disc deserving of its classic status. In 1999, Rhino upgraded *Dusty in Memphis* with a deluxe edition that retained the original album, the three bonus tracks from the same era that appeared on its first CD reissue of the record, and 11 further bonus tracks, the new material dating from 1970-1971. It isn't quite accurate to lump those early-'70s cuts into Dusty's "Memphis" era, since they were recorded in New York and Philadelphia and don't have as much of a soul orientation. "Cherished" and "Goodbye" were produced by Gamble-Huff in early 1970 and are good pop-soul numbers. The rest of the sides were produced by Jeff Barry in 1971, and are more pop in flavor, including covers of Bread's "Make It With You" and Carole King's "You've Got a Friend." These Barry-overseen efforts are okay pop-soul, but lacking in truly memorable songs or inspired playing, especially in comparison to the original *Dusty in Memphis* tracks. *—Ron Wynn & Richie Unterberger*

A Brand New Me / 1970 / Rhino ♦♦♦♦♦
While it's not quite as uniformally excellent as *Dusty in Memphis, A Brand New Me* comes close to recapturing its predecessor's magic and is easily one of Springfield's best albums. *—Stephen Thomas Erlewine*

Anthology / Sep. 23, 1997 / Mercury/Chronicles ♦♦♦♦♦
Weighing in at three discs, *Anthology* sets out to be the definitive Dusty Springfield compilation and it damn near achieves its goal. While the size of this set makes it a little impractical for fans that just want the hits, anyone that wants to dig deeper into her career will discover that she was one of the most consistent interpretive singers of the '60s, capable of sweet girl-group pop, lush orchestral pop, and blue-eyed soul. Bypassing her early records with the Springfields and starting with her solo career in 1963, *Anthology* hits all the high points and features a number of fine forgotten gems as well, making it essential for serious fans of Dusty, '60s pop, and blue-eyed soul. *—Stephen Thomas Erlewine*

★ **The Very Best of Dusty Springfield** / Apr. 21, 1998 / Mercury/Chronicles ♦♦♦♦♦
The Very Best of Dusty Springfield is an ideal compilation, featuring 20 songs from Dusty's prime period of 1963 through 1969. All of the hits—"I Only Want to Be With You," "Wishin' and Hopin'," "Son of a Preacher Man," "I Just Don't Know What to Do With Myself," "A Brand New Me"—are here, along with several lesser-known singles and album tracks that illustrate the full range of her talent. The triple-disc *Anthology* may be more comprehensive and thereby suited for collectors, but this excellent set is the ideal choice for casual fans, since it captures one of the greatest pop singers of the '60s at her very best. *—Stephen Thomas Erlewine*

Dusty in London / Feb. 16, 1999 / Rhino ♦♦♦♦
In the late 1960s and early 1970s, Springfield had an unusual arrangement whereby Philips released her records everywhere in the world except the United States, where they appeared on Atlantic. Atlantic chose to release only 1968-71 material that was recorded in the U.S., meaning that quite a few tracks she recorded in Britain during this time went unreleased stateside. This collects 24 of those songs Springfield recorded in the U.K. between 1968 and 1971, only a few which had appeared in the U.S. before. Although this is not as soul- and R&B-oriented as the material Atlantic recorded with her in America during this era, in truth it's not always that far removed in sound and spirit from what you'll hear on the Atlantic albums *Dusty in Memphis* (1969) and *A Brand New Me* (1970). You can't get much more soulful than "Piece of My Heart," for instance, a good cover of which leads off the collection. Overall, though, it takes in a broader range of pop styles than Springfield did with her American/Atlantic recordings, from covers of the Rascals ("How Can I Be Sure") and Goffin-King ("Wasn't Born to Follow") to Charles Aznavour, Leon Russell, Jimmy Webb, Bacharach-David, and Antonio Carlos Jobim. Most of it's taken from the British albums *Dusty Definitely* (1968) and *See All Her Faces* (1972), and it's lower on standout performances than the familiar Atlantic albums are. The singing is almost always involved and committed, but sometimes the material is pedestrian. The highlights are very good, however, including Randy Newman's "I Think It's Going to Rain Today," the beautiful string ballad "Morning," and the bossa nova spiced "See All Her Faces." This is worth hearing if you like Springfield a lot; just don't gear up for an extraordinarily consistent or essential listen. *—Richie Unterberger*

Simply Dusty / Nov. 7, 2000 / Mercury ♦♦♦♦

Rick Springfield

b. Aug. 23, 1949, Sydney, Australia
Vocals, Keyboards, Guitar / Album Rock, Pop/Rock, Power Pop
Although Rick Springfield's music was frequently dismissed as vapid teen idol fare, his best moments have actually withstood the test of time far better than most critics would ever have imagined, emerging as some of the best-crafted mainstream power pop of the decade. A singer turned soap-opera star turned singer, Springfield worked in a few bands before joining the highly successful Australian teenybopper band Zoot in 1968. He went solo after the band broke up in 1971 and garnered his first U.S. success the following year with a re-recording of his Australian hit "Speak to the Sky." Subsequent '70s albums stiffed however, and he moved to RCA. In the midst of recording his debut for the label, he was signed to the soap opera *General Hospital* in 1981. Springfield's popularity skyrocketed later that year with the release of *Working Class Dog*, powered by the classic chart-topper single "Jessie's Girl" and the Top Ten follow-up "I've Done Everything for You." *Success Hasn't Spoiled Me Yet*, released in 1982, spawned the Top Ten smash "Don't Talk to Strangers," while 1983's *Living in Oz* featured yet another Top Ten, "Affair of the Heart." The soundtrack to his 1984 film *Hard to Hold* spawned his last Top Ten hit to date, "Love Somebody." His career seemed to bottom out afterwards, although he recorded several more albums over the rest of the '80s. In 1999, Springfield returned with a new album, *Karma*. *—Steve Huey*

Beginnings / 1972 / Capitol ♦♦

Comic Book Heroes / 1974 / Razor & Tie ♦♦♦
Springfield grew considerably as a writer between his first record and *Comic Book Heroes*. Although he is still doing some sensitive singer/songwriter material, it no longer sounds as awkward. In fact, a couple tracks, like "Weep No More," are very memorable. On the other hand, "Misty Water Woman" sounds like an overly-melodramatic attempt at being Elton John. Still, the good stuff makes it worth owning. *—Jim Worbois*

Wait for Night / 1976 / Chelsea ♦♦

● **Working Class Dog** / 1981 / RCA ♦♦♦♦♦
Forget that Rick Springfield was a soap star for a moment and listen to his music, because he made some of the finest guitar-driven mainstream pop/rock of the early '80s. *Working Class Dog* is his finest moment, filled with expertly crafted pop songs, highlighted by the massive hit "Jessie's Girl." *—Stephen Thomas Erlewine*

Success Hasn't Spoiled Me Yet / 1982 / RCA ♦♦♦♦♦
Rick Springfield's follow-up to his commercial breakthrough *Working Class Dog* wasn't quite as consistent, but it contained a number of solid power-pop tracks, including "Calling All Girls," "What Kind of Fool Am I," "How Do You Talk to Girls," "The American Girl," and the Top Ten hit "Don't Talk to Strangers." *—Stephen Thomas Erlewine*

Living in Oz / 1983 / RCA ♦♦♦♦

Hard to Hold / 1984 / Razor & Tie ♦♦

Tao / 1985 / RCA ♦♦♦

Greatest Hits / Aug. 1989 / RCA ♦♦♦♦♦
Rick Springfield contributed to some of the most congenial sounding pop that braced radio throughout the 1980s. With 17 singles gracing the Top 40 charts, it was evident that both his charming persona and his hook-induced choruses led to his successful ten-year stint. While his music is lyrical fluff, it's the friendly guitar riffs and contagious three-minute rock formula that sometimes takes on a love song approach and boldly represents the feel-good emptiness of '80s pop. This greatest-hits collection is one of the best that Springfield has to offer, since it doesn't suffer from any unnecessary tracks or lose interest with overkill. His pop fervidness is perfectly outlined by the number one charted "Jessie's Girl" and the staccato rhythm of "I've Done Everything for You," which was penned by Sammy Hagar. His best ballads are represented by the syrupy "Affair of the Heart" and the teenage angst of "State of the Heart." Songs like "Love Is Alright Tonight" and "Love Somebody" show Springfield at his most energetic and are solid checkmarks for him in the rock & roll column. Even later material like "Rock of Life" from 1988 footnotes the type of transparent pop that Springfield produced, held together only by its meaningless but contagious keyboard froth. Other collections do offer more tracks, but none are as substantial as the songs laid out here, which are a truly solid dozen. *—Mike DeGagne*

Karma / Apr. 13, 1999 / Intersound ♦♦♦

VH1 Behind the Music: The Rick Springfield Collection / Sep. 12, 2000 / RCA ♦♦♦♦

Bruce Springsteen

b. Sep. 23, 1949, Freehold, NJ
Vocals, Harmonica, Guitar / Heartland Rock, Album Rock, Pop/Rock, Singer/Songwriter, Rock & Roll
When Bruce Springsteen finally broke through to national recognition in the fall of 1975, after a decade of trying, critics hailed him as the savior of rock & roll, the single artist who brought together all the exuberance of '50s rock and the thoughtfulness of '60s rock, molded into a '70s style. He rocked as hard as Jerry Lee Lewis, his lyrics were as complicated as Bob Dylan's, and his concerts were near-religious celebrations of all that was best in the music. One critic became so enamored that he quit reviewing to become Springsteen's manager. But the hosannas, when piped through the publicity machine of a major record company, were perceived as hype by a significant part of the public as well as the mainstream media—Springsteen landed on the covers of *Time* and *Newsweek*, but both magazines were covering the phenomenon, not the music. Springsteen's album *Born to Run* became a hit, and he jumped to arena status as a live act, but as many people were turned off by the press campaign as turned on by the records and shows. Two decades later, however, Springsteen remained an established star who could look back on a career that had produced one of the best-selling albums of all time, sold-out stadium shows, Grammy Awards and an Oscar, and a group of imitators who constituted their own subgenre of popular music. If he no longer seemed divine, he remained popular enough for his *Greatest Hits* album to enter the charts at number one, and he had won over many of those skeptics from 1975. *—William Ruhlmann*

Greetings from Asbury Park, NJ / Jan. 5, 1973 / Columbia ♦♦♦♦♦
Bruce Springsteen's debut album found him squarely in the tradition of Bob Dylan: folk-based tunes arranged for an electric band featuring piano and organ (plus, in Springsteen's case, 1950s-style rock & roll tenor saxophone breaks), topped by acoustic guitar and a husky

voice singing lyrics full of elaborate, even exaggerated imagery. But where Dylan had taken a world-weary, cynical tone, Springsteen was exuberant. His street scenes could be haunted and tragic, as they were in "Lost in the Flood," but they were still imbued with romanticism and a youthful energy. *Asbury Park* painted a portrait of teenagers cocksure of themselves, yet bowled over by their discovery of the world. It was saved from pretentiousness (if not preciousness) by its sense of humor and by the careful eye for detail that kept even the most high-flown language rooted. Like the lyrics, the arrangements were busy, but the melodies were well-developed and the rhythms, pushed by drummer Vincent Lopez, were breakneck. *— William Ruhlmann*

☆ **The Wild, the Innocent & the E Street Shuffle** / Sep. 11, 1973 / Columbia ♦♦♦♦♦
Bruce Springsteen expanded the folk-rock approach of his debut album, *Greetings From Asbury Park, N.J.*, to strains of jazz, among other styles, on its ambitious follow-up, released only eight months later. His chief musical lieutenant was keyboard player David Sancious, who lived on the E Street that gave the album and Springsteen's backup group their names. With his help, Springsteen created a street-life mosaic of suburban society that owed much in its outlook to Van Morrison's romanticization of Belfast in *Astral Weeks*. Though Springsteen expressed endless affection and much nostalgia, his message was clear: this was a goodbye-to-all-that from a man who was moving on. *The Wild, the Innocent & the E Street Shuffle* represented an astonishing advance even from the remarkable promise of *Greetings;* the unbanded three-song second side in particular was a flawless piece of music. Musically and lyrically, Springsteen had brought an unruly muse under control and used it to make a mature statement that synthesized popular musical styles into complicated, well-executed arrangements and absorbing suites; it evoked a world precisely even as that world seemed to disappear. Following the personnel changes in the E Street Band in 1974, there is a conventional wisdom that this album is marred by production lapses and performance problems, specifically, the drumming of Vini Lopez. None of that is true. Lopez's busy Keith Moon style is appropriate to the arrangements in a way his replacement, Max Weinberg, never could have been. The production is fine. And the album's songs contain the best realization of Springsteen's poetic vision, which soon enough would be tarnished by disillusionment. He would later make different albums, but he never made a better one. The truth is, *The Wild, the Innocent & the E Street Shuffle* is one of the greatest albums in the history of rock & roll. *— William Ruhlmann*

☆ **Born to Run** / Aug. 25, 1975 / Columbia ♦♦♦♦♦
Bruce Springsteen's make-or-break third album represented a sonic leap from his first two, which had been made for modest sums at a suburban studio; *Born to Run* was cut on a superstar budget, mostly at *The Record Plant* in New York. Springsteen's backup band had changed, with his two virtuoso players, keyboardist David Sancious and drummer Vini Lopez, replaced by the professional but less flashy Roy Bittan and Max Weinberg. The result was a full, highly produced sound that contained elements of Phil Spector's melodramatic work of the 1960s. Layers of guitar, layers of echo on the vocals, lots of keyboards, thunderous drums, *Born to Run* had a big sound, and Springsteen wrote big songs to match it. The overall theme of the album was similar to that of *The E Street Shuffle;* Springsteen was describing, and saying farewell to, a romanticized teenage street life. But where he had been affectionate, even humorous before, he was becoming increasingly bitter. If Springsteen had celebrated his dead-end kids on his first album and viewed them nostalgically on his second, on his third he seemed to despise their failure, perhaps because he was beginning to fear he was trapped himself. Nevertheless, he now felt removed, composing an updated *West Side Story* with spectacular music that owed more to Bernstein than to Berry. To call *Born to Run* overblown is to miss the point; Springsteen's precise intention is to blow things up, both in the sense of expanding them to gargantuan size and of exploding them. If *The Wild, the Innocent & the E Street Shuffle* was an accidental miracle, *Born to Run* was an intentional masterpiece. It declared its own greatness with songs and a sound that lived up to Springsteen's promise, and though some thought it took itself too seriously, many found that exalting. *— William Ruhlmann*

Darkness on the Edge of Town / Jun. 2, 1978 / Columbia ♦♦♦♦♦
Coming three years and one extended court battle after *Born to Run, Darkness on the Edge of Town* was highly anticipated. Some attributed the album's embattled tone to Springsteen's legal troubles, but it carried on from *Born to Run*, in which Springsteen had first begun to view his colorful cast of characters as "losers." On *Darkness*, he began to see them as the working class: his characters, some of whom he inhabited and sang for in the first person, had little and were in danger of losing even that. Their only hope for redemption lay in working harder, and their only escape lay in driving. Springsteen presented these hard truths in hard-rock settings, the tracks paced by powerful drumming and searing guitar solos. Though not as heavily produced as *Born to Run, Darkness* was given a full-bodied sound; Springsteen's stories were becoming less heroic, but his musical style remained grand—the sound, and the conviction in his singing, added weight to songs like "Racing in the Street" and the title track, transforming the pathetic into the tragic. But despite the rock & roll fervor, *Darkness* was no easy listen, and it served notice that Springsteen was already willing to risk his popularity for his principles. *— William Ruhlmann*

☆ **The River** / Oct. 10, 1980 / Columbia ♦♦♦♦♦
Imbedded within the double-disc running time of *The River* is a single-disc album that follows up on the themes and sound of *Darkness on the Edge of Town*—wide-screen, mid-tempo rock and stories of the disillusionment of working-class life and the conflicts within families. In these songs, which include the title track, "Independence Day," and "Point Blank," Springsteen's world view is just as dire as it had become on *Darkness*, but less judgmental. "Independence Day," for example, is a father-and-son ballad that has little of the anger of its hard rock counterpart on *Darkness*, "Adam Raised a Cain." Springsteen's heroes again seek to overcome their crushing troubles through defiance and by driving around, and though "The River" repeats the soured love theme of "Racing in the Street," he also posits romance as a possible escape, sometimes combining it with one of the other solutions, as on the eight-plus-minute "Drive All Night." But there is also another album lurking within *The River*, and it is a more light-hearted pop/rock collection of short, sometimes humorous songs like "Sherry Darling" and "I'm a Rocker." At times Springsteen combines elements of the two, as on "Out in the Street," perhaps the album's quintessential song, a catchy, uptempo number that sounds like something from the early '60s and echoes the theme of the Vogues' 1966 hit "Five O' Clock World." "Hungry Heart," which became Springsteen's first Top Ten hit, combines a rollicking musical track with a more sober lyrical theme that emphasizes longing over disappointment. But a better guide to Springsteen's development are the songs "Stolen Car" and the album-closing "Wreck on the Highway," gentle, moody ballads imbued with a sense of hopelessness that anticipate his next record, *Nebraska*. *— William Ruhlmann*

☆ **Nebraska** / Sep. 20, 1982 / Columbia ♦♦♦♦♦
There is an adage in the record business that a recording artist's demos of new songs often come off better than the more polished versions later worked up in a studio. But Bruce Springsteen was the first person to act on that theory, when he opted to release the demo versions of his latest songs, recorded with only acoustic or electric guitar, harmonica, and vocals, as his sixth album, *Nebraska*. It was really the content that dictated the approach, however. *Nebraska*'s ten songs marked a departure for Springsteen, even as they took him farther down a road he had been traveling previously. Gradually, his songs had become darker and more pessimistic, and those on *Nebraska* marked a new low. They also found him branching out into better developed stories. The title track was a first-person account of the killing spree of mass murderer Charlie Starkweather. (It can't have been coincidental that the same story was told in director Terrence Malick's 1973 film *Badlands*, also used as a Springsteen song title.) That song set the tone for a series of portraits of smalltime criminals, desperate people, and those who loved them. Just as the recordings were unpolished, the songs themselves didn't seem quite finished; sometimes the same line turned up in two songs. But that only served to unify the album. Within the difficult times, however, there was hope, especially as the album went on. "Open All Night" was a Chuck Berry-style rocker, and the album closed with "Reason to Believe," a song whose hard-luck verses were belied by the chorus—even if the singer couldn't understand what it was, "people find some reason to believe." Still, *Nebraska* was one of the most challenging albums ever released by a major star on a major record label. *— William Ruhlmann*

★ **Born in the U.S.A.** / Jun. 4, 1984 / Columbia ♦♦♦♦♦
Bruce Springsteen had become increasingly downcast as a songwriter during his recording career, and his pessimism bottomed out with *Nebraska*. But *Born in the U.S.A.*, his popular triumph, which threw off seven Top Ten hits and became one of the best-selling albums of all time, trafficked in much the same struggle, albeit set to galloping rhythms and set off by chiming guitars. That the witless wonders of the Reagan regime attempted to co-opt the title track as an election-year campaign song wasn't so surprising: the verses described the disenfranchisement of a lower-class Vietnam vet, and the chorus was intended to be angry, but it came off as anthemic. Then, too, Springsteen had softened his message with nostalgia and sentimentality, and those are always crowd-pleasers. "Glory Days" may have employed Springsteen's trademark disaffection, yet it came across as a couch potato's drunken lament. But more than anything else, *Born in the U.S.A.* marked the first time that Springsteen's characters really seemed to relish the fight and to have something to fight for. They were not defeated ("No Surrender"), and they had friendship ("Bobby Jean") and family ("My Hometown") to defend. The restless hero of "Dancing in the Dark" even pledged himself in the face of futility, and for Springsteen, that was a step. The "romantic young boys" of his first two albums, chastened by "the working life" encountered on his third, fourth, and fifth albums and having faced the despair of his sixth, were still alive on this, his seventh, with their sense of humor and their determination intact. *Born in the U.S.A.* was their apotheosis, the place where they renewed their commitment and where Springsteen remembered that he was a rock & roll star, which is how a vastly increased public was happy to treat him. *— William Ruhlmann*

Live 1975-1985 / Nov. 10, 1986 / Columbia ♦♦♦♦♦
Long before he sold substantial numbers of records, Bruce Springsteen began to earn a reputation as the best live act in rock & roll. Fans had been clamoring for a live album for a long time, and with *Live 1975-1985* they got what they wanted, at least in terms of bulk. His concerts were marathons, and this box set, including 40 tracks and running over three-and-a-half hours, was about the average length of a show. In his brief liner notes, Springsteen spoke of the emergence of the album's "story" as he reviewed live tapes, and that story seems nothing less than a history of his life, his concerns, and his career. The first cuts present the Springsteen of the early to mid-'70s; these performances, most of them drawn from a July 1978 show at the Roxy in Los Angeles, give us the romantic, hopeful, earnest Springsteen. The second section begins with his first Top Ten hit, "Hungry Heart"—this is the Springsteen of the late '70s and early '80s, an arena rock star with working class concerns. After an acoustic mini-set given largely to material from *Nebraska*—songs of economic desperation and crime—comes a reshuffling of *Born in the U.S.A.*, songs in which the artist and his characters start to fight back and rock out. Finally, he brings it all back home to New Jersey, starting with the unofficial state anthem, "Born to Run." Fans could rejoice in the seven previously unreleased songs, but it wasn't as funny, moving, or exhilarating as a Springsteen show could be. Maybe no single album could have been, but where Springsteen impressed in concert because he tried so hard, here he seemed to have tried a little too hard to make a live album carry the freight of everything he had to say. *— William Ruhlmann*

☆ **Tunnel of Love** / Oct. 9, 1987 / Columbia ♦♦♦♦♦
Just as he had followed his 1980 commercial breakthrough *The River* with the challenging *Nebraska*, Bruce Springsteen followed the most popular album of his career, *Born in the U.S.A.*, with another low-key, anguished effort, *Tunnel of Love*. Especially in their sound, several of the songs, "Cautious Man" and "Two Faces," for example, could have fit seamlessly onto *Nebraska*, though the arrangements overall were not as stripped-down and acoustic as on the earlier album. While *Nebraska* was filled with songs of economic desperation, however, *Tunnel of Love*, as its title suggested, was an album of romantic exploration. But the lovers were just as desperate in their way as *Nebraska*'s small-time criminals. In song after

song, Springsteen questioned the trust and honesty on both sides in a romantic relationship, specifically a married relationship. Since Springsteen sounded more autobiographical than ever before ("Ain't Got You" referred to his popular success, while "Walk Like a Man" seemed another explicit message to his father), it was hard not to wonder about the state of his own 2-year-old marriage, and it wasn't surprising when that marriage collapsed the following year. *Tunnel of Love* was not the album that the ten million fans who had bought *Born in the U.S.A.* as of 1987 were waiting for, and though it topped the charts, sold three million copies, and spawned three Top 40 hits, much of this was on career momentum. Springsteen was as much at a crossroads with his audience as he seemed to be in his work and in his personal life, though this was not immediately apparent. *—William Ruhlmann*

Chimes of Freedom / 1988 / Columbia ✦✦✦

Human Touch / Mar. 31, 1992 / Columbia ✦✦

Lucky Town / Mar. 31, 1992 / Columbia ✦✦✦

In Concert/MTV Plugged / Apr. 1993 / Columbia ✦✦✦

Greatest Hits / Feb. 28, 1995 / Columbia ✦✦✦

Compiling a greatest-hits collection for Bruce Springsteen should be an easy task, yet *Greatest Hits* manages to miss the mark. Nothing from his first two albums is included, and the set includes such non-hits like "Atlantic City" and "The River" instead of hits like "Cover Me," "Tunnel of Love," and "Fade Away." In fact, a good portion of his hits are missing, as are important album tracks like "Backstreets," "Rosalita," and "Candy's Room," making this neither a straight hits collection nor a compilation of his best tracks. What's left are some of his biggest hits and best songs ("Born to Run," "Glory Days," "The River"), but not all of them, as well as four new tracks, the best of which is an outtake from the *Born in the U.S.A.* sessions ("Murder Inc.") Aside from "Murder Inc.," the new tracks follow the synth-laden adult contemporary direction Springsteen began pursuing with "Streets of Philadelphia," only without the lyricism or melody. So, it's a mixed bag, drawing an incomplete portrait of one of the prime rockers of the '70s and '80s. Casual fans would be better served by *Born in the U.S.A.*, which encompasses all of Springsteen's sides. *—Stephen Thomas Erlewine*

The Ghost of Tom Joad / Nov. 21, 1995 / Columbia ✦✦

Tracks / Nov. 10, 1998 / Columbia ✦✦✦✦

For years, decades even, Bruce Springsteen was legendary for the amount of recordings he did not release. Every time he cut an album, he recorded a surplus of songs and left some out, not always on the basis of quality, but often because they simply didn't suit the mood of the record. It was inevitable that dedicated fans and collectors would bootleg these recordings, and for many years, he was one of the most popular bootlegged artists, rivaling even Bob Dylan. Dylan released a box set of unreleased songs in 1991, paving the way for the long-overdue appearance of a similar Springsteen set, *Tracks*, in 1998. Spanning four discs, it isn't entirely devoted to unreleased material—a few B-sides pop up here and there—nor is it truly definitive, since it misses a number of key outtakes, plus his original version of "Because the Night," the sole hit for Patti Smith. Instead, the compilation is an unassuming sampling of what's in the vaults, from his early acoustic demos to polished outtakes from *Human Touch* and *Lucky Town*. Along the way, there are a number of great songs—"Bishop Danced" is every bit as terrific as its legend, as are "Thundercrack," "Give the Girl a Kiss," "Hearts of Stone," "Roulette," and many others. *Tracks* merely offers fans an enjoyably sequenced selection of what was left behind. If the end result isn't as revelatory as some may have expected (even the acoustic "Born in the U.S.A.," powerful as it is, doesn't sound different than you may have imagined it), it's because Springsteen is, at heart, a solid craftsman, not a blinding visionary like Dylan. That's why *Tracks* is for the dedicated fan, where *The Bootleg Series* or *The Basement Tapes* were flat-out essential for rock fans. *—Stephen Thomas Erlewine*

Eighteen Tracks / Apr. 13, 1999 / Columbia ✦✦✦

Squeeze

f. 1974

Group / College Rock, Pop/Rock, New Wave

As one of the most traditional pop bands of the New Wave, Squeeze provided one of the links between classic British guitar pop and post-punk. Inspired heavily by the Beatles and the Kinks, Squeeze was the vehicle for the songwriting of Chris Difford and Glenn Tilbrook, who were hailed as the heirs to Lennon and McCartney's throne during their heyday in the early '80s. Unlike Lennon and McCartney, the partnership betweeen Difford and Tilbrook was a genuine collaboration, with the former providing the music and the latter writing the lyrics. Squeeze never came close to matching the popularity of the Beatles, but the reason for that is part of their charm. Difford and Tilbrook were wry, subtle songwriters that subscribed to traditional pop songwriting values, but subverted them with literate lyrics and clever musical refrences. While their native Britain warmed to Squeeze immediately, sending singles like "Take Me I'm Yours" and "Up the Junction" into the Top Ten, the band had a difficult time gaining a foothold in the States; they didn't have a Top 40 hit until 1987, nearly a decade after their debut album. Even if the group never had a hit in the U.S., Squeeze built a dedicated following that stayed with them into the late '90s, and many of their songs—"Another Nail In My Heart," "Pulling Mussels (From the Shell)," "Tempted," "Black Coffee In Bed"—became pop classics of the New Wave era, as the platinum status of their compilation *Singles—45's and Under* indicates. *—Stephen Thomas Erlewine*

U.K. Squeeze / Mar. 1978 / A&M ✦✦

The band's debut, credited (in the U.S.) to U.K. Squeeze to avoid confusion with a similarly named band, is quite unlike anything that would follow and nearly seems like the work of another band. Much of the reason for this comes from producer John Cale's somewhat warped vision of the band. Cale threw out all of the songs the band came to the studio with and demanded that they write new ones on the spot (he also proposed calling the album *Gay Guys*, and undoubtedly had something to do with the hot pink bodybuilder cover and the shirtless photo of the band on the back). The rough and ragged songs that resulted from the studio writing range from raw, inspired rockers like "Sex Master," "Strong in Reason," and "Get Smart" to the utterly bizarre, near-funk instrumental "Wild Sewerage Tickles Brazil," which features wild shrieks throughout. The band-produced "Take Me I'm Yours" is a fondly remembered hit, but the album in general remains an oddity of the Squeeze catalog. *—Chris Woodstra*

Cool for Cats / Apr. 1979 / A&M ✦✦✦✦✦

After the false start of the debut, Squeeze recast themselves as a quintessentially British band, packing the songs with exaggerated accents, British slang, and incorporating a nearly cinematic narrative style to make incisive observations on British working-class life with a sly, skewed wit and a sex-obsessed thematic undercurrent. Musically, the band often rocks harder than they did on the debut, this time adding synth-driven arrangements while retaining a working-class pub-rock sensibility. *Cool for Cats* stands as the band's first truly great album and boasts arguably their finest song-story in "Up the Junction," a timeless gem, as well as the unforgettable Difford-sung hit title track. *—Chris Woodstra*

☆ **Argybargy** / Mar. 1980 / A&M ✦✦✦✦✦

Where *Cool for Cats* marked a great leap over the debut, *ArgyBargy* improved at least that far over its own predecessor. Still a distinctly British band, Squeeze compensated with an incredibly catchy batch of songs that, despite the subject matter, spoke the universal language of bright, bouncy, instantly endearing pop. The acute observations of the British working class were even more vivid—none so poignant as the classic "Pulling Mussels (From the Shell)," which offers a series of detailed snapshots of the different walks of life on a seaside holiday, or the often-overlooked courting-to-breakup story-song "Vicky Verky," which nearly matched "Up the Junction"'s brilliance. *ArgyBargy* is simply packed with perfect, timeless pop that stands not only as the band's crowning achievement, but also as a landmark recording of the era. *—Chris Woodstra*

East Side Story / May 1981 / A&M ✦✦✦✦✦

East Side Story was originally planned as a double album with each side produced by a different "hot" producer—Elvis Costello, Nick Lowe, Dave Edmunds, and Paul McCartney were the proposed lineup. And while only Elvis Costello (along with Roger Bechirian) ended up doing the job, save for one track by Edmunds, Costello's push for decidedly un-Squeeze-like material and sympathetic production style resulted in not only the band's most diverse but also their most creatively rewarding album to date. *East Side Story* is definitely packed with the band's trademark bouncy Brit-pop numbers like "In Quintessence," "Piccadilly," "Is That Love," and "Mumbo Jumbo," but the standouts come from the unexpected turns—the country lament of "Labeled With Love," the trippy near-psychedelia of "There's No Tomorrow," the lush and delicate "Woman Work" and "Vanity Fair," and the soulful groove of "Tempted" (the song the band is probably best known for, sung by newly added member Paul Carrack). *—Chris Woodstra*

★ **Singles 45's and Under** / 1982 / A&M ✦✦✦✦✦

Above all, Squeeze was a great singles act—among the finest of the era—and *Singles 45's and Under* offers proof of that fact, giving a chronological survey of their biggest hits from their early, pre-breakup period. Most of the songs can be found on the actual albums, aside from the slightly different single version of "Goodbye Girl" and the new "Annie Get Your Gun," but with a perfect collection like this, even those with the albums should purchase this one as well. *—Chris Woodstra*

Sweets From a Stranger / May 1982 / A&M ✦✦

Perhaps the accolades from *East Side Story* and the constant Lennon/McCartney comparisons went to their head, or maybe the strain of constant touring sapped a lot of their energy and better judgment. Whatever the case, *Sweets From a Stranger* suffers from self-conscious sophistication, overambition, and general lack of direction. And though the album is certainly flawed, an average Squeeze album is still pretty good, and when it hits—as in "I've Returned," "His House Her Home," and the favorite "Black Coffee in Bed"—it really hits. With previous albums, Difford and Tilbrook were able to make incisive observations on British life; the same holds true here, but the alcohol-soaked imagery and chaos between the lines of songs also reveals much about the internal problems of the band. Not surprisingly, the group disbanded shortly after the release. *—Chris Woodstra*

Cosi Fan Tutti Frutti / Aug. 1985 / A&M ✦✦✦

Cosi Fan Tutti Frutti marked not only a re-formation of the band but also a reunion with Jools Holland. And while history and a dated production style hasn't been particularly kind to the album, it is not without its merits. True, it is marred by much of the overblown ambition that undercuts *Sweets From a Stranger* and the *Difford and Tilbrook* album, but several of the songs—especially the often overlooked "King George Street"—are real gems in the classic Squeeze tradition, and the move toward "sophistication" is more fully realized and effective. A flawed but certainly worthwhile album, *Cosi Fan Tutti Frutti* deserves reassessment. *—Chris Woodstra*

Babylon and On / Sep. 1987 / A&M ✦✦

Following a brief period of arty, self-conscious indulgence, Squeeze decided to return to the more straight-ahead pop of their classic period. *Babylon and On* strips back a bit and, although the return is a welcomed one, much of the material misses the mark, and the move seems a little forced. Flaws aside, there are some moments of inspiration, and the near-novelty of "Hourglass," unfortunately not one of those moments, became the band's biggest Stateside hit. *—Chris Woodstra*

Frank / Sep. 1989 / A&M ✦✦

A Round & A Bout (Live) / May 1990 / IRS ✦✦

Play / Aug. 1991 / Reprise ✦✦✦

This unfortunately overlooked album finds the songwriting team of Difford and Tilbrook still in strong form through a 12-track song cycle. Now a four-piece band, there is less dependence on keyboards and a focus on more acoustic arrangements. A considerably more subdued mood but no less rewarding on repeated listening. *—Chris Woodstra*

Some Fantastic Place / Sep. 14, 1993 / A&M ✦✦✦

Ridiculous / Nov. 1995 / Ark 21 ♦♦♦
After nearly 20 years of recording, it would be easy to write Squeeze off as spent creative force—certainly their most recent albums have seemed like somewhat forced attempts to recapture the glory days of *Cool for Cats, Argybargy,* and *East Side Story.* With *Ridiculous,* Difford and Tilbrook (the only original members left and still the band's primary songwriters) seem content to have passed the Brit-pop torch on, and, as a result, this effortless album is also one of their most enjoyable in recent years. *Ridiculous* isn't an embarrassing attempt to rewrite previous hits, but rather, a natural progression executed with a dignified maturity rather than resignation. "This Summer" and "Electric Trains," though not candidates for the top of the charts at this point, certainly rank among their finest singles. *—Chris Woodstra*

Picadilly Collection / Aug. 20, 1996 / A&M ♦♦♦
It bills itself as a greatest hits compilation, but *Picadilly Collection* doesn't quite fit that description. Granted, the 18-track disc features some of Squeeze's biggest hits—including "Tempted," "Black Coffee In Bed," "Pulling Mussels (From a Shell)," and "Hourglass"—but the majority of the album consists of songs that will be totally unfamiliar to casual fans. Aside from that handful of hits, *Picadilly Collection* alternates between album tracks from latter-day Squeeze albums like *Frank* and *Some Fantastic Place,* and B-sides that have never before appeared on compact disc. Certainly, dedicated fans will be delighted to have the B-sides on CD, but they would have been better served by a full-fledged rarities collection. Similarly, casual fans would have been better served by a straight singles collection, or a more thorough retrospective—even though this features 18 tracks, it short-changes all of the group's early records, including such classic new wave albums as *Cool for Cats, Argybargy,* and *East Side Story,* in favor of the interminable medley "Squabs on Forty Fab." So, that leaves the question of just who is *Picadilly Collection* for? It's not for casual fans, it's not for diehards—it's just a wasted opportunity, despite the inclusion of many wonderful songs. *—Stephen Thomas Erlewine*

Excess Moderation / Nov. 1996 / A&M ♦♦♦♦♦
Excess Moderation one-ups its American counterpart, *The Picadilly Collection,* by offering two discs worth of mainly rarities and b-sides along with the stray missed album track, complete with track-by-track comments from Chris Difford and Glen Tillbrook. While, even in combination with *The Picadilly Collection,* there are still many B-sides left unavailable on disc, this is certainly a welcome addition for any fan. *—Chris Woodstra*

Domino / Nov. 1998 / Valley ♦♦

The Standells

f. 1962, Los Angeles, CA, **db.** 1983
Group / Garage Rock, Rock & Roll
The Standells made number 11 in 1966 with "Dirty Water," an archetypal garage rock hit with its Stonesish riff, lecherous vocal, and combination of raunchy guitar and organ. In fact, "garage rock" may not have been a really accurate term for them in the first place, as the production on their best material was full and polished, with some imaginative touches of period psychedelia and pop. The Los Angeles band had been playing clubs since the early '60s, hardly typical of the young suburban outfits across America who took their raw garage sound onto obscure singles recorded in small studios. Though they recorded some ordinary albums and singles for Liberty, MGM, and Vee Jay, the group didn't really hit their stride until teaming up with producer Ed Cobb. It was Cobb who wrote "Dirty Water," quite a change of direction from their previous clean-cut image. Their image now considerably toughened, the group churned out four albums during 1966 and 1967, as well as appearing in (and contributing the theme song to) the psychedelic exploitation movie *Riot on Sunset Strip.* After vocalist and drummer Dick Dodd went solo in 1968, the group never recorded again, though they dragged on in one form or another until the early '70s. *—Richie Unterberger*

Dirty Water / 1966 / Sundazed ♦♦♦

Hot Ones / 1966 / Sundazed ♦♦

Why Pick on Me / 1966 / Sundazed ♦♦♦

Try It / 1967 / Sundazed ♦♦

● **The Very Best of the Standells** / May 19, 1998 / Hip-O ♦♦♦♦♦
The Standells were a one-hit wonder, and that hit was "Dirty Water," which appropriately opens and closes this compilation (the second version is in stereo). Among the 15 other tracks are the group's less successful follow-ups to their hit, notably "Sometimes Good Guys Don't Wear White," and LP tracks from their three albums of 1966-67, including their versions of standards like "Hey Joe," "My Little Red Book" and "Ninety-Nine and a Half." Of course, nothing is as good as "Dirty Water," even if many of the tracks echo its snotty garage-rock appeal, especially the taunting "Try It," a single that Cub Koda's entertaining liner notes reveal was banned in Boston, which, for a band that declared (falsely), "Boston, you're my home" on its hit single, must have been traumatic. *—William Ruhlmann*

Edwin Starr

b. Jan. 21, 1942, Nashville, TN
Vocals / Pop-Soul, Northern Soul, Motown, Soul
One of the best soul-shouters to come from the Motown stable, Starr's style was closer to James Brown than to any of the other male Motown artists. Best known for his 1970 hit "War," he made a brief comeback during the disco craze, but he now tours Europe and plays the oldies circuit. Detroit vocalist Edwin Starr returned to the vocal wars in 1984 when he recorded a tribute album to Marvin Gaye for England's Streetwave label. He had relocated to Britain and moved to Warwickshire. Starr signed with Hippodrome and issued a pair of singles on that label in 1985 and 1986. He then recorded briefly for Virgin, being produced by the Stock/Aitken/Waterman trio, and then recorded for Motorcity in England and WEA in Germany. Starr also had some songs featured on the Walt Disney release *Mousersize.* *—Rick A. Bueche*

● **The Very Best of Edwin Starr** / Aug. 25, 1998 / Motown ♦♦♦♦♦
Edwin Starr was at the height of his creative powers in the 1960s and early to mid-1970s, when he did much of his best work for Motown. Released in late 1998, this CD spans 1965-1974 and boasts many of his essential Motown hits. Starr was very much a product of Northern soul, and yet, he sometimes showed an awareness of the sweaty, rough-and-tumble soul that Stax Records was recording down in Memphis. "If My Heart Could Tell the Story," "Stop Her On Sight (S.O.S.)," and "I'm Still a Struggling Man" are pure Detroit; the sweetness and honey-coated harmonies that defined a lot of Motor City and Northern R&B are very much a part of these classics. But Starr's tougher side asserts itself on "25 Miles" and the angry protest song "War," both of which demonstrate that when he wanted, Starr could be every bit as gritty as Memphis shouters like Otis Redding and Sam Moore. If you're seeking an introduction to Starr's talents, this disc would be the best choice by far. *—Alex Henderson*

Ringo Starr (Richard Starkey)

b. Jul. 7, 1940, Liverpool, England
Vocals, Drums / Pop/Rock
Ringo Starr, born Richard Starkey, was the drummer in the Beatles from 1962 to 1970 and thus one of the most famous musicians of the '60s. Though the least prominent member of the quartet, he distinguished himself as an occasional singer of good-natured material and as an actor. Upon the group's split, Starr went solo with two novelty projects: the first, an album called *Sentimental Journey,* found him covering pre-rock standards, and the second, *Beacoups of Blues,* was a country music collection.

Starr then scored Top Ten hits with two nonalbum singles, "It Don't Come Easy" in 1971 and "Back off Boogaloo" in 1972. In 1973 he paired with producer Richard Perry and, with assistance from the three other ex-Beatles, made *Ringo,* which featured two number 1 hits, "Photograph" and "You're Sixteen." "Oh My My," a Top Ten hit, was also included. Almost as successful was the 1974 follow-up, *Goodnight Vienna,* which featured the hits "Only You" and "No No Song."

Starr continued to release albums through 1981, though with diminishing success. His 1983 album *Old Wave* did not find a U.S. distributor. Starr was also suffering from the excesses of his lifestyle, but by the late '80s he had cleaned up, and in 1989 he toured with his "All-Starr Band." In 1992, he signed to Private Music and released a new studio album, *Time Takes Time. Vertical Man,* his first album for Mercury, followed in 1998, as did a disc culled from his performance on the *VH1 Storytellers* series. Starr's first seasonal effort, *I Wanna Be Santa Claus,* appeared a year later. *—William Ruhlmann*

Sentimental Journey / Mar. 27, 1970 / Capitol ♦♦♦

Beaucoups of Blues / Sep. 25, 1970 / Capitol ♦♦♦♦♦

Ringo / Nov. 2, 1973 / Capitol ♦♦♦♦♦
With *Ringo,* Ringo Starr finally put his solo career in gear in 1973, after serving notice with back-to-back Top Ten singles in 1971 and 1972 that he had more to offer than his eccentric first two solo albums. *Ringo* was a big-budget pop album produced by Richard Perry and featuring Ringo's former Beatles bandmates as songwriters, singers, and instrumentalists. On no single track did all four appear, though George Harrison played the guitars on the John Lennon-penned lead-off track "I'm the Greatest," with Lennon playing piano and singing harmony. But it wasn't only the guests who made *Ringo* a success: Ringo advanced his own cause by co-writing two of the album's Top Ten singles, the number one "Photograph" and "Oh My My." The album's biggest hit was a second chart-topper, Ringo's cover of the old Johnny Burnette hit "You're Sixteen." Songs like "Have You Seen My Baby," a Randy Newman song with guitar by Marc Bolan, and Ringo and Vini Poncia's "Devil Woman" were just as good as the hits. Ringo's best and most consistent new studio album, *Ringo* represented both the drummer/singer's most dramatic comeback and his commercial peak. The original ten-track 1973 album got even better in 1991 as a 13-track CD reissue, the bonus tracks including the 1971 gold single "It Don't Come Easy" and its B-side, "Early 1970," a telling depiction of Ringo's perspective on the Beatles breakup. *—William Ruhlmann*

Goodnight Vienna / Nov. 15, 1974 / Capitol ♦♦♦♦
Goodnight Vienna was very much a follow-up to *Ringo,* on which Ringo Starr called upon his bevy of musical buddies. Most prominent among them was John Lennon, who again wrote the lead-off track, "(It's All Da-Da-Down To) Goodnight Vienna," and played on three songs; also included are Elton John, who wrote and played on "Snookeroo," Dr. John, Billy Preston, Robbie Robertson, and Harry Nilsson. Richard Perry again produced, bringing his strong pop sensibility to the diverse material. The only real fall-off was in the songwriting; the album's Top Ten hits were "Only You," the old Platters song, and Hoyt Axton's novelty number "No No Song," which winked at intoxicants, but little else on the set stood out. *Goodnight Vienna* was another enjoyable Ringo record, but it lacked the star power and consistency of its predecessor. Still, compared to the rest of his '70s albums, it was a masterpiece. *—William Ruhlmann*

● **Blast from Your Past** / Nov. 20, 1975 / Capitol ♦♦♦♦♦
Capitol records marked Ringo Starr's impending departure from the label with this ten-song compilation drawn from three of his solo albums, along with the previously non-LP hits "It Don't Come Easy" and "Back Off Boogaloo" and the B-side "Early 1970." As it happened, the set was perfectly timed, since Ringo never threatened the Top Ten again and he was caught here at his 1971-1975 commercial peak, with all seven of his Top Ten hits accounted for, including the gold-selling chart-toppers "Photograph" and "You're Sixteen." *—William Ruhlmann*

Ringo's Rotogravure / Sep. 17, 1976 / Atlantic ♦♦♦

Ringo the 4th / Sep. 26, 1977 / Atlantic ♦♦

Bad Boy / Apr. 21, 1978 / Portrait ♦♦

Stop & Smell the Roses / Oct. 27, 1981 / The Right Stuff ♦♦♦

Old Wave / Jun. 8, 1983 / The Right Stuff ♦♦

Starr Struck: Best of Ringo Starr, Vol. 2 / Feb. 24, 1989 / Rhino ✦✦✦
A follow-up compilation to *Blast from Your Past, Starr Struck* gathered together the better tracks from Ringo Starr's less successful albums originally released between 1976 and 1983. "A Dose of Rock 'N' Roll" and "Wrack My Brain" were Top 40 singles, and the album contained specially written songs by Ringo's Beatle colleagues. The album also marked the first U.S. release for four songs from Ringo's 19B3 album *Old Wave.* The result was a good substitute for five Ringo albums that were out of print when it was released, but no match for the hit-filled *Blast from Your Past.* — *William Ruhlmann*

Time Takes Time / May 22, 1992 / Private Music ✦✦✦✦✦
On his first new studio album to released in the U.S. in 11 years, Ringo Starr made a neo-'60s-sounding record that, if it didn't feature his Beatle-mates, certainly evoked them. Don Was, the king of creative retro, produced half the album, bringing in bands like Jellyfish and the Posies wbo devote their careers to trying to sound like the Beatles of 1965-66. Here, with a real Beatle on drums and vocals, they came much closer. Of course, it's always a little weird when a veteran star makes what is essentially clone music meant to resemble the sound of his glory days. But Ringo remains a distinctive drummer and an engaging singer, so even when he was singing something called "Golden Blunders," it was hard to blame him. Besides, there are worse things to copy than the Beatles. — *William Ruhlmann*

Status Quo

f. 1967, London, England
Group / Boogie Rock, Psychedelic, Hard Rock
Status Quo is one of Britain's longest-lived bands, staying together for over 30 years. During much of that time, the band was only successful in the UK, where they racked up a string of Top Ten singles that ran into the '90s. In America, the group was ignored after they abandoned psychedelia for heavy boogie rock in the early '70s. Before that, the Quo managed to reach number 12 in the US with the psychedelic classic "Pictures of Matchstick Men" (a Top Ten hit in the UK). Following that single, the band suffered a lean period for the next few years, before deciding to refashion themselves as a hard-rock boogie band in 1970 with their *Ma Kelly's Greasy Spoon* album. Over the next 25 years, the Quo have basically recycled the same simple boogie on each successive album and single, yet their popularity has never waned in Britain. If anything, their very predictability has ensured the group a large following. By the mid-'90s, Status Quo had scored 50 British hit singles, which was a greater number than any other band in rock & roll's history. — *Stephen Thomas Erlewine*

Picturesque Matchstickable Messages from the Status Quo / Aug. 1968 / Castle ✦✦✦✦
Status Quo's debut album featured none of the band's better-known boogie rock of the mid-'70s. *Picturesque...* is a psychedelic effort that tries to imitate the sound bands like the Bee Gees or the Beatles were doing at the moment. With this record, Status Quo surprisingly had its first (and last) hit in America, the single "Pictures of Matchstick Men," which peaked at number 12. (It reached number seven on the British charts.) Other highlights from the album are the second single "Ice in the Sun" and the Bee Gees cover "Spicks and Specks." Even if this is not the most representative album from Status Quo, it is a good psychedelic pop exercise that sometimes includes very imaginative guitar phrases (e.g., "Ice in the Sun") and some brilliantly unusual sounds (e.g., the epic "Paradise Flat"). — *Robert Aniento*

● **Whatever You Want: The Best of Status Quo** / 1997 / Polygram ✦✦✦✦✦
In many ways, *Whatever You Want: The Best of Status Quo* is the definitive Quo collection. Spanning two discs, the set features almost all of the band's hits, from "Pictures of Matchstick Men" to "Down Down" and "Rockin' All Over the World," leaving only a couple of cuts behind. For all but the most dedicated fan, this is all the Quo they'll ever need, and it may even be too much for the casual observer. — *Stephen Thomas Erlewine*

Steely Dan

f. 1972, Los Angeles, CA, **db.** 1981
Group / Album Rock, Jazz-Rock, Pop/Rock, Soft Rock
Most rock & roll bands are a tightly-wound unit that developed their music through years of playing in garages and clubs around their hometown. Steely Dan never subscribed to that aesthetic. As the vehicle for the songwriting of Walter Becker and Donald Fagen, Steely Dan defied all rock & roll conventions. Becker and Fagen never truly enjoyed rock—with their ironic humor and cryptic lyrics, their eclectic body of work shows some debt to Bob Dylan—preferring jazz, traditional pop, blues and R&B. Steely Dan created a sophisticated, distinctive sound with accessible melodic hooks, complex harmonies and time signatures, and a devotion to the recording studio. With producer Gary Katz, Becker & Fagen gradually changed Steely Dan from a performing band to a studio project, hiring professional musicians to record their compositions. Though the band didn't perform live after 1973, Steely Dan's popularity continued to grow throughout the decade, as their albums became critical favorites and their singles became staples of AOR and pop radio stations. Even after the group disbanded in the early '80s, their records retained a cult following, as proven by the massive success of their unlikely return to the stage in the early '80s. — *Stephen Thomas Erlewine*

Can't Buy a Thrill / 1972 / MCA ✦✦✦
Walter Becker and Donald Fagen were remarkable craftsmen from the start, as Steely Dan's debut *Can't Buy a Thrill* illustrates. Each song is tightly constructed, with interlocking chords and gracefully interwoven melodies, buoyed by clever, cryptic lyrics. All of these are hallmarks of Steely Dan's signature sound, but what is most remarkable about the record is the way it differs from their later albums. Of course, one of the most notable differences is the presence of vocalist David Palmer, a professional blue-eyed soul vocalist who oversings the handful of tracks where he takes the lead. Palmer's very presence signals the one major flaw with the album—in an attempt to appeal to a wide audience, Becker and Fagen tempered their wildest impulses with mainstream pop techniques. Consequently, there are very few of the jazz flourishes that came to distinguish their albums—the breakthrough single "Do It Again" does work an impressively tight Latin-jazz beat, and "Reelin' in the Years" has jazzy guitar solos and harmonies—and the production is overly polished, conforming to all the conventions of early-'70s radio. Of course, that gives these decidedly twisted songs a subversive edge, but compositionally, these aren't as innovative as their later work. Even so, the best moments ("Dirty Work," "Kings," "Midnite Cruiser," "Turn That Heartbeat Over Again") are wonderful pop songs that subvert traditional conventions, and more than foreshadow the paths Steely Dan would later take. — *Stephen Thomas Erlewine*

☆ **Countdown to Ecstasy** / 1973 / MCA ✦✦✦✦✦
Can't Buy a Thrill became an unexpected hit, and as a response, Donald Fagen became the group's full-time lead vocalist, and he and Walter Becker acted like Steely Dan was a rock & roll band for the group's second album, *Countdown to Ecstasy.* The loud guitars and pronounced backbeat of "Bodhisattva," "Show Biz Kids" and "My Old School" camouflage the fact that *Countdown* is a riskier album, musically speaking, than its predecessor. Each of its eight songs have sophisticated, jazz-inflected interludes, and apart from the bluesy vamps "Bodhisattva" and "Show Biz Kids," which sound like they were written for the stage, the songs are subtly textured. "Razor Boy," with its murmuring marimbas, and the hard-bop tribute "Your Gold Teeth" reveal Becker and Fagen's jazz roots, while the country-flavored "Pearl of the Quarter" and the ominous, skittering "King of the World" are both overlooked gems. *Countdown to Ecstasy* is the only time Steely Dan played it relatively straight, and its eight songs are rich with either musical or lyrical detail that their album-rock or art-rock contemporaries couldn't hope to match. — *Stephen Thomas Erlewine*

☆ **Pretzel Logic** / 1974 / MCA ✦✦✦✦✦
Countdown to Ecstasy wasn't half the hit that *Can't Buy a Thrill* was, and Steely Dan responded by trimming the lengthy instrumental jams that were scattered across *Countdown* and concentrating on concise songs for *Pretzel Logic.* While the shorter songs usually indicate a tendency toward pop conventions, that's not the case with *Pretzel Logic.* Instead of relying on easy hooks, Becker and Fagen assembled their most complex and cynical set of songs to date. Dense with harmonics, countermelodies and bop phrasing, *Pretzel Logic* is vibrant with unpredictable musical juxtapositions and snide, but very funny, wordplay. Listen to how the album's hit single, "Rikki Don't Lose That Number," opens with a syncopated piano line that evolves into a graceful pop melody, or how the title track winds from a blues to a jazzy chorus—Becker and Fagen's craft has become seamless while remaining idiosyncratic and thrillingly accessible. Since the songs are now paramount, it makes sense that *Pretzel Logic* is less of a band-oriented album than *Countdown to Ecstasy,* yet it is the richest album in their catalog, one where the backhanded Dylan tribute "Barrytown" can sit comfortably next to the gorgeous "Any Major Dude Will Tell You." Steely Dan made more accomplished albums than *Pretzel Logic,* but they never made a better one. — *Stephen Thomas Erlewine*

☆ **Katy Lied** / 1975 / MCA ✦✦✦✦✦
Building from the jazz-fusion foundation of *Pretzel Logic,* Steely Dan created an alluringly sophisticated album of jazzy pop with *Katy Lied.* With this record, Becker and Fagen began relying solely on studio musicians, which is evident from the immaculate sound of the album. Usually, such a studied recording method would drain the life out of each song, but that's not the case with *Katy Lied,* which actually benefits from the duo's perfectionist tendencies. Each song is given a glossy sheen, one that accentuates not only the stronger pop hooks, but also the precise technical skill of the professional musicians drafted to play the solos. Essentially, *Katy Lied* is a smoother version of *Pretzel Logic,* featuring the same cross-section of jazz-pop and blues-rock. The lack of innovations doesn't hurt the record, since the songs are uniformly brilliant. Less overtly cynical than previous Dan albums, the album still has its share of lyrical stingers, but what's really notable are the melodies, from the seductive jazzy soul of "Doctor Wu" and the lazy blues of "Chain Lightning" to the terse "Black Friday" and mock calypso of "Everyone's Gone to the Movies." It's another excellent record in one of the most distinguished rock & roll catalogs of the '70s. — *Stephen Thomas Erlewine*

The Royal Scam / 1976 / MCA ✦✦✦
The Royal Scam is the first Steely Dan record that didn't exhibit significant musical progress from its predecessor, but that doesn't mean the album is any less interesting. The cynicism that was suppressed on *Katy Lied* comes roaring to the surface on *The Royal Scam*—not only are the lyrics bitter and snide, but the music is terse, broken and weary. Not so coincidentally, the album is comprised of Becker and Fagen's weakest set of songs since *Can't Buy a Thrill.* Alternating between mean-spirited bluesy vamps like "Green Earrings" and "The Fez" and jazzy soft-rock numbers like "The Caves of Altamira," there's nothing particularly bad on the album, yet there are fewer standouts than before. Nevertheless, the best songs on *The Royal Scam,* like the sneering "Kid Charlemagne" and the gorgeous ballad "Sign in Stranger," rank as genuine Steely Dan classics. — *Stephen Thomas Erlewine*

Aja / 1977 / MCA ✦✦✦✦✦
Steely Dan hadn't been a real working band since *Pretzel Logic,* but with *Aja,* Becker and Fagen's obsession with sonic detail and fascination with composition reached new heights. A coolly textured and immaculately produced collection of sophisticated jazz-rock, *Aja* has none of the overt cynicism or self-consciously challenging music that distinguished previous Steely Dan records. Instead, it's a measured and textured album, filled with subtle melodies and accomplished, jazzy solos that blend easily into the lush instrumental backdrops. But *Aja* isn't just about texture, since Becker and Fagen's songs are their most complex and musically rich set of songs—even the simplest song, the sunny pop of "Peg," has layers of jazzy vocal harmonies. In fact, Steely Dan ignores rock on *Aja,* preferring to fuse cool jazz, blues and pop together in a seamless, seductive fashion. It's complex music delivered with ease, and although the duo's preoccupation with clean sound and self-consciously sophisticated arrangements would eventually lead to a dead end, *Aja* is a shining example of jazz-rock at its finest. — *Stephen Thomas Erlewine*

Gaucho / 1980 / MCA ✦✦✦✦
Aja was cool, relaxed and controlled; it sounded deceptively easy. Its follow-up, *Gaucho,* while sonically similar, was its polar opposite: a precise and studied record, where all of the seams showed. *Gaucho* essentially replicates the smooth jazz-pop of *Aja,* but with none of

that record's dark, seductive romance or elegant aura. Instead, it's meticulous and exacting; each performance has been rehearsed so many times that they no longer have any emotional resonance. Furthermore, Becker and Fagen's songs are generally labored, only occasionally reaching their past heights, like on the suave "Babylon Sisters," "Time Out of Mind" and "Hey Nineteen." Still, those three songs are barely enough to make the remainder of the album's glossy, meandering fusion worthwhile. *—Stephen Thomas Erlewine*

Gold / 1982 / MCA ✦✦✦✦

★ **A Decade of Steely Dan** / 1985 / MCA ✦✦✦✦✦

Citizen Steely Dan / Dec. 14, 1993 / MCA ✦✦✦

Alive in America / Oct. 17, 1995 / Giant ✦✦

Two Against Nature / Feb. 29, 2000 / Giant ✦✦✦✦
Notorious for shunning concert performances, Steely Dan's improbable live reunion in the mid-'90s eventually turned into a full-fledged reunion album. Since Steely Dan fans went two decades without even the hope of a new record, the very prospect was a delight, but it was also a little worrying, since a botched comeback would tarnish the band's legacy. Fortunately, *Two Against Nature* is as seductive and alluring as the best of Steely Dan's later work, with a similar emphasis on classy atmosphere and groove. Pitched halfway between *Gaucho* and the immaculate production of Fagen's solo album *Kamakiriad,* it's a graceful, intricate record that works its subtle charms at its own pace. While that means it isn't a knockout on the first listen, it's a real grower—a quietly addicting album that slowly works its way into the subconscious. It's also an uncannily natural extension of the duo's previous work, but surprisingly, it never sounds nostalgic or dated. It's clear that Becker and Fagen re-teamed because they simply enjoy working together: crafting the songs and arrangements, designing the production, shoehorning in-jokes into the lyrics, finding the exact performances that fit their specifications. In this sense, *Two Against Nature* is no different than any past Steely Dan effort; that's exactly why it's welcome, since they find nearly endless permutations within their signature sound. Lyrically, the album isn't quite as malicious as their '70s work, but they haven't lost their sharp humor, even on some mere throwaway lines. The real payoff, however, is musical. Each song gradually reveals its own identity through small, thrilling touches, giving the record depth and character, and fitting it comfortably into Steely Dan's acclaimed body of work. And that's as delightfully unexpected and peculiarly beautiful as anything else in their career. *—Stephen Thomas Erlewine*

Showbiz Kids: The Steely Dan Story / Nov. 14, 2000 / MCA ✦✦✦✦✦

Steppenwolf

f. 1967, Los Angeles, CA, **db.** 1972
Group / Acid Rock, Psychedelic, Hard Rock
Led by John Kay (born Joachim Krauledat, April 12, 1944), Steppenwolf's blazing biker anthem "Born to Be Wild" roared out of speakers everywhere in the fiery summer of 1968, John Kay's threatening rasp sounding a mesmerizing call to arms to the counterculture movement rapidly sprouting up nationwide. German immigrant Kay got his professional start in a bluesy Toronto band called Sparrow, recording for Columbia in 1966. After Sparrow disbanded, Kay relocated to the West Coast and formed Steppenwolf, named after the Herman Hesse novel. "Born to Be Wild," their third single on ABC-Dunhill, was immortalized on the soundtrack of Dennis Hopper's underground film classic *Easy Rider.* The song's reference to "heavy metal thunder" finally gave an assignable name to an emerging genre. Steppenwolf's second monster hit that year, the psychedelic "Magic Carpet Ride," and the follow-ups "Rock Me," "Move Over," and "Hey Lawdy Mama" further established the band's credibility on the hard-rock circuit. By the early '70s, Steppenwolf ran out of steam and disbanded. Kay continued to record solo, as other members put together ersatz versions of the band for touring purposes. During the mid 80s Kay re-formed his own version of Steppenwolf, grinding out his hits (and some new songs) at oldies shows. Nevertheless, they'll be remembered for generations to come for creating one of the ultimate gas'n'go rock anthems of all time. *—Bill Dahl & Cub Koda*

● **16 Greatest Hits** / 1973 / MCA ✦✦✦✦✦
Just what the name implies; "Born to Be Wild," "Magic Carpet Ride," "The Pusher," and "Rock Me" are just some of the highlights. Everything you're going to want to hear in one neat little package. *—Cub Koda*

Born to Be Wild: A Retrospective / Nov. 5, 1991 / MCA ✦✦✦✦✦
A double-disc collection of Steppenwolf's lengthy career, *Born To Be Wild: A Retrospective* includes more music than anyone but hardcore fans need, but the song selection and packaging are superb, making it essential for those devoted fans. *—Stephen Thomas Erlewine*

Stereolab

f. 1991, London, England
Group / Indie Pop, Ambient Pop, Experimental Rock, Indie Rock, Post-Rock/Experimental, Alternative Pop/Rock
Combining an inclination for melodic '60s pop with an art-rock aesthetic borrowed from Kraut-rock bands like Faust and Neu!, Stereolab were one of the most influential alternative bands of the '90s. Led by Tim Gane and Laetitia Sadier, Stereolab legitimized forms of music that were either on the fringe of rock, or brought attention to a strand of pop music—bossa nova, lounge-pop, movie soundtracks—that were traditionally banished from the rock lineage. The group's trademark sound—a droning, hypnotic rhythm track overlaid with melodic, mesmerizing sing-song vocals, often sung in French and often promoting revolutionary, Marxist politics—was deceptively simple, providing the basis for a wide array of stylistic experiments over the course of their prolific career. Throughout it all, Stereolab relied heavily on forgotten methods of recording, whether it was analog synthesizers and electronics or a fondness for hi-fi test records, without ever sinking to the level of kitsch. *—Stephen Thomas Erlewine*

Peng! / 1992 / Too Pure/American ✦✦✦✦

Switched On / 1992 / Too Pure ✦✦✦

The Groop Played "Space Age Batchelor Pad Music" / 1993 / Too Pure/American ✦✦✦

Transient Random Noise-Bursts With Announcements / Aug. 1993 / Elektra ✦✦✦✦✦
Though it was the group's major-label debut, Stereolab's *Transient Random Noise-Bursts With Announcements* showed no signs of selling out. If anything, it's one of the most eclectic and experimental releases in Stereolab's early career, emphasizing the group's elongated Krautrock jams, instrumentals, and harsh, noisy moments. The album begins and ends with smooth, sensual washes of sound like "Tone Burst" and "Lock-Groove Lullaby" and smoothly bouncy pop songs like "I'm Going Out of My Way." These softer, more accessible moments surround complex and varied compositions such as "Analogue Rock," "Our Trinitone Blast," and "Golden Ball," which, with its distorted vocals and shifting tempos, serves as an appetizer for "Jenny Ondioline." A hypnotic, 18-minute epic encompassing dreamy yet driving pop, a Krautrock groove, forceful, churning guitars, and a furious climax, it's the most ambitious—and definitive—moment of Stereolab's early years. But *Transient Random Noise-Bursts With Announcements* also features quietly experimental pieces such as "Pause," a slightly spooky song that uses distorted whispers as a rhythm track and places fluttery keyboards and Laetitia Sadier and Mary Hansen's sweet, slightly alien harmonies atop it. Likewise, the very sexy, very French "Pack Yr Romantic Mind" reveals the growing influence of '50s and '60s easy listening on the group's musical direction. If *Switched On* and *Peng!* defined the band's essential sound, *Transient Random Noise-Bursts With Announcements* expanded it, reaffirming Stereolab's place as one of the most innovative and evolving groups of the '90s. *—Heather Phares*

Mars Audiac Quintet / Aug. 9, 1994 / Elektra ✦✦✦✦
By the time of 1994's *Mars Audiac Quintet,* Stereolab had already highlighted the rock and experimental sides of its music; now the band concentrated on perfecting its space-age pop. Sweetly bouncy songs like "Ping Pong" and "L' Enfer des Formes" streamline the band's sound without sacrificing its essence; track for track, this may be the group's most accessible, tightly written album. The groove-driven "Outer Accelerator," "Wow and Flutter," and "Transona Five" (which sounds strangely like Canned Heat's "Goin' Up the Country") reaffirm Stereolab's Krautrock roots, but the band's sweet synth melodies and vocal arrangements give it a pop patina. Even extended pieces like "Anamorphose" and "Nihilist Assault Group"—which could have appeared on *Transient Random Noise-Bursts With Announcements* if they had a rawer production—are more sensual and voluptuous than edgy and challenging. It's equally apparent on layered, complex songs such as "New Orthophony" and "The Stars Our Destination," as well as spare, minimal tracks like "Des Etoiles Electroniques," that the members of Stereolab focused their experimental energies on production tricks, vocal interplay, and increasingly electronic-based arrangements. The charming final track "Fiery Yellow" takes the band's fondness for lounge pop and experimentation to the limit; a delicate, marimba-driven piece featuring the High Llamas' Sean O'Hagan, it sounds like the kind of music Esquivel or Martin Denny would be proud to make in the '90s. While it's not as overtly innovative as some of Stereolab's earlier albums, *Mars Audiac Quintet* is an enjoyable, accessible forerunner to the intricate, cerebral direction the group's music would take in the mid- and late '90s. *—Heather Phares*

Music for the Amorphous Body Center [EP] / Apr. 1995 / Duophonic ✦✦✦✦

Refried Ectoplasm (Switched On, Vol. 2) / Jul. 1995 / Duophonic/Drag City ✦✦✦✦✦
Refried Ectoplasm (Switched On, Vol. 2) collects 13 singles and rarities Stereolab released between 1992 and 1995, and it is far more than a mere oddities collection. More than any other album, *Refried Ectoplasm* charts Stereolab's astonishing musical growth between those three years, and offers several definitive songs—including "Lo Boob Oscillator," "French Disko" and "John Cage Bubblegum"—not available on any album. While such items are essential for collectors, the quality and accessiblity of the music is very strong, showcasing Stereolab's complexity and providing an excellent introduction to the group. *—Stephen Thomas Erlewine*

● **Emperor Tomato Ketchup** / Apr. 1996 / Elektra ✦✦✦✦✦
Stereolab was poised for a breakthrough release with *Emperor Tomato Ketchup,* their fourth full-length album. Not only was their influence becoming apparent throughout alternative rock, but *Mars Audiac Quintet* and *Music for the Amorphous Body Center* indicated they were moving closer to distinct pop melodies. The group certainly hasn't backed away from pop melodies on *Emperor Tomato Ketchup,* but just as their hooks are becoming catchier, they bring in more avant-garde and experimental influences, as well. Consequently, the album is Stereolab's most complex, multi-layered record. It lacks the raw, amateurish textures of their early singles, but the music is far more ambitious, melding electronic drones and sing-song melodies with string sections, slight hip-hop and dub influences, and scores of interweaving counter melodies. Even when Stereolab appears to be creating a one-chord trance, there is a lot going on beneath the surface. Furthermore, the group's love for easy listening and pop melodies means that the music never feels cold or inaccessible. In fact, pop singles like "Cybele's Reverie" and "The Noise of Carpet" help ease listeners into the group's more experimental tendencies. Because of all its textures, *Emperor Tomato Ketchup* isn't as immediately accessible as *Mars Audiac Quintet,* but it is a rich, rewarding listen. *—Stephen Thomas Erlewine*

Dots and Loops / Sep. 23, 1997 / Elektra ✦✦✦✦
On *Emperor Tomato Ketchup,* Stereolab moved in two directions simultaneously—it explored funkier dance rhythms while increasing the complexity of its arrangements and compositions. For its follow-up, *Dots and Loops,* the group scaled back its rhythmic experiments and concentrated on layered compositions. Heavily influenced by bossa nova and swinging '60s pop, *Dots and Loops* is a deceptively light, breezy album that floats by with effortless grace. Even the segmented, 20-minute "Refractions in the Plastic Pulse" has a sunny, appealing surface—it's only upon later listens that the interlocking melodies and rhythms reveal their intricate interplay. In many ways, *Dots and Loops* is Stereolab's greatest musical accomplishment to date, demonstrating remarkable skill—their interaction is closer to jazz

than rock, exploring all of the possibilities of any melodic phrase. Their affection for '60s pop keeps *Dots and Loops* accessible, even though that doesn't mean it is as immediate as *Emperor Tomato Ketchup*. In fact, the laid-back stylings of *Dots and Loops* makes it a little difficult to assimilate upon first listen, but after a few repeated plays, its charms unfold as gracefully as any other Stereolab record. *—Stephen Thomas Erlewine*

Aluminum Tunes: Switched On, Vol. 3 / Oct. 20, 1998 / Drag City ✦✦✦✦✦
Stereolab's *Switched On* series is ingenious, one of the best services a band has performed for their fans. Since their inception, Stereolab has made it a practice to release non-LP singles, tour 7"'s, split-singles, special-edition EPs—recordings that were available in small quantities for a limited time. In every case, the limited-edition recordings become very valuable very quickly, often reaching ridiculously exorbitant prices that most fans could never afford. That's where the *Switched On* series comes in. It's where the group gathers the best of these rarities, leaving a couple of tracks on the original single for collectibility's sake. Stereolab may do certain projects as a lark, but they rarely throw away tracks, as each EP and most singles have their own identity, offering a new spin on the group's trademark style. Given that *Aluminum Tunes: Switched On, Vol. 3* spans two discs, it might seem that the compilation will only be of interest to diehards, but it rivals *Refried Ectoplasm: Switched On, Vol. 2* in terms of creativity and consistency. *Aluminum Tunes* is distinguished by the first wide release of the entire sublime easy listening EP *Music for the Amorphous Body Center*, which would be enough to make the compilation essential for all fans, but it also has such minor masterpieces as their swinging duet with Herbie Mann on Antonio Carlos Jobim's "One Note Samba," Wagon Christ's remix of "Metronomic Underground," the horn-spiked "Percolations," and "You Used to Call Me Sadness." There may be a couple of tracks that never rise above the level of good but predictable Stereolab, but the best moments rank among their very best work. Quite simply an essential addition to their catalog. *—Stephen Thomas Erlewine*

Cobra & Phases Group Play Voltage in the Milky Night / Sep. 21, 1999 / Elektra ✦✦✦

First of the Microbe Hunters / May 16, 2000 / Elektra ✦✦

Cat Stevens (Steve Georgiou)

b. Jul. 21, 1947, London, England
Vocals, Keyboards, Piano, Guitar, Synthesizer / Album Rock, Pop/Rock, Folk-Rock, Soft Rock, Pop, Singer/Songwriter
Cat Stevens became interested in folk and rock & roll in his teens and scored his first U.K. hit, "I Love My Dog," before he turned 20. Stevens reached the singles charts four more times, getting to #2 with "Matthew and Son" and releasing the similarly titled Top Ten album before he contracted tuberculosis in 1968 and was forced to retire from music. He re-emerged with a new, mature style in 1970 with the album *Mona Bone Jakon* and hit the U.K. Top Ten with "Lady D'Arbanville." But it was his late 1970 follow-up, *Tea for the Tillerman*, that made him an international success. The album hit the Top Ten and went gold in the U.S., producing the hit "Wild World." *Teaser and the Firecat*, released in 1971, did even better, including the hits "Peace Train" and "Morning Has Broken." Stevens became so successful as an albums artist that, even though his next couple of albums did not generate big hit singles, they were still big sellers. His records were gradually less successful during the second half of the '70s. In 1979, he became a Muslim, adopted the name Yusef Islam, and retired from music. He was not heard from for another ten years, until he shocked admirers at the end of the '80s by supporting the death sentence ordered by the Ayatollah Khomeini against novelist Salman Rushdie for writing the book *The Satanic Verses*. Some "classic rock" radio stations discontinued playing him as a result, though his music remains popular. *—William Ruhlmann*

Matthew & Son / 1967 / Deram ✦✦✦
Released in the late winter of 1967, 19-year-old Cat Stevens' debut album, *Matthew & Son*, contained his breakthrough U.K. hits "I Love My Dog" (28) and the title song (#2), and spawned a third, "I'm Gonna Get Me A Gun" (#6). (The Tremeloes took a cover of the album's "Here Comes My Baby" to U.K. number four.) While it is a precocious effort (Stevens wrote all the songs) and the material is undeniably catchy, it's also wildly overproduced, with gimmicky arrangements typical of the mid-'60s British pop sound around the time of *Sgt. Pepper*. This is especially noticeable, heard in the context of Stevens' later, less-produced, more meaningful efforts. *—William Ruhlmann*

New Masters / 1967 / Deram ✦✦

Mona Bone Jakon / Jul. 1970 / A&M ✦✦✦✦
Cat Stevens virtually disappeared from the British pop scene in 1968, at the age of 20, after a meteoric start to his career. After contracting tuberculosis, Stevens spent a year recovering from both his illness and the strain of being a teenage pop star, and in the spring of 1970—as a very different 22-year-old—he returned to action with *Mona Bone Jakon*. Fans who knew him from 1967 must have been surprised. Under the production aegis of former Yardbird Paul Samwell-Smith, he introduced a group of simple, heartfelt songs played in spare arrangements on acoustic guitars and keyboards and driven by a restrained rhythm section. Built on folk and blues structures, but with characteristically compelling melodies, Stevens' new compositions were tentative, fragmentary statements that alluded to his recent "Trouble," including the triviality of being a "Pop Star." But these were the words of a desperate man in search of salvation. *Mona Bone Jakon* was dominated by images of death, but the album was also about survival and hope. Stevens' craggy voice, with its odd breaks of tone and occasional huskiness, lent these sometimes sketchy songs depth, and the understated instrumentation further emphasized their seriousness. If Stevens was working out private demons on *Mona Bone Jakon*, he was well attuned to a similar world-weariness in pop culture. His listeners may not have shared his exact experience, but after the 1960s they certainly understood his sense of being wounded, his spiritual yearning, and his hesitant optimism. *Mona Bone Jakon* was only a modest success upon its initial release, but it attracted attention in the wake of the commercial breakthrough of its follow-up, *Tea for the Tillerman*. *—William Ruhlmann*

☆ **Tea for the Tillerman** / Nov. 1970 / Mobile Fidelity ✦✦✦✦✦
Mona Bone Jakon only began Cat Stevens' comeback. Seven months later, he returned with *Tea for the Tillerman*, an album in the same chamber-group style, employing the same musicians and producer, but with a far more confident tone. *Mona Bone Jakon* had been full of references to death, but *Tea for the Tillerman* was not about dying; it was about living in the modern world while rejecting it in favor of spiritual fulfillment. It began with a statement of purpose, "Where Do the Children Play?," in which Stevens questioned the value of technology and progress. "Wild World" found the singer being dumped by a girl, but making the novel suggestion that she should stay with him because she was incapable of handling things without him. "Sad Lisa" might have been about the same girl after she tried and failed to make her way; now, she seemed depressed to the point of psychosis. The rest of the album veered between two themes: the conflict between the young and the old, and religion as an answer to life's questions. *Tea for the Tillerman* was the story of a young man's search for spiritual meaning in a soulless class society he found abhorrent. He hadn't yet reached his destination, but he was confident he was going in the right direction, traveling at his own, unhurried pace. The album's rejection of contemporary life and its yearning for something more struck a chord with listeners in an era in which traditional verities had been shaken. It didn't hurt, of course, that Stevens had lost none of his ability to craft a catchy pop melody; the album may have been full of angst, but it wasn't hard to sing along to. As a result, *Tea for the Tillerman* became a big seller and, for the second time in four years, its creator became a pop star. *—William Ruhlmann*

☆ **Teaser & the Firecat** / Oct. 1971 / A&M ✦✦✦✦✦
Even as a serious-minded singer/songwriter, Cat Stevens never stopped being a pop singer at heart, and with *Teaser & the Firecat* he reconciled his philosophical interests with his pop instincts. Basically, *Teaser's* songs came in two modes: gentle ballads that usually found Stevens and second guitarist Alun Davies playing delicate lines over sensitive love lyrics, and uptempo numbers on which the guitarists strummed away and thundering drums played in stop-start rhythms. There were also more exotic styles, such as the Greek-styled "Rubylove," with its twin bouzoukis and a verse sung in Greek, and "Tuesday's Dead," with its Caribbean feel. Stevens seemed to have worked out some of his big questions, to the point of wanting to proselytize on songs like "Changes IV" and "Peace Train," both stirring tunes in which he urged social and spiritual improvement. Meanwhile, his love songs had become simpler and more plaintive. And while there had always been a charming, childlike quality to some of his lyrics, there were songs here that worked as nursery rhymes, and these were among the album's most memorable tracks and its biggest hits: "Moonshadow" and "Morning Has Broken," the latter adapted from a hymn. The overall result was an album that was musically more interesting than ever, but lyrically dumbed-down. Stevens continued to look for satisfaction in romance, despite its disappointment, but he found more fulfillment in a still-unspecified religious pursuit that he was ready to tout to others. And they were at least nominally ready to listen: the album produced three hit singles and just missed topping the charts. *Tea for the Tillerman* may have been the more impressive effort, but *Teaser & the Firecat* was the Cat Stevens album that gave more surface pleasures to more people, which in pop music is the name of the game. *—William Ruhlmann*

Catch Bull at Four / Oct. 1972 / A&M ✦✦✦
Catch Bull at Four began with a statement of purpose, "Sitting," in which Cat Stevens tried to talk himself into believing that he hadn't stalled, beginning to worry that he might be falling behind schedule or even going in circles. It may be that Stevens' recent experiences had contributed to his sense that he was running out of time. Though he was never a directly confessional writer, one got the sense that his disaffection with the life of a pop star was reasserting itself. And while he was touring unhappily around the world, the world was still going to hell in a handbasket. Yet Stevens was still motivated by his urge to help mankind mend its ways. Love provided some comfort, but for the most part, the singer who had seemed so excited on his last album now sounded apprehensive. Stevens set his reflections to a mixture of musical styles that included traces of old English folk songs, madrigals, and Greek folk music along with more typical rock stylings, all performed with the stop-and-start rhythms that added drama to his performances. Nevertheless, *Catch Bull at Four* was a more difficult listen than its three predecessors. Coming off the momentum of *Teaser and the Firecat*, it roared up the charts to number one, but stayed in the Top Ten fewer weeks than its predecessor. Fans who had been stirred by Stevens' rhythmic tunes and charmed by his thoughtful lyrics were starting to lose interest in his quasi-religious yearnings, busy arrangements, and self-absorbed, melodramatic singing. His career still had a ways to go, but as of *Catch Bull at Four*, he had passed his peak. *—William Ruhlmann*

Foreigner / Jul. 1973 / A&M ✦✦✦

Buddha & the Chocolate Box / Apr. 1974 / A&M ✦✦✦

Greatest Hits / Jun. 1975 / A&M ✦✦✦✦✦
Like many of his peers, Cat Stevens made records that were identified by strong, memorable hit singles, but make no mistake: he made albums that were cohesive works onto themselves. For that reason, the very idea of a Cat Stevens' *Greatest Hits* collection may be troublesome to some fans, since they will only notice the missing album tracks, but *Greatest Hits* does its job exceptionally well. With the exception of "The Hurt," all of his hits from the early '70s—"Wild World," "Moon Shadow," "Peace Train," "Morning Has Broken," "Sitting," "Oh Very Young," "Another Saturday Night," "Ready" and "Two Fine People"—are here, along with three other fine album tracks. In short, it is everything that casual fans need—and even fans that find a favorite or two missing will be hard-pressed to deny that this is a solid introduction and a great listen. *—Stephen Thomas Erlewine*

Numbers / Nov. 1975 / A&M ✦✦

Izitso / May 1977 / A&M ✦✦✦

Back to Earth / Dec. 1978 / A&M ✦✦✦

Early Tapes / Jun. 30, 1998 / Spectrum ✦✦✦

• **Very Best of Cat Stevens** / Mar. 28, 2000 / A&M ✦✦✦✦✦
It is impossible to compile a single-disc greatest-hits compilation for Cat Stevens that will come close to satisfying all of his admirers. *The Very Best of Cat Stevens* is the fifth major attempt to do so and, like its predecessors, it is challenged by its subject's success. *Remember Cat Stevens—The Ultimate Collection* is the longest of the five (24 tracks) and may be the most comprehensive. But *The Very Best of Cat Stevens,* released just a year later, has several advantages that make it more appealing. To begin with, it is the only compilation to sequence chronologically songs from every one of Stevens' albums, including the experimental *Foreigner.* It also contains the delightful folk creed "The Wind," which was a glaring omission from the so-called *Ultimate Collection.* Most significantly, it contains the previously unreleased "I've Got a Thing About Seeing My Grandson Grow Old." Stevens recorded a demo of the song during the *Mona Bone Jakon* sessions in 1970, but it never saw the light of day until it was remixed for this collection. Perhaps this was because it was considered too eccentric for public consumption, straddling the line between the hook-rich pop of Stevens' '60s records and the groundbreaking folk-rock of his '70s efforts. If so, the public was vastly underestimated. The song is a buried treasure that fits in perfectly in the company of Stevens' best work. *—Evan Cater*

Al Stewart

b. Sep. 5, 1945, Glasgow, Scotland
Vocals, Keyboards, Trumpet, Guitar / British Folk-Rock, Album Rock, Pop/Rock, Folk-Rock, Soft Rock, Prog-Rock/Art Rock, Singer/Songwriter
Glasgow native Al Stewart began his career playing guitar in Tony Blackburn's band the Sabres, and moved from there to the London folk club scene. After an unsuccessful single on Decca, "The Elf" (which featured Jimmy Page on guitar), Stewart signed with CBS and released a series of albums largely consisting of introspective, confessional love songs beginning in 1967. *Love Chronicles* was the only one to be released in the U.S., and the autobiographical title track, which detailed Stewart's romantic involvements, attracted a bit of attention for the singer's use of the word "fucking" in a song with supposed artistic credibility. On 1973's *Past, Present and Future,* Stewart switched gears, exploring his fascination with historical tales, and was rewarded with his first U.S. chart album. *Modern Times* was even more successful, and *Year of the Cat* was an unqualified hit, selling over a million copies and spawning the Top Ten title single. *Time Passages* duplicated both feats, but Stewart's creativity dried up soon afterwards, and difficulties over his contract and change of labels prevented him from releasing any new material until 1984. *Russians and Americans* was highly political, but sales were disappointing. Even so, Stewart has recorded and toured sporadically in the late '80s and '90s while devoting time to his hobby of wine collecting. *—Steve Huey*

Orange / 1972 / BGO ✦✦✦✦

Past, Present & Future / 1974 / Rhino ✦✦✦
Originally reissued on CD in the late 1980s by Arista, Stewart's breakthrough U.S. album was picked up by Rhino in 1992 in newly remastered form. It features superior sound and extensive new notes by Stephen K. Peeples (writer-producer of *The Lost Lennon Tapes*) with contributions by Stewart himself, including a full account of the sessions and the mixing of the album; Stewart even admits to a few mistakes on his own part. Every CD should get this treatment. *—Bruce Eder*

Modern Times / 1975 / Rhino ✦✦✦✦✦

Year of the Cat / 1976 / Arista ✦✦✦✦✦
Stewart's calm delivery gives his songs a reserved, tasteful sense of understatement, especially on the title track, one of those "mysterious woman" songs, which captivated listeners and turned the album into a million-seller. *—William Ruhlmann*

Time Passages / 1978 / Arista ✦✦✦✦✦
A return to Stewart's historical themes lyrically, though it's still the overall smoothness of his music that connected with another million listeners. *—William Ruhlmann*

24 Carrots / 1980 / Razor & Tie ✦✦✦

Live Indian Summer / 1981 / Arista ✦✦

Russians & Americans / 1984 / Mesa ✦✦

• **The Best of Al Stewart** / 1986 / Arista ✦✦✦✦✦
Eleven songs from Stewart's albums *Past, Present & Future* (1974) through *Live Indian Summer* (1981), remastered in 1992, which gives it more than decent sound. "Roads to Moscow" is drawn from *Past, Present & Future* (the inlay card erroneously lists *Live Indian Summer*), and "Year of the Cat" is the hit studio version, but the producers have chosen live versions of "Nostradamus" (which emphasizes its *Tommy*-like central riff) and "On the Border," rather than their superior originals, probably to retain the value of the original albums. Includes full lyrics (but no instrumental credits) and notes by David Dasch, which may explain too much, removing the mystery from some of the material. *—Bruce Eder*

To Whom It May Concern, 1966-1970 / 1993 / EMI ✦✦✦

Rod Stewart

b. Jan. 10, 1945, London, England
Vocals / Album Rock, Blue-Eyed Soul, Boogie Rock, British Blues, Arena Rock, Pop/Rock, Folk-Rock, Soft Rock, Adult Contemporary, Hard Rock, Singer/Songwriter, Rock & Roll
Despite shifting critical and commercial fortunes, Rod Stewart is one of the greatest interpretative vocalists in rock & roll; when he's on, he's a first-rate songwriter, too. His early '70s recordings remain his strongest, yet he turned into a more than competent mainstream pop/rock star with music that wasn't as distinguished, yet was appealingly professional pop/rock.

Stewart first came to prominence when he joined the Jeff Beck Group at the end of 1966. The group fell apart after two albums, *Truth* and *Beck-Ola,* with Rod and Ron Wood joining the Small Faces, now called the Faces. A boisterous, boozy Stonesy rock & roll band, the Faces couldn't have been more different from Stewart's solo recordings; these albums meshed with his folk, R&B and rock influences, resulting in a distinctive, stripped-down acoustic-based rock & roll. At the beginning of 1971, the Faces released their second album, *Long Player,* yet it was Stewart's third solo album, *Every Picture Tells a Story,* that made him a household name thanks to the number one single, "Maggie May." Stewart's solo success created tension within the band which peaked when 1972's *Never a Dull Moment* was his second solo smash. Following 1973's *Ooh La La* he left the Faces for a solo career. Throughout the late '70s, his celebrity and popularity increased, while his critical respect declined. Stewart's popularity plateaued in the early '80s, then it hit a slump. He had only one gold album and only scored three Top Ten hits between 1982 and 1988. Stewart rebounded with 1988's *Out of Order,* then "Downtown Train," taken from the 1989 four-disc retrospective box set *Storyteller,* became his biggest hit in 10 years. Stewart reunited with Ron Wood to record an *MTV Unplugged* concert and album in 1993. It was his last unqualified hit of the decade, as his next three records failed to capture a sizable audience. He left his longtime home of Warner for Atlantic in 2000, releasing *Human* the following year. *—Stephen Thomas Erlewine*

The Rod Stewart Album / 1969 / Mercury ✦✦✦✦✦
On his debut album (titled *An Old Raincoat Won't Ever Let You Down* in Britain, and *The Rod Stewart Album* in America, presumably because its original title was "too English" or cryptic for U.S. audiences), Rod Stewart essays a startlingly original blend of folk, blues and rock & roll. The opening cover of the Stones' "Street Fighting Man" encapsulates his approach. Turning the driving acoustic guitars of the original inside out, the song works a laid-back, acoustic groove, bringing a whole new meaning to the song before escalating into a full-on rock & roll attack—without any distorted guitars, just bashing acoustics and thundering drums. Through this approach, Stewart establishes that rock can sound as rich and timeless as folk, and that folk can be as vigorous as rock. And he does this not only as an interpreter, breathing new life into Ewan MacColl's "Dirty Old Town" and defining Mike D'Abo's "Handbags & Gladrags," but also as a songwriter, writing songs as remarkable as "Man of Constant Sorrow," "An Old Raincoat Won't Ever Let You Down" and "Cindy's Lament." The music and the songs are so vivid and rich with detail that they reflect a whole way of life, and while Stewart would later flesh out this blueprint, it remains a stunningly original vision. *—Stephen Thomas Erlewine*

☆ **Gasoline Alley** / 1970 / Mercury ✦✦✦✦✦
Gasoline Alley follows the same formula of Rod Stewart's first album, intercutting contemporary covers, with slightly older rock & roll and folk classics and originals written in the same vein. The difference is in execution. Stewart sounds more confident, claiming Elton John's "Country Comfort," the Small Faces' "My Way of Giving" and the Rolling Stones' version of "It's All Over Now" with a ragged, laddish charm. Like its predecessor, nearly all of *Gasoline Alley* is played on acoustic instruments—Stewart treats rock & roll songs like folk song, reinterpreting them in individual, unpredictable ways. For instance, "It's All Over Now" becomes a shambling, loose-limbed ramble instead of a tight R&B/blues groove, and "Cut Across Shorty" is based around a howling, mid-eastern violin instead of a rockabilly riff. Of course, being a rocker at heart, Stewart doesn't let these songs become limp acoustic numbers—these rock harder than any fuzz-guitar workout. The drums crash and bang, the acoustic guitars are pounded with a vengance—it's a wild, careening sound that is positively joyous with its abandon. And on the slow songs, Stewart is nuanced and affecting—his interpretation of Bob Dylan's "Only A Hobo" is one of the finest Dylan covers, while the original title track is a vivid, loving tribute to his adolescence. And that spirit is carried throughout *Gasoline Alley.* It's an album that celebrates tradition while moving it into the present and never once does it disown the past. *—Stephen Thomas Erlewine*

★ **Every Picture Tells a Story** / 1971 / Mercury ✦✦✦✦✦
Without greatly altering his approach, Rod Stewart perfected his blend of hard rock, folk and blues on his masterpiece, *Every Picture Tells a Story.* Marginally a harder-rocking album than *Gasoline Alley*—the Faces blister on the Temptations cover "(I Know I'm) Losing You," and the acoustic title track goes into hyperdrive with Mick Waller's primitive drumming—the great triumph of *Every Picture Tells A Story* lies in its content. Every song on the album, whether it's a cover or original, is a gem, combining to form a romantic, earthy portrait of a young man joyously celebrating his young life. Of course, "Maggie May"—the ornate, ringing ode about a seduction from an older woman—is the centerpiece, but each song, whether it's the devilishly witty title track or the unbearably poignant "Mandolin Wind," has the same appeal. And the covers, including definitive readings of Dylan's "Tomorrow Is Such a Long Time" and Tim Hardin's "Reason to Believe," as well as a rollicking "That's All Right," are equally terrific, bringing new dimension to the songs. It's a beautiful album, one that has the timeless qualities of the best folk, yet one that rocks harder than most pop music—few rock albums are quite this powerful or this rich. *—Stephen Thomas Erlewine*

☆ **Never a Dull Moment** / 1972 / Mercury ✦✦✦✦✦
Essentially a harder-rocking reprise of *Every Picture Tells a Story, Never a Dull Moment* never quite reaches the heights of its predecessor, but it's a wonderful, multi-faceted record in its own right. Opening with the touching, autobiographical rocker "True Blue," awhich finds Rod trying to come to grips with his newfound stardom but concluding that he'd "rather be back home," the record is the last of Stewart's series of epic fusions of hard rock and folk. It's possible to hear Stewart go for superstardom with the hard-rocking kick and fat electric guitars of the album, but the songs still cut to the core. "You Wear It Well" is a "Maggie May" rewrite on the surface, but it develops into a touching song about being emotionally inarticulate. Similarly, "Lost Paraguayos" is funny, driving folk-rock, and it's hard not to be swept away when the Stonesy hard rocker "Italian Girls" soars into a mandolin-driven coda. The covers—whether a soulful reading of Jimi Hendrix's "Angel," an empathetic version of Dylan's "Mama You Been on My Mind" or a stunning interpretation of Etta James' "I'd Rather Go Blind"—are equally effective, making *Never a Dull Moment* a masterful record. He never got quite this good ever again. *—Stephen Thomas Erlewine*

Smiler / 1974 / Mercury ✦✦

Atlantic Crossing / 1975 / Warner Brothers ✦✦✦✦✦
Atlantic Crossing wasn't simply the moment when Rod Stewart left Britain for the greener pasture of America, it was the moment when he accepted his role as a full-fledged, jet-setting superstar. Stewart abandoned the formula of his first five solo records, as well as most of his folk-rock and hard rock undercurrents, trading them for a professionally-polished, rock and soul-inflected pop, courtesy of Muscle Shoals' musicians and producer Tom Dowd. The glossy production doesn't obscure or trivialize Stewart's talents—coming after the tired *Smiler,* the slickness actually accentuated his strength as an interpretive singer. "The fast half" suffers from a couple of weak tracks, but "Three Time Loser" and "Stone Cold Sober" catch fire, and "the slow half" is generally excellent, but Stewart's heart-wrenching rendition of Danny Whitten's "I Don't Want to Talk About It" ranks as one of his finest performances. *—Stephen Thomas Erlewine*

A Night on the Town / 1976 / Warner Brothers ✦✦✦✦✦
After bouncing back to life with *Atlantic Crossing,* Rod Stewart crafted his most self-consciously ambitious record with *A Night on the Town.* The centerpiece of the album, "The Killing of Georgie (Part I and II)," awas a long, winding Dylan-esque tale of the murder of one of Stewart's gay friends and was one of his better songs of the mid-'70s. Even if "The Killing of Georgie" was the conscious artistic focal point of *A Night on the Town,* the true masterpiece of the album was an eloquent rendition of Cat Stevens' "The First Cut Is the Deepest." Apart from the flawed political platitudes of "Trade Winds," the rest of the album was filled with competent, professional pop/rock, highlighted by the number one hit "Tonight's the Night (Gonna Be Alright)," a ballad where the gallant Rod relieves a teenager of her virginity. And, again, the "Slow Half" was more convincing than the frequently perfunctory "Fast Half." *—Stephen Thomas Erlewine*

Foot Loose & Fancy Free / 1977 / Warner Brothers ✦✦✦

Blondes Have More Fun / 1978 / Warner Brothers ✦✦✦
In its simplest terms, *Blondes Have More Fun* is Rod Stewart's disco album, filled with pulsating rhythms and slick, synthesized textures. It's also his trashiest, most disposable album, filled with cheap come-ons and bad double entendres. Of course, that makes *Blondes Have More Fun* one of his most enjoyable records, even if all the pleasures are guilty. With its swirling strings and nagging chorus, "Da Ya Think I'm Sexy?" was the reason the record hit number one and, two decades later, the song stands as one of the best rock-disco fusions. The rest of the record isn't as engaging, but he throws out a handful of winning tracks in the same mould, including "Ain't Love a Bitch," "Attractive Female Wanted," and the title track. *—Stephen Thomas Erlewine*

Foolish Behaviour / 1980 / Warner Brothers ✦✦

Tonight I'm Yours / 1981 / Warner Brothers ✦✦✦✦
Though it lacks a truly great selection of songs, *Tonight I'm Yours* is a fine latter-day effort from Rod Stewart, and one of the last records that makes Rod sound like he's hip. Sporting a shiny new wave production, *Tonight I'm Yours* has a sleek, professional sound that can make even mindless rave-ups like "Tora, Tora, Tora (Out With the Boys)" a guilty pleasure. But the key to the album lays in songs like "Tonight I'm Yours" and the haunting "Young Turks," where Rod sounds totally at ease with a synth-pop beat. They are some of the best examples of mainstream rock co-opting the nervy, quirky appeal of new wave, and they make *Tonight I'm Yours* an enjoyable, if lightweight, listen. *—Stephen Thomas Erlewine*

Body Wishes / 1983 / Warner Brothers ✦✦

Camouflage / 1984 / Warner Brothers ✦✦

Rod Stewart / 1986 / Warner Brothers ✦

Out of Order / 1988 / Warner Brothers ✦✦✦

Storyteller: The Complete Anthology / Oct. 1989 / Warner Brothers ✦✦✦✦✦
Storyteller: The Complete Anthology is a flawed but effective four-disc box set covering Rod Stewart's entire career. Although most of Stewart's biggest hits and best-known songs are on *Storyteller,* the collection is poorly paced, containing too much heistant early material and not enough Jeff Beck Group or Faces selections. Nevertheless, the box traces his evolution from a working-class singer to Rod the Mod to superstar, featuring most of his essential songs—including whole sides of *Every Picture Tells A Story* and *Never A Dull Moment*—along the way. For casual fans looking for an in-depth overview, it's an essential purchase, but more serious fans should stick with individual albums, especially his classic early '70s albums. *—Stephen Thomas Erlewine*

Downtown Train (Selections from the Storyteller Anthology) / Mar. 6, 1990 / Warner Brothers ✦✦✦

Vagabond Heart / Mar. 26, 1991 / Warner Brothers ✦✦✦

The Mercury Anthology / Sep. 22, 1992 / Mercury ✦✦✦✦✦
A two-disc anthology of Rod Stewart's early Mercury recordings, which, in conjunction with the albums he recorded with the Faces, are inarguably his finest (nothing from the Faces records is included). Most of the highlights of his terrific first four albums are here—"Maggie May," "You Wear It Well," "Handbags and Gladrags," "Gasoline Alley"—as well as selections from the lukewarm *Smiler,* a live album recorded with the Faces, and a couple of rare B-sides. *—Stephen Thomas Erlewine*

Unplugged . . . And Seated / May 25, 1993 / Warner Brothers ✦✦✦

Spanner in the Works / Jun. 6, 1995 / Warner Brothers ✦✦✦

If We Fall in Love Tonight / Nov. 12, 1996 / Warner Brothers ✦✦✦

When We Were the New Boys / Jun. 2, 1998 / Warner Brothers ✦✦✦

1964-1969 / Jun. 6, 2000 / Pilot ✦✦✦

Stiff Little Fingers

f. 1977, Belfast, Northern Ireland, **db.** 1982
Group / British Punk, Punk
A taut, explosive Belfast-based punk band, Stiff Little Fingers (named after a Vibrators song) had the dubious distinction of being referred to as "The Irish Clash." What must have seemed like a compliment at the time did little to help their career, only because it made comparisons between the two bands inevitable. Granted, there were many similarities: both bands debuted playing revved-up late-'70s punk rock, both were politically inclined, featured pissed-off lead singers, a love for reggae, and a near-palpable sense of isolation and desperation. But as we all know, the Clash offered complexity, panache, and a consistently breathtaking body of work. Stiff Little Fingers, on the other hand, were simply a very good punk rock band. *—John Dougan*

• **Inflammable Materials** / 1979 / Restless ✦✦✦✦✦
With "Alternative Ulster" and "Suspect Device" leading the way, this is a compelling, raging record that derives most of its style from The Sex Pistols and simply cranks up the personal political issues a notch or two. There is a so-so version of Bob Marley's "Johnny Was" (call it the obligatory reggae cover), but that doesn't hamper the enjoyment, nor does it detract from the record's overwhelming power. Issued on CD by Restless Retro in 1990. *—John Dougan*

Hanx / 1980 / Restless ✦✦✦

Nobody's Hero / Jan. 1980 / Restless ✦✦✦✦✦
It's easy to see why their Rough Trade debut remains so highly rated, but for the discerning fan of second-generation punk, *Nobody's Heroes* is every bit as special. For a start, new drummer Jim Reilly was an improvement on Brian Faloon (who gets a heartwarming tribute on "Wait and See"). Secondly, Jake Burns' songwriting collaborations with journalist Gordon Ogilvie are really beginning to pay off. The cornerstones of the LP are "Gotta Gettaway," "At the Edge" and "Tin Soldiers"—three songs which, in different ways, brilliantly articulate the frustrated ambitions of young men in search of expression and identity, trapped in nowhere jobs/situations. Though "Suspect Device" and "Alternative Ulster" had long since ensured they would always be tagged with the label political punk, in truth SLF were always more interested in their immediate environment, and finding a way out of it. A couple of plausible stabs at reggae are more than an interesting aside. *—Alex Ogg*

Go for It / May 1981 / Cargo ✦✦✦✦

All the Best / 1983 / One Way ✦✦✦✦✦
The best anthology of SLF available. A 30-track chronological overview that's as articulate an argument for SLF's greatness as anything else they released. A perfect way to hear their development from the early punk days to their more "mature" punk-pop period just prior to their breakup: Jake Burns goes from shouter to singer, hooks and riffs replace simple walls of distorted guitars, the reggae influence becomes stronger and is played with greater dexterity; all and all, you simply can't go wrong here. *—John Dougan*

Stephen Stills

b. Jan. 3, 1945, Dallas, TX
Vocals, Keyboards, Guitar, Bass / Pop/Rock, Folk-Rock, Soft Rock, Singer/Songwriter
Famed for his work in Buffalo Springfield and Crosby, Stills & Nash, two of pop music's most successful and enduring groups, Stephen Stills was born in Dallas, Texas on January 3, 1945. He eventually dropped out of college, moving to New York and signing on as a guitar player with the Au Go Go Singers. After a tour of Canada, Stills left the Au Go Go's in 1965 for Los Angeles, where he became enmeshed in the city's burgeoning folk-rock community. In the spring of 1966 Stills joined the Herd, later dubbed the Buffalo Springfield. A year later, the group issued their eponymous debut. Internal problems, ego clashes and drugs were already tearing the band apart, however, and by the release of 1968's *Last Time Around,* the Springfield had already dissolved.

Stills quickly resurfaced with 1968's *Super Session.* A jam session with David Crosby and Graham Nash led to the formation of the vocal harmony supergroup Crosby, Stills & Nash; released in 1969, their self-titled debut was hugely successful. Later that year, Neil Young joined the loose-knit group, and in 1970, as Crosby, Stills, Nash & Young, they issued *Deja Vu,* another major hit.

In late 1970 Stills released his self-titled solo debut. The album was a smash, as was his 1971 follow-up *Stephen Stills 2.* In 1972, Stills began performing with a new backing unit, Manassas; both their debut and 1973's *Down the Road* continued Stills' long string of chart successes.

In 1977, Stills reunited with Crosby and Nash for *CSN,* which sold over four million copies; the band would reunite again several times in the early '80s to tour and produce albums. Stills again went solo for 1984's *Right by You.* In 1985, Crosby was sent to prison on drug possession charges, and Stills spent much of the late 1980s out of the public eye. In 1988 the reconstituted Crosby, Stills, Nash & Young recorded *American Dream,* followed in 1990 by the CSN release *Live It Up.* In 1991, Stills issued the solo LP *Stills Alone,* while CSN's *After the Storm* appeared in 1994. *—Jason Ankeny*

• **Stephen Stills** / 1970 / Atlantic ✦✦✦✦✦

Stephen Stills 2 / 1971 / Atlantic ✦✦✦
Flushed with the success of his first solo effort and the continuing adulation from his role in the supergroup CSNY, Stephen Stills must have felt like he could do no wrong, and in many instances, his second solo disc proves him right. The superb "Marianne" and "Change Partners" more than satisfy the listener, while the dark and brooding "Know You Got to Run" and the prophetic "Fishes and Scorpions" are prime examples of his power as a singer and a songwriter. But when he misses the mark, as on "Ecology Song," he misses it by a mile and then some. Besides that cut, "Bluebird Revisited" is pure self-indulgence that someone of his craft and technique should have known better than to include here—or anywhere. But with compact disc players, one can omit anything offending and concentrate on what's good about *2.*

Cut the disc in half, and you have a very enjoyable listening experience. As for the rest, well, let's just say you've been warned. *—James Chrispell*

Down the Road / 1973 / Atlantic ✦✦✦

Stills / 1975 / Columbia ✦✦

Illegal Stills / 1976 / Columbia ✦✦

Stills Alone / Sep. 11, 1991 / Vision ✦✦✦

Sting (Gordon Sumner)

b. Wallsend, England

Vocals, Bass / College Rock, Album Rock, Adult Alternative Pop/Rock, Pop/Rock, Adult Contemporary

After disbanding the Police at the peak of their popularity in 1984, Sting quickly established himself as a viable solo artist, one obsessed with expanding the boundaries of pop music. Sting incorporated heavy elements of jazz, classical and worldbeat into his music, writing lyrics that were literate and self-consciously meaningful, and he was never afraid to emphasize this fact in the press. For such unabashed ambition, he was equally loved and reviled, with supporters believing that he was at the forefront of literate, intelligent rock and his critics finding his entire body of work pompous. Either way, Sting remained one of pop's biggest superstars for the first ten years of his solo career, before his record sales began to slip. Even before the Police were officially disbanded, Sting began recording his solo debut, 1985's *The Dream of the Blue Turtles*, with jazz musicians Branford Marsalis, Kenny Kirkland and Omar Hakim. The album became a hit, prompting an even more ambitious and successful second album, *Nothing Like the Sun*, which was dedicated to his recently deceased mother. Although 1991's *The Soul Cages* peaked at number two and spawned the Top Ten hit "All This Time," the record was less successful than its predecessor. Two years later, he delivered another hit, *Ten Summoner's Tales*, that showed his audience had shifted from new wave/college rock fans to adult contemporary. Though 1996's *Mercury Falling* stalled at platinum sales and failed to generate a hit single, Sting remained a popular concert attraction, confirming his immense popularity. *—Stephen Thomas Erlewine*

The Dream of the Blue Turtles / 1985 / A&M ✦✦✦✦✦

Sting's early jazz experience was very evident on his solo debut album. Kenny Kirkland (piano), Omar Hakim (drums), Darryl Jones (bass), and Branford Marsalis (sax) contributed greatly to the jazz "feel" of the songs. This captures some of the energy and exuberance of the early Police, like *Regatta de Blanc*, but also maintains some of the somber, serious tone of *Synchronicity*. Sting's first album is his most impressive, boasting such songs as "Love Is the Seventh Wave," "Fortress Around Your Heart," "Children's Crusade," and "Moon over Bourbon Street." *—Iotis Erlewine*

Bring on the Night / 1986 / A&M ✦✦✦

Nothing Like the Sun / 1987 / A&M ✦✦✦✦✦

This album is more somber than *Dream of the Blue Turtles* and light on the jazz influences, focusing more on Brazilian and Hispanic rhythms. Not as lively and concise as *Dream* due to the heavy, political lyrics (on such songs as "They Dance Alone" and "Fragile"), this is a good album, nevertheless. Along with Sting's own songs, the album includes a cover of Hendrix's "Little Wing." This album includes guests Mark Knopfler, Eric Clapton, the Gil Evans Band, former Police bandmember Andy Summers (who plays on "Lazarus Heart"), and, once again, Branford Marsalis featured on sax. *—Iotis Erlewine*

The Soul Cages / Jan. 17, 1991 / A&M ✦✦✦✦

This long-awaited album followed the death of Sting's father, which may explain the melancholy, pained tone of these songs. The focus here is very much on death and dying, making the album a bit of a downer and hard to listen to in a single sitting. Although the material may not be as good overall as Sting's previous work, the song "All This Time" is definitely one of his best. *—Iotis Erlewine*

● **Ten Summoner's Tales** / Mar. 9, 1993 / A&M ✦✦✦✦✦

Ten Summoner's Tales is the most song-oriented, lighthearted collection Sting has delivered since his solo debut. Sting's songs remain densely literate, although the melodies aren't; they are devoid of the jazz pretensions of *Nothing Like the Sun* and the oppressive seriousness of *The Soul Cages*. When he doesn't get carried away by his own cleverness, Sting can deliver the goods with some terrific pop songs ("If I Ever Lose My Faith in You," "It's Probably Me," "Epilogue [Nothin' 'Bout Me]," and "Seven Days"). Those songs help make *Ten Summoner's Tales* one of his strongest solo releases. *—Stephen Thomas Erlewine*

Fields of Gold: The Best of Sting 1984-1994 / Nov. 8, 1994 / A&M ✦✦✦

Early in his solo career, Sting defined himself as a man of taste, choosing to work with jazz musicians instead of rockers. Inevitably, this meant he walked the thin line between sophisticated pop and adult contemporary, but he did it with grace from 1985's *Dream of the Blue Turtles* to 1993's *Ten Summoner's Tales*. Unfortunately, *Fields of Gold: The Best of Sting* doesn't illustrate what a deft trick he pulled off with that quartet of albums. Naturally, *Fields of Gold* concentrates on his hit singles, just like any other greatest hits collection, but Sting's material sounds surprisingly tame in this context. Sure, there is a number of great songs here—enough to state his case as a fine songwriter or to satisfy his casual fans. Still, these songs are safe choices and all share a similar tranquil quality, which means the collection itself becomes a little monotonous. Nevertheless, *Fields of Gold* performs the necessary service of rounding up all of the big hits—"If You Love Somebody, Set Them Free"; "All This Time"; "Fortress Around Your Heart"; "They Dance Alone"; "If Ever Lose My Faith in You"; "Fragile"; and an alternate version of "We'll Be Together"—and offering them on one disc, which is reason enough to make it worthwhile, even with its flaws. *—Stephen Thomas Erlewine*

Mercury Falling / Mar. 12, 1996 / A&M ✦✦✦

Brand New Day / Sep. 28, 1999 / A&M ✦✦✦

Stone Poneys

f. 1964, Los Angeles, CA, **db.** 1968

Group / Folk-Rock, Pop

Before becoming a solo act, Linda Ronstadt was the lead singer of the Stone Poneys, an L.A.-based trio with an acoustic, folkish sound and strong original material. The band's focal point and greatest asset was Ronstadt's clear, powerful vocals. Originally recording in a coffeehouse folk style not far removed from Peter, Paul & Mary, the group rocked up their sound slightly and scored a Top 20 hit with "Different Drum," written by Mike Nesmith of the Monkees, in 1967. *—Richie Unterberger*

● **Stone Poneys Featuring Linda Ronstadt** / 1967 / Capitol ✦✦✦✦

It doesn't have "Different Drum," but the first Stone Poneys album is their folkiest and best, dominated by close harmonies and strong original material by the group's guitarists, Bob Kimmel and Ken Edwards. *—Richie Unterberger*

Evergreen, Vol. 2 / 1967 / Capitol ✦✦✦

Evergreen, Vol. 2 wasn't as strong as their debut album, but it did contain their only hit, "Different Drum," as well as several other pleasant songs in a similar vein. *—Stephen Thomas Erlewine*

Stone Poneys & Friends, Vol. 3 / 1968 / Capitol ✦✦✦

The Stone Poneys broke up during the recording of their final album, leaving Ronstadt to finish the work with various sessionmen (hence the billing "Stone Poneys & Friends"). It's a solid effort, though, of decent if muted Californian folk-rock, with a laid-back (but not offensively so), carefully produced feel. Certainly the material is varied, with selections from the Stone Poneys, Mike Nesmith, and Laura Nyro, and occasional intimations of the country-rock direction that Ronstadt would frequently pursue during the '70s. The inclusion of three Tim Buckley songs serves as evidence that Ronstadt was hipper than some of her detractors have made her out to be. *—Richie Unterberger*

The Stone Roses

f. 1985, Manchester, England, **db.** Oct. 1996

Group / College Rock, Madchester, Alternative Dance, Britpop, Alternative Pop/Rock

Meshing '60s-styled guitar-pop with an understated '80s dance beat, the Stone Roses defined the British guitar-pop scene of the late '80s and early '90s. After their eponymous 1989 debut album became an English sensation, countless other groups in the same vein became popular. However, the band was never able to capitalize on the promise of their first album, waiting five years before they released their second record and slowly disintegrating in the year and half after its release. The Stone Roses emerged from the remains of a band formed by schoolmates John Squire (guitar) and Ian Brown (vocals). In 1987, the Stone Roses' line-up finally coalesced around Squire and Brown, plus drummer Reni (b. Alan John Wren) and bassist Mani (b. Gary Mounfield). At the end of the year, the Stone Roses released the single "Sally Cinnamon," which pointed the way toward the band's hook-laden, ringing guitar-pop. In 1989, the Stone Roses released their eponymous debut album, which demonstrated not only a predilection for '60s guitar hooks, but also a contemporary acid-house rhythmic sensibility. *The Stone Roses* received rave reviews and a single, "She Bangs the Drums," became the group's first Top 40 hit. By the end of the year, they reached the Top Ten with "Fool's Gold."

Though the group returned in 1990 with the single "One Love," the Stone Roses became embroiled in a vicious legal battle with their label. Finally, in 1991 the band signed a multi-million deal with Geffen Records. For the next three years, they worked sporadically on their second album, *Second Coming*, which received mixed reviews and only spent a few weeks in the Top Ten. Forced to cancel a headlining spot at 1995's 25th Glastonbury Festival after John Squire broke his collarbone, the Stone Roses continued to sink in popularity and respect. In the spring of 1996, Squire announced that he was leaving to form a new, more active band and, by the end of the year, the group was finished. Squire's new band, Seahorses, released their debut album in 1997, while Brown released his solo debut in 1998. *—Stephen Thomas Erlewine*

★ **The Stone Roses** / Jul. 1989 / Silvertone ✦✦✦✦✦

Since the Stone Roses were the nominal leaders of Britain's "Madchester" scene—an indie rock phenomenon that fused guitar-pop with drug-fueled rave and dance culture—it's rather ironic that their eponymous debut only hints at dance music. What made the Stone Roses important was how they welcomed dance and pop together, treating it as if it were the same beast. Equally important was the Roses' cool, detached arrogance which was personified by Ian Brown's nonchalant vocals. Brown's effortless malevolence is brought to life with songs that equal both his sentiments and his voice—"I Wanna Be Adored," with its creeping bass line and waves of cool guitar hooks, doesn't demand adoration, it just *expects* it. Similarly, Brown can claim "I Am the Resurrection" and lay back, as if there were no room for debate. But the key to *The Stone Roses* is John Squire's layers of simple, exceedingly catchy hooks and how the rhythm section of Reni and Mani always imply dance rhythms without overtly going into the disco. On "She Bangs the Drums" and "Elephant Stone," the hooks wind into the rhythm inseparably—the '60s hooks and the rolling beats manage to convey the colorful, neo-psychedelic world of acid house. Squire's riffs are bright and catchy, recalling the British Invasion while suggesting the future with their phased, echoey effects. *The Stone Roses* was a two-fold revolution—it brought dance music to an audience that was previously obsessed with droning guitars, while it revived the concept of classic pop songwriting, and the repercussions of its achievement could be heard throughout the '90s, even if the Stone Roses could never achieve this level of achievement ever again. *—Stephen Thomas Erlewine*

Turns Into Stone / Oct. 27, 1992 / Silvertone ✦✦✦

Second Coming / Dec. 1994 / Geffen ✦✦✦

There's no denying that *Second Coming* is a bit of a letdown. None of the songs are quite as strong as the best on their debut, but there is plenty of good music on the band's much-delayed second record. The Stone Roses create a dense tapestry of interweaving guitars and pulsing bass grooves. Ian Brown growls a little more than before, but he isn't the center of the music; John Squire's endlessly colorful riffs are. It's clear that Squire has been listening to a bit of hard rock, particularly Led Zeppelin. While the songs occasionally take a back seat to the grooves, several tracks—"Ten Storey Love Song," "Begging You," "Tightrope," "How Do You Sleep," and "Love Spreads"—rank as true classics. It might not be the long-awaited masterpiece it was rumored to be, but *Second Coming* is a fine sophomore effort. *—Stephen Thomas Erlewine*

The Complete Stone Roses / Jun. 27, 1995 / Silvertone ♦♦♦♦♦
The title's a bit of a misnomer. *The Complete Stone Roses* concentrates on the band's first album, compiling the A- and B-sides of the group's hits from "Elephant Stone" to "One Love." In addition to the familiar material, the disc includes rare, early singles like "So Young" and "Sally Cinnamon" for the first time on compact disc, giving their classic material some context. The loud guitars of "So Young" are clearly the work of a hesitant band, while "Sally Cinnamon" is the first indication of John Squire's gift for ringing, melodic guitar hooks. However, their inclusion—as well as the appearance of the B-sides, which lack the consistent brilliance of "I Wanna Be Adored," "She Bangs the Drums," "Elephant Stone," "Waterfall," etc.—make *The Complete Stone Roses* a flawed introduction to the band. Nevertheless, there's a fair amount of classic pop here and the rarities are necessary for dedicated fans. *—Stephen Thomas Erlewine*

Garage Flower / Nov. 1996 / Silvertone ♦♦♦

Stone Temple Pilots

f. 1992
Group / Grunge, Alternative Pop/Rock, Hard Rock
Stone Temple Pilots were able to make alternative rock into stadium rock; naturally, they became the most critically despised band of their era. Accused by many critics of being nothing more than rip-off artists, pilfering from Pearl Jam, Soundgarden, and Alice in Chains, the band nevertheless became major stars in 1993. And the influences of those bands *are* apparent in their music, but Stone Temple Pilots do manage to change things around a bit. STP are more concerned with tight song structure and riffs than punk rage. Their closest antecedents are not the Sex Pistols or Hüsker Dü; instead the band resembles arena rock acts from the '70s—it's popular hard rock that sounds good on the radio and in concert. No matter what the critics might say, Stone Temple Pilots have undeniably catchy riffs and production; there's a reason why over three million people bought their debut album, *Core*, and why their second album, *Purple*, shot to number one when it was released. Following the success of *Purple* and its accompanying tour, the band took some time off, during which the group's lead singer, Scott Weiland, developed a heroin addiction. *—Stephen Thomas Erlewine*

Core / Sep. 29, 1992 / Atlantic ♦♦♦

● **Purple** / May 31, 1994 / Atlantic ♦♦♦♦
Stone Temple Pilots had hits with *Core*, but they got no respect. They suffered a barrage of savage criticism and it must have hurt, since their second effort seems a conscious effort to distinguish themselves as a band not indebted to grunge. That didn't get them anywhere, as they were attacked as viciously as before, but *Purple* is nevertheless a quantum leap over their debut, showcasing a band hitting their stride. They still aren't much for consistency, and there's more than their fair share of filler over this album's "12 Gracious Melodies." Still, this filler isn't cut-rate grunge, as it was on the debut; it has its own character, heavily melodic and slightly psychedelic. That's a fair assessment of the hits, as well, but there's a difference there—namely, expert song and studiocraft. Yes, they were considerably more mainstream than their peers, but time has proven that that's their primary charm, since they were unafraid to temper their grunge with big arena hooks and swirling melodies. It works particularly well on the tight, concise "Vasoline" and the acoustic-based "Pretty Penny," but it really shines on the record's two masterpieces, "Big Empty" and "Interstate Love Song." "Big Empty" is ominous and foreboding, yet remains anthemic, a perfect encapsulation of mainstream alienation that is surpassed only by "Interstate Love Song," a concise epic as alluring as the open highway. These two songs are so good (really, mainstream hard rock didn't get better than these two cuts) that the unevenness of the rest of the record is all the more frustrating, but the filler here is better than before—and those singles are proof positive that STP was the best straight-ahead rock singles outfit of their time. *—Stephen Thomas Erlewine*

Tiny Music . . . Songs from the Vatican Gift Shop / Mar. 26, 1996 / Atlantic ♦♦♦♦
Purple established that Stone Temple Pilots were not one-album wonders but *Tiny Music... Songs From the Vatican Gift Shop* illustrates that the band isn't content with resting on the laurels. Without abandoning their trademark hard rock, STP have added a new array of sounds that adds depth to their immediately accessible hooks. Dean DeLeo layers his guitar tracks to create distinctive, multi-textured sounds that make his riffs more powerful. Though there are hints of grunge scattered throughout the album, what makes *Tiny Music* impressive is how the band brings in elements of psychedelia, trancy shoegazing, jangle-pop, and other forms of melodic alternative guitar-pop. By accentuating their pop tendencies in both their riffs and melodies, they are able to slip in a number of creative arrangements which manage to expand their musical repertoire significantly. Although the lyrics are nearly as ambitious as the music, they simply don't have the same weight. But with a band like Stone Temple Pilots, the music is what matters and *Tiny Music* showcases the band at their most tuneful and creative. *—Stephen Thomas Erlewine*

No. 4 / Oct. 26, 1999 / Atlantic ♦♦♦♦

The Stooges

f. 1967, Ann Arbor, MI, **db.** 1973
Group / Detroit Rock, Album Rock, Proto-Punk, Glam Rock, Hard Rock
During the psychedelic haze of the late '60s, the grimy, noisy and relentlessly bleak rock & roll of the Stooges was conspicuously out of time. Like the Velvet Underground, the Stooges revealed the underside of sex, drugs and rock & roll, showing all of the grime beneath the myth. The Stooges, however, weren't nearly as cerebral as the Velvets. Taking their cue from the over-amplified pounding of British blues, the primal raunch of American garage rock, and the psychedelic rock (as well as the audience-baiting) of the Doors, the Stooges were raw, immediate and vulgar. Iggy Pop became notorious for performing smeared in blood or peanut butter, diving into the audience. Ron and Scott Asheton formed a ridiculously primitive rhythm section, pounding out chords with no finesse—in essence, the Stooges were the first rock & roll band completely stripped of the swinging beat that epitomized R&B and early rock & roll. During the late '60s and early '70s, the group was an underground sensation, yet the band was too weird, too dangerous to break into the mainstream. Following three albums, the Stooges disbanded, but the group's legacy grew over the next two decades, as legions of underground bands used their sludgy grind as a foundation for a variety of indie-rock styles, and as Iggy Pop became a pop cultural icon. *—Stephen Thomas Erlewine*

The Stooges / 1969 / Elektra ♦♦♦♦♦
While The Stooges had a few obvious points of influence—the swagger of the early Rolling Stones, the horny pound of the Troggs, the fuzztone sneer of a thousand teenage garage bands, and The Velvet Underground's experimental eagerness to leap into the void—they didn't really sound like anyone else around when their first album hit the streets in 1969. It's hard to say if Ron Asheton, Scott Asheton, Dave Alexander, and the man then known as Iggy Stooge were capable of making anything more sophisticated than this, but if they were, they weren't letting on, and the best moments of this record document the blithering inarticulate fury of the post-adolescent id. Ron Asheton's guitar runs (fortified with bracing use of fuzztone and wah-wah) are so brutal and concise they achieve a naive genius, while Scott Asheton's proto-Bo Diddley drums and Dave Alexander's solid bass stomp these tunes into submission with a force that inspires awe. And Iggy's vividly blank vocals fill the "so what?" shrug of a thousand teenagers with a wealth of palpable arrogance and wondrous confusion. One of the problems with being a trailblazing pioneer is making yourself understood to others, and while John Cale seemed sympathetic to what the band was doing, he didn't appear to quite get it, and as a result he made a physically powerful band sound a bit sluggish on tape. But "1969," "I Wanna Be Your Dog," "Real Cool Time," "No Fun," and other classic rippers are on board, and one listen reveals why they became clarion calls in the punk rock revolution. Part of the fun of *The Stooges* is, then as now, the band managed the difficult feat of sounding ahead of their time and entirely *out* of their time, all at once. *—Mark Deming*

☆ **Fun House** / 1970 / Elektra ♦♦♦♦♦
The Stooges' first album was produced by a classically-trained composer; their second was supervised by the former keyboard player with the Kingsmen, and if that didn't make all the difference, it at least indicates why *Fun House* was a step in the right direction. Producer Don Gallucci took the approach that the Stooges were a powerhouse live band, and their best bet was to recreate the band's live set with as little fuss as possible. As a result, the production on *Fun House* bears some resemblance to the Kingsmen's version of "Louie Louie"—the sound is smeary and bleeds all over the place, but it packs the low-tech wallop of a concert pumped through a big PA, bursting with energy and immediacy. The Stooges were also a much stronger band this time out; Ron Asheton's blazing minimalist guitar gained little in the way of technique since *The Stooges*, but his confidence had grown by a quantum leap as he summoned forth the sounds that would make him the hero of proto-punk guitarists everywhere, and the brutal pound of drummer Scott Asheton and bassist Dave Alexander had grown to Heavyweight Champion status. And *Fun House* is where Iggy Pop's mad genius first reached its full flower; what was a sneer on the band's debut had grown into the roar of a caged animal desperate for release, and his primal-scream rants were far more passionate and compelling than what he had served up before. *The Stooges* may have had more "hits," but *Fun House* has stronger songs, including the garage raver to end all garage ravers in "Loose," the primal scream of "1970," and the apocalyptic anarchy of "L.A. Blues." *Fun House* is the ideal document of the Stooges at their raw, sweaty, howling peak. *—Mark Deming*

★ **Raw Power** / 1973 / Columbia/Legacy ♦♦♦♦♦
In 1972, the Stooges were near the point of collapse when David Bowie's management team, MainMan, took a chance on the band at Bowie's behest. By this point, guitarist Ron Asheton and bassist Dave Alexander had been edged out of the picture, and James Williamson had signed on as Iggy's new guitar mangler; Asheton rejoined the band shortly before recording commenced on *Raw Power*, but was forced to play second fiddle to Williamson as bassist. By most accounts, tensions were high during the recording of *Raw Power*, and the album sounds like the work of a band on its last legs—though rather than grinding to a halt, Iggy and the Stooges appeared ready to explode like an ammunition dump. From a technical standpoint, Williamson was a more gifted guitar player than Asheton (not that that was ever the point), but his sheets of metallic fuzz were still more basic (and punishing) than what anyone was used to in 1973, while Ron Asheton played his bass like a weapon of revenge, and his brother Scott Asheton remained a powerhouse behind the drums. But the most remarkable change came from the singer; *Raw Power* revealed Iggy as a howling, smirking, lunatic genius. Whether quietly brooding ("Gimme Danger") or inviting the apocalypse ("Search and Destroy"), Iggy had never sounded quite so focused as he did here, and his lyrics displayed an intensity that was more than a bit disquieting. In many ways, almost all *Raw Power* has in common with the two Stooges albums that preceded it is its primal sound, but while the Stooges once sounded like the wildest (and weirdest) gang in town, *Raw Power* found them heavily armed and ready to destroy the world—that is, if they didn't destroy themselves first. *—Mark Deming*

Metallic K.O. / 1976 / Skydog ♦♦♦♦♦

1970: The Complete Fun House Sessions / 2000 / Rhino Handmade ♦♦♦♦

Stranglers

f. 1974
Group / British Punk, Post-Punk, Punk
As were their contemporaries the Vibrators, the Stranglers were faux-punks; grimy, slightly arty rockers that found the notoriety surrounding punk bands too irresistible to ignore. So armed with short haircuts and reticent about revealing their true ages, the Stranglers became stars of Brit punk's class of 1976-77, garnering headlines for their sexist posturing, drug use

and occasional arrests as well as their music. Their first two albums (*IV Rattus Norvegicus* and *No More Heroes*) featured plenty of taut, guitar-driven songs, rife with urban doom and gloom. After 1978's *Black and White* failed to generate much interest, A&M dropped them, though the Stranglers soldiered on. Prisoners of their own careerist impulses, the Stranglers turned to covering older rock classics in a desperate attempt to win American ears. Trying twice, first with the Kinks' "All Day and All of the Night" and then ? and the Mysterians "96 Tears," the Stranglers sounded as if flogging a dead horse was the best they could do. Gone also was their characteristic gritty and grimy sound replaced by a pop sheen that smelled of adult, new wave marketability (eventually Queen producer Roy Thomas Baker was brought in to help). The saga of the Stranglers is one of a band hanging around far too long. *—John Dougan*

Rattus Norvegicus / Apr. 1977 / A&M ✦✦✦
Like the Vibrators, the Stranglers were an older band which managed to gain visibility and success through association with Britain's punk movement. Musically, the group is much more polished than some of their rawer brethren such as the Adverts and Siouxsie and the Banshees. The Stranglers' early work is most properly described as stripped-down pop played with a hardcore sensibility; fairly lengthy songs with frequent solo breaks, prominent keyboard usage, and occasional employment of vocal harmony sets them apart from their peers. But snarling lead singing that puts forth macho/critical/distasteful lyrics predominates here, clearly showing the group's punk affinity. Most of the songs on this album fit the description of hardcore pop to a tee, but there are a few deviations from this model. "Princess of the Streets" is a slow-tempo selection with blueslike echoes. The ambitious "Down in the Sewer" crosses the concept of episodic numbers like the Who's "A Quick One" with early-'60s instrumentals. And the energetic "London Lady" is almost a true punk song—or at least as close as the band gets to one. While not the equal of their best album, *No More Heroes*, this release is solid and worthwhile, a rewarding listen. *—David Cleary*

No More Heroes / Oct. 1977 / A&M ✦✦✦✦✦
Rattus is hardly a punk rock classic but still is a pretty good chunk of art-punk. Hugh Cornwell's testosterone level is very high here, and the macho preening gets a bit much, but it's still an enjoyable bit of noise that holds up better than anyone would have guessed at the time. Still, it's odd to think of this as a part of the punk rock era—with the exception of the fast and sloppy production by Martin Rushent, and the short songs, there's not much that's overtly punk about it. *Heroes* on the other hand is faster, nastier, and better. At this point the Stranglers were on top of their game, and the ferocity and anger that suffuses these records would never be repeated. *—John Dougan*

Black & White / 1978 / A&M ✦✦✦

● **Greatest Hits 1977-1990** / 1990 / Epic ✦✦✦✦✦
Despite its rather cheeky title, this is a good place to sample the entire Stranglers output. From the squalor of the late-'70s material, to the smoothed out gloom pop of songs like "Skin Deep" and other mid- to late-'80s neo-Goth rock, this is a solid anthology that values substance over style and exhaustive track selection. Trust me, a well-edited Stranglers anthology is the only way to enjoy them, they recorded way too much dross to spend time searching out all of their plentiful, marginal records. *—John Dougan*

Stray Cats

f. 1979, **db.** 1994
Bass (Upright), Vocals, Guitar (Electric), Drums / Rockabilly Revival, New Wave, Rock & Roll
This U.S. rock trio consists of Brian Setzer (b.1960), standup bass slapper Lee Rocker (born Lee Drucher), and drummer Slim Jim Phantom (born James McDonnell). It was formed in 1979 in the midst of the punk/new wave scene, playing retro-rockabilly style. Emigrating to England shortly thereafter, they caught on quickly with a music scene that was always interested in the "next big thing," and their top-notch production by Dave Edmunds quickly moved them into the charts. Visual image and European success augered well for their return to the U.S. just in time to mine the early motherlode of MTV video-land. By the mid-'80s, after much success, the gimmick had worn off, and the band broke up by late 1984. They regrouped in the '90s after various solo projects had fizzled, with their style relatively unchanged, but again disbanded after 1994's *Choo Choo Hot Fish*. *—Cub Koda*

Built for Speed / Jun. 1982 / EMI America ✦✦✦✦✦

Rant N' Rave with the Stray Cats / 1983 / EMI America ✦✦✦✦✦

Rock Therapy / 1986 / EMI America ✦✦✦

Blast Off / 1989 / EMI America ✦✦

● **Greatest Hits [Expanded]** / Jan. 25, 2000 / Capitol ✦✦✦✦✦
One of the great unspoken things about the Stray Cats is that they just didn't have that many hits. In America, they had three Top Ten singles—"Rock This Town," "Stray Cat Strut," "(She's) Sexy and 17"—plus the ballad "I Won't Stand in Your Way," which just scraped the Top 40. The fact that the Stray Cats were so fondly remembered not only by kids of the early '80s, but by older and younger listeners alike, just shows how good those three hits are; they really held their own next to any '50s rockabilly classic. However, they're not all the Stray Cats had to offer, as the 2000 expanded version of *Greatest Hits* illustrates. True, apart from such U.K. hits as "Runaway Boys," they didn't really have original tunes that rivaled their three big hits, but they were a kick-ass rockabilly band, making their newly written genre items sound every bit as convincing as their fine cover of Gene Vincent's "Race With the Devil." The group was fortunate to choose a producer as savvy as Dave Edmunds, the roots-rock trailblazer who captured the Stray Cats' muscular, energetic sound with recordings that would have sounded fine in the '50s, yet managed to sound contemporary in the early '80s. Of course, that production trick wouldn't have amounted to much if that wasn't what the Cats were doing with their music anyway. These 14 songs—plus three bonus tracks—are as good as rockabilly revival has ever gotten. Not only that, these songs also offer a convincing argument that the Stray Cats really did hold their own with their idols. In other words, it's the definitive compilation. *—Stephen Thomas Erlewine*

The Style Council

f. 1983, **db.** 1990
Group / Sophisti-Pop, New Wave
Guitarist/vocalist Paul Weller broke up the Jam, the most popular British band of the early '80s, at the height of their success in 1982 because he was dissatisfied with their musical direction. Weller wanted to incorporate more elements of soul, R&B, and jazz into his songwriting, which is something he felt his punk-oriented bandmates were incapable of performing. In order to pursue this musical direction, he teamed up in 1983 with keyboardist Mick Talbot, a former member of the mod revival band the Merton Parkas. Together, Weller and Talbot became the Style Council—other musicians were added according to what kind of music the duo were performing. With the Style Council, the underlying intellectual pretensions that ran throughout Weller's music came to the forefront. Although the music was rooted in American R&B, it was performed slickly—complete with layers of synthesizers and drum machines—and filtered through European styles and attitudes. Weller's lyrics were typically earnest, yet his leftist political leanings became more pronounced. His scathing criticisms of racism, unemployment, Margaret Thatcher, and sexism sat uneasily beside his burgeoning obsession with high culture. As his pretensions increased, the number of hits the Style Council had decreased; by the end of the decade, the group was barely able to crack the British Top 40 and Weller had turned from a hero into a has-been. *—Stephen Thomas Erlewine*

Introducing the Style Council / 1983 / Polydor ✦✦✦✦✦

Cafe Bleu / 1984 / Polydor ✦✦✦✦✦
Style Council's first proper album *Cafe Bleu* was one of their better efforts, but it indicated the group's fatal flaw—a tendency to be too eclectic and overambitious. Amidst the lazy jazz instrumentals, many of them courtesy of Mick Talbot, Paul Weller inserted several solid soul-tinged pop songs, including "My Ever Changing Moods," "Headstart for Happiness," "You're the Best Thing," and "Here's One that Got Away." However, that doesn't excuse the rap experiment, "A Gospel." The album was later released with a slightly different running order as *My Ever Changing Moods* in the U.S.; the American edition included the U.K. hit "A Solid Bond in Your Heart." *—Stephen Thomas Erlewine*

Our Favourite Shop / 1985 / Polydor ✦✦✦✦✦
Our Favourite Shop, The Style Council's second proper album, was still quite eclectic, but it didn't seem as schizophrenically diverse as *Cafe Bleu.* Weller had been able to incorporate his soul and jazz experiments into his songwriting, writing the fine "Walls Come Tumbling Down," "Come to Milton Keys," "Boy Who Cried Wolf," and "Down in the Seine," which were some of his best songs for The Style Council. The occasional misguided experiment remained—the stiff funk of "The Internationalists" and the self-righteous "The Stand Up Comic's Instructions" were particularly embarrassing—but the record was more cohesive and stronger than the debut. In America, the album was released without "Our Favourite Shop" and retitled *Internationalists. —Stephen Thomas Erlewine*

Home & Abroad / 1986 / Polydor ✦✦

Cost of Loving / 1987 / Polydor ✦✦

Confessions of a Pop Group / 1988 / Polydor ✦

● **The Singular Adventures of The Style Council** / Jun. 1989 / Polydor ✦✦✦✦✦
The Style Council's albums were always weighed down by their far-reaching musical ambitions, which meant that their ideas were usually best heard on their singles. And while this period of Paul Weller's career has been criticized heavily, he wrote several excellent songs during the Style Council, most of which are featured on the fine compilation *The Singular Adventures of the Style Council.* Not all of the 16 songs are first-rate, as it begins to lose steam toward the end of the band's life, but "My Ever Changing Moods," "You're the Best Thing," "Long Hot Summer," "Shout to the Top!," "A Solid Bond in Your Heart," "Money Go Round," "Walls Come Tumbling Down," and "Speak Like a Child" are terrific, and make the collection worthwhile for fans of the Jam and Weller's solo career, as well as fans of New Romantic New Wave and jazzy sophisti-pop. *—Stephen Thomas Erlewine*

Here's Some That Got Away / Feb. 22, 1994 / Polydor ✦✦✦

The Style Council Collection / Mar. 1996 / Polydor ✦✦✦✦✦

The Complete Adventures of the Style Council / Sep. 29, 1998 / Polydor ✦✦✦✦
Given the blockbuster success of the Jam's exhaustive box set *Direction Reaction Creation,* perhaps it was inevitable that Polydor would give the Style Council a similar treatment, but the 1998 release of the five-disc box set, *The Complete Adventures of the Style Council* was still a bit of surprise—there never was much interest in their catalog following their 1990 disbandment. Fortunately, Polydor took a chance and assembled *The Complete Adventures,* a lavish box set containing all of the group's singles and albums, minus the live *Home and Abroad* but including the notorious unreleased 1989 record, *A Decade of Modernism,* which the label allegedly rejected because it found Weller turning toward house music. As it turns out, *A Decade of Modernism* wasn't that far afield from what the Style Council was exploring from their inception, as the chronological running order of the set makes clear. The sequencing is a blessed occurence, since it's easy to trace their development over the years. Instead of an aberration, the Style Council seems like a natural extension of the Jam's final record, *The Gift,* and every one of their subsequent records makes more sense than before. That doesn't mean the music is always compelling. No matter how interesting some of Weller's ideas were, they didn't always work, and he wrote way too many pompous, directionless songs to have *The Complete Adventures* rank with *Direction Reaction Creation.* (There are also too many Mick Talbot instrumentals, but that's another story.) For most listeners, including some serious Weller fans, the Style Council is best appreciated as a singles band, but for the dedicated, *The Complete Adventures* reveals that the Style Council, no matter how maddening they could be, were a group that continually reinvented themselves, occasionally making some remarkable music along the way. *—Stephen Thomas Erlewine*

In Concert / Dec. 28, 1999 / Polydor ✦✦✦

The Stylistics

f. 1968, Philadelphia, PA, **db.** 1980

Group / Smooth Soul, Quiet Storm, Philly Soul, Soul

After the Spinners and the O'Jays, the Stylistics were the leading Philly soul group produced by Thom Bell. During the early '70s, the band had 12 straight Top Ten hits, including "You Are Everything," "Betcha by Golly, Wow," "I'm Stone in Love with You," "Break Up to Make Up" and "You Make Me Feel Brand New." Of all their peers, the Stylistics were one of the smoothest and sweetest soul groups of their era. All of their hits were ballads, graced by the soaring falsetto of Russell Thompkins, Jr. and the lush, yet graceful productions of Thom Bell, which helped make the Stylistics one of the most successful soul groups of the first half of the '70s. After signing to Avco in 1971, the Stylistics began working with producer/songwriter Thom Bell. He crafted a series of hit singles that relied as much on the intricately arranged and lush production as they did on Thompkins' falsetto. Every single that Bell produced for the Stylistics was a Top Ten R&B hit, and several were also Top Ten pop hits. In 1974, the Stylistics replaced Thom Bell with Van McCoy, who helped move the group towards a softer, easy listening style. Though their American sales declined, they remained popular in Great Britain, where they scored four Top Five hits. The Stylistics continued performing into the '90s on oldies shows. *—Stephen Thomas Erlewine*

● **The Best of the Stylistics [Amherst]** / 1975 / Amherst ✦✦✦✦✦

Any of their collections are good, but this one features their biggest and best hits, including "I'm Stone in Love with You," "Rockin' Roll Baby," "Betcha by Golly Wow," and "You Make Me Feel Brand New." *—Cub Koda*

Styx

f. 1970, Chicago, IL

Group / Album Rock, Arena Rock, Pop/Rock, Prog-Rock/Art Rock, Hard Rock

Styx were one of the biggest album-rock bands of the late '70s, capable of producing monster hits with their stadium rock, power ballads, and concept albums. More than any other art-rock band, Styx was able to cross over into the pop charts, scoring hits with "Babe," "Lady," "Come Sail Away," "Too Much Time on My Hands," and "Don't Let It End." Never one for subtlety, their ballads featured sweeping, over-arranged guitars and keyboards while their rockers were long and detailed, with several different sections and gargantuan guitar solos. When MTV rolled around in the early '80s, the hits stopped coming; they broke up in 1984. Six years later, they reunited and released *Edge of the Century;* the record featured "Show Me the Way," which became popular as a Gulf War anthem. The band went on hiatus a couple of years after the album's release, but returned several more times in the late '90s; 1999 saw the release of a new studio album, *Brave New World. —Stephen Thomas Erlewine*

Styx / Sep. 1972 / One Way ✦✦

Styx II / Jul. 1973 / RCA ✦✦✦

The Serpent Is Rising / Feb. 1974 / RCA ✦✦

Man of Miracles / Nov. 1974 / RCA ✦✦✦

Equinox / Dec. 1975 / A&M ✦✦✦

Crystal Ball / Oct. 1976 / A&M ✦✦✦

Crystal Ball wasn't as successful as *Equinox,* but it was a better album, showcasing Styx's increased skill for crafting simple, catchy pop hooks out of their bombastic sound. *—Daevid Jehnzen*

The Grand Illusion / Jul. 1977 / A&M ✦✦✦✦

With *The Grand Illusion,* Styx catapulted to Top Ten and multi-platinum status, thanks to the hit single, "Come Sail Away." Although the group's sound was still based in art-rock, the best moments on the record occur when they fit majestic pomp into the constraints of a pop song like "Fooling Yourself (The Angry Young Man)" or "Come Sail Away." *—Stephen Thomas Erlewine*

Pieces of Eight / Sep. 1978 / A&M ✦✦✦✦

Pieces of Eight continued Styx's winning streak, selling over three million copies over the years. Styx was savvy enough to make their art-rock appear like arena-rock, as the "Blue Collar Man (Long Nights)" single indicates, as well as the hit "Renegade." *—Stephen Thomas Erlewine*

Cornerstone / Oct. 1979 / A&M ✦✦✦✦

"Babe" became Styx's first number one single and its accompanying album, *Cornerstone,* saw the band expanding their pop accessibility without dispensing the art-rock traditions that made them famous. *—Stephen Thomas Erlewine*

Paradise Theater / Jan. 1981 / A&M ✦✦✦✦

Paradise Theater was Styx's masterpiece, filled with conceptually ambitious songs as well as concise pop singles, like the driving hard rocker "Too Much Time on My Hands" and the power ballad "The Best of Times." It perfectly encapsulates both the band's progessive side and their catchy, hard rock leanings. *—Daevid Jehnzen*

Kilroy Was Here / Feb. 1983 / A&M ✦✦✦

An ambitious—and, to be frank, pretty silly—concept album about an Orwellian future controlled by a fascist dictator who has outlawed rock & roll and the rebellion led by an exiled rocker, *Kilroy Was Here* was a pretty odd way for the original lineup of Styx to end their recording career. Some of the album is quite listenable—the ballad "Don't Let It End" is powerful, while "Mr. Roboto" is an infectious pomp-rocker—but the album is hampered by a lack of memorable melodies. *—Stephen Thomas Erlewine*

Caught in the Act / Apr. 1984 / A&M ✦

Classics, Vol. 15 / 1987 / A&M ✦✦✦✦✦

Edge of the Century / Oct. 9, 1990 / A&M ✦✦

● **Greatest Hits** / Aug. 22, 1995 / A&M ✦✦✦✦✦

Replacing the band's volume in A&M's *Classics* series, *Greatest Hits* collects all Styx's major chart and radio hits, from "Lady" to "Show Me the Way." Although they were a definitive album rock band, creating records that were meant to be listened to as a whole, their finest moments were always their singles, making *Greatest Hits* the only Styx disc many fans will need to own. *—Stephen Thomas Erlewine*

Greatest Hits, Part II / Jun. 1996 / A&M ✦✦✦

Greatest Hits, Part II collects all of Styx's radio hits that weren't featured on the first collection, as well as a a handful of newly-recorded tracks. While there are some fine songs on *Part II,* the overall quality isn't as high as that of the first volume, which did have all of the hits. Still, for fans wanting to fill in the holes left by *Greatest Hits* and don't have the desire to dig deep into their back catalog, *Greatest Hits Part II* is a good purchase. *—Stephen Thomas Erlewine*

Suede

f. 1989, England

Group / Neo-Glam, Britpop, Alternative Pop/Rock

Suede kick-started the Brit-pop revolution of the '90s, bringing English indie-rock pop music away from the swirling layers of shoegazing and dance-pop fusions of Madchester, and reinstating such conventions of British pop as mystique and the three-minute single. Before the band had even released a single, the UK weekly music press was proclaiming them as the "Best New Band in Britain," but Suede managed to survive their heavy hype due to the songwriting team of vocalist Brett Anderson and guitarist Bernard Butler. Equally inspired by the glam crunch of David Bowie and the romantic bed-sit pop of the Smiths, Anderson and Butler developed a sweeping, guitar-heavy sound that was darkly sensual, sexually ambiguous, melodic and unabashedly ambitious. At the time of the release of their first single, "The Drowners," in 1992, few of their contemporaries—whether it was British shoegazers or American grunge rockers—had any ambitions to be old-fashioned, self-consciously controversial pop stars and the British press and public fell hard for Suede, making their 1993 debut the fast-selling first-album in UK history. Though they had rocketed to the top in the UK, Suede was plagued with problems, the least of which was an inability to get themselves heard in America. Anderson and Butler's relationship became antagonistic during the recording of their second album, *Dog Man Star,* and the guitarist left the band before its fall release, which inevitably hurt its sales. Instead of breaking up, the band soldiered on, adding new guitarist Richard Oakes, and a keyboardist before returning in 1996 with *Coming Up,* an album that returned them to the top of the British charts.*—Stephen Thomas Erlewine*

★ **Suede** / Mar. 29, 1993 / Nude/Columbia ✦✦✦✦✦

Borrowing heavily from David Bowie and the Smiths, Suede forged a distinctively seductive sound on their eponymous album. Guitarist Bernard Butler has a talent for crafting effortlessly catchy, crunching glam hooks like the controlled rush of "Metal Mickey" and the slow, sexy grind of "The Drowners," but he also can construct grand, darkly romantic soundscapes like the sighing "Sleeping Pills" and the tortured "Pantomime Horse." What brings these elegant sounds to life is Brett Anderson, who invests them with bed-sit angst and seamy sex. Anderson's voice is calculatedly affected and theatrical, but it fits the grand emotion of his self-consciously poetic lyrics. Suede are working-class lads striving for glamour, and they achieve it by piecing together remnants of the past with pieces of the present, never forgetting the value of a strong hook in the process. And while the sound of *Suede* frequently recalls the peak of glam-rock, its punk-influenced passion and self-conscious appropriation of the past makes it thoroughly post-modern. Coincidentally, its embrace of trashy pop helped usher in an era of Britpop, but few bands captured the theatrical melancholy that gave *Suede* such resonance. *—Stephen Thomas Erlewine*

Dog Man Star / Oct. 10, 1994 / Nude/Columbia ✦✦✦✦✦

Instead of following though on the Bowie-esque glam stomps of their debut, Suede concentrated on their darker, more melodramatic tendencies on their ambitious second album, *Dog Man Star.* By all accounts, the recording of *Dog Man Star* was plagued with difficulties—Brett Anderson wrote the lyrics in a druggy haze while sequestered in a secluded Victorian mansion, while Bernard Butler left before the album was completed—which makes its singular vision all the more remarkable. Lacking any rocker on the level of "The Drowners" or "Metal Mickey"—only the crunching "This Hollywood Life" comes close—*Dog Man Star* is a self-indulgent and pretentious album of dark, string-drenched epics. But Suede are one of the few bands who wear pretensions well, and after a few listens, the album becomes thoroughly compelling. Nearly every song on the record is hazy, feverish and heartbroken, and even the rockers have an insular, paranoid tenor that heightens the album's melancholy. The whole record would have collapsed underneath its own intentions if Butler's compositional skills weren't so subtly nuanced and if Anderson's grandiose poetry wasn't so strangely affecting. As it stands, *Dog Man Star* is a strangely seductive record, filled with remarkable musical peaks, from the Bowie-esque stomp of "New Generation" to the stately ballads "The Wild Ones" and "Still Life," which are both reminiscent of Scott Walker. And while Suede may choose to wear their influences on their sleeve, they synthesize them in a totally original way, making *Dog Man Star* a singularly tragic and romantic album. *—Stephen Thomas Erlewine*

Coming Up / Sep. 2, 1996 / Nude/Columbia ✦✦✦✦

Brett Anderson carried on after Bernard Butler's departure, adding a teenage guitarist and restructuring the intent of Suede, if not the sound, for their third album, *Coming Up.* The most striking thing about *Coming Up* is the simplicity. Gone are the grand, sweeping gestures of both *Suede* and *Dog Man Star,* leaving behind the glam, which is now spiked with in invigorating of sense of self-belief—Anderson is out to prove that he's a survivor, and he does give a damn whether you believe he is or not. So *Coming Up* has none of the lush, melancholy and paranoid overtones of *Dog Man Star.* It's about celebrating being young, going out, taking drugs, having sex and living life. And it sounds just like it reads—Richard Oakes pounds out fizzy, fuzzy guitar riffs while the rhythm section lays back with dirty, sexy grooves and new keyboardist Neil Godling exudes a sultry, unattainable cool. Even on the wistful ballads "By the Sea" and "Picnic By the Motorway," there's none of the enveloping melancholy that consumed *Dog Man Star*—they're as optimistic as the buoyant, melodic rockers that comprise the rest of the album. As a statement of purpose, *Coming Up* is unimpeachable. Though it doesn't break any new ground for the band—unless you count the newfound sense of optimism—it's a remarkable consolidation and crystallization of Suede's talents and all the evidence anyone needs that Brett Anderson was always the guiding force behind the band. *—Stephen Thomas Erlewine*

Sci-Fi Lullabies / Oct. 6, 1997 / Nude/Columbia ✦✦✦✦✦
Few debut singles have the impact of Suede's "The Drowners," which helped set the course to Britpop and established Suede as one of the U.K.'s most important bands. In that light, it isn't surprising that the B-sides were considered as important as the A-side—the slow, grinding "My Insatiable One" was covered in concerts by Morrissey weeks after its release, while the band often closed shows with the majestic "To the Birds." The strength of "The Drowners" B-sides wasn't an anomaly—it established a precedent of high-quality B-sides that Suede strived to maintain on their first three albums. The double-disc *Sci-Fi Lullabies* collects the majority of those B-sides, leaving behind the odd live track and remix, as well as the worthy "Painted People" and "Asda Town" and the non-LP single "Stay Together." What's included is stellar, offering an alternate history of Suede. In fact, the first disc—comprised of *Suede* and *Dog Man Star* B-sides, plus the haunting "Europe Is Our Playground"—is as strong as any of their albums, featuring such essentials as the sleazy "He's Dead," "The Living Dead," "My Dark Star," the storming "Killing of a Flash Boy," the sighing "Where the Pigs Don't Fly," and "Whipsnade," all strong enough to be A-sides. Disc two isn't quite as consistent, which might be because they're all drawn from the singles for *Coming Up*, but it does find the band exploring their darker, more adventurous side, which they largely suppressed on that record. Unlike most B-sides compilations, *Sci-Fi Lullabies* is far from extraneous—for any Suede fan, and most fans of contemporary British pop, this absolutely essential material, confirming the group's status as one of the '90s' greatest bands. *—Stephen Thomas Erlewine*

Head Music / Jun. 1, 1999 / Nude/Columbia ✦✦✦

Sugar

f. 1992, **db.** 1995
Group / Alternative Pop/Rock
After two solo albums, ex-Hüsker Dü guitarist/vocalist Bob Mould formed Sugar in 1992, with bassist David Barbe and drummer Malcolm Travis; their first album, *Copper Blue*, was released in the fall of 1992 to enthusiastic reviews and it became Mould's most successful project to date. *Copper Blue* nearly went gold and spawned several alternative radio and MTV hits, including "Helpless" and "If I Can't Change Your Mind." In the spring of 1993, Sugar released the mini-LP *Beaster*, a more abrasive collection than *Copper Blue* that was recorded at the same sessions. Mould wrote the material for the second Sugar album during 1993. The band began recording in the spring of 1994, but the sessions ground to a halt and the tapes were erased. Mould decided to give the album one more try and it was recorded quickly late that spring. *File Under: Easy Listening* appeared in the fall of 1994. Although it received good reviews and was moderately successful commercially, it didn't match the performance of *Copper Blue*. In the spring of 1995, it was announced that Sugar was on hiatus. *Besides*, a collection of rarities and B-sides, was released that summer. By the fall, Mould had broken up the band. *—Stephen Thomas Erlewine*

● **Copper Blue** / Sep. 4, 1992 / Rykodisc ✦✦✦✦✦
Featuring some of Mould's best songwriting, Sugar's debut album is a stunning piece of hook-laden punk-pop, highlighted by the '60s-style "If I Can't Change Your Mind," and the loud, beautiful guitars of "Man on the Moon" and "Helpless," and the tongue-in-cheek Pixies tribute, "A Good Idea." *—Stephen Thomas Erlewine*

Beaster / Apr. 6, 1993 / Rykodisc ✦✦✦

File Under: Easy Listening / Sep. 6, 1994 / Rykodisc ✦✦✦✦✦
Given Bob Mould's reputation for searing electric rock & roll, it may be easy to think that the title is ironic, and it is to a certain extent. But beneath the loud guitars lay the friendliest, most relaxed pop songs Mould has ever written. "Your Favorite Thing" and "Can't Help You Anymore" are two of Mould's most direct, pop-oriented songs, driven by instantly memorable melodies and hooks; they are also the most conventional songs on the record. The best moments come when Sugar push the boundaries a bit, whether it's on the country-rock of "Believe What You're Saying," the swirling "What You Want it To Be" and "Company Book," the searching ballad "Panama City Motel," or "Explode and Make Up," awhich bristles even at its most delicate moments. Mould throws in one classic spite-fueled rocker, "Granny Cool," but the record's finest moment is "Gee Angel," a powerhouse melodic scorcher. *—Stephen Thomas Erlewine*

Besides / Jul. 25, 1995 / Rykodisc ✦✦✦

Sugarcubes

f. 1986, Reykjavik, Iceland, **db.** 1992
Group / College Rock, Alternative Dance, Alternative Pop/Rock
The Sugarcubes were the biggest group ever to emerge from Iceland, which helps explain their off-kilter sense of melody. Their 1988 debut, *Life's Too Good*, attracted terrific reviews and became a college radio hit, but they never were able to recapture that sense of excitement. Taking members from a variety of Icelandic bands, the Sugarcubes formed around vocalists Bjork and Einar Benediktsson plus drummer Siggi Baldursson. After signing to One Little Indian in the UK, the group released their debut album *Life's Too Good* and single "Birthday," an indie hit in Britain and a college radio hit in America. In particular, Björk received a heap of praise, which began tensions between her and Einar. *Here Today, Tomorrow, Next Week!*, the Sugarcubes' second album, was released in 1989. After its release, the band embarked on a lengthy international tour and began recording their third album. Released in 1992, *Stick Around for Joy* received better reviews than *Life's Too Good*, but failed to yield a hit single. Following its release, the Sugarcubes disbanded. In 1993, Björk launched a critically acclaimed and commercially successful solo career that was based in dance music. *—Stephen Thomas Erlewine*

● **Life's Too Good** / 1988 / Elektra ✦✦✦✦✦

Here Today Tomorrow Next Week / Sep. 1989 / Elektra ✦✦✦

Stick Around for Joy / Feb. 18, 1992 / Elektra ✦✦✦

Great Crossover Potential / Jul. 14, 1998 / Elektra ✦✦✦✦
The Sugarcubes were one of the great cult bands of collegiate rock, not only because they had a distinctive sound, but because they were so damn weird. They sounded like nothing else in the late '80s/early '90s or anything that came before, creating an unusual hybrid of pop, dance and the avant-garde. So rabid was their cult that some critics said they could cross over into the mainstream, yet that never really happened, despite their strong English following. However, that notion gives the title to their best-of collection, *The Great Crossover Potential.* The 14-track compilation proves that they could never really have crossed over, mainly because their pop sense is quirky and they're often an acquired taste. Bjork, of course, wound up being a pop star with equally ambitious music, and while her talent is apparent here, it's often submerged by Einar's excruciatingly ridiculous showboating. Einar was often overbearing on the Sugarcubes albums (particularly toward the end of their career), and it is true that he's less irritating here than on the proper records, but casual fans should be aware that *The Great Crossover Potential* is only slightly less uneven than the actual albums, with the exception of the remarkable debut *Life's Too Good.* The collection, however, remains a nice way to round up the highlights, particularly those from *Here Today Tomorrow Next Week* and *Stick Around for Joy.* *—Stephen Thomas Erlewine*

Suicidal Tendencies

f. 1982, Venice, CA
Group / Punk Metal, Skatepunk, Heavy Metal, Thrash, Hardcore Punk
Suicidal Tendencies were formed in Venice, California as a punk/hardcore band and virtually came to define the phrase "skate-punk." Vocalist/bandleader Mike Muir has earned a reputation for addressing various political and personal topics with focused rage and thoughtfulness, and also for his keen sense of humor, which helps set the band apart from its competition. During the '80s, the group was frequently banned in the Los Angeles area, as their gigs often turned into out-of-control melees. Over the years, the band has mixed speed metal, more relaxed alternative rock, and touches of funk into its sound. Muir and bass virtuoso Robert Trujillo formed the metal/funk party band Infectious Grooves as a side project for Muir's non-political side. *—Steve Huey*

● **Suicidal Tendencies** / 1983 / Epitaph ✦✦✦✦✦
Fast, furious, and funny, Suicidal Tendencies' self-titled debut owed much more to hardcore punk than to the later hardcore/heavy metal hybrid they would become known for, but it's still quite possibly their best album. Mike Muir proves himself an articulate lyricist and commentator, delving into subjects like alienation, depression, and nonconformist politics with intelligence and humor. The band behind him is aggressive and speedy, but never sinks into an overly fast sonic blur. Contains the classic rant "Institutionalized." *—Steve Huey*

Join the Army / 1987 / Caroline ✦✦✦

How Will I Laugh Tomorrow When I Can't Even Smile Today / 1988 / Epic ✦✦✦✦✦
Suicidal Tendencies regrouped successfully for one of its best efforts, *How Will I Laugh Tomorrow When I Can't Even Smile Today.* The band's thrashy fusion of its hardcore roots with speed metal was fully developed by this point, and Muir's social commentary and self-analysis were as ragingly compelling and by turns amusing as ever. Highlights include "Trip At the Brain," "One Too Many Times," and the title track. *—Steve Huey*

Controlled by Hatred/Feel Like Shit . . . Deja Vu / 1989 / Epic ✦✦

Lights . . . Camera . . . Revolution! / Jun. 1990 / Epic ✦✦✦

The Art of Rebellion / Jun. 1992 / Epic ✦✦✦

Prime Cuts: The Best of Suicidal Tendencies / Jun. 3, 1997 / Epic ✦✦✦✦✦
Prime Cuts: Best of Suicidal Tendencies is a good overview of the group's career, featuring such hardcore classics as "Institutionalized" and "I Saw Yor Mommy," plus two new songs, "Berserk!" and "Feeding the Addiction." *—Stephen Thomas Erlewine*

Suicide

f. 1971, New York, NY, **db.** 1982
Group / American Punk, New York Punk, Post-Punk, Punk, Electronic
Although they barely receive credit, Suicide (singer Alan Vega and keyboardist Martin Rev) is the sourcepoint for virtually every synth-pop duo that glutted the pop marketplace (especially in England) in the early '80s. Without the trailblazing Rev and Vega, there would have been no Soft Cell, Erasure, Bronski Beat, Yaz, you name 'em, and while many would tell you that that's nothing to crow about, the aforementioned synth-poppers merely appropriated Suicide's keyboards/singer look and none of Rev and Vega's extremely confrontational performance style and love of dissonance. The few who did (Throbbing Gristle, Cabaret Voltaire) were considered too extreme for most tastes.Their approach to music was simple: Rev would create minimalistic, spooky, hypnotic washes of dissonant keyboards and synthesizers, while Vega sang, ranted, and spat neo-Beat lyrics in a jumpy, disjointed fashion. *—John Dougan*

● **Suicide [First Album]** / 1977 / Mute ✦✦✦✦✦
Suicide's debut is extreme, noisy, confrontational, and everything you'd want them to be. A slap in the face of the guitar-oriented punk rock that was coming out of New York and England at this time, Rev and Vega prove they were ahead of their time, even if audiences hated them for it. What doesn't hurt this record is the presence of some of their best material, "Rocket USA" and the deathless "Frankie Teardrop." *—John Dougan*

Suicide [Second Album] / 1980 / Mute ✦✦✦✦✦
Confusingly released in 1980 as *Alan Vega/Martin Rev: Suicide*, Mute reissued Suicide's sec-

ond album as *The Second Album* in 2000. The reissue adds the "Dream Baby Dream" single, as well as a second disc of Vega and Rev's first rehearsal tapes. The Ric Ocasek-produced *Second Album* is less confrontational and more contemporary than the duo's terrifying debut. Vega's rockabilly snarl and Rev's burbling electronics remain, but Ocasek's involvement purges a pop sensibility only hinted at on *Suicide*. Hell, some of the tracks are downright *pretty* ("Shadazz," "Diamonds, Fur Coat, Champagne"). Perhaps it's not as renegade as *Suicide*, but it's an arguably better, more realized work and just as essential. Three of the tracks found on the first rehearsal tapes disc were previously issued on ROIR's *Half Alive* in 1981. The rehearsals are extremely spatial and equally creepy as the proper studio works. Most of the tracks lurch by at a midtempo pace; Vega's distorted vocalisms are rather restrained but highly sinister, and Rev's sonic wizardry is delightfully horrific. *—Andy Kellman*

Half Alive / 1981 / ROIR ✦✦✦✦

Ghost Riders / 1986 / ROIR ✦✦✦
Originally a cassette-only release, this live recording at Walker Arts Center in Minneapolis marked Rev and Vega's 10th anniversary. And while not as deliberately offensive as some of their earlier live gigs (the impossible-to-locate *24 Minutes over Brussels*), this is a compelling, interesting document of their ever-evolving stage show. Not as transcendent as their debut album, but well worth the effort. Reissued on CD by the French Danceteria label in 1990. *—John Dougan*

Donna Summer

b. Dec. 31, 1948, Boston, MA
Vocals / Club/Dance, Urban, Disco
Born Donna Gaines, to a church-going family in the Mission Hill section of Boston, Summer took her name from Helmut Sommer, whom she married while living in Munich, Germany as a member of a travelling cast of *Hair*. Italian electro-pop arranger Giorgio Moroder met her, and in 1975 they recorded "Love to Love You Baby," a 16-minute, riff-driven update of Jane Birkin and Serge Gainsbourg's version of "Je t'aime… moi non plus." But Summer, as it turned out, had a sturdiness quite different from Birkin's short bursts of this and that, and a flair for kitschy show tunes and overproduced slickness, both of which ideally complimented the transparent impersonality of Moroder's electronic rhythms. She and Moroder created entire sub-genres of disco, and there was no stopping them until Summer stopped herself.

Beginning with 1980's *The Wanderer* (except for the title song) she began to sing exactly the kind of pop/rock material her daring impressionism had fought against. She tried to become a pop singer; and when, as in *She Works Hard for the Money*, she drew upon gospel styles, she was listened to. But during the '70s, she wasn't merely listened to, she was a leader. Today Summer tries to catch up, sadly, with a generation whose greatest aesthetic achievement was to catch up with her. *—Michael Freedberg*

The Donna Summer Anthology (Chronicles Series) / Sep. 21, 1993 / Casablanca ✦✦✦✦✦

★ **Endless Summer: The Very Best** / 1995 / Casablanca ✦✦✦✦✦
With '70s and disco nostalgia taking the U.S. by storm in the early to mid-1990s, it wasn't surprising that Mercury/PolyGram saw Donna Summer's recordings as a way to make a quick dollar. What is surprising is that the label came out with this single-disc best-of collection only a year after releasing the two-CD set *The Donna Summer Anthology* in 1993. Why was another greatest-hits package needed? Though not definitive, this CD does contain many of Summer's essential material. From the erotic club diva of "Love to Love You Baby," "Could It Be Magic" and "I Feel Love" to the Vegas-like pop star of "On the Radio," "Last Dance" and "Dim All the Lights," the Queen of Disco is as charismatic as she is cutting-edge. And Summer still sounds incredibly fresh on 1989's infectious "This Time I Know It's For Real" and 1994's previously unreleased "Melody of Love." It would have been preferable to hear many of these songs in their extended versions (as opposed to the shorter ones provided here), but then, a label can only fit so much on a single disc. Although *The Donna Summer Anthology* is more comprehensive, *Endless Summer* can work well as a shorter introduction to her innovations. *—Alex Henderson*

Greatest Hits / Sep. 15, 1998 / Mercury ✦✦✦✦✦
There are Donna Summer collections available for any level of fan. For hardcore fans, there's the double-disc set, *The Donna Summer Anthology*. For casual fans wanting a solid collection that digs a little deeper than a basic hits compilation, there's the very fine *Endless Summer: The Very Best of Donna Summer*. Then there's *Greatest Hits*, a bare-bones collection that contains her 12 biggest hits, from "Love to Love You Baby" to "She Works Hard for the Money," all presented in their single edits. Only listeners who want just the singles will want *Greatest Hits*, since the other compilations provide a better, more thorough overview, but they will be quite pleased with the end result. *—Stephen Thomas Erlewine*

The Sundays

f. 1987
Group / College Rock, Dream Pop, Adult Alternative Pop/Rock, Alternative Pop/Rock
Building on the jangly guitar-pop of the Smiths and the trance-like dream-pop of bands like the Cocteau Twins, the Sundays cultivated a dedicated following in indie-rock circles, both in their native England and in America, in the early '90s. Although the sales of their first two albums were strong, the band never crossed over into the mainstream, as so many observers and critics predicted they would. Vocalist Harriet Wheeler and guitarist David Gavurin, the target of a record-label bidding war soon after their first concert, finally signed to Rough Trade (DGC in the US) and released their first album *Reading, Writing and Arithmetic* in 1990. It entered the UK charts at number four, and became a modern rock hit in America thanks to the single, "Here's Where the Story Ends." After Rough Trade collapsed in 1991, the Sundays moved to Parlophone and released their second album *Blind* in 1992. Although it was initially successful, the album didn't have quite the staying power of the debut. The Sundays were quiet for the next several years, finally returning in 1997 with *Static & Silence*. *—Stephen Thomas Erlewine*

● **Reading Writing & Arithmetic** / Apr. 1990 / DGC ✦✦✦✦✦
The Sundays' debut album built on the layered, ringing guitar hooks and unconventional pop melodies of The Smiths, adding more ethereal vocals and a stronger backbeat. As evidenced by the lilting, melancholy single "Here's Where the Story Ends," it was a winning combination, making *Reading, Writing and Arithmetic* a thoroughly engaging debut. *—Stephen Thomas Erlewine*

Blind / Oct. 20, 1992 / DGC ✦✦✦
Featuring gentle, folk-based guitars and pop melodies, The Sundays' second album isn't much of a sonic departure from their first album. While it does have several fine numbers, it doesn't have as many outstanding songs as *Reading Writing & Arithmetic;* nevertheless, *Blind* will please most fans of the group. *—Stephen Thomas Erlewine*

Static & Silence / Sep. 23, 1997 / Geffen ✦✦✦
It took the Sundays five years to deliver their third album, *Static and Silence*. Five years is a long time, especially in the quicksilver world of pop music, but the Sundays sound totally unbothered by their absence on *Static and Silence*. Instead of sounding labored and forced, the album is gentle and effortless, as if it was recorded five months after *Blind* instead of five years. In some ways, that's a disappointment—it would have been nice for the duo to show some progression, considering all of their time off—but the record delivers the pleasant, endearing jangle-pop that is the Sundays' signature sound. There's certainly nothing as catchy as "Here's Where the Story Ends" on *Static and Silence*, and there aren't many songs that are instantly memorable, yet the album has a quiet charm that should satisfy most longtime fans. *—Stephen Thomas Erlewine*

Sunny Day Real Estate

f. 1992, Seattle, WA
Group / Emo, Indie Rock, Alternative Pop/Rock
Considering their relatively brief existence, Sunny Day Real Estate racked up enough dramatic twists and turns to rank with some of the great rock soap operas. Originally comprised of guitarist-vocalist Dan Hoerner, bassist Nate Mendel and drummer William Goldsmith), Sunny Day Real Estate garnered attention when it added enigmatic lead singer Jeremy Enigk, whose high-pitched, constantly ascending voice complimented their melodic songs. The group was shrouded in mystery from the get-go: they released only one picture to the press, conducted one interview and, for some still-unknown reason, never played a show in the state of California with all four members intact. With the release of their 1994 debut album, Diary, Sunny Day found newfound fame while Enigk found religion, and in 1995 the group broke up. (Goldsmith and Mendel quickly found work with the Foo Fighters.) After much speculation, the group reformed in 1998 minus Mendel, who stayed with the Foo Fighters, and released How It Feels to Be Something On. *—Brian Raftery*

Diary / 1994 / Sub Pop ✦✦✦

● **LP2** / Nov. 1995 / Sub Pop ✦✦✦✦✦
Delivering on the promise Sunny Day Real Estate showed on their 1994 debut *Diary*, the following year's *LP2*—a.k.a. *The Pink Album* for its entirely pink cover—also felt like a posthumous work left by a brilliant writer. Shortly after recording *LP2*, the band spontaneously imploded: Enigk emerged born-again as a Christian, and the rhythm section, Nate Mendel and William Goldsmith, headed off to join Dave Grohl in Foo Fighters, seemingly sabotaging that once-limitless future. As tragic as the turn of events was for fans, the album proved how special the band was and underscored just how lamentable their too-early demise was. From its first ringing guitar tone to its abrupt conclusion, *LP2* is a masterpiece of emotion and evocation, a sprawling musical soundscape that moves effortlessly from tender, unsteady sonic explorations to raging assaults of guitars. At all times, it seems heartbreakingly fragile and moody, ready to spin apart at the apex of one of the band's guitar frenzies or fold in on itself when the music turns serene. There are plenty of both such moments, all of which come together to produce lovely, resplendent songs like "Friday," "5/4," "8," and "J'Nuh," made all the more breathtaking by Enigk's alternately tortured and delicate vocals. It's sometimes difficult to make out what he is warbling about, but the intent seems obvious. *LP2* wears all of its affectations and passions on its sleeve and has a lump in its throat; in the process, it also creates the same sort of longing and desire in the listener. Few post-grunge bands were able to make their tortured souls sound so viscerally appealing, and few albums of the mid-'90s strike as poignant a note as this tour de force. *—Stanton Swihart*

How It Feels to Be Something On / Sep. 8, 1998 / Sub Pop ✦✦✦✦

Live / Oct. 19, 1999 / Sub Pop ✦✦✦✦

The Rising Tide / Jun. 20, 2000 / Time Bomb ✦✦✦✦
Described by Jerermy Enigk as a "wake-up call," Sunny Day Real Estate's fourth album (and their first for Time Bomb) *The Rising Tide* presents the most accomplished version of their gripping, anthemic sound yet. Appropriate to its title, *The Rising Tide* comes in sweeps and swells, ranging from searching, uncompromising rock like "Killed By an Angel" and "One" to gentle, beautiful ballads like "Rain Song" and even pop-tinged songs like "Television," which sounds a bit like a more propulsive version of the Police's early '80s singles. Though the album was recorded with a trio lineup (Jeremy Enigk, Dan Hoerner, and William Goldsmith), it's some of the band's fullest-sounding work, rich with strings and keyboard flourishes that add extra depth to the shimmering, Eastern-inspired drones of "Fool in the Photograph" and "Faces in Disguise." Lou Giordano's production gives *The Rising Tide* an unabashedly big, clean sound that frames Sunny Day's detailed songwriting and arrangements perfectly, giving the restrained, reflective "Tearing in My Heart" and "The Ocean" as much impact as driven tracks like "Snibe" and "Disappear." Best of all is the title track, which blends a beautiful melody, heartfelt vocals, and an insistent rhythm into a sweeping, affecting finale. Expansive and complex without compromising the band's focused, impassioned style, *The Rising Tide* is one of Sunny Day Real Estate's—and 2000's—most impressive albums. *—Heather Phares*

Super Furry Animals

f. 1993, Cardiff, Wales

Group / Indie Pop, Neo-Psychedelia, Britpop, Alternative Pop/Rock

One of the leaders of the mid-'90s Welsh scene, Super Furry Animals fused disparate musical genres—including power-pop, punk rock, techno, and prog-rock—into shimmering, melodic, irreverent and arty rock & roll. Their infectious melodies, irreverent attitude and tendency to sing in their native tongue set them apart, but their unique approach was remarkably popular: their 1996 debut *Fuzzy Logic* and 1999's *Guerilla* became major UK hits, charting in the Top 40 and placing in the Top 10 of many year-end critic's polls.

Super Furry Animals formed in Cardiff, Wales in 1993 and included Gruff Rhys (lead vocals, guitar), Huw "Bunf" Bunford (guitar, vocals), Guto Pryce (bass), Cian Ciaran (keyboards, electronics), and Dafydd Leuan (drums). After the dissolution of Rhys' noise-rock band Ffa Coffi Pawb, the trio he played in with Pryce and Leuan evolved into Super Furry Animals. Initially a techno outfit, they soon became a neo-psychedelic and progressive pop band. In 1995, they signed with the Cardiff-based indie Ankst. Their Welsh-language EPs *Lianfairpwllgywgyllgoger Chwymdrobwlltysiliogoygoyocynygofod (In Space)* and *Moog Droog,* earned them a wide fanbase in Wales and a strong cult following in Britain, which led to a six-album record contract with Creation Records. Prior to signing with Creation, the band decided to sing the majority of their songs in English in order to reach a wider audience. The singles "Hometown Unicorn" and "God! Show Me Magic" became moderate hits in the UK and preceded the summer 1996 release of the band's debut *Fuzzy Logic,* which received uniformly excellent reviews. SFA became one of Britain's hippest acts within a few months; with the release of 1997's *Radiator* and 1999's *Guerilla,* they cemented their place as one of the UK's most entertaining and innovative bands. They secured a US deal with Flydaddy, who released *Radiator, Guerrilla* and 2000's Welsh-language *MWNG* in the States. *—Stephen Thomas Erlewine*

● **Fuzzy Logic** / May 1996 / Creation ✦✦✦✦✦

Super Furry Animals are eclectic, to say the least. Fusing together pop melodies, psychedelia, and art-rock with an impish, punky fury, the band covers more ground on their debut album, *Fuzzy Logic,* than most indie bands do in their entire career. However, the album works better as a series of moments than as a collection, mainly due to their overreaching ambition. Each song floats by on irresistable, catchy vocal harmonies, while the music alternates between glitzy overdriven guitars and sighing, sweeping keyboard, guitar and string backdrops. Over these lush sonic beds, lead vocalist Gruff sings lyrics that are either mystical, nonsensical, or bizarrely funny—none of the songs make much literal sense, but that doesn't quite matter when the music is as free-spirited as this. The songs may start conventionally, but they'll be undercut by wild synthesizers and careening guitar solos, or off-kilter vocal melodies. Taken as individual moments—as the singles "God! Show Me Magic" (relatively straight-ahead punk-pop), "Hometown Unicorn" (gorgeous psychedelia), and "Something for the Weekend" (which finds the middle ground between the first two singles) prove—the music of Super Furry Animals is quite intoxicating, but when assembled together, they don't sustain momentum. However, the individual pleasures of each song become more apparent with each listen and *Fuzzy Logic* suggests that the group could blossom into something quite distinctive and utterly unique within a few albums. *—Stephen Thomas Erlewine*

Radiator / Aug. 21, 1997 / Flydaddy ✦✦✦✦✦

Using the psychedelicized prog-punk of *Fuzzy Logic* as a foundation, Super Furry Animals move even further into left field on their second album, *Radiator.* As before, the group displays a gift for catchy, deceptively complex melodic hooks, but now their songwriting and arrangements are mind-bogglingly intricate and eclectic. Songs boast intertwining melodies and countermelodies, with guitars and keyboards swirling around the vocals. Similarly, the production is dense and heavy with detail, borrowing heavily from prog-rock and psychedelic pop, but pieced together with the invention of techno and played with the energy of punk. It's a heady, impressive kaleidoscope of sounds, but what gives *Radiator* its weight is the way the sonics complement the songwriting. SFA's songs are melodic, accessible, and utterly original—melodically, they may borrow from '60s pop, but they rearrange the clichés in fresh ways. Also, Gruff Rhys has a fondness for revolutionary politics and the bizarre that helps give *Radiator* its intoxicating, otherworldly atmosphere, making it one of the few late-'90s albums that sounds inventive, vibrant, and utterly contemporary. *—Stephen Thomas Erlewine*

Outspaced / Nov. 1998 / Creation ✦✦✦✦

Guerrilla / Jun. 14, 1999 / Flydaddy ✦✦✦✦

It's difficult not to find Super Furry Animals' brand of pop infectious, particularly the collection of numbers compiled for *Guerrilla,* the band's third full-length and arguably most cohesive—albeit pleasingly and consistently unpredictable—one to date. Old-school techno remains in remnants, such as in "Wherever I Lay My Phone (That's My Home)." When it rears its head otherwise, it rests easily beside and within the majority of the fully-fledged pop songs. The High Llamas contribute to the dreamy "Turning Tide"; there's the tropicalia of "Northern Lites", and, as ever, there are shades of punk and distortion in "Night Vision." Amazingly, the super-bouncy-rocker "The Teacher" does not credit a sample to the Who's "Baba O'Riley." *—Denise Sullivan*

mwng / Jun. 20, 2000 / Flydaddy ✦✦✦✦✦

The very fact that Super Furry Animals had the courage to release *Mwng,* an all-Welsh language album, is proof that the group is the great eccentric band of their time. Unfortunately, many critics and listeners may dismiss *Mwng* as a stunt or a wacky joke, which is condescending—especially in light of what a terrific album this is. It doesn't matter that many listeners will not understand the lyrics, since the music is terribly effective in its own right. Ironically, *Mwng* is more of a pop album than its predecessor, *Guerrilla,* which often took fascinating detours into electronica-inspired pure sound. *Mwng* has more than its fair share of evocative sonic textures—it's easy to get lost not just in the surface sound but what's buried beneath the melodies—yet it's also a concise, sharply-written psychedelic-pop record. These are smart, melodic, catchy songs graced with inventive, clever arrangements. Super Furry Animals have tempered their harder-rocking in favor of expanding their prog, psych, and pop inclinations. There are still numbers that rock, but they're unconventional, taking wonderful left turns and being blessed with arrangement that are welcoming, but never predictable. Fuzztone guitars and floating keyboards vie for space in the mix, vocals swoon in reverb, horns sound equally eerie and enthusiastic, and instruments are compressed so they no longer sound normal. Even when it skirts with psych-pop convention, with sitars popping up in the mix, it sounds fresh. *Mwng* is simply intoxicating with its richly melodic songs and dreamlike flow. This is an otherworldly record not because it is sung in Welsh, but because the music is fully realized and visionary. *—Stephen Thomas Erlewine*

Superchunk

f. 1989, Chapel Hill, NC

Group / Indie Rock, Alternative Pop/Rock

Perhaps no band was more emblematic of the true spirit of American indie rock during the 1990s than Superchunk, the pride of Chapel Hill, NC. Following the D.I.Y. ethic to the letter, the group operated solely by their own rules, ignoring all passing trends by sticking to their trademark sound—typified by the buzzing guitars and high, impassioned vocals of frontman Mac McCaughan—and rejecting all major-label advances in favor of their own label, Merge Records. Although Superchunk's resistance to the overtures of the music industry may have deprived them of the wider audience their work clearly deserved, perhaps their greatest legacy remains their unwavering dedication to the indie tradition. With the release of their self-titled debut LP in 1990, Superchunk was widely celebrated among the most promising young bands in America. Label heads scrambling to locate the next alternative rock hotbed after Seattle made Chapel Hill a consensus choice, and Superchunk soon found themselves in the middle of a major-label bidding war. Still, the group remained on Merge for their brilliant 1991 sophomore effort *No Pocky for Kitty.* 1995's *Here's Where the Strings Come In* heralded a subtle refinement of their core sound. As well, McCaughan has also recorded several LPs with his side project Portastatic. *—Jason Ankeny*

No Pocky for Kitty / 1992 / Merge ✦✦✦✦✦

Where Superchunk's self-titled debut otherwise failed to live up to the brilliance of its anti-anthem centerpiece "Slack Motherfucker," the follow-up *No Pocky for Kitty* is a complete and fully realized statement of purpose—opening with the dizzying "Skip Steps 1 & 3," the disc never lets up for a second, crackling with an energy and breathless abandon that underlines the sheer exuberance at the heart of even Mac McCaughan's most superficially bitter songs. Although *No Pocky for Kitty* successfully channels the sound and spirit of punk's heyday, for all their whiplash guitars and spitfire rhythms Superchunk's songs derive their power not from nihilism and ennui but from optimism and passion—implicit in McCaughan's lyrics is a belief in creation over destruction, hope over cynicism, and love over hate. Credit too Steve Albini's no-frills recording for the live-wire snap and crackle of standouts like "Seed Toss," "Punch Me Harder," and "Throwing Things"—for all its earthy simplicity and everyman conviction, *No Pocky for Kitty* positively soars. *—Jason Ankeny*

● **Tossing Seeds (Singles 89-91)** / 1992 / Merge ✦✦✦✦✦

"The single must be a distillation of one's powers, the most exciting slice of noise a person can cram between the lip of the disc and the edge of the label," writes Superchunk frontman Mac McGaughan in the sleeve notes to *Tossing Seeds;* the 13 seven-inch sides which make up this collection deliver everything McGaughan promises and much more, capturing the essence of Amerindie rock in the pre-Nirvana era with an energy and eloquence matched by few other records of the period. As a note-perfect snapshot of minimum-wage angst and attitude, "Slack Motherfucker" justly remains the band's most celebrated moment, but perhaps their most quintessential record is instead "My Noise," a glorious celebration of indie ethos and music's liberating power; add underground classics like "The Breadman" and "Seed Toss" to the mix, and you've got a definitive portrait of arguably the best singles band of the early '90s. *—Jason Ankeny*

On The Mouth / 1993 / Merge ✦✦✦✦

After pushing the buzzsaw abandon of their earliest records to its logical extreme on the masterful *No Pocky for Kitty,* Superchunk begins reinventing itself with their third full-length *On the Mouth,* a record as invigorating as it is frustrating. Without sacrificing any of the energy or conviction of past efforts, many of the disc's 13 songs harness Mac McCaughan's breathless pop-punk melodies into tighter, more demanding contexts—highlights like the singles *Mower* and *The Question Is How Fast* introduce a new arsenal of shifting rhythms and explosively tense dynamics which reveal unexpectedly limitless possibilities within the classic Superchunk approach. The problem is that *On the Mouth* equates to something less than the sum of its parts—while tracks like the blistering *From the Curve* and *Package Thief* barrel forth with the sheer recklessness of old, their adherence to the band's past makes for an ill-fitting match alongside the album's more ambitious moments. More problematic, the slow, plodding *Swallow That*—while an admirable departure from the norm—is simply tedious. Still, more often than not *On the Mouth* comes up with the goods, and remains a pivotal turning point in Superchunk's continued evolution. *—Jason Ankeny*

Foolish / Dec. 1993 / Merge ✦✦✦

Incidental Music / Jun. 20, 1995 / Merge ✦✦✦✦✦

Here's Where the Strings Come In / Sep. 19, 1995 / Merge ✦✦✦

Indoor Living / Sep. 2, 1997 / Merge ✦✦✦

Come Pick Me Up / Aug. 10, 1999 / Merge ✦✦✦✦✦

Actually, *here's* where the strings come in—*Come Pick Me Up* is Superchunk's finest effort in years, a bright, infectious pop record that rejuvenates the group's trademark sound through the addition of producer Jim O'Rourke's candy-colored orchestral flourishes without losing sight of the music's punk roots. Tracks like "Hello Hawk," "1000 Pounds" and "Pink Clouds" achieve a perfect balance between Superchunk's patented brand of hyperkinetic indie rock and O'Rourke's avant-pop aesthetic, drawing upon the talents of Chicago underground notables including saxophonist Ken Vandermark, trombonist Jeb Bishop and cellist Fred Lonberg-Holm to bring galvanizing new dimensions to Mac McGaughan's memorably melodic songs. A stunning and unexpected return to form. *—Jason Ankeny*

Supergrass

f. 1993, London, England

Group / Punk-Pop, Britpop, Alternative Pop/Rock

Like many other British bands of the '90s, Supergrass' musical roots lie in the infectiously catchy punk-pop of the Buzzcocks and the Jam, as well as the post-punk pop of Madness and the traditional British pop of the Kinks and Small Faces. Perhaps because of their age—two of the trio were still in their teens when they recorded their debut single—the band also brings in elements of decidedly un-hip groups like Elton John, as well as classic rockers like David Bowie, the Beatles and the Rolling Stones. With an exuberant, youthful enthusiasm, Supergrass tied all of their influences together in new surprising ways, where a Buzzcocks riff could slam into three-part harmonies out of "Crocodile Rock," or have a galloping music hall rhythm stutter like the best moments of the Who. *—Stephen Thomas Erlewine*

● **I Should Coco** / Jul. 18, 1995 / Capitol ♦♦♦♦♦

Tearing by at a breakneck speed, *I Should Coco* is a spectacularly eclectic debut by Supergrass, a trio barely out of their teens. Sure, the unbridled energy of the album illustrates that the band is young, yet what really illustrates how young the band is how they borrow from their predecessors. Supergrass treat The Buzzcocks, the Beatles, Elton John, David Bowie, Blur, and Madness as if they were all the same thing—they don't make any distinction between what is cool and what isn't, they just throw everything together. Consequently, the jittery "Caught By the Fuzz" slams next to the music-hall rave-up "Mansize Rooster" and the trippy psychedelia of "Sofa of My Lethargy," or the heavy stomp of "Lenny" or the the bonafide teen anthem "Alright." *I Should Coco* is the sound of adolscence, but performed with a surprising musical versatility that makes the record's exuberant energy all the more infectious. *—Stephen Thomas Erlewine*

In It for the Money / May 5, 1997 / Capitol ♦♦♦♦♦

Supergrass' debut album *I Should Coco* rushed by at such a blinding speed that some listeners didn't notice the melodic complexity of its best songs. On their second album, the cleverly-titled *In it for the Money,* Supergrass brought the songs to their forefront, slowing the tempos considerably and constructing a varied, textured album that makes their ambition and skill abundantly clear. From the droning mantra of the opening title track, it's clear that the band has delved deeply into psychedelia and hints of *Magical Mystery Tour* are evident throughout the album, from swirling organs and gurgling wah-wahs to punchy horn charts and human-beat-boxes. In fact, Supergrass has substituted the punky rush of *I Should Coco* for such sonic details, and while that means they only occasionally touch upon the breakneck pace of the debut (the hard-driving "Richard III"), they also deepen its joyful exuberance with subtle songs and remarkably accomplished musicianship. There might not be a "Caught by the Fuzz" or "Alright" on *In it for the Money,* but that's not a problem, since the bright explosion of "Sun Hits the Sky" and the nervy "Tonight" are just as energetic, and the album features introspective numbers like the gorgeous "Late in the Day" and "It's Not Me" that give the album substantial weight. And even with all this musical maturity, they haven't sacrificed their good-natured humor, as the detailed production and the bizarre closer "Sometimes I Make You Sad" makes abundently clear. Sometimes, maturity turns out to be everything it's supposed to be. *—Stephen Thomas Erlewine*

Supergrass / Sep. 20, 1999 / Capitol ♦♦♦

Supertramp

f. 1969

Group / Album Rock, Arena Rock, Pop/Rock, Soft Rock, Prog-Rock/Art Rock

Once upon a time in 1969, a young Dutch millionaire by the name of Stanley August Miesegaes gave his acquaintance, vocalist and keyboardist Rick Davies a "genuine opportunity" to form his own band; he could form the band of his dreams and Miesegaes would pay for it. After placing an ad in *Melody Maker,* Davies assembled Supertramp. Supertramp released two long-winded progressive rock albums before Miesegaes withdrew his support. With no money or fan base to speak of, the band was forced to redesign their sound. Coming up with a more pop-oriented form of progressive rock, the band had a hit with their third album, *Crime of the Century.* Throughout the decade, Supertramp had a number of best-selling albums, culminating in their 1979 masterpiece, *Breakfast in America. Breakfast in America* marked their first album that tipped the scale completely in the favor of pop songs; on the strength of the hit singles "Goodbye Stranger," "Logical Song," and "Take the Long Way Home" it sold over 18 million copies worldwide. After that album, Supertramp continued to develop a more R&B-flavored style; the change in direction was successful on 1982's *Famous Last Words,* but they soon ran out of hits. The band continued to sporadically record and tour into the '90s. *—Stephen Thomas Erlewine*

Supertramp / 1970 / A&M ♦♦

Indelibly Stamped / 1971 / A&M ♦♦

Crime of the Century / 1974 / A&M ♦♦♦♦♦

With *Crime of the Century,* Supertramp established themselves as one of the handful of progressive rock acts that could sell albums and have hit singles. Stripping away the longwinded excesses of their first two albums, *Crime of the Century* featured tighter, more melodic songs, as evidenced by the singles "Bloody Well Right" and "Dreamer." *—Stephen Thomas Erlewine*

Crisis? What Crisis? / 1975 / A&M ♦♦♦

Crisis? What Crisis? wasn't quite as fully-developed as its predecessor, *Crime of the Century,* lacking any instant standouts like "Dreamer" or "Bloody Well Right." Nevertheless, it had a handful of fine songs which signalled that Supertramp was continuing to refine and expand their sound. *—Stephen Thomas Erlewine*

Even in the Quietest Moments / 1977 / A&M ♦♦♦♦♦

Like *Crisis? What Crisis?, Even in the Quietest Moments* is a jumbled affair, alternating between long, unfocused sections and relatively concise pop songs, like the hit "Give a Little Bit." *—Stephen Thomas Erlewine*

● **Breakfast in America** / 1979 / A&M ♦♦♦♦♦

With *Breakfast in America,* Supertramp had a genuine blockbuster hit, topping the charts for four weeks in the U.S. and selling millions of copies worldwide; by the 1990s, the album had sold over 18 million units across the world. Although their previous records had some popular success, they never even hinted at the massive sales of *Breakfast in America.* Then again, Supertramp's earlier records weren't as pop-oriented as *Breakfast.* The majority of the album consisted of tightly-written, catchy, well-constructed pop songs, like the hits "The Logical Song," "Take the Long Way Home," and "Goodbye Stranger." Supertramp still had a tendency to indulge themselves occasionally, but *Breakfast in America* had very few weak moments. It was clearly their high-water mark. *—Stephen Thomas Erlewine*

Paris / 1980 / A&M ♦♦

. . . famous last words . . . / 1982 / A&M ♦♦♦

Even though *. . . famous last words . . .*, Supertramp's follow-up to *Breakfast in America,* was slicker and more pop-oriented than its predecessor, it wasn't quite as successful. Where the singles on *Breakfast* still had a progressive rock edge, most of *. . . famous last words . . .* was light, synthesized pop, with the shimmering "It's Raining Again" being the only song melodic enough to support the lush, layered sound. *—Stephen Thomas Erlewine*

Brother Where You Bound / 1985 / A&M ♦♦

Classics, Vol. 9 / 1987 / A&M ♦♦♦♦♦

This is a fairly good sampler of this band's bigger radio tracks as well as key album numbers. Included are "Bloody Well Right," "Ain't Nobody but Me," "The Logical Song," "Give a Little Bit," "It's Raining Again," "Goodbye Stranger," "Take the Long Way Home," and "Dreamer." Unfortunately, "Even in the Quietest Moments" is curiously omitted. *—AMG*

● **The Very Best of Supertramp** / 1992 / A&M ♦♦♦♦♦

The European compilation *The Very Best of Supertramp* is the closest thing to a definitive overview of the '70s pop-prog group. Certainly, there will be hardcore fans that will notice some favorite album cuts missing—after all, despite their considerable success on the pop charts, Supertramp was as much an album rock band as ELP or Genesis—but all the hits are here, from "Bloody Well Right" to "It's Raining Again," as well as a sizable portion of their blockbuster *Breakfast in America.* That alone will make it worthwhile for all casual fans, but what's really nice about the collection is that it flows very smoothly, even if it isn't in chronological order. There have been other Supertramp compilations, but *The Very Best of Supertramp* stands head and shoulders above the rest. *—Stephen Thomas Erlewine*

The Supremes

f. 1961, Detroit, MI, **db.** 1977

Group / Uptown Soul, Pop-Soul, Girl Group, Motown, Soul

The most successful Black performers of the 1960s, the Supremes for a time rivaled even the Beatles in terms of red-hot commercial appeal, reeling off five number one singles in a row at one point. Critical revisionism has tended to undervalue the Supremes' accomplishments, categorizing their work as more lightweight than the best soul stars' (or even the best Motown stars'), and viewing them as a tool for Berry Gordy's crossover aspirations. There's no question that there was about as much pop as soul in the Supremes' hits, that even some of their biggest hits could sound formulaic, and that they were probably the Black performers who were most successful at infiltrating the tastes and televisions of middle America. This shouldn't diminish either their extraordinary achievements or their fine music, the best of which renders the pop vs. soul question moot with its excellence. *—Richie Unterberger*

☆ **Diana Ross and the Supremes Greatest Hits** / Aug. 1967 / Motown ♦♦♦♦♦

Although all of these 20 songs were credited to The Supremes when they were released between 1963 and 1967, this album marked the first LP on which the group was billed as "Diana Ross and the Supremes." However you credit it, this out-of-print double-LP contains the bulk of the best of The Supremes, no less than 10 number one hits from "Where Did Our Love Go" to "The Happening," and thus some of the most popular music of the 1960s. Ross and the Supremes, together and separately, continued to score afterwards, but this was their peak. *—William Ruhlmann*

☆ **Anthology** / May 1974 / Motown ♦♦♦♦♦

70's Greatest Hits & Rare Classics / 1991 / Motown ♦♦♦

★ **The Ultimate Collection** / Oct. 7, 1997 / Motown ♦♦♦♦♦

The Ultimate Collection nearly lives up to its billing, featuring 25 tracks on a single disc, including all of the Supremes' Top Ten pop and R&B hits with Diana Ross. For most casual fans and those who just want the hits, this will be the definitive collection. *—Stephen Thomas Erlewine*

Supremes / Aug. 29, 2000 / Motown ♦♦♦♦

The Supremes were Motown's most popular act, so there was much anticipation for a comprehensive box set, especially since Motown waited many years to assemble one. So, the question is, was the wait worth it— Almost. It's a lavish set, spanning four discs (five, if you include the limited-edition live bonus disc included with the first 25,000 sets), housed in a red-velvet plated book and boasting a 70-page booklet, plus alternate takes, original 45 mixes, and other rarities. The devil is in the details, though. Rarities are substituted for original hit versions; for instance, the original versions of "Stop! In the Name of Love" and "Love Is Here and Now You're Gone" are not here. Then, there are the little omissions, like noting Elvis Costello's cover of "Remove This Doubt" in a list of great Supremes covers, but not including the original. These curious choices, along with the decision to devote the fourth disc to post-Diana Ross material, makes the set feel a little incomplete even though it covers a tremendous amount of ground. There are some classic cuts missing, and it's not a good thing that some of those missing items are the single versions of the hits. Still, it's hard not to like *The Supremes* as a set for hardcore fans, who will thrill to the different mixes and alternate versions, unreleased photos, Top Ten Lists, and illustrated discographies. But for the listener looking for one exhaustive set containing all the Supremes they'll ever need, this set falls short of the mark. In fact, for that kind of listener, a good double-disc hits compilation remains a preferable choice over this set. *—Stephen Thomas Erlewine*

The Surfaris

f. 1962, Glendora, CA

Group / Frat Rock, Surf, Instrumental Rock

Glendora, CA surf group remembered for "Wipe Out," the number two 1963 hit that ranks as one of the great rock instrumentals, featuring a classic up-and-down guitar riff and a classic solo drum roll break, both of which were emulated by millions (the number is no exaggeration) of beginning rock & rollers. They recorded an astonishing number of albums (about half a dozen) and singles in the mid-'60s; the "Wipe Out" follow-up "Point Panic" was the only one to struggle up to the middle of the charts. The Surfaris were not extraordinary, but they were more talented than the typical one-shot surf group; drummer Ron Wilson was praised by session stickman extraordinaire Hal Blaine, and his uninhibited splashing style sounds like a direct ancestor to Keith Moon. He also took the lead vocals on the group's occasional passable Beach Boy imitations. *—Richie Unterberger*

● **Wipe Out! The Best of the Surfaris** / Jul. 5, 1994 / Varese Sarabande ✦✦✦✦✦

Decent 18-track distillation of their 1962-65 work, including several album tracks and non-LP singles. "Wipe Out" is by far the best cut, of course, but the instrumentals, packed with reverbed guitars, honking saxes, and high-end drums aplenty, usually have an admirably sleek power. Two of the vocal surf tunes were co-written by Gary Usher, who also worked with the Beach Boys during this time. *—Richie Unterberger*

Surfaris Stomp / Jul. 4, 1995 / Varese Sarabande ✦✦✦✦

Aside from the significant drawback of missing "Wipe Out," this second anthology of the Surfaris' best work is just as good as the other Varese Sarabande compilation, *The Best of the Surfaris* (which doesn't duplicate any of the tracks here). Largely taken from rare singles and albums that the group recorded for Decca between 1963 and 1965, it also has a few previously unreleased cuts, some dating from their initial session (the same one that produced "Wipe Out"). If you like *The Best of the Surfaris,* you can't go wrong by adding this one to your collection as well—it's packed with haunting reverb, Ron Wilson's nonstop drum fills rank among the best stickwork of the pre-Keith Moon era, and one of the three vocal cuts is one of the most obscure Brian Wilson compositions ever released ("My Buddy Seat," co-written with Gary Usher). *—Richie Unterberger*

Billy Swan

b. May 12, 1942, Cape Giradeau, MO

Vocals, Keyboards, Guitar, Bass, Producer / Pop/Rock, Country-Rock, Rock & Roll

One of rock's more interesting fringe characters, Billy Swan had been in the music business for more than a decade before he landed a surprise number one neo-rockabilly hit in 1974 with "I Can Help." His composition "Lover Please" was a hit for Clyde McPhatter in the early '60s, and he spent the rest of the decade as a combination roadie, engineer's assistant, and songwriter, penning material for Conway Twitty, Waylon Jennings, and Mel Tillis. He played with Kris Kristofferson, Kinky Friedman, and Billy Joe Shaver in the '70s before the success of "I Can Help," whose swirling organ and classic '50s rockabilly arrangement anchored one of the best hit singles of the mid-'70s. Swan recorded a few albums as a solo act that were well received by critics, but he never hit the Top 40 again. Too eclectic to be characterized as a '50s revivalist, he actually mixed country, soul, and pop into his sound more frequently than out-and-out rockabilly. After a few years, Swan returned to Kristofferson's band, where he stayed until 1992. *—Richie Unterberger*

● **Best of Billy Swan** / Jan. 27, 1998 / Epic/Legacy ✦✦✦✦✦

Epic/Legacy's *The Best of Billy Swan* is a fine 16-track collection that features highlights from his recordings for Monument, Columbia and Epic in the '70s and '80s. Swan's unexpected crossover hit "I Can Help" is here, but the remaining 15 songs veer closer to country, bearing just a slight resemblance to the bouncy pop/rock of the hit. Among the remaining songs are the country hits "Everything's the Same (Ain't Nothing Changed)," "You're the One," "Shake, Rattle and Roll," "I Just Want to Taste Your Wine," "Do I Have to Draw a Picture," "I'm Not Lovin' You," "Stuck Right in the Middle of Your Love," "With Their Kind of Money and Our Kind of Love" and "Your Picture Still Loves Me (And I Still Love You)," as well as "Lover Please," the Clyde McPhatter song Swan wrote when he was in high school. Not all of the songs meet the standards of "I Can Help" and "Lover Please," abut many of them are interesting and are among the better country-pop of their era. *—Stephen Thomas Erlewine*

Sweet

f. 1968, London, England, **db.** 1982

Group / Glitter, Bubblegum, Glam Rock, Hard Rock

In some ways, the Sweet epitomized all the tacky hubris and garish silliness of the early '70s. Fusing bubblegum melodies with crunching, fuzzy guitars, the band looked like a heavy metal band, but were as tame as any pop group. It was a dichotomy that served them well, as they racked up a number of hits in both the U.K. and the U.S., which served as the predecessors for '80s pop-metal. Most of those hits were written by Nicky Chinn and Mike Chapman, a pair of British songwriters who had a way with silly, simple, catchy hooks. Chinn, Chapman and Sweet were smart enough to latch on to the British glam-rock fad, building a safer, radio-friendly and teen-oriented version. Sweet signed to RCA Records in 1971, and Chinn & Chapman wrote a number of lightweight, double-entendre-filled bubblegum pop songs for the group, which included six Top 40 hits. During this time, Sweet were writing their own B-sides and album tracks, which featured crunching hard rock guitars. Consequently, the duo decided to write tougher songs for the group. "Blockbuster," the first result of Chinn & Chapman's glam-rock approach, was the biggest hit Sweet ever had in the U.K., reaching number one in early 1973. By the summer of 1974, the members of Sweet had grown tired of the control Chinn & Chapman exerted over their career and decided to record without the duo. In the spring of 1975, Sweet had their first self-penned hit with "Fox on the Run," which reached the Top Ten in both the U.K. and the U.S.; "Ballroom Blitz" belatedly reached the American Top Ten in the summer of 1975. For the rest of the decade, the group continued to churn out album-oriented rock records, each less successful than its predecessor. Sweet bounced back into the charts in 1978 with "Love Is Like Oxygen," but the single proved to be their last gasp. After several years of little success or attention, Sweet broke up in 1982, reuniting on various occasions in the decade afterward. *—Stephen Thomas Erlewine*

● **The Best of Sweet** / Mar. 1, 1993 / Capitol ✦✦✦✦✦

Nobody played rock & roll trashier or dumber than Sweet, and their best moments shine on this terrific 16-track compilation. Every one of their hits were powered by an irresistibly stupid melody, big dumb guitars, and, on occasion, a whining synthesizer. It was glitter-rock for teens at its best, without the dark sensuality of T. Rex. Even today, Sweet's best songs—"Ballroom Blitz," "Little Willy," "Blockbuster," "Teenage Rampage," and the nearly-perfect "Fox on the Run"—still sound gloriously trashy. *—Stephen Thomas Erlewine*

Matthew Sweet

b. 1964, Lincoln, NE

Vocals, Guitar / Pop Underground, College Rock, Adult Alternative Pop/Rock, Power Pop, Alternative Pop/Rock

After spending the '80s as an unappreciated jangle-pop guitarist with Oh-OK and Lloyd Cole, as well as a solo artist, Matthew Sweet emerged in 1991 as the leading figure of the American power-pop revival. Like his British counterparts Teenage Fanclub, Sweet adhered to traditional songcraft, yet subverted the form by adding noisy post-punk guitar and flourishes of country-rock, resulting in an amalgam of the Beatles, Big Star, R.E.M. and Neil Young. Recorded with guitarists Richard Lloyd and Robert Quine, Sweet's third album, *Girlfriend* (1991), became a word-of-mouth critical and commercial hit over the course of 1992, with its title track reaching the Top Five on the Modern Rock charts. For the next five years, as alternative rock was the dominant commercial force in rock & roll, Sweet was a popular concert attraction, and his reputation as an alternative pop singer-songwriter was at its peak—his next two records, *Altered Beast* (1993) and *100% Fun* (1995), were both critically acclaimed and relatively successful albums, with the latter reaching gold status and making many year-end "Best Of" lists. Beginning with 1997's *Blue Sky on Mars,* Sweet settled into cult status, and while he wasn't enjoying the success of his previous records, most power-pop records of the latter half of the '90s were indebted to *Girlfriend.* *—Stephen Thomas Erlewine*

Inside / 1986 / Columbia ✦✦

Earth / 1989 / A&M ✦✦✦

● **Girlfriend** / Oct. 22, 1991 / Zoo ✦✦✦✦✦

Matthew Sweet's third album is a remarkable artistic breakthrough. Grounded in the guitar-pop of The Beatles, Big Star, Byrds, R.E.M., and Neil Young, *Girlfriend* melds all of Sweet's influences into one majestic, wrenching sound that encompasses both the gentle country-rock of "Winona" and the winding guitars of the title track and "Divine Intervention." Sweet's music might have recognizable roots, but *Girlfriend* never sounds derivative; thanks to his exceptional songwriting, the album is a fresh, original interpretation of a classic sound. *—Stephen Thomas Erlewine*

Altered Beast / Jul. 13, 1993 / Zoo ✦✦✦✦

Compared to the concise songwriting of *Girlfriend, Altered Beast* is all over the place, both emotionally and musically. Ranging from piercing guitar rave-ups ("Dinosaur Act") to gorgeous country-rock ("Time Capsule"), the album not only covers all sides of Sweet's musical personality, but pastes them together haphazardly. Consequently, it takes a bit of time for all of it to make sense, but after a few listens, it falls together, and its best moments equal *Girlfriend.* *—Stephen Thomas Erlewine*

Son of Altered Beast / Mar. 15, 1994 / Volcano ✦✦✦

100% Fun / Mar. 14, 1995 / Zoo ✦✦✦✦

Clocking in at 45 minutes, Matthew Sweet's third record of guitar-dominated, hook-laden power-pop runs through its 12 songs at a classic speed, piling up songs that lovingly conform to the three-minute pop tradition. Richard Lloyd's gnarled guitars save Sweet's melodies and harmonies from being saccharine or sappy. Behind Sweet's bright hooks lies something darker—the self-loathing of "Sick of Myself" and the mental manipulation of "We're the Same" aren't evident from the sound of the record, which obliterates any hidden meanings with its chiming guitars and driving rhythms. It might not have the consistent barrage of great songs like *Girlfriend,* yet it tames the wilder impulses of *Altered Beast* into an album that rocks its worries away without ever getting rid of them. *—Stephen Thomas Erlewine*

Blue Sky on Mars / Mar. 25, 1997 / Zoo ✦✦✦

In Reverse / Sep. 28, 1999 / Volcano ✦✦✦✦✦

Ever since *Girlfriend,* Matthew Sweet made tightly wound guitar-pop, but *In Reverse* takes a different approach, borrowing elements from Phil Spector, Brian Wilson, the Beatles, and Electric Light Orchestra to create a seductive ocean of sound. Vocals, guitars, and pianos are given cavernous reverb, surrounded by grand percussion, backwards guitars, and brass. Unlike many of his '90s pop peers, Sweet isn't aping *Pet Sounds* and *Magical Mystery Tour* just to prove that he can—this rich music is a personal interpretation of lush chamber pop and psychedelia, giving a musical counterpart for lovely melancholy songs of heartbreak and disillusion. *In Reverse* is a song cycle, with songs segueing into one another and playing off each other's themes, each blessed with glorious touches of neo-psychedelia and baroque pop. There's a unity of sound and song which makes *In Reverse* plays like a concept album and, like any good concept album, it ends with a grandiose gesture—a nine-minute suite called "Thunderstruck" which fuses the Beach Boys, Neil Young, and Sweet himself in unpredictable, thrilling ways. In that one song, all of the themes and pretensions of the album brilliantly come together, and that's the most remarkable thing about *In Reverse*—it fulfills its ambitions while delivering the emotional impact of *Girlfriend.* *—Stephen Thomas Erlewine*

Time Capsule: The Best of Matthew Sweet / Sep. 26, 2000 / Volcano ✦✦✦✦✦
One of the most unlikely and endearing successes of the alternative rock era, Matthew Sweet was—and is—one of the most consistent artists to come out of that time period. Compiled by Volcano Records, the same label that released Sweet's 1999 album *In Reverse, Time Capsule: The Best of Matthew Sweet* collects 16 of his best-loved songs and two new ones, "Ready" and "So Far." Not surprisingly, the anthology spends the most time with his strongest albums, especially his breakthrough, *Girlfriend*. A full four songs—"Divine Intervention," "I've Been Waiting," "Girlfriend," and "You Don't Love Me"—come from that 1991 classic, but *Altered Beast, 100% Fun, Blue Sky on Mars*, and even *In Reverse* are well represented with songs like "Time Capsule," "Sick of Myself," "We're the Same," "Where You Get Love," and "What Matters." Sweet's vibrant, vulnerable take on power pop revitalized the genre in the '90s, and this collection of his work still sounds completely fresh and enjoyable. *—Heather Phares*

The Swinging Blue Jeans

f. 1959, Liverpool, England, **db.** 1968
Group / Merseybeat, British Invasion
Although they're only remembered today for their 1964 hit "Hippy Hippy Shake," the Swinging Blue Jeans were actually one of the strongest of the Liverpool bands from the '60s British Invasion. "Hippy Hippy Shake"—a cover of an obscure '50s rocker that was actually done much better by the Beatles on tapes of their BBC performances—was their only Top 30 entry in the U.S. But the band enjoyed some other major and minor hits in the U.K., including a top-notch Merseyization of Betty Everett's (and later Linda Ronstadt's) "You're No Good," which they took into the British Top Five in 1964. They also wrote some catchy and energetic, if slightly sappy, originals in the purest Merseybeat style. While it doesn't add up to an enduring legacy, there's a lot to be said for the naive energy of the best of their early tunes. *—Richie Unterberger*

Blue Jeans A Swinging / 1964 / EMI ✦✦

● **Hippy Hippy Shake: the Definitive Collection** / May 4, 1993 / EMI America ✦✦✦✦✦
All of their U.K. and U.S. hits are included on this compilation. Highlights are "You're No Good," "Hippy Hippy Shake," and their fine (pre-Who) cover of Johnny Kidd's "Shakin' All Over," though even for the Anglophile, about half of this CD is forgettable, especially the dreary post-1966 stuff. This anthology includes several non-LP/rare singles and unreleased songs. *—Richie Unterberger*

T. Rex

f. 1967, **db.** 1978
Group / Album Rock, Proto-Punk, Glam Rock, Hard Rock
Initially a British folk-rock combo called Tyrannosaurus Rex, T. Rex was the primary force in glam rock, thanks to the creative direction of guitarist/vocalist Marc Bolan (b. Marc Feld). Bolan created a deliberately trashy form of rock & roll that was proud of its own disposability. T. Rex's music borrowed the underlying sexuality of early rock & roll, adding dirty, simple grooves and fat distorted guitars, as well as an overarching folkie/hippie spirtuality that always came through the clearest on ballads. While most of his peers concentrated on making cohesive albums, Bolan kept the idea of a three-minute pop single alive in the early '70s. In Britain, he became a superstar, sparking a period of "T. Rextacy" among the pop audience with a series of Top Ten hits, including four number one singles. Over in America, the group only had one major hit—the Top Ten "Bang a Gong (Get It On)"—before disappearing from the charts in 1973. T. Rex's popularity in the U.K. didn't begin to waver until 1975, yet they retained a devoted following until Marc Bolan's death in 1977. Over the next two decades, Bolan emerged as a cult figure and the music of T. Rex has proven quite influential on hard rock, punk, new wave, and alternative rock. *—Stephen Thomas Erlewine*

A Beard of Stars / 1970 / Polygram International ✦✦✦✦

T. Rex / 1970 / Castle ✦✦✦

★ **Electric Warrior** / 1971 / Reprise ✦✦✦✦✦
The album that essentially kick-started the U.K. glam rock craze, *Electric Warrior* completes T. Rex's transformation from hippie folk-rockers into flamboyant avatars of trashy rock & roll. There are a few vestiges of those early days remaining in the acoustic-driven ballads, but *Electric Warrior* spends most of its time in a swinging, hip-shaking groove powered by Marc Bolan's warm electric guitar. The music recalls not just the catchy simplicity of early rock & roll, but also the implicit sexuality—except that here, Bolan gleefully hauls it to the surface, singing out loud what was once only communicated through the shimmying beat. He takes obvious delight in turning teenage bubblegum rock into campy sleaze, not to mention filling it with pseudo-psychedelic hippie poetry. In fact, Bolan sounds just as obsessed with the heavens as he does with sex, whether he's singing about spiritual mysticism or begging a flying saucer to take him away. It's all done with the same theatrical flair, but Tony Visconti's spacious, echoing production makes it surprisingly convincing.

Still, the real reason *Electric Warrior* stands the test of time so well—despite its intended disposability—is that it revels so freely in its own absurdity and willful lack of substance. Not taking himself at all seriously, Bolan is free to pursue whatever silly wordplay, cosmic fantasies, or non sequitur imagery he feels like; his abandonment of any pretense to art becomes, ironically, a statement in itself. Bolan's lack of pomposity, back-to-basics songwriting, and elaborate theatrics went on to influence everything from hard rock to punk to new wave. But in the end, it's that sense of playfulness, combined with a raft of irresistible hooks, that keeps *Electric Warrior* such an infectious, invigorating listen today. *—Steve Huey*

☆ **The Slider** / Jul. 21, 1972 / Mercury ✦✦✦✦✦
Buoyed by two U.K. number one singles in "Telegram Sam" and "Metal Guru," *The Slider* became T. Rex's most popular record on both sides of the Atlantic, despite the fact that it produced no hits in the U.S. *The Slider* essentially replicates all the virtues of *Electric Warrior*, crammed with effortless hooks and trashy fun. All of Bolan's signatures are here—mystical folk-tinged ballads, overt sexual come-ons crooned over sleazy, bopping boogies, loopy nonsense poetry, and a mastery of the three-minute pop song form. The main difference is that the trippy mix of *Electric Warrior* is replaced by a fuller, more immediate-sounding production. Bolan's guitar has a harder bite, the backing choruses are more up-front, and the arrangements are thicker sounding, even introducing a string section on some cuts (both ballads and rockers). Even with the beefier production, T. Rex still doesn't sound nearly as heavy as many of the bands it influenced (and even a few of its glam contemporaries), but that's partly intentional—Bolan's love of a good groove takes precedence over fast tempos or high volume. Lyrically, Bolan's flair for the sublimely ridiculous is fully intact, but he has way too much style for *The Slider* to sound truly stupid, especially after you detect the playful, knowing wink in his delivery. It's nearly impossible not to get caught up in the irresistible rush of melodies and cheery good times. Even if it treads largely the same ground as *Electric Warrior, The Slider* is flawlessly executed, and every bit the classic that its predecessor is. *—Steve Huey*

Tanx / Feb. 1973 / Mercury ✦✦✦✦✦
By 1973's *Tanx*, the T. Rex hit-making machine was beginning to show some wear and tear, but Marc Bolan still had more than a few winners up his sleeve. It was also admirable that Bolan was attempting to broaden the T. Rex sound—soulful backup singers and horns are heard throughout, a full two years before David Bowie used the same formula for his mega-seller *Young Americans*. However, *Tanx* did not contain any instantly recognizable hits, as their past couple of releases had, and the performances were not quite as vibrant, due to non-stop touring and drug use. Despite an era of transition looming on the horizon for the band, tracks such as "Rapids," "Highway Knees," "The Street & Babe Shadow," and "Born to Boogie" contain the expected classic T. Rex sound. The leadoff track, "Tenement Lady," is an interesting Beatle-esque epic, while "Shock Rock" criticizes the early-'70s glam scene, which T. Rex played a prominent role in creating. Other highlights include one of Bolan's most gorgeous and heartfelt ballads, "Broken Hearted Blues," as well as the brief, explosive rocker "Country Honey." *Tanx* marked the close of what many consider T. Rex's golden era; unfortunately, the band members would drift off one by one soon after, until Bolan was the only one remaining by the mid-'70s. Like the 1997 Polygram CD reissue of *The Slider*, the 1997 version of *Tanx* contains seven extra bonus tracks, including such non-album hits as "Children of the Revolution" and "20th Century Boy." *—Greg Prato*

Zinc Alloy & the Hidden Riders of Tomorrow / 1974 / Mercury ✦✦

Bolan's Zip Gun / 1975 / Mercury ✦✦

Futuristic Dragon / 1976 / Mercury ✦✦✦

Dandy in the Underworld / 1977 / Mercury ✦✦✦

T. Rextasy: The Best of T. Rex, 1970-1973 / 1985 / Warner Brothers ✦✦✦✦✦
This is it, T. Rex fans, the best of their greatest hits in a compilation. The only problem is, it's no longer in print. Unlike the T. Rex compilations currently available, *T. Rextasy* contains all the hits prior to *Electric Warrior*, as well as several tracks unavailable anywhere else. This is also the best sequencing job of the T. Rex hits, each song extending to the next, until you feel like you've taken an insightful journey through the dreamy and poetic world of Marc Bolan. You'll also find strong album tracks, like the guitar-fuzz freakout "Jewel," which was one of T. Rex's first "rock" songs (after beginning as a straight folk duo), and an acoustic cover of "Summertime Blues." Also included are unedited versions of such classics as "Get It On (Bang a Gong)" and "Raw Ramp," with unreleased introductions. Every hit is here ("Metal Guru," "Telegram Sam," "Ride a White Swan," etc.), except for "Children of the Revolution," which would have made the anthology complete. If you don't want to buy all of T. Rex's early-'70s albums (which you really should—most of their album tracks were as good as their singles), hunt down *T. Rextasy: The Best of T. Rex 1970-1973*. It will supply you with nearly all of their prime cuts. *—Greg Prato*

The Definitive Tyrannosaurus Rex / Oct. 25, 1994 / Sequel ✦✦✦✦✦

Great Hits 1972-1977, Vol. 1: The A-Sides / Nov. 8, 1994 / Mercury ✦✦✦✦✦
Few other bands have had as many "Best Of" collections released over the years as T. Rex. And for the most part, almost all are missing hits from their 1971 *Electric Warrior* album and before ("Bang a Gong," "Jeepster," "Ride a White Swan," "Hot Love," etc.). As confirmed by the title *Great Hits 1972-1977*, this 1994 collection is no different. While it does contain most of Bolan and company's biggest hits—"Metal Guru," "Solid Gold Easy Action," "Groover," "20th Century Boy" and others—it cannot be considered a definitive "Best Of." What makes this set different than others is the inclusion of A-sides from after 1973, something that most T. Rex compilations fail to do; hence, it's one of the few to contain their forgotten mid-'70s U.K. Top 20 hits "New York City" and "I Love to Boogie." But as most T. Rex fans know, Bolan peaked artistically and commercially in the early '70s, and the majority of his post-1973 work pales in comparison to his early hits. Hopefully one day a record company will finally collect T. Rex's true greatest hits from all eras. *—Greg Prato*

Great Hits 1972-1977, Vol. 2: B-Sides / Nov. 8, 1994 / Mercury ✦✦✦

Take That

f. 1990, **db.** Feb. 13, 1996
Group / Teen Pop, Euro-Pop, Dance-Pop
As the most popular teen-pop sensation in Britain since the '60s, Take That ruled the UK charts during the first half of the '90s. In strict commercial terms, the band sold more records than any English act since the Beatles, though the cultural and musical importance was significantly less substantial. Conceived as a British answer to the New Kids on the Block, Take That initially worked the same territory as their American counterparts, singing watered-down new jack R&B, urban soul, and mainstream pop. Eventually, the group worked their way toward hi-NRG dance music, while also pursuing an adult-contemporary ballad direction. Take That's boyish good looks guaranteed them a significant portion of the teenybopper audience, but in a bizarre twist, most of their videos and promotional photos had a strong homosexual undercurrent—they were marketed to pre-teen girls and a kitschy gay audience simultaneously. Take That was also able to make inroads in the adult audience in Britain

through Gary Barlow's melodic, sensitive ballads. For nearly five years, the group's popularity was unsurpassed in Britain, as they racked up a total of seven number one hits. By the middle of the decade, all of the members were entering their mid-'20s and became disenchanted with each other. Furthermore, the pop music tastes in Britain were shifting toward the classic guitar-pop sounds of Brit-pop bands like Blur and Oasis, who were able to appeal to both the indie-rock and teen-pop audience. Consequently, the group called it quits in 1996, as Oasis began to surpass Take That both in terms of sales and cultural impact. Nevertheless, Take That remained one of the most interesting and popular British teen-pop phenomenons not only of the '90s, but of the rock & roll era. *—Stephen Thomas Erlewine*

Take That & Party / 1993 / RCA ✦✦✦

Everything Changes / Oct. 18, 1993 / RCA ✦✦✦✦✦

Nobody Else / Aug. 15, 1995 / RCA ✦✦✦✦

● **Greatest Hits** / 1996 / RCA ✦✦✦✦✦
Take That disbanded just as they were on the verge of huge success in the U.S., but they never really needed American success—for all of the early '90s, they were undefeatable on the British pop charts. During their six years together, the band racked up seven number one hits, most of them between 1992 and 1996. Every member of Take That sang, but Robbie Williams, Mark Owen, and Gary Barlow were the main vocalists, and they have all of the best moments on the band's *Greatest Hits* collection. Weaving between dance-pop like "Relight My Fire," "Sure," and "I Found Heaven," and ballads like "A Million Love Songs," "Back for Good," and their farewell single, a cover of the Bee Gees' "How Deep Is Your Love, "Take That's *Greatest Hits* is sugary, infectious pop that practically defines the term guilty pleasure. *—Stephen Thomas Erlewine*

Talk Talk

f. 1981, London, England, **db.** 1991
Group / New Romantic, Post-Rock/Experimental, New Wave, Synth Pop
With the exception of a handful of common threads—chief among them the plaintive vocals and haunting lyrics of frontman Mark Hollis—there is little to suggest that the five studio LPs which make up the Talk Talk oeuvre are indeed the work of the same band throughout. After beginning their career with records which virtually epitomize the new wave era which spawned them, the British group never looked back, making significant strides with each successive album on their way to discovering a wholly unique and uncategorizable sound informed by elements of jazz, classical and ambient music; their masterful final recordings, while neglected commercially, possess a timelessness rare among music of any genre, and in retrospect they seem the clear starting point for the post-rock movement of the 1990s. For many casual listeners Eighties-era synth-pop hits like "It's My Life" and "Life Is What You Make of It" remain Talk Talk's enduring legacy, but among more serious fans the group's last two studio LPs, 1988's *Spirit of Eden* and 1991's *Laughing Stock*, are the real deal. *Spirit of Eden* is the breakthrough, rejecting pop conventions in favor of an unprecedented blend of ambient textures, jazz-inspired arrangements and avant-garde musings; complete with frontman Mark Hollis' plaintive vocals and hearftelt, deeply resonant lyrics, it's an album virtually without precedent, existing in its own world and its own time. *Laughing Stock*, meanwhile, refines the experiment, adopting a wider dynamic range while further moving outside the sphere of compositional structure. *—Jason Ankeny*

The Party's Over / 1982 / EMI ✦✦✦
Talk Talk began life as a slavishly derivative, Duran Duran-styled, new romantic synth-pop band, as their debut, *The Party's Over*, clearly shows. Much of the album seems to attempt to recreate Duran Duran's debut, but even with their most blatant ripoffs, like the single "Talk Talk," they do it with a naive charm that makes for some really enjoyable music, even if it isn't particularly innovative or groundbreaking. *—Chris Woodstra*

It's My Life / 1984 / EMI ✦✦✦✦
After an unremarkable debut, Talk Talk regrouped and refashioned themselves more in the style of sophisto-era Roxy Music while developing their own voice. *It's My Life* shows a great leap in songwriting, the band making highly personal statements with a sexy, seductive groove and a diversity that transcends the synth-pop tag. Synthesizers still play a dominant role, but the music is made far more interesting by mixing "real" instruments and challenging world music rhythms seamlessly with the technology. Still pulling off the catchy single (like "Dum Dum Girl" and the title track, as well as the simply sublime "Does Caroline Know?") on *It's My Life*, Talk Talk also proved themselves capable of achieving a cohesive album—a rare feat for the time and an unexpected surprise from a band that seemed to be simply a bandwagon-jumper. *—Chris Woodstra*

The Colour of Spring / 1986 / EMI ✦✦✦✦✦
With *It's My Life*, Talk Talk proved that they could pull off an entire album of strong material. With *Colour of Spring*, they took it one step further, moving to a near-concept song cycle, following the emotional ups and downs of relationships and pondering life in general. Musically, they built on the experimental direction of the previous album with interesting rhythms, sweeping orchestration, complex arrangements, and even a children's chorus to create an evocative, hypnotic groove. Though the songs were catchier on the earlier efforts and the ambient experimentation was more fully achieved later on, *Colour of Spring* succeeded in marrying the two ideas into one unique sound for their most thoroughly satisfying album. *—Chris Woodstra*

Spirit of Eden / 1988 / EMI ✦✦✦✦✦
Compare *Spirit of Eden* with any other previous release in the Talk Talk catalog, and it's almost impossible to believe it's the work of the same band—exchanging electronics for live, organic sounds and rejecting structure in favor of mood and atmosphere, the album is an unprecedented breakthrough, a musical and emotional catharsis of immense power. Mark Hollis' songs exist far outside of the pop idiom, drawing instead on ambient textures, jazz-like arrangements, and avant-garde accents; for all of their intricacy and delicate beauty, compositions like "Inheritance" and "I Believe in You" also possess an elemental strength—Hollis' oblique lyrics speak to themes of loss and redemption with understated grace, and his hauntingly poignant vocals evoke wrenching spiritual turmoil tempered with unflagging hope. A singular musical experience. *—Jason Ankeny*

● **Natural History: The Very Best of Talk Talk** / Oct. 1990 / EMI America ✦✦✦✦✦
During the band's hiatus following *Spirit of Eden*, EMI issued a hits collection, compiling the singles from the first four albums as well as the non-LP "My Foolish Friend," a couple of live tracks, and an edit of "Desire." *Natural History* serves as a nice introduction to the band, showing them as an effective singles act despite their more recent album-concept experiments, and the added rarities make the package a necessary addition for fans as well. *—Chris Woodstra*

Laughing Stock / Nov. 19, 1991 / Polydor ✦✦✦✦✦
Virtually ignored upon its initial release, *Laughing Stock* continues to grow in stature and influence by leaps and bounds. Picking up where *Spirit of Eden* left off, the album operates outside of the accepted sphere of rock to create music which is both delicate and intense; recorded with a large classical ensemble, it defies easy categorization, conforming to very few structural precedents—while the gently hypnotic "Myrrhman" flirts with ambient textures, the percussive "Ascension Day" drifts toward jazz before the two sensibilities converge to create something entirely new and different on "New Grass." The epic "After the Flood," on the other hand, is an atmospheric whirlpool laced with jackhammer guitar feedback and Mark Hollis' remarkably plaintive vocals; it flows into "Taphead," perhaps the most evocative, spacious, and understated piece on the record. A work of staggering complexity and immense beauty, *Laughing Stock* remains an under-recognized masterpiece, and its echoes can be heard throughout much of the finest experimental music issued in its wake. *—Jason Ankeny*

Asides Besides / Apr. 1998 / EMI ✦✦✦✦
Asides Besides can certainly be seen as a cash-in release to coincide with Mark Hollis' first solo release and the reissue of Talk Talk's EMI catalog, but rarely does such a calculated industry move result in such a treat for fans. Over two discs, *Asides Besides* essentially ties up all of the loose ends for the band. Disc one is probably the least essential, bringing out all of the 12" remixes, which are of marginal interest, though all are superior to those found on the unauthorized *History Revisited*. Disc two however, reveals no shortage of prime rarities beginning with three demos from 1981 ("Talk Talk," "Mirror Man" and "Candy"). A handful of singles are included—the not-so-rare single, "My Foolish Friend," the ultra-rare "Why Is it So Hard" (from the film *First Born*), the U.S. remix of "Dum Dum Girl," and the edit of "Eden"—but the real gems are the B-sides, which are anything but "throwaways." In fact, the B-sides are not only in most cases as strong as the ones that made it onto the albums, but they also indicate the more experimental direction the band would take later on. *Asides Besides* may be of interest only to diehard Talk Talk fans, but for that audience this collection is absolutely essential. *—Chris Woodstra*

London 1986 / Apr. 20, 1999 / Blueprint ✦✦✦

Talking Heads

f. 1974, **db.** 1991
Group / College Rock, American Punk, New York Punk, Album Rock, Post-Punk, Pop/Rock, New Wave
At the start of their career, Talking Heads were all nervous energy, detached emotion, and subdued minimalism. When they released their last album about 12 years later, the band had recorded everything from art-funk to polyrhythmic worldbeat explorations and simple, melodic guitar-pop, becoming one of the most critically acclaimed bands of the '80s while still managing to earn several pop hits. While some of their music can seem too self-consciously experimental, clever, and intellectual for its own good, at their best, Talking Heads represents everything good about art-school punks. Vocalist/guitarist David Byrne, drummer Chris Franz, bassist Tina Weymouth literally did meet at art school, adding keyboardist Jerry Harrison just after their New York debut. By 1977, the band had released their first album, *Talking Heads '77*. Working with Brian Eno on a trio of albums during the late '70s resulted in carefully constructed, arty pop songs, distinguished by extensive experimentation and flourishes of African-styled polyrhythms. With mid-'80s albums like *Speaking in Tongues* and *Little Creatures*, the band began emphasizing a more rigid pop-song structure, though they returned to the worldbeat explorations with 1987's *Naked*. Put on hiatus as Byrne pursued solo projects and Franz and Weymouth continued their Tom Tom Club side project, Talking Heads finally broke up in 1991. Five years later, Harrison, Franz and Weymouth formed the Heads for a reunion album; in 1999, all four original members worked together to promote a 15th-anniversary edition of *Stop Making Sense*. *—Stephen Thomas Erlewine*

☆ **Talking Heads '77** / 1977 / Sire ✦✦✦✦✦
Though they were the most highly touted new wave band to emerge from the *CBGB's* scene in New York, it was not clear at first whether Talking Heads' Lower East Side art rock approach could make the subway ride to the midtown pop mainstream successfully. The lead-off track of the debut album, *Talking Heads: 77*, "Uh-Oh, Love Comes to Town," was a pop song that emphasized the group's unlikely roots in late-'60s bubblegum, Motown, and Caribbean music. But the "Uh-Oh" gave away the group's game early, with its nervous, disconnected lyrics and David Byrne's strained voice. All pretenses of normality were abandoned by the second track, as Talking Heads finally started to sound on record they way they did downtown: the staggered rhythms and sudden tempo changes, the odd guitar tunings and rhythmic, single-note patterns, the non-rhyming, non-linear lyrics that came across like odd remarks overheard from a psychiatrist's couch, and that voice, singing above its normal range, its falsetto leaps and strangled cries resembling a madman trying desperately to sound normal. Talking Heads threw you off balance, but grabbed your attention with a sound that seemed alternately threatening and goofy. The music was undeniably catchy, even at its most ominous, especially on "Psycho Killer," Byrne's supreme statement of demented purpose. Amazingly, that song made the singles chart for a few weeks, evidence of the group's

quirky appeal, but the album was not a big hit, and it remained unclear whether Talking Heads spoke only the secret language of the urban arts types or whether that could be translated into the more common tongue of hip pop culture. In any case, they had succeeded as artists, using existing elements in an unusual combination to create something new that still managed to be oddly familiar. And that made *Talking Heads: 77* a landmark album. — *William Ruhlmann*

☆ **More Songs About Buildings and Food** / Jul. 14, 1978 / Sire ✦✦✦✦✦
The title of Talking Heads' second album, *More Songs About Buildings and Food*, slyly addressed the sophomore record syndrome, in which songs not used on a first LP are mixed with hastily written new material. If the band's sound seems more conventional, the reason simply may be that one had encountered the odd song structures, staccato rhythms, strained vocals, and impressionistic lyrics once before. Another was that new co-producer Brian Eno brought a musical unity that tied the album together, especially in terms of the rhythm section, the sequencing, the pacing, and the mixing. Where Talking Heads had largely been about David Byrne's voice and words, Eno moved the emphasis to the bass-and-drums team of Tina Weymouth and Chris Frantz; all the songs were danceable, and there were only short breaks between them. Byrne held his own, however, and he continued to explore the eccentric, if not demented persona first heard on *77*, whether he was adding to his observations on boys and girls or turning his "Psycho Killer" into an artist in "Artists Only." Through the first nine tracks, *More Songs* was the successor to *77*, which would not have earned it landmark status or made it the commercial breakthrough it became. It was the last two songs that pushed the album over those hurdles. First there was an inspired cover of Al Green's "Take Me to the River"; released as a single, it made the Top 40 and pushed the album to gold-record status. Second was the album closer, "The Big Country," Byrne's country-tinged reflection on flying over middle America; it crystallized his artist-vs.-ordinary people perspective in unusually direct and dismissive terms, turning the old Chuck Berry patriotic travelogue theme of rock & roll on its head and employing a great hook in the process. — *William Ruhlmann*

Fear of Music / Aug. 3, 1979 / Sire ✦✦✦✦✦
By titling their third album, *Fear of Music* and opening it with the African rhythmic experiment "I Zimbra," complete with nonsense lyrics by poet Hugo Ball, Talking Heads made the record seem more of a departure than it was. Though *Fear of Music* was musically distinct from its predecessors, mostly because of the use of minor keys that gave the music a more ominous sound. Previously, David Byrne's offbeat observations had been set off by an overtly humorous tone; on *Fear of Music*, he was still odd, but no longer so funny. At the same time, however, the music had become even more compelling. Worked up from jams (though Byrne received sole songwriter's credit), the music was becoming denser and more driving, notably on the album's standout track, "Life During Wartime," with lyrics that matched the music's power. "This ain't no party," declared Byrne, "this ain't no disco, this ain't no fooling around." The other key song, "Heaven," extended the dismissal Byrne had expressed for the U.S. in "The Big Country" to paradise itself: "Heaven is a place where nothing ever happens." It was also the album's most melodic song. Those were the highlights. What kept *Fear of Music* from being as impressive an album as Talking Heads' first two was that much of it seemed to repeat those earlier efforts, while the few newer elements seemed so risky and exciting. It was an uneven, transitional album, though its better songs were as good as any Talking Heads ever did. — *William Ruhlmann*

☆ **Remain in Light** / Oct. 8, 1980 / Sire ✦✦✦✦✦
The musical transition that seemed to have just begun with *Fear of Music* came to fruition on Talking Heads' fourth album, *Remain in Light*. "I Zimbra" and "Life During Wartime" from the earlier album served as the blueprints for a disc on which the group explored African polyrhythms on a series of driving groove tracks, over which David Byrne chanted and sang his typically disconnected lyrics. *Remain in Light* had more words than any previous Heads record, but they counted for less than ever in the sweep of the music. The album's single, "Once in a Lifetime," flopped upon release, but over the years became an audience favorite due to a striking video, its inclusion in the band's 1984 concert film *Stop Making Sense*, and its second single release (in the live version) because of its use in the 1986 movie *Down and Out in Beverly Hills*, when it became a minor chart entry. Byrne sounded typically uncomfortable in the verses ("And you may find yourself in a beautiful house, with a beautiful wife / And you may ask yourself—Well ... how did I get here?"), which were undercut by the reassuring chorus ("Letting the days go by"). Even without a single, *Remain in Light* was a hit, indicating that Talking Heads were connecting with an audience ready to follow their musical evolution, and the album was so inventive and influential, it was no wonder. As it turned out, however, it marked the end of one aspect of the group's development and their last new music for three years. —William Ruhlmann

The Name of This Band Is Talking Heads / Mar. 24, 1982 / Sire ✦✦✦

Speaking in Tongues / Jun. 1, 1983 / Sire ✦✦✦✦
Talking Heads found a way to open up the dense textures of the music they had developed with Brian Eno on their two previous studio albums for *Speaking in Tongues*, and were rewarded with their most popular album yet. Ten backup singers and musicians accompanied the original quartet, but somehow the sound was more spacious, and the music admitted aspects of gospel, notably in the call-and-response of "Slippery People," and John Lee Hooker-style blues, on "Swamp." As usual, David Byrne determinedly sang and chanted impressionistic, nonlinear lyrics, sometimes by mix-and-matching clichés ("No visible means of support and you have not seen nuthin' yet," he declared on "Burning Down the House," the Heads' first Top Ten hit), and the songs' very lack of clear meaning was itself a lyrical subject. "Still don't make no sense," Byrne admitted in "Making Flippy Floppy," but by the next song, "Girlfriend Is Better," that had become an order—"Stop making sense," he chanted over and over. Some of his charming goofiness had returned since the overly serious *Remain in Light* and *Fear of Music*, however, and the accompanying music, filled with odd percussive and synthesizer sounds, could be unusually light and bouncy. The album closer, "This Must Be the Place (Naive Melody)," even sounded hopeful. Well, sort of. Despite their formal power, Talking Heads' last two albums seemed to have painted them into a corner, which may be why it took them three years to craft a follow-up, but on *Speaking in Tongues*, they found an open window and flew out of it. — *William Ruhlmann*

Little Creatures / Jun. 10, 1985 / Sire ✦✦✦✦✦
Talking Heads' most immediately accessible album, *Little Creatures* eschewed the pattern of recent Heads albums, in which instrumental tracks had been worked up from riffs and grooves, after which David Byrne improvised melodies and lyrics. The songs on *Little Creatures*, most of which were credited to Byrne alone (with the band credited only with arrangements) sounded like they'd been written as songs. Perhaps as one result, the band had been streamlined, with extra musicians used only for specific effects rather than playing along as an ensemble. Byrne, who was singing in his natural range for once, frequently was augmented with backup singers. The overall result: ear candy. *Little Creatures* was a pop album, and an accomplished one, by a band that knew what it was doing. True, Byrne's lyrics were still intriguingly quirky, but even his subject matter was becoming more mature. "I've seen sex and I think it's okay," and he sang on "Creatures of Love," and suddenly the geek had become a man. Where he had once pondered the hopes of boys and girls, he was now making observations about children. And even if his impulses remained strange—"I wanna make him stay up all night," he declared about a baby (presumably not his own) in "Stay Up Late"—he retained his charm and inventiveness. *Little Creatures* was, in a sense, Talking Heads lite. It was hard to think of this as the same band that produced "Psycho Killer." But for the band's expanding audience, who made this their second platinum album, that was okay. And their popularity was being accomplished with no diminution in their creativity. — *William Ruhlmann*

True Stories / 1986 / Sire ✦✦

Naked / Mar. 1988 / Fly ✦✦

● **Popular Favorites 1984-1992: Sand in the Vaseline** / Oct. 13, 1992 / Sire ✦✦✦✦✦
Featuring material from every Talking Heads album except the live *The Name of This Band is Talking Heads*, *Sand in the Vaseline* is a terrific double-disc retrospective of the band's long and varied career. Featuring all of their hit singles and trademark songs ("Psycho Killer," "Take Me to the River," "Burning Down the House," "And She Was," "Once In a Lifetime," "Swamp," "Memories Can't Wait," "Crosseyed and Painless," "Road to Nowhere," "(Nothing But) Flowers," "Life During Wartime"), the set also includes five previously unreleased tracks. — *Stephen Thomas Erlewine*

Stop Making Sense [Special Editon] / Sep. 7, 1999 / Sire/Warner ✦✦✦
When the soundtrack for the classic Talking Heads movie *Stop Making Sense* was originally issued in 1984, it was only nine tracks in length, even though a total of 16 were performed on film. So when the film was rereleased in theaters and on home video in 1999, a new version of the soundtrack was issued as well, including all 16 songs and sporting an even better remastered sound. Recorded over three nights at Hollywood's *Pantages Theatre* in December 1983 (during the tour in support of *Speaking in Tongues*, the usual four-piece lineup was supplemented by Parliament-Funkadelic keyboardist Bernie Worrell, percussionist Steve Scales, guitarist Alex Weir, and backup singers Lynn Mabry and Ednah Holt. Songs from all eras of the band are featured. The first four tracks are early selections ("Psycho Killer," "Heaven") performed as bare renditions, plus full-band funky versions of such later hits as "Life During Wartime," "Burning Down the House," "Once in a Lifetime," and "Girlfriend Is Better." Also included are less-known album tracks ("Swamp," "This Must Be the Place," "Crosseyed and Painless"), plus a track from David Byrne's 1981 *Catherine Wheel* album ("What a Day That Was"), and "Genius of Love" by the Tom Tom Club (a side project of drummer Chris Frantz and bassist Tina Weymouth). One of the greatest live albums ever, the 1999 version of *Stop Making Sense* captures the Talking Heads at the height of their powers. A quintessential purchase. — *Greg Prato*

James Taylor

b. Mar. 12, 1948, Boston, MA
Vocals, Guitar / Folk-Rock, Soft Rock, Adult Contemporary, Singer/Songwriter
When people use the term "singer/songwriter" (often modified by the word "sensitive"), in praise or in criticism, it's James Taylor that they're thinking of. Yet in a career now extending three decades, Taylor's biggest hits have come with his cover versions of other people's songs. Go figure. He was signed as a solo artist by the Beatles' Apple label in 1968 and released his debut album, *James Taylor*. But it was his 1970 Warner Brothers LP, the triple-platinum *Sweet Baby James*, with its understated, autobiographical Top Ten hit "Fire and Rain," that was his commercial breakthrough. *Mud Slide Slim and the Blue Horizon* (1971) was another million-seller and contained the number one single "You've Got a Friend," written by Carole King. Taylor married Carly Simon in 1972, around the time that the gold *One Man Dog* was released. *In the Pocket* (1976) was Taylor's last album for Warner Brothers; he moved to Columbia Records for *JT* (1977), a double-platinum comeback that featured a Top Ten cover of Jimmy Jones's "Handy Man." *Flag* (1979) and *Dad Loves His Work* (1981) were Top Ten gold albums. — *William Ruhlmann*

James Taylor / Dec. 6, 1968 / Capitol ✦✦✦✦✦
On this self-titled debut album, James Taylor's reflective lyrics, containing his melancholic observations on life and love, were leavened by his attractive folk melodies, his acoustic guitar fingerpicking, and his warm, rich voice, which was unconsciously reminiscent of the calm crooning school of Bing Crosby and Perry Como. To these, producer Peter Asher added the accomplished but subdued string and brass arrangements, using a few pieces per track, with musical "links" between songs, building up to a full orchestra on the last two songs. The result was an amazingly distinctive effort, all in the service of Taylor's songs, which included "Knocking 'Round the Zoo" (a comic, bluesy reminiscence on life in a mental institution), "Something in the Way She Moves," "Rainy Day Man," and "Carolina in My Mind" (with Paul McCartney on bass), songs that have been concert favorites for decades. However personal Taylor's young angst may have been, it connected strongly with his generation's, and remains among his better efforts. — *William Ruhlmann*

☆ **Sweet Baby James** / Feb. 1970 / Warner Brothers ✦✦✦✦✦
The heart of James Taylor's appeal is that you can take him two ways. On the one hand, his music, including that warm voice, is soothing; its minor key melodies and restrained playing draw in the listener. On the other hand, his world view, especially on such songs as "Fire and Rain," and reflects the pessimism and desperation of the 1960s hangover that was the early '70s. That may not be intentional: "Fire and Rain" was about the suicide of a fellow inmate of Taylor's at a mental institution, not the national malaise. But Taylor's sense of wounded hopelessness—"I'm all in pieces, you can have your own choice," he sings in "Country Road"—struck a chord with music fans, especially because of its attractive mixture of folk, country, gospel, and blues elements, all of them carefully understated and distanced. Taylor didn't break your heart, he understood that it was already broken, as was his own, and he offered comfort. As a result, *Sweet Baby James* sold millions of copies, spawned a Top Ten hit in "Fire and Rain" and a Top 40 hit in "Country Road," and launched not only Taylor's career as a pop superstar but also the entire singer/songwriter movement of the early '70s that included Joni Mitchell, Carole King, Jackson Browne, Cat Stevens, and others. A second legacy became clear two decades later, when country stars like Garth Brooks began to cite Taylor, with his use of steel guitar, references to Jesus, and rural and Western imagery on *Sweet Baby James*, as a major influence. *— William Ruhlmann*

Mud Slide Slim and the Blue Horizon / Apr. 1971 / Warner Brothers ✦✦✦✦
James Taylor's commercial breakthrough in 1970 was predicated on the relationship between the private concerns expressed in his songs and the larger philosophical mood of his audience. He was going through depression, heartbreak, and addiction; they were recovering from the political and cultural storms of the '60s. On his follow-up to the landmark *Sweet Baby James*, Taylor brought his listeners up to date, wisely trying to step beyond the cultural, if not the personal, markers he had established. Despite affirming romance in songs like "Love Has Brought Me Around" and the moving "You Can Close Your Eyes" as well as companionship in "You've Got a Friend," the record still came as a defense against the world, not an embrace of it; Taylor was unable to forget the past or trust the present. The songs were full of references to the road and the highway, and he was uncomfortable with his new role as spokesman. The confessional songwriter was now, necessarily, writing about what it was like to be a confessional songwriter: *Mud Slide Slim and the Blue Horizon* served the valuable function of beginning to move James Taylor away from the genre he had defined, which ultimately would give him a more long-lasting appeal. *— William Ruhlmann*

One Man Dog / Nov. 1972 / Warner Brothers ✦✦✦

Walking Man / Jun. 1974 / Warner Brothers ✦✦✦

Gorilla / May 1975 / Warner Brothers ✦✦✦
Gorilla served notice to anyone expecting James Taylor to continue on in the personal, confessional vein of his first few albums that he did not intend to do so. Recording in Burbank with Warners staff producers Lenny Waronker and Russ Titelman, Taylor used a stellar backup band augmented by such guests as Graham Nash and David Crosby (who harmonized on the chart single "Mexico"), his wife Carly Simon, mandolinist David Grisman, saxophone player David Sanborn, Randy Newman on "hornorgan," and Little Feat slide guitarist Lowell George. This team worked on a set of light, pleasant songs that bordered on the generic—one was called "Music," another "Love Songs"—but were performed and sung with taste and care. Taylor was relentlessly upbeat; even "Angry Blues," which confessed, "I can't help it if I don't feel so good," didn't sound like things were that bad. But then, these songs didn't seem to be about Taylor, or if they were, as in the extended metaphor of the title track, the connection was so oblique that it was hard to say what the point was. Still, one could glide on Taylor's easy vocals and the band's competence, and *Gorilla* was an enjoyable listening experience. "How Sweet It Is (To Be Loved by You)," the first of a series of bleached R&B covers, became a Top Ten hit, and the album restored Taylor's commercial fortunes, setting him on the steady path he would follow for decades after. But who would have thought only a few years before that the king of the confessional song poets would turn into such a lightweight *— William Ruhlmann*

In the Pocket / Jun. 1976 / Warner Brothers ✦✦✦

★ **Greatest Hits** / Nov. 1976 / Warner Brothers ✦✦✦✦✦
James Taylor had scored eight Top 40 hits by the fall of 1976 when Warner Brothers marked the end of his contract with this compilation. One of those hits, the Top Ten gold single "Mockingbird," a duet with his wife Carly Simon, was on Elektra Records, part of the Warners family of labels and presumably available, but it was left off. "Long Ago and Far Away," a lesser hit (though it made the Top Ten on the Easy Listening charts) wasn't used either. In addition to the six hits—"Fire and Rain," "Country Road," "You've Got a Friend," "Don't Let Me Be Lonely Tonight," "How Sweet It Is (To Be Loved by You)," and "Shower the People"—that were included, the album featured a couple of less successful singles, "Mexico" and "Walking Man," the album track "Sweet Baby James," and three previously unreleased recordings—a live version of "Steamroller" and newly recorded versions of "Something in the Way She Moves" and "Carolina in My Mind," songs featured on Taylor's 1968 debut album, recorded for Apple/Capitol. The result was a reasonable collection for an artist who wasn't particularly well-defined by his singles. One got little sense of Taylor's evolution from the dour, confessional songs of his first two albums to the more conventional pop songs of his sixth and seventh ones. But one did hear isolated examples of Taylor's undeniable warmth and facility for folk/country-tinged pop. By the next summer, Taylor was back in the Top Ten on Columbia, and *Greatest Hits* was out of date. But it remains a good sampler of Taylor's more popular early work. And, decades later, it remained the only Taylor compilation in print in the U.S. *— William Ruhlmann*

JT / Jun. 1977 / Columbia/Legacy ✦✦✦✦
On his last couple of Warner Brothers albums, *Gorilla* and *In the Pocket*, James Taylor seemed to be converting himself from the shrinking violet, too-sensitive-to-live "rainy day man" of his early records into a mainstream, easy-listening crooner with a sunny outlook. *JT*, his debut album for Columbia Records, was something of a defense of this conversion. Returning to the autobiographical, Taylor declared his love for Carly Simon ("There We Are"), but expressed some surprise at his domestic bliss. "Isn't it amazing a man like me can feel this way—"he sang in the opening song, "Your Smiling Face" (a Top 40 hit). At the same time, domesticity could have its temporary depressions ("Another Grey Morning"). The key track was "Secret O' Life," which Taylor revealed as "enjoying the passage of time." Working with his long-time backup band of Danny Kortchmar, Leland Sklar, and Russell Kunkel, and with Peter Asher back in the producer's chair, Taylor also enjoyed the playing of music, mixing his patented acoustic guitar-based folk sound with elements of rock, blues, and country. He even made the Country charts briefly with "Bartender's Blues," a genre exercise complete with steel guitar and references to "honky tonk angels" that he would later re-record with George Jones. The album's Top Ten hit was Taylor's winning remake of Jimmy Jones's "Handy Man," which replaced the grit of the original with his characteristic warmth. *JT* was James Taylor's best album since *Mud Slide Slim and the Blue Horizon* because it acknowledged the darkness of his earlier work while explaining the deliberate lightness of his current viewpoint, and because it was his most consistent collection in years. Fans responded: *JT* sold better than any Taylor album since *Sweet Baby James*. *— William Ruhlmann*

Flag / May 1979 / Columbia/Legacy ✦✦✦
James Taylor followed his double-platinum Columbia Records label debut *JT* with this hodgepodge of a record. There are pointless covers of The Beatles' "Day Tripper" and The Drifters' "Up On The Roof" (7 Adult Contemporary, #28 Pop), a remake of Taylor's own "Rainy Day Man," songs written for the failed Broadway musical *Working*, and a few inconsequential new Taylor compositions. The usual brain trust (producer Peter Asher) and the usual backup team (Danny Kortchmar, Dan Grolnick, Leland Sklar, Russ Kunkel) were on board, but the cruise was a snooze. *— William Ruhlmann*

Dad Loves His Work / Mar. 1981 / Columbia/Legacy ✦✦✦✦
James Taylor bounced back from the spotty *Flag* with this all-original album led by his collaboration with J.D. Souther on "Her Town Too" (#11 Pop, #5 Adult Contemporary), his biggest pop hit since "Handy Man" and biggest non-cover hit since his first, "Fire And Rain," in 1970. Also included were "Hard Times" (#72 Pop, #23 Adult Contemporary) and "Summer's Here" (#25 Adult Contemporary), not to mention the unusually impassioned "Stand And Fight." After simmering this long, there wasn't much hope Taylor would ever come to a boil, but that track indicated he could at least heat up now and then. *— William Ruhlmann*

That's Why I'm Here / Oct. 1985 / Columbia/Legacy ✦✦✦

Never Die Young / Jan. 1988 / Columbia/Legacy ✦✦✦

● **Classic Songs** / 1990 / Columbia ✦✦✦✦✦
Classic Songs is the only compilation to feature the original versions of all of James Taylors' classics from his debut up through 1985's *That's Why I'm Here*. Unfortunately, it's only available in Europe, yet it remains the best, most comprehensive collection of his work to date. *— Chris Woodstra*

New Moon Shine / Sep. 24, 1991 / Columbia ✦✦✦

Live / Aug. 10, 1993 / Columbia ✦✦✦✦

Hourglass / May 20, 1997 / Columbia ✦✦✦

Greatest Hits, Vol. 2 / Nov. 7, 2000 / Columbia/Legacy ✦✦✦✦✦
James Taylor's first *Greatest Hits* album, released in 1976 and consisting of his well-known early '70s recordings on Warner Bros. and re-recordings of some of the songs from his 1968 Apple Records debut, is in the rarefied sales category of double-digit millions, so a second volume, taking in his tenure at Columbia Records, was a no-brainer. The only wonder is why it took so long. But the second part of Taylor's recording career has been different from his first, especially when it comes to hits. All of Taylor's Columbia albums have been good sellers, hitting gold or platinum sales. But he has scored only four Top 40 hits on the pop charts: "Handy Man" (his only Top Ten single on Columbia), "Your Smiling Face," "Up on the Roof," and "Her Town Too." It's a different story on the adult contemporary charts, where he has been a mainstay. But *Greatest Hits, Vol. 2* is not so much a collection of Taylor's chart entries as it is a best-of. There are several tracks, among them "Secret O' Life," "Only a Dream in Rio," and "Song for You Far Away," that were never hits but have become audience favorites, frequently played in Taylor's concerts. And there are chart singles, notably "Only One," which got into the adult contemporary Top Ten, and "Hard Times" and "Honey Don't Leave L.A.," which made the pop charts, that have been omitted. That said, this is a well-balanced compilation that should please most of the singer/songwriter's fans and that serves as a good selection of his work, circa 1977-1997. *— William Ruhlmann*

Johnnie Taylor

b. May 5, 1938, Crawfordsville, AR, **d.** May 31, 2000, Dallas, TX
Vocals / Deep Soul, Southern Soul, Retro-Soul, Quiet Storm, Soul-Blues, Disco, Soul
Aptly dubbed the "Philosopher of Soul" by the Stax publicity department, Johnnie Taylor set the ladies' hearts aflutter during the early '70s with his tender brand of Memphis soul. Taylor wasn't always the sincere crooner he developed into. A Sam Cooke protégé who took over with The Soul Stirrers when Cooke went secular, and who retained a hint of his mentor's mellifluous delivery, Taylor took the same pop route via Cooke's SAR label in 1961. Once he got on the Stax label in 1966, the vocalist forged a sublime blues/soul synthesis with a series of absolutely gorgeous efforts. But there was nothing subtle about Taylor's first number one in 1968: "Who's Making Love" was an uncompromising treatise on cheating lovers, with storming brass and slashing guitar. The follow-ups "Take Care of Your Homework" and "Jody's Got Your Girl and Gone" pounded the same message home from different angles. As the decade turned, though, Taylor perceptibly mellowed, turning increasingly to ballads for inspiration—"I Believe in You (You Believe in Me)," "We're Getting Careless with Our Love." By the time he went platinum with the horribly repetitive "Disco Lady" in 1976, the rough edges that made his early work so absorbing were smoothed away, although his latter-day Malaco output sometimes managed to suggest Taylor's glory years. He died of an apparent heart attack on May 31, 2000. *—Bill Dahl*

• **20 Greatest Hits** / 1977 / Malaco ✦✦✦✦✦
Johnnie Taylor's Stax hits were tailored to his gritty voice and tough manner. Taylor's nickname was "The Soul Philosopher," and few were better at dispensing romance formulas and fables, love, wit and wisdom. This collection rivals the two-record *Chronicle* as the best Taylor anthology, containing virtually every significant hit. "Who's Making Love," "Love Bones" and many others accent Taylor's swaggering delivery and the aggressive production and fine instrumental support that augmented his best material. There's no fluff here, just great textbook Southern soul. *—Ron Wynn*

The Best of Johnnie Taylor on Malaco, Vol. 1 / 1984-1992 / Malaco ✦✦✦✦

• **The Best of Johnnie Taylor: Rated X-Traordinaire** / Mar. 12, 1996 / Columbia/Legacy ✦✦✦✦✦
The 16-track *Rated X-Traordinaire* sets out to rescue the reputation of the Johnnie Taylor of 1976-1980, the period that began with his biggest smash, "Disco Lady," but that found him, so the conventional wisdom goes, a Southern soul man set adrift on the disco wave. Annotator Kalamu ya Salaam argues that "Disco Lady" is not a disco song, and backs this up by noting that the track actually was played by members of Parliament-Funkadelic. True enough, though that only applies to Taylor's debut Columbia album, *Eargasm*. Elsewhere, Taylor did drift, from Muscle Shoals tracks that updated his Stax Memphis sound to tracks that sounded like Marvin Gaye. The early years, 1976 and 1977, were more accomplished than the later ones, and that's where compilation producer Leo Sacks focuses, with 12 of the 16 tracks coming from then. In so doing, he ignores R&B chart singles like "Keep on Dancing" and "Ever Ready," but he satisfies the "best of" title. *— William Ruhlmann*

Lifetime / Oct. 24, 2000 / Stax ✦✦✦

The Teardrop Explodes

f. 1978, **db.** 1983
Group / Post-Punk, New Wave
One of the pivotal groups to emerge from the Liverpool neo-psychedelia community during the late '70s, the Teardrop Explodes was a showcase for Julian Cope, a notoriously eccentric figure whose unfashionable love of Krautrock and hallucinogenic drugs set him distinctly apart from the prevailing punk mentality of the era. Cope formed the band in 1978, and recorded their 1979 debut single "Sleeping Gas," a surreal electro-pop effort distinguished by its swirling keyboard washes.

One year later, the Teardrop Explodes issued 1980's infectious "When I Dream," which hit the U.K. Top 50 and even garnered some airplay in the U.S. Finally, the band's debut LP *Kilimanjaro* appeared later that year, to rave reviews and respectable sales. The single "Reward" hit the Top Ten early in 1981, and the ambitious LP *Wilder* was highlighted by the smash "Passionate Friend." A tour of the States followed, with disastrous results to the band's fragile line-up. In the midst of recording their third LP, to be dubbed *Everybody Wants to Shag the Teardrop Explodes*, Cope finally dissolved the band; only a 1983 EP dubbed *You Disappear from View* appeared on schedule, although the unfinished sessions were finally released in full in 1990 under their projected title. In the wake of the Teardrop Explodes' breakup, Cope embarked on a successful and occasionally brilliant solo career. *—Jason Ankeny*

• **Kilimanjaro** / 1980 / Fontana ✦✦✦✦✦
Armed with trumpeters Ray Martinez and Hurricane Smith who add soaring flourishes and energetic blasts throughout, on *Kilimanjaro* the Teardrops explode in a torrent of creative, kicky and often downright fun songs that hotwire garage/psych inspirations into something more. Steering clear of hamhanded attempts to be commercially 'new wave' while at the same time sounding young, bright and alive, the foursome go happily nuts with great results. Cope is already a commanding singer and frontman; his clever lyrics and strong projection result in a series of confident performances, whether his trading lines with himself on the motorik chug of "Sleeping Gas" or his yelps on "Books." For all the bad energy between himself and Balfe, the two sound like they're grafted at the hip throughout, the latter's keyboard washes and staccato melodies adding the fun, nervy vibe. Dwyer's spot-on drumming keeps the pace, while both guitarists, Finkler and his replacement Gill, don't drown the band in feedback to the exclusion of everything else. One listen to many of Gill's pieces, on songs like "Poppies," and Cope's oft-stated claim that early U2 was trying to rip off the Teardrops and other Liverpool/Manchester groups makes sense. Though it was assembled from a variety of different sessions *Kilimanjaro* still sounds cohesive. When it comes to the hit singles, it's no surprise songs like "Treason" and the brilliant "Reward," with its snarky opening line "Bless my cotton socks, I'm in the news today!" were such huge smashes. Perfectly hummable choruses, great arrangements and production and Cope's smiling vibe all add up with fantastic results. The sweet romance of "When I Dream" closes out this entertaining debut. *—Ned Raggett*

Wilder / 1981 / Mercury ✦✦✦
Despite the flux they were going through, the Teardrops somehow got it together to record the heavily-hyped *Wilder*, which unlike its predecessor did nothing in terms of sales or smash singles, outside of the semi-successful shimmering keyboard/crunch of "Passionate Friend." This isn't for lack of talent on the band's part, and the trademark kicky arrangements and horns appear throughout. However, unlike the joyous outpourings of *Kilimanjaro*, *Wilder* sounds distanced. Cope doesn't come across as the lead singer so much as he does someone singing with the music, ironic given that he wrote everything on this album. As a subtler pleasure, though, *Wilder* offers up some good stuff, with more cryptic compositions and performances throughout, while Clive Langer takes over full production after only doing a few on the first album. Strangely, some performances sound like where Sting eventually took the Police on *Synchronicity*, musically if not vocally, like the layered attempts at tribal drumming on "Seven Views of Jerusalem." More measured, sometimes stiff songs like "Falling Down Around Me" make the overall mood more fragmented, while some of Balfe's keyboards sound like they're only there just because. When it connects, though, *Wilder* rocks just fine. The concluding track, "The Great Dominions," is one of Cope's all-time best, with a sweeping, epic sense of scope and sound. The angular funk of "The Culture Bunker" has both some fine guitar and a sharp lyric or two on Cope's part—the 'crucial three' he refers to was his bedroom-only act with Ian McCulloch and Pete Wylie. Other high points include the moody synth shadings on "Tiny Children," where Balfe's work comes through best of all, and Dwyer's generally sharp drumming throughout, keeping the beat well. *—Ned Raggett*

Everybody Wants to Shag the Teardrop Explodes / May 1990 / Fontana ✦✦✦✦✦

Tears for Fears

f. 1981
Group / College Rock, Pop/Rock, New Wave
Tears for Fears were always more ambitious than the average synth-pop group. From the beginning, the duo of Roland Orzabal and Curt Smith were tackling big subjects—their very name derived from Arthur Janov's primal scream therapy, and his theories were evident throughout their debut, *The Hurting*. Driven by catchy, infectious synth-pop, *The Hurting* became a big hit in their native England, setting the stage for international stardom with their second album, 1985's *Songs from the Big Chair*. On the strength of the singles "Everybody Wants To Rule the World" and "Shout," the record became a major hit, establishing the duo as one of the leading acts of the second generation of MTV stars. Instead of quickly recording a follow-up, Tears for Fears labored over their third album, the psychedelic and jazz-rock-tinged *The Seeds of Love*. While the album was a big hit, it was the end of an era instead of a new beginning. Smith left the group early in the '90s, and Orzabal continued with Tears for Fears, pursuing more sophisticated and pretentious directions to a smaller audience. *—Stephen Thomas Erlewine*

The Hurting / Mar. 1983 / Mercury ✦✦✦✦✦

Songs from the Big Chair / 1985 / Mercury ✦✦✦✦✦
If *The Hurting* was mental anguish, *Songs From the Big Chair* marks the progression towards emotional healing, a particularly bold sort of catharsis culled from Roland Orzabal and Curt Smith's shared attraction to primal scream therapy. The album also heralded a dramatic maturation in the band's music, away from the synth-pop brand with which it was (unjustly) seared following the debut, and towards a complex, enveloping pop sophistication. The songwriting of Orzabal, Smith, and keyboardist Ian Stanley took a huge leap forward, drawing on reserves of palpable emotion and lovely, protracted melodies that draw just as much on soul and R&B music as they do on immediate pop hooks. The album could almost be called pseudo-conceptual, as each song holds its place and each is integral to the overall tapestry, a single-minded resolve that is easy to overlook when an album is as commercially successful as *Songs From the Big Chair*. And commercially successful it was, containing no less than three huge commercial radio hits, including the dramatic and insistent march, "Shout" and the shimmering, cascading "Head Over Heels," which, tellingly, is actually part of a song suite on the album. Orzabal and Smith's penchant for theorizing with steely-eyed austerity was mistaken for harsh bombasticism in some quarters, but separated from its era, the album only seems earnestly passionate and immediate, and each song has the same driven intent and the same glistening remoteness. It is not only a commercial triumph, it is an artistic *tour de force*. And in the loping, percolating "Everybody Wants to Rule the World," Tears for Fears perfectly captured the zeitgeist of the mid-'80s while impossibly managing to also create a dreamy, timeless pop classic. *Songs From the Big Chair* is one of the finest statements of the decade. *—Stanton Swihart*

The Seeds of Love / Sep. 1989 / Fontana ✦✦✦
Along with *Songs From the Big Chair, The Seeds of Love* was part of a one-two artistic punch in the late '80s that situated Tears For Fears as one of the decade's more ambitious pop groups. But at the time, Tears was more a platform for Roland Orzabal than a true band—Curt Smith is present only on the smash "Sowing the Seeds of Love" (his only co-writing credit), while Ian Stanley was replaced by Nicky Holland as a keyboardist and Orzabal's songwriting partner. Like their other albums, *The Seeds Of Love* continues the concept of moving from hurting to healing to beginning anew (the hit "Sowing the Seeds of Love") to growing apart. The songs feature expansive melodies instead of blatant hooks, and the sound is more grounded in soul and gospel on songs like "Woman in Chains," the updated Philly-soul strain of "Advice for the Young at Heart" and "Badman's Song." Orzabal's passionate vocals are well matched by Oleta Adams' fervent contributions. The group even dabbles in jazz on "Standing on the Corner of the Third World," the fabulous "Swords and Knives," and the slow-burning "Year of the Knife." As for the title track, it manages to be insanely intricate as well as catchy. Full of arcane references, lovely turns of phrase, and perfectly matched suite-like parts, it updates the orchestral grandiosity—though not the actual sound—of the Beatles' psychedelic period. It's completely different from the polished, atmospheric soul that surrounds it, but paradoxically, it's also the album's cornerstone. "Sowing the Seeds of Love" is the apotheosis of Orzabal and Smith's evolution together, and foreshadowed their impending split: the two parted on bad terms during the album, ensuring yet another change in the band's direction thereafter. *—Stanton Swihart*

• **Tears Roll Down: Greatest Hits 82-92** / Mar. 17, 1992 / Fontana ✦✦✦✦

Elemental / Jun. 22, 1993 / Mercury ✦✦

Raoul and the Kings of Spain / Oct. 10, 1995 / Epic ✦✦

Saturnine Martial & Lunatic / Aug. 1996 / Mercury ✦✦✦

20th Century Masters—*The Millennium Collection: The Best of Tears for Fears/* / *Jun. 27, 2000 / Mercury* ✦✦✦✦

Teenage Fanclub

f. 1989, Glasgow, Scotland
Group / Pop Underground, Indie Pop, Power Pop, Alternative Pop/Rock, Rock & Roll
Teenage Fanclub are a three singer/songwriters from Glasgow and a drummer who make unearthly pop music but remain under-appreciated. So what else is new?

Though Mersey Beat is at the core of their shimmering pop tunes, unlike the Beatles, it's often difficult to distinguish the voices of Norman Blake, Gerry Love and Raymond McGinley as their songs serve the band entity as one very pleasing whole. But like the Beatles, they sing with American accents. Even before their Matador debut, *A Catholic Education,* the indie sensation of 1989, the band had already made a splash as the pick to click in their native U.K.'s trendy music press. It was their second album, *Bandwagonesque* for Geffen that put the Scots on the pop music map. Long before the record was released, insiders talked of how this album was going to blow some minds. Indeed it did, and ended up on most critic's ten-best lists for the year. But not because it was a continuation of the dark and slow indie-trend formula they created for Matador, rather it sounded like a lost Big Star album. The Fanclub made no secret about their love for the obscure American pop band it and was a sound that stuck over the course of their next two albums, *Thirteen* and *Grand Prix.* *—Denise Sullivan*

A Catholic Education / 1990 / Matador ✦✦✦✦
Hard to believe now, but Teenage Fanclub first attracted critical attention for a record far removed from the sparkling power pop on which their fame largely rests—with its gloriously sloppy and sludgy sound, their debut album *A Catholic Education* instead prefigures the emergence of grunge, its viscous melodies and squalling guitars owing far more to Neil Young than Big Star. With not one but two songs dubbed "Heavy Metal," its pretty obvious where *A Catholic Education* is coming from: the title track (also here in duplicate) is a surprisingly snarky attack on the church (at least for a band not exactly renowned for its political agenda), while the great "Everybody's Fool" is a merciless scenester put-down without any of the gentle sarcasm that characterizes similarly themed efforts like *Bandwagonesque's* "Metal Baby." Regardless, for all its glaring differences in attitude and approach, there's no mistaking the effortless melodicism that remains the hallmark of all Teenage Fanclub records—in particular, the opening "Everything Flows," for all its meandering abrasiveness, is still as good as anything the band ever recorded, and that's saying something. *—Jason Ankeny*

● **Bandwagonesque** / Nov. 19, 1991 / DGC ✦✦✦✦✦
The gold standard of the early-'90s power pop revival, in its own way *Bandwagoneque* was as a much a benchmark as contemporary records like *Nevermind* and *Loveless;* though not the generational rallying cry of the former nor the revolutionary sonic breakthrough of the latter, Teenage Fanclub's sophomore album nevertheless heralded the return of melody and craft, coupled with energy and spirit—hallmarks of much of the greatest rock & roll of the past, and virtues as rare as hen's teeth in the years immediately prior to the disc's release. Although its incandescent harmonies, lazily immediate songs, and crunching guitars earned it endless comparisons to vintage Big Star, *Bandwagonesque* is in every way a product of its own time—the thick, grungy sound of the Fannies' debut *A Catholic Education* remains intact for gems like "What You Do to Me" (arguably the most brilliantly simpleminded love song ever penned) and the instrumental "Satan," while the lyrics of other standout moments like "Star Sign" and "Alcoholiday" reflect a *laissez faire* irony and unassuming genius even more emblematic of the moment in question. *—Jason Ankeny*

Thirteen / Nov. 9, 1993 / DGC ✦✦✦✦

Grand Prix / Jul. 3, 1995 / DGC ✦✦✦✦
For all of the brilliance of records like *Bandwagonesque* and the underrated *Thirteen,* at times Teenage Fanclub seemed little more than a showcase for the laconic melodic genius of Norman Blake—fairly or not, the songwriting contributions of bandmates Gerard Love and Raymond McGinley suffered mightily by comparison, mere filler when stacked alongside Blake-penned marvels like "The Concept" and "Norman 3." That said, the superb *Grand Prix* is perhaps the truest group effort in the Fannies' catalog—more than ever before, their democratic approach truly bears fruit, and it's indicative of the disc's uniform excellence that the first Blake composition, the lovely "Mellow Doubt," doesn't even surface until track three, by which time McGinley's "About You" and Love's harmony-rich "Sparky's Dream" have already firmly established the set's ragged-but-right tenor. While new drummer Paul Quinn fails to recreate the buoyantly reckless abandon of the sacked Brendan O'Hare, *Grand Prix* otherwise captures complete creative synergy—in particular, "Don't Look Back" is Love's watershed moment, a gorgeously wistful love song highlighted by wittily lovelorn lyrics like "I'd steal a car to drive you home," as good a pick-up line as anything in the annals of rock & roll. Not everything works (McGinley's "Verisimilitude" goes nowhere fast) and Blake's contributions are still the highlights ("Neil Jung" and "I'll Make It Clear" are simply perfect pop songs), but *Grand Prix* is ultimately the product of a band at the peak of its collective powers, not as much a landmark as *Bandwagonesque* but every bit as good on its own terms. *—Jason Ankeny*

Songs from Northern Britain / Jul. 29, 1997 / Columbia ✦✦✦

Howdy / Nov. 21, 2000 / Columbia ✦✦✦

Television

f. 1973, New York, NY, **db.** 1978
Group / American Punk, New York Punk, Proto-Punk, Punk
Television were one of the most creative bands to emerge from New York's punk scene of the mid-'70s, creating an influential new guitar vocabulary. While guitarists Tom Verlaine and Richard Lloyd liked to jam, they didn't follow the accepted rock structures for improvisation—they removed the blues while retaining the raw energy of garage rock, adding complex, lyrical solo lines that recalled both jazz and rock. With its angular rhythms and fluid leads, Television's music always went in unconventional directions, laying the groundwork for many of the guitar-based post-punk pop groups of the late '70s and '80s. Soon after forming, the band began to build up an underground following. After Television recorded an abortive demo tape in 1975 with Brian Eno for release on Island, bassist Richard Hell left to form the Heartbreakers and later mount a solo career. One year later the band released a British EP on Stiff, then signed with Elektra for their debut album, 1977's *Marquee Moon.* Released to great critical acclaim and a high position on the British charts, it failed to attract a wide audience in America. Television's second album *Adventure* was a Top Ten hit in Britain, though the group broke up scant months later, largely due to tensions between the two guitarists (who both pursued solo careers). Nearly 14 years after their breakup, Television recorded a new album for Capitol and toured to support it, but disbanded again in 1993. *—Stephen Thomas Erlewine*

★ **Marquee Moon** / 1977 / Elektra ✦✦✦✦✦
Marquee Moon is a revolutionary album, but it's a subtle, understated revolution. Without question, it is a guitar rock album—it's astonishing to hear the interplay between Tom Verlaine and Richard Lloyd—but it is a guitar rock album unlike any other. Where their predecessors in the New York punk scene, most notably the Velvet Underground, had fused blues structures with avant garde flourishes, Television completely strips away any sense of swing or groove, even when they are playing standard three chord changes. *Marquee Moon* is comprised entirely of tense garage rockers that spiral into heady intellectual territory, which is achieved through the group's long, interweaving instrumental sections, not through Tom Verlaine's words. That alone made *Marquee Moon* a trailblazing album—it's impossible to imagine post-punk soundscapes without it. Of course, it wouldn't have had such an impact if Verlaine hadn' t written an excellent set of songs that conveyed a fractured urban mythology unlike any of his contemporaries. From the nervy opener "See No Evil" to the majestic title track, there is simply not a bad song on the entire record. And what has kept *Marquee Moon* fresh over the years is how Television fleshes out Verlaine's poetry into sweeping sonic epics. *—Stephen Thomas Erlewine*

Adventure / 1978 / Elektra ✦✦✦✦✦
Television's ground-breaking first album, *Marquee Moon,* was as close to a perfect debut as any band made in the 1970s, and in many respects it would have been all but impossible for the band to top it. One senses that Television knew this, because *Adventure* seems designed to avoid the comparisons by focusing on a different side of the band's personality. Where *Marquee Moon's* was direct and straightforward in its approach, with the subtleties clearly in the performance and not in the production, *Adventure* is a decidedly softer and less aggressive disc, and while John Jansen's production isn't intrusive, it does round off the edges of the band's sound in a way Andy Johns' work on the first album did not. But the two qualities that really made *Marquee Moon* so special were Tom Verlaine's songs, and the way his guitar work meshed with that of Richard Lloyd, whose style was less showy but whose gifts were just as impressive, and if you have to listen a bit harder to *Adventure,* it doesn't take long to realize that both of those virtues are more than apparent here, and while one might wish the sound had a bit more bite on "Foxhole" or "Ain't That Nothin'," the quieter, more layered sound is just what the doctor ordered for "Glory" and "The Dream's Dream." Sure, *Marquee Moon* is a better album, but *Adventure* has one of the greatest guitar bands of all time playing superbly on a set of truly fine songs, and albums like this come along far too infrequently for anyone to ignore music this pleasurable simply on the grounds of relative evaluation; it's not quite a masterpiece, but it's a brilliant record by any yardstick. *—Mark Deming*

Blow Up / 1982 / ROIR ✦✦✦

Television / Sep. 28, 1992 / Capitol ✦✦✦

The Temptations

f. 1960, Detroit, MI
Group / Smooth Soul, Pop-Soul, Motown, R&B, Soul
Thanks to their fine-tuned choreography—and even finer harmonies—the Temptations became the definitive male vocal group of the 1960s; one of Motown's most elastic acts, they tackled both lush pop and politically-charged funk with equal flair, and weathered a steady stream of changes in personnel and consumer tastes with rare dignity and grace. After a series of flop singles, the Tempts' fortunes changed dramatically in 1964 when they entered the studio with writer/producer Smokey Robinson, emerging with the pop smash "The Way You Do the Things You Do," the first in a series of 37 career Top Ten hits. With Robinson again at the helm, they returned in 1965 with their signature song, "My Girl," a Number One pop and R&B hit; other Top 20 hits that year included "It's Growing," "Since I Lost My Baby," "Don't Look Back," and "My Baby." In 1966, the Tempts recorded another Robinson hit, "Get Ready," before forgoing his smooth popcraft for the harder-edged soul of producers Norman Whitfield and Brian Holland for a string of hits including "Ain't Too Proud to Beg," "Beauty's Only Skin Deep" and "(I Know) I'm Losing You." Beginning around 1967, Whitfield assumed full production control, and their records became ever rougher and more muscular, as typified by the 1968 success "I Wish It Would Rain." The Temptations next entered a psychedelic-influenced soul period following the success of the single "Cloud Nine." As the times changed, so did the group, and as the 1960s drew to a close, their music became overtly political; in the wake of "Cloud Nine"—its title a thinly-veiled drug allegory—came records like "Run Away Child, Running Wild," "Psychedelic Shack," and "Ball of Confusion (That's What the World Is Today)." While the Tempts hit the charts regularly throughout 1973 with "Masterpiece," "Let Your Hair Down," and "The Plastic Man," their success as a pop act gradually dwindled as the 1970s wore on, and by the 1990s they were essentially an oldies act. *—Jason Ankeny*

Hum Along and Dance: More of the Best (1963-1974) / Feb. 16, 1993 / Rhino ✦✦✦✦
This 18-track compilation contains Temptations B-sides, non-hit cuts and obscure sides recorded from 1963-1974. It includes such sumptuous ballads as "What Love Has Joined Together" and "Gonna Keep On Trying Till I Win Your Love," plus uptempo wailers and an occasional dud ("Stop The War Now"). The early tracks show the group evolving from its doo-wop roots into soul's premier group. While the cuts on this disc aren't the ones that made The Temptations popular music institutions, they're still a vital part of their legacy. *—Ron Wynn*

Emperors of Soul / Sep. 20, 1994 / Motown ✦✦✦✦✦
The Temptations were unquestionably one of Motown's greatest groups, recording a large number of classic singles. They were also one of the handful of Motown groups that were able to successfully make the transition from the '60s to the '70s, giving them a sizable amount of quality material from both decades. *Emperors of Soul,* a lavishly produced five-CD box set, draws from The Temptations' entire career, treating all aspects of it with equal respect. For the dedicated fan, the box set is a treasure—the sound is great and there are nu-

merous rarities. However, for most listeners, it is simply too much music, featuring too many unfamiliar songs. *—Stephen Thomas Erlewine*

☆ **Anthology [1995]** / May 23, 1995 / Motown ✦✦✦✦✦
There were three versions of this collection (first released in 1973) that provided a comprehensive overview of their career at Motown. The second (1986) collection was an update that featured digitally remastered sound and some later hits that were not featured in the earlier incarnation, like "Shakey Ground," (1975), "Power," (1980), and the excellent "Treat Her like a Lady." (1983). Unfortunately, the updated 1995 collection (like the previously two incarnations) omits many fine tracks recorded and released before their 1964 breakthrough, like "I Want a Love I Can See" (1962) and "Check Yourself" (1963). Even so, *Anthology* is a conciser, less-expensive alternative to the box-set *Emperors of Soul*. *—John Lowe*

★ **Ultimate Collection** / Mar. 25, 1997 / Motown ✦✦✦✦✦
The Ultimate Collection is just that, a superb introduction to the Tempts' greatest hits. Included are 16 of the group's Top Ten smashes, among them "My Girl," "Get Ready," "Ain't Too Proud to Beg," "(I Know) I'm Losing You," "You're My Everything," "I Wish It Would Rain," "I Can't Get Next to You," "Ball Of Confusion," "Just My Imagination," and "Papa Was A Rolling Stone." *—Jason Ankeny*

Lost and Found: You've Got to Earn It (1962-1968) / Sep. 28, 1999 / Motown ✦✦✦✦

10cc

f. 1972, Manchester, England
Group / Album Rock, Pop/Rock, Soft Rock, Prog-Rock/Art Rock
Deriving their name from the metric total of semen ejaculated by the average male, the tongue-in-cheek British art-pop band 10cc debuted in 1972 with "Donna." A sly satire of late-'50s doo wop, the single reached number two on the British charts and established not only a long-running string of major hits but also the quartet's fondness for ironic and affectionate reclamations of musty pop styles. The follow-up, "Rubber Bullets," topped the charts in 1973, and both the subsequent single "The Dean and I" and an eponymously titled debut LP further solidified 10cc as a major force in British pop. While 1974's *Sheet Music* continued 10cc's dominance of the UK charts, they found the American market virtually impenetrable prior to the release of 1975's "I'm Not in Love," which topped the charts at home and climbed as high as number two in the States. After vocalists Kevin Godley and Lol Creme exited the group in 1976, vocalist/guitarists Graham Gouldman and Eric Stewart continued 10cc's success with the 1977 perennial "The Things We Do for Love" and a number one reggae nod "Dreadlock Holiday" one year later. Following a series of unsuccessful efforts, including 1981's *10 Out of 10* and 1983's *Window in the Jungle*, the group disbanded. In 1992, the original lineup reunited for *Meanwhile*, while only Gouldman and Stewart remained for 1993's *Mirror Mirror*. *—Jason Ankeny*

10cc/Sheet Music / 1973 / DCC ✦✦✦✦✦
10cc's first two albums, recorded under the sponsorship of entrepreneur and one-time pop star Jonathan King, are combined on one disc for this CD reissue. 1972's *10cc* shows that from the start, the group had an uncommon command of recording studio technique; the performances are polished, the harmonies superb, and the production flawless and often witty (all the more remarkable from a new band producing themselves, albeit one comprised of music-biz vets). However, the group was still getting up to speed in terms of their songwriting at this point, and while the craft is fine, there isn't a lot of inspiration on hand. Except for the sardonic "Rubber Bullets" and sarcastically sprightly "The Dean and I," the '50s-inspired parodies on side one don't wear well, and most of side two is clever but not terribly distinguished. 1973's *Sheet Music* was where 10cc truly hit their stride; the album is full of effective barbed humor buffered by the superbly polished production, which leans toward pretension without quite falling into the pool. The band began dipping their toes into the elaborate extended narratives that would become Kevin Godley and Lol Creme's hallmark on "Somewhere in Hollywood" and "Hotel," while "Silly Love" and "The Wall Street Shuffle" proved the band could rock when they felt like it, and "The Sacro-Iliac" is one of the great non-dance craze tunes ever. This CD also features a liner essay from Jonathan King on working with the group and tacks on the non-LP single "Waterfall" as a bonus. *—Mark Deming*

The Original Soundtrack / 1975 / Mercury ✦✦✦
10cc's third album, *The Original Soundtrack*, finally scored them a major hit in the United States, and rightly so; "I'm Not in Love" walked a fine line between self-pity and self-parody with its weepy tale of a boy who isn't in love (really!), and the marvelously lush production and breathy vocals allowed the tune to work beautifully either as a sly joke or at face value. The album's opener, "Une Nuit a Paris," was nearly as marvelous; a sly and often hilarious extended parody of both cinematic stereotypes of life and love in France and overblown European pop. And side one's closer, "Blackmail," was an witty tale of sex and extortion gone wrong, with a superb guitar solo embroidering the ride-out. That's all on side one; side two, however, is a bit spottier, with two undistinguished tunes, "Brand New Day" and "Flying Junk," nearly dragging the proceedings to a halt before the band rallied the troops for a happy ending with the hilarious "The Film of Our Love." *The Original Soundtrack*'s best moments rank with the finest work 10cc ever released; however, at the same time it also displayed what was to become their Achilles' Heel—the inability to make an entire album as strong and memorable as those moments. *—Mark Deming*

How Dare You— / 1976 / Mercury ✦✦✦

Deceptive Bends / 1977 / Mercury ✦✦✦

● **The Very Best of 10 CC** / Jun. 17, 1997 / Mercury ✦✦✦✦✦
The Very Best of 10cc is a comprehensive collection, featuring all of the group's biggest hits and best-known songs—including "Neanderthal Man," "Donna," "Rubber Bullets," "The Dean & I," "I'm Not in Love," and "The Things We Do for Love," as well as Godley & Creme's solo hit "Cry"—making it a definitive retrospective and introduction. *—Stephen Thomas Erlewine*

Greatest Hits / Sep. 15, 1998 / Mercury ✦✦✦✦✦

10,000 Maniacs

f. 1981, Jamestown, NY
Group / College Rock, Jangle Pop, Alternative Pop/Rock
10,000 Maniacs (named after the low-budget horror movie *2,000 Maniacs*) was formed in Jamestown, NY, in 1981 by singer Natalie Merchant and guitarist John Lombardo. Other members of the sextet were Robert Buck (guitar), Steven Gustafson (bass), Dennis Drew (keyboards), and Jerry Ausugstyniak (drums). The group gigged extensively and recorded independently before signing with Elektra and making *The Wishing Chair* in 1985. Cofounder Lombardo left the band in 1986, and they continued as a quintet, releasing the second album, *In My Tribe*, in 1987. This album broke into the charts, where it stayed 77 weeks, peaking at #37. *Blind Man's Zoo*, the 1989 follow-up, hit #13 and went gold.

After 1992's *Our Time in Eden* had finished its run on the charts, Natalie Merchant announced that she was leaving for a solo career. *MTV Unplugged* was released a few months after her departure. The remaining 10,000 Maniacs decided to continue performing, adding the folk-rock duo John & Mary (original member Lombardo and violinist/vocalist Mary Ramsey). The new lineup released *Love Among the Ruins*. Merchant released her first solo album, *Tiger Lily*, in the summer of 1995 and a follow-up, *Ophelia* in 1998. In 1999, the remaining Maniacs released *The Earth Pressed Flat* on Bar/None. Sadly a year later lead guitarist and founding member Robert Buck, who co-wrote some of the band's classics like "Hey Jack Kerouac" "What's The Matter Here—"and "These Are Days", died of liver failure. He was 42. *—William Ruhlmann*

The Wishing Chair / 1985 / Elektra ✦✦✦
Put simply, 10, 000 Maniacs sound a lot like Fairport Convention with Sandy Denny, so it's appropriate that Fairport's original producer, Joe Boyd, was brought in to handle their major-label debut. The result is a gentle folk/rock record that highlights the haunting voice of Natalie Merchant. *—William Ruhlmann*

● **In My Tribe** / 1987 / Elektra ✦✦✦✦✦
The band's breakthrough album and creative high point, *In My Tribe* offers a survey in social concerns including child abuse ("What's the Matter Here"), illiteracy ("Cherry Tree"), war ("Gun Shy") and the environment ("Campfire Song")—all tackled subtly and tastefully without too much preaching or pretension and in believable, real-life situations. Producer Peter Asher, whose credits include James Taylor and Linda Ronstadt, provides the perfect sheen—the group's pleasant folk-pop lends itself nicely to the '70s-styled singer/songwriter production. In the end, the album proves powerful not for the ideas (they've been covered before) but rather for the graceful execution and pure listenability. *In My Tribe* has served as one of the soundtracks for P.C. living and was required listening on college campuses in the late-'80s. *—Chris Woodstra*

Blind Man's Zoo / May 1989 / Elektra ✦✦✦
After the success of *In My Tribe*, it would be expected that hordes of bands would take a stab at the market with their own second-rate versions of the album—it's disappointing that 10, 000 Maniacs would be one of them, churning out not only *In My Tribe, Pt. 2*, but an inferior copy at that. It's not that the album is bad—certainly they've perfected their sound and in many cases, the songs are catchier this time out—but in handling the issues (there's no shortage of them), Merchant has become more direct and obvious. For all of its earnestness and good-intentioned teachings, *Blind Man's Zoo* ultimately fails in its heavy-handed and generally uninteresting approach. *—Chris Woodstra*

Hope Chest: The Fredonia Recordings 1982-1983 / Oct. 1990 / Elektra ✦✦✦

Our Time in Eden / Sep. 29, 1992 / Elektra ✦✦✦✦✦
Pushing through the sophomore jinx that gave *Blind Man's Zoo* its preachy feel, 10,000 Maniacs offer up a baker's dozen of wonderful folk-pop songs with hard-hitting messages, nearly matching the brilliance of their debut. Natalie Merchant is a few years older here, a few tribulations wiser, and a few shakes looser, although that's not to say she doesn't have a point (or 13) to make. Whether with old-school R&B horns ablaze or the simple elegance of a piano and strings, she glorifies, condemns, and cherishes the world she witnesses, not excusing herself or anyone else from the part they play. The rest of the band, Rob Buck, Dennis Drew, Steve Gustafson, and Jerome Augustyniak, gives her the superb musical roots and wings from which to grow and soar. The subject matter of the songs is sometimes subtle, sometimes overt, but always graceful. For instance, "These Are Days" is left open to interpretation, though the upbeat tone is unmistakable, while "I'm Not the Man" is a very pointed and poignant story of a jailed man falsely accused and awaiting his death. Merchant's poetry shimmers and tugs at your heart and head. The prophetically titled *Our Time in Eden* spawned modest hits with "These Are Days" and "Candy Everybody Wants," but turned out to be the final chapter for this maniacal five-some, as Merchant departed the band shortly after touring in support of the album. A finer swan song has seldom been heard. *—Kelly McCartney*

MTV Unplugged / Oct. 26, 1993 / Elektra ✦✦

Love Among the Ruins / Jun. 17, 1997 / Geffen ✦✦

Earth Pressed Flat / Apr. 20, 1999 / Bar/None ✦✦✦

Ten Years After

f. 1967, Nottingham, England, **db.** 1974
Group / British Blues, Hard Rock, Blues-Rock
Ten Years After is a British blues-rock quartet consisting of Alvin Lee (b.Dec 19, 1944), guitar and vocals; Chick Churchill (b.Jan 2, 1949), keyboards; Leo Lyons (b.Nov 30, 1944) bass; and Ric Lee (b.Oct 20, 1945), drums. The group was formed in 1967 and signed to Decca in England. Its first album was not a success, but its second, the live *Undead* (1968) containing "I'm Going Home," a six-minute blues workout by the fleet-fingered Alvin hit the charts on both sides of the Atlantic. *Stonedhenge* (1969) hit the U.K. Top Ten in early 1969. Ten Years After's U.S. breakthrough came as a result of its appearance at Woodstock, at which it played a nine-minute version of "I'm Going Home." Its next album, *Ssssh*, reached the U.S. Top 20,

and *Cricklewood Green*, containing the hit single "Love Like a Man," reached #14. *Watt* completed the group's Decca contract, after which it signed with Columbia and moved in a more mainstream pop direction, typified by the gold-selling 1971 album *A Space in Time* and its Top 40 single "I'd Love to Change the World." Subsequent efforts in that direction were less successful, however, and Ten Years After split up after the release of *Positive Vibrations* in 1974. They reunited in 1988 for concerts in Europe and recorded their first new album in 15 years, *About Time*, in 1989. *—William Ruhlmann*

Undead / 1968 / Deram ♦♦♦

Ssssh / 1969 / BGO ♦♦♦♦
This was Ten Years After's new release at the time of their incendiary performance at the Woodstock Festival in August, 1969. As a result, it was their first hit album in the U.S., peaking at number 20 in September of that year. This recording is a primer of British blues-rock of the era, showcasing Alvin Lee's guitar pyrotechnics and the band's propulsive rhythm section. As with most of TYA's work, the lyrics were throwaways, but the music was hot. Featured is a lengthy cover of Sonny Boy Williamson's "Good Morning Little Schoolgirl," with reworked lyrics leaving little doubt what the singer had in mind for the title character. Also included was a twelve-bar blues song with the ultimate generic blues title, "I Woke Up This Morning." *Ssssh* marked the beginning of the band's two-year run of popularity on the U.S. album charts and in the "underground" FM-radio scene. *—Jim Newsom*

● **Cricklewood Green** / Apr. 1970 / Chrysalis ♦♦♦♦♦
Cricklewood Green provides the best example of Ten Years After's recorded sound. On this album, the band and engineer Andy Johns mix studio tricks and sound effects, blues-based song structures, a driving rhythm section, and Alvin Lee's signature lightning-fast guitar licks into a unified album that flows nicely from start to finish. *Cricklewood Green* opens with a pair of bluesy rockers, with "Working on the Road" propelled by a guitar and organ riff that holds the listener's attention through the use of tape manipulation as the song develops. "50,000 Miles Beneath My Brain" and "Love Like a Man" are classics of TYA's jam genre, with lyrically meaningless verses setting up extended guitar workouts that build in intensity, rhythmically and sonically. The latter was an FM-radio staple in the early '70s. "Year 3000 Blues" is a country romp sprinkled with Lee's silly sci-fi lyrics, while "Me and My Baby" concisely showcases the band's jazz licks better than any other TYA studio track, and features a tasty piano solo by Chick Churchill. It has a feel similar to the extended pieces on side one of the live album *Undead*. "Circles" is a hippie-ish acoustic guitar piece, while "As the Sun Still Burns Away" closes the album by building on another classic guitar-organ riff and more sci-fi sound effects. *—Jim Newsom*

A Space in Time / 1971 / Chrysalis ♦♦♦♦

Alvin Lee & Company / 1972 / Deram ♦♦

Greatest Hits / 1977 / Deram ♦♦♦♦
The group's 1968-1970 best, including the hit "Love like a Man" and the Woodstock version of "I'm Going Home." *—William Ruhlmann*

Essential / 1991 / Chrysalis ♦♦♦♦♦

Tenpole Tudor

f. 1974, **db.** 1982
Group / Pub Rock, New Wave
Tenpole Tudor was one the strangest and silliest groups on Stiff Records, a label that was known for its odd-balls. Led by Eddie Tudor (born Edward Tudor-Pole), a former actor that could barely carry a tune, the group played a mixture of punk, roots-rock, pop and British dance-hall music, developing a thoroughly entertaining and ridiculous style. Tudor formed the band in 1974 with guitarist Bob Kingston, bassist Dick Crippen, and drummer Gary Long. Before recording the band's first album, Tudor appeared in the Sex Pistols' movie *The Great Rock 'N' Roll Swindle*, singing "Who Killed Bambi." After releasing a single on Korova records, the group joined the Stiff Roster, releasing "Three Bells in a Row." Tenpole Tudor released their debut album, *Eddie, Old Bob, Dick and Gary* in 1981; it sold well, launching two minor singles in addition to "Three Bells in a Row"—"Wunderbar" and "Swords of a Thousand Men." That same year, the group released their second album, *Let the Four Winds Blow*, which also performed well. The following year, Eddie Tudor broke up Tenpole Tudor; while he led a cajun-inspired version of Tenpole Tudor, the rest of the band became the Tudors. After the new incarnation of Tenpole Tudor failed, Tudor left Stiff Records and began performing in jazz and swing bands, as well as returning to acting; he has since concentrated on acting, although he has assembled new versions of Tenpole Tudor since. *—Stephen Thomas Erlewine*

● **Eddie, Old Bob, Dick & Gary** / 1981 / Stiff ♦♦♦♦♦
Tenpole Tudor's music is so defiantly silly and raucous that it would be easy to dismiss if it wasn't quite so fun. Taking the punk aesthetic to an extreme, no one in Tenpole Tudor, particularly lead vocalist Eddie Tudor, can sing *at all*, so each song turns into a drunken, noisy singalong. And most of these songs are singalongs, filled with rousing choruses, big hooks, and clattering chords that are messy and infectious. What's surprising about the group's debut album, *Eddie, Old Bob, Dick & Gary*, is how many flat-out excellent songs are on the record. Combining ridiculous swords-and-sorcery imagery with laddish party anthems, nearly half of the record is invigorating, noisy rock & roll, with the boozy "Swords of a Thousand Men," "Wunderbar," "Three Bells in a Row," "I Wish," and "There Are the Boys" standing out among the clatter. The rest of the album isn't quite as good, but it has reckless charm that makes *Eddie, Old Bob, Dick & Gary* a thrillingly primitive rock & roll record. *—Stephen Thomas Erlewine*

Let the Four Winds Blow / 1981 / Stiff ♦♦♦

Swords of a Thousand Men / Apr. 21, 1998 / Recall ♦♦♦♦♦

Joe Tex (Joe Arrington, Jr)

b. Aug. 8, 1933, Rogers, TX, **d.** Aug. 13, 1982, Navasota, TX
Vocals / Funk, Soul
Often pausing in the middle of a ballad for a brief but sincere secular sermon on the inherent value of true love or the hazards of cheating, Joe Tex was one of the Southern soul genre's most enduring performers—and one of its most versatile. With a stage surname reflecting his home state, Tex first entered a recording studio in 1955 for King, singing some potent R&B before trying his luck in New Orleans with Ace. Tex joined forces with Nashville producer Buddy Killen (who formed the Dial logo to market the singer's output) and finally scaled the soul playlists in 1965 with his smash "Hold What You've Got." The intense gospel-tinged ballad proved the prototypical Tex track, loaded with sound advice and downhome homilies.

That's not to say that Tex didn't record some hard-driving uptempo soul during the mid-'60s—"A Sweet Woman like You," "S.Y.S.L.J.F.M. (The Letter Song)," and "Show Me" all sizzle, while the hilarious "Skinny Legs and All," another major R&B and pop hit, accurately testifies to Tex's live charisma. With his microphone-stand acrobatics a longtime trademark, Tex's winning streak endured into the next decade with the grunting "I Gotcha," his biggest crossover success in 1972. He eked out another smash in the midst of disco fever with "Ain't Gonna Bump No More (With No Big Fat Woman)," his ebullient sense of humor still intact. Tex died in 1982. *—Bill Dahl*

The Very Best of Joe Tex / 1996 / Rhino ♦♦♦♦♦
Excellent 16-track survey of Tex's best material, from the mid-'60s to the mid-'70s. It favors his country/soul period rather than the disco one, with all but three tracks originating from the '60s, but it does include his biggest '70s hits, "I Gotcha" and "Ain't Gonna Bump No More (With No Big Fat Woman)." *—Richie Unterberger*

● **25 All Time Greatest Hits** / Mar. 21, 2000 / Varese ♦♦♦♦♦
If you're set on having the best available Joe Tex CD anthology and you already have the 1996 16-track Rhino comp *The Very Best of Joe Tex*, it might vex you to learn that all 16 of those songs are on this 25-song anthology, making the Rhino disc redundant should you decide to upgrade. If you *don't* have a Joe Tex CD anthology yet, though, you're in luck, as this definitely supersedes others as the greatest-hits collection of choice. All but one of these songs (the 1965 B-side "Don't Let Your Left Hand Know") was a chart single, and aside from the 1977 hit "Ain't Gonna Bump No More (With No Big Fat Woman)," all are from his prime 1965-1972 period. Of the songs not on the Rhino disc, highlights are the 1965 slowies "You Better Get It" and "A Woman Can Change a Man," and the aforementioned "Don't Let Your Left Hand Know," an odd soul-pop tune with folky guitars and harmonies straight off a Rooftop Singers record. Also, "A Woman's Hands" (a small 1967 hit) is a good example of Tex's preaching style. Then there's 1968's "You Need Me Baby," in which Tex disses a stud who was the best athlete in town and left to become a big success, maintaining that he [Tex] is still a better catch for the woman whom the stud left behind, since he'll love her children. Heck, all of the songs not on the Rhino disc are worthwhile additions. There's no telling if this will remain the definitive Tex compilation if his catalog continues to get passed around, but there's a good chance that it won't be surpassed. *—Richie Unterberger*

The The

f. 1979
Group / College Rock, Post-Punk, Alternative Pop/Rock
The The was the guise of Matt Johnson, a mercurial singer/songwriter whose music ran the gamut from dance-pop to country. Johnson formed the first incarnation of The The in 1979; the group issued its first single, "Controversial Subject," on the 4AD label in 1980. A year later, contractual obligations forced Johnson to issue the LP *Burning Blue Soul* under his own name. In 1982, The The—now essentially a Johnson solo project, backed by a revolving coterie of musicians—recorded the album *The Pornography of Despair*, which a dissatisfied Johnson chose not to release; a 1983 single recorded with Orange Juice's Zeke Manyika, "This Is the Day," formed the centerpiece of The The's proper debut, 1984's *Soul Mining*, an excursion into dance-flavored pop. Illness sidelined Johnson for much of the following year, and The The did not return until 1986's *Infected*, an eclectic commentary on the state of Britain in the modern world that was accompanied by an ambitious album-length video. When The The returned with the dissonant *Mind Bomb* in 1989, they were once again a true band, with Johnson joined by ex-Smiths guitarist Johnny Marr, but 1995's *Hanky Panky* marked yet another new direction—the first in a series of occasional albums celebrating the work of legendary performers, it was a brooding covers collection honoring the music of country great Hank Williams. *—Jason Ankeny*

Burning Blue Soul / 1981 / 4AD ♦♦♦♦
Matt Johnson's work thrives on the tension between accessible pop and dissonant experimentation; between joyful wonder and despairing bleakness. *Burning Blue Soul* was a more disjointed solo album Johnson released under his own name in 1981 before these tensions were fully integrated. This reissue is a valuable sketchbook for The The fans interested in dissecting the early inner workings of Johnson's art, but the meandering tape-collages that serve as framework will leave most others cold. *—Roch Parisien*

Soul Mining / 1983 / Epic ♦♦♦

Infected / 1986 / Epic ♦♦♦♦♦
Infected is such a leap forward from *Soul Mining* that the album hardly seems like the work of the same band. Instead of the light, agreeable dance-pop of the previous album, *Infected* draws a dense, dark sonic landscape that accurately conveys the alienation and despair Matt Johnson sings about. *—Stephen Thomas Erlewine*

● **Mind Bomb** / Jun. 1989 / Some Bizzare/Epic ♦♦♦♦♦
With the addition of former Smiths guitarist Johnny Marr, the The attempted their most ambitious album yet with *Mind Bomb*. Instead of the darkly polished dance-pop stylings of *Infected*, *Mind Bomb* opens up the music to reveal a slow, winding textured world of sound that celebrates its rough edges instead of hiding them. It's serious, dance-influenced rock of the highest order. *—Stephen Thomas Erlewine*

Dusk / Jan. 5, 1993 / Epic ♦♦♦♦
Sixth album *Dusk*—with its themes of desire, fall, redemption, and death—creates both a familiar and dislocating atmosphere, like a well-known film-noir plot for a movie produced on some other planet. Several songs have echoed, phased vocals—as if they were alien trans-

missions being randomly captured by this life-cycle soundtrack. The mutant blues of "Dogs of Lust" is an especially effective example of this unsettling terrain. Even when Johnson gets more conventional, there is no lack of depth. Dusk never looked so convergingly bright—and dark—than on *Dusk*. *—Roch Parisien*

Hanky Panky / Feb. 14, 1995 / 550 Music/Epic ✦✦

NakedSelf / Feb. 29, 2000 / Interscope ✦✦✦

Thee Midniters

f. 1964, **db.** 1972

Group / Latin Rock, Brown Eyed Soul, Frat Rock, Garage Rock, Rock & Roll

Indisputably the greatest Latino rock band of the '60s, Thee Midnighters took their inspiration from both the British Invasion sound of the Rolling Stones and the more traditional R&B that they were weaned on in their native Los Angeles. Hugely popular in East Los Angeles, the group, featuring both guitars and horns, had a local hit (and a small national one) with their storming version of "Land of a Thousand Dances" in 1965. Much of their repertoire featured driving, slightly punkish rock/R&B, yet lead singer Willie Garcia also had a heartbreaking delivery on slow and steamy ballads. In the manner of other local phenomenons like the Rationals (from Detroit), they were equally talented at whipping up a storm with uptempo numbers and offering smoldering, romantic soul tunes. After a few albums and an interesting detour into social consciousness with the single "Chicano Power," the group split in the early '70s, though their legacy is felt in later popular Latino L.A. rock acts like Los Lobos. *—Richie Unterberger*

● **The Best of Thee Midniters** / 1983 / Rhino ✦✦✦✦✦

An excellent compilation of 14 of their best songs, including "Land Of A Thousand Dances" and "Chicano Power." They make a fair Latino Rolling Stones on "Empty Heart," "Everybody Needs Somebody," and "Whittier Blvd." (a thinly disguised reworking of The Stones' "2120 South Michigan Ave."); "That's All," "Dreaming Casually," and "Sad Girl" are exceptional slow R&B ballads, and "Jump, Jive And Harmonize" is a tough garage-punk original. *—Richie Unterberger*

Them

f. 1963, Belfast, Northern Ireland, **db.** 1971, Belfast, Northern Ireland

Group / British Blues, British Invasion, Blues-Rock, Rock & Roll

Not strictly a British group, but packaged as part of the British Invasion, Them forged their hard-nosed R&B sound in Belfast, Ireland, moving to England in 1964 after landing a deal with Decca Records. The band's simmering sound was dominated by boiling organ riffs, lean guitars, and the tough vocals of lead singer Van Morrison, whose recordings with Them rank among the very best performances of the British Invasion. As a hit-making act, their résumé was brief—"Here Comes the Night" and "Baby Please Don't Go" were Top Ten hits in England, "Mystic Eyes" and "Here Comes the Night" made the Top 40 in the U.S.—but their influence was considerable, reaching bands like the Doors, who Them played with during a residency in Los Angeles just before Morrison quit the band in 1966. Their most influential song of all, the classic three-chord stormer "Gloria," was actually a B-side, although the Shadows of Knight had a hit in the U.S. with a faithful, tamer cover version. *—Richie Unterberger*

Them / 1965 / Decca ✦✦✦✦✦

The debut album by the group, also known as *The Angry Young Them*, and half its tracks make it a dead-on rival to the Stones' debut album. This reissue features the album's original British configuration ("Just a Little Bit," "I Gave My Love a Diamond," "Bright Lights, Big City," and "My Little Baby" are here; "One Two Brown Eyes" and "Here Comes the Night" are absent). "My Little Baby" was no huge loss, being a pale imitation of "Here Comes the Night," but the omitted "Just a Little Bit" features a Howlin' Wolf/"Spoonful"-style performance by Van Morrison that would have incinerated a lot of American teens. On the other hand, Morrison's soul-shouting performance on the deleted "I Gave My Love a Diamond," appropriated by Bert Berns from the public domain "Cherry Song," would have shocked any folkie familiar with the original. Morrison's "You Just Can't Win" isn't nearly as impressive, but even as a time-filler it isn't half bad. And then there's "Gloria," rock's ultimate '60s sex anthem, and one of the handful of white-authored songs that can just about hold its own against any blues standard you'd care to name. *—Bruce Eder*

Them Again / Apr. 1966 / Deram ✦✦✦

The group's second and, for all intents and purposes, last full album was recorded while Them was in a state of imminent collapse. To this day, nobody knows who played on the album, other than Van Morrison and bassist Alan Henderson, though it is probable that Jimmy Page was seldom very far away when Them was recording. The 16 songs here are a little less focused than the first LP. The material was cut under siege conditions, with a constantly shifting lineup and a grueling tour schedule; essentially, there was no "group" to provide focus to the sound, only Morrison's voice, so the material bounces from a surprisingly restrained "I Put a Spell on You" to the garage-punkoid "I Can Only Give You Everything." Folk-rock rears its head not only on the moody cover of Dylan's "It's All Over Now, Baby Blue" but also the Morrison-authored "My Lonely Sad Eyes," but the main thrust is soul, which Morrison oozes everywhere—while there's some filler, his is a voice that could easily have knocked Mick Jagger or Eric Burdon off their respective perches. *—Bruce Eder*

● **Them Featuring Van Morrison** / 1987 / London ✦✦✦✦✦

Not to be confused with the identically titled Parrot Records release, which is a 20-track double-LP set, this is a 13-track single CD set and a U.S. reissue of the Decca U.K. LP from 1982. It would have been less confusing if they had called it *Them's Greatest Hits*, since it is primarily a singles compilation. But then, only four of Them's singles were hits, either in the U.K. or the U.S.—"Baby, Please Don't Go," "Gloria," "Here Comes the Night," and "Mystic Eyes," all included here. Also featured are such non-charting singles as "Don't Start Crying Now," "One More Time," "(It Won't Hurt) Half As Much," and "Richard Cory." This is not the ideal Them compilation, but this is the one that contains Them's most familiar material. *—William Ruhlmann*

The Story of Them Featuring Van Morrison / 1997 / Deram ✦✦✦✦✦

Long-overdue double CD, collecting all but one of the 50 songs (only "Mighty Like a Rose" is missing) the legendary British blues band left behind in the English Decca and American London vaults. The sound is a significant improvement over prior reissues—really loud, the way it was meant to be heard—with little touches like "The Story of Them Parts 1 and 2" linked together. It doesn't follow chronological order of release, but the order is entertaining, with alternate takes (stereo single mixes, American single edits, etc.) broken up between the two discs. It would have been nice to have had recording dates and personnel, but considering the fact that the band's lineup, apart from Morrison and bassist Alan Henderson, seemed to change every month, it's conceivable that any session information would be suspect. And one wishes for a coherent essay on the history of the band to go with the spread of photographs of the different lineups that are reprinted here. *—Bruce Eder*

They Might Be Giants

f. 1983, Boston, MA

Group / Pop Underground, College Rock, Post-Punk, Alternative Pop/Rock

Combining a knack for infectious melodies with a quirky, bizarre sense of humor and a vaguely avant-garde aesthetic borrowed from the New York post-punk underground, They Might Be Giants became one of the most unlikely alternative success stories of the late '80s and early '90s. Musically, the duo of John Flansburg and John Linnell borrowed from everywhere, but their free-wheeling eclecticism was enhanced by their arcane, geeky sense of humor. They would reference everything from British Invasion to Tin Pan Alley, while making allusion to pulp fiction and President Polk. Through their string of indie releases and constant touring as a duo, They Might Be Giants built up a huge following on college campuses during the late '80s, switching to a major label in the early '90s. With support from MTV, 1990's *Flood* became a gold album, and with it, the band moved began to reap commercial rewards, elevating them into the status of one of the most popular alternative bands before grunge. However, their whimsical outlook became buried in the avalanche of post-grunge groups that dominated MTV and modern rock radio in the mid-'90s, and the group retreated to its cult following. *—Stephen Thomas Erlewine*

They Might Be Giants / 1986 / Restless-Bar/None ✦✦✦✦✦

They Might Be Giants' eponymous debut album is a wild fusion of new wave pop and arty post-punk experiments borrowed from the New York underground. It runs through a head-spinning 19 songs in just over 45 minutes, running the gamut from the performance-art schtick of "Chess Piece Face" and "Youth Culture Killed My Dog" to the pure pop of "Don't Let's Start" and "Everything Right Is Wrong Again." While there are a lot of geeky jokes and barely developed ideas scattered throughout the album, the sheer kaleidoscopic array of styles is intoxicating, and it helps the best songs—the Costello-esque "Put Your Hand Inside the Puppet Head," the sighing "Hide Away Folk Family," the stomping "(She Was A) Hotel Detective" and the gorgeous "She's an Angel"—stand out in sharp relief. *—Stephen Thomas Erlewine*

● **Lincoln** / 1989 / Restless-Bar/None ✦✦✦✦✦

Cutting away some of the artier aspects of their debut, They Might Be Giants craft another wildly eclectic and geekily fun collection of alterna-pop with *Lincoln*. In general, the album displays greater musical ambition than its predecessor, especially since the duo have trimmed many of the weirder excesses of the debut. Without such arty trappings, their gift for irresistible pop hooks becomes all the more clear, with "Ana Ng," "Purple Toupee," the Latin shuffle of "The World's Address," "Santa's Beard," the surprisingly affecting "They'll Need a Crane" and the lounge jazz of "Kiss Me, Son of God" standing out among the 18 songs. And when They Might Be Giants don't go for the hooks, as on "Pencil Rain" or "Cage & Aquarium," they prove to be expert musical satirists, which means that *Lincoln* is every bit as infectious as the debut. *—Stephen Thomas Erlewine*

Flood / Jan. 1990 / Elektra ✦✦✦✦

On their major-label debut *Flood*, They Might Be Giants exchange quirky artiness for unabashed geekiness and a more varied and polished musical attack. Although the album contains two of the group's finest singles in "Birdhouse in Your Soul" and "Istanbul (Not Constantinople)," the overall record is uneven, since the group's hooks aren't quite as sharp as before and the humor is either too geeky or leavened with awkward social statements like "Your Racist Friend." Even with its faults, *Flood* has a number of first-rate songs, and it's a strong addition to their catalog, even if it isn't as weirdly intoxicating as its predecessors. *—Stephen Thomas Erlewine*

Miscellaneous T / Jul. 1991 / Restless-Bar/None ✦✦✦

Several of They Might Be Giants' finest songs were buried on B-sides, which makes the rarities compilation such a welcome addition to their catalog. While several of these songs are nothing but endearing jokes ("Mr. Klaw," "Lady is a Tramp," "For Science"), there are just as many gems. "We're the Replacements" is a fun homage to the Minneapolis legends, "The Famous Polk" is silly and infectious, "It's Not My Birthday" has a great hook, as does "Nightgown of the Sullen Moon," while "Hey Mr. DJ, I Thought You Said We Had a Deal" is a fun satire. Songs like these often capture the irreverent sense of humor that the group lost when they signed to a major label. *—Stephen Thomas Erlewine*

Apollo 18 / Mar. 24, 1992 / Elektra ✦✦✦

Although it lacks a standout single like "Birdhouse in Your Soul," *Apollo 18* is a more consistent album than *Flood*, overflowing with ideas and pop hooks. The most noteworthy idea may have been "Fingertips," a "suite" of 21 song fragments designed to make each random play a new experience, but the meat of the album lies in pop songs like "I Palindrome I," "My Evil Twin," "She's Actual Size" and "Which Describes How You're Feeling." The album has a slightly darker feeling than its predecessors, but that just gives the album a resonance that was missing on *Flood*. *—Stephen Thomas Erlewine*

John Henry / Sep. 13, 1994 / Elektra ✦✦✦

Factory Showroom / Oct. 8, 1996 / Elektra ✦✦

• **Then: The Earlier Years** / Mar. 25, 1997 / Restless ✦✦✦✦✦
Then: The Earlier Years is a double-disc set containing all of They Might Be Giants' original, independent records—the two albums *They Might Be Giants* and *Lincoln*, plus all of the B-sides and EP tracks that were compiled on *Misc. T*—adding nearly 20 previously unreleased tracks. While the bonus tracks are of varying quality—only "Now That I Have Anything" and demos of "Don't Let's Start," "Which Describes How You're Feeling" and "Hope That I Get Old Before I Die" are of interest to anyone but hardcore collectors—the official releases remain surprisingly fresh, a combination of melodic skills, inventive arrangements, self-consciously clever lyrics, and bizarre, geeky humor. For most listeners, *Then* is the definitive They Might Be Giants, encapsulating all of their charm and quirkiness and capturing them at the height of their career. *—Stephen Thomas Erlewine*

Severe Tire Damage / 1998 / Restless ✦✦✦

Thin Lizzy

f. 1970, Dublin, Ireland, **db.** 1983
Group / Album Rock, British Metal, Heavy Metal, Hard Rock
Despite a huge hit single in the mid-'70s ("The Boys Are Back in Town") and becoming a popular act with hard rock/heavy metal fans, Thin Lizzy are still, in the pantheon of '70s rock bands, underappreciated. Formed in the late '60s by Irish singer/songwriter/bassist Phil Lynott, Lizzy, though not the first band to do so, combined romanticized working-class sentiments with their ferocious, twin-lead guitar attack. As the band's creative force, Lynott was a more insightful and intelligent writer than many of his ilk, preferring slice-of-life working-class dramas of love and hate influenced by Bob Dylan and Bruce Springsteen. As a black man, Lynott was an anomaly in the nearly all-White world of hard rock, and as such imbued much of his work with a sense of alienation; he was the outsider, the romantic guy from the other side of the tracks, a self-styled poet of the lovelorn and downtrodden. His sweeping vision and writerly impulses at times gave way to pretentious songs aspiring to cliched notions of literary significance, but Lynott's limitless charisma made even the most misguided moments worth hearing.

After a few records that hinted at their potential, Lizzy released *Fighting* in 1975, and the band had molded itself into a tight recording and performing unit. Lizzy's big break came with their next album, *Jailbreak*, and its first single, "The Boys Are Back in Town." Never the toast of critics, Lizzy toured relentlessly, building a reputation as a terrific live band, despite the lead guitar spot becoming a revolving door. The records came fast and furious, and Lynott began writing more ambitious songs, wrapping them up in vaguely articulated concept albums. The large fan base the band had built as a result of "Boys" turned into a smaller, yet still enthusiastic bunch of hard rockers. Adding insult to injury was the rise of punk rock, which Lynott vigorously supported, but made Lizzy look too traditional. By the mid-'80s, Thin Lizzy called it a career. Lynott recorded solo records and sadly, became a victim of his longtime substance abuse, dying in 1986 at age 35. *—John Dougan*

Thin Lizzy / 1971 / Deram ✦✦✦

Shades of a Blue Orphanage / 1972 / Deram ✦✦✦

Vagabonds of the Western World / 1973 / Deram ✦✦

Night Life / 1974 / Mercury ✦✦✦

Fighting / 1975 / Mercury ✦✦✦

Jailbreak / 1976 / Mercury ✦✦✦✦✦
On Lizzy's third album with new guitarists Gorham and Robertson, *Jailbreak*, the band perfected their hard rocking, story telling, guitar-laden style, and was rewarded with worldwide breakthrough success. It also marked the first album where the band finally realized they were a true hard rock band, and put a stop to the soft rock that plagued such albums as 1974's *Nightlife*. Although vocalist/bassist Phil Lynott was unfairly criticized as being a Bruce Springsteen soundalike at the time, it was on *Jailbreak* that he came into his own, perfecting his story telling lyric writing and becoming a true poet in the process. Songwise, the album was also Lizzy's first real consistent album, there is simply not a single weak track in the bunch. The hard rocking war tales of "Emerald" and "Warriors," the killer boogie of "Angel of the Coast," the country rocker "Cowboy Song," and a pair of rock's greatest anthems, the title track and the perennial radio favorite "The Boys Are Back in Town," are among Lizzy's best tracks ever. Add to it such strong album cuts as the Dire Straits-esque ballad "Fight or Fall" plus the heartbroken tales "Running Back" and "Romeo and the Lonely Girl," and you have one of the finest hard rock albums of all time. *—Greg Prato*

Johnny the Fox / 1976 / Mercury ✦✦✦

Bad Reputation / 1977 / Mercury ✦✦✦
Although Lizzy's last two albums, 1976's *Jailbreak* and *Johnny the Fox*, were hard rock classics laden with strong songwriting and playing, the production on both releases was anemic. On 1977's *Bad Reputation*, Lizzy hooked up with respected hard rock producer Tony Visconti (David Bowie, T. Rex), who finally helped the band fulfill their potential, sonically speaking. Lizzy had to record the majority of the album as a trio, since guitarist Brian Robertson was forced to bow out and recuperate from a hand injury sustained in a barroom fight. Hence, guitarist Scott Gorham performed double duty on almost all the tracks, and judging by the remarkable guitar harmonies, he rose to the occasion splendidly. Songwriter/singer/bassist Phil Lynott was again equipped with a fine batch of compositions, which comprise Lizzy's third classic album in a row. The tuneful epic "Soldier of Fortune" starts the album off, which quickly gives way to the furiously rocking title track. Lynott's storytelling lyrics take center stage on such tracks as "Opium Trail," "Southbound," and "Dear Lord," while the irresistible dirty funk of "Dancing in the Moonlight" was a U.K. hit single (and later covered by Smashing Pumpkins as a B-side in 1993). Other standouts include the vicious "Killer Without a Cause" and the reflective beauty of "Downtown Sundown." Yet another consistent, stellar Lizzy set. *—Greg Prato*

Live & Dangerous / 1978 / Warner Brothers ✦✦✦✦✦
Along with Kiss' *Alive*, the Who's *Live at Leeds*, and the Rolling Stones' *Get Yer Ya-Ya's Out*, Thin Lizzy's 1978 double album, *Live and Dangerous*, is one of the greatest live rock albums of all time. The band wisely hooked up with producer Tony Visconti, again, and although it's become known in later years that the tracks included extensive overdubbing, many of the performances outshine the original studio versions. Except for a few tracks, the majority of the material spans from 1974's *Nightlife* to 1977's *Bad Reputation*, while the concerts were recorded during Lizzy's last two major tours (1976 and 1977). Few bands have ever matched the explosive energy that Lizzy creates on such tracks as "Jailbreak," "Emerald," "Rosalie/Cowgirl's Song," "Don't Believe a Word," "Are You Ready," and "Sha-La-La," while their sing-along anthem "The Boys Are Back in Town" proves even more vivacious in a live setting. The more serene material—"Southbound" and "Dancing in the Moonlight"—is just as gripping, while the slow blues of "Still in Love with You" contains two of the most heartfelt and lyrical guitar solos ever (a trade-off between both Robertson and Gorham). Add to it such strong album cuts as "Massacre," "Johnny the Fox Meets Jimmy the Weed," "Warrior," "Suicide," and "The Rocker," and you have the ultimate Lizzy album. *Live and Dangerous* is a must-have for fans of powerful hard rock. *—Greg Prato*

Black Rose: A Rock Legend / 1979 / Warner Brothers ✦✦✦✦✦
Black Rose: A Rock Legend would prove to be Thin Lizzy's last true classic album (and last produced by Tony Visconti). Guitarist Brian Robertson was replaced by Gary Moore prior to the album's recording. Moore had already been a member of the band in the early '70s and served as a tour fill-in for Robertson in 1977, and he fits in perfectly with Lizzy's heavy, dual-guitar attack. *Black Rose* also turned out to be the band's most musically varied, accomplished, and successful studio album, reaching number two on the U.K. album charts upon release. Lizzy leader Phil Lynott is again equipped with a fine set of originals, which the rest of the band shines on—the percussion-driven opener "Do Anything You Want To," the pop hit "Waiting for an Alibi" and a gentle song for Lynott's newly born daughter, "Sarah."Not all the material is as upbeat, such as the funky "*S.M.*," as well two grim tales of street life and substance abuse—"Toughest Street in Town" and "Got to Give It Up" (the latter sadly prophetic for Lynott). *Black Rose* closes with the epic seven-minute title track, which includes an amazing, complex guitar solo by Moore that incorporates Celtic themes against a hard rock accompaniment. *Black Rose: A Rock Legend* is one of the '70s lost rock classics. *—Greg Prato*

Chinatown / 1980 / Warner Brothers ✦✦✦

• **Dedication: The Very Best of Thin Lizzy** / Apr. 2, 1991 / Mercury ✦✦✦✦✦
Several Thin Lizzy "best of" collections have surfaced over the years (such as 1981's *Adventures of Thin Lizzy* and 1984's *Lizzy Lives!*), but the best two are undeniably 1996's *Wild One* and 1991's *Dedication*. While not as extensive as *Wild One* (only one track is featured from their '80s work), *Dedication* contains more early selections than the other mentioned titles. But the real attraction for Lizzy buffs is the inclusion of the previously unreleased title track, which was completed by the other members years after Lynott's passing in 1986. Elsewhere, often-overlooked tracks like "She Knows," "Fighting My Way Back" and "Cowboy Song" get to share the spotlight with such familiar faves as "The Boys Are Back in Town," "Bad Reputation," "Jailbreak," "Waiting for an Alibi," "Dancing in the Moonlight" and "Don't Believe a Word." Also included is an essay in which Lynott is quoted as saying that he'd like Lizzy to be remembered as a great guitar band (in the tradition of the Yardbirds, etc.). After hearing the great tracks on *Dedication*, you'll be reminded that there was so much more to this legendary band. *—Greg Prato*

13th Floor Elevators

f. 1965, **db.** 1968
Group / Garage Rock, Psychedelic
Featuring the yelping vocals and visionary, occasionally demented lyrics of Roky Erickson, the 13th Floor Elevators were one of the original acid-rock bands. Formed in Texas in the mid-'60s, the Elevators started as a garage rock outfit, scoring their one and only modest national hit with "You're Gonna Miss Me." While Erickson's loopy persona, along with Tommy Hall's odd "jug" percussion, was the band's most distinguishing feature, several members of the group's original lineup contributed strong material to their albums. Although these inconsistent efforts sometimes wander off into a cloudy haze, they also include sturdy folk-rock tunes and driving psychedelic rockers. Trips to San Francisco established the group as up-and-coming underground favorites, but Erickson's drug problems led to the singer's commission to a state mental hospital in the late '60s, an ordeal from which he has never fully recovered. The band was really only at full power for a couple of albums, although all of their releases for the legendary International Artists label—produced by, of all people, Kenny Rogers' brother Leland—are revered among psychedelic collectors. Live recordings and outtakes of the Elevators continue to surface, though a cogent domestic compilation of the best of these erratic pioneers' work remains overdue. *—Richie Unterberger*

The Psychedelic Sounds of the 13th Floor Elevators / 1966 / Collectables ✦✦✦✦✦
Their first album is their best, although their second (*Easter Everywhere*) also had some good material. Besides "You're Gonna Miss Me," it includes "Fire Engine," "Tried To Hide," "Roller Coaster," and Erickson's best composition, the gentle folk-rocker "Splash 1." *—Richie Unterberger*

Easter Everywhere / 1967 / Collectables ✦✦✦
This is a straight up reissue of the group's second International Artists album. Roky Erickson's vocals sound as wonderfully drug-crazed as ever, and the music is trippy and as true to the psychedelic ideal as these types of records get. With the exception of a drifty version of Dylan's "Baby Blue," pretty much everything on here comes from band members' pens, with Roky and Tommy Hall's "Slip Inside This House," and "She Lives (In a Time of Her Own)" being particular standouts. Anyone wanting a real psychedelic album from the '60s should head right to the counter and grab this one. *—Cub Koda*

Bull of the Woods / 1968 / Collectables ✦✦✦
Guitarist Stacy Sutherland wrote most of the songs on the band's final studio album, as Roky was largely absent due to drugs and problems with the law. Decent psychedelic rock—pretty

straightahead and disciplined for the genre, actually—that doesn't match the inspired heights of their previous material. The closing "May the Circle Be Unbroken," with its wads and wads of reverb, may be the strangest thing the band ever cut. *—Richie Unterberger*

• **The Best of the 13th Floor Elevators** / 1994 / Eva ♦♦♦♦♦
Finally, a best-of compilation for one of the most popular cult psychedelic groups of all time. The 22 tracks draw most heavily upon the first LP, with choice bits from the second and third, as well as some material Roky Erickson cut with his pre-Elevators group the Spades. *—Richie Unterberger*

.38 Special

f. 1975, Jacksonville, FL
Group / Album Rock, Arena Rock, Southern Rock, Hard Rock
Initially, .38 Special was one of many Southern rock bands in the vein of the Allman Brothers and Lynyrd Skynyrd; in fact, the band was led by Donnie Van Zant, the brother of Skynyrd's leader, Ronnie Van Zant. The band later revamped their sound to fall halfway between country-fried blues-rock and driving, arena-ready hard rock. The result was a string of hit albums and singles in the early '80s, beginning with their fifth album, 1981's *Wild-Eyed Southern Boys.* The group's first genuine hit, it went platinum and generated the Top 40 "Hold on Loosely." *Special Forces,* released in 1982, was even more popular, spawning the Top Ten single "Caught Up in You" and "If I'd Been the One." Though 1986's *Strength in Numbers* was quite popular upon release, it didn't stay on the charts as long as its predecessors. *Flashback,* the 1987 greatest-hits album, was moderately successful, but the band took precautions to retain their audience by recording the polished *Rock & Roll Strategy.* Released in 1989, the album slowly became a hit on the strength of "Second Chance," an adult-contemporary-oriented ballad that reached the Top Ten. .38 Special's popularity dipped soon after, and after one failed album in 1991, the group didn't release another until 1997's *Resolution.* *—Stephen Thomas Erlewine*

• **Flashback: The Best of .38 Special** / 1987 / A&M ♦♦♦♦♦
Flashback: Best of .38 Special is a terrific compilation of the Southern rock group's biggest hits, including "Caught Up in You," "If I'd Been the One," "Back Where You Belong," "Wild-Eyed Southern Boys" and the non-LP soundtrack contribution "Teacher Teacher." Since *Flashback* was released in 1987, it doesn't contain their biggest hit, 1989's syrupy ballad "Second Chance," but it remains a comprehensive overview of their best moments, and makes a convincing case that they were the last great Southern rock singles band. *—Stephen Thomas Erlewine*

This Mortal Coil

f. 1983, Wadsworth, London, England, **db.** 1991
Group / Dream Pop, Indie Rock, Alternative Pop/Rock
This Mortal Coil is the brainchild of 4AD's president, Ivo Watts. It's not really a band, it's a way for Watts to explore different musical territory and cover his favorite artists, including Syd Barrett, Alex Chilton, Talking Heads, Tim Buckley, and Gene Clark. Over the years, the lineup has featured various stars from the record label's roster including Kim Deal, Tanya Donelly, Heidi Berry, and Robin Guthrie and Elizabeth Fraser from the Cocteau Twins. Like most 4AD bands, This Mortal Coil is atmospheric, sometimes dreamy, other times haunting. Watts has said that 1991's *Blood* is the last album the outfit will release. *—Stephen Thomas Erlewine*

It'll End in Tears / 1984 / 4AD ♦♦♦
Features the Cocteau Twin's Elizabeth Fraser singing Tim Buckley's "Song to the Siren," and Gordon Sharp singing Rema-Rema's "Fond Affections," and Howard Devoto singing Alex Chilton's "Holocaust." Lisa Gerrard and Brendan Perry of Dead Can Dance are also included on this first collection of covers from 4 AD. *—Heather Phares*

Filigree & Shadow / 1986 / 4AD ♦♦♦♦♦
The second album of This Mortal Coil interpretations includes the vocalist, Jean, doing a version of Van Morrison's "Come Here My Love," and Deidre and Louise Rutkowski singing Tim Buckley's "Morning Glory." Other songs include David Byrne's "Drugs," and Gene Clark's "Strength of Strings." *—Heather Phares*

• **Blood** / May 13, 1991 / 4AD/Warner Brothers ♦♦♦♦♦
The final This Mortal Coil album includes some of the project's finest moments, including a cover of The Byrds' *I Come and Stand at Every Door* by Louise and Deidre Rutkowski, Syd Barrett's *Late Night* sung by Caroline Crawley of Shellyan Orphan, a cover of Gene Clark's *With Tomorrow* and a standout performance of Chris Bell's *You and Your Sister* by The Breeders' Kim Deal and Belly's Tanya Donelly. *—Heather Phares*

1983-1991 / Mar. 30, 1993 / 4AD ♦♦♦
All three of This Mortal Coil's albums packaged in an expensive slipcase, along with a disc of the original versions of the songs they covered. Fans of 4AD bands like Throwing Muses, the Cocteau Twins, and Dead Can Dance will thoroughly enjoy This Mortal Coil's lush, haunting music; some members of these bands play on various tracks on the box, including a standout duet between Kim Deal and Tanya Donelly on Chris Bell's "You and Your Sister." Although the packaging is beautiful, there are no liner notes. *—Stephen Thomas Erlewine*

Carla Thomas

b. Dec. 21, 1942, Memphis, TN
Vocals / Memphis Soul, Southern Soul, Soul
In the glorious decade and a half of sound that was Stax in the '60s and early '70s, Carla Thomas was the Queen of Memphis Soul. She was born in Memphis in 1942, and 18 years later she recorded a duet with her father Rufus Thomas, giving the fledgling Satellite label its first taste of success with the regional hit "Cause I Love You." As her 18th birthday drew nigh, she cut her first solo single, the teen ballad "Gee Whiz (Look at His Eyes)." Written a few years earlier and rejected by Vee-Jay in Chicago, it gave Satellite its first national hit, breaking the Top Ten mark on both the R&B and pop charts. Shortly thereafter Satellite became Stax, and Carla proceeded to claw her way onto the national charts another 22 times with such immortal slices of soul as her answer song to Sam Cooke, "I'll Bring It on Home to You," as well as "Let Me Be Good to You," "B-A-B-Y," "Tramp" (with Otis Redding), and "I Like What You're Doing to Me." Carla released six solo albums and, with Otis Redding, one duet album on Stax between 1961 and 1971. *—Rob Bowman*

Gee Whiz / 1961 / Atlantic ♦♦♦
Carla Thomas's first album was typical fare for the R&B market of the time, combining two chart entries (the title song and "A Love of My Own") with covers of recent chart hits (the Drifters' "Fools Fall in Love" and "Dance with Me," The Five Satins' "To the Aisle"), standards ("The Masquerade Is Over"), and a handful of originals. This was the first album produced by the then-fledgling Stax label and the unique Stax sound was not yet manifest. *—Rob Bowman*

Carla / 1966 / Rhino ♦♦♦♦♦
Paired with Stax writing whiz-kids Isaac Hayes and David Porter, Thomas had her greatest chart run, beginning with the hit "B-A-B-Y" and continuing with "Let Me Be Good to You." Both of those appear here, alongside evocative slabs of country-soul in covers of Hank Williams's "I'm So Lonesome I Could Cry" and Patsy Cline's "I Fall to Pieces." For good measure, Thomas also tries her hand at the blues with covers of Howlin' Wolf's "Little Red Rooster" and Jimmy Reed's "Baby What You Want Me to Do?" *—Rob Bowman*

Comfort Me / 1966 / Rhino ♦♦♦♦♦
A collection of twelve tracks recorded over a year and a half, *Comfort Me* showcases Thomas in the midst of the developed Stax sound. Backed by Booker T. and the MG's and the Mar-Key horns, Thomas turns in fine covers of Baby Washington's "Move on Drifter," and The Marvelettes' "Forever," The Shirelles' "Will You Love Me Tomorrow—," The Everly Brothers' "Let It Be Me," Jackie DeShannon's "What the World Needs Now," The Toys' "Lover's Concerto," and Barbara Mason's "Yes I'm Ready," coupled with a number of efforts by Thomas herself, Steve Cropper, and Eddie Floyd. The highlight is the Cropper-Floyd title cut, with utterly gorgeous backing by Gladys Knight And The Pips. *—Rob Bowman*

Memphis Queen / May 1969 / Stax ♦♦♦

Hidden Gems / 1992 / Stax ♦♦♦

• **Gee Whiz: The Best of Carla Thomas** / Jul. 19, 1994 / Rhino ♦♦♦♦♦
Gee Whiz: The Best of Carla Thomas is a wonderful 22-track collection of her seminal recordings for Atlantic and Stax, featuring all of her biggest hits—"Gee Whiz," "I'll Bring It Home to You," "B-A-B-Y," "Tramp" "I Like What You're Doing (To Me)"—as well as a terrific selection of lesser-known singles and album tracks. *—Stephen Thomas Erlewine*

Irma Thomas

b. Feb. 18, 1941, Ponchatoula, LA
Vocals / New Orleans R&B, Soul
Radiating an outgoing joy that's inevitably at the heart of her infectious vocal delivery, Irma Thomas has no rivals as the Soul Queen of New Orleans. Working at a Crescent City nightery as a waitress in 1959, Thomas sat in one night with Tommy Ridgley's band and made such a favorable impression that the veteran bandleader hustled her into the studio shortly thereafter to wax her first hit for the Ron label, the driving "Don't Mess with My Man." She joined forces with producer Allen Toussaint to make some of her most moving outings for Minit Records during the early '60s, notably "It's Raining," "Ruler of My Heart," and "Cry On," before venturing to the West Coast, where she cut both her biggest seller, the lushly produced "Wish Someone Would Care," and her best-known song, the original "Time Is on My Side." The highly adaptable chanteuse also made some sizzling soul at Muscle Shoals studio for Chess in the summer of 1967 before cooling off for a while during the '70s. But she's back now, as radiant as ever—and for convincing proof, listen to her buoyant 1990 concert performance on Rounder, *Live! Simply the Best.* Now that's truth in packaging! Thomas finally fulfilled a lifelong ambition in 1993 by recording her first gospel release. *Walk Around Heaven* was as magnificently sung and emotionally convincing as any of her classic New Orleans soul cuts. *—Bill Dahl*

★ **Time Is on My Side: The Best of Irma Thomas, Vol. 1** / Apr. 21, 1992 / EMI America ♦♦♦♦♦
Twenty-three sides representing the cream of Irma Thomas's brilliant Minit/Liberty years (1961-1966), when her reputation as "The Soul Queen of New Orleans" was built. Virtually all her best-known tunes are here—"Wish Someone Would Care," "Ruler of My Heart," "It's Raining," and "Time Is on My Side" (covered note-for-note by The Stones). Beautiful singing from one of the first ladies of soul music. Essential. *—Christine Ohlman*

Sweet Soul Queen of New Orleans: The Irma Thomas Collection / Feb. 20, 1996 / Razor & Tie ♦♦♦♦♦
23-track collection of early and mid-'60s sides largely duplicates the material on EMI's *Time Is on My Side* collection, with some additions and subtractions. The EMI set has a very slight edge, though for most listeners either compilation will do the job. It's too bad somebody doesn't take the plunge and issue an 80-minute CD documenting this era; as it is, serious Irma fans will need to get each best-of, as each contains tracks not on the other. *—Richie Unterberger*

Rufus Thomas

b. Mar. 26, 1917, Cayce, MS
Vocals / Memphis Soul, Southern Soul, Electric Memphis Blues, Modern Electric Blues, R&B, Soul
Few of rock & roll's founding figures are as likable as Rufus Thomas. From the 1940s onward, he has personified Memphis music; his small but witty cameo role in Jim Jarmusch's *Mystery Train,* a film which satirizes and enshrines the city's role in popular culture, was entirely appropriate. As a recording artist, he wasn't a major innovator, but he could always be depended upon for some good, silly, and/or outrageous fun with his soul dance tunes. He was

a crucial mentor to many important Memphis blues, rock, and soul musicians. Thomas recorded as early as 1941, but really made his mark on the Memphis music scene as a radio deejay. He had his first recording success in 1953 with the number three R&B hit "Bear Cat," the first national hit for Sun Records. Thomas recorded only sporadically during the 1950s, but then became one of the first and biggest stars—with his daughter Carla—on the Stax label during the '60s. On his own, Rufus wasn't as successful as his daughter, but issued a steady stream of decent dance/novelty singles. The biggest by far was "Walking the Dog," which made the Top Ten in 1963, and was covered by the Rolling Stones on their first album. He hit the R&B Top Five three times during the early '70s, though his recording career basically ended after Stax collapsed later in the '70s. *—Richie Unterberger*

Walking the Dog / 1964 / Rhino ✦✦✦✦✦
One of the artists who defined Memphis soul and put Stax Records on the map, Rufus Thomas is known for liking his R&B hard-edged, gritty and earthy. That approach served him impressively well on his debut album *Walking the Dog.* In contrast to the sleeker, more elaborate production style favored by the Northern soulsters of Motown, Thomas rejects pop elements altogether and thrives on rawness on his hits "Walking the Dog" and "The Dog," as well as inspired versions of "Land of 1000 Dances" (which became a major hit for Wilson Pickett), Lee Dorsey's "Ya Ya" and John Lee Hooker's "Boom Boom." Thomas was in his mid-40s when these fun, infectious recordings were made, and he definitely lives up to his title "The World's Oldest Teenager" (a title later given to Dick Clark as well). Reissued on CD in the early 1990s, *Walking the Dog* is an album Memphis soul aficionados shouldn't overlook. *—Alex Henderson*

Do the Funky Chicken / 1970 / Stax ✦✦✦

Jump Back / 1984 / Edsel ✦✦✦✦✦
The best compilation of his early Stax sides. The 16 tracks include "Walking the Dog," "The Dog," and some lesser-known songs in the same league, some of which ("Jump Back," "All Night Worker," "Sister's Got a Boyfriend," "Sophisticated Sissy") made the rounds via cover versions by both Black and White artists. *—Richie Unterberger*

That Woman Is Poison! / 1988 / Alligator ✦✦✦

Can't Get Away from This Dog / 1992 / Stax ✦✦✦

Did You Hear Me/Crown Prince of Dance / 1995 / Stax ✦✦✦

● **The Best of Rufus Thomas: Do the Funky Somethin'** / Apr. 1996 / Rhino ✦✦✦✦✦
Overdue career-spanning collection of his best material, centering around his Stax hits from the '60s and early '70s. The whole "dog" series of novelty dance songs from 1963-64 is here, as well as the hit "Jump Back" and a clutch of Stax singles that weren't hits, but became pretty well-known anyway, like "Sister's Got a Boyfriend" and "Sophisticated Sissy." There are also the early-'70s funk dance hits "Do the Funky Chicken," "(Do the) Push and Pull," "The Breakdown," and "Do the Funky Penguin," a couple of '60s duets with his daughter Carla, and his 1953 blues single "Bear Cat (The Answer to Hound Dog)," the first hit on Sun Records. A few other compilations have gone into specific phases of his career in greater depth, but this is certainly the best overview of a man who offered some of the funkiest and funniest Memphis soul around. *—Richie Unterberger*

Richard Thompson

b. Apr. 3, 1949, London, England
Vocals, Mandolin, Guitar, Guitar (Acoustic), Dulcimer / British Folk-Rock, Contemporary Folk, British Folk, Folk-Rock, Singer/Songwriter
Richard Thompson is among the most admired guitarists and songwriters in folk-rock music, and in the 1980s and '90s, he moved from a fervent cult following to broader exposure while maintaining critical accolades for his biting guitar work and sardonic songs. He was a founding member of Fairport Convention, the most important British folk-rock group to emerge in the 1960s, and he recorded five albums with them before quitting the group in January 1971. He made his debut solo album, *Henry the Human Fly,* before forming a duo with his wife Linda. The Thompsons released six albums, including the classics *I Want to See the Bright Lights Tonight, Pour Down like Silver* and *Shoot Out the Lights* (1982) before breaking up personally and professionally. In 1981, Thompson had made a second solo album of instrumentals, *Strict Tempo!;* with 1983's *Hand of Kindness,* his first charting album, he relaunched his solo career. *—William Ruhlmann*

Henry the Human Fly / 1972 / Hannibal ✦✦✦✦✦
Fans and critics alike seemed to have a difficult time getting a handle on Thompson's new direction, which, for the most part, eschews the electric guitar that had been an integral part of the British folk-rock he had helped forge with his former band Fairport Convention. With the exception of a couple of short instrumental breaks and various electric shadings, Thompson's Stratocaster defers to accordions, fiddles, whistles, dulcimers, harps and his own acoustic guitar. The songs, which are more idiosyncratic than his Fairport output, are the primary focus. Cuts such as "The Poor Ditching Boy," "The New St. George" and "The Old Changing Way" have the timelessness of the best traditional material Fairport had been mining in the past, while "Roll Over Vaughn Williams," with its swirling electric guitar, and the accordion and electric guitar interplay of the folk-rocker "The Angels Took My Racehorse Away" are prime examples of Thompson's vision of fusing the old and the new. At the time of its release, *Henry the Human Fly,* with its fresh, yet eccentric take on folk and rock, along with tales of "poor ditching boys," racehorses, tinkers, "painted ladies" and weddings where "nobody's wed" was not a fashionable record, but like the bulk of Richard Thompson's work, it transcends times and trends. Linda Peters (Thompson), Sandy Denny, Ashley Hutchings and John Kirkpatrick guest. *—Bruce Eder*

Hokey Pokey / 1974 / Hannibal ✦✦✦✦
With the release of their classic 1974 debut, *I Want to See the Bright Lights Tonight,* Richard and Linda Thompson set an unbelievably high standard for themselves. Although containing many of the same attributes, their follow-up, *Hokey Pokey,* doesn't quite reach the lofty heights of its predecessor, but then again not many records do. The Thompsons, from the opening Irish fiddle derivation of a Chuck Berry riff, through Linda's exquisite performance of "A Heart Needs a Home," to their cover of Mike Waterson's "Mole in a Hole" which closes the record, once again create a timeless amalgam of folk and rock. Recorded at the time of the Thompsons' conversion to Islam, *Hokey Pokey* comes across a bit lighter than *Bright Lights.* Songs such as the playfully suggestive title track, the jaunty "Georgie on a Spree" and the quirky tale of "Smiffy's Glass Eye" make *Hokey Pokey* seem downright cheery for Richard Thompson, although even at its sunniest, themes of sex, cruelty and avarice linger just below the surface. For those more accustomed to the usual straightforward doom and gloom from the Thompsons, there's the rueful "I'll Regret It All in the Morning," the sullen, traditional tone of "The Sun Never Shines on the Poor" and the mournful ballad "Never Again." *Hokey Pokey* is an often overlooked gem in the Thompsons' luminous catalog. *—Brett Hartenbach*

☆ **I Want to See the Bright Lights Tonight** / Apr. 1974 / Hannibal ✦✦✦✦✦
In 1974, Richard Thompson and the former Linda Peters released their first album together, and *I Want To See The Bright Lights Tonight* was nothing short of a masterpiece, the starkly beautiful refinement of the promise of Thompson's solo debut, *Henry The Human Fly.* In Linda Thompson, Richard found a superb collaborator and a world-class vocalist; Linda possessed a voice as clear and rich as Sandy Denny's, but with a strength that could easily support Richard's often weighty material, and she proved capable of tackling anything presented to her, from the delicately mournful "Has He Got A Friend For Me" to the gleeful cynicism of "The Little Beggar Girl". And while Richard had already made clear that he was a songwriter to be reckoned with, on *I Want To See The Bright Lights Tonight* he went from strength to strength. While the album's mood is decidedly darker than anything he'd recorded before, the sorrow of "Withered and Died," & "The End Of The Rainbow," and & "The Great Valerio" spoke not of self-pity but of the contemplation of life's cruelties by a man who, at 25, had already been witness to more than his share. And though Thompson didn't give himself a guitar showcase quite like "Roll Over Vaughn Williams" on *Henry The Human Fly,* the brilliant solos that punctuated many of the songs were manna from heaven for any guitar enthusiast. While *I Want To See The Bright Lights Tonight* may be the darkest music of Richard & Linda Thompson's career, in this chronicle of pain and longing they were able to forge music of striking and unmistakable beauty; if the lyrics often ponder the high stakes of our fate in this life, the music offered a glimpse of the joys that make the struggle worthwhile. *—Mark Deming*

Pour Down Like Silver / 1975 / Hannibal ✦✦✦✦✦
Pour Down Like Silver was the last album Richard & Linda Thompson would release before beginning a self-imposed three-year retirement in order to join a communal Sufi Muslim sect. The cover photographs show the Thompsons dressed in traditional Muslim garb, and while lyrically the album offers few clear signs of the Thompsons' new spiritual direction, the stark asceticism of the music marked a real change from the alcohol-fueled mood swings of *I Want to See the Bright Lights Tonight* and *Hokey Pokey.* The horns, accordion, and ancient instruments that had dotted Richard and Linda's previous albums were used far more sparingly on *Pour Down Like Silver,* and even Thompson's usually astounding electric guitar solos were pared down in favor of a emotionally intimate, bare-wired approach that sounds alternately like a confession and a plea for guidance. *Pour Down Like Silver* is downbeat even by Richard Thompson's less than joyful standards, but it also features some of his most beautiful and compelling songs—the ravaged plea for salvation of "Streets of Paradise," the mysterious and mesmerizing "Night Comes In," the mournful romantic meditations "Beat the Retreat" and "For Shame of Doing Wrong," and the spare but heartfelt love song "Dimming of the Day." And Linda (usually the more pragmatic of the two) breaks the mood near the end of side two with the cynically witty "Hard Luck Stories." *Pour Down Like Silver* is the most severe of the Richard & Linda Thompson albums, but those brave enough to look past its dark surface will find a startlingly beautiful album; it's not an easy album to listen to, but it greatly rewards the effort. *—Mark Deming*

Live (More or Less) / 1976 / Island ✦✦

Guitar & Vocal 1967-1976 / May 1976 / Hannibal ✦✦✦✦✦

First Light / 1978 / Hannibal ✦✦✦

Sunnyvista / 1979 / Hannibal ✦✦✦

Strict Tempo! / 1981 / Hannibal ✦✦✦

★ **Shoot Out the Lights** / 1982 / Hannibal ✦✦✦✦✦
Richard & Linda Thompson's marriage was crumbling as they were recording *Shoot Out The Lights* in 1982, and many critics have read the album as a chronicle of the couple's divorce. In truth, most of the album's songs had been written two years earlier (when the Thompsons were getting along fine) for an abandoned project produced by Gerry Rafferty, and tales of busted relationships and domestic discord were always prominent in their songbook. But there is a palpable tension to *Shoot Out The Lights* which gives songs like "Don't Renege On Our Love" and "Did She Jump Or Was She Pushed" a edgy bite different from the Thompsons' other albums together; there's an subtle, unmistakable undertow of anger and dread in this music that cuts straight down to the bone. Joe Boyd's clean, uncluttered production was the ideal match for these songs are their Spartan arrangements, and Richard Thompson's wiry guitar work was remarkable, displaying a blazing technical skill that never interfered with his melodic sensibilities. Individually, all eight of the album's songs are striking (especially the sonic fireworks of the title cut, the beautiful drift of "Just The Motion", and the bitter reminiscence of "Did She Jump Or Was She Pushed"), and as a whole they were far more than the sum of their parts, a meditation on love and loss in which beauty, passion, and heady joy can still be found in defeat. It's ironic that Richard & Linda Thompson enjoyed their breakthrough in the United States with the album that ended their career together, but *Shoot Out The Lights* found them rallying their strengths to the bitter end; it's often been cited as Richard Thompson's greatest work, and it's difficult for anyone who has heard his body of work to argue the point. *—Mark Deming*

Hand of Kindness / Jul. 1983 / Hannibal ✦✦✦✦✦
Richard & Linda Thompson's final album together, 1982's *Shoot Out the Lights,* was widely seen as a document of their collapsing relationship, despite the fact that both of them

strongly denied that was ever their intention, and when Richard Thompson released *Hand of Kindness* in 1983, it was similarly read as a sad and bitter letter from a lovelorn divorcee, conveniently ignoring the fact that Richard left Linda (not the other way around), and was already involved in a new (and happy) relationship by the time he cut the album. While *Hand of Kindness* is dominated by songs about unhappy relationships, the truth is most of Thompson's albums are full of such songs; if you want to read an autobiographical slant into the album, Thompson's well of anger ("Tear Stained Letter," "A Poisoned Heart and a Twisted Memory") and regret ("How I Wanted To," "Hand of Kindness") seem to run especially deep. But the album's darkest track, "Devonside," is a tragic tale of a dysfunctional relationship that clearly does not involve himself, and the album has a number of solid up-tempo rockers, such as the witty horse-racing tale "Both Ends Burning" and the rollicking, Cajun-flavored "Two Left Feet." Thompson's vocals and guitar work are in splendid shape throughout, and his band is particularly fine fettle, especially drummer Dave Mattacks and John Kirkpatrick on accordion. *Hand of Kindness* lacks a bit of the narrative depth and emotional push-and-pull that made *Shoot Out the Lights* an instant classic (and while "Both Ends Burning" and "Two Left Feet" are lots of fun, it's a stretch to call them great songs), but it certainly confirmed that Richard Thompson had a more than interesting solo career ahead of him. *—Mark Deming*

Small Town Romance / 1984 / Hannibal ✦✦✦✦

Across a Crowded Room / Feb. 1985 / Polydor ✦✦✦✦

Daring Adventures / Mar. 1986 / Polydor ✦✦✦

Amnesia / 1988 / Capitol ✦✦✦✦

Amnesia was Richard Thompson's second album with producer and keyboard player Mitchell Froom, and the two sounded a lot more comfortable with each other than they did on their previous project together, *Daring Adventures*. This being a Richard Thompson album, the high quality of the songs and the guitar playing is a given; while *Daring Adventures* had a few cuts that sounded like padding, Richard comes up aces this time out, and even sounds a bit more upbeat than usual, letting his political side rise to the surface on "Jerusalem on the Jukebox" and "Yankee, Go Home" and rocking out on "Don't Tempt Me" and "Gypsy Love Songs". (Be advised that the gloriously sad "I Still Dream" and "Waltzing's for Dreamers" are on hand to remind us this IS a Richard Thompson album.) Froom's production makes more of a difference this time out; *Amnesia* sounds brighter and cleaner than *Daring Adventures*, with a sharp but glossy mix that truly flatters Thompson's fiery Stratocaster solos (not to mention Jim Keltner and Mickey Curry's drumming), and the blend of British folk-rock stalwarts (John Kirkpatrick, Phillip Pickett, Danny Thompson) and American session veterans (Keltner, Curry, Jerry Scheff, Tony Levin) makes for set of tart and flavorful performances. *Amnesia* is one of Richard Thompson's best-sounding albums, and not a bad place for beginners; he hadn't sounded like he was having this much fun since *Sunnyvista* in 1979. *—Mark Deming*

Rumor and Sigh / May 1991 / Capitol ✦✦✦✦

While Richard Thompson's devotees will tell you the man is a triple-threat genius—passionate vocalist, compelling songwriter, and sterling guitarist—even his most loyal supporters will concede that the dour nature of his songs and the no-frills production of many of his albums make the bulk of his catalog tough sledding for the uninitiated. Given this, 1991's *Rumor and Sigh* is arguably the best album for those wanting to sample Thompson's work for the first time. It captures Thompson at the top of his form on all fronts, but also gives his songs just enough polish to make them approachable for the unconverted, and though it's several shades darker than the average adult-contemporary album, it honors Thompson's obsession with romantic despair and the less pleasant quirks of fate without sounding depressing in the process. Producer Mitchell Froom tricked up Thompson's sound a bit, but his approach added to the material rather than interfering with it; the topsy-turvy keyboards and sharp, snapping drum sound on "Gray Walls" and "You Dream Too Much" actually add to their narrative drama, and Froom coaxed some of Thompson's most soulful vocals on "Why Must I Plead" and "I Misunderstood". Thompson actually gets funny on "Don't Sit On My Jimmy Shands" and the darkly hilarious "Psycho Street", and Thompson fans who like his work straight with no chaser will be knocked flat by "1952 Vincent Black Lightning," perhaps the best traditional-style number in his songbook, and the harrowing "God Loves A Drunk", an unnerving tale of several kinds of addiction. While *Rumor and Sigh* is quite slick by Thompson's standards, its clean lines and bright mix serve both the songs and the bandleader quite well, and make Thompson's tunes sound like the radio hits they've always deserved to be. *—Mark Deming*

Watching the Dark / May 11, 1993 / Hannibal ✦✦✦✦✦

Multi-disc box-sets usually fall into two categories—they're either overstuffed "Greatest Hits" compilations, or packed with enough rarities to ensure loyal fans will part with their money. Since Richard Thompson's career hasn't sent him perilously close to worldwide stardom, the triple-disc anthology *Watching The Dark* was created with the latter market in mind, and if it falls short of being the perfect overview of Thompson's wildly varied career, it's a superb set that manages the not-inconsiderable feat of drawing an accurate picture of the height and breadth of Thompson's body of work, and offers enough buried treasures to leave jaded fans chuckling with glee. Sequenced thematically rather than chronologically, *Watching The Dark* covers Thompson's favorite themes well enough—there's enough spiritual mystery, mortal heartbreak, and British traditionalism to satisfy nearly anyone—and while the first priority appears to be Thompson the songwriter, Thompson the musician is documented with a similar degree of devotion. *Watching The Dark* gives relatively short shrift to Thompson's work with Fairport Convention and his experimental collaborations, but as an overview of his solo work (both with and without former wife and frequent collaborator Linda Thompson), it's remarkably thorough, and packed with fascinating and illuminating rarities. There are copious concert recordings, fascinating studio outtakes, and a handful of otherwise unavailable songs, along with an intelligently-chosen selection of highlights from the first 25 years of his career in music. The sheer bulk of *Watching The Dark* (over three and a half hours of music) makes this a difficult introduction to Richard Thompson's work, but anyone with more than a passing familiarity with his music will be dazzled by it—few box sets that honor their subject with as much intelligence and depth as *Watching The Dark*. *—Mark Deming*

Mirror Blue / Feb. 8, 1994 / Capitol ✦✦✦

You— Me— Us— / Apr. 16, 1996 / Capitol ✦✦✦

Mock Tudor / Aug. 24, 1999 / Bong Load ✦✦✦✦✦

Just how lost Richard Thompson under Mitchell Froom and Tchad Blake's direction during the '90s is made clear by *Mock Tudor*, the brilliant sequel to the botched *You? Me? Us?*. Producers/engineers Tom Rothrock and Rob Schnapf keep the production clean and direct, allowing the songs to breathe and letting Thompson play guitar. That decision alone would have made *Mock Tudor* a satisfying listen, but what elevates it into the first rank of his albums is, naturally, the songs themselves. Thompson structured the album as a portrait of suburbia, tackling a different subject with each song. It's not all about desperation, although there certainly is a lot of that there. Instead, Thompson is at the top of his form, offering subtle shadings in his lyrics and remarkably catchy, memorable melodies throughout the album. As a matter of fact, it's a bit of a tour de force, opening with the rollicking "Cooksferry Queen" and closing with its polar opposite, the hushed, intimate black comedy of "Hope You Like the New Me." Between those two songs, Thompson covers all sorts of emotional textures, resulting in his most affecting effort in years. Since even on his uneven '90s efforts he demonstrated that he still was in full grasp of his talents, it can't be said that *Mock Tudor* is a comeback, but it's certainly the best album he's made in over a decade. *—Stephen Thomas Erlewine*

The Best of Richard & Linda Thompson: The Island Record Years / Jul. 25, 2000 / Island ✦✦✦✦

George Thorogood

b. Dec. 24, 1950, Wilmington, DE

Slide Guitar, Vocals, Guitar / Slide Guitar Blues, Album Rock, Boogie Rock, Hard Rock, Blues-Rock

A blues-rock guitarist who draws his inspiration from Elmore James, Hound Dog Taylor, and Chuck Berry, George Thorogood never earned much respect from blues purists, but he became a popular favorite in the early '80s through repeated exposure on FM radio and the arena rock circuit. Thorogood's music was always loud, simple, and direct—his riffs and licks were taken straight out of '50s Chicago blues and rock & roll—but his formulaic approach helped him gain a rather large audience in the '80s, when his albums regularly went gold. Forming his first band in 1973, Thorogood later moved to Boston and became a regular on the blues club circuit. After signing to Rounder, Thorogood and the Destroyers' eponymous debut was released in early 1977. The group's second album, 1978's *Move It on Over*, entered the American Top 40 thanks to heavy FM airplay of the title track, a Hank Williams cover. A move to EMI brought his major-label debut, 1982's *Bad to the Bone*. The title track became his first major crossover hit, and helped the album go gold. (Its three follow-ups also went gold.) Despite declining record sales by the beginning of the '90s, Thorogood continued to tour and he usually drew large crowds. *—Stephen Thomas Erlewine*

• **The Baddest of George Thorogood and the Destroyers** / Jul. 28, 1992 / EMI America ✦✦✦✦✦

The aptly-titled *The Baddest of George Thorogood and the Destroyers* offers a dozen tracks that cleanse the church of rock'n'roll of all but its most basic elements: guitar, bass, drums, and a pile of Chuck Berry, Bo Diddley and Rolling Stone licks. Delaware's George Thorogood has never quite captured his wildman live presence in the studio, but having all his best material gathered on one disc—including "Bad to the Bone," "Move It on Over," and "One Bourbon, One Scotch, One Beer"—makes for a great party. Steve Morse's liner notes are brief but, like the songs, get right to the point... cut to the bone, you might say. *—Roch Parisien*

Anthology / Aug. 29, 2000 / Capitol ✦✦✦✦

Three Dog Night

f. 1968, Los Angeles, CA

Group / AM Pop, Pop/Rock

Three Dog Night scored a succession of 21 hit singles, including eleven Top Tens, and twelve consecutive gold albums from 1969 to 1975, thanks to the slick, sometimes soulful vocal harmonies of singers Danny Hutton, Chuck Negron, and Cory Wells and an excellent ear for quality material. While often criticized as commercial, the band was noted for its creative arrangements and interpretations, and their cover choices gave exposure (and royalties) to several talented songwriters: Nilsson ("One"), Laura Nyro ("Eli's Coming"), Randy Newman ("Mama Told Me (Not to Come)"), Hoyt Axton ("Joy to the World"), Argent's Russ Ballard ("Liar"), and Leo Sayer ("The Show Must Go On"). "One" became the band's first Top Ten hit in 1969, while "Mama Told Me (Not to Come)" hit number one a year later. "Joy to the World" became the group's biggest hit in 1971, spending six weeks on top of the Billboard charts, and their streak continued with their final number one, 1972's "Black and White" (a U.K. reggae hit for Greyhound), and their final Top Ten, 1974's "The Show Must Go On." *—Steve Huey*

• **The Best of Three Dog Night** / 1983 / MCA ✦✦✦✦✦

Weighing it at a generous 20 tracks, *The Best of Three Dog Night* may be a little much for some casual listeners, yet it's unquestionably the definitive collection, featuring all of their hits, plus a nice selection of album tracks. There isn't anything major missing, and while some of the non-singles material isn't particularly strong, there are enough worthwhile moments to make this a fairly consistent, enjoyable listen, in addition to being the one Three Dog Night album most fans will need. *—Stephen Thomas Erlewine*

Celebrate: The Three Dog Night Story, 1965-1975 / Dec. 7, 1993 / MCA ✦✦✦✦

A comprehensive double-disc anthology, *Celebrate* is necessary for devoted fans of Three Dog Night, but most listeners will be content with *The Best of Three Dog Night*, which features all of the hits on a single disc. *—AMG*

Throwing Muses

f. 1983, **db.** 1997
Group / College Rock, Indie Rock, Alternative Pop/Rock
One of the quietly great college bands from the 1980s, Throwing Muses was formed in 1983 by guitarist/vocalist Kristin Hersh and her half-sister guitarist/vocalist Tanya Donelly. In 1986 the group's debut album was put out by the prestigious British label 4AD; Throwing Muses were the first American band to be released on that label. Throwing Muses' angular, anguished, mercurial sound had much to do with Hersh's mental illness (she suffered from a form of bipolarity that caused her to hallucinate), especially on the early albums like *House Tornado*. 1991's *The Real Ramona* marked a break from the heaviness of the previous albums, with lots of shimmery pop gems penned both by Hersh and Donelly. Creative tensions between the two songwriters rose until Donelly left in 1992 to play with The Breeders and ultimately form Belly. After 1992's *Red Heaven*, Hersh released a solo album and toured extensively, leaving fans to wonder about the status of The Muses. In 1995, however, the group released *University*, one of their most cohesive and accessible efforts; it was followed by *Limbo* in 1996. The group's dissolution was announced soon after, with Hersh continuing on as a solo artist. *—Heather Phares*

Throwing Muses / 1986 / 4AD ✦✦✦✦✦
Throwing Muses' self-titled, 1986 debut is still a startling collision of punk energy, folky melodicism, and Kristin Hersh's mercurial voice and lyrics. The violent, vibrant mood swings on songs like "Call Me" are a testament not only to Hersh's unique talent, but the elasticity of Tanya Donelly, David Narcizo, and Leslie Langston's playing. Even if the volatile moods on songs like "Hate My Way" aren't easily understood, they're easily felt; the twists and turns "Vicky's Box" and "Rabbits Dying" take are guided purely by the intense emotions they carry. *Throwing Muses* is almost as varied musically as it is emotionally, ranging from the scary punkabilly of "America (She Can't Say No)" to "Stand Up"'s angular, acoustic post-punk to the cathartic thrill of "Delicate Cutters"'s unsettling folk. Donelly contributes the surreal, ethereal love song "Green;" even at this early point in the Muses' career, it's clear that she is a more accessible, straightforward songwriter, despite the care taken to make the song sound more like the rest of the album. A powerful debut, *Throwing Muses* puts the work of most self-consciously "tortured" artists to shame; its fluid, effortless emotional shifts may not make for the most accessible music, but they're unquestionably genuine. *—Heather Phares*

House Tornado / 1988 / 4AD/Sire ✦✦✦

Hunkpapa / Oct. 1990 / 4AD/Sire ✦✦

● **The Real Ramona** / Mar. 12, 1991 / Sire ✦✦✦✦✦
The Real Ramona marked the perfect balance of the Muses' angular songwriting and latent pop tendencies. Where *Hunkpapa* tried, somewhat unsuccessfully, to mix these elements, this album succeeds with surreal pop songs like "Counting Backwards" and "Red Shoes." They're catchy and riveting, clearly linked to the band's early material yet more focused and accessible. "Graffiti" and "Two-Step" are two of Kristin Hersh's most appealing pop snippets, but dark, uncompromising tracks like "Say Goodbye," "Ellen West," and "Hook in Her Head" reaffirm that she can still write troubling, fascinating songs like nobody else. And just before she left the Muses to form Belly, Tanya Donelly finally arrived as a full-fledged songwriter with the giddy, gleeful "Not Too Soon" and "Honeychain," proving that she could be a charming foil to Hersh's more challenging style. Their final album as a quartet, *The Real Ramona* highlights the best points of the group's sound, making it a great starting point for new Throwing Muses fans. *—Heather Phares*

Red Heaven / Aug. 11, 1992 / 4AD/Sire ✦✦✦

University / Jan. 17, 1995 / Sire/Reprise ✦✦✦✦✦
Possibly their finest album, Throwing Muses' fifth album *University* blends the rock power of *Red Heaven*, their first effort as a trio, with the shiny, surreal pop of *The Real Ramona*. The result is a collection of songs, like the album opener "Bright Yellow Gun," that are as ferociously kinetic as they are insinuatingly melodic. At first, Tanya Donelly's departure from the group might have been seen as a liability, but on this dreamy yet direct album, it's an asset: it gives Kristin Hersh room for her most wide-ranging collection of songs yet. "Start," "Hazing," "Shimmer," and "Teller" are some of her most immediate, deceptively sweet punk-pop confections, rivalling previous Muses classics like "Counting Backwards" in their hooky intensity. Yet the delicate "Crabtown" and "Fever Few" reaffirm Hersh's finesse with brooding, folky melodies. "That's All You Wanted" and "Snakeface" remain two of the Muses' catchiest songs, and the driven "No Way in Hell" and "Flood" show that Hersh hasn't lost any of her edge. *University*'s smooth, streamlined production adds a bit of sheen to Hersh's jagged, elliptical guitar lines and keening vocals, but doesn't rob either of their impact; if anything, the album's polish just heightens its flowing yet diverse sound. The album the Muses had been trying to make since *Hunkpapa*, *University* is as hypnotic as it is accessible. *—Heather Phares*

Limbo / Aug. 13, 1996 / Rykodisc ✦✦✦✦

In a Doghouse / Jul. 14, 1998 / Rykodisc ✦✦✦✦✦
Throwing Muses' classic first album was never released in the U.S., nor was their follow-up EP, *Chains Changed*. For well over a decade, the two records were only available as imports through 4AD, which meant that Throwing Muses, one of the most influential and individual albums of late-'80s alternative rock, was very hard for anyone outside of devoted record collectors to track down. Rykodisc fortunately remedied that situation in 1998 with the release of *In a Doghouse*, a double-disc set that provides a comprehensive overview of the Muses' early years. The first disc is devoted to *Throwing Muses* and *Chains Changed*, while the second disc contains the group's self-released demo tape *The Doghouse Cassette* and five recordings of Kristin Hersh's earliest songs that the final incarnation of the Muses cut in 1996. Usually, such material would be the province of hardcore collectors only, but the Muses were such an original, unpredictable band in their early days that even the early demos are fascinating. The re-recordings don't quite match the other recordings here, but it's fortunate that Hersh had the foresight to document these songs before they were forgotten. In this context, they are a nice bonus, but the quality of the remaining music—especially the idiosyncratic debut, which remains a fresh, unexpected listen—is why *In a Doghouse* is an essential compilation. *—Stephen Thomas Erlewine*

'Til Tuesday

f. 1983, **db.** 1989
Group / College Rock, Pop/Rock, New Wave
Remembered for their lone hit single "*Voices Carry*," 'Til Tuesday gradually evolved from a New Wave pop band into a vehicle for the songwriting of Aimee Mann. Emerging at the tail end of New Wave, 'Til Tuesday's commercial fortunes were helped dramatically by a stylish video for "Voices Carry," which quickly became an MTV favorite. Mann, involved in Boston's punk scene during the early '80s, formed 'Til Tuesday in 1983. The group signed to Epic one year later and their 1985 debut *Voices Carry* became a hit a few months after its release, as the title track climbed into the Top 10. The band quickly re-entered the studio to record their second album, 1986's *Welcome Home*, though it failed to produce any hits. 'Til Tuesday's third and final album, 1989's *Everything's Different Now*, sold even worse than *Welcome Home* but received strong reviews citing the growth of Mann's songwriting. The group broke up in 1989, though legal problems kept Mann from beginning her solo career until 1993. Her solo debut *Whatever* received strong critical reviews, and she enjoyed a successful cult following throughout the '90s. *—Stephen Thomas Erlewine*

Voices Carry / 1985 / Epic ✦✦✦

Welcome Home / 1986 / Epic ✦✦✦✦✦
It took a lot of guts and integrity for 'Til Tuesday to record *Welcome Home*. Hitting big with 1985's *Voices Carry*, Tuesday became known for a sleek, high-tech style of new wave, and it would have been easy enough for the Boston band to come out with a similar album for a follow-up. But instead of playing it safe, Tuesday gambled with inspiration and moved from new wave to a less keyboard-driven, more folk-influenced approach. Listeners who knew Tuesday for "Love in a Vacuum," "No More Crying" and *Voices Carry's* hit title song found things to be a lot more organic on such personal pop-rock offerings as "David Denies" and "Welcome Home." Lead singer Aimee Mann sounds consistently inspired, and the writing is superb. From a commercial standpoint, the album was too radical a departure from its predecessor. But creatively, *Welcome Home* was quite a triumph for 'Til Tuesday. *—Alex Henderson*

Everything's Different Now / 1988 / Epic ✦✦✦✦✦
As commercially successful as Til Tuesday's debut album was, the Boston band could have easily slipped into formula and continued making infectious, synth-soaked pop-rock. But instead, Tuesday continued to challenge itself and grow with each album. *Everything's Different Now*, the group's third and final album, lacks the immediacy of *Voices Carry* and is even more intimate than *Welcome Home*, but is every bit as rewarding. An often poignant and moving singer/composer, Aimee Mann leaves no doubt that she's coming from the heart on such introspective and personal gems as "Long Gone (Buddy)," "Why Must I" and "(Believed You Were) Lucky." Comparing something as slick as "No More Crying" to much more organic and understated offerings like "Rip in Heaven "and "J for Jules," it becomes obvious just how much Tuesday evolved in the course of three albums. *—Alex Henderson*

● **Coming up Close: A Retrospective** / Sep. 24, 1996 / Epic/Legacy ✦✦✦✦
Just how radically Til Tuesday evolved during its three-album run is illustrated by *Coming Up Close: A Retrospective*. The superb CD kicks into high gear with three sleek, heavily produced new wave gems from the band's debut album of 1985, *Voices Carry:* "Love In a Vacuum," "You Know the Rest" and the hit title song. But as fresh-sounding and popular as that material was, lead singer Aimee Mann was dissatisfied. One hears Tuesday moving from keyboard-driven new wave to a more organic, less produced, folk-influenced sound on "Coming Up Close," "No One Is Watching You Now," "David Denies" and other songs from Tuesday's 1986 sophomore effort *Welcome Home*. And with its finale, *Everything's Different Now*, the Boston residents moved even further in that direction. "J For Jules," "Limits to Love," "Rip In Heaven," "Why Must I" and "Long Gone Buddy" have little in common with the tunes from *Voices Carry*, except for the fact that Mann & Co. always had a great melodic sense. All three of Tuesday's albums are worth having, but for novices, *Coming Up Close* would be the best starting point. *—Alex Henderson*

The Time

f. 1981, Minneapolis, MN
Group / Urban, Funk
From their origins as Prince's first pet project to their self-produced funk-rock oeuvre, the Time has been a fascinating and outrageous congregation. Vocalist Morris Day infused his cocky, swaggering personality into dance hits that would make Rufus Thomas envious, and, unlike most of the competition, the band managed to do something unique with Prince's genre-busting innovations. The Time broke up in the late '80s, with Day going on to a somewhat disastrous solo career, Jesse Johnson crafting two dazzling solo albums, and Jimmy Jam and Terry Lewis becoming one of the most successful production teams this side of Gamble-Huff, working with everyone from Full Force and Janet Jackson to the S.O.S. Band and Human League. The group re-formed in 1990 and released the excellent *Pandemonium*. *—John Floyd*

The Time / 1981 / Warner Brothers ✦✦✦
These Prince proteges became stars in their own right in the early '80s. Their debut album had a smart combination of funk, rock, pop, and punk, with Morris Day the erstwhile lead singer and a cast also including Terry Lewis, Jimmy "Jam" Harris, Jesse Johnson, and Jellybean Johnson. Their early singles "Get It Up" and "Cool" were surly, suggestive, and just as energetic and electric as Prince's. *—Ron Wynn*

● **What Time Is It—** / 1982 / Warner Brothers ✦✦✦✦✦
After a tentative debut, The Time bounced back with one of 1982's best dance albums, full of hilarious stompers and braggadocio ballads. *—John Floyd*

Ice Cream Castle / 1984 / Warner Brothers ✦✦✦✦
Ice Cream Castle finds the band stepping out of Prince's purple shadow and discovering their own personality. The relentless "Jungle Love" is their best song. *—John Floyd*

Pandemonium / Jun. 1990 / Paisley Park ✦✦

Tindersticks

f. 1992, Nottingham, England
Group / Chamber Pop, Indie Rock, Alternative Pop/Rock
Tindersticks were one of the most original and distinctive British acts of the '90s, standing apart from both the British indie scene and the rash of Brit-pop guitar combos that dominated the UK charts. Where their contemporaries were often direct and to-the-point, Tindersticks were obtuse and leisurely, crafting dense, difficult songs layered with literary lyrics, intertwining melodies, mumbling vocals and gently melancholy orchestrations. Essentially, the group filtered the dark romanticism of Leonard Cohen, Ian Curtis and Scott Walker as filtered through the bizarre pop songcraft of Lee Hazlewood and the aesthetics of indie-rock. Though their music was far from casual listening, Tindersticks gained a dedicated cult following in the mid-'90s, beginning with their eponymous 1993 debut album. By the end of the year, the group and the album had won over most of the UK critics, and *Tindersticks* was named Album of the Year by the *Melody Maker.* Tindersticks spent a quiet year in 1994, releasing a live album entitled *Amsterdam 1994.* In the spring of 1995, the group released their untitled second album, which received rave reviews and appeared on nearly every British Top Ten list of the Best of 1995. Late that year, the group released another live album, *Bloomsbury Theatre, 12.3.95.* Tindersticks were quiet for most of 1996, releasing the soundtrack to the Claire Denis film, *Nénette et Boni.* Finally, they re-emerged with 1997's *Curtains.* *—Stephen Thomas Erlewine*

● **Tindersticks [II]** / Mar. 1995 / This Way Up/London ✦✦✦✦✦
Tindersticks' second consecutive eponymously titled double-LP set refines the approach of their debut; while every bit as ambitious and adventuresome, it achieves an even greater musical balance, stretching into luxuriously long compositional structures and more intricate arrangements. While Stuart Staples' songs remain as obsessive and haunted as before, he wards off his demons with fits of pitch-black humor (the narrative "My Sister") and a more tender perspective; similarly, while his funereal vocals remain the focus, there's a new reliance on extended instrumental passages, and even a pair of duets (the centerpiece, "Travelling Light"—a gorgeous collaboration with the Walkabouts' Carla Torgeson—is akin to a Lee Hazlewood & Nancy Sinatra record trapped in emotional purgatory). Another awesome triumph of mood and atmosphere. *—Jason Ankeny*

Curtains / Jun. 24, 1997 / London ✦✦✦✦✦
Curtains finds Tindersticks exploring the same dark, string-drenched territory as their first two albums, and while it shares a surface similarity with its predecessors, there are subtle differences that make it a rewarding listen. The tone of *Curtains* is slightly brighter than that of the second album, with the songs unfolding into lush, affecting laments that recall Scott Walker at his finest. Though the sound is seductive, what is most impressive about *Curtains* is the songwriting. The Tindersticks have become more assured writers, letting the songs gradually develop into intimate epics. Stuart Staples' lyrics are similarly textured and subtle, with alternating layers of pathos and humor. *Curtains,* in many ways, functions as the culmination of what the Tindersticks set out to accomplish with their first two albums, and the results are appropriately stunning. *—Stephen Thomas Erlewine*

Donkeys 92-97 / Aug. 25, 1998 / London ✦✦✦✦
As indicated on the cover, *Donkeys* is a collection of singles, rarities, and unreleased recordings. For the hardcore Tindersticks fan on a budget, it might come as a bit of a disappointment, as the nearly endless well of Tindersticks B-sides from limited releases are barely touched upon here. The absolute gem on *Donkeys* is their (typically brooding) version of Otis Redding's "I've Been Loving You too Long," which was released as a B-side to "Travelling Light." Other highlights include the French version of "No More Affairs" ("Plus de Liaisons"), an orchestral version of Stuart Staples' duet with Isabella Rossellini on "A Marriage Made in Heaven," their single for Sub Pop (a cover of Pavement's "Here"), and their very Velvet Underground-inspired debut single. It's a solid chunk of music, and as an introduction to the band, it serves well. But since Tindersticks are a remarkably consistent band, the beginner can pick their starting point by blindfold and come out a winner every time. *—Andy Kellman*

Simple Pleasure / 1999 / Quicksilver/Island ✦✦✦✦✦

TLC

f. 1991
Group / Club/Dance, Urban, Dance-Pop, Hip-Hop
Comprised of Tionne "T-Boz" Watkins, Rozonda "Chilli" Thomas, and Lisa "Left Eye" Lopes, the Atlanta, Georgia-based hip-hop trio TLC released their first album, *Ooooooh... On the TLC Tip,* in early 1992 to immediate success. Masterminded by the successful R&B producer/singer Pebbles, the group had three consecutive Top Ten hits in 1992, including "Ain't 2 Proud 2 Beg," "What About Your Friends," and "Baby-Baby-Baby." Shortly before the release of their second album, Lopes was arrested for burning down the house of her boyfriend, Andre Rison, then a member of the NFL's Atlanta Falcons. Lopes's arrest didn't affect the sales of their second album, 1994's *Crazysexycool,* which featured three number one singles and sold over four million copies. *Fan Mail* followed in 1999, launching a series of hits including "No Scrubs" and "Unpretty." *—Stephen Thomas Erlewine*

Ooooooohhh . . . On the TLC Tip / Feb. 25, 1992 / La Face ✦✦✦

● **Crazysexycool** / 1994 / La Face ✦✦✦✦✦
On their second album, TLC downplays their overt rap connections, recording a smooth, seductive collection of contemporary soul reminiscent of both Philly soul and Prince, powered by new jack and hip-hop beats. Lisa Lopes contributes the occasional rap, but the majority of *CrazySexyCool* belongs to Tionne Watkins and Rozonda Thomas. While they aren't the most accomplished vocalists—they have a tendency to be just slightly off-key—the material they sing is consistently strong. As the cover of Prince's "If I Was Your Girlfriend" indicates, TLC favors erotic, midtempo funk. Yet the group removes any of the psychosexual complexities of Prince's songs, leaving a batch of sexy material that just sounds good, especially the hit singles. Both "Creep" and "Red Light Special" have a deep groove that accentuates the slinky hooks, but it's "Waterfalls," with its gently insistent horns and guitar lines and instantly memorable chorus, that ranks as one of the classic R&B songs of the '90s. *—Stephen Thomas Erlewine*

Fanmail / Feb. 23, 1999 / La Face ✦✦✦✦
Crazysexycool was one of those records that defined an era. Few records before it combined hip-hop and classic soul songwriting quite as intoxicatingly or gracefully—the performances and productions were utterly seamless. It would have been difficult to top anyway, but TLC had it doubly bad, since a number of behind-the-scenes problems delayed a sequel for nearly five years. As with any eagerly anticipated record, that follow-up, *Fan Mail,* arrived with too many expectations. And initially, it may be disappointing to realize TLC doesn't forge new ground with *Fan Mail,* but after a few spins, it settles in that nobody else makes urban soul quite as engaging as this. Not that it was easy to make this record, as the head-spinning list of collaborators indicates. Almost ten producers worked on the record, all trying to replicate the easy, appealing sound of *Crazysexycool* And "replicate" is the right word, since there are no new innovations on *Fan Mail,* apart from a few lifts from the Timbaland book of tricks. Nevertheless, that may be for the best, since TLC and their army of producers have spent time crafting the songs and productions, turning *Fan Mail* into a record that almost reaches the peaks of its predecessor. By the end of the record, it appears that they can do it all—funky, hip-hop-fueled dance-pop, seductive ballads, and midtempo jams—and they can do it all well. Other groups try to reach these heights, but they don't have the skills or the material to pull it off quite so well. True, the five-year wait felt interminable, and they're now standard-bearers instead of pioneers, but if takes TLC as long to make a sequel to *Fan Mail,* so be it—they have one of the best track records in '90s urban soul. *—Stephen Thomas Erlewine*

Toad the Wet Sprocket

f. 1986, Santa Barbara, CA, **db.** Jul. 27, 1998
Group / College Rock, Adult Alternative Pop/Rock, Pop/Rock
So named in honor of a sketch by the Monty Python comedy troupe, Toad the Wet Sprocket's mellow, melodic folk-pop sound made them one of the most successful alternative rock bands of the early 1990s. Singer Glen Phillips, guitarist Todd Nichols, bassist Dean Dinning (the nephew of '50s hitmaker Mark "Teen Angel" Dinning) and drummer Randy Guss formed the group in 1986 in their native Santa Monica, CA, recording their 1988 debut LP *Bread and Circus* in just eight days at a cost of $650. After years of persistent touring, Toad the Wet Sprocket's commercial breakthrough followed with 1991's *Fear,* as the single "All I Want"—quite nearly left off the album—became a Top 20 hit. Another single from the LP, "Walk on the Ocean," was also a success. Three years later, Toad returned with *Dulcinea,* which generated another Top 40 hit with the single "Fall Down." *Coil,* Toad the Wet Sprocket's fifth proper LP, followed in 1997. The group split in July 1998. *—Jason Ankeny*

● **P.S.: A Toad Retrospective** / Oct. 26, 1999 / Columbia ✦✦✦✦

Tomorrow

f. 1965, **db.** 1968
Group / Freakbeat, British Psychedelia, Psychedelic Pop, Psychedelic
In the early days of British psychedelia, three bands were consistently cited as first-generation figureheads of the London-based underground sound: Pink Floyd, the Soft Machine, and Tomorrow. Pink Floyd became superstars, and the Soft Machine, influential cult legends, but Tomorrow is mostly remembered (if at all) for featuring Steve Howe as their lead guitarist in his pre-Yes days. That's a pity, as Tomorrow were nearly the equal of the two more celebrated outfits. With the early Floyd and Softs, they shared a propensity for flower-power whimsy. Though they were less recklessly innovative and imaginative, their songwriting was accomplished, with adroit harmonies, psychedelic guitar work, and adventurous structures and tempo changes. They never succumbed to mindless indulgence or jamming; indeed, their tracks were rather short and tightly woven in comparison with most psychedelic bands. A couple singles (especially "My White Bicycle") were underground favorites, but the group only managed to record one album before breaking up in 1968. Lead singer Keith West, even before the breakup, had a number two British hit with "Excerpt from a Teenage Opera," which helped inspired Pete Townshend's *Tommy.* Drummer Twink joined the Pretty Things and, later, the Pink Fairies. *—Richie Unterberger*

● **Tomorrow** / 1968 / See for Miles ✦✦✦✦✦
Tomorrow's sole album was a solid effort, with quite a few first-rate tracks. "My White Bicycle" was one of the first songs to prominently feature backwards guitar phasing, "Real Life Permanent Dream" has engaging English harmonies and sitar riffs, "Revolution" is an infectious hippie anthem, and "Now Your Time Has Come" features intricate riffing from Steve Howe. "Hallucinations," with its irresistible melody, gentle harmonies, and affectingly trippy lyrics, was perhaps their best track. The more self-conscious English whimsy—populated by jolly little dwarfs, Auntie Mary's dress shop, colonels, and the like—is less successful, although the band's craftsmanship is strong enough to avoid embarrassment. The 1986 reissue of this album features detailed liner notes and the worthy B-side "Claremont Lake," though unfortunately West's sappy but influential "Excerpt From A Teenage Opera" was deleted. *—Richie Unterberger*

50 Minute Technicolour Dream / 1998 / RPM ✦✦✦
Tomorrow were one of the 1960s' best and most intriguing one-album artists, so this 16-track compilation of additional material comes as quite a welcome bonus to fans, even 30 years after their split. None of these demos, alternates, or live performances were issued in the '60s, although the two respectable mod-psych demos they did for *Blow Up* surfaced elsewhere in the '90s, and the BBC versions of "Revolution" and "Three Jolly Little Dwarfs" have long cir-

culated among collectors. Studio rarities include a fine, slightly sinister unreleased cut "Caught in a Web," a cover of the Byrds' "Why," and considerably different versions of "Revolution" and "Real Life Permanent Dream." Eight songs from their late-1967 concert at the "Christmas on Earth Continued" psychedelic event in London are frustrating: the band plays well and the instruments are decently recorded, but Keith West's vocals suffer heavily from tinny distortion due to poor miking. Nonetheless, these are still interesting to hear, including versions of a bunch of songs from their album (among them "My White Bicycle"), "Why," and the otherwise unavailable "Shotgun & the Duck." The package is enhanced by detailed liner notes with comments from West and Steve Howe. *—Richie Unterberger*

The Tornados

f. 1961, **db.** 1964

Group / Early British Pop/Rock, Instrumental Rock, Rock & Roll

One of the saddest stories in rock & roll history surrounds the Tornados, an instrumental group from Britain. Although there were other groups with the same name, this batch of Tornados were the creation of Joe Meek, England's first independent producer. Equal parts Thomas Edison, Phil Spector and Ed Wood, Meek pioneered such recording techniques as close miking of instruments, distortion and compression. He put together the original Tornadoes in late 1961 as a studio session group; after one single flopped, Meek had the group do one of his compositions, an instrumental called "Telstar." Utilizing willful distortion, cheap tape echo, beeping satellite sound effects, a cheesy-sounding Clavioline (a two-octave keyboard powered by a battery) and massive amounts of tube compression, the resulting production sounded like nothing else at the time, or since. It became the first number one record on the American charts by a British rock group and sold five million copies worldwide. But a French copyright infringement suit kept all royalties tied up for six years, and the Tornados were kept from touring the United States behind their international hit due to a contract employing them as a backup group to U.K. pretty boy Billy Fury. By the time the dust settled, the Tornados had gone hitless for several years, and so had Joe Meek. The copyright infringement suit was ruled in Meek's favor six years later, a year after he had blown his face off with a hunting rifle after murdering his landlady, ending his life in his beloved but debt-ridden studio. *—Cub Koda*

The Very Best of the Tornadoes / May 20, 1997 / Music Club ✦✦✦✦

Away from It All / 1963 / Castle ✦✦

● **Telstar: The Original Sixties Hits of the Tornados** / 1994 / Music Club ✦✦✦✦✦

All you could possibly want to hear: both sides of the nine singles they cut for Decca between 1962 and 1964, along with the small U.S. hit "Ridin' the Wind" and a cut from a soundtrack LP. A fun, if slight, document of one of the most distinctive instrumental rock groups of the early '60s, with thorough liner notes. *—Richie Unterberger*

Tortoise

f. 1990, Chicago, IL

Group / Experimental Rock, Indie Rock, Post-Rock/Experimental, Instrumental Rock

Tortoise revolutionized American indie-rock in the mid-'90s by playing down tried-and-true punk and rock & roll influences, emphasizing instead the incorporation of a variety of left-field music genres from the past 20 years, including Kraut-rock, dub, classical minimalism, ambient & space music, prog-rock, film music and British electronica. At odds as well with the shambling framework of alternative rock's normal song structure, the group—as large as a septet, with at times *two* vibes players—relied on a crisp instrumental aesthetic, tied to cool jazz, which practically stood alone in American indie-rock by actually focusing on instrumental prowess and group interaction. Although the group's unique vision is to an extent the creation of drummer and master producer John McEntire, most of the other members are well-connected—producers and/or participants—in Chicago's fraternal indie-rock community, which consists of numerous side projects and ongoing bands. After debuting in 1993 with several singles and an LP, Tortoise's underground prestige emerged above terra firma with their second album *Millions Now Living Will Never Die;* the 21-minute opening track "Djed" was a sublime pastiche of Kraut-rock, dub and cool jazz. Tortoise then linked themselves with the cream of European electronica (Luke Vibert, Oval, U.N.K.L.E., Spring Heel Jack) to remix the album on a series of 12-inch singles. Despite the band's growing reliance on studio engineering, Tortoise began re-emphasizing their instrumentalist bent in 1998 for third album *TNT. —John Bush*

Tortoise / 1994 / Thrill Jockey ✦✦✦✦✦

★ **Millions Now Living Will Never Die** / Jan. 30, 1996 / Thrill Jockey ✦✦✦✦✦

Tortoise's production expertise hit an early peak with *Millions Now Living Will Never Die,* a work that not only references studio-centric forms like dub and electronica, but actively welds them to the group's aesthetic of sturdily constructed indie rock. The centerpiece is the 21-minute opener "Djed," a multi-part track which brought Tortoise's already impressive compositional abilities to a grand scale. It's almost a history of influences in miniature, first referencing tape music and dub for several minutes, then moving on to Krautrock with a chugging section incorporating wheezing organ and understated guitar chords. Halfway through, the band takes on minimalism with repeating figures of organ and vibes, then return to the green fields of their debut with a final few minutes of moody indie rock (though even this is spiced with a scratchy rhythm and various noise effects). With "Djed," Tortoise made experimental rock do double duty as evocative, beautiful music. The other songs on *Millions Now Living* are hardly afterthoughts, though; highlights "Glass Museum" and "The Taut and Tame" display the band quickly growing out of the angular indie rock ghetto with exquisite music, constructed with more thought and played with more emotion, than any of their peers. *—John Bush*

TNT / Mar. 10, 1998 / Thrill Jockey ✦✦✦✦✦

Expected by many to continue leading the post-rock brigade into a new fusion with dub and electronics, Tortoise instead turned yet another corner with their third album, *TNT.* Adding guitarist Jeff Parker to cement their musicianship as well as their connections to Chicago's fertile jazz/avant-garde scene, the band returned with a record of post-modern cool jazz, only slightly informed by the dub, Krautrock, and electronics of *Millions Now Living Will Never Die.* It shows from the first few seconds—a lazy, slightly free drum solo frames a few tentative guitar chords and some teased effects, before the band kicks in with a no holds-barred jam that encompasses a tremulous solo from trumpeter Rob Mazurek. With engineer/mixer/drummer John McEntire and company adding only a few post-production frills to the mix—and those so complementary and subdued that they rarely even sound like effects—*TNT* comes off as a surprisingly organic record. The evocative Spanish-style guitar on "I Set My Face to the Hillside" plays over an assortment of playground sounds, while "The Suspension Bridge at Iguaz˙ Falls" deconstructs a classically angular Tortoise groove and re-emerges with an evocative, deeply affecting groove over shimmering vibes and precision guitar lines. There are plenty of nods to post-rock touchstones like Krautrock ("Swing From the Gutters"), dub, and minimalism ("Ten-Day Interval"), but Tortoise hardly sounds like a difficult band here. Instead of forcing studio experimentation to become an end to itself, the band mastered—with a single, deft statement—the far more difficult lesson of making technology work for the music. *—John Bush*

Toto

f. 1978, Los Angeles, CA

Group / Album Rock, Pop/Rock, Soft Rock, Adult Contemporary

Toto was formed in Los Angeles in 1978 by David Paich (keyboards, vocals), Steve Lukather (guitar, vocals), Bobby Kimball (vocals), Steve Porcaro (keyboards), David Hungate (bass), and Jeff Porcaro (drums). Paich was the son of arranger Marty Paich. The members had met in high school and at studio sessions in the 1970s, when they became some of the busiest session musicians in the music business. Paich, Hungate, and Jeff Porcaro wrote songs for and performed on *Silk Degrees,* Boz Scaggs' multi-million-selling 1976 album that combined pop, rock, and disco elements into a slick combination which heavily influenced mainstream pop music. Toto released its self-titled debut album in September 1978, and it hit the Top Ten, sold two million copies, and spawned the gold Top Ten single "Hold the Line." The gold-selling *Hydra* (1979) and *Turn Back* (1981) were less successful, but *Toto IV* (1982) was a multi-platinum Top Ten hit, featuring the number one hit "Africa" and the Top Tens "Rosanna" and "I Won't Hold You Back." At the 1982 Grammys, "Rosanna" won awards for Record of the Year, Best Pop Vocal Performance, and Best Instrumental Arrangement with Vocal, and *Toto IV* won awards for Album of the Year, Best Engineered Recording, and Best Producer. In 1984, a third Porcaro brother, Mike, replaced Hungate, then Kimball was replaced by Dennis "Fergie" Frederiksen. Toto's fifth album, *Isolation* (1984), went gold, but was a commercial disappointment. Frederiksen was replaced by Joseph Williams for 1986s' *Fahrenheit.* Steve Porcaro quit in 1988, prior to the release of *The Seventh One.* In 1990, Jean-Michel Byron replaced Williams for the new recordings on *Past to Present 1977-1990,* then left, as Lukather became the lead singer. Jeff Porcaro died of a heart attack in 1992, but was featured on the group's next album, *Kingdom of Desire.* By this time, Toto was far more popular in Japan and Europe then at home. The group added British drummer Simon Phillips. *Tambu,* released in Europe in 1995, appeared in the U.S. in 1996. For 1999's *Mindfields,* Bobby Kimball returned to the lineup after a 17-year absence. *— William Ruhlmann*

Toto / Oct. 1978 / Columbia ✦✦✦✦

Hydra / Oct. 1979 / Columbia ✦✦✦

Turn Back / Jan. 1981 / Columbia ✦✦✦

Toto IV / Apr. 1982 / Columbia ✦✦✦✦✦

It was do or die for Toto on the group's fourth album, and they rose to the challenge. Largely dispensing with the anonymous studio rock that had characterized their first three releases, the band worked harder on its melodies, made sure its simple lyrics treated romantic subjects, augmented Bobby Kimball's vocals by having other group members sing and bringing in ringers like Timothy B. Schmit, and slowed down the tempo to what came to be known as "power ballad" pace. Most of all, they wrote some hit songs: "Rosanna," the old story of a lovelorn lyric matched to a bouncy beat, was the gold, Top Ten comeback single accompanying the album release; "Make Believe" made the Top 30; and then, surprisingly, "Africa" hit number one ten months after the album's release. The members of Toto may have more relatives who are NARAS voters than any other group, but that still doesn't explain the sweep they achieved at the Grammys, winning six, including Album of the Year and Record of the Year (for "Rosanna"). Predictably, rock critics howled, but the Grammys helped set up the fourth single, "I Won't Hold You Back," another soft-rock smash and Top Ten hit. As a result, *Toto IV* was both the group's comeback and its peak; it remains a definitive album of slick L.A. pop for the early '80s and Toto's best and most consistent record. Having made it, the members happily went back to sessions, where they helped write and record Michael Jackson's *Thriller. — William Ruhlmann*

Isolation / Nov. 1984 / Columbia ✦✦✦

● **Past to Present 1977-1990** / Sep. 1990 / Columbia ✦✦✦✦✦

Toto's compilation is to be recommended in that it contains all four of the group's Top Ten hit singles—"Hold the Line," "Rosanna," "Africa," and "I Won't Hold You Back." It also contains four more of Toto's 14 pop chart singles—"Georgy Porgy," "99," "I'll Be over You," and "Pamela." But that means it leaves out six chart entries, including the Top 40 hits "Make Believe," "Stranger in Town," and "Without Your Love." In their place are an album track from the most recent album, *The Seventh One* and four newly recorded songs co-written and sung by the group's fourth lead vocalist, Jean-Michel Byron, who is more soulful than his predecessors, but no more memorable. As such, this is not the ideal Toto best-of and earns its "pick" designation over *Toto IV* only by virtue of its inclusion of the group's first hit, "Hold the Line." *— William Ruhlmann*

Allen Toussaint

b. Jan. 14, 1938, New Orleans, LA

Vocals, Keyboards, Piano / New Orleans R&B, R&B

His inherently funky piano work heavily influenced by his Crescent City forefathers—Professor Longhair, Huey "Piano" Smith, and Fats Domino—and with a heavy dose of Ray

Charles, a young visionary named Allen Toussaint almost singlehandedly fashioned a fresh, vital New Orleans R&B sound for the early '60s. Earning a vaunted reputation as a session pianist, Toussaint debuted on vinyl in 1958 with an obscure RCA album whimsically billed as "A. Tousan." When Joe Banashak inaugurated his Minit label in 1960, Toussaint joined the firm as A&R man and quickly proved himself the ultimate behind-the-scenes wizard on the New Orleans scene. During the early to mid-'60s, Toussaint tirelessly wrote, arranged, produced, and played on hits by Ernie K-Doe, Irma Thomas, Jessie Hill, Chris Kenner, Barbara George, Lee Dorsey, Benny Spellman, the Showmen, and many more, his rolling keyboards vital to the charm of virtually all of them.

After unleashing The Meters on the world, Toussaint finally began to step out as a front man in 1970, although his low-key vocals have never achieved quite the same level of success as his previous productions for others. His brilliant compositions have been covered by everyone from Herb Alpert & the Tijuana Brass to Robert Palmer and Bonnie Raitt. Allen Toussaint's stature as a New Orleans musical giant endures. *—Bill Dahl*

The Wild Sound of New Orleans / 1958 / Edsel ✦✦✦✦✦
His debut album, featuring a killer band, storming second-line instrumentals, and Toussaint's rolling 88s. *—Bill Dahl*

Toussaint / 1971 / Scepter ✦✦✦
New Orleans production and performing wizard Allen Toussaint launched his solo career with this early-'70s release. But for some strange reason, the same performer who's written and produced marvelous material for Irma Thomas, Lee Dorsey, Chocolate Milk, and General Johnson among others, was never able to score the same success working as a lead act. There was nothing on this album even in the same arena as his classic R&B tunes, and throughout Toussaint's run of solo releases, only the song "Southern Nights," which Glen Campbell made a hit, could be even mentioned in the same sentence with Toussaint classics like "Ride Your Pony" or "It Will Stand." *—Ron Wynn*

Motion / Aug. 1978 / Reprise ✦✦✦
A nicely produced, competently performed, but disappointing album by New Orleans giant Allen Toussaint. He seemed unable to find a groove or a sound, dabbling in pop, light R&B, rock, and mild funk, but never coming close to duplicating prior magical productions or compositions. This was perhaps Toussaint's least impressive material, and was especially surprising in light of the artistic success of his prior Warner Bros. album *Homage*. *—Ron Wynn*

● **Allen Toussaint Collection** / Apr. 30, 1991 / Reprise ✦✦✦✦✦
R&B with some meat on its bones from New Orleans songwriter/producer Toussaint. This retrospective collection covers four albums since 1970, including his one album for Scepter, *From a Whisper to a Scream*. The music is often dark, without being depressing, horn driven and loosely propelled along by the rhythm section. It's the sort of music that may not be immediate, but given a few chances it'll work its way right under the skin and stay there. What's sad is that they rarely make music like this anymore—this is music out of blood and bone. *—Steven McDonald*

The Complete 'Tousan' Sessions / 1992 / Bear Family ✦✦✦✦✦
A compilation of instrumentals from 1958 and 1959 featuring Toussaint at the top of his form, *The Complete "Tousan" Sessions* is a wonderful portrait of the seminal New Orleans pianist; it's also the first time this material has ever been available on CD. *—Stephen Thomas Erlewine*

Pete Townshend

b. May 19, 1945, Chiswick, London, England
Vocals, Keyboards, Guitar (Electric), Guitar / Album Rock, Pop/Rock, Prog-Rock/Art Rock, Hard Rock, Singer/Songwriter
Pete Townshend was the guitarist and songwriter for the Who from 1964 to 1982; best known for his conceptual works, he wrote *Tommy* and *Quadrophenia* for the group. Townshend made his first, tentative solo album, *Who Came First*, in 1972. Dedicated to his guru, Meher Baba, the album continued themes pursued in the previous Who album, *Who's Next*, and contained material from an abortive conceptual work, *Lifehouse*. *Empty Glass* (1980) sold half a million copies and featured the Top Ten hit "Let My Love Open the Door," as well as the minor hits "A Little Is Enough" and "Rough Boys." Townshend followed this in 1982 with *All the Best Cowboys Have Chinese Eyes*. Following the demise of the Who, he released *Scoop*, a two-disc collection of demos, in 1983 (a second volume appeared in 1987). In 1985 he returned to thematic efforts with the album *White City—A Novel*, which included the Top 30 single "Face the Face." In 1989, Townshend released an album based on Ted Hughes's children's story, *The Iron Man*. Simultaneous with the album's release, Townshend embarked on a reunion tour with the Who. Four years later, he delivered *Psychoderelict* to mixed reviews and lukewarm sales. By that time, he had successfully reinvented himself as a Broadway tunesmith—the Broadway production of *The Who's Tommy* had become a runaway hit, earning Townshend a Tony and prompting him to pursue more stage musicals. *—William Ruhlmann*

Who Came First / Oct. 1972 / Rykodisc ✦✦✦✦✦
Pete Townshend's first solo album was a homespun, charming forum for low-key, personal songs that weren't deemed suitable for The Who, as well as spiritual paeans (direct and indirect) to his spiritual guru Meher Baba. Who fans will be immediately attracted by the presence of a couple of songs from the aborted Who concept album *Lifehouse* (much of which ended up on *Who's Next*), "Pure & Easy" and "Let's See Action." The Who did eventually release their own versions of both those songs. But Townshend's own versions aren't the highlights of this record, which shows a folkier and gentler side to The Who's chief muse than his albums with the group. "Sheraton Gibson" is a neat tune about rock & roll road life, and "Time Is Passing" takes very subtle inspiration from Baba. Most of the rest of the album contains some of the most unusual pieces Townshend has released: his acoustic cover of Jim Reeves' "There's A Heartache Following Me" (recorded because it was one of Baba's favorite tunes), "Evolution" (which is actually pretty much a solo track by his buddy Ronnie Lane of The Faces), "Parvardigar" (adapted from Baba's Universal Prayer), and "Content" (a philosophical poem by Maud Kennedy that Townshend put to music). The 1993 reissue of this LP for compact disc fleshes out the program considerably with six previously unreleased tracks, including Townshend's demo of The Who single "The Seeker." The other bonus cuts are by no means filler; meditative and melancholy originals, they're just as strong as the tracks on the original release. *—Richie Unterberger*

Rough Mix / Sep. 1977 / Atco ✦✦✦✦

● **Empty Glass** / Apr. 21, 1980 / Atco ✦✦✦✦✦
Pete Townshend was heading toward collapse as the '70s turned into the '80s. He had battled a number of personal demons throughout the '70s, but he started spiraling downward after Keith Moon's death, questioning more than ever why he did what did (and this is a songwriter who always asked questions). Signs of that crept out on *Face Dances*, but he saved a full-blown exploration of his psyche for *Empty Glass*, his first solo album since *Who Came First*, a vanity project released to little notice around *Who's Next* (so limited in its distribution that *Empty Glass* seemed like his solo debut). Some of the songs on *Empty Glass* would have worked as Who songs, yet this is clearly a singer/songwriter album, the work of a writer determined to lay his emotions bare, whether on the plaintive "I Am an Animal" or the blistering punk love letter "Rough Boys." Since this is Townshend, it can be a little artier than it needs to be, as on the pseudo-Gilbert & Sullivan chorus of "Keep on Working," but the joy of *Empty Glass* is that his writing is sharp, his performances lively, his gift for pop hooks as apparent as his wit. Though it runs out of steam toward the end, *Empty Glass* remains one of the highlights of Townshend's catalog and is one of the most revealing records he cut, next to his other breakdown album, *Who By Numbers*. *—Stephen Thomas Erlewine*

All the Best Cowboys Have Chinese Eyes / Jun. 1982 / Atco ✦✦✦✦
If *Empty Glass* could have been performed by the Who, *All the Best Cowboys Have Chinese Eyes* was a solo record in the truest sense, since it's impossible to imagine anyone but Townshend wanting to indulge in this deliberately arty, awkwardly poetic crock. Where his other albums showed an inclination toward classical-influenced art rock, this is defiantly modern art, filled with stagey prose, synthesizers, drum machines, angular song structures, and a heavy debt to new wave—in short, Townshend's vision of what modern music should sound like in 1982. This kind of record taunts cynics and critics, being nearly impenetrable in its content even if the production and the music itself aren't all that inaccessible. The problem is, even if it's autobiographical to a certain extent (how else to read "Somebody Saved Me" or "Stardom in Acton," which drops the Who's home borough?), it's hard to tell exactly what he's on about. So it's easy to see why many listeners are exasperated instead of intrigued, but it's also easy to get fascinated by the album's very obtuseness. This all is very much of a piece and, apart from the gems "North Country Girl" and "Slit Skirts," it's hard to separate individual songs. Indeed, separating *All the Best Cowboys* from its era is even difficult, since the album's surface glistens with new wave synths and guitars; this is clearly a record Townshend could only have made in 1982, emboldened by new wave, the reaction to *Empty Glass*, new sobriety, and general hubris. For these reasons, this is very much loved by a certain portion of Townsend's fan base—and for the same reasons many, many people despise it. And any record that fractures an audience so considerably is worth a spin. *—Stephen Thomas Erlewine*

Scoop / Apr. 1983 / Atco ✦✦✦✦✦
Pete Townshend's demos had grown legendary among Who collectors well before the official release of the double-album *Scoop* in 1983. On each demo, Townshend worked out full arrangements, which the Who would often follow exactly. He also recorded a wealth of songs and instrumental pieces that never made it to record. Over the course of two albums, *Scoop* features 25 of these demos, including both classic Who songs ("So Sad About Us," "Bargain," "Behind Blue Eyes," "Magic Bus," "Love Reign O'er Me") and unreleased gems ("Politician," "Melancholia," "To Barney Kessell," "Mary"). Occasionally, the songs sound better in their demo versions, particularly on latter-day Who songs, which were over-wrought in their official incarnations. But what makes *Scoop* so fascinating is its revelation of the depth and detail of Townshend's imagination, and how he refined his ideas. But even casual fans will find the sheer musicality of the record worthwhile—it's one of the most focused and impressive albums he has ever released. *—Stephen Thomas Erlewine*

White City: A Novel / Nov. 1985 / Atco ✦✦✦
After the experimental *All the Best Cowboys Have Chinese Eyes*, Pete Townshend returned to a more traditional form of concept album with *White City*. Built around a loose narrative concerning urban despair, the album doesn't work very well conceptually, yet a handful of the individual songs are among his finest solo work, including the punchy "Face the Face" and the anthemic "Give Blood." *—Stephen Thomas Erlewine*

Pete Townshend's Deep End Live! / Oct. 1986 / Atco ✦✦✦

Another Scoop / Jul. 8, 1987 / Atco ✦✦✦✦✦
Like its predecessor, *Another Scoop* is a collection of 27 demos Pete Townshend recorded for the Who and, if anything, it surpasses the first volume in terms of quality. *Another Scoop* has a greater percentage of familiar Who classics—including "You Better You Bet," "Pinball Wizard," "Happy Jack," "Substitute," "Long Live Rock," "Pictures of Lily" and "The Kids Are Alright"—and the outtakes are uniformly excellent, ranging from his takes on "Driftin' Blues" and "Begin the Beguine" to neglected gems "Girl In A Suitcase," "Holly Like Ivy" and "Ask Yourself," and even weird experiments like "Football Fugue." For any Townshend fan, *Another Scoop* is necessary listening, containing some of his best and most adventurous work. *—Stephen Thomas Erlewine*

The Iron Man: A Musical / Jun. 27, 1989 / Atlantic ✦✦

Psychoderelict / Jun. 15, 1993 / Atlantic ✦✦✦

The Best of Pete Townshend: Coolwalkingsmoothtalkingstraightsmokingfirestoking / Apr. 23, 1996 / Atlantic ✦✦✦✦

Lifehouse Elements / May 23, 2000 / Redline Entertainment ✦✦✦
Lifehouse Elements is a sampler of Pete Townshend's gargantuan six-disc box set *The Lifehouse Chronicles*, itself the culmination of nearly 30 years of work on his intended follow-up

to *Tommy.* Though much of it was recorded for *Who's Next,* Townshend never abandoned *Lifehouse,* eventually completing it in 1999. It debuted that year as a radio play for the BBC and that play, along with selections of demos, experiments, and orchestrations, were collected on the box (only available through /www.eelpie.com). *Lifehouse Elements* contains highlights from the collection, capturing all the joys and frustrations of the box. There's little question that there's some brilliant music here—not just alternate versions of "Behind Blue Eyes" and "Won't Get Fooled Again", but Townshend-sung demos of "Pure and Easy," "Getting in Tune," "Let's See Action," and "Song Is Over." Still, it's almost as padded as the box, with a formless orchestral version of "Baba O'Riley," a remix called "Baba M1," and a remix of "Who Are You." That doesn't mean it's unsatisfying or unnecessary. If you're a hardcore Townshend fan, it's hard to not hear the demos and works-in-progress of the classic, official *Lifehouse* songs and not get somewhat thrilled, even if that buzz is diminished by the newer recordings. The frustrating thing is, once you hear *Lifehouse Elements,* you'll want to hear *the rest* of the demos and there's no other way to get those without the radio play, orchestrations, experiments, and ramblings that make up the rest of the box. So, *Elements* does whet the appetite for unreleased Townshend while preparing listeners to be a little frustrated by the box's blend of the sublime and stupefying. So, it does its job well. *—Stephen Thomas Erlewine*

Traffic

f. 1967, Midlands, England, **db.** 1975

Group / British Psychedelia, Album Rock, Jazz-Rock, Folk-Rock, Psychedelic, Prog-Rock/Art Rock, Blues-Rock

Though it ultimately must be considered an interim vehicle for singer/songwriter/keyboardist/guitarist Steve Winwood, Traffic was a successful group that followed its own individual course through the rock music scene of the late '60s and early '70s. At a time when electric guitars ruled rock, Traffic emphasized Winwood's organ and the reed instruments played by Chris Wood, especially flute. After Dave Mason, who had provided the band with an alternate folk-pop sound, departed for good, Traffic leaned toward extended songs that gave its players room to improvise in a jazz-like manner, even as the rhythms maintained a rock structure. The result was international success that ended only when Winwood finally decided he was ready to strike out on his own.

Traffic debuted in 1967 with *Mr. Fantasy,* a Top Ten hit. Though Mason left after its release, he later rejoined and contributed heavily to the band's second album, *Traffic.* After a temporary breakup, Winwood began work on a solo record in 1970, but quickly brought in Capaldi and Wood and turned it into the Traffic LP *John Barleycorn Must Die.* Traffic followed with 1971's *The Low Spark of High Heeled Boys,* which reached the American Top Ten, though it didn't even chart back home in Britain. *Shoot Out at the Fantasy Factory,* released in January 1973, also reached the American Top Ten. At the conclusion of a support tour for 1974's *When the Eagle Flies,* Traffic silently disbanded. In 1994, Winwood announced a reunion with Capaldi (Wood had died of liver failure). The two made a new album, *Far From Home,* and toured as Traffic during the summer. Though the album did not sell well, the 1967-1974 era band continued to enjoy significant status as a classic rock act, its albums earning CD reissues along with the release of compilations like *Smiling Phases* (1991) and *Feelin' Alright: The Very Best of Traffic* (2000). *—William Ruhlmann*

Mr. Fantasy / Dec. 1967 / Island ✦✦✦

★ **Traffic** / Feb. 1968 / Island ✦✦✦✦✦

After dispensing with his services in December 1967, the remaining members of Traffic reinstated Dave Mason in the group in the spring of 1968 as they struggled to write enough material for their impending second album. The result was a disc evenly divided between Mason's catchy folk-rock compositions and Steve Winwood's compelling rock jams. Mason's material was the most appealing both initially and eventually: the lead-off track, a jaunty effort called "You Can All Join In," became a European hit, and "Feelin' Alright?" turned out to be the only real standard to emerge from the album after it started earning cover versions from Joe Cocker and others in the 1970s. Winwood's efforts, with their haunting keyboard-based melodies augmented by Chris Wood's reed work and Jim Capaldi's exotic rhythms, work better as musical efforts than lyrical ones. Primary lyricist Capaldi's words tend to be impressionistic reveries or vague psychological reflections; the most satisfying is the shaggy-dog story "Forty Thousand Headmen," which doesn't really make any sense as anything other than a dream. But the lyrics to Winwood/Capaldi compositions take a back seat to the playing and Winwood's soulful voice. As Mason's simpler, more direct performances alternate with the more complex Winwood tunes, the album is well-balanced. It's too bad that the musicians were not able to maintain that balance in person; for the second time in two albums, Mason found himself dismissed from the group just as an LP to which he'd made a major contribution hit the stores. Only a few months after that, the band itself split up, but not before scoring their second consecutive Top Ten ranking in the U.K.; the album also reached the Top 20 in the U.S., breaking the temporarily defunct group stateside. *—William Ruhlmann*

Heaven Is in Your Mind / 1969 / Island ✦✦✦✦✦

In January 1968, United Artists Records released a reconfigured American version of Traffic's debut album *Mr. Fantasy* under the new title *Heaven Is in Your Mind,* but after the first pressing reverted to calling it *Mr. Fantasy.* In 2000, Island reissued two CD versions, one titled *Mr. Fantasy* containing the British track listing in mono, the other titled *Heaven Is in Your Mind* with the U.S. track listing in stereo. Both albums contained bonus tracks, making their contents similar (but not quite identical). Actually, the album originally called *Heaven Is in Your Mind* was the superior version even before this development brought the two editions into stark comparison, since the changes actually improved the record by adding strong singles. But just as important as the substitutions was the sequencing, which banished the British-flavored novelty songs to the middle of Side Two; "Dear Mr. Fantasy," which would turn out to be the best-remembered song on the album, was moved to a climactic position as the penultimate cut on Side Two. The result de-emphasized Traffic's pop-psychedelic style (a hangover from the influence of *Sgt. Pepper*) and promoted its abilities as a jamming blues-rock outfit, talents that were abetted by Jimmy Miller's production and that helped launch them as an album act in the U.S. The 2000 reissue includes as bonus tracks the two deleted Dave Mason songs and two songs from the *Here We Go 'Round the Mulberry Bush* soundtrack. Island's decision to reissue both versions could easily confuse consumers; the U.S. stereo version, once and again known as *Heaven Is in Your Mind,* is really the one to own if you're only buying one. *—William Ruhlmann*

Last Exit / Jan. 1969 / Island ✦✦✦

John Barleycorn Must Die / Jan. 1970 / Island ✦✦✦✦✦

At only 22 years old, Steve Winwood sat down in early 1970 to fulfill a contractual commitment by making his first solo album, on which he intended to play all the instruments himself. The record got as far as one backing track produced by Guy Stevens, "Stranger to Himself," before Winwood called his erstwhile partner from Traffic, Jim Capaldi, in to help out. The two completed a second track, "Every Mother's Son," then, with Winwood and Island Records chief Chris Blackwell moving to the production chores, brought in a third Traffic member, Chris Wood, to work on the sessions. Thus, Traffic, dead and buried for more than a year, was reborn. The band's new approach was closer to what it perhaps should have been back in 1967, basically a showcase for Winwood's voice and instrumental work, with Wood adding reed parts and Capaldi drumming and occasionally singing harmony vocals. If the original Traffic bowed to the perceived commercial necessity of crafting hit singles, the new Traffic was more interested in stretching out. Heretofore, no studio recording had run longer than the 5 minutes of "Dear Mr. Fantasy," but four of the six selections on *John Barleycorn Must Die* exceeded six minutes. Winwood and company used the time to play extended instrumental variations on compelling folk- and jazz-derived riffs. Five of the six songs had lyrics, and their tone of disaffection was typical of earlier Capaldi sentiments. But the vocal sections of the songs merely served as excuses for Winwood to exercise his expressive voice as punctuation to the extended instrumental sections. As such, *John Barleycorn Must Die* moved beyond the jamming that had characterized some of Traffic's 1968 work to approach the emerging field of jazz-rock. And that helped the band to achieve its commercial potential; this became Traffic's first gold album. *—William Ruhlmann*

The Low Spark of High Heeled Boys / Jan. 1971 / Island ✦✦✦✦✦

The Low Spark of High Heeled Boys marked the commercial and artistic apex of the second coming of Traffic, which had commenced in 1970 with *John Barleycorn Must Die.* The trio that made that album had been augmented by three others (Ric Grech, Jim Gordon, and "Reebop" Kwaku Baah) in the interim, though apparently the *Low Spark* sessions featured varying combinations of these musicians, plus some guests. But where their previous album had grown out of sessions for a Steve Winwood solo album and retained that focus, *Low Spark* pointedly contained changes of pace from his usual contributions of midtempo, introspective jam tunes. "Rock & Roll Stew" was an uptempo treatise on life on the road, while Jim Capaldi's "Light up or Leave Me Alone" was another more aggressive number with an unusually emphatic Capaldi vocal that perked things up on side two. The other four tracks were Winwood/Capaldi compositions more in the band's familiar style. "Hidden Treasure" and "Rainmaker" bookended the disc with acoustic treatments of nature themes that were particularly concerned with water, and "Many a Mile to Freedom" also employed water imagery. But the standout was the 12-minute title track, with its distinctive piano riff and its lyrics of weary disillusionment with the music business. The band had only just fulfilled a contractual commitment by releasing the live album *Welcome to the Canteen,* and they had in their past the embarrassing *Last Exit* album thrown together as a commercial stopgap during a temporary breakup in 1969. But that anger had proven inspirational, and "The Low Spark of High Heeled Boys" was one of Traffic's greatest songs as well as its longest so far. The result was an album that quickly went gold (and eventually platinum) in the U.S., where the group toured frequently. *—William Ruhlmann*

Welcome to the Canteen / Feb. 1971 / Island ✦✦✦✦

Shoot Out at the Fantasy Factory / 1973 / Island ✦✦✦

Traffic: On the Road / 1973 / Island ✦✦✦

When the Eagle Flies / 1974 / Island ✦✦✦

Smiling Phases / Nov. 19, 1991 / Island ✦✦✦✦✦

● **Feelin' Alright: The Very Best of Traffic** / Feb. 8, 2000 / Island ✦✦✦✦✦

Though the two-CD set *Smiling Phases* finally put a comprehensive Traffic compilation on the market in 1991, the only readily available single-disc collection had long been *Best of Traffic,* originally issued halfway through the band's career. Thus, *Feelin' Alright: The Very Best of Traffic,* a 77-minute sampler for the CD era, was long overdue. It combines the group's early singles hits like "Paper Sun" and "Hole in My Shoe" with lengthier album tracks like "Dear Mr. Fantasy" and "The Low Spark of High-Heeled Boys." Looking over the song list, any Traffic fan will be able to reel off omissions. But easy as it is to note what's missing, it's not so easy to figure out how such songs could be shoehorned into a single-disc set that is already packed with great material. Except in its first year in England, Traffic was not a band that made hit singles, but it did make a plethora of strong recordings, many of which were lengthy by the standards of the time. Several of the absolute necessities on a collection of their best work run longer than five minutes each; "The Low Spark of High-Heeled Boys" runs close to 12 minutes. Beyond those absolute musts are a bunch of other good songs, many more than could fit on one CD. Compilation producer Bill Levenson has made a reasonable choice among them to construct a well-balanced disc that shows off the band's many talents. Neophytes with a few extra dollars to spend are strongly urged to take the plunge and buy *Smiling Phases,* but as a one-CD collection of some of the highlights of Traffic's career, this album lives up to its title. *—William Ruhlmann*

The Trammps

f. 1973, Philadelphia, PA, **db.** 1980

Group / Disco, Soul

Disco's most soulful vocal group, the Trammps began in the '60s as the Volcanos, and were also called the Moods. A snappy revival of Judy Garland's '40s tune "Zing Went the Strings of My Heart" was their first chart single, reaching number 17 on the R&B list in 1972. Despite their well-deserved reputation and boisterous, jubilant harmonies and sound, the Trammps were never huge commercial successes even during disco's heyday. Indeed, they had only three R&B Top Ten hits from 1972 through 1978, and such wonderful records as "Soul Bones," "Ninety-Nine and a Half," and "I Feel Like I've Been Livin' (On the Dark Side of the Moon)" stiffed on the charts though they were beloved by club audiences and R&B fans alike. Their only huge hit was "Disco Inferno" in 1977, which was a number nine R&B single in 1977 and was also featured in *Saturday Night Fever.* Yet it missed the pop Top Ten, peaking at number 11. But the Trammps' prowess can't be measured by chart popularity; Jimmy Ellis' booming, joyous vocals brilliantly championed the celebratory fervor and atmosphere that made disco both beloved and hated among music fans. *—Ron Wynn*

- **This Is Where the Happy People Go: The Best of Trammps** / 1994 / Rhino ✦✦✦✦✦

Due to all the great funk, R&B, and soul bands of the '70s, it's easy to overlook many of the lesser-known (but just as great) bands. Such is the case with the Trammps. Best known for their smash hit from the *Saturday Night Fever* Soundtrack, "Disco Inferno" (their only Top 20 appearance on the pop charts), the group had many other hits on the R&B charts, which were just as deserving of crossover success. Just about any track from the excellent *This Is Where All the Happy People Go: The Best of the Trammps* compilation is a solid example of '70s R&B at its finest and most expertly crafted. Many overlooked and forgotten gems reside here, such as "Hold Back the Night," "Trammps Disco Theme," "That's Where the Happy People Go," and "Zing Went the Strings of My Heart." Admittedly, the Trammps did seem to jump on the disco bandwagon, like so many other bands from this era, but the quality of the music never suffered. For a representation of some of the finest music the '70s had to offer, *The Best of the Trammps* simply can't be beat. *—Greg Prato*

The Trashmen

f. 1962, Minneapolis, MN, **db.** 1967

Group / Frat Rock, Garage Rock, Surf, Rock & Roll

A Minneapolis rock & roll band, they evolved from Jim Thaxter & the Travelers, recording one single under that name ("Sally Jo"/"Cyclone"). The group comprises Tony Andreason (lead guitar), Dan Winslow (guitar/ vocals), Bob Reed (bass), and Steve Wahrer (drums/vocals). Unfairly depicted as a novelty act, the Trashmen were in actuality a top-notch rock & roll combo, enormously popular on the teen-club circuit, playing primarily surf music to a landlocked Minnesota audience. Drummer Steve Wahrer combined two songs by the Rivingtons ("The Bird's the Word" and "Pa Pa Ooh Mow Mow"), added freakish vocal effects and a pounding rhythm to the mix, and, by early 1964, the group was in the Top Ten nationwide with "Surfin' Bird." Though the group continued to release great follow-up singles and an excellent album, their moment in the sun had come and gone; they disbanded by late 1967/early 1968. They re-formed in the mid-'80s and continued to play locally until Wahrer's death. The Trashmen are revered by '60s collectors as one of the great American teen-band combos of all time, their lone hit exemplifying wild, unabashed rock & roll at its most demented, bare-bones-basic, lone-E-chord finest. *—Cub Koda*

Surfin' Bird / 1964 / Sundazed ✦✦✦✦✦

The only album released by the group during their lifetime actually outstrips most of the Southern California-based competition, due to the ferocious grit of the playing and a vaguely demented, go-for-broke recklessness. A good mix of instrumentals and vocals, though nothing else is on the level of the title cut; the CD reissue adds demos of "Surfin' Bird" and "Bird Dance Beat," and a couple rare singles. *—Richie Unterberger*

Live Bird '65-'67 / 1990 / Sundazed ✦✦✦

- **The Tube City!: The Best of The Trashmen** / 1992 / Sundazed ✦✦✦✦✦

The original *Surfin' Bird* album, plus all the original Garrett singles from that period. The perfect primer set. *—Cub Koda*

The Great Lost Trashmen Album! / Oct. 21, 1994 / Sundazed ✦✦✦✦

The Great Lost Trashmen Album! features some fine unreleased studio recordings. *—Cub Koda*

Bird Call!: The Twin City Stomp of the Trashmen / Sundazed ✦✦✦

The Traveling Wilburys

f. 1988

Group / Pop/Rock

Reversing the usual process by which groups break up and give way to solo careers, the Traveling Wilburys are a group made up of solo stars. The group was organized by former Beatle George Harrison, former Electric Light Orchestra leader Jeff Lynne, Bob Dylan, Tom Petty, and Roy Orbison, thus representing three generations of rock stars. In 1988, the five (who had known each other for years) came together to record a Harrison B-side single and ended up writing and recording an album on which they shared lead vocals. It turned out to be a way to transcend the high expectations made of any of them as individuals, and a delighted public sent the album to number three, with two singles, "Handle with Care" and "End of the Line," hitting the charts. Unfortunately, Orbison died of a heart attack only a few weeks after the album's release.

Two years later, the remaining quartet released a second album, inexplicably titled *Vol. 3.* Although it didn't match the success of the first Wilburys album, it was another million-selling hit. Throughout the '90s, there were rumors of another Traveling Wilburys record in the works, but no new albums from the group surfaced. Harrison and Lynne did reteam in 1995, when Lynne produced and reworked two John Lennon demos with the Beatles for their *Anthology* rarties collection. *—William Ruhlmann*

- **Traveling Wilburys, Vol. 1** / Oct. 1988 / Wilbury ✦✦✦✦✦

The Traveling Wilburys are the only supergroup that lives up to expectations because they underplay them. They never shoot for the moon on their 1990 debut, they simply lay back and have a little fun. Anyone expecting something monumental will be disappointed, yet that's precisely what's fun about it—Dylan, Petty, Harrison, Lynne, and Orbison are having such a good time that it's hard not to get caught up in the spirit of things. The songs— Well, the songs are on one level a mixed bag, a blend of easy rockers, folk-tunes, and silly jokes, but even if these might sound like throwaways on "serious" albums, they sound fresh, lively, funny, even heart-rendering here. Apart from the two singles, "Handle With Care" and "End of the Line," the highlights belong to Dylan, who's having more fun here than he's had since *The Basement Tapes* (check out the Springsteen parody "Tweeter and the Monkey Man" for proof). If Lynne's production is a little lush and lavish for these roots rockers, it's nevertheless warm, welcoming, and appropriate, helping make *Traveling Wilburys, Vol. 1* a unique record, different than anything in any of the members' own catalogs. *—Stephen Thomas Erlewine*

Traveling Wilburys, Vol. 3 / Oct. 19, 1990 / Wilbury ✦✦✦

Travis

f. Glasgow, Scotland

Group / Indie Pop, British Trad Rock, Post-Grunge, Indie Rock, Britpop, Alternative Pop/Rock

Along with Cast, Ocean Colour Scene, Kula Shaker and Embrace, Travis were one of the most prominent British "trad-rock" bands in the mid-to-late '90s. Following Oasis' lead of crafting down-to-earth, heartfelt songs in the vein of classic British bands from the '60s, Travis were more successful and enduring than some of their peers due to their lively, impassioned songwriting and performances.

The group formed in Glasgow around 1990 as something of a lark for its members, singer/songwriter Francis Healy, guitarist Andy Dunlop, drummer Neil Primrose and bassist Douglas Payne. After finishing their studies at art school a few years later, the foursome became more serious about Travis' potential and moved to London in 1996. Their self-released debut EP, *All I Wanna Do Is Rock,* came out in the fall of that year; with its earnest vocals and soaring guitars, it captured the spirit of British rock at the time, which was retreating from some of Britpop's artiness to a back-to-basics sound. Their second single, 1997's *U16 Girls* was released by Independiente Records, the new label headed by former Go! Discs' director Andy MacDonald; a few months later, their critically-acclaimed full-length debut *Good Feeling* arrived. Recorded in a matter of days with top producer Steve Lilywhite, the album included hit singles like "Happy" and "Tied To The '90s" and immediately entered the Top 10 of the UK charts. The following year, Travis began sessions with star producer Nigel Godrich for the follow-up to *Good Feeling,* recording in six studios as many months. Though it was a slower, darker affair, when *The Man Who* appeared in 1999, it eclipsed Travis' previous successes, going platinum six times in the UK and spawning more hit singles such as "Why Does It Always Rain On Me?" and "Writing To Reach You." Nominated Select Magazine's Album Of The Year (and finishing in the top 10 of many other publication's year-end lists), *The Man Who* appeared on US shores in early 2000, just in time for a tour with their musical big brothers, Oasis. *—Heather Phares*

Good Feeling / Oct. 7, 1997 / Indepentente/Epic ✦✦✦✦

Like most post-Oasis bands, Travis is determined to be a classic band, which means they are decidedly classicist in their approach. Travis have the traditional Britpop influences—Beatles, Kinks, Small Faces, etc.—which are filtered through such '90s peers as the Stone Roses, Manic Street Preachers and, of course, Oasis. Fortunately, they aren't tied to the '60s, like Cast or Ocean Colour Scene; they try to revitalize the traditions with harder backbeats and louder guitars, and Fran Healy's voice often strains at the edge of screaming. That approach can keep their conventional aspects entertaining, but what makes *Good Feeling* a successful debut is that Healy can write hooks, whether it's the anthemic "All I Want To Do Is Rock" or the stompy "U16 Girls." There are several slow spots on *Good Feeling* which illustrate that the group's sound has its limits, but it's a promising debut that establishes Travis as one of the better British trad-rock groups. *—Stephen Thomas Erlewine*

- **The Man Who** / 1999 / Epic ✦✦✦✦

The Treniers

f. 1947

Group / Jump Blues, R&B

Featuring twin brothers Cliff and Claude Trenier, the Treniers helped link swing music to rock & roll with their brand of hot jump blues in the late '40s and early '50s. To the latter-day listener, their early-'50s singles can sound closer to swing than rock; indeed, Cliff and Claude had once sung with the Jimmie Lunceford Orchestra. The group did anticipate some crucial elements of rock & roll, though, with their solid, thumping beats, their squealing saxophone solos, and their song titles, such as "Rocking on Sunday Night," "Rockin' Is Our Business," and "It Rocks! It Rolls! It Swings!" The Treniers' brand of swing-cum-R&B was undoubtedly an influence on Bill Haley, who saw them when both acts were playing summer shows at Wildwood, NJ. Their best work was recorded for OKeh in the early '50s; by the middle of the decade, their sound was more R&B-oriented. Like many early R&B pioneers, they were unable to find success in the rock & roll era, though they appeared in a few of the first rock & roll films. *—Richie Unterberger*

- **They Rock! They Roll! They Swing!: The Best of the Treniers** / Feb. 28, 1995 / Epic/Legacy ✦✦✦✦✦

This 20-track compilation has all of their key early- and mid-'50s Okeh singles (only one of which, "Go! Go! Go!," was actually an R&B hit), five previously unreleased songs, and their 1953 version of Bill Haley's "Rock-A-Beatin' Boogie," which must rank as one of the first (if not the very first) covers of a White rock song by a Black artist. *—Richie Unterberger*

Tricky (Adrian Thaws)

b. 1964, Knowle West, Bristol, Avon, England

Vocals, Producer / Electronica, Trip-Hop, Alternative Pop/Rock

Originally, Tricky was a member of the Wild Bunch, a Bristol-based rap troupe that eventually metamorphosized into Massive Attack during the early '90s. Tricky provided pivotal raps on Massive Attack's groundbreaking 1992 album *Blue Lines.* The following year, he released his debut single, "Aftermath." His debut album, *Maxinquaye,* appeared in the spring of 1995.

Not only did the album receive overwhelmingly positive reviews when it was released, but it entered in the UK charts at number two, despite the total lack of daytime radio airplay. Throughout 1995, Tricky was omnipresent in the UK, collaborating with and remixing for a wide variety of artists, including Bjork, Luscious Jackson and Whale. At the end of the year, *Maxinquaye* topped many year-end polls in Britain, including the *Melody Maker* and *NME*. In February of 1996, *Nearly God*—an album featuring Tricky's collaborations with artists as diverse as Terry Hall, Bjork, Alison Moyet, and Neneh Cherry—was released, again to strong reviews; the album was released in the US six months later. Tricky's official second album, *Pre-Millenium Tension*, was released in 1996. Again, he received positive reviews, though there were a few dissenting opinions. *—Stephen Thomas Erlewine*

★ **Maxinquaye** / Apr. 18, 1995 / 4th & Broadway ♦♦♦♦♦
Though he hates the label of trip-hop, Tricky's debut album *Maxinquaye* is one of the finest that the genre has to offer. "Ponderosa," "Suffocated Love," and "Pumpkin" are disturbing and beautiful, with ominous background noises and Martine's soaring vocals, while tracks like the group's cover of "Black Steel" show off their harder side. A striking debut, Tricky's *Maxinquaye* is only the beginning for this innovative artist. *—Heather Phares*

Nearly God / Apr. 29, 1996 / 4th & Broadway ♦♦♦♦♦
Nearly God is Tricky's unofficial second album—he calls it a collection of brilliant, incomplete demos. When Tricky signed his contract with Island, it allowed him to release an album a year under a different name and *Nearly God* is the first of these efforts. Tricky recorded the record with a diverse cast of collaborators—in addition to his partner Martina, there's Terry Hall, Bjork, Neneh Cherry, Cath Coffey, Dedi Madden, and Alison Moyet (Damon Albarn pulled his track just before the album's release). Building on the ghostly, dark soundscapes of Tricky's debut, *Maxinquaye*, *Nearly God* narrows the focus of his first record by making the music slower, hazier, and more distubing. It's not as coherent as *Maxinquaye*, but that's part of its appeal. *Nearly God* is a haunting, fractured, surreal nightmare that doesn't always make sense, but never fails to make an impact. Certain collaborators work better than others—Tricky understands the eeriness of Terry Hall's voice, but he does nothing to tame Alison Moyet's inappropriate bluesy shrieking—but the overall effect of the album is quietly devastating. It gets under your skin and stays there. It's a brilliantly evocative nightmare. *—Stephen Thomas Erlewine*

Tricky Presents Grassroots / Aug. 1996 / ffrr ♦♦♦

Pre-Millennium Tension / Nov. 11, 1996 / 4th & Broadway ♦♦♦♦
Maxinquaye was an unexpected hit in England, launching a wave of similar-sounding artists, who incorporated Tricky's innovations into safer pop territory. Tricky responded by travelling to Jamaica to record *Pre-Millennium Tension*, a nervy, claustrophobic record that thrives in its own paranoia. Scaling back the clattering hooks of *Maxinquaye* and slowing the beat down, Tricky has created a hallucinatory soundscape, where the rhythms, samples, and guitars intertwine into a crawling processions of menacing sounds and disembodied lyrical threats. Its tone is set by the backward guitar loops of "Vent," and continued through the shifting "Christiansands," and the tense, lyrically dense "Tricky Kid," easily Tricky's best straight rap to date. Occasionally, the gloom is broken, such as when the shimmering piano chords of "Makes Me Want to Die" ring out, but nearly as often, it becomes bogged down in its own murk, as in the long ragga rant "Ghetto Youth." While the lyrics are often quite effective in conveying dope-addled paranoia, what ties the album together is its layered rhythms and soundscapes. Though it might not sound that way immediately, *Pre-Millennium Tension* is as much Tricky reaching back to his hardcore rap roots as it is a sonic exploration. As such, it stands as a transition record for Tricky, but its overall effect is only slightly less powerful than *Maxinquaye* or *Nearly God*. *—Stephen Thomas Erlewine*

Angels with Dirty Faces / Jun. 2, 1998 / Island ♦♦♦

Juxtapose / Aug. 17, 1999 / Island ♦♦♦

The Troggs

f. 1964, Andover, Hampshire, England
Group / Frat Rock, British Invasion, Rock & Roll
Remembered chiefly as proto-punkers who reached the top of the charts with the "caveman rock" of "Wild Thing" (1966), the Troggs were also adept at crafting power-pop and ballads. Hearkening back to a somewhat simpler, more basic British Invasion approach as psychedelia began to explode in the late '60s, the group also reached the Top Five with their flower-power ballad "Love Is All Around" in 1968. While more popular in their native England than the U.S., the band also fashioned memorable, insistently riffing hit singles like "With a Girl like You," "Night of the Long Grass," and the notoriously salacious "I Can't Control Myself" between 1966 and 1968. Paced by Reg Presley's lusting vocals, the group—which composed most of their own material—could crunch with the best of them, but were also capable of quite a bit more range and melodic invention than they've been given credit for. *—Richie Unterberger*

Archeology (1967-1977) / Sep. 22, 1992 / Polydor Chronicles ♦♦♦♦♦
A double-CD, 52-track box set that proves there was a lot more to The Troggs than "Wild Thing" and "Love Is All Around." This archetypally primitive British Invasion quartet scored many hits in the U.K. that barely dented the charts in the U.S., like "With A Girl Like You," "Night Of The Long Grass," and the notoriously racy "I Can't Control Myself." They're all here, along with notable album cuts, B-sides, and worldwide post-1968 flops. Primitive they may have been, but The Troggs—who wrote most of their own material—did not lack a flair for hard pop hooks, and could display a surprising delicacy in their ballads. Several of their obscure singles and album tracks are equal in worth to their hits, like the gothic but pretty "Cousin Jane," and the witty light psychedelia of "Maybe the Madman" and "Purple Shades." Some of the '70s hard rockers and glammish novelties are unimpressive, and 52 songs are arguably excessive. But there are a fair number of obscure gems to be found on this well-annotated package. *—Richie Unterberger*

● **The Best of the Troggs** / Oct. 4, 1994 / Fontana ♦♦♦♦♦

Doris Troy

b. Jan. 6, 1937, New York, NY
Vocals (Background), Vocals / Pop-Soul, Soul
Surely one of the most talented one-hit wonders of the rock era, Doris Troy hit the Top Ten with "Just One Look" in 1963, but also recorded many other fine pop-soul sides for Atlantic between 1963 and 1965. Unlike many soul performers of the time, Troy wrote most of her own material (under the pseudonym Payne), and had already written for other artists, and sung backup with Dionne and Dee Dee Warwick and Cissy Houston on New York soul records, before striking out on her own. More melodically ambitious and stylistically eclectic than many of her peers, her Atlantic sides blend elements of gospel, girl group, blues, and pop into a rich New York soul sound. Troy never reached the charts again after "Just One Look," but was more appreciated in England, where she toured occasionally, and where The Hollies covered her "What'cha Gonna Do About It" on their first album. Moving to Britain, she recorded an album for Apple in 1970 with assistance from George Harrison and Billy Preston. In the early '70s, she sang backup vocals for British rock groups, as well as recording a couple more albums. In the '80s, she starred in *Mama I Want to Sing*, a musical based on her life story. *—Richie Unterberger*

Doris Troy / 1970 / Capitol ♦♦♦
An all-star cast supported Troy on her lone Apple effort: George Harrison, Billy Preston, Peter Frampton, Stephen Stills, Klaus Voormann, Jackie Lomax, Eric Clapton, Leon Russell, and Delaney & Bonnie all contributed, and Harrison, Stills, Lomax, Preston, Voormann, and Ringo Starr pitched in on the songwriting, though Troy wrote or co-wrote most of the songs. Well-received by some critics, it really doesn't add up to the sum of its parts. Troy is in great voice, but much of the material is pedestrian, and the heavy rock/soul arrangements often have an over-beefy, early-'70s super-session feel. It works best when Troy puts the brakes on the hard rock to deliver emotional, slower soul tunes. The CD reissue adds five interesting cuts from non-LP singles and outtakes. *—Richie Unterberger*

● **Just One Look: The Best of Doris Troy** / Aug. 23, 1994 / Ichiban Soul Classics ♦♦♦♦♦
This 21-track anthology of her 1963-65 Atlantic sides is as comprehensive as one could ask for. It includes all of her singles, her rare album, three cuts only issued on British singles, and her rare 1965 single for the Calla label, "I'll Do Anything (He Wants Me To Do)." Besides "Just One Look," there are quite a few other downright excellent lost gems here: "What'cha Gonna Do About It," the bluesy "Draw Me Closer," the driving "You'd Better Stop" (with a fierce guitar break that sounds like a young Jimmy Page), and the soulful wall of sound on "I'll Do Anything." "How My Heart Aches" is a special standout that ranks among the very finest wrenching, melancholy soul ever waxed. Much more than a collector's item, this proves Troy to be a genuinely overlooked major talent. *—Richie Unterberger*

Ike Turner

b. Nov. 5, 1931, Clarksdale, MS
Vocals, Guitar (Electric), Piano, Guitar, Producer / Electric Memphis Blues, Soul-Blues, R&B, Soul
It is arguably true that Ike Turner would have never amounted to more than a footnote of rock history if he hadn't joined forces with Tina Turner in 1960. But as a solo artist, he's an important footnote. In 1951, he made a lasting contribution to the music by playing piano on Jackie Brenston's "Rocket 88," which is often cited as one of the very first rock & roll records. That session was one of the first blues/R&B/rock & roll dates produced in Sun Studios in Memphis; Turner learned guitar shortly afterwards, and backed up other R&B artists at Sun in the early '50s. Throughout the decade, the guitarist and piano player was a prolific session player, contributing to records by blues legends Elmore James, Howlin' Wolf, and Otis Rush.

Ike also backed a host of obscure R&B artists in his early years, occasionally issuing discs under his name. Not much of a singer, both his own records and the ones he contributed to and/or produced often showcased his stinging, bluesy licks, and the best of his solo outings tended to be his instrumentals. He continued to put out the occasional solo session and work with other artists after he hooked up with Tina, sometimes under the name Ike Turner's Kings of Rhythm. His career has lurched along in obscurity since he broke up with Tina in the mid-'70s, though he remains active. *—Richie Unterberger*

Trailblazer / 1957 / Charly ♦♦♦♦♦

1958-1959 / May 13, 1993 / Paula ♦♦♦♦♦
Ever the hustler, Ike Turner found himself picking up some extra money on a road trip through Chicago recording for Cobra Records both as a bandleader and sideman. After contributing the sparkle to several Otis Rush classics (an alternate of one of them, "Keep On Loving Me Baby" is found here) and some early Buddy Guy sides, Turner also recorded a handful of sides, scant few of them seeing release until now. This CD collects them all up, including surviving alternate versions and is a delightful fly on the wall invite to a 1950s Chicago blues session. *—Cub Koda*

● **I Like Ike! The Best of Ike Turner** / Nov. 15, 1994 / Rhino ♦♦♦♦♦
18 songs spotlighting Turner's work as a bandleader, guitarist, and solo artist from 1951 to 1972, concentrating heavily on his work in the 1950s and early '60s. Leading off with Jackie Brenston's classic "Rocket 88," it includes rare singles featuring Turner by Dennis Binder, the Sly Fox, Willie King, and others, along with rare Turner solo recordings, some under the pseudonym Icky Renrut, and a 1958 45 with Tina, then known as Annie Mae Bullock, on backing vocals. These singers are usually journeymen, frankly, and the material is rather standard-issue R&B; better are the instrumentals, which give Ike a chance to really strut his distinctive tone. *—Richie Unterberger*

Ike's Instrumentals / 2000 / Ace ♦♦♦♦

Ike and Tina Turner

f. 1959, **db.** 1976
Group / R&B, Soul
There was a time when the Ike and Tina Turner Revue was one of the hottest, most durable, and potentially most explosive of all R&B ensembles. Fronted by Tina, with one of the

rawest, most sensual and impossibly dynamic voices in Black music, the Ike And Tina Revue was an ensemble that dripped musical discipline while manifesting nearly unbearable tension, eventually giving way to wave upon wave of catharsis. They met in 1959 in East St. Louis, where Ike's Kings of Rhythm were the reigning patriarchs of the local R&B scene; their most famous record, "Rocket 88," appeared under the moniker "Jackie Brenston with his Delta Cats" in 1951 and played an integral part in jump-starting the rock & roll revolution. Once Tina joined the Kings of Rhythm, life changed for all concerned. They recorded a demo of "A Fool in Love" in late 1959; by the autumn of 1960 the record was a number two R&B hit on Sue Records. "I Idolize You," "It's Gonna Work Out Fine," "Poor Fool," and "Tra La La La La" all quickly followed, giving the Revue five Top Ten R&B hits in two and a half years. All told, from 1960 to 1975 Ike and Tina Turner placed 25 records on the R&B charts for nine separate record companies. Their most successful pop recording was a reworking of Creedence Clearwater Revival's "Proud Mary" in 1971. *—Rob Bowman*

The Sound of Ike and Tina Turner / 1960 / Collectables ✦✦✦✦✦
Another early-'60s Ike And Tina Turner album, with Tina sounding tentative at times, and other times gaining confidence as the song progressed. They were far from a finished, polished act, especially in the studio. Tina was still determining how much power and sensuality she had in her voice and was developing her delivery and presentation, while Ike was honing the backdrop, and his band learning when to push and when to lay out behind Tina. *—Ron Wynn*

River Deep & Mountain High / 1966 / A&M ✦✦✦✦✦
These sessions, recorded in 1966, were produced by Phil Spector. Spector's production chops and Tina's voice were a match made in heaven. Tina possesses one of the strongest voices ever committed to wax; Spector envelops it in the grandest version of his Wall of Sound that he ever conceived. Besides the title track, Spector cut the Turners redoing their first three chart hits, "A Fool in Love," "I Idolize You," and "It's Gonna Work Out Fine." Although it's a sacrilege to say so, these versions are better than the originals. Finally, Turner's performance of the obscure Holland-Dozier-Holland ditty "A Love Like Yours" is another phenomenal highlight. *—Rob Bowman*

Workin' Together / 1970 / Liberty ✦✦✦

● **Proud Mary: The Best of Ike & Tina Turner** / Mar. 18, 1991 / EMI America ✦✦✦✦✦
Proud Mary—The Best of Ike and Tina Turner is a fine 23-track collection that looks at the Turners' career at the beginning and the end. Their early-'60s hits on Juggy Murray's Sue label are included, as are their early- and mid-'70s successes on Liberty and United Artists. The mid- and late-'60s recordings for Kent, Loma, Modern, Innis, Blue Thumb, and Minit are not here, unfortunately. Superior liner notes round out a fine package. *—Rob Bowman*

Bold Soul Sister: The Best of the Blue Thumb Recordings / Jul. 15, 1997 / Hip-O ✦✦✦✦✦
Make no mistake about it, this 16-track collection culled from their two albums recorded for the Blue Thumb label in 1969 (*Outta Season* and *The Hunter*) is as much Ike's show as it is Tina's—truly the other half of the equation, the blues part of rhythm & blues. His stinging guitar matches Tina's voice lick for nasty lick, and the blues song choices ("Dust My Broom," "Three O'Clock Blues," "Please Love Me," "Five Long Years," "You Don't Love Me," "Mean Old World," "Rock Me Baby," "Honest I Do," "Reconsider Baby") were undoubtedly tunes he and the Kings of Rhythm knew in their sleep, playing them since they were new hits on the charts. These were the last truly pure R&B albums the two of them would ever make, and even the then-current stabs at R&B trends (the title track is little more than Ike's version of a James Brown groove with Tina babbling in true JB incomprehensibility in spots) shine brightly in the spotlight of hindsight. Subtitled "The Best of the Blue Thumb Recordings," this makes a great document of what they must have sounded like in the clubs that dotted the landscape of the chitlin circuit way back when. *—Cub Koda*

The Kent Years / May 16, 2000 / Kent ✦✦✦✦

Tina Turner (Anna Mae Bullock)

b. Nov. 26, 1938, Nutbush, TN
Vocals / Pop/Rock, R&B, Soul
The most dynamic female soul singer in the history of the music, Tina Turner oozed sexuality from every pore in a performing career that began the moment she stepped onstage as lead singer of the Ike & Tina Turner Revue in the late '50s. Her gritty and growling performances beat down doors everywhere, looking back to the double-barrelled attack of gospel fervor and sexual abandon that had originally formed soul in the early '50s. Divorced from Ike in the mid-'70s, she recorded only occasionally later in the decade but resurfaced in the mid-'80s with a series of hit singles and movie appearances. Ike & Tina Turner began hitting the charts in 1960 and notched charting singles for over a decade, including the number four hit "Proud Mary." Increasingly frustrated by Ike's increasingly irrational behavior however, Tina walked out in 1974 and recorded several albums for United Artists, though with little attention. Turner returned in 1983, and hit with "What's Love Got to Do with It," one of the biggest singles of the following year. Her album *Private Dancer* included two more Top Ten singles, the title track and "Better Be Good to Me." She also found a number two hit with the theme to *Mad Max: Beyond Thunderdome*, "We Don't Need Another Hero." Though her chart success began to decline in the late '80s, her high-profile status was assured well into the '90s. *—John Bush*

● **Private Dancer** / Nov. 16, 1984 / Capitol ✦✦✦✦✦
In 1984, a 45-year-old Tina Turner made one of the most amazing comebacks in the history of American popular music. A few years earlier, it was hard to imagine the veteran soul/rock belter reinventing herself and returning to the top of the pop charts, but she did exactly that with the outstanding *Private Dancer*. And Turner did so without sacrificing her musical integrity. To be sure, this pop/rock/R&B pearl is decidedly slicker than such raw, earthy, hard-edged Ike & Tina classics as "Proud Mary," "Sexy Ida" and "I Wanna Take You Higher." But she still has a tough, throaty, passionate delivery that serves her beautifully on everything from the melancholy, reggae-influenced "What's Love Got to Do with It" to the gutsy "Better Be Good to Me" to heartfelt remakes of the Beatles' "Help," Al Green's "Let's Stay Together" and David Bowie's "1984." A reflection on the emptiness of a stripper's life, the dusky title song as poignant as it is depressing. Without question, this was Turner's finest hour as a solo artist. *—Alex Henderson*

Break Every Rule / 1986 / Capitol ✦✦✦

Tina Live in Europe / 1988 / Capitol ✦✦

Foreign Affair / Sep. 13, 1989 / Capitol ✦✦✦

Simply the Best / 1991 / Capitol ✦✦✦✦✦
A solid greatest-hits collection culled from her solo Capitol albums. Includes "Typical Male," "Steamy Windows" (written and produced by Tony Joe White), "I Can't Stand the Rain," and a duet with Rod Stewart on "It Takes Two." *—Cub Koda*

What's Love Got to Do with It / Jun. 15, 1993 / Virgin ✦✦✦

The Collected Recordings—*Sixties to Nineties* / *Nov. 15, 1994 / Capitol* ✦✦✦

Wildest Dreams / Sep. 3, 1996 / Virgin ✦✦

The Turtles

f. 1963, Los Angeles, CA, **db.** 1970
Group / Sunshine Pop, Folk-Rock, Pop
Though many remember only their 1967 hit "Happy Together," the Turtles were one of the more enjoyable American pop groups of the 1960s, moving from folk-rock inspired by the Byrds to a sparkling fusion of Zombies-inspired chamber-pop and straightahead good-time pop reminiscent of the Lovin' Spoonful, infused with beautiful vocal harmonies. Formed as early as 1963, the group's first single was a folk-rock cover of Bob Dylan's "It Ain't Me Babe" that followed the Byrds' own Dylan cover ("Mr. Tambourine Man") into the Top Ten during 1965. After hitting the Top 40 twice more, the Turtles appeared to run out of steam by the beginning of 1967 but stormed back with the infectious number one hit "Happy Together." The group made the expected leap into psychedelia with two Top Ten hits ("Elenore," "You Showed Me") during 1968, and produced an interesting concept LP (*The Turtles Present the Battle of the Bands*) but broke up before the end of the decade. Dual frontmen Howard Kaylan and Mark Volman later appeared with Frank Zappa's Mothers of Invention, and recorded on their own as Flo & Eddie. *—John Bush*

It Ain't Me Babe / Oct. 1965 / Sundazed ✦✦✦✦✦
The Turtles' first album presents them as a folk-rock group covering a lot of Dylan and P. F. Sloan material. They also found "It Was a Very Good Year" on a Kingston Trio album and cut it. Frank Sinatra heard their version and had one of his bigger hits with it, but their version is good too. *—William Ruhlmann*

You Baby / 1966 / Sundazed ✦✦✦
On their second album, The Turtles stuck to the same brand of sunny, commercial folk-rock as their debut. It's pleasant fare, but hardly in the same league as The Byrds, Lovin' Spoonful, or The Mamas & The Papas, and the group's original material is spotty and sometimes awkward. The best cuts are the ones penned by the Barri/Sloan songwriting team, including the hits "You Baby" and "Can I Get to Know You Better." *—Richie Unterberger*

Happy Together / Apr. 1967 / Sundazed ✦✦✦✦✦
The Turtles's best studio album includes the title hit, "She'd Rather Be with Me," "Guide for the Married Man," and then-unknown Warren Zevon's "Like the Seasons," among other songs. *—William Ruhlmann*

The Turtles Present the Battle of the Bands / Nov. 1968 / Sundazed ✦✦✦✦

Turtle Soup / Nov. 1969 / Sundazed ✦✦✦
The group's final album, produced by Ray Davies, is a modestly enjoyable collection of good-time rock, occasionally with a slight progressive or satirical edge. The Turtles always seemed to harbor some serious ambitions, but the fact was that their only true forte was catchy pop/rock singles; when they aimed for more, the results were pleasant but unmemorable. There aren't any hit singles missing in action here, except maybe "You Don't Have to Walk in the Rain," so unless you're a dedicated fan you can pass without remorse. The CD reissue has a couple of bonus tracks. *—Richie Unterberger*

Wooden Head / 1970 / Sundazed ✦✦✦

● **20 Greatest Hits** / 1983 / Rhino ✦✦✦✦✦
A witty and underrated band, The Turtles compiled this fine set themselves. *—Dan Heilman*

Dwight Twilley

b. Jun. 6, 1951, Tulsa, OK
Vocals, Keyboards / Album Rock, Power Pop
Though the Dwight Twilley Band only had one hit (Twilley had another on his own), Twilley and partner Phil Seymour created an enduring and highly memorable brand of power-pop that blended Beatlesque pop and Sun rockabilly "slapback" echo. Only a fraction of the band's early output was made available at the time, but these records are highly revered by power-pop aficionados. The two had recorded together for seven yeras before signing to the Shelter label in 1974. Their first single, "I'm on Fire," became a national hit in 1975, peaking at number 16, with relatively no promotion. Their follow-up single and completed album, *Sincerely*, went unreleased for 18 months due to label problems. *Twilley Don't Mind*, recorded for Arista in 1977, stiffed as well. Seymour left the band the following year, pursuing a brief solo career before lymphoma cut his life short in 1993. Twilley carried on as a solo act, releasing *Twilley* for Arista in 1979, *Scuba Divers* for EMI in 1982, and found success again with *Jungle* in 1984, when he scored his second hit with "Girls." Two newly recorded songs appeared on the "best of" collection *XXI* and he is reportedly working on a new album entitled *The Luck*. *The Great Lost Twilley Album* collects a fraction of the "hundreds" of unreleased songs Twilley and Seymour recorded in the early, ill-fated days. *—Chris Woodstra*

Sincerely / 1976 / The Right Stuff ✦✦✦✦✦
In power pop circles, the Dwight Twilley band's debut album is a classic, revered for its shiny, nervy blend of sparkling British Invasion pop and old-fashioned rock & roll. In other words, it sounds like Big Star, but with a swagger, a sneer, and a tough garage band mentality. Its rocking spirit is all the more remarkable when you realize that the band in question is simply Twilley and cohort Phil Seymour, and the two played every instrument and produced nearly every cut. Musically, the album is undeniably classicist, but there is so much spirit to the recording and songs that it's hard not to get caught up in the record, particularly when the music is as tight as "I'm on Fire" or as evocative as the lightly psychedelic title track. It's easy to see why this is a power pop touchstone—arriving after the twin titans of Badfinger and Big Star, this has sparkling tunes and a do-it-yourself spirit that isn't just great to listen to, it makes you think you can do it, too. Over the years, it has been proven that it's not that easy, and this record remains one of the greatest power pop platters precisely because of that. —*Stephen Thomas Erlewine*

Twilley Don't Mind / 1977 / The Right Stuff ✦✦✦✦
For their second record, Dwight Twilley and Phil Seymour expanded their sound, working with producer/engineer Bob Schaper, adding lead guitarist Bill Pitcock IV, and bringing in guest musicians, including Tom Petty, on occasion, in addition to adding horns and strings on various tracks. Given all these add-ons, it should come as no surprise that *Twilley Don't Mind* isn't as tight or rocking as *Sincerely,* even if the title track that kicks off the record is one of the hardest rocking things they ever cut. Also, the songs, while just a slight notch below those on the original, remain terrific retro-pop tunes, illustrating why this group is held in such high regard among power pop aficionados. Though it may not quite reach the heights of its predecessor, it's a worthy successor and is a large part of Twilley's legacy. —*Stephen Thomas Erlewine*

Twilley / 1979 / Arista ✦✦✦✦✦

Scuba Divers / 1982 / EMI ✦✦✦

Jungle / 1984 / EMI ✦✦✦

The Great Lost Twilley Album / Apr. 1993 / DCC ✦✦✦✦
The rumor had always been that the original Dwight Twilley Band had completed four albums between 1974 and 1978 that were never released due to problems with their label, Shelter Records; the few writers and personal friends who heard the albums claimed the material was superior to much of their released work. *The Great Lost Twilley Album* collects the best "lost" tracks from this era, as well as prime material from the unreleased *Blueprint* album from 1980; true to the myth, the songs are easily as good as the band's classic early albums. The band especially shines on the proposed follow-up to the hit "I'm on Fire," "Shark," an infectious rocker that stands as one of the great "should-have-been-hits." —*Chris Woodstra*

● **XXI** / Mar. 19, 1996 / The Right Stuff ✦✦✦✦✦
Despite critical raves at the time and the undeniable high quality of the songs, the Dwight Twilley Band never quite achieved the success they so sorely deserved. *XXI* collects the finer moments of the band's brief recording career, which only ran from 1976 to 1978, as well as highlights from Twilley's solo work, spanning from 1979 to late 1995. This 21-track compilation offers a good sampling of album favorites, the hits ("I'm On Fire" and "Girls"—both peaked at number 16), some lost should-of-been hits ("Shark" and "Somebody to Love"), a never-before-released song from an aborted 1994 album and a newly recorded track, "That Thing You Do." For fans, the rarities and song-by-song commentary by Twilley make *XXI* an essential addition. For those unfamiliar with Twilley and company's perfect pop, there is no better place to start. —*Chris Woodstra*

Tulsa / Jun. 1, 1999 / Copper ✦✦✦

Between the Cracks, Vol. 1 / Jul. 1999 / Not Lame Archives ✦✦✦

U2

f. 1976, Dublin, Ireland
Group / College Rock, Album Rock, Post-Punk, Pop/Rock, Alternative Pop/Rock
Through a combination of zealous righteousness and post-punk experimentalism, U2 became one of the most popular rock & roll bands of the '80s. Equally known for their sweeping sound as for their grandiose statement about politics and religion, U2 were rock & roll crusaders during an era of synthesized pop and heavy metal. The Edge provided the group with a signature sound by creating sweeping sonic landscapes with his heavily processed, echoed guitars. Though the Edge's style wasn't conventional, the rhythm section of Adam Clayton and Larry Mullen Jr. played the songs as driving hard-rock, giving the band a forceful, powerful edge that was designed for arena rock. And their lead singer, Bono, was frontman who had a knack of grand gestures that played better in arenas than small clubs. It's no accident that footage of Bono parading with a white flag with "Sunday Bloody Sunday" blaring in the background became the defining moment of U2's early career—there rarely was a band that believed so deeply in the rock's potential for revolution as U2, and there rarely was a band that didn't care if they appeared foolish in the process. During the course of the early '80s, the group quickly built up a dedicated following through constant touring and a string of acclaimed records. By 1987, the band's following had grown large enough to propel them to level of international superstars with the release of *The Joshua Tree.* Unlike many of their contemporaries, U2 was able to sustain their popularity in the '90s by reinventing themselves as a post-modern, self-consciously ironic dance-inflected pop-rock act, owing equally to the experimentalism of late '70s Bowie and '90s electronic dance and techno. By performing such a successful reinvention, the band confirmed its status as one of the most popular bands in rock history, in addition to earning additional critical respect. —*Stephen Thomas Erlewine*

Boy / 1980 / Island ✦✦✦✦
From the outset, U2 went for the big message—every song on their debut album *Boy* sounds huge, with oceans of processed guitars cascading around Bono's impassioned wail. It was an inspired combination of large, stadium-rock beats and post-punk textures. Without the Edge's echoed, ringing guitar, U2 would have sounded like a traditional hard rock band, since the rhythm section and Bono treat each song as an anthem. Of course, that's the charm of *Boy:* all of its emotions are on the surface, delivered with optimistic, youthful self-belief, yet the unusual, distinctive guitar textures give it an unexpected tension that makes it an exhilarating debut. The songs may occasionally show some weakness—the driving "I Will Follow," the dark "An Cat Dubh" and the shimmering "The Ocean" stand out among the sonic textures—yet the band's musical and lyrical vision keep *Boy* compelling until the finish. —*Stephen Thomas Erlewine*

October / 1981 / Island ✦✦✦
U2 sounded so confident and assured on their debut that perhaps it was inevitable they would stumble slightly on its follow-up, *October.* The record isn't weaker than its predecessor because it repeats the formula of *Boy,* it's because the band tries too hard to move forward. Bono, in particular, tries too hard to make big political, emotional, and religious statements, but the remainder of the band isn't innocent. In general, the music is too pompous, with the sound overwhelming the actual songs. But when U2 do marry the message, melody and sound together, as on "Gloria," "I Threw a Brick Through a Window" and "I Fall Down," the results are thoroughly impressive. —*Stephen Thomas Erlewine*

☆ **War** / Feb. 28, 1983 / Island ✦✦✦✦✦
Opening with the ominous, fiery protest of "Sunday Bloody Sunday," *War* immediately announces itself as U2's most focused and hardest-rocking album to date. Blowing away the fuzzy, sonic indulgences of *October* with propulsive, martial rhythms and shards of guitar, *War* bristles with anger, despair and, above all, passion. Previously, Bono's attempts at messages came across as grandstanding, but his vision became remarkably clear on this record, as his anthems ("New Year's Day," "40," "Seconds") are balanced by effective, surprisingly emotional love songs ("Two Hearts Beat As One"), which are just as desperate and pleading as his protests. He performs the difficult task of making the universal sound personal, and the band helps him out by bringing the songs crashing home with muscular, forceful performances that reveal their varied, expressive textures upon repeated listens. U2 always aimed at greatness, but *War* was the first time they achieved it. —*Stephen Thomas Erlewine*

Under a Blood Red Sky / Nov. 1983 / Island ✦✦✦

The Unforgettable Fire / 1984 / Island ✦✦✦✦
In many ways, U2 took their fondness for sonic bombast as far as it could go on *War,* so it isn't a complete surprise that they chose to explore the intricacies of the Edge's layered, effects-laden guitar on the follow-up, *The Unforgettable Fire.* Working with producers Brian Eno and Daniel Lanois, U2 created a dark, near-hallucinatory series of interlocking soundscapes that are occasionally punctuated by recognizable songs and melodies. In such a setting, the band both flourishes and flounders, creating some of their greatest music, as well as some of their worst. "Elvis Presley and America" may well be Bono's most embarrassing attempt at poetry, yet it is redeemed by the chilling and wonderful "Bad," a two-chord elegy for an addict that is stunning in its control and mastery. Similarly, the wet, shimmering textures of the title track, the charging "A Sort of Homecoming," and the surging Martin Luther King Jr. tribute "Pride (In the Name of Love)" are all remarkable, ranking among their very best music, making the missteps that clutter remainder of the album somewhat forgivable. —*Stephen Thomas Erlewine*

Wide Awake in America / 1985 / Island ✦✦

★ **The Joshua Tree** / 1987 / Island ✦✦✦✦✦
Using the textured sonics of *The Unforgettable Fire* as a basis, U2 expanded those innovations by scaling back the songs to a personal setting and adding a grittier attack for its follow-up, *The Joshua Tree.* It's a move that returns them to the sweeping, anthemic rock of *War,* but if *War* was an exploding political bomb, *The Joshua Tree* is a journey through its aftermath, trying to find sense and hope in the desperation. That means that even the anthems—the epic opener "Where the Streets Have No Name," the yearning "I Still Haven't Found What I'm Looking For"—have seeds of doubt within their soaring choruses, and those fears take root throughout the album, whether it's in the mournful sliding acoustic guitars of "Running to Stand Still," the surging "One Tree Hill" or the hypnotic elegy "Mothers of the Disappeared." So it might seem a little ironic that U2 became superstars on the back of such a dark record, but their focus has never been clearer, nor has their music been catchier, than on *The Joshua Tree.* Unexpectedly, U2 have also tempered their textural post-punk with American influences. Not only are Bono's lyrics obsessed with America, but country and blues influences are heard throughout the record, and instead of using these as roots, they're used as ways to add texture to the music. With the uniformly excellent songs—only the clumsy, heavy rock and portentous lyrics of "Bullet the Blue Sky" fall flat—the result is a powerful, uncompromising record that became a hit due to its vision and its melody. Never before have their big messages sounded so direct and personal. —*Stephen Thomas Erlewine*

Rattle & Hum / 1988 / Island ✦✦✦

☆ **Achtung Baby** / Nov. 19, 1991 / Island ✦✦✦✦✦
Reinventions rarely come as thorough and effective as *Achtung Baby,* an album that completely changed U2's sound and style. The crashing, unrecognizable distorted guitars that open "Zoo Station" are a clear signal that U2 have traded their Americana pretensions for post-modern, contemporary European music. Drawing equally from Bowie's electronic, avant-garde explorations of the late '70s and the neo-psychedelic sounds of the thriving rave and Madchester club scenes of early '90s England, *Achtung Baby* sounds vibrant and endlessly inventive. Unlike their inspirations, U2 rarely experiment with song structures over the course of the album. Instead, they use the thick dance beats, swirling guitars, layers of effects and found sounds to break traditional songs out of their constraints, revealing the tortured emotional core of their songs with the hyper-loaded arrangements. In such a dense musical setting, it isn't surprising that U2 have abandoned the political for the personal on *Achtung Baby,* since the music, even with its inviting rhythms, is more introspective than anthemic. Bono has never been as emotionally naked as he is on *Achtung Baby,* creating a feverish nightmare of broken hearts and desperate loneliness; unlike other U2 albums, it's filled with sexual imagery, much of it quite disturbing, and it ends on a disquieting note. Few bands as far into their career as U2 have recorded an album as adventurous or fulfilled their ambitions quite as successfully as they do on *Achtung Baby,* and the result is arguably their best album. —*Stephen Thomas Erlewine*

Zooropa / May 1993 / Island ✦✦✦✦
U2 planned to record a new EP before launching the European leg of their ambitious Zoo TV tour in 1993, but the EP quickly turned into the full-length album *Zooropa*. Picking up where *Achtung Baby* left off, *Zooropa* delves heavily into U2's newfound affection for experimental music and dance clubs. While the title track marries those inclinations to the anthems of *The Joshua Tree*, most of the record is far more daring than its predecessor. While that occasionally means it's unfocused and meandering, it also results in a number of wonderful moments, like the quiet menace of "Daddy's Gonna Pay for Your Crashed Car," and the space-age German disco of "Lemon," Edge's droning mantra "Numb," and the gentle, heartbroken "Stay (Faraway, So Close!)," one of U2's very best love songs. As the album winds to a close, it drifts off track, yet the best moments of *Zooropa* rank among U2's most inspired and rewarding music. *—Stephen Thomas Erlewine*

Pop / Mar. 1997 / Island ✦✦✦

Best of 1980-1990/B-Sides / Nov. 3, 1998 / Island ✦✦✦✦

All That You Can't Leave Behind / Oct. 31, 2000 / Interscope ✦✦✦✦
Nearly ten years after beginning U2 Mach II with their brilliant seventh album *Achtung Baby*, U2 eases into their third phase with 2000's *All That You Can't Leave Behind*. The title signifies more than it seems, since the group sifts through their past, working with Daniel Lanois and Brian Eno, all in an effort to construct a classicist U2 album. Thankfully, it's a rock record from a band that absorbed all the elastic experimentation, studio trickery, dance flirtations, and genre bending of *Achtung*, *Zooropa*, and *Pop*—all they've shed is the irony. U2 chooses not to delve as darkly personal as they did on *Achtung* or *Zooropa*, yet they also avoid the alienating archness of *Pop*, returnin to the generous spirit that flowed through their best '80s records. On that level, *All* may be reminiscent of *The Joshua Tree*, but this is a clever and craftsmanlike record, filled with nifty twists in the arrangements, small sonic details and colors. U2 take subtle risks, such as their best pure pop song ever with "Wild Honey"; they're so self-confident, they effortlessly write their best anthem in years with "Beautiful Day"; they offer the gospel-influenced "Stuck in a Moment," never once lowering it to the schtick it would have been on *Rattle & Hum*. Like any work from craftsmen, *All That You Can't Leave Behind* winds up being a work of modest pleasures, where the way the verse eases into the chorus means more than the overall message, and this is truly the first U2 album where that sentiment applies—but there is genuine pleasure in their craft, for the band and listener alike. *—Stephen Thomas Erlewine*

UB40

f. 1978, Birmingham, England
Group / College Rock, Contemporary Reggae, Reggae-Pop, Pop/Rock, Adult Contemporary
Named after a British unemployment benefit form, pop-reggae band UB40 was formed in 1978 with a multiracial lineup that reflected the working-class community its members came from. The band consolidated its street credibility with political topics appealing to dissatisfied youth and got a boost from fans of the waning 2-Tone ska-revival movement. By 1980, their single "Food for Thought" reached the UK Top Ten. UB40's first two albums, *Signing Off* and *Present Arms*, were big sellers in Britain and addressed the political issues of the day with songs like "One in Ten," a Top Ten hit blasting Margaret Thatcher for the country's unemployment rate. 1983's *Labour of Love*, an album of reggae cover songs, gave the group its first chart album in America and first number one UK hit with Neil Diamond's "Red Red Wine." Five years after its initial release, the single entered the American charts and went all the way to the top. Finally having hit on a way to conquer the lucrative American market, UB40 responded with another covers album, *Labour of Love II*, which produced Top Ten singles with versions of the Temptations' "The Way You Do the Things You Do" and Al Green's "Here I Am (Come and Take Me)." The group scored a huge hit in America with Elvis Presley's "Can't Help Falling in Love," and spent seven weeks at number one. A third *Labour of Love* collection followed in 1999. *—Steve Huey*

Signing Off / Nov. 1980 / Virgin ✦✦✦
A hugely popular album in Britain, where it reached number two and stayed in the charts for months, *Signing Off* was the calling card of UB40, a multiracial Birmingham group who took their name from the administrative form used as proof of identity when collecting unemployment benefits. At the time, the post-punk Midlands scene was tinkering with reggae's forerunner, ska, which resulted in the swift rise of 2-Tone. However, the brothers Campbell and their colleagues decided there was a market for a modern Jamaican variant. After touring with the Pretenders, they released their debut single, "Food for Thought," which became an instant hit. The song was reprised on the album, alongside its B-side, "King," and a series of politically inclined, likeable, but musically sanitized cuts. When Graduate decided to excise the polemical "Burden of Shame" from South African copies of the album, UB40 quite rightly dumped the label. *—Alex Ogg*

Present Arms / Jun. 1981 / Virgin ✦✦✦
The popular perception of UB40 as a band who cling to the coattails of true reggae artists is partially merited, given their '90s karaoke-quality interpretations of popular standards in a Jamaican rub-a-dub stylee. But with albums such as their debut and this, admittedly a more uneven effort, their affection for the music was self-evidently genuine and generally well observed. Their conscience-driven lyrics ("One in Ten" especially) are heartfelt and convincing, though Ali Campbell's Rastabrummyfarian voice takes some getting used to. The bottom line? There are dozens of superior reggae albums, but this will do if you're too lazy to find them. *—Alex Ogg*

Present Arms in Dub / Oct. 1981 / Virgin ✦✦

● **Labour of Love** / Sep. 1983 / Virgin ✦✦✦✦✦
Named after the unemployment form in England, UB40 was never the most creative or talented group of musicians. However, what they lacked in talent they made up for with an uplifting spirit and genuine affection for reggae music. This is never more apparent than on their breakthrough album, *Labour of Love*, in which they cover the songs of their heroes. They try to recapture the spirit of early reggae by singing songs originally released before the international success of Bob Marley. They manage to inject their own exuberance into every song; for example, they transform Jimmy Cliff's mournful "Many Rivers to Cross" into an uplifting song of empowerment. The song for which UB40 will always be known is their first number one hit in the U.S., "Red Red Wine," a Neil Diamond-penned tune given a full reggae makeover that miraculously turned the group into an international sensation. Although UB40 relies on standard reggae arrangements, this is their most enjoyable album as a result of the inspired vocal performances and the genuine joy they have for the music. A must-own for reggae fans. *—Vik Iyengar*

Geffery Morgan / 1984 / Virgin ✦✦✦✦✦
UB40 was faced with following up the surprisingly successful covers album *Labour Of Love* (which had topped the U.K. chart and become their U.S. chart debut) with this album of original material. Their own songs were good, but no match for what then seemed a one-of-a-kind collection. "If It Happens Again," which went to number nine in Britain, sounded like a song by The English Beat, while the second single, "Riddle Me" (#59), was a deeper reggae groove tune. It was a good set, but without a classic like "Red, Red Wine" suffered from a certain anonymity, especially in the U.S. *—William Ruhlmann*

Baggariddim / 1985 / DEP Int'l ✦✦✦

Rat in Mi Kitchen / 1986 / Virgin ✦✦✦✦✦
In the U.K., UB40 were major stars, and this album was their sixth Top 10 hit, featuring the singles "Sing Your Own Song" (#5), "All I Want To Do" (#41), and "Rat In Me Kitchen" (#12). In the U.S., the group remained a developing act with a modest following, only able to score a hit by covering a previous hit like "I Got You, Babe." *Rat In The Kitchen* did nothing to change that, although it was, as usual, a tuneful collection of reggae. *—William Ruhlmann*

UB40 CCCP: Live in Moscow / 1987 / A&M ✦✦

Labour of Love II / Nov. 1989 / Virgin ✦✦

Promises and Lies / Jul. 27, 1993 / Virgin ✦✦

The Best of UB40, Vol. 2 / Nov. 7, 1995 / Virgin ✦✦✦

The Best of UB40, Vol. 1 / Nov. 14, 1995 / Virgin ✦✦✦✦

Guns in the Ghetto / Jul. 1, 1997 / Virgin ✦✦

Labour of Love III / Nov. 17, 1998 / EMI ✦✦

● **The Very Best of UB40 1980-2000** / Nov. 21, 2000 / Virgin ✦✦✦✦✦
While the two previous *Best of UB40* collections neatly divided the band's output between their more political early period and their later, covers-oriented pop success, they were also only ten tracks apiece. *The Very Best of UB40 1980-2000* is the first comprehensive single-disc overview of the band's career, and it's a lot more generous at 18 tracks (on the American version). It isn't arranged chronologically, which actually helps the programming by splitting up the covers over the course of the running order. There's a bit more toughness to the earlier songs, both in the lyrics and the punchier performances. Yet in the end, the sonic differences are subtle enough that casual fans should still be able to enjoy them (unless they *only* want to hear the band performing reggae-pop versions of oldies they already know). Skimpy though it is, *The Best of UB40, Vol. 1* is still the compilation for purists enamored of the band's early work, assuming they don't want to spend the money for the original albums. But with its fairly well-balanced selection and inclusion of all the band's U.S. hits, most American listeners who want a UB40 compilation will find *The Very Best of UB40 1980-2000* exactly what they're looking for. [The import version juggles the track listing and running order a bit, excising a couple of *Labour of Love II*'s American cover hits in favor of older songs and reggae covers of Jamaican origin. Also, the version of "Red Red Wine" is the shortened edit, without the toasting break at the end.] *—Steve Huey*

Tracey Ullman

b. Dec. 30, 1959, Buckinghamshire, England
Vocals / Pop/Rock, New Wave
Before she became a famous TV comedienne, Tracy Ullman recorded two albums in the early '80s that effortlessly recalled the classic girl group sound of the '60s. Ullman covered everything from Doris Day ("Move over Darling") to Blondie ("(I'm Always Touched by Your) Presence, Dear"), finding the underlying connections between classic pop songs of all eras. *You Broke My Heart in 17 Places*, her debut album, was a hit in the U.K. and she even managed to have a Top Ten hit in America with a version of Kirsty MacColl's "They Don't Know." Although it had some fine numbers, the follow-up *You Caught Me Out* wasn't as successful, prompting Ullman to return to television. By the end of the '80s, her comedy show, *The Tracy Ullman Show*, was one of the most critically acclaimed television shows in America; she hasn't recorded any music since. *—Stephen Thomas Erlewine*

You Broke My Heart in 17 Places / 1983 / Stiff/Repertoire ✦✦✦✦✦
Ullman's first album, recorded in the middle of the new wave and synth-pop movements, provided a refreshing break with its retro girl group sound. Includes her only U.S. hit, "They Don't Know" (written by Kirsty MacColl) as well as carefully chosen obscure oldies. One of the great lost classics of the new wave era. *—Chris Woodstra*

You Caught Me Out / 1984 / Repertoire ✦✦✦
The second album follows the same formula as the first—a well-chosen collection of covers from obscure oldies to contemporary favorites (Madness' "My Girl"—retitled here as "My Guy") and even another stab at a Kirsty MacColl song ("Terry")—all done in the classic '60s girl group sound. Though it failed to produce the smash hits of the debut, "My Guy" and "Sunglasses" were minor hits in the U.K., and the album is nearly as much fun. Repertoire has released a CD version with six bonus tracks. *—Chris Woodstra*

● **The Best of Tracey Ullman** / 1991 / Rhino ✦✦✦✦✦
This 20-track compilation provides an extensive look at the nearly forgotten singing career of this now famous actress. Combining the entire first LP, *You Broke My Heart in 17 Places*, the highlights from her second effort *You Caught Me Out*, and well chosen B-sides, it more

than lives up to its name. Although this material was recorded in the early '80s, lovers of the classic '60s-girl-group sound will find these retro-gems a familiar delight. *—Chris Woodstra*

Ultravox

f. 1974, London, England, **db.** 1987

Group / New Romantic, New Wave, Synth Pop

Rejecting the abrasive guitars of their punk-era contemporaries in favor of lushly romantic synthesizers, Ultravox emerged as one of the primary influences on the British electro-pop movement of the early '80s. Formed in London in 1974, the group was led by vocalist and keyboardist John Foxx; their obvious affection for the glam rock sound of David Bowie and Roxy Music brought them little respect from audiences caught up in the growing fervor of punk, but in 1977 Island Records signed the quintet anyway, with Brian Eno agreeing to produce their self-titled debut LP. Island dropped the band after 1978's *Systems of Romance*, at which time both Foxx and Simon quit, the former mounting a solo career and the latter joining Magazine. The remaining members of Ultravox tapped singer/guitarist Midge Ure; upon signing to Chrysalis, the new line-up recorded *Vienna*, scoring a surprise smash hit with the single "Sleepwalk," which reached the number two spot on the UK pop charts in 1981 and pushed the LP into the Top Five. Upon completing 1984's *Lament*, Ure left Ultravox to forge a solo career, topping the UK charts a year later with the solo smash "If I Was." *—Jason Ankeny*

Ultravox / 1977 / Island ♦♦♦

John Foxx proves to have an odd, Bowie-influenced vision, here aided and abetted by Brian Eno (then a Bowie crony) and Steve Lillywhite. "My Sex" and "I Want to Be a Machine" are standouts. *—William Ruhlmann*

Vienna / 1980 / Chrysalis ♦♦♦♦♦

The new Ultravox, under Midge Ure, has a dreamy, ethereal sound heard at its best on its debut album, which features the title song, "All Stood Still," "Passing Strangers," and "Sleepwalk," all UK hits. *—William Ruhlmann*

● **Dancing with Tears in My Eyes** / 1997 / EMI ♦♦♦♦♦

Dancing with Tears in My Eyes is a 15-track overview of Ultravox's early-'80s commercial peak, hitting most, but not all, of their biggest hits, including "Sleepwalk," "Vienna," "All Stood Still," and "Reap the Wild Wind." It's not a bad collection, but if it had included hits like "The Thin Wall," it could have been a definitive retrospective. *—Stephen Thomas Erlewine*

Uncle Tupelo

f. 1987, Belleville, IL, **db.** 1994

Group / Americana, Alternative Country, Alternative Country-Rock, Alternative Pop/Rock

With the release of their 1990 debut LP *No Depression*, the Belleville, IL trio Uncle Tupelo launched more than simply their own career—by fusing the simplicity and honesty of country music with the bracing fury of punk, they kick-started a revolution which reverberated throughout the American underground. Thanks to a successful on-line site and subsequent fanzine which adopted the album's name, the tag "No Depression" became a catch-all for the like-minded artists who, along with Tupelo, signalled alternative rock's return to its country roots—at much the same time, ironically enough, that Nashville was itself embracing the slick gloss associated with mainstream rock and pop. Led by singers/songwriters Jay Farrar and Jeff Tweedy, Uncle Tupelo issued *No Depression* in 1990—a reflection of the band's disparate influences, ranging from everyone from Hank Williams to bluesman Leadbelly through to the famed postpunk trio Husker Du, its songs were meditations on small-town, small-time life, candid snapshots of days spent working thankless jobs and nights spent in an alcoholic fog. With the acoustic *March 16-20, 1992*, the group plunged fully into country and folk; signing to Sire/Reprise, in 1993 Uncle Tupelo issued the LP *Anodyne*. Widely regarded as the group's definitive statement, it was a true country-rock hybrid which accented the power of both musical forms; however, the long-standing relationship between Farrar and Tweedy soon dissolved in bitter acrimony, and Uncle Tupelo disbanded. Shortly thereafter, Tweedy formed Wilco, while Farrar resurfaced in Son Volt. *—Jason Ankeny*

No Depression / 1990 / Rockville ♦♦♦♦

Uncle Tupelo's landmark opening salvo is the group's most rock-oriented album, steeped more in breakneck speed, punk crunch and guitar dissonance than any of their subsequent efforts. Indeed, despite the presence of mandolins, fiddles and banjos—as well as inclusion of the title track, a faithful cover of the A.P. Carter classic—the trio's vaunted country leanings are less musical than thematic on *No Depression*, thanks in large part to singers/songwriters Jay Farrar and Jeff Tweedy's acute depictions of rural, blue-collar life. Like the Replacements—never more obvious an influence than on this LP—Uncle Tupelo's songs paint grim, unrelenting portraits of aimless Midwestern existence, split between days working on the opening cut's "Factory Belt" and nights spent blurry-eyed and wasted ("Whiskey Bottle," "Before I Break"). Still, for all of the record's doleful cynicism—virtually every cut nods toward dashed hopes, broken promises and paralyzing fear—there's an undeniable electricity afoot as well; by channeling the mournful clarity of country into the crackling fury of punk, *No Depression* brings new life to both musical camps. *—Jason Ankeny*

Still Feel Gone / Sep. 17, 1991 / Rockville ♦♦♦

Still Feel Gone is Tupelo's transitional record; while it goes far in fusing the band's rock origins with their country aspirations, the alliance is often an uneasy, even schizophrenic, one. Writers Jay Farrar and Jeff Tweedy are rarely in synch; while the former's contributions embrace roots music wholeheartedly, Tweedy's songs journey more deeply into rock than ever before—his opening track, "Gun," ais the most straightforward pop number the trio ever recorded, while "D. Boon," a tribute to the fallen leader of the legendary post-punk trio the Minutemen, borders on thrash. Still, while *Still Feel Gone* lacks the consistency of its predecessor *No Depression*, it's a more wide-ranging record, deeper in maturity, subtlety and texture—all clear evidence of things to come. *—Jason Ankeny*

March 16-20, 1992 / Aug. 3, 1992 / Rockville ♦♦♦♦♦

Produced by R.E.M.'s Peter Buck, *March 16-20, 1992* represents Uncle Tupelo's full evolution into a true country unit; with the exception of the eerie squalls of guitar feedback which haunt Jeff Tweedy's mesmerizing "Wait Up," athere's virtually no evidence of the trio's punk heritage. Instead, the all-acoustic album—a combination of Tupelo originals and well-chosen traditional songs—taps into the very essence of backwoods culture, its music rooted in the darkest corners of Appalachian life. An inescapable sense of dread grips this collection, from the large-scale threat depicted in the stunning rendition of the Louvin Brothers' "The Great Atomic Power" to the fatalism of the worker anthems "Grindstone" and "Coalminers;" even the character studies, including a revelatory "Moonshiner," are relentlessly grim. A vivid glimpse at the harsh realities of rural existence, *March 16-20, 1992* is a brilliant resurrection of a bygone era of American folk artistry. *—Jason Ankeny*

● **Anodyne** / May 1993 / Sire ♦♦♦♦♦

Uncle Tupelo never struck a finer balance between rock and country than on *Anodyne*, their major-label debut and parting shot. For all of the ill will undoubtedly simmering throughout these sessions, Jay Farrar and Jeff Tweedy have never before been more attuned to each other musically; where earlier records often found the band's twin forces moving in opposing directions, *Anodyne* bears the full fruits of their shared vision. Recorded live in the studio, the album encompasses and reinterprets not only country-rock (evidenced by the group's pairing with Doug Sahm on his "Give Back the Key to My Heart") but also traditional country (the tribute to the songwriting legacy of "Acuff-Rose"), rock (the churning "The Long Cut," "Chickamauga") and folk ("New Madrid," "Steal the Crumbs"), the band's reach never once exceeding its grasp. *—Jason Ankeny*

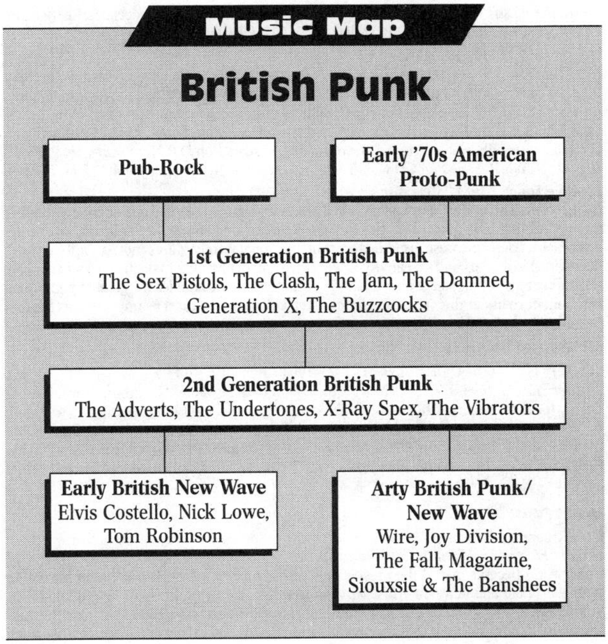

Undertones

f. 1976, Derry, Northern Ireland, **db.** 1983

Group / British Punk, New Wave, Punk

There are those who would disagree vehemently, but in my estimation the Undertones were Ireland's best rock band—ever. Roaring out of Northern Ireland in 1976, the Undertones fused speedy, loud Ramones-inspired walls of guitar racket with irresistible '60s pop hooks, with just a touch of mid-'70s glam rock for good measure. With the singular tenor vocals of frontman Feargal Sharkey making them instantaneously recognizable, Undertones songs tended to eschew punk vitriol for songs about teenage love, girls, snotty cousins, and summertime—life's simple joys (and pains). No more succinct a summation of their style, wit, and power can be found than on their out-of-print debut EP *Teenage Kicks*—a record of startling ebullience, the songs sound as exhilarating today as they did decades ago. However, the Undertones did not go into creative stasis with their winning punk-pop and simply replicate a proven formula over and over. As they grew as musicians, so did their albums change, incorporating some of the Tamla/Motown soul music they loved as kids. Sadly, the Undertones' story ended far too quickly. Growing up meant too much change too fast, and by the time they released their mediocre fourth album, restlessness and "musical differences" were splitting them apart. Sharkey went off to a short-lived solo career, while the guitar-playing O'Neill brothers put together the politically charged That Petrol Emotion. *—John Dougan*

● **The Undertones** / 1979 / Rykodisc ♦♦♦♦♦

An absolutely essential purchase. One of the best albums of the punk era, or any era. Song after song is infused with a liberating joy and intensity that only a handful of rock records at the time equalled. A crucial record, the 'Tones' debut shows how influential '70s commercial pop was on the growing punk community, who embraced it and then tore it all to hell. A record that hasn't lost its luster after hundreds of plays and nearly two decades. Reissued on CD with seven bonus tracks by Rykodisc in 1994. *—John Dougan*

Hypnotised / 1980 / Rykodisc ✦✦✦✦✦
It's ridiculous to not encourage you to purchase the first three Undertones records, because they are such wonderful distillations of all that makes rock and roll great. *Hypnotised* picks up where the debut leaves off, but adds a slightly more sarcastic touch to some of the songs, especially the witty "My Perfect Cousin" and the goofy "More Songs About Chocolate and Girls" (a not-so-subtle parody of the title of Talking Heads' second LP *More Songs About Buildings and Food*). Reissued on CD with five bonus tracks by Rykodisc in 1994. *—John Dougan*

Positive Touch / 1981 / Rykodisc ✦✦✦
By this time, The Undertones had switched labels and made recorded a challenging, slightly arty record that didn't sound much like their first two, and showed an amazing artistic development. There are musical elements not on the previous recordings (horns, Paul Carrack's keyboards); still, the band's creativity, intelligence and personality make this a tremendously rewarding record. Not where one unfamiliar with the 'Tones should start (get that guitar rush first), but once under their spell, *Positive Touch* will become almost as important as the first two albums. Reissued on CD with four bonus tracks by Rykodisc in 1994. *—John Dougan*

All Wrapped Up / 1983 / Rykodisc ✦✦✦

The Very Best of the Undertones / Oct. 25, 1994 / Rykodisc ✦✦✦✦✦
The Very Best of the Undertones collects the cream of the catalog. The group's earliest high-energy teenage anthems (themes of doubt, deceit, yearning, and infatuation) give way, over the course of 25 songs, to the sublime intimacy of "Wednesday Week" and "Julie Ocean," and then the sophisticated, Tamla/Motown layering of "Soul Seven." Group members discuss each track in the informative liner notes. Start here, fall in love, then go find the individual albums. *—Roch Parisien*

Underworld

f. 1988, London, England
Group / Electronica, Techno, Electronic, House
Underworld became one of the most crucial electronic acts of the 1990s via an intriguing synthesis of old and new. The trio's two-man frontline, vocalist Karl Hyde and guitarist Rick Smith, had been recording together since the early-'80s new wave explosion; after two unsuccessful albums released as Underworld during the late '80s, the pair finally hit it big when they recruited Darren Emerson, a young DJ hipped to the sound of techno and trance. Traditional pop song-forms were jettisoned in favor of Hyde's heavily treated vocals, barely-there whispering and surreal wordplay, stretched out over the urban breakbeat trance ripped out by Emerson & Co. while Smith's cascade of guitar-shard effects provided a bluesy foil to the stark music. All in all, the decision to go pop was hardly a concession to the mainstream. The first Underworld album by the trio, *Dubnobasswithmyheadman*, appeared in late 1993 to a flurry of critical acclaim; the trio then gained U.S. distribution for the album with TVT. *Second Toughest in the Infants*, the group's sophomore LP, updated their sound slightly and received more praise than the debut. Unlike the first, the LP also sold well, thanks in part to the non-album single "Born Slippy," featured on the soundtrack to the seminal film *Trainspotting*. Though Underworld's 1999 LP *Beaucoup Fish* was a bit of a disappointment critically and commercially, the band continued to tour the world. *—John Bush*

★ **Dubnobasswithmyheadman** / Dec. 1993 / Wax Trax! ✦✦✦✦✦
From the beginning of the first track "Dark & Long," Underworld's focus on production is clear, with songwriting coming in a distant second. The best tracks ("MMM Skyscraper I Love You," "Cowgirl") mesh Hyde's sultry songwriting with Emerson's beat-driven production, an innovative blend of classic acid house, techno and dub that sounds different from much that preceded it. In a decade awash with stale fusion, Underworld are truly a multi-genre group. *—John Bush*

Second Toughest in the Infants / Mar. 12, 1996 / Wax Trax! ✦✦✦✦✦
On their second album, Underworld continues to explore the fringes of dub, dance and techno, creating a seamless, eclectic fusion of various dance genres. *Second Toughest in the Infants* carries the same knockout punch of their debut, *Dubnobasswithmyheadman*, but it's subtler and more varied, offering proof that the outfit is one of the leading dance collectives of the mid-'90s. *—Stephen Thomas Erlewine*

Beaucoup Fish / Mar. 1, 1999 / Junior Boy's Own ✦✦✦✦

U.N.K.L.E.

f. 1994, London, England
Group / Electronica, Ambient Breakbeat, Ambient Techno, Alternative Rap, Alternative Dance, Trip-Hop
Experimental hip-hop outfit U.N.K.L.E. was one of the original artists releasing material through noted U.K. label Mo'Wax, which helped launch the instrumental mid-'90s downtempo breakbeat revival eventually termed trip-hop. Though hardly the label's highest profile group (at least until the long-delayed release of their debut LP *Psyence Fiction* in 1998), U.N.K.L.E. numbered among its members label-head James Lavelle, who formed Mo'Wax while still in his teens as an antidote to the increasingly stale acid jazz/Northern Soul scene. Stripping the music down to its barest of essentials—bass, percussion, minimal samples and heavy effects—the Mo'Wax sound (best exemplified by the second Mo'Wax label comp, *Headz*, as well as its sequel, the two-part *Headz 2*) quickly gained respectability and a large audience. Although not as prolific as other Mo'Wax artists such as DJs Shadow and Krush, Lavelle's group nonetheless played a crucial role in cementing Mo'Wax's early sound though their *Time Has Come* double EP. Despite the scarcity of released material, U.N.K.L.E. also grew to wider acclaim through remix projects for the Jon Spencer Blues Explosion and Tortoise. *—Sean Cooper*

● **Psyence Fiction** / Sep. 29, 1998 / Mo' Wax/London ✦✦✦✦
James Lavelle and DJ Shadow are unequal partners in U.N.K.L.E., with the former providing the concept and the latter providing music, which naturally overshadows the concept, since the only clear concept—apart from futuristic sound effects, video game samples, and merging trip-hop with rock—is collaborating with a variety of musicians, from superstars to cult favorites Kool G. Rap, Alice Temple, and Mark Hollis (who provides uncredited piano on "Chaos"). Since DJ Shadow's prime gift is for instrumentals, the prospect of him collaborating with vocalists is more intriguing than enticing, and *Psyence Fiction* is appropriately divided between brilliance and failed experiments. Shadow and Lavelle aren't breaking new territory here—beneath the harder rock edge, full-fledged songs, and occasional melodicism, the album stays on the course *Endtroducing* set. Shadow isn't given room to run wild with his soundscapes, and only a couple of cuts, such as the explosive opener "Guns Blazing," equal the sonic collages of his debut. Initially, that may be a disappointment, but U.N.K.L.E. gains momentum on repeated listens. Portions of the record still sound a little awkward—Mike D's contribution suffers primarily from recycled *Hello Nasty* rhyme schemes—yet those moments are overshadowed by Shadow's imagination and unpredictable highlights, such as Temple's chilly "Bloodstain" or Badly Drawn Boy's claustrophobic "Nursery Rhyme," as well as the masterstrokes fronted by Richard Ashcroft (a sweeping, neo-symphonic "Lonely Soul") and Thom Yorke (the moody "Rabbit in Your Headlights"). These moments might not add up to an overpowering record, but in some ways *Psyence Fiction* is something better—a superstar project that doesn't play it safe and actually has its share of rich, rewarding music. *—Stephen Thomas Erlewine*

Urge Overkill

f. 1985
Group / Alternative Pop/Rock, Hard Rock
Few bands ever lusted after rock stardom quite as blatantly as Chicago's Urge Overkill. Although they draped their quest for stardom in a cloak of ironic detachment, it quite clear that the trio expected that if they acted like stars, they would become stars. For a while, their stylish, retro-'70s outfits, matching medallions, and heavy Cheap Trick homages earned the group a popular following in alternative rock circles. *The SuperSonic Storybook* and the *Stull* EP were both underground hits in the early '90s, before alternative rock became big business. Once alternative rock entered the big leagues, it seemed likely that Urge Overkill, with their exceptionally accessible combination of arena rock, power-pop and underground punk, would follow Nirvana to the top of the charts, but mainstream America never quite understood their ironic outlook, embracing the group only after their cover of Neil Diamond's "Girl, You'll Be A Woman Soon" was used in a key scene in *Pulp Fiction*. Instead of breaking down the doors to the stardom, the song proved to be a breaking point. *Exit the Dragon*, the first album released after the hit single, was a bomb, receiving little radio or MTV support, and the band soon fell prey to their widely-documented excesses. *—Stephen Thomas Erlewine*

Americruiser/Jesus Urge Superstar / Oct. 1990 / Touch & Go ✦✦✦
Urge's first two albums were recorded at a time when their visions eclipsed their talents—while there are a lot of good indie-guitar bluster here, there aren't that many memorable songs. With its flat Steve Albini production, *Jesus Urge Superstar* is the weaker of the records. *Americruiser*, with production courtesy of Butch Vig, not only has a fuller sound, but also some real songs. "Ticket to L.A." is a classic rocker, with a locomotive riff and great lyrics. It was a sign of things to come. (The CD also includes their gonzo cover of Jimmy Webb's "Wichitaw Lineman.") *—Stephen Thomas Erlewine*

The Supersonic Storybook / 1991 / Touch & Go ✦✦✦✦
With the addition of drummer Blackie Onassis, Urge Overkill shapes up into a killer rock & roll combo. It also doesn't hurt that the songs are the finest they have written to date. Although the production is a little flat, there's no denying the force of the best tracks. "The Candidate" boasts a huge, stadium-size riff, "The Kids Are Insane" is a frenzied, frenetic rocker, "Today Is Blackie's Birthday" is gleefully stupid, and the band is surprisingly sexy on the old soul song "Emmaline." Things bog down a bit on the second side, but Urge is starting to sound like the rock stars they always knew they were. *—Stephen Thomas Erlewine*

Stull [EP] / Aug. 10, 1992 / Touch & Go ✦✦✦✦✦
It's not the full-throttle rock masterpiece that *Supersonic Storybook* suggested, but the *Stull EP* is almost as remarkable. Opening with a straight cover of Neil Diamond's "Girl, You'll Be a Woman Soon" (which fits Urge Overkill's image perfectly), the EP is an atmospheric guitar workout. While "Stitches" is a salute to their punk roots, the most impressive moments come during the stylish kiss-off to indie-rock "Goodbye to Guyville" and "Stull," with its sly, laid-back groove. As the richness of *Stull* proves, Urge's vision was too large for the independents, and it was time to move on. *—Stephen Thomas Erlewine*

● **Saturation** / Jun. 8, 1993 / DGC ✦✦✦✦✦
When they hit the major labels, Urge Overkill followed through on their promise with the blistering *Saturation*. It's stadium rock by clever post-punkers who are smart enough to not let their carefully crafted image interfere with the music. Every one of the twelve songs is a killer, from the outlandish menace of "Stalker" to the moving ballad "Back On Me," as well as the tongue-in-cheek "Woman 2 Woman" and the radio hit "Sister Havana." *—Stephen Thomas Erlewine*

Exit the Dragon / Oct. 1995 / DGC ✦✦✦✦✦
Sonically falling somewhere between *Supersonic Storybook* and *Stull*, *Exit the Dragon* is a dark, lean album, the flipside of *Saturation*'s glossy celebration of '70s rock & roll excess and easily Urge Overkill's most haunting collection of songs. It kicks off with "Jaywalking," a terse, powerful rocker lamenting "all the evil in this world," which sets the album's tone. *Exit the Dragon* is dominated by Eddie "King" Roeser, with Nash Kato on only six of the 14 songs. As usual, Roeser's songs are more claustrophobic than Kato's, particularly the clenched riffs of "The Break" and the slow crawl of "Tin Foil." Although Kato contributes the flat-out rocker "Need Some Air," amany of his songs are nearly as dark as Roeser's, whether it's the acoustic "View of the Rain" (previously released as "Take a Walk" on the *No Alternative* compilation), the skipping pop of "Somebody Else's Body," athe power-pop of "Monopoly," aor the soaring

closer "Digital Black Epilogue," a duet with an uncredited female soul singer. But the heart of the record is Blackie Onassis's "The Mistake," an eerie tale of a drug overdose which helps *Exit the Dragon* take the form of a loose concept album about a rock & roll band beset by troubles on the road. While the subject is ripe for parody, Urge Overkill performs *Exit the Dragon* without much irony at all. Instead of being a fatal misstep, this choice proves that Urge is a tight, powerful rock & roll band blessed with first-rate songwriters, capable of more emotions than many listeners might have expected. *—Stephen Thomas Erlewine*

Utopia

f. 1974, New York, NY, **db.** 1986
Group / Album Rock, Arena Rock, Pop/Rock, Power Pop, New Wave, Prog-Rock/Art Rock
Stardom was handed to him with *Something/Anything?*, but Todd Rundgren rejected it. He wanted to explore new musical territory instead, and his adventures led him to form Utopia in 1974. Initially, Utopia was a prog-rock septet featuring three keyboardists, but as the '70s progressed, the group evolved into a shiny mainstream rock quartet. As the group evolved, Rundgren retreated into the background, as each of his bandmates contributed songs and lead vocals to the albums. By the early '80s, Utopia had developed into a hit-making entity in their own right, even if much—if not all—of their audience were simply dedicated Rundgren fans, which highlights the problem with Utopia: although they did develop their own signature sound, they were nevertheless always perceived as Rundgren's folly. And to a certain extent that was accurate, since the band's musical evolution often mirrored his own—plus, once he decided he had enough of the group in 1985, it ceased to exist. At that point, Utopia was over a decade old, which made it something more than a folly, but even hardcore Rundgren fans will admit that it's impossible to view Utopia's career as being completely independent from his own. *—Stephen Thomas Erlewine*

Todd Rundgren's Utopia / Oct. 1974 / Bearsville ✦✦

Another Live / Oct. 1975 / Bearsville/Rhino ✦✦✦

RA / Feb. 1977 / Bearsville ✦✦✦

Oops! Wrong Planet / Sep. 1977 / Bearsville ✦✦✦
Abandoning overt prog—thereby leaving behind the operas and extended instrumental sections, but not the organ solos—Utopia became a mainstream rock band with their fourth album, *Oops! Wrong Planet.* Since the group's first two albums were marginally listenable and Ra flirted with outright parody, it comes as a shock to hear Utopia be outright accessible and listenable, two qualities virtually foreign to their previous work. The quartet has been revamped, redesigned as a mainstream arena rock band. And that means that the chores are spread a little more evenly—meaning, not only does everyone get to write, everyone gets to sing, occasionally on songs Todd wrote. Despite his efforts to democratize the group, Utopia still feels very much like Rundgren's baby, mainly because the only songs that really work are ones that he writes and sings. And since Utopia is now merely a hard rock band, Rundgren reserves his more ambitious ideas and complex songs for his solo records. The end result of all this is that *Oops! Wrong Planet* is more consistent than earlier Utopia records, but is not as sporadically brilliant or rewarding as Todd's solo albums. Even the bad moments, such as the very silly "Gangrene," and aren't particularly unlistenable, yet there are simply too many average, undistinguished songs for the record to actually soar. Nevertheless, Rundgren turns in some fine moments—"Love in Action" is a terrific hard rocker, as is "Trapped," and "Love is the Answer" is an ideal stadium anthem—that make the record worthwhile for the cult, even if it will sound like little more than a period piece to most listeners. *—Stephen Thomas Erlewine*

Adventures in Utopia / Jan. 1980 / Bearsville ✦✦✦
Oops! Wrong Planet wrote the blueprint for Utopia, Mach II, but the group didn't deliver the polished, radio-ready follow-up *Adventures in Utopia* until two and a half years later. Granted, leader Todd Rundgren kept busy in the interim, but it was an abnormally long time between records. As it turns out, the wait didn't matter, since Utopia delivered a record that was quintessentially 1980—a shiny, buffed album every bit as pop as *The Hermit of Mink Hollow,* but considerably less introspective and altogether ready for action. It's a bid for the big seats, and Utopia, surprisingly, achieved their goals, as the record climbed into the Top 40 and spawned a hit single with "Set Me Free," a song sung by Kasim Sulton. That fact alone indicates that *Adventures* is the closest Utopia had yet come to its band ideal. It's no surprise that Todd Rundgren still dominates the proceedings, but his presence is not omnipresent, which is to the benefit of the album. Like its predecessor, *Adventures* is consistent but a little bland, but the shiny pop surfaces are more appealing than the arena rock bluster of *Oops!,* which makes the fact that it has about the same number of memorable songs—"You Make Me Crazy," "Second Nature," "Set Me Free," "The Very Last Time" (again, all top-loaded)—not quite as noticeable. It keeps things moving as the record is playing, and if the album as a whole isn't entirely memorable, at least the half that does take hold still sounds as if it was state-of-the-art pop-rock for 1980. *—Stephen Thomas Erlewine*

Deface the Music / Oct. 1980 / Bearsville ✦✦✦✦
Having just scored their first big hits with *Adventures in Utopia,* Utopia inexplicably took a step into arcania with its follow-up, *Deface the Music.* Foregoing the radio-ready style of *Adventures,* Utopia delves deeply into Beatlemania, creating a swift, brutally funny and insanely catchy send-up of the Fab Four's entire career. Clearly, the high (nearly arty) concept makes *Deface the Music* the first Utopia album since *Another Live* to sound like it is solely the work of Todd Rundgren. The music is so savvy, it's clear that these songs are primarily the work of Todd, even if they're credited to Utopia. Rundgren is able to write songs that evoke specific eras of the Beatles' career and have them be funny without being a slave to parody. Like the Rutles, this music works well on its own merits and, unlike the Rutles, Rundgren is as credible with "Penny Lane" psychedelia ("Hoi Poloi") or "Eleanor Rigby" chamber-pop ("Life Goes On") as he is with Merseybeat ("I Just Want to Touch You," "Crystal Ball"). Unlike the Rutles, it sounds like it was recorded in 1980, not the '60s, which intensifies the feeling that *Deface the Music* is merely a curiosity or an exercise for Rundgren, but since the entire thing is finished in just over a half hour, it feels more like a burst of cynical joy that is damn near impossible to resist. *—Stephen Thomas Erlewine*

Swing to the Right / Mar. 1982 / Bearsville ✦✦✦

Utopia / Sep. 1982 / Unidisc ✦✦✦
Utopia followed *Swing to the Right,* their first album for Elektra subsidiary Network, a mere six months after *Swing to the Right,* dubbing the new album *Utopia.* Presumably, an eponymous release signaled a new beginning for the group, which is true to a certain extent. Utopia finally became a true collective here, with each member's contributions sound remarkably similar, in performance and composition. Very few tunes bear an unmistakable Rundgren stamp, and even when they do, it's been processed into a signature Utopia sound—the first time they could truly be said to have a sound of their own. Strangely, this happens on an album where the group makes a self-conscious effort to sound contemporary, dressing in new wave gear for the cover shoot while molding the music after synthesized new wave pop. Granted, that quirkiness masks a fairly traditional set of Utopia arena-pop, yet these songs wind up as the most consistent album in the group's catalog—which is saying a lot, considering that the album spreads over three sides. *Utopia* rarely sags in momentum, and even the weaker songs aren't far removed from the stronger material, highlighted by "Bad Little Actress," "Hammer in My Heart," "Princess of the Universe" and the excellent single "Feet Don't Fail Me Now." They had their moments before, but *Utopia* is where the band finally made a thoroughly enjoyable record; too bad they couldn't extend it through their final two records. *—Stephen Thomas Erlewine*

● **Anthology** / May 1989 / Rhino ✦✦✦✦✦
For all their many attributes, Utopia was notoriously uneven on record. They were just as capable of turning out great pop tunes as they were to wander into meandering jams or directionless hard rock—and this applies not only to their earliest art-rock records, but also to their mainstream pop-rock albums. That's what makes Rhino's *Anthology* such a welcome addition to their catalog. There may be a few great songs missing ("Hammer in My Heart," afor example) and the three prog-rock songs that appear toward the end of the album are a bit of a downer, but the remaining 13 tracks capture Utopia at their absolute best. The group may have attempted to cover more ground in their early prog-rock incarnation, but often those records meandered, which meant that the songs only made sense on the original albums. Once they gave themselves over to pop-rock with 1977's *Oops! Wrong Planet,* they were still uneven, but uneven pop-rock albums can be distilled into one dynamic collection. And that's what happens here. "Crybaby," "The Very Last Time," "Set Me Free," "Love in Action," "Love Is the Answer," "You Make Me Crazy," "Lysistrata," "Feet Don't Fail Me Now" and "I Just Want to Touch You" were undisputed highlights on their respective albums, and hearing them all in a row is a sheer delight. Taken together, they argue that Utopia's records were better and more consistent than they actually were, but the fact is, *Anthology* is "the definitive Utopia album," as Bud Scoppa writes in the liner notes. For Rundgren fans who love his solo records but never quite "got" Utopia, this is the only Utopia record they need. *—Stephen Thomas Erlewine*

Oblivion, POV & Some Trivia / Apr. 9, 1996 / Rhino ✦✦✦

City in My Head / 1999 / Castle ✦✦✦✦

Ritchie Valens

b. May 13, 1941, Pacoima, CA, **d.** Feb. 3, 1959, Clear Lake, IA
Vocals, Guitar / Latin Rock, Rock & Roll
Ritchie Valens will forever be known primarily as one of the two rock stars (along with the Big Bopper) who perished with Buddy Holly when their plane crashed in the midst of a Midwest tour in 1959. At the time, Valens had just established himself as one of the most promising young talents in rock & roll; more than almost any other rock star who died prematurely, it's difficult to assess his unrealized potential—he was only 17 at the time of his death, and had just barely begun to make records.The first Hispanic rock star, Valens was discovered by producer Bob Keane in 1958. Keane signed the guitarist to his Del-Fi label, and they soon had a sizable hit with the brash "Come on Let's Go," which made number 42. It was the pensive, almost awkward "Donna" that got him to number two in early 1959. More innovative was the flipside, "La Bamba," sung entirely in Spanish, and featuring some fierce guitar work, as well as the thick sound of the Danelectro bass, which gave the instrument more electric presence than it had ever previously enjoyed on a rock & roll disc. *—Richie Unterberger*

The Ritchie Valens Story / Jun. 15, 1993 / Del-Fi ✦✦

● **Rockin' All Night: The Best of Ritchie Valens** / Jan. 17, 1995 / Del-Fi ✦✦✦✦✦
There have been a few best-of packages for Valens over the last 20 years, and you're not necessarily better off with this one if you've picked up a collection in the past. As of the mid-'90s, though, this is the best anthology available. The 22 tracks cover all the important bases, including the few hits, several covers, and the best cuts from the remainder of his meager discography. *—Richie Unterberger*

Come On, Let's Go / May 5, 1998 / Del-Fi ✦✦✦✦✦
Considering Valens died about seven months after his first recording session, it's amazing that enough material exists to piece together a three-CD, 62-song box set. It's also amazing that, despite a fair amount of inevitable filler, it's truly a worthwhile collection, recommended to anyone with a deep interest in '50s rock. Besides everything from his two LPs and the *In Concert at Pacoima Jr. High* set (which was actually only half live, anyway), there's a couple dozen home demos and studio outtakes; these are fragmentary and unpolished compared to the official stuff, but the enormous heart in his singing and guitar playing always shines through. While serious collectors probably already have most or all of this, it's never been packaged so thoroughly and thoughtfully: The 64-page booklet includes a long biographical essay and lots of photos, and a 12-page supplemental insert gives more technical notes about the recordings and session musicians. *—Richie Unterberger*

Van Halen

f. 1974, Pasadena, CA
Group / Album Rock, Arena Rock, Heavy Metal, Pop/Rock, Hard Rock
With their 1978 eponymous debut, Van Halen simultaneously re-wrote the rules for rock guitar and hard rock in general. Guitarist Eddie Van Halen redefined what electric guitar could

do, developing a blindingly fast technique with a variety of self-taught two-handed tapping, hammer-ons, pull-offs, and effects that mimicked the sound of machines and animals. It was wildly inventive and over-the-top, equaled only by vocalist David Lee Roth, who brought the role of a metal singer to near performance art standards. Roth wasn't blessed with great technique, unlike Eddie, but he had a flair for showmanship, derived as much from lounge performers as Robert Plant. Together, they made Van Halen into the most popular American rock & roll band of the late '70s and early '80s, and, in the process, set the template for hard-rock and heavy metal for the '80s. Throughout the '80s, it was impossible not to hear Van Halen's instrumental technique on records that ranged from the heaviest metal to soft-pop. Furthermore, Roth's irony-drenched antics were copied by singers who took everything literally. Once of those was Sammy Hagar, an arena-rock veteran from the '70s who replaced Roth after the vocalist had a falling out with Van Halen in 1985. Hagar stayed with the band longer than Roth, helping the group at the top of the charts through the late '80s and early '90s. However, the group's sales began to slide in the mid-'90s, just as tensions between Hagar and Eddie began to arise. In one of the most disastrous publicity stunts in rock history, Hagar was fired (or quit), Roth was brought back on, seemingly as a permanent member, but only for two songs on a greatest hits album. He was subsequently replaced by Gary Cherone, a former member of Extreme. *—Stephen Thomas Erlewine*

★ **Van Halen** / 1978 / Warner Brothers ♦♦♦♦♦
Van Halen's self-titled 1978 debut is undoubtedly one of the all-time best debuts by a hard rock/heavy metal band. All of the components for a classic are represented—excellent songs and high-octane performances (the excitement of their live show was captured perfectly by producer Ted Templeman) are used to create an invigorating, original sound. Like other acclaimed debuts (*Led Zeppelin I, Are You Experienced?*), Van Halen has a raw edge since it was recorded quickly, and every single song is a winner. It's also become one of the ultimate party albums over the years, since the overall mood is excited and celebratory. While singer David Lee Roth's bravado and the steady rhythm section of drummer Alex Van Halen and bassist Michael Anthony were both key ingredients, the main attraction was Eddie Van Halen's guitar playing. Few other guitarists have had such an instant impact on a generation of up-and-coming players, who copied his unorthodox, kamikaze style—especially his trademark tapping technique showcased on the album's legendary solo "Eruption." Almost all of the tracks on *Van Halen* have rightfully become radio staples, such as the scorching rockers "Runnin' With the Devil," "Ain't Talkin' 'Bout Love," "Jamie's Cryin'," "Atomic Punk," and "On Fire," while covers of "You Really Got Me" and "Ice Cream Man" remain awe-inspiring to this day. *Van Halen* proved to be the ultimate coming-of-age soundtrack to many a teenager since its release, resulting in sales of over 10 million in the U.S. alone. Everyone on the planet should own a copy of this landmark release. *—Greg Prato*

Van Halen II / 1979 / Warner Brothers ♦♦♦♦
Rather than take an extended break after spending nearly a year on the road promoting their exceptional 1978 debut, Van Halen went directly back into the studio to record another album. 1979's *Van Halen II* was just as intense as its predecessor, but wasn't as potent compositionally—which is forgivable since it was nearly impossible to top *Van Halen*. A very brief album (barely over 30 minutes in length), *Van Halen II* spawned the group's first true hit single, the aptly titled Top 20 hit "Dance the Night Away," while featuring another strong set of turbo-charged rock. A mid-paced cover of "You're No Good" (originally popularized by Linda Ronstadt) kicks things off, before the band's rowdy party rock regains shape—"Somebody Get Me a Doctor," "Bottoms Up!," "Outta Love Again," "Light Up the Sky," and "D.O.A." are all testosterone-heavy ragers. In addition to the aforementioned "Dance the Night Away," the album closer "Beautiful Girls" showed VH's burgeoning pop sensibilities, while Eddie Van Halen showcases his guitar chops again on the acoustic "Spanish Fly" and the exquisite intro to the sullen "Women In Love." *Van Halen II* confirmed that the band was fast becoming America's premier hard rock/metal band. *—Greg Prato*

Women & Children First / 1980 / Warner Brothers ♦♦♦♦♦
By Van Halen's third release, 1980's *Women and Children First*, the group was a bonafide arena headliner; hence, meaty guitar riffs and a huge, fat sound are featured throughout. While *Van Halen II* was closely rooted both compositionally and sonically to their self-titled debut, *Women and Children First* signaled the band's first (successful) attempt to branch out. The tracks may not have been as immediate as such previous favorites as "Runnin' With the Devil" or "Dance the Night Away," but they were much more ambitious from a songwriting standpoint, resulting in perhaps Van Halen's most underrated record. The anthemic album opener, "And the Cradle Will Rock . . . ," was the first Van Halen track to ever feature keyboards (processed through a guitar amplifier for a heavy sound), while the massive yet spacious sound of such heavy hitters as "Everybody Wants Some!," "Fools," "Romeo Delight," and "Loss of Control" is simply awe-inspiring. Both the intro to "Take Your Whiskey Home" and "Could This Be Magic?" find the band in a loose and fun bluesy mode, while the album-closing epic ballad "In a Simple Rhyme" is one of Van Halen's all-time best and deserved to be a hit. An oft-overlooked hard rock classic. *—Greg Prato*

Fair Warning / 1981 / Warner Brothers ♦♦♦♦
Although Van Halen were enjoying an enormous amount of commercial success by 1981, not all was happy in the VH camp. While the public believed that the euphoric, party-hearty antics of their live show spilled into their personal lives, this proved not to be case. Edward Van Halen was feeling frustrated due to the group's unwillingness to branch out musically as much as he desired, resulting in the group's darkest album, *Fair Warning*. Unlike Van Halen's other Roth-era albums, not a single party anthem was included—in its place was an unmistakable feeling of strife and friction, both lyrically and musically. The album opener, "Mean Street," contains a furious guitar intro by Eddie, before leading into one of VH's funkiest grooves. While the mood is eased from time to time throughout ("Dirty Movies," "Hear About It Later," "Push Comes to Shove"), the album is simply an unapologetic ass-kicker—"Sinner's Swing!," "Unchained," "So This Is Love?," and "One Foot Out the Door" capture the band at their red-hot fiercest. Along with their self-titled debut and *1984*, *Fair Warning* is an undisputed Van Halen masterpiece. *—Greg Prato*

Diver Down / 1982 / Warner Brothers ♦♦♦
Although it went platinum, *Fair Warning* didn't match the multi-platinum standards of Van Halen's first three records, so the group revamped their sound slightly for the follow-up, *Diver Down*. Adding the slightest hints of synthesizers and streamlining both the guitar indulgences of Eddie Van Halen and the vocal excesses of David Lee Roth, the album contained some of the group's most pop-oriented performances—and they were all in the guise of covers. "(Oh) Pretty Woman" and "Dancing in the Street" had the traditional mechanical Van Halen rhythmic pulse, as well as concise solos from Eddie and restrained vocals from Diamond Dave, which helped them become the hits they were designed to be. If they were off-set by more original material like "Hang 'Em High," the concessions would have been acceptable, but the rest of *Diver Down* is filled with covers, including "Big Bad Bill," "Where Have All the Good Times Gone," and a closing "Happy Trails." All of the songs are professionally performed, and the music features more ideas than most previous Van Halen albums, but the lack of strong original material makes *Diver Down* less of an accomplishment than it appears. *—Stephen Thomas Erlewine*

☆ **1984** / 1984 / Warner Brothers ♦♦♦♦♦
Van Halen's *1984* is arguably the best and most defining rock release of the '80s. Eddie Van Halen's guest appearance on Michael Jackson's massive 1983 hit "Beat It" introduced VH to the pop audience, which the band attracted in droves with this expertly crafted set of hard rock with pop leanings, not to mention its imaginative accompanying videos. Musically, *1984* was a gamble that paid off massively—Eddie Van Halen was finally given the green light by his bandmates to incorporate keyboards into their sonic palette, resulting in the number one single "Jump" and the almost new wave-ish Top 15 love song "I'll Wait." But wisely, the keyboards weren't overpowering, and all of the other selections were typical VH hard-rocking heavies—the perennial radio favorites "Hot for Teacher" and "Panama," as well as the highly underrated album tracks "Top Jimmy," "Drop Dead Legs," "Girl Gone Bad," and "House of Pain." While the strong and instantly memorable songs were obviously the main ingredient for the album's success, a string of imaginative and humorous videos really introduced the band to a whole new audience (the hilarious clip for "Hot for Teacher" has to be one of the all-time best). *1984* also opened up the floodgates for many faceless, identical pop-metal bands (something VH was the complete opposite of), who suddenly realized that adding synths to heavy metal could increase their chances of commercial success. Still, it didn't tarnish the fact that *1984* is a timeless hard rock masterpiece, which eventually sold a staggering ten million copies. Unfortunately, the album would be the last Van Halen recording to feature David Lee Roth, who surprisingly left in 1985 at the height of the band's popularity. *—Greg Prato*

5150 / 1986 / Warner Brothers ♦♦♦♦

OU812 / 1988 / Warner Brothers ♦♦♦
Van Halen broke open the pop innovations of *5150* with *OU812*, their second album with Sammy Hagar. On *OU812*, Hagar's direct approach is fully incorporated into the group, as the band churns out straightahead heavy rockers like "Black and Blue" and pulsing power ballads like "Feels So Good." Under Eddie's direction, the group adds a couple of stylistic quirks—from the chicken-picking of "Finish What You Started" and the Hawaiian flourishes of "Cabo Wabo" to the driving, jazz-inflected metallic "Mine All Mine"—which make *OU812* one of the band's most intriguing and rewarding albums. *—Stephen Thomas Erlewine*

For Unlawful Carnal Knowledge / Jun. 17, 1991 / Warner Brothers ♦♦♦

Van Halen Live: Right Here, Right Now / Feb. 23, 1993 / Warner Brothers ♦♦

Balance / 1995 / Warner Brothers ♦♦

The Best of Van Halen, Vol. 1 / Oct. 22, 1996 / Warner Brothers ♦♦♦♦♦
In theory, a Van Halen greatest-hits collection should be easy to assemble, but *The Best of Van Halen, Vol. 1* proves that isn't the case. By trying to give the David Lee Roth and Sammy Hagar eras equal space, they wind up not representing either particularly well. The first eight songs runs through several of Diamond Dave's biggest songs—"Ain't Talkin' 'Bout Love," "Runnin' with the Devil," "And the Cradle Will Rock," "Jump" and "Panama." It's hard to argue with any of the choices, yet significant songs like "You Really Got Me," "Beautiful Girls," "(Oh) Pretty Woman," "I'll Wait" and "Hot for Teacher" are missing. Similarly, the Sammy era has many big hits—"Why Can't This Be Love," "Dreams," "When It's Love," and "Right Now"—but skips over his like "Love Walks In," "Black and Blue," and "Finish What Ya Started." Clearly, the collection would have been better served if it had been assembled as a double-disc set, with Dave and Sammy getting a disc a piece. Furthermore, the much-hyped reunion tracks with Roth, "Can't Get This Stuff No More" and "Me Wise Magic," are a slight disappointment; the band sounds good, but neither track contains a memorable hook. Also, the presence of "Humans Being," one of Van Halen's worst tracks, is an insult, considering how many great songs are missing. Nevertheless, *Best Of, Vol. 1* remains a good single-disc encapsulation of Van Halen's career, even if it isn't a definitive retrospective. *—Stephen Thomas Erlewine*

Van Halen 3 / Feb. 24, 1998 / Warner Brothers ♦♦

Luther Vandross

b. Apr. 20, 1951, New York, NY [The Bronx]
Vocals / Quiet Storm, Urban, Soul
In R&B music, Luther Vandross ranked with Prince, Stevie Wonder, and Michael Jackson as one of the most successful singer-songwriters and producers of the '80s. Amazingly, unlike those peers, for the most part he did not cross over to widespread pop appeal, a situation that finally began to change at the end of the '80s. Vandross had an elastic tenor that made him a natural for backup singing and commercial work in the early '70s, when he became a top session vocalist. In 1981, he signed with Epic and released his debut album *Never Too Much*, which topped the R&B charts and sold two million copies. The title track was also an R&B number one hit single and reached the pop Top 40. His albums were all million-sellers that spawned major R&B hits, but Vandross' pop success was spotty until 1989, when Epic re-

leased *The Best of Luther Vandross… The Best of Love*, a greatest-hits album containing the new track "Here and Now," which became Vandross' first Top Ten pop hit. That proved his breakthrough, and Vandross' next album, *Power of Love* (1991), another million-seller, featured two pop hits, "Power of Love/Love Power" and "Don't Want to Be a Fool." *— William Ruhlmann*

★ **The Best of Luther Vandross** / Sep. 1989 / Epic ✦✦✦✦✦
By the time this way-overdue double-record hits collection came out, Vandross had done many more R&B singles than could fit on it, so *The Best of Luther Vandross… The Best of Love* is inadequate to encompass him. It does, however, contain "Here and Now," which broke Vandross through to the pop Top Ten long after most people had given up hope that he'd ever cross over. *— William Ruhlmann*

Greatest Hits / Nov. 16, 1999 / Epic ✦✦✦✦✦
1999's *Greatest Hits* may not be as generous as 1989's *The Best of Luther Vandross*, which contained 20 tracks on two discs, but it's a good, concise 14-track collection that includes many of his very best songs. There is a lot of overlap with *The Best of*—it shares no less than nine tracks with that collection—but it also has such '90s hits as "Don't Want to Be a Fool" and "Power of Love / Love Power." It is a tight, single-disc collection, which may make it preferable to some listeners. However, *The Best of* does cover Vandross' prime period better, and since *Greatest Hits* covers much of that same territory while missing several big '90s hits, it isn't quite all it could be. Essentially, it's for casual fans that want all the big hits on one disc—serious listeners will want to stick with *The Best of*. *— Stephen Thomas Erlewine*

The Vapors

f. 1978, **db.** 1981
Group / Mod Revival, Power Pop, New Wave
Led by vocalist/guitarist Dave Fenton, the Vapors were a short-lived new wave guitar group that is best known for the spiky pop single "Turning Japanese." Fenton formed the first version of the Vapors in 1978, yet he was the only member to survive that lineup; in 1979, former Ellery Bops members Ed Bazalgette (lead guitar) and Howard Smith (drums) joined the band and bassist Steve Smith came aboard shortly afterward. One of the band's first concert was seen by the Jam's Bruce Foxton, who asked them to perform on his group's *Setting Sons* tour. Before long, the Vapors were managed by Foxton and John Weller, the manager of the Jam, as well as the father of the group's leader, Paul Weller.

The Vapors signed to United Artists, releasing their first single, "Prisoners," at the end of 1979; it failed to chart. "Turning Japanese," the band's second single, became a major hit, reaching number three on the U.K. charts in March of 1980. *New Clear Days*, the band's debut album, was released two months later, which didn't sell as well as the single. In 1981, the Vapors released the more ambitious *Magnets*, yet it received lukewarm reviews and poor sales; the group disbanded shortly after its release. *— Stephen Thomas Erlewine*

New Clear Days / Jun. 1980 / Cargo ✦✦✦✦✦
It's easy to dismiss this band as a one-hit wonder—surely the album has nothing quite as infectious as the single, "Turning Japanese." *New Clear Days* is, however, a fine example of punchy Brit-pop in the vein of The Jam that holds up better than most albums from the period. *— Chris Woodstra*

Magnets / 1981 / Cargo ✦✦✦
David Fenton was obviously growing tired of being written off as light-weight after "Turning Japanese" and responded with the more ambitious and mature *Magnets*. Here he explores the darker side of life, discussing the Kennedy assasination ("Magnets"), police harrassment ("Civic Hall") and even cult leader/mass murder Rev. Jim Jones ("Jimmy Jones," the failed single). Musically the band is more sophisticated, taking the occasional misstep in the arrangements by adding an annoying sythesizer in songs like "Spiders." Virtually ignored by both critics and the buying public, this is a strong follow-up that deserved a better fate. *— Chris Woodstra*

Anthology / May 30, 1995 / One Way ✦✦✦✦
A somewhat misleading title, *Anthology* is a straight reissue of *New Clear Days* with four songs from *Magnets* tacked on to the end. Since the band only made two albums it would have been nice to release both as a two-fer—or at least add some rare tracks to the anthology. Minor complaints aside, this is probably all The Vapors most people will ever need, though Collectables' *Vaporization*, which presents both albums in their entirety, is a better choice. *— Chris Woodstra*

Turning Japanese: The Best of the Vapors / 1996 / EMI ✦✦✦✦✦
A far better collection than its American counterpart (*Anthology*), *The Best of the Vapors* offers a bit more for the fans, combining all of the singles, five rare b-sides, and most of the best album tracks (though the *Magnets* album is still woefully underrepresented). As an introduction, there is no better place to start and for collectors, it's indispensable. *— Chris Woodstra*

● **Vaporized** / Apr. 7, 1998 / Collectables ✦✦✦✦✦
Vaporization is the third Vapors anthology in three years and, for a band who only released two proper albums, that's no small feat. This one rights the wrongs of earlier collections by finally putting out the two albums—1980's *New Clear Days* and 1981's *Magnets*—in their entirety on one CD. Collectors should still seek out the import, *Turning Japanese: the Best of the Vapors* as a supplement, but all but the obsessive can start and stop here. *— Chris Woodstra*

The Vaselines

f. 1986, **db.** 1990
Group / Indie Pop, Twee Pop, Alternative Pop/Rock
Eugene Kelly and Frances McKee were bored with their town, so they decided to form a band; they were called the Vaselines. Adding Charles Kelly on drums and bassist James Seenan, the Scottish quartet began rehearsing in their basements; soon they began recording their rough, simple and highly melodic pop songs in studios in Glasgow and Edinburgh. They recorded about 20 raw, pure pop gems that were barely heard by anyone. The Vaselines would likely have faded away into obscurity if it wasn't for Nirvana, who recorded two of their songs (both appear on the *Incesticide* compilation); Kurt Cobain was very vocal about his admiration for the band and Eugene Kelly in particular. By this time, the Vaselines had broken up and Kelly had formed Captain America, which later became Eugenius; soon, Eugenius became a hip band in alternative circles and the Vaselines' music was reissued. *— Stephen Thomas Erlewine*

● **The Way of the Vaselines** / Jul. 31, 1992 / Sub Pop ✦✦✦✦✦
The Way of the Vaselines collects everything The Vaselines ever recorded; it's a rough gem of raw pop. *— Stephen Thomas Erlewine*

Stevie Ray Vaughan

b. Oct. 3, 1954, Dallas, TX, **d.** Aug. 27, 1990, East Troy, WI
Vocals, Guitar (Electric), Guitar / Album Rock, Modern Electric Texas Blues, Guitar Virtuoso, Electric Texas Blues, Blues-Rock, Modern Electric Blues
With his astonishingly accomplished guitar playing, Stevie Ray Vaughan ignited the blues revival of the '80s. Vaughan drew equally from bluesmen like Albert King, Otis Rush, and Muddy Waters and rock & roll players like Jimi Hendrix and Lonnie Mack, as well as the stray jazz guitarist like Kenny Burrell, developing a uniquely eclectic and fiery style that sounded like no other guitarist, regardless of genre. Vaughan bridged the gap between blues and rock like no other artist had since the late '60s. During the 1980s, he was the leading light in American blues, consistently selling out concerts while his albums regularly went gold. His tragic death in 1990 only emphasized his influence in blues and American rock & roll.

Vaughan began playing guitar as a child, and dropped out of high school to concentrate on playing music. After playing in a band called the Cobras during the early '70s, he formed Triple Threat in 1975, later to become Double Trouble. After the band's 1982 performance at the Montreux Festival caught the attention of David Bowie, Vaughan played on Bowie's *Let's Dance* in 1982. He signed to Epic and soon after, released his debut album *Texas Flood*, a blockbuster blues success and a crossover hit for rock radio. Vaughan's second album *Couldn't Stand the Weather* was even more successful than its predecessor, hitting the Top 40 and going gold.

Though 1985's *Soul to Soul* was also quite successful, Vaughan sank deep into alcoholism and drug addiction. He checked into a rehabilitation clinic in 1988, and performed only sparingly that year. Still, one year later *In Step* became his most successful album, earning a Grammy and going gold. In 1990, Stevie Ray recorded an album with his brother Jimmie, but was killed in a helicopter crash before the record was released. The album, *Family Style*, hit the Top Ten just two months after his death, beginning a series of posthumous releases that were as popular as the albums Stevie Ray released during his lifetime. *— Stephen Thomas Erlewine*

★ **Texas Flood** / 1983 / Epic/Legacy ✦✦✦✦✦
It's hard to overestimate the impact Stevie Ray Vaughan's debut *Texas Flood* had upon its release in 1983. At that point, blues was no longer hip, the way it was in the '60s. *Texas Flood* changed all that, climbing into the Top 40 and spending over half a year on the charts, which was practically unheard of for a blues recording. Vaughan became a genuine star and, in doing so, sparked a revitalization of the blues. This was a monumental impact, but his critics claimed that, no matter how prodigious Vaughan's instrumental talents were, he didn't forge a distinctive voice; instead, he wore his influences on his sleeve, whether it was Albert King's pinched yet muscular soloing or Larry Davis' emotive singing. There's a certain element of truth in that, but that was sort of the point of *Texas Flood*. Vaughan didn't hide his influences, he celebrated them, pumping fresh blood into a familiar genre. When Vaughan and Double Trouble cut the album over the course of three days in 1982, he had already played his set lists countless times; he knew how to turn this material inside out or goose it up for maximum impact. The album is paced like a club show, kicking off with Vaughan's two best self-penned songs, "Love Struck Baby" and "Pride and Joy," then settling into a pair of covers, the slow-burning title track and an exciting reading of Howlin' Wolf's "Tell Me," before building to the climax of "Dirty Pool" and "I'm Crying." Vaughan caps the entire thing with "Lenny," a lyrical, jazzy tribute to his wife. It becomes clear that Vaughan's true achievement was finding something personal and emotional by fusing different elements of his idols. Sometimes the borrowing was overt, and other times subtle, but it all blended together into a style that recalled the past while seizing the excitement and essence of the present. *— Stephen Thomas Erlewine*

Couldn't Stand the Weather / 1984 / Epic/Legacy ✦✦✦✦
Stevie Ray Vaughan's second album, *Couldn't Stand the Weather*, pretty much did everything a second album should do: it confirmed that the acclaimed debut was no fluke, while matching, if not bettering, the sales of its predecessor, thereby cementing Vaughan's status as a giant of modern blues. So why does it feel like a letdown? Perhaps because it simply offers more of the same, all the while relying heavily on covers. Of the eight songs, half are covers, while two of his four originals are instrumentals—not necessarily a bad thing, but it gives the impression that Vaughan threw the album together in a rush, even if he didn't. Nevertheless, *Couldn't Stand the Weather* feels a bit like a holding pattern, since there's no elaboration on Double Trouble's core sound and no great strides forward, whether it's in Vaughan's songwriting or musicianship. Still, as holding patterns go, it's a pretty enjoyable one, since Vaughan and Double Trouble play spiritedly throughout the record. With its swaggering, stuttering riff, the title track ranks as one of Vaughan's classics, and thanks to a nuanced vocal, he makes W.C. Clark's "Cold Shot" his own. The instrumentals—the breakneck Lonnie Mack-styled "Scuttle Buttin'" and "Stang's Swang," another effective demonstration of Vaughan's jazz inclinations—work well, even if the original shuffle "Honey Bee" fails to make much of an impression and the cover of "Voodoo Chile (Slight Return)" is too reminiscent of Jimi Hendrix's original. So, there aren't many weaknesses on the record, aside from the suspicion that Vaughan didn't really push himself as hard as he could have, and the feeling that if he had, he would have come up with something a bit stronger. *— Stephen Thomas Erlewine*

Soul to Soul / 1985 / Epic/Legacy ✦✦✦
By adding two members to Double Trouble—keyboardist Reese Wynans and saxophonist Joe

Sublett—Stevie Ray Vaughan indicated he wanted to add soul and R&B inflections to his basic blues sound, and *Soul to Soul* does exactly that. It's still a modern blues album, yet it has a wider sonic palette, finding Vaughan fusing a variety of blues, rock, and R&B styles. Most of this is done through covers—notably Hank Ballard's "Look at Little Sister," the exquisitely jazzy "Gone Home," and Doyle Bramhall's impassioned soul-blues "Change It"—but Vaughan's songwriting occasionally follows suit, as well. Even if only the tortured blues wailer "Ain't Gone 'N' Give Up On Love" entered his acknowledged canon, he throws in some delightful soul-funk touches on "Say What!," the instrumental wah-wah workout that kicks off the album., and the Curtis Mayfield-inspired closer "Life Without You" captures Vaughan at his best as a composer and performer. It's such a seductive number—such a full realization of his soul-blues ambitions—that the rest of the album pales in comparison. In fact, for all of its positive attributes, *Soul to Soul* winds up being less than the sum of its parts, and it's hard to pinpoint an exact reason why. Perhaps it was because Vaughan was on the verge of a horrible battle with substance abuse at the time of recording or perhaps it just has that unevenness inherent in transitional albums. Still, he has good taste in covers, his originals are sturdy, and there's not a bad performance here, so *Soul to Soul* winds up enjoyable in spite of its flaws, and it clearly points the way to his 1989 masterpiece, *In Step*. —*Stephen Thomas Erlewine*

Live Alive / Jul. 1986 / Epic ✦✦✦

☆ **In Step** / Jun. 1989 / Epic/Legacy ✦✦✦✦✦
Stevie Ray Vaughan had always been a phenomenal guitarist, but prior to *In Step*, his songwriting was hit-and-miss. Even when he wrote a classic modern blues song, it was firmly within the genre's conventions; only on *Soul to Soul*'s exquisite soul-blues "Life Without You" did he attempt to stretch the boundaries of the form. As it turns out, that was the keynote for *In Step*, an album where Vaughan found his own songwriting voice, blending blues, soul, and rock in unique ways, and writing with startling emotion honesty. Yes, there are a few covers, all well chosen, but the heart of the album rests in the songs he cowrote with Doyle Bramhall, the man who penned the *Soul to Soul* highlight "Change It." Bramhall proved to be an ideal collaborator for Vaughan; tunes like the terse "Tightrope" and the dense "Wall of Denial" feel so intensely personal, it's hard to believe that they weren't the product of just one man. Yet the lighter numbers—the dynamite boogie "The House Is Rockin'" and the breakneck blues of "Scratch-N-Sniff"—are just as effective as songs. Of course, he didn't need words to make effective music: "Travis Walk" is a blistering instrumental, complete with intricate fingerpicking reminiscent of the great country guitarist Merle Travis, while the shimmering "Riviera Paradise" is every bit as lyrical and lovely as his previous charmer, "Lenny." The magnificent thing about *In Step* is how it's fully realized, presenting every facet of Vaughan's musical personality, yet it still soars with a sense of discovery. It's a bittersweet triumph, given Vaughan's tragic death a little over a year after its release, yet it's a triumph all the same. —*Stephen Thomas Erlewine*

Live at the El Mocambo / 1991 / Sony ✦✦✦

The Sky Is Crying / Nov. 5, 1991 / Epic ✦✦✦✦
The posthumously assembled ten-track outtakes collection *The Sky Is Crying* actually proves to be one of Vaughan's most consistent albums, rivaling *In Step* as the best outside of the *Greatest Hits* collection. These songs were recorded in sessions spanning from 1984's *Couldn't Stand the Weather* to 1989's *In Step* and were left off of the LPs for whatever reason (or, in the case of *Soul to Soul*'s "Empty Arms," a different version was used). What makes the record work is its eclectic diversity—Vaughan plays slide guitar on "Boot Hill" and acoustic on "Life By the Drop"; he smokes on the slow blues of "May I Have a Talk With You" and the title track just as much as on the uptempo Lonnie Mack cover "Wham"; and he shows the jazzy side of his playing on Hendrix's "Little Wing" and Kenny Burrell's "Chitlins Con Carne." But it's not just musical diversity that makes the record work, it's also Vaughan's emotional range. From the morbidly dark "Boot Hill" to the lilting "Little Wing" to the exuberant tributes to his influences—Lonnie Mack on "Wham" and Albert King on "The Sky Is Crying"—Vaughan makes the material resonate, and in light of his death, "The Sky Is Crying" and the touching survivor-story ballad "Life By the Drop" are two of the most moving moments in Vaughan's oeuvre. —*Steve Huey*

In the Beginning / Oct. 6, 1992 / Epic ✦✦

Greatest Hits / Nov. 21, 1995 / Epic ✦✦✦✦✦
Stevie Ray Vaughan was a great guitarist, but he had trouble making consistent albums. *Greatest Hits* rectifies that problem by collecting all of his best-known tracks, from "Pride and Joy" to "Crossfire." Not only is it a terrific introduction, it's his most consistent album, demonstrating exactly why he was one of the most important guitarists of the '80s. —*Stephen Thomas Erlewine*

Live at Carnegie Hall / Jul. 29, 1997 / Epic ✦✦✦✦

Real Deal: Greatest Hits, Vol. 2 / Mar. 23, 1999 / Epic/Legacy ✦✦✦✦

Blues at Sunrise / Apr. 4, 2000 / Epic/Legacy ✦✦✦

Bobby Vee (Robert Thomas Velline)

b. Apr. 30, 1943, Fargo, ND
Vocals / Brill Building Pop, Teen Idol, Pop
His career launched as a fill-in for the recently deceased Buddy Holly, Bobby Vee scored several pop hits during the early '60s, that notorious period of popular music sandwiched between the birth of rock & roll and the rise of the British Invasion. Though a few of his singles—"Rubber Ball," for one—were as innocuous as anything else from the era, Vee had a knack for infectious Brill Building pop, thanks to his ebullient voice as well as the cadre of songwriters standing behind him. His big break came at the expense of one of his musical idols; the Winter Dance Party package tour, with Buddy Holly, Ritchie Valens and the Big Bopper on their way to Fargo when their plane went down in Iowa, killing all three. Vee's band he Shadows were scheduled to play the date instead of Holly, and several months later, producer Tommy "Snuff" Garrett supervised their first recording session and the release of the single "Suzie Baby" on Soma Records. His third single, "Devil or Angel," hit the Top Ten in mid-1960, followed by "Rubber Ball" later that year. One year later, Vee's biggest hit, "Take Good Care of My Baby," spent three weeks at number one, followed by the number two "Run to Him." His fame appeared to wane after the 1962 Top Ten single "The Night Has a Thousand Eyes," due in large part to the success of the Beatles and other English acts. —*John Bush*

● **Legendary Masters** / 1990 / EMI America ✦✦✦✦✦

Suzanne Vega

b. Jul. 11, 1959, Sacramento, CA
Vocals, Guitar / College Rock, Alternative Folk, Contemporary Folk, Adult Alternative Pop/Rock, Singer/Songwriter
Vega was born in Santa Monica, CA, and moved to New York City at age two. She attended the High School of Performing Arts, then Barnard College. Vega was still at Barnard when she began attracting attention at Greenwich Village folk clubs and was featured on several issues of the songwriters' magazine/record album *The CooP* (later *The Fast Folk Musical Magazine*) in 1982. She was signed to A&M Records in 1984 and released her first album, *Suzanne Vega* in 1985. It was a critical success and a moderate seller. Vega's second album, *Solitude Standing*, featured "Luka," a song about child abuse that became a surprise hit single in 1987. The album itself went gold. Vega took three years to release the follow-up, *Days of Open Hand* (1990), which was a commercial disappointment, though a few months later a couple of British DJs, under the name D.N.A., put out a dance version of her a cappella song "Tom's Diner" from the album *Solitude Standing*, and it became a hit.

On her next album, 1992's *99.9∞ F*, Vega experimented with the dance rhythms that made "Tom's Diner" a hit; although the result was interesting, it didn't give her any hits. Vega's fifth album was scheduled for release in the spring of 1996. —*William Ruhlmann*

Suzanne Vega / May 1985 / A&M ✦✦✦✦
Though early comparisons were made to Joni Mitchell, Suzanne Vega's true antecedents were Janis Ian and Leonard Cohen. Like Ian, she sings with a precise, frequently half-spoken phrasing that gives her lyrics an intensity that seemes to suggest an unsteady control consciously held over emotional chaos. Like Cohen, Vega observes the world in poetic metaphor, her cold urban landscapes reflecting a troubled sense of love and loss. The key track is "Small Blue Thing," in which the singer pictures herself as an object "Like a marble / or an eye," "made of china / made of glass," "lost inside your pocket" and "turning in your hand." The sharply picked acoustic guitar and other isolated musical elements echo the closely observed scenes—everything seems to be in tight closeup and sharp focus. Often, the singer seems to be using the songs to measure an emotional distance; sometimes, as in "Marlene on the Wall," she observes her own actions from a remove. In "Freeze Tag," she tells a companion, "I will be Dietrich / and you can be Dean"; in "Marlene," a poster of the aloof movie star "watches from the wall" observing the singer's succession of lovers, and she tries to emulate her heroine's persona, telling the current one, "Even if I am in love with you / All this to say, what's it to you?" The ten songs on *Suzanne Vega* constitute the self-analysis of a young woman who desires possession without offering commitment; no wonder that, upon its release, it was taken to heart by young women across the country and in Europe. —*William Ruhlmann*

● **Solitude Standing** / Apr. 1987 / A&M ✦✦✦✦✦
The songs on *Solitude Standing*, Suzanne Vega's second album, had years listed beside them on the lyric sheet, so you could see that some of them dated back to 1978. But that bold admission heralded the album's triumph—its diversity was what made it so good. Partially, that was because the old songs were the equal of anything on the first album—tunes like the a cappella slice-of-life "Tom's Diner" and the warmly romantic "Gypsy" simply wouldn't have fit thematically on the debut. On *Solitude Standing*, however, they became part of an album of story songs set in a variety of musical contexts; many had band arrangements, and in fact, members of Vega's touring band often were credited as co-writers. Additionally, Vega had developed more as a singer without losing the focused intonation that had made her debut—one of many compelling elements which helped make "Luka," a character song about domestic abuse, a fluke hit. —*William Ruhlmann*

Days of Open Hand / Apr. 1990 / A&M ✦✦

99.9° F. / Sep. 8, 1992 / A&M ✦✦✦
While this is not the techno album that Suzanne Vega was rumored to be making, *99.9° Fahrenheit* does offer a significant departure from her previous contemporary folk albums. Vega uses more synthesizers and drum machines, often evoking a bizarre carnival-esque atmosphere on the album. Still, *99.9° Fahrenheit* is a folk album at heart; every song is steeped in traditional song form, and Vega's writing is strong. Fans of Vega's previous work might be taken aback, but those willing to listen to the album will find that Vega has produced one of her strongest records yet. —*Stephen Thomas Erlewine*

Nine Objects of Desire / Sep. 10, 1996 / A&M ✦✦✦

Best of Suzanne Vega: Tried and True / Dec. 14, 1999 / A&M ✦✦✦✦✦
This excellent overview of Vega's career contains all the hits and a fair sampling from each of her five albums, though *Days of Open Hand* receives a cold shoulder (only "Book of Dreams" represents it here), being a critical and personal failure. The CD as a whole shows that while Vega has stayed fairly consistent as a songwriter, her growth has been marked in the collaborations with various producers, from the spare, simplistic sound stages of Steve Addabbo and Lenny Kaye to the lush metallurgy of Mitchell Froom and Tchad Blake. The collection also features that bane of fans, the exclusive track, necessitating purchasing the CD when one owns all the other material. However, these two new songs—"Book & a Cover" and "Rosemary"—are quality entries in Vega's songbook, and once again feature the production skills of Froom and Blake. —*Ted Mills*

The Velvet Underground

f. 1964, New York, NY, **db.** 1973
Group / Experimental Rock, Proto-Punk, Rock & Roll
Few rock groups can claim to have broken so much new territory, and maintain such consistent brilliance on record, as the Velvet Underground during their brief lifespan. It was the

group's lot to be ahead of, or at least out of step with, their time. The mid-to-late '60s was an era of explosive growth and experimentation in rock, but the Velvets' innovations—which blended the energy of rock with the sonic adventurism of the avant-garde, and introduced a new degree of social realism and sexual kinkiness into rock lyrics—were too abrasive for the mainstream to handle. During their time, the group experienced little commercial success; though they were hugely appreciated by a cult audience and some critics, the larger public treated them with indifference or, occasionally, scorn. The Velvets' music was too important to languish in obscurity, though; their cult only grew larger and larger in the years following their demise, and continues to mushroom today. By the 1980s, they were acknowledged not just as one of the most important rock bands of the '60s, but one of the best of all time, and one whose immense significance cannot be measured by their relatively modest sales. Historians often hail the group for their incalculable influence upon the punk and new wave of subsequent years, and while the Velvets were undoubtedly a key touchstone of the movements, to focus upon these elements of their vision is to only get part of the story. The group were uncompromising in their music and lyrics, to be sure, sometimes espousing a bleakness and primitivism that would inspire alienated singers and songwriters of future generations. But their colorful and oft-grim soundscapes were firmly grounded in strong, well-constructed songs that could be as humanistic and compassionate as they were outrageous and confrontational. The member most responsible for these qualities was guitarist, singer, and songwriter Lou Reed, whose sing-speak vocals and gripping narratives have come to define street-savvy rock & roll. *—Richie Unterberger*

☆ **The Velvet Underground & Nico** / Jan. 1967 / Verve ✦✦✦✦✦
One would be hard pressed to name a rock album whose influence has been as broad and pervasive as *The Velvet Underground and Nico.* While it reportedly took over a decade for the album's sales to crack six figures, glam, punk, new wave, goth, noise, and nearly every other left-of-center rock movement owes an audible debt to this set. While The Velvet Underground had as distinctive a sound as any band, what's most surprising about this album is its diversity. Here, the Velvets dipped their toes into dreamy pop ("Sunday Morning"), tough garage rock ("Waiting for the Man"), stripped-down R&B ("There She Goes Again"), and understated love songs ("I'll Be Your Mirror") when they weren't busy creating sounds without pop precedent. Lou Reed's lyrical exploration of drugs and kinky sex (then risky stuff in film and literature, let alone "teen music") always received the most press attention, but the music Reed, John Cale, Sterling Morrison, and Maureen Tucker played was as radical as the words they accompanied. The bracing discord of "European Son," the troubling beauty of & "All Tomorrow's Parties," and the expressive dynamics of "Heroin," all remain as compelling as the day they were recorded. While the significance of Nico's contributions have been debated over the years, she meshes with the band's outlook in that she hardly sounds like a typical rock vocalist, and if Andy Warhol's presence as producer was primarily a matter of signing the checks, his notoriety allowed The Velvet Underground to record their material without compromise, which would have been impossible under most other circumstances. Few rock albums are as important as *The Velvet Underground and Nico,* and fewer still have lost so little of their power to surprise and intrigue more than 30 years after first hitting the racks. *—Mark Deming*

☆ **White Light/White Heat** / Nov. 1967 / Verve ✦✦✦✦✦
The world of pop music was hardly ready for The Velvet Underground's first album when it appeared in the spring of 1967, but while *The Velvet Underground and Nico* sounded like an open challenge to conventional notions of what rock music could sound like (or what it could discuss), 1968's *White Light/White Heat* was a no-holds-barred frontal assault on cultural and aesthetic propriety. Recorded without the input of either Nico or Andy Warhol, *White Light/White Heat* was the purest and rawest document of the key Velvets lineup of Lou Reed, John Cale, Sterling Morrison, and Maureen Tucker, capturing the group at their toughest and most abrasive. The album opens with an open and enthusiastic endorsement of amphetamines (startling even from this group of noted drug enthusiasts), and side one continues with an amusing shaggy-dog story set to a slab of lurching mutant R&B ("The Gift"), a perverse variation on an old folktale ("Lady Godiva's Operation"), and the album's sole "pretty" song, the mildly disquieting "Here She Comes Now." While side one was a good bit darker in tone than the Velvets' first album, side two was where they truly threw down the gauntlet with the manic, free-jazz implosion of "I Heard Her Call My Name" (featuring Reed's guitar work at its most gloriously fractured), and the epic noise jam "Sister Ray," 17 minutes of sex, drugs, violence, and other non-wholesome fun with the loudest rock group in the history of Western Civilization as the house band. *White Light/White Heat* is easily the least accessible of The Velvet Underground's studio albums, but anyone wanting to hear their guitar-mauling tribal frenzy straight with no chaser will love it, and those benighted souls who think of the Velvets as some sort of folk-rock band are advised to crank their stereo up to ten and give side two a spin. *—Mark Deming*

☆ **The Velvet Underground** / 1969 / Verve ✦✦✦✦✦
Upon first release, The Velvet Underground's self-titled third album must have surprised their fans nearly as much as their first two albums shocked the few mainstream music fans who heard them. After testing the limits of how musically and thematically challenging rock could be on *The Velvet Underground and Nico* and *White Light/White Heat,* this 1969 release sounded spare, quiet, and contemplative, as if the previous albums documented some manic speed-fueled party and this was the subdued morning after. (The album's relative calm has often been attributed to the departure of the band's most committed avant-gardist, John Cale, in the fall of 1968; the arrival of new bassist Doug Yule; and the theft of the band's amplifiers shortly before they began recording.) But Lou Reed's lyrical exploration of the demimonde is as keen here as on any album he ever made, while displaying a warmth and compassion he sometimes denied his characters. "Candy Says," "Pale Blue Eyes," and & "I'm Set Free" may be more muted in approach than what the band had done in the past, but "What Goes On" and "Beginning to See the Light" made it clear the VU still loved rock & roll, and "The Murder Mystery" (which mixes and matches four separate poetic narratives) is as brave and uncompromising as anything on *White Light/White Heat.* This album sounds less like The Velvet Underground than any of their studio albums, but it's as personal, honest, and moving as anything Lou Reed ever committed to tape. *—Mark Deming*

☆ **Loaded** / 1970 / Warner Brothers ✦✦✦✦✦
After The Velvet Underground cut three albums for the jazz-oriented Verve label that earned them lots of notoriety but negligible sales, the group signed with industry powerhouse Atlantic Records in 1970; label head Ahmet Ertegun supposedly asked Lou Reed to avoid sex and drugs in his songs, and instead focus on making an album "loaded with hits." *Loaded* was the result, and with appropriate irony it turned out to be the first VU album that made any noticeable impact on commercial radio—and also their swan song, with Reed leaving the group shortly before its release. With John Cale long gone from the band, Doug Yule highly prominent (he sings lead on four of the ten tracks), and Maureen Tucker absent on maternity leave, this is hardly a purist's Velvet Underground album. But while Lou Reed always wrote great rock & roll songs with killer hooks, on *Loaded* his tunes were at last given a polished but intelligent production that made them sound like the hits they should have been, and there's no arguing that "Sweet Jane" and "Rock and Roll" are as joyously anthemic as anything he's ever recorded. And if this release generally maintains a tight focus on the sunny side of the VU's personality (or would that be Reed's personality?), "New Age" and "Oh! Sweet Nuthin'" prove he had hardly abandoned his contemplative side, and & "Train Around the Bend" is a subtle but revealing metaphor for his weariness with the music business. Sterling Morrison once said of *Loaded,* "It showed that we could have, all along, made truly commercial sounding records," but just as importantly, it proved the they could do so without entirely abandoning their musical personality in the process. It's a pity that notion hadn't occurred to anyone a few years earlier. *—Mark Deming*

Live at Max's Kansas City / 1972 / Atlantic ✦✦✦
There's a certain amount of disagreement among Velvet Underground scholars regarding whether or not this album, recorded by Andy Warhol associate and longtime fan Brigid Polk on a portable cassette recorder on August 23, 1970, does in fact document Lou Reed's final appearance with the VU. If this wasn't his last stand with the group, it was certainly close to the end of the line, and while the performance is technically strong, it isn't especially inspired, with Reed sounding more than a bit weary. (At this point, the band was near the end of a three month residency at *Max's,* doing recording sessions for *Loaded* during the day, a schedule that would tax most performers.) The absence of Maureen Tucker on drums (who was pregnant and sitting out the *Max's* shows) makes an even bigger difference; the replacement of her steady, tribal pulse in favor of Billy Yule's busy, sometimes sloppy style does these songs no favors. But there are a few lovely moments, including rare live performances of "After Hours" and "Sunday Morning," and Reed and Sterling Morrison lock guitars with their usual authority on "Waiting for the Man" and "Beginning to See the Light." The audio quality isn't great, but given the circumstances it's better than you might expect (it's OK by the standards of an early '70s bootleg), though historical merit seems to be more the issue than high fidelity. And yes, that really is Jim Carroll ordering double Pernods and asking about the availability of Tuinol between songs. Fun for fans, but *1969: Velvet Underground Live* is a much stronger document of this band's onstage prowess. *—Mark Deming*

Squeeze / 1973 / Polydor ✦

1969: Velvet Underground Live, Vol. 1 / 1974 / Mercury ✦✦✦✦✦
Originally a double album and released in two volumes with added songs on CD, *1969: Velvet Underground Live* is a stunning document of the Reed, Yule, Morrison, Tucker edition of The Velvets at their pinnacle. Recorded privately in Texas and San Francisco, The Velvets play extended, intensely driven out and out versions of songs from their first three albums as well as then unreleased material such as "Ocean," "Real Good Time Together," and "Sweet Bonnie Brown." *—Rob Bowman*

1969: Velvet Underground Live, Vol. 2 / 1974 / Mercury ✦✦✦✦✦

☆ **VU** / 1985 / Verve ✦✦✦✦✦
Composed principally of songs that would have appeared on The Velvets' unreleased fourth MGM album, this is only slightly less impressive than their first three LPs, striking a balance between the searing pre-punk of their first two efforts and the calm eloquence of the third. "Lisa Says," "Ocean," and "Stephanie Says" are some of Reed's greatest ballads; "I Can't Stand It" is one of The Velvets' toughest and best conventional hard rock songs. Some of the other tunes are slight (if engaging) in comparison with The Velvets' prime work. Many of the tracks were re-recorded by Reed on his early solo albums, and in every instance, The Velvets' versions are better. *—Richie Unterberger*

Another View / 1986 / Verve ✦✦✦

● **The Best of the Velvet Underground** / Sep. 1989 / Verve ✦✦✦✦✦
The Best of the Velvet Underground: Words and Music of Lou Reed is a 15-track summary of The Velvets' career, borrowing heavily from the debut (six tracks) and featuring "Sweet Jane" and "Rock & Roll," licensed from Atlantic. *—William Ruhlmann*

Live MCMXCIII / Oct. 26, 1993 / Warner Brothers ✦✦

☆ **Peel Slowly and See** / Sep. 26, 1995 / Polydor/Chronicles ✦✦✦✦✦
Does this five-CD box set feature an abundance of essential material? Certainly. It has all four of the studio albums released by the Lou Reed-led lineup, and a wealth of previously unreleased goodies. Is it an essential purchase? That depends on your level of fanaticism. Most serious Velvets fans have all four of the core studio albums already (although the third, self-titled LP is presented in its muffled, so-called "closet" mix), and will be most interested in the previously unavailable recordings, which do hold considerable fascination. The entire first disc is devoted to a drummer-less 1965 rehearsal tape in John Cale's loft, with radically different, almost folky run-throughs of most of the important songs from their classic debut, as well as a song that only made it onto Nico's first LP ("Wrap Your Troubles in Dreams"), and one which makes its first appearance anywhere (the Dylanesque "Prominent Men"). Other big bonuses include no less than seven outtakes from *Loaded,* and other songs re-done by Reed on his early solo albums. And there are sundry other unreleased live and studio items, highlighted by a scorching live 1967 "Guess I'm Falling in Love" and the 1969 demo "Countess from Hong Kong." There are also highlights from *VU* and *Another View,* longer versions of *Loaded*'s "Sweet Jane" and "New Age," and an 80-page booklet. The thing is,

though, that virtually everyone who's interested in this material has already bought the four studio albums, sometimes several times over. A separate release of the two discs or so of truly new material would have been welcomed by the many fans who aren't interested in paying for a five-CD box of stuff when they already have well over half of it. But as a friend of mine is fond of saying, that eats into profit margins real fast. *—Richie Unterberger*

Loaded: Fully Loaded Edition / Feb. 18, 1997 / Rhino ✦✦✦✦✦

The Ventures

f. 1959, Tacoma, WA

Arranger / Surf, Instrumental Rock, Rock & Roll

Not the first but definitely the most popular rock instrumental combo, the Ventures scored several hit singles during the 1960s—most notably "Walk-Don't Run" and "Hawaii Five-O"—but made their name in the growing album market, covering hits of the day and organizing LPs linked thematically and musically. The band put their indelible stamp on each style of '60s music they covered, and they covered many—twist, country, pop, spy music, psychedelic, swamp, garage, TV themes. (In the '70s, the Ventures moved on to funk, disco, reggae, soft rock and Latin music.) And though the band's popularity in America virtually disappeared by the 1970s, their enormous contribution to pop culture was far from over; the Ventures soon became one of the most popular rock groups in the world, with dozens of albums recorded especially for the Japanese and European markets. They toured continually throughout the 1970s and '80s—selling 40 million records in Japan alone and influencing Japanese pop music of the time more than they had American music during the '60s. *—John Bush*

★ **Walk-Don't Run: The Best of the Ventures** / 1990 / EMI America ✦✦✦✦✦

If one looks hard, there are so many CDs out on the Ventures, covering just about every phase of their history, that it's almost impossible to keep track of which numbers appear in what versions on which disc (and that's not even counting some superb Japanese-issued concert videos), but this is still the single best introduction to their work that one can buy. Starting with their second single (and career-establishing hit), "Walk—Don't Run," the 29 tracks on this CD bookend their history from 1960 through 1969, including every chart entry and also significant albums tracks such as the psychedelic era "Underground Fire," all in excellent sound. Producer Ron Furmanek has remixed most of the cuts from the original multitracks, but he's done it true to the originals, with results that transcend the best vinyl copies of much of this material. Understandably, much of the material is weighted toward the early '60s, but the group's hits right up through "Hawaii Five-O" are represented, and Furmanek has even included a few short 1960s-vintage radio spots featuring the band as an extra bonus for fans. *—Bruce Eder*

The Verve

f. 1989, Wigan, Lancashire, England, **db.** Apr. 28, 1999

Group / Dream Pop, Space Rock, Neo-Psychedelia, Britpop, Shoegazing, Alternative Pop/Rock

Long acclaimed among the most innovative and spellbinding bands on the contemporary British pop scene, the Verve finally broke through to the mass international audience in 1997 with the instant classic "Bittersweet Symphony." By no stretch a study in overnight success, the group's rise was instead the culmination of a long, arduous journey which began at the dawn of the decade and went on to encompass a major breakup, lawsuits, and an extensive diet of narcotics; perfecting an oceanic sound fusing the exploratory vision of '60s-era psychedelia with the shimmering atmospherics of the shoegazer aesthetic, the Verve languished in relative obscurity while waiting for the rest of the music world to play catch-up, creating one of the most complex and rewarding bodies of work in modern rock & roll long before most listeners even learned of their existence—only to again fall apart at the peak of their success. Originally formed around vocalist Richard Ashcroft and guitarist Nick McCabe, the band scored with critics and the indie charts with their majestic debut LP, 1993's *A Storm in Heaven*. A lawsuit from the American jazz label also dubbed Verve forced the quartet to officially change their name to "The Verve," and after completing sessions for their 1995 follow-up *A Northern Soul*, Ashcroft exited. He quickly re-assembled the Verve a few weeks later, initially minus McCabe, though the guitarist came back to the fold in early 1997. The result, *Urban Hymns*, was their breakthrough LP, heralded by the smash singles "Bittersweet Symphony" and "The Drugs Don't Work." However, when McCabe pulled out of their 1998 US tour, the group suffered yet another blow, and after months of rumors they officially split the following spring. *—Jason Ankeny*

A Storm in Heaven / Jun. 21, 1993 / Vernon Yard ✦✦✦✦

Whereas future *Verve* masterpieces *A Northern Soul* and *Urban Hymns* would feature succinct song structures (for the most part) and instantly memorable verses and choruses, the group's 1993 full-length debut, *A Storm in Heaven*, was based on buoyant, extended psychedelic passages. Looking back today, it was an interesting and original musical direction, since at the time, angst-ridden Seattle bands (and their many copycats) were all the rage. While a few songs hint at the Verve's future penchant for composing pop gems ("Make It Till Monday," "Blue," "Butterfly"), many of the longer tracks are just as strong, especially the album's best track, the hauntingly beautiful "Already There." Also featured was the album-opening space rocker "Star Sail," the shifting moods of "Slide Away," the misty "Beautiful Mind," and the stark closer, "See You in the Next One (Have a Good Time)." A fine debut, *A Storm in Heaven* proved to be the important connection between the Verve's expansive early work (1992's self-titled EP) and their later worldwide pop hits. *—Greg Prato*

No Come Down / May 17, 1994 / Vernon Yard ✦✦✦

A Northern Soul / Jul. 3, 1995 / Vernon Yard ✦✦✦✦✦

Though shorn of the more overtly shoegazer-styled elements of their debut *A Storm in Heaven*, the Verve's sophomore effort *A Northern Soul* is no less epic in scope, forging a heavier, more traditionally psychedelic sound infused with a chaotic energy which mirrors the emotional upheaval at the heart of Richard Ashcroft's songs. Reportedly produced under the influence of excessive drug use, the album is harrowingly intense, its darkly hypnotic momentum steered by Nick McCabe's spiraling guitar leads and Ashcroft's incantatory vocals; tracks like the remarkable "On Your Own," "So It Goes," and the majestically morose "History" are searing evocations of isolation and desperation, soaring yet heartbreaking anthems of disillusionment and loss. *—Jason Ankeny*

● **Urban Hymns** / Sep. 30, 1997 / Virgin ✦✦✦✦✦

Not long after the release of *A Northern Soul*, the Verve imploded due to friction between vocalist Richard Ashcroft and guitarist Nick McCabe. It looked like the band had ended before reaching its full potential, which is part of the reason why their third album, *Urban Hymns*—recorded after the pair patched things up in late 1996—is so remarkable. Much of the record consists of songs Ashcroft had intended for a solo project or a new group, yet *Urban Hymns* unmistakably sounds like the work of a full band, with its sweeping, grandiose soundscapes and sense of purpose. The Verve have toned down their trancy, psychedelic excursions, yet haven't abandoned them—if anything, they sound more muscular than before, whether it's the trippy "Catching the Butterfly" or the pounding "Come On." These powerful, guitar-drenched rockers provide the context for Ashcroft's affecting, string-laden ballads, which give *Urban Hymns* its hurt. The majestic "Bitter Sweet Symphony" and the heartbreaking, country-tinged "The Drugs Don't Work" are an astonishing pair, two anthemic ballads that make the personal universal, thereby sounding like instant classics. They just are the tip of the iceberg—"Sonnet" is a lovely, surprisingly understated ballad, "The Rolling People" has a measured, electric power, and many others match their quality. Although it may run a bit too long for some tastes, *Urban Hymns* is a rich album that revitalizes rock traditions without ever seeming less than contemporary. It is the album the Verve have been striving to make since their formation, and it turns out to be worth all the wait. *—Stephen Thomas Erlewine*

The Vibrators

f. 1976

Group / British Punk, Punk

One of the great myths in rock & roll is that only serious, dedicated musicians can make great records; a philosophical tract dictating that great rock & roll is not the province of bandwagon jumpers, poseurs, fakes and commercially minded trend groupies. The reality is that great rock & roll can be made by anyone, even accidentally. Case in point, the Vibrators. If you saw a photograph of this "punk" band a few months before they signed a label deal with Columbia in 1976, you would have seen long hair, and bell-bottom trousers—they were bloody hippies! But, by the time they released their debut LP, *Pure Mania*, they had short hair, fake leopard skin pants, safety pins, cheap sunglasses, all the accoutrements a good born-again punk band needed. Did that make them inherently bad— Not really, a tad disingenuous perhaps, but no worse than a punk band (e.g., Generation X) that professed to being real punks all the while secretly harboring the desire of being as commercially viable as the dinosaur bands they purportedly loathed. Sure, *Pure Mania* is a fake though and through, but hating it for that reason alone makes you the boring old fart. Besides, the speedy guitars, irresistible hooks and snappy songs are infectious. *—John Dougan*

Pure Mania / 1977 / Columbia ✦✦✦✦✦

Were the Vibrators real punks— Maybe not, but then again, were the Stranglers— Or Eddie and the Hot Rods— Even more to the point, was Steve Jones— Plenty of rock careerists jumped onto the punk/new wave bandwagon in the wake of the Sex Pistols' success (and more than a few folks, like Jones, stumbled into the new movement by accident), but unlike most of them, the Vibrators took to the fast/loud/stripped down thing like ducks to water, and both Knox (aka Ian Carnarchan) and Pat Collier had a genius for writing short, punchy songs with sneering melody lines and gutsy guitar breaks. If the Vibrators were into punk as a musical rather than a sociopolitical movement, it's obvious that they liked the music very much, and on that level their debut album stands the test of time quite well. *Pure Mania* boasts a bit more polish (and less politics) than many of the albums from punk's first graduating class (such as *Damned Damned Damned* or *The Clash*), but if you're looking for a strong, satisfying shot of chugging four-square punk, cue up "Yeah Yeah Yeah," "No Heart," "Petrol," or "Wrecked on You" and you'll be thrown into a gleeful pogo frenzy. Maybe *Pure Mania* isn't purist's punk, but it's pure rock & roll, and there's nothing wrong with that. *—Mark Deming*

V2 / 1978 / Epic ✦✦✦

Batteries Included / 1980 / CBS ✦✦✦✦✦

The first of several Vibrators compilation albums, this one has the advantage of concentrating heavily on the group's first two albums (with the exception of a couple of bonus cuts). If you think punk was just the Sex Pistols and the Clash, then you're missing out on a lot of fun. And the title is quite funny, too. *—Alex Ogg*

Guilty / 1983 / Anagram ✦✦✦

Alaska 127 / 1984 / Ram ✦✦✦

The Vibrators' second album following their 1982 reunion. The title was taken from producer Pat Collier's studio, which had become their adopted home. It's actually a much better affair than its predecessor, *Guilty*. "Amphetamine Blue" starts things off and is typical of the 12 committed punk-pop efforts on display here. Sadly, there were precious few people prepared to take the Vibrators seriously the first time around; there were next to none now. *—Alex Ogg*

Fifth Amendment / 1985 / Ram ✦✦

Live / 1985 / FM/Revolver ✦✦✦

The Independent Punk Singles / 1996 / Anagram ✦✦✦✦

The Vibrators, much maligned, often wholly dismissed, were nevertheless one of the better U.K. punk bands. Above and beyond anything else, they released a series of great singles—the real marker and currency of punk rock, lest we forget it in this era of digital archiving. This CD, presented in a nice chronological package, contains all of the group's post-reunion work with Cherry Red subsidiary Anagram, which began with 1982's "Baby Baby." Some may not consider that their peak, but there's some good stuff here. *—Alex Ogg*

- **We Vibrate: The Best of the Vibrators** / Aug. 19, 1997 / Cleopatra ✦✦✦✦

Village People

f. 1977, New York, NY

Group / Disco

Part clever concept, part exaggerated camp act, the Village People were worldwide sensations during disco's heyday and keep reviving like the phoenix. Producer Jacques Morali in 1977 assembled a group designed to attract gay audiences while parodying (some claimed exploiting) that same constituency's stereotypes. Songwriters Phil Hurtt and Peter Whitehead were tabbed to compose songs with gay underpinnings, and roles and costumes were carefully selected; among them were a cowboy, biker, soldier, policeman, and construction worker complete with hard hat. The group clicked first in England with the single "San Francisco (You Got Me)" in 1977, then reaped stateside honors with "Macho Man" in 1978. "Y.M.C.A." and "In the Navy" were worldwide smashes, both peaking at number two on the pop charts. After two more successful singles, "Go West" and "Can't Stop the Music," the group's fortunes plummeted, in large part due to their participation in the ill-fated film also titled *Can't Stop the Music.* *—Ron Wynn*

- **The Best of the Village People** / Mar. 22, 1994 / Casablanca ✦✦✦✦✦

Casablanca's *The Best of the Village People* is nearly identical to Rhino's *Greatest Hits,* since it contains all of the big hits, plus a similar selection of club hits. This 14-track collection contains only one remix ("Y.M.C.A.," and which is also present in its original single version) and substitutes "Key West" for "Sodom and Gomorrah," and it also includes "In Hollywood (Everybody Is a Star)." These are such slight differences that the collection will be just as appealing as Rhino's to most fans, and both are first-rate retrospectives. *—Stephen Thomas Erlewine*

Gene Vincent (Vincent Eugene Craddock)

b. Feb. 11, 1935, Norfolk, VA, **d.** Oct. 12, 1971, Los Angeles, CA

Vocals / Rockabilly, Rock & Roll

Gene Vincent only had one really big hit, "Be Bop A Lula," which epitomized rockabilly at its prime in 1956 with its sharp guitar breaks, spare snare drums, fluttering echo, and breathless, sexy vocals. Yet his place as one of the great early rock and roll singers is secure, backed up by a wealth of fine smaller hits and non-hits that rate among the best rockabilly of all time. The leather-clad, limping, greasy-haired singer was also one of rock's original bad boys, lionized by romanticists of past and present generations attracted to his primitive, sometimes savage style and indomitable spirit. Vincent's backing unit the Blue Caps were one of the greatest rock bands of the '50s, anchored at first by the stunning silvery, faster-than-light guitar leads of Cliff Gallup. The slap-back echo of "Be-Bop-A-Lula," combined with Gene's swooping vocals, led many to mistake the singer for Elvis when the record first hit the airwaves in mid-1956, on its way to the Top Ten. Brilliant follow-ups like "Race with the Devil," "Bluejean Bop," and "B-I-Bickey, Bi, Bo-Bo-Go" failed to click in nearly as big a way, although these too are emblematic of rockabilly at its most exuberant and powerful. By the end of 1956, the Blue Caps were beginning to undergo the first of constant personnel changes that would continue throughout the '50s, the most crucial loss being the departure of Gallup. The 35 or so tracks he cut with the band—many of which showed up only on albums or B-sides—were unquestionably Vincent's greatest work, as his subsequent recordings would never again capture their pristine clarity and uninhibited spontaneity. *—Richie Unterberger*

The Capitol Years 1956-63 / 1987 / Charly ✦✦✦✦✦

While Vincent recorded a fair number of overlooked gems during his prime, he also cut a greater number of uninspired tracks. This lavishly packaged and exhaustively annotated ten-album set inadvertently charts the rapidly plummeting quality of his recordings, even as it unearths worthy obscurities. It does manage to gather all of his classic 1956 sessions with guitarist Cliff Gallup in the same place, but Gene's subsequent efforts could have easily been boiled down to a supplementary disc or two. *—Richie Unterberger*

★ **The Screaming End: The Best of Gene Vincent** / Jan. 21, 1997 / Razor & Tie ✦✦✦✦✦

The Screaming End: The Best Of Gene Vincent & His Blue Caps contains 20 of Gene Vincent's very best songs, including all of his hit singles ("Be Bop A Lula," "Race With the Devil," "Lotta Lovin'," "Wear My Ring," "Dance to the Bop") and several lesser-known but equally exciting singles and album tracks ("Bluejean Bop," "Crazy Legs," "Cruisin'," "Cat Man," "Who Slapped John," "Jump Back, Honey, Jump Back," "B-I-Bickey Bi, Bo-Bo Go," "Red Blue Jeans & a Ponytail"). *The Screaming End* may have one less song than *Capitol Collectors Series,* but it contains a stronger selection of material and the original mixes, plus a more infectious, listenable sequence, making it the defintiive single-disc overview of this rock & roll pioneer. *—Stephen Thomas Erlewine*

Violent Femmes

f. 1982, Milwaukee, WI

Group / College Rock, Post-Punk, New Wave, Alternative Pop/Rock

The textbook American cult band of the 1980s, the Violent Femmes captured the essence of teen angst with remarkable precision; raw and jittery, the trio's music found little commercial success but nonetheless emerged as the soundtrack for the lives of troubled adolescents the world over. The Violent Femmes formed in Milwaukee, WI in the early '80s, and comprised singer/guitarist Gordon Gano, bassist Brian Ritchie and percussionist Victor DeLorenzo; Ritchie originated the band's oxymoronic name, adopting the word "femme" from the Milwaukee area's slang for wimps. The trio signed to Slash and issued their self-titled 1983 debut, a melodic folk-punk collection which struck an obvious chord with young listeners who felt a strong connection to bitter, frustrated songs like "Blister in the Sun," "Kiss Off" and "Add It Up." Though never a chart hit, the album remained a rite of passage for succeeding generations of teen outsiders, and after close to a decade in release it achieved platinum status. With 1984's *Hallowed Ground,* Gano's lyrics began to reflect his devout Baptist upbringing, while the group's music approached more traditional folk and country structures, 1986's *The Blind Leading the Naked* advanced towards a more mainstream sound; a cover of the T. Rex chestnut "Children of the Revolution" even became a minor hit. *—Jason Ankeny*

★ **Violent Femmes** / 1983 / Slash/Rhino ✦✦✦✦✦

One of the most distinctive records of the early alternative movement and an enduring cult classic, *Violent Femmes* weds the geeky, child-man persona of Jonathan Richman and the tense, jittery, hyperactive feel of new wave, as well as the band's own raw, amateurish acoustic folk-rock. The music also owes something to the Modern Lovers' minimalism, but powered by Brian Ritchie's busy acoustic bass riffing and the urgency and wild abandon of punk rock, the Femmes forged a sound all their own. The main reason *Violent Femmes* became the preferred soundtrack for the lives of many an angst-ridden teenager is lead singer and songwriter Gordon Gano. Naive and childish one minute, bitterly frustrated and rebellious the next, Gano's vocals perfectly captured the contradictions of adolescence and the difficulties of making the transition to adulthood. Clever lyrical flourishes didn't hurt either; while "Blister In the Sun" has deservedly become a standard, songs like "Kiss Off," with its "count-up" section, "Add It Up," with its pleading "Why can't I get just one..." series of couplets, and "Gimme the Car"'s use of a guitar bend in place of the word "f**k," ensured that Gano's intensely vulnerable confessions of despair and maladjustment came off as catchy and humorous as well. Even if the songwriting slips a bit on occasion, Gano's personality keeps the music engaging and compelling without overindulging in his seemingly willful naiveté. For the remainder of their career, the group would only approach this level in isolated moments. *—Steve Huey*

Hallowed Ground / 1985 / Slash/Rhino ✦✦✦

Though mistaken for a parody when it was released, *Hallowed Ground* features Gordon Gano's serious Christian convictions. The teenage angst is pushed aside on this more mature effort based, for the most part, in traditional American folk—of course, it's slightly skewed. *—Chris Woodstra*

Blind Leading the Naked / 1986 / Slash ✦✦✦✦✦

A more mainstream effort courtesy of producer Jerry Harrison (Talking Heads). Gano returns to his troubled teen persona and the band rocks harder than on the previous two releases. A nice cover of the T-Rex classic "Children of the Revolution" and the yearning "I Held Her in My Arms," complete with a horn section, are highlights. *—Chris Woodstra*

3 / 1989 / Slash ✦✦

Debacle: The First Decade / 1991 / Slash ✦✦✦✦✦

Why Do Birds Sing? / Apr. 30, 1991 / Reprise ✦✦✦

After a several year absence, the Femmes make a comeback of sorts with the charming *Why Do Birds Sing?* Returning to their street-busking roots, the band plays stripped-back acoustic songs as a three piece. Though they can't fight the fact that they have grown up, the songs show that they can still have fun. *—Chris Woodstra*

Add It Up (1981-1993) / Sep. 14, 1993 / Slash/Reprise ✦✦✦✦✦

Add It Up is not quite the definitive Violent Femmes compilation one might hope for, even if it does feature 23 tracks and adds essential later items missing from their first comp, *Debacle: The First Decade.* There are several charming rarities to hook dedicated fans, who will likely find several favorites missing (perhaps another song or two could have been substituted for the between-song bits). The group's self-titled debut does a better job of encapsulating why they were important, and remains the first Femmes album to buy; besides, no compilation that includes live versions of "Kiss Off" and "Add It Up" in place of the original studio cuts can claim to be definitive. However, even casual fans who enjoyed *Violent Femmes* will find post-debut songs like "American Music" and "I Held Her In My Arms" to be essential, so even if *Add It Up* is a little too imperfect to be a necessary first purchase, it's definitely a necessary second purchase. Unless you're a diehard fan, it will likely be the only other Violent Femmes disc you'll need. *—Steve Huey*

New Times / May 17, 1994 / Elektra ✦✦

Rock!!!!! / Jun. 30, 1998 / Cold Front ✦✦

Viva Wisconsin / Nov. 23, 1999 / Beyond ✦✦✦✦

Freak Magnet / Feb. 22, 2000 / Beyond ✦✦✦

Rufus Wainwright

Vocals / Chamber Pop, Adult Alternative Pop/Rock, Singer/Songwriter

A singer/songwriter whose lush, theatrical pop harked back to the traditions of Tin Pan Alley, cabaret and even opera, Rufus Wainwright was the son of folk music luminaries Loudon Wainwright III and Kate McGarrigle. Beginning his piano studies at age six, by thirteen he was touring with his mother, aunt Anna and his sister Martha in a group billed as the McGarrigle Sisters and Family; a year later, Wainwright was nominated for a Juno (the Canadian equivalent of a Grammy) as Most Promising Young Artist, while his "I'm A-Runnin'" was concurrently nominated for a Genie (the Canadian countepart to an Oscar) for Best Song in a Film. After attending the prestigious Millbrook School in upstate New York, he eventually turned away from classical performance towards pop and rock. Becoming a fixture on the Montreal club circuit, Wainwright soon cut a series of demos with producer Pierre Marchand; Loudon Wainwright III then passed a copy of the tape to friend Van Dyke Parks, who in turn handed it on to DreamWorks exec Lenny Waronker. The label signed him soon after, resulting in the release of *Rufus Wainwright* during the spring of 1998. *—Jason Ankeny*

- **Rufus Wainwright** / May 19, 1998 / DreamWorks ✦✦✦✦✦

What separates Rufus Wainwright and the other second-generation singers who sprang up at the same time (Sean Lennon, Emma Townshend and Chris Stills the most notable among them) is that Wainwright deserves to be heard regardless of his family tree; in fact, the issue of his parentage is ultimately as immaterial as that of his sexuality—this self-titled debut cares little for the rock clichés of an earlier generation, instead heralding the arrival of a unique and compelling voice steeped most solidly in the traditions of cabaret. Like his folks, Loudon Wainwright III and Kate McGarrigle, he's a superb songwriter, with a knack for elegantly rolling piano melodies and poignantly romantic lyrics; while the appearance of Van Dyke Parks and his trademark orchestral arrangements hints at an affinity for the pop classicism of Brian Wilson or Randy Newman, the vocals come straight out of opera, and although Wainwright is unlikely to be starring in *La Boheme* anytime soon, he conveys the kind of honest emotion sorely lacking in the ironic posing of many of his contemporaries. Maybe the kids are alright after all. *—Jason Ankeny*

Tom Waits

b. Dec. 7, 1949, Pomona, CA

Vocals, Harmonium, Piano, Guitar, Organ / College Rock, Album Rock, Experimental Rock, Beat Poetry, Singer/Songwriter

In the 1970s, Tom Waits combined a lyrical focus on desperate, lowlife characters with a persona that seemed to embody the same lifestyle, which he sang about in a raspy, gravelly voice. From the '80s on, his work became increasingly theatrical as he moved into acting and composing. Waits' formal recording debut came with *Closing Time* (1973) on Asylum Records, an album that contained "Ol' 55," which was covered by labelmates the Eagles. Waits attracted critical acclaim and a cult audience for his subsequent late-'70s albums, *The Heart of Saturday Night, Small Change, Foreign Affairs* and *Heart Attack and Vine*. His music and persona proved highly cinematic, and starting in 1978 he launched parallel careers as an actor and as a composer of movie music. After moving to Island, Waits made 1983's *Swordfishtrombones*, which found him experimenting with horns and percussion and using more unusual recording techniques. In 1985, he released *Rain Dogs*. An album based on his theatrical debut, *Frank's Wild Years*, was released in 1987. In 1992, he scored the film *Night on Earth* and released the album *Bone Machine*, which won a Grammy Award for Best Alternative Music Album. In 1993, he released *The Black Rider*, the recording of a musical he had co-written with Beat novelist William Burroughs. A long absence from recording ended in 1999 with the release of *Mule Variations*. *— William Ruhlmann*

● **Closing Time** / 1973 / Asylum ✦✦✦✦✦

Tom Waits' debut album was a minor-key masterpiece filled with songs of late-night loneliness. Within the apparently narrow range of the cocktail bar pianistics and muttered vocals, Waits and producer Jerry Yester managed a suprisingly broad collection of styles, from the jazzy "Virginia Avenue" to the uptempo funk of "Ice Cream Man" and from the acoustic guitar folkiness of "I Hope That I Don't Fall in Love with You" to the saloon song "Midnight Lullaby," which would have been a perfect addition to the repertoires of Frank Sinatra or Tony Bennett. Waits' entire musical approach was stylized, of course, and at times derivative—"Lonely" borrowed a little too much from Randy Newman's "I Think It's Going to Rain Today"—and his lovelorn lyrics could be sentimental without being penetrating. But he also had a gift for gently rolling pop melodies, and he could come up with striking, original scenarios, as on the best songs, "Ol' 55" and "Martha," which Yester discreetly augmented with strings. *Closing Time* announced the arrival of a talented songwriter whose self-conscious melancholy could be surprisingly moving. *— William Ruhlmann*

The Heart of Saturday Night / 1974 / Asylum ✦✦✦

If *Closing Time*, Tom Waits' debut album, consisted of love songs set in a late-night world of bars and neon signs, its follow-up, *The Heart of Saturday Night*, largely dispensed with the romance in favor of poetic depictions of the same setting. On "Diamonds on My Windshield" and "The Ghosts of Saturday Night," Waits didn't even sing, instead reciting his verse rhythmically against bass and drums like a Beat hipster. Musically, the album contained the same mixture of folk, blues, and jazz as its predecessor, with producer Bones Howe occasionally bringing in an orchestra to underscore the loping melodies. Waits' songs were sometimes sketchier in addition to being more impersonal, but "(Looking For) The Heart of Saturday Night" and "Semi Suite" were the equal of anything on *Closing Time*. Still, with lines such as "... the clouds are like headlines / Upon a new front page sky" and references to "a 24-hour moon" and "champagne stars," Waits' imagery was beginning to get florid, and in material this stylized, the danger of self-parody was always present. *— William Ruhlmann*

Nighthawks at the Diner / Oct. 1975 / Asylum ✦✦✦

For his third album, Tom Waits set up a nightclub in the studio, invited an audience, and cut a 70-minute, two-LP set of new songs. It was an appropriate format for compositions that dealt even more graphically and, for the first time, humorously, with Waits' late-night world of bars and diners. The love lyrics of his debut album had long since given way to a comic lonely guy stance glimpsed in "Emotional Weather Report" and "Better off Without a Wife." But what really mattered was the elaborate scene-setting of songs like the six-and-a-half-minute "Spare Parts," the seven-and-a-half-minute "Putnam County," and especially the 11Ω-minute "Nighthawk Postcards" that were essentially poetry recitations with jazz backing. Waits was a colorful tour guide of midnight L.A., raving over a swinging rhythm section of Jim Hughart (bass) and Bill Goodwin (drums), with Pete Christlieb wailing away on tenor sax between paragraphs and Mike Melvoin trading off with Waits on piano runs. You could call it overdone, but then, this kind of material made its impact through an accumulation of miscellaneous detail, and who was to say how much was too much? *— William Ruhlmann*

Small Change / Oct. 1976 / Asylum ✦✦✦✦✦

The fourth release in Tom Waits' series of skid-row travelogues, *Small Change* proved to be the archetypal album of his '70s work. A jazz trio comprising tenor sax player Lew Tabackin, bassist Jim Hughart, and drummer Shelly Manne, plus an occasional string section, backed Waits and his piano on songs steeped in whiskey and atmosphere in which he alternately sang in his broken-beaned drunk's voice (now deeper and overtly influenced by Louis Armstrong) and recited jazzy poetry. It was as if Waits was determined to combine the Humphrey Bogart and Dooley Wilson characters from *Casablanca* with a dash of *On the Road's* Dean Moriarty to illuminate a dark world of bars and all-night diners. Of course, he'd been in that world before, but in songs like "The Piano Has Been Drinking" and "Bad Liver and a Broken Heart," Waits gave it its clearest expression. *Small Change* is not Tom Waits' best album. It is, like most of the albums he made in the '70s, uneven, probably because he was putting out one a year and didn't have time to come up with enough first-rate material. But it is the most obvious and characteristic of his albums for Asylum Records. If you like it, you also will like the ones before and after it; otherwise, you're not Tom Waits' kind of listener. *— William Ruhlmann*

Foreign Affairs / Sep. 1977 / Asylum ✦✦✦

Blue Valentine / Oct. 1978 / Asylum ✦✦✦

Heartattack and Vine / Sep. 1980 / Asylum ✦✦✦

Heartattack and Vine, Tom Waits' first album in two years and his last of seven for Asylum Records, was a transitional album, with tracks like the rhythm-heavy title song and "'Til the Money Runs Out" foreshadowing the sonic experiments of the Island albums, while piano with orchestra tracks like "Saving All My Love for You" and "On the Nickel" (written as a motion-picture title tune) harked back to Waits' Randy Newman-influenced early days. It was just as well that Waits never entirely gave up on the ballad material; "Jersey Girl," a Drifters-style song, was a winner, and it was appropriated by Bruce Springsteen on his 1981 tour. Also, at least at this point, the rougher tunes all tended to sound the same. *— William Ruhlmann*

☆ **Swordfishtrombones** / Sep. 1983 / Island ✦✦✦✦✦

Between the release of *Heartattack and Vine* in 1980 and *Swordfishtrombones* in 1983, Tom Waits got rid of his manager, his producer, and his record company. And he drastically altered a musical approach that had become as dependable as it was unexciting. *Swordfishtrombones* had none of the strings and much less of the piano work that Waits' previous albums had employed; instead, the dominant sounds on the record were low-pitched horns, bass instruments, and percussion, set in spare, close-miked arrangements (most of them by Waits) that sometimes were better described as "soundscapes." Lyrically, Waits' tales of the drunken and the lovelorn had been replaced by surreal accounts of people who burned down their homes and of Australian towns bypassed by the railroad—a world (not just a neighborhood) of misfits now had his attention. The music could be primitive, moving to odd time signatures, while Waits alternately howled and wheezed in his gravelly bass voice. He seemed to have moved on from Hoagy Carmichael and Louis Armstrong to Kurt Weill and Howlin' Wolf (as impersonated by Captain Beetheart). Waits seems to have had trouble interesting a record label in the album, which was cut 13 months before it was released, but when it appeared rock critics predictably raved: After all, it sounded weird and it didn't have a chance of selling. Actually, it did make the bottom of the bestseller charts, like most of Waits' albums, and, now that he was with a label based in Europe, even charted there. Artistically, *Swordfishtrombones* marked an evolution of which Waits had not seemed capable (though there were hints of this sound on his last two Asylum albums), and in career terms it re-invented him. *— William Ruhlmann*

★ **Rain Dogs** / Aug. 1985 / Island ✦✦✦✦✦

With its jarring rhythms and unusual instrumentation—marimba, accordion, various percussion—as well as its frequently surreal lyrics, *Rain Dogs* was very much a follow-up to *Swordfishtrombones*, which is to say that it sounded for the most part like *The Threepenny Opera* being sung by Howlin' Wolf. The chief musical difference was the introduction of guitarist Marc Ribot, who added his noisy leads to the general cacophony. But *Rain Dogs* was sprawling where its predecessor had been focused: Waits' lyrics here sometimes were imaginative to the point of obscurity, seemingly chosen to fit the rhythms rather than for sense. In the course of 19 tracks and 54 minutes, Waits sometimes went back to the more conventional music of his earlier records, which seemed like a retreat, though such tracks as the catchy "Hang Down Your Head," "Time," and especially "Downtown Train" (frequently covered and finally turned into a Top Ten hit by Rod Stewart five years later) provided some relief as well as variety. *Rain Dogs* could not surprise as *Swordfishtrombones* had, and in his attempt to continue in the direction suggested by that album, Waits occasionally bordered on the chaotic (which may only be to say that, like most of his records, this one was uneven). But much of the music matched the earlier album, and there was so much of it that that was enough to qualify *Rain Dogs* as one of Waits' better albums. *— William Ruhlmann*

Frank's Wild Years / Aug. 1987 / Island ✦✦✦✦

Tom Waits wrote a song called "Frank's Wild Years" for his 1983 *Swordfishtrombones* album, then used the title (minus its apostrophe) for a musical play he wrote with his wife, Kathleen Brennan, and toured with in 1986. The *Franks Wild Years* album, drawn from the show, is subtitled, "un operachi romantico in two acts," though the songs themselves do not carry the plot. Rather, this is just the third installment in Waits' eccentric series of Island Records albums in which he seems most inspired by German art song and carnival music, presenting songs in spare, stripped-down arrangements consisting of instruments like marimba, baritone horn, and pump organ and singing in a strained voice that has been artificially compressed and distorted. The songs themselves often are conventional romantic vignettes, or would be minus the oddities of instrumentation, arrangement, and performance. For example, "Innocent When You Dream," a song of disappointment in love and friendship, has a winning melody, but it is played in a seesaw arrangement of pump organ, bass, violin, and piano, and Waits sings it like an enraged drunk. (He points up the arbitrary nature of the arrangements by repeating "Straight to the Top," done as a demented rhumba in Act I, as a Vegas-style Frank Sinatra swing tune in Act II.) The result on record may not be theatrical, exactly, but it certainly is affected. It also has the quality of an inside joke that listeners are not being let in on. *— William Ruhlmann*

Big Time / Sep. 1988 / Island ✦✦✦

The Early Years / Jul. 1991 / Bizarre/Straight ✦✦✦✦

Night on Earth / Apr. 1992 / Island ✦✦

Bone Machine / Aug. 1992 / Island ✦✦✦✦✦

Perhaps Tom Waits' most cohesive album, *Bone Machine* is a morbid, sinister nightmare, one that applied the quirks of his experimental '80s classics to stunningly evocative—and often harrowing—effect. In keeping with the title's grotesque image of the human body, *Bone Ma-*

chine is obsessed with decay and mortality, the ease with which earthly existence can be destroyed. The arrangements are accordingly stripped of all excess flesh; the very few, often non-traditional instruments float in distinct separation over the clanking junkyard percussion that dominates the record. It's a chilling, primal sound made all the more otherworldly (or, perhaps, underworldly) by Waits' raspy falsetto and often-distorted roars and growls. Matching that evocative power is Waits' songwriting, which is arguably the most consistently focused it's ever been. Rich in strange and extraordinarily vivid imagery, many of Waits' tales and musings are spun against an imposing backdrop of apocalyptic natural fury, underlining the insignificance of his subjects and their universally impending doom. Death is seen as freedom for the spirit, an escape from the dread and suffering of life in this world—which he paints as hellishly bleak, full of murder, suicide, and corruption. The chugging, oddly bouncy beats of the more uptempo numbers makes them even more disturbing—there's a detached nonchalance beneath the horrific visions. Even the narrator of the catchy, playful "I Don't Wanna Grow Up" seems hopeless in this context, but that song paves the way for the closer "That Feel," an ode to the endurance of the human soul (with ultimate survivor Keith Richards on harmony vocals). The more upbeat ending hardly dispels the cloud of doom hanging over the rest of *Bone Machine*, but it does give the listener a gentler escape from that terrifying sonic world. All of it adds up to Waits' most affecting and powerful recording, even if it isn't his most accessible. *—Steve Huey*

The Early Years, Vol. 2 / Feb. 1993 / Bizarre/Straight ✦✦✦✦✦

The Black Rider / Nov. 2, 1993 / Polygram ✦✦

Beautiful Maladies: The Island Years / Jun. 16, 1998 / Island ✦✦✦

Mule Variations / Apr. 20, 1999 / Epitaph ✦✦✦✦

The Walker Brothers

f. 1964, Los Angeles, CA, **db.** 1967

Group / Baroque Pop, Experimental Rock, Blue-Eyed Soul, Soft Rock, British Invasion, Pop

They weren't British, they weren't brothers, and their real names weren't Walker, but Californians Scott Engel, John Maus, and Gary Leeds were briefly huge stars in England at the peak of the British Invasion. With surprising swiftness, they hit the top of the British charts with "Make It Easy on Yourself" in 1965, and "The Sun Ain't Gonna Shine Any More" the following year. While the Walkers looked the part of British Invaders with their shaggy moptops, in fact they were far more pop than rock and rarely played on their records. They favored orchestrated ballads that were a studied attempt to emulate the success of another brother act who weren't really brothers—the Righteous Brothers. Not quite as soulful, lead singer Scott Walker's deep croon wasn't chopped liver by any means, although it betrayed strong debts to non-rock vocalists like Tony Bennett and Frank Sinatra. In the intensely competitive days of 1967, the Walkers' brand of pop suddenly become passé, and the group disbanded in the face of diminishing success and Scott's increasingly fruitful solo career. Scott ran off a series of Top Ten British solo albums in the late '60s, which have attracted a sizable cult. The Walkers reunited for a while in the mid-'70s, which produced a final British hit ("No Regrets") but disappointing music. *—Richie Unterberger*

Introducing the Walker Brothers / 1965 / Smash ✦✦✦

Take It Easy with the Walker Brothers / 1965 / Fontana ✦✦✦✦✦

The track listing for the Walkers' first British album is similar to the one for their debut American LP (*Introducing the Walker Brothers*), except that it's missing their first single ("Pretty Girls Everywhere"/"Doin' the Jerk") and "My Ship Is Coming In," and adds three cuts not on the U.S. release. As it happens, these three tracks are worth having, particularly the David Gates-penned ballad "The Girl I Lost in the Rain" and "First Love Never Dies," another son-of-Righteous Brothers epic that would have made a reasonable single. The CD reissue is also much preferable to the American LP since it adds eight bonus cuts from the time, including the singles "Love Her" and "My Ship Is Coming In" and their B-sides, as well as the 1966 EP *I Need You*. A couple of the EP tracks are very strong: "Young Man Cried," another booming ballad with Spectoresque production, was one of Scott Walker's first good compositions (co-written with producer John Franz), and "Looking for Me" is a fine dramatic and little-known early Randy Newman song. Unfortunately "Pretty Girls Everywhere" and "Doin' the Jerk" weren't included on this (or any of the other Walker Brothers CD reissues) as bonus tracks; for those you'll still need to look for *Introducing the Walker Brothers*. *—Richie Unterberger*

Portrait / 1966 / Fontana ✦✦✦

Images / 1967 / Fontana ✦✦✦

The Walker Brothers' third and final album of the 1960s was as wildly uneven as their other pair. Affecting pop/rock ballads and operatic crooner vehicles were interspersed with absolutely inappropriate up-tempo blue-eyed soul (always a weak point for the group) and rock covers; the lugubrious reading of "Blueberry Hill" could be the worst track cut by the trio in the '60s. However, Scott Walker's songwriting and singing exhibited a growth that foreshadowed some of the more ambitious aspects of his early solo albums. The almost classical-sounding "Orpheus" was a standout in this arena, and his "Genevieve" was a fine ballad reflecting the encroaching influence of Jacques Brel. "Experience" was a real oddity, with a German oom-pah-like arrangement backing Scott's exhortation "here's to the people who live in a shell"; he also digs into Michel Legrand's "Once Upon a Summertime" and "I Will Wait for You." The gentle John Walker-written and sung "I Can't Let It Happen to You" is one of the Walker Brothers' best songs, and undoubtedly the best thing John Walker contributed to their records. The CD reissue adds the four tracks from their 1967 singles, including their covers of "Stay With Me Baby" and "Walking in the Rain," and a good overlooked Scott Walker-penned B-side, "Turn Out the Moon." *—Richie Unterberger*

No Regrets / 1975 / Columbia ✦✦✦

Lines / 1977 / Columbia ✦✦

Nite Flights / 1978 / Epic ✦✦✦

The difference between the numbing *Lines* and *Nite Flights* is startling. Between the two records, Scott Walker decided to begin writing again, and his new songs ignored all the conventional song structures of pop/rock. With "Shutout," "Fat Mama Kick," "Nite Flight," and the chilling "The Electrician," Walker created a quartet of haunting songs with eerie, electronic arrangements and cryptic, evocative lyrics. It was a far cry from the bland MOR of the Walker Brothers' two reunion albums. John Maus and Gary Leeds sensed this, so they tried to write songs that were just as disturbing as Scott's, but they had no idea how to make titles like "Disciples of Death," "The Fury and the Fire," "Den Haague," and "Child of Flames" into real songs or how to venture into new sonic territory; they simply made their signature folk-pop a little darker. As a result, *Nite Flights* isn't as good as it could have been, suffering from a full side of bad material, but Scott Walker's songs are essential and represent a remarkable artistic comeback. *—Stephen Thomas Erlewine*

● **After the Lights Go Out: The Best of 1965-1967** / 1990 / Fontana ✦✦✦✦✦

20 of their best songs, including all of their hit singles. On original compositions like "Mrs. Murphy," "Archangel," "Orpheus," and "Deadlier Than The Male," Scott Walker unveils the disturbed visions that would characterize his solo work, and John Walker's "Saddest Night In The World" and "I Can't Let It Happen To You" display a solid writing talent that he was sadly unable to develop into a solo career of his own. *—Richie Unterberger*

Junior Walker (Autry DeWalt II)

b. 1942, Blytheville, AR

Vocals, Saxophone / Pop-Soul, Motown, Rock & Roll, Soul

Of all the great musicians who played on scores of Motown records, none of them got label credit, much less a chance to bask in the spotlight. The lone exception was Junior Walker (born Audrey Dewalt), whose tenor sax wailings were made up of equal parts Illinois Jacquet high-note shrieks, Coleman Hawkins growls, and pure Midwest soul. Never much of a vocalist, Walker nonetheless scored hits with his rough-grained chops, though the sax solos remained the definite focal point. Highly influential on the Tom Scott/David Sanborn crowd, Walker should be close to the top of any list of rock & roll's great tenor saxophonists. *—Cub Koda*

Nothing But Soul: the Singles / 1994 / Motown ✦✦✦✦✦

This 40-song double CD includes virtually every Walker track of significance, and then some. Walker is a great player and hits a great groove, but that groove can get tiring over the course of several dozen tracks, especially the similar-sounding early instrumental cuts. Also, the post-'60s selections that take up much of disc two are hampered by material that is inferior to the best output of his '60s heyday. Excellent package and liner notes, but most listeners should be satisfied with the single-disc *Greatest Hits*, leaving this one for the collectors and specialists. *—Richie Unterberger*

● **The Ultimate Collection** / Oct. 7, 1997 / Motown ✦✦✦✦✦

The Ultimate Collection nearly lives up to its billing, featuring 25 tracks on a single disc, including all of Junior Walker & the All Stars' Top Ten pop and R&B hits ("Shotgun," "Do the Boomerang," "Shake and Fingerpop," "Cleo's Back," "(I'm A) Road Runner," "How Sweet It Is (To Be Loved By You)," "Come See About Me," "Hip City, Pt. 2," "What Does It Take (To Win Your Love)," "These Eyes," "Gotta Hold On To This Feeling," "Do You See My Love (For You Growing)," "Walk in the Night"). For most casual fans, those who just want the hits, this will be the definitive collection. *—Stephen Thomas Erlewine*

Scott Walker (Noel Scott Engel)

b. Jan. 9, 1943, Hamilton, OH

Vocals / Baroque Pop, Experimental Rock, Soft Rock, Pop, Avant-Garde

One of the most enigmatic figures in rock history, Scott Walker exited the Walker Brothers in 1967 to launch a hugely successful solo career in Britain with a unique blend of orchestrated, almost MOR arrangements with idiosyncratic and morose lyrics. At the height of psychedelia, Walker openly looked to crooners like Sinatra, Jack Jones, and Tony Bennett for inspiration, and to Jacques Brel for much of his material. None of those balladeers, however, would have sung about the oddball subjects—prostitutes, transvestites, suicidal brooders, plagues, and Joseph Stalin—that populated Walker's songs. His first four albums hit the Top Ten in the U.K.—his second, in fact, reached number one in 1968, in the midst of the hippie era. By the time of 1969's *Scott 4*, the singer was writing all of his material. Although this was perhaps his finest album, it was a commercial disappointment, and unfortunately discouraged him from relying entirely upon his own material on subsequent releases. After a long period of hibernation, he emerged with an album in 1984, *Climate of Hunter*, which drew critical raves for a minimalistic, trance-like ambience that showed him keeping abreast of cutting-edge '80s rock trends. This notoriously reclusive figure, who has rarely been interviewed or even seen in public since his days of stardom, emerged from hibernation in 1995 with a new album, *Tilt*. *—Richie Unterberger*

Scott / 1967 / Fontana ✦✦✦✦✦

Scott Walker's success as a teen idol singer of Spectorish ballads with the Walker Brothers in no way prepared listeners for the mordant, despairing lyrics of his solo debut. To compound the surprise, he does his best to imitate the vocal girth of Tony Bennett and Frank Sinatra on this mix of original tunes and covers, which also features sweeping, bloated orchestral arrangements. It was hardly rock, and pop of a most oddball sort, but it found a surprisingly large audience—in Britain, anyway, where it reached the Top Three in 1967. Poke behind the velvet curtain of the languid MOR arrangements, and one finds a surprisingly literate existentialist at the helm of these proceedings. His lyrical nuances were probably lost on his audience of predominately teenage girls, though they've earned him a small cult audience that endures to this day. Besides presenting three of his own compositions, Walker covers tunes by Weill/Mann, Tim Hardin, and Andre & Dory Previn on this album, as well as three songs by his favorite writer, Jacques Brel. Highlights include his exquisitely anguished rendition of Brel's classic "Amsterdam" and his dramatic cover of the early-'60s Toni Fisher pop ballad "The Big Hurt." *—Richie Unterberger*

Scott 2 / 1968 / Fontana ✦✦✦✦✦

Although Walker's second album was his biggest commercial success, actually reaching number one in Britain, it was not his greatest artistic triumph. His taste remains eclectic, encompassing Bacharach/David, Tim Hardin, and of course his main man Jacques Brel (who is covered three times on this album). And his own songwriting efforts hold their own in this esteemed company. "The Girls From the Streets" and "Plastic Palace People" show an uncommonly ambitious lyricist cloaked behind the over-the-top, schmaltzy orchestral arrangements, one more interested in examining the seamy underside of glamour and romance than celebrating its glitter. The Brel tune "Next" must have lifted a few teenage mums' eyebrows with its not-so-hidden hints of homosexuality and abuse. Another Brel tune, "The Girl and the Dogs," is less controversial, but hardly less nasty in its jaded view of romance. Some of the material is not nearly as memorable, however, and the over-the-top show ballad production can get overbearing. The album included his first Top 20 U.K. hit, "Jackie." *—Richie Unterberger*

Scott 3 / 1969 / Fontana ♦♦♦
Scott Walker's final British Top Ten album was the first to be dominated by his own songwriting. Ten of the 13 tunes on this 1969 LP are originals; the remaining three, naturally, were written by one of his chief inspirations, Jacques Brel. There are some interesting moments here. "Big Louise" talks about a hefty prostitute with shocking explicitness for a pop star album of the era. "Copenhagen" (like much of Walker's '60s work) foreshadows David Bowie. "Funeral Tango" is a particularly vicious Brel song. "30 Century Man" is an uncommonly folkish and focused tune for Walker. "We Came Through" is an oddball cavalry charge featuring one of his occasional forays into Ennio Morricone spaghetti Western-like production. The tension between Walker's dense, foreboding lyrics and orchestral production is unusual, to say the least. But too often, it's too difficult to penetrate Walker's insights through Wally Scott's string-drenched production. It shrouds the lyrics in a fog that's often too syrupy to justify the effort needed to fight through it. *—Richie Unterberger*

Scott 4 / 1969 / Fontana ♦♦♦♦♦
Walker dropped out of the British Top Ten with his fourth album, but the result was probably his finest '60s LP. While the tension between the bloated production and his introspective, ambitious lyrics remains, much of the over-the-top bombast of the orchestral arrangements has been reined in, leaving a relatively stripped-down approach that complements his songs rather than smothering them. This is the first Walker album to feature entirely original material, and his songwriting is more lucid and cutting. Several of the tracks stand among his finest. "The Seventh Seal," based upon the classic film by Ingmar Bergman, features remarkably ambitious (and relatively successful) lyrics set against a haunting Ennio Morricone-style arrangement. "The Old Man's Back Again" also echoes Morricone, and tackles no less ambitious a lyrical palette; "dedicated to the neo-Stalinist regime," the "old man" of this song was supposedly Josef Stalin. "Hero of the War" is also one of Walker's better vignettes, serenading his war hero with a cryptic mix of tribute and irony. Other songs show engaging folk, country, and soul influences that were largely buried on his previous solo albums. *—Richie Unterberger*

Til the Band Comes In / 1970 / BGO ♦♦♦
Walker's sixth album was really the last of his prime eccentric pop crooner era, and in comparison to his previous solo output, it was a bit inconsistent. For one thing, Walker wrote the original material with his manager of the time, Ady Semel; more puzzlingly, after ten original tracks, the album concluded with five covers of pop standards along the lines of "Stormy" and material by Henry Mancini and Michel Legrand. Strangest of all, one of the original cuts was sung not by Walker, but by Esther Ofarim. There's a goodly amount of fine stuff, though, that's characteristic of Walker's unique mix of lounge crooning with morose psychodrama. "Time Operator," a verite monolog of a lonely man's conversation with a telephone operator, may be his most devastating deadpan lyric; "Joe" is Walker in his best pseudo-Tony Bennett voice; and "The War Is Over" and "Little Things" also have a fetching candy-coated melancholy. Even the covers aren't a total loss, featuring as they do some of his trademark masterful balladeering. *—Richie Unterberger*

The Moviegoer / 1972 / Philips ♦♦

Climate of Hunter / 1984 / Virgin ♦♦♦
Walker's only album of the 1980s was both a blow for artistic credibility, and a blow against most of his old fans. The voice of the balladeer was still intact, and still even crooned sometimes. But the arrangements backed brow-furrowing, obtuse lyrics with '80s-oriented rock that incorporated some quasi-classical structures. Walker was seemingly more interested in painting abstracts in which the textures counted more than the content. This made for an album which may have been a hell of a lot more interesting than '80s efforts by other '60s pop stars, but at the same time it was rather impenetrable, and one's attention tended to drift off over the course of the set. Yet it was not half as radical as the avant-garde direction he would stake out with his next album ten years later, *Tilt*. *—Richie Unterberger*

● **Boy Child: The Best of Scott Walker 1967-1970** / 1992 / Fontana ♦♦♦♦♦
This collection of "Scott's best self-composed songs" features 20 Walker originals from his 1967-1970 heyday. While he covered some interesting material on his albums during this period, paying tribute to Jacques Brel with special devotion and frequency, his original compositions are his most enduring achievements. Besides such highlights as "Big Louise," "We Came Through," "The Seventh Seal," "Plastic Palace People," and "The Old Man's Back Again," it includes half a dozen songs that were not included on the four other solo albums that Fontana UK has reissued on CD. Some of those cuts are very strong, especially "The Rope and the Colt," a dramatic Western ballad with an arrangement that would do Ennio Morricone proud; the positively eloquent despair of the ennui-ridden "Time Operator"; and "The Plague," a representative sampling of Walker's taste for the disquieting and bizarre. This is a recommended starting point for those interested in checking out this singularly strange '60s phenomenon, who was a relatively unacknowledged and undetected, but nonetheless substantial, influence on David Bowie and other fashionably decadent British singers. *—Richie Unterberger*

No Regrets: The Best of Scott Walker & the Walker Brothers / 1992 / Fontana ♦♦♦♦♦
Including both of The Walker Brothers' big hits ("The Sun Ain't Gonna Shine Any More," "Make It Easy On Yourself") and highlights from Scott Walker's first four solo albums, *No Regrets: The Best of the Walker Brothers* is a fine overview of Walker's more pop-oriented music, containing the majority of his best-known songs including "Joanna," "Lights of Cincinnati," "Boy Child," "Montague Terrace in Blue," "Jackie" and "If You Go Away," plus the one of the best songs from the Walkers' '70s reunion ("No Regrets,"). *—Stephen Thomas Erlewine*

Tilt / 1995 / Drag City ♦♦

It's Raining Today: The Scott Walker Story (1967-70) / Oct. 15, 1996 / Razor & Tie ♦♦♦
As the first Scott Walker album to be released in the U.S., *It's Raining Today: The Scott Walker Story* is an adequate 17-song overview of his solo career, containing many of the highlights from his first five albums ("Jackie," "Montague Terrace (In Blue)," "The Seventh Seal," "The Old Man's Back Again (Dedicated to the Neo-Stalinist Regime)," "Big Louise," "Lights of Cincinnati," "Joanna"), while overlooking some minor gems, including "Matilda" and the B-side "The Plague." Neverthless, it remains a terrific introduction to Walker's music. *—Stephen Thomas Erlewine*

Stretch/We Had It All / Jun. 24, 1997 / BGO ♦♦

The Wallflowers

f. 1990
Group / American Trad Rock, Adult Alternative Pop/Rock
As part of the mid-'90s revival of roots-rock, the Wallflowers held a special connection to one of the original inspirations: vocalist/songwriter/guitarist Jakob Dylan. Though he is the son of a legend, Jakob's similarities to his father are occasional—in fact, the Wallflowers are more influenced by Tom Petty & the Heartbreakers than original '60s folk-rock, though lyrically, Jakob remains a close companion to the original Dylan. Released in August 1992, the Wallflowers' self-titled debut album sold poorly, and Virgin soon dropped their contract. Undaunted, the group signed to Interscope and recorded its second album with producer T-Bone Burnett, a long-time friend of the Dylan family. *Bringing Down the Horse* was released in May 1996, producing the alternative radio hit "6th Avenue Heartache." Late in 1996, the single "One Headlight" was released, and by the spring of 1997, it had become a Top 10 hit, pushing *Bringing Down the Horse* into the upper reaches of the charts, as well. Early in 1998, "One Headlight" won Grammys for Best Rock Song and Best Rock Performance by a Duo or Group With Vocal. *—John Bush*

The Wallflowers / Aug. 25, 1992 / Virgin ♦♦♦

Bringing Down the Horse / May 21, 1996 / Interscope ♦♦♦♦♦
No sophomore jinx here. Of course, there are only two Wallflowers left from their finest release, so this could be called a whole new band. No matter, because the music here is assured and contemporary with just enough of the past showing through to catch one's eye. Jakob Dylan has been polishing his compositional chops and it really shows on such cuts as "Invisible City," the hit "6th Avenue Heartache" and especially "One Headlight." A fine effort indeed. *—James Chrispell*

● **Breach** / Sep. 26, 2000 / Interscope ♦♦♦♦♦
When Jakob Dylan first debuted with the Wallflowers, nobody expected that he would ever escape the shadow of his famous father, and those doubts hung heavily above the band until their second album, *Bringing Down the Horse,* became an unexpected multi-platinum smash. In light of that success, Dylan became his own man, no longer seen as only Bob's kid. That freedom is evident on the Wallflowers' superb third album, *Breach*. At the time of its fall 2000 release, there was a lot of attention paid to Jakob finally writing about Bob, a subject he steadfastly ignored before, and it is true that several songs do clearly acknowledge his famous father. But that's not the most noteworthy thing about the album. What's remarkable about the album is that he is assured as a songwriter and bandleader. On the surface, there's not much different between this album and its predecessor, but the songs are stronger, sharper, and the performances are lean, muscular, and immediate. Andrew Slater and Michael Penn's clear, surprisingly varied production is a factor, but the credit goes to Jakob Dylan and the Wallflowers; the band has never sounded better and Dylan has never been as convincing as a writer or singer. The result is the finest straight-ahead rock album of 2000. *—Stephen Thomas Erlewine*

War

f. 1969, Long Beach, CA
Group / Latin Rock, Brown Eyed Soul, Funk, Soul
Freewheeling War mixed rock, jazz, and soul influences into a spicy stew throughout the '70s, resulting in a series of R&B and pop hits sporting funky melodies and politically aware messages. Born in Long Beach in 1969, the large combo initially served as rocker Eric Burdon's group, backing the ex-Animal on his 1970 million-seller "Spill the Wine." Bidding Burdon adieu, the band signed with United Artists in 1971 and enjoyed its first smash the next year with "Slippin' into Darkness." Tapping into a sizzling, horn-fueled rock/soul synthesis, "The World Is a Ghetto," "The Cisco Kid," and "Why Can't We Be Friends?" all went gold during the mid-'70s. Despite numerous personnel and label changes, War remained eminent throughout the '80s.

In the early '90s, War experienced a revival, partially due to the fact that all of their albums were reissued. But the group was also acknowledged as a primary influence on contemporary R&B and hip-hop. War returned to recording in 1994 capitalize on their newfound popularity. While 1994's *Peace Sign* wasn't a blockbuster, it was a moderate success, enabling the group to continue recording into the late '90s. *—Bill Dahl*

Eric Burdon Declares War / 1970 / Rhino ♦♦♦
The debut effort by Eric Burdon & War was an erratic effort that hinted at more potential than it actually delivered. Three of the five tunes are meandering blues-jazz-psychedelic jams, two of which, "Tobacco Road" and "Blues For Memphis Slim," chug along for nearly 15 minutes. These showcase the then-unknown War's funky fusion and Burdon's still-

impressive vocals, but suffer from a lack of focus and substance. "Spill The Wine," on the other hand, is inarguably the greatest moment of the Burdon-fronted lineup. Not only was this goofy funk shaggy-dog story one of the most truly inspired off-the-wall hit singles of all time, it was War's first smash—and Eric Burdon's last. The odd closing track, a short piece of avant-garde sentimentality called "You're No Stranger," was deleted from rereleases of this album for years due to legal complications, but was restored for its CD reissue. *—Richie Unterberger*

The Black-Man's Burdon / 1971 / Rhino ✦✦✦✦
Burdon's second and final album with War was a double set that could have benefited from quite a bit of judicious editing. Composed mostly of sprawling psychedelic funk jams, it does find War mapping out much of the jazz/Latin/soul grooves that, cut down to much more economical song structures, would shortly bring them success on their own. Highlights include the soulful vamps "Pretty Colors" and "They Can't Take Away Our Music"; the 13-minute "Paint It Black" medley is the height of their eccentricity, and not one, but two covers of "Nights In White Satin" are absurd low points. *—Richie Unterberger*

War / Jan. 1971 / Rhino ✦✦

All Day Music / Feb. 1971 / Rhino ✦✦✦✦
A great War album, the first where all their influences meshed. They blended gospel-tinged soul, funk, Afro-Latin, and light jazz, with enthusiastic group vocals and interplay, plus just the right amount of instrumental support and occasional solos by Lee Oskar on harmonica, Lonnie Jordan on keyboards, and Charles Miller on saxophones and flute. It also contained the fantastic "Slippin' Into Darkness," one of their best-arranged and performed numbers. *—Ron Wynn*

The World Is a Ghetto / 1972 / Rhino ✦✦✦✦
War hit its peak with this 1972 album, the only one they ever released that topped the pop charts. The title track was a triumphant blend of great exchanges and unison vocals, plus concise and spirited musical contributions all around. It also contained the delightful "Cisco Kid" and elaborate "City, Country, City," plus the curious "Beetles in the Bog." Harmonica player Lee Oskar and percussionist Papa Dee Allen were at their best, as were keyboardist Lonnie Jordan and saxophonist/flutist Charles Miller. *—Ron Wynn*

Deliver the Word / 1973 / Rhino ✦✦✦

War Live / 1973 / Rhino ✦✦

Why Can't We Be Friends / 1975 / Rhino ✦✦✦✦
War returned with a vengeance and new material in the mid-'70s, as the title hit was both a pop and R&B top 10 smash and "Low Rider" did even better, topping the soul surveys and peaking at number seven pop. More importantly, they were once more a carefree, loose, jamming band. Unfortunately, it was the last definitive War album, as ego and production battles would soon undermine their success. *—Ron Wynn*

Galaxy / 1977 / Rhino ✦✦✦

Platinum Jazz / 1977 / Avenue Jazz ✦✦

The Best of War & More / 1991 / Rhino/Avenue ✦✦✦✦

Anthology / Oct. 18, 1994 / Rhino/Avenue ✦✦✦✦✦
A two-disc set collecting the highlights from War's long, prolific career, *Anthology (1970-94)* is the definitive retrospective of the seminal funk band, containing all of their hits as well as most of their best album tracks. *—Stephen Thomas Erlewine*

The Best of War & More, Vol. 2 / Sep. 3, 1996 / Rhino ✦✦✦✦

● **Grooves & Messages: Greatest Hits Of War** / Jun. 15, 1999 / Rhino ✦✦✦✦✦
Grooves & Messages is another compilation from Rhino that recycles War's greatest hits and, like the previous collections, it contains most of the hits, but not all of them. The difference is, it actually has all the Top 10 pop hits and the majority of the Top 10 R&B hits (only "LA Sunshine" is missing), and it's sequenced in chronological order—two important elements that were absent on *The Best of War* and its sequel, *The Best of War & More, Vol. 2.* Sounds perfect, doesn't it— The problem is, *Grooves & Messages* contains a bonus disc of remixes. There are a couple of big-name mixers here, including Armand Van Helden and Ganja Kru, but none of the mixes are of any interest. Furthermore, the casual fans that will want the first disc will have little use for the second. Still, that first disc is the best, most concise collection of War hits on the market, and *Grooves & Messages* is a specially priced double-disc set, so it may be worth the time of some casual fans, those willing to spend a little bit more to get a good hits collection. However, it would have been nicer if the first disc was available individually. *—Stephen Thomas Erlewine*

Billy Ward

b. Sep. 19, 1921, Los Angeles, CA
Vocals, Drums / R&B
The ultra-strict disciplinarian and bandleader of a seminal R&B group, Billy Ward ruled over the Dominoes in a tight-fisted manner. He attempted to regulate everything from onstage harmonies to offstage lifestyles. The group's ranks at one time included Clyde McPhatter and Jackie Wilson, but Ward's insistence on dictatorial control resulted in both of them soon bolting for solo status. The group remained active until the early '60s and scored ten Top Ten R&B hits and two colossal number one singles during its heyday from 1951 to 1957. "Sixty Minute Man" in 1951 was the ultimate innuendo hit, while "Have Mercy Baby" was a landmark uptempo stomper. Each topped the R&B charts for more than two months. All their hits were on either Federal or King, except for their final one, a cover of "Star Dust" in 1957 for Liberty that reached number five R&B and number 12 pop. *—Ron Wynn*

★ **Sixty Minute Men: The Best of Billy Ward & His Dominoes** / Nov. 16, 1993 / Rhino ✦✦✦✦✦
Billy Ward was neither a flamboyant vocalist nor a great instrumentalist; his success came directly from his ability to spot and nurture talent. Unfortunately, Ward was also a taskmaster and couldn't hold onto singers very long after discovering and recruiting them for his groups. But for a short period in the 1950s, Ward and the Dominoes ruled R&B by featuring two of its premier vocalists, Clyde McPhatter and Jackie Wilson. Neither stayed long, but were in the band enough time to make some seminal hits, included in this 20-cut anthology. Ironically, the song the group is remembered for the most featured bass vocalist Bill Brown doing the lead on the title track. *—Ron Wynn*

The Best of the 50's Masters: 1957-1959 / Mar. 21, 2000 / Varese ✦✦✦✦✦
This 19-song anthology covers Ward & the Dominoes' stint with Liberty. Although this was the period that saw them land two of their biggest hits—both "Star Dust" and "Deep Purple" made the Top 20—it's not remembered or written about nearly as much as are their recordings during the first half of the 1950s. That's because their late-'50s material was far less R&B-oriented than their discs for Federal and King, and also because the Dominoes' two best lead singers, Clyde McPhatter and Jackie Wilson, had departed the lineup. Indeed, by this time the group was walking pretty close to the middle of the road, covering numerous pre-rock popular standards and using lots of orchestration. There are still some doo wop and R&B elements involved, but it's far closer to pop than it is to rock & roll. Half a dozen different singers are on lead vocals, though most often taking lead is Eugene Mumford, the voice on "Star Dust" and "Deep Purple." It's not bad as far as harmonized pop vocals go, but often it's rather a throwback to the Ink Spots and the Mills Brothers, and certainly not as innovative as the group's earlier efforts. At times, there's a resemblance to the Platters (they even do "Smoke Gets in Your Eyes"), and for just one moment they turn into a straight R&B/rock group on an unexpected cover of the Jan & Arnie hit "Jennie Lee" that made the middle of the pop charts. Incidentally, five of the tracks (including an earlier vocal take of "Star Dust") were previously unreleased; on one of them, "These Foolish Things (Remind Me of You)," they totally lose the beat going into the second bridge. *—Richie Unterberger*

Dionne Warwick

b. Dec. 12, 1940, East Orange, NJ
Vocals / Pop-Soul, Brill Building Pop, Pop, Soul
The magically melodic voice of Dionne Warwick and the sophisticated pop compositions of Burt Bacharach and Hal David were the proverbial match made in heaven. Warwick proved the prolific songwriting team's favorite interpreter, scaling the pop and soul charts time and again with her soaring renditions of their memorable songs.

Warwick hailed from a musical brood with a strong gospel heritage, and her sister Dee Dee scored a few hits of her own. Dionne's sultry pipes stood out, even on the highly competitive background vocal scene in New York, and she got a chance to step out front in 1963, hitting big on Scepter with the uptown soul classic "Don't Make Me Over."

Under the expert tutelage of Bacharach and David, who doubled as her producers, Warwick's sound soon became smoother and more accessible to pop programming—a formula that resulted in the massive acceptance of her "Walk On By," "I Say a Little Prayer," "This Girl's in Love with You," and a slew of others.

Strangely, Warwick never made it to the top of the pop charts until she broke away from her mentors, traveling to Philadelphia to record the R&B-oriented "Then Came You" with the Spinners in 1974. As elegant and tasteful as ever, Dionne Warwick's breathy vocals still haven't gone out of style—she's managed to remain contemporary while never jeopardizing her appeal. *—Bill Dahl*

★ **The Dionne Warwick Collection: Her All-Time Greatest Hits** / 1989 / Rhino ✦✦✦✦✦
The finest collection of Warwick material compiled by anyone, this excellent set gathered every Warwick gem and smartly remastered them. It's a definitive CD, containing several landmark releases featuring the collaborative compositions of Burt Bacharach and Hal David. These songs underscored Warwick's ability to embody her pop tunes with a soulful, but also light and innocent, quality. It also has excellent liner notes and intelligent sequencing. This is by far the set to get if you want a comprehensive presentation of Warwick's pop/soul greatness. *—Ron Wynn*

Dionne Warwick Greatest Hits (1979-1990) / Oct. 1989 / Arista ✦✦✦
Dionne Warwick enjoyed a career revival in the late '70s and 1980s when she teamed with such producers as Barry Manilow, Barry Gibb, and even Luther Vandross. They returned her to the elaborately arranged and structured soul-tinged pop that had marked her finest hits, although the lyrics and compositions weren't as consistent as they were during the Burt Bacharach/Hal David period. This album collects the biggest hits from this second phase of Warwick's career, including such triumphs as "Deja Vu" and "I Know I'll Never Love This Way Again"; it also introduced a new tune, "Take Good Care of You And Me." *—Ron Wynn*

Hidden Gems: The Best of Dionne Warwick, Vol. 2 / Mar. 24, 1992 / Rhino ✦✦✦✦✦
Turning the spotlight on various rarities, B-sides, and album cuts, *Hidden Gems* reminds us that some of Dionne Warwick's best work with the prolific Burt Bacharach/Hal David team received little or no radio airplay. In retrospect, it's hard to believe that Warwick's versions of "What the World Needs Now Is Love," "The Look of Love" (also recorded by Isaac Hayes, Anita Baker, and countless others), and "Make It Easy on Yourself" (a smash for Jerry Butler) weren't major hits. They certainly deserved to be, as did the hauntingly pretty "Any Old Time of the Day" ("Walk on By"'s B-side) and "They Long to Be (Close to You)." For those who might have overlooked this fine material, *Hidden Gems* is quite a revelation. *—Alex Henderson*

From the Vaults / Oct. 1995 / Ichiban/Soul Classics ✦✦✦

Definitive Collection / Apr. 13, 1999 / Arista ✦✦✦✦

The Very Best of Dionne Warwick / May 23, 2000 / Rhino ✦✦✦✦✦

Jimmy Webb

b. Aug. 15, 1946, Elk City, OK
Singer, Vocals, Keyboards, Piano, Producer, Arranger / Adult Alternative Pop/Rock, Pop, Singer/Songwriter
Jimmy Webb was that rarity in rock music, a professional songwriter; he was also a singer, but his performing career never eclipsed his success as a composer and producer. Indeed, Webb may well have kept the craft of the songwriter in popular music alive and kicking in

a new generation, saving the profession from being ghetto-ized onto the Broadway stage and the world of the commercial jingle. In 1966, Johnny Rivers first recorded "By the Time I Get to Phoenix," which became a modest hit; Glen Campbell later cut it as well, and scored a gold record. Meanwhile, Webb was put in charge of the songs for their first album for a fledgling pop group called the Fifth Dimension; the result was a chart-topping million-selling single, "Up Up and Away." Between them, the two songs won eight Grammy Awards the following year, and turned Jimmy Webb into the most prominent songwriter of his generation. Like many of his peers, Webb had begun thinking of longer compositions and more coherent bodies of songs, and soon wrote "MacArthur Park," which fit into the new spirit of the era—the lyrics, although not remotely "psychedelic," were as rich and ornate as anything the Beatles or the Beach Boys were experimenting with, and the arrangement was as a vast sonic canvas, filled with the combined sounds of a rock combo and a full orchestra and choir. It was placed with his friend, the actor Richard Harris; after Webb recorded the orchestral part in Los Angeles, Harris's voice was added on at a studio in Dublin. Webb tried selling "MacArthur Park" to several major labels, and was rejected—nobody felt that a seven-minute-plus single by an actor scarcely known as a singer had any chance of being played, much less becoming a hit. Instead, "MacArthur Park" climbed to Number Two on the American pop charts over a period of 13 weeks, and in the process shattered every preconception of air-time restrictions on AM radio. *—Bruce Eder*

Jim Webb Sings Jim Webb / 1968 / Epic ✦

Words & Music / Feb. 1970 / Reprise ✦✦✦
Words and Music marked Webb's official debut as a singer of his own songs. Though the second side's experiments (a suite in three movements and a song cycle/medley linking "Let It Be Me," "Never My Love," and "I Wanna Be Free") are a little too ambitious for comfort, side one features the concise, well-crafted pop (such as "P.F. Sloan" and "Love Song") that would feature heavily on later releases. *—Chris Woodstra*

And So On / 1971 / Reprise ✦✦✦
Webb's second album stripped down the excesses of its predecessor for a more consistently enjoyable set, featuring the haunting "Met Her on a Plane" (later covered by Ian Matthews) as well as the equally powerful "If Ships Were Made to Sail," "One Lady" and "All My Love's Laughter." *—Chris Woodstra*

Land's End / 1974 / Asylum ✦✦✦

El Mirage / 1977 / Atlantic ✦✦✦✦✦
Produced by George Martin, *El Mirage* is one of Webb's strongest albums. As always, the songs are perfectly constructed but this time sung with more confidence than ever before. Highlights include "If You See Me Getting Smaller" and "Christian No." *—Chris Woodstra*

Angel Heart / 1982 / Columbia/Legacy/Lorimar ✦✦

● **Archive** / 1993 / WEA International ✦✦✦✦✦
Archive is an excellent 20-track (U.K. import only) overview of Webb's criminally overlooked career as a performer from 1970 to 1977, his most productive period. While he is best remebered as the composer of hits for others, this collection offers proof that he was equally adept at interpreting his own songs—often times bringing more emotion to them. *—Chris Woodstra*

Suspending Disbelief / Sep. 7, 1993 / Elektra ✦✦✦
After a several year absence, Webb returns with one of his most polished efforts to date. His hook-filled melodies are instantly endearing, while he sings a love song to his sports car and remembers a meeting with Elvis. His voice, never one his strong points in the past, has aged particularly well. *—Chris Woodstra*

Ten Easy Pieces / Oct. 15, 1996 / Guardian ✦✦✦✦✦
The idea of releasing a collection of Jimmy Webb's best known songs sung by the author himself may seem like a no-brainer, but it's taken 20+ years for it to happen, apparently mostly because Webb needed to put some distance between himself and most of these numbers, in order to approach them in a fresh manner that makes this disc more than a mere exploitation effort. The result is the best and most accessible of all Webb's albums, featuring his 1990s' takes on "Galveston," "By The Time I Get to Phoenix," "Didn't We," "MacArthur Park," "The Moon Is a Harsh Mistress," "Wichita Lineman," and "All I Know," amongst others. His voice is more expressive than ever, and the performances are generally grittier, with more raw emotion than the better known hit versions display. The arrangements are generally very simple and straightforward, with Webb's piano the primary instrument, and several of the songs are performed in a deeply personal manner, more akin to home recording for Webb's own pleasure than to a commercial release—"Wichita Lineman," in particular, sounds here like the most personal and private of performances, filled with wrenching loneliness at which the Glen Campbell version only hints. The notes are very personal and revealing as well. *—Bruce Eder*

Ween

f. 1984
Group / Comedy Rock, Indie Rock, Alternative Pop/Rock
Ween was the ultimate cosmic goof of the alternative rock era, a prodigiously talented and deliriously odd duo whose work travelled far beyond the constraints of parody and novelty into the hallucinatory heart of surrealist ecstasy. Despite a mastery for seemingly every mutation of the musical spectrum, the group refused to play it straight; in essence, Ween were bratty deconstructionists, kicking dirt on the pop world around them with demented glee. Along with the occasional frat-boy lapses into misogyny, racism and homophobia, the band's razor-sharp satire cut to the inherently silly heart of rock & roll with hilariously acute savagery; fueled by psilocybin mushrooms and an all-consuming craving for hot meals, Ween created its own self-contained universe, a parallel dimension where the only sacred cow was their own demon god, the Boognish. *—Jason Ankeny*

GodWeenSatan: The Oneness / 1990 / Twin/Tone ✦✦✦✦
Dean and Gene Ween were barely out of their teens when they recorded *GodWeenSatan: The Oneness,* and it shows: it's juvenile in the best sense of the word, mixing their sprawling sense of humor with punk, heavy metal, and a surprising amount of pop literacy. At a whopping 23 tracks long, the album features a lot of noodling and lots of whacked-out pop, including "Nan," a dweeby tale of unrequited love, and the jazzy "Never Squeal," which shows off Ween's musical prowess and versatility. *GodWeenSatan: The Oneness* also introduces many of the song styles the band included on their later releases, such as the prog-rock-inspired ballad "Squelch the Little Weasel," the Prince homage "L.M.L.Y.P.," the playful, helium-laced pop of "Don't Laugh" and the funky, soulful "Nicole." "El Camino"'s pseudo-flamenco, "Birthday Boy"'s surprising vulnerability, and the rambling, silly stoner-folk of "Puffycloud" also set the tone for Ween's future work. Though they'd released plenty of cassettes on their own by the time of *GodWeenSatan: The Oneness'* release, Ween still sounds like they're trying ideas on for size. Song snippets like "Cold & Wet," "Fat Lenny," and "I Gots a Weasel" are fun but less successful than some of the band's more developed songs or their more crazed outbursts, such as "You Fucked Up," "Wayne's Pet Youngin'," and "Papa Zit." Stomping rockers like "Old Queen Cole," the sparse weirdness of "I'm in the Mood to Move" and the gospel parody "Up on the Hill"—which introduces Ween's inspiration, the Boognish—make *GodWeenSatan* almost as eclectic and inspired as the albums that followed it. However, the fun Dean and Gene Ween had creating *GodWeenSatan: The Oneness* is palpable, making it more than just a promising debut. *—Heather Phares*

The Pod / 1991 / Elektra ✦✦✦
Another collection of inspired pop pastiche and four-track dementia, 1991's *The Pod* is nearly as long as *GodWeenSatan: The Oneness* but even weirder and more deranged, due in large part to the band's Scotchguard habit and the severe cases of mononucleosis Gene and Dean Ween contracted while recording the album. As a result, *The Pod* is dark and murky, with a slightly distant, fuzzy feel. On some songs, such as the cryptic, prog-inspired "Right to the Ways and the Rules of the World," the psych-tinged "Dr. Rock," and the mystic hard rock of "Captain Fantasy," this sound works well, but on others—like the opening track "Strap on That Jammypac"—it just doesn't fit. Ween flexes their stylistic chops a bit on "Sorry Charlie"'s country-rock, "Sketches of Winkle"'s crazed speed metal, "Oh My Dear"'s cute four-track, and "Pork Roll Egg and Cheese"'s Beatlesque psych-pop, but the majority of *The Pod,* for better or worse, focuses on sludgy weirdness like "Molly," "Awesome Sound," "Laura," and "Can U Taste the Waste?" That most of these songs are grouped together in the middle of the album makes them even more strange and impenetrable—though they may make more sense under the influence of Scotchguard or other, heavier, chemicals. Where *GodWeenSatan: The Oneness'* sense of fun and experimentation was contagious, *The Pod* is insular; you can tell that Dean and Gene had a fun—or at least bizarre—time making the album, but it doesn't translate. Though it does feature a few of Ween's best songs, *The Pod* is easily their most difficult work. However, hardcore fans will still find digging through its messy sprawl worthwhile. *—Heather Phares*

Pure Guava / Nov. 10, 1992 / Elektra ✦✦✦✦
By 1993's major label debut *Pure Guava,* Ween had distilled their unique mix of eclectic pop and crazed humor to its essence. *GodWeenSatan: The Oneness* and *The Pod* were fascinating, but occasionally frustrating albums; at 19 songs, *Pure Guava* is more polished and concise, but it's still sprawling and occasionally sick, featuring the fuzzed-out "Touch My Tooter" and the five-minute noise-burst "Mourning Glory," a tale of pumpkin-smoking gone horribly awry. Though "I Play It Off Legit"—a muttered conversation set to atmospheric keyboards—and the rhythmic, bass-heavy "The Goin' Gets Tough From The Getgo" could have appeared on *The Pod,* most of *Pure Guava's* songs have a poppy, accessible sheen. Fragmented, distorted tracks like "Big Jilm," "Flies On My Dick" and the live favorite "Poop Ship Destroyer" benefit from the album's cleaner production, giddily mixing catchiness and silliness. If *The Pod* was influenced by the band's Scotchguard habit, *Pure Guava* sounds like it was recorded while Dean and Gene were huffing helium; it's fast, shiny and crisp, particularly on the hyper rant "Pumpin' 4 the Man" and the minor alternative rock hit "Push Th' Little Daisies." Ween's prog-rock fascination surfaces on "The Stallion, Pt. 3" and on "Don't Get 2 Close To My Fantasy," which sports wonderfully inane lyrics like "Stare into the lion's eyes / And if you taste the candy / You'll get to the surprise." In the midst of this weirdness, the sweet, seemingly genuine ballad "Sarah" feels like the album's strangest song. With *Pure Guava,* Ween moved away from the snippets of random craziness that defined their first two albums toward a more organized style. Considering Elektra released it, it's just as uncompromising as their previous work, but it hints at just how much further they could go with their music. *—Heather Phares*

● **Chocolate & Cheese** / Sep. 27, 1994 / Elektra ✦✦✦✦✦
A brilliant fusion of pop and gonzo humor, 1994's *Chocolate & Cheese* is arguably Ween's finest moment. Building on *Pure Guava's* more focused approach, the album proved for once and all that, along with their twisted sense of humor and wide musical vocabulary, Dean and Gene are also impressive songwriters. Over the course of *Chocolate & Cheese,* Ween explore virtually every permutation of pop, rock, soul and funk, from the opening song "Take Me Away"'s rootsy rock to "Roses Are Free"'s homage to Prince's shiny Paisley Park era. On the dreamy, British psych-inspired "What Deaner Was Talking About," the Afro-Caribbean funk of "Voodoo Lady" and "Freedom Of '76," their funny, sexy tribute to '70s Philly soul, Ween don't so much parody these styles as reinvent them. Indeed, "Drifter In The Dark"'s surprisingly traditional country and "Joppa Road"'s spot-on soft-rock—foreshadow *12 Golden Country Greats* and *White Pepper,* respectively. Despite *Chocolate & Cheese's* polish and prowess, Ween prove they're still proudly politically incorrect with "Spinal Meningitis (Got Me Down)" and "Mister Would You Please Help My Pony?," two of the creepiest songs about childhood ever recorded. "The HIV Song" revels in its questionable taste and "Don't Shit Where You Eat"'s laid-back pop is one of the album's subtler jokes. Old-school Ween weirdness surfaces on "Candi" (the shouting in the background was recorded from the trunk of Dean Ween's car) and the crazed stomp of "I Can't Put My Finger On It." "Buenas Tardes Amigo," an epic, spaghetti western-inspired tale of murder and revenge, and "Baby Bitch," a wry but stinging retort to an ex-girlfriend, show how good Ween are at taking silly things seriously and serious things lightly. That's exactly what makes *Chocolate & Cheese* such a fun, exciting album. *—Heather Phares*

12 Golden Country Greats / Jul. 1996 / Elektra ♦♦♦
The main problem with *12 Golden Country Greats* (which only contains ten songs, by the way) is that it's Ween's first album to concentrate on a single music genre and such concentration lends the impression that they consider themselves above the genre. But that isn't entirely the case. Ween recorded *12 Golden Country Greats* in Nashville with numerous legendary musicians, including the Jordanaires, Buddy Spicher, Charlie McCoy, Hargus "Pig" Robbins, and Russ Hicks. The presence of these musicians gives the music a very authentic feeling, even though the songs stick to '60s trends like country-pop, country-folk, and polished honky tonk. Some of Ween's songs fit this style perfectly, such as the rolling "You Were the Fool," "I'm Holding You," "Japanese Cowboy," "Fluffy," "Help Me Scrape the Mucus off My Brain," and "Pretty Girl." Even the vulgar honky tonk of "Piss up a Rope" works, turning into a truly delightful gem. The duo runs into trouble on the homophobic "Mister Richard Smoker," as well as with some of the vaguely elitist views that underpin the songs, such as on "I Don't Wanna Leave You on the Farm." Still, Ween's gift for songcraft and the talents of the Nashville musicians prevent the album from being just a joke. In fact, it's as satisfying as any of their record, and gutsier, too. After all, no country fan will want to hear this record and most of their fans are afraid of country music, and that's sort of an admirable move. *—Stephen Thomas Erlewine*

The Mollusk / Jun. 24, 1997 / Elektra ♦♦♦♦♦
On the surface, *The Mollusk* is a return to the panoramic, multi-genre extraganza of *Chocolate and Cheese*, but in its own way, it's as much of a concept album as *12 Golden Country Greats*. It just isn't as explicit about its intentions. Nearly every song on *The Mollusk* has a nautical theme, buoyed by a heavy progressive rock influence. Several songs deviate from the theme—the synthetic new wave pulse of "I'll Be Your Jonny on the Spot" and the frenzied pseudo-country of "Waving My Dick in the Wind" are neither seafaring nor prog—but there's an unmistakable watery undertow to the record. Perhaps the loose concept is the reason why *The Mollusk* is the most concise album in Ween's canon, but it's not what makes the record so impressive. Like *Chocolate and Cheese*, *The Mollusk* could seem like a comedy record to outsiders, but the songwriting and performances are so remarkably accomplished that it is just as listenable after the shock of the humor has faded away. "The Mollusk," "Mutilated Lips," "The Golden Eel" and "Buckingham Green" are all startlingly accurate send-ups of prog-rock, and they are better written than many of their inspirations. Similarly, the vulgar shanty "The Blarney Stone," the faux-Richard Thompson tragedy "She Wanted to Leave" and the sunny, Caribbean-flavored "Ocean Man" are terrific songs offering evidence that Ween are improving as songwriters and musicians with each record. Ironically, this array of silly jokes and musical parody is a richer and more diverse listen than most of its alternative rock contemporaries. *—Stephen Thomas Erlewine*

Paintin' the Town Brown: Ween Live 1990-1998 / Jun. 22, 1999 / Elektra ♦♦♦

White Pepper / May 2, 2000 / Elektra ♦♦♦
White Pepper is Ween's most accessible album to date, lacking their trademark flights of fancy and exuberant bizarreness. By any other standard, *White Pepper is* a weird, wild ride. Let's face it—no other band would even think of recording tracks as diverse as the Brit-pop-styled "Even If You Don't," the Jimmy Buffett parody "Bananas and Blow," a slamming hardcore punk song named after a Burt Reynolds flick ("Stroker Ace"), a tape-warped baroque instrumental called "Ice Castles," and the psych-prog-tinged soft-rock epic "Back to Basom," let alone sequencing all of them in a row. To neophytes, such whiplash shifts in mood may seem alienating (or intriguing, depending on their taste), but to any hardcore fan, it's not surprising and it might not even seem as funny as before. But, if you're listening to Ween just to chuckle, you're missing the point anyway, since they're not just consummate satirists—check out the wonderful "Pandy Fackler," which mimics Steely Dan's lush jazz-pop, down to Gene's deadly Donald Fagen imitation—they're consummate songwriters and musicians. Ween's music rewards multiple plays and *White Pepper* is ample proof. It may not be bracing, nor is it gonzo, yet it's a tight album filled with more pop gems than most bands can hope to achieve in their career. If that seems like hyperbole, especially for a duo that still indulges in silly dirty jokes, it's not. Yes, they may push the boundaries of good taste, but the music is always convincing, from the trippy "Exactly Where I'm At" and "Flutes of Chi" to the minor-key country stomper "Falling Out" and reflective ballad "She's Your Baby." If *White Pepper* isn't as crazy, funny, or sprawling as their previous albums, so be it—it's more satisfying than most records. *—Stephen Thomas Erlewine*

Weezer

f. 1993
Group / Emo, Punk-Pop, Post-Grunge, Alternative Pop/Rock
As one of the most popular groups to emerge in the post-grunge alternative-rock aftermath, Weezer received equal amounts of criticism and praise for their hooky-heavy guitar-pop. Drawing from the heavy power-pop of arena rockers like Cheap Trick and the angular guitar leads of the Pixies, Weezer leavened their melodies with doses of '70s metal learned from bands like Kiss. But what set the band apart was their geekiness. None of the members of Weezer, especially leader Rivers Cuomo, were conventional rockers—they were kids that holed up in their garage, playing along with their favorite records when they weren't studying or watching TV. As a result, their music was infused with a quirky sense of humor and an endearing awkwardness that made songs like "Undone (The Sweater Song)," "Buddy Holly" and "Say It Ain't So" into big modern rock hits during 1994 and 1995. All the singles were helped immeasurably by clever videos, which may have made the songs into hits, but they also made many critics believe that the band were one-hits wonders. Perversely, Cuomo began to feel the same way, and decided that the band would not rely on any visual gimmicks for the second album, 1996's *Pinkerton*. Simultaneously, Cuomo took control of the band, making it into a vehicle for his songwriting. While the album didn't sell as well as their 1994 eponymous debut, it did earn stronger reviews than its predecessor. *—Stephen Thomas Erlewine*

• **Weezer** / May 10, 1994 / DGC ♦♦♦♦♦
Weezer was disparaged from all corners when their 1994 debut became a hit. Hipsters and critics *hated* their raucous, melodic, Pixies-meets-metal geek-pop and the group's clever Spike Jonze-directed videos, proclaiming them as charlatans on the order of Stone Temple Pilots. Time has been kind to Weezer, since they not only turned out a second album that was (no joke) a masterpiece, they wound up being as influential on the emo scene as the purer Sunny Day Real Estate. To top it off, *Weezer* stands the test of time, standing as one of the great records of the post-grunge era. It's not as good or personal as *Pinkerton*, but this is a debut and it's a hell of a debut, too, capturing Rivers Cuomo's skills for effortlessly catchy, bone-crunching alt-pop, best heard on singles like "Buddy Holly," "Undone—The Sweater Song," and "Say It Ain't So," but much of the album is at a similar level excellence. Also, there's something utterly charming about his sensibility and the band itself, who play with spirit, chiming in with tag-team harmonies. This, as much as grunge itself, is the music of outsiders. Specifically, it's the music of geeks, smart kids that loved comics, books, TV, metal, and girls, but were too afraid to talk to them directly. This spirit is what gave Weezer its character and it's the reason why the group remains beloved by a band of outsiders, years after this scaled to the top of the charts. —Stephen Thomas Erlewine

Pinkerton / Sep. 24, 1996 / Geffen ♦♦♦♦♦
From the pounding, primal assault of the opening track "Tired of Having Sex," it's clear from the outset that *Pinkerton* is a different record than the sunny, heavy guitar-pop of Weezer's eponymous debut. The first noticible difference is the darker, messier sound—the guitars rage and squeal, the beats are brutal and visceral, the vocals are mixed to the front, filled with overlapping, off-the-cuff backing vocals. In short, it sounds like the work of a live band, which makes it all the more ironic that *Pinkerton*, at its core, is a singer-songwriter record, representing Rivers Cuomo's bid for respectability. Since he hasn't changed Weezer's blend of power-pop and heavy metal (only the closing song, "Butterfly," is performed acoustically), many critics and much of the band's casual fans didn't notice Cuomo's signficant growth as a songwriter. Loosely structured as a concept album based on *Madame Butterfly*, each song works as an individual entity, driven by powerful, melodic hooks, a self-depricating sense of humor ("Pink Triangle" is about a crush on a lesbian) and a touching vulnerability ("Across the Sea," "Why Bother?"). Weezer can still turn out catchy, off-beat singles—"The Good Life" has a chorus that is more memorable than "Buddy Holly," "El Scorcho" twists Pavement's junk-culture references in on itself, "Falling for You" is the most propulsive thing they've yet recorded—but their endearing geekiness isn't as cutesy as before, which means the album wasn't as successful on the charts. But, it's the better album, full of crunching power-pop with a surprsingly strong emotional undercurrent that becomes all the more resonant with each play. *—Stephen Thomas Erlewine*

Paul Weller

b. May 25, 1958, Woking, Surrey, England
Vocals, Keyboards, Guitar / British Trad Rock, Pop/Rock
As the leader of the Jam, Paul Weller fronted the most popular British band of the punk era, influencing legions of English rockers that ranged from his mod-revival contemporaries to the Smiths in the '80s and Oasis in the '90s. During the final days of the Jam, he developed a fascination with Motown and soul, which led him to form the sophisti-pop group the Style Council in 1983. As the Style Council's career progressed, Weller's interest in soul developed into an infatuation with jazz-pop and house music, which eventually led to gradual erosion of his audience—by 1990, he couldn't get a record contract in the UK, where he had previously been worshipped as a demi-god. As a solo artist, Weller returned to soul music as an inspiration, cutting it with the progressive, hippie tendencies of Traffic. Weller's solo records were more organic and rootsier than the Style Council, which helped him regain his popularity within Britain. By the mid-'90s, he had released three successful albums which were both critically-acclaimed and massively popular in England, where contemporary bands like Ocean Colour Scene were citing him as an influence. Just as importantly, many observers, while occasionally criticizing the trad-rock nature of his music, acknowledged that Weller was one of the few rock veterans that had managed to stay vital within the second decade of his career. *—Stephen Thomas Erlewine*

Paul Weller / Oct. 6, 1992 / Go! Discs/London ♦♦♦♦
Humiliated by Polydor's rejection of the final Style Council album (it remained unreleased until the 1998 box set), Paul Weller retreated from the spotlight, licked his wounds, and redefined his music. He re-emerged with the Paul Weller Movement and the surging trad rock single "Into Tomorrow," a song that may not have been a big hit, but it signaled that he had begun a productive new phase. That same criticism applies to his 1992 solo debut (by this point, he had dropped "Movement," decided to just be "Weller"). Heavily inspired by soul and classic rock (more early Humble Pie than Led Zeppelin, of course), it's a solid effort whose best songs—the opening tryptic "Uh Huh Oh Yeh," "I Didn't Mean to Hurt You," and "Bull-Rush," plus "Into Tomorrow"—demonstrate the virtues of nostalgia, particularly when it's tempered with fine songwriting. If he drifts a bit toward the end, and winds up with some lightweight songs, it's still gritty and effective, displaying a focus absent in the Style Council's last few albums. It's not a full-fledged comeback (that would arrive next), but it's a fine start all the same. *—Stephen Thomas Erlewine*

• **Wild Wood** / 1993 / London ♦♦♦♦♦
Paul Weller deservedly regained his status as the Modfather with his second solo album, *Wild Wood*. Actually, the album is only tangentially related to mod, since Weller picks up on the classicism of his debut, adding heavy elements of pastoral British folk and Traffic-styled trippiness. Add to that a yearning introspection and a clean production that nevertheless feels a little rustic, even homemade, and the result is his first true masterwork since ending the Jam. The great irony of the record is that many of the songs—"Has My Fire Really Gone Out?," "Can You Heal Us (Holy Man)"—question his motivation and, as is apparent in his spirited performances, he reawakened his music by writing these searching songs. Though this isn't as adventurous as the Style Council, it succeeds on its own terms, and winds up being a great testament from an artist entering middle age. And, it helped kick off the trad rock that dominated British music during the '90s. *—Stephen Thomas Erlewine*

Paul Weller Live Wood / 1994 / Go! Discs ♦♦♦

Stanley Road / Jun. 7, 1995 / Go! Discs ♦♦♦
In many ways, *Stanley Road* is *Wild Wood—Part Two,* a continuation of the laidback, soul-inflected rock that dominated his previous albums. Named after the street where he grew up, *Stanley Road* could be seen as a return to Paul Weller's roots, yet his roots were in The Who and the Kinks, not in Traffic. (At this point, the sound of The Jam matters little in what his music sounds like.) Weller's music has always had R&B roots—the major difference with both *Wild Wood* and *Stanley Road* is how much he and his band stretch out. *Stanley Road* in particular features more jamming than any of his previous work. That doesn't mean he has neglected his songwriting—a handful of Weller classics are scattered throughout the album. Unfortunately, too much of it is spent on drawn-out grooves that are self-conscious about their own authenticity. Still, he has the good sense to revive Dr. John's "I Walk on Gilded Splinters" and invite his disciple Noel Gallagher (Oasis) along to jam. *—Stephen Thomas Erlewine*

Heavy Soul / Aug. 5, 1997 / London ♦♦♦

Modern Classics: Greatest Hits / Nov. 24, 1998 / London ♦♦♦♦

Heliocentric / May 9, 2000 / Island ♦♦♦♦♦
Heliocentric a lighter affair than the doggedly traditional *Heavy Soul.* It may be a subtle distinction, since he's using the same musical template he has since *Wild Wood,* plus the same producer and many of the same musicians. So, *Heliocentric* sounds very familiar, yet when it reaches its conclusion with the melancholy psychedelic sweep of "Love-Less," it's clear that it *feels* a lot different than its two immediate predecessors—it's of a similar quality and emotional tenor as *Wild Wood.* It's also his strongest record since then, a remarkably sturdy and varied set of songs and performances. Sadness and regret are scattered throughout the album, but there's also humor, affection, and, ultimately, optimism—three qualities missing on *Heavy Soul. Heliocentric* has many more musical quirks than its predecessor. Strings grace several songs, plus there are extended jams so psychedelic they're almost prog. There really aren't any rockers, but there's the wonderfully jaunty acoustic number "Sweet Pea, My Sweet Pea," one of his most unaffected and, well, sweetest songs. "A Whale's Tale" is his own spin on a sea ballad, while "Back in the Fire" rolls along on a nearly jazzy beat. Those ever-changing moods keep the record fresh and interesting, yet *Heliocentric* still winds up sounding part of a piece, since Weller is focused here, as a songwriter and a record-maker, which he hasn't been since *Wild Wood.* Like that latter-day Weller masterpiece, *Heliocentric* grows stronger with each spin, as the songs catch hold and details in the production and nuances in the performances reveal themselves. That may not constitute a new direction for Weller, but it's certainly a terrific record that signals a creative rebirth, which is the next best thing. *—Stephen Thomas Erlewine*

Mary Wells

b. May 13, 1943, Detroit, MI, **d.** Jul. 26, 1992, Los Angeles, CA
Vocals / Pop-Soul, Girl Group, Motown, Soul
Time and legions of other soul superstars have obscured the fact that for a brief moment, Mary Wells was Motown's biggest star. She came to the attention of Berry Gordy as a 17-year-old, hawking a song she'd written for Jackie Wilson; that song, "Bye Bye Baby," became her first Motown hit in 1961. The full-throated approach of that single was quickly toned down in favor of a pop-soul sound. Few other soul singers managed to be as shy and sexy at the same time as Wells, and the soft-voiced singer hit the Top Ten four times during the early '60s, including the number one hit "My Guy." She left Motown almost immediately afterwards, for a reported advance of over six figures from 20th Century Fox. Though Wells never remotely approached the success of her Motown years (entering the pop Top 40 only once), her '60s singles for 20th Century Fox (whom she ended up leaving after only a year), Atco, and Jubilee were solid pop-soul on which her vocal talents remained undiminished. She wrote and produced a lot of her late '60s and early '70s sessions, exploring a somewhat earthier groove than her more widely known pop efforts. She had trouble landing recording deals in the '70s and '80s, and succumbed to throat cancer in 1992. *—Richie Unterberger*

☆ **Looking Back 1961-1964** / Sep. 7, 1993 / Motown ♦♦♦♦♦
This two-CD, 43-track box set is the most comprehensive retrospective of Motown's biggest female star before Diana Ross. Although her first hit, "Bye Bye Baby," presented Wells as a blues belter, she quickly settled into a sly and sassy groove. Subsequent hits like "You Beat Me to the Punch," "Two Lovers," and "My Guy" (all included here) made the most of her shy, seductive voice by teaming her with some great songs and production by Smokey Robinson. Although many of these tunes were relegated to B-sides, album tracks, or even the can (11 were previously unreleased), the material—written by Motown stalwarts like Berry Gordy, Holland-Dozier-Holland, and Mickey Stevenson when Smokey was unavailable—is not far below the hits in quality. This is as much a testimony to Motown's overflow of prolific talent as Wells', but doesn't detract from the consistency of this set, which includes her duets with Marvin Gaye (as well as a previously unreleased duet with Smokey Robinson). Includes a comprehensive essay in the photo-packed booklet, although the mysterious absence of the excellent "Was It Worth It" is a notable loss. *—Richie Unterberger*

Ain't It the Truth: The Best of Mary Wells 1964-1982 / Aug. 30, 1994 / Varese Sarabande ♦♦♦
It doesn't have anything from her 1965-67 years with Atco (those tracks are compiled on a separate collection), but otherwise this does a good job of assembling the highlights of her post-Motown career. The focus is on her handful of minor mid-'60s hits for 20th Century Fox (which were conscious or half-conscious attempts to emulate her Motown sound) and her grittier 1968-70 recordings for Jubilee (which she co-wrote and co-produced with guitarist and husband/producer Cecil Womack). A couple of unimpressive tracks from her 1981 Epic album round out the collection; Wells is in fine form throughout. *—Richie Unterberger*

Dear Lover: The Atco Sessions / Jan. 1995 / Ichiban Soul Classics ♦♦♦

Never, Never Leave Me: The 20th Century Sides / Feb. 1996 / Ichiban Soul Classics ♦♦♦

● **The Ultimate Collection** / Feb. 10, 1998 / Motown ♦♦♦♦♦
Motown is notorious for recycling their catalog as endless hit collections, but *The Ultimate Collection* is one of the finest series of greatest-hits CDs they have ever assembled. Each disc contains all of the major hits from an artist, plus important B-sides, album tracks and minor hits. Mary Wells' entry in the series is no exception to the rule, boasting all her Top Ten pop and R&B hits. Not only are the familiar Motown singles here—"Bye Bye Baby," "I Don't Want to Take a Chance," "The One Who Really Loves You," "You Beat Me to the Punch," "Two Lovers," "Laughing Boy," "Your Old Stand By," "What's Easy for Two is So Hard for One," "You Lost the Sweetest Boy," "My Guy"—but also her Top Ten hit for Atco, "Dear Lover," a pair of singles from 20th Century and several minor Motown hits and B-sides, resulting in a total of 25 tracks. For anyone who wants a definitive hits collection but is hesitant to invest in the double-disc *Looking Back, The Ultimate Collection* is an ideal choice. *—Stephen Thomas Erlewine*

Wham!

f. 1981, **db.** 1986
Group / Pop/Rock, New Wave, Adult Contemporary, Dance-Pop
Wham! was a U.K. pop-dance duo formed in 1981 by George Michael (born Yorgos Panayiotou, June 26, 1963) and Andrew Ridgeley (b.June 25, 1963). Combining light soul music with slow, romantic ballads, they first hit the U.K. charts in the fall of 1982 with "Young Guns (Go for It)." It hit number three, the first of ten U.K. Top Ten hits for the duo. The first Wham! album, *Fantastic,* topped the U.K. charts in 1983. The group broke through in the U.S. the following year with "Wake Me Up Before You Go-Go," the first of three straight number one hits. The second of those chart-toppers was "Careless Whisper," billed as "featuring George Michael," the first sign that Michael, who sang lead and wrote the songs, was emerging as a solo entity. Nevertheless, Wham! continued through 1986, finishing their career at Wembley Stadium in England, after which Michael went on to a successful solo career. *—William Ruhlmann*

Make It Big / 1984 / Columbia ♦♦♦♦♦
The title was a promise to themselves, Wham!'s assurance that they would make it big after struggling out of the gates the first time out. They succeeded on a grander scale than they every could have imagined, conquering the world and elsewhere with this effervescent set of giddy new wave pop-soul, thereby making George Michael a superstar and consigning Andrew Ridgely to the confines of Trivial Pursuit. It was so big and the singles were so strong that it's easy to overlook its patchwork qualities. It's no longer than eight tracks, short even for the pre-CD era, and while the four singles are strong, the rest is filler, including an Isley Brothers cover. Thankfully, it's the kind of filler that's so tied to its time that it's fascinating in its stilted post-disco dance-pop rhythms and Thatcher/Reagan materialism—an era that encouraged songs called "Credit Card Baby." If this dichotomy between the A-sides and B-sides is far too great to make this essential, the way *Faith* later would be, those A-sides range from good to terrific. "Wake Me Up Before You Go-Go" is absolute silliness whose very stupidity is its strength, and if "Everything She Wants" is merely agreeable bubblegum, "Freedom" is astounding, a sparkling Motown rip-off rippling with spirit and a timeless melody later ripped off by Noel Gallagher. Then, there's the concluding "Careless Whisper," a soulful slow one where Michael regrets a one-night stand over a richly seductive background and a yearning saxophone. It was an instant classic, and it was the first indication of George Michael's strengths as a pop craftsman—which means it points the way to *Faith,* not the half-hearted *Edge of Heaven.* *—Stephen Thomas Erlewine*

Music from the Edge of Heaven / 1986 / Columbia ♦♦♦
More of a hodgepodge of tracks than a coherent album, this still includes the Top Ten hits "I'm Your Man," "A Different Corner," and "The Edge of Heaven." *—William Ruhlmann*

● **The Best of Wham!: If You Were There . . .** / Nov. 1997 / Epic ♦♦♦♦♦
The Best of Wham!: If You Were There . . . is an excellent collection, featuring all the group's biggest hits, including "I'm Your Man," "Club Tropicana," "Wake Me Up Before You Go-Go," "Freedom," "The Edge of Heaven," "Wham Rap!," "Young Guns (Go for It!)," "Last Christmas" and "Everything She Wants '97." Apart from the original version of "A Different Corner" (which was credited to a solo George Michael) and "Everything She Wants," *The Best of Wham!* includes every worthwhile song the duo recorded and makes for a terrific overview for most fans. *—Stephen Thomas Erlewine*

White Zombie

f. 1985
Group / Alternative Metal, Alternative Pop/Rock
All garish colors and trashy noise, White Zombie brought some sleazy fun back to heavy metal, celebrating the sheer schlock of cheap sex and bad horror movies. Although they gathered a cult following with a series of independent albums in the late '80s, it wasn't until their video for "Thunder Kiss '65" was aired on MTV's *Beavis & Butt-head* in 1993 that the band crossed over to a large audience. And they were the rare metal band that could appeal to jaded, post-modern hipsters; with their campy lyrics and theatrics, it was clear that the band didn't take themselves seriously.

White Zombie consolidated their success in 1995 with *Astro Creep: 2000—Songs of Love, Destruction,* which sold over two million copies. In the summer of 1996, the group released a collection of remixes from *Astro Creep* called *Supersexy Swingin' Sounds.* *—Stephen Thomas Erlewine*

● **La Sexorcisto: Devil Music, Vol. 1** / Mar. 17, 1992 / Geffen ♦♦♦♦♦
White Zombie carves out a unique identity for itself in the grunge/thrash genre with this one. The prerequisite loud guitars and shouting vocalist are here, but this album shows an obsession with '60s trash culture, particularly fast cars and grade-B horror movies. The subject matter of Rob Zombie's lyrics, along with frequent movie samples, help this group stand out from their more generic, disaffected brethren. *—Steve Huey*

Astro Creep: 2000—*Songs of Love, Destruction* */ Apr. 11, 1995 / Geffen* ♦♦♦♦
Following the belated surprise success of *La Sexorcisto, Astro-Creep: 2000—Songs of Love, Destruction and Other Synthetic Delusions of the Electric Head* carried the weight of high

expectations, something that White Zombie was never familiar with before. Unsurprisingly, White Zombie plays it safe on *Astro-Creep*, never straying from their white-trash-on-acid metal. While it's undeniably campy, the band genuinely loves the trash they sing about, so they fit right into the tradition of tongue-in-cheek heavy metal bands from Alice Cooper to Kiss. Where those bands relied on songcraft beneath their schtick, White Zombie relies on a full-throttle roar. Borrowing such techniques as distorted vocals and drilling riffs from pseudo-industrial metal like Ministry, the band beefs up their basic sound, making it powerful enough to disguise the lack of solid song structures and memorable riffs. Sonically, *Astro Creep* delivers the initial goods, yet it never develops into trash as substantial as "Thunder Kiss '65." *—Stephen Thomas Erlewine*

Supersexy Swingin' Sounds / Aug. 1996 / Geffen ✦✦✦

Barry White

b. Sep. 12, 1944, Galveston, TX

Vocals, Keyboards, Arranger / Smooth Soul, Urban, Disco, Soul

Barry White has been involved in the popular music industry since age 11, when he played piano on Jesse Belvin's hit single "Goodnight My Love." He recorded with the Upfronts for Lumntone in 1960, then as a lead vocalist for Atlantic in 1964 and for Downey and Veep in 1965 under the name of Barry Lee. He was an A*R* man for Mustang/Bronco Records in 1966 and 1967. White formed the female trio Love Unlimited in 1969, and also became leader of the 40-piece Love Unlimited Orchestra. His solo career was revitalized in the early '70s as his formidable, deep, captivating bass, coupled with pseudo-sophisticated strings and elaborate productions, helped him rack up five number one hits and seven other Top Ten R&B hits from 1973 until 1978 for 20th Century Records. He also scored five Top Ten pop singles and one number one in that same stretch. "I'm Gonna Love You a Little More Baby" started the string in 1973, and his final Top Ten R&B single was "Your Sweetness Is My Weakness," which peaked at number two in 1978. White continued recording for United Gold, 20th Century again, United Gold, and A&M. He scored a mild comeback by being one of the featured vocalists on Quincy Jones' single "The Garden" in 1989 and continues recording for A&M in the '90s. *The Icon Is Love* (1994) marked White's return as a potent commercial force. *—Ron Wynn*

Greatest Hits, Vol. 1 / 1975 / Casablanca ✦✦✦✦✦

Greatest Hits, Vol. 2 / 1981 / Casablanca ✦✦✦✦✦

★ **All Time Greatest Hits** / 1995 / Mercury Funk Essentials ✦✦✦✦✦

Condensing the best moments from the two *Greatest Hits* collections onto one disc, *All Time Greatest Hits* contains all of Barry White's biggest hits, including "I'm Gonna Love You Just A Little More Baby," "Never, Never Gonna Give Ya Up," "Can't Get Enough of Your Love, Babe," "You're the First, the Last, My Everything," and "It's Ecstasy When You Lay Down Next to Me." *All Time Greatest Hits* is the definitive collection of Barry White's '70s heyday, containing all of his truly essential songs. *—Stephen Thomas Erlewine*

Whitesnake

f. 1977, London, England

Group / Hair Metal, Heavy Metal, Hard Rock

After recording two solo albums, former Deep Purple vocalist David Coverdale formed Whitesnake around 1977. In the glut of hard rock and heavy metal bands of the late '70s, their first albums got somewhat lost in the shuffle, although they were fairly popular in Europe and Japan. During 1982, Coverdale took some time off, so he could take care of his sick daughter. When he re-emerged with a new version of Whitesnake in 1984, the band sounded revitalized and energetic. *Slide It In* may have relied on Led Zeppelin and Deep Purple's old tricks, but the band had a knack for writing hooks; the record became their first platinum album. Three years later, Whitesnake released an eponymous album which was even better. Portions of the album were blatantly derivative—"Still of the Night" was a dead ringer for early Zeppelin—but the group could write powerful, heavy rockers like "Here I Go Again" that were driven as much by melody as riffs, as well as hit power ballads like "Is This Love." *Whitesnake* was an enormous international success, selling over six million copies in the U.S. alone. *—Stephen Thomas Erlewine*

Ready An' Willing / 1980 / EMI ✦✦✦✦

Come An' Get It / 1981 / Geffen ✦✦✦

Saints & Sinners / 1982 / Geffen ✦✦✦✦

Slide It In / 1984 / Geffen ✦✦✦✦✦

Whitesnake / 1987 / Geffen ✦✦✦✦✦

David Coverdale built Whitesnake's commercial breakthrough on a collection of loud, polished hard rockers, plus the band's best set of pop hooks. The Led Zeppelin-ish "Still of the Night" offered headbanger appeal, but it was the big chorus of "Here I Go Again"—one of the very small number of non-power ballad '80s hard rock singles to actually top the pop charts—and the quiet ballad "Is This Love" that really sold the album in spades. The rest of the album generally holds interest as well, and it's easily the band's best. *—Steve Huey*

Slip of the Tongue / Feb. 1989 / Geffen ✦✦✦

● **Whitesnake's Greatest Hits** / Jul. 19, 1994 / Geffen ✦✦✦✦✦

Whitesnake's Greatest Hits collects the cream of the band's later '80s efforts, gathering most of its material from *Slide It In*, *Whitesnake*, and *Slip of the Tongue*. Bigger fans will find worthwhile album tracks on the former two efforts, but this collection of Zeppelin-ish rock anthems and hooky power ballads are all most fans will need. *—Steve Huey*

The Who

f. 1964, London, England, **db.** 1983

Group / British Psychedelia, Album Rock, Mod, Pop/Rock, British Invasion, Hard Rock, Rock & Roll

Few bands in the history of rock & roll were riddled with as many contradictions as the Who. All four members had wildly different personalities, as their notoriously intense live per-

formances demonstrated. The group was a whirlwind of activity, as the wild Keith Moon fell over his drum kit and Pete Townshend leaped into the air with his guitar, spinning his right hand in exaggerated windmills. Vocalist Roger Daltrey strutted across the stage with a thuggish menace, as bassist John Entwistle stood silent, functioning as the eye of the hurricane. These divergent personalities frequently clashed, but these frictions also resulted in a decade's worth of remarkable music. As one of the key figures of the British Invasion and the mod movement of the mid-'60s, the Who were a dynamic and undeniably powerful sonic force. They often sounded like they were exploding conventional rock and R&B structures with Townshend's furious guitar chords, Entwistle's hyperactive bass lines and Moon's vigorous, chaotic drumming. Unlike most rock bands, the Who based their rhythm on Townshend's guitar, letting Moon and Entwistle improvise wildly over his foundation, while Daltrey belted out his vocals. This was the sound the Who thrived on in concert, but on record they were a different proposition, as Townshend pushed the group toward new sonic territory. He soon became regarded as one of the finest British songwriters of his era, as songs like "The Kids Are Alright" and "My Generation" became teenage anthems, and his rock opera *Tommy* earned him respect from mainstream music critics. Townshend continually pushed the band toward more ambitious territory, incorporating white noise, pop art and conceptual extended musical pieces into the group's style. At their peak, the Who were one of the most innovative and powerful bands in rock history. *—Stephen Thomas Erlewine*

☆ **The Who Sings My Generation** / 1965 / MCA ✦✦✦✦✦

An explosive debut, and the hardest mod pop recorded by anyone. At the time of its release, it also had the most ferociously powerful guitars and drums yet captured on a rock record. Townshend's exhilarating chord crunches and guitar distortions threaten to leap off the grooves on "My Generation" and "Out in the Street"; Keith Moon attacks the drums with a lightning, ruthless finesse throughout. Some "Maximum R&B" influence lingered in the two James Brown covers, but much of Townshend's original material fused Beatlesque hooks and power chords with anthemic mod lyrics, with "The Good's Gone," "Much Too Much," "La La La Lies," and especially "The Kids Are Alright" being highlights. "A Legal Matter" hinted at more ambitious lyrical concerns, and "The Ox" was instrumental mayhem that pushed the envelope of 1965 amplification with its guitar feedback and nonstop crashing drumrolls. While the execution was sometimes crude, and the songwriting not as sophisticated as it would shortly become, the Who never surpassed the pure energy level of this record. *—Richie Unterberger*

A Quick One (Happy Jack) / 1966 / MCA ✦✦✦✦✦

The group's second album is a less impressive outing than their debut, primarily because, at the urging of their managers, all four members penned original material (though Townshend wrote more than anyone else). The pure adrenaline of *My Generation* also subsided somewhat, as the band began to grapple with more complex melodic and lyrical themes, especially on the erratic mini-opera, "A Quick One While He's Away." Still, there's some great madness on Moon's instrumental "Cobwebs and Strange," and Townshend delivered some solid mod pop with "Run Run Run" and "So Sad About Us." John Entwistle was also revealed to be a writer of considerable talent (and a morbid bent) on "Whiskey Man" and "Boris the Spider." The 1995 CD reissue adds ten bonus tracks: some 1966-67 B-sides, their U.K.-only 1966 *Ready Steady Who!* EP, an acoustic version of "Happy Jack," and a previously unreleased cover of the Everly Brothers' "Man with the Money." *—Richie Unterberger*

☆ **The Who Sell Out** / 1967 / MCA ✦✦✦✦✦

Townshend originally planned this as a concept album of sorts that would simultaneously mock and pay tribute to pirate radio stations, complete with fake jingles and commercials linking the tracks. For reasons that remain somewhat ill-defined, the concept wasn't quite driven to completion, breaking down around the middle of side two (on the original vinyl configuration). Nonetheless, on strictly musical merits, it's a terrific set of songs that ultimately stands as one of the group's greatest achievements. "I Can See For Miles" (a Top Ten hit) is the Who at their most thunderous; tinges of psychedelia add a rush to "Armenia, City in the Sky" and "Relax"; "I Can't Reach You" finds Townshend beginning to stretch himself into quasi-spiritual territory; and "Tattoo" and the acoustic "Sunrise" show introspective, vulnerable sides to the singer-songwriter that had previously been hidden. "Rael" was another mini-opera, with musical motifs that reappeared in *Tommy*. The album is as perfect a balance between melodic mod pop and powerful instrumentation as the Who (or any other group) would achieve; psychedelic pop was never as jubilant, not to say funny (the fake commercials and jingles interspersed between the songs are a hoot). The 1995 CD reissue has over half a dozen interesting outtakes from the time of the sessions, as well as unused commercials, the B-side "Someone's Coming," and an alternate version of "Mary Anne with the Shaky Hand." *—Richie Unterberger*

Tommy / 1969 / MCA ✦✦✦✦✦
The full-blown rock opera about a deaf, dumb, and blind boy that launched the band to international superstardom, written almost entirely by Townshend. Hailed as a breakthrough upon its release, it's critical standing has diminished somewhat in the ensuing decades, because of the occasional pretensions of the concept, and the insubstantial nature of some of the songs that functioned as little more than devices to advance the rather sketchy plot. Nonetheless, the double album has many excellent songs, including "I'm Free," "Pinball Wizard," "Sensation," "Christmas," "We're Not Gonna Take It," and the dramatic ten-minute instrumental, "Underture." Though the album was slightly flawed, Townshend's ability to construct a lengthy conceptual narrative brought new possibilities to rock music. Despite the complexity of the project, he and the Who never lost sight of solid pop melodies, harmonies, and forceful instrumentation, imbuing the material with a suitably powerful grace. *—Richie Unterberger*

☆ **Live at Leeds** / 1970 / MCA ✦✦✦✦✦
A loud, raunchy concert showcase for the group, with surprisingly little material from *Tommy*. The group's R&B roots are showcased here far better than on their post-*My Generation* studio albums, and the only problem for some listeners is the lack of the sophisticated studio sound they'd developed on previous releases. The 1995 CD reissue doubles the length of the original LP, with plenty of additional material from the same performance, including versions of some more of their early singles and unexpected items like "Tattoo" and the R&B standard "Fortune Teller." *—Bruce Eder*

★ **Meaty Beaty Big and Bouncy** / 1971 / MCA ✦✦✦✦✦
Meaty, Beaty, Big & Bouncy has the distinction of being the first in a long line of Who compilations. It also has the distinction of being the best. Part of the reason why it is so successful is that it has an actual purpose. *Meaty* was designed as a collection of the group's singles, many of which never appeared on albums. The Who recorded their share of great albums during the '60s, but condensing their highlights to just the singles is an electrifying experience. "The Kids Are Alright" follows "I Can't Explain," "I Can See for Miles" bleeds into "Pictures of Lily" and "My Generation," "Magic Bus" gives way to "Substitute" and "I'm a Boy"—it's an extraordinary lineup, and each song builds on its predecessor's power. Since it was released prior to *Who's Next*, it contains none of the group's album rock hits, but that's for the best—their '60s singles have a kinetic, frenzied power that the louder, harder AOR cuts simply couldn't touch. Also, there is such a distinct change in sound with *Who's Next* that the two eras don't quite sound right on one greatest-hits collection, as *My Generation* and *Who's Better, Who's Best* proved. By concentrating on the early years—when the Who were fresh and Pete Townshend was developing his own songwriting identity—*Meaty, Beaty, Big & Bouncy* is musically unified and incredibly powerful. *This* is what the Who sounded like when they were a great band. *—Stephen Thomas Erlewine*

★ **Who's Next** / 1971 / MCA ✦✦✦✦✦
Much of *Who's Next* derives from *Lifehouse*, an ambitious sci-fi rock opera Pete Townshend abandoned after suffering a nervous breakdown, caused in part from working on the sequel to *Tommy*. There's no discernable theme behind these songs, yet this album is stronger than *Tommy*, falling just behind *Who Sell Out* as the finest record the Who ever cut. Townshend developed an infatuation with synthesizers during the recording of the album, and they're all over this album, adding texture where needed and amplifying the force, which is already at a fever pitch. Apart from *Live at Leeds*, the Who have never sounded as LOUD and unhinged as they do here, yet that's balanced by ballads, both lovely ("The Song Is Over") and scathing ("Behind Blue Eyes"). That's the key to *Who's Next*—there's anger and sorrow, humor and regret, passion and tumult, all wrapped up in a blistering package where the rage is as affecting as the heartbreak. This is a retreat from the '60s, as Townshend declares the "Song Is Over," scorns the teenage wasteland, and bitterly declares that we "Won't Get Fooled Again." For all the sorrow and heartbreak that runs beneath the surface, this is an invigorating record, not just because Keith Moon runs rampant or because Roger Daltrey has never sung better or because John Entwistle spins out manic bass lines that are as captivating as his "My Wife" is funny. This is invigorating because it has all of that, plus Townshend laying his soul bare in ways that are funny, painful, and utterly life-affirming. That is what the Who was about, not the rock operas, and that's why *Who's Next* is truer than *Tommy* or the abandoned *Lifehouse*. Those were art—this, even with its pretensions, is rock & roll. *—Stephen Thomas Erlewine*

Quadrophenia / 1973 / MCA ✦✦✦✦✦
Pete Townshend revisited the rock opera concept with another double-album opus, this time built around the story of a young mod's struggle to come of age in the mid-'60s. If anything, this was a more ambitious project than *Tommy*, given added weight by the fact that the Who weren't devising some fantasy, but were re-examining the roots of their own birth in mod culture. In the end, there may have been *too* much weight, as Townshend tried to combine the story of a mixed-up mod named Jimmy with the examination of a four-way split personality (hence the title *Quadrophenia*), in turn meant to reflect the four conflicting personas at work within the Who themselves. The concept might have ultimately been too obscure and confusing for a mass audience. But there's plenty of great music anyway, especially on "The Real Me," "The Punk Meets the Godfather," "I'm One," "Bell Boy," and "Love, Reign O'er Me." Some of Townshend's most direct, heartfelt writing is contained here, and production-wise it's a tour de force, with some of the most imaginative use of synthesizers on a rock record. Various members of the band griped endlessly about flaws in the mix, but really these will bug very few listeners, who in general will find this to be one of the Who's most powerful statements. *—Richie Unterberger*

Odds & Sods / 1974 / MCA ✦✦✦
This compilation of outtakes and rarities from the Who's first decade was a rather jumpy listen that harbored few songs that could be termed top-of-the-line. Also, since its 1974 release, several of the tracks have been issued on other compilations, or as bonus tracks to CD reissues of legitimate Who albums. Setting your expectations at the appropriate level, you'll find much of this worthwhile. "Pure and Easy," "Naked Eye," and "Long Live Rock" were all concert favorites of the group in the 1970s; "Glow Girl" introduced some riffs that would resurface in *Tommy;* and "Postcard," Entwistle's tale of rock life on the road, was one of his better compositions. This also has their very first single, "I'm the Face," recorded in 1964 when the group were known as the High Numbers. The 1998 CD reissue is a must-have even if you've got the original LP, as it doubles the album size with a dozen bonus tracks, most previously unreleased. These include some real interesting items: the Motown covers "Leaving Here" and "Baby Don't You Do It" are taken from demos circa late 1964, the latter track featuring some early guitar distortion freakout in the solo; "Mary Anne with the Shaky Hand" is the rare U.S. B-side version; there are late-sixties studio versions of *Live at Leeds* faves "Summertime Blues" and "Young Man Blues"; the Rolling Stones' cover "Under My Thumb" and "Water" are B-sides that weren't on album for a long time; and there are less exciting alternates and outtakes from *Tommy, Who's Next* and *Quadrophenia*. *—Richie Unterberger*

The Who By Numbers / 1975 / MCA ✦✦✦✦
The Who by Numbers functions as Pete Townshend's confessional singer-songwriter album, as he chronicles his problems with alcohol ("However Much I Booze"), women ("Dreaming from the Waist" and "They Are All in Love"), and life in general. However, his introspective musings are rendered ineffective by Roger Daltrey's bluster and the cloying, lightweight filler of "Squeeze Box." In addition, Townshend's songs tend to be under-developed, relying on verbosity instead of melodicism, with only the simple power of "Slip Kid," the grace of "Blue Red and Grey," and John Entwistle's heavy rocker "Success Story" making much of an impact. The 1996 CD reissue adds three live tracks from a 1976 concert. *—Stephen Thomas Erlewine*

Who Are You / 1978 / MCA ✦✦✦
On the band's final album with Moon, their trademark honest power started to get diluted by fatigue and a sense that the group's collective vision was beginning to fade. As instrumentalists, their skills were intact. More problematic was the erratic quality of the material, which seemed torn between blustery attempts at contemporary relevance ("Sister Disco," "New Song," "Music Must Change") and bittersweet insecurity ("Love Is Coming Down"). Most problematic of all were the arrangements, heavy on the symphonic synthesizers and strings, which make the record sound cluttered and over-anxious. Daltrey's operatic tough-guy braggadacio in particular was beginning to sound annoying on several cuts. Yet Townshend's better tunes—"Music Must Change," "Love Is Coming Down," and the anthemic title track—continued to explore the contradictions of aging rockers in interesting, effective ways. Whether due to Moon's death or not, it was the last reasonably interesting Who record. The 1996 CD reissue adds five previously unreleased alternate takes and demos. *—Richie Unterberger*

The Kids Are Alright / 1979 / MCA ✦✦✦

Face Dances / 1981 / MCA ✦✦✦

It's Hard / 1982 / MCA ✦✦

Who's Missing / 1985 / MCA ✦✦✦

Two's Missing / 1987 / MCA ✦✦✦

Thirty Years of Maximum R&B / Jul. 5, 1994 / MCA ✦✦✦

● **My Generation: The Very Best of the Who** / Aug. 27, 1996 / MCA ✦✦✦✦✦
The Who have issued more greatest hits collections than any other major artist, releasing a vast array of compilations while they were together and in the years following their breakup. Released in 1996, *My Generation: The Very Best of the Who* was intended to be the definitive single-disc collection, replacing all the others that preceded it. While it is a very good collection, it just misses being a definitive sampler. Essentially, *My Generation* is a replica of *Who's Better, Who's Best* that adds four tracks that were missing from the previous compilation, including the seminal post-*Tommy* single "The Seeker" and the original single mix of "Magic Bus." *My Generation* isn't strictly a singles collection, since it contains such album rock staples as "Baba O'Riely" and the full-length version of "Won't Get Fooled Again." It also spans the group's entire career, so it has a bit of a scatter-shot feel to it—"You Better You Bet" sounds a little odd next to tense early singles like "Substitute" and "I Can See For Miles." The career-spanning approach doesn't make for a cohesive a collection as *Meaty, Beaty, Big and Bouncy*, but it does mean that *My Generation* is an excellent—even necessary—introduction. There's a lot more in the Who's catalog that needs to be heard, but *My Generation* does boil down the most essential items (even though the abominable "Squeeze Box" is included) to a fine single-disc set. *—Stephen Thomas Erlewine*

Live at the Isle of Wight Festival 1970 / Oct. 29, 1996 / Columbia/Legacy ✦✦✦✦✦

The BBC Sessions / Feb. 15, 2000 / MCA ✦✦✦✦✦
A fine compilation of 1965-73 BBC performances, the majority of the tracks hailing from 1965-67, although some are drawn from 1970 and 1973. As one of the best live bands ever,

the Who as expected come through pretty well in the live-in-the-studio environment, although the arrangements usually stick close to the records. Most of the songs were done by the group for studio releases as well, but there are a few covers that they never put on their albums or singles at the time, making this essential for the fan. Those numbers include the obscure James Brown tune "Just You and Me, Darling," "Dancing in the Street," ""Good Lovin'," and "Leaving Here" (although a mid-1960s studio version of that last song was eventually released). Of the other tracks, particularly worthwhile are "Anyway, Anyhow, Anywhere," with its extensive feedback solo, quite a challenge to do live in May 1965; "The Good's Gone," which has a fuzz solo not on the studio version; and the 1970 performance of "Shakin' All Over," which might be the best rendition of that concert staple that they ever did. This does not have a few BBC songs that have shown up on bootlegs; particularly unfortunate exclusions are "So Sad About Us," "Summertime Blues," and their 1966 cover of the Everly Brothers' "Man with Money." *—Richie Unterberger*

Wilco

f. 1994

Group / Adult Alternative Pop/Rock, Alternative Country-Rock, Alternative Pop/Rock

The alternative country band Wilco rose from the ashes of the seminal roots-rockers Uncle Tupelo, who disbanded in 1994. While Jay Farrar, one of the group's two singer/songwriters, went on to form the band Son Volt, his ex-partner Jeff Tweedy established Wilco along with the remaining members of Tupelo's final incarnation, which included drummer Ken Coomer as well as part-time bandmates John Stirratt (bass) and Max Johnston (mandolin, banjo, fiddle and lap steel). Guitarist Jay Bennett rounded out the group, which in 1995 issued their debut album, *A.M.*, a collection of spry country-rock tunes that followed the course established in Tweedy's earlier work. Wilco's sophomore effort, 1996's two-disc set *Being There*, marked a radical transformation in the group's sound; while remaining steeped in the style that earned Tweedy his reputation, the songs took unexpected detours into psychedelia, power-pop and soul, complete with orchestral touches and R&B horn flourishes. Shortly after the release of *Being There*, which most critics judged to be among the year's best releases, Johnston left the group to play with his sister, singer Michelle Shocked, and was replaced by guitarist Bob Egan of the band Freakwater. At the same time, while remaining full-time members of Wilco, Stirratt, Bennett and Coomer also began performing together in the pop side project Courtesy Move. In 1998, Wilco backed singer-songwriter Billy Bragg on *Mermaid Avenue*, a collection of performances based on unreleased material originally written by Woody Guthrie; their stunningly lush third album, *Summer Teeth*, followed in 1999. *—Jason Ankeny*

A.M. / Mar. 28, 1995 / Sire/Reprise ✦✦✦

● **Being There** / Oct. 29, 1996 / Sire/Reprise ✦✦✦✦✦

While Wilco's debut *A.M.* spread its wings in an expectedly country-rock fashion, their sophomore effort *Being There* is the group's great leap forward, a masterful, wildly eclectic collection shot through with ambitions and ideas. Although a few songs remain rooted in their signature sound, here Jeff Tweedy and band are as fascinated by their music's possibilities as its origins, and they push the songs which make up this sprawling two-disc set down consistently surprising paths and byways. For starters, the opener "Misunderstood" is majestic psychedelia, built on studio trickery and string flourishes, while "I Got You (At the End of the Century)" is virtual power-pop, right down to the handclaps. The lovely "Someone Else's Song" borrows heavily from the Beatles' "Norwegian Wood," while the R&B-influenced boogie of "Monday" wouldn't sound at all out of place on *Exile on Main St.*; and on and on. The remarkable thing is how fresh all of these seeming cliches sound when re-imagined with so much love and conviction; even the most traditional songs take unexpected twists and turns, never once sinking into mere imitation. "Music is my savior/I was named by rock 'n' roll/I was maimed by rock 'n' roll/I was tamed by rock 'n' roll/I got my name from rock 'n' roll," Tweedy sings on "Sunken Treasure," the opener of the second disc, and throughout the course of these 19 songs he explores rock as though he were tracing his family geneology, fervently seeking to discover not only where he came from but also where he's going. With *Being There*, he finds what he's been looking for. *—Jason Ankeny*

Summer Teeth / Mar. 9, 1999 / Warner Brothers ✦✦✦✦✦

Jeff Tweedy once blazed the trail for the American rock underground's embrace of its country and folk roots, but as the decade draws to its close he's spearheading the return of classic pop; simply put, what once were fiddles on Wilco records are now violins—the same instrument, to be sure, but viewed with a radical shift in perception and meaning. While lacking the sheer breadth and ambition of the previous *Being There*, *Summer Teeth* is the most focused Wilco effort yet, honing the lessons of the last record to forge a majestic pop sound almost completely devoid of alt-country elements: the lush string arrangements and gorgeous harmonies of tracks like "She's a Jar" and "Pieholden Suite" suggest nothing less than a land-locked Brian Wilson, while more straightforward rockers like the opening "I Can't Stand It" bear the influence of everything from R&B to psychedelia. Still, for all of the superficial warmth and beauty of the record's arrangements, Tweedy's songs are perhaps his darkest and most haunting to date, bleak domestic dramas informed by recurring themes of alienation, adultery and abuse—even the sunniest melodies mask moments of devastating power. If *Summer Teeth* has a precedent, it's peak-era Band; the album not only possesses a similar pastoral sensibility, but like Robbie Robertson and company before them, Wilco seems directly connected to a kind of American musical consciousness, not only rejuvenating our collective creative mythology, but adding new chapters to the legend with each successive record. *—Jason Ankeny*

Larry Williams

b. May 10, 1935, New Orleans, LA, **d.** Jan. 7, 1980, Los Angeles, CA

Vocals, Saxophone, Keyboards, Piano / Pop-Soul, Rock & Roll, R&B, Soul

A rough, rowdy rock & roll singer, Larry Williams had several hits in the late '50s, several of which—"Bony Maroney," "Dizzy, Miss Lizzy," "Short Fat Fannie," "Bad Boy," "She Said Yeah"—became genuine rock & roll classics and were recorded by British Invasion groups; John Lennon, in particular, was a fan of Williams, recording several of his songs over the course of his career. Singer Lloyd Price hired the teenaged Williams as his valet and introduced him to Robert "Bumps" Blackwell, the Specialty label's house producer. Soon, the label's owner, Art Rupe, signed Williams to a solo recording contract. Just after Specialty signed Larry Williams, the company lost Little Richard, their biggest seller; the label then put all of its energy into making Williams a star, giving him an image makeover and a set of material—ranging from hard R&B, rock & roll, to ballads—that were quite similar to Richard's hits. Williams' first post-Little Richard single was the raucous "Short Fat Fannie," which shot to number one on the R&B charts and number five on the pop charts in the summer of 1957. It was followed in the fall by "Bony Maronie," which hit number four on the R&B charts and number 14 on the pop charts. Williams wasn't able to maintain that momentum, however. "You Bug Me, Baby" and "Dizzy Miss Lizzy," his next two singles, missed the R&B charts but became minor pop hits in late 1957 and early 1958. Despite the relative failure of these singles, Williams' records became popular import items in Britain; the Beatles would cover both sides of the "Dizzy Miss Lizzy" single (the B-side was "Slow Down") in the mid-'60s. However, Williams' commercial fortunes in America continued to decline, despite Specialty's release of a constant stream of singles and one full-length album. *—Stephen Thomas Erlewine*

★ **Bad Boy** / Apr. 6, 1992 / Specialty ✦✦✦✦✦

Bad Boy compiles 23 tracks Larry Williams recorded between 1957 and 1958. The core of the collection are his hit singles—"Bony Maronie," "She Said Yeah," "Lawdy Miss Clawdy," "Just Because," "Dizzy Miss Lizzy," "Short Fat Fannie," "Bad Boy," "Slow Down"—many of which became standards. *—Stephen Thomas Erlewine*

Robbie Williams

b. Feb. 13, 1974, Tunstall, Stoke-on-Trent, Staffordshire, England

Vocals / Britpop, Pop/Rock, Alternative Pop/Rock, Dance-Pop

Out of all the members of Take That, Robbie Williams never really seemed to fit in. Roguishly handsome where his bandmates were merely cute, Williams was tougher and sexier than the rest, which made him more distinctive. He also fought regularly with the other members and their management, primarily because he was occasionally adverse to behing so heavily packaged. So it didn't come as a surprise that he was the first to leave the band, departing early in the summer of 1995 and attempting to boost his credibility by tagging along with Oasis, hoping that Noel Gallagher would give him a couple of songs. He never did, but all of his time with Oasis launched Williams into a world of heavy partying, drinking and drugging. Over the course of 1996, he was only heard from in gossip columns, an occasionally, he was quoted as saying his new music would abandon lightweight dance-pop for traditional Brit-pop, but his first single was a cover of George Michael's "Freedom '90." Released late in 1996, the single was a disaster, but his second single, 1997's "Old Before I Die," was more in the vein of his early pronouncements, featuring a distinct Oasis influence. Williams released his first solo album, *LIfe Thru a Lens*, in 1997. The album became a big hit in Britain, prompting his second *I've Been Expecting You*, in 1998. *The Ego Has Landed*, a US-only compilation designed for breaking Williams to American audiences, was released in the US in 1999. *—Stephen Thomas Erlewine*

● **Life Thru a Lens** / 1997 / Chrysalis ✦✦✦✦✦

One of the best U.K. debuts of the '90s, *Life Thru a Lens* is an uninhibited joyride through all manner of British music, from glam to alternative to soft-rock to dance-pop. Beginning with the joyous "Lazy Days," the album continually betrays overt influences from Oasis and other Britpop stars, but triumphs nevertheless due to gorgeous production, Williams' irresistible personality, and the overall flavor of outrageous, utterly enjoyable pop music. Whether he's romping through aggressive burners like "Ego A Go Go" and "South of the Border," crooning on the ballad "Angels," or offering a slice of life—working-class style—on the title track and "Lazy Days," Williams is a pop star through and through. For those who appreciate great pop with plenty of cheek, *Life Thru a Lens* is an excellent album. *—John Bush*

I've Been Expecting You / Aug. 25, 1998 / Chrysalis ✦✦✦✦

● **The Ego Has Landed** / May 4, 1999 / Capitol ✦✦✦✦

Robbie Williams was an international superstar at the end of the millennium, a recognizable icon in all countries but one—the United States. Traditionally, this is a problem for British superstars, who are able to amass a large global following but are hard pressed to break down the doors to America for a variety of reasons, many of which are inexplicable. For Williams, it was because his records weren't released in the U.S., probably because his former band, Take That, never developed into a commercial powerhouse in America. Once the group split, conventional wisdom suggested that lead singer Gary Barlow would become the star, but after Williams delivered back-to-back smashes (*Life Thru a Lens, I've Been Expecting You*), he seemed like the genuine star. It was time for America to become acquainted with the lovable rock & roll rascal, hence the brilliantly titled *The Ego Has Landed*. Containing six songs from *Life* and eight from *I've Been*, *The Ego Has Landed* isn't a perfect compilation, but it's not half bad either. Since it's culled from just two records, it doesn't have great momentum or pacing, but it does contain a very good cross section of his two albums, leaning a little toward the mid-tempo and ballad side. The pacing is a little off, but the songs are there: the clever showmanship of "Let Me Entertain You," the endearingly silly "Old Before I Die," the crooning "No Regrets," the propulsive "Man Machine," and "Millennium," Willliams' bid for sampadelic hipness—everything that illustrates why he is a perfect post-alternative, post-Brit-pop, post-ironic pop star. *—Stephen Thomas Erlewine*

Sing When You're Winning / Oct. 3, 2000 / Capitol ✦✦✦✦

Chuck Willis (Harold Willis)

b. Jan. 31, 1928, Atlanta, GA, **d.** Apr. 10, 1958, Atlanta, GA

Vocals / R&B

There were two distinct sides to Chuck Willis. In addition to being a convincing blues shouter, Willis harbored a vulnerable blues balladeer side. In addition, he was a masterful songwriter who penned some of the most distinctive R&B numbers of the 1950s. He wrote such gems as "I Feel So Bad" (later covered by Elvis Presley), the anguished ballads "Don't Deceive Me (Please Don't Go)" and "It's Too Late" (the latter attracting covers by Buddy Holly and Otis Redding), and his swan song, "Hang Up My Rock and Roll Shoes." He first recorded in 1951, issuing one single for Columbia before he was shuttled over to its recently reactivated OKeh R&B subsidiary. One year later, he crashed the national R&B lists for OKeh with a typically plaintive ballad, "My Story." He followed up with his own "Don't Deceive Me" and the surging Latin-beat "I Feel So Bad" in 1954. After moving over to Atlantic in 1956, he immediately enjoyed another round of hits with "It's Too Late" and "Juanita." His 1957 revival of the ancient "C.C. Rider" became his first R&B number one hit and a huge pop seller. But the turban-wearing crooner's time was growing short—he had long suffered from ulcers prior to his 1958 death from peritonitis. *—Bill Dahl*

Let's Jump Tonight! The Best of Chuck Willis: 1951-1956 / 1994 / Epic/Legacy ✦✦✦✦✦
Before his brief turn as a rock & roll star with Atlantic, Willis cut a lot of material for Okeh in much more of an R&B/jump blues vein. This 26-cut collection includes all of his early and mid-'50s R&B hits—"My Story," "Goin' to the River," "Don't Deceive Me," "You're Still My Baby," and his most famous number from this period, "I Feel So Bad" (revived by Elvis Presley, among others). The influence of Joe Turner, Charles Brown, early Lloyd Price, and similar performers is strongly felt; Willis could shout competently, but was much better on the emotional R&B ballads. Not as strong or distinctive as his Atlantic material, this includes several cuts that were previously unreleased or previously unavailable in the U.S. *—Richie Unterberger*

★ **Stroll On: The Chuck Willis Collection** / Oct. 19, 1994 / Razor & Tie ✦✦✦✦✦
All 25 of the versatile Atlanta-bred singer's Atlantic Records sides, presented beautifully (every R&B reissue on CD should be packaged so well, with plenty of brilliant stereo). Willis really hit his stride at Atlantic, doing the Stroll with his easy-going "C.C. Rider" and "Betty and Dupree" (both boasting darting sax breaks from Gene Barge), baring his tender soul on a devotional "What Am I Living For," and taking R&B into fresh directions with a jumping "Kansas City Woman," the relentless "Keep A-Drivin'," and a buoyant "Hang Up My Rock and Roll Shoes." *—Bill Dahl*

Jackie Wilson

b. Jun. 9, 1934, Detroit, MI, **d.** Jan. 21, 1984, Mount Holly, NJ
Vocals / Chicago Soul, Uptown Soul, Pop-Soul, R&B, Soul
Jackie Wilson was one of the most important agents of Black pop's transition from rhythm & blues into soul. In terms of vocal power (especially in the upper register), few could outdo him; he was also an electricfying onstage showman. He was a consistent hitmaker from the mid-1950s through the early 1970s, although never a crossover superstar. His reputation isn't quite on par with Ray Charles, James Brown, or Sam Cooke, however, because his records did not always reflect his artistic genius. Indeed, there is a consensus of sorts among critics that Wilson was something of an underachiever in the studio, due to the sometimes inappropriately pop-based material and arrangements that he used. Wilson would score his first big R&B (and small pop) hit in late 1956 with the brassy, stuttering "Reet Petite," which was co-written by an emerging Detroit songwriter named Berry Gordy, Jr. Gordy would also help write a few other hits for Jackie in the late '50s, "To Be Loved," "Lonely Teardrops," "That's Why (I Love You So)," and "I'll Be Satisfied"; they also crossed over to the pop charts, "Lonely Teardrops" making the Top Ten. Most of these were upbeat, creatively arranged marriages of pop and R&B that, in retrospect, helped set the stage both for '60s soul, and for Gordy's own huge pop success at Motown.. In the early '60s, Wilson maintained his pop stardom with regular hit singles that often used horn arrangements and female choruses that have dated somewhat badly. At the same time, he remained capable of unleashing a sweaty, uptempo, gospel-soaked number: "Baby Workout," which fit that description to a T, was a number five hit for him in 1963. In 1966, his career was briefly revived when he teamed up with Chicago soul producer Carl Davis, who had been instrumental in the success of Windy City performers like Gene Chandler, Major Lance, and Jerry Butler. Davis successfully updated Wilson's sound with horn-heavy arrangements, getting near the Top Ten with "Whispers," and then making #6 in 1967 with "Higher and Higher." *—Richie Unterberger*

He's So Fine / 1958 / Brunswick ✦✦✦✦

Jackie Wilson at the Copa / 1962 / Brunswick ✦✦✦
The only live album of Wilson's career was recorded in the early '60s at New York's famous *Copacabana* nightclub. It was an almost obligatory rite of passage for early soul stars breaking into the mainstream, one also enacted by Sam Cooke and several Motown stars. As you'd expect, the cirumstances don't exactly lend themselves to showing Wilson at his greatest advantage, particularly if you're principally a fan of Wilson the soul singer, not Wilson the all-around entertainer. He sounds like an over-the-top lounge lizard throughout much the proceedings, zipping through standards like Leonard Bernstein's "Tonight," "Body and Soul," "St. James Infirmary," and Cole Porter's "Love for Sale," occasionally pausing for some corny between-song patter. He does interject a few of his R&B hits ("That's Why," "Doggin' Around," "To Be Loved," "Lonely Teardrops"), but these too get the casino band treatment, complete with strings and strident female backup vocalists. No, it's not what you play as exhibit A to showcase Jackie Wilson, Rock & Roll Hall of Famer. But taken on its own terms it's enjoyably cheesy entertainment, Wilson's astounding vocal prowess always in evidence. Out of print since 1967, it was reissued on CD in 1995. *—Richie Unterberger*

Higher and Higher / Nov. 1967 / Brunswick ✦✦✦✦

Mr. Excitement / Nov. 10, 1992 / Rhino ✦✦✦✦✦
A three-CD box from the experts of reissue at Rhino, *Mr. Excitement* takes Wilson's career from his first sides with Billy Ward & the Dominoes in 1956 through his final recordings in the early '70s. The former Detroit boxer hit either the R&B or pop chart over 50 times, making him one of the most successful R&B artists ever, in chart terms at least. Every one of those recordings is contained in this set, including such classics as "Reet Petite," "Lonely Teardrops," and "(Your Love Keeps Lifting Me) Higher and Higher." Wilson had an explosive falsetto and a downright weird sense of phrasing that made him utterly unique. Some of his productions were a little overwrought but even in the most extreme cases, that voice was a gift from God. Seminal. *—Rob Bowman*

☆ **The Very Best of Jackie Wilson [Ace]** / Feb. 4, 1993 / Ace ✦✦✦✦✦
Similar to the U.S. greatest-hits collection of the same name (on Rhino), but with substantially more tracks. This 24-song anthology has all the familiar big singles on the Rhino compilation, but goes into his late-'60s-early-'70s material in greater depth. His best stuff was recorded before that, though, so you're not much (if at all) worse off by sticking to the cheaper, more easily available domestic collection. *—Richie Unterberger*

★ **The Very Best of Jackie Wilson [Rhino]** / Jan. 18, 1994 / Rhino ✦✦✦✦✦
This 16-song overview of Wilson's at the peak of his career at Brunswick Records was the best CD of his work available during the 1990s, with the usual care for sound and choice of master tape sources that Rhino is known for. It was also far more entertaining that Rhino's less-than-edifying triple-CD set on Wilson. As of the year 2000, however, it had been deleted and supplanted by Brunswick's own greatest-hits CD, a straight reissue of its 1969 compilation, although anyone finding the Rhino disc as an out of print item should have no reservations about purchasing it. *—Bruce Eder*

This Love Is Real/You Got Me Walking / Jun. 29, 1999 / Edsel ✦✦✦✦

Beautiful Day/Nobody But You / Sep. 27, 1999 / Diablo ✦✦✦✦

Jesse Winchester

b. May 17, 1944, Shreveport, LA
Vocals, Keyboards, Guitar / Contemporary Folk, Folk-Rock, Singer/Songwriter
Jesse Winchester was the music world's most prominent Vietnam War draft-evader, though his renown came from a body of wry, closely observed songs. After growing up in Memphis, Winchester received his draft notice in 1967 and moved to Montreal, Canada, rather than serve in the military. In 1969, he met Robbie Robertson of the Band, who helped launch his recording career. In the same way that James Taylor's history of mental instability and drug abuse served as a subtext for his early music, Winchester's exile lent real-life poignancy to songs like "Yankee Lady." Despite critical acclaim, his inability to tour in the U.S. prevented him from taking his place among the major singer/songwriters of the early '70s, but he made a series of impressive albums before President Jimmy Carter instituted an amnesty that finally allowed him to play in his homeland. By that time, the singer/songwriter boom had passed, though Winchester continued to record and even scored a Top 40 hit with "Say What" in 1981. His most prominently covered songs include "The Brand New Tennessee Waltz," "Biloxi," "Mississippi, You're on My Mind," "Defying Gravity," "Rhumba Girl," "Well-A-Wiggy" and "I'm Gonna Miss You, Girl." *— William Ruhlmann*

Jesse Winchester / 1970 / Stony Plain ✦✦✦✦✦
Jesse Winchester first gained notice as a protégé of the Band's Robbie Robertson, who produced and played guitar on his debut album and brought along bandmate Levon Helm to play drums and mandolin. The album had much of the rustic Southern charm and rollicking country-rock of the Band. Winchester's other immediate appeal was a certain sense of mystery. A Southern American expatriate living in Canada, he was unable to appear in the U.S. to promote the album, which was released in a fold-out LP jacket that featured the same sepia-toned portrait (which looked like one of those austere Matthew Brady photos from the Civil War era) on each of its four sides. Winchester emphasized the dichotomy between his southern origins and his northern exile in songs like "Snow" (which Robertson co-wrote), "The Brand New Tennessee Waltz" ("I've a sadness too sad to be true"), and "Yankee Lady." *Jesse Winchester* was timely: it spoke to a disaffected American generation that sympathized with Winchester's pacifism. But it was also timeless: the songs revealed a powerful writing talent (recognized by the numerous artists who covered them), and Winchester's gentle vocals made a wonderful vehicle for delivering them. (Originally released by Ampex in 1970, *Jesse Winchester* was reissued by Bearsville Records in 1976 and again in 1988 by Rhino/Bearsville). *— William Ruhlmann*

Third Down, 110 to Go / 1972 / Stony Plain ✦✦✦✦✦
If Jesse Winchester's debut album was an auspicious introduction to a powerful new songwriting talent, his two-and-a-half-years-in-the-making follow-up was in some ways even more impressive. Without the influence of Robbie Robertson, Winchester, who produced most of the album himself (three tracks were handled by Todd Rundgren), gave it a homemade feel, using small collections of acoustic instruments, an appropriate setting for a group of short, intimate songs that expressed a deliberately positive worldview set against an acknowledgement of desperate times. Winchester found hope in religion and domesticity, but the key to his stance was a kind of good-humored accommodation. "If the wheel is fixed," he sang, "I would still take a chance. If we're skating on thin ice, then we might as well dance." The album was littered with such examples of aphoristic folk wisdom, adding up to a portrait of a man, cut off from his very deep roots and yet determined to maintain his dignity with grace and even occasionally a goofy sense of humor. *— William Ruhlmann*

Learn to Love It / 1974 / Stony Plain ✦✦✦
As the title suggests, making a virtue of necessity had always been a goal of Jesse Winchester's, and by the time of the release of his third album, the American expatriate had gone ahead and assumed Canadian citizenship. This seemed to free him to comment explicitly on his anti-war exile in "Pharaoh's Army" and especially a version of the old campaign song "Tell Me Why You Like Roosevelt" updated with new lyrics: "In the year of 1967, as a somewhat younger man, the call to bloody glory came, and I would not raise my hand." Elsewhere, Winchester continued to write love songs to his lost South ("L'Air De La Louisiane," "Mississippi, You're on My Mind") and, to a lesser extent, to pursue the wistful philosophizing found on *Third Down, 110 to Go* ("Defying Gravity"). The sense that he was repeating himself was inescapable, however, and with one-third of the album written by others and two of the originals in French Canadian, it was also obvious that Winchester was straining to come up with material. Interestingly, the two Russell Smith songs included, "Third Rate Romance" (which

Smith sang uncredited) and "The End Is Not in Sight," went on to become Top 40 country hits for Smith's group, the Amazing Rhythm Aces, in the next two years. Stoney Edwards took "Mississippi, You're on My Hind" into the country Top 40 in 1975. *—William Ruhlmann*

Let the Rough Side Drag / 1976 / Stony Plain ✦✦✦

Nothing But a Breeze / 1977 / Stony Plain ✦✦✦

A Touch on the Rainy Side / 1978 / Stony Plain ✦✦✦

Talk Memphis / 1981 / Stony Plain ✦✦✦

Humour Me / 1988 / Sugar Hill ✦✦✦

● **The Best of Jesse Winchester** / 1989 / Rhino ✦✦✦✦✦
Jesse Winchester wrote and recorded more than enough great songs for Bearsville to fill a single-disc compilation, which means that some of them were bound to be left off. The trick was to balance the material from the brilliant first two albums with a careful selection from the subsequent five albums, each of which had its virtues. This 14-track album chooses four from *Jesse Winchester,* including the essential "Yankee Lady," "Biloxi," and "The Brand New Tennessee Waltz," and three from its follow-up, *Third Down, 110 to Go.* There are three from *Learn to Love It,* one each from *Nothing but a Breeze* and *A Touch on the Rainy Side,* and two from *Talk Memphis.* Lesser material such as "Tell Me Why You Like Roosevelt" and "Rhumba Man" could have been excised in favor of more from *Third Down,* but the selection is good enough to give a reasonable representation of Winchester's seven Bearsville albums, which contain some of the most impressive songwriting of the 1970s. *—William Ruhlmann*

Gentleman of Leisure / Jun. 22, 1999 / Sugar Hill ✦✦✦✦

Johnny Winter

b. Feb. 23, 1944, Beaumont, TX
Slide Guitar, Vocals, Harmonica, Guitar / Slide Guitar Blues, Album Rock, Modern Electric Texas Blues, Boogie Rock, Arena Rock, Hard Rock, Blues-Rock, Modern Electric Blues
Blues guitarist Winter became a major star in the late '60s and early '70s. Since that time he's confirmed his reputation in the blues by working with Muddy Waters and continuing to play in the style, despite musical fashion. Born in Leland, MS, Winter formed his first band at 14 with his brother Edgar in Beaumont, TX, and spent his youth in recording studios cutting regional singles and in bars playing the blues. His discovery on a national level came via an article in *Rolling Stone* in 1968, which led to a management contract with New York club owner Steve Paul and a record deal with Columbia. His debut album (there are numerous albums of juvenilia), *Johnny Winter,* reached the charts in 1969. Starting out with a trio, Winter later formed a band with former members of The McCoys, including second guitarist Rick Derringer. It was called Johnny Winter And. He achieved a sales peak in 1971 with the gold-selling *Live/Johnny Winter And.* He returned in 1973 with *Still Alive and Well,* his highest-charting album. His albums became more overtly blues-oriented in the late '70s and he also produced several albums for Muddy Waters. In the '80s he switched to the blues label Alligator for three albums, and has since recorded for the labels MCA and Pointblank/Virgin. *Back In Beaumont* was released in 2000. *—William Ruhlmann*

Johnny Winter / 1969 / Columbia ✦✦✦✦✦
Winter's debut album for Columbia was also arguably his bluesiest and best. Straight out of Texas with a hot trio, Winter made blues-rock music for the angels, tearing up a cheap Fender guitar with total abandon on tracks like "I'm Yours and I'm Hers," "Leland Mississippi Blues," and perhaps the slow blues moment to die for on this set, B.B. King's "Be Careful With a Fool." Winter's playing and vocals have yet to become mannered or clichéd on this session, and if you've ever wondered what the fuss is all about, here's the best place to check out his true legacy. *—Cub Koda*

The Progressive Blues Experiment / 1969 / Razor & Tie ✦✦✦

● **Second Winter** / 1969 / Columbia ✦✦✦✦✦
Johnny's second Columbia album shows an artist in transition. He's still obviously a Texas bluesman, recording in the same trio format that he left Dallas with. But his music is moving toward the more rock & roll sounds he would go on to create. The opener, "Memory Pain," moves him into psychedelic blues-rock territory, while old-time rockers like "Johnny B.Goode," "Miss Ann," and "Slippin' and Slidin'" provide him with familiar landscapes on which to spray his patented licks. His reworking of Dylan's "Highway 61 Revisited" is the high spot of the record, a career-defining track that's still a major component of his modern-day set list. This was originally released back in the day as a three-sided vinyl double album, by the way. *—Cub Koda*

Johnny Winter And . . . / 1970 / DCC ✦✦✦✦✦
Winter puts together a new band and takes on the assistance of Rick Derringer, who coproduces and provides such great songs as "Rock and Roll, Hoochie Koo." *—William Ruhlmann*

Johnny Winter And . . . Live / 1971 / Columbia ✦✦✦

Still Alive and Well / 1973 / Columbia ✦✦✦

Saints & Sinners / 1974 / Columbia ✦✦✦

Nothin' But the Blues / 1977 / Blue Sky ✦✦✦✦✦
After a long period making rock records, Winter fronts the Muddy Waters band (with Waters singing) on this Chicago blues workout. He sounds happier than ever before. *—William Ruhlmann*

Guitar Slinger / 1984 / Alligator ✦✦✦✦✦
The first of three blues albums recorded after a four-year studio hiatus finds Winter as fleet-fingered as before and sounding more vocally involved than in some of the later Columbia material. *—William Ruhlmann*

Let Me In / Aug. 1991 / Pointblank ✦✦✦✦

Scorchin' Blues / Jun. 16, 1992 / Epic/Legacy ✦✦✦

A Johnny Winter: A Rock N' Roll Collection / 1994 / Columbia/Legacy ✦✦✦✦✦
A two-CD survey of Winter's recordings for Columbia between 1969 and 1979, the era of his greatest commercial success. This collects many of his most popular tracks, though it doesn't do much to argue a case for artistic diversity. Includes two otherwise unavailable songs: an alternate take of "30 Days," and a previously unreleased 1973 cover of Robert Johnson's "Come on in My Kitchen." *—Richie Unterberger*

Steve Winwood

b. May 12, 1948, Birmingham, England
Vocals, Keyboards, Guitar, Organ / Album Rock, Blue-Eyed Soul, Pop/Rock, Adult Contemporary
Singer/songwriter, keyboardist, and guitarist Steve Winwood was a well-known musician long before he finally embarked on a solo career in the second half of the '70s. Born in Birmingham, England, Winwood joined The Spencer Davis Group with his older brother Muff when he was only 15 years old. His was the soulful, Ray Charles-like voice on such hits as "Gimme Some Lovin'" and "I'm a Man," songs he also co-wrote. In 1967 he formed Traffic, which he led, with time off for the supergroup Blind Faith in 1969, until 1974. Winwood finally released his first solo album in 1977 and, in 1981 had his first million-seller with his second album, *Arc of a Diver. Talking Back to the Night* (1982) was not as much of a success, and Winwood spent four years preparing *Back in the High Life* (1986), which sold three million copies. *Roll with It* (1988) went to number one, but *Refugees of the Heart* (1990) was not up to his usual standard.

After the relative failure of *Refugees of the Heart,* Winwood and Jim Capaldi re-formed Traffic in 1994; although their record and tour were well-received, the reunion wasn't as successful as expected, and Winwood began work on a solo album in 1995. Two years later he presented the result: *Junction Seven. —William Ruhlmann*

Steve Winwood / Jun. 1977 / Island ✦✦✦
Rock fans had been waiting for a Steve Winwood solo album for more than a decade, as he made his way through such bands as the Spencer Davis Group and Traffic. When Winwood finally delivered with this LP, just about everybody was disappointed. Traffic had finally petered out three years before, but Winwood, using such former members as Jim Capaldi and Reebop Kwaku Baah, failed to project a strong individual identity outside the group. That great voice was singing the songs, that talented guitarist/keyboardist was playing them, and that excellent songwriter had composed them, but nothing here was memorable, and the long-awaited debut proved a bust. *—William Ruhlmann*

Arc of a Diver / Jan. 1981 / Island ✦✦✦✦✦
Utterly unencumbered by the baggage of his long years in the music business, Winwood reinvents himself as a completely contemporary artist on this outstanding album, leading off with his best solo song, "While You See a Chance." Winwood also plays all the instruments. *—William Ruhlmann*

Talking Back to the Night / Aug. 1982 / Island ✦✦✦

● **Back in the High Life** / Jun. 1986 / Island ✦✦✦✦✦
Turning to involved percussion tracks and horns, Winwood turns another musical corner on this sophisticated album, which contains echoes of everything from gospel to Caribbean music. Contains the number one hit "Higher Love." *—William Ruhlmann*

Chronicles / Nov. 1987 / Island ✦✦✦✦✦
This isn't an adequate compilation of the years 1977-1986, but it does manage to gather some of the better songs of the period. *—William Ruhlmann*

Roll with It / Jun. 1988 / Virgin ✦✦✦
Winwood manages to reintroduce some of the R&B elements of the Spencer Davis Group and some of the psychedelic effects of early Traffic here, though this is also an effective follow-up to the directions indicated on *Back in the High Life.* Contains the number one title track and "Don't You Know What the Night Can Do?" *—William Ruhlmann*

Refugees of the Heart / Nov. 1990 / Virgin ✦✦✦

The Finer Things / Mar. 21, 1995 / Island ✦✦✦✦✦
Steve Winwood has led a long and varied career, recording everything from straight R&B and jazz-flavored rock to folk and pop. Over the course of four discs, *The Finer Things* chronicles the entirety of his career, beginning with The Spencer Davis Group, through Traffic and Blind Faith, right until his successful solo career. It includes all of the hits and many of his finest album tracks, yet the overall approach is rather exhausting—the rarities are rarely illuminating, they're just there for the sake of being there. Nevertheless, it is a worthwhile purchase for anyone wanting a comprehensive picture of Winwood in all of his various guises. *—Stephen Thomas Erlewine*

Junction Seven / Jun. 3, 1997 / Virgin ✦✦

Wire

f. 1976, London, England, **db.** 1991
Group / British Punk, Experimental Rock, Post-Punk, Alternative Pop/Rock, Punk, Electronic
Wire's brief, fractured songs and minimalistic sound made the band the artiest of all punk bands, as well as one of the most influential. Unlike most other punk bands, their stripped-down approach was not an attempt to get back to rock's roots; it was cutting the music to its raw nerve, so nothing extraneous was left. Their nervy, dissonant avant-pop sound was more art experiment than rock & roll and as a result, their 1977 debut *Pink Flag* was a revolutionary album, a collection of 21 brief songs that displayed a blinding array of ideas. The two follow-ups to *Pink Flag, Chairs Missing* and *154,* were more measured and detailed records, boasting layered productions. Though they weren't as visionary as the band's debut, they refined and expanded the group's sound, earning great critical praise in the process. Just as the group's cult following was growing, Wire suddently broke up in late 1979. After spending several years pursuing various solo projects, the band members reunited in 1986. For the next five years, Wire released a series of experimental pop records which generally received pop-

ular reviews. However, their cult was slowly shrinking, and the group disbanded for good in 1991. All three main members, Colin Newman, Bruce Gilbert and Graham Lewis, pursued solo projects. *—Stephen Thomas Erlewine*

☆ **Pink Flag** / Dec. 1977 / Restless ✦✦✦✦✦
Perhaps the most original debut album to come out of the first wave of British punk, Wire's *Pink Flag* plays like *The Ramones Go to Art School*—song after song careens past in a glorious, stripped-down rush. However, unlike the Ramones, Wire ultimately made their mark through unpredictability. Very few of the songs followed traditional verse/chorus structures—if one or two riffs sufficed, no more were added; if a musical hook or lyric didn't need to be repeated, Wire immediately stopped playing, accounting for the album's brevity (21 songs in under 36 minutes on the original version). The sometimes dissonant, minimalist arrangements allow for space and interplay between the instruments; Colin Newman isn't always the most comprehensible singer, but he displays an acerbic wit and balances the occasional lyrical abstraction with plenty of bile in his delivery. Many punk bands aimed to strip rock & roll of its excess, but Wire took the concept a step further, cutting punk itself down to its essence and achieving an even more concentrated impact. Some of the tracks may seem at first like underdeveloped sketches or fragments, but further listening demonstrates that in most cases, the music is memorable even without the repetition and structure most ears have come to expect—it simply requires a bit more concentration. And Wire is full of ideas; for such a fiercely minimalist band, they display quite a musical range, spanning slow, haunting texture exercises, warped power-pop, punk anthems, and proto-hardcore rants—it's recognizable, yet simultaneously quite unlike anything that preceded it. *Pink Flag's* enduring influence pops up in hardcore, post-punk, alternative rock, and even Britpop, and it still remains a fresh, invigorating listen today: a fascinating, highly inventive rethinking of punk rock and its freedom to make up your own rules. *—Steve Huey*

☆ **Chairs Missing** / Aug. 1978 / Restless ✦✦✦✦✦
Chairs Missing marks a partial retreat from *Pink Flag's* austere, bare-bones minimalism, although it still takes concentrated listening to dig out some of the melodies. Producer Mike Thorne's synth adds a Brian Eno-esque layer of atmospherics, and Wire itself seems more concerned with the sonic textures they can coax from their instruments; the tempos are slower, the arrangements employ more detail and sound effects, and the band allows itself to stretch out on a few songs. The results are a bit variable—"Mercy," in particular, meanders for too long—but compelling much more often than not. The album's clear high point is the statement of purpose "I Am the Fly," which employs an emphasis-shifting melody and guitar sounds which actually evoke the sound of the title insect. But that's not all by any means—"Outdoor Miner" and "Used To" have a gentle lilt, while "Sand in My Joints" is a brief anthem worthy of *Pink Flag,* and the four-minute "Practice Makes Perfect" is the best result of the album's incorporation of odd electronic flavors. In general, the lyrics are darker than those on *Pink Flag,* even morbid at times; images of cold, drowning, pain, and suicide haunt the record, and the title itself is a reference to mental instability. The arty darkness of *Chairs Missing,* combined with the often icy-sounding synth/guitar arrangements, helps make the record a crucial landmark in the evolution of punk into post-punk and goth, as well as a testament to Wire's rapid development and inventiveness. [The CD reissue contains three bonus tracks: the fine non-LP single "A Question of Degree" and the B-sides "Go Ahead" and "Former Airline."] *—Steve Huey*

154 / 1979 / Restless ✦✦✦✦✦
Named for the number of live gigs Wire had played to that point, *154* refines and expands the innovations of *Chairs Missing,* with producer Mike Thorne's synthesizer effects playing an even more integral role; little of *Pink Flag's* rawness remains. If *Chairs Missing* was a transitional album between punk and post-punk, *154* is squarely in the latter camp, devoting itself to experimental soundscapes that can sound cold and forbidding at times. However, the best tracks retain their humanity thanks to the arrangements' smooth, seamless blend of electronic and guitar textures and the beauty of the group's melodies. Where previously some of Wire's hooks could find themselves buried or not properly brought out, the fully fleshed-out production of *154* lends a sweeping splendor to "The 15th," the epic "A Touching Display," "A Mutual Friend," and the gorgeous (if obscurely titled) "Map Ref. 41° N 93° W." Not every track is a gem, as the group's artier tendencies occasionally get the better of them, but *154's* best moments help make it at least the equal of *Chairs Missing.* It's difficult to believe that a band which evolved as quickly and altered its sound as restlessly as Wire did could be out of ideas after only three years and three albums, but such was the case according to its members, and with their (temporary, as it turned out) disbandment following this album, Wire's most fertile and influential period came to a close. [The CD reissue features four bonus tracks from an experimental EP issued with some copies of the vinyl LP.] *—Steve Huey*

The Ideal Copy / 1987 / Mute ✦✦✦
Wire's first new full-length effort in eight years is a stunning comeback picking up where *154* left off while also reflecting the strides made by the members' solo work. Finding its footing in dark, edgy dance rhythms and ominous digital textures, *The Ideal Copy* is experimental and forward-thinking, spanning from the buzzing melodies of "Ahead" and "Ambitious" to the taut minimalism of "Feed Me"; the record has its flaws, but its restless creative spirit and refusal to rest on past glories make it one of the few reunion efforts which actually matters. *—Jason Ankeny*

A Bell Is a Cup . . . Until it Is Struck / 1988 / Mute ✦✦✦

● **On Returning (1977-1979)** / 1989 / Restless ✦✦✦✦✦
On Returning (1977-1979) is a generous 31-song overview of Wire's punk heyday, covering the albums *Pink Flag, Chairs Missing,* and *154,* plus several songs that appeared only on non-album singles. Subsequent CD reissues by Restless have added nearly all of those rarities to the original albums as bonus tracks (the sole exception is the fine "Dot Dash"), so the compilation isn't quite as useful for devoted fans as it once was. Furthermore, even if *On Returning* is a handy way to chart Wire's rapid musical development, their progression is better heard on the individual albums, all of which create their own distinct musical moods. However, *On Returning* does have its advantages: first and foremost, it culls *nearly* all of the group's best songs from the time period ("Mannequin" is missing, and the selection from *154* is somewhat botched—omitting the brilliant "Map Ref. 41°N 93°W," among others, is inexcusable). And listeners with a low tolerance for artiness may find this a more concise and acceptable way to familiarize themselves with this important band: make no mistake, Wire's experiments with sonic texture and song structure are willfully challenging, although ultimately well worth the effort. So, the bottom line is that *On Returning (1977-1979)* is a pretty good overview and likely all the Wire a casual fan will need; however, if you're a neophyte and Wire sounds highly intriguing to you, chances are you'll end up with all three 1977-1979 albums anyway, rendering this compilation redundant. In the latter scenario, the classic *Pink Flag* is the better starting point. *—Steve Huey*

Manscape / May 1990 / Restless ✦✦

The First Letter / Oct. 29, 1991 / Mute ✦✦

1985-1990: The A List / May 18, 1993 / Mute ✦✦✦✦

Bill Withers

b. Jul. 4, 1938, Slab Fork, WV
Vocals / Smooth Soul, Urban, Soul
Songwriter/singer/guitarist Bill Withers is best remembered for the classic "Lean on Me" and his other million-selling singles "Aint No Sunshine" and "Use Me," but he has a sizable cache of great songs to his credit.

Born July 4, 1938, in Slab Folk, WV, Withers was the youngest of six children. After a nine-year stint in the Navy, Withers moved to Los Angeles to pursue a music career in 1967. He recorded demos at night while working at the Boeing aircraft company where he made toilet seats. His debut album, *Just As I Am* included his first charting single, "Aint No Sunshine" which went gold and made it to number six R&B and number three pop in summer 1971, also winning a Grammy as Best R&B Song. Withers wrote "Lean on Me" based on his experiences growing up in a West Virginia coal mining town. His second gold single, "Lean on Me," landed at number one R&B and number one pop for three weeks on *Billboard's* charts in summer 1972. After a legal battle with his label, Sussex, Withers signed with Columbia Records. Columbia later bought his Sussex masters when the label went out of business. His releases on Columbia included *Making Music, Menagerie 'Bout Love* from spring 1979. Teaming with Elektra Records artist Grover Washington Jr., Withers sang the crystalline ballad "Just the Two of Us." It went to number three R&B and held the number two pop spot for three weeks in early 1981. Withers' last charting LP was *Watching You, Watching Me* in spring 1985. He also occasionally did dates with Grover Washington Jr. during the '90s. His songs and recordings have been used as both the source of numerous covers and sampled by a multitude of hip-hop/rap groups. *—Ed Hogan*

Lean on Me: The Best of Bill Withers / Aug. 9, 1994 / Columbia/Legacy ✦✦✦✦✦

● **The Best of Bill Withers: Lean on Me** / May 30, 2000 / Columbia/Legacy ✦✦✦✦✦
Collectors note: This is *not* the same as the very similarly titled *Lean on Me: The Best of Bill Withers,* a 1994 best-of that also came out on Sony (catalog #5294). Each disc has 18 tracks and includes his biggest and best hits, yet only 13 of the songs are found on both CDs, and the 2000 compilation has a new set of liner notes by David Ritz. This is still too light on his earliest Sussex material, which is his best work and is represented by just seven of the tunes. It's also messily sequenced, with six less impressive and poppier mid-1970s Columbia outings leading off the program before you get to the early '70s goodies, including "Ain't No Sunshine," "Lean on Me," and "Use Me." Still, this would have to get the nod over the 1994 best-of just for the inclusion of one of those Sussex tunes alone, the uplifting and earthily bluesy 1971 cut "Harlem." *—Richie Unterberger*

Bobby Womack

b. Mar. 4, 1944, Cleveland, OH
Vocals, Guitar / Blaxploitation, Smooth Soul, Quiet Storm, R&B, Soul
Few careers in American popular music have been as consistently productive and influential as that of singer/songwriter and guitarist Bobby Womack. Sam Cooke, for whom Womack played guitar, financed his first recordings in the early '60s. With his brothers as the Valentinos, he cut two R&B classics, "It's All Over Now" (later a hit for the Stones) and "Lookin' for a Love" (a mega-hit for J. Geils). The Valentinos' combination of shouting lead vocals and blues/gospel harmonies predated late-'60s soul music. Womack knew and championed Jimi Hendrix early on, befriending him during a 1962 soul package tour. Womack's lean, groundbreaking guitar work, so similar in flavor to that of his contemporary Curtis Mayfield, influenced Hendrix. Later, Hendrix would return the favor by popularizing the wah-wah—an effect Womack would use to chilling effect on Sly Stone's *There's a Riot Goin' On* album and its smash single, "Family Affair" (he doubled here on bass). In fact, Womack himself was one of the legendary "wild" soul men, friend and partying companion of Wilson Pickett, for whom he wrote "Midnight Mover" and "I'm in Love." He even scored a movie, *Across 110th Street,* which came out at the same time as the landmark blaxploitation film *Shaft.* He made a stunning 1981 comeback with the number one R&B album *The Poet* and reunited with old Memphis studio friends and producer Chips Moman on 1986's *Womagic.* *—Christine Ohlman*

Communication / Sep. 15, 1971 / The Right Stuff ✦✦✦✦

Understanding / May 30, 1972 / The Right Stuff ✦✦✦✦✦

Across 110th Street / Dec. 16, 1972 / Charly ✦✦✦

The Facts of Life / Jun. 8, 1973 / The Right Stuff ✦✦✦✦✦

Lookin' for a Love Again / Jan. 11, 1974 / The Right Stuff ✦✦✦✦✦

The Poet / 1981 / Razor & Tie ✦✦✦

Poet 2 / 1984 / Razor & Tie ✦✦✦

● **Midnight Mover** / Feb. 1993 / EMI America b ✦✦✦✦✦
Midnight Mover is a double-disc set that offers 44 tracks from Bobby Womack's 1968-1976

stint with United Artists and its related labels. Tracks like "I'm a Midnight Mover," "I'm in Love," and "Broadway Walk" have Womack feeling his way with producer Chips Moman. After parting ways with Moman, Womack himself became one of the more skilled and inventive producers in the Muscle Shoals tradition. "That's the Way I Feel About Cha" and "I Can Understand It" both have plaintive melodies and are punctuated by Womack's guitar skills and his ever broadening and felt vocals. The poignant "Harry Hippie" had him flawlessly singing each line. Disc two covers the years 1973-1976. During this time he had become an even bigger star as his albums became sagacious ruminations on love and life. This set takes six tracks from his classic 1973 album, *Facts of Life*. From his effortlessly revamped and rock-fueled "Nobody Wants You (When You're Down and Out) to his perfect cover of Sam Cooke's "That's Heaven to Me," Womack's interpretive skills were only matched by his rootsy yet polished productions. After the frisky "Check It Out," Womack seemed preoccupied with the darker side of love with a little religion on the side to confuse things. Tracks like "Jealous Love" and "Interlude *1/I Don't Know*" have the message and meaning slipping through his fingers. *Midnight Mover* is a flawless anthology. *—Jason Elias*

The Soul of Bobby Womack / Oct. 29, 1996 / The Right Stuff ✦✦✦✦✦
This solid collection of his best early and mid-'70s work is some of the better (and rootsier) soul music that emerged from the era just prior to disco. Besides the hits "Lookin' For a Love," "Nobody Wants You When You're Down and Out," "Harry Hippie," "You're Welcome, Stop on By," "Daylight," and "That's the Way I Feel About Cha," it adds a few album tracks, minor singles, and an interesting previously unreleased demo of "Across 110th Street." *—Richie Unterberger*

● **Greatest Hits** / Oct. 5, 1999 / The Right Stuff ✦✦✦✦✦
This overview of Womack's solo career features his R&B and pop classics: "Lookin' for a Love," "Welcome Stop on By," "Women Gotta Have It," and "That's the Way I Feel About Cha." Even versions of the folkish "Sweet Caroline" and "Harry Hippie" comes out gritty. The price is right too, a good opportunity to add some gritty, uncut soul to your collection. *—Andrew Hamilton*

Stevie Wonder (Steveland Morris)

b. May 13, 1950, Saginaw, MI
Vocals, Piano (Electric), Keyboards, Piano, Harmonica / Smooth Soul, Album Rock, Pop-Soul, Pop/Rock, Motown, Urban, Funk, Soul

When Stevie Wonder began recording in 1962, he was only eleven years old. Even then, his talent was evident, although there was no sign of how deep it was. After all, the music was the work of a startlingly gifted child; it was all exuberant flash, with few complexities. Soon, Wonder would go far beyond the infectious energy of "Fingertips (Part 2)." In two years, he became one of Motown's finest artists, recording a series of brilliant singles, the overwhelming majority of which he wrote himself. With his creativity growing by leaps and bounds, Wonder soon felt limited by Motown's strict production and publishing contracts. After recording two full albums of material by himself, he gained total artistic control of his career and helped usher in a new era of soul/R&B. Along with Sly Stone and Marvin Gaye, Wonder was responsible for making soul and R&B albums not just collections of singles, but cohesive artistic statements, where artists could extend their music beyond the confines of a three-minute hit single. With the *Talking Book* and *Innervisions* albums, Wonder's music became richly complex and inventive. He sustained his creative peak through the '70s, then moved into more straightforward pop with 1980's *Hotter than July*, his first platinum album. Although his records sold well and he scored the occasional hit—including the smash hit ballad "I Just Called to Say I Love You"—his albums weren't as focused as they were a decade earlier. By the '90s, he was still an immensely respected musician, but his music was no longer on the cutting edge. *—Stephen Thomas Erlewine*

Greatest Hits / Mar. 25, 1968 / Motown ✦✦✦✦✦
When it was released, Stevie Wonder's first hits collection, a 12-track disc tracing his work from 1963 to 1967, served a common function of compilations: It gathered together stray, disparate pieces, from "Fingertip—Pt. 2" to "I Was Made to Love Her," and focused attention on the artist. Wonder had a spotty singles record: five Top Ten hits, but only two of them in succession over the four-and-a-half years, yet *Greatest Hits* made him seem like a consistent hitmaker with an astounding range, from those early harmonica instrumentals to soulful wailers like "Uptight (Everything's Alright)" and even oddball ballads like "A Place in the Sun." By now this set has long since been eclipsed, notably by the *Looking Back* album, but as a demonstration of Wonder's early promise, it is notable. *—William Ruhlmann*

For Once in My Life / Dec. 6, 1968 / Motown ✦✦✦

My Cherie Amour / Aug. 29, 1969 / Motown ✦✦✦

Signed, Sealed & Delivered / Aug. 7, 1970 / Motown ✦✦✦

Where I'm Coming From / Apr. 12, 1971 / Motown ✦✦✦✦✦
Released one month before Stevie Wonder's 21st birthday, *Where I'm Coming From* is really his first adult album, and although it was not a massive hit, it anticipated the musical approach of his commercial breakthrough, *Talking Book*, by a year and a half. The lovely "Never Dreamed You'd Leave in Summer," as the B-side to a cover of the Beatles' "We Can Work It Out," has become a Wonder standard, and the album's real hit, "If You Really Love Me" (number eight pop, number four R&B), marked the first rewards of his alliance with then-wife Syreeta Wright. Elsewhere, Wonder, who produced and composed all the tracks, introduced the funky keyboard style that would take him through the next few years, as well as the social concerns that would absorb him later on. This album was a shot across the bow, fair warning that a major, nearly mature talent had arrived. *—William Ruhlmann*

Greatest Hits, Vol. 2 / Oct. 21, 1971 / Motown ✦✦✦

Music of My Mind / Mar. 3, 1972 / Motown ✦✦✦✦✦
When Wonder turned 21, he renegotiated his Motown contract; the key issue was control. Stevie Wonder had a vision that veered far away from that of the Motown hit-making machine. Influenced by the work of Isaac Hayes in 1969 and 1970 and labelmate Marvin Gaye in 1971, Wonder was no longer content with putting out albums that were a collection of two or three hit singles plus filler; he wanted to record full-length albums that had an integrity unto themselves. *Music of My Mind* was the first such effort. Wonder produced, wrote the songs, and played the majority of the instruments. At the time it was a revelation. Compared with Wonder's subsequent efforts, it pales just slightly. *—Rob Bowman*

★ **Talking Book** / Oct. 27, 1972 / Motown ✦✦✦✦✦
Stevie Wonder came into his own with *Music of My Mind*, but *Talking Book* is where he hit his stride, developing a signature blend of sweet pop, spacy studio experimentation, and hard funk. This wasn't just far removed from what his Motown labelmates were doing, this was far removed from anything his peers were making either, due to his meticulous studiocraft. With a few exceptions, Wonder played everything on the album, relying largely on synthesizers, then piecing it together meticulously in his studio. This gave the music a unique character, warm but insular—this was certainly music of his mind, self-contained and idiosyncratic, yet inviting and generous. Take "I Believe (When I Fall in Love It Will Be Forever)," a psychedelic love song that drifts though its verses before it reaches its anthemic chorus. It's a head trip, yet it pulls the listener in and that's the album—"You Are the Sunshine of My Life" and "Superstition" pull the listener in, setting the stage for such wonderful opposites as the dreamy "You've Got It Bad Girl" or the ominous, funky "Maybe Your Baby." Wonder isn't just a master of mood, he's a tremendous songwriter, and those two elements blend together seamlessly here, kicking off a series of albums that remain among the most impressive in rock, pop, or soul. *—Stephen Thomas Erlewine*

☆ **Innervisions** / Aug. 3, 1973 / Motown ✦✦✦✦✦
The political undercurrents long simmering in Stevie Wonder's work reached their boiling point on the masterful *Innervisions*, a record as potent and insightful in its exploration of contemporary life as Marvin Gaye's *What's Going On* two years earlier. The opening "Too High," an acute condemnation of drug use, quickly establishes the record's forceful yet vibrant tone, which alternates between utopian dreamscapes ("Visions") and tough-minded realism ("Jesus Children of America"); the record's dueling concerns converge on the hit "Living for the City," which is both a brilliant examination of the myriad social ills so endemic to the ghetto experience and a stirring celebration of African-American resilience. And on "Higher Ground," Wonder even points a finger at himself to detail a sinner's second chance at life—a song which took on even greater resonance in the wake of the car crash which nearly killed him just months after the LP's release. *—Jason Ankeny*

Fulfillingness' First Finale / Jul. 22, 1974 / Motown ✦✦✦✦✦
With *Innervisions*, Stevie Wonder eclipsed his peers not just as a musician, but as a social commentator, and it was a hard record to top. If *Fulfillingness' First Finale* doesn't top it, it's nevertheless a fascinating move forward, as Wonder starts to deepen his eclecticism. Despite the portrait of MLK on the back cover, he tempers his social criticism somewhat, though the scathing "You Haven't Done Nothin'" is perhaps his fiercest song. The rest of the record is a little sweet and trippy, a sentiment that infects even such groovers as "Boogie on Reggae Woman." This characteristic means that *Fulfillingness* is perhaps the most idiosyncratic record he released during his classic period, and it demands some serious attention from the listener, since it can drift off in an insular haze. Yet, it's a fascinating, intricate, albeit slightly stoned, record that does reward that bit of intense, concentrated listening. *—Stephen Thomas Erlewine*

☆ **Songs in the Key of Life** / Sep. 28, 1976 / Motown ✦✦✦✦✦
Stevie Wonder's classic period peaked with *Songs in the Key of Life*. Not coincidentally, it's also the peak of his ambition and excess, spreading out over two albums, plus a bonus EP (now part of the last disc on a two-CD set), which gives him plenty of space to explore (or indulge, depending on your charity). And there are some superbly indulgent moments here, yet this is the kind of double album where those excesses add to the overall effect, making the immediate songs—"Sir Duke," "I Wish," "Isn't She Lovely"—shine all the more brightly, and providing little detours to explore on repeated listens. Musically, this is more consolidation than progression, adding elements of the direct *Talking Book* to the pseudo-psychedelic *Fulfillingness' First Finale*, leaving the record as a grand, sprawling demonstration of Wonder at his very peak. Though he tried to move further and farther, he never equaled this, which shines as brightly on its hits as it does in its eccentricities. *—Stephen Thomas Erlewine*

★ **Looking Back** / Nov. 30, 1977 / Motown ✦✦✦✦✦
Between 1963 and the end of 1971, Stevie Wonder placed 25 songs on *Billboard*'s charts. Twenty-four of those—including such radio staples as "Fingertips—Pt. 2," "Uptight (Everything's Alright)," "I Was Made to Love Her," "For Once in My Life," "My Cherie Amour," and "Signed, Sealed, Delivered, I'm Yours"—appear on *Looking Back*. Wonder's recordings in the '60s stand apart from most Motown acts partially because he was paired with producers and writers who very rarely worked with the Temptations, Supremes, et al. In the beginning Wonder was often produced by Clarence Paul and/or William Stevenson; during the golden years, Henry Cosby was usually manning the controls. Then in 1970, Wonder started producing himself, beginning with "Signed, Sealed, Delivered." Most of Wonder's singles were written by Wonder himself in tandem with a variety of others, or by Ron Miller. The hits alternated between stomping barn-burners and mid-tempo, understated ballads. *—Rob Bowman*

Journey Through the Secret Life of Plants / Oct. 30, 1979 / Motown ✦✦✦
Perhaps the most curious album in Stevie Wonder's career, this was ostensibly a soundtrack for a film few people saw (if indeed it was ever released). These were mostly instrumentals, plus a few oddball vocals, but most observers didn't know what to make of it at the time. Wonder was so hot that the record peaked at number four on the pop albums chart, despite the lack of any real singles and confounding almost everyone who heard it. "Outside My Window" was the lone tune to scrape the middle regions of the pop charts, while the R&B community ignored the entire album. *—Ron Wynn*

Hotter Than July / Sep. 29, 1980 / Motown ✦✦✦✦✦
Hotter Than July was Wonder's real follow-up to *Songs in the Key of Life*, even if it took him the then-unconscionably long four years to release it. Wonder had been perhaps the most accomplished and successful pop artist of the years 1972-1977, but his absence had cooled him

off commercially, and this album demonstrated that, artistically, he was also past his peak. Individual moments suggested his earlier triumphs, and Wonder remained a remarkably facile singer/player/composer, but he had lost his ability to amaze his listeners. The album's biggest single was "Master Blaster (Jammin')" (#5 pop, #1 R&B), an adequate but unremarkable reggae number, but the standout track was "Happy Birthday," the theme song for the ultimately successful campaign to make Dr. Martin Luther King, Jr.'s birthday a national holiday. *—William Ruhlmann*

★ **Original Musiquarium I** / May 4, 1982 / Motown ♦♦♦♦♦
Released in 1982, the double-album *Original Musiquarium I* summarizes Stevie Wonder's classic period of the '70s, concentrating primarily on the hits, but adding a few album tracks to hint at the depth of his albums, as well as four new songs (one for each side, all pleasant, none particularly remarkable). Though there could be some dispute about the album tracks, this does wind up as an excellent overview of Wonder's period of greatest activity, and it's a terrific listen to boot—any record that sports such hits as "Superstition," "You Haven't Done Nothin'," "Living for the City," "You Are the Sunshine of My Life," "Higher Ground," "Sir Duke," "Boogie on Reggae Woman," and "I Wish" is guaranteed to be a great listen, and it is. Wonder remains a quintessential albums artist, but this record is a terrific snapshot of the highlights. *—Stephen Thomas Erlewine*

The Woman in Red / Aug. 28, 1984 / Motown ♦♦♦

In Square Circle / Sep. 13, 1985 / Motown ♦♦♦

Characters / Nov. 6, 1987 / Motown ♦♦♦

Jungle Fever / May 22, 1991 / Motown ♦♦♦

Conversation Peace / Mar. 21, 1995 / Motown ♦♦♦

Natural Wonder / Nov. 21, 1995 / Motown ♦♦♦

☆ **At the Close of the Century** / Nov. 23, 1999 / Motown ♦♦♦♦♦
He's been called one of the most influential performers and songwriters of the century, but until 1999 Stevie Wonder didn't even have a box set to call his own. Such was the reissue campaign at Motown that, until very recently, some of the best pop music of the '60s sounded poorer in reissue form than when it was first played on AM radio. In 1996, the long-awaited Stevie Wonder digital-age hits package *Song Review* reached the shelves, but it didn't even follow compilation etiquette (that is, chronological order). Finally, *At the Close of a Century* made everything right—complete with digital remastering, near-perfect sound, complete coverage of his epic career, an attractive design, and copious liner notes and pictures. The box, a four-disc set spanning 1962 to 1996, debuts with "Fingertips, Pts. 1 & 2," the long-unheard seven-minute version of his first hit. The first disc includes every hit that fans can remember, including great-sounding versions of "Uptight (Everything's Alright)" and "Hey Love," plus plenty of moderate hits they may not remember, like his definitive cover of the Beatles' "We Can Work It Out." Disc Two features more than a dozen of his biggest hits, including "Superstition," "You Are the Sunshine of My Life," "Living for the City," "Higher Ground," and "Boogie On Reggae Woman." Disc Three begins with no less than nine tracks from *Songs in the Key of Life*, his standout double album from 1976. Right into the '80s and '90s, Stevie Wonder remained at the top of the charts, with hits like "Rocket Love," "Master Blaster (Jammin')," "Happy Birthday," "I Just Called to Say I Love You," and "Part-Time Lover." It took far too long, but Motown finally issued a box set worthy of Stevie Wonder's continuing artistry. *—John Bush*

Brenton Wood

b. Jun. 26, 1941, Shreveport, LA
Vocals / Brown Eyed Soul, Pop-Soul, Soul
Brenton Wood's charmingly unpredictable phrasing and his infectious sense of good times made the smooth uptown soul of "The Oogum Boogum Song" and "Gimme Little Sign" into hits in 1967. Despite his skill as a pop-soul vocalist, Wood was never able to match such heights again, yet those two songs became genuine R&B classics of their era. Wood formed the Quotations during college, but soon after graduation he became a solo act. Signing with Double Shot Records, Wood had a hit single in the spring of 1967 with "The Oogum Boogum Song," which reached number 19 on the R&B charts and number 34 pop. It was quickly followed by "Gimme Little Sign," which climbed to number nine pop and matched its predecessor's R&B position. It was a promising start to a career, but Wood wasn't able to follow it thorugh. "Baby You Got It" stalled in the bottom reaches of the pop and R&B Top 40 in early 1968 and "Some Got It, Some Don't" failed to make the pop charts later that year. Wood continued to perform and even recorded a duet with Shirley Goodman, but he wasn't able to reach the charts again until 1977, when "Come Softly to Me" registered in the lower reaches of the R&B Top 100. Following its release, Wood faded away, becoming part of the oldies soul circuit. *—Stephen Thomas Erlewine*

● **Brenton Wood's 18 Best** / Jun. 5, 1992 / Original Sound ♦♦♦♦♦
Probably the best collection of Brenton Wood, one of the few voices that rival Sam Cooke's in both quality and content. This collection of 18 songs includes all the hits and shows what a great singer this underappreciated artist is. Songs like "Gimme Little Sign," "Oogum Boogum," and "Baby You Got it" most of us know. But lesser known songs like "I'm the One Who Knows," "Catch You on the Rebound," and "Two Time Loser" make for some great listening. *—Michael Erlewine*

Roy Wood

b. Nov. 8, 1946, Birmingham, England
Multi Instruments, Wind, Vocals, Keyboards, Horn, Cello, Guitar, Bass, Bagpipes / Album Rock, Pop/Rock, Glam Rock, Prog-Rock/Art Rock, Hard Rock, Rock & Roll
Roy Wood has long been regarded as one of the most important, if eccentric, rock musicians to come out of Birmingham, primarily for his role as the leader/cofounder of both the Move and the Electric Light Orchestra. He organized the Move in 1964, and the group hit big three years later with the number two hit "Night of Fear." By 1971 though, Wood had developed ideas and ambitions that were too wide to be embraced by any one band, so he formed an offshoot of the Move called the Electric Light Orchestra. The new band soon attracted more serious attention than the Move, though Wood soon left both groups to form Wizzard. Singles like "Ballpark Incident" and "See My Baby Jive" did very well on the British charts, though the band's first album, *Wizzard's Brew*, didn't fare nearly as well. Wood continued recording and releasing records under his own name in addition to his work with Wizzard, and found hits with 1973's "I Wish It Could Be Christmas Everyday" and "Forever." Meanwhile, Wood's own solo albums, *Boulders* (1970) and *Mustard* (1975) were too idiosyncratic to achieve major followings. After the demise of Wizzard in 1974, his subsequent solo records, *On the Road* (1979) and *Starting Up* (1987) failed to achieve anything like the success of his early-'70s work. *—Bruce Eder*

Wizzard Brew / Mar. 1973 / EMI/Harvest ♦♦♦

● **Boulders** / Jul. 1973 / BGO ♦♦♦♦♦
An intricate, deliberately idiosyncratic record, assembled piece by piece, *Boulders* perfectly captures Roy Wood's peculiar genius, more so than anything else he recorded. All of his obsessions are here—classical music, psychedelia, pre-Beatles pop, pastoral folk ballads, absurdist humor, studio trickery, and good old-fashioned rock & roll—assembled in a gracefully eccentric fashion. Some listeners may find that eccentricity a little alienating, but it's the core of Wood's music. He wrote tuneful, accessible songs, but indulged his passions and weird ideas, so even the loveliest melodies and catchiest hooks are dressed in colorful, odd arrangements. The marvelous thing is, these arrangements never sound self-consciously weird—it's the sound of Wood's music in full bloom. Never before and never again did his quirks sound so charming, even thrilling, as they do on *Boulders*. As soon as "Songs of Praise" reaches its chorus, a choir of sped-up, multi-tracked Roys kick in, sending it into the stratosphere. All nine tunes unwind in a similar fashion, each blessed with delightfully unpredictable twists. It's easy to spot the tossed-off jokes on the goofy "When Gran'ma Plays the Banjo," but it may take several spins to realize that the percussion on "Wake Up" is the sound of Roy slapping a bowl of water. *Boulders* is a sonic mosaic—you can choose to wonder at the little details or gaze at the glorious whole, enjoying the shape it forms. Wood has an unerring knack for melodies, whether they're in folk ballads, sweet pop or old-fashioned rock & rollers, yet his brilliance is how he turns the hooks 180 degrees until they're gloriously out of sync with his influences and peers. *Boulders* still sounds wonderfully out of time and it's easy to argue that it's the peak of his career. *—Stephen Thomas Erlewine*

Introducing Eddy & the Falcons / Aug. 1974 / Edsel ♦♦♦

Mustard / Nov. 1975 / Edsel ♦♦♦♦♦
Unlike *Boulders*, *Mustard* is designed as a full-fledged album instead of a collection of pop vignettes. Outside of Wood's love for Brian Wilson there's no concept, yet it flows smoothly and attractively, since each song sounds like an epic pop extravaganza in miniature. In a typically perverse turn, Wood opens the record with a scratchy parody of the Andrews Sisters, tackling the harmonies with sped-up vocal tapes, but as soon as "Any Old Time Will Do" kicks off, it's clear that this is a shining, glittering pop record. There isn't much of his signature absurdist humor or quirky studio effects, apart from the jaw-dropping "You Sure Got It Now," a masterwork that Wood claims "sounds like the Andrews Sisters backed by John Mayall," yet it isn't missed since the studiocraft on *Mustard* is quite alluring. Where *Boulders* felt homemade, almost pastoral, *Mustard* is unabashedly grand, bolstered by endlessly layered harmonies, chiming keyboards, and cavernous productions. The Beach Boys influences shine brightly on "Why Does a Pretty Girl Sing Those Sad Songs" and "Look Thru' the Eyes of a Fool," and are inescapable on the gorgeous ballad "The Rain Came Down on Everything". Wood never really rocks out until the multi-segmented closer, "Get on Down Home" and even if it's the one misstep, it hardly detracts from the pop wonders that precede it. *Mustard* might not equal the brilliantly maverick *Boulders*, yet it's easily one of the best, most cohesive records Wood ever made and one of the few to capture him as a (relatively) focused pop craftsman. [Edsel's 1999 CD reissue of *Mustard* is graced by no less than seven bonus tracks, all A and B sides of non-LP singles, highlighted by "Oh What a Shame" and "Indiana Rainbow".] *—Stephen Thomas Erlewine*

Singles / 1999 / Repertoire ♦♦♦♦♦
If there's anything wrong with Repertoire's *Singles A's & B's*, it's that Wizzard peaked early, albeit brilliantly, and their B-sides never capitalized on their dazzling, Spector/Beach Boys-tinted rock & roll. It's no coincidence that those B-sides were written by everybody else in the band but Wood, and that most of those were instrumentals. Some are amusing (the mild ELO send-up "Bend Over Beethoven"), some are interesting ("Rob Roy's Nightmare"), but they're all disposable, especially when compared to the A-sides, which are uniformly enchanting. True, they're a little similar—the core is straight-ahead, old-fashioned rock & roll, sort of like Dave Edmunds, graced with wildly ornate arrangements and vocal harmonies—but "Ball Park Incident," "See My Baby Jive," "Angel Fingers," "Rock & Roll Winter," "This Is the Story of My Love (Baby)," and "I Wish It Could Be Christmas Everyday" are all giddy entertainments. The three remaining singles were recorded when Wizzard was trucking as the oldies outfit Eddy & the Falcons, a silly but enjoyable trek into nostalgia highlighted by the *Grease*-soundalike "You Got Me Running". Considering the quality of the nine A-sides, it's easy to wish that they had been combined with Wood's solo A-sides on a dynamite single disc, but that's not what happened—and, perhaps that's appropriate, since with the preponderance of B-sides on both discs are accurate representations of how idiosyncratic Wood is. Even if it is a bit uneven, there's little argument that *Singles* is much, much better and considerably more logical than most Wood/Wizzard compilations. *—Stephen Thomas Erlewine*

● **Exotic Mixture** / Oct. 12, 1999 / Repertoire ♦♦♦♦
Even though it spans two discs and nearly 40 songs, *Exotic Mixture* is hardly the definitive word on Roy Wood. Part of the problem is that it excludes Wizzard recordings (featured on *Singles A's & B's*), but the real problem is that it, like Wood, simply covers too much ground. *Exotic Mixture* is evenly divided, with the first disc devoted to *Boulders* through *Mustard* (plus assorted singles), the second running from 1977's *Super Active Wizzo* to 1987's *Starting Up* (plus assorted singles). The second disc has some fine moments—Roy's duet single

with Annie Haslam, "I Never Believed in Love"/"Inside My Life," isn't bad; "Dancing at the Rainbow's End" is strong; and even 1985's "Sing Out the Old—Bring in the New" is a solid piece of Wizzard-styled Spector/Wilson pop—but, by and large, it's forgettable in comparison to the first disc. Although Wizzard singles are sadly absent from the first disc and the inclusion of instrumental B-sides hurts its momentum, it remains terrific. Over half of *Boulders* is here, as is over half of *Mustard,* as are such spectacular non-LP singles as "Going Down the Road", the Beach Boys tribute "Forever," and "Indiana Rainbow." These songs capture Wood at a pinnacle, and even if they're surrounded by filler when they should be surrounded by Wizzard, no other compilation has managed to summarize his solo work as well as the first disc of *Exotic Mixture.* —*Stephen Thomas Erlewine*

Main Street / May 2, 2000 / Edsel ✦✦

World Party

f. 1986

Group / College Rock, Adult Alternative Pop/Rock, Pop/Rock, Alternative Pop/Rock

World Party began as an outlet for the pop infatuations of vocalist and multi-instrumentalist Karl Wallinger, previously best known for his tenure with the Waterboys. Born October 19, 1957 in Prestatyn, Wales, Wallinger grew up enamored not only of the Beatles but also of the Motown and Merseybeat sounds, and made his professional debut in 1976 as a member of the group Quasimodo. (Years later, after Wallinger had exited to move to London to work as a clerk for ATV/Northern Songs, Quasimodo evolved into the Alarm.)

Following a tenure as the musical director of a West End performance of *The Rocky Horror Picture Show,* Wallinger joined a funk band dubbed the Out before signing on with Mike Scott's Waterboys in 1984 to record the LP *A Pagan Place.* After 1985's superb *This Is the Sea,* Wallinger amicably departed to form World Party, a one-man project heavily indebted to *Revolver*-era Beatlesque pop; recorded in Wallinger's home studio, the 1987 debut *Private Revolution* scored a Top 40 hit with the infectious lead single "Ship of Fools."

After a long-layoff (during which time Wallinger aided Sinead O'Connor in recording her 1988 debut *The Lion and the Cobra*), World Party returned in 1990 with *Goodbye Jumbo,* another successful collection offering the minor hits "Way Down Now" and "Put the Message in the Box." After the 1991 stop-gap EP *Thank You World* (including a cover of the Beatles' "Happiness Is a Warm Gun"), Wallinger recruited guitarist Dave Caitlin-Birch and drummer Chris Sharrock as full-fledged members for 1993's *Bang!,* which reached the number two position on the British album charts. In the late '90s, Wallinger took a three year break from World Party, returning in 2000. —*Jason Ankeny*

Private Revolution / Mar. 1987 / Papillon ✦✦✦

This debut album from World Party is a solid release, even if it is a bit heavy on the synthesized sounds (what can you expect from a one-man band?). Wallinger's insightful songs deal primarily with the responsibility of the individual to recognize and cope with the problems of the world. Features mainly original songs like "Private Revolution," "World Party," and "It's All Mine," as well as a cover of Dylan's "All I Really Want to Do," which remains surprisingly true to the original version. —*Iotis Erlewine*

● **Goodbye Jumbo** / Apr. 1990 / Papillon ✦✦✦✦✦

This excellent follow-up album from World Party is much tighter than the debut. Dealing with issues from the environment ("Take It Up," "Put the Message in the Box") to relationship woes ("And I Fell Back Alone"), these tracks manage to maintain a hopeful, positive mood without becoming trivial. In these songs, Wallinger has developed his own distinct style. A great album, worth checking out just for the uptempo groove of "Way Down Now." —*Iotis Erlewine*

Bang! / Apr. 20, 1993 / Papillon ✦✦✦

Egyptology / Jun. 17, 1997 / Papillon ✦✦✦✦

Karl Wallinger defined the ornate, Beatlesque World Party sound on their debut *Private Revolution,* and he never strayed from that blueprint over the next decade, even if he augmented it with other '60s and '70s pop flourishes. *Egyptology* finds Wallinger at his most conservative, sticking to the basic late-'60s pop and psychedelia that distinguished *Private Revolution* and *Goodbye Jumbo.* As always, his production is tasteful and subtle, revealing new layers of sonic detail on each listen, and his songcraft is sturdy and tuneful, if not remarkable. Few of the songs jump out upon the first few listens, yet there are no weak moments on the record, which makes *Egyptology,* of all things, a workmanlike release. It's not flashy or extravagant, and it may not have the inspiration of *Goodbye Jumbo,* but it does deliver a collection of fine pop tunes without pretension, and that alone makes it a better album than the overly ambitious *Bang!.* —*Stephen Thomas Erlewine*

Dumbing Up / Oct. 31, 2000 / Papillon ✦✦✦✦

Link Wray (Frederick Lincoln Wray)

b. May 2, 1929, Dunn, NC

Vocals, Guitar (Electric), Guitar / Instrumental Rock, Rock & Roll

Link Wray may never get into the Rock & Roll Hall of Fame, but his contribution to the language of rockin' guitar would still be a major one, even if he had never walked into another studio after cutting "Rumble." Quite simply, Link Wray invented the power chord, the major modus operandi of modern rock guitarists. Listen to any of the tracks he recorded between that landmark instrumental in 1958 through his Swan recordings in the early 1960s and you'll hear the blueprints for heavy metal, thrash, you name it. Though rock historians always like to draw a nice, clean line between the distorted electric guitar work that fuels early blues records to the late-'60s Hendrix-Clapton-Beck-Page-Townshend mob, with no stops in between, a quick spin of any of the sides Link recorded during *his* golden decade punches holes in that theory right quick. If a direct line from a black blues musician crankin' up his amp and playing with a ton of violence and aggression can be traced to a young, white guy doing a mutated form of same, the line points straight to Link Wray, no contest. Pete Townshend summed it up for more guitarists than he probably realized when he said, "He is the king; if it hadn't been for Link Wray and 'Rumble,' I would have never picked up a guitar." —*Cub Koda*

Missing Links, Vol. 1: Hillbilly Wolf / 1990 / Norton ✦✦✦✦✦

Missing Links, Vol. 2: Big City After Dark / 1990 / Norton ✦✦✦

Missing Links, Vol. 3: Some Kinda Nut / 1990 / Norton ✦✦✦✦✦

Walkin' with Link / Apr. 1992 / Epic/Legacy ✦✦✦✦✦

After cutting the anthemic instrumental "Rumble" for Cadence Records, Link took his follow-up "Rawhide" over to Epic Records, and this 20-track compilation is the most excellent distillation of his tenure at the label. The honchos at Columbia were trying their level best to tame Link down for mass consumption (Duane Eddy twanged for White teenage America; Link Wray played for hoods). Fortunately here we're spared having to hear "seemed like a good idea at the time" atrocities like "Trail of the Lonesome Pine" and "Clare De Lune" in favor of 20 tracks of solid rockin' mayhem. Casual fans who only think of Wray as a wild-ass guitarist (his tone on the title track is pure, detuned, hacking filth) will be very surprised to find that rebel nature also applies to his vocal cords on such raucous outings as Jimmy Reed's "Ain't That Lovin' You Baby" (in two different takes here), Ray Charles' "Mary Anne," and the previously unissued rocker "Oh Babe Be Mine." This compilation may lack some of the big hits that a best-of collection would have to offer (thus denying it first-purchase status), but as another essential piece in building the perfect Link Wray (or rock & roll guitar gods) collection, one would be very hard pressed to imagine it *not* residing in the pile. Link at his best, and that's just about as wild and crazy as original rock & roll guitar gets. —*Cub Koda*

★ **Rumble! The Best of Link Wray** / May 18, 1993 / Rhino ✦✦✦✦✦

Finally, a multi-label Link Wray collection spanning his lengthy career is available. Starting, appropriately enough, with "Rumble," *Rumble! The Best of Link Wray* illustrates through its 20 tracks (15 on cassette) that Wray was indeed one of the pioneering guitarists of rock & roll, expanding the sonic possibilites of the instrument with a variety of effects. All of the tracks feature some truly warped, genius-caliber fretboard work from Wray, and a few also feature his equally demented vocals. *Rumble! The Best of Link Wray* is the definitive Wray collection. —*Stephen Thomas Erlewine*

Mr. Guitar / Jun. 20, 1995 / Norton ✦✦✦✦✦

While Link cut some great records in the late '50s and early '60s, he really reached his peak during his stay with the Swan label in the early and mid-'60s. This double-CD, 63-song set documents this period with as much thoroughness as anyone is likely to attempt, including great singles like "Jack The Ripper," "Mr. Guitar," "Ace Of Spades," and "The Fat Back," where Link let loose with his dirtiest and most groundbreaking fuzz tones. Including quite a few rarities and tracks that were never previously released in the U.S., as well as a good number of vocal performances (which were never Wray's forte), this is perhaps too exhaustive for the average fan. A single-disc distillation of his best Swan sides would be absolutely killer, but this is still one of the greatest collections of instrumental rock out there, despite its unevenness. —*Richie Unterberger*

Guitar Preacher: The Polydor Years / Aug. 22, 1995 / Polydor ✦✦✦

Missing Links, Vol. 4: Streets of Chicago / 1997 / Norton ✦✦✦

Wreckless Eric

b. Newhaven, England

Vocals, Guitar / British Punk, Pub Rock, New Wave, Rock & Roll

Wreckless Eric gained notoriety as part of Stiff Records' highly eccentric roster of punk and New Wave artists during the late '70s. With his whiny, slurred cockney voice, Eric couldn't carry a tune, but that didn't prevent him from being an enjoyable, if limited, rock & roller. With his early Stiff singles "Whole Wide World," "Semaphore Signals," and "Take the Cash (K.A.S.H.)," Eric bashed out a series of ragged, chaotic, three-chord punk-pop singles driven by his pent-up energy and a knack for melodic pop hooks. Though he never had a big pop hit, his engaging sense of humor and fondness for simple rock & roll helped make him a cult figure that continued to have a following into the '90s. After signing to Stiff in 1977, Eric's debut single was "Whole Wide World," a moderate hit in the punk underground. His 1978 eponymous debut had a boozy sense of charm, though second album *The Wonderful World of Wreckless Eric* demonstrated a previously unknown musical versatility. He fashioned his third album *Big Smash* as a commercial breakthrough, though when it failed he quit the music industry. Eric returned to music during the mid-'80s with two groups, Captains of Industry and the Len Bright Combo, then released the solo album *Le Beat Group Electrique* in 1989. He continued releasing records and performing during the '90s, mostly in France. —*Stephen Thomas Erlewine*

Wreckless Eric / 1978 / Repertoire ✦✦✦✦✦

Wreckless Eric's eponymous debut is a ragged, endearing collection of crude rock & roll. In a way, crude doesn't even begin to describe Eric's music. A muddle of scratchy guitars, pounding drumming, and snarled, indecipherable vocals, the record is pure, primal garage rock in the old-fashioned sense. Although Wreckless Eric has the demeanor of a punk, his music is straight-out rock & roll in the old-fashioned sense—there's even saxophones and organs popping out of the mix. What makes *Wreckless Eric* such fun is its combination of catchy hooks, spirited playing, and downright rudeness. Only a handful of songs are fully formed, and those—"Whole Wide World" and Ian Dury's "Rough Kids"—are punk-inflected pub rock classics, pure pop songs in every sense of the term. The remainder are off-kilter, idiosyncratic pop songs—about everything from "Personal Hygiene" and "Waxworks" to "Telephoning Home" and "Brain Thieves"—performed with sloppy, drunken abandon. Too punk for pub rockers, too straightforward for punk, and too weird for everybody else, Wreckless Eric's debut album is one of the small gems of the punk era. —*Stephen Thomas Erlewine*

The Wonderful World of Wreckless Eric / Nov. 1978 / Stiff ✦✦✦✦

Wreckless Eric had already begun to tire of Stiff's promotion of him as a drunken rebellious lout by the time of his second album, *The Wonderful World of Wreckless Eric.* He hadn't grown strong enough to break free of Stiff's hold, but he was able to clean up his sound enough for *The Wonderful World* to make his music slightly more accessible—which means it just doesn't sound as messy as his debut. Wreckless Eric still has an odd, idiosyncratic point of view, but the sound is streamlined enough to make his snarls and growls palatable. Also, his hooks are getting stronger overall, and while only "Take the Cash" is on the level of "Whole Wide World," the rest of the record is comprised of rockers (and two pointless covers of Tommy Roe and Buddy Holly) that are quite enjoyable. *—Stephen Thomas Erlewine*

- **The Whole Wide World** / 1979 / Stiff ✦✦✦✦✦
The Whole Wide World was an American-only collection of Wreckless Eric singles that provided an excellent distillation of his best moments, from "Whole Wide World" to "Semaphore Signals" and "Take the Cash (K.A.S.H.)." The album was added as a bonus LP to the original pressings of Eric's third album, *Big Smash!*. *—Stephen Thomas Erlewine*

Big Smash / 1980 / Stiff ✦✦✦

Le Beat Group Electrique / 1989 / New Rose ✦✦✦✦✦

Betty Wright

b. Dec. 21, 1953, Miami, FL
Vocals / Quiet Storm, Soul
A consistently strong presence on the Miami music scene throughout the '70s and '80s, Betty Wright was just 15 when she cut the Top 40 "Girls Can't Do What the Guys Do." A child gospel star who switched to R&B at age 13, she put the Miami scene on the map in 1971 with the number six hit "Clean Up Woman," notable for its prominent guitar riff and Wright's swaggering lead vocal. She won a Grammy in 1974 for "Where Is the Love?" (not to be confused with the Roberta Flack/Donny Hathaway tune of the same name). She collaborated with Stevie Wonder in 1981 on the Epic hit "What Are You Gonna Do with It?" Betty continues to live and work in the Miami area. *—Christine Ohlman*

- **The Very Best of Betty Wright** / Jun. 20, 2000 / Rhino ✦✦✦✦✦
Rhino's *Very Best of Betty Wright* collects some of the soul diva's definitive tracks, including her first Top 40 hit "Girls Can't Do What the Guys Do," her 1971 Top 10 hit "Clean Up Woman," "Let Me Your Lovemaker," her 1974 Grammy winner "Where Is the Love," and "I'm Gettin' Tired Baby." Though it's not as extensive as the label's earlier compilation *The Best of Betty Wright*, this album does present most of her major singles as well as a few representative album tracks. *—Heather Phares*

Charles Wright

b. 1942, Los Angeles, CA
Vocals, Guitar / Smooth Soul, Funk, Soul
Charles Wright headed one of the late '60s and early '70s great funk groups, the Watts 103rd Street Band. Wright, who was born in Clarksdale, MS, was a singer, pianist, guitarist, and leader of the eight-member band, recruited from Watts in Los Angeles. They were originally known as the Soul Runners. Bill Cosby helped get the band off the ground by giving them appearances at his gigs. They began recording for Keyman in 1967, then moved to Warner Bros. in 1969. While "Do Your Thing" and "Till You Get Enough" were Top 20 R&B hits, their finest selection was "Express Yourself," a song that expressed the urge for freedom as adroitly as the Isley Brothers' "It's Your Thing" had in the '60s. It has also been among the most sampled funk tracks for hip-hop and rap groups. "Your Love (Means Everything to Me)" was their final R&B hit in 1971, peaking at number nine R&B and number 12 pop. The group's best ballad, "Love Land," did better pop-wise than among R&B fans, many of whom saw it as a bit soft. They continued recording for Dunhill in 1973 before disbanding. Drummer James Gadson and guitarist Al McKay, who later joined Earth, Wind & Fire, were among the instrumental corps of the Watts 103rd Street Rhythm Band. *—Ron Wynn*

- **Express Yourself: The Best of Charles Wright** / 1993 / Warner Archive ✦✦✦✦✦

In the Jungle Babe/Express Yourself / Apr. 8, 1997 / Warner Brothers ✦✦✦✦✦
Released in 1997, this two-fer collects Charles Wright and the Watts 103rd Street Rhythm Band's third and fourth records, 1969's *In the Jungle, Babe* and the following year's *Express Yourself*. A transitional work, *In the Jungle, Babe* captures a group struggling to find its own identity; for every superb workout like the shimmering "Love Land" or the propulsive "I'm a Midnight Mover," there's a redundant cover of the Doors' "Light My Fire" or Sly and the Family Stone's "Everyday People" which falls flat on its face. *Express Yourself*, on the other hand, is the group's masterpiece, a remarkable fusion of funk attitude and soul conviction. Highlighted by the classic title hit—one of the most powerful declarations of independence in the canon, as well as one of the most sampled records of all time—*Express Yourself* is a whirlwind tour through the spectrum of R&B; from the poignance of the Otis Redding-worthy ballad "Tell Me What You Want Me to Do" (arguably Wright's best vocal turn ever) to the supple funk-jazz jam session "High as Apple Pie—Slice I and II," the record is assured and muscular, a primal blast of soul power. *—Jason Ankeny*

O.V. Wright (Overton Vertis Wright)

b. Oct. 9, 1939, Leno, TN, **d.** Nov. 16, 1980
Vocals / Memphis Soul, Deep Soul, Southern Soul, Soul
At first glance, Derek Bailey possesses almost none of the qualities one expects from a jazz musician—his music does not swing in any appreciable way, it lacks a discernible sense of blues feeling—yet there's a strong connection between his amelodic, arhythmic, atonal, uncategorizable free-improvisatory style, and much free jazz of the post-Coltrane era. His music draws upon a vast array of resources, including indeterminacy, rock & roll, and various world musics. Indeed, this catholic acceptance of any and all musical influences is arguably what sets Bailey's art outside the strict bounds of "jazz." The essential element of his work, however, is the type of spontaneous musical interrelation that evolved from the '60s jazz avant-garde. Sound, not ideology, is Bailey's medium. He differs in approach to almost any other guitarist who preceded him. Bailey uses the guitar as a sound-making, rather than a "music"-making, device. Meaning, he rarely plays melodies or harmonies in a conventional sense, but instead pulls out of his instrument every conceivable type of sound using every imaginable technique. His timbral range is quite broad. On electric guitar, Bailey is capable of the most gratingly harsh, distortion-laden heavy-metalisms; unamplified, he's as likely to mimic a set of windchimes. His guitar is much like John Cage's prepared piano; both innovations enhanced the respective instrument's percussive possibilities. *—Chris Kelsey*

- **The Soul of O. V. Wright** / Dec. 22, 1992 / MCA ✦✦✦✦✦
O.V. Wright epitomized gospel-based soul singing. He screamed, roared, belted, hollered, and wailed, proclaiming his need for love. His songs were simple; they were often anguished remembrances of lost loves or pleas that this time things might be different. Occasionally, he did an uptempo dance or novelty number, but Wright was at his best on slow burners. This collection of 1960s and '70s material for Don Robey's Back Beat label includes evocative ballads, lightweight but enjoyable numbers, and songs which returned him to his gospel days. While several foreign anthologies spotlighting Wright have been issued, this 18-track CD stands as the most complete domestic reissue package currently available. *—Ron Wynn*

Hi Masters / Sep. 15, 1998 / Hi ✦✦✦
The *Hi Masters* compiles 15 studio recordings, all from 1977 and 1978 with the exception of the two songs that comprised O.V. Wright's first release on Hi, the 1976 single "Rhymes" (which charted in the R&B Top 100 that year) and it's B-side, "Without You." The collection kicks off strong with the gospel-drenched delivery, decidedly secular subject, and driving momentum of "Into Something (Can't Shake Loose)," his sole hit in 1977 (it reached the Top 50). The following year brought the last two songs by Wright to hit the charts, "Precious, Precious" (R&B Top 50, early 1978) and "I Don't Do Windows" (Top 100). Besides the inclusion of his last four hits, the *Hi Masters* is a collection of the lesser-known material from late in Wright's career. It's not his prime period, but the soft-moving numbers and ballads from this time, including standouts "I Don't Know Why" and "Your Good Thing Is About to End," make *Hi Masters* a relaxed listen that is second priority—but a nice complement—to O.V. Wright's key earlier recordings. *—Joslyn Layne*

Robert Wyatt

b. Jan. 28, 1945, Bristol, England
Vocals, Drums / Canterbury Scene, Prog-Rock/Art Rock
An enduring figure who came to prominence in the early days of the English art-rock scene, Robert Wyatt has produced a significant body of work, both as drummer and vocalist for art-rockers the Soft Machine and as a radical political singer/songwriter. It was not long after his first solo release, 1971's *End of an Ear*, that Wyatt fell from an open window during a party, fracturing his back and permanently paralyzing him from the waist down. After months of painful recuperation, Wyatt re-emerged with the harrowing *Rock Bottom*, which dealt explicitly with his post-accident life. Wyatt shockingly recorded a straight version of the Monkees "I'm a Believer" in 1974 that became a big British hit. Despite his success, Wyatt recorded sparingly during the '70s and released only a handful of singles for the indie label Rough Trade. He returned in the '80s with albums that were lush, at times almost meditative. Wyatt's voice—clear, emotionally charged and always on the verge of breaking—brought great depth and soul to songs that, if recorded by a lesser artist, would have sounded terse and tired. He recorded several albums during the '90s as well, also devoting time to political work. Despite his occasionally strident political posture, he has recorded some stunning music, full of wonder, possibility and pure emotion, that remains undiscovered by many. *—John Dougan*

- **Rock Bottom** / 1974 / Thirsty Ear ✦✦✦✦✦
Rock Bottom, recorded with a star-studded cast of Canterbury musicians, has been deservedly acclaimed as one of the finest art rock albums. Several forces surrounding Wyatt's life helped shape its outcome. First, it was recorded after the former Soft Machine drummer and singer fell out of a five-story window and broke his spine. Legend had it that the album was a chronicle of his stay in the hospital. Wyatt dispels this notion in the liner notes of the 1997 Thirsty Ear reissue of the album, as well as the book *Wrong Movements: A Robert Wyatt History*. Much of the material was composed prior to his accident in anticipation of rehearsals of a new lineup of Matching Mole. The writing was completed in the hospital, where Wyatt realized that he would now need to sing more, since he could no longer be solely the drummer. Many of *Rock Bottom*'s songs are very personal and introspective love songs, since he would soon marry Alfreda Benge. Benge suggested to Wyatt that his music was too cluttered and needed more open spaces. Therefore, Robert Wyatt not only ploughed new ground in songwriting territory, but he presented the songs differently, taking time to allow songs like "Sea Song" and "Alifib" to develop slowly. Previous attempts at love songs, like "O Caroline," while earnest and wistful, were very literal and lyrically clumsy. *Rock Bottom* was Robert Wyatt's most focused and relaxed album up to its time of release. In 1974, it won the French Grand Prix Charles Cros Record of the Year Award. It is also considered an essential record in any comprehensive collection of psychedelic or progressive rock. Concurrently released was the first of his two singles to reach the British Top 40, "I'm a Believer." *—Jim Powers*

Ruth Is Stranger Than Richard / 1975 / Thirsty Ear ✦✦✦✦
There was no way that Wyatt's follow-up to *Rock Bottom* could be as personal and searching, but this album that came barely a year later instead collects some earlier material to be revamped for this release. "Soup Song," for instance, is a rewrite of "Slow Walkin' Talk," written before the forming of Soft Machine. "Team Spirit," written with Phil Manzanera and Bill MacCormick of Quiet Sun, would turn up the same year as "Frontera" on Manzanera's *Diamond Head*. While some of the songs tend to plod along, the dirge-like "Five Black Notes and One White Notes," a lethargic cover of Offenbach's "Baccarole," Charlie Haden's "Song for Che," and Fred Frith's piano team-up with Wyatt on "Muddy Mouth" are magical. As usual, the assembled band, including the underrated Gary Windo on sax and Mongezi Feza on trumpet, never dissapoint. *—Ted Mills*

Nothing Can Stop Us / 1981 / Thirsty Ear ✦✦✦✦✦
This compilation of early-'80s singles includes some of Wyatt's finest work. Aside from "Born Again Cretin" (whose vocals recall the Beach Boys at their most experimental), all of it's non-original material that Wyatt makes his own with his sad, haunting vocals. You could hardly ask for a more diverse assortment of covers: Chic's "At Last I Am Free" (giving an eerie treat-

ment with especially mysterious, spacy keyboards), the a cappella gospel of "Stalin Wasn't Stallin'," political commentary with "Trade Union," the Billie Holiday standard "Strange Fruit," Ivor Cutler's "Grass," and a couple of songs in Spanish. The tracks have since been reissued a few times, with bonus tracks such as the "Shipbuilding" single; the best option for U.S. consumers is *Compilation*, which pairs *Nothing Can Stop Us* with *Old Rottenhat*. *—Richie Unterberger*

Old Rottenhat / 1985 / Thirsty Ear ♦♦♦

Mid-Eighties / 1993 / Gramavision ♦♦♦♦♦
Basically, this is an expanded version of the 1985 album *Old Rottenhat*, with the addition of eight extra tracks from the period: the four-song *Work in Progress* EP, two songs from the B-side of "Shipbuilding," and a couple of cuts from various-artist compilations. These bonus tracks are hardly extraneous, containing as they do some of his strongest work from the time, especially his covers of Peter Gabriel's "Biko" and Monk's "'Round Midnight," which are further evidence of Wyatt as one of contemporary music's most imaginative interpreters. *—Richie Unterberger*

Floatsam Jetsam / 1994 / Rough Trade ♦♦♦

• **Going Back a Bit: A Little History of Robert Wyatt** / 1994 / Virgin ♦♦♦♦♦
A wonderfully compiled 28-track, two-CD set that includes some of Wyatt's work with Soft Machine and his short-lived band of radical politicos Matching Mole (who, frankly, are not very interesting). Also, this generous set includes some outtakes and unreleased material. As for a basic overview of Wyatt's career that's doesn't skimp on the strong stuff and provides a sense of chronology, you can't do much better. The lone drawback is that the set is only available as a pricy English import. But if you've got the time and money, it's well worth the investment. *—John Dougan*

Shleep / Nov. 1997 / Thirsty Ear ♦♦♦♦♦
Wyatt continues to follow his singular musical path with the lovely *Shleep*, delivering another album of considerable quirky charm and understated beauty; a less melancholy affair than much of his recent work, the record is informed by a hazy, dreamlike quality perfectly in keeping with the elements of subconsciousness implicit in the title. *—Jason Ankeny*

X-Ray Spex

f. 1976
Group / British Punk, Punk
One of the great English punk bands of the late '70s, there is only one thing wrong with the careers of X-Ray Spex and lead singer Poly Styrene—they didn't record enough music. X-Ray Spex exploded onto the punk scene with one of the era's great singles, the feminist punk rallying cry "Oh Bondage, Up Yours"—along with the early Sex Pistols and Clash singles, this was one of punk rock's defining moments. So, too, was X-Ray Spex's debut LP *Germ Free Adolescents*, which was great in spite of "Oh Bondage" not being on it (a situation that would be rectified with the 1993 CD reissue). The songs were guitar-driven punk-pop that combined outrage and aggression with a sense of alienation and disenfranchisement about rampant commerciality and an increasingly sterile and artificial world. Poly's songs were more likely to be about drowning in a sea of corporate-designed consumer fantasies than straight-out attacks against the government. This didn't mean the songs were any less political; they simply attacked the zeitgeist from a different vantage point. Tragically, there was no second X-Ray Spex record. But there was Poly Styrene's only full-length solo record, *Translucence*. *—John Dougan*

• **Germ Free Adolescents** / Nov. 1978 / Blue Plate/Caroline ♦♦♦♦♦
Perhaps the most utopian aspect of the U.K. punk scene was that it offered creative, articulate young people the opportunity to express themselves, and to kick up an exuberantly noisy racket in the process. X-Ray Spex certainly came from this wing of the movement, the brainchild of two female schoolmates who re-christened themselves Poly Styrene and Lora Logic. X-Ray Spex was far from the only female-centered British punk act, but they were arguably the best, combining exuberant energy with a cohesive worldview courtesy of singer and songwriter Poly Styrene. As her *nom de punk* hinted, Styrene was obsessed with the artificiality she saw permeating Britain's consumer society, linking synthetic goods with a sort of processed, manufactured humanity. Styrene's frantic claustrophobia permeates the record, as she rails in her distinctively quavering yowl against the alienation she feels preventing her from discovering her true self. *Germ Free Adolescents* is tied together by Styrene's yearning to be free not only from demands for consumption, but from the insecurity corporate advertisers used to exploit their targets (especially in women)—in other words, to enjoy being real, imperfect, non-sterile humans living in a real, imperfect, non-Day-Glo world. Fortunately, the record is just as effective musically as it is conceptually. It's full of kick-out-the-jams rockers, with a few up-tempo thrashers and surprisingly atmospheric pieces mixed in; the raw, wailing saxophone of Rudi Thomson (who replaced Lora Logic early on) gives the band its true sonic signature. The CD reissue of *Germ Free Adolescents* appends both sides of the classic debut single "Oh Bondage Up Yours!," one of the most visceral moments in all of British punk—which means everything you need is right here. *—Steve Huey*

Conscious Consumer / Oct. 24, 1995 / Receiver ♦♦♦

X

f. 1977
Group / American Punk, L.A. Punk, Alternative Pop/Rock, Punk
X were the quintessential L.A. punk rockers before they grew into a world-class rock & roll band and live band; however, enthusiasm for their unique, intelligent and humorous work never quite reached critical mass. Formed in 1977 by John Doe and Exene Cervenka, the band garnered an immediate following via their discovery by ex-Doors keyboardist Ray Manzarek, who recorded their album debut *Los Angeles* in 1980. The record's across-the-board raves earned them stature as California's preeminent punk band, while 1982's *Under the Big Black Sun* began what would be a long career merging hard rock, country and folk into their fiery mix. The band successfully began to mix in their populist politics with an eye toward matters of the heart. As the band began to reach wider audiences, both Doe and Cervenka enjoyed outside careers in the arts—he as an actor in films like *Great Balls of Fire* and *Roadside Prophets*, and she as a poet and spoken-word artist, collaborating with Lydia Lunch and Wanda Coleman. Though the band never broke up, X took some much-needed time off after 1987's *See How We Are*, with Doe and Cervenka continuing their work as solo artists. By 1993, the band got together for the recording of *Hey Zeus!*, a collection of new songs, but the response was underwhelming, and it was back to solo work. X occasionally performed during their frequent hiatuses, recorded the live album *Unclogged* in San Francisco in 1995. *—Denise Sullivan*

Los Angeles / 1980 / Slash ♦♦♦♦♦
By the late '70s, punk rock and hardcore were infiltrating the Los Angeles music scene. Such bands as Black Flag, the Germs, and, especially, X were the leaders of the pack, prompting an avalanche of copycat bands and eventually signing record contracts themselves. X's debut, *Los Angeles*, is considered by many to be one of punk's all-time finest recordings, and with good reason. Most punk bands used their musical inability to create their own style, but X actually consisted of some truly gifted musicians, including rockabilly guitarist Billy Zoom, bassist John Doe, and frontwoman Exene Cervenka, who, with Doe, penned poetic lyrics and perfected sweet yet biting vocal harmonies. *Los Angeles* is prime X, offering such all-time classics as the venomous "Your Phone's Off the Hook, but You're Not," a tale of date rape called "Johnny Hit and Run Paulene," and two of their best anthems (and enduring concert favorites), "Nausea" and the title track. While they were tagged as a punk rock act from the get-go (many felt that this eventually proved a hindrance), X are not easily categorized. Although they utilize elements of punk's frenzy and electricity, they also add country, ballads, and rockabilly to the mix. [In 1988 *Los Angeles* and *Wild Gift* were combined as part of a CD reissue by Slash Records.] *—Greg Prato*

Wild Gift / May 1981 / Slash ♦♦♦♦♦
For X's second release, 1981's *Wild Gift*, the quartet followed the same path they had taken a year earlier on their debut, *Los Angeles*, creating another batch of timeless compositions that merged the energy of punk rock with other musical styles. Former Doors keyboardist Ray Manzarek reprised his role as producer on what would turn out to be X's last independent release before signing to Elektra. Included are such eventual punk standards as "We're Desperate," the melodic hookfest "White Girl" (sampled years later by the Red Hot Chili Peppers in their song "Good Time Boys"), and "Beyond and Back" (which would serve as a title for their 1997 two-CD anthology). Other highlights include the '50s-prom feel of "Adult Books," the punk-pop composition "In This House That I Call Home," and the rapid "Back 2 the Base." While it may be a shade less exceptional than its predecessor, *Wild Gift* is nonetheless a classic effort. [In 1988 *Los Angeles* and *Wild Gift* were combined as part of a CD reissue by Slash Records.] *—Greg Prato*

Under the Big Black Sun / Jul. 1982 / Elektra ♦♦♦♦
X's first album issued on a major label, 1982's *Under the Big Black Sun*, is arguably their finest record. All 11 songs are exceptional, from both a performance and compositional point of view. Ray Manzarek's production is more akin to hard rock bands than their earlier punk works, but the songs still pack quite a punch. Before the recording of the album, singer Exene Cervenka's sister was killed by a drunk driver, and the band decided to work out their grief in the music, as evidenced by two of the album's best tracks: the melodic "Riding With Mary" and the vintage '50s sound of "Come Back to Me." The highlights don't stop there, however; also included are the Led Zeppelin-esque "The Hungry Wolf" (an early video favorite of MTV), the accelerating "Motel Room in My Bed," the rocker "Blue Spark," the spacious title track, and the album closer "The Have Nots." Again, Cervenka and John Doe supply some great vocal harmonies (perhaps the only punk band to ever do so), while Billy Zoom shows off great rockabilly chops throughout. *Under the Big Black Sun* is one of the quintessential rock records from the '80s. *—Greg Prato*

More Fun in the New World / 1983 / Elektra ♦♦♦♦♦
Coming off their 1982 masterpiece *Under the Big Black Sun*, X offered their follow-up *More Fun in the New World* one year later. While its predecessor won the band a slew of new fans, it didn't serve as the major breakthrough that it so deservedly should have. Rightfully, they didn't fool with their already winning formula; they issued another solid set of songs produced, again, by Ray Manzarek. The anthemic album opener "The New World" is still powerful years later, as is the absolutely beautiful ballad "I Must Not Think Bad Thoughts," which perfectly captures the paranoid feeling of Reagen's America in the '80s. X achieved new rough and rocking heights with the vicious "Devil Doll," "Painting the Town Blue," and "Make the Music Go Bang," while returning once again to their retro '50s roots with "Poor Girl." *More Fun in the New World* would prove to be Manzarek's final production credit with X, who would hook up with renowned heavy metal veteran Michael Wagener for their next release two years later, *Ain't Love Grand!*. *—Greg Prato*

Ain't Love Grand! / 1985 / Elektra ♦♦♦♦
After several exceptional (but commercially underappreciated) classic albums, X decided to change their approach on the fifth album, 1985's *Ain't Love Grand*. The most noticeable difference is in the production. Renown heavy metal producer Michael Wagener was on board (whose credits include Motley Crue, Dokken, and Great White), replacing longtime X-ally Ray Manzarek. As usual, the songwriting and performances shine, but the raw sound of their earlier work is noticeably absent—instead of changing his approach for X, Wagener produced them as he would a metal band of the '80s, smoothing out the rough edges. Still, the band scored perhaps their biggest radio and MTV hit ever with "Burning House of Love," and they composed such other highlights as "What's Wrong With Me," "All or Nothing," and "My Soul Cries Your Name." *Ain't Love Grand* would also mark guitarist Billy Zoom's last album with X, retiring from the music biz entirely until a brief X reunion in the late '90s. Not exactly on par with the classics *Under the Big Black Sun* and *More Fun in the New World*, *Ain't Love Grand* still manages to offer a few X standards. *—Greg Prato*

See How We Are / 1987 / Elektra ♦♦♦

Live at the Whiskey a Go-Go / 1988 / Elektra ♦♦♦

★ **Los Angeles/Wild Gift** / Sep. 20, 1988 / Slash ✦✦✦✦✦

Hey Zeus! / Jun. 8, 1993 / Big Life ✦✦✦

Unclogged / Jun. 13, 1995 / Infidelity/Sunset Boulevard ✦✦✦✦

Beyond & Back: The X Anthology / Oct. 28, 1997 / Elektra ✦✦✦✦✦
X cannot be praised enough. The legendary L.A. band wrote countless classics, released consistent albums, and have influenced many along the way (just check out the raves fellow rockers give the band inside *Beyond & Back's* liner notes). It's a testament to their greatness that the material on *Beyond & Back (The X Anthology)* sounds original and fresh in the present day. The group touched on many styles, such as rockabilly, folk and punk, and successfully made each one their own. This two-CD release is a hefty two hours long, and is 50% hits and 50% rarities/unreleased material (demos, outtakes, live takes, etc.). Highlights include the riff-heavy "Hungry Wolf," and the beautiful vocal harmonies of "I Must Not Think Bad Thoughts," and the Nirvana-pop of "White Girl." Some interesting oddities include a cover of the Doors' "Soul Kitchen," a remixed version of their "Blue Spark," and a live take of "Nausea" (a song Jane's Addiction covered). If you're unfamiliar with (or don't own) X's albums, do yourself a favor and get *Under the Big Black Sun, More Fun in the New World,* and/or *Los Angeles/Wild Gift.* Then work your way to *Beyond And Back.* You won't regret it. *—Greg Prato*

XTC

f. 1976, Swindon, England
Group / College Rock, Pop/Rock, New Wave, Alternative Pop/Rock
XTC was one of the smartest—and catchiest—British pop bands to emerge from the punk and new wave explosion of the late '70s. From the tense, jerky riffs of their early singles to the lushly arranged, meticulous pop of their later albums, XTC's music has always been driven by the hook-laden songwriting of guitarist Andy Partridge and bassist Colin Moulding. While popular success has eluded them in both Britain and America, the group has developed a devoted cult following in both countries that remains loyal over two decades after their first records.

Critics praised the angular yet melodic pop of XTC's first two records, *White Music* and *Go 2,* both released in 1978. One year later, the band recorded their first charting single ("Life Begins at the Hop") and released a calmer, more pop-oriented album, *Drums and Wires.* XTC continued to smooth out their edges on 1980's *Black Sea* and the following year's *English Settlement,* featuring more complex arrangements and intellectual lyrics. Nevertheless, *English Settlement* was their biggest success in the U.K., reaching number five on the charts and launching the Top Ten single, "Senses Working Overtime."

After cancelling a tour in 1982, Partridge announced that XTC would never play live again. The first albums recorded by the studio-bound band, *Mummer* and *The Big Express,* were more detailed, well-produced efforts than previous LPs. After a difficult recording session with producer Todd Rundgren, the pastoral *Skylarking* (1986) was hailed as a masterwork by critics and spent over six months on the American charts. *Oranges and Lemons* (1989) featured reworked psychedelia with a Ray Davies-inspired sense of nostalgia, and the single "Mayor of Simpleton" became XTC's only charting U.S. single. Three years later, the group released *Nonsuch,* an album that recalled both *Pet Sounds* and *Revolver.* Years of internal difficulties and label battles kept the group from releasing any new material for much of the decade, however, and not until 1999 did the next XTC album, *Apple Venus, Pt. 1,* finally appear. *Wasp Star Apple Venus, Pt. 2* followed in mid-2000. *—Stephen Thomas Erlewine*

White Music / Jan. 20, 1978 / Geffen ✦✦✦
XTC's first full album shows the band going full-throttle in true punk spirit. More dissonant than their latter period, the young band shines with directionless energy and a good sense of humor. Highlights include the catchy singles, "This Is Pop" and "Radios in Motion" as well as a jumpy version of "All Along the Watchtower." Their first release, *3D EP,* has been appended to the CD version. *—Chris Woodstra*

Go 2 / Oct. 13, 1978 / Geffen ✦✦

Drums & Wires / Aug. 17, 1979 / Virgin ✦✦✦✦✦
Following *Go 2,* keyboardist Barry Andrews left the band and, rather than finding a replacement keyboard player, the band opted to recruit another guitarist (who could also play keyboards), Dave Gregory. The album that followed the lineup change, *Drums and Wires,* marked a turning point for the band, with a more subdued set of songs that reflected an increasing songwriting proficiency. The aimless energy of the first two albums was focused into a cohesive statement with a distinctive voice that retained their clever humor, quirky wordplay and decidedly British flavor. Musically, *Drums and Wires,* titled to reflect the big drum sound they developed for the album, is certainly driven by the powerful rhythms and angular, mainly minimalistic arrangements, but the addition of a second guitarist also allowed for some inventive and interesting guitar work (the "wires") that made up for the lack of Andrews' odd flourishes—the tension between the two sounds creates some truly inspired, nervy pop. Colin Moulding also came into his own as a songwriter, penning their first substantial hit, the new wave classic "Making Plans for Nigel." [The CD reissue contains tracks from the bonus single originally included with the LP—"Limelight" and "Chain of Command"—as well as "Life Begins at the Hop."] *—Chris Woodstra*

Black Sea / Sep. 12, 1980 / Geffen ✦✦✦✦✦
XTC continued on with the big drum sound of *Drums and Wires,* adding more polish and an even heavier-hitting approach for *Black Sea*—their arrangements are fuller and they rock harder than ever before. Where *Drums and Wires* implied social commentary, *Black Sea* more directly addressed sociopolitical concerns, handling them not strictly in a theoretical sense, but rather showing a human response to the circumstances. Of course, the band's skewed outlook and mid-'60s pop sense keeps things from becoming too heavy—included are some of their finest songs, like "Respectable Street," "Generals and Majors," and "Towers of London," as well as the thoroughly enjoyable pop fluff throwaway, "Sgt. Rock (Is Going to Help Me)," to keep the mood light. All in all, there isn't a bad song in the bunch—*Black Sea* was their most consistent album up to that point—and although XTC always operated on the fringes, the album is their most commercial-sounding, fitting in perfectly with the new wave of the late '70s/early '80s. [The CD reissue adds three tracks—"Smokeless Zone," "Don't Lose Your Temper," and "The Somnambulist"—to the middle of the album. And while the extras are welcomed (especially "Don't Lose Your Temper"), they really should have been tacked on to the end rather than disrupting the original.] *—Chris Woodstra*

English Settlement / Feb. 12, 1982 / Geffen ✦✦✦✦
Andy Partridge's discovery of the 12-string guitar set the tone for *English Settlement,* an album which moved away from the pop gloss of *Black Sea* in favor of lighter, though still rhythmically heavy, acoustic numbers with more complex and intricate instrumentation. There are plenty of pop gems —"Senses Working Overtime" stands as one of their finest songs—but the main focus seems to be the more expansive sound; most of the songs are drawn out to near-epic length, ultimately taking some of the impact of the songs away. Despite several terrific tracks, *English Settlement* seems more a transitional album than anything else, although the textural sound of the album is quite remarkable, indicating the direction they would take in their post-touring incarnation. *—Chris Woodstra*

● **Waxworks: Some Singles 1977-1982** / Nov. 1982 / Geffen ✦✦✦✦✦
Though it has been since supplanted by more comprehensive collections—the most notable being *Fossil Fuel,* which repeats all of the *Waxworks* tracks plus the later singles—*Waxworks—Some Singles 1977-1982* remains the classic compilation of the band's first, pre-studio-bound period. Originally, the album was packaged with a second record, *Beeswax—Some B-Sides 1977-1982,* later made available separately. *—Chris Woodstra*

Mummer / Aug. 30, 1983 / Geffen ✦✦✦
Mummer, the first album to follow Andy Partridge's mental breakdown which led to the band's retirement from touring, is very much the work of an eccentric in isolation. The album is a collection that builds on the groundwork of *English Settlement* with gentle, acoustic songs that evoke pastoral images and peaceful times. There are moments of real inspiration, resulting in some of their finest songs to date—"Love on a Farmboy's Wages," "Great Fire," and "Lady Bird"—and the sound sets a pleasingly consistent mood, although the sameness tends to work against the lesser material. Only the out-of-place afterthought of "Funk Pop A Roll," a tirade against the music industry, breaks things up, recapturing the abrasive Partridge of past. [When *Mummer* was reissued on CD, six tracks were added to the middle of the album. While "Jump," "Toys" and "Desert Island" are welcome additions of pop confection, the atmospheric instrumentals "Frost Circus" and "Processions Toward the Learning Land," from the simply bizarre *Homo Safari Series,* serve to disrupt the album's flow.] *—Chris Woodstra*

The Big Express / Oct. 15, 1984 / Geffen ✦✦✦✦
XTC took full advantage of their studio-bound status with *The Big Express,* creating their most painstakingly detailed, multi-layered, sonically dynamic album to date. The more upbeat material and brighter sound recall some of the band's earlier moments, but most of all, *The Big Express* signals a turning point for the band, setting the blueprint for their later approach—a combination of studio perfection matched with impeccable songcraft that results in a thoroughly consistent and enjoyable album beginning to end. *Skylarking,* the album that followed, gets much more glory, and certainly its impact was greater (this one was virtually ignored), but really, *The Big Express* covers much of the same territory and is just as strong an album in many ways. [Three songs were added to the middle of the CD reissue—"Red Brick Dream," "Washaway," and "Blue Overall"—but they fit seamlessly into the complete picture.] *—Chris Woodstra*

★ **Skylarking** / Oct. 27, 1986 / Geffen ✦✦✦✦✦
Working with producer Todd Rundgren didn't necessarily bring XTC a sense of sonic cohesion—after all, every record since *English Settlement* followed its own interior logic—but it did help the group sharpen their focus, making *Skylarking* their tightest record since *Drums and Wires.* Ironically, *Skylarking* had little to do with new wave and everything to do with the lush, post-psychedelic pop of the Beatles and Beach Boys. Combining the charming pastoral feel of *Mummer* with the classicist English pop of *The Big Express,* XTC expands their signature sound by enhancing their intelligently melodic pop with graceful, lyrical arrangements and sweeping, detailed instrumentation. Rundgren may have devised the sequencing, helping the record feel like a song cycle even if it doesn't play like one, but what really impresses is the consistency and depth of Andy Partridge's and Colin Moulding's songs. Each song is a small gem, marrying sweet, catchy melodies to decidedly adult lyrical themes, from celebrations of love ("Grass") and marriage ("Big Day") to skepticism about maturation ("Earn Enough for Us") and religion ("Dear God"). Moulding's songs complement Partridge's songs better than before, and each writer is at a melodic and lyrical peak, which Rundgren helps convey with his supple production. The result is a pop masterpiece—an album that has great ambitions and fulfills them with ease. [The initial release of *Skylarking* didn't feature "Dear God," which was originally the B-side of "Grass." After "Dear God" became an unexpected hit, "Mermaid Smile" was pulled from the album so the hit single could be added to the record.] *—Stephen Thomas Erlewine*

Oranges & Lemons / Feb. 27, 1989 / Geffen ✦✦✦✦
Skylarking was an ambitious yet concise record, one that recalled such graceful concept albums as *Pet Sounds* and *Sgt. Pepper,* so it wasn't entirely a surprise that XTC embraced psychedelia on its double-album follow-up *Oranges and Lemons,* especially if their celebrated Dukes of Stratosphear side project was taken into consideration as well. *Oranges and Lemons* lacks the singular focus of *Skylarking,* but at its best, it's just as impressive as its predecessor. Instead of revelling in the form of psychedelic pop, as they did with the Dukes, XTC bring the genre's sensibility to the mature pop of *Skylarking,* spiking it with a wry, occasionally absurd, sense of humor missing from its predecssor. The result is a record exploding with detail, not the least of which are backward guitars, sound effects and head-spinningly eclectic arrangements. It's sonically rich and filled with immaculately crafted songs, but *Oranges and Lemons* falls just short of being a tour-de-force, since each song feels like an island—they work well as individual tracks, but they don't form a cohesive statement.

However, that's a minor complaint, because Colin Moulding and Andy Partridge in particular are in peak form, contributing some of their very finest songs in "Garden of Earthly Delights," "The Loving," "One of the Millions," "Merely a Man," "Pink Thing" and the elegiac "Chalkhills and Children." Such songs make the relative weaknesses of the album well worth enduring. *—Stephen Thomas Erlewine*

Explode Together: The Dub Experiments 78-80 / Aug. 1990 / Virgin ✦✦

Rag 'N' Bone Buffet / Sep. 24, 1990 / Geffen ✦✦✦
Rag 'N' Bone Buffet collects 24 rarities, B-sides, and side projects, including "Too Many Cooks in the Kitchen" (released under the pseudonym the Colonel), "Thanks for Christmas" (by the Three Wise Men), "Mermaid Smiled," the song dropped from *Skylarking* to make room for "Dear God," "Take This Town," from the film *Times Square*, and a handful of BBC sessions. Finding the complete recorded works of XTC is a collector's nightmare, and *Rag 'N' Bone Buffet* really only scratches the surface of what's out there, but it is a start. Even though these songs were thrown away by the band, there is really some terrific music to be found here—the collection is just as essential as the proper albums. *—Chris Woodstra*

Nonsuch / Mar. 30, 1992 / Geffen ✦✦✦✦✦
Since *Skylarking*, each XTC album was carefully composed and crafted, and *Nonsuch* is no different. Working with producer Gus Dudgeon (Elton John), XTC crafted their most immaculate album to date with *Nonsuch*. A measured and reflective record, recalling the Beach Boys more than the Beatles, the album retains some of their late-'80s psychedelic flourishes, but those have been integrated into an elaborate, lush pop setting that falls somewhere between *Skylarking* and *Oranges and Lemons*. While it lacks the thematic unity of *Skylarking*, as well as the grandstanding eclecticism of *Oranges and Lemons*, *Nonsuch* is in many ways more musically consistent, presenting a set of 17 wonderfully detailed and immediate catchy pop songs, ranging from the relatively rocking "The Ballad of Peter Pumpkinhead" to the sweet "Holly Up on Poppy." Occasionally, the album dips slightly lyrically—Moulding's "The Smartest Monkeys" and "War Dance" are a little too preachy—but never musically, making *Nonsuch* a modest, minor masterpiece. *—Stephen Thomas Erlewine*

★ **Fossil Fuel: The XTC Singles 1977-1992** / 1996 / Virgin/EMI ✦✦✦✦✦
Fossil Fuel: The XTC Singles 1977-1992 is a splendid double-disc set that runs through every one of the group's 31 A-sides, from the nervy "Science Friction" to the lush, sighing "Wrapped in Grey." Between those two songs, XTC's craftsmanship grows remarkably fast—based on the edgy pop of their new wave singles "Statue of Liberty," "This Is Pop," "Are You Receiving Me?," and "Life Begins at the Hop," it's hard to believe that they would later write the subtle, near-pastoral Beatles, Kinks, and Beach Boys pastiches of "Love on a Farmboy's Wages," "Great Fire," and "Grass." And those songs just scratch the surface of the terrific pop singles available on *Fossil Fuel*—"Making Plans for Nigel," "Ten Feet Tall," "Generals and Majors," "Towers of London," "Respectable Street," "Sense Working Overtime," "This World Over," "Dear God," "The Mayor of Simpleton," "King for a Day," and "The Ballad of Peter Pumpkinhead" are wonderful songs and forgotten classics. Although XTC continually made carefully constructed albums, they were a dynamite singles band, releasing songs that were tightly constructed and impossibly catchy. They never had hits, because their unabashed pop was never in fashion; plus, Andy Partridge's voice was too pinched and his lyrics frequently too cerebral. But XTC's music stands as some of the best and most influential pop of their era, and nowhere is that more evident than on *Fossil Fuel*. *—Stephen Thomas Erlewine*

Upsy Daisy Assortment / Jun. 17, 1997 / Geffen ✦✦✦✦

Transistor Blast: Best of the BBC Sessions / Nov. 24, 1998 / TVT ✦✦✦

Apple Venus, Pt. 1 / Feb. 23, 1999 / TVT ✦✦✦✦✦
Seven years is a long time between records, so it shouldn't come as a surprise that *Apple Venus* is a significant step forward from *Nonsuch*, but the sparse strings and circular arrangements of "River of Orchids" nevertheless come as a shock, especially since its slow build-up feels as ominous and intellectual as 20th-century classical music. It provides the keynote for the album, setting the stage for an ambitious, unpredictable and strangely beautiful record. Although there are similarities with the pastoral *Skylarking* or parts of *Nonsuch*, there is really no comparable record in XTC's canon, given its sustained mood, experimentalism and glimpses of confession. Colin Moulding wrote the brightest tunes on the record, and while the bouncy "Frivolous Tonight" and "Fruit Nut" will be endearing to any longtime XTC fan, they don't fit the tone of *Apple Venus*, which feels like an Andy Partridge solo album—not just a confessional, but a grand outpouring of ideas. Partridge insisted that *Apple Venus* be released in two parts—Gregory left partially because he believed the album would be stronger if it was consolidated to one record—presumably because all his songs on *Pt. 1* are of a piece, sharing similar lyrical and musical themes. Split between orchestral and acoustic pop, *Apple Venus* is alternately lush and melancholy, sometimes within one song. Some of Partridge's darkest work is here, such as the vindictive "Your Dictionary," yet the album overall has a hopeful note—the perfect aural encapsulation of their long, bitter struggle of the '90s. The strike was frustrating for the band and fans alike, but perhaps the extended layoff paid off in sharpening Partridge's focus, since *Apple Venus, Pt. 1* easily ranks as one of XTC's greatest works. *—Stephen Thomas Erlewine*

Homespun / Oct. 5, 1999 / TVT ✦✦✦

Wasp Star (Apple Venus, Pt. 2) / May 23, 2000 / TVT ✦✦✦
Anyone expecting *Wasp Star: Apple Venus, Vol. 2* to continue the majestic acoustic-orchestral blends of *Apple Venus* will be disappointed, because it's a straightforward collection of sharp, witty, well-constructed pop songs. Directness is perhaps the oddest thing about *Wasp Star*—it's unassuming pop from a band that operated on a conceptual plain for nearly 20 years. It could be argued that all the songs that fit a dark, introspective mood went to *Apple Venus*, XTC's first album after seven years in exile, while *Wasp Star* wound up as a clearinghouse for everything else. If that is true, it ignores a basic fact—XTC's leftovers are better than most band's keepers. "Leftovers" isn't quite an accurate term, either. These songs are orphans, tunes without a particular project, which may mean that *Wasp Star* is an album of moments, but there's plenty to cherish here. Colin Moulding is in fine shape, with the spare "Boarded Up" and the clever "Standing in for Joe." Andy Partridge has a few tricks up his sleeve—his compositions are heavy on electric guitars, he builds "Wounded Horse" around a blues riff, and "You and the Clouds Will Still Be Beautiful" is just about the breeziest thing he's ever written—but for the most part, he's in pop craftsman mode, turning out expert, layered tunes that may not push his talents but certainly exploit his capabilities to their fullest. After all, most pop bands would give their eyeteeth to have songs as smart, melodic, and memorable as "Playground," "Stupidly Happy," "My Brown Guitar" and "I'm the Man Who Murdered Love" as their *orphans*—and if these constitute an average XTC album, that's a testament to what a terrific band they are. *—Stephen Thomas Erlewine*

The Yardbirds

f. 1963, Surrey, England, **db.** Jul. 1968, London, England
Group / British Psychedelia, British Blues, Psychedelic, British Invasion, Blues-Rock, Rock & Roll
The Yardbirds are mostly known to the casual rock fan as the starting point for three of the greatest British rock guitarists—Eric Clapton, Jeff Beck, and Jimmy Page. Undoubtedly these three figures did much to shape the group's sound, but throughout their career, the Yardbirds were very much a unit, albeit a rather unstable one. And they were truly one of the great rock bands—one whose contributions went far beyond the scope of their half dozen or so mid-'60s hits ("For Your Love," "Heart Full of Soul," "Shapes of Things," "I'm a Man," "Over Under Sideways Down," "Happenings Ten Years Time Ago"). Not content to limit themselves to the R&B and blues covers they concentrated upon initially, they quickly branched out into moody, increasingly experimental pop/rock. The innovations of Clapton, Beck, and Page redefined the role of the guitar in rock music, breaking immense ground in the use of feedback, distortion, and amplification with finesse and breathtaking virtuosity. With the arguable exception of the Byrds, they did more than any other outfit to pioneer psychedelia, with an eclectic, risk-taking approach that laid the groundwork for much of the hard rock and progressive rock from the late '60s to the present. *—Richie Unterberger*

Five Live Yardbirds / Dec. 1964 / Rhino ✦✦✦✦✦
Five Live Yardbirds was the first important—indeed, essential—live album to come out of the 1960s British rock & roll boom. In terms of the performance captured and the recording quality, it was also the best such live record of the entire middle of the decade Cut at a *Marquee Club* show in 1964 , *Five Live Yardbirds* was a popular album, especially once Eric Clapton's fame began to spread after leaving the band. Although the album didn't appear officially in the United States until its CD release by Rhino in the late 1980s, four of its tracks—"Smokestack Lightning," "Respectable," "I'm a Man," and "Here 'Tis"—made up one side of their classic U.S. album *Having a Rave Up*, and the British EMI LP became a very popular import during the early 1970s as a showcase for both the band and the playing of Eric Clapton. That album had astonishingly good sound, which was not the case with any of the reissues that followed, on vinyl or CD—even Rhino's compact disc suffered from blurry textures and noise, though it was an improvement over any release since the original EMI LP. The 1999 Repertoire Records reissue is the first CD that matches the clarity and sharpness of the original LP, and along with that improvement, their original concert has been very sensibly expanded with a half-dozen live cuts from roughly the same period, recorded at *the Crawdaddy Club*. Among them is a killer live version of the Billy Boy Arnold classic "I Wish You Would." There's also a pair of live tracks from German television in 1967—"I'm a Man" and "Shapes of Things"; the two, in a flash, make up for what they lack in perfect fidelity. *—Bruce Eder*

For Your Love / 1965 / Epic ✦✦✦

Having a Rave-Up with the Yardbirds / Nov. 1965 / Epic ✦✦✦✦✦
In its original U.S. vinyl release, this album, comprised of several singles and B-sides plus excerpts off of *Five Live Yardbirds*, was one of the best LPs of the entire British invasion, ranking on a par with the greatest mid-1960s work of the Beatles and the Rolling Stones; it was also just a step away from being a best-of the Yardbirds as well. The contents have reappeared numerous times in many different configurations, but no collection has ever outdone the sheer compactness and high quality of *Having a Rave Up*. One major problem since the 1960s, as with all of the Yardbirds material owned by Charly Records, has been the sound—for years, Charly only had substandard master materials to offer. That situation improved significantly in the mid- to late 1990s, and Repertoire Records is working from sources that are the cleanest and most impressive to have surfaced on these tracks during the CD era; one suspects that there might still be room for improvement, but not nearly as much as was previously the case—a quick comparison of tracks between this and the contents of *Train Kept A-Rollin'* reveals somewhat superior sound here. The Repertoire reissue also adds 11 songs that cut across the group's history: principally outtakes from later in their careers and some odd studio sides from much earlier, plus the B-side "New York City Blues" (a rewrite of "Five Long Years"), the single "Shapes of Things, and their featured number from the Antonioni movie *Blow Up*, the "Train Kept A-Rollin'" rewrite "Stroll On", featuring Jeff Beck and Jimmy Page in the lineup. There are new notes by Chris Welch that, although structured somewhat haphazardly, give a good account of the history of the varied (and overall stunning) contents of this CD. *—Bruce Eder*

Sonny Boy Williamson & the Yardbirds / 1966 / Mercury ✦✦

Roger the Engineer / Jul. 15, 1966 / Edsel ✦✦✦✦✦
Once Jeff Beck joined the Yardbirds, the group began to explore uncharted territory, expanding their blues-rock into wild sonic permutations of psychedelia, Indian music and avant-garde white noise. Each subsequent single displayed a new direction, one that expanded on the ideas of the previous single, so it would seem that *Roger the Engineer*—Beck's first full album with the group and the band's first album of all original material—would have offered them the opportunity to fully explore their adventurous inclinations. Despite a handful of brilliant moments, *Roger the Engineer* falls short of expectations, partially because the band is reluctant to leave their blues roots behind and partially because they simply can't write a consistent set of songs. At their best on *Roger*, the Yardbirds strike a ki-

netic balance of blues-rock form and explosive psychedelia ("Lost Woman," "Over, Under Sideways, Down," "The Nazz Are Blue," "He's Always There," "Psycho Daisies") but they can also bog down in silly eastern drones (although "Happenings Ten Years Time Ago" is a classic piece of menacing psychedelia) or blues tradition ("Jeff's Boogie" is a pointless guitar workout that doesn't even showcase Beck at his most imaginative). The result is an unfocused record that careens between the great and the merely adequate but the Yardbirds always had a problem with consistency—none of their early albums had the impact of the singles, and *Roger the Engineer* suffers from the same problem. Nevertheless, is the Yardbirds' best individual studio album, offering some of their very best psychedelia, even if it doesn't rank among the great albums of its era. *—Stephen Thomas Erlewine*

Over Under Sideways Down / Aug. 8, 1966 / Epic ♦♦♦♦♦
Over Under Sideways Down is American version of *The Yardbirds* (aka *Roger the Engineer*), with a cool cover photo but also stripped of "The Nazz Are Blue" and "Rack My Mind," which means that two of the harder rocking blues tracks are absent, along with some superb Jeff Beck guitar playing and a good Keith Relf performance. Add an extra star for the mono version of this album, which differs markedly from its stereo counterpart, and from the mono and stereo British editions—the mono *Over Under Sideways Down* (LN 24210) featured versions of "Hot House of Omagararshid" and "Lost Woman" with lead guitar parts that are different (or, in the case of "Hot House," missing) from the stereo versions, and longer versions of "He's Always There," "Turn Into Earth," and "I Can't Make Your Way." Those longer, superior mono cuts have surfaced on post-1997 CD issues of the album. *—Bruce Eder*

★ **Greatest Hits, Vol. 1: 1964-1966** / 1986 / Rhino ♦♦♦♦♦
Greatest Hits, Vol. 1: 1964-1966 falls short of being a truly definitive compilation, stopping shortly after Jeff Beck joined the group and thereby leaving off anything from *Roger the Engineer* on. Still, as a collection of early singles, plus highlights from *Five Live Yardbirds*, this is first-rate, containing their tough blues-rock ravers and their first forays into psychedelia. Yes, it would have been stronger if it had post-1966 material, but considering there is no compilation that does, this remains the most essential, accessible overview of the Yardbirds' classic material. *—Stephen Thomas Erlewine*

Vol. 1: Smokestack Lightning / Oct. 1, 1991 / Columbia ♦♦♦♦

Vol. 2: Blues, Backtrack's and Shapes of Things / Oct. 1, 1991 / Columbia ♦♦♦♦

The Yardbirds Little Games Sessions & More / Aug. 25, 1992 / EMI America ♦♦♦

Live at the BBC / Oct. 7, 1997 / Warner Archives ♦♦♦♦
The Yardbirds recorded several live sessions for the BBC between 1965 and 1968, following Eric Clapton's departure from the band. These recordings have previously been released on bootlegs and small independent labels but Warner Archives's *The Yardbirds BBC Sessions* marks the first big-budget, official release of the material. The disc contains 26 tracks—20 featuring Jeff Beck, six featuring Jimmy Page—which is slightly less than some editions of this same material, but that won't matter to anyone but completists since the gist is the same: the Yardbirds were a tough live band that essentially recreated its studio recordings on the BBC stage. There are slight differences in the guitar solos but the songs are so short, neither Beck or Page have the opportunity to completely tear loose. Nevertheless, hardcore Yardbirds fans will relish the few rarities here, which mainly are covers the band never recorded in the studio: "Dust My Broom," "Most Likely You Go Your Way (And I'll Go Mine)," "My Baby" and "The Sun is Shining." *—Stephen Thomas Erlewine*

Yes

f. 1968, Birmingham, England
Group / British Psychedelia, Album Rock, Pop/Rock, Prog-Rock/Art Rock
Far and away the longest lasting and the most successful of the 1970s' progressive rock groups, Yes has proved one of the lingering success stories from that musical genre. The band, founded in 1968, has overcome a generational shift in its audience and the departure of its most visible members at key points in its history to reach the end of the century as the definitive progressive rock band. Where rivals such as Emerson, Lake & Palmer withered away commercially after the mid-'70s, and Genesis and King Crimson altered their sounds so radically as to become unrecognizable to their original fans, Yes—singer John Anderson, guitarist Steve Howe, bassist Chris Squire, keyboardist Rick Wakeman and drummer Bill Bruford in their most celebrated incarnation—has retained the same sound, and performs much of the same repertory that they were doing in 1971—and for their trouble, they find themselves being taken seriously a quarter of a century later. Their audience remains huge because they've always attracted younger listeners drawn to their mix of daunting virtuosity, cosmic (often mystical) lyrics, complex musical textures, and powerful yet delicate lead vocals. Today, their music of almost every era is regarded by fans with undiminished enthusiasm, and by their critics as respectable attempts at doing something serious with rock music. *—Bruce Eder*

Yes / Oct. 15, 1969 / Atlantic ♦♦♦
Yes' debut album is surprisingly strong, given the inexperience of all those involved at the time. In an era when psychedelic meanderings were the order of the day, Yes delivered a surprisingly focused and exciting record that covered lots of bases (perhaps too many) in presenting their sound. The album opens boldly, with the fervor of a metal band of the era playing full tilt on "Beyond and Before," but it is with the second number, a cover of the Byrds' "I See You," that they show some of their real range. The song is highlighted by an extraordinary jazz workout from lead guitarist Peter Banks and drummer Bill Bruford that runs circles around the original by Roger McGuinn and company. "Harold Land" was the first song on which Chris Squire's bass playing could be heard in anything resembling the prominence it would eventually assume in their sound and anticipates in its structure the multi-part suites the group would later record, with its extended introduction and its myriad shifts in texture, timbre, and volume. And then there is "Every Little Thing", the most daring Beatles cover ever to appear on an English record, with an apocalyptic introduction and extraordinary shifts in tempo and dynamics, Banks' guitar and Bruford's drums so animated that they seem to be playing several songs at once. Ths song also hosts an astonishingly charismatic performance by Jon Anderson. There were numerous problems in recording this album, owing to the inexperience of the group, the producer, and the engineer, in addition to the unusual nature of their sound. Many of the numbers give unusual prominence to the guitar and drums, thus making it the most uncharacteristic of all the group's albums. Its first decent-sounding edition anywhere came with the 1997 remastering by Atlantic. *—Bruce Eder*

Time and a Word / Nov. 2, 1970 / Atlantic ♦♦

The Yes Album / Mar. 19, 1971 / Atlantic ♦♦♦♦
The album that first gave shape to the established Yes sound, build around science-fiction concepts, folk melodies, and soaring organ, guitar, and vocal showpieces. "Your Move" actually made the U.S. charts as a single, and "Starship Trooper," "Perpetual Change," and "Yours Is No Disgrace" became much-loved parts of the band's concert repertory for many tours to come. Remastered in 1995 (under the above mentioned catalog number), with significantly improved sound. *—Bruce Eder*

★ **Fragile** / Jan. 4, 1972 / Atlantic ♦♦♦♦♦
The band's breakthrough album, dominated by science-fiction and fantasy elements and new member Rick Wakeman, whose organ, synthesizers, Mellotrons, and other keyboard exotica added a larger-than-element to the procedings. Ironically, the album was a patchwork job, hastily assembled in order to cover the cost of Wakeman's array of instruments. But the group built effectively on the groundwork left by *The Yes Album*, and group had an AM-radio sucker-punch, aimed at all of those other progressive bands who eschewed the notion of hit singles, in the form of "Roundabout," the edited version (sort of "highlights" of the album version) of which pulled in millions of young kids who'd never heard them before. The single clicked, most album-buyers liked the long version and all of the rest of what they found, and the band was made. Remastered in much improved sound and graphics in 1995, under the above catalog number, with a reference to "digital remastering" across the top back of the jewel case. *—Bruce Eder*

☆ **Close to the Edge** / Sep. 13, 1972 / Atlantic ♦♦♦♦♦
For most fans, this album represents the peak of Yes' work. Side-length suites allowed Jon Anderson even more opportunity for vocal acrobatics and Rick Wakeman an even bigger canvas on which to paint his electronic synthesizer swirls, organ arpeggios, and great swathes of Mellotron-generated color. Steve Howe's playing took on a particularly urgent quality here, but never lost sight of its lyricism, while Chris Squire's bass is practically another lead instrument, and Bill Bruford—in his then seeming swansong with the band—contributed some of his most elegant drumming. The 1995 remastering, referred to on the top back of the jewel box, was especially welcome on this album, the new CD version being many steps superior to the old one in terms of sound. *—Bruce Eder*

Yessongs / May 4, 1973 / Atlantic ♦♦♦♦♦
The best live album to emerge from the entire early-'70s art-rock scene, a compendium of blazing performances covering the previous three studio albums by the group and the accompanying solo career of Rick Wakeman. Some of the performances are superior to their studio originals, most notably "Siberian Khatru," although "And You and I" is something of a disappointment next to the version on *Close to the Edge*. Virtually a live "best-of" album. The 1995 remastered version, in the narrow double jewel box with the label stating that it is the remastered version on the top of the back of the jewel box, is the version to own, being far superior to the old edition. *—Bruce Eder*

Tales from Topographic Oceans / Jan. 9, 1974 / Atlantic ♦♦♦♦
Either the finest record or the most overblown album in Yes' output. When it was released, critics and fans raved over its 20-minute-long tracks, each taking up one side of a double album, and it sold very well. By the 1980s, it was being derided by critics as one of the worst examples of progressive rock's over-indulgent nature. Jon Anderson's fascination with Eastern religions never manifested itself more clearly or broadly, but one needn't understand any of that to appreciate the many sublimely beautiful moments on this album, some of the most gorgeous passages ever recorded by the band. The newly remastered version, in the narrow double jewel box, with a reference to the remastering on the top back of the jewel case, is the version to own, with crisp textures, vivid sound, and excellent reproductions of the original art. *—Bruce Eder*

Relayer / Dec. 5, 1974 / Atlantic ♦♦♦

Yesterdays / Feb. 27, 1975 / Atlantic ♦♦♦

Going for the One / Jul. 7, 1977 / Atlantic ♦♦♦

Tormato / Sep. 20, 1978 / Atlantic ♦♦

Drama / Aug. 18, 1980 / Atlantic ♦♦♦

Yesshows / Nov. 24, 1980 / Atlantic ♦♦♦

90125 / Nov. 7, 1983 / Atco ♦♦♦♦♦
A stunning self-reinvention by a band that many had given up for dead, *90125* is the album that introduced a whole new generation of listeners to Yes. Begun as Cinema, a new band by Squire and White, the project grew to include the slick production of Trevor Horn, the new blood (and distinctly '80s guitar sound) of Trevor Rabin, and eventually the trademark vocals of returning founder Jon Anderson. His late entry insured that Rabin and Horn had a heavy influence on the sound. The album also marked the return of prodigal keyboardist Tony Kaye, whose crisp synth work on "Changes" marked the band's definitive break with its art-rock roots. "Owner of a Lonely Heart" was a huge crossover hit, and its orchestral break has been relentlessly sampled by rappers ever since. The vocal harmonies of "Leave It" and the beautifully sprawling "Hearts" are additional high points, but there's nary a duff track on the album. *—Paul Collins*

Big Generator / Sep. 17, 1987 / Atco ♦♦

Union / Apr. 30, 1991 / Arista ♦♦♦

Yesyears / Aug. 6, 1991 / Atco ♦♦♦♦♦

Yesstory / 1992 / Atco ✦✦✦✦✦
Despite the seeming overabundance of Yes compilations and live recordings, this two-CD release does fill an important niche—it's the definitive Yes set for fans who demand more than a single disc, "The Very Best of," but don't want to spring for the bulky box set. Essentially a distillation of the *Yesyears* box set, it benefits from the fine remastering job, while at the same time trimming away less vital tracks like the Tormato B-sides and the tepid '80s live performances. Still, it's shocking that the fine album, *Drama,* was left out entirely, or that *Relayer* was whittled down to the unsatisfying excerpt of "Soon." And only picking the two hit singles from *90125* and *Big Generator* won't fool many true fans of their later work—both could have been passed over for better cuts that didn't pull in the teenyboppers. Still, despite its post-1980 lapses, fans of early Yes may find this an entirely satisfactory compilation. —*Paul Collins*

The Very Best of Yes / Sep. 21, 1993 / Atlantic ✦✦✦✦✦
If you view *The Very Best of Yes* as a singles sampler, not an attempt to offer a thorough overview of Yes' doggedly album-oriented career, this 11-track collection is actually quite successful, offering the bulk of the band's best-known songs, from "I've Seen All Good People," "Roundabout," and "Long Distance Runaround" to "Owner of a Lonely Heart" and "Leave It." It's sequenced chronologically, too, which gives some sense of the band's development. Therefore, for the curious, this offers a nice snapshot of what Yes did throughout the '70s and into the mid-'80s. —*Stephen Thomas Erlewine*

Talk / Mar. 22, 1994 / Victory ✦✦

Open Your Eyes / Nov. 25, 1997 / Beyond ✦✦

The Ladder / Sep. 28, 1999 / Damian ✦✦✦

Yo La Tengo

f. 1984, Hoboken, NJ
Group / Noise Pop, Dream Pop, Indie Rock, Alternative Pop/Rock
Yo La Tengo was in many respects the quintessential critic's band: in addition to their adventurous eclecticism, defiant independence and restless creative ambition—three qualities which virtually guarantee music press acclaim—the group's frontman, Ira Kaplan, even tenured as a rock scribe prior to finding success as a performer. So frequently compared to the Velvet Underground that they even portrayed the legendary group in the 1996 film *I Shot Andy Warhol,* the Hoboken, New Jersey-based unit explored the extremes of feedback-driven noise-rock and sweetly melodic pop, shading their work with equal parts scholarly composure and fannish enthusiasm; prolific and mercurial, Yo La Tengo ultimately transcended its myriad influences to ensconce itself as a beloved institution of the indie community. —*Jason Ankeny*

Ride the Tiger / 1986 / Matador ✦✦✦✦

President Yo La Tengo/New Wave Hot Dogs / 1989 / Matador ✦✦✦✦✦
Two records now available as a single CD, these really show off Yo La Tengo's ability to create musical extremes. *New Wave Hot Dogs* has the firm pop sense and strong songwriting of the debut, but *President Yo La Tengo* offers up a little more free-form skronk in the ten-minute live version of "The Evil That Men Do," a gloriously squalling, over-the-top crash and bash session which proves how liberating and fun sonic dissonance can be. Just in case you don't like that sort of thing, "Evil" also shows up as a straightahead folk-rock track. This is a great collection of material that, as well as anything else they have recorded, gets to the heart of what makes this band tick. —*John Dougan*

Fakebook / 1990 / Bar/None ✦✦✦✦✦
Recommending *Fakebook* as the best place to begin a relationship with Yo La Tengo is slightly disingenuous, mainly because Yo La Tengo has never made another record like it, and perhaps never will. So, as completely wonderful as this record is (and believe me, it is), it's an accurate representation of one side of Yo La Tengo, and assuming that everything sounds like *Fakebook* might be disappointing. A collection of cover songs that lean toward the idiosyncratic (e.g., Peter Stampfel, Daniel Johnston, Jad Fair), *Fakebook* is warm, low-key and lovely, with heartfelt singing and playing that never flags after hundreds of replays. It's impossible to imagine playing this record and not smiling and singing along. A big bonus is a great version of The Flamin' Groovies "You Tore Me Down." —*John Dougan*

May I Sing with Me / Feb. 28, 1992 / Alias ✦✦✦
With song titles like "Mushroom Cloud of Hiss" and "Five-Cornered Drone (Crispy Duck)," *May I* is classic Yo La Tengo merging pop and noise in an awesome aural display. Songs start with Kaplan's repetitive (and very simple) chord changes, as Hubley and (at this juncture) regular bassist James McNew add layer after layer of supportive sound. During the noisier tracks (especially the aforementioned "Mushroom Cloud of Hiss"), the song explodes in paroxysms of feedback and drops the rhythmic pulse altogether, eventually returning the backbeat after a few minutes of white noise. That may not be everybody's cup of tea, but for those who like this adventurousness and recklessness, it's a lot of fun. —*John Dougan*

Painful / Oct. 5, 1993 / Matador ✦✦✦✦✦

Electr-O-Pura / May 2, 1995 / Matador/Atlantic ✦✦✦
After the noisy but dream-like drift of *Painful, Electr-O-Pura* found Yo La Tengo in livelier and more outwardly enthusiastic form; while they had hardly abandoned their more subdued and contemplative side, as evidenced by the lovely "The Hour Grows Late" and "Pablo and Andrea," they seemed eager to once again explore the grittier textures they'd unearthed on *President Yo La Tengo* and *May I Sing With Me* with tunes like the gleefully manic "False Ending" and the bizarre horn-blasted "Attack on Love." Yo La Tengo also served up one of the most perfectly realized pop tunes in their repertoire with "Tom Courtenay" (which not only name checks the Beatles, but boasts a tune the Fab Four would have been happy to come up with themselves), and revisited the concept of the noisy groove jam (which they pioneered on "The Evil That Men Do (Pablo's Version)") with the acetone-powered "False Alarm" and the joyous "Blue Line Swinger." Throughout, Ira Kaplan's simple but forceful guitar lines, Georgia Hubley's steady, subtly inventive drumming, and James McNew's solid, supportive bass add up to a group that prizes intelligence and imagination over flash, and makes it work over and over. Few bands have consistently better ideas than Yo La Tengo, and they make 14 of them work like a charm on *Electr-O-Pura.* (By the way, those incongruous comments about the songs were lifted from an obscure book on the Blues Project, and don't trust those timings on the back cover—they're deliberately inaccurate.) —*Mark Deming*

Genius + Love Yo La Tengo / Sep. 10, 1996 / Matador ✦✦✦

● **I Can Hear the Heart Beating as One** / Apr. 22, 1997 / Matador ✦✦✦✦✦
Functioning as a virtual catalog of mid-'90s indie-rock trends, *I Can Hear the Heart Beating as One* is an astonishing tour de force from Yo La Tengo, establishing their deep talents as songwriters and musicians. Although the album may run a little long for some tastes, there are very few throwaways on the record—even the shoegazer cover of the Beach Boys' "Little Honda" is a revelatory gem. But what truly impresses is the way the songs, ranging from hypnotically droning instrumentals to tightly written and catchy pop songs, hold together to form what is arguably Yo La Tengo's finest and most coherent album to date. —*Stephen Thomas Erlewine*

And Then Nothing Turned Itself Inside-Out / Feb. 22, 2000 / Matador ✦✦✦✦✦

Neil Young

b. Nov. 12, 1945, Toronto, Ontario, Canada
Vocals, Ukulele, Piano, Harmonica, Guitar / Heartland Rock, Album Rock, Folk-Rock, Hard Rock, Singer/Songwriter, Country-Rock
After Neil Young left the Californian folk-rock band Buffalo Springfield in 1968, he slowly established himself as one of the most influential and idiosyncratic singer-songwriters of his generation. Young's body of work ranks second only to Bob Dylan in terms of depth, and he was able to sustain his critical reputation, as well as record sales, for a longer period of time than Dylan, partially because of his willfully perverse work ethic. From the beginning of his solo career in the late '60s until the late '90s, he never stopped writing, recording and performing; his official catalog only represented a portion of his work, since he kept countless tapes of unreleased songs in his vaults. Just as importantly, Young continually explored new musical territory, from rockabilly and the blues to electronic music. But these stylistic exercises only gained depth when compared to his two primary styles—gentle folk and country-rock, and crushingly loud electric guitar rock, which he frequently recorded with the Californian garage band Crazy Horse. Throughout his career, Young alternated between these two extremes, and both proved equally influential; there were just as many simpy singer-songwriters as there were grunge and country-rock bands claiming to be influenced by Neil Young. Despite his enormous catalog and influence, Young continued to move forward, writing new songs and exploring new music in his fourth decade as a performing artist. That restless spirit ensured that he was one of the few rock veterans as vital in his old age as he was in his youth. —*Stephen Thomas Erlewine*

Neil Young / Jan. 1969 / Reprise ✦✦✦
Young's debut, one of his most low-key efforts, went almost unnoticed at the time, but did introduce many of the traits that would characterize much of his work: countryish ballads, medium-tempo rockers with searing lead guitar lines, tasteful strings and female backing vocals, and gentle but disquieting romantic ruminations. The material isn't strong enough to qualify this as one of his better albums, but it has a touching grace, embellished by Jack Nitzsche's elaborate production on a few tracks. The nine-and-a-half-minute closer, "The Last Trip to Tulsa," is Young's most long-winded and Dylanesque surrealist epic. —*Richie Unterberger*

☆ **Everybody Knows This Is Nowhere** / May 1969 / Reprise ✦✦✦✦✦
Neil Young's second solo album, released only four months after his first, was nearly a total rejection of that polished effort. Though a couple of songs, "Round Round (It Won't Be Long)" and "The Losing End (When You're On)," shared that album's country-folk style, they were altogether livelier and more assured. The difference was that while *Neil Young* was a solo effort, *Everybody Knows* marked the beginning of his recording association with Crazy Horse; with them, Young quickly cut a set of loose, guitar-heavy rock songs—"Cinnamon Girl," "Down by the River," and "Cowgirl in the Sand"—that redefined him as a rock & roll artist. The songs were deliberately underwritten and sketchy as compositions, their lyrics more suggestive than complete, but that made them useful as frames on which to hang extended improvisations and to reflect the ominous tone of his singing. Additionally, it set a musical pattern Young and his many musical descendants have followed ever since; almost 30 years later, he was still playing this sort of music with Crazy Horse, and a lot of contemporary bands were playing music clearly influenced by it. —*William Ruhlmann*

☆ **After the Gold Rush** / Aug. 1970 / Reprise ✦✦✦✦✦
In the 15 months between the release *Everybody Knows This Is Nowhere* and *After the Gold Rush,* Neil Young issued a series of recordings in different styles that could have prepared his listeners for the differences between the two LPs. His two compositions on the Crosby, Stills, Nash & Young album *Deja Vu,* "Helpless" and "Country Girl," are turned him to the folk and country styles he had pursued before delving into the hard rock of *Everybody Knows;* two other singles, "Sugar Mountain" and "Oh, Lonesome Me," also emphasized those roots. But "Ohio," a CSNY single, rocked as hard as anything on the second album. *After the Gold Rush* was recorded with the aid of Nils Lofgren, a 17-year-old unknown whose piano was a major instrument, turning one of the few real rockers, "Southern Man" (which had unsparing protest lyrics typical of Phil Ochs), into a more stately effort than anything on the previous album and giving a classic tone to the title track, a mystical ballad that featured some of Young's most imaginative lyrics and became one of his most memorable songs. But much of *After the Gold Rush* consisted of folk-country love songs, which consolidated the audience Young had earned through his tours and recordings with CSNY; its dark yet hopeful tone matched the tenor of the times in 1970, making it one of the definitive singer/songwriter albums, and it has remained among Young's major achievements. —*William Ruhlmann*

Harvest / Feb. 1972 / Reprise ✦✦✦✦✦
Neil Young's most popular album, *Harvest* employs a number of jarringly different styles. Much of it is country-tinged, although there is also an acoustic track, a couple of electric guitar-drenched rock performances, and two songs on which Young is accompanied by the London Symphony Orchestra. But the album does have an overall mood and an overall lyric content, and they conflict with each other: The mood is melancholic, but the songs mostly describe the longing for and fulfillment of new love. Young's concerns are perhaps most explicit on the controversial "A Man Needs a Maid," which contrasts the fears of committing to a relationship with simply living alone and hiring help. Over and over, he sings of the need for love in such songs as "Out on the Weekend," "Heart of Gold," and "Old Man," and the songs are unusually melodic and accessible; the rock numbers "Are You Ready for the Country" and "Alabama" are in Young's familiar style and unremarkable, and "There's a World" and "Words (Between the Lines of Age)" are ponderous and overdone. But the love songs and the harrowing portrait of a friend's descent into heroin addiction, "The Needle and the Damage Done," remain among Young's most affecting and memorable songs. *—William Ruhlmann*

Journey Through the Past / Nov. 1972 / Reprise ✦✦

Time Fades Away / Oct. 1973 / Reprise ✦✦✦
The beginning of Young's mid-'70s descent into decadence, this is part of a trilogy including *Tonight's the Night* and *On the Beach* that explores drug addiction, desperation, and determination, and the subject matter isn't only expressed in the lyrics, it's in the roughly played music and the strained vocals. The most gripping music of Young's career. *—William Ruhlmann*

☆ **On the Beach** / Jul. 1974 / Reprise ✦✦✦✦✦
Following the 1973 *Time Fades Away* tour, Neil Young wrote and recorded an Irish wake of a record called *Tonight's the Night* and went on the road drunkenly playing its songs to uncomprehending listeners and hostile reviewers. Reprise rejected the record, and Young went right back and made *On the Beach,* which shares some of the ragged style of its two predecessors. But where *Time* was embattled and *Tonight* mournful, *On the Beach* was savage and, ultimately, triumphant. "I'm a vampire, babe," Young sang, and he proceeded to take bites out of various subjects: threatening the lives of the stars who lived in L.A.'s Laurel Canyon ("Revolution Blues"); answering back to Lynyrd Skynyrd, whose "Sweet Home Alabama" had taken him to task for his criticisms of the South in "Southern Man" and "Alabama" ("Walk On"); and rejecting the critics ("Ambulance Blues"). But the barbs were mixed with humor and even affection, as Young seemed to be emerging from the grief and self-abuse that had plagued him for two years. But the album was so spare and underproduced, its lyrics so harrowing, that it was easy to miss Young's conclusion: He was saying goodbye to despair, not being overwhelmed by it. *—William Ruhlmann*

☆ **Tonight's the Night** / Jun. 1975 / Reprise ✦✦✦✦✦
Written and recorded in 1973 shortly after the death of roadie Bruce Berry, *Tonight's the Night* was Young's musical expression of grief, combined with his rejection of the stardom he had achieved in the late '60s and early '70s. The title track, performed twice, was a direct narrative about Berry, while the late Crazy Horse guitarist Danny Whitten was heard singing "Come on Baby Let's Go Downtown," a live track recorded years earlier. Performing with the remains of Crazy Horse, bassist Billy Talbot and drummer Ralph Molina, along with Nils Lofgren and Ben Keith, Young performed in the ragged manner familiar from *Time Fades Away*—his voice was often hoarse and he strained to reach high notes, while the playing was loose, with mistakes and shifting tempos. But the style worked perfectly for the material, emphasizing the emotional tone of Young's mourning; it was the work of a man trying to turn his torment into art and doing so unflinchingly. *—William Ruhlmann*

Zuma / Nov. 1975 / Reprise ✦✦✦✦✦
Having apparently exorcised his demons by releasing the cathartic *Tonight's the Night,* Neil Young returned to his commercial strengths with *Zuma* (named after Zuma Beach in Los Angeles, where he now owned a house). Seven of the album's nine songs were recorded with the reunited Crazy Horse, in which rhythm guitarist Frank Sampedro had replaced the late Danny Whitten, but there were also nods to other popular Young styles in "Pardon My Heart," an acoustic song that would have fit on *Harvest,* his most popular album, and "Through My Sails," retrieved from one of Crosby, Stills, Nash & Young's abortive recording sessions. Young had abandoned the ragged, first-take approach of his previous three albums, but Crazy Horse would never be a polished act, and the music had a lively sound well-suited to the songs, which were some of the most melodic, pop-oriented tunes Young had crafted in years, though they were played with an electric-guitar-drenched rock intensity. The overall theme concerned romantic conflict, with lyrics that lamented lost love and sometimes longed for a return ("Pardon My Heart" even found Young singing, "I don't believe this song"), though the overall conclusion, notably in such catchy songs as "Don't Cry No Tears" and "Lookin' for a Love," was to move on to the next relationship. But the album's standout track (apparently the only holdover from an early intention to present songs with historical subjects) was the 7-minute epic "Cortez the Killer," a commentary on the Spanish conqueror of Latin America that served as a platform for Young's most extensive guitar soloing since his work on *Everybody Knows This Is Nowhere.* *—William Ruhlmann*

Long May You Run / Sep. ??, 1976 / Reprise ✦✦✦

American Stars 'N Bars / Jun. 1977 / Reprise ✦✦✦

★ **Decade** / Nov. 1977 / Reprise ✦✦✦✦✦
Given the quirkiness of Neil Young's recording career, with its frequent cancellations of releases and last-minute rearrangements of material, it is a relief to report that this two-disc compilation is so conventional and so satisfying. A 35-track selection of the best of Young's work between 1966 and 1976, it includes songs performed by Buffalo Springfield, Crosby, Stills, Nash & Young, and the Stills/Young Band, as well as solo work. In addition to five unreleased songs, *Decade* offers such key tracks as the Springfield's "Mr. Soul," "Broken Arrow," and "I Am a Child"; "Sugar Mountain," a song that had appeared only as a single before; "Cinnamon Girl," "Down by the River," and "Cowgirl in the Sand" from *Everybody Knows This Is Nowhere;* "Southern Man" and the title track from *After the Gold Rush;* and "Old Man" and the chart-topping "Heart of Gold" from *Harvest.* This is the material that built Young's reputation between 1966 and 1972, although he is more idiosyncratic with the later material, including the blockbusters "Like a Hurricane" and "Cortez the Killer" but mixing in more unreleased recordings as the set draws to a close. He seems intent on making the album a listenable one that will appeal to a broad base of fans, and he succeeds despite the exclusion of much of the harrowing work of 1973-1975. Nevertheless, the album is an ideal sampler for new listeners, and since there is no one-disc Young compilation covering any significant portion of his career, this lengthy chronicle is the place to start. *—William Ruhlmann*

Comes a Time / Oct. 1978 / Reprise ✦✦✦✦✦
Six and a half years later, *Comes a Time* finally was the Neil Young album for the millions of fans who had loved *Harvest,* an acoustic-based record with country overtones and romantic, autobiographical lyrics, and many of those fans returned to the fold, enough to make *Comes a Time* Young's first Top Ten album since *Harvest.* He signaled the album's direction with the leadoff track, "Goin' Back," and its retrospective theme augmented with an orchestral backup and the deliberate beat familiar from his number one hit "Heart of Gold." Of course, Young remained sly about this retrenchment. "I feel like goin' back," he sang, but added, "Back where there's nowhere to stay." Doubtless he had no intention of staying with this style, but, for the length of the album, melodies, love lyrics, lush arrangements, and steel guitar solos dominated, and Young's vocals were made more accessible by being paired with Nicolette Larson's harmonies. Larson's own version of Young's "Lotta Love," released shortly after the one heard here, became a Top Ten hit single. Other highlights included the reflective "Already One," which treats the unusual subject of the nature of a divorced family, the ironic "Field of Opportunity," and a cover of Ian Tyson's folk standard "Four Strong Winds" (a country Top Ten hit for Bobby Bare in 1965). *—William Ruhlmann*

☆ **Rust Never Sleeps** / Jul. 1979 / Reprise ✦✦✦✦✦
Rust Never Sleeps, its aphoristic title drawn from an intended advertising slogan, was an album of new songs, some of them recorded on Neil Young's 1978 concert tour. His strongest collection since *Tonight's the Night,* its obvious antecedent was Bob Dylan's *Bringing It All Back Home,* and, as Dylan did, Young divided his record into acoustic and electric sides while filling his songs with wildly imaginative imagery. The lead-off track, "My My, Hey Hey (Out of the Blue)" (repeated in an electric version at album's end as "Hey Hey, My My [Into the Black]" with slightly altered lyrics), is the most concise and knowing description of the entertainment industry ever written; it was followed by "Thrasher," which describes Young's parallel artistic quest in an extended metaphor that also reflected the album's overall theme—the inevitability of deterioration and the challenge of overcoming it. Young then spent the rest of the album demonstrating that his chief weapons against rusting were his imagination and his daring, creating an archetypal album that encapsulated his many styles on a single disc with great songs—in particular the remarkable "Powderfinger"—unlike any he had written before. *—William Ruhlmann*

Live Rust / Nov. 1979 / Reprise ✦✦✦✦✦

Hawks & Doves / Nov. 1980 / Reprise ✦✦✦

Re-ac-tor / Nov. 1981 / Reprise ✦✦

Trans / Jan. 1983 / Geffen ✦✦

Everybody's Rockin' / Aug. 1983 / Geffen ✦✦

Old Ways / Aug. 1985 / Geffen ✦✦✦

Landing on Water / Jul. 1986 / Geffen ✦✦

Life / Jul. 1987 / Geffen ✦✦✦

This Note's for You / Apr. 1988 / Reprise ✦✦✦
This Note's for You was another installment in Neil Young's '80s tour of genres, recorded with a ten-piece, horn-driven blues band. In terms of style, it was merely another genre exercise, but the songs on the album were his strongest in several years, particularly the haunting "Coupe Deville," and began his late-'80s return to form. *—Stephen Thomas Erlewine*

Eldorado / 1989 / Reprise ✦✦✦

Freedom / Oct. 1989 / Reprise ✦✦✦✦✦
Neil Young is famous for scrapping completed albums and substituting hastily recorded ones in radically different styles; *Freedom,* a major critical and commercial comeback, seemed to be a selection of the best tracks from several different unissued projects. First and foremost was a hard rock album like the material heard on Young's recent EP *Eldorado* (released only in the Far East), several of whose tracks were repeated on *Freedom.* On these songs—especially "Don't Cry" and a cover of the Drifters' "On Broadway"—Young played distorted electric guitar over a rhythm section in an even more raucous fashion than on his Crazy Horse records. Second was a follow-up to *This Note's For You,* which had featured a six-piece horn section; they were back on the lengthy "Crime in the City" and "Someday," each of which contained a series of seemingly unrelated, mood-setting verses. Third, there were tracks that harked back to acoustic-based, country-tinged albums like *Harvest* and *Comes a Time,* including "Hangin' on a Limb" and "The Ways of Love." What made it all work was that Young had once again written a great bunch of songs, bookended by acoustic and electric versions of one of Young's greatest anthems, "Rockin' in the Free World." *—William Ruhlmann*

Ragged Glory / Oct. 11, 1990 / Reprise ✦✦✦✦✦
Having re-established his reputation with the musically varied, lyrically enraged *Freedom,* Neil Young returned to being the lead guitarist of Crazy Horse for the musically homogenous, lyrically hopeful *Ragged Glory.* The album's dominant sound was made by Young's noisy guitar, which bordered on and sometimes slipped over into distortion, while Crazy

Horse kept up the songs' bright tempos. Despite the volume, the tunes were catchy, with strong melodies and good choruses, and they were given over to love, humor, and warm reminiscence. They were also platforms for often extended guitar excursions: "Love To Burn" and "Love And Only Love" ran over ten minutes each, and the album as a whole lasted nearly 63 minutes with only ten songs. Much about the record had a retrospective feel—the first two tracks, "Country Home" and "White Line," were newly recorded versions of songs Young had played with Crazy Horse but never released in the '70s; "Mansion On The Hill," the album's most accessible track, celebrated a place where "psychedelic music fills the air" and "peace and love live there still"; there was a cover of the Premiers' garage rock oldie "Farmer John"; and "Days That Used To Be," in addition to its backward-looking theme, borrowed the melody from Bob Dylan's "My Back Pages" (by way of the Byrds' arrangement), while "Mother Earth (Natural Anthem)" was the folk standard "The Water Is Wide" with new, environmentally aware lyrics. Young was not generally known as an artist who evoked the past this much, but if he could extend his creative rebirth with music this exhilarating, no one was likely to complain. *—William Ruhlmann*

Weld / Oct. 1991 / Reprise ✦✦✦✦✦

Harvest Moon / Oct. 27, 1992 / Reprise ✦✦✦
After 20 years, Neil Young finally decided to release the sequel to *Harvest,* his most commercially successful album. *Harvest Moon* is in some ways a better album, without the orchestral bombast that stifled some of the songs on the first album and boasting a more diverse overall selection of songs. *Harvest Moon* manages to be sentimental without being sappy, wistful without being nostalgic. The lovely "Unknown Legend," "From Hank to Hendrix," and the beautiful "Harvest Moon" are among Young's best songs. Only the overlong (11 minutes) and oversimplified "Natural Beauty" hurts a beautiful album that proudly displays scars, heartaches, and love. *—Stephen Thomas Erlewine*

Lucky Thirteen / Jan. 5, 1993 / Geffen ✦✦✦

Unplugged / Jun. 15, 1993 / Reprise ✦✦✦✦✦

Sleeps with Angels / Aug. 16, 1994 / Reprise ✦✦✦✦
Reportedly spurred by the death of Kurt Cobain (who quoted Young's line, "It's better to burn out than to fade away," in his suicide note), Young turns in an unusually low-key, elegiac effort, its songs worrying about depression, lack of communication, and drive-by shootings, its music (despite the presence of Crazy Horse) slow and meditative (except for the funny change-of-pace rocker "Piece Of Crap"). The result is not as gloomy as *Tonight's The Night* (in which Young seemed past the point of caring and even managed a certain gallows humor), but extremely mournful, with only glimmers of hope. *—William Ruhlmann*

Mirror Ball / Jun. 27, 1995 / Reprise ✦✦✦
Knocked out in about two weeks, Neil Young's collaboration with Pearl Jam is considerably different than *Sleeps with Angels;* the record sounds like a spiritual rebirth after its bleaker predecessor. Playing with the Seattle band has reinvigorated Young. In fact, it has reinvigorated him so much that he hasn't spent much time on the songs, preferring to let the music carry the record. Pearl Jam's grooves are more elastic than Crazy Horse, yet new drummer Jack Irons reigns in the group's tendency to meander. As does Young himself, who dominates the proceedings with his jerky, wailing guitar. A couple of stray, minute-long organ-and-voice fragments from the *Sleeps with Angels* album punctuate the second side, yet the album isn't contemplative—it barrels ahead. *—Stephen Thomas Erlewine*

Dead Man / Feb. 27, 1996 / Vapor ✦✦

Broken Arrow / Jul. 2, 1996 / Reprise ✦✦✦

Year of the Horse / Jun. 17, 1997 / Reprise ✦✦✦

Silver and Gold / Apr. 25, 2000 / Reprise ✦✦✦

Road Rock, Vol. 1 / Nov. 21, 2000 / Reprise ✦✦✦

Paul Young

b. Jan. 17, 1956, Luton, Bedfordshire, England
Vocals / Pop/Rock, New Wave
A soulful U.K. interpretive singer who gained fame in his native country in 1983 with a cover of Marvin Gaye's "Wherever I Lay My Hat (That's My Home)" and in the U.S. with Daryl Hall's "Everytime You Go Away" in 1985. Young found less success writing his own songs, then returned to the U.S. Top Ten with a cover of the Chi-Lites' "Oh Girl" in 1990. In 1992, he left Columbia and moved to MCA. *—William Ruhlmann*

No Parlez / 1983 / Columbia ✦✦✦✦✦
Paul Young's debut album was a strong set of soulful covers of forgotten classics ("Love of the Common People," "Wherever I Lay My Hat [That's My Home]") and contemporary classics ("Love Will Tear Us Apart"), as well as the occasional made-to-order original, like the hit "Come Back and Stay." *—Stephen Thomas Erlewine*

The Secret of Association / 1985 / Columbia ✦✦✦✦✦
The Secret of Association continued the formula of *No Parlez* to fine effect, and thanks to a number one version of Hall & Oates' "Everytime You Go Away" that bettered the original, it was a bigger hit. *—Stephen Thomas Erlewine*

Between Two Fires / 1986 / Columbia ✦✦

Other Voices / Jun. 1990 / Columbia ✦✦✦
Other Voices marked a comeback from the tepid *Between Two Fires,* featuring a set of lush, soulful covers (the Top Ten hit "Oh Girl") and several harder-rocking numbers, including a cover of Free's "A Little Bit of Love." *—Stephen Thomas Erlewine*

● **From Time to Time: The Singles Collection** / Nov. 1991 / Columbia ✦✦✦✦✦
All Young's UK and US hits, among them "Everytime You Go Away," "Come Back and Stay," "I'm Gonna Tear Your Playhouse Down," "Love of the Common People," "Wherever I Lay My Hat (That's My Home)," and "Oh Girl." *—William Ruhlmann*

The Youngbloods

f. 1965, New York, NY, **db.** 1972
Group / Folk-Rock, Pop
The Youngbloods could not be considered a major '60s band, but they were capable of offering some mighty pleasurable folk-rock in the late '60s, and produced a few great tunes along the way. One of the better groups to emerge from the East Coast in the mid-'60s, they would temper their blues and jugband influences with gentle California psychedelia, particularly after they moved to the San Francisco Bay area. For most listeners, they're identified almost exclusively with their Top 10 hit "Get Together," but they managed several respectable albums as well, all under the leadership of singer/songwriter Jesse Colin Young. Comparisons between the Youngbloods and the Lovin' Spoonful are inevitable—both groups offered good-timey folk-rock with much stronger jugband influences than West Coast rivals like the Byrds, though the Youngbloods made greater use of electric keyboards than the Spoonful, courtesy of the enigmatically named Lowell "Banana" Levinger. The Youngbloods didn't craft nearly as many brilliant singles as the Lovin' Spoonful, but (unlike the Spoonful) endured well into the hippie/psychedelic era. The group broke up in 1972, and Jesse Colin Young had a long and moderately successful career as a solo singer/songwriter. *—Richie Unterberger*

The Youngbloods / 1967 / Edsel ✦✦✦✦✦
The New York quartet come off as a mini-Lovin' Spoonful on their engaging debut, with a deeper touch of melancholy and more prominent electric keyboards. As with the Spoonful, they would have been better off leaving the blues alone, but the rest of the material is good, highlighted by "Get Together" and the achingly tuneful "All Over the World (La-La)." *—Richie Unterberger*

Earth Music / 1967 / Edsel ✦✦✦
Similar but a bit inferior to their debut, with the same division between accomplished folk-rock, good-timey ragtime-influenced romps, and pedestrian blues-rock. Includes one of the best versions of Tim Hardin's oft-covered standard "Reason to Believe." *—Richie Unterberger*

Elephant Mountain / 1969 / RCA ✦✦✦✦✦
By the time they made this album, the group had relocated to Northern California from New York and guitarist Jerry Corbitt had departed, leaving the songwriting chores almost exclusively in the hands of Jesse Colin Young. The mellower, more psychedelic sound reflected the group's new surroundings, and despite some weak moments, it remains their strongest and most cohesive LP. Young's acoustic love song "Sunlight" is his best original composition, and the Youngbloods' best track besides "Get Together"; "Darkness, Darkness" and "Smug" are also outstanding. *—Richie Unterberger*

● **The Best of the Youngbloods** / 1970 / RCA ✦✦✦✦✦
It's a bit short at ten songs, but this collection offers a nice overview of this '60s band's growth from good-time ragtimers to laidback jammers. *—Jeff Tamarkin*

Frank Zappa

b. Dec. 21, 1940, Baltimore, MD, **d.** Dec. 4, 1993, Los Angeles, CA
Vocals, Guitar (Electric), Guitar / Album Rock, Experimental Rock, Comedy Rock, Jazz-Rock, Experimental, Prog-Rock/Art Rock, Fusion, Hard Rock
Frank Zappa was one of the most accomplished composers of the rock era; his music combines an understanding of and appreciation for such contemporary classical figures as Stravinsky, Stockhausen, and Varese with an affection for late-'50s doo wop rock & roll and a facility for the guitar-heavy rock that dominated pop in the '70s. But Zappa was also a satirist whose reserves of scorn seemed bottomless and whose wicked sense of humor and absurdity have delighted his numerous fans, even when his lyrics crossed over the broadest bounds of taste.

A band he joined in 1964 evolved into the Mothers by 1966, the year of the group's first album for MGM, a two-LP set called *Freak Out!* Subsequent albums extended the musical and lyrical themes of the debut, and they came frequently. Toward the end of the '60s, Zappa expanded the Mothers lineup, turning more toward instrumental jazz-rock. Zappa assembled a new edition of the Mothers in 1970, moving the group more in the direction of X-rated comedy. During a London performance however, he was pushed from the stage by a demented fan and seriously injured. After he recovered, Zappa re-formed the Mothers with himself as lead singer and made pop/rock albums, such as *Over-nite Sensation,* which were among his best-selling records ever. In the '80s, Zappa gained the rights to his old albums and began to reissue them, at first on his own and then through the pioneering Rykodisc CD label. Zappa died in 1993, two years after he was confirmed as being seriously ill with cancer. *—William Ruhlmann*

☆ **Freak Out!** / Jul. 1966 / Rykodisc ✦✦✦✦✦
One of the most ambitious debuts in rock history, *Freak Out!* was a seminal concept album that somehow foreshadowed both art rock and punk at the same time. Its four LP sides deconstruct rock conventions right and left, eventually pushing into territory inspired by avant-garde classical composers. Yet the album is sequenced in an accessibly logical progression; the first half is dedicated to catchy, satirical pop/rock songs that question assumptions about pop music, setting the tone for the radical new directions of the second half. Opening with the nonconformist call to arms "Hungry Freaks, Daddy," *Freak Out!* quickly posits the Mothers of Invention as the antithesis of teen-idol bands, often with sneering mockeries of the teen-romance songs that had long been rock's commercial stock-in-trade. Despite his genuine emotional alienation and dissatisfaction with pop conventions, though, Frank Zappa was actually a skilled pop composer; even with the raw performances and his stinging guitar work, there's a subtle sophistication apparent in his unorthodox arrangements and tight, unpredictable melodicism. After returning to social criticism on the first song of the second half, the perceptive Watts riot protest "Trouble Every Day," Zappa exchanges pop song structure for experiments with musique concrète, amelodic dissonance, shifting time signatures, and studio effects. It's the first salvo in his career-long project of synthesizing popular and art music, high and low culture; while these pieces can meander, they virtually explode the lim-

its of what can appear on a rock album, and effectively illustrate *Freak Out!*'s underlying principles: acceptance of differences and free individual expression. Zappa would spend much of his career developing and exploring ideas—both musical and conceptual—first put forth here; while his myriad directions often produced more sophisticated work, *Freak Out!* contains at least the rudiments of almost everything that followed, and few of Zappa's records can match its excitement over its own sense of possibility. *—Steve Huey*

Absolutely Free / May 26, 1967 / Rykodisc ✦✦✦✦✦
Frank Zappa's liner notes for *Freak Out!* name-checked an enormous breadth of musical and intellectual influences, and he seemingly attempts to cover them all on the second Mothers of Invention album, *Absolutely Free.* Leaping from style to style without warning, the album has a freewheeling, almost schizophrenic quality, encompassing everything from complex mutations of "Louie, Louie" to jazz improvisations and quotes from Stravinsky's *The Rite of Spring.*

It's made possible not only by expanded instrumentation, but also Zappa's experiments with tape manipulation and abrupt editing, culminating in an orchestrated mini-rock opera ("Brown Shoes Don't Make It") whose musical style shifts every few lines, often in accordance with the lyrical content. In general, the lyrics here are more given over to absurdity and non sequiturs, with the sense that they're often part of some private framework of satirical symbols. But elsewhere, Zappa's satire also grows more explicitly social, ranting against commercial consumer culture and related themes of artificiality and conformity.

By turns hilarious, inscrutable, and virtuosically complex, *Absolutely Free* is more difficult to make sense of than *Freak Out!,* partly because it lacks that album's careful pacing and conceptual focus. But even if it isn't quite fully realized, *Absolutely Free* is still a fabulously inventive record, bursting at the seams with ideas that would coalesce into a masterpiece with Zappa's next project. *—Steve Huey*

Lumpy Gravy / Mar. 1968 / Rykodisc ✦✦✦✦
Initially commissioned by Capitol Records when the Mothers of Invention were signed to Verve, *Lumpy Gravy* was Frank Zappa's first solo album, one on which be continued his tape experiments and employed an orchestra along with members of the Mothers. Snatches of conversation and sound collages make up the bulk of it, so that it is the most exploratory (but not the most accomplished) album Zappa made in the 1960s. *—William Ruhlmann*

★ **We're Only in It for the Money** / Sep. 1968 / Rykodisc ✦✦✦✦✦
From the beginning, Frank Zappa cultivated a role as voice of the freaks—imaginative outsiders who didn't fit comfortably into any group. *We're Only in It for the Money* is the ultimate expression of that sensibility, a satirical masterpiece that simultaneously skewered the hippies and the straights as prisoners of the same narrow-minded, superficial phoniness. Zappa's barbs were vicious and perceptive, and not just humorously so: his seemingly paranoid vision of authoritarian violence against the counterculture was borne out two years later by the Kent State killings. Like *Freak Out, We're Only in It for the Money* essentially devotes its first half to satire, and its second half to presenting alternatives. Despite some specific references, the first-half suite is still wickedly funny, since its targets remain immediately recognizable. The second half shows where his sympathies lie, with character sketches of Zappa's real-life freak acquaintances, a carefree utopia in "Take Your Clothes Off When You Dance," and the strident, unironic protest "Mother People." Regardless of how dark the subject matter, there's a pervasively surreal, whimsical flavor to the music, sort of like *Sgt. Pepper* as a creepy nightmare. Some of the instruments and most of the vocals have been manipulated to produce odd textures and cartoonish voices; most songs are abbreviated, segue into others through edited snippets of music and dialogue, or are broken into fragments by more snippets, consistently interrupting the album's continuity. Compositionally, though, the music reveals itself as exceptionally strong, and Zappa's politics and satirical instinct have rarely been so focused and relevant, making *We're Only in It for the Money* quite probably his greatest achievement. [Rykodisc's 1987 reissue restored passages censored on the LP, but included re-recorded rhythm tracks and sounded quite different. Their 1995 reissue contains both the original music and content edits.] *—Steve Huey*

Cruising with Ruben and the Jets / Oct. 1968 / Rykodisc ✦✦✦
The music of Frank Zappa and the Mothers of Invention always retained roots in soul and doo wop, even at its most satirical. On this, the Mothers' fourth album (and their final release for Verve, now available as a Rykodisc CD reissue), they tried playing it straight, making an affectionate genre album for the low-riding Los Angeles pachucos, although the result is still tongue-in-cheek, as the cover blurb, "Is this the Mothers of Invention recording under a different name in a last-ditch attempt to get their cruddy music on the radio?," makes clear. When Zappa prepared the album for reissue in the 1980s, he re-recorded the rhythm tracks, which mars the original. It is this version that is the only one currently available, however. *—William Ruhlmann*

Burnt Weeny Sandwich / Jun. 1969 / Rykodisc ✦✦✦✦✦
Burnt Weeny Sandwich is another high-quality entry in Zappa's 1969-70 period of largely instrumental works. Like *Weasels Ripped My Flesh,* which immediately followed it, *Burnt Weeny Sandwich* was compiled from studio and concert recordings of the original Mothers of Invention lineup. A bit more on the heavy guitar-rock side than the jazzy *Hot Rats,* and less avant-garde than portions of *Weasels, Burnt Weeny Sandwich* also features stately classical passages and extended solo excursions from Ian Underwood, Don Preston, and Sugarcane Harris, as well as two doo wop covers bookending the record: the Four Deuces' "WPLJ" and Jackie and the Starlites' "Valarie." The other tracks are mostly segued together, and flow into one another quite well. *—Steve Huey*

Uncle Meat / Jun. 1969 / Rykodisc ✦✦✦✦✦
Just three years into their recording career, the Mothers of Invention released their second double album, *Uncle Meat,* which began life as the largely instrumental soundtrack to an unfinished film. It's essentially a transitional work, but it's a fascinating one, showcasing Frank Zappa's ever-increasing compositional dexterity and the Mothers' emerging instrumental prowess. It was potentially easy to overlook Zappa's melodic gifts on albums past, but on *Uncle Meat,* he thrusts them firmly in the spotlight; what few lyrics there are, Zappa says in the liner notes, are in-jokes relevant only to the band. Thus, *Uncle Meat* became the point at which Zappa began to establish himself as a composer and he would return to many of these pieces repeatedly over the course of his career. Taken as a whole, *Uncle Meat* comes off as a hodgepodge, with centerpieces scattered between variations on previous pieces, short concert excerpts, less-realized experiments, doo wop tunes, and comedy bits; the programming often feels as random as the abrupt transitions and tape experiments held over from Zappa's last few projects. But despite the absence of a conceptual framework, the unfocused sprawl of *Uncle Meat* is actually a big part of its appeal. It's exciting to hear one of the most creatively fertile minds in rock pushing restlessly into new territory, even if he isn't always quite sure where he's going. However, several tracks hint at the jazz-rock fusion soon to come, especially the extended album closer "King Kong"; it's his first unequivocal success in that area, with its odd time signature helping turn it into a rhythmically kinetic blowing vehicle. Though some might miss the gleeful satire of Zappa's previous work with the Mothers, *Uncle Meat*'s continued abundance of musical ideas places it among his most intriguing works. *—Steve Huey*

Hot Rats / Oct. 10, 1969 / Rykodisc ✦✦✦✦✦
Aside from the experimental side project *Lumpy Gravy, Hot Rats* was the first album Frank Zappa recorded as a solo artist sans the Mothers, though he continued to employ previous musical collaborators, most notably multi-instrumentalist Ian Underwood. Other than another side project—the doo wop tribute *Cruising With Ruben and the Jets—Hot Rats* was also the first time Zappa focused his efforts in one general area, namely jazz-rock. The result is a classic of the genre. *Hot Rats'* genius lies in the way it fuses the compositional sophistication of jazz with rock's down and dirty attitude—there's a real looseness and grit to the three lengthy jams, and a surprising, wry elegance to the three shorter, tightly arranged numbers (particularly the sumptuous "Peaches en Regalia"). Perhaps the biggest revelation isn't the straightforward presentation, or the intricately shifting instrumental voices in Zappa's arrangements—it's his own virtuosity on the electric guitar, recorded during extended improvisational workouts for the first time here. His wonderfully scuzzy, distorted tone is an especially good fit on "Willie the Pimp," with its greasy blues riffs and guest vocalist Captain Beefheart's Howlin' Wolf theatrics. Elsewhere, his skill as a melodist was in full flower, whether dominating an entire piece or providing a memorable theme as a jumping-off point. In addition to Underwood, the backing band featured contributions from Jean-Luc Ponty, Lowell George, and Don "Sugarcane" Harris, among others; still, Zappa is unquestionably the star of the show. *Hot Rats* still sizzles; few albums originating on the rock side of jazz-rock fusion flowed so freely between both sides of the equation, or achieved such unwavering excitement and energy. *—Steve Huey*

Weasels Ripped My Flesh / Aug. 1970 / Rykodisc ✦✦✦✦✦
A fascinating collection of mostly instrumental live and studio material recorded by the original Mothers, complete with horn section, from 1967-69, *Weasels Ripped My Flesh* segués unpredictably between arty experimentation and traditional song structures. Highlights of the former category include the classical avant-garde elements of "Didja Get Any Onya," which blends odd rhythmic accents and time signatures with dissonance and wordless vocal noises; these pop up again in "Prelude to the Afternoon of a Sexually Aroused Gas Mask" and "Toads of the Short Forest." The latter and "The Eric Dolphy Memorial Barbecue" also show Zappa's willingness to embrace the avant-garde jazz of the period. Yet, interspersed are straightforward tunes like a cover of Little Richard's "Directly From My Heart to You," with great violin from Sugar Cane Harris; the stinging Zappa-sung rocker "My Guitar Wants to Kill Your Mama," and "Oh No," a familiar Broadway-esque Zappa melody (it turned up on *Lumpy Gravy*) fitted with lyrics and sung by Ray Collins. Thus, *Weasels* can make for difficult, incoherent listening, especially at first. But there is a certain logic behind the band's accomplished genre-bending and Zappa's gleefully abrupt veering between musical extremes; without pretension, Zappa blurs the normally sharp line between intellectual concept music and the visceral immediacy of rock and R&B. Zappa's anything-goes approach and the distance between his extremes are what make *Weasels Ripped My Flesh* ultimately invigorating; they also even make the closing title track—a minute and a half of squalling feedback, followed by applause—perfectly logical in the album's context. *—Steve Huey*

Chunga's Revenge / Oct. 23, 1970 / Rykodisc ✦✦✦

Fillmore East: June 1971 / Jun. 1971 / Rykodisc ✦✦✦

200 Motels / Oct. 1971 / Rykodisc ✦✦✦✦

Just Another Band from L.A. / Apr. 1972 / Rykodisc ✦✦

Waka/Jawaka / Jul. 5, 1972 / Rykodisc ✦✦✦

The Grand Wazoo / May 1973 / Rykodisc ✦✦✦✦✦
Like its immediate predecessor, *Waka/Jawaka, The Grand Wazoo* was a largely instrumental jazz fusion album recorded during Zappa's convalescence from injuries sustained after being pushed off a concert stage. While Zappa contributes some guitar solos and occasional vocals, the focus is more on his skills as a composer and arranger. Most of the five selections supposedly form a musical representation of a story told in the liner notes about two warring musical factions, but the bottom line is that overall, the compositions here are more memorably melodic and consistently engaging than *Waka/Jawaka.* The instrumentation is somewhat unique in the Zappa catalog as well, with the band more of a chamber jazz orchestra than a compact rock unit; over 20 musicians and vocalists contribute to the record. While *Hot Rats* is still the peak of Zappa's jazz-rock fusion efforts, *The Grand Wazoo* comes close, and it's essential for anyone interested in Zappa's instrumental works. *—Steve Huey*

● **Over-Nite Sensation** / Sep. 1973 / Rykodisc ✦✦✦✦✦
Love it or hate it, *Over-Nite Sensation* was a watershed album for Frank Zappa, the point where his post-'60s aesthetic was truly established; it became his first gold album, and most of these songs became staples of his live shows for years to come. Where the Flo and Eddie years were dominated by rambling, off-color comedy routines, *Over-Nite Sensation* tightened up the song structures and tucked sexual and social humor into melodic, technically accomplished heavy guitar rock with jazzy chord changes and funky rhythms; meanwhile,

Zappa's growling new post-accident voice take over the storytelling. While the music is some of Zappa's most accessible, the apparent callousness and/or stunning sexual explicitness of "Camarillo Brillo," "Dirty Love," and especially "Dinah-Moe Humm" leave him on shaky aesthetic ground. Zappa often protested that the charges of misogyny leveled at such material missed out on the implicit satire of male stupidity, and also confirmed intellectuals' self-conscious reticence about indulging in dumb fun; however, the glee in his voice as he spins his adolescent fantasies can undermine his point. Indeed, that enjoyment, also evident in the silly wordplay, suggests that Zappa is throwing his juvenile crassness in the face of critical expectation, asserting his right to follow his muse even if it leads him into blatant stupidity (ironic or otherwise). One can read this motif into the absurd shaggy-dog story of a dental floss rancher in "Montana," the album's indisputable highlight, which features amazing, uncredited vocal backing from Tina Turner and the Ikettes. As with much of Zappa's best '70s and '80s material, *Over-Nite Sensation* is ideologically problematic and musically terrific. *—Steve Huey*

Apostrophe / Mar. 1974 / Rykodisc ✦✦✦✦✦
The musically similar follow-up to the commercial breakthrough of *Over-Nite Sensation, Apostrophe'* became Frank Zappa's second gold and only Top Ten album with the help of the "doggy wee-wee" jokes of "Don't Eat the Yellow Snow," Zappa's first chart single (a longer, edited version that used portions of other songs on the LP). The first half of the album is full of nonsensical shaggy-dog story-songs that segué into one another without seeming to finish themselves first; their dirty jokes are generally more subtle and veiled than the more notorious cuts on *Over-Nite Sensation.* The second half contains the instrumental title cut, featuring Jack Bruce on bass; "Uncle Remus," an update of Zappa's critique of racial discord on "Trouble Every Day"; and a return to the album's earlier silliness in "Stink Foot." *Apostrophe'* has the narrative feel of a concept album, but aside from its willful absurdity, the concept is difficult to decipher; even so, that doesn't detract from its entertainment value. *—Steve Huey*

Roxy & Elsewhere / Sep. 10, 1974 / Rykodisc ✦✦✦✦

One Size Fits All / Jun. 25, 1975 / Rykodisc ✦✦✦

Bongo Fury / Oct. 2, 1975 / Rykodisc ✦✦✦
Except for two instrumental studio tracks, *Bongo Fury* was recorded live in Austin, Texas on a reunion tour between Zappa and Captain Beefheart, the latter of whom takes most of the vocals. Many of the tracks feature Beefheart's surreal poetry with musical backing from the Mothers reminiscent of the Flo and Eddie band; Zappa also takes a few guitar solos and pushes some songs into bluesier territory, revisiting the music that originally cemented his and Beefheart's friendship. On this album, Zappa and Beefheart are a decent, if not quite inspiring pairing, with such highlights as "Carolina Hardcore Ecstasy," and the Zappa-sung "Muffin Man," and the country-tinged bicentennial satire "Poofter's Froth Wyoming Plans Ahead." *—Steve Huey*

Zoot Allures / Oct. 29, 1976 / Rykodisc ✦✦✦✦

Zappa in New York / Mar. 3, 1978 / Rykodisc ✦✦✦✦

Studio Tan / Sep. 15, 1978 / Rykodisc ✦✦

Sleep Dirt / Jan. 19, 1979 / Rykodisc ✦✦✦

Sheik Yerbouti / Mar. 3, 1979 / Rykodisc ✦✦✦✦

Joe's Garage: Acts 1-3 / Nov. 19, 1979 / Rykodisc ✦✦✦✦✦
Joe's Garage was originally released in 1979 in two separate parts; *Act 1* came first, followed by a two-record set containing *Acts 2-3.* Rykodisc's reissue puts all three acts together on two CDs. *Joe's Garage* is generally regarded as one of Zappa's finest post-'60s conceptual works, a sprawling, satirical rock opera about a totalitarian future in which music is outlawed to control the population. The narrative is long, winding, and occasionally loses focus; it was improvised in a weekend, some of it around previously existing songs, but Zappa manages to make most of it hang together. Acts 2-3 give off much the same feel, as Zappa relies heavily on what he termed "xenochrony"—previously recorded guitar solos transferred onto new, rhythmically different backing tracks to produce random musical coincidences. Such an approach is guaranteed to produce some slow moments as well, but critics latched onto the work more for its conceptual substance. *Joe's Garage* satirizes social control mechanisms, consumerism, corporate abuses, gender politics, religion, and the rock & roll lifestyle; all these forces conspire against the title protagonist, an average young man who simply wants to play guitar and enjoy himself. Even though Zappa himself hated punk rock and even says so on the album, his ideas seemed to support punk's do-it-yourself challenge to the record industry and to social norms in general. Since this is 1979-era Zappa, there are liberal applications of his trademark scatological humor (the titles of "Catholic Girls," "Crew Slut," "Why Does It Hurt When I Pee?," and 'Keep It Greasey" are self-explanatory). Still, in spite of its flaws, *Joe's Garage* has enough substance to make it one of Zappa's most important '70s works and overall political statements, even if it's not focused enough to rank with his earliest Mothers of Invention masterpieces. *—Steve Huey*

Tinsel Town Rebellion / May 17, 1981 / Rykodisc ✦✦✦

You Are What You Is / Sep. 1981 / Rykodisc ✦✦✦✦✦
You Are What You Is was another of Zappa's periodic post-*Over-Nite Sensation* efforts that concentrated on tight songwriting supported by satirical lyrics. Originally a two-record set featuring 20 songs, *You Are What You Is* skewered a variety of targets, from teenagers, punk rock, disco, and country music to the media, yuppies, the beauty and fitness industry, upper-class vice, religious hypocrisy, suicide, and the military draft—all the trappings of Reagan-era America. Occasionally, Zappa's points seem ill-thought-out, if not unnecessarily malicious; the title track seems to condemn both blacks and whites who overstep their racially defined boundaries and act like each other, and "Jumbo Go Away" is perhaps the most offensive song in Zappa's huge canon of potentially offensive songs, a tale of a whining, VD-riddled groupie who is portrayed as deserving the punch in the face she gets from an irritated musician. Despite its low points, though, *You Are What You Is* is quite ambitious in scope and in general one of Zappa's most accessible later-period efforts, showcasing both his songwriting skills and often acute satirical perspective with less of the smutty humor that some listeners find off-putting. *—Steve Huey*

Ship Arriving Too Late to Save a Drowning Witch / May 1982 / Rykodisc ✦✦✦

Baby Snakes / Mar. 1983 / Rykodisc ✦✦

Man from Utopia / Mar. 1983 / Rykodisc ✦✦

Them or Us / Oct. 1984 / Rykodisc ✦✦✦

Thing-Fish / Nov. 1984 / Rykodisc ✦✦✦

Jazz from Hell / Nov. 15, 1986 / Rykodisc ✦✦✦✦✦

You Can't Do That on Stage Anymore, Vol. 1 / May 16, 1988 / Rykodisc ✦✦✦✦✦
This two-LP set provides a curtain-raiser on the massive *You Can't Do That On Stage Anymore* series and is typical of the approach of the series in that it jumps from one time and band and location to another, leading off, for example, with a version of "Plastic People" recorded by the Mothers of Invention in 1969 and moving immediately to a version of "The Torture Never Stops" by Frank Zappa's band in 1977. Some of Zappa's more entertaining numbers are here, such as "Montana," "King Kong" (a short version from 1982), and "Cosmic Debris," but, as with most of the series, the jumping around gives the album an unfocused feel. *—William Ruhlmann*

Broadway the Hard Way / Oct. 1988 / Rykodisc ✦✦✦✦✦

You Can't Do That on Stage Anymore, Vol. 2 / Oct. 1988 / Rykodisc ✦✦✦✦✦

You Can't Do That on Stage Anymore, Vol. 3 / Nov. 1989 / Rykodisc ✦✦✦✦✦

Frank Zappa Meets the Mothers of Prevention / May 1990 / Rykodisc ✦✦✦

The Best Band You Never Heard in Your Life / Apr. 1991 / Rykodisc ✦✦✦✦✦
This is the second album that Frank Zappa culled from live performances on his final 1988 world tour, the first being *Broadway the Hard Way.* That release contained newly written material; this one, in contrast, contains, as Zappa puts it in his liner notes, "big-band arrangements of concert favorites and obscure album cuts, along with deranged versions of cover tunes and a few premiere recordings." In practice, that means you have the opportunity to hear Zappa treatments of such surprising songs as "Ring of Fire," "I Left My Heart In San Francisco," "Bolero," "Purple Haze," and "Stairway to Heaven." In other words, even for an idiosyncratic artist, this is an idiosyncratic album. (The title derives from Zappa's note that the band "self-destructed" before most of the U.S. could hear it play.) *—William Ruhlmann*

Make a Jazz Noise Here / Jun. 1991 / Rykodisc ✦✦✦

You Can't Do That on Stage Anymore, Vol. 4 / Jun. 21, 1991 / Rykodisc ✦✦✦✦✦

You Can't Do That on Stage Anymore, Vol. 5 / 1992 / Rykodisc ✦✦✦✦✦

You Can't Do That on Stage Anymore, Vol. 6 / Oct. 23, 1992 / Rykodisc ✦✦✦✦✦

Zappa: The Yellow Shark / Nov. 2, 1993 / Rykodisc ✦✦✦✦✦
Released only a month before Frank Zappa's death, *The Yellow Shark* is an album of orchestral treatments of Zappa's compositions done by the 25-piece Ensemble Modern orchestra, conducted by Peter Rundel. It features vintage material like "Dog Breath Variations" as well as more recent work, played with more sensitivity and verve than previous orchestras have brought to Zappa's music. Hence, the "pick" notation should alert fans who want to hear the orchestral Zappa—this is the best executed and most varied of the albums Zappa devoted to his "serious" music. *—William Ruhlmann*

Strictly Commercial: The Best of Frank Zappa / Aug. 22, 1995 / Rykodisc ✦✦✦✦✦

Lost Episodes / Feb. 27, 1996 / Rykodisc ✦✦✦✦✦
A 30-track compilation of rarities, spanning much of his career, but in the main confined to the 1960s and early '70s (some date from as early as the late '50s!). Much of it's previously unreleased, or extremely hard to locate. It's not just a collection of fan-oriented odds and ends, though. The material, for one thing, is extremely diverse, ranging from collaborations with Captain Beefheart and primitive teenage garage recordings to comic dialog to progressive instrumentals and orchestral pieces. The pre-*Freak Out* stuff in particular is revelatory, in the sense that it finds Zappa's sophisticated compositional and arrangement skills in full bloom years before he made his proper debut. There's also good old rock and roll, in an early version of "Any Way the Wind Blows," and an early '60s take of "Fountain of Love" with explosive fuzz bass. The cuts range in duration from 11 seconds to 11 minutes, often connected by amusing bits of spoken patter or nifty instrumental links. The effect is somewhat like *Uncle Meat* or *Lumpy Gravy,* meaning that those who appreciate that period of Zappa's evolution will find an immediate affinity with this anthology. *—Richie Unterberger*

Läther / Sep. 24, 1996 / Rykodisc ✦✦✦
The full saga of *Läther* (pronounced leather) is tangled enough to give a migraine to all but committed Zappaphiles. Basically, what you need to know is that this project was originally conceived of as a four-record box set. When record-company politics prevented its release in that format, much of the material was spread over the albums *Live in New York, Sleep Dirt, Studio Tan,* and *Orchestral Favorites.* This three-CD set presents the album as it was originally conceived, with the addition of four bonus tracks at the end. It mixes previously available material, alternate mixes and edits, and previously unissued stuff, though only the most serious Zappa fans will have a good grip on exactly what has appeared where (the liner notes are surprisingly unexact in this regard). And the music— It's almost like a résumé of Zappa's bag of tricks: *Uncle Meat*-like experimentation, intricate jazz-rock, straight hard rock, orchestral composition, and comedy. Some of those comedy tracks became some of his most notorious routines, like "Punky's Whips" and "Titties 'n Beer," which amounted to avant-rock for drunk frat boys and pot-smoking, underachieving junior-high-school students. The juvenile humor, hamfisted parody of hard rock cliches, and the shaggy-dog opera of the 20-minute "The Adventures of Greggery Peccary" are outshone by the lengthy, more experimental instrumental passages. It's interesting, but exhausting to wade through all at once, and the avant-garde/composerly cuts are not as exceptional as his earlier work in this vein

in the late '60s and early '70s. That means that this will appeal far more to the Zappa cultist than the general listener, though the Zappa cult—which has been craving *Läther* in its original format for years—is a pretty wide fan base in and of itself. *—Richie Unterberger*

Strictly Genteel: A Classical Introduction to Frank Zappa / May 20, 1997 / Rykodisc ✦✦✦✦

Cucamonga / 1998 / Del-Fi ✦✦✦✦

Warren Zevon

b. Jan. 24, 1947, Chicago, IL

Vocals, Keyboards, Piano, Guitar, Bass / Album Rock, Hard Rock, Singer/Songwriter, Rock & Roll

One of the most acute and savagely satiric songwriters of his era, as a youth Warren Zevon focused primarily on classical material, even studying under the tutelage of Igor Stravinsky. However, a disintegrating home life led him into pop music, as well as a few run-ins with the law, and at 16 he hopped into the Corvette his father won in a card game and headed for New York to become a folksinger. His music found little response, however, and he returned to California, eventually releasing his first recordings as part of the duo Lyme and Cybelle. Session work followed before Zevon issued his solo debut *Wanted—Dead or Alive* in 1969; the LP received a poor reception, and so he returned to session gigs and composing advertising jingles. With longtime friend Jackson Browne in the producer's seat, Zevon returned with a self-titled offering which was met with lavish critical praise upon its 1976 release. His 1978 follow-up *Excitable Boy* established him as a wholly unique talent, and earned a sizable hit with its wry single "Werewolves of London." However, Zevon had fallen prey to alcoholism, and his personal demons sidelined him for the next two years; the promise of his early work was finally restored on 1982's brilliant *The Envoy.* The album fared miserably on the charts, however, and Zevon again fell off the wagon. A long period of therapy and counseling followed before, newly sober and revitalized, he issued *Sentimental Hygiene* in 1987. *—Jason Ankeny*

Warren Zevon / 1976 / Asylum ✦✦✦✦✦

Warren Zevon was a ten-year music industry veteran who had written songs for the Turtles, backed up Phil Everly, done years of session work, and been befriended by Jackson Browne by the time he cut his self-titled album in 1976 (which wasn't his debut, though the less said about 1969's misbegotten *Wanted Dead or Alive* the better). Even though Warren Zevon was on good terms with L.A.'s Mellow Mafia, he sure didn't think (or write) like any of his pals in the Eagles or Fleetwood Mac; Zevon's music was full of blood, bile, and mean-spirited irony, and the glossy surfaces of Jackson Browne's production failed to disguise the bitter heart of the songs on *Warren Zevon.* The album opened with a jaunty celebration of a pair of Old West thieves and gunfighters ("Frank and Jesse James"), and went on to tell remarkable, slightly unnerving tales of ambitious pimps ("The French Inhaler"), lonesome junkies ("Carmelita"), wired, hard-living lunatics ("I'll Sleep When I'm Dead"), and truly dastardly womanizers ("Poor Poor Pitiful Me"), and even Zevon's celebrations of life in Los Angeles, long a staple of the soft rock genre, had both a menace and an epic sweep his contemporaries could never match ("Join Me in L.A." and "Desperados Under the Eaves"). But for all their darkness, Zevon's songs also possessed a steely intelligence, a winning wit, and an unusually sophisticated melodic sense, and he certainly made the most of the high-priced help who backed him on the album. *Warren Zevon* may not have been the songwriter's debut, but it was the album that confirmed he was a major talent, and it remains a black-hearted pop delight. *—Mark Deming*

Excitable Boy / 1978 / Asylum ✦✦✦✦

Warren Zevon's self-titled 1976 album announced he was one of the most striking talents to emerge from the Los Angeles soft rock singer/songwriter community, and Linda Ronstadt (a shrewd judge of talent if a sometimes questionable interpreter) recorded three of its songs on two of her biggest selling albums, which doubtlessly earned Zevon bigger royalty checks than the album itself ever did. But if *Warren Zevon* was an impressive calling card, the follow-up, *Excitable Boy,* was an actual hit, scoring one major hit single, "Werewolves of London," and a trio of turntable hits ("Roland the Headless Thompson Gunner," "Lawyers, Guns and Money," and the title track). But while *Excitable Boy* won Zevon the larger audience his music certainly deserved, the truth is it was a markedly inferior album; while it had all the bile of *Warren Zevon,* and significantly raised Zevon's dark-humor factor, it was often obvious where his previous album had been subtle, and while all 11 tracks on *Warren Zevon* were strong and compelling, two of the nine tunes on *Excitable Boy*—"Johnny Strike Up the Band" and "Nighttime in the Switching Yard"—sound like they're just taking up space. Musically, most of *Excitable Boy* is stuck in a polished but unexceptional FM pop groove, and only "Veracruz" hints at the artful intelligence of *Warren Zevon*'s finest moments. It's hard to say if Zevon was feeling uninspired or just dumbing himself down when he made *Excitable Boy,* but while it made him famous, it lacks the smarts and substance of his best work. *—Mark Deming*

Bad Luck Streak in Dancing School / 1980 / Asylum ✦✦✦✦✦

Excitable Boy earned Warren Zevon a hit single ("Werewolves of London") and the mainstream success he richly deserved, but his new fame came with a price; the hard-living Zevon did not react well to the temptations that come with rock stardom, and in the wake of *Excitable Boy* he had developed a severe drinking problem. *Bad Luck Streak in Dancing School* was cut as Zevon was working hard to stay clean and sober and put his career back on track, and it projects an ambition and strength of focus that was decidedly absent from *Excitable Boy.* The album's rockers hit harder and cut deeper than any of his previous work, especially the twisted Southern gothic of "Play It All Night Long" and the mercenary's anthem "Jungle Work," while "Bed of Coals" and "Wild Age" found Zevon bravely addressing his own failings and expressing his need for a greater maturity in his life. While the album was still short on subtlety compared to 1976's *Warren Zevon,* "Empty Handed Heart proved Zevon could still write a straightforward song about love (not a happy one, but no one expected that from him anyway), and the two interludes for orchestra gave credence to Zevon's claims that he planned to write a symphony some day (and that it might even be worth hearing). And if "Gorilla You're a Desperado" was a throwaway, it was a better waste of time than "Midnight at the Switching Yard" on *Excitable Boy.* While *Bad Luck Streak in Dancing School* didn't quite return Zevon to the top of his game, it made clear that the quality of *Warren Zevon* was no fluke, and is a stronger effort than *Excitable Boy* in nearly every respect. *—Mark Deming*

Stand in the Fire / 1981 / Asylum ✦✦✦

The Envoy / 1982 / Asylum ✦✦✦

A Quiet Normal Life: The Best of Warren Zevon / 1986 / Asylum ✦✦✦✦✦

This is an adequate but skimpy best-of covering Zevon's best known songs. Though his self-titled LP and *Excitable Boy* have a lot of terrific music not represented here, *A Quiet Normal Life* still stands as a good introduction. *—John Floyd*

Sentimental Hygiene / 1987 / Virgin ✦✦✦✦✦

After a rather well-publicized fall off the wagon following the release of *The Envoy,* Warren Zevon went five years without releasing an album, but his time in the woodshed seemed to have done him good, as *Sentimental Hygiene* was his strongest album since *Warren Zevon* in 1976. While a few members of the L.A. Mellow Mafia (David Lindley, Waddy Wachtel, Don Henley) made cameo appearances on the album, for most of the sessions Zevon worked with Peter Buck, Mike Mills, and Bill Berry of R.E.M., who were about a year away from their mainstream commercial breakthrough; they made for a solid, no-nonsense rhythm section, and gave the music a passionate, forceful backbone that was largely absent from *The Envoy* (not to mention rocking harder than one might expect from the kings of jangle pop). Zevon put his newly muscular sound to good use; the songs on *Sentimental Hygiene* are Warren Zevon at his flintiest, as he indulges in his usual obsessions with machismo ("Boom Boom Mancini") and bad love (the title cut) while also exploring the media's skewed perspective on his addiction problems ("Detox Mansion," "Trouble Waiting to Happen"), his disgust with the music business ("Even a Dog Can Shake Hands"), and errors in both personal and political judgement ("Bad Karma," "Leave My Monkey Alone"). And Zevon scored three inspired musical guest shots on the album—Neil Young, whose jagged guitar runs embroider the title cut; Bob Dylan, whose howling harmonica is the ideal punctuation for the Springsteen-gone-psychotic "The Factory"; and George Clinton, who adds a bed of menacing funk to "Leave My Monkey Alone." *Sentimental Hygiene* proved that Warren Zevon was still an artist to be reckoned with, and that which didn't kill him had only made stronger (and more bitterly funny). *—Mark Deming*

Transverse City / Oct. 1989 / Virgin ✦✦✦✦

Mr. Bad Example / Oct. 15, 1991 / Giant ✦✦

Learning to Flinch / Apr. 13, 1993 / Giant ✦✦✦

Mutineer / May 23, 1995 / Giant ✦✦

● **I'll Sleep When I'm Dead (An Anthology)** / Sep. 17, 1996 / Rhino ✦✦✦✦✦

I'll Sleep When I'm Dead (An Anthology) covers the bulk of Warren Zevon's career, conviently skipping over his long-forgotten first album and concentrating heavily on his Asylum records, as well as his albums for Virgin and Giant. Over the course of the double-disc set's 44 songs, nearly every one Zevon's greatest songs is featured, including six songs each from *Warren Zevon* and *Excitable Boy,* as well as a number of songs only featured on soundtrack albums, a handful of outtakes, and Hindu Love Gods' cover of Prince's "Raspberry Beret." The quality of Zevon's music declines somewhat as his career progresses, but the compilation captures most of the highlights from his latter-day records. For casual fans that want to dig deeper than *Warren Zevon* or *Excitable Boy, I'll Sleep When I'm Dead (An Anthology)* is an ideal purchase. *—Stephen Thomas Erlewine*

Life'll Kill Ya / Jan. 25, 2000 / Artemis ✦✦✦

The Zombies

f. 1962, St. Albans, Herts, England, **db.** 1967

Group / British Psychedelia, Psychedelic Pop, Psychedelic, British Invasion, Pop

Aside from the Beatles and perhaps the Beach Boys, no mid-'60s rock group wrote melodies as gorgeous as those of the Zombies. Dominated by Colin Blunstone's breathy vocals, choral backup harmonies, and Rod Argent's shining jazz- and classical-influenced organ and piano, the band sounded utterly unique for their era. Indeed, their material—penned by either Argent or guitarist Chris White, with unexpected shifts from major to minor keys—was perhaps too adventurous for the singles market. To this day, they're known primarily for their three big hit singles, "She's Not There" (1964), "Tell Her No" (1965), and "Time of the Season" (1969). Most listeners remain unaware that the group maintained a remarkably high quality of work for several years. Argent's composition "She's Not There" got them a deal with Decca, and the song ended up being their debut release. It was a remarkably confident and original first-time effort, with a great minor melody and the organ, harmonies, and urgent, almost neurotic vocals that would typify much of their work. The tragedy was that throughout 1965 and 1966, the Zombies released a string of equally fine, intricately arranged singles that flopped commercially, at a time in which chart success on 45s was a lot more important to sustain a band's livelihood than it would be a few years down the road. *Odessey and Oracle* was their only cohesive full-length platter (the first album was largely pasted together from singles and covers). A near-masterpiece of pop/psychedelia, it showed the Zombies reaching new levels of sophistication in composition and performance, finally branching out beyond strictly romantic themes into more varied lyrical territory. The album passed virtually unnoticed in Britain, and was only released in the States after some lobbying from Al Kooper. By this time it was 1968, and the group had split for good. *—Richie Unterberger*

The Zombies (Featuring She's Not There and Tell Her No) / Dec. 1964 / Parrot ✦✦✦

The Zombies' first American LP was a rushed, somewhat schizophrenic affair, mixing first-rate originals ("It's Alright," "Sometimes", and the two big hits) with sloppy, ill-suited R&B

covers. There's some very good stuff here, but you're much better advised to pick it up on a number of CD reissue compilations than track down the pricy original vinyl. *—Richie Unterberger*

Begin Here / Apr. 1965 / Decca ✦✦✦
The group's British debut LP repeated a lot of the same tracks from the American version, but as was the habit in those days, deleted some cuts and substituted some others. Unlike the U.S. record, it was reissued, and thus became much easier to find. But as with the American version, you can find all of the tracks on other CD compilations, and almost all of the important ones on the anthologies that concentrate only on their best material. The 1999 CD reissue on Big Beat expands the track lineup substantially with the addition of three songs from their 1965 U.K. EP *The Zombies* and, more interestingly, alternate takes of "Sticks and Stones" and "It's Alright With Me," as well as demos of "I Know She Will" and "I'll Keep Trying." The demos of these last two tunes are notable in that they don't have the overdubs on the versions available on other albums. *—Richie Unterberger*

☆ **Odessey & Oracle** / 1968 / Rhino ✦✦✦✦✦
Odessey & Oracle was one of the flukiest (and best) albums of the 1960s, and one of the most enduring long-players to come out of the entire British psychedelic boom, mixing trippy melodies, ornate choruses, and lush Mellotron sounds with a solid hard rock base. But it was overlooked completely in England and barely got out in America (with a big push by Al Kooper, who was then a Columbia Records producer); and it was neglected in the U.S. until the single "Time of the Season," culled from the album, topped the charts nearly two years after it was recorded, by which time the group was long disbanded. Ironically, at the time of its recording in the summer of 1967, permanency was not much on the minds of the band members. *Odessey & Oracle* was intended as a final statement, a bold last hurrah, having worked hard for three years only to see the quality of their gigs decline as the hits stopped coming. The results are consistently pleasing, surprising, and challenging: "Hung Up on a Dream" and "Changes" are some of the most powerful psychedelic pop/rock ever heard out of England, with a solid rhythm section, a hot Mellotron sound, and chiming, hard guitar, as well as highly melodic piano; "Changes" also benefits from radiant singing. "This Will Be Our Year" makes use of trumpets (one of the very few instances of real overdubbing) in a manner reminiscent of "Penny Lane"; and then there's "Time of the Season," the most well-known song in their output and a white soul classic. Not all of the album is that inspired, but it's all consistently interesting and very good listening, and superior to most other psychedelic albums this side of the Beatles' best and Pink Floyd's early work. Indeed, the only complaint one might have about the original LP is its relatively short running time, barely over 30 minutes, but even that's refreshing in an era where most musicians took their (and our) time making their point, and most of the CD reissues have bonus tracks to fill out the space available. *—Bruce Eder*

Live on the BBC / 1985 / Rhino ✦✦✦

★ **The Singles A's & B's** / 1990 / See For Miles ✦✦✦✦✦
While "She's Not There" and "Tell Her No" are the only well-remembered mid-'60s Zombies singles, they recorded quite a few great non-hit 45s as well during this period. This outstanding collection (now available on CD) features all 22 of the sides they released on singles between 1964-67, and shows the group to be among the most superbly inventive pop-rock composers of their era, exploring moody minor-key melodies more than anyone before or since. Colin Blunstone's delicate, neurotic vocals and Rod Argent's biting electric keyboards pace the band on this set, which features the two big hits and such great lost classics as "Remember When I Loved Her," "I Want You Back Again," "I Must Move," "Indication," and "Gotta Get a Hold of Myself." Essential British Invasion music. *—Richie Unterberger*

Zombie Heaven / Nov. 18, 1997 / Big Beat ✦✦✦✦✦
After years of being under-recognized as the true geniuses that they were, the Zombies finally started getting their due in the 1990s. Artists such as Eric Matthews and Jason Faulkner and others have been profoundly influenced by the group. Lovingly compiled by longtime fan and journalist Alec Palao, this four-CD set offers everything that this fine group ever cut, with numerous outtakes, live versions, and alternate mixes. The sound alone is awesome, especially on the *Odessay and Oracle* album and the outtakes that came from it. The early material such as "I Remember You," "Tell Her No," and "She's Not There" sparkle as well. Add to that that this is essentially a template for *any* box set, and you have one of the finest rock or pop releases of the 1990s. *—Matthew Greenwald*

● **Absolutely the Best** / Jul. 13, 1999 / Varese ✦✦✦✦✦
At the time of its release, *Absolutely the Best* was, indeed, absolutely the best single-disc Zombies collection available in the U.S. Of course the big hits "She's Not There," "Tell Her No," and "Time of the Season" were included, along with the group's minor U.S. chart entries "She's Coming Home," "I Want You Back Again," "Just out of Reach," and "Imagine the Swan," and some good album tracks. With 16 cuts in just over 40 minutes, this is not a comprehensive compilation, but for most fans who know only the three big hits and would welcome some similar sounding material, it's plenty. *—William Ruhlmann*

The Singles Collection: A's & B's, 1964-1969 / Mar. 14, 2000 / Big Beat ✦✦✦✦✦

ZZ Top

f. 1970, Houston, TX
Group / Album Rock, Boogie Rock, Arena Rock, Southern Rock, Hard Rock, Blues-Rock
A sturdy American blues-rock trio from Texas, ZZ Top consists of Billy Gibbons (guitar), Dusty Hill (bass), and Frank Beard (drums). Their first two albums reflected the strong blues roots and Texas humor of the band. Their third album (*Tres Hombres*) gained them national attention with the hit "La Grange," a signature riff tune to this day, based on John Lee Hooker's "Boogie Chillen." Their success continued unabated throughout the '70s, culminating with the year-and-a-half-long Worldwide Texas Tour. Exhausted from the overwhelming work load, they took a three-year break, then switched labels and returned to form with *Deguello* and *El Loco,* both harbingers of what was to come. By their next album, *Eliminator,* and its worldwide smash follow-up, *Afterburner,* they had successfully harnessed the potential of synthesizers to their patented grungy blues-groove, giving their material a more contemporary edge while retaining their patented Texas style. As genuine roots musicians, they have few peers; Gibbons is one of America's finest blues guitarists working in the arena of rock idiom—both influenced by the originators of the form and British blues-rock guitarists like Peter Green—while Hill and Beard provide the ultimate rhythm section support. ZZ Top's music is always instantly recognizable, eminently powerful, profoundly soulful, and 100% American in derivation. *—Cub Koda*

ZZ Top's First Album / 1970 / Warner Brothers ✦✦✦

Rio Grande Mud / 1972 / Warner Brothers ✦✦✦

Tres Hombres / 1973 / Warner Brothers ✦✦✦✦✦
Tres Hombres is the record that brought ZZ Top their first Top Ten record, making them stars in the process. It couldn't have happened to a better record. ZZ Top finally got their low-down, cheerfully sleazy blooze-n-boogie right on this, their third album. As their sound gelled, producer Bill Ham discovered how to record the trio so simply that they sound indestructible, and the group brought the best set of songs they'd ever have to the table. On the surface, there's nothing really special about the record, since it is just a driving blues-rock album from a Texas bar band, but that's what's special about it. It has a filthy groove and an infectious feel, thanks to Billy Gibbons' growling guitars and the steady propulsion of Dusty Hill and Frank Beard's rhythm section. They get the blend of bluesy shuffles, gut-bucket rocking, and off-beat humor just right. ZZ Top's very identity comes from this earthy sound and songs as utterly infectious as "Waitin' for the Bus," "Jesus Just Left Chicago," "Move Me on Down the Line," and the John Lee Hooker boogie "La Grange." In a sense, they kept trying to remake this record from this point on—what is *Eliminator* if not *Tres Hombres* with sequencers and synthesizers?—but they never got it better than they did here. *—Stephen Thomas Erlewine*

Fandango / 1975 / Warner Brothers ✦✦✦

Tejas / 1976 / Warner Brothers ✦✦

● **The Best of ZZ Top** / 1977 / Warner Brothers ✦✦✦✦✦
ZZ Top closed out their tenure with London records in late 1977 with *The Best of ZZ Top,* a basic but terrific ten-song retrospective of highlights from their first five albums (well, four, actually, since the underwhelming *Tejax* is ignored). There are no surprises here, just album rock favorites, which means it does draw heavily on *Tres Hombres* (four songs, total), adds *Fandango*'s "Tush," "Blue Jean Blues," and "Heard it on the X" for good measure, then rounds it out with two songs from *Rio Grande Mud* and a selection from the debut. Yeah, there are a couple good album tracks missing, but as a ten-song summary of their early years, this can't be beat. *—Stephen Thomas Erlewine*

Deguello / 1979 / Warner Brothers ✦✦✦✦✦
ZZ Top returned after an extended layoff in late 1979 with *Deguello,* their best album since 1973's *Tres Hombres.* During their time off, ZZ Top didn't change much—hell, their sound never really changed during their entire career—but it did harden, in a way. The grooves became harder, sleeker, and their off-kilter sensibility and humor began to dominate, as "Cheap Sunglasses" and "Fool for Your Stockings" illustrate. Ironically, this, their wildest album lyrically, doesn't have the unhinged rawness of their early blooze rockers, but the streamlined production makes it feel sleazier all the same, since its slickness lets the perversity slide forth. And, let us not forget, the trio is in fine shape here, knocking out a great set of rockers and sounding stylish all the time. Undoubtedly one of their strong suits. *—Stephen Thomas Erlewine*

El Loco / 1981 / Warner Brothers ✦✦✦

Eliminator / 1983 / Warner Brothers ✦✦✦✦✦
ZZ Top had reached the top of the charts before, but that didn't make their sudden popularity in 1983 any more predictable. It wasn't that they were just popular—they were *hip,* for God's sake, since they were one of the only AOR favorites to figure out to harness the stylish, synthesized grooves of new wave, and then figure out how to sell it on MTV. Of course, it helped that they had songs that deserved to be hits. With "Gimme All Your Lovin," "Sharp Dressed Man," and "Legs," they had their greatest set of singles since the heady days of *Tres Hombres,* and the songs that surrounded them weren't bad either—they would have been singles on *El Loco,* as a matter of fact. The songs alone would have made *Eliminator* one of ZZ Top's three greatest albums, but their embrace of synths and sequencers made it a blockbuster hit, since it was the sound of the times. Years later, the sound of the times winds up sounding a bit stiff. It's still an excellent ZZ Top album, one of their best, yet it sounds like a mechanized ZZ Top thanks to the unflaggingly accurate grooves. Then again, that's part of the album's charm—this is new wave blues-rock, glossed up for the video, looking as good as the omnipresent convertible on the cover and sounding as irresistible as Reaganomics. Not the sort the old-school fans or blues-rock purists will love, but ZZ Top never sounded as much like a band of its time as they did here. *—Stephen Thomas Erlewine*

Afterburner / 1985 / Warner Brothers ✦✦✦

Recycler / 1990 / Warner Brothers ✦✦

● **Greatest Hits** / Apr. 14, 1992 / Warner Brothers ✦✦✦✦✦
An 18-song compilation, it features the greatest hits of ZZ Top's MTV era, including "Gimme All Your Lovin'," "Sharp Dressed Man," "Tush," "Pearl Necklace," "Cheap Sunglasses," "Sleeping Bag," "Rough Boy," and a remixed version of "Legs." It's a good, fun collection that should have been sequenced better and, unfortunately, omits a few good songs. *—AMG*

Antenna / Jan. 18, 1994 / RCA ✦✦✦

Rhythmeen / Sep. 17, 1996 / RCA ✦✦✦

XXX / Sep. 28, 1999 / RCA ✦✦

Various Artists

25 All-Time Greatest Bubblegum Hits: The Ultimate Bubblegum Collection / Jun. 27, 2000 / Varese ✦✦✦✦✦

Ace Story, Vol. 1 / Ace ✦✦✦✦✦

● **Acid Visions: Best of Texas Punk/Psychedelic, Vol. 1** / 1991 / Collectables ✦✦✦✦✦
One of the very best '60s garage compilations, a high compliment given the thousands of competitors, and the very best Texas '60s garage anthology. With the possible exception of California, Texas was home to more fine obscure garage records than any other state, and these 14 cuts are among the finest. Roy Head delivers a fine Johnny Winter tune, "Easy Lovin' Girl," and Winter himself sings a prime slice of folk-rock-acid-punk, "Birds Can't Row Boats" (this version, incidentally, is much better than the one found on the early Winter compilation of the same name). The other names are totally obscure, and some of the tracks weren't even released until the 1980s. But the Things and the Bad Roads come through with fine pop-punk numbers, and A-440's "Torture," Satori's "Time Machine," and The Pandas' "Walk" have been belatedly recognized as some of the best garage psychedelia ever, combining sharp melodic hooks and songwriting with out-and-out dementia. *—Richie Unterberger*

☆ **Atlantic Rhythm & Blues 1947-1974** / 1991 / Atlantic ✦✦✦✦✦
This eight-CD set should be a part of any collection that presumes to take American music—not just rock & roll or rhythm & blues—seriously. Atlantic Records was one of dozens of independent labels started up after the war by neophyte executives and producers, but it was different from most of the others in that the guys who ran it were honest and genuinely loved music. Coupled with a lot of luck and some good judgment, the results trace a good chunk of the history of American music and popular culture. Disc One opens with cuts which slot in somewhere midway between jazz, bop, and "race" music (as the term was used then). Disc Two is pure, distilled R&B, the stuff filling the airwaves of black radio and the jukeboxes in the "wrong" parts of town in 1952-54. Surprisingly, the material on Disc Three, covering 1955-57, isn't very different in content or character from Disc Two, despite the fact that it covers the period when white teenagers were starting to listen to and buy these records in large numbers. It's only with Disc Four that one sees the consequences of the late '50s—Ray Charles in his final days with the label, juxtaposed with the Drifters in their post-1958 incarnation and the start of the company's relationship with Stax/Volt Records. Disc Six (1965-67) is practically a mini-tribute to Stax/Volt, filled with the best-known sides of Eddie Floyd, Otis Redding, Sam & Dave, and Booker T. & the MG's. Discs Seven and Eight run from the late '60s and the heyday of Aretha Franklin to some great early-'70s soul, including Roberta Flack and the Spinners. The booklet, with a full sessionography and biographical notes on each artist, would be worth 20 bucks on its own. *—Bruce Eder*

The Beat Generation / 1992 / Rhino ✦✦✦✦✦

☆ **The Best of Chess Rock & Roll** / Chess ✦✦✦✦✦

☆ **Best of Doo Wop Ballads** / 1989 / Rhino ✦✦✦✦✦

☆ **Best of Doo Wop Uptempo** / 1989 / Rhino ✦✦✦✦✦

★ **The Best of New Orleans Rhythm & Blues, Vol. 1** / 1988 / Rhino ✦✦✦✦✦
The Best of New Orleans Rhythm & Blues, Vol. 1 is an incredible collection of 18 of the greatest Crescent City R&B singles ever released. Divided equally between classics ("Mother-In-Law," "It Will Stand," "I Hear You Knocking," "I'm Gonna Be a Wheel Someday," "Lipstick Traces (On a Cigarette)," "A Certain Girl," "One Night," "Ooh Poo Pah Doo [Pt. 1]") and terrific but frequently underappreciated singles from the likes of the Spiders, Irma Thomas, Aaron Neville, Earl King, and Dave Bartholomew, the collection is a concise and utterly intoxicating overview of New Orleans R&B, one that appeals not only to neophytes, but also to collectors. *—Stephen Thomas Erlewine*

★ **The British Invasion: History of British Rock, Vols. 1-9** / 1991 / Rhino ✦✦✦✦✦
Rhino's nine-volume ^British Invasion: The History of British Rock is the most exhaustive and essential overview of '60s British pop/rock available. Although the collection doesn't include tracks from the Beatles, the Rolling Stones, the Who, Herman's Hermits, the Dave Clark Five, and the early Animals, their absence doesn't hurt the series, since it spotlights several artists who never had more than a handful of hits, plus many forgotten gems. And there are plenty of major acts here, as well: The Kinks, the Small Faces, the Yardbirds, Donovan, the Hollies, the Zombies, the Spencer Davis Group, the Searchers, Manfred Mann, and Them are all represented by their best-known tracks. The collection runs from the beginnings of Merseybeat to the aftermath of psychedelia, meaning that it chronicles the evolution of British pop/rock quite effectively. But *The History of British Rock* shouldn't be thought of as simply an educational overview of one of the most vital eras of pop; each volume is fun and exciting, and sounds more like a good time than a history lesson. The series is one of the cornerstones of any comprehensive pop/rock collection. *—Stephen Thomas Erlewine*

Casablanca Records Story / 1994 / Casablanca/Mercury ✦✦✦✦✦

☆ **Chess Blues-Rock Songbook: The Classic Originals** / Aug. 26, 1997 / Chess ✦✦✦✦✦

☆ **The Complete Stax-Volt Singles 1959-1968** / 1991 / Atlantic ✦✦✦✦✦
At nine discs and 244 tracks, *The Complete Stax-Volt Singles: 1959-1968* is far too exhaustive for casual fans, but that's not who the set is designed for—it's made for the collector. Featuring every A-side the label released during those nine years, as well as several B-sides, the set is a definitive portrait of gritty, deep Southern soul. Many of the genre's major names—Otis Redding, Sam & Dave, Carla Thomas, Booker T & the MG's, William Bell, Rufus Thomas, the Bar-Kays, Albert King—plus many terrific one-shot wonders are showcased in terrific sound and augmented with an in-depth booklet. For any serious soul or rock collector, it's an essential set, since Stax-Volt was not only was a musically revolutionary label, their roster was deep with talent, which means much of the music on this collection is first rate. But if you only want the hits, you'll be better off with a smaller collection, since too much of this set will sound too similar, and sorting through the nine discs will be a monumental task if you only want to hear Otis, Rufus, Carla and Sam & Dave. *—Stephen Thomas Erlewine*

Cowabunga! The Surf Box / 1996 / Rhino ✦✦✦✦✦
Massive, though not quite definitive, four-CD, 82-track box set of surf music. The first three discs are devoted to material from the genre's '60s prime, and the fourth devoted to revivalists from 1977 to 1995. Most listeners are still better off with the several excellent single-disc surf compilations available (the best of which, like this one, are on Rhino). If your interest runs very deep, this should satisfy, placing most of the emphasis on instrumentals rather than vocals (though significant efforts in the latter vein by the Beach Boys, Jan & Dean, and others are included). It has most of the big hits, and quite a few of the ones which were principally popular in Southern California, as well as some neat rarities that are hard to find anywhere, like the Illusions' storming "Jezebel," and the Surfmen's "Paradise Cove," the Latin-surf hybrid of Dave Myers's "Moment of Truth," the Sandals' "Theme from Endless Summer," and the Sunrays' pale Beach Boys xerox, "I Live for the Sun." The fourth disc of modern-day revivalists, alas, was probably unnecessary in the minds of everyone except the compilers; it's the first three that really deal with the heart of the matter, with voluminous annotation in the 66-page booklet. *—Richie Unterberger*

★ **D.I.Y.: Come out and Play: American Power Pop . . .** / Feb. 16, 1993 / Rhino ✦✦✦✦✦
Power-pop benefited from the punk explosion, since it had as much to do with the rock & roll mainstream as with the punks. In the wake of the Ramones and Sex Pistols, straightforward, guitar-driven power-pop bands had a greater audience than before, since more listeners were aware of the existence of such music. And if the ringing pop on *D.I.Y.: Come Out and Play—American Power Pop I* has more to do with the British Invasion than the Damned, it shares the same kinetic energy and vital spirit as punk, especially since many of the bands on this collection were doggedly releasing independent records and touring in the late '70s to a dedicated cult following. There are no hits on *Come Out on Play*—Cheap Trick, the one marquee name on the compilation, is represented by the dynamic album track "Southern Girls"—but that doesn't mean it's a collection of also-rans and mediocrities. Instead, these songs are the foundation of the first wave of power-pop, and many of the artists here—Pezband ("Baby It's Cold Outside"), the Nerves ("Hanging on the Telephone"), Artful Dodger ("Wayside"), Chris Stamey ("Summer Sun"), Tommy Hoehn ("Blow Yourself Up"), the Paley Brothers ("Come Out and Play"), Fotomaker ("Where Have You Been All My Life") and Chris Bell ("I Am the Cosmos"—have become legendary in certain circles. As a result, *Come Out and Play* serves as a terrific introduction to the world of power-pop, but it's better seen as a collection of some of the best and catchiest pop singles that slipped through the cracks in the late '70s. *—Stephen Thomas Erlewine*

★ **D.I.Y.: Blank Generation: The New York Scene (1975-78)** / Jan. 19, 1993 / Rhino ✦✦✦✦✦
From the outset, New York punk rock had more subgenres and styles than its British counterparts. Even the Ramones, who were seemingly the most straightforward band on the scene, had a distinctly arty conceit behind their fusion of garage-rock, bubblegum and pop-culture kitsch. Most of their contemporaries had similar attitudes, whether it was Blondie with their sexy, ironic revision of '60s pop, Television's cerebral guitar rock, Richard Hell's jaggedly atonal rock, Patti Smith's punk poetry, or Suicide's eerie synthesizers. All of those bands are collected on the superb overview *D.I.Y.: Blank Generation—The New York Scene (1975-78)*, along with such cult favorites as the Dictators ("(I Live for) Cars and Girls"), Mink DeVille ("Let Me Dream If I Want To"), Wayne County, the Dead Boys, the Heartbreakers and the Mumps. While Talking Heads are missing from the collection, *Blank Generation* nevertheless is an accurate and nearly flawless portrait of the heyday of New York punk. *—Stephen Thomas Erlewine*

★ **D.I.Y.: Anarchy in the Uk: Uk Punk I (1976-77)** / Jan. 19, 1993 / Rhino ✦✦✦✦✦
With the exception of The Clash, who could not be included because of licensing obstacles, this 19-song collection includes all of the major originators of British punk music. The Sex Pistols are here, of course, with somewhat rawer demo versions of "Anarchy In The U.K." and "God Save The Queen" that have previously appeared on various quasi-legitimate albums. Otherwise, you get the major singles from a posse of leading bands of the movement, including The Damned, the Saints, the Jam, and the Buzzcocks. Cult acts of nearly equal importance, like X-Ray Spex, the Adverts, the Only Ones, Generation X, and Wire also weigh in with trailblazing singles like "Orgasm Addict" and "One Chord Wonders." Major punk fans and collectors won't find anything here that they don't already have. But for those who didn't pick up everything the first time around, or weren't even around the first time around, it's as ideal an introduction as can be imagined to a sound that totally realigned rock with its emphasis on brittle guitars, amphetamine rhythms, and socially charged songwriting. The booklet includes a lengthy, informative essay by Jon Savage, author of the British punk history England's Dreaming. *—Richie Unterberger*

☆ **Disco Box** / Feb. 16, 1999 / Rhino ✦✦✦✦✦
Rhino's four-CD *Disco Box* is the most impressive disco retrospective yet assembled, featuring 80 tracks and exhaustive liner notes which chronicle the music's history, artists, innovations, and subsequent influence. Like many of the best Rhino anthologies of this sort, *The Disco Box* is a mixture of acknowledged classics and neglected yet surprisingly high-quality lesser-knowns (although the emphasis here is more on the former). The result is an enormously infectious, entertaining package that makes the best case yet for the importance and creative viability of disco in its heyday. There are a couple of minor flaws—most disco fans will be able to name a few absent favorites (none of the Bee Gees' historically crucial Saturday Night Fever tracks were available for licensing, for example), and others may bemoan the lack of extended 12" club versions, which simply wouldn't fit into a compilation of this scope. At any rate, *The Disco Box* is still as definitive and well-done an overview as we're ever likely to see, and even at four CDs, it's the perfect introduction. *—Steve Huey*

☆ **Doo Wop Box** / 1994 / Rhino ✦✦✦✦✦

☆ **Frat Rock!** / 1991 / Rhino ✦✦✦✦✦

Rhino's *Frat Rock* series is an excellent overview of '60s rock & roll and R&B party anthems like The Kingsmen's "Louie Louie," "Double Shot of My Baby's Love" (Swinging Medallions), "La La La La La" (Blendells), "Shout" (Isley Brothers), "Do You Love Me?" (The Contours), and "Mony Mony" (Tommy James & The Shondells). *—John Floyd*

Get Hot or Go Home: Vintage RCA Rockabilly '56-'59— *Vols. I & II* / *Country Music Foundation* ✦✦✦✦✦

★ **Golden Age of American Rock 'n' Roll, Vol. 1** / 1991 / Ace ✦✦✦✦✦
For many years, Original Sound's Oldies But Goodies series was acknowledged as the best source for catching up on the many great early rock & roll hits by artists who had only one (or two, or three, or even a few more) classics to offer. Ace's Golden Age of American Rock-'n'Roll series, however, has surpassed Oldies But Goodies as the series of choice in the CD age. Even at an import price, they offer better value (with 30 songs each!); they use the best possible available source tapes for remastering; they also offer lengthy, intelligent liner notes and some photos, where Original Sound have historically offered none. Most important, they offer a wealth of great hits from rock & roll's first decade as a widespread phenomenon (1954-63), some of which are very difficult to find on other recordings, CD or not. There are some huge hits represented, but an equal amount of attention is paid to lower-charting items that have fallen out of rotation at oldies stations, as well as some slight/regional hits that you might not have heard even if you grew up during the era. Volume One, like each installment, reflects the incredible diversity and excitement of rock's first decade: doo-wop, primitive rockabilly, girl groups, instrumental rock, proto-soul, pop-rock, and more, ranging from famous one-shots (the Jaynetts' "Sally Go Round the Roses," the Penguins' "Earth Angel") to semi-forgotten treasures like the Fendermen's "Mule Skinner Blues" and Toni Fisher's "The Big Hurt." *—Richie Unterberger*

☆ **Grandson of Frat Rock!, Vol. 3** / 1991 / Rhino ✦✦✦✦✦

★ **Hardcore Doo-Wop: In the Hallway-Under the Street Lamp** / 1993 / Specialty ✦✦✦✦✦
This compact disc collects 25 doo wop collector's classics from a variety of small West Coast R&B labels who dabbled in the genre. The California version of the streetcorner vocal group phenomena had stronger leanings toward bluesier harmonies and vocal performances bordering on madness. As best exemplified here by groups like Arthur Lee Maye & The Crowns and Byron "Slick" Gipson & the Sliders, the West Coast doo wop movement definitely had a sound all its own. *—Cub Koda*

Hey Drag City / Oct. 24, 1994 / Drag City ✦✦✦✦✦

Hi Times: Hi Records R&B Years / Feb. 21, 1995 / Capitol ✦✦✦✦✦

☆ **Hitsville USA: The Motown Singles Collection 1959-1971** / 1992 / Motown ✦✦✦✦✦

☆ **Just Can't Get Enough: New Wave Hits of the 80s, Vols. 1-5** / 1994 / Rhino ✦✦✦✦✦
Rhino's first five volumes of its 15-disc new wave retrospective are filled with classic tracks from the early '80s, from "Love Will Tear Us Apart" to "867-5309/Jenny." Each disc is loosely chronological and contains a number of obscurities and novelties along with the hits. For sound and content, this is likely to be the best series of new wave hits ever to be released. Start with the fifth volume—which contains "I Want Candy," "Someday, Someway," "The Kids in America," "Love Plus One," "Valley Girl," and other gems—then work your way through the rest of the discs. *—Stephen Thomas Erlewine*

Kill Rock Stars / 1991 / Kill Rock Stars ✦✦✦✦✦

Land of 1000 Dances / Feb. 26, 1999 / Ace ✦✦✦✦✦

☆ **Loud, Fast & Out of Control: The Wild Sounds of the '50s** / May 18, 1999 / Rhino ✦✦✦✦✦
If anyone wanted to prove that original '50s rock & roll was a lot more than just white guys trying to sound black, this deluxe box set would be the perfect flag-waver. Loaded up heavy from top to bottom with the kind of discs that rockabilly collectors consider their personal epiphany, along with obvious hits from Elvis Presley, Jerry Lee Lewis, Little Richard, Bo Diddley and others, this collection burrows right into the heart of what made the first edition of rock & roll so upsetting to staid adults back in the '50s. This is loud, noisy, *dangerous* music, as far away from malt-shop memories and wedding-reception drivel as you could possibly ask for. Encompassing rockabilly, jump R&B, crazed instrumentals, hits and classics that have earned their rep over the intervening decades, this should be a major cornerstone of anyone building a sensible rock & roll collection. *—Cub Koda*

☆ **Millennium Party: Funk** / Jul. 14, 1998 / Rhino ✦✦✦✦✦

Millennium: 80's New Wave Party / Oct. 5, 1999 / Rhino ✦✦✦✦✦

The Minit/Instant Story / Jan. 1, 1996 / Charly ✦✦✦✦✦
This 52-song collection doesn't entirely overlap EMI's *Minit Records Story* box set, which has a few rarities and obscure tracks, but it's a good overview of some of the best and most interesting of the label's output, and also the sheer diversity of the company's output, from the hard blues of Jessie Hill to the smooth, near-pop stylings of Allen & Allen. Joe Banashak, who founded Minit and Instant, was truly in love with the sounds he heard from the clubs in New Orleans, and he seldom seems to have heard any artists expressing confidence and inspiration who he didn't want to release. Thus, hard-rocking numbers like Lee Dorsey's "Lottie Mo" share space on this set with harmony numbers like "The Owl Sees You" by the Showmen (aka the Humdingers) and the sultry, seductive soul of Irma Thomas ("It's Too Soon to Know," "Ruler of My Heart," "It's Raining"). British Invasion fans will find a lot to keep them busy as well, given the originals by several Brit-rock favorites, including "Fortune Teller," "Something You Got," and "I Like It Like That" represented here. Throughout both of these discs, Allen Toussaint is represented as producer, arranger, and frequently songwriter as well; if anyone needed convincing that Banashak had a resident genius under contract, the first few tracks do the job. The second disc moves up through later, post-Toussaint Instant and Seven B label tracks that feature Eddie Lang, Skip Easterling, and Eddie Bo, as well as Bo's production work from the mid- and late '60s. The sound is excellent as well, and one only wishes that a bit more material from Minit's early history was present, and that a few more details were available on some of the lesser-known artists. *—Bruce Eder*

Northern Soul Classics / 2000 / Goldmine/Soul Supply ✦✦✦✦✦

The Northern Soul of Chicago, Vol. 1 / 2000 / Goldmine/Soul Supply ✦✦✦✦

Northern Soul of L.A., Vol. 1 / 2000 / Goldmine/Soul Supply ✦✦✦

Northern Soul Spectrum / Apr. 22, 1997 / Kent ✦✦✦✦

☆ **Nuggets: A Classic Collection From the Psychedelic Sixties** / 1986 / Rhino ✦✦✦✦✦
In its time, in the mid-'80s, Rhino Records' first volume of its *Nuggets* series was one of the basic starting points for a collection of mid-'60s psychedelic and garage punk music, and it still holds up for content. Almost everything here is a musical touchstone of the genres, either a major chart hit or an underground classic, and the little that doesn't really fit entirely into those categories, such as &"Friday on My Mind" by the Easybeats and "Laugh Laugh" and "Just a Little" by the Beau Brummels, is still catchy enough to fit in seamlessly with the rest. The main drawback for new purchasers may be the sound—Rhino's mastering standards were always higher than those of virtually every other company, which means that their '80s CDs have held their value a very long time, but there are better things being done with the sound on most of this material in the early 21st century. As of 1998, thanks to a new licensing agreement, Rhino was able to issue a much-expanded version of that double album as a four-CD box and put out *Nuggets from Nuggets*, a 20-song highlights CD that includes five of the cuts from this CD and 15 choice additions; of the missing tracks, the Chocolate Watch Band's "Let's Talk About Girls" is the only hugely glaring omission, the others being a matter of subjective choice, some of which is dictated by their availability elsewhere and changing perceptions of the music. This remains a superb starting point, however, and even fits in well alongside *Nuggets from Nuggets*. *—Bruce Eder*

☆ **Nuggets: Original Artyfacts from the First Psychedelic Era 1965-1968** / Sep. 15, 1998 / Rhino ✦✦✦✦✦
Compiled by rock critic and future Patti Smith Group guitarist Lenny Kaye, 1972's *Nuggets* was the anthology responsible for reviving interest in mid-'60s American garage rock. After the proliferation of specialized volumes with the Nuggets title by reissue label Rhino, this four-CD box set is intended as the ideal summation/expansion of the Nuggets concept. The first CD reproduces, track-by-track, the original 27-song *Nuggets*, while the other three CDs add what may be considered 91 bonus tracks, from the biggest-selling garage hits ("Louie Louie," "Wooly Bully") to some cuts that only devout '60s specialists will know. All important permutations of the mid-'60s garage style are present: primitive fuzz, folk-rock, horn rock, psychedelic dementia, protest rock, etc. Major heroes the Music Machine, the Seeds, the Shadows of Knight, the Electric Prunes, the Standells, the Sonics, the Chocolate Watch Band, and many others are all represented, often by more than one song. If it's possible to give a five-star rating with reservations, it's tempting to do so here. No one could have possibly satisfied all rabid garage collectors with a mere 118 songs, but that's not really the point here; the object was to provide a wide-ranging box set of '60s garage rock that would entertain, represent the considerable span of garage styles, and be massive—yet affordable—for the committed rock fan who nonetheless doesn't want everything. Rhino has succeeded, while also presenting the songs in the best possible quality (in mono), whether from the master tapes or best existing copies. With a 100-page booklet of new liner notes (Kaye's original annotation is also included), it is the best investment possible for those who thirst for more '60s garage rock than is available on the best single-volume compilations, with a track selection geared toward cream-of-the-crop quality and variety rather than narrow collector prejudices. *—Richie Unterberger*

Oh Yeah! The Best of Dunwich Records / 1992 / Sundazed ✦✦✦✦✦

Oh, Merge: Merge Records 10 Year Anniversary Compilation / Jul. 6, 1999 / Merge ✦✦✦✦

☆ **The OKeh Rhythm & Blues Story 1949-1957** / 1995 / Epic/Okeh/Legacy ✦✦✦✦✦
The three-CD set is a real eye opener. As the most straight-laced and self-consciously upscale of the major labels, Columbia Records isn't usually thought of as having had much to contribute to the history and development of rhythm & blues. That impression was never more than partly true, however, as every track on this three-disc set reminds us. The postwar OKeh label was Columbia's attempt to grab a piece of a market that, as early as 1948, it knew it was losing, and the music is as solid a representation of R&B of the era as that of any major label of the period. It's true that Okeh had only sporadic success and developed a relative handful of R&B stars: Chuck Willis, Big Maybelle, the Treniers, and Screamin' Jay Hawkins. A great many other notable artists passed through, however, either after their biggest successes or in the years prior to their emergence, including LaVern Baker (known at the time as Bea Baker) singing with Maurice King & His Wolverines, Marvin Gaye as a member of the Marquees (working with Bo Diddley), Hadda Brooks, Annie Laurie, and the Ravens. They're all represented here, and there's not a second-rate song anywhere on this set, which also features some of the cleanest, richest remastering heard on a Columbia CD set of truly vintage material up to that time. The booklet is also pretty impressive in its details, listing individual band members and filled with concise encapsulated biographies (where known) of the artists. *—Bruce Eder*

☆ **On Broadway: Hit Songs and Rarities from the Brill Building Era** / Mar. 2, 1999 / West Side ✦✦✦✦✦
There's like two weeks of dazzling analytical listening to be found on this double-CD set, unless you want to try it for the pure pleasure, which is practically infinite. *On Broadway* is a magnificent idea for a multi-artist compilation, and one that no U.S. label could do, because the licensing fees would be too high. The primary focus is the work of the Brill Building-based songwriting teams of Gerry Goffin and Carole King, Barry Mann and Cynthia Weil, and Jeff Barry and Ellie Greenwich, which hardly makes it restrictive. There are at least a dozen revelations for the casual listener among the 25 songs on each CD in this set. One gets to hear alternate (but equally valid) performances, sometimes predating the hits by months, of several dozen songs that became pop standards in other hands. The talent represented here includes period pop music icons (Little Eva) and up-and-coming talent (pre-Phil Spector Ronettes), pop culture footnotes (Vince Edwards, Paul Petersen, Shelley Fabares), sibling acts (Idalia Boyd, sister of Little Eva), forgotten performers (the James Boys, Myrna March),

one future jazz success (Birdie Green), and a future pop/rock superstar (Carole King). There aren't any new horizons in pop music to be discovered here, just some beautiful and mostly forgotten moments, and established hits as well. The Raindrops are here, of course, as are Carole King and a handful of Barry Mann solo numbers, just to give the performing side of their early careers a nod. The notes are thorough and then some, although they're weighted toward the songwriters rather than the performers, especially where the genuinely obscure acts are concerned. And the sound is good to excellent, though a couple of the Freddie Scott numbers (but not "On Broadway") seem slightly compressed. *—Bruce Eder*

Pebbles, Vols. 1-28 / AIP ✦✦✦✦✦
Though 1972's Nuggets compilation reawakened listeners to the sounds of mid-'60s garage rock, it only focused on the tip of the iceberg. Behind those forgotten hits and semi-hits lurked hundreds, if not thousands, of regional hits and flops from the same era, most even rawer and cruder. In the late '70s, the Pebbles compilations came along to fill in the gap and then some. Each volume gathered 15 to 20 obscure 45s, originally issued on tiny labels and remastered right from the excruciatingly rare original vinyl. The featured acts were unknown to anyone but collectors and those who happened to have lived in the areas where the bands played. More than any other factor, these compilations were responsible for the resurgence of interest in garage rock, which remains high among collectors to this day. Though the lyrics are at times downright juvenile and sexist, the main attraction is the sound and stance, which anticipates the outrage of punk rock, but tempers it with tough British Invasion-inspired melodies, harmonies, and hooks, as well as fuzz-toned guitars, Farfisa organs, and wildly manic songwriting and performances. There are a lot of great unknown songs on Pebbles, but there are also a fair number of generic tunes that have little to recommend them beyond an excess of energy, which can make listening to an entire volume at once as much a challenge as a joy. Listeners approaching this series for the first time should search for the first ten volumes; after this initial burst, the well ran increasingly dry, and the later volumes can be a chore. Most of the individual installments don't have themes, but those looking for a concentration of certain items should check out the third (psychedelia) and sixth (British R&B/mod) volumes. Of special interest among the later volumes are installments devoted to wide-ranging obscurities from the European continent. *—Richie Unterberger*

Philly Sound: Kenny Gamble, Leon Huff and the Story of Brotherly Love (1966-1976) / Sep. 30, 1997 / Epic/Legacy ✦✦✦✦✦

Pimps, Players & Private Eyes / Jan. 14, 1992 / Warner Brothers ✦✦✦✦✦

Poptopia! 70's Power Pop Classics / May 27, 1997 / Rhino ✦✦✦✦✦
Named after an annual power-pop festival in the Los Angeles, Rhino's three-disc Poptopia! Power Pop Classics series attempts to chronicle power-pop's evolution from its '70s roots to its '90s incarnation as a cult genre. Power-pop, in many ways, is the ultimate cult music: it has a specific sound, a strict songwriting formula and a small number of classic artists. In other words, it's a genre that lends itself easily to an anthology—it's possible to feature both the classics and a number of obscure gems on one compact disc. The first volume of *Poptopia* proves this point, as it skillfully balances the familiar with the relatively unknown. Over the course of 18 tracks, the album features all of the key power-pop bands, from the Raspberries ("Go All the Way") and Big Star ("September Gurls") to Cheap Trick ("Come On, Come On") and 20/20 ("Yellow Pills"). Nearly every artist is represented by one of their big songs, with the notable exception of Badfinger, whose Capitol material wasn't available due to licensing restrictions. As a result, *Poptopia! Power Pop Classics of the '70s* is a basic primer on the genre, offering every major artist and many of the great songs that provided power-pop with its foundation, including Nick Lowe ("Cruel to Be Kind"), the Dwight Twilley Band ("I'm on Fire"), Flamin' Groovies ("Shake Some Action"), Todd Rundgren ("Couldn't I Just Tell You"), the Knack ("Good Girls Don't"), Bram Tchaikovsky ("Girl of My Dreams"), the Shoes ("Too Late"), Pezband ("Baby It's Cold Outside"), the Rubinoos ("I Wanna Be Your Boyfriend") and the Records ("Starry Eyes"). Any serious power pop fan, and many casual listeners as well, will have everything here, but this is where the curious should start. *—Stephen Thomas Erlewine*

Poptopia! Power Pop Classics of the '80s / May 27, 1997 / Rhino ✦✦✦✦
Poptopia! Power Pop Classics of the '70s presented the roots of power-pop, and its successor, *Power Pop Classics of the '80s,* finds the genre slowly mutating into a classicist style. In the '80s, power-pop didn't have as dedicated an audience as it did in the previous decade (or that it would have in the '90s), and the place to hear catchy guitar-pop was in the ringing jangle-pop of the American underground. As a result, about half of the bands on this collection—including Let's Active, the Bangles, the DB's, Tommy Keene, the Smithereens, Hoodoo Gurus and the La's—had more in common with jangle-pop than power-pop, but they shared the same love of the three-minute single and the pure, catchy melody. Also, their presence makes *Power Pop Classics of the '80s* a bit more diverse than its predecessor, since there's a greater variety of pop styles, from the punchy rock of the Romantics' "What I Like About You" and the British Invasion stylings of the SpongeTones ("She Goes Out With Everybody") to the AOR of Utopia ("Crybaby") and the new wave of Holly & the Italians ("Tell That Girl to Shut Up") and the Plimsouls ("A Million Miles Away"). On the whole, the collection doesn't deliver as many thrills as Power Pop Classics of the '70s, but that's only by a slight margin, since among these 18 tracks are some of the finest pop singles of the '80s. *—Stephen Thomas Erlewine*

Poptopia! Power Pop Classics of the '90s / May 27, 1997 / Rhino ✦✦✦
The compilers of Poptopia! were on solid ground when they assembled the '70s and '80s editions of their series, since there was already an established canon of power pop greats for those decades. However, they ran into problems with Power Pop Classics of the '90s; first, the album was released in 1997, three years before the decade was finished. It's quite likely that all the significant power pop bands of the '90s had already appeared, but the major hurdle the compilers faced was the possibility that some artists might not be available for licensing. That certainly is the case with *Power Pop Classics of the '90s;* there's even a disclaimer in the liner notes that apologizes for the absence of Material Issue, the Gin Blossoms, and Teenage Fanclub. It's hard to believe that Material Issue and Teenage Fanclub were unavailable, considering that Matthew Sweet, the Lemonheads, and the Posies—three acts that sold more than those bands—are present, but their absence accentuates how uneven this collection actually is. There are some wonderful songs on *Power Pop Classics of the '90s,* but the remainder of the record proves that '90s power pop was a classicist genre, caring more about form than content. Most of these songs sound good but just aren't that memorable, an especially frustrating situation in the case of Velocity Girl, the Rembrandts, and the Posies, bands that all have better songs in their catalogs. And that draws attention to the fact that many of the liveliest and best pop bands of the '90s—from Sloan and Sugar to Cast and Fountains of Wayne—are not here. Consequently, Power Pop Classics of the '90s can only be seen as an admirable effort, not a definitive collection. *—Stephen Thomas Erlewine*

Poptronica: Dance / Aug. 10, 1999 / Buddha ✦✦✦✦

Poptronica: Romance / Aug. 10, 1999 / Buddha ✦✦✦✦

Poptronica: Sci-Fi / Aug. 10, 1999 / Buddha ✦✦✦✦

Post Punk Chronicles: Going Underground / Jan. 12, 1999 / Rhino ✦✦✦✦✦
For the most part, *Going Underground* is a coronation of the guitar in the post-punk ethic. With a couple exceptions—like Throbbing Gristle—this volume in the *Postpunk Chronicles* series demonstrates the fusion of distortion and power with rediscovered pop melody. A dollop or two of romantic angst doesn't hurt either. A handful of punk and alternative's most important all-time artists show up here, such as the Smiths, Sonic Youth, Gang of Four, Pere Ubu and the Jam; much of the second tier is represented as well. Highlights are all over the map: the Smiths' still-rousing "What Difference Does It Make?", troubadour Billy Bragg's wistful "A New England," and two of nihilism's all-time greatest hits, the Soft Boys' "I Wanna Destroy You" and Pere Ubu's "Final Solution." The "title track" from the Jam closes the set as both an epitaph and a hint of where this music was largely headed: to the American underground, until bands like Nirvana proclaimed its importance to a wider audience. *—Paul Pearson*

Post Punk Chronicles: Left of the Dial / Jan. 12, 1999 / Rhino ✦✦✦✦✦
One of three initial releases in Rhino's survey of the pop music landscape after it had been redefined by the punk aesthetic. Series producer Jim Neill's goal with each 16-song volume in the series was to simulate "how a typical college radio show might have played out" circa 1979 to 1984.

Left of the Dial concentrates on the architects of dark avant-rock and moody, synthesized new wave. The lineup on this installment omits some key tracks because of licensing snags acknowledged in the liner notes, but the end result is no less enchanting. Key tracks are the original single version of R.E.M.'s "Radio Free Europe," Wire's "Outdoor Miner," and the Church's cover of Paul Simon's "I Am a Rock," an ideally revised anthem for the disenfranchised underground of the '80s. These songs quietly linger long after they've ended. *—Paul Pearson*

Post Punk Chronicles: Scared to Dance / Jan. 12, 1999 / Rhino ✦✦✦✦✦
Of the three initial entries in Rhino's Postpunk Chronicles, this volume might sound the most dated, but in its own way it's the most enjoyable. *Scared to Dance* skews toward faster-tempo landmarks of the early-'80s college underground, particularly the prototypes of synth-pop and dance music. You can hear bands trying to figure out where keyboards and dance might fit in the punk aesthetic, especially in Heaven 17's wry "(We Don't Need This) Fascist Groove Thang" and Pigbag's jungle instrumental "Papa's Got a Brand New Pigbag." These songs were largely created just before MIDI and sampling improved synthesizers' flexibility, and their joyful innocence is retroactively stunning. Other highlights include Magazine's amazing "The Light Pours Out of Me," Iggy Pop's jagged "New Values," and cuts from Orchestral Manoeuvres in the Dark ("Enola Gay") and Simple Minds ("Life in a Day") before they broke it big thanks to contributions to John Hughes movies. *—Paul Pearson*

Psychedelia at Abbey Road: 1965-1969 / Aug. 25, 1998 / EMI ✦✦✦✦
A 22-track single CD seems a bit paltry given the scope of the title—except, of course, that the 1969 cutoff date here puts the material from Harvest (a label started late that year and containing the lion's share of EMI psychedelia) out of reach. Of course, there are no Beatles tracks and, likewise, no Pink Floyd here, but we do get cuts by the Hollies, Donovan, Tomorrow, the Fingers, Focus 3, the Tales of Justine, Simon Dupree & the Big Sound, the Pretty Things, the Aquarian Age, the Koobas, the Nocturnes, Locomotive, the Gods, Mandrake Paddle Steamer, Mark Wirtz, and Syd Barrett. Most of this stuff, apart from "Sunshine Superman," "My White Bicycle," and "King Midas in Reverse," isn't exactly routine material, and two tracks—"Delighted to See You" by the N'Betweens and "Why" by Tomorrow—are previously unissued. The latter, a cover of the Byrds' song, features a tour de force guitar break by future Yes member Steve Howe. Just as revelatory is "Monday Morning," a 1967 single by the largely forgotten the Tales of Justine, featuring David Daltrey, with arrangement and production by Tim Rice and Andrew Lloyd Webber, respectively. Everything on the album has been remastered in 24-bit digital sound, and the long version of Donovan's "Sunshine Superman" has been remixed, bringing out extraordinary detail in the percussion section, from the choppy rhythm guitars and harpsichord down to the exceptionally busy drumming. The annotation by Brian Hogg is detailed without going overboard on trivia, and the entire collection turns out to be great fun. *—Bruce Eder*

Radio Daze: Pop Hits of the 80's, Vols. 1-5 / 1995 / Rhino ✦✦✦✦✦

Rarest Rockabilly & Hillbilly Boogie: The Best of Ace Rockabilly / Ace ✦✦✦✦✦

Risque Rhythm: Nasty 50s R&B / 1991 / Rhino ✦✦✦✦✦

The Rock 'N' Roll Fever!: The Wildest from Specialty / 1994 / Specialty ✦✦✦

Rock Instrumental Classics, Vol. 3 / 1994 / Rhino ✦✦✦

Rock Instrumental Classics, Vol. 4 / 1994 / Rhino ✦✦✦

Rock Instrumental Classics, Vol. 5 / 1994 / Rhino ✦✦✦✦

Rock Instrumental Classics, Vol. 1 / 1994 / Rhino ✦✦✦✦

Rock Instrumental Classics, Vol. 2 / 1994 / Rhino ♦♦♦♦

Rockin' from Coast to Coast, Vol. 1 / 1996 / Ace ♦♦♦

Rockin' From Coast to Coast, Vol. 2 / May 11, 1999 / Ace ♦♦♦

The Roulette Story / Nov. 10, 1998 / West Side ♦♦♦♦♦
This three-CD, 84-track box set brings together the hits and rarities from Morris Levy's New York indie label that closed down in 1977, after being in business for a 20-year period spanning the history of rock & roll's ascendancy to the top of the charts. Starting off with two million sellers on its first two releases (Buddy Knox's "Party Doll" and Jimmy Bowen's "I'm Sticking With You"), Roulette also made inroads in the folk and pop fields with the success of Jimmie Rodgers and artists like Valerie Carr and Georgia Gibbs. The label also released some of the very best in rockabilly, doo wop, and rock & roll with Ronnie Hawkins' "Forty Days" and "Who Do You Love," Tiny Tim and the Hits' "Wedding Bells," and Jimmy Lloyd's "Rocket in My Pocket." But Roulette was much more than just another indie rock & roll label, as the second disc amply proves with stellar jazz offerings from Count Basie, Joe Williams, Sarah Vaughan, Sonny Stitt, Louis Armstrong, and Duke Ellington peppering the catalog. The third disc picks up the pop/rock story from the early '60s to the label's demise in the late '70s, with hitworthy selections from Lou Christie, the Hullabaloos, Tommy James, and Alive and Kicking. The label also knew a good novelty record when it heard one, as all three discs are peppered with items like the Playmates' "Beep Beep" and the Detergents' "Leader of the Laundromat." For true surrealism, one is directed to Jim Nabors doing a rock & roll version of "There's No Tomorrow," an early stab at what Elvis later turned into "It's Now or Never." Excellent notes, stellar sound; this is one great label overview that tells the story of rock & roll and its place in the pop music scheme of things in microcosm. *—Cub Koda*

A Shot of Rhythm & Blues: R&B Era, Vol. 1 / 1990 / Sequel ♦♦♦♦
There are some pretty valuable tracks here, all dating from between 1963 and 1965. The stars include Cyril Davies & His Rhythm and Blues All-Stars ("Country Line Special"), Tony Jackson & the Vibrations ("Fortune Teller"), the Undertakers ("If You Don't Come Back"), and the Kinks ("Milk Cow Blues"), but they're augmented by a brace of worthwhile songs by unknown acts, including the Riot Squad ("Jump"), Felders Orioles ("Turn on Your Lovelight"), Jimmy Powell & the Dimensions ("I'm Looking for a Woman"), and the Chosen Few ("Today Tonight and Tomorrow"). Along the way are glimpses of the early work of future members of Lindisfarne and the Blockheads (the Chosen Few) and the Rutles (Felders Orioles), among other bands from the '70s and '80s. The producers have become a bit too ambitious at 22 tracks, however; Wayne Gibson & the Dynamic Sounds' "Portland Town" is way too folky and Van Dyke & the Bambis' "All I Want Is You" is pretty forgettable. As a result, about half of this CD is priceless, a third is edifying, and about 20 percent fills space and takes your time. *—Bruce Eder*

Smooth Grooves: A Sensual Collection, Vols. 1-9 / 1995 / Rhino ♦♦♦♦♦

☆ **Son of Frat Rock** / 1991 / Rhino ♦♦♦♦♦

The Songs of Tommy Boyce & Bobby Hart / Oct. 24, 1995 / Varese Saraband ♦♦♦
Boyce & Hart, best known as frequent songwriters for the Monkees, were among the more successful West Coast pop/rock composers of the late '60s, also landing some material with other artists and making some records of their own, including the hit "I Wonder What She's Doing Tonight." Only six of these 18 tracks were recorded by the Boyce & Hart duo (another was recorded by Dolenz, Jones, Boyce & Hart). But since Boyce & Hart's principal importance came from their songwriting rather than their performing, this compilation—which matches the most notable Boyce & Hart recordings with the best and most famous cuts by other artists covering Boyce-Hart compositions—is the best representative sampling of their most important music. Other than "I Wonder What She's Doing Tonite," Boyce & Hart's own tracks pale next to the cover versions on this disc, which include the Monkees' "Last Train to Clarksville" and "Valleri"; "(I'm Not Your) Stepping Stone" in its pre-Monkees version by Paul Revere & the Raiders; and relatively rare, gritty versions of "Words" (from 1966, by the Boston Tea Party) and "Tomorrow's Gonna Be Another Day" (from 1965, by the Astronauts), both of which would later be done by the Monkees as well. There are also a bunch of hits that Boyce & Hart did not write on their own, or to which only Boyce or only Hart contributed, like Freddie Cannon's "Action," Curtis Lee's "Pretty Little Angel Eyes," Jay & the Americans' "Come a Little Bit Closer," and Little Anthony & the Imperials' "Hurt So Bad." Overall, it's a decent compilation of the best work of a composing team with a knack for the peppy and catchy melodies typical of the form of LA '60s rock known as sunshine pop, although their songs were usually on the lightweight side. *—Richie Unterberger*

☆ **Soul Hits of the 70s: Didn't It Blow Your Mind! Vol. 1-5** / 1995 / Rhino ♦♦♦♦♦
Soul music began to drift away from gritty, deep sounds in the late '60s, moving back toward smooth, immaculately produced uptown soul, but this time there was a difference. Taking their cue from the pop-oriented records of Motown, the purveyors of early-'70s soul threw everything in the mix. Not only were there impassioned vocals and sexy rhythms, but also pop productions, sound effects, psychedelic flourishes, elements of reggae, and Latin inflections. Soul had not been this ambitious in years and, as the first 15 volumes of Rhino's multi-disc series *Soul Hits of the '70s: Didn't It Blow Your Mind!* illustrate, it was frequently as good as anything released in the '70s. Due to contractual reasons, some big names, including Al Green, Stevie Wonder, and Marvin Gaye, aren't included on *Didn't It Blow Your Mind!*, but they aren't missed because the overall quality of the material is so shockingly strong. The Spinners establish themselves as the finest vocal group of the '70s, but the Delfonics, the Chi-Lites, the Chairmen of the Board, and many others give them a run for their money. And while Curtis Mayfield stands out from the competition, that doesn't diminish the worth of Eddie Holman, Freda Payne, or any of the other lesser-known artists. In fact, one of the main pleasures of this set is discovering so many one-hit wonders who released singles as good as the major artists. There are a few misses on the first 15 volumes but, by and large, each collection is terrific; in addition to being sold separately, the first five volumes were also packaged together in a slipcase, providing a good entryway to one of the finest various-artists collections ever assembled. *—Stephen Thomas Erlewine*

Soul Train: Hall of Fame, 20th Anniversary / 1974-1991 / Rhino ♦♦♦♦

The Specialty Story / 1994 / Specialty ♦♦♦♦♦

☆ **Stax: Top of the Stax, Vol. 1: Twenty Greatest Hits** / Stax ♦♦♦♦♦

☆ **Stax: Top of the Stax, Vol. 2: Twenty Greatest Hits** / Stax ♦♦♦♦♦

☆ **The Stiff Records Box Set** / 1992 / Rhino ♦♦♦♦♦
Stiff Records was a maverick among British independent record labels, partially responsible for starting the punk and New Wave revolution of the late '70s. Under the guidance of house producer Nick Lowe, Stiff turned out an enormous number of seminal punk and new wave singles in their first years, including classic tracks by The Damned, Elvis Costello, Graham Parker, the Adverts, Ian Dury, and Lowe himself. But what really gave the label its wild, original flavor were minor artists like Ian Dury, Wreckless Eric, Tenpole Tudor, the Yachts, Lene Lovich, Rachel Sweet, and Mickey Jupp, who turned out a series of raw pop gems that were everything good rock & roll singles should be—catchy, energetic, and memorable. Over 100 of Stiff's finest tracks are collected on this wonderful four-disc box set. While most of these songs weren't hits, they are classic rock & roll. The first three discs are excellent; the fourth disc contains some bright moments, but by that time, their artists were pretty much spent. However, the box remains one of the most compulsively listenable sets ever assembled, providing the definitive retrospective of arguably the most important and influential British record label of the late '70s. *—Stephen Thomas Erlewine*

Street Corner Serenade: The Greatest Doo Wop of the 1950's and 1960's / Jul. 20, 1999 / Rhino ♦♦♦♦

☆ **The Sun Records Collection** / 1994 / Rhino ♦♦♦♦♦
There have been a lot of Sun compilations over the years; this three-CD, 74-song compilation strikes the medium ground between abridged single-disc highlights and overkill ten-album box sets. What this means is that you get virtually all the key sides of this vastly influential blues, country, and rockabilly label, including the biggest Sun hits cut by Elvis, Carl Perkins, Jerry Lee Lewis, Johnny Cash, Charlie Rich, and Roy Orbison. There's also a lot of the pioneering electric blues cut by label head Sam Phillips before he made rockabilly Sun's focus, including sides by Howlin' Wolf, B.B. King, Rufus Thomas, Junior Parker, and James Cotton. Then there are the interesting small hits and flops by minor rockabilly figures like Warren Smith, Billy Lee Riley, Malcolm Yelvington, Onie Wheeler, and Carl Mann. There aren't any previously unreleased songs, so the Sun specialist most likely already has everything here; it's a better buy for the avid, knowledgeable fan who isn't a completist. *—Richie Unterberger*

☆ **The Sun Story** / 1994 / Rhino ♦♦♦♦♦

Sunshine Days, Vol. 1: 60's Pop Classics / Jul. 29, 1997 / Varese ♦♦♦♦

Sunshine Days, Vol. 2: 60's Pop Classics / Jul. 29, 1997 / Varese ♦♦♦♦

Sunshine Days, Vol. 3: 60's Pop Classics / Jul. 29, 1997 / Varese ♦♦♦♦

Sunshine Days, Vol. 4: 60's Pop Classics / Jul. 28, 1998 / Varese ♦♦♦♦

Sunshine Days, Vol. 5: 60's Pop Classics / Jul. 28, 1998 / Varese ♦♦♦♦

Super Hits of the '70s: Have a Nice Day / 1990 / Rhino ♦♦♦♦♦
Mainstream pop began catching up with the innovations of the late '60s sometime in the early '70s, incorporating watered-down versions of psychedelia, soul, prog rock, country-rock, and folk-rock. The result was well-produced and crafted schlock that gleefully corrupted countercultural values. Along with the schlock was pure trash ranging from bubblegum epics like "The Night Chicago Died" and "I Think I Love You" to soft rock ("Precious and Few"), Jesus rock ("One Toke Over the Line," "Spirit in the Sky"), hard rock ("Mississippi Queen"), and songs like "Gimme Dat Thing" that are simply uncategorizable. What they all had in common was their utter lack of seriousness and big, catchy hooks, which made them perfect singles for AM radio. Rhino's multi-volume various-artists set Have a Nice Day: Super Hits of the '70s (available as individual discs) is an exhaustive overview of such hit singles, containing 12 tracks on each disc. To be sure, there are some outright dogs on some of these discs, but it's remarkable how entertaining the entire series is. Initially, the label intended to only compile ten or 15 collections, taking the set into the mid-'70s, but *Have a Nice Day* proved so successful that it ran a full 25 volumes and extended right until 1979. Consequently, there's a lot of variety here, and every volume may not be entertaining to all listeners, especially since Rhino predictably leans a little too heavily on novelties. Still, it's a terrific series to pick and choose from, and each disc has several "classics" as well as several fun obscurities; it's impossible to imagine a better, more thorough chronicle of this era than *Have a Nice Day*. *—Stephen Thomas Erlewine*

Supernatural Fairy Tales: The Progressive Rock Era / Aug. 20, 1996 / Rhino ♦♦♦
Right down to the Roger Dean-designed sleeve, this five-CD box set overview of 1967-1976 progressive rock is as grandiose as the music itself, which is not necessarily an unconditional recommendation. But give the compilation points for diversity and thoughtful selection. The expected superstars (Yes, Genesis, ELP, Procol Harum) are usually represented by unexpected cuts that haven't been played to death on FM radio. A lot of ground is covered, from Krautrock (Can, Amon Düül II) and symphonic keyboards (Rare Bird, Argent, the Nice's "America") to the Canterbury sound (Caravan, Hatfield & the North) and pop hits with prog overtones (Traffic's "Paper Sun," Golden Earring's "Radar Love," Roxy Music's "Virginia Plain"). A lot of the Continental bands—like Le Orme, Lard Free, Wigwam, Ange, and Samla Mammas Manna—will be fuzzy or unfamiliar names even to progressive rock fans, making cult faves like Van Der Graaf Generator, Curved Air, the Pretty Things, Savage Rose, and Gong (all here as well) famous by comparison. Will the music cause those who dislike prog rock to re-evaluate their feelings— Absolutely not; the more accessible and poppy cuts are balanced by flashy instrumental workouts that—as even the musicians themselves may admit—do not exhibit a trace of humor. And no box that fails to include selections by Pink Floyd, King Crimson, Jethro Tull, Soft Machine, Kraftwerk, Mike Oldfield, early Brian Eno,

and Kevin Ayers (in at least some cases for licensing reasons) can claim to be comprehensive. It *is* an interesting, carefully assembled, and *extremely* wide-ranging and Catholic survey of the much-maligned genre. It's just a bit too much to take in all at once, and its very eclecticism ensures that many listeners (even dedicated prog fans) will feel the urge to skip around to concentrate on the subgenres they find most appealing. *—Richie Unterberger*

The Swingtime Records Story / May 17, 1994 / Capricorn ✦✦✦✦✦
A Black entrepreneur named Jack Lauderdale, for a period of a half dozen years, ran the Swingtime label—and its myriad subsidiaries—and his story is nicely told through the music on this wonderful two-disc box set. Lauderdale was no two bit hustler; he had both vision and ambition. He recorded everything from big band jump blues to piano trios to gospel groups. He released the first major recordings of guitarist Lowell Fulson and discovered a young Ray Charles when he was still in his Nat King Cole phase, although starting to find his own style. Nineteen of the 50 tracks included here are either by Fulson or Charles, the twin historical peaks of Lauderdale's empire. Add to that mix delightful work from Big Joe Turner, pianist Lloyd Glenn, a young Jimmy McCracklin, Percy Mayfield, Johnny Otis, and Charles Brown and you're beginning to get the big picture. In many ways, the tracks included here could easily represent the breadth of late '40s to early '50s in vogue sounds of African-American music. It's that far reaching in its scope. *—Cub Koda*

Teenage Crush, Vol. 3 / Dec. 27, 2000 / Ace ✦✦✦

☆ **There's a Riot Goin' On! The Rock 'N' Roll Classics of Lieber and Stoller** / 1991 / Rhino ✦✦✦✦✦
Sure, you can spend a lot of dough buying CD reissues by all the bands Leiber & Stoller wrote songs for. And while that would give you a great record collection (especially of Drifters and Coasters material), you might want to start with this indispensable 18-track collection. All the big hits are here, as are the songs that show off Leiber & Stoller's melodramatic way with a song ("I Who Have Nothing") and their deft comic touch ("Charlie Brown"). The essence of Leiber & Stoller's genius is here, and you'll likely recognize nearly all of these songs as soon as they start. Memory can be a wonderful thing. *—John Dougan*

This Is Easy / 1996 / Virgin ✦✦✦✦✦

☆ **The Two Tone Compilation: Checkered Past** / Nov. 16, 1993 / Chrysalis ✦✦✦✦✦

The Vee-Jay Story: Celebrating 40 Years of Classic Hits 1953-1993 / 1993 / Rhino Handmade ✦✦✦✦
Most conversations about Vee-Jay Records will usually be limited to a few salient facts: that they put out great, influential blues and R&B records during the '50s and '60s. That they became the most successful African-American-owned record company in the United States, breaking into the pop field with hits by Gene Chandler, Dee Clark, and the early sides by the Four Seasons. That they were the first American company to have the Beatles. And that, with all that success, they went bankrupt by 1966. But the Vee-Jay Records story is, for all its twists and turns, a true American success story that went sour. Admittedly, this three-disc retrospective *does* leave out some important chunks of the company's history due to licensing restrictions; the Four Seasons' masters aren't aboard, as their original appearance on the label was a lease deal. What *is* here are all the important sides, 75 of them, that moved Vee-Jay from a Gary, Indiana storefront to a major corporation. Much of Vee-Jay's reputation rests as much on the records that weren't hits and many of them are here. Disc one takes us back to the beginning of the label, with the label's first two artists, the Spaniels and bluesman Jimmy Reed. Disc two starts in blues and soul land, and brings aboard Dee Clark—the label's first African-American artist to cross over consistently into the pop field—and Jerry Butler, Curtis Mayfield and the Impressions. The third disc runs the hits and classics from 1961 to the label's impending demise in 1965, including quite a few pop-chart successes and even some great jazz sides. Producer/compiler/annotator Billy Vera deserves special mention for a job well done, given the size constraints and licensing restrictions. An important chunk of American musical history served up classy. *—Cub Koda*

The West Coast East Side Sound, Vol. 1 / Jul. 13, 1999 / Varese ✦✦✦
This 16-song collection may be a little too diverse for its own good. Overall, it's a nicely assembled opening volume of a four CD series devoted to the music of Faro, Rampart, and other labels owned and operated by Eddie Davis in Los Angeles from the '50s through the mid-'70s. It opens with the biggest single that Faro ever issued, "Land of 1,000 Dances" by Cannibal & the Headhunters. The rest of the CD jumps around throughout the history of Davis' various labels, back a year earlier for the Romancers' "Don't Let Her Go," and then on to "Darling (Please Bring Your Love)," a doo wop throwback from 1961, and so it goes. One wants to say that the emphasis is on early-'60s dance and novelty tunes ("Olive Oyl" by the Mixtures being the only annoying example of the latter), but then there's the Village Callers' version of "Evil Ways" from 1969, which nearly hit in place of the Santana version. The CD then jumps back to Ron Holden's early-'60s soul showcase "Girl I Love You"; further along is the Motown-flavored "Crazy Little Things" by the Soul-jers. There's very little sense to much of the order, although it plays great. The producers' apologies for some supposedly substandard sources seems uncalled for, since the sound is good to excellent throughout. The majority of the material on this CD will be unfamiliar to all but the most serious West Coast music buffs. One just wishes that it could've been assembled in a more coherent manner, so that the discoveries could be more orderly. *—Bruce Eder*

The West Coast East Side Sound, Vol. 2 / Jul. 13, 1999 / Varese ✦✦✦
If anything, this CD is an improvement over the initial volume in the series, although it shares similar flaws. The emphasis here is almost completely on dance numbers, with no novelty tracks intruding, and it's all to the credit of bands like the Blendells ("La La La La La"), the Romancers ("Take My Heart"), the Premiers ("Get Your Baby"), and the Mixtures ("Rainbow Stomp") that their stuff holds up magnificently today. What's more, the mastering is so good that one really gets to appreciate the playing as well as the songs. And even the one odd track, "Hector" by the Village Callers, fits in perfectly on a stylistic level with everything else, although it's about four years newer than most everything else here. Being slow romantic numbers in these surroundings, the ballads "Karen" by Little Ray & the Mixtures, "My Heart Cries" by the Romancers, and "Girl of My Dreams" by the Majestics have the hardest time fitting in, and 1962's "Destiny" by Larry Tamblyn has him sounding a little too much like Frankie Avalon, but these songs only change the mood without breaking it. The notes are a little fragmentary and, as with this entire series, one must read the insert booklets of all four volumes to get a decent picture of Eddie Davis and his record labels. *—Bruce Eder*

The West Coast East Side Sound, Vol. 3 / Jul. 13, 1999 / Varese ✦✦✦✦
This volume in the series is more cohesive than most, opening with the Premiers' 1964 hit "Farmer John" and generally confining itself to eminently danceable rockers from that same period by the likes of the Atlantics, Larry Tamblyn & the Standells ("The Girl in My Heart"), the Jaguars, the Romancers, the Soul-jers ("Gonna Be a Big Man"), and Sammy Lee & the Summits. As with the other three parts of this series, there's not a weak song here, whether it's Cannibal & the Headhunters (backed by the King Curtis band) doing "Follow the Music", the edgier, less lyrical, but more rousing "Sloop Dance" by the Atlantics, or the soul rave-up "That's Why I Love You" by the Romancers. Maybe the most interesting tracks here are two covers: the instrumental "Chinese Checkers," a piano-dominated version of the Booker T. and the MG's track cut by the Mixtures, and the extroverted rendition of "Love Is Strange" by the Salas Brothers and the Jaguars. And, oddly enough, the Standells, who were more influenced by doo wop in the early '60s, are outclassed in the garage band department by the Romancers' "She Took My Oldsmobile." The sound is excellent throughout. *—Bruce Eder*

The West Coast East Side Sound, Vol. 4 / Jul. 13, 1999 / Varese ✦✦✦
This last volume in the four-CD series is confusing in its content and programming. Opening with a pair of very ethnic sounding numbers, El Chicano's "Viva Tirado" and the Salas Brothers' "Leaving You" (which owes a bit to "Blue Moon"), it has a split personality from the start. The Majestics' "Everything Is Gonna Be Alright" is also a loud, upbeat dance number, but then comes the Romancers' smoothly romantic "She Gives Me Love." And these numbers bounce back and forth across a half-decade or more in terms of recording dates—and are then closely followed by the Premiers' fuzz-laden "Get on This Plane," which deserved a place on the Nuggets box. Somewhere after that comes the smooth soul sound of the East Side Kids' "Listen to the Wise Man" and the Santana-like "Con Safos" by Tocayo. It makes for a very confusing if rewarding 16 songs, linked in the most general terms, some of them very enlightening and all of it good listening. *—Bruce Eder*

The Westbound Sound of Detroit: Sensational Motor City Groups 1969-1975 / 1995 / Westbound ✦✦✦✦

What More Can A Woman Do— Brunswick & Chi-Sound Sisters of Soul / Oct. 26, 1999 / West Side ✦✦✦✦

What's Up Matador / Jul. 1997 / Matador ✦✦✦✦

When a Man Cries / Nov. 9, 1999 / Kent ✦✦✦

Where the Girls Are / 1997 / Ace ✦✦

Where the Girls Are, Vol. 2 / Jul. 27, 1999 / Ace ✦✦✦✦

Where the Girls Are, Vol. 3 / Jul. 11, 2000 / Ace ✦✦✦

Whistle Bait: 25 Rockabilly Rave-Ups / 2000 / Columbia/Legacy ✦✦✦✦
Culled from the CBS vaults, *Whistle Bait* is a very good anthology of 25 rockabilly numbers—or, if not quite rockabilly, tracks by country artists veering close to rockabilly—that for the most part will be unfamiliar to all but the most dedicated rockabilly collectors. Sure, there are some stars and cult faves here, like the Collins Kids, Link Wray, the post-Sun Carl Perkins, the post-Sun Johnny Cash, and Ronnie Self, whose "Bop-A-Lena" (included here) was one of the most certifiably insane rockers ever put out by a major label. You also get a generous helping of country artists trying to board the rockabilly wagon, and actually, they usually acquit themselves quite well. Don't believe it— Listen to Lefty Frizzell's "You're Humbuggin' Me," Rose Maddox's "Wild Wild Young Men," and Little Jimmy Dickens' "I Got a Hole in My Pocket" for evidence. Then there are the cats you've never heard of that managed to put out something quite hep, like Jaycee Hill on his 1956 single "Romp Stompin' Boogie." Johnny Horton draws from the best of both honky tonk and rock & roll on his two numbers, which are a far cry from the corny Americana that would land him big pop hits at the end of the '50s. Although there's undeniable aesthetic purity in collecting anthologies of crude rockabilly by no-hopers on some tiny label operating out of a small Texas oil town, the truth is that this big company vault-clearing exercise is way better than the average such rockabilly collection. It may not be too popular to say so, but one of the reasons is that major label production values usually delivered far better-sounding, tighter performances and secured better material. Put this on your shopping list if you want quality rare rockabilly. *—Richie Unterberger*

Wild Surf! / 1996 / Del-Fi ✦✦✦

Wired Magazine Presents: Music Futurists / Feb. 16, 1999 / Rhino ✦✦✦✦
Covering 38 years, *Music Futurists* is a compilation of tracks from pop artists "on the cutting edge of technology in music," according to the liner notes. That premise would probably make a great multi-disc box set. As a single-disc, 15-track release, though, *Music Futurists* runs into conceptual trouble despite having more than enough to recommend it. Arranged chronologically, these 15 songs move from space age bachelor Esquivel to avant-garde trumpeter Ben Neill. The commonalities linking the selections are deliberately obscure, and that's fine. Some of the inclusions, however, have to be questioned. No doubt Devo belongs here, for example, but why the relatively uneventful "Beautiful World" instead of one of the songs from *Q: Are We Not Men?* Godley & Creme's "Cry" is a sublime pop moment, but how much more innovative was it from other select Top 40 songs that came before? Most mysterious is the inclusion of Beck's "Total Soul Future (Eat It)." With the already rich backlog of work Beck had by this album's 1999 release, the appearance of this very short song feels arbitrary, as if the com-

pilers needed to attach a bigger, contemporary name to the project. Ignore the concept, though, and this music takes subtle and entrancing effect. Better-known innovators like Todd Rundgren and Brian Eno refine their reputations by being heard side by side with less heralded heroes like composer Steve Reich and the painfully underappreciated German experimentalists Can. Laurie Anderson's "O Superman" is a turning point that's good to hear wherever it shows up. *Wired* magazine wanted to make both a historical artifact and a great mix tape with this album. They've at least made the latter, but it's begging for a lot of sequels. —*Paul Pearson*

Woodstock: Three Days of Peace & Music [25th Anniversary] / 1995 / Atlantic ✦✦✦✦
Youth Gone Wild: Heavy Metal Hits of the '80s, Vol. 1 / Mar. 26, 1996 / Rhino ✦✦✦✦✦
Youth Gone Wild: Heavy Metal Hits of the '80s, Vol. 2 / Mar. 26, 1996 / Rhino ✦✦✦✦✦
Youth Gone Wild: Heavy Metal Hits of the '80s, Vol. 3 / Mar. 26, 1996 / Rhino ✦✦✦✦✦
Youth Gone Wild: Heavy Metal Hits of the '80s, Vol. 4 / Jun. 16, 1998 / Rhino ✦✦✦

RAP

Rap has been called the future of popular music for so long that it's a little odd to realize that it's been around long enough to have a rich, diverse history. Hip-hop is its own culture, with its own codes, slang, and meaning. That culture springs forth on record, since music has always been one of its driving forces.

If the history of hip-hop is written on records alone, its story is vivid and clear. It existed prior to the Sugarhill Gang's seminal "Rapper's Delight," played at clubs and block parties in New York, but that record brought hip-hop crashing into the public consciousness. Many dismissed it as a fad at the time, and it did take a while before rap unequivocally conquered the mainstream. Still, the early '80s—to forever be known as the old school—are where the genre coalesced, as rappers concentrated on free-flowing rhymes and rhythms. At times, hip-hop traveled hand in hand with such underground dance trends as electro, but more often it followed its own course, thanks to such trailblazers as Kurtis Blow and, especially, Grandmaster Flash, who pushed lyrics into new, incisive social commentary.

Still, if there's a time where everything changed for hip-hop, it was the emergence of Run-D.M.C., a ferocious trio from Queens, NY. They were the first rap group to seem like a classic, rebellious rock & roll gang, not just through their attitude, but how they sampled rock records. They also made rock records in a classic sense—records that flowed from beginning to end, like a timeless rock album. These records were the first to cross over to a mainstream audience, but they first captured the attention of collegiate suburbanites who found this music every bit as visceral and exciting as anything released on SST. Then, Run-D.M.C. teamed with Aerosmith for a blistering cover of "Walk This Way," and the floodgates burst open. The single rocketed into the Top Ten, bringing the accompanying album *Raising Hell* along for the ride.

From that moment on, rap was firmly embedded into the mainstream and changes started happening immediately. The music entered what's commonly called its golden age, as innovations started flying fast and furiously. There was the hardcore hip-hop with a political bent, spearheaded by Boogie Down Productions and Public Enemy. There was the neo-psychedelic alternative rap of the Native Tongues troupe, led by De La Soul and the Jungle Brothers. Pop-rap never sounded quite so good as it did in the hands of Delicious Vinyl's key acts, Tone-Loc and Young MC. There was the sheer warped brilliance of Biz Markie, the ironic white-trash rebellion of the Beastie Boys.

And then there was gangsta rap, pumping out of the West Coast with an insidiously seductive swagger. At the time, NWA and gangsta fit easily into the kaleidoscope of hip-hop styles—even the notoriously politically correct KRS-One was tagged as gangsta with BDP's debut Criminal Minded—but few could have expected how thoroughly the entire hip-hop landscape would be dominated by gangsta throughout the '90s. There were exceptions to the rule, of course, but once Dr. Dre made gangsta (and ganja) golden with *The Chronic*, the reverberations were similar to Nirvana's *Nevermind*—most of modern music lived in its shadow, either striving to replicate its mass success, or deliberately shying away from it.

Throughout the '90s, much of hip-hop was dominated by artists grabbing for the golden ring, best personified by the defiant slickness of Puff Daddy. But an underground remained, intent on building on the innovations of old school and the golden era. The Wu-Tang clan became so big that it's not quite fair to tag them as underground (especially considering their talent for marketing), but their uncompromising, restless experimentalism certainly qualified them as a good indicator of what the underground had to offer in the '90s. These were hip-hoppers that relied on both lyrical skills and sound, emphasizing prowess on the mic or in the studio. Then, there were the turntablists, the electronica refugees that spun records and sampled brave new soundscapes. They may not have been popular, but they set the groundwork for the mass acceptance of Outkast at the end of the decade, the first hip-hop crew since Public Enemy to capture the public and critics alike.

Within this section, each of these developments can be traced, but just as much can be read between the lines as well. Rap may have a shorter history than soul, jazz, or rock, but it's still undeniably rich, as this section will undoubtedly illustrate. *—Stephen Thomas Erlewine*

Artist Reviews

Arrested Development

f. 1988, Atlanta, GA, **db.** 1996

Group / Southern Rap, Alternative Rap, Urban, Hip-Hop

One of the major success stories of 1992, Arrested Development was a progressive rap collective fusing soul, blues, hip-hop, and Sly and the Family Stone-influenced funk with political, socially conscious lyrics. The group was founded in the late '80s by rapper Speech and DJ Headliner, who decided to make the transition to a more positive, Afrocentric viewpoint after hearing Public Enemy. Arrested Development's debut album took its title from the amount of time it took the group to secure a record contract; *Three Years, Five Months and Two Days in the Life of*... produced the hit single "Tennessee," a strongly spiritual track that hit the Top Ten and sparked the album to sell over four million copies. Its two follow-ups, "People Everyday" (a rewrite of Sly's "Everyday People) and "Mr. Wendal" did likewise. Accolades poured in; Arrested Development won Grammys for Best Rap Album and Best New Artist, and were named *Rolling Stone's* Band of the Year. The group returned one year later with *Zingalamaduni*, which some reviews hailed as a major work, though overall response was more ambivalent. In 1996, contrary to Speech's earlier assertion that the group would be around for ten or twelve years, Arrested Development officially broke up. Speech went solo and recorded a debut album, which failed to make an impact. *—Steve Huey*

● **Three Years, Five Months & Two Days in the Life of . . .** / Mar. 24, 1992 / Chrysalis ✦✦✦✦✦

A crew that became one of 1992's sensations by infusing hip-hop with blues sensibility on their debut, *Three Years, Five Months & Two Days in the Life of*..., especially on the single "Tennessee." *—Ron Wynn*

Unplugged / Mar. 1993 / Chrysalis ✦✦

Zingalamaduni / Jun. 14, 1994 / Chrysalis ✦✦✦

Afrika Bambaataa (Kevin Donovan)

b. Apr. 10, 1960, New York City, NY [South Bronx]

Vocals, DJ, Producer / Old School Rap, Electro, Club/Dance, Urban, Hip-Hop

A seminal Bronx DJ during the '70s, Afrika Bambaataa ascended to godfather status with "Planet Rock," the 1982 hip-hop classic which blended the beats of hip-hop with techno-pop futurism inspired by German pioneers Kraftwerk. Even before he began recording in 1980, Bambaataa was hip-hop's foremost DJ, an organizer and promoter of the large block parties during the mid-to-late-'70s which presaged the rise of rap. After the success of "Planet Rock," he recorded electro-oriented rap only sparingly, concentrating instead on fusion—exemplified by his singles with ex-Sex Pistol John Lydon and fellow godfather James Brown. Bambaataa had moved to the background by the late '80s (as far as hip-hop was concerned), but the rise of his Zulu Nation collective—including De La Soul, Queen Latifah, A Tribe Called Quest and the Jungle Brothers—found him once more being tipped as one of rap's founding fathers. *—John Bush*

Beware (The Funk Is Everywhere) / 1986 / Tommy Boy ✦✦✦✦✦

Another stunning assortment of singles are included, with heavier beats, thicker rhythms, and a blistering cover of The MC5's "Kick Out the Jams." *—John Floyd*

★ **Planet Rock—*The Album* / *1986* / *Tommy Boy*** ✦✦✦✦✦

All the important early 12-inchers from 1982-1984 are here, including "Planet Rock" and "Looking for the Perfect Beat," plus three previously unreleased tracks. (Recorded with Soulsonic Force) *—John Floyd*

The Light / 1988 / EMI America ✦✦

1990-2000: The Decade of Darkness / Jun. 1991 / EMI America ✦✦✦

After several lackluster albums, Bambaataa came back with a record that explored modern-day dance trends without losing his signature sound. Fueled by righteous social commentary throughout the songs, the record showed that he wasn't creatively spent. It wasn't as innovative as his groundbreaking singles from the early '80s, but it was far from being an embarrassment. *—Stephen Thomas Erlewine*

Don't Stop . . . Planet Rock (The Remix EP) / 1992 / Tommy Boy ✦✦

Rob Base (Robert Ginyard)

b. May 18, 1967

Rap, Vocals / East Coast Rap, Club/Dance, Hip-Hop

Best-known for his platinum hip-hop classic "It Takes Two," Rob Base (with DJ E-Z Rock) rode his hit onto R&B radio stations as well as danceclubs, providing a touchstone for the style known as hip-house. The first Profile release, the title-track single from their debut album *It Takes Two,* became a street sensation upon its release in mid-1988. Though the single just barely reached the R&B Top 20 and Pop Top 40, massive club airplay enhanced its impact considerably. Both the single and album eventually went platinum, and Rob Base & DJ E-Z Rock gained Single of the Year honors both in *Spin* and *The Village Voice.* The second single "Get on the Dance Floor" continued Base's dance appeal, though his excellent rapping helped him retain his street credentials. By the end of 1989, however, Rob Base was on his own; his only explanation for the disappearance of DJ E-Z Rock was "personal problems." The release of *The Incredible Base* in 1989 was a bit of a comedown; despite several interesting tracks—including a reworking of Edwin Starr's "War"—neither the album nor any singles connected with listeners. *—John Bush*

● **It Takes Two** / 1988 / Profile ✦✦✦✦✦

Without question, Rob Base & D.J. E-Z Rock had the party anthem of 1988 in "It Takes Two"—

an insanely infectious rap/dance gem using a James Brown/Lynn Collins classic of the same name as a reference point. While the song was a major hit in dance music and club circles, Base won over hip-hop's hardcore with his strong technique as a rapper. Though most of this debut album falls short of that mega-hit's excellence, it's a generally decent effort that has both hip-hop and R&B appeal. A reflection on societal breakdown, the sobering "Times Are Gettin' Ill" is atypical of this album—which favors soul-flavored party music over social and political commentary. From Maze's "Joy & Pain" (which the duo used without Frankie Beverly's permission, inspiring him to threaten legal action) to the house-influenced "Get on the Dance Floor," *It Takes Two* thrives on strong hooks and unapologetic escapism. *—Alex Henderson*

The Incredible Base / Nov. 1989 / Profile ✦✦✦

Beastie Boys

f. 1979, New York, NY

Group / Old School Rap, Alternative Rap, Hardcore Punk, Alternative Pop/Rock, Hip-Hop

As the first White rap group of any importance, the Beastie Boys received the scorn of critics and strident hip-hop musicians, who accused them of cultural pirating, especially since they began as a hardcore punk group in 1981. But the Beasties weren't pirating—they treated rap as part of a post-punk musical underground, where the do-it-yourself aesthetics of hip-hop and punk weren't that far apart. Of course, the exaggerated B-boy and frat boy parodies of their unexpected hit debut album *Licensed to Ill* didn't help their cause. For much of the mid-'80s, the Beastie Boys were considered as macho clowns, and while their ambitious, Dust Brothers-produced second album *Paul's Boutique* dismissed that theory, it was ignored by both the public and the press at the time. In retrospect, it was one of the first albums to predict the genre-bending, self-referential pop kaleidoscope of '90s pop. The Beasties refined their eclectic approach with 1992's *Check Your Head*, where they played their own instruments. *Check Your Head* brought the Beasties back to the top of the charts, and within a few years, they were considered one of the most influential and ambitious groups of the '90s, cultivating a musical community not only through their music, but with their record label Grand Royal and their magazine of the same name. *—Stephen Thomas Erlewine*

☆ **Licensed to Ill** / 1986 / Def Jam ✦✦✦✦✦

The impact of this album in 1987 was about as subtle as a brick through a window. It was the first number number 1 hip-hop album, selling four million copies, and the first album from a White rap group. From the opening kick of John Bonham's drums (taken from "When the Levee Breaks"), The Beasties proceed to steal from every record they can get their hands on and rhyme about an absurd array of macho fantasies. Sure, it's obnoxious—but it's an act, and an insanely humorous one at that; no other rappers brag about being thrown out of White Castle, drinking Budweiser, or having "more rhymes than Phyllis Diller." Even if some of it sounds dated today, the sheer force of the music and the whiny rhymes still make this worth hearing. *—Stephen Thomas Erlewine*

★ **Paul's Boutique** / Jul. 1989 / Capitol ✦✦✦✦✦

Endlessly complex and relentlessly innovative, *Paul's Boutique* is The Beastie Boys' masterpiece. It's very dense, with samples from nearly every genre of music and clever, literate, absurd lyrics dropping references from Jack Kerouac to *Dragnet; Paul's Boutique* is a virtual catalog of pop culture, deeply rooted in the 1970s. As rappers, The Beasties have grown immeasurably, writing lyrics that are both smart-assed and smart. Musically, the album is much richer than *Licenced To Ill*, covering everything from funk and pop to country and hip-hop, with several layers of samples and beats on each track. *Paul's Boutique* is a brilliant, visionary album, and hasn't aged a day since its release. *—Stephen Thomas Erlewine*

☆ **Check Your Head** / Apr. 21, 1992 / Grand Royal/Capitol ✦✦✦✦✦

Check Your Head returned the Beastie Boys to the spotlight, although in the most unlikely manner possible. Refashioning themselves as a loose and gritty groove band, the Beasties picked up their instruments again and made an album of dirty Stax and New Orleans funk, tripped-out reggae, hard hip-hop, blistering hardcore punk, and scores of pop culture references and jokes. In its own way, *Check Your Head* is as trailblazing as *Paul's Boutique;* with its inspired amateurishness, it acknowledges no boundaries or limitations, creating a post-post-punk world where Eddie Harris, Bob Dylan, Cheap Trick, Groove Holmes, Spoonie Gee, and Biz Markie exist together as one music. And, strange as it may sound, it works. *—Stephen Thomas Erlewine*

Some Old Bullshit / Feb. 8, 1994 / Grand Royal/Capitol ✦✦

Ill Communication / May 23, 1994 / Grand Royal/Capitol ✦✦✦✦

More of a refinement and restatement of *Check Your Head* than a bold departure, *Ill Communication* still finds The Beastie Boys in prime form, adding more elements of jazz to their dense, surrealistic sound. From the scores of wah-wah guitars to the short hardcore punk songs, *Ill Communication* is firmly entrenched in '70s worship without ever once sounding like it's recycled. It may offer the same thing as *Check Your Head*, but *Ill Communication* never sounds formulaic or tired. *—Stephen Thomas Erlewine*

Hello Nasty / Jul. 14, 1998 / Grand Royal/Capitol ✦✦✦✦✦

Hello Nasty, the Beastie Boys' fifth album, is a head-spinning listen loaded with analog synthesizers, old drum machines, call-and-response vocals, freestyle rhyming, futuristic sound effects, and virtuoso turntable scratching. The Beasties have long been notorious for their dense, multi-layered explosions, but *Hello Nasty* is their first record to build on the multi-ethnic junk culture breakthrough of *Check Your Head*, instead of merely replicating it. Moving from electro-funk breakdowns to Latin-soul jams to spacey pop, *Hello Nasty* covers as much ground as *Check Your Head* or *Ill Communication*, but the flow is natural, like *Paul's Boutique*, even if the finish is retro-stylized. Hiring DJ Mixmaster Mike (one of the Invisibl Skratch Piklz) turned out to be a masterstroke; he and the Beasties created a sound that strongly recalls the spare electronic funk of the early '80s, but spiked with the samples and post-modern absurdist wit that have become their trademarks. On the surface, the sonic collages of *Hello Nasty* don't appear as dense as *Paul's Boutique*, nor is there a single as grabbing as "Sabotage," but given time, little details emerge, and each song forms its own identity. A few stray from the course, and the ending is a little anticlimactic, but that doesn't erase the riches of *Hello Nasty*—the old school kick of "Super Disco Breakin'" and "The Move"; Adam Yauch's crooning on "I Don't Know"; Lee "Scratch" Perry's cameo; and the recurring video game samples, to name just a few. The sonic adventures alone make the album noteworthy, but what makes it remarkable is how it looks to the future by looking to the past. There's no question that *Hello Nasty* is saturated in old-school sounds and styles, but by reviving the future-shock rock of the early '80s, the Beasties have shrewdly set themselves up for the new millennium. *—Stephen Thomas Erlewine*

The Sounds of Science / Nov. 23, 1999 / Grand Royal/Capitol ✦✦✦✦

Big Daddy Kane (Antonio Hardy)

b. Brooklyn, NY

Rap, Vocals / Pop-Rap, Hardcore Rap, Hip-Hop

Brooklyn-ite Big Daddy Kane (born Antonio Hardy, KANE is an acronym for King Asiatic Nobody's Equal) has nicely been able to balance his image as the ultimate hipster with the requisite solemnity and air of indignation and anger necessary to creditably deliver messages of Afrocentric awareness and Muslim reverence. He's done alternately inspirational, prophetical, ridiculous, and scandalous raps over his career, and has also managed to include duets with the maestro of love Barry White and legendary comedian Rudy Ray Moore, aka Dolemite, who laid waste to Kane in a dozens (insult-swapping) classic.

Big Daddy Kane has been a high profile figure the past couple of years. Not only has he appeared in such films as *Posse* and *Gunmen*, but he also posed in Madonna's controversial photo book *Sex*, and issued a defiant disc *Looks like a Job for Big Daddy Kane* that offered no apologies for past actions and ridiculed unnamed individuals he claimed were fronting as gangsters. After 1994's *Daddy's Home*, he was absent from the studio for four years prior to releasing *Veteranz Day*. *—Ron Wynn*

● **Long Live the Kane** / 1988 / Cold Chillin' ✦✦✦✦✦

Even though he spends a good 90 percent of the album boasting about his skills and abilities on the microphone, and cutting those of other MCs, Big Daddy Kane consistently proves himself a thrilling artist on his debut album, *Long Live the Kane*, one of the most appealing creations from the original new school of rap. This debut captures the Big Daddy Kane who rocked the house at hip-hop clubs and verbally cut up any and all comers in the late '80s with his articulate precision and locomotive power—the Big Daddy Kane who became an underground legend, the Big Daddy Kane who had the sheer verbal facility and razor-clean dexterity to ambush any MC and exhilarate anyone who witnessed or heard him perform. There are missteps here, to be sure—especially "The Day You're Mine," on which Kane casts himself as a loverman over a stilted drum machine and lackluster, cheesily seductive singing (offering a glimpse of the particular corner into which he would eventually paint himself). But there are also plenty of legitimate early hip-hop classics, none of which have lost an ounce of their power, and all of which serve as reminders of a time and era when hip-hop felt immediate, exciting, fresh, and a little bit dangerous (in the figurative, rather than literal, sense), and when hip-hop spawned commercial tastes of the moment rather than surrendering to them. Although his next album would be nearly the artistic equal of the debut—and, in many ways, even bettered it—Big Daddy Kane would never sound as compelling or as fresh as on this first effort. *—Stanton Swihart*

It's a Big Daddy Thing / Sep. 15, 1989 / Cold Chillin' ✦✦✦✦

When it comes to technique, few rappers can rival Big Daddy Kane. Kane hasn't had as much to say as Public Enemy, KRS-One, or Ice-T, but his chops are unquestionable. Nontheless, Kane generally hasn't made remarkable albums—strong, but not remarkable. On his second album, *It's a Big Daddy Thing*, the Brooklyn native spends too much time boasting—a problem he shares with quite a few other rappers—and is at his most interesting when talking about something other than his rhyming skills. Especially noteworthy are "Another Victory," an arresting commentary on racism; the uplifting "Ain't No Stoppin' Us Now," which uses the McFadden & Whitehead classic as a reference point; and "Calling Mr. Welfare," a humorous yet painfully honest commentary on reasons for seeking public assistance. Kane isn't without his contradictions—the same MC who calls for an end to discrimination stoops to homophobic hate-mongering on "Pimpin' Ain't Easy." *—Alex Henderson*

Taste of Chocolate / Oct. 30, 1990 / Cold Chillin' ✦✦✦✦✦

Prince of Darkness / Oct. 29, 1991 / Cold Chillin' ✦✦

Looks Like a Job for Big Daddy / May 25, 1993 / Cold Chillin' ✦✦✦

Biz Markie (Marcel Hall)

b. Apr. 8, 1964, Harlem, NY

Vocals / Comedy Rap, Pop-Rap, East Coast Rap

Biz Markie's inclination toward juvenile humor and his fondness for goofy, tuneless, half-sung choruses camoflouged his true talents as a freestyle rhymer. The Biz may not have been able to translate his wild rhyming talents to tape, but what he did record was worthwhile in its own way. With his silly humor and inventive, sample-laden productions, he proved that hip-hop could be funny and melodic, without sacrificing its street credibility. His distinctive style made his second album, *The Biz Never Sleeps*, a gold hit and its single "Just a Friend" into a Top 10 pop single. While its success made Biz Markie a semi-star, it also cursed him. Not only was he consigned as a novelty act, but it brought enough attention that Gilbert O'-Sullivan sued him over the unauthorized sample of "Alone Again (Naturally)" on Biz's 1991 album, *I Need a Haircut*. The lawsuit severely cut into Markie's career and 1993's *All Samples Cleared* was the last record he released during the '90s. However, his reputation was restored somewhat in the mid-'90s, as the Beastie Boys championed him and other alternative-rap groups showed some debt to his wild, careening music. *—Stephen Thomas Erlewine*

Goin' Off / Feb. 23, 1988 / Cold Chillin' ✦✦✦✦✦

Biz Markie's debut album introduced his absurdly comical and extremely inventive musical style. While he talked about "Pickin' Boogers," and hanging out at "Albee Square Mall," and made music with his mouth, The Biz never kept the music similar, with Marley Marl's production covering all of the bases, concentrating on a deeply funky R&B/dance beat. It was a funny, surrealistic minor masterpiece. *—Stephen Thomas Erlewine*

The Biz Never Sleeps / Oct. 10, 1989 / Cold Chillin' ✦✦✦✦✦
Biz Markie's madcap humor was effectively utilized on this release. Markie relied on puns, quips, bad jokes and his disjointed rap style, creating material quite different from the hard-edged fare that now rules hip-hop. Some of it was funny, some of it stupid, but none of it vicious or offensive. The album contained the hits "Just a Friend" and "Spring Again." *—Ron Wynn*

I Need a Haircut / Aug. 27, 1991 / Cold Chillin' ✦✦✦
Biz Markie, rap's clown prince, can usually be counted on to deliver goofy humor, and *I Need a Haircut* is as wildly entertaining as anything he's ever done. Biz isn't one to rap about his sexual prowess, drive-by shootings near the projects, or Louis Farrakhan's ideology. In contrast to the sobering gangster rap of N.W.A. and Ice-T, the angry political protests of Public Enemy and Boogie Down Productions, and the machismo of L.L. Cool J, Biz Markie seeks only to amuse, entertain, and have fun. Indeed, rap doesn't get much sillier than "T.S.R. (Toilet Stool Rap)" and "Kung Fu." The Brooklyn native's third album also contains "Alone Again," the song that incorporated Gilbert O'Sullivan's pop hit "Alone Again Naturally" (allegedly without the pop singer's permission) and inspired a major lawsuit. *—Alex Henderson*

All Samples Cleared / Jun. 22, 1993 / Cold Chillin' ✦✦

★ **The Best of Cold Chillin'** / Oct. 17, 2000 / Landspeed ✦✦✦✦✦
Much more than just the clown prince of hip-hop during the late '80s and early '90s, Biz Markie was one of the golden age's most talented, distinctive, and inventive rappers whether he was talking about his skills on the mic ("Nobody Beats the Biz") or his favorite brand of spaghetti sauce ("Biz Is Goin' Off"). And like the other acts on the Cold Chillin' label, he benefited from one of the era's greatest producers, Marley Marl. Led by Marl's raw, drum-heavy tracks and great scratching, *The Best of Cold Chillin'* is a definitive look back for rap fans, gathering 17 tracks from the Biz's four LPs for the label and wisely balancing trademark hits like "Just a Friend" and "Vapors" with rare, early material like the solo human-beatbox number "One Two." The compilation also focuses heavily on his first two albums, with tracks from 1988's seminal *Goin' Off* and the following year's breakout *The Biz Never Sleeps*. *—John Bush*

Kurtis Blow

b. Aug. 9, 1959, New York, NY
Vocals, Keyboards / Old School Rap, Hip-Hop
No discussion of early hip-hop would be complete without some mention of Kurtis Blow, whose cocky, flamboyant, in-your-face brand of old school rapping made him an inspiration to Run-D.M.C., Whodini, and many other MCs who emerged in the early '80s. Born in New York on August 9, 1959, Blow grew up in Harlem and was rapping in Charles Gallery (a Harlem club) as early as 1976. In 1977 and 1978, the MC's frequent club appearances earned him a small inner-city cult following in Harlem and the South Bronx. But it wasn't until 1979 that Blow enjoyed his first taste of national exposure. That year, he signed with Mercury (Blow was the first rapper to record for a major label) and provided his debut single, "Christmas Rappin'." The song did OK nationally, but not as well as Blow's second single, "The Breaks," a 1980 gem that went to number 4 on Billboard's R&B singles chart and was certified gold by the RIAA. It was also in 1980 that Blow recorded his self-titled debut album, which was the first rap album to come out on a major label. Several other Mercury LPs followed, including *Deuce* in 1981, *Tough* in 1982 and *Ego Trip* in 1984. By 1984, Blow's rapping style was sounding dated; nonetheless, he had gone down in history as one of hip-hop's most influential pioneers. Blow, who turned 40 in 1999, wasn't as visible in the '90s, although he hosted a hip-hop radio show on L.A.'s KPWR-FM (Power 106) and wrote the liner notes for Rhino's 1997 series *Kurtis Blow Presents the History of Rap*. *—Alex Henderson*

Kurtis Blow / 1980 / Mercury ✦✦✦✦✦
Back in hip-hop's old school era—roughly 1978-1982—albums were the exception and not the rule. Hip-hop became a lot more album-minded with the rise of its second generation (Run-D.M.C., Whodini, the Fat Boys, among others) around 1983-1984, but in the beginning, many MCs recorded nothing but singles. Two exceptions were the Sugarhill Gang and Kurtis Blow, whose self-titled debut album of 1980 was among hip-hop's first LPs and was the first rap album to come out on a major label. Thus, *Kurtis Blow* has serious historic value, although it is mildly uneven. Some of the tracks are superb, including "The Breaks" (a Top Five R&B smash in 1980) and "Rappin' Blow, Part Two," which is the second half of Blow's 1979 debut single, "Christmas Rappin'." And "Hard Times" is a forceful gem that finds Blow addressing social issues two years before Grandmaster Flash & the Furious Five popularized sociopolitical rapping with 1982's sobering "The Message." Some of the other tracks, however, are decent but not remarkable. Switching from rapping to singing, Blow detours into Northern soul on the Chi-Lites-influenced ballad "All I Want in This World (Is to Find That Girl)" and arena rock on an unexpected cover of Bachman-Turner Overdrive's "Takin' Care of Business." While those selections are likable and kind of interesting—how many other old school rappers attempted to sing soul, let alone arena rock—the fact remains that rapping, not singing, is Blow's strong point. And Mercury really screwed up by providing only the second half of "Christmas Rappin'"; that landmark single should have been heard in its entirety. But despite its flaws and shortcomings, *Kurtis Blow* is an important album that hip-hop historians should make a point of hearing. *—Alex Henderson*

Deuce / 1981 / Mercury ✦✦✦✦
Things cooled quickly for Kurtis Blow following the success of "The Breaks" in 1980. He was unable to get any single from this record on the charts, even though "Rockin'" and "It's Gettin' Hot" were well produced and competently delivered. But rap was still far from being a mainstream phenomenon, and this album did very poorly commercially. *—Ron Wynn*

Party Time— / 1983 / Mercury ✦✦✦✦✦

Ego Trip / 1984 / Mercury ✦✦✦

Kingdom Blow / 1986 / Mercury ✦✦

★ **The Best of Kurtis Blow** / Jun. 7, 1994 / Mercury ✦✦✦✦✦
While he made many groundbreaking singles, Kurtis Blow was never a consistent album artist, making this best-of collection his definitive artistic statement. Throughout the early '80s, Blow helped define what rap could do, and these tracks confirm his status as one of hip-hop's legendary acts. *—Stephen Thomas Erlewine*

Bone Thugs-N-Harmony

f. 1993
Rap / G-Funk, Gangsta Rap, Urban, Hip-Hop
When Bone Thugs-N-Harmony first exploded on the rap scene in 1994 with their fast rhymes, harmonious choruses, ominous G-funk, and gangsta attitude, no one knew whether the uncanny Cleveland group were for real or if they were a novelty success. After all, at this point in time, few rap groups outside of New York or California had been able to prove themselves on a commercial level. And Bone Thugs-N-Harmony leap-frogged cult success, instantly rising to the top of the charts with their summer 1994 anthem "Thuggish Ruggish Bone." By the time their first full-length album, *E 1999 Eternal*, dropped a year later, it not only debuted at number one but also proved to be one of the decade's most important and enduring albums. While other rap groups struggled to break away from the clichés first forged by N.W.A., Public Enemy, Boogie Down Productions, 2 Live Crew, and LL Cool J in the late '80s, Bone Thugs-N-Harmony were one of the few groups able to carve out their own stylistic niche, an inimitable myriad of urban sounds with a strong ghetto attitude. Yet following the unprecedented success of *E 1999 Eternal* and, more so, the Grammy-winning success of "Tha Crossroads," Bone struggled to meet unreasonable expectations and also struggled with redundancy, having realized their apparent summit on their debut album. Yet even if the group was unable to repeat their success, they remained a vital group, as few were able to bite on their signature style. *—Jason Birchmeier*

Creepin on Ah Come Up / Jun. 1994 / Ruthless/Epic ✦✦

E 1999 Eternal / Jul. 25, 1995 / Ruthless/Epic ✦✦✦✦
Following the surprise success of their summer 1994 "Thuggish Ruggish Bone," Bone Thugs-N-Harmony returned a year later with their first full-length album, instantly dismissing any notion that the group was a one-hit wonder. From the opening "Da Introduction" to the closing moments of "Shotz to tha Double Glock," there are few weak moments, as DJ U-Neek's smoked-out, gloomy G-funk kept the mood ominous while the Bone Thugs traded off fast-paced, harmonious rhymes and joined together for melodic choruses; in sum, it was a stunning confluence of modified gangsta rap and R&B conventions that never sound derived. Lurking beneath the group's vocal harmonies and DJ U-Neek's synth melodies is a dark and harsh album that paints a dim yet alluring view of ghetto life. Where "Mr. Ouija 2" and "Shotz to tha Double Glock" spoke of street violence, songs such as "Mr. Bill Collector" and "No Shorts, No Losses" spoke of ghetto greed, and "Buddah Lovaz" and "Budsmokers Only" spoke of a celebratory passion for marijuana; other songs such as "Crossroads" and "Eternal" alluded to the group's bleak view of the world. In other words, this is a well-rounded, perfect rap album: It crafts a unique style for itself, features a few catchy hits, covers all the essential gangsta rap themes, and doesn't include any filler. Actually, it is such a perfect rap album that succeeding Bone Thugs albums were initially received with disappointment as they were unable to compare to the flawless *E 1999 Eternal*. *—Jason Birchmeier*

The Art of War / Aug. 5, 1997 / Ruthless/Epic ✦✦✦

● **The Collection, Vol. 1** / Nov. 17, 1998 / Ruthless/Epic ✦✦✦✦
Bone Thugs-N-Harmony had only released two albums and an EP, plus a handful of side projects, when they released *Collection, Vol. 1* in the fall of 1998. Usually, that would be the sign of a ripoff, but since their albums have been notoriously uneven, this functions as a useful summary for both casual and hardcore fans alike, since it contains all of their best songs, from "Thuggish Ruggish Bone" and "For Tha Love of Money" to "1st of Tha Month" and "Tha Crossroads." It also contains their cover of N.W.A's "Fuck tha Police," previously only available on a tribute album. It may be of interest to collectors, but it's a weak cover, and is the only thing marring this otherwise fine compilation. *—Stephen Thomas Erlewine*

BTNHResurrection / Feb. 29, 2000 / Ruthless/Epic ✦✦

The Collection, Vol. 2 / Nov. 14, 2000 / Ruthless/Epic ✦✦

Boogie Down Productions

f. 1986, Brooklyn, NY, **db.** 1993
Group / Hardcore Rap, East Coast Rap, Gangsta Rap, Hip-Hop
Formed in 1986 by Laurence Krisna Parker and Scott Sterling, Boogie Down Productions quickly became one of the most influential and important hip-hop groups. Parker adopted the name KRS-One (an acronym for Knowledge Reigns Supreme Over Almost Every One) and Sterling became DJ Scott LaRock. They released an independent single, "Crack Attack," in 1986. BDP's groundbreaking 1987 debut, *Criminal Minded*, full of blunt, matter-of-fact tales of life on the mean streets, was a prototype for gangsta rap. As the album was building to a massive underground success, LaRock was shot to death in the South Bronx as he tried to settle an argument. Instead of calling it quits, KRS-One continued BDP with *By All Means Necessary* the following year. KRS-One began calling himself "the Teacher," promoting self-awareness and education in his rhymes. It became evident that KRS-One had taken his role as the Teacher too far on 1990's *Edutainment*, where most tracks were lectures pasted over lackluster beats. KRS-One obliterated all concerns that he sold out on 1992's *Sex and Violence*, where he sounds angrier and stronger than he has in years. The following year, KRS-One released his first solo album, *Return of the Boom Bap*, which was even better; many hip-hop critics equated with the seminal *By All Means Necessary*. But by early 1994, it had already dropped off the R&B and hip-hop charts. *—Stephen Thomas Erlewine*

★ **Criminal Minded** / 1987 / Sugar Hill ✦✦✦✦✦
Boogie Down Productions' 1987 debut was a watershed release in an art form poised for mass consumption. South Bronx natives KRS-One and Scott LaRock combined to form not only a signature and celebrated hip-hop group, but a social and political movement; using hip-hop as their medium, BDP gave disenfranchised inner-city citizens a voice. The album's cover and title suggest that *Criminal Minded* glorifies violence. However, this was a ploy to appeal to the reality faced by inner-city youth: self-preservation through sometimes violent means. It was a gateway to BDP's true message: self-knowledge, empowerment, and peace. DJ/producer Scott LaRock sadly became a martyr for that cause, gunned down soon after the album was released after trying to settle an argument. The legacy of BDP was left to KRS-One, the poet, scholar, teacher, and B-boy who became a hip-hop immortal from the moment he clicked on the mic and his voice rang out on the opening cut, "Poetry." On "South Bronx," KRS lays claim to the true genealogy of hip-hop, stating in true battle fashion that hip-hop's Plymouth Rock is located in his South Bronx stomping grounds. "The Bridge Is Over" is further affirmation, the definitive salvo in the Bronx vs. Queens feud and an answer to MC Shan's "The Bridge." Production on *Criminal Minded* is pure, stripped-down, skeletal brilliance. *Criminal Minded* was one of the first rap albums to utilize rock & roll and pop samples and elements; "Dope Beat" uses an AC/DC guitar riff, the *a cappella* opening of the title cut paraphrases the Beatles' "Hey Jude," and the bridge portion of "The Bridge Is Over" embodies Billy Joel's "It's Still Rock N' Roll to Me." *Criminal Minded* is a classic hip-hop album, a manifesto that outlines the essence of the art form. *—Michael Di Bella*

☆ **By All Means Necessary** / 1988 / Jive/Novus ✦✦✦✦✦
When his partner Scott LaRock was murdered in the Bronx in 1987, KRS-One seriously considered discontinuing Boogie Down Productions. But thankfully, the thought-provoking MC decided to keep the group going, and delivered one of 1988's finest rap albums with *By All Means Necessary.* Social and political commentary, long KRS's forte, abounds here—ranging from the anti-drug song "Illegal Business" to "Stop the Violence," a heartfelt condemnation of violence in hip-hop circles, to the humorous yet hard-hitting call for safe sex, "Jimmy." In fact, "Stop the Violence" became a rallying cry for KRS, who passionately spoke out against Black-on-Black crime when he founded the Stop the Violence Movement. A superb follow-up to BDP's debut album, *Criminal Minded, Necessary* made it abundantly clear that as great a loss as LaRock's death was, KRS could be artistically triumphant on his own. Indeed, it turned out to be one of many excellent post-LaRock BDP albums. *—Alex Henderson*

Ghetto Music: The Blueprint of Hip Hop / Jun. 1989 / Jive/Novus ✦✦✦✦✦
With Boogie Down Productions' third album, *Ghetto Music: The Blueprint of Hip Hop,* KRS-One offered additional proof that he had evolved into one of rap's most intelligent voices. When other MCs were content to simply brag about their microphone skills, KRS focused on his strong point: hard-hitting social and political commentary. KRS is angry, but he's also lucid and thoughtful. From police abuse to obsessive materialism, he denounces injustice without becoming an extremist. In the 1990s, fusing rap and reggae isn't out of the ordinary; but such arresting gems as "Bo! Bo! Bo!" and "Jah Rulez" underscore the fact that KRS was among those combining the two before it became so fashionable. *—Alex Henderson*

Edutainment / Jul. 1990 / Jive/Novus ✦✦✦

Live Hardcore Worldwide / Mar. 12, 1991 / Jive/Novus ✦✦✦

Sex and Violence / Feb. 25, 1992 / Jive/Novus ✦✦✦

Brand Nubian

f. 1989, New Rochelle, NY
Group / Jazz-Rap, Alternative Rap
Picking up on the so-called "daisy age" sound of De La Soul, Brand Nubian's cool, funky rap serves as a platform for the group's declarations of Islamic faith and for the teachings of the Five Percent Nation. The group's original lineup was composed of lead rapper Maxwell "Grand Puba" Dixon (formerly of the Masters of Ceremony), Lorenzo "Lord Jamar" Dechelaus, Derrick "Sadat X" Murphy, and his cousin DJ Alamo. Following the group's acclaimed 1990 debut, *One for All,* Grand Puba departed for a solo career, taking DJ Alamo with him. The remaining members added DJ Sincere and have continued to record albums detailing their religious beliefs and promoting self-reliance and peace. After 1994's *Everything Is Everything,* the group was largely silent until returning four years later with *Foundation. —Steve Huey*

● **One for All** / 1990 / Elektra ✦✦✦✦✦
Brand Nubian never sold as many albums as the West Coast rappers burning up the charts in the early 1990s, but the New York group commanded great respect in East Coast rap circles. In Black neighborhoods of New York and Philadelphia, Nubian's debut album, *One for All,* was actually a bigger seller than many of the platinum gangsta rap releases outselling it on a national level. Influenced by De La Soul and the Jungle Brothers, Nubian favored an abstract rapping style, and Eastern rap fans were drawn to the complexity of jams like "Dance To My Ministry," "Ragtime," and "All for One." Grand Puba, Lord Jammer, and Saddat X had a lot of technique, which was what hip-hoppers favored in the East. On the whole, Nubian's Nation of Islam rhetoric isn't as overbearing as some of the recordings that other Five Percenters were delivering at the time. The CD is a bit uneven, but on the whole is likable and exhilarating. *—Alex Henderson*

In God We Trust / Feb. 1993 / Elektra ✦✦✦✦
Their first album after losing talented MC Grand Puba, Sadat X and Lord Jamar were joined by DJ Sincere for this 1993 effort, which earned some notoriety for the homophobic taunts included in "Punks Jump Up to Get Beat Down." Elsewhere the record is a rallying call for Louis Farrakhan's Nation of Islam—notably on "Allah and Justice" and "Meaning of the 5%." If you can get past the religious dogma, the musical platform is tough and compelling and the rhymes are delivered with surprising dexterity and poise in the absence of Puba. *—Alex Ogg*

Everything Is Everything / Nov. 1994 / Elektra ✦✦✦

Foundation / Sep. 29, 1998 / Arista ✦✦✦✦

Neneh Cherry

b. Mar. 10, 1964, Stockholm, Sweden
Vocals / Pop-Rap, Alternative Rap, Alternative Dance, Club/Dance, Urban, Dance-Pop
The stepdaughter of jazz trailblazer Don Cherry, vocalist Neneh Cherry forged her own groundbreaking blend of pop, dance and hip-hop which presaged the emergence of both alternative rap and trip-hop. Cherry dropped out of school at age 14, and in 1980 she relocated to London to sing with the punk group the Cherries. Following brief flings with the Slits and the Nails, she joined the experimental funk outfit Rip Rig + Panic. When the band broke up, Cherry remained with one of the spin-off groups, Float Up CP, and led them through one album, 1986's *Kill Me in the Morning.* After attracting some notice singing back-up on the The's "Slow Train to Dawn" single, she became romantically and professionally involved with composer and musician Cameron McVey, who, under the alias Booga Bear, wrote much of the material that would comprise Cherry's 1989 debut LP *Raw Like Sushi.* One song McVey did not write was "Buffalo Stance," the album's breakthrough single; originally tossed off as a B-side by the mid-'80s pop group Morgan McVey, Cherry's cover was an international smash which neatly summarized the album's eclectic fusion of pop smarts and hip-hop energy. While 1992's *Homebrew* was not as commercially successful as its predecessor, Cherry returned to the charts in 1994 duetting with Youssou N'Dour on the global hit "Seven Seconds." *—Jason Ankeny*

● **Raw Like Sushi** / May 1989 / Virgin ✦✦✦✦✦
Those arguing that the most individualistic R&B and dance music of the late '80s and early to mid-'90s came out of Britain could point to Neneh Cherry's unconventional *Raw like Sushi* as a shining example. An unorthodox and brilliantly daring blend of R&B, rap, pop, and dance music, *Sushi* enjoyed little exposure on America's conservative, urban, contemporary radio formats, but was a definite underground hit. Full of personality, the singer/rapper is as thought-provoking as she is witty and humorous when addressing relationships and taking aim at the less-than-kosher behavior of males and females alike. Macho homeboys and Casanovas take a pounding on "So Here I Come" and the hit "Buffalo Stance," while women who are shallow, cold-hearted, or materialistic get lambasted on "Phoney Ladies," "Heart," and "Inna City Mamma." Cherry's idealism comes through loud and clear on "The Next Generation," a plea to take responsibility for one's sexual actions and give children the respect and attention they deserve. *—Alex Henderson*

Homebrew / Oct. 27, 1992 / Virgin ✦✦✦✦✦

Coolio (Artis Ivey)

b. Aug. 1, 1963
Vocals / Pop-Rap, West Coast Rap, Hip-Hop
Coolio (born Artis Ivey) is a native of Compton, CA, yet his variation of the P-Funk-inspired rap of Dr. Dre is calmer, less violent, and funnier. Recorded with his DJ Bryan "Wino" Dobbs, Coolio's 1994 debut album, *It Takes a Thief* was a smash hit, selling over a million records and featuring the number three single, "Fantastic Voyage." His second record, 1995's *Gangsta's Paradise,* was an even bigger hit, thanks to the title track, which was the biggest rap single of the year. *My Soul* followed in 1997. *—Stephen Thomas Erlewine*

It Takes a Thief / Jul. 19, 1994 / Tommy Boy ✦✦✦✦
Just when it looked like rap would completely succumb to the violent hyperbole and mean-spirited "realness" of gangsta rap, new blood entered the scene in 1994 to nudge the genre back toward friendlier turf. That new blood included Nas, Craig Mack, and Coolio, whose *It Takes a Thief* starts with the easy-rolling funk of Lakeside's "Fantastic Voyage" and goes from there, infusing rap with a much-needed sense of humor and the promise of good times. While Coolio is no simp—"County Line" playfully explores the hassles of welfare, while some tracks dip into gangsta territory—he manages to make rap a cool, inclusive journey. *—Eddie Huffman*

● **Gangsta's Paradise** / Nov. 21, 1995 / Tommy Boy ✦✦✦✦✦
Most of Coolio's hit debut *It Takes a Thief* was fairly upbeat material, but the appearance of the stark single "Gangsta's Paradise" in the summer of 1995 signaled a change in the rapper's music. Driven by an ominously deep bass line and slashing strings, the creeping, threatening funk of "Gangsta's Paradise" was the most chilling thing Coolio had recorded to date, but the menace didn't come at the expense of his considerable talent for immediate, catchy hooks. Consequently, the single shot to the top of the charts and hovered in the Top Ten for many weeks. The album followed shortly afterwards, and it didn't fail to deliver on the promise of the single. Not only did Coolio expand his sound, but his songwriting skills improved, as *Gangsta's Paradise* has very few weak moments. Alternating between slow, funky grooves and elastic, party-ready anthems, *Gangsta's Paradise* is proof that Coolio is one of the most exciting and interesting hip-hop artists of the mid-'90s. *—Stephen Thomas Erlewine*

My Soul / Aug. 26, 1997 / Tommy Boy ✦✦✦✦

Cypress Hill

f. 1988, Los Angeles, CA
Group / Rap-Rock, Latin Rap, West Coast Rap, Hardcore Rap, Alternative Rap
Cypress Hill was notable for being the first Latino hip-hop superstars, but they became notorious for their endorsement of marijuana, which actually isn't a trivial thing. Not only did the group campaign for its legalization, but its slow, rolling bass-and-drum loops pioneered a new, stoned funk that became extraordinarily influential in '90s hip-hop—it could be heard in everything from Dr. Dre's G-Funk to the chilly layers of English trip-hop. DJ Muggs crafted the sound, and B-Real, with his pinched nasal voice, was responsible for the rhetoric that made them famous. The pro-pot position became a little ridiculous over time, but there was no denying that the actual music had a strange, eerie power. Cypress Hill's first hit was their

second album, 1993's *Black Sunday,* which entered the album charts at number one and spawned the crossover hit "Insane in the Brain." With *Black Sunday* and their subsequent tour with the fifth Lollapalooza festival, Cypress Hill's audience became predominantly white, collegiate suburbanites, which caused them to lose some support in the hip-hop community. A darker, gloomier affair than their first two records, 1995's *Temples of Boom* was greeted with mixed reviews and generally disappointing sales. Though the group appeared to be falling apart (second rapper Sen Dog departed soon afterward), another album, *IV,* appeared in 1998. *—Stephen Thomas Erlewine*

★ **Cypress Hill** / Aug. 13, 1991 / Ruffhouse ✦✦✦✦✦
It's hard enough to transform an entire musical genre—Cypress Hill's eponymous debut album revolutionized hip-hop in several respects. Although they weren't the first Latino rappers, nor the first to mix Spanish and English, they were the first to achieve a substantial following, thanks to their highly distinctive sound. Along with the Beastie Boys and Public Enemy, Cypress Hill was also one of the first rap groups to bridge the gap with fans of both hard rock *and* alternative rock. And, most importantly, they created a sonic blueprint that would become one of the most widely copied in hip-hop. In keeping with their pro-marijuana stance, Cypress Hill intentionally crafted its music to sound stoned—lots of slow, lazy beats, fat bass, weird noises, and creepily distant-sounding samples. The surreal lyrical narratives were almost exclusively spun by B-Real in a nasal, sing-song, instantly recognizable delivery that only added to the music's hazy, evocative atmosphere; as a frontman, he could be funny, frightening, or just plain bizarre (again, kind of like the experience of being stoned). Whether he's taunting cops or singing nursery rhyme-like choruses about blasting holes in people with shotguns, B-Real's blunted-gangsta posture is nearly always underpinned by a cartoonish sense of humor. It's never clear how serious the threats are, but that actually makes them all the more menacing. The sound and style of *Cypress Hill* was hugely influential, particularly on Dr. Dre's boundary-shattering 1992 blockbuster *The Chronic;* yet despite its legions of imitators, *Cypress Hill* still sounds fresh and original today, simply because few hip-hop artists can put its sound across with such force of personality or imagination. *—Steve Huey*

Black Sunday / Jul. 27, 1993 / Columbia ✦✦✦✦✦
Black Sunday made Cypress Hill's connection to rock & roll more explicit, with its heavy metal-like artwork and noisier, more dissonant samples (including, naturally, stoner icons Black Sabbath). It's a slightly darker affair than its groundbreaking predecessor, with the threats of violence more urgent and the pot obsession played to the hilt (after all, it was a crucial part of their widespread appeal). Apart from those subtle distinctions, the sound of *Black Sunday* is pretty much the same as *Cypress Hill,* refining the group's innovations into an accessible bid for crossover success. In fact, it's a little startling how often *Black Sunday* recycles musical ideas and even lyrical catchphrases from the endlessly inventive debut. And the rock-derived, verse-chorus song structures start to sound a little formulaic by the end of the record (how many choruses feature Sen Dog repeating part of whatever B-Real just said?). But in spite of that, *Black Sunday* still sounds vital and lively, since the group has a surer sense of craft. Most of the tracks are fleshed out into structured songs, in contrast to the brief sketches that punctuated *Cypress Hill.* The album benefits immensely from the resulting clutch of excellent singles (and songs that could have been), and while a couple of tracks feel redundant and underdeveloped, *Black Sunday* is overall a consistent, engaging listen, especially the flawless first half. Unfortunately, it's also the group's last great album, thanks to the musical recycling operation that began here and would handicap much of their subsequent work. *—Steve Huey*

Cypress Hill III: Temples of Boom / Oct. 31, 1995 / Columbia ✦✦

IV / Oct. 6, 1998 / Columbia ✦✦

Skull & Bones / Apr. 25, 2000 / Columbia ✦✦✦✦

Das Efx

f. 1991, Petersburg, VA
Group / East Coast Rap, Hip-Hop
With their first album, Das Efx caused a minor revolution based on their speedy, quick-tongued stuttering; it helped that they backed their rhymes with thick, funky tracks. The album was a major success, scoring a Top 40 pop single and going gold. On their second LP, *Straight Up Sewaside,* the duo of Drayz and Skoob Effect slightly altered their approach. They downplayed the high speed stuttering, though they continued with the intense rhyming and confrontational themes that made their debut so memorable. *—AMG*

● **Dead Serious** / Apr. 7, 1992 / East West ✦✦✦✦✦
Das EFX—part of EPMD's Def Squad crew, which also included K-Solo and Redman, among others, made such a wide breakthrough in 1992 with their debut album that their hit "They Want EFX" was even referenced in the lily-white teen serial *Beverly Hills 90210.* That *Dead Serious* could have that sort of broad impact and still retain its credibility within the underground hip-hop community says something about its appeal, which was considerable. But the album wasn't just appealing; it was also enormously influential, ushering in an entirely unique rhyming flow that influenced any number of rappers, established and novice alike. What exactly the duo is rapping about is anyone's guess. One thing is for sure: Their lyrics are about as far removed from hardcore realism as they could possibly be, and although there are certain elements of boasting, it is so cut up and contorted that it never sounds like there's even a hint of the humdrum here. None of the lyrical clichés that can occasionally bog down even the finest hip-hop artist are present. Members Dre and Skoob (tellingly, "books" spelled backwards) instead engage in lightning-fast, tongue-twisted word association and stream-of-consciousness rants rich in pop-cultural references and allusions. It was a completely original rhyming style in 1992—one of the reasons it had such an impact both in the insular world of hip-hop and on the wider public—but it also had an invigorating looseness that lent itself to commercial radio. "They Want EFX" is clearly the creative highlight of the album; the other songs work the same basic template, and each one is nearly equal in execution and charm, particularly the jaunty "Mic Checka" and "Jussummen." *—Stanton Swihart*

Straight Up Sewaside / Nov. 16, 1993 / East West ✦✦✦

Hold It Down / Oct. 1995 / East West ✦✦

Generation EFX / Mar. 24, 1998 / Elektra ✦✦✦

De la Soul

f. 1987, Amityville, Long Island, NY
Group / Alternative Rap, Hip-Hop
Long Island's De La Soul—Posdnuos (b. Kelvin Mercer), Trugoy the Dove (b. David Jolicoeur), and Pasemaster Mase (b. Vincent Mason)—formed while attending high school in the late '80s. Their demo tape came to the attention of Stetsasonic leader/producer Prince Paul, who helped the trio land a contract with Tommy Boy Records and produced their 1989 debut album, *3 Feet High and Rising.* With its colorful, neo-psychedelic collage of samples and musical styles, plus the trio's low-key, clever rhymes and goofy humor, the album sounded like nothing else in hip-hop. De La Soul was gentler and more eclectic than most of their contemporaries, and were quickly perceived as the leaders of a contingent of New York-based alternative rappers dubbed the Native Tongues Posse. In the wake of *3 Feet High and Rising's* critical and commercial success, the '60s pop group the Turtles won a lawsuit against De La Soul over an unauthorized sample of their song "You Showed Me." The decision had substantial impact on rap in general—all samples now had to be legally cleared, which delayed the release of De La Soul's second album, *De La Soul Is Dead.* When the record was finally released in the spring of 1991, it received decidedly mixed reviews, and its darker, more introspective tone didn't attract as big an audience. De La Soul's third album, *Buhloone Mindstate,* was harder and funkier than its predecessors, but although it received strong reviews upon its late-1993 release, the album quickly fell off the charts; the same fate greeted 1996's *Stakes Is High.* Four years later, De La Soul initiated what promised to be a three-album series with *Art Official Intelligence: Mosaic Thump;* though reviews were mixed, it was greeted warmly by record buyers, debuting in the Top Ten. *—Stephen Thomas Erlewine*

★ **3 Feet High and Rising** / 1989 / Tommy Boy ✦✦✦✦✦
The most inventive, assured, and playful debut in hip-hop history, *3 Feet High and Rising* not only proved that rappers didn't have to talk about the streets to succeed, but also expanded the palette of sampling material with a kaleidoscope of sounds and references culled from pop, soul, disco, and even country music. Weaving clever wordplay and deft rhymes across two dozen tracks loosely organized around a game-show theme, De La Soul broke down boundaries all over the LP, moving easily from the groovy my-philosophy intro "*The Magic Number*" to an intelligent, caring inner-city vignette named "*Ghetto Thang*" to the free-wheeling end-of-innocence tale "*Jenifa Taught Me (Derwin's Revenge).*" Rappers Posdnuos and Trugoy the Dove talked about anything they wanted (up to and including body odor), playing fast and loose on the mic like Biz Markie. Thinly disguised under a layer of humor, their lyrical themes ranged from true love ("*Eye Know*") to the destructive power of drugs ("*Say No Go*") to Daisy Age philosophy ("*Tread Water*") to sex ("*Buddy*"). Prince Paul (from Stetsasonic) and DJ Pasemaster Mase led the way on the production end, with dozens of samples from all sorts of left-field artists—including Johnny Cash, the Mad Lads, Steely Dan, Public Enemy, Hall & Oates, and the Turtles. The pair didn't just use those samples as hooks or drumbreaks—like most hip-hop producers had in the past—but as split-second fills and in-jokes that made some tracks sound more like DJ records. Even "*Potholes on My Lawn,*" which samples a mouth harp and yodeling (for the chorus, no less), became a big R&B hit. If it was easy to believe the revolution was here from listening to the rapping and production on Public Enemy's *It Takes a Nation of Millions to Hold Us Back,* with De La Soul the Daisy Age seemed to promise a new era of positivity in hip-hop. *—John Bush*

De La Soul Is Dead / May 13, 1991 / Tommy Boy ✦✦✦✦
De La Soul throws a curveball at listeners with its second album, *De La Soul Is Dead,* taking a slightly harder and tougher approach, but remaining highly musical, distinctive, and recognizable. Though not quite as consistently appealing as the debut, De La Soul is still one of rap's most inviting acts, and remain quite experimental and unpredictable. *De La Soul Is Dead* is less lighthearted than *Three Feet High and Rising,* but offerings like "Oodles of O's" and "Pease Porridge" make it clear that the group can still be enjoyably quirky and eccentric. One song that definitely isn't amusing is "Millie Pulled a Pistol on Santa," an unsettling commentary on child molestation that cuts like a knife without preaching. Like the first album, *De La Soul Is Dead* is a very abstract and cerebral effort that requires several listenings to be fully appreciated. *—Alex Henderson*

Buhloone Mindstate / Sep. 21, 1993 / Tommy Boy ✦✦✦✦
Continually trying to live up the revolution that was their debut, *Buhloone Mindstate* is a return to Daisy Age positive vibes. The beats are big, the samples are fresh, and the melodies are enticing. While the first two albums featured intros and sidelights along the way, *Buhloone Mindstate* has only fifteen tracks (eleven songs). With help from friends Guru, Maceo Parker, and Biz Markie, De La Soul approaches the perfection of *3 Feet High and Rising,* if not the initial effect. *—John Bush*

Stakes Is High / Jul. 2, 1996 / Tommy Boy ✦✦✦

Art Official Intelligence: Mosaic Thump / Aug. 8, 2000 / Tommy Boy ✦✦

Digable Planets

f. 1991
Group / Jazz-Rap, Alternative Rap, Urban
Though they were not the first to synthesize jazz and hip-hop, Digable Planets epitomized the laidback charm of jazz hipsters better than any group before or since. The trio's 1993 debut album *Reachin' (A New Refutation of Time and Space)* was a mellow ride packed with samples from Art Blakey, Sonny Rollins, and Curtis Mayfield, and the single "Rebirth of Slick (Cool like Dat)" became a Top 20 pop hit. After embarking on an ambitious tour which included several live musicians, the Planets returned in late 1994 with their best album yet. *Blowout Comb* continued the group's jazz-rap fusion, but also saw them branching out to

embrace the old-school sound of the street as well. Much stronger than its predecessor, it used fewer samples and even included several solos; with no strong single to carry it, however, *Blowout Comb* sold less well than *Reachin'*. —*John Bush*

- **Reachin' (A New Refutation of Time and Space)** / Sep. 27, 1993 / Pendulum ♦♦♦♦♦

Blowout Comb / Oct. 18, 1994 / Pendulum ♦♦♦♦♦

Digital Underground

f. 1987, **db.** 1996

Group / West Coast Rap, Alternative Rap, Hip-Hop

Formed in 1987 by Shock-G (b. Gregory Jacobs), Oakland's Digital Underground built most of their music from sampled Parliament-Funkadelic records, crafting a bizarre, funky homage. They also developed a similarly weird sense of style and humor, highlighted by Shock-G's outrageous costumes, and the whole band's parade of alter egos. Of all these alter egos, Shock-G's Humpty Hump—a ridiculous figure with a Groucho Marx nose and glasses, and a goofy, stuttering voice—was the most famous, since he was immortalized on their loopy breakthrough single, "The Humpty Dance." Their 1990 debut *Sex Packets* was a platinum-selling hit, and while they never scaled such commercial heights ever again, their role in popularizing George Clinton's elastic funk made them one of the most important hip-hop groups of their era. Over the course of their career, Digital Underground featured numerous members, but throughout it all, Shock-G remained at its core. Early 1991's *This Is an EP Release* was their first recording to feature Tupac Shakur; it went gold and set the stage for their second album, *Sons of the P*, which was released that fall. On the strength of the gold single "Kiss You Back," *Sons of the P* also went gold, but it received criticism for its similarity to *Sex Packets*. By the time Digital Underground delivered its third album *The Body Hat Syndrome* in late 1993, hip-hop had become dominated by gangsta rap, particularly the drawling G-funk of Dr. Dre, which ironically was heavily indebted to George Clinton. Consequently, their fan base diminished significantly, and *The Body Hat Syndrome* disappeared shortly after its release. Nearly three years later, Digital Underground returned with *Future Rhythm*, which spent a mere three weeks on the charts; *Who Got the Gravy?* followed in 1998. —*Stephen Thomas Erlewine*

★ **Sex Packets** / Jan. 1990 / Tommy Boy ♦♦♦♦♦
With their debut album *Sex Packets*, Digital Underground kickstarted the Parliament/Funkadelic obsessions that dominated the hip-hop world of the early '90s. Digital Underground essentially created a full-length tribute to George Clinton's warped fantasy world, taking both the elastic bass lines and the goofy, surreal sense of humor and adopting it to their own purposes. With their ridiculous sense of humor and endless, loping synth-laced grooves, the two hit singles, "The Humpty Dance" and "Doowutchyalike," seem to tell the whole story, but that's not the case. Within the album tracks of *Sex Packets* are jazzy experiments, hardcore funk, and loads of innovative rhymes and grooves that set the pace much of the music followed. Furthermore, the Underground has a good-natured, welcoming sense of humor that infuses everything on *Sex Packets*, particularly the tongue-in-cheek sci-fi mini-opera that comprises the title track. Although they made some musical innovations on their two subsequent albums, Digital Underground never made an album as consistently engaging as their debut. —*Stephen Thomas Erlewine*

This Is an EP Release / Feb. 1990 / Tommy Boy ♦♦♦

Sons of the P / Oct. 15, 1991 / Tommy Boy ♦♦♦♦♦

The Body Hat Syndrome / Oct. 5, 1993 / Tommy Boy ♦♦♦

Future Rhythm / Jun. 1996 / Radikal ♦♦

Who Got the Gravy? / Sep. 8, 1998 / Interscope ♦♦♦♦

DJ Jazzy Jeff & The Fresh Prince

Group / Pop-Rap, Urban, Hip-Hop

If you're looking for bubblegum rap, these guys are your best bet. The Prince spins his teen-suburban tales in a pleasant, if facile fashion, and Jeff isn't bad on the turntable. Don't look for anything gritty or street-smart: when Jeff boasts that he can beat Mike Tyson, that's about as menacing as it gets. The Fresh Prince starred in the early-'90s TV sitcom, *The Fresh Prince of Bel Air*. Will Smith, the "Fresh Prince" part of the team, greatly expanded his horizons in the '90s. He appeared in the films *Six Degrees of Separation* and *Bad Boys*, and also tried to expand his hip-hop horizons enough to offset the talk that his raps had become hopelessy whitebread and irrelevant. *Homebase* in 1991 included "Dog Is a Dog" and the Top Ten pop hit "Summertime," with Smith's rap done in a leaner, harder fashion even if the lyrics were pretty much family hour. But by *Code Red* in 1993 it seemed Smith had made peace with his image and was back to laid back, pop-oriented material such as "Boom! Shake the Room," "I Wanna Rock," and "Can't Wait to Be with You" which had a guest stint from Christopher Williams. A *Greatest Hits* collection followed in 1998. —*John Floyd*

- **Greatest Hits** / Apr. 28, 1998 / Jive ♦♦♦♦♦
DJ Jazzy Jeff & the Fresh Prince actually turned out better albums than many of their pop-rap contemporaries, but like their peers, they excelled at singles, not albums. That's what makes the appearance of *Greatest Hits* welcome. Although it has its flaws—the sublime "Summertime" is here twice, but only as an "Extended Club Mix" and a "'98 remix"—it remains an excellent summation of their career, boasting such hits as "Girls Ain't Nothing But Trouble," "I Think I Can Beat Mike Tyson," "Parents Just Don't Understand," "Boom! Shake the Room," "Ring My Bell," "A Nightmare On My Street," and, as a bonus, Will Smith's 1997 solo hit "Men in Black." —*Stephen Thomas Erlewine*

DMX (Earl Simmons)

b. Dec. 18, 197?

Vocals / Hardcore Rap, East Coast Rap, Gangsta Rap, Hip-Hop

It's obvious that hip-hop has finally come into its own when one of its most respected rappers (among all kinds of fans) is also one of its best-selling artists, and a successful crossover act to rock fans as well. DMX built an excellent reputation in the rap game, working the fragile territory between intense, metaphysical lyrical concerns and his image as a canine-obsessed personality who often uses a backing track to bark assent to his own raps. All this from a tremendously successful chart act, whose first three albums debuted at number one and sold well over ten million records in just a year and a half. With Nas and Jay-Z (both of whom also made it on an artistic and commercial level), DMX was the kingpin of hip-hop in the years after the twin giants, Biggie and 2Pac, were gunned down.

A rough-toned Yonkers MC who debuted with hometown friends the Lox on a DJ Clue mix-tape, DMX hit the big time in early 1998 when his single "Get at Me Dog" became a club and radio smash. The rapper had first appeared seven years earlier however, in an "Unsigned Hype" column by *The Source* back in 1991. He was signed to Columbia a few years later, but the deal fell through before recording had even begun. DMX guested on tracks by LL Cool J, Mase, and Mic Geronimo (among others), then signed to Def Jam in 1997. His debut album *It's Dark and Hell Is Hot* debuted at number one in May 1998, and eventually sold platinum four times over. *Flesh of My Flesh, Blood of My Blood* followed just six months later (also debuting at the top), and in late 1999 DMX returned with *... And Then There Was X*. Once again, he entered the charts at number one. —*John Bush*

- **It's Dark and Hell Is Hot** / May 12, 1998 / Def Jam ♦♦♦♦
A startling debut, *It's Dark and Hell Is Hot* catapulted DMX to instantaneous icon status. Before even listening to the album, DMX's persona pervades via the album title and the cover art. And as one song succeeds another, it quickly becomes evident that DMX's most impressive talent isn't so much his lyrics, or his flow, or his songwriting, or his producers; these are all impressive, no doubt, but it is his dramatic stance as the ideological zenith of urban manhood that makes his music so potent. It's no coincidence that DMX stands tattooed and shirtless on his album cover with a grim expression and high-held face—it's all part of his well-crafted persona. And he spends the entirety of this album theatrically illustrating this dramatic persona. On "Intro," he introduces himself via an extended monologue that seems more of an imposing threat than an introduction. Next comes "Ruff Ryders' Anthem," a simple yet powerful summation of his ethic, followed by one song after another that similarly explores DMX's diametric world of dogs and bitches, heaven and hell, respect and pity, power and weakness, and so on. Not only is this persona crafted with perfection, but it's also accompanied by a myriad of talents: DMX's rousing lyrics, aggressive flow, sincere delivery, and producers Swizz Beatz and Dame Grease's inventive beats are all dazzling. Though he would quickly dilute himself with succeeding albums, DMX is at his peak here, succinctly showcasing one of rap's most well-crafted personas ever. —*Jason Birchmeier*

Flesh of My Flesh, Blood of My Blood / Dec. 15, 1998 / Def Jam ♦♦♦♦
On the heels of his multi-platinum debut *It's Dark and Hell Is Hot*, DMX unleashed his dogs again on an album overflowing with raw energy and spiritual catharsis. The irascible Yonkers MC, 27 at the time of this recording, continues the Ruff Ryder legacy on this follow-up release. DMX's canine split-personality flow is like none other, not only rhyming over tracks, but barking expression over explosive beats. Production here—by Swizz Beats, PK, DJ Shok, Dame Grease—is mostly stripped-down, pure high-tech drum machine and synthesizer combinations that are sure to inspire emotional and adrenal responses in listeners. Although DMX is no new jack, he is a part of a no-frills new breed of MCs that hold nothing back on the microphone; emphasis is on emotion rather than on wordbending. Standout cuts include "Blackout," with guest appearances from fellow hip-hop heavyweights the Lox and Jay-Z; "Coming From," a duet with the queen of hip-hop/R&B, Mary J. Blige, which stuns the ears with a haunting piano loop; "The Omen," a bout with the devil featuring the demonic Marilyn Manson on the hook; and the opening cut on Side B, "Slippin'," an introspective look inside DMX's struggle to stay on top of his art while dealing with the perils of his reality.

This is a very spiritual album, a testimony to one artist's struggle with the manifestations of good and evil. The final cut, "Ready to Meet Him," a conversation between DMX and his god, punctuates this realness. —*Michael Di Bella*

And Then There Was X / Dec. 21, 1999 / Def Jam ♦♦♦♦

The D.O.C.

Vocals / West Coast Rap, Gangsta Rap

After the release of his debut album, the career of Texas-born rapper the D.O.C. was shattered by a car crash that almost took his life. Although he could no longer rap like he used to, his former producer Dr. Dre featured the rapper on his groundbreaking album *The Chronic*, which built on the foundation laid by the D.O.C.'s *No One Can Do It Better;* he was also featured on Snoop Doggy Dogg's *Doggystyle*. The D.O.C. returned in early 1996 with *Helter Skelter*, his first album in nearly seven years. The album received mixed reviews and failed to earn a large audience, leaving the charts a few months after its release. —*Stephen Thomas Erlewine*

★ **No One Can Do It Better** / 1989 / Ruthless ♦♦♦♦♦
Despite the D.O.C.'s connection to the members of N.W.A.—including its producer, Dr. Dre and Ruthless Records' founder, the late Eazy-E—not a trace of gangsta rap is to be found on the Dallas rapper's debut album, *No One Can Do It Better*. N.W.A.'s influence on this enjoyable, though not remarkable, disc is musical rather than lyrical. Avoiding social or political commentary, the D.O.C. devotes himself almost entirely to rap's time-honored tradition of boasting. What makes this album come alive is his strong technique and Dre's imaginative production. At a time when so many East Coast rappers were content to sample James Brown over and over—often sounding tired and clichéd in the process—Dre took a much more mu-

sical, though equally aggressive approach, emphasizing melody and harmony as well as beats. On *No One*, everything from reggae to heavy metal is fair game for Dre and the D.O.C. This album was still burning up the charts when a car crash almost killed the D.O.C., greatly hindering his rapping abilities. *—Alex Henderson*

Helter Skelter / Jan. 23, 1996 / Giant ✦✦✦

Dr. Dre (Andre Young)

b. Feb. 18, 1965

Vocals, Keyboards, Producer / West Coast Rap, G-Funk, Gangsta Rap

More than any other rapper, Dr. Dre was responsible for moving away from the avant-noise and political stance of Public Enemy and Boogie Down Productions, as well as the party vibes of old school rap. Instead, Dre pioneered gangsta rap and his own variation of the sound, G-Funk. BDP's early albums were hardcore but cautionary tales of the criminal mind, but Dre's records with N.W.A. celebrated the hedonistic, amoralistic side of gang life. Dre was never much of a rapper—his rhymes were simple and his delivery was slow and clumsy—but as a producer, he was extraordinary. With N.W.A. he melded the noise collages of the Bomb Squad with funky rhythms. On his own, he reworked George Clinton's elastic funk into the self-styled G-Funk, a slow-rolling variation that relied more on sound than content. When he left N.W.A. in 1992, he founded Death Row Records with Suge Knight, and the label quickly became the dominant force in mid-'90s hip-hop thanks to his debut, *The Chronic*. Soon, most rap records imitated its sound, and his productions for Snoop Doggy Dogg, Warren G, and Blackstreet were massive hits. For nearly four years, G-funk dominated hip-hop, and Dre had enough sense to abandon it and Death Row just before the whole empire collapsed in late 1996. Dre retaliated by forming a new company, Aftermath, and while it was initially slow getting started, his bold moves forward earned critical respect. *—Stephen Thomas Erlewine*

★ **The Chronic** / Dec. 15, 1992 / Death Row ✦✦✦✦✦

With its stylish, sonically detailed production, Dr. Dre's 1992 solo debut *The Chronic* transformed the entire sound of West Coast rap. Here Dre established his patented G-funk sound: fat, blunted Parliament-Funkadelic beats, soulful backing vocals, and live instruments in the rolling bass lines and whiny synths. What's impressive is that Dre crafts tighter singles than his inspiration George Clinton—he's just as effortlessly funky, and he has a better feel for a hook, a knack that improbably landed gangsta rap on the pop charts. But none of *The Chronic's* legions of imitators were as rich in personality, and that's due in large part to Dre's monumental discovery, Snoop Doggy Dogg. Snoop livens up every track he touches, sometimes just by joining in the chorus—and if *The Chronic* has a flaw, it's that his relative absence from the second half slows the momentum. There was nothing in rap quite like Snoop's singsong, lazy drawl (as it's invariably described), and since Dre's true forte is the producer's chair, Snoop is the signature voice. He sounds utterly unaffected by anything, no matter how extreme, which sets the tone for the album's misogyny, homophobia, and violence. The Rodney King riots are unequivocally celebrated, but the war wasn't just on the streets; Dre enlists his numerous guests in feuds with rivals and ex-bandmates. Yet *The Chronic* is first and foremost a party album, rooted not only in '70s funk and soul, but also that era's blue party comedy, particularly Dolemite. Its comic song intros and skits became prerequisites for rap albums seeking to duplicate its cinematic flow; plus, Snoop and Dre's terrific chemistry ensures that even their foulest insults are cleverly turned. That framework makes *The Chronic* both unreal and all too real, a cartoon and a snapshot. No matter how controversial, it remains one of the greatest and most influential hip-hop albums of all time. *—Steve Huey*

First Round Knock Out / May 21, 1996 / Triple X ✦

Dr. Dre Presents the Aftermath / Nov. 26, 1996 / Aftermath/Interscope ✦✦✦

2001 / Nov. 16, 1999 / Aftermath/Interscope ✦✦✦✦

The Slim Shady LP announced not only Eminem's arrival, but it established that his producer Dr. Dre was anything but passé, thereby raising expectations for *2001*, the long-anticipated sequel to *The Chronic*. It suggested that *2001* wouldn't simply be recycled *Chronic*, and, musically speaking, that's more or less true. He's pushed himself hard, finding new variations in the formula by adding ominous strings, soulful vocals, and reggae, resulting in fairly interesting recontextualizations. Padded out to 22 tracks, *2001* isn't as consistent or striking as *Slim Shady*, but the music is always brimming with character. If only the same could be said about the rappers! Why does a producer as original as Dre work with such pedestrian rappers? Perhaps it's to ensure his control over the project, or to mask his own shortcomings as an MC, but the album suffers considerably as a result. Out of all the other rappers on *2001*, only Snoop and Eminem—Dre's two great protégés—have character and while Eminem's jokiness still is unpredictable, Snoop sounds nearly as tired as the second-rate rappers. The only difference is, there's pleasure in hearing Snoop's style, while the rest sound staid. That's the major problem with *2001:* lyrically and thematically, it's nothing but gangsta clichés. Scratch that, it's über-gangsta, blown up so large that it feels like a parody. Song after song, there's a never-ending litany of violence, drugs, pussy, bitches, dope, guns, and gangsters. After a full decade of this, it takes real effort to get outraged at this stuff, so chances are, you'll shut out the words and groove along since, sonically, this is first-rate, straight-up gangsta. Still, no matter how much fun you may have, it's hard not to shake the feeling that this is cheap, not lasting, fun. *—Stephen Thomas Erlewine*

Dr. Octagon (Keith Thornton)

Vocals / Underground Rap, Electronica, Trip-Hop, Hip-Hop

After single-handedly redefining "warped" as the mind and mouth behind the Bronx-based Ultramagnetic MCs, "Kool" Keith Thornton headed for the outer reaches of the stratosphere with this solo project. A one-time psychiatric patient at Bellevue, Keith's lyrical thematics are as free-flowing here as they ever were with the NY trio, connecting up complex meters with fierce, layers-deep metaphors and veiled criticisms of those who "water down the sound that comes from the ghetto." The debut Octagon single, "Earth People," was quietly released in late 1995 on the San Francisco-based Bulk Recordings, and the track spread like wildfire through the hip-hop underground, as did the subsequent self-titled full-length released the following year. *Dr. Octagon's* left field fusion of sound collage, fierce turntable work, and bizarre, impressionistic rapping found audiences in the most unlikely of places, from hard-core hip-hop heads to jaded rock critics. Although a somewhat sophomoric preoccupation with body parts and scatology tends to dominate the album, Keith's complex weave of associations and shifting references is quite often amazing in its intricacy. By 1999 however, Keith had "killed off" Dr. Octagon and released one album as Kool Keith (*Black Elvis/Lost in Space*) and one as Dr. Dooom (*First Come, First Served*). *—Sean Cooper*

● **Dr. Octagonecologyst [Dr. Octagon]** / May 6, 1996 / DreamWorks ✦✦✦✦✦

Ultramagnetic MC Kool Keith's best-known solo pseudonym is a psychotic gynecologist with a soft spot for porn samples and lazy, textured production by DJs Automator and Shadow. If the slightly misogynistic lyrics get occasionally tedious, most of the rest of this album is next-style, James-Joyce-on-acid-in-the-medical-textbook-section hip-hop, with expert scratches by DJ Q-Bert and consistently inventive (if somewhat lo-fi) production. Originally released on underground hip-hop imprint Bulk Recordings, *Dr. Octagon* was picked up for U.K. release by trip-hop label Mo'Wax (an instrumental version of the album, *Instrumentalyst* was also issued by the label toward the end of the year). Confusingly, the album was then issued again by Geffen sublabel Dreamworks (with whom Keith signed in 1997), adding a few new tracks. *—Sean Cooper*

Dream Warriors

Group / Old School Rap, Jazz-Rap

Toronto rappers King Lou and Capital Q form Dream Warriors, a crew that pioneered the fusion of jazz and hip-hop. *—Stephen Thomas Erlewine*

● **Anthology: A Decade of Hits 1988-1998** / Jun. 22, 1999 / Priority ✦✦✦✦✦

Though often neglected within the jazz-rap community during their brief, two-album run, Dream Warriors recorded a legion of interesting tracks, and *Anthology* does a better job than either of those albums in summarizing what made them so great. Featuring two versions of their nearest thing to a hit, "My Definition of a Boombastic Jazz Style," the album also scores with a few collaboration tracks including others in the jazz-rap royalty—"It's a Project Thing" with DJ Premier, "I've Lost My Ignorance" with Premier and Guru (i.e. Gang Starr), and "Tricycles and Kittens" with Digable Planets. Elsewhere, Dream Warriors salute their Caribbean influences with tracks like "Sound Clash" with Beenie Man and "Dem No Ready" with General Degree. It's a great look at one of the better hip-hop groups of the '90s. *—Keith Farley*

Eazy-E (Eric Wright)

b. Sep. 7, 1964, Compton, CA, **d.** Mar. 26, 1995

Vocals / Dirty Rap, West Coast Rap, Hardcore Rap, Gangsta Rap

After leaving N.W.A., rapper Eazy-E led a career that was filled with controversy and was considerably successful commercially, even if it never matched the creativity of his previous band. Eazy-E began his solo career in 1988 with *Eazy-Duz-It;* it was his only full-length album.

Eazy-E left N.W.A. after the 1991's *Niggaz4Life* hit the top of the charts. The break-up of N.W.A. was extremely bitter and Eazy in particular earned the wrath of Dr. Dre. Dre and Eazy carried out their feud on record throughout the early '90s.

Even though he released several hit EPs, Eazy's career was in decline when he announced he was suffering from AIDS in early March of 1995; he only learned that he had the disease in the previous month. Three weeks later, the rapper died on March 26, 1995—he was 31 years old. *—Stephen Thomas Erlewine*

● **Eternal E** / Dec. 1995 / Ruthless/Priority ✦✦✦✦

During his short career, Eazy-E only released one full-length album but managed to release a number of tracks on EPs and with N.W.A.; most of the notorious rapper's best moments from these releases are included here on *Eternal E*, which is essentially a greatest-hits collection. Unfortunately, as great as it is to hear some of Eazy-E's best moments—"Boyz-N-the Hood," "8 Ball," "Eazy-Duz-It," "Only If You Want It"—there are several unacceptable exceptions. Most notably, the material from his most realized moment, *It's On (Dr. Dre) 187um Killa*, is nowhere to be found. Furthermore, the majority of his solo material pales in comparison to his work with N.W.A. on tracks such as "Fuck the Police" and "100 Miles and Runnin'," and this collection sadly only features four N.W.A. songs. So it's almost ironic that this greatest-hits collection ignores his greatest hits (most likely for the licensing costs required to secure the absent material). It would also be nice to have some of Eazy-E's posthumously released material from the *Str8 off tha Streetz of Muthaphukkin Compton* sessions included here. So even though this album is still the best introduction to his canon of work for novices, it functions poorly as a comprehensive representation of Eazy-E's short career, as it ignores much of his best work. *—Jason Birchmeier*

Missy Misdemeanor Elliott (Melissa Elliott)

b. Portsmouth, VA

Vocals / Alternative Rap, Urban, Hip-Hop

A female jack-of-all-trades in the hip-hop world, Missy Misdemeanor Elliot rode into the rap mainstream by the usual route for female MCs (guesting on every track in sight) but proved to be so much more than a rapper: a prolific songwriter, a great R&B singer, director of her own videos, and an astute businesswoman who wrangled an entire sub-label out of her initial Elektra Records deal. She first hooked up with a female R&B group called Sista; though Elliott wrote most of the material for their debut album, it went nowhere and they broke up soon after. Elliott continued to write songs, though, and placed one with former *Cosby Show* sprite Raven-Symone. She also began appearing on several popular singles, like SWV's "Can We," Aaliyah's "If Your Girl Only Knew," and a remix of Gina Thompson's "The Things You Do." Granted her own record deal by 1996, Elliott responded with *Supa Dupa Fly*, which featured much of her own songwriting and production by her friend Timbaland. The album peaked at number three on the album charts, and went platinum soon after its release. The duo teamed up again for 1999's *Da Real World*. —*John Bush*

- **Supa Dupa Fly** / Jul. 15, 1997 / The Gold Mind/EastWest/EEG ✦✦✦✦✦

On her debut album, *Supa Dupa Fly*, Missy "Misdemeanor" Elliott skillfully blends classic soul with modern R&B and street hip-hop rhythms. It's funky and melodic, with strong song sense and startlingly fresh production courtesy of Elliott and her partner, Timbaland. It's a refreshingly ambitious and successful urban R&B debut that reveals the weaknesses of her contemporaries as much as it emphasizes her strengths. —*Leo Stanley*

Da Real World / Jun. 22, 1999 / Elektra ✦✦✦✦

It's really not that difficult to hurdle the sophomore blues provided that you're an excellent songwriter and performer, that you have the same, equally excellent producer behind the scenes who contributed to the first album, and most importantly, that you haven't tampered with the hit- making formula from the first. Thankfully, *Da Real World* is clearly a Missy Elliott album in most respects, with Timbaland's previously trademarked, futuristic-breakbeat production smarts laced throughout. The church-going Elliott has often remarked that she wishes she didn't need profanity to get attention, and the album accordingly includes satirical nods to other clichéd notions of hip-hop—the single "She's a Bitch" is the best example, wherein Elliott re-appropriates the insult to refer to strong females. She also takes on the cartoonish Eminem for "Bus a Rhyme," a track that turns out to be one of the best on the album. Da Brat and Aaliyah make repeat appearances, and Redman and Outkast's Big Boi also contribute to this excellent follow-up. —*Keith Farley*

Eminem (Marshall Mathers)

b. Kansas City, MO

Vocals / Underground Rap, West Coast Rap, Hardcore Rap, Gangsta Rap, Hip-Hop

A protege of Dr. Dre, rapper Eminem was born Marshall Mathers in St. Joseph, MO (near Kansas City), spending the better part of his impoverished childhood shuttling back and forth between his hometown and the city of Detroit. Initially attracted to rap as a teen, Eminem began performing at age 14, later earning notoriety as a member of the Motor City duo Soul Intent. He made his solo debut in 1996 with the independent release *Infinite*, soon followed by the *Slim Shady* EP; both records made a huge splash in the hip-hop underground, earning notice not only for Eminem's exaggerated, nasal-voiced rapping style but also for his skin color, with many quarters dubbing him the music's next "great white hope." According to legend, Dr. Dre discovered his demo tape on the floor of Interscope label chief Jimmy Iovine's garage, although it was not until Eminem took second place in the freestyle category at 1997's Rap Olympics MC battle in Los Angeles that Dre agreed to sign him. The best-selling *Slim Shady LP* followed in early 1999, scoring a massive hit with the single and video "My Name Is," plus a popular follow-up in "Guilty Conscience"; over the next year, the album went triple platinum. With such wide exposure, controversy ensued over the album's content, with some harshly criticizing its cartoonish, graphic violence; others praised its edginess and surreal humor, as well as Eminem's own undeniable lyrical skills and Dre's inventive production. In between albums, Eminem appeared on Dre's *Dr. Dre 2001*, with his contributions providing some of the record's liveliest moments. *The Marshall Mathers LP* appeared in the summer of 2000, moving close to two million copies in its first week of release on its way to becoming the fastest-selling rap album of all time. —*Jason Ankeny*

- **The Slim Shady LP** / Feb. 23, 1999 / Interscope ✦✦✦✦✦

In all the press surrounding the release of Eminem's debut *The Slim Shady LP*, journalists, critics, and Em himself went out of the way to clarify that the songs on the record were not autobiographical—he was merely playing a corrupt character called Slim Shady. Such a practice is common in hip-hop, but it seems disingenuous coming from the mouth of Marshall Mathers, a white-trash kid from the streets of Detroit whose fictional creation is a white-trash kid from the streets of Detroit. The line between fact and fiction seems a little blurry, and it would be more so if Eminem's lyrics weren't ridiculous, violent fantasies. That doesn't quite excuse the endless dreams of rape, murder, and dope that provide the core of *The Slim Shady LP*, but the cartoonish exaggerations do explain why certain journalists were eager to embrace the record as an inspired, surrealistic parody of Jerry Springer-fueled pop-culture and gangsta rap. It also helps that Eminem was endorsed by Dr. Dre, not only because he provides a strong, Beasties-meets-Wu-meets-Dr. Octagon musical backdrop, but because his presence is almost code, proving that Mathers is not a racist. Eminem is clearly a gifted rapper, twisting and turning his words with ease, knowing how to accentuate the strengths of the music with the rhythm of his rhymes. Still, that doesn't erase the uneasiness that his grotesque caricatures and stories leave behind. For many discerning listeners—especially the countless teens who have been raised on a diet of *WWF, Faces of Death*, slasher films, porn, and No Limit records—it's clear that this is all intended as a joke. That may be, but it's hard to escape the impression that if a Black artist had released *The Slim Shady LP*, it wouldn't have been embraced as satire. —*Stephen Thomas Erlewine*

The Marshall Mathers LP / May 23, 2000 / Interscope ✦✦✦✦✦

It's hard to know what to make of Eminem, even if you know that half of what he says is sincere and half is a put-on; the trick is realizing that there's truth in the joke, and vice versa. Many dismissed his considerable skills as a rapper and social satirist because the vulgarity and gross-out humor on *The Slim Shady LP* were too detailed for some to believe that it was anything *but* real. To Eminem's credit, he decided to exploit that confusion on his masterful second record, *The Marshall Mathers LP*. Eminem is all about blurring the distinction between reality and fiction, humor and horror, satire and documentary, so it makes perfect sense that *The Marshall Mathers LP* is no more or no less "real" than *The Slim Shady LP*. It is, however, a fairly brilliant expansion of his debut, turning his spare, menacing hip-hop into a hyper-surreal, wittily disturbing thrill ride. It's both funnier and darker than his debut, and Eminem's writing is so sharp and clever that the jokes cut as deeply as the explorations of his ruptured psyche. The production is nearly as evocative as the raps, with liquid bass lines, stuttering rhythms, slight sound effects, and spacious soundscapes. There may not be overpowering hooks on every track, but the album works as a whole, always drawing the listener in. But, once you're in, Eminem doesn't care if you understand exactly where he's at, and he doesn't offer any apologies if you can't sort the fact from the fiction. As an artist, he's supposed to create his own world, and with this terrific second effort, he certainly has. It may be a world that is as infuriating as it is intriguing, but it is without question his own, which is far more than most of his peers are able to accomplish at the dawn of a new millennium. —*Stephen Thomas Erlewine*

EPMD

f. 1987

Group / Hardcore Rap, East Coast Rap

On the surface, Erick Sermon and Parrish Smith had little to recommend themselves—sample-reliant production and a monotone rapping style—but their recordings as EPMD were among the best in hip-hop's underground during the late '80s and early '90s. Over the course of four albums (from the 1988 classic *Strictly Business* to 1992's *Business Never Personal*), they rarely varied from two themes, dissing sucker MCs and recounting sexual exploits. But a closer look reveals that the duo's rhymes were nothing less than incredible, simply under-valued because of their lack of intonation during delivery. EPMD also had a feel for a good groove, and created numerous hip-hop classics, including "It's My Thing," "You Gots to Chill," and "Rampage." —*John Bush*

★ **Strictly Business** / 1988 / Priority ✦✦✦✦✦

Erick Sermon is a classic example of using a disadvantage to one's advantage. Having a lisp and a slight speech impediment didn't prevent Sermon from pursuing a career as a rapper—and in fact, his lisp caught on in a big way and was a key element of EPMD's distinctive sound. In contrast to the hyper, forceful tendencies of many rappers, Erick and partner Parrish Smith's style of rapping is relaxed and deadpan. On *Strictly Business*, their gold debut album, the Long Islanders aren't very substantial lyrically—all they talk about is how strong their rapping skills are and how pathetic sucker MCs are. But their sound was so unique, fresh, and distinctive that such classics as "You Gots to Chill," "Strictly Business," and "The Steve Martin" proved impossible to resist. —*Alex Henderson*

Unfinished Business / 1989 / Priority ✦✦✦✦✦

EPMD avoided the dreaded sophomore curse and kept its artistic momentum going on its second album, *Unfinished Business*. Once again, the duo triumphed by going against the flow—when MCs ranging from Public Enemy to Sir Mix-A-Lot to N.W.A. weren't hesitating to be abrasive and hyper, EPMD still had a sound that was decidedly relaxed by rap standards. For the most part, EPMD's lyrics aren't exactly profound—boasting and attacking sucker MCs is still their favorite activity. However, Erick and Parrish do challenge themselves a bit lyrically on "You Had Too Much to Drink" (a warning against drunk driving) and "Please Listen to My Demo," which recalls the days when they were struggling. But regardless of subject matter, they keep things exciting by having such an appealing, captivating sound. —*Alex Henderson*

Business as Usual / 1990 / Def Jam ✦✦✦

Business Never Personal / Jul. 28, 1992 / Def Jam ✦✦✦✦✦

EPMD's terse, thick-tongued rapping style was back on point with their fourth album. Although behind the scenes turmoil finally split Erick Sermon and Parrish Smith up, they were together and cooking on this 1992 record. They scored their final signature single with "Crossover," a dead-on commentary directed at rappers putting pop hopes ahead of hip-hop values. "Headbanger" and "Can't Hear Nothing But The Music" were other sterling tracks from their last great album. —*Ron Wynn*

Back in Business / Sep. 16, 1997 / Def Jam ✦✦✦

Out of Business / Jun. 29, 1999 / Def Jam ✦✦✦✦

Greatest Hits / Nov. 23, 1999 / Def Jam ✦✦✦✦✦

Eric B & Rakim

f. 1985, **db.** 1992

Group / East Coast Rap, Hip-Hop

One of rap's most influential acts during the '80s, Eric B & Rakim made the sampling of James Brown records the main source for hip-hop's sound during the late '80s and early '90s, beginning with their stellar debut, *Paid in Full*. While Eric B dazzled listeners with his turntable techniques, Rakim pointed the way toward the easy-rollin' style of the '90s with his laidback raps, though forceful in content. Each of the duo's first three albums achieved gold status, and they even managed the Top Five R&B hit "Friends" in 1989.

While working as a mobile DJ for New York's WBLS during 1985, Eric Barrier met William Griffin, a top MC who had grown up on Long Island. The two began recording together and emerged with "Eric B Is President." The single appeared in 1986 on Harlem's Zakia label, and became a street sensation. Signed to 4th & Broadway the following year, Eric B & Rakim released their debut album, *Paid in Full*. The LP's success led to a contract with Uni/MCA in 1988, and their second album, *Follow the Leader*, was released that year. Two more albums followed, *Let the Rhythm Hit 'Em* (1990) and *Don't Sweat the Technique* (1992), after which the duo broke up. By the mid-'90s, Eric B. had emerged as a solo act on his own 95th Street label. —*John Bush*

★ **Paid in Full** / 1987 / 4th & Broadway ✦✦✦✦✦

The 1987 release of *Paid In Full* marked the arrival of a hip-hop legend, Long Island's own Rakim Allah. With one of the rawest and fiercest deliveries on the microphone, Rakim's voice hit listeners' eardrums from somewhere beyond the clouds. Here was an otherworldly MC whose penetrating lyrics flowed seemingly without effort. This album would be a classic purely on the strength of three of hip-hop's all-time top 50 songs (maybe even top 20): opener "I Ain't No Joke," title cut "Paid In Full," and "Eric B. Is President." Volumes could be written on the legacy and import of these three songs alone. On "I Ain't No Joke," Rakim grabs the listener by the throat and illustrates his mastery of the rhyming craft over a simple James Brown loop produced by Eric B. The other half of the dynamic duo, Eric B. was a master of the minimal beat and one of the first producers to truly scratch the surface of James Brown's work. Eric B. just stripped his beats down and let his partner do his thing, and Rakim shows his appreciation on "Eric B. Is President," a track originally recorded in 1986 along with another entry in the hip-hop canon, "My Melody." "Paid In Full" is the theme the album rests on, outlining one of hip-hop's primary objectives: to get paid and stay paid. However, Eric B. & Rakim sought this goal with originality and superior skills, rather than succumbing to trends or sacrificing their creativity. *Paid In Full* demonstrates the importance of getting paid without diluting one's art; in Eric B. & Rakim's era, anything else was unthinkable. *—Michael Di Bella*

☆ **Follow the Leader** / 1988 / UNI ✦✦✦✦✦
On their second album, Eric B. & Rakim deliver an album that expands on the power of their debut. Taking a cue from the Coldcut remix of "Paid In Full" that became a hit after the release of *Paid In Full, Follow the Leader* has a looser, wilder beat than its predecessor. Eric B. uses the spare, James Brown-influenced grooves that dominated *Paid in Full* as a starting point, adding all kinds of production flourishes that flesh out the funk without watering it down. Not only are Eric B.'s musical accomplishments impressive, but so are Rakim's rhymes, which are more detailed and complex than before, even if his subject matter didn't change much. In short, *Follow the Leader* is the second hip-hop classic Eric B. & Rakim delivered in a row—it captures the duo at the top of their game. *—Leo Stanley*

Let the Rhythm Hit 'Em / May 1990 / MCA ✦✦✦

Don't Sweat the Technique / 1990 / MCA ✦✦✦✦
Starting with their 1986 debut, *Paid in Full,* Eric B. and Rakim earned raves for Eric B's often flawless, judicious productions and Rakim's serious yet relentlessly rhythmic rhyming style. This 1992 album finds the duo picking up from where they left off on 1990's *Let the Rhythm Hit 'Em.* "What's on Your Mind" has Rakim with intents to woo under a bubbling track with an adroit interpolation of D Train's 1983 hit of the same name. That track aside, *Don't Sweat the Technique* has Rakim in bleak spirits as thoughts of combat, revenge, and unfortunate "accidents" are not far from his mind. "Casualties of War" has Rakim as an all-purpose psycho with the unsettling hook, "I get a rush when I see blood and dead bodies on the floor." Although it's supposed to be gripping, the thought of a war-ravaged Rakim with his pistols blazing after hearing a truck backfiring is hilarious. All of *Don't Sweat the Technique* would be more disturbing if it wasn't for the brilliant ear of Eric B. who can cut the tension and exact magic out of a going-nowhere track. Although the lyrics and premise of "What's Going On" aren't extremely sharp, the cracking snare drums and low bass riffs are a perfect compliment to Rakim's delivery. The title track is also jazz influenced, but not as potent as the Simon Law and Mr. Lee's Funky Ginger remixes that don't appear here. Like many albums of this type, *Don't Sweat Technique* ends on tracks of little distinction but it is another strong effort from one of rap's most respected acts. *—Jason Elias*

Everlast (Eric Schrody)

Vocals / Rap-Rock, Hardcore Rap, Alternative Rap
Once best known for his tenure in the rap unit House of Pain, Everlast successfully reinvented himself in 1998 with the best-selling *Whitey Ford Sings the Blues,* a largely acoustic, hip-hop-flavored effort in the genre-crossing mold of Beck. Born Erik Schrody, Everlast first surfaced in Los Angeles as a member of Ice-T's Rhyme Syndicate Cartel, issuing his debut album *Forever Everlasting* in 1990. When the album failed to find an audience, he formed House of Pain with MC Danny Boy and DJ Lethal. By carving out an image which drew heavily on Everlast and Danny Boy's shared Irish heritage, the trio managed to overcome the stereotypes facing white rappers and scored a massive hit with their 1992 single "Jump Around." Their self-titled debut LP also went platinum, but when follow-ups including 1994's *Same as It Ever Was* and 1996's *Truth Crushed to Earth Shall Rise Again* failed to repeat House of Pain's early success, the group disbanded. Everlast then returned to his solo career, but while recording *Whitey Ford Sings the Blues* he suffered a massive cardiac arrest stemming from a congenital defect, resulting in heart bypass surgery and an artificial valve implant. Following his recovery, he completed the album, which appeared in the fall of 1998 to strong commercial notices: hitting the Top Ten, going platinum, and launching the Top 40 single "What It's Like." After appearing on Santana's vaunted comeback album *Supernatural,* Everlast began work on a follow-up with an eclectic group of guest artists. Titled *Eat at Whitey's,* the album was released in late 2000. *—Jason Ankeny*

Forever Everlasting / Mar. 27, 1990 / Warner Brothers ✦✦✦

● **Whitey Ford Sings the Blues** / Sep. 8, 1998 / Tommy Boy ✦✦✦✦✦
Saying that Everlast showed a great deal of artistic growth between his first and second solo albums would be a understatement. While 1989/1990's *Forever Everlasting* was a decent, if uneven, debut, Everlast's second solo album, *Whitey Ford Sings the Blues* is an amazingly eclectic gem that finds him really pushing himself creatively. Between those two albums, Everlast joined and left House of Pain, which evolved into one of the most distinctive rap groups of the 1990s. While Pain's albums thrived on wildness for its own sake, *Whitey Ford* has a much more introspective and serious tone. Everlast, who was born with a heart defect, was in the process of recording the album when he needed life-saving open-heart surgery; in fact, he was lucky that he was around to see *Whitey Ford* completed and released. Though not without its share of hardcore B-boy rap, *Whitey Ford* also finds Everlast playing acoustic guitar, doing some singing and exploring folk-rock, Memphis soul, and heavy metal. As a singer, Everlast has a relaxed style that sounds a bit like Gil Scott-Heron. "Today (Watch Me Shine)," "Ends," and "What It's Like" venture into Neil Young/Bob Dylan territory, while "Hot to Death" is blistering metal with industrial touches. And the plot thickens—on "The Letter," he raps over a jazz-influenced piano. Given how rap's hardcore tends to frown on rappers crossing over to rock, it took guts for Everlast to be so diverse. But it's a good thing that he did, for his risk-taking pays off handsomely on this outstanding release. *—Alex Henderson*

Eat at Whitey's / Oct. 17, 2000 / Tommy Boy ✦✦✦✦

The Fat Boys

f. 1982, Brooklyn, NY
Group / Comedy Rap, Old School Rap, Hip-Hop
One of early rap's most successful acts, the Fat Boys parlayed a combined weight of over 750 pounds into a comic novelty act that sustained them through several albums and hit singles. Originally known as the Disco 3, Brooklynites Mark "Prince Markie Dee" Morales, Damon "Kool Rockski" Wimbley, and Darren "Buff the Human Beat Box" Robinson recorded a series of good-time party anthems and songs humorously exploiting their weight; their first few records were produced by Kurtis Blow and feature fusions of hip-hop with reggae and rock. The Fat Boys hit their commercial peak with 1987's platinum LP *Crushin',* a collection of entertaining party tunes that included a hit collaboration with the Beach Boys, "Wipeout." The group took the opportunity to star in the comedy film *Disorderlies* that year. *Coming Back Hard Again* essentially repeated the formula of *Crushin';* the cover this time was "The Twist (Yo' Twist)," which featured backing from Chubby Checker. However, audience tastes were changing, and the Fat Boys' gimmicky novelty act was quickly becoming passe. Robinson died of a heart attack in December 1995. *—Steve Huey*

● **All Meat No Filler: The Best of Fat Boys** / Mar. 18, 1997 / Rhino ✦✦✦✦✦
All Meat No Filler: The Best of the Fat Boys is an excellent 18-track compilation of all of the Fat Boys' biggest hits, including "Fat Boys," "Human Beat Box," "Jail House Rap," "Can You Feel It," "The Fat Boys Are Back," "Hard Core Reggae," "Failling In Love," "Wipeout" (with the Beach Boys), and "The Twist (Yo, Twist!)" (with Chubby Checker). Although some of the latter-day cuts have aged poorly, the Fat Boys' earliest singles are ground-breaking and timeless records, proving that they weren't merely a novelty act. *—Stephen Thomas Erlewine*

Doug E. Fresh

b. Sep. 17, 1966
Vocals / Old School Rap, Hip-Hop
New Yorker Doug E. Fresh (born Doug E. Davis), got his initial notoriety for being the "human beatbox," able to approximate and imitate a rhythm machine. He had a string of hit singles with his then partner Ricky Dee in the early and mid-'80s, notably "The Show (Oh, My God)" in 1985, which included guest stints from jazz veteran trumpeter Jimmy Owens and synthesizer player Bernard Wright. Fresh had a long absence from the scene after 1988's *The World's Greatest Entertainer* and has just resurfaced with a new release on a small independent label. *—Ron Wynn*

Oh, My God! / 1986 / Reality ✦✦✦✦✦

The World's Greatest Entertainer / 1988 / Reality ✦✦✦✦✦

● **Greatest Hits, Vol. 1** / Aug. 1996 / Bust It ✦✦✦✦✦
Greatest Hits, Vol. 1 collects all of Doug E. Fresh's biggest hit singles—including "La Di Da Di," "Keep Risin' to the Top," and "The Show," adding a couple of new tracks produced by Sean "Puffy" Combs for good measure. It's a concise and entertaining retrospective that sums up his career very well. *—Stephen Thomas Erlewine*

The Fugees

f. 1987
Group / East Coast Rap, Alternative Rap, Hip-Hop
The Fugees translated an intriguing blend of jazz-rap, R&B, and reggae into huge success in the mid-'90s, when their sophomore album *The Score* hit number one on the pop charts and sold over five million copies. The trio formed in the late '80s in the New Jersey area, where Lauryn Hill and Prakazrel Michel ("Pras") attended a local high school and began working together. Michel's cousin Wyclef Jean ("Clef") completed the group, whose debut album, *Blunted on Reality* was quite solid, although it reflected a prevailing gangsta stance that may have been forced by the record label. No matter how pigeonholed the Fugees may have sounded on their debut, the group had obviously asserted their control by the time of their second album, *The Score.* With just as much intelligence as their jazz-rap forebears, the trio also worked with surprisingly straightahead R&B on the soulful hit "Killing Me Softly with His Song." Elsewhere, Clef and Pras sampled doo-wop and covered Bob Marley's "No Woman No Cry," giving the record familiarity for the commercial mainstream, but keeping it real with insightful commentary on their urban surroundings. *The Score* became one of the surprise hits of 1996, making the Fugees one of the most visible rap groups around the world. *—John Bush*

Blunted on Reality / Feb. 1, 1994 / Ruffhouse ✦✦✦

★ **The Score** / Feb. 1996 / RuffHouse ✦✦✦✦✦
An open, yet funky, collage of hip-hop, soul, blues, jazz, and reggae, the Fugees' second album, *The Score,* is a great step forward for the New York trio. On their debut, the group had sketched out a pattern similar to the multi-ethnic, edgy music on *The Score,* but they didn't deliver it with the aurhority that they do here. The Fugees cover Bob Marley's "No Woman, No Cry" and Roberta Flack's "Killing Me Softly," which gives an idea of their range, as well as their intent to carry on the soul/R&B tradition. They pull it off with a surprising amount of style and innovation—with intelligent, gritty lyrics and brave eclecticism, *The Score* simply sounds like few rap records of the mid-'90s. *—Stephen Thomas Erlewine*

Warren G. (Warren Griffin III)

b. Nov. 10, 1971
Vocals / West Coast Rap, G-Funk
Born Warren Griffin III, Warren G. exploded out of the burgeoning Long Beach rap scene in 1994 with the smash single "Regulate," a duet with longtime friend Nate Dogg, and its accompanying album, *Regulate… G Funk Era.* As a teenager, he and his friends Nate Dogg and future superstar Snoop Dogg formed a rap group called $213, after their area code. When Snoop cut the demo "Super Duper Snooper," G. played it for his half-brother, Dr. Dre, who

invited all three to his studio and wound up collaborating with Snoop on *The Chronic;* while G. also made several contributions, he opted to develop his talents mostly outside of Dre's shadow. Eventually G. recorded his debut album for Death Row. "Regulate" appeared on the *Above the Rim* soundtrack and was released as a single. It quickly became a massive hit, peaking at number 2 on the *Billboard* charts and pushing the album up to the same position. Warren G. took nearly three years to complete his second album, returning in the spring of 1997 with *Take a Look Over Your Shoulder,* which was greeted with decidedly mixed reviews and weak sales. *—Steve Huey*

● **Regulate . . . G Funk Era** / Jun. 7, 1994 / Def Jam ✦✦✦✦
Dr. Dre's little brother Warren G. proved that he was a talent in his own right with his debut record, *Regulate . . . G Funk Era.* With his music's slow, bass-heavy grooves and layers of synthesizers, Warren G. does sound slightly similar to his older brother, but his album is more relaxed. But that doesn't mean he's soft. In fact, his casual mix of singing and speaking is often more evocative than Dre's standard thundering beats and whining keyboards. Plus, Warren G.'s sly, direct lyrics manage to convey the tragedy of the ghetto. *—Stephen Thomas Erlewine*

Take a Look Over Your Shoulder / Mar. 25, 1997 / Def Jam ✦✦

I Want It All / Oct. 12, 1999 / Restless ✦✦✦✦

Gang Starr

f. 1988
Group / Jazz-Rap, East Coast Rap, Hip-Hop
These Brooklyn rappers are near the top among hip-hop artists influenced by and interested in jazz. In 1989, longtime jazz and Black-pop publicist Elliot Horne placed a poem he wrote with them, and the group used it as the foundation for the song "Jazz Music" on their debut *No More Mr. Nice Guy.* That track was later included on the soundtrack for Spike Lee's *Mo' Better Blues.* The group has also used saxophonist and *Tonight Show* bandleader Branford Marsalis and included acoustic as well as electric instruments on their follow-up release *Step in the Arena.* They've also discussed the jazz/rap connection in such magazines as *The Source* and *The Wire.*

Both Gang Starr and their main man Guru were in the limelight during 1993 and 1994. Guru teamed with old and new jazz types Donald Byrd, Roy Ayers, and Ronnie Foster, as well as vocalist N'Dea Davenport and other guest stars for the session *Jazzmatazz.* He later did some New York club dates with some of the same musicians. Gang Starr issued *Hard to Earn* in March of 1994; it debuted on the *Billboard* R&B charts at number two. After four years of side-projects and inactivity, Gang Starr returned in the spring of 1998 with *Moment of Truth,* and the following year saw the release of the career retrospective *Full Clip. —Ron Wynn*

No More Mr. Nice Guy / 1989 / EMI America ✦✦✦

Step in the Arena / 1991 / Chrysalis ✦✦✦✦✦
This is the album on which DJ Premier and Guru perfected the template that would launch them into underground stardom and a modicum of mainstream success. Guru's deadpan monotone delivery was shockingly different from other early-'90s MCs, many of whom were either substituting charisma for substance or engaging in hardcore "realism" without really commenting on black inner-city life or offering ways to alter the situation for the better. But it is Guru who sounded like the real clarion call of and to the street on *Step in the Arena* ("Why bring ignorance/where we're inviting you to get advancement," he intones on "Form of Intellect"). *Step in the Arena* was the first real mature flowering of his street-wise sagacity. His voice would grow more assured by the next album, but here Guru imparts urban wisdom of a strikingly visible variety. It's easy to allow yourself to get caught up in the fantasy of hardcore rap, but it is somewhat more involving and disorienting to hear truth that avoids exaggeration or glorification. Guru is not easy on any aspect of the inner city, from the "snakes" that exploit the community ("Execution of a Chump") to those that are a product of it ("Just to Get a Rep"), and the result is a surprising but hard-fought compassion ("Who's Gonna Take the Weight?" pleads for the acceptance of responsibility, for not taking the easy path). He seems to have somehow developed a hopefulness out of the bleak surroundings. DJ Premier was already near the top of his game at this early point. His production seems less jazz-fueled on *Step in the Arena* opting more for spare guitar lines and tight beats, as well as his unmistakable vocal cut-up style of scratching for a slightly warped and out-of-phase soundscape. *—Stanton Swihart*

Daily Operation / 1992 / Chrysalis ✦✦✦✦✦
On *Step in the Arena,* DJ Premier and Guru hit upon their mature sound, characterized by spare, live jazz samples, Premier's cut-up scratching, and Guru's direct, unwavering street-wise monotone; but, with *Daily Operation,* the duo made their first masterpiece. From beginning to end, Gang Starr's third full-length album cuts with the force and precision of a machete and serves as an ode to and representation of New York and hip-hop underground culture. The genius of *Daily Operation* is that Guru's microphone skills are perfectly married to the best batch of tracks Premier had ever come up with. Guru has more of a presence than he has ever had, slinking and pacing through each song like a man with things on his mind, ready to go off at any second. Premier's production has an unparalleled edge here. He created the minimalist opening track, "The Place Where We Dwell," out of a two-second drum-solo sample and some scratching, but is also able to turn around and create something as lush and melodic as the jazz-tinged "No Shame in My Game" without ever seeming to be out of his element, making every track of the same sonic mind. For an underground crew, Gang Starr has always had a knack for crafting memorable vocal hooks to go with the expert production, and they multiply both aspects on *Daily Operation.* Every song has some attribute that stamps it indelibly into the listener's head, and it marks the album as one of the finest of the decade, rap or otherwise. *—Stanton Swihart*

Hard to Earn / Mar. 8, 1994 / Chrysalis ✦✦✦✦

Moment of Truth / Mar. 31, 1998 / Noo Trybe/Virgin ✦✦✦

● **Full Clip: A Decade of Gang Starr** / Mar. 23, 1999 / Cooltempo ✦✦✦✦✦
Considering that the only previous hip-hop hits collection to stretch two full CDs came from 2Pac (and only after his death), Gang Starr's *Full Clip* is a surprising release, though it's incredibly welcome. The duo of DJ Premier and Guru has been one of the longest continuous acts on the rap scene, beginning with 1989's *No More Mr. Nice Guy* and a spot on the soundtrack to Spike Lee's 1990 film *Mo' Better Blues.* And as demonstrated by Premier's stunning productions on classic early tracks like "Who's Gonna Take the Weight," "Words I Manifest," and "Just to Get a Rep," Gang Starr hit its stride early, and just kept on hitting peak after peak during the '90s with "Speak Ya Clout," "Code of the Streets," "Tonz 'O' Gunz," and "You Know My Steez." And new tracks, usually the bane of any best-of collection, provide quite a few highlights here—including "Full Clip," "Discipline" (featuring Total), and "All 4 Tha Cah." Also, the set compiles several notable B-sides—"The — Remainz," "Credit Is Due," and "You Know My Steez (Remix)"—as well as soundtrack works like "1/2 & 1/2" (from *Blade*), "Gotta Get Over" (from *Trespass*), and "The Militia II (Remix)" (from *Belly*). Though Guru's monotone raps can grate over the course of two hours, *Full Clip* documents one of the best, most underrated hip-hop groups ever, from their jazzy beginnings into Premier's harder productions from the mid-'90s and beyond. *—John Bush*

Genius (Gary Grice)

b. New York, NY
Vocals / Hardcore Rap, East Coast Rap, Hip-Hop
Inside and outside of the Wu-Tang Clan, the inventive hip-hop supergroup he co-founded, Staten Island, NY native GZA/Genius likes to make his own rules when it comes to his music. GZA/Genius grew up in a large, musically-inclined family that included cousins Ol' Dirty Bastard and RZA; as the eldest of the three, he was the first to absorb hip-hop culture and the first to make a record. 1989's *Words From the Genius* was released on Cold Chillin' Records; when problems with the label stifled record sales, GZA/Genius saw the other side of the record industry. This inspired him to join forces with Ol' Dirty Bastard and RZA among others as the Wu-Tang Clan; the group's clever wordplay, twisted humor and innovative production techniques provided them with platinum-level success on their own terms. It also provided Genius the opportunity to have an equally lucrative solo career, which started with the 1995 album *Liquid Swords* and continued with 1999's *Beneath the Surface.* As with other Wu-Tang side-projects, Genius/GZA's albums featured guest appearances from most of the other Wu-Tang Clan members. *—Heather Phares*

★ **Liquid Swords** / Nov. 1995 / Geffen ✦✦✦✦✦
Contending with Raekwon's *Only Built for Cuban Linx* for the status of being the overall best Wu-Tang solo album of the 1990s, the Genius' *Liquid Swords* ultimately proves so effective due to the synergy of the rapper's ultra-literate rhymes and RZA's consistently foreboding production. What proves to be even more amazing is how both the Genius and RZA maintain their stellar efforts from the album's kung fu flick intro to the album's prophetic conclusion—this album features no filler. In a way, the album is the perfect medium between the cinematic decadence of *Only Built for Cuban Linx* and the lyrical heights of Method Man's *Tical;* it has both the evocative production and the dizzying rhymes that made these two albums so wonderful, with few interruptions by outside producers or outside rappers. It is this very attribute that makes *Liquid Swords* such a consistent album from beginning to end. Yet this consistency ultimately ends up being the album's only debatable flaw; if anything, the Genius' well-conceived rhymes come across almost too clinically, as if he's reciting from a book rather than flowing lucidly. As talented as he is, he could use a partner, similar to how Ghostface Killah accompanies Raekwon on *Only Built for Cuban Linx.* Granted, this is a minor complaint; for the most part, this is a nearly flawless album—surely one of the decade's best—and it stands as a benchmark for all Wu-Tang albums to be judged against. And judging by successive RZA-produced albums and the Genius' long-awaited follow-up, *Below the Surface,* this is an album that even its creators struggled to match. *—Jason Birchmeier*

Beneath the Surface / Jun. 29, 1999 / MCA ✦✦✦✦✦
There were so many Wu-Tang-related projects released during 1998 and 1999 that listeners—and even fans—could be forgiven for a bit of apathy regarding the second solo effort by Wu-Tang's Genius/GZA. The collective's trademark detuned strings had gone from *de rigueur* to downright dated by mid-1999, and except for a well-received RZA solo album earlier in the year, the lead in hip-hop's hype game appeared to have been taken over by Timbaland's brand of future funk. It may not have proved the commercial smash of a proper Wu-Tang LP, but Genius/GZA's *Beneath the Surface* is a worthy continuation and development of the Wu-Tang Clan conglomeration. The best tracks here, "Amplified Sample" and "Crash Your Crew," are quintessentially Wu-Tang, but with important tweaks to the trademark sound. The crisp, clean production—by Wu associates Inspectah Deck, Mathematics, and Arabian Priest—sounds much better than any project that had been recently issued (even RZA's *Bobby Digital*), and GZA's raps prove he's the most innovative and talented vocalist Wu-Tang had to offer. The only failure (at least in terms of sound) is "Victim," a cloying track with a bit of scratched acoustic guitar and some *X Files*-styled strings. Other than a few "skits" that disturb the flow, *Beneath the Surface* is arguably the best thing to come out of the Wu camp since their second proper album, *Forever. —John Bush*

Geto Boys

f. 1986, Houston, TX
Group / Southern Rap, Hardcore Rap, Gangsta Rap
Though the controversial subject matter of gangsta rap wasn't much of a barrier to popular success during the '90s, the Geto Boys' recordings proved almost too extreme for widespread exposure. Based in Houston's 5th Ward, the trio of Scarface, Willie D., and Bushwick Bill signed to Rap-A-Lot Records and recorded their first album in 1990. The group was blocked

from releasing it by distributor Geffen, who insisted that "Mind of a Lunatic," a track dealing with necrophilia as well as murder, was a step too far. By late 1990, another distributor was found and the album was released—as *Grip It! On That Other Level*—in 1990. The controversy, which occurred two years earlier than similar censorship incidents involving Ice-T and 2 Live Crew, gave the Geto Boys a large amount of publicity and their second album *We Can't Be Stopped* eventually hit platinum. The trio of Scarface, Willie D., and Bushwick Bill began to fracture by 1993, and went their separate ways after that year's *'Til Death Do Us Part*. Each mounted several solo projects before reuniting in 1996 for their most praised album yet, *The Resurrection. Da Good, Da Bad & Da Ugly* followed in 1998. *—John Bush*

Geto Boys / 1990 / Rap-A-Lot/Def American ✦✦✦✦
This disturbing CD inspired quite a bit of controversy when Geffen Records refused to distribute it unless the Geto Boys agreed to tone down their violent and profane lyrics. American Records founder Rick Rubin (who had produced everyone from L.L. Cool J to Slayer to the Beastie Boys) countered that the Houston gangsta rappers shouldn't have to compromise their artistic vision, and sought distribution elsewhere. When the Geto Boys was finally released, it hadn't been toned down a bit. Adding a horror-movie element to their accounts of inner-city crime and violence, the Geto Boys paint a brutally honest and sobering picture of urban life. The members of this group grew up in the tough Houston ghetto known as the Fifth Ward, and don't hesitate to inform listeners just how ugly things can get in so oppressive an environment. From "Assassins" (originally released in 1988) to "Mind of a Lunatic" (a shocking depiction of a mental patient's psychopathic terror spree), this album proves that Rubin did the right thing by holding his ground. *—Alex Henderson*

Grip It! On That Other Level / 1990 / Rap-A-Lot ✦✦✦
The Geto Boys hit the national spotlight with this debut, which disgusted many, frightened a few others and won them a niche in hip-hop's growing "gangsta" constituency. From the sheer repulsiveness of "Let A Ho Be A Ho" and "Do It Like A G.O." to the frightening nihilism of "Mind of a Lunatic" and "Life In the Fast Lane," this was one group definitely uninterested in pop/mainstream approval. The rapping ranged from surly to sleazy, the beats were sometimes popping, sometimes slashing, and even the most loyal fan would have a tough time finding something good to say about "Trigga Happy Nigga" or "Scarface." *—Ron Wynn*

We Can't Be Stopped / Jul. 1, 1991 / Rap-A-Lot/Priority ✦✦✦✦✦
The cover of the Geto Boys' *We Can't Stopped* shows a member with his eye poked out. It's grotesque, but realistic—a realistic cover for an album whose violent, profane lyrics paint a vivid and accurate picture of life as the Geto Boys knew it growing up in Houston's tough ghetto known as the Fifth Ward. This CD isn't as though-provoking as Ice-T, N.W.A., or Ice Cube can be—nor is it the Geto Boys' best offering. But it's an engaging, disturbing effort that comes across as much more heartfelt than the numerous gangster rap albums by the N.W.A. and Cube clone and wannabes who jumped on the gangster bandwagon in the early '90s. *We Can't Be Stopped* serves as an unsettling reminder of the type of ugly social conditions that were allowed to fester in poor innercity neighborhoods. *—Alex Henderson*

• **Uncut Dope: Geto Boys' Best** / 1992 / Rap-a-Lot/Priority ✦✦✦✦✦
With various members opting for solo projects and the group disintegrating, Rap-A-Lot Records primed the pump one last time with what was essentially a greatest hits CD. It wasn't totally a retrospective because it included "Damn It Feels Good To Be A Gangsta," the ultimate genre definition piece and the last significant Geto Boys composition. "And My Word," "Actions Speak Louder Than Words," and "The Unseen" were other fresh jams that joined The Geto Boys anthems "Mind Playing Tricks On Me," "Assassins," "Scarface," and "Mind of a Lunatic," among others. The old/new menu made this the one to grab if one Geto Boys CD is all you need. *—Ron Wynn*

Til Death Do Us Part / Mar. 19, 1993 / Rap-A-Lot ✦✦✦

The Resurrection / Apr. 2, 1996 / Rap-A-Lot/Noo Trybe ✦✦✦✦

Da Good Da Bad & Da Ugly / Nov. 17, 1998 / Virgin ✦✦✦

Grandmaster Flash (Joseph Saddler)

b. Jan. 1, 1958, Barbados, West Indies
DJ, Producer / Old School Rap, Electro, Club/Dance, Hip-Hop
DJ Grandmaster Flash and his group the Furious Five were hip-hop's greatest innovators, transcending the genre's party-music origins to explore the full scope of its lyrical and sonic horizons. Flash began spinning records as a teen growing up in the Bronx, and first worked with the Furious Five (rappers Melle Mel, Cowboy, Kid Creole, Mr. Ness, and Rahiem) during 1978-79. After one single on Enjoy, they signed with the famed Sugar Hill label in 1980 and released their first truly landmark recording one year later. "The Adventures of Grandmaster Flash on the Wheels of Steel" introduced Flash's "cutting" techniques to create a stunning sound collage from snippets of songs by Chic, Blondie, and Queen. Flash and the Five's next effort, 1982's "The Message," was even more revelatory—for the first time, hip-hop became a vehicle not merely for bragging and boasting but for trenchant social commentary, with Melle Mel delivering a blistering rap detailing the grim realities of life in the ghetto. Following 1983's anti-cocaine polemic "White Lines," relations between Flash and Melle Mel turned ugly, and the rapper soon left the group. After a series of Grandmaster Flash solo albums during the 1980s, he reformed the original line-up for a charity concert and a new LP, 1988's *On the Strength*. Another reunion followed in 1994, when Flash and the Five joined a rap package tour also including Kurtis Blow and Run-DMC. *—Jason Ankeny*

The Message / 1982 / Sugar Hill ✦✦✦✦✦

The Source / 1986 / Elektra ✦✦✦

Da Bop Boom Bang / 1987 / Elektra ✦✦

On the Strength / 1988 / Elektra ✦

★ **Message from Beat Street: The Best of Grandmaster Flash** / Apr. 19, 1994 / Rhino ✦✦✦✦✦
Grandmaster Flash was one of the most important, groundbreaking rap artists of the early '80s, and all of his most important records—with and without Melle Mel and the Furious Five—are collected on this essential 11-track disc, which includes the classic tracks "The Message" and "White Lines (Don't Don't Do It)." *—Stephen Thomas Erlewine*

Adventures of Grandmaster Flash, Melle Mel & The Furious Five: More of the Bes / Jul. 1996 / Rhino ✦✦✦✦✦
Although many of Grandmaster Flash's best, biggest, and most groundbreaking work was compiled on *Message From Beat Street: The Best Of, The Adventures of Grandmaster Flash: More of the Best* is necessary for any comprehensive rap collection. The rest of Grandmaster Flash's most important singles, many of which have not appeared on compact disc before, are corralled onto this single-disc. On the whole, the album concentrates on the group's latter-day efforts for Elektra Records, but the cream of the album is the handful of singles for Sugarhill, including the pioneering "The Adventures of Grandmaster Flash on the Wheels of Steel," which presents the group at its freshest and most innovative. Some of the Elektra recordings are a little rote and by-the-book, but the Sugarhill songs help make this an essential purchase. *—Stephen Thomas Erlewine*

Guru

b. Jul. 17, 196?
Vocals / Jazz-Rap, Alternative Rap, Acid Jazz
The main cog behind Gang Starr, rapper/composer Guru stepped out on his own in 1993 with the album *Jazzmatazz*. Enlisting support from the hip-hop and jazz communities, he received help from Roy Ayers and Donald Byrd to N'Dea Davenport of Brand New Heavies. Guru later did selected club dates with some of the *Jazzmatazz* personnel, before returning to straighter hip-hop on Gang Starr's *Hard to Earn*. In 1995, he recruited Ramsey Lewis, Branford Marsalis, and Jamiroquai to help out on *Jazzmatazz, Vol. 2: The New Reality*. After a five-year break, Guru's Jazzmatazz released *Streetsoul* in 2000, with collaborative tracks featuring Herbie Hancock, Isaac Hayes, the Roots, Erykah Badu, and Macy Gray, among others. *—Ron Wynn*

• **Jazzmatazz, Vol. 1** / 1993 / Chrysalis ✦✦✦✦
Gang Starr's Guru has put together the best hip-hop/jazz outing issued yet, at least on these shores. Instead of merely wedding rap to recycled jazz samples, Guru and a cast of jazz, fusion, and R&B stars actually converge performance-wise, with the jazz musicians playing and the rappers and vocalists singing fresh material. The results are never less than enjoyable, and occasionally inspirational. Guru's deadpan rap style works, as do N'Dea Davenport's sultry vocals, and Roy Ayers, Donald Byrd, and Lonnie Liston Smith sound more convincing doing these songs than they have on any recent release of their own. *—Ron Wynn*

Jazzmatazz, Vol. 2: The New Reality / Jul. 18, 1995 / Chrysalis ✦✦✦

Streetsoul / Sep. 26, 2000 / Virgin ✦✦✦

Handsome Boy Modeling School

Group / Underground Rap, Alternative Rap, Alternative Dance, Hip-Hop
A collaboration between two of the most innovative producers in hip-hop, Handsome Boy Modeling School united Prince Paul (best known for his work with De La Soul) and Dan "The Automator" Nakamura (the mastermind behind Kool Keith's "*Dr. Octagon*" project). The duo's debut record, *So... How's Your Girl?*, appeared on Tommy Boy Records in the fall of 1999. *—Jason Ankeny*

So . . . How's Your Girl? / Oct. 19, 1999 / Tommy Boy ✦✦✦✦
Handsome Boy Modeling School comes from the mind of Prince Paul and Dan "The Automator" Nakamura, or as their known on this album, Nathaniel Merriweather and Chest Rockwell. Both men were fans of the Fox television comedy *Get a Life*. In one episode the main character (played by comedian Chris Elliott) goes to the handsome boy modeling school. Clips from the television show appear in the songs "Look at This Face" and "Modeling Sucks." Joining producers Prince Paul and Dan the Automator are Del the Funkee Homosapien, Miho Hatori of Cibo Matto, Grand Puba, Sadat X, J-Live, DJ Shadow, De La Soul, Sean Lennon, and Father Guido Sarducci of *Saturday Night Live* fame, among others. Usually when an attempt at such an ambitious project as this is made, the product has a few good songs while the rest miss the mark, but not in this case. From front to back this is a well-produced, creative album. The only song that doesn't work is "Megaton B-Boy"; its blown-speaker beat, produced by Alec Empire, is too distracting to hear the lyrics of El-P. As far as standouts go, this release is full of them, one being "The Truth," during which Roisin of Moloko sings to the jazzy beat; then after almost three minutes, J-Live jumps in to add his touch. The finished product is a great song. *Handsome Boy Modeling School* succeeds where so many compilations fail. It's a great album from start to finish. *—Dan Gizzi*

Heavy D & The Boyz

f. 1986, Mt. Vernon, NY
Group / Pop-Rap, Club/Dance, Urban, Hip-Hop
Jamaican-born Heavy D (b. Dwight Myers) sports a 260-pound frame but can move and dance with agility and verve. He wisely chose sensitivity, rather than obesity or verbosity, as his framework, and many of his lyrics emphasize his search for a mate of similar qualities. He's also done good cover songs and penned cultural awareness tunes and tributes to black women. Heavy D has managed perhaps the ultimate balancing act. He's remained a positive figure with close ties to his mother and is arguably the most admired male rap figure among African-American feminists. At the same time he's been willing to take chances musically, never embracing hardcore gangsta rap, but yet able to include snatches of pop, R&B, reggae, and funk into his music without being assaulted with cries of sellout. *—Ron Wynn*

• **Heavy Hitz** / Sep. 12, 2000 / MCA ✦✦✦✦✦
Heavy Hitz is a near-definitive overview of Heavy D & the Boyz' pop-friendly dance-rap style, featuring not only the group's two big hits—"We Got Our Own Thang" and the Top Ten "Now That We Found Love"—but 13 more of their best tracks as well. And that's not as excessive as it might sound to casual observers; Heavy D had not only a good-natured persona and sense of humor, but also a deceptively nimble delivery on the mic, which helps enliven these

already infectious party tunes. Heavy D also had a socially conscious side, recording the occasional ode to harmony between genders and races, but that isn't explored very much here; nonetheless, *Heavy Hitz* will likely be perfectly satisfactory for most listeners. *—Steve Huey*

Lauryn Hill

b. May 26, 1975

Vocals / Contemporary R&B, Alternative Rap, Urban, Hip-Hop

Call Lauryn Hill the Mother of Hip-Hop Invention: With her 1998 solo debut *The Miseducation of Lauryn Hill*, the Fugees' most vocal member not only established herself as creative force on her own, but also broke new ground by successfully integrating rap, soul, reggae, and R&B into her own sound. Her on-again, off-again stint in the Fugees began at the age of 13, but was often interrupted by both the acting gigs and her enrollment at Columbia University. With the multi-platinum *The Score*, the Fugees (and especially the camera-friendly Hill) achieved international success, though some pundits took shots at their penchant for cover songs. That criticism made *Miseducation* even more of a surprise. Hill wrote, arranged, or produced just about every track on the album, which is steeped in her old-school background, both musically (the Motown-esque singalong of "Doo Wop (That Thing)") and lyrically (the nostalgic "Every Ghetto, Every City"). By the end of the year, as the album topped virtually every major music critic's "best-of" list, she was being credited for helping fully assimilate hip-hop into mainstream music, culminating in the February 1999 Grammy awards, during which Hill took home five trophies—the most ever for a woman. *—Brian Raftery*

● **The Miseducation of Lauryn Hill** / Aug. 25, 1998 / Columbia ✦✦✦✦✦

This highly anticipated album from Lauryn Hill features a mix of soul, rap, and reggae. Hill, who gained national attention by singing in the movie *Sister Act II*, is also a member of the hip-hop trio the Fugees, which consists of her partners Wyclef Jean and Prakazrel "Pras" Michel. This, her first solo album, houses some hip-hop-induced soul numbers. "Ex-Factor" has a bouncing flow, an enticing change-up, and a supplicating vamp accentuated by a soothing melody. The charged rhythm of "Doo Wop (That Thing)" presses on with Hill rapping and singing from verse to chorus augmented by some juiced-up horns and a whopping bass line. "Nothing Even Matters," a duet with soul singer D'Angelo, breezes in its dulcet rhythm. Their vocals maintain that consistent pitch throughout the song as they humbly complement each other from their cries to their lyrical sighs. There is much here to savor for aficionados of rap, reggae, and hip-hop/soul music. The Fugees alumna is eloquent throughout the set with her message of love, education, peace, perseverance, understanding, and patience. While the young talent is fluent in each respective genre she embraces, the ambience she exudes with her singing has a magnetic, mesmerizing feel. A great effort by a rising star. *—Craig Lytle*

House of Pain

f. 1990

Group / Pop-Rap, Hardcore Rap, East Coast Rap, Hip-Hop

"Jump Around," an impossibly infectious and catchy single, instantly elevated House of Pain from an unknown white hip-hop group to near-stars when it became a massive crossover hit in 1992. Released on Tommy Boy Records, the group's eponymous debut was co-produced by DJ Muggs, who masterminded Cypress Hill's groundbreaking debut. Fronted by Irish-American rappers Everlast (b. Erik Schrody) and Danny Boy (b. Daniel O'Connor), along with Latvian-born DJ Lethal, House of Pain celebrated their heritage in a tongue-in-cheek fashion that quickly became schtick—wearing green, drinking prodigious amounts of beer, and swearing constantly. It certainly earned them attention at the outset, particularly when it was tied to a single like "Jump Around," but the bottom quickly fell out of their career, partially because of the band's self-consciously loutish behavior. Throughout their 1993 tour, the group ran into trouble with promoters and the law, culminating in Everlast's arrest for possessing an unregistered, unloaded pistol at Kennedy Airport. Like its predecessor, 1994's *Same As It Ever Was* was produced by DJ Muggs and was greeted with surprisingly strong reviews and sales—the latter of which, however, quickly slowed. Most of the next two years were spent in seclusion, and the group returned in the fall of 1996 with *Truth Crushed to Earth Shall Rise Again*, a record that was ignored by both the press and the public. Everlast returned in 1998 as a solo act, and gained critical acclaim for his debut, *Whitey Ford Sings the Blues*. *—Stephen Thomas Erlewine*

● **House of Pain** / Jul. 21, 1992 / Tommy Boy ✦✦✦✦

It would be hard for nearly anyone to top the explosive, insanely catchy "Jump Around," so it's no great surprise to find that House of Pain isn't up to the task. At times, HOP comes close to duplicating the intoxicating power of their slamming single, but for the most part, their debut album is a repetitive circle of similar beats, misogyny, racism, and posturing lyrics. But the perfection of "Jump Around" almost makes up for the numerous faults. *—Stephen Thomas Erlewine*

Same as It Ever Was / Jun. 28, 1994 / Tommy Boy ✦✦✦✦

House of Pain's self-titled album had its moments, but on the whole, wasn't very memorable. However, the Irish-American group really blossomed on its far superior and much more hardcore second album, *Same as It Ever Was*. With this album, Everlast changed his style of rapping considerably and unveiled a much more distinctive and recognizable approach. Sounding twisted, damaged, and maniacal, Everlast grabs the listener's attention and refuses to let go on such wildly entertaining fare as "Back from the Dead," "Over There Shit," and "Runnin' Up on Ya." House of Pain's subject matter—namely, their superior rapping skills and the threat they pose to sucker MCs—is far from groundbreaking. But an abundance of strong, clever hooks and Everlast's psycho-like rapping make *Same as It Ever Was* consistently appealing. *—Alex Henderson*

Truth Crushed to Earth Shall Rise Again / Oct. 22, 1996 / Tommy Boy ✦✦✦

Ice Cube (O'Shea Jackson)

b. Jun. 15, 1969

Vocals / West Coast Rap, Hardcore Rap, G-Funk, Gangsta Rap

After leaving the seminal N.W.A., Ice Cube quickly established himself as one of hip-hop's best and most controversial artists. As a solo artist, his politics and social commentary sharpened substantially, and his first two records were equally praised and reviled; his lyrical stance was often violent, homophobic, and misogynist, yet it also happened to be considerably more articulate than many of his gangsta peers. Ice Cube (b. O'Shea Jackson) came from a surprisingly straight background, raised in South Central Los Angeles by parents who had jobs at UCLA. He formed the first incarnation of N.W.A. with Eazy-E and Dr. Dre in 1986; their debut album *Straight Outta Compton* became an underground hit over the course of 1989, but Cube's deep conflicts with N.W.A.'s management resulted in his departure late that year. Recorded with Public Enemy's production team, the Bomb Squad, his 1990 solo debut *AmeriKKKa's Most Wanted* was an instant hit; even amidst controversy over his lyrics, the album was hailed as a groundbreaking classic within hip-hop. His 1991 acting debut in John Singleton's acclaimed urban drama *Boyz N the Hood* was widely praised. Released later that year, *Death Certificate* was simultaneously more political and vulgar than *AmeriKKKa*, and several tracks provoked public condemnations of Cube as a racist himself; however, the furor didn't prevent it from reaching number two and going platinum. Following Cube's slot on the second Lollapalooza tour in 1992, *The Predator* became the first album to debut at number one on both the pop and R&B charts. However, with the rise of Dr. Dre's G-funk, his hold on the mass rap audience was beginning to slip. While 1993's *Lethal Injection* went platinum, its funkier sound wasn't well-received, and it was Cube's last official album for several years. He concentrated on producing and writing for other artists, and made amends with Dre on their 1995 duet "Natural Born Killaz"; he also appeared in the films *Higher Learning*, *Friday* (his screenwriting debut), and *Anaconda*. He returned to recording in 1998 with *War and Peace—The War Disc*; its sequel, *The Peace Disc*, followed two years later. *—Stephen Thomas Erlewine*

☆ **AmeriKKKa's Most Wanted** / May 16, 1990 / Priority ✦✦✦✦✦

After leaving N.W.A. on anything but good terms with Dr. Dre and Eazy-E, Ice Cube launched his solo career with the hard-hitting and impressive *AmeriKKKa's Most Wanted*. While the Angelino continued to embrace gangster rap—a style in which MCs provide violent, graphic, first-person portrayals of thugs, gang members, drug dealers, etc.—there's a lot more to this riveting CD than that controversial approach. As much as Cube thrives on the shocking and the profane, it's clear that he isn't glamorizing the harsh urban realities he raps about, but rather, protesting them. "Once Upon a Time in the Projects" is about being arrested for being in the wrong place (a crack house) at the wrong time (during a drug bust), while "Endangered Species" (a duet with Public Enemy leader Chuck D) is a sobering reflection on the high mortality rate among young African-American males. On some of his subsequent recordings, Cube would, artistically speaking, become a victim of his own anger. But on *AmeriKKKa's Most Wanted*, a more lucid Cube quite effectively articulates just how bad things are in America's inner cities—and how badly things need to change. *—Alex Henderson*

Kill at Will / 1990 / Profile ✦✦✦✦

Ice Cube's riveting debut album, *AmeriKKKa's Most Wanted* was still burning up the charts when Priority Records released this EP, which lacks that album's overall excellence but has its moments. With *Kill at Will*, Cube unveiled his engaging "The Product" and "Dead Homiez," a poignant lament for the victims of Black-on-Black crime that is among the best songs he's ever written. Enjoyable but not essential are remixes of "Endangered Species (Tales from the Darkside)" and the outrageous "Get Off My D*** and Tell Yo B**** to Come Here." Clearly, *Kill at Will* was intended for hardcore fans rather than casual listeners—who would do well to stick with *AmeriKKKa's Most Wanted* and *Death Certificate*. *—Alex Henderson*

★ **Death Certificate** / Oct. 31, 1991 / Priority ✦✦✦✦✦

Death Certificate is even harder and angrier than *AmeriKKKa's Most Wanted*, which is both a good and a bad thing, depending on your politics. If you're inclined to see Ice Cube as a spokesman and social commentator, *Death Certificate* will support your claims—it continues the sharp insights and unflinching looks at contemporary urban lifestyles that his solo debut only hinted at; in short, its hardcore without any gangsta posturing. If you're inclined to see Ice Cube as a bigoted, misogynistic rabble-rouser, *Death Certificate* will also support your claims—"No Vaseline" contains explicit anti-semetic taunts directed at his former manager, there are homophobic slurs scattered throughout the album and women are frequently either bitches or whores. However, if you look beyond the surface—no matter what political viewpoint you happen to have—you will find that Cube's rhymes do promote self-awareness and education. In short, they are some of the most incisive raps about life as a young Black man since the advent of Public Enemy. Considering this, it's not surprising that *Death Certificate* bears the mark of Public Enemy's dense, abrasive soundscapes—it's a funkier, noisier, and more musically effective album than *AmeriKKKa's Most Wanted*. Ice Cube had never before created a statement of purpose as coherent and incendiary as *Death Certificate* and, sadly, he never did again. *—Leo Stanley*

The Predator / Nov. 17, 1992 / Priority ✦✦✦

The Predator functions as the point in Cube's career where his albums started to become hit-and-miss collections of miscellaneous singles and filler rather than coherent body's of thematically connected work à la *Death Certificate* and *AmeriKKKa's Most Wanted*. So on the one hand, it's disappointing to find that Cube refrains from his formerly conceptual work in favor of seemingly radio-targeted efforts, yet, on the other hand, *The Predator* does prove successful as a collection of individual tracks, many of which stand as some of his most enthused work. Kicking off the album with force, "When Will They Shoot—" explodes with power, and then "Wicked" continues this aggressive tone. Things begin to falter a bit after that, though, both in terms of songwriting and lyrics as well as production. Of the remaining mediocre tracks, "It Was a Good Day" is an obvious highlight; quite similar in tone to

Cube's previous crossover hit "Dead Homiez" and his subsequent crossover hit "You Know How We Do It," this song finds the rapper slowing down his tempo and trading anger and aggressive beats for modest contemplative indifference and relaxed G-funk production. The Muggs-produced tracks, "We Had to Tear This Motha—?- Up" (the only blatant L.A. riot commentary) and "Check Yo Self," also stand out as some of the few bright moments on this otherwise mediocre album. *—Jason Birchmeier*

Lethal Injection / Dec. 7, 1993 / Scarface ✦✦

Featuring . . . Ice Cube / Dec. 16, 1997 / Priority ✦✦✦

War & Peace, Vol. 1 (The War Disc) / Nov. 17, 1998 / Priority ✦✦✦

War & Peace, Vol. 2 (The Peace Disc) / Feb. 29, 2000 / Priority ✦✦✦

Ice-T (Tracy Morrow)

b. Feb. 14, 1959, Newark, NJ
Rap, Vocals / West Coast Rap, Hardcore Rap, Gangsta Rap
Ice-T (born Tracy Morrow) has proven to be one of hip-hop's most articulate and intelligent stars, as well as one of its most frustrating. At his best, the rapper has written some of the best portraits of ghetto life and gangsters, as well as some of the best social commentary hip-hop has produced. Just as often, he can slip into sexism and gratuitous violence, and even then his rhymes are clever and biting. Ice-T's best recordings have always been made in conjunction with strong collaborators, whether it's The Bomb Squad or Jello Biafra. With his music, Ice-T has made a conscious effort to win the vast audience of white male adolescents, as his frequent excursions with his heavy metal band Body Count show. All the while, he has withstood a constant barrage of criticism and controversy to become a respected figure not only in the music press, but the mainstream media as well. *—Stephen Thomas Erlewine*

Rhyme Pays / 1987 / Sire ✦✦✦
Before Ice-T's ascension, L.A. rappers were known primarily for a synthesizer-dominated sound indebted to Kraftwerk's innovations as well as Africa Bambaataa's 1982 hit, "Planet Rock." While L.A. did have its share of hardcore rappers in the mid-1980s (including Toddy Tee, King Tee, and of course, Ice-T), hardcore rap was dominated by the East Coast. That began to change in 1987, when Ice-T's debut album, *Rhyme Pays*, was released and sold several hundred thousand copies. Hard-hitting offerings like "409," "Make It Funky," and the title song (which samples Black Sabbath's "War Pigs" and underscores the L.A. resident's love of heavy metal) left no doubt that Ice had very little in common with the Egyptian Lover, the World Class Wreckin' Cru, or the L.A. Dream Team. The album doesn't contain as much gangsta rap as some of his subsequent releases, but it did have enough to stir some controversy. On "Squeeze the Trigger," "Pain," and a new version of "Six'N the Mornin'" (which had been the B-side of Ice's 1986 single "Doggin' the Wax" on Techno-Hop), Ice portrays ruthless felons and raps candidly about the horrors of the urban ghetto he'd been only too familiar with. With the release of *Rhyme Pays*, the West Coast was well on its way to becoming a crucial part of hip-hop. *—Alex Henderson*

Power / 1988 / Sire ✦✦✦✦✦
As riveting as *Rhyme Pays* was, Ice-T did hold back a little and avoided being too consistently sociopolitical. But with the outstanding *Power*, the gloves came all the way off, and Ice didn't hesitate to speak his mind about the harsh realities of inner-city life. On "Drama," "Soul On Ice" (an homage to his idol Iceberg Slim), "High Rollers," and other gangsta rap gems, Ice embraces a first-person format and raps with brutal honesty about the lives of gang members, players, and hustlers. Ice's detractors took the songs out of context, arguing that he was glorifying crime. But he countered that in fact, he was sending out an anti-crime message in a subliminal fashion, and stressed that the criminals he portrayed ended up dead or behind bars. Another track that some misconstrued was "I'm Your Pusher," an interpretation of Curtis Mayfield's "Pusherman" that doesn't promote the use of drugs, but uses double entendres to make an anti-drug statement. (Ice has always been vehemently outspoken in his opposition to drugs.) In the next few years, gangsta rap would degenerate into nothing more than cheap exploitation and empty cliches, but in Ice's hands, it was as informative as it was captivating. *—Alex Henderson*

☆ **The Iceberg/Freedom of Speech . . . Just Watch What You Say** / Oct. 1989 / Sire ✦✦✦✦✦
Ice-T threw listeners quite a curve ball with his riveting third album, *The Iceberg/Freedom of Speech . . . Just Watch What You Say*—arguably the closest hip-hop has come to George Orwell's *1984*. Instead of focusing heavily on gangster rap, Ice-T made First Amendment issues the CD's dominant theme. Setting the album's tone is the opener "Shut Up, Be Happy," which finds guest Jello Biafra (former leader of punk band Dead Kennedys) envisioning an Orwellian America in which the goverment controls and dominates every aspect of its citizens' lives. Though there are a few examples of first-rate gangster rap here—including "The Hunted Child" and the chilling "Peel Their Caps Back"—Ice's main concern this time is censorship and what he views as a widespread attack on free speech in the U.S. As angry and lyrically intense as most of *The Iceberg* is, Ice enjoys fun for its own sake on "My Word Is Bond" and "The Girl Tried to Kill Me"—an insanely funny rap/rock account of an encounter with a dominatrix. *—Alex Henderson*

★ **O.G. Original Gangster** / May 14, 1991 / Sire ✦✦✦✦✦
One of gangsta rap's defining albums, *O.G. Original Gangster* is a sprawling masterpiece that stands far and away as Ice-T's finest hour. Taken track by track, *O.G.* might not seem at first like the product of a unified vision; perspective-wise, it's all over the map. There's perceptive social analysis, chilling violence, psychological storytelling, hair-trigger rage, pleas for solutions to ghetto misery, cautionary morality tales, and cheerfully crude humor in the depictions of sex and defenses of street language. But with a few listens, it's possible to assimilate everything into a complex, detailed portrait of Ice-T's South Central L.A. roots—the album's contradictions reflect the complexities of real life. That's why the more intelligent, nuanced material isn't negated by the violence and sexism—both of which, incidentally, are held relatively in check, with the former having been reshaped into a terrifying but inescapable fact of life. That isn't to say that *O.G. Original Gangster* is designed to appeal to delicate intellectual sensibilities; it's still full of raw, street-level aggression that makes no apologies or concessions. That goes for the music as well as the lyrics. The beats are a little too hard-driving and jittery to really breathe like funk, which only adds to the dark, claustrophobic feel of the production. Ice smoothly keeps up with the music's furious pace, and also debuts his soon-to-be-notorious metal band Body Count on one track. That kind of artistic ambition is all over the album, whether in the lean musical attack or the urgent rhymes. *O.G. Original Gangster* is a certifiable gangsta rap classic, and arguably the most realistic, unvarnished representation of a world Ice-T was the first to chronicle on record. *—Steve Huey*

Body Count / 1992 / Sire ✦✦✦
Ice-T's excursion into heavy metal brought him a firestorm of controversy, but the album is actually a tepid collection of '80s-style arena metal that never sounds dangerous. Frequently, it's hard to tell if Ice takes this stuff seriously; tracks like "Body Count" and "Cop Killer" are invigorating stabs at social criticism, but most of the album is filled with stupid attempts at being threatening, like "KKK Bitch" and "Mama's Gotta Die Tonight." Maybe the humor was intentional, but too frequently the record sounded embarrassing. After "Cop Killer" was pulled from the album, it was replaced with a version of "The Iceberg" recorded with Jello Biafra. *—Stephen Thomas Erlewine*

Home Invasion / Mar. 23, 1993 / Priority ✦✦✦

VI: Return of the Real / Jun. 1996 / Priority ✦✦✦

7th Deadly Sin / Oct. 12, 1999 / Coroner/Atomic Pop ✦✦✦

Greatest Hits: The Evidence / Aug. 8, 2000 / Atomic Pop ✦✦✦✦

Jay-Z (Shawn Carter)

b. Dec. 4, 1970, Brooklyn, NY
Vocals / East Coast Rap, Gangsta Rap, Hip-Hop
It's hard to imagine a more perfect success story than Jay-Z's remarkable ascendance to the top of the rap game. After a challenging childhood in a rough Brooklyn neighborhood and some time on the streets as a hustler, the rapper otherwise known as Shawn Carter followed his confident instincts, starting his own record label, Roc-a-Fella, at a time when this practice simply wasn't done on such an ambitious scale. His debut album, *Reasonable Doubt*, became a critical favorite among those in the know and scored a gold single. But it wasn't until his third album, *Vol. 2: Hard Knock Life*, that Jay-Z transcended critically acclaimed status to widespread mainstream success thanks to a string of massive hits, most notably "Can I Get A . . ." Yet never one to be content, Jay-Z then embarked on a large-scale arena tour, elevating his popularity to even more astonishing heights. By the end of the '90s, he was arguably the most successful East Coast rapper, or at least the most recognized. By the time he dropped *The Dynasty* in late 2000, his success was just that—a dynasty on which he had leveraged a recognized label and a roster of burgeoning protégés, including Memphis Bleek and Beanie Sigel. *—Jason Birchmeier*

Reasonable Doubt / Jan. 26, 1999 / Roc-A-Fella/Priority ✦✦✦
Even if Jay-Z's debut album didn't have the polish, the superstar roster, or the hits of his subsequent late '90s albums, it retains an air of irreplaceability. No matter how many trendy producers or how many talented rappers Jay-Z would work with on later albums, he couldn't duplicate this one's naked sincerity and naive ambition. Having abandoned a life of hustling and secured a distribution deal with Priority for his own Roc-a-Fella label, he put everything he had at the time into this record. It's essentially an autobiographical album—as are his subsequent albums to a more self-conscious degree—exploring his enigmatic anti-thug hustler mentality. Where many rappers strike a sometimes contradictory and often hypocritical stance in hopes of impressing fans with their glamorized image, Jay-Z doesn't resort to excessive flossing, instead rapping with sincerity, even if it makes him a less ideal ghetto hero. It's this heartfelt sincerity that makes him so potent here; on subsequent albums he would try to recapture this confessional tone over and over, yet he has never sounded this committed. Furthermore, the album's two standout tracks—"Can't Knock the Hustle," featuring a beautiful chorus by Mary J. Blige, and "Dead Presidents II"—are downright masterpieces. So even if *Reasonable Doubt* isn't graced with a who's who roster of hip-hop talent, it's an unbelievably personal album, something Jay-Z has continually tried to duplicate unsuccessfully. *—Jason Birchmeier*

★ **In My Lifetime, Vol. 1** / Nov. 4, 1997 / Pay Day ✦✦✦✦✦
After the death of friend and compatriot the Notorious B.I.G. in early 1997, Jay-Z made his claim for the title of best \rapper on the \East Coast (or anywhere) with his sophomore shot, *In My Lifetime, Vol. 1*. Though the productions are just a bit flashier and more commercial than on his debut, Jay-Z remained the tough street \rapper, and even improved a bit on his flow, already one of the best in the world of \hip-hop. Still showing his roots in the Marcy projects (he's surrounded by a group of kids in a picture on the back cover), Jay-Z struts the line between project poet and up-and-coming player, and manages to have it both ways. He slings some of the most cutting rhymes heard in \hip-hop, brushing off a legion of \rappers riding his coattails on "Imaginary Player." For "Streets Is Watching," high-tension background strings and vocal samples from the gangster film *Sleeper* emphasize the pitfalls of a \rapper everyone's gunning for ("If I shoot you, I'm brainless/But if you shoot me, then you famous"). The song leads right into "Friend or Foe '98," the sequel to a track from *Reasonable Doubt* that only increases the sense of paranoia. But Jay-Z plays the ghetto celebrity equally well, and continues his slick, Cristal-sipping image with "I Know What Girls Like" (featuring Puff Daddy and Lil' Kim), "(Always Be My) Sunshine" (featuring Babyface and Foxy Brown), and "Lucky Me." Puff Daddy's Bad Boy stable is responsible for almost half the productions, and though they often verge far into \pop territory, Jay-Z usually rescues them from a complete crossover. (Ironically, the most commercial production is actually from Teddy Riley on "The City Is Mine," with an unfortunate interpolation of Glenn Frey's "You Belong to the City.") Having one of the toughest producers around (Premier) as well as one of the slickest (Puff Daddy) sometimes creates a disconnect between who Jay-Z really is and who he wants to be-

come, but he balances both personas with the best \rapping heard in the \rap game since the deaths of 2Pac and Notorious B.I.G. *—John Bush*

Vol. 2: Hard Knock Life / Sep. 29, 1998 / Def Jam ✦✦✦✦
Coming on the heels of two strong records which revealed the extent of Jay-Z's talents, *Vol. 2: Hard Knock Life* (it may be titled *Vol. 2*, but it's his third album, arguably his fourth if you count the *Streets Is Watching* soundtrack) is a little bit of a relative disappointment. Jay-Z had established himself as a savvy, street-smart rapper on those two records, but with *Hard Knock Life* he decided to shoot for crossover territory, for better and for worse. At his best, he shows no fear—witness how the title track shamelessly works a Broadway showstopper from *Annie* into a raging ghetto cry, yet keeps it smooth enough for radio. It's a stunning single, but unfortunately, it promises more than the rest of the album can deliver. Jay-Z remains a first-rate lyricist and MC, but too often his subjects are tired, especially since he winds up with no new revelations. Unfortunately, the same could be said for his music. For every "Hard Knock Life," there are a couple of standard post-gangsta jams that don't catch hold—and that's really too bad, because the best moments (including several tracks produced by such stars as Timbaland, Kid Capri and Jermaine Dupri) are state-of-the-art, R&B-inflected mainstream hip-hop. And that's the problem—before, Jay-Z wasn't trying to play by the rules of the mainstream, but here he's trying to co-opt them. At times he does, but the times that fall flat have less strength or integrity than their predecessors, and that's what makes the entire record not quite as effective, despite its numerous high points. *—Stephen Thomas Erlewine*

Vol. 3: Life and Times of S. Carter / Dec. 28, 1999 / Def Jam ✦✦

The Dynasty: Roc la Familia / Oct. 31, 2000 / Def Jam ✦✦✦

Wyclef Jean

b. Oct. 17, 19??
Vocals, Guitar, Producer / Contemporary R&B, East Coast Rap, Alternative Rap, Urban, Hip-Hop
The Haitian MC and producer who rocketed to fame along with the other two members of the Fugees (Pras and Lauryn Hill), Wyclef Jean was the first to embark on a solo side-project. Born in Haiti, though his family moved to South Florida while he was still a child, Jean grew up in Brooklyn, spending time with his cousin, Pras. After the two hooked up with Lauryn Hill, the Fugees were born and revealed as hip-hop superstars after their second album, 1996's *The Score*. The following year, he went out on his own for *The Carnival Featuring the Refugee All Stars*, though both of his band-mates made appearances. Thanks to the single "We Trying to Stay Alive" (and to the Bee Gees for the sample), the album hit the Top 20 and went gold. *Ecleftic: 2 Sides II a Book* followed in mid-2000. *—John Bush*

• **Presents the Carnival Featuring the Refugee All Stars** / Jun. 24, 1997 / Columbia ✦✦✦✦
The Score was one of those rare hip-hop albums that came out of nowhere and rewrote the rules. In the aftermath of its success, many pundits predicted that rap would move away from gangsta and toward a richer, more varied existence. Given such heady praise, perhaps it was reasonable that Wyclef Jean, the guitarist and male rapper for the Fugees, decided to follow *The Score* with a solo project. However, *Wyclef Jean Presents the Carnival* comes across like Jean presenting his case that he is the *true* genius in the Fugees. And he's partially right. He has the ambition and drive common to many great artists, but he lacks the skills to fulfill his vision. Of course, the very fact that he has an original vision makes Jean one of the more compelling figures of late-'90s hip-hop. Not content to rely solely on hip-hop, Jean adds all manners of influences to his music. You can hear reggae, soul, disco, Caribbean rhythms, worldbeat and opera scattered throughout *The Carnival*, giving the record the riotous atmosphere of its title. Even so, Jean occaisonally tries too hard, forcing disparate genres to mix and spending more time on production than songwriting. But even with all its faults, *The Carnival* delivers great thrills when operating at full strength, demonstrating that Jean is at least half a genius. *—Leo Stanley*

The Ecleftic: 2 Sides II a Book / Jul. 25, 2000 / Columbia ✦✦✦✦
Wyclef Jean serves up another slice of his music and remixing creativity with his latest, *The Ecleftic: Two Sides II a Book*. Loaded with pop culture commentary and often directly naming social names, *The Eclefticis* sure to stir up some emotions from not only the famous, but from the general public as well. The purest example is "Diallo," named after the man who was shot 41 times by patrolling night officers when he reached for his wallet, not a gun as the police had thought. With this, Wyclef shows his refugee camp roots, acting as a 21st-century Bob Marley. As much as it is loaded with serious urban observations, Wyclef also serves up a good party and even some love songs. In the beginning, *The Ecleftic*, is loaded with classic and catchy samples, such as the song about his undying love for a stripper paying her way through college entitled "Red Light District." Though older listeners will probably cringe at the thought of Kenny Rogers singing of turntables, this move is no surprise from a man who introduced the Bee Gees to the hip-hop generation with the sample of "Staying Alive" on his album, *The Carnival*. On *Ecleftic*, Wyclef comes full fisted with commentary on the police system, urban ills, and stereotypes. Though some are merited, after the first dozen they lose their impact and are swallowed by catchy beats. Overall, another commentary and playfully meticulous production by Wyclef Jean who has struggled to separate himself from the Fugees. It is clear, with a good retrospective listen, how much Jean's production style was a large part of the praised trio. With *The Ecleftic: Two Sides II a Book*, Jean takes another strong step towards solidifying his own identity. *—Diana Potts*

Jeru the Damaja (Kendrick Jeru Davis)

b. Brooklyn, NY
Producer, Lyricist / Hardcore Rap, East Coast Rap, Hip-Hop
Speaking out against what he saw as a decline in rap during the mid-'90s, Jeru the Damaja came to the fore as a self-proclaimed prophet and the savior of hip-hop, much as KRS-One had done almost ten years before. Jeru first appeared as a guest on Gang Starr's *Daily Operations* album, and his own deal with Payday/FFRR appeared soon after, resulting in 1994's *The Sun Rises in the East. Wrath of the Math* followed in 1996. Though he made few friends in the rap world—given his outspoken criticism of such popular figures as the Fugees and Sean "Puffy" Combs—he proved a vital force in the emergence of the new rap consciousness of the late '90s. *—John Bush*

• **The Sun Rises in the East** / Dec. 22, 1994 / Payday ✦✦✦✦✦
Resting halfway between the sultry swagger of gangsta and the classy tones of jazz-rap, Jeru began his career guesting for Guru on a few tracks. Although Gang Starr are listed as executive producers, *The Sun Rises in the East* has already established The Damaja as a unique voice in hip-hop. His inner-city lyrics on songs "You Can't Stop the Prophet" and "Ain't the Devil Happy," work well with his flowing sing-speak delivery. "Da Bichez" might offend some, even with the line: "I'm not talking about the queens, but the bitches." Nevertheless, *The Sun Rises in the East* is an amazing debut. *—John Bush*

Wrath of the Math / Oct. 1996 / Payday/London ✦✦✦✦
Wrath of the Math proved almost as effective as Jeru the Damaja's debut LP, even though little had changed—DJ Premier once again provides his customary scratchy, minimalist production and Jeru's lyrical themes focus either on hip-hop itself (as on "One Day") or the state of life on the streets ("Revenge of the Prophet"). *Wrath of the Math* just can't sustain the power of Jeru's message, however, since it includes five more tracks than on his debut. "Ya Playin' Yaself," "Not the Average" and "Me or the Papes" (which attempts to atone for the sins of "Da Bichez" from *The Sun Rises in the East*) are great songs, but the album just runs out of steam by the end. *—John Bush*

Heroz4hire / Sep. 7, 1999 / Knowsavage ✦✦✦

Jungle Brothers

f. 1986, New York, NY
Group / Jazz-Rap, Alternative Rap, Hip-Hop
Although they predated the jazz-rap innovations of De La Soul, A Tribe Called Quest and Digable Planets, the Jungle Brothers were never able to score with either rap fans or mainstream audiences, perhaps due to their embrace of a range of styles—including house music, Afrocentric philosophy, a James Brown fixation, and of course, the use of jazz samples—each of which has been the sole basis for the start-up of a rap act. Signed to a major label for 1989's *Done by the Forces of Nature*, the JB's failed to connect on that album, hailed by some as an ignored classic. Their Afrocentric slant gained the Jungle Brothers entry into the Native Tongue Posse, a loose collective formed by hip-hop legend Afrikaa Bambaataa including Queen Latifah (and, later, De La Soul and A Tribe Called Quest). The Jungle Brothers' chances of mainstream acceptance weren't helped at all by a four-year absence after the release of *Done by the Forces of Nature*, inspired mostly by Warner Bros. marketing strategies. Finally, in the summer of 1993, *J Beez Wit the Remedy* appeared, complete with a sizeable push from Warner Bros.; unfortunately, the large amount of promotion failed to carry the album. Obviously not learning from their earlier mistakes, Warner Bros. also delayed the release of the group's fourth album, *Raw Deluxe*, until mid-1997. *—John Bush*

• **Straight Out the Jungle** / 1988 / Warlock ✦✦✦✦✦
The trio's debut is powered by muscular funk riffs underpinned by an Afrocentric sensibility and a sharp sense of humor. *—John Floyd*

Done by the Forces of Nature / Nov. 1989 / Warner Brothers ✦✦✦✦✦
By injecting some vocal delicacy and some clever samples into their moderately militant message, they made a second album that elaborates on their own winning formula. *—John Floyd*

J. Beez Wit the Remedy / Jun. 22, 1993 / Warner Brothers ✦✦✦
Nearly four years after *Done By the Forces of Nature*, The Jungle Brothers return with a hazy, funky album, filled with their brand of literate hip-hop. Although they've made some stylistic progressions since the last record, it wasn't enough to be a completely groundbreaking release, nor was it commericial enough to break them out of their critically acclaimed/cult status. Instead, it was another solid, inventive album that didn't receive the attention it deserved. *—Stephen Thomas Erlewine*

Raw Deluxe / Jun. 3, 1997 / Gee Street ✦✦✦

V.I.P. / Jan. 4, 2000 / V2 ✦✦✦✦
Even though the JB's originated the highly influential Native Tongues clique (De La Soul, A Tribe Called Quest), their ten-year run of musical mischief has been anything but native. Spearheaded by the acid beats of the Propellerheads' Alex Gifford, their latest foray, *V.I.P.*, is yet another experimental set, one that highlights the exquisite chemistry of group members Baby Bam and Mike G. While the JB's don't fit the traditional hip-hop image, that's part of their appeal, as their innocent, party-oriented raps hold one purpose—to get your back up off the wall. *—Matt Conaway*

Jurassic 5

f. 1993, Los Angeles, CA
Group / Turntablism, Underground Rap, Alternative Rap, Hip-Hop
Though there's actually six of them, Jurassic 5 got everything else right on their self-titled debut EP. Part of the new rap underground of the late '90s (along with Company Flow, Mos Def, Doctor Octagon and Sir Menelik), the sextet—rappers Marc 7even, Chali 2na, Zaakir and Akil, plus producers Cut Chemist and DJ Nu-Mark—came together in 1993 at the Los Angeles cafe/venue named the Good Life. The six members were part of two different crews, Rebels of Rhythm and Unity Committee; after collaborating on a track, they combined into Jurassic 5 and debuted in 1995 with the "Unified Rebellion" single for TVT Records. At the tail end of 1997, the *Jurassic 5 EP* appeared and was hailed by critics as one of the freshest debuts of the year (if not the decade). Both Cut Chemist and Chali 2na are also part of the Latin-hop collective Ozomatli, while Chemist himself has recorded several mix-tapes plus the wide-issue album *Future Primitive Soundsession* (with Shortkut from Invisibl Skratch

Piklz). The year 2000 found the group on tour with Fiona Apple and on the Warped Festival, just in time for the release of *Quality Control* that summer. *—John Bush*

- **Jurassic 5 EP** / Oct. 13, 1997 / Rumble/Pickininny ✦✦✦✦✦

Clocking in at just about one-third the running time of your average rap album circa 1997, Jurassic 5's debut was the most refreshing hip-hop release of the year, and not just because it abandoned the epic-length concepts of the rap mainstream. With old-school vibes to spare, excellent rhythmatic raps, and the production genius of Cut Chemist and DJ Nu-Mark, *EP* finally delivered on all the diverse talents promised by the growing hip-hop underground. "Jayou" is a flute-loop classic, and "Concrete Schoolyard" has that nostalgic "can it all be so simple" vibe so rarely heard from hip-hop. *—John Bush*

Quality Control / Jun. 6, 2000 / Interscope ✦✦✦✦✦

In June 2000, almost seven years after their formation, underground rap's most lauded crew finally hit with a full-length. Great expectations aside, *Quality Control* hits all of the same highs as Jurassic 5's excellent EP of three years earlier, stretching out their resume to nearly an hour with a few turntablist jaunts from resident beat-jugglers DJ Nu-Mark and Cut Chemist. The formula is very similar to the EP, with the group usually going through a couple of lines of five-man harmonics before splitting off for tongue-twister solos from Zaakir, Chali 2na, Akil, or Mark 7even. As expected, there are plenty of nods to old-school rap, from "LAUSD," with its brief tribute to hip-hop classic "The Bridge" by MC Shan, to "Monkey Bars," where the group claim inspiration—yet just a bit of distance—from their heroes ("Now you know us but it's not the Cold Crush, four MC's so it ain't the Furious / Not the Force MCs or the three from Treacherous, it's a blast from the past from the moment we bust"). Though critics and uptight rap purists might fault them for not pushing the progression angle enough, Jurassic 5's rhymes are so devastating and the productions (by Nu-Mark and Cut Chemist) are so unstoppable that it hardly even matters whether the group are really old-school or not. *—John Bush*

Kid 'N Play

f. 1987, **db.** 1993

Group / Party Rap, Pop-Rap, Old School Rap, Hip-Hop

Among the first groups to tame rap's hardcore mentality into a positive, message-oriented music suitable for teens and mass audiences, Kid 'n Play debuted in 1988 with the platinum album *2 Hype*, which the duo later spun into a deal involving films and a Saturday-morning cartoon show, the first involving a rap act. Though their recording activity became limited during the gangsta-dominated '90s—1991's *Face the Nation* was their last album—the group managed two sequels to their original *House Party* film, as well as the 1991 teen flick *Class Act*. Kid (b. Christopher Reid) and Play (b. Christopher Martin) first met while performing in rival high-school groups and initially teamed up as Fresh Force. Play's former bandmate, Hurby "Luv Bug" Azor, became the duo's manager and signed Kid 'n Play to Select Records in 1987. Despite the predominance of James Brown samples during the mid-'80s, Hurby "Luv Bug" Azor gave *2 Hype* a production job more rooted in disco and pop; thanks to the near Top Ten R&B hit "Rollin' with Kid 'n Play," the album eventually reached platinum status. *—John Bush*

- **2 Hype** / 1988 / Select ✦✦✦✦✦

Kid 'N Play's music height came on their debut album, *2 Hype*. This album rode up the charts with its tamed take on late-'80s New York hip-hop and, more importantly, the group's image as teen-friendly, goofy dancers. This album's standout moment and largest hit, "Do This My Way," serves as a perfect summation of the duo's chemistry that proved so important to their commercial success; while these two two are only modest rappers firing off many clichés on this song as well as others, they do it in such a conversational manner that it proved infectiously appealing to mainstream audiences in 1988. The duo also makes sure never to take the tough stance so prevalent in hip-hop at the time (LL Cool J, Rakim, KRS-One, Chuck D, Ice-T), instead reciting rhymes with a clean, carefree appeal often centering around innocent partying and girl chasing. Since this album's cover art is the only real insight to the group's most important assets—their fashion and their dancing (which made them MTV favorites)—it's somewhat hard to see what the appeal was with this album outside of its teen-friendly aim. Still, the album's simplicity and danceable beats still make it a bit infectious in a sugar-coated kind of way. Unfortunately, the group's image would quickly eclipse their music once they became Hollywood stars, making this their only worthwhile album. *—Jason Birchmeier*

Kid 'N Play's Fun House / 1990 / Select ✦✦✦

One of two releases from the twosome in 1990, this one has new cuts with funkier, looser foundations and more ambitious adult lyrics and rapping style. *—Ron Wynn*

Face the Nation / Sep. 24, 1991 / Select ✦✦

Kool Keith (Dr. Dooom)

Vocals / Underground Rap, Hip-Hop

After single-handedly redefining "warped" as the mind and mouth behind the Bronx-based Ultramagnetic MCs, "Kool" Keith Thornton—aka Rhythm X, aka Dr. Octagon, aka Dr. Dooom, aka Mr. Gerbik—headed for the outer reaches of the stratosphere with a variety of solo projects. A one-time psychiatric patient at Bellevue, Keith's lyrical thematics remained as free-flowing here as they ever were with the NY trio, connecting up complex meters with fierce, layers-deep metaphors and veiled criticisms of those who "water down the sound that comes from the ghetto." His own debut single, "Earth People" by Dr. Octagon, was quietly released in late 1995 on the San Francisco-based Bulk Recordings, and the track spread like wildfire through the hip-hop underground, as did the subsequent self-titled full-length released the following year. Featuring internationally renowned DJ Q-Bert (also of the Invisible Skratch Picklz) on turntables, as well as the Automator and DJ Shadow behind the boards, *Dr. Octagon*'s leftfield fusion of sound collage, fierce turntable work, and bizarre, impressionistic rapping found audiences in the most unlikely of places, from hardcore hip-hop heads to jaded rock critics. Although a somewhat sophomoric preoccupation with body parts and scatology tended to dominate the album, Keith's complex weave of associations and shifting references is quite often amazing in its intricacy. The record found its way to the UK-based abstract hip-hop imprint Mo'Wax (for whom Shadow also records) in mid-1996, and was licensed by the label for European release (Mo'Wax also released a DJ-friendly instrumental version of the album titled, appropriately, *The Instrumentalyst (Octagon Beats)*). The widespread popularity of the album eventually landed Keith at Geffen splinter Dreamworks in 1997; the label gave *Dr. Octagon* its third release mid-year, adding a number of bonus cuts. In early 1999 however, Keith's alter-ego Dr. Dooom unfortunately "killed off" Dr. Octagon on the opening track of the 1999 album *First Come, First Served* (released on Thornton's own Funky Ass label). Kool Keith signed to Ruffhouse/MCA for his second album under *that* alias, 1999's *Black Elvis/Lost in Space*. *Matthew* followed a year later. *—Sean Cooper*

Sex Style / Feb. 3, 1997 / Funky Ass ✦✦✦

It's not that Kool Keith's Dr. Octagon project (released less than a year before) completely avoided sex; in fact, it was the focus of several tracks. It's just that the first album to be released under his own name is completely obsessed with it. Besides the obviously X-rated tracks like "Regular Girl," "Little Girls," & "Lovely Lady," and "In Your Face," Keith does address some of his previous themes—his status as an inter-planetary entity, and the mediocrity of the hip-hop world—but even on those songs, he brings up sex. Several songs are his most extreme ever, much closer to $2 Live Crew than his former band Ultramagnetic MC's, and though the production (by Kut Master Kurt) is just as excellent and eclectic as Dr. Octagon, the hardcore themes could be too much for listeners. *—John Bush*

- **Black Elvis/Lost in Space** / Aug. 10, 1999 / Ruffhouse ✦✦✦✦

After killing off his Dr. Octagon alias and resurrecting himself as an intergalactic Little Richard named Black Elvis (coiffured appropriately), Kool Keith returned in 1999 with his much-anticipated debut for Ruffhouse. Compared to the scatological bombast sprayed all over his *First Come, First Served* LP (released as Dr. Dooom on his own Funky Ass label earlier that year), *Black Elvis/Lost in Space* is remarkably tame. And despite jettisoning cohorts the Automator and DJ QBert, the results sound surprisingly similar to the *Dr. Octagon* album: sparse 808 beats, a few bizarre, faintly menacing organ lines for hooks, and a sample or two the likes of which have never been heard on a Dr. Dre record (like the odd banjo pickings on "Livin' Astro"). Also cropping up are a few of Keith's patented psychedelic nightmares (reminiscent of "Blue Flowers" and "Earth People"), including "Lost in Space," "Rockets on the Battlefield," and "I'm Seein' Robots." For "Supergalactic Lover," Keith injects a bit of stuttered Timbaland funk into the mix, though this tale of sexual prowess is appropriately schizoid. If *Black Elvis/Lost in Space* doesn't make quite the splash of 1996's *Dr. Octagon*, it's mostly because there's a distinct sense that Kool Keith is retreading familiar (through incredibly fun) territory. One thing's for sure, DJ QBert's scratching is definitely missed. *—John Bush*

Matthew / Jul. 25, 2000 / Funky Ass ✦✦

Kool Moe Dee (Mohandas Dewese)

b. 1963, Harlem, NY

Vocals / Party Rap, Pop-Rap, Old School Rap

A member of one of the original hip-hop crews, the Treacherous 3, Kool Moe Dee later became a solo star in his own right in 1986 by teaming with a teenaged Teddy Riley (later famed as the king of new jack swing) on the crossover hit "Go See the Doctor." The single earned him a contract with Jive Records, for which he recorded three successful late-'80s albums, dominated by his skillful speed-raps. A long-running feud with LL Cool J—who stole his aggressive stance and rapping style, he claims—gained Kool Moe Dee headlines for awhile, but he began to fade by the early '90s. After several early street hits with the Treacherous 3 (including a few for Sugar Hill), Kool Moe Dee went solo with a 1986 debut album *I'm Kool Moe Dee* on Jive. With the following year's *How Ya Like Me Now*, Dee struck back at the brash young generation who had forsook their forebears; the cover featured a red Kangol hat—the prominent trademark of LL Cool J—being crushed by the wheel of a Jeep. The album went platinum and was followed two years later by the gold-certified *Knowlege Is King*, for which Dee became the first rapper to perform at the Grammy Awards ceremonies. After his fourth album *Funke Funke Wisdom*, Jive/RCA dropped him, though he returned in 1994 with *Interlude*. *—John Bush*

I'm Kool Moe Dee / 1986 / Jive ✦✦✦

How Ya Like Me Now / 1987 / Jive ✦✦✦✦✦

Kool Moe Dee resented the fact that in the mid- to late '80s, most of rap's founding fathers were enjoying little attention. But Dee himself was one of the few exceptions, and the old-school survivor had a major hit with his sophomore effort, *How Ya Like Me Now*. He would have done better to devote more time to storytelling and less time to boasting, but he definitely brings plenty of soul and spirit (as well as technique) to this material. Though not as strong as his first album, it definitely has its share of classics, including "Wild Wild West," a reflection on the nitty-gritty environment that surrounded rap during its early years; his denunciation of materialism "No Respect"; and the infectious title song, which was clearly inspired by Dee's feud with L.L. Cool J. A few years later, much of the rap world was sick to death of hearing about the feud, but in 1987, it was a major topic of conversation in hip-hop. *—Alex Henderson*

★ **Greatest Hits** / 1989 / Jive ✦✦✦✦✦

As much as any single performer, Kool Moe Dee epitomized rap's rise from an East Coast underground genre to a national youth sound, and has been unceasing in his demands for respect and recognition. Dee was also among the first able to bring social significance to his material without being pedantic, and his songs (with the exception of "They Need Money") weren't littered with sexist and misogynistic rhetoric. This 15-song collection covers his biggest recordings, from novelty-type fare ("The Wild Wild West" and "Whosgotdaflava") to the safe sex number "Go See The Doctor," cultural battle cries like "Rise 'N' Shine" and "No

Respect," and his "war" with L.L. Cool J that peaked with "Death Blow" and "How Ya Like Me Now." —*Ron Wynn*

Knowledge Is King / May 1989 / Jive ♦♦♦

Funke, Funke Wisdom / Jun. 4, 1991 / Jive ♦♦♦

Talib Kweli (Talib Greene)

b. Brooklyn, NY

Vocals / East Coast Rap, Hip-Hop

Alongside fellow literate underground New York rappers such as Mos Def and Pharoahe Monch, Talib Kweli represented a second wave of East Coast rappers focusing their aims on inspirational themes, rather than glamour or violence. After the late '80s Native Tongue movement in New York centered primarily on De La Soul and A Tribe Called Quest, few rappers stepped into the remaining void, until Kweli and his peers hooked up with Rawkus Records. Providing an intelligent alternative to mainstream New York rap in the late '90s—*Jay-Z, Nas, Puff Daddy, Mobb Deep, Wu-Tang*—Kweli's rhymes were instantly championed by underground B-boys and eventually by critics once he found himself releasing major-label albums.

Born in Brooklyn to a literate family with a proud taste for African culture, the rapper's first name, Talib, is an Arabian name meaning "The seeker or student" while his last name, Kweli, is a Ghanaian name meaning "of truth or knowledge." So with a name that literally translates to "the seeker of truth and knowledge," it's little surprise that Kweli found himself drawn to studies and eventually well-thought-out rap music such as De La Soul. After meeting DJ Hi Tek in 1994 during a trip to Cincinnati, OH, where Hi Tek was in a hip-hop group named Mood, and then after meeting Mos Def in 1995 while he was studying experimental theater at N.Y.U., Kweli soon found himself aligned with some like-minded talent.

Soon, Kweli teamed up with DJ Hi Tek to form Reflection Eternal and also teamed up with Mos Def to form Black Star. After finding success with the underground rap label Rawkus Records, on 12"s and on compilations such as *Soundbombing, Lyricist Lounge,* and *New York State of Mind,* Kweli first crossed over into the mainstream with the major-label release of the debut *Black Star* album in 1998. Though Mos Def quickly went on to superstar status with a solo album in the wake of Black Star's success, Kweli eventually put out his own album with [Hi Tek, *Reflection Eternal.* The album appeared in late 2000 with substantial enthusiasm within both the rap community and among critics, who championed the album's responsible tone; record buyers were responsive as well, sending *Reflection Eternal* to a Top 20 debut on the charts. —*Jason Birchmeier*

● **Reflection Eternal** / Oct. 17, 2000 / Priority ♦♦♦♦♦

After releasing a handful of essential 12"s on various Rawkus Records projects in the late '90s, Talib Kweli and DJ Hi-Tek were on the verge of becoming one of hip-hop's best-kept secrets. Yet their original incarnation as a duo expanded into a triumvirate with the inclusion of Mos Def and transformed their eventual manifestation into Black Star, thwarting their initial bid for acclaim. While Kweli's stardom may have been initially eclipsed by his more charismatic cohort, Mos Def, *Reflection Eternal* houses enough merit to establish Talib as one of this generation's most poetic MCs. Kweli is a rare MC, as his lyricism resounds with a knowledge that transcends his still tender age. He does not aspire to reprogram the masses with this album, just rehabilitate them, as he laments on "The Blast": "They ask me what I'm writing for/I'm writing to show you what we fighting for." In an effort to celebrate life, Kweli breaks down hip-hop's obsession with death on "Good Mourning" and "Too Late." But it is his varied lyrical content that is most inspiring, effortlessly transitioning from the poignant circle-of-life epic "For Women" to the rugged "Some Kind of Wonderful" and "Down for the Count," featuring Rah Digga and Xzibit. While the unassuming, largely minimalist grooves that Hi-Tek supplied on Black Star's debut longed for a dramatic flair, he displays a remarkable maturation on *Reflection Eternal.* In fact, Tek's loping keyboard wails, soulful staccato claps, and shimmering piano loops are often sublime in their arrangement and outcome. Though Kweli and Hi-Tek's debut harbors over-ambitious tendencies, clocking in at over 70 minutes in length, they are a duo that will undoubtedly stain their memory into hip-hop's collective memory with this noteworthy debut. Welcome to the new generation of Native Tongue speaking. —*Matt Conaway*

Lil' Kim

b. Jul. 11, 1975

Vocals / Hardcore Rap, East Coast Rap, Gangsta Rap, Hip-Hop

After making her presence known on Junior M.A.F.I.A.'s debut album *Conspiracy,* Lil' Kim launched a solo career in 1996 with the release of her first record, *Hard Core.* As the album's title implies, Lil' Kim was a raritiy among female rappers—one that not only concentrated on edgy, hardcore rap, but also explicit sexuality, two territories that had long been the province of male rappers. Of course, Lil' Kim's near-pornographic sexuality and hard-edged rhythms made her an anamoly within hip-hop, but *Hard Core* proved that she was no novelty, as it garnered positive reviews and strong sales. The first single from the album, "No Time," was a duet with Sean "Puffy" Combs, and became a number one rap single. —*Stephen Thomas Erlewine*

● **Hard Core** / Nov. 12, 1996 / Undeas/Big Beat ♦♦♦♦

After making her presence felt on Junior M.A.F.I.A.'s hit debut album, Lil' Kim broke out on her own, refashioning herself as a hardcore and defiantly sexy female rapper. Working with producers like Sean Combs and the Notorious B.I.G., Lil' Kim has developed a sleek but hard sound that is positively dripping with attitude and sex. When she slips into conventional, seductive R&B the record loses some steam, but her filthy, hard-driving tracks are stunning—it's hardcore in more than one sense of the word. —*Stephen Thomas Erlewine*

Notorious K.I.M. / Jun. 27, 2000 / Atlantic ♦♦♦

LL Cool J (James Todd Smith)

b. Jan. 14, 1968, Bayshore, Long Island, NY

Rap, Vocals / Pop-Rap, East Coast Rap, Hip-Hop

Hip-hop is notorious for short-lived careers, but LL Cool J is the inevitable exception that proves the rule. Releasing his first single "I Can't Live Without My Radio" in 1985 when he was just 19 years old, LL Cool J initially was a hard-hitting, street-wise B-Boy with spare beats and ballistic rhymes. He quickly developed an alternate style, a romantic—and occasionally sappy—lover's rap epitomized by his mainstream breakthrough single, "I Need Love." LL's first two albums, *Radio* and *Bigger and Deffer,* made him a star, but he strived for pop stardom a little too much on 1989's *Walking With A Panther.* By 1990, his audience had declined somewhat, since his ballads and party raps were the opposite of the chaotic, edgy political hip-hop of Public Enemy or the gangsta rap of N.W.A., but he shot back to the top of the charts with *Mama Said Knock You Out,* which established him as one of hip-hop's genuine superstars. By the mid-'90s, he had starred in his own televsion sitcom, *In the House,* appeared in several films and had racked up two of his biggest singles with "Hey Lover" and "Doin' It." In short, he had proven that rappers could have long-term careers. —*Stephen Thomas Erlewine*

☆ **Radio** / 1985 / Def Jam ♦♦♦♦♦

Run-D.M.C. was the first rap act to produce cohesive, fully realized albums, and LL Cool J was the first to follow in their footsteps. LL was a mere 17 years old when he recorded his classic debut album *Radio,* a brash, exuberant celebration of booming beats and B-boy attitude that launched not only the longest career in hip-hop, but also Rick Rubin's seminal Def Jam label. Rubin's back-cover credit ("Reduced by Rick Rubin") is an entirely apt description of his bare-bones production style. *Radio* is just as stripped-down and boisterously aggressive as any Run-D.M.C. album, sometimes even moreso; the instrumentation is basically just a cranked-up beatbox, punctuated by DJ scratching. There are occasional brief samples, but few do anything more than emphasize a downbeat. The result is rap at its most skeletal, with a hard-hitting, street-level aggression that perfectly matches LL's cocksure teenage energy. Even the two ballads barely sound like ballads, since they're driven by the same slamming beats. Though they might sound a little squared-off to modern ears, LL's deft lyrics set new standards for MCs at the time; his clever disses and outrageous but playful boasts still hold up poetically. Although even LL himself would go on to more intricate rhyming, it isn't really necessary on such a loud, thumping adrenaline rush of a record. *Radio* was both an expansion of rap's artistic possibilities and a commercial success (for its time), helping attract new multiracial audiences to the music. While it may take a few listens for modern ears to adjust to the minimalist production, the fact that it hews so closely to rap's basic musical foundation means that it still possesses a surprisingly fresh energy, and isn't nearly as dated as many efforts that followed it (including, ironically, some of LL's own). —*Steve Huey*

Bigger and Deffer / 1987 / Def Jam ♦♦

Walking With a Panther / 1989 / Def Jam ♦♦♦♦

Walking With a Panther stands as a key turning point in LL Cool J's long career, when he soon found himself not quite as "bad!" as he once claimed. When he devoted a large portion of his first two albums, *Radio* (1985) and *Bigger and Deffer* (1987), to boasting about his talent in old-school fashion ("Rock the Bells," "I'm Bad"), he had justification—at that point in time he was arguably the undisputed MC of MCs. But by the time *Walking With a Panther* hit the streets in 1989, LL had a roster of contenders, most notably Kool Moe Dee and Ice T, who both ridiculed him on vinyl. It was clear to most that LL had to modify his approach. And, yes, he indeed modified his approach with *Walking With a Panther,* rapping over much more developed and dynamic production featuring a heavy use of samples as was the vogue at the time; furthermore, he started rapping about a host of topics besides himself. But besides "Going Back to Cali," one of LL's perennial moments, he's at his best here when he's rapping about women ("Big Ole Butt," "Jingling Baby"). Still, despite the variety and the improved production, this album never comes across as successfully as it should. While some tracks such as "Going Back to Cali" and "Jingling Baby" are successful, most aren't. At this point in his career, LL's limited—he can rap about himself and ladies but not much else. —*Jason Birchmeier*

Mama Said Knock You Out / Aug. 1990 / Def Jam ♦♦♦♦♦

Increasingly dismissed by hip-hop fans as an old-school relic and a slick pop sellout, LL Cool J rang in the '90s with *Mama Said Knock You Out,* a hard-edged artistic renaissance that became his biggest-selling album ever. Part of the credit is due to producer Marley Marl, whose thumping, bass-heavy sound helps LL reclaim the aggression of his early days. *Mama Said Knock You Out* isn't quite as hard as *Radio,* instead striking a balance between attitude and accessibility. But its greater variety and more layered arrangements make it LL's most listenable album, as well as keeping it in line with more contemporary sensibilities. Marl's productions on the slower tracks are smooth and soulful, but still funky; as a result, the ladies'-man side of LL's persona is the most convincing it's ever been, and his ballads don't feel sappy for arguably the first time on record. Even apart from the sympathetic musical settings, LL is at his most lyrically acrobatic, and the testosterone-fueled anthems are delivered with a force not often heard since his debut. The album's hits are a microcosm of its range—"The Boomin' System" is a nod to bass-loving b-boys with car stereos; "Around the Way Girl" is a lush, winning ballad; and the title cut is one of the most blistering statements of purpose in hip-hop. It leaves no doubt that *Mama Said Knock You Out* was intended to be a *tour de force,* to regain LL Cool J's credibility while proving that he was still one of rap's most singular talents. It succeeded mightily, making him an across-the-board superstar and cementing his status as a rap icon beyond any doubt. —*Steve Huey*

14 Shots to the Dome / 1993 / Def Jam ♦♦

Mr. Smith / Nov. 1995 / Def Jam ♦♦♦

On the strength of the slow-burning Boyz II Men duet "Hey Lover," LL Cool J returned to the top of the charts with *Mr. Smith,* meaning the album is somewhat of a comeback for the veteran rapper. LL Cool J's skills had never deserted him, but his previous album, *14 Shots to the Dome*, was a exercise in hardcore that only worked in fits and spurts. There's a couple of hard moments on *Mr. Smith*, but the album is at its most successful when he concentrates on his seductive, romantic side. LL has gotten a bit dirtier since the teenage days of "I Need Love," but he never steps over into the explicit, lewd come-ons of R. Kelly, preferring to suggest everything with a series of double entendres, metaphors, and analogies. *Mr. Smith* isn't a perfect record—there's too many slack moments for it to qualifty as one of his best—but it proves that LL Cool J remains vital a decade after his debut. —*Stephen Thomas Erlewine*

★ **All World: Greatest Hits** / Nov. 5, 1996 / Def Jam ♦♦♦♦♦
All World: Greatest Hits is an excellent compilation of LL Cool J's greatest hits, featuring 16 of his biggest and best singles, including "I Can't Live Without My Radio," "Rock the Bells," "I'm Bad," "I Need Love," "Going Back to Cali," "Jingling Baby," "The Boomin' System," "Mama Said Knock You Out," "Around the Way Girl" and "Hey Lover." It's the definitive retrospective of one of the greatest rappers to ever record, and if you doubt that statement's true, just take a listen to this collection. —*Stephen Thomas Erlewine*

Phenomenon / Sep. 23, 1997 / Def Jam ♦♦♦
Mr. Smith was the third comeback for LL Cool J, the third time he returned to commerical and creative strengths after being written off by many critics and fans. So, it shouldn't come as a surprise that its followup, *Phenomenon*, finds LL coasting—after all, after his two previous comeback albums, he allowed himself to slacken the pace a little bit and ride on his credentials. Fortunately, *Phenomenon* isn't nearly as weak as *14 Shots to the Dome* or *Bigger and Deffer*, but it simply doesn't have the power of masterpieces like *Radio* and *Mama Said Knock You Out*. Essentially, it's a retread of *Mr. Smith*, offering the same laid-back soul jams and rolling party beats. There's a couple of killer singles, a few dogs and a lot of filler—more so than on *Mr. Smith*, in fact. Still, *Phenomenon* sounds good when it's playing and even if it doesn't leave a lasting impression, it's a solid, professional effort that illustrate why LL is still in the game, 12 years after his first record. —*Stephen Thomas Erlewine*

G.O.A.T. Featuring James T. Smith: The Greatest of All Time / Sep. 12, 2000 / Def Jam ♦♦♦

Main Source

f. 1989
Group / Jazz-Rap, East Coast Rap, Alternative Rap, Hip-Hop
New York rappers Main Source exploded into the hip-hop universe with *Breaking Atoms* for Wild Pitch in 1991. It featured the Large Professor's cutting, often cynical narratives about everything from police brutality to betrayal by friends. The one-time cohort of Producer Paul C., the Large Professor was joined by twin disc jockeys K-Cut and Sir Scratch. The single "Lookin' at the Front Door" proved a sizable hit, and Main Source seemed on its way. But nearly three years later, no second LP had been issued; the group eventually split due to creative differences, after which the Large Professor left and was replaced by another MC. During the mid- to late '90s, the Large Professor began to gain considerable notoriety and album credits for his musical production. Such talented work can be heard on projects like A Tribe Called Quest's *Midnight Marauders* and Nas' *Illmatic*, as well as countless single remixes for groups like Organized Konfusion, the Beastie Boys, and Common Sense. —*Ron Wynn & Qa'id Jacobs*

● **Breaking Atoms** / 1991 / EMI America ♦♦♦♦♦
The chemistry between the Large Professor, Sir Scratch, and K-Cut was sufficiently powerful to make *Breaking Atoms* an appreciated album upon its release in 1991, as well as a historically valued recording after the breakup of the original crew. The production credits on *Breaking Atoms* go to the collective Main Source; listening to the album in hindsight, it is difficult to miss the stylistic trademarks (such as the raspy drum kit of the EMU SP1200 and the soul samples) that typically identify the Large Professor's production. In any case, *Breaking Atoms* featured original concepts, innovative production, and conscientious lyrics. Some of the standout tracks include "Just a Friendly Game of Baseball," a well-developed rhyme in which the Large Professor uses a detailed analogy of baseball to describe—in no subtle way—the brutality with which police treat young black men. "Looking at the Front Door" (one of the three commercial singles released from this album) was very popular and was accompanied by a video which helped Main Source to obtain an audience. The two other commercial single releases were "Peace Is Not the Word to Play" and "Live at the Barbeque." The latter was another very influential track, serving as the launching pad for the careers of both Akinyele and Nas. A die-hard favorite of serious hip-hop fans, it's a classic posse cut which has not only Nas and Akinyele delivering tight lyrics, but Joe Fatal and the Large Professor also adding to the lyrical stew to make this cut historically famous. The tracks on *Breaking Atoms* are infused with lucent instrumentation, creative scratching, entertaining bridges, and proficient lyrics, all of which combine to make this a memorable album sure to live in the annals of hip-hop's influential recordings. —*Qa'id Jacobs*

Mantronix

f. 1984, New York, NY, **db.** 1991
Group / Old School Rap, Electro, Club/Dance, House, Hip-Hop
Over and above their standing as one of the best and most innovative groups from hip-hop's golden age, Mantronix provided rap music with its first man-machine, Kurtis Mantronik. A turntable master who incorporated synthesizers and samplers into the rhythmatic mix instead of succumbing to the popular use of samples simply as pop hooks, Mantronik exploited technology with a quintessentially old-school attitude which had little use for instruction manuals and accepted use. After the hip-hop world began to catch up with Mantronik's developments, he moved from hardcore hip-hop to skirt the leading edge of club music, from electro to ragga, techno and house—boundaries increasingly fragile due to his pioneering efforts. With MC Tee on vocals, Mantronix debuted in 1985 with the single "Fresh Is the Word," a street and club hit around New York. The full-length *Mantronix: The Album* followed in 1986 and was paced by "Ladies" and "Basslines" became big street hits as well, and even crossed over to join the first wave of hip-hop chartmakers in Britain. The increasing popularity of hip-hop gave Mantronix a chance at a major-label contract, and in 1988 the duo released their first album for Capitol, *In Full Effect*. Two additional albums followed, but Mantronix had effectively disbanded by 1991. Kurtis Mantronik began producing other acts, but returned later in the decade with a solo LP. —*John Bush*

★ **Mantronix: The Album** / 1985 / Sleeping Bag ♦♦♦♦♦
Curtis "Mantronik" Khaleel was often quoted as saying that his mission was to "take \rap a step beyond the streets," and the innovative producer/mixmaster accomplished that goal on Mantronix's debut album, *Mantronix: The Album*. This excellent 1985 LP was way ahead of its time; while the rapping of Mantronix's partner MC Tee is pure mid-'80s New York \hip-hop, the production is anything but conventional. On gems like "Needle to the Groove," "Bassline," and the hit "Fresh Is the Word," you can hear the parallels between Tee's rhyming and the East Coast b-boy rhymes that Run-D.M.C., LL Cool J, and the Fat Boys were providing in 1985. But *Mantronix: The Album*'s high-tech, futuristic production sets it apart from other New York \hip-hop of the mid-'80s, and even though one of the LP's tracks is titled "Hardcore Hip-Hop," Mantronix had a hard time appealing to \hip-hop's hardcore. *Mantronix: The Album* actually fared better in \dance music, \electro-funk, and \club circles than it did among hardcore b-boys. But this is definitely a \hip-hop record, and it is also Mantronix's most essential release. —*Alex Henderson*

In Full Effect / 1988 / Capitol ♦♦♦
The Capitol debut for Mantronix, and the final album featuring rapper MC Tee. This album skirted the lower regions of the pop charts and had a less abrasive, smoother sound, although the patented dance/hip-hop/urban contemporary fusion hadn't been affected. But overall, it wasn't quite as risky or spirited as their Sleeping Bag records, despite Mantronik's continuing production excellence. —*Ron Wynn*

This Should Move Ya / 1990 / Capitol ♦♦♦
Mantronix switched labels in the late '80s, moving from the independent Sleeping Bag to the major label Capitol. This was their second Capitol album, and it worked out fine. Although the lineup had now changed, with Bryce Luvah and D.J.D. on board rather than M.C. Tee, the group had another strong single in "Got To Have Your Love," and *Capitol* was providing Curtis "Mantronik" Kahleel with a bigger push and sharper production and sound. But the underground spirit that permeated Mantronix's *Sleeping Bag* albums was missing, as was the quirky air that marked their past singles. —*Ron Wynn*

The Incredible Sound Machine / Mar. 18, 1991 / Capitol ♦♦

The Best of Mantronix 1985-1999 / Mar. 15, 1999 / Virgin ♦♦♦♦♦
A solid Mantronix compilation (though UK only) for all those unable to find the out-of-print originals, *The Best of 1985-1999* includes undeniable hip-hop classics like "Bassline," "Ladies" and "King of the Beats" as well as a new single, "Push Yer Hands Up" (which had first appeared on Mantronik's 1998 solo album). —*John Bush*

Mase

b. Aug. 27, 1978, Jacksonville, FL
Vocals / East Coast Rap, Hip-Hop
Mase is a Brooklyn-based rapper who began his career by appearing as a guest artist on hits like the Notorious B.I.G.'s "Mo Money Mo Problems," Junior M.A.F.I.A.'s "Young Casanova" and Puff Daddy's "Can't Nobody Hold Me Down." In the fall of 1997, Mase released his debut album *Harlem World*, which featured guest spots by Puff Daddy, 8-Ball & MJG, Total, Monifah and the Lox. *The Movement*, credited to Mase Presents Harlem World, follwed in 1997. Two years later, Mase returned with *Double Up*. —*Stephen Thomas Erlewine*

● **Harlem World** / Oct. 28, 1997 / Bad Boy ♦♦♦♦
It's a little ironic that Mase, who made his reputation as a guest rapper on records by Puff Daddy and the Notorious B.I.G., almost seems like a guest himself on his debut album, *Harlem World*. Like many big-budget hip-hop records, *Harlem World* is nearly a various-artists collection, featuring an array of different producers and guest rappers that often obscure Mase himself. Still, all that talent guarantees that the record will be well-crafted, and that certainly is true. With Sean "Puffy" Combs and Jermaine Dupri behind the decks for much of the album, *Harlem World* has a dense, funky sound that is uptempo party-rap at its best. Like any late-'90s hip-hop record, it's a little too long for its own good, but the singles, such as the bouncy "Feel So Good," make it worthwhile. It still would have been nice to hear more of Mase on his own album, though. —*Leo Stanley*

Double Up / Jun. 15, 1999 / Bad Boy ♦♦♦♦
Shortly after he completed his second album, *Double Up*, Mase announced his retirement from hip-hop. He chose to follow the path of the Lord, which didn't just mean that he could no longer rap—he no longer had the desire to do so. Frustratingly, the album finds Mase continuing to improve, but falling short of delivering a stunning farewell that could stand as his last testament. *Double Up* pretty much recycles the same hooktastic pop-rap formulas as *Harlem World*, following Puff Daddy's design of borrowing the best, regardless of the source (for example, Gary Numan provides the basis for one cut), and turning it into radio-ready party music. While this is pleasing to the ear, it tends to be a little monotonous and too predictable, especially when compared to Mase's raps. True, he still favors a flat, slow delivery but there's a growing undercurrent of distaste for hip-hop clichés, a feeling which, ultimately, led to Mase throwing in the towel and turning to God. Certainly, this gives *Double Up* more lyrical drama than the average hip-hop album, and it's often enough to keep it compelling when the music flat-lines. Still, there's still the sneaking suspicion that *Double Up* could have been more—either an excellent pop-rap record with no flab, or a convincing statement of purpose, evidence of why Mase had to leave hip-hop behind. As it stands, it's simply a good sequel to a promising debut. Which, of course, is all that it needed to be, but in light of Mase's retirement, it's hard not to want more. —*Stephen Thomas Erlewine*

Master P. (Percy Miller)

b. Apr. 29, 1970, New Orleans, LA
Vocals, Producer / Southern Rap, Hardcore Rap, Gangsta Rap, Hip-Hop
Master P created a hip-hop empire without registering on any mainstream radar. For several years, he operated solely in the rap underground, eventually surfacing in the mid-'90s as a

recording artist and producer who knew exactly what his audience wanted. And what they wanted was gangsta rap. With his independent label No Limit, Master P gave them gangsta rap at its most basic—violent, vulgar lyrics, hard-edged beats, whiny synthesizers and blunted bass. He wasn't a great rapper, and neither was anyone on No Limit; occasionally, the No Limit rappers were even talentless and clumsy. But in a time when major labels were running away from the controversy that gangsta rap caused and Dr. Dre, the father of the genre, was proclaiming it dead, Master P stayed on course, delivering album after album of unadulterated gangsta. It was recorded cheaply and packaged cheaply, and almost all of the records on No Limit were interchangeable, but that didn't matter, because Master P kept making money and getting paid. *—Stephen Thomas Erlewine*

Get Away Clean / 1991 / No Limit/Priority ✦

Mama's Bad Boy / 1992 / In-A-Minute ✦

Ghetto's Tryin' to Kill Me! / Jul. 15, 1994 / No Limit/Priority ✦✦✦

99 Ways to Die / 1995 / No Limit/Priority ✦✦

Ice Cream Man / Apr. 1996 / No Limit/Priority ✦✦✦

● **Ghetto D** / Sep. 2, 1997 / No Limit/Priority ✦✦✦✦✦
On the surface, *Ghetto D* may look like another piece of product from Master P's No Limit empire, and there's a certain amount of truth to that. Master P is a master marketer and he knows how to create demand for his product, which means informing the public that it is out there. He spreads the word about future No Limit releases throughout *Ghetto D:* artwork for forthcoming albums forms 90 percent of the album's artwork, and No Limit artists rap on the record as much as Master P himself. As a result, *Ghetto D* plays much like one of the *West Coast Bad Boyz* discs—it sounds like a various-artists sampler. And not only does it sound like a various-artists record, it also sounds like a virtual catalog of '90s rap styles, from wimpy Bone Thugs-N-Harmony ballads ("I Miss My Homies") to Wu-Tang craziness ("Let's Get 'Em") to G-funk ("Weed & Money"). Master P is a consummate ripoff artist, capable of copying any number of popular records and styles with flair. He's done this on almost all of No Limit's records, but what makes *Ghetto D* different is the ease of the whole thing. Master P is using better equipment this time around, which helps him make better, more seamless records, thereby making his facsimiles sound similar to the originals. The shameless ripoffs make *Ghetto D* an entertaining listen—it's fun to guess who the No Limit crew is ripping off now—yet it's hampered by its ridiculous 80-minute running time. Theoretically, it gives you more bang for your buck, but by the ninth song, "Captain Kirk," the album seems endless. However, that overindulgence is a hallmark of Master P and No Limit, and that's what makes *Ghetto D* his definitive statement. *—Stephen Thomas Erlewine*

MP Da Last Don / Jun. 2, 1998 / No Limit/Priority ✦✦✦

Only God Can Judge Me / Oct. 26, 1999 / No Limit/Priority ✦✦

Ghetto Postage / Nov. 28, 2000 / No Limit/Priority ✦✦✦✦
It's hard to attribute musical quality to Master P's success in the late '90s, but primarily based upon the quality of *Ghetto Postage* rather than marketing gimmicks or musical trends, the rapper has come close to rivaling his best album of the 1990s, *Ghetto D.* Like that breakthrough album, *Ghetto Postage* is a simplistic tour de force through a myriad of proven gangsta rap motifs. Beginning with the standard "I'm Bout It" variation, this time titled "Bout Dat," Master P and his post-Beats By the Pound production team—primarily Carlos Stephens, XL, Ke-Noe, Myke Diesel, and Suga Bear—move through the motifs without making them seem too clichéd and, more importantly, performing with an aura of confidence and poise, two attributes sorely lacking on *Only God Can Judge Me,* this album's clumsy predecessor. So while *Ghetto Postage* doesn't win any awards for finesse or craft, even if it is one of the best No Limit albums, it does deserve acclaim for not surrendering to the trite stunnin'-bling-bling-flossfest clichés littering rap at the end of 2000 and for at least being a blatant motif exercise with integrity—thug farce or not, Master P is actually a rather *likable* guy here. And more than anything, he does what he does best here: He gives his fans exactly what they want—ultra-simple, call-and-response gangsta rap with charisma—without any self-serving, ego-centric attempts to be an "artist." *—Jason Birchmeier*

MC Hammer (Stanley Kirk Burrell)

b. Mar. 30, 1962, Oakland, CA
Vocals / Pop-Rap, West Coast Rap, Christian Rap, Hip-Hop
Considered either the ultimate success story or consummate fraud, Oakland's MC Hammer, a one-time jack-of-all-trades for the Oakland Athletics baseball team, dominated the charts in 1990 with *Please Hammer Don't Hurt 'Em.* The single "U Can't Touch This," despite a rather feeble rap and recycle job on Rick James's single "Superfreak," was an enormous crossover smash. Hammer live puts on a fine show as far as dancing, sound, light effects, production, and such. But from a technical standpoint, everything, from his rhymes to his enunciation, qualifies as the ultimate in "wack" (weak) performance. He does have great taste in cover songs, picking choice items from Marvin Gaye, B.B. King, The Chi-Lites, and Prince, among others. He's since dropped the MC from his name.

After staying in the limelight as a race horse owner and Evander Holyfield's promoter, Hammer returned to the rap wars in 1994 with *The Funky Headhunter.* It featured a leaner, harder sound, with assistance and material provided by gangsta-rap producers, and featured Hammer sporting a more street look. He previewed the new style on Arsenio Hall's show early in the year, then issued the CD in March. It debuted at number two on *Billboard*'s R&B charts, then dipped the next week to six. Skeptics voiced their doubts about the new Hammer, especially in the hip-hop press. *—Ron Wynn*

● **Greatest Hits** / Oct. 1, 1996 / Capitol ✦✦✦✦✦
Despite being one of the best-selling rappers of all-time, none of MC Hammer's albums were very consistent—the singles stood out like a sore thumb among the filler on each record, which is why *Greatest Hits* is such a good bargain. *Greatest Hits* compiles 12 of Hammer's biggest hits for Capitol Records, including "U Can't Touch This," "Pump It Up," "Turn This Mutha Out," "They Put Me in the Mix," "Have You Seen Her," "Pray," "Here Comes the Hammer," "2 Legit 2 Quit," "Do Not Pass Me By," and "Addams Groove." It's not only an excellent introduction to MC Hammer, it's the best album in his entire catalog. *—Stephen Thomas Erlewine*

Method Man (Clifford Smith)

b. Apr. 2, 196?, Alexandria, VA
Vocals / Hardcore Rap, East Coast Rap, Hip-Hop
Born Clifford Smith on Staten Island, Method Man and his mush-mouthed rapping style electrified the 1993 debut album by the hip-hop collective Wu-Tang Clan. The incredibly dark, raw sound of *Enter the Wu-Tang (36 Chambers)* influenced many rappers, and the album eventually reached gold status. As part of the Wu-Tang Clan's contract, each member had the authority to sign separate solo contracts, so Method Man moved to Def Jam for his solo debut *Tical.* The single "Bring the Pain" just missed the Top 40 in 1994, but the following year "I'll Be There for You/You're All I Need to Get By" (his duet with Mary J. Blige) reached number three in the charts. His second duet, "How High" featuring Redman, hit the Top 15 in August 1995. A single with Wu-Tang mates Raekwon and Ghost Face Killer breached the Top 40 later that year. *Tical 2: Judgment Day* followed in 1998, and a year later Method Man resurfaced with *Blackout!,* his long-awaited collaboration with Redman. *—John Bush*

● **Tical** / 1994 / Def Jam ✦✦✦✦✦
As a quick follow-up to Wu-Tang Clan's debut album *Enter the Wu-Tang,* Method Man's solo debut confirms the rapper's status as the group's undeniable superstar. Never short on charisma, Method Man accentuates his lucid lyrical flow with ample personality on *Tical;* on each song, you listen attentively, forever engaged with the rapper's witty rhymes. Furthermore, RZA shines as a producer here, proving not only that *Enter the Wu-Tang* wasn't a novelty record but also that he can shape his beats and soundscapes to each member's personality. In the case of Method Man, RZA chooses to craft short, up-tempo tracks driven by aggressive beats, particularly on raging songs such as "Bring the Pain" and "Release Yo' Delf." Furthermore, besides these rambunctious moments, the album's other noteworthy moment comes on "All I Need," a similarly thunderous song that uncannily functions as a love ballad, delivered with plenty of wit. Yet Method Man's superstar antics, his one-man showmanship, and RZA's accompanying beats also prevent this album from being as well-crafted as successive Wu-Tang solo albums such as Raekwon's *Only Built 4 Cuban Linx,* the Genius' *Liquid Swords,* and Ghostface Killah's *Ironman.* Where those albums find RZA stepping into the spotlight with highly cinematic production and also find a greater abundance of Wu-Tang guest appearances, resulting in conceptual albums, *Tical* comes off sounding like a collection of radio-aimed singles. Still, even if this album isn't as all-around poetic as the other aforementioned early Wu-Tang solo albums, Method Man is still the group's best MC, and *Tical* succinctly summarizes why. Furthermore, the album's consistent production style makes it a more accessible listen than succeeding albums such as *Tical 2000: Judgement Day.* *—Jason Birchmeier*

Tical 2000: Judgement Day / Nov. 10, 1998 / Def Jam ✦✦✦✦
After attaining superstar status with the short, simple, and to-the-point accessibility of *Tical* (and heavily aided by RZA's rousing production), Method Man took a drastically different approach with *Tical 2000: Judgement Day,* making an epic album full of twisting story lines, countless guest stars, and a revolving roster of producers. So looking at the quite opposite approach Method Man chose for his sophomore album, it's a bit difficult to comparatively rate the two since they have so little in common. On the one hand, where *Tical* suffered a bit with its one-sidedness, *Tical 2000* manages to bring an exceeding amount of variety: an abundance of skits, numerous non-Wu-Tang guest rappers, and a revolving ensemble of producers. Yet on the other hand, where *Tical* was driven by effective consistency, *Tical 2000* is weighed down and ultimately diluted by its far-reaching scope. And the latter of these two views seems the more important attribute to note with this particular album. In his aim to improve upon *Tical*'s few minor weaknesses, Method Man simply went too far; there are just way too many skits here and too many guest appearances to make this a beginning to end, satisfying listen—with variety comes inconsistency. So even if tracks such as the album-concluding "Judgment Day" are magnificent, it's often a chore to get there without skipping tracks. *—Jason Birchmeier*

Blackout! / Sep. 28, 1999 / Def Jam ✦✦✦✦

Mobb Deep

f. 1992
Group / Hardcore Rap, East Coast Rap, Gangsta Rap, Hip-Hop
While most hardcore gangsta rappers and rap groups are quickly written off by seasoned rap fans and critics as lowbrow exploitation, Mobb Deep quickly overcame this initial stereotype in the late '90s, becoming one of the few gangsta rap groups to garner unanimous acclaim from all sides of the rap community. Mobb Deep members Prodigy and Havoc originally met while both attending the prestigious Graphic Arts High School in Manhattan as teenagers. Still in their late teens, the duo released their debut album in 1993, *Juvenile Hell,* on the 4th-n-Broadway label. Though the album wasn't that successful from either a financial or critical standpoint, it did serve as a fitting platform for the duo to launch their careers. Their brutally honest reality rapping and complimentary self-produced melancholy beats landed them a deal with the up-and-coming Loud label in 1995, resulting in their first major-label release, *The Infamous.* Propelled to awareness partially by fellow Queens rapper Nas, who took a similar approach lyrically on his championed *Illmatic* album from 1994, Mobb Deep suddenly found themselves developing a quickly growing cult following. Even critics championed their poetic depiction of New York street life and also their trademark production, the bleak aural equivalent of their sullen rhymes. By the end of the decade, Mobb Deep's *Murda Muzik* debuted at number three on *Soundscan* before quickly going platinum, exemplifying exactly how far they had come within less than a decade without compromising their harsh approach. *—Jason Birchmeier*

The Infamous / Apr. 25, 1995 / Loud ♦♦♦♦
Where Mobb Deep's debut album *Juvenile Hell* garnered the young duo a healthy cult following and scored them a record deal with *Loud Records*, it seems merely an omen of what the Queensbridge rappers would achieve on *The Infamous*. At the time of this album's release, they were relatively unknown. Luckily for them, though, another Queensbridge rapper with a similar poetic style of reality rapping, Nas, had won tremendous acclaim with his debut, *Illmatic*. So when this release hit the streets, the public was hungry for more of what Nas had delivered in such harsh terms; *The Infamous* didn't disappoint. Undeniably even more bleak than *Illmatic*, it functioned as a cinematic portrait of Hellish New York City, the ghetto lifestyle that hadn't yet made its way into East Coast rap in the early 1990s. And with the help of two potent singles that were boosted by substantial radio play—"Shook Ones, Pt. 2" and "Survival of the Fittest"—*The Infamous* eventually made its way into the hands of critics and hip-hop heads outside of New York. As a result, this album set the stage for the breakthrough success of the group's successive album, *Hell on Earth*. Yet where this next album featured a polished, more developed version of *Havoc's* trademark sullen production—chilling piano notes, shimmering melancholy strings, dusty crackling ambience, emotive cries of sadness—*The Infamous'* production was less polished and incredibly raw, making this album what many fans consider to be their finest, as the group slowly ascended to mass-catering commercial popularity. *—Jason Birchmeier*

● **Hell on Earth** / Nov. 19, 1996 / Loud ♦♦♦♦♦
When it came time for Mobb Deep to follow up the duo's acclaimed *The Infamous* album, Havoc and Prodigy chose not to depart from their formula for success, crafting yet another album of foreboding beats, eerie soundscapes, and grim lyrics. Since Havoc handles most of the group's production, duplicating his patented aesthetic—the sound of harsh urban darkness set to symphonic beats—wasn't a problem; similarly, he and his partner, Prodigy, didn't seem short on disturbing reality-based rhymes about the side of street life no one likes to think about. *Hell on Earth* remains Mobb Deep's best '90s album, surpassing the oft-hailed *Infamous* album with its aesthetics. Yes, Havoc and Prodigy are repeating themselves here in terms of both production and MCing, but they polish their style, crafting more evocative soundscapes and reciting more horrifying rhymes. The album's highlights—most notably "Hell on Earth" and "G.O.D., Pt. 3"—prove this, surpassing even *The Infamous'* best moment, "Shook Ones, Pt. 2." Of course, it's debatable whether or not the group's succeeding album, *Murda Musik*, tops this album. That album's shining moment, "Quiet Storm," is Mobb Deep's best moment of the decade, but *Murda Muzik* finds the duo trying to expand by incorporating guest rappers and experimenting with new styles; it is this experimentation, though, that prevents *Murda Muzik* from surpassing *Hell on Earth*, a perfect summation from beginning to end of the group's trademark aesthetic. *—Jason Birchmeier*

Murda Muzik / Apr. 27, 1999 / Loud ♦♦♦♦

Pharoahe Monch

Vocals / Underground Rap, East Coast Rap, Alternative Rap, Hip-Hop
While a member of the New York City duo Organized Konfusion, Pharoahe Monch developed a reputation as one of underground hip-hop's pre-eminent lyricists, crafting intricate and intelligent raps with partner Prince Poetry. After recording three albums together from 1991-1997, the two split up amicably, and Monch pursued a more aggressive solo style with the terrific independent label Rawkus. He made guest appearances on other artists' records and contributed tracks to the Rawkus compilation *Soundbombing II*, which raised expectations for his solo debut. The single/video "Simon Says" was released in the summer of 1999 and became a massive hit among rap and club audiences, setting the stage for a surprising debut—just short of the Top 40—for the full-length *Internal Affairs* upon its release several months later. *—Steve Huey*

● **Internal Affairs** / Oct. 19, 1999 / Priority ♦♦♦♦
Pharoahe Monch, the more dynamic member of the ultra-underground duo Organized Konfusion released *Internal Affairs*, his first solo project, in late 1999. Pharoahe, a lyrical mastermind and card-carrying subterranean hip-hopper for eight years plus, possesses the ability to convey a message through painting clear pictures with his rhymes, even when the palette has a smaller range of colors. On *Internal Affairs*, Pharoahe does well to mix his colors, adding another subtle shade to hip-hop. This album's seismic single, "Simon Says," allowed the legendary Pharoahe Monch to taste from the cup of crossover exposure with only slight alterations in style. Organized Konfusion albums, and Pharoahe's work in particular, were always met with critical acclaim, primarily on the strength of lyrics. In the end, however, taking the road less traveled forced Pharoahe to watch as his less talented contemporaries saturated music culture. On *Internal Affairs*, Pharoahe alternates between the abstract and the formulaic quite seamlessly; the abstract cuts contain commercial aspects and vice versa. There's a lot of experimentation musically here, but nothing that could not reach the ears of the ever-expanding and increasingly salacious masses. Beat jewels are laid by the double-dutied Pharoahe, and Lee Stone and Diamond of DITC fame. The absence of recognizable sampling is an underground rubric, and Pharoah stays true to it. Sequencing on the album is layered and innovative. While both versions of "Simon Says" are hardcore club hits that favor repeat listening, "The Truth" may be the most listenable track for its sound and message alike. *Internal Affairs* inspires a range of impressions with a premillennial buzz of frenetic energy, which is illustrated by its extraterrestrial tone. Here is a mixture of subtle thug-ism, storytelling, and poetry of desperation. *—Michael Di Bella*

Mos Def (Dante Beze)

Vocals / East Coast Rap, Hip-Hop
One of the best in the '90s new school of Native Tongue rappers (alongside Common and the Bush Babees), Mos Def guested with old-school Native Tongues De La Soul and recorded for Rawkus Records, the home of independent-minded rap of the 1990s. Born Dante Beze, he began rhyming at the age of nine and formed his first group, Urban Thermo Dynamics (UTD), with his brother and sister. Invited to join the Native Tongues family founded by Afrika Bambaataa and including A Tribe Called Quest and De La Soul among its members, Mos Def agreed and appeared on the fourth De La Soul LP, *Stakes Is High*. He also contributed a verse on the second Bush Babees album, then released his first single "The Universal Magnetic," for the seminal rap independent Rawkus; A Tribe Called Quest's Q-Tip appeared on his second single, "Body Rock." Mos Def began recording for his debut album (with Talib Kweli), *Black Star*, released in September 1998. *Black on Both Sides* followed in the fall of 1999. *—John Bush*

● **Black Star** / Aug. 26, 1998 / Priority ♦♦♦♦♦
While Puff Daddy and his followers continued to dictate the direction hip-hop will take into the millennium, Mos Def and Talib Kweli surfaced from the underground to pull the sounds in the opposite direction. Their 13 rhymefests on this superior debut show that old-school rap still sounds surprisingly fresh in the sea of overblown vanity productions. There's no slack evident in the tight wordplays of Def and Kweli as they twist and turn through sparse, jazz-rooted rhythms calling out for awareness and freedom of the mind. Their viewpoints stem directly from the teachings of Marcus Garvey, the legendary activist who fought for the rights of blacks all around the world in the first half of the 20th century. Def and Kweli's ideals are sure lofty; not only are they out to preach Garvey's words, but they also hope to purge rap music of its negativity and violence. For the most part, it works. Their wisdom-first philosophy hits hard when played off their lyrical intensity, a bass-first production and stellar scratching. While these MCs don't have all of the vocal pizzazz of A Tribe Called Quest's Phife and Q-Tip at their best, flawless tracks like the cool bop of "K.O.S. (Determination)" and "Definition" hint that *Black Star* is only the first of many brilliantly executed positive statements for these two street poets. *—Jason Kaufman*

Black on Both Sides / Oct. 12, 1999 / Rawkus ♦♦♦♦♦
Mos Def's partnership with Talib Kweli produced one of the most important hip-hop albums of the late '90s, 1997's brilliant *Black Star*. Consciously designed as a return to rap's musical foundations and a manifesto for reclaiming the art form from gangsta/playa domination, it succeeded mightily on both counts, raising expectations sky-high for Mos Def's solo debut. He met them all with *Black on Both Sides*, a record every bit as dazzling and visionary as *Black Star*. *Black on Both Sides* strives to not only refine but expand the scope of Mos Def's talents, turning the solo spotlight on his intricate wordplay and nimble rhythmic skills—but also his increasing eclecticism. The main reference points are pretty much the same—old-school rap, which allows for a sense of playfulness as well as history, and the Native Tongues posse's fascination with jazz, both for its sophistication and cultural heritage. But they're supported by a rich depth that comes from forays into reggae (as well as its aura of spiritual conscience), pop, soul, funk, and even hardcore punk (that on the album's centerpiece, "Rock N Roll," a dissection of white America's history of appropriating black musical innovations). In keeping with his goal of restoring hip-hop's sociopolitical consciousness, Def's lyrics are as intelligent and thoughtfully crafted as one would expect, but he doesn't stop there—he sings quite passably on several tracks, plays live instruments on others (including bass, drums, congas, vibraphone, and keyboards), and even collaborates on a string arrangement. In short, *Black on Both Sides* is a tour de force by an artist out to prove he can do it all. Its ambition and execution rank it as one of the best albums of 1999, and it consolidates Mos Def's position as one of hip-hop's brightest hopes entering the 21st century. *—Steve Huey*

Nas (Nasir Jones)

b. Long Island, NY
Vocals / Hardcore Rap, East Coast Rap, Hip-Hop
Long Island rapper Nas, born Nasir Jones, immersed himself in hip-hop and street culture at age nine, the fruits of which can be heard on his 1994 debut, *Illmatic*. Nas got his big break when former 3rd Bass rapper MC Serch included his "Half Time" on the soundtrack of the film *Zebrahead*, which led to a deal with Serch's production company. *Illmatic* was released on Columbia in 1994 and attracted attention for its depiction of ghetto life and Nas's refusal to include much of the misogyny and violence of standard gangsta-rap, not to mention his admiration of Michael Jackson and the Jackson 5. Nas' second album, *It Was Written*, was an immediate hit upon its release in the summer of 1996, entering the charts at number one, which far eclipsed the number 12 peak of *Illmatic*. *Nastradamus* followed in 1999. *—Steve Huey*

● **Illmatic** / Apr. 19, 1994 / Columbia ♦♦♦♦♦
Nas unexpectedly burst onto the rap scene with little foreshadowing in early 1994, convincingly declaring himself—and subsequently being critically declared—a rap prodigy. Showered with critical acclaim yet modest commercial success, *Illmatic* stands as a near masterpiece, particularly since Nas quickly moved toward an occasionally diluted, dumbed-down commercial approach with subsequent albums. Yet the ghetto-superstar tendencies of Nas' late-'90s work are nowhere to be found here, as the young rapper focuses exclusively on MCing and literate lyrics rather than catchy choruses or pop interpolations. Songs such as "N.Y. State of Mind" and "The World Is Yours" feature staggering lyrics rich in enabling Utopian ghetto ideology and equally rich in a prophetic sense. Based on lyrics such as these and Nas' lucid delivery, it's no surprise the rap community instantly championed the young rapper, quickly propelling his ego towards pomposity. Yet in addition to Nas' lyrics and delivery, *Illmatic's* production team—most notably, DJ Premier and Pete Rock—deserves recognition for making this album so engaging; their production here resembled few others at the time of this album's release in the early to mid-'90s. Yet as championed as this album has become, it still isn't quite the masterpiece most claim it to be. First of all, it's rather brief at only ten tracks, sounding almost like an EP. Furthermore, some of the tracks suffer from second-rate guest appearances (Q-Tip's amazing contribution stands out, though), and some of the tracks such as "One Time 4 Your Mind" aren't quite on par with the album's better moments ("One Love," "Life's a Bitch," "N.Y. State of Mind," "The World Is Yours"). Despite these minor complaints, though, most Nas fans will cherish this album as the only 1990s album by the artist that isn't hampered by blatant radio-crossover attempts ("Street Dreams," "Hate Me Now," "Nastradamus"). *—Jason Birchmeier*

It Was Written / Jul. 2, 1996 / Columbia ✦✦✦✦

I Am . . . The Autobiography / Apr. 6, 1999 / Columbia ✦✦✦
I Am . . . is the third album and fourth stage in the evolution of Queensbridge's living legend Nasir Jones, from Nasty Nas to Nas to Nas Escobar to Nastradamus, the soothsaying mega-thug poet. This third installment is an introspective work from one of hip-hop's made men. Always billed as a hip-hop messiah, Nas rose through the ranks of hip-hop on the strength of powerful poetry. Contrary to the album's title, the scope of the work extends beyond the autobiography as Nas takes on politics, the state of hip-hop, Y2K, race, and religion with his own unique perspective. While *Illmatic* was Nas at his rawest and *It Was Written* was Nas' attempt to reconcile his underground leanings with his newfound fame, acclaim, and wealth, the Nas of *I Am . . .* is honest about his elevated status yet still feels the tension of no longer being ravenous on the mic. Musically, *I Am* is somewhat unimaginative by Nas' stratospheric standards. Tried and true producers, the Trackmasters stamp the album with their signature catchy grooves and samples, but some of these tracks lack the sonic depth to do justice to the prophecies of the pharaoh, Nas. Superproducer Premier comes to save the day on two outstanding tracks: "NY State of Mind, Pt. II" and "Nas Is Like." These two cuts are nothing short of *Illmatic* perfection. "Nas Is Like"'s symphonic composition is the perfect complement for an MC of Nas' supreme vocal quality and precise lyrics. Despite some of the blandness on the production end, Nas still shines as the old soul storyteller and crime rhyme chronicler on cuts like "We Will Survive," a dirge for fallen rappers. Nas also experiments stylistically on "Big Things," sporting a Midwest cadence, and on "You Won't See Me Tonight," a Timbaland-produced duet with R&B songstress Aaliyah. *—Michael Di Bella*

Nastradamus / Nov. 23, 1999 / Columbia ✦✦✦

Naughty by Nature

f. 1991, East Orange, NJ
Group / Pop-Rap, Hardcore Rap, East Coast Rap
One of the finest '90s rap posses received some help from Queen Latifah on their 1991 debut and landed a huge hit with the naggingly incessant "O.P.P." Naughty By Nature scored another huge hit with their next release. *19 Naughty III* featured "Hip Hip Hooray," which rivaled "O.P.P." as a crossover smash and national catchphrase in 1993. They followed with *Poverty's Paradise* in 1995 and *Nature's Fury* in 1999. *—John Floyd*

● **Nature's Finest: Naughty by Nature's Greatest Hits** / Mar. 9, 1999 / Tommy Boy ✦✦✦✦✦
Essential stuff for both die-hards and casual fans alike, *Nature's Finest* is an excellent overview of Naughty by Nature's work to date—the blockbusters "O.P.P." and "Hip Hop Hooray" are here of course, as is their poignant tribute to Tupac Shakur ("Mourn You 'til I Join You"), along with hard-to-find remixes and soundtrack contributions. Even the most devoted fan might be put off by the entirely unnecessary megamix of the group's biggest hits, however. *—Chuck Donkers*

Newcleus

f. 1979, Brooklyn, NY
Group / Old School Rap, Electro
Although they recorded only two albums, Newcleus contributed one true electro classic in "Jam on Revenge (The Wikki-Wikki Song)," which has been immortalized on hundreds of hip-hop mix tapes and often included in even techno DJ's sets. The origins of Newcleus lay in a 1977 Brooklyn DJ collective known as Jam-On Productions, including Ben "Cozmo D" Cenac, his cousin Monique Angevin and her brother Pete (all teenagers and still in high school). Many members—MCs as well as DJs—came and went as the group played block parties all over the borough, and by 1979, the group centered around Cenac, his future wife Yvette "Lady E" Cook, Monique Angevin, and her future husband, Bob "Chilly B" Crafton. (The foursome named their group Newcleus as a result of the coming together of their families.)

By this time, Cenac had begun to accumulate a collection of electronic recording equipment, and the quartet recorded a demo tape of material. With several minutes left at the end of the tape, Newcleus recorded a favorite from their block parties, with each member's vocals sped up to resemble the Chipmunks. The track, "Jam-On's Revenge," impressed producer Joe Webb more than the other Newcleus material, and it became the group's first single, released in 1983 on Mayhew Records. A huge street success, the track became known unofficially as "the Wikki-Wikki song" (after the refrain); when it was re-released later that year on Sunnyview Records, it had become "Jam on Revenge (The Wikki-Wikki Song)."

The single hit Top 40 on the R&B charts in 1983, and its follow-up "Jam on It" did well on even the pop charts. "Computer Age (Push the Button)" was a more mature single, with accomplished rapping and better synthesizer effects, and it also hit the R&B Top 40. The first Newcleus LP, Jam on Revenge, was a bit of a disappointment, and their second album, Space Is the Place, did even more poorly upon release in 1984. Without a single as noteworthy as "Jam on Revenge" or "Computer Age," and with the advent of Run-D.M.C.'s organic, rock-influenced approach to rap music, Newcleus faded quickly. Though the Cenacs and the Craftons continued to record sporadically until 1989, they didn't hit the R&B charts after 1986. —John Bush

● **Jam on This!: The Best of Newcleus** / Jul. 22, 1997 / Rhino ✦✦✦
Newcleus deserve mention in any history of electro/hip-hop of the early '80s because of two certifiable classics: "Jam on Revenge (The Wikki-Wikki Song)" and "Computer Age (Push the Button)." Two tracks hardly fill a major compilation album, and at first glance, the group wouldn't appear to deserve their own best-of set; however, the compilers at Rhino did a good job of selecting tracks from the group's two albums, 1984's *Jam on Revenge* and the following year's *Space Is the Place* (a reference to jazz mystic Sun Ra). Other than the obvious hits, great album tracks include "Auto-Man," "I Wanna Be a B-Boy" and "Let's Jam." *—John Bush*

The Notorious B.I.G. (Christopher Wallace)

b. May 21, 1972, **d.** Mar. 9, 1997
Vocals / Pop-Rap, Hardcore Rap, East Coast Rap, Gangsta Rap, Club/Dance, Hip-Hop
The Brooklyn-born rapper the Notorious B.I.G. (born Chris Wallace) first gained attention for his work on Mary J. Blige's "What's the 411—" When he delivered his debut album, *Ready to Die,* in 1994, it became one of the most popular hip-hop releases of the year. In June of 1995, his single "One More Chance" debuted at number five in the pop singles chart, tying Michael Jackson's "Scream" as the highest-debuting single of all time; *Ready to Die* eventually sold two million copies. With its success, the Notorious B.I.G. became the most visible figue in East Coast hip-hop, and he became a target in the heated feud between the two coasts; especially, he and Tupac Shakur, a former ally, became vicious rivals. As the Notorious B.I.G. was preparing his second album, Shakur was shot and killed in Las Vegas. Many in the media speculated that Biggie's camp was responsible for the shooting, accusations that he and his producer, Sean "Puffy" Combs, vehemently denied. Early on the morning of March 9, the Notorious B.I.G. was returning to his hotel in Los Angeles when another car pulled up aside his car and opened fire, killing him instantly. Shakur had been killed just six months earlier. The Notorious B.I.G.'s second album, the double-disc *Life After Death,* was released three weeks later, debuting at number one on the charts. *—Stephen Thomas Erlewine*

★ **Ready to Die** / Sep. 13, 1994 / Bad Boy ✦✦✦✦✦
Upon considering how realized and mature this album sounds from beginning to end, with literally no lulls or second-rate moments, also keep in mind that this was the Notorious B.I.G.'s debut album. There isn't a moment on this album when Biggie doesn't sound sure of himself; his gangsta tales never seem overly dramatic and his boasts never seem like macho bragging—it all sounds sincere, almost too sincere. No matter whether Biggie was really the man he claimed to be or whether he simply understood the makings of an alluring persona, he crafts for himself one of the most powerful characterizations that rap has ever seen. From the harsh thug posing of "Gimme the Loot" to the grim reality of "Ready to Die" to the glamorous pimpery of "Big Poppa," Biggie never sounds ordinary and transcends any hint of cliché. His mammoth persona is ultimately the most enduring attribute of this beginning-to-end masterpiece, but Puff Daddy's role as producer also should be noted, as he seems nearly as responsible as Biggie for this album's perfection. Granted, *Ready to Die* isn't as epic or as grandiose as the follow-up double album, *Life After Death,* yet it is a bit more accessible and a better starting point for newcomers. *—Jason Birchmeier*

Life After Death / Mar. 25, 1997 / Bad Boy ✦✦✦✦✦
With the Notorious B.I.G.'s debut masterpiece, *Ready to Die,* the gangsta rapper found himself crowned the king of the East Coast. So when it came time to succeed his instant classic, Biggie and executive producer Puff Daddy decided to release the epic 24-track *Life After Death,* figuring that if they couldn't surpass the near-perfect quality of *Ready to Die,* they would at least surpass it in terms of quantity. The result was, and still is, staggering. Often compared to 2Pac's similarly epic *All Eyez on Me* for obvious reasons, *Life After Death* finds Biggie never short on rhymes and never stumbling, as he moves swiftly from one motif to another, forever retaining his sense of gangsta suave. It is this uncanny marriage of urbane sophistication and ruthless aggression that makes Biggie so engaging—he finds a perfect balance. As expected with an album of this scope featuring this high-profile of a rapper, there are numerous collaborators besides fellow Bad Boy Puff Daddy: Bone Thugs-N-Harmony, Lil' Kim, Mase, the L.O.X., Too Short, R. Kelly, Jay-Z, and DMC, along with producers such as Havoc, RZA, and DJ Premier. Furthermore, there are a handful of tracks here such as "Hypnotize" and "Mo Money Mo Problems" that stand as perennial anthems. The only thing that may hold this album back from being an undeniable masterpiece is its bloated size; at 24 tracks and two discs, *Life After Death* is a daunting listen, and some moments are undoubtedly better than others. *—Jason Birchmeier*

Born Again / Dec. 7, 1999 / Bad Boy ✦✦✦
Considering it was released almost three years after his death, it'd be easy to dismiss the Notorious B.I.G.'s third album as a cash-in or merely a tribute album, similar to Puff Daddy's *No Way Out.* Fact is, *Born Again* includes a lot of previously unheard material from Biggie, and guest spots from Busta Rhymes, Redman & Method Man, Missy Elliott, Ice Cube, and Snoop Dogg work better than could be expected. It's difficult to say where all this material came from, but it's probable that the productions were simply arranged around old rhymes from Biggie himself. On most tracks, he takes a spotlight and then the guest rapper comes in. Thanks to executive producer Puff Daddy, it'd be easy to fool those not into hip-hop that Notorious B.I.G. was still alive. The outro, a spoken-word reminiscence by Voletta Wallace (his mother) is a bit touching but also a bit ghoulish. For B.I.G. fans, this is another must-have, but for anyone that thinks the rap industry routinely goes too far in pursuit of the almighty dollar, *Born Again* is yet further proof. *—Keith Farley*

N.W.A.

f. 1986, **db.** 1991
Group / West Coast Rap, Hardcore Rap, Gangsta Rap
N.W.A., the unapologetically violent and sexist pioneers of gangsta rap, is in many ways the most notorious group in the history of rap. Emerging in the late '80s, when Public Enemy had rewritten the rules of hardcore rap by proving that it could be intelligent, revolutionary and socially aware, N.W.A. capitalized on PE's sonic breakthroughs while ignoring their message. Instead, the five-piece crew celebrated the violence and hedonism of the criminal life, capturing it all in blunt, harsh language. Initially, the group's relentless attack appeared to be serious, vital commentary, and it even provoked the FBI to caution N.W.A.'s record company, but following Ice Cube's departure late 1989, the group began to turn to self-parody. With his high-pitched whine, Eazy-E's urban nightmares now seemed like comic book fantasies, but that fulfilled the fantasies of the teenage, White suburbanites that had become their core audience, and the group became more popular than ever. Nevertheless, clashing egos prevented the band from recording a third album, and they fell apart once producer Dr. Dre left for a solo career in 1992. Although the group was no longer active, their influence—

from their funky, bass-driven beats to their exaggerated lyrics—was evident throughout the '90s. *—Stephen Thomas Erlewine*

N.W.A. and the Posse / 1987 / Priority ✦✦

★ **Straight Outta Compton** / 1988 / Ruthless ✦✦✦✦✦
Straight Outta Compton wasn't quite the first gangsta rap album, but it was the first one to find a popular audience, and its sensibility virtually defined the genre from its 1988 release on. It established gangsta rap—and, moreover, West Coast rap in general—as a commercial force, going platinum with no airplay and crossing over with shock-hungry white teenagers. Unlike Ice-T, there's little social criticism or reflection on the gangsta lifestyle; most of the record is about raising hell—harassing women, driving drunk, shooting it out with cops and partygoers. All of that directionless rebellion and rage produces some of the most frightening, visceral moments in all of rap, especially the amazing opening trio, which threatens to dwarf everything that follows. Given the album's sheer force, the production is surprisingly spare, even a little low-budget—mostly DJ scratches and a drum machine, plus a few sampled horn blasts and bits of funk guitar. With the gangsta perspective more familiar today, *Straight Outta Compton*'s insistent claims of reality ring a little hollow, since it hardly ever depicts consequences. But despite the romanticized invincibility, the force and detail of Ice Cube's writing makes the exaggerations resonate. Although Cube wrote some of his bandmates' raps, including nearly all of Eazy-E's, each member has a distinct delivery and character, and the energy of their individual personalities puts their generic imitators to shame. But although *Straight Outta Compton* has its own share of posturing, it still sounds refreshingly uncalculated because of its irreverent, gonzo sense of humor, still unfortunately rare in hardcore rap. There are several undistinguished misfires during the second half, but they aren't nearly enough to detract from the overall magnitude. It's impossible to overstate the enduring impact of *Straight Outta Compton;* as polarizing as its outlook may be, it remains an essential landmark, one of hip-hop's all-time greatest. *—Steve Huey*

100 Miles and Runnin' / Aug. 1990 / Priority ✦✦✦
Released almost two years after the seminal *Straight Outta Compton* and a little less than a year before the flawed *Niggaz4life, 100 Miles and Runnin'* effectively accomplishes what an EP should. It both built upon the lingering hype that had surrounded *Straight Outta Compton*-era N.W.A. and foreshadowed the *Niggaz4life*-era N.W.A., a group that had grown increasingly dissident, yet also much wiser after experiencing seemingly endless controversy. This EP's title track remains one of their best moments—if not their best—and with the accompanying video picturing them fleeing from police, it was a fitting song for them to release at the time; furthermore, the song's thick, heavy production showcases rather brilliantly the fact that Dr. Dre had furthered his production talents immensely. Though hard to stomach, "Just Don't Bite It" is anything but forgettable as well, with Eazy-E and MC Ren's prerogatives transcending farce into much more potent territory, making this their most amusing (in a perverse juvenile sense) yet also their most effectively disturbing venture into misogynistic/pornographic rap. As great as *Straight Outta Compton* was, Dre's beats were still a bit primitive there, and Eazy-E was nowhere near the rapper he is here; furthermore, while *Niggaz4life* finds the group at their most realized, that album's tone often proves far too distasteful. Succinct yet poignant with a heavy use of cinematic skits, this EP showcases N.W.A.'s keys to success flawlessly, making it their most perfect release, balancing their strengths perfectly across five songs, each representing different aspects of the group's tainted ideology. *—Jason Birchmeier*

Niggaz4life / May 30, 1991 / Priority ✦✦✦✦
It couldn't have been easy for N.W.A. to follow up *Straight Outta Compton,* a undoubtedly landmark moment in rap history. So after three years of enormous controversy, inner strife, and anticipation, it wasn't exactly a surprise when the group's follow-up, *Niggaz4life,* found N.W.A. a much different group. They weren't out to rouse people anymore à la "Fuck the Police"; they were out to literally shock! By, for the most part, devoting the first half of this album to minority-orientated aggressive revelation and the second half to merciless misogyny, N.W.A. succeeded in making a truly disturbing if not horrifying album. Unfortunately, in their effort to create what stands as one of the most malicious albums ever, the group eclipsed their talent. For instance, some of Dre's most ominous productions ever lie buried beneath near-inaccessible lyrics; only the most carefree individuals will be able to wade through songs such as "To Kill a Hooker" to hear them. Occasionally, such as in "Automobile" or "I'd Rather Fuck You," Eazy-E does manage to at least integrate some ill-advised humor, but, for the most part, there's just no excuse for this album's blatantly irresponsible lyrics. In the end, N.W.A. dilutes their talent with sharp and thick profanity, exemplifying just how distraught they were with each other and with the world and why their collaborations would quickly come to an end. They had taken their music as far as it could go with this album—too far for it's own good, in fact. *—Jason Birchmeier*

Greatest Hits / Jul. 1996 / Ruthless ✦✦✦✦✦
N.W.A.'s career isn't necessarily one that lends itself well to anthologies. Though they had important singles, especially in the underground hip-hop community in the late '80s, they never received any support from radio or MTV, which meant they never had any official "hits." Instead, their albums were more important, popular and influential than singles, even if individual tracks—"Fuck tha Police," "Straight Outta Compton," "Gangsta Gangsta," "Express Yourself"—became the focus of attention. And, if you notice, all those songs were from *Straight Outta Compton,* the only good album the group ever made. *Greatest Hits* does include all of the high points from that album (the title track is present in a previously unavailable remix), plus a scatter-shot sampling of raw early singles and the highlights from *100 Miles & Runnin'* and *Niggaz4Life.* It's nice to have the good tracks isolated from the group's latter-day efforts, but *Greatest Hits* is unnecessary—all you need is *Straight Outta Compton. —Stephen Thomas Erlewine*

Ol' Dirty Bastard (Russell Jones)

Vocals / Hardcore Rap, East Coast Rap, Hip-Hop
A member of the Brooklyn hip-hop congregation the Wu-Tang Clan, Ol' Dirty Bastard released his first solo album in the spring of 1995, after the Clan imploded. Produced by fellow Wu-Tang member Prince Rakeem, Ol' Dirty Bastard's *Return to the 36 Chambers* sounds identical to the Clan's 1993 debut album, *Enter the Wu-Tang (36 Chambers).* The colorful O.D.B., who also began calling himself Big Baby Jesus, made any number of headlines in the years to follow for his regular run-ins with the law; he finally released his second solo effort, *Nigga Please,* in 1999. *—Stephen Thomas Erlewine*

● **Return to the 36 Chambers** / Mar. 28, 1995 / Elektra ✦✦✦✦✦
As a member of the Wu-Tang Clan, Ol' Dirty Bastard's bizarre, free-form rants added both comic relief and a dangerous unpredictability to the group's chemistry. ODB's RZA-produced solo debut *Return to the 36 Chambers* stretches his schtick over a full album, which if anything makes him sound even more unbalanced. Long before the album ends, it's clear that ODB has emptied his bag of tricks—loose, off-the-beat raps that sometimes don't even rhyme, unbelievably graphic vulgarity, gonzo off-key warbling (which sounds a little like Biz Markie as a mental patient), and general goofing off. Yet within that role as hardcore rap's clown prince of psychosis, ODB is pretty damned entertaining. His leaps in association are often as disturbing as they are funny, whether they're couched in scatological detail or not; they certainly don't make his widely publicized erratic behavior seem at all surprising. And, despite the unstructured feel dominating most of the album, there are a fair share of hooks, and two absolutely killer singles in "Shimmy Shimmy Ya" and "Brooklyn Zoo." Certainly, there's no reason for the album to be as long as it is, considering the dull filler toward the end. But, even though *Return to the 36 Chambers* might not be the most earth-shattering piece of the Wu-Tang puzzle, it's an infectious party record which proves that, despite his limitations, Ol' Dirty Bastard has the charisma to carry an album on his own. *—Steve Huey*

Nigga Please / Sep. 14, 1999 / Elektra ✦✦✦✦
Hollywood may have Austin Powers, but hip-hop has it's own international man of mystery; his name is the Old Dirty Bastard. ODB lives and suffers with the adage that any publicity is good publicity, as he has not spent the greater part of the last two years gaining widespread notoriety for the music he makes. Rather, he has spent a majority of that time turning up on local crime blotters from coast to coast, trying to raise bail money, recuperating from gunshot wounds, rescuing a kid who was struck by a car, and hijacking the 1998 Grammy awards. With that in mind, it should be obvious by now that personalities of ODB's magnitude come around once in a lifetime. And even though he is repetitiously contradictory with his neurotic ramblings, who cares— That's half of his appeal, as there is an irrefutable attraction to ODB's carefree and inebriated outlook on life. With rhymes frequently so garbled that they are barely decipherable, calling ODB a quintessential lyricist would surely insult the intelligence of any hip-hop purist. Yet the dirt dog is indubitably a distinguished emcee and a uniquely abrasive one at that, as he turns an array of voice cracking/bloodcurdling hooks into grisly masterpieces. Examples include the nonsensical crooning of his Rick James interpolations "Cold Blooded" and "You Don't Want to Fuck With Me," and the ridiculously addictive "Rollin Wit You." Despite that ODB's production chores are handled admirably by the Neptunes, Irv Gotti and RZA, the backing acoustics are hardly needed; ODB rarely stays on beat and there is little, or no structure to his rhyme sequences. Safely nestled away in his own little world, there is no containing ODB's free-spirited outlook on life. His is a world that is heavy on shock value, yet undeniably entertaining. *—Matt Conaway*

OutKast

f. 1992, Atlanta, GA
Group / Dirty South, Southern Rap, Alternative Rap, Hip-Hop
OutKast's blend of gritty Southern soul, fluid raps and the rolling G-funk of their Organized Noize production crew epitomized the Atlanta wing of hip-hop's rising force, the Dirty South, during the late '90s. Along with Goodie Mob, OutKast took Southern hip-hop in bold, innovative new directions: less reliance on aggression, more positivity and melody, thicker arrangements, and intricate lyrics. After Dre and Big Boi hit number one on the rap charts with their first single "Player's Ball," the duo embarked on a run of platinum albums spiked with several hit singles, enjoying numerous critical accolades in addition to their commercial success.

Andre Benjamin (Dre) and Antwan Patton (Big Boi) attended the same high school in the Atlanta borough of East Point, and several lyrical battles made each gain respect for the other's skills. They formed OutKast, and were pursued by Organized Noize Productions, hitmakers for TLC and Xscape. Signed to the local LaFace label just after high school, OutKast recorded and released "Player's Ball," then watched the single rise to number one on the rap charts. It slipped from the top spot only after six weeks, was certified gold, and created a buzz for a full-length release. That album, *Southernplayalisticadillacmuzik,* hit the Top 20 in 1994 and was certified platinum by the end of the year. Dre and Big Boi also won Best New Rap Group of the Year at the 1995 *Source Awards.* OutKast returned with a new album in 1996, releasing *ATLiens* that August; it hit number two and went platinum with help from the gold-selling single "Elevators (Me & You)" (number 12 pop, number one rap), as well as the Top 40 title track. *Aquemini* followed in 1998, also hitting number two and going double-platinum. There were no huge hit singles this time around, but critics lavishly praised the album's unified, progressive vision, hailing it as a great leap forward and including it on many year-end polls. Unfortunately, in a somewhat bizarre turn of events, OutKast was sued over the album's lead single "Rosa Parks" by none other than the civil rights pioneer herself, who claimed that the group had unlawfully appropriated her name to promote their music, also objecting to some of the song's language. The initial court decision dismissed the suit in late 1999. Dre modified his name to Andre 3000 before the group issued its hotly anticipated fourth album, *Stankonia,* in late 2000. Riding the momentum of uniformly excellent reviews and the stellar singles "B.O.B." and "Ms. Jackson," *Stankonia* debuted at number two and went triple platinum in just a few months; meanwhile, "Ms. Jackson" became their first number one pop single the following February. *—John Bush*

Southernplayalisticadillacmuzik / Apr. 26, 1994 / La Face ✦✦✦✦

ATLiens / Aug. 27, 1996 / La Face ✦✦✦✦✦
Though they were likely lost on casual hip-hop fans, *Southernplayalisticadillacmuzik* was

full of subtle indications that OutKast were a lot more inventive than your average Southern playas. Their idiosyncrasies bubbled to the surface on their sophomore effort, *ATLiens*, an album of spacy sci-fi funk performed on live instruments. Largely abandoning the hard-partying playa characters of their debut, Dre and Big Boi develop a startlingly fresh, original sound to go along with their futuristic new personas. George Clinton's space obsessions might seem to make P-Funk obvious musical source material, but *ATLiens* ignores the hard funk in favor of a smooth, laid-back vibe that perfectly suits the duo's sense of melody. The album's chief musical foundation is still soul, especially the early-'70s variety, but other influences begin to pop up as well. Some tracks have a spiritual, almost gospel feel (though only in tone, not lyrical content), and the Organized Noize production team frequently employs the spacious mixes and echo effects of dub reggae in creating the album's alien soundscapes. In addition to the striking musical leap forward, Dre and Big Boi continue to grow as rappers; their flows are getting more tongue-twistingly complex, and their lyrics more free-associative. Despite a couple of overly sleepy moments during the second half, *ATLiens* is overall a smashing success thanks to its highly distinctive style, and stands as probably OutKast's most focused work (though it isn't as wildly varied as subsequent efforts). The album may have alienated (pun recognized, but not intended) the more conservative wing of the group's fans, but it broke new ground for Southern hip-hop and marked OutKast as one of the most creatively restless and ambitious hip-hop groups of the '90s. *—Steve Huey*

☆ **Aquemini** / Sep. 29, 1998 / La Face ✦✦✦✦✦
Even compared to their already excellent and forward-looking catalog, OutKast's sprawling third album *Aquemini* was a stroke of brilliance. The chilled-out space-funk of *ATLiens* had already thrown some fans for a loop, and *Aquemini* made it clear that its predecessor was no detour, but a stepping stone for even greater ambitions. Some of *ATLiens'* ethereal futurism is still present, but more often *Aquemini* plants its feet on the ground for a surprisingly down-home flavor. The music draws from a vastly eclectic palette of sources, and the live instrumentation is fuller-sounding than *ATLiens*. Most importantly, producers Organized Noize imbue their tracks with a Southern earthiness and simultaneous spirituality that come across regardless of what Dre and Big Boi are rapping about. Not that they shy away from rougher subject matter, but their perspective is grounded and responsible, intentionally avoiding hardcore clichés. Their distinctive vocal deliveries are now fully mature, with a recognizably Southern rhythmic bounce but loads more technique than their territorial peers. Those flows grace some of the richest and most inventive hip-hop tracks of the decade. The airy lead single "Rosa Parks" juxtaposes porch-front acoustic guitar with DJ scratches and a stomping harmonica break that could have come from nowhere but the South. Unexpected touches like that are all over the record: the live orchestra on "Return of the 'G'," the electronic, George Clinton-guested "Synthesizer," the reggae horns and dub-style echo of "SpottieOttieDopaliscious," the hard-rocking wah-wah guitar of "Chonkyfire," and on and on. What's most impressive is the way everything comes together to justify the full-CD running time, something few hip-hop epics of this scope ever accomplish. After a few listens, not even the meditative jams on the second half of the album feel all that excessive. *Aquemini* fulfills all its ambitions, covering more than enough territory to qualify it as a virtuosic masterpiece, and a landmark hip-hop album of the late '90s. *—Steve Huey*

★ **Stankonia** / Oct. 31, 2000 / La Face ✦✦✦✦✦
Stankonia was OutKast's second straight masterstroke, an album just as ambitious, just as all-over-the-map, and even hookier than its predecessor. With producers Organized Noize playing a diminished role, *Stankonia* reclaims the duo's futuristic bent. Keyboardist/producer Earthtone III helms most of the backing tracks, and while the live-performance approach is still present, there's more reliance on programmed percussion, otherworldly synthesizers, and surreal sound effects. Yet the results are surprisingly warm and soulful, a trippy sort of techno-psychedelic funk. Every repeat listen seems to uncover some new element in the mix, but most of the songs have such memorable hooks that it's easy to stay diverted. The immediate dividends include two of 2000's best singles: "B.O.B." is the fastest of several tracks built on jittery drum'n'bass rhythms, but Andre and Big Boi keep up with awe-inspiring effortlessness. "Ms. Jackson," meanwhile, is an anguished plea directed at the mother of the mother of an out-of-wedlock child, tinged with regret, bitterness, and affection. Its sensitivity and social awareness are echoed in varying proportions elsewhere, from the Public Enemy-style rant "Gasoline Dreams" to the heartbreaking suicide tale "Toilet Tisha." But the group also returns to its roots for some of the most testosterone-drenched material since their debut. Then again, OutKast doesn't take its posturing too seriously, which is why they can portray women holding their own, or make bizarre boasts about being "So Fresh, So Clean." Given the variety of moods, it helps that the album is broken up by brief, usually humorous interludes, which serve as a sort of reset button. It takes a few listens to pull everything together, but given the immense scope, it's striking how few weak tracks there are. It's no wonder *Stankonia* consolidated OutKast's status as critics' darlings, and began attracting broad new audiences: its across-the-board appeal and ambition overshadowed nearly every other pop album released in 2000. *—Steve Huey*

The Pharcyde

f. 1990
Group / Underground Rap, West Coast Rap, Alternative Rap, Hip-Hop
An influential alternative-rap quartet from South Central Los Angeles, the Pharcyde was formed by MCs/producers Tre "Slimkid" Hardson, Derrick "Fatlip" Stewart, Imani Wilcox, and Romye "Booty Brown" Robinson. Hardson, Wilcox, and Robinson were all dancers and choreographers who met on the L.A. underground club circuit in the late '80s, worked together for a while, and served a stint as dancers on *In Living Color*. Stewart, meanwhile, performed at local clubs and eventually hooked up with the others in 1990. Under the tutelage of Reggie Andrews, a local high-school music teacher, the group learned about the music industry and the process of recording an album. They landed a deal with Delicious Vinyl in 1991, and a year later released their eccentric debut album, *Bizarre Ride II the Pharcyde*, which went gold. After support slots for De La Soul and A Tribe Called Quest as well as a successful spot on Lollapalooza's second stage in 1994, the group released its second album, *Labcabincalifornia*, which was calmer than their first but no less warped. After a five-year break which saw little action except for the debut of Fatlip as a solo rapper (his single "What's Up Fatlip" became an underground hit), the Pharcyde returned in late 2000 with their third album, *Plain Rap*. *—Steve Huey*

★ **Bizarre Ride II the Pharcyde** / 1992 / Delicious Vinyl/Rhino ✦✦✦✦✦
The cover shot of a Fat Albert-ized Pharcyde roller coasting their way into a funhouse makes perfect sense, as the L.A.-based quartet introduced listeners to an uproarious vision of earthy \hip-hop informed by P-Funk silliness and an everybody-on-the-mic street-corner atmosphere that highlights the incredible rapping skills of each member. With multiple voices freestyling over hilarious story-songs like "Oh Shit," "Soul Flower," the dozens contest "Ya Mama," and even a half-serious driving-while-black critique named "Officer," *Bizarre Ride II the Pharcyde* proved Daisy Age philosophy akin to De La Soul and A Tribe Called Quest wasn't purely an East Coast phenomenon. Skits and interludes with live backing (usually just drums and piano) only enhance the freeform nature of the proceedings, and the group even succeeds when not reliant on humor, as proved by the excellent heartbreak tale "Passing Me By." The production, by J-Sw!ft and the group, is easily some of the tightest and most inventive of any hip-hop record of the era. Though *Bizarre Ride II the Pharcyde* could have used a few more musical hooks to draw in listeners before they begin to appreciate the amazing rapping and gifted productions, the lack of compromise reveals far greater rewards down the line. *—John Bush*

Labcabincalifornia / Nov. 28, 1995 / Delicious Vinyl/Rhino ✦✦✦
LabCabinCalifornia is a more mature record than The Pharcyde's debut. That's not necessarily a good thing, as the group's playful attitude and comic raps were much of what made them so irresistible. True, age has enlightened The Pharcyde on "Moment in Time" and the single "Runnin'," the former a salute to the past and the latter a description of their flight from South Central's Pharcyde Manor to the Hollywood Hills. But the music is much of the problem here. Though the raps are solid, tempos never vary from the usual mid-tempo jam. The keyboard-driven melodies are good—some better than others—but a little variety is needed. The last three tracks ("The Hustle," "Devil Music," "The E.N.D.") do evoke the spirit of the debut, but by that time it's too late—the sophomore jinx has hit. *—John Bush*

Plain Rap / Nov. 7, 2000 / Edeltone ✦✦✦✦

PM Dawn

f. 1988
Group / Pop-Rap, Alternative Rap, Urban
Comprised of brothers Prince Be (Attrell Cordes) and DJ Minute Mix (Jarrett Cordes), the early-'90s group PM Dawn straddled the gap between hip-hop and smooth '70s-style soul, creating an innovative urban R&B that owed as much to pop as it did to rhythm and blues. The brothers recorded their debut single, "Ode to a Forgetful Mind," in 1988, but PM Dawn didn't release a full-length album until 1991. The record, *Of the Heart, Of the Soul, Of the Cross: The Utopian Experience*, was an immediate hit, thanks to the single "Set Adrift on Memory Bliss," which sampled Spandau Ballet's new wave hit "True." Both the album and the single received glowing reviews, as did the 1993 follow-up *The Bliss Album?*, which featured the hit singles "I'd Die Without You" and "Looking Through Patient Eyes." In 1995, PM Dawn returned with *Jesus Wept*, which received strong reviews but weak sales. *Dearest Christian, I'm So Very Sorry for Bringing You Here. Love, Dad* followed in 1998; by this time, the group had virtually dropped out of sight as a commercial force, even though most corners continued to praise the artistic quality of theri work. A greatest-hits compilation, *The Best of PM Dawn*, appeared in the summer of 2000. *—Stephen Thomas Erlewine*

★ **Of the Heart, of the Soul and of the Cross: The Utopian Experience** / Aug. 6, 1991 / V2 ✦✦✦✦✦
In the wake of De La Soul, rap group P.M. Dawn's first album samples jazz, whitebread pop soul, adds a dash of Prince's mysticism, embraces melody, and turns inward for surreal (and admittedly often sophomoric) psychedelic lyrics. P.M. Dawn may care about matters of the soul, but on their first album they don't ignore the booty: these are carefully assembled songs, layered with many a chorused vocal or a harpsichord, but all backed up with a solid beat. "A Watcher's Point of View (Dont'cha Think)" stands out here: a bumping sample with scratchy guitars, shimmering acoustic strings, and interweaving lyrics and a chorus. But it was "Set Adrift on Memory Bliss," with its sample from Spandau Ballet's "True," that made it into the charts (it then became the blueprint for following singles, for better or worse). Other successful tracks: "Reality Used to Be a Friend of Mine," "In the Presence of Mirrors," and "On a Clear Day." There's a few missteps, especially on "Shake," a pointless house-like workout. But it's a delicate balance between doe-eyed metaphysics and the dancefloor that the album treads, and it's all the better for it. *—Ted Mills*

The Bliss Album . . . ? / Mar. 23, 1993 / V2 ✦✦✦✦✦
After the breakout pop success of their debut album, PM Dawn played up the lush, soothing urban-soul qualities of their sound on the follow-up, *The Bliss Album . . . ?* For all of hardcore rap's hysteria over the duo's gentle demeanor and pop influences, *Of the Heart, of the Soul, and of the Cross* had been a predominantly rap-oriented album. That changes on *The Bliss Album . . . ?*, which downplays Prince Be's rapping (only on about a third of the tracks) in favor of dreamy melodies throughout the songs, not just on the choruses. It's a logical move, since PM Dawn's most unique moments were often also their most reflective, and they had an obvious knack for crafting original hooks. *The Bliss Album . . . ?*'s approach also provides more opportunities for the ethereal, layered vocal overdubs that had become one of the duo's signatures. While the results don't quite re-envision hip-hop the way the debut did, they're still tremendously inventive, playing to PM Dawn's strengths. The musical landscapes are even more lushly arranged, and the pop numbers positively shimmer thanks to the duo's increasing sense of craft. A couple of the more aggressive rap tracks break up the mood a little, as with "Plastic," a sly rebuttal of the charges leveled by the group's macho detractors. It seems unnecessary, though, since PM Dawn's cosmic mysticism and vastly different influ-

ences clearly aren't competing on the same turf. Luckily, *The Bliss Album... ?* refuses to acknowledge any artificially imposed purist boundaries, continuing to chart new sonic territory and expanding the possibilities in PM Dawn's music. *—Steve Huey*

Jesus Wept / Oct. 3, 1995 / V2 ✦✦✦✦✦

The Best of PM Dawn / Jun. 20, 2000 / V2 ✦✦✦✦✦

Public Enemy

f. 1982, Long Island, NY

Group / Hardcore Rap, East Coast Rap, Hip-Hop

Public Enemy rewrote the rules of hip-hop, becoming the most influential and controversial rap group of the late '80s and, for many, the definitive rap group of all time. Building from Run-D.M.C.'s street-oriented beats and Boogie Down Productions' proto-gangsta rhyming, Public Enemy pioneered a variation of hardcore rap that was musically and politically revolutionary. With his powerful, authoritative baritone, lead rapper Chuck D rhymed about all kinds of social problems, particularly those plaguing the Black community, often condoning revolutionary tactics and social activism. In the process, he directed hip-hop towards an explicitly self-aware, pro-Black consciousness that became the culture's signature throughout the next decade. Musically, Public Enemy were just as revolutionary, as their production team the Bomb Squad created dense soundscapes that relied on avant-garde cut-and-paste techniques, unrecognizable samples, piercing sirens, relentless beats and deep funk. It was chaotic and invigorating music, made all the more intoxicating by Chuck D's forceful vocals and the absurdist raps of his comic foil Flavor Flav. With his comic sunglasses and an oversized clock hanging from his neck, Flav became the group's visual focal point, but he never obscured the music. While rap and rock critics embraced the group's late '80s and early '90s records, Public Enemy frequently ran into controversy with their militant stance and lyrics, especially after their 1988 album *It Takes a Nation of Millions to Hold Us Back* made them into celebrities. After all the controversy settled in the early '90s, once the group entered hiatus, it became clear that Public Enemy was the most influential and radical band of its time. *—Stephen Thomas Erlewine*

Yo! Bum Rush the Show / 1987 / Def Jam ✦✦✦✦✦

When their debut was released in 1987, very few rap groups even approached Public Enemy's musical or political stance. Listening to the first album now, it's surprising how few of the songs are actually political—the sheer force of the sound fools the listener into thinking Chuck D is saying more than he actually is. Still, "Megablast," "Public Enemy No. 1," and "Miuzi Weighs a Ton" carry a small amount of political rhetoric. Much sparer than later releases, the album is carried over the top by Chuck D's bulldozer roar. *—Stephen Thomas Erlewine*

★ **It Takes a Nation of Millions to Hold Us Back** / 1988 / Def Jam ✦✦✦✦✦

Arguably the best hip-hop album ever made, *It Takes a Nation of Millions to Hold Us Back* was a huge leap forward not only for Public Enemy, but for all of hip-hop. PE's signature sound—a barrage of found sounds, densely woven samples, and noisy tape loops—was evident for the first time, courtesy of The Bomb Squad. Chuck D's lyrics, full of revolutionary rhetoric yet managing to avoid being hysterical, matched the aural onslaught. The group's political stance would be meaningless if the music didn't put it over the top throughout, and that does happen on "Black Steel in the Hour of Chaos," "Night of the Living Baseheads," "Rebel Without a Pause," "Don't Believe the Hype," and "Bring the Noise," in particular. There isn't a weak moment on the album. A landmark recording. *—Stephen Thomas Erlewine*

☆ **Fear of a Black Planet** / 1990 / Def Jam ✦✦✦✦✦

Public Enemy's artistic and commercial winning streak continued with its third album, *Fear of a Black Planet*. While other East Coast rappers were content to boast and boast about their prowess on the microphone, Public Enemy always had a lot to say. Though a few stinkers are included—the worst offender being the homophobic "Meet the G That Killed Me"—they are by far outnumbered by the gems. From "Burn Hollywood Burn" (a brutally honest attack on racism in the film industry) to the optimistic "Brothers Gonna Work It Out," the politically charged rappers have no problem maintaining the level of excellence they reached on *It Takes a Nation of Millions to Hold Us Back*. A gut-level attack on incompetence in the 911 system, "911 Is a Joke" illustrates just how on-target PE could be—in fact, it should be stressed that the song precedes by several years the incident in which 911 operators in Philadelphia came under attack for doing nothing to help a youth who was being beaten to death. And once again, PE's producers, the Bomb Squad, provide a collage of samples that is as imaginative as it is bombastic. *—Alex Henderson*

☆ **Apocalypse 91 ... The Enemy Strikes Black** / Oct. 1, 1991 / Def Jam ✦✦✦✦✦

Although it falls short of the excellence of *Fear of a Black Planet* and *It Takes a Nation of Millions to Hold Us Back*, PE's fourth album proved that the Long Islanders could still be extremely stimulating—both lyrically and musically. This time, the obvious winners include "Shut Em Down" (a commentary on liquor stores profiting from human suffering in the Black commmunity) and "By the Time I Get to Arizona" (an angry reflection on that state's refusal to celebrate Martin Luther King's birthday in the early '90s) and an invigorating rap/metal remake of "Bring the Noize" featuring thrash headbangers Anthrax. Although produced by the Imperial Grand Ministers of Funk instead of the Bomb Squad, the album boasts exactly the type of production one associates with PE—abrasive, hard and dissonant. Unfortunately, PE's popularity would decline considerably after the album—and considerably less talented N.W.A. clones would be selling a lot more albums. *—Alex Henderson*

Greatest Misses / Sep. 15, 1992 / Def Jam ✦✦

Muse Sick-N-Hour Mess Age / Aug. 23, 1994 / Def Jam ✦✦

He Got Game / Apr. 21, 1998 / Def Jam ✦✦✦✦

Nominally a soundtrack to Spike Lee's basketball drama, but in reality more of an individual album, *He Got Game* appeared in 1998, just the second Public Enemy album since 1991's *Apocalypse 91*. Even though Chuck D was pushing 40, the late '90s were friendlier to PE's noisy, claustrophobic hip-hop than the mid-'90s, largely because hip-hop terrorists like the Wu-Tang Clan, Jeru the Damaja, and DJ Shadow were bringing the music back to its roots. PE followed in their path, stripping away the sonic blitzkrieg that was the Bomb Squad's trademark and leaving behind skeletal rhythm tracks, simple loops, and bass lines. Taking on the Wu at their own game—and, if you think about it, Puff Daddy as well, since the simple, repetitive loop of Buffalo Springfield's "For What It's Worth" on the title track was nothing more than a brazenly successful one-upmanship of Puff's shameless thievery—didn't hurt the group's credibility, since they did it *well*. Listen to the circular, menacing synth lines of the opening "Resurrection" or the scratching strings on "Unstoppable" and it's clear that Public Enemy could compete with the most innovative artists in the younger generation, while "Is Your God a Dog" and "Politics of the Sneaker Pimps" proved that they could draw their own rules. That said, *He Got Game* simply lacked the excitement and thrill of prime period PE—Chuck D, Terminator X, and the Bomb Squad were seasoned, experienced craftsmen, and it showed, for better and worse. They could craft a solid comeback like *He Got Game*, but no matter how enjoyable and even thought-provoking the album was, that doesn't mean it's where you'll turn when you want to hear Public Enemy. *—Stephen Thomas Erlewine*

There's a Poison Goin' On... / Jul. 20, 1999 / Play It Again Sam ✦✦✦

Opening with a sonic collage straight out of *Fear of a Black Planet, There's a Poison Goin' On...* comes out of the gates sounding like classic Public Enemy, which is exactly what Public Enemy intended, since their slight sonic change-up on *He Got Game* didn't result in a hit. In a way, PE's feud with Def Jam over downloadable MP3 music was a good thing, since it brought them media attention, which is rare for a veteran hip-hop band. Such increased exposure also brought a minor controversy over "Swindlers Lust," which some perceived as anti-Semitic, but this outrage was isolated because Public Enemy was now at the margins of hip-hop. They were no longer considered cutting-edge, and younger kids never picked up their records, so the only place for this controversy to reside was among the rock critics and aging fans who remembered when *It Takes a Nation of Millions* changed the world ten years prior. Chuck D must have known that they would be the only ones paying attention to the album, since it consciously copies PE's past and never really breaks from that blueprint. In some respects, that's a disappointment, since *He Got Game* showed that PE could subtly incorporate modern hip-hop and do it better than some modern acts. But *There's a Poison Goin' On* is nevertheless a strong album, even if it is doggedly classicist. It's also dogmatic, with Chuck preaching to the converted about the evils of the record industry and conformity in hip-hop, which does become a little trying by the end of the record. But he delivers lyrically and PE delivers musically, in a manner that's entirely familiar to fans of Public Enemy, offering a solid continuation of *Apocalypse 91*. Ultimately, it's their most satisfying record in several years—which is a subtle difference that only the converted will notice. *—Stephen Thomas Erlewine*

Puff Daddy

b. Nov. 4, 1970, Harlem, NY

Producer / Pop-Rap, East Coast Rap, Urban, Hip-Hop

The biggest hip-hop impresario of the mid-'90s, Sean "Puffy" Combs—or Puff Daddy, as he was known on his own musical projects—created a multi-million dollar industry around Bad Boy Entertainment, with recordings by the Notorious B.I.G., Craig Mack, Faith Evans, $112 and Total, all produced and master-minded by Combs himself. Responsible for over $100 million in total record sales and named ASCAP's 1996 Songwriter of the Year, Combs was, on the other hand, criticized by many in the hip-hop community for watering down the sound of the underground and also for a perceived over-reliance on samples as practically the sole basis for many of his hits. A very successful A*R executive at Uptown Records during the early '90s, responsible for sizeable hit records by Father MC,* Mary J. Blige, and Jodeci, Combs formed his own Bad Boy label, signed Notorious B.I.G., Evans, and Craig Mack, and earned enough hits to cement an alliance with Arista Records. A highly publicized feud with Death Row Records (in which Tupac Shakur and label-head Suge Knight served as West Coast/Dark Side equivalents to the Notorious B.I.G. and Combs) was summarily ended in late 1996, when Shakur was murdered and Knight jailed. Six months later, Notorious B.I.G. was dead as well, and after Combs mourned his friend's death, he hit the pop charts in a big way during his biggest year, 1997. *—John Bush*

• **No Way Out** / Jul. 1, 1997 / Bad Boy ✦✦✦✦

Before releasing his first solo album, Puff Daddy (a.k.a. Sean Puffy Combs) was famous as the producer of the Notorious B.I.G., Junior Mafia, Craig Mack, Lil' Kim and many other rappers. As he was making making his solo debut, the Notorious B.I.G. was murdered, and that loss weighs heavily on Puff's mind throughout *No Way Out*. Even though the album has some funky party jams scattered throughout the record, the bulk of the album is filled with fear, sorrow and anger, and it's not only evident on the tribute "I'll Be Missing You" (a duet with Faith Evans and 112 that is based on the Police's "Every Breath You Take") but also on gangsta anthems like "It's All About the Benjamins." That sense of loss makes *No Way Out* a more substantial album than most mid-'90s hip-hop release, and even if it has flaws—there's a bit too much filler and it runs a little long—it is nevertheless a compelling, harrowing album that establishes Puff Daddy as a vital rapper in his own right. *—Leo Stanley*

Forever / Aug. 24, 1999 / Bad Boy ✦✦✦

It was never much of a contest, but with his second solo album, Puff Daddy retains his crown as the biggest ego in hip-hop, if not popular music. It's an arrogance that asserts itself in the over 20 pictures included in the album booklet (all with different poses and outfits) and in the opening track—"Forever (Intro)"—that updates listeners with all the sordid details of Puffy's personal life. With all this ego strutting around, Puffy's sizable production talents have consistently been underrated. The truth is, he's been one of the best hip-hop producers of the '90s, creator of countless solid party jams, heavy on the groove and quite creative for their crossover potential. Though most of the tracks on *Forever* are co-productions with young lieutenants from his Bad Boy organization, Puffy's productions shine through. And he's downplayed sampling obvious pop hits for the main groove of his songs, perhaps a response to the constant criticism of hip-hop fans. Puffy's also a better rapper than he used to be, almost up to the level of the MC superstars guesting here. There are no tracks as propulsive as the hits from *No Way Out* ("It's All About the Benjamins," "Been Around the World"), and the ballad track "Best Friend," which samples Christopher Cross' "Sailing," is a lame rehash of the Biggie tribute "I'll Be Missing You." The final track (and first single), the Public Enemy-sampling "P.E. 2000," is an apt metaphor for Puff Daddy's second album; it's a solid production, not quite as exciting as it should be, informed by a mindset that uses hip-hop as a ladder to pop success and wealth. *—Keith Farley*

Queen Latifah

b. Mar. 18, 1970, Newark, NJ
Rap, Vocals / Pop-Rap, Alternative Rap, Hip-Hop
Although Queen Latifah was certainly not the first female rapper, she was the first to bring a feminist consciousness to the genre's political agenda with her groundbreaking 1989 debut, *All Hail the Queen*, and its single "Ladies First." Latifah (an Arabic word translating as "delicate" or "sensitive") was born Dana Owens in Newark, New Jersey and served a stint as a human beatbox in the group Ladies Fresh. She recorded a single, "Wrath of My Madness," in 1988 and later released *All Hail the Queen* to strongly favorable reviews; the album showcased her versatility on material ranging from soul, dub reggae and dance to straight hip-hop and established a tough, no-nonsense, intelligent persona. *Nature of a Sista* expanded on that role with some more personal material, but *Black Reign* became her most popular album, probably boosted by Latifah's increased visibility as a cast member of the Fox sitcom *Living Single*. The album was dedicated to her late brother, who was killed in a motorcycle accident in 1992, and produced the hit single "U.N.I.T.Y.," which won a Grammy for Best Rap Solo Performance. In addition to *Living Single*, Latifah has also appeared in the films *Jungle Fever, Juice*, and *House Party 2*. She returned to music in 1998 with *Order in the Court*. *—Steve Huey*

• **All Hail the Queen** / Nov. 1989 / Tommy Boy ✦✦✦✦✦
As strong a buzz as Queen Latifah created with her debut single of 1988, "Wrath of My Madness" and its reggae-influenced B-side "Princess of the Posse," one would have expected the North Jersey rapper/actress' first album, *All Hail the Queen*, to be much stronger. Though not a bad album by any means, it doesn't live up to Latifah's enormous potential. The CD's strongest material includes "Evil That Men Do," a hardhitting duet with KRS-One addressing Black-on-Black crime and other social ills; the infectious hip-house number "Come Into My House"; the rap/reggae duet with Stetsasonic's Daddy-O "The Pros"; and the aforementioned songs. Unfortunately, boasting numbers like "A King and Queen Creation" and "Queen of Royal Badness" aren't terribly memorable. Especially disappointing is "Mama Gave Birth to the Soul Children," a duet with De La Soul that surprisingly, is both musically and lyrically generic. To be sure, Latifah's rapping skills are top-notch—which is why *All Hail the Queen* should have been consistently excellent instead of merely good. *—Alex Henderson*

Nature of a Sista / Sep. 3, 1991 / Tommy Boy ✦✦✦

Black Reign / Nov. 16, 1993 / Motown ✦✦✦✦✦
Black Reign marked Latifah's move to Motown, and was also a return to the tough-talking, lyrically frank, frequently controversial material that established her as arguably the finest female rapper. "Coochie Bang" and "Weekend Love" were harsh and explicit attacks on would-be hit-and-run lovers, while "Just Another Day" and "I Can't Understand" examined the continuing inequities plaguing inner-city youth, and "Superstar" took a pointedly unglamorous view of her situation and the perils of hip-hop supremacy. *—Ron Wynn*

Order in the Court / Jun. 16, 1998 / Motown ✦✦✦

Raekwon (Corey Woods)

b. Jan. 12, 19??
Vocals / Hardcore Rap, East Coast Rap
A member of the Wu-Tang Clan, rapper Raekwon was born Corey Woods; a.k.a. the Chef, he first surfaced on the group's 1993 debut *Enter the Wu-Tang: 36 Chambers*, issuing his first solo single "Heaven and Hell" on the soundtrack to *Fresh* a short time later. On Raekwon's 1995 solo LP *Only Built 4 Cuban Linx* he recast the Wu-Tang crew as an Italian mafioso family dubbed the Wu-Gambinos, rechristening himself "Lou Diamonds" in the process. *Immobilarity* followed in 1999. *—Jason Ankeny*

★ **Only Built 4 Cuban Linx** / 1995 / Loud ✦✦✦✦✦
Raekwon's solo debut remains one of the best, if not the zenith, of the numerous Wu-Tang-affiliated albums of the 1990s, even if it attained only modest commercial success upon its release. *Only Built 4 Cuban Linx* attains such hallowed critical status partially because of the amazing synergy between Ghostface Killah and Raekwon. They team up on 12 of the 18 tracks to create some of the most cinematically engaging lyrics ever collected on a rap album, trading off lucid verses on one track after the next, only occasionally joined by their peers, most notably Method Man and Nas. Yet for the most part, *Only Built 4 Cuban Linx* is lyrically a two-man affair, which prevents it from getting diluted and retains a vital sense of consistency—a problem many 1990s rap albums suffer from. This suturing consistency is only furthered by the eerie production of RZA, who turns in what may be his most impressive performance of the decade. Riddled with violent gangsta film samples, haunting keyboards, an overall foreboding aura, and, of course, phenomenal beats, RZA's production may deserve the acclaim for this album more so than Raekwon and Ghostface Killah's dark gangsta tales, as the Wu-Tang mastermind weaves one long cinematic motif characterized by subtle yet emotive twists. One cannot attribute the genius of this album to Raekwon, Ghostface Killah, or RZA alone, but rather to the synergy resulting from their respective contributions. *—Jason Birchmeier*

Immobilarity / Nov. 16, 1999 / Epic ✦✦✦
It's a rare Wu-Tang solo album that doesn't bear the stamp of the collective's production mastermind, RZA, to some extent, and Raekwon's second full-length is no different. Except for the fact that RZA doesn't actually *appear* on *Immobilarity*, the paranoid synth-strings and soundtrack feel he pioneered on Wu-Tang's *Enter the Wu-Tang: 36 Chambers* and *Forever* are all over this album. The producers, including Raekwon's American Cream Team, Infinite Arkatechz, and Six July Productions, give *Immobilarity* the same sounds RZA gave to Raekwon's first album, *Only Built 4 Cuban Linx*. Though few rappers are more entitled to the sound than Raekwon, most of these songs just don't contribute to the lyrical concerns or delivery (a notable exception is "Sneakers," the only track produced by Pete Rock). And since the album's success depends wholly on Raekwon himself, it's almost impossible for him to trump the excellence of his first album. *—Keith Farley*

Rakim

b. Jan. 27, 196?
Vocals / Hardcore Rap, East Coast Rap, Hip-Hop
Rakim may never have achieved the stardom of peers like Ice-T or Chuck D, but he never lost respect among the hip-hop community, where he was acknowledged as one of the great rappers. Throughout the '80s, he was one of the leading figures in hip-hop as he and his partner, DJ Eric B., released a series of groundbreaking records. In 1992, the two parted ways and Rakim spent the next five years in seclusion, returning in the fall of 1997 with his solo debut, *The 18th Letter*. *The Master* followed two years later. *—Stephen Thomas Erlewine*

The 18th Letter / Nov. 4, 1997 / Uptown/Universal ✦✦✦✦
It took Rakim five years to begin his solo careeer, but the wait was worth it—*The 18th Letter* is one of the strongest records a veteran rapper has released in the late '90s. Working with a variety of producers (Pete Rock, Clark Kent, Father Shaheed, DJ Premier), Rakim sounds sharp, focused and strong, rapping with a force unheard of on his classic albums with Eric B. He still retains his knack for rolling, laidback rhymes, but what's impressive is how he can switch between that style and a more aggressive technique. There are a few slow spots on the record, but in general, few latter-day albums by '80s rappers sound as powerful and vital as *The 18th Letter*. *—Leo Stanley*

• **The Master** / Nov. 30, 1999 / Universal ✦✦✦✦✦
When you've been named the best rapper ever in countless readers' and critics' polls, it must be easy to get a bit complacent. And as a veteran who's been on the mic since 1985 (yes, there are several rappers who weren't even on the earth back then), it also must be easy to make a few concessions to all the rappers and delivery styles that have come since Kangols were all the rage—the first time, that is. Thankfully, Rakim's second solo album shows hip-hop's best rapper outdoing himself yet again, and not conceding a whit to '90s rap. Rakim has always been known for his laid-back flow and, accordingly, he never pushes himself here; his flow is smooth as syrup, and will undoubtedly make hip-hop fans realize just what rhythm is after merely a few tracks. He plays with internal rhymes (one of his trademarks) and constructs the most dense lyrics heard in hip-hop for years. *The Master* also benefits from its stellar cast of producers—Clark Kent, DJ Premier, Ron "Amen-Ra" Lawrence, the 45 King, and even Rakim himself. The productions are tough and catchy (no strings here, thankfully), but they never outshine the rhymes. Rakim praises himself on quite a few tracks ("Flow Forever," "When I B on the Mic," "I Know," "It's the R"), but after a listen or two, listeners will likely agree with every boast he makes. After one album (*The 18th Letter*) to get back into things, Rakim is arguably doing the best work of his career. *—John Bush*

Busta Rhymes

b. 1972, Brooklyn, NY
Rap, Vocals / Hardcore Rap, East Coast Rap, Alternative Rap, Hip-Hop
The most idiosyncratic personality in rap and possessor of its most recognizable delivery—a halting, ragga-inspired style with incredible complexity, inventiveness and humor—Busta Rhymes formed Leaders of the New School in 1990 and released two albums with the group before breaking out with a 1996 solo hit single, "Woo-Hah!! Got You All in Check." Much respected in the hip-hop underground for their Afrocentric philosophy and tough rapping styles, Leaders of the New School debuted in 1991 with *Future Without a Past*, but released only one more album, 1993's *T.I.M.E.*, before breaking up the following year. Out on his own for the first time, Busta Rhymes' first solo album, *The Coming*, proved a huge hit; the single "Woo-Hah!! Got You All in Check" hit the Top Ten and pushed album into gold-record territory. His second album, *When Disaster Strikes*, debuted at number three in September 1997. *—John Bush*

• **The Coming** / Apr. 1996 / Elektra ✦✦✦✦✦
Busta Rhymes delivered his debut album, *The Coming*, three years after the Leaders of the New School unofficially disbanded, and it reflects the change in hip-hop between 1993 and 1996. *The Coming* is indebted to the slow, spare, and quietly menacing funk and soundscapes of the Wu-Tang Clan—in fact, Ol' Dirty Bastard appears on one of the album's most infectious tracks, the single "Woo-hah!! Got You All in Check." Busta Rhymes, like Ol' Dirty, is a surreal, inspired rapper, but his skills are on a whole different level. Though his talents were evident on the Leaders of the New School records, Busta Rhymes has never had such an impressive showcase for his rhymes as he does on *The Coming*. Busta doesn't have a deep message in his raps, but he twists words and phrases around with an insane, invigorating flair. Like many hip-hop albums of the mid-'90s, *The Coming* is padded with too much material, but Busta Rhymes's brilliant raps keeps the record from sinking during its monotonous passages. *—Stephen Thomas Erlewine*

When Disaster Strikes / Sep. 23, 1997 / Elektra ✦✦✦✦✦
Alternately brilliantly inspired and brilliantly confused, Busta Rhymes' second album, *When Disaster Strikes*, isn't perfect, but it's considerably more creative than the bulk of contemporary hip-hop albums. Using the Wu-Tang Clan's haunting soundscapes as a blueprint, Busta Rhymes expands that formula, adding funkier beats and elements of electronica and electric funk. It's a forward-thinking mix, pointing the way to new hip-hop fusions, even when the music falls flat. Busta's lyrics remain startlingly fresh and compelling, and they're given more weight by these dense rhythm tracks. Not everything on *When Disaster Strikes* is successful,

partially because the album runs too long, but the best cuts confirm that Busta Rhymes is a singular talent. *—Stephen Thomas Erlewine*

Extinction Level Event (The Final World Front) / Dec. 8, 1998 / Elektra ✦✦✦✦

Anarchy / Jun. 20, 2000 / Elektra ✦✦✦

The Roots

f. 1989

Group / Jazz-Rap, Alternative Rap, Hip-Hop

Though popular success has largely eluded the Roots, the Philadelphia group showed the way for live rap, building on Stetsasonic's "hip-hop band" philosophy of the mid-'80s by focusing on live instrumentation at their concerts and in the studio. Though their album works have been inconsistent affairs, more intent on building grooves than pushing songs, the group's live shows are among the best in the business. Formed by rapper Black Thought and drummer—uestlove, the Roots began their musical career by recreating classic hip-hop tracks with—uestlove's drum kit backing Black Thought's rhymes. Moving from the street to local clubs, the Roots became popular around Philadelphia and recorded an album, 1993's *Organix*, to sell at shows. Later that year, the group signed to DGC and recorded their major-label debut, *Do You Want More?!!!??!*. Though it was mostly ignored by hip-hop fans, the album made tracks in alternative circles. Early in 1996, the Roots released "Clones," the trailer single for their second album. It hit the Rap Top Five, and created a good buzz for the album. The following September, *Illadelph Halflife* appeared and made number 21 on the album charts. The Roots' third album, 1999's *Things Fall Apart*, was easily their biggest critical and commercial success. *—John Bush*

Do You Want More?!!!??! / Jan. 1995 / DGC ✦✦✦✦

Because the Roots were pioneering a new style during the early '90s, the band was forced to draw its own blueprints for its major-label debut album. It's not surprising then, that *Do You Want More?!!!??!* sounds more like a document of old-school hip-hop than contemporary rap. The album is based on loose grooves and laid-back improvisation, and where most hip-hoppers use samples to draw songs together and provide a chorus, the Roots just keep on jamming. The problem is that the Roots' jams begin to take the place of true songs, leaving most tracks with only that groove to speak for them. The notable exceptions—"Mellow My Man" and "Datskat," among others—use different strategies to command attention: the sounds of a human beatbox , the great keyboard work of Scott Storch, and contributions from several jazz players (trombonist Joshua Roseman, saxophonist Steve Coleman and vocalist Cassandra Wilson). By the close of the album, those tracks are what the listener remembers, not the lightweight grooves. *—John Bush*

Illadelph Halflife / Sep. 24, 1996 / DGC ✦✦✦✦

The Roots always had ambition, which theoretically placed them ahead of many of their mid-'90s hip-hop contemporaries. Where many of their peers settled for gangsta cliches, tedious displays of lyrical skills, alternative hip-hop or half-hearted jazz-rap fusions, the Roots decided to take an entirely different route by merging streetlevel rhythms with jazz and old-school technique, and performing everything on live instruments. While their approach works well in theory, it doesn't always work in practice. Though it is decidedly tougher and more adventurous than the group's debut, *Illadelph Halflife* just misses the mark. Part of the problem with the record is the fact that it doesn't capture the relentless energy of their live show; without the reckless, rampaging momentum of their live show, the record is only sporadically engaging. Still, the best moments of *Illadelph Halflife* demonstrate the Roots are an exciting, inventive band that have great potential—they just haven't quite fulfilled it yet. *—Leo Stanley*

● **Things Fall Apart** / Feb. 23, 1999 / MCA ✦✦✦✦✦

This progressive, Philadelphia, hip-hop band's fourth album grabbed its title from the Chinua Achebe novel of the same name, and numerous guest stars add a welcome spice to the pot. Mos Def lends a mic-clutching hand to the Roots' lyrically precise lead MC, Black Thought, on their old school homage, "Double Trouble." Throughout the complex album, listeners are treated to somber textures ("The Spark" with Malik B) and heavyweight jams like "Adrenaline!" Even through often thankless years of relentless touring, marketing and promotion, hip-hop remains a way of life for the group, and they let you know it on "Act Too (The Love of My Life)" featuring Common. On that stellar track, Black Thought raps about what hip-hop culture means to him, "I remember late nights steady rocking' the mic/hip-hop you the love of my life." *—Craig Robert Smith*

The Roots Come Alive / Nov. 2, 1999 / MCA ✦✦✦✦

Run-D.M.C.

f. 1982, Queens, NY

Group / Hardcore Rap, East Coast Rap, Hip-Hop

More than any other hip-hop group, Run-D.M.C. is responsible for the sound and style of the music. As the first hardcore rap outfit, the trio set the sound and style for the next decade of rap. With its spare beats and excursions into heavy metal samples, the trio was tougher and more menacing than its predecessors Grandmaster Flash and Whodini. In the process, it opened the door for both the politicized rap of Public Enemy and Boogie Down Productions, as well as the hedonistic gangsta fantasies of N.W.A. At the same time, Run-D.M.C. helped move rap from a singles-oriented genre to an album-oriented one—they were the first hip-hop artist to construct full-fledged albums, not just a collection with two singles and a bunch of filler. By the end of the '80s, Run-D.M.C. had been overtaken by the groups they had spawned, but they continued to perform to a dedicated following well into the '90s. *—Stephen Thomas Erlewine*

☆ **Run-D.M.C.** / 1984 / Profile/Arista ✦✦✦✦✦

Undeniably, *Run-D.M.C.* is among the most influential rap albums ever. Before Run-D.M.C.'s ascension in the mid-'80s, rap hits tended to be melodic and danceable. Whether the inspiration for their tracks was Chic, Ashford & Simpson or Kraftwerk, hip-hop recordings were generally more interested in grooving than rocking—that is, until Run-D.M.C. had so enormous an impact on rap with "Rock Box," "Sucker Mcs" and other abrasive classics included on this landmark debut album. When these self-proclaimed "Kings from Queens" took off in the mid-'80s, it became fashionable for rappers to used the type of abrasive, amelodic tracks heard here—many of which consist of little more than a drum machine and the influential Jam Master Jay's cutting and scratching. When they do employ some type of melody on "Rock Box," it isn't a Chic groove—but a crunching, Black Sabbath-like guitar. Run-D.M.C.'s daring rap/metal fusion, in fact, influenced everyone from Whodini to Ice-T to the Beastie Boys. [*Run-D.M.C.* was remastered and reissued in 1999.] *—Alex Henderson*

☆ **King of Rock** / 1985 / Profile/Arista ✦✦✦✦✦

Run-D.M.C.'s artistic winning streak continued with its superb second album, *King of Rock*. The fusion of rap and heavy metal the duo unveiled on "Rock Box" proved equally arresting on "You're Blind" and the title song, and the hip-hoppers' boasts were still among the finest in rap. Though boasting, rap's staple, can wear thin in a hurry, Run-D.M.C.'s boasts are consistently clever and often humorous. From the amusing "You Talk Too Much" to the insistent "Jam-Master Jammin'" to the inventive "Rots, Rap, Reggae," everything on *King of Rock* is a classic. By the end of the 1980s, fusing rap and reggae wasn't out of the ordinary—especially on the East Coast. But when Run-D.M.C: recorded "Roots, Rap, Reggae" in 1985, it was quite daring. [*King of Rock* was remastered and reissued in 1999.] *—Alex Henderson*

★ **Raising Hell** / 1986 / Profile/Arista ✦✦✦✦✦

Run-D.M.C. enjoyed its greatest triumph of all—both artistically and commercially—with its triple-platinum third album, *Raising Hell*. Much of the support that Run-D.M.C. enjoyed came from rock fans, and the MCs made their love of rock more than evident on "It's Tricky" (which samples the Knack's "My Sharona"), the forceful title song, and an inspired remake of Aerosmith's "Walk This Way" featuring Steve Tyler and Joe Perry themselves. Most of the other gems on *Raising Hell*—which range from the humorous "You Be Illin'" to the clever "My Adidas" to the uplifting "Proud to Be Black"—don't employ a screaming rock guitar. But even then, Run-D.M.C. is one of the loudest acts in hip-hop. [*Raising Hell* was remastered and reissued in 1999.] *—Alex Henderson*

Tougher than Leather / 1988 / Profile/Arista ✦✦✦✦

At the end of 1986, *Raising Hell* was rap's best-selling album up to that point, though it would soon be outsold by the Beastie Boys' *Licensed to Ill*. Profile Records hoped that Run-D.M.C.'s fourth album, *Tougher than Leather*, would exceed the Beastie Boys' quintuple-platinum status, but unfortunately, the group's popularity had decreased by 1988. One of Run-D.M.C.'s strong points—its love of rock & roll—was also its undoing in hip-hop circles. Any type of crossover success tends to be viewed suspiciously in the hood, and hardcore hip-hoppers weren't overly receptive to "Miss Elaine," "Papa Crazy," "Mary, Mary" and other rap/rock delights found on the album. Thanks largely to rock fans, this album did go platinum for sales exceeding one million copies—which ironically, Profile considered a disappointment. But the fact is that while *Tougher than Leather* isn't quite as strong as Run-D.M.C.'s first three albums, it was one of 1988's best rap releases. [*Tougher Than Leather* was remastered and reissued in 1999.] *—Alex Henderson*

Back from Hell / 1990 / Profile/Arista ✦✦✦

★ **Together Forever: Greatest Hits 1983-1991** / Nov. 6, 1991 / Profile ✦✦✦✦✦

For the most part, all of Run D.M.C.'s most important singles and biggest hits are included on *Together Forever: Greatest Hits 1983-1991*. That alone makes the compilation an necessary purchase. However, that doesn't mean that it is a perfectly assembled collection. Instead of presenting the singles in chronological order, the sequencing skips back and forth—for example, it opens with "Sucker M.C.'s," tjumps ahead to "Walk This Way," jumps further ahead to "Together Forever," then slams back to "King of Rock." Still, *Together Forever* has 18 of the groundbreaking group's absolutely essential items, from "It's Like That" and "Hard Times" to "It's Tricky" and "Run's House," which makes it an ideal introduction and an enjoyable retrospective. It's just not the definitive collection it could have been. *—Stephen Thomas Erlewine*

Down with the King / May 4, 1993 / Profile/Arista ✦✦✦

Salt-N-Pepa

f. 1985

Group / Pop-Rap, Urban, Hip-Hop

By the late '80s, hip-hop was on its way to becoming a male-dominated art form, which is what made the emergence of Salt N Pepa so significant. As the first all-female rap crew (even their DJs were women) of importance, the group broke down a number of doors for women in hip-hop. They were also one of the first rap artists to crossover into the pop mainstream, laying the groundwork for the music's widespread acceptance in the early '90s. Salt N Pepa were more pop-oriented than many of their contemporaries, since their songs were primarily party and love anthems, driven by big beats and interlaced with vaguely pro-feminist lyrics that seemed more powerful when delivered by the charismatic and sexy trio. While songs like "Push It" and "Shake Your Thang" made the group appear to be a one-hit pop group during the late '80s, Salt-N-Pepa defied expectations and became one of the few hip-hop artists to develop a long-term career. Along with LL Cool J, the trio had major hits in both the '80s and '90s, and, if anything, they hit the height of their popularity in 1994, when "Shoop" and "Whatta Man" drove their third album, *Very Necessary*, into the Top 10. *—Stephen Thomas Erlewine*

Hot, Cool & Vicious / 1986 / Next Plateau ✦✦✦✦✦

One of the earliest female rap groups, they hit the big leagues with this debut that includes the pulsating "Push It" and the salacious "Tramp." *—John Floyd*

A Salt with a Deadly Pepa / 1988 / London ✦✦✦

A concept album musically, if not lyrically, this one fleshes out one terrific single, "Shake Your Thing, " with a sharpening of the trio's sensibilities and talents. *—John Floyd*

● **Blacks' Magic** / Mar. 1990 / London ✦✦✦✦✦
Another concept album, this time the themes celebrate Black education and awareness, with some concise feminism included. *—John Floyd*

Very Necessary / Oct. 12, 1993 / Polygram ✦✦✦✦

Brand New / Oct. 21, 1997 / Red Ant/London ✦✦✦

Sir Mix-A-Lot

b. Aug. 12, 1963
Vocals / Pop-Rap, West Coast Rap
Sir Mix-A-Lot put Seattle on the rap map in the late '80s with catchy, comedic dramas drenched in b-boy culture and punctuated by his whiny vocals. Sir Mix-A-Lot vaulted into the spotlight and into controversy with the single "Baby Got Back." Not only was it an enormous pop and R&B hit, it triggered a backlash against what was widely viewed as both sexist and racist lyrics from Mix-A-Lot in his celebration of rear ends and putdown of women who lacked them. It helped make the *Mack Daddy* album one of 1992's biggest, although 1994's *Chief Booty Knocka* and 1996's *Return of the Bumpasaurus* failed to match its success. In 2000, Rhino released an 18-track best-of titled *Beepers, Benzos and Booty: The Best of Sir Mix-a-Lot*. *—John Floyd*

Swass / 1988 / Def American ✦✦✦

Seminar / Mar. 1988 / Def American ✦✦✦
With his second album, Sir Mix-A-Lot continued focusing primarily on the type of material that made his first reach gold status: escapist, lighthearted pop/rap that fared well among pop, R&B and dance-music circles, but generally wasn't well received in "the hood." What few sociopolitical songs the CD does contain are first-rate, including "The (Peek-A-Boo) Game" (which uses Siouxsie & the Banshees as a reference point) and "National Anthem." An angry number addressing the Iran-contra scandal, the drug plague and the plight of Vietnam vets, the latter is as powerful as anything Public Enemy, KRS-One or Ice-T has done. Nonetheless, what made *Seminar* a hit weren't those gems, but odes to cars, gold chains and "fly girls." As enjoyable as such escapist fare as "My Hooptie" and "Beepers" is, Mix sells himself short by not including more message songs. *—Alex Henderson*

Mack Daddy / Apr. 1991 / Def American ✦✦✦✦✦
Sir Mix-A-Lot scored a huge sleeper hit with his ridiculous paean to large buttocks, "Baby Got Back," in the summer of 1992. For those who want it, the rest of *Mack Daddy* offers more of the same—skeletal raps that verge on the point of parody. Sir Mix-A-Lot can barely rap, and his lyrics are full of posturing tales that never have a dose of reality. But this is the very element that makes *Mack Daddy* fun, because Sir Mix-A-Lot tries so hard and sounds so silly. *—Stephen Thomas Erlewine*

Chief Boot Knocka / Jul. 19, 1994 / Rhyme Cartel ✦✦✦

Return of the Bumpasaurus / Aug. 27, 1996 / Warner Brothers ✦✦✦

● **Beepers, Benzos & Booty: The Best of Sir Mix a Lot** / Jun. 20, 2000 / Rhino ✦✦✦✦✦
Rhino's *Beepers, Benzos & Booty: The Best of Sir Mix-A-Lot* collects the Seattle rapper's definitive tracks, including the infamous "Baby Got Back," "My Hooptie," "Society's Creation," "Just Da Pimpin' In Me", "Posse On Broadway," and "Square Dance Rap." A fun compilation of one of rap's most consistently funny artists. *—Heather Phares*

Slick Rick

b. Jan. 14, 1965, London, England
Vocals / Hardcore Rap, Hip-Hop
Slick Rick foreshadowed and epitomized the pimpster attitude of many rappers during the late '80s and early '90s, with gold chains, his trademark eye-patch, and recordings that were no less misogynistic—"Treat Her like a Prostitute," for example, became an underground hit in 1988 though it was justly criticized for its view of women. His 1989 album, *The Great Adventures of Slick Rick*, was a certified-platinum classic, but before he could record a follow-up, Slick Rick was arrested for attempted murder. Out on bail thanks to Def Jam Records' label-head Russell Simmons, Rick recorded 21 songs in 1991 and hastily released them as as *The Ruler's Back*. The album failed to move at all, though Rick's confession track "I Shouldn't Have Done It" scraped the R&B charts later in 1991. Featured in the rap documentary *The Show* (released in 1995)—in a segment where Russell Simmons actually visits the prison—Slick Rick was released on a work program in 1993, and his *Behind Bars* album appeared in 1994. *Art of Storytelling* was issued in 1999. *—John Bush*

★ **The Great Adventures of Slick Rick** / 1988 / Def Jam ✦✦✦✦✦
Slick Rick first gained an audience by rapping on Doug E. Fresh's "La-Di-Da-Di" and "The Show," two songs that immediately established him as a major talent upon their release in 1985. It may have taken him three years to deliver his full-length debut, but when *The Great Adventures of Slick Rick* arrived in 1988, it was an immediate classic. What makes *The Great Adventures of Slick Rick* such a stunning achievement isn't necessarily the music—in retrospect, it's strong, but unexceptional, street funk—but Rick's rhyming. His style was fluid, but filled with odd cadences and an idiosyncratic phrasing. Furthermore, his story-telling technique is unparalleled, full with detail and dramatic momentum; his skewed, slightly cartoonish view point was nearly as influential. Unfortunately, his rampant misogyny and cool, amoralistic outlook became equally influential on '90s hip-hop. Even though Slick Rick released a series of fairly mediocre followups and spent an extended stay in prison, his failure to live up to the potential of *The Great Adventures* doesn't dilute the impact of the album at all. Years after its release, it still sounds fresh. *—Stephen Thomas Erlewine*

The Ruler's Back / 1991 / Def Jam ✦✦✦✦
It was easy to dismiss *The Rulerís Back* before it was even released, or to assume that there was no way it could live up to *The Great Adventures of Slick Rick*. Of course, it did not attain the same level of artistic success as that debut, and it certainly did not equal that album's commercial success, in fact seemingly passing beneath the radar of the whole hip-hop community, for the most part. At the time of its release, the album received mixed reviews and indifferent reactions even from fans of Slick Rick. That's another unfortunate, ill-fated aspect of *The Rulerís Back*, because, in truth, it is a strong, albeit uneven, progression from the debut, and occasionally strikes a flawless note. To think of the album as anything other than a confused, transitional effort would be inaccurate, but it does not follow that it isn't an intriguing record. The messiness of its execution perfectly encapsulates the sort of turmoil Slick Rick was experiencing in his life at the time, and the music pulls the listener into that sort of tangled experience. Both Vance Wright's production and Slick Rick's rapping sound pressed for time, and they rush through the songs with a whip-lashing intensity. It can be a disorienting listen, but it is also a pure adrenaline rush. Slick Rick was going through a time of hurtling change, and the hurried breathlessness of the music captures that. *The Rulerís Back* is all over the map, lacking the thematic focus that held the first album together, but its frayed-threads, seams-showing immediacy is part of what makes it such an underrated album in the hip-hop canon. *—Stanton Swihart*

Behind Bars / Nov. 22, 1994 / Def Jam ✦✦

The Art of Storytelling / May 25, 1999 / Def Jam ✦✦✦✦
If there's one thing Slick Rick has mastered, it is *The Art of Storytelling*. Ever since his debut, *The Great Adventures of Slick Rick*, he has been known for his literate, winding narratives, but his career was marred by legal troubles that kept him in prison for much of the '90s. Consequently, *The Art of Storytelling* is only his fourth album, but it's the first to rank as a worthy sequel to his classic debut. *The Ruler's Back* came close to capturing the feel of *The Great Adventures*, but *The Art* has a continually stunning set of stories and tales, and the presence of guest artists—even rappers as talented as Outkast, Nas, Raekwon and Snoop Dogg—only emphasizes what a singular talent Rick is. The smooth production may be a little bit mired in contemporary rap cliches, but it's all enjoyable. Besides, Rick is about the lyrics, not the music, and he has written a stellar set of songs here, songs that are continually surprising and thought-provoking. It's a masterful set from one of the true lyrical masters of hip-hop. *—Stephen Thomas Erlewine*

Will Smith (William Smith III)

b. Sep. 25, 1968, West Philadelphia, PA
Vocals / Pop-Rap, Urban, Hip-Hop
Beginning his career during the mid-1980s under the name the Fresh Prince, by the following decade rapper Will Smith was one of the biggest superstars of his time—not only a pop music sensation, he also conquered television and eventually feature films, starring in a string of box-office megahits. He was 16 when he met aspiring DJ Jeff Townes; joining forces as DJ Jazzy Jeff and the Fresh Prince, in 1987 the duo issued their debut record *Rock the House*, scoring a hit with the single "Girls Ain't Nothing But Trouble." Propelled by the smash "Parents Just Don't Understand," DJ Jazzy Jeff and the Fresh Prince broke into the mainstream a year later with *He's the DJ, I'm the Rapper*, one of the first hip hop LPs to achieve double-platinum status. Clean-cut, witty and easygoing, the duo's bubblegum approach was a stark contrast to the dominant, harder-edged rap sound of the period; viewed as a non-threatening alternative to their peers, they received the parental seal of approval, and their appeal spread across racial lines as well. Soon Hollywood began taking notice of Smith's success; in 1990, he was tapped to star in *The Fresh Prince of Bel-Air*, a sitcom for NBC. In 1995, Smith co-starred in the action film *Bad Boys*, a major box office hit; it set the stage for his leading role in 1996's *Independence Day*, the summer's biggest smash. A year later, he starred in *Men in Black*, again the box-office champ of the summer season; recording for the first time under his given name, he also scored a smash with the movie's rap theme. Smith's debut solo LP, *Big Willie Style*, also appeared in 1997, notching the hit "Gettin' Jiggy Wit It." *—Jason Ankeny*

● **Big Willie Style** / Nov. 25, 1997 / Columbia ✦✦✦✦
Will Smith wisely decided not to change his style too much on *Big Willie Style*, the first record he released since becoming a major movie star with appearances on *Independence Day* and *Men in Black*. Instead of trying to toughen his image, Smith continued with the friendly, humorous pop-rap that has been his trademark since *He's the DJ, I'm the Rapper*. Of course, he gives the music a glossy modern sheen (ironically based on early-'80s funk) in order to prove that he's still hip—and it works. Sure, there's filler scattered all the way the through the album, but the best moments—the disco-thumping "Gettin' Jiggy Wit It," the Larry Blackmon duet "Candy," the ballad "I Loved You" and the riotous "Men in Black"—rank among his best singles. *—Stephen Thomas Erlewine*

Willennium / Nov. 16, 1999 / Columbia ✦✦✦✦
By the time Will Smith released *Willennium* in November 1999, it was fashionable to put him down, especially since he was recovering from his first major stumble, the overblown *Wild Wild West*. Probably just the fact that he was everywhere made certain spoilsports long to take him down a notch, but *Wild Wild West* wasn't a mess because of him; in fact, he provided the only glimmers of fun in the whole misguided mess, through sheer star power. And that star power drives *Willennium*, turning it into a bold, brassy delight. Smith just doesn't care what anyone thinks; he knows he's a superstar, and he revels in his status. He likes to make fun music, and he likes to make it on a grand scale. Furthermore, he has no shame about entertaining. Consequently, *Willennium* is a gonzo pleasure in the way only a handful of big-budget pop albums can be: gaudy, giddy, infectiously silly, and proudly over-the-top. Case in point, its de facto title track, "Will 2K." Smith and his producers picked the Clash's "Rock the Casbah" as the foundation for an end-of-the-century party jam, a move so mind-bogglingly unpredictable that it's hard not to smile. And that spirit carries throughout the album, as Smith drops lyrical and musical allusions that are at once well-known and totally out of left field. All of this is done to bright, joyful party music that celebrates its big beats and big hooks. Smith isn't quite as convincing when it comes to slow jams, but still his charm shines through. But the heart of the album lies in the uptempo dance numbers, since they're what make *Willennium* irresistible. And this is one of the rare times that an abundance of cameos enhances the spirit of an album, making *Willennium* feel like a Y2K blowout where everyone is invited. *—Stephen Thomas Erlewine*

Snoop Dogg (Calvin Broadus)

b. Oct. 20, 1972, Long Beach, CA

Rap, Vocals / West Coast Rap, G-Funk, Gangsta Rap

As the embodiment of '90s gangsta rap, Snoop Doggy Dogg blurred the lines between reality and fiction. Introduced to the world through Dr. Dre's *The Chronic*, Snoop Dogg quickly became the most famous star in rap, partially because of his drawled, laconic rhyming and partially because the violence that his lyrics implied seemed real, especially after he was arrested on charges of being a murder accomplice. The arrest certainly strengthened his myth, and it helped his debut album, 1993's *Doggystyle*, become the first debut album to enter the charts at number one, but in the long run, it hurt his career. Snoop had to fight charges throughout 1994 and 1995, and while he was eventually cleared, it hurt his momentum. *The Doggfather*, his second album, wasn't released until November 1996, and by that time, pop and hip-hop had burned itself out on gangsta-rap. *The Doggfather* sold half as well as its predecessor, which meant that Snoop remained a star, but he no longer had the influence he had just two years before. *—Stephen Thomas Erlewine*

• **Doggystyle** / Nov. 23, 1993 / Priority ✦✦✦✦✦
Often compared and undoubtedly related in more ways than one, Snoop Dogg's Dr. Dre-produced debut album, *Doggystyle*, might not be as influential or as historically important as *The Chronic*, but it arguably just might be the better album of the two. For instance, where the second half of *The Chronic* gets bogged down with too many second-rate rappers, and where it also suffers from Dre's so-so rapping, *Doggystyle* finds the Death Row camp's best MCs—Snoop, Kurupt, Daz, Nate Dogg—handling most of the lyrical duties. Considering these factors, *Doggystyle* is a wiser and more well-crafted album than *The Chronic*, even if it is monopolized by Snoop's sometimes too-stoned-for-his-own-good delivery (not necessarily a bad thing). Moments such as the opening montage of "Bathtub" into "G Funk Intro" into "Gin and Juice" (and, to a slightly lesser degree, "Doggy Dogg World" and "Murder Was the Case") are brilliantly cinematic moments on a par with the finest moments of Curtis Mayfield's *Superfly*. And the wit practiced by Tha Dogg Pound posse on playboy songs such as "Ain't No Fun" also helps make this an album of non-stop highlights. As proven with his subsequent mid- to late-'90s solo albums, Snoop may be a talented MC, but the brilliance of this album should be attributed, as much if not more so, to Dre, and to a lesser extent Daz, Kurupt, Nate Dogg, and Warren G. This album is the result of an amazing synergy that would soon dissolve. *—Jason Birchmeier*

Tha Doggfather / Nov. 12, 1996 / Death Row/Interscope ✦✦✦
A lot happened to Snoop Doggy Dogg between his debut *Doggystyle* and his second album, *Tha Doggfather*. During those three years, he became the most notorious figure in hip-hop through a much-publicized murder trail, where he was found not guilty, and he also became a father. Musically, the most important thing to happen to Snoop was the parting of ways between his mentor Dr. Dre and his record label, Death Row. Dre's departure from Death Row meant that Snoop had to handle the production duties on *Tha Doggfather* himself, and the differences between the two records are immediately apparent. Though it works the same G-funk territory, the bass is less elastic and there is considerably less sonic detail. In essence, all of the music on *Tha Doggfather* reworks the funk and soul of the late '70s and early '80s, without updating it too much—there's not that much difference between "Snoop's Upside Ya Head" and "Oops Up Side Your Head." Though the music isn't original, and the lyrics break no new territory, the execution is strong—Snoop's rapping and rhyming continue to improve, while the bass-heavy funk is often intoxicating. At over 70 minutes, *Tha Doggfather* runs too long to not have several filler tracks, but if you ignore those cuts, the album is a fine followup to one of the most successful hip-hop albums in history. *—Stephen Thomas Erlewine*

Da Game Is to Be Sold Not to Be Told / Aug. 4, 1998 / No Limit/Priority ✦✦

Top Dogg / May 11, 1999 / No Limit ✦✦✦
As time keeps on slipping into the future, it becomes apparent that Master P's greatest gift is marketing, particularly when his advertising masquerades as liner notes. Witness P's work for Snoop Dogg, once considered the brightest rapper of the '90s but now merely a general in the No Limit army. The Master began plugging *Top Dogg*, Snoop's second No Limit release, in the liners for his label debut, even mentioning a release date only months away. Clearly, Snoop had indeed been placed on the No Limit production line, and there was every indication that from now on, Snoop would churn out moderately enjoyable, Dirty South-lite records crammed with cameos and appropriated hooks. Turns out he had a trick up his sleeve, because *Top Dogg* is about as individualized an album as possible under the No Limit precepts. Since the outset of his career, Snoop has shown a fondness for early-'80s synth-funk, and for the first time, he lets that form the basis of an album. And while there may be a bit too much recycling for some tastes, the end result isn't just the freshest-sounding Snoop album since his debut, it's easily the freshest-sounding No Limit album. Unfortunately, it's still a No Limit album, which means it runs way too long and is filled with superfluous, even irritating cameos, and also that Snoop is content to haul out low-rent gangsta clichés. Since he's a gifted rapper, he makes the dope n' crimes, sex n' violence rhymes go down easily (compare his delivery to some of his guests if you have any doubts), but his lyrics just aren't as clever as they were five years earlier. But records don't have to be deep; they can be appreciated as a pure sonic experience, and taken on that level, *Top Dogg* satisfies. *—Stephen Thomas Erlewine*

Dead Man Walkin' / Oct. 31, 2000 / D-3 ✦✦✦

Tha Last Meal / Dec. 5, 2000 / Priority ✦✦✦✦
Granted, Dr. Dre only produced three tracks on *Tha Last Meal*, but his influence is *all* over this record. The album's promising young producers—Scott Storch, Jelly Roll, Meech Wells, Battlecat, and Soopafly—all lay down Dre-like beats full of fat bass lines and cosmic synth that are just as effective, if not more inspired, than Dre's. Furthermore, half the songs feature Kokane's P-funkesque vocal hooks, one of the most important changes in Snoop's sound; as quirky as his voice might be, the old-school L.A. rapper brings soulful melody, a quality that only enhances itself on successive listens. In addition, the Doggfather lets the beats ride out a bit, sparsely ad-libbing rather than smothering them with rhymes and guest rappers—another welcome decision. Yet calling this album a masterpiece is a bit erroneous. Master P lets Snoop do what he wants for the most part but does manage to include one blatant No Limit-flavored track, "Back Up Off Me." Also, Timbaland produces two tracks here— "Snoop Dogg (What's My Name Pt. 2)" and "Set It Off"—which are great songs, yet the beats are slightly inconsistent with the rest of the album. Overall though, these are minor flaws that do little to scar this otherwise impressive album. *Tha Last Meal* foreshadows a West Coast rap renaissance driven not so much by rappers but rather by a generation of young funk-obsessed producers weaned on *The Chronic*. *—Jason Birchmeier*

Spoonie Gee (Gabe Jackson)

Vocals / Old School Rap, Hip-Hop

Spoonie Gee was the nephew of veteran rhythm and blues producer Bobby Robinson and one of the earliest rap artists. He was known as the "love rapper," an image that was established by his first record, "Love Rap," released on his uncle's Enjoy label as the flip side of the Treacherous Three's "New Rap Language." The bulk of early rap records reproduced an MC's party routine with a loose sequence of narrative, boasting, and call and response. Spoonie's initial outing, however, organized a hip-hop styled record around a romantic theme, coming closer to the lyrical norms of pop music. The intimate "Love Rap" was accompanied only by drum set and congas, and Spoonie Gee's next record continued in a similarly minimalist vein. The voiceover on 1979's "Spoonin' Rap" stuck to more conventional old school boasting, but looks forward to the gangster attitude in its jailhouse references. "Spoonin' Rap" was also prophetic in its use of flexatone and heavily echoed voice, suggesting the Jamaican connection that was denied in early interviews by some of the rap originators. In 1980, Spoonie Gee collaborated with Sequence on a classic single, "Monster Jam," probably the last word on the series of "Good Times/Another One Bites the Dust" variations, and a classic in the Sugar Hill vein, complete with bone crushing bass line and ecstatic crowd noises. *—Richard Pierson*

• **The Godfather . . . Rap** / 1987 / Tuff City ✦✦✦✦✦
Spoonie Gee was among the earliest old-school rappers, performing in a coarse, terse style over funk beats. He was never a great rapper, but he was an effective one, and this album showcased his functional approach on material ranging from straight come-ons to microphone challenges and message cuts. *—Ron Wynn*

Stetsasonic

f. 1981, **db.** 1992

Group / Hip-Hop

One of the first rap groups to use a live band, Brooklyn's Stetsasonic formed in 1981 and were also among the first to promote a positive black consciousness that found its ultimate expression in the so-called daisy-age sounds of De La Soul and the Jungle Brothers. The group consisted of DJs "Prince Paul" Huston and Leonard "Wise" Roman, keyboardist/drummer/DJ Marvin "DBC" Nemley, and rappers Glenn "Daddy-O" Bolton, Martin "Delite" Wright, and Bobby "Fruitkwan" Simmons. Daddy-O and Delite founded the group as the Stetson Brothers, after the hat company, and began performing in New York hip-hop clubs, picking up other members along the way. Their debut, *On Fire*, was released in 1986, but it was the follow-up, *In Full Gear*, that brought them critical acclaim and an R&B hit, "Sally." 1991's *Blood, Sweat and No Tears* was considered by many to be their best and most diverse album, but Daddy-O decided that they had run out of ideas and broke up the band. He went on to work with Mary J. Blige, Queen Latifah, Big Daddy Kane, and the Red Hot Chili Peppers as a producer and remixer. Meanwhile, Prince Paul had already established himself as a producer for his work with De La Soul and Fine Young Cannibals, and later worked with Fruitkwan in the Gravediggaz. Stetsonic released the full-length *On Fire* in early 2001.—*Steve Huey*

On Fire / 1986 / Tommy Boy ✦✦✦
There weren't many bands utilizing a hip-hop format in the mid-'80s, making Stetasonic quite unique on the pop front in 1986. While their subject matter was invariably light and their raps now hopelessly tame and effete, they were ground-breaking at the time and retain a certain charm. *—Ron Wynn*

• **In Full Gear** / 1988 / Tommy Boy ✦✦✦✦✦
They're not "the world's only hip-hop band" anymore, but this seven-piece group (real drums even!) paved the way. Their second disc documents their innovative best, culminating in the anthemic "Talkin' All That Jazz." *—John Floyd*

Blood, Sweat & No Tears / 1991 / Tommy Boy ✦✦✦

The Sugarhill Gang

f. 1979, **db.** 1985

Group / Old School Rap

Though the Sugarhill Gang inaugurated the history of recorded hip-hop with their single "Rapper's Delight," a multi-platinum seller and radio hit in 1979, the group was cooked up to cash in on a supposed novelty item; music-industry producer and label-owner Sylvia Robinson had become aware of the massive hip-hop block parties occurring around the New York area during the late '70s, so she gathered three local rappers (Master Gee, Wonder Mike and Big Bank Hank) to record a single. Infectious and catchy, "Rapper's Delight" borrowed the break from Chic's "Good Times" and became a worldwide hit, eventually selling over eight million copies. Most industry people figured rap for a short-lived trend, and though they were dead wrong, the Sugarhill Gang certainly didn't carry the torch; despite several modest hits ("8th Wonder," "Apache") the trio faded quickly and were gone by the mid-'80s, returning in 1999 with *Jump on It*, a rap album for children. *—John Bush*

The Sugarhill Gang / 1980 / Sugar Hill ✦✦✦✦
Although the Sugarhill Gang didn't invent hip-hop, it was the first rap act to have a huge international hit. Released in 1979, "Rapper's Delight" was millions of listeners' first exposure to hip-hop—before that, very few people outside of New York even knew what hip-hop was.

The Sugarhill Gang was also among the first rap acts to record a full-length LP; when this self-titled debut album came out in 1980, the vast majority of old school MCs were only providing 12″ singles. So *The Sugarhill Gang* is a historically important album even though it is a bit uneven. While "Rapper's Delight" and "Rapper's Reprise" (which features the Sequence, hip-hop's first all-female group) are excellent, most of the material is merely decent. And the ironic thing is that half of the songs aren't even rap. "Bad News Don't Bother Me" and "Here I Am," both of which find the Sugarhill Gang singing instead of rapping, are romantic R&B slow jams and "Sugarhill Groove" is a sleek disco-funk number that hints at Roy Ayers. So this LP can hardly be called the work of hip-hop purists; in 1980, Sugarhill Records leader Sylvia Robinson (herself a veteran R&B singer) evidently felt that putting out an all-rap album would be risky. But, while *The Sugarhill Gang* isn't a masterpiece, it's still an album that hip-hop historians will find interesting. *—Alex Henderson*

8th Wonder / 1982 / Sugar Hill ✦✦✦

● **The Best of Sugarhill Gang** / Jul. 1996 / Rhino ✦✦✦✦✦
Sugarhill Gang's biggest hits are collected on this single-disc compilation. In addition to "Rapper's Delight"—the first rap single to reach the pop Top Ten—the group's seven other R&B hits are included on the disc, plus three other singles that never made the charts. All of the songs are presented in their original 12-inch versions. Not all of the material is first-rate—in retrospective, the group's old-school groove tended to be a little simplistic, monotonous, and too polished, while their rhymes were frequently stilted and sometimes just outright silly—but this music, especially "Rapper's Delight," is important historically. Most casual fans of old-school hip-hop will be content with purchasing "Rapper's Delight" on a various artists collection, but for those wanting to dig deeper into the trio's history, *The Best of Sugarhill Gang* is a defintive retrospective. *—Stephen Thomas Erlewine*

Jump on It! / Apr. 6, 1999 / Rhino ✦✦✦

3rd Bass

f. 1987, Queens, NY, **db.** 1992
Group / East Coast Rap, Alternative Rap
Along with the Beastie Boys, 3rd Bass stand as the rare White hip-hop act that's actually won respect and credibility among the rap hardcore. Pete Nice, one-time English major at Columbia whose radio program "Top of the Hip-hop" was unceremoniously cancelled by the purportedly progressive WKCR-FM, teamed with MC Serch to offer devastating put-downs of the hip-hop lifestyle and worldview. They have since disbanded, but their two albums were definitive, if at times uneven. *—Ron Wynn*

● **The Cactus Album** / 1989 / Def Jam ✦✦✦✦✦
Besides the upper-middle-class frat-punks-in-rap-clothing shtick of the Beastie Boys and emissary/producer Rick Rubin, who both gained a legitimate, earned respect in the rap community, there were very few white kids in rap's first decade who spoke the poetry of the street with compassion and veneration for the form. That is, until *The Cactus Album*. Matching MC Serch's bombastic, goofy good nature and Prime Minister Pete Nice's gritty, English-trained wordsmithery (sounding like a young Don in training), 3rd Bass' debut album is revelatory in its way. For one, it is full of great songs, alternately upbeat rollers ("Sons of 3rd Bass"), casual-but-sincere disses ("The Gas Face"), razor-sharp street didacticism ("Triple Stage Darkness," "Wordz of Wizdom"), and sweaty city anthems ("Brooklyn Queens," "Steppin' to the A.M.," odes to day and night, respectively), with A-plus production by heavyweights Prince Paul and Bomb Squad, as well as the surprising, overshadowing work of Sam Sever. The duo may not have come from the streets, but their hearts were there, and it shows. The album embodies New York life. Not every single idea plays out successfully—Serch's Louis Armstrong impression on "Flippin' Off the Wall..." is on the wrong side of the taste line, and "Desert Boots" is a puzzling Western-themed insertion—but they are at least interesting stretches that add to the dense, layered texture of the album. *The Cactus Album* was also important because it proved to the hip-hop heads that white kids could play along without appropriating or bastardizing the culture. It may not have completely integrated rap, but it was a precursor to a culture that became more inclusive and widespread after its arrival. *—Stanton Swihart*

Derelicts of Dialect / 1991 / Def Jam ✦✦✦
Although 3rd Bass didn't fully realize their tremendous potential, the Brooklyn rappers offered enjoyable, if uneven, albums. Like the group's 1989 debut, their second and final album, *Derelects of Dialect*, makes it clear that the MCs weren't aiming for the pop charts—and were loyal only to the hip-hop hardcore. When MC Serch and Pete Nice tear into such aggressive and forceful declarations as "Pop Goes the Weasel" (an inflammatory attack on Vanilla Ice), "Portrait of the Artist as a Hood" and "Ace in the Hole," it's clear why they were among the few White MCs who were successful in the young Black community—someone who heard their rapping without seeing their picture could easily assume they were Black. Although the goofy "Herbalz in Your Mouth" shows some De La Soul and Tribe Called Quest influence, 3rd Bass doesn't allow itself to be nearly as light hearted, and keeps things hardcore and intense. *—Alex Henderson*

Tone-Loc

Vocals / Pop-Rap, West Coast Rap
Tone-Loc (born Tony Smith) soared from obscurity into pop stardom in 1989 when his hoarse voice and unmistakable delivery made the song "Wild Thing" (using a sample from Van Halen's "Jamie's Cryin'") a massive hit. The song was co-written by Marvin Young, better known as Young MC, as was the second single smash "Funky Cold Medina." The album *Loc-ed After Dark* became the second rap release to top the pop charts. Tone-Loc expanded his horizons into acting in 1992 and 1993, appearing a few times on the FOX sitcom *Roc*. He was also in the films *Posse* and *Ace Ventura: Pet Detective*, and in 1998 returned to recording with *Cool Hand Loc*. *—Ron Wynn*

● **Loc-ed After Dark** / 1989 / Delicious Vinyl/Rhino ✦✦✦✦
A pop hit—however inventive—can be the kiss of death in hip-hop circles. When Tone Loc's incredibly infectious and highly original rap/rock hits "Wild Thing" and "Funky Cold Medina" took the pop world by storm, his reputation suffered considerably among b-boys. The Angelino maintained that those singles were the exception, not that the rule—and that he was a hardcore rapper first and foremost. Indeed, most of *Loc-ed After Dark* bears that out. While this striking debut album does contain the above-mentioned hits, hardcore rap like "Next Episode," "Don't Get Close" and "Cheeba Cheeba" is in fact dominant. When "Cheeba Cheeba" was first released in 1987, the song took its share of criticism for promoting marijuana at a time when numerous rappers were vehemently protesting drug use. (Unfortunately, pro-drug songs would later become the norm in rap.) Deadpan and relaxed, the distinctive Loc isn't a rapper with much technique—though he certainly has a lot of personality. *—Alex Henderson*

Cool Hand Loc / 1991 / Delicious Vinyl/Rhino ✦✦✦
Aiming for credibility among hardcore hip-hoppers, Delicious Vinyl was careful not to include a lot of pop-influenced material on Tone-Loc's second album, *Cool Hand Loc*. But sadly, the inventiveness he displayed on "Wild Thing" continued working against Loc among b-boys and hip-hop's hardcore, who still resented the success he'd enjoyed in the pop market. Though not quite as strong as the triple platinum *Loc-ed After Dark*—either commercially or artistically—the album is a respectable and satisfying effort. The former L.A. gang member tends to overdue it with boasting lyrics—a problem he shares with quite a few other rappers—but his boasts are often quite clever. Sadly, Tone-Loc didn't have much longevity; after *Cool Hand Loc*, little was heard about him. *—Alex Henderson*

Too hort (Todd Shaw)

b. Apr. 28, 1966, Los Angeles, CA
Vocals / West Coast Rap, Hardcore Rap, G-Funk, Gangsta Rap
Too hort was the first West Coast rap star, recording four albums on his own before he made his major-label debut with 1986's gold album *Born to Mack*. Anticipating much of the later gangsta phenomenon, he restricted his lyrical themes to tales of sexual prowess and physical violence, with the occasional social-message track to mix things up. His second major album, 1989's *Life Is... Too Short*, was his biggest success and earned double-platinum honors. The immense success of Too hort that year made him much more viable for radio airplay, and "The Ghetto"—from 1990's *Short Dog's in the House* hit the R&B charts, and just barely missed the pop Top 40. He continued his hit track-record with 1992's *Shorty the Pimp* and 1993's *Get in Where You Fit In*, both of which went platinum. By the time of 1995's *Cocktails*, however, Too hort began to be drowned out by a glut of similar-sounding West Coasters. Though *Gettin' It (Album Number Ten)* became his fifth platinum album by late 1996, he decided to retire, his status assured as one of the most successful solo rappers of the 1980s and early '90s. Just three years later, he returned with the aptly titled *Can't Stay Away*. *—John Bush*

Born to Mack / 1988 / Jive ✦✦✦

● **Life Is... Too hort** / 1988 / Jive ✦✦✦✦✦
Too Short never had the skills or technique of LL Cool J or Big Daddy Kane, but what the Oakland rapper lacks in technique, he's always more than made up for with irresistible, '70s-inspired funk grooves that simply won't quit. When Short—after enjoying a small cult following for a few years in Northern California—joined a major label with *Life Is... Too Short's* predecessor, *Born to Mack*, too many East Coast MCs were inundanting hip-hop with clichéd tracks consisting of only James Brown samples and a drum machine. Too Short, however, presented an attractive alternative with highly melodic, danceable tracks that made no secret of his love of '70s funk heroes like Parliament, the Ohio Players and Cameo. This CD's X-rated, sexually explicit lyrics received their share of vehement criticism, and the MC responsed that Too Short is an outrageous character who shouldn't be taken too seriously. Be that as it may, his commanding reflection on the drug plague, "City of Dope," underscores the fact that he's cheating himself artistically by not devoting more time to social commentary and less time to exploiting sex. *—Alex Henderson*

Short Dog's in the House / Aug. 1990 / Jive ✦✦✦✦
With *Short Dog's in the House*, Oakland's most sexually explicit MC gave his followers more of what he was known for—X-rated lyrics, a relaxed style of rapping and addictive, melodic tracks recalling the splendor of '70s funk. R&B fans who complained that rap on the whole wasn't sufficiently melodic couldn't make that complaint about the distinctive Too Short. When his raunchy lyrics continued to come under fire, he maintained that he was simply portraying a character—and that he wasn't really the ghetto pimp he portrayed. As entertaining as his albums are, Short's inspired interpretation of Donny Hathaway's "The Ghetto" makes it crystal clear that he would do well to be more lyrically challenging more often. —Alex Henderson

Shorty the Pimp / Jul. 14, 1992 / Jive ✦✦✦✦
Shorty the Pimp was Too Short's seventh album. As one would expect from an entertainer with six albums behind him, Too Short had by now perfected his craft. Though his focus was still on womanizing and pimping, by 1992 the rest of the rap world had "caught up" with the Oakland rapper's explicit brand of boasting and bragging. Aware of this, Too Short had gradually begun adding battle rhymes "In the Trunk", social commentary "I Want to Be Free" and cautionary tales "So You Want to Be a Gangster" to the mix. Never particularly gifted as a rapper, Too Short's proved himself a wily veteran in his ability to squeeze every bit of effect out of his relatively simple style. But what separated *Shorty the Pimp* from the rest of the now crowded rap field was the music. Producer Ant Banks, multi-instrumentalist Shorty B and Too Short, himself, created a satisfying blend of funk samples augmented by live drums and deftly played bass lines. Many of the backing tracks are composed well enough to be successful on their own. *—Mtume Salaam*

Get in Where You Fit In / 1993 / Jive ✦✦

Greatest Hits, Vol. 1: The Player Years, 1983-1988 / Nov. 10, 1993 / In-A-Minute ✦✦✦✦✦
If you've never read the collected works of Chester Himes or Iceberg Slim, simply run through this Too hort anthology and you'll have the general idea. Although never an inven-

tive rapper or clever composer of rhymes, Too hort was smart enough to find his niche and stick to it. Most people who continually mined the pimp arena quickly become merely tedious; Too hort became both tedious and profitable. *—Ron Wynn*

Cocktails / 1995 / Jive ♦♦♦♦

Gettin' It (Album Number Ten) / Jun. 18, 1996 / Jive ♦♦♦

Can't Stay Away / Feb. 23, 1999 / Jive ♦♦♦

You Nasty / Sep. 12, 2000 / Jive ♦♦♦

A Tribe Called Quest

f. 1988, Queens, NY, **db.** 1998

Group / Jazz-Rap, East Coast Rap, Alternative Rap, Hip-Hop

Without question the most intelligent, artistic rap group during the '90s, A Tribe Called Quest jump-started and perfected the hip-hop alternative to hardcore and gangsta-rap. In essence, they abandoned the macho posturing which rap music had been constructed upon, and focused instead on abstract philosophy and message tracks. The "sucka MC" theme had never been completely ignored in hip-hop, but Tribe confronted numerous black issues—date rape, use of the word nigger, the trials and tribulations of the rap industry—all of which overpowered the occasional game of the dozens. Just as powerful musically, Quest built upon De La Soul's jazz-rap revolution, basing tracks around laidback samples instead of the played-out James Brown-fests which many rappers had made a cottage industry by the late '80s. Comprised of Q-Tip, Ali Shaheed Muhammad, and Phife, A Tribe Called Quest debuted in 1989 and released their debut album one year later. Second album *The Low End Theory* was, quite simply, the most consistent and flowing hip-hop album ever recorded, though the trio moved closer to their harder contemporaries on 1993's *Midnight Marauders*. A spot on the 1993 Lollapalooza Tour showed their influence with the alternative crowd—always a bedrock of A Tribe Called Quest's support—but the group kept it real on 1996's *Beats, Rhymes and Life*, a dedication to the streets and the hip-hop underground. Soon after 1998's *The Love Movement* though, the group broke up. *—John Bush*

People's Instinctive Travels and the Paths of Rhythm / Apr. 17, 1990 / Jive ♦♦♦♦

With its superb debut album, A Tribe Called Quest established itself as leaders of alternative rap—a term also applied to De La Soul, Digable Planets and the Pharcyde. Though De La had a strong influence on Quest, the experimental New York group projected a highly appealing personality of its own. Quirky, abstract and cerebral, the album lacks the immediacy of more hardcore rap and wasn't as big a seller as many of the gangster rap CDs released in 1990. In fact, much of its support came from alternative rock aficionados, who were drawn to its complexity. Jazz is a strong influenced here, and like many jazz recordings, this is an album that necessitates several listenings in order to be fully appreciated and absorbed. *—Alex Henderson*

★ **The Low End Theory** / Sep. 24, 1991 / Jive ♦♦♦♦♦

While most of the players in the \jazz-rap movement never quite escaped the pasted-on qualities of their vintage samples, with *The Low End Theory*, A Tribe Called Quest created one of the closest and most brilliant fusions of \jazz atmosphere and \hip-hop attitude ever recorded. The rapping by Q-Tip and Phife Dawg could be the smoothest of any \rap record ever heard; the pair are so in tune with each other, they sound like flip sides of the same personality, fluidly trading off on rhymes, with the former earning his nickname (the Abstract) and Phife concerning himself with the more concrete issues of being young, gifted, and black. The trio also takes on the \rap game with a pair of hard-hitting tracks: "Rap Promoter" and "Show Business," the latter a lyrical sound clash with Q-Tip and Phife plus Brand Nubian's Diamond D, Lord Jamar, and Sadat X. The woman problem gets investigated on two realistic yet sensitive tracks, "Butter" and "The Infamous Date Rape." The productions behind these tracks aren't quite skeletal, but they're certainly not complex. Instead, Tribe weaves little more than a stand-up bass (sampled or otherwise) and crisp, live-sounding drum programs with a few deftly placed samples or electric keyboards. It's a tribute to their unerring production sense that, with just those few tools, Tribe produced one of the best \hip-hop albums in history, a record that sounds better with each listen. *The Low End Theory* is an unqualified success, the perfect marriage of intelligent, flowing \raps to nuanced, groove-centered productions. *—John Bush*

☆ **Midnight Marauders** / Nov. 9, 1993 / Jive ♦♦♦♦♦

Midnight Marauders was an intriguing and smartly paced collection that ranged from descriptive verbal essays on city life to confrontational taunts, comic expositions, denunciations, and even quasi-religious theorizing. While their celebrated hip-hop/jazz roots were often evident, the group also utilized fusion, urban contemporary, Afro-Latin and funk samples, while Q-Tip's rap style could be cool and deadpan, reflective, analytical, satirical, or disgusted and angry. There was precious little gangsta posturing or sexist rhetoric, and such numbers as "Sucka Nigga," "God Lives Through," "Electric Relaxation" and "Award Tour" were cleverly delivered and brilliantly composed. *—Ron Wynn*

Beats, Rhymes & Life / Jul. 30, 1996 / Jive ♦♦♦

With their fourth album *Beats, Rhymes and Life*, A Tribe Called Quest manages to be one of the few hip-hop acts to successfully age by pushing both their music and their lyrics into new directions. Stylistically, the record is closest to its immediate predecessor, *Midnight Marauders*, in the sense that the group's jazz-rap fusion are downplayed and the beat stays surprisingly hard throughout the album. What distinguishes *Beats, Rhymes and Life* from *Marauders* is a deeper sense not only of eclectism, but of spirtuality and maturity. Shortly before the album was written and recorded, Q-Tip converted to Islam and the religion's ideals are an undercurrent in nearly every track on the album. But what really stands out is Tip's unease with the transience of the youth-oriented hip-hop scene and his own urges to settle down. Unlike most rappers, he confronts these feelings in the music, by writing lyrics and helping to create music that illustrates the contradictions of growing old with hip-hop. And by tackling the issue head-on, A Tribe Called Quest sound fresh and suggest that it is possible to sustain a career in rap as you approach a full decade of recording, after all. *—Leo Stanley*

The Love Movement / Sep. 29, 1998 / BMG International ♦♦♦♦

Continuing with the subdued, mature stylistic flow of *Beats, Rhymes and Life, The Love Movement*, the fifth album from A Tribe Called Quest, is the group's most subtle album yet—which may just be a polite way for saying it's a little monotonous. Throughout the record, Tribe mines the same jazz-flavored, R&B-fueled beats that were the hallmark of *Beats*. Although the "love" concept provides a thematic cohesion to the album—almost all of the songs are about love, in one way or another—the overall effect is quite similar to its immediate predecessor: the music is enthralling for a while, but soon it all sounds a little too familiar. Part of the problem is that Tribe functions on a cerebral level, a point made painfully clear by Busta Rhymes and Redman's roaring, visceral cameos on "Steppin' It Up." On their own, Tribe favors craft over raw skills. That means there are plenty of pleasures to be had from careful listening, but they've reached a point where it's easier to admire Ummah's stylish production and the subtle rhymes of Q-Tip, Phife and Shaheed than it is to outright love them, which is ironic for an album bearing the title *The Love Movement*. *—Stephen Thomas Erlewine*

Anthology / Oct. 26, 1999 / Jive ♦♦♦♦♦

For those who haven't discovered that A Tribe Called Quest made several of the best LPs in hip-hop history, *Anthology* is a perfect way to encapsulate the trio's decade-long career into one manageable portion. All of their best and biggest songs are here, from the early neglected joint "Luck of Lucien" to classic jazz-rap from *The Low End Theory* like "Jazz (We've Got)," and their 45-rpm peak with "Award Tour," all the way to their last big hit, "Find a Way," from 1998's *The Love Movement*. Yes, anyone who enjoys hip-hop needs to own at least *Midnight Marauders* and *The Low End Theory*, but *Anthology* succeeds in delivering all the highest points from a great hip-hop group's career. The collection also includes the first solo track from Q-Tip, 1999's "Vivrant Thing." *—John Bush*

2 Live Crew

f. 1986

Group / Party Rap, Dirty Rap, Southern Rap, Bass Music, Hip-Hop

This Florida rap band was organized, supervised, and conceived by Luther Campbell, a promoter, record label owner, and rapper, as an updated version of oldtime X-rated party performers. Campbell's production consists of heavy doses of booming synthesized bass, scratching effects, samples, and explicit sex raps and leers. From their beginnings in 1986, the notoriety of Campbell and the group grew in direct proportion to the lewdness of the material. As their songs attained more national prominence, Campbell has become part of a national controversy involving censorship and lyrics. 2 Live Crew hasn't found the going quite as smooth in the '90s. They've continued recording for Luke Records, but haven't scored as much success with such releases as *Move Somethin'* and *Sports Weekend*. Founder Luther Campbell issued both clean and dirty versions in an effort to defuse criticism, but 2 Live Crew's detractors have moved on to gangsta-rap and the group's later releases have been almost ignored. *—Ron Wynn*

2 Live Crew Is What We Are / 1986 / Luke ♦♦♦

Move Somethin' / 1987 / Luke ♦♦♦♦

As Nasty as They Wanna Be / 1989 / Luke ♦♦♦♦♦

Banned in the USA / Jul. 1990 / Little Joe ♦♦♦

Sports Weekend: As Nasty As They Wanna Be, Pt. 2 / Oct. 8, 1991 / Luke ♦♦♦

● **2 Live Crew's Greatest Hits** / Sep. 29, 1992 / Luke ♦♦♦♦♦

Full of the low-minded humor that made this Miami outfit notorious throughout the country, *Greatest Hits* does contain the best material 2 Live Crew ever recorded; it is all The 2 Live Crew most will ever need to hear. *—Stephen Thomas Erlewine*

2Pac (Tupac Amaru Shakur)

b. Jun. 16, 1971, New York, NY, **d.** Sep. 13, 1996, Las Vegas, NV

Rap, Vocals / West Coast Rap, Hardcore Rap, G-Funk, Gangsta Rap

Tupac Shakur became the unlikely martyr of gangsta rap, and a tragic symbol of the toll its lifestyle exacted on urban Black America. At the outset of his career, it didn't appear that he would emerge as one of the definitive rappers of the '90s—he started out as a second-string rapper and dancer for Digital Underground, joining only after they had already landed their biggest hit. But in 1992, he delivered an acclaimed debut album, *2Pacalypse Now*, which quickly followed with a star-making performance in the urban drama *Juice*. Over the course of one year, his profile rose substantially, based as much on his run-ins with the law as his music. By 1994, 2Pac rivaled Snoop Doggy Dogg as the most controversial figure in rap, spending as much time in prison as he did in the recording studio. His burgeoning outlaw mythology helped his 1995 album *Me Against the World* enter the charts at number one, and it also opened him up to charges of exploitation. Yet, as the single "Dear Mama" illustrated, he was capable of sensitivity as well as violence. Signing with Death Row Records in late 1995, Shakur released the double album *All Eyez on Me* in the spring of 1996, and the record, as well as its hit single "California Love," confirmed his superstar status. Unfortunately, the gangsta lifestyle he captured in his music soon overtook his own life. While his celebrity was at its peak, he publicly fought with his rival the Notorious B.I.G., and there were tensions brewing at Death Row. Even with such conflicts, however, 2Pac's drive-by shooting in September 1996 came as an unexpected shock. On September 13, six days after the shooting, Shakur passed away, leaving behind a legacy that was based as much on his lifestyle as it was his music. *—Stephen Thomas Erlewine*

2Pacalypse Now / 1992 / Interscope ♦♦♦

Strictly 4 My N.I.G.G.A.Z. / Feb. 16, 1993 / Jive ♦♦♦♦

Released a year after *2Pacalypse Now, Strictly 4 My N.I.G.G.A.Z.* finds the young 2Pac further carving out his persona. Instead of seeming unsure of whether he wants to be a self-conscious poet or a iconic thug as he did on his debut album, he chooses the latter with this album, a choice that he would continue to define with successive albums. So even if *Strictly 4 My*

N.I.G.G.A.Z. isn't even close to being as gangsta as Death Row-era 2Pac, it's still a harsh album filled with grim moments. Beginning with "Holler If Ya Hear Me," the hard stance cries for respect, highlighted on tough tracks such as "Last Wordz." Yet even if the rapper spends the majority of the album in thug poses, the standout moments, "Keep Ya Head Up" and "I Get Around," occur when 2Pac stops and raps from the heart. The sometimes shoddy, sometimes inconsistent production stands as one lingering problem with this album that makes it inferior to his two masterpieces, *Me Against the World* and *All Eyez on Me*. *—Jason Birchmeier*

☆ **Me Against the World** / Mar. 14, 1995 / Interscope ✦✦✦✦✦
As 2Pac's finest moment before being jailed and then being initiated into the gangsta world of the cultish Death Row camp, *Me Against the World* stands as a landmark rap album. It showcases a much different 2Pac than the more well-known 2Pac of *All Eyez on Me*—arguably a more sincere portrait of the rapper. Rather than spewing vengeful lyrics with no remorse or reservation, the 2Pac of *Me Against the World* seems uneasy with his hatred. Songs such as "Dear Mama" and "If I Die 2 Nite" remain some of the most heartfelt moments in rap history; in such a theatrical genre, rarely has a rapper spoke with such self-consciousness and sincerity. Yet the album isn't all confessional. Other songs such as "Fuck the World" and "Temptations" showcase another side of 2Pac, a thug persona driven by frustration and anger. Though stellar, this album's production isn't quite as rousing as that found on *All Eyez on Me*, and 2Pac isn't quite as charismatic as he would become on Death Row, but this is his most mannered album, a succinct portrait showcasing both the angry thug side of his character as well as a more heartfelt side which he would eventually suppress. *—Jason Birchmeier*

★ **All Eyez on Me** / Feb. 13, 1996 / Death Row ✦✦✦✦✦
Where most rappers would struggle to find enough subject matter to fill a double album, 2Pac uses the epic scope of *All Eyez on Me* as a forum for his seemingly never-ending rants. Whether ranting about his enemies ("Can't C Me"), women he hates ("Wonda Why They Call U Bytch"), women he loves ("Thug Passion"), his homies ("2 of Amerikaz Most Wanted"), the West Coast ("California Love"), his death ("Heaven Ain't Hard 2 Find"), or himself ("Ambitionz Az a Ridah"), 2Pac never seems short on words. So even if this album features some truly amazing production by some of the West Coast's best producers circa 1996—Dr. Dre, Daz, DJ Pooh—2Pac's literate lyrics highlight this timeless album. It's a fitting farewell album for the artist, since it functions almost as an autobiography; furthermore, his well-crafted lyrics are only enhanced by his liquid flow, his aggression, and his clarity—few rappers will ever compare. Yet despite the amazing epic scope of this album and its no-holds-barred delivery, 2Pac seems almost *too* dramatic. After all, he was a talented actor, and one cannot forget that this is the same man who wrote heartfelt ballads such as "Dear Mama" and "Keep Ya Head Up"; yet this sort of emotion is nowhere to be found here, with the exception of a few foreboding moments where he raps about death. So if there can be any complaints about this otherwise amazing album, 2Pac's one-sided thug outlook and his suppressed emotions keep this album from being more revealing. *—Jason Birchmeier*

Don Killuminati: The 7 Day Theory / Nov. 5, 1996 / Death Row/Interscope ✦✦

Stop the Gun Fight / Apr. 22, 1997 / Intersound ✦✦✦

R U Still Down— (Remember Me) / Nov. 25, 1997 / Jive ✦✦✦

● **Greatest Hits** / Nov. 24, 1998 / Interscope ✦✦✦✦✦
Greatest Hits is a strange release. Sure, Tupac Shakur had more than enough hits to make a terrific compilation, but its appearance in the fall of 1998 felt a bit like another opportunity to milk his catalog, simply because of the plethora of releases from previously unheard recordings to interview discs and bootlegs. Even with these misgivings taken into account, it has to be said that *Greatest Hits* does its job well. Given that it runs 25 tracks and two CDs, some may argue that it does its job a little too well, but the fact of the matter is, this contains all of his big hits, from "Keep Ya Head Up" and "Dear Mama" to "California Love" and "I Ain't Mad at Cha." Some may argue that it would have been more effective if it was sequenced in chronological order, but this remains the best place for casual listeners to get all the 2Pac they need. *—Stephen Thomas Erlewine*

Still I Rise / Dec. 14, 1999 / Interscope ✦✦✦

The Rose That Grew from Concrete / Oct. 17, 2000 / Interscope ✦✦

Ultramagnetic MC's

f. 1984, New York, NY [The Bronx], **db.** 1993
Group / Underground Rap, East Coast Rap, Hip-Hop
Arising from the Boogie Down Bronx in the mid-'80s as a far-flung hip-hop trio with a heap of new ideas to try out, Ultramagnetic's Kool Keith, Ced Gee, and DJ Moe Love occupy something of a singular place in the old-school pantheon. Combining funk-heavy tracks with jeep-rocking beats and obscure lyrical references, Ultramagnetic MC's have a list of firsts to their credit: the first group to employ a sampler as an instrument, the first to feature extensive use of live instrumentation … the first to feature a former psychiatric patient (Keith) on the mic. Early singles like "Something Else" and "Space Groove" were block party staples and created waves in the underground, eventually landing the group on the disco-dominated Next Plateau label, where they released their underappreciated debut. The following years found the group shuffling from label to label, releasing albums on Mercury and Wild Pitch before splitting to pursue various projects. *—Sean Cooper*

★ **Critical Beatdown** / 1988 / Next Plateau ✦✦✦✦✦
Besides being an undeniable hip-hop classic, the first album by the cult crew Ultramagnetic MCs introduced to the world the larger-than-life, one-of-a-kind personality of Kool Keith. That alone would make this some sort of landmark recording, but it also happens to be one of the finest rap albums from the mid- to late-'80s ìnew schoolî in hip-hop that numbered among its contributors Run-D.M.C., Public Enemy, and Boogie Down Productions. *Critical Beatdown* easily stands with the classic recordings made by those giants, and it is, in some ways, more intriguing because of how short-lived Ultramagnetic turned out to be. It would be wrong to assume that the finest thing about the album is its lyrical invention. Lyrically the group is inspired, to be sure, but the production is equally forward-looking. *Critical Beatdown* is full of the sort of gritty cuts that would define hip-hop's underground scene, with almost every song sounding like an instant classic. Although he turns in a brilliant performance, Kool Keith had not yet taken completely off into the stratosphere at this early point. He still has at least one foot planted on the street, and gives the album a viscerally real feel and accessibility that his later work sometimes lacks. His viewpoint is still uniquely and oddly individual, though, and he already shows signs of the freakish conceptualizing persona that would eventually surface fully under the guise of Dr. Octagon. If Kool Keith gives the album its progressive mentality and adrenaline rush, Ced Gee gives it its street-level heft, and is, in many ways, the album's core. Somewhere in the nexus between the two stylistic extremes, brilliant music emanated. *Critical Beatdown* maintains all its sharpness and every ounce of its power, and it has not aged one second since 1988. *—Stanton Swihart*

Funk Your Head Up / Mar. 17, 1992 / Mercury ✦✦✦

The Four Horsemen / Aug. 10, 1993 / Wild Pitch ✦✦✦✦
Back on track and on yet another label. The last album by the group before Keith would head off on his solo Doctor Octagon tangent. *—Sean Cooper*

B-Side Companion / Oct. 7, 1997 / Next Plateau ✦✦✦✦

U.T.F.O.

f. 1983
Group / Old School Rap, Hip-Hop
Doctor Ice, the Kangol Kid, and the Educated Rapper (later joined by Mix-Master Ice) formed the Brooklyn group Untouchable Force Organization (U.T.F.O.) by dreaming up a tune about a gorgeous woman oblivious to their charms and appeals. "Roxanne, Roxanne" dominated the airwaves for much of 1984 and 1985, yielding eventually over 100 answer versions. Their first albums included the hit single plus "Roxanne Part 2" and "The Real Roxanne." The group's popularity and influence waned as the Roxanne fad peaked, and subsequent releases had limited appeal. *—Ron Wynn*

UTFO / 1985 / Select ✦✦✦✦

Skeezer Pleezer / 1986 / Select ✦✦✦

Lethal / 1987 / Select ✦✦

Doin' It! / 1989 / Select ✦✦✦

● **The Best of U.T.F.O.** / Dec. 1996 / Select ✦✦✦✦✦
UTFO never had many hits. During the mid-'80s, the rap group released a series of singles, but only one stood out, and for good reason, because that song, "Roxanne, Roxanne," is one of the classic rap singles of all time. Though "Roxanne, Roxanne" only hit number ten on the R&B charts, it was far more popular than its chart position suggests, spawning a craze of answer records that ran for nearly two years. Unfortunately, UTFO never released anything else that quite matched the quality of "Roxanne, Roxanne," though their follow-up, "The Real Roxanne," was entertaining in its own right. Since the group had an uneven track record, *The Best of UTFO* is the best way to get acquainted with the group, even though it has a number of weak spots itself. Nevertheless, it has all the necessary items UTFO ever recorded, and "Roxanne, Roxanne" is a single that should be heard by all rap and hip-hop fans. *—Leo Stanley*

Whodini

f. 1981
Group / Old School Rap, Hip-Hop
Coming out of the fertile early-'80s New York rap scene, Whodini was one of the first rap groups to add a straight R&B twist to their music, thus laying the groundwork for the new jack swing movement. The group consisted of rappers Jalil Hutchins and John "Ecstasy" Fletcher, adding legendary DJ Drew "Grandmaster Dee" Carter, known for being able to scratch records with nearly every part of his body, in 1986. Whodini made its name with good-humored songs like "Magic's Wand" (the first rap song to feature an accompanying video), "The Haunted House of Rock" (a rewrite of "Monster Mash"), and "Freaks Come Out at Night," and their live shows were the first rap concerts to feature official dancers (U.T.F.O. members Dr. Ice and Kangol Kid). Following 1987's *Open Sesame*, Whodini went on hiatus due to problems with their record company, as well as to concentrate on new families. The group attempted a comeback in 1991 with *Bag-A-Trix* without much success, despite receiving their due as rap innovators. Five years later, Whodini returned with their sixth album, appropriately titled *Six*. The album disappeared shortly after its release. *—Steve Huey*

Whodini / 1983 / Jive ✦✦✦
More singers than straight rappers, Jali Hutchins and Ecstasty made a successful conversion to hip-hop, scoring two hits on their debut with "Rap Attack" and "The Haunted House of Funk," a reworking of "The Monster Mash." *—Ron Wynn*

Escape / 1984 / Jive ✦✦✦✦✦
Their best release, containing "Friends, " "Freaks Come out at Night, " and "Big Mouth." Memorable tunes and state-of-the-art (for that time) production. *—Ron Wynn*

Back in Black / 1986 / Jive ✦✦✦

★ **Greatest Hits** / Jun. 1990 / Jive ✦✦✦✦✦
When funksters and soulsters who reached adulthood in the 1960s and '70s criticize rap, their *1 complaint is usually that too much of it isn't melodic enough. But they seldom make that complaint about $Whodini,* which in the mid-'80s, enjoyed a lot more support from R&B fans than the more forceful and abrasive sounds of Run-D.M.C. or LL Cool J. While those artists rocked hard, Whodini grooved. Many of Whodini's early albums are well worth acquring—including *Escape* and *Back in Black*—but for the more casual listener, *Greatest Hits* serves as a fine introduction. From the poignant rap ballad "One Love" to such addictive and

highly danceable grooves as "Five Minutes of Funk" and "Freaks Come Out at Night," *Greatest Hits* makes it clear why Whodini was so successful in the mid-'80s. *—Alex Henderson*

Bag-A-Trix / Mar. 19, 1991 / MCA ✦✦

Jive Collection Series, Vol. 1 / Jun. 27, 1995 / Jive ✦✦✦✦✦

Wu-Tang Clan

f. 1992

Group / Hardcore Rap, East Coast Rap, Hip-Hop

Emerging in 1993, when Dr. Dre's G-funk had overtaken the hip-hop world, the Staten Island, New York-based Wu-Tang Clan proved to be the most revolutionary rap group of the mid-'90s and only partially because of their music. Turning the standard concept of a hip-hop crew inside out, the Wu-Tang Clan was assembled as a loose congregation of nine MCs almost as a support group. Instead of releasing one album after another, the Clan was designed to overtake the record industry in as profitable a fashion as possible—the idea was to establish the Wu-Tang as a force with their debut album, and then spin off into as many side projects as possible. In the process, the members would all became individual stars, as well as receive individual royality checks. Surprsingly, the plan worked. All of the various Wu-Tang solo projects elaborate on the theme the group laid out on their 1993 debut, the spare, menacing *Enter the Wu-Tang: 36 Chambers.* Taking their group name from an powerful, mythical kung fu sword wielded by an invincible congregation of warriors, the crew is a loose collective of nine MCs. All nine members work under a number of psuedonyms, but they are best known as: the RZA (b. Robert Diggs), Genius/GZA (Greg Grice), Ol' Dirty Bastard (Russell Jones), Method Man (Clifford Smith), Raekwon the Chef (Corey Woods), Ghostface Killa (Dennis Coles), U-God (Lamont Hawkins), Inspecta Deck (Jason Hunter) and Masta Killa (E. Turner) Although he wasn't one of the two founding members—Genius/GZA and Ol' Dirty Bastard were the first—the vision of the Wu-Tang Clan is undoubtedly due to the musical sklls of the RZA. Under his direction, the group—through its own efforts and the solo projects, all of which he produced or co-produced—he created a hazy, surreal and menacing soundscape out of hardcore beats, eerie piano riffs, minimal samples. Over these surrealistic backing tracks, the MCs rapped hard, updating the old school attack with vicious violence, martial arts imagery, and a welcome warped humor. By 1995, the sound was one of the most instantly recognizable in hip-hop. —Stephen Thomas Erlewine

★ **Enter the Wu-Tang (36 Chambers)** / Nov. 1993 / Loud/RCA ✦✦✦✦✦

The Wu-Tang Clan's debut album *Enter the Wu-Tang (36 Chambers)* wasn't an across-the-boards blockbuster like Dr. Dre's *The Chronic,* the other seminal hip-hop record of the early '90s, but its impact was just as wide-spread. Where Dr. Dre was loose, hedonistic and funky, the Wu-Tang was tense, scary and funny. *Enter the Wu-Tang* is a series of intense, surrealistic soundscapes that draws equally from pop culture, martial arts, and gangsta traditions. Other hardcore gangstas simply boasted about their hardness—the Wu-Tang clan boasted, but they supported their inventive rhymes with stripped-down samples and lean, menacing beats that evoked their gritty, urban surroundings more effectively than their words. And that's what makes *Enter the Wu-Tang* so effective—the group's unique lyrical obsessions and the distinctive, innovative production techniques of Prince Rakeem. After releasing this pioneering debut, all the members pursued solo careers that explored various elements of *Enter the Wu-Tang* in more depth—and, occasionally, with more effective results—but this contains the roots of everything that followed. *—Stephen Thomas Erlewine*

Wu-Tang Forever / Jun. 3, 1997 / Loud/RCA ✦✦✦✦✦

The Wu-Tang Clan's long-awaited second album *Wu-Tang Forever* arrived to great anticipation, and the double-disc set does not disappoint. Where contemporaries like 2-Pac and the Notorious B.I.G. issued double-discs cluttered with filler, *Wu-Tang Forever* is purposeful and surprisingly lean, illustrating the immense depth of producer RZA and the entire nine-piece crew. Each rapper has a different lyrical style, from Ol' Dirty Bastard's bizarre rants to Raekwon's story sketches, and RZA subtly shifts his trademark style for each song, creating an album of cinematic proportions. There are no great musical innovations on the album, since the Wu-Tang's signature blend of skeletal beats, scratchy samples, eerie pianos and spectral strings remains intact. Yet the music is more nuanced and focused than ever before, balanced equally between scary soundscapes and darkly soulful tracks. The result is an intoxicating display of musical and lyrical virtuosity, one that reveals how bereft of imagination the Wu-Tang's contemporaries are. *—Stephen Thomas Erlewine*

Wu-Chronicles / Mar. 23, 1999 / Wu-Tang ✦✦✦

The W / Nov. 21, 2000 / Columbia ✦✦✦✦

After a host of disappointing solo albums and quickly diminishing celebrity (most of the latter devoted to the continuing extra-legal saga of Ol' Dirty Bastard), Wu-Tang Clan returned, very quietly, with 2000's *The W.* The lack of hype was fitting, for this is a very spartan work, especially compared to its predecessor, the sprawling and overblown *Wu-Tang Forever.* While the trademark sound is still much in force, group mastermind RZA jettisoned the elaborate beat symphonies and carefully placed strings of *Forever* in favor of tight productions with little more than scarred soul samples and tight, tough beats. The back-to-basics approach works well, not only because it rightly puts the focus back on the best cadre of rappers in the world of hip-hop, but also because RZA's immense trackmaster talents can't help but shine through anyway. Paranoid kung fu samples and bizarre found sounds drive the fantastic streets-is-watching nightmare "Careful (Click, Click)."

Unfortunately, though, *The W* isn't quite the masterpiece it sounds like after the first few tracks. It falls prey to the same inconsistency as *Forever,* resulting in half-formed tracks like "Conditioner," with Snoop Dogg barely saving Ol' Dirty Bastard's lone appearance on the LP, a phoned-in vocal (in terms of sound *and* quality). When they're hitting on all cylinders though, Wu-Tang Clan are nearly invincible; "Let My Niggas Live," a feature with Nas, isn't just claustrophobic and dense but positively strangling, and singles material like "Protect Ya Neck (The Jump Off)" and "Do You Really (Thang, Thang)" are punishing tracks. Paring down *Wu-Tang Forever*—nearly a two-hour set—to the 60-minute work found here was a good start, but the Wu could probably create another masterpiece worthy of their debut if they spent even more time in the editing room. *—John Bush*

Young MC

b. May 10, 1967, London, England

Vocals / Pop-Rap, West Coast Rap, Hip-Hop

Intelligent and middle-class, rapper Marvin Young earned a degree in economics from USC, where he met Michael Ross and Matt Dike, co-founders of the fledgling Delicious Vinyl rap label. He made his debut as Young MC on the single "I Let 'Em Know." In 1989, Young collaborated with Tone Loc on "Wild Thing," the first Top Ten pop hit for a Black rapper, and the follow-up smash "Funky Cold Medina." Young MC stepped out on his own later in the year with the Top Ten smash "Bust a Move," a good-natured examination of romantic successes and failures spiced by his sense of humor and quick-tongued rapping. The song won a Grammy for Best Rap Performance, and its strong pop appeal helped the attendant album *Stone Cold Rhymin'* go platinum. The follow-up, "Principal's Office," was a humorous, everyday high school tale resembling a Chuck Berry plot and also climbed into the Top 40.

Following Young MC's success, he split acrimoniously from Delicious Vinyl, citing restrictions on his work and unwanted tinkering with his album; the label sued him for breach of contract and eventually settled out of court. Young signed with Capitol and released *Brainstorm* in 1991, expanding into message tracks promoting personal responsibility. The album didn't fare as well, and by 1993, audience tastes had shifted towards harder-edged hip-hop, rendering *What's the Flavor?* a flop. In late 2000, he attempted a return with *Ain't Going Out Like That* on the indie label, Young Man Moving.*—Steve Huey*

● **Stone Cold Rhymin'** / 1989 / Delicious Vinyl/Rhino ✦✦✦✦✦

Young MC wasn't given props at the time and he wasn't respected in the years following the release of his debut *Stone Cold Rhymin',* largely because he worked entirely in the \pop-rap/crossover vein. All the same, that's what's great about his debut, since it's exceptionally clever and effective, a wonderful combination of deft rhymes and skillful production. And there's no discounting Matt Dike, Michael Ross, the Dust Brothers, and engineer Mario Caldato Jr. (the latter two names are members of the Beastie Boys' inner circle), who make this record easily accessible, without a trace of guilt, even if it does sample from familiar sources. And, really, Young MC is a gifted rapper, spinning out rhymes with a deft touch and turning out rhymes much more clever than they should be. Yes, *Stone Cold Rhymin'* is a product of its time, particularly in its sound and lyrical references, but divorced from the Bush era, it comes off as one of the catchiest, friendliest \pop-rap records and it's still an infectious party record years after its release. *—Stephen Thomas Erlewine*

Brainstorm / 1991 / Capitol ✦✦✦

In hardcore hip-hop circles, more commercial rappers generally aren't thought of as having a lot of technique—the consensus is that they're getting over on their pop or R&B appeal rather than their rapping skills. After "Bust a Move" became a major hit in the R&B market, Young MC was viewed suspiciously by b-boys. But make no mistake: the clean-cut L.A. rapper has considerable technique and could no doubt hold his own in a microphone battle. While his second album wasn't the hit that *Stone Cold Rhymin'* was, it's a decent, enjoyable effort with strong hooks and definite dancefloor appeal. Such congenial, R&B-ish fare as "That's the Way Love Goes," "Listen to the Beat of the Music," and "After School" obviously wasn't aimed at hardcore rap audiences, but leaves no doubt that Young MC could flow with the best. *—Alex Henderson*

Various Artists

Bad Boy's Greatest Hits / Sep. 29, 1998 / Bad Boy ✦✦✦✦✦

Though albums by Bad Boy Records artists always sold incredibly well, the single productions of Sean "Puffy" Combs lit up the charts. Collected here is the essence of Bad Boy, including all of the label's best tracks: the remix of Craig Mack's "Flava in Ya Ear" that practically made the label, the Notorious B.I.G.'s "One More Chance/Stay with Me," Puff Daddy's "It's All About the Benjamins" and Mase's "Feel So Good." Unless you're a big fan, that's about all the Bad Boy you need. It's a bit of a shame that it doesn't include the B.I.G. tribute "I'll Be Missing You," but *Bad Boy's Greatest Hits* is still an excellent summation of the label's hit production. *—John Bush*

Beats & Rhymes: Hip-Hop of the 90's, Vol. 1 / Oct. 28, 1997 / Rhino ✦✦✦

With the three-volume *Beats & Rhymes: Hip-Hop of the '90s,* Rhino attempts to sketch a history of rap in the early '90s, before gangsta rap dominated the marketplace. Hip-hop was thriving between 1990 and 1993, as both veteran artists like Boogie Down Productions and new crews like A Tribe Called Quest began pursuing adventurous territory, fusing hip-hop with jazz and pop, among other things. There aren't many big crossover hits on any of the three volumes, but there are big names and cuts that were important in the underground. Unfortunately, there's some mediocre stuff mixed in with the prime cuts, but the bulk of each disc is so strong—and the set's budget-line price is so attractive—that the entire series functions as an excellent primer, especially when the liner notes by Harry Allen are added into the equation. Among the highlights on the 15-track *Beats & Rhymes: Hip-Hop of the '90s, Vol. 1* are cuts by A Tribe Called Quest ("Bonita Applebum"), the D.O.C. ("It's Funky Enough"), Main Source ("Looking at the Front Door"), Poor Righteous Teachers ("Rock Dis Funky Joint"), Big Daddy Kane ("I Get the Job Done") and Jungle Brothers ("Doin' Our Own Dang"). *—Stephen Thomas Erlewine*

Beats & Rhymes: Hip-Hop of the 90's, Vol. 2 / Oct. 28, 1997 / Rhino ✦✦✦

Beats & Rhymes: Hip-Hop of the '90s, Vol. 2 picks up where its predecessor left off, running through a number of rap classics and underappreciated gems from the early '90s. Cut for cut, the 15-track *Vol. 2* isn't as consistent as its predecessor, but there are still plenty of terrific moments on the disc—including tracks by Leaders of the New School ("Case of the P.T.A."), A Tribe Called Quest ("Check the Rhyme"), Brand Nubian ("Slow Down"), Eric B. & Rakim ("What's On Your Mind"), DJ Jazzy Jeff & the Fresh Prince ("Summertime") and the UMC's ("Blue Cheese")—that make it an essential history lesson. That said, there's still no reason why there are no less than three Chubb Rock cuts on this disc. *—Stephen Thomas Erlewine*

Beats & Rhymes: Hip-Hop of the 90's, Vol. 3 / Oct. 28, 1997 / Rhino ♦♦♦
The third and final volume of *Beats & Rhymes: Hip-Hop of the '90s* is as effective as its two predecessors, chronicling the period in the early '90s before gangsta rap became the dominant form of hip-hop. Several years after its original release, much of this music retains the excitement and spirit of adventure, and it shames much of the music that followed it in the mid-'90s. *Vol. 3* rivals *Vol. 1* for sheer consistency, boasting cuts by A Tribe Called Quest ("Hot Sex," "Scenario"), Grand Puba ("360 Degrees (What Goes Around)"), Main Source ("Fakin' the Funk"), Naughty By Nature ("Guard Your Grill"), the Pharcyde ("Ya Mama"), Fu-Schnickens ("La Schmoove"), Del tha Funkee Homosapien ("Mistadobalina") and Digital Underground ("No Nose Job"). Not only does it capture the depth and range of the era, it's also an excellent listen. *—Stephen Thomas Erlewine*

The Best of Sugar Hill Records / Oct. 6, 1998 / Rhino ♦♦♦♦♦
If Rhino's massive five-disc summation of the crucial old-school label Sugar Hill makes you cringe, this single-disc set is a much better distillation of the label (and the period) than much else out there. It covers the three tracks that are hands-down classics—"Rapper's Delight" by the Sugarhill Gang plus "The Message" and "White Lines" by Grandmaster Flash & the Furious Five. In addition, there are at least a half-dozen minor standouts like the Sugarhill Gang's "8th Wonder" and "Apache," the Funky 4 + 1's "That's the Joint," Kevie Kev's "All Night Long (Waterbed)," and Grandmaster Flash's "Scorpio" and "New York New York." *—John Bush*

Chuck D Presents: Louder Than a Bomb / Aug. 31, 1999 / Rhino ♦♦♦
The idea behind *Chuck D Presents Louder Than a Bomb* is sound. After all, Chuck D may not have invented political and socially conscious rap, but he sure became the spokesman for it during the peak years of his groundbreaking outfit, Public Enemy. Therefore, he was the perfect choice to present this 17-track compilation, containing many of the greatest protest songs in hip-hop history, including Run-DMC's "Proud to Be Black," Boogie Down Productions' "You Must Learn" (available in a "Live From Caucus Mountains Remix [single edit]"), Grandmaster Flash & the Furious Five's "The Message," Ice-T's "Freedom of Speech," and Public Enemy's "Fight the Power." Most of this dates from hip-hop's golden age, which gives the album some sort of thematic consistency, but not all the tracks are right; for instance, Ice-T's "Freedom of Speech" is the Body Count re-recording with Jello Biafra, not the original from *The Iceberg*. Little differences like this, along with a somewhat tiring sequencing, means that *Louder Than a Bomb* falls short of its promise, but it's still an admirable effort to chronicle the best protest hip-hop in one collection and is thus worth a listen. *—Stephen Thomas Erlewine*

Death Row Greatest Hits / Dec. 1996 / Death Row/Priority ♦♦♦♦
More than any other label, Death Row defined gangsta rap and hip-hop in the early '90s, and the double-disc *Death Row Greatest Hits* captures nearly all of the label's biggest hits from artists like Dr. Dre, Snoop Doggy Dogg and 2Pac. Although the disc bends some rules by including cuts that weren't released on Death Row and containing an abundance of previously unreleased songs, the compilation sums up the feeling of the early and mid-'90s. A single disc would have provided more consistent thrills—and it would have eliminated the annoying remixes on disc two—but the sprawl is also indicative of the self-indulgence of gangsta rap, which is essential to understanding the genre. And *Death Row Greatest Hits* has a string of great songs—"Let Me Ride," "What's My Name," "Gin and Juice," "Nothin' But a G Thang" (but no "California Love")—making it an excellent summation of gangsta rap's glory days. *—Stephen Thomas Erlewine*

☆ **Def Jam Music Group—*Ten Year Anniversary* / *1995* / *Def Jam*** ♦♦♦♦♦
In the '80s, Def Jam Records became the leading rap and hip-hop label in America. Featuring a roster filled with superstars—including Public Enemy, LL Cool J, the Beastie Boys, Slick Rick, and EPMD—Def Jam released many of the most innovative and groundbreaking records of the late '80s and, as the four-CD box Ten Year Anniversary proves, the music has lost none of its impact over the years. Over the course of the four discs, the set runs through a number or hip-hop classics, including "I Can't Live Without My Radio," "Fight the Power," "(You Gotta) Fight for Your Right (To Party)," "Slam," "Don't Believe the Hype," "Rock the Bells," "Regulate," "Crossover," and over 50 other tracks. The one (minor) drawback of the set is the fact that it isn't sequenced chronologically; nevertheless, each disc in the box is compulsively listenable. In sheer musical terms, Ten Year Anniversary is one of the best box sets ever compiled and is essential to any popular music collection. —Stephen Thomas Erlewine

Def Jam's Greatest Hits / Sep. 9, 1997 / Def Jam ♦♦♦♦
Although it doesn't follow any chronological order and doesn't always gel musically, *Def Jam Greatest Hits* is a good cross-section of the pioneering hip-hop label's biggest hits, featuring such classics as Onyx's "Slam," the Beastie Boys' "Brass Monkey," L.L. Cool J's "Around the Way Girl," 3rd Bass's "Gas Face," Domino's "Getto Jam," Slick Rick's "Children's Story" and Warren G's "Regulate." *—Stephen Thomas Erlewine*

Kurtis Blow Presents the History of Rap, Vol. 1: The Genesis / Aug. 19, 1997 / Rhino ♦♦♦♦
The first volume of the three-part *Kurtis Blow Presents the History of Rap* is subtitled *The Genesis*, which means that it covers a period of time when rap was strictly a live art form and rarely made it to record. That means, of course, that the disc is filled with funk records—specifically ones with extended rhythm breaks and grooves that provided ideal instrumental backdrops for rappers. *The Genesis* leans toward the obscure, where even the most familiar names (James Brown, the Isley Brothers, Booker T. & the M.G.'s, the Jackson 5) are represented with unfamiliar songs, and the remainder of the compilation is filled with cult artists (Baby Huey, Michael Viner's Incredible Bongo Band, Black Heat, Rhythm Heritage). While many of these songs may be unfamiliar, there are beats and samples that have been popularized through sampling, which makes listening to the disc fascinating. Unfortunately, it never becomes truly intoxicating, since it's a historical recording that's designed for education, not entertainment, but anyone interested in the birth of hip-hop will find it necessary listening. *—Stephen Thomas Erlewine*

Kurtis Blow Presents the History of Rap, Vol. 2: The Birth of the Rap Record / Aug. 19, 1997 / Rhino ♦♦♦♦♦
As the second installment of Kurtis Blow Presents the History of Rap, *The Birth of the Rap Record* chronicles the moment that hip-hop entered the popular consciousness. The record that broke the doors down was "Rapper's Delight," which is represented here, like the ten other tracks on the compilation, in an extended version that allows both the beats and the rhymes to flourish. Where most early rap compilations focus on records that made an impact on the R&B charts, *The Birth of the Rap Records* is devoted to the underground. There are a number of familiar songs here—"The Breaks," "The Message"—but the majority of the disc is devoted to underappreciated artists like the Sequence, Spoonie Gee, "Love Bug" Starski, Davy DMX and Funky Four Plus One More, or unfamiliar songs by artsits like Afrika Bambaataa and the Treacherous Three. Unlike its predecessor, *The Genesis, Vol. 2: The Birth of the Rap Record* plays smoothly, making it a rare historical release that is as entertaining as it is educational. *—Stephen Thomas Erlewine*

Kurtis Blow Presents the History of Rap, Vol. 3: The Golden Age / Aug. 19, 1997 / Rhino ♦♦♦♦♦
Where Kurtis Blow Presents the History of Rap, Vol. 2: The Birth of the Rap Record chronicled rap's first forays into the mainstream, *Vol. 3: The Golden Age* documents the point when hip-hop culture became an undeniable part of popular culture. There are more hits on *The Golden Age* than on any other disc in *The History of Rap*, featuring classics by such artists as Run-D.M.C. ("Rock Box"), Whodini ("Friends"), the Fat Boys ("Jail House Rap"), UTFO ("Roxanne, Roxanne"), Public Enemy ("Rebel Without a Pause"), Boogie Down Productions ("Criminal Minded"), Big Daddy Kane ("Raw"), Rob Base & DJ E-Z Rock ("It Takes Two") and Biz Markie ("Vapors," "Just a Friend"). At that time, rap was becoming more diverse, boasting different rhyming and production styles—where early rap was similiar stylistically, there was a world of difference between the dizzying hardcore of Public Enemy and the comedy shenanigans on Biz Markie. The musical depth of rap is evident on *The Golden Age*—it certainly does not all sound the same—and while it does overlook some artists, it nevertheless is an invaluable sampler, capturing the essence of the era. *—Stephen Thomas Erlewine*

Lyricist Lounge, Vol. 1 / May 5, 1998 / Priority ♦♦♦♦
Lyricist Lounge, Vol. 1 is an excellent showcase of underground and alternative rappers, including Kool Keith, De La Soul, 88 Keys, Natural Elements, Talib Kweli, Bahamadia, Q-Tip, and Jurassic 5, among many, many others. It's a great way to hear a number of the most talented and underappreciated rappers of the late '90s. *—Leo Stanley*

The Lyricist Lounge, Vol. 2 / Nov. 28, 2000 / Priority ♦♦♦♦
The second installment of *the Lyricist Lounge* compilation takes on a decidedly different direction then its predecessor. While the first segment catered towards breaking new, less-familiar talent, names like Prime, Mike Zoot, and Sarah Jones have been phased out and replaced by Erick Sermon and (gasp) JT Money. Yet, the transition is a fairly smooth one, and considering that ~the Lyricist Lounge has expanded from its open mic night roots into a successful MTV comedy show, this revision is not entirely surprising. Though not without filler material, *LL 2* achieves what most compilations promise but never deliver—a satisfactory LP that will appease both the chest-beating backpacker and the bling-bling tunnel faction. The quest in trying to meet this goal is really half the fun, as some interesting collaborations unfold; fellow Detroit natives Royce 5'9" and Jay Dee hook up on the autobiographical "Let's Grow," and Talib Kweli and Dead Prez revitalize the pro-black ideology over Hi-Tek's spaghetti western guitar riffs on the eye-opening "Sharp Shooters." However, the closest example of what *LL 2* aspires to be is captured on Redman and Saukrates' "WKYA" (Will Kick Your Ass), as the easily accessible but fiery rhymes of Red and Sauk are truly universal in their flavor. Though *LL 2* may not portray the idealism or spirit that ~the Lyricist Lounge was initially founded on, it does successfully represent the differing tastes of all hip-hop fans. That in itself is this compilation's biggest accomplishment. *—Matt Conaway*

MTV Presents: Hip-Hop Back in the Day / Feb. 17, 1998 / Priority ♦♦♦♦
Released to coincide with the first showing of MTV's program #This Is Music: Hip-Hop Back in the Day, *MTV Presents: Hip-Hop Back in the Day* is an excellent collection of early rap hits. While a handful of the songs stretch past old school and into the late '80s (Boogie Down Productions' "South Bronx," L.L. Cool J's "Rock the Bells," Tone Loc's "Funky Cold Medina," MC Shan's "The Bridge"), the majority of the collection is devoted to early and mid-'80s hits like Kurtis Blow's "The Breaks," Grandmaster Flash's "The Message," Afrika Bambaataa's "Planet Rock," the Fat Boys' "Fat Boys," UTFO's "Roxanne, Roxanne," Doug E. Fresh's "The Show," Whodini's "Freaks Come Out at Night" and Heavy D's "The Overweight Lover's In the House." Almost every one of these tracks was a hip-hop milestone, and this isn't a bad way to pick them up on one disc, even if the presence of the bonus 1998 remix of "The Message" leaves a bitter aftertaste. *—Stephen Thomas Erlewine*

Ruffhouse Records Greatest Hits / May 4, 1999 / Ruffhouse/Columbia ♦♦♦♦
Although it never gained the notoriety of Def Jam, Death Row or No Limit, Ruffhouse had its share of excellent artists during the '90s, most notably Cypress Hill, the Fugees, Lauryn Hill, Wyclef Jean and Kris Kross. As a celebration of nearly ten years in the business—or at least as a way of celebrating the massive success of Hill's debut solo album—the label released *Ruffhouse Records' Greatest Hits*, a generous compilation that contains 14 of their biggest hits, along with an interesting but superfluous Jason Nevins remix of "Insane in the Brain." Perhaps that mix was added as incentive to collectors, but the reason to pick up the compilation are the hits themselves; the best of these—"How I Could Just Kill a Man," "Fu-Gee-La," "Killing Me Softly With His Song," "Insane in the Brain," "Doo Wop (That Thing)," "Gone Till November" and "Jump"—sound like contemporary classics, while such lesser

numbers as Tim Dog's silly, silly "Fuck Compton" are great nostalgia trips. It's not perfect, of course—although the Fugees and their side projects are rightly emphasized, it's at the expense of some good music by other artists—but it still is a first-class portrait of the label. —*Stephen Thomas Erlewine*

Street Jams: Hip-Hop from the Top, Vol. 3 / 1994 / Rhino ✦✦✦✦
As rap became more of a commercial property in the 1980s, the artists' major lyrical intention often seemed to be staking out territorial rights and proclaiming their superiority at the mike. Doug E. Fresh & the Get Fresh Crew, The Furious Five, the Boogie Boys, Kurtis Blow and Marley Marl featuring MC Shan all do some variation on these themes on this 12-song anthology. "Romeo (Part 1)" by The Real Roxanne featuring Howie Tee is a putdown of the male romantic predator, while Whodini's "Freaks Come Out At Night" was one of the prime pop-rap hits of its day. While most of these cuts now sound simplistic and old, they were quite influential in helping cement rap's popularity, and Run-D.M.C.'s "Here We Go (The Funhouse)" remains a favorite among hip-hop historians. —*Ron Wynn*

Street Jams: Back 2 the Old Skool, Vol. 1 / Aug. 20, 1996 / Rhino ✦✦✦✦
The *Back 2 the Old Skool* volumes of Rhino's *Street Jams* series concentrates on late '70s and early '80s funk, always presented in their full-length versions. Where the Hip-Hop from the Top and Street Funk editions are more closely related to hip-hop, these songs provided the basis for many hip-hop records, either as the source for samples or as the scratched grooves. *Street Jams: Back 2 the Old Skool, Vol. 1* features songs by Bootsy Collins, Dazz, Fatback, and several other artists. Rhino have presented these songs on other collections—most notably Phat Trax—before, but *Back 2 the Old Skool* remains an entertaining and informative listen. —*Leo Stanley*

Street Jams: Back 2 the Old Skool, Vol. 2 / Aug. 20, 1996 / Rhino ✦✦✦✦
Like its predecessor, *Back 2 the Old Skool, Vol. 2* concentrates on late-'70s and early-'80s funk, and if anything, it's an even stronger collection than *Vol. 1, featuring classic cuts by $Funkadelic* ("Freak of the Week"), Zapp ("Computer Love"), Brick ("Dusic"), Mtume ("Green Light"), Fatback ("Keep Your Fingers Out the Jam") and Slave ("Snap Shot"). —*Leo Stanley*

Street Jams: Back 2 the Old Skool, Vol. 3 / Aug. 20, 1996 / Rhino ✦✦✦✦
Although it isn't quite as consistent as its two predecessors, *Back 2 the Old Skool, Vol. 3* is nevertheless another excellent collection of classic late-'70s and early-'80s funk, featuring cuts from Chic ("Good Times"), Bootsy's Rubber Band ("Body Slam!"), Mtume ("Juicy Fruit"), Fatback ("On the Floor"), Zapp ("Doo Wa Ditty (Blow That Thing)"), Betty Wright ("Tonight is the Night") and Average White Band ("Pick Up the Pieces"). —*Leo Stanley*

Street Jams: Electric Funk, Pt. 1-4 / Jul. 16, 1996 / Rhino ✦✦✦✦✦
Available either as a box set or as individual discs, *Street Jams: Electric Funk, Vols. 1-4* is an excellent, comprehensive overview of the groundbreaking electro-funk of the early '80s. Over the course of four discs, most of the genre's major players, including Afrika Bambaataa and Grandmaster Flash, are represented by their biggest hits and best-known remixes; many of its one-hit wonders are here as well, adding depth and context. Much of this music is presented in 12-inch mixes, which gives a more accurate portrait of electro-funk and how it stretched and played with rhythms and electronics. For casual listeners, the sheer length of some of these songs may be intimidating—some push the 10-minute mark—but any serious collector or listener of hip-hop, urban R&B, electronica or modern music should be familiar with many of these songs and mixes. —*Stephen Thomas Erlewine*

☆ **Street Jams: Hip-Hop From the Top, Vol. 1** / 1992 / Rhino ✦✦✦✦✦
Rhino's first attempt at archiving \old-school rap of the early '80s, *Street Jams: Hip-Hop From the Top, Vol. 1* succeeds by balancing a few undeniable classics (tracks that everyone should have in their collection) with more obscure inclusions that fanatics will appreciate as well. The classics on this debut volume are "Rapper's Delight" by the Sugarhill Gang, "The Breaks" by Kurtis Blow, "The Message" by Grandmaster Flash & the Furious Five, and "Friends" by Whodini. Alongside these are some great obscurities that many rap fans had only heard of, including "One for the Treble (Fresh)" by Davy DMX, "Adventures of Super Rhyme" by Jimmy Spicer, and "Request Line" by Rock Master Scott. Though it misses a few crucial artists (Spoonie Gee, Funky Four Plus One, the Treacherous Three) and it would've been better to lean closer to the classics than the rarities, *Street Jams: Hip-Hop From the Top, Vol. 1* is an excellent collection of early \rap. —*John Bush*

Street Jams: Hip-Hop from the Top, Vol. 2 / 1992 / Rhino ✦✦✦✦✦
The second volume in Rhino's \old school rap series compiles a few more big hits than the first, including Run-D.M.C.'s "It's Like That," Grandmaster Flash's "Scorpio," UTFO's "Roxanne, Roxanne," Whodini's "Five Minutes of Funk," and Kurtis Blow's "Basketball." Consequently, there's less room for obscurities (not necessarily a bad thing for neophytes), but those are selected well, with tracks from Rock Master Scott ("The Roof Is on Fire"), the Boogie Boys ("Fly Girl"), and the Real Roxanne (her self-titled answer track to Roxanne Shanté's "Roxanne's Revenge"). As with the first volume, there's a sense that Rhino concentrated on novelties rather than solid tracks, but a few of these inclusions won't be found easily elsewhere. —*John Bush*

Street Jams: Hip-Hop from the Top, Vols. 1-4 / Aug. 20, 1996 / Rhino ✦✦✦✦
Available either as a box set or as four individual discs, *Street Jams: Hip-Hop from the Top, Vols. 1-4* is a superb collection of old-school rap, featuring most of the major singles and artists from the genre's formative years. Over the course of the series, such classics as "Rapper's Delight, " "The Breaks," "The Message," "It's Like That," "The Roof is on Fire," "Roxanne, Roxanne, " "The Real Roxanne, " "The Show, " "Freaks Come Out at Night," "Nightmares" and "La-Di-Da-Di" are presented, usually in their full-length 12-inch mix. It's comprehensive and surprisingly listenable, illustrating that even from the start all hip-hop did not sound the same. It's an essential collection for any comprehensive urban, rap or pop library. —*Stephen Thomas Erlewine*

★ **The Sugar Hill Records Story** / Jul. 20, 1999 / Rhino ✦✦✦✦✦
Sugarhill Records was the first rap and hip-hop label, giving many listeners their first exposure to the urban rhyming and scratching that transformed pop music during the '80s. Like most indie labels, they had troubles with finances and distribution; eventually, that situation resulted in their records remaining out of print during the rise of hip-hop in the late '80s and '90s. The five-disc *Sugarhill Records Story* remedies this situation by collecting all of the label's classic A-sides, many in their full-length mixes, on one set. Tracks by the Sugarhill Gang, Grandmaster Flash, and the Treacherous Three are commonplace and remain excellent, but the true revelation of the box set is how strong largely forgotten cuts by Spoonie Gee, the Funky Four Plus One, Trouble Funk, the Sequence, Super-Wolf, and West Street Mob are—these are supremely funky, infectious, and inventive cuts which have been made familiar through samples and quotations on modern rap records. Male and female rappers trade lines without hesitation, and there is none of the misogyny or violence that characterized gangsta rap. But that doesn't mean the old-school rap on *The Sugarhill Records Story* sounds dated—much of this bright, elastic electro-funk has provided the foundation for '90s hits by the likes of the Beastie Boys and Dr. Dre. There is the occasional dull spot or oddity, but the most surprising thing of all is how *The Sugarhill Records Story* barely loses momentum over the course of five discs. It was inevitable that *The Sugarhill Records Story* would be an important historical document, but what makes it truly essential is how rich, diverse, and timeless the music actually is. —*Stephen Thomas Erlewine*

Tommy Boy's Greatest Beats 1981-1996 / Oct. 27, 1998 / Tommy Boy ✦✦✦✦
Only one label, Tommy Boy, spans hip-hop's entire recorded history with no loss of hits or perfect beats over the course of those ten years. The five-disc box released to commemorate the label's 15th anniversary includes a wealth of hip-hop classics, everything from "Planet Rock" to "Plug Tunin" to "Humpty Dance" to "Jump Around" to "Play at Your Own Risk" to "Hip Hop Hooray" to "Gangsta's Paradise." The addition of a few dance cuts—from Information Society, Coldcut, and 808 State—don't work quite as well as they should, but on the whole *Tommy Boy's Greatest Beats 1981-1996* is an excellent collection that sums up hip-hop better than any other label could. The fifth disc includes nine Tommy Boy classics given the remix treatment, resulting in intriguing combinations like Grooverider with Jonzun Crew's "Pack Jam," Dimitri From Paris with Stetsasonic's "Talkin' All That Jazz," and DJ Premier with Queen Latifah's "Wrath of My Madness." —*Keith Farley*

☆ **West Coast Rap: The First Dynasty, Vol. 1** / 1992 / Rhino ✦✦✦✦✦
Although it contains too many obscurities and novelties to make it absolutely essential for casual listeners, *West Coast Rap: The First Dynasty, Vol. 1* is an excellent compilation of early-'80s hip-hop from the likes of Ice-T ("The Coldest Rap"), Egyptian Lover ("Egypt, Egypt"), L.A. Dream Team ("Rockberry Jam"), World Class Wreckin' Cru ("Slice"), 2 Live Crew ("2 Live") and Bobby Jimmy & the Critters ("We Like Ugly Women"). Only Timex Social Club's "Rumors" stands out as a stone-cold classic, but the rest of the record is first-rate old-school rap, and worth the time of any serious hip-hop fan. —*Stephen Thomas Erlewine*

☆ **West Coast Rap: The First Dynasty, Vol. 2** / 1992 / Rhino ✦✦✦✦✦
Like its predecessor, *West Coast Rap: The First Dynasty, Vol. 2* is short on indisputable classics, yet the overall quality of the material is quite high. Over the course of 13 tracks, *West Coast Rap* runs through several funky old-school highlights from the likes of Ice-T ("Body Rock"), D.J. Matrix ("Feel My Bass"), Kid Frost ("Rough Cut"), L.A. Dream Team ("Calling on the Dream Team"), Darkstar ("Sexybaby") and Egyptian Lover ("Freak-A-Holic"). Most of this is simply party music, but it's good party music, and the collection is worthwhile for any devoted rap listener, even though its momentum occasionally sags. —*Stephen Thomas Erlewine*

Blues

The blues is big business these days, bigger than ever, and if you don't believe me, just turn on your TV set or radio; the sound and style is seemingly everywhere. The blues, in all its myriad strains, has become party music for the millennium. Just look at the short list of irrefutable facts from the last decade of the 20th century: A chain franchise of blues clubs with weekly syndicated TV broadcasts emanating from them? Howlin' Wolf's and Muddy Waters' faces emblazoned on the front of t-shirts that you can order out of catalogs? A blues chart in *Billboard* magazine? The Pillsbury Dough Boy selling blueberry muffins on TV with a honking blues riff in the background? Robert Johnson guitar picks and polishing cloths with a facsimile of his autograph on one and his picture on the other? Instructional videos for aspiring guitarists and harmonica blowers by the carload? John Lee Hooker doing Pepsi commercials? Do you think *any* of this could have happened—or even have been conceivable—30 years ago? No way.

If you've come to blues from a rock & roll background, we certainly have no intentions of making you feel stupid or ashamed of it, quite the contrary. To be honest, that's where most of us came in. As a matter of fact, one of the really cool things about the blues is its inclusionary nature; there's room for everybody. You don't have to be a walking blues encyclopedia to hear and get its basic message. That rock & roll comes straight from the blues is one of the few facts about its history that you can get a room full of critics, musicians, or fans to agree on. But the blues is far more than just your standard "seminal" genre influence. The music is now so interwoven into the fabric of rock and popular music, we take something like hearing the music of Muddy Waters in a TV commercial or a bunch of child actors attempting to sing the blues while extolling the virtues of Kraft Macaroni and Cheese as nothing out of the ordinary. As rock and country music become more manufactured and fragmented, the blues as a popular music force becomes stronger and stronger. Part of the blues' resiliency stems from it being such a bedrock musical form. The other part of the equation is the fact that blues can run the emotional roller coaster from sounding sad and lonesome one minute to the rockinest party you've ever been to the next, and every place in between.

Of course, like any other self-respecting branch of indigenous American music, it's a genre filled with absolutely great songs. Most of these numbers have stood the test of time, becoming part and parcel of everyone's set list, from the legendary greats that spawned them to the local bar band playing down the street. Now a great song can always come back and find a new audience, sometimes without changing a single note and other times just dressing it up in contemporary clothes. Most of the music's originators didn't live long enough to reap the big paycheck from all this, but it is all of one piece, a taut connecting thread that links it all together. And *that,* dear reader, is where this book comes in.

If you're an old hardliner who's done more than your fair share of excavating into the dark past of American roots music, most of these artists and their work will be as plain as the nose on your face. If you're coming to this guide with an interest in the blues that outweighs your knowledge of its history (which roughly parallels the history of recorded music), you're fully expected to keep smacking the side of your head and exclaiming, "So *that's* where that came from!" while you wade through it all. We'll do our best to turn you on to the good stuff. Then it's up to you to decide which ones *you* want to add to your collection. But in the final analysis, it really doesn't matter who you are or what you know or don't know, because the blues is for *everybody.* This section does not purport to be definitive. As a famous bluesman once told me backstage at a genre-mixed pop festival back in the '70s, "You can't be the best, you just try to be a good 'un," and that's what we have honestly strived for here. There's no didactic axe to grind out of any of the writers; if there was, their revisionist historical opinions would be promptly filed by the editors into the round file cabinet next to their respective desks, if you get my drift. We certainly make no apologies for our various contributors' unabashed passion for certain artists. After all, this *is* a music of and about passion, and when the blues hits you hard, it's easy to get swept up in that passion, too.

Walking into any new disc emporium these days can be a fairly daunting task. Most well-stocked stores have a decent-sized blues section. But there are a hundred Lightnin' Hopkins CDs here; which ones are the *good* ones? Which one should you buy first? That's where we come in; if it's good, we want to steer you straight to it. Also along the way, you'll see the occasional buyer beware alert review listed as well. If it's a stinkburger, there's no sense in you getting stuck with it. We also realize that not everybody has the financial outlay to go purchasing multi-disc box sets just because that's the definitive statement on a particular artist or genre. So wherever possible we've listed single-disc best-of's as well.

The blues is a music of great substance. We've done our best to steer you to the best of it, while giving it a sense of place and time. So please enjoy and don't let anybody tell you different; until time travel is perfected and we can all go back and watch Charlie Patton and Son House jamming in a Mississippi juke joint, *these* are the good old days for the music. Just listen to these blues. *—Cub Koda*

Blues Styles

CLASSIC FEMALE BLUES—The earliest recorded form of the blues. This genre features female vocalists singing material with close connections to pop music of the period (mid-'20s to early '30s) and primarily jazz backings. Main proponents: Mamie Smith, Bessie Smith, Ma Rainey, Lucille Bogan, and Victoria Spivey.

DELTA BLUES—Also known as Mississippi blues, this is the earliest guitar-dominated music to make it onto record. Consisting of performers working primarily in a solo, self-accompanied context, it also embraces the now-familiar string-band/small-combo format, both precursors to the modern-day blues band. Main proponents: Charlie Patton, Robert Johnson, and Son House.

COUNTRY-BLUES—A term that delineates the depth and breadth of the first flowering of guitar-driven blues, it embraces all regional styles and variations (Piedmont, Atlanta, early Chicago, ragtime, folk, songster, etc.). Primarily acoustic guitarists, some country-blues performers later switched to electric guitars without changing their style. Major proponents: Henry Thomas, Skip James, Barbecue Bob, Leadbelly, Mississippi John Hurt, Lonnie Johnson, Blind Blake, and Tommy Johnson.

MEMPHIS BLUES—A strain of country-blues all its own, the Memphis style gives us the rise of two distinct forms, the jug band (humorous, jazz-style blues played on homemade instruments) and the separation of guitarists into solo (lead) and rhythm, a tradition that is now part-and-parcel of all modern-day blues bands. The later, post-WWII electric version of this genre featured explosive guitar work, thunderous drumming, and declamatory vocals. Main proponents: Cannon's Jug Stompers, Furry Lewis, Memphis Minnie, and the early recordings of B.B. King and Howlin' Wolf.

TEXAS BLUES—A subgenre earmarked by a more relaxed, swinging feel than other styles of blues. The earlier, acoustic version embraced both songster and country-blues traditions, while the post-war electric style featured jazzy, single-string soloing over predominately horn-driven backing. Main proponents: Blind Lemon Jefferson, Lightnin' Hopkins, Clarence "Gatemouth" Brown, and T-Bone Walker.

CHICAGO BLUES—Delta blues fully amplified and put into a small-band context. Later permutations of the style took their cue from the lead guitar work of B.B. King and T-Bone Walker. Main proponents: Muddy Waters, Howlin' Wolf, Little Walter, Big Walter Horton, Jimmy Rogers, Elmore James, Jimmy Reed, Otis Rush, Magic Sam, and Buddy Guy.

JUMP BLUES—Up-tempo, jazz-tinged blues, usually featuring a vocalist in front of a large, horn-driven orchestra with less reliance on guitar work than other styles. Main proponents: Amos Milburn, Johnny Otis, Roy Brown, Wynonie Harris, and Big Joe Turner.

NEW ORLEANS BLUES—Primarily (but not exclusively) piano- and horn-driven, this genre strain is enlivened by Caribbean rhythms, party atmosphere, and the "second-line" strut of the Dixieland music so indigenous to the area. Main proponents: Professor Longhair, Guitar Slim, and Snooks Eaglin.

WEST COAST BLUES—More piano-based and jazz-influenced than anything else, the West Coast style (California in particular) also embraces post-war Texas guitar expatriates and jump-blues practitioners. Main proponents: Charles Brown, Pee Wee Crayton, Lowell Fulson, and Percy Mayfield.

PIANO BLUES—A genre that runs through the entire history of the music itself, this embraces everything from ragtime, barrelhouse, boogie-woogie, and smooth West Coast jazz stylings to the hard-rocking rhythms of Chicago blues. Main proponents: Big Maceo Merriweather, Leroy Carr, Sunnyland Slim, Roosevelt Sykes, Albert Ammons, and Otis Spann.

LOUISIANA BLUES—A looser, more laidback and percussive version of the Jimmy Reed side of the Chicago style. Production techniques on most of the recordings utilize massive amounts of echo, giving the performances a "doomy" sound and feel. Main proponents: Slim Harpo, Lightnin' Slim, and Lazy Lester.

R&B/SOUL BLUES—A more modern form, this fuses elements of African-American popular music (the rhythm and blues strain of the '50s and the Southern soul style of the mid-'60s) into a wholly urban blues amalgam of its own.

MODERN ACOUSTIC BLUES—Newer artists reviving the older, more country-derived styles of blues. Main proponents: John Hammond, Rory Block, John Cephas, Taj Mahal, and the earlier recordings of Bonnie Raitt.

MODERN ELECTRIC BLUES—An eclectic mixture, this genre replicates older styles of urban blues while simultaneously recasting them in contemporary fashion. Main proponents: Stevie Ray Vaughan, the Fabulous Thunderbirds, Robert Cray, and Roomful of Blues.

BRITISH BLUES—More than a mere geographical distinction, the British style pays strict adherence to replicating American blues genres, with an admiration for its originators bordering on reverence. Main proponents: Alexis Korner, John Mayall, and the early recordings of Fleetwood Mac and the Rolling Stones. —Cub Koda

Artist Reviews

Johnny Adams

b. Jan. 5, 1932, New Orleans, LA, **d.** Sep. 14, 1998
Vocals / Retro-Soul, New Orleans R&B, New Orleans Blues, Soul-Blues, R&B, Soul
Renowned around his Crescent City homebase as "the Tan Canary" for his extraordinary set of soulfully soaring pipes, veteran R&B vocalist Johnny Adams tackled an exceptionally wide variety of material for Rounder in his later years—elegantly rendered tribute albums to legendary songwriters Doc Pomus and Percy Mayfield preceded forays into mellow, jazzier pastures. But then, Adams was never particularly into the parade-beat grooves that traditionally define the New Orleans R&B sound, preferring to deliver sophisticated soul ballads draped in strings. Early on he waxed some outstanding follow-ups for the Ric label, notably "I Won't Cry," "A Losing Battle," and "Life Is a Struggle." After a prolonged dry spell, Adams resurfaced in 1968 with an impassioned R&B revival of the country standard "Release Me" for SSS that blossomed into a national hit. Even more arresting was his magnificent 1969 country-soul classic "Reconsider Me," his lone leap into the R&B Top Ten; in it, he swoops effortlessly up to a death-defying falsetto range to drive his anguished message home with fervor. Despite several worthy follow-ups ("I Can't Be All Bad" was another sizable seller), Adams never traversed those lofty commercial heights again. *—Bill Dahl*

● **I Won't Cry** / 1959-1963 / Rounder ✦✦✦✦✦
Even on his earliest singles, Adams already had developed a velvety crooning style seemingly at odds with his raucous hometown. This 14-track collection of Adams' 1959-63 work for Ric Records contains some stunning stuff, most of it in the big-voiced ballad mode (with an occasional nod to Ray Charles). "I Won't Cry," "A Losing Battle," and "Lonely Drifter" capture Adams' tender, mellifluous delivery beautifully. *—Bill Dahl*

● **Reconsider Me** / 1969 / Collectables ✦✦✦✦✦
This 22-song British compilation is the only place to find a decent cross-section of Adams' SSS sides, including his two biggest hits, the stately "Release Me" and the truly stunning "Reconsider Me." Not all of Adams' late-'60s waxings were ballads; "South Side of Soul Street" is a sizzling upbeat workout. But it's as a balladeer that Adams has always excelled; some of his finest soul senders are to be found right here. *—Bill Dahl*

From the Heart / 1984 / Rounder ✦✦✦✦
First-class production by Scott Billington, a delicious Crescent City combo led by longtime cohort Walter "Wolfman" Washington on guitar and Red Tyler on tenor sax, and Adams' perennially luxurious pipes tab this as one of his finest contemporary outings. Nice song selection: The pens of Tony Joe White, Percy Mayfield, Sam Cooke, and Doc Pomus were all tapped. Johnny unfurls his "mouth trombone"—an uncanny vocal 'bone imitation—on Mayfield's "We Don't See Eye to Eye." *—Bill Dahl*

There Is Always One More Time / Oct. 31, 2000 / Rounder ✦✦✦
There Is Always One More Time is a compilation of the recordings Johnny Adams made for Rounder Records in the '80s and '90s. The compilation was put together by Scott Billington, who produced all of Adams' Rounder albums. In his liner notes, Billington acknowledges that he had never produced an R&B singer before, so it may not be surprising that he was quick to have Adams sing in styles other than R&B. It was precisely this eclecticism that caused fans and reviewers to reserve their judgment on the Rounder recordings, and Billington has carried it over to the compilation. Drawing from all the albums as well as discs by Ruth Brown and Alvin "Red" Tyler on which Adams guested, he emphasizes novelty material. With Brown, Adams is heard joshing his way through Willie Mabon's "I Don't Know"; "A Lot of Living to Do" (aka "A Lot of Livin' to Do"), on which Adams is accompanied by Harry Connick Jr. at the piano and on which he imitates a horn, is from the Broadway musical *Bye Bye Birdie;* "But Not for Me," also featuring a horn imitation, is the Gershwin standard; and "Never Alone" is an a cappella gospel tune. Of course, there are some bluesy numbers, such as "One Foot in the Blues," and several R&B songs. *There Is Always One More Time* is representative of Adams' later work in that it tries to broaden him stylistically. Clearly, he went along gamely with whatever Billington brought him and added his soulful sound to it. But that didn't mean he did his best work. *—William Ruhlmann*

Luther Allison

b. Aug. 17, 1939, Widener, AR, **d.** Aug. 13, 1997, Madison, WI
Vocals, Guitar / Modern Electric Chicago Blues, Modern Electric Blues
An American-born guitarist, singer, and songwriter who lived in France since 1980, Luther Allison was the man to book at blues festivals in the mid-'90s. Allison's comeback into the mainstream was ushered in by a recording contract with an American record company, Chicago-based Alligator Records. After he signed with Alligator in 1994, Allison's popularity grew exponentially and he worked steadily until his death in 1997. It was while living with his family on Chicago's West Side that he had his first awareness of wanting to become a full-time bluesman, and he went on to "blues college" by sitting in with some of the most legendary names in blues in Chicago's local venues: Muddy Waters, Elmore James, and Howlin' Wolf among them. His first chance to record came with Bob Koester's then-tiny Delmark Record label, and his first album, *Love Me Mama,* was released in 1969. But like anyone else with a record out on a small label, it was up to him to go out and promote it, and he did, putting in stellar, show-stopping performances at the Ann Arbor Blues festivals in 1969, 1970, and 1971. After that, people began to pay attention to Allison, and in 1972 he signed with Motown Records. Meanwhile, a growing group of rock & roll fans began showing up at Allison's shows, because his style seemed so reminescent of Jimi Hendrix and his live shows clocked in at just under four hours! As accomplished a guitarist as he was, Allison wasn't a straightahead Chicago blues musician. What he did so successfully is take his base of Chicago blues and add touches of rock, soul, reggae, funk, and jazz. *—Richard Skelly*

Love Me Mama / Jun. 24, 1969-Jun. 25, 1969 / Delmark ✦✦✦
Although it has its moments—particularly on the title track—Luther Allison's debut album, *Love Me Mama,* is on the whole uneven, featuring more mediocre tracks than killer cuts. Nevertheless, it offers intriguing glimpses of the style he would later develop. *—Thom Owens*

Luther's Blues / 1974 / Motown ✦✦✦✦✦
Luther's Blues is where Luther Allison began to come into his own, developing a fluid, gutsy style full of soulful string bending. There are still a few weak spots, but the album remains an effective slice of contemporary Chicago blues. *—Thom Owens*

● **Love Me Papa** / Dec. 13, 1977 / Evidence ✦✦✦✦✦
Luther Allison is the blues' proverbial little boy with the curl; when he's good, he's great. When he's bad, he's awful. Allison was on throughout most of the nine tracks (three bonus cuts) on this 1977 date recently reissued by Evidence on CD, playing with the ferocity, direction, and inventiveness that is often missing from his more uneven efforts. His covers of Little Walter Jacobs' "Last Night" and "Blues With A Feeling" are not reverential or respectful but are launching pads for high-octane, barreling riffs, snappy phrases, and exciting solos. His vocals are not always that keen, but Allison at least stretches them out and adds verbal embellishments, yells, and shouts of encouragement. *—Ron Wynn*

Serious / 1987 / Blind Pig ✦✦✦✦✦
Serious marks the beginning of Luther Allison's late-'80s/early-'90s hot streak. The more streamlined, rock-oriented approach actually is a benefit, since it gives Allison a shot of energy that makes his guitar simply burn all the way through the record. *—Thom Owens*

Soul Fixin' Man / 1994 / Alligator ✦✦✦✦✦
This new venture, recorded in Memphis, is Allison's finest session since his days at Delmark. He blends blues, soul/R&B, and even occasional funk, and his guitar playing is alternately flashy and refined, sometimes explosive, sometimes carefully measured. His vocals are powerful, convincing, and earnest on all 12 selections. Luther Allison finally gives American blues fans the definitive portrait they wanted. *—Ron Wynn*

Blue Streak / Oct. 1995 / Alligator ✦✦✦✦

The Motown Years 1972-1976 / 1996 / Motown ✦✦✦
Allison's reign as Motown's only bluesman saw the guitarist offer competently executed, but basically unmemorable, blues with some soul and rock influences. This 17-track compilation includes selections from all three of the LPs he issued on the label (drawing most heavily from his second, *Luther's Blues*), and adds a previously unreleased live cut from the 1972 Ann Arbor Blues Festival. Pop influences can be heard in the occasional wah-wah guitar and brass-conscious production; Berry Gordy even co-wrote one of the tracks ("Someday Pretty Baby"), and Randy Brecker arranged the horns on Allison's final Motown full-length. *—Richie Unterberger*

Where Have You Been? Live in Montreux 1976-1994 / 1997 / A&M ✦✦✦✦

Reckless / Mar. 25, 1997 / Alligator ✦✦✦
Luther's third album for Alligator finds the 50-something bluesman truly at the peak of his powers. His superb guitar playing has never been more focused, and his singing shows a fervent shouter in full command. But Allison's songwriting has made giant strides as well, and 10 of the 14 tracks aboard feature him as a co-writer as well. The production by Jim Gaines delivers a modern-sounding album that stays firmly in the blues tradition while giving full vent to Luther's penchant for blending soul, rock and funk grooves into his musical stew. There are really no duff tracks aboard, but special attention should be paid to the sloppy but right slide guitar-meets-rock & roll groove of "Low Down And Dirty," Allison's incredibly hot minor key soloing (at full rock volume) on "Drowning At The Bottom," an acoustic duet with his son Bernard on "Playin' A Losing Game," and the grinding social commentary of "Pain In The Streets." If Allison had made albums like this for Motown 20-some years ago, it would be very interesting to speculate on how the blues history books just might have been rewritten. *—Cub Koda*

Live in Chicago / Aug. 24, 1999 / Alligator ✦✦✦✦
Pulled from performances at the *Chicago Blues Festival,* Buddy Guy's *Legends* club with a couple of strays recorded in Lincoln, NE, that were too good not to include, this two-disc set captures Allison at the absolute peak of his powers. Disc one is the *Chicago Blues Festival* in its entirety with a bonus track of Luther jamming on the finale with Otis Rush and Eddie C. Campbell on a medley of two B.B. King tunes. Disc two is equally potent, a combination of performances pulled from Buddy Guy's *Legends* club and *the Zoo Bar* in Lincoln, NE. Luther simply played his heart and spirit out right to the end and these recordings spotlight it in a very fine manner. One of the label's best. *—Cub Koda*

Pink Anderson

b. Feb. 12, 1900, Spartanburg, SC, **d.** Oct. 12, 1974, Spartanburg, SC
Vocals, Guitar / Piedmont Blues, Country-Blues, Acoustic Blues
A good-natured finger-picking guitarist, Anderson played for about 30 years as part of a medicine show. He did make a couple of sides for Columbia in the late '20s with Simmie Dooley, but otherwise didn't record until a 1950 session, the results of which were issued on a Riverside LP that also included tracks by Gary Davis. Anderson went on to make some albums on his own after the blues revival commenced in the early '60s, establishing him as a minor but worthy exponent of the Piedmont school, versed in blues, ragtime, and folk songs. Anderson also became an unusual footnote in rock history when Syd Barrett, a young man in Cambridge, England, combined Pink's first name with the first name of another obscure bluesman (Floyd Council) to name his rock group, Pink Floyd, in the mid-'60s. *—Richie Unterberger*

- **Carolina Blues Man, Vol. 1** / Apr. 12, 1961 / Prestige/Bluesville ✦✦✦✦✦
Anderson runs through a number of both blues and folk standards on this relaxed and engaging, if somewhat slight, session. The CD reissue adds the bonus track "Try Some of That," previously available on Bluesville's *Bawdy Blues* compilation. *—Richie Unterberger*

Ballad and Folksinger, Vol. 3 / Aug. 14, 1961 / Prestige/Bluesville ✦✦✦✦✦
Anderson is known today—if at all—as one-half of the inspiration for the naming of the rock group Pink Floyd. But his music is far more important than that, a delightful blend of Piedmont fingerpicking and songster sensibilities that works like a charm on this inspirational session. Recorded in one afternoon in Spartanburg, SC, this captures Anderson's strong vocals and propulsive guitar work on staples like "The Titanic," "Wreck of the Old '97," "I Will Fly Away," "John Henry," and "Betty and Dupree," all of it effectively produced by Sam Charters. If you've only heard his name mentioned as part of a rock trivia question, here's a good slice of what the man did so very well. *—Cub Koda*

Medicine Show Man, Vol. 2 / 1962 / Prestige ✦✦✦✦✦
Like volume one and three of the series of LPs Anderson did for Bluesville, this was recorded in 1961 (though it was recorded in New York City whereas the others were recorded in Spartanburg, SC). Volumes one and three were mostly traditional songs; this is *all* traditional songs in the public domain. It follows that if you liked volumes one and three, you'd probably like this too; if you want to choose just one, you're about as well off with any of the individual volumes. If you had to split hairs, it seems that Anderson sounds a bit more comfortable in the studio/recording setting on this one than on the others, and a tad less countrified and more urbane. The tone is cheerful and easygoing, like that of a well-loved man entertaining his neighbors. Which is not to say this is a throwaway; the phrasing and rhythms are crisp, and the ragtime-speckled folk/blues guitar accomplished. *—Richie Unterberger*

Billy Boy Arnold

b. Sep. 16, 1935, Chicago, IL
Vocals, Harmonica / Harmonica Blues, Electric Chicago Blues
Talk about a comeback! After too many years away from the studio, Chicago harpist Billy Boy Arnold returned to action in a big way with two fine albums for Alligator: 1993's *Back Where I Belong* and 1995's *Eldorado Cadillac*. Retaining his youthful demeanor despite more than four decades of blues experience, Arnold's wailing harp and sturdy vocals remained in top-flight shape following the lengthy recording layoff. Still in his teens, Arnold cut "Hello Stranger," his debut 78 for the extremely obscure Cool logo, in 1952. He made an auspicious connection when he joined forces with Bo Diddley and played on the shave-and-a-haircut-beat specialist's two-sided 1955 debut smash "Bo Diddley"/"I'm a Man" for Checker. That led, in a roundabout way, to Billy Boy's signing with rival Vee-Jay Records. Arnold's "I Wish You Would," utilizing that familiar Bo Diddley beat, sold well and inspired a later famous cover by the Yardbirds. That renowned British blues-rock group also took a liking to another Arnold classic on Vee-Jay, "I Ain't Got You." Other Vee-Jay standouts by Arnold included "Prisoner's Plea" and "Rockinitis," but by 1958, his tenure at the logo was over. *—Bill Dahl*

- **I Wish You Would** / Apr. 1955-Sep. 1957 / Charly ✦✦✦✦✦
The harpist's indispensable dozen 1955-1957 waxings for Vee-Jay, it includes the classic "I Wish You Would" and its blues-soaked flip "I Was Fooled" (stinging guitar by Jody Williams), the often-covered (but never bettered, except maybe by Jimmy Reed) "I Ain't Got You," and the vicious "Don't Stay Out All Night" and "You've Got Me Wrong." Also included are a pair of rarities Arnold cut for Chess prior to his exit as Diddley's sideman; "Sweet on You Baby" and "You Got to Love Me" feature big bad Bo on guitar and the ever-dynamic Jerome Green shakin' the maraccas. *—Bill Dahl*

More Blues on the South Side / Dec. 30, 1963 / Original Blues Classics ✦✦✦✦
Over half a decade away from the studio didn't hinder Arnold one bit on this 1963 session. His still-youthful vocals, strong harp, and imaginative songs are very effectively spotlighted, backed by a mean little Chicago combo anchored by guitarist Mighty Joe Young and pianist Lafayette Leake. The CD reissue adds a previously unreleased instrumental, "Playing with the Blues." *—Bill Dahl*

Going to Chicago / Jun. 1966 / Testament ✦✦✦
An uneven but intriguing 1966 collection, most of it previously unreleased. The first half-dozen sides are the best, full of ringing West Side-styled guitar licks by Mighty Joe Young and Jody Williams and Arnold's insinuating vocals (he rocks "Baby Jane" with a Chuck Berry-inspired fury). An odd drumless trio backs Arnold on the next seven selections, which get a little sloppy at times but retain period interest nonetheless. *—Bill Dahl*

Back Where I Belong / 1993 / Alligator ✦✦✦✦
Indeed he is. Recorded in Los Angeles with a crew of young acolytes offering spot-on backing (guitarists Zach Zunis and Rick Holmstrom acquit themselves well), Arnold eases back into harness with a remake of "I Wish You Would" before exposing some fine new originals (the Chuck Berry-styled rocker "Move on Down the Road" is a stomping standout) and an homage to his old mentor Sonny Boy (a romping "Shake the Boogie"). *—Bill Dahl*

Eldorado Cadillac / Nov. 1995 / Alligator ✦✦✦✦
This time around, Arnold recorded in his hometown with another gang of well-seasoned players behind him (guitar duties were ably handled by ex-Muddy Waters bandsman Bob Margolin and the versatile James Wheeler), retaining the same high standards set by his previous offering. Seven impressive new originals are joined by solid covers of Roosevelt Sykes' downbeat "Sunny Road" and Ray Charles' streetwise "It Should Have Been Me." *—Bill Dahl*

Kokomo Arnold (James Arnold)

b. Feb. 15, 1901, Lovejoys Station, GA, **d.** Nov. 8, 1968, Chicago, IL
Vocals, Guitar / Prewar Blues, Acoustic Chicago Blues, Acoustic Blues
A popular recording artist of the '30s, James "Kokomo" Arnold was a left-handed bottleneck guitarist who usually recorded solo, occasionally with piano accompaniment. His first Chicago session (Decca, 1934) produced the widely covered "Milk Cow Blues" and "Old Original Kokomo Blues" (the model for Robert Johnson's "Sweet Home Chicago"), as well as the first appearance on record of the classic "I believe I'll dust my broom" line (in "Sagefield Woman Blues"). Critic Hugues Panassi wrote, "Arnold is one of the greatest blues singers ever recorded." Arnold continued to play for a few years in Chicago after his last session (1938) but later took a job in a steel mill, disillusioned with the music business. Interviewed by two Frenchmen in 1959, Arnold said, "I'm finished with music and that mad way of life." *—Jim O'Neal*

★ **Bottleneck Guitar Trendsetters of the 1930's** / 1934-1938 / Yazoo ✦✦✦✦✦
Bottleneck Guitar of the '30s collects all of Kokomo Arnold's classic tracks from the '30s, including the classic "Milk Cow Blues." It's an essential item for a blues library—within these sides lay the groundwork for the Delta and Chicago blues to come, from Robert Johnson to Elmore James. *—Thom Owens*

Long John Baldry

b. Jan. 12, 1941, London, England
Vocals / British Blues, British Invasion, Blues-Rock
Long John Baldry is one of those peculiarly British phenomenons that doggedly resists American translation. As a historical figure, he has undeniable importance. When he began singing as a teenager in the '50s, he was one of the first British vocalists to perform folk and blues music. In the early '60s, he sang in British blues godfather Alexis Korner's Blues Incorporated, which also served as a starting point for future rock stars Mick Jagger, Jack Bruce, and others. As a member of Blues Incorporated, he contributed to the first British blues album, *R&B at the Marquee* (1962). He then joined the Cyril Davies R&B All Stars, taking over top billing after Davies' death in early 1964 (this band featured Rod Stewart as a second vocalist). He later fronted Bluesology, the band that gave keyboardist Reg Dwight—soon to become Elton John—his first prestigious gig. He was a well-liked figure on the London club circuit, and in fact the Beatles took him on as a guest on one of their 1964 British TV specials. All of these famous assocations, alas, don't change the hard fact that Baldry wasn't much of a singer, possessed of a dry-as-dust, charmless croak. His greatest commercial success came not with blues, but orchestrated pop ballads that echoed Engelbert Humperdinck. The 1967 single "Let the Heartaches Begin" reached number one in Britain, which led Baldry to forsake the blues on record for a few years. He returned to blues and rock in 1971 on *It Ain't Easy*, which contained a tiny American chart item, "Don't Try to Lay No Boogie-Woogie on the King of Rock'n'Roll." Baldry never caught on as an international figure, though, and by 1980 had become a Canadian citizen, but he continued to record and do voiceover work. *—Richie Unterberger*

Long John's Blues/Looking at Long John / 1964 / BGO ✦✦✦✦
Beat Goes On combined Long John Baldry's first two albums—*Long John's Blues* and *Looking at Long John*—on a single CD in 1995. Even if Baldry's music never quite lives up to his historical reputation, this remains the best place for the curious to become acquainted with his restrained British blues, since it has his bluesiest album (*Long John's Blues*). But British blues fans should be forewarned that his second record is more pop-soul than blues. *—Thom Owens*

- **Long John's Blues** / Aug. 1964 / Ascot ✦✦✦✦
Stacked up against other British blues/R&B albums of the time, this is a distinctly lower-echelon effort, much stiffer and more routine than the recordings of the Stones, John Mayall, Graham Bond, Duffy Power, and others. What made early British efforts in this style exciting was the sense of risk-taking, even recklessness. Baldry and the Hoochie Coochie Men are totally lacking in that department, displaying a by-the-numbers approach in arrangements (particularly in the traditional piano rolls) and material selection, which consists almost entirely of overdone standards like "My Babe," "Got My Mojo Working," and "Goin' Down Slow." Stacked up against Baldry's own work, though, this qualifies as his most "essential" effort, if only because it is for his contributions to the British blues scene that he is most remembered. This is the most accurate reflection of his work in that field, and Baldry is in better voice here than he is on much of his later '60s work. The album is still mediocre or worse, although it does feature Geoff Bradford (who played in a very early precursor to the Rolling Stones) on guitar. The BGO CD reissue combines *Long John's Blues* and the 1966 LP *Looking at Long John* on one disc. *—Richie Unterberger*

Looking at Long John / 1966 / United Artists ✦✦✦
Baldry's move from blues into pop/soul for his second album may have been viewed as something of a loss in integrity, given his purist blues stance on his debut. Maybe it wasn't such a bad idea, though, given that the debut LP wasn't very good, and the British blues-rock field was crowded with many greater talents in the mid-'60s. *Looking at Long John*, with a sub-Righteous Brothers sort of approach, is certainly a change in style, but the result really isn't any better. Baldry's vocal limitations are a big handicap whether applied to white-boy blues or blue-eyed soul, and the production is thin in comparison with the American soul/pop it's clearly trying to emulate. If you wanted this kind of stuff, the Righteous Brothers did it many times better. Not only that, if you were British at the time and weren't aware of the Righteous Brothers, you weren't about to turn to John Baldry; the Walker Brothers (American, but based in Britain) also did this kind of stuff much better. The BGO CD reissue combines this and the 1964 LP *Long John's Blues* on one disc. *—Richie Unterberger*

Let the Heartaches Begin / 1968 / Pye ✦✦

Wait for Me / 1969 / Janus ✦✦✦

A Thrill's a Thrill: The Canadian Years / 1996 / EMI ✦✦✦

Marcia Ball

b. 1950, Orange, TX
Vocals, Piano / Swamp Blues, Louisiana Blues, Piano Blues, Modern Electric Blues
Pianist, singer, and songwriter Marcia Ball is a living example of how east Texas blues meets southwest Louisiana swamp rock. Born in Texas but raised across the border in Louisiana, she played in a psychedelic rock & roll band during the late '60s but moved to Austin in 1970 and has remained there. Her piano style, which mixes equal parts boogie-woogie with zydeco and Louisiana swamp rock, is best exemplified on her series of excellent recordings for

the Rounder label. They include *Soulful Dress* (1983), *Hot Tamale Baby* (1985), *Gatorhythms* (1989) and *Blue House* (1994). Also worthy of checking out is her collaboration with Angela Strehli and Lou Ann Barton on the Antone's label, *Dreams Come True* (1990). Ball never records until she feels she's got a batch of top-notch, quality songs. Most of the songs on her albums are her own creations, so songwriting is a big part of her job description. She's established herself as an important player in the club scenes in both New Orleans and Austin, and continues to work at festivals and clubs throughout the U.S., Canada, and Europe. — *Richard Skelly*

Soulful Dress / 1984 / Rounder ♦♦♦

Hot Tamale Baby / Apr. 1985 / Rounder ♦♦♦♦♦
Marcia Ball solidifed the favorable impression made with her debut Rounder effort with this rousing second outing. She dedicated it to the late King of Zydeco, Clifton Chenier, and was backed by a fine band of veteran pros that included saxophonist Alvin Tyler. Ball ripped through Booker T. Jones' soul gem "Never Like This Before" and Chenier's title composition, while also demonstrating her own facility with R&B on "That's Enough Of That Stuff" and "Love's Spell." She came close, but didn't quite hit the mark on O.V. Wright's "I'm Gonna Forget About You," turning in a more than acceptable rendition that still didn't approach the original. But other than that one misstep, which she compensated for with a charged version of "I Don't Know," Marcia Ball proved that her debut was no fluke. —*Ron Wynn*

● **Gatorhythms** / 1989 / Rounder ♦♦♦♦♦
Marcia Ball explored R&B and honky-tonk country on this album, keeping her blues chops in order while expanding her repertoire. She included a pair of tunes by country vocalist Lee Roy Parnell, "What's A Girl To Do" and "Red Hot," doing both in a feisty, attacking fashion. She also was challenging and upbeat on Dr. John's "How You Carry On" and "Find Another Fool." Her third Rounder album was her most entertaining and dynamic, as Ball became less of an interpreter and more of an individualist. —*Ron Wynn*

Dreams Come True / 1990 / Antone's ♦♦♦

Let Me Play with Your Poodle / Jun. 24, 1997 / Rounder ♦♦♦♦♦
This album of snaky swamp rock is one of Ball's best recordings. Great choice of songs (she wrote 5 of the 13) that let her show all her talents, both vocally and instrumentally. Slow-tempo songs display the force of her voice, as in "I Still Love You," and another of the many gems, "For the Love of a Man." Meanwhile, the playfulness of the title cut and "The Right Tool for the Job" allow her to have fun and let the band air it out. Then there is the perfect song to end the disc and an absolute tour de force, Randy Newman's "Louisiana 1927."

Ball has again assembled another top-notch cast of characters who more than hold up their end of the bargain. A few of the many who shine are George Rains on drums, Mark Kazanoff, who does double duty as a co-producer and excels on various saxes, and Derek O'Brien, who also co-produced and shares much of the guitar work with Steve Williams. If you don't know Marcia Ball, this is a fantastic introduction, and if you liked her past work this is a gem you won't want to miss. —Bob Gottlieb

Sing It! / Jan. 13, 1998 / Rounder ♦♦♦

Barbecue Bob (Robert Hicks)

b. Sep. 11, 1902, Walnut Grove, GA, **d.** Oct. 21, 1931, Lithonia, GA
Vocals, Guitar / Prewar Blues, Country-Blues, Acoustic Blues
Barbecue Bob may be a familiar name to some blues fans today because at least two young white musicians have adopted the name, but back in the '20s the original Barbecue Bob (Robert Hicks) was a big name on the Bblack "race-records" scene. Recording for Columbia from 1927 to 1930, Hicks was the most popular of the Atlanta blues guitarists of his time, and Columbia's best-selling bluesman. But Barbecue Bob died of pneumonia at the age of 29, and some of his contemporaries like Blind Willie McTell are much better known to modern-day audiences. Most of Bob's recordings were solo outings featuring rhythmic 12-string bottleneck-guitar work and original lyrical themes. In historian Stephen Calt's opinion, "For sheer musical verve and punch, Hicks easily rivals Charley Patton." —*Jim O'Neal*

Complete Recorded Works, Vols. 1-3 / Mar. 25, 1927-Dec. 8, 1930 / Document ♦♦♦♦
Over the course of three CDs, Document Records compiled every note Barbecue Bob recorded in the late '20s. The first volume covers everything he cut between March 25, 1927, and April 13, 1928; the second, April 21, 1928, to November 3, 1929; the third November 6, 1929, to December 8, 1930. In between the first song on the set—which has been issued as individual volumes—and the last song, there is some incredible country-blues; there was a reason why he was among the most popular bluesmen of his time. Although there is too much music here for anyone but dedicated country-blues fans to be able to digest and the sound quality isn't terrific (which isn't surprising, considering that the series had to be mastered from 78s), Document's *Complete Recorded Works in Chronological Order* is an excellent historical document that happens to contain music that still sounds fresh and vital decades after it was recorded. — *Thom Owens*

● **Chocolate to the Bone** / 1927-1930 / Yazoo ♦♦♦♦♦
Although "Barbecue Bob" recorded over 65 extant sides (three are not known to have survived) in a three-year stretch starting in 1927 up to his death in 1931, the 20 collected here make a perfect introduction to the work of this Atlanta-based artist. He may have played a big-city acoustic 12-string guitar, but Hicks' playing was provincial, down-home, and often modal, reducing any chord progression down to one or two chords. He also played embellishments on this instrument with a bottleneck, a rarity then and a rarity now. Usually tuned to an open chord, Barbecue Bob's playing nonetheless shows great diversity and musical flexibility. The 20 sides collected here (all off of old, scratchy 78s and cleaned up as well as can be expected) gives a nice cross-section of that diversity as a solo artist, along with a pair of sides showcasing Bob in a small band context with Buddy Moss on harmonica and Curley Weaver on second guitar and another with Hicks backing up former gal pal Nellie Florence on a raucous "Jacksonville Blues." Of special merit for collectors are the inclusion of two previously unissued sides struck from slightly better sounding test pressings, "Twistin' Your Stuff" and "She Shook Her Gin." This expanded collection replaces the 14-track vinyl collection of the same name. — *Cub Koda*

Roosevelt "Booba" Barnes

b. Sep. 25, 1936, Longwood, MS, **d.** Apr. 2, 1996, Chicago, IL
Vocals, Guitar / Modern Delta Blues, Delta Blues, Electric Delta Blues, Modern Electric Blues
Booba Barnes and his Playboys band rocked the hardest of all the juke-joint combos in the Mississippi delta during the '80s, and after the release of his debut album (*The Heartbroken Man*, 1990), Roosevelt "Booba" Barnes took his act and his band north to Chicago, following the trail of his idols Howlin' Wolf and Little Milton. In a *Guitar Player* review, Jas Obrecht called Barnes "a wonderfully idiosyncratic guitar player and an extraordinary vocalist by any standard."

Booba began playing music professionally in 1960, playing guitar in a Mississippi band named the Swinging Gold Coasters. Four years later, he moved to Chicago, where he performed in blues clubs whenever he could get work. Barnes returned to his home state of Mississippi in 1971, where he began playing bars and clubs around Greenville.

Barnes continued to play the juke joints of Mississippi for the next decade. In 1985, he opened his own joint, the Playboy Club. With Barnes and his backing band, the Playboys, acting as the house band, the bar became one of the most popular in the Delta. Soon, the band was popular enough to have a record contract with Rooster Blues. Their first album, *The Heartbroken Man*, was released in 1990. After its release, Barnes and the Playboys toured the United States and Europe. They continued to tour, as well as occasionally record, until Barnes died of cancer in April 1996. —*Jim O'Neal & Stephen Thomas Erlewine*

★ **The Heartbroken Man** / 1990 / Rooster Blues ♦♦♦♦♦
Booba didn't record his first album, *Heartbroken Man*, until 1990. By that point, he had become a seasoned blueman, and was well-known in the South as a tough, hard-rocking guitarist. *Heartbroken Man* delivers on the promise of his reputation. It's an astonishing record, filled with gutsy vocals and gnarled, unpredictable guitar. Unlike most modern blues, it's teeming with life, and its raw, unvarnished production is a welcome, bracing contrast to the sterile atmosphere of most modern blues records. But what really counts is the music itself, and Barnes proves to be the heir to such classic bluesmen as Howlin' Wolf and Slim Harpo (both of whom he covers here), as both a performer and songwriter. An instant modern classic. — *Thom Owens*

Carey Bell

b. Nov. 14, 1936, Macon, MS
Vocals, Drums, Harmonica, Guitar, Bass / Modern Electric Chicago Blues, Harmonica Blues, Electric Chicago Blues, Chicago Blues
His place on the honor roll of Chicago blues harpists long ago assured, Carey Bell has truly come into his own as a bandleader with terrific discs for Alligator and Blind Pig. He learned his distinctive harmonica riffs from the Windy City's very best (both Walters—Little and Big—as well as Sonny Boy Williamson 2), adding his own signature effects for good measure (an other-worldly moan immediately identifies many of his more memorable harp rides). He was already playing the harp when he was eight and working professionally with his godfather, pianist Lovie Lee, at 13. The older and more experienced Lee brought Carey with him to Chicago in search of steady musical opportunities in 1956. Finally, in 1969, Bell made his debut album (on harp) for Delmark, and he was on his way. He served invaluable early-'70s stints in the bands of Muddy Waters and Willie Dixon, touring extensively and recording with both legends. The 1990 harmonica summit meeting *Harp Attack!* brought him into the studio with fellow greats James Cotton, Junior Wells, and Billy Branch, while the solo set Deep Down rates as his finest album to date. —Bill Dahl

Carey Bell's Blues Harp / Feb. 12, 1969–May 6, 1969 / Delmark ♦♦♦

Last Night / 1973 / One Way ♦♦♦
Nothing flashy or outrageous here, just a meat-and-potatoes session produced by Al Smith that satisfyingly showcases Bell's charms. Once again, there are hearty tributes to Little Walter ("Last Night") and Muddy Waters ("She's 19 Years Old"), but there's some original stuff too, backed by a combo that boasted a daunting collective experience level: Taylor and Perkins return, along with bassist David Myers and drummer Willie "Big Eyes" Smith. —*Bill Dahl*

Heartaches and Pain / 1977 / Delmark ♦♦♦
Legendary producer Ralph Bass supervised this quickie session back in 1977, but it failed to see the light of day domestically until Delmark rescued it from oblivion. They did the blues world a favor: It's a worthwhile session, Bell storming through a mostly original set list (the omnipresent Little Walter cover this time is "Everything's Gonna Be Alright"). Aron Burton and Sam Lay comprise the rhythm section, and son Lurrie contributes lead guitar. —*Bill Dahl*

Harp Attack! / 1990 / Alligator ♦♦♦♦
Four of Chicago's preeminent blues harpists—Bell, James Cotton, Junior Wells, and relative newcomer Billy Branch—gathered in a downtown studio to wax this historic summit meeting. Bell's vocal showcases include two originals, "Hit Man" and "Second Hand Man," and a Muddy Waters cover, "My Eyes Keep Me in Trouble." —*Bill Dahl*

Mellow Down Easy / 1991 / Blind Pig ♦♦♦♦
The harpist hooked up with a young Maryland-based band called Tough Luck for this disc, certainly one of his better outings. The traditional mindset of the combo pushed Bell back to his roots, whether on the originals "Just like You" and the Horton homage "Big Walter Strut" or revivals of Muddy Waters' "Short Dress Woman" and "Walking Thru the Park" and the classic Little Walter title cut. —*Bill Dahl*

● **Deep Down** / 1995 / Alligator ♦♦♦♦♦
More than a quarter century after he cut his debut album, Bell recently made his finest disc to date. Boasting superior material and musicianship (guitarists Carl Weathersby and Lurrie

Bell and pianist Lucky Peterson are all stellar) and a goosed-up energy level that frequently reaches incendiary heights, the disc captures Bell outdoing himself vocally on the ribald "Let Me Stir in Your Pot" and a suitably loose "When I Get Drunk" and instrumentally on the torrid "Jawbreaker." For a closer, Bell settled on the atmo-spheric Horton classic "Easy"; he does it full justice. *—Bill Dahl*

Good Luck Man / Oct. 7, 1997 / Alligator ✦✦✦

Brought up the Hard Way / Mar. 10, 1998 / JSP ✦✦✦✦

Tab Benoit

b. Nov. 17, 1967, Baton Rouge, LA
Vocals, Guitar / Swamp Blues
Guitarist, singer, and songwriter Tab Benoit makes his home south of New Orleans in Houma, LA. Born November 17, 1967, he's one of a handful of bright rising stars on the modern blues scene. For most of the '90s, he's been working each of his records the old fashioned way, by playing anywhere and everywhere he and his band can play; unlike so many others before him, Benoit understands that blues is not a medium in favor with 50,000 watt commercial rock radio stations. *Nice & Warm,* his debut album for Houston-based Justice Records, prompted some critics to say he's reminiscent, at times, of three blues guitar gods: Albert King, Albert Collins, and Jimi Hendrix. Although the hardworking, modest guitarist scoffs at those comparisons, and doesn't think he sounds like them (and doesn't try to sound like them), Benoit doesn't appear to be one who's easily led into playing rock & roll in favor of his downhome blend of swamp blues and east Texas guitar-driven blues. And since each of his records has surpassed the 50,000 mark (impressive numbers for an independent record label), he's well on his way to a career that could rival the kind of popularity that the late Stevie Ray Vaughan enjoyed in the late '80s. *—Richard Skelly*

● **Nice & Warm** / 1992 / Vanguard ✦✦✦✦✦
Tab Benoit's debut album *Nice & Warm* is a startingly fresh debut. The guitarist has a gutsy, fuel-injected style that adds real spice to his swampy blues. Benoit draws equally from the Louisiana and Texas traditions and *Nice & Warm* proves it; not only does he carry on the tradition, he offers a fresh take on it as well. *—Thom Owens*

What I Live For / 1994 / Vanguard ✦✦✦

Standing on the Bank / 1995 / Vanguard ✦✦✦

Live: Swampland Jam / Sep. 16, 1997 / Vanguard ✦✦✦✦

Homesick for the Road / Mar. 23, 1999 / Telarc ✦✦✦✦
Homesick for the Road provides a showcase for three fine blues singer/guitarists. The recording is clean and crisp, as is typical of the Telarc label, and the music cooks from start to finish. This disc provides an excellent introduction to each performer, with ample opportunities for each to shine. Debbie Davies brings to mind Bonnie Raitt, with her appealing vocal timbre and bluesy delivery. The youthful Benoit sings with an authority beyond his 31 years, making Screamin' Jay Hawkins' classic "I Put a Spell on You" his own. Kenny Neal has the scruffy, soulful delivery of a man who knows what the blues are all about. His "I've Been Mistreated" sounds like a late-'60s slice of Muscle Shoals soul. All three of the co-leaders are excellent guitarists, and the band is solid and tight. *Homesick for the Road* rolls down the car window for an enticing look at three relatively young performers carrying the blues torch into the future. *—Jim Newsom*

These Blues Are All Mine / Oct. 12, 1999 / Vanguard ✦✦✦

Big Maceo Merriweather (Major Merriweather)

b. Mar. 31, 1905, Atlanta, GA, **d.** Feb. 26, 1953, Chicago, IL
Vocals, Piano / Electric Blues, Piano Blues, Chicago Blues
The thundering 88s of Big Maceo Merriweather helped pave the way for the great Chicago blues pianists of the '50s—men like Johnny Jones, Otis Spann, and Henry Gray. Unfortunately, Merriweather wouldn't be around to enjoy their innovations—he died a few years after suffering a debilitating stroke in 1946.

Major Merriweather was already a seasoned pianist when he arrived in Detroit in 1924. After working around the Motor City scene, he ventured to Chicago in 1941 to make his recording debut for producer Lester Melrose and RCA Victor's Bluebird subsidiary. His first day in the studio produced 14 tracks—six of his own and eight more as accompanist to renowned Chicago guitarist Tampa Red. One of his initial efforts, "Worried Life Blues," has passed into blues standard status (Chuck Berry was hip to it, covering it for Chess).

Merriweather remained Tampa Red's favorite pianistic accompanist after that, gigging extensively with him and Big Bill Broonzy on Chicago's South side. The pianist cut a series of terrific sessions as a leader for Bluebird in 1941-42 and 1945 (the latter including his tour de force, "Chicago Breakdown") before the stroke paralyzed his right side. He tried to overcome it, cutting for Victor in 1947 with Eddie Boyd assuming piano duties and again for Specialty in 1949 with Johnny Jones, this time at the stool. His health fading steadily after that, Merriweather died in 1953. *—Bill Dahl*

☆ **The King of Chicago Blues Piano, Vols. 1-2** / 1992 / Arhoolie ✦✦✦✦✦
A slightly truncated CD version of the RCA two-record set that first anthologized the thundering '40s RCA Bluebird sides of pianist Big Maceo (25 cuts on the CD, 32 on the vinyl). The CD opens with Maceo's immortal blues "Worried Life Blues," and closes with his instrumental tour de force "Chicago Breakdown," and boasts a great deal of blues piano magic in between. *—Bill Dahl*

Bluebird Recordings 1941-1942 / Jan. 30, 1996 / RCA ✦✦✦✦✦
Bluebird Recordings 1941-42 contains all 16 tracks Big Maceo Merriweather recorded for the label during that year, including the classic "Worried Life Blues." Merriweather was one of the most influential barrelhouse blues pianists, and these Bluebird recordings form the core of his legacy. While these recordings are available in more thorough anthologies, this single disc remains an excellent introduction to his best work. *—Thom Owens*

★ **Victor/Bluebird Recordings 1945-1947** / Apr. 29, 1997 / Bluebird/RCA ✦✦✦✦✦
Victor/Bluebird Recordings 1945-47 contains all the music Big Maceo Merriweather recorded for the label in those two years. Merriweather was one of the most influential barrelhouse blues pianists, and these Bluebird recordings form the core of his legacy. While these recordings are available in more thorough anthologies, this single disc remains an excellent introduction to his best work. *—Thom Owens*

Big Maybelle (Maybelle Smith)

b. May 1, 1924, Jackson, TN, **d.** Jan. 23, 1972, Cleveland, OH
Vocals / New York Blues, East Coast Blues, Jump Blues, R&B
Her mountainous stature matching the sheer soulful power of her massive vocal talent, Big Maybelle was one of the premier R&B chanteuses of the '50s. Her deep, gravelly voice was as singular as her recorded output for Okeh and Savoy, which ranged from down-in-the-alley blues to pop-slanted ballads. In 1967, she even covered $— & the Mysterians' "96 Tears" (it was her final chart appearance). Alleged drug addiction leveled the mighty belter at the premature age of 47, but Maybelle packed a lot of living into her shortened lifespan. Her first OKeh platter, the unusual "Gabbin' Blues" swiftly hit, climbing to the upper reaches of the R&B charts. "Way Back Home" and "My Country Man" made it a 1953 hat trick for Maybelle and OKeh. In 1955, she cut a rendition of "Whole Lot of Shakin' Goin' On" a full two years before Louisiana piano pumper Jerry Lee Lewis got his hands and feet on it. Maybelle rocked harder than ever at Savoy, her "Ring Dang Dilly," "That's a Pretty Good Love," and "Tell Me Who" benefitting from blistering backing by New York's top sessioneers. *—Bill Dahl*

● **The Complete OKeh Sessions 1952-55** / Oct. 8, 1952-Mar. 21, 1955 / Epic/Legacy ✦✦✦✦✦
Maybelle's entire OKeh output—26 tracks—including her three R&B chart items, "Whole Lotta Shakin' Goin' On," and the risqué slow blues "I'm Getting, 'Long Alright." "Gabbin' Blues," her 1952 OKeh debut smash, is a humorous dialogue between Maybelle and gossiping rival Rosemarie McCoy, the tune's co-writer. Maybelle was no mere copyist; her sandpapery vocals stood in sharp contrast to the many interchangeable thrushes then populating the R&B world. Great support from New York session wizards such as tenor saxist Sam "The Man" Taylor and guitarist Mickey Baker throughout. *—Bill Dahl*

Blues, Candy and Big Maybelle / 1956-1957 / Savoy Jazz ✦✦✦
Two vinyl albums of Maybelle's Savoy recordings on one compact disc makes for a nice 28-track retrospective of her prime work. First up is the album originally issued as *Blues, Candy and Big Maybelle,* a chunk of session work from 1956-1957, with a three-song date from 1959 to round things up. Her takes on "Rockhouse," "Ramblin' Blues," and the title track are the big tickets here. The second anthology, titled simply *Big Maybelle,* features her recordings from 1956-1959, with the balance of it leaning toward her later output for the label. A 1957 session with Kenny Burrell on guitar yields interesting stabs at "White Christmas" and "Silent Night," while a 1959 session finds her big voice framed with a string section on a great read of "Until the Real Thing Comes Along." A very underrated singer, Big Maybelle is a total delight and deserves a much wider hearing. *—Cub Koda*

The Last of Big Maybelle / 1973 / Muse ✦✦

Very Best of Big Maybelle: That's All / Jan. 5, 1998 / Collectables ✦✦✦
Collectables' *The Very Best of Big Maybelle: That's All* features 12 songs that she recorded for Sceptor Records in the '60s. This wasn't the most particularly distinguished period of Maybelle's career, and this collection doesn't put it in perspective, leaving out some of the best records she made for the label, including the minor hit "Yesterday's Kisses." That said, this does have its moments—enough to make it worthwhile to dedictated soul collectors willing to sort the wheat from the chaff. It just isn't a definitive collection, not even of her Scepter recordings. *—Stephen Thomas Erlewine*

The Big Three Trio

f. 1946, Chicago, IL, **db.** 1952, Chicago, IL
Group / Acoustic Chicago Blues, Chicago Blues
For the legendary Willie Dixon, the Big Three Trio was an important launching pad for a fantastic career. Pianist Leonard "Baby Doo" Caston and guitarist Bernardo Dennis (replaced after a year by Ollie Crawford) joined upright bassist Dixon to form the popular trio in 1946. Dixon had previously worked with Caston in the Five Breezes and with Dennis in the Four Jumps of Jive. Sharing vocal (they specialized in three-part harmonies) and writing duties democratically, the trio signed with Bullet in 1946 for a solitary session before making a giant jump in stature to Columbia Records in 1947. Their polished, pop-oriented presentation resulted in one national hit, "You Sure Look Good to Me," in 1948, and a slew of other releases that stretched into 1952. Caston split at the end of 1952, effectively breaking up the trio. But Dixon's destiny was at Chess Records, where he was already making inroads as a session bassist and songwriter. Pretty soon, he'd be recognized as one of the most prolific and invaluable figures on the Windy City scene. *—Bill Dahl*

I Feel Like Steppin' Out / 1946-Jun. 16, 1952 / Dr. Horse ✦✦✦
I Feel Like Steppin' Out compliments the Columbia release *The Big Three Trio,* gathering most of the material that was left off that disc and only duplicating "Signifying Monkey." The Big Three played the blues very loosely, adding bits of jazz and pop to their sound—unlike most blues groups of their time, they all sang in unison. Though this compilation isn't quite as strong as the Columbia disc, it's worthwhile for dedicated fans. *—Thom Owens*

● **The Willie Dixon: The Big Three Trio** / 1990 / Columbia/Legacy ✦✦✦✦✦
The only domestic compilation celebrating this trio's accomplishments is a 21-track affair containing Dixon's "dozens" diatribe "Signifying Monkey," the catchy "Tell That Woman" (later covered by Peter, Paul & Mary as "Big Boat Up the River"), and several crackling instrumentals ("Big 3 Boogie," "Hard Notch Boogie Beat") that show what fine musicianship this triumvirate purveyed. Points off, though, for not including their only legit hit, "You Sure Look Good to Me." *—Bill Dahl*

Scrapper Blackwell (Francis Blackwell)

b. Feb. 21, 1903, Syracuse, NC, **d.** Oct. 27, 1954, Indianapolis, IN

Vocals, Guitar / Prewar Blues, Piedmont Blues, Acoustic Chicago Blues, Acoustic Blues

One of the original blues guitar greats, Scrapper had slinky bent-note, bell-like chord fills and impeccable phrasing laid down a musical gauntlet for proteges from Robert Johnson on. Blues chestnut "Sweet Home Chicago" is derived largely from his knockout solo rendition of "Kokomo Blues," and his riffing behind partner Leroy Carr and other circumscribes the basic vocabulary of the blues lead guitarist. Son of a fiddle player, he grew up in Indianapolis where he taught himself to play guitar on a cigar box instrument and began gigging regularly in his teens. In his early twenties he teamed up with Naptown piano lord Leroy Carr. Their 1928 Vocalion recording of "How Long Blues" was a hit, and one of the most often covered blues motifs. Prized as an accompanist, Blackwell worked with Carr, Tom Dorsey, Chippie Hill, and others until, after Carr's death in 1935, he withdrew from the theater circuit and recording scene until the late '50s when he emerged to gig with Champion Jack Dupree and resume solo recording. His 1961 Bluesville album is a thing of great beauty. His tragic murder in 1962 deprived the blues revival scene of what could have been one of its key figures. *—Steve James*

★ **Virtuoso Guitar 1925-1934** / 1925-1934 / Yazoo ✦✦✦✦✦

It's for recordings like this that a lot of blues guitar fans started listening to the music in the first place. The definitive Blackwell collection to date, featuring not only his best extant solo sides, but also his work in association with Leroy Carr, Black Bottom McPhail, and Tommy Bradley. The 14 songs here all have something to offer in the playing, and generally in the singing as well, that will give the listener pause, a run, an arpeggio, a solo passage that makes you say, "Whoa, what was that?" The sound is surprisingly good, and one only wishes there were more than 14 songs here, although it's hard to imag-ine anything that could follow the last track, Leroy Carr's "Barrelhouse Woman No. 2." *—Bruce Eder*

Scrapper Blackwell, Vol. 2 (1934-1958) / 1994 / Document ✦✦✦✦✦

The second volume of Scrapper Blackwell sides features material he cut solo in 1934, accompanying himself on the piano, and as a solo guitarist from 1935 ("D Blues," "A Blues"), as well as songs cut as part of Pinewood Tom and His Blues Hounds, teamed as a guitarist with Josh White (on vocals and guitar) and pianist Leroy Carr; under the name Frankie Black accompanied by pianist Dot Rice, and some in association with Bumble Bee Slim. These are all first-rate sides, equal to the best of his work with Leroy Carr and among the finest guitar playing in any category of music that you're ever likely to hear. Among the songs, "My Old Pal Blues (Dedicated to the Memory of Leroy Carr)" is a beautiful and poignant piece of personal, topical blues songwriting dealing with Carr's death in April of 1935, with Dot Rice providing excellent, fluid piano accompaniment to Blackwell's voice and guitar. Rice and Blackwell are teamed together again, backing Bumble Bee Slim on "Hey Lawdy Mama," the song that Willie Dixon later transformed into the classic "Meet Me in the Bottom" for Howlin' Wolf. The real treat, however, is the first release on CD of the four songs that Blackwell recorded in 1958, at the outset of his comeback—these little-known tracks are dark, moody, and utterly dazzling. Most of the masters are in surprisingly good condition ("Mean Mistreater Mama" and "She's Alright with Me" from 1934, and "Hey Lawdy Mama" from 1935 are notable and unfortunate exceptions), and this is an indispensable release for any serious fan of blues guitar, or guitar-piano duets. Neither gets any better than this. *—Bruce Eder*

Scrapper Blackwell, Vol. 3 (1959-1960) / 1994 / Document ✦✦✦✦✦

Austria's Document Records apparently had this 22-track, 75-minute CD out in 1994, but it only started coming into the U.S. in 1996, and doesn't even show up in some reference sources. Scrapper Blackwell's all-too-brief comeback at the end of the '50s is well represented by a dozen songs from a live concert at Indianapolis' "1444 Gallery" from September 20, 1959, some teaming Blackwell with singer Brooks Berry, paired off with ten tracks from Blackwell's 1960 British-only album on Dave Dobell's 77 label. Blackwell's technique on the guitar had not suffered at all from his nearly 20-year layoff from performing—he finesses sounds from his acoustic instrument that are soft and glittering, utilizing melody notes and carefully varied rhythms. Six of the tracks here are guitar solos, all of which are fascinating on repeated listening. His piano playing is also represented on one track. Blackwell's voice lacks some of the resonance that it had on his '30s recordings, and if anything the sadness in his persona is even more pronounced this late in his career, but he imbues his work with an intense passion that makes it compelling to hear. The worth of these performances makes his death, during an apparent mugging in 1962, all the more tragic, for more than almost any blues figure—including Memphis Minnie and Big Bill Broonzy—who almost made it to the folk/blues revival, Blackwell shows here how he could have reached millions with his work, had he lived only a couple of years longer. Oh, and the apology made by the producers for the sound quality of the 1959 concert tape (provided by Duncan Schmidt, who also appears on a track or two) is utterly unnecessary. *—Bruce Eder*

Bobby "Blue" Bland

b. Jan. 27, 1930, Rosemark, TN

Vocals / Retro-Soul, Electric Texas Blues, Soul-Blues, R&B, Soul

Bobby Bland earned his enduring blues superstar status the hard way: without a guitar, harmonica, or any other instrument to fall back upon. All Bland had to offer was his magnificent voice, a tremendously powerful instrument in his early heyday, injected with charisma and melisma to spare. Just ask his legion of female fans, who deem him a sex symbol to this day. Most of Bland's savage Texas blues sides during the mid-to-late '50s featured the slashing guitar of Clarence Hollimon, notably "I Smell Trouble," "I Don't Believe," "Don't Want No Woman," "You Got Me (Where You Want Me)," and the torrid "Loan a Helping Hand" and "Teach Me (How To Love You)." But the insistent guitar riffs guiding Bland's first national hit, 1957's driving "Farther up the Road," were contributed by Pat Hare, another vicious picker who would eventually die in prison after murdering his girlfriend and a cop. Later, Wayne Bennett took over on guitar, his elegant fretwork prominent on Bland's Duke waxings throughout much of the '60s. The gospel underpinnings inherent to Bland's powerhouse delivery were never more apparent than on the 1958 outing "Little Boy Blue," a vocal tour de force that wrings every ounce of emotion out of the grinding ballad. He steered into smoother material as the decade turned—the seminal mixtures of blues, R&B, and primordial soul on "I Pity the Fool," the Brook Benton-penned "I'll Take Care of You," and "Two Steps from the Blues" were tremendously influential to a legion of up-and-coming southern soulsters. *—Bill Dahl*

The 3b Blues Boy—*The Blues Years: 1952-59* / Jul. 21, 1952-1959 / Ace ✦✦✦

Bland recorded this 25-track compilation of bluesy material for Duke between 1952 and 1959. Bland had previously released a few sides for Chess and Modern in the early '50s, but these sides represent the era in which he began to find his voice. It still catches him at a relatively early stage in his development, concentrating on jump blues-oriented material, sometimes with horn sections, showing the considerable influence of B.B. King. There's some sharp guitar on these sides (including some by Roy Gaines, who also played with Chuck Willis and Hound Dog Thornton), and the vocals are full and confident, if a bit overripe. But neophytes should begin with his early and mid-'60s sides, when his blend of blues and soul reached a much higher level of maturity. *—Richie Unterberger*

☆ **I Pity the Fool: The Duke Recordings, Vol. 1** / Jul. 21, 1952-1960 / MCA ✦✦✦✦✦

Everything the young Bland waxed for Duke between 1952 and the 1960 date that produced "Cry, Cry, Cry" and the R&B-laced "Don't Cry No More." From 1955 on, this is uniformly seminal stuff, Bland's vocal confidence growing by the session and buttressed by the consistently innovative riffs and solos of guitarists Clarence Hollimon, Wayne Bennett (he's amazing on a torrid "You Did Me Wrong"), Roy Gaines, and Pat Hare. "Farther Up the Road," the exotic ballad "Hold Me Tenderly," "Little Boy Blue," and the title track are but few of the two-disc collection's many standouts. No blues fan should be minus this set! *—Bill Dahl*

The Voice: Duke Recordings 1959-69 / 1959-1969 / Ace ✦✦✦✦✦

A 26-track compilation of Duke sides from Bland's peak decade (1959-1969), MCA's two-volume *The Duke Recordings* covers this period in greater depth, and will be more readily available to most North American consumers. On its own terms, though, it's an excellent collection. Contains most of his biggest R&B hits ("Turn On Your Love Light," "Stormy Monday Blues," "Call On Me," "Ain't Nothing You Can Do"), as well as some cuts that didn't make it onto *The Duke Recordings*. *—Richie Unterberger*

☆ **Turn on Your Love Light/The Duke Recordings, Vols. 1-2** / 1960-1964 / MCA ✦✦✦✦✦

Picking up right where the first volume left off and continuing into 1964, this two-disc compilation (50 tracks!) showcases one of Bland's most appealing periods at Duke. Joe Scott was experimenting boldly with his protegé's repertoire, his brass-powered ar-rangements urging Bland to increased heights of incendiary energy on "Turn on Your Love Light" and "Yield Not to Temptation" (driven by future James Brown drummer Jabo Starks' funky traps) and advanced sophistication levels for the honey-smooth "Share Your Love with Me" and "That's the Way Love Is." Bennett's crackling blues licks invest "Stormy Monday Blues," "The Feeling Is Gone," and "Black Night" with T-Bone-derived tradition, while Bland handles Charlie Rich's "Who Will the Next Fool Be" with just the right amount of bluesy resignation. *—Bill Dahl*

☆ **Two Steps from the Blues** / 1961 / Duke/MCA ✦✦✦✦✦

Including classics like "Don't Cry No More," "I Pity The Fool," and "Little Boy Blue," this early-'60s set captures Bland at the point where his sound had just fully matured into a horn-punctuated blend of blues, gospel, and early soul. All 12 of the songs are included on MCA's *Duke Recordings* series, though, making this unnecessary if you're building a complete collection of Bland on CD. *—Richie Unterberger*

The Soul of the Man / 1966 / MCA ✦✦✦✦✦

Like his two other seminal '60s titles on the Duke label, *Here's the Man* and *Two Steps From the Blues*, Bobby Bland's *The Soul of the Man* features the powerful and gravelly voiced singer mixing it up with a bluesy, soul-tinged blend of swingers and slower, after-hours material. While the up-tempo blues "Reach Right Out" finds Bland vocally playing it cool, ballad cuts like "I Can't Stop" show him seamlessly working his dynamic range of hushed tones and throaty cries. Bland's varied approach is reflected in the album's diverse material, which includes the Stax-inspired groover "Back in the Same Old Bag"; a driving, horns-aplenty instrumental "Soul Stretch"; and the breezy, Northern soul sounding gem "Let's Get Together." Adding to the album's appeal are fine covers of the Jimmy Witherspoon standard "Ain't Nobody's Business If I Do" and Peggy Lee's signature tune "Fever." Bland's longstanding musical director Joe Scott provides his standard mix of tight rhythmic backing and urbane horn and guitar charts, perfectly framing the singer's robust voice with a toasty and slightly rough-hewn backdrop. While *The Soul of the Man* is essential listening for Bland fans, it also serves as a fine introduction to the great blues singer's catalog. *—Stephen Cook*

Touch of the Blues/Spotlighting The Man / 1967 / MCA ✦✦✦✦

Two of Bland's better albums for Duke coupled on one great-sounding CD. Both LPs were issued originally in 1969 but contained tracks from as far back as his 1967 Top Ten R&B hit "That Did It" and its immediate follow-up, "Touch of the Blues." Bland never turned his back on the style that brought him to prominence (he digs into Charles Brown's "Driftin' Blues" aggressively, Bennett providing luscious chording behind him), even if his stately reading of Joe Turner's "Chains of Love" is sweetened considerably by strings. On the other hand, the husky singer's unwise whack at Anthony Newley's Broadway showstopper "Who Can I Turn To" is about as far removed from blues tradition as is imaginable. *—Bill Dahl*

Here's the Man! / 1969 / Duke ✦✦✦

His California Album / 1973 / MCA ✦✦✦

Together for the First Time . . . Live / 1974 / MCA ✦✦✦

Together Again . . . Live / 1976 / MCA ✦✦

Members Only / 1985 / Malaco ✦✦✦

Blues You Can Use / 1987 / Malaco ✦✦✦

Years of Tears / 1993 / Malaco ✦✦✦✦

That Did It!: The Duke Recordings 3 / Jun. 18, 1996 / MCA ✦✦✦
That Did It is the third and final installment in MCA's series of double-disc compilations of Bobby Blue Bland's Duke recordings. This set collects everything he recorded between 1965 and 1972, including two unreleased tracks and several alternate takes. Although the music on *That Did It* isn't quite as strong as the songs on the first two installments of the series, it does collect a full 16 singles that have never appeared on an album before, as well as featuring several top-notch album tracks. For Bland fans, the collection remains a necessary purchase—this is Bland's final set of essential recordings. *—Thom Owens*

★ **Greatest Hits, Vol. 1** / Jun. 16, 1998 / Duke/Peacock ✦✦✦✦✦
This single-disc compilation cherry-picks through MCA's three two-disc anthology sets and puts together 16 tracks of essential Bland, starting with 1957's "Farther up the Road" and ending up with his 1969 reading of Big Joe Turner's "Chains of Love." It gathers up all the biggies: "Turn on Your Lovelight," "I Pity the Fool," "Stormy Monday Blues," "Call On Me," and "I'll Take Care of You," and the transfers are exemplary. While it obviously leaves off a few of the early favorites—"Little Boy Blue" is almost inexcusable in its absence—this and its companion volume will be the best introduction for anyone wanting to explore the Bobby Bland collection. *—Cub Koda*

Greatest Hits, Vol. 2: The ABC-Dunhill/MCA Recordings / Jul. 14, 1998 / MCA ✦✦✦✦✦
Subtitled *The ABC-Dunhill/MCA Recordings*, this picks up the last tenure of Bland working under the corporate MCA umbrella. With tunes aboard from various albums and singles, this 16-track collection covers the highlights from his '70s period, with only 1982's "Recess in Heaven" falling outside the time frame. Bland was a much different vocalist by now, and if anything, these tracks, some of them flirting outright with disco, spearheaded the easy-listening-blues style that he still spearheads. Highlights include "This Time I'm Gone for Good," an uncharacteristically funky "Goin' Down Slow," "I Wouldn't Treat a Dog (The Way You Treated Me)," "Ain't No Love in the Heart of the City," "Yolanda," and Bland's own "The Soul of a Man." Experiments with country show up on "Today I Started Loving You Again" and "I Hate You," and yet Bland's duet with B.B. King on Louis Jordan's "Let the Good Times Roll" still shows that his blues roots were always close at hand. Not the place to start, but it is his last hurrah before going over to Malaco, and a solid collection to investigate nonetheless. *—Cub Koda*

Blind Blake (Arthur Phelps)

b. 1897?, Jacksonville, FL, **d.** 1933
Vocals, Guitar / Prewar Blues, Piedmont Blues, Country Blues, Acoustic Blues
What happened to Blind Blake— His disappearance in 1932 from the Chicago blues scene, where he was undisputed king of the string and recorded 81 solo sides for Paramount, is one of the unresolved mysteries of early blues. Similarly mysterious is Blake's prodigious fingerstyle guitar technique which has plank spankers to this day asking: "How the hell did he do that!—" He broke out in 1926 with his debut release, a finger-buster called "West Coast Blues." Through the late '20s he performed and recorded with banjoists Papa Charlie Jackson and Gus Cannon, chanteuses Ma Rainey and Ida Cox, pianist Charlie Spand and a host of others as first-call guitar on Paramount's studio A-team. His best playing, however, was reserved for solo outings like "Diddie-Wah-Diddie" or "Police Dog Blues." On these he spun off guitar variations so dense they were dubbed "piano sounding" by his label. The hot licks framed lyrics often laced with suggestive double entendre. His hypermetabolic instrumentals were full of diffident spoken asides in an accent that gave credence to his supposed Southern seaboard origins. His subsequent whereabouts, including rumors of his murder or death by mishap, have never been substantiated. It's commonly supposed that, as the Depression knocked the bottom out of the race record industry, Blake simply moved back to the South so beloved in his song lyrics, and died there soon after. *—Steve James*

★ **Ragtime Guitar's Foremost Fingerpicker** / Nov. 1926-Oct. 1931 / Yazoo ✦✦✦✦✦
Ragtime Guitar's Foremost Fingerpicker contains a total of 28 prime tracks from Blind Blake. Alternating between solo acoustic numbers and songs recorded with a string band, the set demonstrates how exceptionally gifted the guitarist was—he's playing arrangements and rhythms that several subsequent generations were never able to completely figure out. Blind Blake was one of the finest acoustic guitarists of the '20s and '30s and this is the definitive compilation. *—Thom Owens*

The Best of Blind Blake / Oct. 10, 2000 / Yazoo ✦✦✦✦
Little is known about Blind Blake, including the date of his birth and death. His recording career lasted six years, from 1926-1932, and included 79 titles. After this, he disappeared. His music, however, has survived. Blake's a distinguished vocalist, with a steady medium range reminiscent of Big Bill Broonzy. His easy delivery on "Too Tight Blues, No. 2" and "Georgia Bound" is immediately accessible. The ragtime flavor of many of the tunes creates a light and happy blues. Even when the songs occasionally turn bare and graphic, covering everything from suicide to sex to murder, Blake's spry delivery comes off as joyful. There are also a number of ragtime-influenced instrumentals like "Southern Rag," "Blind Arthur's Breakdown," and "West Coast Blues" that feature his complicated guitar work. "Blind Arthur's Breakdown" is a tour de force in ragtime guitar that features complicated fingerpicking and multiple changes in pacing. Blake is accompanied on several cuts by other unidentified musicians, including a harmonica player on "Panther Squall Blues" and vibraphonist on "Doggin' Me Mamma Blues." It would have been helpful to know a little more about these musicians, though this information may not be available. The liner notes provide a good overview of Blake's music and try to sort out the fact and fiction of his scant biography. These recordings have been transferred from 78s, scratches, surface noise, and all. This is particularly noticeable on songs like "Ice Man Blues" and "Guitar Chimes," but both Blake's vocals and guitar picking remain discernable, and it's probably fortunate that these recordings have been preserved at all. With *The Best of Blind Blake*, Yazoo has released another fine recording of vintage blues. *–Ronnie D. Lankford, Jr.*

Michael Bloomfield

b. Jul. 28, 1943, Chicago, IL, **d.** Feb. 15, 1981, San Francisco, CA
Vocals, Keyboards, Guitar / Modern Electric Chicago Blues, Blues-Rock, Electric Chicago Blues
Michael Bloomfield was one of the first White players who got right into the Chicago blues scene and could actually play the music. As lead guitar for the Butterfield Blues Band, he exerted a powerful influence with far-reaching effect on young rock guitarists. He almost single-handedly pioneered the extended guitar solo, introducing many Western ears to the sounds of the Far East with his sitar-inspired solos. The Butterfield Blues Band album *East-West* (and the lovely title cut) broke new ground in the progressive rock scene—psychedelic rock was born. Bloomfield also backed Bob Dylan in his move into electric-land on *Highway 61 Revisited*, one of the landmarks of modern rock music. He went on to record albums with his own band, the Electric Flag, and with others (*Super Session* with Al Kooper). These later efforts saw only limited success. He was best at blues, and those first two Butterfield albums marked a high point. Part of Bloomfield's enormous influence on younger rock guitar players was due to his very outgoing and generous spirit. Bloomfield was one of those rare performers who cared as much for sharing his vision with others as he did for the music he loved. *—Michael Erlewine*

Don't Say That I Ain't Your Man / 1964-1969 / Columbia/Legacy ✦✦✦✦✦
15 tracks cover the pioneering blues-rock guitarist's '60s work, which was by far his best and most influential. Bloomfield worked with a bunch of bands during the decade, and the compilation flits rather hurriedly from his contributions to the Paul Butterfield Blues Band and Electric Flag to his collaborations with Al Kooper and some late-'60s solo tracks (none of his groundbreaking mid-'60s work with Dylan is here). Collectors will be interested in the first five songs, which date from previously unreleased sessions produced by John Hammond in late 1964 and early 1965. Featuring Charlie Musselwhite on harmonica, this pre-Butterfield Blues Band outfit plays convincingly, but the material is standard-issue, and Bloomfield's vocals are thin and weak (they didn't improve much over time). As befits Bloomfield's considerable but erratic talent, this is an interesting but erratic compilation; seek out the first two Paul Butterfield albums for a more cohesive showcase of his skills. *—Richie Unterberger*

● **Super Session** / 1968 / Columbia ✦✦✦✦✦
Al Kooper was the mastermind behind this appropriately named album, one side of which features his "spontaneous" studio collaboration with Mike Bloomfield and the other a session with Stephen Stills. The recordings have an off-the-cuff energy that displays the inventiveness of the two guitarists to best advantage. The best-selling recording of Bloomfield's career, it inspired the follow-up *The Live Adventures of Mike Bloomfield and Al Kooper*. *—Jeff Tamarkin*

The Live Adventures of Mike Bloomfield and Al Kooper / 1969 / Columbia ✦✦

It's Not Killing Me / 1969 / Columbia ✦✦

Triumvirate / 1973 / Columbia ✦✦✦

Live at the Old Waldorf / 1976 / Columbia/Legacy ✦✦✦✦
If you've never really experienced Mike Bloomfield just letting loose and playing ripping and inspired guitar, this is a darn good starting point. Recorded live in 1976 and 1977 by producer Norman Dayron at the Old Waldorf nightclub on Bloomfield's home turf in San Francisco with a hand-picked band, the results are startling to say the least. Bloomfield plays with assurance and authority throughout, exploring new ideas with each new chorus from his guitar, arguably at his best since his early Butterfield/Dylan days. He plays a lot of slide guitar here, too, and tracks like "Bad Luck Baby," "The Sky Is Crying," "Dancin' Fool," and "Buried Alive In the Blues" showcase his mighty talents with the bottleneck, taking the lessons learned first hand from Robert Nighthawk to places new and wild. Bloomfield was never much of a singer, and everybody from old pal Nick Gravenites to bassist Roger Troy to drummer Bob Jones end up handling all the vocals on this disc. But one listen to the "Blues Medley" that kicks off the proceedings is reason enough to know why Bloomfield's reputation on his chosen instrument ranks up there with the greats. Consider this disc validation of that rep. *—Cub Koda*

Best of Michael Bloomfield / 1978-1980 / Takoma ✦✦✦✦
By the time the majority of these 12 tracks from various solo projects were recorded, Bloomfield was already well-established as America's first official guitar slinger of the baby boomer generation. The selections on this CD come from the later stages of his career, and as such are a marvelous showcase for his wide ranging versatility. They run the gamut from Mississippi John Hurt-style fingerpicking ("Frankie and Johnny"), Scrapper Blackwell acoustic style flat-picking, and Lonnie Johnson slide playing (with "Mr. Johnson and Mr. Dunn," "Effinona Rag," "See That My Grave Is Kept Clean" featuring him on acoustic slide, piano, accordion, and tipple, and two duets with Little Brother Montgomery, "Pleading Blues" and "Michigan Water Blues") to the red-hot electric solo work he's best noted for. Other highlights include "Between the Hard Place and the Ground" and a stray track with the Woody Herman big band, "Hitch-Hike On the Possum Trot Line." *—Cub Koda*

Between the Hard Place and the Ground / 1979 / Takoma ✦✦

Juke Boy Bonner

b. Mar. 22, 1932, Bellville, TX, **d.** Jun. 29, 1978, Houston, TX
Vocals, Harmonica, Guitar / West Coast Blues, Texas Blues
One-man bands weren't any too common on the postwar blues scene. Joe Hill Louis and Dr. Ross come to mind as greats who plied their trade all by their lonesome as did Juke Boy Bonner, a Texan whose talent never really earned him much in the way of tangible reward.

Born into impoverished circumstances in the Lone Star State during the Depression, Weldon Bonner took up the guitar in his teens. He caught a break in 1947 in Houston, winning a talent contest that led to a spot on a local radio outlet. He journeyed to Oakland in 1956, cutting his debut single for Bob Geddins' Irma imprint ("Rock with Me Baby"/"Well Baby") with Lafayette "Thing" Thomas supplying the lead guitar. Goldband Records boss Eddie

Shuler was next to take a chance in 1960; Bonner recorded for him in Lake Charles, LA, with Katie Webster on piano, but once again, nothing happened career-wise.

Troubled by stomach problems during the '60s, Bonner utilized his hospital downtime to write poems that he later turned into songs. He cut his best work during the late '60s for Arhoolie Records, accompanying himself on both guitar and racked harmonica as he weaved extremely personal tales of his rough life in Houston. A few European tours ensued, but they didn't really lead to much. Toward the end of his life, he toiled in a chicken processing plant to make ends meet. Bonner died of cirrhosis of the liver in 1978. *—Bill Dahl*

● **Life Gave Me a Dirty Deal** / Nov. 30, 1968-May 5, 1969 / Arhoolie ♦♦♦♦♦
This is likely the most consistent and affecting collection you'll encounter by this singular Texas bluesman, whose strikingly personal approach was stunningly captured by Arhoolie's Chris Strachwitz during the late '60s in Houston. Twenty-three utter originals include "Stay Off Lyons Avenue," "Struggle Here in Houston," "I Got My Passport," and the title track. Bonner sang movingly of his painfully impoverished existence for Arhoolie, and the results still resound triumphantly today. *—Bill Dahl*

☆ **The Struggle** / Nov. 30, 1968-May 5, 1969 / Arhoolie ♦♦♦♦♦
Recorded in extreme stereo, with drums on one channel and Bonner's guitar on the other, this is Juke Boy Bonner's most cohesive album. Great songwriting and performances are found throughout. *—Cub Koda*

Legacy of the Blues, Vol. 5 / 1972 / GNP Crescendo ♦♦♦
Juke Boy Bonner remains one of the great hidden treasures of the blues. He was a one-man band who had serious lyrical concerns in all of his blues, creating stark and moving poetry out of the simplest of forms. Working in a Jimmy Reed style of guitar-boogie patterns and blowing an expressive neck-rack harmonica, he never saw much in the way of fame or fortune, but every single session produced music of considerable worth. Add this solo session, produced by Chris Strachwitz for Sonet's *Legacy of the Blues* series, to the list of essential albums to put into your shopping cart, as it's the blues at its most personal and moving. In tracks like "I'm a Bluesman," "Problems All Around," "Tired of the Greyhound Bus," and "Funny Money," you'll hear a bluesman laying his heart on the line for the music, something that should happen every time the "record" button goes on, but rarely does. *—Cub Koda*

James Booker (James Carroll Booker III)

b. Dec. 17, 1939, New Orleans, LA, **d.** Nov. 8, 1983, New Orleans, LA
Vocals, Piano / New Orleans R&B, New Orleans Blues, Boogie-Woogie, Acoustic New Orleans Blues, Piano Blues, R&B
Certainly one of the most flamboyant New Orleans pianists in recent memory, James Carroll Booker III was a major influence on the local rhythm & blues scene in the '50s and '60s. In 1960 he first made the national charts with "Gonzo," an organ instrumental, and over the course of the next two decades played and recorded with artists as varied as Lloyd Price, Aretha Franklin, Ringo Starr, the Doobie Brothers, and B.B. King. In 1967 he was convicted of possession of heroin and served a one-year sentence at Angola Penitentiary, which took the momentum out of an otherwise promising career. The rediscovery of roots music by college students during the '70s (focusing primarily on Professor Longhair) provided the opportunity for a comeback by 1974, with numerous engagements at local clubs. As with "Fess," Booker's performances at the New Orleans Jazz & Heritage Festivals took on the trappings of legendary "happenings." Booker's left hand was simply phenomenal, often a problem for bass players who found themselves running for cover in an attempt to stay out of the way; with it he successfully amalgamated the jazz and rhythm & blues idioms of New Orleans, adding more than a touch of gospel thrown in for good measure. *—Bruce Boyd Raeburn*

King of the New Orleans Keyboard / 1976 / Junco Partner ♦♦♦♦♦
Spectacular date by a great New Orleans pianist whose personal difficulties prevented him from both long life and sustained career achievement. Booker was cited as inspiration by everyone from Dr. John to Harry Connick Jr., and played with array of performers. He seamlessly fused a blues base, jazz touches, and R&B/gospel feeling, and this was among his best (and few) recordings. *—Ron Wynn*

Junco Partners / Oct. 22, 1976 / Hannibal ♦♦♦♦♦
A superb effort from a premier New Orleans piano master who made far too few recordings. The rumbling licks, often astonishing technique, and variety of rhythms and styles that Booker fused were always matched by his energy and exuberance. These sessions have since been reissued on CD. *—Ron Wynn*

New Orleans Piano Wizard: Live! / Nov. 27, 1977 / Rounder ♦♦♦♦

Resurrection of the Bayou Maharajah / 1977-1982 / Rounder ♦♦♦♦
For a man of such talent and influence, New Orleans piano legend James Booker is amazingly underrecorded. This disc, along with its partner (*Spiders on the Keys*) offer up some measure of what the folks of the Big Easy might have heard if they caught James Booker on one of his "on" nights (he was a known drug user and inconsistent in his playing). He is at his best here (recorded at the Maple Leaf between 1972-1982), focused and intense in his playing, wildly passionate on both keyboards and vocals. Some songs are repeated on the companion disc, but each treatment makes the songs new again, so that even his standards are always fresh and vital. Sheer genius at the keyboards and unrestrained, heartfelt vocals on such highlights as Fats Domino's "All By Myself," "The Fat Man," and "St. James Infirmary." *—Bob Gottlieb*

★ **Classified** / Oct. 18, 1982–Oct. 20, 1982 / Rounder ♦♦♦♦♦
While there has suddenly been a flood of CDs featuring masterful New Orleans keyboard wizard and vocalist James Booker, his best release arguably remains *Classified*. The 12-track set was a landmark album, as Booker displayed every facet of his distinctive style. He did uptempo blues, quasi-classical, rock, and R&B, making them all sound easy while performing frequently awesome keyboard feats. His "Professor Longhair Medley: Bald Head/Tipitina" pays homage to a legend while also demonstrating how much farther Booker's pianistic skills had developed. While his vocals sometimes aren't the equal of his brilliant playing, they're never less than effective and are sometimes almost frightening in their intensity. *—Ron Wynn*

Spiders on the Keys / 1993 / Rounder ♦♦♦

Gonzo: More Than All the 45's / Jun. 11, 1996 / Night Train ♦♦♦♦
Numerous discs are available featuring the eccentric and tragic New Orleans R&B pianist James Booker usually performing solo, recorded during live gigs from the '70s and early '80s. This disc provides an amazing collection of the earliest Booker on piano and organ backed by a full band. Booker made his recording debut in 1954 with the Imperial single "Doing the Hambone," backed with "Thinking About My Baby." During the next few years he would release equally exciting, although sporadic, singles on Chess, Ace, Peacock, and Duke, supported by some of New Orleans finest R&B musicians, including the sax section of Lee Allen, Robert Parker, and Red Tyler, drummer Earl Palmer, and bassist Frank Fields. The 1956 Chess singles "You're Near Me" and "Heavenly Angel" find Booker paired up on doo wop vocal duets with Arthur Booker (no relation). The remaining tracks are scorching dance numbers tied in with novelty/twist themes with catchy names such as "Teenage Rock," "Gonzo" (providing a national hit), "Cool Turkey," "The Duck," "The Crown," and "Beale Street Popeye." This is exceptional New Orleans R&B that provides an important piece of the James Booker musical puzzle. *—Al Campbell*

Lost Paramount Tapes / Mar. 11, 1997 / DJM ♦♦♦

Eddie Boyd (Edward Riley Boyd)

b. Nov. 25, 1914, Stovall, MS, **d.** Jul. 13, 1994, Helsinki, Finland
Vocals, Piano / Piano Blues, Electric Chicago Blues, Chicago Blues
Few postwar blues standards have retained the universal appeal of Eddie Boyd's "Five Long Years." Cut in 1951, Boyd's masterpiece has attracted faithful covers by B.B. King, Muddy Waters, Jimmy Reed, Buddy Guy, and too many other bluesmen to recount here. But Boyd's discography is filled with evocative compositions, often full of after-hours ambience. In 1941, he settled in Chicago, falling in with the "Bluebird beat" crowd that recorded for producer Lester Melrose, who produced Boyd's 1947 recording debut for RCA. Boyd reportedly paid for the date that produced "Five Long Years" himself, peddling the track to JOB Records (where the stolid blues topped the R&B charts during 1952). Powerful deejay Al Benson signed Boyd to a contract with his Parrot imprint and promptly sold the pact to Chess, inaugurating a stormy few years with Chicago's top blues outlet. There he waxed "24 Hours" and "Third Degree," both huge R&B hits in 1953, and a host of other Chicago blues gems. But Boyd and Leonard Chess were often at loggerheads, so it was on to the Bea & Baby imprint in 1959 for eight solid sides with Robert Jr. Lockwood on guitar and a slew of lesser labels after that. *—Bill Dahl*

● **Third Degree** / 1951-1959 / Charly ♦♦♦♦♦
Amazingly, this is the only comprehensive overview of Boyd's 1951-1959 Chess stint available on CD. Both "Third Degree" and "24 Hours" are aboard this 20-track compilation, along with the lesser-known standouts "I Got the Blues," "Nothing but Trouble," and "Cool Kind Treatment." Boyd's sturdy, concise piano work and darkly introspective vocals were brilliantly captured on tape by Leonard Chess, even if the two weren't exactly the best of pals. *—Bill Dahl*

Five Long Years / Oct. 20, 1965 / Evidence ♦♦♦♦
One of the first and best of Boyd's many overseas recordings, cut while he was in the midst of that auspicious 1965 American Folk Blues Festival tour of Europe. While the caravan was ensconced in London, young producer Mike Vernon spirited Boyd and a rhythm section (guitarist Buddy Guy, bassist Jimmie Lee Robinson, and drummer Fred Below) off to the studio, where Boyd ran through some of his classics ("I'm Comin' Home," "24 Hours," the title track) and a few less familiar items while alternating between piano and organ. *—Bill Dahl*

7936 South Rhodes / Jan. 25, 1968 / BGO ♦♦♦
Recorded in London in January 1968 with three members of the early lineup of Fleetwood Mac (the one that played blues, not pop/rock): Peter Green (guitar), John McVie (bass), and Mick Fleetwood (drums). It's an adequate setting for Boyd's straight Chicago piano blues, going heavier on the slow-to-mid-tempo numbers than the high-spirited ones, though Green is a far more sympathetic accompanist than the rhythm section. *—Richie Unterberger*

Ishmon Bracey

b. Jan. 9, 1901, Byram, MS, **d.** Feb. 12, 1970, Jackson, MS
Vocals, Guitar / Prewar Blues, Delta Blues
One of the early giants of the Delta blues, Ishmon Bracey often worked with local Jackson, MS legends like Tommy Johnson, Son Spand, and Charlie McCoy. He cut a small handful of sides for the Paramount label in 1930, some of the most coveted discs in blues history. Bracey's best work is marked by a tremulous vibrato to his largely nasal voice and simple but effective guitar work. As a parenthetical note, when Bracey was trying to be coaxed out of retirement to record in the '60s, to get researchers off his back he directed them to the whereabouts of another Delta legend—Skip James. *—Cub Koda*

● **Complete Recorded Works (1928-1929)** / Feb. 4, 1928-Dec. 1929 / Document ♦♦♦♦♦
Bracey's complete recorded works (1928-1929) are presented in chronological order on this single disc, with the bonus of four tracks by the elusive Charley Taylor. Since Bracey only recorded a handful of sides, this compilation is far more accessible than most of Document's *Complete Recorded Works* discs. Furthermore, Bracey was one of the best Delta blues artists of the '20s and his work is consistently engaging. *Complete Recorded Works (1928-1929)* is the best compilation available on Bracey—not only does it work as a concise introduction, it has everything completists will need. *—Cub Koda & Stephen Thomas Erlewine*

Tiny Bradshaw

b. Sep. 23, 1905, Youngstown, OH, **d.** Nov. 26, 1958, Cincinnati, OH
Vocals, Drums, Piano / Jump Blues, Swing, R&B
Tiny Bradshaw really had a two-part career, in the '30s in swing and from the mid-'40s on as a best-selling R&B artist. He majored in psychology at Wilberforce University but chose mu-

sic as his career. Bradshaw sang early on with Horace Henderson's Orchestra (in addition to playing drums), Marion Hardy's Alabamians, the Savoy Bearcats, The Mills Blue Rhythm Band and Luis Russell. In 1934 he put together his own orchestra and they recorded eight spirited numbers for Decca later that year. A decade of struggle lay ahead and, when Bradshaw's big band recorded again in 1944, the music was more R&B and jump-oriented. The majority of Bradshaw's recordings were cut during 1950-54 (all of his post-1947 output was made for King) although there would be one session apiece made in 1955 and 1958. A fine blues singer, Bradshaw had such sidemen along the way as Shad Collins, Russell Procope, and Happy Caldwell (all in 1934), Sonny Stitt (who recorded with Bradshaw in 1944), Big Nick Nicholas, Red Prysock, Bill Hardman, and Sil Austin. *—Scott Yanow*

- **Breakin' Up the House** / 1950-1952 / Charly ♦♦♦♦♦
Sixteen of Tiny Bradshaw's biggest and hardest-swinging King label waxings from 1950-1952, notably "The Train Kept A-Rollin'," "Well, Oh Well," "Two Dry Bones on the Pantry Shelf," "Walkin' the Chalk Line," and the jiving title item. Unfortunately, the torrid big band-styled instrumental arrangements that also defined Bradshaw's output are nowhere to be found on this collection. *—Bill Dahl*

Great Composer / 1959 / King ♦♦♦
Domestic CD collection that duplicates one of the popular jump blues bandleader's early albums from the King catalog. *—Bill Dahl*

EP Collection ... Plus / Dec. 14, 1999 / See For Miles ♦♦♦♦
Another excellent entry in See for Miles' EP series, here are 24 of Bradshaw's sides for the King label pulled from various extended-play 45 albums along with five bonus tracks. By and large, it's a wild collection of honkin' sax-driven big-band sides that trot the fine line between big-band stomps and jump-blues rockers with a few stray pop things (the corny "Butterfly") thrown in to round things out. An excellent introduction to this highly underrated bandleader's work. *—Cub Koda*

Jackie Brenston

b. Aug. 15, 1930, Clarksdale, MS, **d.** Dec. 15, 1979, Memphis, TN
Vocals, Saxophone / Jump Blues, Electric Memphis Blues, R&B
Determining the first actual rock & roll record is a truly impossible task. But you can't go too far wrong citing Jackie Brenston's 1951 Chess waxing of "Rocket 88," a seminal piece of rock's fascinating history with all the prerequisite elements firmly in place: practically indecipherable lyrics about cars, booze, and chicks; Raymond Hill's booting tenor sax; and a churning, beat-heavy rhythmic bottom. Sam Phillips, then a fledgling in the record business, produced "Rocket 88" in Memphis. The singer/saxist was backed by Ike Turner's Kings of Rhythm, an aggregation that Brenston had joined the previous year. Turner played piano on the tune; Willie Kizart supplied dirty, distorted guitar. Billed as by Jackie Brenston & His Delta Cats, "Rocket 88" drove up to the top slot on the R&B charts and remained there for more than a month. But none of his Chess follow-ups sported the same high-octane performance, though "Real Gone Rocket" was certainly a deserving candidate, and Brenston's slide from the spotlight was swift. *—Bill Dahl*

- **Rocket 88** / Mar. 5, 1951-Apr. 17, 1953 / Charly ♦♦♦♦♦
If Brenston's "Rocket 88" was in actuality the very first rock & roll record, as many experts claim, the rest of his brief Chess legacy adds up to quite a definitive rockin' statement. Among these 16 sides dating from 1951-1953 are his amazing sequel "My Real Gone Rocket" (which probably rocks even harder than "Rocket 88" as Ike Turner pounds the keys), "Tuckered Out," the evocative "Fat Meat Is Greasy" (one of several items only out in Japan before the advent of this British CD), and seven sides Brenston cut in Chicago without Sam Phillips to guide him, nor Turner's Kings of Rhythm to back him up. Great stuff. *—Bill Dahl*

John Brim

b. Apr. 10, 1922, Hopkinsville, KY
Vocals, Harmonica, Guitar / Electric Chicago Blues, Chicago Blues
One of the last still-active links to the classic '50s Chicago blues sound that once thrived at Chess Records, John Brim may be best-known for writing and cutting the original "Ice Cream Man" that Van Halen covered on their first album. That's a pity, for the seriously under-recorded Brim made some exceptionally hard-nosed waxings. He met his wife Grace in 1947; fortuitously, she was a capable drummer who played on several of John's records. In fact, she was the vocalist on a 1950 single for Detroit-based Fortune Records that signaled the beginning of her hubby's discography. John recorded for Random, JOB, Al Benson's Parrot logo (the socially aware "Tough Times"), and Chess ("Rattlesnake," his answer to Big Mama Thornton's "Hound Dog," was pulled from the shelves by Chess for fear of a plagiarism suit). Cut in 1953, the suggestive "Ice Cream Man" had to wait until 1969 to enjoy a very belated release. Brim's last Chess single, "I Would Hate to See You Go," was waxed in 1956; after a hiatus of a few decades, he made a welcome return to studio action with a set for Tone-Cool Records, *The Ice Cream Man*. *—Bill Dahl*

- **Whose Muddy Shoes** / 1991 / MCA/Chess ♦♦♦♦♦
First unleashed back in 1969 on vinyl as part of the Chess Vintage Series, this hard-hitting disc couples six of Brim's meanest Parrot and Chess sides with nine Elmore James gems. Brim is at his toughest on the threatening "Be Careful" and "Lifetime Baby." *—Bill Dahl*

Ice Cream Man / 1994 / Tone-Cool ♦♦♦
Brim's vocals don't quite possess the same snap, crackle, and pop that they did in the mid-'50s, but thanks to a savvy song selection and sympathetic backing by the likes of guitarist Bob Margolin and harpist Jerry Portnoy, Brim's comeback album is a generally successful project. *—Bill Dahl*

Hadda Brooks

b. Oct. 29, 1916, Los Angeles, CA
Vocals, Piano / Boogie-Woogie, Piano Blues
In the mid-to-late '40s, black popular music began to mutate from swing jazz and boogie-woogie into the sort of rhythm & blues that helped lay the foundation for rock & roll. Singer and pianist Hadda Brooks was one of the many figures who were significant in aiding that transition, although she's largely forgotten today. While her torch song delivery was rooted in the big-band era, her boogie-woogie piano looked forward to jump blues and R&B. Ironically, her elegant vocals and jazzy arrangements, the same qualities that made her briefly successful, left her ill-equipped to compete when harder-driving forms of rhythm & blues, and then early rock & roll, began to dominate the marketplace in the early '50s. Her first record, the pounding "Swingin' the Boogie," was a sizable regional hit in 1945. Brooks' first records were instrumental, but by 1946 she was singing as well. She had a fair amount of success for Modern in the late '40s, reaching the R&B Top Ten with "Out of the Blue" and her most famous song, "That's My Desire" (which was covered for a big pop hit by Frankie Laine). *—Richie Unterberger*

- **That's My Desire** / 1945-1950 / Virgin ♦♦♦♦♦
Twenty five tracks from her prime, recorded for Modern in the '40s and '50s, includ her hits "That's My Desire" and "Out of the Blue," as well as "Anytime, Anyplace, Anywhere." While Brooks was an important figure of the L.A. '40s R&B scene, latter-day listeners may find this rather tame. Vocally she owed much more to pop-jazz stylings than gritty R&B influences. Her most durable and influential performances were her instrumental ones at the piano bench, especially on the pounding "Swingin' the Boogie," which leads off this collection. *—Richie Unterberger*

Jump Back Honey: The Complete OKeh Sessions / Feb. 11, 1997 / Columbia ♦♦♦♦♦
She was best known as a boogie-woogie piano player in the late '40s, but this first-time CD reissue focuses on Hadda Brooks' brilliantly sophisticated, laidback vocal material in the '50s. These songs don't carry the dirgelike sentiments of most blues, but more of a euphoric look at life and love. There are rocking dancers such as "Jump Back Honey" and "Brooks Boogie" among tasteful ballads such as "I Went To Your Wedding" and saucy mid-tempos like "Time Was When." *—Bill Carpenter*

I've Got News for You / Mar. 9, 1999 / Virgin ♦♦♦
This two-CD set spans Brooks' career from 1945 to 1998 and does a fine job of gathering bits and pieces from the veteran singer/pianist's catalog. Divided into two sections, "Hadda Sings" and "Hadda Swings," it unsuccessfully tries to separate essentially similar patterns in Brooks' style and manner, amounting to a representative, if incomplete, compilation of progressing, artistic achievement. The '90s recordings featured here aren't bad, but it's the late-'40s material—particularly Brooks' sublime take on "That's My Desire"—that gives *I've Got News for You* something to shout about. *—Michael Gallucci*

Lonnie Brooks

b. Dec. 18, 1933, Dubuisson, LA
Vocals, Guitar / Modern Electric Chicago Blues, Electric Chicago Blues, Modern Electric Blues
Having forged a unique Louisiana/Chicago blues synthesis unlike anyone else's on the competitive Windy City scene, charismatic guitarist Lonnie Brooks has long reigned as one of the town's top bluesmen. A masterful showman, the good-natured Brooks puts on a show equal to his recordings (and that's saying a lot, considering there's four decades of wax to choose from). Inaugurating his recording career in 1957 with the influential swamp-pop ballad "Family Rules," the young rock & roller—then billed as Guitar Junior—enjoyed more regional success on Goldband with the rocking dance number "The Crawl" (much later covered by the Fabulous Thunderbirds). When Sam Cooke offered the young rocker a chance to accompany him to Chicago, he gladly accepted. But two problems faced him once he arrived: There was another Guitar Junior in town (precipitating the birth of Lonnie Brooks), and the bayou blues that so enthralled Gulf Coast crowds didn't cut it up north. Scattered session work (he played on Jimmy Reed's Vee-Jay classic "Big Boss Man") and a series of R&B-oriented 45s for Midas, USA, Chirrup, and Chess ensued during the '60s, as Lonnie learned a new style of blues. By the late '70s, Brooks was gaining a deserved reputation as an exceptionally dynamic Chicago bluesman with a fresh perspective. Albums for Alligator and extensive touring have cemented Brooks' standing as a Chicago blues giant. *—Bill Dahl*

The Crawl / 1955-1959 / Charly ♦♦♦♦♦
Lonnie Brooks' pervasive '50s bayou-blues roots are laid bare and rocking hard. "Family Rules" was highly influential to the blossoming swamp-pop movement soon sweeping southern Louisiana; "The Crawl," "I Got It Made (When I Marry Shirley Mae)," "Roll, Roll, Roll," and "Knocks Me Out" (the latter one of his Mercury singles) drive with youthful abandon. The youngster's ears were wide-open—he even covered Harlan Howard's country ditty "Pick Me Up on Your Way Down," investing it with serious swamp angst. *—Bill Dahl*

Live at Pepper's 1968 / 1968 / Black Top ♦♦♦

Let's Talk It Over / Mar. 24, 1977 / Delmark ♦♦♦
Of all the quickie dates produced by Ralph Bass in 1977 for a project that never came to real fruition, Lonnie Brooks's contribution to the series is likely the most satisfying, thanks to a tight band (his working unit at the time) and a sheaf of imaginative originals (notably "Crash Head on into Love," "Greasy Man," and the title cut). An ingenious reworking of Lowell Fulson's "Reconsider Baby" doesn't hurt either. *—Bill Dahl*

- **Bayou Lightning** / Mar. 1979 / Alligator ♦♦♦♦♦
All the promise that Lonnie Brooks possessed was realized on this album, his finest and most consistent to date. The churning bayou groove of "Voodoo Daddy," and a soul-steeped "Watch What You Got," a bone-chilling remake of Junior Parker's "In the Dark," rollicking covers of Tommy Tucker's "Alimony" and Brooks' own "Figure Head," and the swaggering originals "You Know What My Body Needs" and "Watchdog" are among the set's many incendiary highlights. *—Bill Dahl*

Turn on the Night / 1981 / Alligator ♦♦♦

Hot Shot / 1983 / Alligator ♦♦♦♦
A return to rollicking good-time form, boasting the roaring "Don't Take Advantage of Me" and "I Want All My Money Back," relentless rocking revivals of Otis Blackwell's "Back Trail"

and J.B. Lenoir's "One More Shot," and a faithful remake of Lonnie Brooks' own "Family Rules" from the Guitar Junior era. *—Bill Dahl*

Wound Up Tight / 1986 / Alligator ✦✦✦

Live from Chicago / Nov. 5, 1987-Nov. 7, 1987 / Alligator ✦✦✦

Roadhouse Rules / Feb. 27, 1996 / Alligator ✦✦✦

Deluxe Edition / Oct. 28, 1997 / Alligator ✦✦✦✦✦
Deluxe Edition rounds up 15 highlights from Lonnie Brooks' late-'70s and '80s recordings for Alligator. Like many Alligator artists, Brooks made records that were just a little too slick to demonstrate the depth of his talents and the grittiness of his playing, yet they still remained solid, rock-inflected contemporary blues albums. The bulk of the highlights from his records are here, making it a fine introduction to Brooks' most popular recordings. *—Stephen Thomas Erlewine*

Lone Star Shootout / May 25, 1999 / Alligator ✦✦✦✦

Big Bill Broonzy (William Lee Conley Broonzy)

b. Jun. 26, 1893, Scott, MS, **d.** Aug. 15, 1958, Chicago, IL
Vocals, Mandolin, Guitar / Prewar Blues, Blues Revival, Country-Blues, Acoustic Chicago Blues, Acoustic Blues
In terms of his musical skill, the sheer size of his repertoire, the length and variety of his career and his influence on contemporaries and musicians who would follow, Big Bill Broonzy is among a select few of the most important figures in recorded blues history. Among his hundreds of titles are standards like "All by Myself" and "Key to the Highway." In this country he was instrumental in the growth of the Chicago blues sound, and his travels abroad rank him as one of the leading blues ambassadors. After brief stints on the pulpit and in the Army, Broonzy moved to Chicago and began playing with elders like Papa Charlie Jackson. After inaugurating his recording career with Paramount in 1927, he waxed some brilliant blues and hokum in the early '30s for Bluebird, Columbia, and OKeh. In 1938, Broonzy appeared at Carnegie Hall (ostensibly filling in for the fallen Robert Johnson) for John Hammond's revolutionary Spirituals to Swing Series. He continued alternating stints in Chicago and New York with coast-to-coast road work until 1951, when live performances and recording dates overseas earned him considerable notoriety in Europe and led to worldwide touring. Back in the States he recorded for Chess, Columbia, and Folkways. He spent the last year of his life in and out of hospitals and finally succumbed to cancer in 1958. *—Steve James*

☆ **Do That Guitar Rag (1928-1935)** / 1928-1935 / Yazoo ✦✦✦✦✦
This is a marvelous little companion piece to *Young Big Bill Broonzy (1928-35)* on Yazoo. Broonzy's ragtime guitar picking is textbook in its scope and his vocals are as warm as can be. Dubbed from old 78s, the ultra high quality of the music make any audiophile nitpicking a moot point indeed. Broonzy at his youngest and full of pep. *—Cub Koda*

★ **The Young Big Bill Broonzy (1928-35)** / 1928-1935 / Yazoo ✦✦✦✦✦
The young Bill Broonzy was as far removed from his later folk, blues posturings as you could imagine. If you're only familiar with his later work, these early sides will come as quite a jolt. Big Bill whips off some fleet-fingered single note leads and his rhythmic drive is never less than spot on. Great stuff. *—Cub Koda*

★ **Good Time Tonight** / 1930-1940 / Columbia/Legacy ✦✦✦✦✦
If you're following the 30-plus year career of Bill Broonzy and already have the two early compilations available on Yazoo, here's where you go next. These are basically ensemble works covering the time frame between 1930 to 1940 and Broonzy sounds very comfortable in the company of Blind John Davis and Joshua Altheimer. The 20 tracks compiled here (culled from various Vocalion, ARC, and Columbia sessions) sound pretty great, benefitting mightily from modern sound restoration devices. *—Cub Koda*

Big Bill Broonzy Sings Folk Songs / 1956 / Smithsonian/Folkways ✦✦✦✦✦
Two different sessions provided the material for this collection of folk songs, spirituals, and blues standards. Half the disc is previously unreleased material from Broonzy's final Folkways recording session. The other half of the disc was recorded at a live broadcast with Pete Seeger for radio station WFMT Chicago in front of an audience of friends; Seeger joins Broonzy during "John Henry." Although his vocal range is not quite what it used to be, Broonzy sings with authority and vibrance, using the occasional strained notes for effect. His fluid guitar technique remains unhampered. Unlike many of his peers, Big Bill Broonzy was able to utilize the late-'50s folk boom as an opportunity to be recognized while he was still alive. This disc shows Broonzy in his element as one of the classic blues masters. *—Jim Powers*

The Bill Broonzy Story / 1960 / Verve ✦✦✦
This three-CD set (originally five LPs) was a product of three recording sessions, held on July 12 and 13, 1957, immediately before Broonzy entered the hospital for surgery on the lung cancer that would end his career and take his life just a year later. He sounds in good enough spirits, and the voice and guitar are still in excellent form as he runs through the songs that evidently mattered most to him on those two days: "Key to the Highway," "Take This Hammer," "See See Rider," "Alberta," "Frankie and Johnny," "In the Evening (When the Sun Goes Down)," "Swing Low, Sweet Chariot," and more than two dozen others. Producer Bill Randle didn't get a lot of the songs he'd hoped to record, such as "Stack O Lee" and "Night Time Is the Right Time," which Broonzy didn't want to sing, but he got enough for five LPs' worth of music out of the ten hours of recordings. (Did the rest survive, one wonders, and might there be anything that was left off that's worth hearing?) The sound is state of the art, with the singer and his solo acoustic guitar clean and close. The set is a vital and important document, as well as great listening, not only for the music but for Broonzy's between-song banter—he was one of the great raconteurs of the blues—although it isn't quite as indispensable as one might think. *—Bruce Eder*

Complete Recorded Works, Vol. 1 (1927-1932) / 1991 / Document ✦✦✦✦✦
This is a particularly fascinating CD, for it has the first 26 selections ever recorded by Big Bill Broonzy as a leader. The beginning of Document's complete reissuance of all of Broonzy's early recordings, the set starts with four duet numbers that Broonzy cut during 1927-28 with fellow guitarist John Thomas. Although his style was already a bit recognizable, the young guitarist/vocalist really started coming into his own in 1930. There are 15 selections from that year included on this set, with Big Bill often using the pseudonyms of Sammy Sampson or Big Bill Johnson; in fact, even the final seven numbers (from 1932) had him billed as the latter. The CD finds Broonzy evolving from a country-blues musician who already had strong technique into a star of hokum records. Among the many highlights are "Big Bill Blues" (different versions in 1928 and 1932), "I Can't Be Satisfied," "Pig Meat Strut," "Beedle Um Bum," and "Selling That Stuff." Pianist Georgia Tom Dorsey helps out on three numbers. Big Bill Broonzy fans have a right to rejoice about the existence of this wonderful series. *—Scott Yanow*

Complete Recorded Works, Vol. 2 (1932-1934) / 1991 / Document ✦✦✦

Complete Recorded Works, Vol. 3 (1934-1935) / 1991 / Document ✦✦✦

Complete Recorded Works, Vol. 4 (1935-1936) / 1992 / Document ✦✦✦✦✦

Complete Recorded Works, Vol. 5 (1936-1937) / 1992 / Document ✦✦✦✦

Complete Recorded Works, Vol. 6 (1937) / 1992 / Document ✦✦✦✦

Complete Recorded Works, Vol. 7 (1937-1938) / 1992 / Document ✦✦✦✦

Complete Recorded Works, Vol. 8 (1938-1939) / 1992 / Document ✦✦✦✦✦

Complete Recorded Works, Vol. 9 (1939) / 1992 / Document ✦✦✦✦

Complete Recorded Works, Vol. 10 (1940) / 1992 / Document ✦✦✦✦

Complete Recorded Works, Vol. 11 (1940-1942) / 1992 / Document ✦✦✦✦✦

Can't Be Satisfied / Jun. 30, 1998 / Columbia/Legacy ✦✦✦✦✦
Can't Be Satisfied is a terrific collection that contains 16 highlights from Big Bill Broonzy's Columbia recordings, offering an affordable, concise introduction to some of his best material for curious listeners. *—Stephen Thomas Erlewine*

Trouble in Mind / Feb. 22, 2000 / Smithsonian/Folkways ✦✦✦✦
This is something of a best-of for Broonzy's Folkways recordings, done in 1956-57 near the end of his life, all featuring just his voice and his acoustic guitar (although Pete Seeger adds banjo to a live version of "This Train (Bound for Glory)"). Although Broonzy, who died in 1958 of throat cancer, was likely not in peak physical shape by this time, you wouldn't suspect that from the quality of the performances. His vocals are still rich and moving on a relaxed selection of originals and standards, including such well-known favorites as "Trouble in Mind," "Key to the Highway," "Digging My Potatoes," "It Hurts Me Too," and "C.C. Rider." Especially good is his version of "Louise," where the intensity rises to a level higher than most of the other tracks approach. Occasionally Broonzy gets into racial and social comment, as on "When Will I Get to Be Called a Man" and the more controversial "Black, Brown and White Blues." *—Richie Unterberger*

Absolutely the Best / Dec. 5, 2000 / Varese ✦✦✦
A very affordable collection of Big Bill Broonzy's better-known songs, Fuel Records' 15-song collection *Absolutely the Best* serves as a good overview and an excellent starting point for curious blues fans. The album is an assortment of traditional folksongs, reworked blues standards, and eight Broonzy originals. The liner notes give a brief look into the life of this legendary bluesman, and the music deals with his bouncing brand of bare-bones acoustic country-blues, omitting his late career foray into horn-driven R&B. The only complaint with this collection is that the recording quality from the earlier recordings is a little brash and raspy, which is to be expected but is quite noticeable when sequenced right next to cleaner tracks. *—Zac Johnson*

Charles Brown

b. Sep. 13, 1922, Texas City, TX, **d.** Jan. 21, 1999
Vocals, Piano / Urban Blues, West Coast Blues, Piano Blues, R&B
How many blues artists remain at the absolute top of their game after more than a half century of performing? One immediately leaps to mind: Charles Brown. His incredible piano skills and laidback vocal delivery remain every bit as mesmerizing today as they were way back in 1945, when his ultra-mellow, jazz-inflected sound invented an entirely new blues genre for sophisticated postwar revelers. Classically trained on the ivories, Brown recorded his first single "Drifting Blues" as head of the Blazers. After the single hit number two on the R&B charts, the band remained popular during the late '40s until Brown opted to go solo. Recording for Aladdin, he visited the R&B Top Ten no less than ten times from 1949 to 1952, retaining his mournful, sparsely arranged sound for smashes like the chart-topping "Trouble Blues." Brown's mellow approach failed to make the transition to rock's brasher rhythms though, and he soon faded from national prominence. Occasionally recording without causing much of a stir during the '60s and '70s, Brown began to regroup by the mid-'80s with a well-received album (1986's *One More for the Road*) and the support slot on a Bonnie Raitt tour. He then recorded half-a-dozen albums, for Alligator, Bullseye Blues, and Verve. *—Bill Dahl*

1944-1945 / 1944-Sep. 11, 1945 / Classics ✦✦✦✦✦
This Classics CD features pianist/vocalist Charles Brown on his first 22 recordings, when he was a sideman with guitarist Johnny Moore's Three Blazers. Brown already sounded quite distinctive, and as it turned out, the 21st song ("Drifting Blues") was his biggest hit. The music, due to the instrumentation (a trio/quartet with bassist Eddie Williams and sometimes Oscar Moore on second guitar), is a bit reminiscent at times of the Nat King Cole Trio, but it had a special soul and feeling of its own. Frankie Laine makes a couple of early appearances, but Brown takes care of the bulk of the vocals, and there are also eight excellent instrumentals. Recommended. *—Scott Yanow*

☆ **The Complete Aladdin Recordings of Charles Brown** / Sep. 11, 1945-Sep. 4, 1956 / Mosaic ✦✦✦✦✦
Every single brilliant side—some 109 in all—that this elegant, tremendously influential pianist cut for the Mesner brothers' Philo and Aladdin imprints from 1945 to 1956 is housed in this lavishly produced five-disc box set. Mosaic's customary attention to detail is evident

in the packaging and the sound; Brown's brilliance makes the entire box a delight, from his earliest sessions with the Three Blazers through his hitmaking run as a solo star during the late '40s and early '50s. The genesis of the entire West Coast club- blues style resides in this box; its expense is well worth it. *—Bill Dahl*

Snuff Dippin' Mama / 1946-1947 / Night Train ♦♦♦♦♦
Even with the above box, you won't own all of Brown's seminal work. In 1946, he and the Blazers landed at Exclusive Records, which is the era that this collection examines via 19 fine sides including the jivey "Juke Box Lil" and "C.O.D.," a mournful "Sunny Road," and the jazzy "B-Sharp You'll See." Guitarist Johnny Moore and bassist Eddie Williams were indeed sharp in smooth support. *—Bill Dahl*

★ **Driftin' Blues: The Best of Charles Brown** / 1948-1956 / Collectables ♦♦♦♦♦
If your budget only allows the acquisition of a single CD of Brown's Aladdin material, let it be this one. It sports most of the truly important hits that inspired so many West Coasters:"Driftin' Blues," "Black Night," "Trouble Blues," and many others. *—Bill Dahl*

One More for the Road / Aug. 6, 1986-Aug. 8, 1986 / Alligator ♦♦♦
One of the first comeback salvos that the veteran pianist fired after suffering the slings and arrows of anonymity for much too long. Typically delectable in a subtle, understated manner, Brown eases through a very attractive program. *—Bill Dahl*

All My Life / 1990 / Bullseye Blues ♦♦♦♦♦
This is by far Brown's best contemporary effort (and the set that really got his recording career back in high gear). Cameos by Dr. John and Ruth Brown certainly didn't hurt the set's chances, but it's the eternally suave pianist and his excellent road band (especially guitarist Danny Caron and saxist Clifford Solomon) that make this such a delightful collection. *—Bill Dahl*

Blues and Other Love Songs / 1992 / 32 Jazz ♦♦♦
This Charles Brown session from early 1992 finds the singer sounding just as natural as he did in the early '50s. *Blues and Other Love Songs* was originally released on Muse records and is available as a budget title from the excellent reissue label 32 Jazz. Brown is in a typically soulful mood, crooning like a gritty modern day Nat "King" Cole. Backing up the piano and vocals of Brown are soul-groove saxophonist Houston Person, whose smokey tenor chops were an excellent match for Brown's blues. Danny Caron on guitar, Ruth Davies on bass, and Gaylord Birch round out the rhythm section. These ten tracks consist of five originals and five covers featuring a brief version of Thelonious Monk's "Round Midnight," showing off Brown's ability to play straight jazz. Person is also heard with Brown on the 32 jazz reissue *Lost and Found*, which combines the albums *Sweet Slumber* and *Wildflower* on one disc. *—Al Campbell*

Someone to Love / 1992 / Bullseye Blues ♦♦♦
Bonnie Raitt, who played such an integral role in Brown's successful comeback, guests on two tracks on the pianist's *Bullseye Blues* encore, which isn't quite the tour de force that his previous outing was but is eminently solid nonetheless. Caron and Solomon once again shine in support of their leader. *—Bill Dahl*

Just a Lucky So and So / Jan. 24, 1994 / Bullseye Blues ♦♦♦

Honeydripper / Nov. 5, 1996 / Verve ♦♦♦♦
"Soothing" is not a word normally associated with blues, but its the word that best captures the experience of listening to Charles Brown, and *Honey Dripper* is no exception. Listening to it is like sipping a fine bottle of cognac. Seventy-two years old at the time of this recording session, Brown sounds agile, almost ageless. Indeed, time seems to stand still when he plays and sings in that same understated, urbane manner he popularized with Johnny Moore's Three Blazers back in the '40s. Like his other recordings this decade, *Honey Dripper* features Brown's regular working combo, led by guitarist Danny Caron and including saxophonist Clifford Solomon. The songs range from straight-ahead blues to jazz ballads, with some straddling the line. *—Steve Hoffman*

1946 / Feb. 3, 1998 / Classics ♦♦♦♦
With the great success of the slow blues ballad "Driftin' Blues," Johnny Moore's Three Blazers emphasized laidback material on record after record in 1946, looking for another hit. Ironically the main star of virtually all of the records, pianist-vocalist Charles Brown, was given second billing if he was mentioned at all, while guitarist Moore (who is joined by bassist Eddie Williams) was often mistaken as the singer. Brown would stick with Moore into 1947 and was largely responsible for the group's success. The second Classics CD to reissue all of the trio's recordings includes 23 enjoyable titles that mostly have a sameness to them in tempo and mood. All are vocal showcases for Brown except for the two-part "Warsaw Concerto" and "Nutmeg," the lone instrumentals. A worthwhile set but not as essential a release as the earlier volume in this series. *—Scott Yanow*

So Goes Love / May 12, 1998 / Verve ♦♦♦

In a Grand Style / Jul. 20, 1999 / Bullseye Blues ♦♦♦♦

Clarence "Gatemouth" Brown

b. Apr. 18, 1924, Vinton, LA
Vocals, Drums, Violin, Mandolin, Harmonica, Guitar, Bass / Modern Electric Texas Blues, Texas Blues, Electric Texas Blues, Modern Electric Blues

Whatever you do, don't refer to multi-instrumentalist Clarence "Gatemouth" Brown as a bluesman, although his imprimatur on the development of Texas blues is enormous. You're liable to get him riled. If you must pigeonhole the legend, just call him an eclectic Texas musical master whose interests encompass virtually every roots genre imaginable (his father specialized in country, cajun, and bluegrass but not blues). He began recording in 1947, after an appearance at a Houston club owned by Don Robey convinced the music entrepreneur to assume control of Brown's career. Robey inaugurated the Peacock label in 1949 to showcase Gate's blistering riffs, which proved influential to a legion of Houston string-benders (Albert Collins, Johnny Copeland, and Johnny "Guitar" Watson, among others). Though the R&B charts didn't reflect Brown's importance, his blazing instrumentals, horn-enriched rockers, and lowdown Lone Star blues are a major component of the rich Texas postwar blues legacy. The '60s weren't all that kind to Brown and when he began to rebuild his career in the '70s, country, jazz, even calypso began playing a prominent role in his concerts. He turned up on *Hee Haw* with pickin' and grinnin' pal Roy Clark after they cut a sizzling 1979 duet album for MCA, *Makin' Music*. Acclaimed discs for Rounder, Alligator, and Verve over the last 15 years have proven that Gatemouth Brown is a steadfastly unclassifiable American original. *—Bill Dahl*

★ **The Original Peacock Recordings** / 1948-1959 / Rounder ♦♦♦♦♦
Only 12 songs long, this collection remains the best place to begin appreciating why so many young Texas blues guitarists fell in love with Gatemouth Brown's style (until MCA decides to compile the ultimate Brown package, anyway). Listen to the way his blazing axe darts and weaves through trombonist Pluma Davis' jazzy horn chart on 1954's "Okie Dokie Stomp," or the stratospheric licks drenching "Dirty Work at the Crossroads." Brown proves that a violin can adapt marvelously to the blues (in the right hands, anyway) on "Just Before Dawn," and blows a little atmospheric harp on "Gate's Salty Blues." *—Bill Dahl*

Just Got Lucky / Mar. 22, 1973-Jul. 1, 1973 / Evidence ♦♦♦♦
More goodies from the same French 1973 dates (originally issued on Black & Blue). Lots of Jordan covers, along with Brown's own "Here Am I" and "Long Way Home," three Peacock remakes, and a sizzling revival of Bill Doggett's "Honey Boy." The last three titles date from a 1977 session, again cut in France, and are all Brown originals. *—Bill Dahl*

Pressure Cooker / Jul. 23, 1973-Aug. 1, 1973 / Alligator ♦♦♦♦
Before Gate was able to rebuild a following stateside, he frequently toured Europe. He recorded the contents of this inexorably swinging set in France in 1973 with all-star backing by keyboardists Milt Buckner and Jay McShann, saxists Arnett Cobb and Hal Singer, among others. Brown indulges his passion for Louis Jordan by ripping through "Ain't That Just like a Woman" and "Ain't Nobody Here but Us Chickens" and exhibits his immaculate fretwork on the torrid title item. *—Bill Dahl*

Alright Again! / Jun. 2, 1981-Jun. 8, 1981 / Rounder ♦♦♦♦♦
One of the most satisfying contemporary Brown discs of all for the discerning blues fan. Nothing but swinging, horn-abetted blues adorn this album, as Gate pays tribute to an influence and a protégé by covering T-Bone Walker's "Strollin' with Bones" and Albert Collins' "Frosty." Brown's jauntily revives Junior Parker's "I Feel Alright Again" and Percy Mayfield's "Give Me Time to Explain," while his own numbers—a funky "Dollar Got the Blues," the luxurious blues "Sometimes I Slip"—are truly brilliant. *—Bill Dahl*

One More Mile / Oct. 1982 / Rounder ♦♦♦
Considerably more varied than its predecessor, this one nods toward the Louisiana swamp ("Sunrise Cajun Style," complete with pedal steel guitar), sentimental ballads (Cecil Gant's "I Wonder"), and jazz ("Big Yard"). Blues purists will perk up for revivals of Junior Parker's "Stranded" and Roy Milton's "Information Blues." *—Bill Dahl*

Texas Swing / 1988 / Rounder ♦♦♦♦♦

Standing My Ground / 1989 / Alligator ♦♦♦♦
A delightfully eclectic program spotlighting nearly all of Gate's musical leanings—blues, jazz, country, even a hearty taste of "Louisiana Zydeco"—and a revealing glimpse of his multi-instrumental abilities: he plays guitar, violin, drums, and piano! There's a tender remake of the Chuck Willis R&B ballad and a funk-tinged update of "Got My Mojo Working," but everything else is from Brown's own pen. *—Bill Dahl*

No Looking Back / 1992 / Alligator ♦♦♦

Man / 1995 / Verve ♦♦♦
Brown made the big jump to major-label stature for this typically unclassifiable set, which feistily sweeps through zydeco ("Big Mammou"), country ("Up Jumped the Devil"), Louis Jordan ("Early in the Morning"), and even a little blues along its unpredictable course. Cajun accordionist Jo-El Sonnier receives several solos in a guest-starring role. *—Bill Dahl*

American Music, Texas Style / Jun. 29, 1999 / Verve ♦♦♦
Clarence "Gatemouth" Brown was 74 when he recorded *American Music, Texas Style*, and the Texas bluesman made it clear that he still had plenty of energy. On this CD, Brown really emphasizes his love of jazz. Young hard bop players like trumpeter Nicholas Payton and alto saxman Wes Anderson are on board, and the veteran singer/guitarist offers no less than three standards from Duke Ellington's repertoire ("I'm Beginning to See the Light," "Don't Get Around Much Anymore," and son Mercer Ellington's "Things Ain't What They Used to Be") and two classics from Charlie Parker's years with Jay McShann ("Hootie Blues," "Jumpin' the Blues"). Meanwhile, the jazz influence is hard to miss on such fast jump blues as "Rock My Blues Away" and "Without Me Baby." Brown's voice is thinner than it used to be, but his guitar playing is as energetic as ever. While this CD isn't definitive, it's a good, solid effort that Brown can be proud of. *—Alex Henderson*

Nappy Brown (Napoleon Brown Goodson Culp)

b. Oct. 12, 1929, Charlotte, NC
Vocals / Jump Blues, Modern Electric Blues, R&B

Nobody sounded much like Nappy Brown during the mid-'50s. Exotically rolling his consonants with sing-song impugnity (allegedly, Savoy Records boss Herman Lubinsky thought Brown was singing in Yiddish), bellowing the blues with gospel-inspired ferocity, Brown rode rock & roll's first wave for a few glorious years before his records stopped selling. But in the early '80, Brown seemingly rose from the dead to stage a comeback bid. Now he's ensconced once again as a venerable blues veteran who'll stop at nothing (including rolling around the stage in sexual simulation) to enthrall his audience. Brown brought hellfire intensity to his blues-soaked Savoy debut, "Is It True," but it was the next year "Don't Be Angry", that caused his fortunes to skyrocket. The sizzling rocker sported loads of Brown's unique vocal gimmicks and a hair-raising tenor sax solo by Sam "The Man" Taylor, becoming his first national smash. Novelty-tinged upbeat items such as "Little by Little" and "Piddily Patter Patter" defined Nappy's output, but his throat-busting turn on the 1957 blues "The Right Time" remains a highlight of his early heyday. After decades away from the limelight, Nappy resurfaced in 1984 with a very credible album for Landslide Records, *Tore Up*. *—Bill Dahl*

Don't Be Angry! / Feb. 1, 1955-Oct. 4, 1956 / Savoy Jazz ✦✦✦✦✦
Rolling his consonants like a crazed cantor, shouter Nappy Brown brought a gospel-imbued fervor to his rocking mid-'50s R&B that few of his peers could match. Backed by some of New York's finest sessioneers, Brown roars 16 of his best early Savoy sides on this essential purchase. "Don't Be Angry," "Just a Little Love," "Open Up That Door," and "Bye Bye Baby" rate with his hottest jump efforts; "I Cried like a Baby" and "It's Really You" are hair-raising blues; and "Little by Little" rides a bouncy, pop-accessible groove. Now where's volume two? *—Bill Dahl*

Tore Up / Aug. 1984 / Alligator ✦✦✦
After too many years during which he was missing and presumed forever lost in action, Brown returned to prominence with this very credible album, cut with backing by guitarist Tinsley Ellis and the Heartfixers and originally issued on the tiny Landslide logo. He reprises his salacious blues "Lemon Squeezin' Daddy" and rolls his R's like the good old days on dusties by Little Walter, the Midnighters, Howlin' Wolf, and even Bob Dylan and the Allmans. *—Bill Dahl*

Something Gonna Jump out the Bushes / Apr. 1987 / Black Top ✦✦✦✦
Ultra-solid support from guitarists Anson Funderburgh, Eugene Ross, Ronnie Earl, and Earl King and Black Top's superb house horn section make this Dallas-cut set Brown's best contemporary album to date. His lusty shouting style works well on covers of the Dominoes' "Have Mercy Baby," the "5" Royales' title track, a pair of Earl King-penned numbers, and Robert Ward's "Your Love Is Real." *—Bill Dahl*

★ **Night Time Is the Right Time** / Jul. 18, 2000 / Savoy Jazz ✦✦✦✦✦
Night Time Is the Right Time is a two disc collection of 36 gems recorded by R&B singer Nappy Brown. With one foot grounded in the blues and the other stepping toward soul, Brown's mid- to late-'50s recordings are exciting and impressive. The first disc, with classics like "Don't Be Angry," "That Man," and "Two-Faced Woman (And a Lyin' Man)," is probably the best. The tight arrangements, filled with saxophone, piano, and electric guitar, place Brown's voice in the best light. He shouts, croons, and bends words playfully on upbeat numbers like "Just a Little Love" and "Piddily Patter Patter." While his voice is distinctive, it is the exuberant punch of his delivery that keeps his music vibrant some forty years after it was recorded. Even slower numbers, such as "Is that Really You?," find Brown building a soulful intensity, or the "slow burn" as it was called. There are several songs like "I've Had My Fun" on the second disc that fall more comfortably into the blues category. These are fine recordings, but straight R&B seemed to work best for his style. It should also be noted that whatever you call his music—R&B, soul, jump blues—much of it would have fit comfortably into '50s rock & roll, though it is certainly rawer and more exciting than the average Top 40 radio. This is fine R&B and a good collection for Brown fans. A great place to learn more about the roots of soul music. *—Ronnie Lankford, Jr.*

Roy Brown

b. Sep. 10, 1925, New Orleans, LA, **d.** May 25, 1981, San Fernando, CA
Vocals, Piano / Jump Blues, West Coast Blues, Rock & Roll, R&B
When you draw up a short list of the R&B pioneers who exerted a primary influence on the development of rock & roll, respectfully place singer Roy Brown's name near its very top. His seminal 1947 DeLuxe Records waxing of "Good Rockin' Tonight" was immediately ridden to the peak of the R&B charts by shouter Wynonie Harris and subsequently covered by Elvis Presley, Ricky Nelson, Jerry Lee Lewis, and many more early rock icons (even Pat Boone!). In addition, Brown's melismatically pleading, gospel-steeped delivery impacted the vocal styles of B.B. King, Bobby Bland, and Little Richard (among a plethora of important singers). Clearly, Roy Brown was an innovator and from 1948-1951, an R&B star whose wild output directly presaged rock's rise. Though Harris' version of "Good Rockin' Tonight" beat him out for top chart honors, Brown didn't have to wait long to dominate the R&B lists himself. He scored 15 hits from 1948 to 1951 for DeLuxe, ranging from emotionally wracked crying blues to party-time rockers. Strangely, his sales slumped badly during the early '50s, even though his output for Cincinnati's King label rates among his hottest. He briefly rejuvenated his commercial fortunes in 1957 with the single "Let the Four Winds Blow," recorded at Imperial. Inactive during much of the '60s, he'd begun to rebuild his long-lost momentum during the '70s when he died of a heart attack in 1981, his role as a crucial link between postwar R&B and rock's initial rise still underappreciated by the masses. *—Bill Dahl*

★ **Good Rocking Tonight: The Best of Roy Brown** / 1947-1957 / Rhino ✦✦✦✦✦
An unassailable 18-cut cross-section of the monstrously popular and influential New Orleans jump blues shouter's sides for DeLuxe, King, and Imperial labels that spans 1947-1957 and takes in his seminal "Good Rocking Tonight" (where it all began!), "Rockin' at Midnight," "Boogie at Midnight," and "Love Don't Love Nobody"; the almost unbearably tortured "Hard Luck Blues," and the unbelievably raunchy two-parter "Butcher Pete." Looking for the origins of rock? Here they are! *—Bill Dahl*

Mighty Mighty Man! / 1953-1959 / Ace ✦✦✦✦✦
Another British import that really delivers the rocking goods! This time zeroing in on Brown's 1953-59 King sides exclusively, the 22-cut CD shows that Brown actually picked up his tempos to meet rock's rise head on. The clever sequel "Ain't No Rocking No More," "Black Diamond," "Gal from Kokomo," and "Shake 'Em Up Baby" rate with his hottest rockers, with great support from a crew of Crescent City stalwarts. *—Bill Dahl*

The Complete Imperial Recordings / Sep. 27, 1956-Mar. 6, 1958 / Capitol ✦✦✦
In the mid-'50s Brown, like many other early R&B pioneers, was a bit lost at sea amid the rock & roll explosion. From 1956 to 1958, he recorded these 20 tracks for Imperial under the direction of legendary New Orleans R&B producer Dave Bartholomew. Brown and Bartholomew were attempting to update Brown's jump blues/R&B hybrid with a lot of Fats Domino-type Crescent City influence on these sides. The results weren't bad, but with Bartholomew co-writing most of the tunes and using local musicians like saxophonist Lee Allen, Brown sounded more like a journeyman New Orleans R&B singer than an innovative, bluesy forefather of rock & roll. There were a couple of commercial successes; his cover of Buddy Knox's "Party Doll" made the R&B Top 20, and "Let the Four Winds Blow" actually made the pop Top 40, although Fats Domino would have much greater success with the same song when he covered it a few years later. Diluted by occasional pop and rock influences, as well as a substandard variation of "Good Rockin' Tonight," this compilation shouldn't be the first Brown on your shelf. But for those who want to go a little further, it's packaged very well, with thorough liner notes and seven previously unissued cuts. *—Richie Unterberger*

Good Rockin' Tonight / 1978 / Route 66 ✦✦✦✦

Roy Buchanan

b. Sep. 23, 1939, Ozark, AL, **d.** Aug. 14, 1988, Fairfax, VA
Vocals, Guitar / Blues-Rock, Modern Electric Blues
Buchanan's reputation as a hot-shot guitarist extends back to the beginnings of rock & roll itself. On the road and recording with Dale Hawkins by his teens, Buchanan became the law of the land around the Washington, D.C., area by the mid- to late '60s. His use of the Fender Telecaster, using high harmonic squeals in place of feedback and distortion, was part and parcel of rock guitar's vocabulary by the early '70s. A reluctant superstar, Buchanan later became more unfocused as his career waned, but his unique stylings remain etched into his best records.

Sadly, when Buchanan seemed on the verge of a comeback in 1986, he hung himself in a police cell after he was arrested for public intoxication. He left behind a number of records which testify that he was a consummate guitarist, capable of tones and techniques that other guitarists only dream of. *—Cub Koda*

Roy Buchanan / Aug. 1972 / Polydor ✦✦✦✦✦
On his debut album, with a skunk-hot stage band, Buchanan's guitar sizzles on tracks like "Haunted House," "Sweet Dreams," and "The Messiah Will Come Again." *—Cub Koda*

Second Album / 1973 / Polydor ✦✦✦
More blues-based than his debut, this one features great stretched-out jams showcasing some of his best playing. *—Cub Koda*

That's What I Am Here For / Feb. 1974 / Polydor ✦✦✦✦
The late Roy Buchanan is a sadly underrated cult figure in the world of hard rock guitar. His aggressive attack, soulful selection of notes, and general playing attitude made him one of the most respected players of his generation. With heavy competition from musicians such as Eric Clapton, Duane Allman, and Jimi Hendrix, this is quite a feat. *That's What I Am Here For*, one of his earlier Polydor albums, illustrates all of the above artists in fine style. The extended reading of "Hey Joe" is enough to seal Buchanan's reputation, with some lightning fast and super heavy blues runs. Overall, the album suffers from some weak songwriting, but there are some gems, such as an extremely sad "Home Is Where I Lost Her," a tale of the death of a lady friend. Billy Price's vocals are a bit mannered and somewhat dated, but effective nonetheless. Another of the album's highlights is "Rodney's Song," a soulful Southern rocker that would have been at home on an early Allman Brothers album. Buchanan really rips on this one, and proves what an awesome player he really was. *—Matthew Greenwald*

Live Stock / Aug. 1975 / Polydor ✦✦✦✦✦
Brilliant live blues-rock guitar by the legend who turned down a spot in the Rolling Stones is must for guitar-hero fans. *—David Szatmary*

When a Guitar Plays the Blues / Jul. 1985 / Alligator ✦✦✦
This is an excellent example of the blues-rock guitar virtuoso's recent work. *—David Szatmary*

● **Sweet Dreams: The Anthology** / Sep. 22, 1992 / Polydor/Chronicles ✦✦✦✦✦
Over two CDs, *Sweet Dreams* collects the finest moments from Buchanan's '70s albums, including nine unreleased tracks; as a career retrospective, it's the finest collection available. *—Stephen Thomas Erlewine*

Guitar on Fire: Atlantic Sessions / Apr. 20, 1993 / Rhino ✦✦✦

Deluxe Edition / Jan. 30, 2001 / Alligator ✦✦✦✦✦

R.L. Burnside

b. Nov. 23, 1926, Oxford, MS
Vocals, Guitar / Juke-Joint Blues, Modern Delta Blues, Delta Blues, Electric Delta Blues, Electric Blues, Modern Electric Blues
North Mississippi guitarist R.L. Burnside is one of the paragons of state-of-the-art Delta juke-joint blues. He learned his music from his neighbor, Fred McDowell, and the highly rhythmic style that Burnside plays is evident in McDowell's recording as well. Burnside's music is pure country Delta juke-joint blues, heavily rhythm-oriented and played with a slide. Up until the mid-'80s, he was primarily a farmer and fisherman. After getting some attention in the late '60s via folklorists David Evans and George Mitchell, he recorded for the Vogue, Swingmaster, and Highwater record labels. Although he had done short tours, it wasn't until the late '80s that he was invited to perform at several European blues festivals. In 1996, Burnside teamed with indie-rocker Jon Spencer to cut *A Ass Pocket O' Whiskey* for the hip Matador label; he returned to Fat Possum in 1998 for the more conventional *Come on In*. *—Richard Skelly*

● **Too Bad Jim** / 1994 / Epitaph ✦✦✦✦✦
Too Bad Jim is cut from the same cloth as its predecessor, *Bad Luck City*. It features R.L. Burnside fronting a small juke-joint combo, tearing through some greasy blues. However, *Too Bad Jim* is the better album, simply from a performance standpoint. Burnside sounds more relaxed and the band steps back from the spotlight slightly, letting the guitarist burn brightly on his own, showcasing his deep blues roots. *—Thom Owens*

AAss Pocket of Whiskey / Jun. 25, 1996 / Matador ♦♦♦♦
Although he had been playing for years, it wasn't until the '90s that R.L. Burnside's raw electrified Delta blues was heard by a wide audience. His new fans celebrated his wild, unbridled energy, so it made sense for him to team with the Jon Spencer Blues Explosion, the warped indie-rock band that's all about energy. However, the very purists who celebrate Burnside hate Spencer, believing that he mocks the blues. As the blistering *A Ass Pocket O' Whiskey* proves, Spencer may not treat the blues with reverence, but he and his band capture the wild essence of juke-joint blues. And that makes them the perfect match for Burnside, who knows his history but isn't burdened by it. Together, Burnside and the Blues Explosion make raw, scintillating, unvarnished blues that positively burns. *—Thom Owens*

Mr. Wizard / Mar. 11, 1997 / Fat Possum/Epitaph ♦♦♦

Sound Machine Groove / Jul. 22, 1997 / HMG ♦♦♦
Recorded by folklorist David Evans in 1979 and 1980, these are Burnside's first recordings with electric guitar and also his first with a band. That band was the Sound Machine, a band he literally created himself out of members of his own family, blending raw Mississippi blues with soul, funk, R&B, and other urban flavors to make a marvelous amalgam of his own. Contemporary beats and modern themes like "Bad Luck City," "Searching for My Baby," "Can't Let You Go," and "Sound Machine Groove" sit nicely alongside slower, traditional material like "Going Down South" and "Begged for a Nickel," while R.L.'s duets with drummer Calvin Jackson on "Goin' Away Baby" and "Long Haired Doney" show a marvelous empathy and interplay. Especially notable is a version of "Sitting on Top of the World" with Burnside on slide guitar that, with Jackson's help, neatly evokes the sound and feel of a fife and drum band. Although R.L. is presently the darling of the blues crowd and hailed as something of an overnight success, one listen to this disc tells you he was already forging a new chapter in the Mississippi blues tradition with these recordings. *—Cub Koda*

Acoustic Stories / Sep. 23, 1997 / M.C. ♦♦♦

Come on In / Aug. 11, 1998 / Epitaph ♦♦♦

My Black Name A-Ringin' / 1999 / Genes ♦♦♦
R.L. Burnside has been playing the blues since the '50s, but providing for his large family (he would eventually have 13 children) and his love for his hometown kept him from supporting himself with his music until the '80s. These recordings were made in 1969 when blues musician Big Joe Williams led a carload of Adelphi Records filmmakers and sound engineers on a tour through the blues country from Chicago south to Mississippi. Burnside was one of the highlights of the trip, and the crew ended up setting up camp near his home for some time to record. *My Black Name A-Ringin'* presents Burnside in a stripped-down, acoustic form and shows his native north hill country style as well as some early influences. Each song shows off a different facet of his style: "Goin' Down South" is a hypnotic drone with short, repetitive rhythmic sections; "Two Trains Runnin'" features more of a traditional Delta style with its deep, sad harmonica; and "My Black Name A-Ringin'" shows what Burnside could do with a traditional song dating as far back as slavery. Overall, this album presents an interesting prequel to Burnside's recordings with Fat Possum Records and his experimentalism in the '90s. *—Stacia Proefrock*

Mississippi Hill Country Blues / Jul. 11, 2000 / Swingmaster ♦♦♦
It's a pleasure to hear R.L. Burnside's early acoustic blues played the way he learned them in the hill country of Northern Mississippi. Three of these tracks date from 1967 and were recorded in Coldwater, MS by folklorist George Mitchell, while the remaining 16 were recorded in the early '80s by Swingmaster operator Leo Bruin in Groningen, Netherlands. This is Burnside playing solo (and mainly) acoustic country-blues with the only addition to his guitar and voice being the harmonica of Red Ramsey on "Rolling and Tumbling." While you can't go wrong with the purchase of any Burnside recording, these Swingmaster sessions portray a natural relaxed unaccompanied Burnside. Recorded long before the mid-'90s, Fat Possum releases would find him playing in an electric band with his son and son-in-law and occasionally experimenting with sampling and indie rock leanings. *—Al Campbell*

Paul Butterfield

b. Dec. 17, 1942, Chicago, IL, **d.** May 4, 1987, Hollywood, CA
Vocals, Harmonica, Guitar, Flute / Modern Electric Chicago Blues, Harmonica Blues, Blues-Rock, Electric Chicago Blues
The first two Paul Butterfield Blues Band albums are essential from an historical perspective. While *East-West*, the second album, with its Eastern influence and extended solos set the tone for psychedelic rockers, it was that incredible first album that alerted the music scene as to what was coming. Although it has been perhaps over-emphasized in recent years, it is important to point out that the release of *The Paul Butterfield Blues Band* on Elektra in 1965, had a huge effect on the white music culture of the time. Used to hearing blues covered by groups like the Rolling Stones, that first album had an enormous impact on young (and primarily white) rock players. Here is no deferential imitation of black music by whites, but a racially-mixed hard-driving blues album that, in a word, rocked. It was a signal to white players to stop making respectful tributes to black music, and just play it. In a flash the image of blues as old-time music was gone. Modern Chicago, style urban blues was out of the closet and introduced to mainstream white audiences, who loved it. Fueled by guitarist Michael Bloomfield's infatuation with Eastern music and Indian ragas at the time and aided by Billy Davenport's jazz-driven sophistication on drums, there arose in the group a new music form that was to greatly affect rock music—the extended solo. There is little question that here is the root of psychedelic (acid) rock—a genuine fusion between East and West. Those first two albums served as a wakeup call to an entire generation of White would-be blues musicians. Speaking as one who was on the scene, that first Butterfield album stopped us in our tracks and we were never the same afterward. It changed our lives. *—Michael Erlewine*

An Offer You Can't Refuse / 1963 / M.I.L. Multimedia ♦♦♦
An album released on the Red Lightnin' label in 1972 consists of one side of Big Walter Horton and the other side with very early Paul Butterfield (1963) (See: Big Walter Horton). It contains six tracks with Butterfield, Smokey Smothers on guitar, Jerome Arnold on bass, and Sam Lay on drums. This was recorded at *Big Johns*, the North side Chicago club where the Butterfield Band first played in 1963, some two years before the material on the first Paul Butterfield Blues Band album, which was released in 1965. The six tracks include two instrumentals, "Got My Mojo Working" and the Butterfield-authored tune "Loaded." Although this is very early Butterfield, the harp playing is excellent and already in his own unique style. The singing is a little rough and heavy sounding. Butterfield fans will want to find this rare vinyl for musical and historical reasons. *—Michael Erlewine*

The Original Lost Elektra Sessions / Dec. 1964 / Rhino ♦♦♦♦♦
All but one of these 19 tracks were recorded in December, 1964, as Butterfield's projected first LP; the results were scrapped and replaced by their official self-titled debut, cut a few months later. With both Bloomfield and Bishop already in tow, these sessions rank among the earliest blues-rock ever laid down. Extremely similar in feel to the first album, it's perhaps a bit rawer in production and performance, but not appreciably worse or different than what ended up on the actual debut LP. Dedicated primarily to electric Chicago blues standards, Butterfield fans will find this well worth acquiring, as most of the selections were never officially recorded by the first lineup (although different renditions of five tracks showed up on the first album and the *What's Shakin'* compilation). *—Richie Unterberger*

☆ **Paul Butterfield Blues Band** / 1965 / Elektra ♦♦♦♦♦
Butterfield's unique amplified harmonica style is already present on this classic first album—a wakeup call for a generation of young white players used to hearing blues filtered through covers by groups like the Rolling Stones or as a part of music history. Here was a racially mixed group of brilliant young players that rocked—an historic album. Great guitar from Michael Bloomfield and Elvin Bishop comes, with Mark Naftalin (organ), Jerome Arnold (bass), and Sam Lay (drums). *—Michael Erlewine*

★ **East-West** / 1966 / Elektra ♦♦♦♦♦
The second Butterfield album had an even greater effect on music history, paving the way for experimentation that is still being explored today. This came in the form of an extended blues-rock solo (some 13 minutes)—a real fusion of jazz and blues inspired by the Indian raga. This ground-breaking instrumental was the first of its kind and marks the root from which the acid rock tradition emerged. *—Jeff Tarmarkin & Michael Erlewine*

East-West Live / 1966-1967 / Winner ♦♦♦♦
The tune "East-West" from the second Butterfield Blues Band album of the same name made music history. It is arguably the first extended rock solo, a fusing of blues-rock with Eastern scales and tone. Here is the root of psychedelic-acid rock. Now, thanks to Mark Naftalin (the original Butterfield keyboardist), we have three live recordings of "East-West" recorded in 1966-1967 that capture the origin and development of this classic tune. The first example (some 12 minutes) was taped prior to the edited studio version; the second (16 minutes) and third (28 minutes) were recorded after the album cut. There is some great music (and music history) here. *—Michael Erlewine*

The Resurrection of Pigboy Crabshaw / 1967 / Elektra ♦♦♦♦♦

Strawberry Jam / 1996 / Winner ♦♦♦

An Anthology—*The Elektra Years* / Oct. 28, 1997 / *Elektra* ♦♦♦♦♦
An Anthology—The Elektra Years is a double-disc, 33-song set that offers a comprehensive overview of Paul Butterfield's eight years with the label. His first two albums, *Paul Butterfield Blues Band* and *East-West*, were seminal, groundbreaking records that blurred the boundaries between blues, jazz, and rock, suggesting everything from blues-rock to psychedelia. They were stunning achievements which proved to be difficult to match, but Butterfield's remaining albums for the label all had a few good cuts. *An Anthology* does a nice job of rounding up those highlights, picking the best moments from uneven records; consequently, it's quite a valuble package for listeners who simply want a sampling from those later albums instead of purchasing them individually. Butterfield's first two albums remain necessary listens in their own right, but this set offers an excellent summary of his entire stint with Elektra. *—Stephen Thomas Erlewine*

Gus Cannon

b. Sep. 12, 1885, Bed Banks, MS, **d.** Oct. 15, 1979, Memphis, TN
Jug, Kazoo, Piano, Guitar, Fiddle, Banjo / Jug Band, Prewar Blues, Country, Blues, Acoustic Memphis Blues, Acoustic Blues
A remarkable musician (he could play five-string banjo and jug simultaneously!), Gus Cannon bridged the gap between early blues and the minstrel and folk styles which preceded it. His band of the '20s and '30s, Cannon's Jug Stompers, represents the apogee of jug-band style. Songs they recorded, notably the raggy "Walk Right In," were staples of the folk repertoire decades later; and Cannon himself continued to record and perform into the '70s. The early 1900s found him playing around Memphis with songster Jim Jackson and forming a partnership with Noah Lewis whose harmonica wizardry would be basic to the Jug Stompers sound. In 1914, Cannon began work with a succession of medicine shows which would continue into the '40s, and where he further developed his style and repertoire. His recording career began with Paramount sessions in 1927. Side projects included duets with Blind Blake and the first ever recordings of slide banjo. Cannon resumed his stalled recording efforts in 1956 with sessions for Folkways. Subsequent sessions paired him with other Memphis survivors like Furry Lewis. *—Steve James*

Walk Right In / 1962 / Stax ♦♦♦
In June of 1963, 79-year-old Gus Cannon went into the studio in Memphis to cut his first recording in close to seven years, all a result of the Rooftoop Singers having made his "Walk Right In" into a number one single. The producers didn't ask for too much out of Cannon, to judge from the results—just that he sit there with his banjo and old friends Will Shade (jug) and Milton Roby (washboard) backing him, and do his favorite songs. He introduces a few of them in separately indexed spoken passages, and runs through them in leisurely if dedicated fashion: the title track (which is much bluesier than the hit in Cannon's hands), "Salty

Dog" (the best track here), "Gonna Raise a Ruckus Tonight," "Make Me a Pallet on Your Floor," and "Crawdad Hole." The album is almost an audio documentary tour through different corners of Cannon's life and career that, ideally, might've run to several volumes. *—Bruce Eder*

● **The Complete Recordings** / Yazoo ✦✦✦✦✦
Complete Works compiles all of the recordings Cannon's Jug Stompers made in the late '20s. Gus Cannon and the Jug Stompers were the definitive jug band and all of their classic tracks, including "Walk Right In," are featured on this essential single-disc collection. *—Thom Owens*

Leroy Carr

b. Mar. 27, 1905, Nashville, TN, **d.** Apr. 29, 1935, Indianapolis, IN
Vocals, Piano / Piano Blues
The term "urban blues" is usually applied to post-World War II blues-band music, but one of the forefathers of the genre in its pre-electric format was pianist Leroy Carr. Teamed with the exemplary guitarist Scrapper Blackwell in Indianapolis, Carr became one of the top blues stars of his day, composing and recording almost 200 sides during his short lifetime, including such classics as "How Long, How Long," "Prison Bound Blues," "When the Sun Goes Down," and "Blues Before Sunrise." His blues were expressive and evocative, recorded only with piano and guitar, yet as author Sam Charters has noted, Carr was "a city man" whose singing was never as rough or intense as the country bluesmen's; and as reissue producer Francis Smith put it, "He, perhaps more than any other single artist, was responsible for transforming the rural blues patterns of the '20s into the more city-oriented blues of the '30s." *—Jim O'Neal & Stephen Thomas Erlewine*

★ **Blues Before Sunrise** / 1962 / Portrait ✦✦✦✦✦
Despite minimal sound quality, this reissue contains some prime Leroy Carr/Scrapper Blackwell material. They were arguably the greatest piano and guitar duo to emerge in the late '20s and early '30s. You can find these tracks on other import collections, but this was among the first reissues available on a domestic label. *—Ron Wynn*

☆ **Naptown Blues (1929-1934)** / 1988 / Yazoo ✦✦✦✦✦
A seminal piano/guitar duo, Leroy Carr was among the most influential early blues singer/pianists, and Scrapper Blackwell was a remarkably fluid guitarist. *—Mark A. Humphrey*

Bo Carter (Armenter "Bo" Chatmon)

b. Mar. 21, 1893, Bolton, MS, **d.** Sep. 21, 1964, Memphis, TN
Vocals, Guitar, Clarinet, Bass, Banjo / Dirty Blues, Delta Blues, Country-Blues, Acoustic Blues
Bo Carter (Armenter "Bo" Chatmon) had an unequaled capacity for creating sexual metaphors in his songs, specializing in such ribald imagery as "Banana in Your Fruit Basket," "Pin in Your Cushion," and "Your Biscuits Are Big Enough for Me." One of the most popular bluesmen of the '30s, he recorded enough material for several reissue albums, and he was quite an original guitar picker, or else three of those albums wouldn't have been released by Yazoo. (Carter employed a number of different keys and tunings on his records, most of which were solo vocal and guitar performances.) Carter's facility extended beyond the risqué business to more serious blues themes, and he was also the first to record the standard "Corrine Corrina" (1928). Bo and his brothers Lonnie and Sam Chatmon also recorded as members of the Mississippi Sheiks with singer/guitarist Walter Vinson. *—Jim O'Neal*

● **Greatest Hits, 1930-1940** / Feb. 1970 / Yazoo ✦✦✦✦✦
With mostly solo selections by Carter, plus a couple of Mississippi Sheiks songs, it features very fine and distinctive country-blues guitar playing and singing. Most of the songs are of the double-entendre variety—a possible reason why he's not as well known as he deserves to be, since some blues researchers did not deem his material worthy. As with most Yazoo releases, the liner notes include various guitar tunings and chord progressions for each song—fascinating for guitarists. *—George Bedard*

Banana in Your Fruit Basket / 1978 / Yazoo ✦✦✦✦
Bo Carter is the alias for singer/guitarist Bo Chatmon, a member of the famous Chatmon family from Mississippi (which produced 13 musically capable children). Notorious for his double-entendre blues, Carter based his songs around sexual metaphors and the results were, unsurprisingly, widely popular. If there were such a thing as parental warning stickers in the '30s, they would have been applied liberally to Carter's releases. On *Banana in Your Fruit Basket* (the companion to *Twist It Baby*), Yazoo brings together 14 more Carter sides from the '30s. A cursory glance at track titles alone tells a great deal: "Mashing That Thing," "Don't Mash My Digger So Deep," "Pin in Your Cushion," "My Pencil Won't Write Anymore." The themes in Carter's music were certainly pervasive in the country-blues of the period, but they were rarely as explicit. Whereas one singer might ask "Baby, where'd you stay last night? You got the hair all tangled and you ain't talkin' right" (a stock blues verse), few would ask the same woman "Baby, what kind of scent is that?" when she walks through the door. Often, Carter's metaphors are so thin that the results have little value beyond their novelty. Musically, Carter has a relaxed, clear, and fairly indistinct singing style and a fluid, fingerpicking guitar attack to match it. While *Banana in Your Fruit Basket* paints an accurate picture of Bo Chatmon's al-
ter ego, the music is very much a product of its time. Giving insight into what people appreciated in their entertainment, it also feels like proof that not much has changed. *—Nathan Bush*

William Clarke

b. Mar. 29, 1951, Inglewood, CA, **d.** Nov. 2, 1996, Fresno, CA
Vocals, Harmonica / Modern Electric Chicago Blues, Harmonica Blues, Electric Chicago Blues
I have had the very good fortune to hear great Chicago harp (harmonica) players like Little Walter, Junior Wells, Big Walter Horton, and many others playing live in the clubs of Chicago during the mid-'60s. Those days are gone and I had given up hope of ever hearing a new voice on amplified blues harp again in my lifetime. Then came William Clarke. Technically, Clarke was a master of both the cross and chromatic harps. He took blues on the chromatic up to and well beyond where Little Walter left it years ago. But far more important than the technique is the music. Clarke plays straight-ahead blues that is music to the ears—and it rocks. Clarke started playing the harmonica in 1967, and worked with George "Harmonica" Smith, a veteran of the Muddy Waters band, from 1977 until Smith passed away in 1983. Clarke recorded a number of albums prior to releasing his first CD. They are *Hittin' Heavy* (Good Time, 1978), *Blues from Los Angeles* (1980), *Can't You Hear Me Calling* (Watch Dog, 1983), *Tip of the Top* (Satch, 1987—nominated for a Handy award) and *Rockin' the Boat* (Riviera, 1988). Clarke died on an operating table in Fresno, CA on November 2, 1996. He was only 45 years old. His presence in the blues world is missed. William Clarke (along with Big Walter Horton and Paul Butterfield) had an almost impeccable sense of which notes to play. There are a lot of players out there (white and black) that basically play what's on the records of the great Chicago artists. Nothing wrong with this, but no news there either. Clarke was an original. Having heard him play live a number of times, I can testify that here is the real thing—an extension of the classic Chicago-style amplified harp tradition into the present. Just listen to those first two Alligator albums—it's all on the CDs. *—Michael Erlewine*

Tip of the Top / 1987 / King Ace ✦✦✦
Tip of the Top is a loose tribute to William Clarke's mentor, George Harmonica Smith, who taught Clarke many of his tricks. Clarke plays a selection of tracks that were staples in Smith's catalog (including a version of "Hard Times," which features Smith himself), as well as newer songs written in the same style. But what really makes *Tip of the Top* notable is how William Clarke begins to develop his distinctive, idiosyncratic sound on the record. Unlike his debut *Can't You Hear Me Calling, Tip of the Top* explores some new sounds, which would come to fruition in his next few albums. *—Thom Owens*

★ **Blowin' Like Hell** / 1990 / Alligator ✦✦✦✦✦
The title says it all. William Clarke cooks on this one, his first CD. And these are new sounds. Songs like "Lollipop Mama," "Gambling for My Bread," and "Lonesome Bedroom Blues" (all written by Clarke) are just great tunes. "Must Be Jelly" won Clarke a W.C. Handy Award for blues song of the year in 1991. I find myself humming them. Clarke's timing and music are right on the money, with the great Alex Schultz on lead guitar. There is no doubt that Clarke is one of the few modern bluesmen who is exploring and extending the amplified blues harp tradition without violating any of its principles. No one plays chromatic blues harp with this kind of passion and sheer conviction. Hear for yourself. *—Michael Erlewine*

Serious Intentions / 1992 / Alligator ✦✦✦✦✦
His follow-up to *Blowin' Like Hell* burns with a ferocious intensity, particularly for his groundbreaking work on chromatic harp and his ability to cover all styles with remarkable elan. Again, he wrote most of the songs, and "Pawnshop Bound," "Trying to Stretch My Money," and "With a Tear in My Eye" are real songs. Instrumentals like "Chasin' the Gator" feature Clarke with Alex Schultz on lead guitar. *—Cub Koda & Michael Erlewine*

Groove Time / 1994 / Alligator ✦✦✦✦
Here is Clarke, hot again. This time he has added a horn section on some cuts for this recording. No problem. Alex Schultz is there on lead guitar to make sure that this album rocks. Clarke once again writes most of the songs—all 15 fat tracks. By this time, his Alligator albums have a style and feel (all his own) that one looks forward to. Plenty of high-impact amplified chromatic harmonica here of the push-the-band-hard variety that Clarke does so well, plus some tasty acoustic thrown in too. *—Michael Erlewine*

The Hard Way / 1996 / Alligator ✦✦✦✦
His fourth CD from Alligator is his jazziest and bluesist recording to date. Clarke has written half of the compositions and put his own sound and style on those he did not write. Highlights include "The Boss" (inspired by saxophonist Willis Jackson) which is a fast jump that finds chromatic harp riffing along with a horn section—some interesting ideas. Other tunes are the Benny Moten tune "Moten Swing," "My Mind is Working Overtime" (a Latin-tinged tune written by Clarke), and "Letter from Home." *—Michael Erlewine*

Deluxe Edition / Feb. 23, 1999 / Alligator ✦✦✦✦
Clarke was the new harmonica genius for the millennium when his heart gave out on tour in 1996 and he passed away at age 45. This deluxe edition brings together 16 tracks culled primarily from his four Alligator albums along with three previously unreleased tracks from sessions conducted in 1986 and 1995, every track a winner. Clarke's tone is massive and only outdone by the wealth of ideas he constantly poured into his instrument. While others were still trying to imitate Little Walter, Clarke took the lessons he learned from George "Harmonica" Smith and built one of the most original and truly breathtaking styles in modern blues. Consider this disc his lasting legacy. *—Cub Koda*

Willie Clayton

b. Mar. 29, 1955, Indianola, MS
Vocals / Retro-Soul, Chicago Blues
As long as he's been recording (since 1969), one might think that Willie Clayton is an old geezer. No way—he's barely past the age of 40 and is just hitting his commercial stride with a couple of blues-soul albums for Ace that have sold well to the Southern market (where the two interrelated idioms have never been deemed mutually exclusive). After his debut single for Duplex, "That's the Way Daddy Did," went nowhere, Clayton left Mississippi for Chicago in 1971. Like his older Windy City compatriots Otis Clay and Syl Johnson, the young singer ended up contracted to Hi Records in Memphis, where he worked with producer Willie Mitchell and the vaunted Hi rhythm section. Hi issued a series of fine Clayton efforts on its Pawn subsidiary, including "I Must Be Losin' You," "It's Time You Made Up Your Mind," and "Baby You're Ready," but none of them hit. Finally, in 1984, Clayton enjoyed a taste of soul success when his "Tell Me" (produced by General Crook) and "What a Way to Put It" for Compleat Records nudged on to the R&B charts. *Let's Get Together,* Clayton's 1993 album for Johnny Vincent's Ace logo, was a smooth soul-blues hybrid dominated by originals but titled

after Al Green's immortal hit. *Simply Beautiful,* his Ace follow-up, found Clayton mixing dusties by Rev. Al, Aretha Franklin, and Arthur Crudup with his own stuff. *It's About Love* followed in 1999. *—Bill Dahl*

Let's Get Together / 1993 / Ace ✦✦✦
Contemporary Southern deep soul has a strong taste of blues underlying. The clever "Three People (Sleeping in My Bed)" and "Back Street Love Affair," along with the self-penned "Feels like Love" and "Let Me Love You," are attractive showcases for Clayton's warm, assured vocal delivery. *—Bill Dahl*

Simply Beautiful / 1994 / Ace ✦✦✦
this one more of the same—Clayton's intimate confident vocals framed in terms midway between deep soul and contemporary blues. His own "Lose What You Got" and "Crazy for You" rate highly, along with Frank Johnson's "Love Stealing Ain't Worth Stealing" and the singer's delicate revival of Al Green's title cut. *—Bill Dahl*

● **Chicago Soul Greats** / Jul. 18, 1995 / Hi ✦✦✦✦

Ace in the Hole / Feb. 13, 1996 / Ace ✦✦✦✦
The most consistent and satisfying of Clayton's contemporary output for Johnny Vincent's reactivated Ace imprint, thanks to top-flight soul-blues items like "Hurt by Love" and "My Baby's Cheating on Me," the Bob Jones-penned "Equal Opportunity" and "Bartender's Blues," and the singer's own "Happy." *—Bill Dahl*

Albert Collins

b. Oct. 3, 1932, Leona, TX, **d.** Nov. 24, 1993, Las Vegas, NV
Vocals, Guitar / Modern Electric Texas Blues, Electric Texas Blues
Albert Collins, "The Master of the Telecaster," "The Iceman," and "The Razor Blade" was robbed of his best years as a blues performer by a bout with liver cancer that ended with his premature death on November 24, 1993. He was just 61 years old. Collins began performing in the clubs of Houston by the mid-'50s, going after his own style, characterized by his use of minor tunings and a capo. . It was also at this point that he began his "guitar walks" through the audience, which made him wildly popular with the younger white audiences he played for years later in the '80s. He led a ten-piece band, the Rhythm Rockers, and cut his first single in 1958, "The Freeze." The single was followed by a slew of other instrumental singles with catchy titles, including "Sno-Cone," "Icy Blue," and "Don't Lose Your Cool." All of these singles brought Collins a regional following. After recording "De-Frost" b/w "Albert's Alley" for Hall-Way Records of Beaumont, TX, he hit it big in 1962 with "Frosty," a million-selling single. The tune quickly became part of his ongoing repertoire, and was still part of his live shows more than 30 years later. Collins' percussive, ringing guitar style became his trademark, as he would use his right hand to pluck the strings. Collins' big break came about in 1977, when he was signed to the Chicago-based Alligator Records, and he released his brilliant debut for the label in 1978, *Ice Pickin'.* Collins recorded six more albums for the label, culminating in 1986's *Cold Snap.* It was at Alligator that Collins began to realize that he could sing adequately, and working with his wife Gwynn, he co-wrote many of his classic songs, including items like "Mastercharge" and "Conversation with Collins." *—Richard Skelly*

Love Can Be Found Anywhere / 1969 / Imperial ✦✦✦

Truckin' with Albert Collins / 1969 / MCA ✦✦✦✦✦
Truckin' with Albert Collins is a 1969 Blue Thumb reissue of *The Cool Sound of Albert Collins,* which was originally released on TCF Hall Records in 1965. These are the earliest recordings that Collins made and already his trademark sound is in place—his leads are stinging, piercing, and direct. The album features a set of blistering instrumentals (with the exception of the vocal "Dyin' Flu") that would eventually become his signature tunes, including "Frosty" and "Frostbite." Collins doesn't just stick to blues, he adds elements of surf, rock, jazz, and R&B. These songs may not have been hits at the time, but they helped establish his reputation as the Master of the Telecaster. *—Thom Owens*

★ **Ice Pickin'** / 1978 / Alligator ✦✦✦✦✦
Ice Pickin' is the album that brought Albert Collins directly back into the limelight, and for good reason, too. The record captures the wild, unrestrained side of his playing that had never quite been documented before. Though his singing doesn't quite have the fire or power of his playing, the album doesn't suffer at all because of that—he simply burns throughout the album. *Ice Pickin'* was his first release for Alligator Records and it set the pace for all the albums that followed. No matter how much he tried, Collins never completely regained the pure energy that made *Ice Pickin'* such a revelation. *—Thom Owens*

Frostbite / 1980 / Alligator ✦✦✦
Frostbite was the first indication that Albert Collins' Alligator albums were going to follow something of a formula. The album replicated all of the styles and sounds of *Ice Pickin',* but the music lacked the power of its predecessor. Nevertheless, there was a wealth of fine playing on the album, even if the quality of the songs themselves is uneven. *—Thom Owens*

Frozen Alive! / 1981 / Alligator ✦✦✦
Frozen Alive! demonstrates the exuberant power of Albert Collins in concert and contains enough first-rate solos to make it a worthwhile listen for fans of his icy style. *—Thom Owens*

Don't Lose Your Cool / 1983 / Alligator ✦✦✦✦
Keeping up with his "Iceman" moniker, Albert Collins delivers with his fourth Alligator release *Don't Lose Your Cool.* The title cut was one of his first instrumental hits back in the late '50s and here it's given a gritty, organ-driven workout à la one of his heroes and onetime collaborators, Jimmy McGriff. Forging on in this impressively diverse set, Collins revels in the humorous, spoken commentary of Oscar Brown Jr.'s "But I Was Cool" (reminiscent of Collins' spoken interludes on the John Zorn piece "Spillane"), updates the jump-blues antics of Big Walter Price's "Get to Gettin'," and closes the set out with a faithful take on Guitar Slim's "Quicksand." He also adds a few of his own impressive cuts here, including the funky, syncopated New Orleans groove "Melt Down" and the Stax 'n' blues cut "Ego Trip." Throughout, of course, Collins comes up with plenty of his grating, barbed- wire guitar licks and rough-hewn vocals. Riding atop his crack, seven-piece Ice Breakers band (including a fine horn section), Collins certainly keeps things burnin' on this set, while still living up to all the icy allusions with some of the most cool and urbane modern blues on record. *—Stephen Cook*

Live in Japan / 1984 / Alligator ✦✦✦

Showdown / 1985 / Alligator ✦✦✦✦
In a summit meeting between Texas guitar veterans Collins and Johnny Copeland and newcomer Robert Cray, the set is scorching all the way. *—Bill Dahl*

Cold Snap / 1986 / Alligator ✦✦✦

☆ **The Complete Imperial Recordings** / 1991 / EMI ✦✦✦✦✦
Texan Albert Collins was in the very first rank of post-war blues guitarists. This two-CD set is a reissue of all 36 sides he cut for Imperial from 1968 to 1970—representing this artist's second major recording stint. Instrumentals comprise roughly three-fourths of the material. They frame his distinctive guitar work with a tight ensemble of organ, bass, and drums, adding at times a piano and/or second guitar, punctuated by a horn section. About ten of these tunes are as great as anything Collins ever did. They are riddled with the biting, incisive, dramatic, and economical playing that made him a legend. There are also some outstanding vocals. Although this set is not without its clinkers, it is a solid package and a must for any Collins fan. *—Larry Hoffman*

Iceman / 1991 / Virgin ✦✦✦

Collins Mix: The Best / Oct. 5, 1993 / Pointblank ✦✦✦✦
This provided fresh looks at 11 Collins classics, among them such epic numbers as "Don't Lose Your Cool," "Frosty," "Honey Hush," and "Tired Man." There were slow, wailing ballads with blistering solos, electrifying up-tempo wailers with a great horn section answering Collins' phrases with their own bleats, and first-rate mastering and production. Guest stars included B.B. King, Branford Marsalis, Kim Wilson, and Gary Moore, while Collins injected vitality into numbers he'd already made standards years ago. This set is a wonderful tribute to an incredible guitarist and musician. *—Ron Wynn*

Live 92/93 / Sep. 12, 1995 / Pointblank ✦✦✦

Deluxe Edition / 1997 / Alligator ✦✦✦✦✦
Deluxe Edition is a solid, albeit imperfect, 13-track collection of highlights from Albert Collins' latter-day recordings for Alligator. There are only a handful of genuine classics, but there are a lot of great performances that spotlight Collins' stinging guitar work and impassioned vocals. Nevertheless, it's only adequate as an introduction, since *Ice Pickin'* remains the place to become acquainted with Collins' blistering blues. *—Stephen Thomas Erlewine*

Johnny Copeland

b. Mar. 27, 1937, Haynesville, LA, **d.** Jul. 3, 1997, New York, NY
Vocals, Guitar / Modern Electric Texas Blues, Electric Texas Blues
Considering the amount of time he spent steadily rolling from gig to gig, Johnny "Clyde" Copeland's rise to prominence in the blues world in the early '90s isn't all that surprising. A contract with the PolyGram/Verve label put his '90s recordings into the hands of thousands of blues lovers around the world. It's not that Copeland's talent changed all that much since he recorded for Rounder Records in the '80s; it's just that major companies began to see the potential of great, hardworking blues musicians like Copeland. Unfortunately, Copeland was forced to slow down in 1995-96 by heart-related complications, yet he continued to perform shows until his death in July of 1997. His music, by his own reasoning, fell somewhere between the funky R&B of New Orleans and the swing and jump blues of Kansas City. He began recording in 1958 with "Rock 'n' Roll Lily" for Mercury, and moved between various labels during the '60s, including All Boy and Golden Eagle in Houston, where he had regional successes with "Please Let Me Know" and "Down on Bending Knees," and later for Wand and Atlantic in New York. In 1965, he displayed a surprising prescience in terms of the pop market by cutting a version of Bob Dylan's "Blowin' in the Wind" for Wand. Beginning in 1981, Copeland recorded seven albums for Rounder Records; he won a Grammy award in 1986 for his efforts on an Alligator album, *Showdown!* with Robert Cray and Albert Collins. *—Richard Skelly & Bruce Eder*

● **Copeland Special** / 1981 / Rounder ✦✦✦✦✦
This immaculate collection put the veteran Houston axeman among the blues elite; it features searing guitar and soulful vocals. *—Bill Dahl*

Make My Home Where I Hang My Hat / 1982 / Rounder ✦✦✦
This second Rounder Records album has its share of incendiary moments. *—Bill Dahl*

Texas Twister / 1983 / Rounder ✦✦✦✦✦
Johnny Copeland's tenure on Rounder Records was mostly productive. He made several albums that ranged from decent to very good, increased his audience and name recognition and got better recording facilities and company support than at most times in his career. The 15 numbers on this anthology cover four Rounder sessions, and include competent renditions of familiar numbers. But what makes things special are the final three selections; these were part of Copeland's superb and unjustly underrated *Bringing It Back Home* album, recorded in Africa, which matched Texas shuffle licks with swaying, riveting African rhythms. *—Ron Wynn*

Bringin' It All Back Home / 1986 / Rounder ✦✦✦✦

Ain't Nothing But a Party / 1988 / Rounder ✦✦✦
Texas guitarist and vocalist Johnny Copeland didn't turn in a formula job on these six tunes recorded live at the 1987 Juneteenth festival. Indeed, the concert setting seems to put some juice in Copeland's singing; his voice isn't raspy or detached, and he actually seems exuberant about doing the umpteenth version of "Big Time" and "Baby, Please Don't Go." His band, especially saxophonist Bert McGowan, also seem to get new life from the crowd reaction and dig in behind Copeland with renewed vigor. Even Copeland's shuffle licks and patterns, which can become awfully predictable, were executed with some sharp twists and surprising turns. *—Ron Wynn*

Collection, Vol. 1 / 1988 / Collectables ♦♦♦
Fifteen mostly early Johnny Copeland sides, originally released on the Golden Eagle, All Boy, Paradise, and Suave labels, recorded between 1960 and the summer of 1967, including the hit singles "Please Let Me Know" and "Down On Bending Knees" (from 1960 and 1963, respectively). Some of the previously unissued numbers, such as the instrumental "Late Hours," are showcases for Copeland (and especially for his guitar) as good as the released stuff. A close listen reveals Copeland developing great confidence, mostly as a singer but also as a guitarist, between 1960 and 1963 on sides like "Working Man's Blues," while other songs, such as "There's a Blessing," ashow him turning into a top soul shouter, in keeping with the changing times—"It Must Be Love" and "I've Gotta Go Home" are two great unheralded jewels in the latter category on this collection. The
B-side "Wella Wella Baby" clocks in at a near-epic-length five minutes, none of it wasted. His heart-stopping vocal workout on the 1967 Paradise single "(The Night Time Is) The Right Time" is also some of the most worthwhile music from this decade of Copeland's career. His never-issued solo acoustic demo of Arthur Crudup's "That's All Right Mama" is followed by the finished single—on electric instruments, with a girl chorus and a full piano and rhythm section—released on Suave in late 1964. All are pretty cool, with good sound all the way through, too. *—Bruce Eder*

When the Rain Starts Fallin' / 1988 / Rounder ♦♦♦

Boom Boom / 1990 / Rounder ♦♦

Collection, Vol. 2 / 1990 / Collectables ♦♦♦
Another 14 Johnny Copeland sides fill in more holes in his history from before and even during his Rounder Records tenure. "Love Song," which opens the set, is from 1990 and shows him in exceptionally good vocal and instrumental form, while "Daily Bread" dates from 1984. All of the rest is attributed to the late '60s and early '70s (although there's an unreleased version of his 1963 single "Please Let Me Know" here as well), which sounds about right. "May the Best Man Win" is a fine piece of late-'60s soul, with a few dissonant edges and a very active horn section that make it doubly interesting. "Heebie Jeebies" is one of the best dance tunes in Copeland's entire output, while his raunchy cover of B.B. King's "Rock Me Baby" is a killer guitar/piano workout, clocking in at over five minutes and worth every second. The rest lurches between '60s soul influences ("Mama Told Me," "Soul Power") and a slicker '70s sound, but it's all enjoyable if one can adjust to the sudden shifts in style and sound. *—Bruce Eder*

The Three Sides of Johnny Copeland / Sep. 14, 1993 / Collectables ♦♦♦

Jungle Swing / May 1996 / Verve ♦♦

Live in Australia 1990 / Mar. 18, 1997 / Black Top ♦♦♦

James Cotton

b. Jul. 1, 1935, Tunica, MS
Vocals, Drums, Harmonica, Guitar / Modern Electric Chicago Blues, Harmonica Blues, Electric Chicago Blues
At his high-energy '70s peak as a bandleader, James Cotton was a bouncing, sweaty, whirling dervish of a bluesman, roaring his vocals and all but sucking the reeds right out of his defenseless little harmonicas with his prodigious lungpower. Undoubtedly, he had some gargantuan shoes to fill when he stepped into Little Walter's slot as Muddy Waters' harp ace in 1954, but for the next dozen years, the young Mississippian filled the integral role beside Chicago's blues king with power and precision. Of course, Cotton prepared for such a career move for a long time, having learned how to wail on harp from none other than Sonny Boy Williamson himself. By 1966, Cotton was primed to make it on his own. Waxings for Vanguard, Prestige, and Loma preceded his official full-length album debut for Verve Records in 1967. Throwing a touch of soul into his eponymous debut set, Cotton ventured into the burgeoning blues-rock field as he remained with Verve through the end of the decade. Beginning in 1974, Cotton recorded several albums for Buddah and, in the '80s it was Alligator. Cotton still commands a huge following, even though serious throat problems have tragically robbed him of his once-ferocious roar. That malady ruined parts of his last Grammy-nominated album for Verve, *Living the Blues;* only when he stuck to playing harp was the customary Cotton energy still evident. *—Bill Dahl*

Cut You Loose! / 1967 / Vanguard ♦♦♦

The James Cotton Blues Band / 1967 / Verve ♦♦♦
Upbeat, soul-influenced mid-'60s work is by Cotton's initial solo aggregation. *—Bill Dahl*

100% Cotton / Mar. 1974 / One Way ♦♦♦♦
The ebullient, roly-poly Chicago harp wizard was at his zenith in 1974, when this cooking album was issued on Buddah. Matt "Guitar" Murphy matched Cotton note for zealous note back then, leading to fireworks aplenty on the non-stop "Boogie Thing," a driving "How Long Can a Fool Go Wrong," and the fastest "Rocket 88" you'll ever take a spin in. *—Bill Dahl*

Live & on the Move / 1976 / One Way ♦♦♦
Originally released on two vinyl platters in 1976 by Buddah, this set was digitally unleashed anew by the British Sequel label. It faithfully captures the boogie-burning capabilities of the mid-'70s Cotton outfit, fired by its leader's incendiary harp wizardry and Murphy's scintillating licks. *—Bill Dahl*

High Compression / 1984 / Alligator ♦♦♦♦♦
This is the best contemporary Cotton album gracing the shelves today, thanks to its ingenious formatting: half the set places Cotton in a traditional setting beside guitarist Magic Slim and pianist Pinetop Perkins, and a solid rhythm section; the other half pairs him with a contemporary combo featuring guitarist Michael Coleman's swift licks and a three-piece horn section. Both combinations click on all burners. Includes scorching theme song, "Superharp." *—Bill Dahl*

Live at Antone's / 1988 / Antone's ♦♦♦♦
Reuniting Cotton with his former guitarists Matt Murphy and Luther Tucker, pianist Pinetop Perkins, and Muddy Waters' ex-rhythm section (bassist Calvin Jones and drummer Willie Smith) looks like a great idea on paper, and it worked equally well in the flesh, when this set was cut live at Antone's Night Club in Austin, TX. *—Bill Dahl*

Harp Attack! / 1990 / Alligator ♦♦♦♦
Four Chicago harmonica greats make for one eminently solid album. Teamed with Junior Wells, Billy Branch, and Carey Bell, Cotton sings Willie Love's Delta classic "Little Car Blues" and Charles Brown's "Black Night" and plays along with his cohorts on most of the rest of the set. *—Bill Dahl*

Mighty Long Time / 1991 / Discovery ♦♦♦♦
Although the titles are all familiar (most of them a little too much so), Cotton and his all-star cohorts (guitarists Jimmie Vaughan, Matt Murphy, Luther Tucker, Hubert Sumlin, and Wayne Bennett, the omnipresent Perkins on keys) pull the whole thing off beautifully. Cotton's cover of Wolf's "Moanin' at Midnight" is remarkably eerie in its own right, and he romps through Muddy Waters' "Blow Wind Blow" and "Sugar Sweet" with joyous alacrity. *—Bill Dahl*

3 Harp Boogie / 1994 / Tomato ♦♦

Living the Blues / 1994 / Verve ♦♦

● **The Best of the Verve Years** / 1995 / Verve ♦♦♦♦♦
Taken from the high-energy harpist's first three albums for Verve following his split from Muddy Waters (including the entirety of his fine eponymous 1967 debut), this 20-track anthology is a fine spot to begin any serious Cotton collection. In those days, Cotton was into soul as well as blues—witness his raucous versions of "Knock on Wood" and "Turn on Your Lovelight," backed by a large horn complement. Compiler Dick Shurman has chose judiciously from his uneven pair of Verve follow-ups, making for a very consistent compilation. *—Bill Dahl*

Deep in the Blues / Aug. 1996 / Verve ♦♦♦
Deep in the Blues is a fascinating jam session between James Cotton, guitarist Joe Louis Walker, and jazz bassist Charlie Haden. The trio runs through a number of classic blues songs written by Muddy Waters, Percy Mayfield, and Sonny Boy Williamson and a few originals by Walker and Cotton. The sound is intimate and raw, which is a welcome change from Cotton's usual overproduced records. *—Thom Owens*

The Best of the Vanguard Years / Jun. 22, 1999 / Vanguard ♦♦♦♦

Ida Cox

b. Feb. 25, 1896, Toccoa, GA, **d.** Nov. 10, 1967, Knoxville, TN
Vocals / Classic Female Blues
One of the finest classic blues singers of the '20s, Ida Cox was singing in theaters by the time she was 14. She recorded regularly during 1923-29 (her "Wild Woman Don't Have the Blues" and "Death Letter Blues" are her best-known songs). Although she was off- record during much of the '30s, Cox was able to continue working and in 1939 she sang at Cafe Society, appeared at John Hammond's "Spirituals to Swing" concert and made some new records. Ida Cox toured with shows until a 1944 stroke pushed her into retirement; she came back for an impressive final recording in 1961.

Cox left her hometown of Toccoa, GA as a teenager, travelling the south in vaudeville and tent shows, performing both as a singer and a comedienne. In the early '20s, she performed with Jelly Roll Morton, but she had severed her ties with the pianist by the time she signed her first record contract with Paramount in 1923. Cox stayed with Paramount for six years, recording 78 songs, which usually featured accompaniment by Love Austin and trumpeter Tommy Ladnier. During that time, she also cut tracks for a variety of labels, including Silvertone, using several different pseudonyms, including Velma Bradley, Kate Lewis, and Julia Powers.

During the '30s, Cox didn't record often, but she continued to perform frequently, highlighted by an appearence at John Hammond's 1939 "Spirituals to Swing" concert at Carnegie Hall. The concert increased her visibility, particularly in jazz circles—following the concert, she recorded with a number of jazz artists, including Charlie Christian, Lionel Hampton, Fletcher Henderson, and Hot Lips Page. She toured with a number of different shows in the early '40s until she suffered a stroke in 1944. Cox was retired for most of the '50s, but she was coaxed out of retirement in 1961 to record a final session with Coleman Hawkins. In 1967, Ida Cox died of cancer. *—Scott Yanow & Stephen Thomas Erlewine*

Complete Recorded Works, Vol. 2 (1924-1925) / Mar. 1924-Apr. 1925 / Document ♦♦♦♦♦
Unlike most of her contemporaries, who spent at least part of their time singing vaudeville-type material and pop songs, Ida Cox stuck throughout her career to the blues. On the second of four Document CDs that reissue all of her '20s material (although some of the many alternate takes are bypassed), Cox is mostly accompanied by either Lovie Austin's Blues Serenaders (which usually includes cornetist Tommy Ladnier and clarinetist Jimmy O'Bryant, although the great Johnny Dodds is on six selections) or, on one date, members of Fletcher Henderson's Orchestra. The recording quality of these Paramount 78s (which cover a 13-month period) is erratic, but there are a few classics here, including "Chicago Monkey Man Blues" (which has some lyrics that would later be used for "Going to Chicago"), "Blues Ain't Nothin' Else But," "Wild Women Don't Have the Blues" and "Death Letter Blues." Throughout, Ida Cox (who was second to Bessie Smith at the time) is quite consistent, making the most of her limitations. Recommended.
—Scott Yanow

Complete Recorded Works, Vol. 3 (1925-1927) / Apr. 1925-Jul. 1927 / Document ♦♦♦♦
The third of four "complete" Ida Cox CDs from Document has 14 selections from 1925, 6 from 1926, and four from 1927. Most of the sessions feature the masterful blues singer assisted by Lovie Austin's Blues Serenaders, whose personnel was changing during this era—they featured either Tommy Ladnier, the underrated Bob Shoffner, Bernie Young or Shirley Clay on cornet, Jimmy O'Bryant or (on two songs) Johnny Dodds on clarinet, and other unidentified musicians, including a trombonist. In addition, there are three duets with banjoist Papa Charlie Jackson, a couple of numbers in which Cox is joined by cornetist Dave Nel-

son and Jesse Crump on reed organ, and the first four tunes from a lengthy 1927 set that has Cox accompanied only by Crump's piano. Most interesting is "How Long Daddy, How Long," which was the basis of Leroy Carr's famous "How Long Blues." Other highlights include "Long Distance Blues," "Southern Woman's Blues," "Coffin Blues," and Cox's famous "'Fore Day Creep." All four of the discs in this valuable series are easily recommended to serious blues collectors. *—Scott Yanow*

Complete Recorded Works, Vol. 4 (1927-1938) / Jul. 1927-Dec. 24, 1938 / Document ♦♦♦♦
The fourth and final CD in Document's extensive Ida Cox series features the classic blues singer in a variety of settings: backed by her future husband Jesse Crump on eight selections from 1927; accompanied by a variety of mostly unknown players on a dozen numbers from 1928; joined by a trio (including trombonist Roy Palmer) on two 1929 sides; and, finally, assisted by five Count Basie sidemen (trumpeter Shad Collins, trombonist Dickie Wells, tenorman Buddy Tate, bassist Walter Page, and drummer Jo Jones) and pianist James P. Johnson during her two songs at the 1938 *Spirituals to Swing Concert*. Unfortunately, Document did not put out a Vol. 5 to cover Cox's 1939-40 recordings (which were reissued by Affinity). Although none of these individual selections became that famous, she is heard in prime form throughout, and she is at her best during the duets with Crump. In fact, Cox is in such fine form during her 1938 concert appearance that it makes one wonder why she was not more active on records during the '30s and '40s. The first two CDs in this series get the edge, but all four will be wanted by vintage blues fans. *—Scott Yanow*

★ **Blues for Rampart Street** / Apr. 11, 1961-Apr. 12, 1961 / Riverside/OJC ♦♦♦♦♦
Classic blues singer Ida Cox had not recorded since 1940 nor performed regularly since the mid-'40s when she was coaxed out of retirement to record a date for Riverside in 1961. At 65 years old (some books list her as being 72), Cox's voice was a bit rusty and past its prime but she still had the feeling, phrasing, and enough tricks to perform a strong program. With assistance from trumpeter Roy Eldridge, tenor saxophonist Coleman Hawkins, pianist Sammy Price, bassist Milt Hinton, and drummer Jo Jones (swing-era veterans who came up after Cox was already a major name), the singer does her best on such numbers as "Wild Women Don't Have the Blues," "Blues for Rampart Street," "St. Louis Blues," and "Death Letter Blues." Since she passed away in 1967, this final effort (reissued on CD) was made just in time and is well worth acquiring by '20s jazz and blues collectors. *—Scott Yanow*

☆ **Complete Recorded Works, Vol. 1 (1923)** / Apr. 1, 1997 / Document ♦♦♦♦♦
Ida Cox was one of the most powerful blues singers of the '20s, ranking just below Bessie Smith. The Document label has reissued all of Cox's '20s recordings on four CDs, leaving out many of the alternate takes (since there are a great deal from 1923-24) to be put out on a later series. The first CD has the master takes of all of Cox's recordings from 1923, plus four alternates. Except for the closing "Bear-Mash Blues," which finds the singer joined by her future husband Jesse Crump on piano, the music either features accompaniment by pianist Lovie Austin (an underrated blues player) or assistance from Austin, the great cornetist Tommy Ladnier and clarinetist Jimmy O'Bryant. Cox was one of the few singers from this early period who could overcome the technical limitations of the primitive recording equipment and really communicate with the listener. Among the highlights from her first year on records are "Any Woman's Blues," "Graveyard Dream Blues" (which is heard in three versions), "Ida Cox's Lawdy, Lawdy Blues," "Moanin' Groanin' Blues," "Come Right In" (which has some lines that would become quite familiar in later songs), and "I've Got the Blues for Rampart Street." Highly recommended.
—Scott Yanow

Robert Cray

b. Aug. 1, 1953, Columbus, GA
Vocals, Guitar / Retro-Soul, Contemporary Blues, Modern Electric Blues
Tin-eared critics have frequently damned him as a yuppie blues wanna-be whose slickly soulful offerings bear scant resemblance to the real downhome item. In reality, Robert Cray is one of a precious few young (at this stage, that translates to under 50 years of age) blues artists with the talent and vision to successfully usher the idiom into the 21st century without resorting either to slavish imitation or simply playing rock while passing it off as blues. Just as importantly, his immensely popular records helped immeasurably to jump-start the contemporary blues boom that still holds sway to this day. Blessed with a soulful voice that sometimes recalls '60s-great O.V. Wright and a concise lead guitar approach that never wastes notes, Cray's ascendancy was amazingly swift—in 1986 his breakthrough *Strong Persuader* album for Mercury (containing "Smoking Gun") won him a Grammy and shot his asking price for a night's work skyward. Unlike too many of his peers, Cray continues to experiment within his two presiding genres, blues and soul. Sets such as *Midnight Stroll, I Was Warned*, and *Shame –A Sin* for Mercury show that the "bluenatics" (as he amusedly labels his purist detractors) have nothing to fear and plenty to anticipate from this innovative, laudably accessible guitarist. *—Bill Dahl*

Who's Been Talkin' / 1980 / Mercury ♦♦♦♦
The Pacific Northwest-based blues savior's first album in 1980 boded well for his immediate future. Unfurling a sterling vocal delivery equally conversant with blues and soul, Cray offers fine remakes of the Willie Dixon-penned title tune, O.V. Wright's deep soul romp "I'm Gonna Forget About You," and Freddy King's "The Welfare (Turns Its Back on You)," along with his own "Nice as a Fool Can Be" and "That's What I'll Do." *—Bill Dahl*

☆ **Bad Influence** / 1983 / Hightone ♦♦♦♦♦
One of Cray's best albums ever, and the one that etched him into the consciousness of blues aficionados prior to his mainstream explosion. Produced beautifully by Bruce Bromberg and Dennis Walker, the set sports some gorgeous originals ("Phone Booth," "Bad Influence," "So Many Women, So Little Time") and two well-chosen covers, Johnny "Guitar" Watson's "Don't Touch Me" and Eddie Floyd's Stax-era "Got to Make a Comeback." Few albums portend greatness the way this one did. *—Bill Dahl*

False Accusations / 1985 / Hightone ♦♦♦♦
If its predecessor hadn't been so powerful, this collection might have been a little more striking in its own right. As it is, a solid if not overwhelming album sporting the memorable "Playin' in the Dirt" and "I've Slipped Her Mind." *—Bill Dahl*

Showdown [A Collins & J Copeland] / 1985 / Alligator ♦♦♦♦♦
Cray found himself in some pretty intimidating company for this Grammy-winning blues guitar summit meeting, but he wasn't deterred, holding his own alongside his idol Albert Collins and Texas great Johnny Copeland. Cray's delivery of Muddy Waters' rhumba-rocking "She's into Something" was one of the set's many highlights. *—Bill Dahl*

★ **Strong Persuader** / 1986 / Mercury ♦♦♦♦♦
The set that made Cray a pop star, despite its enduring blues base. Cray's smoldering stance on "Smoking Gun" and "Right Next Door" rendered him the first sex symbol to emerge from the blues field in decades, but it was his innovative expansion of the genre itself that makes this album a genuine '80s classic. "Nothing but a Woman" boasts an irresistible groove pushed by the Memphis Horns and some metaphorically inspired lyrics, while "I Wonder" and "Guess I Showed Her" sizzle with sensuality. *—Bill Dahl*

Don't Be Afraid of the Dark / 1988 / Mercury ♦♦

Midnight Stroll / Jun. 1990 / Mercury ♦♦♦
Cray went into a more soul-slanted direction for this solid collection, coarsening his vocal cords for "The Forecast (Calls for Pain)" and the rest of the set. *—Bill Dahl*

Too Many Cooks / Sep. 1990 / Tomato ♦♦♦♦

I Was Warned / Apr. 1992 / Mercury ♦♦♦

Shame – A Sin / Oct. 5, 1993 / Mercury ♦♦♦♦
This time, Cray veered back toward the blues (most convincingly, too), even covering Albert King's "You're Gonna Need Me" and bemoaning paying taxes on the humorous "1040 Blues." Unlike his previous efforts, Cray produced this one himself. Also, longtime bassist Richard Cousins was history, replaced by Karl Sevareid. *—Bill Dahl*

Some Rainy Morning / May 9, 1995 / Mercury ♦♦♦
A typically well-produced and well-played outing includes mostly originals, with smoldering covers of Syl Johnson's "Steppin' Out" and Wilson Pickett's "Jealous Love" for good measure. Cray's crisp, concise guitar work and subtly soulful vocals remain honed to a sharp edge. *—Bill Dahl*

Sweet Potato Pie / May 5, 1997 / Mercury ♦♦♦

Take Your Shoes Off / Apr. 27, 1999 / Rykodisc ♦♦♦♦
It's evident right from the start that Robert Cray's aiming for a Memphis soul groove on *Take Your Shoes Off*. Willie Mitchell of Hi Records fame co-wrote and did the horn arrangements for the lead-off cut, "Love Gone to Waste," and Jim Pugh's burbling organ would have fit snugly into the mix of an early '70s Al Green record. The blues is not missing from this effort, but is most present in Cray's usual assertive blues guitar lines. Otherwise, this is far more appropriately pegged as a blues-soul album, or even just a retro-soul album, than a straight blues one. Cray, indeed, only writes about half of the songs, covering soul classics identified with Mack Rice's "24-7 Man" and Solomon Burke's "Won't You Give Him (One More Chance)," as well as Willie Dixon's "Tollin' Bells." No one would be claiming that this disc plows new territory, but to Cray's credit, he fits the quasi-Hi and (less frequently) Stax-type grooves with an unforced ease. It's a lot harder to do than it sounds—for Cray or anyone in the late '90s—and it's frankly more interesting than a straightahead blues album from the singer-guitarist would have been. *—Richie Unterberger*

Heavy Picks: The Robert Cray Collection / Nov. 16, 1999 / Mercury ♦♦♦♦♦

Pee Wee Crayton (Crayton, Connie C.)

b. Dec. 18, 1914, Rockdale, TX, **d.** Jun. 25, 1985, Los Angeles, CA
Vocals, Guitar / West Coast Blues, Electric Texas Blues
Although he was certainly inexorably influenced by the pioneering electric guitar conception of T-Bone Walker (what axe-handler wasn't during the immediate postwar era?), Pee Wee Crayton brought enough daring innovation to his playing to avoid being labeled as a mere T-Bone imitator. Crayton's recorded output contains plenty of dazzling, marvelously imaginative guitar work, especially on stunning instrumentals such as "Texas Hop," "Pee Wee's Boogie," and "Poppa Stoppa," all far more aggressive performances than Walker usually indulged in. He signed with the L.A.-based Modern logo in 1948, quickly hitting paydirt with the lowdown instrumental "Blues After Hours" (a kissin' cousin to Erskine Hawkins' anthem "After Hours"), which topped the R&B charts. The steaming "Texas Hop" trailed it up the lists shortly thereafter, followed the next year by "I Love You So." But Crayton's brief hit-making reign was over, through no fault of his own. He moved on to Aladdin and, in 1954, Imperial. Under Dave Bartholomew's savvy production, Crayton made some of his best waxings in New Orleans—"Every Dog Has His Day," "You Know Yeah," and "Runnin' Wild" found his guitar turned up to the boiling point over the fat cushion of saxes characterizing the Crescent City sound. *—Bill Dahl*

The Things I Used to Do / 1971 / Vanguard ♦♦♦♦
Pee Wee Crayton, a popular L.A.-based blues singer and guitarist, recorded frequently between 1947-57 but this 1970 session was his first full album and ended an eight-year drought in the studios. At 55, Crayton performed some country-flavored tunes and soul ballads but is at his best on the simpler straight-ahead blues such as a spirited "Let the Good Times Roll," the atmospheric instrumental "Blues After Hours," "Things I Used to Do," and "S.K. Blues" which at 6:24 is easily the longest performance of the brief 41-minute set. Although not a major stylist, Crayton is in good form throughout his date. *—Scott Yanow*

● **The Modern Legacy Vol. 1** / 1996 / Ace ♦♦♦♦♦
As an overview of Crayton's work for Modern from 1948-51, this might not be ideal, as only about half of it appeared on singles during that time; the rest was mostly unissued until the '80s and '90s, some making their first appearance on this CD. It also means that some of his Modern singles, including his biggest hit for the label (the ballad "I Love You So"), aren't here, as they were saved for another Ace volume of Crayton's Modern sides. Those considerations

aside, this is superior Los Angeles jump blues, with the rare vault sides holding up about as well as what came out on singles. Were this the only anthology to appear of Crayton's Modern material—heck, were it the only Crayton material, period—it would still offer convincing proof of his stature as a significant bluesman, one who (like several Modern labelmates) was instrumental in the transition from the earliest electric blues to a harder R&B style. Although his singing and songwriting are good, what really makes this stand out is his incendiary guitar playing. In addition to taking good single-note solos, he made use of insistent, sometimes machine-gun-like jazzy chords that unpredictably shifted keys and pushed the limits of the day's amplification technology. That really comes to the fore on some of the up-tempo instrumentals, like the nearly out-of-control "Pee Wee's Wild." Unlike many blues guitar heroes, though, he doesn't have to wait for the fast tunes to strut his stuff, as the crazily descending solo of the bump-and-grind "Please Come Back" demonstrates. On top of being a quality early electric blues anthology on its own merits, the CD makes a good case for Crayton being one of the more overlooked pioneers of the electric guitar as a whole. *—Richie Unterberger*

Complete Aladdin & Imperial Recordings / Mar. 19, 1996 / Capitol ✦✦✦✦✦
Crayton was fading fast commercially by the time he cut these sides in the '50s, though his vocal and instrumental skills, particularly his stinging guitar, were undimmed. Aside from two 1951 tracks cut for Aladdin in 1951, this 20-song compilation is devoted to his mid-'50s hitch with Imperial. The label had him record in New Orleans with Dave Bartholomew and other local musicians, giving many of these sides a hybrid jump blues/New Orleans R&B feel (Imperial would use the same approach with Roy Brown around this time). It's not his very best work, but even at its slightest this is pleasant. It's most effective, however, when the Crescent City touches are muted in favor of slicing straight-ahead blues riffing, as on the instrumental "Blues Before Dawn." Another obscure cut, "Do Unto Others," is nothing less than a revelation, boasting a light-years-ahead-of-its-time opening riff that sounds almost identical to the blast of notes that opens the Beatles' "Revolution," cut nearly 15 years later. *—Richie Unterberger*

Early Hour Blues / Jun. 22, 1999 / Blind Pig ✦✦✦✦

Modern Legacy, Vol. 2: Blues Guitar Magic / Jun. 26, 2000 / Ace ✦✦✦✦
As a companion volume to *The Modern Legacy Vol. 1* (also on Ace), this wraps up the label's comprehensive overview of Crayton's stint with Modern Records. With material from the end of the '40s and the early '50s, about half of the 25-track CD was drawn from 1949-52 singles, filled out by LP cuts and four previously unreleased items. This might not be quite as good as volume one, recycling some of the same ideas a few times (something, of course, found on many blues albums). But it's in the same league, showing Crayton to be a capable and often exciting performer in both the up-tempo and ballad styles, and on both vocal and instrumental tracks. The highlights, naturally, are the guitar solos, as fiery and innovative as any being done in blues and R&B at the time, even if Crayton has not received the wide recognition granted some of his peers. There's the exhilarating staccato picks on the high end of the neck on the instrumental "Poppa Stoppa," for instance, and his facility for alternating speedy solo lines with crunching, thick chords that rapidly changed keys. "Long After Hours" starts off with an unholy burst of thick distorted chords that no doubt caused some turntable needles to shudder violently upon its first release. Crayton was not just about boogying blues, as demonstrated here by his biggest hit, "I Love You So," a ballad that made the R&B Top Ten in 1949, and "Have You Lost Your Love for Me," which has an almost doo wop-pop influence. Sound quality varies—sometimes this sounds right off the master tape, at other times there's surface noise—but is about as good as could be given the condition of the source materials. *—Richie Unterberger*

Arthur "Big Boy" Crudup

b. Aug. 24, 1905, Forest, MS, **d.** Mar. 28, 1974, Nassawadox, VA
Vocals, Guitar / Delta Blues, Electric Delta Blues, Electric Blues, R&B
Arthur Crudup may well have been Elvis Presley's favorite bluesman. The swivel-hipped rock god recorded no less than three of Big Boy's Victor classics during his seminal rockabilly heyday—"That's All Right Mama" (Elvis' Sun debut in 1954), "So Glad You're Mine," and "My Baby Left Me." Often lost in all the hubbub surrounding Presley's classic covers are Crudup's own contributions to the blues lexicon. He didn't sound much like anyone else, and that makes him an innovator, albeit a rather rudimentary guitarist (he didn't even pick up the instrument until he was 30 years old). Crudup pierced the uppermost reaches of the R&B lists during the mid-'40s with "Rock Me Mama," "Who's Been Foolin' You," "Keep Your Arms Around Me," "So Glad You're Mine," and "Ethel Mae." He cut the original "That's All Right" in 1946, but it wasn't a national hit at the time. In 1961, Crudup surfaced after a long layoff with an album for the Fire logo dominated by remakes of his early hits. Another lengthy hiatus preceded Delmark boss Bob Koester's following the tip of Big Joe Williams to track down the elusive legend (Crudup had drifted into contract farm labor work in the interim). Happily, the guitarist's sound hadn't been dimmed by Father Time: His late-'60s work for Delmark rang true. Finally, Crudup began to make some decent money, playing various blues and folk festivals for appreciative crowds for a few years prior to his 1974 death. *—Bill Dahl*

That's Allright Mama [Relic] / 1961 / Relic ✦✦✦
After a long studio hiatus, Crudup reentered the studio in 1961 at the behest of producer Bobby Robinson of Fire/Fury Records. The results of their brief liaison show that Crudup hadn't altered his approach one whit during the layoff—these remakes of his RCA classics sound amazingly similar to the originals. There are a few unfamiliar titles aboard this 18-song collection to make it all the more worthwhile. *—Bill Dahl*

Mean Ol' Frisco / 1962 / Collectables ✦✦✦✦✦
These are his '60s Fire sessions. It fits into the second stage of his recording career, with *Look on Yonder's Wall* and *Coal Black Mare. —Barry Lee Pearson*

Look on Yonder's Wall / 1969 / Delmark ✦✦✦
This late-'60s Delmark session represents the third stage of his career history. *—Barry Lee Pearson*

★ **That's Allright Mama [RCA]** / 1992 / Bluebird/RCA ✦✦✦✦✦
This may not have been where rock & roll all started, but it's very likely where Elvis Presley's knowledge of blues began: 22 tracks dating from 1941 to 1954 by the guitarist whose "That's All Right" proved Presley's ticket to Sun Records stardom. Crudup was fairly limited on guitar—his accompaniment is rudimentary at best—but his songs were uncommonly sturdy (Elvis also covered "So Glad You're Mine" and "My Baby Left Me," both here in their original incarnations) and his vocals strong. *—Bill Dahl*

Meets the Master Blues Bassists / 1994 / Delmark ✦✦✦
Delmark boss Bob Koester brought Crudup back from obscurity one more time during the late '60s, and by golly, he still sounded pretty much the same. The 1968-69 waxings comprising this disc date from 1968-69 and team the veteran guitarist with two upright bassists of legendary status: Willie Dixon and Crudup's longtime cohort Ransom Knowling. A few remakes are aboard, but plenty of new material as well. *—Bill Dahl*

Charles "Cow Cow" Davenport (Charles Edwards Davenport)

b. Apr. 23, 1894, Anniston, AL, **d.** Dec. 3, 1955, Cleveland, OH
Piano, Organ / Piano Blues
Charles "Cow Cow" Davenport is one of those seldom remembered names in the annals of early blues history. But a little investigation will unearth the salient fact that he played an important part in developing one of the most enduring strains of the music; yes, "Cow Cow" Davenport was one hell of a boogie-woogie piano player. Davenport worked on numerous vaudeville tours on the TOBA circuit in the '20s and early '30s, usually in the company of vocalist Dora Carr. While he's principally noted as the composer of his signature tune, "The Cow Cow Boogie," which would be revived by jazz band vocalist Ella Mae Morse during the boogie-woogie craze of the early '40s, he also claimed to have written Louis Armstrong's "I'll Be Glad When You're Dead, You Rascal You," selling the tune outright and receiving no royalties or composer credits. He recorded for a variety of labels from 1929 to 1946, eventually settling in Cleveland, OH, where he died in 1955 of hardening of the arteries. *—Cub Koda*

Charles "Cow Cow" Davenport 1926-1938 / 1926-1938 / Wolf ✦✦✦✦✦
The material ranges from magnificent Cow Cow Davenport solo tunes to good and not-so-good duets with a host of performers. Ivy Smith and Dora Carr are the artists with whom Davenport works best. Since these were dubbed from 78s, don't expect pristine sound. *—Ron Wynn*

★ **Complete Recorded Works, Vol. 1** / Jun. 2, 1994 / Document ✦✦✦✦✦
The complete output of pianist/singer Cow Cow Davenport as a leader has been made available on two CDs by Europe's Document CD; his sideman dates are also available on two other CDs. Because Cow Cow (named after his famous "Cow Cow Blues") is often categorized as a member of the blues world, it is sometimes overlooked how strong a jazz/blues pianist he was. On this first volume, Davenport is heard collaborating with singer Dora Carr, playing duets with cornetist B.T. Wingfield, interacting with singer Sam Theard, and performing heated solos which are sometimes commented upon by his partner Ivy Smith; in addition, there are a few solo instrumentals that really show what Davenport could do. The highlights include "Chimes Blues," "Atlanta Rag," "Back In the Alley" and four versions of "Cow Cow Blues." *—Scott Yanow*

Complete Recorded Works, Vol. 2 (1929-1945) / Jun. 2, 1994 / Document ✦✦✦✦✦
The second half of the Cow Cow Davenport story (the two Document CDs in this series have all of his recordings as a leader) features Davenport in a variety of settings: solo in 1929; sharing vocal duets with Sam Tarpley and Ivy Smith during 1929-30; sticking to vocalizing on a lone date from 1938; and performing eight selections (six of which are piano solos) in 1945 for what would be his final recordings. Although Cow Cow Davenport ended up quite destitute and forgotten, his music was generally quite joyous, and he was certainly a fine, underrated pianist. Among the more memorable selections on this recommended disc are "Mama Don't Allow No Easy Riders," "Everybody Likes That Thing," "The Mess Is Here," "Jeep Boogie," and "Hobson City Stomp." *—Scott Yanow*

Complete Recorded Works, Vol. 3 / Mar. 2, 1998 / Document ✦✦✦✦

Larry Davis

b. Dec. 4, 1936, Kansas City, MO, **d.** Apr. 19, 1994, Los Angeles, CA
Vocals, Guitar / Electric Texas Blues, Soul-Blues
Anyone who associates "Texas Flood" only with Stevie Ray Vaughan has never auditioned Larry Davis' version. Davis debuted on vinyl in 1958 with the song, his superlative Duke Records original remaining definitive to this day despite Vaughan's impassioned revival many years down the road.

Davis grew up in Little Rock, AR, giving up the drums to play bass. Forging an intermittent partnership with guitarist Fenton Robinson during the mid-'50s, the pair signed with Don Robey's Duke label on the recommendation of Bobby Bland. Three Davis 45s resulted, including "Texas Flood" and "Angels in Houston," before Robey cut Davis loose. From there, Davis was forced to make the most of limited opportunities in the studio. He lived in St. Louis for a spell and took up the guitar under Albert King's tutelage while playing bass in King's band.

A handful of singles for Virgo and Kent and a serious 1972 motorcycle accident that temporarily paralyzed Davis' left side preceded an impressive 1982 album for Rooster Blues, *Funny Stuff,* produced by Gateway City mainstay Oliver Sain. But follow-up options remained hard to come by: Few blues fans could find a copy of the guitarist's 1987 Pulsar LP *I Ain't Beggin' Nobody.*

Finally, in 1992, Ron Levy's Bulleye Blues logo issued a first-class Davis set, *Sooner or Later,* that skillfully showcased his rich, booming vocals and concise, Albert King-influenced guitar. Unfortunately, it came later rather than sooner—Davis died of cancer in the spring of 1994. *—Bill Dahl*

Funny Stuff / 1982 / Rooster Blues ✦✦✦✦
Larry Davis didn't record all that often, but when he did, he certainly made it count. That's

the case with this fine St. Louis recording, not available yet on CD but well worth searching for at your favorite used vinyl emporium. Produced by Oliver Sain (who handled all sax work) and featuring Billy Gayles on drums and pianist Johnnie Johnson, the set is a ringing endorsement of Davis' slashing, tremolo-enriched guitar and booming vocals. *—Bill Dahl*

I Ain't Beggin' Nobody / 1987 / Evidence ♦♦♦♦♦
Only bad luck and the follies of the record industry have prevented Larry Davis from being the well-known blues star he should be. Davis has never received either sustained label support or concentrated marketing and thus is only a footnote when he should be a full chapter. His playing is energetic and varied, while his vocals are animated, soulful, and expressive. He recorded the nine tracks on this 1985 date (newly reissued on CD by Evidence) with longtime blues and soul producer and instrumentalist Oliver Sain at the controls, and Davis demonstrated his convincing appeal on Sain's title track, as well as the defiant "I'm A Rolling Stone" (another Sain original), Davis' own anguished "Giving Up On Love," and "Please Don't Go," a Chuck Willis composition. *—Ron Wynn*

● **Sooner or Later** / 1992 / Bullseye Blues ♦♦♦♦♦
Unless someone has the ultimate Larry Davis album still awaiting release somewhere, the late guitarist's final album also looks to be his best. Sumptuously produced by organist/Bullseye Blues boss Ron Levy with the Memphis Horns providing punchy interjections, Davis roars a finely conceived concoction of covers and his own material ("Goin' Out West," "Little Rock") that represent contemporary blues at its finest. *—Bill Dahl*

Reverend Gary Davis

b. Apr. 30, 1896, Laurens, SC, **d.** May 5, 1972, Hammonton, NJ
Vocals, Guitar, Arranger / Prewar Gospel Blues, Piedmont Blues, Country-Blues, Blues Gospel, Acoustic Blues
The blind, South Carolina-born country-blues/gospel singer and guitarist Reverend Gary Davis was, after Blind Blake, the foremost exponent of the East Coast ragtime school of country-blues guitar. Davis recorded mostly gospel material, with an occasional ragtime or pop instrumental. His impassioned, gravelly vocals drew on his church and preaching experience. He recorded only a handful of sides in the '30s, but after a number of years spent singing on the streets of New York City, he became a fixture of the '50s and '60s folk revival, recording and performing extensively. Using finger-picks, Davis drew a tremendous sound from the jumbo Gibson guitars he favored. His guitar style (simplified and copied by his much-recorded protégé Blind Boy Fuller) enjoyed complex rhythms and countermelodies far more involved than the garden-variety alternating-bass style of finger-picking. To hear Davis perform his spectacular reworking of Blind Willie Johnson's "Samson and Delilah" is an electrifying experience, and humbling for aspiring guitar pickers. *—Richard Lieberson*

Pure Religion & Bad Company / 1957 / Smithsonian/Folkways ♦♦♦♦♦
Moses Asch became the first producer to record Davis in a full-length album release, showcasing his dazzling guitar style more fully than ever before. *—Bruce Eder*

Say No to the Devil / 1958 / Original Blues Classics ♦♦♦♦
Say No to the Devil is Rev. Gary Davis' third Bluesville album and it was originally released in 1961. Davis was in fine form throughout the session, playing some startlingly intricate 12-string guitar licks, blowing some rootsy harp, and singing with conviction. Between the songs, Davis tells some rambling stories, which are just as gripping and fascinating as the music itself. *—Thom Owens*

Rev. Gary Davis at Newport / 1959 / Vanguard ♦♦♦♦
One of the finest single artist albums to come out of Newport, not quite in the league of Muddy Waters' performance but a superb introduction to the range of his repertory, from ragtime and novelty tunes to gospel numbers. *—Bruce Eder*

Harlem Street Singer / Aug. 1960 / Original Blues Classics ♦♦♦♦♦
Recorded during a three hour session on August 24, 1960, Gary Davis laid down 12 of his most impassioned spirituals for *Harlem Street Singer.* Starting off the session with a version of Blind Willie Johnson's "If I Had My Way I'd Tear That Building Down," here renamed "Samson and Delilah," Davis is in fine form. His vocals are as expressive as Ray Charles' while similar in richness to Richie Havens' work. *Harlem Street Singer* features his inspired country-blues fingerpicking as well. Many moods color the selections, from the gentle "I Belong to the Band" to the mournful "Death Don't Have No Mercy," only to be followed by the joyous shouting of "Goin' to Sit Down on the Banks of the River." Overall, the collection is well worth the purchase and should be considered essential listening for fans of country-blues or gospel. *—Matt Fink*

Gospel, Blues & Street Songs / Jul. 1961 / Original Blues Classics ♦♦♦♦♦
Eight of Davis' best-known gospel songs, cut in 1956 in New York, and among the most glowing sides of his career. Paired up with seven tracks cut by Pink Anderson for Riverside in 1950. *—Bruce Eder*

From Blues to Gospel / Mar. 1971 / Biograph ♦♦♦
This particular set was recorded one year before Davis' death, when he was 76 years old. Producer Arnold Caplin has combined two LPs to create this package and believes these to be the artist's very last recordings. Although the master-picker pulls off some prodigious playing here—on both the 6- and 12-string guitars—he is no match for his own earlier work recorded between 1935-60. Listeners already familiar with the younger Davis'playing will feel great affection and gratitude for these last recordings. *—Larry Hoffman*

Blues & Ragtime / 1993 / Shanachie ♦♦♦♦♦
The Rev. Gary Davis forsook his gospel calling for a little while between 1962 and 1966 to set down formal studio versions of many of his most important blues and ragtime repertory. Some of the material here runs over ten minutes, as Davis lays out his best playing and singing voice. The booklet includes a fairly detailed biography as well as musical annotation. *—Bruce Eder*

★ **Complete Works (1935-1949)** / 1994 / Document ♦♦♦♦♦
Bull City Red, who played with the Reverend Gary Davis at various times, turns up on vocals for "I Saw the Light," but the rest of *1935-1949* is all Davis' show. The quality and inventiveness of the playing alone is astonishing, a youthful version of the technique that was still dazzling players 30 years after Davis' rediscovery. Some of the tracks are a little noisy but generally the quality is better than decent for blues of this vintage, and it's startling to hear the '30s versions of numbers like "Twelve Gates to the City," which Davis was still performing better than anyone else in the mid-'60s. On "You Can Go Home," he really does get the guitar to sound like an orchestra, rippling through melodic and harmonic flourishes with the kind of assurance that would have made many a would-be bluesman of the '50s just throw away the guitar in despair.

The Document disc overlaps Yazoo Records' *Complete Early Recordings* and includes three cuts not found there. "Civil War March," a guitar transcription of military marches that Davis cut for Moe Asch in 1945, is by itself worth the purchase price of this disc; one of the most humbling examples of a lighthearted virtuoso piece that one is ever likely to run into, its presence alone makes the disc a potentially better choice than the Yazoo version. However, the two subsequent tracks dating from 1949, "I Cannot Bear My Burden By Myself" and "I'm Gonna Meet You at the Station," are just as alluring, showing Davis still playing and singing brilliantly, patiently waiting to be rediscovered a few years later. *—Bruce Eder*

Complete Early Recordings / 1994 / Yazoo ♦♦♦♦♦
One can't possibly own too much of the Reverend Gary Davis' music from any era, but he made so few recordings in the '30s that the material is represented on several overlapping CDs. The Yazoo collection of his sides cut for the American Record Company is good as far as it goes—which is a long way—giving as complete a picture as one will ever find of Davis' output during that decade, with good sound and a superb set of sleeve notes on his life and work. It is not, unfortunately, as full an account of Davis' pre-'50s career as other discs that are available (especially from Document Records), and purchasers should be aware of one thing that they can be sure of concerning Davis—they will want more of his music. *—Bruce Eder*

O, Glory: The Apostolic Studio Sessions / 1996 / Genes ♦♦♦
Recorded in 1969, *O, Glory: The Apostolic Studio Sessions* is the Rev. Gary Davis' final studio LP, but he went out in style, working under the most state-of-the-art studio conditions of his career. The result is perhaps the best-sounding record in his catalog, even if the performances don't quite capture all the fire of his peak period; equally interesting is another break in tradition—rarely recorded with other artists (outside of a few early-'50s sides cut with Sonny Terry), here Davis is backed by vocalist Sister Annie Davis, harpist Larry Johnson, and the Apostolic Family Chorus. Also worth noting is that Davis performs on a pair of instruments he'd never before recorded with, the piano and the five-string banjo. The cumulative result makes *O Glory* a must for historians, but casual fans will undoubtedly be better served by his earlier material. *—Jason Ankeny*

Paul DeLay

b. Jan. 31, 1952, Portland, OR
Vocals, Harmonica / Electric Harmonica Blues, Modern Electric Blues
Paul deLay was born in Portland, OR, on January 31, 1952, but grew up in Milwaukie, OR, a suburb of Portland. He grew up listening to classical, jazz (big band), Dixieland, barrelhouse piano, and barbershop quartets. He came to blues through rock and the various blues covers of British artists. When he discovered Chess Records and the original blues recordings, he had found his vocation.

DeLay joined the band Brown Sugar in 1970, and the band played a combination of blues, soul, and R&B. They stayed together for about ten years working the local bar scene, dances, and coffeehouses. In 1979, deLay formed his own four-piece Chicago-style blues band. This became the Paul deLay Band. DeLay took Paul Butterfield as his model early on but says of his playing, "I guess, more or less, what I've ended up sounding like is a combination between Big Walter, George Smith, Sonny Boy II, and Toots Thielemans."

In 1990, deLay was arrested on cocaine-related charges and spent three years in federal prison. In the early '90s, the band released two CDs *The Other One* (1990), and *Paulzilla* (1992), both now available on one CD from Evidence. Almost all the songs on these CDs were written by deLay.

While deLay was serving time, his band teamed up with singer Linda Hornbuckle, calling themselves the No Delay Band and waited for Paul to return. Upon Paul's release, they reformed as the Paul deLay Band and released their first post-prison album, *Ocean of Tears,* in September of 1996. The main (long-standing) members of the deLay band include Peter Dammann (lead guitar), Louis Pain (keyboards), and Dan Fincher (sax). Dammann was raised in Chicago and traces his musical roots to the blues scene there.

DeLay has an excellent voice—an apologist-style singer in the manner of Bobby Bland and Junior Parker. As a harp player, he is superb. Not just another white guy playing the records of other bluesmen, deLay is expert on both the standard Marine Band Hohner and the chromatic. He (along with William Clarke) has taken the blues chromatic to new heights. DeLay has received a number of awards, including a Handy Award nomination, and appeared at many blues and jazz festivals.

DeLay's music shows R&B, jazz, and gospel influence, but still hangs more or less in the blues groove. He has written some excellent songs in the apologetic style of singers like Bobby "Blue" Bland. He claims, "I'm really a frustrated Dixieland saxophone player." *—Michael Erlewine*

Paulzilla / 1992 / Criminal ♦♦♦♦♦
Declared the album of the year by the Cascades Blues Association, this was completed just days before deLay's three-year visit to the pen. DeLay wrote most of the songs and there is plenty of first-rate chromatic harp playing here, with Peter Dammann on guitar and Louis Pain on keyboards. *—Michael Erlewine*

● **Take It from the Turnaround** / 1996 / Evidence ♦♦♦♦♦
Combining the best of two albums (1991's *Just This One* and 1992's *Paulzilla*) on one CD, *Take It from the Turnaround* heralds the arrival of a harp player who's been a certified

blues legend in his native region of Portland, OR. DeLay blows with authenticity and a full command of his instrument and way more than a hint of reckless abandon. Traditional blues, even by modern bar-band standards, this ain't, but the high creative level of deLay's songwriting on numbers like "Second Hand Smoke," "Merry Way," and the heartfelt "Just This One" heralds the arrival of a new way of looking at things and bodes well for future recordings. As a parenthetical note, the liner notes that accompany this release are superlative, telling deLay's story in a way that's both horrifying and inspiring. The man has lived a life in the blues and not only lived to tell the tale, but has triumphed over the worst elements a road musician has to suffer through. *—Cub Koda*

Ocean of Tears / Sep. 1996 / Evidence ♦♦♦♦

Nice & Strong / Feb. 3, 1998 / Evidence ♦♦♦♦

DeLay Does Chicago / Jan. 12, 1999 / Evidence ♦♦♦♦

American Voodoo / Criminal ♦♦♦

Burnin' / Criminal ♦♦♦♦

Floyd Dixon

b. Feb. 8, 1929, Marshall, TX
Vocals, Piano / Jump Blues, West Coast Blues, Piano Blues, R&B
Floyd Dixon was an unabashed admirer of Charles Brown's mellow "club-blues" sound, but he added a more energetic, aggressive jump-blues edge to his sound during the early '50s—a formula that made the L.A.-based pianist an R&B star. Dixon was swept up in the late '40s R&B boom, recording for Supreme in 1947 and signing with Modern Records in 1949. He nudged into the R&B Top Ten with "Dallas Blues" and just missed similar lofty stature with "Mississippi Blues" later in 1949. After cutting prolifically for Modern, he switched over to Aladdin and hit in 1950 with "Sad Journey Blues," "Telephone Blues" the next year, and the mournful "Call Operator 210" in 1952. But there was a playfully ribald side to Dixon, too. The double-entendre "Red Cherries," a storming "Wine, Wine, Wine," and the two-sided 1951 live waxing "Too Much Jelly Roll" (penned by a young Jerry Leiber and Mike Stoller) and "Baby, Let's Go Down to the Woods" showcased his more raucous leanings. The hits ceased, but Dixon's West Coast R&B odyssey continued. *—Bill Dahl*

Opportunity Blues / 1976 / Route 66 ♦♦♦♦
Vinyl-only examination of the pianist's early sides for several West Coast R&B indies that spans 1948-1961. Dixon's ballad style was quite reminiscent of Charles Brown's but his jump-blues leanings—here typified by "Wine, Wine, Wine" and "Real Lovin' Mama"—were all his own. *—Bill Dahl*

Houston Jump / 1979 / Route 66 ♦♦♦♦
Another cross-section of Dixon's 1947-1960 output that hasn't made the jump to the digital age as of yet. Surveys a wide array of labels, including a 1954 date for Atlantic's short-lived Cat subsidiary that produced "Roll Baby Roll" and "Is It True." *—Bill Dahl*

Marshall Texas Is My Home / 1991 / Specialty ♦♦♦♦♦
Dixon landed at Art Rupe's Specialty label in 1953, his music jumping harder than ever. These 22 tracks rate with his best; the collection is full of rarities and previously unissued items, many featuring the wailing tenor sax of Carlos Bermudez in lusty support of the pianist. By 1957, when he momentarily paused at Ebb Records, Dixon could do a pretty fair breathless imitation of Little Richard, as the scorching "Oooh Little Girl" definitively proves. Also includes Dixon's best-known number, the often-covered rocker "Hey Bartender" (first out on Atlantic's Cat subsidiary in 1954). *—Bill Dahl*

● **Complete Aladdin Recordings** / Mar. 19, 1996 / Capitol ♦♦♦♦♦
It's a matter of opinion as to whether Dixon's Aladdin output was his peak; many would give his Specialty sides (available on the *Marshall Texas Is My Home* compilation) the nod. Still, his late-'40s and early-'50s work for the label included some of his most popular and best tracks, such as "Wine, Wine, Wine," "Call Operator 210," "Tired, Broke and Busted," "Let's Dance," "Telephone Blues," and "Too Much Jelly Roll" (the last of which was one of Leiber-Stoller's first recorded compositions). This two-CD, 48-track compilation is geared more toward the completist collector than the average fan, especially with the inclusion of five Sonny Parker sides (which Dixon now says he didn't play on, despite some reports to the contrary) and about ten songs that feature Mari Jones on vocals. The best stuff is jump blues at its best, though, with good guitar work by Johnny and Oscar Moore (the latter of who had played with Nat "King" Cole), Dixon's fine piano playing, and witty, knowing vocals and lyrics. *—Richie Unterberger*

Wake up and Live! / May 21, 1996 / Alligator ♦♦♦♦♦

Cow Town Blues / Jan. 25, 2000 / Ace ♦♦♦♦
Twenty-six songs from Dixon's 1948-1950 sessions for Modern are compiled here, mostly taken from singles that appeared on Modern between 1949 and 1951, but also including seven previously unissued tracks. These were Dixon's first recordings, but his style was already in place, both on uptempo jump blues and ballads, sounding like fellow L.A.-based pianist Charles Brown on the slower tunes. This would rate a little below the compilations of his later '50s sides for Specialty and Capitol, as those include his best and best-known recordings, such as "Hey Bartender," "Wine, Wine, Wine," "Call Operator 210," and "Tired, Broke and Busted." This remains quality transitional West Coast blues, from that time when jazz and blues were intersecting to shape R&B, a movement that had Modern artists such as Dixon at the forefront. Modern session musicians such as saxophonist Maxwell Davis and guitarists Tiny Webb and Chuck Norris were sympathetic and sometimes exciting accompanists for Dixon on his Modern dates. As is the case with compilations of Modern R&B from this period, though, the songs do sometimes get too close to each other in arrangement and mood when they're grouped together en masse. This includes his first R&B hit (and biggest for Modern), the slow "Dallas Blues," although the peppier jump blues are definitely more interesting. *—Richie Unterberger*

Willie Dixon

b. Jul. 1, 1915, Vicksburg, MS, **d.** Jan. 29, 1992, Burbank, CA
Vocals, Guitar, Bass / Electric Chicago Blues
Willie Dixon's life and work was virtually an embodiment of the progress of the blues into a recognized and vital part of America's musical heritage. That Dixon was one of the first professional blues songwriters to benefit in a serious, material way from his work—and that he had to fight to do it—also made him an important symbol of the injustice that still informs the music industry. A producer, songwriter, bassist, and singer, he helped Muddy Waters, Howlin' Wolf, Little Walter, and others find their most commercially successful voices. As a youth, Dixon won the Illinois State Golden Gloves Heavyweight Championship, but ultimately turned to music instead, taking up bass as an instrument. The Chess brothers liked Dixon's playing, and his skills as a songwriter and arranger, and he began working regularly for the Chess label. Dixon's real recognition as a songwriter began with Muddy Waters' recording of "Hoochie Coochie Man," and he was soon established as Chess' most reliable tunesmith. During the mid-'60s, he began to see a growing interest in his songwriting from British rock bands like the Rolling Stones and the Yardbirds. Gradually, however, Dixon saw his relationship with Chess Records come to a halt. He was eager to try his hand as a performer again; he recorded an album of his best-known songs, *I Am the Blues*, and organized a touring band to play concerts in Europe. Suddenly, he began making a major name for himself on stage for the first time. During the '70s, Dixon began to understand just *how much* songwriting money he'd been deprived of, by design or just plain negligence; he filed several suits that resulted in generous out-of-court settlements. The '80s saw Dixon working with various organizations to help secure song copyrights on behalf of blues songwriters who, like himself, had been deprived of revenue during previous decades. By that time, Dixon was regarded as something of an elder statesman, composer, and spokesperson of American blues. However, he suffered from increasingly poor health, and lost a leg to diabetes; he died peacefully in his sleep early in 1992. *—Bruce Eder*

Willie's Blues / 1959 / Original Blues Classics ♦♦♦

I Am the Blues / 1970 / Columbia/Legacy ♦♦♦
The material is superb, consisting of some of Dixon's best-known songs of the '60s, and the production is smoothly professional, but none of the performances here are likely to make you forget the hits by Howlin' Wolf, Muddy Waters, and others. Reissued on CD by Mobile Fidelity and more recently by Sony Music—unfortunately, none of the unreleased tracks from the session seem to have survived. *—Bruce Eder*

★ **The Chess Box** / 1989 / MCA/Chess ♦♦♦♦♦
There are a few holes in this collection, but not many. As it is, the material is virtually a best-of-Chess collection, featuring some of the best tracks in the respective outputs of Muddy Waters, Howlin' Wolf, Little Walter, Sonny Boy Williamson, Bo Diddley, Lowell Fulsom, Koko Taylor, and others. *—Bruce Eder*

The Original Wang Dang Doodle / 1995 / MCA/Chess ♦♦♦♦
This is a good collection of hard-to-find and previously unreleased Dixon sides, although there are several Chess tracks that were left off that would have made it much more valuable. The title track is especially worthwhile, as is "Tail Dragger," but it is also easy to see from this collection why Dixon was never quite a star in his own right as a performer—he has a good voice, but not a very memorable or powerful one, compared with Muddy Waters, Howlin' Wolf, and others. *—Bruce Eder*

Poet of the Blues / Jun. 30, 1998 / Columbia/Legacy ♦♦♦♦
Columbia/Legacy's *Poet of the Blues* is a fine 16-track collection that spotlights Willie Dixon's own recordings of such blues standards as "Back Door Man," "I Can't Quit You Babe," "Spoonful," "The Little Red Rooster," and "I Ain't Sperstitious," plus some lesser-known originals like "If the Sea Was Whiskey," "O.C. Bounce," "Money Tree Blues," "Juice-Head Bartender," and "Signifying Monkey." Many of these songs were recorded with his early trio, the Big Three, and while they're of historical interest, they're not quite as good as his Chess recordings. Nevertheless, this is a good, concise sampler of his Columbia recordings for anyone curious about this period of Dixon's career. *—Thom Owens*

K.C. Douglas

b. Nov. 21, 1913, Sharon, MS, **d.** Oct. 18, 1975, Berkeley, CA
Vocals, Guitar / Piedmont Blues, West Coast Blues, Electric Country Blues
K.C. Douglas was a Mississippi bluesman who transplanted himself and his music, not to Chicago but to the San Francisco Bay Area in 1945. He became one of the rare Californians with such a down-home rural style, as many of his recordings were remakes of old blues he knew from Mississippi. (His first album, an obscure item on the Cook label, was entitled *K.C. Douglas, a Dead Beat Guitar and the Mississippi Blues*.) His re-creations of Tommy Johnson's blues were of particular interest to fans of pre-war blues, but his own compositions attracted attention as well (K.C.'s music was introduced to rock listeners when his "Mercury Boogie" was redone by The Steve Miller Band.) *—Jim O'Neal*

● **K.C.'s Blues** / 1961 / Bluesville ♦♦♦♦
Like *Big Road Blues*, *K.C., Blues* was recorded in 1961 during the peak of the blues revival. Unlike that record, which contained a number of songs he learned through Tommy Johnson, *K.C.'s Blues* consists primarily of original compositions that showcase Douglas' easy-rolling, relaxed style perfectly. *—Thom Owens*

Big Road Blues / 1961 / Ace ♦♦♦

Mercury Blues / Oct. 20, 1998 / Arhoolie ♦♦♦
Spare electric blues from 1973-74 with a juke-joint feel, including a version of "Mercury Blues," covered by Steve Miller and Alan Jackson. Originally released on LP on Arhoolie 1073, the CD reissue adds a dozen previously unissued bonus cuts, taken from sessions in 1960, 1963, 1973, and 1974. It's competent but unexceptional country-blues with added electricity and a rhythm section, and pretty similar-sounding most of the way through. "I'm

Gonna Build Me a Web," the 1963 track, stands out here as the piano and sax add some needed texture; the three 1960 songs are solo acoustic performances. *—Richie Unterberger*

Chris Duarte

b. Feb. 16, 1963, San Antonio, TX

Vocals, Guitar / Blues-Rock

Austin-based guitarist, songwriter, and singer Chris Duarte is such a promising young upstart in the world of modern blues that he's already being compared with the late Stevie Ray Vaughan. It's heady stuff for the musician, who plays a rhythmic style of Texas blues-rock that is at times reminiscent of Vaughan's sound, and at other times reminiscent of Johnny Winter. The truth is, Duarte has his own sound that draws on elements of jazz, blues, and rock & roll. Although he is humbled by the comparisons with the late Vaughan, the San Antonio-raised musician began playing out in clubs there when he was 15 years old.

After Duarte moved to Austin when he was 16, he began taking his guitar playing much more seriously, and at that time, Vaughan was still around playing in Austin-area clubs. Duarte was one of those lucky few thousand who got to see Vaughan at the Continental Club before the late guitarist got his first break with David Bowie. After a short stint in an Austin jazz band, Duarte joined Bobby Mack and Night Train, and began getting heavily into blues at that point. He traveled all over Texas with that band before a big break came his way in 1994, when New York-based Silvertone Records released his critically praised debut album, *Texas Sugar Strat Magik. Tailspin Headwhack* followed in 1997 and *Love Is Greater Than Me* appeared three years later. *—Richard Skelly*

● **Texas Sugar Strat Magic** / 1994 / Silvertone ♦♦♦♦

Guitarist Chris Duarte's *Texas Sugar Strat Magik* is an impressive debut album, showcasing his fiery, Stevie Ray Vaughan-derived blues-rock. As a songwriter, Duarte is still developing—he fails to come up with any memorable songs, although he does contribute several competent, unexceptional genre pieces—but as an instrumentalist, he's first-rate, spitting out solos with a blistering intensity or laying back with gentle, lyrical phrases. And that's what makes *Texas Sugar Strat Magik* a successful record—it's simply a great guitar album, full of exceptional playing. *—Stephen Thomas Erlewine*

Tailspin Headwhack / Aug. 26, 1997 / Silvertone ♦♦♦♦

Chris Duarte's debut album, *Texas Sugar Strat Magik*, promised great things, and his second album, *Tailspin Headwhack*, doesn't fail to deliver. Like its predecessor, it's a dynamic collection of hot Texas blues-rock powered by Duarte's muscular, tasteful playing. There's still a lack of distinctive original material, but that doesn't matter, because he infuses each song, from the single "Cleopatra" to a cover of B.B. King's "The Thrill Is Gone," with energy and passion. Most importantly, Duarte is beginning to break away from his Stevie Ray and Hendrix influences and establish himself as a talented stylist in his own right, and that's what makes *Tailspin Headwhack* a successful second record. *—Thom Owens*

Love Is Greater Than Me / Sep. 26, 2000 / Zoe ♦♦♦

Champion Jack Dupree

b. Jul. 4, 1910, New Orleans, LA, **d.** Jan. 21, 1992, Hanover, Germany

Vocals, Drums, Piano, Guitar / New Orleans Blues, Acoustic Chicago Blues, Piano Blues, Acoustic Blues

A formidable contender in the ring before he shifted his focus to pounding the piano instead, Champion Jack Dupree often injected his lyrics with a rowdy sense of downhome humor. But there was nothing lighthearted about his rock-solid way with a boogie; when he shouted "Shake Baby Shake," the entire room had no choice but to acquiesce. He spent his formative years in New Orleans, then lived in Chicago, Detroit, and Indianapolis while boxing during the mid-'30s. He first recorded in 1940, for OKeh and Columbia, exhibiting a strong New Orleans tinge despite the Chicago surroundings. After a stretch in the Navy during World War II (he was a Japanese POW for two years), Dupree cut records for Continental, Joe Davis, Alert, Apollo, and Red Robin, often in the company of Brownie McGhee. King Records corralled Dupree in 1953 and held onto him through 1955 (the year he enjoyed his only R&B chart hit, the relaxed "Walking the Blues"). After a year on RCA's Groove and Vik subsidiaries, he made a masterpiece LP for Atlantic (1958's *Blues from the Gutter*) but left for Europe in 1959, continuing to record prolifically for Storyville, British Decca, and many other firms. Dupree returned to New Orleans in 1990 and recorded three albums of new material before his death in 1992. Jack Dupree was a champ to the very end. *—Bill Dahl*

★ **Blues from the Gutter** / 1958 / Atco ♦♦♦♦♦

The 1958 masterwork album of Dupree's long and prolific career. Cut in New York (in stereo!) with a blasting band that included saxist Pete Brown and guitarist Larry Dale, the Jerry Wexler-produced Atlantic collection provides eloquent testimony to Dupree's eternal place in the New Orleans blues and barrelhouse firmament. There's some decidedly down-in-the-alley subject matter—"Can't Kick The Habit," "T.B. Blues," a revival of "Junker's Blues"—along with the stomping "Nasty Boogie" and treatments of the ancient themes "Stack-O-Lee" and "Frankie & Johnny." *—Bill Dahl*

Sings the Blues / 1961 / King ♦♦♦♦

A domestic no-frills collection of Champion Jack Dupree's aforementioned King label material, albeit containing fewer tracks and little in the way of annotation—but you can't argue with the wonderful music therein! *—Bill Dahl*

1944-1945: The First 16 Side From Joe Davis / 1982 / Red Pepper ♦♦♦

Journeyman blues pianist Champion Jack Dupree took his New Orleans-born, boogie-woogie style north to Chicago and Indianapolis and gave it some blues backbone via meetings with Leroy Carr and Tampa Red. The first fruits of that education were his early '40s sides for OKeh, which are available on Columbia's *New Orleans Barrelhouse Boogie*. While his OKeh sides paired Dupree with a rhythm section, Red Pepper's reissue of his later recordings for the Joe Davis label, *1944-1945*, feature him alone at the piano. The 16 tracks wear a bit thin at times as Dupree recycles many of the same boogie-woogie patterns, but the intimacy of the solo setting and the energy of his swaggering vocal delivery keep these sides engaging. Dupree supplies variety by way of subject matter that takes in domestic strife ("Outside Man"), politics ("F.D.R. Blues"), and drinking ("Rum Cola Blues"). For fans of both Champion Jack Dupree and the blues, *1944-1945* is worth getting; you'll not only get some fine boogie-woogie blues, but also hear how Dupree influenced blues and rock & roll greats like Memphis Slim and Fats Domino. *—Stephen Cook*

Back Home in New Orleans / 1990 / Bullseye Blues ♦♦♦♦♦

By far the best of Dupree's three albums for Bullseye Blues, this collection was cut during the pianist's first trip home to the Crescent City in 36 long years. With his longtime accompanist Kenn Lending on guitar, Dupree sounds happy to be back in his old stomping grounds throughout the atmospheric set. *—Bill Dahl*

Blues for Everybody / 1990 / Charly ♦♦♦♦♦

Although Dupree seldom paused at any one label for very long, the piano pounder did hang around at Cincinnati-based King Records from 1951 to 1955—long enough to wax the 20 sides comprising this set and a few more that regrettably aren't aboard. By this time, Dupree was a seasoned R&B artist, storming through "Let the Doorbell Ring" and "Mail Order Woman" and emphasizing his speech impediment on "Harelip Blues" (one of those not-for-the-politically correct numbers). Most of these tracks were done in New York; sidemen include guitarist Mickey Baker and saxist Willis Jackson. *—Bill Dahl*

Forever & Ever / 1991 / Bullseye Blues ♦♦♦

New Orleans Barrelhouse Boogie (The Complete Champion Jack Dupree) / 1993 / Columbia/Legacy ♦♦♦♦♦

The New Orleans barrelhouse-boogie piano specialist's earliest sides for OKeh date from 1940-1941 and in a few cases sport some fairly groundbreaking electric guitar runs by Jesse Ellery. Dupree rocks the house like it's a decade later on two takes of "Cabbage Greens" and "Dupree Shake Dance," while his drug-oriented "Junker Blues" was later cleaned up a bit by a chubby newcomer named Fats Domino for his debut hit 78 "The Fat Man." *—Bill Dahl*

One Last Time / 1993 / Bullseye Blues ♦♦♦

A Portrait of Champion Jack Dupree / Oct. 31, 2000 / Rounder ♦♦♦

A Portrait of Champion Jack Dupree is a compilation drawn from three albums Dupree recorded for Rounder Records near the end of his life, when he was in his late seventies and early eighties. The first of them, *Back Home in New Orleans*, was released in 1990, the year he turned 80, the last, *One Last Time*, came out in 1993, the year after his death. Even at his advanced age, Dupree remained a formidable barrelhouse pianist and a strong vocal presence. Backed on these sessions by sympathetic New Orleans musicians, he seems to have been simply turned loose to do as he liked. There is a noticeable informality to the recordings, with the artist occasionally stumbling over his words, stopping and starting at will. Some tracks find him playing recognizable songs, while others, such as "Skit Skat" and "Dupree Special," are jams. The album is enjoyable despite this as an expression of Dupree's personality. On several songs, notably "Give Me the Flowers While I'm Livin'" and "You Can Make It" (both of which also appeared on the posthumous *One Last Time*), Dupree makes specific references to death (the former song even pictures him in his coffin). The subject of death is not unknown in the blues, of course, but Dupree seems conscious of his advanced age here and deals with his coming death evenly and even humorously. His last sessions may not be his best work, but they show him to be as distinctive as ever. *—William Ruhlmann*

Snooks Eaglin (Ford Eaglin, Jr.)

b. Jan. 21, 1936, New Orleans, LA

Vocals, Guitar / Swamp Blues, Piedmont Blues, New Orleans Blues, Acoustic New Orleans Blues

When they refer to consistently amazing guitarist Snooks Eaglin as a human jukebox in his New Orleans hometown, they're not dissing him in the slightest. The blind Eaglin is a beloved figure in the Crescent City, not only for his gritty, Ray Charles-inspired vocal delivery and wholly imaginative approach to the guitar, but for the seemingly infinite storehouse of oldies that he's liable to pull out on stage at any second (often confounding his bemused band in the process!). His earliest recordings in 1958 for Folkways presented Eaglin as a solo acoustic folk-blues artist with an extremely eclectic repertoire. His dazzling finger-picking was nothing short of astonishing, but he really wanted to be making R&B with a band. Imperial Records producer Dave Bartholomew granted him the opportunity in 1960, and the results were sensational. Eaglin's fluid, twisting lead guitar on the utterly infectious "Yours Truly" (a Bartholomew composition first waxed by Pee Wee Crayton) and its secpped "Cover Girl" was unique on the New Orleans R&B front, while his brokenhearted cries on "Don't Slam That Door" and "That Certain Door" were positively mesmerizing. Eaglin stuck with Imperial through 1963, when the firm closed up shop in New Orleans, without ever gaining national exposure. *—Bill Dahl*

Country Boy Down in New Orleans / 1958 / Arhoolie ♦♦♦♦♦

Country Boy Down in New Orleans collects 23 tracks Snooks Eaglin recorded in the '50s. During this time, he was a street musician, playing with just one guitar or as a one-man band. On these tracks, he is accompanied by a couple of washboard players and a harpist. As expected, the sound is stripped-down, but it is exciting. Eaglin's early repertoire included a broad variety of blues, folk, and gospel songs and all of these genres are covered thoroughly on this delightful single disc. It may not be the ripping electric blues of his best-known records, but it is just as enjoyable. *—Thom Owens*

That's All Right / 1961 / Prestige/Original Blues Classics ♦♦♦

Recorded during the time in which Eaglin was doubling as a blues/folk singer and a commercial R&B artist (for Imperial), he addresses the acoustic folk and blues side of his repertoire, performing everything solo on 6 and 12-string guitars. Time will probably judge these not to be as interesting as his full-band New Orleans R&B recordings. But this is warm, good-natured acoustic blues, with interpretations of traditional tunes, early blues by Robert Johnson, and then-recent R&B hits by Ray Charles, Arthur Crudup, and Amos Milburn. *—Richie Unterberger*

Baby, You Can Get Your Gun / 1987 / Black Top ✦✦✦✦✦
The first of the masterful guitarist's amazing series of albums for Black Top is an earthly delight; his utterly unpredictable guitar weaves and darts through supple rhythms provided by New Orleans vets Smokey Johnson on drums and Erving Charles Jr. on bass (David Lastie is on sax). Few artists boast Eaglin's "human jukebox" capabilities; his amazingly vast knowledge of eclectic numbers takes in the Four Blazes' "Mary Jo," Tommy Ridgley's "Lavinia," and the Ventures' version of "Perfidia." *—Bill Dahl*

☆ **Teasin' You** / 1992 / Black Top ✦✦✦✦✦
The best of Eaglin's terrific series of Black Top efforts so far—song selection is absolutely unassailable (lots of savage New Orleans covers, from Lloyd Price and Professor Longhair to Willie Tee and Earl King), the band simmers and sizzles with spicy second-line fire (bassist George Porter Jr. and drummer Herman Ernest III are a formidable pair indeed), and Eaglin's churchy, commanding vocals and blistering guitar work are nothing short of mind-boggling throughout the entire disc. *—Bill Dahl*

Soul's Edge / 1995 / Black Top ✦✦✦✦✦
Give this New Orleans master enough studio time, and he'll redo the entire history of postwar R&B his own way. Here he lays his mind to Joe Simon's powerhouse soul ballad "Nine Pound Steel," the Midnighters' "Let's Go, Let's Go, Let's Go," even Bill Haley & the Comets' "Skinny Minnie" and the Five Keys' loopy "Ling Ting Tong," giving each the same singular treatment that he's always brought to his recordings. Porter and Ernest return to lay down their immaculate grooves, and Fred Kemp blows sturdy sax on Eaglin's parade-beat "I Went to the Mardi Gras." *—Bill Dahl*

● **Complete Imperial Recordings** / Oct. 24, 1995 / Capitol ✦✦✦✦✦
Eaglin is apt to be classified as a blues singer with considerable New Orleans R&B influences. This collection of his early-'60s recordings for the Imperial label would be much more appropriately categorized as exactly the opposite. Produced by Dave Bartholomew (who also wrote over half of the material), the thrust of these recordings is most definitely in the classic-'50s/early-'60s New Orleans R&B mold, though Eaglin's vocal delivery may be bluesier than some other practitioners of the sound. It doesn't suffer for this in the least; it's solid stuff betraying the influence of Guitar Slim and Ray Charles (though Eaglin's style is sometimes compared to the latter, it isn't extremely similar, with sparer arrangements and a distinct Creole vocal slur). This compiles 26 tracks (seven previously unreleased) that he cut between 1960 and 1963, none of which were hits, perhaps because the commercial peak of classic New Orleans R&B had already passed. But it's well worth looking into if you like records from the same period by the likes of Bartholomew, Lee Dorsey, and the early Nevilles. *—Richie Unterberger*

Live in Japan / 1997 / Black Top ✦✦✦

Ronnie Earl (Ronald Horvath)

b. Mar. 10, 1953, New York, NY
Guitar / Modern Electric Blues
Guitarist Ronnie Earl (born Ronald Horvath) was born March 10, 1953, in New York City, but later moved to Boston. In 1975, while attending a Muddy Waters concert, he was so moved by what he heard that he decided to learn the guitar and dedicate himself to mastering the blues tradition. He was soon playing in clubs in and around the Boston area as well as backing various blues artists on tour. He claims that his main influences were T-Bone Walker, B.B. King, Magic Sam, and Robert Jr. Lockwood. In 1980, he replaced Duke Robillard in Roomful of Blues and worked with that band for eight years, helping to take the band to national acclaim.

In the '80s, Earl recorded three solo albums with his band the Broadcasters that were very well-received: *Smokin',* (Black Top, 1983) *They Call Me Mr. Earl* (Black Top, 1984), and *I Like It When It Rains* (Antone's, 1990). Earl left Roomful of Blues in 1988 and continues to perform and record. His intense guitar style, somewhat in the style of T-Bone Walker, has made him one of the most respected young players in the business—much in demand as a backup musician for recording dates. *—Michael Erlewine*

Surrounded by Love / May 1991 / Black Top ✦✦✦

● **Test of Time** / 1992 / Black Top ✦✦✦✦✦
Test of Time collects the highlights from Ronnie Earl's six Black Top albums. The 18-song compilation showcases one of the finest blues guitarists of the '80s, picking nearly all of his finest material, which happens to include duets with Robert Jr. Lockwood and Hubert Sumlin. The album is an excellent introduction to Earl, as well as his most consistently entertaining release. *—Thom Owens*

Eye to Eye / 1996 / AudioQuest ✦✦✦

Grateful Heart: Blues and Ballads / Mar. 19, 1996 / Bullseye Blues ✦✦✦✦
Perhaps the smartest move a non-singing guitar-playing virtuoso like Mister Earl could make was ditching the lame singers who permeate most of his earlier efforts and go with an all-instrumental program. On this outing, he surrounds himself with an excellent quartet of players in David "Fathead" Newman on tenor sax, Per Hanson on drums, Rod Carey on bass, and Bruce Katz on keyboards, and the results are simply sublime. Instead of a bunch of Chicago retreads, we are treated to a heady mixture of blues, jazz, soul, swing, you name it, all of it infused with taste, tone, and economy. When Ronnie burns, the results are jaw dropping; when he slows it down, his choice of notes is exquisite. "Welcome Home," "Still Soul Searching," "Drown in My Own Tears," and "Skyman (For Duane Allman)" are just a few of the highlights, but there really isn't a wasted note on this record to be found. Anywhere. *—Cub Koda*

The Colour of Love / Jun. 24, 1997 / Verve ✦✦✦✦

Healing Time / Jan. 1, 2000 / Telarc ✦✦✦✦
Guitarist Ronnie Earl continues his string of all instrumental albums with this stunning follow-up to 1997's critically acclaimed *The Colour of Love.* With sturdy yet subtle assistance from Anthony Geraci on keyboards, Mark Greenberg or Don Williams on drums, Michael "Mudcat" Ward on bass, and, for two tracks, special guest Jimmy McGriff handling the Hammond B-3 in his inimitable fashion, Earl peels off sweet and spicy jazz-blues-gospel licks with the touch of a musician whose heart and soul is intimately infused in his music.

Earl's love of Muddy Waters shines on a sizzling cover of "Catfish Blues" where his guitar alternately screams and moans through the stop-start rhythm of the song as if it's singing the lyrics. But this is primarily a jazz album with a heavy blues influence, and Earl's Kenny Burrell and Grant Green roots are pervasive throughout. His tensile tone ranges from tender and sensitive to biting and majestic, with touches of Carlos Santana's unique phrasing thrown in. Whether digging deep into the achingly soulful slow groove of "Blues for Shawn" or closing out the album with a rapturous "Amazing Grace," Ronnie Earl proves himself to be a master of moods. *Healing Time* effectively moves him into the realm of the guitar greats he idolizes. *—Hal Horowitz*

David "Honeyboy Edwards"

b. Jun. 28, 1915, Shaw, MS
Vocals, Harmonica, Guitar / Delta Blues
Living links to the immortal Robert Johnson are few. There's Robert Jr. Lockwood, of course—and David "Honeyboy" Edwards. Until relatively recently, Edwards was something of an underappreciated figure, but no longer—his slashing, Delta-drenched guitar and gruff vocals are as authentic as it gets.

Edwards had it tough growing up in Mississippi, but his blues prowess (his childhood pals included Tommy McClennan and Robert Petway) impressed Big Joe Williams enough to take him under his wing. Rambling around the south, Honeyboy experienced the great Charley Patton and played often with Robert Johnson. Musicologist Alan Lomax came to Clarksdale, MS, in 1942 and captured Edwards for Library of Congress-sponsored posterity.

Commercial prospects for the guitarist were scant, however—a 1951 78 for Artist Record Co., "Build a Cave" (as Mr. Honey), and four 1953 sides for Chess (that laid unissued until "Drop Down Mama" turned up 17 years later on an anthology constituted the bulk of his early recorded legacy, although Edwards was in Chicago from the mid-'50s on.

The guitarist met young harpist/blues aficionado Michael Frank in 1972. Four years later, they formed the Honeyboy Edwards Blues Band and broke into Chicago's then-fledgling North-side club scene; they also worked as a duo (and continue to do so on occasion). When Frank inaugurated his Earwig label, he enlisted Honeyboy and his longtime pals Sunnyland Slim, Big Walter Horton, Floyd Jones, and Kansas City Red to cut a rather informal album, *Old Friends,* as his second release in 1979. In 1992, Earwig assembled *Delta Bluesman,* a stunning combination of unexpurgated Library of Congress masters and recent performances that show Honeyboy Edwards has lost none of his blues fire. *—Bill Dahl*

● **White Windows** / Sep. 1988 / Evidence ✦✦✦✦✦
David "Honeyboy" Edwards is one of the last surviving Delta-blues warriors and is among the originators of a musical style as evocative and vibrant as any this nation has ever experienced. Edwards' voice, with its ironic, colorful, weary tonal qualities and cutting, keen delivery are contrasted by a crisp, slicing guitar approach. Edwards does not rely on slickness, inventiveness, or niceties; his riffs, lines, phrases, and licks are as aggressive and fiery as his vocals. He showed what real traditional blues singing was all about when he recorded for Blue Suit in 1988. Evidence has reissued that 13-song session in splendid digital glory, as Edwards' triumphant, resounding voice rings through each number. *—Ron Wynn*

I've Been Around / 1995 / 32 Jazz ✦✦✦
This fine solo project features Edwards recorded down in Bruce Iglauer's cellar in 1974. On "Sad & Lonesome," "Take Me in Your Arms," "I Feel So Good Today," and "Big Road Blues," Edwards is backed by Big Walter Horton on amplified harmonica while Honeyboy plays electric guitar. On "Ride With Me Tonight," "Things Have Changed," and "The Woman I'm Loving," Honeyboy's idiosyncratic timing is helped out by the addition of Eddie El on second guitar. A very solid session by this seldom-recorded artist. *—Cub Koda*

Crawling Kingsnake / Jul. 22, 1997 / Testament ✦✦✦✦
Any fan of Delta blues should grab this reissue as fast they can get to it. These are vintage recordings, mostly from 1967, made by scholar-producer Pete Welding when Edwards was 51 years old. Edwards' itinerant lifestyle resulted in his missing many opportunities to record, so that this was only the fifth session he'd had in over 30 years in music, performing solo, with an acoustic guitar on eight of the 13 cuts here. Edwards cuts a daunting figure on the guitar, making the strings sing in several voices at once (check out the playing on "Love Me Over Slow"), and his singing is a match for his playing. The eight solo numbers, dating from 1967, feature the music he was most familiar with, including Robert Johnson's "Sweet Home Chicago" and the title track of this collection. The rest date from a March 1964 session on which Edwards shares the spotlight with singer-harpist John Lee Henley. As a bonus, the last track is an interview from his 1967 solo session in which Edwards talks about Robert Johnson and Tommy Johnson, both of whom he knew personally. The background ambient sound does nothing to detract from the worth of the music, which has a wonderful raw quality. *—Bruce Eder*

World Don't Owe Me Nothing / Dec. 24, 1997 / Earwig ✦✦✦
This is a companion disc to Honeyboy Edwards' autobiography of the same name. It features full-length performances along with interview segments that tell some of the great stories of the blues, particularly trenchant being Edwards' version of the night of Robert Johnson's death. Musical high points include several turns on Johnson material like "Walkin' Blues," "Sweet Home Chicago," and "Crossroads," the latter featuring some slashing slide work from Edwards. Carey Bell contributes some great harp to Edwards' lone guitar, and on other tracks Edwards is ably supported by Rick Sherry on harmonica and washboard. With his timing as idiosyncratic as ever, Edwards also brings a couple of fine originals to the table with "My Mama Told Me" and "Every Now and Then." A great lion-in-winter recording with more than its share of oddball quirks, this is one great listening experience. *—Cub Koda*

Shake 'Em on Down / May 2, 2000 / APO ✦✦✦✦
This 1999 session finds Honeyboy working his acoustic magic in the company of Madison Slim on harmonica and Jimmy D. Lane, son of the late Jimmy Rogers, on second guitar. Recorded at the Blue Heaven Studios (a converted church) in Salina, KS, this is a pretty inspired session with Edwards running through old classics like Charlie Patton's "High Water Everywhere" and "Pony Blues," "Drop Down Mama," "Shake 'Em on Down," "Anna Lee," "Bullfrog Blues," and "Monkey Face Woman." As an added bonus, there's also an interview with this fascinating bluesman, making this session a real keeper. One of his best. *—Cub Koda*

Sleepy John Estes (John Adams Estes)

b. Jan. 25, 1899, Ripley, TN, **d.** Jun. 5, 1977, Brownville, TN
Vocals, Guitar / Prewar Blues, Blues Revival, Memphis Blues, Country-Blues
Big Bill Broonzy called John Estes' style of singing "crying" the blues because of its overt emotional quality. Actually his vocal style harks back to his tenure as a work-gang leader for a railroad maintenance crew, where his vocal improvisations and keen, cutting voice set the pace for work activities. He teamed with mandolinist Yank Rachell and harmonica player Hammie Nixon to play the houseparty circuit in and around Brownsville in the early '20s. Forty years later, the same team reunited to record for Delmark and play the festival circuit. Never an outstanding guitarist, Estes relied on his expressive voice to carry his music, and the recordings he made from 1929 on have enormous appeal and have remained remarkably accessible. Over the course of his career, his music remained simple yet powerful, and despite his sojourns to Memphis or Chicago he retained a traditional down-home sound. One of the true masters of his idiom, he lived in poverty, yet was somehow capable of turning his experiences and the conditions of his life into compelling art. *—Barry Lee Pearson*

The Legend of Sleepy John Estes / 1962 / Delmark ✦✦✦✦
In the late '50s Sleepy John Estes wasn't nearly as visible as he had been before and during World War II—in fact, he had become so obscure that some historians wondered if he had died. But the blues veteran was still very much alive, and in 1962 a 63-year-old Estes (some claimed he was 58 or 57) made an impressive comeback with *The Legend of Sleepy John Estes.* Produced by Delmark president Bob Koester on March 24, 1962, this historic acoustic session finds singer/guitarist Estes joined by Ed Wilkinson on bass, John "Knocky" Parker on piano, and long-time ally Hammie Nixon on harmonica. *Legend* isn't much different from Estes' recordings of the '20s, '30s, and '40s, and the Tennessee native successfully revisits old favorites like "Divin' Duck Blues," "Someday Baby Blues," "Stop That Thing," "Milk Cow Blues," and "Married Woman Blues." Although not the definitive recordings of these songs, Estes' 1962 versions are captivating nonetheless. Delmark has a lot to be proud of, and getting Estes back into the studio after many years of neglect (reunited with Hammie Nixon, no less!) is certainly among the Chicago indie's greatest accomplishments. *—Alex Henderson*

Electric Sleep / 1966 / Delmark ✦✦✦

In Europe / 1966 / Delmark ✦✦✦✦
Having only sporadically left his rural hamlet of Brownsville, TN, for recording trips in Chicago and Memphis, blues guitarist and singer Sleepy John Estes must have found it a bit of a shock to make the 1964 *American Folk-Blues Festival* tour of Europe. Like most contemporary country-blues musicians from the South, Estes did ramble, playing country suppers and plantation parties as a solo act or with a minstrel show, but his exposure to the urban and transatlantic world was still minimal to nonexistent. As evidenced by both reportage and this document of his 1964 trip to Denmark, France, Sweden, Germany, and England, though, Estes mostly enjoyed his first trip abroad, having fun with his international hosts while still living up to his nickname by mysteriously nodding off on several occasions. Traveling with other blues luminaries such as Howlin' Wolf and Sonny Boy Williamson, Estes teamed up with longtime harmonica partner Hammie Nixon (who also plays the jug on a few tunes here) to cut a batch of numbers at studios in Copenhagen and London. The two cover classic Estes material like "Needmore Blues" and "Drop Down Mama" (most of the material here was originally recorded for Decca during the '30s), as well as newer cuts like "Denmark Blues." In fact, throughout the album, Estes updates many of the old songs with references to cities visited and friends made along the tour route. And while Estes' sinuously grainy voice and furtive guitar strumming perfectly reflect the kaleidoscopic nature of the trip, Hammie Nixon's high-lonesome harmonica makes light of the homesickness the two musicians reportedly felt. A great disc that's best heard after first checking out Estes' classic Decca sides. *—Stephen Cook*

Brownsville Blues / 1969 / Delmark ✦✦✦✦
Not to be confused with the *Brownsville Blues* session that Sleepy John Estes recorded for Delmark in the '60s, this *Brownsville Blues* is an Austrian release that focuses on the Tennessee bluesman's early recordings for Victor, Decca, and RCA/Bluebird. Many blues experts will tell you that Estes did his most essential work before World War II, and they speak the truth. The Tennessee country-blues don't get any richer than the 23 selections on this CD, which span 1929-1941 and boast Estes' definitive versions of classics like "Divin' Duck Blues," "Milk Cow Blues," "Married Woman Blues," and "Brownsville Blues." Equally valuable is 1935's "Someday Baby Blues," the gem that became the basis for Big Maceo Merriweather's famous "Worried Life Blues." On these essential recordings, Estes' acoustic guitar playing competent, although not fantastic. But then, one doesn't have to have killer chops to create meaningful music. While Estes was never a great guitarist, he was a compelling storyteller and a most expressive vocalist—and those qualities make *Brownsville Blues* a joy to listen to. For those who don't own any Estes albums and are looking for a single-CD collection of his most essential work, *Brownsville Blues* would be an excellent choice. *—Alex Henderson*

Complete Works, Vol. 1 (1929-1937) / 1990 / Document ✦✦✦✦✦
For completists, specialists and academics, Document's *Complete Works, Vol. 1 (1929-1937)* is invaluable, offering an exhaustive overview of Sleepy John Estes' early recordings. For less dedicated listeners, the disc is a mixed blessing. There are some absolutely wonderful, classic performances on the collection, but the long running time, exacting chronological sequencing, poor fidelity (all cuts are transferred from original acetates and 78s), and number of performances are hard to digest. The serious blues listener will find all these factors to be positive, but enthusiasts and casual listeners will find that the collection is of marginal interest for those very reasons. *—Thom Owens*

Complete Works, Vol. 2 (1937-1941) / 1990 / Document ✦✦✦✦✦
For completists, specialists, and academics, Document's *Complete Works, Vol. 2 (1937-1941)* is invaluable, offering an exhaustive overview of Sleepy John Estes' early recordings. For less dedicated listeners, the disc is a mixed blessing. There are some absolutely wonderful, classic performances on the collection, but the long running time, exacting chronological sequencing, poor fidelity (all cuts are transferred from original acetates and 78s), and number of performances are hard to digest. The serious blues listener will find all these factors to be positive, but enthusiasts and casual listeners will find that the collection is of marginal interest for those very reasons. *—Thom Owens*

★ **Sleepy John Estes 1929-1940: I Ain't Gonna Be Worried No More** / 1992 / Yazoo ✦✦✦✦✦
I Ain't Gonna Be Worried No More compiles 23 songs Sleepy John Estes recorded between 1929 and 1941, capturing the bluesman at the height of his creative powers. Unlike many Delta bluesmen of his era, Estes worked with a full jug band, which gave his music a greater variety of textures. His music swings, with a loose, relaxed feel that isn't heard on many Delta-blues records. Furthermore, his songs are inventive, featuring pseudo-autobiographical lyrics loaded with evocative imagery. Nearly all of his best material is included on *I Ain't Gonna Be Worried No More,* making it as close to a definitive retrospective of Estes' music as possible. *—Thom Owens*

Goin' to Brownsville / Feb. 24, 1998 / Testament ✦✦✦

Frank Frost (Frank Otis Frost)

b. Apr. 15, 1936, Auvergne, AR, **d.** Oct. 12, 1999
Vocals, Piano, Harmonica, Guitar / Juke-Joint Blues, Electric Delta Blues, Soul-Blues, R&B
The atmospheric juke-joint blues of Frank Frost remain steeped in unadulterated Delta funk. But his ongoing musical journey has taken him well outside his Mississippi homebase. Leaving Sonny Boy Williamson's employ in 1959, Frost and drummer Sam Carr settled in Lula, MS. Guitarist Jack Johnson came aboard in 1962 after sitting in with the pair at the Savoy Theatre in Clarksdale. The three meshed perfectly, enough to interest Memphis producer Sam Phillips in a short-lived back-to-the-blues campaign that same year: *Hey Boss Man!* was a wonderful collection of uncompromising Southern blues (albeit totally out of step with the marketplace at the time). Elvis Presley's ex-guitarist Scotty Moore produced Frost's next sessions in Nashville in 1966 for Jewel Records. Augmented by session bassist Chip Young, the trio's tight downhome ensemble work was once again seamless. "My Back Scratcher," Frost's takeoff on Slim Harpo's "Baby Scratch My Back," even dented the R&B charts on Shreveport-based Jewel for three weeks. 1979's *Rockin' the Juke Joint Down,* billed as by the Jelly Roll Kings (after one of the standout songs on that old Phillips International LP), showcased the trio's multi-faceted approach—echoes of R&B, soul, even Johnny & the Hurricanes permeate their Delta-based attack. *—Bill Dahl*

Hey Boss Man / 1962 / Philips ✦✦✦✦✦
On one of the last great blues recordings produced by the legendary Sam Phillips, Frost and his Mississippi cohorts Jack Johnson and Sam Carr play Southern juke, joint blues rough and ready in the classic mold, with plenty of dynamic interplay and nasty, lowdown grooves. *—Bill Dahl*

Jelly Roll Blues / 1991 / Paula ✦✦✦✦
Same band, different producer: this time it was Elvis Presley's legendary guitarist, Scotty Moore, behind the glass as Frost and his pals dished out the lowdown sounds during the mid-'60s for Stan Lewis' Jewel logo. "My Back Scratcher" owes a stylistic debt to Slim Harpo but feels mighty good all the same. The entire 13-song disc reeks of steamy juke-joint ambience. *—Bill Dahl*

Deep Blues / 1992 / Evidence ✦✦✦
Originally issued on Appaloosa, this 1999 reissue teams Frost with producer-guitar, hotshot Fred James, Bob Kommersmith on upright bass, and Gatemouth Brown alumnus Waldo Latowsky on drums. The grooves are straightforward and cleanly played with a true spark of spontaneity plainly evident to the entire session. Even recuts of his old Jewel material like "Ride With Your Daddy Tonight" and "Pocketful of Shells" sound inspired here. A keeper. *—Cub Koda*

Keep Yourself Together / 1996 / Evidence ✦✦✦
This is a nicely put together—if rather unexceptional—set with Frost's vocal and harp ably supported by his long-time drummer Sam Carr, producer Fred James on guitar and Bob Kommersmith on string bass. While nothing on here burns with the smoldering intensity of his early Sun-Phillips International sides or his later sessions for Jewel, a pair of Little Walter tunes ("Everything's Gonna Be Alright," "Just a Feeling") a remake of one of his Sun-P.I. sides ("Come on Home"), and a version of Jimmy Rushing's "Going to Chicago" make this an album more than worthy of a spin or two in the CD player. *—Cub Koda*

The Jelly Roll Kings / Dec. 18, 1998 / HMG ✦✦✦
Recorded in 1998 in the Sonny Boy Williamson *Memorial Music Hall* in Helena, AR, this pares the blues down to a bare-bones sound with Frank Frost on vocals and harmonica (piano on one track) and Sam Carr on drums (vocals on one track, "Owl Head Woman"), tied together with the overdubbed guitar work of producer Fred James, who also provides the unobtrusive bass parts in the background. The result is a very modern-sounding (i.e., powerful) production that nonetheless keeps the format so astoundingly simple, it seems like a throwback to an earlier time. Even better is that all of the material on here is original; only a solid remake of "Jelly Roll King" (previously recorded by Frost for Sun) interrupts the flow of new songs, all of them firmly in the Delta juke-joint tradition. There's something very alive about

these recordings, even with James' overdubbed guitar or bass work, that has as much to do with the sound of the Music Hall as the performances themselves. Highlights include "Let's Go Out Tonight," "Love I Have Is True," "Sittin' On Daddy's Knee," the low-down instrumental "Mess Around," Frost's out-of-tune piano playing behind Carr on "Owl Head Woman" and the Bo Diddley-like closer, "Done With Me," all representative of loose, wonderful, down-home blues playing captured raw, alive, and exciting. *—Cub Koda*

● **Big Boss Man: The Very Best of Frank Frost** / Feb. 2, 1999 / Collectables ♦♦♦♦

Blind Boy Fuller

b. 1908, Wadesboro, NC, **d.** Feb. 13, 1941, Durham, NC

Vocals, Guitar / Prewar Blues, East Coast Blues, Piedmont Blues, Country-Blues, Acoustic Blues

Unlike blues artists like Big Bill or Memphis Minnie who recorded extensively over three or four decades, Blind Boy Fuller recorded his substantial body of work over a short, six-year span. Neverthless, he was one of the most recorded artists of his time and by far the most popular and influential Piedmont-blues player of all time. Fuller could play in multiple styles: Slide, ragtime, pop, and blues were all enhanced by his National steel guitar. Initially discovered and promoted by Carolina entrepreneur H. B. Long, Fuller recorded for ARC and Decca. He also served as a conduit to recording sessions, steering fellow blues musicians to the studio. In spite of Fuller's recorded output, most of his musical life was spent as a street musician and house party favorite, and he possessed the skills to reinterpret and cover the hits of other artists as well. In this sense, he was a synthesizer of styles, parallel in many ways to Robert Johnson, his contemporary who died three years earlier. *—Barry Lee Pearson*

★ **Truckin' My Blues Away** / 1978 / Yazoo ♦♦♦♦♦

For most listeners, Yazoo's *Truckin' My Blues Away* may be a better bet than Columbia/Legacy's *East Coast Piedmont Style*, since it actually has a higher concentration of strong material, capturing the influential bluesman at his peak. All of the 14 tracks were recorded between 1935 and 1938, and there are a number of exceptional performances here, including "Homesick and Lonesome Blues," "Truckin' My Blues Away," "I Crave My Pig Meat, " "Walking My Troubles Away," and "Sweet Honey Hole." It's a nice, concise introduction and, best of all, there's no duplication between this disc and *East Coast Piedmont Style*, making the two discs wonderful, complementary collections that tell a comprehensive story when taken together. *—Thom Owens*

East Coast Piedmont Style / Aug. 1991 / Columbia/Legacy ♦♦♦♦

Blind Boy Fuller, who died in 1940 when he was only 33, recorded extensively during 1935-40. HIs guitar playing was in the tradition of the ragtime-influenced Blind Blake and Blind Willie McTell while his singing was simple and direct. The music on this CD reissue becomes a bit repetitive after awhile for Fuller generally lacked variety but, taken in small doses (as if one were listening to the original 78s and treasuring individual songs), Blind Boy Fuller's performances were often memorable. The reissue is a cross section of his work with the emphasis on his earliest recordings. Guitarist Blind Gary Davis, Bull City Red on washboard, and harmonica wiz Sonny Terry help out on a few numbers; 5 of the 20 selections were previously unreleased. *—Scott Yanow*

Jesse Fuller

b. Mar. 12, 1896, Jonesboro, GA, **d.** Jan. 29, 1976, Oakland, CA

Vocals, Kazoo, Harmonica, Guitar / Blues Revival, Folk-Blues, Country-Blues, West Coast Blues

Equipped with a bandful of instruments operated by various parts of his anatomy, Bay Area-legend Jesse Fuller was a folk-music favorite in the '50s and '60s. His infectious rhythm and gentle charm graced old folk tunes, spirituals, and blues alike. One of his inventions was a homemade, foot-operated instrument called the "footdella" or "fotdella." Naturally, Fuller never needed other accompanists to back his one-man show. His best-known songs include "San Francisco Bay Blues" and "Beat It on Down the Line" (the first one covered by Janis Joplin, the second by the Grateful Dead). Jesse's musical career didn't properly begin until the early '50s, when he decided to become a professional musician—he was 55 years old at the time. Performing as a one-man band, he began to get spots on local television shows and nightclubs. However, Fuller's career didn't take off until 1954, when he wrote "San Francisco Bay Blues." The song helped him land a record contract with the independent Cavalier label and in 1955, he recorded his first album, *Folk Blues: Working on the Railroad with Jesse Fuller.* The album was a success and soon he was making records for a variety of labels. In the late '50s and early '60s, Fuller became one of the key figures of the blues revival, helping bring the music to a new, younger audience. *—Jim O'Neal & Stephen Thomas Erlewine*

Jazz, Folk Songs, Spirituals & Blues / Apr. 1958 / Good Time Jazz ♦♦♦♦♦

Jesse Fuller was among the greatest one-man bands in blues history. The title of this 1958 date adequately described the session's musical width and depth; Fuller handled everything from old spirituals such as as "I'm Going to Meet My Loving Mother" to the rollicking "Memphis Boogie" and "Fingerbuster" and the concluding "Hesitation Blues." As sole performer, melodic, rhythmic, and performing focus, Fuller's energy never wanes through the CD's 11 numbers. He nicely conveys the varying moods, themes, and sentiments, knowing which lyrics to emphasize, when to intensify the pace and when to lower his voice and let the music make the point. *—Ron Wynn*

● **San Francisco Bay Blues** / 1963 / Good Time Jazz ♦♦♦♦♦

By the time *San Francisco Bay Blues* was released in 1963, the title track had long been established as a classic and Jesse Fuller's career had been revived. Nevertheless, the album may be his finest, containing wonderful versions of "San Francisco Bay Blues," "Jesse's New Midnight Special," "John Henry," "I Got a Mind to Ramble," and "Crazy About a Woman," that find Fuller at his easygoing best. *—Thom Owens*

Favorites / 1965 / Prestige/Original Blues Classics ♦♦♦

Jesse Fuller's *Favorites* is a highly enjoyable collection of the singer's favorite blues standards. Performing everything as a solo piece, he runs through classics like "Key to the Highway," "The Midnight Special," and "Brownskin Gal" with humor and warmth. It's a small, but entertaining, gem. *—Thom Owens*

Frisco Bound / 1968 / Arhoolie ♦♦♦♦

A one-man band with guitar, harmonica, kazoo, and "footdella" bass, these are some of his first recordings, ca. 1955. Innocent echoes of turn-of-the-century rural America. *—Mark A. Humphrey*

Lowell Fulson

b. Mar. 31, 1921, Tulsa, OK, **d.** Mar. 6, 1999

Vocals, Guitar / West Coast Blues, Texas Blues, Electric Texas Blues, Soul-Blues

Lowell Fulson has recorded every shade of blues imaginable. Polished urban blues, rustic two-guitar duets with his younger brother Martin, funk-tinged grooves that pierced the mid-'60s charts—clearly, the veteran guitarist, who's been at it now for more than half a century, isn't afraid to experiment. Fulson first hit big in 1948 with "Three O'Clock Blues," later covered by B.B. King. When Swing Time Records snapped him up soon after, the hits really began to flow: the immortal "Every Day I Have the Blues," "Blue Shadows," the two-sided holiday perennial "Lonesome Christmas," and a groovy mid-tempo instrumental "Low Society Blues" that really hammers home how tremendously important pianist Lloyd Glenn and alto saxist Earl Brown were to Fulson's maturing sound (all charted in 1950!). Fulson toured extensively from then on, his band stocked for a time with dazzling pianist Ray Charles and saxist Stanley Turrentine. He inked a longterm pact with Chess in 1954. His first single for the firm was the classic "Reconsider Baby;" the relentless mid-tempo blues proved a massive hit and perennial cover item—even Elvis Presley cut it in 1960. But apart from "Loving You," the guitarist's subsequent Checker output failed to find widespread favor with the public. Baffling, since Fulson's crisp, concise guitar work and sturdy vocals were as effective as ever. 1965's driving "Black Nights" became his first smash in a decade, and "Tramp," a loping funk-injected workout co-written by Fulson and Jimmy McCracklin, did even better, restoring the guitarist to R&B stardom, gaining plenty of pop spins, and inspiring a playful Stax cover by Otis Redding and Carla Thomas only a few months later that outsold Fulson's original. *—Bill Dahl*

★ **Hung Down Head** / 1954 / MCA/Chess ♦♦♦♦♦

The most indispensable collection in Fulson's vast discography. He was hitting on all burners during the mid-'50s when he was with Chess, waxing the immortal "Reconsider Baby," and swinging gems like "Check Yourself," "Do Me Right," and "Trouble, Trouble," and the supremely doomy "Tollin' Bells," here in many truncated false takes before he and the band finally jell. *—Bill Dahl*

I've Got the Blues / 1973 / Fuel 2000 ♦♦♦

Everyday I Have the Blues / 1984 / Night Train ♦♦♦♦♦

The first of two extremely solid compilations of the guitarist's late-'40s/early-'50s output for Jack Lauderdale's L.A.-based Swing Time imprint. You'll need 'em both, since the essentials are spread across them about evenly—Fulson's smashes "Every Day," "Lonesome Christmas," and "Blue Shadows" regally inhabit this 20-cut disc. *—Bill Dahl*

It's a Good Day / 1988 / Rounder ♦♦♦

San Francisco Blues / 1988 / Black Lion ♦♦♦♦♦

Guitarist and vocalist Lowell Fulson helped establish his reputation with a string of fine songs for the Swingtime label in the late '40s and early '50s. Fulson showed he could belt out hard-hitting blues, do sentimental ballads, double-entendre novelty pieces, or irony-filled laments, and also play riveting solos. This '92 CD reissue collects 16 early Fulson numbers, all original compositions, and features Fulson leading a group with Lloyd Glenn, King Solomon or Rufus J. Russell on piano, Ralph Hamilton, Billy Hadnott or Floyd Montgomery on bass, and Bob Harvey or Asal Carson on drums. *—Ron Wynn*

Tramp/Soul / 1991 / Ace ♦♦♦♦♦

The veteran guitarist's two best mid-'60s albums for Kent Records on one packed-to-the-gills CD. Fulson cannily made the leap into soul-slanted grooves while at Kent, scoring a major R&B smash with "Tramp." Also aboard is Fulson's classic "Black Nights," "Talkin' Woman" (later revived most memorably by Albert Collins as "Honey Hush"), and a fine version of Smokey Hogg's enduring "Too Many Drivers." *—Bill Dahl*

Hold On / May 1992 / Bullseye Blues ♦♦♦♦

My First Recordings / Jan. 21, 1997 / Arhoolie ♦♦♦♦

Twenty-six tracks that Fulson cut between 1946 and 1951 for the Swing Time, Big Town, and Down Town labels. This is far more sparsely produced, and less urbane in feel, than the material Lowell would record for Chess throughout the '50s. Indeed, on ten of the cuts, he's supported only by his brother Martin on rhythm guitar; there's a small combo on the remainder of the cuts, but a fairly subdued one. Those who prefer their blues down-home might like this better than the more polished sound that Fulson moved into for the rest of his career. It's city blues just out of the country, with Fulson's high, pleading vocals and sharp, countrified electric licks to the fore. The most famous song, by far, is the original version of "Three O'-Clock Blues," which was covered for a huge R&B hit by B.B. King in the early '50s. *—Richie Unterberger*

The Complete Chess Masters (50th Anniversary Collection) / Nov. 4, 1997 / MCA ♦♦♦♦♦

Two-CD, 45-song compilation covers Fulson's Chess years, which spanned 1954 to 1963. Fulson didn't have a great deal of commercial success at Chess (the big exception being "Reconsider Baby," which leads off this set), and his jazzy West Coast form of R&B/blues was considerably more polished than the electrified Delta blues for which Chess is most renowned. Most of this, in fact, was recorded not in Chicago, but in Los Angeles, where Fulson could work with combos more sympathetic to his style. You'd have to consider this Fulson's peak, however, and the two discs' worth of material is not excessive, due to the consistency of his material and vocal confidence throughout the decade. It's not without its weird moments of rawness, either, as in "Blues Rhumba," the Bo Diddley-esque guitar that opens "Please Don't Go," Willie Dixon's classic dirge moaning blues "Tollin' Bells," and the (deliberately?) out-of-tune guitar licks that open "K.C. Bound" with a bang. "Smokey Room" and "Be On Your Merry Way" were previously unreleased in the U.S.; "Father Time" and the alternate takes of "Lonely Hours" and "Check Yourself" were previously unreleased anywhere. *—Richie Unterberger*

My Baby / 1998 / Jewel ✦✦✦✦
Lowell Fulson always moved with the times, evidenced by the fact that one of his best known tunes was the mid-'60s soul number, "Tramp." This 11-track collection of sides recorded in the late '60s for the Shreveport, LA-based Jewel label finds him moving into blues-rock territory with an eye toward a piece of B.B. and Albert King's turf to call his own. With the Muscle Shoals rhythm section in place on most of the tracks (appearing here uncredited, as this disc features no liner notes, recording dates or personnel, songwriter, and publishing information whatsoever), the accent is more on commercial breakthrough than down-home blues. From the opening slide guitar riff on "Look at You Baby," it's clear that Lowell Fulson is in full command of his blues powers when he needs them. But his stomp, down, noisy version of the Beatles' "Why Don't We Do It in the Road" shares the same seemed-like-a-good-idea-at-the-time territory as Muddy Waters' version of "Let's Spend the Night Together" and is totally devoid of any blues content whatsoever. Fulson plugs in a wah-wah on a couple of tunes and on "Don't Destroy Me," comes up with a solo that recalls both Hendrix and Stevie Ray, a long stretch from Oklahoma. While his potent slide and lead guitar work pop up here and there, this is mostly Fulson letting the band do the lion's share of the work and setting the pace. Certainly not the place to start with this prolific artist, but an interesting chapter in his career nonetheless. *—Cub Koda*

The Tramp Years / May 16, 2000 / Ace ✦✦✦✦✦
The first of a planned series of three compilations devoted to Fulson's '60s Kent sides, this focuses on the chronological middle (and commercial peak) of his Kent output. "Tramp" itself, possibly Fulson's most well-known song (certainly to the pop and soul audience), leads off the disc, whose 24 tracks span 1966 to 1969. Much of the material shows Fulson to be one of the masters of blues-soul crossover (and one of the first to explore that sub-genre), his work the equal of somewhat more renowned artists working the field, like B.B. King, Albert King, and Little Milton. There's a loose and lean feel that sets this off—in a good way—from the beefier, more disciplined blues-soul outings recorded by Stax and some other labels. Possibly because this series is so thorough in its coverage, the material is not always top of the line; some of the outings are routine, going through the blues motions in songwriting if not performance. Still, more often than not this is a pleasure, both for Fulson's relaxed vocals and his contrasting stinging, fluid guitar licks. A half dozen of the tracks are previously unissued, including "It Takes Money," a song recorded right after "Tramp"; In interviews Fulson expressed annoyance that Kent withheld this from release. As another bonus for the committed collector, four songs ("I'm Sinking," "Blues Pain," "What the Heck," and "Price for Love") are presented in extended versions from their original issue. *—Richie Unterberger*

Anson Funderburgh

b. Nov. 15, 1954, Plano, TX
Guitar / Modern Electric Texas Blues, Electric Texas Blues, Modern Electric Blues
Dallas-based guitarist Anson Funderburgh has taken his band the Rockets out of the clubs and onto the festival stages with his critically acclaimed recordings for the Blac Top label out of New Orleans. With Jackson, MS-native Sam Myers delivering the vocals and harmonica treatments, this band mixes up a powerful gumbo of Texas jump blues and Delta blues that can't be found anywhere else. Funderburgh formed the Rockets in 1978, but didn't meet Myers until 1982. Funderburgh recorded with the Fabulous Thunderbirds on their *Butt Rockin'* album, and went solo in 1981, when the New Orleans-based Black Top released *Talk to You by Hand,* the label's first release. *—Richard Skelly*

Sins / 1987 / Black Top ✦✦✦✦✦
Sins is a good fusion of Texas and Delta blues, alternating between rocking shuffles and laid-back ballads. Funderburgh's playing is tasteful—he has an enticing sound, but he never falls into grandstanding—and Sam Myers' voice is rich and his harp playing intoxicating. Furthermore, the selection of material is first-rate, featuring sharp originals and well-chosen covers from the likes of Percy Mayfield and Elmore James. The result— one of Anson Funderburgh's best albums. *—Thom Owens*

Rack 'em Up / 1989 / Black Top ✦✦✦

Tell Me What I Want to Hear / 1991 / Black Top ✦✦✦✦✦
First-rate, contemporary Texas shuffle and blues with tasteful, biting guitar comes from Funderburgh great vocals and harp from Mississippian Sam Myers. This is their most varied and ambitious release to date (the band seems to get better with each album). The title track was used in the movie *China Moon.* "Rent Man Blues" is a humorous dialog between Myers and guest-vocalist Carol Fran. Myers also adds an "answer" song to the blues classic "Sloppy Drunk." *—Niles J. Frantz*

● **Thru the Years: A Retrospective (1981-1992)** / 1992 / Black Top ✦✦✦✦✦
Thru the Years: A Retrospective (1981-1992) collects the highlights from Funderburgh's albums for Black Top, drawing from all the different bands he fronted in that decade or so. The best tracks remain his cuts with Sam Myers or Darrell Nulisch, but the finest songs from his lesser bands are included, making *Thru the Years* an excellent way to get acquainted with the modern blues guitar hero. *—Thom Owens*

That's What They Want / Apr. 15, 1997 / Black Top ✦✦✦✦

Change in My Pocket / Mar. 2, 1999 / Bullseye Blues ✦✦✦

Jazz Gillum (William McKinley Gillum)

b. Sep. 11, 1904, Indianola, MS, **d.** Mar. 29, 1966, Chicago, IL
Vocals, Harmonica / Prewar Blues, Acoustic Chicago Blues
Next to John Lee "Sonny Boy" Williamson, no harmonica player was as popular or as much in demand on recording sessions during the '30s as Jazz Gillum. His high, reedy sound meshed perfectly on dozens of hokum sides on the Bluebird label, both as a sideman and as a leader. Gillum was evidently teaching himself how to play harmonica by the tender age of six, and after running away from home in 1911 he spent the next dozen or so years working a day job and spending his weekends playing for tips on local streetcorners. When he visited Chicago in 1923, he found the environment very much to his liking and put down roots there. There he met guitarist Big Bill Broonzy and the two of them started working club dates around the city as a duo. By 1934, Gillum started popping up on recording dates for ARC and later Bluebird, RCA Victor's budget label. This association would prove to be a lasting as Chicago producer Lester Melrose frequently called on Gillum as a sideman one as part of the "Bluebird beat" house band and to cut sides on his own. His career seemed to screech to a halt when the label folded in the late '40s. *—Cub Koda*

● **The Bluebird Recordings 1934-1938** / Feb. 25, 1997 / Bluebird/RCA ✦✦✦✦✦
The Bluebird Recordings 1934-1938 is the best CD retrospective yet assembled of Jazz Gillum's peak years, offering 22 tracks that find him at his easygoing best ncluding such songs as "Early in the Morning," "Don't Scandalize My Name," "Alberta Blues," "Just Like Jessie James," "Reefer Head Woman," "Worried and Bothered," and "Good Old 51 Highway." Document's multi-volume series may be a more complete overview of his works, but this remains the best summation of his strengths and talents. *—Thom Owens*

Roll Dem Bones 1938-1949 / 1938-1949 / Wolf ✦✦✦✦
Roll Dem Bones 1938-49 rounds up a number of sides not issued on the Document series, offering good insight into the final days of Jazz Gillum's career. While it isn't the first place to go—RCA's concise and comprehensive Bluebird Recordings 1934-1938 holds that title—it nevertheless is a welcome addition to any serious blues historian that has all the Document reissues. *—Thom Owens*

Guitar Shorty (David Kearney)

b. Sep. 8, 1939, Houston, TX
Vocals, Guitar / West Coast Blues
When he's not turning somersaults, doing backwards flips, and standing on his head—all while playing, of course—Guitar Shorty is prone to cutting loose with savagely slashing licks on his instrument. Live, he's simply amazing—and after some lean years, his two recent albums for Black Top have proven that all that energy translates vividly onto tape.

At age 17, David Kearney was already gigging steadily in Tampa, FL. One night, he was perched on the bandstand when he learned that the mysterious "Guitar Shorty" advertised on the club's marquee was none other than he! His penchant for stage gymnastics was inspired by the flamboyant Guitar Slim, whose wild antics are legendary. In 1957, Shorty cut his debut single, "You Don't Treat Me Right," for Chicago's Cobra Records under Willie Dixon's astute direction. Three superb 45s in 1959 for tiny Pull Records in Los Angeles (notably "Hard Life") rounded out Shorty's discography for quite a while.

During the '60s, he married Jimi Hendrix's stepsister and lived in Seattle, where the rock guitar god caught Shorty's act (and presumably learned a thing or two about inciting a throng) whenever he came off the road. Shorty's career had its share of ups and downs—once he was reduced to competing on Chuck Barris' zany *The Gong Show,* where he copped first prize for delivering "They Call Me Guitar Shorty" while balanced on his noggin.

Los Angeles had long since reclaimed Shorty by the time things started to blossom anew with the 1991 album *My Way on the Highway* for the British JSP logo (with guitarist Otis Grand in support). From there, Black Top signed Shorty; 1993's dazzling *Topsy Turvy* and 1995's *Get Wise to Yourself* have been the head-over-heels results so far. *Roll Over, Baby* followed in 1998. *—Bill Dahl*

My Way on the Highway / 1991 / JSP ✦✦✦✦
Until he joined forces with British guitarist Otis Grand's band and waxed this very credible comeback set, David "Guitar Shorty" Kearney's legacy was largely limited to a solitary single for Cobra and a handful of great but legendarily obscure follow-ups for L.A.-based Pull Records during the late '50s. The acrobatic guitarist informed everyone he was alive and lively with this one, exhibiting his Guitar Slim roots on "Down Thru the Years" and slashing with a vengeance on "No Educated Woman" and the title cut (but shouldn't it have read "or the highway?"). *—Bill Dahl*

Topsy Turvy / 1993 / Black Top ✦✦✦✦✦
More impressive than Shorty's British venture thanks to superior production values and a better handle on his past (there's a stellar remake of "Hard Life"), *Topsy Turvy* made it clear that Guitar Shorty was back to stay stateside. Black Top assembled a fine New Orleans combo for the majority of the album, as Shorty proved that his act translates beautifully to record minus the crowd-pleasing acrobatic antics. *—Bill Dahl*

Get Wise to Yourself / 1995 / Black Top ✦✦✦✦
No sophomore jinx for this veteran L.A. blues guitar wildman. Other than the discordant pseudo-New Orleans number "A Fool Who Wants to Stay," this is non-stop red-hot blues axe with a funky Crescent City twist and a skin-tight horn section led by saxist Kaz Kazanoff. *—Bill Dahl*

● **Roll Over, Baby** / Aug. 11, 1998 / Black Top ✦✦✦✦✦

Guitar Slim (Eddie Jones)

b. Dec. 10, 1926, Greenwood, MS, **d.** Feb. 7, 1959, New York, NY
Vocals, Guitar / New Orleans Blues
No '50s blues guitarist even came close to equalling the flamboyant Guitar Slim in the showmanship department. Armed with an estimated 350 feet of cord between his axe and his amp, Slim would confidently stride onstage wearing a garishly hued suit of red, blue, or green—with his hair usually dyed to match! It's rare to find a blues guitarist hailing from Texas or Louisiana who doesn't cite Slim as one of his principal influences; Buddy Guy, Earl King, Guitar Shorty, Albert Collins, Chick Willis, and plenty more have enthusiastically testified to Slim's enduring sway. With the emergence of the stunning "The Things That I Used to Do" on Art Rupe's Specialty logo, Slim's star rocketed to blazing ascendancy nationwide.

Combining a swampy ambience with a churchy arrangement, the New Orleans-cut track was a monster hit, pacing the R&B charts for an amazing 14 weeks in 1954. Strangely, although he waxed several stunning follow-ups for Specialty in the same tortured vein—"The Story of My Life," "Something to Remember You By," "Sufferin' Mind"—as well as the blistering rockers "Well I Done Got Over It," "Letter to My Girlfriend," and "Quicksand," Slim never charted again. *—Bill Dahl*

The Things That I Used to Do / 1964 / Specialty ✦✦

Atco Sessions / Jul. 1988 / Atlantic ✦✦✦
Sometimes a bit subdued compared to his bone-chilling output for Specialty, these 1956-1958 sides for Atco still possess considerable charm, especially the tough "It Hurts to Love Someone" and "If I Should Lose You," which conjure up the same hellfire and brimstone intensity as Slim's earlier work. *—Bill Dahl*

★ **Sufferin' Mind** / 1991 / Specialty ✦✦✦✦✦
His guitar fraught with manic high-end distortion and his vocals fried over church-fired intensity, Eddie "Guitar Slim" Jones influenced a boatload of disciples while enjoying the rewards that came with his 1954 R&B chart-topper "The Things That I Used to Do." This 26-song survey of Slim's seminal 1953-1955 Specialty catalog rates with the best New Orleans blues ever cut—besides the often-imitated but never-duplicated smash, his "Story of My Life," "Sufferin' Mind," and "Something to Remember You By" are overwhelming in their ringing back-alley fury. Slim could rock, too: "Well I Done Got Over It," "Quicksand," "Certainly All," and the raucous introduction "Guitar Slim" drive with blistering power (saxist Joe Tillman was a worthy foil for the flamboyant guitarist in the solo department). *—Bill Dahl*

Buddy Guy

b. Jul. 30, 1936, Lettsworth, LA
Vocals, Guitar (Electric), Guitar / Modern Electric Chicago Blues, Electric Chicago Blues
He's Chicago's blues king today, ruling his domain just as his idol and mentor Muddy Waters did before him. Yet there was a time, and not all that long ago either, when Buddy Guy couldn't even negotiate a decent record deal. Times sure have changed for the better—Guy's first three albums for Silvertone in the '90s all earned Grammys. Eric Clapton unabashedly calls Buddy Guy his favorite blues axeman, and so do a great many adoring fans worldwide. High-energy guitar histrionics and boundless onstage energy have always been Guy trademarks, along with a tortured vocal style that's nearly as distinctive as his incendiary rapid-fire fretwork. His first Chess single in 1960, "First Time I Met the Blues" and its follow-up, "Broken Hearted Blues," were fiery, tortured slow blues brilliantly showcasing Guy's whammy-bar-enriched guitar and shrieking, hellhound-on-his-trail vocals. Although he's often complained that Leonard Chess wouldn't allow him to turn up his guitar loud enough, the claim doesn't wash: Guy's 1960-1967 Chess catalog remains his most satisfying body of work. A shuffling "Let Me Love You Baby," the impassioned downbeat items "Ten Years Ago," "Stone Crazy," "My Time After Awhile," and "Leave My Girl Alone," and a bouncy "No Lie" rate with the hottest blues waxings of the '60s. Guy's reputation among rock guitar gods such as Eric Clapton, Jimi Hendrix, and Stevie Ray Vaughan was unsurpassed, but prior to his Grammy-winning 1991 Silvertone disc *Damn Right, I've Got the Blues*, he amazingly hadn't issued a domestic album in a decade. That's when the Buddy Guy bandwagon really picked up steam—he began selling out auditoriums and turning up on network television (David Letterman, Jay Leno, etc.). Guy, whose club remains the most successful blues joint in Chicago (you'll likely find him sitting at the bar whenever he's in town), is without a doubt the Windy City's reigning blues artist—and he rules benevolently. *—Bill Dahl*

I Left My Blues in San Francisco / 1967 / Chess ✦✦✦✦✦
Guy's last Chess album finds him shifting gears to keep up with the scene. His turns on "Keep It to Yourself," "Crazy Love," "When My Left Eye Jumps," "Leave My Girl Alone," and "I Suffer With the Blues" are some examples of this mercurial guitarist at his explosive best. The rest of the album is filled with groovy, soul-styled workouts; some of them succeed and some sound a bit dated, but overall this is one of Buddy's stronger efforts.
—Cub Koda

A Man and the Blues / 1968 / Vanguard ✦✦✦✦
The guitarist's first album away from Chess—and to be truthful, it sounds as though it could have been cut at 2120 S. Michigan, with Guy's deliciously understated guitar work and a tight combo anchored by three saxes and pianist Otis Spann laying down tough grooves on the vicious "Mary Had a Little Lamb," "I Can't Quit the Blues," and an exultant cover of Mercy Dee's "One Room Country Shack." *—Bill Dahl*

Buddy Guy & Junior Wells Play the Blues / 1972 / Rhino ✦✦✦
Considering the troubled background of this album (Eric Clapton, Ahmet Ertegun, and Tom Dowd only ended up with eight tracks at a series of 1970 sessions in Miami; two years later, the J. Geils Band was brought in to cut two additional songs to round out the long-delayed LP for 1972 release), the results were pretty impressive. Guy contributes dazzling lead axe to their revival of "T-Bone Shuffle," Wells provides a sparkling remake of Sonny Boy's "My Baby She Left Me," and Guy is entirely credible in a grinding Otis Redding mode on the southern soul stomper "A Man of Many Words." *—Bill Dahl*

I Was Walkin' through the Woods / 1974 / MCA/Chess ✦✦✦✦✦
Ten of the mercurial guitarist's best recordings ever for Chess, cut during his early-'60s peak. "First Time I Met the Blues" and "Broken Hearted Blues" are harrowing downbeat blues of enormous power, Guy's shrieks and tremolo-rich guitar bursts boasting an intensity level he's only achieved intermittently ever since. Even better, they're here in stereo—unlike virtually every other Chess collection to follow. *—Bill Dahl*

Live in Montreux / Jul. 9, 1977 / Evidence ✦✦✦

Drinkin' TNT 'n Smokin' Dynamite / 1982 / Blind Pig ✦✦✦

Alone & Acoustic / 1991 / Alligator ✦✦✦

Damn Right, I've Got the Blues / 1991 / Silvertone ✦✦✦✦✦
Grammy-winning comeback set that brought Guy back to prominence after a long studio hiatus. Too many clichéd cover choices—"Five Long Years," "Mustang Sally," "Black Night," "There Is Something on Your Mind"—to earn unreserved recommendation, but Guy's frenetic guitar histrionics ably cut through the superstar-heavy proceedings (Eric Clapton, Jeff Beck, and Mark Knopfler all turn up) on the snarling title cut and a handful of others. *—Bill Dahl*

The Complete Chess Studio Sessions / 1992 / MCA/Chess ✦✦✦✦✦
Here's everything that fleet-fingered Buddy Guy waxed for Chess from 1960 to 1966, including numerous unissued-at-the-time masters, offering the most in-depth peek at his formative years imaginable. Stone Chicago blues-classics ("Ten Years Ago," "My Time After Awhile," "Let Me Love You Baby," "Stone Crazy"), rockin' oddities ("American Bandstand," "$100 Bill," "Slop Around"), even a cut that features guitarist Lacy Gibson's vocal rather than Guy's ("My Love Is Real") are among some 47 sizzling songs. *—Bill Dahl*

★ **The Very Best of Buddy Guy** / 1992 / Rhino ✦✦✦✦✦
Credible attempt to digitally summarize Guy's entire pre-Silvertone career on a single 18-song disc. Encompasses the guitarist's 1957 demo "The Way You Been Treating Me," two killer Cobras, four of his hottest Chess sides, a couple notable Vanguards, a pair of alluring Atlantics, and three tremendously unsubtle 1981 items from Guy's days with the British JSP label. *—Bill Dahl*

Feels Like Rain / 1993 / Silvertone ✦✦✦

Slippin' In / 1994 / Silvertone ✦✦✦✦✦
Now this is more like it: no sign of any superfluous duets, and far fewer hoary standards to contend with (only the Z.Z. Hill title track, in fact). Lots of high-energy guitar fireworks and vocal intensity from the perpetually eager-to-please blues superstar, as he drives through well-chosen numbers first rendered by Bobby Bland, Jimmy Reed, Charles Brown, and Fenton Robinson and Guy's own impassioned "Cities Need Help" and "Little Dab-A-Doo." *—Bill Dahl*

Southern Blues 1957-63 / 1994 / Paula ✦✦✦
Kind of a thrown-together hodgepodge, but still a worthwhile add to your CD collection. Guy's four indispensable 1958 sides for Cobra are here (along with alternates of "This Is the End" and the Guitar Slim-influenced "You Sure Can't Do"), while Guy provides crackling lead guitar on four 1963 outings by singer Jesse Fortune (notably the minor-key rhumba "Too Many Cooks"). Finally, there are two demos that Guy cut at a Baton Rouge radio station back in 1957—or they're supposed to be here, anyway: the crudely engaging "The Way You Been Treatin' Me" is definitely Buddy Guy, but "I Hope You Come Back Home" isn't (no guesses from this corner on exactly who it may be, either). *—Bill Dahl*

Live! The Real Deal / Apr. 1996 / Silvertone ✦✦✦✦

☆ **Buddy's Blues (Chess 50th Anniversary Collection)** / Apr. 8, 1997 / MCA ✦✦✦✦✦
As part of MCA's Chess Records 50th Anniversary series, this sweats his multi-disc retrospective, *The Complete Chess Studio Recordings*, down to a scintillating 15-track package and comes up with a bare-bones winner. There's loads of great guitar on classics like "First Time I Met the Blues," "Let Me Love You Baby," "Pretty Baby," "My Time After Awhile," "Stone Crazy," and Buddy's voice is at its whiplash exuberant best. Unexpected bonuses pop up in the comp's kickoff track, a full-length version of "Worried Mind," that's issued here without the overdubbed applause and crowd noises that accompanied its original release on *Folk Festival Of The Blues* (see Muddy Waters entry). Also noteworthy is Junior Wells' appearance on chromatic harp on "Ten Years Ago," and Guy's stellar guitar behind Lacy Gibson's vocal on a Buddy Guy original, "My Love Is Real." And special note must also be made of the spacious stereo mixes used on this compilation, making these 30-year-old-plus tracks shine like diamonds coming off the laser beam. We also experience all the stylistic turns toward a kinship with the burgeoning soul and rock scenes that Buddy would make toward the end of his Chess tenure, along with the smoking slow burners that are his trademark, some of which clock in at four to six minutes here. With his very best tracks compiled on one disc and with beautiful transfers of them to enhance the listening experience, this should be one of your very first stops in absorbing the sides that made Buddy's reputation among blues fans and guitar aficionados the world over. *—Cub Koda*

Heavy Love / Jun. 2, 1998 / Silvertone ✦✦✦

Buddy's Baddest: The Best of Buddy Guy / Jun. 15, 1999 / Silvertone ✦✦✦
Buddy Guy revitalized his career when he signed with Silvertone Records in the early '90s. His first album for the label, *Damn Right, I've Got the Blues*, was a smash success, earning critical acclaim, awards, and sales hand over fist. Prior to that record, he was a legend only among blues fans; afterward, he was a star. Although it was a bit too rock-oriented and slick for purists, *Damn Right* was a terrific album, setting the pace not only for Guy but for modern electric blues in the '90s. As the decade wore on, Guy continued to make albums for Silvertone, some of them a little complacent, others quite excellent. *Buddy's Baddest: The Best of Buddy Guy* attempts to summarize those years in 14 songs, including three previously unreleased cuts. Not surprisingly, the compilers favor the Guy of *Damn Right*, featuring four songs from the record and three from its soundalike sequel, *Feels Like Rain*. Only two tracks from *Slippin' In*, his hardest blues record for the label, made the cut, while the fine live album *Live! The Real Deal* and the misguided *Heavy Love* are represented by a track apiece. In other words, a lot of good stuff remains on the original albums, which is doubly unfortunate since the three unreleased cuts are all throwaways. By relying so heavily on two records, *Buddy's Baddest* doesn't wind up being an accurate portrait of Guy's Silvertone recordings. That doesn't mean it's a bad listen, since the first ten songs are all very good and quite entertaining. However, anyone who has *Damn Right* but wants to dig deeper into Guy's Silvertone albums may prefer to pick up *Feels Like Rain*, which offers more of the same crossover Chicago blues, or *Slippin' In*, which is the real deal. *—Stephen Thomas Erlewine*

The Complete JSP Recordings: 1979-1982 / Mar. 21, 2000 / JSP ✦✦✦

The Complete Vanguard Recordings / Oct. 31, 2000 / Vanguard ✦✦✦

John Hammond Jr. (John Paul Hammond)

b. Nov. 13, 1942, New York, NY

Slide Guitar, Vocals, Harmonica, Guitar / Folk Revival, Contemporary Blues, Blues-Rock, R&B

With a career that now spans in excess of three decades, John Hammond is one of handful of white blues musicians who was on the scene at the beginning of the first blues renaissance of the mid-'60s. That revival, brought on by renewed interest in folk music around the U.S., brought about career boosts for many of the great classic blues players, including Mississippi John Hurt, Rev. Gary Davis, and Skip James. Some critics have described Hammond as a white Robert Johnson, and Hammond does justice to classic blues by combining powerful guitar and harmonica playing with expressive vocals and a dignified stage presence. Within the first decade of his career as a performer, Hammond began crafting a niche for himself that is completely his own: the solo guitar man, harmonica slung in a rack around his neck, reinterpreting classic blues songs from the '30s,'40s and '50s. Yet, as several of his mid-'90s recordings for the Pointblank label demonstrate, he's also a capable bandleader who plays wonderful electric guitar. This guitar-playing and ensemble work can be heard on *Found True Love* and *Got Love If You Want It*, both for the Pointblank/Virgin label. *—Richard Skelly*

John Hammond / 1963 / Vanguard ✦✦✦✦✦

Big City Blues / 1964 / Vanguard ✦✦✦✦

Hammond's second effort was one of the first electric white blues recordings, and one of the very first that could be said to be blues-rock. Covering a variety of Chess Records classics and electrifying some older tunes, the playing, featuring Hammond, Billy Butler, and James Spruill on electric guitar, is first-rate. But Hammond's vocals are overly mannered and overwrought, and although he would improve, these flaws would keep him from rising to the top rank of white bluesmen. *—Richie Unterberger*

Country Blues / 1964 / Vanguard ✦✦✦✦

Although Hammond had already recorded electric material, he went back to a solo acoustic format for his fourth album, accompanying himself on guitar and harmonica on faithful interpretations of standards by Robert Johnson, Blind Willie McTell, John Lee Hooker, Sleepy John Estes, Jimmy Reed, Willie Dixon, and Bo Diddley. If it sounds a bit unimaginative and routine today, one has to remember that the general listening audience was much less aware of these artists and songs in the mid-'60s. Hammond did a commendable job of rendering them here, with fine guitar work and vocals that were a considerable improvement over his earliest efforts. *—Richie Unterberger*

I Can Tell / 1967 / Atlantic ✦✦✦✦✦

Hot Tracks / 1978 / Vanguard ✦✦✦✦✦

In September of 1979, John Hammond went into Vanguard Records' 23rd Street Studio in New York with the Nighthawks—Jimmy Thackeray, guitar; Mark Wenner, harmonica; Jan Zukowski, bass; Pete Ragusa, drums—and cut this record, one of his best (which might've sold better with maybe some better cover art). The sounds are alternately hot and soulful on the ten-song collection, featuring covers of songs by Little Walter ("You Better Watch Yourself," "Last Night"), Chuck Berry ("Nadine"), Jimmy Reed ("Caress Me Baby," one of Hammond's slowest, most seductive numbers), and Robert Johnson ("Sweet Home Chicago"). Highlights include a stunningly beautiful rendition of Howlin' Wolf's "Who's Been Talkin'," a wailing reconsideration of John Lee Hooker's "Sugar Mama" with a really searing guitar break, a very powerful version of "Howlin' for My Darling," and even the best cover of Dixon's "Pretty Thing" this side of Bo Diddley himself, where Hammond and company manage to be raunchy and smooth at the same time. Nothing's going to make anyone forget Walter, Wolf, or Willie, but this isn't a bad way to spend 40 minutes, especially given the really crunchy guitar sound achieved by Jeff Zaraya and the uncredited producer. A real diamond in the rough, and one of Hammond's best albums. *—Bruce Eder*

● **The Best of John Hammond** / 1989 / Vanguard ✦✦✦✦✦

Vanguard's *The Best of John Hammond* is an excellent collection that features 22 highlights from his early albums, balancing acoustic and electric material, including "My Babe," "Milk Cow Calf's Blues," "Big Boss Man," "See That My Grave Is Kept Clean," "Stones in My Passway," "Key to the Highway," and "Who Do You Love," among others. While his first albums hold up quite well as individual records, this collection does a good job of summarizing his strengths, making it a nice introduction to Hammond's peak years. *—Thom Owens*

Live / Jan. 15, 1992 / Rounder ✦✦✦✦

Trouble No More / Jan. 25, 1994 / Pointblank ✦✦✦

Found True Love / Jan. 23, 1996 / Virgin ✦✦✦

Long as I Have You / Apr. 21, 1998 / Virgin ✦✦✦✦

Best of the Vanguard Years / Feb. 22, 2000 / Vanguard ✦✦✦✦✦

In lieu of a boxed set, the Welk Music Group (which owns the Vanguard Records library) has produced this rock-solid 23-track overview of Hammond's early recordings for Vanguard, covering highlights of the years 1963 through 1967 and his return to the label from 1976 through 1979. The tracks aren't in strict chronological order but are juxtaposed on a more general basis, and you can hear him gain confidence and maturity as this compilation chronologically moves on, from the rough-edged enthusiasm of the opener "32-20 Blues," to the closing "Guitar King." Six of the tracks are from the *So Many Roads* album that featured Mike Bloomfield, Charlie Musselwhite, and members of the Band in the lineup. The producers did more than remaster all of this material in 20-bit sound —they also raided the vaults and found a pair of unissued songs, "Ask Me Nice" and "Hellhound Blues," that they've issued here. Cut with a small, uncredited backing band, "Ask Me Nice" could have fit in easily on either *Big City Blues* or *So Many Roads*, though it's more likely associated with the former, while "Hellhound Blues" is an ominous all-acoustic number, very different in character and texture. The resulting 75 minutes of music is the best (and best-sounding) overview of his work for the label, and if you're going to add some John Hammond to the collection, this is a real good place to start. *—Cub Koda & Bruce Eder*

W.C. Handy

b. Nov. 16, 1873, Muscle Shoals, AL, **d.** Mar. 28, 1958

Piano, Bandleader / Early American Blues

Often referred to as the "father of the blues," William Christopher Handy was born on November 16, 1873, in Muscle Shoals, AL. He studied music early on, starting with the cornet in a brass band, working with a vocal quartet, and eventually playing throughout the South in minstrel and tent shows. It was during his many travels that he began to notate the music he heard, including Delta blues. He would adapt these tunes and sounds to his own performance, in this way popularizing the music he heard, the blues in particular. He was the first to add flatted thirds and sevenths (so-called "blue notes") to published compositions.

He became music director of Mahara's Minstrels in 1896, a group that played rags, popular dance numbers, and even some light classical compositions. They toured the South in the late 1800s and early 1900s. He recorded in New York in 1917 with his Memphis Orchestra.

Handy was the first to compose and publish a tune with the word "blues" in it, "Memphis Blues" in 1912. He composed and published many classic blues tunes including "St. Louis Blues," "Beale Street Blues," "Ole Miss," and "Yellow Dog Blues." Handy's foray into writing and publishing blues songs inspired other writers, including Perry Bradford, the author of "Crazy Blues"—the first blues song ever recorded (1920).

Handy moved himself and his Memphis Orchestra to New York in 1917, started the Handy Record Company (a failure) in 1922, and recorded with his own band until 1923. Throughout the later '20s and '30s Handy, who had developed eye problems, was forced to work less. Still, he continued working with many orchestras. He was on recording sessions with Red Allen and Jelly Roll Morton. His autobiography *Father of the Blues* was written in 1938, the same year that he was given a tribute concert in Carnegie Hall. In his later years, Handy was not very active. He died on March 28, 1958. The movie *St. Louis Blues* was released in 1958, starring Nat King Cole. It is not considered to be very reflective of the facts of Handy's life. A legend in Memphis, Handy has a park named after him there containing a statue of himself. The W.C. Handy Award is the most prestigious honor currently awarded to blues artists. Handy, along with Duke Ellington, appears on a U.S. postage stamp.

Although no one person is the father of the blues, and Handy was not by temperament or cultivation what we might call a bluesman, W.C. Handy did much to popularize and publicize what had been until that time a very personal and local phenomenon. Handy helped to broadcast the blues form to the world. *—Michael Erlewine*

● **Father of the Blues** / 1923-1962 / DRG ✦✦✦✦

In addition to the nine performances of Handy songs included on this Blues Foundation of Memphis-produced document, there is also a wealth of interview excerpts from 1950 to 1955. The music is wide-ranging, from a 1923 instrumental "Memphis Blues" cut by Handy's Orchestra up to a 1962 Louis Armstrong remote. Also included is a 1934 aircheck vocal take of the aforementioned "Memphis Blues" sung by Mae West with the Duke Ellington Orchestra, as well as the 1929 film soundtrack to Bessie Smith's *St. Louis Blues*. *—Jason Ankeny*

Slim Harpo (James Moore)

b. Jan. 11, 1924, Lobdell, LA, **d.** Jan. 31, 1970, Baton Rouge, LA

Vocals, Harmonica, Guitar / Juke-Joint Blues, Blues Revival, Swamp Blues, Louisiana Blues, Harmonica Blues, Electric Blues

In the large stable of blues talent that Crowley, LA producer Jay Miller recorded for the Nashville-based Excello label, no one enjoyed more mainstream success than Slim Harpo. Just a shade behind Lightnin' Slim in local popularity, Harpo played both guitar and neck-rack harmonica in a more down-home approximation of Jimmy Reed, with a few discernible, and distinctive, differences. Slim's music was certainly more laid-back than Reed's, if such a notion was possible. But the rhythm was insistent and overall, Harpo was more adaptable than Reed or most other bluesmen. His material not only made the national charts, but also proved to be quite adaptable for white artists on both sides of the Atlantic, including the Rolling Stones, Yardbirds, Kinks, Dave Edmunds with Love Sculpture, Van Morrison with Them, Sun rockabilly Warren Smith, Hank Williams Jr., and the Fabulous Thunderbirds. *—Cub Koda*

Sings Raining in My Heart / 1961 / Hip-O ✦✦✦✦✦

This was Excello's first album on Slim Harpo and still the one to beat. Besides the title track in all of its original mono and heavily echoed glory, we're treated to the double whammy of "I'm a King Bee" and its original single flip side, "I Got Love If You Want It," along with certified swamp-blues killers like "Buzz Me Babe," "My Home Is a Prison," "Blues Hangover," "Don't Start Crying Now," and "Dream Girl." "My Little Queen Bee (Got a Brand New King)," "Late Last Night," and "Tip on In, Part 2" are the three bonus CD tracks appended to the original track lineup, making this an excellent first purchase and a darn good backup even if you already have a Slim Harpo best-of in the pile. *—AMG*

The Scratch: Rare & Unissued / Feb. 1996 / Excello ✦✦✦✦✦

A 25-track single-disc compilation loaded with previously unissued sides and alternate takes (the title track is an interesting variant of his hit, "Baby, Scratch My Back"), the perfect companion volume to *Hip Shakin'.* This also has the added bonus of more (and even wilder) live recordings from the infamous 1961 frat party dance in Alabama. Dodgy sound on the live sides, but the performances are too great to leave in the can either way. *—AMG*

★ **The Best of Slim Harpo** / Nov. 4, 1997 / Hip-O ✦✦✦✦✦

There have been many Slim Harpo best-of's available over the years, some frustratingly incomplete. This one gets all the chart hits together with several of the obscure singles like "Wonderin' and Worryin'," "Strange Love," "One More Day," and "You'll Be Sorry One Day," along with album tracks like "Snoopin' Around" and "Blues Hangover." Transfers are clean and exemplary, and this makes as good an introduction into his music as any currently available. *—Cub Koda*

Peppermint Harris (Harrison Nelsom)

b. Jul. 17, 1925, Texarkana, TX

Vocals, Guitar / Jump Blues, West Coast Blues

The contemporary-blues boom has resuscitated the career of many a veteran blues artist who's been silent for ages. Take guitarist Peppermint Harris, who in 1951 topped the R&B

charts with his classic booze ode "I Got Loaded." Nobody expected a new Peppermint Harris CD in 1995, but Home Cooking producer Roy C. Ames coaxed one out of old Pep for Collectables nonetheless. *Texas on My Mind* may not be as enthralling as Harris' early-'50s output, but it's nice to have him back in circulation. Harris recorded his debut 78 in 1948 (as Peppermint Nelson). The Sittin' in With label was the vehicle that supplied Harris' early work to the masses—especially his first major hit, "Raining in My Heart," in 1950. These weren't exactly formal sessions—legend has it one took place in a Houston bordello! Nor was Shad too cognizant of Pep's surname—when he couldn't recall it, he simply renamed our man Harris. Harris moved over to Aladdin Records in 1951, cutting far tighter sides for the firm in Los Angeles. After "I Got Loaded" lit up the charts in 1951, Harris indulged in one booze ode after another: "Have Another Drink and Talk to Me," "Right Back On It," "Three Sheets in the Wind." *—Bill Dahl*

Sittin' in With / 1979 / Mainstream ♦♦♦♦
Fifteen well-chosen 1950-1951 masters from Bob Shad's Sittin' in With label by Houston bluesman Peppermint Harris, including his hit "Rainin' in My Heart." Rowdy little bands behind the powerful singer sometimes included Goree Carter on guitar. *—Bill Dahl*

● **I Got Loaded** / 1987 / Route 66 ♦♦♦♦♦
Harris hit his full stride after signing with Aladdin Records in 1951 and moving his recording base to Los Angeles. Under saxist Maxwell Davis' direction, Harris waxed his smash "I Got Loaded" and a few more potent rounds after that ("Three Sheets in the Wind," "Have Another Drink and Talk to Me"). Unfortunately not yet available on CD, these sides comprise Pep's chief claim to fame. *—Bill Dahl*

Texas on My Mind / Dec. 1995 / Collectables ♦♦♦

Penthouse in the Ghetto / Oct. 21, 1997 / M.I.L. Multimedia ♦♦♦
Penthouse in the Ghetto features 20 tracks from Texas bluesman Peppermint Harris, including some of his famed "blues drinking songs." *—Steve Huey*

Being Black Twice / Collectables ♦♦♦
A curious collection of late-1950s and early-'60s recorded titles with unissued mid-'70s sides to pad things out. Oddly enough, Pep sounds the same despite the intervening years; his pleasing baritone rumbles through a set of his originals and standards like "Cherry Red" and "Key to the Highway." Collections of Harris' best are not exactly plentiful, but this one isn't the place to start; seek out his Aladdin sides instead. *—Cub Koda*

Wynonie Harris

b. Aug. 24, 1915, Omaha, NE, **d.** Jun. 14, 1969, Los Angeles, CA
Vocals, Drums / Jump Blues, R&B
No blues shouter embodied the rollicking good times that he sang of quite like raucous shouter Wynonie Harris. "Mr. Blues," as he was not-so-humbly known, joyously related risque tales of sex, booze, and endless parties in his trademark raspy voice over some of the jumpingest horn-powered combos of the postwar era.

Those wanton ways eventually caught up with Harris, but not before he scored a raft of R&B smashes from 1946 to 1952. The shouter debuted in 1945 at an L.A. date for Philo with backing from drummer Johnny Otis, saxist Teddy Edwards, and trumpeter Howard McGhee. A month later, he signed on with Apollo Records, an association that provided him with two huge hits in 1946: "Wynonie's Blues" (with saxist Illinois Jacquet's combo) and "Playful Baby." Harris' own waxings were squarely in the emerging jump-blues style then sweeping the West Coast, and after he joined the star-studded roster of Cincinnati's King Records in 1947, his sales really soared. Few records made a stronger seismic impact than Harris's 1948 chart-topper "Good Rockin' Tonight." Ironically, Harris shooed away its composer, Roy Brown, when he first tried to hand it to the singer; only when Brown's original version took off did Wynonie cover the romping number. With Hal "Cornbread" Singer on wailing tenor sax and a rocking, socking backbeat, the record provided an easily followed blueprint for the imminent rise of rock & roll a few years later. After that, Harris was rarely absent from the R&B charts for the next four years, his offerings growing more boldly suggestive all the time. "Grandma Plays the Numbers," "All She Wants to Do Is Rock," "I Want My Fanny Brown," "Sittin' on It All the Time," "I Like My Baby's Pudding," "Good Morning Judge," "Bloodshot Eyes," and "Lovin' Machine" were only a portion of the ribald hits Harris scored 1952 (13 in all). *—Bill Dahl*

Everybody Boogie! / Aug. 2, 1945-Dec. 1945 / Delmark ♦♦♦♦
This is one marvelous collection of 1945 recordings made for Apollo Records with Harris' powerhouse vocals backed by jump-blues bands led by jazz greats Illinois Jacquet, Oscar Pettiford and Jack McVea. No real honking and bar walking going on here; quite the opposite, as the Pettiford, have bop lines creeping in throughout. But Harris seems oblivious to it all as tracks like "Time to Change Your Town," "Here Come the Blues," "Stuff You Gotta Watch," and "Somebody Changed the Lock on My Door" are on an equal par for sheer bravado and intensity with the best of his later work for King. A welcome compilation. *—Cub Koda*

☆ **Good Rocking Tonight** / 1990 / King ♦♦♦♦♦
Equally splendid compilation of the raspy shouter's King label output from the British Charly logo contains 20 sides, including a few essentials that Rhino didn't bother with: a roaring "Rock Mr. Blues" that grants Harris vocal group backing; the lascivious rocker "I Want My Fanny Brown" and "Lollipop Mama"; and a celebratory "Mr. Blues Is Coming to Town." Harris and King always used inexorably swinging bands—saxists include Red Prysock and David Van Dyke (who duel it out on the amazing "Quiet Whiskey"), Big John Greer, Hal Singer, and Tom Archia. *—Bill Dahl*

★ **Bloodshot Eyes: The Best of Wynonie Harris** / 1993 / Rhino ♦♦♦♦♦
Wynonie Harris was a hard-living, rousing R&B shouter who made some of the most sexually explicit songs in modern popular music history. Harris didn't leave much to the imagination, but he also possessed a booming voice with wonderful tone and range, and the comedic skill to execute these tunes without becoming raunchy. There are many hilarious cuts on this 18-track anthology, among them "I Like My Baby's Pudding," "Grandma Plays The Numbers," and "Good Morning Judge." Harris roars, struts, and wails over equally feverish arrangements, and earns a draw with Joe Turner on "Battle Of The Blues." These songs give a good portrait of a delightful, often spectacular vocalist who could be both provocative and compelling. *—Ron Wynn*

Women, Whiskey & Fish Tails / 1993 / Ace ♦♦♦♦
British compiler Ray Topping focuses on Harris' 1952-1957 King output on this 21-song collection, when he was undeniably on the downslide as far as making hits. But there was still plenty of wind in the shouter's sails, judging from "Greyhound," "Christina," "Shake That Thing" (an update of an ancient blues theme), "Git to Gittin' Baby," and "Mr. Dollar." Harris even supplied a savvy sequel to one of his immortal numbers with "Bad News Baby (There'll Be No Rockin' Tonite)." *—Bill Dahl*

Wilbert Harrison

b. Jan. 5, 1929, Charlotte, NC, **d.** Oct. 26, 1994, Spencer, NC
Vocals, Drums, Piano, Guitar / East Coast Blues, Rock & Roll, R&B, Soul
Perceived by casual oldies fans as a two-hit wonder (his 1959 chart-topper "Kansas City" and a heartwarming "Let's Work Together" a full decade later), Wilbert Harrison actually left behind a varied body of work that blended an intriguing melange of musical idioms into something quite distinctive. He recorded briefly for Miami's Rockin' label and New Jersey's Savoy during the mid-'50s, but didn't find any success until he recorded "Kansas City" in 1959 for the Fury label. With a barbed-wire guitar solo by Wild Jimmy Spruill igniting Harrison's no-frills piano and clenched vocal, "Kansas City" paced both the R&B and pop charts soon after its issue. Contract wrangles with Savoy stalled the momentum for any Fury follow-ups, despite fine attempts with "Cheatin' Baby," the sequel "Goodbye Kansas City," and the original "Let's Stick Together." Harrison bounced from Neptune to Doc to Constellation to Port to Vest with little in the way of tangible rewards before unexpectedly making a comeback in 1969 with his infectious "Let's Work Together" for Sue. The two-part single proved a popular cover item—Canned Heat and Brian Ferry later revived it—though it was an isolated happenstance. After "My Heart Is Yours," a bottom-end chart entry on SSS International in 1971, no more hits were in Wilbert's future. He soldiered on, sometimes as a one-man band, for years to come. *—Bill Dahl*

Let's Work Together / 1969 / Sue ♦♦♦
Quickie album supervised by Juggy Murray to cash in on the unexpected success of Harrison's "Let's Work Together"is not a bad effort all the same. Harrison brings his unique vocal delivery to oldies such as "Blue Monday," "Stagger Lee," "Louie Louie," and "Stand by Me," imparting his own personal stamp to each. This LP deserves digital reissue somewhere down the line. *—Bill Dahl*

Listen to My Song / 1987 / Savoy ♦♦♦♦
Harrison's first label association of any endurance commenced when he signed with Herman Lubinsky's Savoy logo in 1954 for a two-year stretch. Top New York sessioneers like guitarists Mickey Baker and Kenny Burrell and saxists Buddy Lucas and Budd Johnson help out on these 16 Savoy tracks (still unavailable on CD). Terry Fell's "Don't Drop It" is a tremendously catchy hillbilly tune given an R&B flavor by the young singer. *—Bill Dahl*

● **Kansas City** / 1992 / Collectables ♦♦♦♦♦
Finally, paydirt! Harrison smashed the charts in 1959 with his massive hit "Kansas City" for Bobby Robinson's Fury logo. Here we have 22 fine sides from the Fury hookup, some in stereo and many with Wild Jimmy Spruill on lead guitar. "Cheatin' Baby," "C.C. Rider," "1960," and the inevitable sequel "Goodbye Kansas City" are prime examples of Harrison's slightly off-kilter approach to his craft, while his infectious "Let's Stick Together" developed into the more worldly "Let's Work Together" toward the end of the decade. *—Bill Dahl*

Roy Hawkins

Vocals, Piano / West Coast Blues, Piano Blues, R&B
Not only was Roy Hawkins dogged by bad luck during his career (at the height of his popularity, the pianist lost the use of an arm in a car wreck), he couldn't even cash in after the fact. When B.B. King blasted up the charts in 1970 with Roy Hawkins' classic "The Thrill Is Gone," the tune was mistakenly credited to the wrong composers on early pressings.

Little is known of Hawkins' early days. Producer Bob Geddins discovered Hawkins playing in an Oakland, CA nightspot and supervised his first 78s for Cavatone and Downtown in 1948. Modern Records picked up the rights to several Downtown masters before signing Hawkins to a contract in 1949. Two major R&B hits resulted: 1950's "Why Do Things Happen to Me" and "The Thrill Is Gone" the following year. Hawkins recorded for the Bihari brothers' Modern and RPM imprints into 1954. After that, a handful of 45s for Rhythm and Kent were all that was heard of the Bay Area pianist on vinyl. He's rumored to have died in 1973. *—Bill Dahl*

Highway 59 / 1984 / Ace ♦♦♦♦
Early-'50s rarities from the vaults of the Bihari brothers' Modern label, with a good amount of unissued masters recommending this 16-song LP (no CD equivalent yet). Hawkins' cool California blues piano blends well with the tasty little combos Modern provided; of special interest are the title cut and "Would You," a pair of 1952 gems that feature T-Bone Walker's incomparable guitar work. *—Bill Dahl*

● **The Thrill Is Gone** / Aug. 29, 2000 / Ace ♦♦♦♦♦
Twenty-four of Hawkins' 1949-1952 Modern sides, mostly taken from singles that came out during those years. Even by the standards of the Modern roster, Hawkins is a fairly forgotten figure—although he was, according to the liner notes, briefly the label's biggest moneymaker. As with all of Modern's early-'50s recordings, this has a dependable urban, slightly jazzy West Coast groove, very accomplished and not as variable as one might like over the course of a couple dozen numbers. Hawkins was a good piano player and a sufficient, easygoing, slightly foggy-textured vocalist, capable of both rapid jump shuffles and morose ballads. "Gloom and Misery All Around" and "I Don't Know Just What to Do" were entirely typical sentiments of his slower tunes. His band featured an excellent underrated guitarist,

Ulysses James, whose burning tone shines when it's given a little space to strut, as on "Wine Drinkin' Woman." His Modern output was most notable for the self-pitying ballad "Why Do Everything Happen to Me," a Number 3 hit later covered by B.B. King and James Brown, and, more memorably, the original version of "The Thrill Is Gone," which became B.B. King's biggest hit a couple of decades later. The original renditions of both are on this CD, and the gloomy "The Thrill Is Gone," far more piano-based and small band-scaled in its arrangement than King's classic cover, in particular outclasses anything else in Hawkins' discography. Otherwise, Hawkins is not among the first West Coast blues stars of the era, or even among the first such artists on the Modern roster, one should hear, though if you've a jones for that style, this reliably delivers the goods. *—Richie Unterberger*

Ted Hawkins

b. Oct. 28, 1936, Biloxi, MS, **d.** Jan. 1, 1995, Los Angeles, CA
Vocals, Guitar / Contemporary Blues, Singer/Songwriter, Modern Acoustic Blues, Soul-Blues, Soul

Overseas, he was a genuine hero, performing to thousands. But on his L.A. hometurf, sand-blown Venice Beach served as Ted Hawkins' makeshift stage. He'd deliver his magnificent melange of soul, blues, folk, gospel, and a touch of country all by his lonesome, with only an acoustic guitar for company. Passersby would pause to marvel at Hawkins' melismatic vocals, dropping a few coins or a greenback into his tip jar on the way by. That was the way Ted Hawkins kept body and soul together until 1994, when DGC/Geffen Records issued *The Next Hundred Years,* his breakthrough album. Suddenly, Hawkins was poised on the precipice of stardom. And then, just after Christmas that same year, in a bout of cruel irony, he died of a stroke. After growing up in Mississippi, Hawkins moved to L.A. in 1966 and cut his debut 45, the soul-steeped "Baby"/"Whole Lot of Women," for Money Records. He also recorded some material in 1971, which appeared on Rounder in 1982 (as *Watch Your Step*). The album gained a five-star review from *Rolling Stone,* and Hawkins recorded another album, *Happy Hour,* in 1986. He moved to England later that year and became a well-known presence performing around Europe and even Japan. After returning to America in the early '90s, DGC ever so briefly propelled him into the major leagues. *Love You Most of All: More Songs from Venice Beach* was issued posthumously in 1998. *—Bill Dahl*

Watch Your Step / 1982 / Rounder ✦✦✦
Guitarist/vocalist Ted Hawkins was an instant sensation when this session was originally released in 1982. At a time when slick, heavily produced urban-contemporary material was establishing its domination on the R&B scene, Hawkins' hard-edged, rough, cutting voice, plus his crisp acoustic guitar accompaniment and country-blues roots, seemed both dated and extremely fresh. This 15-track CD includes four numbers with Hawkins backed by Phillip Walker and his band, and others ranging from the humorous "Who Got My Natural Comb?" to the poignant "If You Love Me" and two versions of the title track. He also teamed with his wife Elizabeth on "Don't Lose Your Cool" and "I Gave It All I Had" for moving duets. *—Ron Wynn*

Happy Hour / 1986 / Rounder ✦✦✦✦✦
Guitarist/vocalist Ted Hawkins' second Rounder record enhanced his reputation. *Happy Hour* features Hawkins' memorable compositions, plus a wonderful version of Curtis Mayfield's "Gypsy Woman." Hawkins' vocals were even more gritty and striking, as was his acoustic guitar backing and chording. He teamed with his wife Elizabeth on "Don't Make Me Explain It," "My Last Goodbye" and "California Song," and with guitarist Night Train Clemons on "Gypsy Woman" and "You Pushed My Head Away." Hawkins blended soul- and urban-blues stylings with country- and rural-blues inflections and rhythms, making another first-rate release. *—Ron Wynn*

The Next Hundred Years / Mar. 29, 1994 / DGC ✦✦✦

The Kershaw Sessions: Live at the BBC / 1995 / Varese ✦✦✦

Songs from Venice Beach / Oct. 1995 / Evidence ✦✦✦✦
Blending every form of roots music imaginable into his own singular soulful stew, the incomparable Ted Hawkins stuck mostly to R&B covers on this splendid 1985 solo outing—songs by Sam Cooke (his idol), Jerry Butler, Bobby Bland, the Temptations, and Garnet Mimms receive gorgeous readings by the acoustic guitarist. But even though he only contributed one original, the touching "Ladder of Success," to the set, Hawkins wasn't content to remain in one genre—his commanding revival of Webb Pierce's hillbilly weeper "There Stands the Glass" ranks with the disc's very best moments (of which there are many). *—Bill Dahl*

The Final Tour / Jan. 13, 1998 / Evidence ✦✦✦✦✦

● **The Ted Hawkins Story: Suffer No More** / Jan. 13, 1998 / Rhino ✦✦✦✦✦
Taken individually, Hawkins' albums didn't measure up to his critical reputation, due to uneven material, occasionally inappropriate production, and overreliance upon covers. More than most best-ofs, this 20-song compilation is a revelation of sorts. By focusing on his best moments, it's much easier to make a convincing case for Hawkins as a major, if erratic, roots-music performer who sounded like a coarsened, acoustic-oriented Sam Cooke. The set goes all the way back to both sides of his rare (and good) 1966 soul single on the Money label, and highlights the best originals from the '70s and '80s sessions released on Rounder, wisely selecting sparsely from his cover-dominated albums of the mid-'80s. The songs from his major-label finale *The Next Hundred Years* can veer toward production slickness, but there's a pleasing bonus in three acoustic, previously unreleased cuts from the early '90s. It's an intelligently selected, well-rounded disc, presenting several sides of this idiosyncratic artist: composer, folky interpreter of material by Sam Cooke and Brook Benton, and country-tinged soul artist. *—Richie Unterberger*

Z.Z. Hill (Arzell Hill)

b. Sep. 30, 1935, Naples, TX, **d.** Apr. 27, 1984, Dallas, TX
Vocals / Retro-Soul, Modern Electric Blues, Soul-Blues, Soul

Texas-born singer Z.Z. Hill managed to resuscitate both his own semi-flagging career and the entire genre at large when he signed on at Malaco Records in 1980 and began growling his way through some of the most uncompromising blues to be unleashed on black radio stations in many a moon. His impressive 1982 Malaco album *Down Home Blues* remained on *Billboard's* soul album charts for nearly two years, an extraordinary run for such a blatantly bluesy LP. His songs "Down Home Blues" and "Somebody Else Is Steppin' In" have graduated into the ranks of legitimate blues standards (and there haven't been many of those come along over the last couple of decades). His debut single, the gutsy shuffle "You Were Wrong," showed up on *Billboard's* pop chart for a week in 1964. With such a relatively successful showing his first time out, Hill's fine subsequent singles for the Kent logo should have been even bigger. But "I Need Someone (To Love Me)," "Happiness Is All I Need," and a raft of other deserving Kent 45s went nowhere commercially. A 1972 hookup with United Artists resulted in three albums and six R&B chart singles over the next couple of years. From there, Z.Z. moved on to Columbia, where his 1977 single "Love Is So Good When You're Stealing It" became his biggest-selling hit of all. From 1980 until 1984, when he died suddenly of a heart attack, Z.Z. bravely led a personal back-to-the-blues campaign that doubtless helped to fuel the current contemporary blues boom. It's a shame he couldn't stick around to see it blossom. *—Bill Dahl*

Let's Make a Deal / 1978 / Columbia ✦✦✦
One of the most commercial of Hill's albums, this disco-tinged release included the minor hits "This Time They Told the Truth" and "Love Is So Good When You're Stealing It." *—Richie Unterberger*

The Mark of Z.Z. Hill / 1979 / Columbia ✦✦✦
Hill's second and final Columbia LP was essentially a continuation of the first. On both, Hill sounds like a journeyman Southern-soul singer embellished with period disco/mainstream R&B production, which neither added to the quality of the music nor made it unlistenable. *—Richie Unterberger*

Z.Z. Hill / 1981 / Malaco ✦✦✦✦

☆ **Down Home** / 1982 / Malaco ✦✦✦✦✦
On one of the very few classic blues albums of the '80s Hill revitalized the genre among African-American listeners with his "Down Home Blues," which earned instant standard status. But the entire album is tremendously consistent, with the percolating R&B workouts "Givin' It Up for Your Love" and "Right Arm for Your Love" contrasting with an intimate "Cheatin' in the Next Room" and the straight-ahead blues "Everybody Knows About My Good Thing" and "When It Rains It Pours." *—Bill Dahl*

The Rhythm & The Blues / 1982 / Malaco ✦✦✦✦

I'm a Blues Man / 1983 / Malaco ✦✦✦✦

Bluesmaster / 1984 / Malaco ✦✦✦

★ **In Memorium (1935-1984)** / 1985 / Malaco ✦✦✦✦✦
Most of the highlights of Hill's glorious blues-singing stint at Malaco, although the individual albums possess more than their share of worthwhile moments that aren't here. But with hallowed titles like "Down Home Blues," "Someone Else Is Slippin' In," and "Everybody Knows About My Good Thing," this stunning collection neatly summarizes Hill's heart-warming rise to blues power. *—Bill Dahl*

Greatest Hits / 1986 / Malaco ✦✦✦✦✦
When he died in 1984 at the relatively young age of 48, Z.Z. Hill went down in history as a great blues singer. But he was also an excellent soul singer, and this 1990 CD reminds us that he had as much to do with earthy, gospel-drenched southern soul as he did with B.B. King-influenced electric blues. Focusing on Hill's Malaco output, *Greatest Hits* contains some inspired 12-bar numbers (including "Open House at My House," "Shade Tree Mechanic," and Denise LaSalle's "Someone Else Is Steppin' In") but is just as heavy in its R&B content. "Right Arm for Your Love," "Get a Little, Give a Little," and "Cheatin' In the Next Room" serve as fine examples of his unpretentious approach to Stax-influenced soul. And, of course, the CD boasts what became Hill's signature song, the infectious "Down Home Blues." For those who haven't experienced the impressive material Hill was delivering during the last years of his life, this CD would be the appropriate starting point. *—Alex Henderson*

The Best of Z.Z. Hill / 1987 / Malaco ✦✦✦✦✦

The Down Home Soul of Z.Z. Hill / 1992 / Kent ✦✦✦✦✦
Before Hill made his sensational '80s comeback as a blues growler, he sang a slightly sweeter brand of West Coast soul during the mid-'60s at Kent. Under saxist Maxwell Davis' supervision, Hill waxed a series of magnificent R&B ballads—"Happiness Is All I Need," "I Need Someone (To Love Me)"—that should have hit but inexplicably didn't. Gathered on one 22-track import disc, they sound terrific in retrospect. *—Bill Dahl*

The Complete Hill/UA Recordings / Mar. 19, 1996 / Capitol ✦✦✦✦
The gritty singer made three albums for United Artists (mostly under his brother Matt's supervision) from 1972 to 1975, and they were an idiomatically mixed bag. All three LPs are housed in their entirety on this two-disc set, its selections ranging from the deep soul sincerity of "I've Got to Get You Back" and "Your Love Makes Me Feel Good" and the country-soul hybrids "You're Killing Me (Slowly But Surely)" and "Country Love" to the funky Lamont Dozier-produced "I Created a Monster" and an Allen Toussaint-supervised "I Keep on Lovin' You." *—Bill Dahl*

Love is So Good When You're Stealing It / Mar. 26, 1996 / Ichiban Soul Classics ✦✦✦
Much of Hill's 1978-79 output for Columbia was laced with disco rhythms, but there were also plenty of soulful throwbacks to the sort of intense testifying that Hill did best: the surging mid-tempo "That's All That's Left," and a string-enriched "This Time They Told the Truth," an insistent "Need You By My Side," and the smoldering title tale of cheating in the wee hours that hit big for him. Ichiban has cobbled together both of Hill's Columbia LPs, the first being infinitely superior to the brutally formulaic disco-dominated encore. *—Bill Dahl*

This Time They Told the Truth: The Columbia Years / Feb. 17, 1998 / Columbia ✦✦✦✦
The best of Hill's late-'70s stay at Columbia Records, *This Time They Told the Truth* might be

a bit of a shock to listeners not familiar with the period, for Hill's always smooth vocals are embellished with a very disco-fied production, not always disturbing, but definitely obtrusive in several places. The songs themselves are quite good (distilled from 1978's *Let's Make a Deal* and 1979's *The Mark of Z.Z. Hill*), including "Stop by and Love Me Sometime," "A Message to the Ladies," and the title track. *—John Bush*

Willie "Smokey" Hogg (Willie Anderson Hogg)

b. Jan. 27, 1914, Westconnie, TX, **d.** May 1, 1960, McKinney, TX
Vocals, Piano, Guitar / Texas Blues
Smokey Hogg was a rural bluesman navigating a postwar era infatuated by R&B, but he got along quite nicely nonetheless, scoring a pair of major R&B hits in 1948 and 1950 and cutting a thick catalog for a slew of labels (including Exclusive, Modern, Bullet, Macy's, Sittin' in With, Imperial, Mercury, Recorded in Hollywood, Specialty, Fidelity, Combo, Federal, and Showtime).

During the early '30s, Hogg, who was influenced by Big Bill Broonzy and Peetie Wheatstraw, worked with slide guitarist Black Ace at dances around Greenville, TX. Hogg first recorded for Decca in 1937, but it was an isolated occurrence—he didn't make it back into a studio for a decade. Once he hit his stride, though, Hogg didn't look back. Both his chart hits—1948's "Long Tall Mama" and 1950's "Little School Girl"—were issued on Modern, but his rough-hewn sound seldom changed a whole lot no matter what L.A. logo he was appearing on. Hogg's last few sides were cut in 1958 for Lee Rupe's Ebb label.

Smokey's cousin John Hogg also played the blues, recording for Mercury in 1951. *—Bill Dahl*

• **Angels in Harlem** / 1992 / Specialty ✦✦✦✦✦
Angels in Harlem is a wonderful compilation of Smokey Hogg's early-'50s recordings for Specialty Records, containing 22 tracks, including "I Want a Roller," "Nobody Treats Me Right," "Evil Mind Blues," "I Ain't Gonna Put You Down," "Born on the 13th," and "Good Mornin' Baby." *—Thom Owens*

The Holmes Brothers

f. 1980, New York, NY
Group / Retro-Soul, Modern Electric Blues, Soul-Blues
The Holmes Brothers' unique synthesis of gospel-inflected blues harmonies, accompanied by good drumming and rhythm-based guitar playing, gives them a down-home rural feeling that no other touring blues group can duplicate. Brothers Sherman and Wendell Holmes, along with drummer Popsy Dixon are the group's core members. The Holmes Brothers are so versatile, they're booked solid every summer at folk, blues, gospel and jazz festivals, as they play a style of music that is a gumbo of church tunes, blues and soul. Although they'd been performing in Harlem for years, the Holmes Brothers have only recently become international blues touring stars. Thanks to a fair deal at Rounder Records, the group has released three recordings for that label, beginning with a 1989 release, *In the Spirit*. When this album made waves and got them off and running on the festival and club circuit around the U.S. and Europe, they followed it up two years later with *Where It's At*, subsequently issuing *Soul Street* (1993) and *Promised Land* (1997). *—Richard Skelly*

In the Spirit / 1990 / Rounder ✦✦✦✦✦
The Holmes Brothers' voices are too potent, their harmonies too smashing and their love of vintage sounds too immense for them to be content with producer-dominated, softer urban-contemporary sounds. This set included some riveting gospel tunes like "None But The Righteous" and "Up Above My Head," plus a credible (if a little lengthy) version of "When Something Is Wrong With My Baby" and the tighter, hard-hitting tunes "Please Don't Hurt Me," "Ask Me No Questions," and "The Final Round." If straight-ahead, rousing shared leads and booming harmonies interest you, the Holmes Brothers do it the way they used to throughout the South in the '60s and '70s. *—Ron Wynn*

Where It's at / 1991 / Rounder ✦✦✦✦
Their second release contained 11 more wonderful tunes that easily moved from surging R&B to rousing blues with an occasional venture into gospel or country. They covered "Drown In My Own Tears" and "High Heel Sneakers" and had the requisite qualities for each one down pat, as well as "Never Let Me Go," "The Love You Save," and "I Saw The Light." But their own numbers, like "I've Been A Loser" and the title track, were even better, displaying a contemporary sensibility and classic style and sound. *—Ron Wynn*

Jubilation / 1992 / Real World ✦✦✦
Jubilation is a revealing, wonderful collection of the Holmes Brothers' distinctive soul. The brothers tie together a seemingly disconnected array of styles—everything from straightforward blues, R&B, and gospel to worldbeat and country—and come up with a cohesive whole. Even when the group delves into soukous or works with a Chinese flutist, it manages to retain the pure qualities of American blues and R&B. *—Thom Owens*

• **Soul Street** / 1993 / Rounder ✦✦✦✦✦
This album continued the Holmes Brothers' tradition of doing tremendous covers ("You're Gonna Make Me Cry," "Down In Virginia," and "Fannie Mae"), authentic originals ("I Won't Hurt You Anymore," "Dashboard Bar,") and adding gospel ("Walk In The Light") and honky-tonk ("There Goes My Everything") into their blend. There's little to criticize about The Holmes Brothers; their sound, vocals, and harmonies aren't laid-back or restrained, and everything they sing is done with exuberance and integrity. It may not be commercially viable, but it's musically sound. *—Ron Wynn*

Promised Land / Apr. 1996-Jun. 1996 / Rounder ✦✦✦✦
The Holmes Brothers have honed their blend of rock, blues, gospel, and soul to perfection on this, their fifth release. Whether it's Popsy Dixon's stunning interpretation of Tom Waits' "Train Song," the soul, stirring harmonies on the gospel standard "I Surrender All," or an original, gritty guitar workout like "Start Stoppin'," there is simply not a bad song on this album. The Holmes Brothers continue to defy all classifications, except one: damn good music. *—Steve McMullen*

Speaking in Tongues / Jan. 30, 2001 / Alligator ✦✦✦

Earl Hooker (Earl Zebedee Hooker)

b. Jan. 15, 1930, Clarksdale, MS, **d.** Apr. 21, 1970, Chicago, IL
Slide Guitar, Vocals, Guitar / Slide Guitar Blues, Delta Blues, Electric Chicago Blues
If there was a more immaculate slide guitarist residing in Chicago during the '50s and '60s than Earl Hooker, his name has yet to surface. Boasting a fretboard touch so smooth and clean that every note rang as clear and precise as a bell, he was an endlessly inventive axeman who would likely have been a star had his modest vocal abilities matched his instrumental prowess and had he not been dogged by tuberculosis (it killed him at age 41). Hooker made his first recordings in 1952 and 1953 for Rockin', King, and Sun. At the latter, he recorded some terrific sides with pianist Pinetop Perkins (Sam Phillips inexplicably sat on Hooker's blazing rendition of "The Hucklebuck"). Back in Chicago again, Hooker's dazzling dexterity was intermittently showcased on singles for Argo, C.J., and Bea & Baby during the mid to late '50s before he joined forces with producer Mel London (owner of the Chief and Age logos) in 1959. For the next four years, he recorded both as sideman and leader for the producer, backing Junior Wells, Lillian Offitt, Ricky Allen, and A.C. Reed and cutting his own sizzling instrumentals ("Blue Guitar," "Blues in D-Natural"). He also contributed pungent slide work to Muddy Waters' Chess waxing "You Shook Me." *—Bill Dahl*

Two Bugs and a Roach / 1966 / Arhoolie ✦✦✦✦✦
This compact disc reissue of Earl Hooker's debut Arhoolie adds some tracks to the original lineup, making for a much more varied package. In addition to the contents of *Two Bugs and a Roach* (itself a varied lot, with vocals from Hooker, Andrew Odom, and Carey Bell in between the instrumentals, all cut in 1968), there are two tracks from stray sessions in late 1968 and July, 1969, along with four very early sides probably recorded in Memphis in the company of Pinetop Perkins, Willie Nix, and an unknown bass player. Of these, "Guitar Rag" is the least together, hampered by a bass player who can't find the changes, but "I'm Going Down the Line" and "Earl's Boogie Woogie" are both top-notch up-tempo boogies full of fleet-fingered soloing. "Sweet Black Angel" was the A-side of a stray single from the early '50s and appears to be from another session, although it's an excellent example of Hooker playing in the Robert Night Hawk style. All in all, one of the must-haves in this artist's very small discography. *—Cub Koda*

Sweet Black Angel / 1970 / One Way ✦✦✦
Ike Turner co-produced this set with Blue Thumb Records boss Bob Krasnow. It's a wide-ranging collection, as its oddly generic song titles ("Country and Western," "Shuffle," "Funky Blues") would eloquently indicate. *—Bill Dahl*

Blue Guitar / 1981 / Paula/Flyright ✦✦✦✦✦
The slide guitar wizard's immaculate fretwork was never captured more imaginatively than during his early-'60s stay with Mel London's Age/Chief labels. Twenty-one fascinating tracks from that period include Hooker's savage instrumentals "Blue Guitar," "Off the Hook," "The Leading Brand," "Blues in D Natural," and "How Long Can This Go On," along with tracks by A.C. Reed, Lillian Offitt, and Harold Tidwell that cast Hooker as a standout sideman. *—Bill Dahl*

Play Your Guitar Mr. Hooker / 1985 / Black Top ✦✦✦
1964-1967 output by the guitarist that was largely done for the tiny Cuca logo of Sauk City, WI. The normally tight-lipped Hooker proves that he could sing on this romping version of "Swear to Tell the Truth," while A.C. Reed, Little Tommy, Frank Clark, and Muddy Waters Jr. help out behind the mike elsewhere. A pair of live cuts from 1968 find Hooker stretching out in amazing fashion. *—Bill Dahl*

Moon Is Rising / Aug. 18, 1998 / Arhoolie ✦✦✦
The first eight tracks of this 79-minute compilation of late-'60s material originally appeared on Arhoolie's *Hooker'n'Steve* LP; a couple of others showed up on Arhoolie's *His First & Last Recordings*, while the four remaining cuts were previously unreleased. Hooker didn't have long to live when these were laid down in 1968 and (for the most part) 1969, but he's in real good form on guitar, although he only takes an occasional vocal (other band members help out on other tracks, and some are instrumental). Indications are from the liner notes that the sessions were run on a no-frills budget, but it's very respectable '60s Chicago electric blues with a shade of funky soul and a hot live feel, and Hooker's guitar has an upfront bite and presence. Actually, the instrumentals are highlights, particularly "Hooker N' Steve" with its smoking guitar-organ duets. *—Richie Unterberger*

• **Simply the Best: Earl Hooker Collection** / May 18, 1999 / MCA ✦✦✦✦✦
Focusing on his output as a leader as well as his work backing such dynamos as Muddy Waters, John Lee Hooker (his second cousin), Andrew "Big Voice" Odom, and Sonny Terry/Brownie McGhee, this CD spans 1956-1969 and paints an impressive picture of the distinctive guitarist. Most of the tunes from Hooker's own sessions are infectious, groove-oriented instrumentals like the funky "Frog Hop" from 1956, the twangy "Tanya" from 1962, and the playful "Hookin'" from 1969. Hooker's vocal on "You Got to Lose" points to the fact that while he wasn't a fantastic singer—he was a fantastic guitarist, an OK singer—his vocals did have a certain charm. Hooker, of course, backed quite a few first-class singers, and on this compilation, they range from Muddy Waters on "You Shook Me" (a 1962 gem that was covered by Led Zeppelin in 1969) and John Lee Hooker on "Messin' Around with the Blues" (1962) and "If You Miss 'Im,… I Got 'Im…" (1969) to Charles Brown on "Drifting Blues" (1969). Brown was a very different type of singer from Waters and John Lee Hooker, both of whom were, like Earl Hooker, Mississippi natives who started out playing acoustic country-blues in the Deep South before heading north and going electric. The smoother Brown, however, was a jazz singer as well as a blues and R&B singer. But Hooker fits in perfectly in the jazz/blues environment of "Drifting Blues," which finds him playing alongside soul-jazz saxman Red Holloway. Boasting comprehensive liner notes and excellent digital remastering, *Simply the Best* is a collection that blues lovers should go out of their way to obtain. *—Alex Henderson*

John Lee Hooker

b. Aug. 17, 1920, Clarksdale, MS, **d.** Jun. 21, 2001

Vocals, Guitar / Detroit Blues, Blues Revival, Delta Blues, Country-Blues, Electric Delta Blues, Acoustic Blues

He's beloved worldwide as the king of the endless boogie, a genuine blues superstar whose droning, hypnotic one-chord grooves are at once both ultra-primitive and timeless. But John Lee Hooker has recorded in a great many more styles than that over a career that stretches back more than half a century. In 1948, the aspiring bluesman hooked up with entrepreneur Bernie Besman, who helped him hammer out his solo debut sides, "Sally Mae" and its seminal flip, "Boogie Chillen." This was blues as primitive as anything then on the market; Hooker's dark, ruminative vocals were backed only by his own ringing, heavily amplified guitar and insistently pounding foot. He became the point man for the growing Detroit blues scene during the mid-1950s, recruiting guitarist Eddie Kirkland as his frequent duet partner; once tied in with Vee-Jay, the rough-and-tumble sound of Hooker's solo and duet waxings was adapted to a band format. Hooker had recorded with various combos along the way before, but never with sidemen as versatile and sympathetic as guitarist Eddie Taylor and harpist Jimmy Reed, who backed him at his initial Vee-Jay date that produced "Time Is Marching" and the superfluous sequel "Mambo Chillun." Vee-Jay presented Hooker in quite an array of settings during the early '60s. His grinding, tough blues "No Shoes" proved a surprisingly sizable hit in 1960, while the storming "Boom Boom," his top seller for the firm in 1962 (it even cracked the pop airwaves), was an infectious R&B dance number. Eventually, though, the endless-boogie formula grew incredibly stagnant. Much of Hooker's '70s output found him laying back while plodding rock-rooted rhythm sections assumed much of the work load. But Hooker wasn't through—not by a long shot. With the expert help of slide guitarist extraordinaire/producer Roy Rogers, the Hook waxed *The Healer,* an album that marked the first of his guest star-loaded albums (Carlos Santana, Bonnie Raitt, and Robert Cray were among the luminaries to cameo on the disc, which picked up a Grammy). *—Bill Dahl*

Everybody's Blues / 1950-1954 / Specialty ✦✦✦
John Lee Hooker reissues abound, as might be expected of a singer and guitarist who's recorded hundreds of songs for countless labels since the late '40s. What makes the 20 tracks on *Everybody's Blues* different from the mountain of other Hooker material available is the fact that seven of them are newly issued, and most were done in the studio with Hooker wailing and accompanying himself on guitar minus any backing chorus or production armada. Even the cuts with a supporting combo are animated and loose, with the vocal trademarks that are now established Hooker clichés sounding fresh and genuine. *—Ron Wynn*

House of the Blues / 1960 / MCA/Chess ✦✦✦✦
Verbatim CD reissue of a 1959 Chess album that collected 1951-1954 efforts by the Hook. Some important titles here: an ominous "Leave My Wife Alone," and the stark "Sugar Mama" and "Ramblin' by Myself," and with Eddie Kirkland on second guitar, "Louise" and "High Priced Woman." *—Bill Dahl*

That's My Story/John Lee Hooker Sings the Blues / 1960 / Riverside ✦✦✦✦✦
Hooker's earliest Riverside albums presented him playing solo acoustic guitar, in a conscious effort to direct his work to listeners outside the R&B audience. Opinions differ on the matter, but this outing is more interesting than his solo acoustic Riverside records, due to the presence of a supporting rhythm section on most of the tracks. The liner notes (in the fashion of the day) are almost apologetic about this, emphasizing that it's not to create R&B rhythms, but "to free Hooker from the burden of carrying the full rhythm load." To make matters more palatable for the purists, maybe that's why a couple of jazz players were chosen for the job (bassist Sam Jones and drummer Louis Hayes, who formed the rhythm section for Cannonball Adderley at the time). What's important is not how pure the music is, but that it's a decent album, striking a good midpoint between his acoustic and electric sound. *—Richie Unterberger*

The Country Blues of John Lee Hooker / Jan. 1960 / Original Blues Classics ✦✦✦
Hooker was still churning out R&B-influenced electric blues with a rhythm section for Vee-Jay when he recorded this, his first album packaged for the folk/traditional blues market. He plays nothing but acoustic guitar, and seems to have selected a repertoire with old-school country-blues in mind. It's unimpressive only within the context of Hooker's body of work; in comparison with other solo outings, the guitar sounds thin, and the approach restrained. *—Richie Unterberger*

☆ **John Lee Hooker Plays and Sings the Blues** / 1961 / MCA/Chess ✦✦✦✦✦
A 1961 Chess album restored to digital print by MCA is filled with 1951-1952 gems from the Hook's heyday. Chess originally bought "Mad Man Blues" and "Hey Boogie" from the Gone label; the rest first came out on Chess during Hooker's frenzied early days of recording, when his platters turned up on nearly every R&B indie label existant at the time. *—Bill Dahl*

Don't Turn Me from Your Door / 1963 / Atco ✦✦✦

Burning Hell / 1964 / Riverside/Original Blues Classics ✦✦✦

Live at Cafe Au Go-Go (And Soledad Prison) / 1966 / MCA ✦✦✦
This reissue contains the entirety of Hooker's 1966 *Cafe Au Go-Go* set, and adds five bonus tracks from his 1972 album, *Live at Soledad Prison.* Luther Tucker is one of the guitarists for the Soledad portion, which has a somewhat more electric, rock-oriented sound than the Au Go-Go material. The disc only has five of the seven cuts from the original *Soledad* album, but that's okay, as the two missing items featured John Lee Hooker Jr. on lead vocals, rather than Hooker himself. *—Richie Unterberger*

The Real Folk Blues / 1966 / MCA/Chess ✦✦✦
Although the great majority of the albums in Chess's *Real Folk Blues* series were vintage compilations, this disc was cut in 1966 with longtime cohort Eddie Burns on second guitar and an uncredited band behind him. Not exactly essential in Hooker's personal pantheon, but decent nonetheless. *—Bill Dahl*

It Serves You Right to Suffer / Jun. 1966 / Impulse! ✦✦✦
Given Hooker's unpredictable timing and piss-poor track record recording with bands, this 1965 one-off session for the jazz label Impulse! would be a recipe for disaster. But with Panama Francis on drums, Milt Hinton on bass, and Barry Galbraith on second guitar, the result is some of the best John Lee Hooker material with a band that you're likely to come across. The other musicians stay in the pocket, never overplaying or trying to get Hooker to make chord changes he has no intention of making. This record should be played for every artist who records with Hooker nowadays, as it's a textbook example of how exactly to back the old master. The most surreal moment occurs when William Wells blows some totally cool trombone on Hooker's version of Berry Gordy's "Money." If you run across this one in a pile of 500 other John Lee Hooker CDs, grab it; it's one of the good ones. *—Cub Koda*

That's Where It's At! / 1969 / Stax ✦✦✦
A characteristic solo outing with moody compositions and that doomy one-electric-guitar-and-stomping-foot ambience. One of his sparer and more menacing post-'50s outings, highlighted by "Two White Horses" and a seven-minute "Feel So Bad," features extended verbal sparring with an unidentified male partner. *—Richie Unterberger*

I Feel Good / 1971 / Jewel ✦✦✦✦✦
Nine songs recorded double-quick in one session, with Lowell Fulson on lead guitar on most of it—the rare embellishment on a Hooker release makes for unusually complex and rewarding listening, instrumentally speaking, beneath Hooker's ominous vocals. The textures on this reissue are very crisp and vivid, with a crunchiness that should make this a CD of choice for Hooker's rock fans, much more so than, say, the Canned Heat collaborations—Hooker and Fulson make a mean team on "Dazie Mae." Among the other highlights is Hooker's own take on the blues standard "Rollin' and Tumblin'," done here as "Roll and Tumble." The uncredited band that shows up on some of these cuts (which, in some instances, may have originated in Paris) is loose enough to follow Hooker, and he and Fulson play like one person together. *—Bruce Eder*

Alone / 1976 / Rhino ✦✦✦

☆ **The Ultimate Collection (1948-1990)** / 1991 / Rhino ✦✦✦✦✦
The single best place to begin appreciating the Boogie Man's incredible contributions to the blues lexicon, it surveys a wide cross-section of labels and eras. Disc one contains "Boogie Chillen," "Sally Mae," "Huckle Up Baby," "I'm in the Mood," "Dimples," and "It Serves Me Right." The second spottier CD sports "Boom Boom," "One Bourbon, One Scotch, One Beer," a snarling "I'm Bad like Jesse James," and an utterly superfluous finale with Bonnie Raitt from a Showtime TV program. At only 31 songs, it could unequivocally be longer, but this anthology serves as a convenient spot for the neophyte to delve into Hookerology. *—Bill Dahl*

The Best of John Lee Hooker 1965-1974 / 1992 / MCA ✦✦✦
MCA's *The Best of John Lee Hooker* has a misleading title. All of the 16 selections are taken from his recordings for ABC, which were made at the end of the '60s and beginning of the '70s. During this time, his producers were experimenting with his sound, adding contemporary sonic touches like funk rhythms and wah-wah pedals. Needless to say, this sound didn't sit particularly well with Hooker's lean, haunting blues. However, these songs do take the best material from generally poor albums—anyone who wants to sample his ABC material should turn here first and they'll realize that they don't need to explore much further. *—Thom Owens*

Graveyard Blues / 1992 / Specialty ✦✦✦✦
At the beginning of his career, Hooker's sides were leased to several different labels. This 20-song anthology of material from the late '40s and early '50s was originally released on the Sensation and Specialty labels; while the track listings indicate a timespan of 1948-50, the liner notes say that much of it was recorded in 1954. Doesn't anyone proofread these things? Anyway, this was mostly recorded solo, and boasts his characteristic spooky electric-minimalist-boogie sound. *The Legendary Modern Recordings,* covering the same era, is a better place to start for this kind of thing due to its stronger content. If you want more of the same, though, this (and Capitol's *Alternative Boogie*) is the next stop. *—Richie Unterberger*

John Lee Hooker on Vee-Jay, 1955-1958 / Jul. 1993 / Vee-Jay ✦✦✦✦✦
Some of Hooker's finest recordings with a band were also some of his first recordings with a band. The unpredictable guitarist seemed to mesh well with guitarist Eddie Taylor, harpist Jimmy Reed, and the rest of the sidemen he was given on his 1955-58 Vee-Jay output. Includes the classic "Baby Lee" and "Dimples," along with 20 more that crackle with electricity. *—Bill Dahl*

☆ **The Early Years** / 1994 / Tomato ✦✦✦✦✦
Hooker's voluminous output for Vee-Jay Records is scattered across numerous compilations. This double CD contains 31 songs spanning the mid-'50s to the mid-'60s, and is probably the most extensive and satisfying retrospective of his Vee-Jay work (at least domestically). That's not to say it's perfectly assembled; Tomato, as usual, declines to include trimmings like songwriter credits, although Pete Welding's liner notes do (unlike most Tomato releases) provide dates and discuss the sessions in some detail. Hooker's Vee-Jay material was in most ways the most commercially-minded of his early efforts, often employing a rhythm section and R&B-influenced arrangements, and occasionally using horns. It's sometimes been said that this approach diluted Hooker's strengths, but one listen to this collection refutes that notion soundly. This is by and large prime Hooker, with some of his best (and best-selling) songs, like "Boom Boom," "Dimples," "I'm So Excited," and "One Bourbon, One Scotch, One Beer." Hooker may have sometimes sounded a bit ill at ease with a band, but he usually worked with backing musicians very well. Non-purists will find these tracks to be some of his most accessible and dynamic performances. *—Richie Unterberger*

☆ **The Legendary Modern Recordings 1948-1954** / 1994 / Virgin ✦✦✦✦✦
From the beginning of his career, Hooker recorded prolifically, sometimes for several labels at once, sometimes under a number of pseudonyms. That makes his discography a bit difficult for the collector to sort out, but if you want just one document of his early years, this is

the anthology of choice, containing 24 sides from 1948 to 1954 that were issued on the Modern label. These, more than any other, are the recordings that did the most to establish the Hooker protoype—the overamplified electric guitar, the moody boogies, the stomping-foot rhythms, performed without a rhythm section (some sides feature accompaniment by Eddie Kirkland on second guitar). It contains his two most massive early hits, "Boogie Chillen" and "I'm in the Mood," as well as his oft-covered "Crawling Kingsnake." This one can get a bit similar-sounding over the course of two dozen tracks, but little other postwar electric blues can match the stark power here. *—Richie Unterberger*

★ **The Very Best of John Lee Hooker** / Apr. 25, 1995 / Rhino ✦✦✦✦✦
This 16-track collection sweats down Rhino's two-disc anthology to a lean, mean, and essential single disc. Here are the earliest recordings that established Hooker as a major blues artist—"Boogie Chillen," "Hobo Blues," "I'm In the Mood," "Crawlin' Kingsnake," and "Huckle Up Baby"—and they sound better here than on most other collections, reverberating with a clarity that belies their age. The rest of the set follows Hooker's move toward working with bands not always in step with his erratic timing, but still producing classic blues on favorites like "Dimples" and "Boom Boom." If you're going to own only one Hooker collection, add this one to the shopping basket. *—Cub Koda*

His Best Chess Sides (Chess 50th Anniversary Collection) / Jun. 17, 1997 / Chess ✦✦✦
Hooker, as anyone with a decent-sized blues collection knows, recorded for a virtual parade of labels early in his career, including Chess, although his stays with the company were fairly brief. Hooker's best early recordings, most would agree, were issued on Modern and Vee-Jay, not Chess. Still, if the only Hooker extant was his Chess sides, his greatness would be readily apparent. Approached not as a best-of but simply as one of many Hooker compilations, this 15-song disc is fine, leaving heavily on early-'50s material (the source for 11 of the songs). This is typical of his early work in its stress on his great guitar work, walking rhythms, and drumless arrangements (most of it is played solo). It's good stuff, even if much of it is derivative of things he recorded elsewhere, and the mike plainly catches him coughing on "Bluebird." The solo on "Leave My Wife Alone" is almost avant-garde in conception, a series of plucked runs up and down the scale with little relation to convention, even by blues standards. Closing the set are four much more modern-sounding cuts from the mid-'60s, comprising the "I'm in the Mood"/"Let's Go Out Tonight" single and a couple of cuts from the *Real Folk Blues* LP (including his standard "One Bourbon, One Scotch and One Beer"). *—Richie Unterberger*

The Complete 50's Chess Recordings / Jan. 13, 1998 / Chess ✦✦✦
Hooker bounced around between label affiliations like crazy in the '50s, recording under almost as many fake names as he did labels during that decade. His two lasting record company hookups occurred with Chess in the early '50s and Vee-Jay later on in the decade. All of Hooker's Chess masters from that decade (he would later record in the '60s for them as well) are here on this two-disc, 31-track collection. Unlike other Chess artists, Hooker did little of his recording in Chicago, preferring to work out of his Detroit home base, where he continued to record for other labels under a variety of pseudonyms. His 1951 Chicago session excepted, the rest of the tracks emanate from Detroit sessions that also saw issuance on the local Gone, H-Q, and Fortune labels. This is early John Lee at his solo-guitar, foot-stomping best, featuring boogies and introspective, slow blues that rival his best work. Some of the Detroit tracks reveal inbred distortion that can't be overcome even with modern day noise reduction techniques, but don't let that deter you from sampling some of the best John Lee Hooker available on compact disc for a second.
—Cub Koda

The Best of Friends / Oct. 20, 1998 / Virgin ✦✦✦

Lightnin' Hopkins (Sam Hopkins)

b. Mar. 15, 1912, Centerville, TX, **d.** Jan. 30, 1982, Houston, TX
Vocals, Piano, Guitar, Organ / Blues Revival, Acoustic Texas Blues, Electric Texas Blues
Sam "Lightnin'" Hopkins was a Texas country bluesman of the highest caliber whose career began in the 1920s and stretched all the way into the 1980s. Along the way, Hopkins watched the genre change remarkably, but he never appreciably altered his mournful Lone Star sound, which translated onto both acoustic and electric guitar. Hopkins's nimble dexterity made intricate boogie riffs seem easy, and his fascinating penchant for improvising lyrics to fit whatever situation might arise made him a beloved blues troubadour. "Katie May," cut in 1946, was Hopkins' first regional seller of note. He recorded prolifically for Aladdin in both L.A. and Houston into 1948, scoring a national R&B hit for the firm with his "Shotgun Blues." "Short Haired Woman," "Abilene," and "Big Mama Jump," among many Aladdin gems, were evocative Texas blues rooted in an earlier era. But Hopkins's style was apparently too rustic and old-fashioned for the new generation of rock & roll enthusiasts, and he was back on the Houston scene by 1959, largely forgotten. Fortunately, folklorist Mack McCormick rediscovered the guitarist, who was dusted off and presented as a folk-blues artist—a role that Hopkins was born to play. Pioneering musicologist Sam Charters produced Hopkins in a solo context for Folkways Records that same year, cutting an entire LP in Hopkins's tiny apartment (on a borrowed guitar). The results helped introduced his music to an entirely new audience. *—Bill Dahl*

☆ **Lightnin' Hopkins** / Jan. 16, 1959 / Smithsonian/Folkways ✦✦✦✦✦
Originally released as *The Roots of Lightnin' Hopkins*, Smithsonian/Folkways' *Lightnin' Hopkins* was recorded in 1959. Upon its initial release, it was a pivotal part of the blues revival and helped re-spark interest in Hopkins. Before it was recorded, the bluesman had disappeared from sight; after a great deal of searching, Sam Charters found Hopkins in a rented one-room apartment in Houston. Persuading Lightnin' with a bottle of gin, Charters convinced Hopkins to record ten songs in that room, using only one microphone. The resulting record was one of the greatest albums in Hopkins' catalog, a skeletal record that is absolutely naked in its loneliness and haunting in its despair. These unvarnished performances arguably capture the essence of Lightnin' Hopkins better than any of his other recordings, and it is certainly one of the landmarks of the late-'50s/early-'60s blues revival. *—Thom Owens*

Last Night Blues / 1961 / Bluesville/Original Blues Classics ✦✦✦

The Lightnin' / 1961 / Prestige/Original Blues Classics ✦✦✦
Recorded for Prestige's Bluesville subsidiary in 1960 and reissued on CD for Fantasy's Original Blues Classics (OBC) series in 1990, *Lightnin'* is among the rewarding acoustic dates Lightnin' Hopkins delivered in the early '60s. The session has an informal, relaxed quality, and this approach serves a 48-year-old Hopkins impressively well on both originals like "Thinkin' 'Bout an Old Friend" and the familiar "Katie Mae" and enjoyable interpretations of Sonny Terry & Brownie McGhee's "Back to New Orleans" and Arthur "Big Boy" Crudup's "Mean Old Frisco." Hopkins' only accompaniment consists of bassist Leonard Gaskin and drummer Belton Evans, both of whom play in an understated fashion and do their part to make this intimate setting successful. From the remorseful "Come Back Baby" to more lighthearted, fun numbers like "You Better Watch Yourself" and "Automobile Blues," *Lightnin'* is a lot like being in a small club with Hopkins as he shares his experiences, insights and humor with you. *—Alex Henderson*

How Many More Years I Got / 1962 / Fantasy ✦✦✦
Repackaging of three earlier albums, *Walkin' This Road by Myself, Lightnin' & Co.* and *Smokes like Lightnin'.* Lightnin' plays electric with small band support on these sides, which probably come the closest to what he sounded like in the juke joints around Houston in the early '60s. *—Cub Koda*

Goin' Away / 1963 / Bluesville/Original Blues Classics ✦✦✦

Smokes Like Lightnin' / 1963 / Bluesville/Original Blues Classics ✦✦✦

Hopkins Brothers: Lightnin', Joel, & John Henry / Feb. 1964 / Arhoolie ✦✦✦

Swarthmore Concert / Apr. 1964 / Bluesville/Original Blues Classics ✦✦✦✦
A Lightnin' solo concert from his college kiddie-folk period (1964), this languished unissued in Fantasy Records' vaults until its release in the early '90s. That's a shame, because this concert captures Lightnin' at his beguiling best, spinning tales and blues magic with every track. His introductions are half the show, making even shopworn staples like "Baby Please Don't Go" and "My Babe" sound fresh. His guitar work is astounding, pulling off inventive leads while maintaining a constant boogie rhythm that makes other instruments superfluous. If you want a disc that clearly showcases Lightnin' Hopkins at his enchanting best, start your collection with this one; it's a charmer. *—Cub Koda*

Hootin' the Blues / 1965 / Prestige/Original Blues Classics ✦✦✦

The Herald Material 1954 / 1988 / Collectables ✦✦✦✦✦
Lightnin' Hopkins in a heavily amplified mode (especially for 1954!) and tearing it up with some of the wildest licks of his long and storied career! It's hard to fathom a more torrid tempo than the one he employs for "Hopkins' Sky Hop," and "Flash Lightnin'," "Lightnin's Boogie," and "Lightnin' Stomp" aren't far behind. Alas, Hopkins' Herald waxings didn't sell particularly well—though they're downright astonishing in retrospect. *—Bill Dahl*

Drinkin' in the Blues: Golden Classics, Pt. 1 / 1989 / Collectables ✦✦✦✦✦
Almost 70 minutes of Lightnin' Hopkins, some live (no date or location listed) and some studio, but all pretty well indispensable for any fan, from the first words of the extraordinary opening monologue ("Big Black Cadillac Blues") on. He's playing acoustic live, and this sounds like one of his coffeehouse gigs along the folk circuit from the early 1960s, except that the quality is better than on many of those shows, with a close sound on the guitar—the studio stuff is electric, natch. *—Bruce Eder*

The Herald Recordings, Vol. 2 / 1989 / Collectables ✦✦✦✦
Hopkins left a ton of tapes behind at New York-based Herald Records—enough to support this second volume of 1954 gems. *—Bill Dahl*

☆ **The Complete Aladdin Recordings** / 1991 / Aladdin/EMI ✦✦✦✦✦
This is where it all began for the Houston troubadour: 43 solo sides, as evocative and stark as any he ever did, from 1946-1948. The first 13 sides find the guitarist in tandem with pianist Wilson "Thunder" Smith (who handles the vocals on a few tracks), but after that, old Lightnin' Hopkins went the solo route. "Katie May," "Short Haired Woman," "Abilene," "Shotgun"—all these and more rate with his seminal performances. *—Bill Dahl*

Complete Prestige/Bluesville Recordings / 1991 / Prestige/Bluesville ✦✦✦✦✦
This is a seven-CD box set that repackages all 11 LPs that Lightnin' Hopkins recorded for Bluesville and Prestige during the first half of the 1960s: *Last Night Blues, Lightnin', Blues in My Bottle, Walkin' This Road By Myself, Lightnin' and Co., Smokes Like Lightning, Hootin' the Blues, Goin' Away, Down Home Blues, Soul Blues* and *My Life in the Blues.* The very prolific Hopkins (who was never loyal to any one label) also recorded for Candid, Arhoolie, Fire and Vee Jay during the period! The bulk of *My Life in the Blues* is actually a lengthy and rather historic interview that Samuel Charters conducted with Hopkins. A special bonus of the set is 13 often exciting tracks from a previously unissued concert at the Swarthmore College Folk Festival. The music throughout the box covers quite a variety of moods and subject matter (with Hopkins being unaccompanied on 34 of the tracks) and definitively sums up the veteran bluesman's later period. *—Scott Yanow*

Gold Star Sessions, Vol. 1 / 1991 / Arhoolie ✦✦✦✦✦
The first of two discs devoted to Hopkins' extensive recording activities during the late '40s for Bill Quinn's Gold Star logo. *—Bill Dahl*

Gold Star Sessions, Vol. 2 / 1991 / Arhoolie ✦✦✦✦✦
More wonderfully sparse ruminations by the Texas blues troubadour for Quinn's Gold Star label. Hopkins was amazingly prolific during his first few years of recording, and nearly everything he did back then has great artistic merit. *—Bill Dahl*

☆ **Mojo Hand: The Anthology** / May 18, 1993 / Rhino ✦✦✦✦✦
As with its John Lee Hooker two-disc set, Rhino offers a very pleasant way to begin serious appreciation of Hopkins' humongous recorded legacy with this 41-track anthology. His Aladdin, Gold Star, RPM, Sittin' in With, and Mercury output are all liberally sampled on disc one, and there are a half dozen of those electrifying 1954 Herald sides that verged on rock

& roll. Disc two is a less exciting affair, those 1960s folk-blues and later efforts usually paling in comparison to seminal early efforts. Still, for a cogent overview of the guitarist's daunting discography, this is the place to start. *—Bill Dahl*

Jake Head Boogie / Feb. 12, 1999 / Ace ✦✦✦✦✦
In the late 1940s and early 1950s, Hopkins recorded for Houston record producer Bill Quinn, the results appearing on several labels (including Quinn's own Gold Star company). In 1951, Quinn sold unreleased Hopkins masters to Modern, which issued some on its RPM subsidiary. This 31-track disc has all 14 of the Hopkins sides that came out on RPM, plus a bunch of other tracks from the same batch of Modern-by-way-of-Quinn masters; most were not available on CD outside of Japan before this release and were indeed usually hard to find anywhere. The sounds are what you'd expect from Hopkins if you've heard more widely circulated stuff from this period: Texas blues caught between the rural and electric era, done country style and performed solo, but usually played on a harshly amplified electric guitar that adds to the power. The title track especially has some of Hopkins' most effective guitar, getting into some really crunching and raunchy chords in the breaks. "Bad Luck and Trouble," "Beggin' You to Stay," "Mistreater Blues," "War News Blues," "Lonesome Dog Blues," "Everyday I Have the Blues"—it's not always the most optimistic fare, although it's delivered with casual good cheer. Collectors should note that some of these sound different from the actual Modern singles, which added a lot of reverb echo; Ace decided whenever possible to use the original acetates, which had only the natural echo of the room in which Lightning recorded. *—Richie Unterberger*

★ **Blues Masters: The Very Best of Lightnin' Hopkins** / Aug. 15, 2000 / Rhino ✦✦✦✦✦
Pruning 16 tracks from Hopkins' extensive catalog for a best-of meant that some hard choices had to be made. The ones Rhino came up with won't satisfy everyone, but the label did take the correct road by sticking exclusively to the earliest part of his career, 1947-61. Perhaps the decision will offend some fans who feel that his 1960s and '70s work should be represented, but two things should be acknowledged. First, Hopkins, as is the case with most artists, did his most interesting recordings in the earlier part of his career. Second, as is the case with many blues artists, he did not vary his approach substantially throughout the decades. So what you have is a good assortment of his first 15 years on disc, taken from about ten labels, including both originals and covers, and placing the singer/guitarist in various instrumental contexts: with a full electric band (Sonny Terry is on a couple of 1961 cuts), as a solo guitarist, or accompanied by nothing more than a bass or additional guitarist. It's a good deal for those who want only one Hopkins disc, and for those who want a best-of that's more extensive, there's Rhino's own two-disc anthology, *Mojo Hand*. *—Richie Unterberger*

Big Walter Horton

b. Apr. 6, 1917, Horn Lake, MS, **d.** Dec. 8, 1981, Chicago, IL
Vocals, Harmonica / Juke Joint Blues, Harmonica Blues, Electric Memphis Blues, Electric Chicago Blues
Big Walter "Shakey" Horton is one of the all-time great blues harp (harmonica) players. Along with Little Walter, Horton defined modern amplified Chicago-style harmonica. There is no harp player (and that includes Little Walter) with Horton's big tone and spacious sense of time. Horton was not a natural group leader and therefore has produced few solo albums. His best work is as a sideman; his backup harmonica and virtuoso harp solos have graced many great Chicago blues recordings—turning an otherwise good cut into a dynamite jam. Walter is the master of the single note and his characteristic walking bass line (usually with a deep tone and selection of notes that is unsurpassed) is instantly recognizable. As an accompanist, he has few equals. His backup harp is always unobtrusive yet bright and fresh—enhancing whatever else is going on. Give Big Walter a chance to solo and you are in for some of the most tasteful lines Chicago-style harp has ever produced. He made a specialty of playing entire tunes (often in blues style) on the harmonica ("La Cucaracha," "Careless Love," "I Almost Lost My Mind," etc). This might sound trite, but give them a listen. You'll see. As for harmonicas, he used Hohner's Marine Band. He was just as comfortable playing first position (A harp in the key of A) as with the more standard cross harp (D harp in the key of A). He did not do much with chromatic harmonicas. Although Big Walter could play in the style of other harp players (and was often asked to do so), he has no credible imitators. He is one of a kind. Horton's taste in notes and depth of tone is unparalleled in the history of amplified Chicago-style harmonica. As Willie Dixon says, "Big Walter is the best harmonica player I ever heard." I agree. He was the man. *—Michael Erlewine*

The Soul of Blues Harmonica / Jan. 13, 1964 / MCA/Chess ✦✦✦
Big Walter's first album and with an all star cast—Buddy Guy (guitar), Jack Myers (bass), Willie Dixon (vocals), and Willie Smith (drums). Although not definitive, this album is worth seeking out for Horton fans. It features Walter in a variety of musical styles, including a good rendition of "Hard Hearted Woman" and a wild version of "La Cucaracha" *—Michael Erlewine*

★ **Chicago: The Blues Today!, Vol. 3** / 1967 / Vanguard ✦✦✦✦✦
One of the all-time great blues albums. Period. It features Big Walter with the Johnny Shines Blues Band, the Johnny Young South Side Blues Band, and Big Walter Horton's Blues Harp Band (with Charlie Musselwhite). The timing and sense of musical spaciousness is incredible. Walter's backup harp and harmonica solos mark a high point in his career. A must hear. *—Michael Erlewine*

Big Walter Horton with Carey Bell / Jan. 1973 / Alligator ✦✦✦✦
The teacher/pupil angle might be a bit unwieldy here—Bell was already a formidable harpist in his own right by 1972, when Horton made this album—but there's no denying that a stylistic bond existed between the two. A highly showcase for the often recalcitrant harp master, and only his second domestic set as a leader. *—Bill Dahl*

Fine Cuts / Apr. 1979 / Blind Pig ✦✦✦✦✦
Horton was tragically underrecorded as a bandleader; this album certainly attests to his talents in that regard, whether romping through a joyous "Everybody's Fishin'" or elegantly examining the tonal possibilities of the Duke Ellington chestnut "Don't Get Around Much Anymore." John Nicholas provides sympathetic backing on both guitar and piano, and Kaz Kazanoff is the stellar saxman. *—Bill Dahl*

Mouth Harp Maestro / 1988 / Ace ✦✦✦✦✦
Long before he arrived in Chicago, Horton was knocking 'em dead with his amplified harmonica wizardry in Memphis. Sam Phillips produced the classic sides that comprise much of this album in 1951, when Horton was billed as "Mumbles." Sizzling backup by guitarists Joe Hill Louis and Calvin Newborn urged the introverted harp giant on to dazzling heights on his earliest sides as a leader. *—Bill Dahl*

Can't Keep Lovin' You / 1989 / Blind Pig ✦✦✦

Son House (Eddie James House, Jr.)

b. Mar. 21, 1902, Riverton, MS, **d.** Oct. 19, 1988, Detroit, MI
Slide Guitar, Vocals, Guitar / Slide Guitar Blues, Field Recordings, Prewar Blues, Work Songs, Blues Revival, Delta Blues, Acoustic Blues
Son House's place, not only in the history of Delta blues, but in the overall history of the music, is a very high one indeed. He was a major innovator of the Delta style, along with his playing partners Charley Patton and Willie Brown. Few listening experiences in the blues are as intense as hearing one of Son House's original 1930s recordings for the Paramount label. Entombed in a hailstorm of surface noise and scratches, one can still be awestruck by the emotional fervor House puts into his singing and slide playing. Little wonder then, that the man became more than just an influence on some White English kid with a big amp; he was the main source of inspiration to both Muddy Waters and Robert Johnson, and it doesn't get much more pivotal than *that.* Even after his rediscovery in the mid-'60s, House was such a potent musical force that what would have been a normally genteel performance by any other bluesmen in a "folk" setting, turned into a night in the nastiest juke joint you could imagine, scaring the daylights out of young White enthusiasts expecting something far more prosaic and comfortable. Not out of Son House, no sir. When the man hit the downbeat on his National steel bodied guitar and you saw his eyes disappear into the back of his head, you *knew* you were going to hear some blues. And when he wasn't shouting the blues, he was singing spirituals, a cappella. Right up to the end, no bluesman was torn between the sacred and the profane more than Son House. *—Cub Koda*

☆ **Masters of the Delta Blues: the Friends of Charlie Patton** / 1930 / Yazoo ✦✦✦✦✦
If you've only heard Son House's 1965 rediscovery recordings for Columbia (or his excellent 1941-1942 Library of Congress sessions), boy, are you in for a shock. This various-artists compilation collects up House's original 1930 recordings for the Paramount label, some of the rarest and hardest to find 78s in blues history. Recorded in Grafton, WI, House sounds positively demonic on the six issued titles (all of them two-part numbers, each being a separate take, rather than a single performance spread over both sides of a single) and with the inclusion of a previously unissued test acetate of "Walking Blues," this is the most complete document of his first recordings that has survived on this important Delta bluesman. The original Paramount 78s were always considered of inferior pressing quality even back in the days when turntables were called Victrolas and the hailstorm of surface noise on these sides seems by and large resistant to all forms of modern noise reduction devices employed here. But House's performances here cut through the crackles, pops, and hisses like slicing up a cold stick of butter with a soldering iron. Absolutely indispensable. *—Cub Koda*

★ **Delta Blues** / 1991 / Biograph ✦✦✦✦✦
All of the recordings Alan Lomax made of Son House in 1941 and 1942 are collected on this essential CD. *—Stephen Thomas Erlewine*

Father of the Delta Blues: The Complete 1965 Sessions / 1992 / Columbia/Legacy ✦✦✦✦✦
After being rediscovered by the folk-blues community in the early '60s, Son House rose to the occasion and recorded this magnificent set of performances. Allowed to stretch out past the shorter running time of the original 78s, House turns in wonderful, steaming performances of some of his best-known material. On some tracks, House is supplemented by folk-blues researcher/musician Alan Wilson, who would later become a member of the blues-rock group Canned Heat and here plays some nice second guitar and harmonica on several cuts. This two-disc set features alternate takes, some unissued material and some studio chatter from producer John Hammond, Sr. that ocassionally hints at the chaotic nature inherent to some of these '60s "rediscovery" sessions. While not as overpowering as his earlier work (what could be?), all of these sides are so power packed with sheer emotional involvement from House, they're an indispensable part of his canonade.*—Cub Koda*

● **Original Delta Blues** / Jun. 30, 1998 / Columbia/Legacy ✦✦✦✦✦
Columbia/Legacy's *The Original Delta Blues* is a fine distillation of the label's double-disc set *Father of the Delta Blues,* containing 16 highlights from that comprehensive overview of his '60s rediscovery recordings. Curious listeners who are intimidated by the size of the previous set are advised to pick up this terrific sampler instead. *—Stephen Thomas Erlewine*

Howlin' Wolf (Chester Arthur Burnett)

b. Jun. 10, 1910, West Point, MS, **d.** Jan. 10, 1976, Hines, IL
Vocals, Harmonica, Guitar / Electric Chicago Blues
In the history of the blues, there has never been anyone quite like the Howlin' Wolf. Six foot three and close to 300 pounds in his salad days, the Wolf was the primal force of the music spun out to its ultimate conclusion. A Robert Johnson may have possessed more lyrical insight, a Muddy Waters more dignity, and a B.B. King certainly more technical expertise, but no one could match him for the singular ability to rock the house down to the foundation while simultaneously scaring its patrons out of its wits. By 1948, he had established himself as a radio personality. Wolf finally started recording in 1951, when he caught the ear of Sam Phillips; when he entered the Chess studios in 1954, the violent aggression of the Memphis sides was being replaced with a Chicago backbeat and, with very little fanfare, a new member in the band, Hubert Sumlin, who proved himself to be the Wolf's longest-running musical associate. In what can only be described as an "angular attack," Sumlin played almost no chords behind Wolf, sometimes soloing right through his vocals, featuring wild skitterings

up and down the fingerboard and biting single notes. By 1956, Wolf was in the R&B charts with "Evil" and "Smokestack Lightnin'." He remained a top attraction both on the Chicago circuit and on the road. His records, while seldom showing up on the national charts, were still selling in decent numbers down South. But by 1960, Wolf was teamed up with Chess staff writer Willie Dixon and for the next five years, he would record almost nothing but songs written by Dixon. The magic combination of Wolf's voice, Sumlin's guitar and Dixon's tunes sold a lot of records and brought the 50-year-old bluesman roaring into the next decade with a considerable flourish. The mid-'60s saw him touring Europe regularly with "Smokestack Lightnin'" becoming a hit in England some eight years after its American release. Certainly any list of Wolf's greatest sides would have to include "I Ain't Superstitious," "The Red Rooster," "Shake for Me," "Back Door Man," "Spoonful," and "Wang Dang Doodle," Dixon compositions all. While almost all of them would eventually become Chicago blues standards, their greatest cache occurred when rock bands the world over started mining the Chess catalog for all it was worth. *—Cub Koda*

The Real Folk Blues / 1966 / MCA/Chess ✦✦✦✦✦
This was originally released by Chess in 1966 to capitalize on the then-current folk music boom. The music, however—a collection of Wolf singles from 1956 to 1966—is full-blown electric featuring a nice sampling of Wolf originals with a smattering of Willie Dixon tunes. Some of the man's best middle period work is aboard here; "Killing Floor," "Louise," the hair-raisingly somber "Natchez Burning," and Wolf's version of the old standard "Sitting on Top of the World," which would become his set closer in later years. The Mobile Fidelity version sounds as sonically sharp as anything you've ever heard on this artist and its heftier price tag is somewhat justified by the inclusion of two bonus cuts. But those on a budget who just want the music minus the high-minded audiophile concerns will be happy to note that this is also available as a Chess budget reissue. *—Cub Koda*

More Real Folk Blues / 1967 / MCA/Chess ✦✦✦✦✦
This companion volume to the *Real Folk Blues* album was issued in 1967 (after the Wolf had appeared on network television with the Rolling Stones, alluded to in the original liner notes) and couldn't be more dissimilar in content to the first one if you had planned it that way. Whereas the previous volume highlighted middle period Wolf, this one goes all the way back to his earliest Chess sessions, many of which sound like leftover Memphis sides. The chaotic opener, "Just My Kind," sets a familiar Wolf theme to a "Rollin' & Tumblin'" format played at breakneck speed and what the track lacks in fidelity is more than made up in sheer energy. For a classic example of Wolf's ensemble Chicago sound, it's pretty tough to beat "I Have a Little Girl" where the various members of his band seem to be all soloing simultaneously—not unlike a Dixieland band—right through Wolf's vocals. For downright scary, the demonic sounding "I'll Be Around" is an absolute must-hear. Wolf's harp solo on this slow blues is one of his best and the vocal that frames it sounds like the microphone is going to explode at any second. As soul singer Christine Ohlman commented upon hearing this track for the first time, "Boy, I'd sure hate to be the woman he's singing that one to." *—Cub Koda*

The London Howlin' Wolf Sessions / 1971 / MCA/Chess ✦✦

The Back Door Wolf / 1973 / Chess ✦✦✦

Ridin' in the Moonlight / 1982 / Ace ✦✦✦✦
Having moved from his home in Mississippi to Arkansas and eventually West Memphis, Howlin' Wolf recorded his first sides for Sam Phillips at the *Memphis Recording Service* between 1951-1953. These important recordings show that Wolf's gruff, Delta-fashioned and piledriving blues style was already intact before he hooked up with Chess for a successful stretch that would continue into the '60s. Featuring the fractured and menacing guitar work of Willie Johnson (equally celebrated axe man Hubert Sumlin would eventually supplant Johnson as the featured guitarist on Wolf's Chicago sides), the pumping piano of Ike Turner, and the ragged-but-right drumming of Willie Steel, the 16 tracks included on this Ace collection are alternate takes of some of the Memphis material originally released by Modern Records. While most of the master takes can be heard on Flair/Virgin's *Howlin' Wolf Rides Again,* the tracks on *Ridin' in the Moonlight* are certainly worthwhile, especially for collectors. With his permanently hoarse pipes and sour harmonica in the forefront, Wolf leads the band on highlights like the tittle track, "Chocolate Drop," "Keep What You Got," "Drivin' This Highway," and "Passing by Blues." A highly enjoyable release; newcomers, though, are advised to check out one of Wolf's Chess collections or the Flair album first. *—Stephen Cook*

★ **Howlin' Wolf/Moanin' in the Moonlight** / 1986 / MCA/Chess ✦✦✦✦✦
Wolf's first and second Chess albums are essential listening of the highest order. Compiled—as were all early blues albums—from various single sessions (not necessarily a bad thing, either), blues fans will probably debate endlessly about which of these two albums is the perfect introduction to his music. But this CD reissue renders all arguments moot as both album appear on one disc, making this a true best buy. Wolf's debut opus—curiously tacked on here *after* his second album—features all of his early hits ("How Many More Years," "Moanin' at Midnight," "Smokestack Lightning," "Forty Four," "Evil" and "I Asked for Water [She Gave Me Gasoline]") and is a pretty potent collection in its own right. But it is the follow-up (always referred to as 'the rocking chair album' because of Don Bronstein's distinctive cover art) where the equally potent teaming of Willie Dixon and Wolf produced one Chicago Blues classic ("Spoonful," "The Red Rooster," "Back Door Man," "Wang Dang Doodle") after another. It's also with this marvelous batch of sides that one can clearly hear lead guitarist Hubert Sumlin coming into his own as a blues picking legend. The number of blues acolytes, both Black and White, who wore the grooves down to mush learning the songs and guitar licks off these two albums would fill a book all by itself. If you have to narrow it down to just one Howlin' Wolf purchase for the collection, this would be the one to have and undoubtedly the place to start. This and *The Best of Muddy Waters* are the essential building blocks of any Chicago Blues collection. And seldom does the music come with this much personality and brute force. *—Cub Koda*

☆ **Cadillac Daddy: Memphis Recordings, 1952** / 1989 / Rounder ✦✦✦✦✦
You can't possibly fault the material aboard this 12-song collection of Howlin' Wolf's Memphis recordings cut for Sam Phillips. The title track features some truly frightening guitar work from Willie Johnson,and all the material here is loaded with feral energy and a sense that it could fall apart at any second. It's totally intuitive music, with Wolf seemingly making it all up as he went along, which Sam Phillips had the patience to capture as it all went down. These are some of the great moments in blues history, but this part of Wolf's career is better documented on the two Bear Family volumes of the same material and the Flair/Virgin single disc of Memphis and West Memphis recordings. *—Cub Koda*

Memphis Days: Definitive Edition, Vol. 1 / 1989 / Bear Family ✦✦✦✦✦
These are Wolf's earliest and rarest sides recorded at the Sun studios, as raw and explosive as blues records come. Much of this was issued on various European albums during the '70s, always transferred off of muffled-sounding copy tapes. These 21 tracks (all but two of them off the master tapes) feature the amp-on-11 guitar work of Willie Johnson and the cave-man drumming of Willie Steele; they're loose and somewhat chaotic, with Wolf sounding utterly demonic. The real bonus on this volume is the first time inclusion of both sides of the only known acetate of Wolf's first session at Sam Phillip's 706 Union Avenue studio from 1951. With only Johnson and Steele in support (no bass, no piano), these early versions of "How Many More Years" and "Baby Ride with Me (Riding in the Moonlight)" are Wolf at his most primitive. *—Cub Koda*

The Memphis Days: Definitive Edition, Vol. 2 / 1990 / Bear Family ✦✦✦✦✦
The second volume in this series collects up all the known Memphis recordings that were either issued or originally offered to Chess. As such, it stands as a marvelous collection of Wolf's early 78s for that label. But what truly puts it over is the added bonus of a newly discovered acetate featuring several unissued versions of "How Many More Years" and "Baby Ride With Me (Riding in the Moonlight)." Much of this volume is pulled from discs, but the overall sound is good and the performances make it yet another must-have. *—Cub Koda*

☆ **The Chess Box** / 1991 / MCA/Chess ✦✦✦✦✦
This three-CD box set currently rates as the best—and most digestible—overview of Wolf's career. Disc one starts with the Memphis sides that eventually brought him to the label, including hits like "How Many More Years," but also compiling unissued sides that had previously only been available on vinyl bootlegs of dubious origin and fidelity. The disc finishes with an excellent cross section of early Chicago sessions including classic Wolf tracks like "Evil," "Forty Four," "I'll Be Around" and "Who Will Be Next." Disc two picks it up from there guiding us from mid- to late-'50s barnburners like "The Natchez Burnin'" and "I Better Go Now" to the bulk of the Willie Dixon classics. The final disc runs out the last of the Dixon sessions into mid-'60s classics like "Killing Floor" taking us to a nice selection of his final recordings. A really nice bonus on this box set is the inclusion on the first two discs of snippets from a 1968 Howlin' Wolf interview and two performances of Wolf playing solo acoustic. If you've heard the sound of the Wolf, here's where you go to get a lot of it in one place. Definitely *not* the place to start (unless you have money to burn), but maybe just the perfect place to end up. *—Cub Koda*

☆ **Howlin' Wolf Rides Again** / 1993 / Flair ✦✦✦✦✦
While both Bear Family sets deal with a largely unissued wealth of material, this collection is devoted in the main to all the Memphis recordings from 1951 and 1952 that saw the light of day on a number of Los Angeles-based labels owned by the Bihari Brothers, being issued and reissued and reissued again on a plethora of $1.98 budget albums. Featuring recordings done in Sam Phillips' Memphis Recording Service and surreptitious sessions recorded by a young Ike Turner in makeshift studios, these 18 sides are the missing piece of the puzzle in absorbing Wolf's early pre-Chess period. It also helps that this just happens to be some of the nastiest sounding blues ever recorded. With no tracks being duplicated from the two Bear Family *Memphis Days* volumes, and sonics far surpassing all previous issues of this material (every last one of them horribly marred by an annoying 60 cycle hum), this is an essential part of any Wolf collection. Alternate-take freaks will revel in the inclusion of two extra takes of "Riding in the Moonlight" from an earlier and different session than the issued version also included. While not *quite* as essential as his first two Chess albums (and if you were making a judgement call on just passionate performances alone, even *that* would be debatable), this is definitely the next stop along the way in absorbing the raw genius of Howlin' Wolf. *—Cub Koda*

☆ **Ain't Gonna Be Your Dog** / 1994 / MCA/Chess ✦✦✦✦✦
This double-disc set features 42 rare and unissued performances, effectively cleaning out the Chess vaults of all but alternate takes of alternate takes. But these are no bottom-of-the-barrel scrapings here, quite the opposite. The first 14 tunes collect up the remainder of his Memphis recordings for Sam Phillips while the rest does the bootleggers one better, compiling masters that were previously only available on bad-sounding '70s vinyl albums. There's another snippet from his 1968 interview along with four more acoustic numbers from that same session (done, it turns out, as a promotional piece of sorts to preview his "soon-to-be-released psychedelic album," which Wolf always dismissed as "birds**t"), sadly the only time Chess ever tried to record him as a solo artist. A wonderful companion piece to any other Wolf collection you might own. *—Cub Koda*

★ **His Best (Chess 50th Anniversary Collection)** / Apr. 8, 1997 / MCA/Chess ✦✦✦✦✦
With the exception of a vinyl compilation issued in the early 1980s (*His Greatest Sides, Volume 1*), there's never really ever been a single-disc Howlin' Wolf best-of package available. That all changes with this entry in MCA-Chess' 50th Anniversary series, a 20-track retrospective that serves as the perfect introduction to the man and his music, some of the very best the blues has to offer. While some naysayers will always decry the exclusion—or inclusion—of any given number of tracks on any artists' best-of compilation, it's pretty hard to fault what's been collected here. Starting with the two-sided smash that brought him from Memphis to Chicago ("Moanin' At Midnight" b/w "How Many More Years"), this compilation hits all the high points and essential tracks, illustrating how his music developed into the mid-1960s. 11 of the 20 tunes on here are either written or co-written by Willie Dixon, and Wolf's original takes on "Back Door Man," "Spoonful," "The Red Rooster," "Wang Dang Doodle," and "I Ain't Superstitious" are truly the definitive ones, a place where personality and

material symbiotically become as one. Even if you have already have this material, diehard Wolf fans—and audiophiles in particular—will want to investigate this package as the master transfers used here are absolutely stunning, with stereo mixes of "Killing Floor," "Built For Comfort," "Hidden Charms" (with the full-length Hubert Sumlin guitar solo), "Shake For Me," and the long version of "Going Down Slow" being particular standouts. This is a set so essential that it should on everyone's Top Ten first purchases in building the perfect blues collection. While Wolf's music will take you to many places (both musically and spiritually), here's where you start to absorb it all. *—Cub Koda*

Howlin' at the Sun / Aug. 19, 1997 / Charly ✦✦✦✦
In terms of song selection, *Howlin' at the Sun* is an exact replica of the 21 tracks featured on Bear Family's *Memphis Days Vol. 1,* although the liner notes are, predictably, less thorough. In fact, there's nothing here that hasn't been released elsewhere, in better settings. *—Jim Smith*

☆ **His Best, Vol. 2** / Jul. 27, 1999 / MCA/Chess ✦✦✦✦✦
Where Chess' two-volume Muddy Waters anthology *His Best* was divided according to chronological guidelines, the Howlin' Wolf series of the same name follows a different pattern. *His Best, Vol. 1* contained all of the Wolf's best-known songs—as if the label never planned a sequel. Consequently, when it came time to assemble *Vol. 2,* they had two major items ("The Natchez Burnin'," "Down in the Bottom") that didn't make the first cut, a take of "The Red Rooster" with dialogue, plus a host of songs familiar to Wolf fans, but not casual blues fans. Since Chester Burnett was one of the greatest bluesmen in history, these second-tier songs aren't cast-offs—they're forgotten or unappreciated classics. They might not be as monumental as the songs on *His Best, Vol. 1,* yet they're great songs, making *His Best, Vol. 2* an excellent compliment to its essential predecessor. *—Stephen Thomas Erlewine*

Ivory Joe Hunter

b. Oct. 10, 1914, Kirbyville, TX, **d.** Nov. 8, 1974, Memphis, TN
Vocals, Piano / West Coast Blues, Piano Blues, R&B
Bespectacled and velvet-smooth in the vocal department, pianist Ivory Joe Hunter appeared too much mild-mannered to be a rock & roller. But when the rebellious music first crashed the American consciousness in the mid-'50s, there was Ivory Joe, deftly delivering his blues ballad "Since I Met You Baby" right alongside the wildest pioneers of the era. Hunter was already a grizzled R&B vet by that time who had first heard his voice on a 1933 Library of Congress cylinder recording made in Texas. He started his own label, Ivory Records, to press up his "Blues at Sunrise" (with Johnny Moore's Three Blazers backing him), and it became a national hit when leased to Leon Rene's Exclusive imprint in 1945. Another Hunter enterprise, Pacific Records, hosted a major hit in 1948 when the pianist's "Pretty Mama Blues" topped the R&B charts for three weeks. At whatever logo Hunter paused from the mid-'40s through the late '50s, his platters sold like hotcakes. For Cincinnati-based King in 1948-49, he hit with "Don't Fall in Love with Me," "What Did You Do to Me," "Waiting in Vain," and "Guess Who." At MGM, he cut his immortal "I Almost Lost My Mind" (another R&B chart-topper in 1950), "I Need You So" (later covered by Elvis), and "It's a Sin." Signing with Atlantic in 1954, he hit big with "Since I Met You Baby" in 1956 and the two-sided smash "Empty Arms"/"Love's A Hurting Game" in 1957. *—Bill Dahl*

16 of His Greatest Hits / 1958 / King ✦✦✦
Other than ruining his 1949 smash "Guess Who" entirely with hideous stereo overdubs, King has done pretty well by the pianist on this collection of his post-war output for the Cincinnati firm. Hunter was primarily in a sentimental blues ballad bag back then, some of his hits displaying a tinge of country influence. Sound quality is okay if not superlative. *—Bill Dahl*

● **Since I Met You Baby: The Best of Ivory Joe Hunter** / Oct. 19, 1994 / Razor & Tie ✦✦✦✦✦
Bespectacled pianist Ivory Joe Hunter's crooning blues balladry made him a hot commodity from the late '40s through the late '50s, but he could rock reasonably convincingly hard too. He does both on this wonderful survey of his 1949-1958 MGM and Atlantic sides—"I Need You So," "I Almost Lost My Mind," and the title item are sophisticated and mellow, while "Rockin' Chair Boogie," "Love Is a Hurting Game," and "Shooty Booty" find the pianist in decidedly unsentimental moods. *—Bill Dahl*

Ivory Joe Hunter/Sings the Old & the New / Jul. 27, 1999 / Collectables ✦✦✦✦

Mississippi John Hurt

b. Jul. 3, 1893, Teoc, MS, **d.** Nov. 2, 1966, Grenada, MS
Vocals, Harmonica, Guitar / Field Recordings, Prewar Blues, Blues Revival, Delta Blues, Country Blues, Acoustic Blues
The history of Mississippi John Hurt reads like a real Cinderella story. As a young adult, he became a sharecropper or tenant farmer for many years, but finally gave that up and switched to day labor. In the late '20s, a well-known fiddler named Willie Narmour, with whom Hurt often played, was spotted by a talent scout for Okeh Phonograph. When asked about other talented local musicians, Narmour gave them the name of John Hurt and directions on how to find him. Okeh found and interviewed Hurt, had him play a few songs, and decided to record him, provided he was willing to travel to Memphis and New York. Hurt's records did not sell in great numbers, perhaps in the hundreds, and he went back to sharecropping. That could have been the end of Hurt's national career had two young blues musicians from Washington, D.C., Tom Hoskins and Mike Stewart, not come across the original Okeh recording of "Avalon Blues." This was in 1963. Intrigued by John's intricate finger-picking style, they came up with the idea of trying to locate some of the original artists, should they still be alive. On a hope and a whim, the two blues archivists headed south armed with a tape recorder. With the help of the old map, they found Avalon with its single gas station/store and inquired about John Hurt. They were floored to see the attendant point down the road and say that Hurt's house was "About a mile down that road, third mail box up the hill. Can't miss it." Hurt, at 71 years of age, was waiting for them, alive and still able to sing and play about as well as he had before. They recorded John and returned to Washington with the precious taped results and the rediscovery of Mississippi John Hurt. He was a complete and instant success in the folk/blues scene. *—Michael Erlewine*

Avalon Blues / Apr. 1963 / Rounder ✦✦✦✦✦
This is the first in a multiple-volume series devoted to the Piedmont recordings Hurt made upon his rediscovery in the early '60s. They capture him with his playing and singing still intact, untouched by the world around him, a world that had changed so much since he initially recorded back in the '20s. Many of his best-known tunes are here—"Candy Man Blues," "Salty Dog," "Spike Driver Blues," "Louis Collins," "Spanish Fandango," and the title track—and although Hurt was to re-record them for other labels, these versions are as fine as any. There's really no one else in the blues with the gentle wistfulness of John Hurt, and this collection makes a wonderful addition to anyone's blues or folk music collection. *—Cub Koda*

Worried Blues / Apr. 1963 / Rounder ✦✦✦✦✦
This second of two sessions devoted to Mississippi John Hurt's first recordings followed the same pattern as its predecessor. Hurt did mostly blues, with an occasional spiritual number like "Oh Mary Don't You Weep." He sang in a fragile, yet powerful manner, backing his vocals on acoustic guitar in an equally simple, gentle manner with lines and riffs that often surpassed passages with far more intricate voicings. These two CDs restored into public circulation very valuable recordings. *—Ron Wynn*

The Best of Mississippi John Hurt / 1965 / Vanguard ✦✦✦✦✦
Contrary to what its title would make one believe, this record is not a collection of previously available recordings by Mississippi John Hurt—rather, it is a complete concert from Oberlin College on April 15, 1965. Regardless, the title is justified, as the concert features Hurt in excellent form doing most of his best known classic songs from the 1920s as well as newer compositions. *—Bruce Eder*

Last Sessions / 1966 / Vanguard ✦✦✦✦✦
Recorded in New York during February and July of 1966, the 17 songs on this collection represent Mississippi John Hurt's final studio efforts. It is astonishing that this man, in the final months of his life, could do 17 songs that were the equal of anything he had done at his first sessions 45 years earlier, his playing (supported on some tracks with producer Patrick Sky on second guitar) as alluringly complex as ever and his voice still in top form. Hurt is brilliant throughout, his voice overpowering in its mixture of warmth, gentleness, and power, and in addition to the expected crop of standards and originals, he covers songs by Bukka White ("Poor Boy, Long Ways from Home") and Leadbelly ("Goodnight Irene")—all of it is worthwhile, with some tracks, such as "Let the Mermaids Flirt with Me" especially haunting. *—Bruce Eder*

Today! / 1966 / Vanguard ✦✦✦✦
Today is Mississippi John Hurt's first and finest studio release since his "rediscovery" on his Avalon farm by folklorist Tom Hoskins in 1963. Eclipsed possibly only by his earlier *1928 Sessions,* this album shows a more mature Hurt picking his way through standards and originals after the Depression years and Hurt's fall into obscurity before the folk revival of the 1960s. It shows, however, that all that the great bluesman has lost is years; his voice retains its characteristic Buddha-esque warmth and it is still difficult to believe that there is just one man playing on the seemingly effortless guitar work. The music on the album comes from a variety of different influences, from the fun and poppy "Hot Time in Old Town Tonight" and "Coffee Blues," to the bluesy standards "Candy Man" (Hurt's most famous song) and "Spike Driver's Blues" to the soulful spirituals "Louis Collins" and "Beulah Land." Hurt's tranquil guitar work—mixing country, Scottish folk, and Delta blues—strings all of the songs along the same simple and elegant thread. Hurt himself never could explain his guitar playing, as he used to say, "I just make it sound like I think it ought to." Regardless, that sound, along with a mellow and heartfelt voice, wizened here by decades, combine to make *Today* an unforgettable whole. A truly essential album of the folk revival, unrivaled in its beauty and warmth. *—David Freedlander*

The Immortal / 1967 / Vanguard ✦✦✦✦✦
This is the best of Hurt's '60s "rediscovery-era" recordings. *—Mark A. Humphrey*

1928 Sessions / 1988 / Yazoo ✦✦✦✦✦
The 13 original 1928 recordings of Hurt. Justifiably legendary, with gentle grace and power on these understated vocal and fingerpicking masterpieces. These are the ones to hear, although all Hurt is worth listening to. *—Michael Erlewine*

★ **Avalon Blues: The Complete 1928 Okeh Recordings** / Oct. 8, 1996 / Columbia/Legacy ✦✦✦✦✦
Hurt's latter day recordings after his rediscovery have somewhat obscured the importance of these debut sides, the ones that made his rediscovery an idea initially worth pursuing. They are the collector's items that made his rep in the first place and stand as some of the most poetic and beautiful of all country blues recordings. Hurt's playing is sheer musical perfection, with a keen sense of chord melody structure to make his bouncy, rhythmic execution of it sound both elegant and driving. Mississippi John's voice—he was 36 at the time of these recordings—was already a warm and friendly one, imbued with the laidback wistfulness that would earmark his rediscovery recordings half a lifetime later. His best known songs—his adaptions of "Frankie *(Johnny)*" and "Stack O' Lee," "Avalon Blues," "Nobody's Dirty Business," "Candy Man Blues"—are all accounted for in their original incarnations here and the NoNoiser remastering on this collection is superb. Mississippi John Hurt would go on to re-record this material for other labels in the 60s with fine results, but these are the originals and the ones that much of his justifiable reputation rests on. *—Cub Koda*

Legend / Oct. 7, 1997 / Rounder ✦✦✦

Rediscovered / Aug. 11, 1998 / Vanguard ✦✦✦✦
Featuring over 75 minutes and 23 tracks, *Rediscovered* compiles tracks off Hurt's four Vanguard releases— *Today!, The Immortal Mississippi John Hurt, Last Sessions,* and *The Best of Mississippi John Hurt.* The tracks selected are truly first-rate and give a fine cross-section of Hurt's gently rolling country-blues, including many of his better-known tracks such as "It Ain't Nobody's Business" and "Avalon, My Home Town," as well as a few spirituals and

a handful of live tracks. These recordings are some of the last Hurt would make before his death, and are fine evidence of just how good he still was up until his last days. *—Matt Fink*

The Complete Studio Recordings / Oct. 31, 2000 / Vanguard ✦✦✦✦✦

J.B. Hutto (Joseph Benjamin Hutto)

b. Apr. 26, 1926, Blackville, SC, **d.** Jun. 12, 1983, Harvey, IL

Slide Guitar, Vocals, Guitar / Slide Guitar Blues, Electric Chicago Blues

J.B. Hutto—along with Hound Dog Taylor—was one of the last great slide guitar disciples of Elmore James to make it into the modern age. Hutto's huge voice, largely incomprehensible diction and slash and burn playing was Chicago blues with a fierce, raw edge all its own. His recording career started in 1954 with two sessions for the Chance label, resulting in six of the nine songs recorded being issued as singles to scant acclaim. Hutto then worked outside of music for a good decade, part of it spent sweeping out a funeral parlor! He resurfaced around 1964, working regularly at Turner's Blue Lounge and recording blistering new sides for the first time in as many years. From there, he never looked back and once again became a full-time bluesman.Hutto was an incredibly dynamic live performer, dressed in hot pink suits with headgear ranging from a shriner's fez to high-plains-drifters' hats, snaking through the crowd and dancing on tabletops with his 50-foot guitar cord stretched to the max. And this good-time approach to the music held sway on his recordings as well, giving a loose, barroom feel to almost all of them, regardless of who was backing him. *—Cub Koda*

☆ **Chicago: The Blues Today!, Vol. 1** / 1967 / Vanguard ✦✦✦✦✦

Hutto only has five tracks on this album, sharing it with great solo turns by Junior Wells and Otis Spann, but it's truly the place to start, because it doesn't get much better than this; "Too Much Alcohol", "Please Help", "Going Ahead" and "That's The Truth" are all classics and Hutto is in perfect form throughout with swinging support from the Turner's Blue Lounge version of the Hawks, bass-rhythm guitarist Herman Hassell and former Bo Diddley drummer Frank Kirkland. Sound is crystal clear. *—Cub Koda*

● **Hawk Squat!** / 1968 / Delmark ✦✦✦✦✦

The raw-as-an-open-wound Chicago slide guitarist outdid himself throughout an outrageously raucous album (most of it waxed in 1966) anchored by an impossible-to-ignore "Hip-Shakin'," the blaring title cut, and savage renditions of "20% Alcohol" and "Notoriety Woman." Sunnyland Slim augments Hutto's Hawks on organ, rather than his customary piano. *—Bill Dahl*

Slideslinger / Apr. 1, 1982 / Evidence ✦✦✦

While he was not in top shape during the early '80s, J.B. Hutto could still bend strings, churn out whiplash chords, and offer exuberant shouts, which he did on this '82 set, reissued on a '92 CD with two bonus cuts. He did not always hit every note on the fretboard or maintain his vocal depth, but his spirit never flagged. Hutto's jagged lines, energized vocals, and inspiring presence made his originals standouts, while his covers of Little Walter Jacobs' "Tell Me Mama" and Elmore James' "Look At The Yonder Wall" resonated with the quality that only a genuine blues survivor could provide. The backing band of guitarist Steve Coveney, bassist Kenny Krumbholz, and drummer Leroy Pina gave Hutto good support, wisely yielding him the spotlight, where he belongs. *—Ron Wynn*

And the Houserockers Live 1977 / 1991 / Wolf ✦✦✦

Masters of Modern Blues / 1995 / Testament ✦✦✦✦

1966 was a banner year for Hutto and his Hawks—in addition to laying down the lion's share of his killer Delmark album, the slide master also waxed a similarly incendiary set for Pete Welding's Testament logo. Vicious versions of "Pet Cream Man," "Lulubelle's Here," and "Bluebird" are but a few of its charms, with Big Walter Horton's unmistakable harp winding through the proceedings. *—Bill Dahl*

Rock with Me Tonight / Jul. 13, 1999 / Bullseye Blues & Jazz ✦✦✦

Bull Moose Jackson (Benjamin Joseph Jackson)

b. Apr. 22, 1919, Cleveland, OH, **d.** Jul. 31, 1989, Cleveland, OH

Vocals, Saxophone / Dirty Blues, Jump Blues, R&B

Allegedly, Benjamin Jackson resembled a bullmoose. At least, that's what a few wags in Lucky Millinder's band thought—and the colorful monicker stuck as he lit up the R&B charts repeatedly during the late '40s and early '50s. Jackson had a split musical personality—he sang "I Love You, Yes I Do" and "All My Love Belongs to You" like a pop crooner, then switched gears to belt out the double-entendre naughties "I Want a Bowlegged Woman" and "Big Ten Inch Woman" with total abandon. Record buyers loved both sides of the Moose. Jackson dubbed his combo the Buffalo Bearcats due to his frequent gigs at a Buffalo nitery, and hit big for King in 1947 with "I Love You, Yes I Do"; in 1948 with "Sneaky Pete," "All My Love Belongs to You," "I Want a Bowlegged Woman," "I Can't Go On Without You," and two more; and in 1949 with "Little Girl, Don't Cry" and "Why Don't You Haul Off and Love Me." Some of Jackson's hilariously risqué stuff—"Big Ten Inch Record" and the astonishingly raunchy "Nosey Joe" (penned by the young but obviously streetwise Jerry Leiber and Mike Stoller), both from 1952—were probably too suggestive to merit airplay, but they're stellar examples of jump blues at its craziest. *—Bill Dahl*

● **Badman Jackson That's Me** / 1991 / Charly ✦✦✦✦✦

The best representation of saxist Jackson's jump blues activities for King Records during the late '40s and early '50s. The Moose was a smooth ballad crooner, too, but you'll find none of his mellow stuff on this 22-tracker—just horn-leavened blasters, often with hilariously risque lyrics. "Big Ten Inch Record" (here in two takes), "I Want a Bowlegged Woman," the country-rooted "Why Don't You Haul Off and Love Me," and most of all the Leiber & Stoller-penned sleaze-o "Nosey Joe" are party records guaranteed to excite any gathering! *—Bill Dahl*

Elmore James

b. Jan. 27, 1918, Richland, MS, **d.** May 24, 1963, Chicago, IL

Slide Guitar, Vocals, Guitar (Electric), Guitar / Slide Guitar Blues, Electric Chicago Blues

No two ways about it, the most influential slide guitarist of the postwar period was Elmore James, hands down. Although his early demise from heart failure kept him from enjoying the fruits of the '60s blues revival as his contemporaries Muddy Waters and Howlin' Wolf did, James left a wide influential trail behind him. And that influence continues to the present time—in approach, attitude and tone—in just about every guitar player who puts a slide on his finger and wails the blues. As a guitarist, he wrote the book, his slide style influencing the likes of Hound Dog Taylor, Joe Carter, his cousin Homesick James and J.B. Hutto, while his seldom-heard single-string work had an equally profound effect on B.B. King and Chuck Berry. His signature lick—an electric updating of Robert Johnson's "I Believe I'll Dust My Broom" and one that Elmore recorded in infinite variations from day one to his last session—is so much a part of the essential blues fabric of guitar licks that no one attempting to play slide guitar can do it without being compared to Elmore James. Others may have had more technique—Robert Nighthawk and Earl Hooker immediately come to mind—but Elmore had the sound and all the feeling. A radio repairman by trade, Elmore reworked his guitar amplifiers in his spare time, getting them to produce raw, distorted sounds that wouldn't resurface until the advent of heavy rock amplification in the late '60s. This amp on 11 approach was hot-wired to one of the strongest emotional approaches to the blues ever recorded. There is never a time when you're listening to one of his records that you feel—no matter how familiar the structure—that he's phoning it in just to grab a quick session check. Elmore James always gave it everything he had, everything he could emotionally invest in a number. *—Cub Koda*

Whose Muddy Shoes / 1969 / MCA/Chess ✦✦✦✦✦

Elmore had recorded a session for Chess in 1953 before settling down with the Bihari brothers and again in 1960, shortly before starting his final recordings for Bobby Robinson's Fire, Fury and Enjoy labels. This collects up all of them on CD with the bonus addition of an alternate take of "The Sun Is Shining," which can be interpreted as a precursor to his later hit "The Sky Is Crying." The earlier sides from 1953 lack his inimitable slide, but the 1960 session produced classics like "Talk to Me Baby," "Madison Blues" and a powerful reading of T-Bone Walker's "Stormy Monday." These tracks of Elmore working with the Chess production team are delightfully fleshed out with a half dozen gems by the highly underrated John Brim, some of which include stellar harp work by Little Walter ("Rattlesnake," "Be Careful"—on which Walter stops playing in several spots to become an ad-lib backup vocalist—and "You Got Me") as well as the original version of "Ice Cream Man," better known to rock fans from Van Halen's cover version of it from their debut album. *—Cub Koda*

Let's Cut It: The Very Best of Elmore James / 1986 / Ace ✦✦✦✦

Let's Cut It: The Very Best of Elmore James rounds up 18 tracks from his Modern, Flair and Meteor recordings. These are generally considered to be some James' greatest recordings, and there's no denying that there are incendiary performances throughout the record that more than prove James' legendary status is deserved. A few alternate takes are thrown in that are more noteworthy for collectors than general listeners. Then again, fans who only want one disc of Elmore will be best served by Rhino's *The Sky is Crying*, which selects highlights from all of his many labels. This, in turn, is for fans who want to dig a little deeper than that set, since this contains the best of one of his best periods. *—Stephen Thomas Erlewine*

☆ **King of the Slide Guitar** / 1992 / Capricorn ✦✦✦✦✦

Elmore's last great recordings occurred in the 1960s when he was signed by New York producer/label-owner Bobby Robinson. Unlike many of his contemporaries, James seemingly got *better* as the years went by and while none of the sides feature a slide guitar anywhere near as nasty as his early Modern and Flair recordings, he's still obviously giving it all on each and every side. These recordings are the ones most commonly issued on James and have surfaced on so many different compilations—all with varying levels of sound quality—that it would be futile to list them all here. Fortunately, to make things easier we have this two-disc 50-song box set rounding up at least one extant take of everything Elmore recorded with Robinson at the helm. While some of the material are recuts of his best known tunes ("Dust My Broom" resurfaces here in two versions from two different sessions and the version of "It Hurts Me Too" included here—it was originally cut for Chief in the late '50s—became a posthumous hit for him), the majority of it breaks new ground and stands as some of Elmore's most emotion-laden work. Nice essays in the booklet make up for the disgusting art work that adorns the box. *—Cub Koda*

☆ **The Classic Recordings** / 1993 / Flair/Virgin ✦✦✦✦✦

After James hit the national charts with his Trumpet recording of "Dust My Broom," he came to record for the Bihari Brothers, first for their Meteor subsidiary, then later for their Flair and Modern labels. This multi-disc retrospective rounds up every existing master James recorded for the Biharis, plus his backup work behind bandmembers Johnny Jones and J.T. Brown. James' guitar tone is distorted and overamped to the extreme; *this* is the sound that changed the face of slide guitar forever, influencing everyone from Hound Dog Taylor to J.B. Hutto to George Thorogood and everybody in between. The intensity of James' vocals are nothing short of riveting and the material collected here (along with breakdowns, studio chat, etc.) is simply the best of James' early-'50s sides and a box set well worth saving up for.—*Cub Koda*

★ **The Sky Is Crying: The History of Elmore James** / Apr. 6, 1993 / Rhino ✦✦✦✦✦

With the confusing plethora of Elmore James discs out on the market, this is truly the place to start, featuring the best of his work culled from several labels. Highlights include James' original recording of "Dust My Broom," "It Hurts Me Too," "T.V. Mama" (with Elmore backing Big Joe Turner), and the title track, one of the best slow blues ever created. Slide guitar doesn't get much better than this, making this particular compilation not only a perfect introduction to Elmore's music, but an essential piece for any blues collection. *—Cub Koda*

The Best of Elmore James: The Early Years / 1995 / Ace ♦♦♦
This breaks down Elmore's Modern recordings into a single disc retrospective and a damn fine one it is, too. This compiles the A and B sides of every single recorded for the Bihari brothers, with the original Trumpet recording of "Dust My Broom" standing in the place of "1839 Blues." If you really want to hear Elmore at his wildest and most unfettered and don't want to wade through a pile of alternate takes to get to it, we heartily suggest adding this one to the collection. Import. *—Cub Koda*

The Complete Fire & Enjoy Recordings / Sep. 1, 1995 / Collectables ♦♦♦
This three-disc set mirrors Capricorn's double box set of the same material. The Collectables set offers more alternate takes and stray vocals from Sammy Myers and an unidentified female vocalist, recorded at the same sessions, with Elmore contributing guitar, many of the tracks in true stereo. But the liner-note information is scant, and the lack of a proper booklet makes this set an also-ran compared to the more sensibly ordered and far better annotated Capricorn set, garish box graphics and all. Further points are docked for the inclusion of two tracks that certainly aren't Bobby Robinson recordings, the first version of "Make My Dreams Come True" and "I Can't Stop Lovin' You." *—Cub Koda*

Blues Masters: The Very Best of Elmore James / Mar. 14, 2000 / Rhino ♦♦♦♦♦
A good 16-song compilation, but a puzzling one. It essentially duplicates *The Sky Is Crying: The History of Elmore James*, but must be judged as slightly inferior, as that other compilation has 21 tracks. The puzzle is that *The Sky Is Crying*, like *The Very Best Of*, is also on Rhino, and was still in print when this compilation was released in 2000. True, this does have a couple of songs not on *The Sky Is Crying* ("Wild About You Baby" and "Coming Home"), and presents the tracks in chronological order, whereas *The Sky Is Crying* does not. Are these reasons to merit a second compilation in the same label's catalog— One would think not. However, if you could care less about such fine distinctions, this is as good a James anthology as any. And the expected classics are here, including "Shake Your Moneymaker," "The Sky Is Crying," "Dust My Broom," "Madison Blues," "It Hurts Me Too," and "The Sun Is Shining." *—Richie Unterberger*

Etta James (Etta James Hawkins)

b. Jan. 25, 1938, Los Angeles, CA
Vocals / Classic Female Blues, Soul-Blues, R&B, Soul
A growling and purring stylist who is at the top of her genre, Etta James was discovered at the tender age of 16 by bandleader Johnny Otis, fronting an all-girl vocal trio called The Peaches. They quickly hit paydirt with her waxing of an answer record to Hank Ballard's "Work with Me Annie" entitled "The Wallflower." This tune, also known as "Roll with Me Henry," was cleaned up for White cover record chart consumption by Georgia Gibbs as "Dance with Me Henry," its national success prompting a flurry of lawsuits over composer royalties. Though Etta continued to record classic sides for Modern (some with Little Richard's band backing her), nothing clicked until she signed with Chess Records in 1960. It was here that she really hit her stride, charting 24 crossover pop/R&B hits between 1960 and 1970. Her reading of ballads ("All I Could Do Was Cry" and "At Last" being notable examples) and uptempo material (the definitive reading of "Something's Got a Hold of Me") presaged the Soul music movement to come. After several bouts with drugs and drinking, she is recording and touring again, her incredibly soulful voice delivering the goods every time, making her new recordings every bit as satisfying as her old classics. *—Cub Koda*

★ **At Last** / 1961 / MCA/Chess ♦♦♦♦♦
After spending a few years in limbo after scoring her first R&B hits "Dance With Me, Henry" and "Good Rocking Daddy," Etta James returned to the spotlight in 1960 with her first Chess release, *At Last*. James made both the R&B and pop charts with the album's title cut, "All I Could Do Was Cry," and "Trust in Me." What makes *At Last* a great album is not only the solid hits it contains, but also the strong variety of material throughout. James expertly handles jazz standards like "Stormy Weather" and "A Sunday Kind of Love," as well as Willie Dixon's blues classic "I Just Want to Make Love to You." James demonstrates her keen facility on the title track in particular, as she easily moves from powerful blues shouting to more subtle, airy phrasing; her Ruth Brown-inspired, bad-girl growl only adds to the intensity. James would go on to even greater success with later hits like "Tell Mama," but on *At Last* one hears the singer at her peak in a swinging and varied program of blues, R&B, and jazz standards. *—Stephen Cook*

The Second Time Around / 1961 / MCA/Chess ♦♦♦♦
Etta James's second album isn't what you pull off the shelf when you want to hear her belt some soul. Like her debut, it found Chess presenting her as more or less a pop singer, using orchestration arranged and conducted by Riley Hampton, and mostly tackling popular standards of the '40s. If you're not a purist, this approach won't bother you in the least; James sings with gusto, proving that she could more than hold her own in this idiom as well. R&B isn't entirely neglected either, with the rousing "Seven Day Fool" (co-written by Berry Gordy, Jr.) a standout; "Don't Cry Baby" and "Fool That I Am" were R&B hits that made a mild impression on the pop charts as well. *—Richie Unterberger*

☆ **Rocks the House** / 1964 / MCA/Chess ♦♦♦♦♦
Simply one of the greatest live blues albums ever captured on tape. Cut in 1963 at the New Era Club in Nashville, the set finds Etta James in stellar shape as she forcefully delivers her own "Something's Got a Hold on Me" and "Seven Day Fool" interspersed with a diet of sizzling covers ("What'd I Say," "Sweet Little Angel," "Money," "Ooh Poo Pah Doo"). The CD incarnation adds three more great titles, including an impassioned reprise of her "All I Could Do Is Cry." Guitarist David T. Walker is outstanding whenever he solos. *—Bill Dahl*

Call My Name / 1966 / Cadet ♦♦♦♦
Still unavailable digitally, James's 1966 LP is dynamite Chicago soul, with the vaunted Chess house band in uplifting support. Among the many standouts are "I'm So Glad (I Found Love in You)," "It Must Be Your Love," and "Don't Pick Me for Your Fool." *—Bill Dahl*

Tell Mama / 1968 / MCA/Chess ♦♦♦♦♦
Leonard Chess dispatched Etta James to Muscle Shoals in 1967, and the move paid off with one of her best and most soul-searing Cadet albums. Produced by Rick Hall, the resultant album boasted a relentlessly driving title cut, the moving soul ballad "I'd Rather Go Blind," and sizzling covers of Otis Redding's "Security" and Jimmy Hughes' "Don't Lose Your Good Thing," and a pair of fine Don Covay copyrights. The skin-tight session aces at Fame Studios really did themselves proud behind Miss Peaches. *—Bill Dahl*

Come a Little Closer / 1974 / Chess ♦♦♦
James was fighting serious substance-abuse problems when this record was recorded, commuting to the sessions from a rehab center. It was a triumph simply to complete the record at all. But although James' life may have been in rough shape outside of the studio, she delivered a fairly strong set that fused forceful '70s soul arrangements with some rock (Randy Newman and John Kay both contribute compositions), jazz, and New Orleans R&B. Some of the material's routine, but there are some very strong cuts here, like a rousing "Sookie Sookie," and "Out on the Street Again," with its slightly sinister funk groove. "Feeling Uneasy," in fact, counts as one of the unsung highlights of her career, with a wrenching, near-wordless scat-moan vocal over a suitably languorous, melancholy blues-jazz arrangement. The CD reissue adds a couple of interesting bonus tracks: the 1975 single "Lovin' Arms," a good rootsy ballad, and a single edit of one of the tracks from the album, "Out on the Street Again." *—Richie Unterberger*

Deep in the Night / 1978 / Bullseye Blues ♦♦♦♦

Early Show, Vol. 1: Blues in the Night / 1986 / Fantasy ♦♦♦

R&B Dynamite / 1987 / Flair ♦♦♦♦♦
The singer in her precocious formative years, headed by her 1955 R&B smash "Roll With Me Henry" (aka "The Wallflower"). James' follow-ups included the driving "Good Rockin' Daddy," a bluesy "W-O-M-A-N," and the New Orleans raveup "Tough Lover," which found her backed by the gang at Cosimo's (notably saxman Lee Allen). Even though her tenure at Modern Records only produced a handful of hits, these 22 cuts are delightful artifacts of the belter's earliest days. The CD was reissued, with identical (though slightly resequenced) tracks and liner notes, as *Hickory Dickory Dock* on Ace 680. *—Bill Dahl*

How Strong Is a Woman: The Island Sessions / 1993 / 4th & Broadway ♦♦♦

☆ **The Essential Etta James** / 1994 / MCA/Chess ♦♦♦♦♦
Forty-four tracks summarizing the long and brilliant Chess tenure of Miss Peaches, opening with her 1960 smash "All I Could Do Was Cry, " and encompassing her torchy, fully orchestrated ballads "At Last, " "My Dearest Darling, " and "Trust in Me, " and continuing on through her 1962 gospel rocker "Something's Got a Hold on Me, " the Chicago soul standouts "I Prefer You" and "842-3089, " and her 1967 Muscle Shoals-cut smash "Tell Mama." A few of the '70s sides that conclude the two-disc set seem makeweight when compared to what preceded them, but most of the essentials are aboard. *—Bill Dahl*

These Foolish Things / 1995 / MCA/Chess ♦♦♦♦
James has long been a masterful blues balladeer—a talent spotlighted throughout the course of this 14-song collection. Some tracks are cushioned by string-enriched arrangements, others—notably 1965's passionate "Only Time Will Tell"—are melodic Chicago soul. Four tracks are previously unreleased, including her reading of Billie Holiday's "Lover Man." *—Bill Dahl*

★ **Her Best** / 1997 / Chess ♦♦♦♦♦
While several best-ofs from Etta's Chess period have been available over the years—with the two-disc, 44-track *Essential Etta James* at the top of the list in giving the big picture—this 20-track collection sweats *that* bigger picture down to bare essentials. For those wishing to finally sample Etta's classic period at Chess without opening the wallet for box set-anthology expense, this single-disc retrospective will fill the bill quite nicely. Featuring 20 of the tracks that appear on the double-disc *Essential* anthology without anything literally essential left off, this scintillating little disc now officially becomes the one-stop, first-time purchase in connecting with the emotional greatness inherent in Etta's siren song. There's plenty more after this to discover, but *this* is absolutely where you start. *—Cub Koda*

Love's Been Rough on Me / Apr. 29, 1997 / Private Music ♦♦♦

The Heart of a Woman / Jun. 29, 1999 / Private Music ♦♦♦

☆ **The Chess Box** / Jun. 27, 2000 / Chess ♦♦♦♦♦
Etta James is one of the towering figures of the blues, the foremost female blues vocalist of the second half of the 20th century, and the foundation of her legacy is her recordings for Chess Records in the '60s. Despite her reputation and enduring popularity, Etta didn't receive a box set retrospective between 1988 and 1990, the time when Chess was honoring such heavyweights as Chuck Berry, Muddy Waters, Howlin Wolf, Bo Diddley, and Willie Dixon with multi-disc retrospectives. They eased away from box sets during the '90s, only issuing a comprehensive double-disc Little Walter set early in the decade, but they finally returned to the sets in 2000 with a long-overdue *Chess Box* for Etta James. Like before, when they assembled terrific sets on Berry and Waters, they got it right. Collectors may find a favorite side missing, but the great majority of her best work for Argo, Cadet, and Chess is here. Although there are a handful of unreleased tracks, the point behind this set is to provide a thorough overview of the most pivotal years in James' career, and on that level, it succeeds tremendously. Like many career-spanning sets, it does dip slightly in quality on the last disc, but not enough to make this anything less than an essential addition to a thorough blues library, since even on the lesser material, she sounds terrific. As a matter of fact, it's rather astonishing how strong all these recordings are, from her terrific vocals to the songs themselves. It's a shame it didn't come out with the first round of *Chess Box*es, but it was worth the wait. *—Stephen Thomas Erlewine*

Skip James (Nehemiah Curtis James)

b. Jun. 21, 1902, Bentonia, MS, **d.** Oct. 3, 1969, Philadelphia, PA
Vocals, Kazoo, Piano, Guitar, Organ / Blues Revival, Delta Blues, Country Blues, Acoustic Blues
Among the earliest and most influential Delta bluesmen to record, Skip James was the best known proponent of the so-called Bentonia school of blues players, a genre strain invested

with as much fanciful scholarly "research" as any. Coupling an oddball guitar tuning set against eerie, falsetto vocals, James's early recordings could make the hair stand up on the back of your neck. Even more surprising was when blues scholars rediscovered him in the '60s and found his singing and playing skills intact. Influencing everyone from a young Robert Johnson (Skip's "Devil Got My Woman" became the basis of Johnson's "Hellhound on My Trail") to Eric Clapton (who recorded James's "I'm So Glad" on the first Cream album), Skip James's music, while from a commonly shared regional tradition, remains infused with his own unique personal spirit. *—Cub Koda*

Greatest of the Delta Blues Singers / 1964 / Biograph ✦✦✦✦✦
Shortly after his triumphant resurrection at the 1964 Newport Folk Festival, Skip James returned to the recording studio for the first time in over three decades to cut the 12 sides which comprise the superb *Greatest of the Delta Blues Singers,* a career-capping overview which reprises some of the songs from his 1931 Paramount sessions and introduces a half-dozen new compositions as well. Although his guitar skills have lost a step in the intervening years, the passage of time has only made James' vocals that much more expressive; his new material is especially devastating, in particular "Sick Bed Blues" and "Washington D.C. Hospital Center Blues," both detailing the fight with cancer that eventually led to his death. *—Jason Ankeny*

She Lyin' / 1964 / Genes ✦✦✦✦✦
By the time James had been rediscovered in the 1960s, he was still capable of playing entrancing, dynamic music, but was much less consistent and not as striking a vocalist. It was a testimony to his greatness that he still managed to make compelling records, and he was among the best storytellers and dramatic singers in the traditional realm. This mid-'60s CD features songs James recorded for the Adelphi label in 1964 that were never issued. It's hard to understand why this wasn't issued at the time it was recorded; it's just as solid as the albums James recorded for Columbia during the same period. *—Ron Wynn*

☆ **Skip James Today!** / 1965 / Vanguard ✦✦✦✦✦
As quiet as it was kept then, Skip James might have made the best music of anyone who resurfaced during the mid-'60s "rediscovery" era for Mississippi country blues types. Certainly, there weren't many albums made during that time as good as this one; wonderful vocals, superb guitar and a couple of tunes with tasty piano make this essential. *—Ron Wynn*

Devil Got My Woman / Mar. 22, 1966–Mar. 24, 1966 / Vanguard ✦✦✦

★ **The Complete Early Recordings of Skip James** / 1994 / Yazoo ✦✦✦✦✦
The Complete Early Recordings CD showcases a true guitar virtuoso who was no slouch on the piano either. His break on "Illinois Blues" is almost off-putting in the nonchalance with which he twists the notes around, and "How Long 'Buck'" features him giving forth some funky piano in an almost playful manner. This is a remastered edition of an earlier Yazoo collection, and features the same 18 songs that appeared on Document's *Complete Recorded Works,* but the sound quality is still a problem at times. High-quality sources for "What Am I to Do Blues," "4 O'Clock Blues," and several other of the numbers here are simply not known to exist, but these are the best-known editions of the songs until better 78 discs happen to turn up (if ever). Regardless of the surface noise, it is a delight listening to James' rippling guitar run on "4 O'Clock Blues" or his piano improvising (and improvising the percussion by pounding away with his feet) on "20-20 Blues." And his fiercely intense original rendition of "I'm So Glad" makes the repopularized version by Eric Clapton and Cream from the 1960s seem like easygoing pop. Actually, James' vocals tend to suffer under the weight of the surface defects far more than his playing—the source discs distort on high-volume passages, which mostly occurs with his singing rather than his playing. Therefore, fans of blues guitar or piano need have no hesitation in picking this disc up. *The Complete Early Recordings* ought to be heard by anyone who claims an interest in the blues. *—Bruce Eder*

Blues from the Delta / Aug. 11, 1998 / Vanguard ✦✦✦✦
Drawing 18 tracks from Skip James' rediscovery recordings made on Vanguard Records—*Today!* and *Devil Got My Woman,* plus two previously unreleased tracks—*Blues From the Delta* is over 75 minutes of the best tracks James ever recorded. Where the definitive cuts of many of these songs haven't been preserved by modern technology without considerable flaws, these tracks, recorded in 1966 and 1968 (respectively), are clean and crisp, highlighting James' tremendous talents. Though it had been 35 years since James first recording sessions, he still possessed his spooky melodic sense, his distinctive guitar and piano playing, and the eerie falsetto that made his original recordings so sought after. These might not be the most historically relevant versions of James' quintessential works, but they are by no means inferior, and on the whole, are much easier to listen to. *—Matt Fink*

Blind Lemon Jefferson

b. Jul. 11, 1897, Couchman, TX, **d.** Dec. 1929, Chicago, IL
Vocals, Guitar / Prewar Gospel Blues, Field Recordings, Country Blues, Acoustic Texas Blues, Texas Blues, Acoustic Blues
Country blues guitarist and vocalist Blind Lemon Jefferson is indisputably one of the main figures in country blues. He was of the highest in many regards, being one of the founders of Texas blues (along with Texas Alexander), one of the most influential country bluesmen of all time, one of the most popular bluesmen of the 1920s, and the first truly commercially successful male blues performer. Up until Jefferson's achievements, the only real successful blues recordings were by women performers, including Bessie Smith and Ida Cox, who usually sang songs written by others and accompanied by a band. With Jefferson came a blues artist who was solo, self-accompanied, and performing a great deal of original material in addition to the more familiar repertoire of folk standards and shouts. These originals include his most well-known songs: "Matchbox Blues," "See That My Grave Is Kept Clean," and "Black Snake Moan." In all, Blind Lemon Jefferson recorded almost 100 songs in just a few years, before his untimely death in December 1929, when he was found dead following a particularly cold snowstorm. He was only in his thirties at the time. During his life he made his mark on not only the bluesmen of the time (including Leadbelly and Lightnin' Hopkins) but also on music fans in the years to come. The legacy of Jefferson's unique and powerful sound did not fade with the passing decades and in 1980 he was inducted into the Blues Foundation's Hall of Fame. *—Joslyn Layne*

Blind Lemon Jefferson / Mar. 1961 / Milestone ✦✦✦✦✦
Solid collection (73 minutes' worth) of some of Lemon's best. "Jack O'Diamond Blues," "Match Box Blues," and "That Black Snake Moan" are all on board, and with the Sonic Solutions System employed on the audio restoration end, the result is about the best these surviving 60-year-old 78s have ever sounded. *—Cub Koda*

★ **King of the Country Blues** / 1985 / Yazoo ✦✦✦✦✦
King of the Country Blues compiles 28 of Blind Lemon Jefferson's finest songs, all presented in the original '20s versions. It is the finest introduction to the guitarist—as well as the most effective, concise retrospective—ever assembled. *—Thom Owens*

The Best of Blind Lemon Jefferson / Oct. 10, 2000 / Yazoo ✦✦✦✦
Blind Lemon Jefferson's life contains a great deal of mystery. The date of his birth is uncertain, and the cause of his death—heart failure— freezing during a blizzard—is unknown. What is known is that he left behind a number of blues recordings on which he accompanied himself on guitar. His expressive vocals and guitar work shine on well-worn classics like "Match Box Blues" or on unfamiliar songs like "Black Horse Blues." Preserving the fidelity of these recordings has been made difficult by poorly pressed records as well as the condition of the rare 78s. This is evident on "'Lectric Chair Blues" and "Prison Cell Blues," where surface noise cuts into the clarity of the lyrics. Still, both of these songs are effectively edgy because of their subject matter, with "'Lectric Chair Blues" being particularly chilling. Despite difficulties with fidelity, the majority of the vocals and guitar work are easy to discern and enjoy. The laid-back, relaxed quality of songs like "Bed Spring Blues" and "See That My Grave's Kept Clean" are unpretentious and disarming. Jefferson also covers the unusual "He Arose From the Dead" and "I Want to Be Like Jesus in My Heart," two religious blues pieces (one can only hope that neither were recorded in the same session with "Bed Spring Blues"). Blake's guitar work covers a number of styles including boogie runs on "Rabbit Foot Blues" and slide on "Jack O' Diamond Blues." The liner notes cover what little is know about Jefferson and offer a good discussion of his vocal and guitar styles. With *The Best of Blind Lemon Jefferson,* Yazoo has done a fine job of preserving Jefferson's music and of documenting the early history of blues recordings. ~Ronnie D. Lankford, Jr.

Blind Willie Johnson

b. Feb. C. 1, Texas, **d.** 1947, Beaumont, TX
Slide Guitar, Vocals, Guitar / Slide Guitar Blues, Prewar Gospel Blues, Blues Gospel, Acoustic Texas Blues
Seminal gospel-blues artist Blind Willie Johnson is regarded as one of the greatest bottleneck slide guitarists. Yet the Texas street-corner evangelist is known as much for his powerful and fervent gruff voice as he is for his ability as a guitarist. Johnson was born in a small town just South of Waco near Temple, TX, around 1902. His mother died while he was still a baby, and his father eventually remarried. When Johnson was about seven years old, his father and stepmother fought and the stepmother threw lye water, apparently at the father, but the lye got in Willie Johnson's eyes, blinding him. As he got older, Johnson began earning money by playing his guitar, one of the few avenues left to a blind man to earn a living. He was a passionate believer in the *Bible.* So, he began singing the gospel and interpreting Negro spirituals. He became a Baptist preacher and brought his sermons and music to the streets of the surrounding cities. Johnson recorded a total of 30 songs during a three-year period and many of these became classics of the gospel-blues, including "Jesus Make up My Dying Bed," "God Don't Never Change," and his most famous, "Dark Was the Night—Cold Was the Ground."

Over the years, many artists have covered the gospel songs made famous by Blind Willie Johnson, including Bob Dylan, Eric Clapton, and Ry Cooder. Johnson's song "If I Had My Way" was even revived as a popular hit during the 1960s when it was covered by the contemporary folk band Peter, Paul and Mary. Several excellent collections of Blind Willie Johnson's music exist, including Dark Was the Night (on Sony) and *Praise God, I'm Satisfied* (on Yazoo). His music also appears on many compilations of country blues and slide guitar. *—Joslyn Layne*

Praise God I'm Satisfied / 1989 / Yazoo ✦✦✦✦✦
Yazoo's *Praise God I'm Satisfied* is an excellent collection of 14 tracks Blind Willie Johnson recorded in the '30s, including such numbers as "Jesus Make Up My Dying Bed," "Praise God I'm Satisfied," "Rain Don't Fall on Me" and "Jesus Is Coming Soon." These are excellent, haunting recordings, boasting some stellar guitar work, but everything that's on this disc and its companion, *Sweeter as the Years Go By,* is included on Columbia/Legacy's *The Complete Recordings of Blind Willie Johnson,* which makes this unnecessary for any serious listener. *—Stephen Thomas Erlewine*

Sweeter as the Years Go By / 1990 / Yazoo ✦✦✦✦✦
Blind Willie Johnson was perhaps the finest singing evangelist of all time. While the 16 tracks on this CD aren't as striking as those on the seminal *Praise God I'm Satisfied,* they're still invigorating and a vital part of his legacy. Johnson played acoustic rather than slide on several cuts, and didn't take flamboyant solos or add slashing counterpoint. But he demonstrated a skillful use of repetition and outstanding rhythmic and melodic skills. Johnson teamed with Willie B. Harris on several songs, and her rough, cutting voice proved an ideal match with his equally ragged sound. *—Ron Wynn*

☆ **Complete Recordings of Blind Willie Johnson** / Apr. 27, 1993 / Columbia/Legacy ✦✦✦✦✦
If you've never heard Blind Willie Johnson, you are in for one of the great, bone-chilling treats in music. Johnson played slide guitar, and sang in a rasping, false bass that could freeze the blood. But no bluesman was he; this was gospel music of the highest order, full of emotion and heartfelt commitment. Of all the guitar-playing evangelists, Blind Willie Johnson may have been the very best. Though not related by bloodlines to Robert Johnson, comparisons in emotional commitment from both men cannot be helped. This two-CD anthology collects everything known to exist, and that's a lot of stark, harrowing emotional commitment no matter how you slice it. Not for the faint of heart, but hey, the good stuff never is. *—Cub Koda*

● **Dark Was the Night** / Jun. 30, 1998 / Columbia/Legacy ♦♦♦♦♦
Columbia/Legacy's *Dark Was the Night* is an excellent collection that distills 16 of his very best tracks on a single disc, offering a terrific introduction for listeners who don't want to invest in the comprehensive double-disc set *The Complete Recordings of Blind Willie Johnson*. *—Stephen Thomas Erlewine*

Johnnie Johnson

b. Jul. 8, 1924, Fairmont, WV
Piano / Piano Blues, Rock & Roll, R&B
Legendary piano player Johnnie Johnson isn't exactly a household name, even among followers of blues music. That's because for 28 years, he worked as a sideman to one of rock & roll's most prominent performers, Chuck Berry. Berry joined Johnson's band, the Sir John Trio, on New Year's Eve, 1953, and afterward, Berry took over as the group's songwriter and frontman/guitar player. On the strength of a recommendation from Muddy Waters and an audition, Berry got a deal with Chess Records. Johnson's rhythmic piano playing was a key element in all of Berry's hit singles, a good number of which Johnson arranged. The pair's successful partnership lasted a lot longer than most rock & roll partnerships last these days. Johnson's albums under his own name include *Blue Hand Johnnie* for the St. Louis-based Pulsar label in 1988; *Johnnie B. Bad* in 1991 for the Elektra American Explorer label; *That'll Work* in 1993 for the same label, and most recently, *Johnnie Be Back* for the New Jersey-based MusicMasters label in 1995. All four are winners. *—Richard Skelly*

● **Blue Hand Johnnie** / 1987 / Evidence ♦♦♦♦♦
Johnnie Johnson's rolling, barrelling licks are as enticing as ever on this reissued Evidence CD of cuts from '90, but there are some other things that are not so grand. These include barely tolerable vocalists Barbara Carr and Stacy Johnson, whose enthusiasm is commendable, but whose vocals often get in the way. Johnson's covers of Fats Washington's "O.J. Blues" and "Black Nights" are great, as are his versions of "Honky Tonk" and "See See Rider." But he falters on "Baby, What You Want Me To," in part because he does not convey either the original's loping stride or laconic quality, and also because it is not the kind of peppy arrangement and backbeat suited to his style. A decent effort that might have been a superior one with a couple of added touches. *—Ron Wynn*

Johnnie B. Bad / 1992 / Elektra/Nonesuch ♦♦♦♦♦
Keith Richards, Eric Clapton, and various NRBQ members guest on this pianist's inconsistent major-label debut. *—Bill Dahl*

Lonnie Johnson (Alonzo Johnson)

b. Feb. 8, 1899, New Orleans, LA, **d.** Jun. 16, 1970, Toronto, Ontario, Canada
Vocals, Violin, Guitar, Guitar (Acoustic) / Prewar Blues, Blues Revival, Piedmont Blues, Country Blues, Jazz Blues, Classic Jazz, Acoustic Blues
Blues guitar simply would not have developed in the manner that it did if not for the prolific brilliance of Lonnie Johnson. He was there to help define the instrument's future within the genre and the genre's future itself at the very beginning, his melodic conception so far advanced from most of his pre-war peers as to inhabit a plane all his own. For more than 40 years, Johnson played blues, jazz, and ballads his way; he was a true blues originator whose influence hung heavy on a host of subsequent blues immortals. He signed up with OKeh Records in 1925 and commenced to recording at an astonishing pace—between 1925 and 1932, he cut an estimated 130 waxings. The red-hot duets he recorded with White jazz guitarist Eddie Lang (masquerading as Blind Willie Dunn) in 1928-29 were utterly groundbreaking in their ceaseless invention. Johnson also recorded pioneering jazz efforts in 1927 with no less than Louis Armstrong's Hot Five and Duke Ellington's orchestra. Johnson went with Cincinnati-based King Records in 1947 and promptly enjoyed one of the biggest hits of his uncommonly long career with the mellow ballad "Tomorrow Night," which topped the R&B charts for seven weeks in 1948. More hits followed posthaste: "Pleasing You (As Long as I Live)," "So Tired," and "Confused." *—Bill Dahl*

He's a Jelly Roll Baker / Nov. 2, 1939-Dec. 14, 1944 / Bluebird/RCA ♦♦♦♦♦
This 20-song collection covers 1930s and '40s material in which Johnson primarily performs blues tunes, doing salty, sassy, mournful and suggestive numbers in a distinctive, memorable fashion. His vocals on "Rambler's Blues," "In Love Again," the title cut and several others are framed by brilliant, creative playing and excellent support from such pianists as Blind John Davis, Lil Hardin Armstrong and Joshua Altheimer. This is tight, intuitive music in which Johnson set the tone and dominated the songs. If you're unaware of Lonnie Johnson's brilliant blues material, here's an excellent introduction. *—Ron Wynn*

Blues by Lonnie Johnson / Mar. 8, 1960 / Bluesville/Original Blues Classics ♦♦♦♦
After four years off records and in obscurity, Lonnie Johnson launched his final comeback with this release, which has been reissued on CD. Teamed with tenor saxophonist Hal Singer, pianist Claude Hopkins, bassist Wendell Marshall and drummer Bobby Donaldson, Johnson sings and plays guitar on a variety of blues, showing that the layoff (he was working at the time as a janitor) had not hurt his abilities in the slightest. *—Scott Yanow*

★ **Blues & Ballads** / Apr. 5, 1960 / Bluesville/Original Blues Classics ♦♦♦♦♦
This combination works quite well. Guitarist-singer Lonnie Johnson was just starting a successful comeback, and here he is teamed up with acoustic rhythm guitarist Elmer Snowden (who had not recorded since 1934) and bassist Wendell Marshall. Johnson sings smooth blues and sentimental ballads with equal skill, and both guitarists have opportunities to display their complementary but distinctive styles. This CD reissue is easily recommended, as is its more instrumental counterpart, *Blues, Ballads, and Jumpin' Jazz, Vol. 2*. *—Scott Yanow*

Blues, Ballads, and Jumpin' Jazz, Vol. 2 / Apr. 5, 1960 / Bluesville ♦♦♦♦♦
When producer Chris Albertson brought Lonnie Johnson and guitarist Elmer Snowden into a studio for this album on April 9, 1960, both musicians hadn't recorded in a number of years. Indeed, Snowden hadn't seen the inside of a studio in 26 years, but you'd never know it by the fleet-fingered work he employs on the opening "Lester Leaps In," where he rips off one hot chorus after another. Johnson plays a dark-toned electric while Snowden plays acoustic, with Wendell Marshall rounding things out on bass. Given Johnson's reputation as a closet jazzer, it's remarkable that he merely comps rhythm behind Snowden's leads on "C-Jam Blues" and "On the Sunny Side of the Street." Johnson handles all the vocals, turning in an especially strong turn on the second take of "Stormy Weather." Lots of studio chatter make this disc of previously unissued material a real joy to listen to, a loose and relaxed session with loads of great playing and singing to recommend it. *—Cub Koda*

Losing Game / Dec. 28, 1960 / Bluesville/Original Blues Classics ♦♦♦♦
Johnson recorded prolifically for Prestige's Bluesville during his early-'60s comeback; this 1960 set is a typically gorgeous solo outing that ranges from torchy standards of the Tin Pan Alley species ("What a Difference a Day Makes," "Summertime") to bluesier pursuits of his own creation. *—Bill Dahl*

Idle Hours / Jul. 13, 1961 / Bluesville/Original Blues Classics ♦♦♦♦
Johnson and Victoria Spivey had known one another for decades (they duetted on the ribald "Toothache Blues" way back in 1928), so it's no surprise that their musical repartee on 1961's *Idle Hours* seems so natural and playful. Spivey guests on three tracks (including the title number) and plays piano on her one solo entry. Johnson does the majority of the disc without her, benefitting from pianistic accompaniment by Cliff Jackson. *—Bill Dahl*

Another Night to Cry / Apr. 6, 1962 / Bluesville/Original Blues Classics ♦♦♦

The Complete Folkways Recordings / 1967 / Smithsonian/Folkways ♦♦♦♦
An even two dozen solo performances from late in the legendary guitarist's amazing career (1967), but chock full of stellar moments all the same. Artists of Johnson's versatility were rare even then—he brings a multitude of shadings to "My Mother's Eyes" and "How Deep Is Tthe Ocean," then delivers a saucy "Juice Headed Baby" with the same stunning complexity. *—Bill Dahl*

★ **Steppin' on the Blues** / 1990 / Columbia/Legacy ♦♦♦♦♦
Groundbreaking guitar work of dazzling complexity that never fails to amaze—and this stuff was cut in the 1920s!! Johnson's astonishingly fluid guitar work was massively influential (Robert Johnson, for one, was greatly swayed by his waxings), and his no-nonsense vocals (frequently laced with threats of violence—"Got the Blues for Murder Only" and "She's Making Whoopee in Hell Tonight" are prime examples on this 19-cut collection) are scarcely less impressive. Johnson's torrid guitar duets with jazzman Eddie Lang retain their sense of legend nearly seven decades after they were cut. *—Bill Dahl*

Luther "Guitar Jr" Johnson

b. Jul. 15, 1939, Itta Bena, MS, **d.** Boston, MA
Vocals, Guitar / Electric Blues, Modern Electric Blues
Of the three blues guitarists answering to the name of Luther Johnson, this West side-styled veteran is probably the best-known. Adding to the general confusion surrounding the triumvirate: like Luther "Georgia Boy" Johnson, "Guitar Junior" spent a lengthy stint in the top-seeded band of Muddy Waters (1972-1979).

Gospel and blues intersected in young Luther Johnson's life while he was still in Mississippi. But after he moved to Chicago in the mid-'50s, blues was his main passion, working with Ray Scott and Tall Milton Shelton before taking over the latter's combo in 1962. Magic Sam was a major stylistic inspiration to Johnson during the mid-'60s (Johnson spent a couple of years in Sam's band). The West side approach remains integral to Johnson's sound today, even though he moved to the Boston area during the early '80s.

Johnson's 1976 debut album, *Luther's Blues*, was cut during a European tour with Muddy Waters. By 1980, he was on his own, recording with the Nighthawks as well as four tracks on Alligator's second series of *Living Chicago Blues* anthologies. With his own band, the Magic Rockers, and the Roomful of Blues horn section, Johnson released *Doin' the Sugar Too* on Rooster Blues in 1984. Since 1990, Johnson has been signed to Ron Levy's Bullseye Blues logo; his three albums for the firm have been sizzling, soul-tinged blues (with a strong West Side flavor often slicing through). *—Bill Dahl*

Luther's Blues / Nov. 1, 1976 / Evidence ♦♦♦

Doin' the Sugar Too / 1984 / Bullseye Blues ♦♦♦

I Want to Groove with You / 1990 / Bullseye Blues ♦♦♦♦♦
Now this is more like it. Johnson and his New England-based Magic Rockers sizzle the hide off the genre with tough West Side-styled grooves redolent of Johnson's Chicago upbringing but up-to-the-minute in their execution. With this set, Johnson fully came into his own as a recording artist. *—Bill Dahl*

It's Good to Me / 1992 / Bullseye Blues ♦♦♦♦
Another barn-burner mixing the guitarist's West-side roots with soul and blues shadings to present some of the fieriest contemporary blues on the market. Saxist Gordon Beadle and keyboardist Joe Krown distinguish themselves behind Johnson. *—Bill Dahl*

Country Sugar Papa / Mar. 30, 1994 / Bullseye Blues ♦♦♦♦
Johnson's third and final album for producer Ron Levy's Bullseye Blues diskery is every bit as spellbinding as the prior pair. Whether fronting his latest batch of Magic Rockers or going it alone, Johnson is totally convincing. *—Bill Dahl*

● **Slammin' on the West Side** / Apr. 1996 / Telarc ♦♦♦♦♦
Lousy album title, great album. Johnson hasn't been based out of Chicago in years, but that sound remains at the heart of his approach—even when he's recording in Louisiana with a funky New Orleans rhythm section (bassist George Porter, Jr. and drummer Herman Ernest). Jump blues in the form of Buddy Johnson's "A Pretty Girl (A Cadillac and Some Money)," athe Magic Sam tribute "Hard Times (Have Surely Come)," the solo acoustic "Get Up Aand Go," a soul-slanted "Every Woman Needs to Be Loved"—Johnson smokes 'em all. *—Bill Dahl*

Live at the Rynborn / Mar. 3, 1999 / M.C. ♦♦♦♦

Luther "Houserocker" Johnson

b. Atlanta, GA
Vocals, Guitar / Modern Electric Blues
The latest Luther Johnson to add his name to the blues directory is an adept singer/guitarist who is a current favorite on the Atlanta blues scene. Proficient in various shadings of the electric blues idiom, Johnson has recently extended his repertoire from covers of blues standards to his own material, performed with the same '50s/'60s flavor.

Johnson taught himself how to play guitar when he was a teenager in Atlanta by listening to records. Soon, he began playing guitar in pickup bands, which gave him the opportunity to support such touring musicians as Johnny Winter. After several years playing in bar bands, Johnson formed his own group, the Houserockers.

The Houserockers played bars and clubs around Georgia for several years, eventually landing a record contract with Ichiban in 1989. The next year Johnson released his debut album, *Takin' A Bite Outta the Blues*. Two years later, his second record, *Houserockin' Daddy*, appeared. Luther "Houserocker" Johnson continued to tour the U.S. throughout the '90s. *—Jim O'Neal & Stephen Thomas Erlewine*

Takin' a Bite Outta the Blues / 1990 / Ichiban ✦✦✦
Luther "Houserocker" Johnson isn't a huge name in the blues market, although he did enjoy a small following in Atlanta when he recorded *Takin' a Bite Outta the Blues* for Ichiban in April 1990. That album didn't bring him fame, though it did give blues enthusiasts outside of Atlanta (where Ichiban was based) the chance to hear him. Not fantastic but likable and sincere, *Takin' a Bite Outta the Blues* left no doubt that Johnson (who should not be confused with fellow bluesman Luther "Guitar Junior" Johnson) was very much a disciple of the late Chicago blues icon Jimmy Reed. The influence of Reed is impossible to miss on familiar classics like Ray Charles' "What'd I Say," B.B. King's "Rock Me, Baby," and a number of songs that Reed wrote ("Hush, Hush," "Where Can My Baby Be") or defined (Willie Dixon's "Pretty Thing"). Several years after its 1990 release, *Takin' a Bite Outta the Blues* went out of print; however, half of the songs on the album were reissued on Ichiban's 1998 collection, *Retrospectives*. *—Alex Henderson*

● **Houserockin' Daddy** / 1991 / Wild Dog ✦✦✦✦✦
Johnson is a traditional electric bluesman (now living and working in the Atlanta area) who was heavily influenced by Jimmy Reed. The album includes covers of Jimmy Reed, Lightnin' Slim, Howlin' Wolf, and Guitar Slim tunes. It's simple, driving, to the point, streamlined, no-frills blues. *—Niles J. Frantz*

Retrospectives / Jun. 30, 1998 / Ichiban ✦✦✦✦

Luther Snake Boy Johnson

b. Aug. 30, 1934, Davisboro, GA, **d.** Mar. 18, 1976
Vocals, Guitar / Electric Chicago Blues
The confusing plethora of artists working under the name of Luther (nickname here) Johnson can leave even those with a decent knowledge of blues in a major state of confusion. But in this biographical entry, we concern ourselves with the life and times of Luther "Georgia Boy/Snake Boy" Johnson who, to make matters even *more* confusing, also worked and recorded under the names Little Luther and Luther King. (It turns out his real name wasn't even Luther, but Lucius.) Upon his military discharge, he picked guitar as a member of the Milwaukee Supreme Angels gospel group, working the local church circuit. But the blues bug hit and he soon had his own little blues trio together, eventually settling in Chicago by the early '60s. He played for a while with Elmore James and was a regular fixture in the Muddy Waters band by the mid-'60s. He recorded as Little Luther for Chess in the mid-'60s ("The Twirl") and by 1970 was relocated to Boston, MA, working as a solo artist. The next five years found him working steadily on the college and blues festival circuit before cancer overtook him on March 18, 1976, at a mere 41 years of age. *—Cub Koda*

● **Lonesome in My Bedroom** / Dec. 18, 1975 / Evidence ✦✦✦✦✦
This was Johnson's final album before his death in 1976, and it was originally cut for Black and Blue (now reissued with three bonus tracks). While various tracks reflect the influence of Muddy Waters, Jimmy Reed and John Lee Hooker, Johnson's own inimitable vocals, raspy lines and tart guitar eventually create his own aura. He is nicely backed by drummer Fred Below, bassist Dave Myers, guitar burner Lonnie Brooks and the solid rhythm work of Hubert Sumlin. This was a fine session for a good, occasionally outstanding blues artist. *—Ron Wynn*

Get Down to the Nitty Gritty / 1976 / New Rose ✦✦✦

On the Road Again / 1976 / Evidence ✦✦✦
On the Road Again, an early-'70s outing, shows Johnson in fine form, assisted by a tough backing band. Cut in France. *—Bill Dahl*

Robert Johnson

b. May 8, 1911, Hazlehurst, MS, **d.** Aug. 16, 1938, Greenwood, MS
Slide Guitar, Vocals, Guitar, Guitar (Acoustic) / Slide Guitar Blues, Prewar Blues, Delta Blues
If the blues has a truly mythic figure, one whose story hangs over the music the way a Charlie Parker does over jazz or a Hank Williams does over country, it's Robert Johnson, certainly the most celebrated figure in the history of the blues. Of course, his legend is immensely fortified by the fact that Johnson also left behind a small legacy of recordings that are considered the emotional apex of the music itself. These recordings have not only entered the realm of blues standards ("Love in Vain," "Crossroads," "Sweet Home Chicago," "Stop Breaking Down"), but have been adapted by rock & roll artists as diverse as the Rolling Stones, Steve Miller, Led Zeppelin and Eric Clapton. While there are historical naysayers who would be more comfortable downplaying his skills and achievements (most of whom have never made a convincing case as where the source of his apocalyptic visions emanates from), Robert Johnson remains a potent force to be reckoned with. As a singer, a composer and as a guitarist of considerable skills, he produced some of the genre's best music and the ultimate blues legend to deal with. Doomed, haunted, driven by demons, a tormented genius dead at an early age, all of these add up to making him a character of mythology who—if he hadn't actually existed—would have to be created by some biographer's overactive romantic imagination. *—Cub Koda*

☆ **King of the Delta Blues Singers** / 1966 / Columbia/Legacy ✦✦✦✦✦
Reading about the power inherent in Robert Johnson's music is one thing, but actually *experiencing* it is another matter entirely. The official 1998 edition of the original 1961 album was certainly worth the wait, remastered off the best-quality original 78s available, of far superior quality to any of the source materials used on even the 1991 box set. Johnson's guitar takes on a fullness never heard on previous reissues, and except for a nagging hiss in spots on "Terraplane Blues" (the equalization on this disc is extreme to even sport some minute turntable rumble in the low end), this really brings his music alive. If there is such a thing as a greatest-hits package available on Johnson, this landmark album, which jump-started the whole '60s blues revival, would certainly be the one. The majority of Johnson's best-known tunes, the ones that made the legend, are all aboard: "Crossroads," "Walkin' Blues," "Me & The Devil Blues," "Come On In My Kitchen," and the apocalyptic visions contained in "Hellhound On My Trail" are the blues at its finest, the lyrics sheer poetry. And making its first appearance anywhere is a newly discovered-in-1998 alternate take of "Traveling Riverside Blues" that's appended to the original 16-track lineup. If you are starting your blues collection from the ground up, be sure to make this your very first purchase. *—Cub Koda*

☆ **King of the Delta Blues Singers, Vol. 2** / 1970 / Columbia/Legacy ✦✦✦✦✦
This second volume—although made somewhat superfluous by the arrival two decades later of the box set—contains the rest of the issued takes and some, but not all, of the alternate takes. The music is excellent, featuring the first album appearance of "Love in Vain." *—Cub Koda*

☆ **The Complete Recordings** / 1990 / Columbia/Legacy ✦✦✦✦✦
A double-disc box set containing everything Robert Johnson ever recorded, *The Complete Recordings* is essential listening, but it is also slightly problematic. The problems aren't in the music itself, of course, which is stunning and the fidelity of the recordings is the best it ever has been or ever will be. Instead, it's in the track sequencing. As the title implies, *The Complete Recordings* contains all of Johnson's recorded material, including a generous selection of alternate takes. All of the alternates are sequenced directly after the master, which can make listening to the album a little intimidating and tedious for novices. Certainly, the alternates can be programmed out with a CD player, but the set would have been more palatable if the alternate takes were presented on a separate disc. Nevertheless, this is a minor complaint—Robert Johnson's music retains its power no matter what context it is presented in. He, without question, deserves this kind of deluxe box-set treatment. *—Stephen Thomas Erlewine*

★ **King of the Delta Blues** / Oct. 7, 1997 / Columbia/Legacy ✦✦✦✦✦
This 16-track single-disc compilation gathers up the best-known tracks from the two original volumes of *King of the Delta Blues Singers* for a nice entry-level collection of Robert's best. Utilizing the latest in remastering technology, these recordings have never sounded quite this clear and full-bodied before, and the difference between this and the first pressing of the *Complete Recordings* box set is quite noticeable. While sweating down Johnson's best to a 16-track selection is an arbitrary choice at best, it's hard to fault the selection here. It's also a focused set that isn't hampered by the inclusion of the more collector-oriented alternate takes that bog down much of the box set's listenability. *—Cub Koda*

Tommy Johnson

b. 1896, Terry, MS, **d.** Nov. 1, 1956, Crystal Springs, MS
Vocals, Kazoo, Guitar / Prewar Blues, Delta Blues, Country Blues, Acoustic Blues
Next to Son House and Charley Patton, no one was more important to the development of pre-Robert Johnson Delta blues than Tommy Johnson. Armed with a powerful voice that could go from a growl to an eerie falsetto range and a guitar style that had all of the early figures and licks of the Delta style clearly delineated, Johnson only recorded for two years—from 1928 to 1930—but left behind a body of work that's hard to ignore. The legend of Tommy Johnson is even harder to ignore. The stories about his live performances—where he would play the guitar behind his neck in emulation of Charley Patton's showboating while hollering the blues at full throated level for hours without a break—are part of it. So is his uncontrolled womanizing and alcoholism, both of which constantly got him in trouble. Johnson's addiction to spirits was so pronounced that he was often seen drinking Sterno-denatured alcohol used for artificial heat—or shoe polish strained through bread for the kick each could offer when whiskey wasn't affordable or available in dry counties throughout the South. Then there's the crossroads story. Yes, years before the deal with the Devil at a deserted Delta crossroad was being used as an explanation of the other-worldly abilities of young Robert Johnson, the story was being told repeatedly about Tommy, often by the man himself to reinforce his abilities to doubting audiences. Then there's the music. His "Cool Water Blues" got amped up in the '50s by one of his early admirers, Howlin' Wolf, and became "I Asked for Water (She Brought Me Gasoline)." Another signature piece, his "Maggie Campbell," came with a chord progression that was used for infinite variations by blues players dating all the way back to his contemporary Charley Patton through Robert Nighthawk. Two of his best-known numbers have survived into modern times; "Big Road Blues" is probably best known to contemporary blues fans from adaptions by Floyd Jones and others, while his "Canned Heat Blues"—a bone-chilling account of his complete addiction to alcohol and his slavish attempts to score it by whatever means necessary—was the tune that gave a California blues-rock band their name. After awhile, all of the above starts adding up, no matter how you slice it. Tommy Johnson was one tough hombre, and a real piece of work. *—Cub Koda*

★ **Complete Recorded Works (1928-1929)** / 1929 / Document ✦✦✦✦✦

Tommy Johnson (1928-1930) / 1928-1930 / Wolf ✦✦✦✦✦
Austria-based Wolf Records has done a masterful job on this 12-song collection (missing only

two of Johnson's works, which have never turned up), much of it surprisingly clean and crisp. Most of the best sounding material here has already appeared on RCA/BMG's *Canned Heat Blues* compilation, which seems to be headed out-of-print at this writing. "Cool Drink of Water Blues" and "Canned Heat Blues" are by far the best known of Johnson's works, but they've got a lot of worthy pieces surrounding them. "Big Road Blues" is a fine showcase for Johnson's and Charlie McCoy's paired guitars, playing two complex, interwoven figures. And "Bye Bye Blues" and "Maggie Campbell Blues" show off his unique vocal qualities, not the dark heaviness typical of bluesmen at the time, but a more flexible, lighter toned, more relaxed instrument that, coupled with his and McCoy's guitars, made his music as "busy" as it was beautiful. The songs featuring only Johnson's guitar are no less intriguing, if only for his ability to get a lot of sound from some surprisingly simple strumming and picking. The later songs, "I Wonder To Myself," "Slidin' Delta," "Lonesome Home Blues," and "Black Mare Blues," leave something to be desired in terms of sound, but at least they're represented here. *—Bruce Eder*

Eddie "One String" Jones

b. Dec. 10, 1926
Guitar / Slide Guitar Blues, Acoustic Blues
A fascinating anachronism whose story is as interesting as his music, Eddie "One-String" Jones was discovered by Frederick Usher, Jr. and Richard Barlow in Los Angeles' skid row in 1960. Jones was nicknamed "One-String" after his instrument, a relative of the southern single-string diddley bows that functioned as homemade instruments, and emulated the sound of the slide guitar. As Usher wrote in the liner notes to the *One String Blues* album, Jones' instrument consisted of "about three feet of discarded 2 × 4, hacked off at both ends, a steel wire string from a nail at each end and raised off the wood suface by bridges—a wooden block at the open end and a pill bottle at the other end under the resonator, a gallon paint can, wired onto the 2 × 4 and split up the side part way to pass over the string."

Duly impressed by Jones' ingenious sounds, which seemed to reach back into the roots of the blues themselves, Usher and Barlow arranged to record Jones the same day, using a wall plug in a skid-row back alley. Two other sessions followed, and the results—consisting mostly of primitive renditions of standards like "Rolling and Tumbling," "Chauffeur Blues," and "Baby Please Don't Go"—were issued on an album that Jones shared with harmonica player Edward Hazelton (discovered while Usher was trying to locate Jones again on skid row after his first session). A public performance at a private home was apparently a success, but soon afterwards Jones again vanished into vagrancy, leaving behind a fascinating document that has mightily impressed listeners like Captain Beefheart. *—Richie Unterberger*

One String Blues / 1993 / Gazell ✦✦✦✦✦
Jones shares this 15-track compilation with harmonica street player Edward Hazelton, another one of Frederick Usher's elusive Skid Row discoveries, who contributes a half dozen sides featuring a stripped-down Sonny Terry style. The first nine tracks by Jones are primitive in the extreme, untouched by any commercial considerations whatsoever. His instrument—described on the front cover as "a home-made African derived Zither-Monochord"—delivers tones that border on somewhere between keening, rhythmic, and downright eerie. Even repeated listening to any of the early Delta blues slide greats will not prepare you for the sound on this recording, which is trebly, bordering on metallic. Blues as folklore, but a whole lot of fun to explore as well. *—Cub Koda*

Floyd Jones

b. Jul. 21, 1917, Marianna, AR, **d.** Dec. 19, 1989, Chicago, IL
Vocals, Guitar / Acoustic Chicago Blues, Electric Chicago Blues
His sound characteristically dark and gloomy, guitarist Floyd Jones contributed a handful of genuine classics to the Chicago blues idiom during the late '40s and early '50s, notably the foreboding "Dark Road" and "Hard Times."

Born in Arkansas, Jones grew up in the blues-fertile Mississippi Delta (where he picked up the guitar in his teens). He came to Chicago in the mid-'40s, working for tips on Maxwell Street with his cousin Moody Jones and Baby Face Leroy Foster and playing local clubs on a regular basis. Floyd was right there when the postwar Chicago blues movement first took flight, recording with harpist Snooky Pryor for Marvel in 1947; pianist Sunnyland Slim for Tempo Tone the next year (where he cut "Hard Times"), JOB and Chess in 1952-53, and Vee-Jay in 1955 (where he weighed in with a typically downcast "Ain't Times Hard").

Jones remained active on the Chicago scene until shortly before his 1989 death, although electric bass had long since replaced the guitar as his main axe. He participated in Earwig Records' *Old Friends* sessions in 1979, sharing a studio with longtime cohorts Sunnyland Slim, Honeyboy Edwards, Big Walter Horton, and Kansas City Red. *—Bill Dahl*

● **Masters of Modern Blues** / 1994 / Testament ✦✦✦✦✦
Eight priceless 1966 tracks by tragically underrecorded guitarist Floyd Jones are paired for this CD with eight more by sessionmate Eddie Taylor. Produced in both cases by Testament boss Pete Welding with Big Walter Horton on harp, pianist Otis Spann, and drummer Fred Below lending their collective hands, Jones recreates his dour, uncompromising "Dark Road," "Hard Times," and "Stockyard Blues" with an early-'50s sense of purpose. *—Bill Dahl*

Keb' Mo' (Kevin Moore)

b. Oct. 3, 1951, Los Angeles, CA
Slide Guitar, Vocals, Guitar / Contemporary Blues, Modern Acoustic Blues
Keb' Mo' draws heavily on the old-fashioned country blues style of Robert Johnson, but keeps his sound contemporary with touches of soul and folksy storytelling. He writes much of his own material and has applied his acoustic, electric, and slide guitar skills to jazz and rock-oriented bands in the past as well. At 21, Moore joined an R&B band later hired for a tour by Papa John Creach and played on three of Creach's albums. He cut an R&B-based solo album, *Rainmaker,* in 1980 for Casablanca, which promptly folded. In 1983, he joined Monk Higgins' band as a guitarist and met a number of blues musicians who collectively increased his understanding of the music. He subsequently joined a vocal group called the Rose Brothers and gigged around L.A. 1990 found Moore portraying a Delta bluesman in a local play called *Rabbit Foot* and later playing Robert Johnson in a docudrama called *Can't You Hear the Wind Howl?* He released his self-titled debut album as Keb' Mo' in 1994; his second album, *Just Like You,* was well-received. *Slow Down* followed in 1998. *—Steve Huey*

● **Keb' Mo'** / Jun. 3, 1994 / OKeh/550/Epic ✦✦✦✦
Keb' Mo's self-titled debut is an edgy, ambitious collection of gritty country blues. Keb' Mo' pushes into new directions, trying to incorporate some of the sensibilites of the slacker revolution without losing touch of the tradition that makes the blues the breathing, vital art form it is. His attempts aren't always successful, but his gutsy guitar playing and impassioned vocals, as well as his surprisingly accomplished songwriting, make *Keb' Mo'* a debut to cherish. *—Thom Owens*

Just Like You / Jun. 18, 1996 / OKeh/550/Epic ✦✦✦
On his second album, Keb' Mo' begins to expand the borders of his Delta blues by recording with a full band on a couple of tracks and attempting more expansive, rock-based song structures. The attempts aren't entirely successful and it's ironic that he decided to try rock-oriented material after he received such praise for his traditionalist debut. Still, there are a few songs on the album that rank with the best on his first album, which suggests that *Just Like You* is merely a sophomore slump. *—Thom Owens*

Slow Down / Aug. 25, 1998 / OKeh/550/Epic ✦✦✦

The Door / Oct. 10, 2000 / OKeh/550/Epic ✦✦✦

Junior Kimbrough

b. Jul. 28, 1930, Hudsonville, MS, **d.** Jan. 17, 1998
Vocals, Guitar / Modern Delta Blues, Electric Country Blues
Cited as a prime early influence by rockabilly pioneer Charlie Feathers, Mississippi Delta bluesman Junior Kimbrough's modal, hypnotic blues vision remained a regional sensation for most of his career. He finally transcended the confines of his region in the early '90s, when he appeared in the 1991 movie *Deep Blues* and on its Anxious/Atlantic soundtrack, leading to his own debut for Fat Possum Records, *All Night Long.* In 1968, he cut his first single, "Tramp," for the local Philwood label. For the next two decades, Kimbrough didn't have the opportunity to record frequently, and primarily played juke joints throughout Mississippi, which is where music journalist Robert Palmer discovered him in the late '80s. Palmer featured Kimbrough in his documentary film *Deep Blues.* The exposure in the movie led to a national record contract for Kimbrough—he signed with Fat Possum and released his first full-length album, *All Night Long,* in 1992. The record was critically acclaimed by both blues and mainstream publications, as was *Deep Blues* and its accompanying soundtrack. *—Bill Dahl & Stephen Thomas Erlewine*

● **All Night Long** / 1992 / Epitaph ✦✦✦✦✦
A beautifully packaged edition of Junior Kimbrough's first album, recorded live in the converted church that replaced Kimbrough's original wooden shack juke joint. The lineup is Kimbrough on vocals and guitar, Garry Burnside on bass, and Kenny Malone on drums (it's a family business around this area, and you'll find Burnsides and Malones all over Fat Possum's releases). *All Night Long* is a big, scruffy racket of an electric blues album, and it's fantastic material, a mix of charging, biting rhythms, intense slow blues, hollerin', stompin' and moanin'. The lack of studio polish is a big plus here—producer Robert Palmer was absolutely right to give this to us flubs and all—and the energy is wonderful. A great electric blues portrait that's getting widespread attention at last—and deserves it all. *—Steven McDonald*

Sad Days, Lonely Nights / 1993 / Epitaph ✦✦

Most Things Haven't Worked Out / Mar. 25, 1997 / Epitaph ✦✦✦
While this album lacks the revelatory impact of Kimbrough's debut *All Night Long,* or a hair-raising number like that release's "You Better Run," and it is akin to his debut in both its packaging and its production values. With three of the tracks recorded directly from *Junior Kimbrough's Juke Joint,* the sound here is absolutely raw; aside from the ugly drum tone in "Everywhere I Go," it's a perfect evocation of live performance. Indeed, half the fascination in Kimbrough's works are the strange harmonics, "off" notes, and just sheer noise that gives a murky depth to his repetitive looping around a song's tonic note. Even the lyrics are often buried beneath layers of blues grunge, but it hardly matters—the whole album qualifies as a liminal, half-waking Mississippi dream. Highlights include the hypnotic "I'm in Love," and the stomping "Burn in Hell," which Kimbrough introduces by ribbing a bandmate: "If I die before you, I go before you, I'm gonna be there to open the door—come on in, brother!" With less than a year left to live, Kimbrough could still laugh at eternity. *—Paul Collins*

God Knows I Tried / Aug. 25, 1998 / Epitaph ✦✦✦

Meet Me in the City / Sep. 21, 1999 / Epitaph ✦✦

Albert King

b. Apr. 25, 1923, Indianola, MS, **d.** Dec. 21, 1992, Memphis, TN
Vocals, Guitar (Electric), Guitar / Modern Electric Blues, Soul-Blues
Albert King is truly a "King of the Blues," although he doesn't hold that title (B.B. does). Along with B.B. and Freddie King, Albert King is one of the major influences on blues and rock guitar players. Without him, modern guitar music would not sound as it does—his style has influenced both Black and White blues players from Otis Rush and Robert Cray to Eric Clapton and Stevie Ray Vaughan. It's important to note that while almost all modern blues guitarists seldom play for long without falling into a B.B. King guitar cliché, Albert King never does—he's had his own style and unique tone from the beginning. Albert King plays guitar left-handed, without re-stringing the guitar from the right-handed setup; this "upside-down" playing accounts for his difference in tone, since he pulls down on the same strings that most players push up on when bending the blues notes. King's massive tone and totally unique way of squeezing bends out of a guitar string has had a major impact. Many young White guitarists—especially rock & rollers—have been influenced by King's playing, and many players who emulate his style may never have heard of Albert King, let alone heard

his music. His style is immediately distinguishable from all other blues guitarists, and he's one of the most important blues players to ever pick up the electric guitar. *—Daniel Erlewine & Stephen Thomas Erlewine*

☆ **Born Under a Bad Sign** / 1967 / Stax ♦♦♦♦♦
One day this southpaw was playing little clubs in Osceola, AR, the next he was headlining rock ballrooms like the Fillmore. This is the album that changed everything—including seemingly 90% of the blues and rock guitarists on the landscape. Backed by Booker T. & the MG's and the Memphis Horns, Albert proved he was every bit as hip as they, not to mention flexible. In fact, as throughout his career, he used a relatively small vocabulary of licks, but gave them slightly different timing and English, depending on the groove and the surroundings. The result was a whole new language. This LP is one big classic from top to bottom. "Crosscut Saw," "Oh, Pretty Woman," "The Hunter," "As the Years Go Passing By," "Personal Manager," the title tune—every track is a must-have. *—Dan Forte*

Live Wire/Blues Power / 1968 / Stax ♦♦♦♦♦
Live Wire/Blues Power is one of Albert King's definitive albums. Recorded live at the Fillmore Auditorium in 1968, the guitarist is at the top of his form throughout the record—his solos are intense and piercing. The band is fine, but ultimately it's King's show—he makes Herbie Hancock's "Watermelon Man" dirty and funky and wrings out all the emotion from "Blues at Sunrise." *—Thom Owens*

★ **King of the Blues Guitar** / 1969 / Atlantic ♦♦♦♦♦
Atlantic's original vinyl edition of this was comprised of Albert's Stax singles—a few from *Born Under a Bad Sign*, along with "Cold Feet," "I Love Lucy" (two of King's patented monologues), and the beautiful "You're Gonna Need Me." Great stuff. Even greater, though, is the CD reissue, which includes those singles (which didn't appear on any other LPs) and *all* of *Born Under a Bad Sign*. Need I say more— *—Dan Forte*

Years Gone By / 1969 / Stax ♦♦♦♦♦
King cranked out this solid, if typical, album for the Stax label after the success of *Born Under a Bad Sign*. With Booker T. drummer Al Jackson producing, the set includes such staples as "You Threw Your Love on Me Too Strong," "Wrapped up in Love Again," and a powerful version of Howlin' Wolf's "Killing Floor." For fans of King's guitar work, the inclusion of the instrumental workouts on "You Don't Love Me" and "Drowning on Dry Land" are a special bonus. Not an essential Albert King album, but one of his good ones. *—Cub Koda*

Blues for Elvis: Albert King Does the King's Things / 1970 / Stax ♦♦♦
Originally titled *King Does the King's Thing*, here's Albert King adding his own touch to a batch of Elvis Presley tunes. Because King's style is so irreducible, the concept actually works, as he fills this album with his traditional, high-voltage guitar work and strong vocals. That isn't surprising, since four of the nine tunes on here originally started as R&B hits covered by Presley, including an instrumental version of Smiley Lewis' "One Night." No matter what the original sources may be, though, this is a strong showing in King's catalog. *—Cub Koda*

The Lost Session / 1971 / Stax ♦♦

Lovejoy / 1971 / Stax ♦♦♦
This 1970 studio effort teamed up Albert with producer Don Nix, who supplied the majority of the original material here. Kicking off with a typical reading of the Stones' "Honky Tonk Woman" and including Taj Mahal's "She Caught the Katy and Left Me a Mule to Ride," the session is split between a Hollywood date with Jesse Ed Davis, Jim Keltner, and Duck Dunn in the band and one at Muscle Shoals with Roger Hawkins, David Hood, and Barry Beckett in the lineup. Although all of this is well-produced, there's hardly any fireworks out of Albert or any of the players aboard, making this an unessential addition for any but Albert King completists. *—Cub Koda*

I'll Play the Blues for You / 1972 / Stax ♦♦♦♦♦

Tomato Years / 1976-1977 / Tomato ♦♦♦
Albert King enjoyed an erratic but memorable reign at Tomato in the 1970s. The label aimed to continue the success King had enjoyed at Stax mixing blues backing and vocals with pop/soul arrangements and lyrics. He recorded six LPs for Tomato; this anthology culls 14 cuts from his Tomato releases, among them the slashing numbers "Blues At Sunrise" and "I'm Gonna Call You Soon As The Sun Goes Down," which vividly illustrated King's guitar prowess. Others, like "Truckload Of Lovin'" and "We All Wanna Boogie," show how he skillfully crammed moments of inspiration into formulaic outings. *—Ron Wynn*

The Pinch / 1977 / Stax ♦♦♦
One of King's more soul-oriented efforts, from sessions recorded in 1973 and 1974. It's been retitled as *The Blues Don't Change* for its CD reissue. *—Richie Unterberger*

Chronicle (With Little Milton) / 1979 / Stax ♦♦♦
This compilation has a leftover feel; the liner notes provide no sources and dates, admitting only that these are "Stax recordings, some never before available on LP." If you're a big fan of one or both of the artists involved, though, it's not bad, with a quality that's generally consistent with their fully-baked Stax-era albums, though the King half of the program is somewhat superior to the Milton tracks. *—Richie Unterberger*

In San Francisco-Crosscut Saw / Mar. 1983 / Stax ♦♦♦
A reissue of King's 1983 album *San Francisco '83* (a studio album, not a live one), with the addition of two previously unreleased cuts. His first new release in five years, it wasn't one of King's better records. But it did represent a return to a basic five-piece sound, an improvement upon his over-produced outings of the late '70s. *—Richie Unterberger*

I'm in a Phone Booth, Baby / 1984 / Stax ♦♦♦

The Best of Albert King, Vol. 1 / 1986 / Stax ♦♦♦♦♦
"The best of Albert King"— More like the best material that he happened to record for Stax between 1968 and 1973. Even that's debatable, the 13 tracks including covers such as "Honky Tonk Woman," "Sky Is Crying," and "Hound Dog." It does present a reasonable cross-section of his soul-inflected work of the period, drawing from over a half-dozen LPs and a couple of singles, though you might be as well or better off with his more focused individual titles. And for the true "best of Albert King," Rhino's *Ultimate Collection* remains the hands-down winner. *—Richie Unterberger*

Blues at Sunrise: Live at Montreux / 1988 / Stax ♦♦♦

Let's Have a Natural Ball / 1989 / Modern Blues ♦♦♦♦♦
Great compilation of King's Bobbin sides of the late '50s and early '60s. *—Bill Dahl*

Thursday Night in San Francisco: Recorded Live at the Fillmore Auditorium / 1990 / Stax ♦♦♦
Recorded live in San Francisco in 1968, here's Albert King pretty much at the top of his game, blasting out tons of great guitar and singing his heart to an appreciative crowd of young hippies. With a tight four-piece road band backing him, King fires up his Flying V and slams down hard on material like Freddie King's "San-Ho-Zay," "you Upset Me Baby," "Call It Stormy Monday," "Crosscut Saw," and "Drifting Blues." This is one of two volumes from the same *Fillmore* stand and both are absolutely essential to any Albert King collection; in many ways, they're the perfect introduction to this blues giant. *—Cub Koda*

Wednesday Night in San Francisco: Recorded Live at the Fillmore Auditorium / 1990 / Stax ♦♦♦

☆ **The Ultimate Collection** / 1993 / Rhino ♦♦♦♦♦
This two-disc set covers a few early songs, but concentrates on the inspired blend of soul, blues and rock that King made famous in the 1960s and '70s. Many songs, such as "Laundromat Blues," "Crosscut Saw," "I'll Play The Blues For You" and of course "Born Under A Bad Sign," featured simple riffs, catchy lyrics and solid grooves parlayed into memorable performances through King's confident vocals and soaring solos. To be sure, there were formulaic numbers, and after a time King's solos and note choices were as much show biz effect as they were exciting, but the anthology's live cuts show that King was always capable of surprise and invention on the bandstand. The later numbers aren't quite as powerful, but King's rendition of "Phone Booth" shows his successors and imitators what legitimate blues playing is all about. *—Ron Wynn*

Hard Bargain / Feb. 1996 / Stax ♦♦♦

The Very Best of Albert King / Apr. 20, 1999 / Rhino ♦♦♦♦♦
There have been many compilations of Albert King's classic Stax recordings over the years, including the wonderful double-disc set *The Ultimate Collection*, but Rhino's *The Very Best of Albert King* is perhaps the best for curious listeners, since it offers 16 classics on one disc. There may be a few favorites missing, from "The Hunter" to "The Phone Booth," but the disc does a wonderful job of summarizing the classic Stax years while adding some highlights from his latter-day recordings for Tomato. In the end, what matters is that the bare basics—"Let's Have a Natural Ball," "C.O.D.," "Laundromat Blues," "Oh Pretty Woman," "Crosscut Saw," "Born Under a Bad Sign," "Personal Manager," "Blues Power"—are all here, making this ideal for neophytes on a tight budget. (Of course, *Born Under a Bad Sign* remains an excellent introduction on its own terms, as well.) *—Stephen Thomas Erlewine*

In Session / Aug. 17, 1999 / Stax ♦♦♦♦♦

B.B. King (Riley B. King)

b. Sep. 16, 1925, Indianola, MS
Vocals, Guitar (Electric), Guitar / Modern Electric Blues, Soul-Blues
Universally hailed as the reigning king of the blues, the legendary B.B. King is without a doubt the single most important electric guitarist of the last half century. A contemporary blues guitar solo without at least a couple of recognizable King-inspired bent notes is all but unimaginable, and he remains a supremely confident singer capable of wringing every nuance from any lyric (and he's tried his hand at many an unlikely song—anybody recall his version of "Love Me Tender"?).

Yet B.B. King remains an intrinsically humble superstar, an utterly accessible icon who welcomes visitors into his dressing room with self-effacing graciousness. Between 1951 and 1985, King notched an amazing 74 entries on *Billboard*'s R&B charts, and he was one of the few full-fledged blues artists to score a major pop hit when his 1970 smash "The Thrill Is Gone" crossed over to mainstream success (engendering memorable appearances on *The Ed Sullivan Show* and *American Bandstand!*). King's immediately recognizable guitar style, utilizing a trademark trill that approximates the bottleneck sound shown him by cousin Bukka White all those decades ago, has long set him apart from his contemporaries. Add his patented pleading vocal style and you have the most influential and innovative bluesman of the post-war period. There can be little doubt that B.B. King will reign as the genre's undisputed king (and goodwill ambassador) for as long as he lives. *—Bill Dahl*

My Kind of Blues / 1961 / EMI-Capitol Special Markets ♦♦♦
According to his biographer, Charles Sawyer, this is King's personal favorite among his recordings. Unlike most of his albums from this period (which are mostly collections of singles), this was recorded in one session and takes him out of his usual big-band setting, using only bass, drums, and piano for accompaniment. The result is a masterpiece: a sparse, uncluttered sound with nothing to mask King's beautiful guitar and voice. "You Done Lost Your Good Thing Now" (its unaccompanied guitar intro is a pure distillation of his style), "Mr. Pawn Broker," "Someday Baby" (R&B Top Ten, 1961), "Walkin' Dr. Bill," and a great version of "Drivin' Wheel" are highlights. (Out of print.) *—George Bedard*

★ **Live at the Regal** / 1965 / ABC/MCA ♦♦♦♦♦
This is one of the all-time classic live albums. Recorded in 1964, it captures King in his prime playing to a *very* enthusiastic Black audience. He stretches out on guitar in a way he doesn't on his studio recordings—his guitar sound (it's a joy to hear him switching around and playing with different settings and guitar tones) has a vibrancy and, sometimes, a wild edge that doesn't get captured in the studio. This is a must for B.B. King fans. *—George Bedard*

Blues on Top of Blues / 1968 / BGO ♦♦♦♦♦
This isn't his most well-known stuff, but it's a very solid late '60s set. Featuring brassy

arrangements by Johnny Pate (who also worked with many prominent Chicago soul acts during the '60s), it presents King's sound at its fullest without sacrificing any of his grit or sophisticated swing. No famous classics here, but the material is very strong throughout. —*Richie Unterberger*

Lucille / 1968 / MCA ✦✦✦✦
A decent but short (nine songs) late '60s set, with somewhat sparser production than he'd employ with the beefier arrangements of the "Thrill Is Gone" era. Brass and stinging guitar plays a part on all of the songs, leading off with the eight-minute title track, a spoken narrative about his famous guitar. —*Richie Unterberger*

Completely Well / 1969 / MCA ✦✦✦✦
This was B.B.'s breakthrough album in 1969, which finally got him the long-deserved acclaim that was no less than his due. It contained his signature number, "The Thrill Is Gone," and eight other tunes, six of them emanating from B.B.'s pen, usually in a co-writing situation. Hardliners point to the horn charts and the overdubbed strings as the beginning of the end of B.B.'s old style that so identifiably earmarked his early sides for the Bihari brothers and his later tracks for ABC, but this is truly the album that made the world sit up and take notice of B.B. King. The plus points include loose arrangements and a small combo behind him that never dwarfs the proceedings or gets in the way. B.B., for his part, sounds like he's having a ball, playing and singing at peak power. This is certainly not the place to start your B.B. King collection, but it's a nice stop along the way before you finish it. —*Cub Koda*

Live & Well / 1969 / MCA ✦✦✦
Although *Live & Well* wasn't a landmark album in the sense of *Live at the Regal*, it was a significant commercial breakthrough for King, as it was the first of his LPs to enter the Top 100. That may have been because recognition from rock stars such as Eric Clapton had finally boosted his exposure to the White pop audience, but it was a worthy recording on its own merits, divided evenly between live and studio material. King's always recorded well as a live act, and it's the concert tracks that shine brightest, although the studio ones (cut with assistance from studio musicians like Al Kooper and Hugh McCracken) aren't bad. —*Richie Unterberger*

Indianola Mississippi Seeds / 1970 / MCA ✦✦✦✦
B.B. King hasn't made many better pop-flavored albums than this. Besides making Leon Russell's "Hummingbird" sound like his own composition, King showed that you can put the blues into any situation and make it work. Carole King was one of several pop luminaries who did more than just hang on for the ride. —*Ron Wynn*

Live in Cook County Jail / 1971 / MCA ✦✦✦✦✦
B.B. King has cut a lot of albums since the success of *Live at the Regal.* And, like the live shows they document, none of them are any less than solid and professional, hallmarks of King's work aesthetic. But every so often B.B. truly catches fire; his playing and singing comes up an extra notch or two, and the result is a live album with some real sparks to it. *Live in Cook County Jail* is one of those great concerts that the record company was smart enough to be there to capture, documenting B.B. firing on all cylinders in front of an audience that's just damn happy for him to be there. Possibly the best live version of "The Thrill Is Gone" of all its many incarnations, and rock solid renditions of classics like "Everyday I Have the Blues," "How Blue Can You Get—," "Sweet Sixteen" and a great medley of "3 O'Clock Blues" and "Darlin' You Know I Love You." *Live at the Regal* is still the champ of King's live output, but many say this runs a close second, and they just may be right. —*Cub Koda*

Midnight Believer / 1978 / MCA ✦✦✦

Great Moments with B.B. King / 1981 / MCA ✦✦✦✦
Very solid 23-track package culled from some of King's best mid-to-late-'60s ABC-Paramount and BluesWay LPs. Some of the best cuts stem from a sizzling live album; "Gambler's Blues," "Waitin' on You," and a stunning "Night Life" find his reverb level rising to the boiling point. A brassy "That's Wrong Little Mama," "Dance with Me," and "Heartbreaker" connect like consecutive right hooks, and his rousing smash "Paying the Cost to Be the Boss" is also on board. —*Bill Dahl*

Do the Boogie! B.B. King's Early '50s Classics / 1988 / Flair ✦✦✦✦✦
20 killer tracks from B.B. King's 1950s heyday, including quite a few alternate takes and a few tough-to-locate items ("Bye Bye Baby," "Dark Is the Night," "Jump with You Baby"). Many of the titles are familiar ones— "Woke Up This Morning," "Every Day," "Please Love Me," "Whole Lotta Love"—but often as not, compiler Ray Topping unearthed contrasting versions from the same sessions that shed new, fascinating light on King's studio techniques. —*Bill Dahl*

☆ **The Best of B.B. King, Vol. 1** / 1991 / Ace ✦✦✦✦✦
A 20-track hits compilation that should have been a great deal better than it is. The disc embarrassingly uses an inferior remake of King's classic "Whole Lotta Love" instead of the original, while drums and electric bass have been clumsily overdubbed on the original takes of "You Upset Me Baby," "Every Day," and "Please Love Me," absolutely ruining them. What a shame, since two-thirds of the collection is just fine. —*Bill Dahl*

Spotlight on Lucille / 1991 / Flair ✦✦✦✦
From the contemporary-looking cover, this would appear to be recently recorded material. But wait—these are all 1950s/early-'60s instrumentals from the Modern/Kent vaults, spotlighting B.B. King's pristine lead guitar in an often jazzier mode than he usually adopted in the studio. His workout on Louis Jordan's "Just like a Woman" is a tour de force that's been reissued often, but much of the compilation is rare stuff that gives Lucille her full due. —*Bill Dahl*

King of the Blues / 1992 / MCA ✦✦✦✦✦
No way can a mere four discs cover every facet of the blues king's amazing recording career, but MCA makes a valiant stab at it. The first two discs, as expected, are immaculate: opening with his Bullet Records debut ("Miss Martha King"), the box continues with a handful of pivotal RPM/Kent masters before digging into his 1960s ABC-Paramount material ("I'm Gonna Sit in 'Til You Give In" and "My Baby's Comin' Home" are little-recalled gems). The hits—"The Thrill Is Gone," "Why I Sing the Blues," "To Know You Is to Love You"—are all here, and if much of the fourth disc is pretty disposable, it only mirrors King's own winding down in the studio. —*Bill Dahl*

☆ **Singin' the Blues/The Blues** / 1992 / Flair ✦✦✦✦✦
Two great original Crown albums from the '50s appear on one import CD, including most of King's Top Ten R&B hits from the period: "3 O'Clock Blues," "Please Love Me," "You Upset Me Baby," "You Know I Love You," "Woke Up This Morning," and "Sweet Little Angel," plus one of his best, "Crying Won't Help You." This is the stuff that was so hugely influential to other blues guitarists and singers in its original recorded version. Here is lots of the real early, gritty stuff: "That Ain't the Way to Do It," "When My Heart Beats like a Hammer," "Don't You Want a Man like Me—" The guitar intro to "Early in the Morning" is one of the finest examples of King in a jazzy mode. Great guitar! —*George Bedard*

Blues Summit / 1993 / MCA ✦✦✦

How Blue Can You Get—: Classic Live Performances 1964 to 1994 / Jun. 18, 1996 / MCA ✦✦✦

Greatest Hits / Aug. 25, 1998 / MCA ✦✦✦
There's more than one B.B. King best-of out on the racks, but this 1998 issue updates his latest chart achievements and puts it together in a modern, 16-track package for both the novice and casual modern blues listener. Kicking off with a pair of tunes from the influential *Live at the Regal* album ("Sweet Little Angel," "Everyday I Have the Blues"), the set moves through mid- to late-'60s breakthrough hits like "How Blue Can You Get?," "Paying the Cost to Be the Boss," "Why I Sing the Blues," "Don't Answer the Door" and his signature tune, "The Thrill Is Gone." The pop-blues fusions King experimented with in the '70s and '80s show up on "To Know You Is to Love You," "I Like to Live the Love" and "Hummingbird." The modern-day end of things is represented by duets with Robert Cray on "Playin' With My Friends" and rock group U2 on "When Love Comes to Town." Although missing all of his early-'50s hits, this is a good buy for the casual fan coming to his music for the first time and for longtime aficionados looking for a quick-fix update. —*Cub Koda*

Blues on the Bayou / Oct. 20, 1998 / MCA ✦✦✦

RPM Hits 1951-1957 / Feb. 26, 1999 / Ace ✦✦✦✦

Live in Japan / May 18, 1999 / MCA ✦✦✦✦

Let the Good Times Roll: The Music of Louis Jordan / Oct. 5, 1999 / MCA ✦✦✦✦

☆ **The Best of the Kent Singles 1958-1971** / Jun. 26, 2000 / Ace ✦✦✦✦✦
This isn't as straightforward an anthology as you might suppose from the title. Yes, it has King singles released on Kent between 1958 and 1971. King, however, left Kent in 1962, after which the label continued putting out singles from the tracks he had done with the company; often, these singles charted. Therefore, all of the material on this CD is from the late '50s and early '60s—not that this is a drawback. Furthermore, some of the singles were produced by altering the original recordings with newly dubbed instrumentation. Ace has made some judgment calls and, in many instances, used the original undubbed versions, although in the case of "Worry, Worry," the overdubbed single version *is* used. As for the different versions that were omitted due to these judgment calls, Ace promised, upon the 2000 release of this compilation, that all missing sides would eventually be issued on other Ace CDs. Having gotten all that straight, this is a good collection of King's late-'50s, early-'60s material. It includes some of his signature tunes, like "Why Does Everything Happen to Me," "Rock Me Baby," and "Sweet Sixteen (Pts. 1 & 2)," not to mention his crunchy version of "Eyesight to the Blind," the Sonny Boy Williamson song whose lyrics were later adapted by the Who in *Tommy.* King's arrangements were getting jazzier by this time, often employing horns, although they were still somewhat rawer than the ones that would bring him crossover success by the late '60s. It may be unpopular to note that this, like many King compilations, isn't the most diverse listen, and 25 songs at once might be more than enough. At the same time, for King fans, of which there are many, it probably *isn't* enough. —*Richie Unterberger*

☆ **Anthology** / Nov. 7, 2000 / MCA ✦✦✦✦✦
MCA's double-disc set *Anthology* is a bit of a blessing, actually, a welcome entry to B.B. King's extensive catalog, since the last half of his career has not been anthologized often (it was most notably on the box set *The King of Blues*). Once King's career entered the '70s, he never lost his way, but his recordings became uneven. The situation didn't improve in the '80s or '90s, either—he was always reliable, but the records could either be too slick or uninspired or just solid journeyman efforts. *Anthology* does a terrific job of consolidating the years between 1963 and 1998, his time at ABC and MCA, respectively. Smartly, the compilers lean heavily on the '60s and early-'70s material, with only a handful of tracks from 1980-1998. There are certainly some terrific tracks missing, but by concentrating on his great recordings of the mid-'60s, plus the work that just followed it, they wind up with not just a very enjoyable compilation, but one that's a testament to B.B.'s talents as a guitarist, vocalist, stylist, and showman. This, in conjunction with a compilation of early Flair recordings and *Live at the Regal,* provide a better history of the great bluesman's career than his box set. —*Stephen Thomas Erlewine*

Earl King

b. Feb. 7, 1934, New Orleans, LA
Vocals, Guitar / New Orleans R&B, New Orleans Blues, R&B, Soul
Unilaterally respected around his Crescent City homebase as both a performer and a songwriter, guitarist Earl King has been a prime New Orleans R&B force for more than four decades—and he shows no signs of slowing down. The guitarist debuted on wax in 1953 on Savoy with "Have You Gone Crazy" (with pal Huey "Piano" Smith making the first of many memorable supporting appearances on his platters). 1954's "A Mother's Love," Earl's first Specialty offering, was an especially accurate Guitar Slim homage produced by Johnny Vincent, who would soon launch his own label, Ace Records, with King one of his principal artists. King's first Ace single, the seminal two-chord south Louisiana blues "Those Lonely, Lonely

Nights," proved a national R&B hit. King remained with Ace through the rest of the decade, waxing an unbroken string of great New Orleans R&B sides with the unparalleled house band at Cosimo's studio. But he moved over to Imperial to work with producer Dave Bartholomew in 1960, cutting the classic "Come On" (also known as "Let The Good Times Roll") and 1961's humorous "Trick Bag" and managing a second chart item in 1962 with "Always a First Time." King admirably rode out the rough spots during the late '60s and '70s. Since signing with Black Top, his performing career has been rejuvenated; 1990's *Sexual Telepathy* and *Hard River to Cross* three years later were both superlative albums. *—Bill Dahl*

Street Parade / 1981 / Charly ♦♦♦
Funky 1972 tracks that should have fueled a comeback for the Crescent City mainstay but didn't (a lease deal with Atlantic fell through). Allen Toussaint was apparently in charge of the sessions, which produced updates of "Mama and Papa" and "A Mother's Love" as well as a bevy of fresh nuggets (notably the fanciful "Medieval Days," later revived by King on Black Top), and the two-part title item. *—Bill Dahl*

Trick Bag / 1983 / EMI ♦♦♦♦♦
Here's an extremely hard-to-find French LP that remains the only place where King's wonderful early-'60s Imperial Records catalog was gathered in one place (a handful grace EMI's two-disc Dave Bartholomew set; he produced them). Earl changed his sound to fit the funkier Crescent City sound of the time on the two-part "Come On," and the humorous "Trick Bag" and "Mama and Papa," and a passionate "You're More to Me than Gold." *—Bill Dahl*

Sexual Telepathy / 1990 / Black Top ♦♦♦♦♦
Reunited with a more sympathetic New Orleans rhythm section (bassist George Porter, Jr., and drummer Kenny Blevins) and a funkier horn section, King excelled handsomely on this uncommonly strong outing. As we've come to expect from him, he brought a sheaf of new originals to the sessions, from a saucy "Sexual Telepathy" to a heartwarming "Happy Little Nobody's Waggy Tail Dog." Remakes of his "Always a First Time" and "A Weary Silent Night" were welcome inclusions (especially since we can't easily lay our hands on the originals!). *—Bill Dahl*

Hard River to Cross / 1993 / Black Top ♦♦♦♦♦
The quirky guitarist with the endlessly wavy hair made it two winners in a row with this one. Snooks Eaglin guests on guitar for three tracks (including the hilarious "Big Foot" and a joyous "No City like New Orleans," while Porter and drummer Herman Ernest III lay down scintillating grooves behind King's ringing axe and wise vocals. *—Bill Dahl*

Those Lonely, Lonely Nights / 1993 / P-Vine ♦♦♦♦♦
Why must New Orleans guitarist Earl King's 1950s material be so difficult to locate on CD— This expensive Japanese import does the job handily, if you can find it—all eight of King's Guitar Slim-influenced Specialty sides (including "A Mother's Love" and its rocking flip, "I'm Your Best Bet Baby") and 17 of his terrific efforts for Ace, notably the hit title track, the equally moving "My Love Is Strong," and the jumping "Everybody's Carried Away," "Little Girl," and "I'll Take You Back Home." *—Bill Dahl*

● **Earl's Pearls** / May 5, 1998 / Westside ♦♦♦♦♦
This top-notch collection brings together 25 tracks from King's 1955-1960 tenure with Ace Records in Jackson, Mississippi. Classic '50s New Orleans music doesn't come much finer than this, and Earl's contributions to the genre are plentiful on this disc, starting with his big hit, the original "Those Lonely, Lonely Nights." A real treat is hearing Huey "Piano" Smith soloing with complete abandon on tracks like "Nobody Cares," "Little Girl," "I'll Take You Back Home" and "Baby You Can Get Your Gun." Earl's guitar playing is equally fine and his Guitar Slim-derived style is well to the fore on "My Love Is Strong" and "I'm Packing Up." Although King's discography encompasses many labels and sessions, this is a great place to start absorbing this Crescent City genius. *—Cub Koda*

Freddie King

b. Sep. 3, 1934, Gilmer, TX, **d.** Dec. 28, 1976, Dallas, TX
Vocals, Guitar (Electric), Guitar / Electric Texas Blues, Modern Electric Blues
Guitarist Freddie King rode to fame in the early '60s with a spate of catchy instrumentals which became instant bandstand fodder for fellow bluesmen and White rock bands alike. Employing a more down-home (thumb and finger picks) approach to the B.B. King single-string style of playing, King enjoyed success on a variety of different record labels. Furthermore, he was one of the first bluesmen to employ a racially integrated group onstage behind him. Initially, King played rural acoustic blues, in the vein of Lightin' Hopkins. By the time he was a teenager, he had grown to love the rough, electrified sounds of Chicago blues. King didn't cut his own record until 1957, when he recorded "Country Boy" for the small independent label El-Bee. The single failed to gain much attention. Three years later, he signed with Federal Records and cut his first single for the label, "You've Got to Love Her with a Feeling," in August of 1960. The single appeared the following month and became a minor hit, scraping the bottom of the pop charts in early 1961. It was followed by "Hide Away," the song that would become Freddie King's signature tune and most influential recording. Throughout the '60s, "Hide Away" was one of the necessary songs blues and rock & roll bar bands across America and England had to play during their gigs. Throughout 1961, he turned out a series of instrumentals—including "San-Ho-Zay," "The Stumble," and "I'm Tore Down"—which became blues classics. His influence was heard throughout blues and rock guitarists throughout the '60s. *—Stephen Thomas Erlewine & Cub Koda*

Freddy King Sings / 1961 / Modern Blues ♦♦♦♦♦
Great stuff from this influential Texas Bluesman—the haunting "Lonesome Whistle Blues," "I'm Tore Down," and other classics. From the B.B. King school, but with his own searing style of singing and playing, it's a must for fans of modern blues. *—George Bedard*

Let's Hide Away and Dance Away / 1961 / King ♦♦♦♦♦
The classic first, all-instrumental, Freddy King album, it was monstrously influential to succeeding generations of great artists. *—Bill Dahl*

Freddie King Is a Blues Master / 1969 / Atlantic ♦♦♦

Getting Ready / Apr. 1971 / Shelter ♦♦♦
The first of King's three albums for Leon Russell's Shelter label set the tone for his work for the company: competent electric blues with a prominent rock/soul influence. King sings and plays well, but neither the sidemen nor the material challenge him to scale significant heights. Part of the problem is that Freddie himself wrote none of the songs, which are divided between Chicago blues standards and material supplied by Leon Russell and Don Nix. The entire album is included on the compilation *King of the Blues. —Richie Unterberger*

The Texas Cannonball / May 1972 / Shelter ♦♦♦
Similar to his first Shelter outing (*Getting Ready*), but with more of a rock feel. That's due as much to the material as the production. Besides covering tunes by Jimmy Rogers, Howlin' Wolf, and Elmore James, King tackles compositions by Leon Russell and, more unexpectedly, Bill Withers, Isaac Hayes-David Porter, and John Fogerty (whose "Lodi" is reworked into "Lowdown in Lodi"). King's own pen remained virtually in retirement, as he wrote only one of the album's tracks. Reissued in its entirety on *King of the Blues. —Richie Unterberger*

Woman Across the River / Jun. 1973 / Shelter ♦♦♦
King's last Shelter album was his most elaborately produced, with occasional string arrangements and female backups vocals, although these didn't really detract from the net result. Boasting perhaps heavier rock elements than his other Shelter efforts, it was characteristically divided between blues standards (by the likes of Willie Dixon and Elmore James), Leon Russell tunes, and more R&B/soul-inclined material by the likes of Ray Charles and Percy Mayfield. It's been reissued, along with his other Shelter albums, on the *King of the Blues* anthology. *—Richie Unterberger*

Burglar / 1974 / BGO ♦♦♦
This even more rock-oriented album is still quite powerful. *—Bill Dahl*

Just Pickin' / 1986 / Modern Blues ♦♦♦♦♦
Both of Freddy's all-instrumental albums for the King label (*Let's Hide Away and Dance Away with Freddy King* and *Freddy King Gives You a Bonanza of Instrumentals*) on one compact disc. "Hide Away," "The Stumble" and "San-Ho-Zay" are the numbers that made King's rep and influenced guitarists on both sides of the Atlantic. *—Cub Koda*

★ **Hide Away: The Best of Freddie King** / 1993 / Rhino ♦♦♦♦♦
Although not always placed in the upper echelon of blues performers alongside the other Kings (B.B. and Albert), Freddie King was a dynamo. He was both a powerhouse, imaginative guitarist and a glorious, soulful vocalist who could belt out come-ons, shout with gusto or wail in anguish. His instrumentals were also catchy, usually simply structured but vigorous and vividly articulated. This tremendous 20-cut sampler includes familiar hits like "Going Down" and the title cut, plus the shattering "Have You Ever Loved A Woman" and the poignant "Lonesome Whistle Blues." The tracks are exquisitely remastered and intelligently sequenced, and the notes are informative and thorough without being academic or fawning. *—Ron Wynn*

Live at the Electric Ballroom, 1974 / Feb. 20, 1996 / Black Top ♦♦♦

The Best of the Shelter Years / Jun. 20, 2000 / Capitol ♦♦♦♦
King's Shelter years were covered in toto on the 1995 double-CD *King of the Blues,* which had everything from all three of his Shelter albums and then some. Although all of the 18 songs on this single-disc anthology were on *King of the Blues,* this is a more manageable survey of the same era. Not an era, it should be said, that was King's best, with more ordinary material and less canny production than was used on his best earlier work. It does, however, have some of the better cuts from his 1970s recordings, such as "Going Down," "Lowdown in Lodi," the string-drenched Leon Russell tune "Help Me Through the Day," the brassy instrumental "Guitar Boogie," and covers of chestnuts like "Reconsider Baby," "I'd Rather Be Blind," and "Please Send Me Someone to Love." *—Richie Unterberger*

Eddie Kirkland

b. Aug. 16, 1928, Jamaica
Vocals, Harmonica, Guitar / Electric Blues, Modern Electric Blues, Soul-Blues
How many Jamaican-born bluesmen have recorded with John Lee Hooker and toured with Otis Redding— It's a safe bet there's only one: Eddie Kirkland, who's engaged in some astonishing onstage acrobatics over the decades (like standing on his head while playing guitar on TV's *Don Kirshner's Rock Concert*).

But you won't find any ersatz reggae grooves cluttering Kirkland's work. He was brought up around Dothan, AL, before heading north to Detroit in 1943. There he hooked up with Hooker five years later, recording with him for several firms as well as under his own name for RPM in 1952, King in 1953, and Fortune in 1959. Tru-Sound Records, a Prestige subsidiary, invited Kirkland to Englewood Cliffs, NJ, in 1961-62 to wax his first album, *It's the Blues Man!* The polished R&B band of saxist King Curtis crashed head on into Kirkland's intense vocals, raucous guitar and harmonica throughout the exciting set.

Exiting the Motor City for Macon, GA, in 1962, Kirkland signed on with Otis Redding as a sideman and show opener not long thereafter. Redding introduced Kirkland to Stax/Volt co-owner Jim Stewart, who flipped over Eddie's primal dance workout "The Hawg." It was issued on Volt in 1963, billed to Eddie Kirk. By the dawn of the 1970s, Kirkland was recording for Pete Lowry's Trix label; he also waxed several CDs for Deluge in the '90s. *—Bill Dahl*

It's the Blues Man! / 1961 / Original Blues Classics ♦♦♦♦♦
Wildman guitarist/harpist Kirkland brought his notoriously rough-hewn attack to this vicious 1962 album for Tru-Sound, joined by a very accomplished combo led by saxman extarordinaire King Curtis and including guitarist Bill Doggett. As the crew honed in on common stylistic ground, the energy levels soared sky-high, Kirkland roaring "Man of Stone," "Train Done Gone," and "I Tried" with ferocious fervor. *—Bill Dahl*

Have Mercy / 1988 / Evidence ♦♦♦
Kirkland's roaring guitar and garbled, gospel-tinged vocals are pretty much submerged in the mix here, a hodge podge of standard blues readymades and hyperactive funk-blues workouts. *—Cub Koda*

● **Three Shades of the Blues** / 198 / Relic/Original Blues Classics ♦♦♦♦♦
Kirkland's eight sides on this compilation are as hard-driving and intense as you could possibly ask for. It also includes four sides each from B.B. King-disciple Mr. Bo and the Ohio Untouchables, with dazzling guitar work from Robert Ward on the latter. *—Cub Koda*

Some Like It Raw / Sep. 1993 / Deluge ♦♦♦
Recorded live at a blues bar in Vancouver, British Columbia, this finds Kirkland in typical latter day form, full of buzzy guitar, garbled vocals, and loads of intensity. Alternating between original material (most of it in a soul-funk vein) and blues classics (few of which bear much likeness to their original counterparts), Kirkland gets solid support from the young, white backing band here and the recording quality is quite good. *—Cub Koda*

Complete Trix Recordings / Oct. 26, 1999 / 32 Jazz ♦♦♦♦

Koerner, Ray & Glover

f. 196?, Minneapolis, MN
Group / Blues Revival, Acoustic Blues
In today's climate of a blues band seemingly on every corner with "the next Stevie Ray Vaughan" being touted every other minute, it's hard to imagine a time when being a White blues singer was considered kind of a novelty. But in those heady times of the early '60s and the folk and blues revival, that's *exactly* how it was. But into this milieu came three young men who knew it, understood it, and could play and sing it; their names were Koerner, Ray and Glover. They were folkies, to be sure, but the three of them did a lot—both together and separately—to bring the blues to a White audience and in many ways, set certain things in place that have become standards of the Caucasian presentation of the music over the years. Their breakthrough album, *Blues, Rags and Hollers*, released in 1963, sent out a clarion call that this music was just as accessible to White listeners—and especially players—as singing and strumming several choruses of "Aunt Rhody." *—Cub Koda*

● **Blues Rags and Hollers** / 1963 / Red House ♦♦♦♦♦
Blues Rags and Hollers, the first album from Koerner Ray & Glover, follows through on the folk and country-blues leanings of the blues revival. The result is a strong, catchy album that nevertheless sounds closer to folkies than the typical British blues record. *—Thom Owens*

Lots More Blues Rags & Hollers / 1964 / Red House ♦♦♦♦
John Koerner, Dave Ray and Tony Glover, who emerged from the same University of Minneapolis music scene that produced Bob Dylan, were the best white folk blues group of their day. This reissue of one of their influential mid '60s albums—which sounds at times like a cross between the Kingston Trio and Sonny Boy Williamson—provides ample evidence of that. Koerner and Ray were first-rate guitarists, Glover could play harmonica like nobody's business and they all sang with style, enthusiasm, and a dash of humor. Plus, they had great material, some from blues giants like Lead Belly and Memphis Minnie, but much of it original. Three cheers to the folks who put together this reissue so well. The 21 remastered tracks include all of the original album, plus five songs from the same sessions that got bumped from the LP due to the format's space limitations. The liner notes feature all the original commentary from critic Paul Nelson and an extensive new essay by Tony Glover. *—Jeff Burger*

Return of Koerner, Ray & Glover / 1966 / Red House ♦♦♦♦
The last in a series of three reissues of classic, folk-blues albums from Koerner Ray & Glover, this beautifully remastered 1965 collection is filled with the humor, rhythm, soulful vocals and top-notch material that made the outfit such a standout. Among the best of the 15 tracks: a reading of Lead Belly's "Titanic," about how boxer Jack Johnson narrowly avoided being on its doomed voyage; Koerner's irresistibly rhythmic "The Boys Was Shootin' It Out Last Night" and Glover's "Don't Let Your Right Hand Know What Your Left Hand Do," in which—to quote the liner notes—"Tony kicks the bass harp through some places you've never heard." If you like this kind of music, it's a safe bet that you'll love this album. *—Jeff Burger*

Alexis Korner

b. Apr. 19, 1928, Paris, France, **d.** Jan. 1, 1984, London, England
Vocals, Guitar / Blues Revival, British Blues, Blues-Rock, Electric Blues
Without Alexis Korner, there still might have been a British blues scene in the early 1960s, but chances are that it would have been very different from the one that spawned the Rolling Stones, nurtured the early talents of Eric Clapton and made it possible for figures such as John Mayall to reach an audience. The duo of Korner and guitarist Cyril Davies made their first record in 1957, and in early 1962, they formed Blues Incorporated, a "supergroup" (for its time) consisting of the best players on the early '60s British blues scene. In March of 1962 they opened their own club, which quickly began attracting large crowds of young enthusiasts, among them Mick Jagger, Keith Richards, and Brian Jones, all of whom participated at some point with the group's performances—others included Ian Stewart, Steve Marriott, Paul Jones, and Manfred Mann. In May of 1962, Blues Incorporated was invited to a regular residency at London's Marquee Club, where the crowds grew even bigger and more enthusiastic. John Mayall later credited Blues Incorporated with giving him the inspiration to form his own Bluesbreakers group. Record producers began to take notice, and in June of 1962 producer Jack Good arranged to record a live performance by the band. The resulting record, *R&B from the Marquee*, the first full-length album ever made by a British blues band, was released in November of 1962. *—Bruce Eder*

R&B from the Marquee / 1962 / Ace of Clubs ♦♦♦♦♦
Alexis Korner's Blues Incorporated's early, raw, unpretentious British take on American blues. The album shows a multitude of influences, from rural, country blues to the electric sounds of Chess Records, Sleepy John Estes to Willie Dixon and Muddy Waters. Note: The British Decca CD from the late '80s has four bonus tracks not on the original album, but the American Mobile Fidelity CD reissue from 1996 has yet another previously unreleased bonus track, a cover of Willie Dixon's "Built for Comfort," that Decca missed on its CD. *—Bruce Eder*

New Generation of Blues / 1968 / BGO ♦♦♦
A basically competent, though hardly enthralling, effort from the British bluesman that alternates between minimal, acoustic-flavored production and fuller arrangements with jazzy touches of flute and upright bass. Korner wrote about half of the material, leaving the rest of the space open for R&B/blues covers and adaptations of traditional standards. "The Same for You" has a strange, ever-so-slight psychedelic influence, with its swirling flute, fake fadeout, and odd antiestablishment lyrics. Korner's voice is (and always would be) a tuneless bark, but it sounds better here than it did on the first album to prominently feature his vocals (*I Wonder Who*, 1967). As such, this album is one of the best representations of Korner as a frontman. *—Richie Unterberger*

Bootleg Him! / 1972 / Warner Brothers ♦♦♦♦♦
The best of all the Korner anthologies, boasting unreleased tapes and a lot of interesting one-off recordings from the various nooks and crannies of his career. *—Bruce Eder*

Rocket 88 / 1981 / Atlantic ♦♦♦♦♦
This was the best record Korner had made since 1962, and featured a core membership of former acolytes—Charlie Watts, Jack Bruce, and Ian Stewart. The sound is as much jazz as blues-influenced, it was all cut live on tour of Europe, and nobody involved ever sounded better, happier, or more relaxed. Not yet released on CD, and worth its weight in gold on vinyl, this was both Korner's and Stewart's final efforts. *—Bruce Eder*

● **The Alexis Korner Collection** / 1988 / Castle ♦♦♦♦♦
Castle's *Alexis Korner Collection* is a good single-disc collection that does a nice job of summarizing Korner and his various supporting bands throughout his career. Along the way, most of his popular songs and a healthy selection of his best material are showcased, making this an excellent introduction to his prodigious body of work. *—Thom Owens*

Best of Alexis Korner / Jul. 11, 2000 / Castle ♦♦♦♦

Smokin' Joe Kubek

b. Texas
Vocals, Guitar / Modern Electric Texas Blues, Electric Texas Blues, Modern Electric Blues
Another young Texas axeman from the old school, Smokin' Joe Kubek issued his band's debut disc in 1991 on Bullseye Blues, *Steppin' Out Texas Style*. Kubek was already playing his smokin' guitar on the Lone State chitlin circuit at age 14, supporting such musicians as Freddie King. Soon, he formed his own band and began playing a number of bars across Dallas. In the '80s, he met guitarist/vocalist B'nois King, a native of Monroe, LA, and the duo formed the first edition of the Smokin' Joe Kubek Band. The Smokin' Joe Kubek Band began playing the rest of the southwest in the late '80s. In 1991, they signed to Bullseye Blues, releasing their debut *Steppin' Out Texas Style* the same year. Following its release, the band launched their first national tour. For the rest of the '90s, the Smokin' Joe Kubek Band toured the United States and toured frequently and issued records like 1993's *Texas Cadillac*, 1996's *Got My Mind Back* and 2000's *Bite Me*. *—Bill Dahl & Stephen Thomas Erlewine*

● **Steppin' Out Texas Style** / 1991 / Bullseye Blues ♦♦♦♦♦
Smokin' Joe Kubek's debut album is a delight. Kubek leads his band through a set of smoking hot Texas and Memphis blues, delivered with passion—they can play this music with precision, but they choose to be looser and more fun than most traditionalists. Kubek's a skillful guitarist and B'Nois King, his vocalist and rhythm guitarist, can play nearly as well and their duels are the high watermark of an already wonderful album. *—Thom Owens*

Chain Smokin' Texas Style / 1992 / Bullseye Blues ♦♦♦
Smokin' Joe Kubek is pure Texas blues—he's a forceful guitarist and his band rocks with a loose, greasy vibe. What makes the album so much fun is the combination of solid material and piledriving performances—it may follow a tradition, but it manages to be unpredictable. *—Thom Owens*

Texas Cadillac / 1993 / Bullseye Blues ♦♦♦♦♦
Smokin' Joe Kubek's third Rounder album juggles blues-rock originals with faithful, exuberant covers of Jimmy Reed, Willie Dixon, Muddy Waters and Little Walter Jacobs, among others. Kubek is a good, sometimes captivating guitarist and entertaining singer, if not the greatest pure vocalist, and the band rips through the 11 cuts in a relaxed, yet passionate fashion. But it's hard for any longtime blues fan to get excited over hearing another version of "Little Red Rooster" or "Mean Old World"; it's impossible to reinvent Delta, urban, Texas or West Coast blues. The solution is probably to make the best music you can and hope you hook those willing to listen to contemporary blues rather than spurn it for the originals. *—Ron Wynn*

Got My Mind Back / 1996 / Bullseye Blues ♦♦♦♦
There is no need for guest musicians when Smokin' Joe Kubek is around, for the explosive guitarist completely fills up the ensembles with distortions worthy of acid rock. Kubek is a fairly well-rounded player who occasionally leaves space and during at least two songs ("All the Love There Is" and "She's It") on this CD creates some surprising tones on his instrument (sounding like a keyboard on the former and playing 1970s-style wah-wah notes during the latter). With B'nois King contributing smooth but emotional vocals and bassist Paul Jenkins and drummer Mark Hays supporting Kubek, this is a tight group that probably puts on a killer live show. *—Scott Yanow*

Take Your Best Shot / Apr. 7, 1998 / Bullseye Blues ♦♦♦♦

Bite Me / Apr. 4, 2000 / Bullseye Blues ♦♦♦

Jonny Lang

b. Jan. 29, 1981, Minneapolis, MN
Vocals, Guitar / Blues-Rock, Modern Electric Blues
Modern blues in the '90s had a weird phenomenon of teenage blues guitarists rocketing to popularity with their first album. The entire trend culminated with Jonny Lang, a guitarist from Fargo, North Dakota, who released his solo debut album *Lie to Me* when he was 15. At the age of 12, he attended a show by the Bad Medicine Blues Band and began playing with the group. Several months later he had become the leader, and the newly re-named Kid Jonny Lang & the Big Bang relocated from Fargo to Minneapolis and released their debut album, *Smokin*, in 1995. The LP became a regional hit, leading to a major-label bidding war and culminating in Lang's signing to A&M Records in 1996. Early in 1997, his major-label debut, *Lie to Me*, was released to mixed reviews; *Wander This World* followed late the next year. *—Stephen Thomas Erlewine*

Smokin / 1995 / Oarfin ✦✦

Lie to Me / Jan. 28, 1997 / A&M ✦✦✦
Like his peers Kenny Wayne Shepherd and Chris Duarte, Jonny Lang is a technically gifted blues guitarist, capable of spitting out accomplished licks and riffs at an astonishingly rapid rate. That doesn't necessarily mean the album has much emotional weight—Lang can deliver the style, but not the substance, simply because he still needs to grow as a musician. Lang does boast an impressive array of licks and instrumental technique, but he needs something more to make *Lie to Me* a substantive record. *—Stephen Thomas Erlewine*

● **Wander This World** / Oct. 20, 1998 / A&M ✦✦✦✦
When reviewers heard a teenage Jonny Lang's debut album of 1997, *Lie to Me*, many of them commented on how mature the blues singer/guitarist sounded for his age. Similarly, Lang's second album, *Wander This World*, often sounds like it could have been the work of a man of 30. With David Z (known for his work with Prince) producing, the Midwesterner delivers an exciting sophomore effort that has as much to do with soul, funk and rock as it does with actual blues. Far from a purist, Lang takes an approach that is best described as Albert Collins, B.B. King and Luther Allison by way of Otis Redding, Stax Records and Eric Clapton. While "Angel of Mercy" and the moody "Cherry Red Wine" demonstrate his mastery of the 12-bar format, most of the other selections aren't actual 12-bar blues, but rather Southern-style soul, funk or rock with a wealth of blues feeling. Lovers of 1960s Memphis soul should appreciate "Walking Away" and "Second Guessing," while "The Levee" and "Still Raining" have more of a rock orientation. The haunting title song finds Lang singing a little *too* convincingly about loneliness—even though Lang didn't actually write the lyrics, hearing an adolescent sounding so world-weary and isolated is rather disconcerting. There's nothing even remotely bubblegum about this excellent CD, which proves that Lang's supporters had every right to be enthusiastic. *—Alex Henderson*

Lazy Lester

b. Jun. 20, 1933, Torras, LA
Washboard, Vocals, Percussion, Harmonica, Guitar / Swamp Blues, Harmonica Blues
His colorful sobriquet (supplied by prolific south Louisiana producer J.D. Miller) to the contrary, harpist Lazy Lester swears he never was all that lethargic. But he seldom was in much of a hurry either, although the relentless pace of his Excello Records swamp blues classics "I'm a Lover Not a Fighter" and "I Hear You Knockin'" might contradict that statement too. His entree into playing professionally arrived quite by accident: while riding on a bus sometime in the mid-'50s, he met guitarist Lightnin' Slim, who was searching fruitlessly for an AWOL harpist. The two's styles meshed seamlessly, and Lester became Slim's harpist of choice. In 1956, Lester stepped out front at Miller's Crowley, LA studios for the first time. During an extended stint at Excello that stretched into 1965, he waxed such gems as "Sugar Coated Love," "If You Think I've Lost You," and "The Same Thing Could Happen to You." Lester proved invaluable as an imaginative sideman for Miller, utilizing everything from cardboard boxes and claves to whacking on newspapers in order to locate the correct percussive sound for the producer's output. Lester gave up playing for almost two decades (and didn't particularly miss it, either) before inaugurating a comeback that included a nice 1988 album for Alligator, *Harp & Soul*. *—Bill Dahl*

☆ **True Blues** / 196 / Excello ✦✦✦✦✦
His original album collects the best of the early Excello sides. Includes "Sugar Coated Love," " "I Hear You Knockin', " and "I'm a Lover, Not a Fighter." *—Cub Koda*

Harp & Soul / 1988 / Alligator ✦✦✦✦
After a lengthy hiatus from the music business, Lester was in the midst of his comeback when he waxed this album for Alligator. The overall sound is redolent of those Louisiana swamp blues classics, but with a cannily updated contemporary edge that works well. *—Bill Dahl*

Rides Again / 1988 / Sunjay ✦✦✦✦✦
His original rediscovery album pairs him with English blues musicians, with surprisingly great results. *—Cub Koda*

Lazy Lester / 1989 / Flyright ✦✦✦✦
Alternate takes and unissued titles from the cache of producer J.D. Miller, whose tiny Crowley, LA studio was the prime site for recording swamp blues during the '50s and '60s. A fine companion to AVI's essential Lester compilation. *—Bill Dahl*

★ **I Hear You Knockin'!!!** / 1995 / Excello/AVI ✦✦✦✦✦
Southern Louisiana swamp blues doesn't get more infectious or atmospheric than in the hands of Lazy Lester, whose late-'50s/early-'60s catalog for Excello Records (produced by the legendary J.D. Miller) is splendidly summarized with the 30 sides here. Lester's insistent harp and laconic vocals shine brightly on the rollicking "I'm a Lover, Not a Fighter," "Sugar Coated Love," "I Hear You Knockin'," and "If You Think I've Lost You," serving to help define the genre's timeless appeal. *—Bill Dahl*

All Over You / Oct. 6, 1998 / Antone's ✦✦✦✦
The last time Lester released an album was 1988's *Harp & Soul* on Alligator, an uneven affair. This 1999 effort for Antone's is a vast improvement with producer Derek O'Brien providing linchpin guitar support and fronting a band that includes stellar contributions from Mike Buck on drums and Sarah Brown on bass. Although the intervening years have added a bit of rust to Lester's vocal chops, the added graininess just enhances the performances of old chestnuts like "Strange Things Happening," "If You Think I've Lost You," "Irene," "I'm a Lover, Not a Fighter," "I Need Money," and "The Sun Is Shining." The classic Excello is called on for most of the album but the big surprise comes with two solo performances by Lester, singing and playing guitar on Lightnin' Slim's "Nothing but the Devil" and Lonesome Sundown's "My Home Is a Prison." His most cohesive album since his first for Excello. *—Cub Koda*

J.B. Lenoir

b. May 5, 1929, Monticello, MS, **d.** Apr. 29, 1967, Urbana, IL
Vocals, Guitar / Electric Chicago Blues
Newcomers to his considerable legacy could be forgiven for questioning J.B. Lenoir's gender upon first hearing his rocking waxings. Lenoir's exceptionally high-pitched vocal range is a fooler, but it only adds to the singular appeal of his music. His politically charged "Eisenhower Blues" allegedly caused all sorts of nasty repercussions upon its 1954 emergence on Al Benson's Parrot logo (it was quickly pulled off the shelves and replaced with Lenoir's less controversially titled "Tax Paying Blues"). Boogie grooves were integral to Lenoir's infectious routine from the get-go, although his first single for Chess in 1951, "Korea Blues," was another slice of topical commentary. From late 1951 to 1953, he cut several dates for Joe Brown's JOB logo; he waxed his most enduring piece, the infectious (and often-covered) "Mama Talk to Your Daughter," in 1954 for Al Benson's Parrot label. Lenoir's 1954-55 Parrot output and 1955-58 Checker catalog contained a raft of terrific performances, including a humorously defiant "Don't Touch My Head" (detailing his brand-new process hairdo) and "Natural Man." Lenoir's sound was unique: saxes (usually Alex Atkins and Ernest Cotton) wailed in unison behind Lenoir's boogie-driven rhythm guitar as drummer Al Galvin pounded out a rudimentary backbeat everywhere but where it customarily lays. Somehow, it all fit together. *—Bill Dahl*

Natural Man / 1968 / MCA/Chess ✦✦✦✦✦
This collection of J.B.'s mid-'50s tenure at the label—originally issued in the '70s—duplicates two songs from the Parrot collection (a label which Chess later acquired), but the rest of it is more than worth the effort to seek out. The rocking "Don't Touch My Head," the topical "Eisenehower Blues" and the sexually ambiguous, chaotic and cool title track are but a few of the magical highlights aboard. Either this or the Parrot sides will do in a pinch, but I can't imagine being without either one. *—Cub Koda*

★ **The Parrot Sessions, 1954-55: Vintage Chicago Blues** / 1989 / Relic ✦✦✦✦✦
Lenoir's sound really got locked in during this period, using twin saxes, himself on boogie rhythm guitar (with an occasional minimal solo), revolving piano, and bass stools and Al Gavin—certainly the strangest of all Chicago drummers—constantly turning the beat around. This is Lenoir at his creative and performing best, including his best-known songs "Mama Talk to Your Daughter" (with the famous "one note for 12 bars" guitar solo), "Eisenhower Blues," and "Give Me One More Shot," where Gavin starts out the tune on the wrong beat, gets on the right beat by mistake, then "corrects" himself! Lyrics as metaphorically powerful as any in the blues against grooves alternating between low-down slow ones and Lenoir's patented boogie. *—Cub Koda*

His J.O.B. Recordings 1951-1954 / 1991 / Paula/Flyright ✦✦✦✦✦
These are Lenoir's earliest sides in a very stripped down setting compared to the Parrot and Chess sides. Over half of the 14 sides feature Lenoir on guitar with only Sunnyland Slim on piano and Alfred Wallace on drums in support, with J.T. Brown on tenor sax aboard for the next session. They all suffer from a curiously muffled sound, but early delights like "The Mojo (Boogie)" and "Let's Roll" make all audio points mute. This CD also includes seven tracks fronted by Sunnyland Slim recorded the same day with Lenoir in a supporting role. *—Cub Koda*

Vietnam Blues: The Complete L&R Recordings / 1995 / Evidence ✦✦✦✦✦

Furry Lewis (Walter Lewis)

b. Mar. 6, 1893, Greenwood, MS, **d.** Sep. 14, 1981, Memphis, TN
Vocals, Harmonica, Guitar / Blues Revival, Piedmont Blues, Acoustic Memphis Blues, Acoustic Blues
Furry Lewis was the only blues singer of the 1920s to achieve major media attention in the 1960s and '70s. One of the most recorded of Memphis-based guitarists of the late '20s, Lewis's subsequent fame 40 years later was based largely on the strength of those early sides. One of the very best blues storytellers, and an extremely nimble-fingered guitarist right into his seventies, he was equally adept at blues and ragtime, and made the most out of an understated, rather than an overtly flamboyant style. Lewis's musical start took place on Beale Street in the late teens, where he began his career; he later started playing traveling medicine shows, and it was in this setting that he began showing off an uncommonly flashy visual style, including playing the guitar behind his head. Lewis's recording career began in April 1927, with a trip to Chicago to record for the Vocalion label. He seldom played with anyone else, partly because of his loose bar structures, which made it very difficult for anyone to follow him. The interplay of his voice and guitar, on record and in person, made him a very effective showman in both venues. Lewis's records, however, did not sell well, and he never developed more than a cult following in and around Memphis. A few of his records, however, lingered in the memory far beyond their relatively modest sales, most notably "John Henry" and "Kassie Jones—Parts 1 and 2," arguably one of the great blues recordings of the 1920s. His brand of acoustic country blues was hopelessly out-of-

style in Memphis during the postwar years, and Lewis didn't even try to revive his recording or professional performing career. At the end of the 1950s, however, folksong/blues scholar Sam Charters discovered Lewis and persuaded him to resume his music career. In the interim, all of the blues stars who'd made their careers in Memphis during the 1930s had passed on or retired, and Lewis was a living repository of styles and songs that, otherwise, were scarcely within living memory of most Americans. Audiences—initially hard-core blues and folk enthusiasts, and later more casual listeners—were delighted, fascinated, charmed, and deeply moved by what they heard. Gradually, as the 1960s and the ensuing blues boom wore on, Lewis emerged as one of the favorite rediscovered stars of the 1930s. *—Bruce Eder*

☆ **Complete Recorded Works (1927-1929)** / 1927-1929 / Document ✦✦✦✦✦
This release supplants both the Yazoo *In His Prime* and the Wolf Records 1990 *Complete Works* reviewed in the first edition of this book. This time *everything* that Lewis recorded for Victor and Vocalion during those extraordinary two years of work during the 1920's has been gathered together, including both parts of "Kassie Jones." The sound has been improved as well, and the notes are decent if, as is usual with Document, unexceptional. But this is one instance where Document's release of the complete works of an artist are preferable to Yazoo's picking and choosing. *—Bruce Eder*

Back on My Feet Again / Apr. 1961 / Prestige/Bluesville ✦✦✦
An April 1961 session of traditional material such as "Shake 'Em on Down, " "John Henry, " "Roberta, " and "St. Louis Blues." The album has been combined with another 1961 LP, *Done Changed My Mind,* for the CD reissue compilation *Shake 'Em on Down. —Richie Unterberger*

Done Changed My Mind / May 1961 / Prestige/Bluesville ✦✦✦
A May 1961 session of traditional material along the lines of "Casey Jones" and "Frankie and Johnnie." It's been combined with a similar 1961 LP, *Back on My Feet Again,* onto one disc for the CD reissue compilation *Shake 'Em on Down. —Richie Unterberger*

☆ **Shake 'Em on Down** / 1972 / Fantasy ✦✦✦✦✦
A 20-song single CD reissue of Lewis's first modern commercial recordings, done for two Prestige/Bluesville albums (*Back on My Feet Again, Done Changed My Mind*) in April and May of 1961 at Sun Studios in Memphis. Lewis is in brilliant form throughout, his fingers nearly as fast and his voice as rich as they were 30-odd years earlier. The disc includes the definitive version of "John Henry" (not just Lewis's definitive version—*the* definitive version), one of the greatest vocal performances ever put on record and a guitar workout so dazzling that you'd swear there was more than one guy playing. What's more, with the extended running time available on tape (Lewis's sessions in the 1920s having been captured on 78 rpm discs with limited running times), he really stretched out here and obviously loves doing it. The slight reverb in the studio also gives Lewis a larger-than-life stature on this recording. *—Bruce Eder*

Fourth & Beale / 1975 / Lucky Seven ✦✦✦

★ **In His Prime (1927-1928)** / 1988 / Yazoo ✦✦✦✦✦
The best overview of Lewis's classic late-'20s sides, containing 14 songs from the period (though not "John Henry"), all of which are crisply remastered, showing off both his superb guitar playing and his brilliantly expressive singing (the vocal performance on "Falling Down Blues" alone is worth the price of the disc) to excellent advantage. A seminal part of any blues collection, as well as any collection of Lewis's material. *—Bruce Eder*

Jimmy Liggins

b. Oct. 14, 1922, Newby, OK, **d.** Jul. 18, 1983, Durham, NC
Vocals, Guitar / Memphis Soul, Jump Blues, Boogie-Woogie, R&B
Another of the jump blues specialists whose romping output can be pinpointed as a direct precursor of rock & roll, guitarist Jimmy Liggins was a far more aggressive bandleader than his older brother Joe, right down to the names of their respective combos (Joe led the polished Honeydrippers; Jimmy proudly fronted the Drops of Joy).

Inspired by the success of his brother (Jimmy toiled as Joe's chauffeur for a year), the ex-pugilist jumped into the recording field in 1947 on Art Rupe's Specialty logo. His "Tear Drop Blues" pierced the R&B Top Ten the next year, while "Careful Love" and "Don't Put Me Down" hit for him in 1949. But it's Liggins's rough-and-ready rockers—"Cadillac Boogie," "Saturday Night Boogie Woogie Man," and the loopy one-chord workout "Drunk" (his last smash in 1953)—that mark Liggins as one of rock's forefathers. His roaring sax section at Specialty was populated by first-rate reedmen such as Harold Land, Charlie "Little Jazz" Ferguson, and the omnipresent Maxwell Davis.

Liggins left Specialty in 1954, stopping off at Aladdin long enough to wax the classic-to-be "I Ain't Drunk" (much later covered by Albert Collins) before fading from the scene. *—Bill Dahl*

● **Jimmy Liggins And His Drops of Joy** / 1989 / Specialty ✦✦✦✦✦
The music of Jimmy Liggins differs greatly from his elder brother Joe's in many respects. Whereas Joe was a more schooled musician, Jimmy was harder, brasher and altogether from the rougher and cruder side of the street. This 25-track collection brings together all the notable tracks Jimmy recorded for Art Rupe's Specialty label between 1947 and 1954. The music Liggins made during his stay at the label produced several R&B hits, most notably the jump-blues perennial "Drunk" (complete with crudely overdubbed lead vocal) and the proto-rock & roll classic "Cadillac Boogie," which in turn provided the basis for Jackie Brenston's "Rocket 88." *—Cub Koda*

Rough Weather Blues, Vol. 2 / 1992 / Specialty ✦✦✦✦✦
Twenty-five more Specialty cookers, including an undubbed version of "Drunk," plenty of horn-leavened jump blues outings, and several unissued artifacts (including a rare example of the Drops of Joy getting jazzy on "Now's the Time"). *—Bill Dahl*

Joe Liggins

b. Jul. 9, 1915, Guthrie, OK, **d.** Aug. 1, 1987, Lynwood, CA
Vocals, Piano / Jump Blues, R&B
Pianist Joe Liggins and his band, the Honeydrippers, tore up the R&B charts during the late '40s and early '50s with their polished brand of polite R&B. Liggins scored massive hits with "The Honeydripper" in 1945 and "Pink Champagne" five years later, posting a great many more solid sellers in between.

Born in Oklahoma, Liggins moved to San Diego in 1932. He moved to Los Angeles in 1939 and played with various outfits, including Sammy Franklin's California Rhythm Rascals. When Franklin took an unwise pass on recording Liggins's infectious "The Honeydripper," the bespectacled pianist assembled his own band and waxed the tune for Leon Rene's Exclusive logo. The upshot: an R&B chart-topper. Nine more hits followed on Exclusive over the next three years, including the schmaltzy "Got a Right to Cry," the often-covered "Tanya" (Chicago guitarist Earl Hooker waxed a delicious version) and "Roll 'Em."

In 1950, Joe joined his brother Jimmy at Specialty Records. More hits immediately followed: "Rag Mop," the number one R&B smash "Pink Champagne," "Little Joe's Boogie," and "Frankie Lee." During this period, the Honeydrippers prominently featured saxists Willie Jackson and James Jackson, Jr. Liggins stuck around Specialty into 1954, later turning up with solitary singles on Mercury and Aladdin. But time had passed Liggins by, at least right then; later, his sophisticated approach later came back into fashion, and he led a little big band until his death. *—Bill Dahl*

★ **Joe Liggins & the Honeydrippers** / 1989 / Specialty ✦✦✦✦✦
Pianist Joe Liggins presented a fairly sophisticated brand of swinging jump blues to jitterbuggers during the early '50s, when his irresistible "Pink Champagne" scaled the R&B charts. Twenty-five of his very best 1950-1954 Specialty sides grace this collection, including a tasty remake of "The Honeydripper;" "Rhythm in the Barnyard," and the syncopated "Going Back to New Orleans" (recently revived by Dr. John). *—Bill Dahl*

Dripper's Boogie, Vol. 2 / 1992 / Specialty ✦✦✦✦✦
An encore helping of 20 rarities by Joe Liggins from Specialty, dotted with unissued discoveries (including two versions of "Little Joe's Boogie" and "Hey, Betty Martin") from 1950-1954. *—Bill Dahl*

Lightnin' Slim (Otis Hicks)

b. Mar. 13, 1913, St. Louis, MO, **d.** Jul. 24, 1974, Detroit, MI
Vocals, Guitar / Swamp Blues, Louisiana Blues
The acknowledged kingpin of the Louisiana school of blues, Lightnin' Slim's style was built on his grainy but expressive vocals and rudimentary guitar work, with usually nothing more than a harmonica and a drummer in support. Combining the country ambience of a Lightnin' Hopkins with the plodding insistence of a Muddy Waters, Slim's music remained uniquely his own, the perfect blues raconteur, even when reshaping other's material to his dark, somber style. As the first great star of producer J.D. Miller's blues talent stable, the formula was a successful one, scoring him regional hits that were issued on the Nashville-based Excello label for over a decade, with one of them, "Rooster Blues," making the national R&B charts in 1959. After moving to Baton Rouge in the mid-'40s, Slim started to make a name for himself on the local circuit. He was broadcasting over the radio in the '50s when a local disc jockey persuaded the Excello label to record him, and he ended up with the label for 12 years. As the late '60s found Lightnin' Slim working and living in Detroit, a second career blossomed as European blues audiences brought him over to tour, and he also started touring with Slim Harpo as a double act. When Harpo died in 1970, Lightnin' went on alone, recording sporadically, while performing as part of the American Blues Legends tour until his death in 1974. *—Cub Koda*

★ **Rooster Blues** / 1987 / Hip-O ✦✦✦✦✦
When people talk about Louisiana swamp blues, *this* is what they're talking about. Excello Records' first foray into albums came with this wonderful collection of singles by Lightnin' Slim largely issued around the success of the title track, an R&B hit in 1960. "Long Leanie Mama," "My Starter Won't Work," "It's Mighty Crazy," "Hoo-Doo Blues," "Tom Cat Blues," "Lightnin' Troubles," "G.I. Slim" and "Feelin' Awful Blues" are all certified swamp blues classics and about as lowdown as the genre can get possibly get. With Lazy Lester on harmonica for the majority of the tracks here, the stripped-down approach to Slim's brand of blues casts these sides in a decidedly front-porch ambience with the added pulsating tape echo and oddball percussive effects just making everything on here sound even more doom-laden. "Lightnin's Blues," the John Lee Hooker-inspired "Just Made Twenty One" and "Sugar Plum," the A-side and both sides of his first and third singles for Excello, are the three bonus CD tracks appended to the original track lineup on this 1998 CD reissue. An essential blues purchase. *—AMG*

King of the Swamp Blues 1954-61 / 1992 / Flyright ✦✦✦✦✦
Lightnin' Slim true believers will want to take the extra time to search for this one. It's a 20-track collection that brings together a rash of alternate takes, previously unissued sides, studio warm-ups, and the like, all recorded by producer Jay Miller between 1954 and 1961. This is no bottom-of-the-barrel scrapings; Slim's outtakes can sometimes be better than some of the later sides released on Excello. Listeners are treated to an unreleased track from what is believed to be Slim's audition for Miller, a bare-bones reading of Jimmy Rogers' "That's All Right." One of the few examples of Slim recording without a supporting harmonica, the starkness of his guitar and vocal against the rudimentary drums of disc jockey Ray "Diggy Doo" Meaders makes this the track that fans of the lowdown will enthusiastically embrace. Another unreleased song from the same tape is an original, "Love Me for Myself," which features Lightnin's guitar front and center doing rare fills in the upper register between vocal lines. Several more sides emanate from these first sessions in 1954, including a wobbly tape reel alternate of his first record, "Bad Luck," and Slim in support of harmonica ace Wild Bill Phillips. Phillips' amplified harp tone is huge and distorted on the rocking "Paper in My Shoe" and Slim encores the same supporting role behind Schoolboy Cleve on three tracks. Five al-

ternate takes illustrate how Miller and the artists shaped material for release in his Crowley, LA, studio, but mavens of unreleased material will revel in the studio warm-up of "Don't Mistreat Me" where Slim breaks a guitar string in mid-song and starts cussing out his guitar. Certainly not the place to start with this artist, but an interesting addition to his recorded legacy that hardcore fans will definitely want to pick up. *—Cub Koda*

I'm Evil / 1995 / Excello/AVI ✦✦✦✦✦
A goldmine of 27 1950s and '60s obscurities from one of the lonesomest bayou blues greats ever. Filled with alternate takes and outright unissued efforts, *I'm Evil* reverberates with low-down treatises that cut to the the heart and soul of the swamp. "Bad Luck, " "Mean Ol' Lonesome Train, " and "Rock Me Mama" are pure, unadulterated Louisiana blues of the highest order. *—Bill Dahl*

Nothing But the Devil / 1996 / Ace ✦✦✦✦✦
This 24-song collection undoubtedly overlaps with some of the U.S.-issued Excello material—including the same alternate takes of "Rooster Blues" and "It's Mighty Crazy"—but there's just enough that they don't share to make this worth a look, if not a purchase, by owners of the U.S. material. The sound, as is usual with Ace, is excellent, and the stuff is worthy of inclusion with the best of Slim's work. Among the best tracks here are two outtakes unique to this set at this time, "I'm Leavin' You Baby," on which Slim steps over into Howlin' Wolf territory ("Moanin' at Midnight," etc.), and "Sweet Little Woman," where he crosses swords with Sonny Boy Williamson II. *—Bruce Eder*

The Best of Lightnin' Slim / Jul. 27, 1999 / Hip-O ✦✦✦✦
Whether the 16 tracks collected here represent Slim's absolute best is open to debate. Here are 16 performances issued on ten different singles during his heyday at Excello, covering a time frame from of 1956 to 1962. What this package *does* do is provide a nice addition to Slim's *Rooster Blues* record, with only three of the tunes from that album duplicated here. Tracks like "Bad Luck and Trouble," "I'm a Rollin' Stone," "Nothin' but the Devil," and "Cool Down Baby" catch Lightnin' in peak form, and the later tracks like "Winter Time Blues" and "I'm Evil" rock with a heavier guitar intensity. Once you get hooked into Lightnin' Slim, you're going to want it all, and here's a great little stop along the way. *—Cub Koda*

Lil' Ed & the Blues Imperials (Lil' Ed Williams)

f. 1975, Chicago, IL
Vocals, Guitar / Modern Electric Chicago Blues, Modern Electric Blues
Lil' Ed and the Blues Imperials are among the premiere party bands to have come out of Chicago during the '80s. Often compared to Elmore James and Hound Dog Taylor, firey, flamboyant slide guitarist Lil' Ed Williams and his group play dedicated, rough-edged and hard-rocking dance music and have established an international reputation. Signing to Alligator in the mid-'80s, they released their debut album, *Roughhousin',* in 1986 and found themselves receiving national attention. They began playing urban clubs and festivals all over the country and eventually toured Canada, Europe and Japan. They released their second album, *Chicken, Gravy & Biscuits,* in 1989 and the success continued as the Blues Imperials began appearing with such artists as Koko Taylor and Elvin Bishop during the Alligator Records 20th Anniversary Tour. If Ed, half brother Pookie Young, and the latest members of the revamped Blues Imperials never do much to modernize their blues or develop a new sound, that will be just fine with the band's growing legion of followers ("Ed Heads," no less), to whom the raucous, rocking slide guitar heritage of J.B. Hutto (Williams' uncle), Hound Dog Taylor, and Elmore James is blues nirvana. *–Jim O'Neal & Sandra Brennan*

Roughhousin' / 1986 / Alligator ✦✦✦
Wild & greasy blues at its best, a two-song session for an anthology turned into an all-night, live-in-the-studio jam. Sounds like it was great fun. *—Niles J. Frantz*

● **Chicken Gravy & Biscuits** / 1989 / Alligator ✦✦✦✦✦
Wild, raw, rough-edged Chicago slide guitar blues, this is jumpin', partyin' music in the tradition of Hound Dog Taylor and J.B. Hutto (Lil' Ed's uncle). Recorded live in the studio with no overdubs, it includes nine original compositions plus covers of Hutto and Albert Collins tunes. *—Niles J. Frantz*

What You See is What You Get / 1992 / Alligator ✦✦✦
This group fits the bill for listeners who enjoy hard-driving good-time electric blues. Lil' Ed Williams only has an average voice but his slashing guitar works well with rhythm guitarist Mike Garrett and the rest of the quintet (which includes Eddie McKinley on tenor) is well rehearsed and spirited. The result is an above average set of rockish blues that, although not terribly distinctive, is sure to satisfy. *—Scott Yanow*

Get Wild / Jul. 13, 1999 / Alligator ✦✦✦✦

Mance Lipscomb

b. Apr. 9, 1895, Navasota, TX, **d.** Jan. 30, 1976, Navasota, TX
Vocals, Violin, Guitar / Songster, Country Blues
Like Leadbelly and Mississippi John Hurt, the designation as strictly a blues singer dwarfs the musical breadth of Mance Lipscomb. A sharecropper/tenant farmer all his life who didn't record until 1960, "songster" fits what Lipscomb did best. A proud, yet unboastful man, Lipscomb would point out that he was an educated musician, his ability to play everything from classic blues, ballads, pop songs to spirituals in a multitude of styles and keys being his particular mark of originality. With a wide-ranging repertoire of over 90 songs, Lipscomb may have gotten a belated start in recording, but left a remarkable legacy (eight albums in fifteen years) to be enjoyed. *—Cub Koda*

★ **Texas Sharecropper & Songster** / 1960 / Arhoolie ✦✦✦✦✦
Arhoolie's *Texas Sharecropper & Songster* is a recording made in 1960, during the blues revival. Prior to the blues revival, Lipscomb was an unknown, and his discovery was one of the positive by-products of the revival. He was a great country-blues man, and this is perhaps his greatest effort, capturing him running through a number of traditional songs. Most of the songs are augmented by his jackknife slide guitar, and all feature his raw, haunted vocals, which make these classic songs sound timeless. *—Thom Owens*

Mance Lipscomb: Texas Songster, Vol. 2 (You Got to Reap What You Sow) / 1964 / Arhoolie ✦✦✦✦✦
Mance Lipscomb was a great songster, someone who knew hundreds of songs and could deliver any and all of them in different but effective ways. He sang blues, spirituals, old folk numbers, and his own tunes. Lipscomb had few rivals when it came to telling stories, setting up situations, creating characters, and depicting incidents. This 24-song reissued disc from 1964 puts Lipscomb in a perfect context, ripping through various songs and talking about everything from drugs to domestic conflict and police worries to spiritual concerns. *—Ron Wynn*

Texas Blues Guitar / 1994 / Arhoolie ✦✦✦
A 15-cut disc issued in conjunction with the song transcription book *Mance Lipscomb: Texas Blues Guitar,* this is a fine introduction to the Texas bluesman's work, and includes acoustic performances of "Ain't It Hard, " "Motherless Children" and "You Got to Reap What You Sow." *—Jason Ankeny*

Captain, Captain: The Texas Songster / Apr. 21, 1998 / Arhoolie ✦✦✦
Eight of these 24 tracks come from an April 1966 session and were originally released on LP (on Arhoolie); the other 17 are previously unissued, five of them sourced from April 1966, the rest from 1960. It's entirely typical of Lipscomb's output: versatile, relaxed, and samey-sounding acoustic blues with some prominent ragtime and folk influences. The 1960 material doesn't boast fidelity as strong as the 1966 takes (though it's certainly adequate), and has more of a down-home flavor; the 1966 tracks sound more innocuous and front-porch-relaxed by contrast. *—Richie Unterberger*

Little Charlie & the Nightcats

f. 1976, San Francisco, CA
Group / Modern Electric Chicago Blues, Modern Electric Blues
Little Charlie and the Nightcats have been bringing West Coast clubgoers to their feet with their eclectic, blues-infused repertoire since the mid-'70s. Drawing from styles ranging from Chicago and jazzy West Coast blues to Texas swing to rockabilly to surf music and R&B, the Nightcats sing mostly original songs and are noted for their wry, satirical lyrics; they also perform adaptations of obscure older tunes. Although they primarily perform in California and Oregon, the Nightcats frequently tour across the continent, and have also toured Europe. Their lineup centers upon extraordinary harp player/songwriter/singer Rick Estrin and versatile guitarist Little Charlie Baty; Dobie Strange on drums and bass player Ronnie James Weber, who joined the Nightcats in the mid-'90s, round out the current lineup. *—Sandra Brennan*

All the Way Crazy / 1987 / Alligator ✦✦✦
This 1987 outing found the band in fine form with its usual mix of strong originals and choice covers. Estrin's harp work on "Poor Tarzan" shows him to be a blower of chops equal to shining guitar whiz Charlie Baty's mercurial flights. Baty, as usual, struts vintage approved tones and blows hotter than a flamethrower on "Suicide Blues," and sprays Magic Sam licks all over Bobby Guitar's "When Girls Do It." Another solid entry in this band's discography. *—Cub Koda*

Disturbing the Peace / 1988 / Alligator ✦✦✦✦✦
This 1988 outing is another seamless part of the thread that is this eclectic West Coast band, brimming with equal parts good humor and sensational playing. Charlie Baty tears into his guitar on the opener, "That's My Girl," and keeps the heat up throughout this set, turning in jazzy work on "My Money's Green," rockabilly licks galore on "She's Talking," and getting quite bluesy on the slow one, "V-8 Ford." Rick Estrin contributes explosive harp work on "Nervous," "I Ain't Lyin'," and "Don't Boss Me," plus vocals full of sly charm on every track along the line. If you like these guys, add this one to the shopping cart if you haven't already. *—Cub Koda*

The Big Break / 1989 / Alligator ✦✦✦

Captured Live / 1991 / Alligator ✦✦✦
This enjoyable live set captures the group's manic energy. *—Niles J. Frantz*

Night Vision / 1993 / Alligator ✦✦✦

Straight Up! / 1995 / Alligator ✦✦

● **Deluxe Edition** / Oct. 28, 1997 / Alligator ✦✦✦✦✦
Deluxe Edition is a wonderful 15-track collection that compiles all of the highlights from his first six albums for Alligator Records. Although a few of Little Charlie & the Nightcats' albums hold up as individual works, they've all been a little uneven, which means the appearance of this best-of collection is all the more welcome. Not only will it satisfy the needs of the curious, but fans who just want the cream of the crop will be thrilled with this record. *—Thom Owens*

Shadow of the Blues / Oct. 13, 1998 / Alligator ✦✦✦✦

Little Milton (Milton Campbell)

b. Sep. 7, 1934, Inverness, MS
Vocals, Guitar / Retro-Soul, Electric Blues, Electric Chicago Blues, Modern Electric Blues, Soul-Blues, R&B, Soul
One of the great blues guitarists, singers, and composers of all time, Milton began his recording career in Memphis with Sun Records in 1953. Small-label singles followed for Meteor and Bobbin before he landed at Chess records in Chicago in 1961. He became one of the best-selling blues artists of the '60s, with many hit singles, including a 1 R&B hit "We're Gonna Make It" and items such as "Feel So Bad," "If Walls Could Talk," and "Baby I Love You." There may be soap-opera elements in much of Milton's work, but it is always done with flair and good humor. While the mold was pretty much established during his Checker pe-

riod, it also worked with his later affiliations at Stax and Glades. His Malaco recordings (dating from 1984) bring the formula of strings, horns, and background vocals up to date, but the blues artistry of Milton still shines through. *—Bob Porter*

Sings Big Blues / 1968 / Chess ♦♦♦
This is one of the hottest collective blues albums of the '60s. *—Bill Dahl*

If Walls Could Talk / 1970 / MCA/Chess ♦♦♦♦♦
On *If Walls Could Talk* Little Milton continues to fuse blues with soul—if anything, the album leans toward soul more than blues. Supported by a band with a thick, wailing horn section, Little Milton sings and plays with power. Though there a couple of wonderful solos, the focus of the record is on the songs, which all sound terrific, thanks to Milton's compassionate vocals. *—Thom Owens*

Grits Ain't Groceries / Jan. 1970 / Stax ♦♦♦
Grits Ain't Groceries is another set of soul and R&B songs from the blues guitarist Little Milton, highlighted by the scorching title track. *—Thom Owens*

Greatest Hits [Chess/MCA] / 1972 / MCA/Chess ♦♦♦
Greatest Hits offers a good sampling of Little Milton's singles for Chess Records in the '60s, including the hits "We're Gonna Make It" and "If Walls Could Talk." It may be a little brief, but there are no bad songs on the record at all and it's an excellent introduction to the guitarist's talents. *—Thom Owens*

Waiting for Little Milton / 1973 / Stax ♦♦♦
Although Little Milton's Stax recordings aren't as blues-oriented as his classic Chess and Checker recordings, there are still plenty of things to recommend about them. Primarily, they're of interest because they focus on his soulful vocals and those vocals shine on *Waiting for Little Milton.* On the whole, the album is a little uneven—the songs aren't always first-rate and the production is a little too smooth—but the performances make it worthwhile for most dedicated fans. *—Thom Owens*

What It Is / 1973 / Stax ♦♦♦

Blues 'N Soul / 1974 / Stax ♦♦♦

Tin Pan Alley / 1975 / Stax ♦♦♦♦♦
Most of the guitarist's best soul/blues Stax sides of the 1970s with plenty of his crisp guitar. *—Bill Dahl*

Greatest Sides / 1984 / MCA/Chess ♦♦♦♦♦
Greatest Sides contains a few of Little Milton's best cuts—including "We're Gonna Make It"—but the packaging isn't very good and the songs are presented haphazardly. There might be some good music on *Greatest Sides,* but there are far better compilations to purchase. *—Thom Owens*

Playing for Keeps / 1984 / Malaco ♦♦♦

Back to Back / 1988 / Malaco ♦♦♦♦

★ **Sun Masters** / 1990 / Rounder ♦♦♦♦♦
While he was at Sun, Little Milton tried a variety of different sounds and styles—sounding like everybody from Elmore James and B.B. King to Fats Domino—which was all tied together by his raw, manic lead guitar. *The Sun Masters* collects many of Milton's absolute finest moments—he never again sounded quite as wild or reckless, either vocally or instrumentally, as he did here. *—Thom Owens*

Too Much Pain / 1990 / Malaco ♦♦♦

Greatest Hits [Malaco] / Sep. 5, 1995 / Malaco ♦♦♦
For fans of Little Milton's Chess, Checker, and Sun sides, his '80s records for Malaco aren't particularly attractive, since they are slicker and more polished. Nevertheless, he cut several first-rate songs for the label, songs that showcase his considerable guitar and vocal talents, and the majority of those songs are collected on *Greatest Hits.* It's a solid introduction to the latter part of Milton's career. *—Thom Owens*

Live at Westville Prison / Oct. 3, 1995 / Delmark ♦♦♦♦♦

★ **Greatest Hits (Chess 50th Anniversary Collection)** / Jun. 17, 1997 / MCA/Chess ♦♦♦♦♦
Milton Campbell was a blues chameleon in his early recording career for Sun and Bobbin, changing styles seemingly with every record he made. But he found his groove—a Bobby Bland-style R&B with a bluesy edge to it—when he came to Chess Records in 1963. These 16 tracks collect the highlights of his six-year tenure at the label, featuring the hits "We're Gonna Make It," "Who's Cheating Who?" and "If Walls Could Talk." The majority of the sides feature strong horn charts courtesy of Oliver Sain and Gene Barge, the core of Milton's sound during this period. The stylistic connection of Milton to Bland is no more stronger evidenced than on his cover of "Blind Man," but equal mention in the soulful department must go to the heart-wrenching ballad "Let Me Down Easy" and "Poor Man's Song," one of two songs collected here that Campbell had a hand in writing. Interesting updates of Little Willie John's "All Around the World" ("Grits Ain't Groceries"), Chuck Willis' "I Feel So Bad" and Rosco Gordon's "Just a Little Bit" complete the package. As part of MCA's Chess 50th Anniversary Series, this sweats the two-disc *Welcome to the Club: The Essential Chess Recordings* down to a perfect introductory package to this sometimes misunderstood (is he blues— soul— R&B?) artist. *—Cub Koda*

We're Gonna Make It/Little Milton Sings Big Blues / 199 / MCA/Chess ♦♦♦♦♦
This CD of two of Little Milton's classic, early-'60s titles for the Checker label, *We're Gonna Make it* and *Sings Big Blues,* features a nice variety of blues material and some stellar arrangements. Towering above it all, though, is Milton's powerful voice: a solid combination of gospel intensity and fluid phrasing that sprang from Roy Brown, moved through B.B. King, and found its way to both Bobby Bland and Milton, among others. The program features one of Milton's biggest hits "Were Gonna Make It" and other uptempo, blues-soul hybrids, like "Who's Cheating Who?" and "Can't Hold Back the Tears" (all benefiting from Milton's fine, sinewy guitar lines). On more traditional, yet vibrant blues cuts, Milton shows off his tremendous vocal control, seamlessly alternating between soft, earnest tones and guttural shouts on "Blind Man" and expertly blending jazz and blues phrasing on "I'm Gonna Move to the Outskirts of Town." Rounding out the set are some fine blues and soul covers, including B.B. King's "Sweet Sixteen," Lowell Fulson's "Reconsider Baby," James Brown's "Please, Please, Please," and Milton's reconfiguration of Guitar Slim's "Well I Done Got Over It" ("Ain't No Big Deal on You"). Everything is held together nicely by some of the most tasteful and tight arrangements you'll hear on a blues album, compliments of Phil Wright and tenor saxophonist James Carter. This two album CD is a great bargain when in print and a worthwhile purchase even if you already have one of Milton's career retrospectives from Chess. *—Stephen Cook*

Little Walter (Marion Walter Jacobs)

b. May 1, 1930, Marksville, LA, **d.** Feb. 15, 1968, Chicago, IL
Vocals, Accordion, Harmonica / Harmonica Blues, Electric Chicago Blues
Who's the king of all postwar blues harpists, Chicago division or otherwise— Why, the virtuosic Little Walter, without a solitary doubt. The fiery harmonica wizard took the humble mouth organ in dazzling amplified directions that were unimaginable prior to his ascendancy. His daring instrumental innovations were so fresh, startling, and ahead of their time that they sometimes sported a jazz sensibility, soaring and swooping in front of snarling guitars and swinging rhythms perfectly suited to Walter's pioneering flights of fancy. Walter joined forces with Muddy Waters in 1948; the resulting stylistic tremors of that coupling are still being felt today. Along with Rogers and Baby Face Leroy Foster, this super-confident young aggregation became informally known as the Headhunters. By 1950, Walter was firmly entrenched as Waters's studio harpist at Chess as well (long after Walter had split the Muddy Waters band, Leonard Chess insisted on his participation on waxings—why split up an unbeatable combination?). That's how Walter came to record his breakthrough 1952 R&B chart-topper "Juke"—the romping instrumental was laid down at the tail end of a Waters session. Suddenly Walter was a star on his own, combining his stunning talents with those of the Aces (guitarists Louis and David Myers and drummer Fred Below) and advancing the conception of blues harmonica another few light years with every session he made for Checker Records. From 1952 to 1958, Walter notched 14 Top Ten R&B hits, including "Sad Hours," "Mean Old World," "Tell Me Mama," "Off the Wall," "Blues with a Feeling," "You're So Fine," a threatening "You Better Watch Yourself," the mournful "Last Night," and a rocking "My Babe" that was Willie Dixon's secularized treatment of the traditional gospel lament "This Train." Throughout his Checker tenure, Walter alternated spine-chilling instrumentals with gritty vocals (he's always been underrated in that department; he wasn't Muddy Waters or the Wolf, but who was?). *—Bill Dahl*

☆ **The Best** / 1958 / MCA/Chess ♦♦♦♦♦
If there's a blues harmonica player alive today who *doesn't* have this landmark album in their collection, they're either lying or had their copy stolen by another harmonica player. This 12-song collection is the one that every harmonica player across the board cut their teeth on. All the hits are here: "My Babe," "Blues With a Feeling," "You Better Watch Yourself," "Off the Wall," "Mean Old World," and the instrumental that catapulted him from the sideman chair in Muddy Waters' band to the top of the R&B charts in 1952, "Juke." Walter's influence to this very day is so pervasive over the landscape of the instrument that this collection of singles is truly one of the all-time greatest blues harmonica albums, one of the all-time greatest Chicago blues albums, and one of the first ten albums you should purchase if you're building your blues collection from the ground floor up. *—Cub Koda*

Hate to See You Go / 1969 / MCA/Chess ♦♦♦♦♦
Another solid collection of tracks recorded between 1952 and 1960 that originally appeared in 1969 as part of the short lived Chess Vintage Blues Masters series. Three of the tracks overlap with the budget compilation *The Best of Little Walter, Volume 2,* but the other 12 are just too good to pass by because of a minor programming gaffe. Standout cuts abound just about anywhere the laser beam falls, but the set closer, the minor-key masterpiece "Blue and Lonesome," just may be the most emotionally terrifying masterpiece of Walter's illustrious career. *—Cub Koda*

The Blues World of Little Walter / 1988 / Delmark ♦♦♦
If you really want to hear what Little Walter sounded like in his pre-amplified days and early stages of development with the Muddy Waters band, this is the one to get. The title is a bit of a misnomer as Walter is featured more as a sideman to Baby Face Leroy, Muddy Waters and others on early Parkway, Regal and Savoy sides, but it's clear that Walter at this stage of the game should have been paying royalties to both Sonny Boys and Walter Horton in particular. One of the high points features explosive slide work from Waters on a pre-Chess version of "Rollin' & Tumblin'," as crude as a version as you'll ever hear and certainly not to be missed. Although many of these sides have appeared on other compilations (usually taped up off of old scratchy 78s), this one features superior sound taken from the original lacquer masters. *—Cub Koda*

☆ **The Essential** / Jun. 8, 1993 / MCA/Chess ♦♦♦♦♦
In many ways, this supplants the original single disc, *Best of Little Walter,* and appends it with 35 more classics of Chicago blues harp genius, although one track from the original 12-song lineup is (perhaps purposely) left off. If you want to start your Walter collection with a nice generous helping of his best, this one runs the entire gamut of his solo career, from the classic 1952 instrumental "Juke" up to the Willie Dixon-penned "Dead Presidents." 46 tracks, one dynamite booklet, nice remastering, a great value for the cash outlay involved and best of all, an album title that truly delivers the goods. *—Cub Koda*

Blues with a Feeling / Oct. 24, 1995 / MCA/Chess ♦♦♦♦♦
A 40-song double CD of material that didn't appear on *The Essential Little Walter.* Much of this is pretty rare, having only appeared on long unavailable singles or hard-to-get import LPs; almost a dozen, in fact, had not previously been officially released anywhere. Its appeal isn't limited to collectors, though. Anyone who likes a Little Walter greatest-hits anthology will like this almost as much, including as it does some excellent performances ("Flying Saucer," "Teenage Beat," "Who," "Crazy for My Baby," "Thunderbird") that don't appear on

The Essential Little Walter. The dozen or so alternate takes get closer to specialist territory, but even so they're worth hearing even if you're not a fanatic, sometimes varying substantially from the official versions. *—Richie Unterberger*

Confessin' the Blues / Nov. 19, 1996 / MCA/Chess ✦✦✦✦
This release is a little confusing, coming out as it does more than a year after the release of MCA-Chess's Little Walter rarities collection *Blues With A Feeling*, and two years after the double CD anthology set that contains most of the best parts of this collection. Still, for those who can't afford either of those pricey sets, this disc, coupled with the two best-of volumes, and the other Walter compilations, fills in some holes that are well worth filling. Made up of songs cut between 1953 and 1959—none of which had ever appeared on LP before the original 1974 release of this collection—the selection features Walter in his prime, playing alongside Robert Lockwood Jr. and Louis Myers or Luther Tucker on guitar (with Muddy Waters present, on slide, on one indispensable track, "Rock Bottom"), mostly Willie Dixon on bass, and Fred Below on the drums, with Lafayette Leake or Otis Spann on piano. His harp work was never than first rate during the era covered by this collection, and there are some top flight instrumentals featured, but the material (check out "Crazy Legs," with its dazzling interplay between Walter on harp and Louis and Dave Myers on guitars) here also features some of Walter's best singing, including the romantic "One More Chance with You," the quietly raunchy "Temperature," and "Confessin' the Blues." The sound, as is usual on these MCA-Chess reissues, is superb, although certain tracks, such as "I Got to Go," seem slightly compressed. *—Bruce Eder*

★ **His Best (Chess 50th Anniversary Collection)** / Jun. 17, 1997 / MCA/Chess ✦✦✦✦✦
As MCA reconfigures their Chess catalog, this 20-track single-disc compilation now takes the place of their original 12-track *Best of Little Walter* collection, a landmark blues album which had remained in print for over three decades. This collections reprises ten of those seminal tracks (leaving off the echoey "Blue Light" and "You Better Watch Yourself," the latter being available on the two-disc anthology *The Essential Little Walter*) and brings ten others cherry-picked from the catalog to the mix. If you've never experienced the innovative instrumental genius of Little Walter, classics like "Juke," "Off the Wall," "Mean Old World," "Sad Hours," "Blues With a Feeling," "My Babe," "Boom Out Goes the Light," "Last Night," "Mellow Down Easy" and "Roller Coaster" (written by Bo Diddley, who also guests on guitar) will come as a major revelation. These are the recordings that changed the sound and style of blues harmonica forever, and everyone who came after him was as influenced by him as jazz saxophonists were by Charlie Parker. Everyone who fancies themselves a blues harmonica player should have this one in their collection as an textbook instructional tool, while the rest of us can just bask in the glow of his genius. Essential first purchase doesn't even begin to describe it. *—Cub Koda*

Little Willie Littlefield

b. Sep. 16, 1931, Houston, TX
Vocals, Piano / Jump Blues, West Coast Blues, Boogie-Woogie, Piano Blues, R&B
Before he was 21 years old, Texas-born pianist Little Willie Littlefield had etched an all-time classic into the blues lexicon. Only trouble was, his original 1952 waxing of "Kansas City" (here titled "K.C. Loving") didn't sell sufficiently to show up on the charts (thus leaving the door open for Wilbert Harrison to invade the airwaves with the ubiquitous Jerry Leiber/Mike Stoller composition seven years later). Little Willie was already a veteran of the R&B recording wars by the time he waxed "K.C. Loving," having made his debut 78 in 1948 for Houston-based Eddie's Records while still in his teens. After a few more sides, he moved over to the Bihari brothers' Los Angeles-headquartered Modern logo in 1949. There he immediately hit paydirt with two major R&B hits, "It's Midnight" and "Farewell." At Littlefield's first L.A. session for King's Federal subsidiary in 1952, he cut "K.C. Loving," but neither it nor several fine Federal follow-ups returned the boogie piano specialist to the charts. Other than a few 1957-58 singles for Oakland's's Rhythm logo, little was heard from Little Willie Littlefield until the late '70s, when he began to mount a comeback at various festivals and on the European circuit. *—Bill Dahl*

● **It's Midnight** / 1979 / Route 66 ✦✦✦✦✦
Although it may be a little hard to find, *It's Midnight* is a valuable collection that contains the highlights from Little Willie Littlefield's recordings for Modern and Federal between 1949 and 1957. These recordings capture Littlefield at his best, rocking through a number of jump blues, R&B and blues songs, including "K.C. Loving," "It's Midnight," "Farewell" and "I've Been Lost." It's an excellent collection that should be reissued on compact disc. *—Thom Owens*

Going Back to Kay Cee / Feb. 7, 1995 / Ace ✦✦✦✦✦
Littlefield's stint with Federal was brief (1952-1954), and not nearly as commercially successful as his time with Modern prior to that. Nonetheless he did a good amount of recording in that period, from which 19 tracks emerged to form this CD retrospective of his Federal years. It, together with Ace's slightly more extensive overview of Littlefield's Modern era, *Kat on the Keys*, forms a satisfying document of his most productive years. The Modern stuff is a little more well-known, and though it's a close call as to which disc is better (not that you can't get both), the nod might go to *Going Back to Kay Cee* by a whisker, if only for the inclusion of Littlefield's most famous recording, the 1953 single "K.C. Lovin." This is the original model for the song that would be adapted into Wilbert Harrison's number one hit "Kansas City" and become a rock standard. Of course Federal wanted to milk that cow as much as it could, which is why a take of "K.C. Lovin'" was overdubbed with rockier instrumentation and retitled "Kansas City" on a 1959 single. That "Kansas City" single (which is actually not at all bad) is here too, along with a few "Kansas City" soundalikes. Actually, however, this is a pretty strong and (for the early-'50s piano blues genre) a fairly diverse set, including a couple of vocal duets with Little Esther and one with Lil Greenwood; some effectively brooding, but not dragging, blues such as "Blood Is Redder Than Wine"; and the strikingly unusual "(Please Don't Go) O-O-O-Oh," where Littlefield adopts an effective and unique gargling vocal style. Littlefield's vocals are wise and aged beyond his years, and his piano playing is fine throughout; the instrumental showcase for his boogie "Jim Wilson's Boogie" is superb. *—Richie Unterberger*

Kat On The Keys / Nov. 23, 1999 / Ace ✦✦✦✦✦
This is a 25-song compilation drawn from Littlefield's output for Modern between 1949 and 1952, including the sole hit he scored for that label, "It's Midnight (No Place to Go)." Littlefield is somewhat more obscure than many other artists mining a similar blues/R&B crossover field in Los Angeles studios in the early 1950s, such as Charles Brown, Amos Milburn, and Floyd Dixon. On the basis of the music here, Littlefield deserves to be in the same echelon as the aforementioned performers. He was a fine pianist who was skilled in the boogie woogie style and tempered for the times with a modern R&B influence. His use of triplets, according to the liner notes, influenced Fats Domino. He was also more versatile than some piano bluesmen of the era, and was comfortable with slow and melancholy-tinged ballads as well as jumping uptempo R&B tunes (the boasting "I Like It" is a standout). His singing was more easygoing than distinctive, but still had a relaxed charm. Many of the sides here were cut with some of the Los Angeles studio musicians—horn player Maxwell Davis, guitarist Johnny Moore, and others—that were instrumental in setting the paces for the jazzy, urbane R&B music of the early 1950s in L.A. The sound is very good, and is mastered from the original acetate lacquers, with only occasional (and slight) surface noise peeping through. The disc includes five previously unissued cuts (three of which are alternate takes). A second volume of Littlefield's Modern sides was in the works from Ace as of the 1999 issue of this collection. *—Richie Unterberger*

Robert Lockwood, Jr.

b. Mar. 27, 1915, Marvell, AR
Vocals, Harmonica, Guitar, Arranger / Delta Blues, Electric Delta Blues, Acoustic Blues, Chicago Blues
Robert Jr. Lockwood learned his blues first-hand from an unimpeachable source: the immortal Robert Johnson. Lockwood can still conjure up the bone-chilling Johnson sound whenever he so desires, but he's never been one to linger in the past for long—which accounts for the jazzy swing he often brings to the licks he plays on his 12-string electric guitar. Jazz elements steadily crept into Lockwood's dazzling fretwork, although his role as Sonny Boy Williamson's musical partner on the fabled KFFA *King Biscuit Time* radio broadcasts during the early '40s out of Helena, AR, probably didn't emphasize that side of his dexterity all that much. Settling in Chicago in 1950, Lockwood swiftly gained a reputation as a versatile in-demand studio sideman, recording behind harp genius Little Walter, piano masters Sunnyland Slim and Eddie Boyd, and plenty more. Solo recording opportunities were scarce, though Lockwood did cut fine singles for Mercury in 1951 ("I'm Gonna Dig Myself a Hole" and a very early "Dust My Broom") and JOB in 1955 ("Sweet Woman from Maine"/"Aw Aw Baby"). Lockwood's best modern work as a leader was done for Pete Lowry's Trix label, including some startling workouts on the 12-string axe that he daringly added to his arsenal in 1965. *—Bill Dahl*

Steady Rollin' Man / Aug. 12, 1970-Aug. 1970 / Delmark ✦✦✦
Sophisticated, mellow set cut in 1970 that occasionally gets a little too laidback. Lockwood's complex lead guitar work and aged-in-the-wood vocals are a delight, but guitarist Louis Myers asserts himself as soloist more than he should have in such a situation, making one yearn for more Robert Jr. riffs. *—Bill Dahl*

Contrasts / 1974 / Trix ✦✦✦✦✦
Robert Jr. Lockwood has never been a conventional musician or blues artist. This was one of a pair of spectacular albums done for Trix in the 1970s. Johnson's version of "Driving Wheel" maintains the spirit of Roosevelt Sykes' familiar rendition, but has his own compelling twists. Otherwise, the session featured Lockwood songs, and he demonstrated the probing, animated qualities that made him a legend and a survivor. *—Ron Wynn*

Hangin' On / 1979 / Rounder ✦✦✦
Two of the principal keepers of the Robert Johnson flame joined forces for a Rounder LP that's stunning in its non-conformity to what purists might like to hear from the two veterans. Jazz and swing influences invest much of the LP, the pair sharing vocal and guitar duties. *—Bill Dahl*

● **Plays Robert and Robert** / Nov. 28, 1982 / Evidence ✦✦✦✦✦
Lockwood in a beautifully recorded solo context (cut in France in 1982 for Black & Blue), doing what he does best—his own songs and those of his legendary mentor, Robert Johnson. Purists may quiver at Lockwood's use of the 12-string guitar as his primary axe, but he long ago made the instrument his own blues tool of choice, and he handles its nuances expertly. *—Bill Dahl*

Robert Lockwood / 1991 / Paula ✦✦✦✦✦
All 20 of these tracks were recorded for JOB in the early '50s, but only half feature Lockwood; the others are Johnny Shines solo sides. The title is a bit misleading; the Lockwood tracks, recorded in 1951 and 1955, mix genuine Lockwood solo performances with sides on which he supported Sunnyland Slim and Alfred Wallace. It's decent sparse, early Chicago blues, though not as good as the preceding Shines tracks on the disc. *—Richie Unterberger*

I Got to Find Me a Woman / Mar. 17, 1998 / Verve ✦✦✦✦✦
These 14 tracks, cut in 1996 when Lockwood was 81 years old, are among the most accessible music that he has ever laid down. Had this record, with its mix of spare, raw solos and duets, juxtaposed with full band pieces that thunder quietly or roar loud and clear, come out in the late 1960s, it might have been as big and important a record as anything cut by Muddy Waters—maybe more, since Muddy didn't get to make albums as strong and straightforward as this until the 1970s. Lockwood's playing (accompanied by B.B. King on two tracks) is bold yet articulate, on 12-string or six, electric or acoustic, and his singing is unrivaled, recalling Muddy Waters at his late-career peak for expressiveness if not power. The band backing him up really rocks, especially Richard Smith's electric bass, which anchors the rhythm section.

Most of the tracks are Lockwood originals, juxtaposed with new interpretations of songs by Robert Johnson, Roosevelt Sykes, Leroy Carr, et al., but his numbers don't suffer at all from the presence of those classics. *—Bruce Eder*

Complete Trix Recordings / Feb. 23, 1999 / 32 Jazz ✦✦✦

Just the Blues / Jul. 13, 1999 / Bullseye Blues & Jazz ✦✦✦
This brings together all the Lockwood-fronted tracks from his two Rounder albums with Johnny Shines. Lockwood shines on a brace of originals that range from jazzy to bluesy to proto-funk ("Here It Is, Brother") as well as tackling everything from Larry Darnell's swinging "For You My Love" to Leroy Carr's "Mean Mistreater." Featuring Lockwood in duo settings with Shines and with a full band of Cleveland regulars, this is a nice sampling of one of the blues' most exploratory musicians. *—Cub Koda*

Lonesome Sundown

b. Dec. 12, 1928, Donaldsville, LA, **d.** Apr. 23, 1995, Gonzales, LA
Vocals, Guitar / Swamp Blues, Louisiana Blues
Unlike many of his swamp blues brethren, the evocatively monickered Lonesome Sundown (the name was an inspired gift from producer J.D. Miller) wasn't a Jimmy Reed disciple. Sundown's somber brand of blues was more in keeping with the gruff sound of Muddy Waters. The guitarist was one of the most powerful members of Miller's south Louisiana stable, responsible for several seminal swamp standards on Excello Records.

The former Cornelius Green first seriously placed his hands on a guitar in 1950, Waters and Hooker providing early inspiration. Zydeco pioneer Clifton Chenier hired the guitarist as one of his two axemen (Phillip Walker being the other) in 1955. A demo tape was enough proof for Miller—he began producing him in 1956, leasing the freshly renamed Sundown's "Leave My Money Alone" to Excello.

There were plenty more where that one came from. Over the next eight years, Sundown's lowdown Excello output included "My Home Is a Prison," "I'm a Mojo Man," "I Stood By," "I'm a Samplin' Man," and a host of memorable swamp classics preceded his 1965 retirement from the blues business to devote his life to the church. It was 1977 before Sundown could be coaxed back into a studio to cut a blues LP; *Been Gone Too Long,* co-produced by Bruce Bromberg and Dennis Walker for the Joliet imprint, was an excellent comeback entry but did disappointing sales (even after being reissued on Alligator). Scattered live performances were about all that was heard of the swamp blues master after that. *—Bill Dahl*

Been Gone Too Long / 1977 / Hightone ✦✦✦
The Louisiana blues vet's 1977 comeback album was a well-done affair, capturing some of the flavor of his '50s material (but with a modern edge). Producers Bruce Bromberg and Dennis Walker (who doubled on bass) recruited guitarist Phillip Walker, a longtime Sundown cohort, to handle some of the fret load, and the predominantly original songlist was worthy of Sundown's lowdown sound. *—Bill Dahl*

Lonesome Sundown / 1990 / Flyright ✦✦✦✦
Twenty-one sides for producer J.D. Miller's Crowley, LA vaults, dominated by alternate takes of the guitarist's best-known sides and some otherwise unreleased numbers. Backing musicians include keyboardist Katie Webster, harpist Lazy Lester, and drummer Warren Storm. Tough stuff! *—Bill Dahl*

● **I'm a Mojo Man: The Best of the Excello Singles** / 1995 / Excello ✦✦✦✦✦
One of the swamp blues stalwarts in south Louisiana producer J.D. Miller's stable receives the deluxe treatment with a 24-song anthology spanning his 1956-1964 Excello tenure. Sundown's sparse, nasty sound was influenced by Muddy Waters as much as the prevailing bayou beat, giving an extra discernible tang to his "Leave My Money Alone," "My Home Is My Prison," and the title cut. *—Bill Dahl*

Willie Mabon

b. Oct. 24, 1925, Hollywood, TN, **d.** Apr. 19, 1985, Paris, France
Vocals, Piano / Piano Blues, R&B
The sly, insinuating vocals and chunky piano style of Willie Mabon won the heart of many an R&B fan during the early '50s. His salty Chess waxings "I Don't Know," "I'm Mad" and "Poison Ivy" established the pianist as a genuine Chicago blues force, but he faded as an R&B hitmaker at the dawn of rock & roll. Schooled in jazz as well as blues, Mabon found the latter his ticket to stardom. His first sides were a 1949 78 for Apollo as Big Willie and some 1950 outings for Aristocrat and Chess with guitarist Earl Dranes as the Blues Rockers. But Mabon's asking price for a night's work rose dramatically when his 1952 debut release on the Parrot logo, "I Don't Know," topped the R&B charts for eight weeks after being sold to Chess. From then on, Mabon was a Chess artist, returning to the top R&B slot the next year with the ominous "I'm Mad" and cracking the Top Ten anew with the Mel London-penned "Poison Ivy" in 1954. Throughout his Chess tenure, piano and sax were consistently to the fore rather than guitar and harp, emphasizing Mabon's cool R&B approach. He never regained his momentum after leaving Chess but recorded and toured Europe prolifically until his death. *—Bill Dahl*

● **Seventh Son** / 1993 / Charly ✦✦✦✦✦
Since MCA hasn't gotten around to this insinuating character's splendid Chess catalog as yet, we'll have to opt for a 16-song import that encompasses his three major hits "I Don't Know," "I'm Mad" (here in alternate take form, for whatever reason), and the Mel London-penned "Poison Ivy." Mabon's urban R&B approach was something of a departure for the Delta-rooted blues prevalent at Chess at the time, but his laconic vocals on "The Seventh Son," "Knock on Wood," and "Got to Have It" made him a star (albeit briefly). *—Bill Dahl*

Chicago Blues Session! / 1995 / Evidence ✦✦✦
Chicago Blues Session! features a session pianist Willie Mabon cut on Independence Day 1979 with guitarist Hubert Sumlin, guitarist Eddie Taylor, bassist Aron Burton and drummer Casey Jones. The album was originally released on the German LR label, mainly because American labels were shunning the blues. That could be the only reason this album wasn't released at the time, since it's a nice, straightahead Chicago blues record. There are several Mabon originals, all of them strong and memorable, plus several Willie Dixon tracks and a Howlin' Wolf cut. That Howlin' Wolf song is one of a handful of tributes to Chicago blues legends—the others are to Jimmy Reed and Willie Dixon—but the true tribute is the spirit and passion the group puts into their music. That's what makes the album a worthwhile listen for serious fans of Chicago blues. *—Thom Owens*

Lonnie Mack

b. Jul. 18, 1941, Harrison, IN
Vocals, Guitar / Instrumental Rock, Modern Electric Blues, Rock & Roll, R&B
When Lonnie Mack sings the blues, country strains are sure to infiltrate. Conversely, if he digs into a humping rockabilly groove, strong signs of deep-down blues influence are bound to invade. Par for the course for any musician who cites both Bobby Bland and George Jones as pervasive influences. Fact is, Lonnie Mack's lightning-fast, vibrato-enriched, whammy bar-hammered guitar style has influenced many a picker too—including Stevie Ray Vaughan, who idolized Mack's early singles for Fraternity and later co-produced and played on Mack's 1985 comeback LP for Alligator, *Strike Like Lightning.* While doing session work during the early '60s, Mack stepped out front to cut a searing instrumental treatment of Chuck Berry's "Memphis" and watched the single leap all the way up to the Top Five on *Billboard's* pop charts. The follow-up "Wham!" was another hit, though a major-label deal with Elektra led to three inconsistent albums. He worked in AR for awhile, then signed with Capitol to wax a couple of obscure country-based LPs. Finally, Mack returned with two albums on Alligator, 1985's Strike Like Lightning and 1987's Second Sight. Though he left for major-label prestige at Epic in 1988, Mack was back with Alligator for 1990's *Live! Attack of the Killer V.* *—Bill Dahl*

☆ **The Wham of that Memphis Man** / 1964 / Alligator ✦✦✦✦✦
This is a vinyl reissue of Mack's first album for Fraternity in 1964, the one thousands of guitarists cut their teeth on. Muddy Waters once sang, "The blues had a baby and they named the baby rock & roll." This is the album that proves it. Instrumental versions of R&B hits ("Memphis," "Susie Q," "The Bounce") rebound against heartfelt soul numbers ("Farther Down the Road," "Why?") right next to dazzling fretboard blues romps both slow and fast ("Wham!," "Down and Out"). Mack sings his rear end off, the band—with saxes and Hammond organ and pumping soul bass—is right in there and Mack's vibrato-drenched guitar stings, wounds, and amazes. It remains his defining moment. *—Cub Koda*

Glad I'm in the Band / 1969 / Elektra ✦✦✦
With the exception of his comeback album for Alligator, *Strike like Lightning,* nothing Mack has done since leaving Fraternity Records has come close to the wham-fisted brilliance of those seminal sides. This LP isn't bad at all, though—besides passable remakes of "Memphis" and "Why," Mack attacks Frankie Ford's "Roberta," Ted Taylor's "Stay Away from My Baby," and Little Willie John's "Let Them Talk" with a slightly rockier edge than his previous stuff. R&B vet Maxwell Davis did the horn charts. *—Bill Dahl*

Whatever's Right / 1969 / Elektra ✦✦✦

Strike like Lightning / 1985 / Alligator ✦✦✦
Co-produced by Stevie Ray Vaughn, this was Lonnie's ticket back to the show after a few years on the sidelines. To say it was an inspired date would be putting it mildly. With his batteries recharged, Mack was in peak form, playing and singing better than ever. A major highlight is an inspired duet between Stevie and Lonnie on "Wham (Double Whammy)," going toe to toe for several exciting choruses. *—Cub Koda*

Second Sight / 1987 / Alligator ✦✦✦

Attack of the Killer V: Live / 1990 / Alligator ✦✦✦

Lonnie on the Move / 1992 / Ace ✦✦✦✦✦
These 19 Flying V-soaked sides pack the same punch and hail from the same mid-'60s time-frame as Mack's seminal LP *Wham of That Memphis Man.* He unleashes his vibrato-drenched axe on the torrid "Soul Express," "Lonnie on the Move," "Florence of Arabia," and an astonishing instrumental version of "Stand by Me" that'll send aspiring guitarists' jaws crashing to the floor. For a change of pace, "Men at Play" mines a jazzy walking groove to equally satisfying ends. *—Bill Dahl*

★ **Memphis Wham** / Jul. 27, 1999 / Ace ✦✦✦✦✦
At first glance, this might seem like nothing more than a retread of the classic *The Wham of That Memphis Man,* as the disc includes all 14 songs from that album. This is a quality upgrade/supplement to that record, though, adding 11 more tracks of 1963-1967 vintage from both rare singles and previously unreleased outtakes. This is hardly filler that only collectors will care about; it's good stuff, sometimes ace stuff, that's almost all on the same level of *The Wham.* "Oh, I Apologize," a cover of an obscure Barrett Strong track, is white soul singing on par with Mack's best vocal efforts, while "Cry, Cry, Cry" is a great instrumental version of a Bobby "Blue" Bland number; both of these cuts, unbelievably, were not released prior to this CD. The singles "Say Something Nice to Me" and "Save Your Money" (from 1964 and 1967) are more filet of white soul, and "Tension Pts. 1 & 2" (a 1966 single) another cool roadhouse instrumental. Some of the rare add-ons are less essential than others (like the instrumental reading of the Beatles' "From Me to You"), but taken together it's certainly the best Mack collection, enhanced by Bill Millar's informative liner notes. By the way, in one of those inexplicable occurrences bound to cause collectors to run around in circles, the song titled "Farther on Down the Road" on *The Wham of That Memphis Man* recording is here titled "Farther on up the Road" and listed as previously unreleased, although in fact it seems to be the same track as the one given a different title on the LP. (To cause further confusion, Mack definitely sings the lyric "Farther on up the road, " not "Farther on down the road, " as it was originally titled.) *—Richie Unterberger*

Music Map

Blues History

African Roots

Work Songs, Field Hollers

Church & Gospel Music
Standard Quartette (rec. 1894)
Dinwiddie Colored Quartet (rec. 1902)
Apollo Male Quartette (rec. 1912)

Black Entertainment
Minstrel, Ragtime, String Bands

Medicine Shows
Papa Charlie Jackson – Pink Anderson
Daddy Stovepipe

Early Blues Recorders (ca. 1920)
W. C. Handy (1873-1958) – Perry Bradford (1893-1970)
Clarence Williams (1898-1965)

Songsters
Henry Thomas (1874-1950) – Frank Stokes (1888-1955)
Peg Leg Howell (1888-1966) – Leadbelly (1889-1949)
Mance Lipscomb (1895-1976) – Mississippi John Hurt (1893-1966)

Classic Female Blues Singers
Mamie Smith (1883-1946) – Ma Rainey (1886-1939)
Bessie Smith (1894-1937) – Lucille Bogan (1897-1948)
Sara Martin (1884-1955) – Clara Smith (1894-1935)
Ida Cox (1896-1967) – Sippie Wallace (1898-1986)
Victoria Spivey (1906-1976) – Chippie Hill (1905-1950)

Postwar Female Blues
Big Maybelle (1924-1972) – Big Mama Thornton (1926-1984)
Little Esther Phillips (1935)

Religious Music That Influenced Blues
Blind Willie Johnson (1900-1947)

Major Influences
Lonnie Johnson (1889-1970)
Blind Lemon Jefferson (1897-1929)

Piano Blues
Origins – 1890s Barrelhouses, Railroad & Lumber Camps
Clarence "Pine Top" Smith (1904-1929)
Cow Cow Davenport (1894-1955) – George Thomas
Henry Townsend (1929-1971) – Roosevelt Sykes (1906-1983)
Albert Ammons (1907-1949) – Meade "Lux" Lewis (1905-1964)
Big Maceo (1905-1953) – Sunnyland Slim (1907)
Peetie Wheatstraw (1902–1941) – Leroy Carr (1905-1935)
Johnnie Jones (1949-1964) – Otis Spann (1930-1970)
Pinetop Perkins (1913)

Mississippi Blues

Delta-Style Blues
Charley Patton (1887-1934) – Willie Brown (1900-1952)
Son House (1902-1971) – Robert Johnson (1911-1938)
Fred McDowell (1904-1972) – Bukka White (1906-1977)
Big Joe Williams (1903-1982) – Arthur Crudup (1905-1974)
Tommy McClennan (1908-ca. 1962)
John Lee Hooker (1917)

Jackson-Style Blues
Rubin Lacy (1901–1972) Ishmon Bracey (1901–1970)
Charles McCoy (1909–1950) Tommy Johnson (1896–1956)

Bentonia-Blues
Henry Stuckey (1897–1966) Skip James (1902–1969)
Jack Owens (1904)

Regional Down-Home Blues

Atlanta
Barbecue Bob (Robert Hicks) (1902-1931)
Blind Willie McTell (1901-1959) – Curley Weaver (1906-1962)
Buddy Moss (1906)

Piedmont School
Blind Blake (1890-1933) – Blind Boy Fuller (1908-1941)
Sonny Terry (1911-1984) – Brownie McGhee (1915)
Rev. Gary Davis (1896-1972)

Tennessee

Memphis Jug Bands
Gus Cannon's (1885-1979) Jug Stompers – Memphis Jug Band
Will Shade (1898-1966) – Noah Lewis (1895-1961)

Memphis
Furry Lewis (1893-1981) – Frank Stokes (1888-1955)
Robert Wilkins (1896-1987) – Memphis Minnie (1897-1973)

Brownsville, Tennessee
Sleepy John Estes (1899-1977)
Yank Rachell (1910) – Sonny Boy Williamson (1914-1948)

The End of World War II – The Rise of Live Blues Radio – "King Biscuit Time" – KFFA – Helena, Arkansas 1941

Sonny Boy Williamson II (Rice Miller) (1899-1965) – Robert Lockwood Jr (1915) – Willie Love (1906-1953)
Joe Willie Wilkins (1923-1979) – Houston Stackhouse (1910-1981) – Peck Curtis (1912-1970)
Doctor Isaiah Ross (1925) – Elmore James (1918-1963) – Hound Dog Taylor (1917-1975)

Music Map

Blues History

Chicago
The Bluebird Sound (mid '30s-late '40s)
Producer: Lester Melrose
Recorded:
Big Bill Broonzy – Washboard Sam (1935-1964) – Jazz Gillum
Tampa Red – Memphis Minnie – Walter Davis
Sonny Boy Williamson – Big Joe Williams – Arthur Crudup
Tommy McClennan – Henry Townsend (1909)

Chicago – Early Artists
Big Bill Broonzy (1893-1958) – Tampa Red (1900-1981)
Jazz Gillum (1904-1966) – Leroy Carr (1905-1935)
Big Maceo (1905-1953) – Robert Nighthawk (1909-1967)
Scrapper Blackwell (1903-1962) – Kokomo Arnold (1901-1968)
Sonny Boy Williamson (1914-1948)

Chess Records
Producer: Leonard Chess
Recorded:
Muddy Waters – Little Walter – Elmore James
Howlin' Wolf – Buddy Guy – Sonny Boy Williamson II
Jimmy Rogers

The Muddy Waters Band
Muddy Waters (1915-1983) – Little Walter (1930-1968)
Jimmy Rogers (1924) – Otis Spann (1930-1970)

The Howlin' Wolf Band
Memphis ca. 1952
Howlin' Wolf – Willie Johnson – Willie Steele

Chicago ca. 1954-1975
Hubert Sumlin – Henry Gray – Eddie Shaw
Sam Lay – Detroit Jr. – Jody Williams

2nd Generation Chicago Bands
Buddy Guy (1936) – Otis Rush (1934) – Junior Wells (1934)
James Cotton (1935) – Magic Sam (1937-1969)
Hound Dog Taylor (1917-1975) & the Houserockers

Postwar Chicago Harmonica
Little Walter – Big Walter Horton – Snooky Pryor
Jimmy Reed – James Cotton – Billy Boy Arnold
Junior Wells – George "Harmonica" Smith
Sonny Boy Williamson II

Jimmy Reed – Eddie Taylor

Modern Postwar Blues Guitar
T-Bone Walker (1910-1975)
B. B. King – Albert King – Freddy King

Texas Guitar
Clarence Gatemouth Brown (1924) – Lowell Fulson (1921)
Albert Collins (1932) – Johnny Copeland (1937)

Chicago Guitar
Mississippi-influenced:
Elmore James – Eddie Taylor – Johnny Young
Johnny Shines – Homesick James – Hound Dog Taylor
Earl Hooker – Joe Carter – J. B. Hutto – Louis Myers
B. B. King-influenced (West Side School):
Otis Rush – Magic Sam – Buddy Guy – Hubert Sumlin
Magic Slim (1937) – Son Seals (1942) – Lonnie Brooks (1933)

Jump Blues
Big Joe Turner (1911-1985) – Amos Milburn (1927-1980)
Roy Brown (1920-1981) – Wynonie Harris (1915-1969)

Texas Bluesmen
Smokey Hogg (1908) – Lightnin' Hopkins (1912-1982)
Lil Son Jackson (1915-1976) – Frankie Lee Sims (1917-1970)

West Coast
Jimmy McCracklin (1921) – Lowell Fulson (1921)
Percy Mayfield (1920-1984) – Jesse Fuller (1896-1976)
K. C. Douglas (1913-1975) – Floyd Dixon (1929)
Charles Brown (1920) – Johnny Otis (1921)
Jimmy Witherspoon (1923) – Pee Wee Crayton (1914)

Detroit
John Lee Hooker (1917) – Baby Boy Warren (1919-1977)
Bobo Jenkins (1916) – Eddie Burns (1928)
Eddie Kirkland (1928)

The Memphis Sound
Producer: Sam Phillips/Sun Records
Originally Recorded:
B. B. King – Howlin' Wolf – Bobby Bland – Junior Parker
Big Walter Horton – Joe Hill Louis – Willie Nix – Dr. Ross
Ike Turner – Roscoe Gordon

New Orleans
Professor Longhair (1918-1980) – Guitar Slim (1907-1975)

Zydeco
Clifton Chenier (1925-1987) – Boozoo Chavis
Rockin' Dopsie – Fernest Arceneaux

Louisiana (Excello Records)
Lightnin' Slim (1913-1974) – Slim Harpo (1924-1970)
Lonesome Sundown (1928) – Lazy Lester (1933)
Silas Hogan (1911)

Robert Pete Williams (1914-1980)

More Modern Blues – Mid '60s to present:
Country Blues (White Interpreters)
John Hammond (1942) – Dave Van Ronk (1936)
John Koerner (1938) – Rory Block
Some Electric Blues
Paul Butterfield (1942-1987) – Michael Bloomfield (1944-1981)
Taj Mahal (1940) – Johnny Winter (1944)
Elvin Bishop (1942) – Roy Buchanan (1939-1988)
Lil' Ed and the Blues Imperials – Roomful of Blues
Fabulous Thunderbirds – Stevie Ray Vaughan (1956-1990)
Robert Cray (1953) – William Clarke

Soul Blues
Junior Parker – Bobby Blue Bland (1930)
Little Milton (1934) – Little Johnny Taylor (1943) – Otis Clay
Z.Z. Hill (1940-1984)

Magic Sam (Samuel Maghett)

b. Feb. 14, 1937, Grenada, MS, **d.** Dec. 1, 1969, Chicago, IL
Vocals, Guitar / Blues Revival, Modern Electric Chicago Blues, Electric Chicago Blues, Modern Electric Blues, Soul-Blues
No blues guitarist better represented the adventurous modern sound of Chicago's West side more proudly than Sam Maghett. He died tragically young (at age 32 of a heart attack), right when he was on the brink of climbing the ladder to legitimate stardom—but Magic Sam left behind a thick legacy of bone-cutting blues that remains eminently influential around his old stomping grounds to this day. His tremolo-rich staccato finger-picking was an entirely fresh phenomenon when he premiered it on Eli Toscano's Cobra label in 1957. His debut single, "All Your Love," was an immediate local sensation; its unusual structure would be recycled time and again by Sam throughout his tragically truncated career. Sam's Cobra encores "Everything Gonna Be Alright" and "Easy Baby" borrowed much the same melody but were no less powerful; the emerging West side sound was now officially committed to vinyl. Not everything Sam cut utilized the tune; "21 Days in Jail" was a pseudo-rockabilly smoker with hellacious lead guitar from Sam and thundering slap bass from the ubiquitous Willie Dixon. Sam also backed Shakey Jake Harris on his lone 45 for Cobra's Artistic subsidiary, "Call Me If You Need Me." Delmark Records was the conduit for Magic Sam's two seminal albums, 1967's *West Side Soul* and the following year's *Black Magic*. Both LPs showcased the entire breadth of Sam's West side attack. Even now, more than a quarter century after his passing, Magic Sam remains the king of West side blues. That's unlikely to change as long as the sub-genre is alive and kicking. *—Bill Dahl*

Magic Touch / 1966 / Black Top ✦✦✦✦
Another rare glimpse at Magic Sam hard at work, this time at another fabled West side haunt, Sylvio's, in 1966. No saxes this time, but uncle Shakey Jake was around for a few guest shots, while bassist Mac Thompson and drummer Odie Payne provide supple backing as Sam launches into another terrific set of numbers that for the most part he never recorded in the studio—songs by Freddy King, Albert Collins, James Robins, Junior Parker, and Jimmy McCracklin that briliiantly suited his soaring pipes and singular guitar style. *—Bill Dahl*

★ **West Side Soul** / 1967 / Delmark ✦✦✦✦✦
One of the truly essential Chicago blues albums of the 1960s. There's not a weak piece of filler on it—Sam exudes West side sizzle as he busts loose on "I Don't Want No Woman," "I Need You So Bad," definitive covers of "Sweet Home Chicago" and "Mama Talk to Your Daughter," the clippity-clop finger-twisting instrumental "Lookin' Good," and a soul-slanted "That's All I Need." *—Bill Dahl*

Black Magic / 1968 / Delmark ✦✦✦✦✦
With the key addition of raspy saxist Eddie Shaw to urge him on, Sam's Delmark encore was another instant classic, containing his R&B-slanted "You Belong to Me" and "What Have I Done Wrong," the bandstand favorites "Just a Little Bit" and "Same Old Blues," and a personalized treatment of Freddy King's "San-Ho-Zay." The album also proved his swan song; he was dead a year later. *—Bill Dahl*

Live at Ann Arbor & In Chicago / Jul. 1982 / Delmark ✦✦✦

The Late Great Magic Sam / 1984 / Evidence ✦✦✦
The ten 1963-1964 sides that make up the majority of this set have sort of fallen through the historical cracks over the years. They didn't deserve such shoddy treatment—Sam didn't record "Back Door Friend" or "Hi-Heel Sneakers" anywhere else, and he's in top shape throughout. Two live tracks at the set's close from 1969 don't add much to the overall package. *—Bill Dahl*

The Magic Sam Legacy / 1989 / Delmark ✦✦✦✦
Alternate takes and unissued surprises from the *West Side Soul* and *Black Magic* sessions, along with a couple of welcome 1966 sides ("I Feel So Good" and "Lookin' Good") that didn't see the light of day when they were recorded. Sam's versions of Jimmy Rogers's "Walkin' by Myself" and "That Ain't It" are important additions to his immortal legacy. *—Bill Dahl*

Live at the Alex Club / 1990 / Delmark ✦✦✦✦

☆ **2 1957-1966** / 1991 / Paula ✦✦✦✦✦
Never mind Otis Rush and Buddy Guy—this is the bedrock document of Chicago's West side blues guitar movement. Ten seminal numbers that constitute Sam's complete Cobra stash (notably "All Your Love," "Easy Baby," and the rockabilly-tinged "21 Days in Jail"), another pair by his harp-blowing uncle Shakey Jake, five numbers from 1960 that first appeared on Mel London's Chief logo (a tortured cover of Fats Domino's "Every Night About This Time" is the killer), and a couple of solid 1966 outings that reinforce Sam's standing as the king of the West side prior to his untimely demise. *—Bill Dahl*

Give Me Time / 1991 / Delmark ✦✦✦
We now adjourn to Sam's West side living room, where he's holding court in 1968 with only a few friends and family members on hand. Some of the tunes are familiar—"That's All I Need," "You Belong to Me"—but there are other originals only available here, and the super-intimate atmosphere brings out the intimate side of the late guitarist. *—Bill Dahl*

Magic Slim (Morris Holt)

b. Aug. 7, 1937, Grenada, MS
Vocals, Guitar / Electric Chicago Blues, Modern Electric Blues
Magic Slim & the Teardrops proudly uphold the tradition of what a Chicago blues *band* should sound like. Their emphasis on ensemble playing and a humongous repertoire that allegedly ranges upwards of a few hundred songs give the towering guitarist's live performances an endearing off-the-cuff quality—you never know what obscurity he'll pull out of his oversized hat next. Boyhood pal Magic Sam bestowed his magical monicker on the budding guitarist (times change; Slim's no longer slim). Although he managed to secure a steady gig for a while with Robert Perkins's band (Mr. Pitiful & the Teardrops), Slim wasn't good enough to progress into the upper ranks of Chicago bluesdom. So he retreated to Mississippi for a spell to hone his chops. When he returned to Chicago in 1965 (with brothers Nick and Lee Baby as his new rhythm section), Slim's detractors were quickly forced to change their tune. Utilizing the Teardrops name and holding onto his Magic Slim handle, the big man cut a couple of 45s for Ja-Wes and established himself as a formidable force on the South side—his guitar work dripped vibrato-enriched nastiness, and his roaring vocals were as gruff and uncompromising as anyone's on the scene. *—Bill Dahl*

Highway Is My Home / Nov. 19, 1978 / Evidence ✦✦✦

● **Grand Slam** / 1982 / Rooster Blues ✦✦✦✦✦
This raw-boned LP captures Slim's unpretentious houserocking sound about as well as any studio set possibly could. Among its highlights: the hard-shuffling "Early Every Morning," and a surreal "Scuffling," and Slim's tribute to his late pal Magic Sam, "She Belongs to Me." *—Bill Dahl*

Raw Magic / Jun. 1983 / Alligator ✦✦✦
A more consistent studio collection that first came out over in France and translated well to domestic consumption. Only seven titles, including Slim's lusty "Mama Talk to Your Daughter," and a crowd-pleasing "Mustang Sally," and three tunes of the quartet's own making (which is rather rare with this cover-heavy combo). *—Bill Dahl*

Gravel Road / 1990 / Blind Pig ✦✦✦
Another solid Slim set with an additional emphasis on the considerable contributions of second guitarist John Primer, who handles vocals on three cuts (including covers of Otis Redding's "Hard to Handle" and Eugene Church's "Pretty Girls Everywhere"). This was a particularly potent edition of Teardrops, pounding through Slim's own title cut and "Please Don't Waste My Time" and Albert King's shuffling "Cold Women with Warm Hearts" with barroom bravado. *—Bill Dahl*

Black Tornado / May 19, 1998 / Blind Pig ✦✦✦✦
Magic Slim has released a pile of albums, all of them true to his group's house-rocking credo. The idea this time around was to hook him up with producer Dick Shurman and get Slim to record tunes he hadn't committed to wax yet. With a tight version of the Teardrops aboard (the ubiquitous Nick Holt on bass and vocals, Michael Dotson on rhythm, Allen Kirk on drums with Slim's son Shawn Holt making a guest appearance on "Young Man's Blues"), Slim turns in a solid effort here. But perhaps the biggest change this time around is the inclusion of four original tunes from Slim, big news for a combo that many consider to be the ultimate blues cover band. Counting Nick Holt's "Playin' With My Mind" and Shawn Holt's "Young Man's Blues," the original material is up to the 50% mark, making this their most adventuresome outing to date. *—Cub Koda*

Snakebite / Mar. 21, 2000 / Blind Pig ✦✦✦✦✦
Snakebite is the best and most cohesive Magic Slim album to date, where all the things he does best come together in one place. Expertly produced by Dick Shurman, this spotlights all the groove that makes Slim a bandstand favorite, with none of the rough edges that mar his other studio or live efforts. The songs are top-notch (seven of the 11 tunes here are Slim originals), and this version of the Teardrops—Nick Holt on bass, Allen Kirk on drums, and Michael Dotson on second guitar—lay a greasy pocket down behind their leader that fits perfectly. Slim's vocals are spot-on, and his guitar work is his most focused yet. A truly inspired session, this is the perfect introduction to Magic Slim. *—Cub Koda*

Taj Mahal (Henry St. Clair Fredericks)

b. May 17, 1942, New York, NY
Slide Guitar, Vocals, Piano, Harmonica, Guitar, Bass, Banjo / Contemporary Blues, Folk-Blues, Electric Country Blues, Modern Acoustic Blues
Since the mid-'60s, Taj Mahal has played a vital role in the preservation of traditional blues and African-American roots music. He is a singer, songwriter, composer and noted musicologist who through intensive research creates authentic, rootsy compositions that, while remaining true to tradition, are still relevant to modern audiences and always bear his own unique stamp. Although he frequently ventures into different genres, Mahal's heart and soul belongs to the old-time country blues. His passion for the blues began at college, where Mahal began to delve into blues history and later, other forms of Black folk music including West African music, Caribbean, and zydeco, in addition to R&B, rock and jazz. He began playing the Boston folk circuit, and moved to Los Angeles after graduation, teaming up with guitarist Ry Cooder to form the Rising Sons. (Though the band released just one single, more than 20 tracks surfaced on a CD collection in the 1990s.) Mahal recorded several albums for Columbia beginning in 1968, and established himself as a charismatic performer, known for his adventurousness, gentle wit and intelligence. In addition to performing and album work, Mahal also composed for movie soundtracks, television scores and Broadway productions. As the '90s progress, Mahal continued to contribute and add to his discography. *—Sandra Brennan*

☆ **The Natch'l Blues** / 1968 / Columbia/Legacy ✦✦✦✦✦
Taj Mahal's second album, recorded in the spring and fall of 1968, opens with more stripped-down Delta-style blues in the manner of his debut, but adds a little more amplification (partly courtesy of Al Kooper on organ) before moving into wholly bigger sound on numbers like "She Caught the Katy and Left Me a Mule to Ride" and "The Cuckoo"—the latter, in particular, features crunchy electric and acoustic guitars and Gary Gilmore playing his bass almost like a lead instrument, like a bluesman's answer to John Entwistle. Most notable, however, may be the two original closing numbers, "You Don't Miss Your Water ('Til Your Well Runs Dry)" and "Ain't That a Lot of Love," which offer Taj Mahal working in the realm of soul and treading onto Otis Redding territory. This is particularly notable on "You Don't Miss Your Water," which achieves the intensity of a gospel performance and comes complete with a Stax/Volt-style horn arrangement by Jesse Ed Davis that sounds more like the real thing than the real thing. "Ain't That a Lot of Love," by contrast, is driven by a hard electric guitar sound and a relentless bass part that sounds like a more urgent version of the bass line from the Spencer Davis Group's "Gimme Some Lovin'." The fall 2000 CD reissue includes a trio of bonus tracks: a faster-paced rendition of "The Cuckoo" with a more prominent lead guitar, the slow electric lament "New Stranger Blues" featuring some good mandolin-style playing

on the guitar, and the rocking instrumental "Things Are Gonna Work Out Fine," which is a killer showcase for Davis' lead electric guitar and Taj Mahal's virtuosity on the harmonica. *—Bruce Eder*

☆ **Taj Mahal** / 1968 / Columbia/Legacy ✦✦✦✦✦
Taj Mahal's debut album was a startling statement in its time and has held up remarkably well. Recorded in August of 1967, it was as hard and exciting a mix of old and new blues sounds as surfaced on record in a year when even a lot of veteran blues artists (mostly at the insistence of their record labels) started turning toward psychedelia. The guitar virtuosity, embodied in Taj Mahal's slide work (which had the subtlety of a classical performance), Jesse Ed Davis's lead playing, and rhythm work by Ry Cooder and Bill Boatman, is of the neatly stripped-down variety that was alien to most records aiming for popular appeal, and the singer himself approached the music with a startling mix of authenticity and youthful enthusiasm. The whole record is a strange and compelling amalgam of stylistic and technical achievements—filled with blues influences of the 1930s and 1940s, but also making use of stereo sound separation and the best recording technology. The result was numbers like Sleepy John Estes' "Diving Duck Blues," with textures resembling the mix on the early Cream albums, while "The Celebrated Walkin' Blues" (even with Cooder's animated mandolin weaving its spell on one side of the stereo mix) has the sound of a late '40s Chess release by Muddy Waters. Blind Willie McTell ("Statesboro Blues") and Robert Johnson ("Dust My Broom") are also represented, in what had to be one of the most quietly, defiantly iconoclastic records of 1968. *—Bruce Eder*

Giant Step / 1969 / Columbia ✦✦✦
Giant Step/De Old Folks at Home is a two-record set that features one album of Delta blues that was recorded with a full electric band and one album of solo acoustic blues. The electric record is the better collection, but only by a small margin—the acoustic record suffers from poor production that prevents a listener from completely connecting with Taj Mahal's blues. Nevertheless, there are terrific moments on both records and, on the whole, it is one of his finest albums. *—Thom Owens*

Happy Just to Be Like I Am / 1971 / Columbia ✦✦✦✦
With *Happy Just to Be Like I Am,* Taj Mahal offers another (possibly his most effective) course in roots music, this time dabbling in Caribbean rhythms in addition to his more-or-less standard take on acoustic country blues. While his good intentions and craftsmanlike execution can't be denied, one hopes the listener will eventually decide to seek out the inspirations for these recordings. *—AMG*

The Real Thing / 1972 / Columbia/Legacy ✦✦✦
The Real Thing is double-live album featuring a new batch of songs as well as some old favorites augmented by, oddly enough, a four-piece tuba section. The change in arrangements may be a point of curiosity, but in the end, the album is bogged down by directionless jamming. *—AMG*

Recycling the Blues & Other Related Stuff / 1972 / Columbia ✦✦✦
The title *Recycling the Blues & Other Related Stuff* certainly sums up the album quite well—that's exactly what Taj Mahal has been doing for several years by this point. The first side features laidback in-the-studio work with some nice gospel-inflected back-up from the Pointer Sisters. The second (and preferable) side offers a good look at Mahal's stage show. *—AMG*

Ooh So Good 'N' Blues / 1973 / Columbia ✦✦✦

Mo' Roots / Apr. 1974 / Columbia ✦✦✦

Taj's Blues / Jun. 16, 1992 / Columbia/Legacy ✦✦✦✦
Taj's Blues is an entertainingly diverse record, featuring a variety of blues and roots-music styles, all fused together into a distinctive sound of its own. Half of the album is played on acoustic, the other with an electric band (which includes guitarists Ry Cooder and Jesse Davis on a handful of tracks), which gives a pretty good impression of the range of Mahal's talents. It's a good collection, featuring many of his best performances for Columbia, including "Statesboro Blues" and "Leaving Trunk," as well as the unreleased "East Bay Woman." *—Thom Owens*

In Progress & In Motion (1965-1998) / Oct. 13, 1998 / Columbia/Legacy ✦✦✦✦✦
For being a nearly omnipresent figure, Taj Mahal has never quite gotten the respect he's deserved. At the beginning of his career, he earned a significant amount of attention, but as the years passed, he had woven himself into the fabric of blues culture so well that his presence was taken for granted. That is why the 1998 release of *In Progress & In Motion 1965-1998* was so welcome. Spanning three discs and over three decades, the box set accurately summarizes Mahal's career and makes a convincing case for his talents as a roots synthesist. Dedicated fans may notice a favorite or two missing, but they'll be pleased by the 15 unreleased tracks, including two songs intended for his debut album. There are a number of other rarities for the dedicated here, including several unheard live cuts, material from his early group the Rising Sons, and his entire contribution to the Rolling Stones' legendary *Rock & Roll Circus.* Even with this plethora of rarities, *In Progress & In Motion* is primarily for fans who want a solid, comprehensive summary of Mahal's achievements without delving into the particular records, especially since it chooses its songs judiciously, concentrating on his groundbreaking late-'60s/early-'70s work. Indeed, much of his post-Columbia/CBS recordings are quickly recounted on the third disc, but that isn't a problem—the first two discs show how Mahal created his own sound; the third shows how he maintained it. By balancing the music this way, Mahal and his partner, Lawrence Cohn, have created a representative, enlightening retrospective that is appealing to casual and hardcore fans alike. *—Stephen Thomas Erlewine*

Kulanjan / Aug. 3, 1999 / Hannibal ✦✦✦✦

● **The Best of Taj Mahal** / 2000 / Columbia/Legacy ✦✦✦✦✦
Columbia/Legacy's 2000 collection *The Best of Taj Mahal* is a first-rate overview of Taj Mahal's classic late-'60s/early-'70s work for Columbia. Spanning 17 tracks, including a previously unreleased cut "Sweet Mama Janisse" from 1970, this hits many of the key points from the records he released between 1967 and 1974, including "Statesboro Blues," "Leaving Trunk,' "She Caught the Katy and Left Me a Mule to Ride," and "Fishin Blues." Although his albums were constructed and worked as actual albums, this does an excellent job of summarizing these thematic affairs and functions as a nice introduction to Mahal's music. *—Stephen Thomas Erlewine*

Best of the Private Years / Apr. 18, 2000 / Private Music ✦✦✦✦✦
A rockin' good time is guaranteed for all who listen to some of these blistering blues numbers from the legendary singer's best work of the last decade, but the real reward is the depth that goes beyond just the hearty partying. "Blues Ain't Nothin'" is classic bar band rock-blues all the way, with Mahal texturing his raspy voice over his flurrying harmonica and the guitar fire of Johnny Lee Schell and John Porter. "Here in the Dark" captures the more melancholy aspects of Mahal's blues leanings, with his vocals itching for relief over a simmering horn section and the crisp, distorted lines of Eric Clapton. This sort of typical bluesmaking is balanced beautifully by folksy, New Orleans-styled gems like Hank Williams' "Mind Your Own Business" and the aggressive blues meets bebop energy of the Horace Silver tune "Senor Blues." Then its back to the jamming on "Ooh Poo Pah Doo." Mahal has a rich history, and this collection is living proof that a good bluesman gets better with age. *—Jonathan Widran*

Percy Mayfield

b. Aug. 12, 1920, Minden, LA, **d.** Aug. 11, 1984, Los Angeles, CA
Vocals, Piano / Urban Blues, West Coast Blues, Piano Blues, R&B, Soul
A masterful songwriter whose touching blues ballad "Please Send Me Someone to Love," a multi-layered universal lament, was a number one R&B hit in 1950, Percy Mayfield had the world by the tail until a horrific 1952 auto wreck left him facially disfigured. That didn't stop the poet laureate of the blues from writing in prolific fashion, though. As Ray Charles's favorite scribe during the '60s, he handed the Genius such gems as "Hit the Road Jack" and "At the Club." Art Rupe's Specialty logo signed Mayfield in 1950 and scored a solid string of R&B smashes over the next couple of years. "Please Send Me Someone to Love" and its equally potent flip "Strange Things Happening" were followed in the charts by "Lost Love," "What a Fool I Was," "Prayin' for Your Return," "Cry Baby," and "Big Question," cementing Mayfield's reputation as a blues balladeer of the highest order. Mayfield's lyrics were usually as insightfully downbeat as his tempos; he was a true master at expressing his innermost feelings, laced with vulnerability and pathos (his "Life Is Suicide" and "The River's Invitation" are two prime examples). *—Bill Dahl*

My Jug and I / 1962 / Tangerine ✦✦✦✦✦
Mayfield's gentle vocal delivery and the big, brassy sound of Ray Charles's orchestra were a match made in heaven. Mayfield brought some first-class material to this party (which begs for CD reissue): "My Jug and I," "Stranger in My Own Home Town" (later covered by Elvis Presley), the untypically jumping "Give Me Time to Explain," and a handful of Specialty remakes. *—Bill Dahl*

Bought Blues / 1969 / Tangerine ✦✦✦✦
Another elegant, beautifully arranged collection fraught with brilliant, sometimes heartbreaking material: "Ha Ha in the Daytime, " "We Both Must Cry, " "My Bottle Is My Companion." *—Bill Dahl*

★ **Poet of the Blues** / 1990 / Specialty ✦✦✦✦✦
The insightful songwriting skills of this West Coaster were matched by his wry, plaintive vocal delivery (Mayfield was usually his own best interpreter). The 25 sides here date from his hit-laden 1950-1954 stay at Art Rupe's Specialty logo and include his univesal lament "Please Send Me Someone to Love," and the resolutely downbeat "Strange Things Happening" and "Lost Love," and an ironic "The River's Invitation." Saxman Maxwell Davis led the horn-powered combos providing sympathetic support behind Mayfield. *—Bill Dahl*

Percy Mayfield Live / 1992 / Winner ✦✦✦
Although the first-ever release of live Mayfield material is culled from performances between 1981 and 1983, the twilight of the singer's blues career, he remains in fine, laidback voice throughout. The selections draw on all periods of his three decades as a songwriter, and include "Please Send Me Someone to Love," "The River's Invitation" and "Don't Start Lying to Me." Founding Paul Butterfield Blues Band pianist Mark Naftalin backs Mayfield throughout the collection; he also served as the set's producer. *—Jason Ankeny*

Memory Pain / Sep. 17, 1992 / Specialty ✦✦✦✦✦
Ranging from major hits to alternate takes and rarities, this CD (released in 1992) illustrates the prolific nature of Percy Mayfield's Specialty Records output during the 1950s. Though not everything on *Memory Pain* is essential, the collection of early R&B and 12-bar blues is consistently satisfying. The best known song here is the number one hit of 1950, "Please Send Me Someone to Love," and many listeners will also be familiar with such gems as "Strange Things Happening" and the title song. A singer who was flexible as well as charismatic, Mayfield is as convincing on a rare version of the mournful, jazz-tinged "Nightless Lovers" as he is on 12-bar numbers like "My Blues" and "The Big Question." The CD ends on an interesting note with a demo of "Hit the Road Jack" (which became a major hit for Ray Charles). Highly recommended. *—Alex Henderson*

Jerry McCain

b. Jun. 18, 1930, Gadsden, AL
Vocals, Drums, Trumpet, Harmonica, Guitar / Swamp Blues, Harmonica Blues, Electric Harmonica Blues, Modern Electric Blues
Not only is Jerry McCain a terrific amplified harpist, he's also one of the funniest songwriters working the genre. Has been for more than four decades, as anyone who's dug his out-of-control 1950s Excello rockers "My Next Door Neighbor" and "Trying to Please" will gladly testify. In 1953, "Boogie" McCain made his vinyl debut for Trumpet with "East of the Sun"/"Wine-O-Wine." A 1954 encore, "Stay Out of Automobiles"/"Love to Make Up," was

solid Southern blues but barely hinted at the galvanic energy of his subsequent output. McCain signed with Excello in 1955, cutting "That's What They Want" with his usual sidekick, Christopher Collins, on guitar. "Run, Uncle John! Run," "Trying to Please," the torrid "My Next Door Neighbor" and "The Jig's Up" ranked with McCain's best 1955-57 Excello efforts. The harpist is probably best-known for his two-sided 1960 gem for Rex Records, "She's Tough"/"Steady." After too many years spent in relative obscurity, McCain rejuvenated his fortunes in 1989 by signing with Ichiban Records and waxing a series of outings that displayed both his irreverent wit and a social conscience rare on the contemporary circuit. *—Bill Dahl*

Choo Choo Rock / 1981 / White Label ♦♦♦♦♦

Strange Kind of Feelin' / 1990 / Alligator ♦♦♦

● **That's What They Want: The Best of Jerry McCain** / 1995 / Excello ♦♦♦♦♦
McCain has always marched to the beat of a different drummer and the proof of it is right here, 23 recordings that define the place where the blues and rock'n'roll meet at the end of a dark alley. The first 12 tracks are McCain's complete singles output for Excello Records, the sides upon which most of his reputation rests. From the cold hearted bravado of the the title track to the rocking insanity of "Trying To Please," this music is as special as it comes. The following 11 tracks come from homemade demo tapes circa.1955 that were cut in Jerry's living room with a single mike, one track home tape recorder. Featuring grinding, massively distorted guitars, crashing drums and lyrical texts concerning themselves with going crazy to rock'n'roll, rock'n'roll as salvation ("Rock & Roll Ball," "Geronimo's Rock"), or going crazy from outside worldly pressures ("Bell In My Heart," "My Next Door Neighbors"), these masterpieces answer the musical question: what would a rock & roll album by Little Walter have sounded like— *AMG*

Retrospectives / Jun. 30, 1998 / Ichiban ♦♦♦
When Jerry McCain re-emerged on Ichiban in 1989 after many years of not doing nearly enough recording, followers of the Alabama native were delighted to see him back in the studio again. This 1998 CD (which spans 1989-1993) points to the fact that while his Ichiban output may not have been in a class with his great Excello recordings of the 1950s, he could still blow a mean harp and make us laugh with his funny, insightful storytelling. "Brand New Mojo" and "Spoiled Rotten to the Bone" are excellent examples of how witty he can be, and on "Sue Somebody," he takes an amusing jab at Americans who file frivolous lawsuits. Many of the selections have an urban blues outlook, although "Lucy Pearl," "Strut Your Stuff" and "I've Got the Blues All Over Me" are pure Louisiana-style swamp blues. Close your eyes while listening to these tunes, and it's easy to pretend you're in the steamy Louisiana bayous. Although not quite essential, *Retrospectives* paints an enjoyable picture of McCain as he sounded when he was in his late '50s and early '60s. *—Alex Henderson*

Good Stuff! / May 18, 1999 / Varese ♦♦♦♦♦
McCain's career didn't quit with his Excello sides of the 1950s. He went on to cut his most remembered singles ("She's Tough" and "Steady") for the Rex label and kept cutting a steady stream of obscure but inspired 45s and a stray album for labels like Jewel, OKeh, Continental, Gas, Esco, Bad, and Royal American. Sixteen of the best sides are compiled on this one with "What About You" and "Rough Stuff" emanating from the same groove-filled session that produced "She's Tough" and "Steady." "Ting-Tang-Tagalu," "Welfare Cadillac Blues," and the soulful "I'll Come Running Back for More" are all highlights, but the closer "Pussycat A-Go-Go," issued as the Shindigs and supposedly featuring Sam the Sham and the Pharoahs as the backing group, may be the blues at both its hippest and most surreal. Like the title says, good stuff. *—Cub Koda*

Mighty Sam McClain

b. 1941, Monroe, LA
Vocals / Retro-Soul, Modern Electric Blues, Soul-Blues
Vocalist Mighty Sam McClain is a specialist in Southern soul-blues, one of the original masters from the 1960s, when the music enjoyed its peak popularity. Like so many other soul-blues vocalists, McClain began singing gospel in a choir. He left home at 13 and later hooked up with Little Melvin Underwood, working first as a valet but then as a featured vocalist in his road show. While working in Florida, he recorded Patsy Cline's hit "Sweet Dreams." After this, visits to Muscle Shoals yielded singles like "Fannie Mae" and "In the Same Old Way." He also recorded a single for Malaco and two singles for Atlantic in 1971 before falling out of the music scene for over a decade.

He returned in the mid-'80s, recording a single for Orleans Records as part of a band and appearing on *Hubert Sumlin's Blues Party* for BlackTop in 1987. McClain began to re-establish his former reputation as a great soul-blues singer, touring with Sumlin and his entourage. He finally recorded a studio album under his own name with 1992's *Give It Up to Love,* followed by 1995's *Keep on Moving* and *Sledgehammer Soul and Down Home Blues* one year later. Most of the songs on all three albums utilize a full horn section, and on top of this ride McClain's deep, powerful vocals, oftentimes in self-penned songs. Since the late '80s, McClain's career has been on the upswing again, as he's put together some great backing bands and carved a niche for himself in Europe. *—Richard Skelly*

Soul Survivor: The Best of Mighty Sam McClain / Jun. 8, 1999 / AudioQuest ♦♦♦♦
Good overview of McClain's four Audioquest releases, along with two previously unreleased tracks. "Keep on Movin'" should have been included, as its catchy arrangements are ideal bumper music for a late night TV talk show. *—Char Ham*

● **Papa True Love: The Amy Sessions** / Jul. 18, 2000 / Sundazed ♦♦♦♦
This compilation of the singer's prime 1960s work has both sides of his eight 1966-1968 Amy singles, as well as "Nothing but the Truth" from Bell's LP *Bell's Cellar of Soul Vol. 2* and a previously unreleased 1966 cover of Don Gibson's "A Stranger to Me." Mighty Sam was a good 1960s Southern soul singer, but not a great one; the kinds of people who collect this sort of stuff can go back and forth as to whether he was a top-of-the-second-division artist or the best of a journeyman class. Often he sounded like a somewhat bluesier Otis Redding, more apt to break into growly rasps, though not as inclined in that direction as, say, James Brown was. "Sweet Dreams (Of You)" in particular seems like a conscious emulation of the kind of success Otis Redding was having in 1965-1966 with wrenching ballads like "I've Been Loving You Too Long." He did benefit from a few Spooner Oldham-Dan Penn compositions but didn't get the sort of classic material that might have made him more than a cult favorite. All that taken into consideration, this remains a fairly solid platter of little-known soul music, the vocalist shining brightest on mid-tempo tunes that have him pleading a case without getting too sentimental. The production's pretty good as well, with frequent stinging blues-soul guitar licks and eerie organ of the kind made famous on Percy Sledge's "When a Man Loves a Woman." *—Richie Unterberger*

Tommy McClennan

b. Apr. 8, 1908, Yazoo City, MS, **d.** CA. , Chicago, IL
Vocals, Guitar / Delta Blues, Soul-Blues
A gravel-throated back-country blues growler from the Mississippi Delta, McClennan was part of the last wave of down-home blues guitarists to record for the major labels in Chicago. His rawboned 1939-1942 Bluebird recordings were no-frills excursions into the blues bottoms. He left a powerful legacy that included "Bottle It up and Go," "Cross Cut Saw Blues," "Deep Blue Sea Blues" (aka "Catfish Blues"), and others whose lasting power has been evidenced through the repertoires and re-recordings of other artists. Admirers of McClennan's blues would do well to check out the 1941-1942 Bluebird sessions of Robert Petway, a McClennan associate who performed in a similar but somewhat more lyrical vein. McClennan never recorded again and reportedly died destitute in Chicago; blues researchers have yet to even trace the date or circumstances of his death. *—Jim O'Neal*

★ **Bluebird Recordings 1939-1942** / Apr. 29, 1997 / Bluebird/RCA ♦♦♦♦♦
McClennan's hoarse, shouted vocals, spoken vaudeville asides and scrappy guitar work make for a pretty irresistible combination, especially in light of the simple fact that most blues fans have never been exposed to his music in large doses. This double disc rounds up every known extant side recorded for Bluebird between 1939 to 1942, when the label dropped him for problems with alcohol. The music on here comes from five sessions and is uniformly excellent, if a bit samey. But it is blues at its most intense and unfettered, and tracks like "Bottle It Up and Go," "You Can Mistreat Me Here," "Baby Please Don't Tell On Me," "New Shake 'Em On Down," and "Baby Don't You Want to Go?" (the latter his adaption of "Sweet Home Chicago") are full of energy and verses worth requoting. This set is one of the true hidden treasures of the "Bluebird" period in blues history and, as such, deserves a much, much wider hearing. *—Cub Koda*

Delbert McClinton

b. Nov. 4, 1940, Lubbock, TX
Vocals, Harmonica / Americana, Country-Rock, Blues-Rock, Modern Electric Blues
A Texas music institution, McClinton honed his musical chops to razor sharpness as a teenage harmonica man learning firsthand from blues legends traveling through the area. His harp work on Bruce Channel's hit, "Hey Baby," got him on the big time circuit, making it over to tour England and eventually giving harmonica lessons to a young John Lennon. Much behind the scenes work throughout the '60s ensued with McClinton fronting the Rondells, who hit the Hot 100 with "If You Really Want Me To, I'll Go." He hit the charts again in the '70s with Glen Clark as Delbert & Glen. Around this period, McClinton's songs started getting covered by country acts, Waylon Jennings and Emmylou Harris both having hits with his material. The Blues Brothers used his "B-Movie Box Car Blues" on their first album and their hit movie. He has released idiosyncratic solo efforts up to the present time and guested on albums with everyone from Roy Buchanan to Bonnie Raitt. A Texas music treasure, we've not heard the last of Delbert McClinton. *—Cub Koda*

The Best of Delbert McClinton / 1989 / Curb ♦♦♦♦♦
It's only 11 tracks, but *The Best of Delbert McClinton* contains nearly everything you need to know about how the eclectic blues/country/soul performer sounds, even if it doesn't have every good song he recorded. Nevertheless, it has the best moments from his early '70s records—including "Two More Bottles of Wine" and "Let Love Come Between Us"—and is a terrific introduction to his work. *—Thom Owens*

Live from Austin / 1989 / Alligator ♦♦♦♦

Never Been Rocked Enough / 1992 / Curb ♦♦♦

● **The Ultimate Collection** / Jun. 1, 1999 / Hip-O ♦♦♦♦♦
Hip-O's *The Ultimate Collection* comes very close to fulfilling the promise of its title. Over the course of 18 tracks, the compilation traces the evolution of Delbert McClinton's career, concentrating on his recordings for ABC, Capricorn, Captiol and Rising Tide, while hitting almost all of the major highlights. True, there may be a personal favorite or two missing for hardcore fans, but there is no better introduction to this acclaimed Texas musician than this. *—Stephen Thomas Erlewine*

Don't Let Go: The Collection / Mar. 28, 2000 / Music Club ♦♦♦♦

Genuine Rhythm & the Blues / Mar. 28, 2000 / Hip-O ♦♦♦
Far from a comprehensive overview of Delbert McClinton's four decade career, this is an enjoyable yet relatively brief disc focusing entirely on covers of classic R&B material. Compiled from the rugged Texas singer's four early solo albums recorded from 1974 through 1979, it shines a light onto McClinton's varied influences as well as being a consistently enjoyable listen.

At first listen there's not much exciting here. Many of these classics such as Bobby "Blue" Bland's "Turn on Your Lovelight," Fats Domino's "Blue Monday," and Don Covay's "Have Mercy" are well known through either their original versions or numerous renditions throughout the years. Upon closer listen though McClinton's approach to them is effortlessly soulful, and some of his arrangements- in particular transforming Willie Dixon's "Spoonful" from a wailing Chicago blues to a swampy soul stirrer- are refreshingly unique. McClinton's sand and honey inflected vocals flow easily, and his sharp band including horns, female backing vocals and tight ensemble playing, wrap themselves around the songs with loose precision.

The songs of Elvis Presley, Jimmie Rodgers, Chuck Berry, Johnny Ace, Big Joe Turner, The Clovers and Bo Diddley all become McClinton tunes as he latches onto their varied genres and transforms them into rollicking R&B. The anthology shares only one selection with the excellent *Ultimate Collection*, but even though it's cobbled together from albums recorded over five years, McClinton's cohesive style bonds these tracks into a surprisingly unified whole. Thoughtful and informative liner notes explain the source material, and the lack of individual personnel listings, as well as the album's relative brevity, prove to be minor shortcomings. *—Hal Horowitz*

Jimmy McCracklin

b. Aug. 13, 1921, St. Louis, MO
Vocals, Piano / West Coast Blues, Piano Blues, Soul-Blues, R&B
A full half-century from when he started out in the blues business, Jimmy McCracklin is still touring, recording, and acting like a much younger man. In fact, he vehemently disputes his commonly accepted birthdate—but since he began recording back in 1945, it seems reasonable. After moving to the West Coast in the mid-'40s, McCracklin recorded for a daunting array of tiny labels in Los Angeles and Oakland prior to touching down with Modern, Swing Time and Peacock for approximately two-year hitches. By 1954, the pianist was back with Modern logo and really coming into his own with a sax-driven sound. After a few sessions for Irma in 1956 came McCracklin's first major hit "The Walk," a rudimentary dance number on Checker that hit the Top Ten on both the R&B and pop charts. The nomadic pianist returned to the hit parade with the tough R&B workout "Just Got to Know" in 1961 for Art-Tone. McCracklin's songwriting skills shouldn't be overlooked as an integral factor in his enduring success. He penned the funky hit "Tramp" for his old pal, guitarist Lowell Fulson. Ever the survivor, McCracklin made a string of LPs for Imperial and segued into the soul era totally painlessly. Two recent discs for Bullseye Blues prove that McCracklin still packs a knockout punch from behind his piano—no matter what his birth certificate says. *—Bill Dahl*

I Just Gotta Know / 1961 / Imperial ✦✦✦✦✦
It's always a "Shame, Shame, Shame" (to quote one of this LP's best numbers) when a 35-year-old slab of vinyl must be cited as what may be an artist's finest collection—but since no one has yet touched McCracklin's massive '60s Imperial catalog for CD reissue, here you go! Contains his definitive soul-tinged ballad "Just Got to Know," the Amos Milburn-derived jump blues "Club Savoy," and several more late-'50s rockers that Imperial acquired from various small concerns after he began to hit with regularity. *—Bill Dahl*

My Answer / 1966 / Imperial ✦✦✦✦✦
Conveniently enough, Imperial slapped together what amounts to a greatest-hits set here, and it serves as the best available introduction to the pianist's '60s catalog. Contains "Just Got to Know, " "Every Night, Every Day, " "Think, " "Steppin' Up in Class, " and the title item—every one of them occupying an intriguing island midway between blues and soul. *—Bill Dahl*

High on the Blues / 1971 / Stax ✦✦✦
Given that this was co-produced by Al Jackson (of Booker T. & the MG's) and Willie Mitchell (of Hi Records), and adds embellishment by the Memphis Horns, it's unsurprising that this is very much a soul-blues record. It's a workmanlike effort with an early-'70s Stax period feel, including remakes of two of his past R&B singles, "Think" and "Just Got to Know." The CD reissue adds a couple of previously unreleased bonus tracks. *—Richie Unterberger*

My Story / 1991 / Bullseye Blues ✦✦✦✦✦

Jimmy McCracklin: The Mercury Recordings / 1992 / Bear Family ✦✦✦✦
McCracklin's liaison with Mercury was relatively brief, from late 1958 to the fall of 1960, and Bear Family has only managed to locate 13 songs for this CD. But it's a rewarding chapter in the pianist's endlessly nomadic recording career, featuring his original dance tunes "Georgia Slop" and "Let's Do It (The Chicken Scratch)," a New Orleans-cut cover of Johnny Cash's "Folsom Prison Blues," and some smoothly arranged (by Clyde Otis, Brook Benton's collaborator) pop/R&B outings that suggest Mercury had big plans for McCracklin that never quite panned out. *—Bill Dahl*

Taste of the Blues / 1994 / Bullseye Blues ✦✦✦

● **The Walk: Jimmy McCracklin at His Best** / 1997 / Razor & Tie ✦✦✦✦✦
McCracklin has always been one of those artists whose currency always ran higher in the black blues community than it has in the subsequent years of white historical revision. But decent career retrospectives of McCracklin—who had sides issued on almost a dozen labels in as many years—on compact disc are somewhere between few and far between and nonexistent. But this 20-track single-disc compilation goes a long way toward rectifying that situation. Containing his biggest hits (the title track, the original versions of "The Georgia Slop" and "Get Back"—later hits for Big Al Downing and Roy Head, respectively) along with the best of his Art-Tone and Imperial sides ("Just Got to Know" and "Every Night, Every Day," now both staples of the Chicago blues repertoire after being covered in the early '60s by Magic Sam), this makes a perfect introduction to his style as well as a powerful testament to his superb songwriting skills. *—Cub Koda*

Modern Recordings 1948-1950 / Jul. 27, 1999 / Ace ✦✦✦
Although McCracklin had already been recording for a few years, his association with Modern marked his first reasonably long tenure with an established label. This 25-track disc covers his first stay with the company, covering a half dozen singles, three songs that first showed up on the 1981 Ace album *And His Blues Blasters*, and ten demos, outtakes, and alternate takes that were previously unissued. It's solid small-combo West Coast jump blues, sometimes embellished by the tenor saxophone of Maxwell Davis. It's more interesting on the speedy, jumpy numbers, although McCracklin was competent at setting an after-hours vibe on the slower ones. The drums-piano-guitar trio, especially guitarist Robert Kelton, gets into a real frenetic groove on the 1948 instrumental "Blues Blasters' Shuffle"; "Hamburger Joint" is a silly novelty whose spoken repartee verges on sleaziness. In a more serious mood are two previously unissued McCracklin solo piano demos, "Mistreating Me" and "Bad Health Blues." *—Richie Unterberger*

Blast 'em Dead! / Ace ✦✦✦✦
McCracklin's vast catalog is perhaps more fully appreciated overseas than in his home. British Ace assembled 18 of the piano-pounder's Duke waxings for this searing LP, which features frequent interjections from guitarist Lafayette Thomas. Jumping stuff! *—Bill Dahl*

Mississippi Fred McDowell

b. Jan. 12, 1904, Rossville, TN, **d.** Jul. 3, 1972, Memphis, TN
Slide Guitar, Vocals, Guitar / Blues Revival, Delta Blues
When Mississippi Fred McDowell proclaimed on one of his last albums, "I do not play no rock'n'roll," it was less a boast by an aging musician swept aside by the big beat than a mere statement of fact. As a stylist and purveyor of the original Delta blues, he was superb; equal parts Charley Patton and Son House coming to the fore through his roughed up vocals and slashing bottleneck style of guitar playing. McDowell *knew* he was the real deal and while others were diluting and updating their sound to keep pace with the changing times and audiences, Mississippi Fred stood out from the rest of the pack simply by not changing his style one iota. Though he scorned the amplified rock sound with a passion matched by few country bluesmen, he certainly had no qualms about passing any of his musical secrets along to his young, White acolytes, prompting several of them—including a young Bonnie Raitt—to develop slide guitar techniques of their own. Although generally lumped in with other blues "rediscoveries" from the '60s, the most amazing thing about him was that this rich repository of Delta blues had never recorded in the '20s or early '30s, didn't get "discovered" until 1959, and didn't become a full-time professional musician until the mid-'60s. *—Cub Koda*

★ **Mississippi Delta Blues** / Aug. 1964 / Arhoolie ✦✦✦✦✦
Arhoolie's *Mississippi Delta Blues* is one of the definitive Mississippi Fred McDowell albums. Culled from two sessions, recorded in 1964 and 1965 respectively, this blues revival-era recording finds McDowell at his very best, performing powerful versions of traditional Delta blues songs, as well as a handful of originals. McDowell recorded many fine albums, but this is arguably his best. *—Thom Owens*

My Home Is in the Delta / Sep. 1964 / Testament ✦✦✦✦✦
Mississippi Fred McDowell's home may have been in the Delta, but his music belonged to the world. This is heartfelt, raw, glorious country blues, delivered without an ounce of pretension or nostalgia. *—Ron Wynn*

Amazing Grace / 1966 / Testament ✦✦✦✦✦
The connection between rural blues and spiritual music is sometimes overlooked. This 1966 recording, featuring McDowell, his guitar, and the Hunter's Chapel Singers of Como, Mississippi (including his wife Annie Mae), is one of the best illustrations of how closely the styles can be linked. McDowell and company perform what the record subtitle calls "Mississippi Delta spirituals" on this stark and moving set, which includes a version of one of his signature tunes, "You Got to Move." The CD reissue adds three previously unreleased tracks. *—Richie Unterberger*

Long Way from Home / 1966 / Milestone/Original Blues Classics ✦✦✦
Good no-frills set of acoustic solo blues on bottleneck guitar. The accent is on traditional material, including "Milk Cow Blues, " "John Henry, " "Big Fat Mama, " and the title track. *—Richie Unterberger*

I Don't Play No Rock 'N' Roll / 1969 / Capitol ✦✦✦✦✦
Blues purists were disappointed to hear McDowell pick up an electric guitar for the first time on this LP, as well as work with a young, white rhythm section. To the rest of the listeners, this session sounds pretty good, McDowell's vocals, guitar playing, and integrity coming through just as strongly as it had on his acoustic work. The title track, and the rap that opens it up, is a mini-classic in its own right—if McDowell does not play no rock & roll, as he claims, he certainly keeps a beat pretty well. The album, as well as a second one cut at the same sessions (released on the Just Sunshine label) and some previously unreleased tracks, was released as an expanded double CD by Capitol in 1995. *—Richie Unterberger*

☆ **You Gotta Move** / Nov. 30, 1993 / Arhoolie ✦✦✦✦✦
You Gotta Move is an excellent 19-track compilation of McDowell's best-known work, spotlighting his Mississippi Delta slide guitar virtuosity, as well as his superior songwriting skills; perhaps most familiar to many listeners is the title track, which inspired a Rolling Stones cover version on the group's classic *Sticky Fingers* album. *—Jason Ankeny*

This Ain't No Rock N' Roll / 1995 / Arhoolie ✦✦✦✦

I Do Not Play No Rock 'n' Roll: Complete Sessions / Oct. 24, 1995 / Capitol ✦✦✦✦✦
A reissue of his popular 1969 electric album, expanded into a double CD with the addition of other material recorded at the same sessions (most of which was issued on an LP on the Just Sunshine label). It makes more sense to pick this up rather than the original vinyl album, as it rounds up all the material recorded at the *I Do Not Play No Rock 'N' Roll* sessions in November 1969, and adds lengthy liner notes. *—Richie Unterberger*

Steakbone Slide Guitar / Apr. 1996 / Rykodisc/Tradition ✦✦✦

First Recordings / Sep. 9, 1997 / Rounder ✦✦✦✦✦
In September, 1959, these 14 seminal tracks were recorded by Alan Lomax. Traversing the South with a bulky reel-to-reel tape recorder, this part of his field trip documents the very first recordings (and subsequent "discovery" in folk circles) of McDowell. The recordings were captured outdoors on a front porch, and even though Lomax was recording him at a semi-professional speed on his tape deck (7 1/2 inches per second as opposed to the then-standard 15 ips), seldom did McDowell's subsequent recordings capture this much ambience. Loose and informal, these sides showcase Fred solo and working in tandem with guitarist Miles Pratcher ("I'm Going Down the River," "Shake 'Em On Down," "You're Gonna Be

Sorry"), the utterly surreal tissue-paper-and-comb work of Fanny Davis and—at various times—his wife Annie Mae ("Keep Your Lamps Trimmed and Burning"), James Shorty ("I Want Jesus to Walk With Me"), Sidney Carter and Rose Hemphill ("When the Train Come Along") on background vocals. As an added bonus for fans and historians alike, ten of the 14 tracks are previously unissued and include some of the best sides Fred ever recorded. *—Cub Koda*

Levee Camp Blues / Feb. 3, 1998 / Testament ♦♦♦

Brownie McGhee (Walter McGhee)

b. Nov. 30, 1915, Knoxville, TN, **d.** Feb. 23, 1996, Oakland, CA

Vocals, Kazoo, Piano, Guitar / Blues Revival, East Coast Blues, Piedmont Blues, Country Blues

Brownie McGhee's death in 1996 represents an enormous and irreplaceable loss to the blues field. Although he had been semi-retired and suffering from stomach cancer, the guitarist was still the leading Piedmont-style bluesman on the planet, venerated worldwide for his prolific activities both on his own and with his longtime partner, the blind harpist Sonny Terry. Together, McGhee and Terry worked for decades in an acoustic folk-blues bag, singing ancient ditties like "John Henry" and "Pick a Bale of Cotton" for appreciative audiences worldwide. But McGhee was capable of a great deal more. Throughout the immediate post-war era, he cut electric blues and R&B on the New York scene, even enjoying a huge R&B hit in 1948 with "My Fault" for Savoy (Hal "Cornbread" Singer handled tenor sax duties on the 78). McGhee's third marathon session for OKeh in 1941 paired him for the first time on shellac with whooping harpist Terry for "Workingman's Blues."

The pair resettled in New York in 1942. After the end of World War II, McGhee began to record most prolifically, both with and without Terry, for a myriad of R&B labels: Savoy (where he cut "Robbie Doby Boogie" in 1948 and "New Baseball Boogie" the next year), Alert, London, Derby, Sittin' in With and its Jax subsidiary in 1952, Jackson, Bobby Robinson's Red Robin logo (1953), Dot, and Harlem, before crossing over to the folk audience during the late '50s with Terry at his side. One of McGhee's last dates for Savoy in 1958 produced the remarkably contemporary "Living with the Blues," with Roy Gaines and Carl Lynch blasting away on lead guitars and a sound light years removed from the staid folk world. *—Bill Dahl*

Brownie McGhee & Sonny Terry Sing / 1958 / Smithsonian/Folkways ♦♦♦♦

One of the duo's best acoustic folk-blues collaborations, originally issued in 1958. They convincingly run through a very enjoyable series of collaborations marked by affectionate interplay, with drummer Gene Moore adding rhythmic power. *—Bill Dahl*

Back Country Blues / Nov. 1958 / Savoy ♦♦♦♦♦

Brownie McGhee's solo material had a certain charm and compelling quality missing from his collaborations with Terry. For whatever reason, he tended to try more things alone and vary his approach, sound and delivery. This is first-rate country and topical material, delivered without the forced humor that eventually made his dates with Terry more camp than substance. *—Ron Wynn*

The Bluesville Years, Vol. 5: Mr. Brownie & Mr. Sonny / Oct. 6, 1960-Apr. 1962 / Prestige ♦♦♦

The musical partnership of Brownie McGhee and Sonny Terry stood the test of time and quality wise hardly ever wavered below magnificent. This 17-track collection is culled from four excellent Bluesville vinyl albums from the early 1960s and features numerous fine moments. Starting with five selections from Brownie's first solo album for the label, we find the duo augmented with the presence of Bennie Foster on second guitar with Brownie handling all the vocals. Sonny's solo sides emanate from two separate sessions, the first of which features Brownie's famous brother Stick ("Drinkin' Wine Spo-Dee-O-Dee") contributing guitar on three tracks which also include J.C. Burris on second harmonica behind Terry. The second 1960 session features Lightnin' Hopkins as a somewhat chaotic backup guitarist behind Sonny on two cuts. The compilation closes with seven romping, loosely played tracks from a live performance at the Philadelphia folk club, the Second Fret in April of 1962. The oddball instrumentation on several tracks and the guest turns by Stick and Lightnin' makes this a Brownie and Sonny a cut above the usual and worth seeking out. *—Cub Koda*

Brownie McGhee & Sonny Terry at the 2nd Fret / Mar. 1963 / Bluesville/Original Blues Classics ♦♦♦♦♦

Brownie McGhee and Sonny Terry were the ultimate blues duo; McGhee's stylized singing and light, flickering guitar was wonderfully contrasted by Terry's sweeping, whirling harmonica solos and intense, country-tinged singing. They were in great form during the 10 tunes featured on this live date, recently reissued on CD. Sometimes, as on "Custard Pie" or "Barking Bull Dog," they're funny; at other times, they were prophetic, chilling or moving. This is Piedmont blues at its best, and this disc's tremendous remastering provides a strong sonic framework. *—Ron Wynn*

Brownie's Blues / 1971 / Bluesville/Original Blues Classics ♦♦♦

★ **The Folkways Years (1945-1959)** / 1991 / Smithsonian/Folkways ♦♦♦♦♦

Folkways Years (1945-1959) is a wonderful 17-track compilation of Brownie McGhee's Folkways recordings. During this time, McGhee became a staple on the blues-folk revival circuit, and accordingly these recordings find the Piedmont bluesman playing in a folk style, which he excelled at. Many of the most powerful tracks are straight from the rural Piedmont tradition, but the folkier material shows what a rich musician he was. It's an excellent sampler, one that demonstrates the depth and breadth of his Folkways recordings. *—Thom Owens*

☆ **The Complete Brownie McGhee** / 1994 / Columbia/Legacy ♦♦♦♦♦

Well, complete as far as his pre-war country blues waxings for OKeh sans Sonny Terry (except for one or two where the whooping harpist provided accompaniment). McGhee was working firmly in the Piedmont tradition by 1940, when he signed with OKeh and began cutting the 47 enlightening sides here, which represent some of the purest country blues he ever committed to posterity. *—Bill Dahl*

Blues Is Truth / May 21, 1996 / Blues Alliance ♦♦♦♦

A Long Way from Home / Mar. 24, 1998 / MCA ♦♦♦♦

Music from Brownie and Sonny's latter period, circa March and September of 1969. This combines two albums (*A Long Way from Home* and *I Couldn't Believe My Eyes*, both cut in two days) recorded for ABC-Bluesway, with the inclusion of a stray unreleased track, "Beggin' You," from the second session in September. The personnel stays basically the same for both sessions with excellent rhythm section support from drummer Panama Francis and bassist Jimmy Bond, while the September session also includes Earl Hooker on guitar. Solid, relaxed, rockin' grooves are the hallmarks here with both artists in fine form. *—Cub Koda*

New York Blues 1946-1948 / Feb. 15, 2000 / EPM Musique ♦♦♦♦

Invited to Washington, D.C. by Paul Robeson to appear at a civil-rights defense concert along with Leadbelly, Brownie McGhee and Sonny Terry came up north in 1942 and eventually settled in New York where they played all manner of hootenannies and loft parties around Greenwich Village with other big names in the growing folk boom: Leadbelly, Big Bill Broonzy, Woody Guthrie, and Pete Seeger. *New York Blues 1946-1948* includes 22 tracks recorded for the labels Alert, Disc, and Savoy during McGhee's first few years there, with celebrated sidemen like Sonny Terry (on six tracks), his brother Sticks McGhee, Champion Jack Dupree, Baby Dodds, Pops Foster, and others. The music emphasizes not his Village folk-revival style but a bluesy urban R&B for songs like "Sportin' Life Blues," "Big Legged Woman," "Worried Life Blues," "Drinkin' Wine Spo-Dee-O-Dee," and "My Fault." Though the sound quality is inferior, these are great performances. *—John Bush*

Big Jay McNeely (Cecil James McNeely)

b. Apr. 29, 1927, Watts, CA

Sax (Tenor), Saxophone / Jazz Blues, Jump Blues, Soul-Jazz, West Coast Blues, R&B

His mighty tenor sax squawking and bleating with wild-eyed abandon, Big Jay McNeely blew up a torrid R&B tornado from every conceivable position—on his knees, on his back, being wheeled down the street on an auto mechanic's "creeper" like a modern-day pied piper. As one of the titans who made tenor sax the solo instrument of choice during rock's primordial era, McNeely could peel the paper right off the walls with his sheets of squealing, honking horn riffs. His raucous one-note honking on "The Deacon's Hop" gave him and Savoy an R&B chart-topper in 1949, and his follow-up, "Wild Wig," also hit big for the young saxist with the acrobatic stage presence. From Savoy, McNeely moved to Exclusive in 1949, Imperial in 1950-51, King's Federal subsidiary in 1952-54 (where he cut some of his wildest waxings, including the mind-boggling "3-D"), and Vee-Jay in 1955. McNeely's live shows were the stuff that legends are made of—he electrified a sweaty throng of thousands packing L.A.'s Wrigley Field in 1949 by blowing his sax up through the stands and then from home plate to first base on his back! A fluorescently painted sax that glowed in the dark was another of his showstopping gambits. Today, McNeely records for his own little label and tours the country and overseas regularly. This deacon's still hopping! *—Bill Dahl*

Big Jay in 3-D / Aug. 26, 1952-Apr. 8, 1954 / King ♦♦♦♦

Tenor saxophonist Big Jay McNeely swings and honks his way through 12 classic Federal sides from 1952-1954. Joined by brother Robert on baritone, McNeely and his combo work a well-worn jump blues groove on gospel-imbued scorchers like "Hot Cinders" and "The Goof." Equally adept at torrid and moderate tempos, McNeely also shows off his Illinois Jacquet-inspired chops with a dizzying array of bleats, screeches, and guttural smears, even throwing in some svelte lines when appropriate. And while cuts like "Ice Water" presage the coming of rock & roll, classy swingers such as "Hardtack" offer a unique blend of R&B and jazz adorned with bongo accompaniment. And then there's "3-D," the centerpiece of the set and one of the most blistering of R&B instrumentals. Even amidst the almost pneumatic rhythm, McNeely masterfully wails above the band, not missing a beat during his irrepressible call-and-response workout with the other horn players. Whether blowing teenage brains out at LA's *Shrine Auditorium* or with classic records like this, Big Jay McNeely always backed up the hysteria with loads of good music. *—Stephen Cook*

Live at Birdland: 1957 / 1957 / Collectables ♦♦♦♦

An amazing artifact from 1957, when live recordings like this one didn't happen very often. A Seattle engineer with a spanking-new stereo tape recorder captured the contents of this disc while McNeely and his swinging combo were working out at a Seattle nightspot called the Birdland. He gets plenty of room to peel the paper from the gin joint's walls as he wails on "Flying Home," "How High the Moon," and "Let It Roll." *—Bill Dahl*

Swingin' / 1958-1960 / Collectables ♦♦♦♦

Gymnastic sax maniac's output for L.A. deejay Hunter Hancock's Swingin' logo during the late '50s and early '60s. Naturally, his smash "There Is Something on Your Mind" is front and center, alongside the oddly titled "Back... Shack... Track," "Psycho Serenade," and "Blue Couch Boogie." Little Sonny Warner is the vocalist on some sides. *—Bill Dahl*

● **Nervous** / 1995 / Saxophile ♦♦♦♦♦

A thorough 19-track examination of McNeely's early heyday, incorporating a live 1951 reprise of his signature "Deacon's Hop," and the King label classics "3-D," "Nervous Man Nervous," and "Texas Turkey," a handful of live 1957 efforts that include the crazed "Insect Ball," and McNeely's original hit version of the incendiary blues ballad "There Is Something on Your Mind" (with Little Sonny Warner handling the Ray Charles-influenced lead vocal). *—Bill Dahl*

Blind Willie McTell (William Samuel McTell)

b. May 5, 1901, Thomson, GA, **d.** Aug. 19, 1959, Milledgeville, GA

Vocals, Accordion, Harmonica, Guitar, Guitar (Acoustic) / East Coast Blues, Piedmont Blues, Country Blues, Acoustic Blues

Willie Samuel McTell was one of the blues' greatest guitarists, and also one of the finest singers ever to work in blues. A major figure with a local following in Atlanta from the 1920s onward, he recorded dozens of sides throughout the 1930s under a multitude of names—all the better to juggle "exclusive" relationships with many different record labels at once—including Blind Willie, Blind Sammie, Hot Shot Willie, and Georgia Bill, as a backup musician to Ruth Mary Willis. And those may not have been all of his pseudonyms—we don't even know what he chose to call himself, although "Blind Willie" was his preferred choice among friends. He played a standard six-string acoustic until the mid-'20s, and never entirely abandoned the instrument, but from the beginning of his recording career, he used a 12-string acoustic in the studio almost exclusively. Willie's technique on the 12-string instrument was unique. Unlike virtually every other bluesman who used one, he relied not on its resonances as a rhythm instrument, but, instead, displayed a nimble, elegant slide and finger-picking style that made it sound like more than one guitar at any given moment. He worked medicine shows, carnivals, and other outdoor venues, and was a popular attraction, owing to his sheer dexterity and a nasal singing voice that could sound either pleasant or mournful, and incorporated some of the characteristics normally associated with White hillbilly singers. Willie's recording career began in late 1927 with two sessions for Victor records, eight sides including "Statesboro Blues." McTell's earliest sides were superb examples of storytelling in music, coupled with dazzling guitar work. All of McTell's music showed extraordinary power, some of it delightfully raucous ragtime, other examples evoking darker, lonelier sides of the blues, all of it displaying astonishingly rich guitar work. *—Bruce Eder*

☆ **Atlanta Twelve String** / 1949 / Atlantic ♦♦♦♦♦
In 1949, a brief flurry of interest in old-time country blues resulted in this 15-song session by McTell for the newly formed Atlantic Records. Only two songs, "Kill It Kid" and "Broke Down Engine Blues," were ever issued on a failed single, and the session was forgotten until almost 20 years later. McTell is mostly solo here, vividly captured on acoustic 12-string (his sometime partner Curley Weaver may have been present on some tracks), and in excellent form. The playing and the repertory are representative of McTell as he was at this point in his career, a blues veteran rolling through his paces without skipping a beat and quietly electrifying the listener. Songs include "Dying Crapshooter's Blues," "The Razor Ball," and "Ain't I Grand to Live a Christian." *—Bruce Eder*

Last Session / 1960 / Yazoo ♦♦♦♦♦
This recording has a less-than-stellar reputation, principally because it was done so late in McTell's career, and it is true that he lacks some of the edge, especially in his singing, that he showed on his other postwar recordings. On the other hand, his 12-string playing is about as nimble as ever and a real treat. McTell cut these sides for record store owner Ed Rhodes, who had begun taping local bluesmen at his shop in Atlanta in the hope of releasing some of it—McTell took to the idea of recording only slowly, then turned up one night and played for the microphone and anyone who happened to be listening, finishing a pint of bourbon in the process—the result was a pricelessly intimate document, some of the words slurred here and there, but brilliantly expressive and stunningly played. No apologies are needed for "The Dyin' Crapshooter's Blues," "Don't Forget It," or "Salty Dog," however. McTell lived a few more years but never recorded again, which is a pity because based on this tape he still had a lot to show people. Rhodes never did anything with the tapes, and might've junked them if he hadn't remembered how important the McTell material was—they turned out to be the only tapes he saved, out of all he'd recorded. *—Bruce Eder*

The Early Years 1927-1933 / 1989 / Yazoo ♦♦♦
This is one of the few Yazoo records that cannot be recommended as a potential first choice, because it was done relatively early. The sound is okay, but the song selection—all made up of pre-World War II material, as usual for Yazoo—is rather paltry compared with McTell collections that have come out since. It's not a bad choice, just not as good as some others, and it does include a decent, if limited, cross-section of early material, including "Statesboro Blues." *—Bruce Eder*

☆ **Complete Recorded Works, Vol. 1 (1927-1931)** / 1990 / Document ♦♦♦♦♦
Of all the compilations of McTell's early work, this is probably the most rewarding, because it includes both his Victor songs (including "Statesboro Blues") and his Columbia sides (which have been issued separately by Columbia-Legacy), and RCA-BMG seems to be in no hurry to put any of the Victor material out as a comprehensive collection. The songs all have some noise—there are no "masters" to speak of on acoustic blues of this vintage—but none of it is overly obtrusive, and the orderly chronology is very illuminating. Subsequent volumes from Document are also worthwhile, but Sony-Legacy does have superior workmanship in dealing with much of the same material. *—Bruce Eder*

☆ **Pig 'n Whistle Red** / 1993 / Biograph ♦♦♦♦♦
This collection of 20 songs, cut by McTell with Curley Weaver on second guitar and sharing the vocals, was left out of many McTell biographical accounts until it resurfaced in 1993. Cut for Regal Records in 1950, it's a remarkable document, capturing McTell and Weaver in vivid modern sound, and includes remakes of McTell's 1933 "Talkin' to You Mama" and "Good Little Thing" as well as more recent material that the two had been doing, and even outtakes, showing very different interpretations of the 1920s pop standard "Pal of Mine" and the gospel number "Sending Up My Timber." The sheer diversity of material makes this an indispensable (as well as a delightful) recording, and except for some minor tape damage on "A to Z Blues" and one other cut, there are few technical flaws here. The playing is so sharp and crisp, and vocals so delicate in their textures, that this collection has to be considered essential to any serious blues collection. McTell and Weaver were a legendary duo in Atlanta from before World War II, and it is nothing less than a gift to have them still together and in excellent form on this postwar recording. *—Bruce Eder*

★ **The Definitive Blind Willie McTell** / 1994 / Columbia/Legacy ♦♦♦♦♦
This double-CD set is a little misleading. It is definitive, but only in terms of McTell's Columbia and Okeh sides—you won't find "Statesboro Blues" or his other earliest sides here, because they were done for Victor. But the material that is here is all worthwhile, and this is the best single source for McTell's work for those labels (done under a variety of names) from the mid-'30s, very nicely remastered and thoroughly annotated, although producer Lawrence Cohn concedes that even Sony Legacy was unable to locate sources on a handful of songs that McTell is known to have recorded. *—Bruce Eder*

Memphis Jug Band

f. Memphis, TN
Group / Acoustic Memphis Blues
One of the definitive jug bands of the '20s and early '30s, this seminal group was comprised of Will Shade, Will Weldon, Hattie Hart, Charlie Polk, Walter Horton, and others, in various configurations.

Guitarist/harpist Will Shade formed the Memphis Jug Band in the Beale Street section of Memphis in the mid-'20s. A few years after their formation, Shade signed a contract with Victor Records in 1927. Over the next seven years, Shade and the Memphis Jug Band recorded nearly 60 songs for the record label. During this time, a number of musicians passed through the group, including Big Walter Horton, Furry Lewis, and Casey Bill Weldon. Throughout all of the various lineup incarnations, Shade provided direction for the group. The Memphis Jug Band played a freewheeling mixture of blues, ragtime, vaudeville, folk, and jazz, which was all delivered with good-time humor. That loose spirit kept the group and its records popular throughout the early '30s.

Although the group's popularity dipped sharply in the mid-'30s, Will Shade continued to lead the group in various incarnations until his death in 1966. *—Cub Koda & Stephen Thomas Erlewine*

★ **Memphis Jug Band** / 1927-1934 / Yazoo ♦♦♦♦♦
This definitive 28-song collection by the city's finest jug band spans their output from 1927 to 1934. *—John Floyd*

☆ **Complete Recorded Works, Vol. 3 (1930)** / 1990 / Document ♦♦♦♦♦
The third of three Document CDs has all of the Memphis Jug Band's 1930 recordings. Despite the onset of the Depression, the influential band's good-time style was unchanged and actually had improved a bit during the past couple of years. Will Shade was still its leader and alternated between guitar, harmonica and vocals. The other original member was Ben Ramey on kazoo. During 1930, such players as mandolinist Charlie Burse, Hambone Lewis and Jab Jones on jug, singer Charlie Nickerson, Vol Stevens on banjo-mandolin and even guest vocalist/guitarist Memphis Minnie (on "Bumble Bee Blues" and "Meningitis Blues") passed through the band. Among the more memorable selections of their highly enjoyable CD are "Everybody's Talking About Sadie Green," "Cocaine Habit Blues," "Fourth Street Mess Around," "Going Back to Memphis," "Move that Thing" and "He's in the Jailhouse Now." *—Scott Yanow*

Complete Recorded Works, Vol. 1 (1927-1928) / 1990 / Document ♦♦♦♦♦
One of the greatest of all jug bands and possibly the most influential, the Memphis Jug Band recorded extensively from 1927-30. All of its recordings (other than three sessions from 1934) have been reissued by the European Document label on three CDs. The original version of the group consisted of Will Shade on harmonica, guitar and/or vocals; Ben Ramey on kazoo; guitarist/signer Will Weldon; and Charlie Polk on jug. During the year-long period covered in this CD, the only significant personnel change was the addition of Vol Stevens on banjo-mandolin and guitar. The good-time music that they performed ranged from blues to pop numbers and even a couple waltzes. All three of the Document CDs are fairly equal in quality, with the second volume getting a slight edge. Among the highlights of *Vol. 1* are "Memphis Jug Blues," "I Packed My Suitcase, Started to the Train," "Kansas City Blues" (recorded just a few days after Jim Jackson's famous version), the heated "Beale Street Mess Around" and a previously unreleased "She Stays Out All Night Long." Fun music that still communicates to today's listeners. *—Scott Yanow*

☆ **Complete Recorded Works, Vol. 2 (1928-1929)** / 1990 / Document ♦♦♦♦♦
The Memphis Jug Band was quite popular from 1927-30, particularly if one judges the group by its many recordings (which fill up three CDs in this series). The second volume has slightly better material than the other two CDs, but all are easily recommended. During 1928 and 1929 the Memphis Jug Band featured its leader Will Shade on guitar, harmonica and vocals, and guitarist Charlie Burse (guitarist Will Weldon and banjo-mandolist Vol Stevens from the first group departed by 1929). The band also included the highly expressive kazoo playing of Ben Ramey and Jab Jones' enthusiastic jug playing (an improvement on his predecessor Charlie Polk). Additionally, there are two selections included in which the band accompanies singer Minnie Wallace and there are a few guest musicians and singers on various tracks. Among the many high points of the spirited program are "She Stays Out All Night Long," "Lindberg Hop," "Stealin' Stealin'," "Jug Band Waltz," "The Old Folks Started It" and "Memphis Yo Yo Blues." An important if often overlooked genre of vintage American music. *—Scott Yanow*

Memphis Minnie (Lizzie Douglas)

b. Jun. 3, 1897, Algiers, LA, **d.** Aug. 6, 1973, Memphis, TN
Vocals, Guitar, Banjo / Acoustic Chicago Blues, Acoustic Memphis Blues, Classic Female Blues, Acoustic Blues
Tracking down the ultimate woman blues guitar hero is problematic because woman blues singers seldom recorded as guitar players and woman guitar players (such as Rosetta Tharpe and Sister O.M. Terrell) were seldom recorded playing blues. Excluding contemporary artists, the most notable exception to this pattern was Memphis Minnie. The most popular and prolific blueswoman outside the vaudeville tradition, she earned the respect of critics, the support of record-buying fans, and the unqualified praise of the blues artists she worked with throughout her long career. Despite her Southern roots and popularity, she was as much a Chicago blues artist as anyone in her day. Big Bill Broonzy recalls her beating both him and Tampa Red in a guitar contest and claims she was the best woman guitarist he had ever heard. Tough enough to endure in a hard business, she earned the respect of her peers with her solid musicianship and recorded good blues over four decades for Columbia, Vocalion, Bluebird, Okeh, Regal, Checker, and JOB. *—Barry Lee Pearson*

★ **Hoodoo Lady (1933-1937)** / 1933-1937 / Columbia/Legacy ♦♦♦♦♦
Memphis Minnie is a unique figure in blues history, a female country blues singer who

emerged in the late 1920's when the field (at least on record) was exclusively filled by men. But, gender aside, she was one of the most talented blues singer-guitarists of the '30s and '40s. This CD reissue primarily dates from her period between her partnerships with Cousin Joe and Little Son Joe. Minnie is heard mostly playing her variations of goodtime urban blues (a la Bill Broonzy), an even 12 bars to a chorus but with the feeling and emotion of the country blues. Pianist Blind John Davis and Charlie McCoy's mandolin help out on some of the tracks of the accessible set which serves as a fine introduction to Memphis Minnie; five of its 20 selections were previously unreleased. *—Scott Yanow*

Early Rhythm & Blues from the Rare Regal Sessions: 1934-1942 / 1934-1942 / Biograph ✦✦✦✦✦
You can't go wrong with Memphis Minnie at almost any point in her estimable career. During the 1930s and early '40s, she made the adjustment to changing styles, but in the early '30s she *made* the style. The sound quality is pretty good throughout the set, although it's better on the later tunes. *—Ron Wynn*

Queen of the Blues / Oct. 7, 1997 / Columbia/Legacy ✦✦✦✦✦
Eighteen stellar selections recorded between 1929 and 1946 that clearly show what a potent musical force this woman truly was. Working with second and third husbands Kansas Joe McCoy and Ernest "Little Son Joe" Lawlars, this was a prime period for Minnie's creativity, going from the lowdown blues of "Has Anyone Seen My Man?" to the celebratory novelty of "Joe Louis Strut." Three of the tracks here ("Fashion Plate Daddy," "Killer Diller Blues" and "Please Don't Stop Him") are previously unissued, and the disc transfers are clean and sharp throughout. This perfect little primer set also includes the original version of "When the Levee Breaks," later recorded and partially credited to Led Zeppelin. *—Cub Koda*

Memphis Slim (John 'Peter' Chatman)

b. Sep. 3, 1915, Memphis, TN, **d.** Feb. 24, 1988, Paris, France
Vocals, Piano / Piano Blues, Acoustic Blues
An amazingly prolific artist who brought a brisk air of urban sophistication to his frequently stunning presentation, Memphis Slim assuredly ranks with the greatest blues pianists of all time. He was smart enough to take Big Bill Broonzy's early advice about developing a style to call his own to heart, instead of imitating that of his idol, Roosevelt Sykes. Soon enough, other 88s pounders were copying Slim rather than the other way around—his thundering ivories attack set him apart from most of his contemporaries, while his deeply burnished voice possessed a commanding authority. Born and raised in Memphis, he moved to Chicago and began recording as a leader in 1939 for OKeh and later Bluebird. Slim joined Hy-Tone Records in the mid-'40s, cutting eight tracks that were later picked up by King. The Miracle label reeled in the pianist in 1947, and issued his classics "Lend Me Your Love," "Rockin' the House" and "Nobody Loves Me." After moving from Miracle to Peacock to Premium to Chess to Mercury, he stayed put at Chicago's United Records from 1952 to 1954. Before the decade was through, the pianist landed at Vee-Jay Records, where he cut definitive versions of his best-known songs with a stellar combo. In 1962, Slim moved to Paris and remained there until his death in 1988. *—Bill Dahl*

Memphis Slim at the Gate of the Horn / 1959 / Vee-Jay ✦✦✦✦✦
Only this disc's short length (34 minutes) qualifies as something worthy of complaint; otherwise, this is seminal blues piano, performed by a great player and singer, Memphis Slim. This 1959 session had everything: super piano solos, a strong lineup of horn players, clever, well-written and sung lyrics, and a seamless pace that kept things moving briskly from beginning to end. Other than Slim, instrumental honors go to guitarist Matt Murphy, a marvelous accompanist who was able to blend sophistication, technique, and earthiness into one dynamic package. Even at its bargain-basement length, *At the Gate of Horn* belongs in any blues fan's library. *—Ron Wynn*

Memphis Slim / 1961 / MCA/Chess ✦✦✦✦
A straight CD reissue of a vintage Chess LP, its contents dating back to the early '50s and most tracks originally issued on the Premium logo. Includes an early and very nice reading of "Mother Earth;" also sharp as a tack is "Rockin' the Pad." In an unusual move, Slim is joined by a smooth vocal group, the Vagabonds, for "Really Got the Blues." *—Bill Dahl*

All Kinds of Blues / 1963 / Bluesville/Original Blues Classics ✦✦✦
A good-natured 1961 solo piano session, with Slim's mastery of boogie-woogie styles to the fore on both instrumentals and tunes punctuated by folky monologues. The material's mostly traditional in origin, though Slim wrote the lyrics for the most memorable performance, "Mother Earth." *—Richie Unterberger*

The Real Folk Blues / 1966 / MCA/Chess ✦✦✦✦
Lots of duplication with the other Chess reissue CD here, so take your pick. Or pick 'em both up—you can't go wrong with either one of these early-'50s collections. *—Bill Dahl*

I'll Just Keep on Singin' the Blues / 1981 / 32 Jazz ✦✦✦✦
Recorded in 1961 in Chicago just before pianist Memphis Slim was to embark on a European tour and take up permanent residence there. Backed by members of his exciting '50s band the House Rockers (including Matt Guitar Murphy), *I'll Just Keep on Singin' the Blues* is a lost masterpiece. Slim and his band are in great form on this set of originals that ooze gutbucket postwar Chicago blues. This forgotten gem was reissued in 2000 on the budget label 32 jazz. *—Al Campbell*

★ **Rockin' the Blues** / 1981 / Charly ✦✦✦✦✦
The most complete gathering of Slim's 1958-1959 Vee-Jay output available on disc (16 songs to the even dozen on the *Gate of Horn* domestic disc) and the best-sounding too. This is the crowning achievement in Memphis Slim's massive legacy—he delivers his classics one right after another, backed by his unparalleled combo that was anchored by Matt "Guitar" Murphy's startlingly fresh solos. Along with the standbys—"Messin' Around," "Mother Earth," "Wish Me Well"—there's the catchy instrumental "Steppin' Out," later covered by Eric Clapton; the romping "What's the Matter," and a blistering "Rockin' the House" where the band nearly sails right out of the studio! *—Bill Dahl*

The Folkways Years: 1959-1973 / Feb. 22, 2000 / Smithsonian/Folkways ✦✦✦✦✦
These 21 tracks, selected from the recordings Memphis Slim did for Folkways, tend to be in solo piano or sparsely accompanied arrangements, as one would figure since Folkways was a traditionally oriented label. Still, it doesn't sound like a forced or awkward attempt to steer the pianist toward an outdated approach. It's just on the quiet and restrained side, and not different from numerous recordings Memphis Slim did for more commercially minded labels throughout his career. Although half of the material is just Slim alone at the piano (sometimes singing, sometimes not), it does actually show him in a variety of contexts. Willie Dixon accompanies him on bass on a few numbers; Jazz Gillum does the vocal and harmonica for "Key to the Highway" (which is actually a track on which Memphis Slim was the sideman, not the featured artist); Matt Murphy plays electric guitar on a few songs; Pete Seeger joins Memphis Slim and Dixon on "Midnight Special"; and there are actually drums by Jump Jackson on a couple of tunes. It's assured piano blues whatever the situation, not among his very best recordings, but certainly respectable. Unfortunately, the liner notes, quite detailed in most respects, do not give the dates of recordings for the individual tracks; from the sound of things, most of these date from 1959 and the early 1960s, although the title indicates a timespan of 1959-1973. Three of the cuts were previously unreleased, including "Every Day I Have the Blues," the atypical organ instrumental "The Gimmick," and the piano instrumental "The Dirty Dozens." *—Richie Unterberger*

Amos Milburn

b. Apr. 1, 1927, Houston, TX, **d.** Jan. 3, 1980, Houston, TX
Vocals, Piano / Jump Blues, West Coast Blues, Piano Blues, R&B
Boogie piano master Amos Milburn was born in Houston, and he died there a short 52 years later. In between, he pounded out some of the most hellacious boogies of the postwar era, usually recording in Los Angeles for Aladdin Records and specializing in good-natured upbeat romps about booze and its effects (both positive and negative) that proved massive hits during the immediate pre-rock era. After signing with Aladdin in 1946, his first date included a thundering "Down the Road Apiece" that presaged the imminent rise of rock & roll. The first of Milburn's 19 Top Ten R&B smashes came in 1948 with his party classic "Chicken Shack Boogie." With the ascent of "Bad, Bad Whiskey" to the peak of the charts in 1950, Milburn embarked on a string of similarly boozy smashes: "Thinking and Drinking," "Let Me Go Home Whiskey," "One Scotch, One Bourbon, One Beer" and "Good Good Whiskey" (his last hit in 1954). Alcoholism later brought the pianist down hard, giving these numbers a grimly ironic twist in retrospect. He left Aladdin for good in 1957, and recorded a comeback album for Motown in 1962 (even Little Stevie Wonder pitched in on harp for the sessions). Nothing could jump-start the pianist's fading career by then, though. A string of strokes limited his mobility and he eventually died in 1980. *—Bill Dahl*

☆ **The Complete Aladdin Recordings of Amos Milburn** / 1994 / Mosaic ✦✦✦✦✦
Seven discs tracing the entire 1946-1957 Aladdin Records legacy of jump blues pioneer Amos Milburn, whose rippling boogie-based piano talent and predilection of songs about booze made him a postwar R&B superstar. One hundred forty-five tracks in all (including plenty of unissued goodies) tab this as the ultimate collection for Milburn fans. He boogied like a champ at his first L.A. date for Aladdin with a thundering "Down the Road Apiece" and rocked equally hard a decade later down in New Orleans when he was re-cutting "Chicken Shack Boogie" with the crew at *Cosimo's*. Mosaic does their usual elegant presentational job on this R&B legend, not skimping on a thing. Fabulous box set. *—Bill Dahl*

★ **Best of Amos Milburn—*Down the Road Apiece*** */ Jan. 11, 1994 / EMI America* ✦✦✦✦✦
Pianist Amos Milburn mixed boogie-woogie with vocal energy and intensity to forge a style that was among early R&B's most exciting and appealing. Milburn's 1940s and '50s singles were sometimes fiery and sometimes silly, ranging from drinking songs and celebratory uptempo numbers to stomping instrumentals and an occasional blues or love tune. This excellent 26-track anthology contains such classic Milburn anthems as "Chickenshack Boogie," "One Scotch, One Bourbon, One Beer," "Let's Have A Party," and "Bad, Bad Whiskey," as well as lesser-known but just as spirited romps. The mastering bolsters the sound, but doesn't deaden it, while Joseph Laredo's liner notes clearly and completely outline Milburn's musical and cultural/historical significance. *—Ron Wynn*

Blues, Barrelhouse & Boogie Woogie: 1946-1955 / 1996 / Capitol ✦✦✦✦✦
Here's a very reasonable compromise between the pricey Mosaic box and EMI's incomplete single-disc treatment of Milburn's Aladdin legacy: a three-disc, 66-song package that's heavy on boogies and blues and slightly deficient in the ballad department (to that end, his smash "Bewildered" was left off). Everything that is aboard is top-drawer, though—the booze odes, many a party rocker, and a plethora of the double-entendre blues that Milburn reveled in during his early years. The absent 1956 remake of "Chicken Shack Boogie" is a humongous omission, though. *—Bill Dahl*

The Best of the Aladdin Recordings / Mar. 19, 1996 / Capitol ✦✦✦✦✦
Best of the Aladdin Recordings is quite similar to *Best of Amos Milburn—Down the Road Apiece*, which appeared two years before *The Aladdin Recordings*. All the key Milburn tracks are on both collections, and there isn't much difference between the minor cuts, which means either disc is essentially interchangeable and a good addition to a comprehensive R&B collection. *—Thom Owens*

Roy Milton

b. Jul. 31, 1907, Wynnewood, OK, **d.** Sep. 18, 1983, Los Angeles, CA
Vocals, Drums / Jazz Blues, Jump Blues, West Coast Blues, R&B
As in-the-pocket drummer of his own jump blues combo, the Solid Senders, Roy Milton was in a perfect position to drive his outfit just as hard or soft as he so desired. With his stellar sense of swing, Milton did just that; his steady backbeat on his 1946 single for Art Rupe's fledgling Juke Box—later Specialty—imprint, "R.M. Blues," helped steer it to the uppermost reaches of the R&B charts (his assured vocal didn't hurt either). "R.M. Blues" was such a huge seller that it established Specialty as a viable concern for the long haul. Rupe knew a good

thing when he saw it, recording Milton early and often through 1953. He was rewarded with 19 Top Ten R&B hits by the Solid Senders, including "Milton's Boogie," "True Blues," "Hop, Skip and Jump," "Information Blues," "Oh Babe" (a torrid cover of Louis Prima's jivey jump), and "Best Wishes." Milton's resident boogie piano specialist, Camille Howard, also sang on several Milton platters, including the 1947 hit "Thrill Me," concurrently building a solo career on Specialty. After amassing a voluminous catalog as one of Specialty's early bedrocks, Milton moved on to Dootone, King (there he cut the delectable instrumental "Succotash"), and Warwick (where he eked out a minor R&B hit in 1961, "Red Light") with notably less commercial success. *—Bill Dahl*

★ **Roy Milton & His Solid Senders** / Feb. 1978 / Specialty ✦✦✦✦✦
Certainly this is the place to go for Milton's most popular and influential material—a whopping 18 of the 25 cuts made the R&B Top Ten in the late '40s and early '50s. These include such classics as "R.M. Blues," "The Hucklebuck," and "Hop, Skip & Jump" (given a great rockabilly treatment in the 1950s by the Collins Kids). All of the tracks are prime jump blues, Milton occasionally slowing down the boogies into ballads; one number ("Thrill Me") features fellow jump blues star Camille Howard on vocals. *—Richie Unterberger*

Groovy Blues, Vol. 2 / 1992 / Specialty ✦✦✦✦✦
The rarities and unissued material begin to pop up on *Vol. 2*, making it even more of a feast for collectors. Milton's Solid Senders, featuring pianist/singer Camille Howard, guitarist Johnny Rogers, and a crew of roaring saxmen, were one of the tightest and most respected on the Coast. *—Bill Dahl*

Blowin' with Roy / 1994 / Specialty ✦✦✦✦✦
The third and presumably final entry in Specialty's exhaustive Milton reissue series is by no means a makeweight affair. Even when the Solid Senders tackled Tin Pan Alley fare like "Along the Navajo Trail," "Coquette," and "When I Grow Too Old to Dream," they swung 'em. More late-'40s/early-'50s rarities and unissued items galore. *—Bill Dahl*

Mississippi Sheiks

f. 1926, Jackson, MS, **db.** 193?
Group / String Bands, Country Blues, Acoustic Blues
The Mississippi Sheiks were one of the most popular string bands of the late '20s and early '30s. Formed in Jackson around 1926, the band blended country and blues fiddle music—both old-fashioned and risqué—and included guitarist Walter Vinson and fiddler Lonnie Chatmon, with frequent appearances by guitarists Bo Carter and Sam Chatmon, who were also busy with their own solo careers. The musicians were the sons of Ezell Chatmon, uncle of Charlie Patton and leader of an area string band that was popular around the turn of the century. The Mississippi Sheiks (who took their name from the Rudolph Valentino movie *The Sheik*) began recording for Okeh in 1930 and had their first and biggest success with "Sitting On Top of the World," which was a crossover hit and multi-million seller. In fact, the song became a national standard and has been recorded by Howlin' Wolf, Ray Charles and many more. The Mississippi Sheiks' popularity peaked in the early '30s, and their final recording session happened in 1935 for the Bluebird label. By the end of their career, the prolific and influential string band had recorded well over 60 songs, including the successful "Stop and Listen." *—Joslyn Layne*

★ **Stop & Listen** / Yazoo ✦✦✦✦✦
Stop and Listen collects 20 tracks the Mississippi Sheiks recorded in the early '30s, gathering together most of their best-known material (including "Sitting on Top of the World"), plus the previously unreleased "Livin' in a Strain." These records are of significant historical importance and this is the definitive compilation of this groundbreaking—and popular—string band. *—Thom Owens*

Little Brother Montgomery (Eurreal Montgomery)

b. Apr. 18, 1906, Kentwood, LA, **d.** Sep. 6, 1985, Champaign, IL
Vocals, Piano / Piano Blues
A notable influence to the likes of Sunnyland Slim and Otis Spann, pianist "Little Brother" Montgomery's lengthy career spanned both the earliest years of blues history and the electrified Chicago scene of the 1950s.

By age 11, Montgomery had given up on attending school to instead play in Louisiana juke joints. He came to Chicago as early as 1926 and made his first 78s in 1930 for Paramount (the booty that day in Grafton, WI, included two of Montgomery's enduring signature items, "Vicksburg Blues" and "No Special Rider"). Bluebird recorded Montgomery more prolifically in 1935-36 in New Orleans.

In 1942, Little Brother Montgomery settled down to a life of steady club gigs in Chicago, his repertoire alternating between blues and traditional jazz (he played Carnegie Hall with Kid Ory's Dixieland band in 1949). Otis Rush benefitted from his sensitive accompaniment on several of his 1957-58 Cobra dates, while Buddy Guy recruited him for similar duties when he nailed Montgomery's "First Time I Met the Blues" in a supercharged revival for Chess in 1960. That same year, Montgomery cut a fine album for Bluesville with guitarist Lafayette "Thing" Thomas that remains one of his most satisfying sets.

With his second wife, Janet Floberg, Montgomery formed his own little record company, FM, in 1969. The first 45 on the logo, fittingly enough, was a reprise of "Vicksburg Blues," with a vocal by Chicago chanteuse Jeanne Carroll (her daughter Karen is following in her footsteps around the Windy City). *—Bill Dahl*

Tasty Blues / 1960 / Prestige/Original Blues Classics ✦✦✦✦✦
Here's a very attractive example of a pianist with roots dug deep in pre-war tradition updating his style just enough to sound contemporary for 1960. With a little help from bassist Julian Euell and Lafayette Thomas (better-known as Jimmy McCracklin's guitarist), Montgomery swoops through his seminal "Vicksburg Blues" and "No Special Rider" with enthusiasm and élan. *—Bill Dahl*

● **Chicago: The Living Legends** / 1961 / Riverside/Original Blues Classics ✦✦✦✦✦
Chicago: The Living Legends was recorded live at the Birdhouse in Chicago. Much of the record is performed by Montgomery solo, although there's a handful of wonderful cuts that feature him with a small group of traditional jazz musicians. Most of the album is devoted to classic songs from the likes of Duke Ellington and Jelly Roll Morton, yet there are a couple of originals thrown in the mix as well. It's all distinguished by Montgomery's wonderful, laid-back performances, which make this a little gem. *—Thom Owens*

☆ **Complete Recorded Works (1930-1936)** / 1992 / Document ✦✦✦✦✦
This single CD from the European Document label has all of Montgomery's 26 prewar recordings as a leader. Two solo numbers are from 1930, including "Vicksburg Blues"; there are a couple songs from 1931 and four duets with guitarist Walter Vincson from 1935. The remainder of this release features Montgomery during a marathon session on Oct. 16, 1936 that resulted in 18 solo selections. All the numbers except the final three on this CD have vocals by Montgomery, but the most rewarding selections are those three instrumentals. On "Farish Street Jive," "Crescent City Blues" and "Shreveport Farewell," Little Brother Montgomery shows just how talented a pianist he was, making one regret that he felt compelled to sing (in a likable but not particularly distinctive voice) on all of the other numbers. A very complete and historic set. *—Scott Yanow*

Buddy Moss (Eugene Moss)

b. Jan. 16, 1914, Jewel, GA, **d.** Oct. 19, 1984, Atlanta, GA
Vocals, Harmonica, Guitar / East Coast Blues, Piedmont Blues, Country Blues
Eugene "Buddy" Moss was, in the estimation of many blues scholars, the most influential East Coast blues guitarist to record in the period between Blind Blake's final sessions in 1932 and Blind Boy Fuller's debut in 1935. A younger contemporary of Blind Willie McTell and Curley Weaver, from his childhood as one of 12 children of a sharecropper in Warren County, Georgia to his death in 1984, Eugene "Buddy" Moss was part of a near-legendary coterie of Atlanta bluesmen, and one of the few of his era lucky enough to work into the blues revival of the 1960s and '70s. A guitarist of uncommon skill and dexterity, he was a musical disciple of Blind Blake, and may well have served as an influence on Piedmont-style guitarist Blind Boy Fuller. Although his career was halted in 1935 by a six-year jail term, and then by the Second World War, Moss lived long enough to be rediscovered in the 1960s, when he revealed a talent undamaged by time or adversity. Performing both on harmonica and guitar, her recorded several influential sessions with Columbia and the American Record Company. *—Bruce Eder*

● **Buddy Moss 1933-1935** / 1933-1935 / Document ✦✦✦✦✦
Document's *Buddy Moss 1933-1935* does a nice job of collecting the highlights from the Piedmont bluesman's peak years, making it a solid single-disc introduction to the influential guitarist. *—Thom Owens*

Atlanta Blues Legend / 1967 / Biograph ✦✦✦✦✦
Recorded live on June 10, 1966 at a Washington, D.C. concert, this 11-song album (fleshed out to 18 numbers on CD with additional live tracks from elsewhere) was considered miraculous in its own time, and remains so. Moss's fingering was slowed only slightly from the ravages of time, and his voice had aged beautifully. He gets sympathetic harmonica accompaniment (some of it most impressive, especially on "Pushin' It") from Jeff Espina and occasional help (seemingly unneeded) from a second guitarist billed only as "J.J." Moss, who was then either 52 or 60 years old, rises to the occasion, turning in some dazzling acoustic guitar work (check out "Comin' Back"), very moving and expressive singing, and overall a performance that one can only guess is uncannily like the kind he would've done 30 years earlier. Included are fresh renditions of "Oh Lawdy Mama" and Moss's own, unique renditions of "I'm Sitting On Top of the World" and "Key To the Highway" (done as a guitar showcase that would put Eric Clapton and Duane Allman to shame, and referred to here as "I've Got To Keep To the Highway"). One of the most impressive, and maybe the best, of all 1960s rediscovery records by any '30s blues star—64 minutes of pure golden blues. *—Bruce Eder*

Barbecue Bob: Complete Recorded Works, Vol. 3 / Document ✦✦✦✦✦
This disc contains the Georgia Cotton Pickers songs on which Buddy Moss played on December 7, 1930. Although he is playing harmonica rather than guitar, they're necessary for any completists, and Bob's work is so closely related to Moss's music, that it's impossible to overlook any of it. *—Bruce Eder*

Charlie Musselwhite

b. Jan. 31, 1944, Kosciusko, MS
Vocals, Harmonica, Guitar / Harmonica Blues, Electric Harmonica Blues, Electric Chicago Blues, Modern Electric Blues
Harmonica wizard Norton Buffalo can recollect a leaner time when his record collection had been whittled down to only the bare essentials: *The Paul Butterfield Blues Band* and *Stand Back! Here Comes Charley Musselwhite's South Side Band.* Butterfield and Musselwhite will probably be forever linked as the two most interesting, arguably most important, products of the "White blues movement" of the mid-to-late '60s—not only because they were near the forefront chronologically, but because they each stand out as being especially faithful to the style. Each certainly earned the respect of his legendary mentors. No less than the late Big Joe Williams said, "Charlie Musselwhite is one of the greatest living harp players of country blues. He is right up there with Sonny Boy Williams [I], and he's been my harp player ever since Sonny Boy got killed." *—Dan Forte*

★ **Stand Back! Here Comes Charlie Musselwhite's Southside Band** / 1967 / Vanguard ✦✦✦✦✦
Charlie Musselwhite's earliest recording (reissued on CD) features the fine blues harmonica player when he was 22. His repertoire on this set has a few unusual selections including an instrumental version of "Christo Redemptor" (a jazz hit of the period interpreted here similar to a funeral march) and the effective one-chord vamp "Strange Land." Barry Goldberg's organ sounds very dated throughout the set and the musicians are sometimes out-of-tune but Harvey Mandel's guitar playing is consistently creative and Musselwhite (whose gruff

and untrained voice was already recognizable) already showed real maturity in his playing. *—Scott Yanow*

Stone Blues / 1968 / Vanguard ♦♦♦

☆ **Tennessee Woman** / 1969 / Vanguard ♦♦♦♦♦
The addition of jazz pianist Skip Rose gave a new dimension to the ensemble sound, and provided a perfect foil to Charlie's own soloing—especially on the re-take of "Cristo Redentor," extended to 11 minutes, shifting to double-time in spots. Rose's instrumental, "A Nice Day for Something," is a welcome change of pace, and Musselwhite's "Blue Feeling Today" compares favorably to fine covers of Little Walter and Fenton Robinson tunes. *—Dan Forte*

Takin' My Time / 1974 / Arhoolie ♦♦♦♦♦
Another highly talented and original ensemble—Rose still on piano, with the Ford brothers (Pat and Robben), on drums and guitar, respectively. Again, Rose contributes an original departure, the solo piano ballad "Two Little Girls"—and, as usual, it is to Charlie's credit that he welcomed such far-from-blues mood swings. Otherwise, the band's (especially Robben's) jazzier leanings were checked at the studio door, and Robben's guitar is mixed too low throughout. At this stage, Charlie was changing personnel too quickly to give any unit a second chance in the studio, which would have been especially interesting with this outfit. *—Dan Forte*

Memphis Tennessee / 1984 / Crosscut ♦♦♦♦♦
Though steel guitarist Freddie Roulette was pictured on *Tennessee Woman*, he did not play on the album; luckily he is given ample space here, and the combination of his eerie vocal-like sound, Jack Myers's solid but adventurous bass playing, and Skip Rose's jazz piano voicings made this edition of the Musselwhite band one of the most original blues outfits ever. Charlie is in fine form as well, on a rock-solid cover of Muddy's "Trouble No More," and a lyrical reading of "Willow Weep for Me," and his harp tour de force "Arkansas Boogie." *—Dan Forte*

Tell Me Where Have All the Good Times Gone— / 1984 / Blue Rock'it ♦♦♦♦

In My Time / 1993 / Alligator ♦♦♦♦♦
Charlie Musselwhite takes four different approaches on this Alligator release. On two tracks, he turns to guitar, proving a competent instrumentalist and convincing singer in a vintage Delta style. He also does two gospel numbers backed by the legendary Blind Boys of Alabama, which are heartfelt, but not exactly triumphs. Musselwhite reveals his jazz influence on three tracks, making them entertaining harmonica workouts. But for blues fans, Musselwhite's biting licks and spiraling riffs are best featured on such numbers as "If I Should Have Bad Luck" and "Leaving Blues." Despite the diverse strains, Musselwhite retains credibility throughout while displaying the wide range of sources from which he's forged his distinctive style. *—Ron Wynn*

Up & Down the Highway Live: 1986 / May 16, 2000 / Indigo ♦♦♦♦

Blues Never Die / Vanguard ♦♦♦♦
This may be an overview of Musselwhite's career (from the late '60s to the present—with some previously unreleased tracks, including the title cut), but it is not the best introduction to the artist. For that, his Vanguard '60s output is still recommended, along with the 1984 session on Blue Rock'it and Alligator's *In My Time*. *—Dan Forte*

Kenny Neal

b. Oct. 14, 1957, New Orleans, LA
Vocals, Piano, Harmonica, Guitar / Swamp Blues, Modern Electric Blues
The future of Baton Rouge swamp blues lies squarely in multi-instrumentalist Kenny Neal's capable hands— the second-generation southern Louisiana bluesman is entirely cognizant of the region's venerable blues tradition and imaginative enough to steer it in fresh directions, as his albums for Alligator confirm. His dad, harpist Raful Neal, was a Baton Rouge blues mainstay whose pals included Buddy Guy and Slim Harpo (the latter handed three-year-old Kenny an old harp one day as a toy, and that was it). At age 13, Neal was playing in his father's band, and he picked up a bass at 17 for Buddy Guy. In 1987, Neal cut his debut LP for Florida producer Bob Greenlee—a stunningly updated swamp feast initially marketed on King Snake Records as *Bio on the Bayou*. Alligator picked it up the following year, retitled it *Big News from Baton Rouge!!*, and young Neal was on his way. Neal's sizzling guitar work, sturdy harp, and gravelly, aged-beyond-his-years vocals have served him well ever since. *—Bill Dahl*

Big News from Baton Rouge!! / 1987 / Alligator ♦♦♦♦
The debut release for the second-generation bayou blues guitarist/harpist, whose gruff-before-their-time vocals retain their swamp sensibility while assuming a bright contemporary feel that tabs him as a leading contender for future blues stardom. [*Big News from Baton Rouge* was originally released in 1987 as *Bio on the Bayou* on King Snake Records.] *—Bill Dahl*

Devil Child / 1989 / Alligator ♦♦♦♦
Backed by a punchy horn section and sizzling rhythms, Neal didn't suffer from any sophomore jinx. Between Neal, his bass-playing co-producer Bob Greenlee, and drummer Jim Payne, there's some very crafty songwriting going on here—"Any Fool Will Do," "Bad Check," and "Can't Have Your Cake (And Eat It Too)" are among the standouts. *—Bill Dahl*

Bayou Blood / 1992 / Alligator ♦♦♦♦♦
You really can't go wrong with any of the guitarist's fine Alligator albums, but this one sparkles as brightly as any, with memorable outings like "Right Train, Wrong Track," "That Knife Don't Cut No More," and the steamy title track. Neal's albums are invariably dominated by well-chosen originals—no small feat these days. *—Bill Dahl*

Hoodoo Moon / 1994 / Alligator ♦♦♦♦
Neal is one of the most impressive young blues artists on the scene today—a fact borne out by the contents of this collection. Ably backed by a band that includes his brother Noel on bass and keyboardist Lucky Peterson, Neal indulges in a couple of covers this time, but the majority of the disc is original and incendiary. *—Bill Dahl*

● **Deluxe Edition** / Oct. 28, 1997 / Alligator ♦♦♦♦♦
Deluxe Edition is a great compilation of 15 highlights from Kenny Neal's first five albums for Alligator Records. Neal's records were more consistent than those from some of his Alligator peers, but this best-of collection is welcome since it provides a nice introduction for the neophyte. And, since it isolates the cream of the crop on one record, it's also not a bad bet for serious fans who want all the good stuff in one place. *—Thom Owens*

What You Got / Apr. 25, 2000 / Telarc ♦♦♦♦♦

Tracy Nelson

b. Dec. 27, 1947, Madison, WI
Vocals, Keyboards / Retro-Soul, Contemporary Blues
A very versatile and talented vocalist, Tracy Nelson is better known for her role as lead singer of Mother Earth. The Nashville sextet had three albums in a country-rock vein make the charts in the late '60s and early '70s. But Nelson is just as capable in soul, R&B, and blues, though she hasn't released many records in that style. Her albums for Flying Fish were more indicative of her eclecticism, but her R&B and blues roots are really evident on her 1993 release, *In The Here And Now*, and 1995's *I Feel So Good*—both on Rounder Records.

Born in California but raised in Madison, Wisconsin, Nelson began playing music when she was a student at the University of Wisconsin. Nelson began singing folk and blues at coffeehouses and R&B and rock & roll at parties with a covers band called the Fabulous Imitators. In 1964, she recorded an album for Prestige, *Deep Are the Roots*, which was produced by Sam Charters.

Two years after recording *Deep Are the Roots*, Nelson headed out to the West Coast, spending some time in Los Angeles before settling in San Francisco. After arriving in San Francisco, she formed Mother Earth in 1968, moving the group to Nashville the following year. The band stayed together for five years, recording several albums for Mercury Records, among a handful of other labels. Nelson left the band in the mid-'70s, embarking on a solo career that saw her release albums for a variety of labels, including Columbia, Atlantic, and Flying Fish.

Tracy Nelson continued to record and perform into the '90s. In 1993, she released *In the Here and Now*, her first album for Rounder Records and, not coincidentally, her first straight blues record since she began recording in the '60s. Nelson followed *In the Here and Now* with several acclaimed records of gritty blues-rock for Rounder. *—Ron Wynn & Stephen Thomas Erlewine*

● **The Best of Tracy Nelson & Mother Earth** / Sep. 9, 1996 / Reprise Archives ♦♦♦♦♦
Janis Joplin may have gotten all of the fame and glory, but she was far from the only white female blues shouter to emerge from the San Francisco music scene of the mid-1960s; *The Best of Tracy Nelson/Mother Earth* is proof positive of that, providing an excellent introduction to one of the more sadly overlooked talents of her time and place. Despite any number of passing similarites to Joplin, Nelson sings with greater finesse; her style is more adaptable as well, capable of fitting comfortably into R&B, psychedelia and pop ballads, all the while remaining grounded in classic roots music traditions. Highlighted by her perennial "Down So Low"—subsequently recorded by everyone from Linda Ronstadt to Etta James—this 17-track compilation also spotlights performances spanning from a wrenching cover of Little Willie John's "Need Your Love So Bad" to contemporary material like Steve Young's "Seven Bridges Road" and John Hiatt's "Thinking of You," offering a comprehensive overview of her earliest and most enduring work. *—Jason Ankeny*

Robert Nighthawk (Robert McCollum)

b. Nov. 30, 1909, Helena, AR, **d.** Nov. 5, 1967, Helena, AR
Slide Guitar, Vocals, Harmonica, Guitar / Slide Guitar Blues, Acoustic Chicago Blues, Electric Chicago Blues
Of all the pivotal figures in blues history, certainly one of the most important was Robert Nighthawk. He bridged the gap between Delta and Chicago blues effortlessly, taking his slide cues from Tampa Red and stamping them with a Mississippi edge learned first hand from his cousin, Houston Stackhouse. It should be noted that the huge lapses in the man's discography are direct results of his rambling nature, taciturness and seeming disinterest in making records. Once you got him into a studio, the results were almost always of a uniform excellence. But it might be two years or more between sessions. Nighthawk never achieved the success of his more celebrated pupils, Muddy Waters and Earl Hooker, finding himself to be much happier to be working one nighters in taverns and the Maxwell Street open market on Sundays.Robert Nighthawk is not a name that regularly gets bandied about when discussing the all-time greats of the blues. But well it should, because his legacy was all pervasive; his resonant voice and creamy smooth slide guitar playing (played in standard tuning, unusual for a bluesman) would influence players for generations to come and many of his songs would later become blues standards. *—Cub Koda*

Bricks in My Pillow / 1977 / Delmark ♦♦♦
This 14-song collection, consisting of tracks recorded on July 12, 1951 and October 25, 1952, completely transforms the landscape where Robert Nighthawk's music is concerned. Up to now, apart from seeking out his pre-war, unamplified work as Robert Lee McCoy (or McCullum) on Bluebird or grabbing a few tracks from some Chess reissues, there hasn't been a lot of Robert Nighthawk in one place. Now there are 14 hard-rocking tracks, cut for United Records in Chicago and showing Nighthawk in his prime and loving it, playing a mean slide underneath some boldly provocative singing that could have given Muddy Waters a run for his money. The style is there, and the voice and the guitar are there, so why didn't Nighthawk hit it big— Based on this collection, his style with an electric guitar, just wasn't as distinctive as Muddy's playing; additionally, he just didn't have Muddy's (or Chess songwriter Willie Dixon's) way with a catch-phrase—there are some okay songs here ("Kansas City," "You Missed a Good Man," "Bricks In My Pillow") but nothing as catchy or instantly memorable

as "I Can't Be Satisfied," "Hoochie Coochie Man" or "Got My Mojo Working." A pair of instrumentals, "Nighthawk Boogie" and "U/S Boogie," both driven by Nighthawk's guitar and a romping piano, pretty much make this collection worthwhile and show the man in his peak form. Included on this collection are a pair of previously unissued tracks, an alternate take of "Seventy-Four" and a loud, crunchy, but, alas, unfinished version of "The Moon Is Rising." The sound is surprisingly clean and rich, especially given the 1951-52 origins of the tapes. —*Bruce Eder*

★ **Live on Maxwell Street** / 1988 / Rounder ✦✦✦✦✦
Recorded by Norman Dayron live on the street (you can actually hear cars driving by!) in 1964 with just Robert Whitehead on drums and Johnny Young on rhythm guitar in support, Nighthawk's slide playing (and single string soloing, for that matter) are nothing short of elegant and explosive. Highlights include "The Maxwell Street Medley," which combines his two big hits "Anna Lee" and "Sweet Black Angel"; a mind-altering 12-bar solo on "The Time Have Come," which proves that Nighthawk's lead playing was just as well developed as his slide work; and a couple of wild instrumentals with Carey Bell sitting in on harmonica. Nighthawk sounds cool as a cucumber, presiding over everything with an almost genial charm while laying the toughest sounds imaginable. One of the top three greatest live blues albums of all time. The 2000 CD reissue on Bullseye Blues & Jazz adds five previously unreleased bonus tracks, although Nighthawk doesn't have a lead vocal on any of these. "The Real McCoy" is an instrumental, Young sings on "Big World Blues" and "All I Want for Breakfast/Them Kind of People," Bell sings "I Got News for You," and J.B. Lenoir takes a guest lead vocal on "Mama Talk to Your Daughter" (though Peter Gurlanick's liner notes express doubt that the singer is actually Lenoir). —*Cub Koda*

Masters of the Modern Blues / 1994 / Testament ✦✦✦✦

Johnny Otis

b. Dec. 28, 1921, Vallejo, CA
Vibraphone, Vocals, Drums, Piano / Jump Blues, West Coast Blues, R&B
Johnny Otis has modeled an amazing number of contrasting musical hats over a career spanning more than half a century. Bandleader, record producer, talent scout, label owner, nightclub impresario, disc jockey, TV variety show host, author, R&B pioneer, rock & roll star—Otis has answered to all those descriptions and quite a few more. Not bad for a Greek-American who loved jazz and R&B so fervently that he adopted the African-American culture as his own. Otis' influence on L.A.'s R&B scene soared exponentially when he and partner Bardu Ali opened the *Barrelhouse Club* in Watts. R&B replaced jazz in Otis's heart; he pared his big band down and discovered young talent such as the Robins, vocalists Mel Walker and Little Esther Phillips, and guitarist Pete Lewis that would serve him well in years to come. He signed with Newark, NJ-based Savoy Records in 1949, and the R&B hits came in droves: "Double Crossing Blues," "Mistrustin' Blues," and "Cupid's Boogie" all hit number one that year (in all, Otis scored ten Top Ten smashes that year alone!); "Gee Baby," "Mambo Boogie,"and "All Nite Long" lit the lamp in 1951, and "Sunset to Dawn") capped his amazing run in 1952. Otis was a masterful talent scout; among his other platinum-edged discoveries were Jackie Wilson, Little Willie John, Hank Ballard, and Etta James (he produced her debut smash "Roll with Me Henry"). —*Bill Dahl*

The Johnny Otis Show / 1958 / Savoy ✦✦✦✦✦
Some of the R&B bandleader's earliest and best work (1945-51) for Savoy. The cast includes singers Little Esther and Mel Walker, The Robins, and guitarist Pete Lewis. —*Bill Dahl*

Cold Shot / 1968 / J&T ✦✦✦

Live at Monterey / 1971 / Epic ✦✦✦✦✦
An R&B oldies show with a difference, the artists represented the cream of the crop of jump blues, and in 1970, they were still in fine form. The disc stars Otis, Esther Phillips, Eddie Vinson, Joe Turner, Ivory Joe Hunter, Roy Milton, Roy Brown, Pee Wee Crayton, and Johnny's guitar wielding son, Shuggie. —*Bill Dahl*

★ **Original Johnny Otis Show, Vol. 1** / 1994 / Savoy ✦✦✦✦✦
Twenty-seven of the Otis aggregation's best early sides for Savoy and Excelsior, including a slew of the group's early-'50s Little Esther and/or Mel Walker-fronted R&B smashes ("Mistrustin' Blues," "Cry Baby," "Sunset to Dawn"). Jimmy Rushing and the Robins also share vocal duties, as does Otis himself on a jumping "All Nite Long." This is one time when the bonus cuts are on the vinyl version—it contained 32 cuts appearing on a *Completer Disc* that Savoy Jazz reissued at the same time as this CD. The original artwork and liner notes have been reduced so much for the CD that they're unreadable (Pete Welding's essay deserves more respect). —*Bill Dahl*

The Complete Savoy Recordings / Savoy ✦✦✦✦✦
A deluxe three-disc set summing up Otis' pre-*Hand Jive* days as an R&B bandleader of some renown who employed various singers on a number of singles for the Savoy label. The recording debuts of the Robins, Little Esther Phillips, Mel Walker, guitarist Pete Lewis, and Linda Hopkins are all here, and you hear how Otis kept his ear to the ground, changing and moving to keep pace with a big-band scene that was slowly dying out, while making some marvelous DIY records along the way. Incredible notes from Billy Vera make this a box set well worth having in the collection. —*Cub Koda*

Junior Parker (Herman Parker, Jr.)

b. May 27, 1932, Clarksdale, MS, **d.** Nov. 18, 1971, Chicago, IL
Vocals, Harmonica / Soul-Jazz, Electric Memphis Blues, Soul-Blues, R&B, Soul
His velvet-smooth vocal delivery to the contrary, Junior Parker was a product of the fertile postwar Memphis blues circuit whose wonderfully understated harp style was personally mentored by none other than regional icon Sonny Boy Williamson. Little Junior (as he was known then) got his first recording opportunity in 1952 for the Modern label. Parker landed at Sun Records in 1953 and promptly scored a hit with his rollicking "Feelin' Good." Later that year, Little Junior cut a fiery "Love My Baby" and a laidback "Mystery Train" for Sun, though he moved on to the Duke label before the end of the year. He scored big in 1957 with the smooth "Next Time You See Me," an accessible enough number to even garner some pop spins. Parker developed a breathtaking brass-powered sound that pushed his honeyed vocals and intermittent harp solos with exceptional power. Parker's updated remake of Roosevelt Sykes's "Driving Wheel" was a huge R&B hit in 1961, as was the surging "In the Dark." Once Parker split from Robey's employ in 1966, though, his hitmaking fortunes declined. His 1966-68 output for Mercury and its Blue Rock subsidiary deserved a better reception than it got, but toward the end, he was covering the Beatles for Capitol. A brain tumor silenced Junior Parker's magic-carpet voice in late 1971. —*Bill Dahl*

Mystery Train / 1990 / Rounder ✦✦✦✦✦
This excellent little compilation features at least one extant take of everything Junior and his original band, the Blue Flames, recorded at Sun Records between 1952 to 1954. His debut single for the label and his first hit, the classic "Feelin' Good" is aboard as well as the equally fine (but originally unissued) "Feelin' Bad." His leanings toward smoother Roy Brown stylings are evident with tracks like "Fussing and Fighting Blues" and "Sitting and Thinking," but the follow-up to his first Sun single, the original version of "Mystery Train" and two takes of the flip side, "Love My Baby," are the must-hears on this collection. Fleshing out Parker's meager output for Sun are essential early tracks from James Cotton. Cotton doesn't blow harp on any of these, but the sax-dominated "My Baby," and especially "Cotton Crop Blues" and "Hold Me in Your Arms" with Pat Hare on super distorted blistering guitar are Memphis-'50s blues at its apex. Hare himself also rounds out the compilation with two tracks, the prophetic "I'm Gonna Murder My Baby" (Hare did exactly that and spent the rest of his life behind bars as a result) and the previously unissued "Bonus Pay." Don't let the short running time of this CD stop you from picking this one up; the music is beyond excellent. —*Cub Koda*

★ **Junior's Blues/The Duke Recordings, Vol. 1** / 1992 / MCA ✦✦✦✦✦
After the non-success of "Mystery Train" on the R&B charts, Parker jumped contract and signed with Don Robey's Houston-based Duke Records. With his smooth vocal approach, Parker clearly envisioned himself as the next Roy or Charles Brown. But from the evidence of these early sides, it's clear that Robey wanted to piggyback off the success of the Sun sound. Tracks like "I Wanna Ramble" were virtual carbon copies of the "Feelin' Good" riff and Parker's recasting of old favorites like Robert Johnson's "Sweet Home Chicago," Roosevelt Sykes's "Driving Wheel," "Yonder's Wall" and "Mother-In-Law Blues," were all clearly in the down-home vein that Parker felt was too "old timey" for an up-to-date musician/vocalist of his caliber. His first big hit for the label, the horn-driven "Next Time You See Me" is here with others in the same vein, but this otherwise excellent collection is curiously missing "Pretty Baby," Parker's version of Howlin' Wolf's "Riding in the Moonlight," certainly one of his best. —*Cub Koda*

Charley Patton

b. 1887, Edwards, MS, **d.** Apr. 28, 1934, Indianola, MS
Slide Guitar, Vocals, Guitar, Guitar (Acoustic) / Slide Guitar Blues, Prewar Gospel Blues, Prewar Blues, Delta Blues, Country Blues
If the Delta country blues has a convenient source point, it would probably be Charley Patton, its first great star. His hoarse, impassioned singing style, fluid guitar playing and unrelenting beat made him the original king of the Delta blues. Much more than your average itinerant musician, Patton was an acknowledged celebrity and a seminal influence on musicians throughout the Delta. Rather than bumming his way from town to town, Patton would be called up to play at plantation dances, juke joints and the like. He'd pack them in like sardines everywhere he went, and the emotional sway he held over his audiences caused him to be tossed off of more than one plantation by the ownership, simply because workers would leave crops unattended to listen to him play any time he picked up a guitar. He epitomized the image of a '20s "sport" blues singer; rakish, raffish, easy to provoke, capable of downing massive quantities of food and liquor, a woman on each arm with a flashy, expensive looking guitar fitted with a strap and kept in a traveling case by his side, only to be opened up when there was money or good times involved. His records—especially his first and biggest hit, "Pony Blues"—could be heard on phonographs throughout the South. Although he was certainly not the first Delta bluesman to record, he quickly became one of the genre's most popular. By late-'20s Mississippi plantation standards, Charley Patton was a star, a genuine celebrity. His music gives us the first flowering of the Delta blues form, before it became homogenized with turnarounds and 12-bar restrictions, and few humans went at it so agressively. —*Cub Koda*

★ **Founder of the Delta Blues** / 1969 / Yazoo ✦✦✦✦✦
A cornerstone of any blues collection, this is where you start. As compilations go, this originally started life as a double record set featuring all of Patton's best known titles and sound wise was miles above all previous versions. Its compact disc incarnation here trims the tune list to 24 tracks, but all the seminal tracks are here: "Pony Blues," "High Water Everywhere," "Screamin' and Hollerin' the Blues," "A Spoonful Blues," "Shake It and Break It" and the wistful "Poor Me," recorded at his final session in 1934, a scant two months before he died. —*Cub Koda*

Complete Recorded Works, Vol. 1 (1929) / 1990 / Document ✦✦✦✦✦
For completists, specialists and academics, Document's *Complete Recorded Works, Vol. 1 (1929)* is invaluable, offering an exhaustive overview of Charley Patton's early recordings. For less dedicated listeners, the disc is a mixed blessing. There are some absolutely wonderful, classic performances on the collection, but the long running time, exacting chronological sequencing, poor fidelity (all cuts are transferred from original acetates and 78s), and number of performances are hard to digest. The serious blues listener will find all these factors to be positive, but enthusiasts and casual listeners will find that the collection is of marginal interest for those very reasons. —*Thom Owens*

Complete Recorded Works, Vol. 2 (1929) / 1990 / Document ✦✦✦✦✦
For completists, specialists and academics, Document's *Complete Recorded Works, Vol. 2 (1929)* is invaluable, offering an exhaustive overview of Charley Patton's early recordings.

For less dedicated listeners, the disc is a mixed blessing. There are some absolutely wonderful, classic performances on the collection, but the long running time, exacting chronological sequencing, poor fidelity (all cuts are transferred from original acetates and 78s), and number of performances are hard to digest. The serious blues listener will find all these factors to be positive, but enthusiasts and casual listeners will find that the collection is of marginal interest for those very reasons. *—Thom Owens*

☆ **King of the Delta Blues** / 1991 / Yazoo ✦✦✦✦✦
This excellent companion volume to the above pulls together 23 more Patton tracks (including some alternate takes that were for years thought to be lost) to give a much more complete look at this amazing artist. It's interesting here to compare the tracks from his final session to his halcyon output from 1929. Highlights include "Mean Black Cat Blues," Patton's adaption of "Sitting on Top of the World" ("Some Summer Day") and both parts of "Prayer of Death," originally issued under the non de plume of "Elder J.J. Hadley." The sound on this collection is vastly superior from a noise reduction standpoint to its companion volume. *—Cub Koda*

Pinetop Perkins

b. Jul. 13, 1913, Belzoni, MS
Vocals, Piano, Guitar / Boogie-Woogie, Piano Blues, Acoustic Blues
He admittedly wasn't the originator of the seminal piano piece "Pinetop's Boogie Woogie," but it's a safe bet that more people associate it nowadays with Pinetop Perkins than with the man who devised it in the first place, Clarence "Pinetop" Smith. Although it seems as though he's been around Chicago forever, the Mississippi native actually got a relatively late start on his path to Windy City immortality. It was only when Muddy Waters took him on to replace Otis Spann in 1969 that Perkins's rolling mastery of the ivories began to assume outsized proportions. He accompanied Robert Nighthawk on a 1950 session for the Chess brothers that produced "Jackson Town Gal," but Chicago couldn't hold him at the time. Nighthawk disciple Earl Hooker recruited Perkins during the early '50s. They hit the road, pausing at Sam Phillips's studios in Memphis long enough for Perkins to wax his first version of "Pinetop's Boogie Woogie" in 1953. Music gradually was relegated to the back burner until Hooker coaxed him into working on an LP for Arhoolie in 1968. After more than a decade with Waters, Perkins and his bandmates left en masse to form the Legendary Blues Band. Their early Rounder albums (*Life of Ease, Red Hot 'n' Blue*) prominently spotlighted Perkins' rippling 88s and rich vocals. *—Bill Dahl*

● **After Hours** / 1988 / Blind Pig ✦✦✦✦✦
Easy-grooving blues and boogie is backed by the competent New York City-based blues band Little Mike and the Tornadoes. Though Perkins followed Otis Spann as the piano player in the Muddy Waters band, these are the first domestically available recordings under his own name. *—Niles J. Frantz*

Pinetop's Boogie Woogie / 1992 / Discovery ✦✦✦✦
The maze of new and recent discs by this veteran Chicago piano man can be daunting, but rest assured that this is one of his best to date. Many of the songs are Perkins standbys—"Kidney Stew," "Caldonia," and of course, "Pinetop's Boogie Woogie"—but the backing here is so stellar (sidemen include harpists James Cotton and Kim Wilson, guitarists Matt Murphy, Jimmy Rogers, Hubert Sumlin, and Duke Robillard, and several driving rhythm sections)—that the project rises above most of Perkins's output. *—Bill Dahl*

Portrait of a Delta Bluesman / 1993 / Vanguard ✦✦✦✦✦
Considerably more ambitious than just another Perkins set, this solo disc intersperses key songs from his storied history with interview segments that reveal much about the man himself, from his Delta beginnings to when he replaced Otis Spann in Muddy Waters' vaunted band. *—Bill Dahl*

Lucky Peterson

b. Dec. 13, 1964, Buffalo, NY
Vocals, Organ (Hammond), Drums, Piano, Guitar, Bass, Organ / Modern Electric Blues
Child-prodigy status is sometimes difficult to overcome upon reaching maturity. Not so for Lucky Peterson—he's far bigger (in more ways than one) on the contemporary blues circuit than he was at the precocious age of six, when he scored a national R&B hit with the Willie Dixon-produced "1-2-3-4." Little Lucky Peterson was lucky to be born into a musical family. His dad, James Peterson, owned the Governor's Inn, a popular Buffalo, NY, blues nightclub that booked the biggies: Jimmy Reed, Muddy Waters, Bill Doggett. The latter's mighty Hammond B-3 organ fascinated the four-and-a-half-year-old lad, and soon Peterson was on his way under Dixon's tutelage. "1-2-3-4" got Peterson on *The Tonight Show* and *The Ed Sullivan Show,* but he didn't rest on his laurels—he was doubling on guitar at age eight, and at 17, he signed on as Little Milton's keyboardist for three years.Two solo albums for Alligator, 1989's *Lucky Strikes!* and the following year's *Triple Play,* remain his finest recorded offerings. Extensive session work behind everyone from Etta James and Kenny Neal to Otis Rush also commenced during this period. In 1992, Peterson's first Verve label album, *I'm Ready,* found him boldly mixing contemporary rock and soul into his simmering blues stew. *—Bill Dahl*

Ridin' / Mar. 1984 / Evidence ✦✦✦✦✦
As a child prodigy, keyboardist and organist Lucky Peterson's exploits were legendary. The stories grew even more widespread as he became a teen and stints with Little Milton and Bobby "Blue" Bland only added to his fame. But Peterson's records have not always justified or reaffirmed his reputation. That is not the case with the cuts on this 1984 set, recently reissued by Evidence. The spiraling solos, excellent bridges, turnbacks, pedal maneuvers, and soulful accompaniment are executed with a relaxed edge and confident precision. If you have wondered whether Lucky Peterson deserves the hype and major label bonanza, these songs are the real deal. *—Ron Wynn*

Lucky Strikes / 1989 / Alligator ✦✦✦✦
Peterson's real coming-out party as a mature blues triple threat: his guitar and keyboard skills are prodigious (though he's no longer a child prodigy), and his vocals on "Pounding of My Heart," "Can't Get No Loving on the Telephone," and "Heart Attack" (all written by producer/bassist Bob Greenlee) served notice that more than luck was involved in Peterson's adult rise to fame. *—Bill Dahl*

● **Triple Play** / 1990 / Alligator ✦✦✦✦✦
Even more impressive than his previous Alligator set, thanks to top-flight material like "Don't Cloud Up on Me," "Let the Chips Fall Where They May," and "Locked Out of Love," the fine house band at Greenlee's King Snake studios, and Peterson's own rapidly developing attack on two instruments. *—Bill Dahl*

Kelly Joe Phelps

b. Oct. 5, 1959, Sumner, WA
Slide Guitar, Vocals / Contemporary Blues
Portland, Oregon-based acoustic/slide guitar player and singer-songwriter Kelly Joe Phelps has been carving a growing niche for his music throughout the 1990s and *Roll Away The Stone* (Rykodisc, 1997).

Phelps was raised in Washington and learned country and folk songs, as well as drums and piano, from his father. At first, he concentrated on free jazz and took his cues from musicians like Ornette Coleman, Miles Davis and John Coltrane before finding his true calling as a blues musician in the late '80s, when he began listening to acoustic blues masters like Fred McDowell and Robert Pete Williams. He began singing as well, and released his critically praised debut, *Lead Me On,* in 1995. Six original songs showcase Phelps' ability in the blues idiom, but he also tackles, and does justice to, traditional numbers like "Motherless Children" and "Fare Thee Well."

Phelps, as deft and creative an acoustic slide guitarist as you'll hear anywhere in the U.S., also made appearances on Greg Brown's album *Further In,* Tony Furtado's *Roll My Blues Away,* and Townes Van Zandt's *The Highway Kind.* In recent years, he's opened shows for B.B. King, Leo Kottke, Keb' Mo', Robben Ford and Little Feat. He released his second album, *Roll Away the Stone,* in 1997, and followed it up with 1999's *Shine Eyed Mister Zen.* *—Richard Skelly*

Lead Me On / 1995 / Burnside ✦✦✦✦
This is the real deal—Phelps performs with the full authority and authenticity of the Delta bluest tradition without ever once sounding like a Folkways museum piece. There's nothing more to it than the 34-year-old's raspy, swamp-infused vocals, lapstyle acoustic guitar played using fingerpicking and slide, and self-accompanied stomp-box percussion. For the six originals and seven gospel and prewar blues selections on offer here, it's more than enough. File alongside the likes of Ben Harper and Keb' Mo'. *—Roch Parisien*

● **Roll Away the Stone** / Aug. 26, 1997 / Rykodisc ✦✦✦✦
If anything, *Roll Away the Stone* is an even better record than Kelly Joe Phelps' debut, *Lead Me On.* Phelps continues to grow as both a musician and songwriter, and his interpretations of classic blues songs show increased imagination. Although it's based in classic blues, this music doesn't sound ancient—it sounds vital and alive, like any great music should. *—Thom Owens*

Shine Eyed Misted Zen / Jul. 13, 1999 / Rykodisc ✦✦✦✦
Phelps' third album is an accomplished serving of country blues that combines the sweet and sour power of his guitar playing with the equally bittersweet charge of Phelps' wearied voice. *Shine Eyed Mister Zen* features a lot of singing, but most importantly it spotlights the singing of Phelps' slide guitar, which integrates a humid and natural style that invokes the mystery and religion that these mostly original songs lean toward. The dusty delta Phelps conjures here is at once familiar and nostalgic; it's to his credit that Phelps is able to add his own voice to the spiritual mix. A mystical and unaffected recording. *—Michael Gallucci*

Piano Red (William Lee Perryman)

b. Oct. 19, 1911, Hampton, GA, **d.** Jul. 25, 1985, Decatur, GA
Vocals, Piano / Piano Blues
Willie Perryman went by two nicknames during his lengthy career, both of them thoroughly apt. He was known as Piano Red because of his albino skin pigmentation for most of his performing life. But they called him Doctor Feelgood during the '60s, and that's precisely what his raucous, barrelhouse-styled vocals and piano were guaranteed to do: cure anyone's ills and make them feel good. Like his older brother, Rufus Perryman, who performed and recorded as Speckled Red, Willie Perryman showed an aptitude for the 88s early in life. In 1950, Red's big break arrived when he signed with RCA Victor. The typically rowdy "Rockin' with Red," was a number five R&B hit. "Red's Boogie," another pounding rocker from the pianist's first RCA date, also proved a huge smash. Though there weren't many more hits, that didn't stop the firm from producing a live LP by the pianist in 1956 that throbbed with molten energy. Recording for Checker and Jax preceded the rise of Red's new guise, Dr. Feelgood & the Interns, who debuted on OKeh with a self-named hit rocker, 1961's "Doctor Feelgood." The Doc remained with OKeh through 1966, remained ensconced at Muhlenbrink's Saloon in Atlanta through 1979, sandwiching in extensive European tours along the way. He died of cancer in 1985. *—Bill Dahl*

Jump Man, Jump / 1956 / Groove ✦✦✦✦✦

Atlanta Bounce / 1992 / Arhoolie ✦✦✦
Two distinct timeframes are represented on this slightly schizophrenic disc. Much of it is comprised of latter-day barrelhouse and blues waxed by Arhoolie, but there's also a thrilling handful of raucous live items from a 1956 concert at Atlanta's Magnolia Ballroom that capture the albino 88s ace at his most enthralling. *—Bill Dahl*

The Doctor Is In! / 1993 / Bear Family ✦✦✦✦✦
This four-CD set, containing 122 songs (23 of them previously unreleased) cut between 1950 and 1966 for RCA, Groove, Okeh, and Columbia, is, literally, the best of Piano Red, and may be the best box in the entire Bear Family catalog. This is about as good as piano blues and

R&B got, and also some of the best piano-based rock & roll you'll ever hear—rivaling *anything* that Jerry Lee Lewis or Little Richard ever cut—with barely a second-rate track. Even the multiple versions of his signature tune, "Right String But the Wrong Yo-Yo," are welcomed, from its lean, mean piano-bass-drums original 1950 version, to the live 1955 rendition and the broader 1961 remake (at the "Mr. Moonlight" session), because they're each different enough to justify their presence. And, yet, the most amazing thing about the 16 years covered on these four discs is the consistency of the music and performances—Red hardly changed at all until the early '60s, always giving his audience a good show whether he was making records or playing live. Discs Two and Three are arguably the best parts of the set, with Red at the peak of his prowess as a pianist and singer. He made the jump into rock & roll more easily than most bluesmen of his age, with the result that his music from this period is as solid as anything else he ever did. Still later, on Disc Four, once he moves into a more produced, pop-oriented R&B sound, he holds up almost as well. The sound is excellent, the notes are thorough, and the $100 list price of this 122-song set makes it proportionately *more* attractive than any $15/15-song best-of on Red that might ever show up (and there *isn't* one). *—Bruce Eder*

Flaming Hurricane / Sep. 28, 1999 / West Side ✦✦✦

● **Wildfire** / Matchbox ✦✦✦✦✦
Although it's hardly comprehensive, Matchbox's *Wildfire* is the best available single-volume sampler of Piano Red's music, containing 12 of his greatest numbers, including "Red's Boogie" and "Diggin' the Boogie." *—Thom Owens*

Professor Longhair (Henry Roeland Byrd)

b. Dec. 19, 1918, Bogalusa, LA, **d.** Jan. 30, 1980, New Orleans, LA
Vocals, Piano, Arranger / New Orleans R&B, New Orleans Blues, Piano Blues
Justly worshipped a decades after his death as a founding father of New Orleans R&B, Roy "Professor Longhair" Byrd's Latin-tinged rhumba-rocking piano style and croaking, yodeling vocals were as singular and spicy as the second-line beats that power his hometown's musical heartbeat. Byrd brought an irresistible Caribbean feel to his playing, full of rolling flourishes that every Crescent City ivories man had to learn inside out (Fats Domino, Huey Smith, and Allen Toussaint all paid homage early and often). After playing piano at various clubs around New Orleans, Longhair debuted on wax in 1949 and gained his first and only national R&B hit one year later, the hilarious "Bald Head" (credited to Roy Byrd & his Blues Jumpers). The pianist made great records for Atlantic in 1949, Federal in 1951, Wasco in 1952, and Atlantic again in 1953. After recuperating from a minor stroke, Longhair came back on Lee Rupe's Ebb logo in 1957 and Joe Ruffino's Ron imprint in 1959. He hit the skids in the '60s though, abandoning his piano playing until a booking at the fledgling 1971 Jazz & Heritage Festival put him on the comeback trail. He made a slew of albums in the last decade of his life, topped off by a terrific set for Alligator (*Crawfish Fiesta*), but died in 1980. His music is played in his hometown so often and so reverently, you'd swear he was still around. *—Bill Dahl*

New Orleans Piano / 1972 / Atlantic ✦✦✦✦✦
All 16 of the Atlantic sides from 1949 and 1953 (including a handful of alternate takes) on one glorious disc. Longhair's work for the label was notoriously marvelous—this version of "Mardi Gras in New Orleans" reeks of revelry in the streets of the French Quarter; "She Walks Right In" and "Walk Your Blues Away" ride a bedrock boogie, and "In the Night" bounces atop a parade-beat shuffle groove and hard-charging saxes. *—Bill Dahl*

Rock 'n Roll Gumbo / 1977 / Dancing Cat ✦✦✦✦✦

Crawfish Fiesta / 1980 / Alligator ✦✦✦✦✦
Probably the best of all the many albums Longhair waxed during his comeback (and likely the last). A tremendously tight combo featuring three horns and Dr. John on guitar delightfully back the Professor every step of the way as he recasts Solomon Burke's "Cry to Me" and Fats Domino's "Whole Lotta Loving" in his own indelible image and roars, yodels, and whistles out wonderful remakes of his own oldies "Big Chief" and "Bald Head." *—Bill Dahl*

Mardi Gras in New Orleans / 1981 / Nighthawk ✦✦✦✦✦

House Party New Orleans Style / 1987 / Rounder ✦✦✦

Mardi Gras in Baton / 1991 / Rhino ✦✦✦✦
Some of the earliest sides from Longhair's rediscovery period (1971-72), featuring a lot of tunes inexorably associated with him through previous versions and a few ("Jambalaya," "Sick and Tired") that weren't. An added bonus is the magical presence of guitarist Snooks Eaglin, whose approach is every bit as singular as the Professor's was. *—Bill Dahl*

★ **Fess: Professor Longhair Anthology** / Nov. 16, 1993 / Rhino ✦✦✦✦✦
The rhumba-rocking rhythms of Roy "Professor Longhair" Byrd live on throughout Rhino's 40-track retrospective of the New Orleans icon's amazing legacy. Most of the seminal stuff arrives early on: "Bald Head," the rollicking ode Byrd cut for Mercury in 1950, is followed by a raft of classics from his 1949 and 1953 Atlantic dates ("Tipitina," "Ball the Wall," "Who's Been Fooling You"), the storming 1957 "No Buts—No Maybes" and "Baby Let Me Hold Your Hand" for Ebb, and his beloved "Go to the Mardi Gras" as waxed for Ron in 1959. The second disc is a hodge-podge of material from his 1970s comeback, all of it wonderful in its own way but not as essential as the early work. *—Bill Dahl*

Snooky Pryor (James Edward Pryor)

b. Sep. 15, 1921, Lambert, MS
Vocals, Drums, Harmonica / Harmonica Blues, Electric Chicago Blues
Only in the last few years has Snooky Pryor finally begun to receive full credit for the mammoth role he played in shaping the amplified Chicago blues harp sound during the postwar era. He's long claimed he was the first harpist to run his sound through a public-address system around the Windy City—and since nobody's around to refute the claim at this point, we'll have to accept it! He hit Chicago for the first time in 1940, later serving in the Army at nearby Fort Sheridan. Playing his harp through powerful Army PA systems gave Pryor the idea to acquire his own portable rig once he left the service. Armed with a primitive amp, he dazzled the folks on Maxwell Street in late 1945 with his massively amplified harp. Pryor made some groundbreaking 78s during the immediate postwar Chicago blues era. Teaming with guitarist Moody Jones, he waxed "Telephone Blues" and "Boogie" for Planet Records in 1948, encoring the next year with "Boogy Fool"/"Raisin' Sand" for JOB. Pryor made more more classic sides for Parrot (1953) and Vee-Jay ("Someone to Love Me"/"Judgment Day") in 1956, but commercial success never materialized. The 1987 Blind Pig album *Snooky* announced to the world that the veteran harpist was alive and well, his chops still honed. *—Bill Dahl*

● **Snooky Pryor [Flyright]** / 1969 / Flyright ✦✦✦✦✦
These tracks from the JOB label, recorded from the early '50s to early '60s, include the classics "Boogie" and "Stockyard Blues" and the raucous, echo-laden stomp of "Boogie Twist." These are Pryor's finest moments on wax. *—Cub Koda*

Snooky / 1987 / Blind Pig ✦✦✦✦
An outstanding comeback effort by Chicago harp pioneer Snooky Pryor, whose timeless sound meshed well with a Windy City trio led by producer/guitarist Steve Freund for this set. Mostly Pryor's own stuff—"Why You Want to Do Me like That," "That's the Way To Do It," "Cheatin' and Lyin'"—with his fat-toned harp weathering the decades quite nicely. *—Bill Dahl*

Snooky Pryor [Paula] / 1991 / Paula/Flyright ✦✦✦✦✦
If anyone doubts the longevity and journeyman greatness of Snooky Pryor, this collection of sides should do much to quiet them. Starting with the 1947 Floyd Jones (the classic "Stockyard Blues") and Johnny Young sessions for Old Swingmaster with Snooky in support and running right from the early '50s into the early-'60s sides for the JOB label with "Boogie Twist" (his Vee-Jay and Parrot sides are not here), this is ground floor Chicago blues one step removed from Maxwell Street. Lots of unissued sides-all of them great-plus the inclusion of the instrumental "Boogie," which became the blueprint for Little Walter's hit "Juke." Pryor's finest moments on wax. *—Cub Koda*

Shake My Hand / Feb. 9, 1999 / Blind Pig ✦✦✦✦
Veteran harp man Pryor (who claims to be the first to amplify his harmonica) was still capable of some potent blues when he released this album in early 1999. Kicking off with a solo version of Faye Adams' "Shake a Hand" (its lyrics reworked heavily into the title track) that owes a huge debt to idol Sonny Boy Williamson II, Pryor settles into a comfortable groove with a tight little trio behind him consisting of Bob Stroger on bass, Billy Flynn on guitar and Jimmy Tilman on drums. His version of Hank Ballard's "Annie Had a Baby" is so radically different that it almost qualifies as an original, while his covers of Al Dexter's "Pistol Packin' Mama" and Sleepy John Estes' "Someday Baby" stay closer to the originals. The rest of the set features Snooky's great originals, with the minor-keyed "Headed South," "In This Mess," "Jump for Joy" and a nice remake of his "Telephone Blues" being particular standouts. Simple, no-frills production makes this a modern-day blues album that delivers the wallop of the old singles. *—Cub Koda*

Ma Rainey (Pridgett, Gertrude)

b. Apr. 26, 1886, Columbus, GA, **d.** Dec. 22, 1939, Columbus, GA
Vocals / Classic Female Blues
Ma Rainey wasn't the first blues singer to make records, but by all rights she probably should have been. In an era when women were the marquee names in blues, Ma Rainey was once the most celebrated of all—the "Mother of the Blues" had been singing the music for more than 20 years before she made her recording debut (Paramount, 1923). With the advent of blues records, she became even more influential, immortalizing such songs as "See See Rider," "Bo-Weavil Blues," and "Ma Rainey's Black Bottom." Like the other classic blues divas, she had a repertoire of pop and minstrel songs as well as blues, but she maintained a heavier, tougher vocal delivery than the cabaret blues singers who followed. She began singing professionally as a teenager, and performed with a number of minstrel and medicine shows. In 1923, Ma Rainey signed a contract with Paramount Records. Although her recording career lasted only a mere six years—her final sessions were in 1928—she recorded over one hundred songs and many of them became genuine blues classics. After reaching the height of her popularity in the late '20s, Rainey's career faded away in the early '30s as female blues singing became less popular with the blues audience. She retired in 1933, and died of a heart attack six years later. *—Jim O'Neal & Stephen Thomas Erlewine*

★ **Ma Rainey's Black Bottom** / Jun. 1975 / Riverside ✦✦✦✦✦
The archetypical "classic" blues femme belter on 1924-1928 recordings, with Fletcher Henderson on piano and Coleman Hawkins bass sax on two tracks. *—Mark A. Humphrey*

Black Bottom / 1990 / Yazoo ✦✦✦✦✦
The first eight tracks of this 20-track collection date from 1956: "All Aboard," and featuring both James Cotton and Little Walter on twin harmonicas, "Forty Days and Forty Nights," "Just to Be With You," "Don't Go No Farther," "Diamonds at Your Feet," "I Love the Life I Live," "Rock Me," and the studio version of "I Got My Mojo Working." By now, Waters was a rhythm & blues star, as far removed from the Clarksdale plantation he grew up on as you could get. He also had developed the modern-day blues band lineup and by this time had his running like a well-oiled machine. Little Walter (by now a star in his own right) was still on call for studio dates and if not, Walter Horton, Otis Spann, and Jimmy Rogers were still in the lineup. By 1958's "She's Nineteen Years Old," Waters had built up his second great band with James Cotton, Pat Hare, and Luther Tucker on guitars and Francis Clay on drums, the unit he would take to Newport in 1960. It's this unit that contributes so mightily to "Walkin' Thru the Park," "She's Into Something," and Big Bill Broonzy's "I Feel So Good." Two of Muddy's most influential tracks, "You Shook Me" and "You Need Love" (the blueprint for Led Zeppelin's "Whole Lotta Love") curiously feature Earl Hooker on slide guitar, along with A.C. Reed and John "Big Moose" Walker, the core of the Age-Profile label's house band. A pair of tracks from his now-celebrated *Folk Singer* album with Buddy Guy and Willie Dixon ("My Home Is In the Delta" and "Good Morning Little Schoolgirl") offset the collection's final selections, Willie

Dixon's "The Same Thing" and Muddy's classic "You Can't Lose What You Ain't Never Had," a perfect closer for this essential collection. *—Cub Koda*

Complete Recorded Works: 1928 Sessions / Jun. 2, 1994 / Document ♦♦♦♦♦

Jimmy Reed (Mathis James Reed)

b. Sep. 6, 1925, Dunleith, MS, **d.** Aug. 29, 1976, Oakland, CA

Vocals, Harmonica, Guitar / Blues Revival, Electric Harmonica Blues, Electric Chicago Blues, R&B

There's simply no sound in the blues as easily digestible, accessible, instantly recognizable and as easy to play and sing as the music of Jimmy Reed. His best-known songs—"Baby, What You Want Me to Do," "Bright Lights, Big City," "Honest I Do," "You Don't Have to Go," "Going to New York," "Ain't That Lovin' You Baby" and "Big Boss Man"—have become such an integral part of the standard blues repertoire, it's almost as if they have existed forever. Because his style was simple and easily imitated, his songs were accessible to just about everyone from high school garage bands having a go at it to Elvis Presley, Charlie Rich, Lou Rawls, Hank Williams, Jr., and the Rolling Stones, making him—in the long run—perhaps the most influential bluesman of all. His bottom string boogie rhythm guitar patterns (all furnished by boyhood friend and longtime musical partner Eddie Taylor), simple two-string turnarounds, countryish harmonica solos (all played in a neck rack attachment hung around his neck) and mush mouthed vocals were probably the first exposure most White folks had to the blues. And his music—lazy, loping and insistent and constantly built and reconstructed single after single on the same sturdy frame—was a formula that proved to be enormously successful and influential, both with middle-aged Blacks and young White audiences for a good dozen years. Jimmy Reed records hit the R&B charts with amazing frequency and crossed over onto the pop charts on many occasions, a rare feat for an unreconstructed bluesman.This is all the more amazing simply because Reed's music was nothing special on the surface; he possessed absolutely no technical expertise on either of his chosen instruments and his vocals certainly lacked the fierce declamatory intensity of a Howlin' Wolf or a Muddy Waters. But it was *exactly* that lack of in-your-face musical confrontation that made Jimmy Reed a welcome addition to everybody's record collection back in the '50s and '60s. *—Cub Koda*

I'm Jimmy Reed / 1959 / Collectables ♦♦♦♦♦

☆ **Live at Carnegie Hall/The Best of Jimmy Reed** / Aug. 1961 / Vee-Jay ♦♦♦♦♦

This was originally issued as a vinyl double album by Vee-Jay in the early '60s. The first 12 tracks are not "live" at all (the disclaimer is in the liners) but instead are some nice middle-period studio tracks while the following dozen constitutes a "reissue" of the label's *Best of Jimmy Reed* album. Stereophiles will love this as the sound is Mobile Fidelity impeccable, even on the mono masters, while stereo masters of such classics as "Baby What You Want Me to Do" and "Big Boss Man" sound almost revelatory. Not the place to start (even with most of the hits aboard), but if you have to have some classic Jimmy Reed in clean stereo, this is the place to go. *—Cub Koda*

12 String Guitar Blues / 1963 / Collectables ♦♦♦♦♦

This release added yet another wrinkle to Jimmy Reed's mystique. Even most of his fans would concede that Reed's guitar skills were far short of virtuoso level. Yet, Jimmy Reed—not a celebrated 12-string guitar player like Leadbelly or any of the other renowned instrumentalists who came up in Leadbelly's wake—cut this acoustic 12-string instrumental album, which has become an enduring classic of the genre. Reed was as skilled at presenting his guitar work as he was as a singer, and his playing on *12 String Guitar Blues* is smooth, sinewy, lean, and lyrical, with a tight band behind him. Consisting of recognizable Reed originals and a couple of other blues standards thrown in, the music comes off very well, mixing electric guitar with acoustic 12-string and Reed's harmonica substituting for the vocal parts. The harmonica is on a separate track, making use of a natural sounding stereo separation that keeps the sound of the band—featuring Eddie Taylor and Lefty Bates on guitar, Marcus Johnson on bass, and Morris Wilkerson and Earl Phillips on drums—unified. The result is yet another classic album by Reed, and one of the more straightforward and accessible bodies of blues played on 12-string that one can find. This fall 2000 Collectables reissue, licensed through Rhino Records, features impeccable sound and recreates the original album art and jacket notes. *—Bruce Eder*

The Legend, the Man / 1965 / Collectables ♦♦♦♦♦

Jimmy Reed *The Legend, The Man* was originally released in 1965 on Vee Jay records and was reissued by Collectables in 2000. While it contains a number of classics, like "Baby What You Want Me to Do," "Big Boss Man," "Ain't That Lovin' You Baby," and "Bright Lights, Big City," what makes this reissue so compelling are the short interview sections with Reed at the start of each track. Conducted in 1964 by Vee Jay AR man Calvin Carter, we hear Reed discussing his career and trying to put it into chronological and often humorous perspective. This former cotton picker, junk man, butcher, and "shakeout man in the foundry working in 118 degree heat" went on to become a legend of modern blues. This is not only a perfect introduction anthology to his music, but a blues history lesson that anyone interested in Reed or the genre should find fascinating. *—Al Campbell*

Found Love / 1971 / Collectables ♦♦♦

★ **Blues Masters: The Very Best of Jimmy Reed** / Mar. 14, 2000 / Rhino ♦♦♦♦♦

Over the years, many, many Jimmy Reed compilations have been released, including many repackagings of his classic Vee-Jay material. Sometimes, the compilations have been excellent—the 1993 disc *Speak the Lyrics to Me, Mama Reed* is a prime example— other times they've been shabby, and since many of them have featured the same basic songs, it's hard for novices to discern which are worthwhile and which aren't. Fortunately, Rhino's 2000 release *The Very Best of Jimmy Reed* provides first-timers with an ideal introductory package, while satisfying longtime fans by serving 17 of his very best sides for Vee-Jay. All of the classic songs are here—"Ain't That Lovin' You Baby," "You've Got Me Dizzy," "Honest I Do," "Take Out Some Insurance," "Going to New York," "Baby What You Want Me to Do," "Big Boss Man," and "Bright Lights Big City"—along with such stellar, lesser-known items as his first Vee-Jay single "High and Lonesome," "Oh John," the eerie violin-laced "Odds and Ends," and its boogie-minded flip-side "Ends and Odds." It's a well-rounded, compelling collection that proves Reed's music is always satisfying, even if it's all variations on a basic, three-chord boogie. Or, as Reed expert Cub Koda states in the liner notes, it's "nothin' fancy, but it sure hits the spot every single time." *The Very Best of Jimmy Reed* proves his statement true with 17 timeless tracks. This is an essential cornerstone of any blues collection. *—Stephen Thomas Erlewine*

Tommy Ridgley

b. Oct. 30, 1925, New Orleans, LA, **d.** Aug. 11, 1999

Vocals, Piano / New Orleans Blues, Modern Electric Blues, R&B

Tommy Ridgley was on the Crescent City R&B scene when it first caught fire, and he remains a proud part of that same scene today. That's a lot of years behind a microphone, but Ridgley doesn't sound the slightest bit tired; his 1995 Black Top album *Since the Blues Began* rates with his liveliest outings to date. Ridgley cut his debut sides back in 1949 for Imperial under Dave Bartholomew's direction. Sessions for Decca in 1950 and Imperial in 1952 (where he waxed the wild "Looped") preceded four 1953-55 sessions for Atlantic that included a blistering instrumental, "Jam Up," that sported no actual Ridgley involvement but sold relatively well under his name (incomparable tenor saxist Lee Allen was prominent). New York's Herald Records was Ridgley's home during the late '50s. The consistently solid singer waxed "When I Meet My Girl" for the firm in 1957, encoring with a catchy "Baby Do-Liddle." From there, it was on to his hometown-based Ric logo, where he laid down the stunning stroll-tempoed "Let's Try and Talk It Over" and a bluesy "Should I Ever Love Again" in 1960. He recorded intermittently after leaving Ric in 1963, waxing a soulful "I'm Not the Same Person" in 1969 for Ronn. *—Bill Dahl*

● **The New Orleans King of the Stroll** / 1988 / Rounder ♦♦♦♦♦

Tommy Ridgley was a solid R&B vocalist who was quite successful with novelty tunes and silly songs, but was also a good romantic balladeer. This 15-track collection mostly covers Ridgley material from 1960 to 1964 for the Ric label, and ranges from laments like "Please Hurry Home" and "I Love You Yes I Do" to such comic material and dance-based numbers as "Double Eyed Whammy" and "The Girl From Kooka Monga." Ridgley wasn't as booming or dynamic as some other Crescent City vocalists, but made several nice period pieces and soul tunes, several of which are included on this set. *—Ron Wynn*

Duke Robillard

b. Oct. 4, 1948, Woonsocket, RI

Vocals, Guitar / Contemporary Blues

Duke Robillard is one of the founding members of Roomful of Blues, as well as one of the guitarists that replaced Jimmie Vaughan in the Fabulous Thunderbirds in 1990. Between that time, Robillard pursued a solo career that found him exploring more musically adventurous territory than either Roomful of Blues or the T-Birds. On his solo recordings, the guitarist dips into blues, rockabilly, jazz, and rock & roll, creating a unique fusion of American roots musics. In 1967, Robillard formed Roomful of Blues in Westerly, RI. He left the band in 1979, initially signing on as rockabilly singer Robert Gordon's lead guitarist. After his stint with Gordon, Robillard joined the Legendary Blues Band. In 1981, the guitarist formed a new group, the Duke Robillard Band, which soon evolved into Duke Robillard & the Pleasure Kings. After a few years of touring the group landed a contract with Rounder Records, releasing their eponymous debut album in 1984. In 1990, Robillard joined the Fabulous Thunderbirds. Even though he had become a member of the Austin group, the guitarist continued to record and tour as a solo artist, signing with the major label Point Blank/Virgin in 1994. *—Stephen Thomas Erlewine*

You Got Me / 1988 / Rounder ♦♦♦♦

Duke Robillard's sessions have alternated between jazzy, sophisticated, low-key ventures and bluesy, more energetic, rousing dates. This was on the robust side, matching Robillard's guitar and good-natured, celebratory vocals with the talents of a great guest corps that included Dr. John and Ron Levy on keyboards, guitarist Jimmie Vaughan, bassist Thomas Enright and drummer Tommy DeQuattro (The Pleasure Kings). These weren't always musical triumphs, but even the songs that didn't quite work were entertaining, while the more inspirational offerings like "You're the One I Adore" and "Don't Treat Me Like That" nicely balance tremendous instrumental support with energetic vocal performances. *—Ron Wynn*

● **After Hours Swing Session** / May 1990 / Rounder ♦♦♦♦♦

While guitarist Duke Robillard has won widespread popularity for his facility with rocking blues and barrelhouse numbers, he also loves understated, quietly swinging jazz fare. He got a chance to demonstrate his proficiency in this style on this intimate combo session. The eight songs featured on the CD include brisk workouts as well as light-hearted numbers that showcase Robillard's decent, if not great, voice, along with his fluid, tasty fills and crisp, clean acoustic and electric guitar solos. Here's another side of Duke Robillard, one that deserves equal billing with the flashy, burning one. *—Ron Wynn*

Temptation / 1994 / Pointblank ♦♦♦♦

Stretchin' Out / Sep. 29, 1998 / Stony Plain ♦♦♦♦♦

Fenton Robinson

b. Sep. 23, 1935, Minter City, MS, **d.** Nov. 25, 1997

Vocals, Guitar / Modern Electric Chicago Blues, Texas Blues, Chicago Blues, Modern Electric Blues

His Japanese fans reverently dubbed Fenton Robinson "the mellow blues genius" because of his ultra-smooth vocals and jazz-inflected guitar work. But beneath the obvious subtlety resides a spark of constant regeneration—Robinson tirelessly strives to invent something fresh and vital whenever he's near a bandstand. The soft-spoken Mississippi native made his recording debut in 1957 with singles for Meteor and Duke. He moved to Chicago in 1962, playing clubs with Junior Wells, Sonny Boy Williamson, and Otis Rush and laying down a single for USA in 1966. But it was his stunning slow blues "Somebody (Loan Me a Dime)," cut in 1967 for Palos, that insured his blues immortality. Robinson's 1970 waxings in Nashvhille for 77 Records were mostly horrific—he wasn't even invited to play his own guitar on the majority of the horribly unsubtle rock-slanted sides. His 1974 album *Somebody Loan Me a Dime* for Alligator remains the absolute benchmark of his career, spotlighting his rich, satisfying vocals and free-spirited, understated guitar work in front of a rock-solid horn-driven band. By comparison, 1977's *I Hear Some Blues Downstairs* was a trifle disappointing. He also recorded *Nightflight* in 1984 for Alligator, then signed to the Dutch Black Magic label for 1989's *Special Road.* Robinson now resides in downstate Illinois, visiting his old stomping grounds only sporadically. *—Bill Dahl*

★ **Somebody Loan Me a Dime** / 1974 / Alligator ✦✦✦✦✦
One of the most subtly satisfying electric blues albums of the 1970s. Robinson never did quite fit the "Genuine Houserocking Music" image of Alligator Records—his deep, rich baritone sounds more like a magic carpet than a piece of barbed wire, and he speaks in jazz-inflected tongues, full of complex surprises. The title track hits with amazing power, as do the chugging "The Getaway," a hard-swinging "You Say You're Leaving," and the minor-key "You Don't Know What Love Is." In every case, Robinson had recorded them before, but thanks to Bruce Iglauer's superb production, a terrific band, and Robinson's musicianship, these versions reign supreme. *—Bill Dahl*

I Hear Some Blues Downstairs / 1977 / Alligator ✦✦✦
A disappointment in its inconsistency following such a mammoth triumph as his previous set, yet not without its mellow delights. The title track is untypically playful; Robinson's revisiting of the mournful "As the Years Go Passing By" is a moving journey, and his T-Bone Walker tribute "Tell Me What's the Reason" swings deftly. On the other hand, a superfluous remake of Rosco Gordon's "Just a Little Bit" goes nowhere, and nobody really needed another "Killing Floor." *—Bill Dahl*

Special Road / Apr. 1989 / Evidence ✦✦✦
Fenton Robinson is among the second-line blues musicians who have come close but never made it over the hump. He has certainly got the guitar goods, and his vocals are often memorable and anguished. Unfortunately, the 13 songs he did on this 1989 date were mostly good but nowhere as intense as he has delivered on other occasions. Neither is the instrumental work on this Evidence CD; his solos are firmly articulated, often elaborately constructed and paced, but they lack impact. Too many times Robinson falls just short of turning in a triumphant or exciting number, either through a less than emphatic vocal or a mundane solo. This is not necessarily a bad session, just a disappointing one. *—Ron Wynn*

Jimmy Rogers (James A. Lane)

b. Jun. 3, 1924, Ruleville, MS, **d.** Dec. 19, 1997
Guitar / Electric Chicago Blues
Guitarist Jimmy Rogers was the last living connection to the groundbreaking first Chicago band of Muddy Waters (informally dubbed the Headhunters for their penchant of dropping by other musicians' gigs and "cutting their heads" with a superior onstage performance). Instead of basking in worldwide veneration, he was merely a well-respected Chicago elder boasting a seminal 1950s Chess Records catalog, both behind Waters and on his own. Rogers was playing harp with guitarist Blue Smitty when Muddy Waters joined them. When Smitty split, Little Walter was welcomed into the configuration, Rogers switched over to second guitar, and the entire postwar Chicago blues genre felt the stylistic earthquake that directly followed. Rogers made his recorded debut as a leader in 1947 for the tiny Ora-Nelle logo, then saw his efforts for Regal and Apollo lay unissued. Those labels' monumental errors in judgment were the gain of Leonard Chess, who recognized the comparatively smooth-voiced Rogers's potential as a blues star in his own right. Rogers' debut Chess single in 1950, "That's All Right," has earned standard status after countless covers, but his version still reigns supreme. Rogers's artistic quality was remarkably high while at Chess. "The World Is in a Tangle," "Money, Marbles and Chalk," "Back Door Friend," "Left Me with a Broken Heart," "Act like You Love Me," and the 1954 rockers "Sloppy Drunk" and "Chicago Bound" are essential early-'50s Chicago blues. In 1955, Rogers left Muddy Waters to venture out as a bandleader, cutting another gem, "You're the One," for Chess. He made his only appearance on *Billboard*'s R&B charts in early 1957 with the driving "Walking by Myself." Rogers died December 19, 1997. At the time of his death, he was working on an all-star project featuring contributions from Eric Clapton, Taj Mahal, Robert Plant & Jimmy Page, and Mick Jagger & Keith Richards; upon its completion, the disc was issued posthumously in early 1999 under the title *Blues, Blues, Blues.* *—Bill Dahl*

★ **Chicago Bound** / 1976 / MCA/Chess ✦✦✦✦✦
The logical place to inaugurate any Rogers collection is this perennially acclaimed 14-song retrospective of the guitarist's 1950s Chess years. Most of the big ones are here for your perusal: "That's All Right," "Sloppy Drunk," "You're the One," "Walking by Myself," and the thundering title track. Peerless band support from the likes of Muddy Waters, Little Walter, Otis Spann, and Walter Horton. This is a cornerstone of Chicago blues history. *—Bill Dahl*

Feelin' Good / 1985 / Blind Pig ✦✦✦✦
This Blind Pig CD reissues material from 1983-84. The legendary veteran Jimmy Rogers (taking most of the vocals and occasional guitar solos) is heard teamed up with the talented harmonica player Rod Piazza and his jumping group. The results are consistently exciting. Piazza's harmonica serves as a perfect foil to Rogers' voice, and the impressive backup band (which also features Honey Piazza on piano) clearly enjoys jamming on the basic blues changes. The many strong solos and the superior material make this an easily recommended set. *—Scott Yanow*

Complete Shelter Recordings: Chicago Blues Masters, Vol. 2 / Oct. 24, 1995 / Capitol ✦✦✦✦✦
Rogers reemerged after a long layoff with a 1972 album for Leon Russell's Shelter label called *Gold Tailed Bird.* It wasn't the equivalent of his immortal Chess stuff, but the Shelter sides, here in their entirety, are pretty decent themselves (and no wonder, with the Aces, Freddy King, and reliable Chicago pianist Bob Riedy all involved). A few extra numbers not on the original Shelter LP make this 18-song set even more solid. *—Bill Dahl*

Complete Chess Recordings (Chess 50th Anniversary) / Apr. 8, 1997 / Chess ✦✦✦✦✦
While the 1976 issue of *Chicago Bound,* the first collection of Jimmy Rogers' Chess material has been rightly hailed as a definitive cornerstone in absorbing the history of early Chicago blues; sadly, that vinyl album has been out of print for a number of years with virtually nothing in the catalog to take its place. Until now. This two-CD (in a single-disc package) anthology collects up everything that appeared on *Chicago Bound,* a number of notable cuts from a two-vinyl-disc anthology that was barely released in the late 1970s, and no less than ten unreleased alternate takes from a variety of sessions with one of them, "Luedella," emanating from his first solo session in 1950. The singing, playing, and songwriting is virtually a textbook for the early Chicago style, as the players involved include Muddy Waters, Little Walter, Otis Spann, Willie Dixon, and Big Walter Horton, with all but Horton and Dixon regular mainstays of Muddy's original band, the blueprint of the early electric band sound. While some novices will find a two-disc set perhaps more than they want to pop for, this is as good as '50s Chicago blues gets, and no collection should really be without this one. *—Cub Koda*

Roomful of Blues

f. 1967, Providence, RI, **db.** Mar. 11, 1986
Group / Jump Blues, Modern Electric Blues
A nine-piece blues/jump band from Providence, Rhode Island, Roomful of Blues has recorded and toured tirelessly for several decades, while eschewing the standard Chicago blues band/Muddy Waters approach for a horn-dominated style that owes more to jazz leanings and late-'40s blues masters like Wynonie Harris, Roy Brown and Big Joe Turner. More than capable of backing artists like Turner, Eddie "Cleanhead" Vinson (both of whom had Roomful back them for complete albums) as well as delivering the goods on their own, major players who have come through the ranks over the years have included guitarists Duke Robillard and Ronnie Earl, bassist Preston Hubbard and drummer Fran Christina (Fabulous Thunderbirds). They continued performing into the 1990s, issuing LPs including 1994's *Dance All Night,* 1995's *Turn It On, Turn It Up* and 1998's *There Goes the Neighborhood.* Fall 2000 saw the release of *Blues'll Make You Happy, Too.* *—AMG*

● **Let's Have a Party** / Nov. 1979 / Mango ✦✦✦✦✦
Decent to good R&B-influenced jump and party blues. This group has always been great live; their albums have always been mixed affairs, and this was no different. *—Ron Wynn*

Hot Little Mama / 1981 / Varrick ✦✦✦✦
The third album by Roomful of Blues (which they originally put out on their own label; it was later reissued by Varrick) has plenty of exciting moments that should interest blues and jazz fans alike. The nine-piece group in 1980 featured Greg Piccolo on spirited vocals and romping tenor, trombonist Porky Cohen, and the up-and-coming guitarist Ronnie Earl (then known as Ronnie Earl Horvath) as the key soloists. Most of the music consists of blues at various tempos, but there are also a couple of blues ballads and a feature for Cohen on a fairly lengthy "Caravan." The music is accessible, jumping and creative within its genre. Well worth searching for. *—Scott Yanow*

Live at Lupo's Heartbreak Hotel / Nov. 1987 / Varrick ✦✦✦

Dance All Night / May 28, 1994 / Bullseye Blues ✦✦✦✦
This incarnation of Roomful of Blues includes vocalist and harmonica player Sugar Ray Norcia taking the singing spotlight, Matt McCabe now their pianist and Chris Vachon principal guitarist. This CD blends blues and R&B classics with a couple of originals; highlights include a fine reading of Smiley Lewis' "Lillie Mae," a remake of "Hey Now" originally done by Ray Charles and Norcia's fiery vocal and torrid harmonica solo on Little Walter Jacobs' "Up The Line." This is faithful to the classic tradition, but contains enough contemporary qualities to have a fresh and inviting sound. *—Ron Wynn*

Under One Roof / Dec. 2, 1995-Dec. 7, 1995 / Bullseye Blues ✦✦✦

There Goes the Neighborhood / Aug. 18, 1998 / Bullseye Blues ✦✦

Swingin' & Jumpin' / Aug. 3, 1999 / 32 Jazz ✦✦✦✦
32 Jazz's *Swingin' & Jumpin'* is an excellent 12-track compilation of highlights from Roomful of Blues' early recordings, concentrating on their eponymous debut. *—Stephen Thomas Erlewine*

The Blues'll Make You Happy, Too / Oct. 31, 2000 / Rounder ✦✦✦✦✦

Doctor Ross

b. Oct. 21, 1925, Tunica, MS
Vocals, Harmonica, Guitar / Detroit Blues, Juke Joint Blues, Modern Delta Blues, Delta Blues
A triple-threat guitarist, harp blower, and vocalist, Dr. Ross decided to fire his sidemen over thirty years ago and carry on as a one-man band, a tradition that also includes Joe Hill Louis, Daddy Stovepipe, and Jesse Fuller. Ross's music does not depend on novelty effect, yet it has a distinctly recognizable sound, in part because he learned to play his own way and essentially plays everything backwards. His guitar is tuned to open G (like John Lee Hooker and other Delta artists), but Ross plays it left-handed and upside-down. He also plays harmonica in a rack, but it is turned around with the low notes to the right. As an instrumentalist, Ross has perfected the interplay between guitar and harmonica. Unlike other Delta artists who tune in G, Ross doesn't use slide, preferring a series of banjo-like strummed riffs, a percussive approach reminiscent of Atlanta twelve-string guitarist Barbecue Bob. A strong vocalist and excellent songwriter, Ross gained early experience playing Delta jukes and eventually landed radio shows in Clarksdale and Memphis, where he also recorded for Sam Phillips's Sun label.

At the peak of Ross's career, he quit Sun, concerned that his royalties were being used to promote Elvis Presley's recordings. Relocating in Michigan, he recorded for his own label and for several Detroit labels, while working for General Motors. Returning to music as a recording artist, he recently worked the festival circuit. To the present day, Ross's music retains the spirit of his live radio and juke-joint work. I feel the sides he recorded with a band for Sun produced his best material, including classics like "Chicago Breakdown" and "Boogie Disease." As Dr. Ross put it in an interview ten years ago, "I'm kind of like the little boy from the West; I'm different from the rest." Different, yes, but very good. *—Barry Lee Pearson*

● **Boogie Disease** / 1954 / Arhoolie ✦✦✦✦✦
This one will make your teeth rattle. A veteran of the early '50s Sun Studio in Memphis, Ross became known as the "one-man band," a routine gleaned from his mentor Joe Hill Louis. He plays both fine harp (out of the Sonny Boy I mold) and exciting rhythm guitar characterized by churning, mesmerizing rhythms spiced by treble fills. These 22 infectious tracks are the good doctor's very first recordings, and they present him with rhythm section—a style that pre-dates his "one-man" days. *—Larry Hoffman*

Call the Doctor / Jun. 1965 / Testament ✦✦✦✦
If you're looking for one-man blues, this is one of the better efforts in that vein available. Ross is in fine form and strong voice on his first full-length album, sometimes pulling out as many stops as his limbs allow for all-out stompers, at other times just accompanying himself on harmonica. The tracks are largely adaptations of well-worn material like "Good Morning, Little Schoolgirl," "32-20," and "Going to the River"; the opening blast of "Cat Squirrel" is especially good. The one-man band approach gets a bit wearing over the course of 17 songs, though, unless you're a sucker for the style. The CD reissue adds the previously unissued bonus track "Jivin' Blues." *—Richie Unterberger*

Bobby Rush (Emmit Ellis, Jr.)

b. Nov. 10, 1940, Homer, LA
Vocals / Retro-Soul, Modern Electric Blues
The creator of a singular sound which he dubbed "folk-funk," multi-instrumentalist Bobby Rush was among the most colorful characters on the contemporary chitlin circuit, honing a unique style which brought together a cracked lyrical bent with elements of blues, soul and funk. Born Emmit Ellis Jr. in Homer, Louisiana on November 10, 1940, he and his family relocated to Chicago in 1953, where he emerged on the West Side blues circuit of the 1960s, fronting bands which included such notable alumni as Luther Allison and Freddie King. However, as Rush began to develop his own individual sound, he opted to forgo the blues market in favor of targeting the chitlin circuit, which offered a more receptive audience for his increasingly bawdy material; he notched his first hit in 1971 with his Galaxy label single "Chicken Heads," and later scored with "Bow-Legged Woman" for Jewel. He appeared on a wide variety of labels as the decade progressed, culminating in the 1979 LP *Rush Hour*, produced by Kenny Gamble and Leon Huff for their Philadelphia International imprint. During the early 1980s, Rush signed with the LaJam label, where he remained for a number of years; there his work became increasingly funky and deranged, with records like 1984's *Gotta Have Money* and 1985's *What's Good for the Goose Is Good for the Gander*, often featuring material so suggestive he refused to re-create it live. During the mid-1990s, Rush moved to Waldoxy, heralding a return to a soul-blues sound on LPs including 1995's *One Monkey Don't Stop No Show*, 1997's *Lovin' a Big Fat Woman* and 2000's *Hoochie Man*. *—Jason Ankeny*

Rush Hour / 1979 / Philadelphia International ✦✦✦✦
Kenny Gamble and Leon Huff produced *Rush Hour*, Bobby Rush's belated full-length debut album, for the Philadelphia International label. By that time, their patented Philly soul sound was out of favor, and they wisely chose not to impose it on Rush. Nevertheless, the album is considerably slicker than any of his Ichiban albums. Oddly, this is hardly a problem, since Rush always favored soul more than blues and had a fondness for funk. The only real flaw with the record is that the material is a bit uneven, but the quality of the performances carries it over rough spots and helps make the record one of the best in his catalog. *—Thom Owens*

● **Instant Replays: The Hits** / 1992 / Urgent! ✦✦✦✦✦
Instant Replays: The Hits is a good overview of Bobby Rush's '80s recordings for Urgent! and Ichiban, capturing all of the highlights from such funky, greasy blues albums as *Gotta Have Money* and *What's Good for the Goose is Good for the Gander*. *—Thom Owens*

Southern Soul / Sep. 8, 1998 / Cannonball ✦✦✦✦
The king and queen of the Southern soul and blues circuit get a half dozen tracks apiece on this joint effort. Unfortunately, the duo does not team up on this disc, both sessions being produced separately by Willie Mitchell, but these are no leftover cuts by a long shot. Rush smokes and burns on "I Need a Bed Partner," "Funky Way to Treat Your Woman" and "Makin' a Decision (Can Be Hard)," while White is both sexy and assertive sounding on tracks like "Get Your Lie Straight," "Down the Line" and "I Don't Want to Ever See Your Face Again." An excellent introduction to these modern day soul giants. *—Cub Koda*

The Best of Bobby Rush / Jun. 29, 1999 / La Jam ✦✦✦✦

Otis Rush

b. Apr. 29, 1934, Philadelphia, MS
Vocals, Guitar / Electric Chicago Blues
Breaking into the R&B Top Ten his very first time out in 1956 with the startlingly intense slow blues "I Can't Quit You Baby," southpaw guitarist Otis Rush subsequently established himself as one of the premier bluesmen on the Chicago circuit. He remains so today. Rush is often credited with being one of the architects of the West side guitar style, along with Magic Sam and Buddy Guy. It's a nebulous honor, since Otis Rush played clubs on Chicago's South side just as frequently during the sound's late-'50s incubation period. Nevertheless, his esteemed status as a prime Chicago innovator is eternally assured by the ringing, vibrato-enhanced guitar work that remains his stock-in-trade and a tortured, super-intense vocal delivery that can force the hairs on the back of your neck upwards in silent salute. His 1956-58 Cobra legacy is a magnificent one, distinguished by the Dixon-produced minor-key masterpieces "Double Trouble" and "My Love Will Never Die," the nails-tough "Three Times a Fool" and "Keep on Loving Me Baby," and the rhumba-rocking classic "All Your Love (I Miss Loving)." *—Bill Dahl*

Door to Door (With Albert King) / Jun. 1970 / MCA/Chess ✦✦✦✦✦
Although Albert King is pictured on the front cover and has the lion's share of tracks on this excellent compilation, six of the fourteen tracks come from Rush's shortlived tenure with the label and are some of his very best. Chronologically, these are his next recordings after the Cobra sides and they carry a lot of the emotional wallop of those tracks, albeit with much loftier production values with much of it recorded in early stereo. Oddly enough, some of the material ("All Your Love," "I'm Satisfied [Keep on Loving Me Baby]") were remakes—albeit great ones—of tunes that Cobra had already released as singles! But Rush's performance of "So Many Roads" (featuring one of the greatest slow blues guitar solos of all time) should not be missed at any cost. *—Cub Koda*

Cold Day in Hell / 1976 / Delmark ✦✦✦
Inconsistent but sometimes riveting 1975 studio set that hits some high highs (a crunchy "Cut You a Loose," the lickety-split jazzy instrumental "Motoring Along") right alongside some incredibly indulgent moments. But that's Otis—the transcendent instants are worth the hassle. *—Bill Dahl*

Right Place, Wrong Time / Feb. 1976 / Hightone ✦✦✦✦✦
Among the undisputed high points in Rush's checkered career is this 1971 studio set, originally done for Capitol (who astonishingly took a pass on the finished product). Rush has seldom sounded more convincing vocally than on the downtrodden title track, and his surging reading of Ike Turner's "I'm Tore Up" rates with his best up-tempo vehicles. *—Bill Dahl*

Live in Europe / Oct. 1977 / Evidence ✦✦✦✦

★ **Essential Collection: The Classic Cobra Recordings 1956-1958** / Sep. 19, 2000 / Varese ✦✦✦✦✦
The title says it all. This *is* the essential Otis Rush, the singles recorded for Eli Toscano's Cobra label between 1956 and 1958. If Rush had never recorded another note, his legendary status would remain intact based solely on these recordings. Backed by players like Willie Dixon and Little Walter, it's Rush's impassioned vocals and stinging guitar lines that make "I Can't Quit You Baby", "All Your Love (I Miss Loving)," and "Double Trouble" the classics they are. In addition to the A- and B-sides of all eight singles released by Cobra, eight alternate takes are included, four more than the Paula edition of this material released in 1991. Along with a slightly better transfer from the original tapes, this is not only one of the best places to start for someone getting interested in the blues, but a vital part of any blues collection. Outstanding. *—Sean Westergaard*

Saffire the Uppity Blues Women

f. Virginia
Group / Contemporary Blues, Modern Electric Blues
The ladies from Saffire at one point in the early '90s just considered themselves blues historians, but since their performing career has gotten launched on the festival circuit, they've become much more than that. All three have developed into talented songwriters. Since blues fans are always looking for fresh themes or new twists on old themes, this trio is a sought-after club and festival act. Saffire has no shortage of fresh ideas. The group has recorded five albums for the Chicago-based Alligator Records label since 1990, and both *Cleaning House* (1996) and *Old, New Borrowed and Blue* (1994) showcase the trio's songwriting skills, although there are also a few covers, reinterpreted in their own distinctive way. These acoustic musicians inject a sense of humor into their songs and take it with them on stage.The group's fundamental appeal—to growing numbers of music fans who don't know much about blues—is their original songs and their ability to dig up and reinterpret old blues gems from the 1920s and '30s. They specialize in songs made by the sassy original blues divas including Bessie Smith, Ma Rainey, Memphis Minnie and Ida Cox. *—Richard Skelly*

The Uppity Blues Women / 1990 / Alligator ✦✦✦
In 1984 three middle-aged women (guitarist Gaye Adegbalola, bassist Earlene Lewis and pianist Ann Rabson) came together to play blues as Saffire. Their 1990 Alligator CD is still Saffire's best all-around recording. Even overlooking the novelty of three women giving a female and middle-aged slant to the blues, this is a highly enjoyable and musical set. Assisted on three numbers by Mark Wenner's harmonica, Saffire plays spirited versions of such tunes as "Middle Aged Blues Boogie," "Even Yuppies Get The Blues," "Fess Up When You Mess Up," "I Almost Lost My Mind" and their theme "Wild Women Don't Have The Blues." Recommended. *—Scott Yanow*

● **Hot Flash** / 1991 / Alligator ✦✦✦✦
In many ways, *Hot Flash* is the definitive Saffire album. Racy and sassy—and to some tastes cutesy—the album is a fun, free-thinking update of classic female blues, performed with gusto and verve. The instrumentation is sparse—a piano, guitar, bass, harmonica, and kazoo provide the foundation of the music—but the focus of these songs is solely on the vocals, which are vigorous and humorous and if you share Saffire's sense of humor, it's a rollicking good time. *—Thom Owens*

Live and Uppity / Mar. 10, 1998 / Alligator ✦✦✦✦
Saffire has been bringing their "uppity" brand of blues to stages from quite some time, and it was inevitable that a live album would rear its head sooner or later. But recording this one over a three-night stand at the Brans of Wolf Trap is a class-A affair all the way. With the ladies in top form, playing to an adoring audience cheering them on with every line, there's a symbiosis happening on this recording between audience and performers that seldom gets captured on a live album. There's no point in listing highlights simply because every track is a winner, and while the group's strong feminist stance is off-putting to some blues fans, none of them were in the audience on the nights these recordings were made, that's for sure. *—Cub Koda*

Son Seals

b. Aug. 13, 1942, Osceola, AR
Vocals, Drums, Guitar / Modern Electric Chicago Blues, Electric Chicago Blues, Modern Electric Blues
It all started with a phone call from Wesley Race, who was at the Flamingo Club on Chicago's South Side, to Alligator Records owner Bruce Iglauer. Race was raving about a new find, a young guitarist named Son Seals. He held the phone in the direction of the bandstand, so Iglauer could get an on-site report. It didn't take long for Iglauer to scramble into action. Alligator issued Seals's 1973 eponymous debut album, which was followed by six more. When Alligator signed him up, his days fronting a band at the Flamingo Club and the Expressway Lounge were numbered. Seals's jagged, uncompromising guitar riffs and gruff vocals were showcased very effectively on that 1973 debut set, which contained his "Your Love Is like a Cancer" and a raging instrumental called "Hot Sauce." *Midnight Son,* his 1976 encore, was by comparison a much slicker affair, with tight horns, funkier grooves, and a set list that included "Telephone Angel" and "On My Knees." 1994's *Nothing but the Truth* sported some of the worst cover art in CD history but a stinging lineup of songs inside. *—Bill Dahl*

The Son Seals Blues Band / 1973 / Alligator ✦✦✦✦
The Chicago mainstay's debut album was a rough, gruff, no-nonsense affair typified by the decidedly unsentimental track "Your Love Is like a Cancer." Seals wasn't all that far removed from his southern roots at this point, and his slashing guitar work sports a strikingly raw feel on his originals "Look Now, Baby," "Cotton Picking Blues," and "Hot Sauce" (the latter a blistering instrumental that sounds a bit like the theme from *Batman* played sideways). *—Bill Dahl*

● **Midnight Son** / 1976 / Alligator ✦✦✦✦✦
A much more polished set than its predecessor, *Midnight Son* is a particularly effective effort with several numbers that remain in Seals's onstage repertoire to this day—"Telephone Angel," "On My Knees," the jumping "Four Full Seasons of Love." The addition of a brisk horn section enhanced his staccato guitar attack and uncompromising vocals, rendering this his best set to date. *—Bill Dahl*

Live & Burning / 1978 / Alligator ✦✦✦✦
Lives up to its billing. Seals's smoking set, caught live at Chicago's long-gone (and definitely lamented) Wise Fools Pub, finds him attacking a sharp cross-section of material—Detroit Junior's deliberate "Call My Job," Elmore James's "I Can't Hold Out," his own "Help Me, Somebody"—with an outstanding band in tow—saxist A.C. Reed, guitarist Lacy Gibson, pianist Alberto Gianquinto, bassist Snapper Mitchum, and drummer Tony Gooden. *—Bill Dahl*

Bad Axe / 1984 / Alligator ✦✦✦✦
One of Son Seals's finest collections, studded with vicious performances ranging from covers of Eddie Vinson's "Person to Person" and Little Sonny's "Going Home (Where Women Got Meat on Their Bones)" to his own "Can't Stand to See Her Cry" and swaggering "Cold Blood." Top-drawer Windy City studio musicians lay down skin-tight grooves throughout. *—Bill Dahl*

Nothing But the Truth / 1994 / Alligator ✦✦✦✦
The grotesque cover illustration is an abomination, but the contents are right in the growling grizzly bear style that we've come to expect. Only four Seals-penned originals, but the R&B-laced "Life Is Hard" and "I'm Gonna Take It All Back" are quality efforts. So is his heartfelt tribute to Hound Dog Taylor, "Sadie." *—Bill Dahl*

Lettin' Go / Apr. 25, 2000 / Telarc ✦✦✦✦

Marvin Sease

b. Feb. 16, 1946, South Carolina
Vocals / Retro-Soul, Modern Electric Blues
Despite a lack of attention from most print sources and other common avenues of publicity in the blues world, Marvin Sease has turned his smooth, X-rated ladies' man persona into a cottage industry complete with merchandising in the Deep South. Sease straddles the line between blues and gospel-drenched soul, much like fellow Southern singers Johnnie Taylor and Tyrone Davis, but his often racy lyrics and concert performances, coupled with the advantages of major-label distribution, have ensured Sease a strong following, particularly among female fans enamored of his signature song and breakthrough jukebox hit, the provocative, innuendo-laced "Candy Licker." Sease recorded a self-titled LP in 1986 featuring one of his most popular songs, "Ghetto Man," and began working the South's so-called chitlin circuit of ghetto bars, rural juke joints, and blues festivals. While shopping the LP, released on his own Early label, to record stores, Sease stumbled upon a contact who eventually got him a deal with Polygram, which re-released the LP on London/Mercury in 1987 with the addition of the newly recorded, ten-minute track "Candy Licker." The song became an underground success on jukeboxes across the South; it was too explicit for radio airplay, but audiences—especially female ones—flocked to see Sease in concert. *—Steve Huey*

● **The Best of Marvin Sease** / May 20, 1997 / Polygram ✦✦✦✦
The Best of Marvin Sease is the first comprehensive collection of Sease's best bawdy, funky '70s soul, culled from his four albums for Polygram. Among the 15 tracks are the notorious "Candy Licker" and a single that had never been available on an album prior to this collection. *—Stephen Thomas Erlewine*

Kenny Wayne Shepherd

b. Jun. 12, 1977, Shreveport, LA
Vocals, Guitar / Blues-Rock, Modern Electric Blues
Kenny Wayne Shepherd and his group have exploded on the scene in the mid-'90s and garnered huge amounts of radio airplay on commercial radio, which historically has not been a solid home for blues and blues-rock music, with the exception of Stevie Ray Vaughan in the mid-'80s. The Shreveport native began playing at age 7, figuring out Muddy Waters licks from his father's record collection (he has never taken a formal lesson). At age 13, he was invited onstage by New Orleans bluesman Brian Lee and held his own for several hours; thus proving himself, he decided on music as a career. Shepherd's father/manager used his own contacts and pizzazz in the record business to help land his son a major label record deal with Giant Records. *Ledbetter Heights,* his first album, was an immediate hit, selling over 500,000 by early 1996. Most blues records never achieve that level of commerical success, much less ones released by artists that are still in their teens. *—Steve Huey & Richard Skelly*

● **Ledbetter Heights** / Oct. 1995 / Giant ✦✦✦✦
You would never guess from Kenny Wayne Shepherd's fiery playing that the guitarist is still only in his teens. On his debut, *Ledbetter Heights,* Shepherd burns through a set of rather generic blues-rock ravers that are made special by his exceptional technique. It may still be a while before he says something original, but he plays with style, energy, and dedication, which is more than enough for a debut album. *—Thom Owens*

Trouble Is / Oct. 7, 1997 / Revolution/Warner Brothers ✦✦✦
Instead of breaking from his high-energy, high-voltage blues-rock, Kenny Wayne Shepherd offers more of the same on his second album, *Trouble Is.* While the record lacks the surprise and impact of *Ledbetter Heights,* it's clear that Shepherd is growing as a guitarist, developing a cleaner, more nuanced technique. He still suffers from a lack of an original voice, plus a lack of strong material, but his growth as a guitarist compensates for what's missing. *—Thom Owens*

Live On / Oct. 12, 1999 / Warner Brothers ✦✦✦✦
Being a teenage blues guitar prodigy is a double-edged sword. Stunning technique brings attention, but also criticism that it's all style and no soul. This criticism has plagued Kenny Wayne Shepherd since his popular debut album, *Ledbetter Heights,* and it's warranted to a certain extent. It didn't help that Shepherd so strongly recalled Stevie Ray Vaughan. It also didn't help that some of his material was a little too slick, appealing as much to album-rock as to blues-rock audiences. By the time of his third album, 1999's *Live On,* he had begun to reconcile these two sides of his personality, but the best thing about the record is that it's tougher and stronger than its two predecessors. There's still a fair amount of crossover—a Hendrix cover and a cover of Fleetwood Mac's "Oh Well,"—but Shepherd not only seems to be developing a style of his own, the playing of his band has become grittier, or at least it's being captured better on record. Shepherd can still fall prey to excess, but not as often as he used to. He's figuring out how to restrain himself, and his music is all the better for it. *—Stephen Thomas Erlewine*

Johnny Shines (John Ned Shines)

b. Apr. 26, 1915, Frayser, TN, **d.** Apr. 20, 1992, Chicago, IL
Vocals, Guitar / Slide Guitar Blues, Delta Blues, Electric Delta Blues, Electric Chicago Blues
Johnny Shines's best material crackles with energy. In his prime, his slashing slide guitar carried more of the spirit of his onetime running mate Robert Johnson than any other traditional blues artist. Shines, however, was never a Johnson imitator. He had his own sound, his own guitar style, and a voice that can still take you on a roller coaster ride—Shines has too much personal magnetism to be confused with anyone else. Like many artists of his generation, he is also master of the spoken word, a gifted storyteller, a social critic, and a historian dedicated to telling the truth. Shines's distinctive style and songwriting skills should have brought him fame and fortune in music, but such was not the case. During the '40s and '50s, when he was at his peak, he only issued a handful of records. Subsequent recordings, including his collaboration with Robert Jr. Lockwood, have generally maintained a high quality. His later guitar work was hampered by a stroke, but he remained a powerful artist sustained by one of the all-time great blues voices. *—Barry Lee Pearson*

Johnny Shines with Big Walter Horton / Nov. 1969 / Testament ✦✦✦✦✦
Outstanding late-'60s Shines material matching him with a sterling lineup. Big Walter Horton is awesome on harmonica, a young Luther Allison doesn't dissipate his brilliance on haphazard soul and funk, and pianist Otis Spann and drummer Fred Below are super on their cuts. The date combines 1966 and 1969 sessions; there's another LP with a full collection culled from 1966. *—Ron Wynn*

Hey Ba-Ba-Re-Bop / 1978 / Rounder ✦✦✦✦✦
Delta blues vocalist, guitarist and composer Johnny Shines hadn't yet encountered the physical difficulties that made his final years so troubling when he recorded the 13 selections on this CD. He could still sing and moan with intensity and passion, hold a crowd hypnotized with his remembrances and asides, and play with a mix of fury and charm. While the menu includes oft-performed chestnuts "Sweet Home Chicago," "Terraplane Blues" and "Milk Cow Blues," there wasn't anything staid or predictable about the way Shines ripped through the lyrics and presented the music. If you missed it the first time around, grab this one immediately. *—Ron Wynn*

★ **Johnny Shines & Robert Lockwood** / 1991 / Paula/Flyright ✦✦✦✦✦
Shines has half of this 20-track disc, the remainder being devoted to sides from the same era featuring Robert Lockwood. Recorded in 1952 and 1953 for the JOB label, this is Shines at his most primal, working with a drumless trio; Big Walter Horton plays harmonica on the 1953 sides. These tracks decidedly outshine the Lockwood efforts (also recorded for JOB in the early '50s), some of which only feature Robert as a sideman. *—Richie Unterberger*

Traditional Delta Blues / 1991 / Biograph ✦✦✦✦✦

Masters of Modern Blues / 1994 / Testament ✦✦✦✦✦
After stepping away from the music business altogether for a while, Shines came back strong during the mid-'60s, recording far more prolifically than his first time around. This 1966 date is one of his best, spotlighting his booming pipes and sturdy guitar in front of an all-star Chicago crew: Walter Horton on harp, pianist Otis Spann, and drummer Fred Below. *—Bill Dahl*

Siegel-Schwall Band

f. 1964, Chicago, IL, **db.** 1974

Group / Modern Electric Chicago Blues, Electric Chicago Blues, Modern Electric Blues

Paul Butterfield and Elvin Bishop were not the only White dudes that formed a blues band in Chicago in the early '60s. Siegel and Jim Schwall formed the Siegel-Schwall Band in the mid-'60s in Chicago and worked as a duo playing blues clubs like Pepper's Lounge, where they were the house band. All of the great blues players would sit in—all the time. Corky Siegel played harp and electric Wurlizter piano, with an abbreviated drum set stashed under the piano; Jim Schwall played guitar and mandolin. Both sang. Signed by Vanguard scout Sam Charters in 1965, they released their first album in 1966, the first of five they would do with that label. In 1969 the band toured playing the Fillmore West, blues/folk festivals, and many club dates—one of several White blues bands that introduced the blues genre to millions of Americans during that era. They were, however, the first blues band to record with a full orchestra, performing *Three Pieces for Blues Band and Symphony Orchestra* in 1971 with the San Francisco Orchestra. The band broke up in 1974 but reformed in 1987 and produced a live album on Alligator, *The Siegel-Schwall Reunion Concert*. *—Michael Erlewine*

● **Where We Walked (1966-1970)** / 1991 / Vanguard ✦✦✦✦✦
A very nice, fairly thorough, compilation that supersedes the old vinyl collection on several levels; nice mastering, better notes, and nicer selection. For a basic introduction to their sound, this one's hard to beat. *—Cub Koda*

Wooden Nickel Years: 1971-1974 / May 18, 1999 / Varese ✦✦✦✦
Subtitled "the Wooden Nickel years," these are the sides made between 1971 and 1973 for the RCA subsidiary. While the music the group made during this period was blues based, much of it can't really be called straight blues. But Siegel-Schwall always marched to the beat of a different drummer and just how different is collected up nicely here with everything from traditional blues ("Corrina," "Next to You," "Blues for a Lady," "[I Wish I Was on A] Country Road") to New Orleans funk ("Old Time Shimmy") to what can only be described as polka-blues ("Somethin's Wrong," "Sick to My Stomach") in the mix. Grab this one after you digest their earlier Vanguard sides for the full picture. *—Cub Koda*

Frankie Lee Sims

b. Apr. 30, 1917, New Orleans, LA, **d.** May 10, 1970, Dallas, TX

Vocals, Guitar / Juke Joint Blues, Texas Blues, Electric Texas Blues

A traditionalist who was a staunch member of the Texas country blues movement of the late '40s and early '50s (along with the likes of his cousin Lightnin' Hopkins, Lil' Son Jackson, and Smokey Hogg), guitarist Frankie Lee Sims developed a twangy, ringing electric guitar style that was irresistible on fast numbers and stung hard on the downbeat stuff. Sims cut his first 78s for Herb Rippa's Blue Bonnet Records in 1948 in Dallas, but didn't taste anything resembling regional success until 1953, when his bouncy "Lucy Mae Blues" did well down south. The guitarist recorded fairly prolifically for Specialty into 1954, then switched to the Ace label in 1957 to cut the mighty rockers "Walking with Frankie" and "She Likes to Boogie Real Low," both of which pounded harder than a ballpeen hammer. Sims mostly missed out on the folk-blues revival of the early '60s that his cousin Lightnin' Hopkins cashed in on handily. *—Bill Dahl*

● **Lucy Mae Blues** / 1970 / Specialty ✦✦✦✦
This collection of Sims' Specialty sides, primarily in a drums and electric guitar format, is pretty hard to beat. It combines all of the original singles, the extra tracks from his lone album plus unissued material and until further alternate takes come to light, the best overview of his tenure with the label. Some tracks are augmented with harmonica and/or string bass, but it's Frankie Lee's guitar and sly vocals that drive things along. Until his early Bluebonnet and later Ace material is cobbled together to complete the picture, this compilation is all you'll need. *—Cub Koda*

Bessie Smith

b. Apr. 15, 1894, Chattanooga, TN, **d.** Sep. 26, 1937, Clarksdale, MS

Vocals / Classic Jazz, Classic Female Blues

The first major blues and jazz singer on record and one of the most powerful of all time, Bessie Smith rightly earned the title of "The Empress of the Blues." Even on her first records in 1923, her passionate voice overcame the primitive recordinq quality of the day and still communicates easily to today's listeners (which is not true of any other singer from that early period). At a time when the blues were in and most vocalists (particularly vaudevillians) were being dubbed "blues singers," Bessie Smith simply had no competition. Signed by Columbia, her first recording (Alberta Hunter's "Downhearted Blues") made her famous. Bessie worked and recorded steadily throughout the decade, using many top musicians as sidemen on sessions including Louis Armstrong, Joe Smith (her favorite cornetist), James P. Johnson and Charlie Green. However by 1929 the blues were out-of-fashion and Bessie Smith's career was declining despite being at the peak of her powers. Although she was dropped by Columbia in 1931 and made her final recordings on a four-song session in 1933, Smith kept on working; the chances are very good that she would have made a comeback, starting with a Carnegie Hall appearance at John Hammond's upcoming "From Spirituals to Swing" concert, but she was killed in a car crash in Mississippi. "The Empress of the Blues," based on her recordings, will never have to abdicate her throne. *—Scott Yanow*

☆ **The Complete Recordings, Vol. 1** / Feb. 16, 1923-Apr. 8, 1924 / Columbia/Legacy ✦✦✦✦✦
In the 1970s Bessie Smith's recordings were reissued on five double LPs. Her CD reissue series also has five volumes (the first four are double-CD sets) with the main difference being that the final volume includes all of her rare alternate takes (which were bypassed on LP). The first set (which, as with all of the CD volumes, is housed in an oversize box that includes an informative booklet) contains her first 38 recordings. During this early era, Bessie Smith had no competitors on record and she was one of the few vocalists who could overcome the primitive recording techniques; her power really comes through. Her very first recording (Alberta Hunter's "Down Hearted Blues") was a big hit and is one of the highlights of this set along with "'Tain't Nobody's Bizness If I Do" (two decades before Billie Holiday), "Jail-House Blues" and "Ticket Agent, Ease Your Window Down." Smith's accompaniment is nothing that special (usually just a pianist and maybe a weak horn or two) but she dominates the music anyway, even on two vocal duets with her rival Clara Smith. All of these volumes reward close listenings and are full of timeless recordings. *—Scott Yanow*

★ **The Essential Bessie Smith** / Apr. 11, 1923-Nov. 24, 1933 / Columbia/Legacy ✦✦✦✦✦
Although there are a multitude of box sets chronicling Bessie's entire recorded career, this two-disc, 36-song set sweats it down to the bare essentials in quite an effective manner. Bessie could sing it all, from the lowdown moan of "St. Louis Blues" and "Nobody Knows You When You're Down and Out" to her torch treatment of the jazz standard "After You've Gone" to the downright salaciousness of "Need a Little Sugar in My Bowl." Covering a time span from her first recordings in 1923 to her final session in 1933, this is the perfect entry-level set to go with. Utilizing the latest in remastering technology, these recordings have never sounded quite this clear and full, and the selection—collecting her best-known sides and collaborations with jazz giants like Louis Armstrong, Coleman Hawkins and Benny Goodman—is first rate. If you've never experienced the genius of Bessie Smith, pick this one up and prepare yourself to be devastated. *—Cub Koda*

☆ **The Collection** / 1923-1933 / Columbia ✦✦✦✦✦
While there's no denying the importance and quality of Columbia/Legacy's *Complete Recordings* series, nine discs may seem a bit intimidating to the newcomer. *Collection,* a mid-priced, 16-track collection which spans most of Smith's career, ultimately does a better service to the casual listener with a limited budget. This is probably the best introduction—undoubtedly many will seek out the more comprehensive packages afterwards. *—Chris Woodstra*

☆ **The Complete Recordings, Vol. 2 (1924-1925)** / Apr. 8, 1924-Nov. 18, 1925 / Columbia/Legacy ✦✦✦✦✦
Bessie Smith, even on the evidence of her earliest recordings, well deserved the title "Empress of the Blues" for in the 1920s there was no one in her league for emotional intensity, honest blues feeling and power. The second of five volumes (the first four are two-CD sets) finds her accompaniment improving rapidly with such sympathetic sidemen as trombonist Charlie Green, cornetist Joe Smith and clarinetist Buster Bailey often helping her out. However they are overshadowed by Louis Armstrong whose two sessions with Smith (nine songs in all) fall into the time period of this second set; particularly classic are their versions of "St. Louis Blues," "Careless Love Blues" and "I Ain't Goin' to Play Second Fiddle." Other gems on this essential set include "Cake Walkin' Babies from Home," "The Yellow Dog Blues" and "At the Christmas Ball." *—Scott Yanow*

The Complete Recordings, Vol. 5: The Final Chapter / May 6, 1925-Nov. 24, 1933 / Columbia/Legacy ✦✦✦✦✦
Bessie Smith cut 160 sides for the Columbia and OKeh labels between 1923 and 1933, and the four previous two-CD/cassette box sets of her complete recordings released in the 1990s covered 154 of them, which introduces the question, what can a fifth two-CD/cassette box set contain in addition to the remaining six cuts— First, there are five previously unreleased alternate takes; second, there is the 15-minute low-fi soundtrack to the two-reel short *St. Louis Blues,* which constitutes the only film of Smith; and third, taking up all of the second CD/cassette, there are 72 minutes of interview tapes of Ruby Smith, Bessie Smith's niece, who traveled as part of her show. The box contains a "Parental Advisory—Explicit Lyrics" warning because of the nature of Ruby Smith's reminiscences. You won't learn much about Bessie Smith's music from her niece's remarks, but you will learn a lot about her sexual preferences. *—William Ruhlmann*

The Complete Recordings, Vol. 3 / Nov. 20, 1925-Feb. 16, 1928 / Columbia/Legacy ✦✦✦✦✦
On the third of five volumes (the first four are double-CD box sets) that reissue all of her recordings, the great Bessie Smith is greatly assisted on some of the 39 selections by a few of her favorite sidemen: cornetist Joe Smith, trombonist Charlie Green and clarinetist Buster Bailey. But the most important of her occasional musicians was pianist James P. Johnson who makes his first appearance in 1927 and can be heard on four duets with Bessie including the monumental "Back Water Blues." Other highlights of this highly recommended set (all five volumes are essential) include "After You've Gone," "Muddy Water," "There'll Be a Hot Time in the Old Town Tonight," "Trombone Cholly," "Send Me to the 'Lectric Chair" and "Mean Old Bedbug Blues." The power and intensity of Bessie Smith's recordings should be considered required listening; even 70 years later they still communicate. *—Scott Yanow*

The Complete Recordings, Vol. 4 / Feb. 21, 1928-Jun. 11, 1931 / Columbia/Legacy ✦✦✦✦✦
The fourth of five volumes (the first four are two-CD sets) that reissue all of Bessie Smith's recordings traces her career from a period when her popularity was at its height down to just six songs away from the halt of her recording career. But although her commercial fortunes might have slipped, Bessie Smith never declined and these later recordings are consistently powerful. The two-part "Empty Bed Blues" and "Nobody Knows You When You're Down and Out" (hers is the original version) are true classics and none of the other 40 songs (including the double-entendre "Kitchen Man") are throwaways. With strong accompaniment during some performances by trombonist Charlie Green, guitarist Eddie Lang, Clarence Williams's band and on ten songs (eight of which are duets) the masterful pianist James P. Johnson, this volume (as with the others) is quite essential. *—Scott Yanow*

Funny Paper Smith (John T. Smith)

b. 1890, Texas, **d.** 1940

Vocals, Guitar / Prewar Blues, Acoustic Texas Blues

J.T. "Funny Paper" Smith was a pioneering force behind the development of the Texas blues guitar style of the pre-war era; in addition to honing a signature sound distinguished by intricate melody lines and simple, repetitive bass riffs, he was also a gifted composer, authoring songs of surprising narrative complexity. A contemporary of such legends as Blind Lemon Jefferson and Dennis "Little Hat" Jones, next to nothing concrete is known of John T. Smith's life; assumed to have been born in East Texas during the latter half of the 1880s, he was a minstrel who wandered about the panhandle region, performing at fairs, fish fries, dances and other community events (often in the company of figures including Tom Shaw, Texas Alexander and Bernice Edwards). Smith settled down long enough to record some 22 songs between 1930 and 1931, among them his trademark number "Howling Wolf Blues, Parts One and Two"; indeed, he claimed the alternate nickname "Howling Wolf" some two decades before it was appropriated by his more famous successor, Chester Burnett. (The true story behind Smith's more common nickname remains a matter of some debate—some blues archivists claim he was instead dubbed "Funny Papa," with the "Funny Paper" alias resulting only from record company error.) His career came to an abrupt end during the mid-'30s, when he was arrested for murdering a man over a gambling dispute; Smith was found guilty and imprisoned, and is believed to have died in his cell circa 1940. *—Jason Ankeny*

● **The Howling Wolf (1930-1931)** / 1971 / Yazoo ♦♦♦♦♦
This is fine guitar-based Texas country blues by an artist completely unlike the later Howlin' Wolf. *—Mark A. Humphrey*

Complete Recorded Works (1930-1931) / 1991 / Document ♦♦♦♦
For completists, specialists and academics, Document's *Complete Recorded Works (1930-1931)* is invaluable, offering an exhaustive overview of Funny Paper Smith's recordings. For less dedicated listeners, in spite of some of the wonderful, classic performances present, the disc will probably prove more of a chore to get through. The features that make it appealing to academics—long running time, exacting chronological sequencing, poor fidelity (all cuts are transferred from original acetates and 78s), and exhaustive number of performances—will likely impair its overall listenability for more casual audiences. *—Thom Owens*

George Harmonica Smith

b. Apr. 22, 1924, Helena, AR, **d.** Oct. 2, 1983, Los Angeles, CA
Vocals, Harmonica / Juke Joint Blues, Harmonica Blues, Electric Harmonica Blues, West Coast Blues, Electric Blues, R&B
George "Harmonica" Smith began his career as a consistently imaginative amplified harpist with a full, fat tone and ended it as a mentor to a legion of up-and-coming Los Angeles blues harp aces. In between, he spent two stints as Muddy Waters's harpist and made some terrific recordings of his own. Smith was amplifying his harmonica through a public-address system early in his career, when the concept was new and no doubt startling. Influenced by the one and only Little Walter, Smith began working in Chicago at the dawn of the 1950s. His first tour of duty with Waters came in the wake of tragedy; his predecessor, Henry Strong, had just been stabbed to death. He didn't stay for long, journeying to Kansas City for his own gig (where Modern Records prexy Joe Bihari caught his act in 1955). The immediate result was the stunning RPM single "Blues in the Dark"/"Telephone Blues." After being jettisoned by the Biharis, Smith bounced from one tiny L.A. firm to the next, recording as Little Walter Jr. and Harmonica King for Lapel in 1956, under his own name for JM and Carolyn, and as George Allen for Nat McCoy's Sotoplay logo. Smith rejoined Waters in 1966 for a tour and ended up doing a 1968 album for World Pacific, *A Tribute to Little Walter*, with the entire Waters outfit reliving its history behind him. Despite a series of heart attacks that slowed his musical activities during his last few years, Smith continued to provide inspiration and pointers to his young protégés until a final heart attack permanently felled him in 1983. *—Bill Dahl*

Tribute to Little Walter / 1968 / World Pacific ♦♦♦♦♦

● **Harmonica Ace: The Modern Masters** / 1993 / Flair ♦♦♦♦♦
Smith cut these sides for Joe Bihari of Modern Records shortly after he left the Muddy Waters Band in the early '50s. He is featured here with a rhythm section framed by horns arranged by the legendary and prolific Maxwell Davis. Smith's innate sense of drive and swing, coupled with his rich and diverse palette of texture and tone, truly place him in the very first rank of modern harp masters. This disc is aptly described by note-writer Ray Topping as "a lasting memorial to one of the last great harp players of the postwar blues scene." *—Larry Hoffman*

Now You Can Talk About Me / Sep. 29, 1998 / Blind Pig ♦♦♦♦♦
A collection of middle- and late-period Smith with the harmonica genius' '60s sides for the microscopic imprint Sotoplay sampled here with the first five cuts. The remainder of the album is the 1982 session for the Murray Brothers label with Rod Piazza behind the board that produced the *Boogie'n With George* album with the addition of the previously unreleased "Last Chance," and a powerful instrumental slow burner. Junior Watson shines on guitar on these tracks and Smith's tone is big, fat, rich and full of ideas galore on tunes like "Bad Start," "Astatic Stomp," "Sunbird," and the title track. But Smith's use of a chromatic will strike most blues mavens as something unique and out of the ordinary as he tackles such standards as "I Left My Heart In San Francisco" and "Peg O'My Heart" with considerable elan, imparting both with a bluesy feel that Jerry Murad and the Harmonicats could only envision. If you like great blues harmonica playing, you're going to *love* this one. Add Smith's name to the list of all-time greats near the top with this one. *—Cub Koda*

Mamie Smith

b. May 26, 1883, Cincinnati, OH, **d.** Aug. 16, 1946, New York, NY
Vocals / Classic Female Blues
Though technically not a blues performer, Mamie Smith notched her place in American music as the first black female singer to record a vocal blues. That record was "Crazy Blues" (rec. Aug. 10, 1920), which sold a million copies in its first six months and made record labels aware of the huge potential market for "race records," thus paving the way for Bessie Smith (no relation) and other blues and jazz performers. An entertainer who sported a powerful, penetrating, feminine voice with belting vaudeville qualities, as opposed to blues inflections, Smith toured as a dancer with Tutt-Whitney's Smart Set Company in her early teens and sang in Harlem clubs before World War I. Apparently, Smith's pioneering recording session was an accident, since she was filling in for Sophie Tucker, but the success of the record made her wealthy.

Soon thereafter, Smith began touring and recording with a band called the Jazz Hounds, which featured such jazz notables as Coleman Hawkins, Bubber Miley, Johnny Dunn, etc., and she toured with the bands of Andy Kirk and Fats Pichon in the 1930s. She also appeared in several films, including *Paradise in Harlem* late in her life (1939). She recorded several sides for OKeh during her heyday; one unissued take of "My Sportin' Man" is included on Columbia's *Roots N' Blues Retrospective 1925-1950* box set. In the 1980s, all of her recordings were reissued on LP by the imported Document label. *—Richard S. Ginell*

● **Complete Recorded Works, Vol. 1** / Feb. 14, 1920-Dec. 22, 1921 / Document ♦♦♦♦♦
This first volume of a five-volume import set of her complete recordings features her earliest and best sides, including the classic "Crazy Blues." *—Cub Koda*

Complete Recorded Works, Vol. 2 (1921-1922) / May 1921-Oct. 12, 1922 / Document ♦♦♦♦

Otis Spann

b. Mar. 21, 1930, Jackson, MS, **d.** Apr. 24, 1970, Chicago, IL
Vocals, Piano / Blues Revival, Piano Blues, Acoustic Blues, Electric Chicago Blues
An integral member of the non-pareil Muddy Waters band of the 1950s and '60s, pianist Otis Spann took his sweet time in launching a full-fledged solo career. But his own discography is a satisfying one nonetheless, offering ample proof as to why so many aficionados considered him then and now as Chicago's leading postwar blues pianist. He began playing piano by age eight and was inspired by Big Maceo, who took the young pianist under his wing once Spann migrated to Chicago in 1946 or 1947. After hiring with Waters in 1952, he played on Chess classics including "Hoochie Coochie Man," "I'm Ready," and "Just Make Love to Me." Strangely, his own Chess output was limited to a 1954 single, "It Must Have Been the Devil," and sessions in 1956 and 1963 that remained in the can for decades. So Spann looked elsewhere, waxing a stunning album for Candid in 1960 as well as Storyville, British Decca (with Waters and Eric Clapton) and Prestige (with James Cotton). Two mid-'60s albums for Bluesway, *The Blues Is Where It's At* and *The Bottom of the Blues*, were also well-received. He finally turned the piano chair in the Waters band over to Pinetop Perkins in 1969, but fate didn't grant Spann long to achieve solo stardom. He was stricken with cancer and died one year later. *—Bill Dahl*

Otis Spann Is the Blues / Aug. 1960 / Candid ♦♦♦♦♦
He may not have been *the* blues, but he was sure close to being *the blues pianist*. Spann provided wonderful, imaginative, tasty piano solos and better-than-average vocals, and was arguably the best player whose style was more restrained than animated. Not that he couldn't rock the house, but Spann's forte was making you think as well as making you dance. *—Ron Wynn*

☆ **Complete Candid Recordings— *Otis Spann/Lightnin' Hopkins Sessions*** */ Aug. 23, 1960 / Mosaic* ♦♦♦♦♦
With Robert Lockwood, Jr. Two classic Spann albums: *Otis Spann Is the Blues* and *Walkin' the Blues*. Early, potent Spann with flawless liner notes and a complete discography. Also included are the Candid sessions of Lightnin' Hopkins. *—Michael Erlewine*

The Blues Is Where It's At / Aug. 1967 / BGO ♦♦♦♦♦

The Blues Never Die / Oct. 1969 / Prestige/Original Blues Classics ♦♦♦♦♦
Boasting fellow Chicago blues dynamo James Cotton on both harmonica and lead vocals, *The Blues Never Die!* is one of Otis Spann's most inspired albums. When this session was recorded for Prestige's Bluesville subsidiary in 1964, Spann was still best known for playing acoustic piano in Muddy Waters' band. But *The Blues Never Die!* (which Fantasy reissued on CD in 1990 for its Original Blues Classics series) shows that he was as great a leader as he was a sideman. From Willie Dixon's "I'm Ready" (a Chess gem Spann had played numerous times with Waters) and Elmore James' "Dust My Broom" to Cotton's spirited "Feelin' Good" and Spann's dark-humored "Must Have Been the Devil," Spann and Cotton enjoy a very strong rapport on this consistently rewarding date. *—Alex Henderson*

★ **Walking the Blues** / 1972 / Candid ♦♦♦♦♦
Walking the Blues is arguably the finest record Otis Spann ever cut, boasting 11 cuts of astounding blues piano. On several numbers, Spann is supported by guitarist Robert Jr. Lockwood and their interaction is sympathetic, warm, and utterly inviting. Spann relies on originals here, from "Half Ain't Been Told" to "Walking the Blues," but he also throws in a few standards ("Goin' Down Slow," "My Home Is in the Delta") that help draw a fuller portrait of his musicianship. Most importantly, however, is the fact that *Walking the Blues* simply sounds great—it's some of the finest blues piano you'll ever hear. *—Thom Owens*

Down to Earth / 1995 / MCA ♦♦♦♦♦
Both of the great Chicago pianist's albums for ABC-Bluesway, characterized with rippling piano and ruminative vocals. Backed in style by his mates in the Muddy Waters band (including the man himself), Spann responds to a studio full of people on "Popcorn Man," "Steel Mill Blues," and "Nobody Knows Chicago like I Do." Spann's 1967 encore LP united him in the studio with wife Lucille for several vocals. *—Bill Dahl*

Live the Life / Jun. 10, 1997 / Testament ♦♦♦♦

Speckled Red (Rufus Perryman)

b. Oct. 23, 1892, Monroe, LA, **d.** Jan. 2, 1973, St. Louis, MO
Piano, Organ / Jazz Blues, Piano Blues
Pianist Speckled Red (born Rufus Perryman) was born in Monroe, LA, but he made his reputation as part of the St. Louis and Memphis blues scenes of the '20s and '30s. Red was equally proficient in early jazz and boogie woogie—his style is similar to Roosevelt Sykes and Little Brother Montgomery.

Speckled Red was born in Louisiana, but he was raised in Hampton, Georgia, where he learned how to play his church's organ. In his early teens, his family—including his brother Willie Perryman, who is better-known as Piano Red—moved to Atlanta, Georgia. Throughout his childhood and adolescence he played piano and organ and by the time he was a teenager, he was playing house parties and juke joints. Red moved to Detroit in the mid-'20s and while he was there, he played various night clubs and parties. After a few years in Detroit, he moved back south to Memphis. In 1929, he cut his first recording sessions. One song from these sessions, "The Dirty Dozens," was released on Brunswick and became a hit in late 1929. He recorded a sequel, "The Dirty Dozens, No. 2," the following year, but it failed to become a hit.

After Red's second set of sessions failed to sell, the pianist spent the next few years without a contract—he simply played local Memphis clubs. In 1938, he cut a few sides for Bluebird, but they were largely ignored.

In the early '40s, Speckled Red moved to St. Louis, where he played local clubs and bars for the next decade and a half. In 1954, he was rediscovered by a number of blues aficianados and record label owners. By 1956, he had recorded several songs for the Tone record label and began a tour of America and Europe. In 1960, he made some recordings for Folkways. By this time, Red's increasing age was causing him to cut back the number of concerts he gave. For the rest of the '60s, he only performed occasionally. Speckled Red died in 1973. *—Stephen Thomas Erlewine & Michael G. Nastos*

● **Dirty Dozens** / 196 / Delmark ✦✦✦✦✦
If you have trouble keeping track of the "reds," Rufus G. Perryman was "Speckled Red," while William Lee Perryman was either "Piano Red" or "Doctor Feelgood." In addition, Speckled Red's style contained more rag and folk elements than "Piano Red"'s, as this set reveals. But both reds talked a lot trash, and Speckled Red had a lighter barrelhouse approach than his younger brother. *—Ron Wynn*

Complete Recorded Works 1929-1938 / Jun. 2, 1994 / Document ✦✦✦

Victoria Spivey (Victoria Regina Spivey)

b. Oct. 15, 1906, Houston, TX, **d.** Oct. 3, 1976, New York, NY
Vocals, Piano / Acoustic Chicago Blues, Classic Female Blues
Victoria Spivey was one of the more influential blues women simply because she was around long enough to influence legions of younger women and men who rediscovered blues music during the mid-'60s U.S. blues revival brought about by British blues bands as well as their American counterparts, like Paul Butterfield and Elvin Bishop. Spivey could do it all: she wrote songs, sang them well, and accompanied herself on piano and organ, and occasionally ukulele. After working as a pianist in gambling parlors, gay hangouts and whorehouses in Houston with Blind Lemon Jefferson, she recorded her first song, "Black Snake Blues," for the Okeh label in 1926. In the 1930s, Spivey recorded for the Victor, Vocalion, Decca and Okeh labels, and spent time on the road with Louis Armstrong's various bands. She left show business for many years, but then formed her own Spivey label in 1962 (its first release featured Bob Dylan as her accompanist). As the folk revival began to take hold in the early '60s, Spivey found herself an in-demand performer on the folk-blues festival circuit and, unlike others from her generation, continued recording well into the 1970s. Her many albums for Spivey and other labels include the excellent *Songs We Taught Your Mother* (1962), *Idle Hours* (1961), *The Queen and Her Knights* (1965) and *The Victoria Spivey Recorded Legacy of the Blues* (1970). After entering the hospital with an internal hemorrhage, she died a short while later in 1976. *—Richard Skelly*

☆ **Complete Recorded Works, Vol. 1 (1926-1927)** / May 11, 1926-Oct. 31, 1927 / Document ✦✦✦✦✦
The first of four Document CDs that contain all of singer Victoria Spivey's pre-war recordings has her first 23 sides. Spivey made her initial reputation with her series of dark blues that were full of symbolism, such as her trademark "Black Snake Blues"—snakes and tuberculosis were common topics in her lyrics. Her first four selections were recorded in St. Louis from May 11-13, 1926 (she was 19 at the time) and then she relocated to New York. Spivey is heard backed by several ensembles led by pianist John Erby in August 1926 (including her first meetings with guitarist Lonnie Johnson) and on five pieces in October 1927 with Johnson and pianist Porter Grainger. By the time the latter sides were recorded, her style was becoming a little more lighthearted and softer but no less powerful. Among the highlights of this superior set are "Black Snake Blues," "Hoodoo Man Blues," "Spider Web Blues," "Got the Blues So Bad," "The Alligator Pond Went Dry," "T-B Blues" and "Garter Snake Blues." This is highly recommended, as are the other three CDs in this important series. *—Scott Yanow*

● **1926-1931** / 1926-1931 / Document ✦✦✦✦✦
Spivey is in marvelous form throughout. This album features the classics "Steady Grind," "Black Snake Blues," and "Blood Thirsty Blues." *—Cub Koda*

☆ **Complete Recorded Works, Vol. 2 (1927-1929)** / Oct. 31, 1927-Sep. 24, 1929 / Document ✦✦✦✦✦
Victoria Spivey, who made her initial reputation with dark and somewhat scary blues lyrics, altered her style during the period covered by this second of four "complete" Document CDs. She is heard in a series of double-entendre songs (usually issued in two parts) with singer/guitarist Lonnie Johnson, including "New Black Snake Blues," "Toothache Blues," "Furniture Man Blues" and "You Done Lost Your Good Thing Now." Also, Spivey is heard with an all-star group led by pianist Clarence Williams (including cornetist King Oliver and guitarist Eddie Lang) that unfortunately does not get much space to stretch out; on two classic performances ("Funny Feathers" and "How Do You Do It that Way") on which she is joined by Louis Armstrong's Savoy Ballroom Five (with pianist Gene Anderson in Earl Hines' place); and guesting on two versions apiece of those two same songs with Henry "Red" Allen's Octet (which was really Luis Russell's Orchestra). Spivey, who was a strong singer from the start, is featured throughout in peak form, showing that she could not only sing blues but good-time jazz of the era. *—Scott Yanow*

Complete Recorded Works, Vol. 3 (1929-1936) / Oct. 1, 1929-Jul. 7, 1936 / Document ✦✦✦✦✦
Victoria Spivey's ability to evolve with the times and often reinvent her style can be heard throughout the third of four CDs in Document's reissuance of her prewar recordings. She is heard singing classic blues on four numbers with an all-star group drawn from Luis Russell's Orchestra (including trumpeter Red Allen and trombonist J.C. Higginbotham) and on four other songs in which she is just backed by pianist Russell and guitarist Will Johnson. She investigates double-entendre blues with the assistance of pianist/vocalist Porter Grainger and (for the two-part "Mama's Quittin' and Leavin'") with guitarist/singer "Funny Paper" Smith. For a 1931 date, Spivey does her take on hokum (particularly on "He Wants Too Much") with the help of pianist Georgia Tom Dorsey and guitarist Tampa Red. And on "Dreaming 'Bout My Man" she is backed by the pre-swing big band Hunter's Serenaders. This volume concludes by jumping ahead five years and featuring Spivey singing quite confidently with a first-rate Chicago-based swing band (including "Black Snake Swing"). Although not quite as essential as the first two volumes in this series, this set (and *Vol. 4*) is also easily recommended. *—Scott Yanow*

Woman Blues! / Sep. 1961 / Bluesville ✦✦✦✦

Grind It! / 1999 / Total Energy ✦✦✦

Sugar Blue (James Whiting)

b. 1950, New York, NY
Harmonica / Contemporary Blues, Harmonica Blues, Electric Harmonica Blues, Modern Electric Blues
One of the foremost electric blues harpists of the modern era, Sugar Blue was born James Whiting in New York City in 1950. The son of a singer/dancer who regularly performed at the legendary Apollo Theater, he was given his first harmonica at the age of ten, and by his mid-teens had already performed in the company of Muddy Waters; in the early 1970s he made his first recordings, sitting in on sessions by the likes of Johnny Shines and Louisiana Red. Sugar Blue relocated to Paris in 1976, where he was introduced to the Rolling Stones; he went on to play on the group's LPs *Some Girls, Emotional Rescue* and *Tattoo You*, lending his skills to such hits as "Miss You." He also played on jazz dates for Stan Getz and Paul Horn, and in 1979 cut the solo effort *Crossroads*. Upon returning to the U.S. in the mid-1980s, Sugar Blue settled in Chicago; after signing to Alligator, he cut *Blue Blazes* in 1994, followed a year later by *In Your Eyes*. *—Jason Ankeny*

● **Blue Blazes** / Mar. 1994 / Alligator ✦✦✦✦
Harmonica player and vocalist Sugar Blue isn't a singer who doubles on harp; he's an extraordinary instrumentalist who's also a quality vocalist. Blue covers tunes by Willie Dixon, Muddy Waters, James Cotton and Sonny Boy Williamson (II) classics, presents a decent, if disposable version of The Rolling Stones' "Miss You," and adds the good-natured original "Country Blues," co-written with his guitarist Motaoaki Makino. But it's those harmonica lines and phrases that make the CD. One of Alligator's best contemporary albums in a long time. *—Ron Wynn*

In Your Eyes / 1995 / Alligator ✦✦✦

Hubert Sumlin

b. Nov. 16, 1931, Greenwood, MS
Vocals, Guitar / Electric Chicago Blues, Modern Electric Blues
Quiet and extremely unassuming off the bandstand, Hubert Sumlin played a style of guitar incendiary enough to stand tall beside the immortal Howlin' Wolf. The Wolf was his imposing mentor for more than two decades, and it proved a mutually beneficial relationship; Sumlin's twisting, darting, unpredictable lead guitar constantly energized the Wolf's 1960s Chess sides, even when the songs themselves were less than stellar. He grew up near West Memphis, AR, briefly hooking up with another young lion with a rosy future, harpist James Cotton, before receiving a summons from the mighty Wolf to join him in Chicago in 1954. By the dawn of the '60s, Sumlin's slashing axe was a prominent component on the great majority of Wolf's waxings, including "Wang Dang Doodle," "Shake for Me," "Hidden Charms" (boasting perhaps Sumlin's greatest recorded solo) and "Killing Floor." Although they had a somewhat tempestuous relationship, Sumlin remained loyal to Wolf until the big man's 1976 death. Only in later years did Sumlin allow his vocal talents to shine. He's recorded solo sets for Black Top and Blind Pig that show him to be an understated but effective singer—and his guitar continues to communicate most forcefully. *—Bill Dahl*

Heart & Soul / 1989 / Blind Pig ✦✦✦✦
The veteran guitarist sounds more confident and expressive vocally here than on any other of his contemporary recordings. Backing by harpist James Cotton, along with Little Mike & the Tornadoes, is nicely understated, affording Sumlin just enough drive without drowning his easygoing vocals out (no small feat). *—Bill Dahl*

Blues Anytime! / 1994 / Evidence ✦✦✦✦
A remarkable 1964 session produced by Horst Lippmann behind the Iron Curtain in East Germany that found Sumlin trying for the first time on record to sing. He played both electric and acoustic axe on the historic date, sharing the singing with more experienced hands Willie Dixon and Sunnyland Slim (Clifton James is on drums). All three Chicago legends acquit themselves well. *—Bill Dahl*

● **I Know You** / 1998 / AcousTech ✦✦✦✦✦
This is arguably the first musically indispensable album that Hubert Sumlin has done since Howlin' Wolf died some 23 years ago. That isn't to say that he hasn't done some good albums before this, just that *I Know You* has a degree of urgency, coupled with remarkable ease, that makes it a real delight. The result is a record that compares very favorably with Wolf's *London Sessions* record as a mix of old and new. Sumlin will never sound like Wolf as a singer, but he can't help sounding like him in every other way, since it was Wolf's guitar on practically every cut after 1954; but he does his best with a limited voice and a hot guitar to deliver some superb electric blues. Whether he's acknowledging Elmore James, Jimmy Reed, or John Lee Hooker, or paying tribute to Wolf himself ("How Many More Years," in a killer interpretation), Sumlin sounds like he's having great fun grinding and crunching away on his instrument. He even turns in a surprisingly strong vocal and guitar performance on a familiar piece of subdued blues, "That's Why I'm Gonna Leave You." There is a little dross

here—Sumlin doesn't do all that well stepping into John Lee Hooker territory; but generally, *I Know You* is a record that should please any fan of the Wolf or Sumlin (or, for that matter, James or Reed), with two tracks, "I'm Not Your Clown" and "Smokestack" (based on guess which song), indispensable to fans of hot blues guitar. Playing with him are Sam Lay (drums) and Carrie Bell (harp), with Jimmy D. Lane on second guitar and David Krull at the piano and organ. *—Bruce Eder*

Sunnyland Slim (Albert Luandrew)

b. Sep. 5, 1907, Vance, MS, **d.** Mar. 17, 1995, Chicago, IL
Vocals, Piano / Delta Blues, Piano Blues, Acoustic Blues, Electric Chicago Blues
Exhibiting truly amazing longevity that was commensurate with his powerful, imposing physical build, Sunnyland Slim's status as a beloved Chicago piano patriarch endured long after most of his peers had perished. For more than 50 years, the towering Sunnyland rumbled the ivories around the Windy City, playing with virtually every local luminary imaginable and backing the great majority in the studio at one time or another. Though Memphis was his homebase during the late '20s, he moved to to Chicago in 1939 and played for a spell with John Lee "Sonny Boy" Williamson before recording for RCA Victor in 1947. He appeared on over a dozen labels between 1948 and 1956, including Mercury, Apollo, Vee-Jay and Cobra. In addition, his distinctive playing enlivened hundreds of sessions by other artists during the same timeframe. He recorded his first LP, 1960's *Slim's Shout*, for Prestige's Bluesville subsidiary. For a time, he helmed his own Airway label, and continued recording and performing into the '90s. Finally, after a calamitous fall on the ice coming home from a gig led to numerous complications, Sunnyland Slim finally died of kidney failure in 1995. *—Bill Dahl*

House Rent Party / 1949 / Delmark ✦✦✦✦✦
From deep in the vaults of Apollo Records comes this sensational collection of 1949 artifacts by the veteran pianist, along with sides by singer St. Louis Jimmy, young pianist Willie Mabon, and two unissued sides by guitarist Jimmy Rogers (including a pre-Chess rendition of his seminal "That's All Right"). Slim's mighty roar shines on "Brown Skin Woman," "I'm Just a Lonesome Man," and "Bad Times (Cost of Living)," all from the emerging heyday of the genre. *—Bill Dahl*

Midnight Jump / 1969 / BGO ✦✦✦✦✦
Slim cut this session in May 1968 in Chicago (with Mike Vernon producing) as a member of the Chicago Blues All Stars, an ad hoc touring group that consisted of Willie Dixon, Johnny Shines, Walter Horton, and Clifton James. With all that to recommend it, it's still a pretty workmanlike set—no real sparks of any kind, just competently played blues by five old veterans who could knock this stuff out in their sleep, and probably did. Not bad, necessarily, but not essential. *—Cub Koda*

● **Slim's Shout** / 1969 / Prestige/Original Blues Classics ✦✦✦✦✦
You wouldn't think that transporting one of Chicago's reigning piano patriarchs to Englewood Cliffs, NJ would produce such a fine album, but this 1960 set cooks from beginning to end. His swinging New York rhythm section has no trouble following Slim's bedrock piano, and the estimable King Curtis peels off diamond-hard tenor sax solos in the great Texas tradition that also mesh seamlessly. Slim runs through his standards—"The Devil Is a Busy Man," "Shake It," "It's You Baby"—in gorgeous stereo, and two unissued bonus cuts (including another of his best-known tunes, "Everytime I Get to Drinking") make the CD reissue even more appealing. *—Bill Dahl*

Chicago Jump / Apr. 1986 / Evidence ✦✦✦✦
The last of Slim's great band-backed albums, cut with yeoman help from his longtime combo (guitarist Steve Freund and drummer Robert Covington share the vocals). At the heart of the matter are Slim's rolling 88s and still-commanding vocals, invested with experience beyond all comprehension. *—Bill Dahl*

She Got a Thing Goin' On / Oct. 13, 1998 / Blind Pig ✦✦✦✦
Nice collection of sides recorded and produced by Sunnyland Slim for his Airways label in the mid-1970s. Although Slim fronts the various bands here for a few numbers, on this set he's in the main working as a sideman behind vocalists Zora Young, Big Time Sarah and Bonnie Lee. The backup on these sides is superb, with Magic Slim and the Teardrops, Hubert Sumlin, Eddie Taylor and Mack Simmons showing up in various lineups. Highlights include Zora Young's "Bus Station Blues," and Big Time Sarah's "Big Time Operator," and Bonnie Lee's "Sad and Evil Woman." As an extra bonus, the set also includes two previously unissued tracks from the 1979 *Old Friends* sessions, with Sunnyland playing with Floyd Jones, Kansas City and Honeyboy Edwards. *—Cub Koda*

Smile on My Face / Nov. 23, 1999 / Delmark ✦✦✦✦
One of the ten infamous Ralph Bass sessions from 1977, this teams Slim up with guitarist Lacy Gibson and the top-notch rhythm section of Willie Black and Fred Below for a loose and inspired session. The songs are tried-and-true staples from Sunnyland's songbook, and while Gibson sprays more modern licks, it's still the elder piano man who's the real star here. An extra bonus has guitarist Lee Jackson fronting the band on three tunes from the same session. A good one. *—Cub Koda*

Roosevelt Sykes

b. Jan. 31, 1906, Elmar, AR, **d.** Jul. 17, 1983, New Orleans, LA
Vocals, Piano / Acoustic Chicago Blues, Piano Blues, Acoustic Blues
Next time someone voices the goofball opinion that blues is simply too depressing to embrace, sit 'em down and expose 'em to a heady dose of Roosevelt Sykes. If he doesn't change their minds, nothing will. There was absolutely nothing downbeat about this roly-poly, effervescent pianist (nicknamed "Honeydripper" for his youthful prowess around the girls), whose lengthy career spanned the pre-war and postwar eras with no interruption whatsoever. Sykes's romping boogies and hilariously risqué lyrics (his double-entendre gems included "Dirty Mother for You," "Ice Cream Freezer," and "Peeping Tom") characterize his monumental contributions to the blues idiom—he was a pioneering piano-pounder responsible for the seminal pieces "44 Blues," "Driving Wheel," and "Night Time Is the Right Time." Precious few pianists could boast the thundering boogie prowess of Roosevelt Sykes—and even fewer could chase away the blues with his blues as the rotund cigar-chomping 88s ace did. *—Bill Dahl*

Complete Recorded Works, Vol. 1 (1929-1930) / 1929-1930 / Document ✦✦✦✦
All of Roosevelt Sykes's recordings between 1929 and 1942 are collected on this seven-volume series; it is essential for hardcore fans of blues piano. *—AMG*

Complete Recorded Works, Vol. 2 (1930-1931) / 1930-1931 / Document ✦✦✦

Complete Recorded Works, Vol. 3 (1932-1933) / 1932-1933 / Document ✦✦✦

The Return of Roosevelt Sykes / 1960 / Bluesville/Original Blues Classics ✦✦✦✦
Sykes's lyrical images are as vivid and amusing as ever on this 1960 set, with titles like "Set the Meat Outdoors" and "Hangover" among its standouts. Other than drummer Jump Jackson, the quartet behind the pianist is pretty obscure, but they rock his boogies with a vengeance. Contains a nice remake of his classic "Drivin' Wheel." *—Bill Dahl*

Honeydripper [Prestige/Bluesville] / 1961 / Bluesville/Original Blues Classics ✦✦✦✦
Roosevelt Sykes expertly fit his classic downhome piano riffs and style into a fabric that also contained elements of soul, funk and R&B. The nine-cut date, recently reissued by Original Blues Classics, included such laments as "I Hate To Be Alone," "Lonely Day" and "She Ain't For Nobody," as well as the poignant "Yes Lawd" and less weighty "Satellite Baby" and "Jailbait." Besides Sykes' alternately bemused, ironic and inviting vocals, there's superb tenor sax support from King Curtis, Robert Banks' tasty organ and steady, nimble bass and drum assistance by Leonard Gaskins and drummer Belton Evans. *—Ron Wynn*

Roosevelt Sykes Sings the Blues / 1962 / Diablo ✦✦✦
Despite the shoddiness of the recording, this album on the cheaply pressed Crown logo nevertheless impressively captured Sykes's rough-and-tumble boogie and blues prowess in a band setting. *—Bill Dahl*

The Country Blues Piano (1929-1932) / 1972 / Yazoo ✦✦✦✦✦
Featured is this Arkansas-born pianist/songster in some of his best early outings. *—Mark A. Humphrey*

Raining in My Heart / 1987 / Delmark ✦✦✦✦
This fine collection of Sykes's early-'50s sides for Chicago's United Records was reissued on Delmark in 2000. It contains some of the pianist's finest work with his jumping combo, the Honeydrippers (with unusual augmentation from violinist Remo Biondi on one 1952 date). "Toy Piano Blues" finds Sykes switching over to celeste, but "Too Hot to Handle," "Walking the Boogie," and "Fine and Brown" are in the customary Sykes mode. *—Bill Dahl*

★ **Roosevelt Sykes (1929-1941)** / 1988 / Story of the Blues ✦✦✦✦✦
A good sampling of some of Sykes's best tracks, it offers a perfect introduction to this seminal pianist. *—AMG*

Blues by Roosevelt "The Honey-Dripper" Sykes / 1995 / Smithsonian/Folkways ✦✦✦✦
Other than a cameo piano appearance by his producer (and peer) Memphis Slim on the appropriately titled "Memphis Slim Rock," and this is a stellar solo outing by the prolific pianist from 1961. He belts out a booming "Sweet Old Chicago," takes a trip to Chicago's South side on "47th Street Jive," and indulges in a little ribald imagery for "The Sweet Root Man." *—Bill Dahl*

The Honeydripper [Storyville] / Nov. 1997 / Storyville ✦✦✦✦✦

Grind It! / Nov. 23, 1999 / Total Energy ✦✦✦

Boogie Honky Tonk / Oldie Blues ✦✦✦✦✦
Vinyl compilation of the pianist's 1944-1947 output for RCA with his jumping little combo, the Honeydrippers, all of it cut in Chicago. Backed by a myriad of swinging Windy City sidemen (saxists Leon Washington, J.T. Brown, and Bill Casimir; bassist Ransom Knowling, drumemrs Jump Jackson and Judge Riley), Sykes rips through "Peeping Tom," and the wonderfully titled "Flames of Jive," and his often-covered "Sunny Road" with ebullient charm. *—Bill Dahl*

Tampa Red (Hudson Whittaker)

b. Jan. 8, 1904, Smithville, GA, **d.** Mar. 19, 1981, Chicago, IL
Slide Guitar, Vocals, Kazoo, Piano, Guitar / Acoustic Chicago Blues, Acoustic Blues, Electric Chicago Blues
Out of the dozens of fine slide guitarists who recorded blues, only a handful—Elmore James, Muddy Waters, and Robert Johnson, for example—left a clear imprint on tradition by creating a recognizable and widely imitated instrumental style. Tampa Red was another influential musical model. During his heyday in the '20s and '30s, he was billed as "The Guitar Wizard," and his stunning slide work on steel National or electric guitar shows why he earned the title. His 30-year recording career produced hundreds of sides: hokum, pop, and jive, but mostly blues (including classic compositions "Anna Lou Blues," "Black Angel Blues," "Crying Won't Help You," "It Hurts Me Too," and "Love Her with a Feeling"). Listeners who only know Tampa Red's hokum material are missing the deeper side of one of the mainstays of Chicago blues. During Red's prime, his musical venues ran the gamut of blues institutions: downhome jukes, the streets, the vaudeville theater circuit, and the Chicago club scene. Due to his polish and theater experience, he is often described as a city musician or urban artist in contrast to many of his more limited musical contemporaries. Today's listener will enjoy Red's expressive vocals and perhaps be taken aback by his kazoo solos. His songwriting has stood the test of time, and any serious slide guitar student had better be familiar with his guitar wizardry. *—Barry Lee Pearson*

The Complete Bluebird Recordings, Vol. 1: 1934-1936 / Mar. 22, 1934-Apr. 1, 1936 / Bluebird/RCA ✦✦✦✦✦
The Complete Bluebird Recordings: 1934-1936 is a double-disc set containing 46 songs Tampa Red recorded for Bluebird in the mid-'30s, when he was one of the most popular and

influential bluesmen in America. The length of the collection means that it's only of interest to serious blues fans and scholars, which is a shame, because there are many wonderful performances scattered throughout the set that demonstrate Tampa Red's mastery of the guitar and the blues song. *—Thom Owens*

The Complete Bluebird Recordings, Vol. 2: 1936-1938 / 1936-1938 / Bluebird/RCA ✦✦✦✦✦
Bluebird Recordings 1936-1938 is a comprehensive, double-disc set covering the final two years Tampa Red spent at the label. Many classic songs, including "Someday I'm Bound to Win" and "Seminole Blues," are here, but the compilation is primarily of value to blues historians, since its very comprehensiveness makes it a little intimidating for casual fans. Nevertheless, the set is impeccably produced, and any serious fan of Tampa Red or the blues would do well to add it to their collection. *—Thom Owens*

☆ **Bottleneck Guitar (1928-1937)** / 1974 / Yazoo ✦✦✦✦✦
Yazoo's *Bottleneck Guitar (1928-1937)* is a great collection of early recordings from slide guitarist Tampa Red. The 14-track collection has a number of classic solo cuts from Tampa—including "You Gotta Reap What You Sow" and "Seminole Blues"—plus duets with the likes of Georgia Tom and Ma Rainey, making it an excellent overview of his earliest sides. *—Thom Owens*

The Guitar Wizard (1935-1953) / Oct. 1975 / Bluebird/RCA ✦✦✦✦✦
Thirty-two of Red's premier tracks from his RCA Bluebird days dating from 1934-1953 (talk about longevity!) on two slabs of vinyl (with exhaustive liner notes by Jim O'Neal). Red's rousing kazoo blasts power many of these essential sides, which feature legends like pianists Black Bob, Blind John Davis, and Johnny Jones in support roles. Red's last few Victor sides were right in the stylistic heart of the later Chicago sound; the remarkable Latin-tinged "Rambler's Blues" boasts a spine-tingling amplified harp solo from Big Walter Horton. *—Bill Dahl*

The Guitar Wizard / 1994 / Columbia/Legacy ✦✦✦✦✦
Some of the earliest work (1928-1934) by the slide guitar great, ranging from the irresistible hokum he served up with piano-playing partner "Georgia Tom" Dorsey ("Dead Cats on the Line," "No Matter How She Done It") to the gorgeous "Black Angel Blues" (eventually known as "Sweet Little Angel") and the solo guitar masterpieces "Things 'Bout Comin' My Way" and "Denver Blues." *—Bill Dahl*

★ **It Hurts Me Too: The Essential Recordings of Tampa Red** / 1994 / Indigo ✦✦✦✦✦
A magnificent primer on the catalog of this prolific guitar/kazoo ace that spans 1928-1942. Opening with his immortal hokum duet with "Georgia Tom" Dorsey, the bawdy "It's Tight like That," the disc makes clear just how seminal Red's Chicago-cut output was—here are the original versions of "It Hurts Me Too," "Love with a Feeling," "Don't You Lie to Me," and the double-entendre hoots "She Wants to Sell My Monkey" and "Let Me Play with Your Poodle." *—Bill Dahl*

Eddie Taylor

b. Jan. 29, 1923, Benoit, MS, **d.** Dec. 25, 1985, Chicago, IL
Vocals, Guitar / Electric Chicago Blues, Modern Electric Blues, R&B
When you're talking about the patented Jimmy Reed laconic shuffle sound, you're talking about Eddie Taylor just as much as Reed himself. Taylor was the glue that kept Reed's lowdown grooves from falling into serious disrepair. His rock-steady rhythm guitar powered the great majority of Reed's Vee-Jay sides during the 1950s and early '60s, and he even found time to wax a few classic sides of his own for Vee-Jay during the mid-'50s. Taylor was as versatile a blues guitarist as anyone could ever hope to encounter. His style was deeply rooted in Delta tradition, but he could snap off a modern funk-tinged groove just as convincingly as a straight shuffle. Taylor's records didn't sell in the quantities that Reed's did, so he was largely relegated to the role of sideman (he recorded behind John Lee Hooker, John Brim, Elmore James, Snooky Pryor, and many more during the '50s) until his 1972 set for Advent, *I Feel So Bad*, made it abundantly clear that this quiet, unassuming guitarist didn't have to play second fiddle to anyone. When he died in 1985, he left a void on the Chicago circuit that remains apparent even now. They just don't make 'em like Eddie Taylor anymore. *—Bill Dahl*

I Feel So Bad / 1972 / Hightone ✦✦✦✦
One of the Chicago guitarist's most satisfying contemporary albums, this 1972 set (first issued on Advent) was cut not in the Windy City, but in L.A. in 1972 with a combo featuring Phillip Walker on second guitar and George Smith on harp. Taylor was no strict traditionalist; he was as conversant with funk-tinged modern rhythms as with Delta-based styles—and he exhibits both sides of his musical personality on this one. *—Bill Dahl*

☆ **Bad Boy** / 1993 / Charly ✦✦✦✦✦
The Delta-rooted mid-'50s Vee-Jay label classics by perennially underrated Chicago guitarist Eddie Taylor, who stepped out of Jimmy Reed's shadow long enough to leave behind "Bad Boy," "Big Town Playboy," "Ride 'Em on Down," the bouncy "I'm Gonna Love You," and several more brilliant sides. Fifteen songs in all, including five from 1964 that are scarcely less impressive than his previous stuff. *—Bill Dahl*

My Heart is Bleeding / 1994 / Evidence ✦✦✦

★ **Ride 'Em on Down** / Charly ✦✦✦✦✦
An absolutely essential 24-track collection which alternates 12 of Taylor's classic Vee-Jay sides (including "Bad Boy," "Big Town Playboy," "Find My Baby," "Looking for Trouble," and the title track) with a dozen more early Jimmy Reed sides with Taylor in support. As a collection of Taylor's best solo sides, it's as complete as any on the market. As a sample of Taylor's impeccable backup work behind Reed—while containing no hits—it stands by itself as a very nice collection of rarities that shows both artists off to good advantage. As a document of early-'50s Chicago blues, it's a major brick in the wall. As seamless blues groove listening, consider it a must-have. *—Cub Koda*

Hound Dog Taylor (Theodore Roosevelt Taylor)

b. Apr. 12, 1915, Natchez, MS, **d.** Dec. 17, 1975, Chicago, IL
Slide Guitar, Vocals, Guitar / Slide Guitar Blues, Modern Electric Chicago Blues, Electric Chicago Blues
Alligator Records, Chicago's leading contemporary blues label, might never have been launched at all if not for the crashing, slashing slide guitar antics of Hound Dog Taylor. Bruce Iglauer, then an employee of Delmark Records, couldn't convince his boss, Bob Koester, of Taylor's potential, so Iglauer took matters into his own hands. In 1971, Alligator was born for the express purpose of releasing Hound Dog's debut album. We all know what transpired after that. Taylor's pre-Alligator credits were light—only a 1960 single for Cadillac baby's Bea & Baby imprint ("Baby Is Coming Home"/"Take Five"), a 1962 45 for Carl Jones's Firma Records ("Christine"/"Alley Music"), and a 1967 effort for Checker ("Watch Out"/"Down Home") predated his output for Iglauer. Taylor's relentlessly raucous band, the HouseRockers, consisted of only two men, though their combined racket sounded like quite a few more. Second guitarist Brewer Phillips, who often supplied buzzing pseudo-bass lines on his guitar, had developed such an empathy with Taylor that their guitars intertwined with ESP-like force, while drummer Ted Harvey kept everything moving along at a brisk pace. Taylor was the obvious inspiration for Alligator's "Genuine Houserocking Music" motto, a credo Iglauer's firm still tries to live up to today. He wasn't the most accomplished of slide guitarists, but Hound Dog Taylor could definitely rock any house he played at. *—Bill Dahl*

★ **Hound Dog Taylor & the Houserockers** / 1971 / Alligator ✦✦✦✦✦
The first album and the perfect place to start. Wild, raucous, crazy music straight out of the South Side clubs. The incessant drive of Hound Dog's playing is best heard on "Give Me Back My Wig," "55th Street Boogie" and "Taylor's Rock," while the sound of Brewer Phillips' Telecaster on "Phillips' Theme" gives new meaning to the phrase "sheet metal tone." One of the greatest slide guitar albums of all time. *—Cub Koda*

Natural Boogie / 1973 / Alligator ✦✦✦✦✦
Hound Dog's second album was every bit as wild as the first, bringing with it a fatter sound and a wider range of emotions and music. A recut here of Hound Dog's first single, "Take Five," totally burns the original while the smoldering intensity of "See Me In The Evening" and "Sadie" take this album to places the first one never reached. *—Cub Koda*

Beware of the Dog / 1975 / Alligator ✦✦✦✦✦
This was Hound Dog's posthumous live album containing performances that are even steamier than the first two studio albums, if such a notion is possible. For lowdown slow blues, it's hard to beat the heartfelt closer "Freddie's Blues" and for surreal moments on wax, it's equally hard to beat the funkhouse turned looney bin dementia of "Let's Get Funky" or the hopped up hillbilly fever rendition of "Comin' Around The Mountain." *—Cub Koda*

Genuine Houserocking Music / 1982 / Alligator ✦✦✦
With Alligator label prexy Bruce Iglauer recording some 20 or 30 tracks over two nights everytime the band went into the studio, there were bound to be some really great tracks lurking in the vaults and these are it. Noteworthy for the great performance of Robert Johnson's "Crossroads," (previously only available as a Japanese 45) but also for the "rock & roll" inclusion of "What'd I Say" and Brewer Phillips' take on "Kansas City." No bottom of the barrel scrapings here. *—Cub Koda*

Koko Taylor

b. Sep. 28, 1935, Memphis, TN
Vocals / Modern Electric Chicago Blues, Electric Chicago Blues, R&B
She's the undisputed queen of Chicago blues. Has been for decades. And truthfully, no one has even mounted a serious challenge to Koko Taylor's magnificent reign in recent memory. In 1962, Willie Dixon caught Taylor's act and took over as her mentor. He produced her 1963 debut 45 for USA, "Honky Tonky," then got her signed to Chess. There she enjoyed one of the last legitimate Chicago blues hits with her rousing rendition of the Dixon-penned party classic "Wang Dang Doodle." It went all the way to number four on *Billboard*'s R&B charts in 1966. Dixon's role as writer/producer was a prominent one on Taylor's eponymous Chess debut LP, but none of her encores enjoyed the same success level as "Wang Dang Doodle." After a dry spell, Taylor joined Alligator Records in 1975 (she was the fledgling firm's first female artist). Her Grammy-nominated Alligator album debut, *I Got What It Takes*, catapulted her back into the blues limelight. Taylor's raspy growl is a beloved Chicago fixture, just like deep-dish pizza and Michael Jordan. *—Bill Dahl*

Koko Taylor / 1969 / MCA/Chess ✦✦✦✦✦
Straight digital reissue of Taylor's debut Chess album from 1969. Produced by Willie Dixon (who can intermittently be heard as a duet partner), the set is one of the strongest representations of the belter's Chess days available, with her immortal smash "Wang Dang Doodle," and the chunky "Twenty-Nine Ways," "I'm a Little Mixed Up," and "Don't Mess with the Messer." Top-flight session musicians on Taylor's 1965-1969 output included guitarists Buddy Guy, Matt Murphy, and Johnny Shines and saxman Gene "Daddy G" Barge. *—Bill Dahl*

I Got What It Takes / 1975 / Alligator ✦✦✦✦✦
The queen's first album for Alligator, and still one of her very best to date. A tasty combo sparked by guitarists Mighty Joe Young and Sammy Lawhorn and saxist Abb Locke provide sharp support as the clear-voiced Taylor belts Bobby Saxton's "Trying to Make a Living," and Magic Sam's "That's Why I'm Crying," her own "Honkey Tonkey" and "Voodoo Woman," and Ruth Brown's swinging "Mama, He Treats Your Daughter Mean." *—Bill Dahl*

Queen of the Blues / 1975 / Alligator ✦✦✦✦
Co-producer Bruce Iglauer anticipated a future trend by making this a set filled with cameos—but the presence of Lonnie Brooks, James Cotton, Albert Collins, and Son Seals is entirely warranted and the contributions of each work quite well in the context of the whole. Taylor's gritty "I Cried like a Baby" and a snazzy remake of Ann Peebles's "Come to Mama" are among the many highlights. *—Bill Dahl*

★ **What It Takes: The Chess Years** / 1977 / MCA/Chess ✦✦✦✦✦
With 18 tracks spanning 1964-1971, this compilation receives the nod over the shorter *Koko Taylor* (eight cuts double off anyway). Opening with her nails-tough "I Got What It Takes," the disc boasts "Wang Dang Doodle," several sides never before on album, and the strange previously unissued "Blue Prelude." Four 1971 tracks from Taylor's tough-to-find second Chess album, *Basic Soul*, are also aboard (including "Bills, Bills and More Bills" and her queenly version of "Let Me Love You Baby"). Producer Willie Dixon's guiding hand is apparent everywhere. *—Bill Dahl*

The Earthshaker / 1978 / Alligator ✦✦✦✦✦
Koko Taylor's Alligator encore harbored a number of tunes that still pepper her set list to this day—the grinding "I'm a Woman" and the party-down specials "Let the Good Times Roll" and "Hey Bartender." Her uncompromising slow blues "Please Don't Dog Me" and a sassy remake of Irma Thomas's "You Can Have My Husband" also stand out, as does the fine backing by guitarists Sammy Lawhorn and Johnny B. Moore, pianist Pinetop Perkins, and saxman Abb Locke. *—Bill Dahl*

Force of Nature / 1993 / Alligator ✦✦✦✦
A solid contemporary blues album that ranges from Taylor's own "Spellbound" and "Put the Pot On," a rendition of Toussaint McCall's tender soul lament "Nothing Takes the Place of You," and a saucy revival of the old Ike & Tina Turner R&B gem "If I Can't Be First." Gene Barge once again penned the horn charts, Carey Bell contributes his usual harp mastery to Taylor's remake of Little Milton's "Mother Nature," and only Buddy Guy's over-the-top guitar histrionics on "Born Under a Bad Sign" grate. Long may the queen reign! *—Bill Dahl*

Royal Blue / Jun. 6, 2000 / Alligator ✦✦✦
Royal Blue is the first Alligator release from Koko Taylor since 1993's Grammy nominated *Force of Nature*. This is a mainly up-tempo set with excellent support from several guest appearances by B.B. King, Johnny Johnson, Ken Saydak, and Kenny Wayne Shepherd who contributes some scorching guitar on the Melissa Ethridge-penned hit "Bring Me Some Water." Taylor not only co-produced this release but wrote four of the 12 tracks, including the acoustic "The Man Next Door." On this track, the combination of Koko's passionate voice with Keb Mo's gritty Delta slide guitar makes you wish she would move further in this direction on future releases. *Royal Blue* proves Koko Taylor is still the undisputed queen of the blues. *—Al Campbell*

Little Johnny Taylor (Johnny Lamar Taylor)

b. Feb. 11, 1943, Memphis, TN
Vocals / Soul-Blues, R&B, Soul
Some folks still get them mixed up, so let's get it straight from the outset. Little Johnny Taylor is best-known for his two scorching slow blues smashes, 1963's "Part Time Love" and 1971's "Everybody Knows About My Good Thing." He's definitely not the suave Sam Cooke protégé that blitzed the charts with "Who's Making Love" for Stax in 1968; that's Johnnie Taylor, who added to the confusion by covering "Part Time Love" for Stax. Little Johnny came to Los Angeles in 1950 and did a stint with the Mighty Clouds of Joy before going secular. He debuted as an R&B artist with a pair of 45s for the Swingin' logo, but his career didn't soar until he inked a pact with Galaxy in 1963. The gliding mid-tempo blues "You'll Need Another Favor," firmly in a Bobby Bland mode, was Taylor's first chart item. He followed it up with the tortured R&B chart-topper "Part Time Love," which found him testifying in gospel-fired style over Arthur Wright's biting guitar and a grinding, horn-leavened downbeat groove. Taylor's tenure at the Ronn imprint elicited the slow blues smash "Everybody Knows About My Good Thing" in 1971 and a similar witty hit follow-up, "Open House at My House," the next year. *—Bill Dahl*

• **Greatest Hits** / Fantasy ✦✦✦✦✦
The gospel-tinged and decidedly soul-inflected 1963-1968 blues sides of Little Johnny Taylor on Galaxy Records benefitted from marvelous horn-powered arrangements by Ray Shanklin that brilliantly pushed Taylor's melismatic vocals. Naturally, the impassioned "Part Time Love" is included, along with the Bobby Bland-tinged mid-tempo groover "You'll Need Another Favor," a delicious "Since I Found a New Love," and the blistering "You Win, I Lose." Seventeen tracks in all, many of them bolstered by Arthur Wright's stinging guitar. *—Bill Dahl*

Susan Tedeschi

b. Nov. 9, 1970
Vocals, Guitar / Modern Electric Blues
Guitarist, singer and songwriter Susan Tedeschi is part of the new generation of blues musicians looking for ways to keep the form exciting, vital and evolving. Tedeschi's live shows are by no means straight-ahead urban blues. Instead, she freely mixes classic R&B, blues and her own gospel and blues-flavored original songs into her sets. She's a young, sexy, sassy blues belter with musical sensibilities that belie her years. The Susan Tedeschi Band's first album, *Just Won't Burn*, was released on the Boston-based Tone-Cool Records in early 1998. It's a powerful collection of originals, plus a sparkling cover of John Prine's "Angel From Montgomery," a tune often covered by vocalist Phoebe Snow. But Tedeschi and band also do justice to a tune Ruth Brown popularized, "Mama, He Treats Your Daughter Mean," and Junior Wells' "Little By Little." *—Richard Skelly*

• **Just Won't Burn** / Feb. 10, 1998 / Tone-Cool ✦✦✦✦
The very idea of a lady slinging a guitar sets traditional blues fans swooning. But with the release of her debut, Susan Tedeschi slings, aims, and hits her target. What a talent! Singer, songwriter, player, performer and more, the lady from Boston can do it all. Effective, she does justice to John Prine's classic "Angel From Montgomery" while making her own efforts known. Her tunes include "You Need to Be With Me," "Found Someone New" and the title cut. Leading her own band, she has what it takes to keep the boys in line while she wails away. Big Mama Thornton and Bessie Smith must be proud and B.B. King must be impressed, since she has opened for this blues master on several occasions. Just a little taste of things to come, *Just Won't Burn* blazes a trail that Tedeschi is pioneering for herself and younger women in the blues world. A brave heart with spunk and plenty of soul. *—Jana Pendragon*

Better Days / Dec. 15, 1998 / Oarfin ✦✦✦

Johnnie "Geechie" Temple

b. Oct. 18, 1906, Canton, MS, **d.** Nov. 22, 1968, Jackson, MS
Vocals, Guitar, Bass / Prewar Blues, Delta Blues, Acoustic Chicago Blues, Chicago Blues
Johnnie Temple is one of the great unsung heroes of the blues. A contemporary of Skip James, Son House, and other Delta legends, Temple was one of the very first to develop the now-standard bottom-string boogie bass figure, generally credited to Robert Johnson.

Born and raised in Mississippi, Temple learned to play guitar and mandolin as a child. By the time he was a teenager, he was playing house parties and various other local events. Temple moved to Chicago in the early '30s, where he quickly became part of the town's blues scene. Often, he performed with Charlie and Joe McCoy. In 1935, Temple began his recording, releasing "Louise Louise Blues" the following year on Decca Records.

Although he never achieved stardom, Temple's records—which were released on a variety of record labels—sold consistently throughout the late '30s and '40s. In the '50s, his recording career stopped, but he continued to perform, frequently with Big Walter Horton and Billy Boy Arnold. Once electrified post-war blues overtook acoustic blues in the mid-'50s, Temple left Chicago and moved to Mississippi. After he returned to his homestate, he played clubs and juke joints around the Jackson area for a few years before he disappeared from the scene. Johnny Temple died in 1968. *—Cub Koda & Stephen Thomas Erlewine*

• **Complete Recorded Works, Vol. 1** / 1994 / Document ✦✦✦✦✦
Temple's first recordings, beginning with the classic "Lead Pencil Blues" and three other songs (best of all, "Pig Boat Whistle") from his May 14, 1935 sessions for Vocalion. "Lead Pencil Blues" was the first known use on record of the "walking bass" (Temple called it "running bass") figure on the bottom string, which would become a blues commonplace in just a few years, popularized by Robert Johnson. Alas, these were also the most country-sounding records that Temple ever recorded—their lack of success convinced producers that Temple needed a more sophisticated sound, and all of his subsequent sessions, beginning 18 months later with "New Vicksburg Blues," feature a prominent piano sharing the spotlight with the guitar, and the latter instrument played by Charlie McCoy. It's all solid Chicago blues, "Louise Louise Blues," "Snapping Cat," and "So Lonely and So Blue" all being worth the price of the disc by themselves. Much of the later material, especially from the 1938 sessions backed by the Harlem Hamfats, is very smooth, commercial Chicago blues. Most of the sources are in better than decent condition, except for a very noisy "Beale Street Sheik," which can be forgiven as a previously unissued Vocalion side. *—Bruce Eder*

Complete Recorded Works, Vol. 2 (1938-1940) / 1994 / Document ✦✦✦✦✦
Another 23 sides, covering the years 1938 through 1940. The sound on these records is much more jazz than blues, especially in the guitar and clarinet playing, and it sold, "Big Leg Woman" being a major hit and "Mississippi Woman's Blues" repeating the same melody. By the end of the decade, Temple would be working with Lonnie Johnson, one of the jazziest of blues guitarists, and jazz legend clarinetist Buster Bailey, and doing his most mainstream popular music, in terms of sound. The raunchiness of his material was still pronounced and delightful, however, from "Big Leg Woman" and "Grinding Mill" (another musical metaphor for impotence) to "Jelly Roll Bert" (featuring some delightful guitar/voice call-and-response work between Temple and axman Teddy Bunn), "Mississippi Woman's Blues," and "Better Not Let My Good Gal Catch You Here"—it's all surprisingly sophisticated, however, especially with the echo-y piano back-up, and more evocative of a Chicago club than any roadhouse. Temple's guitar playing may have lacked the jazz inflections that his recording manager was looking for, but his voice was one of the best in blues, alternately mournful and leering, with a surprising amount of power and expressiveness. *—Bruce Eder*

Complete Recorded Works, Vol. 3 / May 1, 1995 / Document ✦✦✦

Sonny Terry & Brownie McGhee

f. 1941, **db.** 1975
Vocals, Harmonica / Folk-Blues, Piedmont Blues, Country Blues, Electric Blues, Acoustic Blues
The joyous whoop that Sonny Terry naturally emitted between raucous harp blasts was as distinctive a signature sound as can possibly be imagined. Only a handful of blues harmonicists wielded as much of a lasting influence on the genre as did the sightless Terry (Buster Brown, for one, copied the whoop and all), who recorded some fine urban blues as a bandleader in addition to serving as guitarist Brownie McGhee's longtime duet partner. Terry initially joined forces with Piedmont pioneer Blind Boy Fuller, first recording with the guitarist in 1937 for Vocalion. He recorded for the Library of Congress a year later and cut his first commercial sides in 1940. Terry had met McGhee in 1939, and upon the death of Fuller, they joined forces, playing together on a 1941 McGhee date for OKeh and settling in New York as a duo in 1942. The folk boom of the late '50s and early '60s made Brownie and Sonny household names (at least among folk aficionados). They toured long and hard as a duo, cutting a horde of endearing acoustic duet LPs along the way, before scuttling their decades-long partnership amidst a fair amount of reported acrimony during the mid-'70s. *—Bill Dahl*

Brownie McGhee & Sonny Terry Sing / 1958 / Smithsonian/Folkways ✦✦✦✦

Just a Closer Walk with Thee / Nov. 1960 / Fantasy/Original Blues Classics ✦✦✦
Here's Brownie and Sonny's gospel album, recorded in 1957 at *Jenny Lind Hall* in Oakland, California. Those used to hearing this duo stomp and hoot the blues will be surprised as they tackle material like "What a Beautiful City," "I Shall Not Be Moved," "If I Could Hear My Mother Pray," and Gary Davis' "Get Right Church" in their own inimitable style. But an even bigger surprise comes with the liner notes, penned by major league baseball player Orlando Cepeda! By far the most interesting of all the many recordings this twosome made during their time together. *—Cub Koda*

Sonny & Brownie at Sugar Hill / Dec. 1961 / Fantasy/Original Blues Classics ✦✦✦

Whoopin' / 1984 / Alligator ✦✦✦

Complete Recorded Works, Vol. 1 / Jan. 10, 1996 / Document ✦✦✦✦

● **Blowin' the Fuses** / Apr. 1996 / Rykodisc/Tradition ✦✦✦✦
This mid-priced 12-track compilation album presents six performances from an early-'60s Sonny Terry and Brownie McGhee appearance at *the Troubadour* (the album cover says 1961, the liner notes 1962), two studio recordings from the same era, and four bonus tracks recorded in 1944 and featuring Terry with varying combinations of musicians including Woody Guthrie, Alec Seward, and Cisco Houston. The Terry and McGhee live material is excellent, with McGhee's vocals and guitar playing carrying the tunes, embellished by Terry's inventive harmonica embellishments and occasional harmony singing. The studio tracks are more off the cuff than the live ones, notably the six-minute title track, recorded during a studio blackout. *—William Ruhlmann*

Backwater Blues / Jun. 29, 1999 / Fantasy ✦✦✦✦✦
Songs of whiskey, women, and money—nothing was more important to the repertoire of this classic acoustic blues duo. Good relations on stage were not, but during this 18-tune club date at *Sugar Hill* in San Francisco, Terry and McGhee are in good spirits. The former's finger-picking, good-time guitar strummin', and even-keeled singing, joined by McGhee's frantic harmonica and frequent whoops and hollers were the epitome of this genre's style, and these two performing in their heyday.

They do hits familiar to all like "One Bourbon, One Scotch, One Beer," "Key to the Highway," and "Careless Love," while changing up "Sittin' on Top of the World," making it "Climbin' on Top of the Hill." Advice songs include the poignant "My Father's Words," "(If You) Lose Your Money (Please Don't Lose Your Mind," and "Walk On." There's also a lone instrumental, "Playing With the Blues"; the title track identified by Terry as "Backwater Rising"; and occasionally call-and-response vocalizing as on "Climbin'" or harmony singing on "You'd Better Mind." The clarity of the recording and the singing is pure as the driven snow, with no distortion or compression. It's the way this blues should be heard. Lee Hildebrand's episodic liner notes relating the strained relationship between Terry and McGhee, and the tale of Barbara Dane's involvement in the *Sugar Hill* club is as important a story as the songs the duo sing. The words and music prove a last will and testament accenting this posthumous release, a companion to the *Live at Sugar Hill* Original Blues Classic CD. It's a must buy for those who treasure this type of no-nonsense porch-style get-down blues. *—Michael G. Nastos*

Henry Thomas

b. 1874, Big Sandy, TX, **d.** 1930
Vocals, Guitar / Songster, Prewar Blues, Country Blues
Texas songster Henry Thomas remains a relative stranger who made some great recordings, then returned to obscurity. Evidence suggests he was an itinerant street musician, a musical hobo who rode the rails across Texas and possibly to the World Fairs in St. Louis and Chicago just before and after the turn of the century. Most agree he was the oldest African-American folk artist to produce a significant body of recordings. His projected 1874 birthdate would predate Charley Patton by a good 17 years. Thomas' repertoire bridged the 19th and 20th centuries, providing a compelling glimpse into a wide range of African-American musical genres. The 23 songs he cut for Vocalion between 1927 and 1929 include a spiritual, ballads, reels, dance songs, and eight selections titled blues. "Ragtime Texas," as Thomas was known, provides a welcome inroad to 19th-century dance music, but his music is neither obscure nor merely educational: it has a timeless quality—and while it may be an acquired taste, once you catch on to it, you're hooked. *—Barry Lee Pearson*

★ **Texas Worried Blues: Complete Recorded Works 1927-1929** / 1989 / Yazoo ✦✦✦✦✦
These recordings, dating between 1927 and 1929, are a unique body of work: work songs, minstrel numbers, rags, and what we now define as the blues, all offered in an unpretentious form that would have been every bit as compelling had Henry Thomas cut them this way 40 years later. Songs such as "Arkansas," "Fox and the Hounds" (featuring the reed pipes that Thomas also excelled at playing), and "Little Red Caboose" represent a brand of upbeat dance music associated with late-19th century entertainment, a tradition already largely lost or becoming lost when Thomas cut these numbers. Yet Thomas, who was already in his 50s when he recorded these tracks, sings and plays them with a beguiling ease and honesty, not to mention a dexterity on the guitar that makes him sound every bit as vital and urgent as Big Bill Broonzy or any of the other up-and-coming blues legends just starting out at the time these sides were laid down. The blues numbers, including "Shanty Blues," "Woodhouse Blues," "Honey, Won't You Allow Me One More Chance—," and "Bull Doze Blues" are compelling in their own right—they display musical and lyrical virtuosity and, in the latter two cases, offer a chance to hear the sources for classic works by Bob Dylan and Canned Heat, respectively. Luckily for historians, Henry Thomas recorded for Vocalion and not for one of the truly lost labels like Paramount, and all 23 surviving sides of his work sound very good on this CD. *—Bruce Eder*

☆ **Ragtime Texas: 1927-1929** / Oct. 17, 2000 / Document ✦✦✦✦✦
Many versions of "John Henry" exist, but Henry Thomas's version, because of his use of reeds, is unique. The reeds have a light, radiant air that lifts this song to something joyous. Thomas was born in Texas in 1874 and didn't record his first sessions until he was in his early fifties. His music incorporated blues and patched together songs ("rags") that seemed to come from earlier traditions, including nine pieces on which he uses reeds. The use of them may point to an earlier African-American tradition that had nearly vanished by the time he was recording. These pieces represent the best songs on this collection, with standouts like "The Little Red Caboose" and "Bull-Doze Blues." The later song sounds very similar to Canned Heat's "Goin' Up the Country," including the reed solo that sets the song in motion. Songs like "Don't Ease Me In," would later be performed by the Grateful Dead and many others, while "Honey, Won't You Allow Me One More Chance—" is lyrically related to an early Bob Dylan song with almost the same title. The songs gathered here have been taken from five recording sessions between 1927 and 1929, and are ordered chronologically. The liner notes explain the origins of reeds/quills in African-American music, and help place Thomas in a historical context. The fidelity on certain cuts is scratchy, but his voice and instrumentation are still always discernable. This is a good collection of an early-Texas songster, especially valuable because of Thomas' unique use of reeds. *—Ronnie Lankford, Jr.*

Big Mama Thornton (Willie Mae Thornton)

b. Dec. 11, 1926, Montgomery, AL, **d.** Jul. 25, 1984, Los Angeles, CA
Vocals, Drums, Harmonica / Juke Joint Blues, Texas Blues, Electric Texas Blues, R&B
Willie Mae "Big Mama" Thornton only notched one national hit in her lifetime, but it was a true monster. "Hound Dog" held down the top slot on *Billboard*'s R&B charts for seven long weeks in 1953. Alas, Elvis Presley's rocking 1956 cover was even bigger, effectively obscuring Thornton's chief claim to immortality.

That's a damned shame, because Thornton's menacing growl was indeed something special. Thornton was ensconced on the Houston circuit when Peacock Records boss Don Robey signed her in 1951. She debuted on Peacock with "Partnership Blues" that year, backed by trumpeter Joe Scott's band. But it was her third Peacock date with Johnny Otis's band that proved the winner. With Pete Lewis laying down some truly nasty guitar behind her, Big Mama shouted "Hound Dog," a tune whose authorship remains a bone of contention to this day (both Otis and the team of Jerry Leiber and Mike Stoller claim responsibility) and soon hit the road a star. But it was an isolated incident. Though Thornton cut some fine Peacock follow-ups—"I Smell a Rat," "Stop Hoppin' on Me," "The Fish," "Just like a Dog"—through 1957, she never again reached the hit parade. *—Bill Dahl*

● **Hound Dog: The Peacock Recordings** / 1992 / MCA ✦✦✦✦✦
Let's face it, Big Mama Thornton will always be chiefly recalled for her growling 1952 reading of the Jerry Leiber-Mike Stoller classic "Hound Dog." But the other 17 sides on this collection of her 1952-1957 output for Don Robey's Peacock Records aren't exactly makeweight. Thornton's mighty roar was backed by the jumping combos of Johnny Otis and saxist Bill Harvey, producing additional gems in "My Man Called Me," "They Call Me Big Mama," "The Fish," and a duet with the ill-fated Johnny Ace, "Yes Baby." *—Bill Dahl*

The Complete Vanguard Recordings / Apr. 18, 2000 / Vanguard ✦✦✦✦✦
This wonderful three-disc set brings together everything Willie Mae Thornton recorded for the folk music label in the mid-'70s. It's comprised of her two released albums from 1975, *Jail* and *Sassy Mama*, and a complete unreleased album, *Big Mama Swings*. Thornton was still in good voice on these sessions and while not as powerful as her Peacock sides, the production is solid and these recordings make an excellent addition to her scant discography. *—Cub Koda*

Luther Tucker

b. Jan. 20, 1936, Memphis, TN, **d.** Jun. 18, 1993, San Rafael, CA
Guitar / Electric Chicago Blues
Guitarist Luther Tucker was born on January 20, 1936, in Memphis, TN, but relocated to Chicago's South side when Tucker was around seven years of age. His father, a carpenter, built Tucker his first guitar and his mother, who played boogie-woogie piano, introduced him to Big Bill Broonzy around that time. He went on to study guitar with Robert Jr. Lockwood, for whom he had the greatest admiration and respect. Tucker worked with Little Walter Jacobs for seven years and played on many of Walter's classic sides. He also recorded with Otis Rush, Robben Ford, Sonny Boy Williamson II, Jimmy Rogers, Snooky Pryor, Muddy Waters, John Lee Hooker, Elvin Bishop, and James Cotton.

In the mid-'60s, Tucker was featured in the James Cotton Blues Band and traveled with that band extensively. He relocated to Marin County, CA, in 1973 and formed the Luther Tucker Band. He played in clubs in the San Francisco Bay area until his death on June 18, 1993, in Greenbrae, CA. Luther Tucker, who was soft-spoken and even shy, was one of a handful of backup artists (the Four Aces/Jukes were others) who helped to create and shape the small combo sound of Chicago blues. Unfortunately, they seldom get much credit. Yet, as the history of Chicago blues gets written, there will be more and more time to discover the wonderful understated rhythmic guitar mastery of Luther Tucker. *—Michael Erlewine*

● **Sad Hours** / 1990 / Antone's ✦✦✦✦✦
This album is more of a memorial to late guitarist Tucker (who died in June 1993) than a solo debut (the tracks were recorded three years before his death). Still, it's a very nice, soulful slice of the funkier edge of blues, a good tribute, and showcases some nice guitar work. *—Steven McDonald*

Big Joe Turner (Joseph Vernon Turner)

b. May 18, 1911, Kansas City, MO, **d.** Nov. 24, 1985, Inglewood, CA
Vocals / Jump Blues, Swing, Rock & Roll, R&B
The premier blues shouter of the postwar era, Big Joe Turner's roar could rattle the very foundation of any gin joint he sang within—and that's without a microphone. Turner was a resilient figure in the history of blues—he effortlessly spanned boogie-woogie, jump blues, even the first wave of rock & roll, enjoying great success in each genre. Turner, whose powerful physique certainly matched his vocal might, was a product of the swinging, wide-open Kansas City scene, hooking up with boogie piano master Pete Johnson during the early '30s. Theirs was a partnership that would endure for 13 years. Atlantic picked up his recording contract in 1951, and Big Joe Turner's heyday commenced with a gorgeously world-weary reading to the moving blues ballad "Chains of Love" that restored him to the uppermost reaches of the R&B charts. From there, the hits came in droves: "Chill Is On," "Sweet Sixteen" and "Don't You Cry" were all done in New York, and all hit big. Big Joe Turner had no problem whatsoever adapting his prodigious pipes to whatever regional setting he was in: in 1953, he cut his first R&B chart-topper, the storming rocker "Honey Hush," in New Orleans, and before the year was through, he stopped off in Chicago to record with slide guitarist Elmore James's considerably rougher-edged combo and hit again with the salacious "T.V.

Mama." Prolific Atlantic house writer Jesse Stone was the source of Turner's biggest smash of all, "Shake, Rattle and Roll," which proved his second chart-topper in 1954. Suddenly, at the age of 43, Big Joe Turner was a rock star. His jumping follow-ups—"Well All Right," "Flip Flop and Fly," "Hide and Seek," "Morning, Noon and Night," "The Chicken and the Hawk"—all mined the same goodtime groove. They called him the Boss of the Blues, and the appellation was truly a fitting one: when Big Joe Turner shouted a lyric, you were definitely at his beck and call. *—Bill Dahl*

☆ **Big, Bad & Blue: The Big Joe Turner Anthology** / Dec. 30, 1938-Jan. 26, 1983 / Rhino/Atlantic ♦♦♦♦♦
This three-record anthology shows how Turner, without really ever changing his style, moved from strict Kansas City swing to pioneering rock and roll and back to basic jazzy blues. It contains 62 songs, everything from treasured hits to slow, sweltering ballads, strident uptempo wailers, moaning blues, novelty tunes and fiery pieces with lyrics and sentiments that wouldn't make it in today's environment. A comprehensive, well-written and lavishly prepared and illustrated booklet with numerous anecdotes and remembrances are the icing on a superb cake. *—Ron Wynn*

Have No Fear, Big Joe Turner Is Here / Feb. 2, 1945-Nov. 29, 1947 / Savoy Jazz ♦♦♦♦
Producer Herb Abramson's first encounters with Big Joe Turner weren't at Atlantic, but for the National logo, where Turner paused from 1945 to 1947 and cut the 26 swinging numbers on this collection. For once, the CD format limits the amount of selections rather than enlarging it; the original two-LP version of this package boasted a few more cuts. Pete Johnson returns to run the 88s on the first seven numbers (including a two-part cover of Saunders King's "S.K. Blues"), and familiar names like saxman Wild Bill Moore and drummer Red Saunders also turn up. "Sally Zu-Zazz," "I Got Love for Sale," and "My Gal's a Jockey" capture the peerless shouter at his ribald best. *—Bill Dahl*

Tell Me Pretty Baby / Nov. 1947-1949 / Arhoolie ♦♦♦♦
Lusty, romping jump blues and boogies from 1947-1949 that team Big Joe Turner with his longtime piano partner Pete Johnson and a coterie of solid L.A. sessioneers. The two dozen entries include party rockers like "Wine-O-Baby Boogie," "Christmas Date Boogie," "I Don't Dig It," and an incredibly raunchy two-part "Around the Clock Blues" (where Turner spends his time in a by-the-hour sexual tryst). *—Bill Dahl*

Rhythm & Blues Years / Apr. 17, 1951-Sep. 29, 1959 / Atlantic ♦♦♦♦♦
Picks up the rest of the 1950s Atlantic Records motherlode. The Chicago-cut double-entendre gem "TV Mama" (with Elmore James on guitar), the lighthearted rockers "Rock a While," "Morning Noon & Night," and "Lipstick, Powder & Paint," and a rip-snorting remake of Turner's classic "Roll 'Em Pete," here titled "(We're Gonna) Jump for Joy," that in its own way rivals the original (King Curtis's blistering sax solo doesn't hurt), are among the many highlights on the 28-song collection. *—Bill Dahl*

★ **Big Joe Turner's Greatest Hits** / Apr. 19, 1951-Jan. 22, 1958 / Atlantic Jazz ♦♦♦♦♦
The best single-disc collection available of Turner's seminal 1950s Atlantic sides (21 sides in all). Most of the essential stuff is here—the world-weary blues ballads "Chains of Love" and "Sweet Sixteen," the rockers "Shake, Rattle and Roll," "Flip Flop and Fly," and "Boogie Woogie Country Girl," and a lusty "Well All Right" that rates with Turner's best jump blues outings ever. *—Bill Dahl*

★ **Very Best of Big Joe Turner** / 1951-1959 / Rhino ♦♦♦♦♦
The Very Best of Big Joe Turner is an excellent 16-track collection that features his biggest hits from 1951-1959, including "Chains of Love," "Sweet Sixteen," "Honey Hush," "TV Mama," "Shake, Rattle and Roll," "Well All Right," "Flip Flop and Fly," "Hide and Seek," "The Chicken and the Hawk (Up, Up and Away)," "Boogie Woogie Country Girl," "Corrine Corrina" and "Midnight Special Train." All of his best-known songs in their hit versions are available on this concise, affordable disc, which makes for an ideal introduction to this legendary R&B vocalist. *—Stephen Thomas Erlewine*

☆ **Boss of the Blues** / Mar. 6, 1956-Mar. 7, 1956 / Atlantic ♦♦♦♦♦
During an era when Big Joe Turner recordings were often surprise hits with rock & roll fans (particularly "Shake, Rattle and Roll"), he occasionally recorded no-nonsense blues-oriented jazz dates too. This reissue album matched Turner for one of the last times with the veteran boogie-woogie pianist Pete Johnson and also includes a variety of top swing players: trumpeter Joe Newman, trombonist Lawrence Brown, altoist Pete Brown, tenor saxophonist Frank Wess, guitarist Freddie Green, bassist Walter Page and drummer Cliff Leeman. It is not surprising, considering the number of Basieites on the date, that the band often sounds like a Count Basie combo. Turner is in top form on remakes of some of his early tunes (including "Cherry Red," "Roll 'Em Pete" and "Wee Baby Blues"), a few traditional blues and a couple of swing standards. This music should appeal to many listeners. *—Scott Yanow*

Texas Style / Apr. 26, 1971 / Evidence ♦♦♦
This somewhat obscure Black & Blue session (reissued by Evidence on CD) features the great blues singer Big Joe Turner a year before he hooked up with the Pablo label. Turner is backed by a particularly colorful and supportive trio comprised of pianist Milt Buckner (the master of block chords), bassist Slam Stewart (who takes a few of his trademark solos in which he sings along with his bowed bass) and veteran swing drummer Jo Jones. Turner was still in his prime at the time and, even if his material was not too adventurous, the music (which includes a few newer bluish originals plus such standbys as "Cherry Red" and "'Tain't Nobody's Bizness If I Do") is performed with enthusiasm and solid swing. *—Scott Yanow*

Flip, Flop & Fly / Apr. 17, 1972–Apr. 24, 1972 / Pablo/OJC ♦♦♦♦

Life Ain't Easy / Jun. 3, 1974 / Pablo/OJC ♦♦♦

Stormy Monday / Sep. 19, 1974-Jun. 22, 1978 / Pablo ♦♦♦

The Trumpet Kings Meet Joe Turner / Sep. 19, 1974 / Pablo/OJC ♦♦♦♦

Things That I Used to Do / Feb. 8, 1977 / Pablo/OJC ♦♦♦♦♦

In the Evening / Oct. 1977 / Pablo/OJC ♦♦♦

Nobody in Mind / 1982 / Pablo/OJC ♦♦♦♦

☆ **Jumpin' with Joe: The Complete Aladdin & Imperial Recordings** / Jan. 11, 1994 / EMI America ♦♦♦♦♦
Big Joe Turner's remarkable recordings for Atlantic and Decca have been frequently reissued and evaluated. But his singles for other labels haven't gotten similar treatment, which makes this 18-cut single-disc anthology of Aladdin and Imperial material so welcome. These were recorded in the late '40s and early '50s and were closer to the Kansas City swing Turner had done earlier in his career; there was more emphasis on lyric interpretation, swing, and timing than sheer volume and volcanic, non-stop hollering. Although these songs aren't remembered as fondly as the landmark Atlantic numbers, they're just as important a part of Turner's legacy. *—Ron Wynn*

Joe Turner/Rockin' Blues / Jun. 20, 2000 / Collectables ♦♦♦♦
This reissue from Collectables combines two classic Joe Turner Atlantic sides, *Joe Turner* and *Rockin' the Blues*, originally released in 1957 and 1958, respectively. Featuring 28 tracks, including a number of R&B staples that crossed over into the pop realm: "Shake Rattle & Roll," "Flip Flop & Fly," "Honey Hush," "Chains of Love," and more. This is a sure bet purchase and also sports the addition of the original LP track sequence that highlights jump blues cuts not often heard, which are just as enjoyable as the hits. *—Al Campbell*

Vaughan Brothers

f. 1990
Group / Album Rock, Blues-Rock, Modern Electric Blues
Brothers Jimmie and Stevie Ray Vaughan got together for what would tragically be their first and last studio collaboration in the spring of 1990. That August, just before the release of the album, Stevie was killed in a helicopter crash. The public heard "Tick Tock" for the first time at Stevie's funeral in Dallas. *—Dan Forte*

Family Style / Jan. 1990 / Epic ♦♦♦
With slick production from Nile Rodgers and employing neither guitarist's band (Double Trouble nor the Fabulous Thunderbirds), this is bluesy, but far from purist. Jimmie makes his vocal debut on "White Boots" and "Good Texan," and the brothers blur the lines between their expected guitar styles—Stevie sometimes going for a less sustainy twang, Jimmie moving into Albert King territory. When standard blues is the order of the day (the slow instro "Brothers"), the key word is "standard"—bordering on run-of-the-mill. Instrumentals "D/FW" and "Hillbillies from Outer Space" fare better—offering ZZ Top crunch and Santo & Johnny steel, respectively. *—Dan Forte*

Walter Vinson

b. Feb. 2, 1901, Bolton, MS, **d.** Apr. 22, 1975, Chicago, IL
Vocals, Violin, Guitar, Guitar / Memphis Blues
One half of the legendary Mississippi Sheiks, singer/guitarist Walter Vinson was also among the most noteworthy blues accompanists of his era. Born February 2, 1901 in Bolton, Mississippi, Vinson (also known variously as Vincson and Vincent) began performing as a child, and during his teen years was a fixture at area parties and picnics. Even from the outset, however, he rarely if ever appeared as a solo act, seemingly much more at home in duets and trios; towards that end, during the 1920s he worked with Charlie McCoy, Rubin Lacy and Son Spand before forging his most pivotal and long-lasting union, with Lonnie Chatmon, in 1928. In addition to teaming with Chatmon in the Mississippi Sheiks, Vinson also recorded with him in the Mississippi Hot Footers, and even worked with Chatmon's brothers Bo and Harry. Upon the Sheiks' 1933 dissolution, Vinson recorded with various players in areas ranging from Jackson, Mississippi to New Orleans to finally Chicago; while an active club performer during the early 1940s, by the middle of the decade he had begun a lengthy hiatus from music which continued through 1960, at which point he returned to both recording and festival appearances. Hardening of the arteries forced Vinson into retirement during the early '70s; he died in Chicago in 1975. *—Jason Ankeny*

Complete Recorded Works (1928-1941) / 1991 / Document ♦♦♦♦
For completists, specialists and academics, Document's *Complete Recorded Works (1928-1941)* is invaluable, offering an exhaustive overview of Walter Vinson's early recordings. For less dedicated listeners, the disc is a mixed blessing. There are some absolutely wonderful, classic performances on the collection, but the long running time, exacting chronological sequencing, poor fidelity (all cuts are transferred from original acetates and 78s), and number of performances are hard to digest. The serious blues listener will find all these factors to be positive, but enthusiasts and casual listeners will find that the collection is of marginal interest for those very reasons. *—Thom Owens*

● **Complete Recorded Works in Chronological Order** / Document ♦♦♦♦
Complete Recorded Works in Chronological Order collects all of Mississippi Sheiks leader Walter Vinson's solo recordings from the '30s. While his recordings with the Sheiks are better and more influential, these are nevertheless excellent country-blues recordings that should be sought out by fans of the genre. *—Thom Owens*

Joe Louis Walker

b. Dec. 25, 1949, San Francisco, CA
Vocals, Guitar / Modern Electric Blues
Without a doubt one of the most exciting and innovative artists gracing contemporary blues, guitarist Joe Louis Walker has glowed like a shining blue beacon over the last decade. His 1986 debut album for HighTone, *Cold Is the Night*, announced his arrival in stunning fashion; his subsequent output on HighTone and Verve has only served to further establish Walker as one of the leading younger bluesmen on the scene. He traveled a circuitous route to get to where he is today. At age 14, he took up the guitar, playing blues (with an occasional foray into psychedelic rock) on the mushrooming San Francisco circuit. But by 1975, Walker was burned out on blues and turned to God, singing for the next decade with a gospel group, the Spiritual Corinthians. When the Corinthians played the 1985 New Orleans Jazz & Her-

itage Festival, Walker was inspired to embrace his blues roots again. He assembled a band, the Boss Talkers, and wrote some stunning originals that ended up on *Cold Is the Night.* More acclaimed albums for HighTone—1988's *The Gift, Blue Soul* the next year, and two riveting sets cut live at Slim's in 1990—preceded a switch to the major Verve imprint and three more discs that were considerably more polished than their grittier HighTone counterparts. *—Bill Dahl*

Cold Is the Night / 1986 / Hightone ♦♦♦♦
The Bay Area blues guitarist's debut album sounds underproduced compared to what would soon follow—and that's no knock. Walker's gritty, expressive vocals and ringing, concise guitar work shine through loud and clear in front of his band, the Boss Talkers. Walker and his producers Dennis Walker and Bruce Bromberg wrote virtually the entire set, including the slashing "Cold Is the Night," "Don't Play Games," and "One Woman." *—Bill Dahl*

● **The Gift** / 1988 / Hightone ♦♦♦♦♦
Although it didn't enjoy the major label hype that his current output does, Walker's HighTone encore just may be his finest album of all, filled with soulful vocal performances, bone-cutting guitar work, and tight backing from the Boss Talkers and the Memphis Horns. Honestly, you can't go wrong with any of Walker's remarkably consistent HighTone discs—but give this one the slightest of edges over the rest. *—Bill Dahl*

Blue Soul / 1989 / Hightone ♦♦♦♦♦
Another winner sporting memorable songs ("T.L.C.," "Personal Baby," "City of Angels," "Prove Your Love"), sinuous grooves, and a whole lot of vicious guitar from one of the hottest relatively young bluesmen on the circuit. He goes it alone on the finale, "I'll Get to Heaven on My Own, " sounding as conversant with the country blues tradition as he does with the contemporary stuff. *—Bill Dahl*

Live at Slim's, Vol. 1 / 1991 / Hightone ♦♦♦♦
Walker was hot enough over the course of a two-day stand at Slim's in San Francisco to warrant the issue of two full albums from the dates. The first is a sizzling combination of past triumphs, new items, and covers of Clifton Chenier's "Hot Tamale Baby," Junior Wells' "Little By Little" (with Huey Lewis, no less, on harp), and a saucy duet with Angela Strehli on the old Fontella Bass/Bobby McClure rocker "Don't Mess Up a Good Thing." *—Bill Dahl*

Preacher & The President / Aug. 25, 1998 / Verve ♦♦♦♦

Silvertone Blues / Oct. 5, 1999 / Verve ♦♦♦

T-Bone Walker (Aaron Thibeaux Walker)

b. May 28, 1910, Linden, TX, **d.** Mar. 16, 1975, Los Angeles, CA
Vocals, Guitar (Electric), Guitar / Texas Blues, Electric Texas Blues
Modern electric blues guitar can be traced directly back to this Texas-born pioneer, who began amplifying his sumptuous lead lines for public consumption circa 1940 and thus initiated a revolution so total that its tremors are still being felt today. Few major postwar blues guitarists come to mind that don't owe T-Bone Walker an unpayable debt of gratitude. B.B. King has long cited him as a primary influence, marveling at Walker's penchant for holding the body of his guitar outward while he played it. Aaron Thibeault Walker was a product of the primordial Dallas blues scene; during the early '20s, he led the sightless guitarist Blind Lemon Jefferson from bar to bar as the older man played for tips. After his fascination with electrifying his axe bore fruit, he played L.A. clubs with his daring new toy after assembling his own combo, engaging in acrobatic stage moves—splits, playing behind his back—to further enliven his show. In 1942, Walker cut "Mean Old World" and "I Got a Break Baby"; this was the first sign of the T-Bone Walker that blues guitar aficionados know and love, his fluid, elegant riffs and mellow, burnished vocals setting a standard that all future blues guitarists would measure themselves by. Many of Walker's best sides were smoky after-hours blues, though an occasional up-tempo entry—"T-Bone Jumps Again," a storming instrumental from the same date, for example—illustrated his nimble dexterity at faster speeds. He recorded prolifically for Black & White until the close of 1947, waxing classics like the often-covered "T-Bone Shuffle" and "West Side Baby." In 1950, Walker turned up on Imperial. His first date for the L.A. indie elicited the after-hours gem "Glamour Girl" and perhaps the penultimate jumping instrumental in his repertoire, "Strollin' with Bones." No amount of written accolades can fully convey the monumental importance of what T-Bone Walker gave to the blues. He was the idiom's first true lead guitarist, and undeniably one of its very best. *—Bill Dahl*

☆ **T-Bone Blues** / 1959 / Atlantic ♦♦♦♦♦
The last truly indispensable disc of the great guitar hero's career, and perhaps the most innately satisfying of all—these mid-'50s recordings boast magnificent presence, with Walker's axe so crisp and clear it seems as though he's sitting right next to you as he delivers a luxurious remake of "Call It Stormy Monday." Atlantic took some chances with Bone, dispatching him to Chicago for a 1955 date with Junior Wells and Jimmy Rogers that produced "Why Not" and "Papa Ain't Salty." Even better were the 1956-57 L.A. dates that produced the scalding instrumental "Two Bones and a Pick" (finding Walker duelling it out with nephew R.S. Rankin and jazzman Barney Kessel). *—Bill Dahl*

I Want a Little Girl / 1967 / Delmark ♦♦♦♦♦
This pioneering artist had more influence in the shaping of modern blues guitar styles than anyone on the planet. His was a cross-genre genius that skirted the boundaries of blues, R&B, jump, jazz, and pop. He appears on nearly 50 labels in a studio career that spanned over 30 years, and very little of this output falters even slightly. This tasty set made originally for the Black and Blue label in 1968 features him with a like-minded unit of tenor sax, piano, bass, and drums that provides a solid and excellent groove throughout. Musically, this is truly the genius at home, calling the shots. *—Larry Hoffman*

☆ **The Complete Recordings of T-Bone Walker 1940-1954** / Oct. 1990 / Mosaic ♦♦♦♦♦
A six-CD boxed set—an education in the lineage of urban blues. It appears that T-Bone Walker had a greater influence on urban blues players than any other single talent. His guitar, vocals, song selection, and sheer style live on today in nearly every blues performer. He is the master. *—Michael Erlewine*

☆ **The Complete Imperial Recordings** / 1991 / EMI America ♦♦♦♦♦
Another essential T-Bone Walker stake, this time a two-disc dish with 52 sensational tracks from his stint at Lew Chudd's Imperial Records. Whether waxing with his own jump blues unit in L.A. or Dave Bartholomew's hard-drivers in New Orleans, Walker always stayed true to his vision, and the proof was in the grooves: "Glamour Girl," "The Hustle Is On," "Tell Me What's the Reason," "High Society," "Cold, Cold Feeling," and the immaculate jumping instrumental "Strollin' with Bones" all date from this historic period of Walker's legacy. *—Bill Dahl*

☆ **Complete Capitol/Black & White Recordings** / 1995 / Capitol ♦♦♦♦♦
Three-CD, 75-track box of T-Bone Walker's recordings for the Capitol and Black & White labels in the 1940s. From a historical perspective, this is perhaps the most important phase of Walker's evolution. It was here where he perfected his electric guitar style, becoming an important influence on everyone from B.B. King down. It was also here where he acted as one of the key players in a small combo West Coast bands' transition from jazz to a more jump blues/R&B-oriented sound (though most of these sides retain a pretty strong jazz flavor). These sessions, which include the original version of his most famous tune ("Call It Stormy Monday"), have previously been chopped up into small morsels for reissue, or incorporated into the mammoth limited-edition Mosaic box set; this isolates them more conveniently. At the same time, it may be too extensive for some listeners, especially with the abundance of alternate takes (which are placed right after the official versions). Excellent liner notes, although the discographical information is surprisingly inconsistent. *—Richie Unterberger*

Sings the Blues/Singing the Blues / Nov. 24, 1999 / BGO ♦♦♦♦
This contains straight-up reissues of two of T-Bone's Imperial albums, themselves merely collections of the original 78s. Everything on these 24 sides was recorded between 1950 and 1954—not as trailblazing a period as the one from 1946 to 1947 on Black and White, but still prime T-Bone by any yardstick. The majority of these sides were cut in Los Angeles, with the exception of the New Orleans-recorded "I'm Still in Love With You" and the Windy City cut of "Bye Bye Baby." Loads of great T-Bone guitar and a cool West Coast sound to most everything on here make this an important addition to anyone's blues collection. *—Cub Koda*

★ **The Very Best of T-Bone Walker** / Mar. 28, 2000 / Koch ♦♦♦♦♦
A classic collection of his best Black and White and Imperial recordings from a time frame between 1949 and 1954. T-Bone's in fine swinging and appropriately bluesy form on tracks like "T-Bone Shuffle," "T-Bone Jumps Again," "They Call It Stormy Monday," "Strollin' With Bones," and "The Hustle Is On." If you're only going to add one T-Bone Walker to your collection, this would be the one to get. File under essential blues recordings for sure. *—Cub Koda*

★ **Blues Masters: The Very Best of T-Bone Walker** / Jun. 20, 2000 / Rhino ♦♦♦♦♦
A title as lofty as *The Very Best of T-Bone Walker* begs the question, "Does this CD really contain the seminal Texas bluesman's very best work?" And in fact, this 2000 release (which spans 1945-1957), *does* contain some of Walker's finest, most essential recordings of the '40s and '50s. It isn't the only collection focusing on Walker's recordings of that period—in 1995, for example, Capitol released the comprehensive three-CD set *The Complete Capitol/Black & White Recordings.* But if you need a more concise, single-disc collection of Walker's '40s and '50s classics, *Blues Masters: The Very Best of T-Bone Walker* would be an excellent choice. All of the material is superb—Walker's original 1947 version of "Call It Stormy Monday" (his most famous song) is included, and anyone with even a casual interest in the singer/guitarist's output also needs to hear gems like "The Hustle Is On" (1950), "Tell Me What's The Reason" (1953), "Bobby Sox Blues" (a 3 R&B hit in 1946), and "West Side Baby" (which was recorded in 1947 and made it to 8 on R&B singles charts in 1948). This is primarily a blues collection, but it's a blues collection with a lot of jazz influence. Walker's love of jazz is evident on much of the material, whether he's providing uptempo jump blues and Texas shuffles or becoming an outright torch singer on "Evenin'" and "I'm Still in Love With You" (both from 1945). As rewarding as this CD is, it isn't the last word on Walker's recording career—for the serious blues collector, one Walker album could never be enough. But if you don't own any Walker discs and are exploring his work for the first time, this collection is the most logical place to start. *—Alex Henderson*

Sippie Wallace (Beulah Thomas)

b. Nov. 1, 1898, Houston, TX, **d.** Nov. 1, 1986, Detroit, MI
Vocals / Classic Female Blues
A classic female blues singer from the '20s, Wallace kept performing and recording until her death. She was a major influence on a young Bonnie Raitt, who recorded several of Wallace's songs and performed live with her. Born and raised in Houston, she also spent time in New Orleans before moving to Chicago in 1923; by the end of the year, she had recorded two hits for OKeh including "Shorty George" and "Up the Country Blues." Throughout the '20s, she produced a series of hit singles though her contract expired by the end of the decade. After moving to Detroit, Sippie Wallace was inactive on the blues scene for 30 years, until her friend Victoria Spivey lured her out of retirement to join the thriving blues and folk festival circuit. She began recording again, and released two albums during the '60s. She continued performing even after a stroke in 1970, and landed a contract with Atlantic (with the help of Bonnie Raitt) that resulted in 1983's *Sippie,* which won the WC Handy Award for best blues album of the year and was nominated for a Grammy. She died three years later. *—Stephen Thomas Erlewine & Cub Koda*

★ **1923-1929** / Oct. 26, 1923-Feb. 7, 1929 / Document ♦♦♦♦♦
Document's *1923-1929* is an excellent 18-track collection of Sippie Wallace's first recordings. Many of her very best (and most notorious) songs, such as "I'm a Mighty Tight Woman," are included among these performances, most of which feature Wallace supported by a solitary piano; a few of the cuts have Wallace supported by a small jazz combo. Since Sippie Wallace's classic work has not been widely distributed, this is the best collection simply by default, but

even if there were more discs available, *1923-1929* would still rank among the best compilations, since it has many of her best songs presented in the best fidelity possible. *—Thom Owens*

Complete Recorded Works, Vol. 1 (1923-1925) / 1923-1925 / Document ✦✦✦✦✦
Sippie Wallace was one of the great blues singers of the 1920s. Although she occasionally sang non-blues material on records, the blues was where her powerful voice sounded best. Document, on two CDs, has released all of her recordings prior to 1958. The first disc starts out with impressive performances on the hits "Up the Country Blues" and "Shorty George Blues," which find Sippie backed by Eddie Heywood Sr.'s fluid piano (one of his best records). Wallace is heard accompanied by Clarence Williams' more basic piano during 1924-25 and with bands that include Louis Armstrong (very much in the background on two songs), Sidney Bechet, cornetist King Oliver (for three songs), other Williams associates of the period, plus her young brother, pianist Hersal Thomas. Among the more notable selections are "Mama's Gone, Goodbye," "Leavin' Me Daddy Is Hard to Do," "Baby, I Can't Use You No More," "Walkin' Talkin' Blues," "I'm So Glad I'm Brownskin" and "Devil Dance Blues." Although the second Document volume gets the edge (better recording quality and some exciting contributions by Louis Armstrong), the first CD is well worth getting too by vintage blues collectors. Most of these performances have been difficult to find for decades. *—Scott Yanow*

Complete Recorded Works, Vol. 2 (1925-1945) / 1925-1945 / Document ✦✦✦✦✦
The second half of blues singer Sippie Wallace's early career is fully chronicled on this Document CD, the second of two. All but the last four numbers were recorded from 1925-27. Although the four tunes from the August 25, 1925 session have a cornball gaspipe clarinetist, this is more than compensated for by ten numbers that feature Louis Armstrong in 1926-27. Satch does not get that much space to cut loose, but he clearly inspired Sippie, and vice versa. In addition, Wallace's younger brother, pianist Hersal Thomas, is heard on his last recordings before his early death, while cornetist Cicero Thomas fares well on two songs. Among the high points are "Murder's Gonna Be My Crime," "Suitcase Blues," "Special Delivery Blues" (which has some brief talking by Armstrong), the two earliest versions of Sippie's "I'm a Mighty Tight Woman" (including one from 1929 with clarinetist Johnny Dodds), and "The Flood Blues." Unfortunately, Sippie Wallace apparently lost the desire to record after Hersal Thomas' passing, and she only recorded four selections during the 1928-57 period. There are two cuts here from 1929, plus a pair from 1945 that have the singer backed by a quintet that includes tenor saxophonist Artie Starks, pianist Albert Ammons and guitarist Lonnie Johnson. Highly recommended for blues collectors, as is the first volume. *—Scott Yanow*

★ **Sings the Blues** / Oct. 23, 1966 / Storyville ✦✦✦✦✦
Although Sippie Wallace had begun recording again in 1958 after a long absence (just two 1945 numbers were cut after 1929), she had only recorded a total of 11 selections (including three songs a week earlier in 1966) when she made this album, her definitive LP of her later years. 68 at the time, Sippie was still a powerful singer, as she shows here on such numbers as "Woman Be Wise," "Shorty George Blues," "I'm a Mighty Tight Woman" and "Up the Country Blues." On the latter song, Wallace accompanied herself on piano; otherwise she is backed by either Roosevelt Sykes or Little Brother Montgomery on piano. Other than a 1967 album for the forgotten Mountain Railroad label that also included Jim Kweskin's Jug Band and Otis Spann, her highly recommended Storyville outing was Sippie Wallace's only full-length set during this period. When she cut her next record in 1982, the singer was way past her prime. *—Scott Yanow*

Robert Ward

b. Oct. 15, 1938, Luthersville, GA
Vocals, Guitar / Modern Electric Blues, Soul-Blues
Comeback tales don't come any more heartwarming (or unlikely) than Robert Ward's. Totally off the scene and thought by many aficionados to be dead, Ward's chance encounter with a guitar-shop owner in Ohio set off a rapid chain of events that culminated in Ward's 1990 debut album for Black Top, *Fear No Evil*. Ward's first taste of stardom came during the early '60s as leader of the Ohio Untouchables (who later mutated into the Ohio Players long after Ward's departure). Ward left the Untouchables in 1965, cutting a single for Groove City ("Fear No Evil"/"My Love Is Strictly Reserved for You") circa 1966-67 before working as a session guitarist at Motown. When his wife died in 1977 however, Ward hit the skids. He moved back to Georgia, and served a year in jail at one point (ironically, one of his prison mates was singer Major Lance, whose career was at similarly low ebb). In 1990, that auspicious encounter with guitar-shop owner Dave Hussong started the ball rolling for Ward's return to action. Black Top boss Hammond Scott signed the guitarist and produced the amazing *Fear No Evil* and a credible 1993 follow-up, *Rhythm of the People*. The label also issued a third set, *Black Bottom*, that once again captured Ward's curiously mystical appeal. *—Bill Dahl*

★ **Fear No Evil** / 1990 / Black Top ✦✦✦✦✦
One of the most amazing comeback stories of the modern blues era was ignited by this astonishing album. Robert Ward hadn't recorded as a leader in close to a quarter century, but his melismatic, almost mystical vocal quality and quirky, vibrato-enriched guitar sound utterly vital and electrifying as he revives some of his own obscure oldies ("Your Love Is Amazing," "Forgive Me Darling," "Strictly Reserved for You") and debuts a few new compositions for good measure. One of the classic blues/soul albums of the '90s. *—Bill Dahl*

Black Bottom / Oct. 17, 1995 / Black Top ✦✦✦✦
Now this is more like it. Ward is back in top form for his third Black Top outing, with better songs (most of them originals), skin-tight support from the Black Top house band, and plenty of that singularly gurgly guitar that inspired Lonnie Mack to follow Ward's lead and buy a Magnatone amp when he was starting out. *—Bill Dahl*

Twiggs County Soul Man / Feb. 4, 1997 / Black Top ✦✦✦

Washboard Sam (Robert Brown)

b. Jul. 15, 1910, Walnut Ridge, AR, **d.** Nov. 13, 1966, Chicago, IL
Washboard, Vocals / Acoustic Chicago Blues
A popular hokum blues artist, Washboard Sam recorded hundreds of records in the late '30s and '40s, usually with singer/guitarist Big Bill Broonzy. Out of all the washboard players of the era, Sam was the most popular, which was due not only to his to his washboard talent, but also his skills as a songwriter, as well as his strong voice. As an accompanist, Washboard Sam not only played with Broonzy, but also with bluesmen like Bukka White, Memphis Slim, Willie Lacey, and Jazz Gillum.

Washboard Sam (born Robert Brown) is the illegitimate son of Frank Broonzy, who also fathered Big Bill Broonzy. Sam was raised in Arkansas, working on a farm. He moved to Memphis in the early '20s to play the blues. While in Memphis, he met Sleepy John Estes and Hammie Nixon and the trio played street corners, collecting tips from passer-bys. In 1932, Washboard Sam moved to Chicago. Initially he played for tips, but soon he began performing regularly with Big Bill Broonzy. Within a few years, Sam was supporting Broonzy on the guitarist's Bluebird recordings. Soon, he was supporting a number of different musicians on their recording sessions, including pianist Memphis Slim, bassist Ransom Knowlin, and a handful of saxophone players, who all recorded for Bluebird.

In 1935, Washboard Sam began recording for both Bluebird and Vocalion Records, often supported by Big Bill Broonzy. Throughout the rest of the '30s and the '40s, Sam was one of the most popular Chicago bluesmen, selling numerous records and playing to packed audiences. After World War II, his audience began to shrink, largely because he had difficulty adapting to the new electric blues. In 1953, Washboard Sam recorded a session for Chess Records and then retired. In the early '60s, Willie Dixon and Memphis Slim tried to persuade Sam to return to the stage to capitalize on the blues revival. Initially, he refused, but in 1963 began perfoming concerts in clubs and coffeehouses in Chicago; he even played a handful of dates in Europe in early 1964.

Washboard Sam made his final recordings for the small Chicago-based label Spivey in 1964. The following year, his health quickly declined and he stopped recording and playing shows. In November of 1966, he died of heart disease. *—Stephen Thomas Erlewine & Cub Koda*

● **Washboard Blues 1935-1941** / Feb. 18, 1997 / EPM Musique ✦✦✦✦✦
Washboard Blues 1935-1941 is an excellent overview of Washboard Sam's great tracks, containing all the highlights from his peak years. It's ideal for the curious, or listeners who don't want to dig as deep as Document's multi-volume *Complete Recorded Works* series. *—Thom Owens*

Tuts Washington

b. Jan. 24, 1907, New Orleans, LA, **d.** Aug. 5, 1984, New Orleans, LA
Piano / New Orleans Blues, Boogie-Woogie, Modern Electric Blues
Isidore "Tuts" Washington (also widely known as "Papa Yellow") was 76 years old at the time of the release of his first solo recording. He began playing piano at age ten and worked with a number of famed New Orleans bandsmen—Kid Rena, Papa Celestin, Kid Punch Miller—over the course of his long career. In the late '30s he made trips to California and in 1950 joined the Tab Smith Orchestra in St. Louis for a time. During the better part of the '40s he worked in a trio backing up blues singer Smiley Lewis, which took him to various locations from Oklahoma to Florida. In 1958 he was with the Clyde Kerr Orchestra in New Orleans, and a decade later made several excursions up the Mississippi River on the Delta Queen. From 1968 to 1973 Tuts held forth at the Court of Two Sisters Restaurant in the French Quarter, then moving on to the piano bar at the Caribbean Room of the Pontchartrain Hotel in the early 80s. He died while performing on stage at the 1984 New Orleans World's Fair.

Tuts Washington identified Joseph Louis "Red" Cayou, an itinerant New Orleans pianist, as a prime influence on his early playing. He developed his repertoire by following the brass bands on the streets of New Orleans, memorizing the tunes and working out his own versions at home. He was self-taught at first but eventually took lessons at age 18; apparently his "professor" felt that Tuts was already too advanced to benefit from basic instruction, and at that point he turned to "Red" Caillou, whose hands he described as "like lightning." Washington specialized in instrumental pieces, but he also maintained a number of bawdy blues songs which he delivered with an impish relish. As the recognized "dean" of New Orleans piano players by the mid-century, he is credited frequently as a major influence on Fats Domino, Professor Longhair, James Booker, Dr. John, and Allen Toussaint. *—Bruce Boyd Raeburn*

● **New Orleans Piano Professor** / Apr. 1984 / Rounder ✦✦✦✦✦
Venerable New Orleans pianist Tuts Washington didn't get many chances to record during his lifetime. This 1983 session, now available on CD, was his most extensive project, with 23 songs covering everything from spirituals to traditional jazz numbers, pop pieces, novelty tunes, blues and country. Washington played them all in a seamless manner, displaying the mix of boogie-woogie and barrelhouse riffs, R&B, blues and gospel elements, Afro-Latin and Caribbean rhythmic accents, and jazz phrasing and licks mastered through many decades of playing in bars and clubs. This was his chance in the spotlight, and Washington didn't waste it. *—Ron Wynn*

Walter Washington

b. Dec. 21, 1943, New Orleans, LA
Vocals, Guitar / Soul-Blues
Walter Washington became a local legend in the Black clubs of New Orleans in the '70s and '80s and worked his way up to national status with a series of well-received albums and appearances. His recording affiliations have likewise moved from local to national independent to major label. An innovative guitarist and fine singer who has also done some excellent work with vocalist Johnny Adams, Washington does not perform in the classic New Orleans R&B mold but incorporates soul, funk, jazz, and blues with fluency and power. In the mid-

'60s, Washington formed his own band, the All Fools Band, and began headlining at local New Orleans clubs. By the early '70s, his popularity had grown enough to earn him a slot on a European package tour of New Orleans R&B acts. In the late '70s, he toured Europe on his own with his new band, the Roadmasters. Washington began his recording career relatively late, cutting his first album in 1981. The record, *Rainin' In My Heart*, appeared on a small independent lable called Hep Me; it was later re-released on Maison de Soul. Four years after his debut, Washington landed a contract with Rounder Records, releasing *Wolf Tracks* in 1986. *—Jim O'Neal & Stephen Thomas Erlewine*

Wolf Tracks / 1986 / Rounder ✦✦✦
Guitarist/vocalist Walter "Wolfman" Washington didn't get his shot on a national label until his 1986 debut for Rounder. While the album wasn't flawless, he possessed a strong, often compelling voice and was a skilled guitarist who could play effectively in a blues, R&B or jazz mode. Washington turned in a competent cover of the Tyrone Davis hit "Can I Change My Mind," spun a good yarn on "You Got Me Worried" and sounded weary, forlorn and anguished on various cuts. Although his songs weren't exactly lyrical triumphs, they were earnestly performed, and Washington displayed more than enough talent to justify subsequent followups. *—Ron Wynn*

Out of the Dark / 1988 / Rounder ✦✦✦
Walter "Wolfman" Washington's second Rounder session mixed Crescent City R&B and jazz licks with contemporary and vintage songs and production. Washington's cover of "Ain't That Loving You," while not quite as dramatic as Bobby "Blue" Bland's, was still outstanding, while he was appropriately ironic and bemused on "You Can Stay but the Noise Must Go" and vividly soulful on "Save Your Love for Me" and "Steal Away." Only on "Feel So Bad," a questionable song at best, did he sound strained and unfocused. Washington's guitar playing was sharp, creative, and tasty without being self-indulgent. It wasn't the kind of glossy, trendy work that garners the pop spotlight, but Washington showed progress and fine skills. *—Ron Wynn*

● **Wolf at the Door** / 1991 / Rounder ✦✦✦✦
Most of this CD from Walter "Wolfman" Washington puts the focus on his voice, which is reminiscent of a young Ray Charles. The horn arrangements look back toward 1960s Motown, and five of the six tracks fall squarely into the idiom of pre-disco R&B, with touches of funk and gospel. "Peepin'" is a bit of a surprise, a minor-toned instrumental with Tom Fitzpatrick's soprano in the lead and some nice George Benson-ish guitar by Washington. Even better are the last three tracks: the joyful blues "Tailspin," a minor blues ("At Night In the City"), and a bluesy ballad ("Don't Say Goodbye"). Wolfman Washington's versatility is quite impressive, making this a fairly memorable recording. *—Scott Yanow*

Funk Is in the House / Apr. 7, 1998 / Bullseye Blues ✦✦✦
Walter "Wolfman" Washington, who has an expressive and enthusiastic if not overly memorable voice, is virtually the entire show during this set which mixes together New Orleans funk and 60s soul with aspects of the blues. Although there are pieces by Jerry Butler, Ray Charles and Gamble and Huff, most of the selections are Washington originals. Wolfman's backup group the Roadmasters (a rhythm section with keyboardist Luca Fredericksen plus three guest horn players) is fine in support but fairly anonymous. So this set is primarily recommended to listeners who enjoy Washington's voice and the '60s-soul style in general. *—Scott Yanow*

Muddy Waters (McKinley Morganfield)

b. Apr. 4, 1915, Rolling Fork, MS, **d.** Apr. 30, 1983, Westmont, IL
Slide Guitar, Vocals, Guitar, Arranger / Slide Guitar Blues, Blues Revival, Delta Blues, Electric Chicago Blues, Chicago Blues
A postwar Chicago blues scene without the magnificent contributions of Muddy Waters is absolutely unimaginable. From the late '40s on, he eloquently defined the city's aggressive, swaggering, Delta-rooted sound with his declamatory vocals and piercing slide guitar attack. Like many of his contemporaries on the Chicago circuit, Waters was a product of the fertile Mississippi Delta. After recording a handful of sides for musicologist Alan Lomax, in 1943 he left for the bright lights of Chicago. By the mid-'40s, his slide skills were becoming a recognized entity on the city's South side, where he shared a stage or two with pianists Sunnyland Slim and Eddie Boyd and guitarist Blue Smitty. "I Feel like Going Home" was his first national R&B hit in 1948; he then assembled a band that was so tight and vicious on stage that they were informally known as the Headhunters—they'd come into a bar where a band was playing, ask to sit in, and then "cut the heads" of their competitors with their superior musicianship. Little Walter, of course, would single-handedly revolutionize the role of the harmonica within the Chicago blues hierarchy; Jimmy Rogers was an utterly dependable second guitarist, and Baby Face Leroy Foster could play both drums and guitar. On top of their instrumental skills, all four men could sing powerfully. 1951 found Waters climbing the R&B charts no less than four times, beginning with "Louisiana Blues," and continuing through "Long Distance Call," "Honey Bee," and "Still a Fool." Although it didn't chart, his 1950 classic "Rollin' Stone" provided a certain young British combo with a rather enduring name. By the time of his death in 1983, Muddy Waters's exalted place in the history of blues (and 20th-century popular music, for that matter) was eternally assured. The Chicago blues genre that he turned upside down during the years following World War II would never recover—and that's a debt we'll never be able to repay. *—Bill Dahl*

First Recording Sessions 1941-1946 / 1941-1946 / Document ✦✦✦
The landmark sides which comprise Muddy Waters' *First Recording Sessions* trace the early evolution of one of the blues' most enduring greats, offering invaluable insight into the primal influences which helped shape his musical identity. The profound influence of Waters' idol Son House is most indelibly etched into these early sides, with the bottleneck guitar sound on the first cuts "Country Blues" and "I Be's Troubled"—both recorded by Alan Lomax in 1941—a prime example of the Mississippi blues style of the period. When Lomax returned a year later, he recorded Waters in a string band also including violinist Son Simms, guitarist Percy Thomas and mandolinist Louis Ford; among the tracks they cut is "Take a Walk with Me," in all likelihood inspired by Robert Lockwood. By the final group of songs, dating from 1946, Waters was in Chicago, and here his guitar style began to move toward his future trademark sound, which is most in evidence on the classic closer, the two-part "Rollin' and Tumblin." *—Jason Ankeny*

★ **At Newport** / 1960 / MCA/Chess ✦✦✦✦✦
For many back in the early '60s, this was their first exposure to live recorded blues and it's still pretty damn impressive some 30-plus years down the line. Waters, with a band featuring Otis Spann, James Cotton, and guitarist Pat Hare, lays it down tough and cool with a set that literally had 'em dancing in the aisles by the set closer, a ripping version of "Got My Mojo Working," reprised again in a shorter encore version. Kicking off with a version of "I've Got My Brand on You" that positively burns the relatively tame, in comparison, studio take, Waters heads full bore through impressive versions of "Hoochie Coochie Man," Big Bill Broonzy's "Feel So Good," and "Tiger in Your Tank." A great breakthrough moment in blues history, preserved for posterity. *—Cub Koda*

Muddy Waters Sings Big Bill Broonzy / 1960 / MCA/Chess ✦✦✦✦✦
Waters's tribute album to the man who gave him his start on the Chicago circuit, this stuff doesn't sound much like Broonzy so much as a virtual recasting of his songs into Muddy's electric Chicago style. Evidently the first time Waters and his band were recorded in stereo, the highlights include high voltage takes on "When I Get to Drinkin'" and "The Mopper's Blues," with some really great harp from James Cotton as an added bonus. *—Cub Koda*

Folk Singer / Apr. 1964 / MCA/Chess ✦✦✦✦✦
Muddy's "unplugged" album was cut in September of 1963 and still sounds fresh and vital today. It was Muddy simply returning to his original style on a plain acoustic guitar in a well-tuned room with Willie Dixon on string bass, Clifton James on drums, and Buddy Guy on second acoustic guitar. The nine tracks are divvied up between full rhythm section treatments with Buddy and Muddy as a duo and the final track, "Feel Like Going Home," which Waters approaches solo. What makes this version of the album a worthwhile buy is the inclusion of five bonus tracks from his next two sessions: An April 1964 session brings us Willie Dixon's "The Same Thing" and Muddy's "You Can't Lose What You Never Had," while the October 1964 session features J.T. Brown on sax and clarinet on "Short Dress Woman" and "My John the Conqueror Root," as well as "Put Me in Your Lay Away," another strong side. *Folk Singer* offers both sides of Muddy from the early '60s. *—Cub Koda*

The Real Folk Blues / 1965 / MCA/Chess ✦✦✦✦✦
Once Chess discovered a White folk-blues audience ripe and ready to hear the real thing, they released a series of albums under the *Real Folk Blues* banner. This is one of the best entries in the series, a mixed bag of early Chess sides from 1949-1954, some of it hearkening back to Muddy's first recordings for Aristocrat with only Big Crawford on string in support with some wonderful full band sides rounding out the package to give everyone the big picture. A couple of highlights to pay special attention to are the cha cha/shuffle strut of the band charging through "Walkin' Through the Park" and the "I'm a Man"-derived nastiness of "Mannish Boy." *—Cub Koda*

Live Recordings 1965-1973 / 1965-1973 / Wolf ✦✦✦

Electric Mud / 1968 / MCA/Chess ✦✦

Fathers and Sons / 1969 / Vogue ✦✦✦
This is a 1969 "super session" that actually works, teaming up Muddy with Paul Butterfield, Michael Bloomfield, Duck Dunn, Otis Spann and Buddy Miles and Sam Lay sharing the drum stool. Originally issued as a double album, one disc featured studio remakes while the other disc featured the whole gang live in concert in front of a super enthusiastic audience. No new material to speak of, but some really great performances and the "youngsters" give the old man the backing he deserves. *—Cub Koda*

The London Muddy Waters Sessions / 1971 / MCA/Chess ✦✦

Muddy & the Wolf / 1974 / MCA/Chess ✦✦✦
The title is a bit of a ringer, since this isn't a collaborative effort in any way, shape or form. This contains a half dozen live Waters tracks with Mike Bloomfield, Paul Butterfield, and Otis Spann culled from the *Father & Sons* sessions and also features tracks by Howlin' Wolf from his London sessions with Eric Clapton and Ringo Starr. File under "just okay." *—Cub Koda*

☆ **The Best of Muddy Waters** / 1975 / MCA/Chess ✦✦✦✦✦
If you're building your Muddy Waters collection from the ground up, you can do no better than this compact disc reissue of his first album featuring 12 tightly compacted gems of seminal Chicago blues. This release features the original versions of "I'm Your Hoochie-Coochie Man," "Long Distance Call," "I'm Ready," "Honey Bee," "I Just Wanna Make Love to You," "Still a Fool," and a song called "Rollin' Stone," which provided the name inspiration for a hippie rock magazine and a group of British musicians. Thirty-plus years after its original release, it still stood as the perfect introduction to his music and one of the top five greatest Chicago blues albums of all time. *—Cub Koda*

Woodstock Album / 1975 / MCA/Chess ✦✦✦✦

Hard Again / May 1977 / Blue Sky ✦✦✦✦✦
By the mid-'70s Muddy Waters was all but forgotten as a viable recording entity. But one person who hadn't forgotten—and was willing to put his rock stardom on the line for it—was Johnny Winter. He assembled a crack backing unit with himself, Pinetop Perkins and James Cotton blowing their brains out and fueled the fire even further with top notch material Like "The Blues Had a Baby and They Named It Rock'n'Roll." The end result was the finest latter day album of Muddy's long career and the only one that can sit comfortably on the shelf next to his Chess classics. *—Cub Koda*

King Bee / 1981 / Blue Sky ✦✦✦

Trouble No More/Singles (1955-1959) / 1989 / MCA/Chess ✦✦✦✦✦
This is an excellent compilation of some of Muddy Waters's lesser-anthologized singles, all of them dating from the late '50s. Some of these were surprisingly hard to acquire in *any*

form until this appeared; the original version of "Got My Mojo Working," and for instance, as well as some of his higher-profile tracks, like "Rock Me," "Trouble No More," "Close to You," and "Don't Go No Further." All of these tracks appear on the *Chess Box*, so if you have that one, you don't need this one. But if you don't, you do. *—Richie Unterberger & Cub Koda*

☆ **The Chess Box** / Mar. 1990 / MCA/Chess ♦♦♦♦♦
Multi-disc box sets are a nettlesome proposition for the casual blues fan and even some hard-liners. Most folks just don't have the time or the attention span to stay with one artist over the course of three to four hours of material and because the very best sides are usually spread out over the various discs, just popping one in might not give you the artistic quick fix you're seeking. But if you've decided that Muddy's your main man and you want to build a Chicago blues collection that's comprehensive and expansive, this three-disc box just might be your first stop. While there's a European box that's far more exhaustive (and expensive, sporting both dodgy sound quality and dubious legality), this one is far easier to digest. If you want to go for the big one, this is it. *—Cub Koda*

Blue Sky / Jun. 16, 1992 / Columbia/Legacy ♦♦♦♦♦
This is a nice collection paring down the best of the material Waters recorded for the Blue Sky label between 1976 to 1980. With Johnny Winter in the producer's chair, the backings are sympathetic and the songs are great (some of them remakes of earlier Chess material): these are the tracks that garnered three consecutive Grammy Awards (for Best Ethnic or Traditional Recording) for Waters. And that can't be *all* bad. Not the place to start by any means, but definitely worth a listen or two. *—Cub Koda*

The Complete Plantation Recordings / Jun. 8, 1993 / MCA/Chess ♦♦♦♦♦
At long last, Muddy's historic 1941-1942 Library of Congress field recordings are all collected in one place, with the best fidelity that's been heard thus far. Waters performs solo pieces (you can hear his slide rattling against the fretboard in spots) and band pieces with the Son Sims Four, "Rosalie" being a virtual blueprint for his later Chicago style. Of particular note are the inclusion of several interview segments with Muddy from that embryonic period and a photo of Muddy playing on the porch of his cabin, dressed up and looking sharper than any Mississippi sharecropper on Stovall's plantation you could possibly imagine. This much more than just an important historical document; this is some really fine music imbued with a sense of place, time and loads of ambience. *—Cub Koda*

One More Mile / 1994 / MCA/Chess ♦♦♦♦♦
A double CD of 41 tracks, none of which are found on *The Chess Box*. With only three exceptions, none of them have ever been available on an American album before, and quite a few were never previously released anywhere. During most of his stay at Chess, Muddy's output was remarkably prolific and consistent. If you are interested enough in him to own more than one of his albums, you'll like what you hear on this collection, which matches or nearly matches the standards of his best work. Lots of rarities spanning the late '40s to the early '70s, with some special points of interest: the original 1955 version of "I Want To Be Loved," covered by The Rolling Stones on the B-side of their very first single, finally makes its first appearance on an American album, and the final 11 songs are from a previously unreleased 1972 Swiss radio broadcast, showcasing Muddy in a drummer-less trio. *—Richie Unterberger*

★ **His Best: 1947 to 1955** / 1997 / MCA/Chess ♦♦♦♦♦
This entry into MCA's Chess 50th Anniversary Collection now officially takes the place of *The Best of Muddy Waters* as an essential first purchase in building a Muddy Waters collection, as the original 12-song collection has been forced out of print with the issuance of this 20-tracker. All 12 songs that comprise the budget priced *The Best of Muddy Waters* are aboard, with eight more essential goodies from his first great period of creativity, including great early ones like "Rollin' and Tumblin'," "Train Fare Blues," and "I Feel like Going Home." The one ringer that keeps this collection from being *The Best of Muddy*-plus is an alternate take of "Hoochie Coochie Man" in place of the original issued master, a production error of the highest order. It's a radically different-sounding one, too, with some surprisingly sloppy unthought-out harp work from Little Walter (at one point he simply stops playing), but with a far more intense vocal from Muddy than the issued version. But it is the issued version which by rights *should* have been the one heard here, as this *is* supposed to be a true best-of compilation. That niggling point aside, this collection (part of a two-volume best-of retrospective, the second covering the years 1956 to 1964) sports far superior sound and excellent liner notes, and will now take pride of place as the essential first purchase toward building the perfect Muddy Waters collection. *—Cub Koda*

☆ **His Best: 1956-1964** / May 20, 1997 / MCA/Chess ♦♦♦♦♦
The first eight tracks of this 20-track collection date from 1956: "All Aboard," and featuring both James Cotton and Little Walter on twin harmonicas, "Forty Days and Forty Nights," "Just to Be With You," "Don't Go No Farther," "Diamonds at Your Feet," "I Love the Life I Live," "Rock Me" and the studio version of "I Got My Mojo Working." By now Waters was a rhythm & blues star, as far removed from the Clarksdale plantation he grew up on as you could get. He also had developed the modern-day blues band lineup and by this time had his running like a well-oiled machine. Little Walter (by now a star in his own right) was still on call for studio dates and if not, Walter Horton, Otis Spann and Jimmy Rogers were still in the lineup. By 1958's "She's Nineteen Years Old," Muddy had built up his second great band with James Cotton, Pat Hare and Luther Tucker on guitars and Francis Clay on drums, the unit he would take to *Newport* in 1960. It's this unit that contributes so mightily to "Walkin' Thru the Park," "She's Into Something," and Big Bill Broonzy's "I Feel So Good." Two of Muddy's most influential tracks, "You Shook Me" and "You Need Love" (the blueprint for Led Zepplin's "Whole Lotta Love") curiously feature Earl Hooker on slide guitar, along with A.C. Reed and John "Big Moose" Walker, the core of the Age-Profile label's house band. A pair of tracks from his now-celebrated *Folk Singer* album with Buddy Guy and Willie Dixon ("My Home Is In the Delta" and "Good Morning Little Schoolgirl") offset the collection's final selections, Willie Dixon's "The Same Thing" and Muddy's classic "You Can't Lose What You Ain't Never Had," a perfect closer for this essential collection. *—Cub Koda*

Johnny "Guitar" Watson

b. Feb. 3, 1935, Houston, TX, **d.** May 17, 1996, Chicago, IL
Vocals, Guitar / Modern Electric Texas Blues, Electric Texas Blues, Soul-Blues, R&B
"Reinvention" could just as easily have been Johnny "Guitar" Watson's middle name. The multi-talented performer parlayed his stunning guitar skills into a vaunted reputation as one of the hottest blues axemen on the West Coast during the 1950s. But that admirable trait wasn't paying the bills as the 1970s rolled in. So he totally changed his image to that of a pimp-styled funkster, enjoying more popularity than ever before. His first sides for the King subsidiary found him tinkling the ivories, but by 1954, when he dreamed up the absolutely astonishing instrumental "Space Guitar," the youth (he was two days short of his 17th birthday!) had switched over to guitar. "Space Guitar" ranks with the greatest achievements of its era—Watson's blistering rapid-fire attack, done without the aid of a pick, presages futuristic effects that rock guitarists still hadn't mastered another 15 years down the line. Watson moved over to the RPM label in 1955 and waxed some of the toughest upbeat blues of their timeframe. He scored his first hit in 1955 for RPM with "Those Lonely Lonely Nights." Watson's first released version of "Gangster of Love" emerged in 1957 on Keen; singles for Class ("One Kiss"), Goth, Arvee (the rocking introduction "Johnny Guitar"), and Escort preceded a hookup with Johnny Otis at King during the early '60s. He recut "Gangster" for King, reaching a few more listeners this time, and dented the R&B charts again in 1962 with his impassioned, violin-enriched blues ballad "Cuttin' In." Still, little had been heard of this musical chameleon before he returned decked out in funk threads during the mid-'70s. He hit with "I Don't Want to Be a Lone Ranger" for Fantasy before putting together an incredible run at DJM Records paced by "A Real Mother for Ya" in 1977 and an updated "Gangster of Love" the next year. *—Bill Dahl*

☆ **Gangster of Love** / 1958 / See for Miles ♦♦♦♦♦
The innovative guitar wizard when he was young and wearing his Texas blues roots prominently on his sleeve. Watson spent two stints at King/Federal, both of them sampled here: his 1953-54 output includes the incomparable "Space Guitar," and a sizzling "Half Pint of Whiskey," and a woozy "Gettin' Drunk." The 1961-63 King stuff is headed by the definitive version of "Gangster of Love," the searing soul-tinged "Cuttin' In," and a chunky "Broke and Lonely." *—Bill Dahl*

Johnny Guitar Watson / 1963 / King ♦♦♦♦♦
Fine collection of guitarist's innovative 1950s and '60s stuff. *—Bill Dahl*

Ain't That a Bitch / 1976 / Collectables ♦♦♦♦
The first of Watson's monstrously popular funk-based albums for DJM, and in all likelihood, the best of the lot. The title cut of the 1976 album is a sardonic gem, Watson's sinuous guitar licks a far cry from his brash '50s sound. The intimate "I Want to Ta-Ta You Baby," "Superman Lover," and "I Need It" also rate with Watson's most alluring old school R&B output. *—Bill Dahl*

A Real Mother for Ya / Jan. 1977 / Collectables ♦♦♦
Obviously, the storming funk workout that gives this 1977 gold album its title is the album's principal draw (it's been covered countless times, but never duplicated). As was his wont by this time, the multitalented Watson plays everything except drums and horns. *—Bill Dahl*

Funk Beyond the Call of Duty / Feb. 1977 / Collectables ♦♦♦

Three Hours Past Midnight / 1991 / Flair ♦♦♦♦
Watson's mid-'50s catalog for the Bihari brothers' Flair logo is unassailable with searing rockers like "Oh Baby," "Hot Little Mama," and "Ruben" and the blistering slow blues title cut. Unfortunately, this 16-song collection utilizes inferior alternate takes on several of the most important titles. On the positive side, it contains both sides of his rare 1959 single for Class, "One Kiss"/"The Bear." *—Bill Dahl*

★ **The Very Best of Johnny Guitar Watson** / Apr. 20, 1999 / Rhino ♦♦♦♦♦
Johnny "Guitar" Watson was a blues/R&B/funk pioneer, both in sound and music, and this 18-track collection zeroes in on his bluesiest and earliest sides. Watson a true multi-talent and this set shows it off to great advantage while still staying firmly in the blues mode throughout; he was a blazing boogie woogie pianist (check him out on the earlier version with Chuck Higgins of "Motorhead Baby"), a futuristic guitarist who influenced Bo Diddley and Ike Turner in the instrument-as-noisemaker department (1954's "Space Guitar") and a soulful singer who was both uptown and as gutbucket as you could possibly ask for (1962's "That's the Chance You've Got to Take" and 1955's "Three Hours Past Midnight" which also sports one mean and spare guitar solo), an artist who understood low down blues and bebop jazz and came up with his own melding of it. Watson is the lost genius of the blues and this set is a long overdue tribute to a true pioneer visionary. *—Cub Koda*

Curley Weaver

b. Mar. 26, 1906, Covington, GA, **d.** Sep. 20, 1962, Almon, GA
Vocals, Guitar, Guitar (Acoustic) / Prewar Blues, Piedmont Blues, Country Blues
Curley Weaver, who was known for much of his life as "the Georgia Guitar Wizard," is only just beginning to be appreciated as one of the best players ever to pick up a six-string instrument. Although he recorded a fair number of sides on his own during the 1920s and '30s, Weaver was most commonly heard in performances and recordings in association with his better known colleagues Blind Willie McTell (with whom he worked from the 1930s until the early '50s), Barbecue Bob, and Buddy Moss. Weaver was, by virtue of his virtuosity and the associations that he kept throughout his life and career, a guitarist's guitarist, a virtuoso among a small coterie of Atlanta-based guitar wizards. He never had the renown of Blind Willie McTell, but he was Willie's equal and match in just about every conceivable respect as a player and singer, his six-string being perfectly mated to Willie's 12-string. When he was playing or recording with McTell, Buddy Moss, or Barbecue Bob, the results were the blues equivalent of what rock people later would've called a "super-session" except that, as a listen to the surviving records reveals, the results were more natural and overpowering—these

guys genuinely liked each other, and loved playing together, and it shows beyond the virtuosity of the music, in the warmth and elegance of the playing and the sound. *—Bruce Eder*

★ **Georgia Guitar Wizard (1928-1935)** / 1987 / Story of the Blues ♦♦♦♦♦
Why Atlanta blues guitarist and vocalist Curley Weaver is so obscure when cohorts Blind Willie McTell and Buddy Moss are so well-known is one of those why-ask-why deals. Weaver was an outstanding player and convincing singer, and this collection nicely outlines his attributes. McTell and Moss appear here in accompanying roles. *—Ron Wynn*

☆ **Complete Studio Recordings** / 1990 / Document ♦♦♦♦♦
Weaver's complete recordings, taking into account all of the sessions for Moss, McTell et al. where he played guitar, would comprise a lot more than the 19 tracks here, but that's no reason not to spring for this slightly more expensive collection, which doesn't entirely overlap with the Story of Blues disc. *—Bruce Eder*

Katie Webster (Kathryn Jewel Thorne)

b. Jan. 11, 1936, Houston, TX, **d.** Sep. 5, 1999, League City, TX
Vocals, Piano, Harmonica, Organ / Swamp Blues, Louisiana Blues, Modern Electric Chicago Blues, New Orleans Blues

A piano-pounding institution on the southern Louisiana swamp blues scene during the late '50s and early '60s, Katie Webster later grabbed a long-deserved share of national recognition with a series of Alligator albums before a 1993 stroke temporarily shelved her. Local guitarist Ashton Savoy took her under his wing early on, sharing her 1958 debut 45 for the Kry logo ("Baby Baby"). Webster rapidly became an invaluable studio sessioneer for Louisiana producers J.D. Miller in Crowley and Eddie Shuler in Lake Charles. She played on sides by Guitar Junior (Lonnie Brooks), Clarence Garlow, Jimmy Wilson, Lazy Lester, and Phil Phillips (her gently rolling 88s powered his hit "Sea of Love"). The young pianist also waxed some terrific sides of her own for Miller from 1959 to 1961 for his Rocko, Action, and Spot labels. In 1964, she guested with Otis Redding's band at the Bamboo Club in Lake Charles and so impressed the charismatic Redding that he absconded with her. For the next three years, Webster served as his opening act! The 1970s were pretty much a lost decade for Katie Webster as she took care of her ailing parents in Oakland, CA. But in 1982 a European tour beckoned, and she journeyed overseas for the first of many such jaunts. *—Bill Dahl*

Swamp Boogie Queen / 1988 / Alligator ♦♦♦♦
Lovable Katie Webster had some high-profile help for this impressive comeback album—Bonnie Raitt shares the vocal on "Somebody's on Your Case" and plays guitar on "On the Run"; Kim Wilson duets with Webster for a cover of Johnnie Taylor's "Who's Making Love" (a track that Robert Cray contributes crisp guitar to). Throughout, Webster's vocals are throatier than they used to be (she soulfully covers one-time mentor Otis Redding's "Fa-Fa-Fa-Fa-Fa [Sad Song]" and "Try a Little Tenderness"), while her driving left hand still lays down some powerhouse boogie rhythms. *—Bill Dahl*

Two-Fisted Mama! / 1990 / Alligator ♦♦♦♦
Another impressive showcase for Katie Webster's rollicking 88s and earthy vocals. Other than the Memphis Horns, no special guests this time—just Webster and her tight trio (anchored by guitarist Vasti Jackson). *—Bill Dahl*

Katie Webster / 1991 / Paula ♦♦♦♦♦
Webster is at her full bayou-bred boogie-blues best here, when she was the queen of south Louisiana's swamp sessioneers. Webster's own late-'50s/early-'60s output for producer J.D. Miller was no less captivating; her self-named dance number "The Katie Lee" and "Mama Don't Allow" that uproots the Gary U.S. Bonds party vibe to New Orleans are two of the best items on the 20-track disc. There's also her blues-drenched "No Bread, No Meat" and a nice version of "Sea of Love" (Webster added the gently rolling piano to Phil Phillips's original hit). *—Bill Dahl*

● **Deluxe Edition** / Feb. 23, 1999 / Alligator ♦♦♦♦♦

Junior Wells (Amos Blackmore)

b. Dec. 9, 1934, Memphis, TN, **d.** Jan. 15, 1998
Vocals, Harmonica / Blues Revival, Modern Electric Chicago Blues, Harmonica Blues, Electric Harmonica Blues, Electric Chicago Blues, Modern Electric Blues

He was one bad dude, strutting across the stage like a harp-toting gangster, mesmerizing the crowd with his tough-guy antics and rib-sticking Chicago blues attack. Amazingly, Junior Wells kept at precisely this sort of thing for over 40 years—he was an active performer from the dawn of the 1950s to his death in the late '90s.

After Little Walter left Muddy Waters in 1952, Wells took his place. His debut headlining date produced some seminal Chicago blues efforts, including his first reading of "Hoodoo Man," a rollicking "Cut That Out," and the blazing instrumentals "Eagle Rock" and "Junior's Wail." More fireworks ensued the next year when Wells encored for with a mournful "So All Alone" and the jumping "Lawdy! Lawdy!" (Muddy Waters moonlighted on guitar for the session). In 1957, he hooked up with producer Mel London, who owned the Chief and Profile logos. The association resulted in many of Wells's most enduring sides, including "I Could Cry" and the rock & rolling "Lovey Dovey Lovely One" in 1957; the grinding national R&B hit "Little by Little" (with Willie Dixon providing vocal harmony) in 1959, and the R&B-laced classic "Messin' with the Kid" in 1960 (sporting Earl Hooker's immaculate guitar work). Wells's harp was de-emphasized during this period on record in favor of his animated vocals. With Bob Koester producing, the harpist cut an all-time classic LP for Delmark in 1965. *Hoodoo Man Blues* vividly captured the feel of a typical Wells set at Theresa's Lounge, even though it was cut in a studio. With Buddy Guy (initially billed as "Friendly Chap" due to his contract with Chess) providing concise lead guitar, Wells laid down definitive versions of "Snatch It Back and Hold It," "You Don't Love Me," and "Chittlin' Con Carne." *—Bill Dahl*

★ **Hoodoo Man Blues** / 1965 / Delmark ♦♦♦♦♦
One of the truly classic blues albums of the 1960s, and one of the first to fully document the smoky ambience of a night at a West side nightspot in the superior acoustics of a recording studio. Wells just set up with his usual cohorts—guitarist Buddy Guy (billed as "Friendly Chap" on first vinyl pressings), bassist Jack Myers, and drummer Billy Warren—and proceeded to blow up a storm, bringing an immediacy to "Snatch It Back and Hold It," "You Don't Love Me," "Chitlin Con Carne," and the rest that is absolutely mesmerizing. *—Bill Dahl*

It's My Life, Baby / 1966 / Vanguard ♦♦♦
Partly live from Pepper's Lounge in Chicago, with Buddy Guy and Freddy Below. Junior's first Vanguard album. *—Barry Lee Pearson*

South Side Blues Jam / 1970 / Delmark ♦♦♦
Enjoyable but less electrifying follow-up to *Hoodoo Man Blues,* cut in 1969-1970—looser, with longer songs that afford more room to stretch out instrumentally but don't quite equal the stunning precision of what came before. Buddy Guy returns on guitar; Otis Spann is the pianist, and Fred Below keeps superb time. *—Bill Dahl*

On Tap / Mar. 1975 / Delmark ♦♦♦
Underrated mid-'70s collection boasting a contemporary, funky edge driven by guitarists Phil Guy and Sammy Lawhorn, keyboardist Big Moose Walker, and saxman A.C. Reed. Especially potent is the crackling "The Train I Ride," a kissin' cousin to Little Junior Parker's "Mystery Train." *—Bill Dahl*

Blues Hit Big Town / 1977 / Delmark ♦♦♦♦♦
This 1998 CD reissue of Wells' debut recordings for the States label adds four previously unheard tracks along with the original 13-track vinyl lineup. Wells' legacy begins with these landmark sides, featuring Elmore James, Muddy Waters, Johnnie Jones, Otis Spann, Willie Dixon, and the Aces in the lineup at various points. Whether it's a slow one like his original take on "Hoodoo Man" or a jump number like "Cut That Out," the grooves are classic Chicago and a mile deep. Most telling are the acoustic duets with Louis Myers recorded between the 1953 and 1954 studio sessions and the fine instrumentals like "Junior's Wail" and "Eagle Rock." Although at the start of a long career, it's obvious that Junior Wells was already a young man with a style all his own, ready to make blues history. File under essential. *—Cub Koda*

★ **1957-1966** / 1991 / Paula ♦♦♦♦♦
The indipensable sides for Mel London's Profile, Chief, and Age labels (and a few for USA Records that directly followed). Backed by a modern-sounding crew that included immaculate guitarist Earl Hooker, saxist A.C. Reed, and keyboardist Johnny "Big Moose" Walker. Wells enjoyed a considerable R&B hit with the grinding "Little by Little," glides atop a churning rhythm groove on the original "Messin' with the Kid," rocks "Lovey Dovey Lovely One" and the hokey-but-fun "I Need Me a Car," and blows some husky amplified harmonica on "Cha Cha Cha in Blue" and "Calling All Blues." *—Bill Dahl*

Come on in This House / Feb. 1997 / Telarc ♦♦♦♦♦
Junior Wells' penchant for clowning around sometimes conflicts with his craftsmanship, but he's all business on *Come On In This House,* his most unadulterated blues record since his highly acclaimed *Hoodoo Man Blues* of more than 30 years vintage. This is what has come to be known as an "unplugged" session—that is, predominately, although not exclusively, acoustic instrumentation. Producer John Snyder's concept was threefold: (1) to team Wells with some of the era's top younger traditional blues guitarists—Corey Harris, Alvin Youngblood Hart, Sonny Landreth, Bob Margolin, and John Mooney, (2) to have those musicians, in various combinations, accompany Wells on a variety of slide guitars, and (3) to concentrate on vintage Chicago and Delta blues from the repertoires of Rice Miller, Little Walter, Tampa Red, Arthur Crudup, and Wells himself. The result is a virtual slide-guitar mini-fest and a demonstration of the timeless appeal of classic blues done well. Wells' vocals are deep and manly; his harp playing is high-pitched, like a child's pleading. A surprising highlight is the only contemporary tune on the disc, Tracy Chapman's "Give Me One Reason." New Orleans drummer Herman Ernest III, who appears on 11 of the 14 cuts, does a masterful job laying down understated rhythmic grooves. *—Steve Hoffman*

Live at Buddy Guy's Legends / Jun. 24, 1997 / Telarc ♦♦♦

Bukka White (Booket T. Washington White)

b. Nov. 12, 1906, Houston, MS, **d.** Feb. 26, 1977, Memphis, TN
Slide Guitar, Vocals, Piano, Harmonica, Guitar / Slide Guitar Blues, Prewar Gospel Blues, Prewar Blues, Delta Blues, Acoustic Blues

Achieving a distinctive musical voice is a highly prized blues value, yet few artists develop an easily recognizable vocal and instrumental style that is uniquely theirs. Bukka White was one of those remarkable artists with an overall approach and composition style that were unusual, yet he was a popular houseparty musician and a successful recording artist. Although he had a second career during the blues revival and remained a powerful performer, his best work was on his 1937 and 1940 Vocalion sides. They feature down-home country-blues at its best, personal, moving, and instrumentally compelling. White's percussive approach to his open G-tuned steel National can be imitated but not duplicated. Like other Delta artists, White's sound was melodically simple but rhythmically complex. Sporting an attack vaguely reminiscent of Big Joe Williams, White worked his guitar like a drum, adding rhythmic nuances with his chording hand on the guitar neck. Many of White's pieces employ spoken or chanted passages, especially his train songs, which combined talking blues and train effects. Moody and introspective, his songs let you into his life, detailing his experiences as a prisoner at Mississippi's notorious Parchman Farm or as a hobo riding the rails. *—Barry Lee Pearson*

☆ **Legacy of the Blues** / 1969 / Sonet ♦♦♦♦♦
A CD reissue of the recordings that led to Bukka White's rediscovery, made by Ed Denson and John Fahey at a Memphis rooming house in 1963, nearly a quarter century after his last recordings. White is in astonishingly good form, as both a singer and guitarist—his rendition of "Baby Please Don't Go" is closer to what one by Howlin' Wolf might have sounded like, with an almost palpable fury and desperation, and none of the cultured smoothness of the familiar versions by Big Joe Williams or Muddy Waters. "Aberdeen Mississippi Blues," "New Orleans Streamline," "Parchman Farm Blues," and "Shake 'Em on Down" have an almost

preternatural power, and White gets his one acoustic guitar to make sounds one would expect should require two or three. Of almost equal importance, he reminisces about Charley Patton for several minutes. Denson and Fahey caught this blues master at the right time, just the right moment, rising to the sudden occasion to make a new record, spontaneous and unplanned, and got something about as valuable as any of Alan Lomax's field recordings of the 1940s. *—Bruce Eder*

★ **The Complete Bukka White** / 1994 / Columbia/Legacy ✦✦✦✦✦
Here it is all in one place, all 14 of Bukka White's legendary Vocalion recordings. Kicking off with his lone 1937 single of "Pinebluff, Arkansas" and "Shake "Em on Down," the set continues with the marathon 12-song session from 1940 which produced such classics as "Sleepy Man Blues," "Parchman Farm Blues," "Fixin' to Die Blues," and "Bukka's Jitterbug Swing." This is personal blues, hitting on a number of subjects usually too stark for blues lyrics, but all on open-wound display here. Powerful stuff, indeed. *—Cub Koda*

Big Joe Williams

b. Oct. 16, 1903, Crawford, MS, **d.** Dec. 17, 1982, Macon, MS
Vocals, Guitar / Blues Revival, Delta Blues, Electric Delta Blues, Acoustic Blues
Big Joe Williams may have been the most cantankerous human being who ever walked the earth with guitar in hand. At the same time, he was an incredible blues musician: a gifted songwriter, a powerhouse vocalist, and an exceptional idiosyncratic guitarist. Despite his deserved reputation as a fighter, artists who knew him well treated him as a respected elder statesman. Even so, they may not have chosen to play with him, because—as with other older Delta artists—if you played with him you played by his rules. He recorded through five decades for Vocalion, Okeh, Paramount, Bluebird, Prestige, Delmark, and many others. According to Charlie Musselwhite, he and Big Joe kicked off the blues revival in Chicago in the '60s. *—Barry Lee Pearson*

Nine String Guitar Blues / 1961 / Collectables ✦✦✦✦✦
The title says it all—Big Joe Williams plays a custom-made nine-string guitar, which sounds like no other instrument in existence. That alone would give his stripped-down acoustic Delta blues a new spin, but he brings so much grit and passion to his performances, they would have sounded fresh and vital anyway. *—Thom Owens*

Back to the Country / 1964 / Testament ✦✦✦✦
Fellow Mississippians Jimmy Brown on fiddle and Willie Lee Harris on harmonica augment Big Joe's down-home Delta blues from the blues revival of the 70s. *—Barry Lee Pearson*

● **Early Recordings 1935-41** / 1965 / Mamlish ✦✦✦✦✦
This blues legend and guitar wizard's best initial Bluebird recordings, including the best versions of "49 Highway" and "Baby Please Don't Go" from 1935. *—Barry Lee Pearson*

Stavin' Chain Blues / 1966 / Delmark ✦✦✦✦
A CD reissue of 1958 recordings, it includes four previously unreleased tracks. This is raw but beautiful country-blues, featuring the otherworldly sound of Big Joe's nine-string guitar. *—Niles J. Frantz*

● **Shake Your Boogie** / 1990 / Arhoolie ✦✦✦✦✦
Arhoolie reissued two of Big Joe Williams' seminal rediscovery albums on one disc in 1990. The first, 1960's *Tough Times,* ranks among his best; the second, 1969's *Thinking of What They Did,* isn't as strong, but the two albums provide an excellent introduction to this Delta bluesman. *—Stephen Thomas Erlewine*

Robert Pete Williams

b. Mar. 14, 1914, Zachary, LA, **d.** Dec. 31, 1980, Rosedale, LA
Vocals, Guitar / Blues Revival, Country Blues, Acoustic Louisiana Blues, Electric Blues, Acoustic Blues
Discovered in the Louisiana State Penitentiary, Robert Pete Williams became one of the great blues discoveries during the folk boom of the early '60s. His disregard for conventional patterns, tunings, and structures kept him from a wider audience, but his music remains one of the great, intense treats of the blues. He began playing blues in his late teens, and performed with a homemade guitar at local parties and dances. After he shot and killed a man in 1956, Williams was convicted of murder and sentenced to life in prison (despite his claims of self-defense). While at Angola prison, he was recorded performing several of his own songs, which were all about life in prison. Granted a pardon in 1959, after he had served over three years, Williams was initially able to perform only in Lousiana, though his recordings for Folk-Lyric, Arhoolie and Prestige became popular. Finally, in 1964, he played his first concert outside of Louisiana, at the legendary Newport Folk Festival. Williams' performance was enthusiastically received and he began touring the United States, often playing shows with Mississippi Fred McDowell. During the late '60s and into the '70s, Robert Pete Williams played across America and Europe, and recorded for a handful of small independent labels including Fontana and Storyville. *—Cub Koda & Stephen Thomas Erlewine*

★ **Angola Prisoner's Blues** / Mar. 1961 / Arhoolie ✦✦✦✦✦
Not enough great things to say about this one, one of the finest field recordings ever done anywhere. If Robert Pete's "Prisoner's Talking Blues" doesn't move you, check your heart into your refrigerator's freezer section. *—Cub Koda*

Free Again / Nov. 1961 / Prestige/Original Blues Classics ✦✦✦✦✦

I'm as Blue as a Man Can be / 1994 / Arhoolie ✦✦✦✦✦

When a Man Takes the Blues / 1994 / Arhoolie ✦✦✦✦✦

Homesick James Williamson

b. Apr. 3, 1910, Somerville, TN
Slide Guitar, Vocals, Guitar / Slide Guitar Blues, Electric Chicago Blues
His correct age may remain in doubt (he's claimed he was born as early as 1905), but the slashing slide guitar skills of Homesick James Williamson have never been in question. Many of his most satisfying recordings have placed him in a solo setting, where his timing eccentricities don't disrupt the proceedings (though he's made some fine band-backed waxings as well). Settling in Chicago during the 1930s, Williamson played local clubs and recorded for RCA Victor in 1937. The miles and gigs had added up before Williamson made some of his finest sides in 1952-53 for Art Sheridan's Chance Records (including the classic "Homesick" that gave him his enduring stage name). James also worked extensively as a sideman, backing harp great Sonny Boy Williamson in 1945 at a Chicago gin joint called the Purple Cat and during the 1950s with his cousin, slide master Elmore James. He also recorded with James during the 1950s. Homesick's own output included crashing 45s for Colt and USA in 1962, a fine 1964 album for Prestige, and four tracks on a Vanguard anthology in 1965. Williamson has never stopped recording and touring; he's done latter-day albums for Appaloosa and Earwig. *—Bill Dahl*

● **Blues on the South Side** / 1964 / Prestige/Original Blues Classics ✦✦✦✦✦
Probably the best album the slide guitarist ever laid down (originally for Prestige in 1964). His stylistic similarities to his cousin, the great Elmore James, are obvious, but Homesick deviates repeatedly from the form. Tough as nails with a bottleneck, he goes for the jugular on "Goin' Down Swingin'," "Johnny Mae," and "Gotta Move," supported by pianist Lafayette Leake, guitarist Eddie Taylor, and drummer Clifton James. *—Bill Dahl*

Goin' Back Home / Jun. 1977 / 32 Jazz ✦✦✦
Originally recorded for Pete Lowry's Trix label back in 1974 and 1975, here's Homesick's acoustic album. While his timing (or lack of it) is still firmly in place, it somehow makes these tracks work all the better, keeping a loose time and making the tunes come alive. His voice is unbelievably strong and engaged on the tracks, and as Homesick James sessions go, this is one of his very best. Highly recommended. *—Cub Koda*

Homesick James & Snooky Pryor: Sad and Lonesome / 1980 / Wolf ✦✦✦

Chicago Slide Guitar Legend / 1998 / Official ✦✦✦✦✦
This 26-track overview brings together the early and impossibly rare tracks James recorded for imprints like Chance, Colt, USA and others, from his earliest efforts in 1952 into the mid-1960s before signing with Prestige and producing the *Blues on the South Side* album for them. The first 15 tracks are culled from his 1952 and 1953 sessions for Chance Records (including an alternate take of his first single, "Lonesome Old Train"), and some great harp work from Big Walter Horton on the instrumental "Williamson Shuffle." Along with the surviving Chance material are stray singles for USA (an uptown version of "Crossroads" featuring a droning sax section), Colt ("Set a Date"), UK Decca ("Got to Move"), Spivey ("Can't Hold Out") and a pair of sides shared with Sunnyland Slim ("Sunnyland/Homesick Special"). There are no real session dates or personnel information on here, and only scant liner notes only giving introductory information; the set also leaves off both sides of his 1960 Atomic H single and thus can't be a complete overview. But the music is just as fine as you could possibly ask for, grade-A Chicago blues chock full of raw slide guitar and Homesick's grainy vocals, making this the best overview of this artist's early work available on compact disc. *—Cub Koda*

Sonny Boy Williamson [II] (Aleck Ford "Rice" Miller)

b. Dec. 5, 1899, Glendora, MS, **d.** May 25, 1965, Helena, AR
Vocals, Harmonica / Delta Blues, Harmonica Blues, Electric Chicago Blues
Sonny Boy Williamson was, in many ways, the ultimate blues legend. By the time of his death in 1965, he had been around long enough to have played with Robert Johnson at the start of his career and Eric Clapton, Jimmy Page and Robbie Robertson at the end of it. In between, he drank a lot of whiskey, hoboed around the country, had a successful radio show for 15 years, toured Europe to great acclaim and simply wrote, played and sang some of the greatest blues ever etched into black phonograph records. His delivery was sly, evil and world-weary, while his harp-playing was full of short, rhythmic bursts one minute and powerful, impassioned blowing the next. His songs were chock full of mordant wit, with largely autobiographical lyrics that hold up to the scrutiny of the printed page. Though he took his namesake from another well-known harmonica player, no one really sounded like him. The music Sonny Boy made for Trumpet Records between 1951 to 1954 show him in peak form, his vocal, instrumental, and songwriting skills honed to perfection. Williamson struck paydirt on his first Trumpet release, "Eyesight to the Blind" and though the later production on his Chess records would make the Trumpet sides seem woefully under-recorded by comparison, they nonetheless stand today as classic performances, capturing juke-joint music in one of its finest hours. *—Cub Koda*

Down & Out Blues / 1959 / MCA/Chess ✦✦✦✦✦
Retaining photographer Don Bronstein's cover shot of a disheveled bum lying on the sidewalk (some former Chess artist, perhaps—) Sonny Boy Williamson's original 1959 album made it to digital reissue but has now been supplanted by MCA's exhaustive *The Essential Sonny Boy Williamson.* Still, for a budget price, there's a dozen unforgettable tracks: "Don't Start Me to Talkin'," and his Checker debut; "All My Love in Vain," "Wake Up Baby," "99," "Cross My Heart," "Let Me Explain," and "The Key (To Your Door)." *—Bill Dahl*

The Real Folk Blues / 1965 / MCA/Chess ✦✦✦✦✦
With the exception of "Dissatisfied, " and cut in 1957, everything on this dozen-track comp dates from 1960-63 and holds "One Way Out," "Checkin' Up on My Baby," "Trust My Baby," and the catchy, country-tinged "Peach Tree," which drives along with a pronounced bounce. *—Bill Dahl*

One Way Out / 1968 / MCA/Chess ✦✦✦✦✦
Sly son-of-a-gun that he was, old Sonny Boy Williamson found a way to weld the twist to the blues with his rousing 1961 title track, with guitarists Robert Jr. Lockwood and Luther Tucker positively blazing in supple support. Fourteen more gems make this one a must: 1955's "Good Evening Everybody," "Work with Me" and "You Killing Me," all with Muddy Waters and Jimmy Rogers in support; the sturdy "Keep It to Yourself" from the next year, and a forceful "This Is My Apartment." *—Bill Dahl*

☆ **King Biscuit Time** / 1989 / Arhoolie ✦✦✦✦✦
Sonny Boy's early Trumpet sides, 1951. The original "Eyesight To The Blind", "Nine Below

Zero" and "Mighty Long Time" are Sonny Boy at his very best. Added bonuses include Williamson backing Elmore James on his original recording of "Dust My Broom" and a live KFFA broadcast from 1965. *—Cub Koda*

☆ **The Essential Sonny Boy Williamson** / Jun. 8, 1993 / MCA/Chess ✦✦✦✦✦
Two-disc compilation offering 45 of the wizened harmonica genius' best efforts for the Chess brothers, this is the best domestic Williamson package you'll find. Not everything you might want, but pretty close to it: "Don't Start Me to Talkin'," "Let Me Explain," "The Key (To Your Door)" (an alternate take), "Bring It on Home," "Help Me," "One Way Out," "Your Funeral and My Trial," and plenty more. With Robert Jr. Lockwood and Luther Tucker peeling off sizzling guitar riffs behind him, Williamson always had a trick or two up his sleeve until the end. *—Bill Dahl*

★ **His Best** / May 20, 1997 / MCA/Chess ✦✦✦✦✦
While some hardliners will point to his early 1950s Trumpet recordings as his most undiluted work, Sonny Boy's tenure at Chess Records was his longest and most successful and therefore deserves first look for the novice coming to this remarkable bluesman at ground level. This 20-track collection takes 17 tracks from the excellent two-disc *Essential Sonny Boy Williamson* collection and adds "Sad To Be Alone," "My Younger Days" and an alternate session-second version of "One Way Out" with Buddy Guy on guitar (yes, *this* is the version that the Allman Brothers used as the blueprint for their cover version) to the final mix. This is another entry into MCA's Chess 50th Anniversary Series and the digital transfers here are exemplary, making this an automatic audio upgrade for those who already have this material in their collection. Because his output for the label was of such a uniformly high quality, virtually everything Williamson put down on tape at the Chess studios could make a final cut on any best of package you'd want to put together on the man. So bemoaning the absence of any track here would be minor critical carping, especially in light of no less than five other Sonny Boy Chess packages still being in print at press time. But if you're only going to own *one* of them and your wallet tends to shy away from two-disc anthologies, this makes an excellent first purchase. *—Cub Koda*

Sonny Boy Williamson [I] (John Lee Williamson)

b. Mar. 30, 1914, Jackson, TN, **d.** Jun. 1, 1948, Chicago, IL
Vocals, Harmonica / Harmonica Blues, Acoustic Chicago Blues
Easily the most important harmonica player of the pre-war era, John Lee Williamson almost single-handedly made the humble mouth organ a worthy lead instrument for blues bands—leading the way for the amazing innovations of Little Walter and a platoon of others to follow. If not for his tragic murder in 1948 while on his way home from a Chicago gin mill, Williamson would doubtless have been right there alongside them, exploring new and exciting directions. Already a harp virtuoso in his teens, the first Sonny Boy (Rice Miller would adopt the same monicker down in the Delta) settled in Chicago in 1934. His extreme versatility and consistent ingenuity won him a Bluebird recording contract in 1937 and he commenced his sensational recording career with the seminal "Good Morning School Girl," covered countless times across the decades. Sonny Boy cut more than 120 sides in all for RCA from 1937 to 1947. His call-and-response style of alternating vocal passages with pungent harmonica blasts was a development of mammoth proportions that would be adopted across-the-board by virtually every blues harpist to follow in his wake. But Sonny Boy Williamson wouldn't live to reap any appreciable rewards from his inventions. He died at the zenith of his popularity (his romping "Shake That Boogie" was a national R&B hit in 1947 on Victor), from a violent bludgeoning about the head that occurred during a robbery on the South side. *—Bill Dahl*

Complete Recorded Works, Vol. 3 (1939-1941) / 1991 / Document ✦✦✦✦✦
For completists, specialists and academics, Document's *Complete Recorded Works, Vol. 3 (1939-1941)* is invaluable, offering an exhaustive overview of Sonny Boy Williamson's early recordings. For less dedicated listeners, the disc is a mixed blessing. There are some absolutely wonderful, classic performances on the collection, but the long running time, exacting chronological sequencing, poor fidelity (all cuts are transferred from original acetates and 78s), and number of performances are hard to digest. The serious blues listener will find all these factors to be positive, but enthusiasts and casual listeners will find that the collection is of marginal interest for those very reasons. *—Thom Owens*

Complete Recorded Works, Vol. 2 (1938-1939) / 1991 / Document ✦✦✦✦✦
For completists, specialists and academics, Document's *Complete Recorded Works, Vol. 2 (1938-1939)* is invaluable, offering an exhaustive overview of Sonny Boy Williamson's early recordings. For less dedicated listeners, the disc is a mixed blessing. There are some absolutely wonderful, classic performances on the collection, but the long running time, exacting chronological sequencing, poor fidelity (all cuts are transferred from original acetates and 78s), and number of performances are hard to digest. The serious blues listener will find all these factors to be positive, but enthusiasts and casual listeners will find that the collection is of marginal interest for those very reasons. *—Thom Owens*

Complete Recorded Works, Vol. 1 (1937-1938) / 1991 / Document ✦✦✦✦✦

★ **Sugar Mama** / 1995 / Indigo ✦✦✦✦✦
A well-researched 24-track compendium of the first Sonny Boy Williamson's massively influential Bluebird catalog that spans 1937-1942. Besides being such an innovator on the mouth organ, Williamson's songs themselves have stood the test of time strikingly—"Good Morning School Girl," "Blue Bird Blues," "Decoration Blues," "Sloppy Drunk Blues," and many more on the collection are recognized classics. *—Bill Dahl*

The Bluebird Recordings 1937-1938 / Jan. 28, 1997 / Bluebird/RCA ✦✦✦✦
This 24-track overview of the blues harp master's brief tenure with the Bluebird label includes "Good Morning School Girl," probably Williamson's best known work thanks to subsequent covers by Howlin' Wolf and the Grateful Dead. *—Jason Ankeny*

The Bluebird Recordings 1938 / Apr. 29, 1997 / Bluebird/RCA ✦✦✦✦
Picking up where *Bluebird Recordings 1937-1938* left off, *Bluebird Recordings 1938* features the remaining 18 tracks that Sonny Boy Williamson recorded for the label in '38. These are the recordings that established Williamson's career, and several of his classics, including "Deep Down in the Ground," as well as several duets with Speckled Red are included here. *—Thom Owens*

Chick Willis (Robert Willis)

b. Sep. 29, 1934, Cabiness, GA
Vocals, Guitar / Retro-Soul, Modern Electric Blues, Soul-Blues, R&B
Cousin to the late blues ballad singer Chuck Willis, Robert "Chick" Willis is primarily beloved for his ribald, dozens-based rocker "Stoop Down Baby." The guitarist cut his original version in 1972 for tiny La Val Records of Kalamazoo, MI, selling a ton of 45s for the jukebox market only (the tune's lyrics were way too raunchy for airplay).

The Atlanta-born Willis left the military in 1954, hiring on as valet and chauffeur to cousin Chuck, then riding high with his many R&B hits for OKeh Records. At that point, Chick's primary role on the show was as a singer (he made his own vinyl debut in 1956 with a single, "You're Mine," for Lee Rupe's Ebb Records after winning a talent contest at Atlanta's Magnolia Ballroom), but he picked up the guitar while on the road with his cousin (Chick cites Guitar Slim as his main man in that department).

When Chuck died of stomach problems in 1958, Willis soldiered on, pausing in Chicago to work as a sideman with slide guitar great Elmore James. A few obscure 45s ("Twistin' in the Hospital Ward," cut for Alto in 1962, sounds promising) preceded the advent of "Stoop Down Baby," which Willis has freshened up for countless sequels ever since (he developed the song by teasing passersby with his ribald rhymes while working in a carnival variety show).

Risqué material has remained a staple of Willis's output in recent years. He cut several albums for Ichiban, notably 1988's *Now!, Footprints in My Bed* in 1990, and *Back to the Blues* in 1991. *—Bill Dahl*

● **Stoop Down Baby . . . Let Your Daddy See** / 1972 / Collectables ✦✦✦✦✦
Here's the signifyin' original "Stoop Down Baby" in its long, unexpurgated version as issued on the tiny La Val label in 1972. "Mother Fuyer" travels the same salacious route, but Chick Willis has a serious side too—a pair of Guitar Slim covers spotlight Willis's stinging guitar and sturdy singing. *—Bill Dahl*

Jimmy Witherspoon (James Witherspoon)

b. Aug. 8, 1923, Gurdon, AR, **d.** Sep. 18, 1997, Los Angeles, CA
Vocals / Jazz Blues, Jump Blues, Urban Blues
One of the great blues singers of the post-World War II period, Jimmy Witherspoon was also versatile enough to fit comfortably into the jazz world. As a child he sang in a church choir, and made his debut recordings with Jay McShann for Philo and Mercury in 1945 and 1946. His own first recordings, using McShann's band, resulted in a *1 R&B hit in 1949 with &"Ain't Nobody's Business Parts 1 & 2"* on Supreme Records. Live performances of "No Rollin' Blues" and "Big Fine Girl" provided 'Spoon with two more hits in 1950.

The mid-'50s were a lean time, with his style of shouting blues temporarily out of fashion; singles were tried for Federal, Chess, Atco, Vee Jay, and others, with little success. Witherspoon's album *Live at the Monterey Jazz Festival* (HiFi Jazz) from 1959 lifted him back into the limelight. Partnerships with Ben Webster or Groove Holmes were recorded, and he toured Europe in 1961 with Buck Clayton, perfoming overseas many more times in the decades to follow; some memorable music resulted, but Witherspoon's best '60s album is *Evening Blues* (Prestige), which features T-Bone Walker on guitar and Clifford Scott on saxophone. Despite contracting throat cancer in the early '80s, Witherspoon remained active, a popular attraction until his death in 1997. *—Bob Porter & Scott Yanow*

Ain't Nobody's Business / May 9, 1949-1950 / Jazz Hour ✦✦✦✦✦

Feelin' the Spirit / 1959 / Legacy ✦✦✦

Singin' the Blues / 1959 / Blue Note ✦✦✦✦✦
Jimmy Witherspoon is heard in superior form throughout the two Pacific Jazz sessions included on this 1998 CD reissue. With fine backup and short solos from either Harry "Sweets" Edison (in top form) or Gerald Wilson on trumpet, both Teddy Edwards and Jimmy Allen on tenors, Henry McDode or Hampton Hawes on piano, rhythm guitarist Herman Mitchell, bassist Jimmy Hamilton and drummer Jimmy Miller, Spoon digs into such numbers as "When I've Been Drinkin'," "Then the Lights Go Out," "There's Good Rockin' Tonight" and a remake of his big hit "'Tain't Nobody's Business." The closing "Midnight Blues" is an instrumental, giving the band a chance to stretch out a bit. Recommended. *—Scott Yanow*

☆ **The 'Spoon Concerts** / Oct. 2, 1959–Dec. 2, 1959 / Fantasy ✦✦✦✦✦
This single-CD (which reissues all of the music from an earlier two-LP set) includes the highpoint of singer Jimmy Witherspoon's career. On October 2, 1959 he appeared at the Monterey Jazz Festival and created such a sensation that it caused his career to go through a renaissance. Heard at the peak of his powers, Witherspoon holds his own with a mighty group of veterans (trumpeter Roy Eldridge, both Ben Webster and Coleman Hawkins on tenors, clarinetist Woody Herman, pianist Earl Hines, bassist Vernon Alley and drummer Mel Lewis). Although the five-song set only lasted 25 minutes, Witherspoon's performance was the hit of the festival. The other half of this CD features Witherspoon romping through ten mostly-traditional blues songs two months later with Webster, baritonist Gerry Mulligan, pianist Jimmy Rowles, bassist Leroy Vinnegar and drummer Mel Lewis; the performance is equally exciting. Highly recommended, this CD is the one truly essential Jimmy Witherspoon release. *—Scott Yanow*

Evenin' Blues / Aug. 15, 1963 / Prestige/Original Blues Classics ✦✦✦✦
A good, relaxed (but not laid-back) session, and one of his bluesier ones, with organ, Clifford Scott (who played on Bill Doggett's "Honky Tonk") on sax, and T-Bone Walker on guitar. Nothing too adventurous about the song selection, including well-traveled items like "Good Rockin' Tonight" and "Kansas City," but Witherspoon sings them with ingratiating soul, reaching his peaks on his cover of "Don't Let Go" (perhaps better than the hit version by Roy

Hamilton) and the late-night ambience of the title track. The CD reissue adds previously unissued alternate takes of four of the songs. *—Richie Unterberger*

Jimmy Witherspoon with Panama Francis & the Savoy Sultans Sings The Blues / May 25, 1980 / Muse ✦✦✦✦✦

Rockin' L.A. / Oct. 24, 1988-Oct. 25, 1988 / Fantasy ✦✦✦✦

☆ **Blowin' in from Kansas City** / 1993 / Flair ✦✦✦✦✦
These 20 tunes pair the great Mr. Witherspoon with the finest jazz, jump, and blues talent around. Jay McShann, Maxwell Davis, Tiny Webb, and Chuck Norris are only a few of the first-rate session-men and arrangers who grace the tracks of this essential CD. A special mention must be made of tenor sax legend Ben Webster, whose solo on "I'm Going Around in Circles" is simply magnificent. This is quintessential Kansas City blues. Of all the shouters, Witherspoon is perhaps the greatest singer. *—Larry Hoffman*

Jay's Blues / 1996 / Charly ✦✦✦✦✦
Jays Blues is a fine collection of early-'50s jump blues sides that Jimmy Witherspoon cut for Federal Records. This 23-track collection offers a good retrospective of one of Witherspoon's most neglected—and admittedly, uneven—periods. *—Thom Owens*

'Spoon & Groove / Apr. 1996 / Rykodisc/Tradition ✦✦✦
This was originally released as *Groovin' & Spoonin'* on Olympic (7107). It's a decent if unremarkable set of blues-jazz, heavier on the blues, with organist Groove Holmes being Witherspoon's most important sideman on this date (which also features tenor saxophonist Teddy Edwards). Several of the numbers are shopworn standards like "Take This Hammer," "Key to the Highway," "Please Send Me Someone to Love," and "Since I Fell for You," though everything's performed with taste. If you're looking for Witherspoon blues-jazz with an organ groove, the 1963 album *Evenin' Blues* (1963) is more highly recommended, though *'Spoon & Groove* has no serious flaws. *—Richie Unterberger*

● **Jazz Me Blues: The Best of Jimmy Witherspoon** / May 6, 1998 / Prestige ✦✦✦✦✦
Whether this is truly the "best" of Witherspoon is debatable—there's nothing predating 1956—however, it's a good 20-track sampling of 1956-66 material, favoring (but not limited to) his sessions for Prestige. Witherspoon puts his imprint on a lot of blues/R&B classics—"Good Rockin' Tonight," "Bad Bad Whiskey," "One Scotch, One Bourbon, One Beer," "C.C. Rider," "Money's Gettin' Cheaper, "T'Ain't Nobody's Bizness"—and while not everyone will find these to be his definitive versions, they *are* all good ones. The roster of jazz luminaries heard at one point or another over the course of the disc is staggering, including Coleman Hawkins, Woody Herman, Gerry Mulligan, T-Bone Walker, Kenny Burrell and Pepper Adams. Never do they overshadow the singer, and on the whole this is one of the better jazz/blues vocal collections available, displaying his skill in both small combos and big bands. *—Richie Unterberger*

Jimmy Yancey (James Edward Yancey)

b. 1894, Chicago, IL, **d.** Sep. 17, 1951, Chicago, IL
Piano / Boogie-Woogie, Piano Blues
One of the pioneers of boogie-woogie piano, Jimmy Yancey was generally more subtle than the more famous Albert Ammons, Pete Johnson and Meade Lux Lewis, falling as much into the blues genre as in jazz. Yancey, who could romp as well as anyone, made many of his most memorable recordings at slower tempoes. No matter what key he played in, Yancey ended every song in E flat, leading to some hilarious conclusions to some recordings. He worked in vaudeville as a singer and tap dancer starting at age six and in 1915 settled in Chicago as a pianist. But Yancey spent his last 26 years (from 1925 on) earning his living as a groundskeeper at Comiskey Park for the Chicago White Sox. He played part-time in local clubs and began recording in 1939, on a few occasions backing his wife, singer Mama Yancey. Jimmy Yancey never achieved the fame of his contemporaries but he remained a major influence on all practioners in the genre. *—Scott Yanow*

☆ **Complete Recorded Works, Vol. 1 (1939-1940)** / May 4, 1939-Oct. 25, 1939 / Document ✦✦✦✦✦
The first of three Document CDs that reissue all of pianist Jimmy Yancey's recordings (other than his final Atlantic session) is filled with classic performances. Yancey, a subtle boogie-woogie/blues pianist who was a major influence and inspiration on the better-known players of the 1930s, is featured on his first two solo sessions including "The Fives," "La Salle Street Breakdown," "South Side Stuff," "Yancey's Getaway," "Yancey Stomp" and "State Street Special." Highly recommended as are the two following volumes in this valuable Document series. *—Scott Yanow*

In the Beginning / May 4, 1939 / Solo Art ✦✦✦✦✦
This LP has 12 of the 17 selections that pianist Jimmy Yancey cut during his first recording session. All of the music (plus the missing titles) have been reissued in full on CD by Document but this album has the advantage of also having Rudi Blesh's extensive and informative liner notes. Yancey's subtle boogie-woogie style is heard in prime form on solo performances originally cut for Solo Art. *—Scott Yanow*

☆ **Complete Recorded Works, Vol. 2 (1940-1943)** / Feb. 23, 1940-Dec. 1943 / Document ✦✦✦✦✦
On the second of three CDs that trace virtually his entire recording career, pianist Jimmy Yancey is showcased on a variety of solo tracks. Two number from February 1940 are highlighted by the classic "Bear Trap Blues." There are a couple of numbers made for the tiny Art Center Jazz Gems label, a four-song (plus two alternate takes) definitive set cut for Bluebird (which includes "Death Letter Blues" and "Yancey's Bugle Call") and nine songs (five previously unissued) from 1943; on one version of "How Long Blues," Mama Yancey sings while Jimmy switches to the spooky sounding harmonium. This set also has Jimmy Yancey's only four recorded vocals, which are quite effective even though his voice is limited. All three volumes in this series are highly recommended for the subtle pianist, who made expert use of space and ended every tune in E flat. *—Scott Yanow*

★ **Complete Recorded Works, Vol. 3 (1939-1950)** / Dec. 1943-Dec. 23, 1950 / Document ✦✦✦✦✦
The third of three CDs tracing the recording career of the unique boogie-woogie pianist Jimmy Yancey, whose subtlety could often result in some dramatic music, completes his December 1943 session and also has his December 23, 1950 solo set; his final recordings from July 1951 are available on an Atlantic release. The 1943 titles, three of which were previously unreleased, include two with Mama Yancey vocals (on one Jimmy switches to harmonium) and is highlighted by "White Sox Stomp," "Yancey Special" and two versions of "Pallet on the Floor." After the six fine titles from 1950, this CD finishes off with the only four numbers that Jimmy's older brother, the more ragtime-oriented Alonzo Yancey, ever recorded. Although his style was different, on "Ecstatic Rag" Alonzo does sound a bit like Jimmy. All three of these Document CDs, plus the Atlantic set, are highly recommended and preferable to the piecemeal domestic Bluebird reissues. *—Scott Yanow*

Chicago Piano, Vol. 1 / Jul. 18, 1951 / Atlantic ✦✦✦✦
Jimmy Yancey was one of the pioneer boogie-woogie pianists, but unlike many of the other pacesetters, he had a gentle and thoughtful style that also crossed over into the blues. This Atlantic CD, a straight reissue of the 1972 LP, contains Yancey's final recordings, cut just eight weeks before his death from diabetes. The pianist is in fine form on these introspective and often emotional performances which, with the exception of Meade Lux Lewis's "Yancey Special" and the traditional "Make Me a Pallet on the Floor," are comprised entirely of Yancey's originals. His wife Mama Yancey takes five memorable vocals on this memorable set of classic blues. *—Scott Yanow*

Mighty Joe Young

b. Sep. 23, 1927, Shreveport, LA
Vocals, Guitar / Electric Chicago Blues
Although physical problems curtailed his guitar playing in later years, there was a time during the late '70s and early '80s when Mighty Joe Young was one of the leading blues guitarists on Chicago's budding North side blues circuit. He earned a reputation as a reliable guitarist on Chicago's West side with Joe Little & his Heart Breakers during the mid-'50s, later changing his onstage allegiance to harpist Billy Boy Arnold. After abortive attempts to inaugurate a solo career, Young hit his stride in 1961 with the sizzling "Why Baby"/"Empty Arms" for Bobby Robinson's Fire label. He gigged as Otis Rush's rhythm guitarist from 1960 to 1963 and cut a series of excellent Chicago blues 45s for a variety of firms: "I Want a Love," "Voo Doo Dust," and "Something's Wrong" for Webcor during the mid-'60s; "Something's Wrong" for Webcor in 1966; "Sweet Kisses" and "Henpecked" on Celtex and "Hard Times (Follow Me)" for USA (all 1967); and "Guitar Star" for Jacklyn in 1969. Delmark issued Young's solo album debut, *Blues with a Touch of Soul,* in 1971, but a pair of mid-'70s LPs for Ovation (1974's *Chicken Heads* and an eponymous set in 1976) showcased the guitarist's blues-soul synthesis far more effectively. *—Bill Dahl*

Chicken Heads / 1974 / Ovation ✦✦✦✦
One of Mighty Joe Young's best efforts (and one that's not out on CD), an up-to-the-minute effort that combines soul and blues most effectively. Predominantly original material that suits his booming vocals and stinging guitar well. Nice band, too: bassist Louis Satterfield, drummer Ira Gates, and keyboardist Floyd Morris were all veterans of the '60s soul session scene. *—Bill Dahl*

● **Mighty Joe Young** / 1976 / Ovation ✦✦✦✦✦
Another out-of-print collection that's the crown jewel in Young's album discography. Many of Young's finest originals—"Need a Friend," "Takes Money," "Take My Advice (She Likes the Blues and Barbecue)"—reside in their most memorable recorded forms on this worthwhile LP. *—Bill Dahl*

Mighty Man / May 5, 1997 / Blind Pig ✦✦✦✦
Young embarked on this album in early 1986, financing it himself, determined to finally complete a project his way. But surgery and the subsequent rehabilitation time needed to repair a pinched nerve in his neck (making him unable to play guitar) shelved the project for many years. Young continued writing and recording, however and with the help of musicians, friends, family and Blind Pig's Jerry Del Giudice, the project reached completion a decade later. Guitarist Will Crosby handles all the solo work here (Young plays on the three tracks that were completed before his accident), and the majority of tracks feature his son on rhythm guitar. With co-producer Willie Henderson and Gene "Daddy G" Barge doing the horn charts, Leo Davis on keyboards, and the rhythm section of veterans Bernard Reed and B.J. Jones, the resulting mixture is, in Young's words, "a different sound." Those familiar with his spate of 45s for Webcor, Atomic H, U.S.A., and Celtex from the mid-1960s will recognize the direct link these sides have to classic period Chicago-style soul-blues. Tracks like "Turning Point," "Got My Mind On My Woman," "Got a Hold On Me," and the ballad "Bring It On" are soul music deluxe with strong blues roots, and if his fiery guitar work has been silenced, the 70-year-old bluesman continues to look forward with this release. Billy Branch makes a guest appearance on "Wishy Washy Woman," perhaps the most straightahead thing on here. While comeback albums are usually imbued with nostalgia, this one is as present-time as you could ask for, and in this case, that's a very good thing. *—Cub Koda*

Various Artists

Ace Blues Masters, Vol. 2: 4th and Beale and Further South / Jun. 9, 1998 / West Side ✦✦✦✦✦

American Folk Blues Festival: 1962-1965 / Dec. 1995 / Evidence ✦✦✦✦✦
From 1962 until 1971, the American Folk Blues Festival was responsible for bringing dozens of the most celebrated American blues artists to audiences from England to Poland. For many of the musicians, these were the largest audiences they'd ever played to, and the first (and often only) decent money they ever made. This five-CD set captures the vital early years

of the festival more fully than any prior issues, with previously unreleased bonus tracks (some of which overlaps). The 1962 volume was recorded live in Hamburg, and has no extra tracks, but the material is so vital and robust that this volume, featuring Memphis Slim, John Lee Hooker, T-Bone Walker, Sonny Terry and Brownie McGhee, never needed it. The 1963 disc, recorded live in Bremen, opens with three previously unreleased live Memphis Slim cuts, and follows these with a previously unissued Muddy Waters solo acoustic guitar piece and three more never-issued numbers featuring Muddy backed by Dixon, Otis Spann, and Matt "Guitar" Murphy. The three Sonny Boy Williamson bonus tracks were very late in the day and constitute some of the very last songs left behind by the increasingly ailing harp legend. The 1964 volume is a little less enhanced, with two songs by Willie Dixon and one song each by Sonny Boy Williamson, Sleepy John Estes and Hammie Nixon, and Sugar Pie DeSanto. The 1965 volume was always the odd one in this series; as a studio recording rather than a concert document, it lacks the vibrancy of the earlier volumes, but its eight bonus tracks do include some interesting moments by Buddy Guy, Big Mama Thornton, John Lee Hooker, and Big Walter Horton. The sound quality is good, but given the time that's passed, a full set of notes might have been nice. *—Bruce Eder*

The Atlantic Blues Box / 1986 / Atlantic ✦✦✦✦✦
At the time of its release, this 83-song collection was one of the bolder efforts by a major label at doing a proper survey of major blues categories. The material ranges from old-style big-band jump blues to the leaner, louder guitar sounds of the '60s and '70s, and isn't limited to artists who cut for Atlantic—the producers had to license in a certain amount, especially where Chicago blues was concerned .

Overall, they've done a good job as far as the sheer variety of performers, but trying to summarize any of these areas—blues vocalists, Chicago blues, guitar blues, or piano blues—with only 20 tracks on a single CD each is an exercise in futility. It is a place to start if one has the money, however, showing some of the strong points of a lot of key artists, and the sound was also good for its time. This is also a good chance for the neophyte to hear tracks by certain performers—like Jay McShann and Meade Lux Lewis—who aren't otherwise represented on easy-to-find major label releases.

However, there are other releases on the market now (especially Rhino's blues retrospective series) that can make the same claims and are more thorough and ambitious in scope. Additionally, anyone with a little knowledge and the $60 or so that this box can cost might better spend it on some of the more recent compilations devoted to the top artists on this box's roster, like Muddy Waters or Howlin' Wolf. Those, plus some of the other Chess reissues from MCA, will tell one a lot more about Chicago blues than the one or two tracks by each that show up in this set. *—Bruce Eder*

The Best of Excello Records / 1995 / Excello ✦✦✦✦✦
Although several overviews of the Excello label exist (including Rhino's two-volume set), this single-disc thumbnail collection may be the most digestible and therefore the best of the bunch. With a generous 30 tracks on a single disc to recommend it for openers, this collection tries to hit virtually all popular strains that the label dabbled in, from big city blues to doo wop to rockabilly to rhythm & blues to its best known swamp blues offerings. With hits aboard like Slim Harpo's "Raining in My Heart" and "Baby, Scratch My Back," the Gladiolas' original version of "Little Darlin'," Lillian Offitt's "Miss You So," the Marigolds' "Rollin' Stone," and Guitar Gable's "Congo Mombo," this collection delves far further into collectors' favorites, including "Hey! Baby" by rockabilly Al Ferrier, "Wild Cherry" by Leroy Washington, "Now That She's Gone" by the King Crooners, and the original version of "This Should Go on Forever" by Guitar Gable. The blues quotient inherent in the label's output is also well represented with the inclusion of "Rooster Blues" by Lightnin' Slim, "Baby Let's Play House" by Arthur Gunter, "My Next Door Neighbor" by Jerry McCain, "My Home Is a Prison" by Lonesome Sundown, and "I Hear You Knockin'" by Lazy Lester. All in all, a collection that's hard to beat, especially if your budget doesn't extend to multi-disc retrospectives. *—Cub Koda*

Blow'n The Blues: Best of the Great Harp Players / Jan. 25, 2000 / Vanguard ✦✦✦✦
Subtitled "best of the great harp players," this pulls tracks from various Vanguard releases from the '60s. Kicking off with five tracks from Junior Wells and five more from James Cotton, the set moves to pick up performances of Big Walter Horton behind Johnny Shines and a duet with a very young Charlie Musselwhite. Musselwhite has four tracks as solo artist, followed by two from the Siegel-Schwall Band. But the true highlight is a live at the 1965 Newport Folk Festival recording of the original Paul Butterfield Blues Band. With Mike Bloomfield on slide guitar, Butterfield tears into a version of Little Walter's "Blues With a Feeling" that would challenge his studio recording of the tune until Sam Lay inadvertently short circuits the tune a chorus too early, leaving Butterfield and the band scrambling for the ending—a great moment. A classic compilation, especially if you don't already have these tracks on other sets. *—Cub Koda*

Blue Flames: Sun Blues Collection / 1990 / Rhino ✦✦✦✦✦
If you are curious how the blues helped shape rock & roll, then get this collection of Sun Records' Memphis blues recordings. Stars of Sam Phillips' label and early rock icons Elvis, Jerry Lee Lewis, and Carl Perkins all sighted the influence of many of the performers here, and Elvis even covered one of the songs included on this disc ("Mystery Train" by Little Junior's Blue Flames). A more oblique tie-in to "The King" comes from Rufus Thomas' "Bear Cat," the answer song to Big Mama Thornton's original version of "Hound Dog." Other high-profile cuts include Jackie Brenston's "Rocket 88" (considered by many to be the first rock & roll song) and Roscoe Gordon's "I Found a New Love," as well as numbers by one-time Memphis DJ B.B. King ("B.B. Blues") and one-time Memphis resident Howlin' Wolf ("My Baby Walked Off"). Along the lines of Wolf's electric, Chicago blues sound, there's also James Cotton's "Cotton Crop Blues," Joe Hill Louis' "When I Am Gone (Treat Me Mean and Evil)," and Pat Hare's apparently true-to-life number& "I'm Gonna Murder My Baby." And with the inclusion of Doctor Ross' "Terra Mae" and Sleepy John Estes' "Runnin' Around," country-blues also gets its due. The set is rounded out by fine instrumentals from Jimmy & Walter and Johnny London (aka Alto Wizard) and with an excellent gospel number by the Southern Jubilee Singers. This is an exceptional collection, one that is essential listening for fans of early rock & roll and the blues. *—Stephen Cook*

Blues Hangover / 1995 / Excello ✦✦✦✦
This two disc, 43 track collection collects up a treasure trove of rare and unissued performances from the vaults of Excello Records. All but one of the 17 tracks collected on the first disc were produced by Jay Miller in his Crowley, Louisiana studio, home of Excello's unmistakable 'swamp blues' sound. The first 10 tracks are by Jimmy Anderson, who impersonates the vocal and harmonica style of Jimmy Reed so pervasively, it's downright eerie. Three tracks from Whispering Smith, a stray Lightnin' Slim cut and both sides of the mysterious Blue Charlie single are aboard, as well as rare singles from the equally mysterious Ole Sonny Boy, Little Al (Gunter) and Little Sonny. But the true find here are the first time release of 15 tracks from a 1966 audition tape by one Early Drane. For all intents and purposes, this appears to be the same 'Earl Draines' that recorded for the label as part of The Blues Rockers ("Calling All Cows") in the mid 50s. But these remarkable tapes are the man alone in his living room, singing and playing a quirky collection of original material, blues and gospel covers that careen from brilliant to downright loony. Add to this lineup four tracks by Detroit bluesman Baby Boy Warren (featuring Sonny Boy Williamson on harmonica) and two early 60s stereo swingers by the little known James Stewart and you've got an Excello rarities packages that's pretty hard to beat. *—AMG*

☆ **Blues Masters, Vol. 11: Classic Blues Women** / 1993 / Rhino ✦✦✦✦✦

★ **Blues Masters, Vol. 14: More Jump Blues** / 1993 / Rhino ✦✦✦✦✦

☆ **Blues Masters, Vol. 18: More Slide Guitar Classics** / Jul. 14, 1998 / Rhino ✦✦✦✦✦

★ **Blues Masters, Vol. 4: Harmonica Classics** / 1992 / Rhino ✦✦✦✦✦

☆ **Blues Masters, Vol. 5: Jump Blues Classics** / 1992 / Rhino ✦✦✦✦✦

★ **Blues Masters, Vol. 6: Blues Originals** / 1993 / Rhino ✦✦✦✦✦

The Bluesville Years, Vol. 1: Big Blues Honks and Wails / 1995 / Prestige ✦✦✦✦

The Bluesville Years, Vol. 2: Feelin' Down on the South Side / 1995 / Prestige ✦✦✦✦

☆ **Chess Blues, Vol. 1: 1947-1952** / 1992 / Chess ✦✦✦✦✦

Chess Blues Classics: 1947 to 1956 / 1997 / Chess ✦✦✦✦✦

Chess Blues Classics: 1957 to 1967 / 1997 / Chess ✦✦✦✦✦

The Chess Story: 1947-1975 / Feb. 2000 / MCA International ✦✦✦✦✦
First the good news, which is really good: the sound on this 340-song set is about as good as one ever fantasized it could be, and that means it runs circles around any prior reissues; from the earliest Aristocrat sides right up through Muddy Waters' "Going Down to Main Street," it doesn't get any better than this set. The clarity pays a lot of bonuses, beginning with the impression that it gives of various artists' instrumental prowess. In sharp contrast to the past efforts in this direction by MCA, however, the producers of this set have not emasculated the sound in the course of cleaning it up. When the rock & roll era dawns at Chess as depicted on disc five, the sound is nice and dirty, just really sharp. The contents of the set are largely "limited"—if that's the word for any 340-song collection—to Chess' blues, R&B, rock & roll, and soul output, although Ramsey Lewis gets a nod, as does comedian Pigmeat Markham. What's more, the care lavished on the songs is virtually universal—there was time spent getting all of it right. One wishes that the same could be said for one of the featured bonuses on this set, the CD-ROM that comprises the 15th disc. First, there are the skimpy film clips, misspellings ("Arether Franklin") and incorrect dates. There also would have been enough room to put a complete Chess discography on the CD-ROM, rather than just the MCA reissues of Chess' material. The CDs themselves are conveniently assembled in three fold-out volumes in a slipcase, but identifying individual tracks and artists means constantly referring back to the booklets glued into those volumes; additionally, it would've been nice to have had a sessionography on the songs, or at least the release dates, or even release years. *—Bruce Eder*

★ **Chicago: The Blues Today!** / Aug. 24, 1999 / Vanguard ✦✦✦✦✦
Vanguard's 1999 release of *Chicago: The Blues Today!* combines the three volumes of the legendary series, which were originally all available separately, into one stand-alone triple-disc set. Apart from the cardboard gatefold packaging and some new liner notes from Ed Ward, there isn't much here to interest collectors, but anyone who has yet to pick up these landmark albums—or who have yet to replace their vinyl copies—should consider this set, since it offers all the classic music at a reasonable price. The only drawback is the packaging, which forces the discs into cardboard sleeves, but that's a small price to pay for music this good. *—Stephen Thomas Erlewine*

The Copulatin' Blues Compact Disc / Apr. 29, 1929-Feb. 5, 1940 / Stash ✦✦✦

☆ **Duke-Peacock's Greatest Hits** / 1992 / MCA ✦✦✦✦✦
Don Robey, something of an infamous figure even in the rough-and-tumble world of 1950s R&B labels, owned one of the first successful black-owned labels in the country, and his output was rich and varied. *Duke-Peacock's Greatest Hits* offers a revealing overview of his operation, beginning with major hits by two of the company's humongous female belters, Big Mama Thornton's "Hound Dog" and Marie Adams' "I'm Gonna Play the Honky Tonks." Johnny Ace, Bobby Bland, and Junior Parker are represented by a few of their biggest hits, but it's the relatively unknown "Pack Fair and Square" by San Antonio pianist Big Walter Price that wields a knockout punch. Vocal groups aren't forgotten, with sides by Norman Fox and the Rob Roys and the El Torros, and a foray into rockabilly is recalled by the Original Casuals' "So Tough." *—Bill Dahl*

Excello Story, Vol. 1: 1952-1955 / Feb. 9, 1999 / Hip-O ✦✦✦✦
Twenty sides from the earliest years of Excello, the Nashville-based label best known for Southern-style blues and R&B, though it also recorded some country and gospel. All of these styles are present on this compilation, which may make it an uneven listen for those whose interests don't encompass each of the genres. The quality, however, is good, including a number of rarities that don't make it onto many anthologies. Arthur Gunter's original version of

"Baby Let's Play House," an R&B hit before it was covered by Elvis Presley the following year, is the most famous cut by far; the only other one to be a big hit was Kid King's Combo's "Banana Split," a New Orleans-styled instrumental that made the R&B Top Ten in 1953. A number of the other blues/R&B crossovers here are delights, including the Charlie Dowell Orchestra's jump blues "Wail Daddy"; Del Thorne's jiving "Down South in Birmingham," which sounds familiar enough to be a hit, although it wasn't; the Blues Rockers' "Calling All Cows," which sounds like a bluesier variation of the famous New Orleans tune "Iko Iko"; and the Leap Frogs' "Dirty Britches," with Arthur Gunter on guitar, which like Gunter's "Baby Let's Play House" sounds pretty close to rock & roll. Beyond the blues/R&B realm, there's updated jugband-style blues from the Dixie Doodlers; pretty hot honky-tonk by Rat Batts on "Stealin' Sugar" and early uptempo doo wop on the Peacheroos' "Be Bop Baby." *—Richie Unterberger*

Excello Story, Vol. 2: 1955-1957 / Feb. 9, 1999 / Hip-O ✦✦✦✦
The end of the period covered on the second installment of this Excello retrospective saw the label start to record the Louisiana swamp blues artists for whom it is most famed: Slim Harpo, Lazy Lester, Lightnin' Slim, Lonesome Sundown. While each of those artists is represented here by a cut or two (including Harpo's classic "I'm a King Bee"), much of it's devoted to more urban mid-'50s blues/R&B crossover, most of it recorded in Nashville. A couple of these were big hits: the Marigolds' "Rollin' Stone" made the R&B Top Ten in 1955 (and was covered for a pop hit by the Fontane Sisters), while Louis Brooks made 2 R&B that same year with &"It's Love Baby (24 Hours a Day)" (covered with success by Ruth Brown). Jerry McCain does raw, early electric blues with "Courtin' in a Cadillac; " Guitar Gable does blues with a Mardi Gras rhythm on "Congo Mambo; " a young Johnny Copeland plays "chicken licking" guitar on Clarence Samuels' "Chicken Hearted Woman; " and there are a couple of lowdown blues by Little Al (Arthur Gunter's brother). There's also some rockabilly by Johnny Jano, whose "Havin' a Whole Lot of Fun" is attractively over-the-top, and Al Ferrier, whose "Hey! Baby" is a transparent derivation of "Baby Let's Play House." Like volume one of this fine series, it's a good collection of a variety of sounds on the cusp of becoming rock and roll, though by this point the line was sometimes being crossed into bona fide early rock. *—Richie Unterberger*

Excello Story, Vol. 3: 1957-1961 / Apr. 6, 1999 / Hip-O ✦✦✦✦
Excello was hitting its prime as a good R&B, blues and rock label in this era. This has swamp-blues by Slim Harpo (just one song, but that's okay as he's well-represented by single-artist anthologies), Lightnin' Slim, Lonesome Sundown and Lazy Lester, who's represented by the great "I Hear You Knockin'" and the original version of "I'm a Lover, Not a Fighter" (covered by the Kinks in the '60s). There's more than Louisiana blues, though. For doo wop, there's the Gladiolas' original version of "Little Darlin'" (covered for a big pop hit by the Diamonds), and the one-shot smash "Oh Julie" by the Crescendos. Carol Fran's "Emmitt Lee" is top-notch, early New Orleans soul that will find favor with any Irma Thomas fan, so close is the arrangement to the sound of Thomas' early records. The sound strays closer to straight rock & roll with Lattimore Brown's "Somebody's Gonna Miss Me" and two early sides by swamp pop legend Warren Storm. *—Richie Unterberger*

The Excello Story, Vol. 4: 1961-1975 / Apr. 6, 1999 / Hip-O ✦✦✦
Just from the large chronological span of the final volume of this series, it's obvious that Excello's momentum started to peter out in its later years. Still, over half of this is fine, rock-solid blues that saw the label keep the flame of raw & funky blues with a soul/R&B influence alive better than almost any other company did in the '60s. There are good cuts by Excello, swamp blues stalwarts Slim Harpo (his hits "Baby, Scratch My Back" and "Tip On In"), Lonesome Sundown, Lightnin' Slim and Silas Hogan, but also some decent tracks by less famed bluesmen like Tabby Thomas, Little Sonny and Charles Sheffield (whose "It's Your Voodoo Working" has a snaky modern New Orleans feel). The last 40 percent of the compilation is given over to more modern sounding soul from the '60s and the first half of the '70s, and this isn't nearly as enjoyable, the last few selections in particularly boasting a generic "sweet soul" feel. It's obvious Tiny Watkins is trying to emulate the feel of Percy Sledge's early material with "Soldier's Sad Story," one of the better soul songs here. *—Richie Unterberger*

☆ **The Great Bluesmen at Newport** / 1976 / Vanguard ✦✦✦✦✦
This two-LP, single-CD compilation offers up 21 songs recorded live between 1959 and 1965 at the ~Newport Folk Festival. This is a killer selection of cuts by rediscovered '30s blues legends, many rising to the occasion to perform in front of thousands of people at once. A lot of comebacks and late-in-life careers were sparked by the performances captured on this CD, which is essential listening for anyone who cares about the blues.

Robert Pete Williams, playing his first concert outside Louisiana gave a performance so powerful, energetic, and dexterous, that he built a new career while still a relatively young man at the age of 40. Everyone who has heard Son House's album on Columbia and wondered if they were missing something might better look to the performance on this CD. With Mance Lipscomb accompanying him, the legendary slide player provides a good look at what his playing and singing were like in his prime. Mississippi John Hurt, who made some great records during this era, was at his best working in front of an audience, and had done so in Mississippi for decades. He gives a devastatingly nimble performance on this concert disc, both in his singing and playing. Similarly, Skip James launched a whole new career for himself with his performance on "Hard Time Killing Floor Blues" and "Illinois Blues." Willie Doss appears to have gotten not too much further than his *Newport performances, fine though they were, but $the Reverend Gary Davis* and Mississippi Fred McDowell both reignited their commercial careers with the work heard here. Rounding out the set are contributions from Sonny Terry & Brownie McGhee, John Lee Hooker, and Lightnin' Hopkins, working musicians for decades up to that time, who were simply playing very big outdoor gigs. *—Bruce Eder*

☆ **Harp Blues** / Feb. 26, 1999 / Ace ✦✦✦✦✦
This 25-track collection brings together some of the most inspiring blues harp performances on record. With the exception of John Lee "Sonny Boy" Williamson's "Bring Me Another Half a Pint" (what's better known as Jimmy Rogers' "Sloppy Drunk" and originally penned even earlier by Lucille Bogan) from 1948, everything on here was recorded in the '50s to the late '60s at the height of the electric blues boom. Representative and sometimes definitive performances from Big Walter Horton ("Easy," "Need My Baby" and the solo on Jimmy Rogers' "Walkin' By Myself"), Little Walter ("Roller Coaster"), Jimmy Reed ("Found Love"), Snooky Pryor ("Boogie Twist"), Sonny Boy Williamson ("99"), Jerry McCain (the rare, alternate take of "Steady") and Little Junior Parker ("Sweet Home Chicago") pepper this set. But the rarities from Eddie Hope (the raucous "A Fool No More"), Little Willie Foster ("Little Girl"), Papa Lightfoot (an explosive transfer of "Wine, Women, Whiskey"), Howlin' Wolf ("Howlin' Wolf Boogie"), Sammy Myers ("Sleeping in the Ground") and Joe Hill Louis ("Western Union Man") are every bit as potent as the bigger names aboard. Great selections from Doctor Ross, Billy Boy Arnold, Frank Frost, James Cotton, Junior Wells, George Smith, Shy Guy Douglas and the mysterious Cousin Leroy complete the collection. *—Cub Koda*

I Can't Be Satisfied: Early American Women Blues Singers, Vol. 1: Country / Apr. 22, 1997 / Yazoo ✦✦✦✦✦

● **Juke Joint Jump: Boogie Woogie Celebration** / Nov. 2, 1931-Jul. 7, 1961 / Columbia/Legacy ✦✦✦✦✦
While some purists would like to compartmentalize boogie woogie into a nice, neat box as strictly a form of piano blues, this 18 track collection clearly demonstrates that the form lends itself to a wide variety of treatments. Tracks like "Baby Boogie Woogie" by country picker Curley Weaver, "Boogie Woogie" by Delta Cum. Detroit bluesman Calvin Frazier and jazz visionary Art Tatum's "Tatum Pole Boogie" do much to support that claim, as does the inclusion of tracks from Red Saunders, Adrian Rollini and Harry James. Much of the material reprised here comes from one of the very first Columbia 78 RPM 'albums, ' a collection of boogie woogie classics produced by John Hammond, the man who brought the music into national vogue in the late 30s by simply letting giants like Albert Ammons, Meade Lux Lewis, Pete Johnson and Big Joe Turner do their thing. As a musical flavor of the month, boogie woogie lasted long enough into the 40s to have it rhythms incorporated into Tin Pan Alley fodder, but its influence lasted much longer than that. And here's 18 perfect examples of its timeless appeal, minus the commercial affectations. *—Cub Koda*

Legends of the Blues, Vol. 1 / Feb. 1991 / Columbia/Legacy ✦✦✦✦✦

Living Country Blues: An Anthology / Sep. 28, 1999 / Evidence ✦✦✦✦✦
A three-disc set of recordings produced by music researcher Axel Kuestner and recording engineer Siegfried A. Christmann in 1980. This is one of the last of an exhaustive batch of field recordings made in the 20th century by Christmann. The music is pulled from 14 vinyl LPs issued originally on the L–R label in Germany, and features artists who often never recorded again after these sessions, along with better-known but still peripheral names like Son Thomas, Boogie Bill Webb, Cephas & Wiggins, Hammie Nixon, CeDell Davis, Eddie Cusic, and the late Lonnie Pitchford. The music is uniformly excellent throughout the 60 tracks presented, the sounds varying from acoustic to electric, almost always in a solo setting and literally brimming with raw energy. From broom scrapings to fife and one-string electric guitar playing to more conventional guitar work, there is a phenomenal cross section of styles and some wonderful listening in the four hours of music collected here. A solid recommendation. *—Cub Koda*

☆ **Mean Old World: The Blues from 1940 to 1994** / 1996 / Smithsonian Institution Press ✦✦✦✦✦
A four-CD, 80-song box set that, in line with similar Smithsonian productions, outlines the history of blues spanning over 50 years, with cuts by major performers who represent its stylistic evolution. The set is stuffed with classics by the likes of Muddy Waters, Louis Jordan, T-Bone Walker, Little Walter, Big Mama Thornton, Howlin' Wolf, Elmore James, B.B. King, and Buddy Guy, with plenty of slightly lesser-known artists like Lil' Son Jackson, Billy Branch, Big Maybelle, J.B. Lenoir, Doctor Clayton, and Junior Kimbrough. The selections are a tad conservative (if very good), and it's likely that serious blues fans will have a good share of the tracks in their collections already. The set also concentrates much more heavily on 1940-1970 material (which takes up about 75 percent of the contents) than blues from the 25 years from 1970 onward. If your interest falls somewhere between casual fan and dedicated collector, though, it's a good survey of major blues performers and genres, with an excellent historical overview and notes about each performer in the accompanying 92-page booklet. *—Richie Unterberger*

Mississippi Masters: Early American Blues Classics 1927-1935 / 1994 / Yazoo ✦✦✦✦✦

Motor City Blues / Nov. 10, 1998 / Total Energy ✦✦✦✦✦
When one thinks of Detroit, the kind of musical styles that immediately come to mind are the soulful sounds of Motown and primal hard rock like the Stooges, MC5, and Ted Nugent. While most blues artists are forever associated with the South, Detroit has always been a supporter of blues and roots music. On September 8, 1973, the ~Ann Arbor Blues & Jazz Festival took place at the ~Otis Spahn Memorial Field, and the 1998 release *Motor City Blues* compiles the day's highlights. Over 73 minutes in length, the disc is jam-packed with great performances, featuring many obscure artists that prove to be just as talented as the renowned blues giants (Muddy Waters, Albert King, etc.). Some of the artists stray from the standard blues format and incorporate funky rock sounds into their blues, such as Eddie Kirkland's hyper-jamfest "Mojo In Her Backbone" and Little Junior's "I Got My Eyes On You," while the rest of the featured performances are more straight-ahead blues. Other highlights include *"24 Years" ($Bobo Jenkins)*, "I Call It Love" (Eddie Burns), "Chicago Breakdown" (Dr. Ross), and "Please Mr. Foreman" (Joe L.), among many others. A truly great blues collection. *—Greg Prato*

My Rough & Rowdy Ways, Vol. 2 / Oct. 20, 1998 / Yazoo ✦✦✦
Twenty-three songs from the '30s about badmen and hellraisers, by artists ranging from legends like Uncle Dave Macon, Mississippi John Hurt, and Big Bill Broonzy, obscure music pioneers like George Reneau and groups like the Haywood County Ramblers. The mix of white, country and black, blues artists is one of the better in this series, the music meshing together to form a kind of audio panorama of story-songs dealing with life on the far side of law and order—"Otto Wood the Bandit" by the Carolina Buddies, aka Odel Smith (fiddle) and

Norman Woodlief (guitar), segues into Mississippi John Hurt's "Frankie," followed by Uncle Dave Macon's rip-roaring banjo workout "Railroadin' and Gambin'" (anyone seeking a track that defines Macon's "claw-hammer" style of banjo playing need look no further than this cut). Among the too little heard bluesmen featured here are Waylon "Sloppy" Henry ("Canned Heat Blues") and Joshua "Peg Leg" Howell ("Skin Game Blues"), who also plays on Henry's cut, and Robert Wilkins, whose "Old Jim Canan's" features a superb guitar duet between the singer and Little Son Joe, later the husband of Memphis Minnie. Country highlights include Georgia based fiddle wildman Earl Johnson ("Nobody's Business") and George Reneau's "Jesse James," which features singing by future star crooner Gene Austin. Yazoo has done a generally good job of remastering these cuts, so the sound on most of it (David Miller's "That Bad Man Stackolee" and Uncle Dave Macon's "Late Last Night When Willie Come Home" are the big exceptions) holds together at a decent volume without any excessive artificial processing or distracting noise. The only drawback is the booklet, which is extremely confusing, since it refers extensively to artists and material on Vol. 1 of this collection, a separate CD. *—Bruce Eder*

Raunchy Business: Hot Nuts & Lollypops / Aug. 1991 / Columbia/Legacy ✦✦✦✦

Roots 'N' Blues: The Retrospective 1925-1950 / Jun. 30, 1992 / Columbia/Legacy ✦✦✦✦✦

☆ **Roots of Robert Johnson** / 1990 / Yazoo ✦✦✦✦✦

The Slide Guitar: Bottles, Knives, & Steel, Vol. 1 / Feb. 1991 / Columbia/Legacy ✦✦✦✦✦

● **The Sound of the Delta** / Jun. 1966 / Testament ✦✦✦✦✦

☆ **Texas Music, Vol. 1: Postwar Blues Combos** / 1994 / Rhino ✦✦✦✦✦

Texas blues is harder to define and pigeonhole than, say, Chicago electric blues, or Mississippi Delta country blues. In general terms, the Texas blues of the immediate post-war era often featured hard-driving, jazzy guitar lines, a jump blues influence, occasional brass, and a generally lighter, sunnier attitude than its more famous Chicago cousin. This is a fine 18-song survey of Texas blues from the late '40s to the early '70s, including both giants (T-Bone Walker, Bobby Bland, Freddie King, Albert Collins) and names that are known only to blues collectors (Frankie Lee Sims, Goree Carter, Zuzu Bollin). Some of the selections, even by some of the more well-known names, are damned rare; there are mighty hard-to-find '50s singles by Collins, Gatemouth Brown, and Johnny Copeland (as well as one very well-known single, Ivory Joe Hunter's "Since I Met You Baby"). There are a good variety of styles here, encompassing both bluesy ballads and boogies; the thrilling instrumental string-benders by Clarence Green, Albert Collins, and T-Bone Walker may be the highlights. Whatever your preference, it's a fine survey/introduction to vintage Texas electric blues, and it's a good bet that even listeners with big blues collections won't have a lot of the rarities here. *—Richie Unterberger*

White Country Blues, 1926-1938 . . . / 1993 / Columbia/Legacy ✦✦✦✦

Gospel

Religion has existed for thousands of years, but gospel music is just a few decades old. The term was coined by blues pianist Thomas A. Dorsey in 1920 soon after he wrote "If You See My Savior," his first religious song. After Dorsey established a firm that published his "gospel" songs and those of others (the first such company), the name stuck.

Gospel music was born out of the blood, sweat, and tears of African slaves working on Southern plantations and in cotton fields. They attended segregated Protestant churches, where White ministers led them in worship. Over time, Blacks combined the Southern folk music, Protestant hymns, and European elements of the worship service with their African traditions and Negro spirituals (which were not religious songs but songs of vexation, e.g., "Nobody Knows the Trouble I've Seen"), and the distinct Black gospel sound was born In those early years, gospel was segregated along racial lines: Southern gospel became a catchword for White gospel when Black gospel was equally Southern in its styling. Mahalia Jackson was the primary influence of her era, although the Swan Silvertones, the Clara Ward Singers, the Five Blind Boys, and others made significant contributions to early gospel. In Southern gospel, the Speers reigned "king of the charts," winning contracts on major labels such as Columbia and RCA, where they recorded such standards as "I'm Building a Bridge" and "I'll Meet You in the Morning."

As the '50s approached, there was a greater amalgamation of gospel, folk, and blues styles, which together were the foundation of rock & roll. Elvis Presley, Jerry Lee Lewis, and Little Richard were just a few of the singers with strong gospel backgrounds to make the leap into the secular arena. Groups like the Soul Stirrers and the Pilgrim Travelers supplied secular music with Sam Cooke, Johnnie Taylor, Lou Rawls, and others.

In the '70s, social movements began to influence what the White gospel young adults were recording. Artists such as Larry Norman pioneered "Jesus Rock." When a contemporary Christian music (CCM) magazine writer asked him if his 1969 *Upon This Rock* album was the first Christian rock album, Norman was cautious. "I can't really tell you if it was the first Christian rock album or not," he said. "I had never heard any. I was a Baptist, and the only Christian songs I had ever heard were the hymns and Negro spirituals.... So when Elvis Presley came along in 1956, and all those other boys, I thought, 'That's nothing new.' They were just stealing Black church music... so I decided to steal it back."

A similar revolution was taking place among young Black musicians who had tired of the same old "church" beat. Edwin Hawkins has taken a lot of credit for sparking the contemporary Black gospel movement. Actually, Rance Allen was doing it better, and long before Hawkins. Toward the very late '70s, Andrae Crouch did the unthinkable: he began making music that not only pleased his Black constituency and a progressive White audience but also touched mainstream pop. Amy Grant would pick up on Crouch's theme and run with it.

During the '80s, gospel had its most lucrative decade to date. Many of the biggest hits were by women. Shirley Caesar and Tramaine Hawkins crisscrossed the traditional and contemporary Black audiences. Sandi Patti held down the inspirational arena while Amy Grant held the pop-rock youth market. Grant's success and subsequent influence in pop led to a lot of copycatting An area women did not get into was heavy metal, or heaven's metal, as it's called in CCM. Bands that grew up on Aerosmith, Led Zeppelin, Black Sabbath, and other premier hard rock outfits began to merge Christian lyrics with this type of music. Petra and Stryper are examples.

During the '90s, gospel and CCM began crossing over into the mainstream in a variety of ways. Not only did Amy Grant establish herself as a popular secular vocalist, but Christian acts were able to crossover into the pop charts without abandoning their inspirational roots. Partially, this is because *Billboard* began including Gospel albums on their album charts, which resulted in Michael W. Smith having a Top 20 hit. But it is also because the music opened itself up to contemporary production techniques—by the mid-'90s, CCM bands like the folk-rock Jars of Clay and the hip-hop DC Talk were getting secular play with their inspirational material, and Kirk Franklin & the Family consistently charted in the Top 20 on the R&B charts. The diversity of these successful CCM artists signals the depth and variety within contemporary gospel, as well as proving that gospel music is undergoing a renaissance during the '90s. —*Bil Carpenter*

Gospel Terms

BLACK GOSPEL—An art form that is essentially Black in tone. The term was coined around the popularity of Thomas Dorsey's "Precious Lord." Black gospel is usually traditional music, often choir-oriented. Mahalia Jackson, Clara Ward Singers, James Cleveland, etc.
CONTEMPORARY CHRISTIAN MUSIC—This style of gospel picked up where Jesus rock left off, incorporating more funky and harder music elements, often soft-rock. Amy Grant, Michael W. Smith, and BeBe & CeCe Winans are such performers.
HEAVEN'S METAL—"Heavy metal meets gospel lyrics" is how this style is best defined. Strong bass lines, electric/amplified guitar riffs, and steel drumming. Stryper, Bloodgood, and the latter-day Petra coterie exemplify this form.
INSPIRATIONAL—Not unlike middle-of-the-road (MOR) music in the pop sphere, easy-listening, or adult contemporary. Heavy on strings and grandiose orchestrations. Sandi Patti, Dallas Holm, and Dino fall into this category.
JESUS ROCK—A contemporary "White" music style popularized in the late '60s and early '70s, coinciding with the Jesus movement. Pioneers of the form brought rhythm & blues, rock 'n' roll, and folk elements into standard praise tunes. Larry Norman and Randy Stonehill were among the purveyors of the form.
QUARTET SINGING—Based on the old barbershop quartet styles, with gospel lyrics. Usually four-part harmony performed by traditional Black gospel or Southern gospel musicians. Usually performed by males.
SOUTHERN GOSPEL—A country music gospel art form with emphasis on steel and rhythm guitars as its foundation. Draws on bluegrass, blues, and hillbilly elements. Southern gospel groups tend to use four-part harmony with a high tenor and baritone. The Happy Goodmans, the Speers, and Gold City are examples.
SPIRITUAL— A Black gospel art form rising from the Negro spirituals and blues tradition. Characterized by wailing and guttural sounds. Inez Andrews and Shirley Caesar are examples.
STREET POETRY—Whether the term developed in Christian circles is uncertain; however, Christian rap musicians prefer this term to "rap." An urban, funk style of rap with, in this case, Christian lyrics. —Bil Carpenter

Artist Reviews

Adam Again

Group / Alternative CCM

Adam Again, an alternative rock act from Southern California, anticipated the synthesis of rock and funk to be later expressed by groups like the Red Hot Chili Peppers, Spin Doctors, etc. The band consists of Gene Eugene (lead vocals, guitar, keyboards), Riki Michele (backing vocals), Paul Valadez (bass), and John Knox (drums). Saxophonist Dan Michaels was a full-time member for the first album but has only sporadically appeared as a guest since then. Group leader Gene Eugene is also a talented producer in Christian alternative music. —*Thom Granger*

In a New World of Time / 1987 / Blue Collar ✦✦✦
The original Howard Finster cover let hipsters know something was worth checking out on this first effort. —*Thom Granger*

Ten Songs / 1988 / Broken ✦✦✦
The band's style begins to solidify here. Included is a killer cover of Bill Withers's "Ain't No Sunshine." —*Thom Granger*

● **Homeboys** / 1990 / Broken ✦✦✦✦✦
Urban rock music was met with urban concerns on this excellent collection, including a cover of Marvin Gaye's "Inner City Blues." —*Thom Granger*

Yolanda Adams

b. 1964

Vocals / Contemporary Gospel, Black Gospel, Inspirational

Another in the line of gospel artists putting the soul and fervor back in R&B music, Yolanda Adams was a school teacher in Houston during the mid-'80s and occasionally did modeling work. Her mother had studied music while at college, so Adams grew up listening to jazz and classical music as well as gospel artists such as James Cleveland and the Edwin Hawkins Singers and R&B vocalists like Stevie Wonder and Nancy Wilson.

Yolanda Adams' debut album, *Just as I Am* appeared in 1988 on Sounds of Gospel. Though she was initially criticized in the Christian community for embracing secular music and fashion to accompany her gospel-themed music, the growth of publicly popular gospel in the mid-'90s pushed her into the spotlight; Adams toured with Kirk Franklin & the Family, and her 1996 album *Yolanda Live in Washington* was nominated for a Grammy. *Songs from the Heart* followed in 1998, and a year later she returned with *Mountain High Valley Low* which topped her live album by winning a Grammy. In 2000 she ventured into new territory by issuing a Christmas album, A Yolanda Adams Christmas. *Experience* followed a year later. —*John Bush*

Yolanda Live in Washington / Jun. 1, 1996 / Verity ✦✦✦✦

● **The Best of Yolanda Adams** / Oct. 26, 1999 / Verity ✦✦✦✦
The Best of Yolanda Adams is an excellent survey of the singer's years at Verity, containing 15 songs she recorded during the '90s. Some listeners might spot some personal favorites missing, but the bulk of her greatest hits are here—including "You Know That I Know,"

"Through the Storm," "The Only Way," "Just a Prayer Away," "Let Us Worship Him," "Save the World," "Gotta Have Love," and "What About the Children?"—making it a fine retrospective and introduction. *—Stephen Thomas Erlewine*

Alabama Sacred Harp Singers

Group / Field Recordings, Spirituals, Traditional Gospel, Gospel Choir, Southern Gospel

A rural Alabama choir of "sacred harp" (or shape-note) singing, the Alabama Sacred Harp Singers recorded for Columbia during the late '20s and *the Library of Congress* in the early '40s. The sacred harp tradition, which had journeyed from Britain to the early American colonies and later spread to the southeastern United States, relied on a more stark, Bible-based form of gospel music than traditional black choirs. Led by Paine Denson, A. Marcus Cagle, and "Uncle Dock" Owen, the Alabama Sacred Harp Singers recorded several sides for Columbia in 1928 (two were later compiled on the 1952 folksong compendium *Anthology of American Folk Music*). In 1942, Alan Lomax and George Pullen Jackson recorded the group for *the Library of Congress*, a series of songs that were later reissued on Rounder as *Sacred Harp Singing*. Similar recordings can also be found on volumes nine and ten in the Rounder series known as *Southern Journey*. *—John Bush*

Sacred Harp Singing / Jan. 13, 1998 / Rounder ✦✦✦✦

More riches from the Alan Lomax archives—*Library of Congress: Alabama Sacred Harp Singers* assembles vintage recordings from 1942, spotlighting the tradition of "shape note" singing which originated in the British Isles before spreading to the most remote corners of the southeastern U.S. *—Jason Ankeny*

Rance Allen

b. Detroit, MI

Vocals, / Contemporary Gospel, Black Gospel, Urban

Gospel singer Rance Allen founded the Rance Allen Group in Detroit in the 1960s and has fronted the band with his soulful, soaring vocals ever since. The traditionally trained black gospel group was the first traditional gospel group to incorporate rock, jazz, and soul into their music. They were harbingers for the contemporary Christian music movement popularized in the late '70s by Andrae Crouch, Amy Grant, and the Winans. The Rance Allen Group scored a Top 30 R&B hit in 1979 with "I Belong to You," one of two Stax singles that year to make the charts. The group's recordings for Gospel Truth, Capitol, and Stax proved quite popular among gospel audiences, and had some success attracting soul fans as well. Rance Allen continued singing, recording, and performing with his group up into the next millennium, releasing *Miracle Worker* with the Rance Allen Group in spring 2000. *—Bil Carpenter and Ron Wynn*

Straight from the Heart / 1972 / Stax ✦✦✦

Gospel singer Rance Allen enjoyed some crossover soul success in the early '70s, recording on Stax's Gospel Truth label. His explosive, soaring voice was especially effective on upper-register notes and inspirational ballads. This was one of his biggest albums, especially the single "I Belong To You." *—Ron Wynn*

★ **Soulful Experience** / 1975 / Stax ✦✦✦✦✦

A couple of decades before such stylistic melding would became popular among gospel artists, Rance Allen and his brothers merged the dynamics of soulful rhythms, gospel lyrics, and Rance's testimonial lead vocals. This effort was produced by acclaimed Stax alumnus David Porter, who also co-wrote seven of the selections. The highlight from this album is the proverbial lyric and stirring rhythms of "Ain't No Need of Crying." Rance's versatile vocals sail up and down the register from squeals and cries to riffs and sighs without forsaking solid, cohesive vocals throughout the verses and chorus. The gospel gem peaked on the *Billboard* R&B charts at 61 after a nine weeks. On "Talk That Talk," Rance utilizes his vast vocal reportoire to personify a riveting guitar. The Michigan native slows his delivery on the introspective "Just Found Me." The Allen brothers are consistently excellent on every selection. *—Craig Lytle*

Ain't No Need of Crying / 1985 / Stax ✦✦✦✦✦

Rance Allen's brand of soul-tinged gospel was at its best on this release. The title track cracked the R&B charts, and Allen's soaring voice, coupled with the fine harmonies provided by his brothers Tom, Steve, and Esau, as well as assistance from cousins Judy, Linda, and Annie Mendez, resulted in some arresting songs. *—Ron Wynn*

Best of the Rance Allen Group / 1988 / Stax ✦✦✦✦✦

Infusing traditional gospel music with Memphis soul, Detroit-based singer Rance Allen helped pave the way for the secularized gospel sound of the '80s and '90s. After signing with Stax in 1969, Allen and his group proceeded to bring their hip brand of gospel to the masses by scoring several chart hits and opening concerts for the likes of Isaac Hayes. This hits package covers the group's successful run in the '70s, spotlighting Allen's incredibly flexible and powerful voice (one listens to cuts like "Ain't No Need of Crying" and "Gonna Make It Alright" and it's easy to figure out where Prince picked up his misty falsetto from). The selections include Allen's biggest Stax hit, "I Got to Be Myself," the spiritually reconfigured cover "Just My Imagination (Just My Salvation)," and modern gospel pioneer James Cleveland's "That Will Be Enough for Me." Allen contributes a handful of slick and spirited groovers, like "I Give My All To You" and "I Belong to You," and even goes in for a little disco on another original, "Smile" (considering Allen's devout nature, it's hard to tell if the more commercial elements in the music came from him or hit-minded producers). A bit of unintentional humor also finds its way into the set, with the raucous cut "Hot Line to Jesus." This spirited collection makes Allen's love of the music plain and offers a fine introduction to both his work and to the "new," yet (historically speaking) ancient mix of religious and secular black music. *—Stephen Cook*

Margaret Allison

b. Sep. 25, 1920, McCormick, SC

Vocals, Piano / Traditional Gospel, Black Gospel

The co-founder and lead vocalist of the legendary Angelic Gospel Singers, Margaret Allison was born and raised in Philadelphia, where she first surfaced as a member of a chorus named the Spiritual Echoes. Inspired by the events of a dream, she formed the Angelics in 1944 with her sister Josephine McDowell and fellow Echoes Ella Mae Norris and Lucille Shird; after playing to receptive audiences in the Philadelphia area, the group performed in Shird's hometown of to Asheville, NC, followed by an equally well-received appearance in Norris' native Greenville, SC. Emboldened by their success, the Angelics began touring more and more extensively, and in 1947 they were signed to Gotham Records; their debut single, "Touch Me Lord Jesus," remains a gospel classic. In the face of numerous line-up changes throughout the years which followed, Allison remained the heart and soul of the group, steering them through subsequent tenures on the Nashboro and Malaco labels; in 1994, the Angelics celebrated their golden anniversary. *—Jason Ankeny*

● **Out of the Depths** / 1987 / Malaco ✦✦✦✦✦

An album of traditional cuts featuring "It Could've Been the Other Way" and "Up Above My Head." *—Bil Carpenter*

He's My Ever Present Help / 1992 / Malaco ✦✦✦

An album of new traditional favorites, it features the title song and "I'll Go." *—Bil Carpenter*

The Big Question (Where Will You Spend Eternity?) / Nov. 11, 1997 / Malaco ✦✦✦✦

Margaret Allison and the Angelic Gospel Singers continue in the gentle, disarming tradition of their previous work on the fine *The Big Question (Where Will You Spend Eternity?)* *—Jason Ankeny*

Inez Andrews

b. Oct. 19, 1935

Vocals / Traditional Gospel, Contemporary Gospel, Black Gospel

Inez Andrews's powerful contralto voice has been among gospel's greatest since her days with The Caravans in the late '50s. Andrews's nickname, "Songbird," was taken by Don Robey when he formed a gospel subsidiary label of his Backbeat/Peacock operation. Andrews was among the first gospel artists he signed. She later recorded for Savoy and Spirit Feel. Her most recent release was *Raise up a Nation* with The Thompson Community Singers in 1991 for Word/Epic. *Headline News*, a collection of some of her finest solo work in the '70s, was released in 1999. *—Ron Wynn*

● **Lord Don't Move That Mountain** / 1972 / Jewel ✦✦✦✦✦

Dynamic vocals from this powerful ex-Caravan lead singer. *—Opal Louis Nations*

Raise up a Nation / 1991 / Word ✦✦✦

These traditional Black arrangements are backed with a choir. *—Bil Carpenter*

Vanessa Bell Armstrong

b. Oct. 2, 1953, Detroit, MI

Vocals / Contemporary Gospel, Urban

With a style reminiscent of Aretha Franklin, soulful Vanessa Bell Armstrong has been belting out R&B-flavored contemporary gospel since the '80s. A native of Detroit and mother of five, she got her start working with Dr. Mattie Moss Clark. She has since gone on to work in both gospel and secular music. She did the theme song for the television series *Amen*, where her links to Rev. Al Green (and ultimately to Rev. Claude Jeter) were evident. She's recorded Urban Contemporary ballads and lyrically neutral material for Jive, and done gospel for Muscle Shoals Sound Gospel and Onyx, subsidiaries of Malaco. Albums include the slickly produced *Something on the Inside* (1993) and *The Secret Is Out* (1995). Three years later, she released her first live album, *Desire of My Heart: Live;* a best-of collection appeared in 1999. *—Bil Carpenter and Ron Wynn*

Vanessa Bell Armstrong / 1987 / Jive/Novus ✦✦✦

This contemporary urban gospel has a traditional shouting style and vague lyrics for its gospel content. *—Bil Carpenter*

Greatest Hits / 1990 / Muscle Shoals ✦✦✦✦

Wonderful One / 1990 / Jive/Novus ✦✦✦

While the songs range from spectacular to disapponting, Vanessa Bell Armstrong's singing is uniformly excellent on this '90 collection of crossover gospel and light, urban contemporary pop and R&B. Armstrong's declarative, assertive delivery and triumphant manner make the good songs great and the one or two great ones unforgettable. *—Ron Wynn*

The Secret Is Out / 1995 / Verity ✦✦✦

On *The Secret Is Out*, Vanessa Bell Armstrong turns in one of her most straightforward gospel recordings, with all of the material being written and produced by John P. Kee, whose choir provides musical support. *—Stephen Thomas Erlewine*

Desire of My Heart: Live in Detroit / Apr. 28, 1998 / Verity ✦✦✦✦

● **The Best of Vanessa Bell Armstrong** / Jun. 29, 1999 / Verity ✦✦✦✦

Verity's *The Best of Vanessa Bell Armstrong* collects 14 highlights from the recordings she made for Zomba Records, after she left Benson/Onyx. Musically, these songs are very close to urban contemporary, which means this is hardly traditional gospel. That, of course, won't matter to Armstrong's fans, since they already know that she's one of the leading lights of contemporary gospel, and this collection shows why. At times, the material doesn't quite match the standards of her earlier records, but the collection is still a good portrait of Armstrong at the peak of her powers and popularity, featuring such CCM classics as "Pressing On," "You Bring Out the Best in Me," "You Can't Take My Faith Away," "Father I Stretch," "Good News Blues," and "The Secret Is Out." *—Stephen Thomas Erlewine*

Susan Ashton

Vocals / Adult Contemporary, CCM

Adult contemporary vocalist Susan Ashton's first single gained an audience with CCM radio listeners around America in 1991, and made her album *Wakened by the Wind* the biggest-selling debut in the history of the Sparrow label. Ashton reached number one in the Christian charts two more times that year, received a Dove award for New Artist of the Year and won a CCM readers and reporters poll for Best New Artist. Her second album, *Angels of Mercy* (1992), proved her staying potential: it spawned four CCM number one singles and was nominated for a Grammy in the Best Pop Gospel Album category. In 1993, Ashton released her self-titled third album, with two singles charting number one. She also branched out with *Down the Road* with Margaret Becker and Christine Dente. That album was voted the Favorite Inspirational Album and Favorite Vocal Event in the 1995 readers' polls. *—John Bush*

Wakened by the Wind / 1991 / Sparrow ✦✦✦

Angels of Mercy / 1992 / Sparrow ✦✦✦✦✦

Susan Ashton / Nov. 2, 1993 / Sparrow ✦✦✦

● **So Far, The Best of Susan Ashton, Vol. 1** / Aug. 29, 1995 / Sparrow ✦✦✦✦✦
So Far, The Best of Susan Ashton, Vol. 1 conveniently collects all of the highlights from the inspirational adult contemporary singer. *—Stephen Thomas Erlewine*

Closer / Apr. 20, 1999 / Capitol ✦✦✦✦

Audio Adrenaline

Group / Alternative CCM, CCM
With their fusion of rock, rap and funk, Audio Adrenaline emerged as one of the most popular CCM acts of the 1990s. The group was formed on the campus of Kentucky Christian College by lead vocalist Mark Stuart, guitarist Barry Blair, bassist Will McGinnis, keyboardist Bob Herdman and drummer Brian Hayes; originally named A-180, they recorded an independent single, "My God," which caught the attention of Forefront Records president Dan Brock, and soon after the label issued Audio Adrenaline's self-titled debut LP. *Don't Censor Me* followed in 1993, scoring hits with the singles "Big House" and "Can't Take God Away;" after 1995's *Live Bootleg*, the band resurfaced a year later with *Bloom*, which debuted in the Top 60 on the *Billboard* pop charts. In 1997, Audio Adrenaline—now consisting of Stuart, McGinnis, Herdman and drummer Ben Cissell—resurfaced with *Some Kind of Zombie; Underdog* followed two years later. *—Jason Ankeny*

Don't Censor Me / 1993 / ForeFront ✦✦✦

Audio Adrenaline / 1994 / ForeFront ✦✦✦

● **Bloom** / Feb. 20, 1996 / Forefront ✦✦✦✦✦

Some Kind of Zombie / Nov. 18, 1997 / ForeFront ✦✦✦✦
Some Kind of Zombie continues Audio Adrenaline's hot streak, offering another set of supercharged, funk-punk with religious overtones. Unlike last time, the group's Christian beliefs are underneath the surface, but that's not necessarily a bad thing—their beliefs are delivered forcefully through the heavy, muscular music. The group improves with each record, delivering tougher, catchier riffs and sharper performances, and *Some Kind of Zombie* is no exception to the rule. *—Stephen Thomas Erlewine*

Underdog / Sep. 14, 1999 / ForeFront ✦✦✦
With 1996's *Bloom*, Audio Adrenaline began to really come into its own, getting a handle on their funk/arena-rock hybrid. That hot streak continued through 1997's *Some Kind of Zombie* and its follow-up, 1999's *Underdog*. *Underdog* marks the first time the group itself has helped out with production chores, and the results are largely up to the standard of their previous two records. That's not to say it's perfect—the funk riffs still sometimes feel grafted onto the songs, which are melodic AOR at heart, and there are a few musically awkward moments here and there. But overall, the album will certainly appeal to fans, and the Christian messages are as strong as ever. *—Steve Huey*

Philip Bailey

b. May 8, 1951, Denver, CO
Vocals, Percussion / Contemporary Gospel, Quiet Storm, Black Gospel, Urban, Soul
Philip Bailey first gained fame as the mesmerizing lead falsetto of '70s supergroup Earth, Wind & Fire. The singer/percussionist's four-octave range set a high standard for upper-range pop vocalists. Bailey's shimmering falsetto blended perfectly with Maurice White's charismatic tenor to help the group build a reputation for exciting, live shows (complete with feats of magic) and innovative recordings. Six-time Grammy winners, Earth Wind and Fire had 46 charting R&B singles, 33 charting Pop singles including eight gold singles. The group also won four American Music Awards and earned more than 50 gold and platinum albums. In 1982, while continuing his work with EWF, Philip signed a solo deal with Columbia, releasing his first solo LP *Continuation* Then in October 1984, *Chinese Wall* was issued, an album Bailey co-produced with Phil Collins. The second single, "Easy Lover", a duet with Phil Collins, became a worldwide hit, earning Bailey his first gold solo record. After Bailey's 1986 album, *Inside Out*, he began making a name for himself in the gospel world, releasing four recordings on Word. Shortly after returning to the studio with Earth Wind & Fire to record the band's Grammy-nominated *Millennium*. Bailey collaborated with singer Brian McKnight and members of PM Dawn and Arrested Development to co-write and record another pop/R&B solo project *Philip Bailey* (1994). A single from the LP, "Here With Me" charted #66 R&B, early 1994 In 1998, his album "Life and Love" was released throughout Europe.

In 1999, Bailey took another stylistic turn and signed with Heads Up International released the enhanced CD, *Dreams*, a smooth jazz album that features a "who's who" of contemporary jazz artists, including Gerald Albright, Luis Conte, Everette Harp, Grover Washington, Jr. and Pat Metheny—*Ed Hogan*

Continuation / 1983 / Columbia ✦✦✦

Chinese Wall / 1985 / Columbia ✦✦✦✦
At the time Philip Bailey persuaded Phil Collins to produce his second solo album, *Chinese Wall*, Collins was among the hottest pop stars in the world. The advantage to that, of course, is the exposure it affords, and after the merely modest success of his debut solo album, *Continuation*, Bailey needed the reflected glory. On the other band, it's hard to shine yourself in such a glare, and although Bailey's name was on the gold-selling hit single "Easy Lover," a duet with Collins that helped the album take off, it's Collins' singing and drumming that one remembers. Elsewhere, tunes like "Photogenic Memory" and "Walking On The Chinese Wall" better represent Bailey's ability to handle a variety of material from ballads to techno dance tracks with his elastic falsetto. Still, *Chinese Wall* was a gold-selling standoff that made Bailey a solo hitmaker without really establishing him on his own. *—William Ruhlmann*

Inside Out / 1990 / Columbia ✦✦

● **The Best of Philip Bailey: A Gospel Collection** / 1991 / Word ✦✦✦✦✦
This is a compilation album culled from Philip Bailey's three gospel albums, *The Wonders Of His Love, Triumph*, and *Family Affair*. Bailey brings the same creamy pop production and warm falsetto singing to his inspirational work that he does to his solo albums and to Earth, Wind & Fire, although he is far gentler here (except when he's being religiously righteous on "Call To War"). Note that this is listed as the pick among his gospel albums, not his entire solo catalog. *—William Ruhlmann*

Philip Bailey / Mar. 29, 1994 / Zoo ✦✦✦

Willie Banks

db. Feb. 1, 1993, Raymond, MS
Group / Traditional Gospel, Black Gospel
Gospel legend Willie Banks was born in Raymond, MS, where he started singing at age five; a alumnus of acts ranging from the Jackson Southernaires to the Flying Clouds to the Trumpets of Joy, he formed his own group, the Southernaires, in 1968. Upon signing to the Peacock label, they debuted with the album *Heaven Must Be a Beautiful Place;* in 1972, however, Banks dissolved the group, forming the Messengers and signing on with the small Nashville label HSE; the group's albums, including *God's Goodness, For the Wrong I've Done, Mother Why* and *Still in Charge*, were mainstays of the *Billboard* gospel charts throughout the decade to follow. On July 6, 1981, tragedy struck when the Messengers' tour van plunged off a highway near Atlanta, plummeting nearly 50 feet; one member of the group was killed and Banks' body was thrown from the wreckage, where he lay near death for several days. After a long recovery period, he and the Messengers signed with Malaco in 1988, issuing *Look at the Blessings*. Banks died February 1, 1993, although the Messengers continued performing well after his passing. *—Jason Ankeny*

Look at the Blessings / 1986 / Malaco ✦✦✦
Willie Banks has maintained with the Messengers an awareness of the old gospel style, despite often incorporating lyrics with a more modern tinge. On *Look at the Blessings*, for example, such songs as "Can't Keep From Crying Sometimes" use an image very familiar in soul music, although Banks and company don't even suggest a pop tilt. Other songs, such as "He's Bringing Love to the Nation" and "A Prayer for the Children," could fit into a broad-minded urban or black station's playlist, due to their dual inspirational themes of religious salvation and social emancipation. Banks is a strong, distinctive vocalist; this doesn't compare unfavorably to many of his past gospel releases. *—Ron Wynn*

● **Heaven Must Be a Beautiful Place** / 1990 / MCA Special Products ✦✦✦✦✦

Willie Banks / Mar. 24, 1998 / Music Video Distributors ✦✦

The Barrett Sisters

Vocals / Traditional Gospel, Black Gospel
Delois, Billie, and Rodessa Barrett began singing in the Chicago-based Morning Star Baptist Church in the '40s as children. Under the direction of their aunt, Mattie Dacus, they were originally known as The Barrett and Hudson Singers before becoming The Barrett Sisters. Delois was recruited for The Roberta Martin Singers while a high school senior at Englewood High. After graduation, she joined Martin's group full time and remained a member for 18 years. Rodessa Barrett became a choral director of Galileo Baptist church and Billie Barrett became a church soloist after taking voice lessons at the American Music Conservatory. They formed The Barrett Sisters in 1962 and have remained together ever since. Their first LP was recorded for Savoy in 1963. They currently record for I Am Records in Chicago. *—Ron Wynn*

What Shall I Render Unto God / Dec. 1, 1995 / Sony Special Products ✦✦✦✦
Originally released in 1985, *What Shall I Render (Unto God)* captures the Barrett Sisters at the peak of their formidable powers, delivering electrifying renditions of "He Shall Feed His Flock" and "Waiting for the Lord's Return." *—Chuck Donkers*

● **What Will You Do with Your Life** / Savoy ✦✦✦✦✦
What Will You Do with Your Life is a fine collection of the Barrett Sisters' Savoy recordings that showcases the gospel group at their very best. *—Leo Stanley*

Helen Baylor

b. Tulsa, OK
Vocals / Contemporary Gospel, Urban
Gospel vocalist Helen Baylor began singing in Los Angeles-area clubs while still a child, and by her teens was regularly opening for superstars like Stevie Wonder, B.B. King, and Aretha Franklin. At 17, she won a role in the touring company of *Hair*, and later was a sought-after session vocalist; however, after years of substance abuse, Baylor got sober and left secular music behind, and after four years away from performing she joined her church choir, only becoming a soloist two years later. Her congregation then helped fund a four-song cassette which earned radio play and sold well at local gospel music retailers; she signed to the Word label soon after, and in 1990 issued her debut LP *Highly Recommended*. *Look a Little Closer* followed a year later, and after 1995's *The Live Experience* Baylor signed with Sony, releasing *Love Brought Me Back* in 1996. *—Jason Ankeny*

Highly Recommended / 1990 / Word ✦✦✦✦✦
Modern pop/soul with class, the title says it all. *—Bil Carpenter*

Look a Little Closer / 1991 / Word ✦✦✦
More Southern-R&B-infused than her debut, this set is highly recommended. *—Bil Carpenter*

• **Greatest Hits** / Feb. 16, 1999 / Word ✦✦✦✦

Margaret Becker

Vocals, Guitar / Christian Rock, CCM

Songwriter, electric guitarist, and vocalist Margaret Becker has had no less than fourteen superb number one radio hits, three distinguished Dove Awards, and been nominated for a Grammy four times during her extraordinary Christian rock career—and she's no where near done.

Born to German/Irish parents, Becker was raised in Long Island, New York. When she began performing, she did the coffeehouse circuit, playing where and when she could. In between she studied journalism, taught music, took opera lessons, did odds jobs, even working as a department store bill collector for years, just to pay the rent and keep food on the table.

In 1985, only weeks after moving to Nashville so she could devote all of her energy into her music, Becker was signed by the Sparrow Records label, but as a songwriter, not a singer. Within a year though, she had the recording contract that she had prayed about.

In 1986 Becker, with her husky voice and strong stage presence, began her climb up the stardom ladder when she combined her talents with those of Steve Camp on the album, *One on One*. She also toured with the Rick Cua band, supplying background vocals.

Becker finally saw the release of her own debut album in 1987, *Never for Nothing*. From that first album came her first hit single, "Fight for God." Her next album, *The Reckoning* brought her two more hits, "Light in the Darkness" and "Find Me." Some of her other hits singles are "The Hunger Stays," "You Remain Unchanged," "Clay & Water," and "All I Ever Wanted."

Becker followed *The Reckoning* with several other successful albums, including *Immigrant's Daughter, Simple House*, her best-of album *Steps of Faith, Grace*, and the Spanish language album *Fiel A Ti*. She took a three-year self-imposed sabbatical following the release of *Grace* in 1995. She began several new endeavors, including co-writing a children's series, writing a column for *Campus Life* magazine, and writing a book, *With New Eyes*. She released her next album in 1998, *Falling Forward*, and released another album, *What Kind of Love*, in 1999.

Over the years Becker has toured extensively, including Germany, South Africa, Ireland, Australia, Finland, the U.K., Holland, and all over the United States. She has also been nominated or won awards for New Artist of the Year, Contemporary Album of the Year, Female Vocalist of the Year, Inspirational Song of the Year, Best Pop Gospel Album, Song of the Year, Best Rock/Contemporary Gospel Album, and many others. *—Charlotte Dillon*

Never for Nothing / 1987 / Sparrow ✦✦✦

★ **Steps of Faith 1985-1992** / 1992 / Sparrow ✦✦✦✦✦
Becker's best, with a heavy emphasis on *Immigrant's Daughter* and *Simple House*, shows just what a talented pop stylist she is. The one new cut, "This Love," is essential Becker. *—Brian Mansfield*

Soul / May 18, 1993 / Sparrow ✦✦✦
Shows movement toward European pop/R&B, influenced by artist Annie Lennox and producer Charlie Peacock. *—Thom Granger*

The Belleville a Cappella Choir

Group / Field Recordings, Traditional Gospel, Black Gospel

The Belleville Choir is associated with the Church of God and Saints of Christ, which teaches that the African-American people are descended from the lost tribes of Israel, and incorporates aspects of Judaism into their faith. When recorded by folklorist Alan Lomax in 1960, the choir learned everything by ear, yet was adept at executing vocal arrangements with harmonic complexity that derived more from European musical tradition than much American black gospel. The choir remains active today, over a hundred years after the church was founded. *—Richie Unterberger*

Southern Journey, Vol. 11: Honor the Lamb / Feb. 10, 1998 / Rounder ✦✦✦✦✦
The rather odd title is the result of this album's inclusion in the *Southern Journey* reissue series of Alan Lomax recordings. It's far smoother in execution than the usual Lomax project, which is not to say that it can't be recommended to gospel listeners. The harmonies are rich and rhythmically sophisticated; check the effervescent interplay between the choir and soloist Caleb Garris on "What a Time." *—Richie Unterberger*

The Blackwood Brothers

f. 1934

Group / Traditional Gospel, Country Gospel, Southern Gospel

The Blackwood Brothers have been singing gospel for over 60 years, and from the 1950s to the '70s, they were one of the most popular gospel groups in the U.S. One of their biggest fans was a young Elvis Presley, who auditioned—and was turned down—for the group in 1953. The quartet was formed in 1934 by brothers Roy, Doyle and James Blackwood, along with Roy's 13-year-old son R.W. They sang at churches around their base of Ackerman, MS, during the mid-'30s. By 1937, however, they began working a radio show in Kosciusko, MS. In time they were popular enough to move to KWKH-Shreveport, LA, a regional superstation that broadcast over much of the South. The Blackwoods began recording in 1952, and the increased exposure led to national recognition and a spot on Arthur Godfrey's TV show in 1954. Less than a month later, however, R.W. Blackwood and Bill Lyles (who replaced Roy Blackwood in 1950) were killed in a plane crash. The Blackwoods immediately disbanded and vowed to never perform again. Fortunately they returned several years later. The Blackwoods entered the LP era during the mid-'50s and eventually recorded many albums for RCA and Skylite throughout the 1950s and '60s. They won the first of their eight Grammy Awards for Best Gospel Performance in 1966, and James Blackwood was inducted into the Gospel Music Hall of Fame in 1974. He is still known as "Mr. Gospel Singer of America." *—John Bush*

• **Gospel Classics Series** / Apr. 7, 1998 / RCA ✦✦✦✦✦
Gospel Classic Series is a budget-line series from RCA that was designed to showcase great gospel recordings from individual artists that have yet to appear on compact disc. The Blackwood Brothers were one of the most popular gospel groups of the '50s and '60s, but their recordings were out of print for years. Although it isn't a perfect collection, this budget-line collection is a good overview of their most popular recordings, featuring such songs as "The Old Rugged Cross Made the Difference," "Because He Lives," "Just a Closer Walk With Thee," "How Great Thou Art," "Precious Memories" and "Amazing Grace." It's a nice introduction to the group, even if it is a little brief. *—Stephen Thomas Erlewine*

Ray Boltz

Vocals / CCM

Ray Boltz was one of the most successful Contemporary Christian vocalists of the '90s, selling over a million copies of his first five records. Boltz released his first album, *Seasons Change*, in 1992. The album was an immediate success in CCM circles, and over the next five years he built his fanbase gradually through appearances on Christian radio and a series of well-received albums. *—Rodney Batdorf*

• **Thank You** / Aug. 30, 1994 / Word ✦✦✦✦✦

No Greater Sacrifice / Nov. 12, 1996 / Word/Epic ✦✦✦

Debby Boone

b. Sep. 22, 1956, Hackensack, NJ

Vocals / Inspirational, CCM, Country-Pop

The popular Christian music singer Debby Boone is best known for her 1977 hit "You Light Up My Life," which was number one for 10 weeks and earned Boone a Grammy Award for Best New Artist. The daughter of Pat Boone, she began touring with her three sisters and her father at 14. Her first solo venture was "You Light Up My Life," which earned her instant fame, but Boone found it difficult to repeat her pop success in the '80s. She turned to Christian and inspirational music, and won two more Grammy awards in the Christian and inspirational categories. Aside from a successful music and stage career, Debby Boone is also a children's author, writing *Hours for Little Ones* and *Tomorrow Is a Brand New Day* and producing the children's videos, *Bobby Boone's Hug-A-Long Songs, Vol. 1* and *Bobby Boone's Hug-A-Long Songs, Vol. 2*. She also branched out into acting, playing Rizzo in the Broadway production of *Grease* and portraying Clarissa Hope in the 1984 television movie, *Sins of the Past*. Debby Boone resides in Sherman Oaks, California with her husband and their four children, Gabrielle, Dustin, Jordan and Tessa. Her husband, Gabriel Ferrer, is the son of popular film stars Rosemary Clooney and Jose Ferrer. *—Kim Summers*

The Best of Debby Boone / 1986 / Curb ✦✦✦✦
Best of Debby Boone is a ten-track budget-priced collection that features some of her biggest hits, including "You Light Up My Life," "God Knows," "When You're Loved," "Perfect Fool," "Free to Be Lonely Again" and "Are You On the Road to Love." This isn't a bad budget-priced disc, especially since there aren't really any better Boone collections currently available. *—Stephen Thomas Erlewine*

• **Reflections** / 1988 / Benson ✦✦✦✦✦

Greatest Hymns / Feb. 1, 2000 / Curb ✦✦✦
When her pop career effectively fell by the wayside, Debby Boone turned her focus to something that had been near and dear to her heart for quite some time: gospel music. She launched a successful Christian music career in the mid-'80s, and *Greatest Hymns* collects the best traditional hymns she has recorded over the years. While it doesn't cover her more contemporary songs, *Greatest Hymns* is still a fine introduction to Boone's religious music. *—Steve Huey*

Prof. Alex Bradford

b. 1926, Bessemer, AL, **d.** Feb. 15, 1978, Newark, NJ

Vocals, Piano, Composer, Arranger / Traditional Gospel, Black Gospel

Professor Alex Bradford was among the truly pivotal figures of gospel's golden era; the author of more standards than any other gospel composer of his generation, his music was both reverently traditional and restlessly innovative, true to its spiritual roots but never out of step with the advances of contemporary pop and jazz. A master showman renowned for his theatrical flamboyance, he was not only a gifted singer and songwriter but also a noted pianist, arranger, and group and choral director; like Ray Charles, Little Richard and Sam Cooke—all of whom acknowledged Bradford as a key influence—he walked the tightrope between religious and secular music with rare skill, and through his later compositions for the great LaVern Baker pioneered the fusion of gospel and pop which later evolved into the classic soul sound. *—Jason Ankeny*

Too Close / 1953-1958 / Specialty ✦✦✦✦✦
Rev. Alex Bradford was an amazing singer, prolific composer, and outstanding pianist whose work in the '50s was extremely influential. His flamboyant, exuberant manner and slashing style were imitated by many secular singers and served as a blueprint for the emergence of a sound that would eventually be labeled "soul." This 29-song package includes his biggest hits, particularly the incredible "Too Close To Heaven," a remarkable three-minute piece that merges theatrics, lyrical metaphors, and fire-breathing vocals into a transcendent tour-de-force. There are also seven newly released numbers, including "Move Upstairs," a 1958 duet between Bradford and Bessie Griffin. *—Ron Wynn*

• **The Best of Alex Bradford** / 1982 / Specialty ✦✦✦✦✦
A comprehensive selection of his fiery, stomping cuts with the Bradford Specials all-male quintet on Specialty Records. *—Ron Wynn*

Rainbow in the Sky / 1992 / Specialty ✦✦✦✦✦
A broad range of formats and self-penned songs by one of gospel's greatest writers, producers, and soloists, some are issued for the first time here (ca. 1954-58). *—Opal Louis Nations*

Brooklyn All-Stars

f. 1950

Group / Traditional Gospel, Black Gospel

The Brooklyn All-Stars are an internationally recognized male gospel group who have been performing since 1950. Over their long, fruitful careers, they have won numerous awards and racked up two gold albums. Original members include the group's founder, Thomas J. Spann, Hardie Clifton, and Sam Thomas. They recorded several cuts for Peacock in 1959, including "Rest Awhile" and "Meet Me in Galilee." Their early years were difficult ones; with little money for touring, they often traveled to engagements stuffed into a single car, relying on parishioners' hospitality for food and lodging because they were not permitted inside restaurants and motels. Things improved over the '60s, and they established themselves as a fine traditional gospel act. Between 1971 and 1978, they were annually voted the number one gospel group in the U.S. Their biggest-selling hits are "When I Stood on the Banks of Jordan" and "He Touched Me and Made Me Whole," on Jewel, the label they have been with since 1971. During the '80s, the All-Stars embarked upon a series of world tours. *—Sandra Brennan*

Family Prayer / 1964 / Hob ✦✦✦✦✦
Tight harmonies, fine lead work from Hardie Clifton and Thomas Spann. *—Opal Louis Nations*

The Best of the Brooklyn Allstars / 1995 / Nashboro ✦✦✦✦✦
As the title suggests, truly the quartet's finest moments on Nashboro. *—Opal Louis Nations*

● **Our Greatest Hits** / Nashboro ✦✦✦✦✦
Powerful material drawn from a variety of '60s and '70s Nashboro albums, it's led principally by the soaring tenor of the underrated Hardie Clifton. *—Opal Louis Nations*

Archie Brownlee

d. Feb. 8, 1960, New Orleans, LA
Vocals / Traditional Gospel, Black Gospel
Archie Brownlee's amazing vocal flights and theatrics helped make The Original Five Blind Boys Of Mississippi one of the greatest quartets of all time. They were originally recorded by the Library of Congress in 1937 doing comic and game tunes. Brownlee became a star in the '40s and early '50s until he died of a heart attack in the late '50s. *—Ron Wynn*

● **You Done What the Doctor Couldn't Do** / 1989 / Gospel Jubilee ✦✦✦✦✦
Eighteen stunning hard gospel performances (recorded between 1948-59) by arguably the greatest practitioners of the art. Brownlee was master of controlled vocal pandemonium, his deft leaps from the decorous to the delirious prompting the faithful to "fall out" in ecstatic fits. His "Amazing Grace" becomes an extraordinary plea for deliverance, while The Blind Boys' vamp on the Lord's Prayer ("World Prayer") is a beautifully-tiered tour de force of prayer and song. Anyone wanting to experience the fervor of hard gospel at its intense yet artful best should hear this profoundly heartfelt and masterfully performed music. *—Mark Humphrey, Roundup Newsletter*

Rev. Milton Brunson

d. Apr. 1, 1997, Chicago, IL
Vocals / Traditional Gospel, Black Gospel
In 1948, the Reverend Milton Brunson organized a mass gospel choir at Chicago's McKinley High School; dubbed the Thompson Community Singers, the group—affectionately known as "the Tommies"—would emerge as the nation's oldest existing community choir, celebrating their golden anniversary with the release of 1998's hits collection *50 Blessed Years.* In the interim Brunson and his singers became one of the most honored gospel groups of their era, issuing eight gospel chart-topping LPs and winning a Grammy award in 1995. Their 50th anniversary was also celebrated with the opening of a post office named in Brunson's honor. *—Jason Ankeny*

Available to You / 1988 / Word ✦✦✦✦✦

Open Our Eyes / 1990 / Word ✦✦✦
This includes more of the same as *Available to You. —Bil Carpenter*

● **Greatest Hits** / Jul. 1996 / Word ✦✦✦✦✦
Milton Brunson's *Greatest Hits* collects all of his gospel choir's biggest hits and most popular songs—including "He Cares for You," "I'm Free," "Lord I Believe," and "Jesus Rose"—on one disc, making it a perfect introduction to one of the most successful and acclaimed gospel choirs of the '90s. *—Leo Stanley*

Sit at His Feet & Be Blessed / Mar. 9, 1999 / MCA ✦✦✦✦
Brunson was the head director and organizer of the Thompson Community Singers, a massive choir that spearheaded the modern gospel movement of the '70s. This 10-track compilation features a nice cross-section of their most influential work from 1965 to 1980. Highlights include "God Will Take Care of You," "I Love to Praise Him," "The Lord Is Blessing Me," "All That I Want," "Everything That You Need" and the title track. *—Cub Koda*

Burlap to Cashmere

Group / Alternative CCM, Adult Alternative Pop/Rock
The alternative CCM group Burlap to Cashmere was led by the Brooklyn-based vocal/guitar duo of cousins John Philippides and Steven Delopoulus. Discovered by manager Jamison Ernest while performing in a New Jersey coffeehouse, the duo soon assembled Burlap to Cashmere, recruiting guitarist Mike Ernest, bassist Roby Guarnera, keyboardist Josh Zandman, drummer Theodore Pagano and percussionist Scott Barksdale; drawing on a vast range of folk and world music influences, the group soon began appearing at New York venues including the Bottom Line, Irving Plaza and Tramps, also building a national cult following on the strength of their extensive tour schedule. After independently issuing a live record in 1997, the following year Burlap to Cashmere signed with A&M to release their major-label debut *Anybody Out There? —Jason Ankeny*

● **Live at the Bitter End** / Jan. 27, 1998 / A&M ✦✦✦✦
This is the EP that started it all, showcasing Burlap to Cashmere at their very best—live. Burlap to Cashmere is one of the most innovative bands in CCM, with poetic lyrics and strong musical compositions. Their folky, acoustic guitar-infused sound is both hypnotic and thought provoking. *Live at the Bitter End* includes the poignant "Eileen's Song" and "Basic Instructions," their passionate treatise on salvation. Burlap to Cashmere's velvet sound is alternative CCM as it should be. *—Melinda Hill*

Anybody Out There— / Oct. 27, 1998 / A&M ✦✦✦
Anybody Out There? is Burlap to Cashmere's first full-length release, following *Live at the Bitter End. Anybody Out There?* is difficult to pigeonhole. The percussion is innovative, the guitar work outstanding. Sometimes considered the bad boys of Christian music, their lyrics are alternately poignant, passionate, light hearted, and always original. "Digee Dime," their signature song, is contagiously fun. "Eileen's Song" is soft and sweet, and "Basic Instructions," their Dove Award-nominated song, has point-blank lyrics with a Latin feel. The album slows a bit with the last few numbers, but overall, *Anybody Out There?* is one of the best alternative CCM albums of the '90s. *—Melinda Hill*

Caedmon's Call

Group / Alternative CCM, CCM
Caedmon's Call is a contemporary Christian band that fuses folk-rock with adult alternative rock influences. Cliff Young (vocals, rhythm guitar), Derek Webb (lead guitar, vocals), Danielle Glenn (vocals), Aric Nitzberg (bass), Todd Bragg (drums), Randy Holsapple (organ) and Garett Buell (percussion) formed the Houston, Texas-based band at Texas Christian University in the summer of 1992. The group originally included Aaron Tate, who left the band shortly after its formation, but he continued to write songs with Young. After spending some time playing locally, Caedmon's Call began touring college campuses across the South, steadily building up a dedicated following of young Gen-X singles.

Caedmon's Call self-released their first album in June of 1994. In August of 1995, they released their second record. Both independently released albums sold over 10,000 copies apiece, and were distributed in Canada and the U.K. as well as America. The two albums, plus their live shows, led *Musician* magazine to call Caedmon's Call one of the best unsigned bands in America. Such grassroots success attracted the attention of Warner Brothers, who signed the band in 1996 and released their major-label debut, the Don McCollister-produced *Caedmon's Call,* in the spring of 1997. *Long Line of Leavers* was issued three years later. Stephen Thomas Erlewine

Caedmon's Call / Mar. 25, 1997 / Warner Alliance ✦✦✦✦
This album marks Caedmon's Call's first release with a major label, Warner Alliance, after a string of successful independent releases. The band doesn't compromise their music, though, with most of the songs written by band members Derek Webb and Aaron Tate. "This World" features great harmony between Danielle Glenn and Webb along with honest lyrics. "Bus Driver" is a bouncy tune, and their passionate cover of Rich Mullins' "Hope to Carry On" is a must-hear for any listener of Christian music. "Center Aisle" is poignant look at the reality of suicide and the unanswered questions it leaves behind. This album solidifies the band as one of the premier groups in alternative Christian music with its variety, original lyrics, solid music arrangements, and vocals. *—Melinda Hill*

Intimate Portrait / Nov. 25, 1997 / Warner Brothers ✦✦✦
Intimate Portrait is exactly that—a revealing and candid look at Caedmon's Call and what makes them who they are. It presupposes a great deal of familiarity with the band and interest in the personal lives and struggles of the band. The live acoustic set is particularly nice, with the ballads "Piece of Glass" and "The Truth" and the wry "April Showers," a critique of the church and its separation from the world around it. The "Hope to Carry On" video is well done, with a cameo by premier Christian songwriter Rich Mullins. This enhanced CD might get a little long for casual fans of the band, but is a must-have for any true fan. *—Melinda Hill*

● **40 Acres** / Apr. 13, 1999 / Essential ✦✦✦✦
Caedmon's Call's 1999 effort, *40 Acres,* doesn't disappoint. It shows off the group's broadening concerns, with songs like "Table for Two," which wistfully expresses coming to terms with being single. It also shows off their expanding musical interests, with songs like the rollicking, piano-based "Daring Daylight Escape." This album carries on their trademark honesty through songs like "Petrified Heart" and "Shifting Sand," and encourages with songs like "Climb On (A Back That's Strong)" and "Faith My Eyes." Although by the end the songs start to sound a little bland, *40 Acres* is a fruitful, worthwhile listen. It doesn't have the strength of their previous albums, but it does move Caedmon's Call, and their fans, in some new directions while being faithful to their purpose. *—Melinda Hill*

Shirley Caesar

b. Oct. 13, 1938, Durham, NC
Vocals / Traditional Gospel, Contemporary Gospel, Black Gospel
Most known for her style of singing, Shirley Caesar often shouts her music in order for her messages to be received. Her professional career began in the '60s when she was with the Caravans. In 1966 she began making a name for herself as a solo artist on the gospel music circuit. Shirley Caesar performs with an energetic and boisterous style. She believes that with all the suffering and hardships in the world people will listen to her recordings and be encouraged. Her live album, *He Will Come,* is a testimony to her philosophy of life. The album was recorded with the choir, band and congregation of her church. In the title song "He Will Come," Shirley Caesar transcends the message of hope, that although society is getting worse, the Lord will save us and is coming. Among her other gospel hits with inspiring messages include "God Is Good," "Revive Us Again" and "Time To Be Blessed." Her 1987 hit, "Hold My Mule," was written to encourage people to "fight the good fight." All her songs combine music with ministry to convey her messages. Despite her busy schedule, Shirley Caesar constantly finds time to get her messages of encouragement and peace to people. *—Kim Summers*

★ **The Best of Shirley Caesar with the Caravans** / 1966 / Savoy ✦✦✦✦✦
A truncated but very potent ten-song selection of Caesar's best work with the Caravans. Before going on as a solo artist, Caesar was the group's lead singer, and these are the performances that established her reputation on the gospel music circuit. It's full-blooded, energetic

music with Shirley pouring her heart and soul into numbers like "I Feel Good," "Lord Do Something for Me," "Roll On," "Soul Salvation," and "Choose Ye This Day." The running time may be short on this one, but every track is a winner. This best-of makes for a marvelous introduction to the artist. *—Cub Koda*

Live in Chicago with Rev. Milton Brunson & The Thompson Community Singers / 1988 / Word ♦♦♦

Celebration / 1990 / Myrrh ♦♦♦

☆ **Her Very Best** / 1991 / Word ♦♦♦♦♦
Her Very Best collects highlights from four of Shirley Caesar's albums for Word in the '80s, selecting two from each album and adding two unreleased cuts as incentives for hardcore fans that already have the original albums. The result is a representative introduction to her latter-day recordings. These aren't necessarily her best work, but they're nevertheless strong, offering further proof that Shirley Caesar is one of the great voices in recorded gospel history. *—Leo Stanley*

I Remember Mama / Feb. 25, 1992 / Word ♦♦♦♦♦

Jesus, I Love Calling Your Name / Apr. 28, 1992 / Word ♦♦♦

Sailin' / Apr. 28, 1992 / Word ♦♦♦♦♦
Shirley Caesar and Rev. Al Green made a magnificent team on the title track, which helped win each a Grammy. Caesar's evocative leads and Green's shimmering harmonies and equally spectacular leads were a session highlight, although there were some other fine numbers spotlighting Caesar as well. *—Ron Wynn*

No Charge / Mar. 14, 1995 / Hob ♦♦♦♦

Just a Word / Jul. 1996 / Word ♦♦♦♦

Hallelujah: Collection Of Her Finest Recordings / Aug. 17, 1999 / Music Club ♦♦♦
The recordings compiled here are drawn from Hob Records sessions spanning from 1967 to 1975. On these, a variety of choirs join Shirley Caesar in spreading the gospel, stirring the revival, and joyously praising. This great lady of gospel has a husky preacher's sound and a devout believer's anointment. Her voice is extraordinary, calling to mind the better-known voice of Aretha Franklin and the lesser-known voice of Sister Wynona Carr. The choirs and congregations sing in stirring harmonies and with enough energy to be thrilling. Amazing church organ, piano, and clapping all add to the live service experience. "Satan, We're Gonna Tear Your Kingdom Down" and "Jordan River (I'm Bound to Cross)" are the absolute standouts, with Caesar and different choirs delivering exciting versions of these. The most secular-styled tunes found here are from the later recordings: songs one through three provide moral stories of love and faith and warning, and track number five is wrapped in the music of a classic Marvin Gaye arrangement. This album is a great collection of soul gospel as sung by the tremendous Shirley Caesar. *—Joslyn Layne*

The Campbell Brothers

Group / Black Gospel
The four Campbell brothers—Chuck on pedal steel, Phillip on electric guitar and bass, Carlton on drums, and Darick on lap eight-string steel—play electric gospel music for the House of God, Keith Dominion church. Emphasizing the steel guitar, the group stick to a repertoire that avoids rock and blues, but nonetheless betrays the influences of those forms in their arrangements, which also draw from country, jazz, and other forms. Although their selection of material is spiritual, the guitar work of Chuck Campbell in particular is imaginative and at times even experimental, using a tuning he devised himself and the E-bow to produce eerie sustain. With Kate Jackson on vocals and Charles Flenory contributing electric guitar to some cuts, they recorded an album for Arhoolie's *Sacred Steel* series, *Pass Me Not*, in 1996 and 1997. *— Richie Unterberger*

Pass Me Not / Sep. 16, 1997 / Arhoolie ♦♦♦♦♦
Although the Campbell Brothers are certainly a gospel group and not a secular R&B one, the opening deep soul grooves of "Pass Me Not, Oh Gentle Saviour," followed by quasi-psychedelic wafts of sustain, clue you in that this is not your average gospel act. Certainly it's the guitar work, rather than Kate Jackson's serviceable gospel singing, that makes this worthy of attention for gospel fans, and perhaps for some secular blues and soul listeners as well. Some of the cuts employ steel guitar to some of the most eye-popping ends you'll hear in any kind of 1990s music, such as the jump blues-ish "Jump for Joy" and the curling sustain that colors a lot of this disc (sounding at times like a hybrid of the steel guitar and the theremin). The rollicking instrumental numbers tend to show the playing to its best advantage, yet the languid ballad "End of My Journey" has some of the most moving steel passages. *—Richie Unterberger*

The Caravans

f. 1952, Chicago, IL
Group / Traditional Gospel, Black Gospel
During the period stretching from the late 1950s to the mid-1960s, the Caravans went unrivaled as the nation's most popular touring gospel group; acclaimed as one of the greatest female acts ever to arrive on the spiritual music front, their fluctuating roster was unparalleled as a launching pad for future superstars—Shirley Caesar, Inez Andrews, Bessie Griffin and James Cleveland were just a few of the ensemble's alumni who later went on to solo fame. By 1956, the Caravans were among the most popular acts in all of gospel music, famed for their uncanny—almost telepathic—teamwork. They moved to the Savoy label in 1958, where the combination of the young soprano phenom Caesar and the shrieking contralto Andrews was a powerhouse one-two punch; as the decade drew to a close, the Caravans were the queens of the gospel circuit. *—Jason Ankeny*

The Best of the Caravans / 1977 / Savoy ♦♦♦♦♦
This doesn't necessarily contain their best material, only those songs that garnered either chart success or radio airplay during the 1950s and early '60s. Like all Savoy releases, there's almost no discographical information, although Walker, Andrews, and Caesar are the artists featured most prominently. *—Ron Wynn*

★ **Till I Meet the Lord** / ♦♦♦♦♦
The collection here is taken from the two Vee Jay albums recorded in the early '60s between two lengthy contracts with Herman Lubinsky's Savoy label. Featured singers include founder, manager, and lead Albertina ("Tina") Walker, ably supported by Cassietta George, the great Shirley Caesar, and Josephine Howard, supported by James Herndon and Kenneth Woods on organ and piano. There are some fine high-spirited moments with Walker's raspy wails and Caesar's amazing glissandos. *—Opal Louis Nations, Roots & Rhythm Newsletter*

Michael Card

b. Apr. 11, 1957
Vocals, Violin, Piano, Guitar, Banjo, Dulcimer / Praise & Worship, Inspirational, CCM
Michael Card began writing songs at a Kentucky college, where he would write praise choruses for a local church service. Although pushed to earn his Ph.D. by a professor, he was lured into the recording industry by friends Randy Scruggs and John Thompson, who needed a musician to record for their production company's demos. The record label insisted they produce Card's music as their first project, and his acoustic folk sound appeared from the very start; among his records was 1981's *Present Reality*, 1987's *Life*, 1993's *Come to the Cradle* and 1996's *Brother to Brother*. In 1998, he returned with *Starkindler: A Celtic Conversation Across Time*. *—John Bush*

The Final Word / 1987 / Sparrow ♦♦♦♦♦

The Way of Wisdom / 1991 / Sparrow ♦♦♦
This superb effort has mellow instrumentation and potent lyrics. *—Bil Carpenter*

● **Joy in the Journey: 10 Years of Greatest Hits** / 1994 / Sparrow ♦♦♦♦♦
Card's best known songs are collected here, with the earliest ones newly re-recorded for this album. *—Thom Granger*

Brother to Brother / Jun. 25, 1996 / Word ♦♦♦

Bob Carlisle

Vocals, French Horn / Adult Contemporary, CCM
He began making music by appearing on many vocal sessions from the '70s, and Bob Carlisle finally found a solo career in 1993, singing gospel pop/rock with subtle soul influences. He had appeared with several early Jesus Music acts—including Allies—and sang backup vocals on sessions by Bryan Duncan, Vince Ebo, Sandi Patti and Petra before signing with Sparrow Records in 1993; his self-titled debut album appeared later that year. By 1996, Carlisle was recording for the Diadem label, and that year's *Shades of Grace* became a gospel hit, propelled by the single "Mighty Love." The following year, Carlisle unexpectedly became a crossover success when the single "Butterfly Kisses" became a pop hit. The album was repackaged and reissued in the spring of 1997 under the name *Butterfly Kisses* and it topped the pop charts; *Stories from the Heart* followed in 1998. That same year, Carlisle also issued *Butterfly Kissess & Bedtime Prayers;* its sequel followed in early 1999. *Nothing But the Truth* was released a year later. *—John Bush*

● **Butterfly Kisses** / May 13, 1997 / Diadem/Jive ♦♦♦♦♦
In the spring of 1997, Bob Carlisle unexpectedly had a crossover hit with "Butterfly Kisses," an ode to his love for his daughter which just happened to hit the airwaves around Father's Day. Excited at the prospect of a major hit, the label re-released Carlisle's *Shades of Grace* under the title *Butterfly Kisses*, hoping it would lure in the mainstream audience. Although their gambit worked, it's unclear how many "Butterfly Kisses" fans will be satisfied with the entire album, because it doesn't have that many songs that are equally as catchy. The sound of the record is pleasant enough, since Carlisle has a good voice and the music is smooth and unobtrusive, but there aren't enough strong songs to satisfy pop consumers. Still, *Butterfly Kisses [Shades of Grace]* demonstrates a leap forward for Carlisle, and its best, hook-laden moments make it his best record yet. *—Rodney Batdorf*

Collection / Jul. 29, 1997 / Sparrow ♦♦♦♦
Released after the crossover success of "Butterfly Kisses," *Collection* rounds up 16 of Bob Carlisle's biggest contemporary Christian hits from his previous albums for Sparrow Records. Secular fans of "Butterfly Kisses" won't be disappointed by any of the music on *Collection*, since it all essentially all reworks the same polished, soul-inflected easy listening pop that made that song a hit, even if none of these songs are quite as memorable as that hit. *—Rodney Batdorf*

Ballads of Bob Carlisle / Sep. 2, 1997 / Word ♦♦♦

Butterfly Kisses & Bedtime Prayers / Jan. 27, 1998 / Diadem ♦♦♦♦
Like any of the Bob Carlisle discs to follow in the wake of "Butterfly Kisses," *Butterfly Kisses & Bedtime Prayers* is a collection tied together by a vague theme linked to the hit single. This time, the album is comprised of newly recorded lullabies and children's prayers, which are all narrated by children. *Butterfly Kisses & Bedtime Prayers* is designed to help children learn how to pray, and it succeeds to a certain extent (although it would seem that children would be better off learning to pray from their parents, not a record). Nevertheless, the album is a rousing success on one level—it provides a nice, soothing collection of glossy soft-pop songs with a religious undercurrent that will provide nice background music for sleeping children. *—Rodney Batdorf*

Stories from the Heart / Sep. 29, 1998 / Diadem/Benson ♦♦♦
Bob Carlisle rode the surprise success of "Butterfly Kisses" for nearly two years before moving to new territory with *Stories from the Heart*. In reality, the album isn't all that different from its predecessors—it just happened not to have "Butterfly Kisses" on it. Musically, it's the same ultra-polished CCM and faux-adult contemporary soul that sent *Shades of Grace* to the top of the charts. *Stories from the Heart* also happens to share the same sentiments as "Butterfly Kisses"—almost every song on the record appeals to "the heart," either through tales of family, God, country, Jesus or love. Although nothing stands out like "Butterfly Kisses"

(though, by God, he tries real hard for another grand slam with "Father's Love"), there aren't many weak moments on the record, and that may be enough for many fans of the father-daughter epic. *—Stephen Thomas Erlewine*

Carman

b. Jan. 19, 1956, Trenton, NJ
Vocals / CCM
One of the most successful performers in contemporary Christian music, Carman was born Dominic Licciardello on January 19, 1956; "saved" at an Andrae Crouch concert, he was later discovered by Bill Gaither, eventually founding his own ministry and recording arm. Debuting in 1982 with *Some-O'-Dat*, he issued a series of LPs which gradually launched him to the top of CCM playlists, and between 1987 and 1989 he was named *Charisma* magazine's readers' choice for favorite male vocalist in three consecutive years. In 1990, Carman was also named *Billboard*'s CCM Artist of the Year, with his LP *Revival of the Land* winning Album of the Year honors; he won countless awards in the years to follow, as well as a series of gold and platinum records. On August 15, 1993, in the wake of the release of his *Yo! Kidz: Heroes, Stories and Songs from the Bible*, Carman mounted his "Music For Peace" crusade at Wanderers Stadium in Johannesburg, South Africa, the 50,000 ticketholders in attendance making it the largest solo Christian concert in history; he broke his own mark a year later, appearing before a crowd of 71, 132 at Dallas' Texas Stadium. In 1995 he released *R.I.O.T. (Righteous Invasion of Truth)*, accompanied by a book of the same name; *Mission 3:16* followed in 1998. The double-disc hits compilation *Heart of a Champion* was issued two years later. *—Jason Ankeny*

Live . . . Radically Saved / 1988 / Sparrow ✦✦✦✦✦
A breakthrough album with Christian rap, R&B, and a little rock. *—Bil Carpenter*

Shakin' the House / 1991 / Verity ✦✦✦
A live Black gospel revival set with Commissioned and the Christ Church Choir. *—Bil Carpenter*

The Champion / Jan. 1992 / Word ✦✦

★ **The Absolute Best** / 1993 / Sparrow ✦✦✦✦✦
A collection of what this unconventional artist does best, it spotlights his story-songs and hits and features one new song produced by David Foster. *—Thom Granger*

Revival in the Land / Jan. 4, 1993 / Sparrow ✦✦✦

The Standard / Sep. 27, 1993 / Sparrow ✦✦✦
Carman tries his hand at some new musical directions, with less extended stories and more song-oriented material, alienating some old fans but winning some new ones in the process. *—Thom Granger*

R.I.O.T. (Righteous Invasion of Truth) / Oct. 24, 1995 / Sparrow ✦✦✦

Mission 3:16 / Jan. 27, 1998 / Sparrow ✦

Sister Wynona Carr

b. Aug. 23, 1924, Cleveland, OH, **d.** May 12, 1976, Cleveland, OH
Vocals / Traditional Gospel, Jump Blues, Black Gospel, R&B
Though largely unrecognized during her own lifetime, singer and composer Sister Wynona Carr was among the truly pioneering artists of gospel's golden era; while her music—sophisticated and sensual, distinguished by lyrics of rare metaphorical depth and a progressive sound drawing heavily on jazz and blues—was simply too radical for contemporary listeners, in hindsight she stands as one of the great innovators of her day. In early 1949 Carr traveled to Los Angeles to record her first Specialty label session; her debut 78, pairing the swinging "Each Day" with the torch-like ballad "Lord Jesus," served as an immediate indication of her versatility. Her next studio date was a revolutionary session which yielded "I'm a Pilgrim Traveler"—a reworking of the blues standard "St. James Infirmary"—as well as "I Heard the News (Jesus Is Coming Again)," which updated the 1948 secular hit "Good Rockin' Tonight." Other material, like the Carr original "Our Father," suggested a strong jazz influence; however, while all of the tracks recorded during the session promised to push the singer into new stylistic directions, Specialty apparently felt the songs were all too daring, and none of them were released. Despite all of the frustration and setbacks, Carr forged on; she toured relentlessly, but did not go back into the studio until mid-1952. With "The Ball Game," a vividly metaphorical tale of a showdown between Jesus and Satan, she finally scored a major gospel hit, yet her career continued to flounder—another two years passed prior to her next session. Although she recorded rarely, Carr nevertheless remained a highly prolific songwriter, composing poetic, topical material often inspired by headlines of the day; she cut dozens of demos for Specialty, and ironically enough earned more money from sales of her sheet music than from her actual recordings. *—Jason Ankeny*

Jump Jack Jump! / 1955 / Specialty ✦✦✦✦✦
This 24-track set covers Carr's R&B tunes, with many unissued but fine tunes such as "If These Walls Could Speak," "Finders Keepers," and "Weather Man" finally getting out of the vault. The CD also includes her trademark upbeat, sassy songs, "Jump Jack Jump," "Boppity Bop (Boogity Boop)," "Ding Dong Daddy" and "Nursery Rhyme Rock." Thematic variety wasn't her label's strong suit when it came to material, and they might have done better with more numbers like "Please Mr. Jailer" and "It's Raining Outside" and a few less boogies and jump pieces. *—Ron Wynn*

★ **Dragnet for Jesus** / 1992 / Specialty ✦✦✦✦✦
A must for every fan of soul gospel, *Dragnet for Jesus* compiles all of the gospel songs—many (previously) unreleased—that Wynona Carr recorded for the Specialty label. Spanning 1949 to1954, are many of Carr's original compositions including "I'm a Pilgrim Traveler" and "Nobody But Jesus," as well as her efforts at incorporating pop culture into God's message with the sports-themed "15 Rounds for Jesus" and her most-recognized song, "the Ball Game." The title track is based around a popular TV show of the time, *Dragnet*, opening with a detective office scene. But don't imagine that Carr was making light of, or trying to secularize, the message of salvation. One listen to her earnest, soulful voice and there's no doubt that the woman's heart was in it. Imagine the smoke-and-scotch hoarse edge of Janis Joplin's voice, pour Aretha Franklin's soulful inflections all over it, and you're close to the powerful delivery of Wynona Carr. Carr was, in fact, the gospel choir director of Rev. C.L. Franklin's church (Aretha's father) when Aretha was young. Most of the song's feature a quartet of piano, bass, drums, and either organ or guitar, with Carr usually on the piano. At the end of the disc is a bonus of two demos and a live recording of her leading the previously mentioned church choir in a stunning, hair-raising arrangement of "Our Father." With her out-of-this-world sultry voice, Carr incorporated blues and jazz elements and popular themes, yet she never really took off with the gospel audiences. Regardless, she remains one of the leading ladies of gospel. *—Joslyn Layne*

The Cathedrals

f. 1964
Group / Traditional Gospel, Southern Gospel
Formed in 1965, this traditional Southern gospel vocal group (also known as the Cathedral Quartet) appeared regularly on Rex Humbard's *Cathedral of Tomorrow* broadcast in the '60s. In 1969 they set out on their own, traveling from gig to gig in a converted egg truck until they could afford real tour buses. Over the next decade, the group became one of the most popular Southern gospel groups around. In 1977, they won their first Grammy for Best Gospel Performance, and duplicated the feat in 1978, 1979, and 1982 as well. In 1977, they also won Dove Awards for Male Group of the Year and Best Southern Gospel Album (for *Then . . . And Now*) by the Gospel Music Association. During the '70s and '80s, the Cathedrals had a long stream of number one gospel hits that included "Step Into the Water," "Can He, Could He, Would He," and "I've Just Started Living." In 1988, they became the first Southern gospel group to record in England with the London Philharmonic Orchestra for the album *Symphony of Praise*. In 1989, the group's 25th anniversary, the *Gospel Music Voice* named them Group of the Year, and *Cash Box* named *Goin' in Style* Southern Gospel Album of the Year. The Cathedrals continue to tour extensively in large churches and concert halls. *—Sandra Brennan*

● **Cathedrals Collection, Vol. 1** / 1988 / Benson ✦✦✦✦✦
A fine collection of recent hits, styled in the manner of their old hits. *—Bil Carpenter*

A Farewell Celebration / Nov. 16, 1999 / Spring Hill ✦✦✦✦
Recorded live at Nashville's *Ryman Auditorium* on the Cathedrals' farewell tour, *A Farewell Celebration* is a joyous, star-studded send-off featuring appearances by the Statler Brothers, the Oak Ridge Boys, Bill Gaither, Sandi Patti, and Guy Penrod, to list a few of the most notable names. At a generous 27 tracks, fans aren't likely to be disappointed, and the performances are inspiring and polished. *—Steve Huey*

Gary Chapman

Vocals, Guitar / CCM
Texas-born songwriter Chapman came to early fame with "My Father's Eyes," made popular by Amy Grant, whom he later married. He has also had songs recorded by T.G. Sheppard, Kenny Rogers and other country artists. *—Thom Granger*

Light Inside / 1994 / Reunion ✦✦✦
Grammy-winning producer Michael Omartian teams with Chapman for a comfortably satisfying album, including remakes of two songs from his earlier (and out of print) Lamb & Lion albums. *—Thom Granger*

Outside / Sep. 14, 1999 / Reunion ✦✦✦
Outside continues Gary Chapman's penchant for touching, sentimental paeans to the joys of fatherhood, as well as songs addressing his Christian faith and the subject of love in general. Overall, it's a very positive, affirming outlook that Chapman shares, and fortunately, the songs here live up to the standards of craft that he set on previous releases. *—Steve Huey*

● **Everyday Man** / RCA ✦✦✦✦✦
Chapman's first album in years was prescient in its marriage of pop and country styles on this set, having the unfortunate effect of missing the moment with both audiences. *—Thom Granger*

Steven Curtis Chapman

b. Nov. 21, 1962, Paducah, KY
Vocals, Guitar / Country Gospel, Inspirational, CCM
His music a cross between '70s-style light rock and orchestrated pop, Steven Curtis Chapman has been one of the most prominent performers of contemporary Christian music during the '80s and '90s. Born and raised in Kentucky, Chapman dropped out of college to go to Nashville, where he began writing songs. Soon, many of gospel and country's brightest stars recorded his tunes. He signed to the major Christian music company Sparrow in 1987, and cut his first album, *First Hand*, that same year. The first single, "Weak Days," hit number two on the contemporary Christian chart. His second album, 1988's *Real Life Conversations*, earned him four more hits, including the number one song "His Eyes." Released in 1989, his third album, *More to This Life*, contained four number one hits and in 1990 earned him an unprecedented ten nominations at the GMA Awards (he won five). His next album, *For the Sake of the Call*, contained five number one singles. In 1992, Chapman made a successful bid to attract a more mainstream audience with *The Great Adventure*. Chapman released his seventh album, *Heaven in the Real World*, in 1994 and embarked on a major tour. In 1996, Chapman released *Sign of Life*. *—Sandra Brennan*

First Hand / 1987 / Sparrow ✦✦✦
Chapman's freshman debut is infused with country, soft rock, and pop. *—Bil Carpenter*

Real Life Conversations / 1988 / Sparrow ✦✦✦✦✦

For the Sake of the Call / 1990 / Sparrow ✦✦✦✦✦
Chapman's songwriting voice continues to mature, and the stirring title anthem helped make this his most successful album. *—Brian Mansfield*

The Great Adventure / 1992 / Sparrow ♦♦♦
Chapman flirts with country, rap, and Springsteenian rock on his most ambitious project, both musically and lyrically. Includes guest appearances from Ricky Skaggs, DC Talk, and BeBe Winans. *—Brian Mansfield*

Heaven in the Real World / 1994 / Capitol ♦♦♦
Chapman moves into rockier, more electrified territory with his down-home story songs and values. *—Thom Granger*

Tuesday's Child: The Best of Steven Chapman / Jan. 1, 1996 / Cema Special Markets ♦♦♦

● **Greatest Hits** / Oct. 21, 1997 / Sparrow ♦♦♦♦♦
Greatest Hits is an excellent 14-track overview of Steven Curtis Chapman's Chordant recordings. In addition to Chapman's biggest hits and best-known songs, there are two new songs ("Not Home Yet," "I Am Found In You") and alternate takes of "Lord of the Dance" and "The Walk" that were re-recorded at London's legendary Abbey Road studios. The result is a fine summary of his most popular recordings and an ideal introduction to his music. *—Rodney Batdorf*

Speechless / Jun. 15, 1999 / Sparrow ♦♦♦
Steven Curtis Chapman, Christian music's most awarded artist, returns with 1999's *Speechless*. Songs like the title track and "Drive" will please his fans, who have helped Chapman sell over four million albums, and win 38 Dove Awards and three Grammies. *—Heather Phares*

Rev. Julius Cheeks

b. Aug. 7, 1929, Spartanburg, SC, **d.** Jan. 27, 1981, Miami, FL
Vocals / Traditional Gospel, Southern Gospel, Black Gospel
At the peak of his career, the Reverend Julius Cheeks was the definitive hard gospel singer, famed for a gritty, powerful baritone which influenced not only the next generation of gospel performers but also secular stars including James Brown and Wilson Pickett. Born into abject poverty on August 7, 1929 in Spartanburg, South Carolina, as a child Cheeks was enamored of the recordings of the Dixie Hummingbirds, the Soul Stirrers and others; he began singing in the second grade, quitting school that same year to pick cotton. Later joining a local gospel group dubbed the Baronets, in 1946 he was spotted by the Rev. B.L. Parks, a former Dixie Hummingbird in the process of forming a new group called the Nightingales; upon Cheeks' arrival, he became infamous across the gospel circuit for playing the clown, while each night pushing his voice to its breaking point.

The Nightingales enjoyed considerable success on the road, but they made virtually no money; to make ends meet Cheeks briefly joined the Soul Stirrers, rejoining the Nightingales during the early 1950s. Upon signing to Peacock, the group rattled off a string of hits, among them "Somewhere to Lay My Head" and "The Last Mile of the Way"; they were in fact so popular, and so often the subject of acclaim, that they eventually rechristened themselves the Sensational Nightingales. In 1954, Cheeks offically became a preacher, but he remained a performer, emerging as a gifted writer and arranger as well; a temperamental man, he left the group on numerous occasions, finally quitting for good in 1960 and going into semi-retirement. He soon returned to action with a new group, the Sensational Knights. Cheeks died in Miami on January 27, 1981. *—Jason Ankeny*

● **Somebody Left on That Morning Train** / Savoy ♦♦♦♦♦
Marvelous leads and a good production. This is the best album Cheeks has made as a solo singer. *—Ron Wynn*

We'll Lay Down Our Lives / Savoy ♦♦♦
Representative, but a cut below his best single sessions. *—Ron Wynn*

Chosen Gospel Singers

f. Houston, TX
Group / Traditional Gospel, Black Gospel
Despite notching a series of hits between the early '50s and early '60s, the Chosen Gospel Singers remain one of the most elusive groups of gospel's golden era—plagued by constant lineup changes, the ensemble's proper history remains sketchy at best, and even the exact involvement of their most famous alumnus, Lou Rawls, is something of a mystery. It's known that the Chosen Gospel Singers made their first recordings in 1952 for the Specialty label, yielding the hit single "One-Two-Three." The steady personnel shifts were attributed in large part to the group's status as a semi-professional venture. In 1954, Rawls made his first recordings as a Chosen Gospel Singer but joined the Army prior to the Chosen's final Specialty session, in early 1955. Later that year, the Chosen signed with the Nashboro label, though the group ended when the Texas quartet the Gospel Keynotes joined the Chosen Gospel Singers, then restored the name to the Gospel Keynotes. *—Jason Ankeny*

● **The Lifeboat** / 1954 / Specialty ♦♦♦♦♦
Featured are previously unreleased tracks, alternate takes, and long-out-of-print gems by this major gospel quartet, led at times by Lou Rawls. *—Opal Louis Nations*

Meet the Selah Jubilees / ♦♦♦
The Chosen Gospel Singers were a spiritual group in the sanctified style fronting such vocalists as the sing-and-preach Bob Crutcher, Joe Johnson from The Trumpeteers, jazz-soul singer Lou Rawls and the hard-working Tommy Ellison, who later went on to form The Five Singing Stars. These are exciting selections from various labels, recorded between 1952 and 1963. Side B features the great Thermon Ruth and the Selah Singers, who sang both R&B and gospel under various aliases during the '40s and '50s. The material here from their post-war Arista, Continental, Gotham and Mercury period is entirely gospel—close jubilee harmonies with sparse accompaniment. The songs are taken from rare 45s and 78s. There's good overall sound quality (cassette only). *—Opal Louis Nations, Roots & Rhythm Newsletter*

Chuck Wagon Gang

f. 1936
Group / Country Gospel, Southern Gospel, Traditional Country
Although the Chuck Wagon Gang has been around since 1936—undergoing many personnel changes over the years—its sound and devotion to old-fashioned gospel has remained much the same. Their greatest significance is that the band provides an important link between country music and traditional sacred songs of the South. The original incarnation comprised four members of the Carter family—no relation to *the* Carter Family. Though the group's earliest recording session for ARC produced country singles rather than gospel, by the early '40s they had switched over to gospel completely. Temporarily disbanded during World War II, the family remained primarily a radio band during the late '40s though they began recording again in 1948 for Columbia. After patriarch David (Dad) Carter retired in 1955, non-family members began joining during the '50s and '60s. Through it all, the band kept touring part-time and making records—408 masters by 1975. The Chuck Wagon Gang continued on in a similar vein until 1987, when they once again became a full-time band with new members joining the last of the Carters, Roy and his sister Ruth Ellen Yates. By the late '80s, the Chuck Wagon Gang had been named Gospel Artist or Group of the Year by *Music City News* five years in a row. *—Sandra Brennan*

Family Tradition / 1973 / MCA ♦♦♦

Looking Away to Heaven / 1976 / Columbia ♦♦♦

★ **Columbia Historic Edition** / 1990 / Columbia ♦♦♦♦♦
Columbia Historic Edition compiles highlights from the Chuck Wagon Gang's Columbia recordings between 1936 and 1960. Many of their greatest songs—including "After the Sunrise," "He Set Me Free," "We Are Climbing," and "I Want to See My Jesus"—are featured on this 16-track collection, making it a terrific introduction to this influential country gospel group. *—Thom Owens*

Old Time Hymns, Vol. 2 / 1991 / MCA ♦♦♦
The Chuck Wagon Gang's heartfelt renditions of some well-known traditional hymns are somewhat hampered by the sterile production, but their strong performances carry the disc. *—Stephen Thomas Erlewine*

Chuck Wagon Gang's Greatest Hits, Vol. 1 / MCA ♦♦♦♦
Featuring sixteen tracks, *Greatest Hits* is a solid compilation of some of The Chuck Wagon Gang's best tracks and offers a good introduction to this contemporary country-gospel vocal group. *—Stephen Thomas Erlewine*

The Clark Sisters

Group / Contemporary Gospel, CCM
The Clark Sisters and the top female Gospel group in the United States. Led by organist/vocalist Elbernita "Twinkie" Clark-Farrell, the five sisters have continued to expand the legacy begun by their mother, Dr. Mattie Moss Clark. Dr. Clark, who served as National Music Department president of the Church of God in Christ based in Memphis and founded the Clark Conservatory of Music in Detroit, where the sisters to continue to teach, was the first Gospel artist to be awarded a gold record and introduced the concept of choirs singing in tenor soprano and alto sections. In 1983, The Clark Sisters recorded a cross-over dance hit, "You Bring The Sunshine". In June 1996, the Clark Sisters recorded an album with the FAMU Gospel Choir of Florida A&M College. *—Craig Harris*

● **Heart and Soul** / 1985 / Word ♦♦♦♦♦

Is My Living in Vain— / 1985 / Sony Special Products ♦♦♦
Originally recorded in 1985, *Is My Living in Vain* captures the Clark Sisters at the peak of their formidable powers, delivering electrifying renditions of "Now Is the Time" and "They Were Overcome (By the Word)." *—Chuck Donkers*

Ashley Cleveland

Vocals / Christian Rock, CCM
The earthy Christian rocker Ashley Cleveland began her career during the mid-1980s as a Nashville session vocalist, singing on well over 200 records before cutting her own demo tape with drummer/producer Craig Krampf. The recording won her a contract with Atlantic Records, and in 1991 Cleveland issued her debut album *Big Town*. She moved to the Reunion label for 1993's *Bus Called Desire;* for *Lesson of Love*, issued two years later, she earned her first Grammy award. *—Jason Ankeny*

● **Big Town** / 1991 / Atlantic ♦♦♦
When a major label was releasing as many titles as Atlantic during the late '80s and early '90s, some decent CDs were bound to fall between the corporate cracks. In 1991, one example was *Big Town*, which showed the underexposed Ashley Cleveland to be a passionate, appealing rocker with soul influences. The last thing Cleveland will be accused of is having a soft, girlish voice. Rough, throaty, and hard-edged, Cleveland's delivery brings to mind Melissa Etheridge and Bonnie Tyler. But while she's a pop/rocker first and foremost, melodic cuts such as "Love on the Main Line," "Up From the Ether," and "I Could Learn to Love You" give the impression that she's also spent plenty of time listening to Tina Turner, Aretha Franklin, and other African-American legends. *Big Town* may not contain any outright R&B or funk, but the influences of Turner and Franklin definitely assert themselves in Cleveland's phrasing. Not fantastic but likable on the whole, this CD indicated that Cleveland was someone to watch out for. But, unfortunately, a commercial break would elude the whiskey-voiced singer. *—Alex Henderson*

Rev. James Cleveland

b. Dec. 5, 1932, Chicago, IL, **d.** Feb. 9, 1991, Culver City, CA
Vocals, Trombone, Piano / Traditional Gospel, Contemporary Gospel, Black Gospel
The visionary behind the contemporary gospel sound, the Reverend James Cleveland was a pioneering composer and choral director whose progressive arrangements—jazzy and soulful, complete with odd time signatures—helped push the music past the confines of the traditional Baptist hymnal into new and unexpected directions, infusing elements of the sanctified church style and secular pop to alter the face of gospel forever. His professional career began in 1950, working as a pianist and composer for the Gospelaires, Roberta Martin and the Caravans. With the Gospel Chimes, Cleveland cut a series of records whose harmony

arrangements straddled the line between the current group style and the rapidly developing choir sound. By 1960, he proved himself well ahead of the pack with the breakthrough hit "The Love of God," cut with the Detroit choir the Voices of Tabernacle. Choir directors began mimicking his style, and after signing with Savoy his LP, 1962's live *Peace Be Still*, made history by selling almost a million copies to an almost exclusively black audience without the benefit of mainstream promotion. The success established Cleveland as arguably the most crucial figure to emerge in gospel since Mahalia Jackson. His annual Gospel Singers Workshop Convention helped launch the careers of numerous younger talents, a generation of artists largely inspired by the modernized sound pioneered by Cleveland himself. During the 1970s, he remained a towering figure and recorded prolifically, although his pace began to slow in the decade that followed. Even after his death in 1991, Cleveland's shadow continued to loom large across the gospel landscape. *—Jason Ankeny*

★ **Peace Be Still** / 1962 / Savoy ✦✦✦✦✦
A set of original Cleveland tunes and traditional hymns done in the choir format he pioneered with The Angelic Choir of New Jersey. This live recording, done with crude technology, is helped somewhat by the high-fidelity pressing. It includes "I Had a Talk with God" and "I'll Wear a Crown." Cleveland's gruff vocals appear on most cuts. *—Bil Carpenter*

★ **Hallelujah: Collection Of His Finest Recordings** / Aug. 17, 1999 / Music Club ✦✦✦✦✦
This release compiles selections of the gospel performances that Rev. James Cleveland cut for Hob Records between 1958 and 1967. Cleveland is backed up on most songs by either the Voices of the Tabernacle or the Gospel Chimes, and both Detroit vocal groups add much life and sincerity to the tunes—particularly the Voices, whose large-choir praises round out the songs with an impressive depth. Album standouts are the tunes "It Is Well (With My Soul)" with Rev. Charles Craig, Jr. and "Love of God" with the Voices of the Tabernacle. Cleveland powerfully leads these soul gospel tunes through energetic renditions, and a terrific shoutin' organ adds its musical "amens" throughout. All come together to give the listener a dose of a decently powerful church service. *—Joslyn Layne*

Dorothy Love Coates

b. 1930, Birmingham, AL
Vocals / Traditional Gospel, Black Gospel
Born in Birmingham, AL, Coates started singing in the '40s with The Original Gospel Harmonettes, who had the hits "I'm Sealed" and "Get Away." *—Bil Carpenter*

☆ **Get on Board** / 1956 / Specialty ✦✦✦✦✦
With The Original Gospel Harmonettes, here are 24 exciting songs (circa 1951-56) supported by Herbert "Pee Wee" Pickard, gospel's organist supreme. *—Opal Louis Nations*

★ **The Best of Dorothy Love Coates, Vol. 1-2** / 1957 / Specialty ✦✦✦✦✦
Reissue of the two specialty albums containing the group's best-known songs and hit recordings. *—Opal Louis Nations*

The Original Gospel, Vols. 1 & 2 / 1970 / Specialty ✦✦✦
Dorothy singing ragged with the group on fire circa 1951-57. *—Opal Louis Nations*

The Best of Dorothy Love Coates & the Original Gospel Harmonettes, Vol. 2 / 1991 / Specialty ✦✦✦
Picking up where the first compilation left off, *Best of Dorothy Love Coates/Orig. Gospel Harmonettes, Vol. 2* collects 12 of the gospel group's greatest performances from the '50s—including "Jesus Knows It All, " "These Are They, " "Every Day Will Be Sunday, " "There's a God Somewhere, " "Just to Behold His Face" and "Am I a Soldier"—making it an excellent complement to its predecessor. The album was later combined with *Vol. 1* on a 1991 CD reissue. *—Leo Stanley*

Clay Crosse

Vocals / CCM
One of the top Christian male vocalists of the late '90s, Clay Crosse has recorded half a dozen singles which hit number one on CCM radio charts. Signed to Reunion Records for his 1995 debut album *Time to Believe*, Crosse earned a Dove Award for New Artist of the Year, and did quite well with his second album, 1997's *Stained Glass*. He was nominated for Best Male Vocalist at that year's Dove ceremony. Two years later, he released *I Surrender All: The Clay Crosse Collection, Vol. 1; Different Man* followed in early 2000. *—John Bush*

Stained Glass / Jul. 1, 1997 / Reunion ✦✦✦✦

● **I Surrender All: The Clay Crosse Collection, Vol. 1** / Jun. 1, 1999 / Reunion ✦✦✦✦
I Surrender All: The Clay Crosse Collection may have arrived a little early in Crosse's career—after all, he had only released three albums, with a fourth on the way—but it nevertheless is a good summary of his brief, successful career. Two of the 13 songs are "previews" of his forthcoming album, not scheduled for release until 2000, but the remaining 11 songs contain all of his hits, which makes this the ideal choice for casual fans. *—Stephen Thomas Erlewine*

Andrae Crouch

b. Jun. 1, 1950, San Francisco, CA
Vocals, Piano, Producer, Composer / Contemporary Gospel, Inspirational, CCM
A groundbreaking pioneer in contemporary gospel music, Crouch combined the classic motif of call-and-response, solo with choir approach with pop songwriting techniques and production, resulting in albums accepted by both Black and White audiences. Many of Crouch's early songs are now considered "Jesus Music" standards. After a ten-year hiatus from recording, during which he dabbled in music for film and TV scores, Crouch signed with Quincy Jones' Qwest label for a triumphant return to form with *Mercy*. *Pray* followed in 1997, and two years later *Hall of Fame* was released. *—Thom Granger*

☆ **Andrae Crouch & the Disciples** / 1978 / Light ✦✦✦✦✦
Andrae Crouch & the Disciples—Live in London has all the groundbreaking rock riffs, motifs, and crossover elements that had him labeled a "devil" by conservatives. *—Bil Carpenter*

The Best of Andre Crouch/Disciples / 1982 / Light ✦✦

Let's Worship Him / May 1993 / Arrival/K-Tel ✦✦✦
Featuring driving beats and funky guitars as well as more contemplative slower numbers, *Let's Worship Him* is a good compilation of Crouch's late-'70s and early-'80s work, which was considerably more in touch with modern trends than his earlier records. *—Stephen Thomas Erlewine*

Mercy / 1994 / Qwest ✦✦✦
A potpourri of musical styles from Caribbean to African, laid down with impeccable taste in arrangment and production, exceeded the expectations that come from ten years away from the studio. *—Thom Granger*

● **His Best** / Arrival/K-Tel ✦✦✦✦✦
As the title suggests, *His Best* features some of Crouch's finest moments from the early '70s, including "Jesus is the Answer" and "My Tribute." A good introduction to this popular gospel singer. *—Stephen Thomas Erlewine*

Daniel Amos (Dä)

Producer / Alternative CCM, Christian Rock, CCM
The chameleonic Christian-rock band Daniel Amos started out as a Gram Parsons-influenced country band. By the late '70s, the group had become a rock band, but the collapse of its record label delayed the release of the landmark *Horrendous Disc*. During that time, frontman Terry Taylor discovered Elvis Costello and the Talking Heads. The few fans who stuck around during the band's three-year recording absence were shocked to hear the new wave *Alarma!* released hot on the heels of the mainstream *Horrendous Disc*. The band, also known as Da, now follows its own music with little concern for audiences and marketing. Taylor has become one of the most influential figures in Christian rock, as both a performer and a producer (Randy Stonehill, Jacob's Trouble, Scattered Few). *—Brian Mansfield*

Daniel Amos / 1976 / Maranatha Music ✦✦✦✦✦
Christian country-rock, along the lines of The Flying Burrito Brothers, but hardly *Gilded Palace of Sin*. However, Gram Parsonssideman Al Perkins does contribute pedal steel. *—Brian Mansfield*

Shotgun Angel / 1977 / Maranatha Music ✦✦✦✦✦
This country-rock album, tighter than *Daniel Amos* with added pop harmonies, made them Christian music's answer to The Eagles. It also made *Shotgun Angel* one of the most popular albums of its time. *—Brian Mansfield*

Horrendous Disc / Apr. 23, 1981 / Solid Rock ✦✦✦✦✦
The country influences of *Daniel Amos* and *Shotgun Angel* almost gone, *Horrendous Disc* established Daniel Amos as a rock band with huge melodies and huge guitars, sweetened by Beatles-influenced harmonies. *—Brian Mansfield*

Doppelganger / 1982 / Stunt ✦✦✦✦✦
The Alarma!! Chronicles—Vol. 2 After making (but before releasing) *Horrendous Disc*, Terry Taylor discovered new wave, and Daniel Amos was never the same. *Alarma!!* stripped the band down to bare bones, but *Doppelganger* returned the production values that typified Daniel Amos records. *Doppelganger* is the second of the four-part *Alarma!!* saga, but it works just fine on its own. Stunt's 1992 reissue of the album includes three live bonus tracks. *—Brian Mansfield*

Fearful Symmetry / 1986 / Frontline ✦✦

★ **Kalhoun** / 1991 / Brainstorm ✦✦✦✦✦
"It's the magic word they claim came down from ancient Babylon," Taylor sings by way of explaining the title word. "Don't know exactly what it means, it's just a sacred kind of thing." Satirical, often scathing, this rock brooks no compromise. *—Brian Mansfield*

Motor Cycle / 1993 / Brainstorm ✦✦✦✦✦
A swirling, sonic song cycle, more accessible than most of DA's catalog to a larger audience, has great production and tons of Beatlesque fun. *—Thom Granger*

Bibleland / 1994 / Word ✦✦✦
A return to a harder-edged alternative rock sound, it's less melodic but very much alive. *—Thom Granger*

DC Talk

Group / Christian Rap, CCM
The first gospel act to incorporate hip-hop influences (though the trio rarely departs from standard pop/rock), DC Talk became one of the most popular groups in Christian Contemporary music during the mid-'90s, when their fourth album *Jesus Freak* made the highest debut for a gospel act on *Billboard*'s album charts. Formed in Washington, D.C. during the late '80s, the group first comprised Toby McKeehan and Michael Tait. Adding Kevin Smith to the lineup soon after, the group added elements of hip-hop to their self-titled debut album, which appeared in 1988 on the ForeFront label. Neither McKeehan, Tait nor Smith were comfortable playing instruments on their recordings, so each recorded only vocals by the time of 1991's *Nu Thang*. After the release of *Free at Last* just one year later, DC Talk concentrated on touring for several years, during which a change of image resulted in the group's resemblance to a grunge band. Indeed, 1995's *Jesus Freak* featured more raging guitars, though within the medium of harmonic pop/rock. Upon its release, *Jesus Freak* sold more copies than any gospel album in history, and eventually moved over one million copies. *Supernatural* followed in 1998. *—John Bush*

Nu Thang / 1991 / ForeFront ✦✦✦

☆ **Free at Last** / 1992 / ForeFront ✦✦✦✦✦
Its breakthrough album expands the group's musical boundaries and appeal, with impressive covers of "Jesus Is Just Alright" and "Lean on Me, " and the trio's best original compositions to date. *—Thom Granger*

Jesus Freak / 1995 / Capitol ✦✦✦
After building a dedicated following with three albums of Christian hip-hop, DC Talk makes a play for crossover success with *Jesus Freak*. As the title indicates, the group members haven't abandoned their religious base. What they have done, is expand their musical pallete. Keeping a solid hip-hop foundation, the trio adds elements of soul, psychedelic rock, and pop, making *Jesus Freak* their most ambitious album to date. It also happens to be their best. DC Talk fuses their diverse influences together with style and grace, making the music sound seamless. The lyrics frequently avoid standard cliches, managing to celebrate Christianity without sounding preachy. With its musical diversity and well-crafted lyrics, *Jesus Freak* is the album that will convince secular listeners that DC Talk is worth a listen. *—Stephen Thomas Erlewine*

Welcome to the Freak Show: Live in Concert / Aug. 26, 1997 / ForeFront ✦✦✦
By capturing DC Talk on stage, *Live In Concert—Welcome to the Freak Show* functions as a vital greatest hits album. Despite their many virtues, DC Talk's albums can occasionally sound constrained and guarded. *Welcome to the Freak Show* remedies that situation, as it relies on the group's frentic, kinetic energy and interplay with the audience. The group runs through all of their best-known songs, delivering each with vigor. For the uninitiated, this is the best place to become acquainted with the group, and longtime fans will cherish this document of DC Talk at the peak of their powers. *—Rodney Batdorf*

Supernatural / Sep. 22, 1998 / Virgin ✦✦✦

● **Intermission: The Greatest Hits** / Nov. 21, 2000 / ForeFront ✦✦✦✦✦

Delirious?

f. Jan. 1996, Littlehampton, West Sussex, England
Group / Christian Rock, CCM
One of the most popular Christian rock groups in Britain, Delirious? was formed in early 1996 as the worship band at a monthly outreach sponsored by Arun Community Church of Littlehampton, West Sussex. After the issue of two†independent worship releases, the group began gigging around the area as well and formed their own Furious? label. Furious? released an EP, a live album, and then the band's 1997 studio debut *King of Fools*.

Delirious? received a pleasant shock later that year when the single "Deeper" hit the British Top 20, completely unheard of for an openly religious group. The band signed a contract with EMI, and in 1998 released *The Cutting Edge*, a double-disc compilation of their early worship recordings. Sparrow/Chordant signed the band for American distribution, and released *King of Fools* again in May 1998. *Mezzamorphis*, their Virgin label debut, followed in mid-1999. *Glo*, released on Sparrow Records was issued in fall 2000. *—John Bush*

● **The Cutting Edge** / Jan. 1, 1997 / Sparrow/Chordant ✦✦✦✦

King of Fools / May 19, 1998 / Sparrow/Furious Records ✦✦✦
Like Delirious?'s first album *Cutting Edge*, *King of Fools* has echoes of '80s U2, but the band accentuates the Christian undertones in Bono's lyrics, creating a modern rock record that resonates with spirituality. There are a few awkward moments and underdeveloped songs that prevent the record from being as consistently compelling as its predecessor, but the album offers more proof that Delirious? is a Christian rock band with an edge. *—Stephen Thomas Erlewine*

Mezzamorphis / Jun. 8, 1999 / Virgin ✦✦✦✦

Detroiters

f. Detroit, MI
Group / Traditional Gospel
One of the most successful gospel groups of the late 1940s, the Detroiters were led by Oliver Green, a native of Texas who began his career during the Depression era as a member of the Southern Wonders. Upon settling in the Motor City in 1938, he formed the Evangelist Singers of Detroit; after signing on with local radio station WGC, bandleader Horace Heidt insisted they change their name to the Detroiters, a more secular moniker which by extension would allow the addition of pop and folk material to their repertoire. Their frequent radio appearances led to a steady schedule of live bookings, and on August 14, 1951 the Detroiters entered the studio to record the first of three singles for the Specialty label, "Let Jesus Lead You." A second date from 1952 spawned a rousing "Old Time Religion," but it was their last Specialty effort; for reasons unknown, label chief Art Rupe did not take a shine to the group, and they were soon dropped. Although Barnes later exited to join the Flying Clouds, the Detroiters continued touring regionally into the early 1960s. *—Jason Ankeny*

Old Time Religion / 1992 / Specialty ✦✦✦✦✦
Old Time Religion showcases two great gospel vocal quartets from the '40s and '50s: the Detroiters and the Golden Echoes. The first half of the disc features 15 cuts from the Detroiters, 11 of which are previously unreleased songs recorded at United Sound. The Golden Echoes are represented with 11 songs recorded in 1949, ten of which have never been released. Usually, large sections of unreleased material would mean that the disc is primarily of interest to collectors, but that's not necessarily the case here. Both quartets are excellent examples of impassioned, moving and plain entertaining classic gospel, blessed with remarkable voices—the Detroiters' lineup boasted Oliver Green and Leroy Barnes, while the Golden Echoes featured Paul Foster, Sr. and Wilmer "Little Axe" Broadnax—and true spirit; it's a pleasure to hear them in any setting. Granted, some tastes may find the preponderance of alternate takes a little tedious, but if you program them out, you're left with a sterling collection of classic gospel. *—Leo Stanley*

The Dixie Hummingbirds

f. 193?, Greenville, South Carolina
Group / Traditional Gospel, Southern Gospel, Black Gospel
A pioneering force behind the evolution of the modern gospel quartet sound, the Dixie Hummingbirds were among the longest-lived and most successful groups of their era; renowned for their imaginative arrangements, progressive harmonies and all-around versatility, they earned almost universal recognition as the greatest Southern quartet of their generation. Formed in Greenville, SC by James B. Davis, the Dixie Hummingbirds began their career during the late 1930s as a jubilee-styled act; joined in 1938 by 13-year-old baritone phenom Ira Tucker and bass singer extraordinaire Willie Bobo, a former member of the Heavenly Gospel Singers, the group made their recorded debut a year later on Decca, where they issued singles including "Soon Will Be Done with the Troubles of This World," "Little Wooden Church" and "Joshua Journeyed to Jericho." Upon relocating to Philadelphia in 1942, the Hummingbirds' popularity began to grow—Tucker, in particular, wowed audiences with his flamboyant theatrics, rejecting the long tradition of "flat-footed" singers rooted in place on stage in favor of running up the aisles and rocking prayerfully on his knees. By 1944, he was even regularly jumping off stages—indeed, the frenetic showmanship of soul music may have had its origins in Tucker's manic intensity, itself an emulation of country preaching. At the same time, the Hummingbirds' harmonies continued to grow more sophisticated; the addition of Paul Owens completed the quartet's development, and together he and Tucker honed a style they dubbed "trickeration," a kind of note-bending distinguished by sensual lyrical finesse and staggering vocal intricacy. Their virtuosity did not go unnoticed by audiences, and throughout the mid-1940s—an acknowledged golden age of a cappella quartet singing—the group regularly played to packed houses throughout the south. Tucker continued leading the group at the century's end, recruiting new blood to keep the Dixie Hummingbirds' spirit alive for years to follow and celebrating their 70th anniversary with 1998's *Thank You for One More Day*. *—Jason Ankeny*

Christian Testimonial / 1959 / MCA ✦✦✦
Great Peacock sides led by James Walker and Ira Tucker. *—Opal Louis Nations*

The Best of the Dixie Hummingbirds / 1973 / MCA ✦✦✦✦✦
The Dixie Hummingbirds are generally regarded as one of the finest gospel groups in history, and the material showcased on *The Best of the Dixie Hummingbirds* proves why. Culled from the group's '50s and '60s recordings for Peacock, the compilation contains 12 terrific songs—including "Let's Go to the Programs," "Thank You for One More Day," "What a Friend," "Bedside of a Neighbor," "The Old Time Way" and "Our Prayer for Peace"—all of which are given astonishing, moving performances by the Hummingbirds. Throughout their long career, the Hummingbirds rarely gave anything less than impressive performances, but this remains one of the very best portraits of the superior gospel sextet. *—Stephen Thomas Erlewine*

☆ **Live** / 1976 / Mobile Fidelity ✦✦✦✦✦
With 75 minutes of fine performances, good sound quality and a varied repertoire, this the one to buy. *—Kip Lornell*

In the Storm Too Long / 1991 / Gospel Jubilee ✦✦✦✦✦
Essential Regis, Apollo & Decca sides from the '40s. *—Opal Louis Nations*

In Good Health / Feb. 1, 1993 / Atlanta International ✦✦✦

☆ **Complete Recorded Works (1939-1947)** / Apr. 8, 1997 / Document ✦✦✦✦✦
Essential early sides by this seminal group. *—Opal Louis Nations*

Up in Heaven: The Very Best of the Dixie Hummingbirds & The Angelics / Mar. 3, 1998 / Collectables ✦✦✦✦
Peacock/ABC Paramount sides by this leading group from Philadelphia. *—Opal Louis Nations*

★ **Thank You for One More Day** / Nov. 17, 1998 / MCA ✦✦✦✦✦
Released in conjunction with "The 70th Anniversary of the Dixie Hummingbirds" in 1998, this brings together 14 sides recorded for the ABC label. As one of the oldest of the still-performing groups (alongside the Fairfield Four and the Soul Stirrers), these earlier sides show the group during its hard gospel phase, although still adhering to their original concept of being a five-man gospel group with four-part harmonies surrounding and supporting a lead singer. Highlights anywhere the laser beams falls here, but special note should be paid to "Loves Me Like a Rock," "Let's Go Out to the Program" (where they imitate other groups with uncanny precision), "Two Little Fishes (And Five Loaves of Bread)," "Christian's Automobile," "Mother's Prayer," and "Bedside of a Neighbor." Equally noteworthy are "Ezekial Saw the Wheel," "In the Morning," "If Anybody Asks You," "The Final Edition," "Our Prayer for Peace" and the title track. A nice, bite-sized introduction to this long-standing gospel music tradition. *—Cub Koda*

Rev. Thomas A. Dorsey

b. Jul. 1, 1899, Villa Rica, GA, **d.** Jan. 23, 1993, Chicago, IL
Vocals, Piano, Guitar / Prewar Gospel Blues, Prewar Blues, Traditional Gospel, Blues Gospel, Piano Blues
The acknowleged father of gospel music, Thomas A. Dorsey remains arguably the most influential figure ever to impact the genre. A versatile composer whose material shifted easily from energetic hard gospel to gossamer hymns, he penned many of the best-known songs in the gospel canon, among them "Take My Hand, Precious Lord" and "Peace in the Valley"; the founder of the National Convention of Gospel Choirs and Choruses, he was also a pioneering force in the renowned Chicago gospel community, where he helped launch the careers of legends including Mahalia Jackson and Sallie Martin. A child prodigy, he taught himself a wide range of instruments, and was playing blues and ragtime while still in his teens; under the stage name Georgia Tom, he was a prolfic composer, authoring witty, slightly racy blues songs like the underground hit "It's Tight Like That." In 1928, after suffering his second nervous breakdown in as many years, he opted to retire from the music business. A two-year recovery period followed, during which time a minister convinced Dorsey to return to music, albeit to move from the blues to the church. His first attempt at writing a gospel song, 1921's "If I Don't Get There," had met with some success, and he now returned with a renewed sense of purpose, renouncing secular music to devote all of his talents to the church circuit. Initially, Dorsey resorted to peddling song sheets to make a living; his luck appeared

to be on the upswing by 1932, the year he organized one of the first gospel choirs at Chicago's Pilgrim Baptist Church and also founded the first publishing house devoted exclusively to selling music by black gospel composers. However, tragedy struck when Dorsey discovered that his wife had died while giving birth to their son, who himself died two days later. Devastated, Dorsey locked himself inside his music room for three straight days, emerging with a completed draft of "Take My Hand, Precious Lord," a song whose popularity in the gospel community is rivaled perhaps only by "Amazing Grace." Setting his loss behind him, he enjoyed his most prolific period in the years that followed, authoring dozens of songs with a distinctively optimistic sensibility for audiences held in the grip of the Depression. *—Jason Ankeny*

★ **Precious Lord: The Great Gospel Songs of Thomas A. Dorsey** / 1994 / Columbia/Legacy ✦✦✦✦✦
Precious Lord collects 18 of Georgia Thomas Dorsey's greatest songs, offering a terrific introduction to one of the greatest gospel country blues singers of the '30s. *—Thom Owens*

Phil Driscoll

Vocals, Trumpet / Inspirational, CCM
CCM trumpeter/singer Phil Driscoll was born November 9, 1947 in Seattle, and by the age of three was already playing a plastic trombone and Hawaiian slack guitar. While a freshman at Baylor University he formed the school's first jazz band, and as a sophomore recorded his first album, 1969's *A Touch of Trumpet*, with the Stockholm Symphony Orchestra. During his senior year, Driscoll took top honors on the CBS television talent-search series *The All American College Bowl* for a dozen weeks running, once even beating the aspiring pop duo of siblings Karen and Richard Carpenter; after completing 1970's *Blowin' a New Mind* he moved into secular pop music, composing material for acts including Joe Cocker, Stephen Stills, Blood, Sweat & Tears and Leon Russell. Driscoll returned to the Christian music fold with 1981's *Ten Years After*, and with 1983's *I Exalt Thee* scored a Dove Award for Instrumental Album Of the Year as well as Grammy nomination in the Best Gospel/Pop Album category. Both 1985's *Power of Praise* and 1987's *Make Us One* took home Dove Awards as well, and in the years to follow Driscoll lent his soulful, pop-influenced sound to everything from children's songs (1989's *Gabe and the Good News Gang*) to patriotic material (1990's *Celebrate Freedom*) to R&B (1990's *Innerman*) to seasonal favorites (1993's *The Sound of Christmas*). In 1996 he expanded into the television ministry with the show *The Voice of Praise;* that same year, the album *A Different Man* launched the hit "Christ Remains." Driscoll even turned to country music with 1997's *Shine the Light; Simple Song* followed two years later, and in the spring of 2000 he issued two new LPs, *Plugged In* and *Quiet*. *—Jason Ankeny*

● **I Exalt Thee** / 1983 / Sparrow ✦✦✦✦✦

The Picture Changes / 1992 / Word ✦✦✦
Driscoll trades in his blustery, Joe Cocker-ish vocal style for a more subdued approach that suits his range better. Vocals are featured more than trumpet here, though understated approach is employed instrumentally as well, to good effect. *—Thom Granger*

Simple Song / Jun. 8, 1999 / Mighty Horn ✦✦✦✦
Phil Driscoll's *Simple Song* features the trumpeter's singing and playing on inspirational songs like the title track, "Bless The Lord," "Dance & Sing," "Welcome Holy Spirit," and "Thine Is The Kingdom." *—Heather Phares*

Bryan Duncan

b. Ogden, UT
Vocals / Christian Rap, CCM
It took over twenty years from his entry into the gospel music world, but Bryan Duncan finally became a star during the mid-'90s, hitting number one on Christian radio ten times from 1993 to 1997. He had formed the Sweet Comfort Band in the early '70s and recorded half a dozen LPs with the band, but after the trio agreed to split in 1984, he released his debut solo album *Have Yourself Committed* just one year later. By 1993's *Mercy*, Duncan had begun a parade of hits—the album itself generated five chart-toppers: "Love Takes Time," "You Don't Leave Me Lonely," "Into My Heart," "When It Comes to Love," and "I'll Not Forget You." His major follow-up to *Mercy* was *Blue Skies*, released in early 1997. *—John Bush*

Have Yourself Committed / 1985 / Light ✦✦

Holy Rollin' / 1986 / Light ✦✦

Anonymous Confessions of a Lunatic Friend / 1991 / Word ✦✦✦
Duncan's extroverted comic side, periodically rearing its head on a number of songs over the years, is balanced here with a few tunes featuring a new, more confessional tone that would mark the artist's direction to come. *—Thom Granger*

● **Mercy** / Jan. 19, 1993 / Word ✦✦✦✦✦
Arguably his best album, Duncan digs deep to deal with the things he's been avoiding ... and turns in the best songs and vocal performances of his career. *—Thom Granger*

Slow Revival / 1994 / Myrrh ✦✦✦
Continuing with the themes spotlighted on *Mercy*, this album delivered even better lyrical expressions of the ideas, but is ballad-heavy musically and lacks the variety of earlier work. *—Thom Granger*

My Utmost for His Highest: Quiet Prayers / Jul. 1996 / Word ✦✦✦✦✦
Quiet Prayers is Bryan Duncan's installment in the *My Utmost for His Highest* series and it ranks as one of the best, not only in the series but also in his catalog. Most of the album consists of covers of contemporary Christian songs, but there are also a couple of originals, like "When I Turn to You," thrown in for good measure. No matter who wrote the song, Duncan delivers it convincingly and his smooth, country-tinged mainstream pop style is appealingly melodic on every cut on the record. *—Rodney Batdorf*

Michael English

Vocals / CCM
Michael English's roots are in Southern gospel; he performed with the Singing Americans, the Goodmans, the Gaither Trio and the Gaither Vocal Band before going solo in 1991. English began drawing attention to his powerful tenor when he recorded "I Bowed on My Knees and Cried Holy," first with the Singing Americans, then with the Brooklyn Tabernacle Choir. English has won Dove Awards for Best New Artist and Best Male Vocalist. Among his solo efforts: 1993's *Hope*, 1995's *Healing* and 1996's *Freedom*. He returned in 1998 with *Gospel*, followed two years later by *Heaven to Earth*. *—Brian Mansfield*

● **Michael English** / 1992 / Warner Alliance ✦✦✦✦✦
This wildly successful debut rides the line between adult contemporary and dance-pop. But the real draw is English's eloquent voice, which is showcased to great effect on the likes of "Heaven" and "Solid As the Rock." *—Brian Mansfield*

Hope / 1993 / Warner Alliance ✦✦✦
English traded the sophomore slump for a scandal, as his second solo album made him even more popular, taking home the Dove Award for Artist of the Year in '94, only to leave gospel music a week later as a result of an extramarital affair, after which his label dropped him from its roster. *—Thom Granger*

Freedom / Jul. 1996 / Curb ✦✦✦✦✦

The Fairfield Four

f. Nashville, TN
Group / Hymns, Traditional Gospel, Southern Gospel, Black Gospel
During the 1940s, the Fairfield Four were among the top-ranked gospel quartets, along with the Dixie Hummingbirds, Five Blind Boys, and Soul Stirrers. They recorded for RCA Victor and Columbia and were known for their reinterpretations of standard hymns, featuring bright, close baritone and tenor harmonies. When the Fairfield Four sang, they utilized the full extent of their voices, moving easily from deep, rolling basslines to the staccato upper peaks of the tenor range, all executed with precise, intricate harmonies and ever-shifting leads. The Fairfield Four reached their broadest audience when the Sunway Vitamin Company sponsored a nationally broadcast radio show for them daily at 6:45 a.m. on WLAC, Nashville. In 1942, the quartet recorded for the Library of Congress, but by 1950, it all became too much. Coupled with some financial trouble and a dwindling radio audience, the Fairfield Four broke up, though one member, Reverend Sam McCary, used the group name to perform with other quartets. They continue to perform, though the original members are either deceased or retired. *—Sandra Brennan & Bil Carpenter*

One Religion / 1980 / Nashboro ✦✦✦
This is a prize collection of some of Nashville's Fairfield Four Dot recordings spanning the years 1951 through 1953. The group on these sides is composed of Rev. Sam McCrary—lead, Willie Love—second tenor, James Hill—baritone, and Willie Frank Lewis—bass. Some of these cuts are thought to be alternate takes of earlier Bullet recordings made during the late '40s. Its classic a cappella singing is reminiscent of early Spirit of Memphis material. There's excellent notes by gospel researcher Tony Heilbut. *—Opal Louis Nations, Roots & Rhythm Newsletter*

★ **Angels Watching over Me** / 1981 / P-Vine ✦✦✦✦✦
Angels Watching Over Me is a remarkable collection of classic material the Fairfield Four recorded in the early '50s. Each of the 26 tracks are performed a cappella, yet there's a lot of variety within the music, since the quartet positioned themselves between the classic sound of gospel choirs and the bluesier, harder-edged sound of small vocal combos. The results are stunning and moving, making *Angels Watching Over Me* an essential addition to any serious gospel library. *—Leo Stanley*

Standing in the Safety Zone / 1992 / Warner Alliance ✦✦✦✦✦
The Fairfield Four were once among the finest hard gospel ensembles around. Unfortunately, they didn't stay together as long as their comrades, disbanding in 1950 due to business problems. They reunited 30 years later, then received a National Heritage Fellowship award in 1989. This wonderful '92 release features awesome harmonies, a guest appearance from The Nashville Bluegrass Band on "Roll, Jordan Roll," and soaring, magnificent lead vocals from Walter Settles, Isaac Freeman, and W.L. Richardson. Old-time gospel at its best, vividly presented via contemporary technology. *—Ron Wynn*

I Couldn't Hear Nobody Pray / Sep. 9, 1997 / Warner Brothers ✦✦✦✦✦
Around the time of this album's release, the Fairfield Four reached a new peak in mainstream visibility, complete with an appearance backing Elvis Costello on *The David Letterman Show*. Elvis Costello-led cut ("That Day Is Done") appears here, and there are odd guest appearances by country singer Pam Tillis and Prairie Home Companion narrator Garrison Keillor. But the focus is usually on the singers, who perform a cappella on most of the cuts. They sing full-bodied vocal arrangements with dignified conviction; the low parts are especially vibrant. *—Richie Unterberger*

● **Best of the Fairfield Four** / May 16, 2000 / MCA International ✦✦✦✦

The Bells Are Tolling / Nov. 27, 2000 / Ace ✦✦✦✦
This 1962 LP was actually made in 1960, and was the first time the group recorded with a rhythm section. At this point, the Fairfield Four's ever-changing lineup was comprised of Henry Brown, David Aaron, Willie Williams, and Joseph Henderson. At least, that's what the liner notes on the original LP say; according to the liner notes of the 2000 CD reissue on Ace, most of the leads are taken by Clarence Mills and the Reverend Sam McCrary. Bass singer Henderson, who also played guitar, was in fact the Joe Henderson who would have a Top Ten pop hit in 1962 with "Snap Your Fingers." Regardless of who sang what, *The Bells Are Tolling* is a good gospel record with some trumpet-swallowing leads, particularly on "Don't Let Nobody Turn You Around." Not many copies were pressed the first time around, and although it was reissued in 1973 as *The Famous Fairfield Four With Rev. Samuel McCrary*, it took the 2000 Ace CD reissue to make this album easy to find. *—Richie Unterberger*

The Five Blind Boys of Alabama

f. 1937, Talladega, AL
Group / Traditional Gospel, Southern Gospel, Black Gospel
Evolving out of the Happyland Jubilee Singers, this traditional Black gospel quartet was formed in 1937 at the Talladega Institute for the Deaf and Blind in Alabama. By the '40s they became "The Blind Boys" and recorded for Specialty, Vee Jay, Savoy, Elektra, and other labels. Their first hit was "I Can See Everybody's Mother but Mine" in 1949. Current lineup: Joe Watson, Jimmy Carter, Sam & Bobby Butler, Curtis Foster, Johnny Fields, and Clarence Fountain. They appeared on Broadway in *Gospel at Colonus.* —*Bil Carpenter*

★ **The Sermon** / 1953-1956 / Specialty ✦✦✦✦✦
A treasure trove of previously unreleased material, this brings together 25 new tracks, all recorded between 1953 and 1957. Only two songs, "Heaven on My Mind" and "I'm Going Through," were ever released in any form, but the quality of the material is certainly as high as any of their early sides. Here's one of gospel's greatest groups, singing their hearts out in their absolute prime. —*Cub Koda*

Marching Up to Zion / 1970 / Specialty ✦✦✦✦✦
Essential Blind Boys circa 1952-56. —*Opal Louis Nations*

Oh Lord, Stand by Me / 1970 / Specialty ✦✦✦✦✦
High voltage quartet led by the fiery Fountain, circa 1952-56. —*Opal Louis Nations*

Precious Memories / 1974 / MCA ✦✦✦✦✦
Impassioned vocals matched against stinging guitar and forthright chorus. —*Opal Louis Nations*

Oh Lord, Stand by Me/Marching Up to Zion / 1991 / Specialty ✦✦✦✦✦
Two of this seminal gospel group's Specialty albums on one compact disc. Compiled by musicologist Dr. Demento (under his real name Barret Hansen), this collection offers several of the group's original singles, all of them chock-full of fervent vocalizing from lead singers Clarence Fountain and the Rev. Samuel K. Lewis. This is the perfect introduction to these wonderful musicians and some of the most passionate gospel singing you're likely to encounter. —*Cub Koda*

Deep River / 1992 / Elektra/Nonesuch ✦✦✦✦✦
On their umpteenth release, the Five Blind Boys mix some modern blues and R&B into their core gospel sound. The rhythm section, led by the organ of the legendary Booker T. Jones, keeps the accompaniment simple as the group soars through some traditional material ("Closer Walk with Thee," "Every Time I Feel the Spirit,"), a few originals by lead vocalist Clarence Fountain, and a transcendent version of Bob Dylan's "I Believe in You." —*Jason Ankeny*

Swing Low, Sweet Chariot / Oct. 17, 1994 / Jewel ✦✦✦✦✦

1948-1951 / Dec. 12, 1995 / Flyright ✦✦✦✦✦
Initial recordings by this leading post-war traditional quartet. —*Opal Louis Nations*

Have Faith: The Very Best of the Five Blind Boys of Alabama / Mar. 3, 1998 / Collectables ✦✦✦✦
Pew-burning Vee Jay sides by Clarence Fountain and the boys. —*Opal Louis Nations*

Hallelujah: Collection of Their Finest / May 18, 1999 / Music Club ✦✦✦✦
This 15-track collection brings together both live and studio recordings made for the HOB label. Both of the famous leads with the group—Clarence Fountain and Louis Dicks—are featured on tracks like "Something's Got a Hold on Me," "When I Come to the End of My Journey," "Too Close to Heaven," "Lord's Been Good to Me" and "I Got Jesus on My Mind," their two magnificent voices trading off on "Alone and Motherless," "Running for My Life," and the perennial favorite "I Saw the Light." The live tracks on here literally sweat with emotion and fervor. A nice set. —*Cub Koda*

The Five Blind Boys of Mississippi

f. 193?, Jackson, MS
Group / Traditional Gospel, Southern Gospel, Black Gospel
The Five Blind Boys of Mississippi are among the greatest singing groups in popular music history. Their smashing harmonies and the leads of Archie Brownlee not only influenced numerous gospel ensembles, but such secular artists as Ray Charles. Their origins date back to the '30s, when as The Cotton Blossom Singers they did both spiritual and secular material. Recorded in 1937 by Alan Lomax for the Library of Congress, for a time they performed under dual identities—they were The Cotton Blossom Singers for popular songs and The Jackson Harmoneers for gospel. In the mid-'40s, they became The Five Blind Boys, and made their recording debut for Excelsior in 1946. When they joined Don Robey's Peacock label in 1950, The Five Blind Boys became superstars. The single "Our Father" was a Top 10 R&B hit, and they became a prolific ensemble, recording 27 singles and five albums for Peacock through the '60s. Brownlee died in New Orleans in 1960. His riveting, chilling screams and yells were among gospel's most amazing. —*Ron Wynn*

Soon I'll Be Done / Apr. 1952 / Chess ✦✦✦
Reissue of the group's stunning Chess album with Little Axe and Roscoe Robinson at the helm. —*Opal Louis Nations*

★ **The Original Five Blind Boys** / 1959 / Vee-Jay ✦✦✦✦✦
Considered the finest post-war quartet album ever made. From Peacock singles, 1951-59. —*Opal Louis Nations*

★ **The Best of the Five Blind Boys of Mississippi, Vol. 1** / 1973 / MCA ✦✦✦✦✦
These Specialty recordings truly represent some of the best by this popular group. Arguably the greatest "quartet" ever. Featuring the wondrous Archie Brownlee. —*Kip Lornell & Ron Wynn*

In the Hands of the Lord / 1987 / MCA ✦✦

Counting on Jesus / 1993 / Soul Potion ✦✦✦
The name may be the same, but these are not The Original Five Blind Boys of Mississippi; Archie Brownlee has been dead for many years, and others have departed. No roster list is included here. They still harmonize with exuberance, and the eight numbers on their most recent release are steadfastly traditional in lyrics, production structure, and feel; no huge backing choirs, synthesized backdrops or bombastic settings, but simple stories about spiritual fulfillment and release. —*Ron Wynn*

The Best of the Blind Boys / MCA Special Products ✦✦✦
MCA's *Best of the Blind Boys* is a good, but not exceptional, collection of 12 highlights from the group's Peacock material. There are a number of wondrous performances here—including "Love Lifted Me, " "Jesus Satisfied" and "Speak for Jesus"—but in general, the recordings aren't quite as strong as their recordings for Vee-Jay. Furthermore, the album feels a little skimpy in these days of extensive reissues, making it more of interest for completists and serious fans than listeners seeking out good values or representative collections. —*Leo Stanley*

4 Him

Group / Contemporary Gospel, CCM
Three times voted Gospel Group of the Year, the quartet known as 4Him formed in 1990 as a spin-off from the choral group Truth. Fronted by Kirk Sullivan, the vocal group released its self-titled debut album in 1990 for the Benson label. Four albums followed in the next four years (*Face the Nation, The Basics of Life, 4Him Christmas, The Ride*), after which 4Him toured during 1995 and followed up with 1996's *The Message.* Two years later 4Him delivered *Obvious,* and 2000 saw the arrival of *A Place Of Worship.* The group has also released several videos, including the live document *The Ride Comes Alive.* —*John Bush*

Ride / Oct. 4, 1994 / Verity ✦✦✦
Though the foursome teamed up with super-producer Michael Omartian and others for its fifth album, the results showed nothing particularly new. —*Thom Granger*

Obvious / Apr. 7, 1998 / Benson ✦✦✦✦
By the time 4 Him made *Obvious* in 1998, they were pretty much set in their ways, but instead of getting complacent, the group was refining their sound and getting better. So while there are no real surprises on *Obvious,* the band's craftsmanship has increased. That means the record isn't as immediate or fresh as their early recordings, but the sturdy songs and performances make it worth repeated listens. —*Stephen Thomas Erlewine*

● **The Basics of Life** / Verity ✦✦✦✦✦
The group's breakthough recording has a title song that said it all about returning to traditional values to its growing number of fans. —*Thom Granger*

Kirk Franklin

Vocals, Piano / Contemporary Gospel, Black Gospel, Urban
Since his debut, 1993's *Kirk Franklin and the Family,* Kirk Franklin has been one of the brightest stars in contemporary gospel music. The album spent 100 weeks on *Billboard's* Gospel charts (some of those on top), crossed over to the R&B charts, and became the first gospel album to go platinum. His second album, *Kirk Franklin & the Family Christmas,* became the genre's first Christmas album to make it to number one, and his 1996 album *Whatcha Lookin' 4* went gold as soon as it was distributed. With such phenomenal success, it is small wonder that some have hailed him "the Garth Brooks of Gospel." Still, despite all the adulation and brouhaha, Franklin remains a humble, devout Christian, eschewing the title "entertainer" in favor of labeling himself as just a "church boy." —*Sandra Brennan*

● **Kirk Franklin & The Family** / Jun. 29, 1993 / Sparrow ✦✦✦✦✦
Kirk Franklin & the Family's eponymous debut album is a stunningly assured blend of old-fashioned gospel, contemporary soul and hip-hop. Franklin remains, in his words, a "church boy," but he doesn't hesitate to embrace the conventions and styles of contemporary R&B, which results in some inspired, unexpected fusions. It is truly a record that updates, recontextualizes and redefines what contemporary gospel can mean in the '90s. —*Rodney Batdorf*

Whatcha Lookin' 4 / 1995 / Gospo Centric ✦✦✦
Although it isn't quite as consistent as his debut, *Whatcha Lookin' 4* remains exceptional urban gospel, exhibiting passion, soul and grit. —*Rodney Batdorf*

God's Property / May 27, 1997 / B-Rite/Interscope ✦✦✦✦
The success of God's Property is due to Kirk Franklin's skill as a talent scout and as a producer. Like Franklin's records, *God's Property* is contemporary gospel music that isn't bland or processed; it still has soul and feeling. Not only is the music strong, but so are the songs, making *God's Property* one of the most refreshing contemporary gospel albums of the '90s. —*Rodney Batdorf*

The Nu Nation Project / Sep. 22, 1998 / Interscope ✦✦✦✦

Billy and Sarah Gaines

b. 1981
Vocals / Contemporary Gospel
Spiritual reverance serves as the foundation for the soulful singing of husband and wife duo Billy and Sarah Gaines. Since releasing their self-titled debut duo album in 1986, the duo has reached number one on the Top 40 six times. Their hits include "A Friend Indeed", "How Great His Heart Must Be", "I Found Someone", "Right Here At Home", "The Same All The Time" and "While You Wait". Billy Gaines' musical success is a long way from the days when he told his fourth grade teacher that he was "tone deaf". A year after meeting Sarah in his hometown, Richmond, Virginia, he moved to her hometown, Hampton, and helped form Living Sacrifice, a gospel group that was the opening act and backup band for Danniebelle Hall, the ex-lead singer of Andrea Crouch And The Disciples. Though they began as a duo after the band's breakup in 1981, Billy and Sarah Gaines didn't have their first break until shortly after moving to Nashville three years later. Billy held a series of jobs in Tennessee' s Music City, including janitor and Pinkerton security guard and worked as a songwriter for Nineteenth Street Productions/Lorenz Creativity Services; soon after, the duo signed a five album

deal with the Benson label. The four-time Dove Award nominees received a "Best Inspirational Award" Dove Award for their participation in the "Generation To Generation Project" in 1994. *Come On back*, Billy and Sarah Gaines' first album for Warner Alliance Soundhouse, the label they started with producer Michael O'Martian, featured guest appearances by CeCe Winans, Chris Willis, Kim Fleming, Vickie Hampton, Chris Rodriguez and Eric Millet. —*Craig Harris*

Billy and Sarah Gaines / 1986 / Heartwarming ✦✦✦

● **He'll Find a Way** / 1988 / Heartwarming ✦✦✦✦✦
This R&B, urban CCM collection includes slow and uptempo cuts. —*Bil Carpenter*

Come on Back / Jun. 25, 1996 / Warner Brothers ✦✦✦✦
Billy and Sarah Gaines prove why they are one of the most popular duos in CCM with *Come On Back*, their debut album for Warner Alliance. Under the direction of producer Michael Omartian, the duo crafts an engaging, soothing pop sound that charms the listener with its lilting harmonies and cascading melodies. In short, it's a lovely album. —*Rodney Batdorf*

Gaither Vocal Band

Group / Contemporary Gospel, CCM
One of the premier religious harmony groups, the Gaither Vocal Band was formed by contemporary gospel legend Bill Gaither in the early '90s with Mark Lowry, Jonathan Pierce and Guy Penrod. The group has recorded for Star Song, Benson and Chordant, receiving many Dove awards and several Grammy nominations. The Gaither Vocal Band has released two volumes of *Southern Classics* and *20 Inspirational Favorites*, as well as the live recording *Back Home in Indiana* and 1999's *God Is Good*. *I Do Believe* was issued in fall 2000. —*John Bush*

Peace of the Rock / 1993 / Star Song ✦✦

● **Southern Classics** / 1993 / Benson ✦✦✦✦

Testify / 1994 / Gaither/Chordant ✦✦✦✦
A surprisingly strong release from the GVB, as they get more in touch with their Southern gospel roots, but also allow themselves to delve into calypso, traditional gospel, and even a little rock & roll. Perhaps most importantly, it is obvious on several songs that this group is having a great time singing together. They open with the rollicking "John the Revelator," and show outstanding ensemble work on the wonderfully arranged "I Shall Wear a Crown," and bring it all together with "Send It on Down." They also include several Southern gospel ballads that adequately demonstrate each member's abilities, but it is the upbeat numbers that sets this group apart from the many Southern gospel bands' records: they just have more fun. —*Marc Castellani*

Bill Gaither

b. Mar. 28, 1936, Alexandria, IN, **d.** Los Angeles, CA
Vocals / Contemporary Gospel, CCM
Aside from recording as a duo, Bill and Gloria Gaither have recorded with such other artists as the Gaither Vocal Band and the Bill Gaither Trio. The Gaithers are the most successful songwriters in Christian music. Their songs tend to be praise-and-worship-oriented but often cross various music barriers stylistically; however, their most significant material is contemporary pop. —*Bil Carpenter*

The Gaither Gospel Series: Best of Homecoming, Vol. 1 / Mar. 11, 1997 / Chordant ✦✦✦
Highlights of the 14-volume Gaither Homecoming gospel video series are compiled on this audio companion. —*Jason Ankeny*

● **Live Across America** / 1980 / Word ✦✦✦✦✦
This fine live double album includes their '70s pop-gospel hits. —*Bil Carpenter*

I'll Meet You on the Mountain / Nov. 2, 1999 / Spring House ✦✦✦
Released in both audio and video formats (and aired on the Nashville Network), *I'll Meet You on the Mountain* finds Bill and Gloria Gaither welcoming a variety of guests to a special performance at the Grove Park Inn, near Asheville, NC in the Blue Ridge Mountains. The beautiful setting seems to inspire the Gaithers in their performances, and there are appearances by the Gaither Vocal Band, Kim Hopper, Karen Peck, Bonnie Keen, and Buddy Greene, among others. —*Steve Huey*

Reverend J.M. Gates

b. 1885, **d.** 1941
Vocals / Scriptures, Traditional Gospel
The Baptist preacher J.M. Gates was one of the most prolifically recorded black artists of the early century, with over 200 sides on wax between the mid-'20s and his death in 1940 (he once recorded 23 titles in a week, at just two sessions). His sermons and musical numbers appeared on a variety of labels (Victor, Bluebird, Okeh, Gennett), though Gates often re-recorded his most popular sermons—"Death's Black Train Is Coming," "Oh Death Where Is Thy Sting," "Goin' to Die with the Staff in My Hands"—for multiple labels. Born in 1885, Gates ministered at Atlanta's Calvary Church and first recorded in 1926. Beginning in April, he recorded almost 100 sides by the end of the year. Understandably, his output slowed slightly during the rest of the late '20s, and the advent of the Great Depression resulted in a four-year period off records. He returned in 1934, and recorded about 20 more sides until his death in 1941. Experts estimate that Gates recorded at least a quarter of all the sermons that appeared before 1943. —*John Bush*

● **Complete Recorded Works, Vol. 1 (1926)** / Mar. 5, 1996 / Document ✦✦✦✦

Complete Recorded Works, Vol. 2 (1926) / May 14, 1996 / Document ✦✦✦

Cassietta George

b. Jan. 23, 1929, Memphis, TN, **d.** Jan. 3, 1995, Los Angeles, CA
Vocals / Black Gospel
The potent, clarion voice of Cassietta George rips through crowds with a moving, joyful noise. Though she had a distinguished solo career during the '60s and '70s, many still best remember George for her work with one of the best all-female gospel quartets of all time, the Caravans, in which she was one of the lead singers and a key songwriter.

George was born in Memphis, Tennessee. When she was four, she began singing in her father's church. Before getting involved with the Caravans in 1954, George had experience singing with other quartets, and her style was heavily influenced by that of Clara Ward. While in the seminal group, she sang beside such greats as James Cleveland, Albertina Walker, Inez Andrews, Delores Washington and Shirley Caesar, but only spent a year with them before leaving. George returned to the Caravans in 1960 and sang with them for the next five years. After that, she launched a successful solo career, recording over ten albums in Los Angeles for Audio Arts, Inc., touring constantly and writing over a hundred songs. Along the way, George was twice nominated for a Grammy. —*Sandra Brennan*

Dorothy Norwood Presents / 1994 / Paula/Flyright ✦✦✦✦✦
Fine singing from this ex-Caravan soloist. —*Opal Louis Nations*

Georgia Mass Choir

f. 1983, Macon, GA
Group / Contemporary Gospel, Gospel Choir
Formed in 1983, the 150-voice Georgia Mass Choir came to prominence through highly visible appearances in the Whitney Houston film *The Preacher's Wife* and at the 1996 Olympic Games in Atlanta. Lead voice, songwriter, and founder Rev. Milton Biggham had spent time organizing Savoy Records, but returned to his home state to organize the choir from over 600 applicants. Naturally, the Georgia Mass Choir began recording for Savoy, and released their first album *Yes, He Can* in the mid-'80s. Additional albums followed, and by the early '90s, the group began to be recognized around the nation as one of the leading gospel choirs through Grammy and Dove Award nominations, and the gift of the Keys to the City of Atlanta. Film director Penny Marshall cast them in *The Preacher's Wife* in 1996, and the choir also received a Gospel Music Workshop of America Excellence Award. —*John Bush*

● **Greatest Hits** / Nov. 19, 1996 / Savoy ✦✦✦✦✦
Greatest Hits is an excellent 12-track sampler of the Georgia Mass Choir's career, featuring such staples as "Hold On, Help Is On the Way," "We've Got the Victory," "Joy," "I Sing Because I'm Happy," "Jesus Is a Rock," "You Bring Me Joy" and "I'm Going to Hold Out." For anyone curious about the Choir, this is the perfect way to become acquainted with the group. —*Stephen Thomas Erlewine*

They That Wait / May 25, 1999 / Savoy ✦✦✦✦

Terri Gibbs

b. Jun. 15, 1954, Augusta, GA
Vocals / Urban Cowboy, Country Gospel, Adult Contemporary, CCM, Country-Pop
Singer/songwriter/keyboardist Terri Gibbs was raised on gospel music, and most of her country hits have been gospel-oriented. Blind from birth, as a child and young teen she won several talent contests and sang in various choirs. Chet Atkins helped her launch her career after meeting her backstage at the Bell Auditorium in Augusta, GA. At his request, she sent him a demo tape; he called her on her 18th birthday and suggested she go to Nashville, but the trip was unsuccessful. She founded her own band in 1975 and began playing at a restaurant in Augusta. In 1980, producer/songwriter Ed Penney came to Augusta to hear her and signed her to MCA. Her debut album, *Somebody's Knockin'*, and the title single were well received, the latter becoming a major hit on both pop and country charts in 1981. She released two more albums in 1981 and 1982 and began an extensive tour with George Jones, with whom she sang duets. She continued to make regular chart appearances through 1984. In 1986, Gibbs switched to gospel music and signed with Word Records, and the title track of 1987's *Turn Around* became a minor hit on the country charts. In 1988, Gibbs appeared three times on the contemporary Christian charts with the Top Five hits "Promise Land," "Comfort the People" and "Unconditional Love." —*Sandra Brennan*

● **The Best of Terri Gibbs** / Oct. 22, 1996 / Varèse Vintage ✦✦✦✦✦
All of Terri Gibbs' biggest hits from the early '80s—including "Somebody's Knockin'," "Rich Man," "Mis'ry River," "Ashes to Ashes," and "Anybody Else's Heart But Mine"—are included on this comprehensive, definitive collection. —*Thom Owens*

Jon Gibson

Vocals / Contemporary Gospel, CCM
Blue-eyed soulster Jon Gibson's instincts and songwriting made his too-close-for-comfort Stevie Wonder-like vocals worth tolerating. His later albums are the better, as Gibson evolved into a vocal style more his own. The songs and production are improved as well. —*Thom Granger*

Body & Soul / 1989 / Frontline ✦✦✦

Jesus Loves Ya / 1990 / Frontline ✦✦✦
A solid outing, it features hits like "Love Come Down" and the title cut. —*Thom Granger*

● **Hits** / 1991 / Frontline ✦✦✦✦✦
A good place to start with Gibson, it features most of his hits, a Scott Blackwell remix of "Jesus Loves Ya" and a new Christmas song. —*Thom Granger*

Forever Friends / 1992 / Frontline ✦✦✦
More slammin' blue-eyed soul comes from the still less-than-well-known stylist. —*Thom Granger*

The Man Inside / Oct. 19, 1999 / Interscope ✦✦✦
After taking a few years off of his solo recording career, Jon Gibson returned in 1999 with *The Man Inside*, which continued his approach of blending blue-eyed soul-pop with adult contemporary flavors. Throughout the album, Gibson proves himself a solid craftsman, and his performances are polished enough to make the weaker material not so noticeable. Highlights include the lead single, "God Will Find You." —*Steve Huey*

Gold City

Group / Southern Gospel, CCM
The bible-belt southern gospel group Gold City was formed in Alabama in 1980. Members are bass vocalist Timothy "Tim" Riley, tenor John "Jay" Parrack, baritone Mark Trammell, lead vocalist Jonathan Wilburn, bass vocalist and guitarist Adam Borden, drummer Douglas "Doug" Riley, pianist Channing Eleton, and baritone Daniel Riley. Before joining forcing for Gold City, most of the guys had spent time fine tuning their skills with other gospel bands, like Dixie Echoes, Poet Voices, Arkansas Boys, Greater Vision, the Wilburns, and the Singing Ambassadors.

By the time the new millennium rolled around, Gold City had performed at countless festivals, and appeared on stage at the Southern Baptist Convention, Music City Tonight, the Grand Ole Opry, and Nashville Now. The group had also completed over two dozen remarkable albums, featuring tunes like "There Rose a Lamb," "Getting' Ready to Leave This World," "What a Glad Day," "Be Not Afraid," and "Dearest Friend I Ever Had."

The smooth harmonies the members of Gold City serve up on its albums has earned the group a number of significant awards, including Traditional Male Quartet of the Year and Southern Gospel Music's Band of the Year by *Singing News Magazine*, and Album of the Year and Favorite Group at the acclaimed Voice Diamond Awards.

After two decades of using songs to witness to fans and reach lost souls, Gold City seems completely happy to stay the course and continue forward. *—Charlotte Dillon*

Portrait / 1989 / Heartwarming ✦✦✦✦
Superb harmonies are featured on this camp-meeting-style country music. *—Bil Carpenter*

● **Answer the Call** / Riversong ✦✦✦✦

Golden Eagle Gospel Singers

Group / Black Gospel
An Alabamian a cappella outfit that later developed roots in Chicago, The Golden Eagles were formed in the '30s by Thelma Byrd. On a level with The Golden Gate Quartet, their popularity was strongest in the Midwest. Unlike other groups of the time, who were usually male and Baptist, this one was coed and Sanctified. Much of their music had a fast-paced blues feel, most notably on 1937's "Tone the Bell" and 1940's "He's My Rock," which showcased Hammie Nixon on blues harmonica. They recorded for the Decca label. *—Bil Carpenter*

● **Complete Recordings 1937-1940** / Eden ✦✦✦✦

The Golden Eagle Gospel Singers / Eden ✦✦✦✦
These are gems from the three Chicago sessions (ca. 1937-1940) of this important mixed ten-member aggregation led by Thelma Byrd and supported at times by Hammie Nixon. *—Opal Louis Nations*

Golden Gate Quartet

f. Virginia
Group / Spirituals, Traditional Gospel, Black Gospel
Pioneer Virginia gospel/pop quartet of the '30s and '40s. Calling their innovative approach to sacred hymns "jubilee" singing, the Golden Gate Quartet, propelled by Willie Johnson and William Langford, enjoyed massive acceptance far outside the church. Their smooth Mills Brothers-influenced harmonies made the Gates naturals for pop crossover success, and they began recording for Victor in 1937. National radio broadcasts and an appearance on John Hammond's 1938 "Spirituals to Swing" concert at Carnegie Hall made them coast-to-coast favorites. By 1941 the Gates were recording for Columbia minus Langford, and movie appearances were frequent: *Star Spangled Rhythm, Hollywood Canteen,* and *Hit Parade of 1943,* to name a few. Some experiments with R&B material didn't pan out during the late '40s, and Johnson defected to the Jubilaires in 1948. The group emigrated to France in 1959; led by veteran bass singer Orlando Wilson, the Golden Gate Quartet's vocal blend is as powerful as ever. *—Bill Dahl*

★ **Travelin' Shoes** / Sep. 1992 / Bluebird/RCA ✦✦✦✦✦
Bluebird's *Travelin' Shoes* is a terrific collection that contains 25 tracks the Golden Gate Quartet recorded between 1937 and 1939. During those years, the group was at their peak, and their a cappella harmonies proved to be quite influential on successive generations of gospel singers, as they had enough foresight to add jazz and blues inflections to their harmonies. There's no better place to judge their greatness than this splendid collection. *—Leo Stanley*

Meet Me at the Golden Gate / Aug. 1, 1996 / Collector's Edition ✦✦✦✦
Memorable Columbia and Okeh sides from the 1940s when the group was at its peak. *—Opal Louis Nations*

The Very Best of the Golden Gate Quartet / Apr. 8, 1997 / Blue Note ✦✦✦✦✦
The Very Best of the Golden Gate Quartet is a terrific collection of songs the group recorded in France for EMI Pathe between 1955 and 1969, including versions of "Shadrack" and "Oh Happy Day." Although these aren't the versions that made them stars, they are nevertheless quite good and offer a good sense of what the group is about. *—Thom Owens*

☆ **35 Historic Recordings** / RCA ✦✦✦✦✦
These breathtaking sides from 1937-1939 are largely a cappella, with both gospel and pop music. The album also includes a landmark version of "Stormy Weather" that is at the root of doo wop. *—Hank Davis*

The Gospel Harmonettes

Group / Traditional Gospel, Southern Gospel, Black Gospel
Acknowledged as a prime influence by no less than Little Richard, the Original Gospel Harmonettes was among the greatest and most successful female gospel groups of the '50s; led by soloist Dorothy Love Coates, their music transcended its spiritual foundations to appeal to a secular world on the threshold of the civil rights era. After several early recordings for RCA Victor, a contract with Specialty in 1951 resulted in quick popularity for the singles "I'm Sealed" and "Get Away Jordan." A pure dynamo in seemingly constant motion, the galvanic Coates cut a sharp contrast to her urbane accompanists, and her songs—often updates of traditional numbers tailored to speak to contemporary issues—struck a powerful chord among listeners. Despite the group's enormous popularity during the '50s, the Harmonettes were inactive for several years. Coates re-formed the Harmonettes in 1961, and their comeback record, "Come on in My House," was a hit. Although they never quite recaptured the prominence of their golden era the group continued touring until 1971. In later years, Coates frequently performed at a number of jazz festivals, and even appeared in the 1990 film *The Long Walk Home*. *—Jason Ankeny*

● **Camp Meeting/God Is Here** / Jul. 1993 / Vee-Jay ✦✦✦✦✦
The link between gospel music and the civil rights era has never been clearer than on the two albums that comprise this CD reissue. Both issued in the mid-'60s, the rough-hewn, earthy, bluesy voice of Dorothy "Love" Coates and her inspirational songs were tailor-made to elevate the spirits of those fighting for social justice. Numbers like "Camp Meeting," "I Won't Let Go," "The Righteous on the March," and "Step By Step" don't have overt political lyrics, but certainly speak to the ultimate victories anticipated by civil rights workers. There's also plenty of more traditional spiritual material, sung with passionate belief. *—Ron Wynn*

Gospel Hummingbirds

Group / Traditional Gospel, Black Gospel
The Gospel Hummingbirds play a combination of traditional gospel (in the style similar to the Swan Silvertones, one of the Hummers' chief inspirations) and modern electrified blues- and soul-injected gospel. For the past couple decades, they have performed at religious gatherings, nightclubs, rock concerts and blues festivals, but regardless of where they perform, their joyful praises of God remain the same. The Oakland-based group have been together since the 1970s and were founded by the father of lead vocalist and bass guitarist Joe A. Thomas, who began playing bass with the Hummingbirds when he was only eight. As of 1995, the rest of the lineup included Roy Tyler, Clarence Nichols, James Gibson, Jr. and Mark Smith, Sr. *—Sandra Brennan*

● **Steppin' Out** / 1992 / Blind Pig ✦✦✦✦✦

Taking Flight / Nov. 1995 / Blind Pig ✦✦✦

Amy Grant

b. Nov. 25, 1960, Augusta, GA
Vocals / Adult Contemporary, CCM
Amy Grant is not only one of the most influential singers in contemporary Christian music, but also a successful pop star. She released her self-titled debut album at age 15 after signing with Myrrh/Word Records in 1979. In 1982, she married singer/songwriter Gary Chapman, who was to become her co-writer by the late 1980s. Grant became a bonafide gospel star in 1982 following the release of her acclaimed album *Age to Age*, which won her a Grammy for Best Female Gospel Performance and three Dove Awards, including Artist of the Year. In 1985, *Age to Age* was certified platinum, and her other two albums went gold. Her 1985 album, *Unguarded*, soon followed suit and again won her a Grammy. Grant caused an uproar amongst her loyal gospel audience with this album, which sported two successful pop crossover singles, "Find a Way" and "Wise Up." A year later, she made it to number one on the pop charts with "The Next Time I Fall," a duet with Peter Cetera. Throughout the '80s Grant's success continued, as her albums went gold and platinum and won awards. She signed to A&M in 1990 and began focusing less on her squeaky-clean gospel singer persona, trying to project a more contemporary, sexy (albeit in a wholesome way) pop image. In 1991, she had three big hit singles on the pop charts: the number one "Baby Baby," "Every Heartbeat," and "That's What Love Is For." *—Sandra Brennan*

Amy Grant / 1977 / Reunion ✦✦✦✦✦
Amy Grant's debut album shook the world of contemporary Christian music with a fresh new voice that would quickly become a fixture at the top of the gospel charts. "Beautiful Music," "Old Man's Rubble" and "What a Difference You've Made in My Life" laid the groundwork for the onslaught of hits Grant would produce in the years to come. Before she became a pop star, Amy Grant would reign as the queen of contemporary Christian music for a number of years. *—Michael B. Smith*

My Father's Eyes / 1979 / Reunion ✦✦✦✦✦
With her second album, Amy Grant turns in a fine contemporary Christian album, featuring the award-winning title track, as well as Christian radio staples "Faith Walkin' People," "Never Give You Up," and "There Will Never Be Another." By this time, Amy was becoming the a household name on the youth gospel circuit, playing songs from this and her debut album at venues all across America. Some of Grant's finest non-secular songs grace this release. *—Michael B. Smith*

Never Alone / 1980 / Reunion ✦✦

Age to Age / 1982 / Reunion ✦✦✦✦
Grant's first breakthrough in gospel featured a solid group of songs and players, and was a best-seller for years to come. *—Thom Granger*

Straight Ahead / 1984 / Reunion ✦✦

Unguarded / 1985 / Reunion ✦✦✦
The artist's first foray into crossover featured dance-pop music, and yielded a Top 20 hit, "Find a Way." *—Thom Granger*

Lead Me On / Jun. 28, 1988 / A&M ✦✦✦✦✦

★ **The Collection** / Oct. 17, 1990 / Reunion ✦✦✦✦✦

● **Heart in Motion** / 1991 / A&M ✦✦✦✦✦
In the late '70s and early '80s, Amy Grant enjoyed little exposure outside of Christian circles. But that started to change in the mid-'80s, when A&M promoted her aggressively in the sec-

ular market. And in the 1990s, secular audiences accounted for the vast majority of her sales. Christians were hardly the only ones buying *Heart In Motion*, one of Grant's biggest sellers. Even though she wasn't beating listeners over the head with her beliefs, Grant's wholesome, girl-next-door image was a big part of the appeal of perky pop-rock offerings like "Every Heartbeat," "Galileo" and the major hit "Baby Baby." And it's certainly a key element of another huge single from the album, the idealistic ballad "That's What Love Is For." Grant was a major star, and best of all, she wasn't acting like one. *—Alex Henderson*

House of Love / 1994 / A&M ♦♦♦
After a duo of detours (a youth worship record and a second Christmas offering), Grant returns with an album that doesn't even pretend to be gospel, but still reflects her ideologies. Mellower than *Heart in Motion*, the album sounds more like *Lead Me On*, but doesn't plumb its depths. *—Thom Granger*

Behind the Eyes / Sep. 9, 1997 / A&M ♦♦♦♦♦

Steve Green

Vocals, Bass / Inspirational, CCM
Gospel singer Steve Green began in the gospel industry during the mid-'70s, singing backup vocals and playing bass with Sandi Patti, White Heart and the Gaither Vocal Band. By the early '80s, he had gained a solo contract with Sparrow Records, and his self-titled debut album appeared in 1984. He averaged more than one album per year during the next dozen, with Spanish-language recordings (1987's *Tienen Que Saber*) and Christmas albums (1987's *Joy to the World!* and 1996's *First Noel*) in addition to his usual repertoire. Green has stayed on the Sparrow label for virtually every release, and also concentrates on videos and James Dobson's *Focus on the Family* as part of his musical ministry. *Morning Light* was released in 1999. *—John Bush*

● **For God and God Alone** / 1986 / Sparrow ♦♦♦♦♦

Mighty Fortress / 1987 / Birdwing ♦♦♦

The Faithful / Jan. 13, 1998 / Sparrow ♦♦♦
The Faithful is a typically graceful and melodic collection from Steve Green, highlighting not only his spirituality, but also his strength as a singer. The material is a little uneven, but the best songs—"To God All Praise and Glory," "The Faithful," "I Repent," "The Great Revival"—are equal to anything Green has recorded. *—Stephen Thomas Erlewine*

Morning Light: Songs to Awaken the Dawn / Jun. 15, 1999 / Sparrow ♦♦♦
A lovely, soothing album designed to help set the soul at ease, *Morning Light* is highlighted by "All That You Say," a duet with Twila Paris. *—Steve Huey*

The Greenes

Group / Southern Gospel, CCM
Family gospel group the Greenes emerged from North Carolina's Blue Ridge Mountains region in 1978—comprised of brothers Tim and Tony in tandem with sister Kim, the trio (originally accompanied by their father Everette on piano) toured steadily in the years to follow, finally earning national recognition in 1984 when their single "Gloryland" reached the Gospel Top 40. After Kim's exit from the act, the Greenes employed sopranos Amy Lambert and Milena Parks prior to adding TaRanda Kiser in late 1997; the album *Special Time* appeared a year later, followed in 1999 by *Wonderful Story. So Happy* was issued a year later. *—Jason Ankeny*

Wonderful Story / Sep. 21, 1999 / New Haven ♦♦♦♦
The Greenes' *Wonderful Story* features more of their tight harmonies and energetic performances. Their distinctive style has been popularized by appearances on Gaither videos and television shows such as "*Swan's Place,* " and songs like "The Unexpected Cross, " "Forgiven, Forgotten, Forever, " and "Every Time I Speak His Name" show why they have such a strong following in the gospel community. *—Heather Phares*

Fred Hammond

b. Detroit, MI
Vocals, Bass, Producer / Contemporary Gospel, CCM
A multi-instrumentalist, producer and vocalist for the soulful black gospel group Commissioned during the 1980s and '90s, Fred Hammond also became one of the most popular praise & worship leaders in the field. Born in Detroit, Hammond began singing with his church choir at the age of twelve. He played bass and sang with the Winans during the early '80s, then joined Commissioned later in the decade, showcasing his superb arranging, production and songwriting skill as well as his soaring vocals. Hammond's concurrent solo career began in 1991 with *I Am Persuaded*, and he released additional albums for Benson, gradually embracing an in-concert feel even on his studio recordings. His fifth studio album, *Purpose By Design* was released under the Verity label in 2000. *In Case You Missed It... And Then Some* followed in 2001. *—John Bush*

● **Pages of Life: Chapters 1 & 2** / Apr. 28, 1998 / Verity ♦♦♦♦♦
Pages of Life: Chapters 1 & 2 is a double-disc set: the first disc is a new studio record, the second a live set that captures Fred Hammond & Radical For Christ in concert in Detroit. Both records demonstrate that Hammond is an innovative, exceptional musician, capable of capturing the spiritual fervor of traditional gospel with the smooth rhythms and streetwise attitude of urban R&B. This is especially apparent on the second disc, when the spirit simply surges through the live performance, but the first disc is one of Hammond's better records, filled with great songs and true passion. *—Rodney Batdorf*

The Happy Goodman Family

Group / Traditional Gospel, Country Gospel, Southern Gospel
For nearly four decades, the Happy Goodman Family brightened the world with their gospel songs. They were founded in Alabama in the 1940s by Howard and Gussie Goodman. Over the years, they expanded and changed membership until finally becoming a quartet composed of Ruth, Sam, Rusty and Bob Goodman. They were later joined by Vestal Goodman and the only non-Goodman, tenor Johnny Cook. The family was most successful during the 1960s and '70s; in 1968, their album *The Happy Gospel of the Happy Goodmans* won a Grammy for Best Gospel Album. The following year, Vestal received a Dove Award for Female Vocalist of the Year. The Happy Goodmans were some of the first members of the TV show *The Gospel Singing Jubilee*, which has won numerous Dove Awards. *—Sandra Brennan*

● **Greatest Hits** / 1985 / Canaan ♦♦♦♦♦
A live recording of The Goodman Family's country gospel. *—Bil Carpenter*

Always / Jan. 28, 1997 / Chordant ♦♦♦
Always collects both new material and re-recorded gospel favorites from the Goodman family. *—Jason Ankeny*

The Harmonizing Four

f. Richmond, Virginia
Group / Traditional Gospel, Southern Gospel, Black Gospel
One of the top gospel quartets of the postwar era, the Harmonizing Four was also a relative anomaly of the period; as their contemporaries raced to modernize their sound, rejecting the traditional jubilee style in favor of the intensity of the burgeoning "hard gospel" movement, the Four remained true to their roots, focusing instead on the spirituals and hymns of a time gone by. For all of their renown, little is known about the group's formative years—their leader and manager, Joseph "Gospel Joe" Williams, forbade any of the members to agree to interviews unless they were paid in advance, and as a result the anecdotal information that does exist is sketchy and incomplete. The Harmonizing Four made their recorded debut on Decca in 1943; in all likelihood they came to the label at the behest of Sister Rosetta Tharpe, whom they frequently backed both on record and in concert. Arriving at Vee-Jay in 1957, the group finally began earning the fame long due them, honing their close harmony style to mellow perfection; member Jimmy Jones, in particular, earned renown as perhaps the greatest basso in gospel history, his canyon-deep voice distinguishing hits like "Motherless Child." *—Jason Ankeny*

★ **Gospel in My Soul** / 1974 / Chameleon ♦♦♦♦♦
This truly fine collection of 11 close-quartet gospel songs is from Vee Jay sessions conducted during the late '50s and issued on a Vee Jay LP in the early '60s. This is one of the few worthwhile Vee Jay quartet albums that has never been reissued over the ensuing years. The Richmond group is led here by Thomas Johnson (first tenor) and his son Ellis Johnson (bass). Other members of long standing include Lonnie Smith and Joe Williams.... This is an excellent collection. *—Opal Louis Nations, Roots & Rhythm Newsletter*

Harmonizing Four/God Will Take Care of You / Apr. 1993 / Vee-Jay ♦♦♦♦♦
More beautiful hymn-like renditions from 1958-59 sessions. *—Opal Louis Nations*

I Shall Not Be Moved / Sep. 1, 1995 / Charly ♦♦♦♦♦
Essential 1950s Vee Jay cuts, some with gospel's premier basso, Jimmy Jones. *—Opal Louis Nations*

1950-1955 / Dec. 7, 1995 / Heritage ♦♦♦♦
The quartet's most devout and touching Gotham sides. *—Opal Louis Nations*

When Day Is Done: The Very Best of the Harmonizing 4 / Mar. 3, 1998 / Collectables ♦♦♦♦
The best of the Vee Jay sides featuring Ellis Johnson and Gospel Joe Williams. *—Opal Louis Nations*

Harps of Melody

f. 1950
Group / Traditional Gospel, Contemporary Gospel
A cappella gospel singing with a different twist was the province of the Memphis-based group the Harps of Melody. Throughout their career, their ranks moved between that of a quartet, quintet and a sextet, always led by the strong voice and manner of Clara Anderson. After working her way up through the ranks as a member of the Busyline Soft Singers and their satellite group, the Busyline Junior Girls, Anderson struck out on her own, first forming the Golden Stars, the precursor to the Harps, which featured two of the future charter members of the Golden Harps, lead singer Ruth Youngblood and bass singer Elizabeth Morris.

By 1950, the Golden Harps of Melody had been formed, creating a stir around Memphis with their "soft" harmony, totally at odds with the usual hard singing and screaming in favor in most gospel circles. Never really a professional group, the Harps did a lot of charity work, performing to raise money for various churches in Memphis and surrounding communities, curtailing their travels each winter. They also did regular sustaining radio broadcasts from the '50s into the '80s on stations WDIA, WLOK, WSMS and KWAM. Their recorded legacy consisted of only two singles on the local Philwood and Designer labels (both featuring the only examples of the group singing to backing instruments) with a collection of live and studio a cappella performances from the 1980s finally seeing issuance in 1998. The group stayed together for almost 50 years, their ranks finally decimated by the deaths of Lillian Jones, Ruth Youngblood and Clara Anderson in the mid-1990s, putting an end to one of Memphis' longest-running, and most unique, gospel singing units. *—Cub Koda*

Sing & Make Melody Unto the Lord / Jun. 9, 1998 / Horizon Music Group ♦♦♦♦
The group's only full-fledged album (only two local 45s were their previous recorded legacy), this consists of two sessions recorded both live and in the studio in 1984 and 1985, respectively. On the live tracks recorded at the University of Memphis and on the majority of the studio sides, the Harps are a quartet, but on three tracks, their ranks swell to that of a quintet. Those used to strong singing with lots of shouting and melisma to the vocals will find the work of the Harps totally different, rising in various cascading voicings with consummate ease in a far more 'sweet' and soft style of gospel phrasing. Acapella versions of their

singles, "Lord, Bless the Weary Soldier in Vietnam" and "Two Little Fishes and Five Loaves of Bread" are here along with a baker's dozen of fine standards given the unique Harps of Melody touch. For gospel singing with a decided and wonderful difference, this is a collection well worth seeking out. *—Cub Koda*

Edwin Hawkins

b. Aug. 1943, Oakland, CA

Vocals, Keyboards, Arranger / Traditional Gospel, Contemporary Gospel, Black Gospel

A trailblazing force behind the evolution of the contemporary gospel sound, Edwin Hawkins remains best known for his classic "Oh Happy Day," one of the biggest gospel hits of all time and a major pop radio smash as well. In 1967, Hawkins and Betty Watson co-founded the Northern California State Youth Choir, drawing on the finest soloists from throughout the Bay Area to build the 50-member ensemble. They soon entered the studio to cut the 1968 LP *Let Us Go into the House of the Lord*, its modern, R&B-influenced production pointing the way to a new era in gospel recording. Among the highlights of *Let Us Go into the House of the Lord* was the track "Oh Happy Day," which unexpectedly found a home on underground FM playlists across San Francisco; the single soon began earning airplay on mainstream R&B and pop outlets across the country, and in the spring of 1969 it reached the U.S. Top Five on the on its way to selling an astounding seven million copies and taking home a Grammy award. At this time the choir was rechristened the Edwin Hawkins Singers, although the featured voice on "Oh Happy Day" belonged to singer Dorothy Combs Morrison, who soon exited in pursuit of a solo career. Her loss proved devastating to Hawkins' long-term commercial fortunes, although in 1970 the ensemble did make a return appearance on the pop charts in support of Melanie on her hit "Lay Down (Candle in the Wind)." *—Jason Ankeny*

Oh Happy Day / 1969 / Pair ✦✦✦✦✦

The Best of the Edwin Hawkins Singers [Savoy] / 1985 / Savoy ✦✦✦✦✦

After becoming The Edwin Hawkins Singers, the group became crossover sensations when their single "Oh Happy Day" cracked the Top 10 on both the pop and R&B charts in 1969, peaking at number two R&B (number four pop). It was their biggest hit and one of the seminal tunes in contemporary gospel history. This collection features other successful Hawkins family numbers. Dorothy Morrison later went on to a solo career. *—Ron Wynn*

The Best of the Edwin Hawkins Singers [Capitol] / Jun. 3, 1997 / Capitol ✦✦✦✦✦

The Best of the Edwin Hawkins Singers is a terrific overview of the soulful gospel group's late-'60s/early-'70s heyday, featuring not only the hit "Oh Happy Day, " but also great album cuts like "Jubilation" and inspired covers of such hits as "Lean On Me." *—Stephen Thomas Erlewine*

● **The Very Best of the Edwin Hawkins Singers** / Jun. 16, 1998 / Music Club ✦✦✦✦✦

Tramaine Hawkins

b. Oct. 11, 1957, San Francisco, CA

Vocals / Contemporary Gospel, Black Gospel, Urban

Born Tramaine Davis in San Francisco and raised in Berkeley, Tramaine Hawkins is the granddaughter of Bishop E.E. Cleveland, one of the founders of the Church of God in Christ Church, the largest Black Pentecostal organization in the U.S. She got her start as a teenager in 1968 performing with the Edwin Hawkins Singers during the homemade recording session that produced the crossover smash "Oh Happy Day," the biggest-selling gospel single to date. In the early '70s, she married Walter Hawkins, Edwin's brother, who went on to lead the Berkeley Love Center Church of God in Christ Church. There she sang lead soprano with her husband's Love Center Choir and appeared on the *Love Alive* album, a recorded Sunday session featuring her husband's sermon, Edwin on piano, and Hawkins on lead vocals. It and its follow-up, *Love Alive II*, were both best-sellers.

Hawkins began her solo recording career in the mid-'80s. As a solo artist, she drew from a variety of genres, and her albums demonstrate that she is as much at home shouting traditional tunes as she is belting out the blues, crooning silky-smooth soul numbers, or even doing hard-driving urban funk. Her tendency to utilize popular music has caused controversy amongst conservatives and even caused others to question her faith, but a close listen to her music demonstrates that even though her music has crossed over, her faith and good intentions are rock-solid. *—Sandra Brennan*

● **The Search Is Over** / 1983 / A&M ✦✦✦✦✦

Although Tramaine insisted that she never deserted the church, it was hard to tell the difference between most of this album's songs and standard secular urban contemporary material. They were sung with the same vigor and fire that Tramaine Hawkins brought to her gospel tunes, but only someone with a truly generous definition of gospel would equate *The Search Is Over* with religious or spiritual material. *—Ron Wynn*

Live / 1990 / Sparrow ✦✦✦✦✦

Walter Hawkins

b. May 18, 1949, Oakland, CA

Vocals / Traditional Gospel, Contemporary Gospel, Black Gospel

The younger brother of gospel vocalist and choir director, Edwin Hawkins, Bishop Walter Hawkins is one of gospel's most successful performers and leader of the Love Center Choir, which won two Dove Awards and two Grammy nominations. Love Center Choir's 1975 debut album *Going Up Yonder* spent several months on the Top 40 Gospel charts, *Love III* sold over a million copies and 1989's *Love Alive IV* topped the gospel charts for 39 weeks. Hawkins' musical career began in 1968, when he helped his brother's group, the Ephesian Church Of God in Christ's Youth Choir, record *Let Us Go Into The House of the Lord*, a fundraiser for the group's trip to a convention in Washington, D.C. The album became an international success when a single, "Oh, Happy Days", sold more than a million copies. The group subsequently toured as the Edwin Hawkins Singers. After he earned a masters of divinity degree from the University of California in Berkeley and founded the Love Center Church in Oakland, Hawkins returned to the Ephesian Church Of God In Christ to record *Going Up Yonder* with the Love Center Choir. Throughout the '80s and '90s, he collaborated with his family, joining his brother on an album with the Oakland Symphony and writing and producing *Baby Sis* for his youngest sister, Lynette, in 1985. In 1988, he joined the Hawkins Family to record *Special Gift* and co-produced and arranged 1991's Grammy award-winning *Tramaine Live*, featuring his ex-wife, Tramaine Hawkins. Hawkins and the Love Center Choir also worked with Van Morrison and Lee Oskar; on his own, he worked with Diahann Carroll, Sylvester and Jeffrey Osborne. *—Craig Harris*

Love Alive 1 / 1975 / Platinum ✦✦✦✦✦

Walter and Tramaine Hawkins outsing one another on this contemporary Black gospel recording. *—Bil Carpenter*

● **The Hawkins Family Collection** / 1995 / Platinum ✦✦✦✦✦

Mark Heard

Vocals, Guitar / CCM

A brilliant, poetic singer/songwriter, his work displayed a deep spirituality and an honesty to the human condition uncommon in CCM. Heard died in 1992 of heart failure; *High Noon* recaps best material of his last three albums. *—Thom Granger*

Stop the Dominoes / 1981 / Home Sweet Home ✦✦✦

Victims of the Age / 1982 / Home Sweet Home ✦✦✦

This album continues in much the same vein as 1981's *Stop the Dominoes.* Prior to that, Mark Heard's singer-songwriter style could drum up little more than fortuitous comparisons to James Taylor. With *Victims of the Age*, he combines his acoustic roots with straight up rock & roll and even touches of robotic new wave. While he certainly has a knack for writing catchy melodies, Heard's real gift lies in his ability to convey the mundane and profound aspects of human longing in accessible song lyrics. Also a proficient guitarist, he could lay down a memorable guitar riff in a fraction of the time that showy guitarists require. *—Dave Sleger*

Ashes and Light / 1984 / Home Sweet Home ✦✦✦

Mark Heard always had a preference for acoustic-based pop music, but most of his early said efforts were either wimpy or sketchy affairs that lead to understandable yet unshakable comparisons with James Taylor and other uninteresting singer-songwriter types. After a mediocre *Eye of the Storm* in 1983, Heard took giant steps in perfecting his craft with this album, his most consistent to date. Here he enlists the services of ex-Alpha Band and Bob Dylan picker and future Bruce Hornsby sideman David Mansfield to adorn his intelligent pop songs with acoustic guitar, dobro, and fiddle. While Heard concentrated on rock-oriented material for the next several years, this recording would be the foundation for his early '90s masterpieces *Dry Bones Dance* and *Second Hand.* *—Dave Sleger*

Mosaics / 1985 / Home Sweet Home ✦✦✦

Dry Bones Dance / 1990 / Fingerprint ✦✦✦✦✦

Includes the great "House of Broken Dreams, " the rockin' "Rise from the Ruins" and "Lonely Road." This great acoustic album is very forceful but never forced. Each song has a real drive and committed vocals. *—Richard Meyer*

Second Hand / 1991 / Fingerprint ✦✦✦✦✦

On this album, Heard has adopted a more contemporary electric sound. His songs keep getting stronger. Some key tracks are "Nod over Coffee," "Love Is Not the Only Thing," and "Look over Your Shoulder." Highly recommended. *—Richard Meyer*

Satellite Sky / 1992 / Fingerprint ✦✦✦

Mark Heard has gone into overdrive on this, his third Fingerprint CD. Most songs are arranged around his electrified metal-bodied mandolin. The personal spiritual message is still here in full force, but the songs stand up well. The desparate "Tip of My Tongue," "Love Is So Blind" and "Satellite Sky" are key tracks. *—Richard Meyer*

● **High Noon** / 1993 / Naked Language ✦✦✦✦✦

Excellent collection of tracks selected from Heard's last three recordings, all of which were exemplary. *—Thom Granger*

Reflections of a Former Life / 1993 / Diadem ✦✦✦

The only way to get even a smattering of Heard's early recordings for Home Sweet Home is on this CD collection, unmercifully brief and hardly a substitute for the real things. *—Thom Granger*

The Highway Q.C.'s

f. 194?

Group / Traditional Gospel, Southern Gospel, Black Gospel

Not only among the top gospel groups of the postwar era, the Highway Q.C.'s were also the launching pad for such major secular pop stars as Lou Rawls, Johnnie Taylor and the immortal Sam Cooke. The group was formed in 1945 at Chicago's Highway Baptist Church by a number of teenagers that included Cooke, Creadell Copeland and two pairs of brothers, Marvin & Charles Jones and Curtis & Lee Richardson. Cooke exited in 1951 to join the ranks of hometown heroes the Soul Stirrers; his replacement was Rawls, himself an alumnus of another young Windy City group, the Holy Wonders. In time all of the Wonders' other members—Spencer Taylor, James Walker and Chris Flowers among them—would join the Highway Q.C.'s as well. Rawls remained for just two years, leaving at that time to join the Los Angeles-based Chosen Gospel Singers; his substitute was Johnnie Taylor, previously of the Kansas City group the Melody Kings. The group made their debut on the Vee-Jay label in 1955; in 1956 Spencer Taylor joined, and a year later Johnnie Taylor (no relation) quit to join the Soul Stirrers, ironically enough filling the gap created by the exit of Sam Cooke. Spencer Taylor remained the Highway Q.C.'s leader throughout the decades which followed, continuing to helm the group into the 1990s. *—Jason Ankeny*

Spencer Taylor & the Highway Q.C.'s / 1959 / Vee-Jay ✦✦✦✦✦

Soul-stirring group, has some tracks led by Johnnie Taylor. *—Opal Louis Nations*

★ **Jesus Is Waiting** / 1960 / Vee-Jay ♦♦♦♦♦
The Highway Q.C.'s were considered gospel's greatest farm team, the place where aspiring quartet lead singers would hone their skills before joining a group on the A list. But that doesn't mean the group made inferior music; the songs on *Jesus Is Waiting,* a single-disc collection combining two albums they cut in the mid-'50s and early '60s, can stand with any issued by the better-name ensembles. A youthful Johnnie Taylor soars, whoops, and moans through songs done from 1955-1957, while Spencer Taylor comes on with equal might and ferocity on the later material. They may not have had the reputations or kept their members as long, but at times the Highway Q.C.'s made music that resounded with as much fury as anyone on the gospel trail. *—Ron Wynn*

The Lord Is Sweet / 1965 / Peacock ♦♦♦
Best of the group's late-'60s sides. Includes "Changes at the End" and "Rock Me." *—Opal Louis Nations*

Nearer My God: The Very Best of the Highway QC's / Mar. 3, 1998 / Collectables ♦♦♦♦
The best of the Vee Jay sides featuring Johnnie and Spencer Taylor. *—Opal Louis Nations*

The Best of the Highway / Chameleon ♦♦♦♦♦
A respectable collection for the group that acted as a feeder for The Soul Stirrers and other first-echelon groups. Prior editions included Johnnie Taylor and the unrecorded Sam Cooke and O.V. Wright. *—Ron Wynn*

The Imperials

Group / Inspirational, CCM
The Imperials have been making music since 1964 and have in that time undergone many personnel and stylistic changes before returning to the close harmonies and straight Southern gospel songs that originally made them popular. Over the years, the Imperials have released over 40 albums and had 14 number one songs. They have also won four Grammy Awards and 13 Dove Awards, making the Imperials, despite (or because of) their many style changes, one of the most popular Christian bands ever. But in 1987, they stirred up controversy and lost many of their oldest fans when they exchanged Southern gospel and middle-of-the-road contemporary to adopt a harder rock/techno-pop sound with the album *This Year's Model.* Leader Armond Morales now considers those albums part of an identity crisis for the band, and he brought two ordained ministers, Steve Ferguson and Jeff Walker, on board. Neither had experience in mainstream Christian music and were more interested in spreading the word than selling albums. This proved the very tonic the group needed, and their old fans are slowly starting to return. *—Sandra Brennan*

Let the Wind Blow / 1985 / Myrrh ♦♦

This Year's Model / 1987 / Myrrh ♦♦♦♦
When *This Year's Model* appeared in 1987, there was considerable buzz in the CCM world about the "new" Imperials. Setting aside their image as neatly coifed purveyors of conservative inspirational music, the band's four male vocalists (Ron Hemby, Jimmie Lee, David Will, and Armond Morales) donned leather jackets, laced their hair with styling gel, backed their act with all the musical technology available in the '80s, wrapped it up in shimmering space-themed art direction, and generally sent the message to church youth groups nationwide that this was not their fathers' Imperials. The ultra-sleek pop production, replete with sweeping synthesizers, gritty bass runs, and rockin' electric guitar solos, was courtesy of Brown Bannister, who brought the same big, electronic sound to other '80s CCM records like Michael W. Smith's *The Big Picture,* Amy Grant's *Unguarded,* and Charlie Peacock's *Secret of Time.* As it turned out, *This Year's Model* was aptly titled. By their next album, the new Imperials had gone the way of the moonwalk, as the band turned in the styling gel and retreated to the safer, church-friendly vibe that made them famous. The album was probably destined to be a period piece, but some of the songs, like the opening "Holding On (First Love)" and the breakdanceable "Fallin'," hold up surprisingly well over the years. *—Evan Cater*

● **The Very Best of the Imperials** / Dayspring ♦♦♦♦♦

Mahalia Jackson

b. Oct. 16, 1911, New Orleans, LA, **d.** Jan. 27, 1972, Evergreen Park, IL
Vocals / Spirituals, Traditional Gospel, Black Gospel
General critical consensus holds Mahalia Jackson as the greatest gospel singer ever to live; a major crossover success whose popularity extended across racial divides, she was gospel's first superstar, and even decades after her death remains for many listeners a defining symbol of the music's transcendent power. With her singularly expressive contralto, Jackson continues to inspire the generations of vocalists which follow in her wake; among the first spiritual perfomers to introduce elements of blues into her music, she infused gospel with a sensuality and freedom it had never before experienced, and her artistry rewrote the rules forever. By the time she reached her mid-teens, Jackson's unique vocal style was already fully formed, combining the full-throated tones and propulsive rhythms of the sanctified church and the deep expressiveness of the blues with the note-bending phrasing of her Baptist upbringing. Her provocative performing style—influenced by the Southern sanctified style of keeping time with the body and distinguished by jerks and steps for physical emphasis—enraged many of the more conservative Northern preachers, but few could deny her fierce talent, and she was famous in churches throughout the country for not only her inimitable voice but also her flirtatious stage presence and spiritual intensity. *—Jason Ankeny*

The Power & The Glory / 1960 / Columbia ♦♦♦

Greatest Hits / 1963 / Columbia ♦♦♦♦
Although it's a little skimpy, *Greatest Hits* is a good, basic collection of Mahalia Jackson's best, featuring ten undisputed classics, including "Nobody Knows the Trouble I've Seen," "That's the Way He's Done for Me," "How I Got Over," "The Upper Room" and "Walk in Jerusalem." There are more comprehensive collections on the market, but novices on a strict budget will find this quite useful. *—Stephen Thomas Erlewine*

In the Upper Room / 1965 / 601 ♦♦♦♦♦
Supported by Mildred Falls, the Southern Harmonaires and the Melody Echoes (the two vocal groups are on different tracks), Mahalia Jackson turns in a typically rousing effort with *In the Upper Room.* All of the songs are classic spirituals and sacred songs, and while this was recorded a little later in her career, Jackson nonetheless sings with an incendiary passion that rivals her classic '40s recordings. Anyone looking to round out their Mahalia Jackson collection should look here, as *In the Upper Room* is one of her finest latter-day efforts. *—Leo Stanley*

★ **Gospels, Spirituals & Hymns** / 1991 / Columbia/Legacy ♦♦♦♦♦
Although it's missing some of her classic performances, the double-disc set *Gospels, Spirituals & Hymns* is nonetheless an excellent introduction to Mahalia Jackson, arguably the greatest gospel singer of all time. The box set features 36 performances she recorded for Columbia between 1954 and 1969, offering a comprehensive, but by no means exhaustive, introduction to Jackson and her most popular work. *—Leo Stanley*

☆ **Mahalia Jackson, Vol. 2** / Jul. 28, 1992 / Columbia/Legacy ♦♦♦♦♦
With its excellent sound, solid compiling work, and lengthy liner notes, the second 2-CD box set of Mahalia Jackson's Columbia recordings is just as essential as the first, *Gospels, Spirituals & Hymns.* *—AMG*

☆ **Live at Newport** / 1994 / Columbia/Legacy ♦♦♦♦♦
Live at Newport is a wonderful reissue of the *Newport 1958* album, containing all 15 songs that were on the original record. Jackson was at the peak of her career, and she gave a stunning performance at this show, lifting such songs as "He's Got the Whole World In His Hands," "Lord's Prayer," "Evening Prayer," "I'm on My Way," "Walk over God's Heaven" and "His Eye is on the Sparrow" to glorious heights. It's not only one of the great live gospel albums, it's simply one of the great gospel albums. *—Leo Stanley*

The Best of Mahalia Jackson / 1995 / Columbia/Legacy ♦♦♦♦♦
The Best of Mahalia Jackson is a 16-track collection featuring many of Jackson's very best recordings—"God Put a Rainbow in the Sky," "He's Got the Whole World in His Hands," "Walk in Jerusalem," "God is So Good (To Me)," "Just a Little While to Stay Here"—thereby offering a long overdue single-disc introduction to one of the greatest gospel singers in history. *—Stephen Thomas Erlewine*

★ **16 Most Requested Songs** / Aug. 20, 1996 / Columbia/Legacy ♦♦♦♦♦
If you're looking for something a little less comprehensive and pricey than one of the Mahalia Jackson box sets, this is the best single-disc compilation of her Columbia recordings, spanning the years 1954-1967 in 66 1/2 minutes. It features some amazing performances, including an April 1961 take of "How I Got Over" recorded live in Sweden, a few selections from the 1958 Newport Jazz Festival, and several tracks featuring Billy Preston on organ, among them the seven-minute 1963 version of "In The Upper Room." Jackson is uniformly excellent, and this sampler gives a good sense of the different approaches she took to her music during the Columbia years. Start here, and go on to the more extensive collections. *—William Ruhlmann*

In My Home over There / Oct. 20, 1998 / MCA ♦♦♦♦♦

How I Got Over: The Apollo Records Sessions / Oct. 27, 1998 / West Side ♦♦♦
With three discs featuring a total of 63 tracks, this is Jackson's complete output for the Apollo label from 1946 to 1954. These are the recordings that brought Mahalia to a national audience right up to her breakthrough with Columbia Records and the ones that literally made gospel recording history. Highlights anywhere the laser beam falls on any of these three discs in the set, but her performances of "Go Tell It On the Mountain," "His Eye Is On the Sparrow," "In the Upper Room, Parts 1 & 2" "Move On Up a Little Higher," "What Could I Do," "Ever Me," "I'm Going to Tell God," "Dig a Little Deeper," and "Walk With Me," "In My Home Over There," "Just Over the Hill, Parts 1 & 2," and "Walking In Jerusalem" are too perfect for words and should simply be in everyone's gospel collection as some of the best the genre has to offer. Marvelous transfers of the original master tapes plus great notes by AMG contributor Opal Louis Nations are just extra icing on the cake to this essential addition to anyone's collection. *—Cub Koda*

T.D. Jakes (Thomas Jakes)

b. 1957, Charleston, WV
Vocals / Contemporary Gospel, CCM
One of the most popular Christian preachers in America and a best-selling author who produced over a dozen books in just the first five years of his writing career, Bishop T.D. Jakes began recording in 1997 with a live version of his most popular book, *Woman, Thou Art Loosed!.* Born in 1957 in West Virginia, Jakes was raised as a Baptist, but an experience at a storefront Apostolic church gave him a sense of purpose to preach the unity to a disparate Christian America, whether the issue is denominational, racial or sexual. He attended West Virginia State University and studied psychology, though he later earned a master's as well as a doctorate in the ministry. After marrying in 1980 and working for several years at Union Carbide, he moved into a full-time ministry role with the founding of Charleston's Temple of Faith in 1986.

T.D. Jakes' renown grew during the rest of the decade as he gave several high-profile sermons around the nation, including the Full Gospel Baptist Church Fellowship's convention before 45,000 people. By 1993, he had begun writing Christian books, and in 1995 his *Woman, Thou Art Loosed!* became the second best-selling Christian book of the year. In early 1996, Jakes learned that W.V. Grant's large Eagle's Nest Family Church in Dallas was for sale. He bought the site—as well as its media facilities—and soon gained audiences of over 5,000. *Sacred Love Songs* followed in 1999; *Storm Is Over* appeared two years later. *—John Bush*

● **Woman, Thou Art Loosed!: Recorded Live at the Superdome** / Feb. 11, 1997 / Word ♦♦♦♦

Live from the Potter's House / Nov. 10, 1998 / Word ♦♦♦♦
Woman, Thou Art Loosed! pretty much defined Bishop T.D. Jakes' incendiary style. Its follow-up, *Live from the Potter's House,* is cut from the same cloth, filled with impassioned pleas for

unity and inspiring sermons. It makes for a record that's every bit as impressive as the debut. *—Rodney Batdorf*

Sacred Love Songs / Feb. 23, 1999 / Island ✦✦✦✦
Bishop T.D. Jakes' inspirational, influential vision of love and faith returns with *Sacred Love Songs*. The musical counterpart to his bestselling book *The Lady, Her Lover & Lord*, the album deals with the problems of love and provides spiritual solutions. *Sacred Love Songs'* soulful, relevant gospel is based on the *Bible's* Songs of Solomon, some of the most poetic and romantic texts ever written. As healing as it is entertaining, *Sacred Love Songs* encourages men and women to love each other in God's way with heartfelt musical messages. *—Heather Phares*

Jars of Clay

Group / Alternative CCM, Adult Alternative Pop/Rock, CCM
Jars of Clay's Christian acoustic pop first caused a stir in the religious music industry in 1994, when the group won a nationwide talent contest. Keyboard player Charlie Lowell (b. 10/21/73 Rochester, NY) and vocalist Dan Haseltine (b. 1/12/73 Winter Springs, FL) began playing together at Greenville College in 1993. They formed Jars of Clay with guitarists Steve Mason (b. 7/8/75 Decatur, IL) and Matt Bronleewe, and drummer Scott Savage (for live shows only), playing around the area and campus throughout the year. The group submitted a demo tape to the Gospel Music Association and was invited to participate in the Spotlight '94 talent competition. Jars of Clay took first place and began their major-label courtship, pausing only to let guitarist Matt Odmark (b. 1/25/74 Rochester, NY) join in place of the departed Bronleewe. (Odmark had played with Lowell in a band called Simple Truth from 1987 to 1990.) The group signed to Brentwood Music subsidiary Essential and released a self-titled album with production help on two tracks by Adrian Belew. The album gained a major release in late 1995 on the Silvertone label; that same year Jars of Clay issued a Christmas EP called *Little Drummer Boy*. *Much Afraid* followed in 1997, and two years later the group resurfaced with *If I Left the Zoo*. *—John Bush*

● **Jars of Clay** / Oct. 24, 1995 / Essential/Jive ✦✦✦✦✦
Jars of Clay manage to put a bit of spirit into their rock and roll. But the spirit isn't one of deceased loved ones or demons, but of religious enlightenment. This album revolves around the band's Christian beliefs, but never comes off as preachy or judgemental. It includes the hit "Flood" and also covers such topics as child abuse and the manipulation of modern man. Produced with the help of Adrian Belew, this album shines. *—James Chrispell*

Much Afraid / 1997 / Essential/Silvertone/Jive ✦✦✦
Jars of Clay's second mainstream, adult alternative album, *Much Afraid*, finds the group refining the anthemic, folky neo-jangle that made its predecessor, *Jars of Clay*, a crossover hit. While *Much Afraid* lacks a single as catchy as "Flood," it is a solid, well-crafted collection of alternative folk-rock, highlighted by the single "Crazy Times." *—Thom Owens*

If I Left The Zoo / Nov. 9, 1999 / SIL ✦✦✦✦
If the stripped-down, neo-vaudevillian sound of *If I Left the Zoo's* opener suggests that Jars of Clay is following a different path with their fifth album, that's because it's a little misleading. There are a few new quirks in the group's mature jangle pop, but overall, *If I Left the Zoo* is very much in the same vein as the group's other releases. That's not necessarily a bad thing, however, since Jars of Clay does this kind of thing really well, and with producer Dennis Herring, they have figured out how to add little sonic flourishes that distinguish the album, even if it's stylistically similar to their other efforts. The reason the record works is that the band's songwriting is getting stronger, and Herring has decided to let the music be direct and even a little ragged. The result is a bit like Herring's work with Counting Crows—at its core, it's simple, immediate melodic folk-pop, but there are enough little quirks in the arrangements, from accordions to a toy piano on "Sad Clown," to keep things interesting and flowing smoothly. Consequently, *If I Left the Zoo* is Jars of Clay's strongest since their mainstream, self-titled breakthrough. *—Stephen Thomas Erlewine*

Willie Neal Johnson

Vocals / Traditional Gospel, Black Gospel
Known throughout the gospel circuit as "The Country Boy" for his rootsy, blues-driven style, singer Willie Neal Johnson was born and raised in Tyler, TX; he began performing with his five siblings while still a child, and was still in his teens when he was tapped to join Rev. C.W. Jackson's group the Five Ways of Joy Gospel Singers. A few years later he formed Willie Neal Johnson and the Gospel Keynotes with longtime friends Ralph McGee, Rev. J.D. Talley, Charles Bailey, John Jackson, Lonzo Jackson, and Archie B. McGee; after rising to popularity across the southwest, the group signed to Nashboro Records, where they scored a major hit with "Show Me the Way." The Gospel Keynotes went on to record over 20 LPs for Nashboro; line-up changes were common, and among the more notable talents which passed through the roster in the following years were Paul Beasley, Larry McGowan, Paul Beasley, and Donny Timmons. After Nashboro closed its doors, they signed to Malaco, rechristening themselves Willie Neal Johnson and the New Keynotes; their output for the label includes 1992's *The Country Boy Goes Home*, 1994's *Lord Take Us Through* and 1996's *Help Me to Be Strong*. *—Jason Ankeny*

The Best of Willie Neal Johnson & The Gospel Keynotes / Jan. 31, 1995 / Nashboro ✦✦✦✦✦
Stunning sides by this incendiary quartet. One of today's leading groups. Nashboro sides. *—Opal Louis Nations*

● **Going Back with the Lord** / Malaco ✦✦✦✦✦
Updated material featuring one-time quartet star Johnson with the Gospel Keynotes. *—Ron Wynn*

Cheri Keaggy

Vocals / CCM
The niece-in-law of gospel legend Phil Keaggy, Cheri Keaggy has become a major artist in the Christian music field without using her famous relative as a crutch. She started her career as a worship leader at her church, then in mid-1993 decided to turn recording artist when Sparrow Records offered her a contract. Her debut album, 1994's *Child of the Father*, became quite popular on the Christian charts, leading to Keaggy's nomination for a Dove award as New Artist of the Year in 1995. Her singles "Open My Heart," "Make My Life an Altar" and "You, Oh Lord, Are My Refuge" have all done well on Christian radio, and she has toured with Point of Grace and Phillips, Craig & Dean, as well as appearing on TV shows like *The 700 Club* and *Music City Tonight*. Her second album, *My Faith Will Stay*, was released in 1995, and third album *What Matters Most* appeared two years later. *—John Bush*

Child of the Father / 1994 / Sparrow ✦✦✦

● **What Matters Most** / Oct. 7, 1997 / Sparrow ✦✦✦✦

Phil Keaggy

Vocals, Guitar, Bass / CCM
Phil Keaggy is an excellent all-around guitarist who has been a part of the CCM scene for over two decades. He and his longtime friend, drummer John Sferra, founded Glass Harp in the late '60s; they soon became known as one of the most innovative power trios around—even though they were never together long enough to break through commercially, their growing base of devoted fans was knocked out by Keaggy's lightning-fast guitar riffs and experimental sounds. It being the late '60s, Keaggy was partook of his share of drugs. His life changed dramatically on February 14, 1970. While lying in a hotel room suffering from a bad LSD trip, his parents were involved in a head-on auto crash back in Ohio. His mother died soon afterward, and this spawned a crisis for Keaggy that led to his becoming a born-again Christian. In the early '70s, Keaggy took to testifying before bewildered Glass Harp listeners after their concerts. He left the group in 1972 and the following year recorded his first solo album, *What a Day*. Since then, Keaggy has released well over a dozen albums earning critical acclaim for both his virtuosity on guitar and his songwriting, which ranges from the Beatlesque pop of *Sunday's Child* to more subtle intrumentals. *—Sandra Brennan*

The Wind & The Wheat / 1987 / A&M ✦✦✦

☆ **Phil Keaggy & Sunday's Child** / 1988 / Word ✦✦✦✦✦

Find Me in These Fields / 1990 / Word ✦✦✦✦✦

Love Broke Thru / 1990 / Myrrh ✦✦✦

Town to Town/Ph'lip Side/Play Thru Me / 1990 / Myrrh ✦✦✦

What a Day/Love Broke Thru / 1990 / Myrrh ✦✦✦✦✦
Keaggy's first two solo albums (from 1973 and 1976 reissued here on one CD) remain among his best. Keaggy was one of the first contemporary Christian musicians to bring an original melodic sense to his songs (indebted as it was to Paul McCartney), and his lyrical naivete comes across as refreshing rather than insipid. *—Brian Mansfield*

Beyond Nature / 1991 / Word ✦✦✦

Play through Me / 1991 / Sparrow ✦✦

Blue / 1994 / Myrrh/Word ✦✦✦✦

☆ **Crimson & Blue** / 1994 / Word ✦✦✦✦✦
A tour-de-force of '60s and '70s power trios and extended jams, it has songwriting a few cuts above most of the material that inspired it. The mainstream version titled *Blue* features a cover of Badfinger's "Baby Blue," while both feature the Van Morrison tune, "When Will I Learn (To Live in God)." *—Thom Granger*

★ **Time 1** / 1995 / Myrrh ✦✦✦✦✦
One of two compilations released simultaneously in 1995, this collection does a great job of showcasing Keaggy's strengths (guitar playing and singing) while minimizing his weaknesses (inconsistent material). There is ample evidence of his diversity, as the styles on this album range from the acoustic folk of his first album to his later British invasion rock, with plenty of ballads, pop songs, and instrumentals included. Keaggy's work suffered in the late '70s and early '80s from weak songs, but *Time 1* selects only the strengths from each period. In addition to being a fine introduction to one of CCM's premiere talents, this collection includes enough rare material (an updated version of "Time," a live version of "Do Lord" from his Glass Harp days, and two unreleased songs) to make it an essential collection to longtime fans. Good liner notes as well, with Keaggy sharing his thoughts on each song. Gets a slight edge over *Time 2* based on better overall songs and better unreleased material. *—Marc Castellani*

☆ **Time 2** / 1995 / Myrrh ✦✦✦✦✦
The companion release to *Time 1*, *Time 2* is similarly strong in selection of material, showcasing Keaggy's consistent musicianship through many different styles of music. As on the first volume, this collection pulls from all of Keaggy's different periods and is balanced with rock, ballads, and pop. Includes a live version of "Shouts of Joy" that doesn't vary much from the recorded version and two unreleased songs from Keaggy's early days (including a snippet of "Heaven Is Home," the first song he wrote as a believer). You won't go wrong with either volume from this inspiring and influential artist. *—Marc Castellani*

Acoustic Sketches / 1996 / Sparrow ✦✦✦
This collection will primarily appeal to guitarists who are fans of Keaggy's acoustic work, because while there are a few fully developed songs, many of the pieces are exactly what the title states: sketches. The majority of the songs are performed on solo guitar with the aid of the "Jam Man," a device that allows the guitarist to record a snippet of music and then play along with it. Some of the songs are fully realized and very worthwhile for the casual listener (e.g. "Paka" and "The 50th") and Keaggy also performs a beautiful solo acoustic version of his song "Spend My Life with You." The rest will inspire guitarists with the skill and technique involved, but do little for the average listener. Includes "Swing Low, Sweet Chariot," an outtake from the *Beyond Nature* album that has a good time with the classic spiritual. *—Marc Castellani*

220 / Sep. 3, 1996 / Sparrow ✦✦✦

On the Fly / Jul. 1, 1997 / Canis Major ✦✦✦

Phil Keaggy / Sep. 29, 1998 / Myrrh ✦✦✦✦✦
More than 25 years after the release of his first solo album, Keaggy finally has an eponymously titled work. Appropriately so, because after several instrumental, collaborative, and tribute works, he has brought all his influences together to create music that is diverse in its influences but cohesive in its execution. Stylistically, the album ranges from the opening acoustic pop of "A Sign Came Through the Window" to the Celtic influences of "Beneath the Blood-Stained Lintel" and "Above All Things" to the Beatlesque "Tender Love," but all the songs benefit from stellar arrangments, inspiring and intelligent lyrics, and the best vocals Keaggy has recorded to date. Keaggy's legendary guitar heroics are understated here, reserved more for the intricate rhythm patterns than extended solos or rock jams (although there are several electric cuts on the album). More importantly, perhaps, is that Keaggy wrote or co-wrote every song on the album and participated in its production. This is truly his album, and brings together everything he has been developing during his solo career into a statement of where he is now as a musician and as a Christian. Fans of a particular Keaggy style may want to look elsewhere, but those who want a complete portrait of the artist should start here. *—Marc Castellani*

John P. Kee

b. 1962, Durham, NC
Vocals / Praise & Worship, Contemporary Gospel, Black Gospel, CCM
A religious calling turned John P. Kee (born: John Prince Kee) from a seedy lifestyle to a career as a top-ranked gospel performer, producer and pastor/minister of the New Life Fellowship Church in Charlotte, North Carolina. In a 1996 interview, he exlained, "God delivered me in Charlotte's inner city from a life that mirrors the ills that we still face today." The fifteenth of sixteen children, Kee showed musical talent at a very early age. After studying at a special school for musically gifted children, he launched his musical career at the age of fourteen. Moving to California, he studied music with his older brothers, Al and Wayne, and became involved with the city's top jazz musicians.. His talents didn't save him, however, from difficult times. By his late-teens, he was living a hard-edged street life. Although he returned to his home state, moving to the Double Oaks community, he continued to slide down to a life of drugs and random violence. Kee began to turn his lifestyle around in his early-twenties. Surrendering to the Lord during a revival meeting at the PTL, he became involved with the New Life Fellowship Church. Devoting himself to gospel music, he formed a group, the New Life Community Choir. Together with the choir, Kee recorded his first album, *Yes Lord*, during a 1987 performance at the Brethren In Unity Youth Convention. Kee has continued to balance solo albums and recordings with the choir since then. In 1995, Kee and the choir reached their commercial peak with the gold award-winning album, *Show Up*. Shortly afterwards, he began a full-time ministry. In addition to his own albums, Kee has produced albums by the Victory In Praise Mass Choir, Shawn McClemore And New Image and Drea Randle. *—Craig Harris*

● **Christmas Album** / Sep. 17, 1996 / Verity ✦✦✦✦
This holiday release from Kee and his New Life Community Choir includes gospel performances of chestnuts including "First Noel," "Silent Night," "Tell It on the Mountain," "Let Us Adore Him" and "Joy To The World." *—Jason Ankeny*

Strength / Oct. 28, 1997 / Verity ✦✦✦
Faced with challenges from young upstarts like Kirk Franklin, John P. Kee—one of the major innovators in contemporary gospel—comes back strong with *Strength*. All of the hallmarks of his music are here, but Kee's sense of direction and musical acumen are at a near-peak. His blend of classic gospel, urban soul and traditional R&B sounds as inspired as it ever did. Kee's experiements with hip-hop ("Eastside/Westside") may be a little awkward, but *Strength* overall proves that Kee is a master at contemporary R&B-influenced gospel. *—Rodney Batdorf*

Ron Kenoly

Vocals / CCM
Ron Kenoly began singing in a Baptist church in his hometown, Coffeyville, KS, and after spending time working in the Air Force and raising a family, he became a successful charting singer in the early '70s in Los Angeles, but recommitted his life to being a Christian in 1975. Kenoly then received his master's degree in music at the College of Alameda in California, and became a voice teacher. He began to lead praise & worship services at a local Pentecostal church, and caught the eye of Integrity Records, which signed Ron Kenoly to a contract. His first album, *Jesus Is Alive*, was followed by the fastest-selling praise & worship album ever, *Lift Him Up*. Both that album and the next, *God Is Able*, were nominated for Dove awards. Kenoly has also released *Sing out with One Voice*, and in 1995 passed the one-million mark in total sales. In 1996, he released *Welcome Home*, his major label debut; *Majesty* followed two years later, and in 1999 Kenoly returned with *We Offer Praises*. *—John Bush*

Welcome Home / Nov. 26, 1996 / Word ✦✦✦✦
Ron Kenoly shows no signs of diluting his music on *Welcome Home*, his major label debut. Recorded live at his church in San Jose, the album is an intense piece of traditional gospel, graced by guest appearances from his brother Mark and his sons Samuel and Ronald. *—Rodney Batdorf*

● **High Places: The Best of Hosanna Music** / Oct. 14, 1997 / Word ✦✦✦✦
High Places: The Best of Ron Kenoly is an excellent 15-track retrospective of Kenoly's finest moments, offering a perfect summary of his career to date, plus an ideal introduction to the contemporary Christian singer. Among the highlights are "Lift Him Up," "Sing Out," "Praise the Lord All Nations," "God Is Able," "Mourning into Dancing," "We're Going Up to the Places," "Be Glorified," "Jesus is Alive" and "Use Me." *—Rodney Batdorf*

Rachael Lampa

Vocals / CCM
Christian vocal prodigy Rachael Lampa's sweet singing was first featured on the Word Records release *Live For You*, which was issued on August 1, 2000. Featuring a duet with Aaron Neville, "There is Still a Dream," the album was co-produced by Brent Bourgeois and Brown Bannister, who also discovered Lampa at a music conference in Colorado when she was 14. By the following year, her debut album was released, around the time the young singer was beginning high school. *—Stacia Proefrock*

● **Live for You** / Aug. 1, 2000 / Word ✦✦✦✦
On her debut album *Live for You*, Rachael Lampa mixes her powerful yet sweet voice and pop and Latin elements into a a distinctive twist on CCM. Songs like "Shaken," "Blessed," "My Father's Heart," and the title track showcase the depth of Lampa's faith in a wide array of song styles ranging up-tempo pop to gentle ballads. Though it's hard to believe Lampa was just 15 when she recorded *Live for You*, it makes her debut that much more impressive. *—Heather Phares*

Cristy Lane (Eleanor Johnston)

b. Jan. 8, 1940, Peoria, IL
Vocals / Inspirational, CCM, Country-Pop
Best remembered for 1979's "One Day at a Time," one of the biggest-selling gospel songs of all time, at 17 Cristy Lane made a demo tape which her husband Lee Stoller used to convince a nightclub owner of her talents. After Lane made another demo tape and began sending it to radio stations, the couple moved to Nashville, where she recorded two new songs she had written, "Stop Fooling with Me" and "Heart in the Sand." Stoller then began taking the demo directly to record companies, but had no luck until he decided to market her himself through K-Ark record distributors. Stoller formed LS Records in the mid-'70s and finally found success when Lane's debut single, "Tryin' to Forget About You," and its follow-up, "Sweet Deceiver," appeared on the charts in 1977. That year she also made it to the Top Ten and the Top 20 with "Let Me Down Easy" and "Shake Me I Rattle," respectively. In late 1979, Lane signed to United Artists Records and had three more hits before persuading the label to release "One Day at a Time." After it hit number one on the country charts, she released "Sweet Sexy Eyes," her final Top Ten hit. Lane marketed her 1986 album *One Day at a Time* on television, which helped it become a big seller. *—Sandra Brennan*

One Day at a Time / 1978 / Cema Special Markets ✦✦✦✦✦
A simplistic, soft-pop style of gospel from her gentle voice. *—Bil Carpenter*

● **Footprints in the Sand** / 1983 / Liberty ✦✦✦✦✦
Because of the strong selection of songs and consistent performances, this compilation is the one to get out of the several Lane discs available from Arrival. *—Stephen Thomas Erlewine*

Amazing Grace, Vol. 2 / 1986 / Arrival/K-Tel ✦✦✦
A solid, if unspectacular, set of popular gospel tunes that are nicely performed by Lane, even if she is occasionally dominated by an intrusive synthesizer. *—Stephen Thomas Erlewine*

All in His Hands / 1989 / Heartwarming ✦✦✦
Lane's pristine sounds come through best on the '50s-style "He Loves Me Still." *—Bil Carpenter*

My Best to You / 1992 / Arrival/K-Tel ✦✦✦
A good compilation of some of Lane's most popular gospel material, which is somewhat undermined by the number of tracks duplicated from *Footprints in the Sand*. *—Stephen Thomas Erlewine*

Donald Lawrence

Vocals / Contemporary Gospel, Gospel Choir
One of the most popular gospel choirs of the 1990s, Donald Lawrence and the Tri-City Singers also managed to make waves with the secular media, similar to a handful of other Christian acts during the decade. Comprised of Lawrence plus 34 members—from the "Tri-Cities" of Spartanburg, South Carolina plus Gastonia and Charlotte, North Carolina—the choir debuted with the 1993 album *A Songwriter's Point of View* on the tiny Gospocentric label. The album eventually reached number two on the gospel charts. At the end of the year, the Tri-City Singers had become one of *Billboard*'s Top Ten Gospel Groups, as well as the recipient of several Stellar Awards and a nomination for the NAACP's Image Award. Second album *Bible Stories* followed in 1995 on Crystal Rose/Chordant Records, and the choir released a holidays LP, *Hello Christmas*, in 1997. *—John Bush*

Hello Christmas / Oct. 7, 1997 / Starsong ✦✦✦
Hello Christmas is a lovely, moving holiday album from Donald Lawrence. Supported by the Tri-City Singers, Lawrence runs through many familiar items ("Rudolph the Red Nosed Reindeer," "Little Drummer Boy," "Carol of the Bells"), plus a handful of newly written originals in the contemporary R&B vein, albeit with a religious theme. Occasionally, the sound is a little too slick, but Lawrence is always an engaging vocalist, and there's a real warmth to the record that makes it a satisfying holiday listen. *—Stephen Thomas Erlewine*

Crystal Lewis

Vocals / CCM
CCM singer Crystal Lewis first surfaced as a member of the cast of the youth musical *Hi-Tops*, followed by a stint fronting the rockabilly gospel band Wild Blue Yonder; she subsequently mounted a solo career, issuing a series of commercially-neglected LPs before breaking through with her 1996 Myrrh Records debut *Beauty for Ashes*. The album launched three contemporary Christian chart-toppers, among them "People Get Ready (Jesus Is Comin')," named both the CCM and CRR Song of the Year. *Gold* followed in 1998, and two years later Lewis returned with two albums; the rock-oriented *Fearless*, and the Christmas themed *Holiday*. *—Jason Ankeny*

Simply the Best / 1991 / Frontline ✦✦✦
A compilation of her better Frontline recordings includes one from a reworking of the melodic idea behind "Be My Baby," by Wild Blue Yonder, "Only One." *—Thom Granger*

Bride / 1993 / Metro One ✦✦✦✦
Though still an uneven record (an ongoing problem), her best vocal work is represented here, including an impressive live take on "Amazing Grace." *—Thom Granger*

Crystal Lewis' Greatest Hits / 1995 / Metro One/Diamante ✦✦✦✦✦
Including seven Top Ten CCM singles and a previously unreleased "Come Just as You Are" recorded live at the Harvest Crusade, *The Greatest Hits* includes pop songs alongside traditional hymns. *—John Bush*

★ **Gold** / Oct. 20, 1998 / Interscope ✦✦✦✦✦

Remember / Light ✦✦

Roberta Martin

b. Feb. 12, 1907, Helena, AR, **d.** Jan. 18, 1969, Chicago, IL
Vocals, Piano / Traditional Gospel, Black Gospel
This talented pianist started a quartet with Theodore Frye in the '30s. This aggregation gradually evolved into The Roberta Martin Singers by the '50s. It is now known that she copied the piano style of blind pianist Arizona Dranes, who also influenced The Ward Singers. Martin's singers sang loudly and dramatically. She also wasn't concerned about a harmonious sound; when one member of the group was leading a song, whether male or female, you could easily identify the backing voices. This lack of synchronicity made the group's urgent sound a unique and welcome change amid the repetitive quartets of the time. Robert Anderson was one of Martin's principal singers. She herself was referred to as The Helen Hayes of the Gospel World. She died in 1969. *—Bil Carpenter*

Old Ship of Zion / 1973 / Kenwood ✦✦✦✦✦
Prime Apollo sides from the late '40s/early '50s with fine leads from Roberta, Bessie Folk, Eugene Smith and Norsalus McKissick. *—Opal Louis Nations*

● **The Best of the Roberta Martin Singers** / 1979 / Savoy ✦✦✦✦✦
Most of Martin's best early work from the late '40s through the '50s is out of print, but this is a nice introduction to this dynamic singer and group leader. *—Kip Lornell*

Sallie Martin

b. Nov. 20, 1895, Pittfield, GA, **d.** Jun. 18, 1988, Chicago, IL
Vocals / Traditional Gospel, Black Gospel
Proclaimed "The Mother of Gospel" by the National Convention of Gospel Choirs and Choruses, Sallie Martin is widely credited with introducing spiritual music to the masses; while her rough, unmodulated voice lacked the finesse of many of the singers in her wake, she was an artist who nevertheless commanded absolute respect from both her audiences and peers, and her innovations forever altered not only the music but also the business behind it. Martin had heard about Thomas A. Dorsey, a onetime blues pianist whose original gospel songs were electrifying the Chicago church circuit. Through a mutual friend, she arranged to audition for Dorsey; despite serious misgivings—her style was thoroughly unrefined, complete with whooping, groaning and a great deal of physical movement (the latter a hallmark of the Pentecostal church), and to top it off, she couldn't even read music—he eventually agreed to let her come aboard, and in early 1932 Martin made her debut with his group at the Ebenezer Baptist Church. For all of her lack of polish, Martin nevertheless instantly connected with audiences; over time Dorsey became increasingly aware of her value not only as a performer but also as an entrepreneur, as she took over his music store and within a few months was turning a tidy profit. Their relationship was often adversarial, but quickly it was apparent that neither could succeed without the other. As gospel choruses instructed to sing Dorsey's songs began appearing throughout the Chicago area, Martin traveled to Cleveland in 1933 to organize a chorus there as well; in the years to follow, she helped set up similar groups throughout the South and Midwest, and also joined Dorsey in organzing the annual National Convention of Gospel Choirs and Choruses. In 1940, however, relations between Martin and Dorsey reached their breaking point, and she went solo, teaming with a young pianist named Ruth Jones—later to rocket to fame under the name Dinah Washington—and began touring the country, traveling a gospel circuit which her earlier journeys had helped establish. She later formed her own ensemble, the Sallie Martin Singers; believed to be the first female group in gospel history. *—Jason Ankeny*

★ **Throw Out the Lifeline** / 1950-1952 / Specialty ✦✦✦✦✦
The most instrumentation these tracks ever had was an organ, a piano and an occasional drum. Originally issued on Specialty Records in the 1950-53 period, these 29 tracks are Black congregational styled numbers, 23 of them previously unissued. These sides also include six selections where Brother Joe May joined the singers. Most of the rest finds Sallie and Cora trading leads. A fine example of Sallie's powers shows up on "Ain't That Good News." *—Bil Carpenter*

Precious Lord / 1993 / Vee-Jay ✦✦✦✦✦
Sallie Martin disbanded her famous singing group in the '50s when her daughter told her she didn't want to do any more tours. She briefly resurrected two new editions in the early '60s and cut two albums for Vee-Jay before disbanding them again. Although the 23 songs on this single-disc reissue aren't as glorious or memorable as the group's Specialty recordings, they are still valuable, both to hear Martin's rough but effective leads and harmonizing with new vocalists, and also because the resignation and mournful quality in Martin's singing during the 1963 sessions were an indication that she'd had enough of the performance/recording/touring grind. *—Ron Wynn*

Brother Joe May

b. Nov. 9, 1912, Macon, Mississippi, **d.** Jul. 14, 1972
Vocals / Traditional Gospel, Black Gospel
Dubbed "The Thunderbolt of the Middle West" by his mentor, the legendary Willie Mae Ford Smith, Brother Joe May was arguably the greatest male soloist in the history of gospel music; a tenor whose dramatic sense of showmanship was surpassed only by his unparalleled command of vocal dynamics and projection, he possessed a voice of unimaginable range and power, moving from a whisper to a scream without the slightest suggestion of effort. After graduating high school, May became a protege of the pioneering Smith, and with her aid honed his sense of phrasing, modeling his own vocal acrobatics on hers. In 1949, he signed to the Specialty label and scored a major hit with his debut release, "Search Me Lord." However, despite his popularity—both "Search Me Lord" and 1950's "Do You Know Him—" were estimated to have sold over one million copies each—May never crossed over to white audiences, the ultimate measure of commerical success at that time. His adamant rejection of all musical traditions but gospel likely played a role in his exit from Specialty in 1958. He quickly signed with Nashboro, where he also began recording many of his own original compositions. His fame continued to grow enormously across the Deep South in the years to follow. His health began to fail during the late '60s and he died of a stroke in 1972, en route to a performance. *—Jason Ankeny*

Brother Joe May Story / 1962 / ✦✦✦
Here's a 1972 two-record set of 24 gospel songs made popular by Brother Joe May between 1958, when he joined Nashboro after nine years on Specialty, and the time of his demise in 1974. Macon-born May, also known as "the Thunderbolt of the Middle West," was a Pentacostal practioner of the Willie Mae Ford Smithschool of gospel singing. May's powerful tenor impressed and inspired many. It includes some live church recordings and sides made with the Joe May Singers. Notable cuts include the rousing "I've Been Dipped in the Water." This is a fine collection. *—Opal Louis Nations, Roots & Rhythm Newsletter*

☆ **Thank You Lord for One More Day** / 1967 / Specialty ✦✦✦✦✦
Thank You Lord for One More Day is a wonderful collection of Brother Joe May's Specialty sides, highlighted by collaborations with Sister Wynona Carr and the Pilgrim Travelers. *—Leo Stanley*

★ **In Loving Memory . . .** / 1974 / Specialty ✦✦✦✦✦
In Loving Memory of Brother Joe May is a collection of May's finest shouts and duets on Specialty, supported on some cuts by the Pilgrim Travelers, the Sallie Martin Singers, or a live audience. *—Ron Wynn*

Search Me, Lord / 1974 / Specialty ✦✦✦✦✦
Authoritative gospel and energized vocals with support from the Pilgrim Travelers and the Sallie Martin Singers. *—Ron Wynn*

Thunderbolt of the Middle West / 1974 / Specialty ✦✦✦
Brother Joe May was the male counterpart to Mahalia Jackson, a full-voiced tenor of amazing range and power. Although he recorded prolifically for the Nashboro label for the bulk of his career, this 27-track collection brings together his earliest recordings for the Specialty label. Although many of these tracks feature him working with the Sallie Martin Singers, Sister Wynona Carr, the Pilgrim Travelers, and his daughter Annette May, the real star of the show is Brother Joe, whose voice simply soars no matter what the surroundings. *—Cub Koda*

Brother Joe May Live, 1952-1955 / 1994 / Specialty ✦✦✦✦✦
Brother Joe May earned his "Thunderbolt of the Midwest" nickname with incandescent, riveting vocals that could blow a roof off or reduce listeners to tears, often at the same time. The 16 tracks on this CD were done live, usually at services or during church performances, and they frequently paired him with the Sallie Martin Singers. While they and Prof. Earle Hines are fine, May is in another dimension. His flamboyant, dynamic voice shudders, roars, rises, moans and flails, and he fortifies the songs with commentary that's nearly as inspiring. Even devout atheists will be impressed by the power of Brother Joe May. *—Ron Wynn*

Meditation Singers

f. 1947, Detroit, MI
Group / Traditional Gospel, Black Gospel
Though they never achieved national acclaim like the Ward Singers or the Caravans, the Meditation Singers were Detroit's premier female gospel group in the '50s. The first Motor City act to reject a cappella vocal traditions in favor of instrumental backing, they also produced a pair of secular pop stars in Della Reese and Laura Lee. Formed in 1947 as a product of Detroit's New Liberty Baptist Church's renowned Moments of Meditation choir, the Meditation Singers were led by Earnestine Rundless, wife of onetime Soul Stirrer E.A. Rundless. The group comprised Rundless, Reese, alto Marie Waters (Reese's sister), and soprano Lillian Mitchell. In early 1953, they cut their first session at a local record store; soon after, Reese left the group for pop success, and was replaced by Lee, Rundless' teenage daughter. Their record was licensed to the Deluxe label, and soon they signed to Specialty, though they were dropped due to poor sales. The Meditations toured and worked with the legendary James Cleveland in the mid and late-'50s; his involvement led Specialty to re-sign them. The third Specialty session followed in 1959, but the label left the gospel business altogether; the group signed to Hob, recording once more with Cleveland before he left their ranks. During the '60s, the Meditations recorded and toured constantly, including a 1962 date backing Reese at Las Vegas' Flamingo Casino. This performance caught Frank Sinatra's attention, and he singled out Lee for pop stardom. She left the group in 1965, moving into soul music and scoring the 1971 hit "Women's Love Rights." The Meditations carried on, touring regularly until the early '80s. *—Jason Ankeny*

● **Good News** / 1992 / Specialty ✦✦✦✦✦
This group, centered around the vocal dynamism of founder Ernestine Rundless, often featured the young Della Reese and Laura Lee, who both became popular music luminaries later on. There's piano backing, sporadic lead by the late James Cleveland, and lots of fervent singing. This brings together for the first time the complete, though few in number, 1953-1959 sides by this roof-raising group. *—Opal Louis Nations, Roots & Rhythm Newsletter*

Change Is Gonna Come / Jewel ✦✦✦
Ernestine Rundless and the gals shake up the church. *—Opal Louis Nations*

The Mighty Clouds of Joy

f. 1959, Los Angeles, CA

Group / Traditional Gospel, Southern Gospel, Black Gospel

Contemporary gospel's preeminent group, the Mighty Clouds of Joy carried the torch for the traditional quartet vocal style throughout an era dominated by solo acts and choirs; pioneering a distinctively funky sound which over time gained grudging acceptance even among purists, they pushed spiritual music in new and unexpected directions, even scoring a major disco hit. Over the years, the Mighty Clouds earned a reputation among gospel's greatest showmen; one of the first groups to incorporate choreographed moves into their act, their nimble footwork and bright, color-coordinated outfits earned them the sobriquet "The Temptations of Gospel." More importantly, they were the first group to add bass, drums and keyboards to the standard quartet accompaniment of solo guitar, resulting in a sound which horrified traditionalists but appealed to younger listeners—so much so, in fact, that the Mighty Clouds became the first gospel act ever to appear on television's *Soul Train,* where they performed their disco smash "Mighty High." Their crossover success continued with opening slots for secular pop stars including Marvin Gaye, the Rolling Stones and Paul Simon, whom the group backed during a month-long stint at Madison Square Garden. While lineup changes plagued the Mighty Clouds throughout their career, they remained active through the 1990s. *—Jason Ankeny*

A Bright Side / 1960 / MCA ✦✦✦

The Clouds at their peak. *—Opal Louis Nations*

Sing Live Zion Songs / 1968 / Hob ✦✦✦✦✦

Little Joe Ligon and the group live from Will Rogers Park circa 1958. *—Opal Louis Nations*

The Best of the Mighty Clouds of Joy, Vol. 2 / 1973 / MCA ✦✦

★ **The Best of the Mighty Clouds of Joy** / 1973 / MCA ✦✦✦✦✦

Best of the early Peacock material when the quartet was in their prime. *—Opal Louis Nations*

Live & Direct / 1977 / ABC ✦✦✦✦✦

Live & Direct is a wonderful, inspiring live recording from the Mighty Clouds of Joy. Although the group was past its peak when they recorded this in the late '70s, they nevertheless retained much of their vocal power, and their interplay is simply breathtaking at times. And, since it features all of their classic material, the album functions as a best-of sampler, and it's certainly not a bad way to become acquainted with this extraordinary group. *—Leo Stanley*

Mississippi Mass Choir

Group / Traditional Gospel, Contemporary Gospel, Gospel Choir

The Mississippi Mass Choir was one of the most influential Gospel groups of the late-1980s and '90s. Under the musical direction of David R. Curry, the one hundred-voice choir served their Lord with a sound that made them a constant presence on Billboard's Gospel charts. Each of their recordings have reached the top position on the charts. Their debut album, *Live,* recorded during a 1988 performance at the Jackson, Mississippi Municipal Auditorium, remained on the charts for forty-five weeks and earned the group James Cleveland GMWA awards as 'choir of the year ' contemporary' and 'best new artist of the year ' traditional'. Their second album, *God Gets The Glory,* reached number one two weeks after it was released in 1990. The Mississippi Mass Choir's most successful album, *It Remains To Be Seen* topped the charts for twelve months and received a Soul Train music award as 'best Gospel album of 1993'. The album was the choir's last with founder Frank Williams (June 25, 1947 ' March 22, 1993), a member of the Jackson Southernaires and an executive in the Gospel music division of the Maleco record label. Determined to bring together the best Gospel voices in Mississippi, Williams had convinced Jerry Mannery, the head of Maleco's Gospel division, to sign the band to a record deal and serve as executive director. With their albums released since Williams's passing ' *I'll See You In Rapture, Praise The Lord* and *Emmanuel (God With Us)* ' the Mississippi Mass Choir continues to dedicate itself to its self-described mission of 'serving God through song'. *—Craig Harris*

God Gets the Glory / 1991 / Malaco ✦✦✦

This album is a guaranteed ear-pleaser from the first cut to the last. Whether you're in the mood for rocking, rhythmic praises or meditative, reflective worship, the music contained in this live recording will bless you as well as entertain you. *—Edwin Smith*

● **I'll See You in the Rapture** / May 28, 1996 / Malaco ✦✦✦✦✦

Emmanuel: God With Us / Aug. 3, 1999 / Malaco ✦✦✦✦✦

The powerful, beautiful, contemporary gospel sound of the Mississippi Mass Choir shines on 1999's *Emmanuel:God Is with Us.* Personal and universal messages of faith like "He Can Fix What Is Broke," "The Lord Shall Reign," "They Got the Word," and "Jesus, This Is Jim" make the album a must for gospel fans. *—Heather Phares*

Geoff Moore

Vocals / CCM

The anthemic CCM band Geoff Moore and the Distance emerged from Nashville in 1984 with *Pure and Simple;* the group—its most notable incarnation also featuring guitarist Roscoe Meek, bassist Gary Mullett, keyboardist Geof Barkley and drummer Chuck Conner—resurfaced two years later with *Over the Edge,* followed in 1987 by *The Distance.* With 1988's *A Place to Stand,* Moore signed to Sparrow, although after the following year's *Foundations* he jumped ship to ForeFront for 1992's *Friend Like U. Evolution* appeared a year later, and *Home Run* in 1995; after a 1996 *Greatest Hits* collection, Moore and the Distance issued *Threads.* 1999's *Geoff Moore* was the singer/songwriter's first solo effort. *—Jason Ankeny*

All the Good Music / 1987 / Benson ✦✦✦

This anthology of early music was created for the Benson label. *—Thom Granger*

Pure & Simple / 1990 / ForeFront ✦✦✦✦✦

This set represents a band at its peak as a rock act; later albums would feature more pop-oriented material. *—Thom Granger*

Home Run / 1995 / Forefront ✦✦✦✦✦

Geoff Moore followed up his 1992 Dove award-winning song "The Great Adventure," with *Home Run,* which continued his collaboration with Steven Curtis Chapman on two songs. Throughout *Home Run,* Moore turns in a set of rootsy, driving, inspirational pop/rock. *—Stephen Thomas Erlewine*

● **Greatest Hits** / Sep. 17, 1996 / Forefront ✦✦✦✦✦

Providing an excellent introduction to the acclaimed CCM outfit Geoff Moore & the Distance, the double-disc *Greatest Hits* contains all of the group's biggest hits, as well as a handful of live tracks and two new songs, including the hit single "More than Gold." *—Stephen Thomas Erlewine*

Geoff Moore / Sep. 21, 1999 / ForeFront ✦✦✦✦

Geoff Moore's self titled solo debut focuses on his songwriting skills and a warm, acoustic sound. The album's laid-back, genuine feel is exemplified by tracks like "Out Here, " "Boy Like Me, Man Like You, " "Land Of No Regret" and "Thanks to You, " a duet with Moore's writing collaborator and tour partner Steven Curtis Chapman. Fans of Moore's work with the Distance, as well as fans of inspirational rock in general, will be pleased with *Geoff Moore's* musical and lyrical honesty. *—Heather Phares*

Rev. James Moore

b. Detroit, MI

Vocals / Traditional Gospel, Contemporary Gospel, Black Gospel

Accorded entry into the gospel field thanks to a scholarship received at the 1974 Gospel Music Workshop of America, Rev. James Moore earned a record contract with Savoy that same year and began releasing albums. Born in Detroit, he made his first appearance at the front of church at the age of seven and was introduced to gospel matriarch Mattie Moss Clark by a friend. With the help of Clark—and the tremendous influence of the Revs. James Cleveland and Richard White—Moore entered gospel music with 1974's *I Thank You Master.* He was also invited by Rev. Gerald Thompson to appear on his LP *I Can't Stop Now* that same year.

Rev. James Moore recorded infrequently during the 1980s (for a variety of labels), but returned to Malaco/Savoy in 1988 for *Live: Rev. James Moore.* The album hit the Top Ten on the gospel charts, and earned Moore a Stellar Award for Best Male Solo Performance. He appeared on the debut album by the Mississippi Mass Choir in 1987, and enjoyed the LP's enormous success (over half a year at the top of the gospel charts, almost a dozen awards from GMWA and Dove); the choir returned the favor by appearing on one of his albums, 1991's *Live with the Mississippi Mass Choir.* It also went to number one, prompting live albums recorded in Moore's hometown of Detroit and Jackson State University during the mid-'90s. His 1994 album *I Will Trust in the Lord* earned Rev. Moore his first Grammy nomination. *—John Bush*

● **Live in Detroit** / 1993 / Malaco ✦✦✦✦

Live in Detroit is a ten-track album that captures the Rev. James Moore live in concert in the early '90s. Moore is in great form, adding life to the music when the going gets predictable, even on the overly familiar "He Was There All the Time." Occasionally, Moore gets carried away with preaching and testifying, letting the songs run on a little too long—"He's All I Need" clocks in at nearly 13 minutes—but it's easy to hear that this was captivating live, even if the kineticism is lessened on record. There are better Moore albums and better live Moore albums available, but once you get to listening to *Live in Detroit,* you're likely to get caught up in the infectious spirit of this usually rousing music. *—Thom Owens*

Solid Rock / Jul. 6, 1999 / 601 ✦✦✦

Solid Rock is a solid collection by Rev. James Moore, who utilizes his powerful voice to maximum effect. *—Steve Huey*

Mormon Tabernacle Choir

f. Aug. 22, 1947

Group / Holiday, Choral

The Mormon Tabernacle Choir made their public debut on August 22, 1847, just 29 days after Brigham Young and his 147 followers first settled in the Salt Lake Valley. John Parry was named the choir's first offical conductor in 1949, and two years later construction was completed on the first Tabernacle church, followed in 1867 by the dome-roofed Tabernacle facility which exists to the present. The 150-member choir assembled for the facility's October 6 opening was at that time the largest in the U.S., their voices accompanied by a mammoth organ featuring some 2000 pipes. The Mormon Tabernacle Choir made its first official recordings for Columbia on September 1, 1910; their weekly radio broadcast *Music and the Word* premiered on CBS affiliate KSL on September 15, 1932 and continues to air even today, enjoying the longest uninterrupted network run in American history. In 1959, the choir's recording of "The Battle Hymn of the Republic" earned a Grammy, followed over the years by a number of gold and platinum records; the latter-day Mormon Tabernacle Choir counts 300 members and continues to record and tour on a regular basis. *—Jason Ankeny*

● **More Greatest Hits: 19 Best Loved Favorites** / 1995 / Sony ✦✦✦

More Greatest Hits: 19 Best Loved Favorites finds the Mormon Tabernacle Choir tackling a number of well-known songs. Not only do they sing hymns like "Nearer My God to Thee," but they sing popular favorites like "It's a Grand Night for Singing," "My Favorite Things" and "White Cliffs of Dover," making it an excellent summation of the Choir's far-reaching talent. *—Stephen Thomas Erlewine*

Christmas Carols Around the World / 1996 / Sony Special Products ✦✦✦

Mortification

Group / Christian Metal

Mortification is considered by many to be the most extreme Christian band in existence. Formed in 1990 from the remains of a band called Lightforce, Mortification sought to provide a positive alternative to traditional death metal acts such as Carcass, Death and Obituary. On the strength of their self-titled 1990 debut, Mortification quickly gained a reputation in their native Australia for being one of the loudest and fastest bands around. Their 1992 follow-up, *Scrolls of the Megilloth*, garnered the band some attention from the heavy metal underground and contains some of the most frightening vocals ever recorded. Their later albums were more experimental, combining elements of punk, death and thrash metal; they include 1998's *Triumph of Mercy* and 2000's *10 Years Live, Not Dead*. Bassist/vocalist Steve Rowe has handled most of the songwriting chores for group, and is the only remaining original member. —*Kirk Dombek*

● **EnVision EvAngelene** / Feb. 18, 1997 / Nuclear Blast America ✦✦✦✦

Triumph of Mercy / Oct. 6, 1998 / Metal Blade ✦✦✦

The Hammer of God / Jul. 27, 1999 / Metal Blade ✦✦✦

Rich Mullins

b. Oct. 21, 1955, Richmond, Indiana, **d.** Sep. 19, 1997
Vocals, Piano, Dulcimer / CCM
Rich Mullins was many things to the CCM community: a beloved performer nominated for 12 Dove Awards, an expert on several instruments (including hammered dulcimer, piano, guitar) and a very successful songwriter, responsible for one of the most popular contemporary praise songs in existence, "Awesome God." As part of Zion Ministries, Mullins toured the country and led praise & worship meetings at many retreats. One such meeting, in Nashville, got him signed to a publishing deal by Reunion Records, and Amy Grant recorded his "Sing Your Praise to the Lord" for her 1982 album *Age to Age*. Just two years later, he signed a recording contract with Reunion as well. Even early in his career, Mullins' gift for incisive lyrics and folky, Celtic music revealed itself, as on his 1986 self-titled album and the follow-ups *Pictures in the Sky* and *Winds of Heaven, Stuff of Earth*. Mullins was tragically killed in an Illinois car accident in September 1997. *The Jesus Record* was released posthumously. —*John Bush*

Pictures in the Sky / Dec. 1987 / Reunion ✦✦✦

Winds of Heaven, Stuff of Earth / May 1989 / Reunion ✦✦✦
Mullins's vision begins to take shape, with help from producer Reed Arvin, on the album that featured the now-classic "Awesome God." —*Thom Granger*

The World as Best as I Remember It, Vol. 1 / 1991 / Reunion ✦✦

☆ **The World as Best as I Remember It, Vol. 2** / 1992 / Reunion ✦✦✦✦✦
A near-perfect song cycle, it featured moments worthy of the best in pop music history. —*Thom Granger*

A Liturgy, A Legacy & A Ragamuffin Band / Oct. 26, 1993 / Reunion ✦✦✦✦✦
A brilliant concept, Mullins originals reflecting on concept of legacy are used as liturgical motifs, making for a thoroughly contemporary and powerful worship experience and artistic statement. —*Thom Granger*

★ **Collection of Songs** / Jul. 1996 / Reunion ✦✦✦✦✦
Songs collects 16 of Rich Mullins' best and most popular songs, offering a perfect introduction to one of the most delightful and provocative singer/songwriters in CCM. —*Rodney Batdorf*

Jesus Record / Jul. 21, 1998 / Word ✦✦✦

Songs 2 / Oct. 26, 1999 / Reunion ✦✦✦✦
Songs 2 is the sequel to Rich Mullins' flawless original greatest-hits collection, *Songs*, fleshing out the overview with a selection of high-quality items that didn't quite make the cut the first time around. That's not a knock on the songs, because Mullins' catalog is so full of gems that there simply wasn't room for them; while they aren't the absolutely crucial portions of his output, these songs do help make the case for the breadth and expanse of his talents. The first volume is a better listen, of course, but *Songs 2* is a worthy addition. —*Steve Huey*

Newsboys

Group / Alternative CCM, Christian Rock, CCM
One of the more media-exposed Christian rock bands of the '90s, Newsboys formed in the late '80s around a core of John James, Peter Furler, and Philip Urry. Though early in their career the band was panned for a perceived overreliance on religious clichés in their lyrics, Newsboys later grasped secular music's alternative revolution in the early '90s for an image makeover, with good results. The group gained six number one singles on the Christian charts, and have been featured in more secular media outlets than the average Christian band. *Step Up to the Microphone*, their first album for major label Virgin, followed in 1998; *Love Liberty Disco* appeared a year later. In celebration of the new millennium, the Newsboys also observed their own career with the greatest hits package *Shine... The Hits*, issued in fall 2000. —*John Bush*

Going Public / 1994 / Star Song ✦✦✦✦
For the most part, *Going Public* is a first-rate pop/rock album from this Australian-based band. Although there are traces of dogma in the lyrics, there is enough variety, depth, and cleverness both musically and lyrically to make the album a winner. The first two numbers, "Real Good Thing" (with a great thumping bass line) and "Shine," are extremely hook-laden and musically hard to resist. Lyrically, the album looks at the themes of unmerited grace, being open with one's faith, and the cost of discipleship, among others. Musically, the recording runs the gamut from the ballad "Be Still" to the almost punky "Lights Out" (which is critical of those who are sure of the timing of the Second Coming), with a good balance between slower and uptempo cuts. The best moment on the album is the last cut, "Elle G." It is the story from a survivor's point of view of trying to come to terms with a friend who has committed suicide. What makes this song so outstanding is its honesty, lyrical depth, and the complex musical journey that accompanies the story line. The words reveal both deep compassion and acute anger, in addition to trying to bring a greater meaning to the event in a larger context. The ending guitar solo fits extremely well with the lyrical content, while the entire cut leaves a lasting impression on the listener. The willingness to go deeply into such a subject matter and admit some ambiguity may be seen as a sign of weakness to some believers, but in this case it brings a profundity that is not expected, and most welcome. —*Michael Offord*

Take Me to Your Leader / Feb. 20, 1996 / Chordant ✦✦

Step up to the Microphone / Jun. 30, 1998 / Star Song/Virgin ✦✦✦

Love Liberty Disco / Nov. 16, 1999 / Sparrow ✦✦✦
Contemporary Christian Music (CCM) seems to be chameleonic by nature, always adopting the protective coloration of some pop-music style in order to gain or maintain an audience. In their 12 years of existence, Newsboys have been more changeable than most CCM artists, both geographically (having moved from Australia to Nashville) and stylistically. In 1997, lead singer John James departed, and the group came to be guided by Peter Furler, who assumed the chief vocal chores. The result was 1998's *Step Up to the Microphone*, whose light-pop style found favor with the faithful. Its follow-up, *Love Liberty Disco*, will sound to the uninitiated like a Britpop clone of Oasis and its ilk. Furler emotes in an airy tenor which shades into falsetto over pop/rock arrangements that, like all the Britpop bands, mix the heavy influence of the Beatles with more recent styles. *Love Liberty Disco* successfully follows CCM's basic formula, smartly aping an existing pop style in a Christian context. —*William Ruhlmann*

● **Shine . . . The Hits** / Oct. 24, 2000 / Sparrow ✦✦✦✦
Newsboys' hits compilation is similar to many other such collections circa 2000 in that it is not so much a simple set of the group's most popular songs as a selective history and statement about the band's future. In Newsboys' case, this is complicated by the 1997 departure of lead singer John James; while it may not have been the Christian thing to do, a deliberate attempt seems to have been made to diminish James' role in favor of Peter Furler, who cofounded the group and continued to lead it after his partner left. Many of the major hits of the James era are included, among them "I'm Not Ashamed," "Shine," "Spirit Thing," "Reality," and "Take Me to Your Leader," all of which reached number one on *CCM* magazine's Contemporary Hits chart. But other number one hits—"Real Good Thing," "Truth and Consequences," and "Let It Go"—are missing, and there seems to be a disproportionate number of post-James tracks, including three brand new songs and a remake of "God Is Not a Secret" that recasts it as a rap tune. Newsboys' sound has changed over time, but this collection finds them generally faithful to their U2 and INXS-flavored '80s international pop/rock style, and with a consistently unique lyrical perspective (from "Breakfast," which warns that the devil won't be serving you Cap'n Crunch, to the new "Who—," which describes God as "tender as a burger in your microwave"). Fans will welcome this best-of, but many will notice the omission of favorite tracks. —*William Ruhlmann*

NewSong

f. 1981
Group / CCM
CCM group NewSong was formed in Valdosta, GA in 1981 by Eddie Carswell, Billy Goodwin, Eddie Middleton and Bobby Apon, who met while attending Morningside Baptist Church. The quartet's local popularity quickly swelled, and in 1982 they signed to Covenant Records to issue their debut LP *Son in My Eyes*; a move to the Word label preceded NewSong's 1984 follow-up, *The Word*. Subsequent outings including 1986's *Trophies of Grace*, 1987's *Say Yes!* and 1989's *Light Your World* further expanded the group's growing fanbase, and with their 1993 Benson label debut *All Around the World* NewSong generated four CHR chart-topping hits—"More God," "Got Me Going," "Hero of the Faith," and the title cut. Cofounders Middleton and Apon soon exited, however, and upon adding Charles Billingsley, Russ Lee and Scotty Wilbanks, the revamped group returned in 1994 with *People Get Ready*, which like its predecessor launched no less than four number one singles—"When I'm with You," "This One's with Me," "We Wear His Name" and "My Heart's Already There." Billingsley left NewSong to pursue a solo career prior to 1997's *Love Revolution*, which featured new members Mark Clay and Jack Pumphrey as well as the blockbusters "Rhythm of the World," "Won't Stop Love" and "Miracles." *Sheltering Tree* followed three years later. —*Jason Ankeny*

Arise My Love: The Very Best Of Newsong / Feb. 8, 2000 / Benson ✦✦✦✦
Newsong's *Arise My Love: The Very Best of Newsong* collects a baker's dozen of their hits, including the title track, and adds three new songs: "Can't Keep a Good Man Down," "Jesus to the World (Roaring Lambs)," and "Like Minded, Like Hearted" (which the group recorded with Out of Eden). Other highlights include "Love Revolution," "More God," "Hero of the Faith," and "My Heart's Already There." A worthwhile collection of Newsong music for fans and newcomers alike. —*Heather Phares*

Dorothy Norwood

Vocals / Traditional Gospel, Contemporary Gospel, Black Gospel
Affectionately known as 'The World's Greatest Storyteller', Dorothy Norwood has used her soulful vocals and uplifting delivery to rise to the upper echelon of modern Gospel music. Five of her albums have achieved gold status, while, she's garnered six Grammy nominations and three Stellar Award nominations.

Norwood has been singing most of her life. At the age of eight, she toured and performed with a family group. Moving to Chicago, in 1956, she sang with Mahalia Jackson, the Caravans and Reverend James Cleveland. Launching her solo career, in 1964, she was a hit from the start. With her debut solo album, *Johnny And Jesus*, she earned her first gold record award. Her second album, *Denied Mother*, did equally as well. An opportunity to bring her music beyond the Church came, in 1972, when Norwood was invited to be an opening act for the RollingStones' thirty state American tour.

Norwood continues to share her convictions through music. Her album, *Live With The Northern California GMWA Mass Choir*, released in 1991, reached the top position on the top forty chart compiled by *Billboard*. —*Craig Harris*

Johnny & Jesus / 1960 / Savoy ✦✦✦✦
The great gospel storyteller of grit and conviction. —*Opal Louis Nations*

Denied Mother / 1966 / Savoy ✦✦✦✦✦
Norwood's spectacular vocals are supported by The Combined Choir of Atlanta, GA. One of Norwood's greatest song sermons is the title track. *—Ron Wynn*

● **The Best of Dorothy Norwood** / Jul. 1996 / Intersound ✦✦✦✦✦
All of Dorothy Norwood's biggest hits and most popular songs are collected on *The Best of Dorothy Norwood*, making it a perfect introduction to her career. *—Rodney Batdorf*

Michael Omartian

Vocals, Keyboards, Piano, Producer, Composer / CCM
A solo artist, producer and composer who enjoyed success in both the secular and CCM arenas, Michael Omartian first surfaced during the early 1970s as a top session keyboardist, playing on albums by artists ranging from Steely Dan to the Four Tops to Loggins & Messina before making his solo debut with 1974's Myrrh label release *White Horse*. In 1975 he and producer Steve Barri formed the Los Angeles studio group Rhythm Heritage, topping the pop charts early the following year with their theme to the ABC television series *S.W.A.T.;* "Baretta's Theme (Keep Your Eye on the Sparrow)" appeared in 1976, but was the unit's last effort of note. After helming Alan O'Day's 1977 chart-topper "Undercover Angel," Omartian graduated to the top ranks of producers through his work with singer/songwriter Christopher Cross, collaborating on a series of hits including the Grammy-winning "Sailing," "Ride Like the Wind" and "Arthur's Theme (Best That You Can Do)." From there he produced sessions for Rod Stewart and Donna Summer, focusing increasingly on CCM projects in the years to follow through work with Gary Chapman, Kathy Troccoli and 4 Him. In addition to his solo releases, Omartian also recorded several albums with his wife Stormie. *—Jason Ankeny*

The Race / 1991 / Epic ✦✦✦

★ **White Horse/Adam Again** / 1991 / Myrrh ✦✦✦✦✦

Out of the Grey

Group / CCM
Christine and Scott Dente met while studying at the Berklee College of Music in Boston, where they began to perform in small clubs with Christine on vocals and Scott playing guitar. After getting married, the duo recorded a self-titled debut album which introduced their dreamy alternative-pop sound. Out of the Grey was pushed into the spotlight in 1993 by a national tour with Peacock, four CCM Top 20 singles from their second album *The Shape of Grace* and a readers' poll in *CCM Magazine* which voted the group second-best new artist. In 1994, Christine recorded *Down the Road* with Susan Ashton and Margaret Becker. Out of the Grey's third album, *Diamond Days*, also appeared that year; it was followed in 1995 by *GraVity*. *Remember This: The Out of the Grey Collection 1991-1998* appeared three years later. *—John Bush*

The Shape of Grace / 1993 / Sparrow ✦✦✦✦
Like its debut, the duo works with artist/producer Charlie Peacock to craft a killer collection of songs and hone its sound. *—Thom Granger*

Gravity / Aug. 1, 1995 / Sparrow ✦✦✦✦
Scott and Christine Dente release another strong album under the continued production of Charlie Peacock. The songs are beautiful acoustic pop, with instantly memorable hooks, lilting vocals, and intricate instrumentation. This is a lyrically strong album as well, thoughtful, insightful, and encouraging. *Gravity* is pleasant background music, but is also a very intelligent album that deserves more than a cursory listen. *—Marc Castellani*

See Inside / Apr. 1, 1997 / Sparrow ✦✦

● **Remember This: Out of the Grey Collection 1991-1998** / Nov. 17, 1998 / Sparrow ✦✦✦✦
Remember This is a great representation of Out of the Grey's work over the years. Combining hits from their career with three new tracks, including an instrumental, "Way Late," showcasing Scott Dente's guitar work, *Remember This* shows Out of the Grey at their very best. Particularly noteworthy is the lush, jazzy remix of their 1991 hit, "Wishes." With Christine Dente's ethereal vocals, Scott and Christine Dente's songwriting, and excellent production, *Remember This* is a solid collection worth owning for fans and for those less familiar with Out of the Grey's work. *—Melinda Hill*

Shun Pace-Rhodes

Vocals / Black Gospel
Pace-Rhodes hails from a family of singers active in the Church of God in Christ (COGIC) music movement. She and her siblings formed The Anointed Pace Sisters of Atlanta in the mid-'70s and were known for their contemporary R&B gospel sound. She sang "That Name" on one of Edwin Hawkins's Music and Arts seminal albums in 1987. It was he who personally went to the head of Savoy-Malaco Records and suggested they sign the belting singer as a solo artist, and they did. Rather than cutting her chops on modern styles, Pace-Rhodes sang music that recalls the days of Mahalia Jackson and the Ward Singers. *—Bil Carpenter*

● **He Lives** / 1991 / Savoy Gospel ✦✦✦✦✦
From the most astonishing traditional female gospel soloist in the church today, her powerhouse pipes are supported by The Showers of Blessing Choir and The Voices of Power out of Atlanta, GA. *—Opal Louis Nations*

The Paramount Singers

f. 1936, Austin, TX
Group / Traditional Gospel, Black Gospel
Although eclipsed in popularity by contemporaries including the Soul Stirrers and the Dixie Hummingbirds, the Paramount Singers were among the longest-lived gospel groups of the modern era, upholding the tradition of classic a cappella harmonizing for well over half a century. The Paramounts first recorded for the Library of Congress in 1941, though lineup changes (and a move from Austin to San Francisco) kept the roster in a seemingly constant state of flux. Despite recording for nationally distributed companies like Coral and Duke between the late '40s and mid-'50s, the Paramounts never earned the notoriety of many of their peers, largely because their day jobs and family ties kept their touring activity confined almost exclusively to the West Coast. A 1955 session for Duke was the Paramounts' last commercial recording for close to four decades, but the group continued regularly performing throughout the years to follow. In 1992, the Paramounts—including four-decade members Archie Reynolds and Joseph Dean—issued *Work and Pray On*, their first new record in 37 years. *—Jason Ankeny*

Work & Pray on / 1992 / Arhoolie ✦✦✦✦
Work & Pray On is recorded by a latter-day incarnation of the Paramount Singers. Only two of the members of the sextet were part of the group in the '40s, yet the group still carried on with their classic sound, updated slightly with fresh arrangements. The album suffers from having a few too many undistinguished songs and running a little too long, but it remains an excellent example of how good classic gospel can be. *—Leo Stanley*

● **Paramount Singers** / ✦✦✦✦✦
The Paramounts of San Francisco hail back to the early '40s, when the Library of Congress field unit recorded them. During the '50s they cut sides for Trilon, Olliet, Coral and Duke, and it is this style of close harmony a cappella which, in all its richness and simplicity, is faithfully reproduced here on this excellent recently etched ten-song set. It's great old-time jubilee singing from Doe Dean—first lead (who has a voice like Rev. Claude Jeter), Odie Brown—second lead, Archie Reynolds, Gene Terrell, Clyde Price and J.W. Williams (cassette only). *—Opal Louis Nations, Roots & Rhythm Newsletter*

Twila Paris

b. 1958
Vocals / Inspirational, CCM
Known among fans as "the modern-day hymnwriter," Twila Paris was among contemporary inspirational music's most prolific singers and composers. A native of Arkansas, her grandparents were itinerant preachers, holding outdoor revival meetings and planting churches; her grandmother even wrote songs for use at evangelistic meetings. Paris' father was himself a musician, as well as the leader of an area youth mission; a life of religion and music was seemingly her destiny, and indeed she enjoyed great success as a performer, earning comparison to the legendary Fanny Crosby for her contributions to latter-day hymnody, with songs like "We Will Glorify," "Lamb of God," "How Beautiful" and "Faithful Men" included in millions of hymnals in churches across the globe. Recognized as among the most popular "praise and worship" artists of her generation, Paris also published *In the Sanctuary*, a book co-written with theologian Robert Webber. 1996's *Where I Stand* was her commercial breakthrough, becoming Paris' best-selling record to date; *Perennial: Songs for the Seasons of Life* followed in 1998, and a year later she returned with *True North*. *Bedtime Prayers: Lullabies and Peaceful Worship* appeared in early 2001. *—Jason Ankeny*

Cry for the Desert / 1991 / Star Song ✦✦✦

The Early Works / 1991 / Benson ✦✦✦✦✦
A good anthology of Paris's first few albums, it features songs like "The Warrior Is a Child" and "We Will Glorify." *—Thom Granger*

Sanctuary / 1991 / Star Song ✦✦✦
Produced by contemporary instrumentalist Richard Souther, this album set new musical standards in the inspirational field for arrangement and production ideas. *—Thom Granger*

● **Heart That Knows You** / 1993 / Star Song ✦✦✦✦✦
This best-of collection (radio hits and re-recordings) of early classics serves to introduce the uninitiated. *—Thom Granger*

Beyond a Dream / 1994 / Star Song ✦✦✦
Paris spun a few heads with this one, featuring her most contemporary material to date, and a bit of a new and more confident vocal approach to match it. *—Thom Granger*

Where I Stand / 1996 / Sparrow ✦✦✦✦✦
Twila Paris continues to become more pop-oriented with each of her releases, but that's not necessarily a bad thing. Although *Where I Stand* could be mistaken for any number of records cluttering the adult contemporary radio stations, Paris performs with style and grace, which is what saves the album from being either a sell-out or a wash-out. Some stronger songwriting would have made the album even more enticing, but as it stands, *Where I Stand* is simply another pleasurable record in her deep catalog. *—Rodney Batdorf*

True North / Sep. 21, 1999 / Sparrow ✦✦✦
After detouring into more traditional gospel and hymn-oriented work, Twila Paris returns to the adult contemporary style for which she's best known, and which made 1996's *Where I Stand* her most popular record. *True North* is a solidly constructed record, aimed squarely at radio airplay and highlighted by a few strong, obvious singles, which help make up for the occasional lackluster track. There's no new ground broken here for Paris; it's just another fine album that will appeal to longtime fans. *—Steve Huey*

2nd Chapter of Acts

Group / CCM
This major Christian-rock act, which began in the early '70s, were defined by the sibling harmonies of Annie Herring, Matthew Ward, and Nelly Greisen. Their music brought complex song structures to inspirational music. Their best-known song was 1974's "Easter Song," which achieved moderate mainstream radio airplay (and featured Michael Been, later founder of The Call, on bass). The group's self-deprecating attitudes may have kept them from achieving the renown of some contemporaries. Herring and Ward continued to record solo projects after the group disbanded in 1988. *—Brian Mansfield*

● **20: 1972-1992** / 1992 / Sparrow ✦✦✦✦✦
Twentieth-anniversary retrospective is a 41-track overview of the music of this influential

group. Includes three early singles for MGM and two previously unreleased cuts.—*Brian Mansfield*

The Sensational Nightingales

f. 1942
Group / Traditional Gospel, Southern Gospel, Black Gospel
The Sensational Nightingales were assembled in the '40s. In 1957 they appeared on the Gospel Train tour with The Clara Ward Singers and five other big-name gospel acts. Members included Julius Cheeks (lead), Carl Coates (bass), JoJo Wallace (tenor), Howard Carroll (baritone), and Paul Gwens (tenor). Their noted hit was "See How They Done My Lord." One of the earliest gospel quintets, they recorded and toured throughout the 1990s. Many of their '50s and '60s sides (found on MCA reissues) feature the stunning vocals of Rev. Julius Cheeks. As with Archie Brownlee, Cheeks reaches an intensity that distorts the actual recordings, and his style has been heavily "borrowed" by Bobby Bland, Wilson Pickett, and others. The later recordings by Charles Johnson are smoother and slicker, but still top-notch. —*Bil Carpenter & Billy C. Wirtz*

The Best of the Sensational Nightingales / 1978 / MCA ✦✦✦✦✦
Some of Rev. Julius Cheeks and the group's finest efforts on Peacock from the 1950s. —*Opal Louis Nations*

God Is Not Pleased / Mar. 24, 1998 / Malaco ✦✦✦✦
God Is Not Pleased is a fine latter-day effort from the Sensational Nightingales, who by this point feature a lineup of Jo Jo Wallace, Horace Thompson, and Richard Luster; this triumvirate also handled production duties. —*Steve Huey*

● **Heart & Soul/You Know Not the Hour** / Mobile Fidelity ✦✦✦✦✦
The CD remastering of these two early-'70s albums by this fine harmony quintet is well worth owning. *Heart and Soul* is taken from the better pre-Paramount days (1970-1971), and *You Know Not the Hour* presents the group in a later, more hymnal song setting, both with Charles Johnson on lead. —*Kip Lornell*

The 77's

Group / Christian Rock, CCM
Described by Larry Norman as being "too Christian for the radio, and too radio for the Church," the 77's were formed in Sacramento in the early '80s by Mike Roe (vocals, guitar) Mark Tootle (keyboards, guitar, vocals), Jan Eric Volz (bass, guitar, vocals) and drummer Mark Proctor. Known at first as the Savage Young Scratch Band, the Christian band changed their name and released *Ping Pong over the Abyss* in 1982, and then replaced Proctor with Aaron Smith for *All Fall Down* two years later. Mark Tootle left after the 77's live album *88*, but the group split up after 1990's *Sticks and Stones*. Roe then re-formed the band with Smith and two-thirds of the Strawmen: Mark Harmon (bass, vocals) and David Leonhardt (rhythm guitar, vocals). *Seventy Sevens* (originally titled "Pray Naked") was released in 1992. *Drowning with Land in Sight* appeared in 1994, and was followed by *tom tom Blues*. Roe has also recorded as a solo artist and with the Lost Dogs. In the late '90s, the group formed their own Fools of the World label and reissued many of their older albums, as well as releasing 1999's *EP* and 2001's *A Golden Field of Radioactive Crows* among other new titles. —*John Bush*

The 77's / 1987 / Exit ✦✦✦✦✦
This promising debut shows a band equally influenced by Bob Dylan and blues-rock. Includes their concert favorite, "The Lust, the Flesh, the Eyes & the Pride of Life," and a killer anthem—"Do It for Love." —*Brian Mansfield*

88 / 1988 / BAI ✦✦✦✦✦

★ **Sticks and Stones** / 1990 / Brainstorm ✦✦✦✦✦
After the departure of keyboardist Mark Tootle, Mike Roe emerged as the dominant figure in The 77's. *Sticks and Stones* points the way to The 77's of the future: biting, guitar-dominated rock with provocative lyrics epitomized by "Perfect Blues." Also included are new recordings of the four best songs from *The 77's*. —*Brian Mansfield*

Seventy Sevens / 1992 / Brainstorm ✦✦✦
Originally titled "Pray Naked," the record company went with a self-titled approach instead for this mostly pop collection, with the exception of the Zeppelin-like "Woody" and the unlisted "title" cut, an eight-minute Middle Eastern rave-up. —*Thom Granger*

Drowning with Land in Sight / 1994 / Myrrh ✦✦✦
Again, an uneven but important album, beginning with a dead-on cover of the Led Zep arrangement on "Nobody's Fault but Mine," and evolving into a hard look at some of life's most challenging realities such as a relationship's dissolution, and its effects on the human spirit. —*Thom Granger*

George Beverly Shea

b. Feb. 1, 1909, Winchester, Ontario, Canada
Vocals / Country Gospel
Gospel vocalist George Beverly Shea spent most of his 45-year career closely associated with evangelist Billy Graham. His best-known song is "How Great Thou Art," which was written by Rev. Stuart K. Hine in the 1920s. Shea is also a distinguished writer of popular hymns such as "The Wonder of It All."

Born the son of a Wesleyan Methodist minister in Winchester, Ontario, Shea was raised in the New York area and spent much time as a youth singing in church choirs. Following high school, he briefly attended Houghton College in New York, dropping out only after his family's financial difficulties necessitated it. Shea began working as a clerk, but received voice lessons and sang in churches and on local religious radio stations. The latter led to an audition for the Lynn Murray Singers, but he declined their invitation since they sang secular music. He married his high-school sweetheart in 1934 and moved to Chicago. After ten years in the Windy City, Shea got national exposure when he was hired to appear on *Club Time*, a show he sang with for the next eight years. During this time, Shea also became prominent in the Youth for Christ movement of the 1940s and '50s. He hooked up with Graham in 1947 and signed to RCA Victor in 1951. *Southland Favorites* received a 1965 Grammy for Best Gospel or Other Religious Recording (Musical). Shea was inducted into the Gospel Music Association Hall of Fame in 1978. —*Sandra Brennan*

Echoes of My Soul / Feb. 24, 1998 / Star Song ✦✦✦
Tender Moments, Vol. 1: Echoes of My Soul is a selection of 18 gospel standards that are among George Beverly Shea's favorites, including "The Wonder of It All," "Steal Away," "O Savior Thou Art Mine," "O Love Let Me Go," "I Will Sing the Wondrous Story," "God Leads His Dear Children Along" and "How Great Thou Art." Although Shea recorded this album many decades into his career, his voice remains rich and inviting, which makes it a warm, comforting album. —*Stephen Thomas Erlewine*

● **My Favorite Songs (Best of George Beverly Shea)** / Word ✦✦✦✦✦

Smalltown Poets

f. 1996
Group / Alternative CCM, Adult Alternative Pop/Rock
The alternative CCM group Smalltown Poets was formed in Tifton, GA. by singer/guitarist Michael Johnston, keyboardist Danny Stephens and drummer Byron Goggin, high school pals who'd played in bands together throughout their formative years (including Villanelle, which released an independent-label album titled *Pinwheels and Orange Peels* in 1996). In the spring of 1996, the lineup grew to include guitarist Kevin Breuner and bassist Miguel DeJesus; a year later, the Smalltown Poets signed to Chordant to issue their self-titled debut album. A series of lineup changes followed before the group—now consisting of Johnston, Breuner, DeJesus and drummer Nathan Blackstone—resurfaced with *Listen Closely* in 1999 and *Third Verse* in fall 2000. —*Jason Ankeny*

● **Smalltown Poets** / Mar. 25, 1997 / Forefront ✦✦✦
The Smalltown Poets' eponymous debut album is a pleasant collection of mature, latter-day jangle-pop, sounding like a cross between the Gin Blossoms, Toad the Wet Sprocket and the Rembrandts. Although the group hasn't written anything as catchy as their idols' big hits, *Smalltown Poets*, with its gentle acoustic guitars and harmonies, is an engaging record for fans of those groups. —*Stephen Thomas Erlewine*

Third Verse / Sep. 26, 2000 / ForeFront ✦✦✦
Third Verse, the Smalltown Poets' third album, continues in the vein of its predecessors: smoothed-out, jangly folk-rock with unabashedly Christian lyrics. This sound isn't as prevalent on pop or alternative radio as it was earlier in the '90s, but the group still sounds contemporary thanks to their mostly solid songcraft. —*Steve Huey*

Michael W. Smith

b. Kenova, WV
Vocals, Keyboards / CCM
Michael Whitaker Smith has become one of the most enduringly popular artists on the Christian Contemporary Music front and is also finding considerable success as a mainstream artist. In 1978, a songwriting company expressed interest in his work, and he moved to Nashville, where he played with local bands, including Rose. He was heavily into drugs and continued using until October 1979, when he suffered a sort of emotional mental breakdown that culminated in recommitting to Christ. The next day he auditioned for a new CCM group, Higher Ground, as a keyboardist. While touring with them, Smith cleaned up his act. Over the next few years he provided gospel hits for such artists as Sandi Patti, Kathy Troccoli, Bill Gaither and Amy Grant. He began touring as a keyboardist with Grant in 1982 and the following year, after releasing his first album, *The Michael W. Smith Project*, became her opening act. Smith became a headliner following the release of his second album, *Michael W. Smith 2*. Afterwards, he changed musical directions and began recording more rock-oriented music in order to reach a younger audience. As a result, some of his songs became more secular and began breaking through to mainstream audiences. —*Sandra Brennan*

The Big Picture / Feb. 1986 / Reunion ✦✦✦✦✦
Smith's most rock-oriented project, it garnered him more critical acclaim and less airplay and sales. —*Thom Granger*

The Michael W. Smith Project / Dec. 1987 / Reunion ✦✦✦

I 2 Eye / 1989 / Reunion ✦✦✦

Michael W. Smith 2 / 1989 / Reunion ✦✦

Go West Young Man / 1990 / Reunion ✦✦✦
The artist's first foray into crossover territory includes "Place in This World, " which landed on the pop charts and raised the stakes for a new level of acceptance. —*Thom Granger*

Change Your World / 1992 / Reunion ✦✦✦✦✦
Smith's biggest pop production changed his own world, bringing a bevy of hits in both gospel and pop markets, as well as a new level of touring activity. —*Thom Granger*

Wonder Years / 1993 / Reunion ✦✦✦✦✦
This deluxe two-disc boxed set of Smith's best 35 songs also includes elaborate packaging and commentary from the artist. —*Thom Granger*

● **The First Decade: 1983-1993** / Oct. 12, 1993 / Reunion ✦✦✦✦✦
When Michael W. Smith made a move for a secular audience, he didn't seem to alienate his core contemporary Christian fan base as much as peer Amy Grant did, and the reason might be that he takes the spoonful-of-sugar tack when spreading his message: He seamlessly creates pop music with messages that sometimes subtly and sometimes not-so-subtly hark back to God. On "Go West Young Man" he could just as easily be referring to Israel as California as he advises to go west when evil tempts you east; on "Old Enough to Know" he urges a young

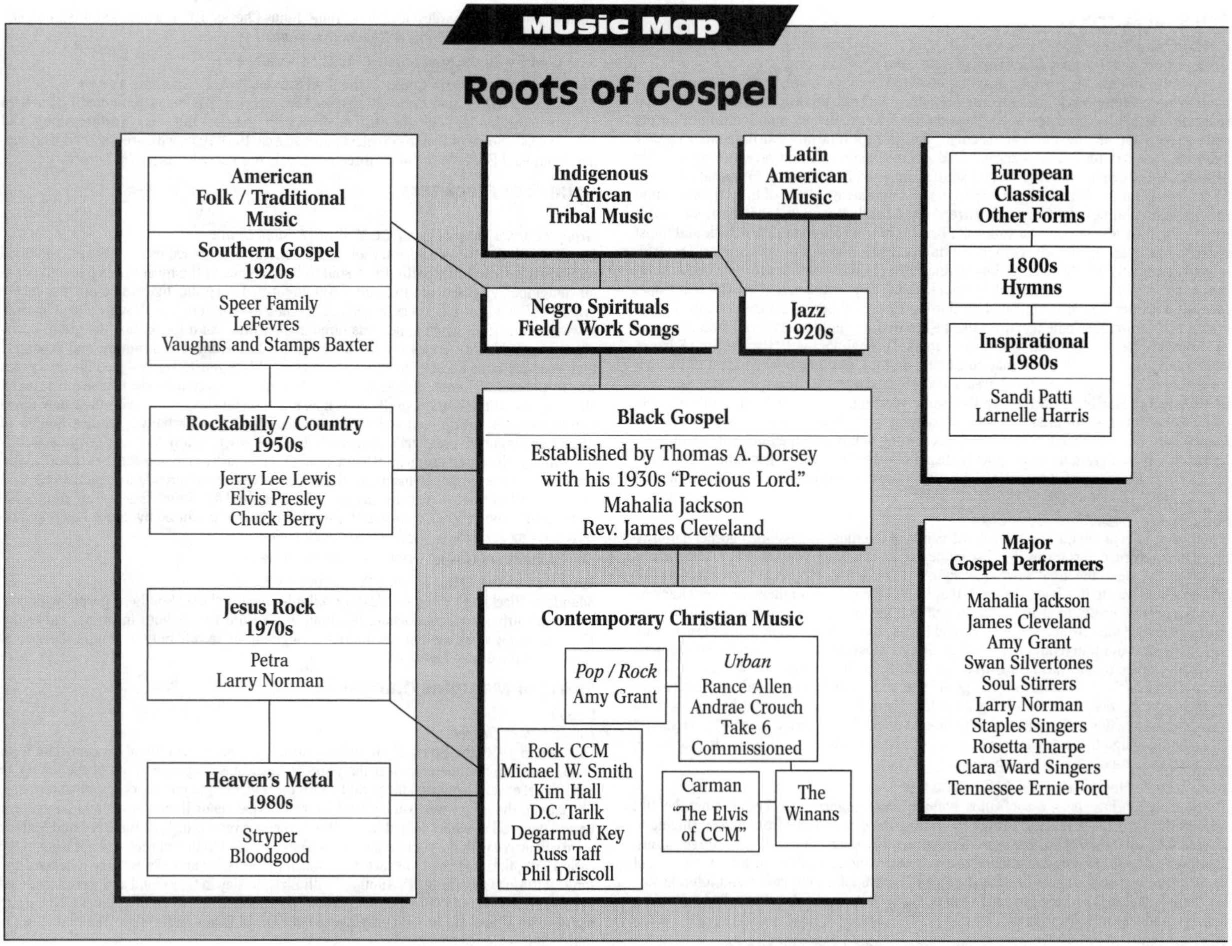

girl to abstain, which is certainly a Christian way of thinking, but it also applies to any teenager in the world; "Rocketown" could be Sodom as well as a seedy part of any town; and his biggest Top 40 hit, "A Place in This World," could refer to simply fitting in or finding God. Much of contemporary Christian music is better pop than most pop, and Smith leads the pack with enviable hooks, production, vocals, and A-list co-writers like Grant, Diane Warren, and Wayne Fitzpatrick. Though it includes some cuts that rely too much on synthesizer-driven production ("Emily," "Friends"), this greatest-hits package is testament to his strengths and his success at spreading the word of God to both Christian and secular audiences. *—Bryan Buss*

I'll Lead You Home / Oct. 1995 / Reunion ✦✦✦✦✦
I'll Lead You Home became the highest-debuting Christian album in chart history and it's easy to see why. Produced by Patrick Leonard, the album consolidates Michael W. Smith's inspirational and pop success, combining gospel songs with glistening, immaculate pop production. Smith had earned pop fans with his previous record, *Change Your World*, and *I'll Lead You Home* will show those listeners his inspirational records are every bit as good as his pop records. That's because they share the same kind of mainstream pop production—the layered synths and guitars speak to the listeners nearly as much as Smith's voice itself. *—Stephen Thomas Erlewine*

Live the Life / Apr. 28, 1998 / Reunion ✦✦✦✦

This Is Your Time / Nov. 23, 1999 / Reunion ✦✦✦✦
Michael W. Smith's 13th studio album *This Is Your Time* features more of the accessible, contemporary Christian rock that has won him a large and increasingly secular audience. Songs like "Hey You It's Me," "I Will Carry You," and "I Will Be Your Friend" blend guitar and synth flourishes with Smith's charismatic vocals, while hook-laden tracks like "Worth It All" and "Everybody Free" demonstrate why his audience continues to expand into the mainstream pop arena. *—Heather Phares*

Willie Mae Ford Smith

b. 1906, Rolling Fort, MS, **d.** Feb. 2, 1994, St. Louis, MO
Vocals / Traditional Gospel, Black Gospel

Considered the greatest of the "anointed singers"—artists who live according to the spirit, and who perform with the ultimate aim of saving souls—Willie Mae Ford Smith was among the most legendary gospel vocalists of her era; rarely recorded, her enormous reputation instead rested almost entirely on her incendiary live performances, where her dramatic, physical style inspired many of the finest soloists to follow in her wake. She was also the first to introduce the "song and sermonette," the act of delivering a lengthy sermon before, during or after a performance. Smith mounted her solo career after performing in a family quartet named the Fords. She was one of the first gospel performers to tour relentlessly, conducting musical revivals in many of the cities she visited. Her arranging skills were almost as influential as her singing, with radical reinterpretations of chestnuts like "Jesus Loves Me," "Throw Out the Lifeline" and "What a Friend We Have in Jesus" galvanizing a new generation of singers to include the songs in their repertoires. By the '40s her music began reflecting the rhythm and energy of the sanctified church; still, she did not finally begin recording until the end of the decade. By the early '50s she had turned to evangelical work; still, she continued to remain a great inspiration, dying on February 2, 1994. *—Jason Ankeny*

● **Mother Smith & Her Children** / 1989 / Spirit Feel ✦✦✦✦
Willie Mae Ford Smith is one of the pivotal figures in gospel; born in 1904, she inspired innumerable younger vocalists. *Mother Smith & Her Children* collects sides by Smith and her spiritual descendents. Among them is Martha Bass, who joins with her own son David Peaston (later a gospel star in his own right) and daughter Fontella, the woman behind the secular hit "Rescue Me" (the best record Aretha Franklin never cut). Brother Joe May, once esteemed as the male Mahalia Jackson, takes the reins for three unreleased and undated performances, while five contributions from Edna Gailmon Cooke round out the collection. *—Jason Ankeny*

Going on with the Spirit / Nashboro ✦✦✦
Of special note: "Give Me Wings" and "I've Got a Secret." *—Bil Carpenter*

Willie Mae Ford Smith / Savoy ✦✦✦✦✦
Includes "I Must Tell Jesus" and "He Never Left Me Alone." *—Bil Carpenter*

The Soul Stirrers

f. 1927, Trinity, Texas

Group / Traditional Gospel, Black Gospel, R&B, Soul

Indisputably among the premier gospel groups of the modern era, the Soul Stirrers pioneered the contemporary quartet sound. Pushing the music away from the traditional repertoire of jubilees and spirituals towards the visceral, deeply emotional hard gospel style so popular among postwar listeners, the group's innovative arrangements—they were the first quartet to add a second lead—and sexually-charged presence irrevocably blurred the lines between religious and secular music while becoming a seminal influence on the development of rock & roll and soul, most notably by virtue of their connection to the legendary Sam Cooke. The Soul Stirrers' classic early lineup included baritone Senior Roy Crain, bass Jesse Farley, baritone T.L. Bruster, second lead James Medlock and, most notably, lead R.H. Harris, whose high, crystalline voice remains the inspiration for virtually all great male quartet leads to follow since. After moving to Chicago, they began shifting away from the signature tight harmonies and compact songs of traditional gospel towards a harder style distinguished by shifting leads and performances elongated to increase their emotional potency; they also began performing new material from the pens of Thomas A. Dorsey, Kenneth Morris and others. Throughout the 1940s, the Soul Stirrers' reputation grew; not only were they constantly on tour, but they booked most of the major gospel programs in the Chicago area. They recorded over two dozen tracks for Specialty in 1950 before Harris quit the group that same year; many predicted a dire future, especially when it was announced that his replacement was a relatively unknown 20-year-old named Sam Cooke. When Cooke made his recording debut with the Soul Stirrers in 1951, however, any reservations were quickly dispelled—blessed with a gossamer voice even sweeter and more graceful than Harris', he would take the group to even greater heights than before. *—Jason Ankeny*

☆ **Shine on Me** / 1950 / Specialty ✦✦✦✦✦

If you want to hear what I humbly submit as one of the most impassioned gospel performances ever recorded, just throw this disc in the player, and brace yourself. Robert Harris was undoubtedly one of the great voices and stylists of the genre, and his performances on this disc go a long way to justifying the claim that he was the greatest of them all. Every track on here is a gem of beauty, tone and commitment. But the kickoff track on this compilation, an alternate take of their two-part single, "By and By," is absolutely devastating in its use of shading, dynamics, and unrelenting fervor in getting its message across. The Soul Stirrers lock the groove down mightily, chiming up on those low seventh chords like twelve feet of concrete. Harris, as the old saying goes, sings his rear end off on this one, and, as transcendent moments go, this one is in a class all by itself. If the issued versions included here are slightly less subdued and don't quite hit as high a quotient on the fervor meter, so what?—we should be grateful enough that this performance has survived. If impassioned gospel is your thing, boy, are you gonna love this. *—Cub Koda*

Heaven Is My Home / 1953-1959 / Specialty ✦✦✦

The Soul Stirrers have been gospel's most honored and recognized vocal group since the '40s, when R.H. Harris made musical history by shifting the genre's focus from unison singing to improvisational theatrics and inter-group dynamics. The selections on their most recent reissue cover a significant and too-often ignored aspect of the ensemble's history; the music of its other premier lead singers besides Harris and Sam Cooke. Paul Foster and Johnnie Taylor, the set's featured vocalists, weren't virtuosos like Harris or Cooke; they relied on timing, delivery, and fervor. *—Ron Wynn*

☆ **The Original Soul Stirrers Featuring Sam Cooke** / 1964 / Specialty ✦✦✦✦✦

The split between the secular and spiritual in black music has not only caused controversy, but has been the springboard for some of the best gospel, R&B, soul, and even hip-hop records to come out in the last 50 years; Ray Charles, Sam Cooke, Little Richard, and Al Green certainly come to mind in relation to seemingly irreconcilable allegiances to God and the commercial spotlight. Cooke's own move into the soul music field (in fact, he practically created the style) certainly caused major problems for fans of his first group and gospel music's own vocal royalty, the Soul Stirrers; it was one thing to sing sexy in church, but to embrace rock & roll with songs like "Having a Party" and "Shake" was tantamount to blasphemy. This fine Soul Stirrers collection reveals what some of the fuss was about, as Cooke is featured on a handful of the group's innovative and highly expressive gospel hits. At times sharing the mike with second lead Paul Foster, Cooke soars with angelic soulfulness on hits like "Wonderful," "Touch the Hem of His Garment," and "I'm So Glad (Trouble Don't Last Always)." Beyond the cuts featuring Cooke, the record also spotlights the talents of Cooke's replacement and future soulster Johnny Taylor as well as veteran group member R.H. Crain. There's also plenty of fine, post-Cooke material like "Feel Like My Time Ain't Long." Check this collection out before picking up Cooke's popular records and see why "soul music" has been a part of the church all along. *—Stephen Cook*

★ **The Soul Stirrers** / 1964 / Specialty ✦✦✦✦✦

Specialty's *Soul Stirrers* is a wonderful, definitive collection that contains the best moments from the seminal gospel group, including material recorded with all four lead vocalists—Sam Cooke, Johnnie Taylor, R.H. Harris and Paul Foster. *—Leo Stanley*

In the Beginning / 1991 / Ace ✦✦✦✦✦

Ace's *In the Beginning* is an excellent collection of recordings the Soul Stirrers made in the early '50s. The disc is augmented by several solo cuts from Sam Cooke, making it an excellent distillation of the essence of the group's stirring, extraordinary music. *—Leo Stanley*

Jesus Gave Me Water / 1992 / Specialty ✦✦✦✦✦

Sam Cooke was one of the most original and influential vocal stylists of all time. You can hear him in all his glory (1951-1955) without edits or overdubs; his peerless soaring melismas are a joy. Catch also the anguished spiritual tones of the great Paul Foster, Sr., as he alternates sparingly with Cooke. The first eight cuts are pure unadulterated a cappella. It includes the "long" version (one of three different unissued renderings) of "All Right Now," sung blazingly by gospel's hardest lead, Rev. "June" Julius Cheeks. This is a once-in-a-lifetime treat. *—Opal Louis Nations, Roots & Rhythm Newsletter*

Sam Cooke with the Soul Stirrers / 1992 / Specialty ✦✦✦

The Gospel Soul of Sam Cooke & the Soul Stirrers, Vol. 2 / Specialty ✦✦✦✦✦

The Gospel Soul of Sam Cooke & the Soul Stirrers, Vol. 2 is being promoted under Sam Cooke's name, but it's really the Stirrers' show with first-class titles like "Farther Along" and "I'm So Glad." Some of Cooke's greatest moments, ca. 1951-1955, with great second-lead support from Paul Foster Sr. Includes three previously unreleased cuts. *—Kip Lornell*

Sounds of Blackness

f. 1971

Group / Contemporary Gospel, CCM, World Fusion, Urban

Sounds of Blackness, a 40-person choir and ten-piece orchestra led by Gary Hines, combined traditional African music with urban soul to become one of the most distinctive and popular contemporary gospel groups. Russel Knight formed the group that would prove to be the origins of Sounds of Blackness in 1969 at St. Paul, Minnesota's Macalester College in 1971. It wasn't until 1971, when Hines was hired as their musical director, that the group developed its own identity. Hines opened the group up to the entire community, and expanded their musical scope to concentrate on all aspects of Black music. He designed the group as a way to embrace all manners of African-American music and create rich, diverse music to celebrate God and the human spirit, as well as make social statements. With their new direction in mind, the group renamed itself Sounds of Blackness. Partially by choice, Sounds of Blackness remained a regional attraction until 1989, when Jimmy Jam and Terry Lewis, the hot Minneapolis-based production team, brought Janet Jackson to one of their concerts. Jackson's enthusiastic response inspired Jam & Lewis, who were already in negotiations with Sounds of Blackness, to sign the group to Perspective/A&M immediately. The group's national debut album, *The Evolution of Gospel,* was largely produced by Jam & Lewis and received strong reviews. *—Stephen Thomas Erlewine*

● **The Evolution of Gospel** / 1991 / Perspective ✦✦✦✦✦

Time for Healing / May 5, 1997 / Perspective ✦✦✦

Sounds of Blackness' *Time for Healing* skillfully blends classic Southern gospel with contemporary urban soul production, resulting in a record that is both inspiring and funky. There are a few weak moments scattered throughout the record, but the group's sheer vocal skills carry the day. *—Leo Stanley*

Spirit of Memphis Quartet

f. 1930

Group / Black Gospel

Founded in 1930, the Spirit of Memphis Quartet are more a continual concept than a set band, changing membership over the years as musicians drop in and out of the lineup. In fact, it's not exactly a quartet; in the mid-1980s there were eight members, five of whom sang. The core of the group was usually lead Jethro Bledsoe, tenor Robert Reed, and bass singer Earl Malone, all of whom joined in the 1930s; Bledsoe retired in 1977, but Reed and Malone were still active with the act into the 1980s. They recorded in the quartet style for King in the early 1950s, then switched to Peacock for much of the 1950s and 1960s. They rehearsed the song "If It Ain't One Thing, It's Another" with Elvis Presley in Graceland and were scheduled to record it with him in 1976, but the session was canceled due to an Elvis illness. The group recorded an album of soul-influenced gospel for David Evans' indie High Water label in the mid-1980s. *—Richie Unterberger*

Spirituals, Vol. 2 / 1958 / King ✦✦✦✦✦

Fine vocals from legendary lead singers Little Ax, Jet Bledsoe and Silas Steele. *—Opal Louis Nations*

If I Should Miss Heaven / 1961 / Peacock ✦✦✦

Great singing featuring Hinton, Willie Jefferson, Jet Bledsoe and Earl Malone. *—Opal Louis Nations*

● **When Mother's Gone** / 1991 / Gospel Jubilee ✦✦✦✦✦

Prime material from King & Peacock labels circa 1949-58. *—Opal Louis Nations*

Traveling On / Oct. 14, 1997 / Highwater ✦✦✦✦✦

This is solid contemporary-electric gospel with blues and soul colorations, sticking to basic guitar-bass-drums instrumentation, and trading lead vocals between five of the members. The definite highlight is "I Believe in God," twhich could pass for a vintage Impressions cut save for the overtly spiritual lyrics. The rewording of the Platters' "Only You" into "Only Jesus," though, is kind of hokey. Mostly group originals, with a few traditional standards as well. *—Richie Unterberger*

Squirt

f. 1997

Group / Alternative CCM

The members of the alternative CCM band Squirt play a fairly typical amalgam of popular late-'90s alternative rock styles—Nirvana-esque post-grunge, punk-pop, a touch of ska—but it's not their sound that sets them apart, it's their extremely young age. At the time their debut album, *Huge,* was released in 1998, drummer and founding member Jordan Dickerson was only 11, while guitarist Chris Fewell (a replacement for original member Blake Kaiser) and bassist Matt Smith (also a replacement, for Torrey Burkum) were both 13. Dickerson's father, former Prince guitarist Dez Dickerson, runs the Absolute record label to which Squirt was signed; the two Dickersons conceived of the group as an opportunity to spread the gospel to young listeners more likely to identify with kids their own age. The band's first single, 1998's "Go!," was recorded with the original lineup of Dickerson, Burkum, and Kaiser; Fewell and Smith joined up in time to complete the recording of *Huge.* *—Steve Huey*

Huge / 1998 / Absolute ✦✦✦
This debut from the very young (ages 12 to 14) Tennessee CCM trio is filled with pop hooks, catchy melodies, and a very strong message dealing with the issue of age and faith. Fronted by Jordan Dickerson, 13, son of Absolute Records President Dez Dickerson (who worked with Prince in the early eighties), the album tackles the issues of being a young Christian and remembering that it is not strictly status that define who we are. A positive release for teens who follow the CCM scene. *—Chris True*

The Staple Singers

f. 1951, Chicago, IL
Group / Traditional Gospel, Country-Soul, Southern Gospel, Black Gospel, Soul
The Staples story goes all the way back to Winona, MS, in 1915. It was then and there that patriarch Roebuck "Pops" Staples entered the world. A contemporary and familiar of Charley Patton, Roebuck quickly became adept as a solo blues guitarist, entertaining at local dances and picnics. Gradually drawn to the church, by 1941 he'd moved to Chicago, playing gospel music with the Windy City's Trumpet Jubilees. A decade later Pops Staples presented two of his daughters, Cleotha and Mavis, and his one son, Pervis, in front of a church audience, and the Staple Singers were born. The Staples recorded in an older, slightly archaic, deeply Southern spiritual style first for United and then for Vee-Jay. In 1960 they signed with Riverside and attempted to move into the then-burgeoning White folk boom. Two Epic releases, "Why (Am I Treated So Bad)" and a cover of Stephen Stills's "For What It's Worth," briefly graced the pop charts in 1967. In 1968 the Staples signed with Memphis-based Stax. The first two albums, *Soul Folk in Action* and *We'll Get Over,* were produced by Steve Cropper and backed by Booker T and the MG's. The Staples were now singing entirely contemporary "message" songs; when Al Bell took over production chores, he took them down the road to Muscle Shoals, and things got decidedly funky. Starting with "Heavy Makes You Happy (Sha-Na-Boom Boom)" and "I'll Take You There," the Staples counted 12 chart hits at Stax. Curtis Mayfield then signed the Staples to his Curtom label and produced a number one hit in "Let's Do It Again." *—Rob Bowman*

Uncloudy Day/Will the Circle Be Unbroken / 1955-1960 / Vee-Jay ✦✦✦✦✦
The Staple Singers brilliantly fused gospel, folk, blues, and soul into a cohesive, commercially potent sound in the '50s and '60s. They perfected this approach during their tenure at Vee-Jay, the first label that fully presented their harmonies and allowed the twangy, expert guitar licks of Roebuck "Pop" Staples to be heard in the group's mix. This single disc contains two pivotal Staples albums; *Uncloudy Day* includes such gospel favorites as "I Know I Got Religion" and "Let Me Ride," while *Will the Circle Be Unbroken* offers the splendid title track, plus masterpieces like "Pray On" and "Come Up in Glory." *—Ron Wynn*

Great Day / 1963 / Milestone ✦✦✦
This two-album Fantasy reissue is an anthology of the material the Staples recorded for Riverside between 1960 and 1963. For Riverside, The Staples recorded mostly gospel but the shouting was toned down a bit. A few modern-day "message" songs make their way into their repertoire as well, including Bob Dylan's "Masters of War." Not quite as cataclysmic as their Vee-Jay material but still essential. *—Rob Bowman*

Freedom Highway / 1965 / Columbia ✦✦✦
Classic live in-church Epic recordings from the height of the civil rights movement of 1965. *—Opal Louis Nations*

Pray On / 1968 / Frank Music ✦✦✦✦✦
The Staple Singers recorded ten 78s over a four-year period for Chicago's Vee Jay. These have been reissued countless times in various forms. The Charly CD is simply the most recent. For Vee-Jay The Staples recorded a number of Pops Staples originals as well as radical rearrangements of standards. Pops Staples and Mavis Staples shared the lead singing chores, with Pervis and Cleotha Staples moaning in the background. Superb gospel shouting. *—Rob Bowman*

We'll Get Over / 1970 / Stax ✦✦✦
Their second Stax release was similar to *Soul Folk in Action.* The album's highlight is Randall Stewart's "When Will We Be Paid—" *—Rob Bowman*

Staple Singers Make You Happy / 1971 / Epic ✦✦

The Staple Swingers / 1971 / Stax ✦✦✦
The Staples' first album produced by Al Bell and recorded in Muscle Shoals hit the winning formula. Other changes saw Pervis Staples departing just before the album was recorded and being replaced by sister Yvonne Staples. Everything was now in place for the Staples' golden years. Three songs, "Heavy Makes You Happy," "Love Is Plentiful," and "You've Got to Earn It," all charted. *—Rob Bowman*

Be Altitude: Respect Yourself / 1972 / Stax ✦✦✦
The Staples' finest single album, containing three Top Ten R&B hits, "Respect Yourself," "I'll Take You There," and "This World." The first two also were pop Top 20s, "I'll Take You There" going all the way to #1. *—Rob Bowman*

Be What You Are / 1973 / Stax ✦✦✦

City in the Sky / 1974 / Stax ✦✦✦

Let's Do It Again / 1975 / Curtom ✦✦✦

Chronicle / 1979 / Stax ✦✦✦✦✦
Released in 1979, *Chronicle* remains a near-definitive overview of the Staple Singers' time at Stax Records, containing 12 tracks including such classic soul singles as "Heavy Makes You Happy (Sha-Na-Boom-Boom)," "You've Got to Earn It," "Touch a Hand (Make a Friend)," "If You're Ready (Come Go with Me)," "Be What You Are," "Respect Yourself" and "I'll Take You There." *—Stephen Thomas Erlewine*

This Time Around / 1981 / Stax ✦✦

★ **The Best of the Staple Singers** / Oct. 17, 1990 / Stax ✦✦✦✦✦
The best and most famous cuts from their glory years at Stax. Includes their massive hits "Respect Yourself" and "I'll Take You There"; less famous but similar gospel-funk fusions like "Touch a Hand (Make a Friend)" and "Heavy Makes You Happy (Sha-Na-Boom Boom)"; and less expected items like a cover of "(Sittin' On) The Dock of the Bay." It does not, however, have their 1975 number one single "Let's Do It Again," which they recorded just after cutting their ties to Stax. *—Richie Unterberger*

The Very Best of the Staple Singers, Vol. 1: Live / Mar. 3, 1998 / Collectables ✦✦✦
1950s Vee Jay classics with Pops' Delta guitar and Mavis's deep, compelling vocals. *—Opal Louis Nations*

The Very Best of the Staple Singers, Vol. 2: On My Way to Heaven / Mar. 3, 1998 / Collectables ✦✦✦
The cream of the cream. Their choice Vee Jay sides. *—Opal Louis Nations*

Too Close / Jun. 15, 1999 / MCA ✦✦✦

Statesmen Quartet

f. 1948
Group
One of Southern gospel's longest-running groups, the Statesmen Quartet was also one of the most influential—their flair for showmanship and jazzy piano accompaniment pointed the way toward the crowd-pleasing CCM of the present. Formed in 1948 by pianist Hovie Lister, the original group also included lead Mosie Lister (no relation), tenor Bobby Strickland, baritone Bervin Kendrick and bass Gordon Hill. Although the Statesmen endured countless lineup changes over the years—alumni included the great Jake Hess—perhaps the most pivotal member (as well as its longest-lived) was pianist Lister; not only was the group among the first Southern gospel quartets to introduce piano into their music, but Lister's soulful, ragtime-influenced style heralded a major shift away from the rigid accompaniment of the past—though an ordained minister, he understood the necessity of updating gospel to appeal to post-war audiences, particularly young people. Throughout the decades to follow, the Statesmen recorded over 100 releases for RCA; at various times, their lineup featured singers including Rozie Rozell, Doy Ott, Buddy Burton, Jim Wetherington, Tommy Thompson and Denver Crumpler, with Lister remaining a roster staple into the 21st century. *—Jason Ankeny*

● **Gospel Classics Series** / Apr. 7, 1998 / RCA ✦✦✦✦✦
Gospel Classic Series is a budget-line series from RCA that was designed to showcase great gospel recordings from individual artists that have yet to appear on compact disc. The Statesmen were one of the most popular gospel groups of the '50s and '60s, but their recordings were out of print for years. Although it isn't a perfect collection, this budget-line collection is a good overview of their most popular recordings, featuring such songs as "What a Savior," "Without Him," "How Long Has It Been," "Brighten the Corner Where You Are," "I Wouldn't Take Nothin' for My Journey," "Just Over in the Glory Land" and "Will the Circle Be Unbroken." *—Stephen Thomas Erlewine*

Stavin' Chain / Mar. 16, 1999 / Platinum ✦✦✦✦
This is a good solid disc that shows a lot of promise—there is nothing groundbreaking or revolutionary here, but the album displays some very good songwriting that sticks within the blues genre. There is a good bit of quality slide and dobro guitar playing, and there are even a couple of tunes on which the producer of the disc, John Mooney, contributes his extraordinary guitar playing. This is the music of the Delta region as sifted through the New Orleans melting pot. The group is comprised of Grayson Capps and John Lawrence, and their sound is fleshed out by an assortment of other musicians on this disc (but predominately by people who have played with Mooney). This is a close and very tight-sounding recording that reflects a similar feel and love for the music. Most of this is composed by Capps, with Lawrence writing two songs; the two collaborated on four others. Capps handles all the vocals on the disc, and plays some rhythm and acoustic guitar. Lawrence is responsible for the exceptionally tasty dobro, slide guitar and most of the electric guitar sounds on the disc. He shows not only great potential but restraint as well—and he doesn't overplay or play too loud. This is the first major label disc for this group and it is an exceptional effort that shows singular good taste with what they chose to present and how they unfurled it. They not only brought in Mooney to produce but got Ron Fraboni to do the mixing, and this disc bears the stamp of quality. An accomplished debut. *—Bob Gottlieb*

Candi Staton

b. Mar. 13, 1940, Hanceville, AL
Vocals / Contemporary Gospel, Quiet Storm, Country-Soul, Urban, Disco, Soul
Candi Staton sang with the Jewell Gospel Trio as a teenager, touring the traditional gospel circuit in the 1950s with the Soul Stirrers, C.L. Franklin and Mahalia Jackson. They recorded several sides for Nashboro, Apollo and Savoy Records between 1953 and 1963. In 1968 Staton launched a solo career as a southern soul stylist, garnering sixteen R&B hits for Rick Hall's legendary Fame Studios and gaining the title of First Lady of Southern Soul for her renditions of country tunes "Stand By Your Man" and "In The Ghetto." In 1975 Staton saw southern soul falling out of fashion and began collaborating with producer Dave Crawford who propelled her into a disco diva with songs such as "Young Hearts Run Free" and "Victim." In 1982 Staton returned to the gospel field. She and husband John Sussewell founded Beracah Ministries in Atlanta with help from Jim & Tammy Bakker's PTL Ministries. In 1992 she was back in the pop mainstream with a Top Ten British hit, "You Got The Love," a club-styled dance hit which sold two million copies abroad. *—Bill Carpenter*

I'm Just a Prisoner / 1969 / Fame ✦✦✦✦✦
Recorded at Rick Hall's Muscle Shoals studios, this set embodies the essence of Southern soul—a hybrid of country, R&B and the blues. This long-out-of-print set features the novelty tune "I'd Rather Be An Old Man's Sweetheart (Than A Young One's Fool)" and a killer cover of O.V. Wright's "That's How Strong My Love Is." *—Bill Carpenter*

Young Hearts Run Free / 1976 / Warner Brothers ✦✦✦
A reissue of Staton's 1976 pop breakthrough which also features her signature song, the title

tune. Recorded at Sound Studios in L.A., it was her first album recorded outside of Muscle Shoals. The set was produced by the late Dave Crawford and marked Staton's exodus from the world of gritty Southern soul to the classy world of urban soul and dance music. The album featured fine ballads such as the whispery "Summertime With You," "What A Feeling," a coming of age tale, and Al Green's "Living For You." The dance tracks "Destiny" and "Run To Me" were too formulaic and similar to "Young Hearts" to merit discussion. The set also featured the rocking "I Know," and the laidback "You Bet Your Sweet, Sweet Love," with background vocals by Deniece Williams, and Ray Parker Jr. on guitar. *—Bill Carpenter*

Stand Up and Be a Witness / 1990 / Beracah ♦♦♦
Produced by John Sussewell and Oliver A. Scott, this nine-track album is on the harder edge of contemporary gospel. For the most part, songs such as the title tune are heavy on synthesizers, percussion and bass. "He's Always There" and "The Glory of Jesus" are oddball traditional Southern gospel fillers. The Richard Smallwood Singers lend their virile background vocals again as they did on *Sing A Song* album. *—Bill Carpenter*

I Give You Praise / 1993 / Beracah ♦♦♦
Staton's usual eclectic routine of putting gospel songs with country, disco and soul styles all on one recording. The best songs are the urban-flavored "Jesus Can't Lie" and the disco beat of "dance," which would presumably have the angels doing the boogie in heaven. *—Bill Carpenter*

★ **The Best of Candi Staton [Warner Archive]** / Nov. 1995 / Warner Archives ♦♦♦♦♦
A long-overdue compilation of the soul siren's best-known '70s dance hits, featuring "Victim," "When You Wake Up Tomorrow," "Run to Me," and her signature tune "Young Hearts Run Free." Also included on the 14-song set is a previously unissued Southern soul ballad entitled "He's Making Love to You (But He's Thinking of Me)." The set also features four of Staton's last recordings with renowned soul producer Rick Hall on the erotic "As Long as He Takes Care of Home" and the torchlike "Here I Am Again" ballad. The set is rounded out with lesser-known dance tracks and album tracks from between 1974 and 1980, such as the quiet storm ballads "One More Chance on Love" and "Halfway to Heaven." The album closes with a very traditional, almost a cappella reading of "Precious Lord" with just piano and background singers. *—Bill Carpenter*

The Best of Candi Staton [A&M] / Jul. 7, 1998 / A&M ♦♦♦♦♦

Randy Stonehill

Vocals, Guitar / CCM
Pioneering Christian rocker Randy Stonehill began playing guitar at age ten, within three years winning grand prize in a citywide talent contest held in his native San Jose, California. He issued his debut LP *Born Twice* in late 1971, and in 1973 recorded *Get Me Out of Hollywood,* which was never officially released; *Welcome to Paradise,* his first major album, followed in 1976. After a four-year hiatus from recording, Stonehill resurfaced with *The Sky Is Falling,* his final collaboration with longtime producer Larry Norman; *Between the Glory and the Flame,* his first release for the Myrrh label, followed a year later. By now one of CCM's elder statesmen, Stonehill enjoyed his most prolific period during the mid-1980s, issuing at least on album annually between 1983 and 1986; after 1988's *Can't Buy a Miracle,* he began work on the next year's *Return to Paradise,* the long-awaited sequel to his breakthrough effort. With 1994's *The Lazarus Heart,* Stonehill inaugurated his own label, Street Level Records. *—Jason Ankeny*

Welcome to Paradise / 1976 / Solid Rock ♦♦♦♦♦
Stonehill's first album to receive widespread distribution, this early "Jesus Rock" masterpiece still stands the test of time, mostly due to top-notch songwriting. Unfortunately, it's out of print. *—Thom Granger*

Between the Glory and the Flame / 1981 / Myrhh ♦♦♦
The first pairing with Daniel Amosleader Terry Taylor producing (and band members playing here), this stripped down pop/rocker reflected the new wave trends of the time. *—Thom Granger*

Equator / 1982 / Myrrh ♦♦♦
The artist's most successful record veers from radio-ready ballads to quirky pop peculiarities. *—Thom Granger*

Wild Frontier / 1986 / Word ♦♦♦
After two unsatisfying forays into the more commercial trappings of pop, Stonehill formed a new association with producer/player Dave Perkins with larger-than-life rock arrangements and vocals. *—Thom Granger*

● **Return to Paradise** / 1989 / Word ♦♦♦♦♦
For someone who is frequently cited as a pioneer in Christian-based pop and rock, his back catalog is extremely weak. Prior to 1989's *Return to Paradise* Randy Stonehill's albums were musically inconsistent and historically insignificant as he dabbled in pop, rock, singer/songwriter, and novelty styles with nothing more than mediocre results. His music was dated, clichéd, and forgettable, and, sadly, even his comedy pieces lacked humor. That all changed for a fleeting moment in 1989 when this album was released. Stonehill enlisted the producing talents of Mark Heard who had a keen ear for arranging acoustic instruments in particular. Presumably what attracted Heard to this project was the quality of Stonehill's songwriting, which was nothing less than superb. Rarely have the oft-used themes of hope, regret, yearning, and conviction been stated in such a sound poetic manner—and Stonehill's poignant melodies complimented his lyrics perfectly. All Mark Heard had to do was introduce the appropriate instrument at the right moment; when it came to accordion, mandolin, fiddle, and acoustic guitars, no one arranged and produced better than him. In addition to the eight self-penned Stonehill songs, Heard lent "Strong Hand of Love," which would surface one year later on his outstanding album *Dry Bones Dance.* In fact, Heard's production skills were significantly sharpened here as he was essentially on musical hiatus for about two years prior to these sessions. Up-and-coming singer/songwriter Pierce Pettis' newly released "I Don't Ever Want to Be Without You" is given second breath here. Randy Stonehill has never sounded better than on this record as he wisely stayed within his own vocal range but also elevated his writing and playing (acoustic guitar) to new heights. *—Dave Sleger*

Wonderama / 1991 / Myrrh ♦♦♦
Randy reunited with Terry Taylor for a psychedelic, Beatlesque song cycle which may have set the stage for Taylor's own version of the same with Daniel Amos, *Motor Cycle.* *—Thom Granger*

Stories / 1993 / Myrrh ♦♦♦
A collection of Stonehill's story-songs, mostly ballads, is culled from his Myrrh releases. *—Thom Granger*

Stryper

f. 1983, Orange County, CA
Group / Christian Metal, Christian Rock
A hard rock/heavy metal CCM quartet founded in Orange County, CA, in 1983. At the time they signed to Enigma Records in 1984, the group consisted of lead singer Michael Sweet, guitarist Oz Fox, bassist Timothy Gaines, and drummer Robert Sweet. Their first recording was the mini-album *The Yellow and Black Attack,* followed by 1985's full-length album, *Soldiers Under Command,* which reached *84 on the charts. $Engima* remixed *The Yellow and Black Attack* and added two songs in 1986, and the new version hit *103. $Stryper's* second (or third) album *To Hell with the Devil* (1986) went gold and earned the band a Grammy nomination. *In God We Trust* (1988) repeated this success. *Against the Law* (1990) was somewhat less of a hit. *—William Ruhlmann*

Soldiers Under Command / 1985 / Hollywood ♦♦♦
While *The Yellow and Black Attack* earned Stryper a fair amount of publicity, it was *Soldiers Under Command* that put the band on the map commercially. The album went gold, and Stryper became a major hit on MTV without abandoning its Christian message. Glossy yet intense pop-metal like "The Rock That Makes Me Roll" and "Surrender" definitely promotes Christianity, but does so without condemning non-Christians or pointing the finger at other religions. Ironically, one of lead singer Michael Sweet's influences is Rob Halford of Judas Priest—although Stryper and the Priest have little in common lyrically. Like *The Yellow and Black Attack, Soldiers Under Command* is decent when it comes to uptempo songs, but weak when it comes to ballads. "First Love" and "Together As One" demonstrate that all too often, Stryper's ballads were much too sugary for their own good. *—Alex Henderson*

To Hell with the Devil / 1986 / Hollywood ♦♦♦
When the majority of Christian artists were going unheard in the secular market, Stryper became even more visible among non-Christian audiences with its third album, *To Hell With the Devil.* This was the first time a Stryper album went platinum—something the headbangers' presence on MTV no doubt played a role in. And the fact that this album boasted Stryper's strongest writing up to that point didn't hurt. The southern Californians sound especially confident and inspired on "The Way," "Sing-Along Song," "More Than a Man" and the infectious title song. But as invigorating as the uptempo numbers are, Stryper's ballads didn't improve a bit; "All of Me" and the hit "Honestly" are as annoying as ever. *—Alex Henderson*

In God We Trust / 1988 / Hollywood ♦♦♦
Unquestionably Stryper's strongest and most rockin' album, *To Hell With the Devil* was a tough act to follow. Instead of following it up with something equally intense, the band stressed its pop side on the uneven and disappointing *In God We Trust.* Though not quite as big a seller as *To Hell With the Devil,* the album quickly went gold and fell short of platinum. *Trust* isn't a terrible album by any means, and it does have its moments (most notably, "Come To the Everlife" and "The Writings On the Wall"), but on the whole, the material isn't very memorable. Quite often, Stryper sounds like just another MTV-friendly arena rock band. Only the more devoted Stryper aficionados should acquire this album. *—Alex Henderson*

Against the Law / 1990 / Hollywood ♦♦♦♦
A definite improvement over *In God We Trust,* the grittier *Against the Law* is not only a more consistently rockin' album, it's also much more focused and inspired. The CD's standout track is an imaginative cover of Earth, Wind & Fire's "Shining Star," which works surprisingly well in a metal/hard rock setting. But originals like "Rock the People," "Caught In the Middle" and "Ordinary Man" aren't anything to be ashamed of either. Because many of the songs don't have overtly Christian lyrics, there was some speculation that Stryper, like Amy Grant, was going secular. But Stryper's members insisted that it was still very much a Christian band. And it's hard to imagine Mötley Crüe, Ratt or Warrant recording a song like "Not That Kind of Guy," which finds Michael Sweet turning down the chance to have casual sex with an attractive woman because he doesn't consider it the moral thing to do. *—Alex Henderson*

★ **Can't Stop the Rock** / 1991 / Hollywood ♦♦♦♦♦
Though *Can't Stop the Rock* isn't the last word on Stryper, it does a decent job of summarizing the Christian rockers' contributions. Drawing on five Stryper albums and providing two new songs ("Believe" and "Can't Stop the Rock"), the CD contains some essential tracks (including "To Hell With the Devil," "Free" and "Soldiers Under Command"), as well as some that listeners can do without. The saccharine, fluffy ballads "Together As One" and "Honestly" may be among Stryper's best-known songs, but neither are even a fraction as exciting as its cover of Earth, Wind & Fire's 1975 funk smash "Shining Star." Nonetheless, if one is checking out Stryper for the first time, *Can't Stop the Rock* is the best place to start. *—Alex Henderson*

J.D. Sumner

d. Nov. 16, 1998
Vocals / CCM
The onetime holder of a Guinness world record honoring the lowest bass note ever reached, gospel pioneer J.D. Sumner was the driving force behind the Stamps Quartet, which earned secular renown as the longtime vocal support for Elvis Presley. Born November 19, 1924, Sumner became the Blackwood Brothers' bass vocalist in 1954, remaining with the group

for a dozen years. At his suggestion, in 1955 the Blackwoods became the first touring act to travel from show to show in their own customized bus, a practice since followed by virtually every live performer. Sumner also befriended the young Presley, then still a high school student who attended the Blackwood Brothers' Memphis-area performances each Saturday night. In 1962, Sumner and bandmate James Blackwood jointly purchased a Dallas-based music publishing company which included among its holdings the rights to the name of the Stamps Quartet, a vocal group originally formed in 1924; within two years Sumner left the Blackwoods to assume leadership of the Stamps, remaining at the helm for over three decades. The Stamps worked regularly with Presley from 1970 onward to the King's 1977 death, backing him live as well as appearing on hit records including "Burning Love." In the wake of Presley's death the group regularly contributed to Graceland's annual Elvis memorial celebrations in addition to maintaining their own rigorous recording and touring schedules; during a concert stay in Myrtle Beach, S.C., Sumner died in his sleep on November 16, 1998, just three days short of his 74th birthday. *—Jason Ankeny*

The Final Sessions / Aug. 3, 1999 / New Haven ♦♦♦
The Final Sessions chronicles the last recording project J.D. Sumner completed with the Stamps Quartet before his death in 1998; it consists mostly of new versions of some of the best and most popular songs in Sumner's repertoire. It isn't up to the level of the recordings Sumner made in his prime—his voice is a little shaky and gravelly, and he sometimes sounds as though he's having trouble keeping up with the music. The production is a little syrupy as well, featuring heavy doses of electric piano which don't seem to fit Sumner's traditional style. However, the package makes a fitting memorial; the booklet is filled with tributes from other artists, friends and relatives. *—Steve Huey*

Swan Silvertones

f. 1938, Coalwood, West Virginia
Group / Traditional Gospel, Southern Gospel, Black Gospel, R&B
The Swan Silvertones are one of the premiere gospel groups of all time. The a cappella quartet Four Harmony Kings was created by tenor Claude Jeter in 1938 in Coalwood, West Virginia, but the name was changed to the Swan Silvertones when they began a 15-minute radio show in Knoxville sponsored by the Swan Bakery Company in 1942. They developed a national reputation during their contract with King Records from 1946 to 1951, recording some 21 songs, mostly in the jubilee gospel style. They joined Specialty Records from 1951 to 1953, but issued only four singles (in a more contemporary, harder style) before they were dropped. The group really came into their own when they signed with Vee-Jay and recorded with that label from 1956 through 1964. During their years at Vee-Jay, the main members of the group were tenor (and falsetto) Jeter, baritone John H. Myles, tenor/arranger Paul Owens and bass William Conner, with a few other singers moving through the group during that time. The smoother Vee-Jay sound is probably due to arranger Owens, who joined the group in 1952. Influenced by jazz vocal groups like the Four Freshmen and the Hi-Los, Owens smoothed out the sound and made it more contemporary, even progressive. Starting in 1956, the group began adding instruments to what had been a purely a cappella sound, including several jazz sidemen. Perhaps their greatest hit was "Oh Mary Don't You Weep," released in 1959; Claude Jeter intones the phrase "I'll be a bridge over deep water, if you trust in my name" that inspired Paul Simon to compose "Bridge Over Troubled Water" some years later. When Vee-Jay closed in 1965, the group moved to Hob Records, where they did one last album before Claude Jeter left to record on his own and focus on his ministry. *—Michael Erlewine*

Heavenly Light / 1952 / Specialty ♦♦♦♦♦
The Swan Silvertones only recorded for Specialty Records from 1952 until 1955, and it's generally not considered a prime period in their tenure. But this set of newly released performances from the early '50s, most of which even the label lacks information about, show that they did turn in some top-flight outings during that period. Ten of the tracks were done live before hollering, celebrating audiences that weren't attending a concert, but participating in a spiritual renewal. The other eight are studio numbers, but they contain the same intensity and spark that make this a memorable Swan Silvertones document. *—Ron Wynn*

Singin' in My Soul / 1960 / Vee-Jay ♦♦♦♦♦
Here is one of the classic Vee-Jay albums (12 tracks) of vintage Swan Silvertones. These tracks came from six sessions for Vee-Jay when the group was at its creative peak. The album includes "End of My Journey," "Jesus is Alright with Me," and their version of "Rock My Soul." *—Michael Erlewine*

☆ **The Swan Silvertones** / 1993 / Specialty ♦♦♦♦♦
Here is perhaps the best of the Vee-Jay albums (12 tracks) of vintage Swan Silvertones. These tracks came from six sessions for VeeJay when the group was at its creative peak—perhaps the single best album they ever put out. It contains their hit "Oh Mary Don't You Weep," "How I Got Over," "My Rock," "The Lord's Prayer," "When Jesus Comes," and "Great Day in December"—all incredible music experiences. *—Michael Erlewine*

★ **Swan Silvertones/Singin' in My Soul** / Oct. 1993 / Vee-Jay ♦♦♦♦♦
Here is one CD with two classic Vee-Jay albums (24 tracks) of vintage Swan Silvertones. The tracks from both albums came from six sessions for Vee-Jay, when the group was at its creative peak. The album *Swan Silvertones* is perhaps the single best album they ever put out, containing 12 tunes including their hit "Oh Mary Don't You Weep," "How I Got Over," "My Rock," "The Lord's Prayer," "When Jesus Comes," and "Great Day in December"—all incredible musical experiences. The music continues from the album *Singin' in My Soul*, featuring 12 more prime Vee-Jay cuts including "End of My Journey," "Jesus is Alright With Me," and their version of "Rock My Soul." *—Michael Erlewine*

Hallelujah: Collection of Their Finest Recordings / May 18, 1999 / Music Club ♦♦♦♦
This 15-track collection brings together both live and studio recordings made for the HOB label. Both of the famous leads with the group—the Rev. Claude Jeter and Louis Johnson—are featured on tracks like "Only Believe," "I Love the Lord," "Home in that Rock," "Call Him Up," "Jesus, I Love You," their two magnificent voices dueting on "Leaning on Jesus," "In My Heart" and "He's My Friend." The live tracks on here literally sweat with emotion and fervor. A nice set. *—Cub Koda*

Southern White Gospel

Gospel songs from the beginning made up a large part of the country music repertoire. Two subgroups quickly formed. First came the traditional British ecclesiastical songs, reflecting a fundamental Protestant view of life as a vale of tears and suffering. But another form of gospel songs, one that tolerated joy in both worlds, became increasingly popular because of the upbeat, optimistic message of its lyrics and its fast-tempo melody. Whatever the mood of the musicians and audience, there was an appropriate gospel song: If you are feeling unreasonably good, "This World Is Not My Home" will bring you crashing back to earth; but if your daily life has so much real woe and suffering that a gospel dirge would be the last nail in your coffin, then request the band to play "I'll Fly Away" or "God Put a Rainbow in the Cloud." Southerners, Black and White alike, found gospel music a contrast to country music's standard fare of songs about family and home, good love and broken love, working men and failures, rambling and jail.

Most of country's great performers learned gospel music first, and a large number returned to it after the pressures of the business drove them to self-destruction—in the old days with alcohol, but more recently with drugs. Thus, gospel songs often have saved not only the audience but the performers, who in the very act of singing "Amazing Grace" have found what the lyrics promise.

Because the church often offered the only opportunity for singing and musicmaking (fiddle and banjo music especially were thought to be the devil's music in the old days), country performers since the '50s have made it standard fare to record a gospel album after "making it" with mass-audience material. The Carter Family, Uncle Dave Macon, Roy Acuff, Bill Monroe, Hank Williams, Red Foley, Tennessee Ernie Ford, Elvis Presley, George Jones, Ricky Skaggs—these are only a few of the legions of country stars who have showcased gospel music in their careers. Bluegrass music, with its base of tradition, emphasizes gospel songs, often sung a cappella. The Lewis Family is the best example of a bluegrass/country group that has established a good reputation over the years by performing gospel and pretty much only gospel. Meanwhile, the Oak Ridge Boys, the epitome of country/rock in the '80s, began as a gospel group. So did the Statler Brothers, who toured as the Kingsmen with Johnny Cash in 1963. Southern gospel is now a subgenre of country music, with its own charts and awards and many groups who perform nothing but gospel. From the earliest country recordings through the most recent, gospel has permeated country music. *—David Vinopal*

Russ Taff

b. 1953
Vocals / CCM
Taff first gained recognition as lead vocalist for The Imperials (1977-1981), but quickly gained a reputation as one of Christian music's most powerful and versatile artists, one whose music could hold its own against the best mainstream acts. His dynamic vocals reflect both the joys and the struggles of The Christian faith. *—Brian Mansfield*

Medals / 1985 / Horizon ♦♦♦
The second solo set showcases '80s pop styles and hooky songs, resulting in a CCM classic. *—Thom Granger*

Russ Taff / 1987 / Word ♦♦♦
This self-titled effort finds Taff trying to find himself. A cathartic album, it's less accessible but deeply felt. *—Thom Granger*

★ **The Way Home** / 1990 / Word ♦♦♦♦♦
Taff serves up his best effort here, a blend of well-crafted acoustic pop and roots-rock that deserved to be heard beyond the walls of CCM. *—Thom Granger*

☆ **Under Their Influence, Vol. 1** / 1991 / Word ♦♦♦♦♦
The musical roots of most CCM artists lie pretty close to the surface, but that's not the case with Taff, the son of a Pentecostal evangelist who preached in California migrant territory. Here Taff pays tribute to Blind Willie Johnson, Brother Joe May, and Mahalia Jackson, among others, with an album that provides the link between gut-level gospel and Southern rock. *—Brian Mansfield*

Right Here Right Now / Nov. 9, 1999 / Benson ♦♦♦♦
In addition to owning a powerful, affecting voice, Russ Taff is among CCM's most versatile performers. *Right Here Right Now* is among his more introspective efforts, exploring issues of strength, frailty, and the trials and joys of maintaining strong religious faith in the face of human imperfection. Taff is more confessional than many of his CCM peers, coming off as all the more effective in his message through his refusal to sugarcoat. Overall, a fine return to the recording arena. *—Steve Huey*

Take 6

f. 1985, Alabama
Vocals / Vocal Jazz, Contemporary Gospel, Acappella, Black Gospel, Urban
With its roots in gospel, doo wop, and the sophisticated jazz-influenced singing groups of mid-century America like the Hi-Los, the a cappella vocal group Take 6 is both a throwback to an earlier, more genteel era of American music and a precursor for a number of black male pop groups of the '90s (most notably Boyz II Men). Its members include David Thomas, Alvin Chea, Cedric Dent, Mark Kibble, Claude V. McKnight III and Joey Kibble (who replaced

Mervyn Warren). McKnight and Mark Kibble caught the a cappella bug at Alabama's Oakwood College in the early '80s, forming a vocal group that solidified into Take 6 when singer/arranger Warren joined up in 1985. They signed a pact with the Reunion label in 1988, recording arrangements of Negro spirituals and newly composed material on their first album, *Doo Be Doo Wop Bop!* They were quickly picked up by Warner Bros.' Reprise label, for whom they started making smooth yet vocally adventuresome albums that defy pigeonholing other than the all-purpose a cappella label. Take 6 has also recorded Christmas carols, toured with Al Jarreau, appeared on Quincy Jones' all-star *Back on the Block* album, and on *Join the Band* (1994), used instrumental backing for the first time. However, 1996's *Brothers* album indicated a turn toward commercial, sound-alike soul music that threatens to rob Take 6 of its unique identity. *So Cool* followed in 1998, with *We Wish You a Merry Christmas* appearing a year later. *—Richard S. Ginell*

Doo Be Doo Wop Bop! / 1988 / Warner Alliance ✦✦✦✦
The vocal sextet's debut release was critically acclaimed, capturing Grammy Awards in both the jazz and gospel categories. In a diverse selection of songs, Take 6 merges an a cappella sound with gospel and big-band jazz arrangements. Of the ten songs recorded, six are from the public domain, two are group collaborations, and the remaining two are from outside sources. Their harmonies and melodies are consistent throughout this outstanding collection of songs. In addition to being the lead vocalists on most of the tracks, Claude McKnight and Mark Kibble also produced the album, along with tenor Mervyn Warren. Moreover, the other three members also exert their vocal versatility by singing lead on at least one selection each. *—Craig Lytle*

★ **Take 6** / 1988 / Reprise ✦✦✦✦✦
The debut recording by Take 6 is still their finest set. Comprised of six singers performing a cappella, Take 6's message was always strictly gospel, but their advanced harmonies, impressive ranges and swinging style often crossed over stylistically to jazz. Some of their ensembles are quite remarkable on this CD, and their interpretations of originals and such songs as "Oh Mary, Don't You Weep," "Get Away, Jordan" and "He Never Sleeps" invigorate both gospel music and the legacy of jazz vocal groups. A classic set. *—Scott Yanow*

So Much 2 Say / 1990 / Warner Alliance ✦✦✦✦✦
Take 6's second recording is almost the equal of their first. The six singers (Mark Kibble, Claude V. McKnight III, Cedric Dent, David Thomas, Mervyn E. Warren and Alvin Chea) perform some near-miraculous ensembles on a variety of original material, all of which contains gospel-oriented lyrics. Take 6's first two CDs are their strongest, before the innovative group started to water down both their message and their jazz-influenced harmony sound with the addition of occasional instruments. *—Scott Yanow*

Join the Band / 1994 / Warner Alliance ✦✦✦
This gospel-infused, jazz-inspired sextet shows all the little boy vocal harmony groups how it's done. The lyrics are geared towards God, but the slick, bubbly production is cool and soulful R&B all the way. Their picture-perfect, rhythmically fascinating voice texturing certainly doesn't need any embellishment; however, on hand to lend support are Stevie Wonder, Ray Charles, Kirk Whalum, and Gerald Albright. In light of all the self-contained artistic brilliance, it's sad that they resorted to the commercialism of a bland David Foster ballad and a Queen Latifah rap. Top cuts include "Biggest Part of Me" (remake of the old Ambrosia hit), "It's Gonna Rain," and "I've Got Life." *—Jonathan Widran*

The Greatest Hits / Jul. 20, 1999 / Reprise ✦✦✦✦

John Michael Talbot

Vocals, Guitar / Inspirational, Christian Rock, CCM
At the peak of his success, John Michael Talbot was the best-selling male performer in the history of Christian music. Born in Oklahoma City in 1954, he began playing piano and drums at the age of six, and later moved on to banjo, guitar and dobro. In 1963, the family moved to Indianapolis; there, Talbot soon made his professional debut as a member of his brother Terry's teen pop band, the Quinchords. The Talbot brothers later co-founded the country-rock band Mason Proffit, which earned a cult following prior to its 1972 breakup; the siblings continued working together, however, with their increasing spirituality pushing them towards contemporary Christian pop. After recording an eponymous 1974 LP as the Talbot Brothers, both went their separate ways; John Michael soon signed to Sparrow, his sound mellowing to combine with his tenor vocals and classical guitar playing. Talbot's first solo LP, a self-titled effort, appeared in 1975; after 1977's *The New Earth,* he withdrew from performing to study Catholicism, with these new beliefs informing 1978's *The Lord's Supper* and its follow-up, *Come to the Quiet.* In the years to follow, Talbot's albums arrived fast and furious, and soon he was the best-selling artist in the history of Sparrow Records. In 1992, he founded his own label, Troubadour for the Lord. *—Jason Ankeny*

The Painter / 1980 / Sparrow ✦✦✦✦✦
The Christian Contemporary Music industry has always been dominated by derivative imitations of secular music, but this 1980 gem by John Michael and Terry Talbot is a genuine original. The record weaves the Talbot Brothers' gorgeous tenor harmonies together with John Michael's complex classical guitar work and tastefully lush orchestral arrangements played by the London Chamber Orchestra to create a beautiful musical tapestry that underscores the album's central motif of Jesus as the "Master Painter." *The Painter* is not, strictly speaking, a holiday record, but many of its songs focus on Christmas themes. Among those songs are the sweeping two-part "Advent Suite" ("There will be living where once there was death, there will be living in Jesus"), the joyful "Jesus Has Come" ("Can you believe the miracle come, come to the city of David"), and "Wonderful Counselor" ("Worship the child come to the world in Bethlehem"), which was included on Sparrow's 1982 collection *25 Songs of Christmas.* Unfortunately, the sound quality of the record leaves something to be desired. The mix tends to wash out John Michael's virtuoso guitar performances and give too much focus to the vocals and the orchestra. But this does little to diminish the pleasure of listening to this exquisitely arranged collaboration between the two talented Talbots. *—Evan Cater*

● **Master Collection, Vol. 1: The Quiet Side** / 1989 / Sparrow ✦✦✦✦✦

Pathways to Wisdom / Jan. 27, 1998 / Chordant ✦✦✦
A change of pace for John Michael Talbot, *Pathways to Wisdom* is a soothing, contemplative collection of new age music with a CCM twist. There's an underlying spirituality to Talbot's layered instrumentals. His classical gutiar takes center stage, naturally, but the wordless backing vocals and interwoven keyboards and percussion gives the music its context, making it the unique CCM experience that it is. *—Stephen Thomas Erlewine*

The Cave of the Heart / Aug. 24, 1999 / Chordant ✦✦✦✦

Ben Tankard

Keyboards, Piano, Synthesizer, Producer / Instrumental Gospel, Contemporary Gospel
He's been called "the Quincy Jones of Gospel," and besides being one of the best-selling instrumentalists in Christian music, keyboard player Ben Tankard has justified his tag, producing many stellar gospel projects as well as serving as an executive vice-president at Tribute Records, for which he has recorded extensively. Born in Florida to a minister father and a missionary mother, he began playing drums in church at the age of three. He later graduated to tuba and was offered several music scholarships to college, though he eventually accepted a basketball scholarship instead.

Tankard endured a rough period of depression and homelessness when a knee injury prevented him from turning professional (though he was drafted by the NBA). A visit to a revival service put him on the right track, an almost overnight, he became a very talented keyboard/organ player. Tankard began his witness in song with 1990's *Keynote Speaker,* recorded for Tribute Records. He continued recording and soon moved into production and arranging as well, calling on his reserves of early musical training to provide impeccable jobs for Yolanda Adams, the Alabama State Mass Choir and Michael Bruce. *—John Bush*

● **Git Yo Prayze On** / Aug. 12, 1997 / Verity ✦✦✦✦

The Minstrel / Jul. 13, 1999 / Verity ✦✦✦

Steve Taylor

Vocals, Guitar / Alternative CCM, CCM
Sometimes referred to as the "clown prince of Christian music," Steve Taylor brought sarcasm and satire to Christian music. His acerbic lyrics engendered enough controversy to place him among the most visible Christian rockers of the mid-'80s. Ultimately he felt stifled by the industry and quit recording for the Christian market, but resurfaced as the lead singer of Chagall Guevara in 1991. He resumed his solo career in 1994. *—Brian Mansfield*

I Predict 1990 / 1987 / Myrrh ✦✦✦✦✦
It's small surprise the Christian community all but disowned Taylor after songs like "I Blew up the Clinic Real Good" and "Since I Gave up Hope I Feel a Lot Better." The songs on *I Predict 1990* don't look for easy answers—they rarely look for answers at all—and they're often unsettling. But half of Taylor's point is that life rarely gives easy answers. The other half is in the final song: "Harder to Believe than Not To." *—Brian Mansfield*

★ **The Best We Could Find** / 1988 / Sparrow ✦✦✦✦✦
This compilation makes an excellent introduction to Taylor's iconoclastic songwriting, with music that frequently sounds like a new-wave Christian sideshow. Taylor gets his licks in on modern culture with "Meltdown (At Madame Tussaud's)," but he more often turns his gaze on the church with songs like "I Want to Be a Clone" and "This Disco (Used to Be a Cute Cathedral)." *—Brian Mansfield*

Squint / 1993 / Warner Alliance ✦✦✦

On the Fritz / Sparrow ✦✦✦
Widely regarded as contemporary Christian music's best lyricist, Steve Taylor resembles Leonard Cohen in that his music takes a definite back seat to his smart and witty word-slinging. Taylor, though, is as much comedian as poet. While *On the Fritz* feels a little less like a novelty record than his previous albums, several of the songs are still essentially satirical sketches with musical accompaniment. In "Lifeboat," for example, Taylor adopts a pepper pot falsetto and portrays a female headmistress who teaches her students the superficial values of a culture obsessed with physical beauty. When Taylor does sing, he usually employs one of two character voices (one a high-pitched, manic nasal yell, the other a sinister deep-throated affectation). The effect is almost that of a substantive Weird Al Yankovic, but Taylor's genius with words extends beyond his razor-sharp comic timing. He also has the ability to communicate insights of some wisdom and depth with originality and power. The Joe Walsh-esque pop on this album doesn't demonstrate that as well as his later albums (particularly the sweepingly cinematic *I Predict 1990* and the fragmented poetry he wrote with Chagall Gueverra). But in moments like the jangly U2 pop anthem "I Forgive," *On the Fritz* shows signs that Taylor's range of expression was steadily expanding. *—Darryl Cater*

Sister Rosetta Tharpe

b. Mar. 20, 1921, Cotton Plant, AR, **d.** Oct. 9, 1973, Philadelphia, PA
Vocals, Guitar / Jump Blues, Black Gospel, Blues Gospel, Classic Female Blues
Alongside Willie Mae Ford Smith, Sister Rosetta Tharpe is widely acclaimed among the greatest Sanctified gospel singers of her generation; a flamboyant performer whose music often flirted with the blues and swing, she was also one of the most controversial talents of her day, shocking purists with her leap into the secular market—by playing nightclubs and theatres, she not only pushed spiritual music into the mainstream, but in the process also helped pioneer the rise of pop-gospel. Born in Arkansas but raised mostly in Chicago, Tharpe signed to Decca in 1938 and right out of the gate recorded two smash hits, "Rock Me" and "This Train." She led an almost schizophrenic existence, remaining in the good graces of her core audience by recording religious material while also appealing to her growing white audience by performing rearranged, uptempo spirituals. In 1946 she teamed with the Sanctified shouter Madame Marie Knight, and their first single "Up Above My Head" was a huge hit. However, in the early '50s Tharpe and Knight cut several straight blues sides that out-

raged their fans and seriously damaged her popularity. Her comeback was slow but steady, and by 1960 she had returned far enough into the audience's good graces to appear at the Apollo Theatre. While not a household name like before, she continued touring for several years even after suffering a major stroke in 1970. *—Jason Ankeny*

Gospel 1938-1943 / 1938-1943 / Frémeaux & Associés ✦✦✦✦✦
Ironically, singer/guitarist Sister Rosetta Tharpe's twin gospel and blues career stunted both, and the fact that she was a woman singing solo in an era of male quartets didn't help. But she was one of the finest of all solo gospel singers and a highly individual one. These stunning, mostly acoustic, performances are pinnacles of the African-American religious tradition. *—John Storm Roberts, Original Music*

Sacred & Secular / 1941-1969 / Rosetta ✦✦✦✦✦
Sacred & Secular is a wonderful collection of 16 tracks that Sister Rosetta Tharpe recorded between 1941 and 1969. Although she recorded both sacred and secular material as the title indicates, this collection favors religious music. All the music here features Tharpe supported by a band, ranging from an orchestra conducted by Leroy Kirkland to small combos led by Lucky Millinder and Sam Price. While many critics and fans prefer Tharpe's solo performances—only one solo performance, a live cut from 1969, is present—these group sessions offer ample proof that Tharpe is compelling in nearly any setting. *—Thom Owens*

Live at the Hot Club de France / 1966 / Milan ✦✦✦
Live at the Hot Club de France was recorded in 1966. At first, Sister Rosetta Tharpe seems a little uneasy in front of the French audience, but she soon loosens up, tearing through a set of spiritual standards (plus a handful of originals). There isn't much guitar on the record, but Tharpe's impassioned voice makes this a concert worth hearing. *—Thom Owens*

★ **Complete Recorded Works, Vol. 1 (1938-1941)** / Feb. 20, 1996 / Document ✦✦✦✦✦
Sister Rosetta Tharpe was an exciting performer and one of the first singers to bring the power of gospel music into the secular world, predating Ray Charles and Aretha Franklin by quite a few years. Unlike those two, Tharpe's main loyalty remained religious music, although her acoustic guitar playing was jazz-oriented, and she spent 1941-43 being featured regularly with Lucky Millinder's Orchestra before returning to work as a solo performer. This Document CD has Tharpe's first 26 recordings. The first 14 numbers are from her unaccompanied solo dates of 1938-41, and despite the similar message of most of the selections, they do hold one's interest due to her exciting delivery. Highlights include her earliest versions of "Rock Me," "That's All," "The Lonesome Road" and "This Train." Next up are eight songs cut with Millinder's big band: five studio numbers (including "Trouble in Mind," "Rock Daniel," "Shout Sister Shout" and "That's All") and three selections taken from the soundtracks of their filmed "Soundies." The CD wraps up with four solo performances from December 1, 1941, including a spirited "Just a Closer Walk with Thee" and "Precious Lord Hold My Hand." This CD and *Volume 2* (which finds the singer-guitarist finishing her Millinder period and resuming her solo career during 1943-44) are highly recommended and contain most of the finest work of Sister Rosetta Tharpe's career. *—Scott Yanow*

Complete Recorded Works, Vol. 2: 1942-1944) / Feb. 20, 1996 / Document ✦✦✦
For completists, specialists and academics, Document's *Complete Recorded Works, Vol. 2 (1942-1944)* is an invaluable overview of Sister Rosetta Tharpe's early recordings. For less dedicated listeners, the disc is a mixed blessing. The disc features a long running time, exacting chronological sequencing, and poor fidelity (all cuts are transferred from original acetates and 78s). While the serious blues listener will find all these factors to be positive, enthusiasts and casual listeners will find that the collection is of marginal interest for those very reasons. *—Thom Owens*

Third Day

f. Ohio
Group / Christian Rock, CCM
Influenced by the Southern rock of Lynyrd Skynyrd and other artists such as U2 and Rich Mullins, Third Day was originally formed by vocalist Mac Powell and acoustic guitarist Mark Lee. The duo added bassist Tai Anderson and drummer David Carr from another local band, and recorded some demos. Third Day's live shows gradually built a loyal fan base, and just after lead guitarist Brad Avery joined, the band signed to Gray Dot Records. Their eponymous debut followed in 1996, with *Conspiracy No. 5* appearing a year later. Third Day returned in 1999 with *Time*, which they followed the next year with *Offerings*, a collection of new and live material. *—John Bush*

Conspiracy No. 5 / Aug. 26, 1997 / Reunion/Silvertone ✦✦✦
Third Day's second album, *Conspiracy, No. 5,* is an intriguing blend of hip-hop and urban soul. While not all of the cuts are successful, the tracks that work are dynamic, funky and soulful, showcasing Third Day's potential. *—Leo Stanley*

Time / Aug. 24, 1999 / Essential ✦✦✦
Third Day's third album, *Time*, delivers more of their Southern rock-influenced Christian music, and rootsy ballads like "I Have Always Loved You" and "Took My Place" broaden the band's sonic palette. *—Heather Phares*

● **Offerings: A Worship Album** / Jul. 11, 2000 / Essential ✦✦✦✦✦
Third Day quickly draws a distinction between entertaining and leading worship on *Offerings*. "King of Kings" starts the release with a fervent longing to know God. "Who is this King of glory with strength and majesty, and wisdom beyond measure, the gracious King of kings." Mac Powell raises the tune to a fervent pitch as the members from Atlanta's Cobb County Mass Choir join in to help the cut reach its pinnacle. "Agnus Dei/Worthy" was written by Michael W. Smith and has been a focal point at Third Day concerts over the past few years. It's easy to see why; the lyrics are inspiring, the energy level high. After distorted guitars and hard hitting drums the song becomes an acoustic sing along as thousands join the band in praise. "Your Everywhere" was written during the *Conspiracy No. 5* sessions but the cut never made the release. The tune is a poignant ballad that displays the bands heartfelt passion. Both "Thief" and "Consuming Fire" have been live Third Day staples since the bands inception. "Thief" tells the account of the criminals crucified with Christ. This piano driven melody is emotionally potent. Equally engaging is "Consuming Fire", which was responsible for launching the band in 1996. You can feel the electricity as Tai Anderson's bass riffs reverberate throughout the arena. Closing *Offerings* is arguably the most requested Third Day song. "Love Song," and is an acoustic gem. The tune reveals the fragile nuances that make Third Day much more than entertainers, and the song is sung by the band's faithful word for word. *—Steven Losey*

Tammy Trent

Vocals / CCM
Gospel pop singer/songwriter Tammy Trent has been making music since the early age of six when she first took up playing drums. Distinctly influenced by gospel music, she was inspired by her mother's constant work as a speaker and performer on the Christian scene. By high school, she undoubtedly knew music was her life journey, already playing in several pop and rock bands. After several bouts with record labels and career moves, Trent signed to Sparrow Records in 1999. Her light R&B flair and glossy pop flavoring is sweet and positive. *Set You Free*, her Sparrow debut, was released in mid-2000. *—MacKenzie Wilson*

Set You Free / Jul. 18, 2000 / Sparrow ✦✦✦
Set You Free is Tammy Trent's Sparrow Label debut. She seems poised to take her career to the next level. Trent offers up likeable pop that doesn't necessarily break new ground but doesn't disappoint either. On the dance pop end Trent is quite apt, at times sounding like Christina Aguilera minus the sexual overtones. Energy levels are high on songs like "If You Need Love" and "My Irreplaceable." Trent seems most comfortable on the slower R&B vibes. On some cuts her sound is poignant, offering spiritual openness (i.e. "Without You" and "Light of Love"). Lyrically it's obvious that Tammy Trent possesses a heartfelt passion for God. *Set You Free* is a testimony of it. *—Steven Losey*

Trin-I-Tee 5:7

Group / CCM
A Christian alternative to the more provocative sights and sounds of acts like TLC and En Vogue, the urban vocal trio Trin-i-tee 5:7 comprised Chanelle Hayes, Terry Brown and Angel Taylor. Their self-titled debut LP appeared in 1998, followed a year later by *Spiritual Love*. *—Jason Ankeny*

Trin-I-Tee 5:7 / Jul. 14, 1998 / Interscope ✦✦✦

● **Spiritual Love** / Oct. 19, 1999 / Interscope ✦✦✦
Spiritual Love, the sophomore effort from urban gospel trio Trin-i-tee 5:7, again features a number of fine moments that equal the best of their debut; the juxtaposition of sexy, slinky, urban R&B grooves with non-secular subject matter still seems a bit odd—form not matching up with content—but Christian music fans will be happy to have a sound they enjoy with the messages they respect. *—Steve Huey*

Kathy Troccoli

b. New York, NY
Vocals / CCM
One of contemporary Christian music's biggest stars during the 1980s, singer Kathy Troccoli was born in Brooklyn, New York on June 24, 1958. She performed her first concert while in junior high, delivering a set of Carole King songs at her school's talent show; she became interested in CCM during the late 1970s, and in 1982 issued her debut LP *Stubborn Love* on Reunion Records, a label formed specifically to release her music. Although some pundits declared Troccoli's smoky voice too "sexy" for Christian audiences, the album became the fastest-selling debut ever by a female CCM artist; however, after just two more releases, 1984's *Heart & Soul* and 1986's *Images*, she quit the music industry, moving back to Long Island after six years in Nashville. Some time later Troccoli resurfaced as a session vocalist, and in 1991 she released *Pure Attraction*, her first new album in five years; after signing to RCA, she issued a self-titled 1994 LP, followed a year later by *Sounds of Heaven. Love & Mercy* appeared in 1997, and a year later she returned with *Corner of Eden*. Troccoli returned in 1999 with the seasonal effort *Sentimental Christmas*. She continued recording and was able to release another solo album, *Love Has a Name* in 2000. *—Jason Ankeny*

Pure Attraction / 1991 / Reunion ✦✦✦✦✦
Troccoli's first recording after a five-year absence was her most commercial, with the Diane Warren-penned "Everything Changes" hitting Top Five on CHR radio. Troccoli had developed her songwriting during her time away; she wrote seven of *Pure Attraction*'s cuts, emphasizing the torch-song style she loves. *—Brian Mansfield*

● **Kathy Troccoli** / 1994 / Reunion ✦✦✦✦✦

Sounds of Heaven / Sep. 26, 1995 / Reunion ✦✦✦
Kathy Troccoli gives a nice balance between soft pop ballads and up-tempo pieces on this inspirational release. The first of ten tracks opens on an upbeat tempo with "I Will Choose Christ" and the pace rarely lets up, even through the ballads. The title track, which is placed in the fourth position, is also a lively song. The seventh track, "Each Moment" is a ballad with a melody that catches and requires full attention, while the eighth track is a dance worthy piece appropriately titled "Fill My Heart." Lots of old-fashioned gospel feel on this album even though the music is more accurately described as inspirational pop. *—Dacia Blodgett-Williams*

The Trumpeteers

db. 1948
Group / Traditional Gospel, Black Gospel
Influenced by The Golden Gate Quartet and led by the spectacular singing of Joe Johnson, this quartet hit the public's consciousness in the late '40s with "Milky White Way," which they recorded for Score Records. Other members included Raleigh Tunrage (tenor), Joseph Arm-

strong (baritone), and James Keels (bass). There were numerous personnel changes, and they disbanded upon Johnson's death in 1948. *—Bil Carpenter & Kip Lornell*

1948-1959 / 1948-1959 / ✦✦✦✦✦
Joe Johnson & The Trumpeteers Quartet were extremely popular during the late '40s and early '50s, due in part to "Milky White Way." The tape mostly covers the Score/Aladdin years 1947-1949 before their appearance on King, Okeh, Gotham, Grand & Jubilee labels. Their style is close harmony jubilee with sparse guitar chordings. Three Nashboro cuts from the late '50s are also included. There's some duplication with a Gospel Jubilee LP. There's good overall sound quality (cassette only). *—Opal Louis Nations, Roots & Rhythm Newsletter*

★ **Milky White Way** / 1956 / Score ✦✦✦✦✦
One of the last great jubilee singing quartets. Score and Grant material. 1947-54. *—Opal Louis Nations*

Michelle Tumes

Vocals, Piano / CCM
CCM singer/songwriter Michelle Tumes was born in Adelaide, Australia, and began studying piano at the age of four. While in her teens, she enrolled in a two-year classical piano program, an experience which left her so disillusioned about performing that she instead turned to studying dentistry. At that point, her little sister gave Tumes $40 she had saved from her paper route in order to convince her older sibling to cut a demo; she agreed, sending the tape unsolicited to a variety of publishing companies. Offers quickly poured in, and after signing a songwriting deal with an Australian publisher she relocated to the U.S., soon authoring Jaci Velasquez's CCM chart-topper "If This World." Tumes' attempts to mount a solo career initially met with frustration, but she eventually signed with the Sparrow, issuing her debut LP *Listen* in 1998 and earning a major hit with the single "Please Come Back." *Center of My Universe* followed in early 2000. *—Jason Ankeny*

Center Of My Universe / Feb. 15, 2000 / Sparrow ✦✦✦
Evoking spiritual emotions through the use of lush, enveloping sonic textures, Michelle Tumes' *Center of My Universe* is an accomplished sophomore effort that refines the sound and style of her debut. Although one can hear echoes of Sarah McLachlan in Tumes' floating, ethereal voice, the closest secular comparison is probably Enya, thanks in part to the lovely, sonically detailed orchestrations of her backing tracks. Fans of *Listen* will be thrilled with this follow-up, which still sounds like little else on the CCM scene. *—Steve Huey*

The Twelfth Tribe

f. 1985
Group / Christian Rap
The California duo of Dave Portillo and Eddie Sierra began rapping in 1985 under the name of Deity. Influenced by soul and heavy metal, they like the rap of Kool Moe Dee, Houdini, and the Fat Boys. They take their name from the twelfth tribe of Israel: the Benjamites, mighty warriors. They portray a tougher image than most Christian rap artists and have a hard street rap sound. *—Bil Carpenter*

● **Knowledge Is the Tribe of Life** / 1991 / Frontline ✦✦✦✦✦
Produced, engineered, and mixed by master urban dance musician Scott Blackwell, who easily moves into the hard, funky side of Christian rap here. There are 15 rhymes on war, peace, and knowing God. The sound is very Black, very hard, with a few metal elements; a good set though not overly original outside of the gospel music industry. *—Bil Carpenter*

Jaci Velasquez

Vocals / CCM, Latin Pop
Jacquelyn Davette Velasquez, born in the early '80s, began singing at the age of ten and performed at the White House just three years later. It's hardly surprising then, that after several more years performing and recording with her family's worship ministry, she gained a record contract on her own. By late 1995, Jaci Velasquez signed with the Christian recording label Myrrh and found a number one hit (on the Christian Contemporary charts) with her Spanish-tinged single, "If This World." Her debut album *Heavenly Place*, produced by Mark Heimermann, continued the Spanish inspiration and made Top Ten on the Christian charts for several months after its May 1996 release. A self-titled follow-up appeared in 1998, and a year later Velasquez resurfaced with *Llegarati*. 2000's *Crystal Clear* emphasized the Latin and pop elements in her style, while retaining her CCM roots. *—John Bush*

● **Heavenly Place** / Oct. 1, 1996 / Word ✦✦✦✦

Jaci Velasquez / Jun. 2, 1998 / Word ✦✦✦✦

Crystal Clear / Sep. 5, 2000 / Word ✦✦✦
It may be unfair to call Hispanic Contemporary-Christian-Music singer Jaci Velasquez CCM's answer to Christina Aguilera, since she got her start well before such secular competitors. But on her fourth album, Velasquez adopts many of the vocal and musical mannerisms of teen-pop's Latin side. In the video interviews on the disc's CD-Rom portion, Velasquez notes that she encountered criticism in the Christian community, who charged she was abandoning CCM with her last album, the Spanish-language release *Llegarati*. She says *Crystal Clear*'s title track makes her religious commitment plain, but like several other songs on the album, the song can be interpreted as a woman's declaration of love to a lover rather than one of faith in God. Though she tosses in the word "Lord" on some songs, Velasquez usually employs the terminology of romantic love rather than religious faith. "There's a union of two becoming one / Deep inside my heart," she sings in "Adore"; such intimacies suggest a highly idealized boyfriend rather than a merciful savior, no matter how many pronouns are capitalized on the lyric sheet. While Velasquez convincingly imitates Britney Spears-style groans, as the album progresses, she and her producers don't maintain the teen-pop sound. Eventually, she begins to sound a lot like the artist who is no doubt her real model, the young Amy Grant. It's no surprise after listening to "Come as You Are," a duet with Louis Fansi, to read the credit "vocals produced by Brown Bannister," Grant's early mentor. Four albums on, Jaci Velasquez still seems to be searching for a style of her own. *—William Ruhlmann*

Albertina Walker

b. Aug. 1930, Chicago, IL
Vocals / Traditional Gospel, Black Gospel
Born the youngest of nine children on August 29, 1929 in Chicago, IL, Albertina Walker grew up on the south side and started singing as a child at Westpoint Baptist Church. She joined several gospel groups before forming the Caravans in 1951 with Ora Lee Hopkins, Elyse Yancey, and Nellie Grace Daniels. They issued a number of classic recordings for the States label between 1952 and 1954. In 1955, they were signed to Savoy Records and by 1956, they were among the most popular acts on the gospel music circuit. Riding high in 1962, the Caravans signed to pioneering Chicago record label Vee-Jay and recorded several hit albums before disbanding in the mid-'70s.

Walker then began her solo career with Savoy releasing such LPs as *Please Be Patient With Me* (her first Grammy-nominated album), *I Can Go to God In Prayer* and *Spread the Word*. By the '80s, Ms. Walker had moved to Word/Epic recording *Let Jesus Come Into Your Heart, I Will Wait on You,* and *Joy Will Come In the Morning*. By this time, she had been nominated 11 times for the Grammy Award. In 1995, she won a Grammy Award for the Best Traditional Gospel Album, *Songs of the Church*. In 1997, she won a Dove Award for Traditional Gospel Album of the Year for *Let's Go Back—Live in Chicago*. Released in summer 1997, the follow-up, *I'm Still Here* was a solid contribution to a catalog that included over 40 albums. As the 21st century began, Albertina Walker was performing on albums by Kurt Carr, the Gospel Music Workshop of America, and the National Baptist Convention. *—Ed Hogan*

Tell the Angels / 1960 / Savoy ✦✦✦

● **God Is Love** / 1975 / Lection/Polygram ✦✦✦✦✦
God Is Love ranks among Albertina Walker's best recordings, capturing the gospel vocalist at her most moving and simply best. It may be a latter-day album from Walker, but her power and influence is readily apparent. *—Thom Owens*

You Believed in Me / 1991 / Benson ✦✦✦

Live / 1992 / A&M ✦✦✦
Albertina Walker's second album for Benson Records finds the former lead singer of the Caravans running through nine of her most popular songs—including "You've Been So Good," "That's the Way Heaven Will Be," "Watch Tower," "He Knows (Just How Much You Can Bear)," "My Best Friend," "I've Got a Feeling," "Day by Day" and "I Can Go to God in Prayer"—in concert. Supported by the Trinity All Nations Choir, Walker turns in a wonderful performance. Even cameos from Ralph Lofton, Derrick Lee and Darius Brooks can't take the spotlight away from Walker, who once again proves why she is considered one of the greatest singers in contemporary gospel. *—Thom Owens*

I'm Still Here / Jul. 1, 1997 / Verity ✦✦✦

Clara Ward

b. Aug. 21, 1924, Philadelphia, PA, **d.** Jan. 16, 1973, Los Angeles, CA
Vocals / Traditional Gospel, Black Gospel
Widely acclaimed among the greatest soloists in gospel history, Clara Ward was also the subject of much criticism from purists—with her backing group the Ward Singers, she pushed gospel out of the church and into the nightclubs, infusing the music with a shot of glitz and glamour the likes of which had never before been seen. Decked out in colorful gowns, towering wigs and dazzling jewelry, the Wards sang only the biggest pop-gospel hits, flamboyantly delivered for maximum commercial appeal; while many observers decried their clownish onstage behavior as demeaning not only to the music but also to their African-American heritage, at their creative peak the group was a true phenomenon, combining superb soloists, exceptional material and innovative arrangements to leave an indelible mark on the generations of spiritual performers who followed. *—Jason Ankeny*

Surely God Is Able / 1955 / Savgos ✦✦✦
The Pilgrim Jubilees were among the greatest of Mississippi quartets: subtle swing, fine guitar, and a terrific time-sense. A treasure trove, it was deleted a while back. The Ward Singers brought free quartet singing to a pinnacle in the 1950s, and this album has some of their most moving songs, among them "Surely God Is Able" and "He Knows How Much I Can Bear." (The cover's claim of mid-price status became history when the label changed hands.) *—John Storm Roberts, Original Music*

Down by the Riverside (Live at the Town Hall, NY) / 1958 / Dot ✦✦✦✦✦
Gospel excitement with the group in full throttle, backed by lap-steel guitar whiz Sammy Fein. *—Opal Louis Nations*

Take My Hand, Precious Lord / Jun. 4, 1996 / MCA Special Products ✦✦✦

Somebody Bigger Than You & I / May 11, 1999 / MCA ✦✦✦
As the woman who mentored Aretha Franklin and had, at one time or another, Della Reese, Marion Williams, and Sarah Vaughn in the ranks of her group, Clara Ward's place in gospel history is assured. To hear what makes her music so very special is right here on this ten-song budget collection that sweats her best down to her very best: "Swing Low Sweet Chariot," "When the Saints Go Marching In," "Joshua Fit the Battle," "Packing Up," "How Great Thou Art," and "Peace in the Valley." Ward has a low-down gospel moan that'll make the hairs on the back of your neck pop right out. Great stuff. *—Cub Koda*

The Best of the Ward Singers / Savoy ✦✦✦✦
The Clara Ward Singers have been called the greatest group, together with The Roberta Martin Singers, produced by gospel. She herself was a magnificent singer—the inspiration for Aretha Franklin—and among those who came out of the group was the superb Marion Williams. Stylistically, the Ward Singers represented an early stage in the move to a deliberate and dramatic use of a fervor that had once been purely religious. *—John Storm Roberts, Original Music*

• **The Clara Ward Singers** / Roulette ✦✦✦
Clara Ward Singers contains 22 tracks the group recorded for Roulette Records in 1963. Although Ward had been a well-known vocalist for nearly 20 years at the time these songs were recorded, she had lost none of her power, and these are as energetic and represenative as any she has ever recorded. The presence of a jumping slide guitarist is slightly surprising, but he gets into the spirit of things, helping propel these sessions to joyful new heights. Highly recommended. *—Leo Stanley*

Ernestine Washington

b. Arkansas, **d.** Jul. 5, 1983, Brooklyn, NY
Vocals / Traditional Gospel, Black Gospel
Born in Arkansas, Madame Ernestine B. Washington grew up on the sanctified gospel of the '20s, singing primarily for her husband's church and denomination, Washington Temple C.O.G.I.C. Though inspired by the controlled Baptist style of the Roberta Martin Singers, she had a strident voice and was known to be a singing shouter in the mode of Mahalia Jackson. Her rare and most important recordings were executed from the late '40s through the '50s. *—Bil Carpenter*

• **In Washington Temple** / 1958 / Collectors Issue ✦✦✦✦✦
Sensational solos are supported rousingly by Brooklyn's Congregation of The Washington Temple C.O.G.I.C. Reissue of material recorded in 1958. *—Opal Louis Nations*

Complete Recorded Works (1943-48) / Sep. 10, 1996 / Document ✦✦✦✦
One of gospel's premier female soloists who recorded with both Bunk Johnson and the Dixie Hummingbirds. *—Opal Louis Nations*

Wayne Watson

b. Wisner, LA
Vocals / Inspirational, CCM
A native of Wisner, Louisiana, CCM singer/songwriter Wayne Watson originally planned to pursue a career playing baseball, but while in college he began dabbling in music, and after graduation regularly performed in area churches. While leading worship at a Christian youth camp, the father of one of the children videotaped Watson's performance and sent it to a Nashville industry rep; his debut LP, *Workin' in the Final Hour,* followed in 1980. A series of albums like 1982's *New Lives for Old,* 1984's *Man in the Middle* and 1985's *Giants in the Land* followed before his breakthrough record, the Grammy-nominated *Watercolor Ponies,* appeared in 1987; Watson also notched well over a dozen Dove Award nominations, and launched a number of CCM chart-toppers including "The Class of '95," "Be in Her Eyes," "A Beautiful Place," "Walk in the Dark," "More of You," "It's Time," "Home Free" and "Almighty." In 1995 he signed to Warner/Alliance to issue *Field of Souls; The Way Home* followed three years later. Appropriately, his song "For Such A Time As This" was used as the theme for the 1999 season premiere of CBS's popular series "Touched By An Angel," reflecting Watson's own growing popularity in the secular music arena. *—Jason Ankeny*

Watercolour Ponies / 1987 / Word ✦✦✦

• **The Fine Line** / 1988 / Word ✦✦✦✦✦

Way Home / Mar. 17, 1998 / Word/Epic ✦✦✦
Although it offers no surprises, *The Way Home* is a fine collection of attractively polished CCM from Wayne Watson. Stylistically, it is essentially the same album that he's recorded throughout the '90s, but there are enough solid songs to make it worthwhile for longtime fans. *—Stephen Thomas Erlewine*

Whitecross

f. 1986
Group / Christian Metal, Christian Rock
Christian rockers Whitecross formed in Chicago in 1986, releasing their self-titled debut LP a year later. Regular line-up changes plagued the group virtually from its inception, but the duo of vocalist Scott Wenzel and guitarist Rex Carroll remained constants throughout; a 1988 tour in support of CCM fan favorite Steve Taylor greatly expanded Whitecross' fanbase, and they soon issued their second album, *Hammer and Nail.* Tours of Europe and South America followed behind the band's third record, the Dove Award-winning *Triumphant Return;* 1991's *In the Kingdom* copped Dove honors as well. In the wake of 1992's *High Gear* Whitecross finally took a break from their relentless touring schedule, not resurfacing with *Unveiled* until two years later; *Equilibrium* appeared in 1995, but after 1996's *Flytrap* the band went on hiatus. *—Jason Ankeny*

Unveiled/Whitecross / Aug. 23, 1994 / REX ✦✦✦✦

Equilibrium / Sep. 12, 1995 / REX ✦✦✦
On *Equilibrium,* Whitecross' seventh album, the band began to back away from the sleek, '80s-styled heavy metal that had distinguished their earlier records, replacing it with a tougher sound that fit right into the mainstream of '90s hard rock. Their songwriting remains solid, however, and they haven't lost any of their power over the years. *—Stephen Thomas Erlewine*

• **One More Encore** / Mar. 10, 1998 / Platinum ✦✦✦✦
On their tenth album, *One More Encore,* Whitecross offer a live retrospective of their greatest hits, tacking on a studio remake of their celebrated 1991 song, "No Second Chances." It's an excellent retrospective of the CCM hard rock group's best material, and often, these versions are better than the studio versions. As a result, it's an excellent introduction to the group. *—Rodney Batdorf*

Whiteheart

Group / Christian Rock
The Christian rock band Whiteheart was formed in 1982 by singer Steve Green, guitarist Dann Huff, bassist Gary Lunn, keyboardists Mark Gersmehl and Billy Smiley, and drummer David Huff, most of the members alumni of Bill Gaither's group. After debuting with a self-titled effort issued on the Home Sweet Home label, a series of roster moves plagued the group, and by the time of 1987's *Emergency Broadcast,* only Gersmehl and Smiley remained from the group's original line-up. By 1997's *Redemption,* Whiteheart offically consisted of Gersmehl, Smiley and vocalist Rick Florian, rounded out by studio players. *—Jason Ankeny*

Freedom / 1989 / Sparrow ✦✦✦
White Heart took the album's name to heart, allowing themselves more creative leeway on this than on any previous album. Most Christian arena rock sounds derivative of its secular counterparts—not *Freedom;* even its weak spots are undeniably original. *—Brian Mansfield*

Powerhouse / 1990 / Star Song ✦✦

Souvenirs / 1990 / Sparrow ✦✦✦✦✦
White Heart found its voice in 1986 with *Don't Wait for the Movie,* the first album with lead singer Rick Florian. *Souvenirs* collects the productive years that followed, including five tracks from *Freedom* and an unusual hard-rock remake of "The Little Drummer Boy." *—Brian Mansfield*

Tales of Wonder / 1992 / Star Song ✦✦✦
The band turns in its most popular album in years, showing continued growth and depth in its songwriting, better than the simplistic anthems that typify the arena rock genre. *—Thom Granger*

• **Highlands** / 1994 / Star Song ✦✦✦✦✦
Another artistic high-water mark for the band, which now includes Adam Again member Jon Knox on drums. The influence of '70s prog-rockers like Yes and Kansas is interwoven with Celtic themes for a Christian rock classic. *—Thom Granger*

Nothing But the Best: Radio Classics / Jan. 24, 1995 / Capitol ✦✦✦✦✦

The Whites

f. 1971
Group / Country Gospel, Contemporary Country, Traditional Bluegrass, Progressive Bluegrass
A part of country music for three decades, the Whites started out in bluegrass, adopted a contemporary country sound and later evolved into a gospel group. Buck White and his daughters Sharon and Cheryl comprise the core of the group, though other members have included Ricky Skaggs and Tim Crouch. Buck White formed his first band in 1947 and played piano and mandolin with the Blue Sage Boys in the '50s. White married Pat Goza in 1951; in 1962, they formed the Down Home Folks with Arnold and Peggy Johnston. Sharon and Cheryl White teamed up with Teddie and Eddie Johnston to form the Down Home Kids in the mid-'60s. In 1971, the Whites moved to Nashville, and the Down Home Folks comprised the entire White family. Pat retired from the group in 1973, but Buck and his daughters continued with the band. Buck White and His Down Home Folks didn't really get their big break until 1979, when they worked with Emmylou Harris on *Blue Kentucky Girl* and later toured with her.

By the early '80s, Buck decided to focus on mandolin playing; after changing their name to the Whites, the group moved away from bluegrass music. In 1982, they made the country Top Ten with "Holding My Baby Tonight" and "Give Me Back That Old Familiar Feeling." The Whites joined the *Grand Ole Opry* in 1984 and had a Top 30 single "It Should Have Been Easy," from their 1986 album *Whole New World.* They moved towards gospel music in 1989 with *Doing It by the Book,* and their '90s releases continued this trend. *—Sandra Brennan*

• **Greatest Hits** / 1987 / Curb ✦✦✦✦✦
This is early '80s sweet harmony from dad and his daughters. *—Mark A. Humphrey*

A Lifetime in the Making / Aug. 15, 2000 / Ceili Music ✦✦✦✦

The Williams Brothers

f. 1960
Group / Traditional Gospel, Southern Gospel, Black Gospel
The group was organized in 1960 by Leon "Pop" Williams, who is the founder and father of the Williams Brothers. They have been writing and arranging most of their music since 1970 and producing since 1979. The group recorded its first album in 1973 on the Songbird label, which included the instant hit, "Jesus Will Fix It." Since then they have recorded over a dozen Top Ten albums, out of which came three #1 records and a Grammy nomination. Their repertoire of hits includes songs such as "Jesus Will Never Say No," "I Won't Let Go My Faith," "He'll Understand," "Sweep around Your Own Front Door," and "A Ship Like Mine," to name a few. In April 1991 the group formed their own record label, Blackberry Records, which is the first Black-owned and-operated label in the state of Mississippi that has major distribution. Their first release on the label, "This Is Your Night," reached #4 on the *Billboard* gospel chart. *—Billy C. Wirtz*

First Class Gospel / 1980 / CBS ✦✦✦
Originally released in 1980, *First Class Gospel* captures the Williams Brothers at the peak of their formidable powers, delivering electrifying renditions of "Take It to the Lord in Prayer" and "So Good to Be Alive." *—Chuck Donkers*

Hold On / Dec. 1, 1995 / Sony Special Products ✦✦✦
Originally issued in 1980, the fiery *Hold On* documents the Williams Brothers in concert, where they deliver powerful renditions of "At the Cross" and "Amazing Grace." *—Chuck Donkers*

★ **Trust in the Lord** / May 11, 1999 / MCA ✦✦✦✦✦
Although they started singing as the Little William Brothers in 1960, the true recording history of the group begins in 1973 with their groundbreaking recordings for the Nashville Nashboro label. This nine-song budget collection brings together some of the very best from that period including "Jesus Will Fix It," "I'll Fly Away," "You Better Check Yourself," and "Try

God." The group's plain country-boy styling still works in a modern context, resonating in a time-worthy manner. *—Cub Koda*

Marion Williams

b. Aug. 29, 1927, Miami, FL, **d.** Jul. 2, 1994, Philadelphia, PA
Vocals, Keyboards / Traditional Gospel, Black Gospel
With an amazing grace, a powerful, yet lyrical voice and unmatched improvisation skills, Marion Williams punctuated her sanctified shouting with gut-wrenching growls, low moans, joyful whoops and soaring, angelic falsettos that made her one of the most influential singers in gospel music. In her heyday she was hailed by some critics as one the greatest singers in the U.S. As a child, on weekends she sang in church programs and on street corners; her extraordinary singing attracted considerable attention, but though attempts were made to steer her into everything from opera to the blues, she was determined to spread the gospel and by 1946 was known as the best gospel soloist in her native Miami. Williams soon joined Clara Ward and the Ward Singers, and remained with them for the next eleven years as their star attraction. During their dynamic performances, it was not uncommon for audience members to fall out in frenzied ecstasy, something Williams encouraged by getting right down into the audience, sashaying about and shouting at the top of her lungs, occasionally sitting demurely upon listeners' laps, and even literally trying to pack up the earthly goods of audience members during her renditions of her second big hit, "Packin' Up." She put so much into her performances with the Ward Singers that in time she began suffering "nervous spells" in which she would yell just to express the remaining energy generated by singing those high notes. Williams and a few others from the group left in 1958 to form Stars of Faith. Williams left the group in 1965 to launch a solo career. *—Sandra Brennan*

O Holy Night / 1959 / Savoy ✦✦✦

Surely God Is Able / 1989 / Spirit Feel ✦✦✦✦✦
A very strong soloist who reworked classic gospel material from the '30s and '40s into a wonderful 1989 album. *—Kip Lornell*

★ **Strong Again** / 1991 / Spirit Feel ✦✦✦✦✦
Eclectic though satisfying 20-cut album by this major singer, her most impressive solo set in recent years. Sparse accompaniment; mainly traditional material. Excellent. *—Kip Lornell*

Can't Keep It to Myself / 1993 / Shanachie ✦✦✦✦✦
Marion Williams has a majesty in her voice, a power in her delivery and a compelling, dynamic quality that underscores her vocals. This new disc features 22 awesome performances recorded with minimal, sympathetic accompaniment and little production support; just mostly Williams' smashing, note-bending, soaring vocals. She flies on slow, bluesy numbers, testifies and shouts on originals like "Ride In The Clouds" and "I'll Never Return No More" and turns old standards such as Roberta Martin's "God's Amazing Grace" and Rev. Thomas A. Dorsey's "Live The Life I Sing About In My Song" into gripping, fresh reaffirmations of her own faith. *—Ron Wynn*

☆ **My Soul Looks Back: The Genius of Marion Williams 1962-1992** / 1994 / Shanachie ✦✦✦✦✦
My Soul Looks Back: The Genius of Marion Williams 1962-1992 is an outstanding 25-track portrait of the legendary gospel singer in all of her glory. Listening to early sides like "Packin' Up" and "Surely God Is Able," it's easy to understand her influence on the likes of Little Richard and Aretha Franklin. These powerful songs are primal blasts of energy with all the cathartic transcendence more commonly attributed to rock & roll. Closer to R&B than any of her contemporaries, Williams also flirts playfully with the blues on cuts like "Dead Cat on the Line" and "It's Your Time Now But My Time After Awhile," and even dabbles in country on a cover of Roy Acuff's "The Great Speckled Bird." Whatever the setting, however, her voice is a marvel of improvisatory brilliance, her soprano never less than devastating. This is gospel at its finest. *—Jason Ankeny*

Born to Sing the Gospel / 1995 / Shanachie ✦✦✦✦
Born to Sing the Gospel returns Marion Williams to her home church, Philadelphia's B.M. Oakley Memorial Church of God in Christ; the material is engagingly varied, spanning from the bluesy original "Sometimes I Ring Up Heaven" to the traditional title track to the medley of the classics "Christ Is All" and "Jesus Is All." Though in fine form throughout, Williams hits her peak on "Death in the Morning," her delivery charged with all of the raw power of a field recording. [Shanachie's CD reissue appends five tracks not included on the original LP.] *—Jason Ankeny*

The Winans

f. Detroit, MI
Group / Contemporary Gospel, Black Gospel, CCM, Urban
These four brothers hail from Detroit, MI. Their contemporary Black gospel style reflects traditional Black gospel roots. They sang gospel all their lives and began their professional careers in the '80s. Marvin, Carvin, Ronald, and Michael have performed several times with the likes of Michael McDonald, Anita Baker, and Vanessa Bell Armstrong. *—Bil Carpenter*

Let My People Go / 1985 / Qwest ✦✦✦

Decision / 1987 / Qwest ✦✦✦

Return / 1990 / Qwest ✦✦

Live at Carnegie Hall / Qwest ✦✦✦
A dynamic concert, with all the hits drawn out, on this double album. *—Bil Carpenter*

● **Tomorrow** / Platinum ✦✦✦✦✦
The title track, a sparkling MOR-style ballad, is the hymn of the '80s. *—Bil Carpenter*

BeBe Winans

b. Detroit, MI
Vocals / Contemporary Gospel, Black Gospel, Urban
Usually working as a duet act with his sister CeCe or working the background on releases by the Winans (four of his older brothers), BeBe Winans released his first solo album in October 1997. It did very well on gospel charts, and even made an impact on the secular charts. He followed it the next year with *Thank You* and 2000's *Love & Freedom*. *—John Bush*

BeBe Winans / Oct. 28, 1997 / Atlantic ✦✦✦
BeBe Winans' long-awaited eponymous solo debut isn't the powerhouse it could have been, but it's nevertheless a first-class set of contemporary soul and gospel. Working with a top-notch set of professional producers—including Rhett Lawrence, Little Louie Vega, Arif Mardin, Manuel Seal and Keith Andes—Winans has created a well-crafted set of smooth urban soul and gospel, one that keeps his remarkable, supple vocals at center stage. The main problem with the record is its inconsistent material—Winans always sounds good, but he often sounds better than what the songs deserve. Still, the very best moments—the single "In Harm's Way," the Eternal duet "I Wanna Be the Only One" and a stirring cover of "Oh Happy Day"—make the album a winning solo debut from one of the best contemporary gospel singers of the '90s. *—Leo Stanley*

● **Love & Freedom** / Aug. 29, 2000 / Motown ✦✦✦✦
Gospel vocalist BeBe Winans follows up 1998's *Thank You* with a decent third release, entitled *Love & Freedom*. He aims to discover his own musical perfection while trying to ignore the massive success of his gospel singing family.

Love & Freedom is spirited with urban loops and heavy soul, but BeBe lacks spark. Known for his incredible collaborations with sister CeCe Winans, Bebe loses such fire found in his previous material. He does, however, bring things to the helm by working with some of R&B's most notable stars. "Jesus Children of America" features songwriting skills of Stevie Wonder, and "Everyday" showcases the vocalic beauty of fellow gospel starlet Stephanie Mills. This may carry the overall material, but noticeably, BeBe is still yearning to break out his well-known, passionate skills. Let's hope it comes sooner than later. *—MacKenzie Wilson*

BeBe and CeCe Winans

f. Detroit, MI
Group / Contemporary Gospel, Black Gospel, Urban
Detroit-born brother and sister BeBe (Benjamin) and CeCe (Priscilla) Winans are part of the gospel-singing Winans family that also includes The Winans, their four brothers. As a duo, BeBe And CeCe maintain the gospel message, although their records have the production values and style of contemporary R&B. They released their debut album, *BeBe & CeCe Winans*, in 1987 and scored a moderate hit (#49) in the R&B charts with the single "I.O.U. Me" scoring on the R&B and adult-contemporary charts. This earned them three Grammy nominations and one award (gospel). Their second album, *Heaven*, came in 1988 and found them scoring three R&B hits with the title track, "Lost without You," and "Celebrate Life." The album reached the R&B Top Ten (#95 in the pop chart) and went gold. 1991's platinum-selling *Different Lifestyles* was their biggest hit yet, topping the R&B album chart and featuring the R&B #1s "Addictive Love" and "I'll Take You There." *—William Ruhlmann*

Lord Lift Us Up / 1985 / PTL ✦✦✦✦✦

Bebe & Cece Winans / 1987 / Capitol ✦✦✦

Heaven / Sep. 1988 / Capitol ✦✦✦✦✦
If you listen carefully, the songs *are* about Jesus rather than love sweet love, but even a casual hearing lets you know this is one of the most soulful duos to come along since Marvin Gaye and Tammi Terrell. Keith Thomas gives the production a contemporary R&B sheen. *—William Ruhlmann*

Relationships / 1994 / Capitol ✦✦✦
The duo's first outing without the involvement of producer Keith Thomas finds them heading toward more downtempo, ballad-heavy R&B, with Cedric Caldwell and BeBe himself at the producer helm, along with mainstream-heavyweights Arif Mardin and David Foster. *—Thom Granger*

● **Greatest Hits** / Nov. 12, 1996 / Sparrow/EMI ✦✦✦✦✦
Greatest Hits contains 12 of BeBe and CeCe Winans' biggest hits, covering nearly every one of their R&B Top 40 hits, including "Lost Without You," "Addictive Love," "I'll Take You There," "It's O.K.," and "Heaven." In addition to the well-known songs, the collection features two new tracks, one of which—"Feels Like Heaven (With You)"—became a hit single upon the album's release. It's an excellent retrospective of one of contemporary gospel's finest groups. *—Rodney Batdorf*

CeCe Winans

b. Detroit, MI
Vocals / Contemporary Gospel, Black Gospel, Urban
The eighth of ten siblings in the musical Winans family, CeCe Winans (b. Priscilla) performed most often with her brother, BeBe, in a duo which recorded gospel material with R&B settings and proved to be the most commercially successful of the Winans groupings (which also includes her older brothers Marvin, Carvin, Ronald and Michael in the Winans and her parents in Mom & Pop Winans). Born in Detroit, she worked with BeBe in a duo called the PTL Singers until 1987, when they released their self-titled debut album (with vocal contributions from nine members of the family). Four albums followed during the next seven years (two of which hit gold) plus 1991's platinum *Different Lifestyles*. The duo's success increased as they added more contemporary forms of production—their two number one R&B singles, "Addictive Love" and "I'll Take You There," both treated spiritual love in fuzzy terms just as conducive to the physical. After 1994's *Relationships*, CeCe began recording her very first solo album. Released in 1995, *Alone in His Presence* found her working her way back to tra-

ditional gospel, singing standards like "Great Is Thy Faithfulness," "Blessed Assurance" and "I Surrender All." *His Gift* followed in 1998, and a year later Winans returned with *Alabaster Box*. *—John Bush*

Alone in His Presence / Oct. 10, 1995 / Sparrow ♦♦♦
The R&B grooves of her earlier recordings with The Winans' give way to a more string-oriented traditional gospel sound (exemplified by "Blessed Assurance" and "Great Is Thy Faithfulness") on her solo debut. *—John Bush*

● **Everlasting Love** / Mar. 17, 1998 / Pioneer ♦♦♦♦♦
For her second solo album, Cece Winans decided to record a full-fledged urban R&B/soul album, enlisting an impressive array of guest artists and collaborators—including Keith Crouch, Tony Rich, Lauryn Hill, Diane Warren, Daryl Simmons and Tommy Sims—to record *Everlasting Love.* All of the guest stars do nothing but enhance Winans' talents. There is no doubt this is her record, and she breathes life even into the weaker material. Fortunately, there isn't much that's weak on *Everlasting Love.* The songwriting is consistently classy, the production is polished without being slick, and Winans' voice simply soars. The only gospel inflections that remain are in her singing, as all of the songs, with the exception of Hill's direct, affecting "On That Day," have a distinct contemporary flavor. It's to Winans' credit that she flourishes in this setting and makes the album as personal as her gospel album *Alone in His Presence. —Stephen Thomas Erlewine*

Alabaster Box / Oct. 19, 1999 / Sparrow ♦♦♦♦
Alabaster Box isn't a box-set package devoted to CeCe Winans, but rather her third non-Christmas solo album, and the first for her own Wellspring label. It's a return to her gospel roots, in contrast to the straight-ahead urban soul of *Everlasting Love,* and it's a triumphant one. Winans sounds invigorated by the spiritual material, delivering committed performances and commanding vocals. The production sounds very contemporary, if a little slick at times, but that's not likely to bother most fans. *Alabaster Box* is an excellent album from a terrific talent. *—Steve Huey*

Various Artists

15 Down Home Gospel Classics / Jan. 20, 1998 / Arhoolie ♦♦♦♦♦
Arhoolie, as is made plain in this 15-song sampler of their gospel catalog, does not favor slick modern spiritual music. (Or, as they say straight-up in the brief liner note, "The selections on this disc... are not by trendy, popular massed choirs.") Much of this is in fact gospel-blues: spiritually oriented numbers by major bluesmen Big Joe Williams, Mance Lipscomb, Robert Pete Williams, Jesse Fuller (a nice slide guitar treatment of "Amazing Grace"), and Fred McDowell, as well as more contemporary steel guitar-flavored gospel by Aubrey Ghent. The arrangements are sparse (sometimes acoustic) and the vocals are soulful, not just by the aforementioned acts, but also by such relative unknowns as the Campbell Brothers, who work more in a contemporary electric vein. It's not being heretical to say that there's more passion and musical quality on this compilation than there is on innumerable glossily produced gospel recordings by feel-good ensembles with higher profiles. By the way, the track by steel guitarist Black Ace, "Farther Along," was previously unissued on CD. *—Richie Unterberger*

1998 Dove Awards Nominees / Apr. 7, 1998 / Brentwood ♦♦♦♦
As is appropriate for a collection that spotlights the most celebrated tunes in all of CCM (at least the most celebrated in 1998), *1998 Dove Awards Nominees* acts as both an effective sampler of the genre's state-of-the-art circa the late '90s and a one-stop introduction for neophytes and the curious. True, some big names are missing on the collection, but there are enough major artists—Michael W. Smith ("Live the Life"), Steven Curtis Chapman ("Let Us Pray"), Bob Carlisle ("Living Water"), Rich Mullins ("Elijah"), Caedmon's Call ("Hope to Carry On"), Crystal Lewis ("People Get Ready... Jesus is Comin'"), Kathy Troccoli ("Baby's Prayer")—to make it a representative sampler, as well as an entertaining listen. *—Stephen Thomas Erlewine*

Absolutely the Best of Gospel, Vol. 1 / Nov. 23, 1999 / Varese ♦♦♦♦
Absolutely The Best Of Gospel Volume 1 pairs classic gospel songs with the genre's most popular performers. The Staple Singers' "Will The Circle Be Unbroken" and "Reach Out And Touch A Hand," the Five Blind Boys Of Alabama's "Just A Closer Walk With Thee," the Caravans' "Lord Don't Leave Us Now" and the Mighty Echoes' "I Found Joy" are some of the album's highlights, and performances by Aretha Franklin and the Carolina Spirituals show that this collection deserves its name. *—Heather Phares*

☆ **Ain't That Good News** / Specialty ♦♦♦♦♦
Super 50s gospel from the Specialty vaults, compiled by Barrett Hanson (aka Dr. Demento). Each cut is a true gem. Of special interest to audiophiles: the tracks carefully segue into each other, with no space between (which could be annoying to some). A spellbinding effect and a great album. *—Barry Lee Pearson*

All God's Sons & Daughters: Chicago Gospel Legends / Mar. 23, 1999 / Shanachie ♦♦♦
A soul stirring collection of Chicago gospel performers belting out their earnest praise in a dramatic fashion. The recordings have a live feel to them which adds to the spiritual honesty, many of them sounding as though they were recorded during sunday services. Featured performers include Gladys Beamon Gregory Thomas, Delois Barrett Campbell Dorsey, and J. Robert Bradley. *—Zac Johnson*

☆ **The Best of Nashboro Gospel** / 1993 / Nashboro ♦♦♦♦♦
Essential collection of quartet and soloist material, unavailable on any other release. *—Opal Louis Nations*

Bless My Bones: Memphis Gospel Radio—*The 50s / Rounder* ♦♦♦♦♦
Bless My Bones: Memphis Gospel Radio—1950s highlights eight stellar ensembles in a stunning set of radio transcriptions from Memphis's WDIA. Includes "99 & 1/2 Won't Do" by The Song Birds of the South and "Milky White Way" by The Spirit of Memphis, as well as tracks by the Dixie Nightingales, Southern Wonders, and Sunset Travelers. *—John Floyd*

Crusade of a Lifetime: A Musical Tribute to Billy Graham / Sep. 17, 1996 / Brentwood ♦♦♦
The one and only Billy Graham is honored on this uplifting Christian music collection, which features performances from vocalists Ralph Carmichael, George Beverly Shea and Kurt Kaiser along with a 250-voice choir. Music includes "Amazing Grace," "I'd Rather Have Jesus" and "How Great Thou Art." *—Jonathan Ball*

Divine Sounds: Best of Classic Gospel / Jan. 12, 1999 / MCA ♦♦♦♦
A ten-track collection that virtually describes itself. Performances include Mahalia Jackson's "Get Away Jordan" and "It Is No Secret," Aretha Franklin's "Precious Lord, Parts 1 & 2" and "He'll Wash You Whiter Than Snow," Reverend Cleophus Robinson's "Because He Lives," Tessie Hill's "Great Things," and the Mighty Clouds of Joy's "Pray for Me." Selections from the Soul Stirrers, the Gospel Keynotes and Jackson Southernaires complete the package. *—Cub Koda*

Elias: The Prayer Cycle / Mar. 23, 1999 / Word ♦♦♦♦♦
The Prayer Cycle is a surprisingly spiritual and moving album masterminded by composer Jonathan Elias, featuring an all-star cast culled from the pop, rock, and world music arenas (including Nusrat Fateh Ali Khan, Alanis Morissette, Perry Farrell, Linda Ronstadt, James Taylor, Ofra Haza, Salif Keita, and more). The album is structured as a nine-movement suite, with each movement dedicated to a different spiritual quality. Elias' material elicits passionate, committed performances from the assembled artists, making it a deeply felt statement on bridging cross-cultural differences. *—Steve Huey*

Free at Last: Gospel Quartets from Stax Records' Chalice Label / May 5, 1997 / Specialty ♦♦♦♦
Stax Records launched a gospel subsidiary called Chalice during the mid-1960s that, although short-lived, recorded some remarkable quartets from Memphis and surrounding areas. This 24-track compilation gathers up some ultra-rare selections from that label's archives, including such then-topical songs as the Dixie Nightingales' "The Assasination" (a harrowing lament for President John F. Kennedy) and the Jubilee Hummingbirds' "Our Freedom Song," all about Dr. Martin Luther King's receipt of the Nobel Peace Prize. What is especially appealing is the crack instrumental support behind these various quartets being provided by Steve Cropper, Al Jackson, Jr., Isaac Hayes and other Stax R&B session stalwarts. Selections from the Stars of Virginia and the Pattersonaires complete the package. Note: this compilation was previously released by Ace Records (U.K.) as Disturb My Soul: Gospel from Stax Records' Chalice Label. *—Cub Koda*

Gospel Sound of Spirit Feel / 1991 / Spirit Feel ♦♦♦♦♦
A generous 27-track sampler, *The Gospel Sound of Spirit Feel* is a well-assembled introduction to the label's vault of classic spiritual performances. While the set's primary emphasis is on the period spanning from 1945 to 1960—gospel's acknowledged golden age—it also includes a number of more traditional performances, with the spirit of the classic Dr. Watts hymns resurfacing in performances by the likes of legends including Mahalia Jackson ("Even Me," "I Gave Up Everything"), Clara Ward ("99 1/2," "The Fountain"), and Marion Williams ("The Lord Will Make a Way Somehow," "Must I Be to Judgment Brought"). Also shining its spotlight on the quartet tradition and the electrifying rockers of the Pentecostal church, this is an excellent primer for beginners. *—Jason Ankeny*

The Gospel Tradition: Roots & Branches, Vol. 1 / 1991 / Columbia/Legacy ♦♦♦♦♦
One of the few gospel collections that ignores the barriers between White and Black gospel music, *The Gospel Tradition: The Roots and the Branches—Vol. 1* contrasts the blues of Bessie Smith and the western swing of Bob Wills, the rough edge of Mitchell's Christian Singers and the smooth polish of The Sons of The Pioneers. Lots of obscure sides dating back to 1927, and a wide range of styles from sanctified women to choral spirituals. *—Brian Mansfield*

☆ **Gospel Warriors: 50 Years of Female Gospel Classics** / 1990 / Spirit Feel ♦♦♦♦♦
Spanning a half century of classic performances, *Gospel Warriors* assembles 16 tracks from some of the church circuit's most renowned female soloists, among them Marion Williams, Bessie Griffin and Sister Rosetta Tharpe. While each vocalist is clearly a singular talent, listening to their music side by side offers real insight into their common gifts for improvisation; all are in total command of melody, tone and lyric, transcending their material to enjoy an unparalleled sense of creative freedom. An ideal introduction for new gospel listeners, the collection's highlights include Tharpe's "Just a Closer Walk with Thee," Williams' "It's Getting Late in the Evening" and Clara Ward's "Precious Lord." *—Jason Ankeny*

The Great 1955 Shrine Concert / 1993 / Specialty ♦♦♦♦
The power and splendor that was gospel in the '50s radiates throughout the performances on *The Great 1955 Shrine Concert.* The Pilgrim Travelers, with twin powerhouse leads Kylo Turner and Keith Barber, get things started in fiery fashion, followed by the dynamic Caravans, whose roster at that time included Albertina Walker and Rev. James Cleveland, who doubled as a pianist. Also on the bill were Brother Joe May, justifying his "Thunderbolt of the Midwest" nickname, The Soul Stirrers with Sam Cooke still in the fold, and The Original Gospel Harmonettes concluding the proceedings with a flourish. Anyone who attended certainly felt the spirit, as will anyone who listens to this magnificent 14-song set. *—Ron Wynn*

☆ **The Great Gospel Men** / 1995 / Shanachie ♦♦♦♦♦
A wide range of magnificent vocals are displayed on *The Great Gospel Men,* a 27-song anthology. Some names such as Brother Joe May, Rev. James Cleveland, and Professor Alex Bradford are familiar even to non-gospel fans; others, like the intense Robert Anderson, Professor J. Earle Hines, Norsalus McKissick, Robert Bradley, and R.L. Knowles are known only to the hardcore, and even they probably haven't heard many songs by any one artist. This collection alternates nicely between slow and fast pieces, giving each artist a chance to demonstrate their skills. *—Ron Wynn*

☆ **The Great Gospel Women** / 1993 / Shanachie ✦✦✦✦✦
Like its male counterpoint, this anthology spotlights contributions from both famous stars (Mahalia Jackson, Marion Williams, Dorothy Love Coates, Sister Rosetta Tharpe) and obscure figures (Mary Johnson Davis, Jessie Mae Renfro, Lucy Smith, and Goldia Haynes, among others), presenting a hefty 31 selections. While some might quibble that celebated stars Jackson and Williams get six tracks apiece, it's hard to argue with the greatness of what's presented by them. Others who give head-turning performances include Frances Steadman, Roberta Martin, and Clara Ward. *—Ron Wynn*

Great Gospel Women, Vol. 2 / 1995 / Shanachie ✦✦✦✦✦
The Great Gospel Women Vol. 2 is a worthy follow-up to the first edition of the series; wisely refusing to mess with a good thing, producer Anthony Heilbut holds over most of the same artists from before, dipping into the well for more classic material from soloists including Mahalia Jackson, Marion Williams, Clara Ward and Sister Rosetta Tharpe. While the overall quality is somewhat diluted this time out, in its favor the disc offers two more tracks than its predecessor, as well as choice cuts from performers making their series debut, among them Bessie Griffin, Ernestine B. Washington, Edna Gallmon Cooke, Imogene Green and Myrtle Scott. An excellent companion piece. *—Jason Ankeny*

Greatest Gospel Gems / 1991 / Specialty ✦✦✦✦✦
An excellent 24-song sampling of '50s and '60s sacred testifying from the vaults of Specialty Records, it includes essential cuts from Dorothy Love Coates, the Swan Silvertones, and Sam Cooke and the Soul Stirrers. *—John Floyd*

The Half Ain't Never Been Told, Vol. 1 / Nov. 16, 1999 / Yazoo ✦✦✦✦
Yazoo has released yet another wonderful compilation chock full of recordings that are essential for roots music fans. *The Half Ain't Never Been Told, Vol. 1* chronicles American rural religious music of the 1920s and 1930s. The moving, heartfelt praise and prayers included here range from a cappella choirs to solo artists with musical accompaniment to gospel groups. Unusually, the collection doesn't separate music from black and white rural music traditions, mixing in bluegrass, prewar gospel blues, sacred harp singing, spirituals, and more. With this variety of styles equally dispersed between two volumes, if you want one, you will want them both. Included on *Volume 1* is Washington Phillips and several sacred harp singing groups, as well as many choirs and congregational recordings. As is always the case with compilations of such early and rare recordings, the sound quality varies widely, with a hiss ranging from barely noticeable to hissing at the same volume as any of the instruments. Nonetheless, this compilation makes an important addition to the library of roots music fans who can overlook sound quality inconveniences for the recordings' historical importance. *—Joslyn Layne*

Hallelujah: Kings of Gospel / Mar. 23, 1999 / Music Club ✦✦✦
Music Club's compilation of male gospel singers from the Hub Records catalog is more varied than the complementary one on females (the concurrently released *Queens of Gospel*). For one thing, there are more groups: Where the distaff disc has three tracks each by five performers, this one has two tracks by seven different acts and one by an eighth. Beyond that, however, where the women's selections lean toward traditional arrangements in which one furiously improvising leader is heard over a harmony backup to ecstatic results, the men's have many different styles. The Dixie Hummingbirds, who lead off the set with "Move Up a Little Higher" and return eight tracks later with "Get Away Jordan," are sweet-voiced a cappella harmonizers. The Five Singing Stars, led by tenor Tommy Ellison, could be soul stars on "Hard to Get Along" and "Heaven to Me" if they weren't in church. Gravel-voiced Dewey Young of the Flying Clouds also has many counterparts in the secular realm, and the Brooklyn All-Stars lean toward pop music. Of course, there are also more traditional sounds, such as a live version of "Amazing Grace" by the Mighty Clouds of Joy complete with screams from the congregation and the same group's rendition of "Old Time Religion." But *Kings of Gospel* is a good album to play as an example of the influence of gospel music on R&B, doo wop, and other popular vocal music of the past 40 years. *—William Ruhlmann*

Hallelujah: Queens of Gospel / Mar. 23, 1999 / Music Club ✦✦✦
This 15-track collection brings together a nice selection of performances from the Hob label, one of the first American labels to heavily champion gospel music and is the companion volume to Music Club's excellent *Kings of Gospel* package. Like its brother-related predecessor, this one is also loaded with top flight selections from the Clara Ward Specials ("How I Got Over," "When the Gates Swing Open," "Happy Over There [Parts 1 & 2]"), the Gospel Harmonettes ("You Must Be Born Again," "The Great Coronation," "Gospel Train"), the Stars of Faith ("I've Got Shoes," "We Shall Be Changed," "Get Away Jordan") the Meditation Singers ("Jesus Be a Fence Around Me," "One More River to Cross," "Get Ready") and the Caravans ("It's Jesus in Me," "To Whom Shall I Turn"). This is some rare and phenomenal material that will be a welcome addition to anyone's gospel music collection. If you're looking for impassioned music sung from the heart, you've come to the right place. Great liner notes from AMG contributor Opal Louis Nations, too. *—Cub Koda*

In the Spirit: The Gospel and Jubilee Recordings of Trumpet Records / 1994 / Alligator ✦✦✦✦
Between 1950 and 1953, the tiny Trumpet label based in Jackson, MS, issued some 30 superb spiritual sides, the best of which are found on this invaluable 16-track set. While the names that make up *In the Spirit* aren't immediately familiar, the performances are uniformly strong; Hugh Dent, a protégé of Brother Joe May, shows off a rich baritone on a group of tracks highlighted by "In the End," while the veteran St. Andrews Gospelaires resurrect the traditional jubilee style on their two cuts, the first ever recorded under the Trumpet banner. Although one wishes Alligator had reissued all of the label's gospel output, perhaps as a two-disc set, this is still essential listening for committed fans of the genre. *—Jason Ankeny*

☆ **Jubilation, Vol. 1 (Black Gospel)** / Jan. 1992 / Rhino ✦✦✦✦✦
Jubilation: Great Gospel Performances, Vol. 1 offers a first-rate introduction and overview of the key players in Black gospel, including stellar performances by Mahalia Jackson, the Soul Stirrers, the Swan Silvertones, Shirley Caesar, Aretha Franklin and James Cleveland, and many other wonderful artists. *—Thom Owens*

☆ **Jubilation, Vol. 2 (More Black Gospel)** / Feb. 1992 / Rhino ✦✦✦✦✦
Like the title says, there's more of the same as the first volume, including The Staples Singers, the Original Gospel Harmonettes, Prof. Alex Bradford, the Harmonizing Four, Sam Cooke with the Soul Stirrers, and more. *—AMG*

Jubilation, Vol. 3 (Country Gospel) / Mar. 1992 / Rhino ✦✦✦✦✦
While the first two volumes in the series spotlighted the history of African-American gospel, this volume peeks over the other side of the fence and sheds the light on six decades' worth of country gospel performances. It's all top-notch, too, with Hank Williams' "I Saw the Light" spearheading an 18-track collection that includes classics from Kitty Wells, Roy Acuff, Bill Monroe, Patsy Cline, Johnny Cash, the Carter Family, the Louvin Brothers, Webb Pierce, and Martha Carson. That gospel is a long-running tradition in country is exemplified by the inclusion of tracks from modern stars like Ricky Skaggs and Tony Rice, Doyle Lawson and Quicksilver, the Nitty Gritty Dirt Band, and old guard like Buck Owens, George Jones and Tammy Wynette, and Ernest Tubb. A delightful set. *—Cub Koda*

Kings of the Gospel Highway / Apr. 11, 2000 / Shanachie ✦✦✦✦✦
Kings of the Gospel Highway presents selections from the top male a cappella groups of the 1940s and '50s, including the Soul Stirrers, the Swan Silvertones, and the Five Blind Boys of Mississippi. Songs range from light and upbeat numbers such as "Does Jesus Care" by R.H. Harris and the Soul Stirrers, to hand-clappers like the jubilee rendition of "Lord Hold My Hand" by the Pilgrim Travelers and Julius Cheeks and the Sensational Nightingales' take on "Lord Have Mercy." The compilation also includes slow and moving numbers, like "The Old Account" by the Swan Silvertones and hard-singing, spirited pieces such as the Silvertones' version of "All Aboard" and Archie Brownlee with the Five Blind Boys of Mississippi singing "I Was Praying." Other highlights include "Jesus Brought Me" by the Spirit of Memphis, with an anointed, hoarse-throated Silas Steele at the front, and the earliest recording on this collection, the Soul Stirrers' 1939 recording of "Walk Around," which has crackly sound quality but rousing spirit, with Harris sounding his best. Besides this one early recording, the rest of the Stirrers' songs come from the mid- to late '40s, while the Sensational Nightingales' tunes span the 1950s. The other groups' selections are drawn from the late '40s through the early '50s. *—Joslyn Layne*

Let Zion Move: Music Of The Shakers / Oct. 26, 1999 / Rounder ✦✦✦✦✦
The spiritual music of the Shakers, as might be expected, is notable for its simplicity and straightforward nature. The vocal music is often (though not always) sung without instrumental accompaniment and without harmony. Most of the sentiments expressed would fit easily in the mainstream of Protestant hymnody, but there's an undercurrent of defiance in songs like "Lion-Hearted, Brave and True" and "My Dear Companions, Let's Move On" that may arise as much from the Yankee heritage of the singers as from the world-denying faith they share. Most of the music on these two discs is taken from a series of ten LPs released in the 1960s entitled The Shaker Heritage, and the performers are members of the Shaker villages in Canterbury, NH and Sabbathday Lake, ME. The first disc is devoted to songs and instrumental performances with brief introductory comments between tracks; the second consists primarily of interviews and narration. The recording quality isn't always very good, but anyone with an interest in American religious music will find the material both interesting and moving. Highly recommended. *—Rick Anderson*

None But the Righteous: Chess Gospel Greats / 1992 / Chess ✦✦✦✦✦
Chess Records was never particularly noted as a gospel label. In the early 1950s, however, the company released more than its share of great gospel recordings, and this 18-track set stands as a testimony to some of the rawest ones that the label put out. While big names like Aretha and Reverend C.L. Franklin, the Soul Stirrers, and the Original Five Blind Boys from Alabama are accounted for, the real gems come from lesser-known acts like the Meditation Singers, the Norfleet Brothers, the Bells of Joy, Sammy Bryant, Elder Beck, and the Southern Stars. A marvelous set of raw gospel music that should be in everyone's collection. *—Cub Koda*

Power Jams / Aug. 31, 1999 / ForeFront ✦✦✦✦
It's difficult to figure out exactly why the CCM sampler *Power Jams* copies so closely the style of ESPN's Jock Jams series aside from the fact that it was a successful repackaging gimmick—you aren't going to hear any of the songs here at sporting arenas, and the play-by-play announcer and cheerleader bits in between songs don't really have anything to do with the music contained herein. Half of *Power Jams* consists of remixes of popular CCM hits; the other half features originals, although all the tracks are strung together in a continuous mix. Thus, listeners wanting a compilation of the familiar versions of these songs won't find it here; however, it may find favor with those who want to hear some newer versions or who would enjoy a Christian music compilation that, for a change of pace, creates a party atmosphere. *—Steve Huey*

Praise the Lord: Gospel Music in Washington D.C. / Jan. 19, 1999 / Smithsonian/Folkways ✦✦✦
These 15 tracks were recorded in 1998 by the Anacostia Museum and Center for African-American History and Culture for an exhibition on contemporary African-American life. It was assembled with an eye toward illustrating diverse forms of gospel, including solo, duet, quartet, and choir performances (though not trio ones), including a couple by the Nannie Helen Burroughs School Choir. The arrangements, too, vary from sparse and traditional, emphasizing piano, to ones which reflect the influence of contemporary soul. The less elaborate tracks sound better; it's pretty unlikely this disc is angling for adult contemporary radio airplay, but that's the effect produced when intrusive synthesizers come into the action. *—Richie Unterberger*

Precious Memories: Favorites from Gospel's Women of Song / 1998 / Peacock ✦✦✦✦
If you were to play *Precious Memories* next to a collection of material by female soul singers, you'd notice some definite parallels. That's because African-American gospel had an enormous influence on soul music. At the same time, quite a few gospel artists were influenced by R&B and blues even if they refused to sing any lyrics that didn't have an overtly Christian message. Released in 1998 for the Peacock Gospel Classics series, this excellent collec-

tion boasts performances by some of gospel's most famous female singers, including Mahalia Jackson ("The Upper Room"), Sister Clara Ward ("When We All Get to Heaven"), Shirley Caesar ("One of These Old Days"), Sister Rosetta Tharpe ("Precious Memories"), Dorothy Love Coates ("I Won't Let Go") and Inez Andrews ("Lord Don't Move the Mountain," "The Healer"). You can be certain that many of the singers on this CD were primary listening for Aretha Franklin, Gladys Knight and so many other R&B greats who sang in church before they became successful in the secular market. Unfortunately, the liner notes don't provide recording dates for all the songs—had Rhino assembled this collection, you probably would have found recording dates or, at the very least, the years in which the songs first came out. But despite that shortcoming, *Precious Memories* is a rewarding compilation that's well worth acquiring. *—Alex Henderson*

Sacred Steel Guitar / Jan. 21, 1997 / Arhoolie ♦♦♦♦
This is one amazing collection. Subtitled "Traditional Sacred African-American Steel Guitar Music in Florida," this multi-artist chronicling of this seldom-heard genre is a musical and emotional delight. The electric lap steel guitar has been the instrument of choice in both the Jewel Dominion and Keith Dominions (both African-American Holiness-Pentecostal churches) since the late '30s, replacing the traditional church organist. This collection showcases the pioneering work of five of its best known and most influential sacred steel practitioners: Willie Eason, Sonny Treadway, Glenn Lee, Henry Nelson, and his son, Aubrey Ghent. Their individual approaches to this style range from crude blues-based slides and slurs (blues table steel master Hop Wilson is called to mind more than once here) to highly technical flourishes bordering on country pedal steel sounds, with all of it played with a sincerity and spirit indigenous to the music, which is nothing short of heartfelt and energetic. Split evenly between instrumentals and the instrument interfacing with the congregation and choir at live religious services, the music runs the gamut from still and beautiful (Sonny Treadway's instrumentals) to the wild and abandoned playing of Aubrey Ghent. This is 75 minutes of music that will appeal to blues and gospel and even retro-minded rock & roll fans willing to take the time to explore this fascinating genre. *—Cub Koda*

Sacred Steel, Vol. 2: Live at the House of God Church / Arhoolie ♦♦♦♦
Incendiary would be one good word to describe this disc, which is one of those rare gems that come along every now and again that works on many different levels. It features various artists captured spreading their joy and faith with their passionate celebratory music, with the electric steel guitar being the dominant instrument in the music of these groups. This disc was recorded at two different House of God churches, a coffeehouse, and the Strawberry Spring Music Festival, and the sound quality is of the high quality that you have come to expect from Arhoolie. The pedal steel guitar is the king on this disc, yet in support of it the singing is equally as strong and unrestrained. Particularly notable is the inspired singing of Katie Jackson and Denise Brown. Then there is Ted Beard making his pedal steel mimic a train in appropriately enough "The Train" and the sharp and biting blues guitar of Phil Campbell stretching out on "Don't Let the Devil Ride." The whole disc from top to bottom is highlight after highlight. *—Bob Gottlieb*

Sacred Voices: An A Capella Gospel Collection / Sep. 28, 1999 / Sugar Hill ♦♦♦♦♦
The Sugar Hill label's roster of bluegrass, folk, and country artists is rich with outstanding singing ensembles, and this compilation shows them off at their best, performing traditional gospel music without instrumental accompaniment. The styles vary. Doyle Lawson & Quicksilver and the Nashville Bluegrass band both dip into the African-American gospel tradition with "Climbing Up the Mountain" and "Father I Stretch My Hand to Thee," respectively. Tony Rice and Ricky Skaggs deliver "Talk About Suffering" from their celebrated duo album, in a style that harks back to that of brother duos like the Blue Sky Boys and the Delmore Brothers. And Don Rigsby teams up with Ralph Stanley and a host of helping voices in a hair-raising version of "Vision of a Golden Crown." Perhaps the most impressive performance, though, is Doc Watson's solo rendition of "What a Friend We Have in Jesus," a traditional hymn whose simple and unadorned melody floats effortlessly on Watson's voice. Highly recommended. *—Rick Anderson*

The Soul of Chicago / 1993 / Shanachie ♦♦♦♦
Distinguished gospel music critic, author, producer and label executive Anthony Heilbut has provided many wonderful anthologies. For this one, he has taken 11 surviving artists from the golden age and recorded them in a traditional setting with their familiar spare backings (mostly piano, guitar and organ). The results are both impressive and memorable; Robert Anderson, Delois Barrett Campbell, Rev. Samuel Patterson, Gladys Beamon Gregory and the Gay Family, among others, don't just sound good, but almost as fabulous as they did in their heyday. They have the spirit just as if they were performing and recording all the time, yet many of them have not sung regularly in decades. The quality of this masterful session blows most contemporary gospel out of the water. *—Ron Wynn*

Southern Gospel's Top 20 Songs of the Century / Apr. 18, 2000 / New Haven ♦♦♦♦
Southern Gospel's Top 20 Songs of the Century includes the songs most often named by respondents to a survey done by the New Haven label. The results include many songs that charted on The Singing News' Top 40, including number one hits "Jesus Is Coming Soon" (it topped the charts in January 1970 with a version by the Oak Ridge Boys), "I Know" (Febrary 1971, the Blue Ridge Quartet), "Touring That City" (November 1973, the Inspirations), "When He Was on the Cross" (August 1985, the Florida Boys), and "Midnight Cry" (January 1988, Gold City). Also included are other songs that charted by the Hinsons, the Rambos, the Kingsmen, and more, and well-known songs like "We Shall See Jesus," "Sweet Sweet Spirit," and the oldest inclusion, "The Church in the Wildwood," which was penned in 1857. -Joslyn Layne

★ **Storefront & Streetcorner Gospel (1927-1929)** / Jun. 2, 1994 / Document ♦♦♦♦♦
Assembling the complete recorded works of A.C. & Blind Mamie Forehand, Washington Phillips and Luther Magby, *Storefront and Streetcorner Gospel (1927-1929)* offers a fascinating glimpse into the kind of spiritual music commonly heard throughout the urban areas of the south during the last years of the pre-Depression era. The common thread among these performers is their choice of unusual accompaniment—the Dallas-based Phillips is backed by the dolceola, an ethereal variant of the dulcimer, while the Forehands employ antique cymbals and Magby uses a harmonium; little or nothing is known about the various artists, yet their music still packs a punch all these decades later. *—Jason Ankeny*

Strong Hand of Love: A Tribute to Mark Heard / 1994 / Word/Epic ♦♦♦
This is a tribute to the late Mark Heard; songwriter, instrumentalist and producer. A devoted Christian, Heard was able to infuse his sense of faith in his songs without their being limited soley to that audience. His intricate lyrics show a high poetic intelligence combined with a frenzy of rock & roll and textured acoustic music. It is from Heard's own final three albums that most of these songs are drawn. Some of the heartfelt performances are "Nod over Coffee" sung by Pierce Pettis (who had been produced by Heard), Victoria Williams's "What Kind of Friend," and Bruce Cockburn's mature interpretation of "Strong Hand of Love." As with the best tributes, this collection stands on its own, but sends you back to Mark Heard's own great performances. *—Richard Meyer*

Testify!: The Gospel Box / Jun. 15, 1999 / Rhino ♦♦♦
It seems like it would be easy to compile a definitive gospel box set, much like Rhino's definitive Doo Wop Box. After all, much classic gospel was never widely distributed and has been out of print for years, and many listeners would like one sweeping set that captures the best of the music. Still, the three-disc set *Testify!: The Gospel Box* suffers from two perennial Rhino curses: a desire to tell a full chronology and a yen for novelty. First, Testify runs from the beginning of the '40s to the end of the '90s. This is an enormous amount of time to consolidate into one set, especially when most casual fans of gospel (i.e., rock fans) have, at best, a passing interest in gospel recorded after the early '70s, which accounts for the last two discs of the set. To be sure, there's some great music on the first disc (covering recorded gospel's peak years), but it's marred by novelty tunes—"Praise the Lord and Pass the Ammunition," "Stalin Wasn't Stallin'"—that are of interest to collectors, but hardly provide the basic introduction that the set intends to provide. Disc two is devoted to music recorded in the '70s and early '80s; disc three picks up where that left off, taking listeners all the way to the end of the century. Some listeners may even want a set that runs through the history of recorded gospel, but *Testify!* isn't satisfying listening; it's merely a textbook, tracing the evolution of gospel. Instructive it may be, but like many textbooks, it doesn't bring the music to life, which is a sad irony for such a joyous music. *—Stephen Thomas Erlewine*

Through the Years / 1998 / Peacock ♦♦♦♦
As another volume in Peacock's Gospel Classics series, this entry is subtitled "A Collection of Songs From Great Gospel Choirs." Like the other entries, the material is pulled from the multi-label gospel material holdings of parent company MCA Records. Highlights include the L.A. Mass Choir's "He Lives Today," the CME Community Choir's "Jesus Will Make a Way," the New Jersey Mass Choir's "I Will Sing Allelujah to the Lord" and Rev. Milton Brunson & The Thompson Community Choir's "I Love To Praise Him." Equally stellar selections from The Chicago Mass Choir ("The Lord Is Alright"), the North Carolina Mass Choir ("Jesus Will Fix It"), the Dallas Academy Youth Choir ("Standing In the Need of Prayer"), the BC&M Mass Choir ("I Made a Vow") and Father Hayes and Univers Kingdom ("Tell Me How Do You Feel") finish out this fine gospel choir compilation. *—Cub Koda*

★ **Wade in the Water, Vol. 1: African American Gospel—*The Concert Tradition* / *May 1, 1994* / *Smithsonian/Folkways*** ♦♦♦♦♦
This four-disc set, drawn from the musical examples to Bernice Johnson Reagon's outstanding National Public Radio series on African-American gospel music, deals respectively with the concert tradition in spiritual singing, the 19th-century roots of African-American congregational singing, the pioneering composers, and community gospel. As ballet music lacks a dimension without the dance, the CDs lack a dimension without the powerful mind tying the whole thing together. And to have included some of the non-African-American roots Professor Reagon illustrated in the programs would also have made this more than just another fine gospel set. But "just another fine gospel set" is pretty fine in its own right. *—John Storm Roberts, Original Music*

☆ **Wade in the Water, Vol. 2: African American Gospel—19th Century Roots** / May 1, 1994 / Smithsonian/Folkways ♦♦♦♦♦
Wade in the Water, Vol. II: African American Congregational Singing offers a glimpse into the long history of black congregational vocals and worshiping practices, a tradition dating back centuries which once accounted for much of the oral transmission passed from generation to generation. Fascinatingly, the songs are never rehearsed—singers learn while they perform; and while organized gospel choirs have since become more widely recognized, the congregational style still thrives, with six of the modern era's most stirring representatives—among them the McIntosh County Shouters, the Seniorlites and the Rev. C.J. Johnson & Family—featured on this disc. *—Jason Ankeny*

☆ **Wade in the Water, Vol. 3: African American Gospel—*The Pioneering Composers*** / 1994 / Smithsonian/Folkways ♦♦♦♦♦
Wade in the Water, Vol. III: African American Gospel focuses on six of the pioneering composers of the genre—Rev. Charles Albert Tindley, Lucie Eddie (Elizabeth) Campbell, Rev. William Herbert Brewster, Roberta Martin, Kenneth Morris and the incomparable Thomas A. Dorsey. Recorded between 1992 and 1993, the disc features new renditions of such perennials as "Just a Closer Walk with Thee," "Precious Lord," "How I Got Over" and "We'll Understand It Better By and By." *—Jason Ankeny*

Wade in the Water, Vol. 4: African American Community Gospel / 1994 / Smithsonian/Folkways ♦♦♦♦♦
The final release in the series, *Wade in the Water, Vol. 4: African American Community Gospel* focuses on the sacred music of two vastly different areas of the U.S.—Washington D.C. and rural Alabama—to illustrate the differences brought about by local perspective. The eight Alabama tracks run the gamut from newly arranged renditions of traditional favorites to popular hits to original compositions; all are in the quartet style, which remains the primary gospel vehicle throughout the state—group anniversary celebrations are even regularly held, with other quartets traveling from miles around to perform in their peers'

honor. In D.C., the trend is toward performances connected with the worship services of the urban church community; again, however, the scope is vast, including traditional styles, processional praise songs and a contemporary reading of "Peace in the Valley." —*Jason Ankeny*

Warrior on the Battlefield: A Capella Trail Blazers—1920s-1940s / Oct. 21, 1997 / Rounder ✦✦✦✦
Twenty-five performances by African-American gospel quartets of the South, recorded between 1927 and 1942. The Silver Leaf Quartette of Norfolk and the Golden Gate Quartet get the most airtime (six and five tracks respectively), though there's also space for less familiar names like the Davis Bible Singers and the T.C.I. Womens Four. This documents Black gospel music in its transition from barbershop quartets to more polished forms, and while the sound quality isn't as dynamic as what you'll find on contemporary releases, the performances are generally much less showy. *—Richie Unterberger*

Women of Gospel's Golden Age, Vol. 1 / 1994 / Specialty ✦✦✦✦✦
Although women have been at the forefront of gospel innovation since the beginning, the domination of male quartets may have fooled some into thinking they weren't that important. Anyone holding that mistaken impression will surely know better after hearing the 28 remarkable cuts on this valuable anthology. New Orleans' wondrous Bessie Griffin, whose vibrant, dazzling voice was overlooked due to Mahalia Jackson, gets the spotlight with six amazing numbers. She's not alone there, however; everyone from the famous Clara Ward Singers and Dorothy Love Coates to the lesser-known Sallie Martin Singers sounds fantastic. *—Ron Wynn*

★ **WOW Gold** / Jun. 20, 2000 / Brentwood ✦✦✦✦✦
Spanning the '70s through the '90s, *WOW Gold* styles itself as a compact history of contemporary Christian music (CCM), seeking not to define, but to sum up the genre, and showcase the range of music it encompasses in the process. One CCM star after another parades across the compilation's two discs; the only flaw is that they aren't always represented by their best-known or most popular songs. Some choices are no-brainers: Rich Mullins' "Awesome God," Stryper's "To Hell With the Devil," or Bob Carlisle's "Butterfly Kisses," for example. But others might bemoan the selection of DC Talk's "What If I Stumble?" over "Jesus Freak," or Michael W. Smith's "Friends" over the pop Top Ten hit "Place in This World." But even if it isn't, ultimately, a one-stop best-of-CCM collection, *WOW Gold* does achieve its aim of displaying the variety and quality of the best contemporary Christian music. *—Steve Huey*

● **WOW The 90's: 30 Top Christian Songs of the Decade** / Jul. 20, 1999 / Word ✦✦✦✦✦
Wow: The 90s: 30 Top Christian Songs of the Decade is an excellent basic survey of CCM in the '90s, collecting 30 of the decade's biggest Christian radio hits over the course of two discs. Long-time CCM fans will probably have some, if not most, of these tracks already, but newcomers to the genre couldn't ask for a much better introduction than *Wow: The 90s*. Featured artists include Michael W. Smith, Amy Grant, dc Talk, Rich Mullins, Jaci Velasquez, Sandi Patty, Steven Curtis Chapman, Newsboys, Point of Grace, Chris Rice, and many more. *—Steve Huey*

COUNTRY

The 1990s were one of the most successful periods for country music, with country albums routinely reaching the upper sections of the pop charts and musicians like Garth Brooks and Shania Twain becoming full-fledged pop stars. Then again, even if this was extreme popularity, it wasn't all that different than what came before. Country has always been popular. Record charts reflected this at times—witness how countrypolitain catapulted to the top of the pops early in the '70s—and at times it didn't (in the immediate wake of MTV, country was nonexistent on the pop charts), but it's never been far removed from the forefront of popular consciousness, and it's inextricably tied to American popular music.

Country has been there since the beginning of recorded music, standing alongside blues and jazz as some of the first recorded music. Where both of those musics were embraced by scholars, country always remained a bit of a bastard cousin, even when its earliest incarnations are celebrated as the roots of American music. That's because it's always been a populist music, from its old-timey roots to Garth's cinematic spectacles. It's never been music that has been readily accepted by the cultural elite or the critics, and the greats were only showered in praise in retrospect, when they were not regularly visiting the top of the charts.

A nice side effect of this is how country winds up being quintessentially of its time, yet transcends it. From the beginning, this has been music that's been recorded according to contemporary standards, but its themes are inarguably timeless, which is why the songs themselves transcend their time, or can sound fresh, vital in new recordings. This maxim has been proven throughout country's history—witness how certain sounds and songs have continually worked their way to the foreground of country's consciousness, whether it's Hank Williams' timeless tunes or the sound of Western swing.

This was the dichotomy that surfaced in the '90s, as country music followed several different directions. In one sense, it was bigger than ever, as icons like Garth and Shania were as big as any pop icon. Then again, these musicians were unapologetically commercial, with Brooks covering his idol Billy Joel and Twain teaming with husband John Mutt Lange, the architect behind such arena-rockers as Def Leppard and AC/DC. Not surprisingly, there was a reaction to this, much like there was a reaction to the slick pop/rock of the '70s. First, there were the new traditionalists, a legion of musicians that loved straightforward honky tonk—a group that Garth actually was associated with at the beginning. More importantly, there were the alt-country refugees, musicians enamored with Gram Parsons, Hank Williams, Neil Young, the Carter Family, Johnny Cash, and Merle Haggard in about equal measure. Most of these artists didn't seem, and weren't classified as, country to begin with, since they were aesthetically closer to many underground rockers of the pre-Nirvana early '90s. But, as the '90s wore on, alt-country, or Americana as it was often called, became a vital genre of its own, supporting its own magazines (the excellent *No Depression*) and filled with artists that were either more forward-looking than mainstream country, or backwards-looking—and always more adventurous. Then, there were the factions that devoted themselves to the steady stream of reissues of classic country. Unlike rock, this never was a deluge (unless you count the tidal waves of comprehensive box sets from Bear Family), since country reissues unfortunately did not sell in mass numbers. Such is the curse of a music that thrives on popular songs, where the tunes themselves become classics, not the albums they're featured on.

All this makes the task of the collector, and the guide that helps them, a little more difficult. There are artists that made great albums that you simply can't find on record in the store. Many contemporary artists can only deliver a song or two on each record and are in desperate need of a hits compilation. Then, there are titans and movers and shakers, such as Wynn Stewart, who only have gargantuan multi-disc boxes on the market. It's hard to know where to start, even for the fan that knows all the names. This section helps sort through the multitude of deluxe and budget-line compilations on the market, pointing the way to classic proper albums wherever possible. It may not be complete, but it gives the neophyte a roadmap, while providing fascinating detours for the dedicated. There's a lot to discover and cherish in country music, and much of it is highlighted here. *—Stephen Thomas Erlewine*

Country Styles

BAKERSFIELD SOUND— Bakersfield was the first genre of country music to rely heavily on electric instrumentation, as well as a defined backbeat—in other words, it was the first to be significantly influenced by rock 'n' roll. Named after the town of Bakersfield, CA, where a great majority of the artists performed, the sound was pioneered by Wynn Stewart and popularized by Buck Owens and Merle Haggard. Using Telecaster guitars, the singers developed a clean, ringing sound that stood in direct opposition to the produced, string-laden Nashville sound. The Bakersfield sound became one of the most popular—and arguably the most influential—country genres of the '60s, setting the stage for country-rock and outlaw, as well as reviving the spirit of honky tonk.

CONTEMPORARY COUNTRY— Contemporary country followed the Urban Cowboy movement and preceded the rise of Garth Brooks. It incorporated subtle pop-production techniques, occasionally using synthesizers but always sounding slick and polished. At times, the country roots of contemporary country were fairly well-hidden beneath pop trappings, but new traditionalists like George Strait and Randy Travis also fit into the genre.

COUNTRY-FOLK— Country-folk is a hybrid of country music and folk. Generally, the music is based on acoustic guitars and is gentler than most country music. Also, country-folk is dominated by singer-songwriters who write and record their own material in the manner of most folk singer-songwriters.

COUNTRY-POP— Country-pop uses country instrumentation and song structures but adds a greater inclination toward pop melody on a lusher, more orchestrated production.

COWBOY— Cowboy songs include both traditional western songs and songs from western movies. Most of the songs are performed on acoustic guitars (though movie songs have much more elaborate instrumentation, frequently featuring orchestras) and are about Western themes.

HONKY TONK— Honky tonk is the most recognizable genre of country music. It's spare and direct, with acoustic guitars, steel guitars, fiddles, and a high, lonesome vocal. Ernest Tubb was the first honky tonk musician to popularize the genre, but Hank Williams, George Jones, and Lefty Frizzell became the definitive artists in the '50s.

NASHVILLE SOUND/COUNTRYPOLITAN— Countrypolitan, an outgrowth of the Nashville sound of the '50s, is among the most commercially-oriented genres of country music. The Nashville sound emerged in the '50s as a way to bring country music to a broad pop audience. The movement was led by Chet Atkins, who was the head of RCA Records country division. Atkins designed a smooth, commercial sound that relied on country song structures but abandoned all of the hillbilly and honky tonk instrumentation. He hired session musicians and coordinated pop-oriented, jazz-tinged productions. Similarly, Owen Bradley created productions—most notably with Patsy Cline—that featured sophisticated productions and smooth, textured instrumentation. Eventually, most records from Nashville featured this style of production and the Nashville sound began to incorporate strings and vocal choirs. In the late '60s, the Nashville Sound evolved into countrypolitan, which emphasized these kinds of pop production flourishes. Featuring layers of keyboards, guitars, strings, and vocals, countrypolitan records were designed to crossover to pop radio and they frequently did. The sound dominated the country charts in the '70s and stayed popular until the early '80s.

NEW TRADITIONALIST— New traditionalists refers to the legions of young country singers that emerged in the late '80s. These artists reworked and updated the classic sounds of honky tonk and traditional country, adding contemporary production touches to make it more commercially viable—even with the flourishes, the music was essentially hardcore country. After the first wave of new traditionalists (George Strait, Randy Travis, Dwight Yoakum), the genre became a bit slicker and demonstrated more overt rock influences, but the new traditionalists continued to dominate the country charts in one form or another until the mid-'90s.

OUTLAW COUNTRY— Outlaw country was one of the more significant trends in country music in the '70s. During that decade, many of the most popular hardcore country singers of the '60s— from George Jones to Merle Haggard—softened their sound slightly, moving away from their honky tonk roots. While the outlaws weren't strictly honky tonk—they were as much storytellers in the tradition of folk songwriters as they were honky tonk vocalists—they kept that spirit alive. Outlaws didn't play by Nashville's rules. They didn't change their music to fit the heavily-produced, pop-oriented Nashville sound, nor did they go out of their way to fit into the accepted conventions of country music. Instead, they created an edgy form of hardcore country that was influenced by rock 'n' roll, folk, and blues. Ironically, two of the leading figures of the movement—Waylon Jennings and Willie Nelson—had their roots in the music industry, but by the time they came into their own as recording artists in the mid-'70s, they had developed a unique, defiant way of performing. Several other musicians—including David Allan Coe, Billy Joe Shaver, and Tompall Glaser—followed in their footsteps, and the outlaws were quite popular for a period of three to four years. At the end of the '70s, the urban cowboy movement easily eclipsed the outlaw movement in terms of commercial appeal, but the outlaws had a lasting influence. During the '80s, certain neo-traditionalists owed a bit of their sound to the outlaws, while a whole breed of songwriters, led by Steve Earle, demonstrated a massive debt to the outlaws and their fusion of country, folk, and rock.

WESTERN SWING— Western swing was the most eclectic form of country music and in its free-wheeling diversity, it set the stage for rock 'n' roll. Based in traditional string band music, Western swing also incorporated traditional pop melodies, jazz improvisation, blues and folk, creating a wildly entertaining and eclectic form of American music. Bob Wills and Milton Brown popularized the genre in the '30s and Wills became known as the father of the genre, since he remained popular for several decades, and had a remarkable string of hit singles. Although it sometimes faded from view, Western swing remained popular throughout the 20th century, occasionally experiencing upswings in popularity, such as the early '70s and the early '90s.

Artist Reviews

Roy Acuff

b. Sep. 15, 1903, Maynardsville, TN, **d.** Nov. 23, 1992
Vocals, Violin, Harmonica / Honky Tonk, Traditional Country
Roy Acuff was called the King of Country Music, and for more than 60 years, he lived up to that title. If any performer embodied country music, it was Roy Acuff. Throughout his career, Acuff was a champion for traditional country values, enforcing his beliefs as a performer, a music publisher, and as the Grand Master of the Grand Ole Opry. Acuff was the first country music superstar after the death of Jimmie Rodgers, pioneering an influential vocal style that complimented the spare, simple songs he was performing. Generations of artists, from Hank Williams to George Jones have been influenced by Acuff, and countless others have paid respect to him. At the time of his death in 1992, he was still actively involved in the Grand Ole Opry, and was as popular as ever, that same year becoming the first living performer to be inducted to the Country Music Hall of Fame. Several months later, he passed away, leaving behind a legacy that isn't limited to his music. Through his records, his performances and his publishing company Acuff-Rose, Roy Acuff has had an enormous effect on shaping the role of country music in the 20th century; it is hard to imagine the music without him. *—Stephen Thomas Erlewine*

The Best of Roy Acuff [Capitol] / 1970 / Capitol ♦♦♦
Recorded when Acuff was in his fifties, *The Best of Roy Acuff* was a reissue of the 1955 *Songs of the Smoky Mountains*, repackaged and re-released in 1963 in the wake of his becoming the first living artist elected to the Country Music Hall of Fame. Whatever its title, *The Best of Roy Acuff* captures the "King of Country Music" still near his prime, covering his classic songs anew in a slower, more dignified, and, in many ways, equally satisfying phase of his career. The voice is more mellow, darker but also a bit richer, and the modern sound (straight, pure mono) helps some, especially because his backing band is really good. "Pins and Needles (In My Heart)" works better here, and "Wabash Cannonball" and "The Great Speckled Bird" are slowed down only marginally. Not one's first choice, and from a purely historical view certainly not one's only choice for an Acuff CD, but a good adjunct to the classic stuff on Columbia. Other songs include "Fire Ball Mail," "Night Train to Memphis," "The Wreck On the Highway," "I'm Building a Home," "This Precious Jewel," "The Great Titanic," and "Lonely Mound of Clay." *—Bruce Eder*

☆ **Steamboat Whistle Blues** / 1985 / Rounder ♦♦♦♦♦
Steamboat Whistle Blues makes a nice companion to Columbia's *The Essential Roy Acuff (1936-1949)*. The Rounder Records release contains late-'30s cuts by Acuff and his Crazy Tennesseeans (later the Smoky Mountain Boys) not found on the *Essential* collection and provides an excellent overview of Acuff's early and varied repertoire, including fiddle breakdown tunes ("Shout Oh Lulu), pop covers ("Yes Sir, That's My Baby"), countrified rags ("Smokey Mountain Rag"), and some mountain blues ("Honky Tonk Mamas"). There's also a fine example of Acuff's church-hymn style here in the endearing, "modern-day" gospel tune "The Automobile of Life." Crazy Tennesseeans and Smoky Mountain Boys alike (guitarist James Clell Summy and harmonica player Sam "Dynamite" Hatcher in particular) provide Acuff with rough-hewn yet tight backing on all the numbers. If you'd like a good record of Acuff's career before his star rose as both a Grand Ole Opry fixture and a country music publishing giant, then pick up a used copy (sorry, it's out of print) of *Steamboat Whistle Blues*. Listening to these great songs one can certainly understand how Acuff, along with Jimmie Rodgers and Hank Williams, have come to define what country music used to be. *—Stephen Cook*

★ **The Essential Roy Acuff (1936-1949)** / 1992 / Columbia/Legacy ♦♦♦♦♦
The Essential Roy Acuff (1936-1949) contains the original versions of "The Great Speckled Bird, " "Night Train to Memphis, " "The Precious Jewel, " and "Wabash Cannon Ball, " and 16 other tracks that were cut for Columbia Records at the peak of his recording career — *Stephen Thomas Erlewine*

King of Country Music (1936-1947) / Aug. 18, 1998 / ASV/Living Era ♦♦♦♦♦
King of Country Music is an affordably-priced import collection of some of Acuff's prime recordings, including three with the Crazy Tennesseans (before the Opry urged them to change their name to the Smoky Mountain Boys). 25 tracks from 1936-47 are presented in chronological order, including some of Acuff's signature songs: "Wabash Cannon Ball, " "Great Speckle Bird" and "The Streamlined Cannon Ball, " as well as several chart hits from the mid '40s. Offering a greater number of tracks than Columbia's *Historic Edition*, *The King of Country Music* provides a generous retrospective of Acuff's peak years. *—Greg Adams*

Trace Adkins

b. Jan. 13, 1962
Vocals, Guitar / New Traditionalist, Contemporary Country
With one foot in the honky tonks and the other planted squarely in a gospel-quartet background, Trace Adkins and his warm baritone gained fans of Nashville's new-traditional movement in the mid-'90s. Born on January 13, 1962, in the small Louisiana town of Sarepta, he grew up playing the guitar and listened to classic country, soul and rock & roll. After high school, Adkins enrolled at Louisiana Tech; he studied music and played football while there, but found himself on an offshore oil rig for several years after graduation. Adkins decided to get back into music and joined a gospel quartet named the New Commitments. He toured the region and recorded two albums with the group, but became a solo performer in the early '90s. Adkins began playing honky tonks throughout Tennessee and Texas, and later moved to Nashville to make it in the country music. At one gig, Capitol Nashville president Scott Hendricks approached him after a set and signed him to the label on the spot. Hendricks, the producer of Brooks & Dunn, Alan Jackson and Faith Hill, oversaw Trace Adkins' debut album *Dreamin' Out Loud*. Released in 1996, the album hit the Country Top 20, thanks to the number three single, "Every Light in the House Is On." *Big Time* followed in 1997, and in 1999, Adkins returned with *More*. *—John Bush*

● **Dreamin' Out Loud** / 1996 / Capitol ♦♦♦♦
Trace Adkins' debut *Dreamin' Out Loud* illustrates that he does indeed have a powerhouse voice, one that's big and strong and capable of handling both honky tonk and ballads. It's a voice that makes singers into stars, and his producers must have realized this. Unfortunately, they wanted to ensure that Adkins became a star, so they gave *Dreamin' Out Loud* a production that's a little too clean and songs that are a little too predictable, when it's clear that he is capable of so much more. Even so, *Dreamin' Out Loud* remains a satisfying debut. Adkins sings his heart out on even the lesser songs, and when he does have a good number ("That's a Bad Way of Saying Goodbye," "There's a Girl in Texas"), he sounds like one of the finest new traditionalists of the late '90s. *—Thom Owens*

Big Time / Oct. 21, 1997 / Capitol ♦♦♦
While Trace Adkins' second album, *Big Time*, isn't as consistently strong as his debut, *Dreamin' Out Loud*, it nevertheless establishes him a vocal talent. There are moments where the songwriting rings a little flat, but the best cuts on *Big Time*, such as the single "The Rest of Mine," are well-crafted contemporary country showcasing his booming baritone to fine effect. *—Thom Owens*

More / Nov. 2, 1999 / Capitol ♦♦♦♦

Alabama

f. 1977, Fort Payne, AL
Group / Urban Cowboy, Contemporary Country, Country-Pop, Country-Rock
Before Alabama, bands were usually relegated to a supporting role in country music. In the first part of the century, bands were popular with audiences across the country, but as recordings became available, nearly every popular recording artist was a vocalist, not a group. Alabama was the group that restored made country bands popular again. Emerging in the late '70s, the band had roots in both country and rock; in fact, many of their musical concepts, particularly the idea of a performing band, owed more to rock and pop than hardcore country. However, there is no denying that Alabama is a country band—their pop instincts may come from rock, but their harmonies, songwriting and approach are indebted to country, particularly the Bakersfield sound of Merle Haggard, bluegrass, and the sound of Nashville pop. Their sleek, country-rock sound made the group the most popular country group in history, selling more records than any other artist of the '80s and earning stacks of awards. *—Stephen Thomas Erlewine*

My Home's in Alabama / 1980 / RCA ♦♦♦♦♦
This is the album that started it all for Alabama. Their Southern rock influences are obvious but encased in a country context. The title track's sentiment is overwhelming, whether you're from Alabama or Iowa. *—Tom Roland*

Mountain Music / 1982 / RCA ♦♦♦♦♦
This is their best effort. The group hadn't quite fallen into any formulas, and as a result, they cover the stylistic gamut pretty well. The title track practically defined what country groups have strived to accomplish, and the group slides easily from sentiment, to social relevance, to out-and-out partying. *—Tom Roland*

The Closer You Get / 1983 / RCA ♦♦♦♦

Roll On / 1984 / RCA ♦♦♦
The title track and "If You're Gonna Play in Texas (You Gotta Have a Fiddle in the Band)" make this entertaining but slightly formulaic album worth pursuing. *—Stephen Thomas Erlewine*

40 Hour Week / 1985 / RCA ♦♦♦♦♦
Opening with the driving title track, *40 Hour Week* encapsulates why Alabama was the top country group of the '80s. Alternating between restrained rockers and well-crafted ballads, it captures the band at its peak. Nevertheless, it isn't quite as strong as their first albums—the performances and production are a bit too mannered—but its professionalism is appealing. And that professionalism made *40 Hour Week* the group's most popular album, as it crossed over into the pop Top Ten. *—Stephen Thomas Erlewine*

★ **Greatest Hits** / 1986 / RCA ♦♦♦♦♦
This batch of hits made them the most successful country act of the 1980s. More than the best available sampler of their much-imitated group sound, it also reflects state-of-the-art Nashville Sound the moment before Randy Travis hit. *—Dan Cooper*

Greatest Hits, Vol. 2 / 1991 / RCA ♦♦♦♦♦
Greatest Hits, Vol. 2 contains a 11-track cross-section of Alabama's hit singles from the mid- and late '80s, including the number one singles "Dixieland Delight," "Lady Down On Love," "The Closer You Get," "Roll On (Eighteen Wheeler)," "Fallin' Again," "Song of the South," "High Cotton," and "Take Me Down." On the, this second volume is even stronger than the first and represents some of the best mainstream rock-influenced country of the '80s. — *Thom Owens*

Greatest Hits, Vol. 3 / 1994 / RCA ♦♦♦♦♦
Like most country artists, Alabama made better singles than albums, rarely releasing a bad song for a single. Their third greatest hits compilation collects their biggest and best hits of the late '80s and early '90s—including "I'm In A Hurry (And Don't Know Why)," "Tennessee River," "Angels Among Us," and "When We Make Love" —, making it a worthwhile addition to a contemporary country library. *—Stephen Thomas Erlewine*

★ **For the Record** / Aug. 25, 1998 / RCA ♦♦♦♦♦
Even though the title should be taken with a grain of salt—an enormous number of these 44 songs did reach number one, but a handful only peaked at two or three—there's no denying that *For the Record: 41 Number One Hits* is an impressive achievements. Spanning two discs and two decades, *For the Record* contains nearly every great song Alabama recorded, plus three new tunes. If any single album provides definitive proof as to why Alabama is the most popular country band of all time, this is it—they make this appealingly polished, hook-heavy, radio-ready mainstream pop sound easy as pie. Alabama may have had a couple of

album cuts every now and then that were quite good, but they were at their best turning out hits as a singles band, as such contemporary classics as "Tennessee River," "Mountain Music," "The Closer You Get," "Forty Hour Week (For a Livin')," "Jukebox on My Mind" and "Down Home" illustrate. Consequently, it's hard not to view *For the Record*, with its virtual cornucopia of hits, as the definitive Alabama collection, maybe even the definitive Alabama album. *—Stephen Thomas Erlewine*

Rex Allen

b. Dec. 31, 1922, Wilcox, AZ, **d.** Dec. 1999
Vocals, Guitar / Cowboy
Better-known as the Arizona Cowboy, Rex Allen was the last of Hollywood's singing cowboys. Between 1950 and 1954, Allen starred in 19 movies for Republic studios. The films launched a popular recording career for Allen, as he had several hit singles and albums in the early '50s, before the singing cowboys slowly disappeared from the charts. After getting his start on Chicago's WLS National Barn Dance, Allen was one of the first country-western artists signed by Mercury. Success in Hollywood soon led to a hit record, 1951's "Sparrow in the Tree Top," though the biggest hit of his career, "Crying in the Chapel," came two years later. Besides appearing on the TV series *Frontier Doctor*, he recorded a few hits during the '60s for Mercury and Decca but was more prominent in this era as a narrator for Walt Disney films and cartoons. *—Stephen Thomas Erlewine*

Voice of the West / Aug. 1986 / Bear Family ♦♦♦♦
Voice of the West collects songs Rex Allen recorded in the early '70s with producer Jack Clement, who cut away the cinematic strings that dominated Allen's previous recordings. Instead, he leaves the singing cowboy with simple, straight-forward production that accentuates the western roots of his music. Not only does he play tradtional cowboy classics, he does a handful of contemporary country numbers. It might not have his classic hits, but *Voice of the West* gives a good sense of the scope of Allen's talents. *—Stephen Thomas Erlewine*

● **Lonesome Letter Blues** / Feb. 27, 1996 / Collectables ♦♦♦♦
Rex Allen cut these 12 sides in association with his friend Johnny Henderson in the early '60s (probably before "Don't Go Near the Indians") with producer E. J. Henke, and Collectables has them courtesy of Home Cooking Records. This is nice, slightly rough-hewn country-pop mixed with a little blues and traditional-sounding stuff, at its best a little more authentic than the kind of stuff that Roy Rogers or Jimmy Wakely did as solo recording acts. "Lonesome Letter Blues" shows off Allen's voice to best advantage and is a solid piece of country-blues; a few other numbers, such as Johnny Henderson's "The Bell in the Steeple," feature more elaborate vocal backing, with a pretty prominent chorus. Other notable songs include covers of Floyd Tillman's "I'll Keep on Lovin' You" (a great showcase for Allen's smoothest romantic baritone), "Cold Cold War," and "Gotta Have My Baby Back"; Johnny Bond's "Love Gone Cold"; plus a pair of surprisingly lively, almost rockin' little numbers, "Sure As Your Name's Kate" by Marty Robbins and a cover of "Sixteen Hundred Miles." The sound is good, and the notes are surprisingly honest in their sketchiness about these sessions. *—Bruce Eder*

Terry Allen

b. May 7, 1943, Wichita, KS
Vocals, Keyboards / Alternative Country, Country-Rock
There may be no greater maverick than Terry Allen in all of late-20th century country music. Along with Jimmie Dale Gilmore, Joe Ely, and Butch Hancock—all of whom he's known and collaborated with—Allen is a standardbearer of the Lubbock, Texas country scene. Though not widely heralded, this is perhaps the most progressive movement in all of contemporary country, digging into modern-day concerns with a gutsy, liberal perspective, while maintaining a firm musical grounding in regional country and folk traditions. Allen is perhaps the most ambitious of them all, writing complex song cycles that are performed with the help of fellow eclectics ranging from Lowell George to David Byrne.

Allen's audience, like those of the other Lubbock pioneers, is not the country mainstream. Indeed, his principal appeal may not lie with the country audience at all (though his music definitely *is* country), but with open-minded alternative folk and rock listeners. Unlike most current country artists, his words aim to question and confront hard day-to-day realities, rather than offer conservative cliches or maudlin comforts to shield listeners from those very day-to-day realities. He does so with a humor and irreverence that will also find little sympathy in Nashville or Middle America. *—Richie Unterberger*

● **Lubbock (On Everything)** / 1979 / Sugar Hill ♦♦♦♦♦
In the view of most critics this is Allen's definitive statement, examining mundane and eccentric small town lives with a sympathetic but penetrating wit that is rare in country music. The musical arrangements are much plainer than the ones Allen would craft on his much more recent *Human Remains*. Still, you won't find songs about a wolfman of Del Rio, a football star who ends up in the pen after a series of post-high school failures, or middle-aged women fighting fading beauty on many other country albums. *—Richie Unterberger*

Human Remains / Jan. 23, 1996 / Sugar Hill ♦♦♦♦♦
The conceptual scope of *Human Remains* is not nearly as ambitious as *Lubbock*. But the gutsier and more varied musical arrangements—crafted with help from Lloyd Maines, David Byrne, Joe Ely, Lucinda Williams, and many others—may make this a better introduction to Allen's world. There's certainly no shortage of interesting character sketches, like a one-legged dancing woman, memories of "flower children and their shit-eating grins," and 13-year-olds well on their way to reform school. "Gone To Texas" especially is a refreshing blast of true anti-establishment sentiment, Allen singing in even-mannered tones that he doesn't need a chickenshit (his term) business man telling him what to do, and dissing some country star who thinks that all it takes to be special is wear a hat and win Grammies. *—Richie Unterberger*

Smokin' the Dummy/Bloodlines / Apr. 22, 1997 / Sugar Hill ♦♦♦♦

Bill Anderson

b. Nov. 1, 1937, Columbia, SC
Vocals / Nashville Sound/Countrypolitan, Country-Pop, Traditional Country
Singer Bill Anderson was one of the most enduring and talented songwriters in country music. Born in South Carolina and raised in Georgia he began writing songs professionally while working as a disc jockey in Commerce, GA. He wrote "City Lights" in 1958, and it became a major hit for Ray Price. Later that year he had his own success with his debut single, "That's What It's Like to Be Lonesome."

Anderson came into his own during the 1960s when he had 24 hit songs on the national charts; among them was "Tips of My Fingers" (1960) and "Po Folks" (1961). He joined the *Grand Ole Opry* in 1961. He had his first number one country hit in 1962 with "Mama Sang a Song,". The next year he had a cross-over hit with "Still," which reached number one on the country charts and made it to the Top Ten on the pop charts. During the '60s, Anderson also hosted a syndicated music show.

During the 1970s, Anderson continued to find success with such hits as "Love Is a Sometimes Thing" (1970) and the number one "World of Make Believe" (1973). He also cut a series of popular duets that included the smash "For Loving You" with Jan Howard in 1967. He also became a successful television producer and hosted ABC's game show *The Better Sex;* he later appeared regularly on that network's soap opera *One Life to Live*. Throughout his long career, Anderson won scores of awards including 50 songwriting awards from BMI. In a *Billboard* magazine poll he was named one of the "Three Greatest Country Music Songwriters" and in 1975 was inducted into the Nashville Songwriters Hall of Fame. In addition to releasing new material throughout the 90's, Anderson continued to appear regularly on the *Grand Ole Opry* and tour with his band Po Folks. *—Sandra Brennan*

● **Bill Anderson's Greatest Hits** / 1967 / Varese Vintage ♦♦♦♦♦
Bill Anderson's Greatest Hits contains 18 of his biggest hits and best-known songs, including "Mama Sang a Song," "Still," "I Get the Fever," "My Life (Throw It Away If You Want To)," "The Corner of My Life," and "8 X 10." Compiled by Anderson himself, the compilation hits almost all of the highlights, and represents the first thorough retrospective assembled on the country-pop crooner during the CD era. *—Stephen Thomas Erlewine*

Greatest Hits, Vol. 2 / Oct. 7, 1997 / Varese ♦♦♦♦♦
Bill Anderson had a few more hits in him than his standard greatest-hits package on Decca would lead you to believe, and this second volume of country chart goodies from Varese Sarabande makes a nice bookend companion to its original volume. Highlights on this 15-track collection include "Walk Out Backwards," "For Loving You" (a number one duet with Jan Howard), "Happy State of Mind," "Quits," "World of Make Believe," "If You Can Live With It (I Can Live Without It)" and "Liars One, Believers Zero," Top Ten charters all. Whispering Bill's smooth style also works well in two duets with Mary Lou Turner, "That's What Made Me Love You" and "Sometimes." *—Cub Koda*

John Anderson

b. Dec. 12, 1955, Apopka, FL
Vocals, Guitar, Bass / New Traditionalist, Outlaw Country, Honky Tonk
Growing up in Apopka, Florida, John Anderson was enamored with the Beatles and the Rolling Stones, like most of his peers. But, when he heard a Merle Haggard album at age 15, he found his true calling. Anderson headed for Nashville, where he showed up unannounced on his sister's doorstep. He took low-paying club jobs in Music City's Printer's Alley for experience, and worked a variety of places for money in the early '70s. In one of those jobs, he actually helped do roofing on the Grand Ole Opry House, before its opening in 1974. Signed to Warner Brothers in the late '70s, Anderson's first album hit the streets in 1980, bringing with it critical acclaim for his attention to country tradition. Adding a vocal strain to the phrasing he picked up from Haggard and Lefty Frizzell, Anderson captured the Country Music Association's Horizon award for 1983, given to an artist who makes the most career progress. "Swingin'," which, at 1.4 million in sales, is the best-selling country single in Warner history, also reeled in the CMA's Single of the Year trophy. Unfortunately Anderson fell out of favor with country radio within two years and future albums failed to capitalize on his earlier momentum. *—Tom Roland*

John Anderson 2 / 1981 / Warner Brothers ♦♦♦♦♦
His second album (obviously), this traditionally minded package contrasted with the bulk of the material released in the same *Urban Cowboy*-influenced time period. His cover of Lefty Frizzell's "I Love You a Thousand Ways" shows his roots nicely, and "I'm Just an Old Chunk of Coal (But I'm Gonna Be a Diamond Someday)" is simply classic. *—Tom Roland*

Wild & Blue / 1982 / Warner Brothers ♦♦♦♦
The occasional use of strings in this album was probably master-minded by former Don Law protege Frank Jones, who co-produced it. Twin fiddles and steel guitar dominate, though, especially in a remake of Ferlin Husky's "The Waltz You Saved for Me," featuring Emmylou Harris. It includes "Swingin'" and a new version of Lefty Frizzell's "Long Black Veil"—the very last track recorded in the legendary Columbia Studio B. *—Tom Roland*

★ **Greatest Hits** / 1984 / Warner Brothers ♦♦♦♦♦
Greatest Hits covers John Anderson's biggest hits from the early '80s, including the Top Ten singles "I Just Came Home to Count the Memories," "She Sure Got Away With My Heart," "Chicken Truck," "1959," "Would You Catch a Falling Star," "I'm Just An Old Chunk of Coal (But I'm Gonna Be A Diamond Someday)" and the number one hits "Wild and Blue," "Swingin'," and "Black Sheep." *—Thom Owens*

Greatest Hits, Vol. 2 / 1990 / Warner Brothers ♦♦♦♦♦

Seminole Wind / 1992 / RCA ♦♦♦♦

Lynn Anderson

b. Sep. 26, 1947, Grand Forks, ND
Vocals / Nashville Sound/Countrypolitan, Country-Pop
Vocalist, songwriter, and guitarist Lynn Anderson is best remembered for her gigantic 1971 crossover hit "Rose Garden." She recorded her first single at the end of 1965 with Jerry Lane;

her first solo single, "In Person," followed in 1966, and a year later, Lawrence Welk invited her to become a regular on his show. Anderson was named Most Promising Female Vocalist in a *Cash Box* deejay poll, which led to her debuting at the Grand Ole Opry and releasing her first album, *Ride, Ride, Ride.* Recording for Chart until 1970, she cut over 100 songs; some of them, such as "Big Girls Don't Cry" (1968) and "That's a No-No," made it to the Top Ten. For Columbia, she released three singles before "Rose Garden," an international hit which topped both the country and pop charts. Anderson continued her affiliation with Columbia until 1981 and had numerous Top 10 hits; some of her tunes, such as "Even Cowboys Get the Blues" (1980), became country music standards. *— Sandra Brennan*

● **Golden Classics Edition** / Jul. 1, 1997 / Collectables ✦✦✦✦✦

Eddy Arnold

b. May 15, 1918, Madisonville, TN
Vocals, Guitar / Nashville Sound/Countrypolitan, Honky Tonk, Country-Pop, Cowboy, Traditional Country
Eddy Arnold moved hillbilly music to the city, creating a sleek sound that relied on his smooth voice and occasionally lush orchestrations. In the process, he became the most popular country performer of the century, spending more weeks at the top of the charts than any other artist. Arnold not only had 28 number one singles, he has more charting singles than any other artist. More than any other country performer of the post-war era, he was responsible for bringing the music to the masses, to people that wouldn't normally listen to country music. Arnold was initially influenced by cowboy singers like Gene Autry, but as his career progressed, he shaped his phrasing in the style of Pete Cassell. Nevertheless, he was more of a crooner than a hillbilly singer, which is a large reason why he was embraced by the entertainment industry at large, and frequently crossed over to the pop charts. Arnold's career ran strong into the '90s. Although his records didn't dominate the charts like they did during the '40s and '50s, he continued to fill concert halls and reissues of his older recordings sold well. *— Stephen Thomas Erlewine*

Cattle Call/Thereby Hangs a Tale / 1961-1963 / Bear Family ✦✦✦✦✦

★ **The Best of Eddy Arnold** / 1967 / RCA ✦✦✦✦✦
His smooth, lushly produced crossover hits upset the traditional crowd, but they represent some of the most romantic country recordings of the era. Featured is "Make the World Go Away, " "Anytime, " "Bouquet of Roses," "The Last Word in Lonesome Is Me, " and a re-recording of his classic "Cattle Call." *— Michael McCall*

The Best of Eddy Arnold, Vol. 2 / 1970 / DCC ✦✦✦✦✦
Best of Eddy Arnold, Vol. 2 collects a generous portion of Arnold hits not covered on the first volume, making it an ideal supplement for the casual fan who wants to dig a little deeper. *— Steve Huey*

Last of the Love Song Singers: Then & Now / 1993 / RCA ✦✦✦✦✦
The double-disc box set *Last of the Love Song Singers: Then and Now* is a wasted opportunity. The first disc, called *Then,* is a quick overview of some of Arnold's biggest hits that doesn't offer enough songs. The second disc, titled *Now,* is a collection of new recordings. Though they aren't bad, the new recordings devalue the set's worth as a retrospective and as an introduction. . *— Stephen Thomas Erlewine*

The Essential Eddy Arnold / Jun. 18, 1996 / RCA ✦✦✦✦✦
The Essential Eddy Arnold contains the majority of Eddy Arnold's biggest hits, including "Make the World Go Away" and "Cattle Call." It's the only single-disc retrospective that offers a reasonably thorough overview of his hit singles, making it an ideal introduction and—considering that the two-disc box set *Last of the Love Song Singers* contained an entire disc of newly recorded material—the only currently available retrospective that could be considered definitive. *— Thom Owens*

☆ **The Tennesse Plowboy & His Guitar** / Aug. 11, 1998 / Bear Family ✦✦✦✦✦
The 120 tracks on these five CDs constitute a group of Eddy Arnold songs with which few people under the age of 50 could be familiar—only about a half-dozen of them ever appeared on LP, much less CD. Recorded between 1944 and 1950, they represent his rise to country stardom (but not yet to pop stardom), and also the evolution of country music in the period immediately after the war. His performances on the early sides were heavily influenced by the work of Gene Autry, but they were much closer to hillbilly music, with thin, twangy guitars and fiddle. With the help of producer Steve Sholes, Arnold and his group (the Tennessee Plowboys) achieved a fine, lean sound that was a good compromise between hillbilly authenticity and commercial country music. Disc Two, covering 1947-48, shows Arnold consolidating his earlier success, and acquiring a greater range in the process. Disc Three shows Arnold's voice mellowing into the fine instrument that it became as he later emerged into pop stardom; his low range is richer, and he reaches those high notes more easily. This was all of a piece with making Arnold accessible to the widest possible audience; what no one realized at the time was that Arnold was helping to change country music in the process. While Disc Four shows Arnold moving toward an ever more mainstream sound, Disc Five has a number of religious songs that come off extremely well—largely due to the quality and sincerity of Arnold's singing. By this time, Arnold's voice had evolved into a wonderfully polished baritone, turning him into almost a countrified Bing Crosby. The sound is excellent, and the notes are extremely informative, although there is relatively little about the recording sessions themselves. The booklet is filled with wonderful photos as well. *— Bruce Eder*

Early Hits of "The Tennessee Plowboy" / Apr. 11, 2000 / ASV/Living Era ✦✦✦✦✦
An excellent entry in ASV's *Living Era* series, this brings together the 25 early hits of Eddy Arnold, when he earned his nickname of "The Tennessee Plowboy" honestly. This is Arnold before he went countrypolitan in the mid- to late '50s, with stripped-down instrumentation and him singing and yodeling his heart out. Indelibly stamped with Little Roy Wiggins' signature steel guitar, these tracks—cut between 1944 and 1949—reflect Eddy's breakthrough into the country & western scene, and show the five-year development of the music itself. If you've only heard Arnold's smoother, more pop influenced work, this set will come as a real eye-opener. *— Cub Koda*

Asleep at the Wheel

f. 1970, Paw Paw, WV
Group / Western Swing Revival, Neo-Traditionalist Country
The Western Swing revivalist band Asleep at the Wheel helped popularize the genre in the '70s and went on to enjoy an eclectic, freewheeling career which earned the group a dedicated following of both fans and critics. Over the course of their career, a number of musicians passed through the group—more than 80, to be precise—but throughout the years, the vision of vocalist/guitarist Ray Benson kept the band together. Their first album, *Comin' Right At Ya,* was released in 1973. In 1974, they had their first minor hit, a remake of Louis Jordan's "Choo Choo Ch'Boogie." *Texas Gold,* was Asleep At The Wheel's breakthrough, reaching the pop charts and spawning the hit single "The Letter That Johnny Walker Red." The album generated four more hits, and later that year they released *Wheelin' and Dealin'.* For the rest of the decade, Asleep At the Wheel was one of the most popular country artists in America; however, 1980's *Framed* was their last release for over half a decade. *Asleep at the Wheel 10,* the group's first album for Epic, was released in 1987 and became the hit they needed: the album launched several hit singles, including "House of Blue Lights," "Way Down Texas Way," and the Grammy-winning "String of Pars." Their next Epic album, *Western Standard Time,* came out in 1988 and led to a Grammy for the instrumental "Sugarfoot Rag." *— Sandra Brennan*

Asleep at the Wheel [Epic] / 1974 / Epic ✦✦✦
Texas guitarist and singer Ray Benson started this band in the early '70s as a "longhair" tribute to Bob Wills, and they've been swinging ever since. This is their first Epic album. *— Mark A. Humphrey*

Texas Gold / 1975 / Capitol ✦✦✦

Asleep at the Wheel [MCA] / 1985 / Dot ✦✦✦✦✦
Benson by now is revealing a romantic baritone as well as his usual sublime swing. Guest appearances come from Bonnie Raitt and Willie Nelson. *— Michael McCall*

Pasture Prime / 1985 / Stony Plain ✦✦✦✦

● **Live & Kickin': Greatest Hits** / Aug. 1991 / Arista ✦✦✦✦✦
Recorded at an Austin roadhouse, *Live and Kickin': Greatest Hits* showcases Asleep at the Wheel running through their best-known material in a kinetic live setting. It's a great introduction to the band—they are never better than they are in concert, and the selection brings out the best in the musicians. *— Stephen Thomas Erlewine*

The Best of Asleep at the Wheel / 1992 / CEMA Special Markets ✦✦✦✦✦
The Best of Asleep at the Wheel is a concise introduction to the group's early years, including their first hit "Choo Choo Ch'Boogie, " as well as favorites like "The Letter That Johnny Walker Read" and "Bump Bounce Boogie" which launched the band into the country mainstream during the mid-1970s and still sound fresh today. *— Jason Ankeny*

A Tribute to the Music of Bob Wills & the Texas Playboys / Oct. 25, 1993 / Liberty ✦✦✦✦✦
Benson and The Wheel invite a bus full of guests to pay homage to the King of Western Swing and do so with joyful, rollicking fun. Garth Brooks, Vince Gill, George Strait, Dolly Parton, Marty Stuart and Suzy Bogguss are among those enjoying themselves on this exemplary album. *— Michael McCall*

Ride with Bob / Aug. 10, 1999 / DreamWorks ✦✦✦✦

Chet Atkins

b. Jun. 20, 1924, Luttrell, TN, **d.** Jun. 30, 2001
Vocals, Guitar (Electric), Guitar, Fiddle, Producer, Arranger / Country Boogie, Instrumental Country, Nashville Sound/Countrypolitan, Country-Pop, Traditional Country
Without Chet Atkins, country music may never have crossed over into the pop charts in the '50s and '60s. Although he is an exceptionally talented guitarist with hundreds of solo records to his credit, Atkins' largest influence came as a session musician and a record producer. During the '50s and '60s, he helped create the Nashville sound, a style of country music that owed nearly as much to pop as it did to honky tonk.

Atkins became RCA's house guitarist for all Nashville sessions in 1949. While he worked for RCA, he played on many hit records, fashioning the lush Nashville sound. In 1953, he was made a consultant to RCA's Nashville division; that same year, he started to release solo instrumental albums. His first hit arrived in 1955, when "Mr. Sandman" charted, followed by "Silver Bell," a duet with Hank Snow. By the late '50s, Atkins's reputation was secure—not only did his records sell, but he designed guitars for Gibson and Gretsch. Atkins became the manager of RCA's Nashville division in 1957, as his performing career gained momentum; "Yakety Axe," his first Top 5 hit, arrived in 1965. During the '60s, he produced hits for the majority of RCA's Nashville acts, including Elvis Presley and Eddy Arnold, and discovered a wealth of talent, such as Don Gibson, Waylon Jennings, Charley Pride and Bobby Bare. Atkins His solo popularity faded in the early '70s and he turned to the Nashville String Band, a trio he formed with Homer and Jethro; they released five albums between 1970 and 1972. Atkins continued to record for RCA throughout the '70s. He left the label in 1982, signing with Columbia, where he released *Work It Out With Chet Atkins,* in 1983. During his time at Columbia, Atkins departed from his traditional country roots, concentrating on jazz instead. He returned to country on occasion, notably on duet albums with Mark Knopfler and Jerry Reed. During the '90s, he was relatively quiet, recording infrequently. *— Stephen Thomas Erlewine*

Stay Tuned / 1985 / Columbia ✦✦✦✦

Neck & Neck / Oct. 1990 / Columbia ✦✦✦✦

The RCA Years / Oct. 1992 / RCA ✦✦✦✦✦

Galloping Guitar: The Early Years / 1993 / Bear Family ✦✦✦✦✦
A wonderful multi-disc boxed set retrospective of Atkins's earliest recordings. Casual fans

will be surprised to hear that Chet was originally marketed as a vocalist/guitarist, much the same as then popular Merle Travis was on Capitol. His eventual move over to strict instrumentals doesn't come until the end of this box set, with guest vocalists flitting in and out of the picture, but Atkins's guitar is solid throughout. *— Cub Koda*

● **Guitar Legend: The RCA Years** / Apr. 4, 2000 / Buddha ✦✦✦✦✦
Considering the incredible amount of influence and prestige Chet Atkins has pumped into country music in the last 50 years, it's strange that there aren't more greatest-hits packages on the market of real value. While RCA's *Essential Chet Atkins* attempts the near-impossible task of condensing the guitarist's vast 30-year output onto a single disc, Bear Family's four-disc box is characteristically too exhaustive and expensive to be practical. With 50 tracks spanning from his first recordings in 1947 to the Nashville Guitar Quartet sessions 30 years later, the two-disc retrospective *Guitar Legend* is arguably the first affordable collection to paint a comprehensive picture. Despite the inclusion of a vocal track, "Tellin' My Troubles to My Old Guitar," the set is focused on the stylistic innovations Atkins brought to Travis-picking, and thus, country music. Each phase of his development is documented, with an emphasis on his classic early group recordings. His saccharine '60s output receives minor attention, as do his ventures into straight jazz, allowing plenty of room for his trademark fingerpicking to be heard without the strings and other excesses that tended to clutter his albums. Most of his hits are here, as well as a few tracks previously unissued in the U.S. *— Jim Smith*

Gene Autry

b. Sep. 29, 1907, Tioga Springs, TX, **d.** Oct. 2, 1998
Vocals, Guitar / Cowboy, Traditional Country
The biggest selling country & western singer of the middle of the century, Gene Autry was more than a musician. His music, coupled with his careers in movies and on radio and television, made him a part of the mythos that has made up the American identity for the past hundred years—John Wayne with a little bit of Sam Houston and Davy Crockett all rolled into one, with a great singing voice and an ear for music added on. He defined country music for two generations of listeners, and cowboy songs for much of this century, and American music for much of the world. He was country music's first genuine "multi-media" star, the best known country & western singer on records, in movies, on radio, and television from the early-'30s until the mid-'50s. His 300 songs cut between 1929 and 1964 include nine gold-record awards and one platinum record; his 93 movies saved one big chunk of the movie industry, delighted millions, and made millionaires of several producers (as well as Autry himself); his radio and television shows were even more popular and successful; and a number of his songs outside of the country & western field have become American pop-culture touchstones. *— Bruce Eder*

Columbia Historic Edition / 1982 / Columbia ✦✦✦✦
This 10-song low-mid-priced collection covers yet more Autry songs that aren't on the other budget Autry releases—and, like them, includes only minimal annotation. Originally released by the Vocalion, Okeh, Banner, and Columbia labels between 1935 and 1944, this would be a chunk of an Autry best-of set, featuring his cover of Bob Nolan's "Tumbling Tumbleweeds," the gentle western swing-styled "I'll Go Ridin' Down That Texas Trail," "Don't Fence Me In" (which is best-remembered today as the title of a Roy Rogers B-western), the ravishingly romantic "Amapola" (which makes "South of the Border" seem tepid), and the previously unreleased romantic ballad "There's A New Moon Over My Shoulder," one of the catchiest, bounciest, most well-played songs in Autry's output. In the absence of a complete Gene Autry set from Bear Family (which would require at least 8 CDs), it's worth springing for this collection, which was prepared with the assistance of the Country Music Foundation, along with the others. *— Bruce Eder*

★ **The Essential Gene Autry** / Aug. 18, 1992 / Columbia/Legacy ✦✦✦✦✦
This would be a perfect Autry collection but for the fact that it has only 18 songs, when there was room for about 25, and the producers evidently think that "South of the Border" and "Blueberry Hill" aren't "essential." But you do get "The Yellow Rose of Texas," "The Last Round-up," "Take Me Back To My Boots and Saddle," "The Call of the Canyon," "It Makes No Difference Now," "Deep In the Heart of Texas," "Tumbling Tumbleweeds" (featuring Jimmy Long and Smiley Burnette) and "Maria Elena," among others. And for a change, there are decent, detailed notes, though as soon as Bear Family gets around to it, their release will probably put all of these to shame. *— Bruce Eder*

● **Portrait of an Artist** / 1995 / Sound Exchange ✦✦✦✦✦
Now this is more like it: The notes still aren't much, but there are 22 songs here, including most of the best material of the existing budget collections, except for the early-'30s-focused *Back in the Saddle Again* (yet another, different, even more lively version of that song is present here), and a few odd items like "Buttons and Bows" that just aren't around elsewhere. The sound is about as good as it gets, and this would be the collection to go out and buy, except that it's a mail-order item from Time Warner on its Sound Exchange imprint, and, thus, you can't find it in stores, except maybe as a used item. And who would sell anything this goo *— Bruce Eder*

Blues Singer 1929-1931: Booger Rooger Saturday / Oct. 8, 1996 / Columbia/Legacy ✦✦✦✦✦
If your concept of a blues singer embraces the sound of country music singer Jimmie Rodgers, as well as a Muddy Waters sideman like Jimmy Rogers, then this collection will make perfect sense to you. This superlative collection of Autry's earliest recordings for various Columbia budget labels like Melotone, Banner, Velvet Tone, Diva, and Oriole cast the latter day cowboy hero in direct competition with Rodgers, sometimes recording covers of well known hits by the Singing Brakeman. While seven of the 23 tracks collected here are Rodgers tunes (and superlative covers they are, too), 10 of them are from Autry's pen, an indication that he not only had his own ideas to impart but had figured the game out early from a business standpoint as well. On the majority of tracks, Autry is only accompanied by his yodeling and his acoustic guitar, but the addition on certain tracks of Roy Smeck on steel guitar or banjo certainly spices things up while allowing Gene to play some nifty fills in tandem. The biggest surprise, of course, is how comfortable Autry sounds on all of this material, clearly enjoying himself while finding his own voice as the sessions progress toward his "cowboy singer" breakthrough, only a year away from the last of these recordings. Yes, Gene Autry sang the blues and was pretty good at it, too. A landmark in country music's history while clearly demonstrating the cross genre appeal of the blues as a musical form accessible to everyone. *— Cub Koda*

Sing Cowboy Sing: The Gene Autry Collection / Mar. 18, 1997 / Rhino ✦✦✦✦✦
Sing, Cowboy, Sing!: The Gene Autry Collection is a comprehensive overview of the most famous singing cowboy in Hollywood history. Spanning three CDs and 84 tracks, the box set contains every one of Autry's biggest hits, plus several unreleased cuts from his *Melody Ranch* radio show and a handful of rarities from his classic Columbia recordings. Though the set is far too exhaustive for the casual listenter, *Sing, Cowboy, Sing!* is a loving tribute to Autry, and it is worth the investment of any devoted fan. *— Stephen Thomas Erlewine*

Gene Autry with the Legendary Singing Groups of the West / Sep. 23, 1997 / Varese ✦✦✦✦✦
The companion to Autry's movie song collection works far better, opening with one of the most extraordinary team-ups of its kind, Gene Autry and Roy Rogers with the Sons of the Pioneers doing "Silent Trail." The use of dialogue elsewhere is a mistake, however, especially on "Wild and Wooley West," from *The Big Show,* which is too laden with support singers. Autry's work with the Cass County Boys on "Yours" and "That's My Home" is less than exceptional, though the Cass County Boys do well on their own "The Cowboy," "Cowboy Blues," and "Great Grandad"—in fact, this is a better showcase for them than it is for Autry or the Pioneers. Autry's collaboration with the Jimmy Wakely Trio (including Johnny Bond) is bright and distinctive, but his work with the Sons of the Pioneers on "Old Pinto" is wasted, as their harmonies don't come in until very late in the song. The sound is surprisingly good, given the age of the recordings, but this is primarily a release for serious fans. *— Bruce Eder*

Hoyt Axton

b. Mar. 25, 1938, Duncan, OK, **d.** Oct. 26, 1999, Victor, MT
Vocals, Guitar / Country-Pop, Traditional Country
Hoyt Axton enjoyed an amazingly diverse career as a songwriter, recording artist and movie actor. While rooted equally in the folk and country traditions, his pop smarts enabled him to land substantial hits with numerous artists; as a performer, Axton released a string of remarkably consistent albums featuring his warm baritone and wry, earthy lyrical style. Axton was inspired to become a songwriter and performer by his mother, herself a distinguished songwriter whose best work, "Heartbreak Hotel," was immortalized by Elvis Presley in 1956. He had his first real success in 1962 with "Greenback Dollar," a song he had co-written with Ken Ramsey. Though it didn't make much money for him, it did lead to his signing with Horizon Records. His debut album was *The Balladeer.* Axton didn't really hit it big until he began opening for the pop group Three Dog Night in 1969. When they recorded his song "Joy to the World," he found himself with a gigantic international crossover hit.. Axton first hit the charts in 1974 with two Top 10 tunes: "When the Morning Comes" and "Boney Fingers." He moved to MCA in 1977 where he produced one of his best albums, *Snowblind Friend.* He left the label to found his own Jeremiah Records in 1978. The following year, his *Rusty Old Halo* album produced two major hits, "Della and the Dealer" and the title track. *— Sandra Brennan and Rick Clark*

Saturday's Child / 1963 / Vee-Jay ✦✦

My Griffin Is Gone / 1969 / Edsel ✦✦✦
One of Axton's less interesting albums—though, considering the consistent quality of this fine songwriter's work, this shouldn't deter anyone interested in it. *— Jim Worbois*

Joy to the World / 1971 / Capitol ✦✦✦
Songwriter Hoyt Axton lets loose with a batch of original songs that have been heavily covered (resulting in hits) by artists as varied as Three Dog Night, Steppenwolf, and Waylon Jennings. Axton has a distinctive style which makes his original versions as interesting as the better-known covers. *— Jim Worbois*

Road Songs / 1977 / A&M ✦✦✦✦✦
Featuring instrumental support from James Burton and backing vocals from Linda Ronstadt, *Road Songs* has a good cross-section of Axton's best-known songs, including "Boney Fingers" and "The No-No Song," making it a good introduction to the songwriter. *— Stephen Thomas Erlewine*

Snowblind Friend / 1977 / Edsel ✦✦✦

● **The A&M Years** / 1998 / A&M ✦✦✦✦✦
The A&M Years is a U.K. import that collects Hoyt Axton's four albums for the label—*Less Than the Song, Life Machine, Southbound,* and *Fearless*—on two CDs. This period of Axton's career (1973-1976) is often considered his peak as a recording artist, and some of his best-known performances are here, including "Boney Fingers," "When the Morning Comes," "Flash of Fire," and "Geronimo's Cadillac." This package marks the only appearance of his classic A&M material on CD; for some, that may justify its high import price (which, in reality, is no more expensive than these four albums would cost if they'd been reissued domestically on individual CDs). *— Greg Adams*

Moe Bandy

b. Feb. 12, 1944, Meridan, MS
Vocals, Guitar / Honky Tonk, Contemporary Country, Traditional Country
Moe Bandyhad a series of hits in the late '70s that elevated him to the front rank of modern honky tonk vocalists, while making him one of the most popular singers of his era. Bandy's songs never strayed far from the traditional bar-room fare yet he delivered them with warmth and a knowing sense of humor that gave them character. Bandy released his first record, "Lonely Lady," on the Texas independent label Satin Records in 1964. It re-

ceived little attention, yet Bandy continued to perform. Nearly 10 years later, the self-financed "I Just Started Hatin' Cheatin' Songs Today" became his first hit. Footprint Records only made 500 copies for distribution in Texas in 1973, but the record took off. GRC released the record nationally, and it went into the country Top 20. Bandy released several more singles on GRC, including the Top 10 hits "It Was So Easy to Find an Unhappy Woman" (1974) and "Bandy the Rodeo Clown" (1975). Bandy signed with Columbia Records in 1975 and his star continued to rise during the next few years, reaching a peak in 1979. That year, he not only had two solo hits ("I Cheated Me Right Out of Her," "Barstool Mountain"), but he had a successful duet with Janie Fricke ("It's a Cheatin' Situation"), while *Just Good Ole Boys*, the record he recorded with Joe Stampley, became one of the year's most popular albums. Bandy regularly charted in the Top 20 during the first half of the '80s, both as a solo act and with various duet partners. He signed with MCA/Curb in 1986, abandoning longtime collaborator Ray Baker for Jerry Kennedy in the process. Appropriately, the sound of the singer's records changed as well, turning slicker and pop-oriented. For a brief time, Bandy continued to have Top Ten hits, yet as his music became smoother, he lost his mass audience. In 1991, he opened the Moe Bandy Americana Theatre in Branson, MO. He spent much of the '90s performing there, recording only occasionally. *—Stephen Thomas Erlewine*

★ **Honky Tonk Amnesia: The Best of Moe Bandy** / Feb. 20, 1996 / Razor & Tie ✦✦✦✦✦
Honky Tonk Amnesia is the first comprehensive collection of Moe Bandy's career, featuring all of his biggest hits on Columbia, plus a couple of his his duets with Joe Stampley. Bandy's strength is his conviction—at his best, he was a straightahead, no-frills honky tonker and there is nothing but his best on this disc. It's the essential Bandy album. *—Stephen Thomas Erlewine*

Bobby Bare

b. Apr. 7, 1935, Ironton, OH
Vocals, Guitar / Nashville Sound/Countrypolitan, Country-Folk, Progressive Country, Traditional Country
Bobby Bare fought to secure control of his own recordings years before Waylon Jennings and Willie Nelson pulled their outlaw coup, and, after Johnny Cash, he was among the first country artists to look at the album as a thematic collection rather than simply a hodgepodge of hits and throwaway tunes. In the 1960s, he concentrated on folk-tinged country, and in the 1970s he mixed novelty songs, rowdy honky tonkers and casual working-class tributes. He helped Waylon Jennings secure his first record deal, and was among the first to champion such singer/songwriters as Kris Kristofferson, Billy Joe Shaver, Guy Clark, Townes Van Zandt, Shel Silverstein and Rodney Crowell. His low-key, laidback personality may be one of the reasons he hasn't received the recognition he deserves. *—Michael McCall*

Sings Lullabys, Legends & Lies / 1973 / Bear Family ✦✦✦
This two-album set features 14 Shel Silverstein songs, all performed in a room of rowdy friends who sing along and comment when the mood strikes. *—Michael McCall*

Cowboys & Daddys / 1975 / RCA ✦✦✦✦✦
Instead of singing about outlaws and rhinestone cowboys, Bare's songs speak of the struggles and joys of those who truly make their home on the range. *—Michael McCall*

Sleeper Wherever I Fall / 1978 / Columbia ✦✦✦
Some of Bare's best albums barely registered on the radio charts, but they're rich in unusual songs and distinct performances. Selections here include a cover of The Rolling Stones' "The Last Time" and a Rodney Crowell gem, "On a Real Good Night." *—Michael McCall*

Mercury Years / 1987 / Bear Family ✦✦✦✦✦
Bear Family has issued Bobby Bare's entire recordings for Mercury on a three-disc box set. Bare was only at Mercury for two years, but that time did produce a handful of his finest singles, including "How I Got to Memphis," "Please Don't Tell Me How the Story Ends," and "Come Sundown," a duet with Kris Kristofferson. Though the music is quite good, the set remains of interest only to completists, since there is simply too much music for casual listeners. Nevertheless, it's a necessary purchase for devoted Bare fans. *—Stephen Thomas Erlewine*

All-American Boy / 1994 / Bear Family ✦✦✦✦✦
The four-disc box set *The All-American Boy* contains all of Bobby Bare's RCA recordings between 1962 and 1970, including the Top 10 hits "Detroit City," "500 Miles Away from Home," "Miller's Cave," "Four Strong Winds," "A Dear John Letter," "It's Alright," "The Streets of Baltimore," "The Game of Triangles" and "(Margie's At) The Lincoln Park Inn." In addition to all of the master recordings, the set also includes several alternate takes, unreleased tracks, incomplete takes, duets and rarities. Certainly, box sets that are this comprehensive only appeal to dedicated fans, yet *The All-American Boy* is more listenable than the average all-encompassing Bear Family release because Bare's RCA recordings were of consistently high quality. Of course, that doesn't mean casual fans should purchase the set—it means that the set is worthwhile for serious fans. *—Thom Owens*

★ **The Best of Bobby Bare** / 1994 / Razor & Tie ✦✦✦✦✦
The 21-track, single-disc collection *The Best of Bobby Bare* offers the first comprehensive overview of his big hits from the '60s and early '70s, including "Detroit City, " "The Long Black Veil, " and "500 Miles from Home." Featuring nearly all of his essential tracks, the disc is a near-definitive retrospective, and a perfect introduction to Bare's music. *—Stephen Thomas Erlewine*

Essential / Jan. 28, 1997 / RCA ✦✦✦✦✦
Like all the other volumes of RCA's *Essential* series, *The Essential Bobby Bare* contains a cross-section of Bare's hits, lesser-known singles, rarities and album tracks. Though it is a useful and entertaining collection, Razor & Tie's compilation remains a more definitive retrospective. *—Thom Owens*

Mandy Barnett

b. Sep. 28, 1975, Crossville, TN
Vocals / Neo-Traditionalist Country, Contemporary Country
Born Amanda Carol Barnett, Mandy Barnett began singing as a child, winning the Best Country Act at Dollywood when she was only ten, and her mother started bringing her on trips to Nashville. As a teenager, she was signed by renowned talent scout and producer Jimmy Bowen, and eventually Asylum Records. An uncompromising singer whose style was rooted in the classic country of Patsy Cline, Jim Reeves, Webb Pierce and Brenda Lee, Barnett's keen interpretive sense enabled her to delve into a song, study the intricacies of its emotional content, and render a powerful performance through her full-bodied voice. Her torchy delivery on her contemporary, yet retro-sounding, country and pop-tinged material recalled Patsy Cline; it's no wonder then that while waiting to record her self-titled debut, she paid her bills by playing the legendary singer four nights a week and 26 weeks a year in the musical production *Always... Patsy Cline* at the Ryman Auditorium. She left Asylum for Sire Records with 1999's *I've Got a Right to Cry*. *—Jack Leaver*

Mandy Barnett / 1996 / Elektra/Asylum ✦✦✦✦✦
Tennessee native Mandy Barnett has already been busy bringing Patsy Cline back to life by playing (and singing the songs of) the rowdy, legendary vocalist in the stage production *Always... Patsy Cline*. Now Barnett, who's not yet even 21 years old, has taken that experience and used it to power her self-titled debut album for Asylum Records. Cline's influence is out front on Barnett's handling of Willie Nelson's 1962 classic "Three Days" and the brand-new Kostas/Richard Bennett song "I'll Just Pretend." The downside of Barnett's album is that the production tends toward clean and safe territory (such as the overabundance of strings on the syrupy "Rainy Days"). The upside is that, even during her album's most middle-of-the-road moments, Barnett's voice remains strong, smooth, and confident. And a few of the songs shine with real promise—Barnett's delicate handling of Jim Lauderdale's "Planet of Love," for example, and the traditional "Wayfaring Stranger," which closes the album on a comfortable, unhurried note. *—Kurt Wolff*

Traveller Songs / 1997 / Asylum ✦✦✦✦✦
While Mandy Barnett may not exactly be a household name, her Asylum Records debut is one of the finest country-pop records to come out of the 1990s. Producer Andy Paley (the Paley Brothers, Brian Wilson) frames Barnett's exquisite vocals with subtle and emotional backings that truly spotlight her wonderful, Patsy Cline-influenced vocals. The record contains an excellent cover of "Dream Lover," revisiting the classic with a new country dimension that sounds as if it was originally written for Barnett. *—Matthew Greenwald*

● **I've Got a Right to Cry** / Apr. 13, 1999 / Sire ✦✦✦✦✦
If ever there was a singer who was born to sing the torch and twang style that Patsy Cline created, it is Mandy Barnett. A soft-spoken performer who belts 'em out with all the guts and grit of the founding mothers of traditional country music, Barnett is amazing. Producer Owen Bradley, a legend himself, is known for his classic production style for country music's true stars like Cline, Bill Monroe, Ernest Tubb and Brenda Lee. Working at his studio, Barnett was given the kind of support an artist of her caliber deserves. However, Owen Bradley passed away suddenly during the course of production, leaving the project unfinished. Barnett, along with Owen's brother and longtime partner Harold, as well as Harold's son Bobby, forged ahead; the result is a lasting and honorable tribute to Owen Bradley's distinguished career, as well as the harbinger of a great career about to blossom.

Songs as traditional as the title cut and as jazz-infused as "Who" show off Barnett's talents. Able to rip and roar with the boys, Barnett distinguishes herself on the pure honky tonk of "Trademark" while being very cool as she performs "Falling, Falling, Falling." Barnett pays homage to Cline on "Mistakes" and swings hard on "Don't Forget to Cry." A remarkable feat in the face of Owen Bradley's passing, Mandy Barnett is most certainly one of the few women recording as a country artist who can actually sing country music. She does so with flair and with a sense of history, while still being firmly grounded in who she is and the music she wants to make. *I've Got a Right to Cry* is lush and breathtaking, fulfilling the promise of the country & western genre and providing the listener great satisfaction. *—Jana Pendragon*

The Bellamy Brothers

f. 1958, Darby, FL
Vocals / Contemporary Country, Country-Pop, Country-Rock
Although the Bellamy Brothers are the most successful duo in country music history, they have never been favored by the critics. That doesn't mean their music was rote, by-the-books formulaic country pop. More than most acts of the late '70s and '80s, the Bellamys pushed the borders of country music, adding strong elements of rock, reggae, and even rap. Nearly a decade after their first hit—the 1975 pop chart-topper, southern-rock tinged "Let Your Love Flow"—the brothers had earned a stack of best-selling records, as well as critical respect came by the late '80s. By that time, they had firmly established themselves as the top duo of the '80s, both in terms of popularity and musical diversity. They may not have sustained their popularity throughout the '90s, yet they continued to perform and record (on their own label, Bellamy Brothers Records), to a faithful fan base. *—Stephen Thomas Erlewine*

● **Greatest Hits** / 1982 / MCA ✦✦✦✦✦
This contains such hits as "Dancin' Cowboys, " "Redneck Girl, " "Let Your Love Flow, " "Lovers Live Longer, " and others. *—AMG*

Greatest Hits, Vol. 2 / Sep. 5, 1995 / Curb ✦✦✦✦✦
Picking up where the first installment left off, *Greatest Hits, Vol. 2* captures the Bellamy Brothers maturing, both in terms of music and message. *Greatest Hits, Vol. 2* collects ten of their biggest singles—including "Feelin' the Feelin'," "When I'm Away From You," "I Need More of You," "Old Hippie," "Lie to You for Your Love," and "Too Much Is Not Enough"—all of which hit the charts between 1982 and 1986. The production and arrangements on these songs borrow from soft rock and folk-rock, taking away most of the duo's country edge. Of course, this is what their fans wanted to hear and these singles dominated the charts during the '80s. *—Thom Owens*

Matraca Berg

b. 1964, Nashville, TN
Vocals / Contemporary Country, Country-Pop
The daughter of country songwriter and session singer Icee Berg, Matraca Berg has written songs for Reba McEntire ("The Last One to Know"), Suzy Bogguss ("Hey Cinderella"), Trisha Yearwood ("Wrong Side of Memphis") and Pam Tillis ("Calico Plains"). Matraca got her start while still a teen, when her mother took her to several music publishing houses. At Tree Publishing, Berg met and teamed up with Bobby Braddock. Their first song, "Faking Love," became a number one hit in 1983 for T.G. Sheppard and Karen Brooks. She then became a keyboardist for the rock-oriented Kevin Stewart Band. Two years later, Berg returned to Nashville and continued to write songs, but never considered singing them herself until 1990, when she released her first album, *Lying to the Moon*, which spawned the Top 40 single "Baby, Walk On." The following year, four more singles from the album made respectable showings on the chart. RCA Nashville refused her second album, so the songwriter moved to the label's pop music division, releasing *Bittersweet Surrender* in 1991 and *The Speed of Grace* in 1993. *—Sandra Brennan*

The Speed of Grace / Nov. 1993 / RCA ✦✦✦

Sunday Morning to Saturday Night / Sep. 23, 1997 / Rising Tide ✦✦✦✦✦

● **Lying to the Moon & Other Stories** / Aug. 10, 1999 / RCA ✦✦✦✦✦
Joe Galante at RCA was the moving force behind this reissue of Berg's splendid RCA debut album "Lying to the Moon," recorded in 1990. Berg has added several new tunes to the original tracks, resulting in a sort of hybrid re-release that recalls old favorites while introducing some outstanding new material. Berg is one of the premier tunesmiths in Nashville, having authored hits for the likes of Deana Carter, Reba McEntire, Pam Tillis, and Suzy Bogguss. Berg is, however, quite capable of delivering her own material in a convincing fashion. As the listener will hear, these aren't just cool tunes; they're cool tunes performed by a pretty cool singer. Special moments include the elemental blues of "I Got It Bad," the melancholy, mountain soul of "Appalachian Rain," the marvelous rollercoaster metaphor of "Along for the Ride," the witty, easy-going groove of "Eat at Joe's," and the sexual semantics of "Back in the Saddle." This is a welcome reincarnation of an excellent album from an artist whose level of talent is way beyond her level of recognition. *—Philip Van Vleck*

John Berry

b. Sep. 14, 1959, Aiken, SC
Vocals / Contemporary Country
Country artist John Berry was born in South Carolina but raised in Atlanta, Georgia. Before signing to Liberty Records, he released a few solo albums; his 1993 eponymous major-label debut featured the Top 30 song "Kiss Me in the Car." In 1994, a hectic tour schedule was interrupted when Berry underwent brain surgery to remove a cyst. On the same day of the surgery, his single "Your Love Amazes Me" hit number one on the country charts. Berry's next album, *Standing on the Edge*, appeared in 1995, as did a Christmas album, *O Holy Night*. *Faces* followed in 1996, with *Crazy for the Girl* appearing a year later. In 1998, he returned with *Better Than a Biscuit*, followed a year later by *Wildest Dreams* and *My Heart is in Bethlehem* in fall 2000. *—Sandra Brennan*

John Berry / Jun. 7, 1993 / Liberty ✦✦✦

Saddle the Wind / Nov. 15, 1994 / EMI-Capitol Special Markets ✦✦✦✦

Standing on the Edge / 1995 / Patriot/Liberty ✦✦✦✦

Faces / Sep. 17, 1996 / Capitol ✦✦✦

Better Than a Biscuit / Sep. 8, 1998 / Capitol Nashville ✦✦✦

● **Greatest Hits** / Mar. 28, 2000 / Capitol ✦✦✦✦

Clint Black

b. 1962, Long Branch, NJ
Vocals, Harmonica, Guitar / New Traditionalist, Contemporary Country
A country music traditionalist from Texas, Clint Black was one of the first artists to kick-start the mass-market popularity of country in the '90s. Black also is one of the first artists of a generation that was equally inspired by rock-oriented pop—like '70s singer/songwriters and '60s rock & roll—as well as country artists like Merle Haggard, Bob Wills, and George Jones. He offered a shiny, marketable version of traditional country and in the process, paved the way for a new generation of country artists, particularly Garth Brooks. After Brooks broke through into the pop mainstream, Black's career began to fade somewhat, but he remained one of the most popular and acclaimed vocalists of the '90s. *—Stephen Thomas Erlewine*

☆ **Killin' Time** / 1989 / RCA ✦✦✦✦✦
Black's accessible brand of Texas country burned up the charts upon its release, selling two million copies and yielding the hit singles "Better Man," "Killin' Time," "Nobody's Home," and "Walkin' Away," and "Nothing's News." *—Brian Mansfield*

Put Yourself in My Shoes / 1990 / RCA ✦✦✦
Put Yourself in My Shoes never approaches the perfection of Black's debut, but it still produced a number of singles, including "Put Yourself in My Shoes," "Loving Blind," "Where Are You Now," and "This Nightlife." *—Brian Mansfield*

The Hard Way / 1992 / RCA ✦✦✦✦✦
Back to form, Black put some of his most exciting singles on his third album. "We Tell Ourselves" rocked without resorting to Southern boogie, and "When My Ship Comes In" contained a masterful chorus. The album also included the hit "Burn One Down." *—Brian Mansfield*

No Time to Kill / Jul. 1993 / RCA ✦✦✦
Black's albums seems to alternate between the remarkable and the merely pretty good. *No Time to Kill*, which plays off the title of his first album, is one of the latter. All of this is acceptable, though little matches quality of the title track. Black does a duet with Wynonna Judd called "A Bad Goodbye." *—Brian Mansfield*

One Emotion / 1994 / RCA ✦✦✦
One Emotion continued Clint Black's streak of uneven albums, featuring a handful of exemplary tracks, including the Merle Haggard collaboration "Untanglin' My Mind," but just as many mediocre songs, like "You Made Me Feel," which was writen with Michael McDonald. Nothing on *One Emotion* is particularly bad, but it doesn't sound like Black is pushing himself into new territories, either. *—Stephen Thomas Erlewine*

★ **Greatest Hits** / Sep. 24, 1996 / RCA ✦✦✦✦✦
Clint Black's 16-song *Greatest Hits* is a comprehensive collection, featuring eight number one hits—including "Killing Time," "Where Are You Now," and "Nobody's Home"—four additional hits, plus four new songs ("Like the Rain," "Half Way Up," "Cadillac Jack Favor," and a live version of the Eagles' "Desperado"). Though the collection is missing a handful of essential tracks, it still provides a convincing argument that Clint Black was one of the finest new traditionalist singers of the early '90s. *—Stephen Thomas Erlewine*

Nothin' but the Taillights / Jul. 29, 1997 / RCA ✦✦✦

D'Lectrified / Sep. 28, 1999 / RCA ✦✦✦✦✦

Blackhawk

f. 1992
Group / Contemporary Country
Comprised of a trio of seasoned professional musicians, Blackhawk became one of the most successful new country groups of the mid-'90s, scoring a string of Top 10 hits from their first two albums. Featuring Henry Paul (lead vocals, mandolin), Van Stephenson (guitar, vocals), and Dave Robbins (keyboards, vocals), the band formed in the early '90s, releasing their first single, "Goodbye Says It All," on Arista Records in late 1993. "Goodbye Says It All" sailed to number one, quickly followed in 1994 by the number two "Every Once In A While," the number nine "I Sure Can Smell the Rain," the number 10 "Wherever You Go" and their eponymous debut album, which would eventually go platinum. *Strong Enough*, Blackhawk's second album, was released in the fall of 1995 and was equally successful, spawning the hit singles "I'm Not Strong Enough to Say No," "Like There Ain't No Yesterday," "Almost A Memory Now," and "King of the World." *Love & Gravity* followed in 1997, with *The Sky's the Limit* appearing a year later. After just four albums, Blackhawk issued its first hits collection in mid-2000. *—Stephen Thomas Erlewine*

Blackhawk / 1994 / Arista ✦✦✦

Strong Enough / Sep. 12, 1995 / Arista ✦✦✦✦✦

Love & Gravity / Jul. 29, 1997 / Arista ✦✦✦✦

The Sky's the Limit / Sep. 29, 1998 / Arista ✦✦✦✦

● **Greatest Hits** / May 16, 2000 / Arista ✦✦✦✦
How appropriate for a greatest hits album to begin with a song that was such a huge hit that it made the band a household name. In this case, *Goodbye Says It All*, Blackhawk's very first release, lands at the top spot. This *Greatest Hits* album plays like a career retrospective and tribute to co-founder, collaborator, and friend, Van Stephenson who not only fought but won a battle against melanoma and decided to leave the road in favor of spending time with his family. Fans will go nuts for all the oldies but goodies on this fine compilation: "I'm Not Strong Enough to Say No," "Every Once in a While," "Almost a Memory Now," and eight memorable others. *Greatest Hits* introduces three new songs, including the very last song on the album, "Ships of Heaven," written by Stephenson while he was facing his continually declining health. Those songs represent more than just new music; they represent the future of Blackhawk without Stephenson. And the future looks pretty bright. *—Maria Konicki*

Suzy Bogguss

b. Dec. 30, 1956, Aledo, IL
Vocals / New Traditionalist, Contemporary Country, Country-Pop
Early in his career, Earl Thomas Conley's music picked up the label "thinking man's country." An accurate description—Conley looks into the heart and soul of his characters, finding the motivations for their actions and beliefs. In the process, the astute listener can find fragments of him/herself in nearly any Conley creation. Born into poverty in Portsmouth, Ohio, Conley struggled with the limits of his social class. He aspired to be a painter or actor but found that his aspirations for music lingered after the other interests died down. Influenced by everything from Hank Williams to the Eagles, Conley delved into the details of writing, trying to learn the craft by following the rules and regulations of the Music Row songwriting community. Eventually, torn by the limits of the "law," he found his own niche by breaking many of those same rules. His public self-analysis—in both his songs and his interviews—has proven inspirational to some, bothersome to others, but Conley has evolved stylistically, even though the thinking-man label continues to follow him. He's admittedly chased a more commercial sound, with a certain degree of success, but the run for the dollars also put him into a financial bind. He spent part of the late '80s and early '90s overworking himself to pay off his debts. Although he has been a hitmaker for more than a decade, his contributions to country have often gone almost unnoticed. *—Tom Roland*

★ **Somewhere Between** / 1988 / Liberty ✦✦✦✦✦
A fabulous, truly surprising debut, this album firmly plants one foot in the past and the other in the Nashville mainstream. The best songs here come from country legends. Merle Haggard penned the powerhouse title cut "My Sweet Love Ain't Around" came from Hank Williams, and "I Want To Be a Cowboy's Sweetheart" was an old Patsy Montana tune. The new stuff was pretty danged good, too: "Cross My Heart," written by Verlon Thompson and Kye Fleming, was the album's highest-charting single. *—Brian Mansfield*

Moment of Truth / 1990 / Liberty ✦✦✦
Under the wing of producer and new label-head Jimmy Bowen, Bogguss relinquished her cow-

boy's sweetheart role and began recording more polished records that often burnished singer/songwriter material. This album didn't do so well, though: it produced only two weakly performing singles, "Under the Gun" and "All Things Made New Again." *—Brian Mansfield*

Aces / 1991 / Liberty ✦✦✦✦✦

Voices in the Wind / 1992 / Liberty ✦✦✦
This sounded like one of those white-bread pop albums folks occasionally try to pawn off as country—until you started listening to the lyrics. *Voices in the Wind* may have been bigger on string sections than twin fiddlers, but Bogguss' choice in covers remained just off-center enough to be exciting, with Cheryl Wheeler's "Don't Wanna" and Lowell George's "Heartache." She revived John Hiatt's "Drive South" for a hit. The more risky material—especially the bleary-eyed blues of "Eat at Joe's" and the troubled alcoholic haze of Bogguss' own "In the Day"—shows why the Country Music Association gave her its Horizon Award just before the release of this album. *—Brian Mansfield*

Somethin' up My Sleeve / Sep. 13, 1993 / Liberty ✦✦✦

Greatest Hits / Mar. 8, 1994 / Liberty ✦✦✦✦
Capping off the first wave of her career, this compilation spotlights Suzy Bogguss' clear, emotive voice on adult contemporary-flavored ballads ("Letting Go"), plucky country ("Outbound Plane"), and even yodeling odes to the rodeo ("I Want to Be a Cowboy's Sweetheart"). Her strengths have always been her consummate vocals and strong material, and this album shows both off to their fullest extent. "Aces" covers the dynamics of a friendship taxed by success; "Drive South" is sexy and carefree; and only Bogguss could make lyrics like "he loves his damned old rodeo/as much as he loves me" swooningly romantic in "Someday Soon." But as much territory as this covers, letting every facet of her talent shine, this is a compilation of a talent in growth, only hinting at what she has. *—Bryan Buss*

Simpatico / Oct. 1994 / Liberty ✦✦✦
Simpatico is a laidback, charming duet album with Chet Atkins. The duo covers a lot of ground, beginning with Jimmie Rogers's "In the Jailhouse Now," and running through Elton John's "Sorry Seems to Be the Hardest Word," and playing a couple of nice, understated originals. Although it isn't a strict country record—there's quite a bit of pop flourishes scattered throughout the record—it's a charmingly low-key listen. *—Stephen Thomas Erlewine*

Give Me Some Wheels / Jul. 23, 1996 / Liberty ✦✦✦

Nobody Love, Nobody Gets Hurt / Jun. 2, 1998 / Liberty ✦✦✦

Suzy Bogguss / 1999 / Platinum ✦✦✦

Boxcar Willie (Lecil Travis Martin)

b. Sep. 1, 1931, Sterret, TX, **d.** Apr. 12, 1999
Vocals, Guitar / Country Comedy, Traditional Country
Boxcar Willie is perhaps the most successful invented character in the history of country music. With his kitschy persona and stage act—highlighted by his amazingly accurate impersonation of a train whistle—Willie played into the stereotype of the loveable, good-natured hobo that spent his life riding the rails and singing songs. Since his popularity had more to do with his image than his music, it makes sense that he was massively successful in England, where he personified Americana. Willie's English success carried him over to American success in the early '80s, where he ironically was perceived as carrying the torch for traditional country, because he kept the stereotypes alive. Initially, Boxcar Willie wasn't very successful, but he had a lucky break in 1976 when he was called in to replace a sick George Jones at a Nashville club. During that performance, he was spotted by Drew Taylor, a Scottish booking agent. Taylor brought Boxcar Willie over to England for a tour, where he was enthusiastically received. Later that year, he released his first album which was a moderate success in the U.K. Through the rest of the '70s, Willie toured Britain and every tour was more successful, culminating in a performance at the International Country Music Festival at Wembley in 1979. After his Wembley show was finished, he received a standing ovation—the performance established Boxcar Willie as a star. By the end of 1980, Willie had become the most successful country artist in England and his American success had just begun. *—Stephen Thomas Erlewine*

● **The Collection** / 1987 / Castle ✦✦✦✦✦
Castle's *The Collection* is the best Boxcar Willie compilation ever assembled, featuring his signature hit, "Train Medley," as well as several other songs in a similar vein. Appropriately, *The Collection* was only released in England, the country that made Boxcar Willie famous. *—Stephen Thomas Erlewine*

King of the Road / Planet Entertainment ✦✦✦✦✦
King of the Road is the album that made Boxcar Willie famous. Advertised on English television, the record wound up climbing to number five on the U.K. charts, setting the stage for his breakthrough success in the United States and Canada. *King of the Road* consists of a number of traditional country songs, including "Wabash Cannonball," "San Antonio Rose," "You Are My Sunshine," "Mule Train," "Rolling in My Sweet Baby's Arms," and three Hank Williams songs, with a couple of cute originals thrown in for good measure. Although it doesn't have his signature song, "Train Medley," it remains his best album. *—Stephen Thomas Erlewine*

BR5-49

Group / Americana, Neo-Traditionalist Country, Alternative Country
Blending rock and country with a vigorous energy, BR5—49 became one of the most critically acclaimed country-rock bands of the mid-'90s. For the first half of the decade, the group carved out a dedicated following in Nashville's downtown district on Lower Broadway, playing for a variety of music fans, ranging from honky tonkers to punk rockers. Eventually, the group landed a record contract with Arista Records. Their first release was a live EP, appropriately called *Live at Robert's*, which was released in the spring of 1996. It was followed later that fall with an eponymous full-length record that was greeted with overwhelmingly positive reviews in both the country and rock press. In 1998, BR5-49 returned with *Big Backyard Beat Show; Coast to Coast* followed two years later. *—Stephen Thomas Erlewine*

Live at Robert's EP / 1996 / Arista ✦✦✦

● **BR5-49** / Sep. 17, 1996 / Arista ✦✦✦✦
BR5-49 carries through on the promise of their debut EP with their eponymous full-length album. The band slams together a variety of country styles, ranging from traditional ballads to edgy country-rock, and delivers them with a bracing energy that's one part honky tonk grit, one part rock & roll hell-raising. While the energy is impressive, what makes *BR5-49* an album worth returning to is the group's musicality. It's not just that they can play a variety of different styles and play them well, it's that they can fuse them together seamlessly. *—Thom Owens*

Big Backyard Beat Show / Jul. 14, 1998 / Arista ✦✦✦✦
When BR5-49 was first signed by a Nashville major, eyebrows were raised on both sides of the country music border. Traditionalists wondered how and what it would cost the hillbilly boys who gained fame while playing in the window of Robert's Western Wear on Lower Broad in Music City. On the other side of the fence, the cats in the suits were shaking their heads, predicting that BR5-49 would be a short-lived novelty act. With some moderate success, no thanks to country-pop radio, and several years on the road, BR5-49 has endured. This, their third release, shows a maturing quintet ready to come into their own. With their integrity intact, the boys have learned a thing or two about writing songs, and display their own material proudly. Sandwiched between a Buck Owens' cover, "There Goes My Love" and ending with Billy Joe Shaver's forever powerful, "Georgia on a Fast Train," Gary Bennett and Chuck Mead provide the band with some worthy tunes. "Storybook Endings (If You Stop Believin')," "My Name Is Mudd," "You Are Never Nice to Me" and "Change the Way I Look" all score big. "Goodbye Maria" is the band's effective salute to the Tex-Mex sound of C&W music. They even present listeners with a fast-moving truck drivin' song, "18 Wheels and a Crowbar."

With Don Herron's magnificent musicanship providing steel, fiddle, dobro, mandolin and almost anything else that is required, BR5-49 deserve more than just a modicum of respect for hanging in there despite predictions. If the infinitely listenable *Big Backyard Beat Show* is any indication of their future, they should be around for a long time. *—Jana Pendragon*

Coast To Coast / Apr. 2000 / Arista ✦✦✦✦

Brooks & Dunn

Group / New Traditionalist, Contemporary Country, Country-Pop
Kix Brooks and Ronnie Dunn were the most popular country duo since the Judds and, in the process, became one of the biggest country artists of the '90s. Their music ran from hard-edged honky-tonk to radio-ready contemporary ballads. The duo met through a Nashville publishing firm, and began not only writing together, but also performing. DuBois was pleased by the new duo and offered them a recording contract. The two started out with a bang in 1990 when their debut single "Brand New Man" hit number one, as did their follow up "My Next Broken Heart." In 1992, they had a double-sided number one hit with "Neon Moon" and the flip-side "Boot Scootin' Boogie," the latter their biggest hit to date. By 1993, their first album had gone triple platinum; that same year, they also released their second album *Hard Workin' Man*, and their string of hits continued. In 1996, they released their fourth album *Borderline* and had a major hit with their cover of B.W. Stevenson's old pop hit "My Maria" (one of the few hits they did not write). *If You See Her* followed in 1998. *—Sandra Brennan*

Brand New Man / 1991 / Arista ✦✦✦✦✦
The title tale of love and redemption was a classic single for all the same reasons that made this would-be modern cowboy duo such a winner: tightly constructed choruses; a perfect balance between romance, macho swagger, and Wild-West imagery; and bracing harmonies that'll clear the trail dust out of your throat quicker than a shot of good whiskey. Four singles from *Brand New Man* topped the country charts: the title tune, "My Next Broken Heart, " "Neon Moon" and "Boot Scootin' Boogie." *—Brian Mansfield*

Hard Workin' Man / 1993 / Arista ✦✦✦
As with most second albums, the successful traits started to isolate themselves on *Hard Workin' Man:* Macho stuff like "Hard Workin' Man" and "Rock My World (Little Country Girl)" rocked harder than anything on *Brand New Man*, though BD made sure their women came off as good as they did (catch the "and women too" tag on "Hard Workin' Man"). The slower songs ("That Ain't No Way to Go," "She Used to Be Mine") tended toward the sort of evocative images that ran all through the debut. The pair never put all the elements together they way they did the first time, but they came close enough that few people noticed. *—Brian Mansfield*

Waitin' on Sundown / Sep. 27, 1994 / Arista ✦✦✦
Waitin' On Sundown didn't depart from Brooks & Dunn's formula much, but the fans didn't mind—it sold over three million albums anyway. By this point, the duo's albums have become a handful of solid singles—this time out, they were "Little Miss Honky Tonk," "She's Not the Cheatin' Kind," and "You're Gonna Miss Me When I'm Gone"—surrounded by filler, but the hits will make the fans forgive the filler. *—Thom Owens*

Borderline / Apr. 1996 / Arista ✦✦

● **Greatest Hits** / Sep. 16, 1997 / Arista ✦✦✦✦✦
Greatest Hits is a thorough overview of one of the most popular country acts of the '90s, containing 11 of Brooks & Dunn's biggest hits—including "Brand New Man," "My Next Broken Heart," "Boot Scootin' Boogie" and "She Used to Be Mine"—plus three new songs which are nearly as good as their older hits. It's an excellent summation of the first part of their career, and an ideal place to become acquainted with the duo. *—Thom Owens*

If You See Her / Jun. 2, 1998 / Arista ✦✦✦

Tight Rope / Sep. 14, 1999 / Arista ✦✦✦
Seven is a lucky number for Brooks & Dunn. The seven-time winners of duo awards from

the Country Music Association and the Academy of Country Music have bestowed on listeners their seventh album (including *The Greatest Hits Collection*.) As always, 12 of *Tight Rope's* 13 songs were written by the duo (six by Kix and six by Ronnie), but what adds to the mix this time is the addition of producer Byron Gallimore (Tim McGraw, Faith Hill, and Jodee Messina), who has stirred things up a bit with a more progressive, technical edge and new-sounding instrumentation to some of the songs. And love is the predominant theme of this album with the longing lyrics of "Goin' Under Gettin' Over You, the sorrowful "Too Far This Time," and the can't-go-wrong re-release of John Waite's 1984 "Missing You." *—Maria Konicki*

Garth Brooks

b. Feb. 7, 1962, Tulsa, OK

Vocals, Guitar / New Traditionalist, Contemporary Country, Country-Pop

Garth Brooks is a pivotal figure in the history of country music, no matter how much some country purists would like to deny it. With his commercially savvy fusion of post-Merle Haggard country, honky tonk, post-folk-rock sensitive singer/songwriter sensibilities, and '70s arena-rock dramatics, Brooks brought country music to a new audience in the '90s—namely, a mass audience. Before Brooks, it was inconceivable for a country artist to sell a million copies. He shattered that barrier in 1991, when his second album, *No Fences*, began its chart domination and its follow-up, *Ropin' the Wind*, became the first country album to debut at the top of the pop charts; *No Fences* would eventually sell a record-shattering 13 million copies. After Garth, country music had successfully carved a permanent place for itself on the pop charts. In the process, it lost a lot of the traditionalism that had always been its hallmark, but that is precisely why Brooks is important. *—Stephen Thomas Erlewine*

Garth Brooks / Apr. 12, 1989 / Liberty ✦✦✦

On Garth Brooks's self-titled debut, his fusion of rock & roll and traditional country genres like honky tonk and Western swing was already fully formed, as was his gift for extended metaphors. One listen to his signature song and breakthrough hit, "The Dance," and proves that, which is why he broke away from the hat acts that he was initially grouped with. Nevertheless, *Garth Brooks* is the most straightforward of all of his albums—Brooks sticks with neo-traditional country on about half of the tracks. He sings traditional country quite well—"Not Counting You" is a particularly effective honky tonk number, demonstrating a debt to both George Jones and George Strait—but what makes the album an exciting debut are songs like the genre-bending ballads "The Dance" and "If Tomorrow Never Comes," and that is the style that brought him mass success with his next album, *No Fences*. *—Stephen Thomas Erlewine*

☆ **No Fences** / Aug. 27, 1990 / Liberty ✦✦✦✦✦

Essentially, Garth Brooks's second album *No Fences* follows the same pattern as his debut album, but it is a more assured and risky record. Brooks still performs neo-traditional country, such as the honky tonk hit "Friends in Low Places," but now he twists it around with clever pop hooks. Those pop/rock influences are most apparent on the ballads, which alternate between sensitive folk-rock and power-ballad bombast. But what made *No Fences* such a success is how seamlessly he blends the two seemingly opposing genres, and how he chose a set of material that makes his genre-bending sound subtle and natural. Of course, it doesn't hurt that the songs are consistently entertaining, either. *—Stephen Thomas Erlewine*

☆ **Ropin' the Wind** / Sep. 1991 / Liberty ✦✦✦✦✦

With *Ropin' the Wind*, Garth Brooks began to make his '70s rock influences more explicit. Naturally, that was most notable in his reworking of Billy Joel's "Shameless," which he transformed from a rock power ballad into contemporary country. But that influence is also evident on ambitious epics like "The River" and even the honky tonk ravers of "Papa Loved Mama" and "Rodeo." Some might say that those rock influences are what made Brooks a crossover success, but he wouldn't have been nearly as successful if he didn't have a tangible country foundation to his music—even when he comes close to standard arena rock bombast, there a gritty steel guitars or vocal inflections that prove he is trying to expand country's vocabulary, not trying to exploit it. *—Stephen Thomas Erlewine*

The Chase / Oct. 1992 / Liberty ✦✦✦✦

The Chase is Garth Brooks' most ambitious and personal album. Not coincidentally, it is one of his least popular releases, selling about half of what the previous *Ropin' the Wind*. But in its own way, *The Chase* is more rewarding and deeper than *Ropin' the Wind*. That's partially due to Brooks' naked ambition—not only does he record "We Shall Be Free" with a gospel choir, but he tackles deeper social and personal issues than he has before. However, the true key to the album is Garth's conviction—even when his musical experiments don't quite work, it's easy to admire and respect his ambition. Although there are light moments like "Night Rider's Lament" and a cover of Little Feat's "Dixie Chicken," *The Chase* is a more sombre, reflective record than his previous three albums, but given a bit of a time, it's as satisfying as anything he's ever recorded. *—Stephen Thomas Erlewine*

In Pieces / Aug. 23, 1993 / Liberty ✦✦✦✦

After the relative commercial disappointment of *The Chase*, Garth Brooks toned down his experimental eclecticism on *In Pieces*. Alternating between heavily rock-influenced numbers, dramatic ballads, and revamped honky tonk, *In Pieces* appeals to the audience that found *The Chase* too pretentious and overly serious. That doesn't mean Brooks abandoned his desire to bend the rules—he's just masked his more ambitious material with crowd-pleasing uptempo numbers like "American Honky-Tonk Bar Association" and "Ain't Going Down (Til the Sun Comes Up)." *In Pieces* is an album that was made for the fans, and it shows—it is one of Brooks' most energetic and exciting collections. *—Stephen Thomas Erlewine*

★ **The Hits** / 1994 / Liberty ✦✦✦✦✦

The Hits is exactly what it says it is—18 of Garth Brooks's biggest hits, including his first 14 number one singles. Although he has good album tracks on each of his records, this is the essential Garth Brooks album—it gives a good sense of the singer's talents, especially his under-appreciated eclecticism. *The Hits* was only in print for a year, but it sold in excess of eight million copies, so it could hardly be called a limited edition. *—Stephen Thomas Erlewine*

Fresh Horses / Nov. 21, 1995 / Capitol Nashville ✦✦✦

Sevens / Nov. 25, 1997 / Capitol ✦✦✦

Double Live / Nov. 17, 1998 / Capitol ✦✦✦

In the Life of Chris Gaines / Sep. 28, 1999 / Capitol ✦✦✦

When his popularity reached a plateau in the late '90s, Garth Brooks knew it was time to try something new, deciding to *become* somebody new: Chris Gaines, a brooding, leather-clad rock star. When Brooks' new persona and his album was revealed to the public, they were unforgiving—they didn't think that he was playing a role, they simply though he'd lost his mind. Granted, the story behind Chris Gaines—both the invented biography and the reasons why Brooks decided to become Gaines—is more interesting than the record itself. Instead encapsulating mainstream pop from the mid-'80s through the end of the '90s, thereby sounding like a true "greatest hits," it's basically the state of adult pop at the close of the '90s. Essentially, the record is anchored in the acoustic balladry Babyface constructed for Eric Clapton's "Change the World," with little touches of Mellencamp rock, lite Prince funk, and Beatlesque pop-craft. While the tunes might not have much flair, they're all sturdy, whether it's the silky ballad "Lost in You," the self-conscious Beatles tribute "Maybe," the folky "It Don't Matter to the Sun," or the Wallflowers-styled "Unsigned Letter." Judged as Brooks' first pop album, it's pretty good, and if it had been released that way, it likely would have been embraced by a wide audience. As it stands, it's an album more fascinating for what it is than for the music itself. *—Stephen Thomas Erlewine*

Jim Ed Brown (James Edward Brown)

b. Mar. 1, 1934, Sparkman, AR

Vocals / Nashville Sound/Countrypolitan, Honky Tonk, Traditional Country

Jim Ed Brown came to fame as a member of the '50s vocal group the Browns, where he was the band's lead male vocalist. In 1965, when the group was still together, he embarked on a solo career that would eventually eclipse the success of the Browns. He began his solo run in 1965, two years before the Browns disbanded. Once the Browns disbanded, Brown began to have more substantial hits, beginning with the Top 20 single "You Can Have Her" and capped off by the number three beer-drinking anthem "Pop A Top." Brown didn't return to the upper reaches of the charts again until 1970, when "Morning" hit number four. A pair of Top 10 hits followed in 1973, though Brown had his greatest success in the late '70s, when he regularly dueted with Helen Cornelius. The duo had six Top 10 hits between 1976 and 1980, including their debut single, "I Don't Want to Have to Marry You," which hit number one in 1976. After the duo broke up, Jim Ed Brown pretty much retired from recording. He made an occasional appearance on the Grand Ole Opry, hosted a few TV game shows and opened his own theater near Opryland. *—Stephen Thomas Erlewine*

● **The Jim Ed Brown & the Browns** / Jan. 30, 1996 / RCA ✦✦✦✦✦

Since this set features none of Brown's duets with Cornelius, it must be assumed that there is a compilation in the works based solely on that aspect of his career. As for this set, it opens with three mellow Jim & Maxine hits, including the 1956 smash "Looking Back To See." There are four songs by the Browns, including the dreamy ballad "Send Me The Pillow You Dream On." The remainder of the album is devoted to Brown's solo material. While he was smooth, Brown could lay down a good honky tonk too, as on "Pop A Top," "Southern Loving" and "Barroom Pals And Goodtime Gals." Also included is his slick, finger-popping read of "You Can Have Her." "Bottle, Bottle" is an ode to drinking his pain away: "You give me the strength to go on day to day, you help keep the memories of a lost love away..." After calling it his crutch, he asks, "Bottle, bottle why do I love you so much—" There are also plenty of pretty love ballads to go around, such as "Gently Comes Love" and "You're The Part of Me." *—Bill Carpenter*

Anthology / Apr. 4, 2000 / Renaissance ✦✦✦✦✦

Jim Ed Brown & Helen Cornelius' *Anthology* collects many of their most memorable duets, including "I Don't Want to Marry You," "Saying Hello, Saying I Love You, Saying Goodbye," "You Don't Bring Me Flowers," "Don't Bother to Knock," and "One Man Woman, One Woman Man." A welcome retrospective of one of the '70s most popular country duos. *—Heather Phares*

Junior Brown

Slide Guitar, Vocals, Guitar (Steel), Guitar / Americana, Neo-Traditionalist Country, Alternative Country

A singer and demon guitarist whose raucous blend of country and rock & roll helped make him a successful crossover act, Junior Brown became a professional musician at the tail end of the 1960s, while still in his teens. After honing his guitar skills in relative anonymity throughout the 1970s, Brown became an instructor at the Hank Thompson School of Country Music, teaching under the auspices of steel guitar legend Leon McAuliffe, a onetime member of Bob Wills' Texas Playboys. A dream prompted Brown to set about creating an instrument fusing a six-string guitar with its steel counterpart. After contacting guitar maker Michael Stevens, in 1985 he developed the "guit-steel," a double-necked guitar combining the standard instrument with the steel. (A decade later, the two men reunited to update the "guit-steel," and Brown's cherry axe 'Big Red' was born.) After moving to Austin, Texas, Brown and his group became the house band at the city's Continental Club, where strong word-of-mouth eventually earned them a record deal. He made his long-awaited album debut in 1993 with *12 Shades of Brown*. *Guit With It* followed later in the year, and like its predecessor was met with consderable critical acclaim. *—Jason Ankeny*

12 Shades of Brown / 1989 / Curb ✦✦✦✦✦

Brown's debut deck shines like gold with standout original material like "They Don't Choose to Live That Way," "My Hillbilly Hula Gal" and "My Baby Don't Dance to Nothing but Ernest Tubb" being particular noteworthy. Possessing a voice that will curl the hair on the back of your neck while picking both single-string picking and slide stylings on his twin neck 'guit-steel,' this is a mighty-talented fella, neo-traditionalist or not. *—Cub Koda*

● **Guit with It** / Aug. 24, 1993 / Curb ✦✦✦✦✦
Junior Brown's rumbling, strikingly deep voice, tasty electric and steel guitar playing, and splendid honky-tonk and Western swing songs have made him a sensation in country circles. There's nothing phony or clichéd about Brown's music; this is the genuine, untutored, undiluted article. Brown can sing tunes requiring sincerity, ache or irony with equal flair. The CD's 12 cuts include the nearly 12-minute "Guit-Steel Blues," and a sharp cover of Hank Garland's "Sugarfoot Stomp," and the bittersweet "Doin' What Comes Easy to a Fool" and "Holding Pattern." Brown is as vital and refreshing as early John Anderson or Randy Travis. *—Ron Wynn*

Junior High / Jul. 18, 1995 / Curb ✦✦✦

Semi-Crazy / May 1996 / Curb ✦✦✦✦
On *Semi-Crazy,* Junior Brown's third full-length album, the suit-and-tied Texas singer's clever lyrics, Ernest Tubb-like voice, and virtuoso guitar playing (on his custom-made, double-necked "guit-steel," which allows him to switch quickly between picking and steel playing) are once again intact and on the mark. *Semi-Crazy* may not bowl Brown fans over immediately—he offers no new twists as either a writer or player. On the other hand, because Brown is one of country music's most stunning guitarists (imagine Ornette Coleman crossed with Speedy West)—not to mention possessing a truly original sound—it's hard not to fall for the classic Brown sound of "I Hung It Up" (a standout for the guitar work), "Gotta Get Up Every Morning," and the fun-loving title track (his duet partner, Red Simpson, penned Brown's earlier song "Highway Patrol"). *—Kurt Wolff*

Long Walk Back / Aug. 18, 1998 / Curb ✦✦✦✦
Just as much fun and as satisfying as he always is, Junior Brown once more gits gone with all the energy and punch that has come to be expected of this hardcore honky tonker. While the title cut is good, he really revs things up on the all-instrumental "Peelin' Taters" and "I'm All Fired Up." "Stupid Blues," "Just a Little Love" and "Read 'Em and Weep" display the interesting blend of Brown's own Texas swing/Bakersfield/honky tonk brand of country & western music. For a little spice, Junior adds a cover of the Elvis hit "Rock-A-Hula Baby" and the Hunter/Vincent tune "(I'm Just) Looking for Love." As always, Tanya Rae provides the complementary backing vocals that make the Brown sound so unique. One of traditional country music's favorite good ol' boys, Junior Brown hits the nail directly on the head once again. *—Jana Pendragon*

Milton Brown

b. Sep. 8, 1903, Stephenville, TX, **d.** Apr. 13, 1936, Crystal Springs, TX
Vocals / Western Swing
Milton Brown was one of the fathers of Western Swing, a vocalist and bandleader who was one of the first to fuse country, jazz, and pop together into a unique, distinctly American hybrid. Along with Bob Wills—who he performed with at the beginning of this career—Brown developed the sound and style of Western Swing in the early '30s and for a while he and his Musical Brownies were as popular as Wills and his Texas Playboys.

Brown joined Bob Wills' Fiddle Band as a vocalist in 1930, staying with the group as they evolved into the Light Crust Doughboys. Playing a diverse repertoire of jazz, blues, cowboy and pop songs, the Doughboys were one of the most popular bands in the Texas/Oklahoma area, but Brown left in September of 1932, following an argument with their manager. He formed the Musical Brownies, who were similar to the Doughboys but with a harder dance edge. Almost immediately, they were a huge success, drawing large crowds at Texas dances and playing regularly on KTAT radio. In April of 1934, the band recorded eight songs for Bluebird, followed by another ten four months later. Toward the end of 1934, the Brownies added steel guitarist Bob Dunn—the first musician to play an electric instrument in country music. The following January, the band recorded 36 songs for Decca. Released as singles during 1934, they established the band as Texas' most popular Western Swing band. The Brownies recorded about 50 new songs for Decca in March 1936; by this time, Cliff Bruner had become their fiddler. The next month, Brown suffered a major car accident, dying five days after the crash from pneumonia. Durwood Brown kept the Musical Brownies together for two years, recording a dozen sides for Decca in 1937. At the time of his death, Milton Brown rivaled Bob Wills in popularity. Although he never became as famous as Wills, he was equally important in the development of Western Swing—without him, the genre as we know it wouldn't exist. *—Stephen Thomas Erlewine*

★ **Pioneer Western Swing Band (1935-1936)** / Jan. 1935+Mar. 1936 / MCA ✦✦✦✦✦
This out of print LP from MCA's early-'80s *Collectables* series has been superceded by Texas Rose's complete reissuance of all of the recordings of Milton Brown and his Brownies on a five-CD set, but at the time it served as a good sampler of Brown's music. The singer, who led the first important Western swing band on record, heads an impressive octet (which also includes the fiddles of Cliff Bruner and Cecil Brower, the steel guitar of Bob Dunn, and banjoist Ocie Stockard) through a swing-oriented set. Two of the selections are from January 1935 while the other ten are taken from a marathon session in March 1936. Highlights of the spirited program include "The Sheik of Araby," "Yes Suh," "Hesitation Blues," "When I Take My Sugar to Tea," and "Easy Ridin' Papa." *—Scott Yanow*

☆ **Complete Recordings of the Father of Western Swing: 1932-1937** / 1996 / Texas Rose ✦✦✦✦✦
Singer Milton Brown led the first Western swing band, beating Bob Wills on record as a bandleader by one year. Milton Brown's Musical Brownies, which consisted of the leader/vocalist, guitarist Derwood Brown, violinist Cecil Brower, pianist Fred Calhoun, bassist Wanna Coffman, banjoist Ocie Stockard, and, in its later period, the steel guitar of Bob Dunn and violinist Cliff Bruner, could play swing, sentimental waltzes, country stomps, and novelties with equal skill. Cary Ginell, who wrote a definitive book on Brown, produced this masterful five-CD set which contains not only all 102 recordings by the Brownies (seven marathon sessions held during 1934-1936) but Milton Brown's two numbers with the Fort Worth Doughboys in 1932 (a unit that includes Bob Wills on fiddle), Derwood Brown's 1937 session with the Brownies after his brother Milton's death, and a couple numbers by Roy Lee Brown (one with a reunion band) in 1984 and 1987. Add to that an extensive 40-page booklet and this is certainly the one Milton Brown set to get. Essential music, available from the small Texas Rose label. *—Scott Yanow*

The Browns

f. 1955, **db.** 1967
Vocals / Nashville Sound/Countrypolitan, Traditional Country
During the '50s and '60s, the Browns offered up some of the finest harmonies in country music. The group was originally comprised of brother and sister Jim Ed Brown and Maxine Brown, and earned national recognition and a guest spot on Ernest Tubb's televison show for their novelty song "Looking Back to See," which hit the Top Ten and stayed on the charts throughout the summer of 1954. The Browns were then joined by younger sister Bonnie and by the end of 1955 had another Top Ten hit with "Here Today and Gone Tomorrow." *Ozark Jubilee* producer Sid Siman arranged for them to sign with RCA Victor in 1956, and soon afterward they had two major hits, "I Take the Chance" and "I Heard the Bluebirds Sing." They scored one of their biggest hits in 1959 with the inspirational, folk-oriented "The Three Bells," which not only spent ten weeks on top of the country charts, but also crossed over and spent four weeks at number one on the pop charts. As a result, the Browns remained in the folk mode for their two follow-up hits, "Scarlet Ribbons" and "The Old Lamplighter," both of which did extremely well on the country and pop charts. Their string of hits continued until 1961, when the national folk craze died out. *—Sandra Brennan*

Rockin' Rollin' Browns / Sep. 1984 / Bear Family ✦✦✦
The Browns didn't really rock or roll, so the title refers to the fact that the album consists of the group's more pop-oriented material, like "The Three Bells," "Buttons and Bows," and "Tobacco Road." Several tracks on the record are previously unreleased and most are album cuts, making the collection necessary only for serious fans that would rather sample from the group's extensive back catalog instead of listening to all of it. Casual fans would be better served with a greatest hits collection. *—Stephen Thomas Erlewine*

● **20 of the Best** / 1985 / RCA ✦✦✦✦✦
20 of the Best collects the great majority of the Browns' biggest hits. Even though it by-passes early hits like "Looking Back to See," "Here Today and Gone Tomorrow," "I Take the Chance," and "I Heard the Bluebirds Sing"—which were all recorded under the name Jim Edward, Maxine & Bonnie Brown (with the exception of "Looking Back to See," which was recorded without Bonnie)—the compilation is the only recent set to attempt a concise retrospective of the vocal group. *—Stephen Thomas Erlewine*

The Three Bells / 1993 / Bear Family ✦✦✦✦✦
Eight CDs and over 240 songs is overkill, except that there's a lot worth hearing here. Disc One opens in 1954 with Jim Ed and Maxine Brown's debut recordings for the Fabor label, including "Looking Back to See," which was successful enough to get them a touring slot with a young Elvis Presley. The sound, while primitive in comparison to their subsequent RCA recordings is very pleasing, with bright harmonies and simple, straightforward accompaniment. As soon as they got to RCA , their sound bloomed—the textures of the instruments became more vivid, with the "voices" of the guitars nearly as crisp as those of the singers themselves. By this time, they were one of country music's great mixed harmony groups, and were applying those vocal talents to bluesy numbers, as well as softer country and bluegrass material. "The Three Bells" was the massive hit that turned the trio toward pop material in 1959. Their repertory on Disc Three was broadening to include more overt folk material and pop standards. By the time of Disc Four, Hank Garland and John D. Loudermilk were playing most of the guitar, though Atkins was still producing, and the results remained impressive. Disc Five is dominated by a brace of inspirational tunes cut for their *Little Brown Church Hymnal* album, and also includes their cover of "They Call the Wind Maria," one of Jim Ed Brown's best performances. Disc Six is probably the only 1964-vintage archive to feature songs by Hank Snow and Bob Dylan coming from the same outfit. Discs Seven and Eight leave the group at the end of their time as a trio, prior to Bonnie's retirement late in 1967—highlights include a ton of beautifully sung country, pop, and folk numbers. *—Bruce Eder*

Ed Bruce

b. Dec. 29, 1939, Keiser, AR
Vocals / Outlaw Country, Rockabilly, Progressive Country, Traditional Country, Rock & Roll
Like so many other artists, singer Ed Bruce got his start as a rockabilly act for Memphis' famed Sun Records; however, he was probably best known for his songwriting acumen. He cut his first sides for Sun at the age of 17, but his career as a frenetic rockabilly performer was largely unsuccessful and by 1964 Bruce had moved to Nashville to become a member of the Marijohn Wilkins Singers. In 1966, he signed with RCA, notching his first chart hit with the single "Walker's Woods." More singles and a change of labels followed, but the singer struggled until 1975, when he took his composition "Mammas Don't Let Your Babies Grow Up to Be Cowboys" into the Top Twenty. The song, Bruce's best-known, was later a monster hit when covered by the duo of Waylon Jennings and Willie Nelson in 1977. Bruce achieved his greatest commericial success with MCA in the 1980s. "The Last Cowboy Song," featuring guest vocals from Willie Nelson, hit #12 in 1980; both "Girls, Women and Ladies" and "(When You Fall in Love) Everything's a Waltz" also fell just short of entering the Top Ten. In 1981, Bruce hit Number One with "You're the Best Break This Heart Ever Had; " other Top Five singles included "Ever, Never Lovin' You" (#4, 1982), "After All" (#4, 1983), "You Turn Me On (Like a Radio)" (#3, 1984) and "Nights" (#4, 1986). *—Jason Ankeny*

● **The Best of Ed Bruce** / 1995 / Varese Sarabande ✦✦✦✦✦
18 songs from 1975 to 1986, all but two of which were country hits, a half dozen making the Top Ten. Includes the original 1975 version of "Mammas Don't Let Your Babies Grow Up To Be Cowboys," a number one duet for Waylon Jennings and Willie Nelson a few years later; "The Last Cowboy Song," which features a guest vocal by Nelson, and the "Theme From Bret Maverick." *—Richie Unterberger*

Cliff Bruner

b. Apr. 25, 1915, Houston, TX, **d.** Aug. 25, 2000
Fiddle / Honky Tonk, Western Swing, Traditional Country
A jazz-influenced fiddler who found his greatest success in the 1930s, Cliff Bruner's place in country music history was assured thanks to his 1939 version of Ted Raffan's "Truck Driver's Blues," the first trucker song ever recorded. In 1934, Bruner joined the Western swing band Milton Brown and His Musical Brownies, cutting close to 50 songs with the group before Brown was killed in an auto accident in April 1936. Shortly thereafter, Bruner returned to Houston, where he formed a group called the Texas Wanderers which fused traditional and contemporary roots music with elements of 1920s and '30s pop and jazz. Included among the group's roster were the honky-tonk pianist Aubrey "Moon" Mullican and Bob Dunn, the creator of the amplified steel guitar. In 1938, the band released its biggest hit, a rendition of Floyd Tillman's "It Makes No Difference Now." While continuing to perform during and after World War II, Bruner's visibility began to slip, and by the early '50s he had left the music industry for a career selling insurance. *—Jason Ankeny*

★ **Cliff Bruner's Texas Wanderers** / 1983 / Texas Rose ✦✦✦✦✦
This is a fine compilation covering the years 1937-44. Beaucoups chops from the aformentioned Bruner, Dunn and Mullican, as well as Leo Raley, the first Western swinger to "plug in" a mandolin. *—Dan Cooper*

Cliff Bruner & His Texas Wanderers / Mar. 18, 1997 / Bear Family ✦✦✦✦✦
This five-CD set is the only extant collection by this legendary Western swing outfit. At $140 list, it's a hefty investment, but it's such solid music that it's difficult not to justify on the basis of quality. Disc One, covering sessions from 1937, is justified by the presence of the greatest version ever of "Milk Cow Blues," with a vocal by Leo Herbert Raley that will curl every hair you have; an awesome Western swing version of "You Got to Hi De Hi"; the bluesy, fiddle-driven "Can't Nobody Truck Like Me"; the smooth yet touching "Under the Silvery Moon"; and a trio of distinctive alternate takes of three of the best numbers here, only uncovered in 1997. Disc Two has even more of a freewheeling feel to it, and some of the best rags and dances ever cut by anybody. By the late 1939 sessions that open Disc Three, the group isn't as much of a blues band, no less lively but playing more straight dance material. Disc Four moves us into the 1940s, and topicality is reflected by the presence of the rollicking "Draft Board Blues," the disc also encompassing the extended periods of recording inactivity by the group, including a gap from 1941 and 1944, and then, again, until 1947. By this time, Bruner and his band were losing the edge that had made their earlier music such a delightfully intense listening experience. Their playing was as good as (and more polished than) ever, but as they moved into the late '40s and the dawn of the 1950s—covered on Disc Five—their overall sound lacked sharpness, although it was still eminently listenable. The notes and discography are both exceptionally detailed. *—Bruce Eder*

Jimmy Bryant

b. Mar. 5, 1925, Moultrie, GA, **d.** Sep. 22, 1980
Guitar / Instrumental Country, Traditional Country
With steel guitar wizard Speedy West, guitarist Jimmy Bryant formed half of the hottest country guitar duo of the 1950s. With lightning speed and jazz-fueled taste for improvisation and adventure, Bryant's boogies, polkas, and country swing—recorded with West and as a solo artist—remain among the most exciting instrumental country recordings of all time. Bryant also waxed major contributions to the early recordings of singers like Tennessee Ernie Ford, Merrill E. Moore, Kay Starr, Billy May, and Ella Mae Morse, and has influenced country guitarists like Buck Owens, James Burton, and Albert Lee. While he enjoyed a career that spanned several decades, it was his sessions with Capitol Records in the early '50s that allowed him his fullest freedom to strut his stuff. *—Richie Unterberger*

Country Cabin Jazz / 1960 / Capitol ✦✦✦✦✦
Featuring Speedy West on steel guitar and Billy Strange on rhythm, Bryant runs through a dozen swinging instrumentals with panache on this "country jam session." *—Richie Unterberger*

● **Guitar Take-Off** / 1989 / See For Miles ✦✦✦✦✦
Undisputably the best Bryant compilation. 20 tracks from 1951 to 1955, many taken from rare singles, and many also featuring Speedy West. Also includes cuts by Ella Mae Morse, Tennessee Ernie Ford, Merrill E. Moore, and Billy May that feature Jimmy as a sessionman. "Stratosphere Boogie" and "Catfish Boogie" are breathtaking Bryant/West duels. *—Richie Unterberger*

Tracy Byrd

b. Dec. 18, 1966, Vidor, TX
Vocals, Guitar / New Traditionalist, Contemporary Country
Singer/songwriter/guitarist Tracy Byrd was part of a movement of contemporary country performers trying to move away from the trend toward pop/country and back towards the more traditional sounds of the genre; his popularity seemed to show that many fans had similar feelings. He began his career in Beaumont, TX, in a rather odd way—he sang "Your Cheatin' Heart" in a shopping mall "recording studio," and the saleswoman was impressed enough to invite him to perform in a monthly amateur talent show. He then got a job playing with Mark Chesnutt at a nightclub in Beaumont. After Chesnutt became a success and hit the road, Byrd formed a new group, Only Way to Fly, which became the club's house band. Showcased in Nashville, he did a successful solo audition for MCA executives Bruce Hinton and Tony Brown. The first single from his self-titled debut, "That's the Thing About a Memory," made it to the charts as a minor hit in 1992. The next single, "Someone to Give My Love To," made the Top 50, but the third single, "Holdin' Heaven," climbed all the way to number one in 1993. Byrd released his second album, *No Ordinary Man*, in 1994; the single "Lifestyles of the Not So Rich and Famous" made the Top 20. *—Sandra Brennan*

Tracy Byrd / Apr. 27, 1993 / MCA ✦✦✦

No Ordinary Man / 1994 / MCA ✦✦✦✦✦
No Ordinary Man, Tracy Byrd's second album, was his breakthrough record and its easy to see why. While he was still sorting out the ins and outs of recording on his debut album, Byrd sounds raw, vibrant, and confident throughout *No Ordinary Man*, which is clear from the record's first single, "Lifestyles of the Not So Rich and Famous" and the first-rate weeper "The Keeper of the Stars." Byrd plays ballads and uptempo dance numbers equally well and his set of material on the album is fairly consistent, making the album his best to date. *—Thom Owens*

Love Lessons / 1995 / MCA ✦✦✦

Big Love / Oct. 22, 1996 / MCA ✦✦✦✦
Tracy Byrd doesn't change his formula much with *Big Love*. He still works the same new-traditionalist ground that he did with his debut album, only with more confidence—his voice is more assured and, more impressively, his selection of material is stronger and more adventurous. On the whole, *Big Love* is the equal to *No Ordinary Man*. *—Thom Owens*

I'm from the Country / May 12, 1998 / MCA ✦✦✦✦
With *I'm From the Country*, Tracy Byrd continues his streak of sturdy, well-crafted neo-traditionalist contemporary country. With each album, Byrd grows more confident in his delivery and choice of material, which naturally makes the albums stronger. There are still a couple of filler numbers on *I'm From the Country*, but the key to the record's success is that he takes pains in proving the title true—and by the end of the record, you have no questions that he is indeed country. *—Thom Owens*

● **Keepers: Greatest Hits** / Feb. 23, 1999 / MCA ✦✦✦✦

Glen Campbell

b. Apr. 22, 1936, Delight, AR
Vocals, Guitar, Banjo / Urban Cowboy, Nashville Sound/Countrypolitan, Soft Rock, Pop, Country-Pop
Glen Campbell may not be "pure country," yet his smooth fusion of country mannerisms and pop melodies made him the leading country-pop musician of the late '60s and '70s. He had a steady string of Top Ten singles, highlighted by "By the Time I Get to Phoenix," "Wichita Lineman," "Galveston," "Rhinestone Cowboy" and "Southern Nights." These songs crossed over to the pop charts as well, which was appropriate, since he began his career as an LA session musician, playing on hits by the Monkees and Elvis Presley. His solo career began with "Kentucky Means Paradise," a 1962 Top 20 single by the one-off group the Green River Boys. Despite its success, Campbell returned to studio work, joining the Beach Boys as a touring member in 1965. A few months later, he signed to Capitol. Two years of unsuccessful singles followed, but in 1967, Capitol pushed Campbell to the country market, leading to his breakthrough "Gentle on My Mind," a Top 40 hit on the country and pop charts. By the end of the year, "By the Time I Get to Phoenix" was his second crossover hit. Campbell continued to have country hits and he hosted a variety show called *The Glen Campbell Good Time Hour* for CBS TV in 1969. Throughout the late '60s and early '70s, he racked up hit singles, but in 1972, his sales started slipping and his television show was cancelled. As his career slowed, he sank into drug and alcohol addiction. He returned in 1975 with "Rhinestone Cowboy," a country and pop number one. Over the next two years, he had several hits, culminating in 1977's chart-topper "Southern Nights." Following this hit, Campbell stopped regularly reaching the country Top 10, yet he remained a popular performer. By the mid-'80s, he was clean and had become a born-again Christian. Campbell continued to hit the charts until the end of the '80s. He recorded infrequently in the '90s, gradually moving into semi-retirement, concentrating on golf and performing at his Goodtime Theater in Branson, Missouri. *—Stephen Thomas Erlewine*

Big Bluegrass Special / 1962 / Capitol ✦✦✦✦✦

By the Time I Get to Phoenix / 1967 / Capitol ✦✦✦✦
Campbell's commercial breakthrough came by way of the title track, which was the direct precursor in production terms to "Wichita Lineman," and by the same writer. The cover of Paul Simon's "Homeward Bound" is sincere if a little perfunctory, but Campbell's rendition of Ernest Tubb's "Tomorrow Never Comes" is a bravura performance, rich and soulful, as well as recalling Rodgers & Hammerstein's "You'll Never Walk Alone" as done by Gerry and the Pacemakers. "Cold December In Your Heart" harks back to Campbell's country-folk material, a piece of mid-tempo country-pop. Material like that and the similar "Back in the Race," Dorsey Burnette's "Hey Little One," Jerry Reed's "You're Young and You'll Forget," and Bill Anderson's "Bad Seed" hold up better than more pop-focused numbers like "My Baby's Gone," though the string backings on most of these very much date them. The final number here, the touching "Love Is a Lonesome River," makes a brilliant coda. *—Bruce Eder*

Gentle on My Mind / 1967 / Capitol ✦✦✦✦✦
The best of Campbell's early albums, and also his first real commercial success. Ironically, the title track (written by John Hartford) which started Campbell on the road to stardom, was never intended for release—he had submitted it as a demo, and Capitol issued it, to everybody's profit. Campbell's cover of "Catch the Wind" is one of the finest covers of a Donovan song ever done, stripping away any hint of the composer's sub-Dylan pretensions and bringing out the song's genuine beauty—it's folk-pop, in the same manner that Peter, Paul and Mary's cover of Dylan's "Blowin' in the Wind" was, but excellent folk-pop. This is Campbell's folksiest album, albeit with string orchestra accompaniment, as he covers "Bowling Green," "Mary in the Morning," and the title tune, and you get to hear him do a solo guitar and voice number, his own "Just Another Man." Even the most overproduced stuff here, "You're My World" and Rod McKuen's "The World I Used to Know," come off well, and Campbell is in excellent voice throughout, most especially on a wonderfully restrained and beautiful rendition of Roy Orbison's "Crying." *—Bruce Eder*

Hey, Little One / 1968 / Capitol ✦✦✦

Wichita Lineman / 1968 / Capitol ✦✦✦✦

Galveston / 1969 / Capitol ✦✦✦✦
Galveston continued Glen Campbell's strong string of hits supplied to him by Jimmy Webb. Here, though, he includes fine tunes from other writers, such as Buffy Sainte-Marie's "Until It's Time For You To Go" and Randy Sparks' "Today," as well as some of his own compositions. But the big draws on *Galveston* are the Webb tunes "Where's The Playground, Susie—" and the title track, a big hit on both the pop and country charts. *—James Chrispell*

★ **The Very Best of Glen Campbell** / Mar. 20, 1987 / Capitol ✦✦✦✦✦
The Very Best of Glen Campbell features 15 of his biggest hits, from "Gentle on My Mind" and "Wichita Lineman" to "Rhinestone Cowboy," making it the place to get acquainted with Campbell's career. *—Stephen Thomas Erlewine*

★ **Glen Campbell Collection (1962-1989): Gentle on My Mind** / Feb. 18, 1997 / Razor & Tie ✦✦✦✦✦
Gentle On My Mind: The Collection is an excellent double-disc collection that contains all of Glen Campbell's biggest hits, from "By the Time I Get to Phoenix" and "Gentle On My Mind" to "Rhinestone Cowboy" and "Country Boy (You Got Your Feet In L.A.)," making it the definitive retrospective of the extremely popular country-pop vocalist. *—Thom Owens*

Reunited With Jimmy Webb / 1999 / Raven ✦✦✦
Reunion With Jimmy Webb is an Australian import that pairs Campbell's complete 1974 album of Jimmy Webb compositions, *Reunion*, with 14 songs from later albums, all of which were also written by Webb. Webb was the songwriter behind some of Campbell's biggest hits, including "Galveston" and "Witchita Lineman," so their collaboration on *Reunion* would seem to have been a commercially promising move. As it turned out, the album wasn't a big seller, although it did spawn the Top 40 country single "It's a Sin (When You Love Somebody)." The liner notes suggest that *Reunion* may be Campbell's finest hour, and although that overstates its excellence, it is a very good, consistent album that sits somewhere between Elton John and John Denver in the country music spectrum. The additional tracks, some of which were recorded as late as 1988, are generally less good, sometimes much less. *—Greg Adams*

20 Greatest Hits / Feb. 29, 2000 / Capitol ✦✦✦

Mary-Chapin Carpenter

b. Feb. 21, 1958, Princeton, NJ
Vocals, Guitar / Country-Folk, Singer/Songwriter, Contemporary Country
Mary-Chapin Carpenter was part of a small movement of folk-influenced, country singer/songwriters of the late '80s. Although many of these performers never achieved commercial success, Carpenter was able to channel her anti-Nashville approach into chart success and industry awards by the early '90s. She entered the music world by involving herself in Washington, D.C.'s folk scene after her parents moved there in 1974. Part of a folk duo with guitarist John Jennings, Carpenter gained a contract with Columbia in 1987 after recording a demo tape. Her first two albums, *Hometown Girl* and *State of the Heart*, earned her a dedicated cult following, as well as two Top Ten singles, "Never Had It So Good" and "Quittin' Time." Though country radio was hesitant to play her soft, folky, feminist material, she received good reviews and airplay on more progressive country stations, as well as college radio. Her breakthrough album, 1992's *Come On Come On*, resulted in several hit singles—including her first number one, "He Thinks He'll Keep Her"—and eventually sold over three million copies. Though 1994's *Stones in the Road* concentrated on the folkier material, it was still a major success, selling over a million copies. *Place in the World* followed in 1996. *—Stephen Thomas Erlewine*

Hometown Girl / Feb. 1987 / Columbia ✦✦✦

State of the Heart / 1989 / Columbia ✦✦✦
Carpenter, a folkie, eventually turned to the country market, especially on her third album, *Shooting Straight in the Dark*. On this, her second, she's still in transition, which makes her more thoughtful than the average country singer and catchier than the average folkie, especially on her breakthrough country hit, "Never Had It So Good." Also includes "Quittin' Time," "Something of a Dreamer," and "How Do." *—William Ruhlmann*

Shooting Straight in the Dark / 1990 / Columbia ✦✦✦✦✦
Carpenter's third album expanded on the promise of her breakthrough, with The Searchers-style pop of "Going out Tonight" and a guest spot from Beausoleil on the Cajun-rooted "Down at the Twist and Shout." It also held some of her most penetrating, introspective songs, with payoff lines that would impress Elvis Costello. The album contains the singles "You Win Again" and "Right Now." *—Brian Mansfield*

• **Come on Come on** / 1992 / Columbia ✦✦✦✦✦
The ultra-serious *Shooting Straight in the Dark* left Carpenter in need of a breather, which she took by covering Dire Straits' "The Bug" and Lucinda Williams' "Passionate Kisses." On "I Feel Lucky," she won the lottery and flirted with Dwight Yoakam and Lyle Lovett in a bar. It's tough to say which she enjoyed more. The line about winning the lottery might have been prescience on Carpenter's part—*Come on Come on* sold more than 2 million copies and generated six hit singles, including "Not Too Much to Ask" with Joe Diffie, "The Hard Way," and the Geritol-inspired "He Thinks He'll Keep Her," her first number one. *—Brian Mansfield*

Stones in the Road / 1994 / Columbia ✦✦✦✦
With *Stones in the Road*, Mary Chapin Carpenter stripped her sound down and returned to the core of her music—namely, her singer/songwrter roots. Although the lyrics are among her best, Carpenter unfortunately cut back the number of hooks and melodies in her songs. Previously, she found a nice balance between the two, but here, she concentrates on the lyrics to the detriment of the actual songs. The sound of *Stones in the Road* is pleasant, but there aren't any songs that stick in your head after the record is finished. *—Thom Owens*

A Place in the World / Oct. 22, 1996 / Columbia ✦✦✦

Party Doll / Columbia ✦✦✦✦✦
Mary Chapin Carpenter has always eschewed the schlock material that often plagues country artists, avoiding the trappings of Nashville in favor of a more independent approach to her music. *Party Doll*, a greatest-hits collection, stays in line with Carpenter's approach of giving listeners substance rather than gloss. Instead of releasing the typical "best-of" collection that includes only the standard radio hits, Carpenter has put enough thought and imagination into *Party Doll* that even familiar fans will be surprised. Her career making hits are here, but often in an alternate form such as the live version of "Down at the Twist and Shout" recorded at Super Bowl XXXI or the version of "Quittin' Time" from *the Ryman Auditorium*. Also included are songs from soundtracks and tribute albums and an achingly beautiful cover of the Mick Jagger song that serves as the album's namesake. While some may be disappointed they can't buy one CD that includes all her hits the way they first heard them, Carpenter's true fans will appreciate the effort that went into this greatest-hits package. *—Steve Kurutz*

The Carter Family

f. 1926, Virginia, **db.** 1943
Vocals, Autoharp, Guitar, Fiddle / Field Recordings, Traditional Country, Old-Timey
The most influential group in country music history, the Carter Family switched the emphasis from hillbilly instrumentals to vocals, made scores of their songs part of the standard country music canon, and made a style of guitar-playing, "Carter-picking," the dominant technique for decades. Along with Jimmie Rodgers, the Carter Family were one of the first country music stars. Comprised of a gaunt, shy gospel quartet member called Alvin P. Carter and two reserved country girls—his wife Sara and their sister-in-law Maybelle—the Carter Family sang a pure, simple harmony that influenced not only the numerous other family groups of the '30s and the '40s, but folk, bluegrass and rock musicians like Woody Guthrie, Bill Monroe, the Kingston Trio, Doc Watson, Bob Dylan and Emmylou Harris, to mention just a few. It's unlikely that bluegrass music would have existed without the Carter Family. A. P., the family patriarch, collected hundreds of British/Appalachian folk songs and, in arranging these for recording, both enhanced the pure beauty of these "facts-of-life tunes" and at the same time saved them for future generations. Those hundreds of songs the trio found around their Virginia and Tennessee homes, after being sung by A.P., Sara, and Maybelle, became *Carter* songs, even though these were folk songs and in the public domain. Among the more than 300 sides they recorded are "Worried Man Blues," "Wabash Cannonball," "Will the Circle Be Unbroken," "Wildwood Flower," and "Keep on the Sunny Side." The Carter Family's instrumental backup, like their vocals, was unique. On her Gibson L-5 guitar, Maybelle played a bass-strings lead (the guitar being tuned down from the standard pitch) that is the mainstay of bluegrass guitarists to the present. Sara accompanied her on the autoharp or on a second guitar, while A.P. devoted his talent to singing a haunting though idiosyncratic bass or baritone. Although the original Carter Family disbanded in 1943, enough of their recordings remained in the vaults to keep the group current through the '40s. Furthermore, their influence was evident through further generations of musicians, in all forms of popular music, until the end of the century. *—David Vinopal*

Diamonds in the Rough / 1990 / Copper Creek ✦✦✦
Subtitled *Heart Songs, Hymns & Ballads as Featured on Border Radio in 1941*, this radio transcriptions reissue of The Carter Family's appearances on the legendary Del Rio border radio stations in 1938 is a fine representation of their repertoire of songs about home, hearth, and heartbreak. *—Mark A. Humphrey*

☆ **Country Music Hall of Fame** / 1991 / MCA ✦✦✦✦✦
After ending an eight-year association with Victor Records, the Carter Family recorded 60 sides for Decca between 1936 and 1938; 15 of those recordings are collected here. Decca wanted to emphasize new material; this posed no problem for A.P. Carter, who was long accustomed to taking copyright credit for minor rewrites of other people's songs. The Decca songs are less familiar than the recordings for Victor or, later, Okeh, but they're worth hearing. *—Brian Mansfield*

★ **Anchored in Love: Their Complete Victor Recordings (1927)** / 1993 / Rounder ✦✦✦✦✦
No American label (except perhaps Arhoolie) deserves a shot at reissuing the treasured Carter Family recordings more than Rounder. The Carter Family's sessions are seminal country music, raw and wonderfully unsophisticated with an emotional directness and honesty that makes a mockery of the slick, overproduced rock/folk now being marketed as country. Charles Wolfe's notes are an ideal combination of insight, historical overview, and musical examination. These are only the first 16 songs in the series, but they get things off to a rousing start. The menu is a sensational mix of originals, mountain and folk tunes, and old-timey hymns. *—Ron Wynn*

☆ **My Clinch Mountain Home: Their Complete Victor Recordings (1928-1929)** / Oct. 1, 1993 / Rounder ✦✦✦✦✦
The second volume in the Carter Family reissue series brings things forward to 1928 and 1929. The 16 selections provide family views of their life, home and background and include a rare topical number, "The Cyclone of Rye Cove," plus prophetic tunes like "The Grave on the Green Hillside" and the reflective selections "The Homestead on the Farm" and the title cut. Rounder plans nine volumes in the line; the first two only make you eager for more. *—Ron Wynn*

On Border Radio, Vol. 1 / 1995 / Arhoolie ✦✦✦✦✦

☆ **When the Roses Bloom in Dixieland: Their Complete Victor Recordings (1929-30)** / Oct. 31, 1995 / Rounder ✦✦✦✦✦
The third volume in Rounder's projected eight-disc series of the Carter Family's 1927-1941 recordings for RCA Victor picks up in Atlanta in November 1929, where the family records ten tracks, including "Motherless Children," "Wabash Cannonball," and "Jimmy Brown the Newsboy," among other country classics, then travels to Memphis for six tracks from the Carters' fifth recording session in May 1930. *—William Ruhlmann*

☆ **Worried Man Blues: Their Complete Victor Recordings (1930)** / Oct. 31, 1995 / Rounder ✦✦✦✦✦
The fourth volume in Rounder's projected eight-disc series of the Carter Family's 1927-1941

recordings for RCA Victor picks up in Memphis in May 1930 and continues in the same city in November for 16 sides, including the title track and "Lonesome Valley." There are an unusually large number of three-part harmony vocals in this set, much of which is given over to gospel songs. The only complaints about this brilliant chronological series are that it could be accomplished faster: This disc runs less than 48 minutes, and Rounder seems to be doling out the albums at a rate of two every two years, which means that it could take until the end of 1999 to hear them all. (The fifth volume, *Sunshine in the Shadows– The Complete Victor Recordings 1931-1932* was scheduled for release June 18, 1996, speeding up the schedule somewhat.) *—William Ruhlmann*

Sunshine in the Shadows: Their Complete Victor Recordings (1931-32) / 1996 / Rounder ✦✦✦✦✦
Sixteen tracks from 1931 and 1932, originally recorded for Victor, most penned by A.P. Carter. It displays the Carters' usual unadorned consistency, moving harmonies, and accomplished picking; "Picture on the Wall," "Where We'll Never Grow Old," and "Lonesome for You" are just some of the more striking examples of their skill with material that is both humble and mournfully evocative. Of special interest are a few songs (and a couple corny sketches) on which the clan is joined by Jimmie Rodgers, the most influential country act of the day bar the Carters themselves. *—Richie Unterberger*

On Border Radio, Vol. 2: 1939 / 1997 / Arhoolie ✦✦✦

Give Me the Roses While I Live: Their Complete Victor Recordings 1932-133 / Feb. 11, 1997 / Rounder ✦✦✦

Gold Watch and Chain: Their Complete Victor Recordings (1933-34) / Feb. 10, 1998 / Rounder ✦✦✦✦
The seventh of what is scheduled to be a nine-disc series of recordings, *Gold Watch and Chain* picks up the Carter Family's catalog in June 1933, by which time the Depression had devastated the record business and the Carters' sales along with it, such that, notes annotator Charles K. Wolfe, "For all practical purposes, many of the sides included in this album... were unheard by the general public at the time.... "In fact, many actually were unheard, not being released until decades later. But the Carters' usual combination of hymns, traditional folk songs, and other old material continues to fascinate in their renditions, with their rough, expressive singing and innovative playing. The Rounder series has been doling out the recordings in 16-track, LP-length CDs since 1993; if one might wish for greater speed and more economical configurations, the music's quality nevertheless holds up *—William Ruhlmann*

Last Sessions: Their Complete Victor Recordings (1934-41) / Apr. 7, 1998 / Rounder ✦✦✦✦✦

Longing for Old Virginia: Their Complete Victor Recordings (1934) / Apr. 7, 1998 / Rounder ✦✦✦✦✦

On Border Radio, Vol. 3: 1939 / Mar. 23, 1999 / Arhoolie ✦✦✦
There's apparently a wellful of transcription discs of late-1930s Carter Family broadcasts on XET in Monterrey, Mexico, as this series enters its third volume with no drops in quality. Again it shows the Carters in various combinations, sometimes featuring Jeanette Carter, sometimes the then-young Carter children, sometimes A.P. There are a bunch of famed standards on board here, like "You Are My Sunshine," "Worried Man Blues," "Great Speckled Bird," "I Shall Not Be Moved," "Wade in the Water," "Something Got a Hold on Me," "I've Been Working on the Railroad" and "Oh, Susanna," though many of the 20-odd tracks are less familiar. It, and other discs in the series, are less recommended than their studio recordings because the songs (including some station IDs) are often extremely short and the presentation less consistent than on the average Carter Family compilation. For serious Carter Family fans, though, they're valuable additions to the act's discography. *—Richie Unterberger*

★ **Can the Circle Be Unbroken—: Country Music's First Family** / Jul. 4, 2000 / Columbia/Legacy ✦✦✦✦✦
The second half of the Carter Family's recorded output largely rests with the contents of this CD. It's their output for Columbia's OKeh and Conqueror labels, 17 of the 20 recorded over five days in May 1935 and the final three from an October 1940 session. In typical Carter Family fashion, the material is wide ranging and eclectic, running from British folk music ("Black Jack David," "Sinking in the Lonesome Sea") to gospel ("On the Rock Where Moses Stood," "River of Jordan") to blues ("Worried Man Blues") and beyond. Along the way we're treated to re-cuts of notable Carter "hits" like "Can the Circle Be Unbroken," "Wildwood Flower," and "Keep on the Sunny Side." After you collect all of their Victor recordings from the 1920s, here's your next stop, an indispensable addition to any basic country collection. *—Cub Koda*

In the Shadow of Clinch Mountain / Sep. 12, 2000 / Bear Family ✦✦✦✦✦

Carlene Carter

b. Sep. 26, 1955, Nashville, TN
Vocals, Piano, Guitar / Neo-Traditionalist Country, New Wave, Roots Rock, Contemporary Country
Carlene Carter has always straddled the line between country and rock. Beginning her career as a rock singer in the mid-'70s, she became immersed in the new wave in the late '70s, before emerging as a new country singer in the late '80s, Throughout it all, her music has always infused roots music—whether its country or rock & roll—with a nervy, edgy energy. The daughter of June Carter and Carl Smith, she obviously developed a musical interest at an early age, and after her mother married Johnny Cash when Carlene was 12, she became a backup singer in the Carter/Cash touring show. In 1978, she recorded her eponymous debut album with Graham Parker's backing band, the Rumour. The following year, her second album, *Two Sides to Every Woman,* featured support from the Doobie Brothers. That same year she married singer/songwriter/producer Nick Lowe, who helped Carter shape her musical direction with 1980's *Musical Shapes* and the following year's *Blue Nun.* After their marriage collapsed in the mid-'80s, Carter returned to the states but didn't release an album until 1990's *I Fell in Love.* The most straightforward country record of her career, it became a hit and two singles, "I Fell In Love" and "Come on Back," climbed all the way to number three. Her 1993 follow-up *Little Love Letters* was equally successful, though 1995's *Little Acts of Treason* enjoyed only moderate success on the country charts. *—Stephen Thomas Erlewine*

Carlene Carter / 1978 / Warner Brothers ✦✦✦
This album was released in the middle of the new wave movement and is interesting, in part, because of the meeting of the artist with the country music background and new wavers Graham Parker and the Rumour. Somewhat uneven but still worth owning. *—Jim Worbois*

Two Sides to Every Woman / 1979 / Warner Brothers ✦✦✦

Musical Shapes / 1980 / F Beat ✦✦✦✦✦

Blue Nun / 1981 / F Beat ✦✦✦
Carter's American label passed on this one, and it's too bad. While it's not one of her best albums, when she's on, she's dead on. It's interesting from a historical point because it somewhat chronicles her musical associations with former-husband Nick Lowe and Paul Carrack (ex-Ace, Squeeze, Mike + the Mechanics). *—Jim Worbois*

C'est C Bon / 1983 / Razor & Tie ✦✦

I Fell in Love / 1990 / Reprise ✦✦✦✦✦
This comeback album has a perfect mix of old (A. P. Carter's "My Dixie Darlin'") and new (guest spots from Dave Edmunds, David Lindley, and Albert Lee). If Carter hasn't come to terms with her love for rock and her duty to heritage, she's at least learned to balance them. *—Brian Mansfield*

Musical Shapes/Blue Nun / 1992 / Demon ✦✦✦✦✦
Demon Records reissued Carlene Carter's *Musical Shapes* and *Blue Nun* on one disc in 1992. Neither album is straight country—with their propulsive rhythms and jangling guitars, they exhibit the influence of her then-current husband Nick Lowe—but *Musical Shapes* is one of her best records, and worth getting in any form. *—Stephen Thomas Erlewine*

Little Love Letters / 1993 / Giant ✦✦✦✦✦
This is the album fans always dreamed she would make. While it shows off her love of, and ability to handle, various styles of music, she never loses her direction. *—Jim Worbois*

Little Acts of Treason / Oct. 1995 / Giant ✦✦✦
Carlene Carter's *Little Acts of Treason* doesn't break much new ground for the singer, but that's not necessarily a bad thing. While she continues in the same vein as *Little Love Letters,* the music is done well, even if the album isn't as infectious and catchy as her previous album. *—Stephen Thomas Erlewine*

★ **Hindsight 20/20** / Sep. 9, 1996 / Giant ✦✦✦✦✦
Hindsight 20/20 is a comprehensive overview of Carlene Carter's career, concentrating on country hits like "Every Little Thing" and "I Fell in Love," but also touching on her earlier recordings like "Never Together But Close Sometimes." The compilation offers an excellent introduction and encapsulation of one of the finest female country singers of the '80s and '90s. *—Stephen Thomas Erlewine*

Deana Carter

b. 1964
Vocals / Neo-Traditionalist Country, Country-Folk, Singer/Songwriter, Contemporary Country
Though she didn't begin her musical career into relatively late, Deana Carter managed to defy conventional expectations and unexpectedly shot to the top of the country charts upon the release of her 1996 debut, *Did I Shave My Legs for This?* Carter's success was equally unexpected considering how she didn't follow quite fit into the mold of a standard female contemporary country singer. Melding the popular appeal of country chanteuses with folky singer-songwriters like Mary Chapin-Carpenter, Carter racked up both positive reviews and healthy sales with *Did I Shave My Legs for This?,* becoming one of the most pleasant success stories of the post-Garth Brooks generation. *Everything's Gonna Be Alright* followed in late 1998. *—Stephen Thomas Erlewine*

● **Did I Shave My Legs for This—** / 1995 / Capitol Nashville ✦✦✦✦✦
Deana Carter's *Did I Shave My Legs For This?* is an excellent debut, full of catchy melodies and clever lyrics. While she occasionally strays into new country territory, she shines on folky country ballads, but ever song on the album demonstrates she is an artist of enormous potential. *—Thom Owens*

Everything's Gonna Be Alright / Oct. 20, 1998 / Capitol ✦✦✦✦
Deana Carter's debut album *Did I Shave My Legs for This?* was a surprise hit, considering that its grace, subtletly and wit were largely qualities unheard of in contemporary country in 1996, the year it climbed up the charts. It immediately marked her as a major artist, placing great expectations on her second album, *Everything's Gonna Be Alright.* Lacking the surprise element of *Legs, Everything's* is nevertheless in many ways its equal, since Carter has chosen to expand its sound, not to replicate it. There are more laid-back rock and pop elements to her style this time around, which fits well with her folky, melodic country. Even the presence of Lynyrd Skynyrd as the support band for "The Train Song" (earthy, not rowdy), works better than it reads. Furthermore, her songwriting is melodic and memorable, and her choice of covers, including Melanie's "Brand New Key," is inspired. As long as Carter continues to deliver albums as enchanting as *Everything's Gonna Be Alright,* things are going to be just fine for her and her fans. *—Thom Owens*

Wilf Carter (Montana Slim)

b. Dec. 18, 1904, Guysboro, NS
Vocals, Guitar / Yodeling, Cowboy, Traditional Country
Also known as Montana Slim, Wilf Carter was a Canadian cowboy who managed to make inroads in America during the late '30s, setting the stage for a long, prolific career that ran

over 60 years. Throughout his career, he never departed from the style that made him famous—traditional cowboy and country music, in the vein of Gene Autry and Jimmie Rodgers. Born and raised in Guysboro, Nova Scotia, Carter became fascinated with music as a child, when he he a travelling musician named the Yodeling Fool play a local concert. However, it took him several years before he began a musical career. In his late teens, he moved to Boston with the intention of becoming a carpenter, but soon left for Calgary, Alberta where he became a cowboy.

Wilf spent the next several years as a cowboy, before beginning a musical career in 1930, when he landed his own radio show on Calgary's CFCN. Around the same his show started, Carter began singing on trail rides in the Rockies, which led to him being hired by C.P.R. to sing on thier cruise ship, the Empress of Britain, on a West Indies voyage in 1933. While on cruise, Carter stopped in Montreal to make his recording debut: a two-song single for Canadian Bluebird. Within a year, he was signed by CBS to do his own show in New York. Upon accepting the offer, Wilf began using the nickname "Montana Slim." Shortly after the show began, RCA Victor began releasing his records in America under the stagename; in Canada, they were still credited to his stage name.

Before World War II, Carter recorded nearly 200 songs, with nearly every track seeing an official release. During the war, his recording slowed considerably, because of rationing and because of health problems due to a car accident. In 1947, he began recording activily for Victor, employing a full band for the first time. Seven years later, he left the label for Decca, where he was produced by Owen Bradley. These singles, which were released on Apex in Canada, were more commercial than his previous recordings, which made Victor interested Carter again. Since he considered Victor his home, he retruned to the label.

Carter's second stint at Victor resulted in records that were primarily released in Canada, although several singles and albums did appear in the US. During the mid-'60s, Wilf briefly recorded for Starday, but he essentially spent the rest of his career at Victor, releasing records well into the '80s. Carter's career was always more successful in his native Canada than in the United States, but his legacy of nearly 500 original songs were enough to have him inducted into the Nashville Songwriters Hall of Fame in 1971. Carter continued to tour into the early '90s, when he essentially retired from music. *—Stephen Thomas Erlewine*

● **The Golden Years** / 1996 / Collectors' Choice Music ✦✦✦✦✦
The Golden Years—a collection compiled by the mail-order record catalog, Collector's Choice—contains 24 of Wilf Carter's RCA Victor tracks from the '30s and '40s, capturing the essence of the Canadian singing cowboy on wone disc. Included on the set are such classic western songs as "Goodnight Irene," "Blue Canadian Rockies," and "There's a Love Knot in My Lariat." *—Thom Owens*

A Prairie Legend / 1996 / Bear Family ✦✦✦✦
Four CDs containing more than 100 songs recorded by Wilf Carter aka Montana Slim between 1944 and 1952, and his self-produced sessions from 1959. Disc One features more than a dozen tracks with Carter accompanied primarily by his own acoustic guitar, and they're pretty fair cowboy songs. Carter's voice is a pleasing one, reminiscent at times of Gene Autry, but his repertory generally doesn't intersect much with Autry's—the early electric accompanied sides from 1947 are also very spare, and have more of a raw quality than one would expect from this era. Disc Two captures Carter at the beginning of his most commercial period for RCA, doing romantic ballads as well as his usual cowboy songs. Disc Three covers the tail end of his RCA period, when Carter was trying for more of a pop sound, in keeping with the declining public response to cowboy songs—the stuff is more sentimental, but Carter never strays too far from the playful mood of his best work. Disc Four closes out the RCA years with numbers like the shockingly upbeat "Goodbye Maria (I'm Off to Korea)," probably the most cheerful song ever done about that war and "Mockingbird Love," the song Carter believes helped cost him his RCA contract. The real highlight of this disc, however, is the stuff that Carter cut himself at the end of the 1950s, which mostly consists of really good cowboy material, all originals and all played in a spare, eloquent style with Carter's voice showing tremendous vigor. With his spoken introduction to the first of these numbers, these could have been the basis for a radio show, if only the time had been right, and they capture the spirit of Carter's earliest work in Alberta and on the CBC. *—Bruce Eder*

Johnny Cash

b. Feb. 26, 1932, Kingsland, AR
Vocals, Guitar / Country Gospel, Rockabilly, Country-Pop, Cowboy, Traditional Country, Rock & Roll

With his deep, resonant baritone and spare, percussive guitar, Johnny Cash combined the emotional honesty of folk, the rebelliousness of rock & roll, and the weariness of country. Cash was inherently rebellious and his simple, direct music was similar to rock, yet his deep sense of history kept him tied to country—and he was indeed one of country's biggest stars, racking up well over 100 hit singles.

Cash began his career at Sun Records, having a number 14 hit with his 1955 debut single, "Cry Cry Cry." Other classics, such as "Folsom Prison Blues" and "I Walk the Line," followed in 1956 and his success kept rolling throughout 1957 and 1958. He left Sun for Columbia Records in 1958 and his second single there, "Don't Take Your Guns to Town," topped the country charts in early 1959. During the early '60s, his career was hampered by his burgeoning drug addiction. Cash returned to the top of the charts with "Ring of Fire" in 1963, yet his comeback was shortlived, as he sank further into addiction. Several lawless years followed, before Cash moved to Nashville and fell in love with June Carter; she helped him clean up and they married in 1968.

Cash's career bounced back in 1967, capped off by the 1968 release of his most popular album, *Johnny Cash at Folsom Prison*. The following year, he released a sequel, *Johnny Cash at San Quentin*, which had his only Top Ten pop single, "A Boy Named Sue." Cash maintained his popularity through the early '70s, partially due to his television show. In the mid-'70s, Cash's sales slowed, yet still hit the charts, but his sales declined steadily in the '80s. He signed with Mercury Nashville in 1986, releasing a series of unsuccessful albums there. In 1993, he signed with American Records and his first album for the label, *American Recordings* revived his career critically and brought him in touch with a younger, rock-oriented audience. Though he stopped performing regularly, he did release two other acclaimed albums for America during the '90s. *—Stephen Thomas Erlewine*

The Fabulous Johnny Cash / 1958 / Columbia ✦✦✦✦✦
The Fabulous Johnny Cash was Cash's first album for Columbia Records and one of his best for the label. Unlike some of his latter-day albums, there wasn't much filler on the record. At the time of its recording, Cash had just been freed from his contract with Sun. Instead of recording these songs for his last Sun sessions, he wound up saving much of his best material for his Columbia album, and that's what makes *The Fabulous* so consistent. The album builds on his basic, spare sound, but it is slightly more polished than his Sun records. But what makes it so entertaining are the songs themselves. From "Don't Take Your Guns to Town" and "Frankie's Man, Johnny," to "Pickin' Time" and "The Troubadour," the album is filled with first-rate songs, with only a handful of mediocre songs like "Supper-Time," that don't distract from the overall quality of the album at all. *—Stephen Thomas Erlewine*

Now, There Was a Song! / 1960 / Columbia/Legacy ✦✦✦✦✦

Ride This Train / 1960 / Columbia ✦✦✦✦✦
Ride This Train was the first explicit Americana concept album that Johnny Cash recorded. As the title implies, the album is about railroads, how they developed and how they changed the land. Apart from a couple of songs, *Ride This Train* isn't comprised of traditional folk ballads—they are songs that tell the history of trains and rails, offering an educational lesson. Cash expounds on the songs with brief spoken narratives. Though it is hard to fault Cash's intentions, the songs aren't very good (although "The Shifting Whispering Sands" is a standout) and the history is a bit simplistic and silly. On the whole, *Ride This Train* sounds as if it is of a piece with the Walt Disney educational features produced at the same time, and like those films, it is more interesting as an historical artifact than a piece of art. *—Stephen Thomas Erlewine*

Blood Sweat & Tears / 1963 / Columbia/Legacy ✦✦✦
Where *Ride This Train* was about railroads and how they shaped America, *Blood, Sweat and Tears* is not only about the folklore of trains, it's about the fables of the American working man. That means there are classic ballads like "Casey Jones" and "The Legend of John Henry's Hammer," but also relatively recent blues like "Busted," the field song "Pick A Bale of Cotton" and the worker's lament "Tell Him I'm Gone." The delivery is plain, simple and never overly sentimental, but the thing that makes the record really work is the fact that the album consists almost entirely of first-rate material, without much of the unintentionaly corny history lessons that weigh down most of Cash's Americana records. *—Stephen Thomas Erlewine*

Bitter Tears / 1964 / Columbia/Legacy ✦✦✦✦✦
Though on the surface *Bitter Tears* is just another installment in the seemingly endless series of Americana albums that Johnny Cash released in the '60s, it was a more daring collection than any of its predecessors or successors. Where Cash's previous Americana albums had previously concentrated on cowboys and Western Pioneers, *Bitter Tears* is all about Native Americans and their trials and tribulations. It isn't a crass move—it's a sensitive, cleareyed take on the unfair treatment of the American Indian that uses traditional folk ballads and newly-written songs in the same vein. It's stark and moving, perhaps his best Americana album of the '60s. *—Stephen Thomas Erlewine*

Mean as Hell / 1965 / Columbia ✦✦✦✦✦
Mean As Hell! Ballads From the True West is Johnny Cash's gunslinger album: a collection of songs about cowboys and their myths. That means there are classic Western ballads like "Bury Me Not on the Lone Prairie" and "The Shifting Whispering Sands," there are fables like "The Blizzard" and the title track, history lessons like "Remember the Alamo," and jokey satires like "25 Minutes to Go." *Mean As Hell* has a handful of good songs—usually the straight ballads, but some of the myths are fun too—but for the most part, there's too much unintentional kitsch on the record to make it necessary. *—Stephen Thomas Erlewine*

☆ **At Folsom Prison** / 1968 / Columbia/Legacy ✦✦✦✦✦
At Folsom Prison was one of two legendary live albums Johnny Cash recorded in front of a prison audience in the late '60s. Part of the appeal of the records is the way Cash plays to the audience, selecting a set of songs that are all about prison, crime, murder, regret, loss, mother, God, and loneliness. Cash stimulates the audience's emotions, which in turn stimulates his performance, especially since he delivers the songs with the conviction of someone who has lived through it. There aren't many hits on the record—"Folsom Prison Blues," "I Still Miss Someone," "Jackson," "Give My Love to Rose," and "I Got Stripes" are the familiar items—but few albums come as close to capturing the darkness and rage that lays deep in Cash's music, as well as the depth of his talent. [The 1999 CD reissue of *At Folsom Prison* presents the complete concert, including three previously unreleased tracks: "Busted," "Joe Bean," and "The Legend of John Henry's Hammer."] *—Stephen Thomas Erlewine*

Hello, I'm Johnny Cash / 1969 / Columbia ✦✦✦✦

Sunday Morning Coming Down / 1972 / DCC ✦✦✦

Rockabilly Blues / 1980 / Columbia ✦✦✦
Not as earth-shaking as his work with The Tennessee Two, and not really true rockabilly, it's still a convincing album of country-rock songs with more depth than nearly anything else coming from Nashville at the time. *—Michael McCall*

Johnny 99 / 1983 / Koch International ✦✦✦✦
If the Springsteen tunes hadn't been included, this would still have been a good album. But Cash sinks his teeth into "Highway Patrolman" and the title tune and gives them the guts that Springsteen only dreamed of. *—Jim Worbois*

★ **The Sun Years** / 1990 / Rhino ✦✦✦✦✦
The Sun Years collects all the big hits from Johnny Cash's Sun recordings, including the classics "I Walk the Line," "Hey Porter," "Cry Cry Cry," "Get Rhythm," "Ballad of A Teenage Queen," "Give My Love to Rose," and "Guess Things Happen That Way," plus 11 other songs, which aren't quite as familiar, but just as compelling. *—Stephen Thomas Erlewine*

The Man in Black: 1954-1958 / Sep. 1990 / Bear Family ✦✦✦✦✦
The Man In Black: 1954-1958 is a five-disc box set that includes everything Johnny Cash recorded for Sun Records, plus the fruits of his first year with Columbia Records. In addition to all of the classic singles—from "Hey Porter" to "Don't Take Your Guns To Town," they're all here—there is a wealth of unreleased material and alternate takes, including a disc that captures an entire recording session from his early days with Columbia. The problem with the set is its very comprehensiveness—only dedicated fans or historians can listen to this much music, especially with all of the alternate takes mixed in with the official versions. And the disc with the recording session isn't interesting—it's a curiosity that makes for tedious listening. Certainly anyone that is willing to invest in this expensive box will find it rewarding, but only serious listeners should consider purchasing the set. *—Stephen Thomas Erlewine*

Come Along and Ride This Train / 1991 / Bear Family ✦✦✦✦✦
It's a statement of Johnny Cash's longevity that the eight albums collected here—each one a concept collection devoted to American historical themes—were considered worthy and viable commercial releases back when, and that most were very successful. This four-CD set assembles *Ride This Train, Blood, Sweat and Tears, Bitter Tears, Ballads of the True West, Mean as Hell! (Johnny Cash Sings Ballads from the True West), America: A 200 Year Salute in Story and Song, From Sea to Shining Sea,* and *The Rambler,* all in one place. They fit together as a body of work, and he put a lot of heart into all of these songs individually. He also engendered a good deal of enmity from members of his core audience of white Southerners, for the sympathies he displayed for the plight of Native Americans on 1964's *Bitter Tears. America: A 200 Year Salute* is the strongest of the other albums, covering the widest scope and allowing Cash to tie together several singing and songwriting traditions. Cash's two Western-song albums make a natural pairing, as do his two albums of railroad-related songs. The last of the four discs, encompassing *From Sea to Shining Sea* and *The Rambler,* is a logical pairing, the latter album being the realistic, somewhat theatrical contemporary equivalent to the former's folk music/history travelogue. Most of the dialogue sequences don't work too well, but the best of the songs come up to Cash's highest standard. Unlike other Bear Family boxes, the book in this one forgoes a detailed sessionography in favor of reprinting original album jacket notes and a good essay by Bob Allen. *—Bruce Eder*

The Man in Black: 1959-1962 / 1991 / Bear Family ✦✦✦✦✦
Picking up where the previous set left off, *The Man In Black: 1959-1962* collects all of the recordings Johnny Cash made for Columbia between '59 and '62; the only music that was left off are his historical albums, which Bear Family had already released on *Come Along on Ride Train.* Like the other set, it has an abundance of alternate takes and outtake, plus a disc that captures an actual recording sessions. Again, it is primarily of interest for historians and dedicated fans willing to take the time to delve deeply into this music—since the songs are presented in chronological order according to their session date, it doesn't make for casual listening. *—Stephen Thomas Erlewine*

☆ **The Essential Johnny Cash 1955-1983** / 1992 / Columbia/Legacy ✦✦✦✦✦
A three-CD set, this one traces his career from his Sun beginnings with "Hey Porter" and "Cry! Cry! Cry!" through the close of his Columbia association. It includes the obvious high points along the way ("Folsom Prison Blues," "Ring of Fire," etc.), but also packs in more obscure hits (like "Blistered" and "Singin' in Vietnam Talkin' Blues"), plus material from some of his later albums, and several appropriate gospel tracks. *—Tom Roland*

The Gospel Collection / Jul. 14, 1992 / Columbia/Legacy ✦✦✦

American Recordings / 1994 / American/Sony ✦✦✦✦✦

Wanted Man / 1994 / Mercury ✦✦✦

The Man in Black: 1963-1969 / Feb. 1996 / Bear Family ✦✦✦✦✦
The Man in Black: 1963-1969 is Bear Family's fourth box set of Johnny Cash recordings and the third in *The Man In Black* series. *1963-1969* picks up where the previous *Man In Black* box left off—in the beginning of the '60s, after Cash established himself as a hitmaker for Columbia. It collects all of the music Cash made for Columbia Records between 1963 and 1969, including outtakes and alternate versions but not the albums that were issued on the *Come Along and Ride This Train* set. Again, this collection is more for collectors and scholars than fans. There is terrific music here, but the strict chronological order—sequenced by the session date, not release date—makes listening to each disc somewhat tiring. *—Stephen Thomas Erlewine*

Unchained / Nov. 5, 1996 / Warner Brothers ✦✦✦

★ **Man in Black: Greatest Hits** / Mar. 2, 1999 / Columbia/Legacy ✦✦✦✦✦
There have been no shortage of Johnny Cash compilations over the years, particularly of his classic Columbia recordings. There's something for whatever your taste—single disc compilations with just the hits and extravagant multi-disc box sets tracing his entire career. *Man In Black: Greatest Hits* falls somewhere in between, presenting a comprehensive 30-song overview of (primarily) Cash's work for Columbia. That means the bulk of his groundbreaking Sun work his missing—"I Walk the Line," "Ballad of a Teenage Queen" and "Guess Things Happen that Way" are here, but classics such as "Get Rhythm," "Cry! Cry! Cry!" and "Folsom Prison Blues" (included in a later live version) aren't—but they're all available on Rhino's excellent *Sun Years* collection; this is notable for being an affordable and relatively exhaustive overview of the Columbia years, which is something that hasn't been attempted before this collection. There may be a few hits and cult favorites missing from this compilation, but it does a stellar job in featuring the best, most important cuts from Cash's prolific years with the label, and it makes an excellent companion to *The Sun Years* for the serious Cash fan on a budget. *—Stephen Thomas Erlewine*

☆ **The Complete Sun Singles** / Sep. 21, 1999 / Varese ✦✦✦✦✦
Two-CD, 40-song set with both sides of all 20 of the singles released by Johnny Cash on Sun through 1964. (Even though Cash left the label in 1958, Sun plundered its vaults for more Cash singles for about five years, with some of the 45s doing quite well on the country charts and denting the lower reaches of the pop ones.) This is really an excuse for a compilation that's more comprehensive than the usual greatest hits set, but more affordable and digestible than the box sets of his Sun stuff. There's nothing wrong with that, either. It's well-packaged, the music is good-to-classic, and it's an excellent compromise for listeners who want a lot of Johnny Cash at Sun, but not everything. *—Richie Unterberger*

☆ **Sings the Ballads of the True West** / Feb. 22, 2000 / DCC ✦✦✦✦✦
One of the projects Johnny Cash wanted to do when he was on Sun Records was to record an album of songs from the Old West. Of course, Sam Phillips wouldn't hear of it, but the idea—along with concept albums of gospel, train songs, and others—all came to fruition when he moved to Columbia Records. This concept album is a 25-track set that combines songs and narrations, the bulk of which were recorded in 1965 (the lone exception is Carl Perkins' "The Ballad of Boot Hill," which originates from a 1959 session). The booklet includes Johnny's original liner notes to the album, along with song-by-song comments. One of Cash's best concept albums. *—Cub Koda*

Love, God, Murder / May 23, 2000 / Columbia/Legacy ✦✦✦✦
Each of the three CDs in this box set are comprised of 16 songs devoted to a single theme: love, God, and murder, of course. And each of the three CDs is available separately should you not have a yen for one or two of the discs. Certainly there is a lot of notable music on this box, as it was personally chosen by Cash himself from recordings spanning the mid-'50s to the mid-'90s, mostly heavily weighting the 1955-70 period. There are a few well-known classics here that virtually anyone considering buying this will already know (and probably have), like "I Walk the Line," "I Still Miss Someone," "Ring of Fire," "Folsom Prison Blues," and "The Long Black Veil." The emphasis, however, is on LP tracks, B-sides, and live recordings that probably won't be familiar to the moderate Cash fan; there are also three mid-'60s tracks previously unreleased in the U.S., though none of them are particularly outstanding. Some of those obscure songs are excellent ("Oh, What a Dream," the brutal hangman humor of "Joe Bean," "Mister Garfield") and almost all of them are worth hearing. And each of the CDs is decorated by liner notes from Cash and a celebrity (his wife June Carter for *Love,* Bono of U2 for *God,* and director Quentin Tarantino for *Murder*). The question still nags: who exactly will find this box wholly satisfying— Not the average Cash fan, who wants a smaller greatest-hits set with more familiar tunes. Not the rabid Cash fan, who probably already has much of this, and might want more well-balanced and thorough boxes, such as those issued on Bear Family of Cash's early material. It's for the in-betweeners, who certainly find the more conventional box retrospective *The Essential Johnny Cash 1955-1983* the essential first stop. *—Richie Unterberger*

☆ **Complete Live at San Quentin** / Jul. 4, 2000 / Columbia/Legacy ✦✦✦✦✦
With all due respect to Cash's breakthrough Sun recordings, this 1969 live album may be his finest moment. Recorded two days before his 37th birthday, this captures Cash and company in loose and unedited form from the original issue, heavily fortified with the addition of nine previously unreleased tracks from the same concert. With a best selling album and hit TV show under his belt, Cash dispenses charisma galore on this set, intermingling with the prisoners in an almost conversational manner. With the addition of the previously unreleased material, the concert (which was originally televised for the BBC) has a much better flow than the original material and the whole shebang finds Cash at the absolute top of his game. After you collect up all his important Sun recordings, this one should be your next stop. *—Cub Koda*

American III: Solitary Man / Oct. 17, 2000 / American ✦✦✦

Rosanne Cash

b. May 24, 1955, Memphis, TN
Vocals, Guitar / Neo-Traditionalist Country, Singer/Songwriter, Contemporary Country
The history of popular music is littered with the careers of the children of famous artists, performers who manage to carve out some small measure of success based far less on talent than on the recognition that their famous names afford them. Perhaps no greater exception to this trend was Rosanne Cash, the daughter of Johnny Cash, whose idiosyncratic and innovative music made her one of the pre-eminent singer/songwriters of her day. Rosanne was raised by her mother after her parents separated in the early '60s. Largely uninfluenced by her father's music until she joined his Road Show following high school, she long remained unsure of a career in music, but finally released an eponymously-titled solo record—later disavowed—in Germany in 1978. She then signed with Columbia Records, and found a hit with her American debut, 1979's *Right or Wrong.* Her commercial breakthrough, 1981's *Seven Year Ache,* yielded three number one singles. 1985's *Rhythm and Romance* was her most significant artistic statement yet, a deft fusion of country and pop that won wide acclaim from both camps. Two years later, she issued *King's Record Shop,* a meditation on country music traditions which generated four successive number one hits. Cash's next two albums, *Interiors* and *The Wheel,* earned great critical acclaim for their unflinchingly confessional examination of the dissolve and eventual failure of her marriage to Rodney Crowell (who had produced many of her records). Cash returned in 1996 with *10 Song Demo,* a collection of stark home recordings released with minimal studio gloss. *—Jason Ankeny*

Right or Wrong / 1979 / Columbia ✦✦✦

★ **Seven Year Ache** / 1981 / Columbia ✦✦✦✦✦
Cash was arguably the most important artist to emerge in country music in the early 80s, and this was her breakthrough album, which introduced a new, assertive, passionate stance to women in country and also helped foster the crossover between folk, rock, and country. Cash's songwriting (the title track and "Blue Moon with a Heartache") was first-rate, and her choices from others, notably Leroy Preston's "My Baby Thinks He's a Train," were equally strong. *—William Ruhlmann*

Somewhere in the Stars / 1982 / Columbia ✦✦✦
A terrific collection, including Rodney Crowell's "Ain't No Money," and Tom T. Hall's "That's How I Got to Memphis." *—William Ruhlmann*

Rhythm & Romance / 1985 / Columbia ♦♦♦
Cash expected criticism for this album, and got it but didn't deserve it. The orange hair and pink fingernails on the cover visually illustrate the musical risks she took in working with Eddie Rabbitt's former producer, David Malloy, and the result is a scorcher. Best cuts: Grammy-winner "I Don't Know Why You Don't Want Me" and "Halfway House." *—Tom Roland*

King's Record Shop / 1988 / Columbia ♦♦♦
After writing most of 1985's *Rhythm & Romance*, Cash returned to largely interpretive work on this powerful collection highlighted by Eliza Gilkyson's feminist anthem "Rosie Strike Back" and her father Johnny Cash's "Tennessee Flat Top Box." *—William Ruhlmann*

Hits 1979-1989 / 1989 / Columbia ♦♦♦
Rosanne Cash recorded many worthwhile albums in the years after *Hits 1979-1989* was released, but this compilation covers the time when Cash was a country star and reliable hitmaker—namely, the '80s. At only 12 tracks, the collection doesn't feature all of her hits, but it does contain what are arguably the cream of the crop—"No Memories Hangin' Around," "Seven Year Ache," "My Baby Thinks He's a Train," "Blue Moon with Heartache," "I Wonder," "I Don' t Know Why You Don't Want Me," "Never Be You," "Hold On," "The Way We Make a Broken Heart," "Tennessee Flat Top Box" and "I Don't Want to Spoil the Party." With a catalog as rich as Cash's, a compilation this brief can only skim the surface, but the end result is a terrifically engaging listen for the devoted and the curious alike. *—Stephen Thomas Erlewine*

★ **Interiors** / 1990 / Columbia ♦♦♦♦♦
What makes *Interiors* brilliant isn't that Cash produced herself for the first time nor that she wrote all the songs. It's that *Interiors*—the last album Cash made for Columbia's Nashville division—meticulously chronicles the unraveling of a terribly dysfunctional relationship, namely Cash's marriage to Rodney Crowell. Cash gets at the psychology behind country's cheating and drinking themes—the emotional anesthetic of addictions, the desperate grasping for love in affairs. The arrangements are stripped as bare as Cash's soul, but *Interiors* is country at its core. *—Brian Mansfield*

The Wheel / Jan. 19, 1993 / Columbia ♦♦♦♦♦
Like the dark, cathartic *Interiors*, *The Wheel* is an introspective, soul-searching set of confessional songs revolving around love and relationships. While many of the themes and emotions of *Interiors* are repeated on *The Wheel*, Roseanne Cash hasn't repeated herself, either lyrically or musically. Working from the same combination of folk and country that has fueled her songwriting throughout her career, she has created an album of subtle, melodic grace that helps convey the deep feelings of her lyrics. It's an immaculately-produced album, but that never detracts from the emotional core of Cash's music. *—Stephen Thomas Erlewine*

Retrospective / Nov. 7, 1995 / Columbia ♦♦♦
Retrospective is an odd overview of Rosanne Cash's later recordings for Columbia, featuring a combination of hits, album tracks, rarities, and new songs. Which means, the album does contain hits like the number one "Runaway Train," but it concentrates on the lesser-known material, whether it was the minor hit "On the Surface" or Elvis Costello's "Our Little Angel." It's a good compilation, but it's a little unnecessary, since the albums it is culled from—*Interiors, The Wheel*—function better as individual albums, and don't lend themselves well to collections. *—Thom Owens*

10 Song Demo / Apr. 2, 1996 / Capitol ♦♦♦♦

Beth Nielsen Chapman

b. Harlington, TX
Vocals / Country-Folk, Singer/Songwriter, Contemporary Country
A Nashville-based singer-songwriter who has written several Number One country hits, her own work leans more toward contemporary adult pop. Her songs are melodic, her themes mostly romantic and obsessed with inner journeys. Comparable to Carole King or the earnest side of Elton John, her range covers insistent pop rock, intimate ballads, sensual soul, and solemn spirituals, all done with an undercurrent of revelation and intelligence. *—Michael McCall*

Hearing It First / 1980 / Capitol ♦♦♦
Produced by Barry Beckett, the album reveals a young, raw talent. *—Michael McCall*

● **Beth Nielsen Chapman** / Sep. 25, 1990 / Reprise ♦♦♦♦♦
Beth Nielsen Chapman had established herself as a Nashville-based songwriter and session vocalist by the time of her self-titled debut in 1990. Although much of her previous work was more country oriented, *Beth Nielsen Chapman* reveals more pop-minded sensibilities and she is backed by an array of top session players from Nashville and L.A. "Life Holds On" is a wide-eyed affirmation of life graced by Mark Casstevens mandolin playing. The scope of most of the album is more focused on relationships, and Chapman delivers songs like "All I Have," "Avalanche," and "Down on My Knees" with a beautiful, crystal-clear voice. Intelligent and mature, she is a gifted artist who comfortably fits alongside '70s singer/songwriters like Carole King and Carly Simon. *—Tom Demalon*

You Hold the Key / 1993 / Reprise ♦♦♦♦
The arrangements are peppier, but the subject matter as intensely internal as on her previous album. *—Michael McCall*

Sand and Water / Jul. 15, 1997 / Reprise ♦♦♦♦
Although the arrangements on *Sand and Water* are slicker than anything on Beth Nielsen Chapman's previous albums, boasting everything from country to pop influences, her songwriting remains incisive, melodic and altogether striking, resulting in another stunningly accomplished record. *—Thom Owens*

Greatest Hits / Mar. 23, 1999 / Reprise ♦♦♦♦♦

Kenny Chesney

Vocals, Guitar / Neo-Traditionalist Country, Contemporary Country
Born in 1968 in Knoxville, TN, Kenny Chesney was raised in Luttrell, the home of Chet Atkins. However, country music never played a big part in his youth; in fact, Chesney plays in an uptempo, mainstream rock-influenced style. Country became his love when he heard Merle Haggard's "That's the Way Love Goes" on the car radio while driving home from East Tennessee State (where he received a marketing degree). He began practicing his guitar up to seven hours per day and gigged around campus. After graduation, Chesney moved to Nashville to make it in the country music business. Associating himself with the New Traditionalists, he signed a writing contract with Acuff-Rose, which got his foot in the door for a deal with Capricorn Records. His debut, *My Wildest Dreams*, appeared in late 1993 followed by *All I Need to Know* in 1995 and *Me & You* in 1996. Chesney's prolific tradition continued in 1997 with *I Will Stand* and resumed two years later with *Everywhere We Go*, which generated the smash "You Had Me from Hello." BMG Entertainment pulled together all of Chesney's favorites for his *Greatest Hits* CD in late 2000—*John Bush*

In My Wildest Dreams / 1994 / Capricorn ♦♦♦

All I Need to Know / Jun. 13, 1995 / BNA ♦♦♦♦

Me & You / 1996 / BNA ♦♦♦

I Will Stand / Jul. 15, 1997 / BNA ♦♦♦♦♦

Everywhere We Go / Mar. 2, 1999 / BNA ♦♦

● **Greatest Hits** / Sep. 26, 2000 / BNA ♦♦♦♦
The culmination of seven years' work, Kenny Chesney's *Greatest Hits* CD is a good overview of his career and also throws in four unreleased tracks and a live version of "Back Where I Come From." His unique blend of traditional country vocal stylings and contemporary, slick pop orchestration is showcased on songs like "She's Got It All" and "All I Need to Know." Among these songs of heartache and loss, there hides a little sunny gem of a song in "She Thinks My Tractor's Sexy," in which Chesney reveals that his girl is kinda crazy about his farmer's tan and how she brings him a "basket 'a chicken and a big cold jug 'a sweet tea." *Greatest Hits* stands as a good introduction to one of the most popular country artists of the '90s or a worthwhile addition to the die-hard fan's collection. *—Zac Johnson*

Mark Chesnutt

b. Sep. 6, 1963, Beaumont, TX
Vocals / New Traditionalist, Contemporary Country
Mark Chesnutt was a major force in the revival of the old-fashioned honky tonk sound made famous by such stars as George Jones and Merle Haggard. The son of country singer Bob Chesnutt, he made his professional debut around age 16 when he began performing with his father's band. Chesnutt began playing throughout Texas for the next decade; he and his group, which included future solo star Tracy Byrd, eventually became the house band at Cutters nightclub in Beaumont. Chesnutt made his recording debut on the AXBAR label in San Antonio, releasing a number of local singles. After signing to MCA, he released "Too Cold at Home," a Top Five hit. He had his first number one hit with Paul Craft's "Brother Jukebox" in 1991.Over the next two years, the album produced three more Top Ten hits. Chesnutt's second album, *Longnecks and Short Stories*, went gold less than seven months after its 1992 release and contained several hits, including the number one singles "Old Flames Have New Names" and "I'll Think of Something," and had his first crossover hit with "Bubba Shot the Jukebox." *—Sandra Brennan*

Too Cold at Home / 1990 / MCA ♦♦♦♦♦
An impressive traditional country debut that often drew on George Jones and Texas swing, *Too Cold at Home* started Chesnutt off strong with the hits "Too Cold at Home," "Brother Jukebox," "Blame It on Texas," and "Your Love Is a Miracle." It also included a version of "Friends in Low Places" that came out at almost exactly the same time Garth Brooks's did. *—Brian Mansfield*

Longnecks & Short Stories / 1992 / MCA ♦♦♦♦♦
Longnecks heralded the emergence of a Texas voice that contained both the knack for humor ("Old Flames Have New Names, " "Bubba Shot the Jukebox"), and the depth for heartache ("I'll Think of Something"). *—Brian Mansfield*

Almost Goodbye / Jun. 22, 1993 / MCA ♦♦♦
Weak material weighs down Chesnutt's third release, though he still sings them like the most romantic western swinger since George Strait. "Almost Goodbye" is backed by a string arrangement as powerful as the one on "I'll Think of Something," but songs like "Texas Is Bigger" and "My Heart's Too Broke" aren't the attention-grabbers "Old Flames Have New Names" and "Bubba Shot the Jukebox" were. One of Chesnutt's biggest strengths is his casual delivery, but *Almost Goodbye* sounds too easy. "Almost Goodbye" and "It Sure Is Monday" both topped the singles charts. *—Brian Mansfield*

What a Way to Live / 1994 / MCA ♦♦♦
Like its predecessor *Almost Goodbye, What A Way To Live* is dogged by inconsistent material, but Chesnutt's fine singing manages to save most of the weaker material from being a bore. *—Stephen Thomas Erlewine*

Wings / Oct. 3, 1995 / Decca ♦♦♦♦♦
Mark Chesnutt's *Wings* is one of his most impressive efforts, showing the singer expanding his sonic template by stepping away from the commercial leanings of his recent material, yet leaving a slight pop and rock influence to his straightforward traditional country. What really makes the album rank among his best is the consistent quality of songwriting. Featuring songwriters like Jim Lauderdale and Todd Snider, *Wings* is filled with first-rate material that pushes at the borders of contemporary country while preserving its heritage. Ranging from romantic ballads to Bakersfield-type raveups, the record showcases Chesnutt at his finest. *—Stephen Thomas Erlewine*

● **Greatest Hits** / Nov. 19, 1996 / MCA Nashville ♦♦♦♦
Mark Chesnutt's *Greatest Hits* does a fair job of summing up the neo-traditionalist's biggest hits, adding two new songs—"It's A Little Too Late" and "Let It Rain"—to the collection. Though his biggest hits are showcased on the album, many of his proper albums offer a better representation of his talent. *—Thom Owens*

Thank God for Believers / Sep. 23, 1997 / MCA Nashville ✦✦✦✦

I Don't Want to Miss a Thing / Feb. 9, 1999 / MCA ✦✦✦✦

Lost in the Feeling / Oct. 17, 2000 / MCA Nashville ✦✦✦

Guy Clark

b. Nov. 6, 1941, Monahans, TX

Vocals, Guitar / Alternative Country, Outlaw Country, Country-Folk, Singer/Songwriter, Progressive Country

Guy Clark doesn't just write songs, he crafts them with the kind of hands-on care and respect that a master carpenter (a favorite image of his) would have when faced with a stack of rare hardwood. Clark works slowly and with strict attention to detail—he's only recorded eight albums since he was first signed to RCA in the early '70s—but he has produced an impressive collection of timeless gems, leaving very little waste behind. Though his albums never met with much commercial success, the emotional level of his work consistently transcends sales figures; he remains the kind of songwriter whom young artists study and seasoned writers (and listeners) admire. Clark worked as a songwriter in Nashville for several years, until RCA signed him for two albums. After switching to Warner Brothers in the late '70s, Clark recorded three albums that were marginally popular; a number of his songs were made into hits by country stars such as Johnny Cash, David Allen Coe, Ricky Skaggs (who took "Heartbroke" to number one), George Strait, Vince Gill, and the Highwaymen. Clark continued to work as a writer but didn't record again until 1988's *Old Friends*. He then switched labels once more, this time to Asylum, who released his 1992 album *Boats to Build* as part of their acclaimed American Explorer series. His eighth album, *Dublin Blues*, came out in 1995. *—Kurt Wolff*

★ **Old #1** / 1975 / Sugar Hill ✦✦✦✦✦

Boasting an excellent set of original songs—including the contemporary classics "L.A. Freeway," "She Ain't Goin' Nowhere," and "Desperados Waiting for the Train"—and stripped-back, honest arrangements, Guy Clark's debut album *Old #1* set the tone for his career. Though he crafted several fine albums after *Old #1*, he never quite matched its consistency, both in terms of songwriting and performance. *—Thom Owens*

Texas Cookin' / 1976 / Sugar Hill ✦✦✦✦

The songs here are more Nashville, hitting many emotions. "Texas Cookin'," "Virginia's Reel," and "Broken Hearted" are all great songs. What a way to finish the album, as Clark and Waylon Jennings sing "The Last Gunfighter Ballad." *—Chip Renner*

Guy Clark / 1978 / Warner Brothers ✦✦✦

This very-overlooked album is more country than his first two RCA albums. Just listen to the vocals (with the Whites, Rodney Crowell, Don Everly, Gordon Payne) and the words. You'll find this album grows on you. *—Chip Renner*

The South Coast of Texas / 1981 / Warner Brothers ✦✦✦✦

A good solid album. Check out Rosanne Cash's vocals on "Cystelle." Vince Gill, Ricky Skaggs, and Rodney Crowell give this album a real polished sound. *—Chip Renner*

Better Days / 1983 / Warner Brothers ✦✦✦✦

Old Friends / 1989 / Sugar Hill ✦✦✦

Boats to Build / 1992 / Elektra/Nonesuch ✦✦✦

Craftsmen / 1995 / Philo ✦✦✦✦✦

Craftsman compiles all three of Clark's Warner Bros. albums—*Guy Clark, The South Coast of Texas,* and *Better Days*—on two CDs. A great collection if you already have *Old No. 1* and want to dig deeper. *—Kurt Wolff*

Dublin Blues / Apr. 4, 1995 / Elektra ✦✦✦

Clark's skill as a singer and songwriter has a long way to go before it fades. "Baby Took a Limo to Memphis" is a silly throwaway, but "Stuff That Works" and the title track are classic Clark. Includes a new version of "The Randall Knife." *—Kurt Wolff*

Keepers / 1997 / Sugar Hill ✦✦✦

Recorded at Nashville's Douglas Corner in the fall of 1996, this is not only Clark's first live album, but his first with a full band in over a decade. "L.A. Freeway," "Texas—1947," "South Coast of Texas," and "Better Days" are some of the longtime Clark favorites included here, along with a couple of new songs, such as "Out in the Parking Lot." *—Kurt Wolff*

● **Essential** / Jan. 28, 1997 / RCA ✦✦✦✦✦

Featuring many of Guy Clark's finest songs, as well as a handful of excellent lesser-known gems, *Essential* is a terrific introduction to one of the best, if under-appreciated, songwriters of the '70s. *—Thom Owens*

Cold Dog Soup / Oct. 26, 1999 / Sugar Hill ✦✦✦✦

Roy Clark

b. Apr. 15, 1933, Meherrin, VA

Vocals, Guitar, Fiddle, Banjo / Instrumental Country, Nashville Sound/Countrypolitan, Country-Pop, Traditional Country

In the '70s Roy Clark symbolized country music in the US and abroad. Between guest-hosting for Johnny Carson on *The Tonight Show* and performing to packed houses in the Soviet Union on a tour that sold out all 18 concerts, he used his musical talent and his entertaining personality to bring country music into homes across the world. As one of the hosts of TV's *Hee Haw* (Buck Owens was the other) for more than 20 years Clark picked and sang and offered country corn to 30 million people weekly. He is first and foremost an entertainer, drawing crowds at venues as different as Las Vegas, Atlantic City, and the Opry. His middle-of-the-road approach has filled a national void, with Clark offering country that was harder-edged than Kenny Rogers but softer and more accessible than Waylon Jennings. Among his numerous vocal hits are "Yesterday When I Was Young" and "Thank God and Greyhound." Instrumentally he has won awards, for both guitar and banjo. Clark has also co-starred on the silver screen with Mel Tillis, in the comedy *Uphill All the Way*. *—David Vinopal*

The Lightning Fingers of Roy Clark / 1963 / Razor & Tie ✦✦✦✦

Originally recorded for Capitol Records in his pre-*Hee-Haw* days (1963), this is Roy's instrumental album, an all-guitar fest that showcases the country artist's amazing chops. Kicking off with a warp-speed version of "Twelfth Street Rag" that actually gets doubles in tempo by the final chorus, this album features a brace of generic "twistin'" instrumentals (read: public domain tunes given a twist beat) like "Texas Twist," "Weeping Willow Twist," "Wildwood Twist" ("Wildwood Flower"), "Golden Slippers" and "Over the Waves," rocked up cha cha's like "Pink Velvet Swing" and Bob Wills' "A Maiden's Prayer," and boogies like the closing "Chicken Wire." Produced by Ken Nelson and sounding for all the world like it was cut in a single afternoon session, this should open up anyone's eyes and ears who think of Roy Clark only as a belly scratchin' fool, telling corny jokes and singing sappy love ballads. *—Cub Koda*

● **Greatest Hits** / Sep. 12, 1995 / Varese Vintage ✦✦✦✦

By concentrating on his biggest straight country hits for Capitol and Dot Records ("Tips of My Fingers," "Yesterday, When I Was Young," "I Never Picked Greyhound," "Thank God and Greyhound," "Come Live With Me") and sidestepping many of the novelty numbers that were associated with *Hee-Haw,* the 14-song *Greatest Hits* makes a case for Roy Clark's talents as songwriter and performer, providing a good introduction to his career. *—Stephen Thomas Erlewine*

Greatest Hits, Vol. 2 / Oct. 7, 1997 / Varese Vintage ✦✦✦✦

Roy Clark had his first brace of hits for the Capitol label in the mid- to late 1960s. But his second batch came with a brace of hit singles and charting albums for the Dot label the following decade with charters on the small Churchill label into the 1980s. This 15-track compilation gives the rest of the story of Roy's country charting hits, including "The Great Divide," "Then She's a Lover," "I Have a Dream, I Have a Dream," "September Song" and "Do You Believe This Town." And Roy's famous guitar chops are well highlighted on "Wildwood Flower" and "Alabama Jubilee." *—Cub Koda*

Terri Clark

Vocals / Neo-Traditionalist Country, Contemporary Country

Like her contemporary Shania Twain, Terri Clark came storming out of Canada and captured the attention of America's country music industry in the mid-'90s. Where Twain incorporated more rock & roll into her music, Clark pretty much stayed close to her country roots, even those roots were more new country than hardcore honky tonk. Following her high school graduation in 1987, she moved to Nashville, and for the next seven years sang at clubs and worked odd jobs, all the while trying to land a record contract. In 1994, she landed an audition for Mercury Records. After seeing a live performance from Clark, the label's president signed the singer. Clark's eponymous debut album was released in the summer of 1995; a hit upon its release, it spawned the Top Ten hits "Better Things to Do," "When Boy Meets Girl" and "If I Were You." Her second album, *Just the Same,* was released in the fall of 1996, preceded by the hit single "Poor Poor Pitiful Me." *—Stephen Thomas Erlewine*

● **Terri Clark** / 1995 / Mercury Nashville ✦✦✦✦

Terri Clark's self-titled debut established the vocalist as a promising singer and songwriter. Working from a basic, traditional country foundation, Clark adds in slight elements of pop and rock, making her music more immediately accessible. Though there are some flaws in the songs—occasionally, the melodies fail to stick—her impassioned, powerful singing make the album consistently entertaining. *—Stephen Thomas Erlewine*

Just the Same / Nov. 5, 1996 / Mercury ✦✦✦

Terri Clark's second album, *Just the Same,* exhibits a slightly stronger country-rock influence, as evidenced by the choice of "Poor, Poor, Pitiful Me"—a Warren Zevon cover as recorded by Linda Ronstadt—as the first single. Clark has the voice and power to make these rocking updates of traditional country convincing, yet the material is slightly too uneven and the production is slightly too slick to make the album the equal of the debut. Nevertheless, *Just the Same* isn't much of a sophomore slip—in fact, the best moments eclipse the finest parts of *Terri Clark*. You just wish there were more great moments than there are. *—Thom Owens*

How I Feel / May 19, 1998 / Mercury ✦✦✦

With her third album, *How I Feel,* Terri Clark confirms that she's one of the stronger female contemporary country singers of the late '90s. Unlike such peers as Shania Twain, Clark keeps things country, even when the production is clean and glossy. Although there's still a pronounced country-rock feel, *How I Feel* moves her back toward honky tonk and straight. She excels in this setting, and the album contains some of her best singing to date, even if some of the songs are a little weak. Nevertheless, Clark pulls through with the strength of her voice, which makes *How I Feel* another solid entry in her catalog. *—Thom Owens*

Ugly Duckling / Jun. 23, 1998 / Virginia ✦✦✦

Fearless / Sep. 19, 2000 / Polygram ✦✦✦✦

Influenced by the likes of Bob Dylan, Joan Baez, and Janis Joplin, Clark served as co-producer on *Fearless* to create an album that showcases those influences. Recorded in the basement of her Nashville home, she also co-wrote eight of the album's 12 inviting tunes. With her crisp vocals and other co-writing credit going to the likes of Mary Chapin Carpenter, Beth Nielsen Chapman, Carlene Carter, and Kim Richey to name a few, *Fearless* is an album pleasantly out of the ordinary for Clark. Fans will overlook her absence from the country music scene for two years to revel in the songs on this 12-track collection, including Clark's version of the classic Emmylou Harris song "Easy From Now On," complete with Harris singing background vocals. *—Maria Konicki*

Patsy Cline (Virginia Patterson Hensley)

b. Sep. 8, 1932, Gore, VA, **d.** Mar. 5, 1963, Camden, TN

Vocals, Piano / Nashville Sound/Countrypolitan, Rockabilly, Traditional Country

One of the greatest singers in the history of country music, Patsy Cline also helped blaze a trail for female singers to assert themselves as an integral part of the Nashville-dominated country music industry. Cline began recording in the mid-'50s, and although she recorded quite a bit of material between 1955 and 1960 (17 singles in all), only one of them was a hit. That song, "Walkin' After Midnight," was both a classic and a Top 20 pop smash. Things took a radical turn in 1960, when—with the help of producer Owen Bradley (who had worked on her sessions all along)—Cline began selecting material that was both more suitable and of a higher quality than her previous outings. "I Fall to Pieces," cut at the very first session where Cline was at liberty to record what she wanted, was the turning point in her career. Reaching number one in the country charts and number 12 pop, it was the first of several country-pop crossovers she was to enjoy over the next couple of years. More important, it set a prototype for commercial Nashville country at its best. Owen Bradley crafted lush orchestral arrangements, with weeping strings and backup vocals by the Jordanaires, that owed more to pop (in the best sense) than country. Cline remained hot through 1961 and 1962, with "Crazy" and "She's Got You" both becoming big country and pop hits. Although her commercial momentum had faded slightly, she was still at the top of her game when she died in a plane crash in March of 1963, at the age of 30. She was only a big star for a couple of years, but her influence was and remains huge. While the standards of professionalism on her recordings have been emulated ever since, they've rarely been complemented by as much palpable, at times heartbreaking emotion in the performances. —*Richie Unterberger*

Patsy Cline Showcase / 1961 / MCA ✦✦✦
One of only three albums released in her lifetime, *Showcase* was the first set of sessions after her near-death in a car crash in 1961. The recordings teamed her up with the Jordanaires and produced the hits "Crazy" and "I Fall to Pieces" as well as new, more stylized versions of "Walkin' After Midnight" and that single's original flip, "A Poor Man's Roses (Or a Rich Man's Gold)." This release features the second cover photo that was issued after her death, replacing the original cover art. —*Cub Koda*

The Patsy Cline Story / 1963 / MCA ✦✦✦
The Patsy Cline Story is a double-record, 24-track collection that Decca released in 1963, shortly after her tragic death. The compilation remains one of the strongest and most thorough retrospectives ever assembled, featuring most of her biggest hits—"Walking After Midnight," "She's Got You," "Crazy," "I Fall to Pieces," "Sweet Dreams"—plus a number of lesser-known gems like "Why Can't He Be You" and "Leavin' On Your Mind." The presence of these relatively unfamiliar tracks means that the album gives a more rounded and complete picture of Cline's career than *12 Greatest Hits*, even if it isn't as thorough as the subsequent four-disc box set *The Patsy Cline Collection*. In short, *The Patsy Cline Story* is the ideal introduction for a listener who wants a little more than the basics, but doesn't want to invest in a box set. —*Stephen Thomas Erlewine*

★ **12 Greatest Hits** / 1988 / MCA ✦✦✦✦✦
12 Greatest Hits is exactly what it says it is—12 of Patsy Cline's biggest hits, including all of her classic singles: "Walkin' After Midnight," "I Fall to Pieces," "Sweet Dreams," "Crazy," "She's Got You," "Faded Love," and "Leavin' On Your Mind." There's also a number of lesser-known gems like "Why Can't He Be You," which are as good as the big hits. *12 Greatest Hits* may be brief, but it contains abosolutely no filler and leaves no gaps, making it the perfect introduction to one of the greatest singers in country music history. —*Stephen Thomas Erlewine*

Live at the Opry / 1988 / MCA ✦✦✦
As everyone who listened to the Ryman opry knows, even a good singer can sound pretty bad live over the radio. Cline sounds simply great, with no studio effects and a sometimes pedestrian backup. —*George Bedard*

Her First Recordings, Vol. 2: Hungry for Love / 1989 / Rhino ✦✦✦✦✦
The second installment of *Her First Recordings*, with 14 tracks from 1957-59, is more pop-oriented than volume one, and perhaps less interesting because of that. It does show Cline and producer Owen Bradley beginning to develop the Nashville sound that would serve her well in the '60s, with contributions from such regulars as the Anita Kerr Singers, the Jordanaires, Floyd Cramer, Grady Martin, and Hank Garland. With some more work and better material, the prototype would pay big dividends just a year or two down the road. —*Richie Unterberger*

Her First Recordings, Vol. 3: Rockin' Side / 1989 / Rhino ✦✦✦✦✦
Patsy Cline—rocker— Well, sort of. At the outset of her recording career in the late '50s, Cline tried a variety of approaches, including rockabilly and uptempo hillbilly. This disc assembles 13 of her rockabilly-flavored recordings from 1956-59. It's not bad, but rockabilly was not Cline's forte—she was much more at ease with ballads and midtempo numbers with a heavier pop/country feel. In comparison with '50s female rockabilly singers like Brenda Lee (who shared Cline's producer), Patsy comes off as rather stiff and inhibited. "Stop, Look and Listen" (1956) is the clear highlight here, with a natural snare-paced groove absent from the other tracks. —*Richie Unterberger*

Her First Recordings, Vol. 1: Walkin' Dreams / 1989 / Rhino ✦✦✦✦✦
Although Cline recorded quite a bit during the last half of the 1950s, it was a frustrating period for her, both commercially and artistically. Commercially, there was only one hit; artistically, she had yet to perfect her delivery, and didn't have access to nearly as much first-rate material as she would later on. Rhino's three-part *Her First Recordings* series presents a few dozen sides from this era. While they aren't as impressive as her more widely known '60s recordings, they're worthwhile both for the occasional first-rate performance and the illustration of the various approaches Cline and producer Owen Bradley attempted in her formative days. Volume one, focusing on recordings from 1955-1957, is variable in both style and quality, as Cline tries out spirituals, melodramatic ballads, and upbeat country-pop. Includes "Walkin' After Midnight," which is the original pop Top 20 version, not the later re-recording that is featured on many compilations. —*Richie Unterberger*

Live, Vol. 2 / 1989 / MCA ✦✦✦✦✦
A sequel to *Live at the Opry*, it's not called *Live at the Opry Vol. 2* because it wasn't taken from Opry broadcasts, but from radio shows produced for the U.S. Navy and Armed Forces. The twelve performances date from 1956 to 1962, and are of special interest in that they include five songs that she never recorded in the studio for commercial release, including numbers by Roger Miller, Webb Pierce, and Sonny James. Cline's in good form throughout, the fidelity is very good, and the arrangements are on the whole considerably sparer than her studio recordings were wont to employ. The straightahead reading of "Strange," a top-notch 1962 Mel Tillis composition that went on the B-side of "She's Got You," is a particular highlight. A good album that will appeal to most country fans, not just Cline collectors. —*Richie Unterberger*

☆ **The Patsy Cline Collection** / 1991 / MCA ✦✦✦✦✦
If Hank Williams remains the undisputed King of Country Music, then surely the passage of time has made the Queen of Country Music crown lay just as easy on the head of Patsy Cline's memory. Since her death in 1963, Patsy Cline has always had an audience. Selling 75,000 copies a year, year in and out, 17 years after you're dead is no small achievement, just ask Sid Vicious. But since her movie deification in the '80s, you can take that 75,000 copies a year and multiply it by ten. Patsy Cline is an official growth industry, just like Elvis or poor ol' Hank. So even though MCA has some 20-odd Patsy Cline packages in the catalog already, it makes more than a little sense to release this excellent four-CD box, produced by the Country Music Foundation. The sound, except for the live radio transcription disc stuff, is as cozy, warm and appealing as you could want. The track lineup, in chronological order, follows Cline's days from hard-line honky tonk belter to the ballad smoothies that made her reputation. There is no place in the four and a half hours of music here that you don't find yourself enjoying what you're hearing and in the world of box sets, that's saying a lot. In other words, there's not a single level at which this release does not mightily succeed. Because the major reason for Cline's enduring legend and growth-industry status is that the girl just flat sang her ass off and here's 104 perfect examples of it. —*Cub Koda*

Crazy Dreams: The Four Star Years / 1996 / Magnum ✦✦✦✦✦

Crazy Dreams: The Classic Early Years / May 20, 1997 / Music Club ✦✦✦

☆ **The Ultimate Collection** / Oct. 17, 2000 / MCA Nashville ✦✦✦✦✦

David Allan Coe

b. Sep. 6, 1939, Akron, OH
Vocals, Guitar / Outlaw Country, Progressive Country, Traditional Country
A life-long renegade, singer/songwriter David Allan Coe was one of the most colorful and unpredictable characters in country music history. One of the pioneering artists of the outlaw country movement of the '70s, he didn't have many big hits—only three of his singles hit the Top Ten—but he was among the biggest cult figures in country music throughout his career. After first getting into trouble with the law at age nine, Coe spent most of the next 20 years inside various correctional facilities. Finally released from prison in 1967, he went to Nashville and released his debut album *Penitentiary Blues* just one year later. His big break came in 1973, when Tanya Tucker recorded his "Would You Lay with Me (in a Field of Stone)" for an number one hit. The exposure gained him a recording contract with Columbia, and "You Never Even Called Me by My Name" cracked the Top Ten in 1975. Two years later, Johnny Paycheck took his "Take This Job and Shove It" to number one. Though Coe never excelled on the singles charts, he released 26 albums for Columbia, including 1984's double album set *For the Record… The First Ten Years*, 1986's *Son of the South* (featuring Willie, Waylon, Jessi Colter and other "outlaws") and 1987's highly regarded *Matter of Life…. and Death*. Problems with the conservative Nashville elite as well as the IRS curtailed his career though he remained a popular concert attraction during the '90s. —*Sandra Brennan*

Castles in the Sand / 1983 / Columbia ✦✦✦✦✦
By far one of David Allan Coe's best albums, *Castles in the Sand* is filled with exceptional songs. The title track is excellent, as is the number one country hit "The Ride," a tale of one man's encounter with the ghost of Hank Williams. Coe and Lacy J. Dalton evoke images of Bob Dylan and Janis Joplin at one point, and there's a cover of Dylan's "Gotta Serve Somebody." —*Michael B. Smith*

● **For the Record: The First 10 Years** / 1985 / Columbia ✦✦✦✦✦
For the Record: The First 10 Years gets a slight edge over its counterpart *17 Greatest Hits*, not just because it contains three more songs, but because it gives a greater context for David Allan Coe's achievements. Yes, his redneck tendencies sound a little disturbing to PC-leaning ears, but Coe was a great, unashamed country singer, singing the purest honky-tonk and hardest country of his era, making even Waylon and Willie seem a little conventional. There is an undeniable reactionary streak to his music yet, especially in retrospect, this makes it stronger, since he seems like one of the lone voices fighting for traditional country values. Did he win the fight— Well, in a way, he did, since he created pure, hardcore country, as this set of songs proves. This is Coe at his very best, from covers of "Please Come to Boston" to his trademarks "Longhaired Country," "Willie, Waylon and Me," "Jack Daniels, if You Please," and "Mona Lisa Lost Her Smile." He winds up relying on covers a bit much, but his attitude makes him stand apart from his brethren. He may not be the most original outlaw, but there's none more outlaw than him. —*Stephen Thomas Erlewine*

Recommended for Airplay / Mar. 30, 1999 / Columbia ✦✦✦

Mark Collie

b. Jan. 18, 1956, Waynesboro, TN
Vocals, Guitar / New Traditionalist, Contemporary Country
The music of singer/songwriter Mark Collie was a lively blend of straight-ahead rock & roll and traditional country. In 1982, Collie, encouraged by his wife, moved to Nashville to become a full-time songwriter at a publishing house. When no one hired him, he began singing his own songs to live audiences and picked up a following when he began doing monthly performances at the Douglas Corner Cafe. A 1989 showcase led MCA/Nashville to sign him. Collie's first single, "Something with a Ring to It," made it to the Top 60 in 1990. His next single, "Looks Aren't Everything," made it to the Top 40; both songs appeared on his first album, *Harden County Line*. He made it to the Top 20 for the first time in 1991 and then re-

leased his second album *Born and Raised in Black & White*, which produced two Top 40 hits, including "She's Never Coming Back." The following year, the album produced the Top Five single "Even the Man in the Moon Is Crying." *—Sandra Brennan*

Born & Raised in Black & White / 1985 / MCA ✦✦✦

Hardin County Line / 1990 / MCA ✦✦✦✦✦
This honky tonk rebel's debut evokes the heart of '50s country, with detailed and compassionate songwriting, wildcat vocals, and guitar by James Burton. One song, "Looks Aren't Everything," hit the Top 40, while two others, "Hardin County Line" and "Something with a Ring to It," didn't fare quite so well. *—John Floyd & Brian Mansfield*

● **Mark Collie** / 1993 / MCA ✦✦✦✦✦
At once a move to the mainstream and a return to Collie's West Tennessee rockabilly roots, the album worked fairly well. "Even the Man in the Moon Is Crying" and "Born To Love You" were Collie's first Top 10 hits, and "Shame Shame Shame Shame" rocked as hard as anything he'd done. *—Brian Mansfield*

Unleashed / 1994 / MCA ✦✦✦
In the same vein as *Mark Collie*, this album is more aggressive. "It Is No Secret" followed in Collie's tradition of midtempo romantic singles, while he rocks it up elsewhere. *—Brian Mansfield*

Tennessee Plates / Jul. 18, 1995 / Giant ✦✦✦

Tommy Collins (Leonard Raymond Sipes)

b. Sep. 28, 1930, Bethany, OK, **d.** Mar. 14, 2000, Ashland City, TN
Vocals, Guitar / Bakersfield Sound, Honky Tonk, Traditional Country
Along with his contemporary Wynn Stewart, Tommy Collins was one of the first country musicians to establish a distinctive Bakersfield, California sound. During the course of the '50s, he released a series of hit singles that lightened up the tone of honky tonk with bouncing back beats, novelty lyrics and electric guitars. Collins explored a more serious side with his ballads, yet they continued to sound slightly different than his peers—though they weren't as polished as the countrypolitain coming out of Nashville, they didn't have the grit of honky tonk. Legions of West Coast country performers—most notably Buck Owens, who played guitar on several of Tommy's hit singles, and Merle Haggard—built on the sound that Collins established in the early '50s. Collins wasn't able to cash-in on the Bakersfield craze of the '60s. By then, he had already quit the music business once, and was mounting a marginally successful comeback. Nevertheless, his influence loomed large, particularly on Haggard, who took Collins' "Carolyn" and "The Roots of My Raising" to the top of the charts in the early '70s. *—Stephen Thomas Erlewine*

● **Leonard** / 1992 / Bear Family ✦✦✦✦✦
Spanning five discs and well over one hundred tracks—featuring all of the songs he cut for Capitol in the late '50s and early '60s, including alternate takes and unreleased material—*Leonard* contains too much Tommy Collins for anyone but completists and historians. Nevertheless, it is the only collection of Collins' prime material to appear on CD. Collins was very influential and he deserves this deluxe box set treatment, but a single disc collection is needed—it would make his music available to country fans that simply can't afford a box set of this magnitude, but still want to hear the singer. If you can afford *Leonard*, it's a worthwhile investment for dedicated country music fans, but there isn't enough first-rate material on the box to justify the expense for listeners that want to explore the roots of the Bakersfield sound. *—Thom Owens*

Jessi Colter (Miriam Johnson Eddy)

b. May 25, 1947, Phoenix, AZ
Vocals, Keyboards, Piano / Outlaw Country, Country-Pop, Traditional Country
Perhaps best known in conjunction with her husband Waylon Jennings, Jessi Colter was the only significant female singer/songwriter to emerge from the mid-'70s "outlaw" movement. Colter in fact affiliated herself with outlaw imagery long before the musical movement blossomed, adopting her stage name in honor of ancestor Jess Colter, a real-life train robber. A vocalist and songwriter married to Duane Eddy for several years, Colter met Waylon Jennings in the late '60s. Jennings co-produced her 1970 debut, and the two married that same year. Under the name Waylon and Jessi, they also hit the Top 40 with a cover of the Elvis Presley hit "Suspicious Minds" and "Under Your Spell Again." Colter's commercial breakthrough came in 1975 when her composition "I'm Not Lisa" hit number one on the country charts and the Top Five on the pop charts. One year later, she teamed with Jennings, Willie Nelson and Tompall Glaser for the album *Wanted! The Outlaws*, which became the most popular album in country history. In between spending much of the remainder of the decade on tour with her husband and Nelson, she also released albums in 1977 and 1978. Her hits tapered off in the '80s and by the early '90s, she had begun directing her energies towards performing children's music. *—Jason Ankeny*

● **Jessi** / 1976 / Capitol ✦✦✦✦✦
After the success of "I'm Not Lisa" it's surprising that this record wasn't more popular than it was. Many of these songs are better than her big hit. *—Jim Worbois*

Leather and Lace / 1981 / RCA ✦✦

Collection / Apr. 4, 1995 / Capitol ✦✦✦✦
Collection is a brief ten-song compilation of Jessi Colter's hits for Capitol, including her number one hit "I'm Not Lisa" and number five hit "What's Happened to Blue Eyes." Her remaining two Top 40 hits on Capitol are included in addition to other select tracks. Colter was often associated with the outlaw movement because of her marriage to Waylon Jennings and her appearance on *Wanted! The Outlaws*, but none of her music here fits with the image. The tempos are generally slow and Colter's music is more reminiscent of Crystal Gayle than Waylon Jenning. *—Greg Adams*

Confederate Railroad

f. 1987
Group / Neo-Traditionalist Country, Southern Rock, Contemporary Country
Georgia-based Confederate Railroad was the contemporary cousin to such outlaw southern rockers as the Allman Brothers, Lynyrd Skynyrd, and Hank Williams, Jr. The group, with their scruffy biker clothes and hard-edged good-time music, got their start as a club band in the late '80s, founded by lead vocalist/guitarist Danny Shirley, who had been playing the club circuit since the early part of the decade. Confederate Railroad—comprised of drummer Mark Dufresne, bassist Wayne Secrest, keyboardist Chris McDaniel, lead guitarist Michael Lamb and steel guitarist Gates Nichols—released their self-titled debut in 1992. It produced several hits including "Jesus and Mama" (Top 5) and "Queen Memphis" (Top 3), but it was "Trashy Women,' the B-side of their "When You Leave That Way You Can Never Go Back," that really gained notoriety. Both the song and the resulting video for "Trashy Women" got considerable media exposure, and made it to the Top 10 on the country charts. In 1994, they released *Notorious* and within less than two months, it went gold. *When and Where* followed a year later, and in 1998 Confederate Railroad returned with *Keep on Rockin': Rockin' Country Party Pack* was issued two years later. *—Sandra Brennan*

● **Greatest Hits** / Jun. 18, 1996 / Atlantic ✦✦✦✦✦
Greatest Hits compiles Confederate Railroad's biggest hits, including all of their Top 10 singles, as well as several singles that never made it quite as far up the charts. As an added bonus, the group has added two new songs—which aren't particularly noteworthy—to lure fans that already own all the band's albums to the new collection. Even with the addition of the new songs, *Greatest Hits* remains the province of casual fans—it's a serves up all the hits in an engaging, concise manner. *—Stephen Thomas Erlewine*

Earl Thomas Conley

b. Oct. 17, 1941, Portsmouth, OH
Vocals / Urban Cowboy, Neo-Traditionalist Country, Country-Pop
Early in his career, Earl Thomas Conley's music picked up the label "thinking man's country." An accurate description—Conley looks into the heart and soul of his characters, finding the motivations for their actions and beliefs. In the process, the astute listener can find fragments of him/herself in nearly any Conley creation. Born into poverty in Portsmouth, Ohio, Conley struggled with the limits of his social class. He aspired to be a painter or actor but found that his aspirations for music lingered after the other interests died down. Influenced by everything from Hank Williams to the Eagles, Conley delved into the details of writing, trying to learn the craft by following the rules and regulations of the Music Row songwriting community. Eventually, torn by the limits of the "law," he found his own niche by breaking many of those same rules. His public self-analysis—in both his songs and his interviews—has proven inspirational to some, bothersome to others, but Conley has evolved stylistically, even though the thinking-man label continues to follow him. He's admittedly chased a more commercial sound, with a certain degree of success, but the run for the dollars also put him into a financial bind. He spent part of the late '80s and early '90s overworking himself to pay off his debts. Although he has been a hitmaker for more than a decade, his contributions to country have often gone almost unnoticed. *—Tom Roland*

Blue Pearl / 1980 / Sunbird ✦✦✦
This is the album that earned Conley the thinking-man label. "Middle-Age Madness" and "Blue and Green" stand out as classically written profiles of people in pain. "Silent Treatment," "Fire and Smoke," and "You Don't Have to Go Too Far" possess a captivating, slick sheen that belies their raw approach. *—Tom Roland*

Don't Make It Easy for Me / 1983 / RCA ✦✦✦✦✦
Conley speaks of "programming" himself to write, and in setting the tone for this album—as well as the followup, *Treadin' Water*—he programmed "radio records" into his consciousness. The result: a driving, rock-inflected package that yielded four number one singles—the first time an album did that in any format. The title track and "Your Love's on the Line" are particularly listenable, but there's not a bad cut on it. *—Tom Roland*

Greatest Hits / 1985 / RCA ✦✦✦✦
Some of his biggest songs are here, including "Angel in Disguise," "Silent Treatment," "Holding Her and Loving You," "Once in a Blue Moon," and others. *—AMG*

The Best of Earl Thomas Conley, Vol. 1 / 1988 / RCA ✦✦✦✦✦
As much as any of his '80s peers, Conley might have benefited from moving his sound toward harder country. The hits he did score ("Fire & Smoke," "Somewhere Between Right and Wrong," among the ones on this album) projected a voice ideally suited to a more Whitley-esque setting. *—Dan Cooper*

Greatest Hits, Vol. 2 / 1990 / RCA ✦✦✦✦
Conley was one of the hottest recording artists of the '80s. While this album isn't quite as strong as the first hits package, it shouldn't be ignored. Also features two new tracks. *—Jim Worbois*

● **The Essential** / Apr. 1996 / RCA ✦✦✦✦✦
Featuring the great majority of his hits plus an intriguing batch of rarities, *Essential* offers the best retrospective of Earl Thomas Conley's career. *—Stephen Thomas Erlewine*

Spade Cooley (Donell C. Cooley)

b. Feb. 22, 1910, Grand, OK, **d.** Nov. 23, 1969, Vacaville, CA
Cello, Fiddle / Western Swing
A musician and actor whose often sordid private life tended to overshadow his career as an entertainer, Spade Cooley was the self-proclaimed "King of Western Swing," an innovator who at his peak led the largest band ever assembled in the annals of country music. By the time he was eight years old, he was performing professionally at square dances, and he moved to Los Angeles by the time he was 20. In 1942, Cooley took control of the house band at the Venice Pier Ballroom in Santa Monica, and their western swing music began attract-

ing thousands of fans each Saturday night. The first single by Spade Cooley and His Orchestra, 1945's "Shame on You," lasted nine weeks atop the country charts. Though the group broke up after singer Tex Williams demanded more money, Cooley began a career in television in 1947, hosting a program that soon gained an estimated 75 percent of all televisions in the L.A. area each Saturday night. After the group's popularity waned in the early '50s, Cooley descended into alcoholism and suffered a series of minor heart attacks. In 1961, his wife Ella Mae left him; after an argument, he stomped her to death while the couple's daughter looked on in horror. The resulting trial and media circus culminated in a sentence of life imprisonment. He was a model prisoner, and thus was allowed to perform at a sheriff's benefit in Oakland in 1969. After playing, Cooley returned to his dressing room, suffered yet another heart attack, and died. *—Jason Ankeny*

★ **Spadella: the Essential** / 1994 / Columbia/Legacy ✦✦✦✦✦
Spadella: The Essential Spade Cooley collects 20 highlights from Cooley's stint as one of the most popular Western swing bandleaders in America. All of the selections on the album were recorded between 1945 and 1946, when Cooley and his group scored six straight Top Ten singles, all of which are included here ("You Can't Break My Heart" is in an alternate version). This is when the group was at its peak, and vocalist Tex Williams was always in stellar form. Although it doesn't cover his entire career, *Spadella* remains the one essential Cooley compilation. *—Stephen Thomas Erlewine*

King of Western Swing / 1997 / Collectors' Choice Music ✦✦✦
There's not a lot of Spade Cooley available—only a fraction of what one can find on Bob Wills—so this live performance from his first radio show, on July 21, 1951, is a welcome release. This was done five years or more after the contents of Sony's collection, after Cooley had become a major media star on television. The music includes solo spots for steel guitarist Noel Boggs and vocalists Becky Barfield, Ginny Jackson, and Phil Gray. Unfortunately, in contrast to Bob Wills' work, the performances and arrangements are more swing than Western, and they don't really swing that well—the resident bands on television shows such as *The Old American Barn Dance* did better. It's fun, but clunky, lacking the smoothness one expects and remembers. Luckily, the special guest is Jimmy Wakely, who performs three numbers including his then new release, "The Solid South," and it's amazing to hear the band come to life on his numbers. The disc includes three comedy routines from the show—luckily, they're indexed and can be bypassed on repeated listening (the jokes were old then, and haven't aged well). The sound is fair, without the crisp resolution of the best radio transcriptions. *—Bruce Eder*

Shame on You: The Western Swing Dance Gang / Apr. 20, 1999 / Bloodshot ✦✦✦✦
Shame On You collects 25 previously unreleased radio transcriptions recorded in 1944-1945, nine of which feature Tex Williams on vocals. The title track is a version of Cooley's number one hit from 1945, and the other material runs the gamut from polkas ("Cowbell Polka," "Yodeling Polka") and hillbilly hoe-downs ("Down Home Rag") to tunes that have become instrumental standards ("Steel Guitar Rag," "Silver Bell.") The sound quality is excellent, and *Shame on You* is a fine companion piece to *Spadella!*, Columbia's collection of Cooley's classic OKeh sides. *—Greg Adams*

1941-1947 / Apr. 11, 2000 / Country Routes ✦✦✦
This collection straddles several different eras and facets of Cooley's career, from his pre-bandleader days working with Cal Shrum to mid-'40s transcriptions featuring his regular band to some 1947 sides. Cooley's fiddle work is showcased nicely on tunes like "MacGregor Swing" and "MacGregor Blues" while Tex Williams does the vocal honors on classics like "Sweethearts or Strangers." The 1947 tracks feature stalwarts like Noel Boggs and Jimmy Wyble along with vocalists Ginny Jackson, Red Egner, and even ex-Spike Jones City Slicker Del Porter. The quality of these transcription discs is pretty decent, taking into factor their age and rarity, and this is a delightful set that showcases the talents of one of Western swing's best. *—Cub Koda*

Stoney Cooper

b. Oct. 16, 1918, Harman, WV, **d.** Mar. 22, 1977
Vocals, Fiddle / Traditional Country, Traditional Bluegrass
Dale Troy "Stoney" Cooper and his wife Wilma Lee were one of the premier husband-and-wife duos in country music. Staples of the *Grand Ole Opry* for twenty years, they performed together for close to four decades, and helped old-time music evolve into modern country music. Stoney and Wilma began singing together and were married in 1941. The couple began their career together singing at various radio stations around the country, ending up on the *Wheeling Jamboree* and staying there for the next 10 years as one of the show's most enduringly popular acts. The duo signed to Columbia in 1949 and remained for five years, releasing several classic singles, including "Sunny Side of the Mountain" and the devotional "Walking My Lord Up Calvary Hill." Their most successful year was 1959, when they released three Top Five hits: "Come Walk With Me," "Big Midnight Special," and "There's a Big Wheel." They scored their last chart appearance in 1961 with the Top Ten hit *Wreck on the Highway*. Stoney suffered a heart attack in 1963 and was forced to slow down considerably. The two moved to Decca in 1965 and tried to update their sound, without much success. *—Sandra Brennan*

● **Classic Early Recordings** / County ✦✦✦✦✦
Originally recorded between 1949 and 1953, the wife-and-husband duo let it fly with passionate zeal on these old-time mountain and gospel songs. Wilma Lee could shake the coal out of the hills with her raw and full-throated voice, and she didn't bother with nuance. *—Michael McCall*

Billy "Crash" Craddock

b. Jun. 16, 1939, Greensboro, NC
Vocals, Guitar / Honky Tonk, Rockabilly, Traditional Country
People often associate the "Crash" nickname with auto racing, but Craddock actually got it as a halfback in high school, crashing into linemen who were twice his size. Growing up in Greensboro, NC, he pantomimed Grand Ole Opry shows in the family's barn with a broomstick as a microphone, alternately pretending he was Hank Williams, Faron Young, or Carl Smith. But when he signed a recording contract in the late '50s, Columbia tried to mold him as a teen idol, much like Elvis Presley or Fabian. It didn't work in the U.S., but "Crash" did pick up a trio of hits in Australia. Fifteen years later, he finally got his chance in country music when record producer Ron Chancey signed him to his Cartwheel label. With a knack for making re-makes of pop hits like "Knock Three Times" and "Ruby Baby"—and for adding a certain energy to the country idiom—Craddock picked up the nickname "Mr. Country Rock." *—Tom Roland*

Boom Boom Baby / 1992 / Bear Family ✦✦✦✦✦
Although Billy "Crash" Craddock claims that he's "always" been country, there's no evidence of it on these late-'50s rock & roll recordings. Sounding very much like Elvis, Craddock tackles 21 rockers, novelties and teen ballads on this collection of his complete Columbia recordings. A few of these tracks charted in Australia, but Craddock's success in the U.S. was limited. Some of these songs, including "Blabbermouth," "Sweetie Pie" and "Ah, Poor Little Baby," seem to have had hit potential, but it wasn't to be. Fans of Elvis and '50s rock in general should check this one out. *—Greg Adams*

● **Crash's Smashes: The Hits Of Billy "Crash" Craddock** / Feb. 20, 1996 / Razor & Tie ✦✦✦✦✦
Drawing from three different labels—Cartwheel, ABC, and Capitol—*Crash's Smashes: The Hits of Billy "Crash" Craddock* is the definitive compilation of Craddock's career. All of his biggest hits—from "Knock Three Times" and "Dream Lover" through "Rub it In," "Easy as Pie" and "Broken Down in Tiny Pieces" to "If I Could Write A Song As Beautiful As You"—are included on the 19-track single disc, making it both a perfect introduction and retrospective. *—Stephen Thomas Erlewine*

Floyd Cramer

b. Oct. 27, 1933, Samti, LA, **d.** Dec. 31, 1997
Piano, Session Musician / Nashville Sound/Countrypolitan, Instrumental Pop, Country-Pop
A distinctive pianist whose unique, slip-note playing style came to typify the pop-oriented "Nashville Sound" of the late 1950s and early 1960s, session and solo musician Floyd Cramer began his career appearing on the radio program *The Louisiana Hayride*, where he performed with the likes of Jim Reeves, Faron Young, Webb Pierce and, in his debut, Elvis Presley. While Cramer cut a few solo sides in 1953, his most important work in the early 1950s was as a session musician, where he first met Chet Atkins. As the house pianist at RCA Records, he began developing what would ultimately be recognized as the Nashville Sound, a style shorn of the elements associated with traditional country and honky-tonk which instead favored a more polished, progressive sheen. With Atkins behind the production boards, Cramer began to perfect his unique style of playing, a method not dissimilar to guitar-picking in that he would hit one key and then slide his finger onto the next, creating a blue, lonesome sound. Under Atkins' guidance, Cramer played on hundreds of sessions, including many for Presley, among them "Heartbreak Hotel." In 1957, Cramer released his own solo debut, *That Honky-Tonk Piano*, and in the next year scored a minor pop hit with the single "Flip, Flop and Bop." As his solo career was largely secondary in relation to his session work, he recorded his own music sporadically, but in 1960 notched a significant country and pop hit with the self-penned instrumental "Last Date." *—Jason Ankeny*

★ **The Essential** / Aug. 1, 1995 / RCA ✦✦✦✦✦
Although it isn't necessarily a definitive retrospective, *Essential* is the best CD compilation of Floyd Cramer's solo recordings yet assembled. Containing 20 tracks, including his hits "Last Date," "San Antonio Rose" and "Stood Up," the disc captures Cramer's signature stride piano style in all of its glory on a variety of country, pop and R&B numbers. Cramer was as well-known as a sideman as he was a solo artist, and even if *Essential* contains none of his session work, it contains a good portion of his very best recordings, making it a fine introduction to one of the most influential pianists in country and pop history. *—Stephen Thomas Erlewine*

Rodney Crowell

b. Aug. 7, 1950, Houston, TX
Vocals, Guitar / Neo-Traditionalist Country, New Traditionalist, Folk-Rock, Pop, Singer/Songwriter, Contemporary Country, Country-Rock, Progressive Country
While Rodney Crowell first gained widespread recognition as a leader of the "New Traditionalist" movement of the mid-'80s, he in fact was a singer, songwriter and producer with roots and ambitions extending far beyond the movement's parameters. Crowell moved to Nashville in 1972 to become a professional musician. He wrote a few songs, then moved to Los Angeles to join Emmylou Harris' Hot Band as a guitarist and songwriter. In 1978, he formed his own group the Cherry Bombs, released his first solo album, and began producing tracks for the album *Right or Wrong*, the American debut from Rosanne Cash; he and Cash later married. In between recording his own 1980 sophomore record and producing Cash's commercial breakthrough *Seven Year Ache*, Crowell's songwriting career took full flight when "Leavin' Louisiana in the Broad Daylight" hit number one hit for the Oak Ridge Boys in 1980. Crystal Gayle, the Nitty Gritty Dirt Band and Highway 101 also gained number ones with Crowell's songs. He continued recording on his own as well, and after helming Cash's 1985 masterpiece *Rhythm and Romance*, finally broke through commercially in 1988 with *Diamonds and Dirt*, which generated an unbroken string of five number one singles. After Crowell and Cash divorced in 1991, he documented the marriage's dissolution with a starkly confessional album, 1992's *Life Is Messy*. He remained a prolific performer throughout the decade, issuing *Let the Picture Paint Itself* in 1994 and two albums the following year. *—Jason Ankeny*

Ain't Living Long Like This / 1978 / Warner Brothers ✦✦✦✦✦
Rodney Crowell's auspicious 1978 debut, *Ain't Living Long Like This*, not only showcases his songwriting prowess, but also his ability to deliver a song, whether it's one of his own or the work of another writer. Crowell possesses a sort of Everly Brothers, Nashville soul in his

strong, emotive tenor, that's equally effective on the country-blues of Dallas Frazier's "Elvira", as it is on the rocking title cut or a country-folk ballad such as the self-penned "Song for the Life". Along with producer Brian Ahern (Emmylou Harris), Crowell employs a who's who of country and rock'n'roll session players, including James Burton and Glen D. Hardin, both of whom played with Elvis Presley and Gram Parsons, as well as enlisting the aid of artists such as Dr. John, Ry Cooder, Nicolette Larson, Emmylou Harris, Ricky Skaggs and Willie Nelson. As a writer, Crowell, who chose to include three terrific covers over any of his backlog of excellent original material, has the knack for mixing a pop sensibility and rock'n'roll vitality, with the heart and reverence of a traditionalist. A song such as "California Earthquake (A Whole Lotta Shakin' Goin' On)", sounds as if it could've been written decades before, while "Voila, An American Dream" hit the pop charts the following year for *the Dirt Band. Ain't Living Long Like This* became a mining-ground of material for others. Nearly every one of Crowell's tunes from the album was covered within the next few years, spawning at least a couple of major hits. Even "Elvira", which he had resurrected, became an early-'80's smash for the Oak Ridge Boys . *—Brett Hartenbach*

But What Will the Neighbors Think / 1980 / Warner Brothers ✦✦

Rodney Crowell / 1981 / Warner Brothers ✦✦✦
Crowell plays down his performance on this album. Yes, he's a bit cool toward the material vocally on occasion, but the overall effect is raw, energetic, and natural, in the best garage-band tradition. A good mix of club rock & roll and country-rock, with, incidentally, his own renditions of "Till I Gain Control Again" and "Shame on the Moon." *—Tom Roland*

Street Language / 1986 / Columbia ✦✦

☆ **Diamonds & Dirt** / 1989 / Columbia/Legacy ✦✦✦✦✦
This reissue adds three previously unreleased bonus tracks to Crowell's watershed 1988 album, which produced five chart-topping country hits. The songs range from soft acoustic ballads to twangy, uptempo slices of neo-rockabilly. *Diamonds & Dirt* functions as a song cycle of romantic relationships, from the bliss of "I Couldn't Leave You If I Tried" to the regret of "I Didn't Know I Could Lose You." The three added tracks were recorded during a demo session for the album. The best of the bonus tracks, "Lies Don't Lie" and the Buck Owens-styled "I've Got My Pride But I've Got My Kids to Feed" would have fit in perfectly on the original album line-up. *—Mary Grady*

Keys to the Highway / 1989 / Columbia ✦✦✦
The success of Rodney Crowell's *Diamonds & Dirt* was a surprise, if only because Crowell had been making records for ten years with only modest sales. It was more country-oriented and less challenging than his previous recordings, but the album threw off a record-setting five number one country hits while remaining in the charts more than two years. *Keys to the Highway,* therefore, should have consolidated Crowell's status as a major country star; instead, it was a commercial disappointment from which he did not recover. Though Crowell had bowed to a traditional approach somewhat on *Diamonds & Dirt,* he remained essentially a stylist as interested in folk, rock, and R&B as he was in country. At the same time, emboldened by his success, Crowell apparently wanted to try to recover some of his critical standing, and he also seems to have been influenced by the death of his father to be true to himself. Momentum pushed the leadoff single, the slow, thoughtful folk-rock ballad "Many a Long and Lonesome Highway," into the country Top Five, but it was not what fans of *Diamonds & Dirt* were expecting, and despite the neo-Nashville sound of second single "If Looks Could Kill," which reached the country Top Ten, *Keys to the Highway* failed to make the country Top Ten or go gold. It's a much better album than that history suggests, however, carefully balanced between exercises in early rock & roll and rockabilly, country-soul, mainstream '60s-style rock, and even dyed-in-the-wool country. *Keys to the Highway* didn't have the songwriting depth of Crowell's early albums, but it was more substantial and more varied than *Diamonds & Dirt,* and if handled well, it might have been even more successful. Instead, it remains an album yet to be really discovered. *—William Ruhlmann*

● **The Rodney Crowell Collection** / 1989 / Warner Brothers ✦✦✦✦✦
Rodney Crowell was one of the premier songwriters of the 1980s. Although his albums were not commercially successful, the high quality of Crowell's songs did not escape the attention of the music community. This compilation collects the best moments from his early albums, and most of these songs will sound instantly familiar to people who listened to country radio in the 1980s. Many of the songs featured on this album were made into hits, including "Queen of Hearts" (Juice Newton), "Stars on the Water" (Jimmy Buffett), "I Ain't Living Long Like This" (Waylon Jennings), and "Shame on the Moon" (Bob Seger). As is often the case when songwriters sing their own material, the songs carry more emotional weight under the care of the original author. Although Rodney Crowell does not have a powerful or distinctive voice, he has a genuine warmth in his delivery and a lyrical directness that gives his songs universal appeal. The finest tracks are the relationship songs, whether it's rising above the pain of heartbreak ("Ashes By Now") or finding romance in the simple pleasures of everyday life ("An American Dream"). Given the uneven nature of his solo albums, this album is a terrific introduction to a respected songwriter. *—Vik Iyengar*

Life Is Messy / May 12, 1992 / Columbia ✦✦✦✦
After the commercial fall-off of *Keys to the Highway,* Rodney Crowell took 2Ω years crafting his seventh album, *Life Is Messy,* in the interim going through a divorce from his wife Rosanne Cash. The most notable characteristic of *Life Is Messy* was that it marked a complete return to his original style. With nary a steel guitar or fiddle to be heard, and featuring top pop session musicians as well as a slew of pop guest stars (Linda Ronstadt, Don Henley, Steve Winwood, etc.), *Life Is Messy* wasn't really a country record at all. A couple of songs had a country-rock, honky tonk feel, but the dominant musical style was a pastiche of late-'50s/early-'60s pop. The title song was a somewhat abstract meditation on romantic discord and career disappointment that was followed by the equally despairing "I Hardly Know How to Be Myself," which actually had been co-written with Cash. These songs sounded so pained and deeply felt that some of the more uptempo songs came off as trivial, even if they made for a change of pace. But other songs came up to their standard without being quite so low in mood. "Alone But Not Alone" found the singer beginning to find his way, and "It's Not for Me to Judge" revealed the non-committal feelings one can have when emotional certainties are uprooted. Taken together, the songs on *Life Is Messy* made for a fascinating portrait of an artist at a personal and professional crossroad—but it didn't have much to do with commercial country music circa 1992, which is what it was primarily marketed as. After a few months, Columbia Records pulled the plug on promotion and parted ways with Crowell, who moved on to MCA Records. *—William Ruhlmann*

● **Greatest Hits** / 1993 / Columbia ✦✦✦✦✦
The music on *Greatest Hits* is taken from an era when Rodney Crowell actually had hits, including the number ones "I Couldn't Leave You If I Tried," "She's Crazy for Leavin'," and "After All This Time." Those songs and several more are collected on *Greatest Hits,* making it a fine introduction to the singer/songwriter. *—Stephen Thomas Erlewine*

Let the Picture Paint Itself / 1994 / MCA ✦✦✦
So much of Crowell's best work has been co-produced by MCA executive Tony Brown, it seemed inevitable he would wind up at MCA himself. This, his first release for his new label, emphasizes Crowell, the thoughtful songwriter, over Crowell the neo-honky tonk bandleader. It's a fair trade, but requires repeat listening to fully appreciate. *—Dan Cooper*

Jewel of the South / 1995 / MCA ✦✦✦

Dick Curless

b. Mar. 17, 1932, Fort Fairfield, ME
Vocals / Truck Driving Country, Bakersfield Sound
Dick Curless was best known for singing truck-drivin' songs such as "Drag 'Em Off the Interstate, Sock It to 'Em J.P. Blues; " a tall man with an eye-patch and rich baritone voice, Curless was often called the "Baron of Country Music," after one of his popular songs, "The Baron." He got his big break when he won on *Arthur Godfrey Talent Scouts.* Afterward Curless began performing in Las Vegas and Hollywood; a record contract followed, but his budding career was interrupted by an illness. He finally reached the country charts in 1965 with the Top Five hit "A Tombstone Every Mile," followed by nine more chart hits including the highly successful "Six Times a Day (the Trains Came Down)." In 1970, Curless signed to Capitol and scored a Top 30 hit based on the classic "Wabash Cannonball," titled "Big Wheel Cannonball." The follow-up "'Hard, Hard Traveling Man," (1970) made it to the Top 40. During his career, he had a total of 22 hits. In the '70s and '80s, Curless recorded infrequently, and eventually became a born-again Christian. He recorded an album in Norway in 1987, and by 1992 was a regular at the Cristy Lane Theater in Branson, MO. Curless died in 1995. *—Sandra Brennan*

A Tombstone Every Mile / 1996 / Bear Family ✦✦✦✦✦
A Tombstone Every Mile is a seven-disc, 191-track box set that contains all of Dick Curless' classic Tower recordings from the '60s, his first sides for Standard, several albums he cut for Tiffany, his duets with guitarist Lenny Breau on Event, and several unreleased, non-commercial Korean war recordings. In short, the set collects everything Curless recorded during the '50s and '60s, stopping when he signed to Capitol in 1970. Curless never had many hits and was always somewhat of a cult artist, which means that a box the size of *A Tombstone Every Mile* plays right into his cult. His dedicated following of fans will treasure all of the rarities, the excellent biography, and the stellar sound on this collection, but the length of the set means that it won't convert neophytes into fans. Nevertheless, any historian or hardcore fan that wants to invest in the box will not be disappointed by the results. *—Thom Owens*

● **Drag 'Em off the Interstate, Sock It to Em: The Hits of Dick Curless** / May 19, 1998 / Razor & Tie ✦✦✦✦✦
Clocking in with 21 tracks, *The Drag 'Em Off the Interstate, Sock It to 'Em Hits of Dick Curless* is a superb career retrospective, an ideal introduction for listeners unable or unwilling to shell out for Bear Family's seven-disc *A Tombstone Every Mile* box set. Though best known for his trucker material, Curless was in fact a versatile performer capable of moving easily from traditional ballads to country-pop to blues; this well-assembled collection underscores that versatility, with highlights including the hits "The Baron," "Six Times a Day," "Nine Pound Hammer," "I Ain't Got Nobody," "Tater Raisin' Man" and of course "A Tombstone Every Mile," his best-known recording. *—Jason Ankeny*

Hard Hard Traveling Man / Sep. 12, 2000 / Bear Family ✦✦✦✦✦

Billy Ray Cyrus

b. Aug. 25, 1961, Flatwoods, KY
Vocals, Guitar / Contemporary Country
Billy Ray Cyrus will forever be known for the catchy, lightweight single "Achy, Breaky Heart," which became a line-dancing anthem upon its 1992 release. "Achy, Breaky Heart" made Billy Ray Cyrus famous, but it also proved to be his undoing. No matter how he tried, he could not escape the song, nor could he replicate the success. Cyrus' music was never particularly innovative—it owed as much to the country-rock of the Eagles as it did to the new traditionalism of George Strait, and the new country of Clint Black and Garth Brooks—but his musical worth became irrelevant in the wake of the success of "Achy, Breaky Heart" and its accompanying album, *Some Gave All.* The album became a crossover success after the single became a hit, spending 17 weeks on the top of the album charts. Part of Cyrus' success was due to his handsome, hunky good looks, and part of it was due to the catchiness of "Achy, Breaky Heart." However, both his good looks and the single were soon forgotten, and just two years after *Some Gave All* ruled the charts, Cyrus virtually disappeared from both the pop and country charts, and became part of the long history of one-hit wonders. *—Tom Roland & Stephen Thomas Erlewine*

● **Best of Billy Ray Cyrus: Cover To Cover** / Jun. 24, 1997 / Mercury ✦✦✦✦
Billy Ray Cyrus recorded only four albums before releasing *The Best of Billy Ray Cyrus,* which indicates his status as a one-hit wonder. "Achy Breaky Heart" was the hit that made

his career, but it also ruined it, since its jokey refrain and his good looks meant that no one took him seriously. There's not much evidence on *The Best of Billy Ray Cyrus* that those critics were wrong, but there are more enjoyable songs here than you might expect, especially since it whittles all four albums down to just the highlights. For every casual fan, this is the one Cyrus disc they'll want to own, even if *Some Gave All* functions fairly well as an album itself. *—Thom Owens*

Lacy J. Dalton

b. Oct. 13, 1948, Bloomsburg, PA

Vocals, Guitar / Neo-Traditionalist Country, Contemporary Country, Country-Pop

Lacy J. Dalton, who has a voice one writer described as "honey laced with whiskey," took a circuitous route to Nashville. Born Jill Byrem in Bloomsburg, PA, she attended Brigham Young University but dropped out to become folk singer. She kicked around Utah, Minnesota, Pennsylvania, and New York before winding up in front of a psychedelic rock band in San Francisco in the late '60s. She married the group's manager, who died as the result of injuries sustained in a swimming-pool accident. Dalton kept performing, and a tape of her music eventually reached producer Billy Sherrill, who signed her to Columbia in 1979. The Academy of Country Music named her Best New Female Vocalist in 1979 on the strength of her debut, "Crazy Blue Eyes." Dalton's distinct sound and far-ranging musical interests may have kept her from being the star she could have been, but her records helped open doors for new sounds in country. *—Brian Mansfield*

● **Greatest Hits** / 1983 / Columbia ✦✦✦✦✦

Dalton's best songs weren't always her hits, but *Greatest Hits* is still a good sampler, including "Crazy Blue Eyes," her first hit; "Hard Times"; remakes of "Tennessee Waltz" and "Dream Baby"; and the music-biz anthem "16th Avenue." *—Brian Mansfield*

Charlie Daniels

b. Wilmington, NC

Vocals, Violin, Guitar, Fiddle / Urban Cowboy, Country Gospel, Southern Rock, Country-Rock, Traditional Country

A talented and showy fiddler, Charlie Daniels and his band fuse hardcore country with a hard-edged southern rock boogie and blues. The group—which has had a rotating cast of musicians over the years—has always been known for their instrumental dexterity, but they were also notorious for their down-home, good-old boy attitude; in the early '80s they became a virtual symbol of conservative country values. Charlie Daniels played fiddle and guitar as a teenager, forming an instrumental rock band named the Jaguars as well as working on songwriting (Elvis Presley recorded his "It Hurts Me" in 1963). By the late '60s, he was working as a Nashville sessionman, and in 1972, he formed the Charlie Daniels Band, using the southern rock of the Allman Brothers as a blueprint. In 1974, *Fire on the Mountain* became a gold record within months of its release, thanks to the Top 40 country hit "Texas." In the late '70s, Daniels refashioned the band as a more straightforward country band. The change paid off in 1979 when the single "The Devil Went Down to Georgia" became a number one hit and crossed over to hit number three on the pop charts. Although he continued to sell respectably throughout the '80s, he never had as big a hit. He remained a popular concert draw. *—Stephen Thomas Erlewine*

John, Grease & Wolfman / 1972 / Epic ✦✦✦

On this, Charlie Daniels' second release, there are obvious signs of a bright future for the guitar- and fiddle-playing hillbilly rocker. Along for the ride is Joel "Taz" DiGregoria, Charlie's longtime bandmate and keyboard wizard. Taz even takes lead vocal duties on one song, "Billy Joe Young," and his ivory tickling is a highlight of this historical Southern-rock document. Daniels rocks with the intensity of a downbound train on "Great Big Bunches of Love," and on his cover of the Jerry Lee Lewis chestnut "Drinkin' Wine, Spo-Dee-O-Dee." A true Southern poet, Charlie Daniels is seen here in the infancy of his artistic development, but even at this early stage, the poet is alive and well. *—Michael B. Smith*

☆ **Fire on the Mountain** / 1975 / Epic ✦✦✦✦✦

Fire on the Mountain is the Charlie Daniels Band's finest moment. Daniels finds the perfect middle ground between southern-rock boogie and hillbilly honky tonk, creating a sound that rocked hard but still had down-home roots. Although he would delve deeper into country, he would never make a stronger, more enjoyable album. *—Thom Owens*

Nightrider / 1975 / Epic/Legacy ✦✦✦✦

Charlie Daniels was faced with a challenge following the success of 1974's *Fire on the Mountain.* With two moderate hits under his ample cowboy hat, Daniels decided to pull out all the stops once again, inviting Volunteer Jam buddies Toy Caldwell of the Marshall Tucker Band, Jaimoe of the Allman Brothers Band, and Paul Hornsby, a noted Capricorn Records session man who not only produced the LP but played keyboards on it, to join the party. The result is another moderate hit, "Texas," and another string of Charlie Daniels Band classics, including "Funky Junky" and "Damn Good Cowboy." *—Michael B. Smith*

High Lonesome / 1976 / Epic ✦✦✦

Saddle Tramp / 1976 / Epic ✦✦✦

Volunteer Jam / 1976 / Capricorn ✦✦✦

When Charlie Daniels held his first-ever Volunteer Jam in his home state of Tennessee, the tapes were rolling and the cameras were as well. Sections of the jam were filmed and released theatrically in 1975. The Volunteer Jam was scheduled to go on the road in 1999, with the film being screened prior to each show. This live recording serves as a good cross-section of the music that was created onstage that day; there is also an EP included in Daniels' *Fire On the Mountain* album, taken from the same show. The Charlie Daniels Band burns white-hot on the first three numbers before turning the show over to the Marshall Tucker Band for a smoking version of "The Thrill is Gone." The CDB backs Dickey Betts of the Allman Brothers Band on the J.J. Cale tune "Sweet Mama," and the stage fills for the finale, "Mountain Dew," with Betts, Mylon LeFevre, Jimmy Hall of Wet Willie, and Ronnie Stoneman on banjo—a down-home hoedown. This album serves as a landmark, the beginning of a Charlie Daniels tradition that would continue into the 21st century. *—Michael B. Smith*

● **A Decade of Hits** / 1983 / Epic/Legacy ✦✦✦✦✦

More than half of the songs from The Charlie Daniels Band's compilation *A Decade Of Hits* were chart successes, especially the fiery "*Devil Went Down To Georgia*", a boot kickin' mix of rock and country fiddle that proved to be this group's biggest hit. Played on both country and rock radio, it hit number three on Billboard's Top 40 in 1979 thanks to it's hard based rhythm and entertaining narrative. *A Decade Of Hits* puts together ten of their most solid songs that integrate both a country and rock feel. "The South's Gonna Rise Again" unleashes Daniels pride of being from North Carolina and the attributes of being a good ol' boy. "Long Haired Country Boy" does much of the same, but with a more generous amount of countrified fervor. "Still In Saigon" leans on a more rock oriented style, and loosely deals with one veteran's flashbacks to the Vietnam War. As a story song, "The Legend Of Wooley Swamp" basks in the southern slang of Daniels drawl which aids in it's bayou campiness. The most delightful aspect of The Charlie Daniels Band's music is the way in which Daniels uses his fiddle to liven up his music, customizing it to the drums and guitar. Most of the tunes on this album contain a feisty mix of instruments that gives this band a different feel and a slightly unique sound. Not the typical country norm, this collection of their best songs will satisfy anyone who is interested. *—Mike DeGagne*

Same Ol Me / Sep. 12, 1995 / Capitol ✦✦✦

Roots Remain / Oct. 29, 1996 / Epic/Legacy ✦✦✦✦✦

Roots Remain is a three-disc box set covering the Charlie Daniels Band's entire career. Over the course of 45 songs, the box touches upon all of his hits—including "The Devil Went Down to Georgia," "Long-Haired Country Boy," and "Uneasy Rider"—plus key album tracks, B-sides, and several unreleased and rare gems, such as his take on Eric Clapton's "Layla." *Roots Remain* is the most comprehensive compilation of Charlie Daniels recordings ever assembled and it misses very few important tracks, making it the one definitive retrospective. *—Stephen Thomas Erlewine*

Fiddle Fire: 25 Years of the Charlie Daniels Band / Aug. 18, 1998 / Blue Hat ✦✦✦✦

Tailgate Party / Mar. 9, 1999 / Blue Hat ✦✦✦✦✦

Road Dogs / May 30, 2000 / Blue Hat ✦✦✦✦

Gail Davies

b. Sep. 1, 1948, Broken Bow, OK

Vocals, Guitar / Neo-Traditionalist Country, Country-Folk, Singer/Songwriter, Country-Pop

Gail Davies, a member of the first wave of intelligent female country-rock songwriters of the '70s, influenced such artists as Mary-Chapin Carpenter and the Judds. After attempting a careers in a rock group and as a jazz singer, Davies returned to country music in the early '70s and gained a songwriting contract. The exposure got her signed to Lifesong/CBS, which released her self-titled debut album in 1978. After signing with Warner Bros. later that same year, "Blue Heartache" hit number seven and her album *The Game* was applauded by critics. Gail Davies' biggest hit, though, was the title track from her 1980 LP *I'll Be There.* It reached number four on the country charts early in 1981, and was followed by three Top Tens: "It's a Lovely, Lovely World," "Grandma's Song" and "'Round the Clock Lovin'," from *Givin' Herself Away.* She recorded for RCA and MCA during the 1980s though a lack of success made her gradually move into production during the late '80s. She accepted a position at Liberty Records as country music's first female staff producer, working with a teenaged Mandy Barnett. She left Liberty to record the 1995 album *Eclectic* for her own Little Chickadee Records, and re-recorded all her biggest singles for 1998's *Greatest Hits.* *—John Bush*

I'll Be There / 1980 / Warner Brothers ✦✦✦✦✦

Here's another consistently strong album. At a time when Barbara Mandrell and Crystal Gayle were country's biggest female stars, Davies was creating albums as distinctive and progressive as Rosanne Cash. *—Michael McCall*

The Game / 1980 / Warner Brothers ✦✦✦

Her second album was the first in which she displayed her commanding vocals on a blend of folk-influenced ballads and punchy, melodic pop-country. *—Michael McCall*

Giving Herself Away / 1982 / Warner Brothers ✦✦✦✦✦

Davies brought in such outside of Nashville help as guitarist Albert Lee, bassist Leland Sklar and pianist Bill Payne of Little Feat to create an excellent album that blends Southern California folk-pop with the cutting edge of modern country. Includes the hit "Hold On" as well as a popular version of Joni Mitchell's "You Turn Me On (I'm a Radio)" and "Round the Clock Lovin'," written by a then-unknown K.T. Oslin. *—Michael McCall*

What Can I Say / 1983 / Warner Brothers ✦✦✦

It's lighter-hearted than her others, but even when in a playful mood Davies sounds feisty, as on "Boys like You" and "You're a Hard Dog (To Keep Under the Porch)." Covers come from Rodney Crowell, Harlan Howard, Mark Knopfler and Ray Charles. *—Michael McCall*

Where is a Woman to Go / 1984 / RCA ✦✦✦✦✦

Her fiercest album, as far as emotional content, is her most consistently forceful, as far as musical arrangements. It's an unheralded classic. *—Michael McCall*

Wild Choir / 1986 / RCA ✦✦✦

Billed as a band, Wild Choir's songs and spirit were pure Davies, but the arrangements took on mild new wave/rock tendencies. The record proved to be too progressive at the time, and it still sounds fresher than most Nashville bands of the 1990s. "Walls" and "Never Cross That Line" rank with Davies's best compositions. *—Michael McCall*

Pretty Words / 1989 / MCA ✦✦✦

A touching combination of songs, some seeking spiritual strength, others drenched in melancholy without sinking into bathos. *—Michael McCall*

● **The Best of Gail Davies** / Jan. 21, 1991 / Liberty ✦✦✦✦✦
A substantial collection of radio hits and crowd favorites, including the poignant "Grandma's Song," "'I'll Be There (If You Ever Want Me)," "'Round the Clock Lovin'" and "It's A Lovely, Lovely World." *—Michael McCall*

Greatest Hits / Jun. 16, 1998 / Koch ✦✦✦✦

The Davis Sisters

f. 1949, Lexington, KY, **db.** 1953
Group / Traditional Country
Known to country fans mainly as the act in which Skeeter Davis originally rose to fame, the Davis Sisters' career would have surely been much more influential and successful if tragedy hadn't derailed them just after their first hit. Although they only had one big single ("I Forgot More than You'll Ever Know," in 1953), their outstanding close dual harmonies helped link the Appalachian harmonies of the Delmore Brothers with the more modern ones of subsequent acts like the Everlys. They were also among the earliest female country singing stars of the post-World War II era, and occasionally went into a boogie mode that foreshadowed the rockabilly movement by a year or two.

The Davis Sisters were in fact not sisters at all. Betty Jack Davis and Mary Frances Penick met in high school in Kentucky in the late '40s, soon forming a close friendship and musical partnership. Penick changed her name to Skeeter Davis for professional purposes, so that the duo could be billed as a sister combination. By the early '50s they'd performed regularly on radio shows in Cincinnati and Detroit, and made their first studio recordings in Detroit. By 1953 they were recording for RCA, backed by Nashville session players such as Chet Atkins. The mournful "I Forgot More than You'll Ever Know" was a big hit that made them immediate stars; just as interesting, in retrospect, was the flip side, "Rock-A-Bye Boogie," which anticipated the rockabilly revolution with its frenetic rhythms and Les Paul-influenced electric guitar runs.

That first RCA session was to be Betty Jack's last, as the pair were involved in a serious auto accident in August 1953; Betty Jack died instantly, though Skeeter would recover. With the support of the Davis family, Skeeter continued the act with Betty Jack's older sister, Georgie. The reconstituted Davis Sisters continued to record through 1956, performing in the same harmony style that Skeeter had formulated with Betty Jack. These outings were quite respectable mixes of traditional country ballads with slicker, more uptempo fare, but there were no more hits, and Skeeter couldn't fully re-create the artistic and personal spark she had enjoyed with Betty Jack. While Georgie retired from music, Skeeter would by the 1960s become one of the most successful women singers in the country-pop field. *—Richie Unterberger*

★ **Memories** / 1993 / Bear Family ✦✦✦✦✦
Bear Family does its usual astonishingly thorough job on this double-CD compilation, which has no less than 59 tracks recorded by both incarnations of the Davis sisters between 1952 and 1956 (as well as a brief 1957 Skeeter Davis solo take on "It Wasn't God Who Made Honky Tonk Angels)." The RCA singles are embellished by numerous outtakes, alternates, pre-RCA acetates of radio broadcasts, an unreleased tape of spirituals at a Kentucky Baptist Church, and their rare pre-RCA singles for the Fortune label; in fact, half of this collection was previously unreleased. The fidelity isn't always stellar on the non-RCA tracks, but most of the material is strong, and the harmonies always affecting, whether on the sad ballads, spirituals, or the occasional proto-rockabilly outings ("Rock-A-Bye Boogie," "Rag Mop," "Gotta Git A-Goin'"). While Skeeter understandably bemoaned the loss of original partner Betty Jack Davis, the sides with her replacement Georgie Davis (which actually comprise over half the package) are on about the same level as the earlier ones. Chet Atkins' guitar can be heard on most of the tracks. *—Richie Unterberger*

Jimmie Davis

b. Sep. 11, 1902, Quitman, LA, **d.** Baton Rouge, LA
Vocals, Guitar / Traditional Country
In a performing career spanning eight decades of the 20th century, Jimmie Davis embraced both risqué country-blues and later traditional gospel, meanwhile maintaining a concurrent public-service career that saw him twice elected governor of Louisiana. In fact, his greatest musical successes came during his two terms as governor, once in the mid-'40s and again in the early '60s. First recorded in 1928, Davis recorded a few hits during the mid-'30s but found big success in 1940 with what is arguably his own composition, "You Are My Sunshine." Elected governor of Louisiana in 1944, he continued to record and scored five Top Five singles during his first term. He moved back to full-time recording in 1948, and gradually moved to a more sacred style. He returned to the governorship in 1960 on a segregationist platform, but to his credit prevented much of the unrest apparent in the South through his moderate position. Though he hadn't recorded a hit since his first term, Davis reached the Top 20 in 1962 with "Where the Old Red River Flows." By 1964, he was back to gospel music, and he recorded heavily throughout the '70s and continued to perform into the 1990s. *—John Bush*

● **Country Music Hall of Fame** / 1991 / MCA ✦✦✦✦✦
Country Music Hall of Fame contains 16 tracks Jimmie Davis recorded between 1934 and 1954 for Decca Records. The material ranges from country blues and novelties to gospel, Western swing, and honky tonk with a few pop crossovers like his signature hit "You Are My Sunshine" and "Nobody's Darling but Mine" thrown in for good measure. Though some of his biggest hits are missing—including "Is It Too Late Now," "Bang Bang," and "There's a Chill on the Hill Tonight"—the collection nevertheless draws a representative portrait of Davis and his career, making it a nearly definitive retrospective. *—Stephen Thomas Erlewine*

Nobody's Darling But Mine: 1928-1937 / May 20, 1998 / Bear Family ✦✦✦✦✦

You Are My Sunshine: 1937-1946 / May 20, 1998 / Bear Family ✦✦✦✦✦

Mac Davis

b. Jan. 21, 1942, Lubbock, TX
Vocals, Guitar / Nashville Sound/Countrypolitan, Soft Rock, Pop, Country-Pop
At his commercial peak in the mid-'70s, Mac Davis was one of America's most popular entertainers, a countrypolitan-styled singer and actor who found considerable success in both fields. He began in the music business as a songwriter, writing several hits for Elvis Presley including "Memories" and "In the Ghetto," the latter a number three single from the landmark *From Elvis in Memphis* LP. Davis gained his own recording contract in 1970, and first hit the charts with a single from his debut album *Song Painter.* In 1972, he scored a number one pop hit with "Baby, Don't Get Hooked on Me," which also reached the country Top Twenty. His crossover success continued throughout the decade, with singles like "Stop and Smell the Roses," "Burnin' Thing" and "Forever Lovers" scoring with listeners in both camps. Davis' success continued in the early '80s; "It's Hard to Be Humble" was the first of four consecutive Top Ten country hits that culminated with his biggest country single, "Hooked on Music." Though his last Top Ten hit came in 1985, he made a comeback as a songwriter, co-authoring Dolly Parton's 1990 hit "White Limozeen." *Will Write Songs for Food,* his first LP in nearly a decade, appeared in 1994. *—Jason Ankeny*

Greatest Hits / 1979 / Columbia ✦✦✦✦✦
In addition to '70s smashes like "Baby Don't Get Hooked on Me" and "Stop and Smell the Roses," *Greatest Hits* also includes the Davis-penned "In the Ghetto," a major hit for Elvis Presley. *—Jason Ankeny*

Very Best & More... / 1984 / Casablanca ✦✦✦✦
All of Davis' hits from his 1980-1984 tenure at Casablanca Records are included in the collection *Very Best and More...* In addition to "Hooked on Music," and his biggest-seller, the album includes "You're My Bestest Friend," "Texas in My Rear View Mirror," "Let's Keep It That Way," and "It's Hard to Be Humble." *—Jason Ankeny*

Baby Don't Get Hooked on Me/Stop and Smell the Roses / Jul. 1, 1997 / Collectables ✦✦✦✦
Two of Mac Davis' most popular albums from the early '70s, *Baby Don't Get Hooked on Me* and *Stop and Smell the Roses,* were combined on this single-CD reissue by Collectables. Although the sound and the packaging could be a little better, this still is a fine way for collectors to pick up these two records on disc. *—Stephen Thomas Erlewine*

● **The Best of Mac Davis** / Oct. 24, 2000 / Razor & Tie ✦✦✦✦✦
Razor & Tie's *The Very Best of Mac Davis* overlooks some late-'70s and early-'80s hits, but they're not missed, since this winds up as a first-rate chronicle of Davis at his peak. Davis walked the thin line between \country and \AM pop with his lavishly produced, sweet \soft rock, delivering the melodies with just a hint of twang. This is unabashedly mainstream stuff, but it's so well done that it's hard to resist, especially since Davis' warm baritone is the perfect foil for is evocatively corny tales. This concentrates on his late-'60s/early-'70s material, when he was at the peak of his powers. The compilers were savvy, and this doesn't slow as it winds through his biggest hits of the time, along with a couple lesser-known hits. It's an excellent compilation, and even if it doesn't have "I Believe in Music," it will make you a believer. *—Stephen Thomas Erlewine*

Skeeter Davis (Mary Frances Penick)

b. Dec. 30, 1931, Dry Ridge, KY
Vocals / Nashville Sound/Countrypolitan, Pop, Country-Pop, Country-Rock, Traditional Country
Skeeter Davis has never gotten a lot of critical attention, but in the '50s and '60s, she recorded some of the most accessible crossover country music, occasionally skirting rock & roll. Born Mary Penick, Davis took her last name after forming a duo with Betty Jack Davis, the Davis Sisters. Their 1953 single "I Forgot More than You'll Ever Know" was a big country hit; its B-side, the remarkable "Rock-A-Bye Boogie," foreshadowed rockabilly. That same year, however, the duo's career was cut short by a tragic car accident in which Betty Jack Davis was killed, and Skeeter was severely injured. In the early '60s, she followed the heels of Brenda Lee and Patsy Cline to become one of the first big-selling female country crossover acts, although her pop success was pretty short-lived. The weepy ballad "The End of the World," though, was a massive hit, reaching number two in 1963. "I Can't Stay Mad at You," a Top Ten hit the same year, was downright rock & roll; penned by Goffin and King, it sounded like (and was) an authentic Brill Building girl group-styled classic. Usually she sang sentimental, country-oriented tunes with enough pop hooks to catch the ears of a wider audience, such as "I Will." *—Richie Unterberger*

Here's the Answer / 1961 / RCA International ✦✦

The End of the World / 1962 / RCA ✦✦✦
Recorded at the peak of Davis' brief stardom, this emphasizes the weepy country-pop that gave her a number two pop hit with the title track. Nothing here measures up to that wonderful smash, but it's tasteful enough period Nashville country, with producers Anita Kerr and Chet Atkins ensuring that the LP measured up to state-of-the-art country-pop production by double-tracking Davis' vocals against a background of strings and lazy barroom piano runs. They did let her loose on Little Eva's "Keep Your Hands off My Baby," which is replete with primitive fuzzy guitar. Though it may sound enticing, the result is actually kind of lousy and ill-fitting. *—Richie Unterberger*

The Best of Skeeter Davis / 1965 / RCA ✦✦✦✦✦
Skeeter fused country, pop, and even occasional girl-group sounds during her commercial peak in the early '60s, which found her at her most fetching and tuneful. This has twelve of her most successful recordings of the era, including the huge ballad "The End Of The World," which hit 2 on the pop charts in 1963, and Goffin/King's irresistible girl-group composition "I Can't Stay Mad At You," which reached the Top Ten the same year. *—Richie Unterberger*

My Heart's in the Country / 1966 / RCA ✦✦✦
The cover art, with Davis fondling farm animals in front of the barn and extolling the rural

life in the liner notes, makes a pretty determined effort at presenting Davis in as much of a pure country light as possible. The actual music, by and large, follows suit. Produced by Felton Jarvis in Nashville, it's plainer and more traditional in mood than her work with Chet Atkins and Anita Kerr. The strings are banished and the guitar picking and fiddles are at the forefront, although the vocals are still double-tracked. It's kind of an average effort, without any particular flaws or standout material. Includes compositions by Dolly Parton and Loretta Lynn, as well as Davis' rendition of the traditional "Goin' Down the Road (Feelin' Bad)." —*Richie Unterberger*

Skeeter Davis Sings Buddy Holly / 1967 / RCA ✦✦✦
Twelve Holly covers, produced by Felton Jarvis in Nashville and featuring Waylon Jennings on guitar, at a time when neither Davis nor Holly were exactly in the forefront of pop's collective consciousness. A modest accomplishment, this LP is nevertheless fairly worthwhile, with a much more upbeat sound than Davis' early-'60s recordings. The arrangements are pretty straightforward and close to the originals, with solid country-rock backing and occasional light, tasteful strings. —*Richie Unterberger*

The Best of Skeeter Davis, Vol. 2 / 1973 / RCA ✦✦✦

She Sings, They Play / 1985 / Rounder ✦✦✦

● **The Essential Skeeter Davis** / 1996 / RCA ✦✦✦✦✦
Featuring 20 tracks, *The Essential Skeeter Davis* collects all of her big hits from both the country and pop charts, making it the one definitive compilation. —*Stephen Thomas Erlewine*

Jimmy Dean

b. Aug. 10, 1928, Plainview, TX
Vocals, Accordion, Piano, Guitar / Nashville Sound/Countrypolitan, Country-Pop, Traditional Country
To the general public, singer/songwriter Jimmy Dean was best known as the star of commercials promoting the sausages and processed meats which bore his name. However, he also had a string of country hits in the early '60s; most of his material consisted of narrative songs. In 1952 he made his debut single, "Bumming Around," which peaked at number five on the country charts. He signed to Columbia Records in 1957 and though he released ten singles, he didn't have a hit until 1961's "Big Bad John," the story of a courageous ex-con turned miner which was the first song he'd ever written. The song topped the country and pop charts and even made it to number two in Great Britain. A follow-up, "Dear Ivan," came out in 1962 and was a more moderate crossover success. In 1963, Dean launched a TV show on ABC. It aired daily and was very successful; in 1964, he tried a nightime version as well, although both shows folded in 1966. In the meantime, he had three more hits, including a cover of Hank Williams' "Mind Your Own Business." Dean continued hitting the charts through the early '70s, and in 1976 had a gold record when his narrative song "I.O.U." became a Top Ten country hit. Beginning in the late '70s, Dean turned his concentration to his business ventures, eventually building the company into a multi-million dollar empire. —*Sandra Brennan*

Big Bad John and Other Fabulous Songs and Tales / 1993 / Bear Family ✦✦✦✦✦
This 26 song single disc collection covers the highlights of Jimmy Dean's 1961-62 recordings for Columbia Records—not everything, but most everything that counts. The sheer diversity of material demonstrates some of the problems that Dean had finding and following up on hits—he was a passable singer and likable personality, but he would follow up a pop-rock piece like "Little Black Book" with a blues piece such as "Gonna Raise A Ruckus Tonight." But apart from the hokiest of these tracks ("A Day That Changed The World"), it all holds up, including the title track, the freewheeling "Smoke, Smoke, Smoke That Cigarette," the weirdly topical "Dear Ivan"; his cover of Merle Travis's "Sixteen Tons"; the sentimental father-to-daughter soliloquy "To A Sleeping Beauty"; the rough-hewn "Big Bad John" follow-up "The Cajun Queen"; the delightful sequel to both songs, "Little Bitty Big John"; "P.T. 109," a tribute to John Kennedy's World War II exploits written in the same vein as Johnny Horton's "Sink The Bismarck"; the wryly cynical "Walk On Boy"; the workers' anthem "Steel Men"; the pop-rock ballad "Little Black Book"; the old Texas blues "Gonna Raise A Ruckus Tonight"; the strange D-day remembrance "A Day That Changed The World"; the breezily folky "Gotta Travel On"; the sad dog (and war) song "Oklahoma Bill"; the effective sub-Elvis "Night Train To Memphis"; and two previously unissued numbers, the slow blues "Lonesome Road" and the swamp ballad "Cajun Joe." —*Bruce Eder*

● **Greatest Hits** / Jan. 27, 1998 / Columbia ✦✦✦✦✦
Jimmy Dean's Greatest Hits remains an excellent summation of his years at Columbia Records, containing the hit singles "Big Bad John," "The Cajun Queen," "To a Sleeping Beauty," "P.T. 109," "Little Black Book," "The First Thing Ev'ry Morning (And the Last Thing Every Night)" and "Harvest of Sunshine." For the 1998 CD reissue, Columbia/Legacy added the 1962 Top Ten hit "Dear Ivan," making the record a near-definitive overview of Dean's peak years. —*Stephen Thomas Erlewine*

The Delmore Brothers

f. 1926, Elkmont, AL, **db.** 1952
Group / Close Harmony, Honky Tonk, Traditional Country, Old-Timey
The Delmore Brothers are not nearly as well-known as such early country giants as the Carter Family, Jimmie Rodgers, Bob Wills, and Hank Williams. The reasons for this, upon close inspection of their work, are not readily apparent. They were one of the greatest early country harmonizers, drawing from both gospel and Appalachian folk. They were skilled songwriters, penning literally hundreds of songs, many of which have proven to be durable. Most important, they were among the few early traditional country acts to change with the times, and pioneer some of those changes. Their recordings from the latter half of the 1940s married traditional country to boogie beats and bluesy riffs. In this respect they laid a foundation for rockabilly and early rock & roll, and rate among the most important White progenitors of those forms. Their music emphasized their beautiful soft harmonies, accomplished guitar picking, and strong original compositions. Unusually for that time (or any other), the Delmores would switch high and low harmony parts from song to song (or even within the same song), although Alton would usually sing lead. Whether performing their own songs, traditional ones, or gospel, they brought a strong bluesy feeling to both their music and their vocals. It's that element, perhaps, that enables the Delmores, more than many other acts of the time, to speak to listeners of subsequent generations. Not to be underestimated either are their down-to-earth lyrical concerns, which address commonplace struggles and lost love with grace and redeeming, good-natured humor, rarely resorting to cornball tears. —*Richie Unterberger*

When They Let the Hammer Fall / 1984 / Bear Family ✦✦✦✦✦
Contains 18 of the boogie sides this great country duo cut (with harmonica player Wayne Raney) between 1945 and 1952, though it inexplicably fails to include their biggest hit from this time, "Blues Stay Away From Me" (later recorded by Johnny Burnette and Gene Vincent). This is the bluesiest and most raucous material cut by the harmonizing siblings. These tunes sound about as close to rock & roll as any other music recorded by white musicians prior to the 1950s, and still makes fine party music today, with its thumping shuffle beats, bluesy solos, and loose abandon. The great "Beale Street Boogie," cut in 1947 (and unissued at the time), is one of the dozens of songs which could make a strong case for being the first rock & roll record. There's a classic opening bluesy call-and-response riff, a long electric guitar solo duel, and appropriate homage to Memphis' famed Beale Street, certainly one of the locales most responsible for brewing together the basic ingredients of rock & roll—"the Beale Street Boogie is eight beats to the bar," they sing in unison, just in case you don't get the point. Compared to their early recordings, the Delmores seem less pious and devout on these sessions and more concerned with celebration than lamentation. —*Richie Unterberger*

Early Sacred Songs / 1985 / Old Homestead ✦✦✦✦✦
Fourteen of their more spiritually inclined tracks, mostly cut between 1935 and 1940. Those who favor secular material over gospel or traditional spirituals shouldn't be wary of this release because of its lyrical content. If you enjoy early country harmonizing, or any of the other material the Delmores cut in their early days, you'll like this as well. Aside from the nominally different lyrical concerns (presented here with humility and without preaching), the basic strengths of the pair remain intact: peerless close harmonizing, fine acoustic guitar playing, and strong songs that can be enjoyed regardless of what your faith (or lack thereof) may be. —*Richie Unterberger*

Lonesome Yodel Blues / 1985 / Old Homestead ✦✦✦✦✦
18 of their early sides, recorded between 1933 and 1940, focusing on the more traditional elements of their repertoire. As the title implies, the brothers do often actually yodel throughout the proceedings, although in a more restrained fashioned than many of their peers. Remastered nicely from original copies of these rare singles, though some unavoidable surface noise is evident. —*Richie Unterberger*

Sand Mountain Blues / 1986 / County ✦✦✦✦✦
The Delmores' recordings for King in the mid-'40s found them shifting away from traditional sounds into more energetic boogies that foreshadowed—however faintly—the blend of R&B and country that would give birth to rock & roll. This has 14 sides from 1944-49, some of which feature such stellar sidemen as guitarist Merle Travis, mandolinist Jethro Burns, and harmonica player Wayne Raney. —*Richie Unterberger*

★ **Freight Train Boogie** / 1993 / Ace ✦✦✦✦✦
It's kind of a toss-up as to whether this or the German *When They Let the Hammer Down* is the best compilation of the Delmores' best work from the late '40s and early '50s. *When They Let the Hammer Down* is more raucous and uptempo; the 20-track *Freight Train Boogie,* though, has more variety. *Freight Train Boogie* is much easier to locate in the U.S. than *When They Let the Hammer Down.* In addition, there's a fair amount of duplication between the anthologies, though each includes several noteworthy songs not on the other. In any case, you won't be disappointed by *Freight Train Boogie,* whether it's your first exposure to the Delmores or not. Featuring King material from 1946-1951, it has plenty of high-spirited country boogies, balanced by more traditionally folk-oriented material ("Sand Mountain Blues," "Weary Day") and bluesy, slower numbers, including their biggest hit (and one of their best), "Blues Stay Away From Me." These sides were not only some of the finest country music of the era, but important building blocks of rockabilly and early rock & roll. —*Richie Unterberger*

Brown's Ferry Blues / County ✦✦✦
The Delmores recorded a great wealth of material in the 1930s and early 1940s, encompassing both country and sacred songs; many of these sides have been reissued on the County label. All of them are good. *Brown's Ferry Blues* may be recommended as an introductory volume because of its range of material (ranging from 1933 to 1941), much of which is bluesy in nature. —*Richie Unterberger*

Iris Dement

b. Jan. 5, 1961, Paragould, AR
Vocals, Guitar / Americana, Neo-Traditionalist Country, Contemporary Folk, Alternative Country, Country-Folk, Singer/Songwriter
One of the most celebrated country-folk performers of her day, singer/songwriter Iris Dement was born on January 5, 1961 in rural Paragould, Arkansas, the youngest of 14 children. At the age of three, her devoutly religious family moved to California, where she grew up singing gospel music; during her teenaged years, however, she was first exposed to country, folk and R&B, drawing influence from Loretta Lynn, Johnny Cash, Bob Dylan and Joni Mitchell. Upon graduating high school, she relocated to Kansas City to attend college.

After a series of jobs waitressing and typing, Dement first began composing songs at the age of 25. Honing her skills at open-mike nights, in 1988 she moved to Nashville, where she contacted producer Jim Rooney, who helped her land a record contract. Dement did not make her recording debut until 1992, when her independent label offering *Infamous Angel* won almost universal acclaim thanks to her pure, evocative vocal style and spare, heartfelt songcraft. Despite a complete lack of support from country radio, the record's word-of-mouth praise earned her a deal with Warner Bros., which reissued *Infamous Angel* in 1993 as well as its follow-up, 1994's stunning *My Life*. Her third LP, 1996's eclectic *The Way I Should*, marked a dramatic change not only in its more rock-influenced sound but also in its subject matter; where Dement's prior work was introspective and deeply personal, *The Way I Should* was fiercely political, tackling topics like sexual abuse, religion, government policy and Vietnam. *—Jason Ankeny*

• **Infamous Angel** / 1992 / Warner Brothers ✦✦✦✦✦
Dement emerges as a wonderfully gifted performer with this debut, a loose concept record about family, innocence and maturity. Though largely a country/folk outing, the bluesy "Sweet Forgiveness" hints at the eclecticism of her later work; already firmly ensconced is her remarkable voice, which evokes the emotional upheaval of her songs with stunning clarity. *—Jason Ankeny*

My Life / 1993 / Warner Brothers ✦✦✦✦
Since her beautiful debut record on Philo, Iris DeMent has graduated to the majors with her style intact. She has a confessional spirit and maintains her perspective as a free thinker all the while. The album is dedicated to her father and it is lovely throughout. These are songs that sound like they've always been around. *—Richard Meyer*

The Way I Should / Oct. 8, 1996 / Warner Brothers ✦✦✦
The introspective scope of DeMent's first two records expands to tackle global topics like religion, sexual abuse and war on the tough-talking *The Way I Should Be,* a more rock-influenced offering including cameo appearances from Mark Knopfler, Lonnie Mack and Delbert McClinton (who duets on "Trouble"). *—Jason Ankeny*

Desert Rose Band

f. 1985, Southern California
Group / Contemporary Country, Country-Rock
The Desert Rose Band formed in 1985. One of the founders was Chris Hillman, a former member of the Byrds and the Flying Burrito Brothers, who sang lead vocals, played guitar and mandolin and functioned as the group's primary songwriter. The original line-up included banjoist/guitarist Herb Pederson, guitarist John Jorgenson, pedal steel guitarist Jay Dee Maness, bassist Bill Bryson, and drummer Steve Duncan. Nearly all of the members were professional studio musicians before joining the group.

In 1986, the Desert Rose Band released a cover of Johnnie and Jack's hit "Ashes of Love." The song hit the Top 30 the following year, as did their self-titled debut album, which also produced three Top Ten singles, including the number one "He's Back and I'm Blue." In 1988, the group released their second album, *Running;* among their subsequent hits were "Summer Wind" and the chart topper "I Still Believe in You." The band's 1989 album *Pages of Life* spawned three more major hits including the Top Ten "Story of Love," which would prove to be their last major hit. In 1992, the group's lineup underwent a few changes when Duncan was replaced by Tim Grogan, Maness was replaced by Tom Brumley, and Jeff Ross replaced Jorgenson. The new lineup of the Desert Rose Band recorded three more albums, *True Love* (1992), *Traditional* and *Life Goes On* (both 1993), before breaking up in 1994. *—Sandra Brennan*

The Desert Rose Band / 1987 / Curb ✦✦✦✦
The Desert Rose Band's eponymous debut demonstrated that Chris Hillman's new band could continue his country-rock tradition effortlessly. Throughout the record, the Desert Rose Band turns in tight performances, highlighted by brief, tasteful instrumental solos and yearning vocals. *—Thom Owens*

Running / 1988 / Curb ✦✦✦✦✦

Pages of Life / 1990 / Curb ✦✦✦
This contains "In Another Lifetime, " "Time Passes Me By, " "Start All Over Again, " and other favorites. *—AMG*

• **A Dozen Roses: Greatest Hits** / 1991 / Curb ✦✦✦✦✦
A showcase for Hillman's pop-country vocals and the considerable chops of bandmembers such as Herb Pedersen. Together they made some of the best country singles of the late 80s, all collected here. *—William Ruhlmann*

True Love / 1991 / Curb ✦✦✦
True Love proves that the Desert Rose Band has a knack for mixing a country-pop attack with pure bluegrass harmonies, making music that is accessible to both mainstream country fans and hardcore bluegrass fanatics. Though *True Love* has too much mediocre material to make it rank among their best, it is nevertheless a very good collection, featuring a wonderful version of Peter Rowan's "Undying Love" that features gorgeous duet vocals between Chris Hillman and Alison Krauss. *—Stephen Thomas Erlewine*

Diamond Rio

f. 1984
Group / Neo-Traditionalist Country, Contemporary Country
Diamond Rio was a '90s country band with bluegrass sensibilities noted for its exceptional musicianship. Each of the four members—lead vocalist/guitarist Marty Roe, lead guitarist/banjo player Jimmy Olander, mandolin player/singer Gene Johnson, keyboardist Dan Truman, bassist Dana Williams and drummer Brian Prout—were involved in music long before the band's formation: Roe began performing professionally and touring at age 12 with Windsong, while Jimmy Olander was a veteran of the Nitty Gritty Dirt Band and Foster & Lloyd. Johnson, meanwhile, had worked with David Bromberg and J.D. Crowe; Williams' uncles were the famed Osborne Brothers, and Truman, a classically trained pianist, got his start playing with Brigham Young University's Young Ambassadors.

In time, each future member of Diamond Rio ended up playing at Nashville's Opryland as the Tennessee River Boys. After performing bluegrass there for seven years, the band managed to snag a contract with Arista, taking their current band name from a passing truck. Diamond Rio released their self-titled debut album in 1991. "Meet Me In the Middle," the first single, became a number one single; both follow-up singles, "Mirror Mirror" and "Mama Don't Forget to Pray for Me," were also substantial hits. Later that year, their second album, *Close to the Edge,* came out and their string of successes continued. *Love a Little Stronger* appeared in 1994, followed by *IV* in 1996. Diamond Rio returned with *Unbelievable* in 1998. *One More Day* was issued three years later. *—Sandra Brennan*

Diamond Rio / 1991 / Arista ✦✦✦✦✦
One of the most successful debut albums in country music, *Diamond Rio* sparked plenty of hits—"Meet in the Middle," "Mama Don't Forget to Pray for Me," "Nowhere Bound," "Norma Jean Riley"—by combining bluegrass harmonies, old-fashioned country virtues, and just enough rock to keep things moving. *—Brian Mansfield*

Close to the Edge / 1992 / Arista ✦✦✦
On *Close to the Edge,* Diamond Rio took the cue of the debut's best songs and created an entire album cut from the same cloth. Diamond Rio's strongest material emphasizes the virtues of God, family and honest living—traditional stuff, no doubt influenced by the members' bluegrass background. But while most folks who'd claim divine intervention in their relationship sound sappy at best, Marty Roe comes off earnest and convincing. Unfortunately, amid hits like "In a Week or Two" and "Oh Me, Oh My, Sweet Baby," *Close to the Edge* reveals such weaknesses as a penchant for bad puns ("This Romeo ain't got Julie yet"—ouch!). *—Brian Mansfield*

Love a Little Stronger / 1994 / Arista ✦✦✦
Spurred by the relatively lackluster performance of *Close to the Edge* (it barely went gold compared to the debut's platinum), Diamond Rio explored the musical possibilities of its talents rather than digging for easy commercial success. The instrumentalists, particularly Jimmy Olander and mandolinist Gene Johnson, assume larger roles on songs like "Love a Little Stronger" and the instrumental "Appalachian Dream," but they rarely show off. The band members even tap into an acoustic jazz-rock mode for "Kentucky Mine," one of the best songs they've ever recorded. *—Brian Mansfield*

IV / Feb. 27, 1996 / Arista ✦✦✦✦
Though the group wasn't able to regain its commercial status with *Love A Little Stronger,* Diamond Rio decided not to play things safe with *IV.* Taking its cue from its predecessor, *IV* explores a number of different country subgenres, thereby demonstrating the versatility and depth of its musicians. However, there's a problem when musicians are this talented—the music is impressive on the surface, but it rarely gels into something memorable. *—Thom Owens*

• **Greatest Hits** / Jul. 15, 1997 / Arista ✦✦✦✦✦
Greatest Hits is a fine collection of the hit singles from Diamond Rio's first four albums, featuring such hits as "Meet in the Middle," "Mirror Mirror," "Norma Jean Riley," "In a Week or Two," "Oh Me, Oh My, Sweet Baby," "Love a Little Stronger," "Night Is Fallin' In My Heart," "Walkin' Away," "That's What I Get for Lovin' You," "Holdin'" and two new songs, inlcuding the single "How Your Love Makes Me Feel." *—Thom Owens*

Unbelievable / Jul. 28, 1998 / Arista ✦✦✦

Little Jimmy Dickens

b. Dec. 19, 1925, Bolt, WV
Vocals, Guitar / Nashville Sound/Countrypolitan, Traditional Country, Novelty
Little Jimmy Dickens is the master of the country novelty songs, as well as a renowned ballad singer. He also known for his diminutive stature—he's less than five feet tall—and his affection for flamboyant, rhinestone-studded outfits and country humor. Although he never had a consistent presence on the charts, he managed to have hits in every decade between the 1940s and the 1970s, and became one of the *Grand Ole Opry*'s most popular performers. He began performing professionally on radio shows around the Midwest during the late '30s and '40s, became a permanent member of *the Grand Ole Opry* in 1949, and found a hit with his first single for Columbia, "Take an Old Cold Tater and Wait." The song launched a string of hit novelty, ballad and honky tonk singles that lasted for a year. Dickens bounced back to the Top Ten in 1962, and recorded his biggest hit, "May the Bird of Paradise Fly Up Your Nose," three years later. The single topped the country charts and crossed over to number 15 on the pop charts. He found moderate success with Decca and United Artists during the '60s and '70s, but began concentrating on touring and performing at *the Grand Ole Opry* by the '90s, becoming one of the most beloved characters in country music. *—Stephen Thomas Erlewine*

• **I'm Little But I'm Loud: the Little Jimmy Dickens Collection** / May 21, 1996 / Razor & Tie ✦✦✦✦✦
I'm Little But I'm Loud: The Little Jimmy Dickens Collection is a thorough retrospective of Dickens' prime years, running from the 1949 Top 10 hit "Take and Old Cold 'Tater (And Wait)" to the 1967 Top 40 hit "Country Music Lover." In between those two songs are no less than 20 tracks, including all of his Top 10 hits ("Country Boy," "My Heart's Bouquet," "A-Sleeping At the Foot of the Bed," "Hillbilly Fever," "Out Behind the Barn," "The Violet and A Rose," and the number one "May the Bird of Paradise Fly Up Your Nose"). In short, *I'm Little But I'm Loud* is the only comprehensive retrospective ever assembled on Jimmy Dickens. *—Stephen Thomas Erlewine*

Joe Diffie

b. 1958, Tulsa, OK
Vocals / New Traditionalist, Contemporary Country
Joe Diffie was among the generation of artists who blended traditional country sounds with '90s sensibilities. Born to a musical family in Tulsa, Diffie was a member of his high school's gospel group Genesis II, local rockers Blitz, and the bluegrass band the Special Edition. After college, the Special Edition began to gain an audience and appeared in several festivals. Diffie then began playing country music with his aunt Dawn Anita and his sister Monica. Soon, one of his early songs, "Love on the Rocks," was recorded by Hank Thompson. Diffie

soon moved to Nashville and began working for Gibson Guitars while continuing to write songs. Holly Dunn recorded one of his collaborations, "There Goes My Heart Again," in 1989.

Diffie's debut single, "Home," climbed to number one in 1990; that year he also debuted at the *Grand Ole Opry*. This was followed by three Top Five hits, all of which he co-wrote, as well as a 1990 debut album, *A Thousand Winding Roads*. Diffie's second album, *Regular Joe*, contained several hits, including "Is It Cold in Here." In 1993, he released his third album, *Honky Tonk Attitude*. *Third Rock from the Sun* appeared in 1994 and both *Life's So Funny* and *Mr. Christmas* were released the following year. A *Greatest Hits* collection appeared in 1998, yielding the new single "Texas Size Heartache." Diffie returned in 1999 with *A Night to Remember*. *—Sandra Brennan*

A Thousand Winding Roads / 1990 / Epic ♦♦♦♦♦

● **Regular Joe** / 1992 / Epic ♦♦♦♦♦
Diffie's second album has all the cliches of country music, and all the good stuff too. If "Ain't That Bad Enough" is a run-of-the-mill song, Diffie rescues it by tearing the melody loose from its mooring. He's also willing to push the line: of all Diffie's country heroes—and you'll be able to name them after one listen—maybe only Merle Haggard would rock out as hard as Diffie does on the title track. *—Brian Mansfield*

Honky Tonk Attitude / Apr. 20, 1993 / Epic ♦♦♦
Taking a cue from some of his peers, balladeer Diffie makes a point to get rowdy on this, his most commercially successful album to date. Besides the title track, it includes the hits "Prop Me up Beside the Jukebox (If I Die)" and "John Deere Green." *—Dan Cooper*

Third Rock from the Sun / 1994 / Epic ♦♦♦♦♦
Third Rock from the Sun represents a bit of a musical departure for Joe Diffie. Though he keeps his basic honky tonk roots, he experiments more, adding more rock flourishes to his sound. Not all of his attempts are successful, but his ballads are frequently compelling. Nevertheless, it's a little distressing that he has only written one song on the album—there's no reason for his well to dry up by only his fourth record. *—Thom Owens*

Life's So Funny / 1995 / Epic ♦♦♦
Led by the tongue-in-cheek single "Bigger Than the Beatles," Joe Diffie's fifth album *Life's So Funny* delivers the relaxed, funny contemporary country that fans have come to expect from the singer. *Life's So Funny* isn't as consistently engaging as his previous *Third Rock From the Sun*, yet its warm sense of humor and varied collection of ballads and mid-tempo rockers makes it a worthy followup to the most popular record Diffie ever released. *—Thom Owens*

Twice upon a Time / Apr. 22, 1997 / Epic ♦♦♦

Greatest Hits / Jun. 9, 1998 / Epic ♦♦♦♦
Greatest Hits is an excellent summation of Joe Diffie's first six albums, offering 12 of his biggest hit singles, including "Third Rock from the Sun," "John Deere Green," "Texas Size Heartache," "Prop Me Up Beside the Jukebox (If I Die)," "Honky Tonk Attitude" and "Bigger Than the Beatles." It's ideal for casual fans and neophytes, but even hardcore fans may want the collection, since it's the most consistently enjoyable record in his catalog. *—Stephen Thomas Erlewine*

A Night to Remember / Jun. 1, 1999 / Epic ♦♦♦♦

Dillard & Clark

Group / Country-Rock, Progressive Bluegrass
Dillard & Clark, a duo featuring former Byrd Gene Clark and Doug Dillard of the Dillards, was one of the first country-rock groups. They formed in 1968 and became one of pioneers of country-rock, releasing two albums before dissolving. Their debut album, *The Fantastic Expedition of Dillard and Clark*, was recorded with Bernie Leadon (guitar), Don Beck (dobro, mandolin), and David Jackson (bass). Dillard & Clark toured following the release of the album; their supporting band featured former Byrd Michael Clarke on drums. Dillard & Clark began recording a second album early in 1969 with a new supporting band. The new lineup featured Leadon, fiddler Byron Berline, drummer Jon Corneal, and guitarist Donna Washburn; the resulting record, *Through the Morning, Through the Night*, appeared later in the year. After its release, Leadon left the duo; he would join the Eagles soon after. Clark decided to pursue a solo career in early 1970. Dillard continued his solo career, using the remaining members of the duo's backing band as the core of his new outfit, the Expedition. Dillard and Clark continued to pursue solo careers throughout the '80s and '90s, with Dillard garnering more success and critical acclaim than Clark. *—Stephen Thomas Erlewine*

★ **The Fantastic Expedition of Dillard & Clark/Through the Morning, Through the Night** / 1968-1969 / Mobile Fidelity ♦♦♦♦♦
The duo's two albums are combined on one CD, making for more than an hour of great listening. Mastered in state-of-the-art sound that still holds up years later, this is the version of the two albums to get (although it is now out of print). The Dillard & Clark duo was Gene Clark's most artistically successful post-Byrds collaboration, and his best venture into country-rock as well. With Chris Hillman and Bernie Leadon playing behind the duo throughout the first album, in many ways it is as much an offshoot of the Flying Burrito Brothers' work as it is of the Byrds, with more of the Burritos' feel. The standard of playing and singing on both albums is extremely high, but the ten songs on *The Fantastic Expedition of Dillard & Clark* are more impressive, both as recordings and compositions. The ten songs from *Through the Morning, Through the Night* fail to match the joyous quality or the originality of their predecessors and the sound is less unified, mostly due to the presence of a third singer in the guise of Donna Washburn. The mix of rollicking bluegrass (such as "Rocky Top" which is sung by Washburn) and covers like the Beatles' "Don't Let Me Down" and the Everly Brothers' "So Sad" is also less successful. But combined together, these 20 songs are an essential addition to any country-rock collection and are also indispensible to fans of the Byrds or the Flying Burrito Brothers. *—Bruce Eder*

Dixie Chicks

f. Maryland
Guitar, Fiddle, Banjo / Neo-Traditionalist Country, Contemporary Country, Country-Pop, Progressive Bluegrass
The Dixie Chicks rose from relative obscurity in 1998 to become one of the most popular acts in contemporary country music. Their origins date back nearly a decade earlier to 1989, when fiddler Martie Seidel and her banjo-playing sister Emily Erwin formed the group in Dallas with bassist Laura Lynch and guitarist Robin Lynn Macy; originally, the Dixie Chicks promoted a classic cowgirl image, complete with a sound inspired by traditional country, folk and bluegrass, but with 1992's *Little Ol' Cowgirl*, they began moving towards a more contemporary sound. By the time the Chicks signed with Sony's newly-revived Monument imprint in 1995, both Lynch and Macy were out of the group—according to a December 10, 1998 feature in the Dallas *Observer*, both were likely victims of Seidel and Erwin's desire to foster a more youthful image. Their replacement was then-21-year-old lead vocalist Natalie Maines, and while the line-up switch brought with it a new contemporary wardrobe and an equally modernized country sound, few predicted the enormous success of the Dixie Chicks' 1998 major label debut *Wide Open Spaces*. After the album's advance first single "I Can Love You Better" became the group's first Top Ten hit, both "There's Your Trouble" and the title track went on to top the country charts. Within a year of *Wide Open Spaces'* release, the record had gone quadruple-platinum, and the Dixie Chicks had become superstars. *—Jason Ankeny*

Little Ol' Cowgirl / 1992 / Crystal Clear ♦♦♦
Their non-stop performance schedule quickly tightened the band's sound, and their musical ability leaps forward in confidence and flair. They're still willing to try anything, at least once, which results in a collection that's uneven but entertaining. *—Michael McCall*

Thank Heavens for Dale Evans / 1992 / Crystal Clear ♦♦♦
Their first album captures their charm and eclectic tastes in its early, amateurish stages. Ragged in spots, but gloriously enthusiastic. *—Michael McCall*

Shouldn't a Told You That / 1993 / Crystal Clear ♦♦♦
Down to a trio, the sound is more focused now, but only slightly less varied. With Laura Lynch taking lead vocals, and with help from producer Steve Fishell, the band sounds more professional and as delightful as ever. *—Michael McCall*

● **Wide Open Spaces** / Jan. 27, 1998 / Monument ♦♦♦♦♦
When sisters Martie Seidel and Emily Erwin founded the Dixie Chicks in 1989, could they have possibly known the success that would someday be theirs— After three independent records and several lineup changes, the group was re-energized by new lead singer Natalie Maines and the support of a major label, and exploded onto the contemporary country scene with the release of *Wide Open Spaces*. As always, their strengths lie in their honey-sweet harmonies and superb musicianship, now topped off by the sassy power of Maines' lead vocals. Apparently, they know how to pick songs as well, with "I Can Love You Better," "Wide Open Spaces," and "There's Your Trouble" all breaking into the Top Ten and pushing album sales into the multi-platinum category. *Wide Open Spaces* is a wonderful blend of traditional elements such as banjo, fiddle, and steel guitar, and contemporary attitude, most notably a strong female perspective. As far as subject matter goes, they cover all the bases by tossing in a great honky tonk/bar/broken-heart song with "Tonight the Heartache's on Me," several touching ballads including "I'll Take Care of You," "Loving Arms," and "You Were Mine," and an in your face, unapologetic breakup anthem ("Let 'Er Rip"). When choosing tunes to cover, they tip their hat to some great, though perhaps surprising, women songwriters in Maria McKee and Bonnie Raitt with the last two tracks on the record. The charm and talent of the Dixie Chicks earned them well-deserved popularity across genre borders, and rightly so. *Wide Open Spaces* is a highly enjoyable listen. *—Kelly McCartney*

Fly / Aug. 31, 1999 / Monument ♦♦♦♦
With more than six million copies of the Chicks' first album *Wide Open Spaces* sold, the highest ever by a country group, it's reasonable to have pretty imposing expectations of their sophomore album. But *Fly* delivers. When you watch Natalie, Martie, and Emily being interviewed on TV or performing in front of an audience, they always look they are having a blast. And that fun shines through in their songs, particularly in "Goodbye Earl," a song about spousal abuse and getting even. If someone like Patty Loveless or Faith Hill sang it, it'd seem silly, but with Natalie's sassy vocals and Emily and Martie's spirited harmonies, it's just good, plain, ol' fun. From the first track, the ebullient "Ready to Run," to the final track, the wistful "Let Him Fly," the Chicks know how to belt out a tune with confidence and flair and have a good time doing it. *—Maria Konicki*

Jimmie Driftwood (James Morris)

b. Jun. 17, 1917, Mountain View, AR, **d.** Jul. 12, 1998
Vocals, Guitar / Traditional Country
Jimmie Driftwood was almost an anachronism in the years he was at his commercial peak, from 1957 through 1961. A schoolteacher by training, he originally started writing songs as a way of helping his students learn about history, and subquently composed (or collected and re-composed) over 5000 songs, many of them dealing with some element of America's past and its history, telling old folk tales, or preserving some aspect of the daily lives of the people who sang them. Only one modern figure in folk music remotely approaches his contribution to American song and the popular undertanding of its roots, and that is Lee Hayes of the Weavers—Driftwood was never the activist that Hayes was, however, being more concerned with teaching than political causes, and, thus, never engendered either the blacklisting or the subsequent canonization by the Left that Hayes received. And Hayes, for all of his leftist sympathies, was never invited to sing before Soviet Premier Nikita Khrushchev on the occasion of the first visit of any Soviet leader to the United Nations, as Driftwood was. *—Bruce Eder*

● **Americana** / 1991 / Bear Family ♦♦♦♦♦
Comprising Jimmie Driftwood's complete recordings for RCA, cut between 1957 and 1961,

this three-CD set opens with Driftwood's most famous song, "The Battle of New Orleans," and the ten other songs that comprised the classic country-folk collection *Newly Discovered Early American Folk Songs*. The material here, when compared to the music of the Weavers or the Kingston Trio, seems like a field recording from 100 years earlier, with Driftwood's rural Arkansas pronunciation, twangy intonation, and spare backing. *The Wilderness Road* is every bit as good and even more entertaining, since Driftwood seems even more comfortable with the recording process. Disc Two opens with Driftwood's September 1959 sessions for *The Westward Movement*, a series of songs about the beginnings of the great American migration west, which features a somewhat more sophisticated sound. The second half of the disc is made up of *Tall Tales in Song*, Driftwood's series of songs about myths and tall tales from history and local legend. The last five songs come from a Time-Life LP, *How the West Was Won*, and deal with such figures as General Custer, Jesse James, and Billy the Kid. Disc Three opens with the Grammy-winning album *Billy Yank and Johnny Reb*, which returns Driftwood to his more familiar backing band (including John D. Loudermilk), accompanied in surprisingly restrained manner by the Anita Kerr singers. The last half of the disc includes *Sea Shanties*, Driftwood's final album from 1961. The sound throughout is excellent, and the music is all priceless, whether one's taste runs toward country or folk. The booklet transcends Bear Family's usual standard, with extremely detailed notes and essays (some by the man himself), as well as the usual full sessionography. —*Bruce Eder*

Dave Dudley (Dave Pedruska)

b. May 3, 1928, Spencer, WI

Vocals, Guitar / Truck Driving Country, Bakersfield Sound, Honky Tonk, Traditional Country

Dave Dudley is the father of truck-driving country music. With his 1963 song "Six Days on the Road," he founded a new genre of country music—a variation of honky tonk and rock-inflected country that concentrated lyrically on the lifestyles of truck drivers. Dudley had a string of hit singles that ran well into the '70s, establishing himself as one of the most popular singers of his era. After working as a DJ, Dudley began performing and led combos in Idaho and Minneapolis before signing his first recording contract. Two years later, his breakthrough hit "Six Days on the Road" peaked at number two on the country charts and made the pop Top 40. After moving to Mercury, he had a long string of truck-driving singles, including "Truck Drivin' Son-of-A-Gun," "Trucker's Prayer" and "Anything Leaving Town Today." By the end of the decade, he was also making conservative, good-old-boy anthems, as well. By the beginning of the '80s, he was no longer a presence on the charts though he remained a popular concert draw. And truck drivers still loved him—the Teamsters Union awarded him an honorary, solid gold membership card. —*Stephen Thomas Erlewine*

● **20 Great Truck Hits: Dave Dudley** / 1983 / EMI ✦✦✦✦✦

Steve Earle

b. Jan. 17, 1955, Fort Monroe, VA

Vocals, Guitar / Heartland Rock, Americana, Alternative Country, New Traditionalist, Roots Rock, Singer/Songwriter

Steve Earle emerged in the mid-'80s, after Bruce Springsteen and John Mellencamp popularized populist rock & roll, and Dwight Yoakam and Randy Travis kick-started country's neo-traditionalist movement. His unwillingness to conform to either side's rules meant that he never broke through into the mainstream, instead cultivating a dedicated following from both audiences. Raised near San Antonio, Earle was a wild child, dropping out of school after completing the eighth grade. After a stint playing bass in Guy Clark's backing band, Earle penned several country hits in the early '80s. With his reputation growing, Earle wanted to become a recording artist in his own right. His 1986 debut *Guitar Town* became a hit, producing two Top Ten singles. Earle was grouped into country's new traditionalist movement, but also gained the attention of rock critics and fans, and 1987's *Exit O* indeed bore a more rock-oriented direction. Though his career was taking off, Earle's personal life was becoming a wreck, with several divorces pushing him deeper and deeper into drug and alcohol abuse. Album-rock radio embraced 1988's *Copperhead Road*, which helped make it his highest-charting effort. But his newfound success quickly began to collapse, as his addictions and fondness for breaking rules began spinning out of control. The tough, dark sound of 1990's *The Hard Way* reflected his problems, but it quickly fell off the charts, and MCA decided not to renew Earle's contract. For the next several years, Earle was severely addicted to cocaine and heroin, and had several run-ins with the law, culminating in his 1994 arrest for possession of heroin. After serving a year in a rehab center, he signed to Winter Harvest and released the acoustic *Train A Comin'*, which received terrific reviews and strong sales. The attention led to a contract with Warner Brothers, who released *I Feel Alright* in early 1996 and *El Corazon* in 1997, both to strong reviews and respectable sales. Re-established as a vital artist, Earle founded his own E-Squared label and released *The Mountain*, a bluegrass record cut with the Del McCoury Band in 1999. A year later, he returned with *Transcendental Blues*. —*Stephen Thomas Erlewine*

● **Guitar Town** / 1986 / MCA ✦✦✦✦✦

Steve Earle rode a suspiciously rocking band into Nashville and up to the top of the country charts with this album, after which it was decided he was just a little too extreme for the country market, which means this record is "on the edge" in more ways than one. —*William Ruhlmann*

Early Tracks / 1987 / Koch International ✦✦✦

Exit O / 1987 / MCA ✦✦✦

Exit O essentially follows the same formula as *Guitar Town*, and while it isn't as uniformly excellent as his debut, Steve Earle has come up with a couple of his best songs, including the yearning "I Ain't Ever Satisfied." The major difference between the two albums is the fact that Earle insisted on working with his road band the Dukes, which gives *Exit O* a tougher sound. If the material had matched the sound of the album, the record would have surpassed *Guitar Town*, but since the songs are uneven, it's just a respectable followup. —*Thom Owens*

Copperhead Road / 1988 / MCA ✦✦✦

Steve Earle always played hard country music with the swagger of a rock & roll star, so it made sense that he would take a detour out of Nashville, both literally and figuratively. On *Copperhead Road*, Earle opted to record in Memphis and veered away from mainstream country in several directions at once—into potent hard rock (most notably on the superb title song, which became his first rock radio hit), as well as Irish folk (with The Pogues backing Earle on "Johnny Come Lately"), and even bluegrass (virtuoso acoustic pickers Sam Bush and Jerry Douglas sit in on "Nothing But a Child"). If *Copperhead Road* lacked a bit of the tight focus of his acclaimed debut *Guitar Town*, it had energy, firepower, and smart-ass humor to spare (along with Earle's always-superb songs), and it made clear that Steve Earle had the stuff to be a contender in rock & roll, if that was what he wanted. —*Mark Deming*

The Hard Way / 1990 / MCA ✦✦✦

Shut Up and Die Like an Aviator (Live) / 1991 / MCA ✦✦

The Essential Steve Earle / 1993 / MCA ✦✦✦✦✦

Steve Earle lives up to the title billing here. While some of Earle's recent work (and live shows) have inclined to excess, this disc collects lean, mean and vital material from Earle's first three outings—the country-rock masterpiece *Guitar Town*, the inward-looking *Exit O*, and the angry lashing out of *Copperhead Road*. *Essential* is topped off by "Continental Trailways Blues," previously available only on a 1987 compilation. 13 tracks is a little skimpy; some rarities from the vaults would have been a nice touch. —*Roch Parisien*

● **Train a Comin'** / 1995 / Warner Brothers ✦✦✦✦✦

1995's *Train A-Comin'* signaled Steve Earle's final declaration of independence from the Nashville assembly line. At last liberated from his personal demons, Earle found himself exiled from mainstream Nashville. So instead of releasing an album designed to appeal to honchos in Nashville or L.A., Earle released an album that appealed first and foremost to Earle. The result was a stupendous album, a foreshadowing of the renaissance of his career. The disc has the air of a "lost album" that somehow found it's way to market. A crack band of Nashville string kings (Peter Rowan, Norman Blake, and Roy Huskey Jr., with Emmylou Harris singing harmony) tears into quasi-legendary tunes that had been lying around Earle's repertoire, neglected for years. Earle's narrative genius is showcased on three numbers—"The Mercenary Song," the Civil War ballad "Ben McCulloch," and the classic outlaw tune "Tom Ames' Prayer," all of which sound as if they were branded into leather rather than written on paper. "Tom Ames' Prayer" especially takes the breath away with its killer final stanza: "And then he cocked both his pistols/spit in the dirt/And walked out in the street." The album is not all a history lesson, of course. The semi-autobiographical "South Nashville Blues" alarms with its deadpan musings from his self-described two-year "vacation in the ghetto," while "Goodbye" ranks with "My Old Friend the Blues" as one of his teariest weepers. *Train A-Comin'* has proven to be just that—the locomotive that Earle drove through some dark tunnels, pulling behind it a boxcar or two of the finest music of his career. —*John Lomax*

I Feel Alright / Mar. 5, 1996 / Warner Brothers ✦✦✦✦✦

"Be careful what you wish for friends, I've been to hell and now I'm back again," Earle sings on the title track of *I Feel Alright*, immediately drawing us into one of the finest albums of his career. This is the Steve Earle we've been waiting for, as unadorned, unashamed, and plain-faced honest about his roots, dreams, and dirty past lives as any of country music's most heralded singers From the drifting, hard-loving woman in "Now She's Gone" to with-drawn junkie in the ghostly "CCKMP" ("cocaine cannot kill my pain") to the teenage outlaw in "Billy and Bonnie," Earle's characters are a string of loners, often down and out but at the same time loyal, self-aware, and romantics right to the bitter end. Few artists can give us a picture of life's other side with such electrifying clarity. But despite its subject matter, "I Feel Alright" is imbued with a true moments of hope. The closing duet with Lucinda Williams, "You're Still Standin' There," for example, is as strong a statement of faith as any Earle has written. —*Kurt Wolff*

Ain't Ever Satisfied: The Steve Earle Collection / Jul. 1996 / Hip-O ✦✦✦✦✦

Although his personal life was plagued with troubles during the late '80s, Steve Earle wrote a wealth of first-rate songs during that time and the majority of those tunes are collected on the double-disc set, *Ain't Ever Satisfied*. Spanning his career from 1985's *Guitar Town* to 1991's *The Hard Way*, *Ain't Ever Satisfied* hits nearly every high point from his studio albums and throws in a handful of rarities, including live covers of the Rolling Stones and Bruce Springsteen, for good measure. It's an excellent retrospective, illustrating exactly why Earle was one of the most acclaimed country singer/songwriters of the latter half of the '80s. —*Thom Owens*

Johnny Too Bad [EP] / Apr. 8, 1997 / E-Squared ✦✦✦

El Corazon / Oct. 7, 1997 / Warner Brothers ✦✦✦✦

I Feel Alright capped off Steve Earle's comeback, restoring his position as one of the most critically acclaimed roots songwriters of the '80s and '90s. *El Corazon*, the follow-up to *I Feel Alright*, doesn't stray far from its predecessor's formula, offering a blend of introspective folk, gritty country and pile-driving rock & roll. If anything, Earle sounds looser than he did before, tearing into these songs with pure passion. He may be surrounded by guest artists—Emmylou Harris offers harmonies on "Taneytown," and the Fairfield Four are on "Telephone Road," the Del McCoury Band supports him on "I Still Carry You Around," and the Supersuckers kick him in the ass on "N.Y.C."—but he remains the focal point of the music. While *El Corazon* isn't quite as consistent as *I Feel Alright*, it nevertheless confirms Earle's status as one of the finest roots songwriters of the '80s and '90s. —*Stephen Thomas Erlewine*

The Mountain / Feb. 23, 1999 / E-Squared ✦✦✦✦

Transcendental Blues / Jun. 6, 2000 / Artemis ✦✦✦✦

Steve Earle is a rebel. Not in the Hollywood/James Dean/*Easy Rider*/rebel-against-society sense but rather in a real and personal way. Throughout his life and career he has rebelled against the very industry that surrounded him and did not find the freedom he sought until he started his own label (E-Squared). He rebelled against his common sense and his health in search of true American artistry and did not find the freedom he sought until he hit the bottom of addiction, and he continues to rebel against mainstream American culture and politics with his attitudes and songs; *Transcendental Blues* is no exception.

Transcendental Blues walks the line between Steve Earle the country-rock rebel who gave the world *Copperhead Road* and *Guitar Town* and Steve Earle the traditionalist who opened a new chapter in bluegrass with his last release *The Mountain.* This album rocks with songs like "Everyone's in Love With You" and "All My Life." It soothes with "The Boy Who Never Cried" and "Lonelier Than This" and it two-steps with new country like "The Galway Girl" and "Until the Day I Die."

Fans of alternative country music sing the praises of artists like Charlie Robison, Jack Ingram, and Robert Earle Keen Jr., but Steve Earle proves again and again that he is the original alternative to the glossy side of Nashville. Steve Earle cut the path that all his followers thankfully hike along avoiding the weeds and branches that made him what he is today. — *Michael Cusanelli*

Joe Ely

b. Feb. 9, 1947, Amarillo, TX

Vocals, Guitar / Americana, Outlaw Country, Country-Rock, Progressive Country

In the '70s, C&W was full of artists referred to as "outlaws," mavericks who bucked the stodgy Nashville music establishment by writing their own songs, recording with their road bands, and producing their own records. The genre produced a slew of acts, but Amarillo, Texas native Joe Ely epitomized the form. Unlike most of that era's big names, Ely remains a viable artist. He got his start back in the early '70s, working with Butch Hancock and Jimmie Dale Gilmore in a group called The Flatlanders. Their only album didn't go far, and the group broke up. (Rounder reissued the album in 1990.) Around the mid '70s, Ely formed an eclectic group that was able to swing from Cajun and Western to honky-tonk stomps and rockabilly; it was signed to MCA in 1977. Ely released an eponymous debut that year, using songs written by ex-Flatlanders Gilmore and Butch Hancock and throwing in some of his own road-worn, oddly poetic originals. The next year brought *Honky Tonk Masquerade,* the cornerstone of Ely's legacy and one of modern country's most ambitious albums. Further albums (especially *Live Shots,* recorded during his European tour with The Clash) brought Ely to the attention of rock fans and netted ecstatic reviews in country and pop magazines (but, mysteriously, produced no hits). MCA dropped Ely in 1983, and he woodshedded until 1987, when the independent Hightone label signed him and released *Lord of the Highway.* Another Hightone album followed before Ely (whose influence was being felt by the new breed of country neo-traditionalists) re-signed with MCA, releasing another live set and *Love and Danger. Twistin' in the Wind* followed in 1998, and *Live At Antone's* arrived two years later along with MCA/Nashville's *Best Of* collection. He's yet to top his late-'70s achievements, but Ely remains an energetic and passionate live performer and an occasionally inspired songwriter. —*John Floyd*

Joe Ely / 1977 / MCA ✦✦✦✦✦

Ely's first album came out while country's outlaw movement was in full swing, but *Joe Ely* took it one better. This is a roots-rocking country album with tunes by Jimmie Dale Gilmore ("Treat Me Like a Saturday Night") and Butch Hancock ("She Never Spoke Spanish to Me," "If You Were a Bluebird") that deserve the near-classic status their cult of fans has bestowed on them. —*Brian Mansfield*

☆ **Honky Tonk Masquerade** / 1978 / MCA ✦✦✦✦✦

Ely's best album, *Honky Tonk Masquerade* contains everything from Texas weepers ("Because of the Wind") to roadhouse rockers ("Fingernails"). Among the best tunes are Jimmie Dale Gilmore's "Tonight I Think I'm Gonna Go Downtown" and Butch Hancock's "West Texas Waltz." Nobody made country records like this in 1978. Come to think of it, they still don't. —*Brian Mansfield*

Down on the Drag / 1979 / MCA ✦✦✦

Simply another set of decent country songs. Ely's momentum was gone: his band, for the first time, sounded like tired and bored pros. —*John Floyd*

Live Shots / 1980 / MCA ✦✦✦✦✦

Ely partakes of the musical diversity of his hometown, Lubbock, TX, freely mixing country, rock, Tex-Mex, and hard honky-tonk music in excellent songs he writes himself or borrows from his friend Butch Hancock. This is a live best-of covering his first three albums, recorded on tour in England. — *William Ruhlmann*

Musta Notta Gotta Lotta / 1981 / MCA ✦✦✦

If you're making a tape of Ely's greatest hits, *Musta Notta Gotta Lotta* is a must—"Dallas" and "Wishin' for You" ensure its necessity. But anyone who has shed tears (and danced them away) to *Honky Tonk Masquerade* will feel cheated by such obvious covers as Roy Brown's "Good Rockin' Tonight" and Buddy Holly's "Rock Me My Baby." —*John Floyd,*

Hi-Res / 1984 / MCA ✦✦

Lord of the Highway / 1987 / Hightone ✦✦✦

After a long recording layoff, Ely picked up where he'd left off in 1984 with this typical collection, whose best songs—"Me and Billy the Kid" and "Are You Listenin' Lucky—"—were Ely originals. — *William Ruhlmann*

Dig All Night / 1988 / Hightone ✦✦✦

Live at Liberty Lunch / Sep. 1990 / MCA ✦✦✦

Love & Danger / Sep. 29, 1992 / MCA ✦✦✦✦✦

Ely is stark and restless... His muse still roams the highways in search of whatever, his romance doomed by a twist of fate. He's a more objective observer; a storyteller who captures the tragic side to the well-defined characters of "The Road Goes on Forever" and "Every Night About This Time." Ely conveys much—if not most—of a song's emotion through his inspired electric guitar playing. The string-bending is at high-pressure intensity for "Love Is the Beating of Hearts," then drops deep, sonorous and echoed for "Slow You Down." —*Roch Parisien*

Letter to Laredo / Aug. 29, 1995 / MCA ✦✦✦✦✦

Flamenco guitarist Teye is the dominant instrumentalist on a Joe Ely album that fits the "unplugged" tag—drums, electric bass and various, mostly acoustic guitars and occasional accordion and harmonica—and that could be played without complaint in any cantina along the Rio Grande. Ely is joined in his story songs about Southwest life and romantic devotion by Raul Malo, Jimmie Dale Gilmore, and Bruce Springsteen, while Butch Hancock and Tom Russell contribute the strongest material; Hancock's is a sequel, "She Finally Spoke Spanish To Me," and Russell's is the tragic story of a man who bets his future on a cock fight. *Letter To Laredo* is a mood piece with less of the raw energy of many of Ely's albums, but the singer is in his element and his mastery of the form is obvious. — *William Ruhlmann*

Twistin' in the Wind / May 12, 1998 / MCA ✦✦✦✦

Live at Antone's / Jun. 6, 2000 / Rounder ✦✦✦✦

★ **The Best of Joe Ely** / Nov. 21, 2000 / MCA ✦✦✦✦✦

For all his critical hosannas, Joe Ely is something of an acquired taste, since his rebellious \neo-traditionalist country fluctuates between heartfelt \honky tonk evocations, self-conscious modern-day mocking, and material that falls somewhere in between. He did cut a series of albums that were acclaimed and influential, including the rollicking *Live Shots,* one the great \country live albums of its time, but MCA Nashville's 2000 *The Best of Joe Ely* is the best introduction to his sound and aesthetic. Spanning his career from his 1977 debut to 1995's *Letter to Laredo,* this touches on every defining moment Ely had, including songs that he initially cut with the Flatlanders. In this setting, his blend of \honky tonk, \folk, and \rock & roll is remarkably effective and consistent, with "She Never Spoke Spanish to Me," "Tonight I Think I'm Gonna Go Downtown," "Musta Notta Gotta Lotta," and "Letter to Laredo" all standing out as \progressive/\alternative country classics. Given his cult status—the kind of cult where all his recordings are acclaimed equally—this is the best way for outsiders to fall in love with Ely. —*Stephen Thomas Erlewine*

Sara Evans

b. 1971

Vocals / Neo-Traditionalist Country, Contemporary Country, Country-Pop

A female country traditionalist during a time when they were quite rare around Nashville, Sara Evans gained her RCA contract in 1996 after her rendition of Buck Owens' perennial chestnut "I've Got a Tiger by the Tail" impressed its songwriter, Harlan Howard, so much he considered it his bound duty to help her. While growing up poor in rural Missouri, Evans performed with her family's band—at the age of four—and even recorded in Nashville several years later.

She eventually married and moved to Oregon in 1992, but continued to perform, as Sara Evans & North Santiam. The group opened for Willie Nelson and Tim McGraw, among others, but Evans eventually returned to Nashville to try to re-make her career. There she impressed Howard enough to recommend her to RCA executives, who connected her with producer Pete Anderson (a veteran of many albums by Dwight Yoakam). After her debut album *Three Chords & the Truth* was released in July 1997, Evans earned a special honor by being hand-picked by George Jones to open a special show in Nashville. *No Place That Far* followed a year later, and in 1999 she resurfaced with *Girls Night Out; Born to Fly* was issued the next year. —*John Bush*

Three Chords & the Truth / Jul. 1, 1997 / RCA ✦✦✦✦

Coming on like an up-to-date version of Patsy Cline, Sara Evans tosses her hat into the ring for best new female country artist of 1998. Surprisingly, with *Three Chords and the Truth,* she just may win. This disc rings out with an air of originality helped along by great tunes and solid backup musicianship. Producer Pete Anderson (of Dwight Yoakam fame) helps keep things pared down and centered, giving Evans the opportunity to shine. The title cut is a must for new country fans, while "Imagine That" calls to mind Billie Holiday. All in all, the title of this disc says it all. —*James Chrispell*

No Place That Far / Oct. 27, 1998 / RCA ✦✦✦

● **Born to Fly** / Oct. 10, 2000 / RCA ✦✦✦✦✦

The third time's a charm for the delightful Sara Evans. Bound to make her a household name, *Born to Fly* is, simply put, a great album. Whether it's her new mom status, or the fact that she co-produced for the first time and had a hand in writing six of the album's 11 enjoyable songs, Evans' confidence radiates in each and every song, from the playful title track "Born to Fly" to the unbreakable spirit of "I Learned That From You" about a love gone wrong even though they tried to make it work. She puts her own spin on distinguished renditions of Edwin McCain's "I Could Not Ask for More" and Bruce Hornsby's "Every Little Kiss." What must have added to her confidence was having her family (sister Ashley, sister Lesley, sister-in-law Melody) sing background vocals on some songs and brother Matt playing bass. Sara Evans has found herself musically and entertains country fans with an album they can be proud of. —*Maria Konicki*

Exile

f. 1963, Lexington, KY

Group / Urban Cowboy, Soft Rock, Contemporary Country, Country-Pop

Although the Kentucky-based group Exile's first hit "Kiss You All Over" was a major pop smash, they experienced their greatest success as a country band in the latter half of the '80s. Exile was co-founded by J.P. Pennington, the son of former Coon Creek Girl Lily May Ledford, in 1963. A decade later, they had their first minor chart success with "Try It On." They followed it up with "Kiss You All Over," which hit number one on the U.S. pop charts in 1978. After delivering several unsuccessful follow-ups to their hit single, Exile reemerged onto the country music scene in the 1980s, having gone from mellow pop band to high-voltage Southern rockers. The group signed to Epic Records in 1983 and their first country single, "High Cost of Leaving," reached number 27. An eponymous album followed and it produced two chart-toppers, "Woke Up in Love" and "I Don't Wanna Be a Memory." In 1984, Exile's second country album *Kentucky Hearts*, provided three more number one hits, including "Crazy for Your Love." Released in 1985, *Hang on to Your Heart* was even more successful, producing four number one singles, including the title track and "I Could Get Used to You." Although 1987's *Shelter from the Night* contained the number one hit "I Can't Get Close Enough," the album wasn't as successful as its predecessors. *—Sandra Brennan*

● **Greatest Hits** / 1986 / Epic ✦✦✦✦✦
Exile– Greatest Hits offers a good cross-section of the band's late '70s and early '80s country-rock hits, including "Kiss You All Over" and "Woke Up In Love." *—Stephen Thomas Erlewine*

Donna Fargo (Yvonne Vaughn)

b. Nov. 10, 1949, Mount Airy, NC
Vocals, Guitar / Nashville Sound/Countrypolitan, Country-Pop
In the early '70s, Donna Fargo was an unusual country star for a couple of reasons. She was one of the few female country singers to write her own material, and one of the few country singers of any sort to cross over to the pop charts in a big way, which she did in 1972 with "The Happiest Girl In The Whole U.S.A." (#11) and "Funny Face" (#5). She never made the pop Top 40 again, but placed over a dozen more singles in the country Top Ten in the '70s, most written by herself. As an artist, she was squarely in the mainstream, her slightly lisping voice delivering upbeat, sweetly produced homilies to romance, home, and America. She faded after developing multiple sclerosis in 1979, although she continued writing and performing. *—Richie Unterberger*

● **The Best of Donna Fargo [Varese Vintage]** / 1995 / Varese ✦✦✦✦✦
18 songs, all but one from dating from her 1972-75 prime, when she recorded for Dot. Contains ten Top Ten country hits, including of course "Funny Face" and "The Happiest Girl In The Whole U.S.A." *—Richie Unterberger*

Freddy Fender (Baldemar Huerta)

b. Jun. 4, 1937, San Benito, TX
Vocals, Guitar / Tex-Mex, Country-Pop, Traditional Country, Rock & Roll
Freddy Fender was one of the few Hispanic stars in country music, a singer and songwriter whose work was defined largely by its strong Latin sensibility. He began recording in the late '50s, but a prison sentence (for possession of marijuana) derailed his career. He worked as an auto mechanic during the '60s, but began recording again after meeting producer Huey P. Meaux. In 1975, "Before the Next Teardrop Falls" hit the top of the country and pop charts, and Fender became an overnight star. He notched his second straight country chart-topper with a re-recording of his early single "Wasted Days and Wasted Nights," and followed with yet another 1975 number one, "Secret Love." Throughout the remainder of the '70s, Fender's success continued. As the 1980s dawned, however, his popularity began slipping. Except for a scattered acting career, he remained largely silent until 1990, when he formed the Tex-Mex supergroup Texas Tornados with Doug Sahm, Flaco Jimenez and Augie Meyers. After three albums, the group disbanded, and Fender again resumed his solo career. *—Jason Ankeny*

Early Years: 1959-1963 / 1986 / Krazy Kat ✦✦✦
These 16 sides are taken from rare regional singles that were cut for tiny labels in the days when Fender was only known in Texas and Louisiana. While Fender's earliest recordings were in Spanish, he only sings in English on these cuts of decent, though not thrilling, early swamp pop. Fender takes his inspiration from rockabilly, doo wop, Tex-Mex, and smoldering R&B ballads on these singles, which include his first (and possibly best) version of "Wasted Days & Wasted Nights." One of the relatively few early rock performers to flavor his sound with Texas border music, these sides were most likely influential on Doug Sahm, although they were unheard by a national audience. *—Richie Unterberger*

Collection / 1991 / Reprise ✦✦✦✦✦
The Freddy Fender Collection is a 10 track compilation that contains his biggest hits, from the country-pop crossovers "Wasted Days and Wasted Nights" and "Before the Next Teardrop Falls" to country chart-toppers "Secret Love" and "You'll Lose A Good Thing." It's a brief but consistent collection, featuring nearly every one of his best singles from the mid-'70s, making it an excellent introduction to his long, prolific career, even if isn't as comprehensive as it could have been. *—Stephen Thomas Erlewine*

Canciones de Mi Barrio: The Roots of Tejano Rock / 1993 / Arhoolie ✦✦✦
Fender's earliest Tejano rock recordings are compiled on *Canciones de Mi Barrio,* a fine collection of singles first issued between 1959 and 1964 on the tiny San Benito, Texas label Ideal. Sung mostly in Spanish, these "canciones" bear a large debt to Elvis Presley's hits—there's even a cover of "Devil in Disguise"—although Fender's clear, sweet voice and the music's strong Latin roots combine to give his formative efforts their own distinct identity. *—Jason Ankeny*

● **Greatest Hits** / Apr. 20, 1999 / Edsel ✦✦✦✦✦

Flatlanders

Group / Alternative Country, Outlaw Country, Country-Folk, Progressive Country
The Flatlanders became legends long after they broke up because the band's three primary members—Jimmie Dale Gilmore, Joe Ely, and Butch Hancock—each attracted a large, loyal cult following as solo performers. In 1972, when their lone album was recorded, they were part-time musicians who hooked up after each returned to their native Texas after exploring some different region of the world. The record wasn't released, and they went their separate ways, each abandoning music briefly. Their careers continued to intertwine in the ensuing decades with great results. *—Michael McCall*

● **More a Legend than a Band** / 1990 / Rounder ✦✦✦✦✦
The title refers to the status these "lost" tapes acquired as time passed and the reputations of Ely, Gilmore and Hancock grew. The music itself is odd and effective, a blend of old-time acoustic music (including a musical saw) matched with lyrics that look at the world as only modern Texas mystics could. Gilmore takes most of the lead vocals. It features the first recorded versions of two of his classics, "Dallas" and "Tonight I'm Gonna Go Downtown." *—Michael McCall*

Rosie Flores

b. Sep. 10, 1950, San Antonio, TX
Vocals, Guitar / Americana, Rockabilly Revival, Neo-Traditionalist Country, Alternative Country
Since the late '70s, guitarist, singer, and songwriter Rosie Flores has been a steady figure on the alternative country scene in both Austin, Texas and Los Angeles. She's a hard-working, independently minded artist who's well-respected for her gritty, energetic vocals and fiery guitar solos.

Flores's first band was Rosie and the Screamers—based in Southern California during the punk-rock era of the late 1970s—who played hard country and rockabilly material, much of it written by Flores. A few years later she began working as a solo acoustic artist, but eventually formed an all-female band, The Screaming Sirens, who recorded the album *Fiesta* in 1984.

In 1987 Flores recorded her first solo album, *Rosie Flores,* produced by Pete Anderson (Dwight Yoakam's producer and guitarist) and released by Warner Bros. Flores eventually parted ways with Warner Bros. and signed to the indie label HighTone. In 1992 she released her second solo album, *After the Farm,* followed by *Once More with Feeling* a year later. Flores then spent the better part of 1994 playing lead guitar in Butch Hancock's band.

In 1995 Flores recorded *Rockabilly Filly,* a spirited tribute to the music she grew up with. The album featured duets with her longtime idols Wanda Jackson and Janis Martin, both of whom Flores brought out of retirement for the project. The album led to a cross-country tour with Jackson, who hadn't played in nightclubs in over 20 years. *Dance Hall Dreams* followed in 1999. *—Kurt Wolff*

● **Rosie Flores** / 1987 / Reprise ✦✦✦✦✦
Produced by Pete Anderson, Rosie Flores's debut made her out to be the female answer to Dwight Yoakam. Flores probably felt like that image straitjacketed her, but from a musical standpoint, it worked beautifully, incorporating Flores's San Antonio roots into Anderson's California country vision. Includes "Crying over You," "Somebody Loses, Somebody Wins," and "Blue Side of Town," which Patty Loveless wouldn't do nearly as well the following year. *—Brian Mansfield*

After the Farm / 1992 / Hightone ✦✦✦✦

Once More with Feeling / 1993 / Hightone ✦✦✦
Closer to modern commercial country than *After the Farm, Once More with Feeling* doesn't have the sleekly professional touch of *Rosie Flores,* but it's not without its charms. It includes a duet with Joe Ely ("Love and Danger," which Flores wrote with Jason & The Scorchers' Jason Ringenberg). Other songs contributed by Wendy Waldman ("Ruin This Romance") and Katy Moffatt ("Real Man"). *—Brian Mansfield*

Rockabilly Filly / Oct. 1995 / Hightone ✦✦✦

Honky Tonk Reprise / Jun. 4, 1996 / Rounder ✦✦✦✦

A Little Bit of Heartache / Jan. 21, 1997 / Watermelon ✦✦✦✦✦

Dance Hall Dreams / Mar. 2, 1999 / Rounder ✦✦✦

Red Foley (Clyde Julian Foley)

b. Jun. 17, 1910, Blue Lick, KY, **d.** Sep. 19, 1968, Fort Wayne, IN
Vocals, Guitar / Country Gospel, Honky Tonk, Traditional Country
Red Foley was one of the biggest stars in country during the post-war era, a silky-voiced singer who sold some 25 million records between 1944 and 1965 and whose popularity went far in making country music a viable mainstream commodity. He gained his big break in 1930, singing for the house band on the WLS radio program *National Barn Dance* and also earned his own show, *Renfro Valley Barn Dance.* In 1941, he signed a lifetime contract with Decca and his first chart single, 1944's "Smoke on the Water," topped the charts for 13 consecutive weeks. Beginning in 1946, Foley began emceeing and performing on a segment of the *Grand Ole Opry* radio program, establishing the *Opry* as country's pre-eminent radio show. He also earned more number one singles during the late '40s including "New Jolie Blonde (New Pretty Blonde)," "Tennessee Saturday Night" and the song that would become his trademark tune, "Chattanoogie Shoe Shine Boy." After his wife Eva Overstake committed suicide, reportedly over the singer's affair with another woman, Foley cut back on performing in order to devote the majority of his time to raising a family. He continued to release hit after hit in a variety of musical styles, including rockabilly, gospel and R&B. Foley also spent the last six years of the 1950s hosting the hit television program, *The Ozark Jubilee.* Although Foley continued recording throughout most of the 1960s, his hit-making days were largely behind him. After a performance in 1968, Foley died of a heart attack. *—Jason Ankeny*

★ **Country Music Hall of Fame** / 1991 / MCA ✦✦✦✦✦
Country Music Hall of Fame contains a good cross-section of Red Foley's heyday in the late '40s and early '50s. All of the selections of this 16-track, single-disc compilation were recorded for Decca Records. While not all of his hits are present—even some of his biggest singles, including "Smoke On Your Water," are missing—but most of the essential items ("Chattanoogie Shoe Shine Boy," "Tennessee Saturday Night," "Peace In the Valley") are here, making it an essential introduction to one of country's biggest stars. *—Stephen Thomas Erlewine*

Tennessee Ernie Ford

b. Feb. 13, 1919, Bristol, TN, **d.** Oct. 17, 1991, Los Angeles, CA
Vocals / Country Boogie, Country Gospel, Nashville Sound/Countrypolitan, Country-Folk, Traditional Country
Tennessee Ernie Ford was a beloved personality and performer during the '50s and '60s whose best known song was his version of Merle Travis' "Sixteen Tons." During his long ca-

reer, Ford recorded over 100 albums and earned numerous honors and awards, including the distinguished Medal of Freedom. His potential as a singer was first recognized by Cliffie Stone, who hired Ford as a featured act on two of his radio shows. From there, he signed to Capitol Records in 1949. Five singles were released that year, including "Tennessee Border" and "Smokey Mountain Boogie" (both Top Ten) and his first number one single, "Mule Train." Early in 1951, "The Shot Gun Boogie" became his second number one, spending 14 weeks at the top of the country charts. By the beginning of 1953, Ford wasn't having as many hits, but he remained popular not only in America, but also in England; he became the first country singer to star at the London Palladium. Ford had two Top Ten country hits in 1955 with "Ballad of Davy Crockett" and his biggest success, "Sixteen Tons," which spent ten weeks at number one on the country charts and eight weeks at number one on the pop charts. He also had great success with his first gospel album, *Hymns* (1956), which became the first religious album to go gold. *—Sandra Brennan*

☆ **16 Tons of Boogie: The Best of Tennessee Ernie Ford** / 1990 / Rhino ♦♦♦♦♦
In his later years, Ford's little pea-pickin' heart was closely associated with gospel and patriotic music, but in earlier years he knew how to—as the album title says—boogie. This includes all the essential material from that period: "Sixteen Tons," "The Shot Gun Boogie," "Mule Train," and "Blackberry Boogie," for starters. *—Tom Roland*

Sixteen Tons / Oct. 10, 1995 / Bear Family ♦♦♦♦♦
Though named after Tennessee Ernie Ford's biggest hit, *Sixteen Tons* was released five years after the single was a hit. The large gap of time between the release of the single and album is inconsequential—in essence, the album is a compilation of Ford's greatest hits of the '50s, containing not only the title track, but also "Mule Train," "The Cry of the Wild Goose," and "The Shot Gun Boogie." Though more comprehensive compilations of Ford's work were later released, *Sixteen Tons* remains an entertaining listen from start to finish; in fact, in terms of sheer listenability, it rivals any of the latter-day collections. *—Stephen Thomas Erlewine*

Vintage Collections Series / Mar. 11, 1997 / Capitol ♦♦♦♦♦
Capitol's stellar *Vintage Collections Series* continues with this excellent overview of Tennessee Ernie Ford's far-ranging 27-year tenure with the label. Along with the singer's hits, the 20-track collection also includes a number of rare performances; featured are "Sixteen Tons," "Smokey Mountain Boogie," "I'll Never Be Free" (with Kay Starr) and "Hey, Good Lookin'" (with Helen O'Connell). *—Jason Ankeny*

★ **The Ultimate Collection (1949-1965)** / Mar. 18, 1997 / Razor & Tie ♦♦♦♦♦
The Ultimate Collection is a definitive 40-song, double-disc set containing nearly all of Ford's biggest hits, from "Tennessee Border" and "Mule Train" through "The Shot Gun Boogie" to "Sixteen Tons" and "Hicktown." For some, the set may simply be too much music, but *The Ultimate Collection* lives up to its billing as the most comprehensive and listenable retrospective ever assembled on Tennessee Ernie Ford. *—Stephen Thomas Erlewine*

Foster & Lloyd

f. 1987, **db.** 1990
Group / New Traditionalist, Contemporary Country
During the mid to late 1980s, Foster & Lloyd were a popular songwriting and singing duo. As singers, they were known for their close harmonies and lively country-rock sound that is reminiscent of Poco or the Eagles. Radney Foster and Bill Lloyd first teamed around 1986, co-writing such successful songs as "Since I Found You," which became a hit for the Sweethearts of the Rodeo. The two turned to singing the following year and signed with RCA. Foster and Lloyd were given free-rein with their eponymous first album; their debut single "Crazy Over You," made it to the Top 5 where it stayed for over four months. In 1988, their second single "Sure Thing" made it to the Top 10 and its follow up made it to the Top 20. Their third single, "What Do You Want from Me This Time," was a Top 10 hit for several months. They released their second album *Faster and Llouder* in 1989. The album produced a Top 5 and a Top 50 hit. Foster and Lloyd released *Version of the Truth*, their final album, in 1990. They amicably split to pursue solo careers after that. *—Sandra Brennan*

Foster & Lloyd / 1987 / RCA ♦♦♦

Faster & Llouder / 1989 / RCA ♦♦♦♦♦

Version of the Truth / 1990 / RCA ♦♦♦

● **The Essential Foster and Lloyd** / Apr. 1996 / RCA ♦♦♦♦♦
The Essential Foster & Lloyd groups together 19 tracks by this influential duo who scored several hits in the 1980s. The two merged Lloyd's melodic pop smarts with Foster's Texas literary soul, giving them catchiness and substance in the same package. They also could rock out, leaning toward a rockabilly energy that didn't carry a trace of the redneck swagger of Southern rock. Instead, this was solid, clean-rocking fun with brains. The duo split in 1990 after three albums, but this collection is a good reminder that they anticipated the country youth movement that followed them. *—Michael McCall*

Janie Fricke

b. Dec. 19, 1952, South Whitney, IN
Vocals, Guitar / New Traditionalist, Contemporary Country, Country-Pop
Janie Fricke came to Nashville in 1975 to sing backup vocals, appearing on albums by artists like Ronnie Milsap, Charley Pride, Loretta Lynn and England Dan & John Ford Coley. In total, she sang on over 1, 200 albums before getting her big break from producer Billy Sherrill, who paired her with Johnny Duncan. During 1977, the duo had three successful singles: "Stranger," "Thinkin' of a Rainbow," and "It Couldn't Have Been Better." The latter two singles hit number one, and their success convinced Sherrill to sign Fricke as a solo artist. She released her first solo single, "What're You Doin' Tonight," in 1977, and it made the Top 30. Under Sherrill's direction, Fricke made three successful albums during the late 1970s and had several hits, including a number one duet with Charlie Rich, "On My Knees" (1978). In 1979 she and Duncan recorded the album *Nice 'n' Easy*. In 1981, she had three hits from her album *Sleeping with Your Memory*. In 1982, she had a number one hit with "Don't Worry 'Bout Me Baby." That year she moved away from soft songs to show another, more hard-driving side of her talent on the album *It Ain't Easy*. It too was successful, and she continued to rack up hits through the 1980s, periodically changing styles. *—Sandra Brennan*

It Ain't Easy / 1982 / Columbia ♦♦♦

Somebody Else's Fire / 1985 / Columbia ♦♦♦

● **Anthology** / Mar. 16, 1999 / Renaissance ♦♦♦♦♦
The most generous single-disc collection of Janie Fricke's late-'70s and 1980's chart hits, *Anthology* offers eight number one country hits and 14 others. Fricke was a background vocalist on hundreds of sessions before becoming a solo artist, and her success as a background vocalist might explain her weakness as a lead singer: her voice is very professional, precise, and generic, lacking the character that makes so many great vocalists immediately identifiable, although she does have a slight Southern accent. Her music is slick and smooth pop-oriented country that recalls both Barbara Mandrell and Juice Newton. Certainly Fricke is a talented vocalist who has sold many records, but she has not forged a unique identity with her music, and consequently the real allure of these singles is in the songwriting rather than the uniqueness of the performances. *—Greg Adams*

Lefty Frizzell (William Orville Frizzell)

b. Mar. 31, 1928, Corsicana, TX, **d.** Jul. 19, 1975, Nashville, TN
Vocals, Guitar / Honky Tonk, Traditional Country
Lefty Frizzell was the definitive honky-tonk singer, the vocalist that set the style for generations of vocalists that followed him. Frizzell smoothed out the rough edges of honky tonk by singing longer, flowing phrases—essentially, he made honky tonk more acceptable for the mainstream without losing its gritty, bar-room roots. In the process, he changed the way country vocalists sang forever. From George Jones, Merle Haggard, and Willie Nelson to George Strait, John Anderson, Randy Travis, and Keith Whitley, hundreds of artists have emulated and expanded Lefty's innovations. Frizzell's singing became the foundation of how hard country should be sung. Despite his influence, there was a time when Lefty Frizzell wasn't regarded as one of country's definitive artists. Unlike Hank Williams—the only contemporary of Lefty that had greater influence—he didn't die young, leaving behind a romantic legend. After his popularity peaked in the early and mid-'50s, Frizzell continued to record, without having much success. However, his recordings continued to reach new listeners and his reputation was restored by the new traditionalists of the '80s, nearly 10 years after Lefty's death. *—Stephen Thomas Erlewine*

Sings the Songs of Jimmie Rodgers / 1960 / Koch International ♦♦♦♦♦

★ **The Best of Lefty Frizzell** / 1991 / Rhino ♦♦♦♦♦
These 18 tracks cover 15 years (1950-65) in the career of a singer whom Merle Haggard once called "the most unique thing that ever happened to country music." Included are such timeless Frizzell gems as "If You've Got the Money, I've Got the Time," "I Love You a Thousand Ways," "I Want to Be with You Always," "Always Late (With Your Kisses)," and "The Long Black Veil." This is a must-hear for anyone interested in the origins of a vocal style so influential it rules country radio to this very day. *—Dan Cooper*

Life's Like Poetry / 1992 / Bear Family ♦♦♦♦♦
Life's Like Poetry is a gigantic, 12-disc box set that includes all of Lefty Frizzell's recordings for Columbia and ABC, plus early demos, a session with Jay Miller, and several radio transcriptions—everything he recorded between 1950 and 1975. Certainly, the box is designed for collectors—no one but the most devoted fan could listen to all 330 tracks. Though all of his classic material is included, there is also a fair share of mediocre material, including some ill-advised attempts at country-pop. Nevertheless, there are gems sprinkled throughout the collection and it offers proof of his far-reaching talents and influence, as well as demonstrating that several of Lefty's later recordings were as worthwhile as his early singles. For any serious fan, it is an indispensible collection. *—Stephen Thomas Erlewine*

That's the Way Love Goes: The Final Recordings of Lefty Frizzell / Oct. 22, 1996 / Varese Sarabande ♦♦♦♦
That's the Way Love Goes: Final Recordings of Lefty Frizzell collects the highlights from Lefty's latter-day recordings for ABC Records, including the minor hit singles "Life's like Poetry," "Lucky Arms" and "I Never Go Around Mirrors." Though his material for ABC wasn't as consistently compelling as his early recordings, *That's The Way Love Goes* salvages his finest moments from this era, making a convincing argument that Frizzell's vocal abilities had not deteriorated much at all. In fact, the best moments on this compilation stand with Lefty's best work ever. It just happens that not every song on the collection is terrific, but enough songs are brilliant to make it a worthwhile purchase. *—Stephen Thomas Erlewine*

★ **Look What Thoughts Will Do** / Jan. 28, 1997 / Columbia/Legacy ♦♦♦♦♦
Look What Thoughts Will Do: The Essential Lefty Frizzell, 1950-1963 is a double-disc set covering all of Lefty's biggest hits ("If You've Got the Money I've Got the Time," "I Love You A Thousand Ways," "I Want To Be With You Always," "Always Late (With Your Kisses)," "Give Me More, More More (Of Your Kisses)," "Run 'Em Off," "The Long Black Veil," "Saginaw, Michigan"), plus several lesser-known singles, B-sides and album tracks. Essentially, the compilation is an expanded version of Rhino's excellent single-disc *The Best of Lefty Frizzell*, featuring all of that disc's 18 tracks. What makes *Look What Thoughts Will Do* exciting for fans that already have the older compilation is the wealth of gems that haven't made it to compact disc in the past. For neophytes, the double-disc is an excellent introduction, since it draws a full portrait of one of the greatest honky tonk singers to ever live. Casual listeners will want to stick with the Rhino compilation, but *Look What Thoughts Will Do* is the definitive overview of Frizzell's heyday, making it an essential addition to any serious country collection. *—Stephen Thomas Erlewine*

Robbie Fulks

Vocals, Guitar / Neo-Traditionalist Country, Alternative Country
After spending his childhood years living in Pennsylvania, Virginia and Creedmoor, NC, Robbie Fulks attended Columbia University in New York City, before relocating to Chicago

in 1983. He sang and played guitar with the Special Consensus Bluegrass Band and appeared on their 1989 Grammy-nominated album *Hole in My Heart,* before becoming a cast member in the award-winning *Woody Guthrie's American Song.* Forming the Trailer Trash Revue, a four-piece rock band complete with go-go dancers, Fulks independently released a 45-rpm single with two country-flavored originals "Little King" and "Jean Arthur," which garnered some regional radio airplay. When Bloodshot Records released its 1994 *For a Life of Sin: A Compilation of Insurgent Chicago Country* a Fulks' original "Cigarette State," which was recorded by Steve Albini was included. When the label released its 1995 follow-up compilation *Hell Bent: Insurgent Country Volume 2* they used another Albini-recorded Fulks original, entitled "She Took a Lot of Pills (And Died)." Fulks subsequently signed with the label and in 1996, working again with Albini at the recording console, he released his first album *Country Love Songs.* Featuring 13 Fulks originals, the album featured musical backing by the Skeletons along with legendary pedal steel guitarist Tom Brumley, a former Buck Owens sideman. *Let's Kill Saturday Night* followed in 1998. *—Jack Leaver*

• **Country Love Songs** / 1996 / Bloodshot ♦♦♦♦
Fulks is cleverly twisted, deliciously irreverent and one the best of the new country singer/songwriters. Musically, *Country Love Songs* supplies plenty of hardcore, bottle-tippin, ' honky-tonk country, with a '50's production that sounds like it's supposed to be there. Fulks writes and sings country music that bears little or no resemblance to what dominates the airwaves, rather his material harkens back an era when humor and dark subject matter shared the same page of a writer's composition book. Paying homage to the classic Bakersfield sound, with former Buckeroo Tom Brumley shining on pedal steel, Fulksdelivers "The Buck Starts Here," which just might be the best country song since "He Stopped Loving Her Today." Lyrically, Fulks can travel some pretty spooky highway, like in the descriptive ballad "Barely Human," a drinking song, that's as tortured as they get, with the song's character "barely human from twilight 'till dawn." Other strong tracks include the saga of an aging movie starlet who loses it in "She Took A Lot Of Pills (And Died)"—which first appeared on the second volume of the label's Insurgent Country compilations—and the swingin' "Every Kind Of Music But Country." *—Jack Leaver*

South Mouth / Oct. 7, 1997 / Bloodshot ♦♦♦
Fulks uses a backing musician cavalcade on each track in this exploration of "the dark side of country music." Not strictly downbeat, there is plenty of humor here, too ("I Told Her Lies," etc.). Especially noteworthy are the steel guitar players (Steve Byam and Buck Owens' Tom Brumley) and the solid bass guitar from Lou Whitney of the Skeletons. These arrangements, bolstered by a mob of electric and acoustic guitarists, make for the salient entertainment on this disc. Fulks is no Hank Williams, in that Fulks can't often hold your attention with merely his material, voice, and guitar. However, the variety on this disc, from ballads like "Forgotten but Not Gone" to real insurgency like "F*ck This Town," and the rich instrumentation make it a fine contribution to alternative country music. *—Thomas Schulte*

Let's Kill Saturday Night / Sep. 15, 1998 / Geffen ♦♦♦♦
Robbie Fulks' *Let's Kill Saturday Night* reflects not only his love of traditional country and early rock & roll, but also his appreciation for British new wave popsters with similar tastes (Nick Lowe, Graham Parker, Elvis Costello). A number of fine musicians make guest appearances, including Lucinda Williams, Al Anderson (NRBQ), Bill Lloyd, Sam Bush, and John Hughey. *—Steve Huey*

The Very Best of Robbie Fulks / Jan. 18, 2000 / Bloodshot ♦♦♦♦
Indicative of Fulks' sly sense of humor, *The Very Best of Robbie Fulks* is nothing of the sort, but a collection of tracks culled from EPs, promos, limited release 45s, soundtracks, and various obscure compilations. While much of the material is probably meant to be a little more fun than serious, with Fulks adding humorous self-effacing humor in the liner notes, there is some truly first rate material here. The very strong country ballad "I Just Want to Meet the Man," and the frantic mock rockabilly of "Roots Rock Weirdoes" make for very entertaining listening. "Parallel Bars," a nice duet with Kelly Willis, and the catchy straightforward rock of "Wedding of the Bugs" also should not be missed. "That Bangle Girl," which Fulks mentions as being a personal favorite, is an absolutely essential piece of sharp country-rock bliss that ranks well with anything he's ever written. While everything here may not always be in the best taste, the rather low-brow "White Man's Bourbon" comes to mind, the material is generally consistent enough for it to be possible that a few first-time listeners could mistake this for an actual greatest hits collection. *—Matt Fink*

Larry Gatlin

b. May 28, 1948, Seminole, TX
Vocals, Guitar / Urban Cowboy, Neo-Traditionalist Country, Country-Pop
Larry Gatlin was the founder of the Gatlin Brothers, but before starting the popular 1980s trio, he had a successful career of his own.

Gatlin was raised listening to and performing gospel music. As a child, he teamed with his brothers to sing on a local radio station. After college, he joined the gospel-oriented Imperials as part of Jimmy Dean's Las Vegas show in the 1960s. While there he met Dottie West and she became his friend and mentor. Later he sent her a demo of his songs. She was so impressed that she sent him plane tickets to Nashville in her reply. After West recorded two of those songs, "Once You Are Mine," and "You're the Other Half of Me," Gatlin moved to Music City and began singing with West's newly formed First Generation Music Company. Soon afterward, he began singing back up for Kris Kristofferson, and it was he who helped Gatlin get a contract with Monument Records in 1973.

Gatlin's first single, "Sweet Becky Walker," reached the country Top 40 and his third single, "Delta Dirt," made it to the Top 15 in 1974. In late 1975, he gathered his brothers and a few others to form Larry Gatlin with Family and Friends. In 1978, he recorded a few solo singles and two of them—"Night Time Magic" and "I've Done Enough Dyin' Today"—reached the Top Ten. In 1979, he created the Gatlin Brothers Band, and for the next five years had great success with them.

The Gatlin Brothers continued recording and touring regularly until 1991; for the rest of the decade, the Gatlins performed regularly, sometimes at their theatre in Myrtle Beach, South Carolina. In 1993, Larry played the part of Will Rogers in the *Will Rogers Follies* on Broadway. Later that year, he and his brothers returned to the recording studio to record a tribute to their favorite musicians, entitled *Moments to Remember.* The solo gospel release *In My Life* appeared in 1998. *—Sandra Brennan*

Night Time Magic / 1978 / Sony Special Products ♦♦♦

Straight Ahead / 1979 / Columbia ♦♦♦♦♦
Occasionally overstated but predominantly satisfying, it's got a little jazz, a little gospel, a little pop, and a little country. Every country fan knows "All the Gold in California, " but the best cuts are the controversial "Midnight Choir (Mogen David)" and a sweet little piece of ear candy: "Taking Somebody with Me When I Fall." *—Tom Roland*

Greatest Hits / 1980 / Columbia ♦♦♦♦♦

Help Yourself / 1980 / Columbia ♦♦♦
Heavy on ballads that effectively show off The Gatlins' trademark genetic harmony. As always, all ten cuts are written by Larry; "Daytime Heroes," a nod to Prince Valium and the soaps, is most inspired. The Gatlin Brothers recorded "Songwriter's Trilogy" live—whether insightful or self-indulgent depends on the listener's viewpoint. *—Tom Roland*

Greatest Hits, Vol. 2 / 1983 / Columbia ♦♦♦♦

17 Greatest Hits / 1985 / Columbia ♦♦♦

The Best of the Gatlins: All the Gold in California / 1996 / Columbia/Legacy ♦♦♦♦♦

Houston to Denver/Not Guilty / Jun. 6, 2000 / Collectables ♦♦♦

• **16 Biggest Hits** / Jun. 13, 2000 / Columbia/Legacy ♦♦♦♦♦
There's only one thing wrong with this album, but it's a big thing. The title notwithstanding, Larry Gatlin & the Gatlin Brothers' *16 Biggest Hits* actually contains 16 of their 17 biggest hits, with one important omission: the number one hit "I Just Wish You Were Someone I Love." It' s hard to think of any excuse other than an error on the part of somebody at Columbia/Legacy to explain why one of the Gatlins' three biggest hits isn't on this collection. Certainly, Larry Gatlin and company were way overdue for a compilation of this sort, not having had any hits albums on the market since a series of three inadequate LPs in the late 1970s and early '80s. (The 1996 collection *The Best of the Gatlins: All the Gold in California* excludes Larry Gatlin's most successful solo recordings, making it another flawed compilation, and more expensive.) The Gatlin discography was subject to a dizzying series of varied billings, with different singles variously credited to: Larry Gatlin; Larry Gatlin with Family & Friends; Larry Gatlin With Brothers and Friends; Larry Gatlin & the Gatlin Brothers Band; Larry Gatlin & the Gatlin Brothers; Larry, Steve, Rudy: the Gatlin Brothers; and the Gatlin Brothers. But no matter what the credit, all of the major Gatlin country hits from 1975's "Broken Lady" to 1988's "Love of a Lifetime" are here, all except "I Just Wish You Were Someone I Love," that is. At a mid-line price, and containing more of the Gatlins' hits than any other disc, this album must be rated their first pick. But somebody at the record company should correct the obvious mistake and then reissue this reissue. *—William Ruhlmann*

Greatest Hits/Straight Ahead / Jan. 16, 2001 / Collectables ♦♦♦

Crystal Gayle (Brenda Gail Webb)

b. Jan. 9, 1951, Paintsville, KY
Vocals / Urban Cowboy, Soft Rock, Adult Contemporary, Country-Pop
With her rich voice and trademark long hair, Crystal Gayle was a popular performer of mainstream country ballads during the '70s and '80s. She was the younger sister of country legend Loretta Lynn, a relationship which both boosted and hindered her career. (Though they shared the same biological father, Gayle and Lynn had very different upbringings.) Gayle's first single was a cover of her sister's song "I've Cried the Blue Right Out of My Eyes" that became a hit but made it difficult to move out from her bigger sister's shadow. Her eponymous 1975 debut album provided her with three hits and by the time of her first number one country hit (1976's "I'll Get Over You"), she had begun to develop her own fan base. Her biggest hit, 1977's "Don't It Make My Brown Eyes Blue," not only spent four weeks topping the country charts, it also reached number two on the pop charts. Gayle had three other number one hits—"Ready for the Times to Get Better," "Talking in Your Sleep," and "Why Have You Left the One You Left Me For." During the early '80s, she continued to rack up number one hits until the late '80s. During the '90s, she recorded infrequently, preferring to concentrate on touring America and Europe. *—Sandra Brennan*

• **Classic Crystal** / 1979 / EMI ♦♦♦♦♦
Of Gayle's many overlapping hits collections, this one's the best. Given her crossover success ("Don't It Make My Brown Eyes Blue," included here, hit number two pop) it's interesting to note that all of these tracks were produced by Allen Reynolds, known these days for his work with Garth Brooks. *—Dan Cooper*

True Love / 1982 / Elektra ♦♦♦♦♦
When Gayle delivered the album to then-Elektra-division-head Jimmy Bowen, he complained that it rocked too much. Producer Allen Reynolds refused to make changes, so Bowen produced three new tracks that seem out of place. Yeah, the Reynolds tracks do rock. So what— Gayle gives some of her best performances ever on "Our Love Is on the Faultline" and "Deeper in the Fire." *—Tom Roland*

Crystal Gayle's Greatest Hits / 1983 / Columbia ♦♦♦♦♦
Always greatly influenced by pop sounds, Gayle embraced that aspect of her musical heritage more in the late '70s and early '80s than any other period. This set covers it well ("Half the Way" is classic), and provides a nice cover photo too. *—Tom Roland*

50 Original Tracks / 1993 / EMI Country ♦♦♦♦
50 Original Tracks is a two-CD import that offers every Top 40 country hit *Gayle* recorded for United Artists in the '70s, including "Don't It Make My Brown Eyes Blue" and several other number ones. She signed with Capitol Nashville in 1990, and a sampling of tracks from

that period are collected as well. The quality is high throughout this very listenable anthology, and many of the non-hits and album tracks are nearly the equal of the better-known hits. Given the quantity of material, there is inevitably a bum track here and there (most notably the bizarre futuristic fantasy of "We Must Believe in Magic"), but in terms of sheer length, this generous import compilation far surpasses anything available domestically. Gayle's music during this era hovers somewhere between the pop-country of, say, Glen Campbell, and the smooth easy listening of the Carpenters, but an occasional strain of pure(r) country sometimes emerges, along with a faint echo of Gayle's hard country sibling, Loretta Lynn. *—Greg Adams*

Bobbie Gentry (Roberta Streeter)

b. Jul. 27, 1944, Chickasaw County, MS

Vocals, Guitar / Blue-Eyed Soul, Nashville Sound/Countrypolitan, Soft Rock, Pop, Country-Pop

Bobbie Gentry was best-known for the late-'60s hit "Ode to Billy Joe"—her debut single, it was a tremendous hit and stayed at the top of the pop charts for a month in 1967 and then crossed over to become a Top 20 hit on the country charts. The follow-up, "I Saw an Angel Die," was a flop but "Okolona River Bottom Band" made it to the Top 60. By late 1968, it looked as if the suspicions that Gentry was only a "one-hit wonder" were true. However, "Mornin' Glory"—a duet with Glen Campbell—reached the Top 75 on the pop charts while the B-side of the single, "Less of Me," nearly reached the Top 40 on the country charts. It set the stage for their hit cover of the Everly Brothers' "Let It Be Me," which reached number 14 on the country charts in 1969; a year later, the duo took "All I Have to Do Is Dream" to number six on the country charts. She and Campbell continued recording together until 1979. Gentry also had a number one hit in the United Kingdom in 1970 with her cover of Burt Bacharach's "I'll Never Fall in Love Again." While her popularity was declining in America, her star in Great Britain was on the rise. She began appearing on numerous TV shows there, including an appearance on the *Tom Jones Show* which led to her own self-titled British variety show. After a brief marriage to Jim Stafford in the late '70s, she basically retired from the music industry and became involved in television production. *—Sandra Brennan*

Ode to Billie Joe / 1967 / Capitol ✦✦✦

Gentry's debut LP, which went to number one on the pop charts, was a promising but not wholly satisfying disc, with the singer penning all but one of the songs. Inevitably, the title track dwarfed everything else by comparison, but a greater problem was that several of the other tunes recycled variations of the "Ode to Billie Joe" riff. On the other hand, "Mississippi Delta" is gloriously tough, throaty swamp rock; few other women pop singers have sounded as raw. Other good cuts were "I Saw an Angel Die," an effective mating of Gentry's country-blues guitar riffs and low-key orchestration, and the jazz waltz-timed "Papa, Woncha Let Me Go to Town With You." Her vocals are poised and husky throughout the record, on which she was definitely on the right track—one that she was quickly diverted from, into more MOR-oriented sounds. *—Richie Unterberger*

The Delta Sweete / 1968 / Capitol ✦✦✦

Delta Sweete was Bobbie Gentry's 1968 follow-up to her hugely popular *Ode to Billie Joe* record—the title track topped the pop charts and made the country Top 20. Although it doesn't quite match the quality of *Ode, Delta Sweete* does contain a good selection of Gentry originals and some fine covers. The "*Sweete*" in the title refers to both Gentry's southern-belle good looks (her publishing company was called Super Darlin') and the album's suite structure. The 12 segued songs detail Gentry's idyllic Mississippi childhood and include portraits of home and church life ("Reunion," "Sermon"), as well as recollections of blues and country hits she certainly heard as a youngster ("Big Boss Man," "Tobacco Road"). In fact, the prevailing sound on both *Delta Sweete* and *Ode to Billy Joe* is a swampy, folk-tinged combination of blues and country, with uptown touches like strings and horns seemingly added to reflect the then modern styles of soul and the Nashville sound. Gentry also includes some dreamy, pastoral originals like "Morning Glory" and "Courtyard," songs that could've been written by melancholy folkster Nick Drake. In light of all the album's good qualities, then, it's a shame it's out of print. Collectables' *The Golden Classics of Bobbie Gentry* combines the *Ode to Billie Joe* album with a few tracks from *Delta Sweete*, including the hits "Okolona River Bottom Band" and "Louisiana Man." *—Stephen Cook*

Touch 'em with Love / 1969 / Capitol ✦✦✦✦✦

Touch 'Em with Love is Bobbie Gentry's finest studio effort, a fascinatingly eclectic and genuinely affecting record which broadened her musical horizons far beyond the limitations of the Nashville Sound. Its unexpectedly gritty, soulful production makes it something of a spiritual twin to Dusty Springfield's *Dusty in Memphis*, also released in 1969 (both even feature renditions of "Son of a Preacher Man"): Gentry's husky, sensual delivery proves as ideally suited for the Southern-fried funk of the opening title track as it does for the bluegrass-flavored "Natural to Be Gone," deftly moving from genre to genre to encompass everything from faux-gospel ("Glory Hallelujah, How They'll Sing") to lushly orchestrated pop ("I Wouldn't Be Surprised," athe disc's centerpiece). Even more eye-opening is that Gentry's originals stand tall alongside material from composers including Burt Bacharach ("I'll Never Fall in Love Again," which earned her a chart-topping single in the U.K.) and Jimmy Webb ("Where's the Playground, Johnny—")—her folky "Seasons Come, Seasons Go,"an acute tale of lost love, offers *Touch 'Em with Love's* most profoundly beautiful moment. A truly great and tragically underrecognized album. *—Jason Ankeny*

The Golden Classics of Bobbie Gentry / Jan. 5, 1998 / Collectables ✦✦✦✦

Collectables' *The Golden Classics of Bobbie Gentry* is an expanded edition of her debut album *Ode to Billie Joe*, featuring all the songs from the original album plus eight bonus tracks, all of which were hits: "Louisiana Man," "Okolona River Bottom Band," "He Made a Woman Out of Me," "Fancy," "Apartment," plus the Glen Campbell duets "All I Have to Do is Dream," "Let It Be Me" and "Mornin' Glory." The presence of the album tracks from *Ode to Billie Joe* prevents it from being a straight-ahead greatest-hits album, but *The Golden Classics* comes closer to filling that bill than any other disc on the market. *—Stephen Thomas Erlewine*

● **Capitol Years: Ode to Bobbie** / Nov. 28, 2000 / EMI ✦✦✦✦✦

Don Gibson

b. Apr. 3, 1928, Shelby, NC

Vocals, Guitar / Nashville Sound/Countrypolitan, Country-Pop, Traditional Country

Singer/songwriter Don Gibson was one of the most popular and influential forces in '50s and '60s country, scoring numerous hit singles as a performer and a songwriter. Gibson's music touched on both traditional country and highly-produced country-pop, which is part of the reason he had such a broad audience. For nearly a decade after his first hit single, "Sweet Dreams," in 1956, he was a reliable hitmaker and his songs have become country classics—they have been covered by a wide range of artists, including Patsy Cline, Ray Charles, Kitty Wells, Emmylou Harris, Neil Young, and Ronnie Milsap. After being signed to MGM (as part of a songwriting deal), he recorded the Top Ten hit "Sweet Dreams" in 1956. One year later, Chet Atkins signed Gibson to RCA and became his producer for the next seven years, resulting in the blockbuster hit "Oh Lonesome Me" (eight weeks at the top of the country charts and a pop Top Ten as well) plus ten other country Top Ten hits between 1958 and 1961. His career took a dive during much of the '60s (partially due to alcoholism and drug addiction), but he cleaned up and hit number one again with 1973's "Woman (Sensuous Woman)." After two Top Ten hits in 1974, he settled into a string of minor hits and continued to tour and perform at the Grand Ole Opry during the '80s and '90s. *—Stephen Thomas Erlewine*

★ **A Legend in My Time** / 1988 / Bear Family ✦✦✦✦✦

A Legend In His Time contains 26 tracks from Don Gibson's peak years of 1957-1965, including all of his country Top 10 hits ("Oh Lonesome Me," "I Can't Stop Lovin' You," "Blue Blue Day," "Sweet Dreams," and several others), as well as a selection of lesser-known material that is all first-rate. It's the definitive retrospective. Although hardcore fans will want Bear Family's box sets and casual fans might want a collection that's a little more concise, *A Legend In His Time* has every essential item from the classic singer/songwriter. *—Stephen Thomas Erlewine*

18 Greatest Hits / 1991 / Curb ✦✦✦

Gibson's best-known hits were recorded in the late '50s and early '60s for RCA with Chet Atkins producing. This recording are drawn from his work for Hickory Records in the early '70s. They include "Woman, Sensuous Woman," "Country Green" and several remakes of his earlier hits. *—Michael McCall*

The Singer, the Songwriter (1949-1960) / 1991 / Bear Family ✦✦✦✦✦

Singer Songwriter, 1961-1966 / Jun. 28, 1994 / Bear Family ✦✦✦✦✦

Oh Lonesome Me / Jan. 5, 1998 / Collectables ✦✦✦✦

Collectables' reissue of *Oh Lonesome Me* contains the original track listening, which boasts hits like "Oh Lonesome Me, " "Bad, Bad Day" and "I Can't Stop Lovin' You, " and it adds several singles as bonus tracks, which only enhances a collection that was pretty great to begin with. There's some filler on the record, but it contains a number of gems among its lesser-known songs. *—Stephen Thomas Erlewine*

Vince Gill

b. Apr. 12, 1957, Norman, OK

Vocals, Guitar / New Traditionalist, Contemporary Country, Progressive Bluegrass

Vince Gill was one of the most popular mainstream country performers of the early '90s. After moving from Kentucky to Los Angeles in the late '70s, he joined the country-rock band Pure Prairie League and soon became the band's lead singer, sparking their return to the Top 40 with "I'm Almost Ready." He later joined Rodney Crowell's Cherry Bombs, then began his solo career in 1984. One year later, he hit the Top Ten twice, also singing harmonies and playing guitar on countless records. After he signed with MCA in 1989, his career fired up again—"Never Knew Lonely" began a string of Top 10 hits that ran for five straight years and he began a string of platinum albums with 1989's *When I Call Your Name.* By the time he was asked to joined the *Grand Ole Opry* in 1992, Gill had become a bonafide superstar; his 1994 album *When Love Finds You* made the Top Ten of the pop album charts and sold three million copies. In 1996, Gill released *High Lonesome Sound*, followed by *The Key* two years later. *—Sandra Brennan*

The Things That Matter / 1984 / Buddha ✦✦✦

The Way Back Home / 1987 / Buddha ✦✦✦

When I Call Your Name / 1989 / MCA ✦✦✦✦✦

"Oklahoma Swing," Gill's duet with Reba McEntire, announced his return to a rootsier sound after leaving RCA. But it was the title cut, with Patty Loveless providing the harmonies, that soared highest from car radios and announced the arrival of a major star. *—Dan Cooper*

Pocket Full of Gold / 1991 / MCA ✦✦✦✦✦

I Still Believe in You / 1992 / MCA ✦✦✦✦✦

Lots of folks inject a shot of R&B cliches into their honky-tonk and call it country soul. Vince Gill is country's real soul man, and not because of a familiarity with black artists' catalogues (though "Nothin' Like a Woman" comes close to sounding what lovers imagine Percy Sledge's "When a Man Loves a Woman" to be). It's because Gill's voice captures pain and promise, love and loneliness—all in a distillation so smooth that you don't even notice it sneaking up to blindside you. With his high tenor harmonies on songs like "Tryin' to Get Over You" and "No Future in the Past," you might even call this bluegrass soul—and you know that's gotta be lonesome. *—Brian Mansfield*

I Never Knew Lonely / Mar. 1992 / RCA ✦✦✦

One of Gill's more pop-oriented efforts, *I Never Knew Lonely* features the title tune, "Everybody's Sweetheart" and "True Love." *—Jason Ankeny*

Let There Be Peace on Earth / 1993 / MCA ✦✦

When Love Finds You / 1994 / MCA ♦♦♦
That Vince Gill—he sure is a nice guy. But at this point, we sure would welcome some serious nastiness from him to keep us awake. *—Dan Cooper*

● **The Essential Vince Gill** / 1995 / RCA ♦♦♦♦♦
The Essential Vince Gill collects highlights from the singer's pop-inflected material for RCA in the early '80s. While Gill didn't have as many hits during this era, the best songs stand up well next to his better-known songs. *—Thom Owens*

● **Souvenirs** / Nov. 21, 1995 / MCA Nashville ♦♦♦♦♦
Souvenirs collects the greatest hits from Vince Gill's most popular period—his recordings for MCA in the late '80s and early '90s. As such, it contains a wealth of first-rate songs and hits—including the number ones "I Still Believe In You" and "Don't Let Our Love Start Slippin' Away"—and functions as a good introduction to his music. *—Thom Owens*

High Lonesome Sound / Jun. 1996 / MCA ♦♦♦

The Key / Aug. 11, 1998 / MCA ♦♦♦♦♦

Let's Make Sure We Kiss Goodbye / Apr. 18, 2000 / MCA ♦♦♦♦

Mickey Gilley

b. Mar. 9, 1937, Ferriday, LA
Vocals, Piano / Urban Cowboy, Honky Tonk, Country-Pop, Traditional Country
For most of his career, pianist/vocalist Mickey Gilley lived in the shadow of his cousin, Jerry Lee Lewis, playing a similar fusion of country, rock, blues, and R&B. In the early '70s, he managed to breakthrough into country stardom, but it wasn't until the late '70s, when he became associated with the Urban Cowboy movement, that he became a superstar. Gilley had recorded a few singles (including a minor hit in 1968) before opening Gilley's Club in 1970 in Pasadena. Four years later, he had his first big hit, "Room Full of Roses," which became a number one country hit and launched a string of 16 number one hits that ran for just over a decade. In 1979, the film *Urban Cowboy*—based on Gilley's Club and featuring a cameo by Mickey, as well as several of his songs—brought him to national attention, which resulted in a string of six straight number one singles. He continued to have Top Ten hits until 1986, when his career began to slip. Though he was forced to close his club in the late '80s, Gilley turned his career around in the early '90s, opening a theater in Branson, Missouri and recording a few albums. *—Stephen Thomas Erlewine*

That's All That Matters to Me / 1980 / Epic ♦♦♦♦♦
This is the album that benefited most from Gilley's *Urban Cowboy* associations, and there's a perfunctory back-cover shot of some cowboy riding a mechanical bull at Gilley's night club. Though Gilley the Balladeer became pretty formulaic during the progression of the '80s, it was a new wrinkle with this album, and he delivers it convincingly. Gilley says the title track is his best performance ever. *—Tom Roland*

● **Ten Years of Hits** / 1984 / Epic ♦♦♦♦♦
It's a shame people have such a hard time dissociating Mickey Gilley from Stepford bulls. At his best, Jerry Lee Lewis's cousin has proven himself a legitimately soulful country singer, as evidenced here on number one hits like "That's All That Matters to Me" and "A Headache Tomorrow (Or a Heartache Tonight)." *—Dan Cooper*

Live at Gilley's / 1985 / Epic ♦♦♦

Crazy Cajun Recordings / Feb. 18, 1999 / Edsel ♦♦♦
Although the liner notes say that the recording dates of Mickey Gilley's sessions for the Crazy Cajun label are unknown, the presence of a twist song, "Whole Lot of Twistin' Going On," puts them in the ballpark of the early '60s. Gilley sounds more like his cousin Jerry Lee Lewis on these tracks than he would later, and many of the songs were recorded Jerry Lee/Sun Records style with just piano, drums, and vocals. *The Crazy Cajun Recordings* sound like demos, but 18 tracks of early rockin' Gilley is a rare and welcome thing. *—Greg Adams*

Jimmie Dale Gilmore

b. May 6, 1945, Tulia, TX
Vocals, Guitar / Alternative Country, Country-Folk, Singer/Songwriter, Progressive Country
With his warm, warbling tenor voice and folksy, friendly approach, Jimmie Dale Gilmore has earned the praise of many critics, even though Nashville has shown little interest in his rich blend of traditional country, folk, blues, and rock styles. Since moving to Austin, Texas and reviving his career in the 1980s, Gilmore in many ways came to represent the latter-day Austin music scene the way Willie Nelson once reigned as king of the town's cosmic cowboys in the 1970s. Growing up in Lubbock, Gilmore met Butch Hancock when they were both 12; later, another casual friend of Gilmore's, Joe Ely, turned him on to the music of Townes Van Zandt. Gilmore eventually hooked up with Ely and Hancock and formed the short-lived, now-legendary Flatlanders, who recorded an album in 1972 that mixed acoustic folk, string-band country, and country-blues. Gilmore moved to Denver, playing music only as a hobby. Ely, meanwhile, won a record contract and recorded some of Gilmore's songs. In 1980, Gilmore moved back to Austin, where he began playing regular gigs in local clubs. Finally, in 1988, Gilmore released his debut solo album, *Fair and Square,* on HighTone, Ely's label. This and his 1989 follow-up, *Jimmie Dale Gilmore,* featured a more straightforward honky-tonk style than anything Gilmore has done previously or since. Gilmore was soon signed to Elektra, which released *After Awhile* in 1991; the album retained a country feeling, but was less honky-tonk in nature, and attracted even more acclaim. His next album, *Spinning Around the Sun,* came out in 1993 and again featured a mix of contemporary and traditional country-flavored songs, plus a fuller instrumental sound. In 1996 he released *Braver Newer World,* produced by T-Bone Burnett; *One Endless Night* followed in early 2000. *—Kurt Wolff*

Fair and Square / 1988 / Hightone ♦♦♦
Jimmie Dale's debut solo album is straight-ahead honky-tonk, featuring two Gilmore originals along with songs by Hancock (including the great "Just a Wave, Not the Water"), Ely, David Halley, and Townes Van Zandt ("White Freight Liner Blues"). Gilmore's sweet, warbling, nasal-inflected tenor voice takes center stage, where it belongs. *—Kurt Wolff*

Jimmie Dale Gilmore / 1989 / Hightone ♦♦♦♦♦
This followup album is sharper and tighter than Gilmore's debut, with a traditional honky-tonk sound that's as raw and visceral as anything in his repertoire. It contains a new version of "Dallas" and an excellent Hancock song "When the Nights Are Cold." This album helped gain Gilmore national attention and place him firmly at the forefront of a new generation of alternative country artists. *—Kurt Wolff*

● **After Awhile** / 1991 / Elektra/Nonesuch ♦♦♦♦♦
While traditionalism is still a driving force, Gilmore's hardcore honky-tonk is toned down. The album is somewhat quieter and more introspective in tone. The songs shift between the playful and the spiritual, Gilmore's vocals enhanced by a rich assortment of acoustic and electric instruments. The album contains a new version of Gilmore classics "Tonight I Think I'm Gonna Go Downtown," from the Flatlanders album, and "Treat My Like a Saturday Night," formerly covered by Ely. *—Kurt Wolff*

Spinning Around the Sun / 1993 / Elektra ♦♦♦
Recorded in Nashville instead of Austin, this album continues where "After Awhile" left off in terms of instrumental depth and a refined, contemporary feeling. The production is shinier, but thankfully no one can take the earthiness out of Jimmie Dale's voice. The album contains another version of Hancock's "Just a Wave" and a beautiful duet with Lucinda Williams ("Reunion"). *—Kurt Wolff*

Braver Newer World / Jun. 25, 1996 / Elektra ♦♦♦
T-Bone Burnett produced this album, which spins Gilmore's music even further away from his honky-tonk roots. This is a sophisticated album, full of sensual, textural beauty and with a heavier emphasis on rhythm and percussion. The mysticism is more prominent, but Gilmore's voice warbling twang keeps the experience grounded. *—Kurt Wolff*

One Endless Night / Feb. 29, 2000 / Rounder ♦♦♦

Tompall Glaser

b. Sep. 3, 1933, Spalding, NE
Vocals / Outlaw Country, Traditional Country
Of all the "outlaw" singers of the mid-'70s, Tompall Glaser was the one who most exploited his newfound moniker. He even titled one album *The Great Tompall and His Outlaw Band,* which brazenly featured a huge picture of him, shirt unbuttoned halfway down his chest, on the cover. It's ironic, then, that even though he had numerous chart records alone and with his brothers, Chuck and Jim, into the 1980s, he's the least remembered of the four artists—Willie Nelson, Waylon Jennings, Jessi Colter, and Tompall—who were packaged together on the immensely popular 1976 album *Wanted! The Outlaws.* Originally a part of the folk trio Tompall and the Glaser Brothers, he began recording as a solo artist in the early '70s and released one of the finest outlaw albums ever, 1973's *Charlie.* Two of his songs were also included on the style's watershed album *Wanted! The Outlaws.* He reunited with his brothers in 1980 for several years, but returned again to a solo career with 1986's *Nights on the Borderline.* *—Kurt Wolff*

● **Charlie** / 1973 / MGM ♦♦♦♦♦
By far Tompall's best release as a solo artist or otherwise, *Charlie* is one of the true classics of outlaw country. "Gideon Bible," the title track, and a knockout version of Kinky Friedman's "Sold American" are just the highlights. Tompall sings about lonliness and staring at closed doors like a true pro. *—Kurt Wolff*

Tompall / 1974 / MGM ♦♦♦♦
On this collection of songs written by Shel Silverstein, the arrangements are outlaw sparse, the players are top-notch, and there's some great material among the typical (and often annoying) Silverstein novelty numbers. "Put Another Log on the Fire" turned into a hit for Tompall (and was later included on the compilation *Wanted! The Outlaws*). *—Kurt Wolff*

Great Tompall and His Outlaw Band / 1976 / MGM ♦♦♦♦
The first of two albums to feature Tompall's hot new band that included acclaimed guitarist Mel Brown. Blues, soul, barroom country, and Western swing are among the subtle but solid moods on this well-crafted and superbly arranged collection. *—Kurt Wolff*

The Outlaw / 1977 / Bear Family ♦♦♦♦♦

Gosdin Brothers

f. 1961, **db.** 1973
Group / Neo-Traditionalist Country, Progressive Bluegrass
Vern and Rex Gosdin were always on the cutting edge of bluegrass and country-rock, yet they never quite broke through the mainstream audience they deserved. In 1961, the Alabama natives moved out to California, where they began playing in the bluegrass band, the Golden State Boys. The Gosdins' time in the Golden State Boys earned the attention of Chris Hillman, who asked them to join his group, the Hillmen. Within a few years, Hillman had joined the Byrds, while Vern found work as a session musician and continued to play duos with Rex.

In 1966, the Gosdin Brothers supported former Byrd Gene Clark on the record *Gene Clark with the Gosdin Brothers.* The following year, the duo had a minor hit with "Hangin' On," but they were not able to deliver another hit single. Following this frustrating lack of success, Vern grew frustrated with the music business and retired from performing for several years. Vern made a comeback in 1976 with a new version of "Hangin' On" and once again hit the road with Rex. While Vern at last found some success, charting more than 27 records over 12 years, Rex was not as lucky. Of the three chart records he had before his death in 1983, the biggest hit was a duet with Waylon Jennings' brother Tommy. Following Rex's death, Vern continued to tour and perform well into the '90s. *—Jim Worbois*

Sounds of Goodbye / 1968 / Capitol ♦♦♦♦
The Gosdin Brothers' obscure 1968 LP *Sounds of Goodbye* is an overlooked country-rock milestone, and one that owes as much to the sound of the 1966-1967 era Byrds as it does to country music. That's unsurprising, perhaps, given that the Gosdins helped out a lot on Gene

Clark's debut solo album in 1967, and sometimes shared bills with the early Byrds, as they shared the same management. In truth, this will appeal far more to the early Byrds fan than to the straight country fan. That's not damning with faint praise, far from it; it's actually high praise. It's a fair guess, too, that anyone who likes Gene Clark's early work will enjoy this record, as it has a similar low-key, hurt, vulnerable mystique to the melodies, vocals, and harmonies. The material, though sometimes average, is also sometimes outstanding, as on "Love at First Sight," which actually comes quite close to the classic 1966 Byrds jangle rock sound; the melancholy, graceful "She's Gone," with the kind of unexpected compelling chord changes you'd expect from the Gene Clark songwriting school; and "The Victim," with its pungent burned-by-love lyrics, and an odd (though not displeasing) dash of psychedelic echo on the chorus. The covers cast an eclectic net ("Catch the Wind," "Let It Be Me," the Everly Brothers' "Bowling Green") and are not as distinctive as the originals, but even so there's an excellent reading of Ewan MacColl's "The First Time Ever I Saw Your Face." As the new millennium begins, it's very hard to find, and is of a high enough caliber to demand CD reissue. *—Richie Unterberger*

Vern Gosdin

b. Aug. 5, 1934, Woodland, AL

Vocals, Guitar / Traditional Country, Traditional Bluegrass, Progressive Bluegrass

Vern Gosdin was one of the best and most subtle traditional vocalists in country music. He entered music when his family began hosting a gospel radio program, and after moving to California Vern and brother Rex teamed up to sing country music as the Gosdin Brothers. Though they had a Top 40 country hit in 1967 with "Hangin On," they broke up soon after. After almost a decade out of music, Vern re-recorded "Hangin On" for Elektra. The single hit the country Top 20, and its B-side, "Yesterday's Gone," reached the Top Ten. The following year he had seven major hits including "Till the End," "Never My Love," and "Mother Country Music." During 1983-84, Gosdin had three Top Five hits—"If You're Gonna Do Me Wrong (Do It Right)," "Way Down Deep" and the number one hit "I Can Tell By the Way You Dance (You're Gonna Love Me Tonight)." Though his career hit a lull in the mid-'80s, he bounced back into the Top Ten in 1987, and hit number one again one year later with "Set 'Em Up Joe." In the early '90s, Gosdin's popularity declined but he continued recording and performing. *—Sandra Brennan*

Till the End / 1977 / Elektra ♦♦♦♦♦

This is probably one of Gosdin's strongest records overall. Additionally, it netted him four hits. *—Jim Worbois*

If Jesus Comes Tomorrow / 1984 / Compleat ♦♦♦

If Jesus Comes Tomorrow (What Then) is part gospel standards, part complementary originals, all sung by a honky-tonk voice hoping for heaven. *—Brian Mansfield*

There Is a Season / 1984 / American Harvest ♦♦♦♦

Throughout the album, Emmylou Harris provides nice harmonies reminiscent of Rex Gosdin's style. Additionally, Roger McGuinn adds vocals (Background and accompanying) and the 12-string instrumental break to "Turn Turn Turn"; very different from the break on The Byrds' version. *—Jim Worbois*

Chiseled in Stone / 1988 / Columbia ♦♦♦♦♦

Chisled in Stone is Vern Gosdin's late '80s comeback album, a record that confirms his vocal talents and, arguably, delivers more than any of his other records. Gosdin's voice is gorgeously worn, and the material is stellar, divided between classics and new songs that sound as old as the hills. Even though it was recorded late in his career, few albums explain the appeal of Vern Gosdin as *Chiseled in Stone. —Thom Owens*

Alone / 1989 / Columbia ♦♦♦

Written and released directly after a painful divorce, *Alone* is a moving set of honky tonk that works better in theory than it does in practise. Though Gosdin's performance is frequently sublime, his songs aren't always strong. However, when he has a good song at his disposal—such as "Right in the Wrong Direction," "I'm Only Going Crazy," "That Just About Does It" and "I'm Still Crazy"—his heart-felt delivery and tortured lyrics makes for some truly memorable music. *—Thom Owens*

● **The Best of Vern Gosdin** / 1989 / Warner Brothers ♦♦♦♦♦

The Best of Vern Gosdin contains 10 of his his late '70s hits, which were originally released in the '70s. Although they bear all the hallmarks of the era—these are slick, string-laden productions—they remain pure, impressive country. Gosdin sounds especially good when Emmylou Harris or Janie Fricke provide harmonies. *—Thom Owens*

10 Years of Hits—*Newly Recorded* / *1990* / *Columbia* ♦♦♦♦

Out of My Heart / 1991 / Columbia ♦♦♦♦

Lee Greenwood

b. Oct. 17, 1942, Los Angeles, CA

Vocals, Saxophone, Piano, Guitar, Bass, Banjo / Urban Cowboy, Adult Contemporary, Contemporary Country, Country-Pop

Born with a good voice and a wide range, Lee Greenwood turned it into a unique voice accidentally, by over-working it in a less-than-healthy setting. Hailing from Sacramento, he used his musical training on the casino circuit, working in the green-felt jungles of Reno and Las Vegas, where he dealt cards by day and sang in dark lounges by night. The physical toll of two jobs, the vocal strain of performing six nights a week, and the damaging endeavor to sing in smoky nightclubs before the advent of smoking ordinances brought Greenwood a permanent hoarseness. He's used it to his advantage, becoming one of country music's premier balladeers. Discovered by Mel Tillis' road manager, Larry McFaden, Lee paid for his own ticket to fly to Nashville and cut a few demos, and it took more than a year for that effort to payoff. When it finally did, Greenwood broke through in late 1981 with "It Turns Me Inside Out," in which his exaggerated vibrato brought frequent comparisons to Kenny Rogers. In short order, Greenwood disposed of the "Kenny clone" image, but he continued to mine romantic material for the bulk of his hits. Occasional exceptions include "Touch and Go Crazy" and "Mornin' Ride," but the biggest exception is also his signature song, the self-written "God Bless the U.S.A.," which earned Song of the Year honors from the Country Music Association. *—Tom Roland*

● **Greatest Hits** / 1985 / MCA ♦♦♦♦

The extent to which Greenwood relies on ballads is fully evident here, although his departures—"Dixie Road" and "Ain't No Trick"—are most memorable. "God Bless the U.S.A." is the last track; if you're not inclined to ultra-patriotism, you can simply lift the needle or push "Stop." *—Tom Roland*

American Patriot / 1992 / Liberty ♦♦♦

Spurred on by George Bush's unofficial adoption of "God Bless the USA" as the new American anthem, Lee Greenwood recorded *American Patriot* in the midst of the President's (ultimately unsuccessful) re-election campaign in 1992. *American Patriot* sealed Greenwood's stance as American songteller extraordinaire. Every song on the album is, unsurprisingly, about America, from "The Pledge of Allegiance" and "The Star Spangled Banner" to "God Bless America" and "God Bless the USA." Of course, Woody Guthrie's populist anthem "This Land Is Your Land" takes on a different meaning in this context, but that's not surprising—*American Patriot* is a slick, satisfied album designed for the modern-day patriot and conservative, not for dustbowl activists or smugly sophisticated liberals. In other words, if you've been a fan of "God Bless the USA" since its first incarnation in the early '80s, you'll be happy with this full-blown sequel. *—Stephen Thomas Erlewine*

Rex Griffin

b. Aug. 12, 1912, Gasden, AL, **d.** Oct. 11, 1959

Vocals / Honky Tonk, Traditional Country

For many country fans, Rex Griffin is an unknown, yet there is no denying the significant role he played in the music's history. Griffin began his career in the '30s singing traditional music in the vein of Jimmie Rodgers, but his music quickly metamorphosized into a prototype for honky tonk, complete with rougher vocals and instrumentation. Although he never had any hits, he was influential on number of musicians in the '40s, most notably Hank Williams, who learned Emmett Miller's "Lovesick Blues" from Griffin. Furthermore, many of his songs—including "Just Call Me Lonesome," "The Last Letter" and "Everybody's Trying to Be My Baby"—became country and pop standards, and he was elected to the Nashville Songwriter's Hall of Fame.

Griffin (born Alsie Griffin, August 12, 1912; d. October 11, 1959) began his career in the early '30s, making appearances at radio stations across the country, including Atlanta, Chicago, Memphis, Dallas, Nashville and Birmingham, which is where he was given his nickname Rex. At the start of his career, he sounded remarkably similar to Jimmie Rodgers, and this is the sound that appeared on Rex's first recordings. Griffin signed to Decca in March of 1935 and over the next four years, he recorded 38 songs for the label. None of the singles became major hits, but the songs themselves—"Over the River," "The Last Letter," "Everybody's Trying to Be My Baby"—grew to be standards. At the end of his stint at Decca, he recorded Emmett Miller's "Lovesick Blues." The song became a minor hit for Rex, but it was more important in providing the basis for Hank Williams' 1949 version, which became his breakthrough hit single. Williams learned the song from Griffin, and then used the recorded version as the template for his own single.

During the '40s, Griffin retired from recording, concentrating on radio performances. Rex remained close friends with Ernest Tubb throughout the decade, yet he couldn't use his connections to restart his recording career. Furthermore, his health was declining rapidly, as he suffered from both diabetes and alcoholism. Griffin finally succumbed to his illnesses on October 11, 1959. After his death, he was inducted to the Nashville Songwriter's Hall of Fame, and his songs continued to be performed and recorded by several generations of country musicians. *—Stephen Thomas Erlewine*

☆ **Last Letter** / 1996 / Bear Family ♦♦♦♦♦

Many Bear Family releases seem like overkill, but this one is easy to justify. This triple CD is a truly wonderful collection, including every one of the 64 sides that Rex Griffin recorded between 1935 and 1946, and also 16 songs recorded as demos by his brother Buddy between 1948 and 1955. The repertory runs the gamut from Jimmie Rodgers-style yodel pieces to highly effective white blues ("I'm Ready to Reform"), and even the future rock & roll standard "Everybody's Tryin' to Be My Baby." Griffin only had six series recording sessions in his whole career, none lasting more than a day or two, and he recorded as many as ten songs at a time, in effect creating an album's worth of songs, more than 90% of it original material. The strange thing is that, despite the fact that each of these sessions pretty much meant using the same backgrounds on each song, they would work as albums—the material is that strong, that it didn't have to be trickled out as singles. The other thing that one notices about these sides is that, along with the quality of the material, the playing is also first-rate. The 1944 sides, radio transcription discs recorded with a band that may have included Red Foley on guitar, intended for broadcast, capture some of the excitement of a Griffin stage performance with his own early-'40s band. These are brisk, rippling, immediate "live-in-the-studio" honky-tonk style renditions of "Everybody's Tryin' to Be My Baby," "An Old Faded Photograph," "Mean Woman Blues" and other 1930s vintage songs, as well as newer material. The set is worth the investment, even if that means saving up for it. *—Bruce Eder*

Nanci Griffith

b. Jul. 6, 1953, Austin, TX

Vocals, Guitar / Contemporary Folk, Country-Folk, Singer/Songwriter, Contemporary Country, Progressive Country

Striding the fine line between folk and country music, Nanci Griffith has become as well-known for her brilliant confessional songwriting as her beautiful voice. A self-styled "folkabilly" singer, Griffith began as a kindergarten teacher and inaugurated her recording career in 1978 with the folk album *There's a Light Beyond These Woods.* After two more albums during the early '80s, the country scene took her to heart in the mid-'80s, giving her a reputation as a quality Nashville songwriter through hit covers of Griffith's songs by Kathy Mattea and Suzy Bogguss. Her most celebrated album, 1986's *The Last of the True Believers,* was nominated for a Grammy and earned her a major-label contract with MCA. Griffith abandoned Nashville to begin recording her major debut, *Lone Star State of Mind,* though the title track ironically proved to be her first country Top 40 hit. MCA paired her with noted rock producer Glyn Johns for 1989's *Storms;* the album became her best-seller, though it featured no successful singles. After a move from rock to pop on 1991's *Late Night Grande Hotel,* Griffith moved to Elektra and returned to her folk influences for 1993's *Other Voices, Other Rooms.* The following year, Griffith's tenth studio album *Flyer* continued her dedication to folk. In March of 1997, Griffith released *Blue Roses from the Moons; Other Voices, Too (A Trip Back to Bountiful)* followed a year later. *—John Bush*

There's a Light Beyond These Woods / 1978 / Philo ✦✦

Poet in My Window / 1982 / Philo ✦✦

Once in a Very Blue Moon / 1984 / Philo ✦✦✦✦✦
Nanci Griffith finds her voice on her third studio album, *Once in a Very Blue Moon.* This is the album where she established her musical identity—she is at home in many genres (which perhaps explains why she never gets played on formatted radio stations), and seamlessly blends folk, bluegrass, and country with a group of stellar musicians, including guitarist Pat Alger and a young banjo player named Béla Fleck. While the music is well-textured with cello, mandolin, Dobro, and fiddle, it is Griffith's lyrics that distinguish her from her peers. Although not a concept album, the main theme explored is travel. She sings about the joys and excitement of the road as well as the longing that comes with extended periods away from home. Nanci Griffith is an excellent storyteller, with detailed, insightful lyrics that vividly portray the hopes and dreams of her characters ("Mary and Omie"). She sprinkles the album with songs of others, as she pays homage to folk veterans such as Bill Staines ("Roseville Fair") and sings a tune by newcomer Lyle Lovett ("If I Were the Woman You Wanted"). This album marks the emergence of a major talent. *— Vik Iyengar*

★ **The Last of the True Believers** / 1986 / Philo ✦✦✦✦✦
Griffith hit her peak as a songwriter here with classics such as "Love at the Five & Dime" and "Banks of the Pontchartrain," while singing over an always-appropriate backup provided by the '80s new bluegrass specialists Bela Fleck, Mark O'Connor, and others. The album earned her a major-label contract with MCA and provided the basis of country singer Kathy Mattea's entire career, but it is also a pivotal 80s folk album. *— William Ruhlmann*

Lone Star State of Mind / 1987 / MCA ✦✦✦

Storms / 1987 / MCA ✦✦✦

Little Love Affairs / 1988 / MCA ✦✦✦✦✦
All of Griffith's albums have songs to recommend them; of her country-folk albums, this one has the most written by her, as well as good tunes by Harlan Howard and fellow Texan Robert Earl Keen Jr. The first half's prime Griffith, and the second suggests that, if she'd stuck with country, she might have started outselling her press—Suzy Bogguss later turned "Outbound Plane" into a hit, and there's probably at least one more of those tucked away here. *—Brian Mansfield*

One Fair Summer Evening / 1988 / MCA ✦✦✦
Recorded in Houston, *One Fair Summer Evening* captures a live 1988 performance from Nanci Griffith, as she runs through solo arrangements of several of her best songs, including "Love at the Five and Dime" and "From a Distance." Griffith's performance is subtle and her voice is frequently beautiful, making it a worthwhile momento for dedicated fans. *— Stephen Thomas Erlewine*

Late Night Grande Hotel / 1991 / MCA ✦✦✦
Two albums out of Nashville and Griffith doesn't even resemble the new-country/folkie role in which she was once cast. Britishers Rod Argent and Peter Van Hooke insulate Griffith with strings and moody atmospheres that complement her wallflower fantasies. She's likely partial to "Power Lines" and "Down 'n' Outer," both tales of folks who fall through society's cracks. Probably, come to think of it, because she identifies with them. *—Brian Mansfield*

The MCA Years: a Retrospective / 1993 / MCA ✦✦✦✦✦

Other Voices, Other Rooms / 1993 / Elektra ✦✦✦✦✦
Griffith pays homage to a wide cut of folk music heroes, from Woody Guthrie to Townes Van Zandt, from Bob Dylan to Kate Wolf, from Malvina Reynolds to John Prine. She sounds looser and more spirited than usual, and her earnest adoration for the songs shines through in these compelling remakes. *—Michael McCall*

Flyer / 1994 / Elektra ✦✦✦✦

Blue Roses from the Moons / Mar. 25, 1997 / Elektra ✦✦✦

Other Voices, Too (A Trip Back to Bountiful) / Jul. 21, 1998 / Elektra ✦✦✦✦✦
Trailing five years behind the release of *Other Voices, Other Rooms,* Nanci Griffith's second collection of covers is that rare sequel which actually surpasses its predecessor. Boasting an even stronger and wide-ranging set of songs, *Other Voices, Too (A Trip Back to Bountiful)* captures the singer at her most radiant and expressive—moving easily from the Stephen Foster perennial "Hard Times Come Again No More" to sixties-pop hits like "You Were on My Mind" to British folk-rock chestnuts like Richard Thompson's "Wall of Death" and Sandy Denny's "Who Knows Where the Time Goes"—Griffith stamps each of these 19 tracks with her own indelible signature, revitalizing not only her material but herself in the process. *— Jason Ankeny*

The Dust Bowl Symphony / Sep. 14, 1999 / Elektra ✦✦

Merle Haggard

b. Apr. 6, 1937, Bakersfield, CA
Vocals, Guitar, Fiddle / Western Swing Revival, Bakersfield Sound, Honky Tonk, Traditional Country
As a performer and a songwriter, Merle Haggard was the most important country artist to emerge in the 1960s. Haggard became one of the leading figures of the Bakersfield country scene in the '60s. While his music remained hardcore country, he pushed the boundaries of the music quite far. Like his idol Bob Wills, his music was a melting pot that drew from all forms of traditional American music—country, jazz, blues, and folk—and in the process, developed a distinctive style of his own. As a performer, singer, and musician, he was one of the best, influencing countless other artists. Not coincidentally, he was the best singer/songwriter in country music since Hank Williams, writing a body of songs that became classics. Throughout his career, Haggard has been a champion of the working man, largely due to his rough and tumble history. Even when success eluded him, Merle Haggard's music remained some of the most consistently interesting and inventive in country music. Not only have his recordings remained fresh, but each subsequent generation of country singers show a great debt to his work. That fact stands as a testament to his great talent even more than his induction to the Country Music Hall of Fame. *— Stephen Thomas Erlewine*

Strangers / 1965 / Koch International ✦✦✦

☆ **Swinging Doors/The Bottle Let Me Down** / 1966 / Koch International ✦✦✦✦✦
Merle Haggard's third album, *Swinging Doors / The Bottle Let Me Down,* was assembled from a variety of singles and session like its two predecessors, but it contained a stronger overall selection of material than either album. In addition to the two masterpieces from which the album took its name, the record included a terrific version of Tommy Collins' "High On A Hilltop," and plus excellent songs like "The Girl Turned Ripe," "If I Could Be Him," and "Someone Else You've Known." There's a few weak tracks, but Haggard and his band are in fine form, making the filler enjoyable. *— Stephen Thomas Erlewine*

Branded Man/I Threw Away the Rose / 1967 / Koch International ✦✦✦✦✦
Like *Swinging Doors* before it, *Branded Man/I Threw Away the Rose* is merely a collection of songs pieced together to cash in on a couple of hit singles. Nevertheless, the intent of an album such as this doesn't really matter when the songs are this fine. In addition to the two title tracks, Haggard co-writes "You Don't Have Very Far to Go" and "Somewhere Between" (with Red Simpson and Bonnie Owens, respectively). While the latter isn't as good as his three other original songs ("Branded Man," "I Threw Away the Rose," "You Don't Have Very Far to Go"), the remainder of the album is comprised of outside material that ranks among some of Haggard's finest performances ("Go Home," "Long Black Limousine," "I Made the Prison Band," "Don't Get Married," "Loneliness Is Eating Me Alive"). *— Stephen Thomas Erlewine*

I'm a Lonesome Fugitive / 1967 / Capitol ✦✦✦

Sing Me Back Home / 1968 / Koch International ✦✦✦✦✦
Sing Me Back Home follows the blueprint of Merle Haggard's first three albums, balancing a hit single with album tracks and a couple of covers, but there is a difference. Where the previous album *Branded Man* was a transitional album, hinting that Haggard's talents were deepening substantially, *Sing Me Back Home* is the result of the flowering of his talent. Like any '60s country album, there are a couple of throwaways (like "The Bottle Let Me Down" rewrite "I'll Leave the Bottle On the Bar"), but the majority of the album is full of rich material, from "The Son of Hickory Holler's Tramp," "Good Times," and "Wine Take Me Away." *— Stephen Thomas Erlewine*

☆ **Same Train, Different Time** / 1969 / Bear Family ✦✦✦✦✦
Same Train, Different Time is Merle Haggard's affectionate tribute to Jimmie Rodgers. Haggard provides narration between the songs, offering tales of Rodgers' life and music. While the album is rooted in the past, the key to its success is how Haggard updates these traditional songs without losing sight of their roots. There are contemporary folk, country and blues influences scattered throughout the record, adding depth to the music and proving that Rodgers' music is indeed timeless. *— Stephen Thomas Erlewine*

☆ **A Tribute to the Best Damn Fiddle Player** / 1970 / Koch International ✦✦✦✦✦
After releasing his tribute to Jimmie Rodgers, Merle Haggard immediately set about working on a tribute to his other major musical idol, Bob Wills. Haggard learned how to play fiddle and, within a month, he had recruited many of the original Playboys to augment the Strangers and began recording the album that became *A Tribute to the Best Damn Fiddle Player: My Salute to Bob Wills.* Where *Same Train, Different Time* was a measured, heartfelt tribute, *Best Damn Fiddle Player* is a ragged, enthusiastic good-time. Haggard, the Strangers and the Playboys play their hearts out, breathing in life to Wills' warhorses like "Right or Wrong," "Stay A Little Longer," "Time Changes Everything," and "San Antonio Rose" while bringing attention to lesser-known songs like "Brain Cloudy Blues," "I Knew the Moment I Lost You" and "Old-Fashioned Love." The fact that Western Swing re-established itself as a viable country genre after the release of *A Tribute to the Best Damn Fiddle Player,* is a testament to the power and charm of this record. *— Stephen Thomas Erlewine*

Serving 190 Proof / 1979 / MCA ✦✦✦
Haggard appears here in the midst of what he admitted was a mid-life crisis. That's no reason to dismiss this record, however, as crisis introspection served him well. Possibly the best of his MCA albums, it includes "Red Bandana," "My Own Kind of a Hat," and a brooding meditation on the emptiness of stardom called "Footlights." *—Dan Cooper*

The Way I Am / 1980 / MCA ✦✦✦

Big City / 1981 / Epic/Legacy ✦✦✦✦
Coming on the heels of a short-lived semiretirement, Haggard's Epic debut is an appropriate group of songs that celebrates relaxation and expresses discontent with the situation forced on blue-collar America. Ironically, he puts plenty of energy into his work here. [The 1999 CD reissue contains two bonus tracks: "Call Me" and "I Won't Give Up My Train."] *— Tom Roland*

Going Where the Lonely Go / 1982 / Epic ✦✦✦

A Taste of Yesterday's Wine / 1982 / Epic ✦✦✦

Pancho & Lefty / 1983 / Epic ✦✦✦✦

His Epic Hits: First Eleven to Be Continued / 1984 / Epic ✦✦✦
As the title implies, *His Epic Hits: First Eleven* covers the first 11 hits Merle Haggard had on Epic Records, including "Are the Good Times Really Over (I Wish A Buck Was Still Silver)," "Pancho & Lefty," "Reasons to Quit," "That's the Way Love Goes," "My Favorite Memory," "What Am I Gonna Do (With the Rest of My LIfe)," and "You Take Me for Granted." Since most of his early Epic albums were uneven, *His Epic Hits* is especially useful, gathering his best material onto one disc. It should be supplemented by *Greatest Hits of the '80s*, which covers his mid-'80s hits for Epic, as well as a few fine cuts that didn't make this collection. —*Stephen Thomas Erlewine*

Chill Factor / 1988 / Epic ✦✦✦✦

Greatest Hits of the 80's / 1990 / Epic ✦✦✦

1994 / Mar. 22, 1994 / Curb ✦✦✦

★ **Lonesome Fugitive: The Merle Haggard Anthology (1963-1977)** / 1995 / Razor & Tie ✦✦✦✦✦
Lonesome Fugitive: The Merle Haggard Anthology is an excellent double-disc retrospective of Hag's Capitol Records. Over the course of the 40-track set, every hit country single Haggard had between 1963 and 1972 is included, as is the majority of his hits between 1973 and 1976. While not every great performance and song Merle recorded during this era is included—he was so prolific it would have been impossible to condense *everything* on to a double-disc set—*Lonesome Fugitive* remains a definitive collection. It has all of the hits, most of his greatest songs, and illustrates the depth of his music in the most concise manner possible. Furthermore, *Lonesome Fugitive* is the only place all of Haggard's classic hits are available on one collection, which means it is both the perfect introduction and a career-defining retrospective. —*Stephen Thomas Erlewine*

☆ **Untamed Hawk: The Early Recordings of Merle Haggard** / 1995 / Bear Family ✦✦✦✦✦
In typical Bear Family fashion, the German record company compiled all of his early Capitol recordings (1962-1968)—including unreleased tracks and alternate takes—over the course of a five disc box set called *Untamed Hawk*. Like any Bear Family set, *Untamed Hawk* is too exhausting to listen to in a single sitting. In fact, with the company's insistence in presenting all the music in session order instead of how it was actually released makes listening to any of individual discs rather difficult—the box plays like a history lesson, not as an album. Nevertheless, there is a wealth of wonderful, timeless music on *Untamed Hawk* and no Haggard completist should be without it, even if it is essentially a library piece. However casual fans—even those who enjoy the original '60s albums like *Sing Me Back Home*—should leave *Untamed Hawk* on the shelf —*Stephen Thomas Erlewine*

☆ **Down Every Road** / Apr. 1996 / Capitol ✦✦✦✦✦
Merle Haggard has been served by a countless number of compilations, but *Down Every Road* is the first multi-disc box set to attempt to give an overview of his career. Spanning from his first singles for Tally, through his glory days on Capitol to his scattershot later career, *Down Every Road* features every one of Haggard's necessary songs, as well as a couple of more obscure gems, including a handful of unreleased songs. Though most casual fans will be better-served by *The Lonesome Fugitive*, a lean double-disc set that contains all of his essential songs, *Down Every Road* is ideal for listeners that want to dig a little deeper. It gives an excellent picture of the full scope of Haggard's talents as a songwriter and musician. —*Stephen Thomas Erlewine*

If I Could Only Fly / Oct. 10, 2000 / Epitaph ✦✦✦✦
For all the '90s, Merle Haggard was stuck in a kind of exile, recording albums that were strangely perched between familiar Haggard material and futile compromises to a modern country radio that would never play material from veterans. Hag knew that he hadn't lost it, so when he finally ran out his contract for Curb, he smartly signed to Anti-, a subsidiary of the indie punk label Epitaph. Finally at a label that would let him record a traditional Haggard album, he seized the opportunity with *If I Could Only Fly*, a gentle, understated, largely acoustic album that's easily his best in over a decade. It's easy to draw comparisons to Johnny Cash's Rick Rubin-produced *American Music*, but this is actually a better fit, since nothing here is forced. There's no mention of his wild ways or outlaw posturing; instead he, dwells on being old, not wanting to leave home, and writes frequently about his family. This is not sad and melancholy, it's a sweet, soothing record, filled with intimately autobiographical songs, delivered with ease and subtle shading through Haggard's always superb vocalizing. *If I Could Only Fly* benefits considerably from its sheer, warm musicality, and it's easy to be charmed by its stripped-back, organic sound. It sounds so good that it's also easy to overlook that the album is shy a couple of great songs it needed to be an unqualified triumph. Only the sublime "Wishing All These Old Things Were New," "If I Could Only Fly," and "Listening (To the Wind)" are truly significant additions to Haggard's canon. Ultimately, that may be a bit of nitpicking—*If I Could Only Fly* is the first album in years that deserves to be compared to Haggard's classic work. —*Stephen Thomas Erlewine*

Tom T. Hall

b. May 25, 1936, Olive Hill, KY
Vocals, Guitar / Country-Folk, Singer/Songwriter, Country-Pop, Progressive Country
Tom T. Hall is known as a storyteller, a songwriter with a keen eye for detail and a knack for narrative. He also has racked up a number of solo hits, including seven number one singles. The first singer to have a hit with one of Tom's songs was Jimmy Newman, who brought "DJ for a Day" to number one on the country charts in 1963. In early 1964, Dave Dudley took "Mad" to the Top Ten. The back-to-back success convinced Hall to move to Nashville, and after Johnnie Wright had a number one hit with Hall's "Hello Vietnam," the music industry was pressuring Tom to become a performer. He decided to take the plunge in 1967, and his first single, "I Washed My Face in the Morning Dew," became a minor hit. In the late summer of 1968, Jeannie C. Riley had a major hit with Tom's "Harper Valley P.T.A.," which spent three weeks at the top of the charts and was voted the Single of the Year by the Country Music Association. Its success brought attention to Hall's own recording career, which was evident from the performance of "Ballad of Forty Dollars." The song became his first Top Ten hit, and throughout 1969, he had a string of hit singles, culminated by the release of the number one "A Week in a Country Jail" at the end of the year. The following year was just as successful, as "Shoeshine Man" and "Salute to a Switchblade" both hit the Top Ten. In 1971, he had his second number one single and his biggest hit, "The Year That Clayton Delaney Died," which was based on his childhood hero. For most of the early '70s, Hall was a consistent hit-maker as well as a popular concert attraction. Although he continued to have the occasional Top Ten hit in the late '70s—most notably the number four "You Man Loves You, Honey" (1977)—Hall didn't deliver hit singles as consistently as he did the first half of the decade. In 1996, he issued *Songs from Sopchoppy*, his first album in ten years. —*Stephen Thomas Erlewine*

Ballad of Forty Dollars / 1969 / Mercury ✦✦✦✦✦
Ballad of Forty Dollars and *Homecoming*, two of Tom T. Hall's excellent late '60s albums, are combined on this single compact disc. Although many of the best songs were featured on *Greatest Hits* and *Storyteller, Poet Philosopher*, these albums work well as individual records and they're well worth acquiring for any Hall fan. —*Thom Owens*

☆ **In Search of a Song** / 1971 / Mercury ✦✦✦✦✦
Hall gathered his material while driving solo through rural America, and his songs are literal and compassionate—but not romantic or sentimental. Instead, he fills his heartland stories with extraordinary realism and humanity. —*Michael McCall*

Greatest Hits, Vol. 1 / 1972 / Mercury ✦✦✦✦✦
Greatest Hits contains the bulk of Tom T. Hall's biggest hits from the late '60s and early '70s, including all his Top 10 hits from that era—"Ballad of Forty Dollars," "Homecoming," "A Week In A Country Jail," "Shoeshine Man," "Salute to a Switchblade," "The Year That Clayton Delaney Died," and "Me and Jesus"—but the record only hints at the his talent as a songwriter. Many of his best songs are on *Greatest Hits* and the collection does avoid his tendency for cuteness (with only a couple of exceptions), making *Greatest Hits* a good introduction, even though it does bypass plenty of fine songs. —*Thom Owens*

Tom T Hall . . . The Storyteller / 1972 / Mercury ✦✦✦✦
It seemed like Hall could do no wrong in the early '70s, and this album adds more fuel to that idea. Another fine album of Hall originals (plus one by Billy Joe Shaver); including one of Hall's finest in "Old Dogs, Children and Watermelon Wine." —*Jim Worbois*

We All Got Together And . . . / 1972 / Mercury ✦✦✦
More great songs from Hall including "Pamela Brown" which was later covered by Leo Kottke and the political satire of "Monkey That Became President"; a song which is still as potent today. Not to be missed. —*Jim Worbois*

The Rhymer and Other Five and Dimers / 1973 / Mercury ✦✦✦✦✦
More great songs from the man called "The Storyteller"; including one from Billy Joe Shaver. This record picked up a little negative publicity when the folks in Spokane took exception with "Spokane Motel Blues." Still, no one else will find anything to complain about. —*Jim Worbois*

Greatest Hits, Vol. 2 / 1975 / Mercury ✦✦✦
Where *Greatest Hits* had the bulk of Tom T. Hall's greatest story songs, *Greatest Hits, Vol. 2* concentrates on his silly, cutesy songs, like "Sneaky Snake," "I Like Beer," "I Love," and "Old Dogs, Children and Watermelon Wine," among seven others. For fans of his detailed narratives, these songs can be quite grating, but for listeners that want all of these hits in one package, *Greatest Hits, Vol. 2* functions quite nicely. —*Thom Owens*

Greatest Hits, Vol. 3 / 1978 / Mercury ✦✦✦
Beginning with 1976's "Faster Horses" and running through 1977's "Your Man Love You, Honey" and "It's All in the Game," *Greatest Hits, Vol. 3* collects the remainder of Tom T. Hall's '70s hit singles for Mercury Records. It does feature his biggest hit singles from the mid-'70s, as well as some less interesting, lesser-known songs, but the material on *Greatest Hits, Vol. 3* isn't quite as strong as his two previous hit collections. The album does pick up some highlights from a number of weaker albums, but casual fans will be better served by the first two *Greatest Hits* collections or, better yet, the box set *Storyteller, Poet Philosopher*. —*Thom Owens*

★ **The Essential Tom T. Hall: Story Songs** / 1988 / Mercury ✦✦✦✦✦
Tom T's songs are stories filled with interesting characters. And, some of his most interesting characters are gathered on this record which celebrates the first 20 years of Hall's career as a performer. (Hall was a writer first with his most famous pre-performer song being "Harper Valley PTA.") Whether you're looking for a hits package (which this isn't, strictly speaking) or just want to learn more about Hall, this is a fine place to start. —*Jim Worbois*

100 Children/I Witness Life / 1992 / Bear Family ✦✦✦✦✦

Ballad of Forty Dollars/Homecoming / 1992 / Bear Family ✦✦✦✦✦

☆ **Storyteller, Poet, Philosopher** / Nov. 14, 1995 / Mercury ✦✦✦✦✦
The double-disc box set *Storyteller, Poet, Philosopher* concentrates on Tom T. Hall's talents as a narrative songwriter, eschewing some of his better-known novelties for lesser-known, but better-written, serious songs. That doesn't mean the box is devoid of hits—all of the important ones are here. What that does mean is that *Storyteller, Poet, Philosopher* is the first Tom T. Hall compilation to accurately convey the scope of his talents, as well as his achievements. —*Thom Owens*

Songs from Sopchoppy / 1996 / Mercury ✦✦

Home Grown / Sep. 16, 1997 / Mercury ✦✦✦

George Hamilton IV

b. Jul. 19, 1937, Winston-Salem, NC

Vocals, Guitar / Nashville Sound/Countrypolitan, Country-Folk, Pop, Country-Pop, Traditional Country

Proclaimed the International Ambassador of Country Music thanks to his world tours in the '70s, George Hamilton IV began his career in the late '50s as a teen-oriented pop star. After his first hit, "A Rose and a Baby Ruth," hit number six on the pop charts in 1956, he toured with Buddy Holly and the Everly Brothers. However, his later pop efforts stalled on the charts, and in 1959, Hamilton joined the *Grand Ole Opry*. Top ten country singles like "Before This Day Ends", "Three Steps to the Phone (Millions of Miles)" and "If You Don't Know I Ain't Gonna Tell You" paved the way for 1963's "Abilene," which topped the country charts for four weeks and hit 15 on the pop charts. The following year, Hamilton charted three singles and returned to the Top Ten with "Fort Worth, Dallas or Houston." Folk music inspired Hamilton's late-'60s hits, including the Gordon Lightfoot-penned "Steel Rail Blues" and Joni Mitchell's "Urge For Going." Except for 1970's number-three hit "She's a Little Bit Country", chart success eluded him during the '70s, so George Hamilton IV took country music around the world. Besides more than ten tours of Great Britain and several BBC-TV productions, Hamilton became the first country artist to perform behind the Iron Curtain; he also toured Africa, the Orient, New Zealand, Australia, and even the Middle East. For the rest of his career, Hamilton concentrated on gospel recordings. His son, George Hamilton V, toured with his father's backup band and charted a single in 1988. *—John Bush*

Abilene / 1963 / Collectables ♦♦♦♦

Collectables' reissue of George Hamilton IV's *Abilene* contains the original album, plus three bonus tracks which include the hits "Why Don't They Understand" and "A Rose and a Baby Ruth." The hits augment an album that, as its subtitle suggest, leans more toward folk songs. Of course, these songs aren't given folk arrangements—they are folk songs and standards, like "The Roving Gambler" and "You Are My Sunshine," given appealingly pop arrangements. There are a few dull spots on the record, but on the whole it's quite entertaining, and it's made even better with the bonus tracks. *—Stephen Thomas Erlewine*

● **Country Boy: The Best of George Hamilton IV** / Dec. 2, 1996 / BMG International ♦♦♦♦

Wayne Hancock

Vocals / Americana, Rockabilly Revival, Neo-Traditionalist Country, Alternative Country

Wayne Hancock is something of a throwback in modern country: an unrepentant hillbilly who appropriates the elder Hank Williams' aversion to the Nashville machine, as well as bits of his style. Hancock's music is hardcore country, a mix of honky tonk, swing, and rockabilly that seems retro but has actually never been thrown together in quite such a way. Hancock's first album, *Thunderstorms and Neon Signs*, was released by DejaDisc in 1995; *That's What Daddy Wants* followed in 1997, and two years later Hancock returned with *Wild, Free & Restless*. *—Steve Huey*

Thunderstorms and Neon Signs / Oct. 1995 / Ark 21 ♦♦♦♦

This, Wayne Hancock's debut album, showcases the artist as a true country music maverick. Hancock's attitude, stance, and general thrust grasp the essence of country music, and his is a record that really captures the Sun Records vibe accurately—much more effectively than any of his "contemporaries." An awesome debut. *—Matthew Greenwald*

● **That's What Daddy Wants** / Aug. 26, 1997 / Ark 21 ♦♦♦♦

Hancock approaches classic country themes with a modern flair. Hank Williams couldn't have gotten away with singing about finding his lover with another on "those damp, slick, sticky satin sheets." And Hancock does branch out a bit, utilizing a drummer as well as the occasional horn or accordion. But his most radical departure, a cover of the Clash's "Brand New Cadillac," is a surf music screamer that advances his sound to state of the art circa 1963. You can almost picture Jethro and Granny out twistin' by the cement pond. This music is something of an anachronism, and that is perhaps that greatest criticism one could levy against it. Hancock swings and moans with the best, but don't expect his '90s themes to modernize this sound. Retro is perfectly fine when it's done as well as this. *—Brian Briscoe*

Wild, Free & Reckless / Jul. 27, 1999 / Ark 21 ♦♦♦

Wayne Hancock's third album, *Wild, Free and Restless*, is another richly eclectic melting pot of vintage American sounds with a distinctly rural orientation. Yet, in spite of the fact that Hancock is an unabashed revivalist, his music never comes off as academic or as mere preservationism; these songs breathe with a lively energy, and the juxtapositions of styles seem natural and unselfconscious. The spirits of Hank Williams, Jimmie Rodgers, and Bob Wills hang the heaviest over Hancock's music, but there's also blues, big-band jazz, and some rockabilly insanity; plus, Hancock covers both Ernest Tubb ("Kansas City Blues") and Carl Perkins ("Blue Suede Shoes") this time out. Another fine effort from a singular stylist. *—Steve Huey*

Emmylou Harris

b. Apr. 2, 1947, Birmingham, AL

Vocals, Guitar / Folk-Rock, Contemporary Country, Country-Rock, Progressive Country, Traditional Country

Though other performers sold more records and earned greater fame, few left as profound an impact on contemporary music as Emmylou Harris. Blessed with a crystalline voice, a remarkable gift for phrasing and a restless creative spirit, she travelled a singular artistic path, proudly carrying the torch of "Cosmic American music" passed down by her mentor, country-rock pioneer Gram Parsons. With the exception of only Neil Young—not surprisingly an occasional collaborator—no other mainstream star established a similarly large body of work as consistently iconoclastic, eclectic or daring; even more than three decades into her career, Harris' latter-day music remained as heartfelt, visionary and vital as her earliest recordings. Indeed, as late as 1995—at a stage in her career at which most performers retreat to the safety of rehashing their greatest hits again and again—Harris issued the Daniel Lanois-produced *Wrecking Ball*, perhaps her most adventuresome record to date. *—Jason Ankeny*

Gliding Bird / 1968 / Amos ♦♦

Elite Hotel / 1975 / Reprise ♦♦♦♦♦

While much of Harris' career has been spent carrying on the legacy of Gram Parsons, *Elite Hotel* ranks among her most overt tributes to his genius, thanks to its covers of the Flying Burrito Brothers' "Sin City" and "Wheels," along with "Ooh Las Vegas" from the *Grievous Angel* album. In addition to the usual eclectic mix of covers—which includes the Beatles' "Here, There and Everywhere" and Hank Williams' "Jambalaya" this time out—*Elite Hotel* offers renditions of the country perennials "Together Again" and "Sweet Dreams," which were, respectively, Harris' first two number one chart hits. *—Jason Ankeny*

★ **Pieces of the Sky** / 1975 / Reprise ♦♦♦♦♦

Harris' major-label solo debut quickly establishes the pattern that the vast majority of her subsequent work would follow: *Pieces of the Sky* is bravely eclectic, impeccably performed, and achingly beautiful. Amidst a collection of songs which ranks among her most well-chosen—ranging from the catalogs of the Beatles ("For No One") to Boudleaux & Felice Bryant ("Sleepless Nights") and the Louvin Brothers (the hit "If I Could Only Win Your Love")—the record's centerpiece is one of Harris' rare original compositions, "Boulder to Birmingham," her stirring tribute to fallen mentor Gram Parsons. *—Jason Ankeny*

Luxury Liner / 1977 / Reprise ♦♦♦♦♦

Luxury Liner ranks as Harris' best-selling solo record to date, and it's one of her most engaging efforts as well; her Hot Band is in peak form, and the songs are even more far afield than usual, including Chuck Berry's "(You Never Can Tell) C'est La Vie" and Townes Van Zandt's painterly tale of aging outlaws, "Pancho & Lefty." *—Jason Ankeny*

☆ **Profile (The Best of Emmylou Harris)** / 1978 / Reprise ♦♦♦♦♦

Profile (The Best of Emmylou Harris) collects 12 of Harris' biggest hits from the mid-'70s, including the number one hits "Together Again," "Sweet Dreams," "Two More Bottles of Wine," and the Top 10 hits "One of These Days," "If I Could Only Win Your Love," "You Never Can Tell," "Making Believe," and "To Daddy." *—Stephen Thomas Erlewine*

A Quarter Moon in a Ten Cent Town / 1978 / Warner Brothers ♦♦♦♦

Quarter Moon in a Ten Cent Town is a transitional effort which bridges the curveballs of Harris' earliest solo work with the more traditional country albums which comprise the bulk of the second phase of her career. For the first time, she covers no Gram Parsons tunes or pop music chestnuts, relying instead on newly-exited Hot Band member Rodney Crowell for two songs ("Leaving Louisiana in the Broad Daylight" and "I Ain't Living Long like This") and Dolly Parton for another (the devastating "To Daddy"); the highlight is a gorgeous cover of Jesse Winchester's "Defying Gravity." *—Jason Ankeny*

Blue Kentucky Girl / 1979 / Reprise ♦♦♦

In response to criticism that her records weren't "country" enough, Harris recorded *Blue Kentucky Girl*, one of her most traditional outings. Relying on a more acoustic sound, the album largely forsakes contemporary pop songs in favor of standard country fare, including the Louvin Brothers' "Everytime You Leave" and Leon Payne's "They'll Never Take His Love from Me." The cover of Dallas Frazier's "Beneath Still Waters" earned Harris her fourth number one single. *—Jason Ankeny*

Roses in the Snow / 1980 / Reprise ♦♦♦♦♦

Combining acoustic bluegrass with traditional Appalachian melodies (and tossing one contemporary tune, Paul Simon's "The Boxer," into the mix), *Roses in the Snow* ranks among Harris' riskiest—and most satisfying—gambits. *—Jason Ankeny*

Evangeline / 1981 / Reprise ♦♦

Cimarron / 1981 / Reprise ♦♦♦

Last Date / 1982 / Reprise ♦♦♦

White Shoes / 1983 / Reprise ♦♦♦

Harris' final album with longtime producer (and husband) Brian Ahern is among her most surprising and diverse, perhaps the closest she's ever come to a straightahead rock LP. Among the unusual cover choices: Johnny Ace's "Pledging My Love" and Donna Summer's "On the Radio." *—Jason Ankeny*

Profile II: The Best of Emmylou Harris / 1984 / Reprise ♦♦♦♦♦

Harris' second hits collection is highlighted by a pair of chart-toppers, "Beneath Still Waters" and "(Lost His Love) On Our Last Date." It also includes the Top Five smashes "Born to Run," "I'm Movin' On" and "Save the Last Dance for Me." *—Jason Ankeny*

The Ballad of Sally Rose / 1985 / Reprise ♦♦♦

Thirteen / 1986 / Reprise ♦♦

Angel Band / 1987 / Reprise ♦♦♦♦

Angel Band is yet another fascinating left turn, an acoustic record comprised of country-gospel songs like "We Shall Rise, " "If I Be Lifted Up" and "Someday My Ship Will Sail, " performed with great subtlety and nuance. *—Jason Ankeny*

Bluebird / 1988 / Reprise ♦♦♦

Like most of Emmylou Harris' albums, *Bluebird* is an expertly performed album, featuring some truly startling and affecting tour-de-forces by Harris. However, the material—while featuring a handful of truly great songs, like John Hiatt's "Icy Blue Heart" and her original "A River for Him"—is too uneven to rank among her finest efforts. *—Thom Owens*

Brand New Dance / 1990 / Reprise ♦♦♦

Duets / Jul. 24, 1990 / Reprise ♦♦♦

On the heels of *Trio*, Harris' smash studio collaboration with Dolly Parton and Linda Ronstadt, comes the compilation *Duets*, which collects previously-released performances recorded in conjunction with Neil Young, Willie Nelson and others. Obviously intended to cash in on the success of *Trio*, the record is by no means an essential addition to the Harris ouevre: virtually everything included is readily available on other albums, and the selections are erratic at best—by and large, Harris' finest material is her solo work, although the power of "Love Hurts," recorded during her all-too-brief period with Gram Parsons, remains undeniable. *—Jason Ankeny*

At the Ryman / 1992 / Reprise ♦♦♦♦
This is the album debut of the Nashville Ramblers, her acoustic backing band featuring Sam Bush and Roy Huskey Jr, recorded over three nights in the former home of the Grand Ole Opry. Harris's choice of songs strikes a balance between hillbilly classics and folk-influenced rock, with Bill Monroe receiving heaviest tribute but sharing space with Tex Owens, Bruce Springsteen, and John Fogerty. *—Brian Mansfield*

Cowgirl's Prayer / 1993 / Elektra/Asylum ♦♦♦♦

Songs of the West / 1994 / Warner Western ♦♦

Wrecking Ball / Sep. 26, 1995 / Elektra ♦♦♦♦♦
Wrecking Ball is a left-field masterpiece, the most wide-ranging, innovative and daring record in a career built on such notions. Rich in atmosphere and haunting in its dark complexity, much of the due credit belongs to producer Daniel Lanois; best known for his work with pop superstars like U2 and Peter Gabriel, on *Wrecking Ball* Lanois taps into the very essence of what makes Harris tick—the gossamer vocals, the flawless phrasing—while also opening up innumerable new avenues for her talents to explore. The songs shimmer and swirl, given life through Lanois' trademark ringing guitar textures and the almost primal drumming of U2's Larry Mullen, Jr. The fixed point remains Harris' voice, which leaps into each and every one of these diverse compositions—culled from the pens of Neil Young, Bob Dylan, Jimi Hendrix, Steve Earle and others—with utter fearlessness, as if this were the album she'd been waiting her entire life to make. Maybe it is. *—Jason Ankeny*

Portraits / Oct. 8, 1996 / Warner Archives ♦♦♦♦♦
Portraits is a three-disc, 61-track box set covering Emmylou Harris' entire career for Reprise and Warner Records, which spans from 1974 to 1992. Not only does the box select highlights from classic albums like *Luxury Liner, Roses in the Snow,* and *Blue Kentucky Girl,* but it also features her early duets with Gram Parsons and selections from the *Trio* album she recorded with Dolly Parton and Linda Ronstadt. *Portraits* doesn't dwell too long on unreleased material—there are only five unearthed tracks on the entire set—preferring to sketch out a full overview of her career. While there might be a few favorite tracks missing, the box nevertheless fulfills its goals quite nicely—anyone looking for a comprehensive compilation of Emmylou's career will not be disappointed. *—Thom Owens*

Spyboy / Aug. 11, 1998 / Eminent ♦♦♦♦

Singin' with Emmylou, Vol. 1 / 2000 / Reprise ♦♦♦
Singin' With Emmylou, Vol. 1 collects Emmylou Harris' collaborations with friends like Glen Campbell, Rosanne Cash, and George Jones. Harris joins Willie Nelson on "Angel Eyes," Vince Gill on "Oh Carolina," Dan Fogelberg on "Only the Heart May Know," and Waylon Jennings on "Spanish Johnny." A worthwhile compilation of supporting performances from one of country's most gifted female vocalists. *—Heather Phares*

Red Dirt Girl / Sep. 12, 2000 / Elektra ♦♦♦♦

John Hartford

b. Dec. 30, 1937, New York, NY, **d.** Jun. 4, 2001
Vocals, Guitar, Fiddle, Banjo / Country-Rock, Progressive Country, Traditional Country, Old-Timey
John Hartford was one of country music's true eccentrics. Best-known for the pop standard "Gentle on My Mind," he was a multi-talented musician who played a variety of stringed instruments, and was also an author and riverboat captain. As a songwriter he was known for a sharp, off-beat wit and music wavering between folk, modern country, and old-timey string music. In the early '60s, Hartford cut a few unsuccessful singles and became involved with songwriters like Kris Kristofferson and Mickey Newbury. He found a hit single in 1967 with "Gentle on My Mind," from his second album *Earthwords & Music.* After Glen Campbell's cover of the song became a Top 40 country and pop hit, Hartford became a star of sorts, appearing regularly on television and even the Byrds' 1968 album *Sweetheart of the Rodeo.* In 1971, Hartford formed a bluegrass band featuring guitarist Norman Blake and master fiddler Vassar Clements. He continued to record solo albums during the '70s, one of the best being *Mark Twang.* He began performing with his son Jamie in the late '80s and also became involved with Opryland, where he helped launch an old-fashioned steamboat ride. He also recorded and re-issued his earlier work on his own Small Dog Barking label. *—Sandra Brennan*

Earthwords and Music / 1967 / RCA ♦♦♦
Aside from the obvious bonus of containing Hartford's own version of his classic "Gentle on My Mind," this record also contains other gems such as "Washing Machine" on which he imitates the difference in the sounds made by both the old and new machines (using only his voice) and his "rap" about the many uses of baking soda. Also contains some fine straight songs. Good stuff. *—Jim Worbois*

Aereo-Plain / 1971 / Rounder ♦♦♦♦♦

Down on the River / 1972 / Flying Fish ♦♦♦
John Hartford's *Down on the River* is an old-timey tribute to the Mississippi River and its steamboats, casinos and saloons, filled with campy salutes to a forgotten lifestyles, as well as surprisingly affectionate paens to a lost era. Hartford's approach may be too kitschy for some—after all, there are several songs driven by calliope—yet its a thoroughly entertaining album for listeners that share his obsessions, or at least his fondness for fine, old-timey banjo. *—Thom Owens*

Morning Bugle / 1972 / Rounder ♦♦♦♦♦
One of Hartford's finest records. Done mostly live in the studio with virtually no over-dubs, this is a fine collection of song covering a variety of subjects. Two of the most poignant are "Howard Hughes Blues" and "Nobody Eats at Linebaugh's," which addresses country music's abandonment of the Ryman and downtown Nashville in favor of "the park." *—Jim Worbois*

Mark Twang / 1976 / Flying Fish ♦♦♦♦♦

● **Me Oh My, How the Time Does Fly** / 1982 / Flying Fish ♦♦♦♦♦
Me Oh My, How the Time Flies is an 18-song compilation that culls from Hartford's nine Flying Fish albums, which were recorded between 1976-1987. The collection gives a good sense of his depth as a songwriter and instrumentalist. *—Thom Owens*

Gum Tree Canoe / 1987 / Flying Fish ♦♦♦♦♦
The best-rounded of all the Flying Fish albums, it has everything from bluegrass to Civil War songs. *—Charles S. Wolfe*

Wild Hog in the Red Brush / 1996 / Rounder ♦♦♦♦
John Hartford would just grin crookedly at you if you brought up the subject of virtuosity in his presence. Half the charm of his music is his loopy sense of humor—he often counts a tune in by grunting rhythmically or by singing the title, and his fiddling is always just a hair away from wobbling off the side of the road. But his knowledge of the traditional repertoire is encyclopedic, and he can fiddle in more idioms than most can recognize. On his latest outing he's joined by banjoist Bob Carlin, guitarist Ronnie McCoury, mandolinist Mike Compton and bassist Jerry McCoury for a sprawling tour of obscure tunes, a number of which Hartford learned from old recordings by Ohio fiddler Ed Haley. Each track is annotated and pedigreed (sample: "French and Solly Carpenter who were friends of Ed Haley's played this according to Wilson Douglas"). The whole thing's a hoot and a joy, and is recommended strongly. *—Rick Anderson*

Good Old Boys / Sep. 14, 1999 / Rounder ♦♦♦♦

Hawkshaw Hawkins

b. Dec. 22, 1921, Huntington, WV, **d.** Mar. 5, 1963, Camden, TN
Vocals, Guitar / Honky Tonk, Traditional Country
Hawkshaw Hawkins was a country singer, guitarist, songwriter, and entertainer. A large man (6 ft., 6 in.) with a deep singing voice, Hawkins was an immensely popular performer in country music for many years without the benefit of big record success. Described as "the man with eleven and a half yards of personality," Hawkins was a warm and engaging performer both onstage and on records, able to pull off a wide variety of material from maudlin weepers to uptempo novelties. He started on radio, becoming a regular on WWVA's *Wheeling Jamboree* by 1946 and releasing the minor hit "The Sunny Side of the Mountain," the song that would eventually become his signature tune. Between 1948 and 1951, he had five Top Ten singles including "Pan American," "Dog House Boogie," "I Love You a Thousand Ways," "I'm Waiting Just for You," and "Slow Poke." In 1953, he left King and signed with RCA, but he had no hits for the label. In 1955, Hawkins became a member of the *Grand Ole Opry* and the exposure earned him a spot on Columbia's roster by 1959. After re-signing to King in 1963 and releasing "Lonesome 7-7203" as a comeback single early that spring, it became a number one hit. Hawkins didn't live to see it reach the top of the charts, though—he tragically died in the same 1963 airplane crash that killed Patsy Cline and Cowboy Copas. *—Cub Koda*

Hawk / 1953-1961 / Bear Family ♦♦♦♦♦
This collection, featuring 63 songs, isn't a cross-section of Hawkins' history, because it's limited to his RCA and Columbia recordings, thus leaving out his pre-1953 and post-1961 hits for King Records. It is, however, a dazzling array of some of the best honky tonk-based country music this side of Hank Williams. The first thing one notices is what a stunning voice Hawkins had, and also his range as a performer—he could do a lovesick ballad and make it seem like the words came right from his heart, but was equally engaging doing playful novelty numbers. Disc One covers his first two years at RCA, one perfect track after another, great singing backed by crisp, tight playing and note-perfect arrangements across a dazzling range of material. It runs the gamut from the sentimental to some of the brightest dance-type tunes and novelty numbers of their period, and even some not-half-bad efforts at hooking into the new rock craze. Disc Two opens with maybe the prettiest, most haunting song that Hawkins ever recorded, the previously unissued "I've Had It Before," a moody country-blues driven by Hawkins' own acoustic guitar. His re-recording of "Sunny Side of the Mountain," Hawkins' signature tune beginning in the late '40s, is also here. Disc Three is given over to Hawkins' stay at Columbia Records, which marked a major change in his repertory. The sound isn't as crisp, but the material is the real curiosity; Hawkins' arrival coincided with Marty Robbins' huge success with Western songs, and Johnny Horton's mega-hit "The Battle of New Orleans," so Columbia had him do half a dozen folk-based and historical songs and Western numbers. It took a year for Hawkins to return to his old sound, which closes out this set. *—Bruce Eder*

● **I'm A Rattlesnakin' Daddy: The King Anthology, 1946-1963** / Feb. 8, 2000 / West Side ♦♦♦♦♦
Subtitled "The King Anthology 1946-1963," this brings together his earliest recordings as well as two versions of his final single. Kicking off with a previously unissued undubbed version of his biggest hit, "Lonesome 7-7203," the set goes back to the dawn of Hawkins' career with sides like "I Ain't Goin' Honky Tonkin' Anymore," "I've Got the Blues," "Sunny Side of the Mountain," and "You Nearly Lose Your Mind," all distinguished by sparse string backing and bluesy vocals. It isn't until 1949's "Pan American" that normal country instruments (fiddles, steel guitar) start showing up in Hawk's music, as he covers everything from Hank Williams to current R&B hits like Ruth Brown's "Teardrops From My Eyes" and John Greer's "Got You on My Mind." Hawkins further blurs the line between country and blues with proto-rockabilly tracks like "Doghouse Boogie," "Back to the Dog House," and "Rattlesnakin' Daddy." Hawkshaw left King in 1953, and the rest of his career is chronicled on an exhaustive Bear Family box set entitled *Hawk,* but these are some of his very best and earliest sides and are absolutely essential to getting the big picture on this highly underrated artist. *—Cub Koda*

Lee Hazlewood

b. Jul. 9, 1929, Mannford, OK
Vocals, Producer / Obscuro, Baroque Pop, Pop, Country-Pop, Country-Rock
Lee Hazlewood has had his hand in so many pies it's hard to know where to start in describing his long and varied music career. He's recorded an impressive number of pop and

country albums himself—immediately distinguished by his deep, dark vocal style and playfully existential lyrics—but he's best known for two accomplishments: Discovering Duane Eddy (he created Eddy's trademark twangy guitar sound), and producing and writing the song "These Boots Are Made for Walking" and other hits for Nancy Sinatra, which turned her into a 1960s icon of sassy miniskirt pop. Initially, it was songwriting success that enabled Hazlewood to form his own Phoenix-based Jamie label in the '50s, which became the launching pad for Eddy's career. (Hazlewood wrote and produced most of the guitarist's major hits.) By the late '60s, Hazlewood had begun working as a producer for Reprise, where he eventually hooked up with Nancy Sinatra and turned her career into a goldmine with songs like "Boots" and "Sugar Town." The pair also recorded several singles together, eventually released on the album *Nancy and Lee*. Hazlewood's own solo singles and albums are some of the era's most unique pop and country creations, with material walking the line between dark, philosophical introspection and wry, playful humor (often on the same song). Hazlewood retreated into obscurity in the 1970s, but continued recording and performing in Europe. He briefly resurfaced in 1995 to tour with Nancy Sinatra, then four years later he released *Farmisht, Flatulence, Origami, ARF!!! and me . . .*, his first proper solo album in over 20 years. *—Kurt Wolff*

Trouble Is a Lonesome Town / 1963 / Smells Like ✦✦✦
Trouble Is a Lonesome Town was Lee Hazlewood's first proper solo album, following his prosperous late-'50s partnership with Duane Eddy and prior to his mentoring and making of '60s boot-walker Nancy Sinatra. Hazlewood considered it a "writer's album" from which other artists could cull songs, but *Trouble* is a perfectly legitimate effort in its own right, and characteristically wonderful Hazlewood. The songs are succinct, country-drenched cowboy ballads given a certain undeniable authority by Hazlewood's warm, bottomless baritone, which booms out of the music like a voice amplified from the heavens. The album runs through jail songs ("Six Feet of Chain"), railroad songs ("The Railroad"), traveling songs ("Long Black Train"), and cold-hearted love songs ("Look at That Woman") peppered with outlaws, itinerants, dead-end women, card players, and beat-down heroes, too. Between the songs, Hazlewood shows his storyteller's gift by offering up bits of narration, and the album itself is a storyteller's record. *Trouble* is like a cross between a novel full of idiosyncratic character studies (a la Faulkner) and a John Wayne western, with Hazlewood—looking a lot like a dharma bum on the album cover, sitting on the railroad tracks with his guitar and a dangling cigarette—spinning out intricate yarns about all manner of interesting souls with names like Orville Dobkins and Emory Zickfoose Brown, all residents of the hard-scrabbled fictitious town Trouble ("nothing with a railroad running through it"), which is loosely based on his birthplace. The music is as somber and loping as such subject matter demands, mostly consisting of strummed acoustic guitars and woeful harmonica wails that weep the blues. But it is in the purposefully humorous, sympathetic, and colorful storytelling that the distinct, dead-on Americana heart of *Trouble* lays. *—Stanton Swihart*

Love and Other Crimes / 1968 / Reprise ✦✦✦✦✦
If you're looking for evidence of Lee Hazlewood the weirdo, this album will not disappoint. As pure music it's another story. Hazlewood usually sounds like Johnny Cash gone pop, after gargling with razor blades; sometimes he sounds like a drunk taking over the cocktail piano, with soused accompaniment by such estimable session greats as guitarist James Burton and drummer Hal Blaine. Check out "She's Funny That Way," which suddenly fades into a silly excerpt of Ray Charles' "Drown in My Own Tears"; there's also "Pour Man'" (sic), a jaunty ballad sung by a convicted murderer on his last night of life. "Forget Marie" is reasonably solid country-pop in the style of the material he fashioned for Nancy Sinatra, but overall this has the ambience of a tax write-off or a vanity project, knocked off with a bit of extra studio time. *—Richie Unterberger*

Nancy & Lee / 1968 / Reprise ✦✦✦✦✦
Lee's first duet album with Nancy Sinatra is a classic of '60s pop. He plays the leering, deep-throated, trail-worn cowboy to her bright-eyed girl-child, and the match on songs like "Summer Wine," "Sand," "Jackson," and "Some Velvet Morning" is a smart, sexy, lip-smacking bowl of mind candy. *—Kurt Wolff*

The Cowboy & the Lady / 1969 / Smells Like ✦✦

Forty / 1969 / LHI ✦✦✦
Another dearth of Hazlewood originals in lieu of medircre showtunes ("It Was a Very Good Year," "September Song"); nonetheless the hardcore downer "The Bed" and his dark, turgid, but almost saucy take on Randy Newman's "Let's Burn Down the Cornfield" are stellar. *—Kurt Wolff*

Cowboy in Sweden / 1970 / Smells Like ✦✦✦✦
At the turn of the '60s, Lee Hazlewood decided to leave America for Sweden. He had already spent time in the country, appearing as an actor in two television productions, so his decision wasn't completely out of the blue—especially since he had become close with the Swedish artist/filmmaker Torbjörn Axelman. The year that he arrived in Sweden, he starred in Axelman's television production *Cowboy in Sweden* and cut an album of the same name. Judging by the album alone, the film must have been exceedingly surreal, since the record exists in its own space and time. At its core, it's a collection of country and cowboy tunes, much like the work he did with Nancy Sinatra, but the production is cinematic and psychedelic, creating a druggy, discombobulated sound like no other. This is mind-altering music—the combination of country song structures, Hazlewood's deep baritone, the sweet voices of Nina Lizell and Suzi Jane Hokom, the rolling acoustic guitars, ominous strings, harpsichords and flutes, eerie pianos and endless echo is stranger than outright avant garde music, since the familiar is undone by unexpected arrangements. Though the songs are all well-written, *Cowboy in Sweden* is ultimately about the sound and mood it evokes—and it's quite singular in that regard. *—Stephen Thomas Erlewine*

Requiem for an Almost Lady / 1971 / Smells Like ✦✦✦✦

13 / 1972 / Smells Like ✦✦✦
One of the rarest of Lee Hazlewood's original LPs, *13* is a surprisingly swinging album completely indicative of the year of its recording, 1972. But though it's undeniably a period piece, in many ways it's dated in all the right ways. The opener, "You Look Like a Lady," is a gem, complete with soaring horn section, a roving bassline, and scads of wah-wah guitar. Oddly, over-production never hurt Hazlewood's gravelly, off-key delivery, and though the arrangements here aren't always sympathetic to the songwriting ("Tulsa Sunday" is particularly jarring), they're usually entertaining. "She Comes Running," a song originally recorded for 1968's *Love and Other Crimes*, makes another appearance, though with a much more commercial production. The lyrics are vintage Hazlewood, and "Ten or 11 Towns Ago" is a highlight: "Met a girl in Baltimore / Nothing less and nothing more / She was rich and I was poor / So I let her take me on a small vacation" and "One week in San Francisco, existing on Nabisco / Cookies and bad dreams / Sad scenes and dodging paranoia." Not all of the songs are up to Hazlewood's level; "Toocie and the River" and "Rosacoke Street" are both, relatively speaking, duds. But Hazlewood fans will love to hear these songs, especially since none have been collected on the quasi-legal compilations available at the nation's better record stores. Out of print for decades, *13* returned in early 2000 thanks to a reissue campaign by Smells Like Records. *—John Bush*

Poet, Fool or Bum / 1973 / Capitol ✦✦✦✦✦
The title track mixes black humor, clever rhymes, and cowboy existentialism; "The Performer" is a stark and somewhat autobiographical picture of a singer who's sick of the game; and the epic "Nancy and Me" is some sort of fantasy-ramble that likely never happened, but stands among the best songs Lee ever wrote. Includes a drawling version of Tom Waits' "Those Were Days of Roses (Martha)." *—Kurt Wolff*

● **The Many Sides of Lee** / 1991 / Request ✦✦✦✦✦
Twenty-five-song import compilation of rare Hazlewood tracks, most or all dating from the 1960s, including solo numbers and collaborations with Suzi Jane Hokom, the Shacklefords, and Mark Robinson. The most country-ish cuts are like a debauched Johnny Cash; the bullfighter narrative "Jose" is Hazlewood at his most compellingly cheesy and melodramatic; and there are shades of his Duane Eddy roots in the more rock-oriented cuts, like the grungy "Della" and the rockabilly tinged "Pretty Jane." There are also solo renditions of several songs that he produced for Nancy Sinatra, although Sinatra's versions are uniformly better. You could justifiably call this the work of an idiot savant, or (at its worst) just a plain idiot, but it is, like much of Hazlewood's stuff, intriguing in its blend of banal '60s pop-country and eccentric production, lyrics, and vocals. It would have been nice to have even a shred of documentation as far as dates and sources, and there's no question that his collaborations with Nancy Sinatra offer a much better context for his work as a songwriter and producer. But this is the best available distillation of the man's erratic and large solo output into one place, if you can find it. *—Richie Unterberger*

Farmisht, Flatulence, Origami, ARF!!! and me . . . / Apr. 27, 1999 / Smells Like ✦✦✦

Ty Herndon

Vocals / New Traditionalist, Contemporary Country
Like many new country singers of the mid-'90s, Ty Herndon fused neo-traditionalist country with a slick, rock-oriented sense of style and production. Like many of his contemporaries, his blend of genres proved commercially successful, as his first album became one of the biggest hits of 1995. Herndon was a little wilder, at least offstage, than many of his peers, but his records had a down-to-earth sense of sentimentality that gave him a broad fan base. Initially, he had difficult time gaining a foothold in the music industry, spending 10 years in Nashville without making any real headway. Ty left the Music City and headed to Texas, where he began slogging it out in local honky tonks. In 1993, he signed to Epic Records. Herndon's first single "What Mattered Most" hit number one in the spring of 1995. An album of the same name was released in April and it became a Top 10 country hit. The second single, "I Want My Goodbye Back," became a number seven hit. His first year of stardom was a difficult one, as he was arrested for drug possession in mid-1995 in Fort Worth, Texas. Nevertheless, the arrest didn't halt his career. The third single, "Heart Half Empty" was a hit and Herndon's second album, *Living In A Moment*, debuted at number six upon its summer 1996 release. *—Stephen Thomas Erlewine*

● **What Mattered Most** / Apr. 18, 1995 / Epic ✦✦✦✦

Living in a Moment / Aug. 13, 1996 / Epic ✦✦✦
Although he is in fine voice throughout the album, Ty Herndon's *Living in a Moment* is bogged down by mediocre material that fails to given him a proper showcase for his talents. Herndon doesn't write his own material, which might not necessarily be a bad thing—after all, hundreds of country singers don't write their own songs—but he doesn't have the best ear for selecting songs. When he does have a strong song—like the title track or "Don't Tell Mama"—he sounds terrific, but otherwise Herndon simply sounds adequate. Furthermore, on the undistinguished numbers, the production sounds generic and canned, which also hurts the record. Although Herndon still shows promise, it's hard to avoid that *Living in a Moment* sounds like a sophomore slump. *—Thom Owens*

Big Hopes / May 26, 1998 / Epic ✦✦✦
Like its predecessor *Living in a Moment*, Ty Herndon's third album *Big Hopes* comes as close to MOR rock and pop as it does to country. Beneath the glossy production, the music has subtle country roots, but often Herndon is closer to Don Henley than Haggard. That may upset some purists, but by this point in his career, anyone interested in Herndon should know he isn't pure country. Those fans should be pleased by some of the cuts on this disc—"A Man Holdin' On (To a Woman Lettin' Go)" is a good ballad, and "The Only Way I Know is better, and "Hands of a Working Man" are about as gritty as Herndon gets—but they may be dismayed that the filler once again slightly outweighs the good stuff. *—Thom Owens*

Steam / Nov. 2, 1999 / Epic ✦✦✦
A bit of a departure from his previous work, *Steam* is an appealing collection of songs from a man who wanted to make "feel-good music." And feel good we do with suggestive lyrics like, "Tonight when we get together, we're gonna make some steam" from the album's title

song or "My heart stops when you touch me" from the uptempo "A Love Like That." With a new production team in tow, Herndon has played a bigger part in selecting the album's songs, which have a spritual undertone, and it's clear he sings from the heart, as he always has. He includes a fan favorite from his live show, the sexy remake of Joe Cocker's "You Can Leave Your Hat On." This fourth album is a step in the right direction for an artist whose career boasts two gold albums and three number-one singles. *—Maria Konicki*

Highway 101

f. 1986, Los Angeles, CA
Group / Contemporary Country
The country-rock band Highway 101 formed in 1986 when Nitty Gritty Dirt Band manager Chuck Morris decided to create a showcase for his newest discovery, Paulette Carlson, a talented singer and guitarist from Minnesota. Carlson wrote Highway 101's debut single, "The Bed You Made for Me," which became a number four hit in early 1987. The band's eponymous debut album, also released in 1987, produced two more hits—the number three "Whiskey, If You Were a Woman" and "Somewhere Tonight," which became their first number one hit. Highway 101 went on to score numerous Top Ten singles, including three other number one hits, in the latter half of the '80s. In 1990, Carlson left the band to pursue a solo career, and Nikki Nelson was brought in to replace her. Their first single with Nelson was the title cut from *Bing Bang Boom* (1991), which became a Top 15 single. However, the group wasn't as popular following the departure of Paulette Carlson—by the end of 1992, they could no longer crack the Top 40. In 1995, Carlson rejoined Highway 101 to celebrate their ten-year anniversary; the following year they released the aptly titled *Reunion*. *—Sandra Brennan*

Highway 101 / 1987 / Warner Brothers ♦♦♦♦
The main thing that this country-rock quartet had going for it was lead singer Paulette Carlson, who approximated the throaty, torn vocal style of Stevie Nicks, but with a Southern accent. The group was heard best on its debut album, which included such characteristic hits as "Whiskey, If You Were a Woman" and "The Bed You Made for Me." *— William Ruhlmann*

Highway 101, Vol. 2 / 1988 / Curb ♦♦♦
Highway 101's second album followed the same rocking country formula that made their debut a success, but its best songs—"Setting Me Up" and "Honky Tonk Heart"—are as good as anything on the first album. *—Thom Owens*

Paint the Town / 1989 / Warner Brothers ♦♦♦
Highway 101 was beginning to show signs of stagnation on *Paint the Town*. Although there were still some good songs on it—particularly the number one single "Who's Lonely Now"—the quality of material wasn't as strong as their first two albums and the group was sounding tired, verging on the formulaic. *—Thom Owens*

● **Greatest Hits (1987-90)** / 1990 / Warner Brothers ♦♦♦♦
Highway 101 teetered on the edge of country-pop in the late '80s. This ten-song compilation gathers the biggest and best of their hits ("Who's Lonely Now," "Somewhere Tonight," "Cry, Cry, Cry," "[Do You Love Me] Just Say Yes"), proving that ultimately they were just a product of '80s obsession with everything huge. *—Michael Gallucci*

Bing Bang Boom / 1991 / Warner Brothers ♦♦

The New Frontier / Sep. 13, 1993 / Liberty ♦♦

Reunited / Feb. 27, 1996 / WillowTree ♦♦♦

The Highwaymen

f. Middletown, CT
Group / Traditional Country
The Highwaymen is a country supergroup featuring Johnny Cash, Willie Nelson, Waylon Jennings and Kris Kristofferson. The group formed in 1985, the same year they released their eponymous debut. *The Highwaymen* went to number one on the country charts, spawned the hit single "Desperados Waiting for a Train" and went gold within a year of its release. In the years immediately following the release of the record, the group was quiet, choosing to reconvene in 1990 to record and release their second album. *Highwaymen 2* wasn't quite as successful, yet it still launched the Top 30 hit, "Silver Stallion." Another five years later, the group reunited to record their third album, *The Road Goes on Forever*. The album was their least successful effort to date, failing to yield any hit singles. *—Stephen Thomas Erlewine*

● **The Highwaymen** / 1985 / Columbia ♦♦♦♦♦
These old friends have appeared together in various combinations, but never as effectively as on the epic title song here, written by Jimmy Webb. And the rest of the record, including Guy Clark's "Desperados Waiting for a Train" and Woody Guthrie's "Deportee," lives up to the lead-off hit. *— William Ruhlmann*

Live! / 1986 / Image ♦♦

Highwaymen 2 / 1990 / Columbia ♦♦♦

Road Goes on Forever / 1995 / Liberty ♦♦♦
For their third album *The Road Goes On Forever,* the Highwaymen hired Don Was to produce. Was had previously worked with every member of the group but Johnny Cash, so he was theoretically a natural choice and, on the surface, *The Road Goes On Forever* has all the trappings of being the classic Highwaymen album. It has great material, from standards like Dallas Frazier's "True Love Travels On A Gravel Road" to contemporary favorites by Steve Earle ("The Devil's Right Hand") and Billy Joe Shaver ("Live Forever"), to new cuts from all four members. It has a crisp sound and a focused production, with fine performances from everyone involved. The problem is, the whole thing sounds too damn serious—Was and the Highwaymen may have all the right cards, but they don't know how to play them. Instead of capturing a kinetic energy or intense introspection, *The Road Goes On Forever* just sounds studious and overlabored, as if the group wanted to produce music that lived up to their mythological legacy, not the music itself. *—Stephen Thomas Erlewine*

Faith Hill

b. Sep. 21, 1967, Jackson, MS
Vocals / Adult Contemporary, Contemporary Country, Country-Pop
Faith Hill was one of the '90s' most popular female singers. Raised in Star, Mississippi, she grew up idolizing Reba McEntire, and sang anywhere she could. When Hill was 19, she left Jackson and headed for Nashville, where she got a job selling T-shirts at Fan Fair. Eventually, she landed a job at Gary Morris' Nashville company, and worked there one year before making her professional debut with songwriter/musician Gary Burr, who went on to become her co-producer. Hill released her debut single, "Wild One," in the fall of 1993; the song became a major hit, spending four weeks at number one on the country charts. Hill released her debut album, *Take Me As I Am*, in 1994. The record reached the Top Ten on the country charts and went gold within a year of its release. Also in 1994, her second single, "Piece of My Heart," also became a number one hit. *It Matters to Me,* Hill's second album, was released in 1995. The following year, she married fellow Nashville star Tim McGraw. Hill's third album, *Faith,* was released in the spring of 1998, generating the hit "The Secret of Life." *Breathe* followed in 1999, containing the title track which proved to be her most widely recognized song to date and earning her an even broader crossover audience. This fact (paired with her fairytale marriage and glamorous looks) helped to turn her into a bonafide American celebrity. *—Sandra Brennan & Brian Mansfield*

● **Take Me As I Am** / 1994 / Warner Brothers ♦♦♦♦
Whether she's singing songs associated with Janis Joplin ("Piece of My Heart") or Maura O'-Connell ("I Would Be Stronger Than That"), Faith Hill sounds every bit like the new-generation Reba McEntire heir her press makes her out to be. Hill sings with with a natural tear in her voice that recalls McEntire without ever mimicking her. Hill sounds like a star on all 10 cuts, whether she's fronting minimal acoustic accompaniment on "Just Around the Eyes" or rocking out on "Wild One." *—Brian Mansfield*

It Matters to Me / 1995 / Warner Brothers ♦♦♦♦
On her second album, Faith Hill confirmed that *Take Me as I Am* was no fluke. Like her debut album, *It Matters to Me* is an ambitious, diverse set of contemporary country that proves Hill can tackle virtually every subgenre of country, singing rockers, ballads, socially-aware stories, and love songs with an equal amount of grace. The singles "Let's Go to Vegas" and "It Matters to Me" aren't the only stong songs here—the entire album is rich with first-rate songs, as well as superb singing from Hill, one of the most promising female vocalist of the mid-'90s. *—Stephen Thomas Erlewine*

Faith / Apr. 21, 1998 / Warner Brothers ♦♦♦
Faith Hill moves toward mainstream pop on her third album, *Faith.* Without abandoning the polished contemporary country that defined her first two efforts, she's exanded her sonic palette, evidently with the hope of getting an MOR audience—that's the only reasonable explanation behind the Diane Warren and Sheryl Crow songs on the album. Hill gives it her all, and there are some very nice performances here; anyone who doubted her vocal prowess will be impressed with her showcase performance here. Still, it's a little disconcerting to hear the heavy-handed arrangements that dominate the album—she may never have been a country singer in the classic sense, but here she's hanging to the genre by the most tenuous of strings. *—Thom Owens*

Breathe / Nov. 9, 1999 / Warner Brothers ♦♦♦♦
Being married to a sexy country superstar and mom to two little baby girls, along with her sultry new image and a huge crossover hit have all changed not only the way Faith Hill sounds, but also the things she sings about. There's no more spousal abuse, heartbreak, or letting go as heard on all three of her previous albums. On *Breathe,* Hill sings of love, making love, kissing, and simply love (In fact, five of the albums 13 tracks have love in the title), and it works for her. Country music fans might be a bit disappointed that there's very little about this album that sounds country, but Faith Hill fans will never feel an ounce of disappointment over this outstanding album. With each release, Hill's voice gets more and more confident and producers Byron Gallimore and Dann Huff (in addition to herself) utilize that confidence by choosing songs that complement her vocal strengths. And of course, what's a Faith Hill album about love without a duet with husband Tim McGraw— Fans won't be able to take a breath from this album—at least not on the first listen. *—Maria Konicki*

Chris Hillman

b. Dec. 4, 1944, Los Angeles, CA
Vocals, Mandolin, Bass / Country-Rock, Progressive Country, Progressive Bluegrass
Along with frequent collaborator Gram Parsons, Chris Hillman was the key figure in the development of country-rock, virtually defining the genre through his seminal work with the Byrds and the Flying Burrito Brothers. During the mid-1960s, the Byrds ranked as one of the most successful and influential American pop groups, issuing a string of massive hits like "Mr. Tambourine Man," "Turn! Turn! Turn!" and "Eight Miles High." Internal strife dogged the band, however, and by late 1967 only Hillman and frontman Roger McGuinn remained from the original roster. At about the same time, Gram Parsons entered the picture, and his mastery of country soon became the Byrds' dominant focus, much to Hillman's delight, and the album they ultimately recorded, 1968's *Sweetheart of the Rodeo,* became the blueprint for all country-rock efforts released in its wake. When Parsons quit the Byrds in July 1968, months later Hillman followed suit, and joined Parsons as a vocalist and guitarist in the Flying Burrito Brothers. Further honing their hybrid sound by combining the energy and instrumentation of rock with the issues and themes of country, the Burritos recorded the landmark *Gilded Palace of Sin,* followed in 1970 by *Burrito Deluxe.* After Parsons left the group in 1971, Hillman stayed on for two less successful records before joined Stephen Stills' Manassas, where he remained until 1973. In 1974, Hillman teamed with singer/songwriters John David Souther and Richie Furay to form Souther Hillman Furay; after recording two LPs with the trio, Hillman issued a pair of solo albums, 1976's *Slippin' Away* and 1977's *Clear Sailin'.* In 1982 he issued a straigtforward country record, *Morning Sky.* Two years later, he released *Desert Rose,* which contained the minor country hits "Somebody's Back in Town" and "Run-

ning the Roadblocks; " the album's title proved indicative of things to come, and in 1986 he formed the Desert Rose Band, a country-rock outfit of Nashville session aces which proved to be Hillman's most commercially successful post-Byrds project. —*Jason Ankeny*

The Hillmen / 1971 / Together ✦✦✦✦✦
This album does as much to explain his background as The Byrds' *Sweetheart of the Rodeo* album. This fine bluegrass band also featured the Gosdin brothers, who not only had country hits during the '70s and '80s, but also made a fine record with Gene Clark. Worth looking for, not only for these reasons but also for some fine music. —*Jim Worbois*

Slippin' Away / 1976 / Line ✦✦✦
Having recently departed Souther, Hillman, & Furay, this album more heavily reflects his association with Manassa than anything he did with SHF. A nice batch of songs overall but the high point for me is the killer version of the bluegrass standard "Take Me in Your Lifeboat" that closes the album. —*Jim Worbois*

Clear Sailin' / 1977 / Asylum ✦✦

● **Morning Sky** / 1982 / Sugar Hill ✦✦✦✦✦
A back-to-the-roots album (of sorts), Hillman has given up the bass in favor of the mandolin and acoustic guitar for this mostly acoustic album of other people's tunes. The band is made up of people with whom Hillman has worked over the years and it's obvious they are comfortable together. Listening to this album is almost like eavesdropping on a group of friends making music in their living room. —*Jim Worbois*

Desert Rose / 1984 / Sugar Hill ✦✦✦✦✦
Bluegrass, country, and country-rock, Hillman played mandolin on this album, but his main instrument (with the Byrds and Desert Rose Band is bass. —*Mark A. Humphrey*

Bakersfield Bound / May 21, 1996 / Sugar Hill ✦✦✦✦

Like a Hurricane / Jun. 16, 1998 / Sugar Hill ✦✦✦

Homer & Jethro

f. 1932, **db.** 1971
Group / Country Comedy, Traditional Country
The duo of Homer and Jethro ranked among country's most successful satirists, a comedy act whose devil-may-care attitude towards popular music often belied the fact that both were serious and talented players. Homer (born Henry D. Haynes on June 27, 1920) and Jethro (born Kenneth C. Burns on March 10, 1920) first met in 1932 at a talent show organized by radio station WNOX in the boys' native Knoxville, Tennessee; there, young mandolinist Burns was performing as half of a duo with his brother, while guitar player Haynes was part of a trio. Neither group won, but instead were brought together by station manager Lowell Blanchard to form one group, the swing-oriented String Dusters, to serve as the house band for the program *Mid-day Merry-Go-Round*. Blanchard also gave each member a stage name, and thus Homer and Jethro were born.

The boys became fast friends within the String Dusters, and began making up nonsensical songs off stage. Soon, the duo of Homer and Jethro began performing as comic relief while the remainder of the group took a break; gradually, their popularity with listeners grew, and after five years at WNOX, they broke off to go solo. Having developed their stage personas, which combined a humorous hayseed sensibility with ill-fitting yokel costumes, they joined the Kentucky-based program *Renfro Valley Barn Dance* in 1939, and again were a big hit with audiences. A string of appearances on both CBS and NBC programs soon followed, but their career went on hiatus in 1941 when both men were drafted to serve in World War II.

After the war ended, Homer and Jethro resumed their partnership, signing on with the Cincinnati, Ohio station WWLW's *Midwestern Hayride* from 1945 to 1947 while also recording some sides with the local King label. In 1949, they scored their first chart hit with "I Feel That Old Age Creeping On," and also signed on to tour with musical comedy genius Spike Jones. In addition, they earned a significant hit with "Baby, It's Cold Outside," which featured June Carter. In 1950, the duo joined the prestigious Chicago-based program *National Barn Dance*, and performed on the show each Saturday through 1958. They also appeared frequently on Don McNeil's *Breakfast Club*.

In the early 1950s, Homer and Jethro abandoned their hillbilly personas in favor of a more genteel look that often found them wearing suits; even their onstage repartee grew more sophisticated, although they remained musical parodists. In 1953, they released their biggest hit, "(How Much Is) That Hound Dog in the Window," as well as *Homer and Jethro Fracture Frank Loesser*, the first of almost three dozen albums they would generate between 1953 and 1969. The duo also toured constantly, graduating from fairs to nightclubs to the Las Vegas stage and television. In 1962, Homer and Jethro released *Playing It Straight*, a serious instrumental homage to their beloved swing music. A series of mid-Sixties TV and radio ads for Kellogg's Corn Flakes also brought the group considerable attention.

In 1970, Homer and Jethro joined forces with the latter's brother-in-law, Chet Atkins, to form the Nashville String Band. The trio recorded several LPs worth of material before Homer suffered a fatal heart attack on August 7, 1971. Jethro retreated from the music industry for a number of years following his partner's passing, but in the late 1970s, singer-songwriter Steve Goodman lured him out of retirement. At that point, Jethro Burns began a renaissance as an acclaimed jazz mandolinist, and issued a number of records before succumbing to cancer on February 4, 1989. —*Jason Ankeny*

★ **America's Song Butchers: The Weird World Of Homer & Jethro** / Feb. 18, 1997 / Razor & Tie ✦✦✦✦✦
America's Favorite Song Butchers: The Weird World of Homer and Jethro is the first comprehensive single-disc overview of the country comedy duo's career, featuring all of their biggest hits and best-known songs. In the process, it showcases not only the duo's sense of humor, but also their amazing instrumental virtuosity. Their dual talents meant that Homer & Jethro were never just another run-of-the-mill cornball comedy team—it meant that they were the defintiive comedic country duo, with instrumental talents that could run rings around their competitors. While some of the songs and jokes on *America's Favorite Song Butchers* have dated, the sheer musicality of the album remains awe-inspiring. —*Thom Owens*

Johnny Horton

b. Apr. 30, 1925, Los Angeles, CA, **d.** Nov. 5, 1960, Milano, TX
Vocals / Country Boogie, Nashville Sound/Countrypolitan, Honky Tonk, Rockabilly, Traditional Country
Johnny Horton was one of the best and most popular country singers of the late '50s, infusing honky tonk with an urgent rockabilly underpinning. His career may have been cut short by a fatal car crash in 1960, but his music reverberated throughout the next three decades.

Horton cut several independent singles in the first half of the '50s and was a regular on the Louisiana Hayride, but he made his first major impression in the spring of 1956, when "Honky Tonk Man," his first single for Columbia, reached the country Top 10. Wearing a large cowboy hat to hide his receding hairline, he became a popular concert attraction and racked up three more hit singles—"I'm a One-Woman Man," "I'm Coming Home," "The Woman I Need"—in the next year, yet the hits dried up as quickly as they arrived. Horton cut some rockabilly before bouncing back in the fall of 1958 with the Top Ten "All Grown Up." His comeback was sealed in early 1959, as "When It's Springtime in Alaska (It's Forty Below)" climbed to number one and its sequel, "The Battle of New Orleans," surpassed its success, spending weeks on the top of the pop and country charts. Following these successes, Horton concentrated solely on folky saga songs in the same vein—"Johnny Reb," "Sink the Bismarck" and "North to Alaska" all reached the Top 10 in 1959/1960, with the latter reaching number one.

On November 4, 1960, Johnny Horton died from complications sustained in a car crash. Although he died early in his career, he left behind a recorded legacy that proved quite influential. Artists like George Jones and Dwight Yoakam have covered his songs, and echoes of Horton's music can still be heard in honky tonk and country-rock music well into the '90s. —*Stephen Thomas Erlewine*

The Spectacular Johnny Horton / 1960 / Columbia/Legacy ✦✦✦
Horton's brief flurry of country-pop mega-stardom coincided with some of his less interesting music, as this 1960 album proves. Corny Americana became his meal ticket after "The Battle of New Orleans" (which leads off the disc), and more of the same follows on the gold-prospecting tales "Sam Magee" and "When It's Springtime in Alaska." Those songs are country-pop with a banjo for a whiff of (not quite genuine) authenticity. On several of the other tracks, he didn't bother with the banjo, leaving average or below-average country-pop balladry to remain. Yet he hadn't forgotten how to play and sing gutsy rockabilly cum honky tonk, as shown on the album's best cuts. His self-penned "The First Rain Headin' South" is certainly the best of the crop; the cover of "Cherokee Boogie," like Warren Smith's "Ubangi Stomp," flirts with imagery that will strike many as un-PC these days; and "Got the Bull by the Horns" and the cover of Hank Snow's "The Rocket" are respectable up-tempo numbers. Half a good album, then, and Horton wouldn't have a chance to resolve his conflicting directions, dying in the same year as the LP's release. The 2000 CD reissue adds three bonus tracks: the lame 1958 ballad "Counterfeit Love," the mild 1958 rockabilly number "All Grown Up," and a bizarre version of "The Battle of New Orleans" cut especially for the English market, in which the *rebels* flee from the *British* instead of vice versa. —*Richie Unterberger*

Johnny Horton's Greatest Hits / 1961 / Columbia ✦✦✦
Johnny Horton's Greatest Hits concentrates on the singer's historical story songs throwing in a handful of ballads and honky tonk numbers. It's not a bad listen—most of these songs were hits—but it doesn't accurately represent Horton's career, especially his hard country roots and his way with a ballad. —*Stephen Thomas Erlewine*

Rockin' Rollin' Johnny Horton / 1981 / Bear Family ✦✦✦✦✦
Although several of his hits are featured—including "Honky Tonk Man," "The Woman I Need," and "All Grown Up"—most of *Rockin' Rollin' Johnny Horton* is comprised of obscurities, culled from his early career. The album veers between is rockabilly experiments and honky tonk, and the entire CD is highly enjoyable compilation for fans of his harder-edged music, even though a handful of tracks haven't aged particularly well. —*Stephen Thomas Erlewine*

1956-1960 / 1991 / Bear Family ✦✦✦✦✦
Johnny Horton's complete recorded works for Columbia Records, as well as all of his demos, are collected on this four-disc box set. Although it certainly designed for collectors and die-hards, there is enough first-rate music on the set to make it a worthwhile investment for serious honky tonk fans. —*Stephen Thomas Erlewine*

★ **Honky Tonk Man: The Essential Johnny Horton 1956-1960** / 1996 / Columbia/Legacy ✦✦✦✦✦
This 36-track double-CD set, running just under an hour and a half, effectively chronicles Johnny Horton's Columbia Records career. The first disc, which is in mono, traces Horton's honky-tonk work of 1956-1957, starting with "Honky Tonk Man." Though lacking the crossover appeal of his later work at the time, this is the material on which his reputation stands today, with people like Dwight Yoakam resurrecting it. The end of the first disc and the beginning of the second (which is in stereo) present the stylistic fishing expedition of Horton's commercially unsuccessful middle period, as be goes looking for a bit. He finds it, of course, with the martial rhythms and historical theme of "The Battle of New Orleans," a chart-topping novelty that leads to a string of similar productions. By the end, in songs like "The Mansion You Stole," Horton seems headed toward the lush, string-filled Nashville Sound, though he died before it gained dominance. Along the way, all of Horton's Country chart singles and most of his pop chart singles are included, along with two tracks, previously unreleased in the U.S. Of course, the set could have been considerably longer (or, better yet, shaved by a few tracks and fit onto a single disc), but nothing essential is missing. —*William Ruhlmann*

David Houston

b. Dec. 9, 1938, Bossier City, LA, **d.** Nov. 30, 1993

Vocals, Guitar / Nashville Sound/Countrypolitan, Honky Tonk, Country-Pop, Traditional Country

Houston apparently came from good stock: his lineage includes Sam Houston and Gen. Robert E. Lee. Born and raised in Bossier City, Louisiana, Houston became a regular on the Louisiana Hayride as a teenager. Apparently his soaring tenor voice wasn't totally appreciated; he found trouble getting work in the music business, and ended up as an insurance underwriter. But record producer Billy Sherrill brought Houston into the fold when Epic Records was still a young label (the early '60s), and Houston brought the company its first real hit with "Mountain of Love." In 1966 he broke through to major status with "Almost Persuaded," which netted a pair of Grammy awards and brought pop recognition as well. A member of the Grand Ole Opry since 1971, he racked up 28 hit records over a decade, including duets with Tammy Wynette and Barbara Mandrell. *—Tom Roland*

● **The Best Of David Houston** / Oct. 19, 1999 / Collectors' Choice Music ✦✦✦✦✦

Ray Wylie Hubbard

b. Nov. 13, 1946, Soper, OK

Vocals / Singer/Songwriter, Progressive Country

A leading figure of the progressive country movement of the 1970s, singer/songwriter Ray Wylie Hubbard remains best known for authoring the perennial anthem "Up Against the Wall, Redneck Mother." Born November 13, 1946 in Soper, Oklahoma, Hubbard and his family relocated to Dallas during the mid-1950s; there he learned to play guitar, eventually forming a folk group with fellow aspiring musician Michael Martin Murphey. Befriended by the likes of Jerry Jeff Walker and Ramblin' Jack Elliott, Hubbard performed with several ensembles in the southwest while building a growing collection of songs.

In 1973 Walker recorded Hubbard's most famous composition, "Up Against the Wall, Redneck Mother," on his acclaimed *Viva Terlingua* LP. The success of the album guaranteed Hubbard instant cult status within progressive country circles. At much the same time he organized a new backing band, dubbed the Cowboy Twinkies. Considered by many the first cowpunk group, their regular set lists included everything from Merle Haggard songs to a show-stopping cover of Led Zeppelin's "Communication Breakdown".

Released in 1975, their debut album, *Ray Wylie Hubbard and the Cowboy Twinkies.* suffered from label-imposed over-production and fared poorly; Hubbard did not resurface prior to 1978, when he issued *Off the Wall.*The following year Hubbard began working with the Lost Gonzo Band, previously Walker's supporting group; they recorded the live LP *Caught in the Act.* By 1984 Hubbard was backed by the Bugs Henderson Trio, which featured guitarist Henderson, bassist Bobby Chitwood and drummer Ron Thompson; with them he cut another live effort, *Something About the Night.* Hubbard did not record for another eight years, instead building a small but loyal following through constant touring, finally issuing a series of albums in the '90s. *—Jason Ankeny*

Off the Wall / 1978 / Lone Star ✦✦✦✦

Loco Gringo's Lament / 1994 / Dejadisc ✦✦✦✦✦

With *Loco Gringo's Lament,* this Texas troubadour plants himself firmly in the thick of life and love, delivering a deeply introspective and honest album that rivals his best work. Poignant songs chronicling the self-discovery that comes as a result of living hard and surviving are presented with solid instrumental backing that adds to their power and emotional impact. "After the Fall" is a masterpiece of song, a journey of struggle and enlightenment sung over a prominent choppy guitar vamp, while "Wanna Rock and Roll" rocks hard underneath Hubbard's brilliant telling of a dark and murderous tale. "I've Seen That Old Highway" is a spirited observation in Texas country style, and the title track is a song for musicians, outlaws, and people of the road—a mournful saga of the life. *—Jack Leaver*

Lost Train of Thought / 1995 / Dejadisc ✦✦✦✦✦

● **Dangerous Spirits** / Aug. 5, 1997 / Philo ✦✦✦✦✦

Crusades of the Restless Nights / Jul. 20, 1999 / Philo ✦✦✦✦✦

"I wanted to be a folk singer," Ray Wylie Hubbard told annotator Geoffrey Himes of his early goal in the liner notes of his second Philo album, *Crusades of the Restless Knights,* and the record bore out the renewal of that ambition. Although the arrangements of Hubbard's tunes usually found several pickers playing stringed instruments (acoustic and electric guitars, steel guitar, bass, mandolin, Dobro), the simple song structures and restrained lyrics gave them the feel of old folk songs. Even when he waxed verbose, on "Conversation With the Devil," Hubbard was employing the talking blues form that dated back to Woody Guthrie and beyond. More typically, he would sing an entire song about a woman getting dressed up for a night on the town ("Red Dress"), each verse describing another article of clothing or makeup. There was a lot deliberately left out of such songs, but the suggestions of meaning were filled in by Hubbard's world-weary persona and rough, south-Texas-accented singing voice. It was music for anyone who liked his peers, especially Jimmie Dale Gilmore and the name-checked Townes Van Zandt, using a similar language and attitude. The strain of '70s-era Texas singer/songwriters turned out to be amazingly rich, and even this late-breaking legend lived up to his reputation after surviving to sobriety. *—William Ruhlmann*

Ferlin Husky

b. Dec. 3, 1927, Flat River, MO

Vocals, Guitar / Nashville Sound/Countrypolitan, Bakersfield Sound, Honky Tonk, Country Comedy, Country-Pop, Traditional Country

Ferlin Husky had three separate careers. Of the three, he's best-known as a country-pop crooner of the late '50s, but he was also known as a honky tonk singer called Terry Preston and a country comic named Simon Crum. Following several sides under the Preston name, Husky came to prominence singing on Jean Shepard's number one "A Dear John Letter," yet he didn't have a hit of his own until 1955, when "I Feel Better All Over (More Than Anywhere's Else)" reached the country Top Ten. Around the same time, he started releasing records as Simon Crum. Ferlin racked up a string of hits during the late '50s, reaching a peak in 1957, when "Gone" spent ten weeks at number one and reached number four pop. That same year, he began an acting career with a spot on the *Kraft TV Theatre* television program and the film *Mr. Rock & Roll.* In 1958, Crum had a number two hit with "Country Music Is Here to Stay." In 1960, the gospel song "Wings of a Dove" gave Husky his biggest hit, spending 10 weeks at the top of the country charts. Despite its massive success, Husky couldn't sustain a presence on the country charts during the '60s. He remained a popular concert attraction, but he had no Top Ten hits between "Wings of a Dove" and "Once," which hit number four in 1966. A year after "Once," Ferlin had his final Top Ten hit with "Just for You." In the late '60s, Husky incorporated the slicker, heavily-produced sounds of contemporary country-pop into his music, which resulted in his brief career revitalization. Husky kept racking up minor hits until 1975. In 1977, he had heart surgery and briefly retired from performing. During the '80s and '90s, he performed regularly at the Grand Ole Opry, as well as Christy Lane's Theater in Branson, MO. *—Stephen Thomas Erlewine*

Capitol Collectors Series / 1989 / Capitol ✦✦✦✦✦

Although *Capitol Collector's Series* is a fairly comprehensive overview of Ferlin Husky's hit-making peak, it's missing a couple of essential items, most notably hit first hit, "A Dear John Letter." It concentrates on his country-pop hits, picking up the great majority of his hits, including "Wings of A Dove," "Gone," "A Fallen Star," "Just for You," and 16 other songs. *—Stephen Thomas Erlewine*

Greatest Hits / 1990 / Curb ✦✦✦✦

Although it's brief and cheaply-produced, *Greatest Hits* contains many of the essential Husky tracks, including "A Dear John Letter," and which isn't on *Capitol Collector's Series,* "Gone," and "Wings Of A Dove." For the budget-conscious it isn't a bad purchase, although *Capitol Collector's Series* offers a greater selection for an equivalent price. *—Stephen Thomas Erlewine*

● **Vintage** / 1996 / Capitol ✦✦✦✦✦

Vintage contains nearly all of the essential items from Ferlin Husky's peak years at Capitol Records. Featuring almost 20 tracks—including the hits "Wings of a Dove," "A Dear John Letter," "Once," "Stormy Weather" and "Gone," which is included in both in its hit single version and the original version released under the name "Terry Preston"—it's the closest thing to a definitive retrospective yet assembled. *—Thom Owens*

Feelin' Better All Over / Apr. 18, 2000 / Jasmine ✦✦✦✦

Alan Jackson

b. Oct. 17, 1958, Newnan, GA

Vocals, Guitar / Neo-Traditionalist Country, New Traditionalist, Contemporary Country

Through the '80s and '90s, Alan Jackson quietly worked to become one of the most popular modern honky tonkers of his era. Music was just a hobby for Jackson until he moved to Nashville, working on sessions and his own songwriting to get by. After he recorded a demo tape, Arista signed him and released his debut album, 1990's *Here in the Real World.* The album produced three chart-toppers including "I'd Love You All Over Again" and "Someday." His second album *Don't Rock the Jukebox* went double-platinum within its first year of release. In 1992, he released *A Lot About Livin' (And a Little About Love),* his most successful release to date. The album spawned five major hits, including the number ones "Love's Got a Hold on You," "She's Got the Rhythm (And I Got the Blues)," and "Chattahoochee." His follow-up *Who I Am* spawned an incredible four number one singles—"Summertime Blues," "Gone Country," "Livin' on Love," and "I Don't Even Know Your Name." *The Greatest Hits Collection,* released in 1995, went triple-platinum within a year of its release. *Everything I Love* surfaced in 1996, followed two years later by *High Mileage.* *—Sandra Brennan*

Don't Rock the Jukebox / 1991 / Arista ✦✦✦

The album art is really ugly, but the music isn't—"Don't Rock the Jukebox," "Someday," "Love's Got a Hold on You," and "Dallas" all hit the top of the singles charts. And "Midnight in Montgomery," which details a ghostly encounter with Hank Williams's spirit, became a video classic. *—Brian Mansfield*

☆ **A Lot About Livin' (& a Little 'bout Love)** / 1992 / Arista ✦✦✦✦✦

By this third album—when many artists start to run out of ideas—Jackson sounds like he's just starting to hit his stride with songs like "Tonight I Climbed the Wall," "She's Got the Rhythm (And I Got the Blues)" (co-written with Randy Travis), and "Chattahoochee," one of country's great summer singles. He also continues a proud tradition of country artists covering blues tunes by singing "Mercury Blues" by a minor Bay Area bluesman named K.C. Douglas. *—Brian Mansfield*

Who I Am / 1994 / Arista ✦✦✦✦✦

The huge singles aren't as readily apparent here, but Jackson begins to reveal more of himself with his album. "Gone Country" is a subtly brilliant jab at people who discover country music only when there's money to be made. The joke is that Jackson leads the album with Eddie Cochran's teenage-angst anthem "Summertime Blues." Jackson pulls out chesnuts from the catalogues of Con Hunley and the Kendalls, and writes "Job Description" to explain to his daughter why daddy's never home. In a time when even artists had trouble telling all the young hat acts apart, a personal statement like *Who I Am* was possibly the smartest move Jackson could have made. *—Brian Mansfield*

★ **Greatest Hits Collection** / Nov. 21, 1995 / Arista ✦✦✦✦✦

As the title indicates, all of Alan Jackson's greatest hits—including the number one singles "Chattahoochee," "She's Got the Rhythm (And I Got the Blues)," "I'd Love You All Over Again," and "Don't Rock the Jukebox"—are collected on this single disc, making it the perfect introduction to the singer. *—Stephen Thomas Erlewine*

Everything I Love / Oct. 29, 1996 / Arista ✦✦✦✦

High Mileage / Sep. 1, 1998 / Arista ✦✦✦✦

Under the Influence / Oct. 12, 1999 / Arista ♦♦♦♦

When Somebody Loves You / Nov. 7, 2000 / Arista ♦♦♦

Stonewall Jackson

b. Nov. 6, 1932, Tabor City, NC

Vocals, Guitar / Nashville Sound/Countrypolitan, Honky Tonk, Traditional Country

A descendant of the famed Confederate general, Stonewall Jackson was one of the more popular country music stars of the early '60s, scoring a handful of Top Ten country hits and becoming a fixture at the *Grand Ole Opry.* The first entertainer to join the *Opry* without a recording contract, Stonewall finally signed with Columbia Records, and cut his first record, "Don't Be Angry," in early 1957. The follow-up, Jackson's cover of George Jones' "Life to Go," became the singer's first major hit, peaking at number two in early 1959. It was followed by "Waterloo," which became his first number one hit, spending five weeks at the top of the country charts and hitting number four on the pop charts. Jackson then had a string of Top 40 hits that was highlighted by "Why I'm Walkin'," "A Wound Time Can't Erase" and "Loeona." His second number one hit, "B.J. the D.J.," arrived in early 1964. During the latter half of the '60s, he reached the upper reaches of the Top 40 less frequently, scoring only one Top Ten hit—1967's "Stamp Out Loneliness"—during the last five years of the decade. By 1970, he wasn't even hitting the Top 40. He bounced back briefly in 1971, when he covered Lobo's "Me and You and a Dog Named Boo." In 1973, he had his last hit with "Herman Schwartz," which reached number 41. *—Sandra Brennan*

● **American Originals** / 1989 / Columbia ♦♦♦♦♦

A re-packaging of many of Jackson's best-known songs includes the great "Don't Be Angry," "A Wound Time Can't Erase," and "Smoke Along the Tracks," the latter revived by Dwight Yoakam. For some unfathomable reason, "I Washed My Hands in Muddy Water" is missing. These kinds of omissions were standard place in this half-hearted oldies series. *—Michael McCall*

Sonny James (Jimmy Loden)

b. May 1, 1929, Hackleburg, AL

Vocals, Guitar / Nashville Sound/Countrypolitan, Pop, Country-Pop

Sonny James, the Southern Gentleman, used the popular Nashville sound of the '60s to countrify pop hits of the past into a form accessible to many, broadening country music's appeal across the nation. James even moved over to the pop charts for a time in the late '50s, but found the secret of his success by the time he returned to the country. During the late '60s, he scored an incredible five-year run of number-one singles which locked up the top spot for a combined 45 weeks during the late '60s. James' first single, "That's Me Without You," hit the Country Top Ten in early 1953, but it was three years before "For Rent (One Empty Heart)" became his second big hit. His biggest hit, "Young Love," spent nine weeks at number one during 1956-57, and crossed over to top the pop charts also. Beginning in 1957, James began to focus his attention on the popular charts. "First Date, First Kiss, First Love" made the Top 25, but no follow-up placed as high. Several of his failures had still managed to go Top Ten on the Country charts, so James returned to country with a vengeance in 1964. "You're the Only World I Know" hit number one Country late that year, and spent four weeks atop the chart. That began one of the greatest tears country music has ever known: 21 of his next 25 singles hit number one (and the other four were near-misses either two or three). Sonny James completely dominated the chart from 1964 to 1972, though only several singles crossed over for modest placements on the popular charts. Even after James' number one streak ended in January 1972, he continued to place high on the charts. *—John Bush*

● **Young Love: The Classic Hits** / Aug. 19, 1997 / Razor & Tie ♦♦♦♦♦

Young Love: The Classic Hits is a definitive 21-track collection that contains all of Sonny James' big hits from the late '50s and '60s—"Young Love," "First Date, First Kiss, First Love," "Uh-Huh-Mm," "Born to Be With You," "Only the Lonely," "Running Bear," "You're the Only World I Know," "I'll Never Find Another You," "Empty Arms," "Bright Lights, Big City"—plus a number of lesser-known singles and album tracks that are as good as the hits. *—Stephen Thomas Erlewine*

Waylon Jennings

b. Jun. 15, 1937, Littlefield, TX

Vocals, Guitar / Outlaw Country, Country-Folk, Progressive Country, Traditional Country

If any one performer personified the outlaw country movement of the '70s, it was Waylon Jennings. Though he had been a professional musician since the late '50s, it wasn't until the '70s that Waylon, with his imposing baritione and stripped-down, updated honky tonk, became a superstar. Jennings rejected the conventions of Nashville, refusing to record with the industry's legions of studio musicians and insisting that his music never resemble the string-laden, pop-inflected sounds that were coming out of Nashville in the '60s and '70s. Many artists, including Willie Nelson and Kris Kristofferson, followed Waylon's anti-Nashville stance and eventually the whole "outlaw" movement—so-named because of the artists' ragged, maverick image and their independence from Nashville—became one of the most significant country forces of the '70s, helping the genre adhere to its hardcore honky tonk roots. Jennings didn't write many songs, but his music—which combined the grittiest aspects of honky tonk with a rock & roll rhythm and attitude, making the music spare, direct and edgy—defined hardcore country, and it influenced countless musicians, including members of the new-traditionalist and alternative country subgenres of the '80s. *—Stephen Thomas Erlewine*

Folk Country / 1966 / Razor & Tie ♦♦♦♦

If the title of Waylon Jennings' full-blown debut is a little misleading, it is true that *Folk Country* finds him leaning on both and folk and country, creating a pretty terrific blend that may not be the full-blown culmination of Waylon's sound, but certainly hints at where he's going. The single "Stop the World and Let Me Off" indicates what the record is like; fairly mainstream in its own way (at least circa 1963), it is a country song, perhaps with some folk tinges. Much of the record is ever so slightly dated, but that's part of its charm. Compared to other debuts of the time, *Folk Country* is quite strong indeed. *—Stephen Thomas Erlewine*

Love of the Common People / 1967 / Buddha ♦♦♦♦

Love of the Common People is where Waylon Jennings began to come into his own, delivering country, folk, pop, and rock in a distinct blend. To a certain extent, he's still searching here, overpowering on Beatles covers but effective on the title track. There's a certain tendency for country albums of this era to be uneven, and if that's the case on *Love of the Common People,* it isn't because of bad material, but because Jennings is searching the entire time, testing things out, finding that some things work and others don't. It may not be a perfect album, but there are enough remarkable moments to make it nearly essential. *—Stephen Thomas Erlewine*

☆ **The Taker/Tulsa** / 1971 / Mobile Fidelity ♦♦♦♦♦

The Taker/Tulsa essentially began the progressive country and outlaw movements of the early '70s. The record represents the discovery of Kris Kristofferson by Waylon Jennings; though it isn't entirely a repertoire album, most of the songs on the album were written by Kristofferson, who worked outside of the conventions of Nashville. The result is one of Jennings' first major statements. Although there are a couple of weak spots on the record, there's no denying that it helped spark a movement that revolutionized the country music industry. *—Thom Owens*

Ladies Love Outlaws / 1972 / RCA ♦♦♦

★ **Honky Tonk Heroes** / 1973 / Buddha ♦♦♦♦♦

When Waylon Jennings hooked up with songwriter Billy Joe Shaver, he found the perfect author for his obsessions, his fascinations, and his very image. Waylon had always been looking, perhaps unintentionally, for a common ground between country and rock, and Shaver's songs—sketching an outlaw stance with near defiance and borrowing rock attitude to create the hardest country tunes imaginable—were perfect. On his previous album, Waylon had sung that "ladies love outlaws," but now he found the music that would soon be called outlaw country, a defiant, ballsy blend of mythmaking and truth-telling. Shaver never had a better voice for his songs, and Jennings never had better songs for his style. *Honky Tonk Heroes* arrived at a crucial moment, a time when true honky tonk was fading, so only a dose of rock & roll could save it. And, no matter how much rock attitude is here, this is pure country in its stance and attitude—yet *Honky Tonk Heroes'* very defiance makes it a perfect discovery album for listeners who never thought they would like country music. And the songs! Shaver earned his stripes here, with songs that were emotional, funny, and clever, utterly bringing the mythic outlaw ethic to life. "Black Rose," "You Asked Me To," and "Honky Tonk Heroes" remain among the greatest things Waylon ever cut, and every other song here matches them. Few country albums have ever been this consistent, and few records, from any genre, have been as consistently compelling. A wonderful album—one that's hard to tire of. *—Stephen Thomas Erlewine*

The Ramblin' Man / 1974 / Buddha ♦♦♦♦♦

If you look at the cover of *The Ramblin' Man,* you would think that Waylon Jennings had been a ramblin' man, riding the top of the charts, for years, maybe decades. He looks worn out, whether it's on the close-up on the cover, or the back-cover shot of him drunkenly playing solitaire. In truth, it would be another album before he hit the top of the country charts and before outlaw country became hip. Still, this is the record where it all came home. If he had created a sketch of outlaw on *Honky Tonk Heroes,* he perfected the marketable version of it here, making it a little slicker, a little more commercial, and a whole lot more unstoppable. If the songs aren't the equal of *Honky Tonk Heroes* or even *This Time, The Ramblin' Man* has a wilder sound and a greater diversity of songs that make it seem more unruly than its immediate predecessor and more blatantly outlaw. This contains, after all, his first flat-out rock cover, with a good take on the Allman Brothers' "Midnight Rider," plus songs that play into the image of what an outlaw country singer is. There are moments of reflection, yet even those feed into the outlaw picture. Too bad many of the album tracks wind up being agreeable filler instead of knockouts. There aren't any bad cuts, and the entire thing holds together quite well, but it doesn't add up to a moment of trancedence the way *Honky Tonk Heroes* or its successor would. Still, with "I'm a Ramblin' Man," "Rainy Day Woman," and the heartbreaking "Amanda" on its side, plus highlights like "Oklahoma Sunshine," this is a first-rate Waylon Jennings record. [The 1999 Buddha reissue contains three bonus tracks.] *—Stephen Thomas Erlewine*

This Time / 1974 / Buddha ♦♦♦♦

This Time appeared just as outlaw hit its stride, thanks in large part to the excellent *Honky Tonk Heroes.* If this record isn't its equal, it's still pretty wonderful all the same. Part of the record's flaw is its heavy reliance on Willie Nelson—actually, not just on Willie, but on *Phases and Stages,* which is the source of no less than four of this record's six songs. Granted, these are great songs, and Waylon's versions are hard to fault, but they nevertheless give the record a slightly recycled feeling. Fortunately, these songs are surrounded by excellent material, such as the number one single "This Time." Overall, *This Time* is fairly muted and deliberate, surprising for an album coming on the heels of the defiant *Honky Tonk Heroes.* Even the songs that swagger, like Billy Joe Shaver's "Slow Rollin' Low," are laid-back, and the whole thing is fairly reflective (appropriate, if it uses a divorce album as its template). It's not that the monochromatic makes it a lesser affair than its predecessor, yet the whole thing does feel a bit reserved and not quite as overpowering as a sequel to *Honky Tonk Heroes* should be. Still, it's a first-rate record—perhaps not a classic, but a subdued, understated album unlike anything in his catalog. [The 1999 Buddha reissue contained five bonus tracks featuring Waylon supported by the Crickets, running through (mostly) highlights from Buddy Holly's catalog. Though incongruous with *This Time,* these are highly entertaining cuts, packing more immediacy than the album itself.] *—Stephen Thomas Erlewine*

☆ **Dreaming My Dreams** / 1975 / DCC ♦♦♦♦♦

Dreaming My Dreams was Waylon Jennings' first number one record, and deservedly so. He had created outlaw country with *Honky Tonk Heroes,* and then delivered two further albums that subtly developed its themes, even if they weren't quite as consistent. *Dreaming My Dreams* maintains the consistency, increasing the country quotient while subtly making it more sentimental than before. This is an unabashedly romantic album, not just in its love songs, but in its tributes to Waylon's heroes. "Are You Sure Hank Done It This Way" opens and "Bob Wills Is Still the King" closes the album—making Jennings an heir apparent to their legacies. Between those two extremes, Waylon appropriates Jimmy Rodgers ("Waymore's Blues"), covers Roger Miller ("I've Been a Long Time Leaving [But I'll Be a Long Time Gone]"), ups the outlaw ante ("Let's All Help the Cowboys [Sing the Blues]"), and writes and records as many sentimental tunes as possible without seeming like a sissy. At times, the emotional undertow may seem a bit much, yet the whole thing adds up as Waylon's best album since *Honky Tonk Heroes*, and one of the few of his prime outlaw period to deliver from beginning to end. *—Stephen Thomas Erlewine*

☆ **Waylon Live** / 1976 / Buddha ✦✦✦✦✦
As one of the great live albums, *Waylon Live* is nearly flawless, a snapshot of Waylon Jennings at the height of his powers and, not so coincidentally, at the peak of the outlaw movement. At this time, he was popular and powerful, creating a mythos out of his performances and songs, delivering first-rate material both on record and in concert. This is where it all came together, since a set list limited Waylon to his best songs, whether his own hits or carefully selected covers. This is especially true of 1999's Buddha reissue that included nine bonus tracks (all put into the middle of the record), restoring *Waylon Live* to the double-LP running time it was designed to have. With the restoration of this section—containing such perennials as "Lovin' Her Was Easier (Than Anything I'll Ever Do Again)," "Lonesome, On'ry and Mean," "The Taker," "Look Into My Teardrops," and "Never Been to Spain"—the record really becomes a definitive statement on outlaw country and how it bent the rules, borrowing from country and rock and twisting them into something thoroughly distinctive. On top of it all, Waylon and his band give a bracing, terrific performance, investing these songs with more passion than they had previously seen on record. It winds up as one of the great country records and one of the great live albums, capturing a movement at its peak and transcending it. *—Stephen Thomas Erlewine*

Ol' Waylon / 1977 / DCC ✦✦✦
Ol' Waylon was released when Waylon Jennings had become a superstar. Outlaw was still popular, perhaps at its peak, but it was no longer the movement that it had been just a few short years before. As if offering proof, Waylon cut his most formulaic album since the early '60s, a record that satisfied the demands of outlaw without ever stretching them. Since this was recorded at a near-peak of not only his popularity but his power, there are some great moments on *Ol' Waylon*, particularly on the lead single "Luckenbach, Texas (Back to the Basics of Love)," a wonderful reminiscence of times back, "If You See Me Getting Smaller," and "I Think I'm Gonna Kill Myself." The rest of the record is a little formulaic and reliant on covers, sometimes enjoyably (including a version of Little Richard's "Lucille"), sometimes not as much ("Sweet Caroline" was never suited for Waylon's style). Overall, *Ol' Waylon* is pretty enjoyable, but it winds up feeling a little hollow, as if Jennings was trying to give the audience what it wanted. There are enough good moments to make it worthwhile, not just to the dedicated but for some casual fans enamored of the outlaw years, but it's still an album that gets by more on its style than substance. *—Stephen Thomas Erlewine*

Waylon & Willie / 1978 / Buddha ✦✦✦

☆ **Greatest Hits** / 1979 / RCA ✦✦✦✦✦
Jennings's career dates back to his days as a Cricket in the '50s, but it wasn't until the '70s that he began to define a particular hard-edged subgenre of country music with his rock shuffles and his deep, sardonic voice on songs like "Lonesome, On'ry and Mean" and "Luckenbach, Texas," the best of which are included here. (A second volume, released in 1984, is also recommended.) *—William Ruhlmann*

WW 2 / 1982 / Buddha ✦✦

Will the Wolf Survive / 1985 / MCA ✦✦✦

★ **Only Daddy That'll Walk the Line: The RCA Years** / 1993 / RCA ✦✦✦✦✦
You wouldn't think that two CDs with 40 cuts could adequately summarize a career as important as his, but quite the opposite is true. If anything, this box set highlights more than you might want to know of his creative rise, peak, and artistic decline. The first disc, covering the years 1965-1974, will be as a revelation to anyone unfamiliar with his luminous early work. On cuts like "Stop the World (And Let Me Off)" and "Just to Satisfy You," his struggle to free himself of the suffocating Nashville sound is palpable. On "Lonesome, On'ry and Mean" and "I'm a Ramblin' Man," his success at doing the same is vicariously liberating. Disc two picks up in the midst of the revolution ("Are You Sure Hank Done It This Way—," "Bob Wills Is Still the King") and carries on through the Napoleonic expansion ("Luckenbach, Texas," a Top 40 pop hit). But the last quarter of the set is really quite depressing, as the performances become more and more self-consciously outlaw. Call "Theme From the Dukes of Hazzard" Waterloo, if you will. The one gem from the 1980s, Jessi Colter's lovely "Storms Never Last," can be taken more than one way. *—Dan Cooper*

Right for the Time / May 21, 1996 / Buddha ✦✦✦

The Essential Waylon Jennings / Jun. 18, 1996 / RCA ✦✦✦✦✦
The Essential Waylon Jennings may not contain every hit Jennings every recorded or every fine album track he cut, but—as the title implies—it does have the bare-bone essentials ("Only Daddy That'll Walk the Line," "Are You Sure Hank Done It This Way," and several others), making it the best single-disc retrospective assembled on the groundbreaking country singer. *—Thom Owens*

☆ **The Journey: Destiny's Child** / 1999 / Bear Family ✦✦✦✦✦

☆ **The Journey: Six Strings Away** / Dec. 14, 1999 / Bear Family ✦✦✦✦✦

Johnnie & Jack

f. 1938, Nashville, TN, **db.** 1963
Group / Close Harmony, Traditional Country, Traditional Bluegrass
Johnnie and Jack mined the familiar turf of singing brother duos in the late '40s through the late '50s with a few distinct twists. For openers, they weren't blood brothers, just brothers in law. Secondly, they brought a new rhythmic strain to country music, both in their use of Latin beats and the unfettered drive of their combo, the Tennessee Mountain Boys. And of all the singing duos, they were the most inclined to stretch the boundaries of their sound, from bluegrass to sacred to amazing covers of R&B tunes with none of their country soul diluted in the bargain. But for all their melding of outside influences, few artists—even in the mid-'50s—were as wholesale committed to sounding as "country" as they were. Whatever they played, sang, or wrote, it *always* sounded like Johnnie & Jack.

Johnnie & Jack's first hit, "Poison Love," arrived in 1951. What they had done to crack the charts was to take their straight bluegrass harmonies and wed them to a distinct rhumba beat. The combination proved a winner, one that the duo would return to on several recordings. Within a couple of years, their sound would change again, as they countrified a batch of R&B recordings; this meant they handled the onslaught of rock & roll better than most country artists while keeping the roots of their sound intact. By the late '50s, Johnnie & Jack's records were being mainstreamed into the Nashville Sound, with the Anita Kerr Singers, saxophones and full rhythm sections burying their plaintive vocals beneath layers of pop sugar coating. Dissatisfied, the duo let their contract run out and signed with Decca Records in 1961. Their new company changed the spelling of their name to 'Johnny & Jack,' and while they didn't have many hits, they had all the road work it could handle. It all came to a tragic end, however, when Jack Anglin died in a car crash on his way to a memorial service for Patsy Cline, Hawkshaw Hawkins and Cowboy Copas. *—Cub Koda*

● **All the Best of Johnnie and Jack** / 1970 / RCA Victor ✦✦✦✦✦
All the Best of Johnnie and Jack is a double LP that contains 24 of Johnnie & Jack's biggest hits for RCA Records, which were all recorded during the '50s and early '60s. The hit singles "(Oh Baby Mine) I Get So Lonely," "Poison Love," "Cryin' Heart Blues," "Three Ways of Knowing," "Goodnight, Sweetheart, Goodnight," and "Stop the World (And Let Me Off)" are all included, as are several other, lesser-known gems, making it an excellent, concise retrospective. It's the perfect introduction to one of the finest, and most underappreciated, groups in all of bluegrass and it is a shame that it isn't available on compact disc. *—Thom Owens*

And the Tennessee Mountain Boys / 1992 / Bear Family ✦✦✦✦✦
Multi-disc box set of everything this country duo ever recorded. From their early bluegrass and gospel sides (some featuring Kitty Wells) to their rhumba beat hits of the '50s, it's all here. With heartfelt singing and playing, great songwriting and much good humor in abundance, all box set retrospectives should be this much fun to listen to. Highly recommended. *—Cub Koda*

At KWKH / 1994 / Bear Family ✦✦✦✦✦

George Jones

b. Sep. 12, 1931, Saratoga, TX
Vocals, Guitar / Country Gospel, Nashville Sound/Countrypolitan, Honky Tonk, Country-Pop, Traditional Country
George Jones is generally acknowledged as the finest vocalist in the recorded history of country music, a hardcore honky tonker that also had a nuanced ballad style. Only Eddy Arnold had more Top Ten hits than Jones, and George always stayed closer to hardcore country.

Producer Pappy Daily signed Jones to Starday in 1953. Two years later, "Why, Baby, Why," became his first hit, followed by two Top Ten hits in 1956; that year, he also recorded a handful of rockabilly singles as Thumper Jones. Pappy moved George to Mercury in 1957 and over the next few years, he regularly landed near the top of the country charts, highlighted by the number ones "White Lightning" (1958) and "Tender Years" (1960). Daily became a staff producer for United Artists in 1962 and Jones followed; "She Thinks I Still Care, " his first single for the label, went to number one. George and Pappy moved to Musicor in 1965. Between 1965 and 1970, Jones recorded almost 300 songs for Musicor, including 17 Top Ten hits highlighted by "Love Bug," "Walk Through This World with Me," and "A Good Year for the Roses." In 1969, Jones married singer Tammy Wynette. Two years later, he joined her label, Epic, where he worked with Billy Sherrill, the producer behind Tammy's hit albums. Jones entered a period of great success, charting regularly as a solo artist and duet partner with Wynette during the early '70s. Tammy divorced George in 1975 (they continued to perform together), and his career spiraled downward. During the next five years, he rarely hit the Top Ten solo hits and he became notorious for drunken rampages and disappearances. In 1979 alone, he missed 54 shows, illustrating why he called "No-Show Jones."

Jones' had a comeback in 1980 when "He Stopped Loving Her Today" started a new streak of Top Ten hits that ran through 1986. Following 1988's *One Woman Man*, Jones signed to MCA. Although his MCA records were well-reviewed, they didn't have much chart success. Jones moved to Elektra/Asylum in 1998, releasing *Cold Hard Truth* in 1999. *—Stephen Thomas Erlewine*

George Jones Salutes Hank Williams / 1960 / Mercury ✦✦✦✦
George Jones Salutes Hank Williams was recorded at Mercury Records, toward the beginning of Jones' career. At this stage, George still sounded similar to Hank Williams, but he had begun to incorporate much of Williams' vocal techniques into a distinctive vocal style of his own. If Jones had recorded these songs while still at Starday, they wouldn't be as exciting as they are now—since he had moved beyond mimicking into his own style, he's able to invest Williams' songs with grit and passion, instead of just copying Hank. It's an affectionate, entertaining tribute, featuring some of the greatest songs ("Cold Cold Heart," "Hey Good Lookin'," "Half As Much," "Jambalaya," "Why Don't You Love Me," "Honky Tonkin'," "Settin' the Woods on Fire") in country music. (The 1984 reissue is slightly shorter than the original issue and features liner notes by Elvis Costello). *—Stephen Thomas Erlewine*

George Jones Sings Bob Wills / 1962 / Razor & Tie ✦✦✦

Homecoming in Heaven / 1962 / Razor & Tie ✦✦

My Favorites of Hank Williams / 1962 / Razor & Tie ✦✦✦

The New Favorites of George Jones / 1962 / Liberty ✦✦✦
The New Favorites of George Jones, the Possum's first album for United Artists, is a mixed

bag that is highly indicative of the crossroads country music faced in the early '60s. Stylistically, *New Favorites* is all over the place, as it tries to appeal to not only Jones' hardcore honky tonk audience, but also to country-pop fans and those listener that had been seduced by the burgeoning rock & roll audience. So, honky tonk weepers like "She Once Lived Here" and "She Thinks I Still Care" sit next to up-tempo country-pop cuts like "What Am I Worth" and "Imitation of Love," and that only scratches the surface of what's here. There's also folk ballads ("Open Pit Mine"), crossover attempts ("Poor Little Rich Boy," "Running Bear"), the requisite novelties ("Best Guitar Picker"), and the ridiculous "White Lightnin'" rewrite, "Root Beer." Even the dated material like the novelties and crossovers are enjoyable, but Jones is at his best when he's singing honky tonk or country-pop. Still, the wide range of material on *New Favorites* does prove that neither artists, producers, or labels knew how to retain the splintering country audience of the '50s. *—Stephen Thomas Erlewine*

The Sings the Hits of His Country Cousins / 1962 / Razor & Tie ✦✦✦

George Jones Sings Like the Dickens! / 1964 / Razor & Tie ✦✦✦
Given George Jones's love for novelty songs, it isn't surprising that he recorded a tribute album to the king of country novelties, Little Jimmy Dickens. What is surprising is his approach. On *George Jones Sings Like the Dickens!* Jones bypasses all of Dickens's biggest hits, choosing to concentrate on personal favorites, which happen to be songs that Dickens interpreted, not ones that he wrote (only two of the 12 songs were co-written by Dickens). Jones realizes that although Dickens was famous for his novelties, he was a first-rate balladeer and he patterns his own album according to his idol's strengths. George gives a fine performance, but it's a bit too laidback to make a lasting impression. There are handful of gems (particularly "We Could," "It Scares Me Half to Death," "Making the Rounds," and "I've Just Got to See You Once More") scattered throughout *Sings Like the Dickens!* and the album is never anything less than enjoyable, even though nothing on the record approaches the transcendent. ["It Scares Me Half to Death" and "Take Me as I Am (Or Let Me Go)" also appear on *The Race Is On*.] *—Stephen Thomas Erlewine*

The Race Is On / 1965 / Razor & Tie ✦✦✦
The title track to *The Race Is On* is one of George Jones's biggest hits. With its gallopping beat and clever, funny lyrics, the single gives the impression that the rest of the record is a return to Jones's honky tonk roots. Although there are several uptempo numbers, *The Race Is On* is dominated by ballads, like the majority of his UA albums. But *The Race Is On* boasts a stronger, more varied set of songs than most of his '60s albums, ranging from ballads like "They'll Never Take Her Love from Me," and the Western Swing of "Time Changes Everything," and the skittering honky tonk of "Don't Let the Stars Get in Your Eyes." There's a couple of weak moments—ironically, one is "She's Mine," which was co-written by George—but the album remains one of his strongest from the mid-'60s. ["It Scares Me Half to Death" and "Take Me As I Am (Or Let Me Go)" also appear on *Sings Like the Dickens!* and "Time Changes Everything" appears on *Sings Bob Wills*.] *—Stephen Thomas Erlewine*

Sings the Songs of Dallas Frazier / 1968 / Musicor ✦✦✦✦✦
Since his beginnings at Musicor, George Jones covered countless songs by Dallas Frazier—Frazier's songs would frequently occupy more than half of an album—so an entire album devoted to his songwriting comes as no surprise. And while the big production numbers, complete with back-up by the Jordanaires, may put off some country purists, the album serves as a true testament to both the singer and the songwriter. In light of the label's constant recycling and repackaging of material, the most surprising thing about this record is that none of the songs have appeared on any previous album. *—Chris Woodstra*

☆ **George Jones with Love** / 1971 / Musicor ✦✦✦✦✦
By 1970, George Jones's stay at Musicor had been marked by a glut of sloppy releases that would continually repackage and repeat material into different thematically based "concept" albums; Initially it would seem that *George Jones With Love*, with its all-love-based-songs lineup, would fall into this disposable category. One listen, however, shows this to be an exception to the rule. Beginning with the wonderful "A Good Year For the Roses" (one of his all-time greatest performances) George tackles affairs of the heart from all directions—from joy and excitement of newfound love to the warmth of a settled relationship to the pain and despair of separation and its aftermath—he's clearly focused on each song, pouring the proper emotion and passion into each performance. It still may not be a "concept album" by rock & roll standards but it does serve as not only a high point for Jones' Musicor period but also as one of his greatest, most consistent albums. *—Chris Woodstra*

The Great Songs of Leon Payne / 1971 / Musicor ✦✦✦✦✦
One of many songbook albums that George Jones recorded while at Musicor Records, *The Great Songs of Leon Payne* is one of the finest minor gems in the Possum's catalog. Though Payne's reputation as a terrific honky tonk songwriter was well-known among country music fans, he only had a handful of hits, which were often recorded by other artists. Granted, the biggest of those were Hank Williams' versions of "Lost Highway" and "They'll Never Take Her Love From Me" as well as his own "I Love You Because," but the depth of Payne's songwriting is not well-known to many casual country fans. George Jones' tribute album remedies that fact. Apart from "They'll Never Take Her Love From Me" and George's hit single "Things Have Gone to Pieces," these songs are all rather obscure and there's not a bad one in the bunch. From ballads like "Blue Side of Lonesome" to uptempo honky tonkers like "Brothers of A Bottle," all of the cuts on *The Great Songs of Leon Payne* are first-rate and Jones brings each of them to life. It's a forgotten album in George's catalog—and Leon Payne's reputation has faded somewhat in the decades following his death—but that doesn't change the fact that *The Great Songs of Leon Payne* is one of his best records of the '60s. *—Stephen Thomas Erlewine*

We Go Together / 1971 / Epic ✦✦✦

George Jones (We Can Make It) / 1972 / Epic ✦✦✦

Me and the First Lady / 1972 / Epic ✦✦✦
The second chapter in the George and Tammy saga still finds the couple pretty happy, settling into a mostly imaginary domestic life. Not all is well though, as told in "A Lovely Place to Cry" and "The Great Divide," which contemplate fading love and the possibility of divorce. The two continue to hold on, still in love, and even go as far as to recreate their wedding ceremony in the album closer, "The Ceremony," seemingly to reaffirm their vows. *—Chris Woodstra*

We Love to Sing About Jesus / 1972 / Razor & Tie ✦✦

The Grand Tour / 1974 / Razor & Tie ✦✦✦
The Grand Tour is arguably the peak achievement of George Jones and Billy Sherrill in the early '70s. By the time the album was recorded, Sherrill had moved Jones' distinctive ballad styles into a more commercial setting, complete with strings, layered guitars and pianos, and even sound effects. Though the pair had recorded several classic singles in the two years preceding *The Grand Tour*, the album was the culmination of this lavish production style. There's very few weak spots on the record, and the best material—the epic title track, the heart-tugging "Once You've Had the Best" and the wonderful "She Told Me So"—are genuine showstoppers, demonstrating not only Jones' rich voice, but Sherrill's grandly textured production. And it's not just the ballads that cut deep, but novelties like "The Weatherman" and the blazing anti-gossip tirade "Our Private Life" make a lasting impression. *The Grand Tour* is a consistently engaging, always entertaining album and one of his best records of the '70s. *—Stephen Thomas Erlewine*

My Very Special Guests / 1979 / Epic ✦✦✦

Double Trouble / 1980 / Razor & Tie ✦

I Am What I Am / 1980 / Epic/Legacy ✦✦✦✦
I Am What I Am announced that George Jones had officially returned to form artistically and, in the process, became his biggest hit album ever. It's easy to see why—the production is commercial without being slick, the songs are balanced between aching ballads and restrained honky tonk numbers, and George gives a nuanced, moving performance. "He Stopped Loving Her Today," "I'm Not Ready Yet," and "If Drinkin' Don't Kill Me (Her Memory Will)" were the hits, but the remaining seven album tracks are exceptionally strong, without a weak track in the bunch. It's mature country, both in the laid-back approach and subject matter, but that doesn't mean it's dull—like the best country music, these are lived-in songs that are simple, direct and emotionally powerful, even with the smooth production. *I Am What I Am* is the sound of George Jones at his peak and his the highlight of his later years. Four bonus tracks—"Am I Losing Your Memory Or Mine—" "The Ghost Of Another Man," "It's All In My Mind" and "I'm A Fool For Loving Her"—give the 20th anniversary version of the album an added richness. *—Stephen Thomas Erlewine*

Together Again / 1980 / Razor & Tie ✦✦✦

Still the Same Ole Me / 1981 / Epic ✦✦✦

★ **Anniversary: Ten Years of Hits** / 1982 / Epic ✦✦✦✦✦
This covers the first ten years of Jones's two-decade association with Epic Records and, more importantly, record-producer Billy Sherrill. Owing much to Sherrill's knack for locating quality material, the hits range from amusing ("Nothing Ever Hurt Me," "Her Name Is...") to morbid ("He Stopped Loving Her Today") to classic ("The Grand Tour," "A Picture of Me Without You"). Best cuts include "Bartender's Blues," "The Door," and "Still Doin' Time." *—Tom Roland*

Don't Stop the Music / 1987 / Ace ✦✦✦✦
The most extensive look at Jones' early Starday and Mercury recordings available, *Don't Stop the Music* is a perfect compliment to Rhino's collection. The disc's 22 tracks document the formative years (1954-61) where he grew from a Hank Williams sound-alike to one of the most distinctive voices in country music. Essential listening worth seeking out. Import only. *—Chris Woodstra*

Live at Dancetown U.S.A. / 1987 / Ace ✦✦✦✦
There have been very few live recordings of George Jones, particularly of his early years, which makes *Live at Dance Town USA* so valuable. Recorded in June of 1965, the compact disc features 26 tracks—including nine songs performed by Jones' supporting vocalist Don Adams—that capture Jones running through his biggest hits, plus a couple of left-field covers like "Bony Moronie" and "Jole Blon." Jones is wired and energetic, breathing fire into the songs; one of the biggest joys of the entire disc is his between-song patter, such as when he tells the audience that he's taking a "liquor mission" halfway through the set. Not only is the music superb—on this date, the Jones Boys featured steel guitarist Buddy Emmons and Cajun fiddler Rufus Thibodeaux—but it illustrates exactly what a honky tonk concert was like in the '60s. For hardcore George Jones fans, it's an essential addition, one that's revelatory and highly entertaining. *—Stephen Thomas Erlewine*

One Woman Man / Feb. 1989 / Epic ✦✦✦

★ **The Best of George Jones 1955-1967** / 1991 / Rhino ✦✦✦✦✦
The 18-track *The Best of 1955-1967* is a good overview of George Jones' early career, containing most of the necessary hits from his first decade or so of hits. It's skewed toward his Mercury hits, featuring everything from "Why Baby Why" to "Aching Breaking Heart," picking up "Just One More," "The Window Up Above," and "Tender Years" along the way. Five wisely-chosen United Artists tracks are featured, as are four Musicor tracks. It doesn't have every hit from 1955-67, but *The Best Of* does contain every truly necessary item Jones recorded during that time. *—Stephen Thomas Erlewine*

Bradley Barn Sessions / 1994 / MCA ✦✦✦

☆ **Cup of Loneliness: The Mercury Years** / 1994 / Mercury ✦✦✦✦✦
Jones was still developing his style on the earliest tracks on *Cup of Loneliness*, but this is the music that established him as one of the great vocalists of the 20th century, country or otherwise. *Cup of Loneliness* gathers together most of his Mercury recordings, as well as several highlights from his time at Starday. These recordings feature Jones at his purest—no strings, no backing vocals, only pure honky-tonk. At the beginning of the double-disc set, traces of Hank Williams can be detected in Jones' vocals, but by the end of the first disc, Jones had become one of the most distinctive and popular country vocalists. His classic ballad style

doesn't begin to develop until the end of the second disc. Mercury released two different versions of *Cup of Loneliness*—a standard two-disc set in a jewel box and a collector's edition that features extra songs; naturally, most fans will want the songs on the collector's edition, simply because they were recorded at a peak in Jones' career. *—Stephen Thomas Erlewine*

★ **The Essential George Jones: The Spirit of Country** / Nov. 1, 1994 / Epic/Legacy ♦♦♦♦♦

George Jone & Gene Pitney / 1995 / Bear Family ♦♦♦♦
When George Jones left United Artists to join Musicor in 1965, it was decided to start off with a duet recording session with teen idol (and labelmate) Gene Pitney. The session resulted in two duet albums—*George Jones and Gene Pitney* and *It's Country Time Again*—as well as a solo country album by Pitney, *The Country Side of Gene Pitney*. Bear Family's *George Jones & Gene Pitney* collects the 31 songs recorded during these sessions. For a seemingly unlikely pairing, the two complemented each other well, with Pitney proving himself not only a fan of the genre but also a competent country singer as well. Though only two hits came from the albums ("Love Bug" and the brilliant "Thing Have Gone to Pieces"—the latter absent from this collection for some reason), this disc captures some truly inspired moments by both artists. In light of the scarcity of good CD collections of George Jones' Musicor recordings, this disc is essential to anyone who wants a complete picture of Jones' career. *—Chris Woodstra*

Vintage Collections Series / Jan. 23, 1996 / Capitol ♦♦♦♦
Vintage collects nearly all of George Jones and Melba Montgomery's duets for United Artists. These songs, originally released on *What's In Our Hearts* and *Bluegrass Hootenanny*, illustrate how well-suited the pair was for each other—there may be a couple of weak songs, but there are no weak performances. In fact, *Vintage* makes a good argument that Montgomery was Jones' best duet partner. *—Stephen Thomas Erlewine*

I Lived to Tell It All / Aug. 13, 1996 / MCA ♦♦♦

She Thinks I Still Care: The George Jones Collection (The United Artists Years) / Apr. 22, 1997 / Razor & Tie ♦♦♦♦♦
She Thinks I Still Care: The George Jones Collection (The United Artists Years) is a comprehensive double-disc retrospective of Jones' four years with UA, featuring 40 songs, including 21 country Top 40 hits. His time with United Artists was essentially a transitional period, as he moved from the hardcore honky tonker of his Starday-Mercury years to the country crooner of his Musicor era, which means there are several cuts on the set that fall somewhere between the two extremes. It also means that there is a handful of mediocre cuts on the collection, but some of George's absolute best is here—not only familiar hits like "The Race is On," "She Thinks I Still Care," "A Girl I Used To Know," "Your Heart Turned Left (And I Was On the Right)," "You Comb Her Hair" and his remarkable bluegrass duets with Melba Montgomery, but also lesser-known gems like "Open Pit Mine," "My Tears Are Overdue" and "Wrong Number." Although his United Artists recordings are on the whole his most uneven work—the Musicor albums may have been inconsistent, but they were usually interesting—he made a number of terrific records for the label, and *She Thinks I Still Care* is easily the best way to hear them. The set is more thorough, represenative and listenable than *All-Time Greatest Hits*, and the original albums contain so much duplication that they're frustrating for anyone but diehard fans. *—Stephen Thomas Erlewine*

Nothing Ever Hurt Me/A Picture of Me (Without You) / Oct. 20, 1998 / Koch ♦♦♦♦♦
On the back cover of Koch's two-fer reissue of *A Picture of Me (Without You)/Nothing Ever Hurt Me (Half as Bad as Losing You)*, George Jones is quoted as saying: "I am so excited about the release of two of my all time favorite albums. I hope you enjoy every song contained on this special release." This is one of the rare times that the Possum's self-evaluation is entirely accurate, since these are two of Jones' very best records, albums that may still follow the pattern of singles-n-filler, but are of higher quality than many of his other albums, regardless of the era they were released. True, if you scan the track listing, only a few titles will pop out—certainly the title tracks, but also "The Man Worth Lovin' You" and definitely "What My Woman Can't Do"—but what makes these records remarkable is that the rest of the albums are comprised of material that is firmly solid. These are not classics, but they're good songs all the same and producer Billy Sherrill gives them a uniform, appealing production that makes them gel into something that's greater than the sum of their parts. And, when paired on this two-fer, they seem all the stronger—they complement each other, with their professional production, fine songwriting, and passionate performances from Jones. So, even if this doesn't have a lot of classics in the traditional sense, it's essential listening for the dedicated George fan all the same. *—Stephen Thomas Erlewine*

The George Jones Collection / Jun. 1, 1999 / MCA ♦♦♦

The Cold Hard Truth / Jun. 22, 1999 / Elektra ♦♦♦♦

Memories of Us/Battle / Jul. 20, 1999 / Koch ♦♦♦♦
So paired because they appear to be reminiscences and elegies to George Jones' legendary failed marriage to Tammy Wynette, this two-fer of *The Battle* and *Memories of Us* reveals that the records aren't all that thematic, no matter what the *Rolling Stone Record Guide* may claim. If anything, these two records are more formulaic than the two records comprising the two-fer of *A Picture of Me (Without You)/Nothing Ever Hurt Me (Half as Bad as Losing You)*, which isn't necessarily a bad thing—it just is. Even if these two records don't just have their share of filler, they have more than their share of novelties, which Jones always loved, and that gives the records the impression of being slightly off-kilter, even if those tunes are pretty good. Even if these two albums don't gel the way the records on Koch's other 1998 two-fer do, each record has not only its share of hits, it has its share of underappreciated songs, resulting in a two-fer that may not be as essential as its counterpart, but is still quite good. *—Stephen Thomas Erlewine*

Wynonna Judd (Christina Ciminella)

b. May 30, 1964, Ashland, KY
Vocals, Guitar / Neo-Traditionalist Country, Contemporary Country
Wynonna Judd launched a solo career after the Judds disbanded in 1992. On her own, Wynonna has been more eclectic—drawing not only from country, but rock, pop, and folk—than she was as part of the duo that made her famous. With mother Naomi, she began performing in Kentucky in the early '80s. They soon went to Nashville, where they landed a recording contract in 1984. The Judds became the most popular duo in country music history during the '80s. In 1991, Naomi was forced to retire after she was diagnosed with a chronic liver disease. Instead of retiring with her mother, Wynonna launched a solo career in 1992 with her eponymous solo album. *Wynonna* featured three consecutive number one singles—"She Is His Only Need," "I Saw the Light," "No One Else On Earth"—and went triple platinum. The following year, she delivered her second album, *Tell Me Why*, which went platinum and spawned four Top Ten songs—"Tell Me Why," "A Bad Goodbye" (a duet with Clint Black), "Girls with Guitars," and "Rock Bottom." In early 1996, she released her third album, *Revelations*. It went platinum within four months of its release. *—Stephen Thomas Erlewine*

Wynonna / 1992 / Curb/MCA ♦♦♦
Daughter Judd stakes out her own territory. It's probably safe to say that she had more in her than most people guessed. From the tender "She Is His Only Need" to the Southern rock 'n' soul of "No One Else on Earth," Wynonna sings with a smoldering sensuality that pulsed beneath the surface of the duo's best records—even "Live with Jesus" sounds sexy. After a few more albums like this, folks may not even remember The Judds. It also includes "I Saw the Light" and "My Strongest Weakness." *—Brian Mansfield*

Tell Me Why / May 11, 1993 / Curb/MCA ♦♦♦♦♦
Wynonna's second album, *Tell Me Why*, is a more confident and diverse collection than her debut. Drawing from sources as varied as gospel, folk, and blues-rock, Wynonna doesn't necessarily deliver a pure country album, but her blend of roots genres does qualify as a cleverly constructed contemporary country record. The selection of material is first-rate, but what makes *Tell Me Why* her best solo effort is how she ties all of the songs together with her assured—and surprisingly subtle—vocals. *—Thom Owens*

Revelations / 1996 / Curb/MCA ♦♦♦♦
Wynonna has no problem with the spotlight—or, as the tabloids regularly reveal, with opening up her private life for all to poke through and ponder. For all of her cultivating of celebrity, her albums continue to turn down the lights and focus on the softer glow of emotional verities her albums. *Revelations* is another worthy solo effort by the younger member of the Judds, the mother-daughter duo through which she first found massive fame. Often somber, and just as often right on the money, she casts a blue tint to several reflective songs that examine spirituality (without sermons) and the quiet discoveries that come with mature relationships. Ballads like "Don't Look Back," "Love By Grace" and "My Angel Is Here"—all album highlights—prove how sympathetic her rich, expressive voice can be when applied to a well-written, sensitive lyric. As in the past, she's equally convincing on uptempo, R&B-infused strutters, such Delbert McClinton's "Somebody to Love You" or the gospel rave-up, "Dance! Shout!" It's a mystery as to why she would include her version of "Free Bird," which previously was released as part of a Lynyrd Skynyrd tribute album. (Maybe someone should tell her that those people who yelled it out during encores were kidding.) Otherwise, *Revelations* is just that—a revealing next step by a country music star who understands the power of subtlety in an age that tends to prefer over-statement. *—Michael McCall*

● **Collection** / Apr. 8, 1997 / MCA ♦♦♦♦♦
Collection conains all of the highlights and big hits from Wynonna's three albums (*Wynonna, Tell Me Why, Revelations*), including "Tell Me Why," "Rock Bottom," "Girls With Guitars," and the number one singles "She Is His Only Need," "I Saw the Light," and "No One Else On Earth." *—Thom Owens*

The Other Side / Oct. 21, 1997 / MCA ♦♦♦

New Day Dawning / Feb. 1, 2000 / MCA ♦♦♦♦
Southern gospel and soul, rockers, and ballads all grace Wynonna Judd's fifth release as a solo artist and her first as co-producer. One of the most recognizable voices in country music, the depth and range of her voice can be heard from the first track, the rhythmic "Going Nowhere," to the last, the soulful "I Can't Wait to Meet You." Fans will be delighted to hear Judd put her rock-influenced country-pop spin on Joni Mitchell's "Help Me." And of course, what's a good Wynonna album without her signature growl— As a bonus for Judd fans, *New Day Dawning* includes a special second CD, *Big Bang Boogie*, available in limited quantities with four new tracks from Wynonna and Naomi. The Judds reunion CD, however brief, is an exciting extra to the already electrifying *New Day....* *—Maria Konicki*

The Judds

f. 1979, **db.** 1991
Group / Contemporary Country
Naomi Judd and her daughter Wynonna were one of the most popular country acts of the 1980s, eventually becoming the most successful duo in the genre's history. With Wynonna's strong bluesy style and Naomi's exquisite harmonies, the Judds presented an arresting image that was both home-spun and city slick. During the eight years they performed together, they had many hits, including 14 number one singles. The Judds arrived in Nashville in 1979, and in late 1983, they released their first single "Had a Dream (For the Heart)" and reached the country the Top 20. With "Mama He's Crazy" in early 1984, they began a streak of eight consecutive number one hits. "Why Not Me," their second number one, won the Country Music Association's Single of the Year award for 1984. Between 1985 and 1990, the duo issued hit after hit; their albums proved equally successful, with *Rockin' With the Rhythm* (1985), *Heartland* (1987), *Greatest Hits* (1988) and *Love Can Build a Bridge* (1990) all reaching platinum-selling status. At the turn of the decade, however, Naomi had contracted chronic, acute hepatitis, an incurable, life-threatening disease which led the duo to their disbandment in 1991. Early in 1992, Wynonna released her eponymous debut album, which became a multi-platinum success. *—Sandra Brennan*

The Judds / 1983 / RCA ♦♦♦♦♦
Though it lacked a strong set of songs, the Judds' eponymous debut album established that the vocals of Wynonna and Naomi played off of each other beautifully, and songs like the hit

"Had A Dream (For the Heart)" provide the foundation for their later hit singles. The best moments on *The Judds* have been compiled on their numerous hit compliation, yet it remains a pleasant listen for most dedicated fans. *—Thom Owens*

Why Not Me— / 1984 / RCA ✦✦✦✦✦
On their second album, Wynonna establishes herself as a fearsome and sultry belter. The production is built around an essentially acoustic base. *—Mark A. Humphrey*

Rockin' with the Rhythm / 1985 / RCA ✦✦✦
On the third album, "Have Mercy" and the title track (among others) kick with a funky glee that makes this the most plainly joyous Judds album. *—Mark A. Humphrey*

Heartland / 1987 / RCA ✦✦✦

★ **The Greatest Hits** / 1988 / RCA ✦✦✦✦✦
These singles document the rise of Naomi and Wynonna Judd, a mother-daughter team who seemed, at times, to be singing for every bank teller, teacher, and struggling single mama in every small town in America. Songs like "Why Not Me," "Mama He's Crazy," and "Girl's Night Out" were more than country hits; they're like validation for every woman brave enough to believe in innocence even when she knows better. *—Dan Cooper*

River of Time / 1989 / RCA ✦✦✦
River of Time earned the Judds two more number one singles, "Young Love" and "Let Me Tell You About Love." *—Jason Ankeny*

Love Can Build a Bridge / Sep. 11, 1990 / RCA ✦✦✦

The Judds Collection 1983-1990 / 1992 / RCA ✦✦✦✦✦
The three-disc box set *The Judds Collection 1983-1990* is an example of a wasted opportunity. Instead of providing a thorough, exhaustive overview of the duo's immensely popular career, the set simply combines their first two *Greatest Hits* albums with a disc of demos, which are only of interest to hardcore fans, who will already have all of the music on the first two discs. That leaves the set as being useful to no one—casual fans are better served by the individual collections, while dedicated fans are being ripped off by being forced to purchase two discs they already have if they want to get the rarities, which aren't that revelatory in the first place. *—Thom Owens*

☆ **The Essential Judds** / Oct. 1995 / RCA ✦✦✦✦✦
The Essential Judds contains a great majority of the duo's biggest hits, as well as a wisely-chosen selection of rarities, making it a definitive compilation. *—Stephen Thomas Erlewine*

Greatest Hits, Vol. 2 / Nov. 19, 1996 / RCA ✦✦✦✦✦
While songs like "Young Love" and "Love Can Build a Bridge" continue to emphasize The Judds' warm and fuzzy middle-American sensibilities, several other hits—"Let Me Tell You About Love," for instance—showcase the side of Wynonna that admires Bonnie Raitt. *—Dan Cooper*

Kentucky Headhunters

f. 1986, Edmonton, KY
Group / Southern Rock, Contemporary Country
The Kentucky Headhunters marked a change of pace from the new traditionalists and country-pop that dominated the country charts at the end of the '80s. Instead of conforming to Nashville traditions, the Headhunters created a hybrid of honky tonk, blues and southern rock that appealed to both rock and country artists as well as music critics. The group only recorded a few albums, but during their time together, they were one of the most popular fringe country acts of the era. After close to 20 years playing in bands, the members of the Headhunters began recording for a major label in 1989 with the album *Pickin' on Nashville.* The single "Dumas Walker" reached number 15 in the spring of 1990, followed by the group's biggest hit, the number six "Oh, Lonesome Me." After several members left to form the Brothers Phelps, the remaining Headhunters released *Rave On* in 1993. WIth *Rave On,* the Kentucky Headhunters began refashioning themselves as a bluesy southern rock act and followed that direction on their subsequent album, *That'll Work.* In 1996, Doug Phelps returned to the group to take over lead vocal duties; in 1997, the band issued *Stompin' Grounds.* *—Sandra Brennan*

Pickin' on Nashville / 1989 / Mercury ✦✦✦✦✦
As their album title suggests, The Headhunters aren't entirely comfortable with the country tag, which is appropriate when you hear their guitar-heavy, rambunctious music. The vocals have that twang, but these good old boys are often closer to Lynyrd Skynyrd than they are to Merle Haggard, and all the better for it. *—William Ruhlmann*

Electric Barnyard / 1991 / Mercury ✦✦✦
The Kentucky HeadHunters aren't a remarkable country mutation, just a top-notch Southern rock band with a sense of humor. "The Ballad of Davy Crockett" is the kind of clever novelty that won't work twice; "Big Mexican Dinner" is a novelty that doesn't even work the first time. Once again, the country and bluegrass covers—"Only Daddy That'll Walk the Line," "With Body and Soul"—are the highlights, and most of the originals (the Beatlesque shuffle "Always Makin' Love" aside) are offbeat, adequate filler. *—Brian Mansfield*

Rave On! / 1993 / Mercury ✦✦

● **The Best of the Kentucky Headhunters: Still Pickin'** / 1994 / Mercury ✦✦✦✦✦
The Best of the Kentucky Headhunters is a first-rate compilation of the highlights from the group's first three albums. Although their debut remains a worthwhile purchase, this collection salvages the good songs from the band's two uneven followups to their exciting breakthrough first album. *—Thom Owens*

Stompin' Grounds / Apr. 29, 1997 / BNA ✦✦✦

Songs from the Grass String Ranch / Jun. 13, 2000 / Audium Entertainment ✦✦✦

Sammy Kershaw

b. Feb. 24, 1958, Kaplan, LA
Vocals / Neo-Traditionalist Country, New Traditionalist, Contemporary Country
Sammy Kershaw's blend of honky tonk and southern-rock made him a popular recording artist in the early '90s. The third cousin of legendary Cajun fiddler Doug Kershaw, Sammy debuted professionally at age 12 with J.B. Perry, a popular local musician. With Perry, Kershaw toured the South, playing clubs and opening for several major acts; he later joined Blackwater, which played the club circuit in the South and West. He also cut some independent solo singles. Eventually, songwriter Barry Jackson suggested that Kershaw send a demo and picture to Nashville. In 1991, he did a showcase there and was signed to Mercury Records. His first album, *Don't Go Near the Water,* contained the song "Cadillac Style," which peaked at number three and spent five months on the charts. Kershaw's next two singles—"Don't Go Near the Water" and "Yard Sale"—reached the Top 20 and the fourth single, "Anywhere But Here," peaked at number ten. *Haunted Heart,* his second album, was released in 1993. The first single, "She Don't Know She's Beautiful," became his first number one hit. *—Sandra Brennan*

Don't Go Near the Water / 1991 / Mercury ✦✦✦
"Cadillace Style," Kershaw's first single, started him off strong. This album, which made his Jones influence explicit with a cover of "What Am I Worth," also produced the hits "Don't Go Near the Water," "Yard Sale" and "Anywhere but Here." *—Brian Mansfield*

Cadillac Style / 1992 / Mercury ✦✦

Haunted Heart / 1993 / Mercury ✦✦✦✦✦
The more you know about Sammy Kershaw, the more there is to like about his albums. Though Kershaw doesn't write his songs, he makes some of the most autobiographical albums to come from Music Row. If you know that Kershaw quit performing for a year and a half when it threatened his marriage, "Still Lovin' You" assumes greater significance. Even a song as strange as "Queen of My Double Wide Trailer" makes more sense when you learn that Kershaw still owns a trailer in Louisiana, "in case things don't work out." Sure, he still sounded a lot like George Jones with a South Louisiana accent. But *Haunted Heart* showed that Kershaw was coming into his own as a vocalist. Just as important, he was choosing songs that set him apart from the pack. If some of those were as offbeat as "Double Wide" and "Neon Leon," well, that's just part of what made him distinctive. *—Brian Mansfield*

Feelin' Good Train / 1994 / Mercury ✦✦✦

● **Hits: Chapter 1** / Sep. 12, 1995 / Mercury Nashville ✦✦✦✦✦
Sammy Kershaw had only been recording for four years when he released *The Hits, Chapter 1,* but its appearance didn't seem premature. During that time, he had racked up a considerable number of Top Ten country hits, including the number ones "National Working Woman's Holiday" and "She Don't Know She's Beautiful." Both of those songs are included, as well as eight others that prove why he was one of the most popular country singers in the early '90s. *—Stephen Thomas Erlewine*

Politics, Religion and Her / 1996 / Mercury ✦✦

Labor of Love / Nov. 4, 1997 / Mercury ✦✦✦

Maybe Not Tonight / Apr. 13, 1999 / Mercury ✦✦✦
This record is pure Nashville by the numbers. Not a displeasing affair, but certainly not inspired either. Covering all bases, there is a romantic duet with Lorrie Morgan (the title track), the requisite honky-tonk rocker ("Louisiana Hot Sauce"), a re-vamped cover of the old Leo Sayer hit, "More Than I Can Say," and plenty of heartbreak songs thrown in for the sensitive crowd. Present throughout *Maybe Not Tonight* are catchy melodies and tasteful playing, but in Nashville, where many of the best studio musicians and writers reside, those elements are a given and the difference between a good album and a great one is a wide bridge to cross. *—Steve Kurutz*

Coverin' the Hits / Jun. 20, 2000 / Mercury ✦✦✦
The title pretty much explains it all on Sammy Kershaw's *Coverin' the Hits.* This is not a collection of his hit singles, it's a compilation of covers Kershaw cut throughout the '90s, including songs from his own albums and selections from tribute albums. That it all sounds like it came from the same session says as much about Kershaw's consistency as it does for his taste. Consider this: the closest he comes to straight country here is "Third Rate Romance," the 1975 classic from country-rockers Amazing Rhythm Aces. It's either that or Chuck Berry's "Memphis, Tennessee," which many a country singer, including Buck Owens, has tackled over the years. No, this reveals that Kershaw is as much a fan of '70s soft rock as he is of country, which is to his benefit. He never treats this material with contempt, he has fun with it, and delivers sincere, effective versions of "More Than I Can Say," "Chevy Van," "Fire and Rain," "Angie," "I Got a Name," and "Little Bit More," plus a respectable version of Lynyrd Skynyrd's rocking "I Know a Little." That might not make *Coverin' the Hits* a major item per se in Kershaw's catalog, but it sure is a lot of fun. *—Stephen Thomas Erlewine*

Hal Ketchum

b. Apr. 9, 1953, Greenwich, NY
Vocals, Drums / Neo-Traditionalist Country, Contemporary Country
Singer/songwriter/drummer Hal Ketchum was raised in the Adirondack Mountains in upstate New York. He began drumming at age 15 and soon joined an R&B trio. At age 17, Ketchum moved to Florida and then to Texas, where he quickly got involved playing at a local dance hall and began to hone his songwriting skills. He went to Nashville in 1986 to write songs, and three years later released his debut album, *Threadbare Alibis;* soon after, Ketchum signed with Forerunner Music, which eventually led to a record contract with Curb. He released his first Curb album, *Past the Point of Rescue,* in 1991. "Small Town Saturday Night, " the first single, reached number two and the second single, "I Know where Love Lies," reached number 13. In 1992, he scored two more hits and released his third album, *Sure, Love,* which produced three Top 20 hits, including the number two "Hearts Are Gonna Roll." The following year, Ketchum joined the Grand Ole Opry. In 1994, he released his fourth al-

bum, *Every Little Word,* which, while not quite as successful as its predecessors, still produced two Top 40 hits. In 1995, he released *Greatest Hits;* a collection of vintage 1977 sessions titled *Hal Yes* was due in 1998 but postponed until the following year, when it was finally released as *Awaiting Redemption.* —*Sandra Brennan*

Threadbare Alibis / 1988 / Watermelon ♦♦♦
Recorded as Hal Michael Ketchum in Austin before he moved to Nashville, it's folkier and less musically focused than his country recordings. But the thoughtfulness that informs his best work is in place, as is the willingness to take chances with his songwriting. —*Michael McCall*

Past the Point of Rescue / 1991 / Curb ♦♦♦♦♦
Hal Ketchum writes simple, sometimes moving songs about relationships and/or life's dilemmas, and communicates them in an attractive, unadorned vocal package. But although many of these numbers espouse country themes, Ketchum's delivery, as well as the arrangements and sensibility, lean toward easy-listening pop and light folk. Certainly every country artist isn't a honky-tonking, tough-talking, drinker whining about lost love, but Ketchum comes perilously close on "Past The Point Of Rescue" or his cover of The Vogues' "Five O'Clock World" to the super-smooth "Nashville Sound" of days past. —*Ron Wynn*

Sure Love / 1992 / Curb ♦♦♦
Ketchum was surprised by the success of his major-label debut, and he followed up with a slicker, peppier album. The melodies are stout, and he's at his best on the working-class tributes "Mama Knows the Highway" and "Daddy's Oldsmobile." —*Michael McCall*

Every Little Word / 1994 / Curb ♦♦♦♦♦
Ketchum reconciles the thoughtfulness of his folkie heart with the verve of modern country, tapping into the directness and earthiness that ties them together. His most country album, it's his most consistent. —*Michael McCall*

● **Greatest Hits** / Mar. 26, 1996 / Curb ♦♦♦♦♦
Although it doesn't collect every worthwhile cut Ketchum recorded, *Greatest Hits* has the great majority of his big hits, making it a good introduction to the vocalist. —*Stephen Thomas Erlewine*

I Saw the Light / May 19, 1998 / Curb ♦♦♦

Awaiting Redemption / May 18, 1999 / Curb ♦♦♦

Claude King

b. Feb. 5, 1933, Shreveport, LA, **d.** 1983
Vocals / Nashville Sound/Countrypolitan, Country-Pop, Traditional Country
Singer/songwriter and actor Claude King will best be remembered for his one big crossover hit, "Wolverton Mountain," the song that attracted him international attention and made him a bona fide country star. King recorded his first singles in 1952, but none of them were released. In 1961, King signed to Columbia and released "Big River, Big Man." The song became a Top Ten country hit, as well as a minor pop hit. The follow-up "The Comancheros," also made it to the Top Ten in 1962. King then released "Wolverton Mountain," which spent nine weeks at the top of the country charts and peaked at number six on the pop charts. Two more hits—the Top Ten "The Burning of Atlanta" and the number 11 "I've Got the World By the Tail"—followed that year, and he and his band, the Nashville Knights, became hot tickets. Through 1964, he continued his string of successes with singles like "Hey Lucille!," "Sam Hill," and "Building a Bridge," but his hits became more sporadic in the latter half of the '60s. —*Sandra Brennan*

American Originals / 1990 / Columbia ♦♦♦♦♦
Though he had been recording for since the late '40s, Claude King didn't rise to national attention until the early '60s, when Columbia Records positioned the vocalist as the heir to the departed Johnny Horton's legacy of story-songs. *American Originals* contains all of King's country-pop hits, including "Wolverton Mountain," "Big River, Big Man," "The Comancheros," "The Burning of Atlanta," and "All for the Love of a Girl," among many others, making it the perfect retrospective of his hit-making heyday. —*Thom Owens*

More Than Climbing That Mountain / 1994 / Bear Family ♦♦♦♦♦
Wolverton Mountain is a five-disc box set containing all of Claude King's recordings for Columbia Records, from 1961's "Big River, Big Man" to 1972's "He Ain't Country." In addition to all of the released masters and hit singles, the box also features a number of unreleased songs, rarities, alternate takes and King's early recordings for Gotham Records. Certainly, a box set of this size is only of interest to historians and hardcore fans—there is simply too much marginal material for casual fans—but for those devoted listeners, *Wolverton Mountain* is the definitive retrospective. —*Thom Owens*

● **16 Original Classics** / Aug. 24, 1999 / Collectables ♦♦♦♦

Sid King

f. 1952, Denton, TX, **db.** 1958
Group / Country Boogie, Rockabilly, Western Swing
One of the first White rock & rollers to record for a major label (Columbia), Sid King was also one of the first young Southern musicians to travel the line from western swing to rockabilly in the mid-'50s. He never quite jumped into rock head over his heels, though; nor did he ever break through to a national audience. The only vintage King available on CD domestically is an interesting, but not wholly representative, set of radio broadcasts from the mid-'50s that fall closer to hillbilly than rockabilly; his Columbia recordings have been reissued in Germany on Bear Family's *Gonna Shake This Shack Tonight.* —*Richie Unterberger*

● **Gonna Shake This Shack Tonight** / 1991 / Bear Family ♦♦♦♦♦
Sid King and the Five Strings were one of the weirdest and most enjoyable of the pre-rock & roll hillbilly country bands. Not only did King and the Five Strings play country boogie and nervy honky tonk, they tore their way through R&B and blues, performing all their songs with a wild, backwoods humor. *Gonna Shake This Shack Tonight* contains all 29 songs the group recorded between 1953 and 1959. Primarily, this is music for collectors—though there is a lot of really weird, wonderful proto-rock & roll here, you have to have a taste for the obscure to truly appreciate it. For those that have a taste for the obscure, the music on *Gonna Shake This Shack Tonight* is a true treasure. —*Thom Owens*

Rockin' on the Radio / Mar. 19, 1996 / Schoolkids ♦♦♦
Sixteen tracks broadcast live on Texas radio stations in 1954 and 1955. With muffled (though listenable) fidelity, this is more of a historical document than a sampling of King at his best; it also finds him and his group much more grounded in hot Western swing (complete with steel guitar) than rock & roll. As an archival glimpse of the first stirrings of hillbilly turning into rockabilly, though, it's not bad. The group runs through the country boogies and ballads with zesty, unpolished flair, and edge close to rockabilly with their covers of "That's All Right," "Maybellene," and "Flip, Flop & Fly." —*Richie Unterberger*

Kris Kristofferson

b. Jun. 22, 1936, Brownsville, TX
Vocals, Guitar / Outlaw Country, Singer/Songwriter, Progressive Country, Traditional Country
The '70s was a decade ripe and waiting for rebels. Still, the Nashville establishment wasn't quite ready for this former soldier and Rhodes Scholar who, with long beard and dressed in jeans, in 1970 walked onstage at the Country Music Association awards and got his songwriting award for "Sunday Mornin' Comin' Down," which his friend Johnny Cash had turned into a number one hit. When in the next year, Janis Joplin had a hit with "Me and Bobby McGee" and Sammi Smith's version of "Help Me Make It Through the Night" became a hit on both the country and pop charts, he was on his way, anti-establishment or not. In 1973, the year he and singer Rita Coolidge married, two of his albums, *The Silver Tongued Devil and I* and *Jesus Was a Capricorn* (the latter containing his first number one hit as a singer, "Why Me"), went gold. Meanwhile his duets with Coolidge sold well and produced two Grammys for them. Kristofferson's acting career also took off in the early '70s. He continued to have minor chart hits into the 1980s, but nothing like his phenomenal sales of the previous decade. In the mid-'80s Kristofferson teamed up with pals Johnny Cash, Waylon Jennings, and Willie Nelson. In 1995, Kristofferson released his first album on the Justice label, the solo effort *A Moment of Forever.* —*David Vinopal & Kurt Wolff*

☆ **Kristofferson** / 1970 / Columbia/Legacy ♦♦♦♦♦
On the evidence of his first collection of songs, Kristofferson was ahead of his country music peers in realizing that, despite Nashville's conservative political tilt, there was a natural affinity between the country archetype of a hard-drinking, romantically independent loner and the rock & roll archetype of a drug-taking, romantically free hippie. A sleeve note suggested that Kristofferson had been reluctant to record, but while he didn't have much range as a singer, he brought a conviction to his vocals and a complete understanding of the nuances of the lyrics. The songs were so personal that they seemed to demand a personal interpretation, and established the persona of a poor songwriter struggling against despair. Nashville, as it turned out, didn't have much use for his countercultural songs, but the country music community could recognize a good love song, and Ray Price quickly cut "For the Good Times," which topped the country charts. Then Johnny Cash covered the first-person hangover narrative "Sunday Mornin' Comin' Down" for a number one country hit, and Sammi Smith gave a twist to "Help Me Make It Through the Night" by recording it as a woman's song for yet another country number one. The finishing touch to Kristofferson's sudden renown was Janis Joplin's cover of the classic on-the-road song "Me and Bobby McGee," released shortly after her death, which topped the pop charts. When it was released in 1970, *Kristofferson* did not reach the charts. By the following year, however, its creator was on his way to becoming a major star, and after his second album broke into the pop charts in July 1971, Monument retitled the first album *Me and Bobby McGee* and reissued it. This time around, it made the pop and country charts and went gold. —*William Ruhlmann*

☆ **The Silver Tongued Devil and I** / 1971 / Monument ♦♦♦♦♦
By the time Monument came to release Kristofferson's second album, *The Silver Tongued Devil and I,* in July 1971, he was the author of four songs that had topped the country or pop charts for others. Kristofferson himself had not yet reached the charts with a recording of his own, but his spectacular success as a songwriter made *The Silver Tongued Devil and I* a much-anticipated record. One consequence of this was that Monument was willing to spend more money; three of the album's songs boasted strings and another a horn section. But the key, of course, was still the songwriting, and though there were several excellent songs, the album could not live up to its predecessor, which was the culmination of years of writing. Typically for a second album, Kristofferson reached back into his catalog, presenting his own treatments of "Jody and the Kid" and "The Taker," which had been hits for Roy Drusky and Waylon Jennings, respectively. In his newly written material, Kristofferson continued to examine the lives of society's outcasts, but the antiestablishment tone of some of *Kristofferson* was gone along with much of the wry humor, and in their place were touches of morbidity and sentimentality. Kristofferson retained his gift for intimate love songs, and the album's most memorable selections turned out to be "Loving Her Was Easier (Than Anything I'll Ever Do Again)" (which became a semi-standard) and "When I Loved Her." And even if his observations seemed less acute, his talent for wordplay often rescued the songs from banality. On its way to becoming a gold record, *The Silver Tongued Devil and I* reached the pop Top 20, Kristofferson's career high on that chart, and the country Top Five; thus, Kristofferson made the transition from being a successful songwriter to a successful recording artist. —*William Ruhlmann*

Border Lord / Feb. 1972 / One Way ♦♦♦♦♦
While the quality of the songwriting remains high on this album, the overall feel of the record is more "down." Monument seemed to be showing some faith in Kristofferson as an artist by releasing "Josie" as a single. Unfortunately, it wasn't a hit. Still, this album should not be missed. —*Jim Worbois*

Jesus Was a Capricorn / Nov. 1972 / Monument ♦♦♦
After a visit to the church of Jimmy Snow, Kristofferson was inspired to write the song that was his first hit as a performer: "Why Me," and includes his cover of Larry Gatlin's "Help Me. Another strong album worth looking for. *—Jim Worbois*

Full Moon / Sep. 1973 / A&M ♦♦

Spooky Lady's Sideshow / May 1974 / One Way ♦♦♦

Breakaway / Dec. 1974 / Monument ♦♦

Who's to Bless and Who's to Blame / Nov. 1975 / One Way ♦♦

Surreal Thing / Jul. 1976 / One Way ♦♦♦♦

A Star Is Born / Nov. 1976 / Monument ♦♦

• **The Songs of Kristofferson** / Apr. 1977 / Monument ♦♦♦♦♦
This greatest-hits collection features most of the songs he wrote but that others turned into hits, including "Sunday Morning Coming Down, " "For the Good Times, " and "Help Me Make It Through the Night." His idiosyncratic versions aren't pretty, but they're intimate and often powerful. *—Michael McCall*

Easter Island / Mar. 1978 / One Way ♦♦

Shake Hands with the Devil / 1979 / One Way ♦♦

Natural Act / Jan. 1979 / A&M ♦♦

To the Bone / 1981 / One Way ♦♦

Music from Songwriter / Oct. 1984 / Monument ♦♦♦

Third World Warrior / Mar. 6, 1990 / Mercury ♦♦

Singer/Songwriter / 1991 / Monument ♦♦♦♦♦
An interesting concept: a two-disc set, one featuring Kristofferson's version of 17 of his songs, the other featuring covers of the same songs by Ray Price, Janis Joplin, Bob Dylan, Johnny Cash and others. *—Michael McCall*

Live at the Philharmonic / 1992 / Monument ♦♦♦♦
Recorded in New York City on December 2, 1972, but not released until two decades later, this live concert showcases Kristofferson during his most musically creative period. The impressive set list includes John Prine's "Late John Garfield Blues," and the soul classic "Rainbow Road," the overlooked "Billy Dee," and an update on "Okie from Muskogee." Willie Nelson, Rita Coolidge, and Larry Gatlin help him out, as does an excellent band that includes Donnie Fritts and Stephen Bruton. *—Kurt Wolff*

A Moment of Forever / 1995 / Buddha ♦♦♦♦♦
An impressive batch of new songs, including "New Mister Me," fills what's easily Kristofferson's best album in years. His voice is even rougher around the edges than it was 25 years ago, but the production (by Don Was) and Kristofferson's soul (dustier but wiser) are both honest and easy. The stellar band of L.A. session players includes Jim Keltner, Benmont Tench, Waddy Wachtel, and Danny Timms. *—Kurt Wolff*

The Austin Sessions / Aug. 24, 1999 / Atlantic ♦♦♦

k.d. lang (Kathryn Dawn Lang)

b. Nov. 2, 1961, Consort, Alberta, Canada
Vocals / Neo-Traditionalist Country, Alternative Country, Adult Alternative Pop/Rock
k.d. lang caused considerable controversy in the traditional world of country music with her vaguely campy approach, androgynous appearance, and edgy, rock-inflected music; very few observers knew what to make of her, although no one questioned her considerable vocal talents. That confusion never quite dissipated over the course of her career, even when she abandoned country music for torchy adult contemporary pop. Born in Alberta, Canada, lang formed a band named the re-clines in 1983 with the help of guitarist/co-songwriter Ben Mink, and recorded two small-label albums that led to national attention. Sire signed lang in early 1986; her first record, *Angel with a Lariat*, was a mix of '50s-styled ballads, kitschy rockabilly and honky tonk numbers. It had heavy support from college radio as well as cutting-edge country stations, though Nashville resisted lang and her tongue-in-cheek concerts. In 1987, lang duetted with Roy Orbison on his old hit "Crying," which marked her first appearance on the country charts. *Shadowland*, her second Sire album, made her debt to Patsy Cline explicit. Recorded with Cline's producer Owen Bradley, the album's lack of campy humor helped it become a sizable word-of-mouth hit, both in modern country and alternative circles. The following year lang released the harder-edged *Absolute Torch and Twang*, which increased her mainstream country audience. Before the 1992 release of her fourth album, lang declared that she was a lesbian in an interview in *The Advocate*, which could have been a risky proposition in Nashville circles. However, the new album, *Ingenue*, was a set of adult contemporary pop that owed very little to country. *Ingenue* went platinum in several countries and won lang a new audience. It wasn't until 1995 that lang delivered the true follow-up *All You Can Eat*, which continued the pop direction of its predecessor. The album didn't enjoy the mass commercial acceptance of *Ingenue*, but it was a moderate success, proving that she had a dedicated cult following. Subsequent efforts included 1997's smoking-themed covers album *Drag*, and 2000's lush, smooth *Invincible Summer*. *—Stephen Thomas Erlewine*

A Truly Western Experience / 1984 / Bumstead ♦♦♦

Angel With a Lariat / 1987 / Sire ♦♦♦
On her debut album, big-voiced k.d. lang took a rockabilly approach, with Dave Edmunds as her perfect producer choice. Edmunds brought out the sharp, rhythmic aspects of her band The Reclines, and lang wailed over them. The record, which was underappreciated at the time of its release, was an amazingly confident first effort. *—William Ruhlmann*

Shadowland / 1988 / Sire ♦♦♦♦♦
k.d. lang is not an ordinary country singer: Born in Canada, she has neither the pedigree nor the charisma of the average female country star. By 1988, she had only released one original album, and it was commercially unsuccessful. Despite the long odds against her, she had not escaped the notice of Owen Bradley, a veteran Nashville producer who had worked with the likes of Loretta Lynn, Brenda Lee, and Patsy Cline. In fact, lang brought Bradley out of retirement with *Shadowland*, and it's easy to understand why he was eager to work with her. lang's wonderful voice is showcased throughout the album, as she sings cover tunes that remain true to the originals while receiving her indelible vocal stamp. The versatility of her voice allows her to tackle heartache ballads ("Lock, Stock and Teardrops") and playful tunes ("Don't Let the Stars Get in Your Eyes") with equal effectiveness. This album also reveals lang's connection to the past and her genuine affection for Owen Bradley—their friendship and collaboration clearly paved the way for her breakthrough album *Ingenue*, released a few years later. Although this is an album of country standards, the production and arrangements (which include strings) indicate her shift toward a more polished pop sound. An excellent introduction to her early music. *—Vik Iyengar*

• **Absolute Torch and Twang** / 1989 / Sire ♦♦♦♦♦
Just as the title implies, *Absolute Torch and Twang* marks a crossroad in k.d. lang's transition from country romper to sensitive balladeer. She and co-writer/co-producer Ben Mink have obviously mastered this genre, as each song could be plucked out and plunked into any era of country music without sounding out of place. A bunch of classics in the making right here. Yet, even as she moves toward a more accessible pop troubadour style, she doesn't quite relinquish what has brought her this far. There are still songs that need singing. So, with voice a-soaring, she gives winks and nods to her roots at every turn. Putting the twang *in* the torch, lang and Mink incorporate western imagery and landscapes into "Trail of Broken Hearts" and "Pullin' Back the Reins"—two exquisite original ballads. Then, in typical lang fashion, she cuts loose on tunes like "Big Boned Gal" and "Big Big Love." She's having so much fun you can hear her smiling. It's a shame country radio couldn't see its way past her activism and personal life to acknowledge her artistry. "Luck in My Eyes" and "Three Days" could have served their airwaves well. No matter, even without the establishment's accolades, lang has a lot to be proud of on *Absolute Torch and Twang*. But let's face it, her voice and persona are so captivating, she could sing her way through the phone book and it would be enchanting. *—Kelly McCartney*

Ingenue / 1992 / Sire ♦♦♦♦
Canada's angel with a lariat has chucked the spurs for *Ingenue* in favor of a classic, Tin-Pan-Alley pop approach. lang's turnaround is a great success. *Ingenue* is an achingly beautiful work, all melancholy longing and heartbreak that strikes a perfect balance between the pain and pleasure of love. To stake out her own individual territory somewhere between Patsy Cline and Billie Holiday without relying on pop standards is a feat in itself. The 10 original compositions allow full reign to lang's spectacularly expressive voice. One misses the sense of humor and playful spirit that has infused lang's music in the past, but that can wait until next time 'round when she's recovered from whatever major personal crisis served as inspiration for *Ingenue*. For now, listen and weep. *—Roch Parisien*

All You Can Eat / Oct. 10, 1995 / Sire ♦♦♦♦
k.d. lang followed through on the promise of her adult contemporary changeover *Ingenue* with *All You Can Eat*. A more experimental and realized record than its predecessor, there are more daring production touches on *All You Can Eat*—it's clear that she has been listening to contemporary pop, not just torch songs. It isn't immediately accessible—the production is low-key, the melodies are gentle and subtle (although her cutesy, tongue-in-cheek song titles suggest otherwise), and lang gives a nuanced, sophisticated performance. Though it lacks a standout song like the aching "Constant Craving," *All You Can Eat* has a more consistent set of songs and, given time, is a more rewarding listen. *—Stephen Thomas Erlewine*

Drag / Jun. 10, 1997 / Warner Brothers ♦♦♦
Returning, however tentatively, to the torch stylings that made *Ingenue* her most successful album, k.d. lang crafted an odd commercial comeback with *Drag*. A collection of covers that are somehow related to smoking, *Drag* is by far more ambitious than the average cover record. She recasts Steve Miller's "The Joker" and the Hollies' "The Air That I Breathe" as slow, bluesy cabaret numbers, while traditional '50s pop like "Don't Smoke In Bed" and "Smoke Rings" act as seductive counterpoints. lang's rich voice and the measured arrangements make *Drag* a ringer for *Ingenue* in places, but the tone is considerably lighter and more humorous, which certainly makes it an enjoyable listen. Nevertheless, the very presence of a tongue-in-cheek, all-covers tribute to smoking is a little disheartening in the wake of the wonderful, if severely underappreciated, *All You Can Eat*, which found lang pushing herself forward. *Drag*, in comparision, can't help but sound like a retreat. *—Stephen Thomas Erlewine*

Invincible Summer / Jun. 20, 2000 / Warner Brothers ♦♦♦
The k.d. lang who played tribute to Patsy Cline in her band the Reclines seems a millennium away from the smooth, pop-infused chanteuse on this album. Glowing with happiness and lovey bliss, this lush album is dripping with the kind of bright, slick production that hasn't seen much light since the Brill Building's heyday. Swelling strings, electronic bubbles and warbles, and the occasional mandolin combine to create a sound that manages to evoke a warm feeling of nostalgia without sounding retro. Topping it all off is lang's smooth-as-maple-syrup voice, which shows even greater range than before, occasionally issuing the bell-like tones more often heard from fellow Canadians Jane Siberry and Sarah McLachlan. If there is a fault to this album, it is that it is too smooth; while the listener is surfing these waves of happiness and cushiony pop, an occasional desire for edges and bones surfaces. While "The Consequences of Falling," "Love's Great Ocean," and "Simple" are all fine songs, this recording also lacks the kind of hooky, knockout singles that have been featured on her best albums. *—Stacia Proefrock*

Tracy Lawrence

b. Jan. 27, 1968, Atlanta, TX
Vocals / New Traditionalist, Contemporary Country
Tracy Lawrence was a new traditionalist honky tonk singer of the mid-'90s, producing a string of hit singles and critically-acclaimed albums. He released his debut album *Sticks and*

Stones in 1991. That May 31, he was celebrating the album's release with his former girlfriend. As he walked her to the hotel door, three gun-toting youths robbed them and tried to force the two into the woman's room. Lawrence, fearing that his friend would be raped, resisted and was shot four times while she escaped. Two of the shots nicked him, but a third had to be surgically removed from his knee and the fourth remained deeply embedded in his pelvis, dangerously close to a major artery. Fortunately, he recovered quickly and performed benefit shows to help with his tremendous medical bills and ensuing physical therapy. His debut single, "Sticks and Stones," made it to number one on the strength of the publicity surrounding the shooting, and began a streak of Top 10 singles. His second album, *Alibis*, went gold 17 days after its release and soon went platinum. The record spawned three straight number one singles—"Alibis," "Can't Break It To My Heart," and "My Second Home." Lawrence's third album, *I See it Now*, was released in 1994; like its predecessors, it was a platinum success. *—Sandra Brennan*

Sticks and Stones / 1991 / Atlantic ✦✦✦
Lawrence's first two chart-toppers, "Sticks and Stones" and "Today's Lonely Fool," are included on this debut outing. *—Jason Ankeny*

Alibis / 1993 / Atlantic ✦✦✦✦
While not as consistent as his debut *Sticks and Stones*, Lawrence's strong baritone is still well-served on *Alibis*. *—Jason Ankeny*

I See It Now / Sep. 20, 1994 / Atlantic ✦✦✦✦

Live and Unplugged / Sep. 19, 1995 / Atlantic ✦✦

Time Marches On / Jan. 23, 1996 / Atlantic ✦✦✦
Tracy Lawrence's *Time Marches On*, the singer's fourth album, is another crowd-pleasing set of contemporary country. Like his previous albums, the song selection is a hit-or-miss affair, with about half of the songs failing to make much of an impression. The remainder, however, proves why Lawrence is one of the most popular singers in Nashville. *—Stephen Thomas Erlewine*

Coast is Clear / Mar. 18, 1997 / Atlantic ✦✦✦✦
The Coast is Clear again demonstrates that Tracy Lawrence was one of the finest new honky tonkers of the '90s. Lawrence can wring tremendous emotion out of a song, adding nuances that give each line heart-tugging resonance. Unfortunately, his material is not the equal of his skills. Although there are bright spots, such as "Livin' in Black and White," about half of the record is saddled with pedestrian material performed without style. Try as he may, Lawrence cannot bring material of this level to life. Still, *The Coast Is Clear* remains a winning record, since Lawrence sings well no matter what the material, and when he is given a good song, the results are first-rate. *—Thom Owens*

● **The Best of Tracy Lawrence** / Sep. 1, 1998 / Atlantic ✦✦✦✦

Lessons Learned / Feb. 1, 2000 / Atlantic ✦✦✦
Given the three years separating it from its predecessor, it's a little disappointing that *Lessons Learned* isn't a little livelier, or at least a little different from his previous records. It's not. It's not bad, however. Lawrence sticks with the polished, modern-day honky tonk that made him a star, toning down the rough edges and adding gloss to the surface. That means the record heavily favors ballads, and even the peppier material is midtempo. The most exciting it gets is "Up All Night," a credible, mild-spirited rocker, graced by a moment of genius when the music stops and Lawrence sings "I Been Up, I Been Up, I Been Up" in mesmerizing cadence. In other words, it's a well-crafted, adult album. How that plays is a matter of taste. Strictly speaking, this isn't really a straight-up country record, but it's hardly the country-pop of Shania Twain either. It falls between the two extremes, borrowing the form of hardcore country, but the sound and attitude of country-pop. This isn't out of character for Lawrence, but it's a little surprising just how measured *Lessons Learned* is. It's certainly pleasant, yet it tends to fade into the background. It doesn't help that the material is, by and large, not particularly distinguished. A few tunes jump out, and there's nothing bad here, but there's nothing particularly noteworthy. It's the kind of record only a veteran could produce: accomplished, professional, and modestly—yet only mildly—entertaining. *—Stephen Thomas Erlewine*

Chris LeDoux

b. Oct. 2, 1948, Biloxi, MS
Vocals, Guitar / Urban Cowboy, Neo-Traditionalist Country, Contemporary Country, Cowboy
Chris LeDoux was not only a successful country singer and songwriter, but also a champion rodeo rider. He reached the pinnacle of his rodeo career in 1976 when he became World Champion Bareback Rider. While riding and traveling, he began writing rodeo songs such as "Rodeo Life," "Bareback Jack," and "Bull Rider."

In 1980, he left the cowboy circuit to focus on a music career. His debut album was released on Lucky Man, a subsidiary of his family's music business American Cowboy Songs. For the next two decades, LeDoux recorded 22 albums on independent labels which contained a blend of originals and traditional cowboy songs. Many of the albums were sold on the rodeo circuit, and over the years he developed a loyal following. Between 1979 and 1980, he had three minor hits with "Lean, Mean and Hungry," "Ten Seconds in the Saddle" and "Caballo Diablo." In 1992 LeDoux teamed up with longtime friend Garth Brooks—who helped popularize LeDoux by mentioning his name in his 1989 hit "Much Too Young (To Feel This Damn Old)"—to sing the title track of *Watcha Gonna Do with a Cowboy*. The song became LeDoux's only Top 10 hit. *—Sandra Brennan*

● **20 Greatest Hits** / Jun. 8, 1999 / Capitol ✦✦✦✦
20 Greatest Hits may not cover Chris LeDoux' entire career, but it does provide a definitive summary of his recordings for Liberty in the '90s. Over the course of the album, all of his big hits, plus a selection of fine album tracks and rarities, are hauled out. It may run a little long for some listeners, but it's nevertheless the ideal LeDoux record for casual fans, since it captures the best from the peak of his popularity. *—Stephen Thomas Erlewine*

Brenda Lee (Brenda Mae Tarpley)

b. Dec. 11, 1944, Lithonia, GA
Vocals / Nashville Sound/Countrypolitan, Pop, Rockabilly, Country-Pop, Rock & Roll
One of the biggest pop stars of the early '60s, Brenda Lee hasn't attracted as much critical respect as she deserves. She is sometimes inaccurately characterized as one of the few female teen idols. More crucially, the credit for achieving success with pop-country crossovers usually goes to Patsy Cline, although Lee's efforts in this era were arguably of equal importance. While she made few recordings of note after the mid-'60s, the best of her first decade is fine indeed, encompassing not just the pop ballads that were her biggest hits, but straight country and some surprisingly fierce rockabilly. A child prodigy, Lee's first few Decca singles from 1956 make a pretty fair bid for the best pre-teen rock & roll performances this side of Michael Jackson. "BIGELOW 6-200," "Dynamite" and "Little Jonah" are all exceptionally powerful rockabilly performances, with robust vocals and white-hot backing. Between 1960 and 1962, she began tempering the rockabilly with teen-idol pop and had a stunning series of huge hits. While she still had hits through the mid-'60s, these became smaller and less frequent with the rise of the British Invasion (although she remained very popular overseas). Like so many early White rock & roll stars, she returned to country music in the '70s and made the country Top Ten half a dozen times. She remained active as a recording and touring artist. *—Richie Unterberger*

★ **Anthology, Vols. 1 & 2 (1956-1980)** / 1991 / MCA ✦✦✦✦✦
A 40-song, two-CD collection, tihs proves Lee was the best White female rock singer of the pre-Beatles '60s. By the time she turned 18, Lee had hit the pop Top Ten 11 times. All of those cuts are here, from the innocently salacious "Sweet Nothin's" to the string-laden "I'm Sorry" and her remake of Earl "Fatha" Hines's "You Can Depend on Me." Her best country singles, "Johnny One Time" and "Big Four Poster Bed," are also included. The compilers wisely passed over some minor hits in favor of obscure sides like the odd rockabilly "Let's Jump the Broomstick," a cover of Edith Piaf's "If You Love Me (Really Love Me)," and "Is It True—" a middling hit from 1964, which features guitarist Jimmy Page (who is 11 months older than Lee). *Anthology* thoroughly traces Lee's development as a vocalist, from early-childish exuberance to mature, graceful phrasing. *—Brian Mansfield*

Rock the Bop / 1995 / Radio Archives ✦✦✦✦✦

Little Miss Dynamite / 1997 / Bear Family ✦✦✦✦
Five hours of pure gold on four CDs, covering the 127 songs that Brenda Lee recorded during the years 1956 through 1962, with the added allure of an 84-page hardcover book. What's more, there's hardly a second-rate song or performance here, and Lee's singing style evolved so far that there are surprises throughout. Her early rockabilly sides are among the best in the field, and Disc One covers her evolution from country-rockin' teen rockabilly queen to an astonishingly precocious pop star with rock roots. Even Lee's early sides, whether hot rockabilly or slow ballads, are all intense experiences—there's just something eerily compelling about 12-year-old Brenda Lee delivering "Your Cheatin' Heart" and sounding like she means all of the yearning and torment behind it. By 1957, her voice and her style had evolved more toward mainstream pop, virtually paralleling Elvis Presley's musical moves of the same era, but, like Elvis, Lee occasionally burst out with hard-rocking sides as late as 1959. Disc Two shows off Lee's mid-teen years, when she was doing pop standards that shouldn't have worked with anyone less than 30, but making them pay off—her hot, raspy voice made even her pop stuff work better than Elvis's and outclassed the work of any other female singer who made that same jump to mainstream music. Disc Three may be the best of the four here, her rock sides alternating with equally compelling pop performances. Much of Disc Four is on the softer side, but even here she comes up with exciting pop/rock songs. By this time, she was nearing 18 years old, and already had a catalog of recordings behind her that would have been the envy of any veteran. As usual with Bear Family, the book is as fascinating as the music. *—Bruce Eder*

In the Mood for Love: Classic Ballads / Aug. 11, 1998 / Hip-O ✦✦✦
She can sing rockers and turn around and sing Hank Williams songs as well as anyone. But nobody can put across a ballad the way Brenda Lee can, and this 18-track collection proves it in a most musical way. Drawn from 11 different albums and recorded between 1961 and 1971, this collection foregoes the usual hits and formulaic choices and instead concentrates on Brenda's interpretations of standards and cover versions of then-current hits by the likes of Dusty Springfield and others. Perhaps it's Owen Bradley's uniformly excellent production that helps to band it all together around Brenda's pipes, but everything on here works together as a whole concept, solid as a brick. Great songs, great singing, and production that still sounds crisp some 35-40 years after it was cut. A noteworthy addition to anyone's Brenda Lee collection, covering material not found on her box set anthologies. *—Cub Koda*

Johnny Lee (John Lee Harn)

b. Jul. 3, 1946, Texas City, TX
Vocals, Guitar / Urban Cowboy, Adult Contemporary, Contemporary Country, Country-Pop
Like many his age, Johnny Lee grew up on the music of Chuck Berry, Elvis Presley, and Jerry Lee Lewis. Raised on a dairy farm in Alta Loma, Texas, he formed his first band, Johnny Lee & the Road Runners, during high school. He tricked his way into playing on stage with Mickey Gilley at a Houston club called the Nesadel, and that shot brought him a long-term run at Gilley's clubs. When *Urban Cowboy* was shot at Gilley's, record executive Irving Azoff offered Lee an opportunity to sing in the picture, and he ended up with a song that more than 20 artists had previously rejected. In his hands, that song— "Lookin' for Love"—became a million-seller and the musical centerpiece of the movie. Stardom occurred practically overnight for Lee, but it was a mixed bag. He and Gilley toured steadily; Lee got a substantial string of hits for about three years and ended up marrying *Dallas* starlet Charlene Tilton. But the marriage soured, he found his name constantly in the tabloids, and he was forced to record a large amount of same-sounding material. Nevertheless, Johnny Lee had an important role in a huge era for country music, and his easygoing vocal style still makes him very listenable. *—Tom Roland*

- **Greatest Hits** / 1983 / Full Moon ✦✦✦✦✦
Lots of mid-tempo love songs are here, much in the vein of "Lookin' for Love." Too bad Lee couldn't break out of that mold a little sooner—"Sounds like Love" and "Hey Bartender" show some real teeth. *—Tom Roland*

The Best of Johnny Lee / 1990 / Curb ✦✦✦

Little Texas

f. 1984, **db.** 1997
Group / Contemporary Country
Drawing from country and rock & roll, Little Texas was one of the more popular country bands of the early '90s. Named after their old rehearsal spot on Little Texas Road, by the end of 1990, they had enough material to record their debut album, *First Time for Everything.* The album was released in the summer of 1991, after the band's debut single, "Some Guys Have All the Love," became a Top Ten hit. The band really began to take off in 1994 with the release of their second album, *Big Time.* The album produced the number two country hit "What Might Have Been," which also became a minor pop hit. This was followed by "God Blessed Texas," a line-dancing favorite which reached the Top Five. In early 1994, Little Texas scored its first number one hit with "My Love," and *Big Time* went platinum. Later in 1994, the group released their third album, *Kick A Little,* which went platinum and produced two Top 10 singles in the title track and "Amy's Back in Austin." In 1995, Little Texas released *Greatest Hits,* which featured two new songs, including the number five hit "Life Goes On." *—Sandra Brennan*

First Time for Everything / Mar. 3, 1992 / Warner Brothers ✦✦

Big Time / 1993 / Warner Brothers ✦✦✦

Kick a Little / 1994 / Warner Brothers ✦✦✦✦

- **Greatest Hits** / Oct. 1995 / Warner Brothers ✦✦✦✦✦
Collecting all of Little Texas's best numbers, *Greatest Hits* is the perfect introduction to the country-pop band, as well as being their most consistent and enjoyable album. *—Stephen Thomas Erlewine*

Little Texas / Apr. 22, 1997 / Warner Brothers ✦✦✦✦

Hank Locklin

b. Feb. 15, 1918, McLellan, FL
Vocals, Guitar / Nashville Sound/Countrypolitan, Honky Tonk, Traditional Country
Hank Locklin (b. Lawrence Hankins Locklin), one of country music's great tenors, was born February 15, 1918 in the small town of McLellan located in the lumbering district of the Florida Panhandle. Locklin ended up based in Houston and signed to Four Star, where he had his first major regional hits with such songs as "The Same Sweet Girl" and "Send Me The Pillow That You Dream On." In those days, Locklin's sound was that of Texas-style dance band, and lacked the smooth, romantic commercial veneer of his later Nashville-based recordings for RCA. In 1953, he finally achieved national recognition with a number one country hit, "Let Me Be The One." His success, however, was still sporadic, particularly in the face of an awkward contractual arrangement that had Locklin recorded by Decca but belonging to Four Star and largely restricted to recording Four Star-owned songs. This didn't change until 1955. His career took off when he joined the RCA Victor label in the Spring of 1955. Locklin's work with RCA has the added advantage that almost all of it was produced by Chet Atkins, often with Atkins himself on rhythm or lead guitar and with the added trills and fill-ins of Floyd Cramer on piano. The extreme simplicity of his early works makes this combination of his clear voice and these particular sidemen very effective. Everyone knows Hank's big hits—"Send Me the Pillow That You Dream On," "Geisha Girl," and "Please Help Me I'm Falling"—but real Locklin fans are in love with his very simple heartfelt tunes like "Who Am I to Cast the First Stone," "A Good Woman's Love," "Seven or Eleven," "I'm Tired of Bummin' Around," "Golden Wristwatch," "Sitting Alone at a Table for Two," and many others. These early songs are characterized by Locklin's crystal clear tenor, the ultra-simplicity of the songs themselves, and their straight-to-the heart emotional plea. *—Michael Erlewine*

☆ **Please Help Me I'm Falling [Box]** / Dec. 1995 / Bear Family ✦✦✦✦✦
This is a four-disc retrospective of Locklin's years with RCA Victor from 1955 through the mid 1960s. Of course Hank's big popular hits "Send me the Pillow that you Dream On" (written by Locklin), "Geisha Girl," and "Please Help Me I'm Falling" are there. While a great many important early Locklin songs are missing from this collection ("I'm Tired of Bummin' Around," "Sitting Alone at a Table for Two," and "Golden Wristwatch"), many fine songs are included that have been unavailable for many years. Songs like "Who Am I to Cast the First Stone," "A Good Woman's Love," "Seven or Eleven." It is this precious early material that has been unavailable, most produced by Chet Atkins, often with Atkins on guitar and almost all with the excellent piano accompanment of Floyd Cramer. Also included are a number of Locklin's concept albums: *Foreign Love, Irish songs, Country Style,* plus his album tribute to Roy Acuff, *A Tribute to Roy Acuff, King of Country Music.*

Of course his early material on Four Star Records (pre RCA) and his later material on MGM and Plantation are not here. Most of these songs in this box set are taken from albums that appeared on Camden and RCA. They are *My Kind of Country Blues* (Camden CAL 912), *Hank Locklin* (Camden CAL 905), *Please Help Me I'm Falling* (RCA LPM 2291), *Foreign Love* (RCA LPM 1673), *This Song Is Just For You* (Camden CAL 765), *Happy Journey* (RCA LSP 2464), *A Tribute to Roy Acuff King of Country Music* (RCA LSP 2597), *The Ways of Life* (RCA LSP 2680), and *Irish Songs, Country Style* (RCA LSP 2801). Unless RCA decides to release all the early Camden material, this fine box set from Bear Family is what we have for now. *—Michael Erlewine*

☆ **Send Me the Pillow You Dream On** / 1997 / Bear Family ✦✦✦✦✦
This triple-CD set is fascinating as well as priceless—66 sides cut by Hank Locklin between 1948 and 1954 for Gold Star, Four Star, and Decca. The majority of the tracks here will be new to most listeners, never having been reissued in any form (or in redubbed form) from their original 78 rpm appearances. They present Locklin doing a rougher, harder honky-tonk brand of music, derived from Texas dance-band roots, but different from the Nashville countrypolitan sound with which he achieved lasting fame—compared to his later, softer material, this stuff rocks. The early Gold Star and Royalty sides come from decent masters, with a certain amount of noise (the bass tends to boom) that is unavoidable, but otherwise they're pretty impressive. Of his early Four Star releases, the most unexpected treats are "Knocking at Your Door," Locklin's theme song in his Texas period, and the heavily Hank Williams-influenced "Born to Ramble." The latter is a revelation, showing Locklin to be a talented yodeler, among other surprises. "Send Me the Pillow That You Dream On" is also here in its original version, a lot less slick than the 1957 hit version off of RCA. Even at this point, Locklin's music was weighted toward ballads, although he interjected bright dance numbers. Disc Two is still honky-tonk-based but slicker, with better players all around. Disc Three opens with Locklin's move to Nashville in 1952, under the aegis of Owen Bradley—the sound on those first sessions is smooth, almost elegant compared with the Texas-based stuff, and shows Locklin hitting his stride as a singer and bandleader, predating the full bloom of his Nashville period. The music on this disc flows seamlessly into the RCA period covered by the next Bear Family box, and Locklin's better-known RCA sides. *—Bruce Eder*

- **Please Help Me I'm Falling [Collectables]** / Jan. 5, 1998 / Collectables ✦✦✦✦✦
This is a strange collection, not to be confused with Bear Family's multi-disc set of the same name. It's not a best-of or a greatest hits, despite the presence of some monster sellers—the title-track and "Send Me the Pillow You Dream On" are present in their hit versions, along with "Livin' Alone," "It's a Little Bit Like Heaven," and "Geisha Girl." The rest are good songs, but hardly hits, including the spritely "Seven Days" (written by Locklin), which could've been a great song for Buddy Holly to cover; the mournful "Blues in Advance," the comical "Why Don't You Haul Off and Love Me" and "Foreign Car," and John D. Loudermilk's angst-filled "When the Band Plays the Blues." The sound is bright and loud, although some of the textures seem harsh, especially the reverb on certain tracks, and the notes are a little haywire, claiming that Locklin wrote "Send Me the Pillow You Dream On" in 1958, when he'd previously recorded it twice for other labels, and had already charted with it. Sad to say, this 14-song CD is the only alternative to Bear Family's four-disc set covering Locklin's post-1955 career—one can only figure that either BMG or Razor & Tie has plans for a proper retrospective on Locklin, and that this will have to do in the meantime. *—Bruce Eder*

The Louvin Brothers

f. Jul. 4, 1940, Knoxville, TN, **db.** Aug. 18, 1963
Vocals / Bluegrass-Gospel, Close Harmony, Traditional Country, Traditional Bluegrass
From the close-harmony brother acts of the '30s evolved Charlie and Ira Louvin, ranking among the top duos in country music history. With Ira's incredibly high, pure tenor and Charlie's emotional and smooth melody tenor, they learned well from the Bolick brothers (the Blue Sky Boys), the Monroe Brothers, the Delmore Brothers and other major family duos of the previous generation, preserving the old-time flavor, while bringing this genre into the '50s, when country music moved to a newer sound. Whatever type of songs they recorded—gospel, folk, hillbilly, or '50s pop—those songs became the Louvins. Add to the list the many Louvin compositions (for example, "If I Could Only Win Your Love," Emmylou Harris' first hit), and you have an act that is outstanding in country music history. Their career took a while to get going, partly because of interruptions from WW II and the Korean War. In the early '50s, after making a reputation for unexcelled gospel singing, the Louvins broadened their repertoire, recording "The Get Acquainted Waltz" (with Chet Atkins adding another guitar to Charlie's and to Ira's mandolin), a fair hit that showed success was reachable with nonreligious music. The electric guitar, with the duo's unique harmony and Ira's exceptional tenor, created a sound that fans asked for in increasing numbers. In 1955, after ten unsuccessful auditions, they finally joined the Opry, where they performed to great acclaim until 1963, when they broke up. They had a number of hits, including the much-covered "When I Stop Dreaming" and "Cash on the Barrel Head." Following the duo's breakup, Ira and Charlie both pursued solo careers. *—David Vinopal*

My Baby's Gone / 1960 / Stetson ✦✦✦✦✦
The Louvins' Capitol output was extremely consistent, and this 1960 LP (reissued on LP in England by Stetson) is no exception. Working under producer Ken Nelson, the traditional core of their harmonies and guitar remained intact, updated only very slightly with some fuller arrangements and mild pop touches. Most of the material is love laments, with "I Wish It Had Been a Dream" and "She Didn't Even Know I Was Gone" (mournfully heartbreaking even by country standards) being standouts. *—Richie Unterberger*

Satan Is Real / 1960 / Capitol ✦✦✦
Much of *Satan Is Real's* reputation stems from its cover, a bizarre photo depicting the Louvins—awkwardly posed and in gleaming white suits—standing amidst the flames of hellfire, a 12-foot-tall plywood Lucifer looming behind them. The jacket is so notorious, in fact, that it merited inclusion in the second volume of the *Incredibly Strange Music* book series. It's a shame the album has acquired such a high kitsch quotient, because in reality *Satan Is Real* is one of the Louvins' finest and most impassioned recordings. The duo's second all-gospel LP, its songs—most of them originals—explore the brothers' deeply-held beliefs without pulling any punches. The title track, in which Ira preaches that any acknowledgment of a higher power demands a similar nod to the reality of darker forces, sets a haunting tone which carries throughout the course of the set; from "The Christian Life" (later covered by the Byrds on their country-rock landmark *Sweetheart of the Radio*) to the stinging "Are You Afraid to Die," these tales of death, sin and despair resonate with raw power and stark beauty. *—Jason Ankeny*

A Tribute to the Delmore Brothers / 1960 / Capitol ✦✦✦✦✦
You could listen to music for 50 years and not hear harmonies as sweet or playing as nimble as what's on this CD. The album was one top-flight brother harmony duo paying tribute to the first great brother harmony duo in recording history. It sometimes seems like every

country duo did tribute records to Alton and Rabon Delmore, and Capitol has at least one other (by Johnny Bond and Merle Travis), but this is the best one, recorded in three days, with Ira Louvin using the late Rabon Delmore's own guitar, former Delmore collaborators Grandpa Jones and Merle Travis standing by, and Chet Atkins on hand. The execution of the record is dazzling, with soaring harmonies and exquisite instrumental textures throughout—stereo was invented just for acts like the Louvins. The song selection is also impeccable (chosen with help from Alton Delmore), including "Brown's Ferry Blues," "Weary Lonesome Blues," "Midnight Special," "When It's Time For the Whippoorwill To Sing," and the hauntingly nostalgic "Put Me On the Trail to Carolina." Also included is "Blues Stay Away From Me," a future part of Bob Dylan's repertory, and a rockin' version of "Freight Train Boogie." It's only a pity that there weren't any leftover tracks from the session to include on the CD. —*Bruce Eder*

Songs That Tell a Story / 1981 / Rounder ✦✦✦✦✦
Arguably the greatest duet and brother act in country history, Ira and Charlie Louvin made remarkably moving, simply performed songs about their faith and lives, with only guitar and mandolin backing, and reflecting the values of country with more sincerity and genuine feeling than hundreds of elaborately produced and packaged albums have since. Rounder issued these numbers on album in the late '70s, and reissued them on CD in 1991. The digital backdrop doesn't drain the authority from their voices; instead, it simply reaffirms the glory and splendor of The Louvins on 15 short, but brilliant gospel numbers. —*Ron Wynn*

Radio Favorites 1951-57 / 1987 / Country Music Foundation ✦✦✦✦✦

☆ **Close Harmony** / 1992 / Bear Family ✦✦✦✦✦
A gargantuan, eight-disc box set *Close Harmony* is essential for serious country fans and scholars. Collecting everything the Louvin Brothers recorded for Capitol, Apollo, Decca, and MGM, the set may have too much music for casual fans, but those willing to delve deeply into these 219 tracks will learn much not only about the duo, but about the evolution of country music in the '50s—many of the roots of contemporary country and rock & roll are apparent throughout the set. —*Stephen Thomas Erlewine*

★ **When I Stop Dreaming: The Best of the Louvin Brothers** / 1995 / Razor & Tie ✦✦✦✦✦
Razor & Tie's single-disc collection *When I Stop Dreaming: The Best of the Louvin Brothers* contains all of the absolute essentials from the groundbreaking country duo, including all of their biggest hits from the '50s. For most casual fans, it's not only the perfect introduction, it's the definitive compilation. —*Stephen Thomas Erlewine*

Patty Loveless (Patty Lee Ramey)

b. Jan. 4, 1957, Pikeville, KY
Vocals / Neo-Traditionalist Country, Contemporary Country
Patty Loveless was one of the most popular female country vocalists of the late '80s and early '90s. Her music drew from country's honky tonk tradition, while also adding a slight rock & roll edge. Loveless got her first break upon meeting Doyle and Teddy Wilburn, who were searching for a singer to replace Loretta Lynn in the Wilburn Brothers. She became their featured singer for three years and signed to their publishing company, Surefire Music, as a songwriter after she graduated from high school. In 1985, Loveless signed with MCA, and in 1987, she broke into the Top Ten and Top Five respectively with "If My Heart Had Windows" and "A Little Bit of Love." In 1988, Loveless' career rose meteorically when she released the album *Honky Tonk Angels,* which produced five tremendously successful singles, including the number one hits "Timber I'm Falling in Love" and "Chains." In 1993, she released *Only What I Feel,* her first album for Epic Records. Within a year, the album went gold and produced several hits, including the number one "Blame It On Your Heart." In 1994, she released *When Fallen Angels Fly,* which also went gold and yielded several Top 10 hits. —*Sandra Brennan*

Honky Tonk Angel / 1988 / MCA ✦✦✦
The song subjects hardly classify Loveless as a honky-tonk angel, at least by Hank Thompson's definition. But this was the album that established Loveless as a major presence, and it includes two of her biggest singles—"Chains," "Timber I'm Falling in Love"—and two of her best—"Blue Side of Town" and "Don't Toss Us Away," a duet with Rodney Crowell. —*Brian Mansfield*

If My Heart Had Windows / 1988 / MCA ✦✦✦✦✦

On Down the Line / May 15, 1990 / MCA ✦✦✦
Patty Loveless entered the 1990s with *On Down the Line,* an excellent album that contained such major hits as "The Night's Too Long," the gutsy "Blue Memories" and the infectiously rockin' "I'm That Kind of Girl." Despite all the talk about Loveless being part of a neo-traditionalist movement in country, this isn't an album for purists—there's plenty of pop and rock influence here, and a 33-year-old Loveless is undeniably folky on the haunting ballad "Some Morning Soon." Loveless still found herself being compared frequently to Patsy Cline, who was no stranger to pop and rock elements either. Not that Loveless excludes more hard-core country—"I've Got To Stop Loving You (And Start Living Again)" is a honky-tonk gem. Unpredictable and consistently inspired, *On Down the Line* remains one of Loveless' finest albums. —*Alex Henderson*

Up Against My Heart / 1991 / MCA ✦✦✦
Loveless gets a little more adventurous with each album, though she never forgets to include sure-fire hits like "Hurt Me Bad (In a Real Good Way)" and "Jealous Bone." This time she invites comparisons to Patsy Cline with "Can't Stop Myself from Loving You" and implies that God is female by switching the pronouns in Lyle Lovett's "God Will." —*Brian Mansfield*

Only What I Feel / Apr. 20, 1993 / Epic ✦✦✦✦✦
Loveless underwent throat surgery and switched labels before creating this album, and both helped. She sounds stronger and more impassioned than she had in years, and her artistic drive seemed more confident and determined. "Nothin' but the Wheel" ranks with her best ballads. —*Michael McCall*

Greatest Hits / May 11, 1993 / MCA ✦✦✦✦✦
The inevitable hits compilation chronicling Patty Loveless's five years and five albums at MCA is, in the Nashville tradition, not exactly generous: It contains only ten tracks and runs 31 1/2 minutes. In that space, though, you get most of Loveless's big hits between 1988 and 1992, from "If My Heart Had Windows" to "Jealous Bone," and including the chart toppers "Timber I'm Falling In Love" and "Chains." Oddly, "A Little Bit In Love," which just missed hitting number one, is not included. The set traces Loveless's rise as part of the neo-traditionalist movement of the 1980s, a movement that had faded, and that Loveless was ready to move beyond, by the time she ended her tenure at MCA. The music included here is fine, bedrock country, but a little faceless for all its authenticity. This is one artist whose second hits collection is likely to be more interesting than her first. —*William Ruhlmann*

When Fallen Angels Fly / 1994 / Epic ✦✦✦✦✦

Trouble with the Truth / Jan. 23, 1996 / Epic ✦✦✦✦

Long Stretch of Lonesome / Sep. 30, 1997 / Epic ✦✦✦✦

● **Classics** / Mar. 23, 1999 / Epic ✦✦✦✦✦
As expected, Patty Loveless's second hits compilation, covering her first five years on Epic Records, was even better than her earlier *Greatest Hits* on MCA, showing off a more confident singer who rocked out convincingly and was comfortable on weepy ballads, even if the latter tended not to be the best compositions she got to sing. Typical of country hits collections, this one was on the skimpy side, containing only 12 tracks, and typical of nearly all contemporary hits collections, it failed to contain all the hits while tossing in a few new songs. The most serious omission was "Halfway Down." But Loveless's biggest hits of the era, "You Can Feel Bad," "Lonely Too Long," and "Blame It On Your Heart" were included, and there was enough here to justify all those Female Vocalist of the Year awards she won during the half-decade. At the same time, the selection reflected the recent downturn in the singer's fortunes, containing nothing from the commercially disappointing 1997 album *Long Stretch of Lonesome.* As so many hits collections do, this one seemed a summing up that confirmed the artist's past triumphs, while she herself stood at a crossroads. —*William Ruhlmann*

Strong Heart / Aug. 29, 2000 / Epic ✦✦✦✦✦

Loretta Lynn

b. Apr. 14, 1934, Butcher's Hollow, KY
Vocals, Guitar / Nashville Sound/Countrypolitan, Honky Tonk, Traditional Country
Loretta Lynn is one of the classic country singers. During the '60s and '70s, she ruled the charts, racking up over 70 hits as a solo artist and a duet partner. Lynn helped forge the way for strong, independent women in country music.

Lynn released her debut single, "I'm a Honky Tonk Girl," in 1960. The honky tonk ballad became a number 14 hit thanks to the insistent, independent promotion of her and her husband. She moved to Nashville in late 1960, signing to Decca Records where she worked with producer Owen Bradley.Lynn's first Decca single, "Success," went to number six in 1962, beginning a string of Top Ten singles that would run over a decade. Throughout the first half of the '60s, she was a honk tonk vocalist. Although she still sang honky tonk in the second half of the decade, her sound became more personal, varied and ambitious. Beginning with 1966's number two hit "You Ain't Woman Enough," Lynn began writing songs that had a feminist viewpoint, which was unheard of in country music, and her lyrical stance became more autobiographical and realistic as time wore on. Between 1966 and 1970, Loretta Lynn racked up 13 Top Ten hits, including four number one hits. In 1971, she began a professional partnership with Conway Twitty and the duo had five consecutive number one hits between 1971 and 1975, becoming one of the most successful duos of country history. Lynn published her autobiography, *Coal Miner's Daughter,* in the mid-'70s. In 1980, the book was adapted for the screen, with Sissy Spacek winning an Academy Award for her performance as Lynn.

Lynn was a popular concert attraction throughout the '80s, yet she wasn't able to continue her domination of the country charts; her last Top 40 single was in 1985. Although she continued to record during the late '80s and '90s, she concentrated on live performances instead. —*Stephen Thomas Erlewine*

Hymns / 1965 / King ✦✦✦

You Ain't Woman Enough / 1966 / MCA ✦✦✦✦

☆ **Greatest Hits** / 1968 / MCA ✦✦✦✦✦
She had a big hand in raising Nashville's perception of women as capable and competent (although the city still has a way to go). "Don't Come Home A-Drinkin'" and "You Ain't Woman Enough" are particularly representative: sassy, honest, and aggressive. —*Tom Roland*

Your Squaw Is on the Warpath / 1969 / Decca ✦✦✦✦
Boasting one of the classic politically incorrect album covers—which depicts Loretta as a sexy, tomahawk wielding Native American—*Your Squaw is on the Warpath* takes its title from the equally inappropriate track that begins the album. And while it may seem that this album's real value comes from its now kitchy artifact status, the rest of the album stands as a good collection, showcasing Lynn's talents as singer and interpreter of others' songs. —*Chris Woodstra*

Coal Miner's Daughter / 1971 / MCA ✦✦✦✦✦
Unlike the song, autobiography and film of the same name, the album *Coal Miner's Daughter* isn't a reflection on Loretta Lynn's upbringing. Instead, it's merely a standard, early '70s collection of originals and covers, all performed with gusto by Lynn. *Coal Miner's Daughter* boasts a stronger, more consistent selection of material than most of her other albums from the period, and contains a number of her classics, like the title song and "I'm a Honky Tonk Girl," plus a handful of lesser-known gems. —*Thom Owens*

Greatest Hits, Vol. 2 / 1974 / MCA ✦✦✦✦✦
In the liner notes, Pete Axthelm cites "the range of her personality," and that range is in evidence here: reflective ("Coal Miner's Daughter"), feisty ("Fist City"), humorous ("One's on the Way"), and sentimental ("Love Is the Foundation"). —*Tom Roland*

★ **Country Music Hall of Fame** / 1991 / MCA ✦✦✦✦✦
Few greatest-hits packages pack the wallop of these 16 performances, which were all recorded for Decca Records between 1961-1976. This album includes duets with Ernest Tubb and Conway Twitty, men who knew to stand clear when Lynn wailed "Your Squaw Is on the Warpath" or "Fist City." *—Mark A. Humphrey*

☆ **Honky Tonk Girl: Collection** / 1994 / MCA ✦✦✦✦✦
Loretta Lynn's three-disc box set *Honky Tonk Girl* has the requisite rarities, but the real strength of the collection is how it offers all of her essential tracks—from 1960's "I'm A Honky Tonk Girl" to 1988's "Who Was That Stranger"—in one place. Not only are her classic hits like "Fist City" and "Coal Miner's Daughter are included," but so are most of her hit duets with Conway Twitty, such as "After the Fire Is Gone" and "As Soon As I Hang Up the Phone." A few hits are missing—notably "Louisiana Woman, Mississippi Man"—but *Honky Tonk Girl* remains the one comprehensive and essential Loretta Lynn collection. *—Stephen Thomas Erlewine*

Shelby Lynne (Shelby Lynne Moorer)

b. Oct. 22, 1968, Quantico, VA
Vocals, Fiddle / Americana, Adult Alternative Pop/Rock, Alternative Country-Rock, Singer/Songwriter, Contemporary Country
Tipped as a hot country newcomer in the early '90s, Shelby Lynne has yet to become a commercial force, though her albums have shown a unique progression from contemporary country to incorporate elements of the blues and even big-band jazz. She was born October 22, 1968, in Quantico, Virginia to a very musical family. Lynne's father was a local singer, and her mother taught vocal harmony to Shelby and her sister Allison. A promising mother-daughter duo career was stopped short in the mid-'80s when Lynne's father shot his wife during an argument and turned the gun on himself also.

Shelby Lynne was forced to raise her sister alone, and raised money around their southern Alabama home by performing in clubs and singing contests. She recorded a few demos in 1987, and they were heard by the Nashville Network. After one performance on TNN's *Nashville Now,* four major labels showed interest and no less a figure than George Jones asked her to sing a duet with him, "If I Could Bottle This Up." The single scratched the Country Top 50 in September 1988, and Lynne signed with Epic.

Though her debut single as a solo act, "Under Your Spell Again," barely hit the Top 100 in 1989, critics praised Lynne's *Sunrise* album. The singer toured as a support act for Jones, Willie Nelson and Randy Travis, and two singles from second album *Tough All Over* hit the Top 30, "Things Are Tough All Over" and "I'll Lie Myself to Sleep." *Tough All Over* made the best-of lists of many critics, who likened her emotional power to the Queen of Country, Patsy Cline.

Shelby Lynne became frustrated with Epic after 1991's *Soft Talk,* and moved to Morgan Creek two years later for *Temptation,* an album that first included Lynne's affection for big band and jazz. Two years later, another label change—this time to Magnatone—resulted in *Restless,* and the single "Slow Me Down" made the Top 60. After a prolonged hiatus, she returned in early 2000 with *I Am Shelby Lynne.* *—John Bush*

Sunrise / 1989 / Epic ✦✦✦

Tough All Over / Aug. 1990 / Epic ✦✦✦✦

Soft Talk / 1991 / Epic ✦✦✦

Temptation / Jul. 6, 1993 / Morgan Creek/Mercury ✦✦✦

Epic Recordings / 2000 / Lucky Dog ✦✦✦
Shelby Lynne's early career on Epic Records frustrated fans of her rich, soulful contralto because, though she placed three albums and nine singles in the country charts between 1988 and 1991, she never scored the big hit needed to propel her to star status. Not all collections are hit oriented, of course, but *Epic Recordings* makes a particular point of second-guessing Epic's singles choices. Of the 16 tracks drawn from the 30 recordings released on her three Epic albums, *Sunrise, Tough All Over,* and *Soft Talk,* only one, "I'll Lie Myself to Sleep," was released as a single. That leaves the compilers plenty of room to emphasize Lynne's diversity, from her Western swing renditions of Duke Ellington's "Don't Get Around Much Anymore" and the Louis Armstrong hit "I'm Confessin'" to a stirring country-rock version of Charlie Rich's "Lonely Weekends" and a fierce performance of Johnny Cash's "I Walk the Line." There are also plenty of lesser album tracks, but it remains odd that the opportunity of an anthology did not inspire Lucky Dog to put Lynne's non-LP chart singles "Under Your Spell Again" and "Don't Cross Your Heart" on disc or to select some of her better-known material. You can't help wondering whether parent label Sony denied Lucky Dog the right to use those songs, preferring to hold them for a Lynne release in its popular *Super Hits* or *16 Biggest Hits* series. It's significant that this album is not billed as a "best-of"; what it really constitutes is "the rest of Shelby Lynne." *—William Ruhlmann*

● **I Am Shelby Lynne** / Jan. 25, 2000 / Mercury ✦✦✦✦✦
After years of kicking around Nashville to great acclaim but nonexistent sales, Shelby Lynne got fed up with the system and reinvented herself as a tough, sexy singer equal parts Bonnie Raitt and Sheryl Crow, with *I Am Shelby Lynne.* Though this undeniably classicist in approach, borrowing from classic R&B, country, soul and rock & roll, it's cleverly constructed, as producer Bill Bottrell gives it a wonderful, warm production graced by slight contemporary flourishes (such as the rolling rhythms behind "*Thought It Would Be Easier*") that keep It fresh, not entrenched in history (even though its succinct 10 tracks and half-hour running time are welcome hold-overs from classic rock). Ultimately, of course, the triumph of the record belongs to Lynne, who finally sounds comfortable in her writing and voice. This music is so warm and welcoming, it's easy to overlook the darker themes running through the songs, particularly because Lynne's greatest strength is that she never over-sings, shading her phrasing and drawing listeners in with her easy confidence and sexy rasp. This isn't an album that flaunts its strengths—it's expertly constructed, subtle music that grows in stature with each spin, as it reveals Lynne as a trad-rocker of uncommon skill and charm. It may have taken her years to finally find her groove, but *I Am Shelby Lynne* is so good, the wait seems worthwhile. *—Stephen Thomas Erlewine*

Uncle Dave Macon

b. Oct. 7, 1870, Smart Station, TN, **d.** Mar. 22, 1952, Readyville, TN
Vocals, Banjo / Field Recordings, Traditional Country, Old-Timey
David Harrison Macon, born in Smartt Station, TN, didn't perform professionally until he was past 50, but he became one of the first superstars of country music. A talented banjoist and comic (and sometimes preacher and farmer), Uncle Dave Macon was the Grand Ole Opry's first major star and an audience favorite from 1925 until his death in 1952. He derived much of his repertoire and stage patter from vaudeville and minstrel shows, but his songs reflected on a wide variety of subjects from political corruption to current events like the advent of the automobile. His presence affected country music like none before it; even today a three-day festival, Uncle Dave Macon Days, is held in Murfreesboro, TN, the site of the National Old-Time Banjo Championship. *—Brian Mansfield*

★ **Country Music Hall of Fame Series** / 1992 / MCA ✦✦✦✦✦
"Shout if you are happy!" Uncle Dave Macon exclaims during "Tom and Jerry" as Mazy Todd saws away at her fiddle. "Kill yo'self!" That's the kind of enthusiasm Macon brings to these 16 fine examples of string-band music, recorded between 1926 and 1934 for the Vocalion, Brunswick, and Champion labels. Macon, who was 55 at the first of these recording sessions, frequently starts the songs with a spoken anecdote (including a plug for his Macon Midway Mule and Wagon Transportation Company). This collection is essentially an expanded version of *Uncle Dave Macon: First Featured Star of the Grand Ole Opry,* a retrospective issued in 1966 after his posthumous election to the Country Music Hall of Fame. *—Brian Mansfield*

Travelin' Down the Road / 1995 / County/BMG ✦✦✦✦✦
This CD is a reissue containing many of Uncle Dave Macon's best sides. All these tunes were transfers from original 78s recorded in 1935. The sound is still quite clear and enjoyable. There is a good selection of religious and secular tunes, all performed with vitality. You can really hear what draws people to old-timey music after listening to these records. *—Richard Meyer*

The Maddox Brothers & Rose

f. 1933, **db.** 1956
Group / Bakersfield Sound, Traditional Country
The Maddox Brothers (Cliff, Cal, Fred, Don, and "friendly Henry, the working girl's friend") and their sister Rose called themselves "America's Most Colorful Hillbilly Band." They weren't kidding. It wasn't just a matter of hillbilly couture—though with their matching Turk suits and spangles the family had style in spades. But colorful described their sound, as well. On the air in Modesto, California by 1937, the group made their first records, for the 4-Star label, in 1946. From 1951 till 1956, they recorded for Columbia. At that point, the family act broke up, though Rose maintained a successful solo career for many years after. But throughout the 1940s and 50s, the Maddox Brothers and Sister Rose tore down the honky-tonks from the Pacific Northwest to the Gulf Coast with slap-bass boogie and an iconoclastic attitude towards the stiffer mores of conventional country. In other words, they rocked the house. *—Dan Cooper*

★ **The America's Most Colorful Hillbilly Band: Their Original Recordings 1946-1951, Vol. 1** / 1961 / Arhoolie ✦✦✦✦✦
The Maddox Brothers and Rose first started recording in 1946 for the tiny 4-Star label, and it was there that they cut their most uninhibited sides, in the years immediately after World War II, freely mixing comedy, raw hillbilly sounds (including elements of what would later evolve into rockabilly), and mainstream country. The sides here move freely from hillbilly to blues to honky tonk to what we would later call rock & roll. Their version of "Move It on Over" is one of the hottest tracks of its era—and all the most amazing since the lead singer is Rose Maddox, and white women performers in those years seldom got to express themselves with the lack of inhibition displayed here. They romp and stomp their way through 27 songs that were so wild and raw, that by the early '50s they made many country music producers cringe at their lack of couth. The CD is worth it just for Rose Maddox's performance on "Milk Cow Blues," a dissolute, cackling, ultimately compelling piece of work that stands next to any other rendition of the song that one cares to name. The group also has savage fun at the expense of sentimental numbers like the ballad "Brown Eyes," and it's hard to listen to too much of this collection without breaking into laughter. The sound is generally excellent and the notes are thorough, although one wishes that there were more information to be found on the history of these actual recordings, which is barely touched upon. *—Bruce Eder*

The America's Most Colorful Hillbilly Band: Their Original Recordings 1946-1951, Vol. 2 / 1995 / Arhoolie ✦✦✦✦✦
Like *Maddox Brothers & Rose, 1946-1951, Vol. 1,* this has a wealth of material—30 cuts in all—from their early four-star era. The quality is on the same level as the first volume, and it's difficult to imagine that anyone who enjoyed the previous installment will be dissatisfied with this collection. The recording quality has the odd effect of making the records seem older than they actually are, but the music is actually as adventurous as any in country in the time, particularly on the fast boogies. Even collectors who kept up with Arhoolie's various vinyl reissues of pre-Columbia Maddox material may want this CD anthology too, as it has eight previously unissued acetates from the same era. *—Richie Unterberger*

On the Air: The 1940's / 1996 / Arhoolie ✦✦✦
These 1940s radio broadcasts have been issued on previous Arhoolie vinyl albums and cassettes, and without those original releases handy as reference, it's difficult to say whether this 32-track compilation gathers every bit of material from these sources that has seen the light of day. Should you still be building your Maddox Brothers collection, however, it's certainly good value, with tracks from 1940, 1945, and 1949, as well as some from a similar vintage whose exact year of broadcast is not known. What matters most is the content, which is good,

and sometimes actually of better fidelity than their 4-Star recordings from the same era; Cal Maddox's harmonica in particular seems more prominent here than in their other early work. *—Richie Unterberger*

Barbara Mandrell

b. Dec. 25, 1948, Houston, TX

Vocals, Guitar (Steel) / Urban Cowboy, Contemporary Country, Country-Pop

Thanks to a string of hit singles and a popular television variety series, vocalist Barbara Mandrell was arguably the biggest female star in country music in the late '70s and early '80s. Mandrell was phenomenally adept at playing the steel guitar before even reaching her teenage years, and became the showpiece when her family formed its own group. After a period during the '60s spent out of the music business, she signed a solo contract with Columbia in 1969 and notching her first Top 40 hit ("Playin' Around with Love") soon after. In 1975, Mandrell jumped to the ABC/Dot label, and reached the Top Five for the first time with "Standing Room Only." Her first number one came with 1978's "Sleeping Single in a Double Bed," and she eventually notched five chart-toppers between 1979 and 1983. In 1980, she gained a TV program with her sisters. Though vocal strain forced her to pull the plug in 1982, two LPs appeared that year, as well as her own Las Vegas stage show. In 1984, a nightmarish head-on car crash involving Mandrell and two of her children necessitated a long period of recovery. When she finally returned to performing a year later, the country music landscape had changed dramatically, with the "New Traditionalist" movement gaining dominance while the glitzier, more pop-influenced music Mandrell favored began falling out of favor. She began focusing almost exclusively on live performing, where she remained a significant draw. *—Jason Ankeny*

- **The Best of Barbara Mandrell** / 1979 / MCA ✦✦✦✦✦

The Best of Barbara Mandrell collects her biggest hits from the late '70s, including "After the Lovin'," "Married But Not to Each Other," "Tonight," "Woman to Woman," and "Sleeping Single in a Double Bed." *—Stephen Thomas Erlewine*

Joe Maphis (Otis Wilson Maphis)

b. May 12, 1921, Suffolk, VA, **d.** Jun. 27, 1986

Guitar, Session Musician / Instrumental Country, Bakersfield Sound, Honky Tonk, Rockabilly, Traditional Country

Joe and Rose Maphis were a popular husband-and-wife act in the late '40s and early '50s, singing traditional material backed by the amazing instrumental talent of Joe, who played everything with strings on it, especially the twin-neck guitar. The honky-tonk anthem "Dim Lights, Thick Smoke (And Loud, Loud Music)" was their big hit. Until his death in 1986, Joe was a sessions instrumentalist, backing such stars as Rick Nelson, Tex Ritter, and Wanda Jackson. *—David Vinopal*

Flying Fingers / Mar. 25, 1997 / Bear Family ✦✦✦✦✦

Along with Chet Atkins and Merle Travis, Joe Maphis was one of the most widely heard session guitarists from the 1940s until the 1980s, but his solo recordings weren't nearly as popular—which doesn't mean they weren't good. The 24 brisk, crisp instrumental tracks on this CD (running under one hour) were cut mostly for Columbia between 1955 and 1960; the 1955-57 stuff was recorded between sides by Rose Lee Maphis, and she is present there playing guitar, with Larry Collins (featured on four numbers, on top of which his sister Lorrie is the subject of the title of the Maphis original "Lorrie Ann"), Johnny Bond, and Leon Silby joining the guitar accompaniment on the later sessions. In addition to guitar, Maphis himself plays banjo and autoharp on various tracks. The best showcase to date of Maphis' work, the music features what seem like superhuman feats of dexterity, reminiscent of Jascha Heifetz's 1930s recordings on the violin, only better—every note is hit spot-on, but the playing never loses its warmth or seems mechanical. Listeners may swear that the masters of "Flying Fingers," "Fire on the Strings," and "Floggin' the Banjo" *must* have been sped up, but they weren't. While they may constitute highlights, they're not alone. Other high spots include "Katy Warren Breakdown," by session fiddle player Fiddlin' Kate Warren, and the cover of "Sweet Fern" by A.P. Carter. There's also a lot of variety, especially with the presence of the four Larry Collins sides, which rock pretty hard; "Early American" shows some strong blues elements. *—Bruce Eder*

Kathy Mattea

b. 1959, Cross Lane, WV

Vocals, Guitar / Country-Folk, Contemporary Country

Singer/songwriter Kathy Mattea primarily worked in a country tradition, but her songs were tinged with the confessional folk of songwriters like Joni Mitchell, Buffy Sainte-Marie, and James Taylor. In 1984, she released her eponymous debut album. Her first two singles, "Street Talk" and "Someone is Falling in Love," both reached the Top 30, and "You've Got a Soft Place to Fall" and "That's Easy for You to Say" both went on to make the Top 50. The 1985 album *From My Heart* produced three more hits, with "He Won't Give In" making it to the Top 25. Her third album, 1986's *Walk the Way the Wind Blows,* provided her with her first Top 10 country hits, "Love At the Five & Dime," "Walk the Way the Wind Blows," "You're the Power," and "Train of Memories." *Untasted Honey,* released in 1987, elevated Mattea to the status of a genuine star, producing the back-to-back number one hits "Goin' Gone" and "Eighteen Wheels and a Dozen Roses." Mattea continued to have Top 10 hits into the early '90s, highlighted by 1989's "Where've You Been," which became a crossover hit on the adult contemporary charts. *—Sandra Brennan*

Walk the Way the Wind Blows / 1986 / Mercury ✦✦✦✦✦

An injection of brash, bluegrass-style energy gave her music a needed lift. This is her strongest collection, matching her folkie sensitivity with an innocent verve that is truly catchy. It includes her hit version of Nanci Griffith's "Love at the Five and Dime." *—Michael McCall*

Untasted Honey / Sep. 28, 1987 / Mercury ✦✦✦

Featured is one of her best uptempo tunes, "Untold Stories," and one of her most wistful ballads, "Life as We Knew It." *—Michael McCall*

Willow in the Wind / 1989 / Mercury ✦✦✦

- **A Collection of Hits** / 1990 / Mercury ✦✦✦✦✦

Kathy Mattea has risen to near the top of the Nashville ranks because of a haunting, soulful voice, well-produced recordings that have a simple, folkie directness, and, most especially, an amazing talent for picking the best songs being written for the country market, among them "Eighteen Wheels and a Dozen Roses," "Goin' Gone," and the heartbreaking "Where've You Been." *—William Ruhlmann*

Time Passes By / 1991 / Mercury ✦✦✦✦

On her most ambitious album, Mattea gets impeccably chosen songs (as usual) and strong supporting performances (from Emmylou Harris, Dougie MacLean, and the Roches). She doesn't write her own stuff, so she may not be the romantic dreamer of "Asking Us to Dance," but she sure sounds like it. Songs like "Time Passes By," co-written by husband Jon Vezner, suggest there's more honesty here than image. She can even make the half-baked "From a Distance" convincing. *—Brian Mansfield*

Lonesome Standard Time / 1992 / Mercury ✦✦✦✦✦

Mattea had vocal-cord surgery that threatened to end her career before she made *Lonesome Standard Time,* but you couldn't prove it by listening: her voice hasn't lost a bit of its deep alto warmth. *Lonesome Standard Time* isn't as ambitious as *Time Passes By,* but it's filled with lovely performances from Mattea's favorite sources: bluegrass ("Lonesome Standard Time"), gospel-influenced country ("Standing Knee Deep in a River (Dying of Thirst)") and Nanci Griffith ("Listen to the Radio"). *—Brian Mansfield*

Good News / 1993 / Mercury ✦✦✦

Mattea's outing is delightfully true to her folk-country style: 10 moving, original pieces scoring a big zero on the saccharine and hackneyed front. A gorgeous voice, pristine production, and a true highlight of the season. *—Roch Parisien*

Walking Away a Winner / Oct. 1993 / Mercury ✦✦✦✦✦

Tired of having critics rave while radio programmers yawned, Mattea enlisted contempo-country producer Josh Leo to help brighten her sound for commercial consumption. It worked. The title cut was a hit right out of the box. *—Dan Cooper*

Love Travels / Feb. 4, 1997 / Mercury ✦✦✦

The Innocent Years / May 16, 2000 / MCA ✦✦✦

The Mavericks

f. 1990

Group / Americana, Neo-Traditionalist Country, Contemporary Country

Fusing traditional country with traditional rock & roll and relying on their own songwriting, the Mavericks became one of the most critically acclaimed and commercially successful groups of the early '90s. After forming in the late '80s around singer/songwriter Raul Malo, bassist Robert Reynolds and drummer Paul Deakin, the Mavericks played an assortment of clubs around the Miami area and released an eponymous independent album in 1990. The record gained the attention of nearly every major record label in Nashville, and led to a contract with MCA. Though their second album, 1992's *From Hell to Paradise,* earned critical acclaim, it wasn't a commercial success. The Mavericks' commercial fortunes turned around with their second major label album, *What a Crying Shame.* A more streamlined and focused record, it became a hit upon its release early in 1994, with the title track becoming a Top 40 hit. By the spring of 1995, *What a Crying Shame* had gone platinum. During the first half of 1995, the Mavericks recorded their fourth album, *Music for All Occasions,* which appeared in the fall of the year. Like its predecessor, it was critically acclaimed and a commerical success. By the spring of 1996, the album had gone gold. *Trampoline* followed in 1998. *—Stephen Thomas Erlewine*

Mavericks / 1990 / Hip-O ✦✦✦

From Hell to Paradise / 1992 / MCA ✦✦✦✦

In spite of Malo's Cuban heritage and the band's Miami roots—*because* of them, in fact—The Mavericks understand outsiders like Buck Owens and Hank Williams (both of whom the group covers) better than most of country's recent comers. And originals like "I Got You," "This Broken Heart," and the scathing title track, about Malo's aunt's escape from Cuban oppression, are so good the covers don't really matter. *—Brian Mansfield*

- **What a Crying Shame** / 1994 / MCA ✦✦✦✦✦

Superb, highly accessible follow-up to *From Hell to Paradise* included songs that made overt comparisons between Raul Malo and Roy Orbison ("I Should Have Been True," Jesse Winchester's "O What a Thrill"). Those who didn't realize the power of Malo's voice knew after those, when he didn't come off looking like a fool. Plenty of hot rockabilly shuffles are included, and the title track, with its Byrdsian guitar hook and bittersweet melody, became the first single by an "alternative" country act since Dwight Yoakam to break radio's Top 30. *—Brian Mansfield*

Music for All Occasions / Oct. 1995 / MCA ✦✦✦

With their third album, The Mavericks added slick country-pop to their arsenal of retro-country styles. The result straddles the line between affection and camp, since the band never goes completely overboard by drenching their songs with strings, and Raul Malo retains his aching Orbisonesque voice. However, that doesn't mean their songwriting has slipped, as all 11 originals are first-rate updated honky-tonk ravers or countrypolitan numbers. And the closing cover of "Somethin' Stupid," recorded with Trisha Yearwood, is a fun, kitschy delight. *—Stephen Thomas Erlewine*

Trampoline / Mar. 10, 1998 / MCA ✦✦✦✦✦

Super Colossal Smash Hits of the 90's: The Best of the Mavericks / Nov. 9, 1999 / MCA ✦✦✦✦

The Mavericks were one of the most acclaimed country bands of the '90s and, for a brief moment, they were among the most popular. With their third album, *What a Crying Shame,* they were at the zenith of their creative powers, and they were rewarded with great reviews and sales. They maintained a high level of creativity with its two follow-ups, 1995's *Music for All Occasions* and 1998's *Trampoline*, but their audience shrank somewhat, turning into a cult following much like Lyle Lovett's—they were popular, going gold with their new albums, but they didn't have crossover hits. That was a crying shame, because as the 1999 singles collection *Super Colossal Smash Hits of the 90's: The Best of the Mavericks* proves, they kept a high level of quality. That doesn't mean that *Super Colossal* is a perfect collection, however. Like most '90s hits compilations, it's baited with unreleased material. Usually, that means there's just one or two new cuts. This time, there are no less than four new tracks, which means there are only eight hits on the record. The new material—including covers of "Here Comes My Baby" and "Think of Me (When You're Lonely)"—isn't bad, and Tex-Mex-flavored "Pizziricco" in particular is pretty good, but the fact that a quarter of the album is devoted to new material means that there's a lot of good stuff missing here. Still, it's a good roundup of the best of the best, and a nice reminder to casual fans that haven't paid attention since *What a Crying Shame* that the Mavericks have a lot more to offer. *—Stephen Thomas Erlewine*

Martina McBride

b. Jul. 29, 1966, Sharon, KS

Vocals / New Traditionalist, Contemporary Country

A Kansas native who sang with power and tenderness, Martina McBride started out in a more traditional country vein in the early '90s, then kicked up the beat and the tempo as her career progressed. After graduating from high school, she began touring her native Kansas with a variety of country bands. She later married soundman John McBride and in 1990 moved with him to Nashville, where he worked for such stars as Charlie Daniels and Ricky Van Shelton while she waited tables and sang demos. John then produced a demo tape of her work which led to a contract with RCA at the end of 1991. Around the same time, John became Garth Brooks' production manager, and Martina became the singer's opening act. She released her debut album, *The Time Has Come*, in 1992. It spent six months in the country album Top 50. The title track was released as her first single and it stayed on the charts for five months, while her next two, "That's Me" and "Cheap Whiskey," nearly cracked the Top 40. *The Way That I Am*, McBride's second album, was released in 1993, and became her breakthrough. The record's first single, "My Baby Loves Me," reached number two and "Life #9" also became a Top 10 hit. Her third album, *Wild Angels*, was released in the fall of 1995; the title track later became her first number one hit. *—Sandra Brennan*

The Time Has Come / 1992 / RCA ✦✦✦
Her bold debut blends traditional country ("Cheap Whiskey, " "That's Me") with acoustic rave-ups, as in the title song. *—Michael McCall*

● **The Way That I Am** / 1993 / RCA ✦✦✦✦✦
McBride revamps her image, flashing a new haircut and a more forceful, uptempo style. She matches the music with a feisty, daring collection of distinguished songs, including the hit "My Baby Loves Me" and the remarkable "Independence Day," about an abused wife who takes justice into her own hands. *—Michael McCall*

Wild Angels / Sep. 26, 1995 / RCA ✦✦✦

Evolution / Aug. 26, 1997 / RCA ✦✦✦✦
Evolution is an appropriate title; it's clear that Martina McBride has grown—evolved—between *Wild Angels* and this terrific follow-up. That's not to say *Wild Angels* wasn't wonderful in its own right—its blend of rootsy country and contemporary production was clever, and her singing and songs were spot-on—but *Evolution* is different and special in its own way. It is true that it's smoother than its predecessor, especially with polished duets like "Valentine" (with Jim Brickman) and "Still Holding On" (Clint Black). What makes *Evolution* work is the purity and power of McBride's voice—she is one of the few contemporary country singers that can pull off this kind of country-pop. And that's not all she can do, as the rocking "Keeping My Distance" or the gospel-inflected "A Broken Wing" prove. Furthermore, McBride's songs remain staunchly independent and strong-willed, with clear feminist overtones, which helps make *Evolution* a rarity among contemporary country albums—it's catchy and it has a heart. *—Thom Owens*

Emotion / Sep. 14, 1999 / RCA ✦✦✦✦
Emotion is the fifth installment in a series of platinum albums from one of the most underrated voices in country music. After two years since the release of her double platinum *Evolution*, Martina McBride tears into these tracks showcasing the range and power of her incomparable voice. *Evolution* was a big-sounding record with lots of overdubbing and production. *Emotion* scales back musically using a very small band and the result is fresh and authentic, allowing McBride to captivate us with her resounding vocals. Aptly titled, *Emotion*, with lyrics like "anything's better than feelin' the blues" and "love's the only house big enough for all the pain in the world," tugs at the heart strings at times. But it's in "Do What You Do" that McBride lets us know that she's just doing what she does: "If you want to give them something different—something to sink their teeth into—well baby, you just do what you do." *—Maria Konicki*

C.W. McCall (William Fries)

b. Nov. 15, 1928, Audubon, IA

Vocals / Truck Driving Country, Urban Cowboy, Bakersfield Sound, Country Comedy, Country-Pop, Novelty

Essentially a character created by advertising executive William Fries, C.W. McCall was the instrumental figure behind the truck-driving craze that swept America in the mid-'70s. Fries was born November 15, 1928, in Audubon, Iowa, and while he displayed musical promise as a child, he was more interested in graphic design. While attending the University of Iowa, Fries studied music and played in the school's concert band, but his major was in fine arts, and after graduation he began handling the art chores at an Omaha, Nebraska television station. After five years there, he was hosting his own program, on which he drew caricatures of celebrities.

Fries signed on as the art director for an Omaha advertising agency in the early 1960s, and it was there that he created the character C.W. McCall as a selling tool for an area bakery. A trucker for the fictional Old Home Bread company who spent much of his time in a diner called "The Old Home Filler-Up-an'-Keep-On-a-Truckin' Cafe," the McCall character was a huge hit with viewers, and the radio campaign won Fries the advertising industry's prestigious Clio Award. In 1974, Fries decided to cut a record under the McCall moniker, and the single, a monologue with country backing titled after the aforementioned cafe, was a Top Twenty hit. A follow-up, "Wolf Creek Pass," was even more successful.

In 1975, McCall released the album *Black Bear Road;* the single "Convoy" hit Number One on both the pop and country charts, and a national craze was born. The song proved so successful that it influenced the famed filmmaker Sam Peckinpah to direct the 1978 film *Convoy*, starring Kris Kristofferson. By the time of the film's release, however, McCall's career was largely over. He released two more LPs, 1975's *Wolf Creek Pass* and 1977's *Roses for Mama*, which did spawn a major hit in its title track. But shortly after the latter album's release, McCall turned his back on the music industry to focus on the burgeoning environmental movement and moved to the small town of Ouray, Colorado, of which he was elected mayor in 1982. An attempt at a comeback in 1990 proved unsuccessful. *—Jason Ankeny*

● **Greatest Hits** / 1990 / Polydor ✦✦✦✦
No other artist took advantage of the CB craze of the '70s better than CW McCall. Chock full of trucker lingo, his songs bordered on the \novelty type and would have been classified as just that if it wasn't for the popularity it gained from radio play. While much of McCall's material is either out of print or extremely hard to find, his *Greatest Hits* more than suffices. Although outdated, there is still some humor left to be found in some of his campy tunes. His hillbilly drawl is front and center on "Wolf Creek Pass," while terms like "smoky" and "10-4" are hilariously rekindled on "'Round the World With Rubber Duck." His claim to fame, the mighty "Convoy," which was loosely based on protests by truck drivers on state-issued border tolls, hit number one on *Billboard*'s Top 40 back in 1975. McCall rarely sang, as his long-tongued songs usually involved him spinning the yarn while a chorus of females with high-pitched voices sang the middle. "Roses for Mama" was a serious attempt for McCall that was in the same vein as Red Sovine's "Teddy Bear," and "Crispy Critters" sounds like a Jeff Foxworthy offering. The music, which is a light spattering of countrified guitar and banjo, helps to guide the *Hee-Haw* whimsy of the songs to the height of 18-wheel silliness. Still fun to listen to, but undoubtedly dated, this disc will still conjure up the odd chuckle. *—Mike DeGagne*

Neal McCoy

b. Jul. 30, 1963, Jacksonville, TX

Vocals / Neo-Traditionalist Country, Contemporary Country

Neal McCoy had a string of hit singles of hit singles in the early '90s with his brand of revivalist honky tonk. McCoy was born and raised in Jacksonville, Texas, to Irish-Filipino parents who enjoyed a wide assortment of music. After graduating from high school, he began playing the Texas honky-tonk circuit and won a nightclub talent contest, where he was seen by Janie Fricke, who later arranged for McCoy to replace her as Charlie Pride's opening act when she left to pursue a full-fledged solo career in the early '80s. McCoy remained with Pride for seven years before releasing his 1988 debut single, the minor hit "That's How Much I Love You," as "Neal McCoy." In 1991, he released his debut album, *At This Moment;* it produced two Top 50 singles—"If I Built a Fire" and "This Time I Hurt Her More (Than She Loves Me)." McCoy released his second album, *Where Forever Begins*, in 1992 but he didn't have a genuine hit until 1994's *No Doubt About It*, which produced the number one singles "No Doubt About It" and "Wink." His success continued with 1995's *You Gotta Love That!*, which went platinum within a year of its release, and 1996's eponymous album. *Be Good at It* followed a year later, and in early 1999 McCoy resurfaced with *Life of the Party*. A year later, *24-7-365* was released. *—Sandra Brennan*

At This Moment / 1990 / Atlantic ✦✦✦

Where Forever Begins / 1992 / Atlantic ✦✦✦
It includes the singles "Where Forever Begins, " "There Ain't Nothin' I Don't Like About You, " and "Now I Pray for Rain." *—Brian Mansfield*

No Doubt About It / 1994 / Atlantic ✦✦✦✦✦
This Barry Beckett-produced disc was the first to capture the rock-influenced sound of McCoy's stage show (which usually included a rap version of *The Beverly Hillbillies* theme). Though McCoy had never had a single chart above 21, the album gave the singer his first two number one hits: "No Doubt About It" and "Wink." *—Brian Mansfield*

You Gotta Love That / 1995 / Atlantic ✦✦✦✦

Neal Mccoy / Jun. 1996 / Atlantic ✦✦✦
Neal McCoy's eponymous album is another set of immaculately crafted contemporary country music. From McCoy's polished but heartfelt performacne to the slik, seamless selection of songs, there isn't an obvious flaw on the album. Some may complain that McCoy's approach is getting a bit to pat and predictable, but the highlights—including the longtime stage favorite "Hillbilly Rap," and which features segments of "Day-O," "The Ballad of Jed Clampett," and "Rapper's Delight"—are well worth the time of any fan. *—Thom Owens*

● **Greatest Hits** / Jun. 10, 1997 / Atlantic ✦✦✦✦✦
Greatest Hits contains all of Neal McCoy's biggest contemporary country hits, including "Wink," "For a Change," "They're Playing Our Song," "You Gotta Love That" and "Then You Can Tell Me Goodbye," plus the new song "The Shake." *—Thom Owens*

Be Good At It / Oct. 28, 1997 / Atlantic ✦✦✦
The first album to follow a *Greatest Hits* collection usually provides an artist the opportunity to break free from his formulas and pursue a new path. It can also mean nothing, the artist just continuing to turn out the kind of music that supplied hits in the first place. That's what Neal McCoy chooses to do with *Be Good At It*, a perfectly fine collection of smoothed-over honky tonk and slick contemporary country ballads. McCoy has considerable charm—he's so engaging that he can effortlessly sell the weaker material here—and that's what makes the unadventurous nature of *Be Good At It* forgivable. Simply put, McCoy may have the po-

tential to achieve more than this kind of contemporary country, but he's very good at this kind of music and it's still entertaining to hear him at the top of his form. *—Thom Owens*

The Life of the Party / Jan. 19, 1999 / Atlantic ✦✦✦

24-7-365 / Aug. 22, 2000 / Warner Brothers ✦✦

Mindy McCready

Vocals / Contemporary Country

Mindy McCready's debut album *Ten Thousand Angels* elevated her into Nashville's music spotlight and established her as a promising singer.

Born and raised in southern Florida, Mindy McCready (b. Malinda Gayle McCready) graduated from high school at the age of 16 with the intention of beginning her musical career early. Following her graduation, she took a part-time job in her mother's ambulance company and began concentrating on performing her music. When she was 18 years old, she moved to Nashville. She had made her mother a promise that she would go to college if she failed to break into the music industry within the space of a year. After a few months in Nashville, she met producer/songwriter Norro Wilson, who directed her demo tapes to producer David Malloy. Impressed with her tapes, Malloy agreed to work with McCready. For the next year, McCready and Malloy refined the singer's style and crafted a high-class demo tape. Eventually, Malloy took the tape to RLG Records who signed Mindy McCready after seeing her perform a live concert; she completed the deal exactly 51 weeks after she moved to Nashville.

Mindy McCready released her debut album *Ten Thousand Angels* in April of 1996 to positive reviews. Within six months of its release, it had gone gold. *If I Don't Stay the Night* followed in 1997, trailed two years later by *I'm Not So Tough*. *—Stephen Thomas Erlewine*

Ten Thousand Angels / Apr. 1996 / BNA ✦✦✦✦

If I Don't Stay the Night / Nov. 4, 1997 / BNA ✦✦✦✦

I'm Not So Tough / Aug. 10, 1999 / BNA ✦✦✦

● **Super Hits** / Jan. 11, 2000 / BNA ✦✦✦✦

Super Hits may be a budget-line compilation—usually a sign of cut-rate product—but it's nevertheless an excellent summation of Mindy McCready's two hit country albums for BNA. It bypasses her third and final record for the label, *I'm Not So Tough*, but that's fine, since that was a pop crossover move that didn't quite work out. That means that *Super Hits* contains nothing but the cream of *Ten Thousand Angels* and *If I Don't Stay the Night*—10 songs, including the hits "Ten Thousand Angels," "Guys Do It All the Time," "A Girl's Gotta Do (What a Girl's Gotta Do)," "Maybe He'll Notice Her Now," "What if I Do," "You"ll Never Know," and "The Other Side of This Kiss," plus a handful of album tracks. It may not be packaged like a first-rate compilation, but that's its only flaw, since *Super Hits* contains everything most McCready fans could want. *—Stephen Thomas Erlewine*

Ronnie McDowell

b. Mar. 26, 1950, Fountain Head, TN

Vocals, Guitar / Urban Cowboy, Country-Pop

Raised in rural Portland, Tennessee, north of Nashville, McDowell didn't take performing seriously until he was stationed in the Philippines with the navy. The first song he performed in public: "It's Now or Never," appropriate since Elvis Presley has had a huge impact on his career. McDowell wrote his first hit, "The King Is Gone," the day that Elvis died. Enough people shared his grief that a reported three million copies were sold. McDowell did all the Elvis vocal imitations for a 1979 Elvis TV movie, starring Kurt Russell, and he began to take on the image of an Elvis imitator. McDowell consciously distanced himself from those comparisons, which became easier when record producer Buddy Killen took over the reins of his career, bringing in solid uptempo material that consistently showcased McDowell's strong (though a bit nondescript) vocal talents. Now comfortable with his reputation, he's returned on occasion to more "Elvis" work, providing the vocal parts for the short-lived ABC series *Elvis* in 1990. *—Tom Roland*

● **Older Women and Other Greatest Hits** / 1987 / Epic ✦✦✦✦✦

McDowell fell into this "clone" thing for a couple of years where he remade his own hits; and all three soundalikes ("Older Women," "Wandering Eyes," "Watchin' Girls Go By") are curiously placed back-to-back. His later material is the most emotive, especially "I Dream of Women like You," "In a New York Minute," and "Love Talks," recorded with Exile. *—Tom Roland*

The Best of Ronnie McDowell / 1990 / Curb ✦✦✦✦

Along with "The King Is Gone," the song which forever established McDowell's remarkable vocal similarities to Elvis Presley, this hits collection includes "I Love You, I Love You, I Love You," "All Tied Up" and "It's Only Make Believe." It does not, however, feature either of his chart-topping hits, "Older Women" and "You're Gonna Ruin My Bad Reputation." *—Jason Ankeny*

Reba McEntire (Reba Nell McEntire)

b. Mar. 28, 1955, Chockie, OK

Vocals, Guitar / Neo-Traditionalist Country, Contemporary Country

It may have taken her several years to reach the top of the country charts, but once Reba McEntire got there she stayed there—scoring a consistent stream of Top Ten singles and a grand total of 18 number one singles, McEntire was the single most successful female country vocalist of the '80s and '90s. She recorded her first album in 1975, though she really didn't make any headway until 1980, when "(You Lift Me) Up to Heaven" made it to number eight. Her first number one single, "Can't Even Get the Blues," followed two years later and soon established herself as one of the decade's most popular artists, selling over 20 million albums. McEntire also began toying with rock and pop influences, both in her music and in her image. In the '90s, Reba stayed as popular as she was in the previous decade, as both her albums and her singles consistently charted in the Top Ten, frequently at number one. *—Stephen Thomas Erlewine*

Reba McEntire / 1977 / Mercury ✦✦✦✦✦

The average listener of Reba McEntire's first album will most likely have one of two minds about it. On the one hand, fans of McEntire's later recordings might reject this album on the grounds that it is more tradition-oriented and less contemporary-sounding than the material for which she is best known, while traditionalists might embrace it as the one Reba McEntire album to own. Whatever the listener's bias, this album has more to do with the early-'70s sounds of Tanya Tucker and Tammy Wynette than the contemporaneous pop-country hits of, say, Barbara Mandrell. Although such individual tracks as "Glad I Waited Just for You" and McEntire's version of "Right Time of the Night" hardly constitute hard country, her recording of Roger Miller's "Invitation to the Blues" is probably as close as she comes. Ironically, it is the very listeners who would likely dismiss any Reba McEntire album out of hand that might find this the most surprising and enjoyable, whereas only the most accepting fans of her later recordings will react so positively. This is a strong album that rewards exploration. *—Greg Adams*

Out of a Dream / 1979 / Mercury ✦✦✦

The Best of Reba McEntire / 1985 / Mercury ✦✦✦✦✦

The Best of Reba McEntire contains 10 of her biggest hits from the early '80s, which were all recorded for Mercury Records. These hit singles—including "(You Lift Me) Up to Heaven," "Today All Over Again," "I'm Not That Lonely Yet," "Can't Even Get the Blues," "You're the First Time I've Thought About Leaving," and "Why Do We Want (What We Know We Can't Have)"—represent the first songs where McEntire truly found a voice of her own. Occasionally, Jerry Buckler's productions are a little too sanitary, but McEntire overcomes any overly-commercial flourishes with her gritty, gutsy vocals, and the best of these songs are as good as her finest moments for MCA. *—Thom Owens*

My Kind of Country / 1986 / MCA ✦✦✦✦✦

McEntire's celebration of the back-to-basics movement in country has many country shuffles. These are her purest country performances and most straightforward production. *—Mark A. Humphrey*

What Am I Gonna Do About You / 1986 / MCA ✦✦✦✦✦

The chart-topping title cut highlights *What Am I Gonna Do About You*, which also features the number one hit "One Promise Too Late." *—Jason Ankeny*

Whoever's in New England / 1986 / MCA ✦✦✦✦✦

This is the album that elevated McEntire from pretty good country singer to megastar. A number of the melodies have pop sensibilities, but the production is decidedly country. *—Tom Roland*

★ **Greatest Hits** / 1987 / MCA ✦✦✦✦✦

Reba McEntire's first collection of hits on MCA Records draws entirely from the beginning of her string of Top Ten hits in the mid-'80s. *Greatest Hits* cover her singles from 1984, 1985, and 1986 and features nearly every Top Ten hit she had, including the number one hits "How Blue," "Somebody Should Leave," "Whoever's In New England," "Little Rock," "What Am I Gonna Do About You," and "One Promise Too Late." *—Stephen Thomas Erlewine*

The Last One to Know / 1987 / MCA ✦✦✦

Recorded as McEntire went through the process of divorce from first husband Charlie Battles, it's understandably heavy on songs about breakups and the uncertainty of the future, "The Stairs"—about domestic violence—is particularly moving. Despite her personal pain, she still holds out hope in "Love Will Find Its Way to You." *—Tom Roland*

Reba Live / 1989 / MCA ✦✦✦

☆ **For My Broken Heart** / 1991 / MCA ✦✦✦✦✦

Only the quietly moving "If I Had Only Known" might be considered a tribute to the members of McEntire's band who died in a 1990 plane crash, but the tragedy creeps into McEntire's voice and her song selection. Throughout the album, McEntire dwells on regrets, unvoiced feelings, and missed chances. The best songs aren't the hits "For My Broken Heart" and "Is There Life out There" but a group of evocative story-songs which unfold slowly, leaving loose threads and developing complex emotional undercurrents. *For My Broken Heart* may be the strongest album of McEntire's career; it's certainly her most heartbreaking. *—Brian Mansfield*

It's Your Call / 1992 / MCA ✦✦✦

McEntire possesses one of the most undeniably emotional voices in country music—one well-phrased word in her Oklahoma accent can start hearts breaking. The overwhelming number of ballads on *It's Your Call* take maximum advantage of that talent, especially on "Straight from You" and "The Heart Won't Lie," a duet with label mate Vince Gill. While *It's Your Call* may have the same intensity of emotion as the double-platinum *For My Broken Heart*, it lacks similar depth—taken as a whole, these songs make McEntire sound like a victim, a role she no longer plays well. The ballads leave few places for McEntire's strength of character, and the bluesy "Take It Back" and "Go Down Easy" only serve as breaks in the despair. McEntire showed her best on *For My Broken Heart;* while she's not holding back here, only casual or partial listeners will be moved as much. *—Brian Mansfield*

☆ **Greatest Hits, Vol. 2** / Oct. 1993 / MCA ✦✦✦✦✦

Greatest Hits, Vol. 2 collects Reba McEntire's biggest hits of the late '80s, including the number one singles "You Lie," "For My Broken Heart," and her biggest hit, "Is There Life Out There," and seven other songs. *—Stephen Thomas Erlewine*

Starting Over / Oct. 3, 1995 / MCA ✦✦✦

If You See Him / Jun. 2, 1998 / MCA ✦✦✦

So Good Together / Nov. 23, 1999 / MCA ✦✦✦✦

It hasn't been hard to notice that Reba McEntire's usually reliable stream of number one hits has slowed lately. But *So Good Together* re-examines McEntire's artistry and puts fans back in touch with the Reba we know and love. No one sings emotion better than McEntire, and the relaxed warmth of her voice produces one of the finest vocal performances she's bestowed on listeners since before *Starting Over. So Good Together*'s first release, the introspective "What Do You Say," has been making its way up the charts in glowing Reba style. *—Maria Konicki*

Tim McGraw

b. May 1, 1967, Delhi, LA

Vocals / Neo-Traditionalist Country, Adult Contemporary, Contemporary Country, Country-Pop

Tim McGraw was best-known for his hit single, "Indian Outlaw," a controversial single that made him a star in the mid-'90s.

The son of the baseball player Tug McGraw, Tim was raised in Start, Louisiana, where he listened to country, Motown, rock & roll and R&B. Like his father, he was a natural athlete and attended college on sports scholarships. McGraw didn't become interested in performing music until he bought a pawn shop guitar while attending school. He moved to Nashville in 1989 and later played gigs in the Deep South. In 1992 he released his first single, "Welcome to the Club," which reached the country Top 50. In 1993, he released his eponymous debut, which produced two more minor hits. In 1994, McGraw released his second album, *Not A Moment Too Soon*, which contained "Indian Outlaw." The song reached number eight on the country charts and number 15 on the pop charts admist controversy over the Native American stereotypes presented in the lyrics. Nevertheless, *Not A Moment Too Soon* became a crossover hit—the album hit number two on the pop charts and went triple-platinum within months of its release. "Don't Take the Girl," the follow-up single, was another crossover success, reaching number 17 on the pop charts and number one on the country charts. In 1995, McGraw released his third album, *All I Want*, which became another multi-platinum hit. *Place in the Sun* was released in 1999, topping the country charts with the single "Something Like That." *—Sandra Brennan*

Tim McGraw / 1993 / Curb ♦♦♦

At a time when most Nashville releases were a blend of redneck resilience and glossy sentimentality, the ever-improving Tim McGraw uses an abundance believability and strong melodies on *A Place in the Sun*. Songs such as "Seventeen" and "My Next Thirty Years" may carry clichéd messages of youth's optimism, but the vocal hooks that house them more than make up for it. No longer relying on hokey material like "Indian Outlaw," *Sun* finds McGraw developing into a quality country crooner. *—Steven Kurutz*

Not a Moment Too Soon / Mar. 22, 1994 / Curb ♦♦♦♦

"Indian Outlaw," with its controversy and its resemblance to The Raiders' "Indian Reservation," made McGraw a star, and the ballad "Don't Take the Girl" reinforced the image. *Not a Moment Too Soon* contained better hooks than its predecessor, but it also belabored the obvious with songs like "It Don't Get Any Countrier Than This" and "Give It to Me Strait." *—Brian Mansfield*

All I Want / Sep. 19, 1995 / Curb ♦♦♦

Tim McGraw's albums always suffer from uneven material, but *All I Want* is a surprisingly consistent record that consolidates his strengths while expanding him into new territory. He hasn't abandoned the honky tonk and jokey country-rock that made his famous, but he's made it harder and more believable. Similarly, his ballads are heartfelt, delivered with convincing sincerity. In other words, he has grown musically and developed into a thoroughly entertaining vocalist. And that growth is what makes *All I Want* his best record. It is still fairly uneven, with several weak songs, but McGraw now knows how to disguise the flaws in the material with his singing. *—Stephen Thomas Erlewine*

Everywhere / Jun. 3, 1997 / Curb ♦♦♦

Place in the Sun / May 4, 1999 / Curb ♦♦♦

Everywhere may have continued Tim McGraw's streak of hit albums, but it also suggested that he was falling into a bit of a rut. That doesn't seem to have bothered McGraw, since *Everywhere*'s sequel, *A Place in the Sun*, is much like its predecessor in its balance of polished ballads, country-pop and uptempo ravers, which are supposed to sound like honky-tonk but are closer to country-rock. Since he's a professional and works with professionals, *A Place in the Sun* sounds good and has a number of highlights, from ballads like "My Best Friend" and the Patty Loveless duet "Please Remember Me" to harder numbers like "Something Like That," "My Next Thirty Years" and "She'll Have You Back." The problem is, there's nothing new here—not only is the music in the same vein as his previous efforts, it has nearly the same ratio of hits to misses. Since the moments that do work are very good, and since it is a stronger overall record than its predecessor, it will be worthwhile for fans, but it doesn't help erase the impression that McGraw won't deliver a truly satisfying album until a greatest-hits compilation comes along. *—Stephen Thomas Erlewine*

● **Greatest Hits** / Nov. 21, 2000 / Curb ♦♦♦♦

Greatest Hits lives up to its title, offering the bulk of Tim McGraw's big hits over the course of its 15 tracks. Thankfully, there are no new recordings to bait hardcore fans—just "Let's Make Love," the duet with Faith Hill that originally appeared on her *Breathe* album. Consequently, this is one of the rare modern-day incidences of a *Greatest Hits* that really offers all the hits, and nothing but, which not only makes it a boon to fans, but also makes it the most consistent record in McGraw's catalog. *—Stephen Thomas Erlewine*

Jo Dee Messina

Vocals (Background), Vocals / Neo-Traditionalist Country, Contemporary Country

Jo Dee Messina's eponymous 1996 album established the vocalist as one of the most popular new female country singers of the year.

During her teens, she sang in country bands around her New England homebase. At the age of nineteen, she left for Nashville. For several years, Messina played local talent contests. By chance, she met an Curb Records executive at a Fan Fair and joked that she would be a good addition to the label. Producer James Stroud persuaded Curb that her demo tape was worth listening to and, by the end of 1994, she had signed to the record label.

Messina recorded her first album with producers Tim McGraw and Byron Gallimore over the course of 1995. The resulting record, *Jo Dee Messina*, was released in the spring of 1996 and was a hit upon its release. *I'm Alright* followed in 1998, scoring the hit "Lesson in Leavin'." *Burn* followed a year later. *—Stephen Thomas Erlewine*

Jo Dee Messina / Mar. 26, 1996 / Curb ♦♦♦♦

I'm Alright / Mar. 17, 1998 / Curb ♦♦♦

Released two years after her breakthrough debut, Jo Dee Messina's second album, *I'm Alright*, essentially follows the same polished country-pop formula as her first. Messina again worked with producers Byron Gallimore and Tim McGraw, who supply arrangements that are just a little too clean. Nevertheless, many of the songs are solid contemporary country tunes, even if they lean a little close to adult contemporary pop, and her delivery is assured and convincing. Like many country albums, *I'm Alright* essentially features a handful of very, very good singles, surrounded by filler that's either pleasant or forgettable, but the best moments on the record ("Bye, Bye," "I'm Alright," "Silver Thunderbird") prove that Messina's debut was no flash in the pan. *—Thom Owens*

● **Burn** / Aug. 1, 2000 / Wea International ♦♦♦♦

Messina's third release with Curb, *Burn* is a riveting collection of 11 songs guaranteed to make even the faintest of heart feel energized. Bryan Gallimore and Tim McGraw throw their hats into the ring again as co-producers putting out an album that speaks volumes to Messina fans. "Downtime," the album's lead track, is an upbeat song about needing a little space in order to mend a broken heart; "Burn," the title track and one of the album's slower songs, is about being what you want to be in life; the soulful "Bring on the Rain" is the culmination of the McGraw/Messina friendship with McGraw singing background vocals about those days in life when you're feeling like everything's going wrong; and perhaps part auto-biographical is "Dare to Dream," a snappy song with lyrics like "Live, love, seize the day, and dare to dream." Having taken two years to make this album was worth it; the third time's a charm. *—Maria Konicki*

Emmett Miller

b. Feb. 2, 1900, Macon, GA, **d.** Mar. 29, 1962, Macon, GA

Vocals / Minstrel, Old-Timey

Although his vocal delivery was influential on several major country singers, Emmett Miller was basically a vaudeville singer, with far stronger aural links to Al Jolson than Merle Haggard. A White man performing in blackface, Miller was an exponent of the minstrel school of performance, touring widely with minstrel shows for several decades. The most influential aspect of his recordings were his yodeling trill, and there can be no doubt that it heavily influenced country singers such as Jimmie Rodgers, Lefty Frizzell, and Hank Williams (who learned "Lovesick Blues" from a Miller record). Bob Wills asked his early lead singer to copy Miller's style, and a bit of Miller's easygoing ragtime sensibility can be heard in Leon Redbone. But Miller, to quote Donald Sutherland's description of John Milton in *Animal House*, does not speak well to our generation. That's not just because the vaudeville arrangements of his 1920s recordings will strike most modern-day listeners as quaint. It's also because the blackface minstrel tradition—which was just part of the scene in Miller's heyday—strikes us as somewhat distasteful in the post-segregation era in its perpetuation of some disagreeable Black stereotypes. *—Richie Unterberger*

● **Minstrel Man from Georgia** / Feb. 6, 1996 / Columbia/Legacy ♦♦♦♦

God knows what this is doing in Legacy's Roots N' Blues series; it's a long way from Blind Willie McTell and Bukka White to this. Anyway, this has 20 of his OKeh sides from the late '20s, including a "Lovesick Blues" that served as the model for Hank Williams' hit with the same song in 1949. The Georgia Crackers accompany Miller on every cut, with a cast including Tommy & Jimmy Dorsey (present on every track), Jack Teagarden, and Gene Krupa. More of historical interest and musical significance than anything else, with a thorough sleeve note from country music authority Charles Wolfe. *—Richie Unterberger*

Roger Miller

b. Jan. 2, 1936, Fort Worth, TX, **d.** Oct. 25, 1992

Vocals, Guitar / Nashville Sound/Countrypolitan, Honky Tonk, Country Comedy, Country-Pop, Traditional Country

Roger Miller's humourous novelties overshadow his considerable songwriting talents, as well as his hardcore honky tonk roots. These are the songs that brought Miller fame in the mid-'60s, but he also wrote a number of hits for other artists in the '50s and '60s that, like his novelty numbers, became country and popular classics.

Miller made his first impression as a songwriter, when Ray Price had a number three hit with "Invitation to the Blues" in 1958. It was followed by other successful versions of his songs, including Jim Reeves' "Billy Bayou." After a few unsuccessful sides for Decca, Miller had two moderate hits for RCA in 1961, then dropped off the charts. Miller moved to Hollywood in 1963, becoming a regular on *The Jimmy Dean Show* and *The Merv Griffin Show*, where he showcased his new goofy persona, singing silly songs. "Dang Me," his first single for Smash, was a huge hit in 1964, spending six weeks at the top of the country charts and reaching the pop Top 10. Following another Top 10 country and pop hit, "Chug-A-Lug," Miller had his biggest hit in early 1965 with "King of the Road." This sparked his most successful year, as each single he released reached the Top 10. Miller's momentum slowed down almost immediately and between 1966 and 1969, he didn't have many hits, even if he remained popular. In the early '70s, he started writing music for movies, notably Walt Disney's 1973 animated adaptation of *Robin Hood*. That year, he left Smash/Mercury for Columbia Records, where he spent four years with only one hit—his first single. Miller didn't record much during the late '70s and early '80s, but he had a career resurgence in the mid-'80s, when he wrote the music for *Big River*, a Broadway adaptation of Mark Twain's works; it won seven Tony Awards, including Best Musical and Outstanding Score. In 1992, Roger Miller died of throat cancer. During the '90s, his legacy remained strong, as new generations of country singers found songs in his catalog to reinterpret. *—Stephen Thomas Erlewine*

★ **Golden Hits** / 1965 / Smash ♦♦♦♦♦

Years before Waylon Jennings and Willie Nelson grew their hair long, Miller took country to the counterculture with these hipster twists on the Nashville sound. No tunesmith in Music City had ever tossed off songs like "Dang Me," "King of the Road," "Chug-A-Lug," and "Engine Engine #9." No one has since. *—Dan Cooper*

☆ **The Best of Roger Miller, Vol. 1: Country Tunesmith** / 1991 / Mercury ♦♦♦♦♦
Downplaying his humorous muse in favor of showing off his skill as a straightahead country writer, these 21 tracks (including some strongly Ray Price-influenced fare from 1957) were either written or co-written by Miller. It's well worth the money to hear his own versions of such standards as "Invitation to the Blues," "Half a Mind," and "Don't We All Have the Right." *—Dan Cooper*

☆ **The Best of Roger Miller, Vol. 2: King of the Road** / Aug. 4, 1992 / Mercury ♦♦♦♦♦
Where *The Best of Roger Miller, Vol. 1: Country Tunesmith* concentrated on Miller's lesser-known honky tonk numbers and hits he wrote for other artists, *Best of Roger Miller, Vol. 2: King of the Road* is strictly Miller's biggest hits. From the novelties of "Dang Me," "Chug-A-Lug," "Do-Wacka-Do," and "Kansas City Star" to the relatively straightforward "King of the Road" and "Engine Engine 9," all of Miller's big hits from the mid-'60s are included, as are selected lesser hits from the late '60s like "Little Green Apples" and "Me and Bobby McGee." Combined, *Country Tunesmith* and *King of the Road* offer a definitive overview of Roger Miller's career that even eclipses the subsequently released box set, *King of the Road.* *—Stephen Thomas Erlewine*

★ **King of the Road** / 1995 / Mercury ♦♦♦♦♦
Over the course of three discs, the box set *King of the Road* contains every essential item Roger Miller ever recorded. Unfortunately, the compilation isn't a consistent one—although there are more great songs than weak ones, there are still too many lesser numbers to make the set a truly essential purchase. All of the necessary items are available on Mercury's two-volume *Best of Roger Miller* collection (*Country Tunesmith* and *King of the Road*), which are leaner, more consistent collections that are preferable to this slightly padded three-disc box. *—Thom Owens*

Ronnie Milsap

b. Jan. 16, 1944, Robbinsville, NC
Vocals, Piano / Urban Cowboy, Contemporary Country, Country-Pop
Ronnie Milsap was one of the major figures of country music in the 1970s, developing a hybrid of country and pop which brought him a large audience. Born blind from congenital glaucoma, he underwent classical training in violin, piano, guitar and many other instruments. After becoming interested in rock & roll, he worked in J.J. Cale's band during the early '60s and formed his own group in 1965. Session work in Memphis followed during the late '60s, and in 1970, he recorded a pop hit, "Loving You Is a Natural Thing." After signing to RCA Victor, he hit the Top Ten with his first single for the label, 1973's "I Hate You." The following year, he had three number one hits in a row—"Pure Love," "Please Don't Tell Me How the Story Ends," and "(I'd Be) A Legend in My Time." Then, Milsap enjoyed a string of six number one hits in a row during 1976. Between 1980 and 1982, Milsap earned an incredible ten more consecutive number one hits including the crossover smashes "Smoky Mountain Rain," "No Gettin' Over Me" and "Any Day Now." Milsap had yet another string of uninterrupted number one hits (eight) between 1985 and 1987, though his commercial appeal began to decline in the '90s. Nevertheless, he continued to record and perform successfully throughout the '90s. *—Sandra Brennan*

Inside / 1982 / Buddha ♦♦♦♦♦
Inside is arguably the strongest album Ronnie Milsap released at the peak of his slick contemporary country hit-making streak. The key to the album is that its consistency is married to a thoroughly appealing production equal parts Nashville and Californian soft-rock. Make no mistake, this is glossy, slick music, but that's its charm—the surface is seductively slick, giving Milsap's warm baritone a sympathetic musical bed. Though he does dip outside of adult contemporary-oriented country-pop on "I Love New Orleans Music," this truly soars when its feet are planted firmly in the mainstream and he has melodic tales of heartbreak, whether it's on the hits "Any Day Now" and "He Got You" or album tracks like "Hate the Lies—Love the Liar" or "It's Just a Room." These are corny and slick, but they work thanks to their production and Milsap's performances. He had a number of number one singles and albums, but few were better than *Inside.* *—Stephen Thomas Erlewine*

One More Try for Love / 1984 / RCA ♦♦♦
In his effort to expand the boundaries of country, Milsap pushes the edge harder here than in any other album. The electronically altered vocals in the tracks "She Loves My Car" and "Suburbia" have a winning effect—tasteful, not overdone. *—Tom Roland*

True Believer / Jun. 7, 1993 / Liberty ♦♦♦
If only the whole album had the energy of the John Hiatt title track (not to mention the wit of The Hoss Allen intro), Milsap's Liberty debut would have been a record to reckon with. *—Dan Cooper*

The Essential Ronnie Milsap / 1995 / RCA ♦♦♦♦♦
The Essential Ronnie Milsap isn't necessarily a definitive collection—Milsap simply had too many big hits to fit on a single-disc compilation, for starters—but it does come close. Many of his biggest hits are included on *Essential,* as well as a handful of obscurities, including album tracks and lesser-known hits. Consequently, the compilation is a nice cross-section that offers a good representation of Milsap's sound, even if it doesn't come close to being a definitive retrospective. *—Thom Owens*

★ **40 #1 Hits** / Jun. 6, 2000 / Virgin ♦♦♦♦♦
Those who pay attention to record labels are liable to assume that this two-disc compilation consists of re-recordings of Ronnie Milsap's hits. Surprisingly, however, *40 #1 Hits* is an exception to this supposition; it does contain Milsap's original RCA Victor recordings, digitally remastered.

There are actually 43 tracks on *40 #1 Hits.* "Stranger in My House," which is one of those extra recordings, didn't get to number one by anybody's estimation, but it did hit the country Top Five and the pop Top 40, and it won the Best New Country Song Grammy Award for 1983. The other two are newly recorded songs, "Livin' on Love" and "Time, Love and Money," both of which rock a little harder than Milsap usually does.

All told, Ronnie Milsap's *40 #1 Hits* is a compilation that exceeds expectations and stands as the definitive collection of the most popular work by one of the most successful country artists of the 1970s and '80s. *—William Ruhlmann*

Patsy Montana (Ruby Blevins)

b. Oct. 30, 1914, Hot Springs, AR, **d.** 1996
Vocals / Cowboy, Traditional Country
One of the true pioneers of country music was Patsy Montana, the original yodeling cowgirl. She was the first woman in country music to have a million-selling single—1935's "I Want to Be a Cowboy's Sweetheart"—and was a mainstay on WLS Chicago's *National Barn Dance* for over 25 years. In the '30s and '40s she was the sweetheart of many a movie cowpoke, appearing in numerous Western films, and her success encouraged the traditionally male-oriented country music business to welcome and respect the scores of female performers that followed her. Influenced early on by Jimmie Rodgers, she learned to yodel and play organ, guitar, and violin. After appearing on several radio programs, she made her recording debut in 1932 for Victor. Though 1935's "I Want to Be a Cowboy's Sweetheart" became her signature song, it was not her only hit; others included "Rodeo Sweetheart," "I Wanna Be a Western Cowgirl," "Back on the Montana Plains," and "I Want to Be a Cowboy's Dream." Montana moved to Decca in 1941 and released only 12 songs over the next four years. Following World War II, she made few appearances but still appeared weekly on the *Louisiana Hayride.* Montana remained active in the music industry, appearing on many country music shows and recording into the '90s before her death in 1996. *—Sandra Brennan*

The Cowboy's Sweetheart / 1988 / King ♦♦♦♦
These are late recordings by the Western radio star. The title track, from 1935, was the first million-selling female country vocal performance. *—Mark A. Humphrey*

● **Columbia Historic Edition** / Columbia ♦♦♦♦

John Michael Montgomery

b. Jan. 20, 1965, Danville, KY
Vocals / New Traditionalist, Contemporary Country
Even though his music leaned closer to pop music than most honky tonkers, John Michael Montgomery was at the forefront of the new traditionalists movement in the early '90s. Montgomery was born in Danville, Kentucky, to a guitar-playing father and a mother who played the drums, and made his debut at age five during one of his parents' concerts. He began playing in local bands at age 15, and when his parents divorced two years later, he began playing in a group with his father and brother. He first gained notice while playing at the Austin City Saloon in Lexington, Kentucky. By 1991, he had signed with Atlantic Records. Montgomery's debut, *Life's a Dance,* was released in 1992 to positive reviews and strong sales, climbing into the Top Five on the country album charts and the Top 30 on the pop album charts. It produced several hits, including the title cut and "I Love the Way You Love Me, " which became a number one country and a moderate pop hit as well. His second album, *Kickin' It Up,* came out in 1994 and contained the chart-topper "I Swear, " which remained number one for over a month. The album reached number one within a month of its release; it quickly went multi-platinum as well. In the spring of 1995, he released his eponymous third album. *What I Do Best* was released in late 1996, and was followed two years later by *Leave a Mark,* which sustained his popularity.

Montgomery's sixth album, *Home to You,* was released in the spring of 1999, and *Brand New Me* followed in a year later. *—Sandra Brennan*

Life's a Dance / 1992 / Atlantic ♦♦♦

Kickin' It Up / Jan. 25, 1994 / Atlantic ♦♦♦♦♦
As the title suggests, Montgomery kicks up the tempos and reveals a stronger country-rock bent. He still leans heavily on contemporary ballads ("I Swear," "Rope the Moon"), but proves just as capable on the brawnier songs. It became a number one album on the pop charts shortly after its release. *—Michael McCall*

John Michael Montgomery / Mar. 28, 1995 / Atlantic ♦♦♦♦♦
It doesn't really matter that *John Michael Montgomery* replicates the formula of its hit predecessor, *Kickin' it Up.* Even though it has the same country-pop ballads, slick country-rock and honky tonk numbers that made *Kickin' It Up* a monster commercial success, the record doesn't sound dull or repetitive. Most of the album's success is due to the clean, commercial production, which makes even the weak material entertaining. *—Stephen Thomas Erlewine*

What I Do the Best / Sep. 24, 1996 / Atlantic ♦♦♦
John Michael Montgomery's fourth album, *What I Do the Best,* doesn't tamper with his hit-making blueprint at all. Essentially, it follows the same pattern as its three predecessor, relying equally on heart-tugging ballads and clean, uptempo neo-honky tonk and country-rock. Occasionally, the material is below par and Montgomery's delivery doesn't quite save the weaker songs, yet the best moments of *What I Do the Best* are among his best, blending well-written songs with crisp production and assured singing. *—Stephen Thomas Erlewine*

● **Greatest Hits** / Oct. 14, 1997 / Atlantic ♦♦♦♦♦
After only four albums and five years of recording, it may be a little soon for John Michael Montgomery to release a *Greatest Hits* album, yet this collection does everything it should do—it features all of Montgomery's biggest hits and best-known songs in one place, providing an excellent summary of the first part of his career, as well as an ideal introduction for listeners unacquainted with his brand of contemporary country. *—Thom Owens*

Leave a Mark / May 5, 1998 / Atlantic ♦♦♦♦
John Michael Montgomery didn't take the release of his career summary *Greatest Hits* as an opportunity to change direction and explore new musical territory. Instead, he continues with the slick contemporary country that made him his reputation. Often, Montgomery's bal-

lads are indistinguishable from MOR pop, and his uptempo numbers a similarly clean and well-produced. When the material is subpar, this can all sound homogenous, and there are times on *Leave a Mark* where everything blends together. Still, Montgomery is a professional vocalist, and he delivers a handful of surefire hits, like "Love Working on You," which makes the album worthwhile for longterm fans, even if they suggest he'll have to work harder to ensure career longevity. *—Thom Owens*

Home to You / May 25, 1999 / Atlantic ✦✦✦

Brand New Me / Sep. 19, 2000 / Atlantic ✦✦✦

George Morgan

b. Jun. 28, 1925, Waverly, TN, **d.** Jul. 7, 1975
Vocals, Guitar / Nashville Sound/Countrypolitan, Traditional Country
The Candy Kid—as George Morgan was known after his first hit "Candy Kisses" spent three weeks at the top of the country chart—was a grand country crooner in the tradition of Eddy Arnold, whom he replaced on the *Grand Old Opry* in 1948. Although "Candy Kisses" proved Morgan's only chart-topper, he placed six of his next seven singles in the Country Top Ten. "Please Don't Let Me Love You," the B-side of "Candy Kisses," reached the Top Five soon after, and another double-sided hit, "Rainbow in My Heart"/"All I Need Is Some More Lovin'" continued the success. Three Top Ten singles in the span of a month was simply astonishing for a debut artist, and Morgan proved he was no fluke by closing out 1949 with three more Top Five hits: "Room Full of Roses," "Cry-Baby Heart," and "I Love Everything About You." It was almost inevitable that Morgan's chart success would taper somewhat, though the three-year gap between hits from late 1949 to 1952 was surprising. "Almost" reached number two in April 1952, however, and Morgan's performances on the *Grand Old Opry* sustained his reputation. He returned in 1959 with "I'm in Love Again," which hit number three. Early the following year, "You're the Only Good Thing (That's Happened to Me)" hit number four, but it was his last Top 20 entry. Morgan witnessed his daughter Lorrie's debut on the *Opry,* but didn't live to see her musical success in the late '80s. *—John Bush*

Candy Kisses / 1996 / Bear Family ✦✦✦✦✦
Candy Kisses contains George Morgan's complete recordings for Columbia between 1949 and 1966. Spanning eight discs and 200 songs, all of Morgan's major hits—"Candy Kisses," "Almost," "I'm In Love Again," "Room Full of Roses," "Please Don't Let Me Love You" and "You're the Only Good Thing (That's Happened to Me)"—are included on this extensive compilation, which is designed for hardcore fans. The consistency of Morgan's material is somewhat uneven, which makes the set a little tedious for any listener that isn't a fanatic or a historian, yet the box—with its excellent biography, sound and sessionography—is worthwhile for anyone willing to invest the time and money. *—Stephen Thomas Erlewine*

● **Room Full of Roses: The Best of George Morgan** / 1996 / Razor & Tie ✦✦✦✦✦
Room Full of Roses contains a generous selection of George Morgan's hits from the late '40s and '50s, including "Candy Kisses," "Please Don't Let Me Love You," "Almost," "I'm In Love Again" and the title track. Every cut is presented in its original hit versions, making the compilation the definitive single-disc retrospective of his hit-making peak at Columbia Records. *—Stephen Thomas Erlewine*

Lorrie Morgan

b. 1960, Nashville, TN
Vocals / Neo-Traditionalist Country, Contemporary Country
Although she spent most of her life singing, Lorrie Morgan didn't become a star until the early '90s, when she scored a string of Top 10 country hits. The daughter of Grand Ole Opry star George Morgan, she made her professional debut at age 13 on the *Opry,* and when her father died in 1975, she took over his band and began leading the group through various club gigs. Within a few years, she disbanded the group, and in 1977, she went on to play with the Little Roy Wiggins band. In 1979 she had a minor hit with "I'm Completely Satisfied," an electronically dubbed duet with her late father. In 1984, Morgan scored another small hit with "Don't Go Changing." That year she became the youngest singer ever to join the *Grand Ole Opry.* She married Keith Whitley in 1986 and two years later had a Top 20 hit, "Trainwreck of Emotion." Morgan's popularity was blossoming and she had just scored a major hit with "Dear Me" when Whitley died suddenly in 1989. Though devastated, she continued to work, and that year her album *Leave the Light On* went gold. In 1990 she had her first number one single, "Five Minutes," along with several other Top 10 hits. *Something in Red,* her second album, was released in 1991; it went platinum and spawned the number one single "What Part of No." *—Sandra Brennan*

Leave the Light on / 1989 / RCA ✦✦✦✦✦

Something in Red / 1991 / RCA ✦✦✦
Morgan backs off the sad songs for her second album—a wise move. (She went through the first part of her life known as George Morgan's daughter; she wouldn't want to spend the rest of it as Keith Whitley's widow.) Instead she concentrates on laidback country and ballads like the title track, which is about the dress colors during different stages of a woman's life. Dolly Parton duets on "Best Woman Wins." *—Brian Mansfield*

Watch Me / Oct. 1992 / RCA ✦✦✦✦✦
Morgan's second and third albums each improved on the last. *Watch Me* contains more good songs than the first two combined, including "I Guess You Had to Be There" and "From Our House to Yours" but not "What Part of No" or the remake of Bonnie Tyler's 1978 hit "It's a Heartache." *—Brian Mansfield*

War Paint / May 10, 1994 / BMG Special Products ✦✦✦

● **Greatest Hits** / Oct. 1995 / BNA ✦✦✦✦✦
As the title implies, *Greatest Hits* contains all of Lorrie Morgan's biggest hits. Morgan's albums tend to be slightly inconsistent, yet her singles have been quite strong. Consequently, *Greatest Hits* is useful both for the casual and the dedicated fan—by featuring nothing but singles, it is her most entertaining album. *—Stephen Thomas Erlewine*

Greater Need / Jun. 1996 / BNA ✦✦✦

Shakin' Things Up / Aug. 12, 1997 / BMG Special Products ✦✦✦✦

The Essential / Jun. 2, 1998 / BNA ✦✦✦✦
Although it falls short of being a definitive collection, *The Essential Lorrie Morgan* contains a handful of her greatest hits—including "Dear Me, " "Back in Your Arms Again" and "I Didn't Know My Own Strength"—plus a number of great album tracks and rarities that give a good idea of her artistic range. As a result, it's a nice sampler and not a bad introduction, but it isn't ideal for listeners just looking for a concise hits collection. *—Thom Owens*

To Get to You: Greatest Hits Collection / Feb. 22, 2000 / BNA ✦✦✦✦
To Get to You: The Greatest Hits Collection weighs in at a generous 17 tracks, but it falls short of being definitive. In fact, it's not necessarily even a hits collection, although it contains a fair share of big singles, including "We Both Walk," "Half Enough," "Good as I Was to You," "Go Away," and "He Talks to Me." Instead, it's a bit haphazard, containing the aforementioned hits, some smaller hits, previously released material that never charted, unreleased recordings (including a fine reading of Tammy Wynette's "Another Lonely Song"), and new recordings (including a live version of Sarah McLachlan's "Angel"). That means *To Get to You* is hardly a greatest-hits collection, but it nevertheless is a fine, fairly representative sampler, showcasing Morgan's terrific voice and ability to tackle everything from straight country to smooth ballads. It should satisfy casual fans, even if it may not have everything they're looking for, and the rarities make it worthwhile for longtime followers. *—Stephen Thomas Erlewine*

Moon Mullican

b. Mar. 29, 1909, Corrigan, Polk County, TX, **d.** Jan. 1, 1967, Beaumont, TX
Vocals, Piano / Instrumental Country, Honky Tonk, Western Swing, Traditional Country
A piano-pounding honky-tonk man, born and raised deep in the heart of East Texas, Aubrey "Moon" Mullican is said to have had a significant musical influence on Jerry Lee Lewis, among others. Throughout the Depression and war years, he cut his ivory teeth on western swing, most notably as vocalist and piano player in Cliff Bruner's Texas Wanderers. In 1946, he signed with the emerging independent powerhouse King Records. A performer of wide-ranging tastes, Mullican was comfortable singing straight country, treacly pop or white boy boogie. Indeed, many of his King sides, cut with black producer Henry Glover, jumped to the beat of hardcore R&B. *—Dan Cooper*

Seven Years to Rock: The King Years, 1946-56 / Sep. ??, 1946-Jan. 26, 1956 / Western ✦✦✦✦✦
Not a hits compilation, it's still a good sampling of Moon in his boogie phase. His take on Tiny Bradshaw's "Well, Oh Well" is required listening for anyone who thinks Elvis invented the hillbilly/R&B cover. *—Dan Cooper*

Moon Mullican Sings His All-Time Greatest Hits / 1958 / King ✦✦✦✦✦
Originally released in 1958, *Sings His All-Time Greatest Hits* is Moon Mullican's first album and, essentially, it *is* a greatest-hits collection, featuring 12 of his hit singles from the late '40s and '50s. Drawn entirely from his King Recordings, this collection contains the bulk of his signature songs—including "I'll Sail My Ship Alone," "Cherokee Boogie," "Mona Lisa," "You Don't Have to Be a Baby to Cry," "Pipeliner's Blues," and "I Was Sorta Wondering"—which means it's a fine introduction and retrospective. There is one slight problem: The compact disc reissue is a little cheaply packaged and contains slightly poor sound, but the music is good enough to make those flaws forgivable. *—Stephen Thomas Erlewine*

Moon's Rock / 1992 / Bear Family ✦✦✦✦
This draws from Mullican's later years, after his career had gone into commercial decline. *—Dan Cooper*

★ **Moonshine Jamboree** / 1993 / Ace ✦✦✦✦✦
The "king of the hillbilly piano players" shows up at his best on these 24 tracks, cut during his prime years, 1946 through 1954, when he was associated principally with King Records. It's easy to hear the roots of Jerry Lee Lewis's (as well as elements of Carl Perkins') sound in early cuts like "Cherokee Boogie", on which Moon Mullican and his band find room for a rippling, pounding performance on piano as well as a short, hot guitar solo around a jaunty, funny honky tonk core, and most of the rest of what's here is as good as that. Indeed, 90 percent of this collection would have passed as rock & roll a few years later, with "Rocket to the Moon" so suggestive as to have had the potential to be banned—the latter also features one of the rare sax solos heard on this collection, which mostly features hot piano and guitar. There is some purer country here as well, including "I'll Sail My Ship Alone," Mullican's one serious hit, a ballad of lost love made special primarily by his flashy piano solo and its catchy chorus; the jaunty "Downstream," a lament about a life misspent; and a country waltz version of Leadbelly's "Goodnight Irene." There also a fair amount of country blues, including "I Done It" and "Moonshine Blues," both showcases for the artist's piano. The sound is excellent and the programming generous, and if there is one flaw, it's the lack of information about the recordings or the sessions in the notes, but that doesn't detract from the music at all. *—Bruce Eder*

Showboy Special: The Early King Sides / May 16, 2000 / West Side ✦✦✦✦✦
This gathers the first 18 sides cut by Moon and his Showboys at their first session for King Records in 1946, plus another five from his first sessions of 1947. The Showboys were a wild Western-swing band that played equal parts blues and jazz, mixed in with polka, weepers, and other Texas dancehall fare. They rocked hard on sides like "Shoot the Moon," "Don't Ever Take My Picture Down," "Showboy Special," and "Let Me Rock You Baby," while getting effectively sentimental on tunes like "I Didn't Think You'd Ever Really Go," "When a Soldier Knocks and Finds Nobody Home," and "There's a Chill on the Hill Tonight." Classic Texas honky tonk music from the late '40s, and an essential part of Moon's catalog. *—Cub Koda*

The EP Collection / Jul. 12, 2000 / See For Miles ♦♦♦♦

Michael Martin Murphey

b. Mar. 13, 1945, Dallas, TX

Vocals, Piano, Harmonica, Guitar / Neo-Traditionalist Country, Singer/Songwriter, Country-Rock, Progressive Country, Cowboy

In many ways, Michael Martin Murphey has the career that Michael Nesmith of the Monkees—with whom Murphey performed early in both of their careers—might've had if he'd never been picked for the NBC series. A guitarist/songwriter, Murphey led the country-rock group The Lewis And Clark Expedition in the middle-late 1960's and had some pop success, and even got one song, "What Am I Doin' Hangin' Around," recorded by the Monkees (with Nesmith singing lead, natch). His songs were cut by the likes of Flatt & Scruggs, Kenny Rogers, Roger Miller, and Bobbie Gentry, and he eventually began recording for A&M Records, and later for Epic Records, where he enjoyed a huge pop hit in the 1970's with "Wildfire." For a time he was known as the "Cosmic Cowboy" after one of his early songs. Murphey moved to Liberty Records in the early 1980's, and later jumped to Warner Bros., where his interest in cowboy and Native American subjects led to the foundation of the Warner Western imprint, a subsidiary label devoted to cowboy music and poetry. —*Bruce Eder*

Cosmic Cowboy Souvenir / 1973 / A&M ♦♦♦

For his second A*M album, $Murphey* continues to celebrate the Texas music scene. The band on this record also includes a couple members of Jerry Jeff Walker's Lost Gonzo Band. With songs like "Prometius Bound," Murphey shows he is deeper than the Cosmic Cowboy thing would indicate. All in all, a good record. —*Jim Worbois*

Michael Murphey / 1973 / Epic ♦♦♦

Despite titles that still promote the Texas movement, this record was done in Nashville with Nashville Cats. Songs like "Nobody's Gonna Tell Me How..." and "You Can Only Say So Much" seem to indicate this has worn thin for Murphey. Still, there is some good stuff on here. —*Jim Worbois*

● **Blue Sky-Night Thunder** / 1975 / Epic ♦♦♦♦♦

His best record of the '70s includes "Wildfire" and "Carolina in the Pines." —*Kenneth M. Cassidy*

The Best of Michael Martin Murphey / 1982 / EMI America ♦♦♦♦♦

A good collection of Murphey's music, featuring the original recordings of his Liberty hits and note-perfect re-recordings of his earlier successes on A&M and Epic (including "Carolina In the Pines," "Wildfire" and "Geronimo's Cadillac"), with something of an all-star lineup on a few of the songs. A very good place to start getting to know Murphey's music before his move to Warner and his move into cowboy music. —*Bruce Eder*

River of Time / 1988 / Warner Brothers ♦♦♦♦♦

Murphey's best includes "From the Word Go," "I'm Gonna Miss You Girl," "Talking to the Wrong Man," and "What Am I Doing Hanging Around," a song Murphey originally wrote for The Monkees. —*Kenneth M. Cassidy*

The Best of Country / 1990 / Curb ♦♦

Cowboy Songs / 1990 / Warner Brothers ♦♦♦♦♦

Sagebrush Symphony / Sep. 12, 1995 / Warner Brothers ♦♦

Wildfire (1972-1984) / Oct. 13, 1998 / Raven ♦♦♦♦♦

Anne Murray

b. Jun. 20, 1945, Springhill, Nova Scotia, Canada

Vocals, Ukulele / Soft Rock, Adult Contemporary, Country-Pop

Nova Scotia-born Anne Murray built her musical influences from the pop sounds that her parents listened to (Rosemary Clooney, Perry Como) and the Top 40 sounds that AM New York radio stations piped into Canada (Buddy Holly, Elvis Presley, Brenda Lee). Originally she intended to work as a physical-education instructor, but she continued to pursue an interest in music. After she was turned down for a spot on a national TV show called *Singalong Jubilee*, she received a call from the show's producer two years later. He offered her a chance to make records, and when she agreed, she found herself with a million-selling crossover single in 1970, "Snowbird." Murray was frequently at odds with the trappings of success—she even performed barefoot in Las Vegas—and when she got married in 1975, she seemingly dropped out of the business. With her family established, she started working in 1978 with a new producer, Jim Ed Norman, who returned her to prominence with "Walk Right Back" and the million-selling follow-up "You Needed Me." Throughout the late '70s and early '80s, Murray successfully walked the line between country and pop with a rich alto voice and a knack for romantic material. —*Tom Roland*

● **Greatest Hits** / 1980 / Liberty ♦♦♦♦♦

It covers Murray's first decade in the international limelight, beginning with "Snowbird" and concluding with "Could I Have This Dance—," a track from the 1980 movie *Urban Cowboy*. It ranges from the folky "Danny's Song" to her cover of The Beatles' "You Won't See Me," but the middle-of-the-road approach is quite obvious. —*Tom Roland*

Greatest Hits, Vol. 2 / 1989 / Liberty ♦♦♦♦

With her country base firmly established, Murray grew restless in the early and mid-'80s, very much desirous of conquering the pop market. It never quite happened, though she made a nice stab at it in her duet with Dave Loggins, "Nobody Loves Me like You Do." She may not be country in the classic sense, but good music is good music and it's hard not to like "Time Don't Run Out on Me" or "Now and Forever (You and Me)." —*Tom Roland*

Now & Forever / 1994 / Capitol ♦♦♦♦♦

This three-disc box contains an excellent booklet and 64 freshly remastered tracks, with a generous helping of alternate mixes, live recordings, and previously unreleased material, including several early, pre-fame nuggets. —*Roch Parisien*

The Best... So Far / 1994 / Capitol ♦♦♦♦♦

A serviceable 20-song distillation of the biggest hits from the box set. However, here's the kicker: the single disc includes "Over You," a new-old track from the vaults (released as a single) which is not included in the box set. So if you want to have it all... —*Roch Parisien*

Willie Nelson

b. Apr. 30, 1933, Fort Worth, TX

Vocals, Guitar, Bass / Outlaw Country, Nashville Sound/Countrypolitan, Country-Pop, Progressive Country, Traditional Country

As a songwriter and a performer, Willie Nelson played a vital role in post-rock & roll country music. Although he didn't become a star until the mid-'70s, Nelson spent the '60s writing songs that became hits for stars like Ray Price ("Nite Life"), Patsy Cline ("Crazy"), Faron Young ("Hello Walls") and Billy Walker ("Funny How Time Slips Away"), as well as releasing a series of records on Liberty and RCA that earned him a small, but devoted, cult following. During the early '70s, Willie aligned himself with Waylon Jennings and the burgeoning outlaw country movement which made him into a star in 1975. Following the crossover success of that year's *The Red Headed Stranger* and "Blue Eyes Crying in the Rain," Nelson was a genuine star, as recognizable in pop circles as he was to the country audience; in addition to recording, he also launched an acting career in the early '80s. Even when he was a star, Willie never played it safe musically. Instead, he borrowed from a wide variety of styles, including traditional pop, western swing, jazz, traditional country, cowboy songs, honky tonk, rock & roll, folk and the blues, creating a distinctive, elastic hybrid. Nelson remained at the top of the country charts until the mid-'80s, when his lifestyle—which had always been close to the outlaw cliches his music flirted with—began to spiral out of control, culminating in an infamous battle with the IRS in the late '80s. During the '90s, Nelson's sales never reached the heights that he experienced a decade earlier, but he remained a vital icon in country music, having greatly influenced the new country, new traditionalist and alternative country movements of the '80s and '90s, as well as leaving behind a legacy of classic songs and recordings. —*Stephen Thomas Erlewine*

Country Willie: His Own Songs / 1965 / Buddha ♦♦♦♦♦

The back of this record says, "Willie writes the songs... You make them into hits" and proceeds to talk about some of the artists who have had hits from the pen of Willie Nelson. While some of these tunes showed up in their original versions on the United Artist album *Best of Willie Nelson*, this is still worth tracking down. —*Jim Worbois*

Country Favorites, Willie Nelson Style / 1966 / Buddha ♦♦♦♦

It may be hard to believe but Willie Nelson wasn't always a national icon. In the mid-'60s, he regularly hit the charts but from behind the scenes as a busy and acclaimed songwriter. His own recordings were less successful until, in 1966, *Country Favorites Willie Nelson Style* became his first album to enter *Billboard's* country album charts, staying there 17 weeks and eventually reaching number nine. Perhaps because the album is a collection of familiar songs, Nelson's idiosyncratic vocals went over better—or maybe his time had just come—but in any case, it's certainly a small treasure.

Supporting Nelson was Ernest Tubb's wonderful band the Texas Troubadours who went uncredited because they were under contract to a different record label. The Troubadours' experience and sympathetic ears made a reliable backing for Nelson as they tackled such material as "San Antonio Rose," "My Window Faces the South," "Heartaches By the Number," and "Columbus Stockade Blues." There's nothing cynical or calculated to their light swing and open-hearted feeling, despite such a potentially unpromising album concept. Nelson had already learned how to handle his unconventional voice effectively, giving these songs the honest freshness and sharp sense of rhythm that would characterize his later work. Like many rebels, Nelson has always shown a deep respect for tradition; here he shares his affection with everyone. —*Lang Thompson*

Yesterday's Wine / 1971 / Justice ♦♦♦♦

☆ **Shotgun Willie** / 1973 / Atlantic ♦♦♦♦♦

Transferring his allegiance to Atlantic (where he would record two remarkable albums that would get him kicked off the label), for his debut Willie Nelson offered his finest record to date—possibly his finest album ever. *Shotgun Willie* encapsulates Willie's worldview and music, finding him at a peak as a composer, interpreter, and performer. This is laid-back, deceptively complex music, equal parts country, rock attitude, jazz musicianship, and troubadour storytelling. Nelson blurs the lines between his own tunes and covers to the point that "Whiskey River," this record's best-known song, seems thoroughly original, yet it was written by Johnny Bush and Paul Stroud. This, along with two songs apiece by Leon Russell and Bob Wills, provides context for his originals, with *Shotgun Willie* becoming a musical autobiography, offering not only insights into his musicality (witness how he slows down "Stay All Night [Stay a Little Longer]" to a slow shuffle) but, seemingly, into himself (most notably on the title track and the wonderful, funny travelogue "Devil in a Sleepin' Bag"). Nelson wasn't just at a peak of performing here—he also wrote some of his greatest songs, highlighted not just by the previously mentioned tunes but also by the lovely slow waltz "Slow Down Old World" and "Sad Songs and Waltzes." All of it adds up to possibly the finest record in a career filled with hits and highlights. —*Stephen Thomas Erlewine*

☆ **Phases and Stages** / 1974 / Atlantic ♦♦♦♦♦

If *Shotgun Willie* played a bit like a concept album, *Phases and Stages* was a full-blown one, tracing the dissolution of a marriage and devoting one side to the wife's perspective, the second to the husband's. If anything, Willie overplays his hand a bit, insisting on grafting the "Phases and Stages Theme" between crucial songs to the point of genuine irritation. But, pretend that never happened, erase it from your mind, and *Phases and Stages* is easily the equal of its remarkable predecessor, a wonderful set of music that resonates deeply, as deeply as the words. Make no mistake—the deceptively relaxed arrangements, including the occasional strings, not only highlight Nelson's clever eclecticism, but they also heighten the emotional impact of the album. And this is a hell of an emotional record, where even each side's celebratory honky tonk numbers (the medley "Sister's Coming Home/Down at the Corner

Beer Joint" and "Pick Up the Tempo," respectively) are muted by sadness. Then, there are the centerpieces: "Walkin'," where the woman decides it's time to move on; "Pretend I Never Happened," perhaps the coldest ending to a relationship ever written; "Bloody Mary Morning," a bleary-eyed morning-after tale that became a standard; "It's Not Supposed to Be That Way," a nearly unbearably melancholy account of a love gone wrong; and "Heaven and Hell," a waltz summary of the relationship. Any two of these would have formed a strong core for an album but, placed together in a narrative context, their impact is even more considerable. As a result, this is not just one of Willie Nelson's best records, but one of the great concept albums overall. *—Stephen Thomas Erlewine*

☆ **Red Headed Stranger** / 1975 / Columbia/Legacy ♦♦♦♦♦
Red Headed Stranger perhaps is the strangest blockbuster country produced, a concept album about a preacher on the run after murdering his departed wife and her new lover, told entirely with brief song-poems and utterly minimal backing. It's defiantly anti-commercial and it demands intense concentration—all reasons why nobody thought it would be a hit, a story related in Chet Flippo's liner notes to the 2000 reissue. It was a phenomenal blockbuster, though, selling millions of copies, establishing Nelson as a superstar recording artist in its own right. For all its success, it still remains a prickly, difficult album, though, making the interspersed concept of *Phases and Stages* sound shiny in comparison. It's difficult because it's old-fashioned, sounding like a tale told around a cowboy campfire. Now, this all reads well on paper, and there's much to admire in Nelson's intimate gamble, but it's really elusive, as the themes get a little muddled and the tunes themselves are a bit bare. It's undoubtedly distinctive—and it sounds more distinctive with each passing year—but it's strictly an intellectual triumph and, after a pair of albums that were musically and intellectually sound, it's a bit of a let-down, no matter how successful it was. *—Stephen Thomas Erlewine*

The Troublemaker / 1976 / Columbia ♦♦♦♦
The Troublemaker is a fascinating effort from Willie Nelson, an album that is essentially a \contemporary gospel effort, but isn't nearly as blindly devotional as that implies. Religion has had a large part in Nelson's music, notably on the *Red-Headed Stranger*, but here, it functions as the centerpiece and he delivers a really good record that's far more detailed and imaginative than you might imagine. It's also more realized musically than *Red-Headed Stranger* even if it isn't as undeniably classic. Still, it's a worthy album and a nice little gem in his catalog. *—Stephen Thomas Erlewine*

To Lefty from Willie / 1977 / Columbia ♦♦♦
To Lefty from Willie is an affectionate and thoroughly enjoyable salute to Lefty Frizzell, featuring stellar versions of a number of Lefty's best-known songs—including "Always Late (With Your Kisses)," "She's Gone, Gone, Gone," "I Never Go Around Mirrors" and "That's the Way Love Goes"—plus revealing takes on a number of obscurities from the influential vocalist's catalog. Nelson is respectful without being overly reverential, giving his own spin to each song without abandoning their honky tonk roots. *—Stephen Thomas Erlewine*

☆ **Stardust** / 1978 / Columbia/Legacy ♦♦♦♦♦
At the height of outlaw country, Willie Nelson pulled off perhaps the riskiest move of the entire bunch. He set aside originals, country and folk and recorded *Stardust*, a collection of pop standards produced by Booker T Jones. Well, it's not entirely accurate to say that he put away country and folk, since these are highly idiosyncratic interpretations of "Georgia on My Mind," "All of Me," "Moonlight in Vermont" and "Don't Get Around Much Anymore," blending pop, country, jazz and folk in equal measures. It's not that Willie makes these songs his own, it's that he reimagines these songs in a way that nobody else could and, with his trusty touring band, he makes these version indelible. It may be strange to think that this album, containing no originals from one of America's greatest songwriters, is what made him a star and it continues to be one of his most beloved records, but it's appropriate, actually. *Stardust* showcases Nelson's skills as a musician and his entire aesthetic—where there is nothing separating classic American musical forms, it can all be played together—perhaps better than any other album, which is why it was a sensation upon its release and grows stronger with each passing year. *—Stephen Thomas Erlewine*

Willie and Family Live / 1978 / Columbia ♦♦

Sings Kris Kristofferson / 1979 / Columbia ♦♦♦

One for the Road / 1980 / Columbia ♦♦

★ **Greatest Hits (& Some That Will Be)** / 1981 / Columbia ♦♦♦♦♦
This capsulizes Nelson's first five years in the spotlight, with lots of classics: "On the Road Again," "Blue Eyes Crying in the Rain," "Heartbreak Hotel" (a duet with Leon Russell), as well as the smartly produced "My Heroes Have Always Been Cowboys." *—Tom Roland*

Always on My Mind / 1982 / Columbia ♦♦♦

Half Nelson / 1985 / Columbia ♦♦♦
This is an appropriate collection, since Nelson has recorded more duets with more fellow performers than any other country singer in history. This runs the gamut, from traditional country singers Merle Haggard and George Jones, to soulman Ray Charles, to Latin-lover Julio Iglesias, and the rock band Santana. It even has a duet with the late Hank Williams, arranged through modern studio recording technology. *—Tom Roland*

Me and Paul / 1985 / DCC ♦♦♦♦

★ **Nite Life: Greatest Hits and Rare Tracks, 1959-1971** / 1989 / Rhino ♦♦♦♦♦
Nite Life: Greatest Hits and Rare Tracks collects material Willie Nelson wrote and recorded while he was trying to launch a career as a professional songwriter during the '60s. At this time, he also made two albums and several singles for Liberty, and many recordings for RCA. These songs, including some rarities, are compiled for this flawless single-disc collection. *Nite Life* runs through all of the songs other performers had hits with and made standards, including the title tracks, "Crazy," "Funny How Time Slips Away," and "Hello, Walls." Not only does it have the songs that established Nelson's reputation, the disc shows that even early in his career, he was creating an eclectic, far-reaching music that never stayed within the boundaries of traditional country. *—Stephen Thomas Erlewine*

Who'll Buy My Memories . . . / 1992 / Columbia ♦♦♦♦♦
Commonly known as *The IRS Tapes* because it was made to help pay for Willie Nelson's IRS debts, *Who'll Buy My Memories* is a double disc, 25-track collection of demos, outtakes and stripped-down recordings that feature only Nelson and his guitar. Over the course of the set, Nelson plays a handful of unusual tracks, several new tunes, and a few of his most familiar songs. The result is one of Nelson's most direct and affecting albums, featuring several of his finest vocal performances. *—Thom Owens*

Across the Borderline / 1993 / Columbia ♦♦♦♦

☆ **The Early Years: The Complete Liberty Recordings Plus More** / May 3, 1994 / Liberty ♦♦♦♦♦
Not only a fine compilation, it was a gutsy move. Nelson's 1962-1964 sessions for Liberty Records, the first label to sign him as an artist, have never been held in high regard by his fans. On many cuts, the strings were poured on so thick even Eddy Arnold would have protested. But if one dispenses with prejudice and gives this two-CD box set an open-minded listen, there's a wealth of fine work to appreciate among the 61 singles, album cuts, and alternate takes. And no matter the production—lush or spare—his songwriting is a continual joy. Besides the familiar (including a riveting, pre-Liberty version of "Night Life" that opens the set) are any number of near-forgotten songs that would have been another writer's best work. Excellent liner notes are provided by Joseph F. Laredo, who deserves credit for not pretending the strings aren't there. *—Dan Cooper*

A Classic & Unreleased Collection / 1995 / Rhino ♦♦♦
Originally released as a mail-order-only release through the Home Shopping Network, the three-disc *A Classic and Unreleased Collection* compiles a selection of unreleased and rare material recorded between 1957 and the mid-'80s. Considering that all of the set is composed of rarities, the "classic" in the title is a little dubious. Nevertheless, the music throughout the box is fine and occasionally excellent. Opening with Nelson's first independently-released single, the set runs through a number of music-publishing demos he made for Pamper Music, unreleased Atlantic recordings, a complete unreleased live album (*Live at the Texas Opry House*) from 1974, the unreleased *Sugar Moon* from the mid-'80s, a handful of tracks from the scrapped record *Willie Alone* and, finally, *Willie Sings Hank Williams*, another unreleased album from the '80s. Since it covers such a large time-frame, it isn't surprising that the set features a bit of everything that made Nelson famous—his Western Swing and honky tonk roots, as well as his fondness for pop standards, jazz, country-pop, and folk. Even though there is music on the box that would please the casual fan, *A Classic and Unreleased Collection* remains a treasure chest for collectors, who will find plenty of rough gems within the set. *—Stephen Thomas Erlewine*

☆ **Revolutions of Time, The Journey 1975-1993** / 1995 / Columbia/Legacy ♦♦♦♦♦
Compiling material from Willie Nelson's later career, the box set *Revolutions of Time: The Journey 1975-1993* provides a through overview of the singer's most popular recordings, as well as some of his most obscure. Divided into three thematic discs—*Pilgrimage, Sojourns, Exodus*—the box contains most of his hits from the era, including selections from *The Red Headed Stranger* and *Stardust*. These songs are on *Pilgrimage*. *Sojourns* concentrates on his duets, while *Exodus* is filled with songs from the late '80s and early '90s. It doesn't round up all of his best songs of the era—there are still several gems hidden away on the original albums—but it does provide an effective and throughly entertaining portrait of Nelson's later career. *Revolutions of Time* could be all that the casual fan needs to hear from Nelson's later career, and every country fan should be familiar with much of these songs. *—Stephen Thomas Erlewine*

Spirit / Jun. 1996 / Island ♦♦♦

Nashville Was the Roughest / Jun. 10, 1998 / Bear Family ♦♦♦♦♦
Willie Nelson's '60s recordings for RCA have long been the subject of critical disdain due to the supposed ill fit between Nelson's idiosyncratic style and the conventions of the Nashville sound era. In fact, Nelson's RCA material is largely of high quality, his modest hits from this period were often excellent, and his uniqueness comes through no matter how syrupy the orchestration (which isn't always the case—the production on many of these tracks is quite spare). This deluxe eight-CD box set compiles everything Nelson recorded during his eight years with RCA, including a complete live set, unreleased recordings, rough takes of songs that would later surface on his A*M* albums, and his few early-'60s recordings for Monument. Nelson covers Western swing, pop country, ballads, and versions of classic country songs in minimalist fashion with his jazzy phrasing fully developed. In fact, those who have been frightened away from these recordings by critics may be surprised by how little they differ from his '70s sound. Fans will delight over the LP-sized hardback book that accompanies this set and the opportunity to review a neglected episode in the Willie Nelson saga. *—Greg Adams*

Teatro / Sep. 1, 1998 / Island ♦♦♦♦
One of Willie Nelson's best albums of the '90s also happens to be one of the most haunting and lyrical works of his entire career. A companion piece of sorts to Emmylou Harris' equally haunting and lyrical *Wrecking Ball* (which ultimately is a better album), *Teatro* paints an aural landscape that's simultaneously barren and full of life. Like he did with *Wrecking Ball*, producer Daniel Lanois shapes *Teatro* as a veteran's somewhat scarred, but finally optimistic, take on the American experience (which in Nelson's case is flamenco-influenced and Mexican-flavored in nature, reflecting his never-shed Texan roots). *Teatro*'s spare reflections on the past (Nelson reworks several of his old tunes here), as well as its cozy interplay between instruments and singers (Harris provides backing vocals on 11 of the album's 14 tracks), add up to something very much unlike anything Nelson has attempted in the past: a collaborative album that celebrates a life in music but sounds oddly distanced from its musical soul. Still, a creative resurgence for its main author. *—Michael Gallucci*

Night & Day / Jul. 13, 1999 / Free Falls Entertainment ♦♦♦♦

Milk Cow Blues / Sep. 19, 2000 / Island ♦♦♦

Mickey Newbury

b. May 19, 1940, Houston, TX

Vocals, Guitar / Outlaw Country, Singer/Songwriter, Progressive Country

Along with fellow songwriters such as Kris Kristofferson, Willie Nelson, and Tom T. Hall, Mickey Newbury helped revolutionize country music in the 1960s and '70s by bringing new, broader musical influences as well as a frank, emotional depth to the music—while at the same time never losing respect for tradition. Newbury infused his country music with haunting beauty and spiritual melancholy, creating an impressive collection of introspective, emotionally complex songs that are more spiritual cousins of the work of Leonard Cohen than that of Roy Acuff. (Newbury, in fact, calls himself a folksinger, and has never toured with a band, prefering the ambience of a quiet coffeehouse.) The fact that many of his songs became hits for singers from Don Gibson to Elvis Presley was proof that the industry and the public were hungry for a change. Like many of his generation, however—such as his friend Townes Van Zandt Newbury is better known as a songwriter than as a singer. Newbury has recorded 15 albums over a nearly 30 year period—right up to 1996's "Lulled By the Moonlight," a limited-edition release sold by mail order—but his soft, beautiful tenor voice has rarely reached the charts. *—Kurt Wolff*

Looks Like Rain / 1969 / Mountain Retreat ✦✦✦✦✦

In sonic terms, *Looks Like Rain* sounds as far from the studio slickness of the "countrypolitan" machine rock and roll was from Lawrence Welk. In fact, Newbury's sound held more in common with that of Tim Buckley's or Simon and Garfunkel's. But even here, comparisons fail miserably. Aided by co-producers Bob Beckham and guitarist Jerry Kennedy, Newbury created an album haunting, so elegant, full of melancholy and mystery, it sounds out of time, out of space. It is a sound that seemingly comes from inside the mind of the listener than from the speakers on the stereo. When the sound of thunder and rain appears at the beginning of "She Even Woke Me Up To Say Goodbye," we are hardly surprised. Newbury's stories are movies; all the settings are in place before the story begins. He can move back and forth in time while changing images to suit the evolving narrative. "San Francisco Mable Joy," is a long tale of dispossession, dislocation, failure, and death, but so poetically beautiful, it can't help but be heard then echoed, deep in the heart of the listener. The thunderstorm is in full flood now, running through each track, from speaker to speaker in one long line, sheets of rain pouring down around the place the singer emotes from. Suddenly a gunshot cuts just loudly enough to jar us from the reverie. At six minutes and forty-three seconds, there is plenty of room for the song's drama to create a tension so mournful it becomes nearly unbearable. And even though we know what's coming as the story winds down, the song's ending is totally devastating. *Looks Like Rain* is so fine, so mysterious in its pace, dimension, quark strangeness and charm, it defies any attempt at strict categorization or criticism; a rare work of genius. *—Thom Jurek*

'Frisco Mabel Joy / 1971 / Mountain Retreat ✦✦✦✦✦

Newbury jumped from Mercury to Elektra and in 1970 recorded the second of his amazing trilogy that concluded with *Heaven Help The Child.* Produced by Dennis Linde, a songwriter, and recorded at the same converted garage studio (Cinderella Sound) *Looks Like Rain* had been, 'Frisco Mabel Joy adapts its title from a song on the previous album. Once again, texture, atmosphere ands above all mood and mystery were the central tenets of what would become Newbury's trademark sound. The album opens with Newbury's arrangement of what he called "The American Trilogy," a suite containing three songs that have their origin in the Civil War. If this sounds familiar, it is: Elvis Presley made a much more bombastic version of this the centerpiece of his Vegas shows. Newbury's version, full of soft strings, guitars, Charlie McCoy's haunting harmonica bleeding into a muted brass section, is full of drama and pathos. *Looks Like Rain* moves into an entire series of songs that talk of dislocation, emptiness and endless searching through regret, remorse, and ultimately acceptance and resignation. And Newbury's vocal abilities are just astonishing. He has a different voice for literally every song. It is tempting to write about every single song here, but it would be fruitless. Newbury's tunes are so slippery and mercurial. They shift shape and disappear into a puff of smoke the minute you think you have them pinned down. And if the stories and arrangements aren't enough to confound the listener, the melodies, all of which have their roots in country music, are so much more deceptive, they turn in on themselves and extend each measure with complex phrasing and mode changes. *—Thom Jurek*

● **Heaven Help the Child** / 1973 / Mountain Retreat ✦✦✦✦✦

After issuing two solid critical successes that went nowhere commercially, Newbury was more determined than ever to get his idea of what music was across to a the American public. He was also hell bent on changing Nashville's stolid, conservative way of recording, producing, marketing and selling music. He failed on both counts but left another stunner of an album along the way. *Heaven Help The Child* opens with the title track, a wondrously arranged, and gorgeously sung, three-generational American Odyssey that offered, with all of its tragedy the clearly visible line of hope on the horizon. Also included here are three definitive interpretations of songs from his very first album, *Harlequin Melodies:* "Sunshine" "Sweet Memories," and "Good Morning Dear." These songs haven't been re-recorded so much as reinvented from the ground up. Newbury changes pace with an awesome dobro-drenched, country rock sing along, "Why You Been Gone So Long." "Cortelia Clark" a tale of a young man and an older, blind black musician coming to the train yards in Georgia, is one of Newbury's great achievements as a songwriter. Acoustic guitars and strings woo each other through Newbury's glorious tenor and offers a coming of age tale that is both morally instructive and imagistic ally evocative; only Newbury could tell a story that echoed both the blues of the 20s and 30s and the folk songs of the 40s and 50s. The album closes with the Bob Beckam-produced reinvention of "San Francisco Mabel Joy" and it's a punch-in-the-guts way to end an album. With *Heaven Help The Child,* Newbury, for the third time in as many recording sessions, came up with a record that defied categorization or gentrification. And for the third time in a row, he had done the impossible, created a masterpiece, a work of perfection. –Thom Jurek

Live at Montezuma Hall / 1973 / Mountain Retreat ✦✦✦✦

This is Newbury's first live set and it's revelatory to hear him in front of an audience with nothing but an acoustic guitar. It's obvious that Newbury has his audience from the opening of "How I love Them Old Songs" and by the time he tells the heartbreaking story of "Cortelia Clark," they are falling apart and Newbury is soaring with the inspiration he's taking from the songs and the audience entranced in front of him. The second part of the album begins with a long, rambling story that ends in "Bugger Red Blues," is a kind of ruse to break the tension. Newbury is a master showman here (the set was not edited in any way), carrying his audience through "How Many Times (Must The Piper Be Paid For His Song)," and a raggedly beautiful rendition of "American Trilogy." It sounds like the place is coming apart at the seams! But it's in the encores that Newbury reveals just who he is as an artist. Newbury does a soulful cover of Percy Mayfield's "Please Send Me Someone To Love." It's as if Ray Charles and Charlie Rich met each other in New Orleans barroom and sang together. And while that may be the scenario, the delivery is all Newbury's. He breaks the song-and himself-down and builds it back up again before taking the set out with his own "She Even Woke Me Up To Say Goodbye." Man, there must not have been a dry eye in the place because I can't get through it straight after hearing it over a hundred times! Newbury has recorded numerous live records since Montezuma Hall, but none have come even close to matching its power and intensity. In fact, there are few live records by anybody that can hold a candle to this classic. *—Thom Jurek*

I Came to Hear the Music / 1974 / Mountain Retreat ✦✦✦✦

Produced by Chip Young, *I Came to Hear the Music* is Newbury's most diverse recording from his early period. Along with the bittersweet love songs that defy categorization, there are bona fide country waltzes like "You Only Live Once in a While,", rock & roll songs such as "Dizzy Lizzy" and "1 X I Ain't 2," and some blues and gospel. The rain and thunderstorms are back, and there are appearances by the Jordanaires and Bobby Emmons. The lushly orchestrated "countrypolitan" sound of "Yesterday's Gone" and the folk-country "If You See Her" mark two ends of the acoustic spectrum for Newbury. The last half of the album features the most diversity; it begins and ends with the aforementioned rock tracks, and Newbury, with his killer guitar pickers and piano player, could rock with anybody. Traffic sounds open "Organized Noise," which could have been a vintage Neil Diamond track, with its African percussion and off-meter rhyme. It's full of drama, of bitter reverie, of remorse, and as the orchestra swells behind the singer and the cut begins to open itself up, it just abruptly ends… a squandered idea, an emotion best left unexplored. There is also the ballad "Love Look (At Us Now)," which was covered by no less than five different artists, none of them coming close to Newbury's bone honest, tell-it-like-it-is delivery. The song is full of shame and bewilderment, unable to resolve the emotions contained within it (with the strings swelling repeatedly to underscore this) or stand against them. An amazing tome that lasts less than three minutes! Alas, this album sold only as well as its predecessors, but it pointed its creator in new directions, or at least revealed the many simultaneous directions he'd been capable traveling all along. *—Thom Jurek*

Lovers / 1975 / Elektra ✦✦✦

Rusty Tracks / 1977 / Hickory ✦✦✦✦

Newbury hooks up with Bobby Bare as a producer and puts out *Rusty Tracks,* a record full of pedal steel guitars, fiddles, cut time rhythms, and lyrical darkness, for his first album for ABC/Hickory. This concentration on one music and its classic themes and rougher-edged production proved to be as great as anything he had done since his early records. "Makes Me Wonder if I Ever Said Goodbye" answers in true loner fashion his early '70s classic "She Never Even Woke Me Up to Say Goodbye," and the whispering gospel prayer "Bless Us All" takes the darkness Newbury held so firmly in his grasp and opens it up for all of us to be a part of; it expresses our own longing and wish for fulfillment. But it's the close of the album that knocks the listener out of her chair. Mirroring his own "American Trilogy" of half a decade before, Newbury strings together—once more without seams—four pieces of classic Americana with breathtakingly gorgeous arrangements: "Shenandoah," "That Lucky Old Sun," "Danny Boy", and "In the Pines." On this set, the orchestra appears and Newbury's singing is as good as anybody's ever was. He doesn't merely sing these songs—he *is* them, a part and parcel of the fabric of the notes themselves and what they represent. Just when Americans were trying to forget who they were by embracing European disco and punk rock as well as dumbed-down versions of both country and jazz, Newbury reveals—much to his own commercial detriment—who and what we are as a nation. There is no more stunning finish to a Newbury record—maybe anybody's record. *—Thom Jurek*

His Eye Is on the Sparrow / 1978 / Hickory ✦✦✦✦

His Eye Is on the Sparrow is one of Newbury's prettiest records. It's intimate in a way that none of his others are; it's a lonely but not world-weary set. The songs are fraught with a more fragile and tender beauty, and are underscored by his production team's subtle nuances and textures. The album shows a return to the sound effects (particularly the rainstorm) of his earliest sides. "Westphalia Texas Waltz" is a country waltz showcasing a beautiful chamber string section set against Charlie McCoy's harmonica and the endless sound of rain falling. Newbury's version of the title track—arranged here by film score producer Alan Moore—is an American classic in the public domain. It's a gospel song that isn't gospel, a sacred song that is secular enough to include the sounds of gulls (and, one supposes, sparrows). "The Dragon and the Mouse" 's deep metaphorical narrative is missed because of the deceptive simplicity of the arrangement, instrumentation. Another pleasant weirdness is the brief "St. Cecelia," with its church bell and stacked choirs courtesy once again of the Nashphilharmonic. It's a country hymn to everything that has passed away except for the burden of inspiration to do what's right. The disc closes with a reprise (of sorts) of its opener. But "Juble Lee's Revival Shout" is no gospel song; it's a small, bleak testament to the most intimate kind of loneliness—the kind found in the mirror at the end of the day. It's a chilling way to end a record than began so tenderly, so simply, if not optimistically. But that's Newbury. The most horrible truths are the ones that are gorgeously told to us by sages and well-meaning hucksters, and he's both. It is a truly awesome and off-putting finish. *—Thom Jurek*

The Sailor / 1979 / Hickory ✦✦✦✦✦

Who would have thought that Mickey Newbury would issue a 100%, crackling fresh country-pop record in 1979— Produced by Ronnie Gant with (massive) string arrangements by Alan Moore at Cowboy Jack Clement's studio, *The Sail* reveals that Newbury knew what it took all the time, but by the time he let his muse follow him down the commercial country rabbit hole, it was too late. The first track, "Blue Sky Shinin'," is a country love song arranged and exquisitely performed as if written for Patsy Cline. Next, "Let's Have a Party" is perhaps Newbury's anthem, not because of its title, but because it's one of the most beautiful confessional songs he's ever written. The production by Gant is straightforward and Newbury's voice is clearly in the foreground. The sound effects are replaced with layers of instrumentation and backing vocals. Newbury's relaxed delivery offers the listener a way to see just *how* sincere these songs are. While there are no weak cuts, the aforementioned stand out. So does "Let It Go," done in 2/4 time, beginning as a country song and ending by transforming itself inside out into a gospel shouter. *The Sailor*, once again, refused to sell, perhaps because it was too late, perhaps because it was too early—Merle Haggard and George Jones made records that sounded exactly like this only three years later and scored big. As great as this record is, and as good as Newbury knew it was, it was the same old story. Nashville's radio machine wasn't having it, and therefore the public never got the chance to make up its mind. In fact, the way Newbury's entire career was handled by Nashville is evidence enough to raze the entire town and start over. *— Thom Jurek*

After All These Years / 1981 / Mercury ✦✦✦✦

In a New Age / 1988 / Airborne ✦✦

Nights When I Am Sane / 1994 / Winter Harvest ✦✦✦✦
Released by the tiny Nashville label Winter Harvest, *Nights When I Am Sane* was Newbury's first album in six years and his first live album since *Live at Montezuma Hall* 20 years earlier. Those decades may have deepened Newbury the singer's voice a bit, but it only made him a more powerful performer. As one would expect, *Nights When I Am Sane* is comprised of a batch of Newbury's most well-known songs but the power these performances hold make them the definitive versions. With one guitar or at most one accompanist, Newbury has always been able to convey what most others would need an entire band to try to get to. Songs like "Just Dropped In (To See What Condition My Condition Was In)" (bet you didn't know he wrote that, did ya—) come across with so much feeling, pathos, and depth that it's possible to see clear into the darkness in the soul of the man when he wrote it. When Newbury gets to his famous refrain on "Nights When I Am Sane," he's telling a hidden truth, one so obscured by legend and the grime of time and music business bullshit that it almost slips though in its gentleness. "We would sweat and moan/Until the need in us was gone/In one another's arms all through the night," begins "What Will I Do Now," the track that ends this set. A song of a lover left to bear his grief in the darkness now that she's gone. Newbury's falsetto conveys the grief with so much empathy, it's hard to believe this isn't some man crying on his best friend's shoulder. Only Newbury would have the naked, unpretentious honesty to end a concert with a song like this, and only he could get away with it. *— Thom Jurek*

The Mickey Newbury Collection / 1998 / Mountain Retreat ✦✦✦✦✦
The Mickey Newbury Collection is an eight-CD box set containing ten albums originally released between 1969 and 1981. (The first six discs contain one album each, while the last two each combine two albums.) They are: *Looks Like Rain* (1969), *'Frisco Mabel Joy* (1971), *Heaven Help the Child* (1973), *Live at Montezuma Hall* (1973), *I Came to Hear the Music* (1974), *Lovers* (1975), *Rusty Tracks* (1977), *His Eye Is on the Sparrow* (1978), *The Sailor* (1979), and *After All These Years* (1981). While this is not a complete set of Newbury's recordings, it constitutes the bulk of his work as a recording artist, tracing the most productive periods of one of popular music's most impressive, if least known, singer-songwriters. *The Mickey Newbury Collection* uses transfers from vinyl records, the master tapes having long-since disappeared. (The resulting sound quality is good, though the occasional click can be heard in quiet passages.) At his best, Mickey Newbury is an original, compelling singer-songwriter who ranks with the best to come out of Nashville; at his worst, he is a highly competent writer of generic country songs. He may have been too well compensated for the latter to feel challenged sufficiently to be the former with any consistency, but one hears many examples of his great and only good work in this lengthy collection. *— William Ruhlmann*

Juice Newton

b. Feb. 18, 1952, Virginia Beach, VA
Vocals, Guitar / Urban Cowboy, Adult Contemporary, Country-Pop
Juice Newton was part of the first wave of country singers raised on rock, folk-rock, and singer/songwriters, which is evident from her hit singles, "Angel of the Morning" and "Queen of Hearts." Newton's first professional recordings were with Juice Newton & Silver Spur, a band she formed with collaborator Otha Young. They signed to RCA Records and released an eponymous debut, which spawned the minor hit single "Love is a Word" in early 1976. RCA dropped the group after their second record, *After the Dust Settles*, stiffed. One more record, the Capitol-released *Come to Me*, appeared in 1978 before the group disbanded. Newton still had a contract with Capitol and she began work on her solo debut with Young. The result, *Juice*, was a crossover in 1981, with "Angel of the Morning" and "Queen of Hearts" reaching the pop Top 10 and the country Top 25; the record's third single, "The Sweetest Thing (I've Ever Known)," peaked at number one country. *Quiet Lies*, her second record, became a hit in 1982 thanks to the pop Top 10 "Love's Been A Little Bit Hard on Me" and the number two country hit "Break It To Me Gently." After *Dirty Looks* failed to have any singles crack either the pop or country Top 40 in 1983, she signed with RCA. At RCA, she concentrated on country and her 1985 album *Old Flame* was her country breakthrough, spawning three number one hits, plus three additional Top 10 hits. This was her only major country hit, as both 1987's *Emotion* and 1989's *Ain't Gonna Cry* didn't generate much interest. Newton then abandoned recording for concerts, finally returning with *The Trouble with Angels*, a collection of re-recordings and new songs, in 1998. *— Stephen Thomas Erlewine*

• **Greatest Hits (And More)** / 1984 / Liberty ✦✦✦✦✦
One of a series of single-artist CD anthologies on Liberty sharing this title, this collection compiles 15 of Juice Newton's hits and album tracks. Her best-known songs such as "Queen of Hearts" and "Love's Been a Little Bit Hard on Me" are included, as well as interesting items such as a cover version of the Zombies' "Tell Her No." The hits are the highlights here; although the fusion of new wave, power pop, and country may sound dated, the hooks are timeless. *Greatest Hits (and More)* makes for enjoyable listening, and provides an excellent and concise overview of Newton's early-'80s output. *— Greg Adams*

The Nitty Gritty Dirt Band

f. 1965, Long Beach, CA
Group / Country-Rock, Progressive Country, Progressive Bluegrass
Founded in California during 1965, the Nitty Gritty Dirt Band has lasted longer than virtually any other country-based rock group of their era. Younger contemporaries of the Byrds, they played an almost equally important role in the transformation from folk-rock into country-rock, and have been an influence on such bands as the Eagles and Alabama. Formed in late 1965, they soon began playing jug band music at local clubs. At that time, Southern California was undergoing a musical renaissance, courtesy of the folk-rock movement and the Nitty Gritty Dirt Band fit in with these other folkies-turned-rockers. By mid-1968 the group had gone electric, and also added drums to their sound. Their first electric album, *Rare Junk*, released in June of 1968, was a commercial failure. 1970's *Uncle Charlie and His Dog Teddy* was rooted tightly in their jugband sound, with a country feel but no trace of the vaudeville and novelty numbers that had appeared on their earlier records. The album yielded what is the group's best-known single, their cover of Jerry Jeff Walker's "Mr. Bojangles." Their next album, *All The Good Times*, released in early 1972, had an even more countrified feel. The Nitty Gritty Dirt Band then went to Nashville and recorded a selection of traditional country numbers with the likes of Roy Acuff, Earl Scruggs, Mother Maybelle Carter, and other members of country and bluegrass music's veteran elite. Some of the veteran Nashville stars were skeptical and suspicious at first of the bandmembers and their amplified instruments, but the ice was broken when they saw how respectful the band was toward them and their work, and their music, as well as how serious they were about their own music. The resulting triple album, *Will the Circle Be Unbroken*, released in January of 1973, became a million-seller and elicited positive reviews from both the rock and country music press. *— Bruce Eder*

Ricochet / 1967 / BGO ✦✦✦✦
The Nitty Gritty Dirt Band's second album is a masterpiece. From the opening bars of Jackson Browne's "Shadow Dream Song," and the high spirits overflow the grooves (or ones and zeros, on the CD) of the record. The singing and playing are more confident, and some of the songs, including the bluesy "Ooh Po Pe Do Girl" and the hook-laden "I'll Search The Sky" by Jeff Hanna, and Copeland and Noonan's (the "Buy For Me The Rain" team) "Tide Of Love," is as solid as anything coming out of California. Even the kazoo-dominated "Coney Island Washboard" and "Happy Fat Annie," and the nostalgic 20's styled Jackson Browne-written "It's Raining Here In Long Beach" , fit well into the mix, reflecting the full range of the band's influences. As to why this record never caught on, it could be the timing—released late in 1967, in the wake of *Sergeant Pepper* (which had its own music hall influences, albeit of the English variety, and covered with lots of psychedelic overdubbing) and the Summer of Love, it just wasn't what college kids starting their search for the Lost Chord were looking for. Maybe a kazoo or two less would've helped, and a real drug song or two wouldn't have hurt, but these guys would play a jug-band number ahead of a drug anthem anytime. Their cover of Brewer and Shipley's "Truly Right" is pretty spacy in its production, though, but "The Teddy Bear's Picnic"—an adaptation of an old children's song—was probably beyond the pale of most listeners. Beyond NGDB completists, anyone looking for a companion to *Notorious Byrd Bros.* or the Monkees' *Aquarius, Capricorn Pisces & Jones Ltd.*, or a precursor to Crazy Horse's *At Crooked Lake* need look no further. (British import) *— Bruce Eder*

Pure Dirt / 1968 / BGO ✦✦✦✦
The group's first compilation album, made up of six songs from the first album and eight from Ricochet, assembled and released by Liberty Records in England (where neither of the original albums had appeared). A fair representation of the original Nitty Gritty Dirt Band, though serious fans would be more advised to pick up the complete albums. "Buy For Me The Rain" is here, along with some of the more rousing cuts off of the first LP. (British import) *— Bruce Eder*

Rare Junk / 1968 / Liberty ✦✦✦✦
This, the group's third album release, was actually an odds-and-sods type compilation of leftover tracks and singles that formed a respectable 10-song 30-minute plus LP. As a sign of just how strong the band was, it still represented a step forward from their second album, and is one of the great unknown albums of 1968. *— Bruce Eder*

Alive / 1969 / Liberty ✦✦✦✦
How many live albums—forget decent ones—were left behind by bands in 1967/68— This is one, and it's better than decent, and almost a gift from heaven, capturing an early incarnation of the group (circa 1967) on a good night at the L.A. Troubadour. Someone has earned a place in musical heaven for seeing to recording the show. *— Bruce Eder*

Uncle Charlie & His Dog Teddy / 1970 / Liberty ✦✦✦✦
The first album issued by the Nitty Gritty Dirt Band after they had temporarily disbanded in 1969, this greatly expanded their \pop audience, due primarily to the Top 10 hit cover of Jerry Jeff Walker's "Mr. Bojangles" (which actually wasn't a hit until early 1971). The group moved into a more accessible \rock-oriented fusion of \country, \bluegrass, \pop, and \rock & roll, relying primarily on smartly chosen covers of tunes by the likes of Walker, Mike Nesmith, Randy Newman, and Kenny Loggins. Few bands had incorporated instruments more commonly associated with \country and \bluegrass, particularly mandolin and banjo, as comfortably into a \rock setting prior to this release, and their well-crafted harmonies help put the songs over for those not-steeped-in backwoods sounds. It was an extremely diverse program for a \country-rock album, too, moving from rustic instrumentals and snippets of tapes of elderly musicians performing rural \Americana to the Buddy Holly cover "Rave On." The group were actually at their best, though, when doing softer, melodic \pop tunes. "Mr. Bo-

jangles" was a deserved huge success in that regard, but Nesmith's "Some of Shelley's Blues" and Loggins' "House at Pooh Corner" were almost as catchy and appealing. *—Richie Unterberger*

★ **Will the Circle Be Unbroken** / 1972 / EMI America ✦✦✦✦✦
With all due respect to the Byrds and the Flying Burrito Brothers, it took the Nitty Gritty Dirt Band with this album to come up with a merger of rock and country music that worked for both sides and everyone involved. The opening number, "The Grand Ole Opry Song," set the tone for the album, showing that this band—for all of their origins in rock and popular music—was willing to meet country music on its terms, rather than as a vehicle for embellishment as rock music. The result, without a false or strained note anywhere among its 37 songs, was an all-star country project that worked (and transcended its country and rock origins), with the Nitty Gritty Dirt Band serving as catalyst and intersecting point for all of the talent involved, all of who gave superbly of themselves. Not only did this album result in new exposure to a new and wider audience for the likes of Mother Maybelle Carter, Roy Acuff, Earl Scruggs, Merle Travis, and others, but this was the first real country album that a lot of rock listeners under the age of 30 ever heard. Thus, it opened up pathways and dialogue in all directions, across several generations and cultural barriers; the dialogue between Doc Watson and Merle Travis alone was almost worth the price of admission. This was also one of rock's very few multi-disc sets to be fully justified in its length and content; at a time when unnecessary double-LPs were all the rage, the Nitty Gritty Dirt Band and company gave a triple album that, if anything, left audiences asking for more. *—Bruce Eder*

Stars & Stripes Forever / 1974 / Capitol ✦✦✦✦✦

Dream / 1975 / United Artists ✦✦✦

Dirt Band / 1978 / United Artists ✦✦

American Dream (Dirt Band) / 1979 / United Artists ✦✦

20 Years of Dirt . . . / 1986 / Warner Brothers ✦✦✦✦✦
20 Years of Dirt: The Best of the Nitty Gritty Dirt Band. This album traces the development of The Nitty Gritty Dirt Band from a pop outfit with folk and country edges into a contemporary country band. Their version of "Mr. Bojangles" remains memorable, as does "American Dream;" other tracks are sturdy, middle-of-the-road, 80s Nashville. *—William Ruhlmann*

More Great Dirt (Best, Vol. 2) / 1989 / Warner Brothers ✦✦✦✦✦
Tight harmonies and infectious arrangements are the staple of this compilation. "I've Been Lookin'," "Fishin' in the Dark," and "Baby's Got a Hold on Me" are the musical equivalent of a good book—you can't put 'em down. *—Tom Roland*

Will the Circle Be Unbroken, Vol. 2 / 1989 / Universal ✦✦✦

Live Two Five / Jul. 8, 1991 / Liberty ✦✦✦

Alive/Rare Junk / 1995 / BGO ✦✦✦✦✦

Bang Bang Bang / Apr. 21, 1998 / DreamWorks ✦✦✦
While it pales in comparison with their classic early '70s releases, *Bang Bang Bang* is far from being a lesser latter-day effort from the Nitty Gritty Dirt Band. The group are seasoned professionals, capable of making even second-rate material sound fine, which is fortunate since there's a little bit too much filler on the record. Nevertheless, it's a pleasure to hear the group play, and there are moments where they nearly recapture the magic of yesteryear, which may make the album worthwhile for dedicated fans. *—Thom Owens*

The Oak Ridge Boys

f. (, Oak Ridge, TN
Group / Country Gospel, Country-Pop
Over the course of their long career, the Oak Ridge Boys became a country music institution. The vocal group went through a number of personnel changes over the years, but their sound remained the same, as they never strayed from their gospel-inflected country-pop. The group's origins go all the way back to the mid-'40s and the Oak Ridge Quartet, one of the top gospel groups in America by the '50s. After a namechange to the Oak Ridge Boys in 1961, the group flip-flopped between gospel and pop before returning to the secular world with two 1977 hit singles, "Y'All Come Back Saloon" and "You're the One. " Almost immediately, the Oak Ridge Boys became a fixture in the country Top Ten; for the next eight years, they had a string of 13 number one hits including the crossover smash "Elvira." By the mid-'80s, the group's commercial success had slowed. In 1987, longtime group icon and baritone vocalist William Lee Golden was fired by the rest of the group, who believed that his burly appearance and long beard didn't fit their image. Though the move appeared just a little crass, it paid off with four number one hits over the next three years. The Oak Ridge Boys continued to tour and record throughout the '90s. *—Sandra Brennan*

Y'all Come Back Saloon / 1977 / MCA ✦✦✦✦✦
"You're the One" and the title cut are the featured selections on *Y'All Come Back Saloon.* *—Jason Ankeny*

Room Service / 1978 / MCA ✦✦✦✦✦
Room Service includes the Oaks' first number one single, "I'll Be True to You," as well as the Top Three hits "Come on In" and "Cryin' Again." *—Jason Ankeny*

Greatest Hits, Vol. 1 / 1980 / MCA ✦✦✦✦✦
Earliest package of hits, with gospel roots showing on material like "Y'All Come Back Saloon." *—Cub Koda*

Fancy Free / 1981 / MCA ✦✦✦✦✦
This is their best-selling album, thanks to the presence of "Elvira." Each of The Oaks gets a turn at the lead part, although Duane Allen is easily best suited to that role. Includes some quasi-folk and straightahead country, but the best track is the obligatory gospel tune "I Would Crawl All the Way (To the River)." *—Tom Roland*

Bobbie Sue / 1982 / MCA ✦✦✦✦✦

● **Greatest Hits, Vol. 2** / 1984 / MCA ✦✦✦✦✦
This covers The Oaks at their peak, with repetitive, singalong choruses predominating in "American Made," "Love Song," and "Everyday." The delicate "I Guess It Never Hurts to Hurt Sometimes" is a nice change of pace, but why did MCA hold out "Bobbie Sue" until *Greatest Hits 3*? *—Tom Roland*

Greatest Hits, Vol. 3 / 1989 / MCA ✦✦✦✦✦
This contains "Gonna Take a Lot of River," "Take Pride in America," "This Crazy Love," and other hits from the mid- and late '80s. *—AMG*

20th Century Masters— ***The Millennium Collection: The Best of the Oak Ridge Boys /*** *Aug. 15, 2000 / MCA Nashville* ✦✦✦✦
The Millennium Collection: The Very Best of the Oak Ridge Boys gathers highlights from the country-pop group's body of work, including number one hits like "Elvira," "Leavin' Louisiana in the Broad Daylight," "American Made," and "It Takes a Little Rain (To Make Love Grow)." Choice album tracks and radio favorites make up the rest of this concise, affordable hits collection from one of the most popular country acts of the '70s and '80s. *—Heather Phares*

Molly O'Day (LaVerne Williamson)

b. Jul. 9, 1923, Pike County, KY, **d.** Dec. 5, 1987
Vocals, Guitar / Honky Tonk, Traditional Country
A pioneering vocalist whose soulful, gut-wrenching performances helped redefine the role of the female country solo artist, Molly O'Day's career was relatively brief, but her influence was lasting. Born Lois LaVerne Williamson to a coal mining family living in a remote Appalachian community in eastern Kentucky, she spent her childhood enamored of cowgirl singers like Patsy Montana and Lily May Ledford. She sang and played guitar with her brothers Cecil ("Skeets") on fiddle and Joe ("Duke") on banjo in a string band. In 1939, Skeets began playing on a radio station in Charleston, West Virginia, and his sister soon followed, performing as "Mountain Fern." Under the name "Dixie Lee Williamson" she joined guitarist Lynn Davis' band the Forty-Niners; she married Davis in 1941. The Forty-Niners toured the South south extensively and built a substantial fanbase, and by 1946, the name "Molly O'-Day" was firmly entrenched. Her heartfelt solo performances led writer/publisher Fred Rose to sign O'Day to Columbia Records. That year, she recorded several songs by Hank Williams, who taught O'Day her best-loved song, "Tramp on the Street." Already, O'Day was having trouble coping with her success; in 1949, she suffered a nervous breakdown and was hospitalized. In the early '50s, she turned her back on show business and focused on church performances. Davis became an ordained minister, and the couple preached throughout the coal mining communities of West Virginia through the '50s,'60s and '70s. O'Day recorded for a few small gospel labels in the '60s; in 1973 she and Davis began hosting a daily gospel program on a West Virginia radio station. Molly O'Day died of cancer December 5, 1987. *—Jason Ankeny*

★ **And the Cumberland Mountain Folks** / 1992 / Bear Family ✦✦✦✦✦
Molly O'Day and the Cumberland Mountain Folks is a double-disc, 36-track collection that compiles all of the recordings O'Day made for Columbia Records between 1946 and 1951. Though her music presages the upcoming honky tonk era, O'Day was more closely tied to the mountain music that dominated country music in the first half of the 20th Century. As such, her music can be a little difficult for contemporary ears—her thick nasal twang is something that modern listeners will have to accomodate. For country historians, however, *Molly O'Day and the Cumberland Mountain Folks* is a worthwhile. Not only did she bridge the gap between string bands and honky tonk with her old-timey banjo playing and twang, but she was one of the first country artists to record a Hank Williams song. As such, this double-disc set is worth investigation for serious musicologists. *—Stephen Thomas Erlewine*

Molly O'Day & The Cumberland Mountain Folks / 1996 / Bear Family ✦✦✦✦✦
The double-disc set *Molly O'Day & the Cumberland Mountain Folks* contains all 36 tracks that O'Day recorded for Columbia Records between 1946 and 1951. O'Day was one of the most important female country singers of the '40s, but she never attained the stardom she deserved because she retired from the business in 1951. Nevertheless, her music has come to be regarded as some of the finest of her era, especially considering how she could make traditional mountain music, both sacred and secular, come alive. *Molly O'Day & the Cumberland Mountain Folks* preserves her classic sides in a classy fashion, and any musicologist or dedicated fan of string bands needs the compilation in their collection. *—Thom Owens*

Orion (Jimmy Ellis)

b. 1945, Orrville, AL
Vocals / Rockabilly, Country-Pop, Traditional Country, Rock & Roll
The music industry is filled with many strange tales of artists whose lives took unexpected turns on the winding road to success, but the saga of singer Jimmy Ellis is perhaps one of the weirdest of them all. He was professionally known as Orion, and his double-edged claim to fame was that his natural speaking and singing voice sounded almost exactly like that of Elvis Presley. Ellis hailed from Orrville, Alabama and began his recording career in 1964. In 1972, he worked for Sun Records (Presley's label) with producer Shelby Singleton in Nashville. His first two singles were covers of two of the King's former hits, "That's All Right" and "Blue Moon of Kentucky."

The strange part of the tale began in January, 1979 when author Gail Brewer-Giorgio received a bizarre early morning phone call. Two years before she had begun a novel about a musical superstar, Orion, who faked his own death to find much-needed peace and privacy, based on the circumstances surrounding Elvis' death. The mysterious phone call came from a stranger with a Presley-like voice, claiming to be Orion. A year prior, Jimmy Ellis' voice had been overdubbed with Jerry Lee Lewis on an old single from the Sun archives, "Save the Last Dance for Me;" on it, Ellis was billed only as "Friend." The single made the Top 20 and caused quite a stir as listeners tried to guess the mysterious "Friend's" identity. An album featuring the duet came out and the controversy really heated up when *Good Morning America* had the Friend's voice "scientifically scanned and analyzed" and concluded that it could be no one but Presley. Giorgio's book had just come out, so Singleton decided to cash in on its popularity and transform Jimmy Ellis into the mysterious "Orion" who had phoned the author earlier that year. Ellis' hair and long sideburns were dyed black, and he dressed in a loud, bejeweled polyester jumpsuits, with a mask to protect him from crazed fans.

"Orion" recorded a single, "Ebony Eyes," for Sun in 1979, which became part of his debut album, *Reborn.* The album cover itself generated controversy because it depicted a phantom singer rising from a coffin, and was later withdrawn. He released two more albums in 1980; the third, *Trio Plus,* featured Orion's voice overdubbed on old cuts with Lewis, Carl Perkins, and Charlie Rich. The albums were quite popular, and Orion had three Top 70 hits, including "Am I That Easy to Forget." He had four minor hits the following year, including the contemporary rockabilly song "Crazy Little Thing Called Love," originally recorded by the rock group Queen. Ellis continued recording and performing through 1983 as Orion, and scored only one more minor hit before trying to break his Sun contract to become a recognized performer in his own right.

While performing at *the Eastern States Exposition,* Ellis took off the mask and swore to never wear it again. Unfortunately, despite the fact that most of the songs he recorded were not covers of Elvis songs, he could not escape the uncanny similarities between their natural voices. At one point he even released the single "I'm Trying Not to Sound Like Elvis." During his time with Sun, Ellis/Orion cut over 11 albums and toured with the Oak Ridge Boys, Jerry Lee Lewis, and other stars like Dionne Warwick. As Jim Ellis, he released an album in 1987 and continued to tour North America; interestingly, he resumed wearing his mask. — *Sandra Brennan*

● **Who Was That Masked Man?** / Jun. 23, 1999 / Bear Family ♦♦♦♦♦
Let's call a spade a spade. Orion is an Elvis impersonator. No more, no less. That he's a good Elvis impersonator is important, since if he wasn't, Sun probably wouldn't have tried to promote his recordings as if they were genuine Elvis material, even going to the extremes of overdubbing Orion's voices on recordings by such Sun stalwarts as Jerry Lee Lewis and Carl Perkins. This doesn't make him any better, but it sure makes him fascinating, particularly because he is gifted at mimicry and these are pretty good evocations of Elvis at his peak. Bear Family's four-disc box *Who Was That Masked Man?* contains all of his '70s masterworks, including original recordings and fake duets, and it's a singularly fascinating listen. Really, it's pretty good music, but for God's sake, the blatant charlatanism behind this can grate even those with an inclination for kitsch. Taken on surface value, it's enjoyable, but dig a little deeper and it becomes a little silly and a little creepy and completely fascinating. That's not necessarily justification for a four-disc set, but if you're inclined to purchase this on the basis of what Orion is, you won't be disappointed, no matter how uneven the music is. — *Stephen Thomas Erlewine*

K.T. Oslin

b. 1942, Crossett, AR
Vocals / Contemporary Country, Country-Pop
During the late '80s, K.T. Oslin had a string of hit singles with her pop-inflected modern country. Most of Oslin's material was directed at—in the words of her breakthrough single—"80's Ladies," which meant her songs were about modern women and were recorded with modern equipment, including synthesizers. For a brief time, she was one of the most popular singers in country music, earning four number one singles and two platinum albums. Her first musical experience came with a folk trio featuring Guy Clark and David Jones in the '60s. After moving to New York to appear in a Broadway version of *Hello Dolly!,* she began performing and recorded a minor hit with her debut single, 1981's "Clean Your Own Tables." Signed to RCA, she released her first album, *'80s Ladies,* in 1987. Thanks to the Top Ten title track, it became the highest-charting debut album for a female since Loretta Lynn's in 1964. She hit number one with its follow-up, "Do Ya." In the next two years, she recorded three albums and had four more Top Ten hits. Oslin released the compilation *Greatest Hits: Songs from an Aging Sex Bomb* in 1993. Three years later she released the covers album *My Roots Are Showing.* — *Sandra Brennan*

80's Ladies / 1987 / RCA ♦♦♦♦♦

This Woman / 1988 / RCA ♦♦♦

Love in a Small Town / 1990 / RCA ♦♦♦♦♦

● **Greatest Hits: Songs from an Aging Sex Bomb** / Apr. 27, 1993 / RCA ♦♦♦♦
You'll find K.T. Oslin in the country section, but don't be fooled. This music is to country as Kenny G is to jazz—a slicker, poppier variation on a familiar formula. And Kenny G's example to the contrary notwithstanding, there's nothing necessarily wrong with that. Oslin's reedy alto doesn't have much of that mountain twang to it (her singing owes much more to Phoebe Snow than to Loretta Lynn, whether she knows it or not) and you're not going to hear any tear-jerking steel guitar on this collection. But you will certainly hear lots of snappy pop music with good melodies and slick production. Country radio listeners will recognize staples like "Hold Me" and "80s Ladies," but if no one told you that "You Can't Do That" was a country song, you'd never guess. And who cares— This is great pop music, no matter what bin you find it in. — *Rick Anderson*

My Roots Are Showing / Oct. 1, 1996 / BNA ♦♦♦

Buck Owens (Alvis Edgar Owens)

b. Aug. 12, 1929, Sherman, TX
Vocals, Saxophone, Trumpet, Guitar / Bakersfield Sound, Honky Tonk, Traditional Country
Buck Owens, along with Merle Haggard, was the leader of the Bakersfield Sound, an twangy, electrified, rock-influenced interpretation of hardcore honky tonk that emerged in the '60s. Owens was the first bonafide country star to emerge from Bakersfield, scoring a total of 15 consecutive number one hits in the mid-'60s, including "Act Naturally," "Love's Gonna Live Here" and "Tiger by the Tail." In the process, he and his band the Buckaroos, led by guitarist Don Rich, provided an edgy alternative to the string-laden country-pop that was being produced during the '60s. Later in his career, his musical impact was forgotten by some as he became a television personality through the country comedy show *Hee Haw.* Nevertheless, several generations of musicians—from Gram Parsons in the late '60s to Dwight Yoakam in the '80s—were influenced by his music, which wound up being one of the key blueprints for modern country music. — *Stephen Thomas Erlewine*

Buck Owens / Jan. 30, 1961 / Capitol ♦♦♦
This is a reissue of Buck's debut album, originally issued on Capitol in 1961. Featuring Owens' early development of the Bakersfield sound (the classic Buckaroos lineup had yet to be assembled and Don Rich is only listed as the fiddle player on "Excuse Me [I Think I've Got a Heartache]"), this opening salvo sports his early hits "Above and Beyond," "Under Your Spell Again" and "Second Fiddle." This 14-track reissue also sports two extra bonus tracks in addition to the original album, "High as the Mountain" (a 1961 single) and the first recorded version of "Nobody's Fool But Yours," originally issued on a Capitol country compilation. Transfers are astonishingly crisp and clear, showing producer Ken Nelson's touch to good advantage. The sound that became the legend starts right here. — *Cub Koda*

Buck Owens Sings Harlan Howard / Aug. 28, 1961 / Sundazed ♦♦♦♦

On the Bandstand / Apr. 29, 1963 / Sundazed ♦♦♦
One of Buck's rootsier '60s Capitol albums, including only one hit ("Kickin' Our Hearts"), and giving plenty of instrumental and vocal space to the rest of the band. It's not as heavy on original material as some of his other Capitol LPs, including numbers by Wanda Jackson, Willie Nelson, Leadbelly, and John D. Loudermilk, as well as an arrangment of "Orange Blossom Special." The CD reissue adds two cuts from a 1963 Top 20 duet single he recorded with Rose Maddox. — *Richie Unterberger*

Buck Owens Sings Tommy Collins / Nov. 11, 1963 / Sundazed ♦♦♦♦
Buck Owens Sings Tommy Collins is a straight CD reissue of the 1963 album of the same name, without the bonus tracks that appear on many of Sundazed's Buck Owens reissues. Tommy Collins' hillbilly novelties are well-suited to Owens, and he tackles a slew of them here, including "It Tickles" (with Bonnie Owens), "I Always Get a Souvenir," "You Gotta Have a License," "Whatcha Gonna Do Now—," and that perennial fave "Down, Down, Down." In recording an album of *Collins'* songs, Owens honors a fellow Bakersfield pioneer and pays tribute to an artist who deserves wider recognition. — *Greg Adams*

☆ **Together Again/My Heart Skips a Beat** / Jul. 20, 1964 / Sundazed ♦♦♦♦♦
Named after his double-sided number one hit single of early 1964, *Together Again/My Heart Skips a Beat* is one of Buck Owens' strongest albums of the '60s, as well as one of his few records to stick firmly in the honky tonk camp. Despite the rolling drums of "My Heart Skips A Beat," the jumpy "Truck Drivin' Man," the jokey "Ain't It Amazin' Gracie" and a Bakersfield overhaul of "Save the Last Dance for Me," the majority of the album is straight-ahead honky tonk. Whether it's Buck's excellent weepers "I Don't Hear You" and "Getting Used to Losing You," or terrific versions of classics like "Close Up the Honky Tonks" and "A-11," the record is filled with superb, pure honky tonk. Sundazed's CD reissue adds the singles "Love's Gonna Live Here" and "Act Naturally," which don't follow in the honky tonk theme of the album, but since both are classics, it's not worth complaining. — *Stephen Thomas Erlewine*

I Don't Care / Nov. 2, 1964 / Sundazed ♦♦♦

I've Got a Tiger by the Tail / Mar. 1, 1965 / Sundazed ♦♦♦♦♦

Before You Go/No One But You / Jul. 26, 1965 / Sundazed ♦♦♦
When it comes to Owens's mid-'60s Capitol LPs, there really isn't much to choose between. If you like his Bakersfield sound, you'll like all of them; if you're trying to zero in on just one or two collections, you'd be better off with greatest-hits surveys, because the individual albums sound rather interchangeable to the non-enthusiast. This has the usual competent original material and accomplished guitar picking, paced by the number one title track, with occasional instrumentals thrown in for a change of pace. The CD reissue adds a couple of instrumental bonus cuts from his 1966 album, *The Buck Owens Songbook.* — *Richie Unterberger*

☆ **The Carnegie Hall Concert** / Jul. 25, 1966 / Sundazed ♦♦♦♦♦
Buck Owens & the Buckaroos' 1966 concert at *Carnegie Hall* was a landmark not only for the band, but for country music: It signaled that country had firmly integrated itself not only into America's popular music mainstream, but also urban centers like New York. Owens and the Buckaroos had to deliver a stellar performance, and they did—the group sounded like dynamite, tearing through a selection of their classic hits with vigor. Several decades removed from the performance itself, what really comes through is how musical and gifted the Buckaroos were, particularly Don Rich. For dedicated fans, it's a necessary addition to their collection. — *Stephen Thomas Erlewine*

It Takes People Like You to Make People Like Me / Jan. 2, 1968 / Sundazed ♦♦♦

☆ **The Buck Owens Collection (1959-1990)** / 1992 / Rhino ♦♦♦♦♦
Spanning three discs, *The Buck Owens Collection* is the most comprehensive compilation ever assembled on one of the founders of the Bakersfield sound. Although his earliest recordings aren't included, all of his greatest Capitol hits are present, as is his 1988 duet on "Streets of Bakersfield" with Dwight Yoakam and its followup single, "Hot Dog." The box is a necessary purchase, simply because it presents all of Buck's biggest hits in one place. There might not be many rarities on *The Buck Owens Collection,* but with an artist as consistent as Buck, all you need is the good stuff and that is all on this essential set. — *Stephen Thomas Erlewine*

★ **The Very Best of Buck Owens, Vol. 1** / 1994 / Rhino ♦♦♦♦♦
The Very Best of Buck Owens, Vol. 1 contains a great deal of Buck's most essential songs, including "Under Your Spell Again," "Act Naturally," "I've Got A Tiger By the Tail," and "Waitin' In Your Welfare Line." The set runs from 1959 to 1971, picking up a good cross-section of his biggest hits along the way. The compilation is a perfect introduction and what songs it doesn't cover are readily available on *The Very Best of Buck Owens, Vol. 2.* Of course, listeners that want the most comprehensive set available should invest in the triple-disc box set, *The Buck Owens Collection.* — *Stephen Thomas Erlewine*

☆ **The Very Best of Buck Owens, Vol. 2** / 1994 / Rhino ✦✦✦✦✦
The Very Best of Buck Owens, Vol. 2 contains all the essential Owens songs the first volume didn't cover, including "Above and Beyond," "Love's Gonna Live Here," "My Heart Skips A Beat," "Cryin' Time," "Buckaroo," and "Big in Vegas." Like its predecessor, the collection spans from 1959 to 1971, and features an excellent cross-section of his biggest hits along the way. Not only is it a perfect supplement to *The Very Best of Buck Owens, Vol. 1,* the compilation works as a good introduction, even though the first collection is a better choice for a new fan. Of course, listeners that want the most comprehensive set available should invest in the triple-disc box set, *The Buck Owens Collection.* — *Stephen Thomas Erlewine*

In Japan! / Nov. 11, 1997 / Sundazed ✦✦✦✦✦
Long one of the finer efforts in the Buck Owens album catalog and also one of the finest live country records of all time, *In Japan!* shines in its compact disc reissue. Originally released by Capitol in 1967, this finds Buck and the Buckaroos in the prime of their chart-topping existence and playing like a well-oiled machine, firing exquisitely on all cylinders. The opening and closing remarks and between song translating banter to the audience from emcee Tetsuo Otsuka makes for wonderful ambience throughout, and Buck's good-natured master-of-ceremonies turns work hand-in-glove with him. Musically, the Buckaroos, led by Don Rich, are at the top of their game, and the live versions here of "Open Up Your Heart," "Roll Out the Red Carpet" and "Where Does the Good Times Go" sometimes eclipse their better-known hit studio versions. Although his *Live at Carnegie Hall* album is considered by most fans as definitive, here's another one that shouldn't dismissed for a second. — *Cub Koda*

Brad Paisley

Vocals, Guitar / Western Swing Revival, Neo-Traditionalist Country, Contemporary Country
Contemporary country singer/songwriter Brad Paisley was born October 28, 1972 in Glen Dale, WV; given his first guitar at age eight, he delivered his first public performance at church two years later. With his 50-something guitar teacher Clarence "Hank" Goddard and two of the older man's seasoned musician buddies, the teenaged Paisley formed his first band, the C-Notes, and at age 12 began writing his own material. After performing in front of the local Rotary Club, he was invited to appear on Wheeling, WV station WWVA's famed Saturday night broadcast *Jamboree USA;* Paisley's debut was so well-received that he was invited to join the program full-time, and in the years to follow he opened for the likes of the Judds, Roy Clark and Little Jimmy Dickens. He later attended Nashville's Belmont University, serving an internship with ASCAP; the contacts Paisley made there helped him land a songwriting deal with EMI, and he also appeared on countless demos. Signing to Arista, he issued his debut solo album *Who Needs Pictures* in 1999. — *Jason Ankeny*

● **Who Needs Pictures** / May 18, 1999 / Arista ✦✦✦✦
It's easy to glance at Brad Paisley and assume that he's another in a long line of contemporary country artists that get by on their good looks instead of their talent, but his debut album *Who Needs Pictures* suggests otherwise. Paisley follows the pattern set by such neo-traditionalists as George Strait, Randy Travis, and Alan Jackson, yet he adds a bit of a pop sheen—never as much as John Michael Montgomery, but similar to Tim McGraw. Although it boasts a shiny, clean production, *Who Needs Pictures* keeps itself firmly within country territory, even if it doesn't feel like its roots dig that deep. Similarly, Paisley's voice is a little thin, lacking the resonance of a Travis, but it is appealing, as are his songs, all of which he co-wrote with a host of collaborators (most notably Chris DuBois and Kelley Lovelace). His material may be a little cutesy, but it's catchy, particularly on the faster numbers. Those tunes are surprisingly diverse, ranging from the Western swing-styled "It Never Woulda Worked Out Anyway" and the breezy "I've Been Better" to the skittering Bakersfield instrumental "The Nervous Breakdown," the rocking contemporary country opener "Long Sermon," and the winning honky tonk of "Sleepin' on the Foldout." And even if his ballads tend to drag, "He Didn't Have to Be" is strikingly autobiographical and heartfelt, showcasing his potential in that area, as well. So, even if *Who Needs Pictures* is a little uneven, it hits considerably more than it misses, and those hits suggest Brad Paisley is an artist worth following. — *Stephen Thomas Erlewine*

Lee Roy Parnell

b. Dec. 21, 1957, Abilene, TX
Slide Guitar, Vocals, Guitar / Western Swing Revival, New Traditionalist, Contemporary Country
Singer/songwriter and slide guitarist Lee Roy Parnell sang with a Texas-style Western swing enlivened with just a hint of blues. In addition to having a string of Top 10 singles of his own, Parnell wrote songs for artists as diverse as Sweethearts of the Rodeo, Jo-El Sonnier, and David Wills & Johnny Lee. As a youngster, Parnell made his debut singing "San Antonio Rose" on Bob Wills' radio show in Fort Worth; following high school, Parnell moved to Austin and set about touring for the next dozen years. While playing in a local cafe, he was heard by Tim Dubois, the head of Arista Records, who signed the aspiring singer to the label. Parnell released his eponymous debut album in 1990 and the record yielded three minor hits. Released in 1992, his second album *Love Without Mercy* produced the number two smash "What Kind of Fool Do You Think I Am." Following its success, he had four consecutive Top 10 hits—"Love Without Mercy," "Tender Moment," "On the Road," and "I'm Holding My Own." The latter two were taken from his third album *On the Road,* released in the fall of 1993. In 1995, he returned back to the Top 10 with "A Little Bit of You," taken from his fourth album, *We All Get Lucky Sometimes.* — *Sandra Brennan*

Lee Roy Parnell / 1990 / Arista ✦✦✦✦

Love Without Mercy / 1992 / Arista ✦✦✦✦

On the Road / Oct. 26, 1993 / Arista ✦✦✦

We All Get Lucky Sometimes / 1995 / Career ✦✦✦

Every Night's a Saturday Night / Jun. 17, 1997 / Arista ✦✦✦✦

● **Hits And Highways Ahead** / Aug. 24, 1999 / Arista ✦✦✦✦
Hits and Highways Ahead compiles the majority of Lee Roy Parnell's hits from his first five albums, adding two new songs ("She Won't Be Lonely Long," "Long Way to Fall") plus "John the Revelator," taken fro, the various-artists album *Peace in the Valley: A Country Music Journey Through Gospel.* It isn't quite definitive—not only are there a handful of hits missing, there are also some good album tracks absent, and nothing is taken from his fine debut—but it's nevertheless a strong, entertaining hits collection, blessed with two strong new entries and such highlights as "Tender Moments," "Love Without Mercy," "On the Road," "I'm Holding My Own," and "What Kind of Fool Do You Think I Am." For casual fans and the curious, this is the ideal choice. — *Stephen Thomas Erlewine*

Dolly Parton

b. Jan. 19, 1946, Locust Ridge, TN
Vocals, Guitar, Banjo / Urban Cowboy, Honky Tonk, Country-Folk, Contemporary Country, Country-Pop, Progressive Country, Traditional Country
It's difficult to find a country performer who has moved from country roots to international fame more successfully than Dolly Parton. Her autobiographical single "Coat of Many Colors" shows the poverty of growing up one of 12 children on a run-down farm in Locust Ridge, Tennessee. At 12 years old she was appearing on Knoxville television; at 13 she was recording on a small label and appearing on the Grand Ole Opry. Her 1967 hit "Dumb Blonde" (and she's not) caught Porter Wagoner's ear, and he hired Parton to appear on his television show, where their duet numbers became famous. By the time her "Joshua" reached number one in 1970, Parton's fame had overshadowed the boss's, and she had struck out on her own, though still recording duets with him. During the mid-'70s, she established herself as a country superstar, crossing over into the pop mainstream in the early '80s, when she smoothed out the rough edges in her music and began singing pop as well as country. In the early '80s, she also began appearing in movies, most notably the hit *9 to 5.* Though her savvy marketing, image manipulation—her big, dumb blonde stage persona is an *act*—extracurricular forays into film, and her flirtations with country-pop have occasionally overshadowed her music, at her core Dolly Parton is a country gal and a tremendously gifted singer/songwriter. Among her classics are "Coat of Many Colors," "Jolene," "Kentucky Gambler," "I Will Always Love You," "But You Known I Love You" and "Tennessee Homesick Blues," and they give a hint to why her contribution to bringing country music to a wide audience, not only in America but throughout the world, cannot be underestimated. — *David Vinopal*

Just Because I'm a Woman / 1968 / RCA ✦✦✦✦✦
It's a measure of how impressed producer Bob Ferguson must have been with Parton that he (and possibly Porter Wagoner in the background) made no attempt to crowd her with strings or choruses on her first RCA album. In fact, it's almost frightening to hear how fully realized her talent was in 1968. — *Dan Cooper*

Coat of Many Colors / Oct. 1971 / Buddha ✦✦✦✦✦
Dolly Parton had a number of hits in the late '60s as Porter Wagoner's duet partner, yet solo success eluded her until her 1971 album, *Coat of Many Colors.* The title track was a Top 10 single, and it effectively became her signature song, largely because it was a sweetly autobiographical tune about her childhood. That song, along with its two hit predecessors "Traveling Man" and "My Blue Tears," were evidence that Parton was a strong songwriter, but the full album reveals the true depth of her talents. She wrote seven of the ten songs (Wagoner wrote the other three), none of which are filler. There isn't really a theme behind *Coat of Many Colors,* even if its title track suggests otherwise. Instead, it's a remarkably consistent album, in terms of songwriting and performances, but also remarkably diverse, revealing that Dolly can handle ballads, country-rockers, tearjerkers, and country-pop with equal aplomb. And while it is very short, clocking in at under a half hour, there isn't a wasted moment on the album. It's a lean, trim album that impresses because of succinctness—with its ten songs, it announced Parton as a major talent in her own right, not merely a duet partner. — *Stephen Thomas Erlewine*

Jolene / 1974 / Buddha ✦✦✦

The Best of Dolly Parton / 1975 / RCA ✦✦✦✦✦
She projects an admirable child-like sense of hope and positivism, which is matched to some degree by her thin, girlish vocal quality. It translates well in her pre-Hollywood, unencumbered productions, notably "Coat of Many Colors," "Love Is like a Butterfly," and "The Bargain Store." — *Tom Roland*

My Tennessee Mountain Home / 1975 / RCA ✦✦✦

9 to 5 and Odd Jobs / 1980 / Buddha ✦✦✦✦✦
Dolly Parton has never been an albums artist, and RCA has always been adept at shoving poorly organized products onto the market (look how they've treated Elvis Presley). Hence, though she is an important country figure, most of Parton's albums are hard to recommend. This one contains the title hit, plus a few other Parton originals and a version of Woody Guthrie's "Deportee" among its eight tracks. But that's enough to put it a notch above most of Parton's RCA catalog. — *William Ruhlmann*

Greatest Hits / 1982 / RCA ✦✦✦✦✦
This is a good sampling of Parton's work in the first few years that she deliberately chased a crossover career in Hollywood. The country-pop stuff might offend purists, but it still gets the toe tappin'. "Hard Candy Christmas" and her updated version of "I Will Always Love You" (both from *The Best Little Whorehouse in Texas*) show her growth as an interpreter. — *Tom Roland*

White Limozeen / 1989 / Columbia ✦✦✦✦✦

Eagle When She Flies / 1991 / Columbia ✦✦✦

Slow Dancing with the Moon / 1993 / Columbia ✦✦✦

★ **The RCA Years 1967-1986** / May 25, 1993 / RCA ✦✦✦✦✦
The long-overdue box set turns out to be a cursory two-CD set that cheats on her better early

years in favor of latter-day hits. Still, it's the best retrospective available, and it emphasizes her stature as a truly significant songwriter, which is easy to forget in the shadow of her Daisy Mae in Hollywood image. *—Michael McCall*

Honky Tonk Angels / Nov. 2, 1993 / Columbia ✦✦✦

Something Special / 1995 / Columbia ✦✦✦

The Essential Dolly Parton, Vol. 1: I Will Always Love You / Mar. 28, 1995 / RCA ✦✦✦✦✦
This set kicked off RCA's long-overdue "essential" reissue series with a package by country's best-known ambassador, Dolly Parton. The volume one imprint on the album implies that there will be another Parton set, which is good news, considering that this set is geared toward her late-seventies and thereafter pop recordings. Parton fans must demand a respectful set featuring Parton's very early hits, when she was hungry to establish herself—songs like "Mule Skinner Blues," "Try Being Lonely," "Joshua," "She Never Met A Man (She Didn't Like)," "Coat of Many Colors," "Touch Your Woman," "Dumb Blonde," "The Bargin Store" or "Just Because I'm A Woman." And how about throwing in a couple of Porter Wagoner duets like "If Teardrops Were Pennies" or "Please Don't Stop Loving Me" for good measure—

That those tracks aren't included here shouldn't inhibit anyone from picking this set up. There's not a rotten apple in this bunch. There's the 1982 version of her 1974 country smash "I Will Always Love You" which was used in the film *The Best Little Whorehouse In Texas*, the equally familiar "Islands In The Stream" duet with Kenny Rogers and the title song from the 1980 film "9 To 5." The rest of the material is divided between what RCA hoped to cross over to the pop charts and what they planned to program to Parton's base country audience. Of the former there is the spirited "Think About Love" and the all-out MOR ballads "Starting Over Again" and "You're The Only One." As for the latter, there are the fun, snappy "Do I Ever Cross Your Mind," "Sweet Summer Lovin'" and "Heartbreak Express" among others. *—Bill Carpenter*

☆ **The Essential Dolly Parton, Vol. 2** / Apr. 29, 1997 / RCA ✦✦✦✦✦
The Essential Dolly Parton, Vol. 2 doesn't cover the late-'60s and early-'70s pure country hits that were also ignored by its predecessor, choosing to concentrate on her '70s crossover hits. Although that still leaves a large portion of her best work unanthologized, *Vol. 2* is still a very good compilation. It's true that including the original version of "I Will Always Love You"—which was presented in a re-recorded take from 1982 on *Vol. 1*—is a bit redundant, but the remainder of the disc is filled with hits, from her faithful cover of Jimmie Rodgers' "Mule Skinner Blues" to the soft-rock of "Here You Come Again." Such diversity doesn't make for a coherent collection, but it does illustrate exactly why Dolly had such a large fan base. *—Stephen Thomas Erlewine*

Hungry Again / Aug. 25, 1998 / MCA ✦✦✦✦✦

The Grass Is Blue / Oct. 26, 1999 / Sugar Hill ✦✦✦✦✦
It was inevitable, especially considering her recent albums, that Dolly Parton would eventually go all the way back to the mountains with a bluegrass project.

A child of the southern Appalachians, Parton would have absorbed this music straight through her skin during her formative years. And, indeed, her performance on this CD is impeccable, as is her choice of material. Producer Steve Buckingham has taken care to bring together a group of accomplished bluegrassers to accompany Parton. Alison Krauss, Stuart Duncan, Dan Tyminski, Jerry Douglas, Rhonda Vincent, and Bryan Sutton are major contributors, as is Patty Loveless. Parton wrote two songs for the CD—the title tune and "Endless Stream of Tears"—and she also reworked two of her previously recorded numbers, "Will He Be Waiting for Me" and "Steady As the Rain" as bluegrass pieces. She convinced her producer that Billy Joel's "Travelin' Prayer" and Blackfoot's hard-rocking "Train, Train" could work as bluegrass songs and, sure enough, they do. She also reached into the traditional folk repertoire and crafted a beautiful, haunting version of "Silver Dagger." Parton shows a terrific knack for this genre and, as always, her approach is a bit eccentric, but that's one of her gifts as a musician. She's always followed her own muse; this time it has led her to a singular interpretation of bluegrass that is one of the important bluegrass releases of 1999. *—Philip Van Vleck*

Little Sparrow / Jan. 23, 2001 / Sugar Hill ✦✦✦✦

Johnny Paycheck (Don Eugene Lytle)

b. May 31, 1938, Greenfield, OH
Vocals, Guitar (Steel), Guitar, Bass / Outlaw Country, Honky Tonk, Traditional Country
The first that many people ever heard of Johnny Paycheck was in 1977, when his "Take This Job and Shove It" inspired one-man wildcat strikes all over America. The next time was in 1985, when he was arrested for shooting a man at a bar in Hillsboro, Ohio. That Paycheck is remembered for a fairly amusical novelty song and a violent crime (for which he spent two years in prison) is a shame, for it just so happens that he is one of the mightiest honky-tonkers of his time. Born and raised in Greenfield, Ohio, Paycheck was performing in talent contests by the age of nine, and riding the rails as a drifter by the time he turned fifteen. After a Navy stint landed him in the brig for two years, he arrived in Nashville, where he performed in the bands of Porter Wagoner, Faron Young, Ray Price and George Jones. He recorded several singles under the name Donny Young, then, in 1965, cut his first sides as Johnny Paycheck for the Hilltop label. A year later, he and gadfly producer Aubrey Mayhew started the Little Darlin' label, for which Paycheck recorded his greatest work. Marked by Lloyd Green's knockout steel guitar and Paycheck's broad, resonant vocals (not to mention his rounder's sense of humor) his Little Darlin' records of the 1960s have since become cult favorites. After splitting with Mayhew (and after running his life into the gutter) Paycheck made a celebrated comeback on Epic in the 1970s. "Take This Job and Shove It" was the most famous result, though ballads like "She's All I Got" and "Someone to Give My Love To" are far more indicative of his stylistic range. *—Dan Cooper*

She's All I Got / 1971 / Koch ✦✦✦✦✦

Take This Job & Shove It / 1978 / Epic ✦✦✦

● **Biggest Hits** / 1983 / Epic ✦✦✦✦✦
Heavy on the late-'70s outlaw sound, this is where to find the original "Take This Job and Shove It" on CD. *—Dan Cooper*

● **The Real Mr. Heartache: The Little Darlin' Years** / 1996 / Country Music Foundation ✦✦✦✦✦
For the casual country fan who only knows Johnny Paycheck from his late-'70s outlaw period ("Take This Job and Shove It," a hit song so huge that its title was made into a major film), these 24 sides from the mid-'60s will come as a major revelation. Paycheck has always come by his outlaw image honestly and he had been knocking around Nashville since 1958, cutting rockabilly country singles under the name Donny Young when he came to the attention of producer-record executive Aubrey Mayhew in 1962. Forming a partnership, they produced a spate of hard country singles for Hilltop before starting up their own label, Little Darlin'. Figuring the easiest way to get noticed was to be as wild as possible, they uncorked a rash of singles (and a couple of albums) that pushed the darkest side of honky tonk lyrics to their limits while simultaneously widening the limits of 45-rpm reproduction with stinging, high-end mixes perfect for AM country radio stations and truck-stop jukeboxes alike. These weren't merely honky tonk records bucking the tide of the '60s Nashville Sound; this was country music with a wild-hair unrepentant redneck attitude to it. This dissolute persona is reflected in many of the titles alone, from "If I'm Gonna Sink (I Might as Well Go to the Bottom)," to "He's in a Hurry (To Get Home to My Wife)," to the absolutely scary "(Pardon Me) I've Got Someone to Kill," the mood getting blacker and blacker with each keening wail of Lloyd Green's steel guitar. Paycheck may have had bigger (much bigger) hits than the 24 tracks collected here, but he never made any greater music than this. *—Cub Koda*

Webb Pierce

b. Aug. 8, 1926, West Monroe, LA, **d.** Feb. 24, 1991, Nashville, TN
Vocals, Guitar / Honky Tonk, Traditional Country
Webb Pierce was one of the most popular honky tonk vocalists of the '50s, racking up more number one hits than similar artists like Hank Williams, Eddy Arnold, Lefty Frizzell, and Ernest Tubb. For most of the general public, Pierce—with his lavish, flamboyant Nudie suits—became the most recognizable face of country music, as well as all of its excesses; after all, he boasted about his pair of convertibles lined with silver dollars and his guitar-shaped swimming pool. For all of his success, Pierce never amassed the reputation of his contemporaries, even though he continued to chart regularly well into the '70s. Webb's weakness for gaudy ornaments of his wealth, as well as his reluctance to break away from hardcore honky tonk meant that he had neither supporters in the industry, nor the ability to sustain the ever-changing tastes of a popular audience. Nevertheless, he remains one of the cornerstone figures of honky tonk, both for his success and his artistic achievements. *—Stephen Thomas Erlewine*

☆ **The Wondering Boy (1951-1958)** / 1990 / Bear Family ✦✦✦✦✦
For the devout, Germany's Bear Family offers a 4-CD boxed set of Pierce's primal honky tonk, a total of 113 songs by one of the seminal post-war country artists, including duets with Kitty Wells, Red Sovine, and the Wilburn Brothers. This is the best sound quality and presentation available of this influential music. *—Mark A. Humphrey*

★ **King of the Honky-Tonk: From the Original Master Tapes** / 1994 / Country Music Foundation ✦✦✦✦✦
No one ever accused Pierce of being a singer's singer; neverthless, his classic country oeuvre is totally individualistic, which is really more important. Any fan of '50s fiddle-and-steel honky tonk will want this collection, which features such Pierce immortals as "There Stands the Glass," "Slowly," a rollicking 1954 remake of Jimmie Rodgers's "In the Jailhouse Now," and the to-the-point "Honky Tonk Song." The latter is one of several cuts from the pen of a young Mel Tillis. *—Dan Cooper*

Sandy Posey

b. Jun. 18, 1947, Jasper, AL
Vocals / Nashville Sound/Countrypolitan, Girl Group, Country-Pop
Despite having several moderate hits in both the country and pop charts, Sandy Posey was never fully embraced by either audience and is far from being a household name. Her clear voice was perfectly suited for the ultra-slick Nashville "countrypolitan" sound of the day, and MGM records signed her at age 18 to a solo deal on the strength of her demo recording of "Born a Woman." Despite her country roots and the country feel of her material, MGM marketed her as a pop singer—in retrospect, a wise decision. "Born a Woman" and "Single Girl" became her first two hits (both reached number 12 in the pop charts in 1966). Posey had two more pop hits with the Top 40 "What a Woman in Love Won't Do" and the number 12 "I Take It Back." By 1968, Posey's woman-as-a-helpless-victim themes were decidedly out of touch with the times and the hits stopped coming. She returned in 1970 for phase two of her career—"the country years." At Columbia, she had another string of hits—this time in the country charts including the Top 20 Vietnam War-inspired "Bring Him Home Safely to Me," the slightly risque "Why Don't We Go Somewhere and Love," "Happy Birthday Baby" and "Don't." Her last hit was in 1979 with "Love Is Sometimes Easy." *—Chris Woodstra*

Born a Woman / 1966 / MGM ✦✦✦✦
Sandy Posey's debut record starts off with her signature hit song, "Born A Woman" and the rest of the songs, which are mostly laments on lost love and loneliness, set the blueprint she would follow for her pop phase with MGM. The ultra-slick Nashville pop gloss of the arrangements helped secure a pop audience but Posey clearly demonstrated that she had the soul of a country singer. *—Chris Woodstra*

I Take It Back / 1967 / MGM ✦✦✦
Posey's third album features a mix of originals and covers, including songs that had been hits for Miss Toni Fisher ("The Big Hurt"), Tony Orlando ("Halfway to Paradise"), and The Fleetwoods ("Come Softly to Me"). *—Jim Worbois*

Single Girl / 1967 / MGM ♦♦♦
Posey's defiant stance on the cover and the title are slightly deceptive—this isn't a testament to the independence and joy of being a "single girl" but rather another case of Sandy mourning her life without "her man." The title track preaches, "A single girl needs a good hearted man to lean on." Aside from outdated anti-feminist statements, the album's real strengths lie in the haunting, slightly skewed arrangements which cross "countrypolitan" with pure '60s pop best exemplified in the overlooked classic, "Hey Mister." *—Chris Woodstra*

● **The Best of Sandy Posey** / 1996 / Collectables ♦♦♦♦♦
The Best of Sandy Posey is a 14-track collection covering Posey's first recording period for MGM, including the classic forgotten hits, "Born a Woman," "Single Girl" and "I Take It Back"—oddly, all three peaked at number 12. Posey's mid-'60s songs, almost all depicting a woman helpless without—or alternately, trapped with—"her man," were slightly out-of-touch at the time and are artifacts now, but the slick pop-country arrangements have a timeless charm. Posey would have later success in the country charts in the '70s but unfortunately, those hits are not represented here. Though the album appears to be a straight reissue of the MGM's *The Best of Sandy Posey,* this package actually expands on it by three tracks. *—Chris Woodstra*

Ray Price

b. Jan. 12, 1926, Perryville, TX
Vocals, Guitar / Nashville Sound/Countrypolitan, Honky Tonk, Country-Pop, Traditional Country
Ray Price has covered—and kicked up—as much musical turf as any country singer of the postwar era. He's been lionized as the man who saved hard country when Nashville went pop, and vilified as the man who went pop when hard country was starting to call its own name with pride. Actually, he was—and still is—no more than a musically ambitious singer, always looking for the next challenge for a voice that could bring down roadhouse walls. Circa 1949, Price cut his first record for Bullet at the Famous Jim Beck in Dallas. In 1951, he was picked up by Columbia, the label for which he would record for more than twenty years. After knocking around in Lefty Frizzell's camp for six months or so (his first Columbia single was a Frizzell composition) Price befriended Hank Williams. The connection brought him to the Opry and profoundly effected his singing style. After Hank died, Price starting stretching out more as a singer and arranger. His experimentation culminated in the 4/4-bass driven "Crazy Arms," the country song of the year for 1956. The intensely rhythmic sound he discovered with "Crazy Arms" would dominate his—and much of country in general's—music for the next six years. To this day, people in Nashville refer to a 4/4 country shuffle as the "Ray Price beat." Heavy on fiddle, steel, and high tenor harmony, his country work from the late '50s is as lively as the rock & roll of the same era. Price tired of that sound, however, and started messing around with strings. His lush 1967 version of "Danny Boy," and his 1970 take on Kris Kristofferson's "For the Good Times," were, in their crossover way, landmark records. But few of his old fans appreciated the fact. In the three decades following "For the Good Times," Price's career was often an awkward balancing act in which twin Texas fiddles are weighed against orchestras. *—Dan Cooper*

Talk to Your Heart / 1958 / Columbia ♦♦♦♦♦

Night Life / 1962 / Koch International ♦♦♦♦♦
Depending upon which lens of the historical perspective you view this, this 12-song collection is the last gasp of true honky tonk, the first stab at mainstreaming it into the Nashville sound of the 1960s or country music's first concept album. In 1962, Ray Price was at the peak of his form as a honky tonker of major repute. His regular touring band, the Cherokee Cowboys, were the finest of their kind and Ray's voice was an instrument of wonder, full of reflection with every lyrical reading. As a traveling musician, Price knew well of the 'night life' depicted in Willie Nelson's title track, a life spent on the road full of hotels, bar rooms, one-night stands, heartache and regrets. This album, full of well-written songs paying homage to that sinful life and its road to nowhere, evokes the sound, feel, and ambience of classic honky tonk music like few others do. As the decade wore on, Price would go on to major superstardom as a mellow balladeer, working with full string sections, reaching audiences that never heard this music or the other honky tonk classics that preceded it. More's the pity, for this album just may be Price's defining moment as an artist. *—Cub Koda*

San Antonio Rose / 1962 / Koch International ♦♦♦♦♦
Fans of Ray Price or Bob Wills won't want to miss the Price's 1961 album, *San Antonio Rose: A Tribute to the Great Bob Wills.* Price, who acknowledged Wills as a primary influence, became the first of many to devote an album to covering the songs of the renowned master of Southwestern dance music. Price recorded the album in a nine-hour period, utilizing many of Nashville's best musicians, including guitarist Grady Martin, fiddler Tommy Jackson, pedal steel specialist Jimmy Day and pianist Pig Robbins (in one of his first Nashville sessions). Also sitting in on acoustic guitar was a new Music City arrival, a little-known songwriter named Willie Nelson, who had just been hired to crank out songs for Price's publishing company. The record finds Price crooning with smooth, easy richness while the band lets it fly. *—Michael McCall*

The Other Woman / 1965 / Koch International ♦♦♦♦♦
The Other Woman was Ray Price's follow-up to his classic *Night Life* album and on it he continued to work the seasoned Texas honky tonk he and the Cherokee Cowboys had been perfecting since the mid-'50s—this in the midst of his initial foray into the country pop style he would eventually embrace. With Cherokee alumni Buddy Emmons on guitar and pedal steel, Tommy Jackson on fiddle, and Buddy Harmon handling the drums, Price works some choice country terrain including a lazy shuffle rendition of the perennial "Born to Lose" and a show-stopping version of Floyd Tillman's "This Cold War With You." He turns in a smoldering version of the classic, blues-tinged "Funny How Time Slips Away," penned by one-time Cherokee Cowboy Willie Nelson. Price's famous shuffle beat style is still intact here, too, on the chart-topping title track, Hank Cochran's codependency nugget "Don't You Ever Get Tired of Hurting Me," and a pair of Fred Carter gems—"Too Much Love is Spoiling You" and "Rose Colored Glasses"—all benefiting from Emmons' stellar pedal steel work. The album is rounded out by a touching version of the Patsy Cline hit "Unloved, Unwanted" and the beautiful waltz "The Last Letter." *The Other Woman* does not quite match the variety or song quality of *Night Life,* but the steady delivery of fine country material as well as the spacious Grady Martin production make for very enjoyable listening. *—Stephen Cook*

The Best of Ray Price / 1976 / Columbia ♦♦♦♦♦
This compilation presents the highlights of Price's string-laden years. "For the Good Times" is simply one of the most mature singles ever recorded. "She's Got to Be a Saint" has somehow gotten lost over the years. *—Tom Roland*

★ **The Essential Ray Price (1951-1962)** / 1991 / Columbia/Legacy ♦♦♦♦♦
A not-completely-accurate title, this 20-track compilation excludes a few later necessities like "Night Life" and "For the Good Times." The important stuff from Price's hard-country heyday is all here, however, from the teetering rise-and-fall of "Crazy Arms" (the first of a thousand country songs to employ a walking bassline and modified swing beat, which became known as the "Ray Price shuffle") to Harlan Howard's "Heartaches by the Number." The fake stereo that marred earlier reissues of his '50s material is happily absent here. This is essential country music. *—Brian Mansfield & Mark A. Humphrey*

The Honky Tonk Years (1950-1966) / 1996 / Bear Family ♦♦♦♦♦
The Honky Tonk Years (1950-1966) is an accurate title for this mammoth 10-disc set. Tracing Ray Price's career through his heyday in the '50s and stopping in the late '60s, just as he abandoned honky tonk for country-pop, the set documents one of the finest singers and bandleaders in country music. During this era, Price had a long, impressive string of Top 10 singles—including "Don't Let the Stars Get in Your Eyes," "I'll Be There (If You Ever Want Me)," "My Shoes Keep Walking Back to You," "City Lights," and the massive hit "Crazy Arms"—and led a band that featured, at various times, such musicians as Willie Nelson, Johnny Paycheck and Roger Miller. Price and his band were talented enoguht to make weak material, which helps make this exhaustive set interesting; after all, there's bound to be a few lesser cuts in a box that runs over 260 tracks. Though the strict chronological session order is occasionally tedious, the quality of the music far outweighs the flaws in presentation. For serious listeners and musicologists, *The Honky Tonk Years* is an essential purchase, since it offers a complete picture of one of the biggest figures in country music. Neophytes and casual listeners, however, are advised to stick with the single-disc collection, *The Essential Ray Price,* simply because it is far easier to digest. *—Stephen Thomas Erlewine*

Prisoner of Love / May 16, 2000 / Buddha ♦♦♦

For the Good Times/I Won't Mention It Again / Columbia ♦♦♦

Charley Pride

b. Mar. 18, 1938, Sledge, MS
Vocals, Guitar / Country-Pop, Traditional Country
With 36 number one hits under his belt, Charley Pride, who is black, has helped prove how little race matters to the majority of country music fans. It's taken a long time to understand that, though. His first single, "Snakes Crawl at Night," was released without publicity photos, as some in the industry feared listeners would automatically reject a black country singer. Since then, Pride's 12 gold albums in the United States, combined with 30 gold and 4 platinum internationally, place him in the top 15 all-time country record sellers. His easy-going singing style and easy-to-listen-to voice show why these honors have come his way. From picking cotton in his native Mississippi, Pride ended up working in a smelting plant in Montana, after a stint as a semi-pro baseball player. At the suggestion of Red Sovine, Pride moved to Nashville, where he was signed by Chet Atkins of RCA. In 1966, "Just Between You and Me" brought Pride a Grammy nomination and national fame. At the end of the '60s and the early part of the '70s, he had five number one singles in a row, including "All I Have to Offer Is Me" and "Is Anybody Goin' to San Antone— "Numerous awards came in 1971 and 1972, with many more hits following, among them "She's Too Good to Be True," "Kiss an Angel Good Mornin'," and "Night Games." Pride's warm baritone voice and relaxed style made him the highest-selling act for RCA since Elvis Presley. *—David Vinopal*

The Pride of Country Music / 1967 / RCA Victor ♦♦♦♦♦
Charley Pride returns to the studio with another collection of edifying songs. The hit "Just Between You and Me" is included, as is "Apartment 9," which was also recorded by Tammy Wynette. Pride seems to have begun gaining his confidence in the recording studio, and is more willing to experiment a bit with his vocal style. *—Michael B. Smith*

Songs of Pride: Charley, That Is / 1968 / Koch ♦♦♦
Songs of Pride... is a straight CD reissue of a 1968 album by Charley Pride, and the hit on this record was "The Easy Part's Over," which went to number two the same year. Produced by Chet Atkins, Felton Jarvis, and Jack Clement, *Songs of Pride*... features love songs and hurtin' tunes with more fiddle and steel than might be expected. None of these tracks overlap with the *Essential* disc, providing fans with a mid-priced opportunity to delve more deeply into the work of Pride. *—Greg Adams*

In Person / 1969 / Koch ♦♦♦♦♦
Recorded live at Panther Hall in Fort Worth, Texas, *In Person* gained Charley Pride a gold record in 1969, thanks in part to the abundance of early RCA hits included, like the highlight "Kaw-Liga." *—John Bush*

★ **The Essential Charley Pride** / Apr. 29, 1997 / RCA ♦♦♦♦♦
Charley Pride's significance in the history of country music isn't entirely tied to the quality of his music, although his warm baritone and adherence to "tradition" certainly provided the listening public with a wealth of enjoyable music. But his immense popularity with what is often assumed to be a conservative (read racially-intolerant) country audience in spite of (or because of) his skin color, will provide country music scholars with points to ponder for years to come. Beyond the curious phenomenon, though, is the music, which is often simply great. "Kiss an Angel Good Mornin'" and "Is Anybody Goin' to San Antone" are enduring classics, and his live version of Hank Williams' "Kaw-Liga" demonstrates the rural charm that helped

make Pride a star. This 20-song collection is a good distillation of hits from the late '60s through the late '70s, including the aforementioned tracks as well as a number of other hits. Charley Pride had too long and too successful a career to sum up with a single disc, but until he is granted his deserved and overdue box set, *The Essential Charley Pride* will do. —*Greg Adams*

★ **RCA Country Legends** / Nov. 7, 2000 / Buddha ✦✦✦✦✦
Don't think of this as a definitive hits compilation. Instead, think of it as a perfect introduction to Charley Pride at his peak, proof that he was a genuine \country talent, not just a hitmaker. He had a powerful baritone that worked equally well with \hard country and \country-pop, which may be the reason why he leaned toward the latter as his career progressed. This, however, captures him at the peak of his powers, concentrating primarily on the harder material but adding some \pop for balance. This may dilute the portrait of his career somewhat, but it does a terrific job in summarizing his skills and importance. Yes, some familiar items are missing, but for the curious listener looking for confirmation of Pride as a \country singer, this is the compilation to get. —*Stephen Thomas Erlewine*

Eddie Rabbitt (Edward Thomas)

b. Nov. 27, 1941, Brooklyn, NY, **d.** May 7, 1998
Vocals, Guitar / Urban Cowboy, Soft Rock, Country-Pop
One of country music's most innovative artists during the late '70s and early '80s, Eddie Rabbitt has made contributions to the format that have often gone overlooked. Especially in songs like the R&B-inflected "Suspicions" and the rockin' "Someone Could Lose a Heart Tonight," Rabbitt challenged the commonly recognized creative boundaries of the idiom. Though it took a few years to get his recording career off the ground, he paid the rent through songwriting, authoring Elvis Presley's "Kentucky Rain" and Ronnie Milsap's "Pure Love." Eddie continued to write professionally until 1975, when he signed with Elektra. Initially, Rabbitt made recordings that were decidedly country—mostly uptempo material, like "Two Dollars in the Jukebox" and "Drinkin' My Baby (Off My Mind)"—with thick, inimitable harmonies. However, Rabbitt's records became "progressively progressive." In 1976, he started a string of Top Ten hits that ran uninterrupted until 1989. During that time, he had 16 number one singles, including "Drinkin' My Baby (Off My Mind)" (1976), "You Don't Love Me Anymore" (1978), "Every Which Way But Loose" (1979), "Drivin' My Life Away" (1980), "I Love a Rainy Night" (1980), "Step By Step" (1980), and "You and I," a 1982 duet with Crystal Gayle. —*Tom Roland*

The Best of Eddie Rabbitt / 1979 / Elektra ✦✦✦✦✦
Strong melodies are enhanced by Rabbitt's searing harmonies. The instruments are "hotter" in the final mix than in other productions from the same period, so even the mainstream country fare is a little different from that of his mid-'70s contemporaries. —*Tom Roland*

Loveline / 1979 / Elektra ✦✦✦
Fellow reviewers will cringe at this choice, but it displays Rabbitt at his most daring. Lots of R&B influence—even a bit of a "disco" feel on a couple of tracks—inspired melodies and unusual chord progressions throughout. Lyrically lightweight, but hey, this is music not poetry. —*Tom Roland*

Horizon / 1980 / Elektra ✦✦✦✦
This is Rabbitt's rockabilly release. "I Love a Rainy Night" and "Drivin' My Life Away" set the pace for side one: Sun-inspired, guitar-based productions, heavy on the echo. Side two is a bit ballad-heavy, though most of the tracks stand up well individually. "That's Just the Way It Is" is something of a forerunner for "Someone Could Lose a Heart Tonight." —*Tom Roland*

Step by Step / 1981 / Liberty ✦✦✦✦

The Best of Eddie Rabbit: Greatest Hits, Vol. 2 / 1983 / Warner Brothers ✦✦✦✦✦

● **All Time Greatest Hits** / Mar. 12, 1991 / Warner Brothers ✦✦✦✦✦
The 10 track collection *All Time Greatest Hits* covers Eddie Rabbitt's most commercially productive period—the late '70s and early '80s. "Drivin' My Life Away," "I Love a Rainy Night," and "Step by Step" were all Top Ten pop hits, in addition to hitting number one country. "Drivin'" and "Rainy," in fact, were million-sellers. —*Dan Cooper*

Marvin Rainwater (Marvin Karlton Percy)

b. Jul. 2, 1925, Wichita, KS
Vocals / Nashville Sound/Countrypolitan, Rockabilly, Traditional Country
Few artists in country music ever made music as quirky and just plain weird as that of one Marvin Rainwater. His recorded cannonade—featuring his strong, rumbling baritone—showed that he was equally adept at Western ballads, pop confections with breathtaking go for broke forays into rockabilly.

Marvin started recording for MGM Records in the mid-'50s. Solemn Americana recitations ("Pink Eyed Stallion") sat alongside novelty fluff like "Tennessee Hound Dog Yodel," which were B-sided by straightahead country weepers. At his next recording session in 1956, Rainwater cast his lot with the emerging rockabilly sound. Marvin had his first genuine hit with "Gonna Find Me A Bluebird," a number three country hit that reached the pop Top 20. Flush with success, Rainwater moved to New York, ready to take on the world, but his follow-ups were as diverse and quirky as his pre-hit output and his slide from the charts, coupled with one bad business deal after another, was swift and sure.

In order to stay on *any* kind of chart, Rainwater had taken on a personal appearance schedule that would reduce lesser individuals to babbling protoplasm. By 1961, Marvin showed up for several recording sessions with his voice so burned out from show dates that he was unrecordable. After a nine month layoff, he signed with Warwick Records and with Link Wray and the Raymen backing him, put out a pair of singles as fine as anything he had recorded in his heyday, yet these sides fell stillborn at the presses. Going for it one more time, Rainwater and new partner Bill Guess built a studio in Chicago and started up Brave Records, solely devoting its catalog to new songs from the singer. Aside from a brief stay with United Artists in 1964 and a one off session for Warner Brothers in 1969, the Brave singles document Marvin's last commercial sides. Rainwater may not have become a big name, but he left behind a great number of sides that showed musical depth and originality. And that's got to count for something. —*Cub Koda*

Classic Recordings / 1992 / Bear Family ✦✦✦✦✦
This four-CD set puts Marvin Rainwater's recording career from 1953 through 1969 into sharp relief, most notably his inability to fix on a sound, either country or rockabilly, and stick with it. In a fairer world, he wouldn't have had to decide, because he was good at both. Disc One opens with his earliest officially released sides, which ran the gamut from rockabilly to faux-western to upbeat comic country-pop to country-blues, and one good dog song ("Tennessee Hound Dog Yodel"). Rainwater's best numbers here, however, may be the raucous rocker "Hot and Cold" and the only slightly more restrained "Mr. Blues," both of which show off Roy Clark's lead guitar in the strongest light. Disc Two is more consistent, with fewer of the pop efforts of the prior years. The rockabilly sides, especially "(There's Always) A Need for Love," really spark this disc and provide the real drive around more convention pop/rock & roll numbers like "I Dig You Baby." Disc Three has its great moments, such as "It Wasn't Enough," amid a series of duets with singer Bill Guess that present Rainwater at his most commercial and accessible. Disc Four contains Rainwater's earliest sides, cut as demos in 1953 and 1954, and while the quality of the sound is a little shaky, the stuff goes to the core of Rainwater's music-making, freewheeling studio performances without looking for the next big hit or trying to catch the wave of public fancy. The real joy here, however, are five live numbers recorded in 1962—Rainwater, already gone from MGM and disillusioned, still loved playing to an audience, as these sides show, and the only pity is that there isn't more of this stuff, especially since the sound is unexpectedly good. —*Bruce Eder*

● **Whole Lotta Woman** / 1994 / Bear Family ✦✦✦✦✦
A superb single disc of Rainwater's most rocking sides, 26 in all, although inexplicably leaving off his biggest hit, "Gonna Find Me A Bluebird." But there's much here to love, including the chugging "Mr. Blues" and "Hot and Cold" featuring explosive guitar from Roy Clark and "Boo Hoo," "Tough Top Cat," and "There's A Honky Tonk In Your Heart," which features backing from Link Wray and the Raymen. Marvin at his quirkiest and if you can live without his big hit, this is the package to grab. —*Cub Koda*

Rascal Flatts

Group / Contemporary Country
The contemporary country group Rascal Flatts features second cousins Gary Levox and Jay Demarcus along with Joe Don Rooney. Demarcus and Rooney met while they were playing in Chely Wright's backing band, and Levox was a back-up singer for Michael English. The trio began playing and writing songs together, eventually performing in Nashville's Printers Alley and signing a deal with Lyric Street Records. The group's self-titled debut album arrived in mid-2000. —*Heather Phares*

● **Rascal Flatts** / Jun. 6, 2000 / Hollywood ✦✦✦✦
Rascal Flatts are three average, nice guys. They make contemporary country-pop that's nice, but ever so slightly and satisfyingly a cut above average. Nothing on their eponymous debut deviates from the norm—it's squarely down the center of the mainstream, edging closer to pop than it does to real country—but it's sweetly endearing and unassuming. Take the lead song and single, "Prayin' for Daylight," for example. It's almost defiantly square, but the trio doesn't ever realize that it's not hip to be square—the very quality that makes it so much fun. They revel in their warm harmonies, bright production, catchy mid-tempo pop tunes, and ballads of heartbreak and love that always seem happy. Rascal Flatts never really changes their approach at any point during the album—many of the zippier songs sound a lot like "Prayin' for Daylight" and the slower numbers are just slower variations of that tune—but that doesn't matter, since this is an amiable, well-crafted, professional record. Are there some slow moments? Well, yes, but they pass by easily, thanks to the surface gloss and the boys' cheerful attitude. *Rascal Flatts* may not be weighty, but it's not supposed to be. It's designed to be a sunny, pleasing modern country-pop album, and that's exactly what it is. —*Stephen Thomas Erlewine*

Collin Raye

b. Aug. 22, 1959, DeQueen, AR
Vocals / New Traditionalist, Contemporary Country
Singer/songwriter Collin Raye's blend of Western swing, rockabilly, country-rock and sentimental ballads brought him a string of hit singles in the early '90s. Billing himself as "Bubba," Collin and sibling Scott founded the country-rock Wray Brothers Band in the late '70s and moved west to perform. The brothers made their recording debut in 1983 and had some chart success with their first single "Reason to Believe." In 1987, they had a Top 50 hit with "You Lay a Lotta Love on Me." Following the single's success, the band broke up. After the Wrays disbanded, Collin signed to Epic and released his solo debut, *All I Can Be.* Raye's first single, "All I Can Be (Is a Sweet Memory)," reached the country Top 40 but it was his second single, "Love, Me," that made him a star when it climbed to number one in early 1992, kick-starting a string of Top 10 hits that ran for a number of years. Raye's second album, *In This Life* (1992), went gold and produced three hits, including "Somebody Else's Moon." He released his third album *Extremes* in 1994 and it went gold by the end of the year, spawning the Top 10 hits "Little Rock," "Man of My Word," and "My Kind of Girl." —*Sandra Brennan*

All I Can Be / Dec. 1990 / Epic ✦✦

In This Life / Aug. 25, 1992 / Epic ✦✦✦
The soft-focus, yet rugged, album art helps establish Raye as the heartthrob his silky smooth tenor makes him out to be. Inside, it's an even smoother mix than *All I Can Be,* with Raye indulging his tendencies at every turn, including a revival of The Everly Brothers' make-out classic "Let It Be Me." The hit "I Want You Bad (And That Ain't Good)" put some sweat and muscle into Raye's image, but even the trucker song, "Latter Day Cowboy," sounds like it was written for the women back home. The album also includes "In This Life," a number one hit; "Somebody Else's Moon;" and "That Was a River." —*Brian Mansfield*

Extremes / 1994 / Epic ✦✦✦✦✦
Tired of the balladeer image "Love, Me" and "In This Life" had tagged him with, Raye set out to show that he was made of stronger material. The first single, the rollicking "That's My Story," was a Lee Roy Parnell tune that Raye roared through. *Extremes*, as its title suggested, caromed recklessly from that type of song to, of course, ballads—but "Little Rock," about a recovering alcoholic, and "Dreaming My Dreams with You," earlier cut by Waylon Jennings, were two of the most powerful recordings of Raye's career. *—Brian Mansfield*

I Think About You / 1995 / Epic ✦✦✦✦
After attempting a somewhat rougher approach with *Extremes*, Collin Raye returned to his smooth ballad stylings on *I Think About You*. Though he still sings the occasional honky tonk raver, the high points on his fourth album come when he slows the pace down. *I Think About You* does suffer from a few bland tracks, but the album does demonstrate why Raye was one of the most popular country singers of the mid-'90s. *—Stephen Thomas Erlewine*

● **The Best of Collin Raye: Direct Hits** / Mar. 11, 1997 / Epic ✦✦✦✦✦
The Best of Collin Raye contains all of the contemporary country singer's biggest hits and best-known songs—including "Every Second," "That Was A River," "Little Rock," "One Boy, One Girl," "Not That Different," and the number one singles "Love, Me," "In This Life," and "My Kind of Girl"—making it an excellent introduction to the popular vocalist. *—Thom Owens*

The Walls Came Down / Jul. 14, 1998 / Epic ✦✦✦

Tracks / May 2, 2000 / Epic ✦✦✦

Jerry Reed

b. Mar. 20, 1937, Atlanta, GA
Vocals, Guitar, Session Musician / Instrumental Country, Rockabilly, Country-Pop, Progressive Country, Traditional Country
Known throughout country music as "The Guitar Man," singer/songwriter Jerry Reed gained recognition not only for a successful solo career but also as an actor and ace session player. He began by releasing a stream of country and rockabilly singles to little notice, until Gene Vincent and Brenda Lee both covered Reed's songs. Though he recorded steadily during the '60s as well, it wasn't until 1967's "Guitar Man" (which Elvis Presley soon covered) that he finally gained a chart hit. In 1971, Reed issued his biggest hit, the chart-topper "When You're Hot, You're Hot" (also the title track of his first solo album). He also teamed with Chet Atkins for two LPs, 1971's *Me and Jerry* and 1972's *Me and Chet*. In 1973, he scored his second number one, "Lord, Mr. Ford," though in the mid-'70s, Reed's recording career began to take a backseat to his acting aspirations. His greatest visibility was as a motion-picture star, almost always in tandem with headliner Burt Reynolds. He appeared in all three of the *Smokey and the Bandit* films, and landed a number two hit in 1977 with "East Bound and Down," from the soundtrack to the first. He topped the charts again in 1982 with the novelty hit "She Got the Goldmine (I Got the Shaft)," though after an unsuccessful 1986 LP (*Lookin' at You*), Reed focused on touring until 1992, when he and Atkins reunited for the album *Sneakin' Around*. *—Jason Ankeny*

Alabama Wild Man / 1968 / RCA Victor ✦✦✦✦
Actor, singer, and guitar man Jerry Reed blurred the line between country and pop music from the late '60s through the '70s while occasionally throwing in the odd novelty record for good measure. Released in 1968, *Alabama Wild Man* was one of the earliest examples of his crossover appeal. Reed played what he liked, had a good time doing it, and made records strictly to entertain. However, that didn't mean he was creating one-dimensional music, proven here by the contemplative lyrics of "Today Is Mine" and "Losing Your Love," the Jimmy Reed-inspired instrumental "Twelve Bar Midnight," and the autobiographical title track featuring punchy boogaloo horns with country pickin'. As a side note, the addition of Reed's laid-back version of the Monkees' hit "Last Train to Clarksville" was recorded three decades before Cassandra Wilson would do the same for the song in the jazz world in 1995. *—Al Campbell*

Jerry Reed Explores Guitar Country / 1969 / RCA ✦✦✦✦
Jerry Reed Explores Guitar Country is an overlooked 1969 concept album that updated traditional folk and country tunes with modern pop-country arrangements. Classics like "St. James Infirmary," "Blue Moon of Kentucky," "In the Pines," and "John Hardy" were assembled utilizing unconventional combinations of organ, banjo, congas, and jazz guitar. Much of the exploratory credit goes to the pop-country hybrid production mastery of Chet Atkins. *Jerry Reed Explores Guitar Country* is quietly influential in helping to map out the area where many alternative country artists now reside. *Explores Guitar Country* is available with *Alabama Wild Man* on a One Way two-fer CD. *—Al Campbell*

Ko-Ko Joe / 1971 / RCA ✦✦

When You're Hot You're Hot / 1971 / RCA ✦✦✦✦✦

● **The Essential Jerry Reed** / Aug. 1, 1995 / RCA ✦✦✦✦✦
The Essential Jerry Reed contians over 20 of the singer/songwriter's greatest htis, from "Amos Moses" to "East Bound and Down," hitting the number ones "When You're Hot, You're Hot," "Lord, Mr. Ford," and "She Got the Goldmine (I Got the Shaft)." In addition to the hits, there's a handful of obscurities, but it remains the best single overview of Reed's career. *—Thom Owens*

Guitar Man / 1997 / Camden ✦✦✦✦✦
Guitar Man is a 22-song U.K. import that consists mainly of album tracks from the late '60s through the early '80s, as opposed to hit singles. There are a few hits in the mix, including "Amos Moses," "When You're Hot, You're Hot," and Jerry Reed's 1983 cover of Creedence Clearwater Revival's "Down on the Corner," but listeners in search of a greatest hits package should look elsewhere. That said, *Guitar Man* offers a more balanced view of Reed's music than the *Essential* disc, since there is less of a focus on his novelty hits and a broader sampling of the ballads, instrumentals, and otherwise serious material that made up a large portion of his catalog. For fans, the real appeal of this set is the wealth of material that is otherwise difficult—if not impossible—to find on CD, including versions of "500 Miles Away from Home," "Sixteen Tons," and "The Devil Went Down to Georgia," which Reed recasts as a guitar duel with the devil. *—Greg Adams*

When You're Hot You're Hot/Ko-Ko-Joe / Jul. 1, 1997 / Collectables ✦✦✦

Here I Am / Sep. 15, 1999 / Bear Family ✦✦✦✦
Many fans of Jerry Reed may not realize that his recording career began in the mid-'50s when, as a teen, he signed to Capitol records. *Here I Am* collects his complete recordings for Capitol (30 songs), most of which were originals. "If the Good Lord's Willing and the Creek Don't Rise" was later covered by Johnny Cash during his tenure at Sun, and a few of the other tracks here occasionally surface on rockabilly compilations, but many of these recordings have been unavailable since they were originally waxed (and a few are previously unreleased). Reed's music at this stage was stylistically varied, from rockabilly to honky tonk to teen pop, and he had yet to develop the unique fingerpicking style that characterized his later recordings. Although the quality of the material is inconsistent, *Here I Am* chronicles the earliest phase of an important artist's career. Fans of Reed as well as those with a broad interest in rockabilly and '50s pop and country will likely enjoy this set. *—Greg Adams*

Jim Reeves

b. Aug. 20, 1924, Galloway, Panola County, TX, **d.** Jul. 31, 1964, Nashville, TN
Vocals, Guitar / Nashville Sound/Countrypolitan, Country-Pop
Gentleman Jim Reeves was perhaps the biggest male star to emerge from the Nashville Sound. His mellow baritone voice and muted velvet orchestration combined to create a sound that echoed around his world and has lasted to this day. Detractors will call the sound country-pop (or plain pop), but none can argue against the large audience that loves this music. Reeves was capable of singing hard country ("Mexican Joe" went to number one in 1953), but he made his greatest impact as a country-pop crooner. From 1955 through 1969, Reeves was consistently charted in the country and pop charts—an amazing fact in light of his untimely death in an airplane accident in 1964. Not only was a presence in the American charts, but he became country music's foremost international ambassador and, if anything, he was even more popular in Europe and Britain than he was in his native America. After his death, his fanbase didn't diminish at all, and several of his posthumous hits actually outsold his earlier singles; no less than six number one singles arrived in the three years following his burial. In fact, during the '70s and '80s, he continued to have hits with both unreleased material and electronic duets like "Take Me in Your Arms and Hold Me" with Deborah Allen and "Have You Ever Been Lonely—" with his smooth-singing female counterpart of the plush Nashville Sound, Patsy Cline, who also perished in an airplane crash, in 1963. But Reeves' legacy remains with lush country-pop singles like "Four Walls" (1957) and "He'll Have To Go" (1959), which defined both his style and an entire era of country music. *—David Vinopal*

He'll Have to Go & Other Hits / 1960 / RCA ✦✦✦✦✦
There may have been other country crooners as smooth, but no one else in his era had the hand-in-glove marriage of great songs and appropriate "countrypolitan" production. This brief collection doesn't contain all of his biggest hits, but the most essential singles— "He'll Have to Go," "Four Walls," "Billy Bayou," and "Anna Marie," among others—are included. *—Mark A. Humphrey*

Kimberley Jim / 1964 / Soundies ✦✦✦✦

The Jim Reeves Way / 1965 / RCA Victor ✦✦✦

Distant Drums / 1966 / DCC ✦✦✦

Live at the Grand Ole Opry / 1987 / Country Music Foundation ✦✦✦

Gentleman Jim: 1955-1959 / 1989 / Bear Family ✦✦✦✦✦
This four-disc set, which contains 110 tracks, has Reeves's first ventures into pop as well as some of his best country performances of such favorites as "Am I Losing You—," "Just Call Me Lonesome," "According to My Heart," and others. A discography accompanies the set. *—AMG*

☆ **Four Walls: The Legend Begins** / Aug. 1991 / RCA ✦✦✦✦✦
Four Walls—The Legend Begins collects 20 songs Jim Reeves recorded between 1953 and 1957, including his earliest hits, "Mexican Joe," "Bimbo," "According to My Heart" and "My Lips Are Sealed." *—Stephen Thomas Erlewine*

★ **Welcome to My World: The Essential Jim Reeves Collection** / Mar. 1993 / RCA ✦✦✦✦✦
Welcome to My World: The Essential Jim Reeves Collection is a double disc box set that offers an overview of his entire career, even if its balance is a bit uneven. Beginning with his early '50s hit, the box runs through most of his biggest hits, concentrating on his smooth countrypolitan '60s hits. Though fans of his early honky tonk material will feel that side of Reeves is overlooked, *Welcome to My World* is the best overall Reeves retrospective available. *—Stephen Thomas Erlewine*

★ **The Essential Jim Reeves** / Aug. 1, 1995 / RCA ✦✦✦✦✦
The Essential Jim Reeves runs through 20 of Reeves' biggest hits, throwing a couple of rarities along the way. It's by no means definitive, but it offers a good introduction to his countrypolitan sound. *—Stephen Thomas Erlewine*

Welcome to My World / 1996 / Bear Family ✦✦✦✦✦
The sheer size of *Welcome to My World* is intimidating. Spanning a full 16 discs and 446 tracks, the box set covers every recording Jim Reeves ever made—certainly, it's a set designed for the fanatic, not the neophyte. All of Reeves' classic hits for RCA are present, as are his recordings for Macy's, Fabor, Abbott, several demos and undubbed singles, and they're all presented in chronological order, according to when they were recorded. For fanatics, the set is essential, since it comes with a detailed biography and sessionography, as well as first-rate sound, but the very size of the compilation makes it difficult to digest, even for the serious fan. *—Thom Owens*

Best of the Best of Jim Reeves / Jan. 6, 1998 / Koch ✦✦✦✦

Charlie Rich

b. Dec. 14, 1932, Colt, AR, **d.** Jul. 24, 1995, Hammond, LA

Vocals, Piano / Nashville Sound/Countrypolitan, Rockabilly, Country-Pop, Progressive Country, Traditional Country

Charlie Rich was one of the most acclaimed country singers of the post-war era, skillfully fusing country, jazz, blues, gospel, rockabilly, and soul. Though he had 45 country hits in a career that spanned nearly four decades, he's best-known for his lush countrypolitan hits of the early '70s.

Rich first recorded for Sun in the late '50s, yet he didn't have a hit until 1960, when "Lonely Weekends," reached the pop Top 30. None of its follow-ups were hits and signed with Groove, a division of RCA, in 1964. He didn't have any hits there and when the label folded in 1965, Rich signed with Smash, where he had a Top 30 hit with "Mohair Sam." No other hits were forthcoming and Rich again switched labels, cutting a series of unsuccessful sides for Hi. In 1967, Rich moved to Epic and producer Billy Sherrill refashioned him as a smooth balladeer. The makeover didn't pay off until the summer of 1972, when "I Take It On Home" hit number six, setting the stage for the blockbuster 1973 album, *Behind Closed Doors*. The album contained two crossover hits in the title track and its followup "The Most Beautiful Girl," and then the hits started to flow, as re-released material from Smash and Groove competed with his new Epic recordings for chart prominence. Despite his popularity, Rich was drinking heavily, causing problems off-stage, highlighted by an incident at the 1975 CMA ceremony where he set fire to a certificate proclaiming John Denver Entertainer of the Year. Fans and industry insiders were outraged, and he didn't return to the Top Ten until late in 1977. Early in 1978, he signed with United Artists. Shortly afterward, the hits dried up, though a switch to Elektra in 1980 resulted in a final Top 20 hit. Not long afterward, Rich retreated to semi-retirement. He returned in 1992 with the acclaimed *Pictures and Paintings*, which turned out to be his last record. Charlie Rich died from a blood clot in his lung in the summer of 1995. *—Stephen Thomas Erlewine*

Big Boss Man: The Groove Sessions / 1966 / Koch International ♦♦♦♦♦

After a sporadic career at Sun Records in the late '50s, Charlie Rich hooked up with Nashville sound architect Chet Atkins in 1963 to record for RCA's R&B subsidiary, Groove. Rich proceeded to cut his usual mix of country, rockabilly, blues, and pop sides but with added, Nashville-sound touches like choral backing and strings; it was a style that landed somewhere between the raw sound of his Sun hits ("Rebound") and the pop-crossover tone of his Epic smashes ("Behind Closed Doors"). Fortunately, the glossier elements of the Groove sides collected on *Big Boss Man* are neutralized by Rich's powerful tenor voice and solid, jazz-tinged piano work. The mixed set includes blues-rockers like "Big Boss Man" and "Big Jack," as well as swinging, lounge treatments of "River Stay Away From My Door" and "Ol' Man River." Rich also applies his varied musical approach to many excellent originals here, like the driving, shuffle-beat tune "The Ways of a Woman in Love," the sanctified ballad "Rosanna Now," and the straight-pop song "Are You Still My Baby." Throw in a fine, Ray Charles-style number like "Tomorrow Night" and the touching country ballad Rich co-wrote with wife and tune-smith Margaret Rich, and you have a completely satisfying set. Multifaceted artists are usually not tended to by a record industry comfortable with distinct categories, and this certainly explains why it took Rich so long to achieve stardom. Rich's fans, though, love his ability to forge a very distinct sound out of all kinds of music; this excellent Koch reissue of many of his Groove sides certainly proves the point. *—Stephen Cook*

Set Me Free / 1968 / Koch ♦♦♦♦♦

Set Me Free was Charlie Rich's first album for Epic Records and the first record he ever cut with Nashville producer Billy Sherrill. Previously, Rich's producers hadn't known what to do with his eclectic style, although his sessions for Smash came close to capturing all sides of his personality. With Sherrill, Rich had a producer whose musical tastes were nearly as eclectic as his own, and that is captured on the freewheeling, diverse sounds of *Set Me Free*. Purists may be uncomfortable with Sherrill's lush production—he sets Rich's voice in a bed of strings, keyboards, horns, and backing vocals. Consequently, the sound of *Set Me Free* is laid-back and relaxed; occasionally, Rich sounds *too* relaxed, as if he didn't connect with the material. Although there are a handful of poor songs and half-hearted performances on the record, *Set Me Free* has an overall tone lacking on Rich's previous records that makes up for its assorted weaknesses. The songs come from a variety of sources, ranging from country and blues to jazz and pop, but they're all given a cohesive Nashville production by Sherrill, which is what makes *Set Me Free* one of Rich's best, most consistent albums. *—Stephen Thomas Erlewine*

☆ **The Fabulous Charlie Rich** / 1969 / Koch ♦♦♦♦♦

The Fabulous Charlie Rich follows the same formula as its predecessor *Set Me Free*, but to more successful results. For starters, the record has a more consistent set of material—these are songs that Rich can really sink his teeth into, as evidenced by the beautiful, melancholy "Life Has It's Little Ups and Downs" (written by his wife, Margaret Ann) and his own "Sittin' and Thinkin'." Furthermore, the core of each song—from the bluesy of "July 12, 1939" and "Bright Lights, Big City" (which is done essentially as a Jimmy Reed medley, performed in the style of Ray Charles) to the soulful "I Almost Lost My Mind" and the country-pop stylings of "San Francisco Is A Lonely Town" and "Love Waits for Me"—are more apparent, thanks to Sherrill's relatively trimmed-down production. There are still strings, vocal choruses, and horns, throughout the album, but Sherrill has incorporated them into Rich's style more effectively. Occasionally, there is a fairly uninspired number, but *The Fabulous Charlie Rich* does capture the eclectic nature of Rich's music better than the great majority of his albums, even if the sumptuous production will make it less palatable for country purists. *—Stephen Thomas Erlewine*

Boss Man / Aug. 1970 / Koch International ♦♦♦♦♦

Charlie Rich and Billy Sherrill reached a peak with *The Fabulous Charlie Rich*, creating a perfect middle ground between Rich's rootsier tendencies and Sherrill's country-pop leanings. Like any of Rich's records, it didn't sell and that might have been one of the reasons its followup, *Boss Man*, was their weakest effort to date. Although there are quite a few high spots and the album essentially follows the same formula as their previous efforts, the material isn't consistent, alternating between bluesy shuffles and country weepers; both styles range from the brilliant to the boring. What's even worse is the fact that Rich sound uninspired himself, giving competent but unenthusiastic performances. There's enough prime material to make *Boss Man* an enjoyable listen, pariticularly for Rich fans that know that he rarely comes up with consistent albums. However, it didn't have the spark of *The Fabulous Charlie Rich*, nor did it have the immaculate sheen of *Behind Close Doors*, the country-pop masterpiece that followed *Boss Man*. Nevertheless, *Boss Man* had enough fine songs to make it an essential purchase for true Rich fans. *—Stephen Thomas Erlewine*

☆ **Behind Closed Doors** / 1973 / Epic/Legacy ♦♦♦♦♦

Charlie Rich finally had a genuine hit with *Behind Closed Doors*, an exceedingly lush expansion of the sound he had essayed with producer Billy Sherrill on his first Epic albums. Here, Sherrill ups the ante considerably by adding layers of strings and choirs, and the two move the material toward the mainstream. The key to the record's success, is that Rich's signature blend of country, jazz, blues, rock and pop retains its character throughout it all, resulting in an album that's a twin peak—the pinnacle of Sherrill's countrypolitan sound, while standing as one of Rich's great albums. The hit singles—"*Behind Closed Doors*," "*The Most Beautiful Girl*," "*I Take It On Home*"—deservedly receive most of the attention, but the record is filled with great songs, including two from his wife Margaret Ann ("*A Sunday Kind of Woman*," "*Nothing in the World (To Do With Me)*") that stand as highlights. Throughout it all, Rich delivers the kind of shaded, nuanced performances that earned him a devoted a cult—a cult that might not cherish *Behind Closed Doors* as much as some of his other records because of its lushness, but if that lushness introduced a new audience to the wonders of Charlie Rich, it can't be bad at all. [The 2001 CD reissue contains four bonus tracks, culled from the 1972 album *We Love Each Other*.] *—Stephen Thomas Erlewine*

Greatest Hits / 1976 / Epic ♦♦♦♦♦

Pictures and Paintings / 1992 / Sire ♦♦♦♦♦

Charlie Rich's comeback album *Pictures and Paintings*—which would turn out to be his final recording—is one of his most rewarding records. It is stripped-down, relaxed album that captures Rich running through a mixture of covers, originals, and new versions of his classics, like "Don't Put No Headstone on My Grave." It's one of the few albums he made that captures all facets of his talent, featuring jazzy playing, bluesy singing, and simple, straightforward country. *—Stephen Thomas Erlewine*

☆ **The Complete Smash Sessions** / Aug. 4, 1992 / Mercury ♦♦♦♦♦

The Complete Smash Sessions contains everything that Charlie Rich recorded and released for Smash during the mid-'60s. Many of these songs forshadows the music Elvis Presley would make during his comeback in 1968, as well as the country-pop of the early '70s. Skillfully mixing rock, blues, R&B, country, and soul, Rich was at the top of his form when he made this music. He may have only had one hit during this period—"Mohair Sam" reached number 21 in 1965—but his tenure at Smash remained one of his most fruitful and creative periods. *—Stephen Thomas Erlewine*

Charlie Rich Sings the Songs of Hank Williams Plus the R&B Sessions / 1994 / Diablo ♦♦♦

☆ **Lonely Weekends: Best of the Sun Years** / Mar. 19, 1996 / AVI ♦♦♦♦♦

While the casual fan will only remember Charlie Rich for his later country MOR hits, if you really want to get in on the ground floor and experience some of the wide variety and depth of the man's prodigious talents, here's exactly where you go to get straight. Sam Phillips pretty much let Rich do whatever he wanted to do at 706 Union, making a "Complete Sun Sessions" a real unlikely vote-getter on the reissue horizon simply because Rich had so much talent in so many different directions (jazz vs. country, blues vs. crass banality) that putting it all out almost makes no sense at all. Which is why this compilation is so refreshing; no filler, no dumb stuff, just the hits and the best tracks from a five- or six-year period when Rich was one of the last glimmers of hope for the label. All the early hits like "Lonely Weekends," "Sittin' and Thinkin'," and "Who Will the Next Fool Be" are aboard, along with several stereo tracks remixed from the original multi-track masters for the first time ever with sparkling sound. Charlie Rich was one talented man and here's where you find some of his best. *—Cub Koda*

★ **Feel Like Going Home: The Essential Charlie Rich** / Jan. 28, 1997 / Columbia/Legacy ♦♦♦♦♦

Though it bypasses his late '70s and early '80s records for United Artists and Elektra, the double-disc, 36-track set *Feel Like Going Home: The Essential Charlie Rich* covers Rich's best (and best-known) work for Sun/Phillips, Groove, Smash and Epic, making it the first cross-licensed compilation ever assembled on the idiosyncratic vocalist and pianist. The multi-label approach works wonders in illustrating the depths of Rich's talents, since the compilation showcases all of his stylistic detours and his rich musical eclectism. The song selection also helps showcase his versatility. While *Feel Like Going Home* contains all of his best-known songs in their original hit versions ("Lonely Weekends," "Who Will the Next Fool Be," "Sittin' and Thinkin'," "Big Boss Man," "Mohair Sam," "I Washed My Hands in Muddy Waters," "Set Me Free," "Don't Put No Headstone On My Grave," "Life's Little Ups and Downs," "Behind Closed Doors," "The Most Beautiful Girl"), it overlooks several big country hits from the mid-'70s in favor of lesser-known '60s and early '70s recordings, which are stronger performances. As a consequence, *Feel Like Going Home* is the only compilation that truly shows the scope of Rich's talent, and it works both as an introduction and as a definitive retrospective. *—Stephen Thomas Erlewine*

Sun Years 1958-1963 / Mar. 25, 1998 / Bear Family ♦♦♦♦♦

The Complete Charlie Rich on Hi Records / Oct. 17, 2000 / Hi ♦♦♦♦

Riders in the Sky

f. 1977

Group / Western Swing Revival, Cowboy, Traditional Country

Beginning each performance with their trademark greeting "Mighty fine and a great big Western 'Howdy,' all you buckaroos and buckarettes," Riders in the Sky simultaneously paid tribute to and poked gentle fun at classic B-movie cowboy songs from the '40s and '50s, particularly the work of Roy Rogers and Gene Autry. During the '70s and '80s, the group built a strong cult following in America, especially on college campuses. The trio formed in the mid-'70s, playing a weekly gig at a Nashville nightclub which led to a job with TNN's *Tumbleweed Theater.* In the early '80s, they released five albums before signing to MCA in 1987, releasing their first album for the label—*Riders Radio Theater*—a year later. The record was a success, which led to the program *Riders Radio Theater* on National Public Radio. They recorded two more albums with MCA and in 1991 moved to Columbia where they recorded the children's album *Harmony Ranch,* which led to a short-lived CBS-TV Saturday-morning television show. *—Sandra Brennan*

Three on the Trail / 1979 / Rounder ✦✦✦✦✦
Three on the Trail, the Riders in the Sky's debut album, established their tongue-in-cheek tribute to cowboys and western music. Though the humor is piled on a little thicker here than on their later releases, the music is often quite good and they never deviated from this formula—slightly ironic covers, affectionate jokes and made-to-order originals—on any of their subsequent records. They also rarely did it any better. *—Thom Owens*

● **The Best of the West** / 1988 / Rounder ✦✦✦✦✦
Best of the West contains 25 highlights from the Riders in the Sky's first five album for Rounder Records, including such western standards as "Tumbling Tumbleweeds," "Here Comes the Santa Fe," "Don't Fence Me In," "Blue Montana Skies," and the group's namesake, "Ghost Riders in the Sky." *—Thom Owens*

Live / Mar. 15, 1992 / Rounder ✦✦✦

Always Drink Upstream from the Herd / Oct. 31, 1995 / Rounder ✦✦✦✦

Public Cowboy #1: The Music of Gene Autry / Oct. 22, 1996 / Rounder ✦✦✦✦✦
The Riders in the Sky cut this record in the wake of their performing a Gene Autry medley in a television appearance with Autry himself in the audience. The songs are done reverently but with a real sense of fun, essentially the same balancing act that has made them a success on stage and television. Their main innovations are the harmony singing, which works well throughout, and a jazzy approach to Jimmie Rodgers' "Can't Shake The Sands of Texas From My Shoes." Autry's versions have held up magnificently well, but this loving tribute album is a necessary addition to any fan's collection. *—Bruce Eder*

The Best of the West Rides Again / Rounder ✦✦✦✦✦
Picking up where the first compilation left off, *Best of the West Rides Again* contains many of the best-known and most popular songs from the campy western revival band, Riders in the Sky. *—Stephen Thomas Erlewine*

Jeannie C. Riley (Jeanne Stephenson)

b. Sep. 19, 1945, Anson, TX
Vocals / CCM, Country-Pop
Best known for her international crossover hit "Harper Valley P.T.A.," Jeannie C. Riley made her first public performance as a teen, appearing on her uncle's jamboree show. She also made a few demos that led to her debut recording "What About Them" as Jean Riley; the single wasn't successful. Her manager Paul Perry hooked Riley up with producer Shelby Singleton, with whom she recorded "Harper Valley P.T.A." The song became an instant hit, reaching number one on both the pop and country charts. Later in 1968, Riley debuted on the *Grand Ole Opry* and released "The Girl Most Likely," which reached number six on the country charts. During the early '70s, she had a string of minor hits and five other Top Ten singles, including "Country Girl," "Oh, Singer" and "Good Enough to Be Your Wife." Around 1974, Riley became a born-again Christian and formed a new band, Red River Symphony, which had a minor hit in 1976, "The Best I've Ever Had." *—Sandra Brennan*

● **The Best of Jeannie C. Riley** / Oct. 22, 1996 / Varese Sarabande ✦✦✦✦✦
Fifteen-song compilation concentrating on her late-'60s/early-'70s prime; everything's from 1968-71, except for a couple of inessential '80s cuts tacked onto the end. Sometimes thought of as a one-shot artist, Riley was one of the better unsung country singers of her era, with a far saucier delivery than was the norm. The material, much of it penned by the songwriting team of Myrna Smith and Margaret Lewis, is almost schizophrenic in its reach. "The Rib" could be heard as an early, dignified plea for women's rights; "The Generation Gap" had some muted anti-establishment undertones; and of course Tom Hall's "Harper Valley P.T.A." poked fun at small-town hypocrisy. At the same time, she also released bathetic ballads like "Things Go Better with Love"; "There Never Was a Time" is as corny an ode to family, God, and honest struggle as you can find in the country field. At any rate, the anthology as a whole is above average, also including the hits "Oh, Singer," "Good Enough to Be Your Wife," "Country Girl," and "The Girl Most Likely." *—Richie Unterberger*

Leann Rimes

b. Aug. 28, 1982
Vocals / Adult Contemporary, Contemporary Country
In 1996, LeAnn Rimes burst out of nowhere with her debut single "Blue," which immediately captured the attention of country fans across America. It wasn't just the fact that her rich, powerful vocals were remarkably similar to Patsy Cline—it was the fact that LeAnn Rimes was only 13 years old. Like Tanya Tucker and Brenda Lee before her, she had a hit with her debut single and was barely a teenager at the time. At the age of 11, she released her first album on an independent label. That same year, record promoter Bill Mack began cultivating a plan to break Rimes into the mainstream. The cornerstone of Mack's plan was a song called "Blue" which he had written in the '60s. He claimed that he had written the tune for Patsy Cline, but she had died before she was able to record the song and he had been waiting over 30 years to find the right vocalist. The story was an exaggeration: "Blue" had been recorded by no less than three different artists, as late as 1993. Nevertheless, the story was repeated throughout the country, adding to the growing myth that Rimes was the successor to Cline's tradition. "Blue" and its accompanying album of the same name became major hits in the summer of 1996. After two quickie 1997 releases—*Unchained Melody: The Early Years* and *You Light Up My Life: Inspirational Songs*—she issued her second proper LP, *Sittin' on Top of the World,* in 1998. *—Stephen Thomas Erlewine*

● **Blue** / 1996 / Curb ✦✦✦✦
With her debut single "Blue," the 13 year-old Leann Rimes made a major impression on Nashville. Although her age made her a novelty, what made a lasting impression was the depth and richness of her voice, which sounded for all the world like that of a young Patsy Cline. Stylistically, "Blue" is the closest Rimes gets to Cline on her debut album, which is also titled *Blue.* Though Cline's twangy countrypolitan is an undercurrent throughout *Blue,* Rimes' music is designed for mid-'90s listeners, so there are flourishes of commercially oriented new country, new traditionalism, and country-pop. Naturally, the quality of the songs is somewhat uneven, but Rimes' vibrant voice sounds exquisite throughout the album and suggests that she'll be able to develop her talent into something truly unique. *—Thom Owens*

Unchained Melody: The Early Years / Feb. 11, 1997 / Curb ✦✦

You Light Up My Life: Inspirational Songs / Sep. 9, 1997 / Curb ✦✦✦

Sittin' on Top of the World / May 5, 1998 / Curb ✦✦✦

LeAnn Rimes / Oct. 26, 1999 / Curb ✦✦✦✦
Essentially, *LeAnn Rimes* is a covers album, with one new song ("Big Deal") tacked onto the end, which makes it a return to her roots—which, in turn, means that it's sort of a salute to her main influence, Patsy Cline. Rimes tackles no less than five songs from Cline's *12 Greatest Hits,* plus "Lovesick Blues," which Cline also recorded. It's a tricky situation for a singer pegged as a Cline soundalike with her first hit single, "Blue." If those comparisons bother Rimes, it's impossible to tell from her performance, since she sings these six songs *exactly* like Cline does. As it turns out, imitation is a crutch Rimes uses quite often, since she mimics Janis Joplin on "Me and Bobby McGee" and pretty much uses Marty Robbins as a guide vocal on "Don't Worry." Since she has a good voice and these are, by and large, great songs, it's hard to complain—given the best set of songs of her career, she delivers good, professional performances, stumbling only on "Me and Bobby McGee" with Joplin-like histrionics. So, *LeAnn Rimes* winds up being one of her better efforts, even if her vocals are fairly mannered and the arrangements are fairly predictable. But the most curious thing about this covers album is that Rimes turns in her best performance on the lone new track. She sounds loose, confident and exciting on "Big Deal," and even more importantly, she never sounds like one of her idols—she sounds like herself. And since it comes at the end of the record, you can't help but wish she'd recorded an album of new, pure country songs as good as "Big Deal" instead of a collection of covers, no matter how well she sang those covers. *—Stephen Thomas Erlewine*

I Need You / Jan. 30, 2001 / Curb ✦✦✦

Tex Ritter (Woodward Maurice Ritter)

b. Jan. 12, 1907, Murval, TX, **d.** Jan. 2, 1973, Nashville, TN
Vocals, Guitar / Cowboy, Traditional Country
Singing cowboy Tex Ritter stood as one of the biggest names in country music throughout the postwar era, thanks to a diverse career that led him everywhere from the Broadway stage to the political arena. Ritter was playing cowboy songs on the radio when he travelled to New York in 1931 to act in the Broadway production *Green Grow the Lilacs;* during scene changes, he also performed on his guitar. Thanks to his success on the stage, he began hosting radio programs like *Tex Ritter's Campfire* and *Cowboy Tom's Roundup* before entering the studio with producer Art Satherley in 1933, where his deep, lived-in voice graced songs like "Rye Whiskey." He caught the attention of Hollywood producer Edward Finney, who was searching for a cowboy singer in the mold of the highly successful Gene Autry, and was tapped to star in the 1936 Western *Song of the Gringo.* Over the next two years, Ritter starred in a dozen films, including 1937's *Trouble in Texas* (co-starring a young Rita Hayworth), before Finney's studio Grand National Pictures folded. Ritter then switched to Monogram Studios, for whom he made some twenty Westerns, including 1940's *Take Me Back to Oklahoma* with co-star Bob Wills; work at Columbia and Universal followed, and by the time of his movie swan song, 1945's *The Texas Rangers,* he had appeared in a total of 85 films. In 1942, he became the first country artist signed to Capitol Records, where he recorded everything from traditional folk tunes to patriotic material to sentimental songs. In 1944, Tex Ritter and His Texans topped the charts with the single "I'm Wastin' My Tears on You." The record's flip side, "There's a New Moon Over My Shoulder," peaked at Number Two, as did the follow-up "Jealous Heart." 1945's "You Two-Timed Me One Time Two Often" proved to be Ritter's greatest success, holding at Number One for 11 consecutive weeks. *—Jason Ankeny*

Country Music Hall of Fame / 1991 / MCA ✦✦✦✦✦

● **High Noon** / 1992 / Bear Family ✦✦✦✦✦
The single best collection of Tex Ritter's Capitol recordings isn't quite complete, but it's a lot better than Capitol's own Collector Series release on Ritter, and it's the best we're likely ever to see on this extraordinary artist, at least until a boxed set is forthcoming. The 28 songs here include most of the important tracks that he cut for Capitol between 1942 and 1956, including the ultra-rare 1952 British recording of "High Noon" (bar none, the best version of the song that Ritter ever did, and one that has a very unusual history to it) as well as the undubbed (i.e. drumless) original Capitol release; "Blood On the Saddle," "Jingle, Jangle, Jingle," "Goodbye, My Little Cherokee," the pop-western "Boogie Woogie Cowboy," and Ritter's definitive 1946 version of "Rye Whiskey." The range of styles here is daunting, as Ritter moves from early 1940's pop with a western twang ("Jingle, Jangle, Jingle") through authentic folk material ("Rye Whiskey") and into the western screen mythos—"Gunsmoke" is unexpectedly beautiful, but so is "Wichita," and Ritter's version of "The Searchers" is the best recording ever done of that Stan Jones movie theme song. There's also one previously unreleased track, Ritter's gorgeous rendition of "When It's Springtime in the Rockies." The notes and the detailed sessionography are up to Bear Family's usual daunting standards of excellence. *—Bruce Eder*

Capitol Collectors Series / Feb. 17, 1992 / Capitol ♦♦♦♦
Now deleted, this 25-song collection is as close as Capitol has gotten so far to doing a definitive collection on one of the label's founding artists. Ritter spent 31 years on the label, with successful singles in each decade of his relationship with Capitol from 1942 until 1973, and one would think that Capitol could do someone with a record like that some justice. There are some classics here, including "Rye Whiskey" and "Blood on the Saddle," as well as the obligatory "High Noon," but, like the rest of the *Capitol Collectors Series*, this disc was unsatisfying to true fans, leaving out more than a few worthy album tracks, not to mention a single or two that should be represented, even as it was too ambitious for the casual listener. (Out of print.) *—Bruce Eder*

Blood on the Saddle / Jun. 23, 1999 / Bear Family ♦♦♦♦♦
Blood on the Saddle is a deluxe four-disc box set which collects Tex Ritter's recordings from 1932 to 1947, including his complete ARC and Decca sides, and everything from his first five years at Capitol. Over this period, Ritter progressed from spare, folksy readings of cowboy material to his mellow take on Western swing. Perhaps the earthiest of the singing cowboys, Ritter's rich personality and flair for the dramatic come through on these classic recordings. Hits such as "Jealous Heart" and "There's a New Moon Over My Shoulder" are represented, as well as alternate takes, unreleased songs, and rarities, including a number of recordings for children with spoken intros in the style later adopted by Merle Travis for his folk albums. Tex Ritter's catalog has been under-represented in the CD era, so collectors and serious fans will no doubt be thrilled by this loving presentation of his earliest recordings. *—Greg Adams*

The Very Best of Tex Ritter / Jul. 25, 2000 / Varese ♦♦♦♦
Exactly half of these recordings previously appeared on the Hollywood Records compact disc *Conversation With a Gun*, including excellent remakes of "The Boll Weevil" and "Green Grow the Lilacs," both of which were recorded by Ritter for Capitol in the '40s. These recordings are said to be from a 1964 session for overseas radio broadcast, and Ritter remakes a number of his well-known songs. An answer to Lefty Frizzell's "Saginaw Michigan" is included ("Son of a Saginaw Fisherman"), along with the Harlan Howard's "The Gallows Pole" and an instrumental treatment of Johnny Bond's "Cimarron." *The Very Best* isn't Tex Ritter's very best—not even close—but fans will greatly enjoy a number of these tracks. *—Greg Adams*

Marty Robbins

b. Sep. 26, 1925, Glendale, AZ, **d.** Dec. 8, 1982, Nashville, TN
Vocals, Guitar / Nashville Sound/Countrypolitan, Pop, Rockabilly, Country-Pop, Cowboy, Traditional Country
No artist in the history of country music has had a more stylistically diverse career than Marty Robbins. Never content to remain just a country singer, Robbins performed successfully in a dazzling array of styles during more than thirty years in the business. To his credit, Robbins rarely followed trends, but often took off in directions that stunned both his peers and fans. Plainly Robbins was not hemmed in by anyone's definition of country music. Although his earliest recordings were unremarkable weepers, by the mid-'50s Robbins was making forays into rock music, adding fiddles to the works of Chuck Berry and Little Richard. By the late '50s, Robbins had pop hits of his own with teen fare like "A White Sport Coat (And a Pink Carnation)." Almost simultaneously, he completed work on his *Hawaiian Songs of the Islands* album. In 1959, Robbins stretched even further with the hit single "El Paso," thus heralding a pattern of "gunfighter ballads" that lasted the balance of his career. Robbins also enjoyed bluesy hits like "Don't Worry," which introduced a pop audience to fuzztone guitar in 1961. Barely a year later, Robbins scored a calypso hit with "Devil Woman." Marty Robbins also left a legacy of gospel music and a string of sentimental ballads, showing that he would croon with nary a touch of hillbilly twang. *—Hank Davis*

Gunfighter Ballads & Trail Songs / 1959 / Columbia/Legacy ♦♦♦♦♦
Gunfighter Ballads and Trail Songs was Marty Robbins' first album to consist entirely of western and cowboy music. Containing the hit single "El Paso," the album was divided between originals, traditional cowboy songs, and contemporary western songs. The result was a successful and thoroughly entertaining celebration of cowboy songs and western movies, particularly since the songs are alternately idealistic and adventerous. Sure, *Gunfighter Ballads and Trail Songs* doesn't deal in reality, but it is grounded in myth. It just happens to be one of the most effective and romantic statements of the cowboy mythology recorded in the late '50s and early '60s. [The 1999 CD reissue contains three bonus tracks: "The Hanging Tree," "Saddle Tramp" and "El Paso."] *—Stephen Thomas Erlewine*

More Gunfighter Ballads & Trail Songs / 1960 / Columbia ♦♦♦♦♦
Marty Robbins' sequel to *Gunfighter Ballads and Trail Songs* followed the same formula as its predecessor, dividing traditional cowboy songs with original numbers by Robbins. Though the album didn't feature any hit singles, it was the equal to its predecessor—"San Angelo" is one of Robbins' best cowboy songs, while his version of "Streets of Laredo" boasts one of his finest vocals. *—Stephen Thomas Erlewine*

Hawaii's Calling Me / 1963 / Bear Family ♦♦♦

The Drifter / 1966 / Koch International ♦♦♦♦♦
Based of Marty Robbins' syndicated television series of the same name, *The Drifter* was one of the purest cowboy albums Robbins ever made. Though Robbins had made several cowboy albums before—indeed, his love of western music informed much of his music—the instrumentation and song selection on *The Drifter* was stripped-down and direct, concentrating almost entirely on epic western narrative sagas. The lack of concise songs resulted in a less successful album by commerical standards—only "Mr. Shorty" was a hit, while the "El Paso" sequel "Feleena" ran over eight minutes—but *The Drifter* was of Robbins' most artistically ambitious albums, as well as one of his most accomplished. *—Stephen Thomas Erlewine*

★ **All-Time Greatest Hits** / 1972 / Columbia/Legacy ♦♦♦♦♦
Released in 1972, the double-album/single-CD *All-Time Greatest Hits* remains one of the best compilations ever assembled on Marty Robbins. Featuring 20 tracks—including most of his big hits—there are very few essential tracks missing from the collection. As an introduction, this relatively concise compilation is a bit more managable than the double-disc *Essential Marty Robbins* and, therefore, is more attractive to neophytes. *—Stephen Thomas Erlewine*

Country 1951-1958 / 1991 / Bear Family ♦♦♦♦♦
Listeners charmed by his pre-*El Paso* country have a motherlode to explore in this five-disc boxed set filled with dewy-eyed weepers (his earliest recordings), his rockabilly (he cut the first cover of "Maybellene"), ancient country-folk accompanied solely by acoustic guitar ("The Dream of the Miner's Chill"), Hawaiiana ("Aloha Oe"), and a handful of his country-pop outings arranged by Ray Conniff. *—Mark A. Humphrey*

☆ **The Essential Marty Robbins: 1951-1982** / 1991 / Columbia/Legacy ♦♦♦♦♦
The double-disc set *The Essential Marty Robbins: 1951-1982* effectively presents an overview of Robbins' long, prolific career, taking in nearly every style he tried out during that time. There are honky tonk and hillbilly numbers and cowboy songs, country-pop, rockabilly and Hawaiian tunes—in all, there are 50 songs, including the great majority of his big hit singles. In short, it's the perfect place to begin exploring his long, prolific and varied career, and it's a necessary addition to any country music library. *—Stephen Thomas Erlewine*

Musical Journey to the Caribbean & Mexico / 1994 / Bear Family ♦♦♦♦

Country (1960-1966) / 1996 / Bear Family ♦♦♦♦♦
Cutting away all of Marty Robbins' rock & roll, Hawaiian and cowboy recordings, Bear Family's four-disc box set *Country (1960-1966)* contains nothing but his straight country and country-pop recordings of the early '60s. During that era, Robbins was one of the most popular performers in country music, scoring an impressive series of Top 10 hits and pop crossovers like "Don't Worry" and "Devil Woman," which are all included on this set. Where many Bear Family sets are so thorough and complete, they merely wind up being exhausting, *Country (1960-1966)* is entertaining from start to finish, since it is sequenced in a logical, listenable order and doesn't dwell on the rarities. Any serious fan of Robbins will find the set an essential addition to their library, and it is arguably the finest Robbins box Bear Family has released. *—Stephen Thomas Erlewine*

☆ **The Story of My Life: The Best of Marty Robbins** / 1996 / Columbia/Legacy ♦♦♦♦♦
This 18-track compilation covering the first half of Marty Robbins's recording career is almost an exact duplication of a chronological list of Robbins's biggest country hit singles of the period, the only exception being "I Can't Quit Her (I've Gone Too Far)," and which, while a Top Ten entry, was not as big a hit as "She Was Only Seventeen (He Was One Year More)," which has been left out. (No one seems to have told annotator Rick Kienzle, who mentions the missing track and not the included one.) That means Robbins's 11 chart toppers are here, from "I'll Go on Alone" to "Ribbon of Darkness," with such massive hits as "Singing the Blues," "El Paso," "Don't Worry," and "Devil Woman" in between. The songs, 11 of which were written by Robbins himself, are amazingly diverse, covering country, western, pop, and folk styles, but the set is held together by Robbins's warm, country-tinged voice. The only objection to this set is that, at only 49+ minutes, it could have been longer by half. *—William Ruhlmann*

Under Western Skies / Feb. 1996 / Bear Family ♦♦♦♦♦
Four CDs covering Marty Robbins' complete Western recordings, 99 songs in all from 1958 until 1979. As a concept, *Under Western Skies* is cohesive and enjoyable, largely because Robbins' music, regardless of the particular year in which it was recorded, is unified thematically. It's also a superb showcase for Robbins' voice, one of the most versatile in country & western—he was equally adept at rock & roll, traditional country, or Western ballads dating back 100 years or more, but he had a way of extending the latter genre's melodic beauty and lyricism without ever seeming repetitive. Thus, it wasn't just that Robbins was covering this repertory, but that he was doing it in ways that, as a solo artist of his era, were just about definitive. Disc One contains songs from *Gunfighter Ballads and Trail Songs* and parts of the follow-up record, *More Gunfighter Ballads and Trail Songs*. Disc Two is devoted to songs from *Return of the Gunfighter* and the rest of *More Gunfighter Ballads*, filled out with songs that only appeared previously in 1984 on a Bear Family vinyl release. By the mid-'60s, Robbins' voice was even better, richer and more confident on this material, and Disc Three reflects this. Disc Four extends up through 1979, and it's something of a tribute to Robbins' success with this repertory that precious little was left in the vaults for Bear Family or anyone else to unearth and issue for the first time. The accompanying booklet is 60 pages long, and while it does seem as though the essay is not as well organized as it might have been, it's interesting overall, highlighted with excellent photographs and accompanied by lyrics to each of the songs and a full sessionography. *—Bruce Eder*

Jimmie Rodgers

b. Sep. 8, 1897, Meridian, MS, **d.** May 26, 1933, New York, NY
Vocals, Guitar, Banjo / Yodeling, Traditional Country
His brass plaque in the Country Music Hall of Fame reads, "Jimmie Rodgers' name stands foremost in the country music field as *the man who started it all*." This is a fair assessment. The "Singing Brakeman" and the "Mississippi Blue Yodeler," whose six-year career was cut short by tuberculosis, became the first nationally known star of country music and the direct influence of many later performers from Hank Snow and Ernest Tubb and Hank Williams to Lefty Frizzell and Merle Haggard. Rodgers sang about rounders and gamblers, bounders and ramblers—and he knew what he sang about. At age 14 he went to work as a railroad brakeman, and on the rails he stayed until a pulmonary hemorrhage sidetracked him to the medicine show circuit in 1925. The years with the trains harmed his health but helped his music. In an era when Rodgers' contemporaries were singing only mountain and mountain/folk music, he fused hillbilly country, gospel, jazz, blues, pop, cowboy, and folk; and many of his best songs were his compositions, including "TB Blues," "Waiting for a Train," "Travelin' Blues," "Train Whistle Blues," and his thirteen blue yodels. Although Rodgers wasn't the first to yodel on records, his style was distinct from all the others. His yodel wasn't merely sugar-coating on the song, it was as important as the lyric, mournful and plaintive

or happy and carefree, depending on a song's emotional content. His instrumental accompaniment consisted sometimes of his guitar only, while at other times a full jazz band (horns and all) backed him up. Country fans could have asked for no better hero/star—someone who thought what they thought, felt what they felt, and sang about the common person honestly and beautifully. In his last recording session, Rodgers was so racked and ravaged by tuberculosis that a cot had to be set up in the studio, so he could rest before attempting that one song more. No wonder Jimmie Rodgers is to this day loved by country music fans. —*David Vinopal*

☆ **First Sessions** / Jan. 1991 / Rounder ✦✦✦✦✦
The opening volume in Rounder's mammoth eight-disc Jimmie Rodgers reissue series presents his earliest, and in some cases, most tentatively performed material from 1927 and 1928. Rodgers quickly makes the leap from raw, if engaging singer to emphatic, distinctive artist, and midway through has established a singular sound and riveting delivery, with his trademark yodel and mastery of blues inflection and sensibility in place. These cuts include the signature track "Blue Yodel," aplus other classics such as "In The Jailhouse Now," "Treasures Untold" and "Memphis Yodel," as well as "The Brakemen's Blues." Things would never be the same for Rodgers, and these were the songs that helped make him an institution. —*Ron Wynn*

☆ **Vol. 5: America's Blue Yodeler 1930-31** / May 1991 / Rounder ✦✦✦✦✦
This fifth set of vintage Jimmie Rodgers performances included some spectacular collaborations. While neither sounded fully comfortable, the meeting of Rodgers and Louis Armstrong on "Blue Yodel No. 9" is a landmark date in music annals, two immortals finding a way to make seemingly disparate styles mesh on a short tune. Armstrong's wife at the time, Lil Hardin, accompanied the pair on piano. Rodgers also teamed frequently with Lani McIntire's Hawaiians on this set, often on throwaway tunes that Rodgers' vocals made enjoyable. There's another collaboration with a blues artist, this time Clifford Gibson on "Let Me Be Your Side Track," a great bawdy/innuendo number. Rodgers was paired with The Carter Family on two wonderful classic country numbers, the heartbreak tune "Why There's A Tear In My Eye" and the gospel song "The Wonderful City." —*Ron Wynn*

☆ **Vol. 6: Down the Old Road 1931-32** / 1991 / Rounder ✦✦✦✦✦
This CD features songs with Jimmie Rodgers working in fresh formats as producer Ralph Peer attempted to break a sales slump. Rodgers recorded with The Louisville Jug Band on "My Good Gal's Gone Blues" and teamed with The Carter Family again in both Kentucky and Texas in 1931. They made four songs together, but three were unissued until after Rodgers' death. They're pleasant and often nicely sung, but not among either artist's finest. Rodgers teamed with steel guitarist Cliff Carlisle and guitarist Wilber Ball on three songs, with Rodgers added ukulele backing. The final four cuts saw Rodgers return to his trademark railroad numbers and yodeling blues in 1932. For the most part, these weren't great tunes, as they show Rodgers experimenting and finally opting to do comfortable, familiar material rather than try new things. —*Ron Wynn*

☆ **The Early Years 1928-1929** / Feb. 1991 / Rounder ✦✦✦✦✦
The second disc in the Jimmie Rodgers series covers 1928 and 1929, the years in which Rodgers solidified his stature as a premier performer. These 16 tracks saw him doing both his brilliant solo yodeling blues and also working with bands on some cuts. "Desert Blues" featured Rodgers backed by a group with cornet, clarinet, tuba and piano among the instrumentation. Steel guitarist John Westbrook provided tingling accompaniment on "I'm Lonely and Blue," "My Carolina Sunshine Girl" and "Blue Yodel No. 4." But once more, it's such cuts as "Daddy and Home," "You and My Old Guitar" and "Never No Mo' Blues" that are the triumphs, with Rodgers simply wailing, singing and yodeling, displaying the emotional clout and memorable style that turned these numbers into anthems. —*Ron Wynn*

☆ **On the Way Up 1929** / Mar. 1991 / Rounder ✦✦✦✦✦
This third Jimmie Rodgers disc in the eight-CD line covers arguably his greatest year, 1929. Rodgers scored huge hits doing popular novelty cuts like "Frankie and Johnny" and railroad numbers like "Train Whistle Blues," and continued cutting yodeling tunes, as well as cowboy songs and bawdy blues. The 17 cuts include the marvelous "Everybody Does It in Hawaii," with Weldon Burkes on ukulele and Joe Kapo on steel, and the memorable "Hobo Bill's Last Rides." The session also contains alternate takes of "The Land Of My Boyhood Dreams" and "Frankie and Johnny." Rodgers was now ably mixing identities and personas, alternating between yodeling blues singer, railroad narrator and carefree cowboy. —*Ron Wynn*

☆ **Riding High 1929-1930** / Apr. 1991 / Rounder ✦✦✦✦✦
Jimmie Rodgers was enjoying the fruits of his labors in 1929 and 1930, the years covered on this fourth CD in Rounder's historic eight-disc retrospective series. The 17 numbers highlighted here were done either during his final 1929 session or in Hollywood the next year. They're primarily yodeling blues tunes, with Rodgers backed by guitarist Billy Burkes. There are two versions of "Anniversary Blue Yodel (Blue Yodel No. 7)," "Mississippi River Blues" and "Why Did You Give Me Your Love—," as well as stark, marvelous numbers like "She Was Happy Till She Met You," "A Drunkard's Child" and "Why Should I Be Lonely." This set also includes Rodgers working with Lani McIntire's Hawaiians on two tunes and with Bob Sawyer's Jazz Band on the finale, "My Blue-Eyed Jane." —*Ron Wynn*

☆ **No Hard Times, 1932** / Jul. 1991 / Rounder ✦✦✦✦✦
Although he was nearing the end, Jimmie Rodgers kept going in 1932, turning out several sterling numbers; among them were the dynamic "Blue Yodel No. 10" and riveting "No Hard Times" and "Long Tall Mama Blues," with Oddie McWinders on banjo. Rodgers also displayed his affection for his mother on "Mother, the Queen of My Heart" and the interesting confessional number "I've Only Loved Three Women." Rodgers teamed effectively with guitarist Slim Bryant on "Prairie Lullaby," "Miss the Mississippi and You" and "In The Hills of Tennessee," and once more sang frankly and movingly about his illness on "Whippin' That Old T.B.," although it wasn't as triumphant as "The T.B. Blues." —*Ron Wynn*

☆ **Last Sessions, 1933** / Aug. 1991 / Rounder ✦✦✦✦✦
Illness ravaged Jimmie Rodgers during his final days, as he attempted to record as much as possible. There's an eerie quality to such tunes as "The Yodeling Ranger," "Years Ago" and "Somewhere Down The Line," as it's evident that Rodgers was far from top vocal form. But despite the shortness of breath, lack of range and weak quality, he could still deliver emotionally gripping performances. The earlier cuts on the disc, "Blue Yodel No. 13," "Dreaming With Tears In My Eyes" and "I'm Free (From The Chain Gang Now)" have a hypnotic finality and edge, even when his vocals falter. Rodgers died 48 hours after he finished his final song, not turning in a particularly great performance, as might be expected. But his accomplishments had long ago established him as one of the most memorable performers in American music annals. —*Ron Wynn*

★ **The Essential Jimmie Rodgers** / Apr. 29, 1997 / RCA ✦✦✦✦✦
As the first serious attempt at a single-disc Jimmie Rodgers retrospective in the CD-era, *The Essential Jimmie Rodgers* isn't bad at all. Over the course of 20 songs, nearly all of his best-known songs—including "Blue Yodel, No. 1," "In the Jailhouse Now" and "Blue Yodel, no. 8 (a.k.a. Mule Skinner Blues")—are featured, and while some good things remain in the vaults, it's hard to argue with what's here. After all, *Essential* isn't designed for historians or completists—it's for the curious, who are reluctant to invest in either Rounder's multi-volume series or Bear Family's comprehensive box. For those listeners, *The Essential Jimmie Rodgers* is an invaluable introduction. —*Stephen Thomas Erlewine*

The Singing Brakeman / Bear Family ✦✦✦✦✦
The Singing Brakeman is a six-disc set that compiles every song that Jimmie Rodgers ever recorded. It covers the same ground as Rounder's eight-disc set, but Bear Family's set condenses the material into six CDs and adds a large booklet that features a thorough discography and biography. Although it essentially has the same material, adding a few alternate takes that weren't on the Rounder series, *The Singing Brakeman* has a more scholarly approach—the discs are designed not as a casual listening experience, but intense, concentrated listening. In the end, however, it's neither superior or inferior to Rounder's series. No matter how they are presented, Rodgers' recordings constitute essential listening. —*Stephen Thomas Erlewine*

Kenny Rogers

b. Aug. 21, 1938, Houston, TX
Vocals, Guitar, Bass / Urban Cowboy, Soft Rock, Adult Contemporary, Country-Pop
It took several tries before Kenny Rogers became a star. As a member of the First Edition (and the New Christy Minstrels before that), he shared in some million-sellers, among them "Reuben James" and "Ruby, Don't Take Your Love to Town," an excellent Mel Tillis song about a disabled veteran. But superstardom lay ahead for this Texan, and it arrived in the late '70s. His experience with the two previous pop groups had prepared him well: he knew the easy-listening audience was out there, and he supplied them with well-done middle-of-the-road songs with a country flavor. Having gone solo, in 1976 Rogers charted with "Love Lifted Me." But it was with an outstanding song by writer Don Schlitz, "Lucille," that his star shot upward. The rest (as they say) is history: award-winning duets with Dottie West and Dolly Parton, 12 TV specials, another song-of-the-year with "The Gambler," "Daytime Friends," "Coward of the County," "We've Got Tonight," "Crazy," "Lady" (his first pop number one), etc., etc., etc. And that's just the musical side of Kenny Rogers. In 1980, the made-for-TV movie *The Gambler* blasted the competition, followed quickly by *Coward of the County*, then enough sequels to *The Gambler* to get him to Roman numeral IV. Throughout the '80s, Rogers remained a celebrity, even when his sales were declining. Even the '90s, when he rarely charted, his name, face and music was recognizable in a series of concerts, television specials, films and even fast food resturaunts. –*David Vinopal and Stephen Thomas Erlewine*

Ten Years of Gold / 1979 / EMI America ✦✦✦✦✦
Ten Years of Gold is a fine starting point for anyone looking for an overview of Kenny Rogers' early career, spanning from his early hits with the First Edition like "Just Dropped In (To See What Condition My Condition Was In)" to later solo hits like "Lucille" and "Love Lifted Me." —*James Chrispell*

Greatest Hits [EMI America] / 1980 / EMI America ✦✦✦✦✦
This shows off both Rogers the storyteller ("Lucille," "The Gambler," "Coward of the County") and Rogers the hero of easy listeners ("She Believes in Me," "Lady"). —*Dan Cooper*

25 Greatest Hits / 1987 / EMI America ✦✦✦✦✦
This two-CD set includes much the same material as *Greatest Hits*, but also has "Daytime Friends," "Love or Something like It," and "Love Will Turn You Around." —*Dan Cooper*

Greatest Hits [Hip-O] / Sep. 24, 1996 / Hip-O ✦✦✦✦✦
Kenny Rogers & the First Edition's *Greatest Hits* contains all of the group's greatest hits, including "Ruby, Don't Take Your Love to Town" and "Just Dropped In (To See What Condition My Condition Is In)," plus a number of lesser-known singles. Though the group didn't have enough strong material to make the compilation consistently entertaining, this single-disc collection is nevertheless the definitive retrospective of Rogers' early years. —*Stephen Thomas Erlewine*

Decade of Hits / Mar. 25, 1997 / Warner Brothers ✦✦✦
With the exception of "Islands in the Stream," Rogers' chart-topping duet with Dolly Parton, this compilation of the singer's mid-1980s and 1990s work for RCA and Reprise concentrates primarily on forgettable, minor hits including "Morning Desire," "The Vows Go Unbroken (Always True to You)," "Tomb of the Unknown Love" and "What About Me?," recorded with Kim Carnes and James Ingram. —*Jason Ankeny*

● **Through the Years: A Retrospective** / Jan. 26, 1999 / Capitol ✦✦✦✦✦
Through the Years: A Retrospective doesn't take its duties lightly—it truly does attempt to present a full portrait of Kenny Rogers, from struggling musician to bonafide superstar. Helpfully, it breaks down his career into four easily digestible discs, containing 20 tracks each. The first disc is dubbed "The Vintage Years" and it doesn't just feature songs from the First Edition—it contains revelatory material from his early groups the Scholars, the Bobby Doyle

Three and the Kirby Stone Four. The second disc is what most casual fans will treasure—an entire disc devoted to "The Number One Hits." The third disc rounds up various singles, album tracks and duets Rogers recorded during his late '70s and early '80s peak. Which, of course, leaves the fourth disc like any other final disc in a box set—a collection of highlights from the years when the artist faded away from the spotlight. Certainly, this results in a thorough and accurate overview of his career, but that doesn't mean it's entirely listenable. Yes, hardcore fans and collectors will be interested in the first disc, but for many listeners, only the First Edition tracks will be noteworthy. Similarly, the final disc is extraneous for most tastes, leaving this little more than a very good two-disc summary of Rogers' hitmaking years. Naturally, single and double disc retrospectives of the hits are available elsewhere, for less money and without two extra discs, and that's what most fans will want. Nevertheless, anyone wanting a thorough summary of Rogers' entire career can't go wrong with *Through the Years.* —*Stephen Thomas Erlewine*

The Greatest Hits: 1983-1988 / Jun. 15, 1999 / Music Club ✦✦✦✦

Roy Rogers (Leonard Slye)

b. Nov. 5, 1911, Cincinnati, OH, **d.** Jul. 6, 1998
Vocals, Guitar / Country Gospel, Cowboy, Traditional Country
When Cincinnati-born Leonard Franklin Slye headed west in the spring of 1931, it was as a would-be musician, working jobs ranging from driving a gravel truck to picking fruit in California's Central Valley. In less than two years, he'd co-founded the greatest western singing group of all time, the Sons of the Pioneers, and barely four years after that, he'd started a career as a movie star under the new name Roy Rogers. Ultimately he found great fame as a movie and TV cowboy, and even founded a very successful chain of restaurants. The early 1940's saw Rogers turn into a national institution, and he became the undisputed "King of the Cowboys" after Gene Autry joined the U.S. Army Air Force in 1942. By 1944, however, the movies and records represented only a small part of the success that Rogers had achieved. The merchandizing of Roy Rogers memorabilia and other items—not just toys, but cereals and electric ranges—coupled with a syndicated radio show made him one of the most familiar figures in popular culture throughout the war years. Rogers' sessions on his own recordings with the Sons of the Pioneers little resembled his earlier work as a member of the group, for his was now the lead voice. His music quickly took on the aura of more typical Hollywood western songs, pleasant but not generally profound. His covers of songs such as "Don't Fence Me In" are probably the best remembered versions, thanks to his movies, and as songs like "San Fernando Valley" or "Home In Oklahoma" reveal, he had an extremely appealing tenor voice, not as memorable as Autry's voice but very pleasing to the ear nonetheless. Perhaps the most well known of all Rogers' songs was one written by wife Dale Evans and originally recorded by them together, "Happy Trails," which became the theme of the *Roy Rogers Show.* From the 1950's onward, his repertory included country music as well as western songs and spirituals, the latter often recorded with Evans. Rogers continued to record into the 1970's, and he scored a hit in 1972 with "Candy Kisses." —*Bruce Eder*

Country Music Hall of Fame Series / 1992 / MCA ✦✦✦✦✦
When Gene Autry got into a contract dispute with Republic Pictures in 1937, the studio replaced him with Sons of the Pioneers member Len Slye, whose name they changed to Roy Rogers. These Decca tracks, which range from 1934 to 1942, cover Rogers's output just before he became "King of the Cowboys" with the release of *Ridin' Down the Canyon.* Two of these cuts were recorded with The Sons of the Pioneers; the rest are solo. —*Brian Mansfield*

King of the Cowboys / Jan. 19, 1999 / ASV/Living Era ✦✦✦✦
A fine compilation of Rogers' early songs with the Sons of the Pioneers and his sessions from the following decade, in all covering 1936-1947. He's at his best when only accompanied by the Sons, such as in the classic wanderlust anthem "Tumbling Tumbleweeds" and the gleeful guitar riffs of "When the Golden Train Comes Down." The orchestral tracks often show a pop influence that pales next to the restless energy of the rawer early tracks, and numbers like "Make-Believe Cowboy" can be a bit too sugary, but the later tracks nonetheless have some keepers like "Don't Face Me In" and the moody harmonies of "Blue Shadows on the Trail." When combined with the Rhino *Happy Trails* compilation, the release makes for an ideal overview of his early career. —*Paul Collins*

● **Happy Trails: The Roy Rogers Collection 1937-1990** / May 18, 1999 / Rhino ✦✦✦✦✦
This box is a brilliant achievement, and all the more surprising for what it does to elevate Roy Rogers' musical reputation. Essentially, Roy Rogers had two distinct musical periods—the first, in the Sons of the Pioneers from 1931 to 1937, is considered the more important; the second, as the singing cowboy star, far less important even though he became a cultural icon. *Happy Trails: The Roy Rogers Collection* offers a complete reconsideration of Rogers' post-Sons of the Pioneers musical career, offering a vast selection of previously lost songs, which greatly expand the range of music with which he is associated. Rather than assembling a collection of his commercial recordings, which concentrated on the most marketable side of Roy Rogers, Rhino producer James Austin went to Rogers' own archives and retrieved dozens of radio broadcasts, rehearsal tapes and live performances by Rogers, Dale Evans, the Sons of the Pioneers, the Riders of the Purple Sage, Pat Brady, and Gabby Hayes, that have been unheard for 50 years. The repertory they performed on those shows was infinitely wider ranging than Rogers' official record releases: traditional country songs of the 19th century, established country hits, older Pioneer hits reprised, Tin Pan Alley, bluegrass, swing and jazz, and even classical elements get a hearing. The pacing of these performances is also marvelous—Rogers' solo material, often featuring his inimitable yodelling, is sandwiched between Rogers/Sons of the Pioneers performances that are a match for any of their classic '30s work. The notes give us not only the background of the particular recordings by Rogers and company, but also the history of the songs themselves. The booklet is well annotated and illustrated, and the sound is pretty much beyond reproach, especially considering the half-century age of much of the unissued material. —*Bruce Eder*

Beginnings: Hillbilly, Old-Time, and String-Band Music

If your experience of country music has consisted of playing the latest Garth Brooks or Barbara Mandrell CD, you'll be needing to set aside considerable time to listen to and appreciate the original country music— but it will be time well spent. Though this music from the '20s can be an acquired taste, depending on what you're accustomed to hearing, the enthusiasm, charm, and simplicity of the music and its performers will transport you back to a decade when country music was facts-of-life music, no more and no less.

The band names give a fair taste of the early performers and of their zest for playing: Gid Tanner and the Skillet Lickers, Al Hopkins and the Hill Billies, the Aristocratic Pigs, the Possum Hunters, the Fruit Jar Drinkers (Uncle Dave Macon's band), the Gully Jumpers, and the Dixie Clodhoppers, all string bands that flourished in the late '20s. The fiddle was the dominant instrument in the beginning; Texan Eck Robertson, who cut six songs for Victor in 1922 (including the classic "Sally Gooden"), is credited with the first recording in country music. The standard repertoire ranged from drinkin'-and-cuttin'-up songs to minstrel/medicine-show standards to gospel and spiritual numbers—something for everyone.

But by no means were hillbilly bands the only show in town in the '20s, nor the fiddle the only instrument: old-time music featured guitars (including the Hawaiian slide guitar), banjos, mandolins, and harmonicas, which soon backed up singers as diverse as Buell Kazee and Bradley Kincaid (folksingers) on one hand and Vernon Dalhart (a reformed opera singer) on the other. It was Dalhart who had the first country hit—"The Prisoner's Song," a 1924 million-seller. In the late '50s and early '60s, hillbilly/old-time/string-band music was rediscovered by the folkniks who, in listening to the New Lost City Ramblers, resurrected the popularity of country music's original genre.—*David Vinopal*

Sawyer Brown

f. 197?
Group / Contemporary Country, Country-Pop
Country rockers Sawyer Brown got their big break with a victory on the nationally syndicated talent show *Star Search.* Named in tribute to the Nashville street where they used to rehearse, the band performed on the show and wound up earning $100,000. The subsequent publicity helped them land a contract with Capitol/Curb in 1984. Later that year, they released their self-titled debut album and had a Top 20 hit with their debut single "Leona." The following year, the band had its first number one hit with their second single "Step That Step." Despite their initial success, Sawyer Brown experienced a backlash from many country radio stations who found their music a bit too slickly produced. By 1987, their singles had plummeted to the bottom half of the charts, until "This Missin' You Heart of Mine" became a number two hit in early 1988. Their next major hit came in 1989 with "The Race Is On." In late 1991, they burst back onto the country music scene with *The Dirt Road,* which produced two Top Five hits. Following its release, the group enjoyed their greatest period of success, as they produced a string of Top 10 hits and successful albums like 1993's *Outskirts of Town* and 1995's *This Thing Called Wantin' and Havin' It All.* —*Sandra Brennan*

Greatest Hits / Aug. 27, 1990 / Curb ✦✦✦✦✦
Curb's *Greatest Hits* is a ten-track budget-priced collection that features some of Sawyer Brown's biggest hits, including "Step That Step," "Heart Don't Fall Now," "Betty's Bein' Bad," "The Race is On," "When Love Comes Callin'," "Used to Blue" and "Shakin'." Although this isn't a bad budget-priced disc, there are better collections available, offering more songs, more hits and better sound for not much more money. —*Stephen Thomas Erlewine*

● **Greatest Hits 1990-1995** / 1995 / Curb ✦✦✦✦✦
Greatest Hits 1990-1995 is a solid retrospective of Sawyer Brown's career highlights, featuring nearly all of their biggest hits. —*David Jehnzen*

Jack Scott (Jack Scafone Jr)

b. Jan. 24, 1936, Windsor, Ontario, Canada
Vocals, Guitar / Rockabilly, Traditional Country, Rock & Roll
Jack Scott sounded tough, like someone you wouldn't want to meet in a dark alley unless he had a guitar in his hands. When he growled "The Way I Walk," wise men stepped aside. Despite his snarling rockabilly attitude, Scott hailed from Ontario and grew up near Detroit, developing a love for hillbilly music along the way. His pronounced emphasis on acoustic guitar distinguished his atmospheric rockers, though his principal pop success came with tear-in-your-beer ballads. After recording for ABC during 1957, he found a hit with "My True Love" after signing to Carlton. The single reached number three and became a British Top Ten hit. After switching labels again, to Top Rank, he hit the Top Five twice during 1959 with "What in the World's Come Over You" and "Burning Bridges." Those two singles were his peak, though Scott also recorded with Capitol during 1961. He continued to vacillate between cowboy crooner and rough-edged rocker throughout the remainder of the '60s and '70s. During the '80s and '90s, Scott occasionally turned up on the oldies circuit, still looking and sounding like a man you seriously didn't want to mess with. —*Bill Dahl*

Scott on Groove / 1989 / Bear Family ✦✦✦✦✦
The music on *Scott on Groove* was recorded after Jack Scott's hit-making era on Capitol was

finished. Scott recorded for Groove in the early '60s. During this time, he was trying to refashion his sound into a rock & roll/rockabilly direction. Not all of the attempts were successful, but the set is interesting for dedicated fans, but they would probably rather acquire this material on the more comprehensive box set, *Classic Scott.* —*Stephen Thomas Erlewine*

● **Greatest Hits** / 1990 / Curb ♦♦♦♦♦
Curb's *Greatest Hits* was the only American Jack Scott compilation available in the mid-'90s, after Capitol pulled its *Collector's Series* from the market. Although *Greatest Hits* only has 11 tracks—including a recently-recorded version of "Running Scared"—it has the essential big hits ("My True Love," "Goodbye Baby," "Burning Bridges," "Leroy," "The Way I Walk," "What in the World's Come Over You") and is a servicable collection, even if it is frustratingly brief. —*Stephen Thomas Erlewine*

Classic Scott / Jun. 27, 1994 / Bear Family ♦♦♦♦♦
With the exception of Roy Orbison and Elvis, no white rock & roller of the time ever developed a finer voice with a better range than Jack Scott, or cut a more convincing body of work in rockabilly, rock & roll, country-soul, gospel, country-pop, or blues. And it's all here on this five-CD set, which probably seems at first like more Jack Scott than most of us need. Its 134 tracks include very, very few songs that aren't worth hearing at least twice (and most a lot more), and have more than their share of surprises. Anyone who laments Scott's failure to remain a rockabilly artist will be surprised at just how much he brought to country ballads and gospel, as well as the convincingly bluesy approach to rock & roll that he maintained years into his recording career. The handful of rockabilly tracks here, confined to the first half of the first disc (with their stereo mixes appearing on the last one), show Scott as a potential rival to Elvis Presley and Gene Vincent. He found success as more of a ballad singer, however, and never returned to his rock & roll roots for more than a song at a time. At the end of the 1950s, he moved back into the haven of country music, where he'd started in his teen years. The fit wasn't an ideal one, although Scott was good enough to make an album's worth of Hank Williams songs a worthwhile venture. This box has it all, mastered about as well as it's ever likely to be. Moreover, good as everything else is, the producers of this box have saved the best for last—unissued, undated demos a few of which are worth the price of a CD themselves. —*Bruce Eder*

The Way I Walk / Roller Coaster ♦♦♦
Jack Scott cut a couple of great rockabilly 45s for ABC/Paramount to begin his career, and Scott's two biggest hits, "What in the World's Come Over You" and "Burning Bridges," were recorded directly after his stay at Carlton Records. But it's generally conceded by rockabilly fans that the majority of his best and most lasting work was cut for that label between 1958 and 1960. This 26-track compilation makes a nice one-stop for the casual Scott fan who doesn't want to opt for Bear Family's massive multi-disc box set, as it's loaded with great rockers like "The Way I Walk," "Leroy," "Goodbye Baby," and his first big hit, "My True Love." But the non-inclusion of his two biggest hits and his early rockabilly singles keep this one from being the definitive package, although it's great listening all the way. —*Cub Koda*

Dan Seals

b. 1948, McCamey, TX
Vocals, Guitar / Soft Rock, Adult Contemporary, Country-Pop
One of the most popular members of the musical Seals family, singer/songwriter Dan Seals had a string of hit singles in the '70s as part of the duo England Dan and John Ford Coley and as a solo performer in the '80s with his country-inflected soft rock. After a few years spent in garage bands, Seals and Coley formed a soft-rock duo as early as 1969, though they didn't break through until 1976's "I'd Really Love to See You Tonight" hit number two on the US pop charts. Throughout the late '70s, the group had a string of pop and adult contemporary hits. Seals left in 1980 to pursue a solo career on Atlantic, though he was still billed as England Dan. His first solo single was only a moderate hit, so in 1983, he began to focus his efforts on breaking the country market. The shift in style worked—he had three Top 40 hits that year, including "Everybody's Dream Girl." He had three Top Ten hits in 1984, and in 1985 began a streak of nine straight number one hits with "Meet Me in Montana," a duet with Marie Osmond. Seals continually charted in the Top Ten until the end of 1990, when mainstream country shifted away from his pop-inflected soft country. After a 1991 album for Warner Brothers failed to do well, the vocalist effectively retired from recording in the mid-'90s, choosing to concentrate on touring instead. —*Sandra Brennan*

● **The Best of Dan Seals** / 1987 / Liberty ♦♦♦♦
The Best of Dan Seals contains 11 of Seals' smooth contemporary country hits from the mid- and late '80s, including the number one singles "Three Time Loser," "You Still Move Me," "Bop," "Everything That Glitters (Is Not Gold)," "Meet Me in Montana," "I Will Be There" and "One Friend." A couple of hits are missing, yet every truly essential item is here, making it the best retrospective of Seals' hit-making peak. —*Thom Owens*

Billy Joe Shaver

b. Aug. 16, 1939, Corsicana, TX
Guitar / Americana, Outlaw Country, Honky Tonk, Singer/Songwriter, Progressive Country
Shaver is a rough-hewn Texan with a rounder's sensibilities, a prophet's humility, and a poet's tongue. He first arrived in Nashville during the freewheeling 1970s, when he fell under the influence of ambitious songwriters like Kris Kristofferson. He combined their artful earthiness with his own colorful way of looking at the world, and came up with a string of honky tonk classics that express the uncommon yearnings of common people. Waylon Jennings' classic *Honky Tonk Heroes* album consists solely of Shaver originals, and Willie Nelson, Johnny Cash, John Anderson and others enjoyed hits with his songs. Despite several exceptional, critically acclaimed albums, he never found the larger audience he deserved. *Tramp On Your Street,* however, gave his late-blooming career a much-deserved lift. —*Kurt Wolff*

Old Five & Dimers Like Me / 1973 / Koch ♦♦♦♦♦
Billy Joe Shaver's debut *Old Five & Dimers Like Me* is full of songs that Shaver wrote and artists like Waylon Jennings, Tom T. Hall, and Johnny Cash scrambled to record. Though his readings of these songs weren't quite commercial enough to be hits, these were important songs that effected the way country music developed in the '70s. It's a must for anyone interested in good songwriting, as well as the development of outlaw country. —*Jim Worbois*

When I Get My Wings / 1976 / Capricorn ♦♦♦♦
Here's proof that his blend of sawdust-floor honkers and spiritually endowed ballads were in place from the start. —*Michael McCall*

I'm Just an Old Chunk of Coal / 1981 / Koch International ♦♦♦♦♦
Again, he combines straight-from-the-soul spirituals like the title cut with some of the most colorful honky tonk ever written, including "Fit to Kill and Going Out in Style" and "Saturday Night," as well as an astounding "Ragged Old Truck," in which he begins by contemplating suicide before deciding all he needs is a good, hard night on the town. —*Michael McCall*

Billy Joe Shaver / 1982 / Columbia ♦♦♦
As with the title, this is his most straightforward collection of Texas soul music. It includes a few remakes of earlier classics. —*Michael McCall*

Salt of the Earth / 1987 / Lucky Dog ♦♦♦

Tramp on Your Street / Aug. 10, 1993 / Volcano ♦♦♦♦♦
His rawest, rockingest setting comes courtesy of his guitarslinging son, Eddie Shaver, who gooses his old man in all the right places. Then, on the more introspective tunes, the father dispenses his hard-earned wisdom in unforgettable fashion. It's a true classic. —*Michael McCall*

Honky Tonk Heroes / 1994 / Bear Family ♦♦♦♦

Unshaven: Live at Smith's Olde Bar / Jun. 27, 1995 / Volcano ♦♦♦♦♦

● **Restless Wind: The Legendary Billy Joe Shaver 1973-1987** / Oct. 1995 / Razor & Tie ♦♦♦♦♦
Restless Wind: The Legendary Billy Joe Shaver 1973-1987 covers the highlights of Shaver's acclaimed career effectively, providing a fine introduction to a distinctive, idiosyncratic singer/songwriter. —*Thom Owens*

Highway of Life / 1996 / Justice ♦♦♦♦♦

Victory / Jul. 14, 1998 / New West ♦♦♦♦♦

Electric Shaver / May 4, 1999 / New West ♦♦♦

SHeDAISY

Group / Contemporary Country
The contemporary country trio SHeDAISY comprised sisters Kristyn, Kelsi, and Kassidy Osborn, natives of smalltown Magna, UT. They began their performing career as children, regularly appearing at county fairs and the like; continuing to hone their soaring three-part harmonies throughout their formative years, the Osborns eventually relocated to Nashville, adopting the name SHeDAISY from a Native American word for "my sisters." Upon signing to the Lyric Street label, they issued their debut album *The Whole Shebang* in the spring of 1999. In fall 2000, the trio released the seasonal effort *Brand New Year.* —*Jason Ankeny*

Whole Shebang / May 11, 1999 / Hollywood ♦♦♦
Shedaisy is one of those contemporary country acts that are country in name only. Using the work of Faith Hill, Shania Twain and the Dixie Chicks as a starting point, the three Osborn sisters—Kristyn, Kelsi and Kassidy—have created an appealingly polished collection of modern country-pop, which means it sounds as much (if not more) like mainstream, radio-ready adult contemporary pop as it does contemporary country. For purists, that will be a problem, but the fact of the matter is, Shedaisy does this music very well and their debut *The Whole Shebang* is every bit as winning as Hill's *Faith* and Twain's *Come on Over,* even if it doesn't quite match the Dixie Chicks' *Wide Open Spaces.* The key to the record's success is not only the sisters' harmonies, which are very good, but Kristyn Osborn's fine songwriting skills. She wrote or co-wrote every song on the album, and while there's a few tunes that feel like filler, most of them are well-crafted, melodic, memorable songs which are distinctive enough to give the group their own identity. *The Whole Shebang* may not be pure country, but its glossy pop sheen and big hooks, along with Shedaisy's charismatic vocals, is enough to make it a winning debut. —*Stephen Thomas Erlewine*

● **Brand New Year** / Sep. 26, 2000 / Hollywood ♦♦♦♦
The Osborn sisters and producer Dan Huff put a new spin on holiday music and put some funk in Christmas. Anything but country, *Brand New Year* is truly a treat for all music listeners. The incomparable harmonies of Kristyn, Kassidy, and Kelsi grace every song on the 12-song collection of new and old holiday music. But the Osborn sisters give their own delicious sound to tradition. "Deck the Halls," "Jingle Bells," and "Sleigh Ride" have all been consecrated with the melodious sound that is uniquely SheDaisy. And the girls give the Andrews Sisters a run for their money on "Santa's Got a Brand New Bag," sounding much like "The Boogie Woogie Bugle Boy." Although Christmas albums generally do little to further a career, SheDaisy better be prepared—*Brand New Year* is sure to be under every tree, making them a household name. —*Maria Konicki*

Jean Shepard

b. Nov. 21, 1933, Pauls Valley, OK
Vocals, Bass / Bakersfield Sound, Honky Tonk, Traditional Country
Few country singers—let alone female country singers—working since the 1950s have produced a large body of work as enduring as Jean Shepard's. Her voice is pure country—accent on both words. She cut one great record after another, mostly on Capitol Records. Nearly all of them crackle, no matter the topic, with honky-tonk angel spunk. Discovered by Hank Thompson, Shepard's first chart appearance came in 1953 (as a duet partner with Ferlin Husky), and she hit the Top Ten in her own right two years later with "A Satisfied Mind." Another Top Ten hit, "Beautiful Lies," led to an invitation to join the Grand Ole Opry in 1956; that same year, she wrote each of the songs for and recorded *Songs of a Love Affair,* arguably

the first concept album in country music history. Though she continued to record and tour during the late '50s and early '60s, she didn't return to the Top Ten until 1964—one year after her husband Hawkshaw Hawkins died in the same plane crash that killed Patsy Cline—with "Second Fiddle (To an Old Guitar)." The song began a string of hits that continued into the 1970s. Shepard continued to record during the '80s and '90s, particularly in the UK, where she had a strong fan base.—*Dan Cooper & Stephen Thomas Erlewine*

- **Honky Tonk Heroine** / Dec. 1995 / Country Music Foundation ✦✦✦✦✦
At a time when most of her contemporaries were heading down the country-pop route, Jean Shepard was one of the few female honky tonk singers to stay true to the genre in the '50s and '60s. The definitive *Honky Tonk Heroine: Classic Capitol Recordings, 1952-1962* is a terrific anthology of her peak years. Most of her biggest hits are included, as are a handful of rarities that should delight casual fans as much as dedicated fans. —*Stephen Thomas Erlewine*

T.G. Sheppard (Brian Stacy)

b. Jul. 20, 1944, Humboldt, TN
Vocals, Guitar / Urban Cowboy, Country-Pop
After working his way through the record industry, T.G. Sheppard emerged in the mid-'70s as one of the leading country-pop singers, bringing the music closer to the rock-influenced, cosmopolitain sounds of urban cowboy. A native of Humboldt, Tennessee, Sheppard headed off to Memphis after high school, getting involved in the record business on several different levels. He tried recording as a pop artist, and even signed with Atlantic Records under the name Brian Stacy, opening shows for the Beach Boys. A few years later, he took a job with a Memphis record distributor, then ended up in record promotion, where the job entailed calling radio stations and trying to persuade them to play his company's records. In that capacity for RCA, he helped break Elvis Presley's "Suspicious Minds," Perry Como's "It's Impossible," and John Denver's "Take Me Home Country Roads." After "going independent," he came across a demo tape of "Devil in the Bottle." He tried to talk a number of artists into doing the song, and when no one was interested, he decided to do it himself on Motown's fledgling country division, Melodyland Records. Primarily a recitation, "Devil in the Bottle" became a number one hit in 1975, but within three years, the company folded, and Sheppard's career was in limbo. Connecting with record producer Buddy Killen, he signed with Warner, and starting in 1979, the two churned out some of country's best-crafted singles over a four-year period. Sheppard gradually moved away from recitations and grew significantly as a vocalist, though the press often ignored his achievements. He changed producers several times in the mid-'80s and, after a divorce in 1987, took a couple of years off for personal reflection. When he returned, Sheppard found it difficult to regain his earlier momentum. —*Tom Roland*

- **The Best of T.G. Sheppard** / 1992 / Curb ✦✦✦✦✦
You'll have to look for this one at used-record stores. A sampler released only to radio, it covers the half-dozen years up to and including "I Loved 'Em Every One." Some of the performances are a little stiff but it lends appreciation for his improved, later work. —*Tom Roland*

Red Simpson

b. Mar. 6, 1934, Higley, AZ
Vocals / Truck Driving Country, Bakersfield Sound, Traditional Country
Best known for his string of trucking songs, Red Simpson was raised in Bakersfield, California, the youngest of a dozen children. At age 14, he wrote his first song—about chickens—and sang it to his family's fowl. During the Korean War, he served aboard a naval hospital ship, the *Repose*, where he found relief by forming the Repose Ramblers, who played any instruments they could scrounge up. He bought better ones in Japan and began to practice in earnest, and became a professional musician in California after his discharge.

Simpson was working at the Wagon Wheel in Lamont when Fuzzy Owens saw him and arranged for Simpson to work at his Clover Club as a piano player. He then got a job replacing Buck Owens at the Blackboard Club on weekends. Simpson was influenced by Owens, Merle Haggard and Bill Woods, who asked Red if he would write a song about driving trucks. (By the time Simpson handed him four truck songs, however, Woods had stopped recording.) Simpson began writing songs with Buck Owens in 1962, including the Top Ten hit "Gonna Have Love."

In 1965, Capitol's Ken Nelson was looking for someone to record some songs about trucking. His first choice was Haggard, who wasn't interested, but Simpson readily agreed. His first, Tommy Collins's "Roll, Truck, Roll," became a Top 40 country hit and Simpson recorded an album of the same name. That year he offered up two more trucking songs, both of which made it to the Top 50 or beyond. As a songwriter, he scored his first number one hit with "Sam's Place," recorded by Buck Owens. After th3at, Simpson decided to become a full-time writer. He returned to performing in 1971 with his Top Five hit "I'm a Truck," which had been written by postman Bob Staunton.

In 1972, he debuted on the *Grand Ole Opry* and had two more "truck" hits for Capitol. In 1976, Simpson signed to Warner Brothers and released "Truck Driver's Heaven." The following year, he teamed up with Lorraine Walden for a series of duets that included "Truck Driver Man and Wife." In 1979, Simpson appeared for the last time on the charts with "The Flying Saucer Man and the Truck Driver." Haggard recorded his song "Lucky Old Colorado" in 1988; later that year Simpson was diagnosed with skin cancer and underwent surgery, but he fully recovered and continued his writing and performing career. —*Sandra Brennan*

- **The Best of Red Simpson: Country Western Truck Drivin' Singer** / Aug. 24, 1999 / Razor & Tie ✦✦✦✦✦
Country Western Truck Drivin' Singer is an excellent single-disc overview of the '60s and '70s recordings of Red Simpson. His best-known tracks are here, "Highway Patrol" and "I'm a Truck," in addition to 18 others, nearly all of which are about truck driving. If you enjoy trucking songs, there is no better place to go than here; Simpson's nearly single-minded dedication to the genre may be numbing to some, but the entertainment value of these tracks cannot be denied. The possible trials and tribulations of trucking are thoroughly explored, from the logistics of making a U-turn in a big rig to dealing with brake failure while hauling explosives. Those who know "Highway Patrol" from Junior Brown's remake might enjoy the similarities between these two artists. —*Greg Adams*

Ricky Skaggs

b. Jul. 18, 1954, Cordell, KY
Vocals, Mandolin, Guitar, Fiddle, Banjo / Bluegrass-Gospel, New Traditionalist, Progressive Country, Traditional Bluegrass, Progressive Bluegrass
By the time he was in his mid-30s, Kentuckian Ricky Skaggs had already produced a career's worth of music. At age seven he appeared on TV with Flatt & Scruggs; at 15 he was a member of legendary Ralph Stanley's bluegrass band (with fellow teenager, the late Keith Whitley). None of his '80s peers, male or female, had better musical credentials than Ricky. The term "multi-talented" lacks the power to characterize this extraordinary singer and instrumentalist. Not only can he sing and pick with the best in progressive country, his broad and deep experience in traditional music separates him from the crowd. In the estimation of many, he is without peer as a combination vocalist and intrumentalist (guitar, mandolin, fiddle, banjo). After playing with Ralph Stanley for three years, Ricky moved on to progressive bluegrass bands, the Country Gentlemen and J.D. Crowe & the New South. With his own band, Boone Creek, he mixed the old and the new, adding Django Reinhardt. Ricky took Rodney Crowell's place in Emmylou Harris' Hot Band in 1977, and the band's excellent *Roses in the Snow* album showcased Ricky's versatility. Two number one hits came out of his 1981 album *Waiting for the Sun to Shine*, and the awards started arriving. Skaggs is largely responsible for a back-to-basics movement in country music. He showed many that a bluegrass tenor with impeccable taste and enormous talent could sell traditional country in the '80s, a time when pop music had invaded the land of rural rhythm. —*David Vinopal*

Sweet Temptation / 1979 / Sugar Hill ✦✦✦✦✦
With guest vocals by then-boss Emmylou Harris, Skaggs' first solo effort (not counting the Boone Creek project) is equal parts bluegrass and Harris-styled new traditionalism. —*Dan Cooper*

Skaggs & Rice / 1980 / Sugar Hill ✦✦✦✦✦
Skaggs & Rice is a lovely duet album between Ricky Skaggs and Tony Rice. The two musicians run through a number of bluegrass classics, performing them in a spare, simple old-timey style, backed only by their guitar and mandolin. Not only are the performances breathtaking, but the song selection—featuring Bill Monroe classics like "Mansions for Me" and "Tennessee Blues," as well as other standards like "Talk About Suffering" and "Have You Someone in Heaven Awaiting." —*Thom Owens*

Waitin' for the Sun to Shine / 1981 / Epic ✦✦✦
His first album after signing with Epic Records, this one took Skaggs into the mainstream, in effect beginning the new-traditionalist movement. It has a simple, mountain approach, with lots of remakes and Skaggs's mournful vocal tones. The best cut is the plaintive title track. —*Tom Roland*

Family & Friends / 1982 / Rounder ✦✦✦
Skaggs' last breath of pure bluegrass was recorded with help from the Whites, guitarist Peter Rowan, dobroist Jerry Douglas, and others. Included are two songs by Carter Stanley, one by Bill Monroe, and some fine examples of Appalachian gospel, including a stunning a cappella trio vocal on "Talk About Sufferin'." —*Brian Mansfield*

Highways & Heartaches / 1982 / DCC ✦✦✦✦✦
Long a sideman or supporting vocalist in previous situations, Skaggs wasn't totally comfortable with his role as a lead vocalist when he signed with Epic Records. Thanks to a year of touring and greater support from his record label (when Epic signed him, the company honestly didn't think he'd sell more than 100,000 copies of his Epic debut), he had greater confidence vocally the second time around. And the material is more upbeat. —*Tom Roland*

Don't Cheat in Our Hometown / 1983 / Epic ✦✦✦

Country Boy / 1984 / Epic ✦✦✦✦✦
Every one of Ricky Skaggs' albums is a pickin' festival and a country delight. Not only is this one no exception, but it also includes Bill Monroe's "Wheel Hoss" with Monroe himself picking along on mandolin, which earns it a listing here. If you like this album, you'll probably like every other one Skaggs has made. —*William Ruhlmann*

Live in London / 1985 / Epic ✦✦✦✦✦
This is the one Skaggs album to own if you can only have one. Because it's a live recording, the picking is just that much more exciting, and the album serves as an unofficial best-of, its highlights including "Heartbroke," "Uncle Pen," and a version of "Don't Get Above Your Raising" that features noted country fan Elvis Costello. —*William Ruhlmann*

Love's Gonna Get Ya / 1986 / Epic ✦✦✦
Skaggs continued to inch closer to modern mainstream country on *Love's Gonna Get Ya*, which features the hit "Love's Gonna Get You Someday." —*Jason Ankeny*

Comin' Home to Stay / 1988 / Epic ✦✦✦
Comin' Home to Stay marks Skaggs' return to traditional country, and includes "I'm Tired," "Thanks Again" and "(Angel on My Mind) That's Why I'm Walkin'." —*Jason Ankeny*

Kentucky Thunder / 1989 / Epic ✦✦✦
This contains such Skaggs favorites as "Let It Be You, Heartbreak Hurricane," and more. —*AMG*

My Father's Son / 1991 / Epic ✦✦✦
A concept album about families, *My Father's Son* is the Skaggs album that owes the least to bluegrass. Skaggs is concerned with the legacies fathers leave their sons, both the wisdom ("Father Knows Best") and the limitations ("My Father's Son"). He also sees materialism for the distracting, destructive force it is. His duet with Waylon Jennings on "Only Daddy That'll

Walk the Line" fits neatly, though perhaps not the way the writer intended. And because Skaggs' background is bluegrass rather than honky-tonk, every father image is inextricably bound to God. *—Brian Mansfield*

Life Is a Journey / Jul. 29, 1997 / Atlantic ♦♦♦

That's It / Oct. 8, 1997 / Rebel ♦♦♦♦

Bluegrass Rules! / Oct. 21, 1997 / Rounder ♦♦♦♦♦

★ **Country Gentleman: The Best of Ricky Skaggs** / Jan. 27, 1998 / Epic/Legacy ♦♦♦♦♦
Country Gentleman: The Best of Ricky Skaggs is a terrific double-disc set that traces Skaggs' years at Epic Records, which spanned from 1981 to 1991. All of his charting singles are featured on this 32-track collection, including the number one singles "Crying My Heart Out Over You," "I Dont' Care," "Heartbroke," "I Wouldn't Change you If I Could," "Highway 40 Blues," "Uncle Pen" and "Cajun Moon," as well as the Mark O'Connor/New Nashville Cats duet "Restless." Skaggs was one of the few country artists of his era to make albums as good as his singles, but boiling his career down to his singles does him no disservice—in fact, it accentuates the consistant brilliance of his music, not to mention its depth. It's a definitive portrait of one of the most important country musicians of the '80s, capturing him at his peak. *—Stephen Thomas Erlewine*

Ancient Tones / Jan. 26, 1999 / Skaggs Family ♦♦♦♦♦

Soldier of the Cross / Sep. 14, 1999 / Skaggs Family ♦♦♦♦♦

Big Mon / Aug. 29, 2000 / Skaggs Family ♦♦♦

● **16 Biggest Hits** / Sep. 12, 2000 / Epic/Legacy ♦♦♦♦♦
Does *16 Biggest Hits* really contain Ricky Skaggs' 16 biggest hits as measured in the country singles charts— No, it doesn't. It contains his 13 biggest hits, plus three other songs that have special significance for the artist and his audience. Among his top 16 singles are "You Make Me Feel Like a Man," "Love's Gonna Get You Someday," and "Let It Be You," none of which are included here. In their place are "Don't Get Above Your Raising," Skaggs' first Epic single and first significant hit; "You May See Me Walkin'," his first Top Ten hit; and "Wheel Hoss," an album track from his *Country Boy* album written by his mentor, Bill Monroe. It's hard to argue with such substitutions, except to note that they rob the album's title of strict accuracy. The music contained here helped define the new traditionalist movement in country music in the 1980s. Skaggs, a top instrumentalist steeped in bluegrass, found a formula at the start of that decade which combined a heavy emphasis on traditional playing with a fresh approach that didn't violate the old-time sound so much as extend it. Trends come and go, and after Skaggs' style passed from mass popularity he predictably returned to the traditional style from which he had emerged, but not before he had reinvigorated country music with the hits heard on this album, which stands as an excellent introduction to his most popular work. *—William Ruhlmann*

Carl Smith

b. Mar. 15, 1927, Maynardsville, TN
Vocals, Guitar / Western Swing Revival, Honky Tonk, Traditional Country
Known as "Mr. Country," Carl Smith was one of the most popular honky tonkers of the '50s, racking up over 30 Top Ten hits over the course of the decade. Smith was also able to sustain that popularity into the late '70s, during which time he had a charting single for every year except one. Smith had a talent for singing smooth ballads which polished the rough edges of hardcore country. Neverthless, he could sing pure honky tonk with the best of them, and his hardest country was made tougher by the addition of a drum kit. Smith was one of the very first country artists to regularly perform with a drummer, and though it earned him criticism at the time, the hard-driving sound of those uptempo numbers proved to be influential. Smith also occasionally dabbled in Western Swing, and as he continued to record, he delved deeper into the genre. Since he specialized in honky tonk ballads and western swing, Smith rarely crossed over into the pop audience. Still, he was one of the most popular and best-known country singers of his era, recording several classics—including "Let's Live a Little," "Let Old Mother Nature Have Her Way," "This Orchard Means Goodbye," "Cut Across Shorty," "Loose Talk," "(When You Feel like You're in Love) Don't Just Stand There" and "Hey Joe!"—appeaing a handful of movies, and hosting his own television show. By the time he retired in the early '80s, he had hit the country charts nearly 100 times. *—Stephen Thomas Erlewine*

The Best of Carl Smith / 1991 / Curb ♦♦♦

★ **The Essential Carl Smith (1950-1956)** / 1991 / Columbia/Legacy ♦♦♦♦♦
The Essential Carl Smith (1950-1956) collects 20 tracks from the height of Smith's career, including classics like "Are You Teasing Me," "If Teardrops Were Pennies," "(When You Feel Like You're In Love) Don't Just Stand There," "Hey, Joe," "Back Up Buddy," and "Loose Talk." Smith bridged the gap between raw honky tonk and smoother Nashville pop and these sides capture him at his very best. *—Stephen Thomas Erlewine*

Satisfaction Guaranteed / 1996 / Bear Family ♦♦♦♦♦
Every song that Carl Smith recorded during the '50s is included on *Satisfaction Guaranteed*, a five-disc, 143-track box set that stands as the most comprehensive retrospective of the honky tonk star's peak period. During the era that *Satisfaction Guaranteed* covers, Smith scored more Top 10 hits than either Hank Williams or Lefty Frizzell, and many of his best songs—"Loose Talk," "Let Old Mother Nature Have Her Way," "Hey Joe!," "Are You Teasing Me," and "(When You Feel Like You're In Love) Don't Just Stand There," among them—are stone-cold honky tonk classics. For serious Smith and honky tonk fans, the set is essential, but the sheer length of the box—not to mention its strict chronological sequence—is tedious for anyone that isn't willing to dedicate the time to plow through the abundance of material here. *—Stephen Thomas Erlewine*

Connie Smith

b. Aug. 14, 1941, Elkhart, IN
Vocals, Guitar / Country Gospel, CCM, Country-Pop
In less than a year, Connie Smith moved from being a small-town Ohio housewife to country stardom with a number one single to her credit. Perhaps overly compared to and identified with Patsy Cline, Smith is still considered by many to be one of the best, most underrated, vocalists in country history. Her lonely desperation came straight from the heart, also: her father was abusive when she was a child, causing Smith to suffer a mental breakdown while she was in her teens. Discovered by Bill Anderson in 1963, she signed to RCA and earned a number one hit—for eight weeks running—with her first single, "Once a Day" (written for her by Anderson). Her Top Ten streak continued unabated until late 1968, including big hits like "If I Talk to Him," "Ain't Had No Lovin'" and "The Hurtin's All Over." That year, she cut her schedule back due to the pressures of being a country star, but continued to hit the Top Ten occasionally during the early '70s. She also began incorporating more gospel into her act and signed with Columbia to record straight gospel songs. Though she has not been a commercial force since the '70s, Connie Smith continued to perform with the *Grand Ole Opry*, and in 1998 returned with her first LP in many years, a self-titled effort issued on Warner Bros. *—John Bush*

Connie Smith [RCA] / 1965 / RCA ♦♦♦♦♦
Cut in Music City, Smith's first LP (which includes "Once a Day") features her blowing through the Nashville Sound production like a down-home Streisand fronting The Lennon Sisters. *—Dan Cooper*

Soul of Country Music / 1968 / RCA ♦♦♦
More of the same unearthly sound, but this has Smith covering—at times burying—other singers' hits. Her version of Rex Griffin's "The Last Letter" is almost literally to die for. *—Dan Cooper*

Back in Baby's Arms / 1969 / RCA ♦♦♦♦♦
If any Thomas ever doubted Smith's religious convictions (which are as much a part of her story as her voice is) one listen to this LP's "How Great Thou Art" should take care of that mistrust. *—Dan Cooper*

★ **The Essential Connie Smith** / Apr. 1996 / RCA ♦♦♦♦♦
The Essential Connie Smith is the only thorough compilation of her '60s hits for RCA, featuring all of her Top 10 hits—including the number one "Once A Day," "If I Talk to Him," "Ain't Had No Lovin'," "Then and Only Then," "Burning A Hole in My Mind," "Just One Time," and "Nobody But A Fool (Would Love You)"—and a selection of her lesser-known material. *—Thom Owens*

Sammi Smith

b. Aug. 5, 1943, Orange, CA
Vocals / Outlaw Country, Country-Pop, Progressive Country
In the tradition of Waylon Jennings and Willie Nelson, singer/songwriter Sammi Smith was considered a country music outlaw, unafraid to sing songs that reflected the sometimes gritty realities of modern life. She first came to fame singing Kris Kristofferson's "Help Me Make It Through the Night" and was noted for her husky voice, the result of spending many years singing in smoke-filled clubs.

She was born Jewel Fay Smith in California, but spent her childhood living in different southwestern states. At age 11, Smith dropped out of school and the following year began singing professionally in clubs. She married at age 15 and produced four children. At songwriter Gene Sullivan's urging, a newly-divorced Smith moved to Nashville in 1967. A year later she had her first minor hit, "So Long, Charlie Brown, Don't Look for Me Around." In 1970, she had another minor hit, but it was not until the end of the year that she had her first major smash with "Help Me Make It Through the Night," which made it to the top of the country charts and also became a Top Ten pop hit. Later that year, she wrote "Cedartown, Georgia," which became a major hit for Waylon Jennings.

In 1973, Smith moved to Dallas to join Jennings and Willie Nelson and become an "outlaw." Through 1975, she had several hits including "Then You Walk In" and "Today I Started Loving You Again." She moved to Elektra in 1975 and remained with them for three years. During that time, she had several chart entries with such songs as "Loving Arms," "Days That End in 'Y'" (both 1977) and "Norma Jean" (1978), a tribute to Marilyn Monroe. In 1979, she signed to the independent label Cyclone and had a Top 20 hit with "What a Lie," In 1980, she moved to Sound Factory and had one Top 40 and two Top 20 hits including "I Cry When I'm Alone." Her last hit came in 1986 with "Love Me All Over." *—Sandra Brennan*

● **The Best of Sammi Smith** / Oct. 22, 1996 / Varese Sarabande ♦♦♦♦
The 16-track *The Best of Sammi Smith: Help Me Make it Through the Night* is the most comprehensive retrospective of Smith's prime hit-making years of the early '70s, featuring all of her biggest hits, including "Help Me Make It Through the Night" and "Then You Walk In." *—Stephen Thomas Erlewine*

Hank Snow (Clarence Eugene Snow)

b. May 9, 1914, Liverpool, Nova Scotia, Canada, **d.** Dec. 20, 1999
Vocals, Guitar / Country Boogie, Honky Tonk, Cowboy, Traditional Country
Canada's greatest contribution to country music, Hank Snow was famous for his "travelling" songs. It's no wonder. At age 12 he ran away from his Nova Scotia home and joined the Merchant Marines, working as a cabin boy and laborer for four years. Once back on shore, he listened to Jimmie Rodgers records and started playing in public, building up a following in Halifax. His original nickname, the Yodelling Ranger, was modified to the Singing Ranger when his high voice changed to the great baritone that graced his hit records. In 1950, the year he became an Opry regular, his self-penned "I'm Moving On" (the first of his many great travelling songs) became a smash hit, reaching number one and remaining their for 21 weeks. "Golden Rocket" (also 1950) and "I've Been Everywhere" (1962), two other hits, show his life-long love for trains and travel. But he was as much at home with two other styles, the ballad and the rhumba/boogie. Among his many great ballads are "Bluebird Island" (with Anita Carter, of the Carter Family), "Fool Such as I," and "Hello, Love" a hit when Snow was 60 years old. Snow appeared regularly on the Opry into the '90s, proving that his incredible

voice suffered no loss of quality over the last half-century, as well as what a tasteful, understated guitar stylist he is. With small stature and huge voice, Snow is a country traditionalist who has given much more to the business than he's taken. *—David Vinopal*

The Singing Ranger: 1949-1953 / 1989 / Bear Family ✦✦✦✦✦
Bear Family's *The Singing Ranger: 1949-1953* contains every song Hank Snow recorded for RCA in the beginning of his career. Not only are career-making songs like "I'm Movin' On," "Marriage Vow," and "The Rhumba Boogie" included, but so is a wealth of unreleased songs and alternate takes. For diehard Hank Snow fans, this first volume of *The Singing Ranger* series is the most essential of the three. *—Stephen Thomas Erlewine*

★ **I'm Movin' On & Other Country Hits** / 1990 / RCA ✦✦✦✦✦
I'm Movin' On & Other Hits doesn't have all the hits Hank Snow had over the course of his career, but it has 20 essential tracks from the early '50s, including "The Rhumba Boogie," "Silver Bell," "The Wreck of the Old '97," "Marriage Vow," and the title track. These are the songs that made his career and while he had decades worth of other hits, this disc gives you an accurate sense of what Snow accomplished. *—Stephen Thomas Erlewine*

The Singing Ranger, Vol. 2 / 1990 / Bear Family ✦✦✦✦✦
Running from 1953 to 1958, the four-disc box set *The Singing Ranger, Vol. 2* contains everything Hank Snow recorded during those five years, including all the hits and a bevy of outtakes. Again, the set is not for the fairweather fan—there's plenty of brilliant music here, but its very scope makes it appealing only to completists, who will find much to treasure. *—Stephen Thomas Erlewine*

The Thesaurus Transcriptions / 1991 / Bear Family ✦✦✦✦✦
Bear Family's five-disc box set *The Thesaurus Transcriptions* contains 138 radio transcriptions that Hank Snow cut during the early '50s, when he was one of the biggest stars in country. Many of these songs were never recorded in the studio, and Snow is in superb voice throughout the set. It's not a set for neophytes or casual fans, but those diehard fans and historians willing to invest in such a mammoth box will find it fascinating. *—Stephen Thomas Erlewine*

The Singing Ranger, Vol. 3 / 1994 / Bear Family ✦✦✦✦✦
Singing Ranger, Vol. 3 picks up where the second box set left off and presents the final recordings Hank Snow ever made. The box is extremely lengthy, running a total of 12 discs and spanning all of his '60s output, and contains less first-rate material than Bear Family's other three box sets, but it remains necessary for completists. *—Stephen Thomas Erlewine*

Yodelling Ranger (1936-1947) / 1994 / Bear Family ✦✦✦✦✦
The Yodelling Ranger (1936-1947) is a five-disc box set containing all of Hank Snow's early recordings, including all of his material for RCA Canada and several unreleased songs, alternate takes and rarities. This material is primarily of interest to hardcore Snow fans—there aren't many well-known hits on the collection, but there are good versions of contemporary hits, as well as several answer records—but for those dedicated listeners, the set's comprehensiveness and loving liner notes are a worthwhile investment. Consumer warning: the fifth disc contains just four tracks—a two-part "Life Story" and two demos. *—Thom Owens*

★ **The Essential Hank Snow** / Apr. 29, 1997 / RCA ✦✦✦✦✦
In 1997, *The Essential Hank Snow* replaced *I'm Movin' On & Other Country Hits* as the one essential, single-disc retrospective of Snow's classic hits currently on the market. While it isn't quite as listenable as its direct predecessor, *The Essential* still captures all of Snow's styles, from Hawaiian music and country boogie to his famous traveling songs, featuring most of his best-known songs ("I'm Moving On," "The Rhumba Boogie," "Yellow Roses," "Silver Bell," "The Gal Who Invented Kissin'") along the way. *—Stephen Thomas Erlewine*

Yodelling Ranger: Young Hank Snow 1936-1943 / Mar. 16, 1999 / Bear Family ✦✦✦✦

The Sons of the Pioneers

f. 1934
Group / Cowboy, Traditional Country
The Sons of the Pioneers were the foremost vocal and instrumental group in Western music and cowboy songs, setting the standard with their superb harmonies and brilliant arrangements. They were also one of the longest-surviving country vocal groups in existence, going into their seventh decade. Formed in Los Angeles, the earliest group consisted of Leonard Slye, Bob Nolan, and Tim Spencer on vocals, with Nolan playing string bass and Slye on rhythm guitar. Fiddle player Hugh Farr joined early in 1934, adding a bass voice. Thanks to radio syndication, the Sons of the Pioneers' fame spread quickly, and it wasn't long before they made their first commercial recording for Decca. In 1935, Farr's brother Karl was added on lead guitar; Lloyd Perryman joined in 1936 and eventually did most of their vocal arrangements. In 1938, Slye—renamed Roy Rogers—won a starring role in a Western film; he was replaced by singer and comic Pat Brady. This version of the group, which lasted until 1942, became the "classic," most familiar Pioneers lineup. In 1941, Republic Pictures signed the Pioneers to appear in Roy Rogers' movies, and in 1944, the group moved to RCA-Victor. Previously, they'd been a self-contained outfit, but RCA provided additional backup, including small-scale orchestration. The Pioneers re-recorded several of their standards (including "Cool Water" and "Tumbling Tumbleweeds") with new arrangements; many fans regard these as the best versions. They also recorded a number of new Western classics and hit country singles, and continued working on Roy Rogers' movies through 1948. However, time and changing public tastes took their toll. Spencer and Nolan both left in 1949; RCA attempted to push the Pioneers into the pop vocal market, but these efforts failed, and lost part of their country audience. Still, the group remained a going concern. In 1976, the Sons of the Pioneers were inducted into the Country Music Hall of Fame, a last hurrah for the early members—many had passed away by the early '80s. Dale Warren, who had joined in 1952, carried the group into the '90s; they continued to perform and record. *—Bruce Eder*

☆ **Columbia Historic Edition** / 1982 / Columbia ✦✦✦✦✦
The Sons of the Pioneers' sides for the American Record Company are their least-known body of material—in contrast to their Decca and RCA Victor sides, which have been heavily exploited on CD at various times. This ten-song collection is still the only way to hear their work for the American Record Company, representing not a third of their output on the label. All sides of the group's output are represented, including cowboy and trail songs, gospel tunes and one hot instrumental. Although he'd officially left the group earlier, Leonard Slye (aka Roy Rogers) sang on several of the numbers recorded during the October and December 1937 sessions from which these songs were drawn. Bob Nolan's lead singing makes him a dominant presence (and he gets a solo vocal number here too), but Slye's singing and especially his yodeling on "The Devil's Great Grandson" and his solo number "Cowboy Night Herd Song" give him a chance to show off his abilities to great advantage. Hugh Farr and Karl Farr get to stand in the spotlight with their instrumental virtuosity as well, most notably on "When the Golden Train Comes Down" and "Cajun Stomp," which is essentially their number. The restoration job on these masters—held by the Country Music Foundation—is extraordinary, and the fidelity is a match for recordings made decades later. Columbia Legacy, which owns the American Record Company library, could find a way to be more generous in the programming, but this is one killer CD as it is. *—Bruce Eder*

★ **Country Music Hall of Fame** / 1991 / MCA ✦✦✦✦✦
The most perfect collection of the Sons of the Pioneers' early work—which is their best work—currently available, 16 songs, half of which were recorded during the early and mid-1930's by the original group of Bob Nolan, Tim Spencer, and Roy Rogers (then known as Leonard Slye), and Lloyd Perryman, and Hugh and Karl Farr. No collection of theirs could open with anything stronger than the first two songs the Pioneers ever cut, "Way Out There" and the original, never-to-be-duplicated versions "Tumbling Tumbleweeds." They and the original version of "Cool Water" all rely on the Pioneers' three-part harmonies and their own instruments (acoustic guitars, fiddle, upright bass) and sounding like musical gold pouring out of a portal from another age. Some of the songs are topical and, in their way, rather poignant reminders of the Great Depression, such as "When Our Old Age Pension Check Comes To Our Door." Other highlights include "There's A Round-Up In the Sky," "Ride Ranger Ride," "Private Buckaroo" (a topical song about World War II), "When the Moon Comes Over Sun Valley," and one previously unreleased gospel gem from their 1954 stay at Coral Records, "Somebody Bigger Than You and I." *—Bruce Eder*

Wagons West / 1996 / Bear Family ✦✦✦✦✦
Wagons West is a thorough four-disc box set containing 115 songs the Sons of the Pioneers recorded for RCA/Victor during the '40s, when the group was at the height of their popularity. Containing all of their best-known songs and hits like "Cool Water," "Stars and Stripes on Iwo Jima," and "Tumbling Tumbleweeds," plus several unreleased tracks and alternate takes, the set is the most complete portrait of the group's peak that has ever been drawn. Of course, the sheer length and weight of the set means that only musicologists and diehard fans will find *Wagons West* consistently compelling, yet it still stands as one of the most essential—and comprehensive—western and cowboy box sets ever assembled. *—Thom Owens*

Songs of the Prairie / Nov. 25, 1998 / Bear Family ✦✦✦✦
The title of this stunning five-CD set is a bit misleading, for it contains gospel, Civil War, blues, square dance and classic (19th century) popular tunes, as well as cowboy songs. And it's an extraordinary addition to the Sons of the Pioneers' output, 151 transcriptions done for Standard Radio, of Los Angeles, between 1934 and 1936, the prime early years in the group's history—it's as though 151 Beatles songs from their first year of existence had suddenly turned up—and these have almost all been unheard for more than 60 years. The first four discs offer Sons of the Pioneers as a quartet, Bob Nolan, Tim Spencer, Len Slye and Hugh Farr, in their first flourish of success, beginning in August of 1934. The performances here are different from, and usually more spirited than, the group's Decca recordings. "Way Out There" is a number that the group cut commercially several times over as its lineup changed, but it never sounded fresher than the version here. Another joy of this set is the spotlight given to Hugh Farr—the violinist is showcased in a series of instrumentals, including "Milenburg Joys," "Fire in the Mountains," and "Whistlin' Rufus." And then there is the treat of the fourth and fifth discs, which feature the five-man group line-up, with guitar virtuoso Karl Farr; all of a sudden, the group's playing rises to the level of its singing, from impressive to downright dazzling as the Farr brothers become a pair of dual spark plugs in the instrumental mix. Some tracks are in slightly rough condition, but considering that these discs, according to the contracts under which they were licensed, were supposed to be destroyed at the end of their licensing term, just having them around to hear is something close to miraculous. *—Bruce Eder*

Souther Hillman Furay Band

f. 1973, Los Angeles, CA
Group / Country-Rock
Formed in 1973 at the urging of Asylum Records president David Geffen, Souther-Hillman-Furay was the offspring of just about every notable country-rock band. Richie Furay was a founding member of both Buffalo Springfield and Poco; Chris Hillman had been with the Byrds, the Flying Burrito Brothers, and Stephen Stills' Manassas; and J.D. Souther formed Longbranch Pennywhistle with Eagle Glenn Frey, as well as recording a solo record for Asylum and penning tunes for artists like Linda Ronstadt, Bonnie Raitt, and the Eagles. S-H-F's supporting cast also came with impressive credentials, including studio stalwart Paul Harris on piano, Al Perkins (Flying Burrito Brothers, Manassas) on pedal steel guitar, and former Derek & the Dominos drummer Jim Gordon, who also wrote the piano piece that concludes "Layla."

Although the band, which was meant to be a sort of country-rock version of Crosby, Stills & Nash, received a great deal of hype and promotion, things never really gelled. Their debut sold reasonably well, but the aptly titled *Trouble in Paradise* was poorly received. S-H-F broke up shortly thereafter with each member going on to solo careers. Souther released a couple of solo efforts, achieving a minor success with "You're Only Lonely"; Hillman recorded unsuccessfully for Asylum before teaming with former Byrd-mates Roger McGuinn and Gene Clark in McGuinn, Clark, and Hillman, and then forming the popular country-rock

Desert Rose Band; and Furay, who became a minister in Colorado, made three Christian-influenced abums, as well as rejoining Poco for their 20th-anniversary recording. *—Brett Hartenbach*

● **The Souther, Hillman, Furay Band** / 1974 / Asylum ♦♦♦♦
An occassionally pleasant, but for the most part disappointing debut. The chemistry is never really there between the three, but Furay probably comes closest to living up to his past accomplishments with the Poco-like rocker, "Fallin' in Love," and the ballad "Believe Me." *Souther-Hillman-Furay Band* is a relatively lightweight country-rock, singer/songwriter affair that may appeal to fans. *—Brett Hartenbach*

Trouble in Paradise / 1975 / Line ♦♦♦

Red Sovine

b. Jul. 17, 1918, Charleston, WV, **d.** Apr. 4, 1980, Nashville, TN
Vocals, Guitar / Honky Tonk, Traditional Country
Though he had a long, distinguished career in country music, singer/songwriter and guitarist Red Sovine is best remembered for his earnest, funny and, at times, highly sentimental odes to the life of the American trucker. After several unsuccessful starts to his music career, Sovine developed a large following as a radio host in Alabama. With help from none other than Hank Williams, he landed a contract with MGM Records in 1949. Though he never hit the charts, he signed to Decca in 1954 and hit number one a year later as a duet with friend Webb Pierce on George Jones' "Why Baby Why." A few minor hits followed, but Sovine never really found his niche until 1966, when he recorded "Giddy-up Go," his very first spoken-word truck driver song. The single spent six weeks atop the country charts and even crossed over to become a minor pop hit. Subsequent truck-driving hits included the ghost story "Phantom 309" and the tearjerking tale of a crippled child's CB-radio relationship with caring truckers, "Teddy Bear." The latter was his biggest hit since "Giddyup Go," spending three weeks at the top of the country charts in 1976 and reaching number 40 on the pop charts. His last big hit was "Little Joe," after which Sovine died in 1980 as the result of a heart attack on the road. *—Sandra Brennan*

● **The Best of Red Sovine** / 1995 / TeeVee ♦♦♦♦
A true mixed blessing here. Oh, the packaging is an absolute disgrace, nothing past the gnarly photo of Red adorning the cover, no liner notes, recording, or publishing information to be found anywhere—just a cryptic listing of the 20 tracks on the back. But once you pop the disc into the player, you're rewarded with 20 of Red's best Starday sides, all presented in the most sparkling sound, the majority of them sporting vivid stereo mixes. If you run across this one in a budget bin somewhere, it's definitely worth the investment, crummy packaging and all. *—Cub Koda*

Jim Stafford

b. Jan. 16, 1944, Eloise, FL
Vocals, Keyboards, Guitar, Banjo / AM Pop, Country Comedy, Country-Pop
Multi-talented entertainer Jim Stafford remains best remembered for the novelty songs he released in the 1970s, particularly the single "Spiders & Snakes," which made him an international star. He started out playing dance clubs, where he offered humorous running commentaries on the skills of the go-go dancers. He was performing in Clearwater, FL when he reunited with Nashville friend Lobo; Stafford asked him to perform his song "Swamp Witch," but Lobo convinced Stafford to perform it himself. The song eventually made its way to Mike Curb, who signed Stafford to MGM Records. The single was released in 1973 and became a Top 40 pop hit. Stafford then released "Spiders & Snakes," which was a smash hit on both the pop and country charts and went gold in 1974. His next hit was the playful "My Girl Bill," which did better on the pop charts than the country charts. He had two more hits, "Wildwood Weed" and "Your Bulldog Drinks Champagne." In 1975, he hosted the summer replacement series *The Jim Stafford Show;* although Stafford's quirky songs brought him fame, the show gave him a chance to showcase his exceptional ability as a guitar player. *—Sandra Brennan*

● **Jim Stafford** / 1974 / Polydor ♦♦♦♦♦

Joe Stampley

b. Jun. 6, 1943, Springhill, LA
Vocals / Urban Cowboy, Honky Tonk, Country Comedy, Country-Pop, Traditional Country
Joe Stampley has had a career that spans the genres and styles of music and entertainment. Born in Louisiana and raised on his father's Hank Williams records, Stampley began playing piano before the age of ten, and by the age of 15 he was recording demos with a local DJ named Merle Kilgore. The demos went nowhere, however, and neither did a 1961 session with the Chess label, but Kilgore was able to score a smooth R&B hit with a group he had formed called the Uniques. The song, 1966's "Not Too Long Ago," was a regional hit in the south, but the group was unable to capture any momentum and soon Stampley was changing gears again and making in-roads into the country music establishment. A Nashville publishing house, Algee Music, gave Stampley a contract and Algee head Al Gallico helped get the singer a recording contract with Paramount. Blending country and soul, Stampley had hits with 1971's "Take Time to Know Her" and "If You Touch Me You've Got to Love Me." Though his smooth sound virtually defined the countrypolitan movement of the mid-'70s, Stampley changed gears once more when he started writing rougher, hard-edged honky tonk songs such as "Whiskey Chasin." Yet Stampley still had other tricks up his sleeve, and in 1979 he teamed up with Moe Brandy to form a tongue-in-cheek comedy duo. The pair, known as Moe and Joe, had hits with songs such as "Just Good Ole Boys" and the ridiculous "Hey Joe (Hey Moe)" before falling off the cultural radar. *—Steve Kurutz*

● **The Best of Joe Stampley** / 1995 / Varese Sarabande ♦♦♦♦♦
18 songs from the '70s, most of them big country hits, drawing primarily from his recordings for Dot in the early part of the decade (including his version of "The Most Beautiful Girl"). Also includes the number-one hits he cut after leaving Dot for Epic, "Roll On, Big Mama" and "Just Good Ol' Boys." *—Richie Unterberger*

Good Ol' Boy: His Greatest Hits / 1995 / Razor & Tie ♦♦♦♦♦
While Varese's *The Best of Joe Stampley* covers his ABC/Dot recordings, Razor & Tie's *Good Old Boy: The Greatest Hits* concentrates on the singer's big hits for Epic Records during the latter half of the '70s. Though his Dot and ABC records were harder country and bigger hits, the Epic singles were often just as good, as this collection demonstrates. Boasting such hits as "Red Wine and Blue Memories," "If You've Got Ten Minutes (Let's Fall in Love)," "Do You Ever Fool Around," "Put Your Clothes Back On," and the Moe Bandy duet "Just Good Ol' Boys," *Good Old Boy* is an excellent overview of the latter half of Stampley's career. *—Stephen Thomas Erlewine*

The Statler Brothers

f. 1955, Staunton, VA
Vocals / Country Gospel, Country-Pop, Traditional Country
Named after a brand of tissues, the four members of the Statler Brothers did not in fact share a fraternal bond; what they did share, however, was the distinction of being one of the most successful vocal harmony groups in the history of country music. The Statlers signed to Columbia Records in 1964, and a year later scored a huge country and pop hit with "Flowers on the Wall." 1967's *The Statler Brothers Sing the Big Hits* held true to its title's promise, generating a pair of Top Ten singles in "Ruthless" and "You Can't Have Your Kate and Edith, Too." In 1969, the quartet moved to Mercury Records, where they remained for over two decades; their first single for the label, 1970's "Bed of Rose's," was a Top Ten hit. Throughout the first half of the 1970s, the Statlers remained fixtures on the Top 40 charts thanks to a string of nostalgic singles like 1972's "Do You Remember These" and "The Class of '57," 1973's "Carry Me Back," and 1974's "Whatever Happened to Randolph Scott." They earned their first chart-topper in 1978 with "Do You Know You Are My Sunshine." In 1982, co-founder Lew DeWitt was forced to leave the group as a result of Crohn's disease; the illness ultimately killed him on August 15, 1990. The remaining Statlers tapped Jimmy Fortune as his successor, and immediately Fortune earned the group its second Number One with his "Elizabeth." Their next two LPs, 1984's *Atlanta Blue* and 1985's *Pardners in Crime,* were credited to simply the Statlers; each record generated a Number One hit—"My Only Love" and "Too Much on My Heart," respectively—again composed by Fortune. 1989's "More Than a Name on the Wall," which peaked at Number Six, was their last significant hit. They continued releasing albums, however, and in addition to remaining a popular touring act in the 1990s, the Statler Brothers also hosted a long-running variety show on TNN. *—Jason Ankeny*

Bed of Rose's / 1971 / Mercury ♦♦♦♦♦
In addition to the hit title track, the Statlers' Mercury debut *Bed of Roses* features the quartet's takes on Kris Kristofferson's "Me and Bobby McGee" and Ernest Tubb's "Tomorrow Never Comes." *—Jason Ankeny*

☆ **The Best of the Statler Brothers** / 1975 / Mercury ♦♦♦♦♦
The Statlers' first decade of recording is recalled in their initial *Best Of* collection. The compilation includes all of the quartet's biggest Mercury hits from the first half of the 1970s, including "Do You Remember These," "I'll Go to My Grave Loving You," and "Bed of Rose's." However, only one song from their late-'60s tenure at Columbia—the classic "Flowers on the Wall"—makes the cut. *—Jason Ankeny*

The Best of the Statler Brothers, Vol. 2 / 1980 / Mercury ♦♦♦♦♦
Released just four years after their first hits collection, *The Best of the Statler Bros. Rides Again Volume II* collects their biggest singles from the bottom half of the 1970s. In addition to "Do You Know You Are My Sunshine, " and the group's first number one, the collection features "Who Am I to Say," "How to Be a Country Star," and "The Official Historian on Shirley Jean Berrell." *—Jason Ankeny*

30th Anniversary Celebration / Nov. 21, 1995 / Mercury ♦♦♦♦♦
A 30th Anniversary Celebration is three-disc compilation covering the Statler Brothers' entire career, from their early days at Columbia to their hit-making peak at Mercury. Over the course of 62 tracks, all 27 of their Top 10 hits—including "Flowers on the Wall," "Do You Remember These," "The Class of '57," "Do You Know You Are My Sunshine," "Who Am I To Say," "Oh Baby Mine (I Get So Lonely)," "Elizabeth," "My Only Love" and "Too Much On My Heart"—are featured, as are a handful of lesser-known gems. For any fan of the group, this is an essential purchase, since it is a lovingly-produced, definitive retrospective of the Statlers' best-known material. In fact, it may be all the Statlers most listeners will ever need to own. *—Thom Owens*

★ **Flowers on the Wall: The Essential Statler Brothers** / Mar. 1996 / Columbia/Legacy ♦♦♦♦♦
The Statler Brothers started their recording career at Columbia Records and cut eight albums for the label in five years, scoring eight country singles chart entries, including the Top Ten hits "Ruthless," "You Can't Have Your Kate and Edith, Too," and the pop Top Ten crossover "Flowers on the Wall." This 18-track compilation includes all those hits, along with standards like "The Wreck of the Old '97," "Green Grass," and the gospel pop song "Oh Happy Day," and one previously unreleased track, "Half a Man," which, despite having been recorded two years later, sounds like the logical follow-up to "Flowers on the Wall." The influence of the Statlers' employer, Johnny Cash, is apparent, especially on "Hammer and Nails," on which he appears. At this early stage, without losing the sound of the classic country quartet, the Statlers also sang pop, folk, and gospel well. The only complaint to be made about this set is that, in the CD age, a running time of 42:15 is short for a compilation (if typical of country music). But nothing essential is missing. *—William Ruhlmann*

Ray Stevens (Harold Ray Ragsdale)

b. Jan. 24, 1939, Clarkdale, GA
Vocals, Piano / AM Pop, Country Comedy, Country-Pop, Novelty
Singer/songwriter/multi-instrumentalist Ray Stevens found fame as a performer of novelty and parody songs. Stevens hooked up with Mercury in 1961 and had his first chart success with the advertising parody "Jerimiah Peabody's Poly Unsaturated Quick Dissolving Fast Act-

ing Pleasant Tasting Green and Purple Pills," which climbed to the Top 40 on the pop charts. His next release, "Ahab the Arab" (1962), made Stevens a bonafide star and was a Top Five pop hit. His career really didn't take off until 1969 with the Top Ten pop parody "Gitarzan," which became his first gold record and was followed by the Top 30 hit "Along Came Jones." In the early '70s, Stevens had an international chart-topper with "Everything Is Beautiful," which became his second gold record and made the pop and country charts. In 1971, he had a major country hit with a more serious tune, "Turn Your Radio On," and his novelty number "Bridget the Midget" was also successful. He also had a number one pop and number three country hit with "The Streak." His final pop hit was "I Need Your Help, Barry Manilow" (1979). In 1980, he began to concentrate on country novelty songs, and had a big hit with "Shriner's Convention." Other major hits from the '80s included "Mississippi Squirrel Revival" and "It's Me Again Margaret." *—Sandra Brennan*

Gitarzan / 1969 / Varese Sarabande ♦♦♦
Stevens plies his stock-in-trade pop novelties on this 1969 album, replete with hayseed monologues, skilled mimicry of various voices (spoken and sung), and Vegas-soul female backup singers. It sounds hokey now—and probably sounded hokey then—but not to everyone, as the title track made the Top Ten, and the remake of the Coasters' "Along Came Jones" made the Top Thirty. The rest of the album's divided between Stevenized covers of vintage rock novelties ("Yakety Yak," "Alley Oop") and satirical originals that ensured his stature as the Top 40's answer to *Hee Haw.* The CD reissue adds three bonus tracks, including "Bridget the Midget," a small hit from 1970, and "The Streak," his number one single from 1974. Better than anything else on the disc, though, is his 1974 single "The Moonlight Special" (included here). This satire of DJ Wolfman Jack's TV show is actually genuinely funny in places, complete with spot-on send-ups of Jerry Lee Lewis and a Gladys Knight-type soul group. *—Richie Unterberger*

His All-Time Greatest Comic Hits / 1990 / Curb ♦♦♦

● **The Best of Ray Stevens** / Sep. 16, 1997 / Rhino ♦♦♦♦
Rhino's *The Best of Ray Stevens* is a thorough overview of the vocalist/comedian's peak, containing 20 tracks recorded between 1961 and 1977. All of his best-known songs, from "The Streak" to "Everything Is Beautiful," are included on this single disc, making it the one definitive Ray Stevens compilation. *—Stephen Thomas Erlewine*

B.W. Stevenson

b. Oct. 5, 1949, Dallas, TX, **d.** Apr. 28, 1988
Vocals, Guitar / AM Pop, Soft Rock, Country-Pop, Country-Rock
Best remembered for his 1973 smash "My Maria," singer/songwriter B.W. Stevenson (the "B.W." reportedly stood for "Buckwheat"—his real first name was Louis) was born October 5, 1949 in Dallas, TX. As a teen he played in a variety of local rock bands before attending college, eventually joining the U.S. Air Force; upon returning from duty Stevenson settled in the Austin area, where he became a frequent attraction on the city's thriving club circuit. Upon signing to RCA he was marketed primarily to country listeners, enjoying little success with either his 1972 self-titled debut or its follow-up *Lead Free;* the title track of 1973's *My Maria,* however, became a Top Ten pop favorite, although ironically it missed the country charts altogether. Stevenson never again recaptured the single's success, and after 1974's *Calabasas* he landed at Warner Bros. to issue *We Be Sailin'* a year later. "Down to the Station," from 1977's *Lost Feeling,* was his last chart hit, and after 1980's *Lifeline* his recording career was over. Sadly, Stevenson died on April 28, 1988 shortly after undergoing heart surgery; he was just 38 years old. *—Jason Ankeny*

● **The Very Best of B.W. Stevenson** / Feb. 8, 2000 / Collectables ♦♦♦♦

Gary Stewart

b. May 28, 1945, Letcher County, KY
Vocals, Piano, Guitar, Bass / Honky Tonk, Country-Rock, Progressive Country, Traditional Country
While much of what passes for contemporary country music these days sounds like reheated Eagles and Lynyrd Skynyrd, what's really annoying is what a youth-driven market it has become, leaving many great country performers of the '60s and '70s out in the cold. This is especially irritating when considering the career of Gary Stewart, one of the greatest of the hardcore honky-tonk school who, at his peak in the mid- to late '70s, could write and sing circles around just about any contemporary country star you can mention. With his huge, vibrato-laden tenor voice (which sounds a bit like Jerry Lee Lewis's), Stewart released 1975's *Out Of Hand,* one of the finest honky-tonk records of all time. Another conspicuous high point came with 1977's *Your Place or Mine,* a hard-driving slice of aggressive honky-tonk. In the early '80s, he hooked up with Dean Dillon and made a couple of terrible two-good-ol'boy records, then stopped recording for most of the '80s. After descended into alcoholism and drug use, Stewart returned, clean and sober, with a strong comeback record, 1988's *Brand New.* Considering that most folks had given him up for dead, this was a remarkable turn of events. His heyday was in the '70s, but Gary Stewart deserves to be celebrated for his considerable talent, tenacity and influence. *—John Dougan*

You're Not the Woman You Used to Be / 1973 / MCA ♦♦♦
MCA put this album out in an attempt to capitalize on Gary's RCA success. Except for two tracks, all this material had been released while he'd been signed with Kapp and, in most cases, shows that Stewart hadn't yet found his voice or his style. The title track, though, is nearly as good as anything he did at RCA. *—Jim Worbois*

★ **Out of Hand** / 1975 / Hightone ♦♦♦♦♦
Stewart's best album and one of the greatest honky-tonk records ever recorded, *Out of Hand* has "Drinkin' Thing," "She's Actin' Single (I'm Drinkin' Doubles)," and "I See the Want To In You Eyes," as strong a grouping of songs as on any Stewart record. Few, if any, country performers have made a better hard honky-tonk record (although Joe Ely came the closest). If you get tired of the songs about drinking and want something a little less self-pitying and uplifting, this won't be for you, but a true fan of country music better own this. *—John Dougan*

Steppin' Out / 1976 / RCA ♦♦♦
Not one of Stewart's strongest efforts but worth the price of admission just to hear him cover Willie Nelson's "I Still Can't Believe You're Gone." The original album came with an iron-on patch (or in the case of my copy, two) featuring Gary playing his guitar. *—Jim Worbois*

Your Place or Mine / 1977 / RCA ♦♦♦♦♦
If anything has hurt this record since its release, it's that some of the tracks ("Rachel" and "Broken Hearted People") sound a bit pro forma, and the drinking songs sound a little tired. But the best tracks (the title cut and "Ten Years of This") are as good as anything on *Out of Hand.* The record's diamond is Stewart's version of Rodney Crowell's "Ain't Living Long Like This," which he sings as if his life depended on it. It's a truly transcendent moment, perhaps Stewart's best single moment on record (although his vocal on the title track comes pretty close). One of the great hard country records of all time, *Your Place or Mine* (though few will admit it) is one of the records that contemporary country artists borrow from shamelessly. *—John Dougan*

Cactus & Rose / 1980 / RCA ♦♦♦
This is not the kind of record most people would associate with Gary Stewart, one of the finest honky tonk singers ever. For this effort, he has teamed up with people like Allman Brother members Gregg Allman and Dicky Betts as well as Bonnie Bramlett (ex-Delaney, Bonnie & Friends) and Randy Scruggs. And, what do we learn— That Stewart could have easily fronted the Allman Brothers or Marshall Tucker or, vocally kicked Charlie Daniels' southern rock butt from here to Pascagoula as a great honky tonk singer. *—Jim Worbois*

☆ **Gary's Greatest-17 Original Hits** / 1981 / Hightone ♦♦♦♦♦
Featuring material recorded from 1973 to 1990—including songs from both his RCA and HighTone days—*Gary's Greatest* has 17 of Stewart's best songs and is an excellent introduction to the under-appreciated singer/songwriter. *—Thom Owens*

Brand New / 1988 / Hightone ♦♦♦
Stewart ends a lengthy recording hiatus, showing a newfound maturity while tackling songs that are still rife with tortured self-revelation. His voice has lost little of its edge. *—Michael McCall*

I'm a Texan / Oct. 15, 1993 / Hightone ♦♦♦
More impassioned than ever, Stewart continues to excel at raw-boned honky tonk and revved-up country-rock. The songs don't all live up to his treatment, but when they do, as on "Honky Tonk Hardwood Floor" or the inviting "Come on In," he reveals the timidity that undercuts the new traditionalists of the modern country era. *—Michael McCall*

The Essential Gary Stewart / Jan. 28, 1997 / RCA ♦♦♦♦♦
Gary Stewart's *Essential* is an excellent cross-section of hit singles, rarities, and album tracks that demonstrates his talents as a songwriter and as a gritty honky tonk performer. *Gary's Greatest* remains a better way to become acquainted with Stewart's entire catalog, but *Essential* is still a fine sampler. *—Thom Owens*

Wynn Stewart

b. Jun. 7, 1934, Morrisville, MO, **d.** Jul. 17, 1985, Hendersonville, TN
Vocals / Bakersfield Sound, Traditional Country
Wynn Stewart was one of the leading figures of West Coast country music, developing in the early '50s the style that would later become known as the Bakersfield sound. Along with Tommy Collins and Buck Owens, Stewart stripped down the sound of honky tonk, taking away the steel guitars and relying on electric instruments, a driving beat and loud, energetic performances. For most of the late '50s and early '60s, Wynn released a series of independent singles that performed respectably, yet failed to break him into the mainstream. By the end of the '60s, he had modified his sound slightly, bringing himself closer to country-pop territory. The shift in style was successful, resulting in his lone number one hit single "It's Such a Pretty World Today," but Stewart wasn't able to become a genuine country star, despite his steady stream of records during the '70s and '80s. At the time of his sudden death in 1985, he was preparing for another comeback, which may have resulted in some long-overdue critical and popular acclaim. Even though he never received those accolodes while he was alive, his early singles like "Wishful Thinking" and "Big, Big Love" clearly inspired contemporaries like Owens and Haggard, as well as '80s neo-traditionalists and alternative country musicians like Dwight Yoakam and k.d. lang, which guarantees him a place in the history of contemporary country music. *—Stephen Thomas Erlewine*

★ **California Country: The Best of the Challenge Masters** / 1995 / AVI ♦♦♦♦♦
This masterful collection is the best of Wynn Stewart, the early years. Twenty-nine cuts that range from the hits to some of the more obscure numbers he recorded in California while signed to both Jackpot and Challenge are included here: "Come On," a rockabilly tune; "Wishful Thinkin'"; and two of the three big Challenge hits, "Big, Big Love" and "Another Day, Another Dollar." As good as anything recorded since, Wynn Stewart's voice was always notable. Best described as a "rolling chord style," Stewart continues to be praised as one of the outstanding vocalists of the genre. His contribution to the West Coast country scene and to the Bakersfield sound makes him one of the founding fathers of that musical ilk. Tunes that demonstrate this include "Playboy," "Falling for You," a Ralph Mooney tune, and "Heartaches for a Dime." His duets with Jan Howard, then married to Harlan Howard, convinced the young woman to pursue a singing career. "How the Other Half Lives," "Wrong Company," and "We'll Never Love Again" continue to set a standard for couple's duets. Ending with the bleak "The Black Limousine" seems fitting since Stewart's career was cut short in 1985 when he died of a heart attack just as he was about to make another bid for success. Underappreciated, especially in the States, Wynn Stewart and the songs he wrote and recorded continue to draw attention to a talent and a career that never quite took off, yet is more remarkable than most of the artists who find themselves sitting at the top of the charts with their pockets full of gold. This is an exceptional introduction to Wynn Stewart as well as a remarkable collection for Wynn Stewart fans to savor and enjoy. *—Jana Pendragon*

Wishful Thinking / Aug. 22, 2000 / Bear Family ♦♦♦♦♦
Bear Family's *Wishful Thinking* compilation gathers virtually everything that Bakersfield

sound pioneer Wynn Stewart ever recorded, summarizing his three-decade career over the course of ten discs. "Keeper of the Keys," "It's Such a Pretty World Today," "Sing a Sad Song," "Waltz of the Angels," and the title track are some of the many highlights from this 279-song collection, which traces Stewart's evolution from his hard-driving, rockabilly tinged sound in the '50s to a more pop-oriented country style in the '60s, '70s, and '80s. His complete works for labels such as Jackpot-Challenge, Copre, Playboy, and his own Win and Pretty World imprints are also included. As with all Bear Family releases, *Wishful Thinking* also includes extensive liner notes, and the first full-length Wynn Stewart biography is part of the package as well. Though the *California Country: The Best of the Challenge Masters* collection is probably still the best introduction to Stewart's work, *Wishful Thinking* is a treasure for his long-time fans. *—Heather Phares*

Doug Stone

b. Jun. 19, 1956, Newnan, GA

Vocals / New Traditionalist, Contemporary Country

Doug Stone's sensitive Deep South baritone has made him one of country's premier romantic balladeers. This Georgian can sing hard traditional country and easy country with equal ease. For years diesel mechanics was his day job, and he hated it. This dissatisfaction carries over into his music and his stage presence, which presents him as distant and alone; he knows what he's singing about. With the release of his first album, his record company announced the dawning of a new "Stone Age." They weren't far off, as acceptance from country's female-dominated audience was almost immediate; his second album, 1991's *I Thought It Was You,* overdid the self-pity but yielded a couple of hits, including the title cut. "I'd Be Better Off (In a Pine Box)" was his breakthrough song. Shortly before the release of his third album, *From the Heart,* in 1992, 35 years of Southern-fried food sent Stone under the surgeon's knife for quadruple bypass surgery. He returned a year later with *More Love,* but after 1995's *Faith in Me, Faith in You* he largely disappeared from sight, finally resurfacing in 1999 with *Make Up in Love. —Brian Mansfield & David Vinopal*

● **Greatest Hits, Vol. 1** / 1995 / Epic ✦✦✦✦✦
Greatest Hits, Vol. 1 does an effective job of chronicling all of Stone's biggest hits from the early '90s. Most of his Top Ten hits are featured, including the number one singles "In a Different Light," "A Jukebox With a Country Song," "Too Busy Being In Love," and "Why Didn't I Think of That." *—Thom Owens*

George Strait

b. May 18, 1952, Pearsall, TX

Vocals, Guitar / Western Swing Revival, New Traditionalist, Contemporary Country

Out of all the new country singers to emerge in the early '80s, George Strait stayed the closest to traditional country. Drawing from both the honky tonk and western swing traditions, Strait didn't refashion the genres; instead, he revitalized them for a new decade. In the process, he beccame one of the most popular and influential singers of the decade, sparking a wave of neo-traditionalist singers from Randy Travis and Dwight Yoakam to Clint Black, Garth Brooks and Alan Jackson. He began playing country music while in the Army and formed his own band in the late '70s. Signed to MCA in 1980 as a solo act, his first single "Unwound" climbed into the Top Ten. In 1982, "Fool Hearted Memory" became the first of his astonishing 31 number one singles.

Unsurprisingly, he dominated the country singles charts throughout the '80s and his albums consistently went platinum or gold. Strait rarely abandoned hardcore honky tonk and western swing, and he was also one of the few '80s superstars to survive the generational shift of the early '90s. Just one year after its release, Strait's four-disc box set career retrospective, *Strait Out of the Box,* had become one of the five biggest-selling box sets in popular music history. *Blue Clear Sky,* his 1996 album, debuted on the country charts at number one and the pop charts at number seven. *—Stephen Thomas Erlewine*

Strait Country / 1981 / MCA ✦✦✦

Strait from the Heart / 1982 / MCA ✦✦✦

Right or Wrong / 1983 / MCA ✦✦✦

☆ **Does Fort Worth Ever Cross Your Mind** / 1984 / MCA ✦✦✦✦✦
Does Fort Worth Ever Cross Your Mind? is George Strait's first full-fledged masterpiece, signalling that his fusion of honky tonk, western swing and post-outlaw contemporary country had reached its fruition. Strait's performance is confident and assured, while producer Jimmy Bowen helps bring the music into focus, bringing subtle dynamic shades to a set of excellent swing numbers, ballads and honky tonk ravers. The record includes several of Strait's best songs, includng "Honky Tonk Saturday Night," "Fireman" and the title track. *—Thom Owens*

Something Special / 1985 / MCA ✦✦✦✦✦
Something Special is another excellent George Strait record from the mid-'80s, featuring new traditionalist classics like "Left's Gone" and "The Chair." Occasionally, the album wanders into softer, more sentimental territory than Strait has explored in the past, yet that only makes the straight country more effective. *—Thom Owens*

★ **Greatest Hits** / 1986 / MCA ✦✦✦✦✦
A good overview of Strait's first round of MCA chartbusters from the early '80s, it includes "Right or Wrong," "Amarillo by Morning," "You Look So Good in Love," "Fool Hearted Memory," "A Fire I Can't Put Out," "Let's Fall to Pieces Together," and several other hits. *—Mark A. Humphrey*

☆ **Greatest Hits, Vol. 2** / 1987 / MCA ✦✦✦✦✦
Greatest Hits, Vol. 2 picks up George Strait's string of hits in 1984 and includes 10 of his biggest singles from the mid-'80s, including "Does Fort Worth Ever Cross Your Mind," "The Fireman," "The Chair," "Nobody In His Right Mind Would've Left Her," "It Ain't Cool to Be Crazy About You," "Ocean Front Property," and "All My Ex's Live in Texas." *—Stephen Thomas Erlewine*

Ocean Front Property / 1987 / MCA ✦✦✦✦✦

If You Ain't Lovin' (You Ain't Livin') / 1988 / MCA ✦✦✦

Beyond the Blue Neon / Feb. 6, 1989 / MCA ✦✦✦
Beyond the Blue Neon doesn't really alter George Strait's formula at all, but it is remarkable for its consistent quality. Over the course of its 10 tracks, nothing on the album rings false. Strait's voice is pure and gorgeous, while the material—particularly "Ace in the Hole," "Hollywood Squares," and "Baby's Gotten Good at Goodbye"—is first-rate. In short, it is one of his finest albums ever. *—Thom Owens*

Livin' It Up / May 15, 1990 / MCA ✦✦✦

Chill of an Early Fall / 1991 / MCA ✦✦✦

2 Ten Strait Hits / Dec. 31, 1991 / MCA ✦✦✦✦✦
Ten Strait Hits covers ten straight Top 10 singles (including eight number one hits) that George Strait had between 1988 and 1990, all of which are presented in chronological order. Several of his most popular songs—including "Famous Last Words of a Fool," "Ace in the Hole," "Baby Blue," "Baby's Gotten Good At Goodbye," "I've Come to Expect it from You" and his biggest hit, "Love Without End, Amen"—are featured on this collection. Though Strait did make very good albums, his singles compilations remain excellent albums in their own right, showcasing some of the very best country music made in the '80s and '90s. *—Thom Owens*

Holding My Own / 1992 / MCA ✦✦✦

Pure Country / 1992 / MCA ✦✦✦
The soundtrack to the movie of the same name starring George Strait himself. The songs are a little larger than life if you are a Strait fan, but very nice nevertheless. Some were put together just for this movie. "Where the Sidewalk Ends" and "The King of Broken Hearts" stand out, but the version of "I Cross My Heart" recorded here is just one great song. *—Michael Erlewine*

★ **Strait out of the Box** / Sep. 12, 1995 / MCA ✦✦✦✦✦
A truly comprehensive four-CD compilation covering the years 1976-1995, including all 31 of his number one hits, 11 more chart singles of great musical significance, 19 LP tracks, and 11 more rare tracks, plus a brace of unreleased songs that are anything but leftovers. The opening three tracks, all written by Strait and dating from 1976-1979, show a lot of potential on his part as a singer fronting a competent band. 1981's "Unwound" was where his career lifted off, and his singing takes on serious depth and range. Beyond "Unwound," there's a lot here that could've done well as singles, displaying his early sound as a mix of traditional country and country-pop. Strait ultimately rebelled against the latter, but the songs off of his first two LPs show a prodigious talent in any milieu he'd have chosen to work. Disc Two opens with the Bob Wills number "Right or Wrong," which became central to Strait's sound and image and, in the early '80s, was a reminder that as smooth as those early MCA songs had been, Strait had a genuine commitment to Western swing and traditional country music. Disc Three divides its space between ballads and honky tonk numbers, with some comedy and some bracing Western swing. Disc Four is all '90s material, right up through April 1995. The cut that helped sell this set is Strait's never-issued 1993 duet with Frank Sinatra on "Fly Me to the Moon," which never should have been left off the *Duets* album—the two singers' voices sound right together, and the song works as is. The producers have provided a booklet with an extensive biographical essay, a full sessionography, and comments from Strait himself on each of the songs included. *—Bruce Eder*

Blue Clear Sky / Apr. 1996 / MCA ✦✦✦✦✦
Country's most consistent traditionalist, George Strait, scores again with *Blue Clear Sky,* one of the best albums of his 15-year career. *Blue Clear Sky* shows off Strait's range with a well-chosen sweep of material. "Rockin' in the Arms of Your Memory" and "I'd Just as Soon Go" prove that well-written, mainstream adult ballads can carry an insinuating strength when performed with the subtle grace of a master. On "Need I Say More," Strait reveals, again, that he's also a wonderful jazz-tinged crooner. "I Ain't Never Seen No One Like You" swings with the joyful ease of a youngster on a backyard set, and "Do the Right Thing" gives Strait the chance to show casually that he can navigate an eccentric meter, masking how difficult the inventive arrangement might have been for a lesser vocalist. Strait, an experienced calf-roping competitor, also includes "I Can Still Make Cheyenne." Instead of creating a deadly dramatic situation or joking about the macho manner of the lifestyle, the song uses a telephone call between a struggling rider and his lover to convey the dreams, the fears, the financial hardships and the difficulties of life on the road that surround the sport. Just like the singer, the song relies on quietly reserved emotion to convey enormously important sentiments. *—Michael McCall*

Carrying Your Love with Me / Apr. 22, 1997 / MCA ✦✦✦
Blue Clear Sky was a defining moment in George Strait's career, illustrating that he could still deliver a masterpiece in the latter half of his career. Its follow-up, *Carrying Your Love With Me,* isn't quite as strong, yet it still has a number of very nice moments, making it a worthwhile endeavor for fans, even if it lacks its predecessor's resonance. *—Thom Owens*

One Step at a Time / Apr. 21, 1998 / MCA ✦✦✦✦
One Step at a Time continues the hot streak George Strait began with *Blue Clear Sky.* It's not on par with that latter-day masterpiece, yet equals its follow-up, *Carrying Your Love With Me,* by offering a uniformly excellent set of songs that are all delivered with conviction from Strait. If anything, Strait is getting better with age, as he's able to give even mediocre material nuanced, impassioned performances, which is a trick younger country artists need to learn if they're ever going to have a catalog as rich and consistently rewarding as his. *—Thom Owens*

Always Never the Same / Mar. 2, 1999 / MCA ✦✦✦

Latest Greatest Straitest Hits / Mar. 7, 2000 / MCA ✦✦✦✦✦
With a career that spans nearly 20 years, 26 albums that have been certified platinum or multi-platinum, and countless number-one and Top-Ten hits, it's probably easy for George Strait to gather some songs for a greatest-hits album. The cream of the crop turn up here,

drawn from his four most recent studio albums. "Carrying Your Love With Me," "Adalida," "Blue Clear Sky," and "Today My World Slipped Away" are just a few of the celebrated songs that grace this prodigious 15-song anthology. But no country artist's greatest-hits album is complete without the obligatory addition of at least two new songs, and Strait fulfills this obligation with a slightly appealing duet with fellow country artist Alan Jackson, crooning about "Murder on Music Row," and "The Best Day," which has filled the airwaves of country radio. It takes only one listen to *Latest Greatest Straitest Hits* to remind listeners that George Strait continues to hit them out of the park and will go down in history as one of the top country entertainers of all time. *—Maria Konicki*

George Strait / Sep. 19, 2000 / MCA ♦♦♦
George Strait continues his foray into the neo-traditionalist country style that he helped to pioneer on his 24th album, the simply titled *George Strait.* His voice has deepened over the years but he sounds just as alive as he did on his 1981 debut, and his songs hold just as much pain. The stark "If It's Gonna Rain" and the rich "She Took the Wind From His Sails" are testaments to the years that Strait has put into his craft and his unique ability to infuse a song with honest heart and soul. While some fans of "young country" might wonder where the screaming guitar solos and distorted fiddles are, fans of traditional country will no doubt be able to tell them where to go. *—Zac Johnson*

Marty Stuart

b. Sep. 30, 1958, Philadelphia, MS
Vocals, Mandolin, Guitar / New Traditionalist, Contemporary Country, Country-Rock, Traditional Bluegrass
Fusing honky tonk with a gritty rockabilly backbeat and a fondness for bluegrass, Marty Stuart became one of the most popular country performers of the early '90s, as well-known for his edgy music as he was for his flamboyant, glittery Nudie suits. By the age of 13, he had joined Lester Flatt's band as a guitarist; in 1973, Stuart became Flatt's mandolin player after Roland White left the band, and soon he was also singing lead vocals and harmonies. In 1982, Stuart released his first solo effort, *Busy Bee Cafe;* an eponymous 1985 album yielded four minor hits, including the Top 20 "Arlene." Stuart's first album for MCA, *Hillbilly Rock,* generated several hit singles, including "Don't Leave Her Lonely Too Long" and the title track, his first Top Ten hit. *Tempted* was his breakthrough album, producing Top Ten hit singles in "Little Things" and the title track. Late in 1991, Stuart duetted with Travis Tritt on the number two hit "The Whiskey Ain't Working;" the following year, the two singers embarked on the popular "No Hats Tour." Also in 1992, Stuart released *This One's Gonna Hurt You* and had two Top Ten hits and three additional Top 20 singles. *—Sandra Brennan*

Let There Be Country / 1988 / Columbia ♦♦♦♦♦
This early recording gives a clear idea of just who Marty Stuart is. Without all the hype and over production of many of the MCA recordings, *Let There Be Country* displays Stuart's traditional hillbilly bent. Only his 1982 Sugar Hill debut, *Busy Bee Cafe,* defines him better. Self-produced, it is obvious that the artist knows what he is doing in terms of material and performance. With the inclusion of only two original songs, the rest of the tunes are strong statements by Stuart concerning country music. Merle Haggard's "Mirrors Don't Lie" is strong evidence of Stuart's affiliations. Also good is Bill Monroe's "Get Down on Your Knees and Pray." Stuart's version of the Johnny Horton hit "One Woman Man" is priceless and the sincere sweetness he reflects on the Harlan Howard-Max D. Barnes number "I'll Love You Forever (If You Want Me To)" is stunning. A worthy addition to any Stuart collection. *—Jana Pendragon*

Hillbilly Rock / 1989 / MCA ♦♦♦♦♦
This first MCA project is the epitome of what the adult Marty Stuart is all about. With a new groove that runs just left of center, while still retaining a classic C&W-bluegrass flair, *Hillbilly Rock* is a wild ride to what surely must be honky tonk heaven. On par with Dwight Yoakam's debut, *Hillbilly Rock* sets the tone for a whole new faction of neotraditionalists. Opening with the title cut, an infectious romp that demands your attention, and ending on a high note with a love song, "Since I Don't Have You," acrafted by Stuart and another tragically overlooked supernova, Mark Collie, this is one heck of an album. "Western Girls," a favorite of the numerous cowgirls who follow his career, and the Merle Kilgore-Tillman Franks tune, "The Wild One," all demonstrate how effective Marty Stuart is. "Cry, Cry, Cry," a Johnny Cash hit, is made new again. While this release displays more of Stuart's own songwriting skills, it also displays how deeply involved he is with the music he plays. *—Jana Pendragon*

Tempted / 1991 / MCA ♦♦♦♦♦

Once upon a Time / 1992 / CMH ♦♦♦

This One's Gonna Hurt You / 1992 / MCA ♦♦♦♦
With a snappy duet of the title with his buddy Travis Tritt, and an interesting prologue that explains how Stuart and Hank Sr. got together somewhere in outer space, this is a fun experience. "High on a Mountain Top" is outstanding as is "Hey Baby." His paean to country music, "Now That's Country" explains why this is a gold album. But, Stuart's edge is verging on the pedestrian in places. *—Jana Pendragon*

Love and Luck / 1994 / MCA ♦♦♦♦

● **Marty Party Hit Pack** / 1995 / MCA ♦♦♦♦♦
This is a hits package that shows off Marty Stuart's hard-earned success with tongue firmly planted in cheek. The man is a precious commodity and the songs presented here include his contribution to the Mercury tribute album to Elvis, *It's Now or Never.* "Don't Be Cruel" is handled expertly and given a little panache by the Don Was Band and the Jordanaires. The Staple Singers join Stuart for a gospel version of "The Weight," produced by Was. As for the known hits, they are all here, including the Tritt-Stuart duet that appeared on Tritt's album of the same name, "This One's Gonna Hurt You (For a Long, Long Time)." Another classic from the man who also penned "The Whiskey Ain't Workin'" with Ronny Scaife. "Western Girls," "Hillbilly Rock" and two previously unreleased cuts, "If I Ain't Got You" and "The Likes of Me," round things out. Hoopin' it up Marty style is whole lot of fun. *—Jana Pendragon*

Honky Tonkin's What I Do Best / Jun. 18, 1996 / MCA ♦♦♦

The Pilgrim / Jun. 15, 1999 / MCA ♦♦♦

Sweethearts of the Rodeo

f. 1973, California
Group / New Traditionalist, Contemporary Country
Drawing from country-rock, bluegrass, and pop, the harmony duo Sweethearts of the Rodeo—Janis Oliver Gill and Kristine Oliver Arnold—made a series of records in the late '80s and early '90s which received positive reviews and earned the group a dedicated cult following. The sisters began performing country and bluegrass music in high school and played various clubs along the California coast; Kristine sang leads, while Janis harmonized and played guitar. In 1983, Janis and her husband, Vince Gill, moved to Nashville to began work on his career. Soon after he signed to RCA, producer Steve Buckingham encouraged Janis to continue with her own career. When Kristine and her husband, Blue Steel's Leonard Arnold, also moved to Nashville, the sisters resumed their act. In 1986, the duo scored a Top 30 hit with their debut single "Hey Doll Baby." Their second single, "Since I Found You," hit the Top Ten, and "Midnight Girl" hit the Top Five. The Sweethearts released their second album, *One Night, One Time,* in 1988 and had two Top Five hits, "Satisfy You" and "Blue to the Bone." *—Sandra Brennan*

Sweethearts of the Rodeo / 1986 / Columbia ♦♦♦♦♦

One Time, One Night / 1988 / Columbia ♦♦♦

Buffalo Zone / 1990 / Columbia ♦♦♦

Sisters / 1992 / Columbia ♦♦

Rodeo Waltz / 1993 / Sugar Hill ♦♦♦

Beautiful Lies / Aug. 20, 1996 / Sugar Hill ♦♦♦

● **Anthology** / Apr. 4, 2000 / Renaissance ♦♦♦♦♦
Anthology collects many of Sweethearts of the Rodeo's finest moments, from their first single "Hey Doll Baby" to subsequent hits like "Midnight Girl," "Satisfy You," "Chains of Gold," and "Blue to the Bone." The sisters' sweet harmonies also soar on "Since I Found You," "This Heart," and "A Woman Can Tell Every Time." This 20-track compilation is a welcome overview of the Sweethearts' pop-tinged country sound. *—Heather Phares*

Sylvia (Sylvia Kirby Allen)

b. Dec. 9, 1956, Kokomo, IN
Vocals / Urban Cowboy, Soft Rock, Country-Pop
Growing up in Kokomo, Indiana, Sylvia moved to Nashville around Christmas of 1975 with a definite gameplan: get a job as a secretary, get to know influential people in town, and build a career as a recording artist. The plan worked. She picked up a job as the receptionist for Pi-Gem Music, headed by record producer Tom Collins. She started singing on demo sessions, and Collins helped her secure a recording contract with RCA.

Since she'd never performed live before, Sylvia ended up learning to do concerts at the same time she was making hit records. With an engaging voice, a bubbly personality, and a beautiful appearance, Sylvia was practically a marketing dream, and Collins built her sound around catchy melodies and strong backbeats. Songs like "Drifter" (number one, 1981), "The Matador" (1981), "Nobody" (number one, 1982) and "Like Nothing Ever Happened" (1982) became big hits; "Nobody" even crossed over into the pop Top 40. The material was often lyrically shallow, however, and Sylvia grew increasingly frustrated. She left Collins and recorded a pair of albums with record producer Brent Maher. The second was never released. Sylvia, instead, was dropped by RCA in 1987.

She used the opportunity for personal growth (she toured almost constantly during the height of her career and was emotionally drained) and to develop as a songwriter. In 1992, she re-emerged as a touring artist and pursued a recording deal with self-penned material that was inner-directed and uplifting. *—Tom Roland*

● **Anthology** / Nov. 18, 1997 / Renaissance ♦♦♦♦♦
The 24-track budget-priced *Anthology* paints a definitive portrait of Sylvia's country career, compiling each and every one of the chart entries the singer notched between 1979 and 1989. Thanks to the disc's chronological sequencing, it's possible to chart Sylvia's evolution from early hits like "You Don't Miss a Thing" to later chart-toppers like "Drifter" and the pop crossover smash "Nobody"; other highlights include "Like Nothing Ever Happened," "I Never Quite Got Back (From Loving You)" and "Fallin' in Love." *—Hank Small*

Gid Tanner

f. 1925, Monroe, GA, **db.** 1934, Dacula, GA
Group / String Bands, Old-Timey
The Skillet Lickers were one of the most important and influential string bands of the '20s and '30s. Led by fiddler Gid Tanner, the band combined old-timey country music with a wacky sense of humor and showmanship that made the group one of the most popular country bands in America. The original lineup of the band featured the dexterous and stunning interplay of Tanner, guitarist Riley Puckett, fiddler Clatyon McMichen, and banjoist Fate Norris. From 1926 to 1931, the Skillet Lickers were the most popular country band in the country. Following the original band's dissolution, Puckett and latter-day fiddler Bert Layne led various bands called the Skillet Lickers, but the group wasn't relaunched until 1934, when Tanner formed a new lineup that recorded one final session that yielded their biggest hit, "Down Yonder." Following Tanner's death hin 1960, his son Gordon continued fiddling, preserving the tradition of his father and the Skillet Lickers. *—Stephen Thomas Erlewine*

● **The Skillet Lickers** / 1996 / County ♦♦♦♦♦
The single-disc compilation *Skillet Lickers* contains 16 tracks that the hillbilly musical comedy group recorded between 1926 and 1931, including "Ride Old Buck to the Water," "Dixie," and "Leather Breeches." The Skillet Lickers were one of the most popular groups of their time, and although their music and humor has dated considerably in the decades since, the

musical talents of fiddler Gid Tanner remain impressive, and this compilation is the best way to hear him and his group. *— Thom Owens*

B.J. Thomas (Billy Joe Thomas)

b. Aug. 7, 1942, Houston, TX

Vocals / Pop/Rock, Soft Rock, Pop, CCM, Country-Pop

B.J. Thomas straddled the line between pop/rock and country, achieving success in both genres in the late '60s and '70s. At the beginning of his career, he leaned more heavily on rock & roll, but by the mid-'70s, he had turned to country music, becoming one of the most successful country-pop stars of the decade. His first big success came with a cover of Hank Williams' "I'm So Lonesome I Could Cry" that hit the Top Ten in 1966. By the end of the '60s, he scored his biggest hit with Burt Bacharach and Hal David's "Raindrops Keep Fallin' on My Head," a chart-topper taken from the hit film *Butch Cassidy and the Sundance Kid.* After a string of soft-rock hits, Thomas hit a dry period at his new label Paramount and moved to ABC to pursue a new country-pop direction. "(Hey Won't You Play) Another Somebody Done Somebody Wrong Song," his first single for the label, became his second number one record on the pop charts. For the next decade he continued to perform well on the country charts, including two mid-'80s number ones—"Whatever Happened to Old Fashioned Love" and "New Looks from an Old Lover." He also recorded a number of hit gospel records for Myrrh. The hits began to dry up at the end of the '80s, but he continued to tour and record occasionally. *— Stephen Thomas Erlewine*

● **Greatest Hits [Rhino]** / 1990 / Rhino ✦✦✦✦✦
Rhino's *The Very Best of B.J. Thomas* is a definitive collection, chronicling Thomas' peak of popularity in the late '60s and early '70s. All of his big hits are here—"I'm So Lonesome I Could Cry," "Hooked on a Feeling," "Raindrops Keep Fallin' on My Head," "I Just Can't Help Believing," "No Love at All," "Rock & Roll Lullaby," "(Hey Won't You Play) Another Somebody Done Somebody Wrong Song"—along with a generous selection of lesser-known singles and album tracks. The end result may not change anybody's mind about Thomas—he was simply a good mainstream pop singer, which pleases some listeners but not others—but there's no denying that this is the ultimate Thomas collection. *— Stephen Thomas Erlewine*

The Best of B.J. Thomas: New Looks and Old Fashioned Love / Jan. 25, 2000 / Razor & Tie ✦✦✦✦
Razor & Tie's 18-track *New Looks and Old Fashioned Love: The Best of BJ Thomas* concentrates on BJ Thomas' country-pop work for Columbia and Cleveland International Records in the '80s. Not every hit he had during this era is here but all the big hits are: "Whatever Happened to Old Fashioned Love," "New Looks From an Old Lover," "Two Car Garage," "The Whole World's in Love When You're Lonely," "The Girl Most Likely To," and "Night Life." The first half of the disc eases on by on its slick commercialism—which is a compliment. This is well-constructed, contemporary country-pop, melodic and polished tunes about modern concerns. They do sound a little dated, thanks to the synths and production techniques, but they're entertaining, unabashedly commercial period pieces from the early '80s. The second half of the record draws heavily from Thomas' 1986 covers album *Night Life,* which may have been more straight-ahead than its immediate predecessors, yet the production was too sterile (the drums are entirely too big) to give it the country grit it needs. Still, these covers lend credence to Thomas' skills as an interpretative singer, and they help make this a strong retrospective of the third act of his career. The last song—"As Long as We Got Each Other (Theme from Growing Pains)," which happens to be a duet with Dusty Springfield—doesn't really fit the rest of the collection, aside from the fact that it was also cut in the '80s, but it's enjoyable and it's nice to have it included on a hits compilation. *— Stephen Thomas Erlewine*

Greatest Hits, Vol. 1 [Varese] / Apr. 4, 2000 / Varese Sarabande ✦✦✦✦
Greatest Hits, Vol. 1 was originally released in 1969, not in time to have BJ Thomas' first number one single, "Raindrops Keep Fallin' on My Head," be included on the collection. Other than that significant omission, the compilation is an excellent overview of Thomas' first few years of hit-making, made even better on Varese Sarabande's 2000 reissue, which includes the three charting singles that didn't make the original release—"Tomorrow Never Comes," "It's Only Love," and "Pass the Apple Eve." If you can overlook the absence of "Raindrops Keep Fallin' on My Head," this is a really nice compilation of his '60s work, but many casual fans might want to seek out Rhinos' *The Very Best of BJ Thomas,* which covers all of his Scepter recordings up until 1972, not just the '60s cuts. *— Stephen Thomas Erlewine*

Hank Thompson

b. Sep. 3, 1925, Waco, TX

Vocals, Guitar / Bakersfield Sound, Honky Tonk, Western Swing, Traditional Country

Country Hall of Famer Hank Thompson has had chart hits in five different decades. Between Bob Wills and Asleep at the Wheel, there was Thompson with his Brazos Valley Boys, keeping the sound of Western swing alive. His swing music and well-written honky-tonk songs produced 21 Top 20 charters from 1949 and 1958. His signature song, "The Wild Side of Life" (1952), was his biggest hit, prompting Miss Kitty Wells to defend bar-life females in "It Wasn't God Who Made Honky Tonk Angels." Much of his best music was set in the dim lights and thick smoke of the honky-tonk, with such hits as "Hangover Tavern," "On Tap, in the Can, or in the Bottle," "Smokey the Bar," "A Six-Pack to Go," and "Honky-Tonk Girl." While music tastes changed during his career, he kept on touring world-wide with his band, keeping true honky-tonk and western swing in the public's ear. He's often seen on Ralph Emery's *Nashville Now* TV show. *— David Vinopal*

Hank! / 1957 / Capitol ✦✦✦✦
This is a surprise, with Thompson and company covering swing standards ("Don't Be That Way") as well as adding their own parts of the repertory ("Prosperity Special," featuring Merle Travis on steel guitar). Also included is a cover of Bob Wills' "Hang Your Head In Shame" and Ernest Tubb's "Don't Look Now (But Your Broken Heart Is Showing"). The band was nearing its peak from this point in its history. *— Bruce Eder*

☆ **Dance Ranch** / 1958 / Capitol ✦✦✦✦✦
One of the group's best albums, filled with western swing standards ("Bubbles In My Beer," "Drivin' Nails In My Coffin"), honky tonk ("Lawdy, What A Gal"), and originals by Thompson. The Brazos Valley Boys also contribute four instrumentals, including numbers associated with Bob Wills ("Beaumont Rag"), Artie Shaw ("Summit Ridge Drive"), and Woody Herman ("Woodchopper's Ball"). *— Bruce Eder*

☆ **Songs for Rounders** / 1959 / Capitol ✦✦✦✦✦
Maybe Thompson's best LP, made up of songs about the rougher, raunchier sides of life, including "Cocaine Blues," "Little Blossom," "Deep Elem" (a real hot rocking number), and "Rovin' Gambler." This record was considered very controversial within conservative country music circles at the time, and in many ways broke a lot of ground within the field. This was also his first stereo album. *— Bruce Eder*

At the Golden Nugget / 1961 / Capitol ✦✦✦✦✦
At the Golden Nugget was not only the first live album ever recorded for commercial release by a single country artist, but is arguably Hank Thompson's best album, representing his amalgam of honky tonk and Western swing better than any other long-player in his history. Most country artists of his generation responded better to the enthusiasm of an audience than to the cold, usually tense, often retake-laden ambience of a studio, and Thompson had a very satisfied audience that night in March of 1961. The record is made all the more alluring by the presence of Merle Travis (who had played on Thompson's recordings since 1953) on lead guitar, and two numbers out of Travis' repertory ("Nine Pound Hammer," "John Henry") are included among the 13 songs here. The CD transfer, from 1995, is state of the art, and the historical notes are an extra treat. Along with Capitol's 1996 *Vintage Collections* compilation, this is essential to own, and not just for country music fans—rock & rollers (and not just Flying Burrito Bros. aficionados) can also learn a few things from Thompson. *— Bruce Eder*

Capitol Collectors Series / 1989 / Capitol ✦✦✦✦✦
Hank Thompson's *Capitol Collector's Series* contains a good cross-section of his big hits and lesser-known singles, making it an excellent single-disc introduction to one of the finest honky tonk vocalists of the late '40s and early '50s. *— Thom Owens*

Country Music Hall of Fame Series / 1992 / MCA ✦✦✦✦✦
These 1968-1978 recordings from Dot Records document a past-his-prime Thompson still capable of turning out good singles when the Nashville Sound didn't smother him. *— Brian Mansfield*

Hank Thompson & His Brazos Valley Boys (1946-1964) / 1996 / Bear Family ✦✦✦✦✦
It's 12 CDs, 321 tracks, and lists for over $300, but for those with the budget or the discipline to save up for it, this box set is it—not only every record that Hank Thompson cut for Capitol between 1947 and 1964, but also his ultra-rare, never-before-reissued sides for Globe and Blue Bonnet from 1946 and 1947. Disc One opens with those early jewels—there's not a less-than-first-rate recording on this 30-song CD, and the playing, while a little crude compared to Thompson's later work, is a match for anything being recorded at the time. Disc Three begins Thompson's history as an album artist, and the character and quality of the material changes somewhat—there are a few more slow numbers, and some slight sameness begins to intrude into the music, but the quality of the performances is undiminished. Disc Four has the major part of his second album along with a ton of singles, and the latter are generally more brisk and upbeat than the LP material. Disc Five includes the first extensive re-records of Thompson's older stuff, and also includes Thompson's brief foray into rock & roll, as well as lots of Western swing standards. Disc Seven opens real hot, with the stuff off of *Songs for Rounders,* and a bunch of instrumentals that round out the 1958 material, then jumps ahead a year to his next session. Discs Nine and Ten jump ahead a bit to Thompson's last studio work for Capitol, released through 1965. Discs Eleven and Twelve are devoted to Thompson's live albums from the early 1960s. And to top it off, this set comes with an oversized *hardcover* book, featuring not only a biography and sessionography, but recollections by Thompson about every recording session. *— Bruce Eder*

★ **Vintage** / 1996 / Capitol ✦✦✦✦✦
Twenty songs, containing nearly all of the essential items from Thompson's history with Capitol Records from 1947 through 1961, from "(I've Got A) Humpty Dumpty Heart" through "Oklahoma Hills." In addition to containing all of the expected hits, such as "The Wild Side of Life," there are a few nice bonus tracks, such as the Brazos Valley Boys' instrumental "Big Beaver," and excellent notes, depicting Thompson's arrival at the label, the founding of the Brazos Valley Boys, the beginning of his long and profitable relationship with producer Ken Nelson, and the background on each song's recording and history. *— Bruce Eder & Thom Owens*

The Best of Hank Thompson: 1966-79 / Oct. 22, 1996 / Varese Sarabande ✦✦✦✦✦
The Best of Hank Thompson: 1966-79 contains the great majority of his biggest hits from the latter half of his career. Drawing from his recordings for Warner and Dot, the 16-track compilation features singles like "On Tap, In the Can, Or in the Bottle," "Next Time I Fall in Love (I Won't)," and "Smoky the Bar." A few hits are missing, but the compilation nevertheless draws a full portrait of Thompson's latter-day career. *— Stephen Thomas Erlewine*

Hankworld: The Unissued World Transcriptions / Aug. 24, 1999 / Bloodshot ✦✦✦

☆ **Dance Ranch/Songs for Rounders** / Sep. 21, 1999 / Koch ✦✦✦✦✦

Seven Decades / Jul. 18, 2000 / Hightone ✦✦✦✦
Seven Decades is an impressive album any way you look at it: Thompson sounds almost as good as ever, he's still writing some great material (the album is more than half original), and the songs he chose to cover are interesting and even ambitious. "Condo in Hondo" and "Lobo the Hobo" indulge Thompson's trademark wordplay, while "Medicine Man" celebrates the bygone days of the medicine show. Tex Williams' hit "The Night Miss Nancy Ann's Hotel for Single Girls Burned Down" gets an entertaining run-through, while "Dinner for One, Please James" and the Kingston Trio's "Scotch and Soda" are smoky sounding and ready-made for the supper club. Thompson even breathes some fire into such well-worn covers as "In the

Jailhouse Now" and "Wreck of the Old '97." With crystal clear sound, tasteful production, and lots of great Merle Travis-style picking by Thom Bresh, *Seven Decades* is sturdy enough to stand alongside Thompson's best. *—Greg Adams*

Mel Tillis

b. Aug. 8, 1932, Tampa, FL
Vocals, Guitar / Country-Pop, Traditional Country
In light of all the attention given Mel Tillis' infamous speech impediment—he even named his autobiography *Stutterin' Boy*—the polished, sincere vocal delivery and songwriting skills that first earned him fame were often lost in the shuffle; nonetheless, throughout the course of his many decades in country music, Tillis remained one of Nashville's most enduring personalities. In 1957, Webb Pierce reached number three with Tillis' composition "I'm Tired," earning the aspiring artist a songwriting contract with Pierce's Cedarwood Music. Tillis soon cut his first single, a cover of the standard "It Takes a Worried Man to Sing a Worried Song;" the B-side, the self-penned "Honky Tonk Song," quickly became a chart-topper for Pierce. After a few excursions into rock 'n' roll territory, Tillis earned his first Top 40 hit with 1958's "The Violet and a Rose." In 1965, Tillis recorded his first Top 15 hit, "Wine." A string of successes followed, including 1966's "Stateside," "Life Turned Her That Way" and his first Top Ten, 1968's "Who's Julie." At the same time, his stature as a songwriter continued to grow thanks to hit covers of his "Ruby, Don't Take Your Love to Town" (by both Johnny Darrell and Kenny Rogers & the First Edition) and "Mental Revenge" (Waylon Jennings). At the end of the 1960s, Tillis and his esteemed new backing band the Statesiders came into their own as performers; after two 1969 Top Ten hits, "These Lonely Hands of Mine" and "She'll Be Hanging Around Somewhere," he scored back-to-back Top Five hits in 1970 with "Heart Over Mind" and "Heaven Everyday." 1972's "I Ain't Never" became his first chart-topper, and the remainder of the decade which followed was Tillis' most fertile period as an artist, as evidenced by a series of Top Five smashes like "Neon Rose," "Sawmill," "Midnight, Me and the Blues," "Stomp Them Grapes" and "Memory Maker." Between 1976 and 1980, he scored five more Number Ones—"Good Woman Blues," "Heart Healer," "I Believe in You," "Coca Cola Cowboy," and "Southern Rains." *—Jason Ankeny*

American Originals / 1989 / Columbia ♦♦♦♦♦
American Originals compiles material from Tillis' brief time at Columbia Records. He was with the label at the beginning of his career, and while he was there, he primarily recorded his own material. *American Originals,* though too brief at 10 tracks, gives a good sense of his developing talents. *—Thom Owens*

Greatest Hits / 1991 / Curb ♦♦♦♦♦
Featuring a selection of his late '70s and early '80s hits—including the number one "Coca Cola Cowboy," "Lying Time Again," "Southern Rains," "Your Body Is an Outlaw," "New Patches," and "Blind In Love"—Curb's *Greatest Hits* is a servicable, but not thorough, retrospective that does work as an effective introduction to Mel at the height of his popularity. *—Thom Owens*

● **Memory Maker** / 1995 / Mercury ♦♦♦♦♦
Although he reached his commercial peak in the latter half of the decade, Tillis hit his creative stride in the early 1970s, the period compiled on *The Memory Maker.* Leading off with "I Ain't Never," and his first number one, the collection also features "Sawmill," "Mental Revenge," "Neon Rose," and "Midnight, Me and the Blues." *—Jason Ankeny*

Pam Tillis

b. 1957, Plant City, FL
Vocals / Urban Cowboy, Contemporary Country, Country-Pop
Like many children of famous fathers, Pam Tillis was forced to overcome an amount of prejudice to establish herself as an individual artist and not simply the daughter of country vocalist Mel Tillis; eventually, she earned her own identity, which led to a string of country hits in the early '90s. Despite a natural affinity for country, she also found herself drawn to other genres—she performed in a folk duo with Ashley Cleveland, worked as a songwriter and founded the band Freelight, an experimental free-form jazz and rock outfit. Tillis made her own recording debut in 1983, releasing *Beyond the Doll of Cutey.* Throughout the '80s, she had a string of minor country hits and stayed busy with her songwriting. She also flirted with pop music for a time, but then returned to her country roots in 1990 and recorded the Top Five single "*Don't Tell Me What to Do.*" For the next few years, she had a steady stream of hit singles, highlighted by "*Maybe It Was Memphis.*" In 1994, her album *Sweetheart's Dance* reached the country Top Ten. After an album in 1995, Tillis waited until 1998 to release her sixth album, *Every Time. —Sandra Brennan*

Put Yourself in My Place / 1991 / Arista ♦♦♦♦♦
The album that established Tillis as a performer in her own right has a traditional country base cut with bluegrass, folk and rock. It all creates the same sort of mixed breed she sings about in "Melancholy Child": "You take a black Irish temper, some solemn Cherokee, a Southern sense of humor, and you got someone like me." Her characters are the awkward dancers of "I've Seen Enough To Know": bruised, tentative, and needing to be cajoled back to love. Even the throwaway songs are of a high standard; the best ones ("Maybe It Was Memphis," "Don't Tell Me What to Do") are truly enticing. *—Brian Mansfield*

Homeward Looking Angel / 1992 / Arista ♦♦♦

Pam Tillis Collection / Feb. 1, 1994 / Warner Brothers ♦♦♦♦♦
Before hitting big with Arista Records and "Don't Tell Me What to Do," Tillis had recorded rock-influenced country for Warner Bros. She had minor success with the likes of "There Goes My Love" and "These Memories of You," but what makes *Collection* interesting is early versions of "One of Those Things" and "Maybe It Was Memphis" as well as a version of "Five Minutes," later a hit for Lorrie Morgan. *—Brian Mansfield*

Sweetheart's Dance / Apr. 26, 1994 / Arista ♦♦♦♦♦
Producing herself for the first time (along with Steve Fishell), Tillis found the magic blend of Nashville Sound, California country-rock and post-Beatles pop. She released the heady "Spilled Perfume" as her first single, but the riches of *Sweethearts Dance* go much deeper: the Bo Diddley/Tejano rhythms of "Mi Vida Loca (My Crazy Life)," the lilting waltz of "In Between Dances," and a playfully romantic title cut. A charming album without a bad cut, *Sweethearts Dance* ranks with the best of Trisha Yearwood, Wynonna Judd and Carlene Carter. *—Brian Mansfield*

All of This Love / Nov. 7, 1995 / Arista ♦♦♦

● **Greatest Hits** / Jun. 3, 1997 / Arista ♦♦♦♦♦
Greatest Hits contains all of Pam Tillis' biggest singles, including the Top Ten country hits "Don't Tell Me What To Do," "One of Those Things," "Maybe It Was Memphis," "Shake the Sugar Tree" and "Let That Pony Run," plus two new songs, "Land of the Living" and "All the Good Ones Are Gone." *—Thom Owens*

Every Time / Jun. 30, 1998 / Arista ♦♦♦♦

Floyd Tillman

b. Dec. 8, 1914, Ryan, OK
Vocals, Guitar / Honky Tonk, Traditional Country
Floyd Tillman is probably best known for writing "It Makes No Difference Now," a country classic that he sold to Jimmie Davis for $300 in 1938, only to watch it become a hit for Davis, Bob Wills, Bing Crosby, and Gene Autry. Tillman was born in Ryan, Oklahoma, but raised in Post, Texas. He began playing guitar and performing as a back-up musician for local fiddlers while he was still a child. In 1933, at age 19, Tillman joined Adolph and Emil Hofner's house band at Gus' Palm Garden in San Antonio. Two years later, he became the leader of the Blue Ridge Playboys. In 1936, he began singing and playing electric guitar, mandolin and banjo with the Mark Clark Orchestra. He also wrote songs and occasionally sang them with the band. Tillman began a solo recording career in the late '30s, and had his first number one hit in 1944 with "They Took the Stars Out of Heaven," which he followed up with two Top Five hits, "G.I. Blues" and "Each Night at Nine," with his Favorite Playboys. In the late '40s he had more hits, "Slippin' Around" and "I Love You So Much It Hurts." His Western swing/honky tonk mixture and easy vocal delivery, with its distinctively bent notes, made Tillman a much-imitated performer, and he continued writing songs through the 1960s; his last solo success came in 1960 with "It Just Tears Me Up." *—David Vinopal & Sandra Brennan*

Country Music Hall of Fame Series / 1991 / MCA ♦♦♦♦♦
Tillman had his biggest hits in the late '40s while recording for Columbia, but these World War II-era sides for Decca show him as a leader of a Texas dance band that's not afraid to mix it up with some jazz playing. Moon Mullican plays piano on a number of these sides. *—Brian Mansfield*

★ **Best of Floyd Tillman** / Apr. 20, 1999 / Collectors' Choice Music ♦♦♦♦♦
Country Music Hall of Famer Floyd Tillman finally gets a fair showing on this, a 24-track anthology of his greatest recordings for Columbia from 1946-1954, including such classics as "Drivin' Nails in My Coffin" and "Slipping Around" (plus its follow-up, "I'll Never Slip Around Again"). All of Tillman's hits for the label are included and much more, offering a thorough picture of *Tillman* at his peak . *The Best of Floyd Tillman* is an excellent and essential anthology of this influential artist's smooth, Western swing-inflected honky tonk. *—Greg Adams*

Aaron Tippin

b. 1958, Pensacola, FL
Vocals / New Traditionalist, Contemporary Country
Aaron Tippin was part of the 1990's new traditionalist wave of honky tonk singers; although his music was among the rootsiest of the new traditionalists, he became massively popular—his singles regularly charted in the Top 10, and his albums went platinum. At age 20, he was working as a commercial pilot, but switched to music, writing songs for various Nashville publishing outfits. In 1986, Tippin permanently moved to Nashville, where he eventually became a staff writer at Acuff-Rose. Eventually, his demo tape arrived at RCA, who offered him a contract. Tippin's debut single, "You've Got to Stand for Something," reached the Top Ten in 1991 and was followed by an album of the same name which spawned two other minor hit singles and peaked at number 25 on the country charts. *Read Between the Lines,* his second album, was released in 1992 and contained his first number one single, "There Ain't Nothing Wrong with the Radio." *Read Between the Lines* climbed to the Top Ten and crossed over to the Top 50 on the pop album charts; it went platinum in 1993 and produced two more hits, including the Top Five "I Wouldn't Have It Any Other Way." In 1993, Tippin released his third album, *Call of the Wild,* which went gold four months after its release. *—Sandra Brennan*

You've Got to Stand for Something / 1991 / RCA ♦♦♦♦♦

Read Between the Lines / 1992 / RCA ♦♦♦♦

Call of the Wild / Aug. 1993 / RCA ♦♦♦

Lookin' Back at Myself / Nov. 8, 1994 / RCA ♦♦♦♦♦

Tool Box / Nov. 21, 1995 / RCA ♦♦♦

● **Greatest Hits... and the Some** / Mar. 25, 1997 / RCA ♦♦♦♦♦
Greatest Hits and Then Some contains all of Aaron Tippin's best-known songs and biggest hits from the early '90s, including "I Wouldn't Have It Any Other Way," "My Blue Angel," "Working Man's Ph.D.," "I Get It Honest," and the number one singles "You've Got to Stand for Something" and "That's As Close As I'll Get to Loving You." *—Thom Owens*

What This Country Needs / Oct. 6, 1998 / Hollywood ♦♦♦♦

People Like Us / Jul. 25, 2000 / Lyric Street ♦♦♦

Merle Travis

b. Nov. 29, 1917, Rosewood, KY, **d.** Oct. 20, 1983, Tahlequah, OK

Vocals, Guitar (Electric), Guitar / Country Boogie, Instrumental Country, Traditional Country

Merle Travis was virtually without peer as a guitarist and songwriter. A unique stylist, he was respected and prominent enough to have an instrumental style ("Travis picking") named after him, and only Chet Atkins even comes close to the influence that Travis had on the way the guitar is understood and played in country music. As a songwriter, he wasn't far behind, with originals such as "Sixteen Tons" crossing over as popular standards in the hands of other artists. Travis was born in 1917 in Rosewood, Kentucky, and lived on the bare edge of poverty. Travis learned a three-finger guitar style native to the area, and grew astonishingly proficient in a repertory that included blues, ragtime, and popular tunes. After joining the Drifting Pioneers in 1938, Travis acquired a national following through radio. In 1946 he released the topical song "No Vacancy" and earned a hit. His next major project was 1947's *Folk Songs of the Hills*, which was intended to compete with Burl Ives' folk recordings. It was a failure, but introduced several standards and classic Travis originals. 1947 began a boom period in Travis' career, launching a string of half a dozen Top Ten records. Travis also devised the first solid-body electric guitar, which, when perfected by Leo Fender, would become a key element in early rock & roll. In 1955, Tennessee Ernie Ford had his crossover hit with "Sixteen Tons," and Travis acolytes such as Chet Atkins and Scotty Moore were making a major impact on music themselves. However, Travis was never able to ascend the charts himself again. Much of the problem lay in his personal life; he was arrested for public intoxication, drunk driving (on his motorcycle), and assaulting his wife. During the early '60s, he did one new folk-style album, *Songs of the Coal Mines*, which failed to sell, but his other, mostly instrumental albums proved much more significant and influential. He still played occasionally, and became something of a star on the college folk circuit in the '70s. At age 65, he suffered a massive heart attack and died the following morning. *—Bruce Eder*

Walkin' the Strings / 1960 / Capitol ✦✦✦✦✦
Although originally issued on LP in 1960 (it was reissued on CD in 1996), these 22 songs were actually recorded in the late '40s and early '50s for Capitol's *Electrical Transcription* series. This showcases Travis's fingerpicking abilities at their best, on unaccompanied acoustic vocal and instrumental numbers; most of the material is original, with a few standards by the likes of Stephen Foster and Georgia Tom Dorsey. *—Richie Unterberger*

Merle Travis Story—24 Greatest Hits / 1989 / CMH ✦✦✦✦✦
Although *The Merle Travis Story?24 Greatest Hits* consists of re-recordings from the late '70s, it gives a better sense of why Travis was important than Rhino's *The Best of Merle Travis*. Unlike Rhino's set, CMH concentrates on Travis' guitar playing, which is why he was an important musician. Therefore, the it gives a far better sense of why the guitarist was a revered, influential artist than the vocal hits of Rhino's collection, even if the music was recorded late in his career. *—Thom Owens*

The Best of Merle Travis / 1990 / Rhino ✦✦✦✦✦
Rhino's *The Best of Merle Travis* may contain all of his big chart hits, but it's a misleading collection. Instead of focusing on Travis' revolutionary playing, the set runs through his hits and novelty songs, which all emphasize his vocals. Therefore, it isn't quite as comprehensive—or essential—as it initially appears. The album hints at his greatness, but never shows why Travis' playing was so groundbreaking. *—Thom Owens*

Folk Songs of the Hills [Expanded] / 1996 / Capitol ✦✦✦✦✦
In 1946, Capitol approached Travis with the idea of cutting a folk album, and although he wasn't an especially folk-oriented artist, he agreed to give it a go. Although the resulting 1947 record (released as a 78 rpm album) didn't sell well, it was a respectable effort performed by Travis on solo acoustic guitar. Folksy introductions embellish the songs, which include standbys like "John Henry" and "Nine Pound Hammer." Travis added a few songs of his own penned in the folk style, and one of these, "Sixteen Tons," would prove to be his most famous composition, reaching number one when it was covered by Tennessee Ernie Ford in the 1950s. The CD reissue combines the eight songs from the 1947 release with four songs from the Capitol *Electrical Transciption* series that were added to the batch when the album was reissued as *Back Home* in 1957; it also adds a song from the 1946 sessions that was previously unreleased in the U.S., "This World Is Not My Home." *—Richie Unterberger*

★ **The Best of Merle Travis: Sweet Temptation 1946-53** / Apr. 18, 2000 / Razor & Tie ✦✦✦✦✦
The Best of Merle Travis: Sweet Temptation (1946-1953) is an excellent compilation featuring 20 tracks from Travis' golden-era recordings for Capitol, including his biggest hit singles from the period as well as his original version of "Sixteen Tons," later a smash hit for Tennessee Ernie Ford. Anyone familiar with Travis knows what a great guitarist he is, and his skills are on ample display here, but the collection also illustrates what a fine, underappreciated songwriter he was. It's both a stellar introduction and a definitive single-disc overview of this most important part of Travis' career. *—Steve Huey*

☆ **Guitar Rags & a Too Far Past** / Bear Family ✦✦✦✦✦
Containing five CDs and 141 songs, and runs nearly seven hours, this set is pure gold, whether you like Travis's instrumental string dazzlers or his novelty hits of the late '40s—and it's just about 100% indispensable to anyone who likes good folk, hillbilly, country, or blues. Disc One is worth half the cost by itself, 20 of its 28 tracks drawn from Travis's early/mid-'40s career on King, Capitol, and a handful of forgotten labels, in duets and group settings. This includes his recordings with Grandpa Jones (on guitar, no less) as the Sheppard Brothers from 1943, and his topical (anti-Axis) songs recorded under aliases. All of this stuff features not only Travis's superb guitar, but excellent harmony singing by him as well. The first Travis solo track as we would know it, "That's All," is worth the wait, and later selections find him slipping into the sound recognized from his familiar recordings. Part of Disc Two is given over to *Folk Songs of the Hills*, but Travis's full band sound is also well represented. Disc Three contains more of Travis's full-band pop numbers, and a similar new discovery in an alternate take of "Merle's Boogie Woogie," the first multi-tracked country recording ever done. Disc Four, with 31 tracks, covers 1950 to 1953, when Travis's sound became more varied—there were still full-band pop numbers; his group was stripped down, and there were fewer novelty numbers. Disc Five is a mix of superb instrumentals and rousing pop numbers, along with some blues and a few reworked old standards. It may be the strongest of the five. The book is excellent—all 80 pages of it—and the sound on all but a handful of tracks is as good as being at the session. *—Bruce Eder*

Randy Travis (Randy Traywick)

b. May 4, 1959, Marshville, NC

Vocals, Guitar / Neo-Traditionalist Country, New Traditionalist, Country Gospel, Contemporary Country

Like the Beatles in rock, Randy Travis marks a generational shift in country music. When his *Storms of Life* came out in 1986, country music was still wallowing in the post-*Urban Cowboy* recession, chasing elusive crossover dreams. Travis brought the music back to its basics, sounding like nothing so much as a perfect blend of George Jones and Merle Haggard. He became the dominant male voice in country until the rise of "hat acts" like Garth Brooks and Clint Black, releasing seven consecutive number one singles during one stretch. He won the CMA's Horizon Award in 1986 and was the association's Male Vocalist of the Year in 1987 and '88. Warner Brothers signed Randy in 1985; "On the Other Hand," his first single for the label, was released in the summer of that year and climbed to number 67. Despite its lackluster performance, radio programmers were enthusiastic for Travis, as evidenced by the number six placing of "1982," which was released late in the year. "1982" was followed by a re-release on "On the Other Hand" in the spring of 1986 This time, the song hit number one. *Storms of Life*, Travis' full-fledged debut album, was released in the summer of 1986 and became a huge success, eventually selling over three million copies. Travis was the first country artist to go multi-platinum; before his success, most country artists had difficulty achieving gold status. With his mass appeal, he set the stage for country music's cross-over success in the early '90s. However, Travis dominated the late '80s. The last two singles from *Storms of Life*, "Diggin' Up Bones" and "No Place Like Home," with number one and two, respectively. "Forever and Every, Amen"—the first single from Randy's second album, 1987's *Always & Forever*—began a streak of seven straight number one singles that ran through 1989. *—Brian Mansfield & Stephen Thomas Erlewine*

☆ **Storms of Life** / 1986 / Warner Brothers ✦✦✦✦✦
His first and best album features astonishing Lefty Frizzell-style pipes, excellent material, and sympathetic production. Easily the most impressive country debut of the '80s, it includes "1982," "On the Other Hand," "Diggin' up Bones," and "No Place like Home." *—Mark A. Humphrey*

Always & Forever / 1987 / Warner Brothers ✦✦✦✦✦
This one stayed at the top of the country charts for 10 months and sold five million copies. Well, of course he was huge. If you had songs as good as "Forever and Ever, Amen" you'd be a star too. *—Brian Mansfield*

Old 8x10 / 1988 / Warner Brothers ✦✦✦✦✦
Almost on a par with *Storms of Life*, *Old 8x10* lacks the monster hits of his debut but wears just as well. When Travis sings of love, he doesn't mean romance; there's a permanence in his voice that sounds like settling down. The album contains "Honky Tonk Moon," "Deeper than the Holler," and "Is It Still Over—" *—Brian Mansfield*

No Holdin' Back / 1989 / Warner Brothers ✦✦✦✦✦
Though it essentially a formulaic album from Randy Travis, *No Holdin' Back* is nevertheless an exceptional formula record, demonstrating both the strengths of traditionalist country songwriting and Travis' classically honky tonk voice. *No Holdin' Back* is filled with remarkable songs and performances, highlighted by a version of Brook Benton's "It's Just A Matter of Time." Occasionally, the lack of musical experimentation is a little frustrating, yet there's no denying that the album offers many pleasures, particularly for listeners who thought the spirit of traditional country had died out in the late '80s. *—Thom Owens*

Heroes and Friends / 1990 / Warner Brothers ✦✦✦
This duets album includes the obvious influences (George Jones, Conway Twitty, Tammy Wynette) as well as a few surprises (B.B. King, Clint Eastwood). The Jones song, "A Few Ole Country Boys," and the title track were hit singles. *—Brian Mansfield*

High Lonesome / 1991 / Warner Brothers ✦✦✦
With young whippersnappers like Clint Black and Garth Brooks breathing down his neck, Travis realized he needed to be more than just a pretty voice. On *High Lonesome* he proved he could write, too, helping pen five of the album's 10 songs, including "Forever Together" for his manager-turned-wife Lib Hatcher, and the country-gospel "I'm Gonna Have a Little Talk," sung a cappella with Take 6. It also includes "Better Class of Losers," written with Alan Jackson. *—Brian Mansfield*

Wind in the Wire / 1992 / Warner Brothers ✦✦

★ **Greatest Hits, Vol. 1** / Sep. 15, 1992 / Warner Brothers ✦✦✦✦✦
When Travis finally got around to releasing a greatest-hits collection, he realized he had almost enough material for two albums. So, adding two new songs to each, he put them out simultaneously. Volume one gets the edge for including those first two hits, "1982" and "On the Other Hand"; the best of the new songs, "If I Didn't Have You"; and the shattering "Reasons I Cheat," which proved as early as 1986 that Travis could write 'em as well as sing 'em. *—Brian Mansfield*

☆ **Greatest Hits, Vol. 2** / Sep. 15, 1992 / Warner Brothers ✦✦✦✦✦
Eleven more Travis classics are included here, among them "Diggin' Up Bones," "Forever and Ever, Amen" and a fabulous remake of Brook Benton's "It's Just a Matter of Time." The new songs are "Look Heart, No Hands" and "Take Another Swing at Me." *—Brian Mansfield*

This Is Me / 1994 / Warner Brothers ✦✦✦✦✦
The vanity project *Wind in the Wire* excepted, Travis hadn't released an album of new music in three years, and some people were wondering what had happened to the man who

started the neo-traditionalist boom. *This Is Me*, which included the wildly funny "Before You Kill Us All" and a stunning song called "Whisper My Name" that synthesized countrypolitan with gospel, silenced most of the questioners and showed the young whippersnappers what all the fuss had been about in the first place. *—Brian Mansfield*

Full Circle / Aug. 1996 / Warner Brothers ♦♦♦♦

You and You Alone / Apr. 21, 1998 / DreamWorks ♦♦♦

Greatest #1 Hits / Aug. 25, 1998 / Warner Brothers ♦♦♦♦♦
When you have as many number one hits as Randy Travis, it's possible to have a collection called *Greatest #1 Hits*—you can select the best of the best. And, despite the presence of "1982," which never went past number six, that's pretty much what this is—a selection of ten (nine, if you discount "1982") songs that are the best of his best. Which means that "On the Other Hand," "Diggin' Up Bones," "Forever and Ever, Amen," "Too Gone Too Long," "I Told You So," "Deeper Than the Holler," "It's Just a Matter of Time," "Hard Rock Bottom of Your Heart" and "Look Heart, No Hands," are on one disc. Which means in turn that it's a bargain for most casual fans. *—Stephen Thomas Erlewine*

A Man Ain't Made of Stone / Sep. 21, 1999 / DreamWorks ♦♦♦

Inspirational Journey / Oct. 31, 2000 / Warner Brothers ♦♦♦

Travis Tritt

b. 1963, Marietta, GA
Vocals, Guitar / New Traditionalist, Contemporary Country
Travis Tritt was one of the leading new country singers of the early '90s, holding his own against Garth Brooks, Clint Black, and Alan Jackson. He was the only one not to wear a hat and the only one to dip into bluesy Southern rock. Consequently, he developed a gutsy, outlaw image that distinguished him from the pack. Throughout the early '90s, he had a string of platinum albums and Top Ten singles, including three number one hits.

Though Tritt was determined to have a musical career from an early age, he worked several jobs before testing the performing waters. He began by recording several demo tapes, and finally signed to Warner's Nashville division for his first album, released in 1990. Two subsequent singles, "Help Me Hold On" and "I'm Gonna Be Somebody," hit number one and two respectively. Despite his success, the Nashville music industry was hesitant to embrace Tritt's rock & roll image. Nevertheless, Travis' second album, 1991's *It's All About to Change*, appealed to both country fans as well as mass audiences and became a multi-platinum breakthrough success. The singles "Can I Trust You with My Heart" and "Foolish Pride" also hit number one. *Restless Kind* was released in 1996, followed two years later by *No More Looking Over My Shoulder*. *—Stephen Thomas Erlewine*

Country Club / 1990 / Warner Brothers ♦♦♦
Tritt proclaimed his influences early with "Put Some Drive in Your Country," which paid homage not only to Roy Acuff and George Jones but to Hank Williams, Jr. and Duane Allman as well. It was the lowest-charting single off Tritt's debut, but it sold him a ton of albums. Radio programmers preferred the ambitious "I'm Gonna Be Somebody" and the ballads "Help Me Hold On" and "Drift off to Dream." *—Brian Mansfield*

It's All About to Change / 1991 / Warner Brothers ♦♦♦♦♦
Better production means ballads like "Anymore" sound bigger and rockers like "Bible Belt" (with Little Feat) and a cover of bluesman Buddy Guy's "Homesick" rock harder. Tritt brought in Marty Stuart for a duet on "The Whiskey Ain't Workin'" and revived "Here's a Quarter (Call Someone Who Cares)" as a catchphrase. *—Brian Mansfield*

T-r-o-u-b-l-e / 1992 / Warner Brothers ♦♦♦
Tritt's covers of Buddy Guy ("Leave My Girl Alone") and Elvis Presley ("T-R-O-U-B-L-E") are nice touches and show deeper roots than the Gary Rossington cowrite ("Blue Collar Man") or the last album's Little Feat remake. Beyond that, *T-r-o-u-b-l-e* is almost indistinguishable from *It's About to Change:* a good novelty song masquerading as more, a couple of ballads with big flourishes, and a large helping of Southern. That's a good formula, granted, but it still sounds like a formula. *—Brian Mansfield*

Ten Feet Tall & Bulletproof / 1994 / Warner Brothers ♦♦♦♦
Tritt's most personal album is the one in which he feels most comfortable with his Southern rock/outlaw mantle. ("Outlaws like Us," in fact, features the voices of Hank Williams Jr. and Waylon Jennings.) Tritt poked fun at his own foibles in the title track and co-wrote "Wishful Thinking" and "No Vacation from the Blues" with Lynyrd Skynyrd's Gary Rossington. "Wishful Thinking" and "Foolish Pride" are ballads that rival "Anymore" for power and Skynyrd and Bob Seger for production values. *—Brian Mansfield*

● **Greatest Hits—*From the Beginning*** / *Sep. 12, 1995 / Warner Brothers* ♦♦♦♦♦
Greatest Hits—From the Beginning features 15 of Travis Tritt's biggest hits, including "Country Club," "Help Me Hold On," "Here's a Quarter (Call Someone Who Cares)," and "Tell Me I Was Dreaming." Although there are a couple of hits missing, nothing essential has been overlooked and it's a first-rate introduction. *—Stephen Thomas Erlewine*

Restless Kind / Aug. 27, 1996 / Warner Brothers ♦♦♦♦♦

No More Looking over My Shoulder / Oct. 13, 1998 / Warner Brothers ♦♦♦

Down the Road I Go / Oct. 3, 2000 / Columbia ♦♦♦

Ernest Tubb

b. Feb. 9, 1914, Crisp, TX, **d.** Sep. 6, 1984, Nashville, TN
Vocals, Guitar / Honky Tonk, Traditional Country
The incomparable Ernest Tubb ("E.T." to all who knew him) became a legend as much for what he was personally as for the half-century career that stretched from his first radio date in 1932 to his death in 1984. Though other singers with better voices and more raw musical talent have come and gone, none has inspired greater love of the fans over six decades. Along with such performers as Jimmie Rodgers, Roy Acuff, Bill Monroe, Hank Williams, Lefty Frizzell and George Jones, E.T. is country music personified. Tubb was among the first of the honky-tonk singers and the first to achieve national recognition. His first recording was "The Passing of Jimmie Rodgers," a tribute to his hero. His long association with Decca began with "Blue Eyed Elaine" in 1940. Three years later his self-penned "Walkin' the Floor over You," a country classic, was a hit, leading to the Opry, movie roles, and stardom. In 1947 he opened his Nashville record store and began the *Midnight Jamboree*, which followed the Opry on WSM and advertised the shop while showcasing stars and those on the rise. By that time, he had become one of the most recognizable musical stars in the world, bringing country music to the widest audience it had ever seen. Over the years, Tubb toured widely with his Texas Troubadours, pressing the flesh with fans after shows that featured his many hits, including "Slippin' Around," "Two Glasses Joe," "Tomorrow Never Comes," "Drivin' Nails in My Coffin," "Rainbow at Midnight," "Let's Say Goodbye like We Said Hello," and "Driftwood on the River." In 1975, after 35 years with Decca/MCA, he was let go, the allegiance of company executives not matching that of his multitude of fans. Because of a lung disease Ernest Tubb had to rest in pain on a cot between takes, ending his career just as his hero Jimmie Rodgers had 50 years earlier. Quoting one of his album titles, Tubb left a legend and a legacy. *—David Vinopal*

★ **Country Music Hall of Fame** / 1987 / MCA ♦♦♦♦♦
Boasting 16 tracks, *Country Music Hall of Fame* is the most complete single-disc Ernest Tubb compilation available. All of the songs—which range "Walking the Floor Over You" in 1941 to "Waltz Across Texas" in 1965—are the original hit versions, not the remakes that tend to flood the budget-line collections. That alone would make *Country Music Hall of Fame* a necessary purchase, but the compilers have also done an excellent job of whittling down Tubb's extensive career to 16 tracks that show neophytes exactly how and why the vocalist was important. Not every one of Tubb's biggest hits are included on *Country Music Hall of Fame*, to be certain, but many of the most important—"Soldier's Last Letter," "You Nearly Lose Your Mind," "Seaman's Blues," "It's Been So Long Darlin," and "Letters Have No Arms"—are present, making the disc an essential addition to any basic country record collection. *—Stephen Thomas Erlewine*

Let's Say Goodbye Like We Said Hello / 1991 / Bear Family ♦♦♦♦♦
These 119 songs over five CDs represent Ernest Tubb at the very peak of his career musically and commercially, from 1947 until 1953. Disc One is filled with winners; Tubb's voice on these and the rest of the songs in this collection is at its richest and most expressive, not exactly soaring (it never did that) but never straining into the top of his range, and the results, coupled with Jerry Byrd's steel guitar and Tubb's and Jimmie Short's guitars, are exceptionally satisfying, crisp and well-articulated playing bringing out his singing at its best. Disc Two is highlighted by the presence of several duets featuring Tubb with the Andrews Sisters, which work beautifully, the Andrews Sisters crossing over from pop to country rather than Tubb moving in the other direction; here also is Red Foley, along with an album of religious songs and some great solo numbers. (By itself, this disc would have made a great single-platter release.) Disc Three features a bunch of duets with Red Foley, and even a pair of cuts with the trio of Tubb, Foley, and Minnie Pearl. Disc Four has more work with Foley, all of it worthwhile, and also includes Tubb's tribute records to Hank Williams and Jimmie Rodgers, as well as his topical Korean War songs and his first covers of compositions by his son Justin. Disc Five is a mixed bag, nearly half of it comprised of good duets with Red Foley and a few prime solo numbers, and the other half dominated by a dozen religious songs and Christmas numbers recorded for a theme album. The notes are informative and nicely thorough, though the booklet also has a few more photos than is typical on these sets. *—Bruce Eder*

Yellow Rose of Texas / 1993 / Bear Family ♦♦♦♦♦
This five-CD/150-song collection, covering the end of 1954 up through 1960, is the only way to hear any of this material, other than finding his old albums (which isn't such a bad idea). By 1955, Ernest Tubb was one of the most popular and beloved country artists in Nashville, adored by the public and revered by his fellow musicians. His work as host and player on the radio (and short-lived television) broadcasts of the *Grand Ole Opry* and the *Midnight Jamboree*, made him a familiar figure to millions, his genial presence punctuated by an easygoing sense of humor. Disc One of this set includes numerous highlights in a wide range of styles. The second disc is more consistent in tone and content, mixing blues and midtempo ballads, most of which are compiled here for the very first time, including four priceless cuts pairing Tubb off with the Wilburn Brothers. By this time, Tubb's backing band included Hank Garland sharing electric lead guitar chores with Grady Martin, with Tommy Jackson still on the fiddle and Floyd Kramer at the piano, and all of it is among the best-played country music of its era. By the fourth disc, Tubb is settling comfortably into musical middle age; the settling down comes not a moment too soon for a man whose second marriage produced its fourth child in 1958, about the same time his first grandchild was born. Disc Five opens with Tubb at his most mature and sophisticated, freely moving between honky tonk, country-pop, and modern country sounds, his voice at its richest. His band, however, is lacking its edge, with lead guitarist Billy Byrd replaced by Leon Rhodes, and the later songs from this period show Tubb slackening off as well, a somewhat less interesting singer and interpreter. *—Bruce Eder*

Walking the Floor over You / 1996 / Bear Family ♦♦♦♦♦
Okay, it's eight 70-minute-plus CDs and over $200 retail, and that would dissuade even loyal fans from springing for this set. But there's not a bad cut here, nor more than a dozen tracks that have been heard in 50 years, or are ever likely to be heard elsewhere. And most of the 200+ songs, covering 1936 until early 1947, never showed up on LP. The first six songs on Disc One are of special interest, since they feature Tubb with only his own guitar as accompaniment—since his voice is the dominant instrument, before age and smoking hardened it, the stuff is all worthwhile. The first Decca sessions from 1940 are also of extraordinary interest—the playing is sharper and anticipates his later recordings with a band, and Tubb's newly narrowed, deeper voice has a freshness that his later singing gradually lost. His subsequent sessions were even more successful, accompanied by Dick Ketner on electric guitar,

which gave Tubb a more assertive sound and a backing against which his voice worked even better—here are the roots of honky tonk music. Disc Two is where honky tonk comes into the world fully formed, with a comparatively loud, jaunty backup and Tubb's vocals acquiring the smooth, deep, emotive quality that characterized his peak performance. This disc is Ernest Tubb lean and mean, creating a popular music genre as he goes along. Disc Three and the three that follow are made up of the rarest, largest body of work in Tubb's entire career—the World Broadcasting Service recordings, made during the musicians' strike. Disc Seven returns to Tubb's formal Decca recordings, while Disc Eight contains 26 previously unreleased cuts. The notes, photos, and sessionography on this volume are as overwhelming as the musical contents. *—Bruce Eder*

Complete Live 1965 Show / Dec. 15, 1998 / Lost Gold ♦♦♦♦♦

Waltz Across Texas / Jan. 26, 1999 / Bear Family ♦♦♦♦♦
Not to be confused with any other collection using the same title, Bear Family's five-CD *Waltz Across Texas* continues the label's comprehensive release of Ernest Tubb's complete recordings. The highlights for most fans will be the dozen 1964-65 duets with Loretta Lynn, which are considered essential listening, but there's a lot more here worth owning. Tubb's vocal range had narrowed considerably in the ten years or so leading up to the 1960s, but he and producer Owen Bradley had worked out recordings that made his range sound greater than it was. For a lot of real fans, the highlights on Disc One will be the raw studio performances of cuts that were later mixed with applause for release as the fake "live" *On Tour* album, which might have been a cheat but did present Tubb and the band playing loose and free-wheeling. Disc Three has a generally jauntier selection of material, including a dozen songs by the Texas Troubadors; its last two songs mark the beginning of the Ernest Tubb-Loretta Lynn collaborations. The quality of Tubb's music held steady even coming up on his 30th year in the recording business, mostly by virtue of his continuing to find good songs and Owen Bradley's way of recording him to the best advantage—his voice on much of his mid-'60s output sounds like a finely aging instrument, and far more comfortable and pleasing than some of his late '50s material. Disc Five presents the balance of the early Lynn duets, as well as the title track, Tubb's last major hit. The sound throughout is state-of-the-art, and the annotated booklet is worth owning by itself, for what it tells us about the man and the band. *—Bruce Eder*

Tanya Tucker

b. Oct. 10, 1958, Seminole, TX
Vocals / Contemporary Country, Country-Pop, Country-Rock
Tanya Tucker had her first country hit in 1972, when she was just 13 years old. Over the succeeding decades, Tucker became one of the few child performers to mature into adulthood without losing her audience, and during the course of her career, she notched a remarkable streak of Top Ten and Top 40 hits. Her career began with a contract for CBS, and her first single ("Delta Dawn") hit the country Top Ten. Tucker's age quickly made her a sensation and she followed three number one singles "What's Your Mama's Name," "Blood Red and Goin' Down" and "Would You Lay with Me (In a Field of Stone)." She also had a string of hit singles for MCA during the late '70s, but decided to radically change her image with the rock crossover *T.N.T.* Despite the controversy over the record and its sexy cover, it went gold the following year. After another switch, to Arista Records, she signed to Capitol and returned in 1986 with "One Love at a Time," which rocketed to number three. For the rest of the decade, she scored a constant stream of Top Ten singles, including four number one hits. Her success continued in the early '90s, even though her sales began slumping as the decade wore on. *—Sandra Brennan*

★ **Greatest Hits [MCA]** / 1978 / MCA ♦♦♦♦♦
No matter how far Tucker's come the last 20 years, it all comes back to "Delta Dawn," "What's Your Mama's Name—," and the other hillbilly-gothic hits of her youth. Producer Billy Sherrill is best known for his work with George Jones and Tammy Wynette, but how he turned an underage, waifish Southwest homegirl into a singer to make old boys sweat is surely his most notable, if unsettling, career achievement. *—Dan Cooper*

The Best of Tanya Tucker / 1982 / MCA ♦♦♦
Later '70s material for the blooming of a belter, honky tonk style. *—Mark A. Humphrey*

Greatest Hits [Liberty] / 1989 / Liberty ♦♦♦♦♦
Tanya, undergoing her second coming as a commercial country queen, appears here with her 1986-1991 hits. *—Mark A. Humphrey*

Can't Run from Yourself / Sep. 28, 1992 / Liberty ♦♦♦
Edgier and more consistent than *What Do I Do with Me, Can't Run from Yourself* runs the range of Tucker's abilities, from the slow-blues burn of Marshall Chapman's "Can't Run from Yourself" to the wistful melancholy of Hugh Prestwood's "Half the Moon." A rollicking duet with Delbert McClinton on "Tell Me About It" is matched by the fine romance of "Two Sparrows in a Hurricane"; which one you like best will depend strictly on personal preferences. Switch one song on each side, and you've got a side of rockers and a side of ballads. *—Brian Mansfield*

Greatest Hits 1990-1992 / Apr. 20, 1993 / Liberty ♦♦♦♦♦
As the title says, *Greatest Hits 1990-1992* contains all of the biggest hits Tanya Tucker had in the early '80s, including the number two singles "Down to My Last Teardrop," "(Without You) What Do I Do With Me," "Some Kind of Trouble," and "Two Sparrows In A Hurricane," among others. *—Stephen Thomas Erlewine*

★ **What's Your Mama's Name/Would You Lay with Me** / Nov. 9, 1999 / Collectables ♦♦♦♦♦

20 Greatest Hits / Sep. 26, 2000 / Capitol ♦♦♦♦♦

Shania Twain

b. Aug. 28, 1965, Timmins, Ontario, Canada
Vocals / Adult Contemporary, Contemporary Country
Emerging in the mid-'90s, Shania Twain (pronounced shu-NYE-uh) became the most popular country music artist since Garth Brooks. Skillfully fusing mainstream, AOR rock production with country-pop, Twain and her producer/husband Robert John "Mutt" Lange created a commercial juggernaut with her second album, *The Woman In Me*. The record became a multi-platinum phenomenon, peaking at number five on the pop charts and eventually selling over nine million copies in America alone. Twain might have sold a lot of records, but like other mega-selling acts before her, she earned few good reviews—most critics accused her of diluting country with bland, anthemic hard rock techniques and with shamelessly selling her records with sexy videos. Fans ignored such complaints, mainly because her audience was comprised of many listeners that had grown accustomed to such marketing strategies by constant exposure to MTV. And Twain, in many ways, was the first country artist to fully exploit MTV's style. She created a sexy, video-oriented image—she didn't even tour during the year when *The Woman In Me* was on the top of the country charts—that appealed not only to the country audience, but also to pop fans. In turn, she became a country music phenomenon. *—Stephen Thomas Erlewine*

Shania Twain / Apr. 20, 1993 / Mercury ♦♦♦
Shania Twain's eponymous debut album was a bland set of contemporary country that demonstrated her considerable vocal abilities, but none of the spark that informed her breakthrough, *The Woman In Me*. Part of the problem is that none of the songs are well-constructed and each leans toward soft-rock instead of country or country-rock. By and large, the songs are lacking in strong melodies, so they have to rely on Twain's vocal skills and, although she is impressive, she is too showy to make any of these mediocre songs stick. It's a promising debut, largely because it showcases her fine vocal skills, but it isn't engaging enough to be truely interesting outside of a historical context. *—Thom Owens*

The Woman in Me / 1995 / Mercury ♦♦♦♦♦
Shania Twain's second album broke down the doors of stardom for the singer, selling over four million copies by the beginning of 1996. Like many country artists of the mid-'90s, Twain's music combined country conventions with mainstream rock flourishes, creating a sound that appealed to both audiences. *The Woman in Me* isn't necessarily flawless product—the material is a bit inconsistent, and the music plays it a bit too safe—but it all sounds convincing, thanks to the dynamic charisma of Shania Twain. *—Stephen Thomas Erlewine*

★ **Come on Over** / Nov. 4, 1997 / Mercury ♦♦♦♦♦
Shania Twain's second record *The Woman in Me* became a blockbuster, appealing as much to a pop audience as it did to the country audience. Part of the reason for its success was how producer Robert John "Mutt" Lange—best-known for his work with Def Leppard, the Cars and AC/DC—steered Twain toward the big choruses and instrumentation that always was a signature of his speciality, AOR radio. *Come on Over*, the sequel to *The Woman in Me*, continues that approach, breaking from contemporary country conventions in a number of ways. Not only does the music lean toward rock, but its 16 songs and, as the cover proudly claims, "Hour of Music" breaks from the country tradition of cheap, short albums of 10 songs that last about a half hour. Furthermore, all 16 songs and Lange-Twain originals and Shania's sleek, sexy photos suggest a New York fashion model, not a honky tonker. And there isn't any honky tonk here, which is just as well, since the fiddles are processed to sound like synthesizers and talk boxes never sound good on down-home, gritty raveups. No, Shania sticks to what she does best, which is countrified mainstream pop. Purists will complain that there's little country here, and there really isn't. However, what is here is professionally crafted country-pop—even the filler (which there is, unfortunately, too much of) sounds good—which is delivered with conviction, if not style, by Shania and that is enough to make it a thoroughly successful followup to the most successful country album by a female in history. *—Stephen Thomas Erlewine*

Come on Over [International] / Nov. 23, 1999 / Mercury ♦♦♦♦♦
The week the *Come on Over: The International Version* appeared in the States, *Come on Over* was still in the Top 20 after spending over two years on the charts and selling over 14 million copies. That is massive success and it's all the more remarkable because the hits on pop radio were not on the album. Each single was remixed and refurbished—most notably the dance reworking of "That Don't Impress Me Much"—with an eye on Top 40 and adult contemporary radio, plus foreign markets that wanted Shania the pop diva, not Twain the country crooner. Actually, the original versions weren't all that country to begin with; they were adult contemporary pop tunes with the occasional violin or steel guitar—enough to make *Come on Over* seem like country on the surface, but at its heart, it was pop music. That's why the single remixes were so successful—they revealed the true nature of the song. Similarly, *The International Version* feels more genuine than the original, since it has no qualms embracing the gaudy thrills of pop. Every cut on *Come on Over* has been remixed for this version and the sequencing has changed. Each track benefits from this tinkering, since these versions are giddily infectious and present Shania as the pop diva she really is. In this incarnation, *Come on Over* stands as the best pop diva album of the late '90s—playful, funny, tuneful, catchy, amusing, sexy. No diva has delivered a record this consistently fun in years—not Mariah, not Whitney, not Madonna (who abandoned the whole idea of fun during the '90s, anyway). Sure, almost all of its best qualities are on the surface but that's precisely why it's irresistible. *—Stephen Thomas Erlewine*

Conway Twitty (Harold Lloyd Jenkins)

b. Sep. 1, 1933, Friars Point, MS, **d.** Jun. 5, 1993, Branson, MO
Vocals, Guitar / Nashville Sound/Countrypolitan, Rockabilly, Country-Pop, Traditional Country
Originally a '50s rock & roll singer, Conway Twitty became the reigning country superstar of the '70s and '80s, racking up a record 40 number one hits over the course of two decades. With his deep, resonant down-home voice, Twitty was one of the smoothest balladeers to work in Nashville during the country-pop era, but he was also one of the most adventurous. More than any other singer, he was responsible for selling country as an "adult" music, slipping sexually suggestive lyrics into his lush productions, yet never singing misogynist lyrics—by and large, his songs were sensitive and sensual, which is part of the reason why he achieved such a large success. Once Twitty reached the top of the country charts in the

late '60s, he stayed there for years on end, releasing a consistent stream of Top 10 hits that both defined and expanded the limitations of country-pop by adding subtle R&B, pop, and rock & roll influences. Though he had some pop success, Twitty remained country to the core—occasionally, his song titles were simply too corny—which was why he retained his popularity until his death in 1993. *—Stephen Thomas Erlewine*

Conway Twitty Sings / 1965 / Decca ♦♦♦

Hello Darlin' / 1970 / Decca ♦♦♦♦♦
This is Twitty's finest hour as a country singer and songwriter. The great title track is included, plus "Up Comes the Bottle" and "I'm So Used to Loving You." He's at his C&W vocal peak on this one, and almost all of the material is good—even forgive the inclusion of "Rocky Top." *—George Bedard*

☆ **Conway Twitty's Greatest Hits, Vol. 1** / 1972 / MCA ♦♦♦♦♦
Every one of these songs were Top 10 hits and this 1972 package goes a long way to explain Twitty's appeal. There's not a weak track on this record and smaller hits like "I Wonder What She'll Think About Me Leaving—" and "Image of Me" are every bit as good as the monster hits. *—Jim Worbois*

Greatest Hits, Vol. 2 / 1976 / MCA ♦♦♦♦♦
Greatest Hits, Vol. 2 is a fine summation of Conway's early '70s hits, including "You've Never Been This Far Before," "There's A Honky Tonk Angel (Who'll Take Me Back In)," and "I See the Want To In Your Eyes," among others. *—Thom Owens*

☆ **20 Greatest Hits** / 1987 / MCA ♦♦♦♦♦
20 Greatest Hits covers a large portion of Conway Twitty's biggest hits from the '70s and '80s, from "Hello Darlin'" to "Red Neckin' Love Makin' Night," making it an excellent retrospective and introduction to his long, prolific career. *—Stephen Thomas Erlewine*

Number One's: The Warner Brothers Years / 1988 / Warner Brothers ♦♦♦
This greatest-hits set shows (with the exception of "The Rose") an artist in command of his own performance, with a clear grasp on quality material and a strong sense of powerful arrangements. *—Tom Roland*

Greatest Hits, Vol. 3 / 1990 / MCA ♦♦♦
Greatest Hits, Vol. 3 runs through Conway Twitty's big hits from his second stint at MCA Records in the late '80s. The collection includes the Top 10 hits "Julia," "I Want To Know You Before We Make Love," "That's My Job," "Goodbye Time," "Saturday Night Special," "I Wish I Was Still In Your Dreams," and "She's Got A Single Thing In Mind." *—Stephen Thomas Erlewine*

☆ **Silver Anniversary Collection** / 1990 / MCA ♦♦♦♦♦
25 hits from Twitty's work for MCA and Warner Bros. are contained on this album, from "Guess My Eyes Were Bigger than My Heart" (1966) to "She's Got a Single Thing in Mind" (1989). It's an excellent introduction to one of the most popular singers in country music history. *—AMG*

The Best of Conway Twitty, Vol. 1: The Rockin' Years / 1991 / Mercury ♦♦♦♦♦
The Best of Conway Twitty, Vol. 1: The Rockin' Years contains all of the recordings he made for Mercury Records in the late '50s, when he was trying to follow in the footsteps of Elvis. Naturally, there's a lot of rockabilly on this collection—which he did very well—as well as some ballads that hint at his future country career. In between are some of his very best moments, including "It's Only Make Believe," "Mona Lisa," "Is A Bluebird Blue," and "Lonely Blue Boy." *—Stephen Thomas Erlewine*

☆ **The Conway Twitty Collection** / 1994 / MCA ♦♦♦♦♦
The Conway Twitty Collection is a stellar four-disc box set that contains every essential track he ever recorded. Beginning with some early recordings—including a cut from when he was a pre-teen—the set runs through every hit from 1958's "It's Only Make Believe" to 1993's "I'm the Only Thing (I'll Hold Against You)." Several rarities are scattered throughout, but the true treasure of the compilation is the simple fact that it contains the great majority of his Top 10 hits, including his duets with Loretta Lynn. It is a lasting testament to his considerable talents. *—Stephen Thomas Erlewine*

Rock 'N' Roll Years / Jun. 24, 1997 / Bear Family ♦♦♦♦
Fans of Conway Twitty's pre-country recordings will rejoice with this massive eight-disc, 192-track collection, collecting every track from an eight-year period encompassing 1956 to 1964. Here's Conwayfrom his start as a scrapping rockabilly to his early hit-making triumphs right up to the cusp of his even more popular change in direction. The first disc collects his 1956 recordings for Sam Phillips in Memphis. Although Conwaywith his band, the RockHousers never saw a release on Sun Records, it certainly wasn't for lack of trying. The disc kicks off with his original recording of the band's theme, "Rockhouse," which became Roy Orbison's second Sun single. Although few titles seemed to survive, several full sessions featuring multiple takes did, and they're here. Disc two is where the hits begin, kicking off with "It's Only Make Believe." With a career-making tune under his belt, Twitty quickly moved in to a groove of recording teen ballads like "The Story of My Love" while still cutting growly rockers like "I Vibrate (From My Head to My Feet)." Disc three and four continue the trend with the hits "Mona Lisa" and "Danny Boy." The next two discs find Twitty exploring the 1950s rock & roll catalog, but Conway's move to country is presaged with the inclusion of "Walk On By." There's also a nice duet with Roy Orbison on "I'm In a Blue, Blue Mood." The final two discs show Twitty trying on R&B and blues numbers for size, plus rockers like "The Pickup," whose beat and storyline presaged Orbison's "Oh, Pretty Woman" by a couple of years. Glossy, uptown versions of "City Lights," "Faded Love" and 17 raw demos of hard country material close the set. Those who only know Conway's later, lacquer-haired country period will find this massive box a major revelation. *—Cub Koda*

The Ultimate Collection / Aug. 10, 1999 / Hip-O ♦♦♦♦♦
The Ultimate Collection may be missing some big hits—after all, Conway Twitty ruled the country charts throughout the '70s and '80s—but it comes surprisingly close to fulfilling the promise of its title. Many of his best-known songs are here—"It's Only Make Believe," "Lonely Blues Boy," "Hello Darlin," "You've Never Been this Far Before," "Louisiana Woman, Mississippi Man," "Linda on My Mind," "I'd Love to Lay You Down," "Tight Fittin' Jeans," "That's My Job"—and they date from all eras of his career. A collection that spotlights his prime years in the '70s is still the better introduction, since it contains nothing but great songs, but this is nevertheless a good sampler of his entire career that would be very useful for neophytes. *—Stephen Thomas Erlewine*

★ **The #1s Collection** / Sep. 12, 2000 / MCA Nashville ♦♦♦♦♦

Leroy Van Dyke

b. Oct. 4, 1929, Spring Fork, MO
Vocals / Nashville Sound/Countrypolitan, Country-Pop, Traditional Country
Singer/songwriter Leroy Van Dyke was best known for penning the country novelty standard "Auctioneer" and the country-pop smash "Walk on By," his biggest hit. Born in Missouri, Van Dyke originally wanted to be a farmer, and earned a BS in agriculture at the University of Missouri, which was where he first began playing guitar. Following graduation, Van Dyke worked as a newspaper reporter and later as an auctioneer. While stationed in Korea, he began performing for his peers and wrote "Auctioneer," which was dedicated to his cousin. Following military service, Van Dyke returned to journalism in Chicago. In 1956, he entered WGN Chicago's talent contest, and sang "Auctioneer." Deejay Buddy Black signed up as Van Dyke's manager and slipped in a document giving him co-writing credits and half the royalties for the song, which made the pop charts later that year and appeared on the country charts in early 1957, where it climbed to the Top Ten. The following year, Van Dyke began appearing on Red Foley's *Ozark Jubilee* television show.

In 1961, Van Dyke went to Nashville and signed to Mercury, where he released "Walk on By." It went right to the top of the country charts and remained there for 19 weeks; it also crossed over to the Top Five on the pop charts. Its success was followed up with another major crossover hit, "If a Woman Answers (Hang Up the Phone)," and the Top 40 "Black Cloud." In 1962, Van Dyke joined the *Grand Ole Opry.* His next few Mercury releases only reached the middle of the charts, and in 1965, he signed to Warner Brothers and had Top 40 success with "Roses from a Stranger." In 1967, Van Dyke appeared in the film *What Am I Bid—* He recorded throughout the decade, but only hit the charts with "Louisville" in 1968. In 1977, he notched one final minor hit, "Texas Tea." Later that year he also released two albums, *Gospel Greats* and *Rock Relics,* both produced by old friend Shelby Singleton. In 1982, he resurfaced with a self-titled effort. *—Sandra Brennan*

● **Hits & Misses** / 1994 / Bear Family ♦♦♦♦♦
While *The Auctioneer* contained the highlights of Leroy Van Dyke's '50s hits for Dot, *Walk On By* concentrates on his early '60s singles for Mercury, including "If A Woman Answers (Hang Up the Phone)," "Black Cloud," "Happy to Be Unhappy" and the title track, which spent an extraordinary 19 weeks at the top of the country charts. By and large, the material on *Walk On By* is stronger than that on *The Auctioneer,* making it an excellent introduction to this talented singer. *—Thom Owens*

Ricky Van Shelton

b. 1952, Danville, VA
Vocals, Guitar / Contemporary Country
Noted for his rich baritone voice, Ricky Van Shelton became an overnight country music sensation in the late '80s—between 1987 and 1994, he had over 13 number one hits. Van Shelton was raised in Grit, Virginia and grew up listening to gospel music. As a teen, he was interested in pop music and had little interest in country music until his brother convinced him to become the lead vocalist in his country band. After his wife got a job in Nashville, he moved to the city in the mid-'80s; shortly after his arrival, he began playing local clubs. In 1986, he signed with Columbia Records. Van Shelton's debut single, the title track from his album *Wild Eyed Dream,* hit the Top Ten, beginning a streak of Top Ten hits that ran for several years. During this time, he had number one hits with "Somebody Lied" (1987), "I'll Leave This World Loving You" (1988), "From a Jack to a King" (1989), and "I've Cried My Last Tear for You" (1990). In 1991, he and Dolly Parton had a chart-topper with "Rockin' Years." Van Shelton's first four albums went platinum. By the mid-'90s, his popularity had slipped somewhat, however, and he had trouble cracking the country Top 40. Despite his declining record sales, he remained a popular concert attraction. In 2000, he released *Fried Green Tomatoes* *—Sandra Brennan*

Wild-Eyed Dream / 1987 / Columbia ♦♦♦
This debut from this country hunk balladeer, with occasional thumpin' at the hop contains "Working Man Blues," "Crime of Passion," and more. *—Mark A. Humphrey*

Loving Proof / 1988 / Columbia ♦♦♦♦♦
Here are stabs at rockabilly alongside the ballads at which Shelton excels. Some of the songs on the album are "From a Jack to a King" and "Hole in My Pocket." *—Mark A. Humphrey*

RVS III / 1990 / Columbia ♦♦♦
The third album puts out more sounds in the winning Shelton formula, such as "I Still Love You," "I've Cried My Last Tear for You," "Oh Pretty Woman," and more. *—Mark A. Humphrey*

Greatest Hits Plus / 1992 / Columbia ♦♦♦♦♦
Despite rocking hits like "Wild Man" and "I Am a Simple Man" (or even the new cover of Elvis Presley's "Wear My Ring Around Your Neck"), Ricky Van Shelton's greatest-hits collection shows that he's made his best records as a balladeer raised on stone-country gospel. For proof, just listen to "Just As I Am," "I'll Leave This World Loving You" or "Keep It Between the Lines." *—Brian Mansfield*

● **16 Biggest Hits** / Feb. 2, 1999 / Columbia/Legacy ♦♦♦♦♦
Ricky Van Shelton scored 16 Top Ten country solo hits between 1987 and 1993, and they are all on this appropriately named compilation, which is sequenced in hit order: first the ten number ones, then the three number twos, and so on. Van Shelton came in on the neo-traditionalist wave of the mid-'80s, and his hits spotlight such veteran country songwriters

as Harlan Howard, Roger Miller, and Boudleaux and Felice Bryant and include revivals of standards like "From a Jack to a King." They also exhibit the sentiment and wordplay typical of the country songwriting craft on such newly composed works as the philosophical "Keep It Between the Lines" and the romantic twist of "I Meant Every Word He Said." As country veered toward pop in the Garth-and-Shania era of the '90s, sturdy talents like Van Shelton struggled, but this thorough collection of his most popular material confirms his veneration of traditional country and his status as one of its latter day masters. *—William Ruhlmann*

Porter Wagoner

b. Aug. 12, 1927, West Plains, MO

Vocals / Nashville Sound/Countrypolitan, Country-Pop, Traditional Country

Porter Wagoner, the Thin Man from West Plains, Missouri is among the most immediately recognizable figures in country music, largely due to his exploiting TV—and flashy costumes—a good 20 years before the video boom. As for his music, since signing with RCA in 1952 he has produced a wealth of superb hard country, and just as much of the most wretchedly oversentimentalized tripe you'll ever want to hear. The latter, of course, is half the reason we love him.

Though he had several hits in the late '50s, most notably 1955's "A Satisfied Mind", Wagoner's career truly took of in 1961 when he began hosting his own syndicated television show; it turned into the most popular country show of the '60s. The look of Porter's television show defined country music for much of America's general public during the '60s. In 1967, his female duet partner Norma Jean was replaced by Dolly Parton. Not only did exposure on Wagoner's program kick-start Parton's career, it provided a boost for Porter's as well. Their first joint single, 1968's "The Last Thing on My Mind," launched a string of Top 10 hits that ran more or less uninterrupted until 1975, when the duo stopped working together.

Porter continued to have solo hits during the late '60s and early '70s, though none of them were as big as his songs with Parton. She parted ways with Wagoner in late 1974, yet they continued to duet occasionally. Porter continued to film his TV show and to chart singles after she left, but all of his hits were minor. In 1976, he retired from touring. Porter had several minor hits in the early '80s, but he effectively retired from recording in 1983, two years after leaving RCA Victor. In the late '80s and early '90s, he became increasingly active on the Nashville Network, eventually becoming the regular host of *the Grand Ole Opry.* In July 2000, he released his first new album in many years, *The Best I've Ever Been. —Dan Cooper & Stephen Thomas Erlewine*

The Thin Man from West Plains: The RCA Sessions 1952-1962 / 1989 / Bear Family ✦✦✦✦✦

From a cover of "Settin' the Woods on Fire" in September 1952 to "Blue House Painted White" in August of 1962, this four-CD set is a priceless overview of the best part of Porter Wagoner's career. Disc one features his earliest stuff, most of which is solid honky tonk material sung in Hank Williams' style. Most of it disappeared without a trace at the time, but it's all extremely enjoyable and shows some of Wagoner's versatility. His own sound, as it developed on the later songs on disc one and all of disc two, is more backwoods, with a strong folk component, but also beautifully harmonized. Wagoner's most striking attribute was the sheer joy evident in his singing and playing, whether he was doing a deeply religious number ("What Would You Do") or a loving tribute to Bill Monroe ("Uncle Pen"). He was equally comfortable with bluegrass and also country-blues, as is clear from the previously unissued "My Brand of Blues," where he sounds a lot like Johnny Cash. Disc three shows Wagoner working in a smoother, more sentimental and commercial country-pop-oriented vein, but as late as 1959, he was still doing wonderfully exuberant numbers. Disc four covers the early '60s, the period during which Wagoner continued to merge the stripped-down country of his roots and the smooth Nashville sound. Among the outtakes released for the first time is "Private Little World," featuring a killer guitar solo totally unexpected in a romantic number like this. The accompanying book is informative, though not as well organized as the usual Bear Family notes. *—Bruce Eder*

★ **The Essential Porter Wagoner and Dolly Parton** / Jun. 1996 / RCA ✦✦✦✦✦

The Essential Porter and Dolly contains all of Wagoner and Parton's Top 10 hits, including "The Last Thing on My Mind," "Holding on to Nothin'," "Just Someone I Used to Know," "If Teardrops Were Pennies," "Please Don't Stop Were Pennies," and "Say Forever You'll Be Mine." In addition to the hits, a handful of interesting obscurities are included, making this the definitive retrospective of Porter and Dolly's partnership. *—Thom Owens*

★ **The Essential Porter Wagoner** / Apr. 29, 1997 / RCA ✦✦✦✦✦

The Essential Porter Wagoner is the first thorough CD-era collection of his greatest hits, and while it misses a few items, all of the essential songs—from "Company's Comin'" and "A Satisfied Mind" to "The Carroll County Accident" and "Uncle Pen"—are here, making it a necessary addition to any country collection. *—Stephen Thomas Erlewine*

Jimmy Wakely

b. Feb. 16, 1914, Mineola, AR, **d.** Sep. 25, 1982, Mission Hills, CA

Vocals, Piano, Guitar / Cowboy

Jimmy Wakely was one of the last singing cowboys to transform a movie contract into a successful recording career. A protege of Gene Autry, he was never remotely as successful as Autry in movies, but found recording success with country and pop audiences.

James Clarence Wakely was born in Arkansas on February 16, 1914, but was raised in Oklahoma. He formed the Jimmy Wakely Trio in 1937. Having achieved some recognition locally, they managed to parlay that into a meeting with Gene Autry and they became regulars on Autry's Melody Ranch radio show and also began appearing in his films. Wakely got a recording deal in 1942 and had his first hit a year later with a cover Elton Britt's "There's A Star-Spangled Banner Waving Somewhere."

Monogram Pictures approached Wakely with a contract in 1944, and his first picture, *Song of the Range,* was a modest success, leading to a five-year stint in front of the cameras and 28 films. His first major cross-over hit song followed in 1948 with "One Has My Name (The Other Has My Heart)," which reached the top spot on the country-and-western charts and the top 10 on the pop charts. He then teamed up with songstress Margaret Whiting. The effervescent Whiting and the smooth, laid-back Wakely had ten hits together. In 1952, he became the star of *The Jimmy Wakely Show* on the CBS radio network. After co-hosting the ABC television network series *Five Star Jubilee* in 1961 with Tex Ritter, he continued to record for his own Shasta Records label. He continued to perform live in an act that included his son and daughter, and remained popular during the 1970s, until age and health problems began taking their toll. Wakely died of emphysema in 1982. *—Bruce Eder*

● **The Very Best of Jimmy Wakely** / Jul. 25, 2000 / Varese Sarabande ✦✦✦✦✦

The Very Best of Jimmy Wakely includes singles like "Slipping Around," "Beautiful Brown Eyes," "I Love You So Much It Hurts," and "One Has My Name (The Other Has My Heart)" along with 12 other hits. "I'll Never Let You Go, Little Darlin'" and "Too Late" are also featured on this worthwhile collection from one of the '40s and '50s most popular singing cowboys. *—Heather Phares*

Clay Walker

b. Aug. 19, 1969, Beaumont, TX

Vocals, Guitar / New Traditionalist, Contemporary Country

With his first two singles reaching number one upon their release, Clay Walker immediately established himself as a commercial success. Unlike most of his new country contemporaries of the mid-'90s, he was able to sustain that success over a couple of years, racking up no less than five number one singles in the first three years of his career. While appearing as the house singer at the Neon Armadillo bar in Beaumont, TX, Walker was discovered by producer James Stroud, who helped Clay secure a contract with Giant Records; the pair soon began working on the vocalist's debut album. "What's It To You" became a number one hit upon its release in August of 1993, with "Live Until I Die" following it into the pole position later that same year. "Dreaming With My Eyes Open" became his third number one hit in the summer of 1994, helping make his self-titled debut record a platinum album. *If I Could Make A Living* was not quite as successful as his debut, yet it still yielded the number one title track. *Hypnotize the Moon,* Walker's third album, appeared in the fall of 1995, preceded by the number two single "Who Needs You Baby." *—Stephen Thomas Erlewine*

Clay Walker / 1993 / Giant ✦✦✦✦✦

If I Could Make a Living / Sep. 27, 1994 / Giant ✦✦✦✦✦

Hypnotize the Moon / Oct. 17, 1995 / Giant ✦✦✦✦

Rumor Has It / Apr. 8, 1997 / Giant ✦✦✦

● **Greatest Hits** / Jun. 9, 1998 / Giant ✦✦✦✦✦

Greatest Hits is an excellent summation of Clay Walker's first four albums, featuring all of his big hits, including "What's It to You—." Not only is it a great introduction to Walker, it is his most consistently enjoyable record to date. *—Thom Owens*

Live, Laugh, Love / Aug. 24, 1999 / Giant ✦✦✦

Jerry Jeff Walker (Paul Crosby)

b. Mar. 16, 1942, Oneonta, NY

Vocals, Guitar / Outlaw Country, Singer/Songwriter, Progressive Country

Jerry Jeff Walker is best known as the writer of "Mr. Bojangles," an enduring pop classic he wrote at the beginning of his career. He's also strongly associated with the progressive ("outlaw") country scene that centered around Austin, Texas, in the 1970s and included such figures as Willie Nelson, Guy Clark, and Townes Van Zandt. Born in upstate New York, he recorded his first few albums while there but moved to Austin in 1971. That same year, the Nitty Gritty Dirt Band's rendition of "Mr. Bojangles" made the Top Ten of the pop charts. In 1972 he signed with MCA and released a self-titled album. His best-known album however, is 1973's *Viva Terlingua,* which went gold. He released a couple albums on Elektra/Asylum in the late '70s, but remained mostly with MCA until his 1982 album *Cowboy Jazz*—a record that became his last for any major label. In 1985, however, he showed the industry he could live without their help and released the first of a series of self-made cassettes, *Gypsy Songman.* In 1987 Walker worked out a deal with Rykodisc to release his CDs, but he still sells the cassettes himself through his own company, Tried & True Music. *—Kurt Wolff*

Mr. Bojangles / 1968 / Rhino ✦✦✦✦✦

Walker's debut introduced his dry vocals and narrative songwriting style, with support from many session musicians, the most notable of whom were Ron Carter and David Bromberg. The influence of Dylan and other singer-songwriters of the time is felt fairly strongly on this extremely low-key release (especially on the seven-minute "Desolation Row"-like "The Ballad Of The Hulk"), but Walker favored the country and folk side of folk-rock much more than the rock side. The title track, taken into the Top Ten by The Nitty Gritty Dirt Band, remains his most famous song. The CD reissue includes the original mono single version of "Mr. Bojangles" and its flipside, as well as liner notes with comments on the songs by Jerry Jeff himself. *—Richie Unterberger*

Driftin' Way of Life / 1969 / Vanguard ✦✦✦✦✦

A beautifully simple album of country-flavored original songs, mostly from the point of view of the sentimental roustabout, this great record sounds as though the players just went in, knocked it off, and hit the road. *—Richard Meyer*

Viva Terlingua / 1973 / MCA ✦✦✦✦✦

Ridin' High / 1975 / MCA ✦✦✦✦

The Best of Jerry Jeff Walker / 1980 / MCA ✦✦✦✦✦

The Best of Jerry Jeff Walker is a concise, ten-track collection of tunes from his years on the MCA label. It includes all the Jerry Jeff favorites while never being anything more than a straightforward greatest-hits compilation, thereby making it a fine record for those wishing an overview of his career. *—James Chrispell*

- **Great Gonzos** / 1991 / MCA ✦✦✦✦✦
Great Gonzos is a good cross-section of 14 of Jerry Jeff Walker's best-known songs, including "Mr. Bojangles," "Old Five and Dimers Like Me," "Desperados Waiting for the Train" and "Sangria Wine." It's not necessarily definitive—several of his actual charting hits did not make the collection, including "Jaded Lover," "It's A Good Night for Singing," and "Got Lucky Last Night"—but it cuts to the essence of Walker, making it an excellent introduction. —*Thom Owens*

Lone Wolf: The Best of Jerry Jeff Walker / 1998 / Warner Archives ✦✦✦
This compilation draws seven tracks each from the two albums Jerry Jeff Walker released on Elektra Records: *Jerry Jeff* (1978) and *Too Old to Change* (1979). Walker moved to Elektra after a successful run on MCA and promptly got lost. While that can in part be attributed to record company convulsions, it's also apparent listening to the performances of these songs of dissolution that their singer was taking their themes to heart—he sounds hung over most of the time. Of course, that's an appropriate condition for titles that include Guy Clark's "Comfort and Crazy," Keith Sykes' "I'm Not Strange" and Rodney Crowell's "I Ain't Living Long Like This." Sometimes on these songs, Walker recalls the easygoing hedonism of Jimmy Buffett, but unlike Buffett, he sounds like he was still living the life he was singing about and is the worse for wear. It's good to have this material back in print, and it is a significant chapter in Walker's history, but it isn't Walker at his best. —*William Ruhlmann*

Best of the Vanguard Years / Mar. 23, 1999 / Vanguard ✦✦✦✦
Jerry Jeff Walker's *Best of the Vanguard Years* collection includes some of his finest songwriting for Circus Maximus as well as his early solo efforts. This album features two versions of his ballad "Fading Lady," one recorded with Circus Maximus and one with the players Walker worked with in Nashville while recording his solo album *Driftin' Way of Life. Best of the Vanguard Years* also features songs like "Trying to Live Right," "Negative Dreamer Girl" and "No Roots in Ramblin'," which hint at the influence Walker would have on country and folk-rock groups for years to come. —*Heather Phares*

Steve Wariner

b. Dec. 25, 1954, Noblesville, IN
Vocals, Guitar, Bass / Western Swing Revival, Neo-Traditionalist Country, Country-Folk, Contemporary Country
One of country music's most versatile performers, Steve Wariner grew up in suburban Indianapolis. At age 17, he joined Dottie West's band, and signed a singles deal with RCA Records in 1976. His career developed slowly, and in the beginning, the low-tuned guitars and wide range of his singles brought frequent comparisons to early Glen Campbell. His first really successful single was "Your Memory," which peaked in the country Top Ten in early 1981. Wariner's career really took off when he left RCA for MCA in late 1984, setting off a string of 18 consecutive Top Ten hits that included eight chart-toppers. This run took him into 1990, when he switched to Arista Records. He had considerable initial success, with his first Arista album, *I Am Ready,* going platinum (none of his previous albums had even gone gold). But by 1993, his record sales were declining. In 1997, he sang with Anita Cochran on "What If I Said," and the single topped the country charts in early 1998, just after Garth Brooks' recording of Wariner's "Longneck Bottle" had gone to *1. This twin success reinvigorated his career. He signed to Capitol Records* and released "Holes in the Floor of Heaven," which made the country Top Five and won CMA awards for song of the year and single of the year. *Burning the Roadhouse Down,* his debut album for Capitol, reached the country Top Ten, went gold, and crossed over to the Top 50 of the pop charts. He followed it with 1999's *Two Teardrops,* which also went gold; his third Capitol album, *Faith in You,* was released in May 2000. —*William Ruhlmann and Tom Roland*

- **Steve Wariner** / 1982 / Buddha ✦✦✦✦✦
RCA waited until they had a veritable greatest-hits package before releasing Wariner's first album. Bright arrangements have lots of dovetailing instruments, and Wariner shows off a substantial vocal range. —*Tom Roland*

It's a Crazy World / 1987 / MCA ✦✦✦✦✦
Wariner's in charge vocally, and seems to glide through the album effortlessly. He's received more responsibility for his own direction, and—with one or two exceptions—has upgraded every aspect of his record, particularly in song selection and musicianship. —*Tom Roland*

Greatest Hits / Sep. 7, 1987 / RCA ✦✦✦✦✦
Many of Steve Wariner's best moments were his singles and *Greatest Hits* contains many of his best and biggest hits, including the number ones "Some Fools Never Learn," "You Can Dream of Me," and "Life's Highway." —*Thom Owens*

Laredo / 1990 / MCA ✦✦✦
After nine years and nine *1 singles, $Wariner* had basically established himself as Mr. Consistency. *Laredo* proved, again, that he could sing any type of country well—swing ("L-O-V-E, Love"), rock ("The Domino Theory"), and heartbreak ballads conveying genuine pain ("She's in Love," "There for Awhile"). —*Brian Mansfield*

Greatest Hits, Vol. 2 / 1991 / MCA ✦✦✦✦✦

I Am Ready / 1991 / Arista ✦✦✦✦
Wariner, a master of the subtle touch, builds this album's impact quietly and methodically, with songs like Bill Anderson's "The Tips of My Fingers" and Wariner's own "Like a River to the Sea." "Leave Him out of This" is a masterpiece of smoldering intensity, its raging anger and pain barely held in check. The only time Wariner lets it loose is at the end, where he locks his guitar in mortal combat with Mark O'Connor's fiddle in the cathartic "Crash Course in the Blues." —*Brian Mansfield*

Burnin' the Roadhouse Down / Apr. 21, 1998 / Capitol ✦✦✦✦

The Hits / Oct. 6, 1998 / MCA ✦✦✦✦
With mentors like the late Dottie West, singer Bob Luman and fellow guitar great Chet Atkins, Wariner has managed to remain vital in the music business since 1977. His deal with MCA, signed in 1984, has resulted in a career of some stature. An excellent technician, his guitar playing makes him a standout. Known for his soft touch in selecting material, songs like "The Weekend," "Can I Come Over Tonight" and "The Domino Theory," his most country country hit, built his reputation. Less obvious is his ability to pull out the stops, as he does on "Lynda," showing off his first recorded guitar solo, and "Life's Highway." —*Jana Pendragon*

Two Teardrops / May 4, 1999 / Capitol ✦✦✦

Faith in You / May 9, 2000 / Capitol ✦✦✦

Ultimate Collection / Aug. 29, 2000 / Hip-O ✦✦✦✦
Steve Wariner's *Ultimate Collection* gathers some of the best sides he recorded for RCA, MCA Nashville and Arista Nashville, including number one country hits like "All Roads Lead to You," "Some Fools Never Learn," "Where Did I Go Wrong" and "Small Town Girl." The collection also includes his duets with Nicolette Larson ("That's How You Know When Love's Right") and Glen Campbell ("The Hand That Rocks the Cradle") as well as hit singles such as "The Tips of My Fingers," "I Should Be With You" and "Life's Highway." The most complete collection of Wariner's work available, *The Ultimate Collection* emphasizes both the depth and diversity of his enduring career. —*Heather Phares*

Dale Watson

b. Oct. 7, 1962
Vocals, Guitar / Americana, Alternative Country
Dale Watson is a singer/guitarist who writes and plays original material in the tradition of 1950s and '60s honky tonk—which makes him something of an outsider in the 1990s country music market. Watson began writing songs at age 12, and recorded his first at age 14. By the time he graduated from high school, he was performing locally. He spent the next seven years playing the clubs and honky tonks around Pasadena. In 1988, Watson moved to L.A., seeking the Bakersfield sound of Buck Owens and Merle Haggard, two of his major inspirations. Watson recorded two singles for Curb, "One Tear at a Time" and "You Pour It On," which were released in 1990. He also contributed one track to volume three of the L.A. country compilation *A Town South of Bakersfield,* released in 1992. That same year he moved to Nashville, where he worked as a staff writer for Gary Morris Music. Eventually, however, he settled in Austin, TX. He landed a recording deal with HighTone Records, who released Watson's debut album, *Cheatin' Heart Attack,* in 1995. Watson and his band, Lone Star, released a follow-up, *Blessed or Damned,* in 1996; *The Truckin' Sessions* appeared two years later. —*Kurt Wolff*

- **Cheatin' Heart Attack** / 1995 / Hightone ✦✦✦✦✦
Watson's hearty, down-to-earth honky tonk makes *Cheatin' Heart Attack* one of the most exciting country debuts this side of Junior Brown's *12 Shades of Brown.* Watson and his band Lone Star burn through 14 no-nonsense songs that prove the genre can be vital and fun at the same time. Watson's voice is pure, deep, and strong, and his songs feature guitar and pedal steel prominantly. He's a veteran of the Texas honky tonk circuit, which shows in his sharp arrangements on songs like "List of Reasons," "Holes in the Wall," and "Nashville Rash"—the latter mixing heartfelt commentary on the current country market with a smart sense of humor. —*Kurt Wolff*

Blessed or Damned / 1996 / Hightone ✦✦✦✦
Blessed or Damned pretty much picks up where Watson's 1995 debut, *Cheatin' Heart Attack,* left off. He pines for "A Real Country Song" on modern radio, sings praises for his adopted state on "That's What I Like About Texas" (a good-natured duet with Johnny "Whiskey River" Bush), and wonders at the fate of his chosen musical genre on the moving title track. Watson may have no surprise ace in the hole on *Blessed or Damned,* but it's nonetheless a solid hand of fresh, invigorating material. —*Kurt Wolff*

I Hate These Songs / Jun. 10, 1997 / Hightone ✦✦✦
Dale Watson's third album, *I Hate These Songs,* is a little tamer than *Blessed or Damned* or *Cheatin' Heart Attack,* but it remains a solid collection of neo-honky tonk. Watson writes sturdy, memorable songs in the tradition of Merle Haggard and Waylon Jennings, and he delivers them with conviction and humor that compensate for his resistance to move the form forward. —*Thom Owens*

The Truckin' Sessions / Aug. 18, 1998 / Koch ✦✦✦✦✦
Dale Watson is one of the strongest country & western vocalists around. As always, he is very convincing, and his tribute to truckin' tunes is a delight. All originals, the 14 cuts presented here would make Bakersfield bard Red Simpson proud. Mostly upbeat, Watson manages to tip his hat to his home state of Texas with some swing on "You've Got a Long Way to Go" and the Bakersfield sound on the humorous "I'm Fixin' to Have Me a Nervous Breakdown." Straight-down-the-pike truckin' songs like "Have You Got It On," "Makin' Up Time" and "...Loose Nut Behind the Wheel" keep this project moving along at a nice pace. A more melancholy Watson displays his soft center on the touching "Big Wheels Keep Rollin'." All in all, a great ride. —*Jana Pendragon*

Kitty Wells (Muriel Deason)

b. Aug. 30, 1918, Nashville, TN
Vocals, Guitar / Nashville Sound/Countrypolitan, Honky Tonk, Traditional Country
One of the few country stars born in Nashville, Kitty Wells (born Muriel Deason) had a string of hits from the '50s to the early '70s that earned her the title "Queen of Country Music." She made her radio debut on Nashville's WSIX, where she met her future husband, Johnnie Wright of Johnnie And Jack. She began touring as part of Johnnie And Jack's show; Wright gave her the stage name, taken from a folk song called "I'm A-Goin' to Marry Kitty Wells." Wells recorded unsuccessfully for RCA before switching to Decca, where she hit with 1952's "It Wasn't God Who Made Honky Tonk Angels," a response to Hank Thompson's "The Wild Side of Life." Its controversial pre-feminist lyrics, which blamed unfaithful men for creating unfaithful women, paved the way for Loretta Lynn and Tammy Wynette and established Wells as the first major female country star. Wells recorded a number of answer songs and

remakes, but she has top-notch original material as well, including some of Harlan Howard's earliest hits. *—Brian Mansfield & Stephen Thomas Erlewine*

☆ **Country Music Hall of Fame Series** / 1991 / MCA ✦✦✦✦✦
Country Music Hall of Fame contains 16 of Kitty Wells' best songs, giving a reasonably thorough overview of her career by combining big hits like "It Wasn't God Who Made Honky Tonk Angels" with minor hits like "A Woman Half My Age." The songs on this single disc were recorded for Decca Records between 1952 and 1965, so it naturally touches on many of the highlights from her artistic heyday, including "Release Me," "Making Believe," "I Can't Stop Loving You," "Mommy for a Day," and "Heartbreak, USA." It's an excellent retrospective, even though several important cuts—including most of her up-tempo material—is missing. Nevertheless, it's collects many of her most important songs and provides a terrific introduction to one of the most important vocalists in country music history. *—Stephen Thomas Erlewine*

★ **God's Honky Tonk Angel: The First Queen of Country Music** / Aug. 15, 2000 / Edsel ✦✦✦✦✦
No one ever sang a cheatin' song better than Kitty Wells, and this collection of her peak-period material (25 songs recorded for Decca between 1952 and 1965) is as good an introduction as one could ask for to one of country & western's seminal artists. Wells was one of Nashville's first major female stars, and if she often sang as a wife who strayed, she also gave a voice to every woman who had been led into shame by a no-good man, and her strong, rich voice was the perfect instrument for a gal wrestling with the shame, remorse, and anger of infidelity. And while Wells could take the grief, she could also dish it out; "Will Your Lawyer Talk to God," in particular, is possessed of a righteous wrath the Louvin Brothers would have envied. The earlier sides on this disc (especially her first hits "It Wasn't God Who Made Honky Tonk Angels" and & "Paying for That Back Street Affair") are tough, flinty honky tonk at its best, with Wells' superb vocals buoyed by great (though unfortunately uncredited) fiddle and steel guitar accompaniment, and while the later selections are arranged and produced in a manner more befitting the countrypolitan slant of the day, Wells' performances are as tough and pure as ever, and she's a joy to listen to throughout. While the sheer breadth of Kitty Wells' career would prevent any single-disc collection from being definitive, as an overview of her most important period, *God's Honky Tonk Angel* is an ideal starting place. *—Mark Deming*

Queen of Country / Bear Family ✦✦✦✦✦
The Queen of Country is an exhaustive four-disc box that covers all of Kitty Wells' recordings for RCA and Decca between 1949 and 1958. For the diehard fan, it's an essential collection, but the casual fan will find its thoroughness overwhelming. *—Stephen Thomas Erlewine*

Dottie West

b. Oct. 11, 1932, McMinnville, TN, **d.** Sep. 4, 1991, Nashville, TN
Vocals, Guitar / Nashville Sound/Countrypolitan, Country-Pop
Dottie West was one of the most successful, and controversial, performers to rise to popularity during the Nashville Sound era; like her friend and mentor Patsy Cline, West's battles for identity and respect within the male-dominated country music hierarchy were instrumental in enabling other female artists to gain control over the directions of their careers. West earned her first Top 40 hit in 1963 with "Let Me Off at the Corner," followed a year later by the Top Ten "Love Is No Excuse," a duet with Jim Reeves (who had scored a major success with her "Is This Me—"). Also in 1964, she auditioned for producer Chet Atkins, the architect of the Nashville Sound, who agreed to produce her composition "Here Comes My Baby; " the single made West the first female country artist to win a Grammy Award, leading to an invitation to join the *Grand Ole Opry*. In Atkins, West found the perfect producer for her plaintive vocals and heart-wrenching songs, scoring her biggest hit yet in "Would You Hold It Against Me." Around the time of 1971's *Have You Heard… Dottie West*, she left husband Bill West, and in 1972 married drummer Bryan Metcalf, who was a dozen years her junior. Suddenly, West's image underwent a huge metamorphosis; the woman who once performed dressed in conservative gingham dresses and refused to record Kris Kristofferson's "Help Me Make It Through the Night" because it was "too sexy" began appearing in skin-tight stage attire. As the sexual revolution peaked, so did West's career; after the 1973 success of the crossover smash "Country Sunshine," written for Coca-Cola, her material became far more provocative and, much to the chagrin of country purists, more commericially successful as well. *—Jason Ankeny*

● **The Essential Dottie West** / Jan. 30, 1996 / RCA ✦✦✦✦✦
Truly overdue is the Dottie West collection. Most of these tracks have been long out of print even prior to the CD revolution. The set opens with a smooth duet between crooner Jim Reeves and West on "Love Is No Excuse." It must have been difficult to decide on twenty songs for what will probably be the only release on West in this series. In addition to recording several big original hits, she left a body of excellent cover songs, such as her haunting rendition of Don Gibson's "A Legend In My Own Time," which is sadly absent here. Two upbeat, but so-so Gibson duets are presented here, "There's A Story (Goin' Round)" and "Rings of Gold."

Barring those couple of tracks, the song selection is flawless. Hank Cochran's slightly honky tonk "Me Today And Her Tomorrow" is featured, as is a warm duet with Jimmy "The Sausage King" Dean on "Slowly." There are three songs from what may well be West's best album, 1966's *Suffer Time*. Two superb B-side singles show up—the quiet "Childhood Places" and the uptempo "Reno," which carries a storyline similar to Linda Ronstadt's "Desperado" or Judy Collins' "Someday Soon." West's stellar rendition of "His Eye Is On The Sparrow" is simple and seemingly divinely inspired. When she pays homage to her rural roots on "Country Girl" or bemoans her role of absentee mother on "Six Weeks Every Summer (Christmas Every Other Year)" it's hard to imagine West ever topping these records in substance or passion. *—Bill Carpenter*

Are You Happy Baby: Collection (1976-1984) / Nov. 18, 1997 / Razor & Tie ✦✦✦✦

Speedy West

b. 1924, Springfield, MO
Guitar (Steel), Pedal Steel Guitar / Instrumental Country, Traditional Country
One of the greatest virtuosos that country music has ever produced, Speedy West bridged the western swing and rockabilly eras with eye-popping steel guitar. Besides contributing to literally thousands of country sessions, West cut many of his own instrumentals, as a solo act and with his guitarist partner Jimmy Bryant. Adept at boogie, blues, and Hawaiian ballads, West played with an infectious joy and daring improvisation that, at its most adventurous, could be downright experimental. It's doubtful whether anyone could collect all of Speedy's solos under one roof, but it was his sessions of the 1950s and early 1960s—especially those with Jimmy Bryant—that found his genius at its most freewheeling and dazzling. *—Richie Unterberger*

Steel Guitar / 1960 / Capitol ✦✦✦✦✦
A twin album to the set released by his partner Jimmy Bryant at the same time (*Country Cabin Jazz*), both featuring the same bands. Twelve virtuosic steel guitar showcases, ranging from frenetic boogie to Hawaiian-like tranquil moods. *—Richie Unterberger*

Steel Guitar from Outer Space / 1989 / See For Miles ✦✦✦✦✦
Together with the 1960 *Steel Guitar* LP, this is West at his peak. This compilation gets the nod not because of superior quality, but because of sheer quantity—24 tracks, half from rare '50s singles, the other half comprising the entirety of his 1963 album *Guitar Spectacular*. The appeal of these skyrocketing boogies and swing tunes is not at all limited to country fans; even in the 1990s, it sounds quite advanced and cutting-edge. *—Richie Unterberger*

● **Stratosphere Boogie** / 1995 / Razor & Tie ✦✦✦✦✦
The 16-track *Stratosphere Boogie: The Flaming Guitars of Speedy West and Jimmy Bryant* collects highlights from the duo's early '50s records, picking out selected album tracks and singles. It's an excellent retrospective, demonstrating the depth of their mind-bending instrumental genius. *—Thom Owens*

Swingin' on the Strings: The Speedy West & Jimmy Bryant Collection, Vol. 2 / Mar. 9, 1999 / Razor & Tie ✦✦✦✦✦
Speedy West and Jimmy Bryant recorded a wealth of quality material in the 1950s, in enough quantity to dispel any notions of regarding them as a novelty act. Those who want more West/Bryant instrumentals after hearing their *Stratosphere Boogie* collection (also on Razor & Tie) but don't want to spring for *the Bear Family* box set will be happy to own this second volume of 1951-56 tracks. The caliber of these 20 selections is almost uniformly high, whether it's the blazing leads and slightly dissonant accents of "Frettin' Fingers," the faster-than-bejesus run-through of Rodgers/Hart's "Lover" (one of five cuts previously unavailable in the U.S.), the pre-exotica jungle/bird noises created on West's steel for "West of Samoa" or the six-minute "China Boy," on which Bryant disregarded the producer's gestures to "cut." The slow numbers tend to impress less than the flashier workouts, but even on those they can throw in some head-spinning licks, like the steel guitar facsimile of a train whistle that opens "Railroadin'." *—Richie Unterberger*

Bryan White

Vocals / Contemporary Country
With his big voice, easy-going manner and streamlined mainstream country-pop, Bryan White easily fit into the post-Garth Brooks climate of the mid-'90s. His first album, *Bryan White*, began a string of number one hits that ran into 1996.

White was born and raised in Oklahoma City, where he became involved in music in an early age. Both of his parents were professional local musicians and when Bryan was five, his father taught him how to play drums. As a teenager, he played drums in both of his mother and father's band—his mom sang rock & roll, his father country—which gave him a broad musical knowledge and skill. Eventually, he formed his own trio. At first, he only drummed but during a soundcheck his mother heard him sing "Stand By Me." After the song was over, his mother was in tears and she encouraged him to become a vocalist himself. In no time, he learned how to play guitar and began writing songs.

Following his graduation from high school, White headed to Nashville, where he hooked up with Billy Joe Walker, Jr., a family friend that happened to be a session musician in the Music City. Over the next two years, Walker helped White hone is act and helped him land a job as a demo singer. Eventually, producer Kyle Lehning, who worked with Randy Travis and Dan Seals in the past, began working with Walker and White. The three crafted Bryan's debut album and landed the singer a record contract with Asylum. The self-titled debut appeared in 1994.

The first two singles from the record—"Eugene You Genius" and "Look At Me Know"—didn't gather much attention, with the latter peaking at number 24. However, in the spring of 1995 "Someone Else's Star" rocketed to number one, followed by "Rebecca Lynn" in the fall. In the spring of 1996, his second album, *Between Now and Forever*, was released, accompanied by the number one single 'I'm Not Supposed to Love You Anymore." "So Much for Pretending"became his fourth number one single in a row in the fall of 1996. Also in the fall, he won the Country Music Association's 1996 Horizon Award, as well as their award for Best New Touring Artist. *The Right Place* followed in 1997, and two years later White resurfaced with *How Lucky I Am*. His first seasonal release, *Dreaming of Christmas*, appeared in 1999. Warner Bros. pulled together his four #1 hits and a handful of top 20s for a *Greatest Hits* album, released in late 2000. *—Stephen Thomas Erlewine*

Bryan White / 1994 / Elektra ✦✦✦

Between Now and Forever / Mar. 26, 1996 / Elektra/Asylum ✦✦✦✦

The Right Place / Sep. 23, 1997 / Elektra ✦✦✦

How Lucky I Am / Aug. 24, 1999 / Elektra ✦✦✦

● **Greatest Hits** / Oct. 31, 2000 / Elektra ✦✦✦✦
As demonstrated on this compilation, which contains his ten biggest hits and two new tracks, Bryan White never made really compelling country music. In fact, the music is only country-

flavored pop, the real antecedents for which lie in early '70s folk-rock. When White performs a ballad like "I'm Not Supposed to Love You," it sounds like the Eagles doing "Desperado"; when he turns to a rhythm song like "So Much for Pretending," it recalls Stephen Stills' "Love the One You're With." Clearly, White is more pop than country, and he has paid the price by apparently becoming a has-been before his 25th birthday. The two new songs, "How Long" and "The Way You Look at Me," are typically pleasant, but they don't sound like what's needed to turn things around. As it stands, *Greatest Hits,* which manages to encapsulate all of White's popular material without including anything from his 1999 album *How Lucky I Am,* sums up a representative career in the pop-oriented country music of the '90s with no indication that that career will flourish in the future. *—William Ruhlmann*

Lari White

b. 1966, Dunedin, FL

Vocals / Contemporary Country

Most contestants on televised talent shows never are able to forge a lasting career, but Lari White is the exception that proves the rule. After winning on the Nashville Network's *You Can Be A Star,* White went on to become one of the most popular female new country singers of the mid-'90s, breaking through into the big time in 1994. Her 1988 appearance on *You Can Be a Star* led to a record contract with Capitol, and before the end of the year, she had released a single, "Flying Above the Rain," which became a regional hit in the South but failed to break into the big time. Later that same year, she joined Ronnie Milsap's publishing house and began taking acting lessons. For the next few years, White continued in this vein, waiting for another break. That break arrived in 1991—after an ASCAP showcase revived interest in her talents, Rodney Crowell asked her to sing backup vocals in his live band. In 1992, Lari signed a record contract with RCA and Crowell produced her debut album, *Lead Me Not,* which produced three minor hit singles—"What A Woman Wants," "Lead Me Not," and "Lay Around and Love You." *Wishes,* White's second album, became her breakthrough release, producing the Top 10 singles "That's My Baby," "Now I Know" and "That's How You Know (When You're In Love)." *—Stephen Thomas Erlewine*

Lead Me Not / Apr. 27, 1993 / RCA ✦✦✦✦✦

Wishes / Jun. 1994 / RCA ✦✦✦✦✦

Don't Fence Me In / Feb. 13, 1996 / RCA ✦✦✦

● **The Best of Lari White** / Jan. 28, 1997 / RCA ✦✦✦✦✦

Lari White didn't have that many big hits—she didn't begin having Top 10 singles until 1995—but that doesn't mean she didn't record a wealth of strong music, as *The Best of Lari White* proves. By selecting the highlights from her three albums, the compilation helps neophytes get up to speed with her past, but *Lead Me Not* and *Wishes* remain terrific albums in their own right. *—Thom Owens*

Stepping Stone / Jul. 28, 1998 / Hollywood ✦✦✦✦

Keith Whitley

b. Apr. 1, 1955, Sandy Hook, KY, **d.** May 9, 1989, Nashville, TN

Vocals, Guitar / New Traditionalist, Progressive Country, Progressive Bluegrass

Keith Whitley's legacy loomed large over the country music landscape of the '90s. A talented new country singer and songwriter, Whitley was just beginning to emerge as a superstar at the time of his death in 1989. Throughout the next decade, his reputation as both a performer and writer continued to grow, as other artists had hits with his songs and posthumous recordings climbed into the Top Ten. Whitley began a full-fledged solo career after leaving J.D. Crowe's band the New South in 1982. Signing with RCA Records, he released his debut album, *Hard Act to Follow,* in 1984. A record of pure honky tonk, it didn't attract much of an audience. The following year, he released *L.A. to Miami,* a more commercial affair which spawned three back-to-back Top Ten hits—"Ten Feet Away," "Homecoming '63," and "Hard Livin'." Although *L.A. to Miami* was a success, its slick production didn't please Whitley, and he convinced RCA to let him work with a new producer, Garth Fundis. 1988's *Don't Close Your Eyes* was the result, solidifying Keith's commerical standing: its first three singles—"Don't Close Your Eyes," "When You Say Nothing At All," and "I'm No Stranger to the Rain"—were all number one hits. Things may have been going smoothly on the surface for Keith Whitley, but behind the scenes he was being torn apart by alcoholism. On May 9, 1989, he suffered from a fatal case of alcohol poisoning; he was 34 at the time of his demise. Just before his death, he completed his fourth album, *I Wonder Do You Think of Me.* The record was released shortly after his death and its first single, which was the title track, reached number one, as did its follow-up, "It Ain't Nothin'." *—Stephen Thomas Erlewine*

Hard Act to Follow / 1984 / RCA ✦✦

L.A. to Miami / 1985 / RCA ✦✦

Don't Close Your Eyes / 1988 / RCA ✦✦✦✦✦

Don't You Close Your Eyes was more successful than Keith Whitley's two previous albums and it's easy to see why. Though the record still suffered from a handful of mediocre songs and a slightly soft production, the overall album was leaner and more direct than Whitley's earlier solo work, showcasing his talent for heartfelt honky tonk singing and his skill for crafting excellent barroom ballads. "Don't Close Your Eyes," "When You Say Nothing At All," and "I'm No Stranger to the Rain" were the hits, but there's a wealth of excellent material here, including a haunting version of Lefty Frizzell's "I Never Go Around Mirrors." The sheer strength of the best numbers make the handful of weaker songs perfectly excusable. After all, country in the late '80s rarely got better than *Don't You Close Your Eyes* at its best. *—Thom Owens*

★ **I Wonder Do You Think of Me** / 1989 / RCA ✦✦✦✦✦

Though Keith Whitley displayed his immense talents on his previous albums, it was only in small measures. It wasn't until *I Wonder Do You Think of Me,* his fourth and final album, that he truly came into his own. The difference between this album and its predecessors is focus. The essential style remains the same, but Whitley has decided to concentrate only on a heart-tugging, gritty honky tonk and to give the record an appropriately straightforward, simple production. The direct approach gives more weight to the sad tales of lost love and drinking and when Whitely died shortly before the record's release, these songs gained even more gravity. Still, *I Wonder Do You Think of Me* stands as an excellent testament—songs like "It Ain't Nothin'," "I'm Over You" and the title track only begin to suggest the depth and appeal of this album. *—Thom Owens*

☆ **Greatest Hits** / 1990 / RCA ✦✦✦✦✦

Assembled shortly after Keith Whitley's death, *Greatest Hits* contains nine of his biggest hits—including the Top 10 singles "Ten Feet Away," "Don't Close Your Eyes," "When You Say Nothing At All," "I'm No Stranger to the Rain," "I Wonder Do You Think of Me," "It Ain't Nothing" and "I'm Over You"—plus two unreleased songs: a duet with wife Lorrie Morgan on "'Til A Tear Becomes A Rose" and a demo of "Tell Lorrie I Love Her." It's an excellent compilation, but it is a bit unbalanced, drawing almost entirely from *Don't Close Your Eyes* and *I Wonder Do You Think of Me.* Granted, those are his two best albums, but it would have been nice to have collected the highlights from his uneven first two solo records as well as the obvious hits. Nevertheless, *Greatest Hits* is the perfect record for fans that just want the hits. *—Thom Owens*

Kentucky Bluebird / 1991 / RCA ✦✦✦

The Best of Keith Whitley / Jun. 1993 / RCA ✦✦✦

Although it only contains one big hit with "I Wonder Do You Think of Me," the nine-track, budget-line collection *The Best of Keith Whitley* is a passable sampler of Whitley's career, featuring such highlights as "Brother Jukebox," "Day in the Life of a Fool," "Lady's Choice," "Some Old Side Road," "On the Other Hand" and "Turn This Thing Around." *—Stephen Thomas Erlewine*

The Essential Keith Whitley / Jun. 18, 1996 / RCA ✦✦✦✦✦

The Essential Keith Whitley is an excellent single-disc retrospective of the late country singer/songwriter, including such classic songs as "I Wonder Do You Think of Me," "If You Think I'm Crazy Now," "I'm Losing You All Over Again," and "Miami, My Amy." Although it concentrates on his earlier recordings, it is stil the best, most comprehensive collection assembled on the tragically short-lived country star. *—Thom Owens*

Sad Songs and Waltzes / Sep. 12, 2000 / Rounder ✦✦✦✦

The origins of Keith Whitley's "new traditionalist" roots are readily evident on *Sad Songs and Waltzes,* a collection of some of classic country's most prolific songwriters' grittiest contributions. Available for the first time on CD, this album pulls together tracks from Whitley's 1982 LP *Somewhere Between* and adds five previously unreleased songs, each filled with twang and heartache. Tastefully remixed by J.D. Crowe, the 15-song CD features Alison Krauss, Carl Jackson, and Diamond Rio's Gene Johnson and really captures the essence of Keith Whitley not only as a performer, but also as a true fan of country music. *—Zac Johnson*

Slim Whitman (Otis Dewey Whitman Jr)

b. Jan. 20, 1924, Tampa, FL

Vocals, Guitar / Country-Folk, Folk-Pop, Country-Pop, Cowboy, Traditional Country

Once known as "America's Favorite Folksinger," Slim Whitman was more famous in Europe than in the United States for the majority of his career. An excellent yodeler known for singing mellow, romantic and clean-cut songs, Whitman got his first big break after Colonel Tom Parker—who was managing Eddy Arnold at the time—heard him singing on radio station WFLA. Parker landed Whitman a contract with RCA by the end of 1948. His first single, "I'm Casting My Lasso Towards the Sky," was released in early 1949, and eventually became his theme song. He made his national debut on the Mutual Network's *Smokey Mountain Hayride* in the summer of 1949, and the following year joined the *Louisiana Hayride.* In the early '50s, he released a cover of Bob Nolan's "Love Song of the Waterfall," which became his breakthrough hit, peaking at number ten on the country charts; the follow-up single, "Indian Love Call," made him a star, peaking at number two on the country charts and crossing over into the pop Top Ten. Both sides of his next single—"Keep It a Secret" / "My Heart Is Broken in Three"—were also major hits and he continued to have a string of Top Ten hits into the mid-'50s. In 1955, his title song for the film *Rose-Marie* became a smash on both sides of the Atlantic; following its success, Whitman joined the *Grand Ole Opry,* and then went to Britain in 1956 as the first country singer to play the London Palladium. After 1954's "Singing Hills," however, he had only two Top 40 hits in the course of a decade. In 1965, he bounced back into the country Top Ten with "More Than Yesterday." Until the early '70s, he continued to have minor hits, but in 1974, he retired from active recording. *—Sandra Brennan*

● **The Best of Slim Whitman (1952-1972)** / 1990 / Rhino ✦✦✦✦✦

Over its 17 tracks, *The Best of Slim Whitman (1952-1972)* runs through all of his Top 10 hits—from "Love Song of the Waterfall" to "Something Beautiful (To Remember)"—adding significant hit singles like "Cattle Call," "The Twelfth of Never," and "Rainbows Are Back In Style." Out of all the Whitman collections, nothing surpasses this one for selection and sound—it's the definitive compilation. *—Thom Owens*

Rose Marie / 1996 / Bear Family ✦✦✦✦✦

Rose Marie is a six-disc, 162-track box set containing all of Slim Whitman's recordings between 1949 and 1959, including all of his early sides for RCA Victor and his classic singles ("Singing Hills," "Indian Love Call," "Rose-Marie," "Love Song of the Waterfall") for Imperial Records. For any dedicated Slim Whitman fan, this lovingly assembled collection is necessary, though, due to its size, it is probably only of interest to devoted fans. Nevertheless, the box stands as the most comprehensive set ever assembled on Whitman's heyday, and it is unlikely to ever be surpassed in terms of sheer quantity and comprehensiveness. *—Stephen Thomas Erlewine*

Vintage Collections Series / Mar. 11, 1997 / Capitol ✦✦✦✦

For fans, *Vintage Collections* offers a concise view of Slim Whitman's hits; for the uninitiated, here is a chance to experience his otherworldly falsetto at a mid-level price. Although

Capitol's *Vintage Collections* discs typically offer 20 tracks, the volume devoted to Whitman compiles only 15 songs. This compilation features all of his Top 40 hits (including "Indian Love Call" and "Rose-Marie"), two tracks previously unreleased in the U.S., and a few later hits from the '60s and '70s. *—Greg Adams*

The Wilburn Brothers

f. 1953

Group / Traditional Country

As members of the larger Wilburn Family group (mother, father, elder brothers, sister), nine-year-old Teddy (b. 1931) and ten-year-old Doyle (1930-1982) appeared on the Opry in 1940; 13 years later, when they had grown up, they became part of the Opry's regular cast. With Jim and Jesse McReynolds and Bobby and Sonny Osborne, the Wilburns continue the tradition of brother duets in country music. Their wide choice of material is shown by the traditional "Knoxville Girl," a hit in 1959, and the more modern sound of "Hurt Her Once for Me" (1966). *—David Vinopal*

● **Retrospective** / MCA ✦✦✦✦✦
This nice overview of The Wilburn Brothers' smooth Decca hits of the '50s and '60s features 12 songs. *—Mark A. Humphrey*

Don Williams

b. May 27, 1939, Floydada, TX

Vocals, Guitar / Country-Pop, Traditional Country

With his laidback vocals and imposing build, Don Williams was known as "the Gentle Giant." That nickname was bestowed on him in the early '70s, when he began a string of country-pop hits that ran into the early '90s. Williams was never known as an innovator, but his ballads were immensely popular—in the course of his career, he had a total of 17 number one hits.

Williams formed his first group, the folk-pop the Pozo-Seco Singers, with friends Lofton Kline and Susan Taylor in 1964. The next year, the band signed with Columbia Records and over the next three years, they had several minor hits. The group disbanded in 1971 and Williams pursued a songwriting career in Nashville. By the end of 1972, he had returned to performing. His first big hit was 1974's "We Should Be Together," a number five hit that led to a contract with ABC/Dot. "I Wouldn't Want to Live If You Didn't Love Me" became his first number one in the summer 1974. launching a series of Top Ten hits that ran more or less uninterrupted until 1991—during that time, only four of his 46 charting singles didn't make the Top Ten. Williams not only crossed over into the American pop mainstream, he earned fans in England and Europe. He began acting in the late '70s, appearing primarily Burt Reynolds films, including and *Smokey and the Bandit II.*

In the early '80s, Williams slowed down the pace of his career slightly, yet he continued to rack up number one hits. In 1986, he signed with Capitol and he continued to hit the Top Ten with regularity. Two years later, Williams moved to RCA. Initially, he continued to have hits, but his Top Ten streak came to an end in early 1992. Although he continued to perform in the mid-'90s, he had effectively retired to his Nashville farm, returning to recording in 1998 with *I Turn the Page.* *—Stephen Thomas Erlewine*

★ **Anthology** / Oct. 17, 2000 / Hip-O ✦✦✦✦✦
Spanning two discs, 20 years, and 40 songs, Hip-O's *Anthology* is a definitive overview of Don Williams' hit-making peak, containing the cream of his chart-topping \country smashes. It's neatly divided, with the first disc devoted to his '70s work, the second to his '80s, and if the first is a bit stronger, it's only because it's more interesting to hear an artist hit his stride than settling into a signature sound. Still, there are great moments throughout both discs, all offering definitive proof that Williams' laid-back, warm \country-pop was as good as mainstream \country-pop got—it was lush and accessible, but with real \country roots, unlike many of his peers. *—Stephen Thomas Erlewine*

Hank Williams (Hiriam King Williams)

b. Sep. 17, 1923, Mount Olive, AL, **d.** Jan. 1, 1953, Oak Hill, WV

Vocals, Guitar / Honky Tonk, Traditional Country

Hank Williams is the father of contemporary country music. Williams was a superstar by the age of 25; he was dead at the age of 29. In those four short years, Williams wrote and recorded a body of work that established the rules for all the country performers that followed him and, in the process, set the standard for most popular music.

"Move It On Over," Williams' first single for MGM, was an immediate hit in early 1947, climbing into the country Top Five. Two other singles followed in 1948, but "Lovesick Blues" was the song that made him a star. Upon its spring release in 1949, it was a smash hit, staying at number one for 16 weeks and crossing over into the pop Top 25. Williams had seven other hits in 1949 and another string of hits followed in 1950; that same year, Hank recorded a series of spiritual records as Luke the Drifter. Williams racked up more hits in 1951, beginning with the number one "Cold Cold Heart." Tony Bennett had hit with "Cold, Cold Heart" that year, opening the doors for mainstream artists to cover Williams.

Though his career was soaring, Williams's personal life was spinning out of control. He had descended into drug and alcohol addiction and in January 1952, his wife Audrey left him. Despite this, the hits kept coming, with no less than six Top 10 singles in 1952. Soon, his reckless behavior caught up with him, as he started missing concerts or playing drunk, losing friends and band members in the process. On his way to a concert in Canton, OH, on January 1, 1953, Hank Williams died in the backseat of his new Cadillac, the victim of a drug and alcohol overdose. "I'll Never Get Out of This World Alive," the last single he released in his lifetime, reached number one immediately after his death. Decades after his death, Hank Williams remains a towering figure in contemporary music. His songs are classics, his recordings timeless, and his life story is legendary. *—Stephen Thomas Erlewine*

I Saw the Light / 1956 / Mercury ✦✦✦✦✦
Every bit as essential as his country hits, *I Saw the Light* is an excellent testament to the songwriting genius of Hank Williams. A very spirited and, at times, utterly beautiful collection that has to rank with the best country-gospel albums ever made; these perfectly crafted songs might take Williams out of the honky tonk, but they can't take the honky tonk out of Williams' sound, as the tracks sound contemporary to anything else in his catalog. Standout harmonies on "How Can You Refuse Him Now" and "Jesus Remembered Me" to the just plain frightening "Angel of Death" and the poignant "Wealth Won't Save Your Soul" rank with Williams' best work. Overall, a truly essential piece in the viewing of Hank Williams' entire body of work. *—Matt Fink*

24 of Hank Williams' Greatest Hits / 1970 / MGM ✦✦✦✦✦
24 of Hank Williams' Greatest Hits was originally released as a set of overdubbed recordings, where the spare original recordings were augmented by a fuller band and, occasionally, strings. In the '80s, Mercury reissued the album with the original, undubbed versions of the songs and this version stands as an excellent retrospective of Williams' finest moments, containing a wealth of tremendous, timeless songs like "Your Cheatin' Heart," "I'm So Lonesome I Could Cry," "Honky Tonk Blues," "Cold, Cold Heart," "Mind Your Own Business," "Hey Good Lookin'," and "Jambalaya," among others. It's an excellent introduction, but *40 Greatest Hits* offers a deeper selection and, therefore, is an even better starting point. *—Stephen Thomas Erlewine*

★ **40 Greatest Hits** / 1978 / Mercury ✦✦✦✦✦
Over the course of two CDs, *40 Greatest Hits* runs through all of Hank Williams' essential songs, presented in their original, undubbed versions. It is the perfect place to start listening to Williams. *—Stephen Thomas Erlewine*

Rare Demos: First to Last / 1990 / Country Music Foundation ✦✦✦✦✦
Rare Demos: First to Last compiles all 24 publisher's demos that the country Music Foundation originally released as *The First Recordings* and *Just Me and My Guitar.* These are stark, moving recordings that cut to the core of each songs. Though the master takes are masterpieces in their own right, the demo versions are equally essential for dedicated fans, since they offer new insights to Williams' songwriting, as well as his performance technique. *—Stephen Thomas Erlewine*

☆ **Original Singles Collection . . . Plus** / 1992 / Mercury ✦✦✦✦✦
The title of *The Original Singles Collection... Plus* is slightly misleading. Although PolyGram marketed the three-disc, 84-song set as a complete collection, it doesn't feature all of the singles Hank Williams released during his lifetime. Several singles Williams released under the pseudonym "Luke the Drifter" as well all of the duets he cut with Audrey Williams aren't present. Despite these handful of songs, *everything* else is included in their original, undubbed versions and are presented in the best sound possible. For a fan that wants all the essential songs without springing for the eight disc series of complete recordings, *The Original Singles* collection is invaluable. *—Stephen Thomas Erlewine*

Health & Happiness Shows / 1993 / Mercury ✦✦✦✦✦
The double-disc set *Health & Happinesss Shows* collects eight complete radio shows that Hank Williams recorded in 1949, when his career was just taking off. Throughout the collection, Williams sounds energetic and vibrant, even during his between-song stage patter which is nearly fascinating as the music. It's a set that is designed for collectors, but even casual Williams fans will find much to treasure on the *Health & Happiness Shows.* *—Stephen Thomas Erlewine*

☆ **The Complete Hank Williams** / Sep. 22, 1998 / Mercury ✦✦✦✦✦
Between 1986 and 1987, Mercury launched its first effort to chronicle Hank Williams' complete recorded works, releasing a series of eight double-albums/single CDs which were later collected as a box set. Both the individual compilations and the box set were pulled from the market in the '90s, clearing the way for *The Complete Hank Williams,* a 10-disc box set which purported to contain all of Hank's recordings. Mercury, however, played it a little loose with their terms, deciding that "complete" covers the studio recordings, demos and selected live performances, leaving overdubbed tracks and many live cuts (including much of *The Health and Happiness Shows,* which was released as a separate collection) in the vaults. This is bound to frustrate some collectors, but it makes for a better listen, actually. Instead of piling all the recordings into an impenetrable chronological trawl through Hank's recording life, the compilers logically devoted specific discs to the studio sessions, live cuts and demos. In particular, the studio discs are quite compelling, but for hardcore fans, the previously unheard live performances (including several songs that Williams only performed in concert) are the real treasures. Then again, only hardcore fans will invest in such a lavish, extensive box set as *The Complete Hank Williams,* and there's little question that they'll be quite pleased with it. *—Stephen Thomas Erlewine*

Live at the Grand Ole Opry / Sep. 28, 1999 / Mercury ✦✦✦
This two-disc set brings together every extant performance from Hank Williams' brief hookup with the *Opry.* The first disc collects 21 performances, both musical and in the company of *Opry* comedy regulars Minnie Pearl and Rod Brasfield. To give a sense of how his presence worked in the format of the show, the second disc is a complete *Opry* broadcast from 1950 with Williams as part of the cast that also features Red Foley, Wally Fowler and the Oak Ridge Quartet (forerunners of today's Oak Ridge Boys), Minnie Pearl, Claude Sharpe and the Old Hickory Singers, and blackface comedians Jamup and Honey. Whether he's singing one of his famous hits or an old gospel favorite, or playing straight man to Brasfield or Pearl, it's obvious that here was a performer with personality aplenty, and it comes across on these old acetates with amazing impact. *—Cub Koda*

Hank Williams, Jr. (Randall Hank Williams)

b. May 26, 1949, Shreveport, LA

Vocals, Guitar / Urban Cowboy, Outlaw Country, Southern Rock, Traditional Country

The offspring of famous musicians often have a hard time creating a career for themselves, yet Hank Williams, Jr. is one of the few to develop a career that is not only successful, but markedly different from his legendary father. Originally, Hank Jr. simply copied and played his father's music, but as he grew older, he began to carve out his own niche and it was one that owed as much to country-rock as it did to honky tonk. In the late '70s, he retooled his image to appeal both to outlaw country fans and rowdy southern rockers, and his makeover worked, resulting in a string of Top 10 singles—including the number one hits "Texas Women," "Dixie on My Mind," "All My Rowdy Friends (Have Settled Down)," "Honky Tonkin'" and "Born to Boogie"—that ran into the late '80s. Hank Jr. never was above capitalizing on his father's name, yet his tributes and name-dropping often seemed affectionate, not crass. Also, Bocephus—as his father nicknamed him when he was a child—was a passionate cheerleader for patriotic American values; he even wrote a pro-Gulf War song during 1991. All of these actions helped make him an American superstar during the '80s, becoming one of the most recognizable popular culture figures of the era. As new country took over the airwaves in the '90s, Williams slowly disappeared from the charts and his concerts stopped selling as well as they did ten years earlier, yet he retained a devoted core audience throughout the decade. *—Stephen Thomas Erlewine*

★ **Bocephus Box Set [2000]** / Aug. 29, 2000 / Curb ✦✦✦✦✦
The years covered on Curb's *The Bocephus Box (1979-1999)* are the 20 years where Hank Jr. was an American icon, the larger-than-life rowdy man of country. His rise began in the early '80s, when he hit upon a terrific blend of honky tonk, Southern rock, blues, and country that appealed to rock and country audiences alike—rednecks of all persuasions, as less charitable critics would say. Throughout the '80s, he ruled the country charts, as every single one of his new albums went gold. For some observers, he slipped into self-parody halfway through that reign, but as this three-disc box set proves, the best of his music was remarkably consistent. Yes, the individual albums sagged somewhat (especially in the mid-'90s), but he remained true to his vision and had a good choice of material, whether it was newly written songs or rock covers. Early on in *The Bocephus Box,* it dawns on you that while some have replicated his style—and while he has spent a long time working the same ground—nobody really did this rowdy, rockin' country before Hank, and nobody has done it better since. Country purists may deny it, but he was a distinctive stylist, and while he got a little silly even when he was good, he usually delivered, especially in a concentrated setting like this. During those two decades, he released an album almost every year, which were distilled to 65 songs and three discs with almost no duds—which means he must have been doing something right. For doubters and fans alike, this is the place to really absorb Hank Jr. at the height of his powers. *—Stephen Thomas Erlewine*

☆ **Hank Williams Jr. & Friends** / 1975 / Polydor ✦✦✦✦✦
The breakthrough record of Williams's career. On his first mature record (made in his mid 20s), Williams teamed with Southern rockers Charlie Daniels, Toy Caldwell (Marshall Tucker Band), and Chuck Leavell (Allman Brothers Band), among others, for a session that opened his musical vistas to folk, blues, and rock, and incidentally introduced his mature persona in songs like "Stoned at the Jukebox" and "Living Proof." *—William Ruhlmann*

Family Tradition / 1979 / Warner Brothers ✦✦✦

Whiskey Bent and Hell Bound / 1979 / Warner Brothers ✦✦✦

Rowdy / 1981 / Warner Brothers ✦✦✦
In 1981, Hank Williams Jr was one of the hottest acts in country music, starting the year with this album, which spawned the number one hits "Texas Women" and "Dixie on My Mind" and the striking "Are You Sure Hank Done It This Way." *—William Ruhlmann*

★ **Hank Williams Jr's Greatest Hits** / 1982 / Warner Brothers ✦✦✦✦✦
Hank Williams, Jr. established himself as a country superstar in the late '70s and early '80s with a fusion of outlaw country and southern rock. *Hank Williams, Jr.'s Greatest Hits* contains his 10 biggest hits from that era, including "Family Tradition," "Whiskey Bent & Hell Bound," "Women I've Never Had," "Texas Women," "Dixie on My Mind," "A Country Boy Can Survive" and "All My Rowdy Friends (Have Settled Down)." It's not only some of the best music Williams ever made, but it's some of the definitive work of the era. *—Thom Owens*

Major Moves / 1984 / Warner Brothers ✦✦✦

Greatest Hits, Vol. 2 / 1985 / Warner Brothers ✦✦✦✦✦
A well-chosen hits collection covering 1983 to 1985, including "Leave Them Boys Alone" and "All My Rowdy Friends Are Coming Over Tonight." *—William Ruhlmann*

Greatest Hits, Vol. 3 / 1989 / Warner Brothers ✦✦✦✦✦
This chronicles Williams's ongoing '80s success, 1985-1989, featuring the number one hits "I'm for Love," "Ain't Misbehavin'," "Mind Your Own Business," and "Born to Boogie." *—William Ruhlmann*

America (The Way I See It) / 1990 / Warner Brothers ✦✦✦

The Bocephus Box: Hank Williams Jr. Collection '79-92 / 1992 / Capricorn ✦✦✦✦✦
A box set covering much the same turf as the Warner Brothers greatest-hits volumes, it does have additional outtakes and live cuts for the completist to enjoy. *—Dan Cooper*

American Legends: The Best of the Early Years / Sep. 1, 1995 / Polygram Special Markets ✦✦

Stormy / Aug. 31, 1999 / Curb ✦✦✦✦

Tex Williams (Sol Williams)

b. Aug. 23, 1917, Ramsey, Fayette County, IL, **d.** Oct. 11, 1985
Vocals, Guitar / Western Swing, Traditional Country
Although not nearly as well known as figures like Bob Wills, the Maddox Brothers, and Merle Travis, Tex Williams was an important western swing performer. Like all of the aforementioned musicians, he helped develop country music from its rural, acoustic origins to a more danceable, citified, and electrified form with a much wider popular appeal. At his peak in the late '40s, he also recorded some of the most enjoyable country swing of his time, distinguished by his talking-blues vocal delivery. Originally a member of Spade Cooley's Orchestra, Williams was later offered a solo contract by Capitol, while most of Cooley's band opted to follow Tex rather than remain with their difficult boss. Numbering about a dozen members, Tex's renamed backing band, the Texas Caravan, attained an enviable level of fluid interplay between electric and steel guitars, fiddles, bass, accordion, trumpet, and other instruments (even occasional harp). The single "Smoke! Smoke! Smoke! (That Cigarette)" emphasized Tex's talking-blues delivery and heavier boogie elements, becoming a monstrous number one pop hit in 1947, and indeed one of the biggest country hits of all time. That set the model for several of Williams' subsequent hits: hot western swing backup, over which Tex would roll his deep, laconic, easygoing narratives of humorous, slightly ridiculous situations. Williams continued to record often in the 1950s, mostly for Decca, without much success. He had one final country hit, the memorably titled "The Night Miss Ann's Hotel for Single Girls Burned Down," which entered the Top 30 in 1971. *—Richie Unterberger*

★ **Vintage Collections Series** / Jan. 23, 1996 / Capitol ✦✦✦✦✦
Vintage collects most of Tex Wiliams' best and most popular western swing hits, including "Smoke Smoke Smoke That Cigarette," making it a perfect introduction to of the most innovative country artists of the late '40s. *—Stephen Thomas Erlewine*

The Very Best of Tex Williams / Jul. 25, 2000 / Varese ✦✦✦✦
The Very Best of Tex Williams collects 13 of the Western swing star's most memorable songs and includes three previously unreleased performances: "Love Carefully," "Giddy-Up Go," and "Shakespeare Cha-Cha." "The Battle of New Orleans," "I'll Hold You in My Heart," "Little Ol Wine Drinker Me," and "Yankee Go Home" are some of the entertaining songs included on this collection, but its lack of definitive tracks like "Smoke! Smoke! Smoke! That Cigarette" and "Never Trust a Woman" makes it a less than ideal starting point. *—Heather Phares*

Kelly Willis

b. Oct. 2, 1968, Annandale, VA
Vocals / New Traditionalist, Contemporary Country
Although the music of singer/songwriter Kelly Willis earned widespread critical acclaim, she found little in the way of comparable commercial success; her sound, a smart hybrid of country and rock, simply assimilated both styles too well to gain acceptance in either camp. She began performing around Washington, D.C. in her boyfriend (and future husband) Mas Palermo's band at the age of 16. Her powerhouse vocals were so popular with club audiences that soon the group was renamed Kelly and the Fireballs in her honor. After Willis graduated high school, the band moved to Austin, TX, only to break up six months later. She and Palermo soon started a new band, Radio Ranch; one of their performances so impressed singer Nanci Griffith that she began lobbying her label MCA to sign to group, leading to Willis' 1990 debut *Well-Travelled Love.* In an attempt to capitalize on Willis' stunning looks, she was marketed as a girl-next-door type, and despite the presence of the full band, only her name appeared on the album jacket. Despite the glowing reviews, the LP fared poorly, and so for her 1991 sophomore effort *Bang Bang,* she was depicted as a coquettish pin-up, again to poor sales. For her third album, Willis joined forces with pop producer Don Was; the self-titled 1993 effort suffered the same fate as its predecessors, however, and she was dropped by MCA shortly after its release, finally resurfacing in 1999 with What I Deserve. *—Jason Ankeny*

Well Travelled Love / 1990 / MCA ✦✦✦

Bang Bang / 1991 / MCA ✦✦✦✦✦

Kelly Willis / 1993 / MCA ✦✦✦✦✦

What I Deserve / Feb. 23, 1999 / Rykodisc ✦✦✦
ThIs effort from country singer Kelly Willis has a number of important things going for it. First of all, there's her voice, which is an almost archetypally perfect blend of sweetness and grit. Then there are her backing musicians—in particular guitarist Mark Spencer, who makes a recognizably country sound without overdoing it or descending into bathos and stereotype. Last, and very importantly, there's producer Dave McNair, who has crafted a beautifully balanced and full-bodied sound for the album without allowing things to get too slick and prettified. What's lacking, for the most part, are melodies strong enough to grab your interest and hold it. There are some hooks—"Take Me Down" is quite singable, and there's a great version of Nick Drake's "Time Has Told Me"—but they're relatively few and far between, and scarcity of hooks can be death for a country album. In this case the lack is far from fatal, but it's noticeable. Recommended with reservations. *—Rick Anderson*

● **One More Time: The MCA Recordings** / Sep. 12, 2000 / MCA Nashville ✦✦✦✦✦
MCA Nashville's *One More Time: The MCA Recordings* was released on the heels of the independent success Kelly Willis enjoyed in 1999 with *What I Deserve.* Though it may have appeared after a success, the compilation isn't really a cash in. It's really quite useful, as a matter of fact, since it summarizes her three MCA albums—1990's *Well Travelled Love,* 1991's *Bang Bang,* and 1993's *Kelly Willis*—while adding "Little Honey," her contribution to the *Thelma & Louise* soundtrack. For anyone looking to catch-up after *What I Deserve,* this is an excellent place to go (especially since two of her three MCA albums were out of print at the time of *One More Time's* release), and it's a satisfying listen in its own right. *—Stephen Thomas Erlewine*

Bob Wills (James Robert Wills)

b. Mar. 6, 1905, Kosse, TX, **d.** May 13, 1975, Fort Worth, TX
Vocals, Fiddle / Western Swing, Traditional Country
Bob Wills' name will forever be associated with Western Swing. Although he did not invent the genre singlehandedly, he did popularize the genre and changed its rules. In the process, he reinvented the rules of popular music. Bob Wills and his Texas Playboys were a dance band with a country string section that played pop songs as if they were jazz numbers. Their music expanded and erased boundaries between genres. It was also some of the most popular music of its era. Throughout the '40s, the band was one of the most popular groups in the country and the musicians in the Playboys were among the finest of their era. As the popularity of Western Swing declined, so did Wills's popularity, but his influence is immeasurable. From the first honky tonkers to Western Swing revivalists, generations of country artists

owe him a significant debt, as do certain rock and jazz musicians. Bob Wills was a maverick and his spirit infused American popular music of the 20th century with a renegade, virtuosic flair. *—Stephen Thomas Erlewine*

☆ **Bob Wills Anthology** / 1973 / Columbia ♦♦♦♦♦
This two-LP set gives listeners a very good overview of the highly influential recordings of Bob Wills and the Texas Playboys. Many of Wills' best-known recordings of his prime years are included among the 24 selections with highlights including "Spanish Two Step," "Maiden's Prayer," "Steel Guitar Rag," "New San Antonio Rose," and "Twin Guitar Special." Programmed loosely in chronological order, the music is split fairly evenly between the 1935-1938 and 1940-1941 period with two later performances wrapping up the compilation. Wills was the most famous of the Western swing bandleaders, leading a very strong outfit that featured the steel guitar of Leon McAuliffe, guitarist Eldon Shamblin, fiddlers Jesse Ashlock and Louis Tierney, and vocalist Tommy Duncan, among others; some selections also include horns. Wills' band found the perfect blend between country music and swing-oriented jazz, and this set can serve as an excellent introduction to his enjoyable music. *—Scott Yanow*

For the Last Time / 1974 / United Artists ♦♦♦
Wills and the Texas Playboys reunited for the last swinging session of his life. Sitting in on fiddle and vocals is one of his biggest fans, Merle Haggard. *—Dan Cooper*

☆ **Tiffany Transcriptions, Vol. 1** / 1982 / Rhino ♦♦♦♦♦
The first of ten volumes (produced for CD by Jeff Alexson and Tom Diamant) of radio transcriptions done by Wills and his band in the mid-1940s is the strongest of the bunch. Done for the Tiffany Music Company—a concern formed by Wills, songwriter Clifford Sundin, and radio personality Clifton Johnson (Cactus Jack)—between 1946 and 1947, these recordings were intended as the basis for a syndicated radio series, but soon after the initial distribution of some of the recordings, the company was dissolved and the music withdrawn. Sundin had possession of the recordings, along with the relevant business files and promotional materials, until his death in 1981, after which the release of the music became possible through Kaleidoscope Records (which also handles records by Kate Wolf, Tiny Moore and Jethro Burns, the Bobs, the Sundogs, and the Zazu Pitts Memorial Orchestra), distributed by Rhino. The music features Wills and his band performing in a freer atmosphere than the typical recording session, not trying for a perfect take as much as a lively flow to each of the songs that would make the radio listener continue to tune in each week. The music is closer to a live performance than anything else Wills and his band ever recorded, with the members very informal and obviously enjoying themselves. Volume One gives a good idea of the entire ten-disc set, a mix of country, dance, jazz, folk, and blues standards (including a version here of "What's the Matter With the Mill," a song equally well known in versions by Moon Mullican and Muddy Waters), with vocalist Tommy Duncan at the top of his form. The sound is astonishingly good as well, given the age of the masters and the fact that they were never intended to be preserved for posterity. *—Bruce Eder*

☆ **Tiffany Transcriptions, Vol. 5** / 1986 / Rhino ♦♦♦♦♦

★ **Tiffany Transcriptions, Vol. 2** / Sep. 1986 / Rhino ♦♦♦♦♦
Containing the great majority of Bob Wills' most familiar songs—including "Take Me Back to Tulsa," "Faded Love," "Right or Wrong," "Cherokee Maiden," "Stay A Little Longer," "Time Changes Everything," "Corrine, Corrina" and "San Antonio Rose"—*Tiffany Transcriptions, Vol. 2* is the place for casual fans to get acquainted with this extraordinary multi-volume series of radio transcriptions. *—Stephen Thomas Erlewine*

☆ **Tiffany Transcriptions, Vol. 3** / Sep. 1986 / Rhino ♦♦♦♦♦

☆ **Tiffany Transcriptions, Vol. 4** / Sep. 1986 / Rhino ♦♦♦♦♦

Fiddle / 1987 / Country Music Foundation ♦♦♦
As the title suggests, *Fiddle* concentrates on Bob Wills' sometimes neglected Western fiddle style. Over the course of 20 tracks, which were recorded between 1935 and 1942, Wills and his colleagues—including Jesse Ashlock, Louis Tierney, Joe Holley, Clifton Johnson and Art Haines—run through a number of styles, ranging from direct fiddle and guitar duets to Cajun and jazzy big band numbers. For dedicated fans, it's an excellent addition to a library, even if it is a bit specialized for some tastes. *—Stephen Thomas Erlewine*

☆ **Tiffany Transcriptions, Vol. 6: Sally Goodin'** / 1987 / Rhino ♦♦♦♦♦

☆ **Tiffany Transcriptions, Vol. 7: Keep Knockin'** / 1987 / Rhino ♦♦♦♦♦

☆ **Tiffany Transcriptions, Vol. 8: More of the Best** / 1988 / Rhino ♦♦♦♦♦

Tiffany Transcriptions: For Collectors Only / 1990 / Rhino ♦♦♦♦♦

★ **Anthology 1935-1973** / 1991 / Rhino ♦♦♦♦♦
The only comprehensive retrospective of Bob Wills & the Texas Playboys, the double-disc set *Anthology 1935-1973* contains material from every label the Playboys recorded for and features the hit version of each of Wills' most famous songs, including "Right or Wrong," "Time Changes Everything," "Corrine, Corrina," "New San Antonio Rose," "Take Me Back to Tulsa," "Cherokee Maiden," "Roly-Poly," "Stay A Little Longer," "Big Beaver," "Bubbles in My Beer," "Faded Love," and many others. It's the rare compilation that functions both as a definitive overview and an excellent introduction. *—Stephen Thomas Erlewine*

☆ **Tiffany Transcriptions, Vol. 9: 1946-47** / 1991 / Rhino ♦♦♦♦♦

Country Music Hall of Fame Series / 1992 / MCA ♦♦♦♦♦

The Essential Bob Wills & His Texas Playboys / Aug. 25, 1992 / Columbia/Legacy ♦♦♦♦♦
A basic 20-track primer to some of the Western swing master's best sides. Acknowledged classics like "Steel Guitar Rag," "Take Me back to Tulsa," and "Stay a Little Longer" are all here, with the players and arrangements that made Wills and his Texas Playboys legends in country music. *—Cub Koda*

Longhorn Recordings / 1993 / Bear Family ♦♦♦♦♦
These mid-'60s Dallas sessions feature Wills in both large band and small rootsy combo settings. *—Dan Cooper*

☆ **San Antonio Rose** / Dec. 13, 2000 / Bear Family ♦♦♦♦♦

Lee Ann Womack

Vocals (Background), Vocals / Neo-Traditionalist Country, Adult Contemporary, Contemporary Country

After spending several years as a professional songwriter, Lee Ann Womack became one of the breakout contemporary country stars of 1997 with her eponymous debut album.

Born and raised in Jacksonville, Texas, Womack became infatuated with music at an early age, which is appropriate for the daughter of a disc jockey. Her father often took her to work, where she picked out records to play on the air. Following high school graduation, she attended South Plains Junior College in Levelland, Texas. The school was one of the first in the country to offer degrees in country and bluegrass music, and Womack soon became a member of the college's band, Country Caravan. She traveled throughout the South and California with Country Caravan and stayed with the group until she left South Plains to study music business at Belmont University in Nashville. That led to an internship in MCA's A&R department.

By 1990, she had settled in Nashville, where she married and became a mother. She continued to attend Belmont, as well as write songs. Soon, she began singing on songwriting demos and performing her own showcase concerts. Eventually, Womack was spotted by Tree Publishing at one of her showcases. In 1995, the company signed her after listening to one of her original demos. While she was a staff writer at Tree, she co-wrote songs with Ed Hill, Bill Anderson, Sam Hogin and Mark Wright. Her songs were recorded by Anderson and Ricky Skaggs.

Within a year after signing to Tree, Lee Ann Womack signed to Decca Records as a recording artist. Wright was hired as the producer for Womack's debut album, which was comprised of both original material and songs written by professional songwriters. Mark Chesnutt, Ricky Skaggs, Sharon White and Tony Brown all appeared on the record, which created a buzz in the industry.

Lee Ann Womack's eponymous album was released in May of 1997, and shortly after its release, it reached the Top Ten on the country chart. *I Hope You Dance* followed in mid-2000. *—Stephen Thomas Erlewine*

Lee Ann Womack / May 13, 1997 / MCA Nashville ♦♦♦
Lee Ann Womack's eponymous debut showcases a promising country vocalist who is more comfortable with ballads and pop than down-home honky tonk. The slick, professional production helps make the album a pleasant listen, despite the fairly uneven songwriting, and Womack certainly has a voice that can make the mediocre sound appealing, which results in a winning debut. *—Thom Owens*

Some Things I Know / Sep. 22, 1998 / MCA ♦♦♦

● **I Hope You Dance** / May 23, 2000 / MCA ♦♦♦♦
After a platinum-selling self-titled debut and a gold follow-up with *Some Things I Know*, Lee Ann Womack just keeps getting better. *Billboard* calls it "a career record." *I Hope You Dance* is one of the finest albums to hit country music post Shania Twain. Womack possesses such a sweet, melodious voice and its distinctiveness graces every one of the 12 tracks like they were chosen just for her vocals. But it's the album's title track, a dedication to Womack's daughters (and featuring the Sons of the Desert) that will leave you feeling swept away. (Her daughters, Aubrie and Anna Lise, who were ages 9 and 1 [respectively] at the time, appear in the video with her.) "Don't let some hardened heart leave you bitter/When you come close to selling out, reconsider/Give the heavens above more than a passing glance/And when you get the choice to sit it out or dance, I hope you dance." Listeners will undoubtedly dance to *I Hope You Dance*. *—Maria Konicki*

Sheb Wooley (Ben Colder)

b. Apr. 10, 1921, Erick, OK

Vocals / Country Comedy, Cowboy, Traditional Country, Novelty

Among pop-culture scholars, Sheb Wooley is best remembered for his late 1950's rock 'n roll/comedy hit "Purple People Eater," which sold over three million copies. But among country music afficianados, especially fans of cowboy songs, Sheb Wooley is the real article, or as near as one gets to it in modern times. A rodeo rider from the time that he was a boy, he was making a living on the circuit as a teenager, before he ever turned to music as a career. He turned to music and then acting, appearing in such westerns as *High Noon*, before he was ever well known as a singer, and later spent six seasons playing cowhand Pete Nolan on the television series *Rawhide*, even as he pursued a career in country music. In addition to cowboy songs, his repertory includes traditional country music and hillbilly tunes, along with the ubiquitous "Purple People Eater." Later on in 1960's, he also developed a drunken comic persona named Ben Colder, whose success in satirizing various elements of country music, its audience, and its sensibilities actually threatened to eclipse Sheb Wooley. *—Bruce Eder*

● **The Very Best of Sheb Wooley** / 1965 / MGM ♦♦♦♦♦

Rawhide/How the West Was Won / Feb. 1996 / Bear Family ♦♦♦♦
This isn't an ideal compilation, in the sense that none of the material on it was ever a hit, so the general public might not care for it—and people looking for anything like "Purple People Eater" or the Ben Colder material will be disappointed. But Bear Family has gathered together Wooley's two early '60s country-western albums, and they're very fine, even including a few originals that are quite good. He does a good job with the *Rawhide* title song, and also deeply evocative pieces like "Enchantment of the Prairie" and "The Story of Billy Burdell," backed by the likes of Earl Palmer on drums. *How The West Was Won* includes numbers such as "High Lonesome" and "Plowin' In The New Ground," and the sentimental "Papa's Old Fiddle," all of which come off well, in the manner of Gene Autry/Johnny Western/Sons of the Pioneers-style western songs. The backing musicians include Charlie McCoy on harmonica and Earl Palmer on drums. *—Bruce Eder*

That's My Pa / Mar. 25, 1998 / Bear Family ♦♦♦♦♦
This box and its 113 songs cover the years 1945 through 1972, and the least known side of Sheb

Wooley's career, but the one where he started out—as a country singer and songwriter, first fronting a Western swing-style band and later working in the straight commercial Nashville style. Warning to casual Sheb Wooley fans—there's no "Purple People Eater" here, or any sign of Wooley's "Ben Colder" comedy alias. Most were never on LP, and only a handful have been available in decades. The first ten cuts on this box, dating from 1945 and 1947, reveal him as a talented, smooth Gene Autry-type singer with more depth and range, with a good Western swing band behind him. On the MGM sides, beginning in 1948, the music is more polished, and the mix of songs is weighted more toward sentimental ballads. The middle section of this box shows us a fascinating set of possibilities—starting at the dawn of the 1950s, Wooley began merging Western swing with some components of R&B; his music could easily have moved toward rock & roll, but Wooley evidently wasn't comfortable making that jump. The material from the 1960s and early 1970s is utterly polished, and some of it is beautiful, commercial country music, using all of the smooth Nashville techniques. The assembly of the discs is also strange, mostly owing to the fact that after 1961, a huge amount of Wooley's studio time was given over to comedy tracks as "Ben Colder," leaving big gaps in his "straight" output for years at a time. The accompanying booklet contains a finely detailed account of Wooley's career. *—Bruce Eder*

Tammy Wynette (Virginia Wynette Pugh)

b. May 5, 1942, Itawamba County, MS, **d.** Apr. 6, 1998
Vocals, Guitar / Nashville Sound/Countrypolitan, Honky Tonk, Country-Pop, Traditional Country

In many ways, Tammy Wynette deserves the title of the First Lady of Country Music. During the late '60s and early '70s, she dominated the country charts, scoring 17 number one hits. Along with Loretta Lynn, she defined the role of female country vocalists in the '70s. Her career began in the mid-'60s, when she began performing to raise money for her treatment of her son's spinal meningitis. After moving to Nashville in 1966, she signed to Epic through producer Billy Sherrill and found her first number one hit with just her third single, "My Elusive Dreams." During 1968 and 1969, Tammy had five number one hits—"Take Me to Your World," "D-I-V-O-R-C-E," "Stand By Your Man," "Singing My Song" and "The Ways to Love a Man." In 1968, she started a relationship with George Jones, which would prove to be extremely stormy. Beginning in 1971, Wynette and Jones recorded a series of duets—the first was the Top Ten "Take Me"—which were as popular as their solo hits. However, the marriage was difficult and the couple divorced in 1975; they continued to record sporadically over the next two decades. Wynette's career began to slow down in the '80s, though she still had occasional hit singles and remained a popular concert attraction. She had been hospitalized several times during the mid-'90s before her death in 1998. *—Stephen Thomas Erlewine*

Your Good Girl's Gonna Go Bad / Apr. 1967 / Epic/Legacy ✦✦✦✦✦

D-I-V-O-R-C-E / Dec. 1967 / Koch International ✦✦✦✦✦
Tammy Wynette's third album, D-I-V-O-R-C-E features the number one C&W hit by the same name in addition to a bevy of album tracks, including covers of "Gentle on My Mind," "The Legend of Bonnie and Clyde," and the Beatles' "Yesterday." Amazingly, Wynette's version of "Yesterday" actually succeeds, and it's far less cloying than might be expected. Other tracks include "Kiss Away," co-written by producer Billy Sherrill, and "Honey (I Miss You)," an answer to Bobby Goldsboro's "Honey." The vocal performances are excellent even on the more disposable material, and although nothing here approaches the level of the title track, the album is ultimately rewarding for those whose interest in Tammy Wynette extends beyond her greatest hits. *—Greg Adams*

Stand by Your Man / 1968 / Epic/Legacy ✦✦✦✦✦
"Stand by Your Man" became a number one C&W hit as well as Tammy Wynette's signature song, and the album that shares its name topped the C&W album chart and crossed over to the pop chart, achieving platinum sales status along the way. Others in the music industry must have been paying attention, considering that two album tracks, "I Stayed Long Enough" (written by Wynette) and "Forever Yours," soon became hits for Billie Jo Spears and Dottie West respectively. Unlike Wynette's previous album, *D-I-V-O-R-C-E, Stand by Your Man* does not rely heavily on material associated with other artists, the most notable exception being a recording of Webb Pierce's 1957 hit "It's My Way." Although the result is a consistent album by '60s standards, the commercial importance of *Stand By Your Man* is more significantly tied to the strength of the title track than to its overall quality. Two years after Koch's CD-release of *Stand By Your Man,* Sony Legacy reissued it with bonus tracks. *—Greg Adams*

Take Me to Your World/I Don't Wanna Play House / Jan. 5, 1968 / Koch International ✦✦✦✦
Built around the two big hits comprising the title, this was a strong outing from Wynette, sensitively and sparely produced by Billy Sherrill (who co-wrote those two hits and one of the other better tracks, "Good"). Wynette is in good plaintive voice throughout the record, showing her interpretive skills to good effect on her version of Johnny Ray's "Cry," although the reading of "Ode to Billie Joe" is too jaunty (especially when compared with Bobbie Gentry's magnificent original). "It's My Way," with its sad melody, multi-tracked vocals, and spare steel guitar, is a standout. The CD reissue on Koch adds historical liner notes. *—Richie Unterberger*

☆ **Tammy's Greatest Hits** / 1969 / Epic ✦✦✦✦✦
This follows Wynette's trail of tears right out of the chutes on classics like "Stand by Your Man" and "D-I-V-O-R-C-E." Producer Billy Sherrill's less-than-light touch never found a better instrument to work with than her voice. *—Dan Cooper*

Kids Say the Darndest Things / 1973 / Epic ✦✦✦
Wynette and Sherrill join forces for a concept album, including "Listen, Spot," "My Daddy Doll," "Buy Me a Daddy," and "Too Many Daddies." Sound funny— It is. Except "Too Many Daddies" will still rip your heart out. *—Dan Cooper*

★ **Anniversary: 20 Years of Hits** / 1987 / Epic ✦✦✦✦✦
"Stand by Your Man" and "D-I-V-O-R-C-E" speak for themselves. But not to be overlooked are the less honored likes of "Apartment 9," her debut hit, written by Johnny Paycheck; and "Your Good Girl's Gonna Go Bad," in which her freedom (instead of little J-O-E's tears) are at stake. Also included are three duets with George Jones. *—Dan Cooper*

Tears of Fire: the 25th Anniversary Collection / Nov. 3, 1992 / Epic ✦✦✦✦✦
Tears of Fire: 25th Anniversary, a three-disc box set covering Wynette's entire career, contains most of her hits as well as rarities and oddities like her lead vocal on KLF's "Justified and Ancient." It's hard to fault a collection that includes such classics as "Stand By Your Man" and "D-I-V-O-R-C-E," but casual fans might want to stick with the single-disc *Anniversary—20 Years of Hits* collection. *—Thom Owens*

16 Biggest Hits / Feb. 2, 1999 / Epic/Legacy ✦✦✦✦✦
Unlike "greatest" hits or "best-of" compilations, whose titles imply a qualitative element, *16 Biggest Hits* is measurable solely by commercial success. And by that measure, *Tammy Wynette's 16 Biggest Hits* is exactly what it says it is, presenting the singer's 16 number one country hits from 1967 to 1976 in chronological order, from "I Don't Wanna Play House" to "You and Me," with standards like "D-I-V-O-R-C-E," "Stand By Your Man," and "'Til I Can Make It on My Own" in between. (Her chart-topping duets with David Houston and George Jones were not included.) Wynette was the queen of the plaintive heartbreak ballad on many of these tracks (five of which she co-wrote), though there were occasional expressions of domestic contentment such as "He Loves Me All the Way" and "My Man (Understands)," and more pieces of womanly advice in the tradition of "Stand By Your Man," such as "Run, Woman, Run" and the cautionary "Good Lovin' (Makes It Right)." Released only a couple of months before her death, *16 Greatest Hits* was a fitting tribute to Tammy Wynette. *—William Ruhlmann*

Trisha Yearwood

b. Sep. 19, 1964, Monticello, GA
Vocals / Contemporary Country, Country-Pop

Trisha Yearwood exploded onto the country scene in the early '90s with her chart-topping smash single "She's in Love with the Boy," which kick-started a string of hits and albums that established her as one of the most popular country performers of the '90s. After moving to Nashville in 1987, she began hanging out with such developing artists as Garth Brooks. For a while Yearwood worked as a demo singer, and then began singing back-up for Brooks, who promised her that if he became successful, he would help her career. While singing at a local bar she was discovered by producer Garth Fundis, who got her the showcase that led to her signing with MCA Records. Her debut single came out in 1990, and was followed by "That's What I Like About You," which appeared on her self-titled first album. She was later tapped to become Brooks' opening act, and her next two albums, *Hearts in Armor* (1992) and *The Song Remembers When* (1993), provided her with an impressive string of hits. In 1994, she again hit number one with "XXXs and OOOs (An American Girl)" from the album *The Sweetest Gift.* *—Sandra Brennan*

Trisha Yearwood / 1991 / MCA ✦✦✦✦
This impressive debut brought everybody to lend a hand: Vince Gill, Mac McAnally, keyboardist Al Kooper, and more. Garth Brooks co-wrote two songs and helped sing one, the tentatively tender "Like We Never Had a Broken Heart." Yearwood is more at home with blue-collar romance than sweltering Texas nightlife, but her big Georgia range lets her sing just about anything, from the ballad "When Goodbye Was a Word" to Pat McLaughlin's saucy "That's What I Like About You." *—Brian Mansfield*

★ **Hearts in Armor** / Sep. 1, 1992 / MCA ✦✦✦✦✦
Take away the bluesy hit "Wrong Side of Memphis," and this is practically an emotional diary of Yearwood's divorce (which happened just as she hit the big time). In light of that event, "Nearest Distant Shore" and "Hearts in Armor" assume devastating significance and the cover of Emmylou Harris' "Woman Walk the Line" couldn't be more appropriate. As before, she's got the big-name back up singer—Harris, Don Henley, Vince Gill, and Garth Brooks—but not one steals the spotlight. *Hearts in Armor* is strictly Yearwood's show, and she's marvelous in it. *—Brian Mansfield*

The Song Remembers When / 1993 / MCA ✦✦✦✦✦
Yearwood shares common ground with peers Nanci Griffith and Mary-Chapin Carpenter by walking the line between country, folk, and pop, appealing to those who elevate the song above category limitations. Yearwood doesn't write her own material, but she and producer Garth Fundis have impeccable taste, securing contributions from the likes of Rodney Crowell, Willie Nelson (both also guest on backing vocals), and Matraca Berg. Ballads are Yearwood's forte: pure, sweet, sparsely rendered gems like "One In a Row" and "Lying to the Moon." *—Roch Parisien*

Thinkin' About You / 1995 / MCA ✦✦✦
Although there are a couple of high points on *Thinkin' About You,* the record is weighed down with mediocre material and slick, commercially oriented prodcution. Occasionally, Yearwood's vocals save the day, but there are times where she oversings the songs, giving them emotion they don't deserve. In all, it's one of the few Trisha Yearwood albums that can be called a disappointment. *—Thom Owens*

Everybody Knows / Aug. 27, 1996 / MCA ✦✦✦

Songbook: A Collection of Hits / Aug. 26, 1997 / MCA ✦✦✦✦✦
(Songbook) A Collection of Hits is a terrific overview of Trisha Yearwood's hit singles of the early and mid-'90s, containing such songs as "She's in Love With the Boy," "Like We Never Had a Broken Heart," "The Woman Before Me," "Walkaway Joe," "The Song Remembers When," "XXX's and OOO's (An American Girl)," "Thinkin' About You" and "I Wanna Go Too Far." It's a near-definitive collection that shows why Yearwood was one of the most popular contemporary country vocalists of the '90s. *—Thom Owens*

Where Your Road Leads / Jul. 14, 1998 / MCA ✦✦✦✦
Trisha Yearwood is a pop diva who knows how to play her instrument, her voice. Perhaps one of the most gifted contemporary pop vocalists, Yearwood continues to explore the vast

expanses of her talent. Displaying only traces of her early work as a country music artist, she sings with yearning on songs like "Powerful Thing." Buddy Miller's backing vocals on "Bring Me All Your Lovin'" are a highlight of this project. Yearwood's brilliance is adequately displayed on "I Don't Want to Be the One" and "I'll Still Love You More," a Diane Warren composition. She is at her best when she inhabits the world of emotional ballads and snappy, uptempo tunes about the emotional life of modern women. While she is no country singer by any stretch of the imagination, she is still an important element in pop music. *—Jana Pendragon*

Real Live Woman / Mar. 28, 2000 / MCA ✦✦✦

Dwight Yoakam

b. 1956, Pikeville, KY

Vocals, Guitar / Alternative Country, New Traditionalist, Bakersfield Sound

With his stripped-down approach to traditional honky tonk and Bakersfield country, Dwight Yoakam helped return country music to its roots in the late '80s. Like his idols Buck Owens, Merle Haggard, and Hank Williams, Yoakam never played by Nashville's roots; consequently, he never dominated the charts like his contemporary Randy Travis. Then again, Travis never played around with the sound and style of country music like Yoakam. On each of his records, he twists around the form enough to make it seem like he doesn't respect all of country's traditions. Appropriately, his core audience was composed mainly of roots-rock and rock & roll fans, not the mainstream country audience. Nevertheless, he was frequently able to chart in the country Top Ten, and he remained one of the most respected and adventurous recording country artists well into the '90s. *—Stephen Thomas Erlewine*

Guitars, Cadillacs, Etc., Etc. / 1986 / Reprise ✦✦✦✦✦

Who would have guessed when this album was released, with its uncompromisingly basic, honky-tonk approach, that it would not only be a success but would help move the country music industry back from its crossover ways of the early '80s to a new renaissance based on its most traditional sounds— Maybe Yoakam, who doggedly stuck to that approach and wrote a bunch of songs that fit in with covers like Johnny Horton's "Honky Tonk Man." *—William Ruhlmann*

Hillbilly Deluxe / 1987 / Reprise ✦✦✦

Hillbilly Deluxe essentially follows the same formula as *Guitars, Cadillacs, Etc., Etc.* and is just slightly less successful than Yoakam's breakthrough debut. The record is quite enjoyable—not only are updated honky tonk originals like "Little Ways" first-rate, but so are covers like Elvis Presley's "Little Sister" and Lefty Frizzell's "Always Late (With Your Kisses)." So the problem with the album lies in the fact that it doesn't move forward signficantly, it is just Yoakam treading water. It's an enjoyable record, yet it still ranks as a minor work in his canon. *—Thom Owens*

Buenos Noches from a Lonely Room / 1988 / Reprise ✦✦✦✦✦

The first five cuts constituted a cold-blooded cycle that ran from possessive love to murderous rage with alarming quickness. The rest was subsequently a letdown but still gave Yoakam a couple of big hits in "I Sang Dixie" and "Streets of Bakersfield," a duet with Buck Owens. *—Brian Mansfield*

★ **Just Lookin' for a Hit** / 1989 / Reprise ✦✦✦✦✦

A strong 10-track singles collection with a typically sarcastic title, paced by duets with K.D. Lang on Gram Parsons' "Sin City" and with Buck Owens (a match made in heaven) on "Streets of Bakersfield." *—William Ruhlmann*

☆ **If There Was a Way** / 1990 / Reprise ✦✦✦✦✦

Dwight Yoakam began a new decade with *If There Was A Way* and, along with it, a new approach to recording. Working from the foundation he laid with *Buenas Noches from a Lonely Room,* Yoakam lightens the tone somewhat with abandoning the gut-wrenching emotional impact or ambitious musical eclecticism. If anything, he's even more eclectic, bringing in touches of R&B and '50s rock & roll that make his honky tonk tales of despair cut even deeper. Of particular note is the Dwight Yoakam and Roger Miller collaboration, "It Only Hurts When I Cry." *—Thom Owens*

La Croix D'Amour / 1992 / Reprise ✦✦✦✦✦

An international-only compilation, *La Crois D'Amour* is worth searching out for its rarities: two songs that appeared on other collections (Elvis Presley's "Suspicious Minds" and The Grateful Dead's "Truckin'") and four new tracks, among them covers of The Beatles' "Things We Said Today" and Them's "Here Comes the Night." *—Brian Mansfield*

☆ **This Time** / 1993 / Reprise ✦✦✦✦✦

Heartbroke fool that he is, Dwight Yoakam knows all the words for loneliness. He doesn't let up once he starts on the self-pity binge of *This Time:* he begins as the devastated lover and winds up 11 songs later the desolate loner. Musical traditionalist that he is, he knows all the styles, too, from Buck Owens' Bakersfield country ("This Time") to Gene Pitney's mini-soundtracks ("A Thousand Miles from Nowhere") to rock's spite fantasies ("Fast as You"). He knows so many that *This Time* sounds more like a collection of individual songs than the single-minded work that it is. He understands them, too: That's why Yoakam gets good mileage from campy gimmicks like the ooh-wah background vocals on "Pocket of a Clown." There's plenty of hardcore country here—"This Time," "Home for Sale," "Lonesome Road"—but the best stuff allows for Yoakam's pop roots, too. *—Brian Mansfield*

Dwight Live / May 23, 1995 / Reprise ✦✦

Gone / Nov. 1995 / Reprise ✦✦✦

With *Gone,* Dwight Yoakam continued to push the boundaries of country music, adding elements of rock & roll, Tex-Mex, Stax R&B, strings and even sitar to his already eclectic Bakersfield country. However, what makes *Gone* distinctive is the directness of the songwriting. For the first time, Yoakam has written the majority of the album alone and the results are riviting. He is able to fuse together disperate elements into an emotional and daring whole. Ten years into his career, Dwight Yoakam remains one of country's most exciting and restless talents. *—Stephen Thomas Erlewine*

Under the Covers / Jul. 15, 1997 / Reprise ✦✦✦

A Long Way Home / Jun. 9, 1998 / Reprise ✦✦✦

☆ **Last Chance for a Thousand Years: Greatest Hits from the 1990's** / May 18, 1999 / Reprise ✦✦✦✦✦

dwightyoakamacoustic.net / May 30, 2000 / Reprise ✦✦✦

Faron Young

b. Feb. 25, 1932, Shreveport, LA, **d.** Dec. 10, 1996

Vocals, Guitar / Nashville Sound/Countrypolitan, Honky Tonk, Country-Pop, Traditional Country

Originally known as the "Hillbilly Heartthrob" and the "Singing Sheriff," Faron Young had one of the longest-running and most popular careers in country music history. Emerging in the early '50s, Young was one of the most popular honky tonkers to appear in the wake of Hank Williams' death, paritially because he was able to smooth out some of the grittiest elements his music. At first, he balanced honky tonk with pop vocal phrasing and flourishes. This combination of grit and polish resulted in a streak of Top 10 hits—including "If You Ain't Lovin'," "Live Fast, Love Hard, Die Young," "Sweet Dreams" "Alone With You" and "Country Girl"—that ran throughout the '50s. During the '60s, Young gave himself over to country-pop, and while the hits weren't quite as big, they didn't stop coming until the early '80s. Through that time, he was a staple at the Grand Ole Opry and various television shows, including *Nashville Now,* and he also founded the major country music magazine, *Music City News.* Most importantly, he continued to seek out new songwriters—including Don Gibson, Willie Nelson, and Kris Kristofferson—thereby cultivating a new generation of talent. *—Stephen Thomas Erlewine*

The Classic Years 1952-62 / 1992 / Bear Family ✦✦✦✦✦

Swashbuckling Louisiana honky tonk, much of Faron Young's early work on Capitol is marked by an undertone of grinning lasciviousness. That's not a bad thing, given how many of his industry pals completely hid their wolfishness behind apple-pie lyrics. In any case, Bear Family has here collected the entirety of Young's Capitol output on five CDs. Besides the swaggering stuff ("If You Ain't Lovin'," "Live Fast, Love Hard, Die Young," and the amazing "Alone with You") one can hear the hit version of "Sweet Dreams" he cut seven years before Patsy Cline's. It comes with a beautiful 48-page book. *—Dan Cooper*

☆ **Live Fast, Love Hard: Original Capitol Recordings,1952-1962** / Oct. 1995 / Country Music Foundation ✦✦✦✦✦

Faron Young was one of the most popular honky tonk stars of the '50s and *Live Fast, Love Hard: Original Capitol Recordings, 1952-1962* is an excellent, 24-song overview of the peak of his career. Featuring his big hits like "If You Ain't Lovin' (You Ain't Livin')" as well as more obscure tracks (a radio transcription of "Three Days"), the album is the most thorough and listenable single-disc retrospective ever assembled on Young. For honky tonk fans, it's an essential listen. *—Stephen Thomas Erlewine*

★ **The Complete Capitol Hits of Faron Young** / Oct. 17, 2000 / Collectors' Choice Music ✦✦✦✦✦

As the title suggests, *The Complete Capitol Hits of Faron Young* collects all 41 of the honky tonk star's hits for the label, including "If You Ain't Lovin'," "Goin' Steady," "For the Love of a Woman Like You," "Turn Her Down," and "I Hear You Talkin'." Grammy Award-winning writer Colin Escott provides thoughtful liner notes for this comprehensive anthology of Young's years with Capitol, which were arguably his most fruitful. Richer than 1995's collection *Live Fast, Love Hard,* which covers the same territory, *The Complete Capitol Hits* captures Young's appealingly pop-tinged take on honky tonk. *—Heather Phares*

Various Artists

16 Down Home Country Classics / Jan. 20, 1998 / Arhoolie ✦✦✦✦✦

This is in effect a sampler of Arhoolie's country-related catalog, with cuts from 16 different releases. It's country of the old-timey and early honky tonk variety, not of the produced country-pop sort, though that's not a drawback. Highlights include the Maddox Brothers & Rose's raucous "George's Playhouse Boogie," the Carter Family's "Hello Stranger" (from a 1939 radio broadcast), the Strange Creek Singers' "No Never No" (with Alice Gerrard and Hazel Dickens duetting on vocals), and Toni Brown's "You Turned Your Back," a lost modern hillbilly classic of sorts (and also the rarest cut, previously issued on an Arhoolie 45-rpm single). Also including selections by Del McCoury, J.E. Mainer, the Any Old Time String Band, and many others, this may be too old-timey/Appalachian in nature for those with modern country tastes. *—Richie Unterberger*

All-Time Legends of Country Music / Nov. 1, 1994 / Columbia/Legacy ✦✦✦✦

All-Time Legends of Country Music is an excellent cross-section of country classics recorded or owned by Columbia and Epic Records. The 22-track disc spans several decades and styles, from the traditional country of Roy Acuff's "Wabash Cannon Ball" to the outlaw duet of Merle Haggard and Willie Nelson's "Pancho & Lefty." Since there's such a variety of styles, the disc doesn't quite gel as a cohesive listening experience, but there are so many great songs here that it doesn't really matter. It's just nice to have Patsy Montana's "I Want to Be a Cowboy's Sweetheart," Bob Wills' "Take Me Back to Tulsa," Bill Monroe's "Rocky Road Blues," the Stanley Brothers' "I'm a Man of Constant Sorrow," Carl Smith's "Hey Joe," Flatt & Scruggs' "Foggy Mountain Special," Johnny Horton's "Honky Tonk Man," Marty Robbins' "El Paso," Johnny Cash's "Ring of Fire," the Statler Brothers' "Flowers on the Wall," Jim & Jesse's "When I Stop Dreaming," Jim & Jesse's "When I Stop Dreaming," Lynn Anderson's "I Never Promised You a Rose Garden," Willie Nelson's "My Heroes Have Always Been Cowboys" and Willie & Merle's "Pancho & Lefty" all in one place. *—Stephen Thomas Erlewine*

Best of Austin City Limits: Country Music's Finest Hour / 1996 / Columbia/Legacy ✦✦✦

☆ **The Bristol Sessions** / 1991 / Country Music Foundation ✦✦✦✦✦

It's common knowledge that Ralph Peer's open recording session in Bristol, TN, launched the careers of The Carter Family and Jimmie Rodgers, but as this double CD proves, they weren't the only worthwhile musicians to turn up. In fact, Peer recorded 21 other acts, including the Stoneman Family and Blind Alfred Reed in what turns out to be an amazing display of rural talent and the birth of country music. *—William Ruhlmann*

Cattle Call: Early Cowboy Music and Its Roots / 1996 / Rounder ✦✦✦✦✦

☆ **Columbia Country Classics, Vol. 1: The Golden Age** / 1990 / Columbia ✦✦✦✦✦

● **Columbia Country Classics, Vol. 2: Honky Tonk Heroes** / 1984 / Columbia ✦✦✦✦✦

Columbia Country Classics, Vol. 3: Americana / 1990 / Columbia ✦✦✦✦✦

Columbia Country Classics, Vol. 4: The Nashville Sound / Columbia ✦✦✦✦✦

Don't Fence Me In: Western Music's Early Golden Era / Feb. 1996 / Rounder ✦✦✦✦✦

From Where I Stand: The Black Experience in Country Music / Jan. 27, 1998 / Warner Brothers ✦✦✦✦✦

An ambitious three-CD mini-box that is not 100% successful in its attempt to document the history of black country music, *From Where I Stand* is quite worthy and admirable nonetheless. Each disc is assembled thematically: disc one concentrates on pre-World War II stringband and folk acts, disc two has soul singers' interpretations of country material, and disc three spotlights black artists working more or less within the country mainstream from the late '60s onward. Disc one is interesting in its illustration of how early rural white and black musicians drew from such similar material that they could sound far closer to each other stylistically than historians might lead one to believe. Three of Grand Ole Opry harmonica player DeFord Bailey's rare cuts are here; other highlights are numbers by Leadbelly and artists (Peg Leg Howell, Bo Chatmon) who have been more commonly categorized into the blues idiom. Disc two has country-oriented material by Solomon Burke, Arthur Alexander, the Supremes, Ray Charles, Joe Tex, Etta James, and others, mostly from the golden age of soul. Disc three has cuts by modern black country acts, as well as outings into country by soul singers. Artistically, it's the least successful of the discs—a black singer doing faceless country-pop is just as boring as a white singer doing it. There are so many covers of country tunes by soul singers on the final two discs that one gets the sense the compilers stretched the definition of black country as far as they could simply to fill this out to the length of a box set, which isn't necessarily such a bad thing. The soul cuts are probably the best in the box, and the historical connections between the artists and their country influences are made clearer by a fine 60-page booklet. *—Richie Unterberger*

Hank Williams: Songwriter to Legend / Sep. 16, 1998 / Bear Family ✦✦✦

Songwriter to Legend is an essential addendum to the *Complete Hank Williams* box set, as it collects a bevy of songs that Williams wrote but did not record in the studio. Williams had a good sense of quality control and did not give away his best material, so there are no forgotten masterpieces among these recordings. But there are some worthwhile tracks, particularly Red Sovine's recording of "You're Barking Up the Wrong Tree Now" and Braxton Shooford's "Rockin' Chair Daddy." In addition to these "lost" songs written or co-written by Williams, there are ten tributes recorded after his death by such artists as Marvin Rainwater, Ernest Tubb, Johnnie & Jack, and Jimmie Skinner, as well as Kitty Wells' "answer" song, "My Cold, Cold Heart Is Melted Now" and Rex Griffin's 1939 version of "Lovesick Blues," which served as the template for Williams' recording. As a dubious bonus, there is a "mystery bonus track" with an unidentified artist relating tales of Williams' shortcomings to the tune of "The Battle of New Orleans." Fascinating. *—Greg Adams*

Hillbilly Boogie / 1994 / Columbia/Legacy ✦✦✦✦✦

A find for fans of Western swing and honky tonk music, Hillbilly Boogie's 20 selections from 1946-1954 mirror the carefree postwar years with a rousing blend of vocal numbers and instrumentals. The selections include everything from fiddle and pedal-steel combo swingers like Paul Howard & His Cotton Pickers' "Drinking All My Troubles Away" to big-band country numbers like Al Dexter & His Troopers' "New Broom Boogie." Even the South's unsung Eastern European musical heritage is given its due on a handful of accordion-heavy polkas, including Spade Cooley's "Yodeling Polka" and Louise Massey & the Westeners' "Squeeze Box Polka." Plenty of boogie-woogie rhythm is also on hand with Curley Williams & His Georgia Peach Pickers' "Georgia Boogie" and Andy Reynolds & His 101 Ranch Boys' "Fiddlin' Boogie." Other fine cuts are contributed by country stars Bob Wills, Lefty Frizzell, and Little Jimmy Dickens. Topped off with excellent transfers from the original lacquers, plenty of humor ("Hamburger Hop"), and fine playing throughout, Hillbilly Boogie is a must for devotees of the golden era of pre-Nashville sound country music. *—Stephen Cook*

☆ **Hillbilly Fever, Vol. 1** / 1995 / Rhino ✦✦✦✦✦

Where most country various-artists collections are designed with dollars, not sense, in mind, Rhino's five-disc Hillbilly Fever series was thoughtfully compiled and intelligently executed. Hillbilly Fever concentrates on the classic era of recorded country music, running from 1933 to 1975, spotlighting nearly all the important artists (usually with one of their best-known songs) along the way. The first volume of the series, *Legends of Western Swing,* is an 18-track compilation that encapsulates the genre. Featuring cuts by the Fort Worth Doughboys, Milton Brown, the Light Crust Doughboys, Cliff Bruner, Johnnie Lee Wills, Bob Wills, Spade Cooley, Tex Williams, Leon McAuliffe, and Hank Thompson, the disc contains all of the most important musicians in the genre, as well as a handful of terrific obscurities. As a result, Legends of Western Swing functions as a definitive, essential introduction to one of the most infectious genres in country music. [None of the five discs in the Hillbilly Fever series sold in its initial release, probably because its title was too smug to appeal to either hardcore record collectors or casual country fans. A year after the release of Hillbilly Fever, Rhino reissued the entire series under the title Heroes of Country Music. Unfortunately, the second time around, they pulled several essential tracks from each disc. But even in its edited form, the series is worth getting.] *—Stephen Thomas Erlewine*

★ **Hillbilly Fever, Vol. 2** / 1995 / Rhino ✦✦✦✦✦

Hillbilly Fever, Vol. 2: Legends of Honky Tonk is an essential primer in country music's most enduring genre, boasting some of the greatest barroom tunes ever recorded during the genre's heyday. Beginning in 1937 with Al Dexter's "Honky Tonk Blues" and ending 30 years later with Jim Edward Brown's "Pop A Top," the disc contains definitive cuts from nearly all of honky tonk's major players, including Rex Griffin ("The Last Letter"), Ernest Tubb ("Walking the Floor Over You"), Floyd Tillman ("Drivin' Nails in My Coffin"), Hank Williams ("Honky Tonkin'"), Leon Payne ("I Love You Because"), Hank Thompson ("The Wild Side of Life"), Lefty Frizzell ("Just Can't Live That Fast [Any More]"), and George Jones ("A Girl I Used to Know"). Though several additional songs and artists could have been included, Legends of Honky Tonk is nevertheless an essential overview and introduction to country's defining genre. [None of the five discs in the Hillbilly Fever series sold in its initial release, probably because its title was too smug to appeal to either hardcore record collectors or casual country fans. A year after the release of Hillbilly Fever, Rhino reissued the entire series under the title Heroes of Country Music. Unfortunately, the second time around, they pulled several essential tracks from each disc. But even in its edited form, the series is worth getting.] *—Stephen Thomas Erlewine*

☆ **Hillbilly Fever, Vol. 3** / 1995 / Rhino ✦✦✦✦✦

"The Nashville sound" commonly refers to the lushly orchestrated country-pop sound also called countrypolitan, which came to prominence in the late '50s. Hillbilly Fever, Vol. 3: Legends of Nashville bypasses that era, choosing to concentrate on the classic days of the Grand Ole Opry. As a result, Legends of Nashville has a wide range of styles, from honky tonk to country-pop, but it all sounds unified because it captures the essence of pre-rock & roll country music (1945-1956). Though the collection doesn't have a story to tell like its two predecessors, Legends of Nashville is just as essential to any comprehensive country collection, simply because of the number of classics available on the disc: Eddy Arnold's "Bouquet of Roses," Ernest Tubb's "It's Been So Long Darling," Pee Wee King's "Tennessee Waltz," Hank Williams' "Lovesick Blues," George Morgan's "Room Full of Roses," Webb Pierce's "Wondering," Slim Whitman's "Indian Love Call," Kitty Wells' "It Wasn't God Who Made Honky Tonk Angels," Faron Young's "If You Ain't Lovin' (You Ain't Livin')," the Louvin Brothers' "I Don't Believe You've Met My Baby," Ray Price's "Crazy Arms," Marty Robbins' "Singing the Blues," and Patsy Cline's "Walkin' After Midnight." [None of the five discs in the Hillbilly Fever series sold in its initial release, probably because its title was too smug to appeal to either hardcore record collectors or casual country fans. A year after the release of Hillbilly Fever, Rhino reissued the entire series under the title Heroes of Country Music. Unfortunately, the second time around, they pulled several essential tracks from each disc. But even in its edited form, the series is worth getting.] *—Stephen Thomas Erlewine*

☆ **Hillbilly Fever, Vol. 4** / 1995 / Rhino ✦✦✦✦✦

Hillbilly Fever, Vol. 4: Legends of the West Coast doesn't just cover the Bakersfield sound of the late '50s and early '60s, but also traces its development through the late '40s and '50s. The disc begins with a selection of cowboy songs (Jack Guthrie's "Oklahoma Hills," Gene Autry's "You Are My Sunshine," Sons of the Pioneers' "Cool Water"), before moving toward Western swing (Al Dexter's "Too Late to Worry," Spade Cooley's "Shame on You") and country-boogie (Tennessee Ernie Ford's "Mule Train"). By the end of the disc—after Skeets McDonald's "Don't Let the Stars Get in Your Eyes," Jimmy Wakely's "One Has My Name (The Other Has My Heart)," Tex Ritter's "High Noon (Do Not Forsake Me)," and Joe Maphis Rose Lee's "Dim Lights Thick Smoke (And Loud, Loud Music)" have all been heard—the electrified honky tonk of Bakersfield begins to emerge in the form of Jean Shepard ("A Dear John Letter"), Tommy Collins ("You Better Not Do That"), Ferlin Husky ("Gone"), Wynn Stewart ("Wishful Thinking"), Buck Owens ("Second Fiddle"), and Merle Haggard ("Sing a Sad Song"). Since it covers so many different styles, Legends of the West Coast is a little inconsistent. Nevertheless, it tells its story well and contains a wealth of classics, making it another essential addition to any comprehensive country library. [None of the five discs in the Hillbilly Fever series sold in its initial release, probably because its title was too smug to appeal to either hardcore record collectors or casual country fans. A year after the release of Hillbilly Fever, Rhino reissued the entire series under the title Heroes of Country Music. Unfortunately, the second time around, they pulled several essential tracks from each disc. But even in its edited form, the series is worth getting.] *—Stephen Thomas Erlewine*

● **Hillbilly Fever, Vol. 5** / 1995 / Rhino ✦✦✦✦✦

If you're a big country-rock fan, you're probably familiar with most of the work on this compilation. If you're not, it's a good introductory survey of the genre; if you're a fan but not passionate enough about the style to actively collect country-rock recordings, it may satisfy more basic needs. Focusing exclusively on music from country-rock's heyday in the late '60s and early '70s, it has cuts by most of the leading lights of the scene, including the Flying Burrito Brothers, the International Submarine Band, the Byrds, the Everly Brothers, Poco, the Nitty Gritty Dirt Band, Michael Nesmith, and the New Riders of the Purple Sage. The compilation also briefly visits the mid-'70s with Pure Prairie League and Marshall Tucker. There are also off-the-beaten tracks by Linda Ronstadt and Bob Dylan, as well as country-rock outings by name acts not primarily affiliated with the style, such as the Lovin' Spoonful, the Youngbloods, and Delaney & Bonnie. It's a good mix of the familiar and the unfamiliar, though it doesn't include important work in the field by Buffalo Springfield, the Grateful Dead, the Beau Brummels, and Rick Nelson, mostly because of licensing restrictions. *—Richie Unterberger*

☆ **Hillbilly Jazz** / 1975 / Flying Fish ✦✦✦✦✦

The name *Hillbilly Jazz* might sound like an oxymoron to some, but when you think about it, jazz and "hillbilly music" have made for a healthy combination from time to time. The seminal country singer Jimmie Rodgers featured Louis Armstrong as a vocalist on some of his classic 1920s recordings, and Western swing came about when, in the 1930s, Bob Wills and others combined jazz with country and bluegrass. Then, in the 1950s and early 1960s, jazz and pre-rock pop influenced country-pop stars like Patsy Cline and Willie Nelson. Hillbilly Jazz was a project that, in 1991, drew on jazz, bluegrass, Western swing, blues and country. With such talented players as fiddle great Vassar Clements, guitarist David Bromberg, drummer D.J. Fontana and singer Gordon Terry on board, Hillbilly Jazz successfully turns its attention to everything from Wills' "San Antonio Rose" (a natural choice) to Duke Ellington's

"C-Jam Blues," Benny Goodman's "Breakfast Feud" and Les Brown's "Sentimental Journey." Improvisation is a high priority for *Hillbilly Jazz,* and a love of improvisation is one thing that jazz, bluegrass and Western swing players have in common. This rewarding but little-known CD reminds us that jazz and "hillbilly music" can fit together quite nicely. *—Alex Henderson*

Home on the Range / 1992 / Pavilion ✦✦✦✦✦
It's sort of embarrassing that a collection of early cowboy songs as good as this has to come out of England. Gene Autry is represented by his stripped-down, mournful 1930 ballad "No One to Call Me Darling," the delightful 1938 "I've Got the Jailhouse Blues," the equally bluesy "I'll Always Be a Rambler," and two other seldom reissued numbers. Roy Rogers is here with "Colorado Sunset," but the really good material comes from the other side of the tradition, in the guise of Jimmie Rodgers and "Round Up Time Out West," "I've Only Loved Three Women," and "Any Old Time." The rarities here include superb tracks by the little-known Hillbillies (including a version of "Home on the Range" with a delightful trilling banjo) and Carson Robison & His Pioneers doing the sentimental "There's a Bridle Hangin' on a Wall" and the more upbeat "Blue River Train." The sound is very good, with most of the material drawn from British sources (especially EMI's Regal Zonophone label) pressed in the 1930s. *—Bruce Eder*

Insurgent Country, Vol. 1: For a Life of Sin / 1994 / Bloodshot ✦✦✦✦

Insurgent Country, Vol. 2: Hell-Bent / 1995 / Bloodshot ✦✦✦

● **Insurgent Country, Vol. 3: Nashville—*The Other Side of the Alley*** / 1996 / Bloodshot ✦✦✦✦✦

Jamie/Guyden Story / 1995 / Bear Family ✦✦✦✦
The double-disc set *Classic Jamie Masters* contains a selection of highlights from the Jamie vaults, boasting 60 tracks from the late '50s and early '60s. Jamie didn't really have a signature sound, which means that *Classic Jamie Masters* is all over the place in terms of sound and style, flipping between rock & roll, country, pop and R&B in the blink of the eye. Furthermore, the set doesn't contain many hit singles. While there are a number of famous names, only two of them—Duane Eddy and Barbara Lynn—are represented by big hits. Nevertheless, the set is a quite entertaining, especially for listeners who are looking for rarities, obscurities and arcane items from big names. *Classic Jamie Masters* contains tracks by Duane Eddy ("Rebel Rouser," "Because They're Young," "40 Miles of Bad Road"), Barbara Lynn ("You'll Lose A Good Thing," "(I Cried At) Laura's Wedding"), Titus Turner ("Sound Off"), Barbara Mason ("Yes I'm Ready"), Bruce Channel ("Going Back to Louisiana"), Johnny Rivers ("Hole In the Ground"), Mac Davis ("I'm a Poor Loser"), Danny & the Juniors ("Oh-La-La Limbo"), Neil Sedaka ("Ring A Rockin'"), Maureen Gray ("Dancing the Strand"), Lee Hazlewood ("Words Mean Nothing"), Sanford Clark ("Son of A Gun"), Harold Melvin & the Blue Notes ("Get Out"), and Barbara Mason ("Oh How It Hurts"). *—Stephen Thomas Erlewine*

Songs of the West / 1993 / Rhino ✦✦✦✦✦
This "definitive collection of cowboy songs" covers both famous and obscure odes to the high lonesome plains by Gene Autry, Roy Rogers, Tex Ritter, Marty Robbins, Slim Pickens, Bob Wills, and others. Spanning the 1930s to the present, the 72-track, 4-CD collection is broken into four separate thematic discs. Volume One features "Cowboy Classics" like "Back In The Saddle Again," "Mule Train," and "Happy Trails." The real find here has to be the ultradramatic narrative by Walter Brennan describing the "Gunfight At The O.K. Corral." Volume Two, "Silver Screen Cowboys," features tunes from Hollywood Westerns; Volume Three is devoted exclusively to performances by the kingpins of the genre, Gene Autry and Roy Rogers. The final disc is perhaps the most fun of the batch, presenting movie and television themes like "Bonanza," "Gunsmoke," "The Good, The Bad, And The Ugly," and "Rawhide." The box comes with a 60-page color booklet that includes detailed essays, photos, and reproductions of movie posters. *—Richie Unterberger*

Stampede! Western Music's Late Golden Era / 1996 / Rounder ✦✦✦✦✦
The third installment of Rounder's four-volume cowboy music series contains the songs most likely to be familiar to the general listener: Tex Ritter's "High Noon," Vaughn Monroe's "Riders in the Sky," Marty Robbins' "El Paso," Johnny Western's "The Ballad of Paladin," Eddy Arnold's "Cattle Call." Taken from the years spanning 1945-1960, it presents the form at its most pop-oriented, but it's not less enjoyable for that. Filling out the 14-track set are numbers by the likes of Elton Britt, Jimmy Wakely, and the Sons of the Pioneers (one of whose tracks is the theme to one of the definitive cowboy western films, The Searchers). *—Richie Unterberger*

Swingwest!, Vol. 1: Bakersfield / 1999 / Razor & Tie ✦✦✦✦✦
Part one of Razor & Tie's three-part series of Bakersfield country from the '50s and '60s leans heavily (though not exclusively) on Ken Nelson-produced cuts for Capitol. Perhaps this 20-track overview is a bit too casual in its sweep for the country fanatic, but it's a good sampler of key sounds for most listeners. Many of the style's important figures are represented here, including Ferlin Husky, Jean Shepard, Tommy Collins, Wynn Stewart, Rose Maddox and Merle Haggard. The selections often dig past obvious hits to less obvious items, like Husky's 1952 recording of "Gone" with Speedy West on guitar (which he would re-record a few years later in Nashville for a big hit), Jan Howard's "I Wish I Was a Single Girl Again" (written by husband Harlan), the "Please Mr. D.J." 1964 B-side by Merle Haggard, and Bobby Austin's "Apartment 9" (covered with greater success by Tammy Wynette). There's also one of country's most ridiculous hit novelties, Red Simpson's "I'm a Truck." *—Richie Unterberger*

Swingwest!, Vol. 2: Guitar Slingers / 1999 / Razor & Tie ✦✦✦✦✦
Recorded between 1947 and 1972, with the accent on pre-1965 material, this 20-song compilation highlights the instrumental skills of country guitarists working on the West Coast in the heyday of the L.A.-Bakersfield country sound. Like the other *SwingWest!* volumes, it's largely drawn from the Capitol vaults, but that's no great drawback, as Capitol's roster included such ace pickers as Jimmy Bryant, Joe Maphis, Merle Travis, Roy Clark and Speedy West, not to mention odds and ends in the country style by James Burton, Glen Campbell and Les Paul. All of those names are found on this anthology, along with stellar work by sidemen on tracks bearing the name of star bandleaders Merle Haggard and Hank Thompson. To be honest, you'll get as much quality swinging country virtuosity, with considerably more daring and invention, on Razor & Tie's Speedy West-Jimmy Bryant compilations. But if you're looking for a wider historical perspective, this is a good disc. A previously unreleased 1965 version of "Caravan," credited to Ferlin Husky but probably a jam by session musicians between songs, is not extraneous but a real highlight. It, and the cuts by Joe Maphis and Joe Clark, boast dazzlingly fast yet tasteful playing. *—Richie Unterberger*

Swingwest!, Vol. 3: Western Swing / 1999 / Razor & Tie ✦✦✦✦✦
Although country swing originated in Texas and Oklahoma, by the '40s and '50s many of its best performers were playing and recording in Southern California. In part, this was because many Texans and Oklahomans moved west during this time; in part, it was also because major record companies were starting to record country in Los Angeles. This is a first-rate collection of 20 Hollywood-recorded western swing, or heavily western swing-derived, tracks from 1945-64, mostly done for Capitol, and most done between 1954-55. There are fine cuts by Bob Wills, Spade Cooley, Tommy Duncan, Hank Thompson, Merle Travis and Tex Williams (the massive hit "Smoke! Smoke! Smoke! (That Cigarette)"). Of equal stature are selections by less famed names like boogying pianist Merrill Moore (with a version of "Down the Road Apiece"), Woody Guthrie's cousin, Jack Guthrie, early rockabilly-type music by Cliffie Stone, and steel guitar virtuoso Leon McAuliffe. This was a time at which country music was gracefully incorporating influences from a wide variety of genres: blues, swing jazz, pop, cowboy music and boogie. That eclecticism made this one of the most interesting points of country's evolution, and this compilation captures some high points of this phase well. *—Richie Unterberger*

☆ **Texas Music, Vol. 2: Western Swing & Honky Tonk** / 1994 / Rhino ✦✦✦✦✦
Not just valuable to Texas music fans, but also to country music enthusiasts of all kinds, this 18-track compilation is heaviest on western swing classics from the 1930s and 1940s, and also has a bit of 1950s honky tonk and western swing revival from the 1970s. Bob Wills, Milton Brown, the Light Crust Doughboys, and Floyd Tillman are all represented with classics, and there are less expected highlights like Roy Newman's "Everybody's Trying to Be My Baby," which Carl Perkins would record (with considerable alteration to the music and the words) in the 1950s, providing in turn the basis for the Beatles' cover version. The Light Crust Doughboys' "Knocky-Knocky" and Cliff Bruner's "Milk Cow Blues" show how close blues could roam to the center of western swing. Renowned tunes by Ernest Tubb, Lefty Frizzell, and Hank Thompson signify honky tonk's golden years; Ted Daffan offers the 1942 version of "Born to Lose," now a country standard; and zydeco even creeps in with Harry Choates' "Harry's Blues." Johnny Gimble, Asleep at the Wheel, and Alvin Crow bring the disc to a close with cuts from the 1970s. An excellent overview of the best in vintage Texas country sounds, with something to offer both the novice and the collector. *—Richie Unterberger*

Wanted! the Outlaws / 1996 / RCA ✦✦✦✦✦
The term "outlaw" had been bandied about after Jennings's 1972 hit "Ladies Love Outlaws," but it didn't permanently gel until the release of the album *Wanted! The Outlaws* in 1976. The songs in this packaged product weren't new—the album contained previously released material by Nelson, Jennings, Glaser, and Jennings's wife, Jessi Colter, (who had hit the charts a year earlier with "I'm Not Lisa"). But it marked the industry's recognition of the changing times, and as the centerpoint of a campaign to publicize Nashville's new "progressive" breed it worked like a charm. It quickly became the first country album to sell more than a million copies, and it boosted the careers of all involved. In 1996, RCA re-issued *Wanted! The Outlaws* on CD for the first time, adding one new Waylon and Willie recording (a lively reading of Steve Earle's "Nowhere Road") and nine "lost" tracks. But "lost" isn't really correct: Like the original 11 selections, such songs as Waylon's "Slow Movin' Outlaws" and Willie's "Healing Hands of Time" have been previously released. They do, however, sweeten the package, making this 20th anniversary edition a decent (though by no means definitive) sampler of outlaw country. *—Kurt Wolff*

☆ **When I Was a Cowboy, Vol. 1** / 1996 / Yazoo ✦✦✦✦✦
These are the records that gave everyone from Gene Autry through Marty Robbins the basis for their careers, bridging the gap between nineteenth century reality and twentieth century nostalgia. These 23 songs are the real article from the mid-to-late 1920's, a time when the singers had ridden the range, and the events they sung of were often within living memory. This material is the white equivalent of recordings by Blind Lemon Jefferson, Papa Charlie Jackson et al, and anyone owning their records—even if they don't like cowboy songs—ought to own this as well; J.D. Farley's "Bill Was A Texas Lad," could even pass for blues. Alas, there is no information included about Farley, the Cartwright Brothers, Harry McClintock ("Sam Bass"), Edward L. Crain ("Bandit Cole Younger"), the Crowder Brothers, Taylor's Kentucky Boys ("The Dixie Cowboy"), Carl Sprague ("The Last Longhorn"), Billie Maxwell, Watts & Wilson, Lonesome Luke & His Farm Hands (who give us an authentic square dance), or Patt Patterson & His Champion Rep Riders, and the only name that will be recognizable to modern listeners is rider-actor Ken Maynard, whose "Lone Star Trail" is one of the best things here. All of it is stripped down, sometimes with no more than a guitar accompaniment; the singing is raw and unaffected, but some of it displays surprising virtuosity, most notably the Arkansas Woodchopper's dexterous guitar playing on "I'm A Texas Cowboy" and "Texas Ranger" by the Cartwright Brothers, with a droning fiddle accompaniment that emphasizes the British origins of the melodies behind some of these songs. The sound is also unusually good. *—Bruce Eder*

Bluegrass

There are many wonderful moments in the Coen brothers' 2000 film *O Brother Where Art Thou*, but perhaps what's most surprising about the film is how it made old-timey music seem alive in a way that hasn't been heard in years. The strange thing about *O Brother* is that it documented a time before bluegrass proper existed—it actually documents the era that led to bluegrass, the time that string bands and old-timey country ruled the South, before honky tonk dives cluttered the highways and before Nashville turned out enticingly lush country-pop. That happened after World War II, when the record industry consolidated, but what also happened after WWII is that the country musicians that wanted to keep it real splintered off into a separate faction, called bluegrass.

Bluegrass has always been about tradition, so it shouldn't be a surprise that it often sounds similar, even in its progressive incarnations. But it's undeniably distinctive, standing as a distinct musical form outside of country. Its basics have always derived from old-timey country, but as it matured, bluegrass revealed itself to be as much about a musician's prowess as it is about the song. Like jazz, the core standards—*Blue Moon of Kentucky, Uncle Pen*, etc.—became foundations for explorations into instrumental virtuosity, ways for musicians to simply shred. Part of this arises from the acknowledged father of bluegrass, Bill Monroe, who was equally skilled at songs and shredding. Monroe's backing band not only brought the phrase bluegrass into the popular music lexicon, but this band established the very sound and style of bluegrass. Backed by such stellar musicians as Lester Flatt and Earl Scruggs, who later became a duo of their own reknown, Monroe's reign began in 1945, and he remained the main bluegrass figure throughout his life, which lasted into the '90s. They set the sound, relying on banjo, fiddle, guitar, and mandolin, playing at tempos much faster than traditional country, harmonizing on the verses, and tearing it up on the solos.

Bluegrass in this style exists to this very day—this, after all, is a music with a foundation that is doggedly traditionalist, preserving a tradition at the very point it started to develop. But, like any musical style, it did mutate itself, particularly in the '60s, when everything mutated. Newgrass, as it popularly became known, sprung its head, as newer bluegrass musicians decided to experiment with the form, amplifying instruments and adding elements of folk and rock to the template. This wasn't particularly well-received at the time—rock fans embraced it more enthusiastically than country fans—but it undoubtedly laid the groundwork for bluegrass' sustained popularity throughout the 20th century.

One of the most successful bluegrass outfits of the last two decades of the 20th century was Old & in the Way, a collective of ex-hippies (fronted by Jerry Garcia and David Grisman) that proved bluegrass and old-timey music was still relevant. The interesting thing about the group was that they played it straight—their most radical move was making rock and R&B songs sound bluegrass, not vice versa—thereby establishing bluegrass as a viable, vibrant music, not something that was ancient. This was as important as any newgrass record, since this, like newgrass, illustrated that old-timey music wasn't simply for the old times, that it could thrive in the modern world.

Ever since the development of newgrass in the late '60s, bluegrass remained on the periphery of popular conscious, slowly gaining a large following. In the '80s, its revival was spearheaded by Ricky Skaggs, who revitalized the music (and traditional country) with his invigorating, barebones music. Then, Béla Fleck emphasized the virtuosity and jazziness inherent in bluegrass with his freewheeling, evocative fusion. Finally, Alison Krauss brought the music into the mainstream in the late '90s, successfully scoring a crossover hit with her melodic, measured bluegrass—something that was unthinkable in the early '90s, when the most successful country was that primed for crossover.

Still, the popular image of bluegrass remained that of old-timey music, the kind that was featured in the surprise 2001 hit of the *O Brother Where Art Thou* soundtrack. Though technically not bluegrass (except in a couple of places), it was the most current manifestation of how old-timey music keeps revitalizing itself, and how it continued to sound fresh, even when its tunes were decades, perhaps even a century, old. This section fills in the gaps, pointing out why it's seemed like its always been here. *— Stephen Thomas Erlewine*

Artist Reviews

Eddie Adcock

b. Jun. 21, 1938, Scottsville, VA
Guitar, Banjo / Traditional Bluegrass, Progressive Bluegrass
Among the major-league talent that emerged from the folk music boom of the late '50s were the Country Gentlemen, a DC-based quartet that introduced bluegrass to a generation of city folks and college students, people who had never heard of Flatt & Scruggs or Bill Monroe or the Stanley Brothers. The Gentlemen, in playing the old bluegrass standards but playing them "different," were in a sense the first newgrass group. Eddie Adcock was the band's banjo player and he was a player of distinction. Raised in a musical family, Adcock didn't begin his professional musical career until 1953, when he joined Smokey Graves and his Blue Star Boys, who had a regular show at a radio station in Crewe, VA. Bill Monroe offered a job to Adcock in 1957, and he played with the Blue Grass Boys for a short time—Monroe had to let him go because the band simply wasn't earning enough money to employ him. Adcock returned to working day jobs but that was short-lived. After he started working in a sheet metal factory, Jim Cox, John Duffery, and Charlie Waller asked him to join their new band, the Country Gentlemen.

The Country Gentlemen became one of the most popular and respected bluegrass bands of the late '50s and '60s, as well as one of the most progressive. They expanded the repertoire of bluegrass bands to include contemporary country, folk, and rock songwriters, most notably Bob Dylan; usually they added this material at the urging of Adcock. At the end of the '60s, Adcock began to feel constrained by the Country Gentlemen. He wanted to experiment with different musical genres, which he felt the band wasn't willing to do, eventually leading to his departure from the group. Through the following decades Adcock worked with several bands (most notably II Generation with his wife Martha Hearon), and after nearly 50 years in the music business, he has remained as popular as ever. *—Stephen Thomas Erlewine & David Vinopal*

• **Spirited** / May 6, 1998 / Pinecastle ✦✦✦✦✦
Eddie Adcock boasts stints with the "classic" Country Gentlemen, Mac Wiseman and Bill Monroe on his glittering bluegrass resume. His wife, vocalist and guitarist Martha, joins the banjoist as well. The title track is a fiery instrumental that showcases the virtuoso picking ability of these two players trading leads. A cunning dip in tempo brings the foray to a close. The meat of the recording is the 11 other songs that are ostensibly bluegrass hymns, still feature the stunning playing and singing (mostly from Martha) that make this collection a hallmark of contemporary bluegrass, regardless of topic. A particularly memorable track is in the Eddie-penned "What Love Can't Do." Eddie picks the melody and supports Martha with baritone harmonies as she provides guitar rhythm. The lyrics are poetic and insightful, the music skilled and melodic. *— Thomas Schulte*

Red Allen

b. Feb. 12, 1930, Perry County, KY, **d.** Apr. 3, 1993
Vocals, Guitar / Traditional Bluegrass
Appalachia-born Red Allen had a voice that personified the "high lonesome sound" of traditional bluegrass music. In 1954, Allen made his recording debut on an independent Kentucky label. Later he joined the Osborne Brothers, recording such classics as "Ruby" and "Wild Mountain Honey." Allen stayed with the Osbornes until 1958 and then left music for a time. In 1959, he moved to Washington, DC, where he formed the Kentuckians, and in 1969, Allen formed a band with his four teen-aged sons. As Red Allen and the Allen Brothers, they began playing the *Wheeling Jamboree*, and recording for King Bluegrass and Lemco. Throughout the '70s, he toured America and Europe, usually playing bluegrass and folk festivals. A decade later, Allen recorded two albums for Folkways. He continued to be play clubs and festivals near Dayton until his death from cancer in 1993. *— Sandra Brennan*

Red Allen & The Kentuckians / 1991 / County ✦✦✦✦
Red Allen & The Kentuckians is an album the bluegrass pioneer Red Allen recorded for County Records in 1966. The record is one of his best, capturing his pure and intense style through both instrumental showcases and a selection of fine material, such as "Milk Cow Blues," "I Wonder Where You Are Tonight," "Maiden's Prayer" and "If That's the Way You Feel." *— Thom Owens*

• **The Kitchen Tapes** / 1994 / Acoustic Disc ✦✦✦✦
Red Allen and Frank Wakefield were recorded here by Wakefield's future student David Grisman in 1963. *The Kitchen Tapes* captures the two of them jamming and improvising informally—at the time, Peter K. Siegel and David Grisman were college students who had simply been allowed to capture one of Allen and Wakefield's private sessions, sitting in a kitchen in Hyattsville, Maryland. This was purely for Siegel and Grisman to learn from, but the tapes proved so valuable through the years that 31 years later, arrangements were made to issue it commercially. Lines are blown and notes are slurred here and there, and not every harmony is as smooth as it might be with some rehearsal, but this is still a priceless document, showing off these two legends in an informal, private session playing for their own pleasure. The 25 numbers include "I'm Just Here to Get My Baby Out of Jail," "Bluegrass Breakdown," "Muskrat Song," "Crying Heart Blues," "Billy In the Lowground" (in maybe the best version of its era), "Nine Pound Hammer," "'Tis Sweet to Be Remembered," and "Swing Low Sweet Chariot." Grisman studied copies of these tapes for years, and has now shared them with the world. *— Bruce Eder*

Darol Anger

Cello, Violin, Mandolin, Guitar, Fiddle / New Acoustic, Chamber Jazz, Adult Alternative, Progressive Bluegrass

Violinist Darol Anger has made his mark on new acoustic music with a number of different groups.

From 1975-84, Anger was a key member of new-acoustic pioneers the David Grisman Quintet, whose blend of folk, bluegrass, and jazz virtually defined the new acoustic genre, as well as advancing the harmonic and instrumental frontiers of traditional musics; as a member of the Turtle Island String Quartet in the late '80s and early '90s, Anger also helped bring virtuosic improvisation and boundless eclecticism to what had been an essentially classical, strictly composed musical format. Additionally, Anger co-founded the Montreux Band, a folk- and jazz-influenced group which recorded for Windham Hill in the mid- to late '80s and had an impact on the formation of so-called New Adult Contemporary radio, and with Grisman alumnus Mike Marshall founded the progressive bluegrass outfit Psychograss, which carried on the eclectic Grisman tradition in the 1990s. Again teaming up with Marshall in the late '90s, Anger co-founded the Anger/Marshall Band, which kept him busy along with his work on the Heritage Folk Music project, his continued appearances with his previous groups, and his work as a producer and arranger for other artists. *—Steve Huey*

Fiddlesticks / 1981 / Kaleidoscope ✦✦✦

Fiddlistics includes an all-star cast of new-grass musicians, and in many ways it is a continuation of the excellent *David Grisman Quintet* album. In fact, there is a slowed-down version of the composition "Blue Midnight" which first appeared on the innovative Grisman album, and the new-grass suite "Megatones" could easily have been from that session. However, the uniqueness of this album stems from its eclecticism. Anger and mandolin legend Tiny Moore joyfully swing through Charlie Parker's "Moose the Mooche," and Anger takes two duets: one quiet and meditative with pianist Barbara Higbie, and the other a traditional bluegrass romp, at first, which slowly becomes more progressive with George Stavis on banjo. Fans of the David Grisman Quintet, Mike Marshall, Tony Rice, or any of the other participating musicians will not be disappointed because this album is well-worth searching for. *—Wilson McCloy*

● **Chiaroscuro** / 1985 / Windham Hill ✦✦✦✦✦

This 1985 release is still one of the finest examples of new-acoustic music's appeal. Some fiery ensemble pieces are balanced by a few slower, moodier works and even some down-home versions of melodies by J. S. Bach. *—Linda Kohanov*

Jam / Apr. 20, 1999 / Compass ✦✦✦

Darol Anger and Mike Marshall reunite with 1999's *Jam*, another fine example of their skillful fusion of folk, jazz and classical idioms. Primarily acoustic, with flourishes of electric bass here and there, *Jam* features Anger's violin and fiddle virtuosity, as well as his composing and producing skills. Marshall provides intelligent, inspired accompaniment on a number of string instruments, and the duo are joined by Anger/Marshal Band newcomers Derek Jones, an electric and acoustic bass virtuoso, and drummer Aaron Johnston, who add to *Jam's* festive fusion of styles and sounds. *—Heather Phares*

The Diary of a Fiddler / Jul. 20, 1999 / Compass ✦✦✦✦

Brand New Can / Jul. 25, 2000 / Compass ✦✦✦

Dave Apollon

b. 1898

Mandolin / Traditional Bluegrass

On the mandolin, Dave Apollon was, in a word, a virtuoso. The late Jethro Burns (of Homer And Jethro) said that Dave Apollon was the best that he had ever heard, and he ought to know, for Burns himself was the best mandolin player of the last quarter-century. Born in Russia, Apollon made many recordings, the first in 1932, and became a celebrity through these and also through his movies. He was to the mandolin what Benny Goodman was to the clarinet. *—David Vinopal*

● **Man with the Mandolin** / Oct. 21, 1997 / Acoustic Disc ✦✦✦✦✦

Mike Auldridge

b. Dec. 30, 1938, Washington, D.C.

Slide Guitar, Vocals, Pedal Steel Guitar, Guitar, Dobro / Traditional Bluegrass, Progressive Bluegrass

Generally considered one of the masters of bluegrass dobro, Mike Auldridge was raised in Kensington, Maryland, where he began playing guitar at age 12, banjo at 16, and dobro at 17. In 1954, he made his first appearance on local radio, playing in a band with his brother Dave. In 1967, he graduated from the University of Maryland and became a commercial artist, continuing to play dobro occasionally at local clubs. In 1969 he joined the New Shades of Green; within a year, the bluegrass group had gained a stong following, and Auldridge was considered an innovator in the relatively new field of bluegrass dobro.

He became a member of the Seldom Scene in 1971, but still did session work, playing on albums by such as Emmylou Harris, Jonathan Edwards, Linda Ronstadt, and Jimmy Arnold. He also recorded several solo albums, including *Dobro* (1972) *Blues & Bluegrass* (1974), and *Eight-String Swing* (1982). Auldridge teamed with singer/mandolin player Lou Reid and bassist T. Michael Coleman in 1989 for the album *High Time*. Also in 1989, he released a solo album, *Treasures Untold*. Auldridge continued to play concerts and record as a session musician in the '90s. *This Old Town*, his first solo album in a decade, appeared in early 2000. *—Sandra Brennan*

● **Dobro/Blues & Bluegrass** / 1974 / Takoma ✦✦✦✦✦

Two of Mike Auldridge's early '70s albums, *Dobro* and *Blues & Bluegrass*, are combined on this single disc, which provides an excellent introduction to the dobroist. *—Thom Owens*

Eight String Swing / 1988 / Sugar Hill ✦✦✦

As the title suggests, Mike Auldridge recorded *Eight String Swing* with a specially-made, eight-string dobro, which helped him ease his music out of traditional bluegrass and into country, jazz, western swing, and folk. Auldridge is joined by several of his Seldom Scene cohorts and fiddler Jimmy Arnold on the album, and the sympathetic support adds depth to both the originals and the eclectic covers (Duke Ellington's "Caravan," Willie Nelson's "Crazy," Benny Goodman's "Stompin' at the Savoy"). *—Stephen Thomas Erlewine*

Treasures Untold / 1989 / Sugar Hill ✦✦✦✦✦

Treasures Untold is comprised entirely of traditional country & western songs, ranging from cowboy standards ("Deep Water," "Shenandoah Waltz") to honky tonk ("Walking the Floor Over You," "Drivin' Nails in My Coffin"). Most of the record features lead vocals by Doc Watson, Tony Rice and John Starling, while Auldridge simply plays some stunning dobro, but he does step to the mike for a couple of songs, including the title track. *—Thom Owens*

This Old Town / Jan. 25, 2000 / Rebel ✦✦✦

Austin Lounge Lizards

f. 1980

Group / Progressive Bluegrass

Regarding their name, Austin Lounge Lizards guitarist and founding member Conrad Deisler said: "I think it was a slang term I'd heard my grandmother use to describe gentlemen of easy virtue who hung around in bars. When we started out, that's just what we were doing—hanging out and playing for beer and tips and stuff like that." The Lounge Lizards trace their origins back to the late '70s, when Deisler, then a Princeton student, hooked up with Hank Card to indulge their shared interest in folk and country by playing in progressive folk bands. The two landed in Austin in 1980, where they met Tom Pittman, a banjo and pedal-steel player who'd just moved to town from Georgia. They combined the sounds of Pittman's bluegrass heritage with the folk and country forms from Deisler and Card's college-band days up north. Unsatisfied with playing bluegrass and traditional country covers, the Lizards found they had a knack for writing bizarro social and politically themed songs, overflowing with tongue-in-cheek twang.

The band has gone through its share of mandolin players, bassists, and fiddlers, but the core of the group has remained Pittman, Deisler, and Card, with long stints from bassist Boo Resnick, drummer Paul Pearcy, and multi-instrumentalist Richard Bowden. Whatever its lineup, the Austin Lounge Lizards have long been known for their Texas-sized twisted tales and humorous songs, charming their fans for over twenty years. In their own words, "Our accents are the drawliest, our howdies are the y'alliest/Our Lone Star flag's the waviest, our fried steak's the cream graviest."

The group's first album, *Creatures From the Black Saloon*, was released in 1984, and was followed by 1988's *The Highway Cafe of the Damned*, 1991's live album *Lizard Vision*, 1993's *Paint Me on Velvet*, 1995's *Small Minds*, and 1998's *Employee of the Month*. *Never an Adult Moment* was issued in late summer 2000. *—Zac Johnson*

● **Creatures from the Black Saloon** / 1984 / Watermelon ✦✦✦✦✦

Imagine tradition-steeped Texas swing fused to Monty Python, and you have an idea what's in store with the Austin Lounge Lizards. The Lizards can serve up the tastiest country licks imaginable while at the same time trashing every old West cliche/tradition in the book. The group's debut *Creatures from the Black Lagoon* revealed such classics as "The Car Hank Died In," "Kool Whip" (Devo meets The Bonzo Dog Band), and "Saguaro" (wailing pedal steel and mock heroic baritone rendering the tale of a twerpy urban cowpoke duelling a gang of desperado cacti—and losing). *—Roch Parisien*

The Highway Cafe of the Damned / 1988 / Watermelon ✦✦✦✦

Lizard Vision / 1991 / Flying Fish ✦✦✦

Combine country and bluegrass melodies with the type of irreverent, authority-questioning lyrics you'd expect from a rock & roll or folk act, and you've got the Austin Lounge Lizards, whose sense of humor is impossible to miss on *Lizard Vision*. Recorded live at *the Waterloo Ice House* in Austin, TX, in January 1990, this CD illustrates the Lizards' vitality and makes it clear they're far from typical of country and bluegrass acts. The band might sound a bit like the Statler Brothers at times, but lyrically, they're in a class by themselves. "Dan Stepford" has a good laugh at the expense of Dan Quayle (who was the U.S. vice president when this CD was recorded), while the doo-wop-influenced "Jesus Loves Me (But He Can't Stand You)" takes aim at the hypocrisy of religious fanatics. Not all of the songs have sociopolitical references; on "He's Just a Friend" and Roger Waters' "Brain Damage," for example, the Lizards simply enjoy some healthy, good-natured goofiness for the sake of goofiness. Arguably, *Lizard Vision* is the band's most essential release. *—Alex Henderson*

Small Minds / 1995 / Watermelon ✦✦✦

There's nothing more demented than a country band with a sense of humor, unless it's a country band with a sense of humor *and* a sense of irony. The Austin Lounge Lizards have humor, irony and satire going for them, a pretty deadly combination altogether. Targets on *Small Minds* range from Newt Gingrich (in the acidic "Gingrich the Newt," which has this Newt giving the humble newt species a bad name) to the intelligentsia of the art world. For all the bent edges, *Small Minds* is a finely played and sung album that's a pleasure to listen to and gets a definite recommendation. *—Steven McDonald*

Employee of the Month / Feb. 17, 1998 / Sugar Hill ✦✦✦✦

They're light, they're fluffy, they're as funny as all get out. Whether it's a lampoon of Very Big Texan Things in "Stupid Texas Song," a parody of Leonard Cohen in "Leonard Cohen's Day Job" (which gets funnier the more you listen to it) or acknowledging the family of the '90s ("Hey, Little Minivan"), they're sharp and smart. The satire isn't quite as biting as on *Small Minds*, their 1995 release, but they sure are funny. *—Steven McDonald*

Never an Adult Moment / Aug. 29, 2000 / Sugar Hill ✦✦✦✦

Bashful Brother Oswald

b. Dec. 26, 1911, Sevier County, TN

Vocals, Guitar, Dobro, Banjo / Traditional Country, Old-Timey

For nearly 60 years, Bashful Brother Oswald was one of the most influential and talented dobro players in country music. For the majority of his career, he was the dobroist for Roy

Acuff's Smoky Mountain Boys, becoming the leading dobroist in country as well as one of the most popular members of the band. Over the course of his career, Oswald released only a handful of solo recordings, but left behind enough music to illustrate why he was one of the most influential players of his era. As a vocalist, he first gained recognition for singing a few lines on Acuff's classics "Precious Jewel" (1940) and on "Wreck on the Highway" (1942). Acuff later named him "Brother Oswald," and the dobroist happily complied in creating the Oswald character, wearing a floppy mountain hat, tattered overalls, and enormous shoes while adopting a braying horse laugh. He began a solo career beginning with 1962's *Bashful Brother Oswald.* In 1972, guitarist and dobro player Tut Taylor produced Oswald's *Brother Oswald* album. Later in the decade, he began playing in the Opryland theme park with former Smoky Mountain bandmate Charlie Collins. Following Acuff's death in 1992, he and Collins earned a regular slot on the Opry's main stage. *—Sandra Brennan*

● **Brother Oswald** / 1972 / Rounder ✦✦✦✦✦
Roy Acuff's dobroist since the '30s, in a pleasant set of Hawaiian-inspired old-time country songs. *—Mark A. Humphrey*

Don't Say Aloha / 1998 / Rounder ✦✦✦✦

Byron Berline

b. 194?, Caldwell, KS
Violin, Mandolin, Fiddle / Bluegrass, Progressive Bluegrass
Like his contemporary Vassar Clements, fiddler Byron Berline expanded the sonic possibilities of bluegrass, adding elements of jazz, pop, blues, rock and traditional country to the genre. In addition to being a popular solo act, he performed as a session musician on a number of albums, including records by the Flying Burrito Brothers, Stephen Stills, the Dillards, Gram Parsons, the Nitty Gritty Dirt Band, Emmylou Harris, Kris Kristofferson, and James Taylor. He was briefly a member of Bill Monroe's Blue Grass Boys during 1967, but was drafted into the US Army. After reentering civilian life, he played with the Dillard and Clark Expedition and the Flying Burrito Brothers, also forming his own bands, the Country Gazette, Sundance, the LA Fiddle Band and BCH (a trio with Dan Crary and John Hickman). His long-awaited solo debut *Outrageous* was released in 1980, and he recorded several additional albums for Sugar Hill throughout the 1980s. BCH later added bassist Steve Spurgin and mandolinist/guitarist John Moore to the lineup, renaming itself California. *—Sandra Brennan*

And the L.A. Fiddle Band / 1980 / Sugar Hill ✦✦✦✦
Put together three fiddles and some great acoustic bluegrass music and you have *Byron Berline & the L.A. Fiddle Band,* a great album. Guests are Vince Gill and John Hickman. *—Chip Renner*

● **Double Trouble** / 1986 / Sugar Hill ✦✦✦✦
Byron Berline is a fiddler whose talents have been employed by artists as diverse as Bill Monroe and the Rolling Stones; Hickman has stayed closer to the bluegrass mainstream, but his playing is melodically adventurous and highly inventive. "Double Trouble" is a reissue of a 1986 session which finds Berline and Hickman playing a stripped-down, but still innovative, style of bluegrass that may come as a surprise to fans of the influential Berline/Crary/Hickman ensemble and of California, the band in which both currently play. There are several Berline originals here as well as standards like "Blackberry Blossom" and "Sugar in the Gourd." Everywhere Hickman's picking is supple, slippery and crystalline, and Berline shows more humor and intelligence in his playing than just about any ten other fiddlers you could think of. These guys have been playing together so long that they almost share a brain, and this disc is a pleasure. *—Rick Anderson*

Jumpin' the Strings / Sugar Hill ✦✦✦
While the fiddle playing of Byron Berline sets him squarely within the realm of bluegrass, the melodic originality of his work seems to almost transcend the genre over the course of the 21 self-penned songs that make up *Jumpin' the Strings.* While Berline is the star attraction, a fine backing band comprised of banjoists Alan Munde and John Hickman, guitarists Howard Yearwood and Joe Carr and dobro player Skip Conover is also given the chance to cut loose on this fine release. *—Jason Ankeny*

Norman Blake

b. Mar. 10, 1938, Chattanooga, TN
Slide Guitar, Vocals, Mandolin, Guitar, Fiddle, Dobro / Traditional Bluegrass, Progressive Bluegrass
Although he is proficient with a variety of stringed instruments, Norman Blake is famous for his acoustic guitar skills—he was one of the major bluegrass guitarists of the '70s. Blake came into view in the late '60s, when he began performing as a sideman with artists as diverse as June Carter and Bob Dylan. During the '70s, he began a solo career which quickly became one of the most popular and musically adventurous within bluegrass. Blake began playing professionally in the mid-'50s, and he played with numerous groups during the '50s and '60s until his recording debut in 1962, the Lonesome Travelers' *12 Shades of Bluegrass.* He later joined Johnny Cash's band and gained additional exposure on the television program Cash hosted. After playing on sessions for Bob Dylan, Kris Kristofferson and Joan Baez, Blake returned to his bluegrass roots in 1971 and recorded his first solo album, *Back Home in Sulphur Springs,* one year later. During the 1970s and '80s, he released more than an album per year for Rounder and Flying Fish, many recorded with wife Nancy on cello. *—Kurt Wolff*

Back Home in Sulphur Springs / 1972 / Rounder ✦✦✦✦
Reissued and remastered, this 1972 album from guitarist/vocalist Blake, here in cahoots with dobro master Tut Taylor, is utterly delightful, comfortably mixing up several varieties of folk with guitar rags and a little bit of bluegrass picking that somehow fits right in. The music is a mixture of traditional pieces and cover versions, alongside some Blake originals, all recorded beautifully—the guitar and dobro tones on this album are absolutely magnificent. Blake's voice is as worn as an old shoe, comfortable, friendly and familiar, lacking in pretension or artifice, just fine for the songs here. If you're looking for a dose of unalloyed folk music, it would be hard to go wrong with this set. *—Steven McDonald*

Blackberry Blossom / 1974 / Flying Fish ✦✦✦✦✦

The Norman & Nancy Blake / 1986 / Rounder ✦✦✦✦✦
Norman & Nancy Blake Compact Disc combines Norman's *Lighthouse on the Shore* and Nancy's *Grand Junction* on one 21-track compact disc, offering neophytes a good introduction the duo's distinctive style of acoustic country and bluegrass. *—Thom Owens*

★ **Natasha's Waltz** / 1987 / Rounder ✦✦✦✦✦
Natasha's Waltz is a compilation of highlights from the albums Norman and Nancy Blake recorded for Rounder during the '80s, giving an excellent overview of one of the finest bluegrass and new acoustic duos of the era. *—Thom Owens*

Slow Train through Georgia / 1987 / Rounder ✦✦✦✦✦
Slow Train Through Georgia collects 22 tracks from Norman Blake's early '70s albums, making it an excellent retrospective of the beginning of his solo career. *—Thom Owens*

Blind Dog / 1988 / Rounder ✦✦✦✦
Blind Dog is a fine summation of bluegrass guitarist's Norman Blake's career and aesthetics, a largely- instrumental collection of favorites from his own catalog as well as from his influences'. The covers include songs by A.P. Carter and Woody Guthrie, while Blake dips into his own back pages to re-do fan-favorite "Billy Gray." The focus of the record, however, is Blake's playing; a tasteful, economical picker, he shadows the melodies to allow the songs to speak for themselves. *—Jason Ankeny*

Just Gimme Somethin' I'm Used To / 1992 / Shanachie ✦✦✦
Just Gimme Somethin' I'm Used To is another charming album by Norman and Nancy Blake, featuring an excellent selection of old-timey country and traditional folk like "Wabash Cannonball" and "Georgia Railroad." There's not much that separates *Just Gimme Somethin' I'm Used To* from the rest of the duo's catalog, yet it remains a thoroughly enjoyable listen. *—Stephen Thomas Erlewine*

The Hobo's Last Ride / Aug. 20, 1996 / Shanachie ✦✦✦✦✦

Chattanooga Sugar Babe / Jan. 20, 1998 / Shanachie ✦✦✦

Be Ready Boys: Appalachia to Abilene / Jun. 22, 1999 / Shanachie ✦✦✦✦
Bringing together the musical traditions of the Appalachian Mountains and Texas, Norman Blake and Rich O'Brien convened in Denver, CO, in July of 1998 to collaborate on a beautiful recreation of traditional instrumentals and early country forms. A very loose and impromptu feel pervades the 16 tracks, as Blake provides guitar, six-string banjo, mandolin, fiddle, and viola, with O'Brien adding guitar on both combining for classic country harmonies on tracks like "When It's Lamplighting Time in the Valley," A.P. Carter's "Homestead on the Farm," and the spiritual "Heavenly Sunlight." As is to be expected, the instrumentals are outstanding, incorporating rags, waltzes, and even Spanish elements. O'Brien's own "Grandpa's Barn" is guaranteed to be a tearjerker for anyone with rural roots. *—Matt Fink*

Far Away, Down on a Georgia Farm / Nov. 16, 1999 / Shanachie ✦✦✦
Far Away Down on a Georgia Farm is a collection of the newest offerings from veteran folk musician Norman Blake. Capitalizing on Blake's recent notoriety (he is prominently featured on Johnny Cash's 1999 release and the soundtrack for Joel and Ethan Coen's film *O Brother, Where Art Thou?,* as well as collaborating with Michelle Shocked), this album is another example of his hard work—allowing him to step to the forefront and really show what he can do. *—Stacia Proefrock*

Blue Highway

Group / Traditional Bluegrass, Progressive Bluegrass
A traditional bluegrass group comprised of five experienced musicians, the members of Blue Highway have played in the bands of such notable artists as Alison Krauss & Union Station, Ricky Skaggs, Larry Sparks and Doyle Lawson. Guitarist and vocalist Tim Stafford played on the Grammy-winning album *Everytime You Say Goodbye,* by Alison Krauss & Union Station, while dobro player Rob Ickes earned one for his contribution to the various-artists project *The Great Dobro Sessions* and another for his playing on *I Know Who Holds Tomorrow,* the collaborative album project by Krauss & the Cox Family. Other Blue Highway members include: Shawn Lane on tenor vocals, mandolin and fiddle; bassist, vocalist and songwriter Wayne Taylor and Jason Burlesonon banjo, mandolin and vocals. The Tennessee-based group has been nominated for four International Bluegrass Music Association Awards, including 1996 Album of the Year for their debut release *It's a Long, Long Road,* with both the title-track single and album staying at number one on the national bluegrass chart for five months. After 1996's *Wind to the West,* in 1998 Blue Highway issued *Midnight Storm;* the following year, their self-titled fourth album appeared. *—Jack Leaver*

● **Wind to the West** / Jul. 1996 / Rebel ✦✦✦✦
Traditional bluegrass at its best, this album contains masterful playing, inspired singing and memorable songwriting. Blue Highway turns in an affecting vocal and instrumental performance on guitarist Tim Stafford's haunting "The Rounder," and as well as ripping through a cover of Merle Haggard's "Huntsville," and showcasing their gospel side on a soul-stirring arrangement of the traditional "God Moves in a Windstorm." Shawn Lane's lonesome tenor is pleasing, as well as the harmony blend and the lead vocals of the rest of the band. Ace dobro player Rob Ickes—voted 1996 Dobro Player of the Year by the International Bluegrass Music Awards—shines throughout, rounding out this band's second effort and making it more than a worthwhile choice. *—Jack Leaver*

Blue Highway / Jul. 13, 1999 / Ceili Music ✦✦✦✦
This is Blue Highway's first album for the Ceili label and it's an auspicious piece of work. The group members are all reaching the peak of their musical powers, both in terms of their instrumental prowess and their vocal skill. Factor in the strong songwriting of Shawn Lane and Tim Stafford and it all adds up to one of the most polished acts in bluegrass. The album features not only fiery instrumental work, as in "Lonesome Hearted Blues," but also a wonder-

ful a cappella, rhythmic gospel number, "I Am Near the Gate" (written by Lane), a couple of tunes that approximate country music rather well ("Lonely Old Town" and "That Could Be You"), an evocative folklike version of Stafford's "Clay and Ottie," and the Western-flavored bluegrass sound of "I Hung My Head," a song written by Sting. Dobro player Rob Ickes is the primary IBMA award winner in this group but, as this self-titled release indicates, Blue Highway is a versatile and creative outfit. This album clearly ups the ante, but there's reason to believe that Blue Highway will achieve results at this level for some time to come. *—Philip Van Vleck*

The Bluegrass Album Band

f. 1980

Group / Progressive Bluegrass

The Bluegrass Album Band was a bluegrass supergroup formed in 1980. Originally, the band featured J.D. Crowe, Doyle Lawson, Tony Rice, Bobby Hicks, and Todd Phillips. All of the members were known as progressive bluegrass musicians, but the Bluegrass Album Band was designed to showcase the traditional side of their talents. Their first album, *The Bluegrass Album,* was intended as a one-shot project but it proved so successful the group recorded four other albums over the course of the decade. Over the years, the lineup of the Bluegrass Album Band shifted, but Crowe, Lawson, and Rice remained its core members. The group's final album, *The Bluegrass Album, Vol. 5: Sweet Sunny South,* was released in 1989 and featured Crowe, Lawson, Rice, Vassar Clements, Jerry Douglas, and Mark Schatz. *—Stephen Thomas Erlewine*

The Bluegrass Album, Vol. 1 / 1981 / Rounder ♦♦♦♦♦

The debut from this superstar bluegrass band featuring Tony Rice, J. D. Crowe, Doyle Lawson, Bobby Hicks, Todd Phillips, and Jerry Douglas. A superstar bluegrass band. *—Chip Renner*

The Bluegrass Album, Vol. 2 / 1982 / Rounder ♦♦♦♦

The Bluegrass Album Band's second record reiterates all of the strong points of their debut—the group's interaction and harmonies are so natural, they're breathtaking. *—Thom Owens*

The Bluegrass Album, Vol. 3 (California Connection) / 1983 / Rounder ♦♦♦♦♦

On their third album, the Bluegrass Album Band adds some more country-rock to the mix, in the form of the Flying Burrito Brothers' "Devil In Disguise," but they largely stick to bluegrass classics from the likes of Bill Monroe and Flatt & Scruggs. Like the group's two previous albums, *California Connection* is filled with graceful, stunning musicianship that continues to astonish after several listens. *—Thom Owens*

The Bluegrass Compact Disc / 1986 / Rounder ♦♦♦♦♦

● **The Bluegrass Compact Disc, Vol. 2** / 1987 / Rounder ♦♦♦♦♦

A collection of the group's first four releases. There are 21 songs in all. *—Chip Renner*

The Bluegrass Album, Vol. 5: Sweet Sunny South / 1989 / Rounder ♦♦♦

The Bluegrass Cardinals

f. 1974, **db.** 1991

Group / Traditional Bluegrass, Progressive Bluegrass

During the '70s and '80s, the Bluegrass Cardinals were one of the premiere bluegrass bands in America, noted for performing both contemporary and traditional bluegrass with tight, intricate vocal harmonies and dynamic, precise musicianship. Banjoist Don Parmley and his then 15-year-old son David founded the Cardinals in 1974. Earlier, Don had played banjo for *The Beverly Hillbillies,* and had been part of the Golden State Boys and the Hillmen, both featuring the Gosdin Brothers. In 1976, the Cardinals—which also featured Mike Hartgrove, Norman Wright, John Davis, and Dale Perry—moved from California to Virginia in 1976, where they recorded their eponymous debut album for Briar. The following year, they recorded *Welcome to Virginia.* The Bluegrass Cardinals eventually released five more albums, in addition to touring America and Europe. In 1991, Don and David Parmley left the group, and recorded *Parmley and McCoury* with Del McCoury and his two sons Ronnie and Robbie. Later, after some solo work, David Parmley performed in Continental Divide with Scott Vestal. *—Sandra Brennan*

● **Cardinal Class** / 1983 / Sugar Hill ♦♦♦♦♦

A very good, solid, tight album. The Cardinals at their best. Highly recommended. *—Chip Renner*

Bray Brothers

db. 1971

Group / Contemporary Bluegrass, Contemporary Folk, Traditional Bluegrass

One of the more talented, though little known, traditional bluegrass bands of the early 1960s, The Bray Brothers, usually accompanied by guitarist Red Cravens, were typical of the many regional artists who began to take up playing bluegrass outside of the South. Hailing from Champaign-Urbana, IL, The Bray Brothers have very little to point to in the way of a recording legacy, as the majority of their performances were at unrecorded festivals and on the Cornbelt Country Style radio show of WHOW in Clinton, IL, from which few tapes have survived. What has survived, however, points to an outstanding traditional bluegrass band, with lead vocalist and mandolinist Nate Bray leading brothers Francis and Harley Bray in a very tight bluegrass ensemble. Early on, under the direction of Red Cravens, being both older and more experienced and knowledgeable in the ways of bluegrass, pointed the young Brays in the direction of the classic sounds of Bill Monroe and Flatt & Scruggs. The four would eventually combine for tight, though not overpowering harmonies, and increasingly impressive instrumental skills. Soon Nate Bray would become so accomplished on the mandolin that Monroe himself would pay considerable respect to his talents, as the Bray Brothers would serve an apprenticeship by becoming Monroe's house band in his *Bean Blossom festivals.* It was after those appearances that the Brays landed the aforementioned radio gig, which soon resulted in a *Grand Ole Opry* appearance and a contract with Liberty Records. When their debut failed to make any considerable noise, the band was forced to go back into the workforce as performances became few and far between. In 1971, Nate Bray would die of Hodgkin's disease and a tribute entitled *419 W. Main* was compiled of the Bray Brothers radio performances. Further compiling led to 1976's *Prairie Bluegrass,* which was re-released by Rounder in the spring of 2000 with long lost bonus tracks. *—Matt Fink*

● **Prairie Bluegrass** / Rounder ♦♦♦♦♦

These homemade radio broadcasts from 1961 and 1962 capture this Central Illinois bluegrass group in prime form. A young John Hartford sits in with the band on "Harley's Breakdown," but it's ultimately the Bray Brothers' show. Bluegrass doesn't come much better than this. *—Cub Koda*

Alison Brown

Banjo / Traditional Bluegrass, Progressive Bluegrass

A Harvard graduate who quit a fast-track career as an investment banker to dedicate herself to her music, Brown came to prominence as a stand-out member of Alison Krauss' Union Station band and later was musical director for Michelle Shocked. Her instrumental albums are melodic and graceful and manage to sound both accessible and adventurous. She wrote all but one song on her first three albums—1990's *Simple Pleasures,* 1992's *Twilight Motel* and 1994's *Look Left* and her compositions owe more to the influence of David Grisman (who produced her debut) and Bela Fleck than to Earl Scruggs or Alan O'Bryant. *Quartet* appeared in 1996, followed by *Out of the Blue* in early 1998. Brown resurfaced two years later with *Fair Weather.* *—Michael McCall*

Simple Pleasures / 1990 / Vanguard ♦♦♦♦♦

Her all-instrumental debut instantly earned respect among progressive acoustic music fans. Produced by David Grisman, and featuring guests Mike Marshall and Alison Krauss, Brown weaves cello, flute and congas into her hybrid string sound, and she maintains an innate elegance amid the tricky arranging. *—Michael McCall*

● **Twilight Motel** / 1992 / Vanguard ♦♦♦♦♦

Produced by Mike Marshall, Brown moves in several new directions, showing off the breadth of her talent while keeping the composition at the center of her playing. Jazzier, yet also more relaxed, than her debut. Maura O'Connell provides vocals on a traditional Irish song. *—Michael McCall*

Look Left / 1994 / Vanguard ♦♦♦♦

Brown criss-crosses the globe sonically, taking on Cajun, Celtic, Native American and Australian Aboriginal music with characteristically relaxed proficiency. *—Michael McCall*

Alison Brown Quartet / 1996 / Vanguard ♦♦♦

Alison Brown, believe it or not, is a five-string banjo player. The rest of her quartet is a standard jazz ensemble consisting of piano, bass and drums, and you can be confident that there's nary a bluegrass lick anywhere on this album. Like her compadre Bela Fleck (to whom she must be absolutely sick of being compared), Brown figured out some time ago that the banjo is a fully chromatic instrument with every bit as much melodic flexibility as a guitar, and that its clear, crisp tone is perfectly suited to jazz. It works especially well as a bebop instrument, which Brown demonstrates on this album's opening track, the rollicking, Charlie Parker-ish "G Bop." It also works pretty well as a cool jazz instrument, which Brown demonstrates on the album's second track, the loping, Bill Evans-ish "Red Balloon." This sort of stylistic variety is grist for Brown's mill, but it doesn't always work in her favor: "My Favorite Marsha" (one of several tracks on which she switches to guitar) is nice but borders on new-acoustic sappiness—her guitar playing is good but not exceptional. However, "Without Anastasia" draws nicely on classical influences without sounding pedantic, and "Banjo Mambo" is a very fun Latin romp. Strongly recommended overall. *—Rick Anderson*

Out of the Blue / Feb. 17, 1998 / Compass ♦♦♦

Fair Weather / May 9, 2000 / Compass ♦♦♦♦

Banjo virtuoso Alison Brown, whose primary group is a jazz quartet, returns to her bluegrass roots on this beautiful and exhilarating album. Well, sort of. The instrumental format is certainly bluegrass, given guest artists like Stuart Duncan and Darol Anger on fiddles, guitarists Mike Marshall and Tony Rice, and mandolinist Sam Bush, and with Brown's fiery five-string picking front and center. But much of this is bluegrass music of a type that Bill Monroe might not recognize; while "Late on Arrival" is a good old-fashioned Scruggs-style banjo showcase and "Fair Weather" a modern bluegrass song with all the standard accouterments, the twin mandolins and easy-swinging rhythm of "Poe's Pickin' Party" sound kind of like an old-time string band playing turn-of-the-century salon music. And then there are the cover tunes, which include a gently winning rendition of the old Elvis Costello hit "Everyday I Write the Book." The album's most thrilling moments come on the complex and exhilarating "Leaving Cottondale," which is both one of the prettiest and one of the most technically impressive of Brown's compositions. Here she's joined by fellow banjo maverick Bela Fleck for one of the most jaw-dropping passages of twin-banjo counterpoint ever put on tape. Call it bluegrass, call it newgrass, call it jazzgrass, whatever. This is one of the best albums of 2000 in any genre. *—Rick Anderson*

Sam Bush

b. Apr. 15, 1952, Bowling Green, KY

Vocals, Mandolin, Fiddle / Contemporary Bluegrass, Instrumental Country, Country-Folk, Progressive Bluegrass

Sam Bush extended the musical capabilities of the mandolin and the fiddle to incorporate a seamless blend of bluegrass, rock, jazz and reggae both in his solo work and with his innovative musical ensembles.

A child prodigy on the fiddle, he placed first at the national fiddle contest in Weister, Idaho three times in a row. Together with childhood friends Wayne Stewart and Alan Munde, later of Country Gazette, he formed a band and recorded his first album, *Poor Richard's Almanac,* in 1969. The same year, he made his debut appearance on the *Grand Ole Opry.*

In 1972 he formed the New Grass Revival. Over the next seventeen years, Bush and the New Grass Revival, with their constantly changing cast of musicians, including John Cowan and Bela Fleck, revolutionized the music of the hill country, incorporating everything from gospel and reggae to rock and modern jazz to their tradition-rooted sound.

In 1984,Bush recorded his debut solo album, *Late As Usual.* In 1989, he and Fleck joined Mark O'Connor, Jerry Douglas and Edgar Meyer in an all-star bluegrass band, Strength In Numbers, at the *Telluride Bluegrass Festival* in Colorado. When Fleck and Cowan elected to leave the New Grass Revival in 1989, Bush disbanded the group and joined Emmylou Harris' Nash Ramblers. He toured and recorded with Harris and the band for the next five years.

Bush recorded his second solo album, *Glamour and Grits,* in 1996. In the winter of 1997, Bush and the New Grass Revival reunited for an appearance on the *Conan O'Brien Show* as the backup band for Garth Brooks. On March 28, 1998, Bush's hometown of Bowling Green, Kentucky honored him with a special "Sam Bush Day" celebration. Soon after, he released yet another solo album, *Howlin' at the Moon* which featured guest appearances from Emmylou Harris, Bela Fleck and J.D. Crowe.
—Craig Harris

Late as Usual / 1985 / Rounder ♦♦♦♦

● **Glamour & Grits** / Apr. 1996 / Sugar Hill ♦♦♦♦

Howlin' at the Moon / Apr. 21, 1998 / Sugar Hill ♦♦♦
A wildly talented multi-instrumentalist (mandolin, fiddle, banjo, guitar, pretty much anything with strings), Bush weaves an eclectic blend of bluegrass, country, folk and jazz on this solo release from Sugar Hill. With such gifted cohorts as Bela Fleck, Jerry Douglas and J.D. Crowe on hand, the musicianship here is frequently dazzling. The album is evenly split between instrumental and vocal numbers, with the instrumentals faring better. Bush and John Cowan handle the vocal duties, and while both are good enough singers, several of the songs tend lyrically toward a new-agey sort of earnestness. *—Joel Roberts*

Ice Caps: Peaks of Telluride / Jul. 25, 2000 / Sugar Hill ♦♦♦♦
With the release of *Ice Caps: Peaks of Telluride,* Bush pays tribute to the legendary music festival, pulling together some of his finest live performances from the event, all taped during the 1990s. Accompanied by longtime compatriot Jerry Douglas on Dobro, Bush turns in an unparalleled rendition of Bob Dylan's "Girl From the North Country" and the music just keeps flowing free and pure. Speaking of special guests, the album is chock full of them, from New Grass bandmates Béla Fleck and John Cowan, guitarists Darrell Scott and Jon Randall Stewart, bassist Byron House, drummer Larry Atamanuik, and Subdudes alumnus John Magnie.

One of the album's finest moments—and there are many—comes at the end, as Bush joins John Cowan in a bass, mandolin, and vocal song on Lowell George's Little Feat staple, "Sailing Shoes." This one just has to be heard. It defies any journalistic description. If that isn't reason enough to check out *Ice Caps,* Sam Bush covers "Celebration" by Kool and the Gang on mandolin. Oddly enough, Bush pulls it off with his usual class and style, where many would fall flat on their face in a puddle of disco mud. *Ice Caps: Peaks of Telluride* is another stellar release from one of acoustic music's true innovators. *—Michael Smith*

Vassar Clements

b. Apr. 25, 1928, Kinard, SC
Violin, Fiddle / Traditional Bluegrass
Combining jazz with country, Vassar Clements became one of the most distinctive, inventive and popular fiddlers in bluegrass music. Clements first came to prominence as a member of Bill Monroe's band in the early '50s, but he never limited himself to traditional bluegrass. Over the next four decades, he distinguished himself by incorporating a number of different genres into his style. In the process, he became not only one of the most respected fiddlers in bluegrass, he also became a sought-after session musician, playing with artists as diverse as the Monkees, Hank Williams, Paul McCartney, Michelle Shocked, Vince Gill, and Bonnie Raitt. During the 1950s, spent six years with Bill Monroe during the 1950s, then joined Jim & Jesse for four years. Though sidelined from alcoholism during the early '60s, he returned to playing in 1967 and played with with Faron Young, John Hartford and the Earl Scruggs Revue. Much session work followed during the early '70s, and Clements capitalized on the exposure with his first solo album, 1973's *Crossing the Catskills.* He recorded two albums for Mercury, one for MCA, then began a long-running agreement with Flying Fish. During the '80s and '90s, Clements continued to record sporadically, but he cut numerous sessions for other artists and played numerous concerts every year. *—Stephen Thomas Erlewine*

Crossing the Catskills / 1973 / Rounder ♦♦♦♦♦

Vassar / 1980 / Flying Fish ♦♦♦
This album features Clements strutting his stuff on jazz fiddle with sympathetic backing from his band. Clements is one of the very best on his instrument, and the album showcases his talent. *—AMG*

Hillbilly Jazz Rides Again / 1987 / Flying Fish ♦♦♦
Hillbilly Jazz Rides Again is a collection of Western Swing revival by Vassar Clements, a former sideman for Bill Monroe. With pianist Bob Hoban and guitarists Dave Salyer and Doug Jemigan in tow, the album actually veers closer to swing than Western, which isn't necessarily a bad thing. However, the performances aren't always inspired, which becomes even more noticeable on the numerous mediocre original songs by Hoban. *—Stephen Thomas Erlewine*

Vassar Clements, John Hartford, Dave Holland / 1988 / Rounder ♦♦♦♦
Vassar Clements is the star here, but John Hartford and Dave Holland hold their own. Besides each contributing tunes, Hartford and Holland combine on the wonderful "Till Something Better Comes Along. Hartford's singing is almost comic relief, but nobody's really going to sweat it on this charming little gem. Put it on and let your mind roam to the hills and the streams and the simple life. *—Mark Allan*

Grass Routes / 1991 / Rounder ♦♦♦
This recent album shows why Clements is one of the greatest fiddlers in modern country music. *—Mark A. Humphrey*

Once in a While / 1993 / Flying Fish ♦♦♦
Violinist Vassar Clements has demonstrated the improvisatory link between bluegrass and jazz, and this was another example of the two styles' affinity. Clements' soaring phrases and adept solos were right at home on such standard jazz tunes as "Perdido," "Cherokee" and "Sonnymoon For Two," but he didn't stray far from his favorite breakdown riffs or signature country sound. The results were the kind of loose, joyous jam date where labels meant nothing, and musicianship rather than genre ruled. *—Ron Wynn*

● **Back Porch Swing** / Nov. 30, 1999 / Cedar Glen ♦♦♦♦
Vassar Clements has always been one of the most recognizable fiddlers in bluegrass. When he steps to the mic to take a solo, the most foursquare traditional breakdown or reel takes on a jazzy, swinging flavor—one that generally disappears as soon as his solo ends. On this album, he moves well away from the whole bluegrass genre, opting instead for the accompaniment of a jazz band and a program of undiluted swing, jazz, and R&B. Opening with a burning rendition of Jelly Roll Morton's "King Porter Stomp," Clements delivers one original (the thoroughly charming "Hillbilly Jazz"), several standards ("That Old Black Magic," "String of Pearls"), and a handful of numbers by his pianist, Fred Bogert. Bogert's "If That's Love" sounds like it came straight out of Muscle Shoals, with Clements' slinky fiddle weaving in, out, and around the sturdy drumming and funky bass. "Ezra's Holler" is a sort of modified bossa nova on which Clements plays the head in unison with sax player Paul Martin Zonn, to very fine effect. Just about everything on this album is both musically interesting and lots of fun. Highly recommended. *—Rick Anderson*

Bill Clifton

b. 1931, Riderwood, MD
Vocals, Autoharp, Piano, Guitar / Traditional Country, Traditional Bluegrass
Few contributed as much to the preservation and performance of traditional bluegrass music as Bill Clifton. He began recording as a solo act in the late '50s, releasing five albums over the next seven years. In 1967, he was hired by the Peace Corps and spent three years in the Philippines. While there, he visited New Zealand, recording an album with the Hamilton County Bluegrass Band. Clifton occasionally returned to the U.S. to record, and also kept recording in Europe. In 1972, he returned briefly to America to play his first bluegrass festival circuit. Encouraged by the experience, he began visiting the U.S. more frequently and recorded more regularly, signing a contract with County Records. On his third album for the label, he formed the First Generation with mandolinist Red Rector and banjoist Don Stover. After the album's release, the trio toured the bluegrass circuit for the remainder of the 1970s. In the early '80s, Clifton and his family moved to Virginia, where he worked as a businessman. However, Clifton continued to perform at bluegrass festivals and occasional concerts into the '90s. *—Sandra Brennan*

★ **The Early Years (1957-1958)** / Jun. 15, 1992 / Rounder ♦♦♦♦♦
Bill Clifton was one of bluegrass's finest guitarists and also an underrated vocalist. He was especially gripping on slow, aching tunes like "Lonely Heart Blues" or gospel numbers like "I'm Living The Right Life Now" and "When You Kneel At Your Mother's Grave." Clifton's late-'50s singles were collected on this CD, featuring him working alongside such musicians as Curley Lambert on mandolin and Johnny Clark on banjo, as well as fiddler Tommy Jackson, Ralph Stanley on banjo and Gordon Terry on fiddle. These songs are light-years away from the polished, intricate newgrass and contemporary bluegrass sounds of the 1980s and '90s. The harmonies, leads, solos and arrangements reflect simpler, more innocent times, but don't lack intensity or musical quality. *—Ron Wynn*

Coon Creek Girls

f. 1937, **db.** 1957
Group / Old-Timey, Traditional Bluegrass
One of the most famous all-female string bands in country, the Coon Creek Girls were also among the first female groups to play their own instruments and focus on authentic mountain music, instead of sentimental and cowboy songs. The founding member of the long-lived group was Lily May Ledford, and on October 9, 1937, they made their live radio debut from Cincinnati Music Hall. Shortly after their debut, the group began appearing on the *Renfro Valley Barn Dance;* they would sing on the program for the next 15 years. In 1938, the Coon Creek Girls cut their first session, although their records, which featured traditional mountain songs, never proved as popular as their radio performances. The Coon Creek Girls kept performing together in various incarnations until 1957. After the group broke up, Lily May launched her own solo career. *—Sandra Brennan*

● **Early Radio Favorites** / Old Homestead ♦♦♦♦♦
Early Radio Favorites contains all of the music that the Coon Creek Girls recorded during the '30s, including "Banjo Picking Girl" and "How Many Biscuits Can You Eat?" Not only were the Coon Creek Girls one of the last mountain string bands of their era, they were the only female old-timey group, which made them unique. If they were just unique, the band would simply be a historical curiosity, but the girls also made good music, as evidenced by this stellar collection. For fans of string bands, *Early Radio Favorites* is an essential addition to their record collections. *—Stephen Thomas Erlewine*

The Country Gazette

f. 1971, USA, **db.** 1988
Group / Progressive Bluegrass
One of the most infuential bluegrass acts of the '70s—as well as one of that decade's most popular country artists in Europe—Country Gazette blended bluegrass with country-rock and, in the process, sowed the seeds for the newgrass movement of the '80s. Formed by fiddler Byron Berline, bassist Roger Bush, and banjoist Billy Ray Latham (all former members

of Dillard & Clark), the trio released their debut *A Traitor in Our Midst* in 1972. Opening spots for Steve Miller, Crosby & Nash, and Don McLean indicated that the group was aiming for a more rock-oriented audience. Following 1973's *Don't Give Up Your Day Job*, the band signed with the European-based Ariola, which released *Bluegrass Special* later in 1973. As the location of their record label indicated, the band was more popular in Europe than America. Though Berline and Bush both left in 1975, the band continued on with guitarist Kenny Wertz, multi-instrumentalist Roland White and fiddler Dave Ferguson. Two albums—1977's *What a Way to Earn a Living* and 1979's *All This and Money Too* followed on Ridge Runner. After 1982's *America's Bluegrass Band*, Country Gazette temporarily disbanded but reunited to tour America and Europe during the '80s. The group broke up for a second and final time in 1988. *—Stephen Thomas Erlewine*

Don't Give Up Your Day Job / 1973 / United Artists ✦✦✦✦✦
Country Gazette's second studio album is a stunner. Highlighted by the likes of such great songwriters as Stephen Stills, whose "The Fallen Eagle" is on a par with Manassas' Graham Nash, whose "Teach Your Children" gets a great bluegrass treatment here, and Elton John, whose "Honky Cat" finds a home where it belongs, everything seems to work on *Don't Give Up Your Day Job*. Original tunes, the likes of "Deputy Dalton" and "Huckleberry Hornpipe," only add to this fine disc. With the help of such friends as Herb Pederson, Clarence White, and Leland Sklar, Country Gazette puts on an amazing array of music that tickles you in all the right places. It's no wonder these guys were looked upon as stars by bluegrass-crazy Europeans. *Don't Give Up Your Day Job* is as wonderful as it gets. *—James Chrispell*

Live / 1975 / Transatlantic ✦✦✦
Live was released after Byron Berline had left Country Gazette, but that shouldn't deter music fans from seeking out this fine bluegrass disc. From the opener, "Black Mountain Rag" on through to "Down In the Bluegrass" there is much for listeners to sink their teeth into. Highlights also include "Never Ending Song of Love" courtesy of Delaney & Bonnie, along with such bluegrass staples as "Sally Goodin" and the Louvin Bros.' "My Baby's Gone" are all aided in the club atmosphere which helps *Live* show off Country Gazette's charm. It's Hard to find, but well worth seeking out. *—James Chrispell*

Strictly Instrumental / 1981 / Flying Fish ✦✦✦✦✦
The Country Gazette's impassioned bluegrass goes instrumental on this release, with assistance from fiddler Billy Joe Foster, guitarist David Grier and bassist Kathy Chiavola. Still, the show belongs to Alan Munde's banjo work, which articulately navigates the rest of the group through the dozen traditional tunes contained here. *—Jason Ankeny*

● **Hello Operator . . . This Is Country Gazzette** / 1991 / Flying Fish ✦✦✦✦✦
Hello Operator . . . This Is Country Gazette covers the group's five Flying Fish records, which were made between 1976 and 1987. During that time, a number of excellent musicians made their way through the band, but Country Gazette retained a distinctive progressive bluegrass style, as this compilation demonstrates. Certainly, anyone wanting an idea of what the group achieved during the height of their career should pick up *Hello Operator*, since it sums up their music succinctly and effectively. *—Thom Owens*

The Country Gentlemen

f. Jul. 4, 1957, Washington, D.C.
Group / Contemporary Bluegrass, Traditional Bluegrass, Progressive Bluegrass
The Country Gentlemen expanded the definition of "bluegrass"—they were progressive bluegrass before the term existed. The Gentlemen came along with the first wave of the folk-music revival in the late '50s and quickly made a name for themselves as a band who could not only play traditional material straight but who also brought Bob Dylan and contemporary country material into the genre. Because of their exceptional singing and virtuoso instrumentals, The Gentlemen attracted a broad audience, ranging from traditional country/bluegrass fans to folk and soft-rock lovers. Led by guitarist/vocalist Charlie Waller through all of its numerous incarnations, the group debuted with an album for Starday. Their breakthrough album, Country Songs Old & New, came after a move to Folkways. After their stint at Folkways, the group moved to Mercury in 1963, where they released *Folk Session Inside*. The following year, they began a long association with Rebel Records. During the '60s, the Country Gentlemen built up a dedicated fan base in America through constant touring. Although their lineup shifted rapidly, their sound pretty much stayed the same. For the next 20 years, various lineups of the Country Gentlemen, which were are led by Waller, remained popular on the bluegrass festival circuit. *—Stephen Thomas Erlewine & David Vinopal*

The Country Gentlemen / 195 / Smithsonian/Folkways ✦✦✦✦✦
MCA Special Products' *Country Gentlemen* culls ten country hits from the MCA vaults, including other labels that were acquired later. There may be no rhyme or reason to the featured tracks, but there's really no fluff on the record—Porter Wagoner's "Green, Green Grass of Home," Cal Smith's "Country Bumpkin," Ned Miller's "From a Jack to a King," Ray Price's "Make the World Go Away," Don Gibson's "Sea of Heartbreak," Faron Young's "It's Four in the Morning," Jimmy Dean's "To a Sleeping Beauty" and Hank Locklin's "Please Help Me, I'm Falling" guarantee that this is a worthwhile budget-priced collection. —Stephen Thomas Erlewine

★ **Country Songs Old & New** / 1960 / Smithsonian/Folkways ✦✦✦✦✦
This is a reissue of the 1960 Folkways album that launched their career. Includes "The Little Sparrow, " "The Long Black Veil, " "Under the Double Eagle, " and 13 other classic cuts. A magic album. *—Michael Erlewine*

☆ **Award Winning Country Gentlemen** / 1972 / Rebel ✦✦✦✦✦
Not only does *Award Winning Country Gentlemen* culminate a major shift in direction for the Country Gentlemen, it is also quite possibly their finest album. Charlie Waller had to reassemble the group in the early '70s, bringing in a new lineup—including mandolinist Doyle Lawson, bassist Bill Yates and banjoist Bill Emerson—that helped move the Country Gentlemen even further into contemporary music. On *Award Winning*, the band covers songs by rock and folk songwriters like Bob Dylan and Gordon Lightfoot, bringing a bluegrass attitude and instrumentation to the contemporary numbers. The result is a stunning record, with a great selection of songs and simply stunning musicianship. *—Thom Owens*

Calling My Children Home / 1978 / Rebel ✦✦✦
Thanks to the superb direction of mandolinist Doyle Lawson, *Calling My Children Home* is an excellent bluegrass gospel album, highlighted by a handful of tremendous a cappella quartets. *—Thom Owens*

Live in Japan / 197 / Rebel ✦✦✦✦
Live in Japan captures a strong early '70s concert from the Country Gentlemen, spotlighting much of their best-known material, as well as their excellent harmony and instrumental skills. *—Thom Owens*

☆ **25 Years** / 1980 / Rebel ✦✦✦✦✦
25 Years was released in 1980, when the Country Gentlemen were celebrating their 25th anniversary. The compilation covers the group's recordings for Rebel Records, which began in the mid-'60s. Over the course of *25 Years*, various incarnations of the Country Gentlemen are displayed. Each one has its own merits, but the the classic lineup of Eddie Adcock, John Duffey, Tom Gray and Charlie Waller does stand out in particular. Though the other incarnations aren't quite as accomplished as this lineup, the compilation nevertheless remains an excellent purchase and introduction, since it gives a fine overview of the group's career. *—Thom Owens*

Bluegrass at Carnegie Hall / 1988 / Hollywood ✦✦✦✦✦
Originally released on Starday in 1962, *Bluegrass at Carnegie Hall* isn't a live album, even though the title suggests that it is. Instead, it is a collection of excellent studio recordings made around the same time as their 1961 appearance at Carnegie Hall, that rank among their finest early recordings. *—Thom Owens*

Folk Songs & Bluegrass / 1988 / Smithsonian/Folkways ✦✦✦✦✦
Folk Songs & Bluegrass is one of the Country Gentlemen's best releases, featuring the classic lineup of Eddie Adcock, John Duffey, Tom Gray and Charlie Waller at the height of their power. Both the songs—which are divided between standards and newer folk numbers—and the performances are first-rate, making *Folk Songs & Bluegrass* an essential purchase for any bluegrass collection. *—Thom Owens*

Sit Down Young Stranger / 1988 / Sugar Hill ✦✦✦✦✦

The Country Gentlemen Feat. Ricky Skaggs / 198 / Vanguard ✦✦✦
Featuring Ricky Skaggs on Fiddle collects material drawn from Skaggs' early-'70s tenure with the band, and features "House of the Rising Sun," "The City of New Orleans," and "Catfish John." *—Jason Ankeny*

Let the Light Shine Down / 1991 / Rebel ✦✦✦
Let the Light Shine Down is a fine compilation of gospel and inspirational songs the Country Gentlemen recorded between 1962 and 1976, including several tracks that have never been available before on compact disc. *—Thom Owens*

Sugar Hill Collection / 1995 / Sugar Hill ✦✦✦✦✦
As the title suggests, *Sugar Hill Collection* compiles the highlights from the Country Gentlemen's recordings for the independent label Sugar Hill. Although these were made later in their career, the group sounds as good as they ever have. *—Thom Owens*

☆ **The Early Rebel Recordings 1962-1971** / 1998 / Rebel ✦✦✦✦✦
This is an especially pleasing four-CD set, comprising most of the Country Gentlemen's recordings for the Rebel label over a period of nine years, when they used bluegrass music as a vehicle for innovation by way of country, folk, and rock. The influence of the Osborne Brothers can be heard throughout their early work (along with more mainstream country sources), but then they start cutting Dylan and Tom Paxton songs. The odd early individual tracks lead into the contents of the *Bringing Mary Home* album, which established their reputation nationally as a bluegrass act to be reckoned with. Disc One ends with the controversial "Big Bruce," a gay parody of Jimmy Dean's "Big Bad John" that skirts a fine line between satire, burlesque, and slur. Disc Two features several previously unissued songs, and also shows the group growing artistically amid a flurry of concert activity—a surprising number of songs from this period were cut on the fly at semi-pro and improvised studios, as the band fit recording in anywhere they could. Disc Three picks up in 1969—the group by this time was freely adapting popular as well as folk tunes, thus the presence of "Mrs. Robinson" amid the bluegrass standards. By Disc Four, the group was nearing a summit of popularity and creativity. The irony was that, even as they were achieving success, the group was nearing a decision to leave Rebel. This collection isn't quite ideal, since it is missing a key mid-'60s live recording; the booklet and annotation are very thorough, as is the session information, all of it pitched at the Bear Family level. *—Bruce Eder*

The Cox Family

f. 1976
Group / Traditional Bluegrass, Progressive Bluegrass
The singing Cox Family from Cotton Valley, LA, was comprised of father Willard, son Sidney, and daughters Evelyn and Suzanne, who derived their sound from combining country, bluegrass and gospel styles. They first began performing together in 1976, and were a popular draw at fairs and festivals, but their career was given a big boost when in the early '90s they met Alison Krauss, who brought them to the attention of Rounder Records. They also gained massive exposure when in 1994 they caught the ear of the multiplatinum-selling Counting Crows' frontman Adam Duritz, who was so impressed with the group he invited them to open for the band during its North American tour. The Cox Family recorded two records of their own on Rounder Records: *Everybody's Reaching Out Ffor Someone* (1993) and *Beyond the City* (1995), which earned them a Grammy nomination for Best Bluegrass Album. They also collaborated with Krauss on an album entitled *I Know Who Holds Tomorrow*, which won a Grammy in 1994 for Best Country/Gospel/Bluegrass Album. The Cox Family released their major-label debut *Just When We're Thinking It's Over* on Asylum Records in 1996. *—Jack Leaver*

Beyond the City / 1995 / Rounder ✦✦✦✦✦

● **Just When We're Thinking It's Over** / Jul. 1996 / Elektra/Asylum ✦✦✦✦✦
The smooth and effortless vocal blend of the Cox Family make this a pleasurable experience throughout. And although their angelic four-part harmonies are based in bluegrass, to categorize the family in that genre solely, would be to pigeonhole them. The performances here also mix in country, gospel and a touch of blues, with top-notch session players providing a sound foundation that employs electric, as well as acoustic instruments and includes producer Alison Krauss' fiddle and viola playing on a couple of cuts. All four family members take turns singing lead, and there isn't a weak link in the group, nor a weak song on the album. Highlights include a great bluegrass reworking of Del Shannon's 1961 hit "Runaway" and the beautiful ballad "Nothing Else I Can Do," penned by Sidney and Suzanne Cox. —*Jack Leaver*

J.D. Crowe

b. Aug. 27, 1937, Lexington, KY
Vocals, Banjo / Traditional Bluegrass, Progressive Bluegrass
Banjoist J.D. Crowe was one of the most influential progressive bluegrass musicians of the '70s. Initially influenced by Earl Scruggs, as well as rock & roll and the blues, Crowe worked his way through several bands during the '60s, developing a distinctive instrumental style that melded country, bluegrass, rock, and blues. Crowe didn't receive national exposure until the early '70s, when he formed the New South but after the release of the band's eponymous debut in 1972, he became a fixture on the bluegrass scene for the next 20 years.

Born and raised in Lexington, KY, Crowe picked up the banjo when he was 13 years old, inspired by one of Flatt & Scruggs' performances on the Kentucky Barn Dance. After that show, he regularly attended the duo's performances, sitting down in the front row to study Scruggs' revolutionary picking. Soon, Crowe was playing with various groups in Kentucky, including an outfit that also featured Curley Parker and Pee Wee Lambert. The young banjo player frequently played on local radio stations and that is where he got his first major break in 1956. Jimmy Martin was driving through Lexington when he heard Crowe on the radio station and was so impressed with what he heard, he drove to the station and asked him to join his band, the Sunny Mountain Boys. Crowe immediately accepted and began touring with Martin. While he was in the Sunny Mountain Boys, J.D. didn't stick to a strict bluegrass set list—he often added rock & roll songs to his repertoire.

After spending six years with Martin, Crowe left the Sunny Mountain Boys in 1962 to pursue a solo career. For a while, he played Lexington bars and hotels, developing a new, progressive direction for bluegrass which incorporated stronger elements of folk, blues and rock. In the mid-'60s, he formed the Kentucky Mountain Boys with Red Allen and Doyle Lawson, which released their first album, *Bluegrass Holiday,* in 1968 on Lemco Records. The Kentucky Mountain Boys had a varied repertoire, but played solely acoustic instruments. Two other records followed—*Ramblin' Boy* and *The Model Church* before the group broke up in the early '70s.

Following the disbandment of the Kentucky Mountain Boys, J.D. Crowe formed the New South, which was the most revolutionary bluegrass outfit of its time. Originally, the band consisted of guitarist Tony Rice, mandolinist Ricky Skaggs, dobroist Jerry Douglas, and fiddler/bassist Bobby Sloan and they played a wildly eclectic brand of bluegrass on electric instruments. When they released their debut, *J.D. Crowe & the New South* in 1975 on Rounder Records, it caused an instant sensation—it marked a genuine turning point in the sound of the genre. All of the musicians in the original lineup of the New South were acclaimed and they would later go on to popular solo careers—in fact, most of them had left within a few years of the debut. By the end of the decade, the band featured guitarist/vocalist Keith Whitley, mandolinist Jimmy Gaudreau, fiddler Bobby Slone, and bassist Steve Bryant.

During the '80s, the New South featured an ever-revolving lineup, as former members came back for guest appearances and Crowe discovered fresh, developing talents—the group became known as a source for new musicians that would later go on to individual success. In 1980, Crowe formed the Bluegrass Album Band with Tony Rice, Bobby Hicks, Doyle Lawson, and Todd Phillips. The Bluegrass Album Band toured and recorded sporadically throughout the course of the decade, always to great critical and popular acclaim. J.D. continued with the New South until 1988, when he decided to retire from the road. Following his decision, he appeared at special, one-shot concerts—including a tour with Tony Rice—but he concentrated on studio work, particularly producing records for developing bands. —*Stephen Thomas Erlewine*

☆ **The Model Church** / 1969 / Rebel ✦✦✦✦✦
This gospel album was recorded and originally released in the early 1970s on the Lemco label. When Rebel acquired the rights to Lemco's catalog several years later, it reissued this and two other J.D Crowe albums (*Bluegrass Holiday* and *Ramblin' Boy,* retitled *Blackjack*). What may be most noteworthy about *The Model Church* is the fact that it's the first gospel album to feature singer Doyle Lawson, who would later make some of the best bluegrass gospel recordings to date at the head of his own band Quicksilver. With J.D. Crowe on banjo and vocals, Larry Rice on mandolin and vocals, and Bobby Slone on bass, this quartet delivers a lovely set of gospel songs, some of which have since become standards. Highlights include the hauntingly beautiful title track "Goin' Up," a the Gosdin Brothers classic, and a fine version of Jim & Jesse's "Look for Me." The echoey production is a little bit strange for a bluegrass album; it won't satisfy everyone's tastes, but there's no denying the power of these performances. —*Rick Anderson*

☆ **J. D. Crowe & The New South** / 1975 / Rounder ✦✦✦✦✦
J.D. Crowe & the New South's eponymous debut album is one of the most influential and pioneering records in the history of bluegrass. For the first edition of the New South, Crowe assembled a stellar group of musicians—including Ricky Skaggs (fiddle, mandolin, vocals), Tony Rice (lead vocals, guitar), and Jerry Douglas (dobro)—and gave them each equal weight. Consequently, this is vibrant collaborative music, not just a leader with some faceless studio hacks. Furthermore, Crowe pushed the music in new direction with his section of material, taking songs from contemporary singer/songwriters like Gordon Lightfoot, adding a couple of originals, as well as standards. With such an eclectic selection of songs, plus the band's trailblazing instrumental style, *The New South* did indeed offer a new kind of bluegrass and its impact could still be felt years after its release. —*Thom Owens*

My Home Ain't in the Hall of Fame / 1978 / Rounder ✦✦✦
Crowe, on banjo and baritone, moves closer to country in the company of Keith Whitley and Doug Jernigan. —*Mark A. Humphrey*

Live in Japan / 1982 / Rounder ✦✦✦

Blackjack / 1987 / Rebel ✦✦✦
Blackjack is one of J.D. Crowe and the New South's best albums, featuring a mixture of bluegrass standards and contemporary country-rock and folk songs, like the Flying Burrito Brothers' "Sin City." It's a stunning display of ambition, progression and heritage, highlighted by Crowe's excellent instrumental work and Doyle Lawson's wonderful lead vocals. —*Thom Owens*

★ **Flashback** / 1994 / Rounder ✦✦✦✦✦
FlashBack is a first-rate retrospective of J.D. Crowe's groundbreaking, innovative career and an excellent way to get acquainted with all aspects of his music. —*Thom Owens*

Come on Down to My World / Jan. 12, 1999 / Rounder ✦✦✦✦
This 1998 release found Crowe and his band, the New South, at their creative best and definitely at the top of their game. Always skirting the fine line between what is traditional bluegrass and what is country, Crowe and his band stick close to tradition while alternately blazing new trails in the genre. That said, this album probably has a higher quotient of straight country done up Crowe style than any previous outing. From its remake of Charley Pride's "I'm So Afraid of Losing You Again" to Merle Haggard's "Back to the Barrooms" to Townes Van Zandt's "White Freightliner," the band takes on this type of material with considerable elan, imparting a fresh slant to all of them. The more traditional instrumentals, "J's Tune" and "Careless Love," individually call to mind the work of Bill Monroe and Earl Scruggs, respectively. Mandolinist and lead singer Dwight McCall's original "I Don't Know" is another highlight falling into that nether region between bluegrass and country. "Come Back Sweetheart" and "You Didn't Say Goodbye" are more traditional pieces and serve as musical anchors throughout this album, an album that shows the wide range of Crowe's music and his unbelievable facility on his instrument. —*Cub Koda*

Doug Dillard

b. Mar. 6, 1937, Salem, MO
Vocals, Guitar, Banjo / Country-Rock, Traditional Bluegrass, Progressive Bluegrass
Doug Dillard's music blended bluegrass, country-rock, and pop. Throughout his long and varied career, he was one of the leading banjoists in country and bluegrass music, pioneering a distinctive instrumental style. With younger brother Rodney, he formed the Dillards in 1962, issuing the first in a series of successful LPs a year later. In addition to work with the

The Banjo

With the possible exception of pedal steel guitar, the banjo is that one instrument most identified with country music, especially bluegrass music. Beginning as a four-stringed fretless instrument, the banjo became much more versatile with an added fifth string (the shorter "drone" string). In the South after the Civil War, banjos of many configurations—some with four strings (the tenor and plectrum banjo), others with five strings (since the '20s the country banjo)—were plentiful; in fact, in the '20s the banjo/fiddle combination formed the basis of country music instrumentals.

Uncle Dave Macon, the first real star of the Opry, in the '20s played five-string in the old style, often called frailing, clawhammer, or simply "thumping." In this style, the backs of the fingernails pick out the melody, while the thumb catches the drone string, thus creating a regular beat and rhythm. (Grandpa Jones is no doubt the most famous living player of the frailing banjo.)

Although the banjo didn't die out in the '30s, the many guitar/mandolin duets put it on the back burner for the decade. String bands, precursors to Bob Wills and other Western swing bands of the '40s, used the tenor banjo for volume and rhythm. Meanwhile, a banjo picker from North Carolina, Charlie Poole, had developed his own style of playing, three-finger picking instead of frailing; he was in fact paving the way for another North Carolinian, Earl Scruggs, who may not have invented the banjo but certainly reinvented it. Bill Monroe's Blue Grass Boys, formed in 1939, were without a five-string banjo until 1942, when Dave "Stringbean" Akeman added his frailing style to the band. But it wasn't until 1945, when Earl Scruggs joined the Blue Grass Boys, that what is now known as bluegrass banjo was invented.

It's nearly impossible to overstate the effect of Earl Scruggs on banjo playing. Live audiences gaped and gasped in disbelief when they heard the flood of careful notes that rolled off Earl's fingers. Many banjo pickers who rose to prominence admit to giving up the old style the same night they heard the new "Scruggspicking" style on the Grand Ole Opry. This new sound absolutely dominated, in large part because of Scruggs's signature songs "Foggy Mountain Breakdown" (recorded with Flatt and the Foggy Mountain Boys around 1951 and later the chase music for the movie Bonnie and Clyde) and "The Ballad of Jed Clampett" (on TV's "Beverly Hillbillies"). Further reinforcement came in the form of "Dueling Banjos" in the weirdly memorable version from the 1973 film Deliverance.

Though Earl Scruggs will rightly be remembered as the reinventor of the banjo, other musicians, all beholden to Earl, have taken the instrument in yet different directions: Buck Trent electrified it; Bill Keith invented the chromatic/melodic style; and Bela Fleck adds jazz, classical, and other difficult-to-label influences.—*David Vinopal* side-project the Folkswingers, in 1966 Doug played with ex-Byrd Gene Clark and the Gosdin Brothers on their self-titled collaboration. In 1967, Doug left the Dillards to form a duo with Gene Clark. Dillard & Clark released their debut album, *Fantastic Expedition*, in 1968. After Clark left the band in 1970, Dillard continued with the group, renaming them Dillard and the Expedition. His first solo effort was the soundtrack to *Vanishing Point*. In 1973 and 1974, Dillard released two albums, *Dueling Banjos* and *Douglas Flint Dillard—You Don't Need a Reason to Sing*. In 1978 he formed the Doug Dillard Band, which featured fiddler Byron Berline. *—Sandra Brennan*

The Banjo Album / 1969 / Together ✦✦✦✦✦
The Banjo Album is first, and foremost, an album of traditional bluegrass played by musicians firmly rooted in the work of pioneers like Flatt and Scruggs, the Stanley Brothers and Bill Monroe. These same musicians, however, are all top-notch, second generation players influenced by the rock scene. Consequently, Dillard and crew manage to breathe genuine new life into many standards without sacrificing the integrity of the originals. In fact, the musicians not only play ferociously, but often completely reinterpret the old chestnuts, occasionally making them sound even better. In many cases, Dillard employs droning harmonic tonalities characteristic of Indian music and Indian-influenced psychedelic rock guitar. The record also features atypical bluegrass instruments such as harpsichord, harmonica, drums, dembek, and tablas. Rather than coming off as gimmicky, though, the use of exotic instrumentation serves to add exciting new textures and moods to music which, during this pre-"Newgrass" period, rarely deviated from very strict stylistic guidelines. Plus, nearly every performance here is simply an all-out jam, with Dillard playing particularly explosively. Special mention should be made of his fantastic version of "Clinch Mountain Backstep," which shows a confidence, boldness and energy that rivals even the definitive version by Clarence White's Kentucky Colonels. *—Pemberton Roach*

Heaven / 1979 / Flying Fish ✦✦✦
A gospel album featuring Dan Crary, Byron Berline, John Hartford, Herb Pedersen. It includes an excellent cover of "Turn Your Radio On." *—Chip Renner*

● **Jackrabbit** / 1980 / Flying Fish ✦✦✦✦✦
A live album from the Telluride Bluegrass Festival, with guests Sam Bush and Byron Berline. *—Chip Renner*

The Dillards

f. 1962, Missouri, **db.** 1980
Group / Country-Rock, Traditional Bluegrass, Progressive Bluegrass
During the '60s, the Dillards helped bring bluegrass to a wider audience, both through their records and their appearances on television and film. For the next three decades, the band continued to perform in various incarnations, all the while remaining one of the most popular bluegrass bands in America. Missouri-born brothers Doug and Rodney Dillard formed the core of the original lineup of the Dillards. The siblings headed to California in 1962, and less than a week after their arrival, Jim Dickson saw them jamming with the Greenbriar Boys and he signed the group to Elektra. In 1963, the Dillards released their first album, *Back Porch Bluegrass*, followed a year later by *Live... Almost!* By the time the latter album was released, the group had amplified their instruments, angering the purists that formed the core of the American bluegrass audience. Nevertheless, they developed a strong fan base. In 1965, they released the album *Pickin' and Fiddlin'*, which featured fiddler Byron Berline; two years later, Doug left the band to form the Dillard & Clark Expedition with former Byrd Gene Clark.He was replaced by banjo player Herb Peterson and the group recorded their fourth album, *Wheatstraw Suite;* released in 1968, it featured an increasingly adventurous musical approach, as did its followup, 1970's *Copperfields*. On these two albums, the Dillards added drums and steel guitar to their sound and began covering rock and folk songwriters like Bob Dylan, Lennon & McCartney, Gordon Lightfoot, John Prine and Tim Hardin. Although neither record was a commercial success, they opened the doors for progressive bluegrass bands in the '70s. *—Sandra Brennan*

Wheatstraw Suite / 1968 / Elektra ✦✦✦✦✦
It never got any better than this. In 1968, as the Byrds were making valiant (if unappreciated) efforts to bring rock and country music closer together, the Dillards were trying to do some of the same for bluegrass and rock. The result was 13 all-but-perfect tracks mixing some pretty laid-back topicality ("Hey Boys") and humor ("The Biggest Whatever"), cowboy songs ("Single Saddle," which Gene Autry should have covered), just plain gorgeous poetry ("Lemon Chimes"), and a couple of unexpected covers ("I've Just Seen a Face," "Reason to Believe"), with arrangements that exude a delicate, subdued lushness ("Listen to the Sound") and an element of electric rock (courtesy of Joe Osborn on electric bass and Jim Gordon on drums) that worked perfectly. In many ways, this is a finer rural/rock fusion album than *Sweetheart of the Rodeo*, the first Flying Burrito Brothers album, or the Beau Brummels' efforts during this same period, and an indispensable part of any collection of '60s music. *—Bruce Eder*

Homecoming & Family Reunion / 1979 / Flying Fish ✦✦✦
This is a pleasant album of several Dillard generations live at a picnic. *—Mark A. Humphrey*

Let It Fly / 1991 / Vanguard ✦✦✦
Produced by Herb Pedersen of the Desert Rose Band, *Let It Fly* is a strong collection of traditional bluegrass with an electric twist. The album is one of the best records from the late '80s and '90s incarnation of the Dillards. *—Thom Owens*

★ **There Is a Time (1963-70)** / 1991 / Vanguard ✦✦✦✦✦
Twenty-nine tracks drawn from the Dillards' first five albums (originally on Elektra), which are otherwise unavailable. The CD is assembled not in chronological order, but with musical coherence as the main determining factor, so tracks from different albums get juxtaposed together. From *Back Porch Bluegrass* we get five songs, including "Banjo In the Hollow" and "Dooley" (another version of which they performed with Andy Griffith on his TV show), while *Pickin' and Fiddlin'* is represented by the bracing "Hamilton County Breakdown" and "Sally Johnson." *Live!!! Almost!!!* gets six tracks, including the group's version of Dylan's "Walkin' Down the Line." There are five numbers (including the title track and the Beatles' "Yesterday") off of their 1970 release *Copperfields*, and the legendary *Wheatstraw Suite*, from two years earlier, has nine songs, among them the group's loving covers of the Beatles' "I've Just Seen a Face" and Tim Hardin's "Reason to Believe." *—Bruce Eder*

Take Me Along for the Ride / 1992 / Vanguard ✦✦
This latter-day effort from the Dillards features new material molded in the band's late-'60s electric bluegrass sound. *—Jason Ankeny*

Roots and Branches/Tribute to the American Duck / Mar. 19, 1996 / BGO ✦✦✦✦
After leaving Elektra Records in the early '70s, but before signing with Flying Fish, the Dillards released two albums, *Roots and Branches* and *Tribute to the American Duck*, on independent labels. Neither was particularly remarkable, but they're of interest to hardcore fans. Beat Goes On reissued the pair on one CD in 1996. *—Stephen Thomas Erlewine*

The First Time Live / Nov. 2, 1999 / Varese ✦✦✦✦
Varese's *First Time Live* compiles 16 live performances recorded in 1962 by the original lineup of the seminal bluegrass band. As should be expected, this is a gem in the rough, capturing the band as they're finding their distinctive voice. Even though this music was recorded within the band's first year of existence, the band is still surprisingly assured, yet their very newness keeps this fresh, vital, and exciting. A priceless dip into the vaults that's sure to thrill diehard Dillards fans. *—Stephen Thomas Erlewine*

Dixie Gentlemen

f. 1956, **db.** 1966
Group / Traditional Bluegrass, Progressive Bluegrass
During the folk revival of the early '60s, the Dixie Gentlemen were one of the most original bluegrass bands performing. The Alabama-based band was formed in the mid-'50s by mandolinist/vocalist Herschel Sizemore and banjoist/vocalist Rual Yarbrough, who met while playing in the Alabamains. When their guitarist friend Jake Landers was discharged from the military, the three formed the Dixie Gentlemen. During the late '50s, the group played in clubs throughout the South and appeared on local television shows. In 1959, the Dixie Gentlemen released their first singles—the gospel songs "Pray for Me" and "Three Steps." Later that year, the group recorded two albums of classic bluegrass songs, *Hootenanny N' Blue Grass* and *Blue Grass Down Home*, under the name the Blue Ridge Mountain Boys. In 1966, the Dixie Gentlemen made their final album, *Blues and Bluegrass*. Following its release, the members pursued careers as sidemen for popular artists like Jimmy Martin. The original Dixie Gentlemen reunited in 1972 to record *Together Once More*. Close to twenty years later, they again took time out from their solo careers to make *Take Me Back to Dixie*. *—Sandra Brennan*

● **Country Style of the Dixie Gentlemen** / 1963 / United Artists ✦✦✦✦✦

Jerry Douglas

b. 1955, Columbus, OH
Slide Guitar, Dobro / Contemporary Bluegrass, Progressive Bluegrass
As one of the premiere dobro players in bluegrass, new-acoustic, and country music, Jerry "Flux" Douglas toured and recorded with everyone from Emmylou Harris, Ricky Skaggs, and the Nitty Gritty Dirt Band to mandolin sensation David Grisman and banjo innovator Bela Fleck. Douglas' albums as a leader fully exploited the dobro's resonant guitar sound, his aggressive touch, incredibly fast finger picking and deft use of the steel bar giving the instrument a bright, cutting tone-quality. In 1978, Douglas made his solo debut with *Fluxology*. His next album, *Tennessee Fluxedo* came out two years later. He began playing and recording with the Whites in 1983, and eventually left to focus on his solo career and much sought-after session work. He recorded three albums for MCA in the late 1980s, most notably 1989's *Plant Early*, which marked a change toward a calmer, more textured direction. *—Sandra Brennan & Linda Kohanov*

Fluxology / 1979 / Rounder ✦✦✦✦
A good bluegrass album with Tony Rice, Darol Anger, Todd Phillips, and Ricky Skaggs. *—Chip Renner*

Fluxedo / 1982 / Rounder ✦✦✦
A smoother sound, which has become his trademark with Strength in Numbers. Featuring Sam Bush, Bela Fleck, the Whites, Mark Shatz, and Russ Barenberg. *—Chip Renner*

Under the Wire / 1986 / Sugar Hill ✦✦✦
Though all of his releases are dobro tour-de-forces, this is a highly sophisticated ensemble album with some of the best players in the new- acoustic realm, including Mark O'Connor, Russ Barenberg, Bela Fleck, and Sam Bush. With seven of the ten tracks written by Douglas, the album is also a tribute to his inventive compositional style. *—Linda Kohanov*

Everything Is Gonna Work out Fine / 1987 / Rounder ✦✦✦✦
Everything Is Gonna Work Out features Jerry Douglas' first two albums—*Fluxology* and *Fluxedo*—on one compact disc. The two records showcase the dobroist at his rootiest, and contain some wonderful traditional bluegrass, which is occasionally spiked by jazzy flourishes. *—Thom Owens*

● **Slide Rule** / 1992 / Sugar Hill ✦✦✦✦✦
On *Slide Rule*, Jerry Douglas moves away from the the jazz experiments of *Plant Early*, returning to the straightforward bluegrass of his early work. The result is a stunner, featuring not only a remarkable performance from Douglas, but also from an impressive list of guest musicians, including Alison Krauss, Sam Bush, Maura O'Connell, Stuart Duncan, and Tim O'Brien. *—Thom Owens*

Skip, Hop & Wobble / 1994 / Sugar Hill ✦✦✦✦
This excellent 1993 Sugar Hill CD features three of the top artists playing newgrass today. Entirely instrumental, entirely enjoyable, the tracks on this CD run the gamut of musical expression from the humorous play of "Why Don't You Go Back to the Woods" to the slow,

beautiful "Hymn to Ordinary Motion." The liner notes discuss the creative process around each song, as well as the group's union and the challenges/rewards of playing as a trio. Sam Bush does a couple of very nice guest spots on mandolin. If you are tired of the musical simplicity and inane lyrics of much of today's music, this CD cleanses the palate. *—Jeff Crooke*

Yonder / 1996 / Sugar Hill ✦✦

Restless on the Farm / May 19, 1998 / Sugar Hill ✦✦✦

Dry Branch Fire Squad

f. 1976

Group / Bluegrass-Gospel, Traditional Bluegrass, Progressive Bluegrass

The Dry Branch Fire Squad was a modern bluegrass band committed to keeping the old-time Appalachian traditional music alive. This southern Ohio bluegrass group was fronted by Ron Thomason, a mandolinist and comedian who grew up in Russell County, Virginia. While working as a high school English teacher and administrator in the Springfield area, he also played in a local bluegrass band with Frank Wakefield and later went on to spend a year touring with Ralphy Stanley's Clinch Mountain Boys.

Thomason formed the Dry Branch Fire Squad in 1976, after he spent time with Lee Allen's Dew Mountain Boys. The earliest incarnation of the band included guitarist John Baker, banjo player Robert Leach, and bass player John Carpenter. Two years later, Mary Jo Leet became the group's vocalist. During the late 1970s, the Fire Squad recorded a series of independent records, and were later joined by bassist Dick Erwin and banjoist John Hisey, who would remain with the band for the next ten years. During that time, the Dry Branch Fire Squad became favorites on the festival circuit. Over the years the band underwent many subsequent personnel changes, but remained dedicated to preserving the old mountain sounds. *—Sandra Brennan and David Vinopal*

Born to Be Lonesome / 1978 / Rounder ✦✦✦

Good. Featuring Kenny Baker, Bobby Osborne. A nice cover of "Brand New Tennessee Waltz." *—Chip Renner*

● **Good Neighbours & Friends** / 1985 / Rounder ✦✦✦✦✦

Long Journey / 1991 / Rounder ✦✦✦✦

Old timey—in a modern way. Very good. *—Chip Renner*

Live at Last / Oct. 8, 1996 / Rounder ✦✦✦✦✦

Live At Last captures the mid-'90s incarnation of the Dry Branch Fire Squad in concert, running through most of their favorites. Thanks to the group's buoyant, joyous performance, this isn't just a rote concert affair—it's a testament to the band's talent and taste, and arguably one of their best albums ever. *—Thom Owens*

Memories That Bless & Burn / Oct. 26, 1999 / Rounder ✦✦✦✦✦

With *Memories that Bless and Burn* Dry Branch Fire Squad has made the kind of music that the alt-country folks are copying, but a few steps closer to the real thing. Sweet gospel harmonies exist side-by-side with episodes of banjo madness and the vocalists, especially Mary Jo Leet and Ron Thomason, sometimes sound like they are singing right on top of their last raw nerve. This is not to say that the members of Dry Branch Fire Squad lack talent—rather their sound is stripped down to a kind of pure mirror of the music of their grandparents, something which helps make their faith-driven lyrics sound sincere and evokes the sound of the church itself, with its shouting preachers and passionate bursts of praise.

This album functions as sort of a greatest-hits album—the first three songs are new material—including the excellent title track, which features the sweet singing of Suzanne Thomas and helps set the mood for the rest of the album. Tracks 4-10 are from previous Rounder recordings and provide a profile of the band's earlier work. Tracks 4 and 5 are two versions of the same song, interesting because they show the evolution of both the band's technique and the quality of the equipment that they recorded on (the second version is amazingly clearer, as well as featuring a more powerful vocal). Tracks 11-13 are songs that had been featured on other albums but were re-recorded for this one, and 14-16 are songs that have long been a part of their gospel shows but are being recorded for the first time. "Touch the Hem of His Garment," provides a beautiful closing to this album, evoking the gentle despair and hope that echo all throughout this fine work. *—Stacia Proefrock*

Flatt & Scruggs

f. 1948, **db.** 1969

Group / Traditional Bluegrass

Probably the most famous bluegrass band of all time was Flatt And Scruggs and the Foggy Mountain Boys. They made the genre famous in ways that not even Bill Monroe, who pretty much invented the sound, ever could. Because of a guitar player and vocalist from Tennessee named Lester Flatt and an extraordinary banjo player from North Carolina named Earl Scruggs, bluegrass music has become popular the world over and has entered the mainstream in the world of music.

Like so many other bluegrass legends, Flatt And Scruggs were graduates of Bill Monroe's Blue Grass Boys. Because of the unique sound they added ("overdrive," one critic called it), Monroe felt let down after Flatt's quality vocals and Scruggs's banjo leads left in 1948. Quickly the two assembled a band that in the opinion of many was among the best ever, with Chubby Wise on fiddle and Cedric Rainwater on bass; a later band, with Paul Warren on fiddle and Josh Graves on dobro, was equally superb. With so many extraordinary musicians and the solid, controlled vocals of Flatt, it's no wonder The Foggy Mountain Boys was the band that brought bluegrass to international prominence. From 1948 until 1969, when Flatt And Scruggs split up to pursue different musical directions, they were *the* bluegrass band, due to their Martha White Flour segment at the Opry and, especially, their tremendous exposure from TV and movies. *—Stephen Thomas Erlewine & David Vinopal*

☆ **Foggy Mountain Banjo** / 1961 / Columbia ✦✦✦✦✦

The album that secured their standing among folk music enthusiasts in the 1960s, it focuses on Scruggs's instrumental prowess as well as his sharp interplay with dobroist Josh Graves, fiddler Paul Warren and Flatt's flat-picking guitar. The album also features drummer Buddy Harman, whose appearance shocked purists. *—Michael McCall*

Songs of the Famous Carter Family / 1961 / Columbia/Legacy ✦✦✦

Live at Vanderbilt University / 1964 / Columbia ✦✦✦

Strictly Instrumental / 1967 / Columbia ✦✦✦✦

Strictly Instrumental is a delightful duet album between Flatt & Scruggs and Doc Watson, giving the three musicians an opportunity to flaunt their exceptional instrumental talents. Sticking to a selection of songs that is traditional in approach, but are not played frequently ("John Hardy Was a Desperate Little Man," "Pick Along," "Spanish Two-Step"), Flatt & Scruggs and Watson play with a startling fluidity—these instrumentals are so rich and skillful that vocals would have been superfluous. For lovers of instrumental bluegrass, this album is a must-hear. *—Thom Owens*

The Golden Era 1950-55 / 1977 / Rounder ✦✦✦

Golden Era: 1950-55 contains a selection of highlights from Flatt & Scruggs' early days at Columbia. *—Thom Owens*

Blue Ridge Cabin Home / 1979 / County ✦✦✦✦

Blue Ridge Cabin Home contains a selection of Flatt & Scruggs' finest recordings from the '50s, material that demonstrates why they had to leave Bill Monroe's band. Where Monroe wanted to keep the music pure, Flatt & Scruggs were constantly pushing the boundaries of what bluegrass could do, bringing in heavy elements of country, folk, gospel and even pop. The recordings on this compilation helped popularize bluegrass, and while it is available on more comprehensive collections, *Blue Ridge Cabin Home* remains a terrific single-disc sampler of their sound. *—Thom Owens*

☆ **20 All Time Great Recordings** / 1983 / Columbia ✦✦✦✦✦

Three-part gospel-style harmonies, breakneck banjo, flinty Americana, and "a bubblin' crude" are the cornerstone collection of bluegrass at its best. *—Mark A. Humphrey*

☆ **1949-1959** / 1992 / Bear Family ✦✦✦✦✦

1949-1959 is a four-disc box set filled with the very best Flatt & Scruggs tunes recorded during their peak years at Decca.. A Bear Family import with superb liner notes, and music beyond compare. *—Michael Erlewine*

☆ **1959-1963** / 1992 / Bear Family ✦✦✦✦✦

Although the material covered on the five-disc box set *1959-1963* isn't as innovative as the music on Bear Family's first Flatt & Scruggs box, *1949-1959*, it's quite nearly as good. During these five years, the duo brought bluegrass into the mainstream and this collection shows why. Over the set's 129 tracks—which includes a wealth of unreleased material and alternate takes, most notably the complete Carnegie Hall concert from December of 1962—Flatt & Scruggs runs through a selection of originals and standards, including some re-recorded versions of their earlier Mercury hits. They might not sound quite as lively as they did a decade earlier, but this remains classic bluegrass. *—Thom Owens*

Don't Get Above Your Raisin' / 1992 / Rounder ✦✦✦

Flatt's song became a back-to-basics anthem when Ricky Skaggs waxed it ca. 1981. The original is here, along with other greats from the '50s, on this 15-track compilation of material that was originally released on Columbia Records. *—Mark A. Humphrey*

★ **The Complete Mercury Sessions** / Aug. 4, 1992 / Mercury ✦✦✦✦✦

The integral early recordings of this seminal bluegrass band. Included is their classic "Foggy Mountain Breakdown," "Roll in My Sweet Baby's Arms," "Old Salty Dog Blues" and others. It's indispensable for bluegrass fans. *—Michael McCall*

1964-1969, Plus / Feb. 1996 / Bear Family ✦✦✦✦✦

Bear Family's third box set of Flatt & Scruggs material is necessary for completists and historians, but it doesn't have the revelatory spark of the first box, nor the crossover appeal of the second. There is plenty of enjoyable music on the set, but the completist approach—all of the released studio recordings are included, plus alternate takes and unreleased tracks—makes listening to the box somewhat difficult. Nevertheless, for diehard Flatt & Scruggs fans, *1964-1969, Plus* is as essential a purchase as the first two Bear Family boxes. *—Thom Owens*

★ **The 'Tis Sweet to Be Remembered: Essential Flatt & Scruggs:** / Jan. 28, 1997 / Columbia/Legacy ✦✦✦✦✦

Tis Sweet to Be Remembered: The Essential Flatt & Scruggs is a double-disc set that covers all of the essential items that the ground-breaking bluegrass duo recorded for Columbia Records, including the hit singles "'Tis Sweet to Be Remembered," "Cabin in the Hills," "Go Home," "The Ballad of Jed Clampett," "Pearl Pearl Pearl," and "Foggy Mountain Breakdown." Though the compilation is a little too extensive for casual listeners, for dedicated bluegrass fans it's an essential purchase—it may not be as thorough as the Bear Family box sets, but it considerably more digestable, which means it gives a better sense of Flatt & Scruggs' career and their considerable accomplishments. *—Thom Owens*

Flatt and Scruggs at Carnegie Hall!: The Complete Concert / 1998 / Koch ✦✦✦✦

Lester Flatt

b. Jun. 19, 1914, Overton County, TN, **d.** May 11, 1979, Nashville, TN

Vocals, Mandolin, Guitar / Traditional Bluegrass

After Lester Flatt and Earl Scruggs parted ways in 1969, Flatt reassembled many of the Foggy Mountain Boys, renamed the group Nashville Grass, and toured very successfully until his death in 1979. Unlike Scruggs, who with his sons moved on to music that was only marginally country, Flatt and the Grass stuck to traditional bluegrass material. Even without Scruggs, the band shone, and Flatt's vocals, musical direction, and taste received the credit they had so long deserved. *—David Vinopal*

● **Greatest Bluegrass Hits, Vol. 1** / 1982 / CMH ✦✦✦✦✦

This is a good overview of Flatt's post-Scruggs recordings with Nashville Grass, a band that included a young Marty Stuart on mandolin. *—Mark A. Humphrey*

Lester Raymond Flatt / 1989 / Flying Fish ♦♦♦
Here this bluegrass legend turns to more basic music. *—AMG*

Josh Graves

b. Tellico Plains, TN
Slide Guitar, Dobro / Contemporary Bluegrass, Traditional Bluegrass, Progressive Bluegrass
For over five decades, the legendary Josh Graves remained one of the major forces keeping the unique sounds of the dobro alive in both country and bluegrass music. In 1942, Graves joined the Pierce Brothers. Later he played with Esco Hankins and Mac Wiseman before becoming a member of the *Wheeling Jamboree* with Wilma Lee and Stoney Cooper, where he remained through the mid-'50s. During a performance with the Coopers at the *Grand Ole Opry*, Graves made a big impression upon Lester Flatt and Earl Scruggs who invited him to join their Foggy Mountain Boys. In the late '50s, acoustic instruments were out of favor, due to the popularity of rock & roll; the survival of the dobro as an important instrument in country can largely be attributed to Graves, who electrified audiences with a red-hot picking style and then cooled them down with bluesy, sweet mellowness. He remained a primary member of the Foggy Mountain Boys until the group disbanded in 1969. In 1971, he began playing with the Earl Scruggs Review; three years later, he went solo with the LP *Alone at Last*. *—Sandra Brennan*

● **King of the Dobro** / 1982 / CMH ♦♦♦♦♦
This is the man who created bluegrass-style dobro with his bluesy hound-dog slide playing. *—Mark A. Humphrey*

Josh Graves / Sep. 29, 1998 / Rebel ♦♦♦♦
On this album of mostly traditional bluegrass, split evenly between instrumental and vocal numbers (nicely handled by Terry Eldredge), Graves proves he is still one of the world's great dobro masters. The set includes familiar tunes from the catalogs of the Carter Family, Bill Monroe, the Delmore Brothers, and Flatt & Scruggs, plus a handful of Graves originals. Occasionally, Graves and fellow septuagenarians Kenny Baker (longtime fiddler with Monroe) and Curly Seckler (former mandolinist and vocalist with Graves in the Foggy Mountain Boys) push things into overdrive, embarking on some blazing runs that would challenge players of any age. Who says old dudes can't rock— *—Joel Roberts*

The Puritan Sessions / Rebel ♦♦♦♦
Longtime fiddler Kenny Baker appears in an uncharacteristic role as a fingerstyle guitarist in a delightfully low-key set of tunes and songs with dobroist (and sometime-singer) Graves. *—Mark A. Humphrey*

David Grier

Guitar / Traditional Bluegrass, Progressive Bluegrass
David Grier stands at the forefront of progressive bluegrass guitarists, following in the footsteps of Clarence White and Tony Rice. Three-time winner of the Best Guitar Player of the Year award by the Bluegrass International Music Association, Grier began playing guitar at age eight. His father, Lamar Grier, played banjo with Bill Monroe's Blue Grass Boys and Grier had an opportunity to learn from a number of musicians, including legendary guitarist Clarence White. Although surrounded by bluegrass musicians, Grier counts Ry Cooder, Jimi Hendrix, and Eric Clapton as influences.

Grier played bluegrass with the the Country Gazette and Doug Dillard in the '80s, but he began recording his own projects in 1988 with *Freewheeling* followed by 1991's *Climbing the Walls* with mandolin player Mike Compton. By the mid-'90s Grier had become a valued session player, working with quality musicians like fiddler Stuart Duncan, banjoist Tony Furtado, and working on projects like the Grammy-winning *Great Dobro Sessions*.

Grier has shown a willingness to play in a variety of styles, and he has refused to be confined to any musical genre. From the potpourri of his 1995 release *Lone Soldier* to the progressive bluegrass of Psychograss' *Like Minds*, Grier has continued to develop as an artist. Both of these projects, plus 1997's *Panorama*, have been purely instrumental projects, a feast for lovers of acoustic music.

In 1998, *Hootenanny* was released on his own recording label, Dreadnought, and the following year he recorded the jazzier *Phillips, Grier & Flinner* with mandolin player Matt Flinner and bassist Todd Phillips. He has been recognized by *Acoustic Guitar* as one of the ten most influential artists of the '90s. Grier's inventive and occasionally unorthodox style along with his ability to hop from genre to genre continue to keep his music fresh and vital. *—Ronnie D. Lankford, Jr.*

● **Freewheeling** / 1991 / Rounder ♦♦♦♦♦
After working with Doug Dillard and the Country Gazette in the early '80s, David Grier made his first album in 1988. With Grier's reputation as a flat-picker on the rise, he attracted an outstanding cast of musicians for this recording, including mandolin players Sam Bush and Roland White and fiddler Stuart Duncan. The first thing a listener will notice on the opening cut "Wheeling" is that, while this may be Grier's album, the other musicians are given plenty of room for lengthy solos. *Freewheeling* is based more in bluegrass and tradition than Grier's later efforts like *Lone Soldier* and *Panorama*. Grier has also written seven of the 12 instrumentals on this all-acoustic outing, including the lingering "A Blue Midnite Star," a melancholy piece that evokes a lonely starry night in the Appalachians. "Shadowbrook" flows openly, with a lovely fiddle solo by Duncan, and multiple solos by Grier that continue to develop fresh phrasings. Grier is a complicated soloist, never satisfied to complete speedy runs to gain attention; instead, he varies his solos with chords, unique phrasings, and straight-out picking. His solos are never scattered affairs, but colored and textured to create a whole. "If I Knew Her Name," also written by Grier, is a relaxed instrumental that ventures away from the more traditional material on this album, hinting at explorations to come on later albums. The last three cuts feature Grier solo and include a light and airy version of "Gold Rush." For lovers of traditional music and of great flat-picking, *Freewheeling* is sure to please. *—Ronnie Lankford, Jr.*

Lone Soldier / 1995 / Rounder ♦♦♦♦
Although *Lone Soldier* is a fairly typical slice of David Grier's supercharged blend of bluegrass and jazz, many of the tracks find him in a somewhat more pensive mood. His always superb flatpicking, while as fast and firey as ever, seems especially light, airy and imbued with a somewhat more relaxed feel. That's not to say, however, that Grier leaves behind his characteristically unstoppable rhythmic drive. Many have suggested that Grier is the spiritual heir to the great Clarence White, and such comparisions are wholly justified on this record if just for Grier's supremely supportive and driving approach to playing rhythm guitar. Of course, David Grier's leads are what set jaws to dropping, and *Lone Soldier* is filled with mind-boggling technique. Like all Grier's recorded work, however, speedy fingers are only secondary to a pure musicality that would seem almost impossible to surpass if not for the existence of Grier's even more sublime 1997 album *Panorama. Lone Soldier* contains standout performances from the usual crew of young bluegrass and "new acoustic" music all-stars, plus appearances on several tracks by Flecktones electric bassist Victor Wooten, who turns in some of his most sensitive work on record. *—Pemberton Roach*

Panorama / Oct. 21, 1997 / Rounder ♦♦♦♦♦
Ever since the release of *FreeWheeling*, David Grier's debut Rounder Records album, he has been recognized as one of the true giants of bluegrass guitar. On *Panorama*, though, his playing reaches new levels of technical and stylistic fluidity that few guitarists in any genre even attempt. Although he often fuses country, bebop, classical, traditional jazz, funk and just about every other style imaginable in the course of a single song or solo, Grier never incorporates a lick for the sake of pure experimentation or to show off his chops. Both his rhythm and lead playing are unerringly musical and always supportive of the song. That's not to say, however, that those listeners who are just in it for the shredding will be disappointed. The delicacy and speed of his playing on some tunes is less like traditional guitar picking and more like a hummingbird in flight. Of course, Grier's sidemen (a misnomer, really, because each one is a virtuoso in his own right) on *Panorama* all share the limelight with dazzling solos of their own. The work of mandolinist Sam Bush is particularly awe-inspiring, and he blazes through several tunes less like Bill Monroe than a young Al DiMeola. Grier, though, is unquestionably the leader on this effort, his flawless feel and sophisticated compositions leading the way for his talented compatriots. Although the album may be a little too ambitious for some fans of straight-ahead bluegrass, *Panorama* will certainly appeal to lovers of "Dawg Music," progressive bluegrass or imaginative, expertly played instrumental music of any sort. *—Pemberton Roach*

Hootenanny / 1998 / Dreadnought ♦♦♦

Tone Poems, Vol. 3: The Sounds of the Great Slide & Resophonic Instruments / Aug. 22, 2000 / Acoustic Disc ♦♦♦♦
Tone Poems, Vol. 3 is part of a series of fascinating recordings by the Acoustic Disc label featuring vintage guitars. On this entry, David Grisman, founder of the David Grisman Quintet, National guitar expert Bob Brozman, and former Seldom Scene member Mike Auldridge utilize 53 slide guitars, dating from 1915 to 1998, on 21 instrumentals. The fidelity of this recording is astounding, and each instrument's tone is pure and clean. The accompanying booklet provides pictures of the guitars used on each cut and a wealth of information on instrument makers such as Herman Weissenborn and John Dopyera. On the majority of the material, the listener can hear Auldridge on the left speaker, Brozman on the right, and Grisman in the center. Standout tunes include "St. Louis Blues," with a lively tempo that fluctuates between slow blues and New Orleans-styled jazz, and the upbeat "Trash Can Stomp," which finds everyone trading leads and squeezing in an incredible amount of guitar work within the two-minute structure. The Hawaiian origins of slide guitar are also recognized by the inclusion of "Akaka Falls" and "Kohala March." It should also be noted that while this album features slide guitars, this is a quiet album, tastefully presented. It's somewhat surprising that albums like *Tone Poems, Vol. 3* are made at all because the market for resophonic guitar music is surely limited. But Acoustic Disc seems unconcerned by this. Grisman, Brozman, and Auldridge have set forth to create great music while representing a historical link between acoustic guitars and electric ones. In this goal, they have succeeded admirably. *—Ronnie Lankford, Jr.*

David Grisman

b. 1945, Hackensack, NJ
Mandolin / Progressive Bluegrass
David Grisman is normally associated with the bluegrass wing of country music, but his music owes almost as much to jazz as it does to traditional American folk influences. Because he couldn't think of what to call his unique, highly intricate, harmonically advanced hybrid of acoustic bluegrass, folk and jazz without leaning toward one idiom or another, he offhandedly decided to call it "dawg music"—a name which, curiously enough, has stuck. A brilliant mandolinist, with roots deep in the Hot Club Quintette of France, Grisman's jazz sensibilities were strong enough to attract the admiration of the HCQ's Stephane Grappelli, who has toured and recorded with Grisman on occasion. *—Richard S. Ginell*

★ **The David Grisman Quintet** / Nov. 1977-Dec. 1976 / Rhino ♦♦♦♦♦
The David Grisman Quintet's eponymous debut was a stunning achievement, capturing a pivotal point in newgrass history. It was a record that opened up new rhythmic textures and instrumental textures, specifically new, jazzier ways to solo. Grisman—who wrote the majority of the compositions—arranged each number as a way for his quintet to shine instrumentally, as a way for each musician to demonstrate their innovative skills. It's not traditional bluegrass—these instrumental recordings draw equally from folk, rock and country as they do from bluegrass—but it's was a thrilling new variation on the form that broke down countless doors for the genre. *—Thom Owens*

Quintet '80 / 1980 / Warner Brothers ♦♦
Throughout his career, mandolinist David Grisman has performed music that crosses between many boundaries, from "new acoustic" folk to bluegrass and swing-oriented jazz. This set features Grisman's string group (which also includes violinist Darol Anger, Mike Marshall on mandolin, guitar and violin, Mark O'Connor on violin and guitar, and bassist Rob Wasserman) playing six of Grisman's diverse originals, an obscure tune, and a brief rendi-

tion of John Coltrane's "Naima." The music is excellent, but Grisman's more jazz-oriented projects would be in the future. *—Scott Yanow*

Mondo Mando / Jul. 7, 1981-Jul. 16, 1981 / Warner Brothers ✦✦✦✦✦
David Grisman's desire to break or extend the boundaries of string music, folk, and bluegrass resulted in recordings that are also of interest to jazz listeners. The mandolinist performs seven colorful originals (including "Dawg Funk"), plus Django Reinhardt's lesser-known "Anouman" with various string players, including Mike Marshall on mandolin, violinists Darol Anger and Mark O'Connor, guitarist Tony Rice, and bassist Rob Wasserman; the Kronos String Quartet helps out on "Mando Mando." Unpredictable and fairly unique music. *—Scott Yanow*

Mandolin Abstractions / 1983 / Rounder ✦✦✦
Despite the musicianship and some colorful moments, this duo set by mandolinists David Grisman and Andy Statman (essentially melodic free improvisations) misses a rhythm section. The song titles (which include "Two White Boys Watching James Brown at the Apollo," "Journey to the Center of Twang" and the two-part "March of the Mandolas") are more colorful than the music, and although not without interest, this is one of David Grisman's least memorable recordings. *—Scott Yanow*

Svingin' with Svend / Nov. 5, 1986-May 21, 1987 / Zebra ✦✦✦✦✦
Despite his popularity, mandolinist David Grisman has made relatively few recordings since this CD. Matched with the great veteran swing violinist Svend Asmussen, Grisman holds his own on one of his most jazz-oriented dates. With guitarist Dimitri Vandellos, bassist James Kerwin and drummer George Marsh completing the quintet, Grisman and Asmussen jam on the title cut, two of the violinist's originals, "It Don't Mean a Thing," "Jitterbug Waltz," Milt Jackson's "The Spirit Feel," and a pair of Django Reinhardt-Stephane Grappelli tunes. Highly recommended. *—Scott Yanow*

Home Is Where the Heart Is / 1988 / Rounder ✦✦✦
A more traditional country and bluegrass album than his "dawg" sessions, Rounder issued this Grisman session in 1988. He's playing with J.D. Crowe, Ricky Skaggs, and Doc Watson, among others. There's little jazz here, but there are some superb bluegrass, country, and folk selections, plus marvelous playing. *—Ron Wynn*

Dawg '90 / 1990 / Acoustic Disc ✦✦✦✦✦
This CD marked the beginning of mandolin master David Grisman's own label, giving him the complete freedom he had sought so long to record as he wished. His continuously fascinating blend of elements of jazz, Gypsy music and bluegrass with additional influences help all ten compostions remain fresh after numerous hearings. The campy "Learned Pigs" and the delightful "Hot Club Swing" (with the obvious flavor of Django Reinhardt & Stephane Grappelli) are among the many strong tracks. The supporting cast includes guitarist John Carlini, fiddlers Mark O'Connor and Matt Glaser, and a trio of incredible musicians who continued to make a number of great recordings with Grisman after this gem: flautist Matt Eakle, bassist Jim Kerwin and the unbelievably talented Joe Craven, who is not only the perfect percussionist for Grisman's "Dawg" music, but is also an outstanding fiddler as well. Anyone who enjoys masterful music should forget about trying to pigeonhole Grisman into any preconceived category and just go out and buy this incredible release. *—Ken Dryden*

Tone Poems / 1994 / Acoustic Disc ✦✦✦✦✦
While mandolin master David Grisman and the equally talented guitarist Tony Rice may be better known in the world of bluegrass, jazz fans need to check out this excellent collection of mandolin/guitar duets, performed with different vintage instruments on each track. The improvising by both men is never less than brilliant, transforming traditional folk tunes like "Grandfather's Clock" and "I Am a Pilgrim," plus the unlikely "O Sole Mio," into masterpieces. The lone track that's very familiar to jazz listeners is "Swing '42," played very convincingly by two men who are well versed in jazz even if they don't play it exclusively. *—Ken Dryden*

Dawganova / 1995 / Acoustic Disc ✦✦✦

Tone Poems 2 / Oct. 31, 1995 / Acoustic Disc ✦✦✦✦✦
David Grisman doesn't stick exclusively to mandolin on this top notch duo date with guitarist Martin Taylor, playing mandola, mandocello, tenor guitar and guitar as well. Like its predecessor, the two artists play a different vintage instrument on each track, though the music this time is much more familiar to jazz fans. The interpretations of such classics as "Swanee," "Anything Goes," "Blue Moon," and "Over the Rainbow" are consistently both stunning and fresh. The gems among the jazz compositions include Django Reinhardt's "Tears" and a tour de force arrangement of Chick Corea's "Crystal Silence." Two surprising tracks are the usually trite "Mairzy Doats" (an irritating song that was a huge hit in the '40s) and the very snappy take of of the often tedious "Besame Mucho"; when musicians the caliber of Grisman and Taylor can make something out of unpromising songs like these, it demonstrates how gifted they are. Highly recommended. *—Ken Dryden*

DGQ-20 / 1996 / Acoustic Disc ✦✦✦✦
Back in 1976, mandolinist David Grisman was one of the pioneers of what would come to be called "New Acoustic Music," and a groovy, swinging fusion of bluegrass, hot jazz and pop played primarily by young virtuosos from California. It was a scene that gave rise to such giants as Tony Rice, Bela Fleck, Sam Bush and Mark O'Connor, and brought established artists like fiddler Vassar Clements and French jazz violinist Stephane Grappelli to new prominence. But David Grisman's mandolin was the signature sound of the genre, and still is—that's him you hear picking away between NPR news segments, and you've heard him in movie soundtracks and on hundreds of other people's records over the last twenty years. Of all the musicians who emerged from the New Acoustic Music scene, only Grisman had a subgenre named after him: "Dawg Music."

This three-disc set brings together live recordings, alternate takes and previously unreleased compositions from Grisman's tape vault. It charts the changes in his quintet from the earliest days, when it nurtured the fiery talents of the young guitarist Tony Rice and fiddler Darol Anger, to its modern incarnation, which features a percussionist and flutist. Some of the titles—"Swing '39," "Ricochet," "Rattlesnake"—will be familiar to NAM aficionados, as will Grisman's penchant for punning titles based on his nickname ("Dawgma," "Dawggy Mountain Breakdown"). Others are more obscure, some of them deservedly so, as in the case of "Shasta Bull," an ill-conceived soda jingle. But most of these 39 tracks are delightful; among them are the two numbers the DGQ performed with Stephane Grappelli on the *Tonight Show* in 1979, a beautiful three-mandolin arrangement of "Ricochet," and a live version of "Mondo Mando" that features Jethro Burns and the young Kronos Quartet. Highly recommended. *—Rick Anderson*

Dawg Duos / Oct. 19, 1999 / Acoustic Disc ✦✦✦

Aubrey Haynie

Fiddle / Contemporary Country, Traditional Bluegrass, Progressive Bluegrass
Born in 1974, Aubrey Haynie has wasted no time in establishing himself as one of the most talented fiddle and mandolin players in contemporary country music. Haynie has been one of the most sought after session players in Nashville, having appeared on releases by George Jones, Porter Wagoner, Trisha Yearwood and Bryan White among others, and with tours in the bands of Aaron Tippin and Clint Black padding his resume, as well. Comfortable in a variety of traditional musical genres, from bluegrass and country to more swing and jazz oriented styles, Haynie has drawn comparisons to swing and bluegrass fiddler Chubby Wise, who served as something of a mentor to Haynie in his youth, and accolades from Ricky Skaggs, who contributed vocals on Haynie's debut. Released in 1997, *Doin' My Time*, an excellent mix of traditionals, covers, and original instrumentals mixed with the occasional vocal track, was well received in the bluegrass community and netted Haynie a nomination from the International Bluegrass Music Association for Instrumental Album of the Year. The similarly impressive, *A Man Must Carry On* followed in the spring of 2000 and only added to Haynie's growing reputation. *—Matt Fink*

● **Doin' My Time** / Sep. 16, 1997 / Sugar Hill ✦✦✦✦
Aubrey Haynie's debut, recorded at the ripe old age of 23, is a tour de force in bluegrass, country, and Western swing instrumentals. Taking the title track from Haynie's version of the Flatt & Scruggs classic, *Doin' My Time* never disappoints, as the young artist effortlessly tosses off amazing renditions of traditionals like "Cherokee Shuffle," "Dark Hollow," and "Turkey in the Straw." The jazzy "Cracker Jack" and the Texas swing of "Foolin' Around" are also exceptional. Just as impressive are Haynie's own entries into the genre, with the solemn "Leavin' Rosine," featuring Bela Fleck and Jerry Douglas, "Montgomery Bell," and the gorgeous "Austin's Dream," on which Haynie adds tenor guitar to his fiddle. Given time, these could be the songs that the next generation of bluegrass musicians will be learning, and Haynie's, being young enough, will still be around to teach them firsthand. *—Matt Fink*

A Man Must Carry On / Mar. 21, 2000 / Sugar Hill ✦✦✦✦
Once again joined by members of the bluegrass elite, the ridiculously talented Aubrey Haynie's second Sugar Hill release *A Man Must Carry On* is an exceptional extension of Haynie as an artist, as he composed 11 of the 16 tracks here, with most sounding so familiar that it's hard to think they were written by someone born in 1974. From the gently mournful "Sam's Creek Blues" to the Spanish elements of "Thonotosassa," this is the sound of an artist truly coming into his own. More traditional elements, like the straightforward bluegrass of "Homesick & Lonesome" and the more contemporary country of "Can I Get an Amen" go along perfectly with toe-tapping instrumental workouts like "Buffalo Gals" and "Yeehaw Junction" to make a well-rounded set. *—Matt Fink*

Hot Rize

f. 1976, **db.** 1992
Group / Traditional Bluegrass, Progressive Bluegrass
The eclectic Colorado progressive bluegrass band Hot Rize also played traditional bluegrass, jazz, and rock. They came together in 1976 and were named after the secret ingredient of Martha White Self-Rising Flour, the product Flatt & Scruggs promoted early in their careers. The band members were Tim O'Brien on lead and harmony vocals, mandolin and fiddle; Pete Wernick on banjo and harmony vocals; and Charles Sawtelle on bass guitar, guitar, harmonies and lead vocals. Mike Scap departed in 1976 and was replaced by bass player, guitarist and vocalist Nick Forster, who also became the group's emcee. Hot Rize recorded its self-titled debut album, a blend of traditional and new material, in 1979. Their second album, *Radio Boogie*, came out in 1981. A year later, their alter ego Red Knuckles and the Trail Blazers, a parody of hardcore '50s country music, recorded their own album, *Hot Rize Presents Red Knuckles and the Trail Blazers*. In 1984, Hot Rize released a concert album largely comprised of traditional hits, and in 1985 released *Traditional Ties*. In 1991 another Red Knuckles album, *Shades of the Past*, followed. Their final album, *Take It Home*, came out in 1992; O'Brien and Wernick subsequently went on to pursue solo careers. *—Sandra Brennan*

Hot Rize / 1979 / Flying Fish ✦✦✦✦✦
Hot Rize's debut album demonstrated that traditional bluegrass bands could bring the music into the modern era without turning totally progressive or losing the music's roots. Over the album's 14 tracks, Hot Rize turns in consistently engaging and exciting performances, particularly from vocalist/fiddler/mandolinist Tim O' Brien and banjoist Pete Wernick. It's a terrific debut. *—Thom Owens*

Radio Boogie / 1981 / Flying Fish ✦✦✦✦
No sophomore highjinks on this release. Solid album, highly recommended. *—Chip Renner*

Traditional Ties / 1986 / Sugar Hill ✦✦✦✦
Traditional Ties is the first album Hot Rize recorded for Sugar Hill, and it is arguably their best effort ever, capturing their skill for both traditional material, originals (Tim O'Brien's "Walk the Way the Wind Blows," which became a Top 10 hit for Kathy Mattea), and progressive bluegrass (Keith Whitley's "You Don't Have to Move the Mountain"). *—Thom Owens*

● **Untold Stories** / 1989 / Sugar Hill ✦✦✦✦✦
It all comes together on this CD, Tim O'Brien's swan song. *—Chip Renner*

Take It Home / 1992 / Sugar Hill ✦✦✦✦
Take It Home, Hot Rize's final album, demonstrates that the group continued to improve the longer they stayed together. The group's instrumental interplay is astonishing and their harmonies are quite beautiful—their performances are effortlessly graceful, making it a farewell album to treasure. *—Thom Owens*

Snuffy Jenkins

b. Oct. 27, 1908, Harris, NC, **d.** Apr. 30, 1990
Banjo / Old-Timey, Traditional Bluegrass
Bluegrass banjo pioneer DeWitt "Snuffy" Jenkins was born in Harris, North Carolina on October 27, 1908; the youngest of ten children, all of whom excelled in music, he began playing the fiddle as a child, but was too small to use the bow and as a result picked the instrument like a mandolin. He later turned to guitar, and by 1927 was playing in a trio with banjo players Smith Hammett and Rex Brooks; Jenkins copied their three-finger style, and in the years to follow the banjo became his primary instrument, honing his skills playing square dances throughout the western North Carolina region. At this time he began mentoring the young Earl Scruggs; while Jenkins' technique bridged the gap between jagged, old-timey picking and the more fluid contemporary style, Scruggs soon surpassed his teacher, forging a thoroughly modernized sound distinguished by its subtlety and grace.

Jenkins relocated to Columbia, South Carolina in the spring of 1937, soon joining a string band which performed on local radio station WIS; despite the inevitable line-up changes, the group—later dubbed the Hired Hands—remained active for over half a century. Joining in 1939 was Jenkins' longtime foil, fiddler Homer "Pappy" Sherrill, a onetime member of the Blue Sky Boys; eight years later the Hired Hands welcomed lead guitarist Julian "Greasy" Medlin and bassist Ira Dimmery, followed in 1955 by the arrival of second guitarist Bill Rey. This five-piece line-up cut the first Hired Hands recordings in 1962, released by Folklyric in 1970 and subsequently reissued on Arhoolie as *Pioneer of the Bluegrass Banjo*. In 1971, Jenkins and Sherrill also recorded an LP for Rounder, and in 1989 also cut material for Old Homestead; Jenkins died on April 30, 1990. *—Jason Ankeny*

Pioneer of the Bluegrass Banjo / Aug. 18, 1998 / Arhoolie ✦✦✦
Although credited to Snuffy Jenkins, this is actually an 18-song set by the full Hired Hands band, several of whom also take vocals, recorded at WIS in Columbia, South Carolina in October 1962. It's straightforward bluegrass with some versatility to the approach, going into instrumentals, old-timey tunes, comic numbers, and a couple tracks ("Step It Up and Go" and "Born in Hard Luck," both sung by "Greasy" Medlin) with a bluesy skiffle flavor. *—Richie Unterberger*

Jim & Jesse

f. 1945
Group / Close Harmony, Traditional Bluegrass
One of the great bluegrass bands in history, brothers Jim (b. 1927) and Jesse (b. 1929) McReynolds and their Virginia Boys remained at the top by changing with the times. Starting as a traditional brothers duet, Jim on guitar and Jesse on mandolin showed their versatility by following country's changing tastes, moving to country/folk when necessary to keep a road band going. Whatever style they played (including *Berry Pickin' in the Country*, an album of bluegrass versions of Chuck Berry tunes), they retained a pure country core, due in no small part to Jim's pure, high tenor and Jesse's virtuoso, cross-picking mandolin playing.

Raised in Virginia, Jim & Jesse were born into a musical family. Their grandfather Charles McReynolds was a fiddler that had recorded a single for Victor in 1927 with the Bull Mountain Moonshiners. The brothers learned to play a number of stringed instruments while they were children, occasionally playing local dances and events as teenagers. However, the duo didn't begin playing professionally until they were in their 20s and Jim left the Army—by this point, Jim was playing guitar and Jesse played mandolin. In 1947, they landed a daily 15-minute spot on a local Norton radio station. For the next few years, they played on a variety of southern radio stations, securing a regular spot on Augusta, Georgia's WGAC in 1949. After staying at the station for a year, they moved to the midwest where they played stations in Iowa and Kansas without gaining much of a following. In 1951, they relocated to Middletown, Ohio where they had a regular spot at WPFB. While they were at the station they cut 10 songs with vocalist Larry Roll under the name the Virginian Trio; the records didn't gain much attention.

For the remainder of 1951 and much of 1952, Jim & Jesse played at a variety of radio stations throughout the country. Finally, in 1952, the group secured a major label deal with Capitol Records. However, their career was interrupted when Jesse was drafted into the Army to serve in the Korean War. After he was discharged in 1954, he rejoined Jim, who was still playing the Tennessee Barn Dance in Knowville, Tennessee. For the rest of the decade, they played radio and television stations across the country—including ones in Alabama, Georgia, and Florida—building up a fan base. During this time, their band the Virginia Boys, included such musicians as fiddler Vassar Clements and banjoist Bobby Thompson. In 1958, they recorded a handful of sides for Starday Records.

Martha White Mills flour company became Jim & Jesse's sponsors in 1959; the duo was the company's second major sponsorship, following Flatt & Scruggs. In 1961, they debuted at the Grand Ole Opry; three years later, they became members of the Opry. Jim & Jesse switched record labels in 1962, signing with Epic Records. The change in labels resulted in success for the duo, as "Cotton Mill Man" became their first charting country single in the summer of 1964. For the next few years, they continued in a straight bluegrass direction, scoring the occasional hit. In the late '60s, Jim & Jesse adopted a more country-oriented direction, which resulted in their biggest hit singles, including the number 18 "Diesel On My Tail."

In 1970, Jim & Jesse re-signed to Capitol Records and the first album they released under their new contract featured electric instruments. However, the duo quickly returned to a traditional bluegrass sound, since a bluegrass revival had gripped the attention of many country fans and college students across the United States. For the next two decades, the duo was a staple on the bluegrass festival scene, and they recorded for a variety of independent labels, including CMH, Rounder, and their own Old Dominion and Double J labels. In 1982, they had a minor hit single with "North Wind," which was recorded with Charlie Louvin. *—Stephen Thomas Erlewine & David Vinopal*

☆ **Bluegrass Special/Bluegrass Classics** / 1963 / Epic ✦✦✦✦✦
Bluegrass Special/Bluegrass Classics is a double-LP set containing 24 tracks Jim & Jesse cut for Epic Records. These songs were recorded in the early '60s, during the era when folk and bluegrass were experiencing a revival in popularity. The bluegrass boom happened to coincide with a time that Jim & Jesse were reaching their musical peak, at least according to many observers. These Epic songs—including many of their popular favorites ("Drifting and Dreaming of You," "Stoney Creek") but none of their hits from that era—feature an accomplished, streamlined band that effortlessly plays dazzling instrumental leads. It's a fine introduction to one of the best duos in bluegrass; while missing some hits, it captures Jim & Jesse at their best. *—Thom Owens*

Jim & Jesse Saluting the Louvin Brothers / 1969 / Epic ✦✦✦
Here are the best of the duo's recordings with electric country, rather than bluegrass accompaniment. *—Richard Lieberson*

The Jim & Jesse Story: 24 Greatest Hit / 1980 / CMH ✦✦✦✦✦
The Jim & Jesse Story: 24 Greatest Hits contains the majority of the duo's biggest hits and most familiar numbers, including "Diesel on My Tail," "Paradise," "Cotton Mill Man," "Better Times A-Coming" and "Are You Missing Me." However, the disc does *not* contain original recordings—it is all re-recordings from the early '90s. Nevertheless, the album does boast a number of excellent performances, since the duo is supported by several of the finest former Virginia Boys, and they themselves sound energetic and surprisingly lively, making *The Jim & Jesse Story* a fine introduction to the duo's sound. *—Thom Owens*

Music Among Friends / 1991 / Rounder ✦✦✦✦✦
A celebration of this bluegrass duo's 25 years on the Grand Ole Opry includes guest appearances by Bill Monroe, Emmylou Harris, Porter Wagoner, and others. *—Mark A. Humphrey*

★ **Jim & Jesse: 1952-1955** / 1992 / Bear Family ✦✦✦✦✦
Bear Family's *Jim & Jesse: 1952-1955* contains 20 recordings the duo recorded for Capitol in the prime of their career. Among the highlights are "I'll Wash Your Love from My Heart," "Just Wondering Why," "Virginia Waltz," "Look for Me (I'll Be There)," "Purple Heart," "Air Mail Special," "My Little Honeysucke Rose," "My Darling's in Heaven," "Memory of You," "I'll Wear the Banner" and "My Garden of Love." The duo's harmonies never sounded better than they did on these Capitol recordings, and their instrumental work is equally impressive. *—Stephen Thomas Erlewine*

Y'All Come: The Essential Jim & Jesse / Jan. 27, 1998 / Epic/Legacy ✦✦✦✦✦
Y'All Come: The Essential Jim & Jesse is a 20-track collection that culls highlights from the duo's decade at Epic Records in the '60s, featuring such hits and favorites as "Better Times A-Coming," "Ballad of Thunder Road," "Yonder Comes a Freight Train," "She Left Me Standing on the Mountain," "Stay a Little Longer," "Memphis Tennessee" and "Truck Drivin' Man." This isn't the set for traditional bluegrass fans, although there is plenty of that. Instead, the set is divided between bluegrass and the duo's brief flirtation with straight-ahead country, giving a good picture of their time at Epic. Either way, it's a fine set, showcasing some of the best music Jim & Jesse ever recorded, and it's one of the best anthologies of their Epic years yet assembled. *—Stephen Thomas Erlewine*

The Old Dominion Masters / Mar. 9, 1999 / Pinecastle ✦✦✦✦✦
This four-disc set compiles material from nine Jim & Jesse albums originally released on their own record label in the 1970s and 1980s, as well as a few radio show recordings and some previously uncompiled singles. In 1972, tired of the pressure they were feeling from the major labels to modernize their sound with drums and electric guitars, the brothers Jim & Jesse McReynolds formed the Old Dominion label and began producing and releasing their own albums. Among the nine collected here (some, but not all, in their entirety), there are two gospel albums, a collection of patriotic songs released during the U.S. bicentennial, and an album recorded live in Japan. All feature the McReynolds brothers' winning combination of tradition and innovation; the irony of the Jim & Jesse story is that even as they were resisting the more crass modernizations urged on them by record executives, they were developing a sound that was really quite progressive in bluegrass terms. They adopted the electric bass early on, their banjo players were typically well-versed in the melodic Tony Trischka/Bill Keith approach, and, along with traditional bluegrass standards like "Live and Let Live" and "Blue Ridge Mountain Blues," they frequently performed material with more complicated, country-derived structures. Jesse's own "Jesus Is the Key to the Kingdom" is one good example of that tendency, as is a surprising cover version of Chuck Berry's "Back in the U.S.A." This outstanding box set provides an excellent overview of one of bluegrass music's finest ensembles working at the peak of its powers. *—Rick Anderson*

Honor the King of Country Music, Roy Acuff / Double J ✦✦✦✦✦
This stunner of an album—a pleasure just to hear—features the pair in excellent voice, achieving an extraordinary elegance in their singing and playing. Recorded after Acuff's death in 1992, the music naturally has a high degree of reverence, but it's never dull or predictable. The harmony singing is, of course, the main appeal of Jim & Jesse's work, but their instrumental backing also honors the man and his songs; in addition to the duo's own guitar and mandolin, their backup musicians include Pete Kirby on dobro, Raymond McLain on banjo, and Dan Kelly on fiddle, all at the top of their form. The songs include "Wabash Cannonball," "The Precious Jewel," "Write Me Sweetheart," "That Glory Bound Train," "Night Train to Memphis," "Great Speckled Bird," and "Roll On Buddy," all sung about as well as they're likely ever to be. *—Bruce Eder*

The Johnson Mountain Boys

f. 1978, **db.** 1988
Group / Traditional Bluegrass, Progressive Bluegrass
During the 1980s, the Johnson Mountain Boys were contemporary masters of traditional bluegrass music who remained faithful to the old styles while keeping the songs fresh and

original. The band was founded in the suburbs of Washington, D.C. by vocalist/banjoist/guitarist Dudley Connell, banjoist Richie Underwood, mandolinist David McLaughlin, fiddler Eddie Stubbs, and Larry Robbins on bass. The personnel changed over the years, but the group's sound remained consistent. The Johnson Mountain Boys made their recording debut with a single in late 1978; an EP soon followed and helped build a loyal audience in the D.C. area. They became festival favorites after the release of their self-titled debut. Their second album, *Walls of Time*, came out in 1982 and featured Connell, McLaughlin, Stubbs and vocalist/banjoist/mandolinist Tom Adams. The same lineup recorded four more albums during the early '80s. In 1988, the Johnson Mountain Boys announced that they planned to retire after a farewell concert in Lucketts, Virginia. Two years later, the Boys reunited briefly to play two festivals. Eventually, the band became an active performing outfit in the early '90s and released a new album, *Blue Diamond*, in 1993. *—Sandra Brennan*

Walls of Time / 1982 / Rounder ♦♦♦♦

Working Close / 1983 / Rounder ♦♦♦♦♦
Dudley Connell's chilling, high-lonesome lead vocals were only one of the delights of this militantly traditional, young bluegrass band. Any of their albums are among the best bluegrass of recent decades. *—Mark A. Humphrey*

● **Favorites** / 1987 / Rounder ♦♦♦♦♦
Favorites features a terrific cross-section of highlights from the Johnson Mountain Boys' early-'80s Rounder albums and is the perfect introduction to their traditionalist bluegrass. *—Thom Owens*

Let the Whole World Talk / 1987 / Rounder ♦♦♦
One of the finest records the Johnson Mountain Boys ever recorded, *Let the Whole World Talk* is an audaciously accomplished set of modernized bluegrass. The group slips a couple of excellent contemporary folk songs onto the record, but it is mainly notable for the way they make traditional songs into vibrant, vital and undeniably contemporary music. For its instrumentals, harmonies and arrangements, *Let the Whole World Talk* is one of the finest contemporary bluegrass albums of the late '80s. *—Thom Owens*

At the Old Schoolhouse / 1989 / Rounder ♦♦♦♦
At the Old Schoolhouse was recorded on the Johnson Mountain Boys' intended "farewell tour" of the late '80s. The group later decided to stick together, perhaps because they knew they were giving performances as good as this. Throughout *At the Old Schoolhouse*, the group gives lively, invigorating performances that prove traditional bluegrass isn't boring. It's a terrific live album, and one of the Johnson Mountain Boys' finest moments. *—Thom Owens*

Blue Diamond / 1993 / Rounder ♦♦♦
Blue Diamond is an excellent newgrass album that juxtaposes contemporary folk songs by Bob Dylan with standards by Carter Stanley, and country songs by Buck Owens. It proves that the Johnson Mountain Boys remain one of the best progressive bluegrass combos of the '70s and '80s. *—Thom Owens*

Bill Keith

b. Dec. 20, 1939, Boston, MA
Guitar (Steel), Banjo / Instrumental Country, Progressive Bluegrass
Bill Keith had great impact on modern banjo playing, particularly in the direction of "newgrass." He even had a picking style informally named after him—the melodic, chromatic or "Keith" picking style was borne of his desire to play fiddle melodies on his instruments. Following graduation and a brief stint in the US Air Force Reserve, Keith began learning to make banjos with Tom Morgan. Later he, guitarist Jim Rooney, mandolin player Frank Wakefield and guitarist Red Allen formed the Kentuckians. In 1963, Earl Scruggs contacted Keith to lay out the tablature for the instructional book *Earl Scruggs and the 5-String Banjo*. Later that year, Keith and his former Amherst classmate Dan Bump developed a new kind of tuning peg that was adopted by Scruggs who provided a name for the resulting company in 1964. In the mid-'60s, Keith joined Bill Monroe's Blue Grass Boys, where he was listed as Brad Keith. He left the band after only eight months to do more session work and by the year's end had joined Jim Kweskin's Jug Band where he would stay for four years. He abandoned the banjo for a while in 1968 to become a pedal steel guitarist. He and long-time cohort Rooney also toured together in both the U.S. and in Europe during the '70s and '80s, with Keith developing a particularly large following in France. *—Sandra Brennan*

● **Something Auld, Something Newgrass, Something Borrowed, Something Bluegrass** / 1976 / Rounder ♦♦♦♦
Catch Tony Rice, David Grisman, Jim Rooney, Tom Grey, Vassar Clements, Ken Kasek, and Al Jones on this album. The bluegrass is top-notch, and Bill Keith struts his stuff. *—Chip Renner*

The Kentucky Colonels

f. 1963
Group / Traditional Bluegrass, Progressive Bluegrass
Progressive bluegrass band the Kentucky Colonels had a short but legendary career during the folk revival of the late '50s and early '60s. As the Country Boys, the group recorded their first single, "I'm Head Over Heels in Love with You." They began appearing on *Town Hall Party* and *Hometown Jamboree* and recording on Gene Autry's label. The Boys then recorded *Songs, Themes & Laughs from the Andy Griffith Show* for Capitol. The group then cut its first album on Briar, which disliked the band's moniker and suggested a series of names, the best of which was the Kentucky Colonels. By this time, the Colonels had begun to gather a following through their U.S. tours, and appeared at both the UCLA and Newport Folk Festivals in 1964. The band recorded several albums and appeared in the movie *The Farmer's Other Daughter*, but broke up in 1965. *—Sandra Brennan*

☆ **Appalachian Swing!** / 1964 / World Pacific ♦♦♦♦♦
Appalachian Swing! is one of the most influential albums in the whole of bluegrass music, primarily because of the stunning playing of Clarence White. With his vibrant, innovative flat-picking, White helped pioneer a new style in bluegrass; namely, he redefined the acoustic guitar as a solo instrument instead of confining it to just background status. The sound was revolutionary upon its release in 1964 and the music still sounds alive, even timeless, because of the strength of White's vision and talent. He was one of the greatest musicians in bluegrass history and the fact that *Appalachian Swing!* still sounds fresh makes his tragic death all the more painful. *—Thom Owens*

★ **Long Journey Home** / 1964 / Vanguard ♦♦♦♦♦
These great recordings from a 1964 live performance at the Newport Folk Festival feature Clarence White and many others, including duets with Doc Watson. *—Richard Lieberson & Mark A. Humphrey*

The Kentucky Colonels 1965-1966 / 1979 / Rounder ♦♦♦♦♦

Laurel Canyon Ramblers

f. 1994
Group / Bluegrass-Gospel, Contemporary Bluegrass, Singer/Songwriter, Traditional Bluegrass
Virtuosic instrumentation and ultra-smooth vocal harmonies have made the Laurel Canyon Ramblers one of the most successful groups performing tradition-rooted bluegrass. Led by banjo, guitar and dobro player and vocalist Herb Pederson, the Laurel Canyon Ramblers represent over one hundred years of bluegrass experience.

The Laurel Canyon Ramblers, named after a street in Los Angeles that crosses Hollywood Boulevard, were brought together when Pederson returned to bluegrass in 1994. The son of a policeman who was born in 1944 and raised in Berkeley, California, Pederson had filled in for an ailing Earl Scruggs in the mid-1960s and had replaced influential banjo Doug Dillard in the Dillards in 1968. Since leaving the Dillards in 1971, Pederson had recorded three solo albums, been a founding member of Country Gazette, and played on recordings by such artists as Linda Ronstadt, John Denver, Jerry Garcia, David Grisman, Diana Ross, Nicolette Larson, Gordon Lightfoot, Stephen Stills, John Prine, Johnny Rivers, Emmylou Harris, Jackson Browne and Dan Fogelberg. Together with Chris Hillman (the Byrds, the Flying Burrito Brothers), Pederson had recorded six albums with California country-rock band, Desert Rose, and a duo tribute album to the early-'60s sounds of Buck Owens-style country music, *Bakersfield Bound*, in 1996. In addition to writing such standard bluegrass tunes as "Old Train" and "Wait A Minute," Pederson contributed to the soundtracks of films and television shows including *Smokey & The Bandit, City Slickers, Maverick, The Fire Down Below, The A Team, The Rockford Files* and *The Dukes of Hazzard*.

The remaining members of the Laurel Canyon Ramblers have resumes nearly as impressive. Mandolin player and vocalist Kenny Blackwell, who studied with the late Jethro Burns, was a member of Richard Greene's The Grass Is Greener. Guitarist and vocalist Richard Reed, a former member of Byron Berline's Fiddle Band and Sundance, recorded with Earl Scruggs, Tony Trischka and with his brothers, Dennis, Terry and Ronnie. Fiddler Gabe Witcher continues to be a longtime member of a family group, the Witcher Brothers. The Academy of Country Music's Bass Player of the Year in 1990, Bill Bryson was a member of Desert Rose, Country Gazette and the Bluegrass Cardinals and toured with Dan Fogelberg and the Doug Dillard Band. A talented songwriter, Bryson wrote several tunes for the Bluegrass Cardinals including "Riding On the L & N" and "Girl at the Crossroads," which was also covered by Larry Sparks and Jerry Garcia. The Ramblers reconvened in 1998 for *Back on the Street Again*. *—Craig Harris*

● **Back on the Street Again** / Jul. 21, 1998 / Sugar Hill ♦♦♦♦
This West Coast bluegrass outfit is fronted by Bill Bryson and Herb Pedersen, well-respected country and roots artists from Los Angeles. And their West Coast edge is displayed proudly, as evidenced on "It Hurts to Know," apenned by Red Allen and Tommy Sutton, and the Louvin Brothers tune "When I Stop Dreaming." The standard "Please Come Back, Sweetheart" and the band's newer songs, "Hold On" and "Move On," all have a strong traditional magic that defines the continuous appeal of the Laurel Canyon Ramblers. Breathtaking in every way. *—Jana Pendragon*

Doyle Lawson

b. Apr. 20, 1944, Kingsport, TN
Vocals, Mandolin / Country Gospel, Traditional Bluegrass
Doyle Lawson was considered one of the premiere bluegrass mandolin players by his peers; his bluegrass-gospel band Quicksilver was equally respected. Lawson made his recording debut with Red Allen and bassist Bobby Slone on *Bluegrass Holiday* and subsequently recorded two albums with J.D. Crowe. In 1971, Lawson joined the Country Gentlemen—he remained with the band for several years and recorded ten albums with them. Lawson also recorded an album of mandolin instrumentals, *Tennessee Dream*, in 1977. In 1979, he put Quicksilver together; they released their self-titled debut album in 1980 and followed it up with *Rock My Soul*. They also released a gospel album, *Heavenly Treasures*. *—Sandra Brennan*

Rock My Soul / 1981 / Sugar Hill ♦♦♦♦
Rock My Soul is the first gospel album that Doyle Lawson recorded and it's a wonderful record of simple, graceful beauty. The key to the success of *Rock My Soul* is that Lawson has opened up bluegrass gospel by incorporating elements of country and southern gospel, which made it accessible to a wider audience. *—Thom Owens*

I'll Wander Back Someday / 1988 / Sugar Hill ♦♦♦
Relying primarily on traditional songs and standards, *I'll Wander Back Someday* is another excellent effort from Doyle Lawson and Quicksilver, highlighting the group's innovative vocal arrangements and accumen for driving, straight-edged instrumental support. *—Thom Owens*

I Heard the Angels Singing / 1989 / Sugar Hill ♦♦♦
Lawson returns to gospel on *I Heard the Angels Singing*, which features his rendition of Carl Jackson's "The Little Mountain Church House." *—Jason Ankeny*

Never Walk Away / 1995 / Sugar Hill ♦♦♦
This album is crystal clear from the first notes of the Buck Owens tune "Rosie Jones" to the end of "Ancient History." It is a tight ensemble album where the instrumental playing is all the more impressive for being excellent but not showy. Strong songs include "Jealous," "In the Gravel Yard" and "Your Crazy Heart." There's nothing groundbreaking here, just a solid rootsy bluegrass band album, and that's not bad. *—Richard Meyer*

There's a Light Guiding Me / Feb. 20, 1996 / Sugar Hill ♦♦♦♦
Doyle Lawson and Quicksilver are among bluegrass music's most heavenly harmonizers, as they prove once again on the timeless music featured in *There's a Light Guiding Me.* Largely a cappella, and completely focused on spirituals, these songs will fill the soul with warmth. No matter what one believes, this music—just like that of spiritual singers from Tibet, Hungary, Pakistan or Cambodia—strikes a resonant chord deep within. *—Michael McCall*

Once & For Always/News Is Out / Feb. 16, 1999 / Sugar Hill ♦♦♦♦
This disc was released simultaneously with *The Original Band,* and, like its counterpart, it combines the contents of two Quicksilver albums from the early '80s. If this one is the less consistently satisfying of the two compilations, it's probably due in part to the stress of a constantly-changing lineup-bassist and singer Lou Reid had left by the time *Once and for Always* was recorded, and by the following album the entire band was different with the exception of Lawson. There was a slight but noticeable drop in vocal quality during this period; while the ensemble singing is still uncannily tight, no member of the band emerges as an outstanding lead singer. Nor is the song quality as consistent. There are still great moments, such as the a capella gospel number "A Lover of the Lord" and the very high and lonesome "I've Heard These Words Before." But "The Grass that I'm Playing Is Really Blue" is a complete clunker and there are just a few too many others like it. This one's worth owning, but if you have to choose between it and *The Original Band,* the latter's your best bet. *—Rick Anderson*

Original Band / Feb. 16, 1999 / Sugar Hill ♦♦♦♦
What has always set Doyle Lawson's groups apart from other progressive bluegrass outfits is their equal focus on both vocal and instrumental virtuosity. Where colleagues like the Country Gentlemen, the Seldom Scene and the New Grass Revival tended to emphasize unusual repertoire and instrumental pyrotechnics, Lawson's band, even with its kaleidoscopically shifting membership, has always maintained a consistent dual focus on fiery playing and tight, rich, gospel-flavored harmonies. *The Original Band* compiles the first two albums (*Doyle Lawson & Quicksilver* and *Quicksilver Rides Again*) that Lawson made with his own group after leaving the Country Gentlemen in 1979, and it will probably stand as the definitive document of his early work as a bandleader. There are blistering versions of Bill Monroe's "On and On" and the traditional "Shady Grove," the forward-looking "A Touch of Pennsylvania," and several absolutely stunning gospel numbers, including the standard "He Put a Rainbow in the Clouds for Me" and "Calm the Storm." If you had to limit your bluegrass collection to only twenty discs, this would have to be one of them. *—Rick Anderson*

● **Winding Through Life** / Jul. 27, 1999 / Sugar Hill ♦♦♦♦♦
It almost doesn't seem fair—not only is Doyle Lawson's band arguably the finest in traditional bluegrass, but he seems to be determined to lead the best gospel group as well. Several things set his ensemble apart from the pack. It's not just the consistently high quality of his singers (though that alone would be enough to put Quicksilver in the top rank of gospel groups)—it's also the group's surprising stylistic variety. On their latest release, they move easily from upbeat bluegrass tunes like "The Lord Will Answer Thee" and "Gladness, Peace and Love" to a more modern country sound on "Just Let Me Fly" and "River of Tears." But most impressive of all is "If Jesus Is There," which sounds like it draws equally on barbershop and shape-note influences, and "Do Right and Come Smiling Thru," which comes squarely from the African-American gospel harmony tradition. "Closer I Must Be" sounds like a Louvin Brothers tune (although it isn't). Everything is delivered with an effortless blend that somehow manages to reconcile the conflicting qualities of creamy smoothness and mountain astringency. Excellent. *—Rick Anderson*

Just Over in Heaven / Jun. 20, 2000 / Sugar Hill ♦♦♦♦
Doyle Lawson & Quicksilver, without doubt the finest bluegrass gospel group performing today, seems unable to make a bad album, and Lawson's current lineup may be the best one he's ever had. *Just Over in Heaven* combines band arrangements with a cappella numbers, but even when the instruments are playing the vocal arrangements are at the center of the group's sound; where most bluegrass bands use standard parallel harmonies in their gospel arrangements, Lawson's approach is far more complex and is rooted equally in shape, note, and African-American gospel traditions. On tracks like "I Am Glad" and "We Need the Light" the parts move in intricate counterpoint, like cogs in a perfectly designed watch; the sound borders on that of a barbershop quartet. In fact, that effect is a little bit cloying on one or two tracks (notably "Listen to the Bells"), but, for the most part, this album succeeds spectacularly and is highly recommended. *—Rick Anderson*

Laurie Lewis

b. 1950, Berkeley, CA
Vocals, Violin, Fiddle / Traditional Bluegrass, Progressive Bluegrass
Playing a unique blend of old-time country, bluegrass, Western Swing, Cajun and Tejano, Laurie Lewis and her Grant Street String Band were not easy to pigeonhole. Lewis, a key figure in helping female musicians break into the traditionally male-dominated genre, was an exceptional, versatile fiddler and a singer blessed with a smooth, musical voice. She also wrote well-crafted, thought-provoking songs, some of which were recorded by singers like Patsy Montana and Kathy Mattea. She and friend Kathy Kallick, a veteran of the Phantoms of the Opry and Arkansas Sheiks, teamed up to form the all-woman band Good Ol' Persons, who soon developed a large West Coast following. Lewis left the group in 1979 to found her Grant Street String Band, which released their critically-acclaimed eponymous debut album in the early '80s. Lewis also made her solo debut, *Restless Rambling Heart,* in 1986, and continued dividing her time between her solo and group work for the next several years. *—Sandra Brennan*

● **Restless Rambling Heart** / 1986 / Flying Fish ♦♦♦♦♦
The first solo album from this Bay Area singer and fiddler is sweet but not saccharine, a mix of old-time, bluegrass, and rootsy contemporary folk. *—Mark A. Humphrey*

Singin' My Troubles Away / 1990 / Flying Fish ♦♦♦♦
With *Singin' My Troubles Away,* Laurie Lewis balances her music between folk-tinged country and progressive bluegrass. Though Lewis' fiddle certainly takes the center-stage, she has assembled a first-class backing band—featuring guitarist Scott Nygaard, banjoist Tony Furtado, bassist Tammy Fassaert and mandonlinist Tom Rozum—that keeps the music vibrant and alive. *—Thom Owens*

True Stories / 1993 / Rounder ♦♦♦
Laurie Lewis has enjoyed most of her support from traditional bluegrass and folk audiences, and yet, she's hardly a slave to tradition. A varied release, *True Stories* ranges from the traditional Irish song "Singing Bird" to the country gems "Who Will Watch the Home Place," "Still a Fool" and "Val's Cabin" to folk-pop numbers like "Knocking On Your Door Again" and "Swept Away." The Bay Area native is as excellent a songwriter as she is a vocalist, and it isn't hard to imagine "Val's Cabin" or "You'll Be Leaving Me" being big country hits with slicker production and some of Nashville's promotional muscle. Lewis' audience is a small one, but her music is definitely well worth getting to know. *—Alex Henderson*

Seeing Things / May 5, 1998 / Rounder ♦♦♦♦
While previous albums have explored Lewis' prodigious fiddle talents and her ability to put a new spin on bluegrass music, *Seeing Things* zeroes in on her glorious voice and her ability to tell a story with it. Eight of the 11 tunes come from her pen; tunes like "The Refugee," "Kiss Me Before I Die," "Angel On His Shoulder," and "Bane and Balm" all show tremendous growth as a writer, while the opening "Blues Days, Sleepless Nights" bears strong comparison to her best bluegrass work. Tom Russel's "Manzanar" (the story of a World War II Japanese POW), her duet with Cris Williamson on "Let the Bird Go Free" and the traditional "The Blackest Crow" set moods bleak, somber and ethereal. But mostly it comes down to Lewis' voice, an instrument of uncommon beauty, depth and versatility. This is one special album. *—Cub Koda*

Laurie Lewis & Her Bluegrass Pals / May 4, 1999 / Rounder ♦♦♦
Laurie Lewis comes full circle and brings a batch of her friends together for an inspired session of straight-ahead bluegrass. There's an empathy to the playing of Lewis with mandolinist Tom Rozum, banjoist Craig Smith, bassist Todd Phillips, and rhythm guitarist Mary Gibbons that grows on you as the album unfolds with the strong trio singing of Lewis, Gibbons, and Rozum that's equally as seductive. Highlights include "Tall Pines," Jimmy Martin's "Stepping Stones," Jean Ritchie's "Black Waters," "Acony Bell," and Lewis' own "Wind at Play," "Blow, Big Wind," and "Big Eddy." An inspired session. *—Cub Koda*

The Lilly Brothers

f. 1938, Clear Creek, WV, **db.** 1980
Group / Traditional Bluegrass
The Lilly Brothers, Everett and B., played old-time/bluegrass music together for over three decades. They may best be remembered in New England, where they were a fixture in the downtown Boston music scene from the early '60s through 1980. The Lillys debuted in 1938 singing old-time country on a West Virginia radio station; in 1939, they began performing regularly at the newly-established WKLS Beckley. They made their recording debut in 1948, and recorded fairly frequently during the 1950s. The Lilly Brothers remained intact through 1970. In addition to playing downtown Boston, they also played the local festival circuit and were instrumental in the development of urban bluegrass. *—Sandra Brennan*

Bluegrass Breakdown / 1963 / Rounder ♦♦♦♦

★ **Early Recordings** / 1971 / Rebel ♦♦♦♦♦
These driving, late-'50s performances have breathtaking banjo from Don Stover and hand-in-glove vocal harmonies. It is one of the best bluegrass albums ever. *—Mark A. Humphrey*

Prestige/Folklore Years, Vol. 5: Have a Feast Here Tonight / Jan. 26, 1999 / Prestige ♦♦♦♦♦
In 1999, Fantasy reissued two classic Lilly Brothers albums on *Vol. 5* of its *Prestige/Folklore Years* series: *Bluegrass Breakdown* (recorded in either late 1962 or early 1963) and *Country Songs* (recorded in 1964). Hearing the albums back to back on a single 75-minute CD, the listener is exposed to two very different but equally appealing sides of vocalist/mandolin player Everett Lilly and vocalist/guitarist Bea Lilly. On one hand, they're heard playing some very passionate, hot-blooded bluegrass; the siblings' versions of Bill Monroe's "Bluegrass Breakdown," Charlie Monroe's "Rollin' On," and Earl Scruggs' "Foggy Mountain Breakdown" aren't exactly short on exuberance. Much of the CD, however, finds them focusing on the gentle, old-time, pre-Hank Williams country styles of the 1920s and 1930s. The influence of the Carter Family and Jimmie Rodgers (country's most important pre-Williams stylists) can be heard on Everett's "Beneath the Old Southern Skies" as well as such Carter gems as "Rosewood Casket" and "The Storms Are on the Ocean." The Lilly Brothers' treatment of Lefty Frizzell's "The Long Black Veil" is especially interesting; Frizzell, one of the top electric honky tonkers of the 1950s, didn't record the ballad until 1959, but the Lilly Brothers give it an acoustic 1930s-style makeover. This is a CD that lovers of bluegrass and unplugged, pre-World War II country should make a point of obtaining. *—Alex Henderson*

Lonesome Pine Fiddlers

f. 1938, **db.** 1966
Group / Traditional Bluegrass
The Lonesome Pine Fiddlers were an enduring force in the development of bluegrass music for over three decades. Over the years, the band underwent many personnel changes and played a variety of styles, ranging from old-time string music to bluegrass to country. The

group was founded in 1938 by Ray Cline in Baisden, WV. By 1950, they had become a full-fledged bluegrass band, and in 1953 began playing at WJR in Detroit. There they cut six sides for Victor in Chicago, among them their best-known song, "Dirty Dishes Blues." The Lonesome Pine Fiddlers then moved to WLSI Pikeville, Kentucky, and stayed there the rest of their career. They recorded eight singles in 1954, including two bluegrass classics, "Windy Mountain" and "No Curb Service." By 1966, the members of the Lonesome Pine Fiddlers had gone their separate ways. *—Sandra Brennan*

• **Windy Mountain** / 1992 / Bear Family ✦✦✦✦✦
Windy Mountain contains all of the material the Lonesome Pine Fiddlers recorded for Cozy and RCA Records during the early '50s. Though the 26-track collection is exhaustive, it is also exhausting; no matter how good these tracks are as individual songs, the relentless chronological sequencing of the material on this compact disc makes the record more of a history lesson than a casual listen. Nevertheless, *Windy Mountain* functions as the definitive retrospective of one of the finest and most important bluegrass bands of the '50s, and features great performances by Bobby Osborne, Charline Cline, Paul Williams, and Curly Ray Cline. For bluegrass historians, it's essential. *—Stephen Thomas Erlewine*

The Lonesome River Band

f. 1983
Group / Contemporary Bluegrass, Traditional Bluegrass, Progressive Bluegrass
The Lonesome River Band has withstood numerous personnel changes to merge as one of the best respected bands in bluegrass. Although rooted in the traditional sounds of Flatt & Scruggs and Bill Monroe, the Lonesome River Band continues to set standards of its own. The recipients of the SPBGMA award as "vocal group of 1997," The Lonesome River Band continues to fuse ultra-tight, vocal harmonies with virtuosic musicianship and well-conceived arrangements.

The original line-up of the Lonesome River Band was assembled by banjo player-turned-lead vocalist and rhythm guitarist Tim Austin and featured Steve Thomas on mandolin and fiddle, Rick Williams on banjo and Jerry McMillan on bass. After attracting attention on the local bluegrass circuit in Virginia, The Lonesome River Band released their debut album, *I Guess Heartaches Are in Style This Year,* in 1985, on the regional label, Shar-Lynn. Their national debut came with a self-titled album, released by rebel, the following year.

The Lonesome River Band has been evolving at a steady clip since the early-1990s with the arrival of lead vocalist and bass player Ronnie Bowman and banjo ace Sammy Shelor. North Carolina-born Bowman sang with Gospel music with a family group from the age to three until his late-teens and is equally effective singing traditional bluegrass tunes as he is voicing songs by contemporary singer-songwriters$. Shelor, who inherited his love of the banjo from his grandfathers, began to play the five stringed instrument at the age of five. Although he learned his early technique from an old timey clawhammer banjo player Carp Ayers, Shelor's approach to the instrument has been as much influenced by the playing of Earl Scruggs, J.D. Crowe, Ben Eldridge, Allen Shelton, Pete Wernick and Bela Fleck. Shaping his performance skills with local bluegrass bands in North Carolina and Virginia, Shelor was a founding member of The Virginia Squires in 1983. He remained with the Squires until 1989 when he was joined The Lonesome River Band.

The reorganized Lonesome River Band hit their stride with their first album together, *Carrying The Tradition,* which debuted at the top slot on the best selling charts compiled by *Bluegrass Unlimited.* It remained on the charts for five months before being subplanted by the band's next release, *Old Country Town,* which remained at the number one position for six months.

In the aftermath of their success, founding member Tim Austin left The Lonesome River Band to devote more time to working in his home recording studio, Doobie Shea. Although he was replaced by Kenny Smith, of Claire Lynch's Front Porch String Band, Austin continued to work with The Lonesome River Band on their albums. The newest member of The Lonesome River Band, Don Rigsby, who sings tenor vocals and plays mandolin, is a veteran of such bands as J.D. Crowe & The New South, The Bluegrass Cardinal and previously worked with Vern Gosdin. The first album by the reconstructed line-up, *One Step Forward,* was released in 1996.

Each member of the current Lonesome River Band has recorded memorable solo albums. Bowman, who was named "Vocalist of the year" by the International Bluegrass Music Association (IBMA) in 1995, delivered the most successful of the solo albums, *Cold Virginia Night,* which won the IBMA award as "best album of the year" in 1997. Bowman followed it with a second solo album, *The Man I'm Trying To Be* in 1998. Shelor, who was namd the IBMA's "banjo player of the year" in 1995 and 1998, released *Leading Roll* in 1997 with guest appearances by Tony Rice, Sam Bush, Jerry Douglas and Alan O'Bryant of the Nashville Bluegrass Band. Rigsby's solo debut, *A Vision,* celebrated his religious views and featured a duet with Ralph Stanley. Smith's *"Studebaker,"* released in 1997, spotlighted his songwriting talents and featured instrumental and vocal support from the other members of the Lonesome River Band.

The Lonesome River Band were featured on several tracks of John Fogerty's 1997 album, *Blue Moon Swamp.* Their *Finding the Way* album followed a year later, and in mid-2000 the group returned with *Talkin' to Myself.* *—Craig Harris*

• **Old Country Town** / 1994 / Sugar Hill ✦✦✦✦
High-speed playing and high lonesome vocals characterize this quartet's smooth bluegrass album. *—Richard Meyer*

Finding the Way / Aug. 18, 1998 / Sugar Hill ✦✦✦✦✦
Certainly, the Lonesome River Band is one of the most significant proponents of traditional bluegrass music to canoe down any river in a long while. And this project is reflective of their status as a band of integrity and purpose. In every way, musicianship, vocals, harmonies, performance and execution, this is a solid outing. "Love's Come Over Me," an upbeat tune that highlights Sammy Shelor's banjo and the harmony vocals of Don Rigsby and Kenny Smith, recalls the best of the Louvins and the Stanleys. In fact, "Sweet Sally Brown," penned by Wandell M. Smith and Dr. Ralph Stanley, displays the intensity and talent of the Lonesome River Band in full bloom. They could very well stand side by side with Ralph and Carter Stanley. The Tommy Morse tune "Perfume, Powder and Lead" is filled with all the dark mystery that many classic bluegrass tunes are known for. Again, Rigsby and Smith provide the harmony vocals that make this performance so haunting. Jason Carter's fiddle underscores the moaning quality of a song sung high upon a hill into a dark, unknown holler as the protagonist reaches out to eternity. "Baby Come Home," "Another By My Side," "Don't Worry 'Bout Daddy" and "Up On the Shelf" are all high steppin', while "Finding Your Way" is a nod of the head to the softer side of bluegrass music. Ending with the traditional tune "Devil Chased Me Around the Stump" places this project among the finest in the annals of bluegrass history. Produced by Jerry Douglas, it is a fine introduction to the Lonesome River Band or to the more contemporary forms of bluegrass music. *—Jana Pendragon*

Talkin' to Myself / Jun. 20, 2000 / Sugar Hill ✦✦✦✦
Since their debut in the mid-'80s, the Lonesome River Band has spent time both in the middle of the bluegrass road and along its margins, experimenting with newer, more progressive sounds while periodically returning to their traditional bluegrass roots. *Talkin' to Myself* finds them in the latter mode, running through a program of bluegrass standards ("Are You Afraid to Call Me Darlin'," the Stanley Brothers' classic "Dog Gone Shame") and tradition-minded originals and covers (bassist Ronnie Bowman's "Talkin' to Myself," Bill Castle's "Swing That Hammer"). This lineup may be the strongest vocal ensemble the group has had yet: Mandolinist Don Rigsby is one of the best tenors in bluegrass right now, and Bowman is just as good singing lead. Dan Tyminski's production offers just the right balance of slickness and grit. This is one of those rare bluegrass albums that is likely to appeal equally to fans of the traditional and progressive schools. *—Rick Anderson*

Longview

f. 1995
Vocals, Mandolin, Guitar, Bass, Banjo / Traditional Bluegrass
Named after the recording studio where they spent a week recording their debut album, Longview was a supergroup comprised of six top-ranked traditional bluegrass musicians and vocalists. With a sound that recalled the bluegrass bands of the 1940s and '50s, the sextet produced a memorable tribute to the roots of the hill-country sound.

Longview was first conceived during a late night jam session at the Denton, North Carolina Bluegrass Festival in 1994. A celebration of Rounder Records' 25th anniversary, the session featured James King, Dudley Cornell and Don Rigsby. King, who had recorded with Ralph Stanley in the 1980s, had garnered acclaim with his solo albums including *Lonesome And Then Some* in 1997 and *These Old Pictures* in 1995. Cornell, whose father had played with the Johnson Boys in the Washington, D.C. area in the 1950s, had sung lead and played guitar with the Johnson Mountain Boys and had replaced the late John Duffey in the Seldom Scene. Rigsby had played mandolin and sang high tenor vocals in a lengthy list of bands, including the Bluegrass Cardinals, J.D. Crowe & the New South and the Lonesome River Band.

The magic generated during the jam session was reinforced a few months later during a similar jam session at a bluegrass festival in Ohio that featured Cornell, fiddler Glen Duncan and banjo player Joe Mullins. Duncan, who co-led Lonesome Standard Time from 1991 to 1995, was a veteran of recording sessions with Bill Monroe, Jim & Jesse, the Osborne Brothers, Reba McEntire and Barbara Mandrell, while Mullins had been a member of Traditional Grass from 1983 until 1995.

At the encouragement of Ken Irwin, co-owner of Rounder, the five musicians came together with bass player Marshall Wilborn of the Lynn Morris Band for a week in December 1995 at the Long View Recording studio complex in North Brookfield, Massachusetts. Recording most tunes live without overdubs, the group cut three songs per day for five consecutive days and performed a live show for a small audience. With a focus on traditional-sounding songs by the Louvin Brothers, Don Reno and Ralph Stanley, the week-long session resulted in an album of tight ensemble playing and emotionally rich vocal harmonies. *High Lonesome* followed in mid-1999. *—Craig Harris*

• **Longview** / Sep. 9, 1997 / Rounder ✦✦✦✦✦

High Lonesome / Jun. 8, 1999 / Rounder ✦✦✦✦✦
Longview proves that traditional bluegrass need not sound archaic. The key to Longview's success is that the band returns not to the traditional songs that everyone knows, but instead discovers unheralded tunes from the classic period of bluegrass while reworking contemporary songs into music that sounds classic. All the while, the focus remains on the songs themselves, with emphasis on close harmonies and surging emotions over instrumental technique. On paper, it doesn't sound that difficult, but few traditional bluegrass bands sound as unselfconscious and gleeful as Longview. That was the difference that made the group's eponymous debut an award-winning hit, and it's what makes the second record, *High Lonesome,* every bit its equal. Some may be disappointed that *High Lonesome* simply delivers more of the same, but that's all that Longview needed to do, since the band is skillfully reviving sounds and spirits, not trying to innovate. Longview has again done a wonderful job of finding songs, whether Gretchen Peters' title track or tunes from Mac Martin and the Lonesome Pine Fiddlers, and making them sound like stone classics. Not only are the songs uniformly terrific, they're delivered with gusto, and the production is clean yet organic, not sterile like many contemporary bluegrass albums. It feels as if the music has been given room to breathe, which is a blessing in bluegrass. Taken all together, the songs, sounds, and performances make *High Lonesome* a rare sequel that matches its praised predecessor. *—Stephen Thomas Erlewine*

The Lost & Found

f. 1973
Group / Progressive Bluegrass
Formed in 1973, the original lineup of the Lost & Found bluegrass band consisted of bass fiddler Allen Mills, banjo player Gene Parker, mandolin player Dempsey Young and guitarist

Roger Handy. The band became quite popular playing bluegrass festivals, with Mills' exceptional songwriting contributing much to the group's fame; "Love of the Mountains," recorded by the original lineup, has become a contemporary bluegrass standard. In addition to contemporary songs, the band also recorded more traditional fare, such as "The Man Who Wrote 'Home Sweet Home' Never Was a Married Man." Most of their albums feature similar material, and the band continues to be a strong positive force in contemporary bluegrass music. By the mid-'90s, only Mills and Young had stayed, recruiting guitarist Ray Berrier and banjo player Lynwood Lunsford as replacements. *—Sandra Brennan*

● **The Best of Lost and Found** / 1984 / Rebel ✦✦✦✦✦

New Day / 1989 / Rebel ✦✦✦✦✦
New Day features a new lead vocalist/guitarist in Ronnie Bowman, plus new banjoist Jody King. The addition of the two new members has reinvigorated Lost & Found, giving them a new kick which is evident both on the covers (particularly a tough version of Buck Owens' "Trouble"), but also on their original numbers. *New Day* does indeed represent a new beginning for Lost & Found. *—Thom Owens*

Jimmy Martin (James Henry Martin)

b. 1927, Sneedville, TN
Vocals, Guitar / Truck Driving Country, Traditional Bluegrass
Blessed with a great tenor voice, this traditional bluegrass singer and guitarist mastered his craft as lead vocalist for Bill Monroe's Blue Grass Boys for much of 1949-1951 and again in 1952-1953. Martin's vocals and his dynamic guitar playing both complemented Monroe perfectly, and in the opinion of many, he was the finest lead singer and guitarist Bill Monroe ever had. In 1951, between stints with Monroe's band, Martin joined with The Osborne Brothers, forming The Sunny Mountain Boys. Though this association lasted only until 1955, Martin has used this band name up to the present. In keeping up such high standards over the years, Martin has hired numerous major-league musicians, including banjo players J. D. Crowe, Bill Emerson, Vic Jordan, and Alan Munde, and mandolin player Paul Williams, all of whom subsequently made it big in bluegrass. Jimmy Martin is required listening for anyone with more than a passing interest in bluegrass. *—Stephen Thomas Erlewine & David Vinopal*

★ **You Don't Know My Mind (1956-1966)** / 1990 / Rounder ✦✦✦✦✦
This is a Monroe band veteran with astonishing high pipes and a penchant for blending bluegrass and honky-tonk. *You Don't Know My Mind (1956-1966)* is a 14 track collection that boasts many highlights from his 10-year stint at Decca Records. These are great bands, great songs, and classic sides. *—Mark A. Humphrey*

Jimmy Martin and the Sunny Mountain Boys / 1994 / Bear Family ✦✦✦✦✦
This five-CD set covers Jimmy Martin's complete recorded output from 1954 until 1974, 20 years and 146 tracks cut primarily for Decca-MCA, with a handful for RCA at the very outset. Disc One covers the early days, from his sides with the Osborne Brothers to his formation of a band of his own—once Martin gets people like banjo man J.D. Crowe and fiddler Gordon Terry, the sound tightens up and gets smoother, and Martin's singing grows in power and confidence. Disc Two represents Martin and the Sunny Mountain Boys at their peak, at least in the studio—these tracks display a range of singing, emotion, and restrained instrumental virtuosity that are almost overpowering. By that time, Martin had managed to incorporate the best components of Nashville's "countrypolitan" sound into his bluegrass work, and was reaping rewards both musical and financial. Disc Three is a direct continuation, with a growing body of fare that country-rock bands would later pick up from Martin and others. Disc Four, gets into the middle/late '60s, when Martin's music achieved an incredibly high level of dexterity. His fourth distinct lineup of Sunny Mountain Boys are as good as any but the originals; different, with a more brittle, dexterous approach. This disc is dominated by the 1966 instrumental album *Big and Country Music;* as it will probably never be issued as a CD, this material alone may justify the purchase of this box. Disc Five goes into the mid-1970s, when Martin had a more obviously smooth and commercial sound than his earlier work—the music is more sentimental and a little less impressive technically, but still worth hearing. The sound is all high quality, and the essay by Chris Skinker and the discography are impressive in their own right. *—Bruce Eder*

Del McCoury

b. Feb. 1, 1939, Bakersville, NC
Vocals, Guitar / Traditional Bluegrass
Among the most distinguished practitioners of traditional bluegrass, for over three decades Del McCoury's voice was the epitome of the "high lonesome sound." He got his start as a five-string banjo picker with Keith Daniels and the Blue Ridge Ramblers. Later he played with Jack Cooke's Virginia Mountain Boys in Baltimore. McCoury got his first big break in 1963 when Bill Monroe hired the Virginia Mountain Boys to play a few New York gigs. Monroe was impressed by the young banjo player and invited him to join his Blue Grass Boys. Shortly after accepting Monroe's offer, McCoury became the group's lead vocalist and took up rhythm guitar. McCoury then began playing and recording with the Shady Valley Boys; after leaving the group in 1967, he founded the Dixie Pals. In 1987, the unit was renamed the Del McCoury Band. *—Sandra Brennan*

I Wonder Where You Are Tonight / 1968 / Arhoolie ✦✦
McCoury's first album (the CD reissue includes a number of previously unreleased cuts). A favorite of purists, McCoury still hadn't developed the vocal style that would make him great in the '90s. *—Brian Mansfield*

Don't Stop the Music / 1988 / Rounder ✦✦✦✦✦
Don't Stop the Music is a typically entertaining and surprisingly bluesy release from the Del McCoury Band, featuring a selection of originals and covers, including a version of the George Jones title track. *—Thom Owens*

★ **Classic Bluegrass** / 1991 / Rebel ✦✦✦✦✦
Rebel label recordings from the '70s by the man who sometimes sounds more like Bill Monroe than Monroe himself. Stunning, pure, high-lonesome pipes and mountain bluesy songs. Beautiful. *—Mark A. Humphrey*

Blue Side of Town / May 15, 1992 / Rounder ✦✦✦✦✦
Named for his version of the Patty Loveless hit "The Blue Side of Town," McCoury covers Steve Earle's "If You Need a Fool" and Arthur "Big Boy" Crudup's "That's Alright Mama." When it comes to song choice, he may be the most well-rounded man in bluegrass. *—Brian Mansfield*

☆ **Deeper Shade of Blue** / 1993 / Rounder ✦✦✦✦✦
A classic from the word go, McCoury's love affair with blues is never more explicit than here, where songs with the titles like "Cheek to Cheek with the Blues," "A Deeper Shade of Blue," and "The Bluest Man in Town" are the order of the day. Never a purist when it comes to songs, McCoury covers Kevin Welch's "True Love Never Dies," Willie Nelson's "Man with the Blues," and the Jerry Lee Lewis hit "What Made Milwaukee Famous." His version of Lefty Frizzell's "If You've Got the Money Honey" is downright piercing. *—Brian Mansfield*

Cold Hard Facts / Sep. 17, 1996 / Rounder ✦✦✦

Family / Feb. 9, 1999 / Ceili Music ✦✦✦✦
Del McCoury has one of those high tenor voices that seems to be enriched, rather than undermined, by age. Although you'd never mistake him for a youngster, he can still let the high notes fly with the confidence of a singer half his age. And in collaboration with his mandolin-playing son Ronnie, he has built a top-notch traditional bluegrass band that manages to keep itself firmly rooted in the verities while still conducting such (largely successful) experiments as collaborating with punk-country icon Steve Earle and recording songs by commercial folkie John Sebastian. The band's latest finds McCoury covering Bill Monroe ("Get Down on Your Knees and Pray") and Jimmy Martin ("She's Left Me Again"), as well as the aforementioned Sebastian (the cute and clever "Nashville Cats"), and delivering a few fine originals as well. Highlights include Ronnie McCoury's vinegary instrumental "Red Eyes on a Mad Dog" and a great version of Verlon Thompson' s "Backslidin' Blues," not to mention the group's spookily beautiful rendition of "Get Down on Your Knees and Pray." *—Rick Anderson*

John McEuen

b. Dec. 19, 1945, Garden Grove, CA
Vocals, Violin, Mandolin, Guitar, Banjo / Progressive Country, Progressive Bluegrass
Best known for his long tenure as a key member of the venerable Nitty Gritty Dirt Band, John "the String Wizard" McEuen was one of the most influential figures in contemporary American country, bluegrass and even pop music. Credited with introducing both the banjo and the mandolin to pop, he was a master string player who developed a devoted fan base on the festival circuit. In 1965 he hooked up with Michael Martin Murphey for a year and subsequently performed on all five of Murphy's albums. One year later, he joined the Nitty Gritty Dirt Band and remained with them for over two decades, singing and playing banjo, mandolin, fiddle and other stringed instruments through the watershed period that produced such classic albums as *Uncle Charlie and His Dog Teddy* (1970) and the landmark compilation *Will the Circle Be Unbroken* (1972). He abruptly left the Dirt Band in 1987, and in 1992, released the album *String Wizards,* an all-star venture featuring such illustrious artists as Earl Scruggs, Vassar Clements, and Byron Berline. A follow-up, *String Wizards II,* appeared in 1994, at about the same time McEuen founded his own label—named, appropriately enough, String Wizard. *Acoustic Traveller* was released in 1996. *—Sandra Brennan*

String Wizards / 1991 / Vanguard ✦✦✦
Considering the bluegrass superstars who drop in, maybe the expectations are unfairly raised. But with players that include Josh Graves, Vassar Clements, Earl Scruggs, Sam Bush, Byron Berline, and Jerry Douglas, it's hard to not anticipate more than what is delivered here. The high points such as "Return to Dismal Swamp" are high indeed, but too much is too laid back. Perhaps the players were too respectful of each other. "Miner's Night Out" is a delightful little surprise that would sound more at home in the English North Country than in the Appalachians. Much as Doc Watson and Merle Watson did for "Take Me out to the Ballgame," this album gives "Stars and Stripes Forever" a new life as a bluegrass anthem. *—Mark Allan*

● **Acoustic Traveller** / 1996 / Vanguard ✦✦✦✦✦
John McEuen plays a variety of stringed instruments, including mandolin, guitar, banjo, dulcimer, lap steel guitar, and even a Japanese koto on this accomplished album of folk-, country-, bluegrass-, and Western-flavored traditional-sounding original instrumentals, with one vocal track, "I Am A Pilgrim." There are many familiar sounds from McEuen's long career, including "Mr. Bojangles (suite)." *—William Ruhlmann*

Round Trip: Live in L.A. / Nov. 30, 1999 / Cedar Glen ✦✦✦✦
This delightful live recording finds John McEuen (former leader of the Nitty Gritty Dirt Band) onstage in his hometown, obviously completely at ease and spinning out a long program of tunes both standard ("I Am a Pilgrim," "Sheik of Araby") and original ("Good Old Boys Texas," "Night Flight"). The focus is on instrumentals, with McEuen taking the lead on guitar and banjo, but he also sings a few (including the inevitable "Mr. Bojangles") in his agreeably undistinguished voice. Surprises include a very attractive banjo arrangement of an old Muzio Clementi piano etude and a boot-stomping version of "Kiss" that probably makes the diminutive purple artist formerly known as Prince go into convulsions whenever (if ever) he hears it—young Jonathan McEuen approximating a soul falsetto is not something you'd want to hear without a good night's rest and a fully functioning sense of humor. Best of all are the Merle Travis songs and stories; McEuen's renditions of "Cannonball Rag" and "I Am a Pilgrim" are warm and wonderful. Highly recommended. *—Rick Anderson*

The Monroe Brothers

f. 1932, **db.** 1938
Group / Close Harmony, Country-Folk, Traditional Country, Old-Timey, Traditional Bluegrass
The Monroe Brothers began as a trio of Birch, Charlie, and Bill Monroe on fiddle, guitar and mandolin respectively, performing square dance songs as well as traditional and gospel

numbers. By 1932, Bill and Charlie began touring professionally, appearing with the Hoosier Hot Shots and Red Foley among others, and in 1934 secured the sponsorship of the Texas Crystals Company, a manufacturer of laxatives. The association provided the Monroes with a steady stream of radio work for over a year until competing laxative maker Crazy Water Crystals took over sponsorship of the duo while they continued working on many of the same stations. The radio appearances made the Monroe Brothers a popular live act, which prompted the interest of RCA to recording the two. In mid-February the Monroe Brothers made their first recordings for RCA's Bluebird imprint, and went on to wax 60 sides in the following two years. Their music at this point was firmly within the brother duo tradition and exhibited only hints of the style Bill Monroe would later pioneer as the Father of Bluegrass. They were set apart from other harmony duos by Bill's piercing harmonies and mandolin leads, as well as the energy and often fast tempos of their performances. The very use of the mandolin as a lead instrument would revolutionize its application in country music, as would Bill's unique fiddle-influenced style. It would be silly to label them the "rock & roll of the '30s," but certainly there was an excitement and an edge to their music that put them on the frontier of hillbilly innovation in their day. In early 1938, Bill and Charlie parted ways due to personality conflicts and business disagreements, and each formed his own band shortly thereafter. Charlie formed a group called the Kentucky Pardners, and by 1941 (after a short stint with a band called the Kentuckians and an abortive attempt at recreating the Monroe Brothers sound with partner Cleo Davis) Bill Monroe was recording again for RCA with a band he named the Blue Grass Boys. In this new group, Monroe built upon his earlier innovations and developed the distinctive and enduring style that came to be known as bluegrass. *—Greg Adams*

★ **The Legendary the Monroe Brothers** / 1997 / BMG Japan ✦✦✦✦✦
Available only as a pricey Japanese import, this three-CD collection contains the Monroe Brothers' complete 1936-1938 recordings. The historical importance of this package cannot be overstated, providing, as it does, a link between the brother duo sound and the birth of bluegrass. Although the seeds of bluegrass can be heard among these 86 recordings, and some of the material would later surface as standards of bluegrass repertory, the music of the Monroe Brothers is unique in its own right. Bill Monroe's high harmonies and aggressive mandolin leads were revolutionary at the time, and the influence of the brothers' choice of material and presentation would resonate throughout country music for decades to come. Some of the recordings on this set have been mastered from off-center or damaged 78s, but most of the material is quite listenable. Despite the high import price, *The Legendary Monroe Brothers* is essential for serious fans of Bill Monroe or anyone with a deep interest in the history of country music. *—Greg Adams*

What Would You Give in Exchange for Your Soul, Vol. 1 / May 16, 2000 / Rounder ✦✦✦✦✦
This is the first of a four-volume set covering the entirety of the 60 sides the duo recorded for RCA/Bluebird. It would have been nice if dates, even estimated ones, were included with the tracks in the liner notes, but it can be gathered that the 15 cuts represent the first chronological fourth of the Monroe Brothers' RCA/Bluebird material. Again it's not certain from Charles Wolfe's liners (which are, it should be added, in the main excellent), but most or all of them date from 1936. There was no run up the ramp to a level of musical accomplishment when the brothers started recording. Right from the start, they were tight instrumentalists and harmonizing vocalists. The guitar (Charlie Monroe) and mandolin (Bill Monroe) blended in a way that foreshadowed, indeed virtually was, bluegrass on the rapid "My Long Journey Home" and "Nine Pound Hammer Is Too Heavy," the latter getting heavy exposure in 2000 via its inclusion on *Harry Smith's Anthology of American Folk Music, Vol. 4.* Much of the material on this disc was gospel in origin; they were also able interpreters of both traditional folk songs and contemporary compositions (some of which were their own). Although this was mastered from old 78s, the sound is pretty good, certainly about as good as it's going to get via the remastering process. *—Richie Unterberger*

Bill Monroe

b. Sep. 13, 1911, Rosine, KY, **d.** Sep. 9, 1996, Springfield, TN
Vocals, Mandolin, Guitar, Fiddle / Bluegrass-Gospel, Traditional Bluegrass
Bill Monroe is the father of bluegrass. He invented the style, invented the name and, for the great majority of the 20th century, embodied the art form. Beginning with his Blue Grass Boys in the '40s, Monroe defined a hard-edged style of country that emphasized instrumental virtuosity, close vocal harmonies and a fast, driving tempo. The musical genre took its name from the Blue Grass Boys and Monroe's music forever has defined the sound of classical bluegrass—a five-piece acoustic string band, playing precisely and rapidly, switching solos and singing in a plaintive, high lonesome voice. Not only did he invent the very sound of the music, Bill Monroe was the mentor for several generations of musicians. Over the years, Monroe's band hosted all of the major bluegrass artists of the '50s and '60s, including Flatt and Scruggs, Reno and Smiley, Vassar Clements, Carter Stanley, and Mac Wiseman. Though the lineup of the Blue Grass Boys changed over the years, Monroe always remained devoted to bluegrass in its purest form. *—Stephen Thomas Erlewine*

Live Duet Recordings 1963-1980 / 1963-1980 / Smithsonian/Folkways ✦✦✦✦
Any time two greats who admire each other and are musically compatible team together, the results are usually mutually beneficial. That was true for Bill Monroe and Doc Watson, whose spirited union on this 17-song disc is a sampler of American musical styles. They ripped through bluegrass, folk, blues, spirituals, mountain tunes, work songs, reels and breakdowns. Monroe's mandolin and Watson's guitar playing were masterful, wondrous and performed without any trace of self-indulgence. Their vocals were also delivered with ease, fluidity and conviction, the product of two performers completely at ease with themselves and only interested in spotlighting the material. *—Ron Wynn*

Columbia Historic Edition / 1989 / Columbia ✦✦✦✦✦
Columbia Historic Edition has a nice selection of 10 songs that Bill Monroe cut for Columbia in the early '40s, including "Kentucky Waltz," "Blue Yodel No. 4 (California Blues)," "Bluegrass Special." Several hits are missing and there are several compilations released in the '90s that cover the same ground more thoroughly, but this record remains an enjoyable listen. *—Thom Owens*

Live at the Opry: Celebrating 50 Years on the Grand Ole Opry / 1989 / MCA ✦✦✦
Recorded live in 1989, Monroe has by this time turned over a majority of lead vocal turns to guitarist Tom Ewing. But the music proves how vibrant and aggressive Monroe's mandolin skills remain. It also features one fantastic cut from a 1948 Opry date. *—Michael McCall*

☆ **Bluegrass 1950-1958** / 1990 / Bear Family ✦✦✦✦✦
Bluegrass 1950-1958 is a 109-track, four-disc box set that contains all of Bill Monroe's recordings for Decca during that era. Though there are no charting hits on this set, these recordings are is among the finest and most accomplished music that Monroe ever made; it is the sound of the master perfecting the style of bluegrass. Though it is too extensive for casual fans, there are no other reissues that explain why Monroe was important—and what bluegrass music actually is—more convincingly than this four-disc set. *—Thom Owens*

☆ **Bluegrass 1959-1969** / 1991 / Bear Family ✦✦✦✦✦
This, the companion set to the above, comprises over 100 tracks on four CDs, including such hits as "The Long Black Veil," "Midnight on the Stormy Deep," "Big River," "Dusty Miller," and many other Monroe favorites, and also several recordings released here for the first time. *—AMG*

★ **Country Music Hall of Fame** / 1991 / MCA ✦✦✦✦✦
Bill Monroe made his most famous and popular—and arguably his best—recordings after he signed to Decca Records in 1950. For the next 40 years, he cut a number of classics, and 16 of his finest tracks are collected on *Country Music Hall of Fame.* The original versions of many of Monroe's best-known songs, including "New Mule Skinner Blues" and "Uncle Pen," are included, as well as his popular remake of his standard "Blue Moon of Kentucky." Of course, with a career as long and varied as Monroe's, it's hard to boil it down to just 16 tracks and, inevitably, some of the latter-day cuts won't please some dedicated fans. Nevertheless, it's hard to beat *Country Music Hall of Fame* as a single-disc introduction to one of the greatest musicians in country music history. *—Stephen Thomas Erlewine*

Cryin' Holy Unto the Lord / 1991 / MCA ✦✦✦
An all-gospel album propped up with some stellar guests, it includes Ricky Skaggs, Ralph Stanley, the Osborne Brothers, Jim & Jesse McReynolds, and Mac Wiseman. *—Michael McCall*

Mule Skinner Blues / 1991 / Roadracer ✦✦✦
Mule Skinner Blues contains the first recordings that Bill Monroe made with the Blue Grass Boys in 1940 and 1941 for RCA. On these recordings of the earliest and loosest bluegrass band, Monroe is wearing his blues, old-time, and even swing influences on his sleeve. *—Mark A. Humphrey*

☆ **The Essential Bill Monroe (1945-1949)** / 1992 / Columbia/Legacy ✦✦✦✦✦
On the surface, *The Essential Bill Monroe: 1945-49* seems like the perfect compilation, containing 40 tracks of Monroe and the Blue Grass Boys' Columbia recordings. However, the set wasn't executed with care—no less than 16 of these songs are represented with alternate takes, not the original versions. Though these alternates are interesting, they don't have a place in a set like this, which purports to be an extensive *introduction,* not an exhaustive compilation of Monroe's complete recordings; the alternates would have been more acceptable if they were placed in conjuction with the master takes. Still, *The Essential Bill Monroe* is a necessary set for bluegrass historians, since it does contain the bulk of his groundbreaking '40s recordings, including versions of "Blue Moon of Kentucky," "Kentucky Waltz," and "Rocky Road Blues." It's just not quite as good as it could have been. (The 16 master takes that were not included on this box were later issued by Columbia as the single-disc *16 Gems* collection). *—Stephen Thomas Erlewine*

Blue Moon of Kentucky / 1993 / MCA ✦✦✦

Live Recordings 1956-1959 / 1993 / Smithsonian/Folkways ✦✦✦
The 27 numbers presented here offer Monroe in more intimate settings, including workshops, jam sessions and live performances where he's casually swapping yarns, offering anecdotes, and displaying the blistering, yet folksy and down-home style that's made him a musical legend. His group included a number of marvelous players and future stars, such as Del McCoury, Peter Rowan, Bill Keith, and Tex Logan. Monroe was also playing with brothers Charlie and Birch. This is 75 minutes of breakdowns, folk tunes, railroad and work songs, such classics as "Blue Grass Stomp" and "Blue Moon of Kentucky" and many others performed in a loose, next-door neighbor atmosphere. *—Ron Wynn*

☆ **The Music of Bill Monroe** / 1994 / MCA ✦✦✦✦✦
A four-disc set covering his entire career from 1936 to 1994, this is a meticulously remastered and researched four hours and 20 minutes of music and features important recordings from seven decades of recordings for RCA, Columbia, Decca and MCA. It's an exceptional box set, put together with great care and knowledge, and it's essential for any fan of bluegrass or traditional country music. *—Michael McCall*

Bluegrass (1970-1979) / 1995 / Bear Family ✦✦✦✦✦
Bluegrass (1970-1979) is a four-disc box set containing all of Monroe's '70s recordings for Decca, including several unreleased cuts and a live album featuring Jim & Jesse, James Monroe, Jimmy Martin, Lester Flatt, and Carl Jackson. By the time he made these recordings, Monroe was no longer making any innovations with his music. Instead, he just demonstrated his skill and artistry—the music on *Bluegrass (1970-1979)* is for afficianados, the kind of listener that can discern subtle differences between supporting bands and solos. Overall, the material on the box isn't as strong as the previous two box sets, but any Monroe completist will not be disappointed by the set. *—Stephen Thomas Erlewine*

☆ **16 Gems** / 1996 / Columbia/Legacy ✦✦✦✦✦
Sony's decision to use 16 alternate takes for the double-CD *Essential* collection was disagreeable to some completists. That omission is rectified by *16 Gems,* which makes all 16 of the official versions of those tunes available on CD, and creates a useful adjunct to the *Es-*

sential set for collectors. On its own merits, it's hardly dismissable, with an appeal not limited to Monroe obsessives. Spanning 1945-49, it includes such notable cuts as "Kentucky Waltz" and "Blue Grass Special." *—Richie Unterberger*

The Essential Bill Monroe & Monroe Brothers / Apr. 29, 1997 / RCA ✦✦✦✦✦
The Essential Bill Monroe and the Monroe Brothers chronicles Monroe's very first recordings from the late '60s. Selecting 24 highlights, including nine selections from the Monroe Brothers, from the 60-plus tracks he recorded for Bluebird, *The Essential* is the best single-disc overview of the beginning of Monroe's career and the roots of bluegrass, featuring such classics as "Mule Skinner Blues," "In the Pines" and "Crying Holy Unto My Lord." These are neither the best nor the best-known versions, yet they are historically invaluable, demonstrating the birthing pangs of bluegrass. *—Stephen Thomas Erlewine*

The Early Years / Jul. 14, 1998 / Vanguard ✦✦✦
Featuring an excellent cross section of tracks from the definitive 1945-1949 period, *The Early Years* charts Bill Monroe's evolving sound through Western swing-influenced pieces, waltzes, blues, spirituals, ballads, and instrumentals. Though there are definitely far more comprehensive collections on the market, and the tracks here aren't particularly rare, *The Early Tapes* does a good job of representing Monroe's early recordings, the inclusion of Flatt & Scruggs, and the period following their departure. The material included is first rate, with "Blue Moon of Kentucky," "Toy Heart," and the sharp "Blue Grass Breakdown" among the 14 tracks included. Good liner notes also make this an excellent introductory collection. *—Matt Fink*

Live from Mountain Stage / May 11, 1999 / Blue Plate ✦✦✦

20th Century Masters—*The Millennium Collection: The Best of Bill Monroe* / *Oct. 5, 1999 / MCA* ✦✦✦
MCA's *20th Century Masters: The Millennium Collection* is a good, basic collection of many of the best-known recordings of Bill Monroe's best-known songs, including "Blue Moon of Kentucky," "In the Pines," "New Mule Skinner Blues," "Uncle Pen," "I'm Sitting on Top of the World," "I Saw the Light," and "My Sweet Blue-Eyed Darlin'." These may not be his most historically important recordings, and undeniably there are some classic songs missing, but this should satisfy casual listeners on a tight budget. *—Stephen Thomas Erlewine*

The Nashville Bluegrass Band

f. 1984
Group / Traditional Bluegrass, Progressive Bluegrass
The Nashville Bluegrass Band was made up of several excellent musicians more interested in preserving their group sound than showing off their individual expertise. The band favored a traditional, earthy sound that led one critic to call them the band that "put the blues back in bluegrass." The Nashville Bluegrass Band came together in 1985 and released *My Native Home,* which featured production by Bela Fleck. In 1987, they released another Fleck-produced album, *Idle Time,* and before the end of the year released a bluegrass/gospel album, *To Be His Child.* In 1990, the Nashville Bluegrass Band released *The Boys Are Back in Town.* A series of albums followed, including 1993's *Waiting for the Hard Time to Go* and 1998's *American Beauty.* *—Sandra Brennan*

The Nashville Bluegrass Band / 1987 / Rounder ✦✦✦✦✦
The Nashville Bluegrass Band selects highlights from the group's first two albums for Rounder Records. Though the band's music would improve with time, this is a terrific overview of the group's origins. *—Thom Owens*

To Be His Child / 1987 / Rounder ✦✦✦✦✦
To Be His Child is an affecting sampling of the Nashville Bluegrass Band's gospel material, featuring both their string work and several tracks that feature an a capella quartet. *—Thom Owens*

The Boys Are Back in Town / 1990 / Sugar Hill ✦✦✦✦
Very well performed, highly recommended. These vocals are on the mark. Produced by Jerry Douglas. *—Chip Renner*

Home of the Blues / 1991 / Sugar Hill ✦✦✦
Home of the Blues is one of the Nashville Bluegrass Band's finest albums, boasting a handful of excellent originals like "Blue Train," and interpretations of standards like "Old Daingerfield," and, as a bonus, a live cut with the black gospel group the Fairfield Four. *—Thom Owens*

★ **Waitin' for the Hard Times to Go** / 1993 / Sugar Hill ✦✦✦✦✦
Waitin' for the Hard Time to Go is an excellent collection from a stellar bluegrass band. Instead of choosing to follow either a traditional or progressive direction, the Nashville Bluegrass Band decide to alternate between the two approaches, which makes it a considerably richer and eclectic record than most contemporary bluegrass albums. *Waitin' for the Hard Time to Go* won the 1993 Grammy Award for Best Bluegrass Album. *—Thom Owens*

Unleashed / Oct. 1995 / Sugar Hill ✦✦✦
The new CD from the all-star Nashville Bluegrass Band is a jaunty, highly musical collection of contemporary tunes with a few trads. thrown in for good measure. The bluegrass and light gospel singing is very agreeable, unforced and as always with this band, it seems completely natural. Too often this style of country singing is adopted but not lived in. Not the case here. This is a very strong album. Instrumentalists trade licks back and forth with casual authority. Some of the highlights are "I Got a Date," "Tear My Stillhouse Down" and "The Doorstep of Trouble." *—Richard Meyer*

American Beauty / Jul. 21, 1998 / Sugar Hill ✦✦✦✦
Always a delight, this band is one of the best in any genre. Pure and true to the music, they pull off such classics as the Flatt & Scruggs song "The Johnson Boys" and Ralph Stanley's "Holiday Pickin'" with finesse. They do a wonderful cover of Bob Dylan's "Livin' the Blues" and make the Gillian Welch-David Rawlings tune "Red Clay Halo" feel almost ancient. "All Alone," penned by Candice Randolph, is outstanding, with Alan O'Bryant's banjo calling out to the faithful. *—Jana Pendragon*

New Coon Creek Girls

f. 1979
Group / Traditional Folk, Traditional Bluegrass
The New Coon Creek Girls carried on the bluegrass traditions that made the original Coon Creek Girls a popular act between the late '30s and early '50s. The band was the brainchild of producer John Lair, who was trying to recreate the magic of the original group. The New Coon Creek Girls remained on Lair's show through 1983 and then moved out on their own; during the '80s and '90s, they were a popular concert attraction on the bluegrass and folk festival circuit. In addition to performing, the group occasionally recorded, releasing *The L&N Don't Stop Here Anymore* in 1994. A year later, a line-up including guitarist Vicki Simmons, lead singer/rhythm guitarist Dale Ann Bradley, mandolinist/vocalist Pam Perry, and banjoist Ramona Church Taylor issued *Ain't Love a Good Thing.* In 1996, they released *Everything You Do.* *—Sandra Brennan*

● **So I'll Ride** / 1991 / Turquoise ✦✦✦✦✦
This well-crafted album features a high energy level. Jesse McReynolds, Dempsey Young, Mike Stevens, Edgar Meyer, and Raymond McLain were guests on the album. *—Chip Renner*

Our Point of View / 1998 / Pinecastle ✦✦✦✦✦
The New Coon Creek Girls is a bundle of bluegrass talent. Foremost, we have the dulcet vocals of Dale Ann Bradley—she makes "Danny Boy" sound fresh as she expresses it here. The instrumentalists step out and tear it up with lightning exchanges like the fiddle-mandolin-banjo frenzy of "On Fire." Other standards they give new life to are Jimmie Rodgers' "Muleskinner Blues" and "Sassafras." The combined chops in this band simply cannot be overlooked. After nearing 20 years of performance, three-way harmonies and stunning melodies mark *Our Point of View* as a stellar bluegrass album of skill and tradition. *—Thomas Schulte*

The New Grass Revival

f. 1972, **db.** 1990
Group / Progressive Bluegrass
The New Grass Revival, formed in 1972 by four former members of the Bluegrass Alliance, flourished in a decade when numerous groups took traditional bluegrass and changed it to varying degrees. The group was successful enough to have the group's name become a generic label: "newgrass." The band's image, with long hair and occasionally electrified instruments, as well as its musical material, contrasted greatly with the standard (traditional) bluegrass of Bill Monroe, Ralph Stanley and Lester Flatt. In terms of longevity, popularity, and exposure, the Revival, with its hip reputation, was perhaps the most successful in competition against II Generation, Seldom Scene, the Country Gentlemen, and others. The band released their debut *Arrival of the New Grass Revival* later that year on Starday Records, but recorded most of their '70s output for Flying Fish Records. The addition of banjoist Bela Fleck in 1981 gained moderate commercial fortunes for the group; their eponymous debut for EMI proved to be a breakthrough of sorts, including two country hits and a Grammy award for Fleck's showcase "Seven by Seven." *Hold on to a Dream* and *Friday Night in America* also proved popular (the latter featured their first Top 40 single, "Callin' Baton Rouge"). Even though the band was more popular than ever, nominal leader Sam Bush decided to pull the plug after the release of *Friday Night In America.* Bush became a session musician and Fleck went onto a very successful and respected solo career. *—Stephen Thomas Erlewine & David Vinopal*

Fly through the Country / 1975 / Flying Fish ✦✦✦✦✦
This first version of New Grass was not so polished as their second era, but they had good chemistry. You've gotta love "These Days," "Skippin'," "All Night Train," and "Fly Through the Country." *—Chip Renner*

When the Storm Is Over / 1977 / Flying Fish ✦✦✦
New Grass Revival's *When the Storm is Over* is one of the group's earliest albums and as the record demonstrates, the group had developed a distinctive sound even at this formative stage. *When the Storm is Over* is combined on one compact disc with *Fly Through the Country.* *—Thom Owens*

Barren County / 1979 / Flying Fish ✦✦✦✦✦
The first incarnation of this band was never better than on this one. Strong songs and vocals. *—Chip Renner*

Live / 1984 / Sugar Hill ✦✦
Live captures a boisterous, lively performance from the New Grass Revival, as they tear through their best material. The new additions to the band—banjoist Bela Fleck and guitarist Pat Flynn—have energized the band, and vocalist John Cowan helps spur the band on to truly remarkable performances. *—Thom Owens*

Friday Night in America / 1989 / Southern Music ✦✦✦
Their last album covers John Hiatt's "Angel Eyes," and Jesse Winchester's "Let's Make a Baby King," and Bela Fleck's "Big Foot." Hot! These guys will be missed. *—Chip Renner*

New Grass Anthology / Aug. 27, 1990 / Liberty ✦✦✦✦✦
Culling tracks from the first three New Grass Revival discs cut for Capitol Records, *Anthology* has all the highlights, including "Callin' Baton Rouge," later made world famous by one Garth Brooks. It also includes one unreleased gut, "Reach" which adds to *Anthology's* charm. Good compile. *—James Chrispell*

● **The Best of New Grass Revival** / Mar. 8, 1994 / Liberty ✦✦✦✦✦
Best of New Grass Revival is a first-rate, 18-track collection of the band's biggest hits of the late '80s, plus a number of significant album tracks. It's the perfect way to get acquainted with the group. *—Thom Owens*

Tim O'Brien

b. Mar. 16, 1954
Mandocello, Vocals, Mandolin, Guitar, Fiddle, Bouzouki / Contemporary Folk, Country-Folk, Singer/Songwriter
Tim O'Brien is one of the spearheads of contemporary bluegrass. As co- founder and lead vocalist of Hot Rize and Red Knuckles & The Trailblazers, O'Brien served as a bridge between

the traditional sounds of the hill country and the modern styles of bluegrass in the 1980s. Since the band's break-up, O'Brien has continued to expand the music's borders as a soloist, a duo partner with his sister Mollie and with his band, The O'Boys. O'Brien's songs have additionally been recorded by Kathy Mattea, The Seldom Scene, The New Grass Revival and The Johnson Mountain Boys. O'Brien also joined with his sister, Mollie, to record an album of old-timey country songs, *Take Me Back*, in 1988. Although they had sung together in church and school choirs, they had spent most of their later teens apart. Since being reunited, they've collaborated on three albums. *—Craig Harris*

Take Me Back / 1988 / Sugar Hill ✦✦✦✦✦
Mollie and Tim O'Brien's vocals blend perfectly. A masterpiece. *—Chip Renner*

★ **Away Out on the Mountain** / 1994 / Sugar Hill ✦✦✦✦✦
If you ever wished you could hear brand new music with the conviction and flawless vocal vork of the classic Everly Brothers recordings this album by brother and sister Mollie and Tim O'Brien is for you. The cuts are mostly contemporary gospel-bluegrass sounding tunes with an A.P. Carter and Leadbelly song tossed in. There is not a misplaced note. *—Richard Meyer*

When No One's Around / 1997 / Sugar Hill ✦✦✦✦✦
This is one of Tim O'Brien's most engaging projects. Known as a writer, he chooses here to co-write with others, including sister Mollie O'Brien, Hal Ketchum, and the elusive Danny O'Keefe. The songs range from celebratory ("Out On the Rolling Sea") to sardonic ("How Come I Ain't Dead") to reflective ("First Days of Fall"). In spite of his attempts to the contrary, O'Brien is still his own best writer, with kudos especially to "Think About Last Night" and "First Days of Fall." The feel of this music is more mainstream country than some of his other albums. The players are quite good, with high praise for drummer John Gardner for his accents and exclamation marks. *—William Ashford*

The Crossing / May 4, 1999 / Alula ✦✦✦✦
It might be a cliché to say that to understand where you are and where you're going, you must know where you've been, but it's a very accurate cliché—especially when it comes to music. If you're going to have a thorough understanding of the history of country, bluegrass and Anglo-American folk, it's important to have some knowledge of the music that paved the way for those forms—namely, the music that immigrants from the British Isles brought with them to the U.S. On *The Crossing*, singer/instrumentalist Tim O'Brien does a fine job reminding us how great a role Celtic music played in the development of Anglo-American styles. As a vocalist, O'Brien shows us how Irish and Scottish ballad traditions have influenced American folk and country, and as an instrumentalist, O'Brien (who plays fiddle, mandolin, guitar and other instruments) shows us how the jigs and reels of Ireland and Scotland paved the way for Appalachian bluegrass. A fine storyteller, he describes the experiences of Irish immigrants to the U.S. on gems like "The Crossing" and "Lost Little Children"—and on the humorous, Bob Dylan-influenced "Talkin' Cavan," O'Brien (himself an Irish-American from West Virginia) recalls traveling to Ireland in 1998 to visit the land of his ancestors. This CD is not to be missed. *—Alex Henderson*

Real Time / Apr. 18, 2000 / Howdy Skies ✦✦✦✦
Music has occasionally been born of a couple of friends playing both new and familiar songs in a relaxed setting. Words that are often used to describe the music they make are "natural" or "unaffected." Examples would include John Hartford's *Morning Bugle*, Hartford, David Grisman, and Mike Seeger's *Retrograss*, and Tim O'Brien and Darrell Scott's *Real Time*. The songs on *Real Time* were recorded in Scott's living room over the period of a week. Both musicians play multiple instruments including banjo, mandolin, guitar, and bouzouki; they also exchange lead vocals and sing some very fine harmony. Both the song choice and songwriting add to this project. Hank Williams' "Weary Blues from Waiting" receives an acoustic revision, with both singers sharing lead vocals and providing affecting harmony. O'Brien sings a charged version of "Little Sadie" driven by Scott's aggressive guitar playing. Part of the beauty of this album is how fresh and vital these traditional songs become with these simple and straightforward arrangements. *Real Time* also contains a handful of refined originals, including O'Brien's "Walk Beside Me" and "I'm Not Gonna Forget You." Scott has written the impressive "There Ain't No Easy Way," complete with the same soulful singing found on his last release, *Family Tree*. There are even moments when Scott's vocal style reminds one of the soulful delivery of Little Feat's Lowell George. *Real Time* brings together two artists who love to make music and who give the impression that making good music is as simple as hanging out with friends. While this may not be how all good music is made, it has produced a gem of an album in the hands of Scott and O'Brien. Fans of both artists, and fans of good traditional and folk music, should enjoy this one. *—Ronnie Lankford, Jr.*

Old & In the Way

f. 1973, California
Group / Traditional Bluegrass
Old & In the Way was a one-shot bluegrass band whose legacy lasted far longer than the band. Led by Grateful Dead member Jerry Garcia (banjo, vocals), the band also featured David Grisman (mandolin, vocals), Vassar Clements (fiddle), Peter Rowan (guitar, vocals), and John Kahn (bass). Garcia formed the band in 1973 as a way to revisit his bluegrass roots and demonstrate his affection for the music. To round out the lineup, he recruited Clements and Kahn, as well as Grisman and Rowan, who were both West Coast session musicians that had previously played together in the band Muleskinner. Taking their name from a Grisman composition, Old & In the Way played a handful of gigs, most of them at the Boarding House in San Francisco in October. An album, also called *Old & In the Way*, was culled from these shows but not released until 1975 on the Grateful Dead's own record label, Round. The record combined standards and Rowan originals, which later became standards. Although the album was the only one the lineup released during the 1970s, the members continued to play together in various permutations over the next two decades and the record continued to sell steadily. The group reunited after Garcia's death in 1995, releasing a second album (actually composed of 1973 recordings) *That High Lonesome Sound*, in early 1996. A third album of 1973 vintage appeared at the end of 1997. *—Stephen Thomas Erlewine*

★ **Old & In the Way** / Oct. 1973 / Grateful Dead ✦✦✦✦✦
This release was one of the greatest things to happen to bluegrass music, in that it exposed a whole new audience to bluegrass music and acoustic music. *—Chip Renner*

That High Lonesome Sound / Feb. 20, 1996 / Acoustic Disc ✦✦✦✦✦
Twenty-one years after the first album Old & In the Way came the second, an amazing development for a group that existed for only nine months and about 30 gigs in 1973. *That High Lonesome Sound*, like its predecessor, *Old & In the Way*, was drawn from the group's stand at the Boarding House in San Francisco in October 1973. And like that release, it combined traditional bluegrass material, in this case standards like "Orange Blossom Special" and "Uncle Pen," with interpolations from the world of rock & roll ("The Great Pretender") and new originals that touched on contemporary issues (Peter Rowan's "Lonesome L.A. Cowboy," a comment on the Southern California country-rock scene of the time). *Old & In The Way* was a great crossover album, largely because the bandmembers had enjoyed careers in rock, especially banjo player and singer Jerry Garcia, moonlighting from his day job in the Grateful Dead. What was less-well-known was that the group had real roots in the music, as Neil V. Rosenberg pointed out in the second album's liner notes. Four of the five members had experience in bluegrass, and two had been members of Bill Monroe's Blue Grass Boys. Old And In The Way was a hybrid, but it was far more bluegrass than rock. *—William Ruhlmann*

Breakdown: Live Recordings 1973 / Nov. 18, 1997 / Acoustic Disc ✦✦✦✦✦
Breakdown: Live Recordings 1973 collects 18 unreleased tracks from the group's legendary 1973 concerts, including two Jerry Garcia banjo songs that aren't available on any other disc and six alternate takes of songs like "Panama Red," "Pig in a Pen," "*Wild Horses*" and "Midnight Moonlight." In short, it's quite similar to their second record *That High Lonesome Sound*, a compilation of leftovers from the original *Old & In The Way* album that was released the year before *Breakdown*, but when music is as joyous as this, there's no reason to complain. Old & In The Way were one of the greatest progressive bluegrass bands of the early '70s, and each subsequent release proves that they were a special band. Even if you are intimately familiar with its two predecessors, it's unlikely you'll be disappointed with *Breakdown*. *—Thom Owens*

Osborne Brothers

f. 1956, Hyden, KY
Group / Close Harmony, Traditional Bluegrass, Progressive Bluegrass
The Osborne Brothers were one of the most popular and innovative bluegrass groups of the post-war era, taking the music into new directions and gaining a large audience. Among their most notable achievements are their pioneering, inventive use of amplification, twin harmony banjos, steel guitars and drums—they were the first bluegrass group to expand the genre's sonic palette in such a fashion.

Born in Kentucky but raised in Ohio, guitarist Bobby and banjoist Sonny Osborne played (together and apart) with a variety of bluegrass groups, including the Lonesome Pine Fiddlers, the Stanley Brothers and Bill Monroe's Blue Grass Boys. The pair finally formed their own band in 1956 and two years later, recorded a Top 20 country hit, "Once More." In 1960, the Osbornes became the first bluegrass act to play a college campus, ushering in a new era for bluegrass and creating a new, younger audience for the music. After moving to Decca in 1963, they began experimenting more with their music by adding piano, steel guitar, and electric instruments to their music. Although their experimentation angered many bluegrass traditionalists, the Osbornes were the only bluegrass group to consistently hit the country charts during the '60s and '70s. The duo returned to a more traditional sound later in the '70s and stuck to the sound during the '80s and '90s, remaining an active act in the mid-'90s. *—Stephen Thomas Erlewine*

☆ **The Osborne Brothers** / 1971 / Rounder ✦✦✦✦✦
Great vocal harmonies and tightly woven banjo-mandolin conversations come together on this, the best early material from 1959-1963. *—Mark A. Humphrey*

★ **The Best of the Osborne Brothers** / 1975 / Sugar Hill ✦✦✦✦✦
Their 1963-1967 Decca hits blend smooth bluegrass with then-contemporary country production. A unique sound, it's radical for its time. *—Mark A. Humphrey*

The Bluegrass Collection / 1978 / CMH ✦✦✦✦✦
Recorded in 1978, *Bluegrass Collection* is the Osborne Brothers' tribute to the fathers of bluegrass—Bill Monroe, Flatt & Scruggs, and the Stanley Brothers. The duo throws in nice, but unremarkable, remakes of their older hits as well, making the album a pleasant exercise in nostalgia. *—Thom Owens*

★ **The Essential Bluegrass Album** / 1979 / CMH ✦✦✦✦✦
The Essential Bluegrass Album features 24 of the finest songs Mac Wiseman and the Osborne Brothers recorded together in the '60s and '70s. Instead of adhering to the rigid traditionalism of Bill Monroe, the Osbornes and Wiseman open the music up, bringing in a drummer and elements of Western swing, Tex-Mex and traditional country. It's an excellent collection, epitomizing the best of progressive bluegrass in the '60s and '70s. *—Thom Owens*

Bluegrass 1956-1968 / 1995 / Bear Family ✦✦✦✦✦
Bluegrass 1956-68 is a multi-disc box set that contains everything the Osborne Brothers recorded between those years. During that time they recorded for two major labels, MGM and Decca Records. All the songs the duo released on those two labels, plus alternate takes and unreleased tracks, are included on the box. With all of that material, the set is simply too large for anyone but historians and completists to enjoy. Nevertheless, there's lots of wonderful music on the collection and anyone with the patience (and the funds) to invest in the box will not be disappointed. *—Thom Owens*

Greatest Bluegrass Hits / 1996 / CMH ✦✦✦
Greatest Hits, Vol. 1 is an excellent cross-section of the Osborne Brothers' finest material for MGM Records, including the hits "Poison Love," "Rocky Top" and "Pain in My Heart," making it an excellent introudciton to one of the finest bluegrass bands of the late '50s. *—Thom Owens*

Psychograss

f. 1993

Group / Progressive Bluegrass

Psychograss was one of the most eclectic bands in the history of American string music. Although rooted in the modern sounds of contemporary bluegrass, Psychograss incorporated everything from folk, jazz and classical music to Latin-American rhythms and pop tunes.

A supergroup of top-rated acoustic musicians, Psychograss was conceived by fiddler Darol Anger and mandolin player Mike Marshall. Former members of the innovative David Grisman Quintet, Anger and Marshall had since collaborated as a duo and as members of the chamber music/folk band Montreux, along with pianist Barbara Higbie and bassist Michael Manring. Anger had gone on to form the Turtle Island String Band, while Marshall had formed the Modern Mandolin Quartet. Recruiting string bassist Todd Phillips, a founding member of the Grisman Quintet, Tony Rice's Bluegrass Album Band and Montreux, and current Grisman Quintet percussionist Joe Craven, Anger and Marshall recorded Psychograss' self-titled debut album in 1993. In addition to original instrumentals by Anger and Marshall, the album included a folk-pop rendition of Procol Harum's "A Whiter Shade of Pale" featuring the lead vocals of Tim O'Brien, and a newgrass instrumental by Tony Trischka, "Flanders Rock," with Trischka playing five-string banjo. Anger and Marshall reunited to record a second Psychograss album, *Like Minds*, in 1996 with Trischka and flatpicking guitar virtuoso David Grier added to the group. With each band member contributing an original tune, the album was all originals except for a bluegrass-inspired interpretation of Jimi Hendrix's "Third Stone From the Sun." *—Craig Harris*

• **Psychograss** / 1993 / Windham Hill ✦✦✦✦

Featuring members of the Modern Mandolin Quartet, the David Grisman Quintet, the Turtle Island Quartet and Montreux, the one-shot bluegrass super-group Psychograss turns in a freewheeling, exciting newgrass record with their eponymous album. The group pushes the boundaries as they swing between bluegrass, jazz, country, pop and classical, as they cover everything from bluegrass standards to Procul Harum. It's an unconventional bluegrass album, and all the better for it. *—Thom Owens*

Like Minds / May 21, 1996 / Sugar Hill ✦✦✦✦

If you wanted to take a group of excessively talented musicians and put them together to play inventive instrumental music, you would have something a lot like Psychograss. *Like Minds* offers 60 minutes of jazz, bluegrass, and progressive bluegrass provided by Tony Trischka, David Grier, Todd Phillips, Mike Marshall, and Darol Anger. A traditionally styled reel "Tree King Creek" opens the album, while the lively "Jeremy Reel" continues in this vein. But tradition is left far behind when the band launches into Jimi Hendrix's experimental "Third Stone From the Sun." Psychograss' version is quintessential progressive bluegrass, allowing every member the space to display imaginative lead work within the six-minute structure. Another important element of the group's sound is that, while each player is an accomplished soloist, they are also fully capable of adding textured and resourceful accompaniment. This album is more aggressive and also more willing to explore traditional music than Psychograss' debut; this places it closer in spirit to David Grisman than contemporary jazz. Trischka and Todd Phillips have also written more material on this effort, and the addition of guitarist David Grier has added spice to the mix. Grier provides fresh and occasionally unorthodox solos, full of energy without overplaying. He has also written two songs for the album, including the graceful instrumental "Fuzzy Navel." The song begins slowly, then moves into a rolling pace that ebbs and flows for seven minutes as the musicians trade leads. *Like Minds*' eclectic choice of material is one of the elements that makes acoustic instrumental music so fascinating. Many acoustic musicians have shown a willingness to play in multiple settings as opposed to being associated with one band; Psychograss' second effort shows just how captivating these experiments can be. *—Ronnie Lankford, Jr.*

Reno & Smiley

f. 1951, **db.** 1964

Group / Traditional Bluegrass

Don Reno, Red Smiley, and the Tennessee Cutups were a bluegrass band of such high quality that they gave serious competition to Flatt and Scruggs in the '50s. Don Reno, an unsurpassed master of the banjo, played for Bill Monroe in 1948, replacing Earl Scruggs. With a smooth and mellow baritone, Red Smiley made a perfect partner to Don, singing lead to Don's high harmony part. Don's incredible talent carried over to guitar playing and songwriting—among his compositions are the exquisite "Emotions," as well as "Feuding Banjos." Though both had grown up in rural North Carolina and played with the Morris Brothers, it wasn't until 1949 that Reno and Smiley actually met. Two years later, they formed a band and found moderate success with several sides cut for King early in 1952. By 1956, they were secured a daily morning television show in Roanoke, as well as various shows for a station in Harrisonburg, Virginia. The pair made a handful of recordings for Dot in 1957, but they continued their relationship with King until 1964, recording a wealth of material. At the end of 1964, the pair parted ways after Smiley decided to retire from active performance. Reno remained active in the bluegrass community, cutting numerous records and playing with a variety of collaborators. *—Stephen Thomas Erlewine & David Vinopal*

Instrumentals / 1958 / King ✦✦✦✦

• **Good Old Country Ballads** / 1959 / King ✦✦✦✦✦

Good Old Country Ballads is an original King album from 1959 that collects several singles that the bluegrass Reno & Smiley recorded durign the '50s. There's not any weak tracks on the record, and several songs, including "Country Boy Rock 'n' Roll," rank among their very best. It would ahve been nice to see the compact disc reissue fleshed out with bonus tracks, liner notes or even credits, but it's nice to have the music in any form. *—Thom Owens*

Variety of Country Songs / 1959 / King ✦✦✦✦✦

Like *Good Old Country Ballads*, *A Variety of Country Songs* is an original King album from 1959 that contains several singles Reno & Smiley recorded during the '50s. Where the predecessor concentrated on mid-tempo numbers, the songs on *A Variety* are generally speedier and more infectious, whether it is straightforward bluegrass or country gospel. Taken together with *Good Old Country Ballads*, *A Variety of Country Songs* gives a good idea of the depth of Reno & Smiley's talents. *—Stephen Thomas Erlewine*

16 Greatest Gospel Hits / 1987 / Rounder ✦✦✦✦

16 Greatest Gospel Hits is a solid collection of traditional country gospel tunes—"How I Miss My Darling Mother," "There's a Highway to Heaven," "My Mother's Bible"—as performed by Reno & Smiley. While these perofrmances aren't breathtaking, they're sturdy and engaging and make a nice addition to any comprehensive bluegrass collection. *—Stephen Thomas Erlewine*

Early Years 1951-1959 / 1994 / King ✦✦✦✦✦

Early Years: 1951-1959 is a four-disc box set that presents all of Reno & Smiley & the Tennessee Cutups' recordings for King Records in chronological order, as well as four sides they recorded for Federal as supporting musicians for Tommy Magness. The set contains many of Reno & Smiley's finest and most influential moments, most of which feature the support of bassist John Palmer and fiddler Mack MaGaha. As a historical recording, *Early Years: 1951-59* is invaluable, since it documents the greatest recordings from one of the best bluegrass groups in history. However, it is difficult listen—this is educational listening, and is not intended for entertainment. For musicologists and dedicated fans, it's a necessary purchase, but country and bluegrass fans intending to build a basic bluegrass collection don't need to purchase this set. *—Thom Owens*

On Stage / May 14, 1996 / Copper Creek ✦✦✦✦✦

Tony Rice

b. Jun. 8, 1951, Danville, VA

Vocals, Guitar, Guitar (Acoustic) / Progressive Bluegrass

Tony Rice is one of bluegrass' most inventive flatpicking guitar players. Although he's displayed a mastery of genre's traditions, Rice set the standard for more contemporary styles. A former member of the Bluegrass Alliance, The David Grisman Quintet, J.D. Crowe's New South and The Bluegrass Album Band, Rice has continued to reflect his eclectic approach on solo recordings, two albums with flatpicking guitar ace Norman Blake and two albums, recorded with his brothers Larry, Ron and Wyatt, as The Rice Brothers. In 1996, Rice joined with Chris Hillman, Herb Pederson and his brother Larry to record a tradition-rooted album, *Out of the Woodwork*. *—Craig Harris*

Tony Rice / 1977 / Rounder ✦✦✦✦

This was the first of Tony Rice's many albums for the Rounder label, and hardcore bluegrass fans will probably consider it his best. Joined by an impressive roster of sidemen representing both the old and new schools of bluegrass playing (including David Grisman, J.D. Crowe, Jerry Douglas, and Darol Anger), Rice runs through a program consisting primarily of bluegrass standards but also including a number of forward-thinking modern compositions, such as David Nichtern's *Plastic Banana* and Grisman's swinging *Rattlesnake*. This album is one of the early landmarks in the development of what came to be called New Acoustic Music, an instrumental genre that drew almost equally on bluegrass, jazz, and classical traditions and came to be championed by Rice, Grisman, Anger, and a few others in their circle. But as Rice's warm singing on *Hills of Roane County* and *Banks of the Ohio* and his fiery flatpicking on *Big Mon* and *Farewell Blues* attest, this is also a very fine straight bluegrass album. It's difficult to pick out highlights, but the joyful *Eighth of January* and the wonderful twin fiddle arrangement on *Big Mon* are both definite show-stoppers. *—Rick Anderson*

Acoustics / 1979 / Rounder ✦✦✦✦

Acoustics was released in 1979, some two years after Tony Rice's involvement with the David Grisman Quintet's debut album. Like the Grisman recording, *Acoustics* proved to be a groundbreaking album for progressive bluegrass musicians. The music on *Acoustics* is all instrumental and features an incredible group of musicians including Sam Bush, Richard Greene, Mike Marshall, Todd Phillips, and, on one cut, David Grisman. Perhaps the first thing a listener will notice is that an instrumental like "Swing 51" has very little to do with bluegrass. The essence of "Swing 51" is—as the title suggests—swing jazz. This is a romantic music, inspired by the spirit of Stephane Grapelli and Django Reinhardt and perfectly suited for acoustic instruments. "Blues for Paradise" is a lovely melody, set in motion by Rice's subtle flat-picking and brought to full beauty by Sam Bush's violin. Bush and Greene share violin duties on *Acoustics*, proving especially apt at defining melodies and setting the mood. The highlight of this disc is the quick paced "So Much," a piece bursting with vitality. "So Much" was written by Rice and, like the other songs on *Acoustics*, features open structures with fascinating chord progressions. Emphasis throughout this album is placed on instrumental dexterity, with each musician given the chance to build and develop each lead at length. The musicians also provide unadorned accompaniment, leaving lots of quiet space around the lead player. The glue holding this project together is Rice, who also played a primary role in the original David Grisman Quintet. On this album Rice expands the role of the guitar, building each lead faultlessly through intricate succession. *Acoustics* gives notice that acoustic musicians, like jazz musicians, possess the skills required to create spontaneous and vital music. *—Ronnie D. Lankford, Jr.*

Still Inside / 1981 / Rounder ✦✦✦✦✦

Still Inside is the fourth recording by the Tony Rice Unit and like their previous recordings, it is all acoustic and all instrumental, with emphasis centered on the skill of the individual musicians involved. *Still Inside* features some of the best acoustic musicians on the scene, including mandolin player John Reischman, violinist Fred Carpenter, and bassist Todd Phillips. The strength of the Tony Rice Unit albums also depend on the quality of the material, and on *Still Inside*, Rice draws on more diverse sources than he had on 1980's *Mar West*. This variety spices things up. Standouts include Earl Klugh's "Vonetta," a Latin-tinged instrumental with superb bass work by Phillips, and a relaxed-paced "Tzigani," a David Grisman piece that begins playfully slow, then flies into high gear. Rice's own material, as on the relaxed "Delvin" and the beautifully tender "Moses Sole," is stronger than on the previous album. Another difference this time is that Carpenter and Reischman are new to the group.

Carpenter's violin adds a warm tone while defining melodies, and Reischman follows in the giant footsteps of Sam Bush and Mike Marshall without faltering. Reischman also adds his songwriting talents to the mix on "Birdland Breakdown," creating an odd but rewarding blend of Eastern European and bluegrass music. Rice's flat-picking thrives on the variety of melodies present on *Still Inside,* creating fresh expressions and romantic coloring at his usual swift pace. This album will please Rice fans as well as fans of acoustic music. *—Ronnie Lankford, Jr.*

☆ **Backwaters** / 1982 / Rounder ✦✦✦✦✦
Is it jazz— Is it bluegrass— Is it early new age— At the time of this album's release, Rounder Records was lumping it into a category called "new acoustic music." Call it whatever you choose, this is excellent music, impeccably played by a group of guys who are all virtuosos on their respective instruments. Even the most diehard jazz cop would appreciate the playing, but one needn't be a critic to simply enjoy this collection. Tony Rice may be the finest acoustic guitar picker on the planet, and he also has written some beautiful pieces for this recording. Accompanied by Fred Carpenter and Richard Greene on violins, John Reischman on mandolin, with support from Todd Phillips on standup bass and brother Wyatt Rice on rhythm guitar, Tony Rice takes his music to a whole new place. Every note sounds right, and each member of the ensemble plays with exceptional taste and class. Dave Grusin's "A Child Is Born" is absolutely gorgeous, and the quintet's bluegrass-paced take on "My Favourite Things" is an obvious, but reinvigorating, string-picker's nod to John Coltrane. "On Green Dolphin Street" is reminiscent of Stephane Grapelli and Django Reinhardt on their *Hot Club of France* recordings. After this release, Tony Rice returned to more traditional-sounding folk and bluegrass music, but *Backwaters* is his masterpiece. So, what label can you place on this genre-defying music— How about Rice's own term, "spacegrass." *—Jim Newsom*

River Suite for Two Guitars / 1995 / Sugar Hill ✦✦✦

Rice, Rice, Hillman, and Pedersen / Oct. 5, 1999 / Rounder ✦✦✦✦
With a country and bluegrass music pedigree as long as your right arm, Tony and Larry Rice team up again with Chris Hillman and Herb Pedersen for another musical go-round that finds them all at the top of their game. On the other hand, despite the formidable musical chops of all the players involved, this is not an album full of flashy soloing, but rather a laid-back, reflective session of superlative music that draws from a multitude of sources. Hillman provides a quartet of new compositions and Larry Rice weighs in with "The Side Effects of Life" and "The Year of El Niño," but just as telling are the covers, roping in such diverse sources as the Grateful Dead, Delaney & Bonnie, and Flatt & Scruggs. Every bit as in the pocket as their first outing (1997's *Out of the Woodwork*), this second go-round is solid American music every note of the way. *—Cub Koda*

● **Devlin** / Rounder ✦✦✦✦✦
Devlin collects a selection of material from his Rounder albums of the '70s and '80s, making it a perfect introduction to his music. *—Thom Owens*

Peter Rowan

b. Jul. 4, 1942, Boston, MA
Vocals, Mandolin, Guitar / Contemporary Folk, Progressive Bluegrass
Peter Rowan was one of the major cult bluegrass artists of the '80s, winning a devoted, international fan base through his independent records and constant touring. A skilled singer/songwriter, Rowan also yodeled, and played numerous stringed instruments and the saxophone. After college, he decided to become a professional musician, and in 1963 joined the Cambridge-based Mother Bay State Entertainers as a mandolin player and singer, appearing on their LP *The String Band Project.* In 1964, Rowan became a rhythm guitarist and lead singer with Bill Monroe and his Blue Grass Boys. He remained with them through 1967, leaving to join mandolinist David Grisman in the folk-rock band Earth Opera. After leaving Earth Opera, he became a part of Seatrain, a rock-fusion unit whose records were produced by George Martin. Rowan left the band in 1972 to form the Rowan Brothers with siblings Chris and Lorin, and recorded one eponymous album. After the group disbanded Rowan then recorded *Old & in the Way* with Grisman, Jerry Garcia, Vassar Clements and John Kahn. In 1974, Rowan, Grisman, Clarence White and Richard Greene formed Muleskinner, a bluegrass band. He then reunited the Rowan Brothers, who this time played together until the early '80s. He founded the Nashville-based Wild Stallions in 1983, and throughout the '80s and '90s continued to work with a variety of musicians and tour as a solo act. *—Sandra Brennan*

Peter Rowan / 1978 / Flying Fish ✦✦✦
The solo debut album of this bluegrass vocalist features an original mixture of styles and backing from Flaco Jimenez, Richard Greene, and Tex Logan. *—AMG*

The Walls of Time / 1982 / Sugar Hill ✦✦✦
Walls of Time is a fine slice of traditional bluegrass and country, performed by several of the finest newgrass performers, including Sam Bush, Ricky Skaggs, and the Rowan siblings. Though the album focuses on vocal material, not instrumental, it remains an enjoyable, heartfelt evocation of classic bluegrass by some of the very best progressive bluegrass musicians of the '70s and '80s. *—Thom Owens*

Red Hot Pickers / 1984 / Sugar Hill ✦✦✦
Joining Rowan on this 1995 release are the Red Hot Pickers, a group comprised of Richard Greene, Roger Mason, Andy Statman, and Tony Trischka. The record marks a reunion for Rowan and Greene, both of whom were Blue Grass Boys with Bill Monroe before joining forces in Earth Opera, Sea Train and Muleskinner. *—Jason Ankeny*

The First Whippoorwill / 1985 / Sugar Hill ✦✦✦
The Fisrt Wippoorwill is a tribute album by Peter Rowan to his mentor, Bill Monroe, and it is one of the most moving salutes ever recorded in country music. It isn't moving purely in sentimental terms, either—what makes the record so successful is how Rowan affectionately demonstrates his debt to Monroe with invigorating, lively performances instead of treating the music as a museum piece. Rowan assembled a crackerjack backing band—featuring Buddy Spicher, Sam Bush, Roy Huskey Jr., Bill Keith and Richard Greene—which helps him make one of the best, most focused records of his career. *—Thom Owens*

● **New Moon Rising** / 1988 / Sugar Hill ✦✦✦✦✦
Tight album. Rowan is backed by The Nashville Bluegrass Band. Maura O'Connell sings harmony vocals on "Meadow Green" and Jerry Douglas is featured on dobro. This release set the tune for some real good music. *—Chip Renner*

All on a Rising Day / 1991 / Sugar Hill ✦✦✦✦✦
An all-around fine release. Rowan picks up where he left off on *Dust Bowl* but improves on the idea with some great backup musicians—Stuart Duncan, Sam Bush, Jerry Douglas, Alison Krauss, Roy Husky Jr, Alan O'Bryant, Edgar Meyer. The result is a highly recommended album, boasting 12 solid songs. *—Chip Renner*

Earl Scruggs

b. Jan. 6, 1924, Flint Hill, NC
Vocals, Guitar, Banjo / Traditional Bluegrass
Earl Scruggs is to the five-string banjo what Paganini was to the violin. After more than 20 years with the Foggy Mountain Boys, forming the most famous band in bluegrass history, Scruggs and Lester Flatt parted company in 1969 because of artistic differences, with Flatt pursuing more traditional sounds and Scruggs forming the Earl Scruggs Revue with his two sons. The Revue appealed more to a young and urban audience and, with dobro player Josh Graves, played rock and other non-country music. Scruggs has made many albums since his parting with Flatt (including *The Storyteller and the Banjoman* with Tom T. Hall in 1982) and is seen on TV, often for reunion appearances. *—David Vinopal*

● **Dueling Banjos** / 1973 / Columbia ✦✦✦✦✦

The Seldom Scene

f. 1971
Group / Contemporary Bluegrass, Progressive Bluegrass
"Old-fashioned" was never a word used to describe Seldom Scene's take on bluegrass. Since their inception in 1971, the Washington D.C.-based group remained a driving force in "newgrass" and was considered among the finest modern bands around. The band's founder, John Duffey, had spent 12 years as a charter member of the Country Gentlemen. A rather flamboyant character onstage, he was noted for playing amazing solos on the mandolin, dobro and guitar, and also for his powerful, exceptionally flexible voice. Banjoist Ben Eldridge was a veteran of Cliff Waldron's New Shades of Grass, as was Mike Auldridge, considered among the top dobro players in the world. These three distinguished musicians formed the band's core and remained together through the mid-'90s. Other charter members included former Country Gentleman Tom Gray and John Starling, a former army surgeon. By the summer of 1971 the group was touring on the bluegrass festival circuit and soon found themselves quite popular on the East Coast. The original lineup of the Seldom Scene recorded seven albums for independent Rebel Records in the first half of the '70s. *—Sandra Brennan*

At the Scene / 1983 / Sugar Hill ✦✦✦
Highlighted by a cover of Jackson Browne's "Jamaica, Say You Will" and two original inspirational numbers, *At the Scene* is a typically impressive effort by the Seldom Scene that emphasizes their considerable instrumental and vocal skills. *—Thom Owens*

Blue Ridge / 1985 / Sugar Hill ✦✦✦✦
Songwriter and vocalist Jonathan Edwards ("Sunshine") teams with The Seldom Scene's flawless playing. Featuring Edwards, John Duffey, Mike Auldridge, Phil Rosenthal, Ben Eldridge, Tom Gray, Robbie Magruder, and Kenny White. *—Chip Renner*

● **The Best of Seldom Scene, Vol. 1** / 1987 / Rebel ✦✦✦✦✦
The Best of Seldom Scene, Vol. 1 contains a sampling of the band's best songs from their first four albums and gives a good sense of what the band is about. *—Thom Owens*

15th Anniversary Celebration / 1988 / Sugar Hill ✦✦✦✦✦
This all-star tribute to America's finest progressive bluegrass band took place at *the Kennedy Center* in November of 1986, and featured performances by artists as prominent as Emmylou Harris and Linda Ronstadt and as influential as Charlie Waller, Ricky Skaggs, and Tony Rice. The program is a delight from beginning to end, and includes the band's own renditions of classic material ("Workin' on a Building," "Rose of Old Kentucky") as well as a number of tribute performances by the guest artists. Ricky Skaggs and Sharon White deliver a gorgeous duet version of Townes Van Zandt's "If I Needed You," while Harris and Ronstadt team up on "The Sweetest Gift." Original lead singer John Starling joins the Scene on several songs, and the resulting sound will make longstanding fans of the band wistful for the old days; though mandolinist and tenor singer John Duffey is beginning to sound his age at this point, the old magic is still there on "You Don't Know My Mind" and "Rose of Old Kentucky." The band's rollicking rendition of the traditional gospel classic "Take Me in Your Lifeboat" is the perfect finale. *—Rick Anderson*

Scenic Roots / 1990 / Sugar Hill ✦✦✦
With *Scenic Roots,* Seldom Scene returned to their traditional bluegrass roots. Although the music occasionally sounds forced, much of it is lively and wonderful, making the disc a worthwhile purchase for long-time fans, even if it isn't the place to start with this perrenial bluegrass favorite. *—Thom Owens*

Scene 20: 20th Anniversary Concert / 1991 / Sugar Hill ✦✦✦
For their 20th anniversary, Seldom Scene held a concert and invited all of the former members of the group to join them on stage. Everyone turned up and the results are captured on the splendidly entertaining *Scene 20: 20th Anniversary Concert.* Seldom Scene runs through a wide variety of material, playing everying from traditional bluegrass numbers to Wilson Pickett's "In the Midnight Hour." For fans of the group, this album is an unexpected and totally delightful treat. *—Thom Owens*

Like We Used to Be / 1994 / Sugar Hill ♦♦♦

Dream Scene / Sep. 24, 1996 / Sugar Hill ♦♦♦
In 1995 the Seldom Scene split apart and three of its members left to form the progressive bluegrass band Chesapeake. The remaining members re-formed with Dobro player Fred Travers, lead singer Dudley Connell, and bassist Ronnie Simpkins to record what would be John Duffey's last album. The album begins with the spirited "Dry Run Creek" which tips its hat toward traditional bluegrass. Connell's vocals have a more country flavor than earlier Seldom Scene vocalists like John Starling and Phil Rosenthal, and this quality helps create a more traditional effort from a band known for its progressive tendencies. Despite these changes, the band retains much of its trademark sound and a good deal of credit for this should be given to Fred Travers's excellent Dobro playing. The song choice is also solid, including an excellent version of Jean Ritchie's "Blue Diamond" and "Creedence Clearwater Revival's "Bad Moon Rising." There are lovely moments as when Duffey sings lead on "The Boatman," though it should be noted that his voice lacks the range it once had. The harmony singing on "The Little Sparrow (Fair and Tender Ladies)" even recalls the earlier sound of Duffey's first group, the Country Gentlemen. It is perhaps tempting to use such comparisons to suggest that Duffey is looking back over his long career on *Dream Scene;* but it would be closer to the truth to say that Duffey and the re-formed Seldom Scene are only trying to make good music. Toward that end, they have succeeded. *Dream Scene* is a fine effort for both old and new fans. *—Ronnie Lankford*

Scene It All / May 16, 2000 / Sugar Hill ♦♦♦♦
With the gradual departure of most of its original members and the sudden and untimely death of mandolinist/singer/founder John Duffey in late 1996, one might forgive the Seldom Scene if it had just given up the ghost. But instead, the sole remaining original member (banjoist Ben Eldridge) gathered some of the more recent participants around him (guitarist Dudley Connell, mandolinist Lou Reid, bassist Ronnie Simpkins, and Dobro player Fred Travers) and made one of the better Seldom Scene albums of the last 20 years. The band's reputation as a "progressive" bluegrass band remains intact, though now with a tighter focus: no synthesizers, no electric instruments. But the unusual song selections are still there, from Bruce Springsteen's "One Step Up" to Muddy Waters' "Rollin' and Tumblin'" and the Chuck Berry chestnut "Nadine." As it turns out, those are not the album's high points. Although the band's rendition of "Rollin' and Tumblin'" works very well, the Springsteen tune doesn't sit very comfortably in its arrangement, and "Nadine" is a disaster—the banjo has to play painfully slowly to support the song's rhythm. But the Bill Monroe ("Blue and Lonesome") and Jim & Jesse ("I Will Always Be Waiting for You") numbers are standouts, and the funky bluegrass gospel of "You Better Get Right" is also superb. Maybe it's time for the Seldom Scene to go "acid grass" for good. *—Rick Anderson*

Larry Sparks

b. Sep. 15, 1947, Lebanon, OH
Vocals, Guitar / Traditional Bluegrass, Progressive Bluegrass
One of the finer lead singers in contemporary bluegrass, Larry Sparks filled in with Ralph Stanley's band after the death of the great Carter Stanley, and later went on to head the traditional bluegrass group the Lonesome Ramblers. Sparks was born and raised in Lebanon, Ohio, and began learning to play guitar as a child. In his teens, he played in bluegrass, country and rock bands. In 1966 he cut his first bluegrass single and began his association with the Stanley Brothers' Clinch Mountain Boys. He recorded five albums with the band and stayed through 1969. After that he formed the Lonesome Ramblers. After the mid-'80s, he began recording less frequently and eventually moved to Richmond, Indiana, where he continued to perform on the bluegrass circuit; earning a reputation as one of the premiere bluegrass players, he remained dedicated to preserving the traditional styles of the Stanley Brothers. *—Sandra Brennan & David Vinopal*

Ramblin' Bluegrass / 1972 / Starday ♦♦♦♦

Larry Sparks Sings Hank Williams / 1977 / Rebel ♦♦♦♦♦
Larry Sparks expertly recasts several of Hank Williams' finest songs as bluegrass numbers in *Sings Hank Williams,* one of the finest records he ever released. Of special interest is the supporting band, which features a terrific performance from a young mandolinist named Ricky Skaggs. *—Thom Owens*

The Best of Larry Sparks / 1983 / Rebel ♦♦♦♦♦
Best of Larry Sparks is an adequate collection for this fine traditional bluegrass singer. *—Mark A. Humphrey*

★ **Classic Bluegrass** / 1989 / Rebel ♦♦♦♦♦
Classic Bluegrass collects the highlights of Larry Sparks '70s and '80s albums, which were recorded for a variety of different labels. The compilation hits all the high points of the records, providing a definitive retrospective of his career, as well as an excellent, concise introduction to one of bluegrass' best singers. *—Thom Owens*

Special Delivery / Oct. 10, 2000 / Rebel ♦♦♦♦
Larry Sparks has managed to remain within the fold of traditional bluegrass while also forming a unique style. This style includes hot flatpicking guitar, distinctive vocals, and a steady release of albums. *Special Delivery* finds Sparks with a good batch of songs and strong supporting players. The songs have been penned by a number of writers, but the themes are unified in outlook. Each lyric is imbued with a Southern, rural point of view, which includes championing the virtues of rural living, true love that transcends death (for a girlfriend or mother), and nostalgia for "the way things used to be." "Ghost Stories" tells of driving past abandoned farmhouses and overgrown gardens and leaves the listener with a sense of loss. This song, written by Bill Cook, Bo Jamison, and Jim Benson, captures something deep and elusive, much like Sparks' classic, "John Deere Tractor." "Timberline" is about having a quiet place to go and sort out one's thoughts, a place to "get it straight and head on home again." "Lovin' on Borrowed Time" is a defiant sendoff to a lover who's left for someone new (bluegrass musicians seem to lose women to other men almost as frequently as blues players do). Two instrumentals, "Around the Carousel" and "San Antonio Rose," give Sparks, mandolinist Scott Napier, and banjoist Josh McMurry room for a little picking and grinning. In fact, there really isn't anything bad to say about *Special Delivery,* though one should note its short length (33 minutes). Sparks is in good voice, his friends are in good form, and the 12 songs/instrumentals are good ones. This performance should be a real treat for lovers of traditional bluegrass. *—Ronnie Lankford, Jr.*

The Stanley Brothers

f. 1947, **db.** 1966
Group / Traditional Bluegrass
If you even *think* you know bluegrass, you have to know Ralph (b. 1927) and Carter Stanley (b. 1925), The Stanley Brothers. Parallel to Flatt And Scruggs and Bill Monroe's Blue Grass Boys, though not with their renown, were Virginians Ralph and Carter, mountain boys who took those mountains and their traditions and their songs and wove them into a traditional bluegrass sound of utter purity, simplicity, and astonishing beauty. Their first band, formed around 1947, played more of a mountain/folk music reminiscent of the old string bands, changing to their style of ultra-traditional bluegrass when Bill Monroe's band became popular. Even on their recordings in the early '50s, the Stanleys' unmistakable sound is there, with guitarist Carter singing lead and banjo player Ralph singing tenor harmony. In the opinion of many, Carter possessed the best lead voice in bluegrass history—rich, emotional, and (in the best sense of the word) lonely. He took a happy song and sang it sad; he took a sad song and sang it sadder. And Ralph's unworldly mountain tenor matched his brother's voice perfectly, soaring above and often lightening the emotional load of the lyrics, creating a duet unsurpassed in country history. *—Stephen Thomas Erlewine & David Vinopal*

Hymns and Sacred Songs / 1959 / King ♦♦♦
Hymns and Sacred Songs is an original album that the Stanley Brothers recorded for King Records in 1959. Comprised entirely of classic country gospel numbers, the music on the album is completely beautiful and haunting, thanks the brothers' extraordinary harmonies. *—Thom Owens*

Long Journey Home / 1961 / Rebel ♦♦♦
Long Journey Home features 16 songs that the Stanley Brothers recorded in the early '60s for the Wango record label. Originally released under the name of John's Country Quartet, the songs on the album consist entirely of classic old-timey songs, all of which are delivered with gusto by the brothers and a supporting duo. *—Thom Owens*

Early Years 1958-1961 / 1994 / King ♦♦♦♦
The Early Starday-King Years: 1958-1961 is a 109-track, four-disc box set that compiles every track the Stanley Brothers cut for Starday and King during that era. At the time, the group were releasing albums both on Starday and King, so there was an immense amount of confusion between the releases; the box set helps clarify the matters, by gathering all of the music together and presenting it in chronological order. This way, it's possible to hear their progression, as well as the differences between the recordings for the two labels; on the King recordings, the Stanley Brothers tended to be more experimental, working in electric instrumentation. Though there is plenty of fine music on the set, *The Early Starday-King Years* is, overall, too thorough and extensive for anyone but bluegrass historians. *—Thom Owens*

☆ **Stanley Brothers & The Clinch Mountain Boys 1953-59** / 1994 / Bear Family ♦♦♦♦♦
The Stanley Brothers & the Clinch Mountain Boys, 1953-1958 & 1959 is a double-disc containing everything the group recorded during the latter half of the '50s for Mercury, Starday, and King Records. These recordings are generally considered to be among their best work and this set is the only one to make complete sense of the recordings. All of the group's best moments, plus many forgotten but equally fine gems, are included on the collection, making it a comprehensive retrospective. Nevetheless, it also functions as a good, if rather lengthy, introduction to the Stanley Brothers, since it showcases the richness and depth in their music. In short, it's an essential addition to any serious bluegrass collection. *—Thom Owens*

★ **Angel Band: The Classic Mercury Recordings** / 1995 / Mercury Nashville ♦♦♦♦♦
Angel Band collects the bulk of the Stanley Brothers' mid-'50s recordings, when they were expanding their sound slightly. Although it isn't always straight bluegrass, it shows how versatile and talented the Stanleys were. It's an essential purchase for a bluegrass collection. *—Thom Owens*

★ **Complete Columbia Recordings** / Mar. 1996 / Columbia/Legacy ♦♦♦♦♦
While this doesn't have the two alternate takes that surfaced on the nearly identical Bear Family collection *(1949-1952),* this does have all 22 of the sides they officially released on Columbia, and will be much easier to find in the U.S. It's classic bluegrass of great historical importance, featuring mostly original compositions. *—Richie Unterberger*

Earliest Recordings: Complete Rich-R-Tone 78s (1947-1952) / Jul. 15, 1997 / Revenant ♦♦♦♦♦
This collection gathers the Stanley Brothers' earliest recordings: 78s they cut for the Rich-R-Tone label between 1947 and 1952. Included are traditional gospel songs, breakneck-paced bluegrass ("Molly and Tenbrooks"), and songs of their own that would later become staples ("Little Maggie"). There's some variation in the sound quality, but it isn't bad overall: a light hiss and some mild distortion of the high levels is as bad as it gets. Historic and wonderful, this Stanley Brothers release is a must-have for fans. *—Joslyn Layne*

The Stanley Brothers (1949-1952) / Bear Family ♦♦♦♦♦
All 22 of the their Columbia recordings are here, superbly remastered, including the issued and alternate takes of two classics, "The Fields Have Turned Brown" and "Little Glass of Wine." Carter Stanley's dramatic story songs are underpinned by chilling vocal harmonies and an ensemble sound that bore their unique signature. *—Mark A. Humphrey*

Ralph Stanley

b. Feb. 25, 1927, Stratton, VA
Vocals, Banjo / Truck Driving Country, Contemporary Bluegrass, Traditional Bluegrass, Bluegrass-Gospel
Ralph Stanley and his older brother Carter formed the Stanley Brothers and the Clinch Mountain Boys.Their music, which was inspired by their Virginia mountain home, was en-

couraged by their mother, who taught Ralph the claw-hammer style of banjo picking that he and Carter became famous for. They recorded for such companies as the small Rich-R-Tone label and later Columbia, a relationship that lasted from 1949 until 1952. These classic sessions defined the Stanleys' own approach to bluegrass and made them as important as Bill Monroe. In December of 1966, Carter Stanley died at just 41 years old. After much consideration and grief, Ralph carried on without Carter. Already their haunting mountain melodies made them stand apart from other bluegrass bands, but Ralph expanded upon this foundation and took his own "high lonesome" vocals to a new plane. As far as west as California and even up in the hollars of Kentucky, people were drawn to the poignant, mournful sound of Ralph Stanley's style. Different from all the rest, Ralph's ability to hit the right notes and chords made him a singer of trailblazing proportions. With his raw emotions and Mother Stanley's three-fingered banjo technique, he helped bring the mountain style of bluegrass music to mainstream audiences. —*Jana Pendragon*

I'll Answer the Call / 1987 / Rebel ✦✦✦✦

☆ **Bound to Ride** / 1991 / Rebel ✦✦✦✦✦
This disc collects 20 recordings made in the early 1970s by the legendary Ralph Stanley with his Clinch Mountain Boys, who included, at various times, Ricky Skaggs, Roy Lee Centers, and even the late John Duffey. The fierce, elemental purity of Stanley's sound is captured beautifully on these sessions, many of which feature him playing clawhammer banjo in the style he learned from his mother. But though his banjo playing is very good, it's Stanley's singing that has always set him apart from the rest of the bluegrass pack: his piercing mountain tenor voice and his sanctified delivery almost sound like something from another world. When he sings "Pretty Polly," "Riding the Midnight Train" or, especially, the hair-raising "Man of Constant Sorrow," the effect is visceral and spiritual at the same time. Listening to him blow out the microphone with John Duffey and Roy Lee Centers on "The Lonesome River" is almost literally a religious experience. This is mountain music at its finest. —*Rick Anderson*

Almost Home / 1992 / Rebel ✦✦✦

● **Saturday Night & Sunday Morning** / 1992 / Freeland ✦✦✦✦✦
This 31-cut, two-disc project is a masterpiece reflecting both the secular and spiritual sides of Ralph Stanley's artistry. It is also a concept he mulled over in his mind for some time before executing it. The idea was to include performers from both the country and bluegrass worlds doing songs that somehow fit into the Stanley Brothers' tradition. With the inclusion of some Stanley originals as well as tunes written by Bill Monroe, Dwight Yoakam, Tom T. Hall, and Roy McMillan, this is not only a diverse compilation of material, but also one that never fails to interest the listener. Certainly the start-off number, McMillan's "Mountain Folks," which is done up just right by Ralph Stanley & the Clinch Mountain Boys, sets the tone. Followed by a duet between Stanley and Yoakam on the infectious "Down Where the River Bends," it quickly moves through to Stanley's final secular duet with fellow bluegrasser Bill Monroe. Their teamwork on "Letter From My Darling" is monumental. The spiritual numbers include Stanley and Tom T. Hall on the well-known gospel number "Rank Stranger" and Carter Stanley's sadly descriptive "The Fields Have All Turned Brown." But the most beguiling track is the fervent version of Yoakam's tribute song to his coal mining grandfather, Luther Tibbs. "Miner's Prayer" is given a gospel overhaul, making what was already a brilliant creation into an even more ageless tune that will be played, loved, and remembered for many generations to come. Ralph Stanley's high lonesome sound fits in perfectly here and is endlessly effective. Outstanding performances in both categories come from Patty Loveless, Allison Krauss, George Jones, Jimmy Martin, and Emmylou Harris, to name just a few. A concept that works well for Ralph Stanley and his many friends, this is certainly a project that belongs in every bluegrass or gospel collection. —*Jana Pendragon*

Back to the Cross / Aug. 15, 1992 / Freeland ✦✦✦
Like Bill Monroe, Ralph Stanley maintained his skills and spirit into the 1990s, still singing and picking classic bluegrass. He joined Freeland in 1992, and appropriately made his label debut a gospel session with the Clinch Mountain Boys. You wouldn't expect any surprises, and there weren't any; nor were there low points. The CD contained 12 wonderful renditions of traditional hymns and praise songs performed with the humility, grace and down-home artistry that has always characterized Ralph Stanley's music. —*Ron Wynn*

1971-1973 / Jul. 11, 1995 / Rebel ✦✦✦✦✦
This four-CD set is a collection of the entire output of Ralph Stanley and the Clinch Mountain Boys during an astonishing three-year period in the early '70s. The albums collected here include the first appearance of Stanley's signature a cappella bluegrass gospel, and feature the outstanding lead singing of the late Roy Lee Centers. The strong incarnation of the Clinch Mountain Boys features Curley Ray Cline on fiddle, Jack Cooke on bass, and Ricky Lee on lead guitar. Teenage Stanley disciples and future country stars Keith Whitley and Ricky Skaggs make their first recorded appearances here also, and Country Gentleman John Duffey stops by to max out the needles on the Stanley Brothers classic *The Lonesome River.* The band runs through straight bluegrass, gospel, old-time banjo songs, fiddle tunes, and Stanley Brothers classics, all with great confidence and style. Songs are pulled from multiple and diverse sources, including the Carter Family, old country, Bill Monroe, and even a beautiful Jesse Winchester song, "Brand New Tennessee Waltz." This set is for purists more than bluegrass neophytes, but no fan of Ralph Stanley or the Stanley Brothers should be without it. These albums broke new stylistic ground at a time when there was some concern whether Ralph Stanley could continue in the wake of Carter Stanley's death. —*Ben O'Connor*

My All and All / Jun. 3, 1997 / Rebel ✦✦✦✦

Songs My Mother Taught Me & More: Clawhammer Style Banjo / May 12, 1998 / Freeland ✦✦✦✦
Ralph Stanley is one of very few bluegrass banjo players who still take off the steel fingerpicks occasionally and play in the older, more traditional clawhammer (or "frailing") style. It's a more percussive, less intricate approach, one that carries with it the rough-hewn charm of old-time string band music rather than the flashier, more commercial appeal of bluegrass. This disc collects 18 live and studio recordings in that mode by bluegrass legend Ralph Stanley, some made just a few years ago and others dating as far back as the early 1970s. Many of the tunes will be familiar to Stanley fans—he's recorded "Shout Little Lulie" and "Little Birdie" many times—but others are more obscure. While all of these performances are a delight, it' s the live ones that work the best, partly because he sings more on those; the live performance of "Little Birdie" may be definitive. And the disc ends with an onstage interview in which an unidentified MC gets Stanley to explain his technique in detail. Musician credits would have been helpful to those interested in this recording as a historical document, but the music couldn't be better. —*Rick Anderson*

Clinch Mountain Country / May 19, 1998 / Rebel ✦✦✦✦✦
This two-disc set is a treasure that amazes and inspires at every turn. Dr. Stanley is one of the true greats of American music. Kicking off with an all-time favorite, "How Mountain Girls Can Love," features Stanley's signature claw-hammer banjo style and the distinctive mountain harmonies perfected by himself and his brother, the late Carter Stanley. Other guests from the music world include Dwight Yoakam, Marty Stuart, Bob Dylan, Patty Loveless, BR5-49, Rhonda Vincent, Gillian Welch, Laurie Lewis, Junior Brown, Vern Gosdin, Vince Gill and many others.

One of the most poignant tracks is Stanley, the Clinch Mountain Boys and C*W master $George Jones* singing "The Window up Above." The meeting of Stanley and Jones is a monumental moment in music history. Together their voices blend effortlessly on a song that Jones wrote so many years ago. Also significant is the prominence of Ralph II, the man who will carry on the legacy his father and uncle began in the mountains of Virginia. Ralph Stanley's high lonesome vocal style is unlike any other sound and Dr. Stanley is without peer in the world of bluegrass music. This collection of tunes, many written by Carter and/or Ralph, is evidence of the heartfelt, soul nourishing music the Carters brought out of the western Virginia Highlands and gave to the world. A worthy follow-up to the 1992 two-CD release, *Saturday Night and Sunday Morning.* —*Jana Pendragon*

Carl Story

b. May 29, 1916, Lenoir, NC, **d.** Mar. 30, 1995
Vocals, Fiddle / Country Gospel, Traditional Bluegrass
Fiddler Carl Story was a key figure in the development of gospel bluegrass music throughout his decades-long career. In the mid-'30s, he and teen-age banjoist Johnnie Whisnant joined the Lonesome Mountaineers. From there the two founded the Rambling Mountaineers, playing at various radio stations and making the occasional record until Story left to become a fiddler for Bill Monroe and his Blue Grass Boys. In 1943, he left Monroe to join the Navy. Following his discharge, Story reassembled the Rambling Mountaineers; as they moved from station to station, the membership changed and many of the members, such as Tater Tate and the Brewster Brothers, went on to become important bluegrass figures. Story and his group began recording secular and gospel songs for Mercury in 1947, and remained with the label until 1952. He moved to Columbia the following year and recorded over a dozen singles. Although his music was close to bluegrass, Story and his band did not become full-fledged bluegrass players complete with banjo, mandolin and dobro until 1957. Story began recording less frequently during the '70s, but still continued touring. On occasion, he also worked as a deejay at WSEC Greenville, South Carolina —*Sandra Brennan*

Late and Great Carl Story / 1995 / Kingdom ✦✦✦
The Late and Great Carl Story features 14 bluegrass renditions of such gospel standards as "Old Time Religion," "Cry Holy Unto the Lord," and "Unclouded Day." A cover of "Daddy Sang Bass" displays a sense of humor, and the performances in general are spirited and affecting. The packaging offers minimal liner notes and no recording information, so it is difficult to say when these recordings were made, but the collection is an otherwise pleasing anthology of recordings by an under-recognized bluegrass heavyweight. —*Greg Adams*

● **16 Greatest Hits** / Starday ✦✦✦✦✦

IIIrd Tyme Out

f. 1991
Bass (Electric), Mandolin, Guitar, Fiddle / Contemporary Bluegrass, Contemporary Folk
IIIrd Tyme Out is one of the leading bluegrass vocal groups of the 1990s. Formed in 1991 by lead vocalist and guitarist Russell Moore, fiddler Mike Hargrove and bass vocalist and electric bass player Ray Deaton, shortly after they left Doyle Lawson & Quicksilver, the Georgia-based quintet has received numerous "vocal group of the year" awards from the International Bluegrass Music Association (IBMA) and the Society For The Preservation Of Bluegrass Music In America (SPBGMA). While most of their repertoire centers around the bluegrass and country songs of Bill and Charlie Monroe, The Delmore Brothers, The Carter Family, Hank Williams and Jimmie Rodgers, the group has been equally effective with Gospel material. Their 1996 album, *"Living On The Other Side,"* was an all-Gospel recording that included the Lester Flatt tune, "I'm Working On A Road To Gloryland," with guest Earl Scruggs on guitar. The song became a top ten country hit and was named "Song of the year" by the IBMA. In addition, IIIrd Tyme Out was named "Best Contemporary Gospel Group" by the SPBGMA in 1997 and 1998.

Strengthened by the soulful singing of Moore, a three time winner of the SPBGMA's award for "Best Contemporary Male Vocalist" and the recipient of the IBMA's award as "Best Male Vocalist' in 1994 and 1997, and the deep vocal tones of Deaton, IIIrd Tyme Out is the product of a group effort. Mandolin player and harmony vocalist Wayne Benson replaced Alan Bibey and banjo player Barry Abernathy replaced Terry Baucom shortly before the band recorded their third album, *"Grandpa's Mandolin"* in 1993. Abernathy was subsequently replaced by Steve Dilling. IIIrd Tyme Out continues to set the pact for bluegrass singing. The group was named "Vocal Group Of The Year" by the IBMA in 1998, returning in 1999 with *John and Mary.* —*Craig Harris*

● **Living on the Other Side** / 1996 / Rounder ✦✦✦✦✦
IIIrd Tyme Out is a great group. Their warmth, subtlety, and rollicking spirit have earned

them tremendous praise from all corners of the country music industry. It is well deserved, for there isn't a song on *Living on the Other Side* that doesn't capture the glory of bluegrass' greatest acts while simultaneously strengthening the genre for the next century. Their first all gospel album features Earl Scruggs on a cover of "I'm Working on the Road to Gloryland" and traditional tunes in outstanding arrangements. IMBA awarded them Vocal Group of the Year in 1994, 1995, and 1998. *—Jim Smith*

John & Mary / Oct. 5, 1999 / Rounder ✦✦✦
One of the first albums to feature a number of Third Tyme Out originals, *John & Mary* marks the band's baby steps away from tradition. The well-crafted vocal harmonies are still there (sometimes singing doo wop), as well as tight bluegrass-style instrumentation. A number of gospel classics also make appearances. The addition of Blue Highway's Rob Ickes excellent Dobro playing adds texture to about half of the songs. A few songs stand out as favorites: their cover of the Loretta Lynn song "I Pray My Way Out of Trouble" sounds spare and hopeful, and "Milk Cow Blues" provides one more turn for a song that has had a long history of interpretation. Among the original songs on the album, "Bobby and Millie" stands out (even with its somewhat precious lyrics) as a beautiful example of what this band will be capable of in the future. *—Stacia Proefrock*

Tony Trischka

b. Jan. 16, 1949, Syracuse, NY
Banjo / Contemporary Bluegrass, Progressive Bluegrass
The avant-garde banjo sylings of Tony Trischka inspired a whole generation of progressive bluegrass musicians; he was not only considered among the very best pickers, he was also one of the instrument's top teachers, and created numerous instructional books, teaching video tapes and cassettes. In 1965, he joined the Down City Ramblers, where he remained through 1971. That year, Trischka made his recording debut on *15 Bluegrass Instrumentals* with the band Country Cooking; at the same time, he was also a member of Country Granola. Between 1974 and 1975, he recorded two solo albums, *Bluegrass Light* and *Heartlands.* After one more solo album in 1976, *Banjoland,* he went on to become musical leader for the Broadway show *The Robber Bridegroom.* In the early 1980s, he began recording with his new group Skyline, which recorded its first album in 1983. *—Sandra Brennan*

Fiddle Tunes for Banjo / 1981 / Rounder ✦✦✦✦
What unites these three banjo players is their shared status as stylistic innovators on an instrument that, to most people, embodies strict traditionalism. There's still debate as to whether Trischka or Keith originated the "melodic" style of bluegrass banjo playing, one which tends to follow the melody exactly and fill in the spaces with scalar embellishments, rather than hitting occasional melody notes from within cascades of arpeggios, as is the practice in traditional, Scruggs-style picking. Neither Trischka nor Keith has proved willing to claim precedence over the other, so the debate may never be settled. At the time of this recording, Bela Fleck (who would later go on to great fame playing a sort of banjo-based jazz fusion) was a young player expanding the boundaries of the Trischka/Keith school. On most of the program, the banjoists take turns leading separate groups through bluegrass standards such as "Black Mountain Rag" and "Fiddler's Dream" (as well as unusual fare like the Irish tune "Paddy Kelly's Jig"), but on the two bonus cuts provided on this CD reissue, the three team up for barnstorming trio arrangements of "Bill Cheatham" and "John Hardy." Needless to say, the playing is amazing, but you don't have be a banjo player to enjoy the rapport these guys share or the music they make. *—Rick Anderson*

Skyline Drive / 1986 / Flying Fish ✦✦✦✦
With *Skyline Drive,* Tony Trischka injects progressive bluegrass techniques into the smooth, post-Urban Cowboy country-pop. While Trischka isn't as technically skilled as Bela Fleck or Ricky Skaggs, he is more accessible to a mainstream country audience on this album. For most bluegrass fans, of both traditional and progressive persuasions, the pop concessions are a bit hard to swallow, yet there are some very strong—mainly instrumental—that make it a worthwhile listen. *—Thom Owens*

● **Dust on the Needle** / 1988 / Rounder ✦✦✦✦✦
A good collection of Trischka's six Rounder albums, featuring Sam Bush, Marc O'Connor, and David Grisman. *—Chip Renner*

World Turning / 1993 / Rounder ✦✦✦
One man's exploration of the history of the banjo, *World Turning* is not for the bluegrass purist. The styles here vary as widely as the guests, from the dusty afternoon of William Burroughs' voice narrating the simple playing of "The Boatman's Dance/Over the Mountains" to the Violent Femmes helping out on "Down In the Cider House," which sounds remarkably like the Velvet Underground at times. In such an ambitious project, there are bound to be moments not to an individual's taste, but on the whole, this experiment is a success, with Trischka's grasp of his instrument complete. *—Jeff Crooke*

Bend / May 4, 1999 / Rounder ✦✦✦
Bend is an accurate title, since if Tony Trischka does anything, he bends the conventions of bluegrass. He's been doing that for years, but that doesn't mean that later records such as *Bend* are any less interesting than his earlier efforts. Although the music is essentially in the same vein as his '70s and '80s work, Trischka still finds way to make his blend of bluegrass, jazz, folk and country sound new. *Bend* may not be as consistent as some of his other albums, but the best moments illustrate that he's still an inventive, compelling musicians and a fine songwriter to boot. *Bend* will not surprise anyone familiar with his music, but it will sound fresh to neophytes—and that's quite a claim indeed. *—Stephen Thomas Erlewine*

Frank Wakefield

b. Jun. 26, 1934, Emory Gap, TN
Vocals, Mandolin / Instrumental Country, Traditional Bluegrass, Progressive Bluegrass
One of the chief innovators on the mandolin, Frank Wakefield played straight bluegrass with a number of well-known bands, including Red Allen and the Greenbriar Boys. Born into a musical family in Emory Gap, Tennessee, by age eight he already knew how to play harmonica, guitar and bass. In 1950, his family moved to Dayton, Ohio and soon afterward, he took up the mandolin and formed the gospel-oriented Wakefield Brothers with sibling Ralph, who played guitar. In 1951, the brothers made their first radio appearance in Dayton. After the duo split up, Frank teamed with Red Allen in 1952 to form Red Allen & Frank Wakefield and the Kentuckians. They remained partners through 1972, occasionally pursuing side-projects as well. It with Allen that Wakefield mastered the banjo and dobro, and when he moved with Allen to Washington, D.C. in 1960 he began offering private mandolin lessons; his star pupil was a young David Grisman. Wakefield joined the Greenbriar Boys in 1965 and remained with them through 1970. He also founded the Good Ol' Boys, and in 1971 recorded *The Frank Wakefield Band.* He cut *Pistol Packin' Mama* in 1974 with Don Reno, Jerry Garcia, Dave Nelson and Chubby Wise. He also continued to teach, and released an instructional video. *—Sandra Brennan & David Vinopal*

Pistol Packin' Mama / 1974 / Round ✦✦✦✦✦
Wakefield and David Nelson (New Riders) give a more San Francisco sound to this album, with Jerry Garcia producing "Ashes of Love," "Dim Lights, Thick Smoke," and "Glendale Train." All excellent. *—Chip Renner*

Blues Stay Away from Me / Rounder ✦✦✦
While John Delafose & the Eunice Playboys are zydeco's finest traditional band, they're also gifted at doing blues and R&B hybrids. They find a comfortable middle ground on this release, mixing modern numbers like the title track, "Make Me Yours," and "Don't You Leave Me" with such vintage tracks as "Old Time Two Step," "Oh 'Tit Fille," and "Mamou Two Step." Delafose and his son Geno alternate lead vocals and accordion support, with John having the stronger, more authoritative voice, but Geno steadily gaining in experience, depth, and intensity. The band offers everything from swaying waltzes to brisk two-steps and hard-hitting blues/R&B, all done with passion and distinction. *—Ron Wynn*

● **Frank Wakefield with Country Cooking** / Rounder ✦✦✦✦✦
A fine bluegrass album. Wakefield is backed by Country Cooking, featuring Peter Wernick, Tony Trischka, Russ Barenberg, and Kenny Kosek. *—Chip Renner*

Clarence White

b. Jun. 7, 1944, Lewiston, ME, **d.** Jul. 14, 1973, Palmdale, CA
Vocals, Guitar / Country-Rock, Progressive Country, Traditional Bluegrass, Progressive Bluegrass
Clarence White was a gifted guitarist who was one of the pioneers of country-rock in the late '60s. Although he died young, his work with the Byrds and the Kentucky Colonels, among others, remained celebrated among country-rock and bluegrass aficionados in the decades following his death. White began playing the guitar at an early age, joining his brothers' band, the Country Boys, when he was just ten years old. The band eventaully evolved into the Kentucky Colonels. Clarence left the Colonels in the mid-'60s, becoming a session musician; Clarence recorded a solo album for Bakersfield International which the label didn't release. In 1968, White joined Nashville West, which recorded an album for Sierra Records, but the record didn't appear until 1978. White was invited to join the Byrds in the fall of 1968, fitting into the revamped band's country-rock direction. He played on the group's untitled album, which spawned the single "Chestnut Mare." Once the Byrds disbanded in 1973, White continued his session work and joined Muleskinner. He had only completed four tracks for a projected solo album when he was killed by a drunken driver while loading equipment onto a van; he died on July 14, 1973. *—Stephen Thomas Erlewine*

● **Clarence White & the Kentucky Colonels** / 1980 / Rounder ✦✦✦✦✦
Clarence White & the Kentucky Colonels includes 1964-1967 live performances that are musts for bluegrass guitar enthusiasts. White was a member of The Byrds and a session player for Linda Ronstadt and the Everly Brothers. *—Richard Lieberson*

Vern Williams

b. 1930
Vocals, Mandolin / Traditional Bluegrass
Vern Williams is one of the great unheralded masters of bluegrass music, a mandolin virtuoso who was a star in California throughout the 1960s, '70s, and '80s, and an influence on an entire generation of players, but who is little known beyond the confines of the Golden State. His relative handful of recordings, either as a member of Vern & Ray in the 1960s or leading the Vern Williams Band in the 1970s, don't begin to indicate his importance to bluegrass music.

Williams grew up in rural Newton County, Arkansas. Raised as a member of a musical family, he played guitar until receiving his first mandolin at the age of 17. His professional experience began in 1959 when he met fiddle-player Ray Park and the two formed a duo. Vern & Ray thrived in California, became known as one of the best bluegrass outfits in the region, and got a contract with Nashville-based Starday Records in the early '60s. The group found little opportunity to perform in Nashville, where traditional bluegrass acts were usually kept at arm's length. The group stuck it out for more than a decade, but disbanded in 1974. After the break-up of Vern & Ray, Williams formed a new group with his son and a handful of bluegrass musicians, calling themselves the Vern Williams Band. In less than a year after their debut, they were pegged as one of the powerhouse bluegrass outfits on the West Coast. In 1980, they were signed to Rounder Records and their 1981 release, *Bluegrass from the Gold Country,* was a regional success. The group also toured as Rose Maddox' backing band, but this did little to bring them to the attention of a national audience. Finally, in 1986, the Vern Williams Band broke up. *—Bruce Eder*

Bluegrass from the Gold Country / 1996 / Rounder ✦✦✦✦✦
An expanded version of the Vern Williams Band's only Rounder album, containing the complete original LP as released in 1981 and nine additional cuts recorded by the group in 1980. A very solid representation of the group's repertory, from bluegrass standards like A.P. Carter's "Foggy Mountain Top" and "When the Springtime Comes Again" and Bill Monroe's "You Better Get Right," to Stephen Foster's "Oh, Susannah" and "Old Black Joe," as well as

traditional numbers like "The Arkansas Traveler." It's nearly an hour of some of the best West Coast bluegrass music to show up since Chris Hillman gave up the mandolin and the Hillmen in favor of playing bass with the Byrds, all very nicely remastered and thoroughly annotated. *—Bruce Eder*

Mac Wiseman (Wiseman, Malcolm B.)

b. May 23, 1925, Waynesboro, VA

Vocals, Guitar / Truck Driving Country, Contemporary Bluegrass, Traditional Bluegrass, Progressive Bluegrass

Famed for his clear and mellow tenor voice, Mac Wiseman recorded with many great bluegrass bands, including those of Molly O'Day, Flatt and Scruggs, Bill Monroe, and the Osborne Brothers; his command of traditional material made him much in demand by bluegrass and folk fans alike. Possessing one best tenor voices in bluegrass, Wiseman differed from Monroe and Flatt & Scruggs in that he usually sang alone, with little or no harmonizing. After forming his own group, the Country Boys, in the '50s, Wiseman recorded many popular local singles and had his first national Top Ten hit with his version of "The Ballad of Davy Crockett." The song's success steered him away from bluegrass and more towards pop and country. During the '60s, Wiseman recorded for Dot and Capitol before moving to Nashville in 1969. He signed with RCA Victor, and recorded three well-received bluegrass albums with Lester Flatt. From the mid-'70s on, he concentrated on bluegrass, becoming a fixture at festivals and releasing a series of records on independent records that ran into the '90s. In 1992, Wiseman narrated the documentary *High Lonesome,* a chronicle of bluegrass music, and in 1993 was inducted into the Bluegrass Hall of Fame. *Mac, Doc and Del* followed in 1998. *—Sandra Brennan & David Vinopal*

The Mac Wiseman Story / 1976 / CMH ✦✦✦✦✦
The best of Mac Wiseman. A good place to start. *—Chip Renner*

Early Dot Recordings, Vol. 1 / 1985 / County ✦✦✦✦✦
Early Dot Recordings, Vol. 1 contains the earliest recordings Mac Wiseman made for Dot Records, including "Ballad of Davy Crockett," and while they aren't quite as consistently terrific as the material that comprises the two later volumes, there still plenty of first-rate songs here. *—Thom Owens*

Classic Bluegrass / 1987 / Rebel ✦✦✦
Classic Bluegrass captures a 1976 recording session where Mac Wiseman re-recorded many of his earlier hits, plus a handful of new material. Instead of being tired retreads, these new versions nearly equal the originals, since Wiseman's voice has matured and is rich with nuance. *Classic Bluegrass* may not be the definitive Mac Wiseman album, yet it comes very close to fulfilling that bill. *—Thom Owens*

Early Dot Recordings, Vol. 2 / 1988 / Rebel ✦✦✦✦✦
Early Dot Recordings, Vol. 2 picks up where the first volume left off, featuring some of the best early recordings Mac Wiseman made, including the hit "Jimmy Brown the Newsboy." *—Thom Owens*

Grassroots to Bluegrass / 1990 / CMH ✦✦✦
Grassroots to Bluegrass is a 22-track album which feature some outstanding vocals from Wiseman. A Grammy nominee and a tasty one at that. *—Chip Renner*

● **Early Dot Recordings, Vol. 3** / 1992 / Rebel ✦✦✦✦✦
Early Dot Recordings, Vol. 3 (the first two volumes were released only on vinyl) is a compilation of highlights that Mac Wiseman recorded for Dot Records in the early '50s, and contain some of his finest performances. *—Thom Owens*

20 Old-Time Country Favorites / Jul. 22, 1997 / Rural Rhythm ✦✦✦
The 20 tracks on this CD (recorded in the mid-'60s) aren't bluegrass, but rather mostly-acoustic country with drums and occasional flourishes such as electric guitar leads with effects. As the title suggests, the songs include standards such as "Corina Corina," "Rovin' Gambler," and "Turkey in the Straw" in brief renditions; most tracks are under two minutes in length, and a few songs are barely over a minute long. The performances are interesting and entertaining, and will certainly please those who don't get too worked up over modern influences creeping into "old time" music. *—Greg Adams*

Mac, Doc & Del / 1998 / Sugar Hill ✦✦✦✦
Joined by Alison Krauss, Jerry Douglas and Rob and Ronnie McCoury, among others, this is a treasure created by three of very recognizable voices from the world of bluegrass music. And these Groovegrass Boyz never sounded better! An exciting adventure that includes some pretty fancy fiddle work by Jason Carter. The senior McCoury is bright and meaningful on "The Old Accent" and solidly traditional on "Speak to Me Little Darlin." Wiseman is superb vocally on "When a Soldier Knocks." These three masters blend their voices effortlessly throughout, as "Live and Let Live" displays. The McCoury family is unstoppable as they join Carter and bassman Mike Bubb to perform an energetic rendition of "I've Endured." Don Reno's notable tune "Talk of the Town" is a masterpiece, when McCoury, Wiseman and Watson team up to create a stunning moment. The standard "I Wonder Where You Are Tonight" is exceptional as their clear harmonies rise and fall magically. Emotionally satisfying, this is a special project within the scope of traditional American music. *—Jana Pendragon*

Various Artists

☆ **Appalachian Stomp: Bluegrass Classics** / 1995 / Rhino ✦✦✦✦✦
Like many Rhino compilations, this is geared more to the novice or the casual fan than the aficionado, but that's not a criticism. If someone wants a basic primer of the bluegrass sound past and present that manages to be accessible and avoid unduly clichéd track selection, this 18-song compilation fits the bill well. Most of the biggest names are here (Bill Monroe, Flatt & Scruggs, the Dillards, the Stanley Brothers, the Kentucky Colonels, J.D. Crowe, Ricky Skaggs, Alison Krauss), as are some of the genre's top standards ("Blue Moon of Kentucky," "Orange Blossom Special," "Uncle Pen," "Foggy Mountain Breakdown"). The inclusion of Flatt & Scruggs' "The Ballad of Jed Clampett," Eric Weissberg & Steve Mandell's "Dueling Banjos," and The Nitty Gritty Dirt Band's "Will the Circle Be Unbroken" may rankle purists, but it clears the path to listeners who are only familiar with the idiom through these songs, and may find a lot more that they'll like on the less overexposed performances on this anthology. *—Richie Unterberger*

Appalachian Stomp: More Bluegrass Classics / Apr. 20, 1999 / Rhino ✦✦✦✦
With some of the genre's most recognizable songs having already been used, *Appalachian Stomp: More Bluegrass Classics* isn't quite up to the level of the first *Appalachian Stomp* collection, which remains one of the best introductory bluegrass surveys available. However, it does maintain a similarly high standard of quality, featuring selections by legends like Bill Monroe, Flatt & Scruggs, Ralph Stanley, J.D. Crowe, Alison Krauss, the Stanley Brothers, and many others. It's a great way for bluegrass neophytes to sample more top-notch material after being hooked in by the first volume. *—Steve Huey*

Bluegrass Essentials / Apr. 7, 1998 / Hip-O ✦✦✦✦
18-track collection featuring selections from everyone from Bill Monroe to Vince Gill. With selections from Jim and Jesse, J.D. Crowe, Ricky Skaggs, Allison Krauss, Jimmy Martin, the Dillards (who played the Darlings on the *Andy Griffith Show*), *Reno & Smiley,* Flatt and Scruggs, the Stanley Brothers, Claire Lynch, Del McCoury, Jonathan Edwards, Chesapeake and the Country Gentlemen, it's extremely hard to find fault with any of the artists or selections aboard. A great value in the midline field. *—Cub Koda*

Bluegrass Masters / 1996 / Vanguard ✦✦✦✦✦
The title doesn't lie—this disc has 21 tracks by three of the best acts in the field (Bill Monroe, Flatt & Scruggs, and Jim & Jesse McReynolds), recorded live at the 1965 and 1966 Newport Folk Festivals. The sound and performances are good, and each act presents some familiar favorites—the McReynolds offer "Dueling Banjos" and "Sugarfoot Rag," Monroe does "Shady Grove" and "Cotton-Eyed Joe," and Flatt & Scruggs play "Orange Blossom Special," "Foggy Mountain Chimes," and "The Ballad of Jed Clampett." A youthful Peter Rowan, then a guitarist with Monroe, does a duet vocal with the bandleader on "Walls of Time." *—Richie Unterberger*

Mountain Music of Kentucky / Mar. 19, 1996 / Smithsonian/Folkways ✦✦✦✦✦
In 1959, John Cohen of the New Lost City Ramblers made field recordings in the mountains of Kentucky of Appalachian folk performers who were virtually unknown to the record-buying public. This is no-nonsense, sometimes raw stuff, with fiddlers, banjos, a cappella singers, and Baptist church choirs presenting folk standards, blues-influenced numbers, stomping bluegrass, even the odd country song. It's got as much of the unadulterated American white folk feel as the older recordings on Harry Smith's *Anthology of Folk Music* box (to use a celebrated example), though the material here is of better fidelity. Although some of these artists would make other recordings, only Roscoe Holcomb–the most passionate and arresting of them—would gain anything like substantial recognition. This is too basic and unschooled, not to mention too long, to hold the attention of the average folk or bluegrass fan, but scholars and roots aficionados will value its no-frills authenticity. Originally issued as a single LP in 1960, the two-CD reissue adds an hour of previously unreleased material, and lengthy historical liner notes by John Cohen. *—Richie Unterberger*

Poor Man, Rich Man: American Country Songs of Protest / 1989 / Rounder ✦✦✦✦✦
Recorded between 1923 and 1936, these 16 country and old-timey songs comment upon the conditions of the time, particularly the struggles of workers, miners, and the Depression. The "protest" factor is muted in comparison with, say, 1960s folk singers or even Woody Guthrie; these are more like reflections of the difficulties of the common man than statements of anger or defiance. Whether you're in this for the social commentary or not, it's a pretty respectable collection of vintage country and folk on purely musical terms, with selections by major figures such as Uncle Dave Macon, Fiddlin' John Carson, Gene Autry, the Dixon Brothers, Ernest Stoneman, and Blind Alfred Reed, along with several less famed performers. *—Richie Unterberger*

That's Bluegrass!: CMH Records 20th Anniversary Collection / Jul. 11, 1995 / CMH ✦✦✦✦✦
Two discs, 40 cuts, 20 years of bluegrass selections from CMH. Just about every bluegrass style you can think of is represented here, with examples from Lester Flatt, the Stonemans, the Eddie Adcock Band, Joe Maphis, Mac Wiseman, Vassar Clements, Bill Monroe and more. It's a spectacular collection (to say the least), lots of fun, and a great introduction to the art and science of bluegrass. *—Steven McDonald*

FOLK

In its widest possible application, "folk music" refers to music composed and performed by amateurs and passed down in an oral tradition devoid of formal training. In this sense, folk music is not only the ballads that derive from the Scots and the Irish and that have descended from the Appalachian Mountains, it is also the rural blues of the Mississippi Delta and the drum-heavy music of northwestern Africa, not to mention any other tribal or traditional genres.

In the 20th century in the US, however, the definition of folk music has tended to narrow over time, as other musical styles have encroached on it. Thus, though the Carter Family was an obvious influence on Woody Guthrie, and though they played their traditional music on acoustic instruments and sang it with untrained voices, we think of them as country musicians, not folk ones. Woody Guthrie, however, is resolutely categorized as folk, even though he introduced two main innovations to the form: first, he moved to the city, and second, he wrote his own songs.

It is probably the second factor that's the most important. By the early post-WWII era, Guthrie's songs were getting pop treatments in the hands of the Weavers, and by the mid-'50s, two distinct camps had sprung up, both of whom benefited from the boomlet of popular interest in folk music that lasted roughly from the 1955 Weavers comeback concert at Carnegie Hall (after years of blacklisting) to the summer day in 1965 when Bob Dylan turned up on stage at the Newport Folk Festival with an electric guitar in his hands.

The first camp followed in Guthrie's footsteps, writing their own songs and singing them in some approximation of Guthrie's Oklahoma accent. This camp tended to be more political and artistic, and most of them were individuals. Dylan was the most prominent of them, though Phil Ochs, Tom Paxton, Dave Van Ronk, and many others were included The second camp followed in the footsteps of the Weavers, singing the songs of others (including many of the Child ballads, but also songs written by those in the first camp) in sweet harmonies and clearly enunciated phrases. This camp tended to be apolitical and entertainment-oriented, and most of them were singing groups. Peter, Paul, and Mary were preeminent in this camp, along with the Kingston Trio, the Limeliters, and others. Joan Baez started in the second camp and gradually moved to the first.

After 1965, the first camp merged with pop and rock 'n' roll, especially the "sensitive singer/songwriter" school of the early '70s, and the second camp retreated into a nostalgic past. By the end of the '70s the folk boom was over, but folk music remained healthy, continuing to flourish in the places it always had—in hundreds of small clubs spread across the US and Europe and at dozens of summer festivals. A new crop of singer/songwriters was emerging, and if they didn't have the clear road to national recognition enjoyed by their '60s forebears, they were nevertheless gradually able to build up reputations on a viable circuit, record their own tapes, and even eventually move up to independent labels like Flying Fish and Rounder.

You will find in the listings that follow, therefore, records by the old hands (many of them reissued on CD in recent years) and a healthy sampling of those younger artists operating in what is now, as perhaps it always should have been, a highly decentralized field. It's likely that many of those names will be unfamiliar, but the reader is encouraged to try out a recording or two by the new folk acts and to keep an eye out for their appearances in local venues. That's where folk music lives today. *—William Ruhlmann*

Artist Reviews

Pat Alger

Vocals, Guitar / Contemporary Singer/Songwriter, Contemporary Folk, Contemporary Country

Pat Alger, who is among the most successful country songwriters of the late '80s and early '90s, comes from a folk background, and that colors the unusually thoughtful, articulated songs he writes. He first turned up on record himself playing guitar and singing with the loosely constructed Woodstock Mountains Revue on the album *More Music from Mud Acres* in 1977. Alger really began to gain recognition as a songwriter with the release of Nanci Griffith's third album, *Once in a Very Blue Moon,* in 1985. Alger co-wrote the title song, which reached the country charts in 1986. Alger was co-author of the title song on Griffith's 1987 album, *Lone Star State of Mind,* and that song became a Top 40 country hit. In 1988, Kathy Mattea's version of his "Goin' Gone" hit the top of the country charts. In 1990, Mattea took Alger and Fred Koller's "She Came from Fort Worth" to number two. It's no surprise, then, that when Alger came to record his debut album, *True Love & Other Short Stories,* in 1991, he was able to call on the help of the cream of the young Nashville writers and performers. Trisha Yearwood, Nanci Griffith, Mary Black, Ashley Cleveland, Kathy Mattea, and Lyle Lovett all turn up, though Alger himself is the focus, singing his best-known songs. *—William Ruhlmann*

● **True Love & Other Short Stories** / 1991 / Sugar Hill ✦✦✦✦✦
This country/folk songwriter sings his own versions of such hits as "Lone Star State of Mind" and "Goin' Gone." Guests include Nanci Griffith and Kathy Mattea. *—William Ruhlmann*

Seeds / 1994 / Sugar Hill ✦✦✦
Produced by Jim Rooney, this album contains a baker's dozen of new Alger songs, including his Garth Brooks hit "The Thunder Rolls." Alger is supported by such artists as Tim O'Brien, Trisha Yearwood, Kathy Mattea and the solid Roy Husky Jr. While most of these tracks are good, straight, coverable country-folk songs, some have a deeper irony such as the final song, "Unanswered Prayers." *—Richard Meyer*

Almanac Singers

f. 1941, New York, NY, **db.** 1942
Group / Political Folk, Traditional Folk

The Almanac Singers lasted for barely a year and only left behind three dozen songs, and their work was at least as controversial as it was popular. But they were among the very first folk music groups organized for political purposes to record, and their lineup—Pete Seeger, Lee Hayes, Woody Guthrie, and Millard Lampell—was a virtual "who's who" of topical and popular folk music for the next 20 years. They were the group where Seeger first hooked up officially with Hayes, as well as the first direct link in the careers of Seeger, Hayes, and Guthrie, and their influence lingers more than 50 years after they disbanded.

The Almanac Singers had their start in 1940, when Pete Seeger, Lee Hayes, and Millard Lampell first got together informally. Woody Guthrie signed on in 1941, and the group became a popular fixture at union meetings and fund-raising events for various left-wing political groups. They also entered the studio, and recorded two albums (Songs for John Doe, Talking Union) that spring. In July, the group cut a new series of songs of a somewhat less political nature, to raise money to make a trip to California. The resulting songs later appeared in two albums, initially issued on 78 r.p.m. disc and later as LPs, and finally on a single CD, entitled Sod Buster Ballads and Sea Chanties.

After the group was featured in the 1942 radio broadcast *This Is War,* it looked as though a national radio contract and a recording deal with a major label would follow. But then newspapers began running stories about the group's political history and isolationist position, and any radio or recording deals were forgotten. The members became scattered to the needs of the American war effort, and the Almanacs dissolved, although Seeger and Hayes later formed the Weavers. Ironically, despite his being crippled by Huntington's disease, which ended his career after the mid-'50s, Guthrie went on to have the greatest influence of all, with the help of self-proclaimed disciple Bob Dylan. —Bruce Eder

☆ **Talking Union & Other Union Songs** / 1973 / Smithsonian/Folkways ✦✦✦✦✦
This is the most readily available collection of the recordings made by the influential Almanac Singers, including the title track, "The Union Maid," "Which Side Are You On," and other standards of the union struggle. Pete Seeger's idea for a folk group would take more permanent form a decade later with the Weavers, and the concept would help give birth to the folk boom of the late '50s and early '60s. But it was all here in the simple instrumentation and vibrant harmony singing of the Almanacs. This is one of the essential recordings of American folk music. Note, however, that the album contains only six Almanac Singers tracks, recorded in May 1941, paired with seven tracks recorded in 1955 by Pete Seeger and a chorus dubbed "the Song Swappers" that included Erik Darling, later of the Weavers, and Mary Travers, later of Peter, Paul and Mary. *—William Ruhlmann*

★ **Their Complete General Recordings** / Oct. 22, 1996 / MCA ✦✦✦✦✦
The 14 surviving songs from the group's 1941 session for General Records, which could sound like a set of Weavers demos but for the absence of any female voice. The repertory is a mix of songs about the land and the sea, mixed with some political barbs ("The Dodger Song"), all displaying harmonies that are surprisingly well-sung and preserved, given the haste with which they were sung (in single takes) and the age of the recordings (55 years). "Hard, Ain't It Hard" is necessarily of interest as a number that later became a signature tune for the Weavers, and a version of "House of the Rising Sun" is another highlight, but there isn't a bad song here. Seeger (who originally participated on these sessions as "Pete Bowers"), Hayes, Lampell, and Guthrie are joined by sometime Almanac Pete Hawes on vocals and guitar, although the dominant instrument throughout is Seeger's banjo and, occasionally, Guthrie's harmonica. The notes are the only flaw, presenting an oversimplified history of the Almanacs that is a bit vague on details. *—Bruce Eder*

Eric Andersen

b. Feb. 14, 1943, Pittsburgh, PA
Vocals, Harmonica, Guitar / Contemporary Singer/Songwriter, Contemporary Folk, Singer/Songwriter

Eric Andersen has maintained a career as a folk-based singer/songwriter for 30 years. In contrast to such peers as Tom Paxton and Phil Ochs, Andersen's writing has had a romantic/philosophical/poetic bent for the most part, rather than a socially conscious one, though one of his best-known songs, "Thirsty Boots," has as its background the Freedom Rides of the early '60s. (The song has been recorded by Judy Collins and others.)

After emerging from the Northeast folk-club circuit, Andersen began to record in 1965 with *Today Is the Highway*. His second album, *'Bout Changes & Things*, contained some of his most accomplished writing, including the highly poetic "Violets of Dawn," "Thirsty Boots," and "I Shall Go Unbounded." All were sung in Andersen's flexible tenor (he shaded toward a baritone later), backed by rapid, intricate fingerpicking. In the late '60s and early '70s, Andersen experimented with country, pop, and rock music, settling on an amalgamation by the time of his masterpiece *Blue River* in 1972. This was also his most commercially successful album, but Andersen, like friends Leonard Cohen and Townes Van Zandt, was always too serious-minded for the mainstream. In the '70s and '80s, he recorded sporadically while playing folk clubs around the U.S. and especially in Europe, where he took up residence. His later material, including 1989's *Ghosts Upon the Road*, recalls his work in the '60s as it ruefully reflects on that decade. The '90s saw Andersen collaborate with friends like Rick Danko and Jonas Fjeld on *Danko/Fjeld/Andersen*, as well as release a solo album, 1998's *Memory of the Future;* Andersen also oversaw the release of *Stages: The Lost Album* as well as a 1999 re-issue of *Blue River*. *You Can't Relive the Past* followed early the next year. *—William Ruhlmann*

Today Is the Highway / 1965 / Vanguard ✦✦✦
Andersen's debut album presented him playing in a folkie style that was just starting to become passé upon its release in 1965. It's an inoffensive set of originals (except for a cover of "Baby Please Don't Go") in the early-'60s Greenwich Village style, accompanied only by his own guitar and harmonica (and, on two songs, by Debby Green on second guitar). Whether by coincidence or intention, or some combination thereof, it's highly reminiscent in spots of early Bob Dylan, although Andersen is gentler and more subdued. At times it especially recalls the *Freewheelin'*-era Dylan, or at least Dylan on that album's most reflective and low-key cuts, such as "Girl from the North Country." Andersen fills a lot of these early compositions with imagery of bumming around the country (hence the title "today is the highway"), adding some love songs. Certainly, however, it's not as forceful or original as the best singer-songwriter folk of the era, not just in comparison to Dylan, but also in comparison to others, such as his friend Tom Paxton. Nor is it as accomplished as his best material on subsequent 1960s recordings. The finest composition here is "Looking Glass," an elaborate first-person narrative-fantasy with a melody similar to folk tunes such as "Scarborough Fair." *—Richie Unterberger*

'Bout Changes & Things / 1966 / Vanguard ✦✦✦✦
On his second album, Andersen took considerable strides toward finding his own voice as a writer, and establishing himself as a noted singer/songwriter. The record featured several songs that would endure among his most renowned compositions. The pretty "Violets of Dawn" was an obvious candidate for a hit record if it was given a folk-rock arrangement, though it never was a hit, in spite of several artists trying. "Thirsty Boots," inspired by the '60s civil rights movement, is one of the better known social commentary \folk tunes of the period, although it wasn't that typical of Andersen's repertoire. "Close the Door Lightly When You Go" was one of Andersen's best bittersweet romantic tunes, and covered to good effect by Fairport Convention and the Dillards. At other points, Andersen still sounded a good deal like early Bob Dylan, but on the whole he was outgrowing that early persona, nonetheless often sounding like a gentler and more romantic counterpart to Dylan, with a more conventionally pretty voice. While Debbie Green added second guitar to a couple of songs and Harvey Brooks played electric bass on a couple of others, the album was otherwise just Andersen with his guitar and harmonica, which in 1966 was becoming an old-fashioned way of doing things among contemporary songwriters. Perhaps for that reason, the entire album was redone with electric arrangements and resequenced (although with the exact same 12 songs), and the results were released as Andersen's next album, *'Bout Changes & Things Take Two*. *—Richie Unterberger*

Tin Can Alley / 1968 / Vanguard ✦✦✦✦✦
This record, which contains "Hello Sun" and "Rollin' Home," is one of his most solid early albums. It begins and ends with the title cut played by a great junkyard band. *—Richard Meyer*

The Best of Eric Andersen / 1970 / Vanguard ✦✦✦✦
Between 1965 and 1969, Eric Andersen made his mark as the resident romantic of the East Coast folk scene. He also drifted through various musical styles and phases during this period. *The Best of Eric Andersen* (originally two LPs, reissued on one CD) covers his journeys through Woody Guthrie-style folk ("Dusty Box Car Wall," "My Land Is a Good Land"), Dylanesque imagery ("The Hustler," a diatribe written for Dylan), folk-rock (he rerecorded his most popular album of the time, *'Bout Changes and Things*, with a three-piece band), country ("Just a Country Dream") and poetic love songs ("Violets of Dawn"), and it's a good introduction to Andersen's inconsistent early career. All of his best-known songs from the Vanguard years are here, including "Thirsty Boots," inspired by civil rights organizer Gil Turner, the country-folk "Close the Door Lightly," the exquisite "Violets of Dawn" and the tradition-based American folk of "Dusty Box Car Wall." Andersen, whose long and varied career has ranged from brilliant to lackluster, is an artist desperately in need of a comprehensive anthology. Of the three collections of his material released over the years (two concentrate on his work with particular labels), only the long-deleted *The Best Songs* (1977) included tracks from his best record, *Blue River* (1972), which is indispensable on its own and a must for any Eric Andersen retrospective. *—Brett Hartenbach*

★ **Blue River** / 1972 / Columbia ✦✦✦✦✦
With mid-'60s gems like *Violets of Dawn, Thirsty Boots,* and *Close the Door Lightly,* Eric Andersen became the archetypal, literate romantic before the likes of James Taylor and Jackson Browne had even cut their first records, but at the same time seemed to lack direction from album to album. With his eighth album, *Blue River*, recorded in Nashville in 1972, he found the perfect setting for his gentle, poetic songs. After nearly seven years of dabbling in folk, folk-rock, pop, and country, Andersen found a smart, sympathetic ear in producer Norbert Putnam. Putnam, whose production here is rarely extraneous, utilizes subtle touches of bass, drums, accordion, and organ along with Andersen's own guitar, piano, and harmonica to frame the material. The record, Andersen's first effort for Columbia, also featured his best collection of tunes to date.

Blue River, with its themes of uncertainty and struggle, is by no means a casual record, although songs such as the bittersweet "Is It Really Love at All" and the title track, featuring Joni Mitchell's ethereal supporting vocal, will draw the listener in with their sheer beauty. Andersen, then in his late twenties, was dealing with questions of love, life, and desire with a maturity matched only by a handful of songwriters at the time. Never overly precious or maudlin, nearly every cut resonates with eloquence and grace. Although continuing to grow as a writer in the years to come, *Blue River* remains Eric Andersen's masterwork and one of the true classics of the genre. *—Brett Hartenbach*

Sweet Surprise / 1976 / Arista ✦✦✦

Stages: The Lost Album / Apr. 23, 1991 / Columbia/Legacy ✦✦✦✦
Eric Andersen's long-thought lost album *Stages* features superior versions of six tunes which were reworked for *Be True to You*, as well as three previously unavailable tracks. The record's centerpiece, the 8-minute meditation "Time Run Like a Freight Train," and is as good as anything Andersen has written, while "Woman, She Was Gentle" (with Joan Baez on backing vocals) and "Moonchild River Song" (presented for the first time on record with all three verses) are exquisite examples of his romanticism at its best. He also shows a tougher side here with cuts like the Beat-inspired paean to Patti Smith, "Wild Crow Blues," and the tongue-in-cheek rocker "I Love to Sing My Ballad Mama (But They Only Wanna Hear Me Rock and Roll)." Also included along with the nine original tracks, is the entrancing "Dream to Rimbaud," recorded around the time of *Blue River*, and three new songs—the Band-inspired ballad "Make It Last (Angel in the Wind)" (featuring Garth Hudson and Rick Danko), the tender "Lie With Me" and "Soul of My Song," an English translation of a song by Norwegian singer/songwriter Jonas Fjeld. The new tunes which fit nicely on the record, also featured appearances by Fjeld, Shawn Colvin, Willie Nile and Eric Brazilian of the Hooters.

Whether or not *Stages* would have boosted Eric Andersen into mainstream acceptance is anybody's guess, but it does give us a chance to hear a timeless piece of work by an artist at the height of his craft. *—Brett Hartenbach*

The Collection / Sep. 2, 1997 / Archive ✦✦✦✦

Memory of the Future / Nov. 17, 1998 / Appleseed ✦✦✦✦✦

Violets of Dawn / Jul. 7, 1999 / Vanguard ✦✦✦✦
Vanguard Records' 1999 Eric Andersen compilation *Violets of Dawn* differs in only four tracks out of 18 from its 1970 compilation *The Best of Eric Andersen*, and the selection is marginally improved. (The major difference is that *Violets of Dawn* contains two rare tracks, "Boots of Blue" and "Rambler's Lament," from the 1964 compilation *New Folks, Vol. 2*.) The sound, remastered from the original analog tapes, is much improved. Like its similar predecessor, *Violets of Dawn* collects the most impressive efforts from Andersen's 1960s Vanguard recordings, including the title track, "Thirsty Boots," "Close the Door Lightly When You Go," and "Come to My Bedside." It also traces Andersen's musical development from acoustic folk to folk rock and country, a development that shadowed Bob Dylan's progression during the same period. And it stops short of the excellent work Andersen did with *Blue River* (1972) on Columbia and *Be True to You* (1975) on Arista. *—William Ruhlmann*

You Can't Relive The Past / Feb. 22, 2000 / Appleseed ✦✦

Asylum Street Spankers

f. 1995, Austin, TX
Group / Americana, Contemporary Folk, Acoustic Blues
The Asylum Street Spankers, from Austin, Texas, are a unique band led by vocalist/washboard player/poet Wammo and vocalist Christina Marrs. They're finding a growing cult following for their unique brand of acoustic blues and early jazz. While much of their material is blues from the '20s and '30s, the band also performs original songs in their live shows and on their debut album for Watermelon Records, *Spanks for the Memories*. The band's live shows are performed without amplifiers or microphones, usually including tunes from Bessie Smith, Robert Johnson and other standard, traditional blues tunes. In addition to Wammo and Marrs, members of the Asylum Street Spankers have included guitarist Colonel Josh, guitarist Jeff Ross, banjo and mandolin player Pops Bayless, drummer Jimmie Dean, guitarist and saw player Olivier, kazoo player Mysterious John, Guy Forsyth, and bassist Kevin Smith.

The genesis of the eight-member band occurred in the early '90s at a hotel outside of Austin. After an all-night acoustic tune swap, the musicians realized they were on to something, getting back to basics and playing acoustic music. After several phone calls and circulated tapes, the band met again for a rehearsal, and the chemistry took over from there.

The band began attracting growing crowds after playing steady Wednesdays at the Electric Lounge, a bar in Austin, and from that following, they took the next step and recorded their debut album for a local label, Watermelon Records. While many of the melodies and progressions on *Spanks for the Memories* are old, some of the band's lyrics are straight out of contemporary America. Songs like "Funny Cigarette," "Trade Winds," "Lee Harvey" and "Hometown Boy" are funny and entertaining to most audiences. *—Richard Skelly*

Spanks for the Memories / Nov. 5, 1996 / Watermelon ✦✦✦✦

Live / Jun. 24, 1997 / Watermelon ✦✦✦

● **Hot Lunch** / Feb. 23, 1999 / Cold Spring ✦✦✦✦
This, Asylum Street Spankers' sophomore recording, breezes in on acoustic guitar and ukulele strains and the words "Life ain't a cakewalk, it's a waltz/And they're playing my music out of time"—and it only gets better from there. Indeed, the Asylum Street Spankers, a loose, unplugged collective of Austin, TX, pickers and *bon vivants*, seem to have little trouble, on *Hot Lunch*'s 16 cuts, deftly blending virtuosic musicianship with seemingly ef-

fortless musical and lyrical wit. The band flits between ragtime, country, old-style am radio pop tunes, swing, and country-blues with equal ease. The Spankers are—particularly on such puckish, narrative cuts as "Trippin' Over You," "Sad Bomber," and others—manage to walk the razor thin line between novelty and just plain fun-lovin' jamboree frolics. It's this graceful self-awareness that separates Asylum Street Spankers from such less graceful musical revivalists as the Squirrel Nut Zippers. In fact, on the cut *Smells Like Thirty-Something*, the Spankers seem to, well, spank the mid-'90s swing revival craze on its rump, chiding, atop a rollicking, bluesy riff, *I like martinis/and I like cigars/But I hate martini and cigar bars.* Somewhere between that sense of humor and vocalist/instrumentalist (for every Spanker is a multi-instrumentalist) Christina Marrs' sublime vocals lies the charm of Asylum Stret Spankers as expressed in these grooves. A beautiful, rocking, and rollicking unplugged beer-and-pot party populated with the most unpretentious, heartbreaking characters you're ever likely to meet. *—Chris Handyside*

Joan Baez

b. Jan. 9, 1941, Staten Island, NY
Vocals, Guitar / Folk Revival, Contemporary Folk, Folk-Rock, Singer/Songwriter, Traditional Folk
The most accomplished interpretive folksinger of the '60s, Joan Baez has influenced nearly every aspect of popular music in a career still going strong after more than 35 years. Baez is possessed of a once-in-a-lifetime soprano, which, since the late '50s, she has put in the service of folk and pop music as well as a variety of political causes.Baez first gained recognition at the 1959 Newport Folk Festival, then cut her 1960 self-titled debut album for Vanguard Records. It was made up of 13 traditional songs given near-definitive treatment. A moderate success on release, the album took off after the breakthrough of *Joan Baez, Vol. 2* (Sep. 1961), and both albums became huge hits, as did her third album, *Joan Baez in Concert.* From 1962 to 1964, Baez was the popular face of folk music, headlining festivals and concert tours and singing at political events, including the August 1963 March on Washington. During this period, she began to champion the work of folk songwriter Bob Dylan, and gradually her repertoire moved from traditional material toward the socially conscious work of the emerging generation of '60s artists like him. Like other popular folk performers, Baez was affected by the changes in popular music wrought by the appearance of the Beatles in the U.S. in 1964 and Dylan's introduction of folk-rock in 1965, and she began to augment her simple acoustic guitar backing with other instruments. Baez continued to experiment in the late '60s, releasing *Baptism: A Journey Through Our Time* (Jun. 1968), in which she recited poetry, and *Any Day Now* (Dec. 1968), a double album of Dylan songs done with country backing, which went gold. Baez switched record-label affiliation to A&M Records with *Come from the Shadows* (May 1972), which moved her in a more pop direction. *—William Ruhlmann*

☆ **Joan Baez** / 1960 / Vanguard ✦✦✦✦✦
At the time of its release, Joan Baez's debut album was something of a revelation. The folk music revival was beginning to gather steam, stoked on the popular side by artists such as the Kingston Trio and the Easy Riders, as well as up-and-coming ensembles such as the Highwaymen, and on the more intense and serious side by the Weavers. The female singers on the scene were mostly old-time, veteran activist types like Ronnie Gilbert and Malvina Reynolds, who was in her 60s. And then along comes this album, by a 19-year-old who looked more like the kind of coed every mother dreamt her son would come home with, displaying a voice from heaven, a soprano so pure and beguiling that the mere act of listening to her—forget what she was singing—was a pleasure. Baez's first album, made up primarily of traditional songs (including a startling version of "House of the Rising Sun"), was beguiling enough to woo even conservative-leaning listeners. Accompanied by the Weavers' Fred Hellerman and a pair of session singers, Baez gives a fine account of the most reserved and least confrontational aspects of the folk revival, presenting a brace of traditional songs (most notably "East Virginia" and "Mary Hamilton") with an urgency and sincerity that makes the listener feel as though they were being sung for the first time, and opening with a song that was to become her signature piece for many years, "Silver Dagger." The recording was notable at the time for its purity of sound, but like a lot of Vanguard releases from this period reissued in the '80s), it could do with a fresh remastering on the CD, which is not quite up to modern standards. *—Bruce Eder*

Joan Baez 2 / 1961 / Vanguard ✦✦✦✦
Joan Baez's second album, recorded when she was 20 years old, is a hearty helping of folk masterpieces that give ample evidence to exactly how she was established as a leader of the contemporary folk scene of the day. The material chosen is truly exceptional, from the beautifully stark British ballad "The Trees They Do Grow High" to the tragic tales of death and lost love in "Engine 143" and "Banks of the Ohio," which recall the Carter Family in presentation as much as spirit. Without a doubt, Baez's version of "Pal of Mine" is every bit as vibrant as when the Carters recorded it, though here given a more bluegrass sound by the banjo and backup vocal accompaniment of the Greenbriar Boys. The traditional Christmas tune "The Cherry Tree Carol" is presented perfectly by Baez's gorgeous arrangement. Baez is a true master of her craft, and though she hasn't always made the best choices for material, the 14 interpretations here are as timeless as the songs themselves. Similar to Bob Dylan's self-titled debut, this is an album that all fans of traditional folk music should seek out. *—Matt Fink*

Farewell, Angelina / 1965 / Vanguard ✦✦✦
Baez moves toward contemporary work, with songs by Donovan and Woody Guthrie. She sings four songs by Bob Dylan, including the title track. *—William Ruhlmann*

Noël / 1966 / Vanguard ✦✦✦✦✦
An album of stately beauty, Baez's pure, soaring soprano is accompanied by a consort of recorders and viols, lute, harpsichord, baroque organ, winds, strings, and percussion. Her rendition of the "Coventry Carol" is stirring, and Baez pours her heart into "The Carol of the Birds." Considering Baez's politics, one would never know she recorded this album in the Vietnam War era. *—Dennis MacDonald*

Joan / 1967 / Vanguard ✦✦✦
Ornate, heavily orchestrated versions of other people's songs. Over-produced, but quite beautiful. *—Bruce Eder*

Any Day Now / 1968 / Vanguard ✦✦✦
Any Day Now is an all-[Dylan album which includes a definitive performance of "Love Is Just a Four-Letter Word." *—William Ruhlmann*

● **The First Ten Years** / 1970 / Vanguard ✦✦✦✦✦
The First Ten Years is an excellent overview of Joan Baez's first decade of recording, balancing her work as an interpreter of both traditional and contemporary folk songs. There may be a few fan favorites missing, but the all the essentials are here, making it an excellent introduction for the novice. *—Stephen Thomas Erlewine*

One Day at a Time / 1970 / Vanguard ✦✦✦✦

Blessed Are / 1971 / Vanguard ✦✦✦✦

Carry It On / 1971 / Vanguard ✦✦✦

Come from the Shadows / 1972 / A&M ✦✦✦
After recording for the folk label Vanguard for more than a decade, Baez moved to AM. On this label debut, she maintained her interest in country music, recording in Nashville with some of the city's session aces. She also continued to dedicate herself to radical politics, from her set opener "Prison Trilogy," which pledged, "We're gonna raze the prisons to the ground," to the closer, John Lennon's "Imagine." In between were her call on Bob Dylan to return to protest music ("To Bobby") and her sister Mimi Farina's touching tribute to Janis Joplin, "In the Quiet Morning." *—William Ruhlmann*

Hits the Greatest & Others / 1973 / Vanguard ✦✦✦

Where Are You Now, My Son? / 1973 / A&M ✦✦✦
This isn't only *not* the place to start listening to Joan Baez, it's the album that separates the true fans from the, um, fellow travelers. Side 2 is taken up by the title song, a musical account of Baez's trip to Hanoi over Christmas of 1972, complete with the sound of US bombs falling on the city. Side 1, on the other hand, contains one of Baez's best original songs, "A Young Gypsy," and two by her sister, "Mary Call" and "Best of Friends." *—William Ruhlmann*

★ **Diamonds & Rust** / 1975 / A&M ✦✦✦✦✦
Baez's peak as a songwriter (title track) and folk/rock interpreter, singing songs of Jackson Browne, John Prine, and Bob Dylan. *—William Ruhlmann*

From Every Stage / 1976 / A&M ✦✦✦✦
Recorded on the *Diamonds & Rust* tour, *From Every Stage* is a satisfying portrait of Joan doing what she does best. Performing selections from every stage of her career, this live release is a testament to Baez's long and illustrious career. Divided into acoustic and electric sets, highlights include "Blowin' in the Wind, "The Night They Drove Old Dixie Down" and "Diamonds & Rust." Faithful to her ideals, Joan Baez is here at one of the peaks of her long career. *—James Chrispell*

Honest Lullaby / 1979 / Portrait ✦✦✦

Very Early Joan Baez / 1983 / Vanguard ✦✦✦✦
This Vanguard release is a heartwarmingly intimate look at Joan Baez during her most influential period (1960-1963). The album's 22 tracks are all live, performed before audiences held in silent and rapt attention in packed concert halls. The singer's trademark politically tinged folk songs are charmingly blended with a few pop interpretations like the Jerry Ragovoy early soul classic "She's a Trouble Maker" and a fun version of the Diamonds' "Little Darlin'," revealing a rarely seen lighthearted side of the activist. Baez's voice never sounded better than during this era, and her live performances resonate with a confident honesty.

The only detractions of this CD are in the production: the whole album is mixed very quietly (requiring the listener to crank up the volume) but the applause between songs seems brashly loud. The other nitpick is that, for some reason, the album's engineer fades Baez's voice from left to right within the songs; this isn't a tremendous problem but listening on headphones to the sound bobbing back and forth can create a feeling of seasickness. However, these minor flaws should not discourage anyone from picking up *Very Early Joan Baez,* a shining example of the bridge from the traditional Weavers/Kingston Trio folk singing of the fifties and the youthful fire of the political folk of the '60s. *—Zac Johnson*

Recently / 1988 / Gold Castle ✦✦✦✦✦
Baez returned to US record shops with a vengeance here, delivering her interpretations of songs by Dire Straits, Johnny Clegg, U2, and Peter Gabriel, performers whose political consciousness had been formed by listening to old Joan Baez albums. And on the title track, a stunning original, she boldly answered ex-husband David Harris' downbeat memoir of the '60s, *Dreams Die Hard,* as well as other 80s revisionists. *—William Ruhlmann*

Play Me Backwards / 1992 / Virgin ✦✦✦

Rare, Live & Classic / Sep. 1993 / Vanguard ✦✦✦✦✦
Spanning three discs, the box set *Rare, Live & Classic* is an odd mix of Baez's best-known songs and rarities. For the hardcore collector, there are plenty of interesting items here, including previously unreleased duets with Bob Dylan, Donovan, Bill Wood, and Jeffrey Shurtleff, but for the casual fan, there's too much material; they would be better off with her original albums or single-disc compilations. *—Stephen Thomas Erlewine*

Greatest Hits / May 7, 1996 / A&M ✦✦✦✦✦

Best of Joan Baez / Sep. 30, 1997 / Vanguard ✦✦✦
Vanguard's *Best of Joan Baez* is a solid, if brief, collection that features a handful of her best-known songs—"The Night They Drove Old Dixie Down" "There But for Fortune," "I Am a Poor Wayfaring Stranger," "Joe Hill," "Silver Dagger," "Pack up Your Sorrows," "We Shall Overcome"—but it leaves just as many off the disc. It's a serviceable, but hardly definitive, introduction to her career, and there are far better collections on the marketplace. *—Stephen Thomas Erlewine*

Vanguard Sessions: Baez Sings Dylan / Jun. 9, 1998 / Vanguard ♦♦♦♦
Culling 15 tracks from her 1968 release of *Any Day Now* and adding five tracks taken from her releases of the early '60's, *Vanguard Sessions: Baez Sings Dylan* is a wonderful example of Joan Baez's ability to transcend the work of other songwriters. Though it could be said that the genius of Dylan's songcraft can occasionally be obscured by the understated starkness of his presentation, Baez's use of slightly countrified arrangements to compliment her powerful vocals succeeds in recasting these classics in a slightly prettier package. Baez takes few liberties, so most tracks don't count as surprises, though a bluesy a cappella rendition of "Tears of Rage" and a funky, soulful "Dear Landlord" nearly qualify as such. More than anything, Baez's renditions make the listener realize just how incredibly nuanced Dylan's delivery can be. Though standards like "You Ain't Goin' Nowhere," "It Ain't Me Babe," and "I Shall Be Released" are covered, just as many tracks are of a lesser-known variety, such as "Walkin' Down the Line," "Love Is Just a Four-Letter Word," and "Walls of Red Wing." Of course, bringing out the genius in Dylan's work isn't exactly akin to pulling teeth, but the timeless quality of Baez's thoughtful renditions more than does the work justice. *—Matt Fink*

20th Century Masters—*The Millennium Collection: The Best of Joan Baez* / *Oct. 19, 1999 / A&M* ♦♦♦
It may not be a definitive collection—after all, it bypasses all of her influential '60s recordings—but the Joan Baez installment of *20th Century Masters: The Millennium Collection* is a good overview of her recordings for A*M*, featuring such highlights as "Diamonds and Rust," "Fountain of Sorrow," "Hello in There," "Dida," "Jesse," "In the Quiet Morning (For Janis Joplin)," "Gracias a la Vida," "Forever Young," and a live version of "The Night They Drove Old Dixie Down." There may be some good songs missing, but this isn't a bad choice for budget-minded casual fans. *—Stephen Thomas Erlewine*

Robbie Basho

Vocals, Guitar / Progressive Folk, Experimental
Robbie Basho was the least celebrated of the trio of '60s acoustic guitar virtuosos who established themselves as innovators on the Takoma label (the other two were John Fahey and Leo Kottke). It's not hard to surmise why Basho found a natural home on Takoma. Like Fahey and Kottke, he was determined to expand the horizons of the acoustic steel-string guitar by utilizing dissonance, unusual tunings, and influences from all over the world. At the same time, it's not hard to see why Basho attracted a smaller, more specialized audience than Fahey and Kottke. His work requires a little more time and effort to absorb, and is more colored by Eastern and Indian modal influences.

"Haunting" is an overused adjective for Basho's instrumentals (as it has often been for Fahey's records), but entirely appropriate. Difficult to pigeonhole and categorize, Basho's strums were characterized by a tension between spiritual, meditative moods and bursts of restlessness. In addition to American folk and Middle Eastern influences, traces of classical, Irish, koto, medieval, and other musics could be heard in his material (and he had notably little pure blues influence when compared to his Takoma label-mates). Occasionally he would add some eerie whistling, or even eerier, not to say unsettling, singing; even dedicated Basho fans concede that his vocals weren't what you came to hear.

From the mid-'60s to his death in 1986, Basho recorded several respected if little-heard albums for Takoma, Windham Hill, and other labels. Windham Hill founder Will Ackerman, who wrote some appreciative liner notes on the 1996 reissue *Guitar Soli*, was a big fan of Basho. Like John Fahey, Basho's solo instrumental approach helped lay the groundwork for the meditative new age sounds that Windham Hill and others would make a specialty. And also like Fahey, Basho's work is far darker and more challenging than most of what is now categorized as new age music. *—Richie Unterberger*

The Grail and the Lotus / 1966 / Takoma ♦♦♦♦♦
A fine, innovative album of six extended pieces that blend American, Asian and other forms of folk/acoustic styles. All of the tracks are now available on the *Guitar Soli* reissue CD, which also features five other selections from Basho's mid-'60s Takoma records. *—Richie Unterberger*

The Falconers Arm 1 / 1967 / Takoma ♦♦♦
Five instrumentals, mostly performed on solo acoustic guitar (Susan Graubard played flute on "Tassajara"). It's a satisfying continuation of the ground Basho laid out on his first Takoma albums, playing dense (often 12-string), often busy guitar lines in unusual tunings influenced by both blues and Indian music. This frequently explores minor and modal moods evoking blustery, rainy fall days with leaves swirling around on the ground. Somber and serious, yes, but not quite depressed, although the melancholy pieces ("Lost Lagoon Suite" and "Tassajara") are the ones that make the most lasting impression. It's similar in some respects to labelmate John Fahey's work of the time, but not so much so that it sounds imitative or like a lesser derivation. *—Richie Unterberger*

The Voice of the Eagle / 1972 / Vanguard ♦♦♦
Basho's guitar playing is of his habitual high standard on this LP, "dedicated to Avatar Meher Baba, and in the spirit of love and respect to the American Indian." Those who value Basho mostly for his instrumental skills—which would include most Basho fans—need to be aware, however, that all but one of these nine songs is a vocal. The songs are mostly inspired by Native American music and culture. While Basho was no doubt sincere, taking pains to explain the Native American elements in the liner notes, his voice will be hard for many listeners to take; no one sang with more vibrato than Robbie. The song structures are sometimes more like Native American chants and ceremonies than conventional folk numbers. *—Richie Unterberger*

● **Guitar Soli** / 1996 / Takoma ♦♦♦♦♦
A superb reissue of the cream of Basho's earliest work, mostly recorded in 1965 for his first two Takoma LPs, *Seal of the Lotus/Guitar Soli*... and *The Grail and the Lotus* (one cut from a 1966 album, *Basho Sings/Vol. 3*, is also included). Whether you decide to use this as background mood music or thinking-person's acoustic folk, it's moving music, the constant shifts in tone and style remaining fresh and inventive. By the standards of 1965 folk, it was rather radical in its form, both in its length (with cuts that usually lasted between five and ten minutes) and its breadth of style (encompassing American, Indian, Far Eastern, and other musics). Basho's unorthodox vocal delivery, the aural equivalent of a leaf shaking on a tree, is most emphatically not for everyone, but that's not much of an issue here, as most of the pieces are instrumental. With 78 minutes of music and extensive liner notes, it's excellent value. *—Richie Unterberger*

The Big Three

Group / Folk Revival, Folk-Pop
Remembered today mostly for featuring a pre-Mamas & Papas Cass Elliot, the Big Three recorded a couple of pleasant pop-folk albums around 1963. Elliot was flanked by notable partners Tim Rose (who went on to become a minor but noteworthy singer/songwriter in the late '60s, most famous for performing the version of "Hey Joe" that provided a loose blueprint for Jimi Hendrix's) and James Hendricks. The Washington, D.C. trio were typical of many of the acts working the East Coast coffeehouse circuit in the first half of the '60s, stressing clean and full harmonies, somewhat in the mold of the Kingston Trio. The Big Three were a little (but not much) funkier than the Kingstons, and also occasionally made stabs at a more pop-oriented sound with full band instrumentation. Most of their material, though, was solidly in the acoustic stream, and their repertoire emphasized then-contemporary versions of folk standards, although they did compose some of their own material (which was usually by Rose). The Big Three disbanded in 1964, when Rose left to go solo; Elliot and Hendricks joined Zal Yanovsky and Denny Doherty in the short-lived folk-rock precursors the Mugwumps, which in turn helped spawn two of the biggest folk-rock groups, the Mamas & the Papas (with Elliot and Doherty) and the Lovin' Spoonful (with Yanovsky). *—Richie Unterberger*

● **The Big Three Featuring Mama Cass Elliot** / 1995 / Sequel ♦♦♦♦
Twenty-one tracks from their two albums, recorded circa 1963. Their brand of cleanly arranged pop-folk may sound dated these days, with a set list heavy on standbys like "Down in the Valley," "Silkie," and "All the Pretty Little Horses." But it's still reasonably soothing and soaring stuff, historically interesting for the glimpse it allows us of Cass Elliot's budding vocal skills, which are already accomplished and assertive at this formative stage. *—Richie Unterberger*

Luka Bloom (Barry Moore)

b. May 23, 1955, Newbridge, Ireland
Vocals, Guitar / Alternative Folk, Contemporary Folk, Singer/Songwriter, Urban Folk
Before making his American debut, Barry Moore recorded three albums in Ireland. Perhaps because his brother is the revered Irish singer Christy Moore, he changed his name to Luka Bloom—Luka is taken from Suzanne Vega's song, Bloom from James Joyce's *Ulysses*. With his literate, melodic original songs and impassioned live performances, Bloom earned a devoted following in the New York area, which led to his record contract with Reprise. While he can occasionally suffer from over-worked lyrics and a cloying cuteness, Bloom is one of the best post-punk folk performers and songwriters.

His album roster includes his 1998 self-titled debut, the critically acclaimed *Riverside* (1990), 1992's *The Acoustic Motorbike*, 1994's *Turf*, and 1999's *Salty Heaven*.

Keeper of the Flame followed in fall 2000. *—Stephen Thomas Erlewine*

Luka Bloom / 1988 / Mystery ♦♦

● **Riverside** / Feb. 1990 / Reprise ♦♦♦♦♦
Expatriate Irishman Luka Bloom cloaks his Celtic folk songs in furious strumming on his "electro-acoustic" guitar, added instrumentation, and echo effects on everything, but he is still a folkie, blowing up his feelings to heroic proportions, whether it's the autobiography of "The Man Is Alive" or the romantic fantasy of "An Irishman In Chinatown." But the content is less convincing than the expression, which is more a characteristic of rock than folk. It isn't that Bloom has much to say, it's that he's so passionate about saying it: he's more Bono than Bob Dylan. Maybe it's an Irish thing. *— William Ruhlmann*

The Acoustic Motorbike / Jan. 1992 / Reprise ♦♦♦♦
Having made his mark in America and moved back home to Ireland, Luka Bloom attempted to incorporate some of the spirit of the country where he spent four years into his Irish folk-rock, covering LL Cool J's "I Need Love" and the Elvis Presley hit "Can't Help Falling In Love." But in his own songs, he didn't go much beyond such surface aspects of the U.S. as Elvis and rap, preferring to devote himself to vague, cliched lyrics of love and longing (some of them not so much rapped as recited), once again set for the most part against his aggressive guitar strumming, various acoustic instruments, and a bottom provided by an Irish bodhran, sometimes played by his brother, Christy Moore. While Bloom's second album expanded somewhat on his first record's stylistic range and maintained its urgency, it lacked the debut's exuberance—Bloom was getting more serious when what he needed to do was to get more substantive. *— William Ruhlmann*

Turf / Jun. 14, 1994 / Reprise ♦♦♦
A portrait of the Irishman as an American neo-folkie. Having experimented with extra instrumentation on his first two albums, Luka Bloom made a man-with-guitar record his third time out, the better to emphasize his songs, which combined a strong folk traditionalism (one was called "Black Is The Colour [of my true love's hair]," another described an encounter with a mermaid) with an Amer-Irish social concern ("Freedom Song" mixed the stories of political activists from each country, "Background Noise" was a tale of violence applicable anywhere, even if it referred to the Irish Troubles). All of this made for a more focused record than Bloom's second album, although his debut remained his most satisfying effort. *— William Ruhlmann*

Salty Heaven / 1999 / Shanachie ♦♦♦

Keeper of the Flame / Nov. 28, 2000 / Skip ♦♦♦♦

David Blue (S. David Cohen)

b. Feb. 18, 1941, Providence, RI, **d.** Dec. 2, 1982
Vocals, Guitar / Folk-Rock, Singer/Songwriter
Born in Providence, RI, as S. David Cohen (a name he returned to for one of his albums), David Blue was a member of the folk singer/songwriter community of Greenwich Village in the '60s and a close friend of Bob Dylan's (he recounts this period of his life in Dylan's movie *Renaldo & Clara*). Blue made several albums for Elektra, Reprise, and Asylum in the '60s and '70s, and is best remembered for his songs "I Like to Sleep Late in the Morning" and "Wanted Man" (recorded by the Eagles). *— William Ruhlmann*

- **David Blue** / 1966 / Asylum ✦✦✦✦✦
Blue's debut album features the first recording of his remarkable "Grand Hotel" and other well-written folk/rock songs. *— William Ruhlmann*

Stories / 1972 / Line ✦✦✦
Once known as one of the "new Dylans," David Blue signed to Asylum Records and released this collection of tunes that are harrowing, yet fulfilling. From the drugged images of "House of Changing Faces" to the longing of "Looking For a Friend," Blue spins his *Stories* with verve. Fans of the singer-songwriter genre should keep an eye out for this one. *— James Chrispell*

Nice Baby and the Angel / 1973 / Asylum ✦✦✦✦✦
Blue is joined by an all-star California cast (Dave Mason, Graham Nash, David Lindley, and Glenn Frey) for this excellent 70s singer-songwriter collection, which includes his "Outlaw Man." *— William Ruhlmann*

Hugh Blumenfeld

b. 1958
Vocals, Guitar / Contemporary Folk, Singer/Songwriter
Brooklyn-born but now residing in Connecticut, Hugh Blumenfeld was a mainstay in the late '80s Greenwich Village scene, an associate editor and contributor of songs to the *Fast Folk Musical Magazine,* winner of the Kerrville New Folk Competition, featured performer on Christine Lavin's *On a Winter's Night* compilation and was the first artist signed to the new 1 800 Prime CD label. He has a Ph.D. in poetry but doesn't let that get in the way of honest songwriting on records like 1987's *Strong in Spirit,* 1989's *Barehanded* and 1996's *Mozart's Money. Rocket Science* followed in 1998. *— Richard Meyer*

The Strong in Spirit / 1987 / 1-800-Prime ✦✦✦✦✦
Hugh's first collection contains some of his signature tunes including "Brothers," "Sailing to the New World" and "Rising Moon." Its simple production showcases his intimate vocal style very well. *— Richard Meyer*

Barehanded / 1991 / 1-800-Prime ✦✦✦
Originally released independently in cassette, *Barehanded* was remixed with some additional parts and crisper sound on this 1 800 Prime CD release. Blumenfeld's songwriting continues to mature as evidenced by "Bring Stones," "Watertowers" and "Jerusalem." *— Richard Meyer*

- **Mozart's Money** / 1996 / 1-800-Prime ✦✦✦✦✦
Hugh Blumenfeld's third album is his strongest album so far. Titled *Mozart's Money,* this record is produced by David Seitz with a radio-ready sound that is never overbearing. For any who have heard Blumenfeld's two earlier albums and found them a little on the safe side, do take the time to check this record out. On this album he delivers his songs with a confident assurance of someone who knows he has made a quantum leap in his singing dynamics and the consistent focus of his songwriting. Hugh takes on a wide range of subjects beginning with a humorous musing where all the money Mozart's work earned has gone, since it certainly didn't go to the composer, and that artists of all levels still have to do their work for its own sake. There is a wonderful vocal support throughout from Lucy Kaplansky, Madwoman in the Attic and Judith Zweiman. The arrangements are distinctive and make no concessions for a folk audience although the singer/songwriter nature of the material will still probably still appeal to that audience. "Talking Island" sounds like he dropped in on the Turtle Island Quartet, "What Is You Do Nothing" sounds like Hugh is channeling Steve Goodman, while "Mr. Rain," an ode to Kurt Cobain, rocks out and hammers the hook into your head with a great guitar part and Hugh's strongest vocal yet. *— Richard Meyer*

Rocket Science / Jul. 7, 1998 / 1-800-Prime ✦✦✦

Dock Boggs (Moran Lee Boggs)

b. Feb. 7, 1898, West Norton, VA, **d.** 1971
Vocals, Banjo / Appalachian Folk, Folk Revival, Country Blues, Traditional Folk, Old-Timey
Dock Boggs was just one of the primeval hillbillies to record during the '20s, forgotten for decades until the folk revival of the '60s revived his career at the twilight of his life. Still, his dozen recordings from 1927 to 1929 are monuments of folk music, comprised of fatalistic hills ballads and blues like "Danville Girl," "Pretty Polly," and "Country Blues." Born near Norton, Virginia in 1898, Boggs was the youngest of ten children. (He gained his nickname at an early age, since he was named after the doctor that delivered him.) Boggs began working in the mines at the age of twelve. In what remained of his spare time, he began playing banjo, picking the instrument in the style of blues guitar instead of the widespread clawhammer technique.

Boggs began picking up songs from family members and the radio. He married in 1918, and began subconctracting on a mine until his wife's illness forced him to move back to her home. He worked in the dangerous moonshining business, and made a little money playing social dances.

His big break finally came in 1927, when executives from the Brunswick label arrived in Norton to audition talent. He passed (beating out none other than A.P. Carter), and recorded eight sides in New York City for the label. Though they didn't quite flop, the records sold mostly around Boggs' hometown. He signed a booking agent, and recorded four more sides for W.E. Myer's local Lonesome Ace label. The coming of the Great Depression in late 1929 put a hold on Boggs' recording career, as countless labels dried up. He continued to perform around the region until the early '30s however, until his wife forced him to give up his music and go back into the mines. Boggs worked until 1954, when mechanical innovations forced him out of a job.

Almost a decade later, in 1963, folklorist Mike Seeger located Boggs in Norton and convinced him to resume his career. Just weeks after their meeting, Boggs played *the American Folk Festival* in Asheville, North Carolina. He began recording again, and released his first LP, *Legendary Singer & Banjo Player,* later that year on Smithsonian/Folkways. Two more LPs followed during the '60s though, like his original recordings, they too were out of print not long after his death in 1971.

The revival of interest in early folk music occasioned by a digital reissue of Harry Smith's *Anthology of American Folk Music* finally brought Boggs' music back to the shelves. In 1997, John Fahey's Revenant label released *Complete Early Recordings (1927-1929),* and one year later *His Folkways Years (1963-1968)* appeared. *— John Bush*

Country Blues: Complete Early Recordings (1927-1929) / Oct. 21, 1997 / Revenant ✦✦✦✦✦
Released on John Fahey's Revenant label, this Dock Boggs collection includes all 12 of his 1927-29 recordings, plus five alternate takes and four cuts by Bill and Hayes Shepherd, friends and fellow players of Boggs. Included with the set is a 64-page book with essays by Greil Marcus, among others, and this is undoubtedly the best Dock Boggs collection ever assembled. *— John Bush*

- **His Folkways Years (1963-1968)** / Sep. 15, 1998 / Smithsonian/Folkways ✦✦✦✦✦
After Boggs, the Appalachian singer-banjoist who had released a dozen sides in the late 1920s, was rediscovered by Mike Seeger in 1963, he did some recording for Folkways Records. This double-CD, 50-song set contains the material from three Boggs LPs for Folkways: *Legendary Singer & Banjo Player* (1963), *Vol. 2* (1965), and *Vol. 3* (1970). The unearthly qualities of his '20s recordings that caused critics such as Greil Marcus to get wet were not in such exotic force on these later efforts; Boggs had only recently started playing music again after a gap of about 30 years. He's in fairly good form on this extensive compilation, dominated by old folk and blues tunes (some traditional, some learned from mundane sources such as commercial records and a Banker's Life Insurance ad). His singing and banjo playing are the definition of "stark," an overused adjective when applied to traditional Appalachian music. He's much easier to take than even starker proponents such as Roscoe Holcomb, however, with vocals that are effectively plaintive and rough-hewn without sounding unduly pinched, although they sometimes crack and strain. His best tunes are the ones with a spooky undercurrent, like "Danville Girl," which shares the same melody as the famous standard "St. James Infirmary," and "Oh Death." The reissue has excellent, lengthy historical liner notes from Barry O'Connell, and fascinating recollections of Boggs' rediscovery by Mike Seeger. *— Richie Unterberger*

Oscar Brand

b. Feb. 7, 1920, Winnipeg, Manitoba, Canada
Vocals, Guitar / Singer/Songwriter, Traditional Folk
Oscar Brand is one of the stalwart American folksingers, writers, and interpreters. Over the course of his 60-some-year career he has released 93 albums. He roamed the country with Woody, concertized with Leadbelly, promoted folk of all kinds like Pete Seeger and has hosted the Folk Song Festival on New York's WNYC for 50 years. Many of his recordings contain parodies on single subjects such as holidays, car songs, or political satire. He is well known for his many collections of bawdy songs. Generally the recording style is simple; Oscar and his guitar and a few back-up players. Oscar's records are totally directed toward the songs. *— Richard Meyer*

- **Best of Oscar Brand** / 1975 / Tradition ✦✦✦✦✦

Presidential Campaining Songs: 1789-1996 / May 18, 1999 / Smithsonian/Folkways ✦✦✦✦✦
One of the most thoroughly unique folk records released in 1999, *Presidential Campaigning Songs* is also a thorough and unique look at America's political history. Folk singer Oscar Brand sings campaign songs for each president, from "Follow Washington" to Clinton's campaign theme, Fleetwood Mac's "Don't Stop Thinking About Tomorrow" (simply titled "Don't Stop" on Mac releases). Along with tracing America's political currents, *Presidential Campaigning Songs* also documents the changing importance of songs in a campaign. The earliest songs, like "For Jefferson and Liberty" and John Q. Adams' "Little Know Ye Who's Coming," reflect the newness of the U.S. and how fresh the struggle for liberty was in people's minds at the time. Similarly, the songs from the Roaring '20s era, such as "Keep Cool and Keep Coolidge" and Warren G. Harding's "If He's Good Enough for Lindy" evoke the decade's free-and-easy prosperity. An important and well-crafted historical document, *Presidential Campaigning Songs* educates and entertains in equal measure. *— Heather Phares*

The Brandywine Singers

f. 1962, **db.** 1965
Group / Progressive Folk, Folk Revival, Folk-Pop
From 1962 through 1965 the Brandywine Singers were one of the hottest acts on the college folk circuit. Then life, the Viet Nam War, and other careers intervened. The Brandywines reformed in 1992 with original members Rick and Ron Shaw and Les Clark joined by multi-instrumentalist, multi-talented Taylor Whiteside. The result is pure magic, folk music as we remember it in its popularity heyday and still able to send chills up and down one's spine. Folk favorites, beautifully sung, played, and arranged, spiced with a couple of originals. *— Allan Shaw*

- **World-Class Folk** / 1993 / Folk Era ✦✦✦✦
Here's the group you've never forgotten and never can forget. *— Mike Fleischer*

David Bromberg

b. Sep. 19, 1945, Philadelphia, PA

Vocals, Mandolin, Guitar, Fiddle, Dobro, Session Musician / Contemporary Folk, Singer/Songwriter

Often referred to as a musician's musician throughout his career, Bromberg has spent almost as much time being a sideman to people like Bob Dylan and Jerry Jeff Walker as he has fronting his own band. Session credits for albums by Tom Paxton and Jerry Jeff Walker started getting Bromberg attention in the mid-'60s, and he began making the transition from sideman to frontman in the early '70s, when he was signed to record for Columbia records.

The key to appreciating Bromberg is to realize he has an equal passion for blues, folk, country and western, bluegrass and rock & roll. This diverse range of influences is reflected on all his recordings for Columbia, Fantasy, and Rounder, and in his performances as well. His musical eclecticism over the years may have cost him some fans, but a typical Bromberg concert can be a musical education. *—Richard Skelly*

David Bromberg / 1971 / Columbia ✦✦✦✦✦

David Bromberg was already a well-known folk instrumentalist before this album proved he was also a top-notch songwriter and an appealing vocalist as well. The styles mix folk, blues, rock, and jug-band music, and the songs alternate from the painfully sensitive ("Sammy's Song") to the rib-tickling "The Holdup," which was cowritten by George Harrison. *—William Ruhlmann*

Wanted Dead or Alive / 1974 / Columbia ✦✦✦✦

This is a reissue of Bromberg's 1974 album. Backing musicians include several members of The Grateful Dead as well as Andy Statman on mandolin and tenor sax. Some of Bromberg's strongest and best-loved material can be found here, including "The Holdup," "Danger Man," "Send Me to the 'Lectric Chair," "The New Lee Highway Blues," and Bob Dylan's "Wallflower." *—Roundup Newsletter*

Midnight on the Water / 1975 / Columbia ✦✦✦

A big-band blowout album with guest appearances by Bonnie Raitt, Linda Ronstadt, Emmy Lou Harris, it features "The Jokes on Me" and "Don't Put that Thing on Me." *—Richard Meyer*

How Late'll Ya Play 'til— / 1976 / Fantasy ✦✦✦

Bromberg's band, with two horns and a fiddle player, is capable of playing just about any style of popular music, and most of them are here on a double album, half recorded in the studio and half live. (Fantasy has also issued the two discs separately.) The standout inclusion is Bromberg's "Will Not Be Your Fool," which became his onstage showstopper from here on out. *—William Ruhlmann*

Out of the Blues: Best of David Bromberg / 1977 / Columbia ✦✦✦

Out of the Blues: Best of David Bromberg is a solid ten-track collection that features many highlights from Bromberg's '70s recordings, including both originals ("The Holdup," "The Joke's On Me," "The New Lee Highway Blues," "Demon in Disguise," "Sharon") and covers ("Send Me to the 'Lectric Chair," "Mr. Bojangles," "Kansas City," "(What A) Wonderful World"). It's a good summation of his prime period and, therefore, a good introduction to his music. *—Stephen Thomas Erlewine*

Reckless Abandon / 1977 / Fantasy ✦✦✦

Long Way from Here / 1987 / Fantasy ✦✦✦

Sideman Serenade / 1990 / Rounder ✦✦

● **The Player: Retrospective** / May 5, 1998 / Columbia/Legacy ✦✦✦✦✦

The Player: A Retrospective is an incomplete but effective summary of David Bromberg's career, containing the majority of his best songs. It is true that some personal favorites such as "The New Lee Highway Blues" may be missing—and this may be a sticking point, since Bromberg fans are very dedicated—but most of the important songs—"Sharon," "The Hold Up," "Mr. Bojangles," "Sammy's Song," "The Joke's On Me," "Wallflower"—are here, making this a fine replacement for the earlier compilation, *Out of the Blues*, as well as a good introduction for the curious. *—Stephen Thomas Erlewine*

Reckless Abandon/Bandit in a Bathing Suit / Jun. 9, 1998 / Fantasy ✦✦✦

My Own House/You Should See the Rest of the Band / 1999 / Fantasy ✦✦✦✦✦

The Brothers Four

f. 1958, Seattle, WA, **db.** 1970

Group / Folk Revival, Traditional Folk

The band was formed in 1958 by four University of Washington students (Bob Flick, Michael Kirkland, John Paine, and Dick Foley) who met in a fraternity. The group signed to Columbia in 1959 and immediately hit the charts with "Greenfields." Between 1961-1963, they toured over 300 college campuses and in 1961 performed on the Academy Awards Show. The Brothers also made TV appearances on *The Ed Sullivan Show, The Pat Boone Chevy Showroom*, and *Mitch Miller's Singalong*. They recorded their last Columbia album in 1967. *—David Szatmary*

The Best of the Brothers Four / Apr. 1996 / Vanguard ✦✦✦✦✦

● **Greatest Hits** / Columbia ✦✦✦✦✦

Greatest Hits is a fine, 13-track collection that contains the bulk of the Brothers Four's folk-pop hits, including "Green Fields," "Yellow Bird," "I Am a Roving Gambler," "Lafayette," "Summer Days Alone," "Nobody Knows," "Green Leaves of Summer" and "Nine Pound Hammer." *—Stephen Thomas Erlewine*

Greg Brown

Vocals, Guitar / Contemporary Singer/Songwriter, Contemporary Folk

With his sandpaper-coarse but sensitive baritone, Greg Brown offers keen insights into the realities and foibles of modern life tinged with a hefty dose of common sense. He began singing around age 18 in New York where he ran hootenannies at Gerdes Folk City, later working with Garrison Keillor on the *Prairie Home Companion* live radio program. Brown had founded his own record label, Red House, a few years back, and had issued the albums *44 & 66* and *The Iowa Waltz*, but had turned over control to Bob Feldman to concentrate on writing and performing. He recorded his first widely available album, *In the Dark with You*, in 1985 to widespread critical acclaim. With his own songwriting, Brown expresses many moods in a variety of styles and with vivid imagery. Many of his songs tell stories, both humorous and sad. In addition to recording folk albums for adults, Brown has also recorded an intelligent children's album, *Bathtub Blues*, featuring songs he wrote in conjunction with elementary school students. *—Sandra Brennan*

Iowa Waltz / 1983 / Red House ✦✦✦

One More Goodnight Kiss / 1986 / Red House ✦✦✦✦

Singer/songwriter Greg Brown delivers his first classic on his fourth studio album, *One More Goodnight Kiss*, where he uses a keen observer's eye and his acoustic guitar to conjure up vivid images from his idyllic childhood. Born in Iowa, Greg Brown offers his reflections on small town life, from descriptions of the community characters hanging around the corner store to the importance of family bonds in keeping one's life grounded. This album is his tribute to his roots, and he brings these songs to life with a deep baritone voice that is surprisingly expressive for its limited range. The centerpiece of the album is "Canned Goods," a song dedicated to his grandmother that may catch you daydreaming about eating fresh produce on a perfect summer day. Greg Brown really shines on the up-tempo songs, where he gets to demonstrate his chops and let his guitar playfully duet with his gravelly voice. This is a great introduction to his early catalog and the birth of an important contemporary folk artist. *—Vik Iyengar*

Dream Cafe / 1992 / Red House ✦✦✦

Poet Game / 1994 / Red House ✦✦✦

Greg Brown's latest release is somber and streetwise with more political undertones than his previous CDs. The simple 1964 "Dodge" is a most powerful song about the impending destruction of faith in America after the Kennedy assassination; and it does not even mention the event. Production is simple and in a few cases one would have liked to hear a bit more thought given to the instrumental arrangement, but still this is a fine stripped-to-the-bone songwriter album by one of the premiere contemporary writers. *—Richard Meyer*

The Live One / Oct. 11, 1995 / Red House ✦✦✦✦

On this concert disc recorded at JR's Warehouse in Traverse City, MI, we get to hear Brown's commanding, but casually relaxed, solo performances of some of his old and new songs. His gravelly voice is remarkably expressive, especially when he is conveying the humorous side of some serious subject. He also includes covers of Richard Thompson's "1952 Vincent Black Lightning" and Van Morrison's "Moondance." This is very informal recording with bits of tuning and chit-chat. The songs, of course, carry the day. "Spring Wind" is heartbreaking and lovely as is his classic "Canned Goods." *—Richard Meyer*

● **Further In** / Sep. 24, 1996 / Red House ✦✦✦✦✦

Wonderfully and sparsely produced by guitarist Bo Ramsey, *Further In* may be the best outing yet from old-fashioned folkie Brown—which is saying plenty. Brown's warm baritone has never sounded better, and slide-guitar-spiced numbers like "China" are addictive ear candy. Typically, Brown wrote every track; typically, too, the moods range from somber or even depressing ("Small Dark Movie") to positively ebullient ("Hey Baby Hey"). The latter mood predominates, though: most of the time, Brown comes across as genuinely happy, and the disposition inspires him. Unlike, say, Bob Dylan, who appears to produce his best recordings when he's facing a personal crisis, the introspective Brown seems to deliver his most striking verse, effusive melodies, and heartfelt singing when he's satisfied. A line in the irresistible "Two Little Feet" sums up his apparent state of mind: "Oh man, what am I trying to say—/It's a messed up world but I love it anyway." *—Jeff Burger*

Slant 6 Mind / Oct. 21, 1997 / Red House ✦✦✦✦

One Night / May 18, 1999 / Red House ✦✦✦✦✦

Covenant / Aug. 8, 2000 / Red House ✦✦✦✦

If you still haven't discovered Greg Brown, this is as good a place to start as any. His deep, vibrant voice—as instantly recognizable as that of Fred Neil, Tim Buckley, or Van Morrison—remains a national treasure, and so does his songwriting, which has gone from great to better over the years. Wisely keeping the production simple and his voice upfront on this release, he unveils some of his best songs about love, life, friendship, dreams, and the American scene. There are no major departures from form here, but hope and love—not to mention hummable melodies—are perhaps in greater evidence than in the past. There's not a rotten apple in the bunch, but highlights include the effusive "Rexroth's Daughter"; "Lullaby," about a long-married couple; and the lilting "Walkin' Daddy." And stay tuned after the album's official end for a "hidden" track, the very funny "Marriage Chant," whose lyrics offer a sort of modern variation on Rodgers and Hart's "I Wish I Were in Love Again." *—Jeff Burger*

Richard Buckner

b. 1967

Vocals, Guitar / Americana, Alternative Country, Country-Folk, Singer/Songwriter

A husky-voiced country/folk singer-songwriter very much in the mold of the Lubbock, TX school of mavericks, including Butch Hancock, Terry Allen, and Jimmie Dale Gilmore. Richard Buckner is actually based in San Francisco, but the Lubbock connection is no accident. His debut album *Bloomed* was recorded in Lubbock, for one thing, with producer Lloyd Maines, who has also worked with Hancock, Allen, Joe Ely, and Uncle Tupelo. Buckner's principal following, however, is not with the country audience, but the alternative rock one. Like Allen and Hancock, the guitarist's work is based in rootsy country traditions, but his lyrics are far too personal and ambitious for those who think of country music as virtually synonymous with Nashville. So, like those Lubbock musicians, he tends to appeal to open-minded rock fans, or adventurous general music fans, more than country ones. Appearing on a small Texas independent label, his album won good critical notices, and his signing to a major company for 1997's acclaimed *Devotion and Doubt* probably means that both rock and country listeners will be much more widely exposed to him in the future. *Since* followed in 1998 and *The Hill*, an interpretation of Edgar Lee Masters' *Spoon River Anthology*, was issued two years later. *—Richie Unterberger*

Bloomed / 1994 / Dejadics ♦♦♦
Buckner's debut is an accomplished but subdued affair with hardly a trace of rock in sight. The emphasis is on his rich-but-weary vocals and sober tales of romance and restlessness, with dignified Texas prairie backup by such esteemed regionals as Lloyd Maines (who produced) and Ponty Bon. Very much in the vein of Butch Hancock, but much more ordinary at this point, without the eccentricity and boisterousness that characterizes much of Hancock and fellow Lubbockite Terry Allen's work. [The 1999 reissued of *Bloomed* contains five previously unreleased bonus tracks.] *—Richie Unterberger*

● **Devotion + Doubt** / Mar. 11, 1997 / MCA ♦♦♦♦
Buckner's second album of cross-country folk is an exploration of love's paranoia and its resulting desperation and hopelessness. Stemming from the singer-songwriter's divorce, the 13 songs on *Devotion + Doubt* reflect and, to a lesser degree, celebrate both his newfound independence and loneliness. His road-weary voice (often calmed to a whisper here), coupled with the sparing strums of his acoustic guitar, strikes a point of intimacy within the songs, giving the best of them ("Pull," "4am") the feeling that they were reluctantly cribbed from personal diary entries. But Buckner never sounds defeated on *Devotion + Doubt*, only a bit haunted, as if he's convinced himself—based on past attempts at love and their eventual failures—that he's destined to make the same mistakes again and again, no matter how hard he tries to make the relationships work. *—Michael Gallucci*

Since / Aug. 11, 1998 / MCA ♦♦♦
Richard Buckner's follow-up to his 1997 divorce odyssey *Devotion + Doubt* is a more upbeat affair, with questions of faith and being tossed into the electric mix. Moving from contemplative singer-songwriter treks ("Once") to blurry guitar rave-ups ("Believer"), *Since* is the picking-up-and-getting-on antidote to *Devotion + Doubt's* downer trip. Buckner still seems troubled by life's little hang-ups, but instead of falling into an acoustic-drenched funk, he rages against his blues with his guitar. That doesn't mean *Since* isn't without its distressing moments; there are plenty of hushed and fragile songs here that recall the breaking tone of his previous two albums. Yet, for all of the creeping positivity going on within the grooves, Buckner sounds more weary than ever, his already delicate voice cracking under the pressure as he trudges his way through his own brand of electric folk music. *—Michael Gallucci*

Hill / Oct. 3, 2000 / Overcoat ♦♦♦

Sandy Bull

b. 1941, New York, NY, **d.** Apr. 11, 2001
Guitar / Contemporary Folk, Folk-Rock, World Fusion
Long before Ry Cooder, Leo Kottke, Richard Thompson, and others were impressing us with their ability to hop from genre to genre, Sandy Bull glided from classical and jazz to ethnic music and rock & roll with grace and verve on his first two albums. Accompanied on his first two albums by renowned jazz drummer Billy Higgins, Bull produced some of the first extended instrumental compositions for guitar that incorporated elements of folk, jazz, and Indian and Arabic-influenced dronish modes. Not "rock" by any stretch of the imagination, it's nevertheless easy to see that it could have had an influence on the rock musicians who began incorporating eclectic and Middle Eastern sensibilities into their music a few years later. After his debut, Bull expanded his arsenal from the acoustic guitar and banjo to include oud, bass, and electric guitar. After his second album, however, his recordings were less focused and less impressive. In the 1970s, he dropped out of music altogether due to drug problems, although he began recording again in the late '80s. *—Richie Unterberger*

Fantasias for Guitar & Banjo / Aug. 1963 / Vanguard ♦♦♦

● **Inventions for Guitar & Banjo** / 1964 / Vanguard ♦♦♦♦♦
On his second and best album, Bull added more instruments and a bit of electricity. The centerpiece of the record is "Blend II." Like "Blend" from his first album, it is a melange (somewhat more electric in tone) of folk, jazz, and the Middle East, this time 24 minutes' worth. Also included on this 54-minute LP are two versions (electric and acoustic) of a Bach passage, a composition from the 14th century (Guillaume de Machaut's "Triple Ballade"), and Luiz Bonfa's "Manha de Carnival." A heavily reverbed (with drums), extended version of Chuck Berry's "Memphis, Tennessee" closes the set with an unexpected blast of rock & roll. *—Richie Unterberger*

E Pluribus Unum / 1968 / Vanguard ♦♦

Re-Inventions: The Best of Vanguard Years / Jan. 26, 1999 / Vanguard ♦♦♦♦
Sandy Bull's technical skills have always been correlated with his vision. As a guitarist, he could often slip into repetitive drags of both time and space; but as a musical theorist, those crawls into other dimensions were often fascinating excursions that were years ahead of their time. *Re-Inventions: Best of the Vanguard Years* gathers eight songs from three of the four albums Bull recorded for Vanguard for a decade beginning in 1963. It's Bull's most productive and exciting period, and this splendidly assembled compilation serves it well. His mastery of the acoustic and electric guitar, bass, banjo and oud is prominently on display here. And on his most sublime track, the 21-minute "Blend," Bull constructs a psychedelic folk song that meanders through several glorious fields before slamming into an open crevice for a rejoicing journey home. It's a straight take, with no overdubs or edits, and it's Bull—with drummer Billy Higgins—at his most poetic and timeless. *—Michael Gallucci*

Andrew Calhoun

b. Nov. 30, 1957
Vocals, Guitar / Contemporary Folk, Singer/Songwriter, Urban Folk
Sensitive lyricism is set to gentle, acoustic melodies by Chicago-based singer/songwriter and record company owner/producer Andrew Calhoun. Influenced by early John Prine, Leonard Cohen and Martin Carthy, Calhoun brings a poetic approach to his unique style of songwriting.

Although he continues to perform and record as a soloist, Calhoun has expressed his love of acoustic music as much through his record label, Waterbug Records, which has released more than forty albums by such artists as Chuck Brodsky, Diane Ziegler, Kat Eggleston, Sloan Wainwright, Kate McDonnell, Rick Lee, Michael Jerling, Michael McNevin and Steve Fisher.

The son of a Bell Laboratories technician and a high school teacher, Calhoun grew up listening to traditional songs recorded by folk singers including Ewan MacColl and Richard Dyer Bennett. When he was a youngster, his mother opened her home to problem-struck teenagers and runaways, including several who played acoustic guitar. By the age of ten, Calhoun had taught himself to play the six-stringed instrument, and after attending a concert by John Prine at the age of twelve, he began writing his own songs.

Calhoun moved with his family to the suburbs of Chicago in 1968. Nine years later, he moved on his own to Evanston, Illinois, where he continues to reside with singer/songwriter Kat Eggleston. Sharpening his performance skills in folk music coffeehouses, Calhoun recorded his debut album, *Water Street*, in 1983. After releasing two albums on Flying Fish, he launched Waterbug Records in August 1992 to issue efforts including *Hope*, 1996's *Phoenix Envy* and 1999's *Where Blue Meets Blue*. *—Craig Harris*

● **Hope** / Waterbug ♦♦♦♦♦
This album finds Calhoun in fine form. He is humorous in the face of domestic disaster; "Better Get a Lawyer," and passionate in "I Love You All the Time." His rich voice lends a traditional sound to all he does, but his songs are rooted in a modern poetic sensibility that is uncluttered and powerful. *—Richard Meyer*

Terry Callier

Vocals, Guitar / Chicago Soul, Folk-Jazz, Singer/Songwriter, Soul
For far too long, folk-jazz mystic Terry Callier was the exclusive province of a fierce but small cult following; a singer/songwriter whose cathartic, deeply spiritual music defied simple genre categorization, he went all but unknown for decades, finally beginning to earn the recognition long due him after his rediscovery during the 1990s. In 1964, he recorded his debut album *The New Folk Sound of Terry Callier;* upon the completion of the session, however, producer Samuel Charters traveled to Mexico with the master tapes in tow, and the album went unreleased before finally appearing to little fanfare in 1968. With producer Charles Stepney, Callier finally returned to the studio in 1973 for *Occasional Rain*, a beautiful fusion of folk and jazz textures which laid the groundwork for the sound further explored on the following year's *What Color Is Love?* Despite earning strong critical notices and building up a devoted fanbase throughout much of urban America, Callier failed to break through commercially, and after 1975's *I Just Can't Help Myself* he was dropped by the Cadet label. Upon signing to Elektra's Jazz Fusion imprint at the behest of label head Don Mizell, Callier resurfaced in 1978 with the lushly orchestrated *Fire on Ice;* with the follow-up, 1979's *Turn You to Love*, he finally cracked the pop charts with the single "Sign of the Times." He largely disappeared from music around during the early 1980s—a single parent, he instead accepted a job as a computer programmer, returning to college during the evenings to pursue a degree in sociology. His cult bloomed in the years to follow, however, and in 1998 Callier released his Verve Forecast debut *Timepeace*, his first major-label effort in close to two decades. *—Jason Ankeny*

The New Folk Sound of Terry Callier / 1964 / BGP ♦♦♦♦
The New Folk Sound of Terry Callier was not released until 1968, about three years after the project was originally completed; while the long delay almost certainly crippled the momentum of Callier's fledgling career, the impact on the music itself was at most minimal—while not the singer's best album, it's his most timeless and inviting, adhering closely to the folk stylings addressed by the title while largely ignoring the mystical jazz dimensions which texture his later material. Surprisingly, none of the album's eight songs are originals, relying instead on traditional tunes like "900 Miles" and "Cotton Eyed Joe"; while Callier's spiralling acoustic guitar lines and the use of two bassists (Terbour Attenborough and John Tweedle) reflect his admiration of John Coltrane, *New Folk Sound* is for the most part stark and simple, possessed of a subtle grace which spotlights his remarkably moving vocals to excellent effect—it's a debut which holds all the promise fulfilled by his classic recordings for Cadet. *—Jason Ankeny*

● **Occasional Rain** / 1972 / Cadet ♦♦♦♦♦
Recorded more than six years after *The New Folk Sound*, this was the first album to feature Terry Callier's unusual hybrid sound. The combination of a rich baritone voice and his unique blues/folk/jazz songwriting are met by just a touch of Andy Williams' zim, making *Occasional Rain* the best of his albums from the early '70s. Often prone to expansive, wandering melodies, Callier has written a tightness into most of the songs here that would generally be abandoned on the records to follow. Two of his most recognizable songs, "Ordinary Joe" and "Lean on Me," make their appearance and are joined by fragments of "Go 'Head On," which are interspersed throughout and provide a conceptual framework for the album as a whole. Highly accessible, this album conjures an intimate and relaxed mood, perfect for that lazy weekend morning. *—Joshua David Shanker*

What Color Is Love / Mar. 1973 / Cadet ♦♦♦♦♦
Like the artist himself, the music on this brilliant album defies all categories, embracing Callier's wide range of influences and experiences. Callier's musical kaleidoscope is filled with funk, rock, folk, jazz and even classical influences. "Dancing Girl" opens the album with Charles Stepney's majestic orchestration. This opus is the album's pinnacle, moving with soft intensity toward soul-stirring crescendos. Songs like "What Color Is Love" and "Ho-Tsine Mee (A Song of the Sun)," an elegant anti-war prayer of confusion, somehow avoid clichés or take them to another level. "You Goin' to Miss Your Candyman" was made popular by Urban Species when they sampled it on "Listen" in the early 1990s, and not surprisingly, it sounds better in its original form. No matter where you turn, Callier's passionate voice captures the

sweeping drama of the human condition. A lost romantic amidst "concrete front yards," this album is a must-have for any music connoisseur. *—Ryan Randall Goble*

I Just Can't Help Myself / 1975 / Universal ✦✦✦✦✦
Terry Callier's third and final album for the Cadet label is the most soulful and supple of the bunch—Marvin Gaye's classic Motown LPs from the same early 1970s period serve as a good reference point, both in their richly-detailed arrangements as well as their thoughtful political and social messages. Despite its contemporary feel, however, much of the material on *I Just Can't Help Myself* dates back several years—both the powerful "Alley-Wind Song" and the John Coltrane tribute "Can't Catch the Trane" were initially recorded during the 1969 sessions which later comprised the *First Light* collection, while the graceful reading of Duke Ellington's "Satin Doll" was and would remain a longstanding highlight of Callier's live set. Under the circumstances, then, the cohesive beauty and power of *I Just Can't Help Myself* is all the more remarkable—possessed of a subtlety and shading absent from his other Cadet dates, the disc simmers with quiet intensity, its underlying confidence and serenity occasionally giving way to moments of soul-searching angst. Certainly Callier's later records have much to recommend them, but the conclusion of his Cadet stint was nevertheless the end of an era—he never reached quite the same peaks again. *—Jason Ankeny*

First Light: Chicago 1969-71 / 1998 / Premonition ✦✦✦✦✦
Despite the lag between the 1965 recording of his debut album *The New Folk Sound of Terry Callier* and his 1972 sophomore effort *Occasional Rain*, Callier was far from inactive—in addition to regularly playing on the Chicago club circuit, he also cut a series of extraordinary demos which have finally surfaced almost three decades later as *First Light*. In the nine studio tracks which comprise the collection—a superb 1971 solo benefit date is also included—it's possible to hear the foundations of the aesthetic perfected on his classic Cadet recordings of the mid-1970s; on early renditions of songs like "Ordinary Joe" and "Alley Wind Song," all the pieces are already in place, as the haunted soulfulness of Callier's vocals blends perfectly with waves of acoustic folk guitar and subtle jazz textures. "Can't Catch the Trane," a tribute to his hero John Coltrane, barrels forward with appropriate locomotive force, spurred on by an incendiary tenor sax solo, while "Lean on Me" is beautifully delicate, a ballad of remarkable warmth and tenderness. Essential stuff. *—Jason Ankeny*

Timepeace / Jan. 27, 1998 / Verve ✦✦✦✦
Where has Terry Callier been all of our lives— Outside of the lucky few collectors fortunate enough to possess copies of his 1968 debut *The New Folk Sound of Terry Callier* and the series of brilliant records he cut for the Cadet label during the mid-1970s, the Chicago singer/songwriter has otherwise slipped through the cracks of contemporary music; his resurrection has been a long time in coming, and *Timepeace* is indeed well worth the wait. Long ago tagged with the label "folk-jazz," Callier's music eludes easy description; cosmic and spiritual, it also bears the influence of gospel and soul, yet synthesizes its disparate elements in unprecedented and breathtaking ways. Sparked by Callier's spiralling guitar leads, highlights like "Lazarus Man" and "Java Sparrow" seem to tap a higher consciousness, his yearning vocals channeling unfathomable power; the stark opener "Ride Suite Ride" matches the grace of Curtis Mayfield with the poignancy of Nick Drake, while "Coyote Moon" captures an ethereal yet pastoral beauty best likened to extraterrestrial country music. It's wonderful to have Callier back again—we need him now more than ever. *—Jason Ankeny*

● **Essential: The Very Best of Terry Callier** / May 4, 1998 / Universal ✦✦✦✦✦
Despite his fervid cult following, Terry Callier never sold many records, which meant his albums were frequently out of print. In 1998, he released his first album in nearly 20 years, and on the strength of the strong reviews, Universal released *Essential: The Very Best of Terry Callier*, a collection that featured highlights from his legendary '70s albums. Although those records are well worth the search, this compilation is necessary for any fan that can't find the original albums, and it's also a good introduction for the curious. *—Stephen Thomas Erlewine*

LifeTime / Sep. 6, 1999 / Talkin' Loud ✦✦✦

Terry Callier Live at Mother Blues: 1964 / Feb. 15, 2000 / Premonition ✦✦✦✦

Eliza Carthy

b. 1975
Vocals, Fiddle / Progressive Folk, Contemporary Folk, British Folk, Traditional Folk
The daughter of British guitarist/vocalist Martin Carthy and vocalist Norma Waterson, Eliza "Liza" Carthy has continued in her parents' footsteps. Carthy and her solo work have showcased her ability to breathe new life into England's traditional folk music. According to *Dirty Linen*, Carthy "has turned into a marvelous vocalist who has drawn equally from the craft and the idiosyncrasies of both her parents' distinctive styles." Carthy's earliest performances came as leader of her own band, the Kings of Calcutta, in 1990. Although they recorded a self-titled album, with producer John McCusker of the Battlefield Band, in her mother's home in 1994, it wasn't released until three years later. By that time, Carthy's debut solo album, *Heat, Light and Sound*, had been available for a year. In 1992, Carthy began to play in a highly technical duo with Nancy Kerr. Their first duo album, *Eliza Carthy and Nancy Kerr*, released in 1993, was followed by *Shape of Scrape* in 1995. Occasionally performing with her parents in the Watersons, since the early '90s, Carthy has been active with a traditional folk trio, Waterson Carthy, formed in 1994. The trio has recorded two albums, *Waterson: Carthy* in 1994 and *Common Tongue* in 1996. Carthy has also recorded with a Basque band, Hirutruku. In 1998, she released the critically acclaimed *Red Rice*, which received a Mercury Music Prize nod, and two years later she returned with *Angels and Cigarettes*. *—Craig Harris*

Eliza Carthy & The Kings of Calicutt / Aug. 5, 1997 / Topic ✦✦✦✦

Red Rice / May 19, 1998 / Topic ✦✦✦✦

● **Angels & Cigarettes** / 2000 / Warner Brothers ✦✦✦✦
Eliza Carthy comes from a family steeped in traditional folk, so it may seem somewhat disconcerting to see her with blue-streaked hair and pierced nose. While the music itself shows that Carthy hasn't completely turned her back on her roots, she is clearly determined to make her own path. Grounded in the folk and singer/songwriter school, she doesn't mind lacing her sound with pop rhythms, keyboards, and even trip-hop. Call it experimental folk. "Beautiful Girl" pushes forward with electronics and driving drums, creating a catchy beat that wouldn't be out of place on a Madonna album. However, the difference is the words, with biting lyrics like "Beautiful girl I know you're probably dead clever/But you're only gorgeous once and you'll be clever forever." The opening track, "Whispers of Summer," is much more folky, with Carthy's fiddle rising above the drum track to create a danceable melody. This cut is more upbeat than much of the material on the album. "The Company of Men" begins with a lyric about giving sexual favors "to men who didn't want me anymore"; the more oblique "Poor Little Me" is about a death, perhaps an abortion. Songs like "Train Song" and "Fuse" explore love and lust, themes that run throughout *Angels & Cigarettes*. These lyrics are at times emotionally bare, and everyone may not be comfortable with Carthy's revelations. But she seems determined to purge these emotions by turning them into art. The result is ten well-written songs, filled with searching lyrics and an innovative sound. For those who enjoy folk that's willing to take musical chances, *Angels & Cigarettes* is a gratifying release. *—Ronnie Lankford Jr.*

Slaid Cleaves

Vocals / Contemporary Singer/Songwriter, Contemporary Folk
The music of Austin-based singer/songwriter and guitarist Slaid Cleaves is rooted in country and traditional folk songs, but it is unusual enough to hold interest in what appears to be a sea of singer-songwriters in the 1990s. Working with former Lucinda Williams guitarist Gurf Morlix, Cleaves combines his passion for folk songs, blues and traditional country music on his debut into an amalgamation of styles known as "Americana" music. After many years in Portland, Maine, he sought new mountains to climb, and found some of them after moving to Austin, Texas in 1992. Despite the echelon of great singer/songwriters like Jimmie Dale Gilmore, Lucinda Williams, Robert Earl Keen, Guy Clark and Joe Ely all centered around the Austin scene, Cleaves was able to make a name for himself there. In 1995, he recorded an independent album for Rock Bottom Records entitled *Life's Other Side*. In 1996, he began his collaboration with Morlix, who liked Cleaves demo tape a whole lot and ended up serving as producer for 1997's *No Angel Knows*. *—Richard Skelly*

Promise / 1990 / Rock Bottom ✦✦✦

● **Life's Other Side** / 1992 / Play Hard ✦✦✦✦✦
This simply produced CD contains songs of wandering and wanderers. Many of the lyrics have an underlying theme of mystery. "Willie of the Wind" is one of the highlights. *—Richard Meyer*

For the Brave & Free / 1993 / Slaid Cleaves ✦✦✦✦✦
The songwriting here is darker than the previous two releases. Like Springsteen's *Nebraska*, this album is comprised of sparse sketched-out stories. The band is simple and tight. *—Richard Meyer*

No Angel Knows / Feb. 11, 1997 / Philo ✦✦✦

Broke Down / Jan. 25, 2000 / Rounder ✦✦✦
Austin-based singer-songwriter Slaid Cleaves writes about losers. Sherry, in the title song of his second album, *Broke Down*, abandons a "love grown cold" with "Billy" in favor of a pretty boy who treats her even worse. The narrator of "Cold and Lonely" reflects on his lost children and wife. "I lost my wife, I lost my home / Quit my job, and set out alone," notes the singer of "Key Chain," while Sandy Gray in "Breakfast in Hell" loses his life in a logjam and the title character of "Lydia" (written by Karen Poston), remembers the husband and son lost in a mine collapse. Needless to say, *Broke Down* is not the cheeriest of albums, though Cleaves usually employs some religious imagery and pledges on which to build some hope by song's end. Still, it seems odd that he has included a song with lyrics by Woody Guthrie that he has set to music, "This Morning I Am Born Again." After all, it was Guthrie who once wrote, "I hate a song that makes you think that you are just born to lose.... I am out to fight those songs to my very last breath of air and my last drop of blood." His lyric is a typical example of his flinty defiance and stubborn optimism, but it stands in stark contrast to the rest of this album, and one can't help wondering what he would have thought about being in the company of these lose-lose propositions. *—William Ruhlmann*

Judy Collins

b. May 1, 1939, Seattle, WA
Vocals, Keyboards, Guitar / Folk Revival, Folk-Rock, Singer/Songwriter
Judy Collins was one of the major interpretive folksingers of the '60s. She released her first album, *A Maid of Constant Sorrow*, in 1961 when she was 22. That album and its follow-up, *The Golden Apples of the Sun*, consisted of traditional folk material, with Collins's pure, sweet soprano accompanied by her acoustic guitar playing. By the time of *Judy Collins #3*, she had begun to turn to contemporary material and to add other musicians. Collins' musical horizons were expanded further by 1966 and the release of *In My Life*, which added theater music to her repertoire and introduced her audience to the writing of Leonard Cohen; it was one of her six albums to go gold. Her first gold-seller, however, was 1967's *Wildflowers*, which contained her hit version of "Both Sides Now" by the then-little-known songwriter Joni Mitchell. By the '70s, Collins had come to be identified as much as an art song singer as a folksinger and had also begun to make a mark with her original compositions. Her best-known performances cover a wide stylistic range: the traditional gospel song "Amazing Grace," the Stephen Sondheim Broadway ballad "Send in the Clowns," and such songs of her own as "My Father" and "Born to the Breed." *—William Ruhlmann*

Maid of Constant Sorrow / 1961 / Elektra ✦✦✦
Collins's talent is to sing these traditional chestnuts, even at the time, without the prissiness of so many female folk singers. Her phrasing has enough strength to stand up to the "Prickile Bush" and give in to "Wild Mountain Thyme." *—Richard Meyer*

Golden Apples of the Sun / 1962 / Elektra ✦✦✦
Collins takes on such diverse repertoire as Gary Davis' "Twelve Gates to the City," "Crow on the Cradle" and her setting of "Golden Apples of the Sun." *—Richard Meyer*

3rd Album / 1963 / Elektra ✦✦✦
Having established herself as one of the foremost interpreters of traditional material, Collins did the same for contemporary folk songwriters on this album, which mixed standards with pristine covers of compositions by Dylan, Bob Gibson, Pete Seeger, Ewan MacColl, and Shel Silverstein. With Jim McGuinn arranging and playing second guitar and banjo, this album, which included a fine version of Seeger's "Turn! Turn! Turn!," had a clear (if overlooked) influence on the folk-rock he pioneered with The Byrds a couple years later. *—Richie Unterberger*

Judy Collins' Concert / 1964 / Elektra ✦✦✦
On this live set recorded at Town Hall in New York in 1964, Collins stirs up the audience with a rich mixture of traditional and contemporary covers, including Billy Ed Wheeler's "Coal Tattoo" and Paxton's "Ramblin' Boy." *—Richard Meyer*

5th Album / 1965 / Elektra ✦✦✦✦✦
Collins took a major stride forward with this fine, consistent album, tailoring both her material and arrangements to reflect contemporary changes shaking folk and folk-rock. Features stellar interpretations of songs by several major '60s songwriters (Dylan, Eric Andersen, Phil Ochs, Gordon Lightfoot, Malvina Reynolds, Richard Farina), and first-rate accompaniment by some of the day's finest folk and folk-rock musicians, including Eric Weissberg, Bill Lee, Danny Kalb, John Sebastian, and Richard Farina (although no drums are present). *—Richie Unterberger*

In My Life / 1966 / Elektra ✦✦✦✦✦
Collins, who by this point has moved from the acoustic renderings of traditional folk ballads to more extensive instrumentation and the work of contemporary folk writers, takes another step here, turning to tasteful string arrangements by Joshua Rifkin and adding theater music from *Threepenny Opera* and *Marat/Sade* to the Bob Dylan covers. She also starts covering Leonard Cohen ("Suzanne," "Dress Rehearsal Rag"). *— William Ruhlmann*

Wildflowers / 1967 / Elektra ✦✦✦
Passionate and filled with memorable passages. Includes her hit "Both Sides Now" and her first major original composition "Since You Asked." Leonard Cohen's "Priests" has not appeared elsewhere. *—Bruce Eder and William Ruhlmann*

Who Knows Where the Time Goes / 1968 / Elektra ✦✦✦
Rock and country leanings are found on this album featuring guitarists James Burton and Stephen Stills. Includes the hit "Someday Soon" and Collins' own brilliant "My Father." *— William Ruhlmann*

Recollections: The Best of Judy Collins / 1969 / Elektra ✦✦✦✦✦
Collins sings "Tomorrow Is a Long Time," "Early Mornin' Rain" and "Winter Sky." This is a best-of compilation. *—Richard Meyer*

Whales & Nightingales / 1970 / Elektra ✦✦✦

Living / 1971 / Elektra ✦✦✦

● **Colors of the Day: The Best of Judy Collins** / 1972 / Elektra ✦✦✦✦✦
An excellent collection of some of the best tracks from Judy Collins' early Elektra albums, *Colors of the Day* will both entertain and leave you wanting more. Lovingly programmed (it leads off with her excellent country-pop hit, "Someday Soon," an Ian Tyson classic), this is Collins at her finest. Earlier explorations into folk-pop ("Both Sides Now"), British folk ("Sunny Goodge Street," "In My Life") and gospel ("Amazing Grace") clearly show her eclecticism. Some of the record's finest moments are from her exquisite 1968 album, *Who Know Where the Time Goes* (such as that album's title track and the aforementioned "Someday Soon"). This anthology brings the "best of" collection to a new art form. *—Matthew Greenwald*

True Stories and Other Dreams / 1973 / Elektra ✦✦✦

Judith / 1975 / Elektra ✦✦✦

☆ **So Early in the Spring . . . The First 15 Years** / 1977 / Elektra ✦✦✦✦✦
This two-LP, 23-song set was the second Judy Collins compilation in five years and the third in under a decade. However, in contrast to the folk-oriented *Recollections* or *Colors of the Day*'s focus on her best-known popular tracks from the late '60s, this was a more comprehensive retrospective covering all phases of her career. Unfortunately, it came out at a point when Collins' career momentum was slowing, and a little too long after her unexpected chart hit "Send in the Clowns." In addition, all of Collins' albums were still in print at the time, and there was nothing here that wasn't on those LPs. This collection could be of little interest to anyone but hardcore fans—and they were the people who needed it least. Fans of her post-folk era didn't need the summary of the early period, and fans of the folk period didn't want the pop/rock material. However, as a career overview it was the only place to go, and as of the year 2000 *So Early in the Spring . . .* is still available as a cassette. It can be considered superior in aspects of its programming to *Forever: An Anthology*; indeed, there has never been a definitive anthology of Collins' work. Maybe they should let Lenny Kaye try his hand at that, since he's been so good at repackaging so many Elektra releases. *— Bruce Eder*

Live at Newport, 1959-1966 / Oct. 25, 1994 / Vanguard ✦✦✦
A 13-song compilation of material recorded at the 1959, 1963, 1964, and 1966 Newport Folk Festivals; it would have been nice if they'd been able to document what year each song was recorded. In any case, it does reflect Collins' artistic growth during this period, from an interpreter of strictly traditional fare to more contemporary material by Bob Dylan, Richard Farina, and others. Highlights include her versions of "Turn, Turn, Turn," "Blowin' In the Wind," "Hey, Nelly Nelly," "Get Together," "Hard Lovin' Loser," and "The Great Silkie," which has the same melody the Byrds used for "I Come and Stand at Every Door" on their *Fifth Dimension* album. All of the songs are previously unreleased, except "The Greenland Whale Fisheries," a duet with Theodore Bikel; on some tracks, Collins is accompanied on upright bass by Bill Lee, and on second guitar by Steve Mandell or Eric Weissberg. With good sound, a nice if not essential addition to the Collins catalog. *—Richie Unterberger*

Forever: An Anthology / Oct. 28, 1997 / Elektra ✦✦✦✦✦
Forever: An Anthology is a good but flawed double-disc overview of Judy Collins' long, prolific and productive career at Elektra/Asylum Records. Over the course of 35 tracks, nearly all of Collins' best-known songs are showcased ("Someday Soon," "Who Knows Where the Time Goes," "Send in the Clowns," "Both Sides Now," "Hard Lovin' Loser," "Amazing Grace"). Scattered throughout the collection are four new songs—including, inexplicably, a re-recorded version of "Chelsea Morning"—that may not live up to the quality of her classic songs, but still are quite strong. It might have been more appealing if the songs were sequenced in chronological order, and if "Chelsea Morning" was present in its original version, but *Forever: An Anthology* remains an ideal compilation for the serious Collins fan. *— Stephen Thomas Erlewine*

Classic Broadway / Sep. 21, 1999 / Madacy ✦✦✦

Christine Collister

b. Dec. 28, 1961
Vocals / Contemporary Singer/Songwriter, Contemporary Folk, British Folk
Christine Collister is one of the most respected female vocalists in contemporary British folk-rock. Although she first attracted attention as a member of Richard Thompson's band in the late 1980s and then in a duo that she shared with Clive Gregson, the former leader of British rock band Any Trouble, she's continued to make her presence felt since embarking on a solo career in 1992.

Collister made her earliest mark as the singer of the theme song of the popular BBC Television series *The Life and Loves of a She Devil*. Meeting Gregson, who was playing backup guitar in Thompson's band, in 1985, she was quickly recruited as a harmony singer, touring with the group until 1988. Gregson and Collister's debut album as a duo, *Home and Away*, was a homemade cassette sold at their shows; it was later reissued by Flying Fish. The duo released their first full-fledged album, *Mischief*, in 1987, following it with the all-original album *A Change in the Weather* in 1989, and *Love is a Strange Hotel*, a collection of their favorite songs, in 1990. Their final album together, *The Last Word*, was released in 1992.

Collister has continued to balance her solo career with a variety of projects. In 1992, she joined with Barb Jungr, Michael Parker and Ian Shaw in a four-part harmony show, *Hell Bent Heaven Bound*. In addition to a crowd-rousing performance at the *Winnepeg Folk Festival* in 1993, the show was presented during a sold-out tour of the United Kingdom. After touring with Richard Thompson in 1995, Collister joined a supergroup of British female performers, Daphne's Flight, that also featured Melanie Harrold, Julie Matthews, Helen Watson and Chris While. The group recorded a self-titled album in 1996.

Collister's debut solo album, *Live*, was recorded during a 1994 concert in her hometown. Her solo studio debut, *Blue Aconite*, was released in 1996 and featured guest appearances by Thompson and Watson. *Horizon* was released in 1997. Collister's fourth solo album, *The Dark Gift of Time*, released the following year, featured guests B.J. Cole (pedal steel), Danny Thompson (double bass), Jacqui McShee (vocals) and John Surman (bass clarinet and saxophone), in addition to Thompson (electric guitar). *Songbird* appeared in early 2000. *—Craig Harris*

● **Dark Gift of Time** / Sep. 15, 1998 / Koch ✦✦✦✦
The Dark Gift of Time is Christine Collister's second solo album since beginning her solo career in 1992. Prior to that time, she built a name for herself as vocalist for Richard Thompson and one half of Gregson and Collister. Collister is a talented, impassioned song stylist. As such there are only two original tracks here. One is Collister's moving duet, "The Irish Sea," which is augmented by John Surman on bass clarinet. Elsewhere, we are invited to recognize her ability in the way she possesses a song and infuses it with her soul. Her treatment of "The Whole Night Sky" (Bruce Cockburn) paints the entire twinkling canopy a somber hue. The mood of Tom Waits' crisp, sanguine ballad "Dirt in the Ground" becomes redeeming in her gospel-like delivery. A brighter glint of hope shines through Collister's stark and abandoned take on "Deeper Well" (Emmylou Harris). Her equally downbeat jazz ensemble shows up in various lineups for these tracks. On "I Want to Vanish" (Elvis Costello), only double bass and baritone saxophone are required for maximum effect of her spare treatment. The simplicity of each approach spells intimacy and authenticity upon listening. Combined with an even tone and approach, *The Dark Gift of Time* is an exquisite, smoky jazz approach to a well-chosen contemporary repertoire. Collister also provides excellent versions of "Black Eyed Dog" (Nick Drake), "God Bless the Child" (Billie Holiday), and an excellent theme for her musical Weltanschauung, Colin Linden's "Sad & Beautiful World." *—Tom Schulte*

Mike Cross

b. 1946
Vocals, Guitar, Fiddle / Contemporary Singer/Songwriter, Contemporary Folk
Mike Cross is one of folk music's most energetic performers. From the time he hits the stage to his closing tune, he serves up a turbo-charged collection of humorous songs, sensitive ballads, Will Rogers-like tales, Delta blues and Appalachian and Celtic fiddle tunes. Cross' first three albums—*Child Prodigy, The Bounty Hunter* and *Born in the Country*—made him a fixture on the Southern folk circuit. He garnered most of his fame for his humorous songs. He poked fun at Southern hillbilly culture with such tunes as "Mountain Mean," "Liquor in the Well," "Rocky Top Bar-B-Que" and "Elma Turl." However, not all of Cross' songs aim at the tickle bone; "Leon McDuff" was performed by the Dirt Band as the theme song of Farm Aid, "Twelve Disciples" has been used in Sunday schools as an aid to learning the names of the apostles, and "Not for the Love I Can Take" is a romantic masterpiece. *—Craig Harris*

Carolina Sky / 1975 / Sugar Hill ✦✦✦
Another well-done studio album of Cross's energetic songs is played with a crack band. *— Richard Meyer*

● **Prodigal Son** / 1989 / Sugar Hill ✦✦✦✦✦

Irregular Guy / Sugar Hill ✦✦✦
A solid collection of instrumental rave-up and fun songs from this multi-instrumentalist, it includes "Carolina Calling" and the tongue-twisting "Directions." *—Richard Meyer*

Live & Kickin' / Sugar Hill ✦✦✦✦✦
Cross mixes country, folk, bluegrass, and Scots/Irish music, playing fiddle and guitar and singing on material ranging from spirited dance tunes to off-the-wall novelties. He is thus best heard in a live setting, especially one that includes the infectious "Whiskey 'Fore Breakfast." *—William Ruhlmann*

Cumberland Three

f. 1960, USA, **db.** 1960
Group / Traditional Folk
John Stewart (b. Sep. 5, 1939, San Diego, CA) started out playing professionally in rock & roll in the late 1950s. He moved toward folk music while in college, however, and hooked up with John Montgomery. They formed a banjo/guitar duet, John and Monty, and in 1960 added bassist Gil Robbins (b. Rubin) to their lineup, forming the Cumberland Three, a group modeled after the Kingston Trio, and signed to Roulette Records. Every label was looking for its own Kingston Trio, but the Cumberland Three succeeded better than most by virtue of the talent involved—their first album showed promise, but it was their second and third albums, *Civil War Almanac Vol. 1 (The Yankees)* and *Civil War Almanac Vol. 2 (The Rebels)*, both issued in 1960, that have lingered longest in memory.

The group broke up after less than a year of existence. In June of 1960, Stewart announced that he was leaving the Cumberland Three, at approximately the same time that Kingston Trio co-founder Dave Guard decided that he was leaving that group. Stewart was already a fan of the Kingston Trio and had sold some songs to them; in early 1961, he was chosen to become Guard's successor. Gil Robbins went on to join the Highwaymen, another folk group modeled after the Kingston Trio that had several successful singles during the early 1960s, and continues to work in music as a vocal arranger in the 1990s. John Stewart has had a long and thriving career as a country-rock solo star and songwriter. *—Bruce Eder*

● **Folk Scene, U.S.A.** / 1960 / Collectors' Choice Music ✦✦✦✦✦
The debut album by the Cumberland Three was also an attempt by Morris Levy's Roulette Records to get in on a piece of the folk-music action spurred by the success of the Kingston Trio. The album compares very favorably with the work of the Kingston Trio—no less a figure than the latter group's co-founder, Dave Guard (who was to be succeeded by Cumberland Trio co-founder John Stewart), endorses the Cumberland Three on the original jacket—and may even be preferable to some listeners, because the Cumberland Three don't let overt humor and comic relief play too large a role in their recordings. Not that they don't have fun, but they concentrate on the music, which ranges from traditional folk to faux Civil War songs and calypso-influenced numbers. The vocals are impeccable, and even more alluring as they aren't too perfect—John Stewart's singing on "New Land" is rough-hewn and affecting in a very serious way, and the rousing follow-up, "Nine Hundred Miles," makes them a perfect match-up on the original album. The 1999 Collectors' Choice reissue has been extended with three bonus tracks, a surprisingly soulful version of Leadbelly's "Cotton Fields," a lyrical and touching "You Can Tell the World," and a slow but not too mournful "Old Dog Blue," all familiar songs from other venues that come to life anew here. *—Bruce Eder*

Songs of the Civil War / Rhino ✦✦✦
The Cumberland Three's second and third albums combined on one CD, and reissued in the wake of Ken Burns' *Civil War* series. These are spirited performances, based on arrangements by Oscar Brand or the group members, with only one original ("Bessie") by John Stewart, that fits in perfectly with the period material. The original order of release put the North's volume first, but the CD puts the South's songs first among the 23 tracks. The material holds up remarkably—some of the more familiar songs include "The Yellow Rose of Texas," "Hold Our Glasses Steady," "Story of the Lamb" (aka "Rally Round the Flag Boys"), "Bring the Good Old Bugle" (aka "Marching Through Georgia"), "Back to Home," and "Battle Hymn of the Republic." The singing and playing are of a very high caliber, with "Gonna Get You" being perhaps the best sung song here, followed closely by "Shipmates Come Gather," stunningly moving performances of "The Boys Are Home" (aka "When Johnny Comes Marching Home"), and "Battle Hymn of the Republic." And "Bring the Good Old Bugle" offers Stewart's best banjo work. *—Bruce Eder*

Erik Darling

b. Sep. 25, 1922, Baltimore, MD
Vocals, Guitar, Banjo / Folk Revival
Erik Darling was an important influence on the folk scene in the late 50s and early 60s. Inspired by The Weavers, in the 50s he formed The Tunetellers, later called The Tarriers. Darling left that group to replace Pete Seeger in The Weavers, staying with them from 1958 through 1962. He then formed The Rooftop Singers (see separate entry in this section). His solo album *True Religion* for Vanguard was influential on younger folksingers in the 60s. *—Michael Erlewine*

● **True Religion** / 1961 / Vanguard ✦✦✦✦✦
Darling performs all the styles named in the title on banjo, 6- and 12-string guitar. He has good command of the idiom, more than many other contemporaries, on such tunes as "Moanin' Dove" and "Blackeyed Susan." *—Richard Meyer*

The Deighton Family

f. 1980
Group / Traditional Folk, Traditional Bluegrass
An eclectic range of music serves as the repertoire of the Yorkshire, England-based Deighton Family. Led by father, Dave, who plays melodeon, harmonica, fiddle and guitar and sings lead, and, mother, Josie, who plays acoustic guitar and bodhran, the seven-piece group blends Cajun two-steps, bluegrass breakdowns, folk ballads, blues and roots rock and roll into their infectious, good-natured, sound. In a review of their second album, *Acoustic Music to Suit Most Occasions*, released in 1988 and named National Public Radio's "record of the year," *The San Francisco Bay Guardian* wrote, "no matter what mood has hold of you when you approach this approach, the breezy, giddy, feeling will take over." CMJ took a similar view, writing, "From dad, Dave, to six year old, Angelina, the Deightons play with an unaffected spirit and feeling that shines right through the processed cheese that poses for music most of us are used to hearing." *The Roundup Newsletter* referred to the group as "The Carter Family of the global village." In addition to Dave and Josie Deighton, the group features their five children—*Maya (tin whistle, flute), Arthur (mandolin, electric guitar), Kathleen (fiddle), Rosalie (vocals, percussion, mandolin) and Angelina (boogie, percussion).* —Craig Harris

Mama Was Right / 1980 / Philo ✦✦✦✦✦
With more fun performances with squeezebox, tin whistles, and mandolin, it includes a wiggy take on George Harrison's "Tax Man." *—Mark A. Humphrey*

★ **Acoustic Music to Suit Most Occasions** / 1988 / Philo ✦✦✦✦✦
This delightful British folkabilly band defies easy pigeon-holing. National Public Radio named this its Album of the Year. *—Mark A. Humphrey*

Sandy Denny

b. Jan. 6, 1947, Wimbledon, England, **d.** Apr. 21, 1978
Vocals, Piano, Guitar / British Folk-Rock, British Folk, Folk-Rock
Maddy Prior, Jacqui McShee, and June Tabor all give her a run for her money, but the late Sandy Denny remains the pre-eminent British folk-rock singer. In addition to recording several albums of her own, Denny was an integral force behind the best work of the most respected British folk-rock band of all, Fairport Convention, and also contributed mightily to recordings by the Strawbs and Fotheringay. It's impossible for words to fully evoke the haunting, spectral presence of her powerful and penetrating alto voice, which seemed to bring the mythology of English moors and folktales to life in contemporary, 20th-century settings. Her composition "Who Knows Where the Time Goes." gave Sandy her first international recognition when Judy Collins recorded it in 1968; that same year Denny was tapped to replace Judy Dyble in Fairport Convention in 1968, and is prominently featured on their late-'60s albums *What We Did on Our Holidays, Unhalfbricking*, and *Liege and Lief.* These are not only recognized as Fairport's best work, but as some of the finest British folk-rock records of all time. Denny left Fairport Convention in 1970, and while both she and Fairport would produce some worthwhile work in the future, it's fair to say that neither band nor singer would reach the same peaks again. Much of the best of Denny's later solo work, oddly, is found on live and BBC recordings, some of which surfaced on the box set *Who Knows Where the Time Goes?* Her final LP, *Rendezvous*, came out in 1977; the following year, she died from injuries sustained in a fall down a flight of stairs. *—Richie Unterberger*

North Star Grassman and the Ravens / 1971 / Hannibal ✦✦✦
Following the breakup of the short-lived Fotheringay, Sandy Denny returned with her first post-Fairport solo album, *The North Star Grassman and the Ravens.* Produced with ex-bandmate Richard Thompson and longtime engineer John Wood, who would go on to produce the bulk of Thompson's work with Linda Thompson, the record consists of eight evocative Denny originals, along with the traditional "Blackwaterside" and a pair of borrowed rockers. There's a looseness and roominess to the sound, with acoustic guitar, piano, and Thompson's electric guitar leading the sparse backing from former members of Fotheringay, along with the occasional accordion, violin, pedal steel, and strings. Songs such as "Late November," "John the Gun," and "Next Time Around" are among her best, while "Blackwaterside," featuring Thompson's guitar and accordion, continues to show her mastery of traditional music. Because her songs tend to lean towards the melancholy, and are primarily on the slow to mid-tempo side, Denny had to look elsewhere for upbeat material. Choices such as Brenda Lee's "Let's Jump the Broomstick" and a ragged, yet somewhat effective, duet with Thompson on Bob Dylan's "Down in the Flood," are good ones, though both sound as if they were afterthoughts. Her best record was still a year away, but *The North Star Grassman* is a solid effort from Sandy Denny's sadly shortened solo career. *—Brett Hartenbach*

The Bunch / 1972 / A&M ✦✦

Sandy / 1972 / A&M ✦✦✦✦✦
Sandy Denny's second post-Fairport solo offering, produced by (then-future) husband Trevor Lucas, is a beautiful blend of the traditional style with which she is most often associated and a slightly more lavish sound that would become more prevalent in her later work. Lucas does an excellent job of balancing the two and creating an exquisite backdrop for Denny's gorgeous songs and majestic voice. Nearly every track has the radiance and timelessness of her best Fairport work, along with an accessibility she had merely hinted at prior to this. "Listen, Listen," and with its soaring chorus and bed of strings and mandolin, the lovely "The Lady," and the layered a cappella vocal arrangement of Richard Farina's "Quiet Joys of Brotherhood" (featuring Dave Swarbrick's haunting solo violin coda) are perfect examples of Denny's enormous talents, and only a few of the many pleasures found here. Touches such as lush strings, Allen Toussaint's horn arrangement on "For Nobody to Hear," Sneaky Pete Kleinow's steel guitar and former Fairport partner Richard Thompson's guitars and mandolin, bring out the many dimensions in Denny's music without obscuring it. *Sandy* also boasts her best collection of original material, as well as terrific covers of Dylan's "Tomorrow Is a Long Time," featuring Linda (Thompson) Peters on backing vocals, and the aforementioned "Quiet Joys of Brotherhood." If you're simply looking for a quick introduction to a wonderful songwriter and one of the finest voices in popular music, go for the single disc best-of collection, but if you would like to hear Sandy Denny's definitive (solo) musical statement, search out *Sandy. —Brett Hartenbach*

Like an Old Fashioned Waltz / 1973 / Hannibal ✦✦

Rendezvous / 1977 / Hannibal ✦✦✦
With a sublime voice and a catalog full of beautiful songs, Sandy Denny left an indelible mark on British folk and popular music in her 31 years. Released in 1977, less than one year before her untimely death, the overwrought *Rendezvous*, unfortunately stands as her final musical statement. Producer Trevor Lucas' use of cumbersome strings, backup singers and bloated lead guitars weigh things down and bury some otherwise fine writing. One of her

best, "I'm a Dreamer," is nearly ruined by the chorus of singers and anthemic guitar at the end, while the heartfelt "One Way Donkey Ride" and the poignant "Full Moon," though more successful, never seem to quite reach their potential. Even some choice covers—including Richard Thompson's "I Wish I Was a Fool for You" (aka "For Shame of Doing Wrong"), Elton John's "Candle in the Wind," and a somber working of "Silver Threads and Golden Needles"—lack the impact she brought in the past to works by the likes of Thompson, Bob Dylan, Joni Mitchell, Richard Farina and Buddy Holly, as well as the many traditional tunes that she made her own. Few, if any of the exquisite touches that Lucas brought to Denny's superb 1972 release *Sandy* are evident here. Originally released by Island Records in the U.K., and not available in the U.S. until the mid-'80s, *Rendezvous* seems to be a flawed attempt at gaining a wider audience, by an artist who deserved better and was capable of the best. *—Brett Hartenbach*

Sandy Denny & The Strawbs / 1985 / Hannibal ✦✦✦✦
Sandy Denny was only with the Strawbs for a short period of time, but she was around long enough to make some very memorable contributions to the band. An expressive jewel of a folk singer with a rich, angelic voice, the pre-Fairport Convention Denny is clearly the main attraction on this CD. In contrast to the progressive-rock and art-rock elements the band would later embrace, these sides are acoustic-oriented and unmistakably British-sounding folk-pop. Gems like "Tell Me What You See In Me," "Nothing Else Will Do" and "Who Knows Where the Time Goes" not only illustrate how superb and moving a singer Denny was, they also demonstrate how prolific a composer Dave Cousins was. One can only speculate as to what direction the Strawbs would have taken had Denny stayed, but what we know with certainty is that her short-lived association with Cousins was lucrative and valuable. *—Alex Henderson*

Who Knows Where the Time Goes? / 1986 / Hannibal ✦✦✦✦✦
This magnificently produced multi-disc boxed set presents a complete portrait of Sandy Denny, the haunting singer, the melodic, mournful songwriter, and the mesmerizing bandleader of Fairport Convention and Fotheringay. Much of the material is previously unheard, but it's all of a piece with Denny's accomplished work on her solo albums and in her groups. The album makes the case for Denny as a major folk artist. *—William Ruhlmann*

The Best of Sandy Denny / 1989 / Hannibal ✦✦✦✦✦

Original Sandy Denny / 1991 / Trojan ✦✦✦
Denny's first recording, originally released in 1967, is her most traditional effort. Backed only by her own acoustic guitar, Denny's voice is assured, pure, and powerful on her debut. The album features traditional folk staples like "This Train," "Make Me A Pallet On Your Floor," and "Pretty Polly," as well as covers of Tom Paxton's "Ramblin' Boy" and "Milk And Honey." There are also a couple of songs by the obscure American songwriter Jackson Frank, one of which she would soon perform with Fairport Convention ("You Never Wanted Me"). Although this has little of the folk-rock cross-pollination that Denny would soon master with Fairport and others, it is still an impressive collection that shows her voice in as haunting and commanding form as her more renowned recordings. *—Richie Unterberger*

Attic Tracks 1972-1984 / 1995 / Raven ✦✦✦✦✦
The perfect—and we do mean *Perfect*—complement to Hannibal Records' *Who Knows Where the Time Goes* box. *Attic Tracks* (so named to distinguish it from Dylan's *Basement Tapes*) is an 18-song collection from Australia's Raven Records consisting of unreleased songs, outtakes, and extreme rarities, recorded by Sandy Denny and her former husband, the late Trevor Lucas. Included are tracks from Fairport's 1974 tour ("The Ballad of Ned Kelly"); Denny's beautiful, passionate French version of "Listen, Listen," entitled "Ecoute, Ecoute"; a pair of Denny demos ("One More Chance," "Rising for the Moon") given to Fairport Convention for their recording of the *Rising for the Moon* album; the lost 1975 Lucas/Fairport track "Tears"; "Losing Game," a Flying Burrito Bros. track recorded by Denny and Lucas, in a broad, brassy, hard-rocking version in 1972 and finished in 1976, but never released; the forgotten 1977 Denny B-side "Still Waters Run Deep"; Lucas' version of Bob Dylan's "Forever Young"; three songs from the last concert that Denny ever gave, including one of her longest, liveliest versions of "Who Knows Where the Time Goes" on record; and Denny's fiery reading of the Little Feat song "Easy to Slip," recorded during the making of her *Rendezvous* album. The big surprise, however, is Lucas' gently soulful cover of the Australian hit "Girls on the Avenue," on which his voice has an extraordinary "haunt count" and the accompaniment is nothing less than ravishing, in a mid-'70s pop vein—Paul McCartney should only make such records! A unique collection, and a necessary addition to the possessions of any fan of Fairport Convention or Sandy Denny. *—Bruce Eder*

The BBC Sessions 1971-1973 / 1997 / Strange Fruit ✦✦✦✦✦
This 20-track CD was available only super-briefly in the spring of 1997 before Island Records prevented further copies from being distributed. The several thousand copies that had already been released, however, were allowed to remain in circulation, meaning that this disc is difficult but not impossible to find. And if you like Sandy Denny, you need to find it, because it's some of her best material. Most of the tracks are BBC versions of songs that appeared on her first three solo albums, and most are her own compositions; all but four are performed solo on piano or guitar. In a sense, it's Sandy unplugged, although that term didn't exist in those days. Denny arguably sounds much better on these spare versions that she does on the official takes, when she had to contend with often humdrum, over-arranged session accompaniment. In this context, she comes off much more like a kindred spirit to early-'70s singer/songwriters, especially Joni Mitchell and Judy Collins, than she does a British folk troubadour. You could, indeed, make a strong argument for this as her best solo recording, with fidelity that ranges from good to excellent. While eight of these tracks previously appeared on the fine bootleg *Dark the Night*, the remaining 12 did not, making it an essential addition for Denny fans. *—Richie Unterberger*

Gold Dust: Live at the Royalty / Jun. 9, 1998 / Island ✦✦✦

● **No More Sad Refrains: The Anthology** / Jul. 25, 2000 / A&M ✦✦✦✦✦
Like fellow Briton Nick Drake, Sandy Denny is one of the rare lesser-known artists whose extraordinary talents have been duly represented on disc over the years. *No More Sad Refrains: The Anthology* joins or replaces a number of previously available compilations, including an excellent box set, a couple of single disc best-of's, and *Attix Tracks*, an assortment of archival recordings. Though it may not be as expansive as the multiple disc set *Who Knows Where the Time Goes*, *No More Sad Refrains* may be the best introduction to Sandy Denny's career to hit the market: more affordable, while still covering 34 songs over two discs (as opposed to 43 over three), including a few rarities. And though the collections overlap on nearly two-thirds of the songs selected, less than a third are the same recordings, and these have been digitally remastered. The tracks are arranged chronologically from her first record with Fairport Convention in 1969 to 1977's *Rendezvous*, concentrating on her exquisite songwriting, along with a handful of well-chosen covers ("Banks of the Nile" is curiously the only true traditional song included). And while it may emphasize her solo years, her work with Fotheringay and the one-off \rock & roll tribute the Bunch, is given a good overview as well. In regards to her time with Fairport Convention, with the exception of two cuts and an outtake from their seminal British \folk-rock record *Liege and Lief*, it seems to be presented merely as a reference point (one song from each of her first two albums with the group), completely skipping her second time around with the band (only a pair of solo demos from this period are included). Fans who will have a majority of the material included here will be enticed by the previously unreleased demo version of "Stranger to Himself" and rarities such as "Here in Silence" and "Man of Iron," which were taken from the soundtrack to the movie *Pass of Arms* and issued as a single in 1972. Still, *No More Sad Refrains* is seemingly aimed more at the uninitiated than devotees, though it does a admirable job of covering a lot of territory and trying to please both. Either way, this is a fine retrospective of a terrific songwriter and what may well have been the most stunningly beautiful voice in British folk and pop. Included is a 22-page booklet featuring musician credits, photos, and informative liner notes by Denny biographer Clinton Heylin (-No More Sad Refains: The Story of Sandy Denny), who is also responsible for compiling a book documenting her recordings *Sad Refrains: The Recordings of Sandy Denny*. *—Brett Hartenbach*

Hazel Dickens

b. Jun. 1, 1935, Mercer County, WV
Vocals / Political Folk, Traditional Folk, Old-Timey
Protest and folk singer Hazel Dickens grew up the eighth of eleven children in a large, poor mining family in West Virginia, and she has since used elements of country and bluegrass to spread truth about two causes close to her heart: the plight of non-unionized mineworkers and feminism, born not of the '60s movement but traditional values. Her family's dire poverty forced Dickens to move to Baltimore when she was 19, where she worked in factories with her sister and two brothers. The four displaced siblings often attended old-timey festivals and gatherings, watching others and performing themselves. At one of these festivals, Dickens met Mike Seeger, and the two formed a band with her brothers. Over the ensuing decade, Dickens became active in the folk/bluegrass movement around the Baltimore/Washington, D.C. area, playing bass and singing with several bands, including the Greenbriar Boys. Around this time she met Seeger's wife, Alice Gerrard, and the two began researching early feminist songs and then incorporated them into their own repertoire. The duo recorded two albums for Folkways, *Who's That Knocking (And Other Bluegrass Country Music)* (1965) and *Won't You Come and Sing for Me* (1973). Dickens also recorded a series of solo albums for Rounder which include old-timey country alongside protest songs and songs in a more contemporary country style. *—John Bush*

Hazel & Alice / May 1973 / Rounder ✦✦✦✦✦
Although Dickens and Gerrard had recorded a couple of albums as a duo in the mid-1960s, those were more traditional-minded bluegrass recordings than this 1973 effort. Several of the songs documented women's experiences in personal terms that struck a chord in many listeners involved in the women's movement, a constituency that the performers were not consciously addressing and somewhat surprised (though pleased) to reach. In fact, about half of this was devoted to traditional numbers by the likes of the Carter Family and Wilma Lee Cooper, but the original numbers brought a still-rare feminist viewpoint to folk and bluegrass music, particularly Dickens' "Don't Put Her Down, You Helped Put Her There." The songs make their points about women's struggles without being doctrinaire; the vocals (both solo and harmony) are impassioned, particularly on the Dickens a cappella showcase "Pretty Bird," and the musicianship appropriately spare. The CD reissue features extensive historical liner notes and track-by-track commentary by country music authority Charles Wolfe. *—Richie Unterberger*

Hard Hitting Songs for Hard Hit People / 1980 / Rounder ✦✦✦

★ **By the Sweat of My Brow** / 1983 / Rounder ✦✦✦✦✦
A great record, which features "By the Sweat of My Brow," "Old & in the Way," "The Ballad of Ira Hayes, " and "Your Greedy Heart." *—Chip Renner*

Hard to Tell the Singer from the Song / 1987 / Rounder ✦✦✦✦

Pioneering Women of Bluegrass / May 21, 1996 / Smithsonian/Folkways ✦✦✦✦✦
Dickens and Gerrard recorded a couple of albums in the mid-1960s that are now acknowledged as groundbreakers in demonstrating that women could play and record quality bluegrass. This collection remasters and resequences 26 tracks from the sessions, as well as adding lengthy historical liner notes, much of them contributed by the performers themselves. Historical significance aside, it's pretty good bluegrass, the two singers and instrumentals supported by other good musicians, including a young David Grisman. Their set leaned heavily on covers of tunes by the Carter Family and Bill Monroe (who specifically gave "I Hear a Sweet Voice Calling" to the duo), with additional items by the Delmore Brothers, the Stanley Brothers, and the like. Alice Gerrard's low vocals give this a greater gravity than much bluegrass. A special highlight is the cover of the magnificently mournful "The One I Love Is Gone," another tune that Monroe donated to the pair. Inverting the usual bluegrass cliché, one might call it an example of the *low* and lonesome sound. *—Richie Unterberger*

It's Hard to Tell the Singer From the Song / Jul. 11, 2000 / Rounder ✦✦✦✦✦

A Few Old Memories / Rounder ✦✦✦

Richard Dyer-Bennett

b. Oct. 6, 1913, Leicester, England, **d.** Dec. 4, 1991

Vocals / Traditional Folk

Singer/songwriter Richard Dyer-Bennet was among the leading performers of the folk music renaissance of the early '40s; a classically-trained talent with a pitch-perfect, high lyric tenor, he was also an uncompromising proponent of creative rights, even founding his own highly-influential independent record label. All told, he learned over 600 songs over the course of his lifetime, an eclectic catalog including English sea shanties, spirituals, cowboy songs, French love ballads, American and European folk songs dating as far back as the 13th century, and more than 100 of his own compositions.

Growing up with an interest in opera and theater, as a youth he traveled widely; performing in choirs and investigating folk music in Germany. In 1942 began a lengthy stay at the Village Vanguard where he developed a large and loyal fanbase. In 1944 Dyer-Bennet became the first folk performer ever presented in solo concert at a major venue—in this case, New York's Town Hall; the show was a sell-out, a feat soon repeated at his Carnegie Hall debut. Dyer-Bennet weathered the McCarthy era by enjoying an extended return stay at the Village Vanguard; there he met television producer Harvey Cort, and in 1955 the two men agreed to form their own recording company. Dyer-Bennet, his first release, titled simply *Richard Dyer-Bennet #1* was the subject of considerable critical acclaim, and sold remarkably, and ultimately released 14 more albums on the label.

Dyer-Bennet remained a notable presence on the folk music landscape throughout the 1960s. After suffering a cerebral hemorrhage in 1972 (which severely limited the use of his left hand, making it virtually impossible to play guitar), Dyer-Bennet's performance career was essentially finished, but he still remained involved in music until his death in 1991. —*Jason Ankeny*

With Young People in Mind / Jan. 25, 2000 / Smithsonian/Folkways ✦✦✦

Ostensibly this might have been geared toward children, but it's actually for the most part traditional English ballads and American folk songs that were pretty typical of Dyer-Bennet's repertoire. Thus it's a folk album that could be appropriate for either kids (not necessarily real young ones) or adults, sung and performed plainly by Dyer-Bennet on guitar. There are a few selections more suited for children's singing than others, like "The Tailor and the Mouse," a traditional English children's song, "Little Pigs" (with the animal noises common to several children's folk albums, such as those by Pete Seeger), and "The Hole in the Bottom of the Sea." It's dated in its stilted 1950s folk way, but is pleasant, and differentiated from some other similar recordings of the era by the gentle British Isles lilt in Dyer-Bennet's vocals. Could famous British radio DJ John Peel, who changed his name from John Ravenscroft, have gotten the idea from the English fox-hunting song "John Peel," performed here— The album was reissued on CD by Smithsonian Folkways in 2000. —*Richie Unterberger*

• **Dyer-Bennet, Vol. 1** / Oct. 21, 1997 / Smithsonian/Folkways ✦✦✦✦✦

The first of Richard Dyer-Bennet's releases on his eponymous independent label is also among his very best; beautifully sung and impeccably crafted, *1* is also a landmark recording as one of the earliest and most successful artist-owned albums ever issued. Smithsonian Folkways' excellent reissue sports extensive liner notes and superbly remastered sound. —*Jason Ankeny*

Richard Dyer-Bennett, Vols. 1-7 / DYB ✦✦✦✦✦

These comprehensive collections of Dyer-Bennett form the most complete collection of his work, recorded in the mid-to-late '50s. —*Richard Meyer*

Fred Eaglesmith

Vocals / Americana, Country-Folk, Singer/Songwriter

Country-folk singer/songwriter Fred J. Eaglesmith was one of nine children born to a farming family in rural southern Ontario. Often employing his difficult upbringing as raw material for his heartland narratives, he issued his self-titled debut LP in 1980. He recorded infrequently throughout the remainder of the decade, releasing only two more albums, *The Boy That Just Went Wrong* and *Indiana Road.* However, Eaglesmith gradually became an underground favorite in his native Canada, thanks largely to a relentless touring schedule in tandem with bassist Ralph Schipper and mandolinist Willie P. Bennett. In 1991, he released the double live collection *There Ain't No Easy Road,* followed two years later by *Things Is Changin'.* Another live set, *Paradise Motel,* appeared in 1994, and in 1995 Eaglesmith returned with *Drive-In Movie.* 1999 saw the release of *50-Odd Dollars.* —*Jason Ankeny*

Drive-In Movie / 1996 / Vertical ✦✦✦✦✦

It's no big surprise that the majority of Canadian songwriters don't get their due in the United States, but listening to *Drive-In Movie* from Ontario native Fred Eaglesmith, you have to wonder just how much we're missing. Eaglesmith's vivid lyrics, simple arrangements, and plaintive but sturdy voice echo the rural landscape and the wide, clear, Northern skies he grew up with. In the tradition of Texas songwriters such as Guy Clark and Robert Earl Keen—who evoke images of their home state with masterful clarity—he sings with the honest and sometimes mournful tone of a man who recognizes that the lifestyle he grew up with and loved is now drifting into the past. —*Kurt Wolff*

• **Lipstick, Lies & Gasoline** / Oct. 21, 1997 / Razor & Tie ✦✦✦✦✦

50 Odd Dollars / Jun. 15, 1999 / Razor & Tie ✦✦✦

Anyone who's come to know Fred Eaglesmith as one of the most brilliant folk-rock songwriters of the '90s can't help but be disappointed by *50 Odd Dollars*' middle-of-the-road country-rock crunch. Then again, it depends on what you like to hear. Fans of his trailer-trash tales of fast trains and drunken nights will probably enjoy this album's loud guitars and pounding beat, whereas folks who live for his wistful early work will be disappointed in its lack of clemency. The lone ballad flits by so unremarkably that it feels like a weak link, which is sad because Eaglesmith's sentimental poetry, like Dylan's, has always been a strong anchor for his records and the perfect foil for his folky comedy. Without it, songs like "Mighty Big Car" just sound tired. —*Jim Smith*

Cliff Eberhardt

Vocals, Guitar / Contemporary Singer/Songwriter, Contemporary Folk

Guitarist, singer and songwriter Cliff Eberhardt, often referred to as one of the "new folk" artists on the scene, comes from suburban Philadelphia, historically a strong folk music area. Raised in a musical family in the 1960s, the self-taught guitarist began performing at age eight and performed with his brother while in high school. In the mid-1970s, he relocated to southern Illinois and found a singer-songwriter scene there. He continued to hone his skills as a performer, singer, guitarist and songwriter. Since the late 1970s, he's been based in New York, one of the early pioneers in Greenwich Village's 1980s folk music revival.

Eberhardt's debut recording, *The Long Road,* was released on Windham Hill Records in 1990; the title track is a duet with his longtime friend and mentor, Richie Havens. Other releases include his 1993 debut for the Cachet subsidiary of Shanachie Records, *Now You Are My Home,* where he's backed by people like John Gorka, Nanci Griffith and Patty Larkin. More recently, he released *Mona Lisa's Café* (1995), for Shanachie. A gifted songwriter, Eberhardt's songs have been covered by everyone from Buffy Sainte-Marie to Carl Perkins. He also has a track on the recent Rounder Records release, *Big Time In a Small Town: The Vineyard Tapes,* produced by fellow New York singer-songwriter Christine Lavin. —*Richard Skelly*

Live At Speakeasy / Aug. 12, 1988 / ✦✦✦✦✦

The Long Road / 1990 / Windham Hill ✦✦✦✦✦

Cliff Eberhardt was one of those singer/songwriters who took a long time to make a formal album (one of the copyrights here was 1974), and you could hear the years, the miles, and the struggle in his songs. "White Lightning" commented on the need of the singer to escape a provincial existence; "My Father's Shoes" dealt with separation from family; and the title song (a duet with strong influence Richie Havens) reflected on the length of the journey. For the most part, however, Eberhardt was concerned with romance, usually with a sense of idealized commitment in songs whose titles sometimes told the story: "Always Want to Feel Like This," "(Just To) Walk Down the Street With You." Singing in a gruff, earnest tenor, he always seemed to have come through a long period of difficulties to this one, perfect love, even if, as in the beautiful "Your Face," he was still writing from a distance. In his solo concerts, Eberhardt could seem even more impassioned; on record, with a backing band to blend into, his mannerisms were less pronounced (and one got less of a sense of his impressive guitar playing); he recalled Bruce Springsteen (especially in the *Darkness on the Edge of Town* cadences of "Right Now" and the small-town reminiscences of "White Lightning") more than Ray Charles. "If you let your passion loose," he sang in "White Lightning," "you would run like fire." But passion remained his ruling emotion. —*William Ruhlmann*

• **Now You Are My Home** / Nov. 2, 1993 / Shanachie/Cachet ✦✦✦✦✦

Cliff Eberhardt recorded his first cover song on his second album, cutting Smokey Robinson's "You Really Got a Hold on Me" with harmony vocals by John Gorka, Patty Larkin, and Judy Dunleavy. It was an appropriate choice for a songwriter so concerned with romantic obsession. The character depicted in his songs was a traveler (references to the road and motels abounded), who had been looking for love a long time: "I've been searching," was a phrase used in both "Now You Are My Home" and "Every Time I See Your Face." This person alternated between expressions of unabashed devotion ("Now You Are My Home," "Every Time I See Your Face," "Now That You Are Mine") and bitter recriminations about lost love ("Ever Since I Lost Your Love," "I'm Not Quite Over You," "Baton Rouge"). There were also a few variations. In "Not Alone in This World," a man with a new girlfriend can't help thinking about an old one, while "I Thought That You Should Know" and "One or Two Things (You Don' t Know)" find him tentatively proposing a relationship. Throughout, the singer wore all his emotions on his sleeve, whether love, anger, or regret: "I believe that nothing comes to those who hesitate," he declared, which gave his expression a raw immediacy. He backed up these explosions of feeling with his rough tenor on tracks less produced than those on his debut album and therefore more dominated by his guitar work and singing. At times, his song construction and performance transcended the material, especially on "Baton Rouge" (which someone in Nashville should get a hold of) and "Make Me Believe," turning them into powerful statements of feeling. But the album was uneven and repetitive, and Eberhardt's angst and fervor could be wearing. —*William Ruhlmann*

Mona Lisa Cafe / Aug. 11, 1995 / Shanachie ✦✦✦

12 Songs of Good & Evil / Aug. 19, 1997 / Red House ✦✦✦✦

Front and center are Cliff Eberhardt's expressive voice and his effective string work on guitar and dobro, making this the first real folk-sounding album this singer/songwriter had ever made. Eberhardt had backed away somewhat from his romantic obsessions on his previous album, *Mona Lisa Café,* but without replacing them effectively with other subjects. On *12 Songs of Good and Evil,* he expanded those obsessions from merely interpersonal love relationships to general behavior. The title didn't imply that there were songs about good and songs about evil; rather, Eberhardt made clear that the line between the two was very thin and that most of his characters, the singer very much included, managed some of both. In the album's most striking song, "Joey's Arms," he marveled at the emotional attachment an addict could show toward his drug, and even contrasted it with a reflection on his own romantic travails that revealed surprisingly confessional insight: "I loved but I was unfaithful/I loved but I never stayed/But Joey knows about commitment/He loves the needle in the vein." If the album had a fault, it was that it was so downbeat. Only "Someone Like You," which sounded like a lost '60s pop/rock song, really broke the mood. But the disc showcased some of Eberhardt's strongest performing talents, and it demonstrated that he was finding new avenues for his songwriting. —*William Ruhlmann*

Borders / Mar. 23, 1999 / Red House ✦✦✦

Eddie from Ohio

Group / Contemporary Folk

This folk-rock quartet from the Washington, D.C./suburban Virginia area was only formed in 1991, but they've quickly become favorites on the folk festival circuit with their jazzy, rootsy blend of folk-rock. The group's popularity grew with the growth of Triple A (adult album alternative) radio stations in the 1990s, and their crossover appeal prevented them from being labeled purely a folk act.

Composed of Julie Murphy (vocals), Robbie Schaefer (guitar and vocals), Eddie Hartness (percussion and vocals) and Michael Clem (guitar, bass, harp and vocals), the quartet came together in northern Virginia when longtime friends Schaefer and Clem decided to form an acoustic rock trio with Murphy, a mutual friend from high school choir. Hartness was recruited soon after the group's formation to add percussion treatments. A year later, Clem and Murphy were able to leave their day jobs and the band began to attract growing crowds to its residency show on Tuesday nights at Bad Habits Grille in Arlington, VA. They got the name Eddie from Ohio from Hartness, whose girlfriend started calling him "Eddie from Ohio" after eD fROMOHIO, a member of the now-defunct group fIREHOSE.

In their relatively brief existence, the neo-folk/folk-rock band's sound has been compared to 10, 000 Maniacs, the Indigo Girls, Crosby, Stills and Nash, and Shawn Colvin, but their eclectic approach has appealed to well-educated music fans: they artfully blend bluegrass, folk, calypso, jazz, acoustic blues and pop and rock melodies. Their eclectic philosophy is a reflection of their influences: Clem and Schaefer cite Bruce Cockburn, Lyle Lovett and Shawn Colvin, while Hartness' tastes run toward alternative rock, including the Red Hot Chili Peppers and Pearl Jam. Lead vocalist Murphy grew up listening to 1940s jazz, including Billie Holiday and the music of the Gershwins.

In its six years of existence, the group has played to festival crowds from New York to Colorado and produced four albums for their own Virginia Soul Records label. Eddie From Ohio released its fourth album in 1997, *Big Noise*. Their earlier releases include *I Rode Fido Home* (1995), *Actually Not* (1993), and *A Juggler On His Blades* (1992). *—Richard Skelly*

I Rode Fido Home / Aug. 1, 1995 / Virginia Soul ✦✦✦

Big Noise / Jan. 1, 1997 / Virginia Soul ✦✦✦

● **Portable EFO Show** / Feb. 12, 1998-Feb. 21, 1998 / Virginia Soul ✦✦✦✦

"I like your albums, but they just don't compare to your live show." This is what Eddie from Ohio's audiences have been telling them for years, they admit, and it's not hard to understand why by listening to this double live album. The group's music, propelled by percussionist Eddie Hartness, proves energetic and kinetic onstage in a way it doesn't without an audience cheering along. Songs that seem slight in terms of musical and lyrical content turn out to be crowd pleasers. Mildly amusing novelties become laugh-out-loud funny. And by mixing in covers of everything from Lyle Lovett's "If I Had a Boat" to the Grateful Dead warhorse "I Know You Rider"/"Turn On Your Lovelight," the group makes use of material that is more clever and rocking than their own. Michael Clem's novelty songs (including three new ones: "Jack Can't Cook," "Not Enough Gold in the World," and "Smoke") come off better onstage than Robbie Schaefer's more earnest ones. But if Hartness is the secret weapon, the best all-around performer is the much-improved (and recently married) singer, Julie Murphy Wells, who often betters her studio versions of the songs. A group like this makes its money on the road, not on records, and *Portable EFO Show* will be a terrific enticement to listeners to go out and see them in person. *—William Ruhlmann*

Looking out the Fishbowl / May 18, 1999 / Virginia Soul ✦✦✦✦

Songwriters Michael Clem and Robbie Schaefer, who separately write the songs for Eddie From Ohio, share an interest in small, quirky subjects: Clem writes from the perspectives of fish and dogs on "Fifth of July," pens an ode to his home state of Virginia on "Old Dominion," and describes the awkwardness of a visit home by a priest long stationed in India in "From Dacca"; Schaefer, a master of odd romantic pairings, explores the difficulties of a multinational couple in "Stupid American," an interracial one in "Minnesota 1945," and reflects on lost opportunities in "Good at That." Singer Julie Murphy Wells makes the most of the songs' possibilities, whether comic or wistful, aided by the band's sprightly acoustic arrangements. Typical of a group that makes its own records for its own label, some of the references are too local or obscure for anyone who doesn't follow them around their mid-Atlantic haunts. But when the songwriters really let themselves go, the results are both hilarious and moving. For Schaefer, that would be on "Maylee, I Had a Dream," in which the singer worries about the dangers posed by a lover who isn't yet ready to break up, but may be violent, and for Clem it's the album's best song, "Eddie's Concubine," in which a woman laments her relationship with a bar owner. In this case, the references may be local, but they're clear. You can't hear a couplet like "Eddie makes a pretty good living, stealing from the college bands/Eddie pulls locals with the Skynyrd groups, but only serves the beer in cans," without thinking that the author knows his subject well. *—William Ruhlmann*

Actually Not / Sep. 7, 1999 / Virginia Soul ✦✦

A Juggler on His Blades / Sep. 7, 1999 / Virginia Soul ✦✦✦✦

Mid-Atlantic folk quartet Eddie From Ohio recorded their debut album for their own Virginia Soul label by turning up at their favorite venue, *the Birchmere* in Alexandria, VA, with only producer Billy Wolf as an audience, playing their concert repertoire into a tape recorder. The two-acoustic-guitars-and-conga-drum sound, topped by frequent lead singer Julie Murphy, allowed for sharp, fresh arrangements of the songs, two-thirds of them written by Michael Clem, with the remainder contributed by Robbie Schaefer. Clem's lyrics told stories from a 20-something suburban perspective, whether he was musing about the partying that accompanies payday ("Payday in The Village"), a city's sinking into the mud ("Our Fair City"), or the funeral of a relative nobody liked very much ("A Very Fine Funeral"). His songs were full of the details of contemporary life: 7-11s, "Stairway to Heaven" on the radio, *The Flintstones* and *The Jetsons* on TV. And, of course, there was romantic discord, whether in the various secret signals that make infidelity too difficult in "Porchlight" or "lying by your 13th lover" in "Long Walk Home." Schaefer's songs often complement Clem's, but don't cut as deep. It doesn't much matter whether Murphy is singing Clem's lyrics or he or Schaefer sings them, except that the male voices tend to emphasize his debt to Paul Simon, especially in the city observations of "The Ghosts of St. George's Drive." *A Juggler on His Blades* was very much a debut album, more a collection of random songs than a cohesive effort, but it introduced a songwriter with a particular perspective and a group with its own sound. [The 1994 CD reissue added three songs.] *—William Ruhlmann*

Jonathan Edwards

b. Jul. 28, 1946, Aitkin, MN

Vocals, Harmonica, Guitar / Folk-Rock, Singer/Songwriter, Progressive Bluegrass

Best remembered for his crossover hit "Sunshine," country and folk singer/songwriter Jonathan Edwards got his start in the blues band Sugar Creek, debuting with the 1969 LP *Please Tell a Friend*. Wanting to pursue acoustic performing, he left the group to record a solo album. Near the end of the 1970 sessions, one of the finished tracks, "Please Find Me," was accidentally erased, forcing Edwards to instead record a brand new composition. The song was "Sunshine," and when it was released as a single the following year, it quickly became a Top Five pop hit. With the release of 1972's *Honky-Tonk Stardust Cowboy*, Edwards' music began gravitating towards straight-ahead country; his label was at a loss as to how to market the record, however, and over the course of two more albums, 1973's *Have a Good Time for Me* and the following year's live *Lucky Day*, his sales sharply declined. A cameo on Emmylou Harris' *Elite Hotel* resulted in a new record deal and the LP *Rockin' Chair*, recorded with Harris' Hot Band. Edwards eventually moved to Nashville; his 1989 album *The Natural Thing* generated his biggest country hit, "We Need to Be Locked Away." *—Jason Ankeny*

● **Jonathan Edwards** / 1971 / Atco ✦✦✦✦✦

This album is best known for Edwards's hit, "Sunshine" and the song "Shanty," which radio stations around the country call "The Friday Song." If either of these songs is as far as you've gotten with this album, you are missing a great deal. Edwards has a great sense of melody, which means there is not a weak track on this record. Aside from the previously mentioned numbers, one or two of the songs on the record have taken on a life of their own. "Don't Cry Blue," for instance, has been knocking around bluegrass circles for some years. One listen and you'll know why this album has never gone out of print. *—Jim Worbois*

Honky-Tonk Stardust Cowboy / 1972 / Atco ✦✦✦✦

Edwards continues where the first record left off and continues to grow as an artist. In addition to his own fine songs, Edwards chose to include a few covers like Jesse Colin Young's "Sugar Babe," The Mills Brothers' "Paper Doll" (complete with faux "trombone" solo), and the title track. The title track did receive some airplay on country radio in 1972 but was never the hit it should have been. If you find a copy of this one, grab it. *—Jim Worbois*

Have a Good Time for Me / 1973 / Atco ✦✦✦

Lucky Day / 1974 / Atco ✦✦✦

Rockin' Chair / 1976 / Reprise ✦✦

Sailboat / 1977 / Reprise ✦✦

Cruising America's Waterways / Media Artists ✦✦✦✦

Little Hands: Songs for and About Children / American Melody ✦✦✦✦

Ramblin' Jack Elliott

b. Aug. 1, 1931, Brooklyn, NY

Vocals, Guitar / Folk Revival, Singer/Songwriter, Traditional Folk

Ramblin' Jack Elliott is one of folk music's most enduring characters. Since he first came on the scene in the late 1950s, Elliott has influenced everyone from Bob Dylan and Pete Seeger to the Rolling Stones and the Grateful Dead. The son of a New York doctor and a onetime traveling companion of Woody Guthrie, Elliott has used his self-made cowboy image to bring his love of folk music to one generation after another. Pressured by his parents to follow in his father's footsteps and become a doctor, Elliott resisted their urging. Instead, inspired by the rodeos he attended at Madison Square Garden, he became fascinated with the image of the American cowboy. Elliott's recording debut came in the mid-1950s when he recorded three songs for a multi-artist compilation, *Bad Men, Heroes and Pirates*, released by Elektra. He was so influenced by Guthrie (whom he had met during a Greenwich Village picking session in 1950) that he began his musical career by mimicking the legendary folk singer. England provided the setting for Elliott's early success; his first album on his own, *Woody Guthrie's Blues*, was recorded in England for the Topic label. In addition to recording four more albums for Topic, he attracted attention with his peformances with Derroll Adams, a banjo player he had met in California. The duo barnstormed throughout Europe and had a profound influence on the British music scene. After living in Europe for six years, Elliott returned to the United States in 1961. The day after he returned, he visited Guthrie in the hospital and was introduced to Bob Dylan. (In the mid-1970s, Elliott joined Dylan's Rolling Thunder Revue and was featured in Dylan's film *Renaldo and Clara*.) *—Craig Harris*

Sings the Songs of Woody Guthrie / 1960 / Monitor ✦✦✦✦✦

Elliott interprets many of the most popular items in the Guthrie repertoire, including "So Long," "This Land Is Your Land," "Pretty Boy Floyd," "Talking Dust Bowl," and "Philadelphia Lawyer," on the recording that is most representative of his role in popularizing the work of his hero. It's been combined with another early-'60s Prestige album, *Ramblin' Jack Elliott*, on Fantasy's *Hard Travelin'* CD reissue. *—Richie Unterberger*

Ramblin' Jack Elliott / 1961 / Prestige ✦✦✦

A solidly traditional set of interpretations of standards like "The Cuckoo," "Rollin My Sweet Baby's Arms," "East Virginia Blues," and "Railroad Bill," as well as occasional blues covers ("Candyman," "San Francisco Bay Blues"). John Heard (second guitar) and Ralph Rinzler (mandolin) help out occasionally on this set, which has been combined with another early-'60s Prestige album, *Sings the Songs of Woody Guthrie*, on Fantasy's *Hard Travelin'* CD reissue (with one song, "I Love You So/I Got a Woman," omitted for space reasons). *—Richie Unterberger*

At the Second Fret / 1962 / Prestige ✦✦✦
Recorded at a Philadelphia club on May 18, 1962, this has a good cross-section of the cowboy- and country-oriented folk Elliott liked to sing: Jimmie Rodgers' "Mule Skinner Blues," the Sons of the Pioneers' "Cool Water," "Boll Weevil," "How Long Blues," "Hobo's Lullaby," "Rock Island Line"; and, of course, a couple of "talking" Woody Guthrie tunes. It's perhaps a little more fun to hear than the average early 1960s Jack Elliott album, because the live ambience and spoken introductions and asides give it a warmer atmosphere than the earnest but plain studio recordings. It's been paired with another 1962 Prestige LP, the studio *Country Style,* on the single-disc Fantasy CD reissue *Country Style/Live.* —*Richie Unterberger*

Country Style / 1964 / Prestige ✦✦✦
A two-for-one single-disc reissue of two 1962 albums: the studio date *Country Style* and the live club recording *At the Second Fret* (here retitled *Live*). With a couple dozen songs in all, you get a good representation of Elliott's repertoire of the time: old country songs ("The Wreck of the Old 97," "Mule Skinner Blues"), old-school country tunes ("Wabash Cannonball," Ernest Tubb's "Take Me Back and Try Me One More Time"), blues ("How Long Blues"), and naturally a few Woody Guthrie tunes. He's trying to sound like Guthrie a lot of the time, of course, and as an inadvertent consequence, sounds similar to very early Bob Dylan (who at the very beginning of his career was also trying to sound like Woody Guthrie). He's not as good a singer as Guthrie or Dylan, and contributed no original material to these sets. That gives this something of a dry historical artifact feel, although the live portion of the disc has a slightly warmer atmosphere than *Country Style.* —*Richie Unterberger*

★ **The Essential Ramblin' Jack Elliott** / 1970 / Vanguard ✦✦✦✦✦
Elliott was the complete folksinger of the 60s, singing and yodeling traditional material derived from folk, country, and blues sources and (especially) carrying on the tradition of Woody Guthrie. This two-pocket set, some of which is taken from a 1965 concert, provides a representative sampling of his repertoire and style. — *William Ruhlmann*

Hard Travelin' / 1989 / Fantasy ✦✦✦✦✦
Elliott's early-'60s Prestige LPs *Sings the Songs of Woody Guthrie* and *Ramblin' Jack Elliott* are combined onto a single 77-minute disc on this CD reissue, with one song ("I Love Her So/I Got a Woman") deleted for space reasons. It's not as good as hearing Guthrie himself, and may strike contemporary listeners as a bit tame and dated. Elliott played an important role in the '60s folk revival as a popularizer of Guthrie's songs and style, though, and this is one of the best places to hear him at his best, on both Guthrie covers and interpretations of various traditional and blues songs. —*Richie Unterberger*

Kerouac's Last Dream / Sep. 16, 1997 / Appleseed ✦✦✦

☆ **America** / Nov. 11, 1997 / A World of Music ✦✦✦✦✦
Recorded by Derroll Adams and Ramblin' Jack Elliott, this legendary collection—in 1998 the only extant body of Derroll Adams' music on CD—has held up miraculously well over more than 31 years. It might not be the ideal showcase for Adams as an artist, as he has the deeper voice, and to some extent is overshadowed by Elliott's twangier singing (and yodeling), but his banjo drives a good deal of the music here, and their voices mesh nicely. There's not a bad or weak track among the 18 here, but among the most extraordinary is a rolicking rendition of Jimmy Rodgers' "Muleskinner's Blues" (which also includes one of the longest sustained yodels in modern recording, by Elliott). Other songs include Jessie Fuller's "San Francisco Bay Blues," Roy Acuff's "Precious Jewel," A. P. Carter's "Worried Man Blues," "Rich And Rambling Boy," and "East Virginia Blues," Woody Guthrie and Lee Hayes' "I'm Going Down The Road," Guthrie's "More Pretty Girls Than One" and "900 Miles," and Leadbelly's "Ain't It A Shame"—the latter, along with the traditional "Cigarettes and Whiskey," give Adams a lead vocal, showing off a rough-hewn instrument with a dark, rich tone. There are no notes on this budget-priced release, but it has been carefully treated with the CEDAR noise-reduction system, and all sounds astonishingly clean and crisp. —*Bruce Eder*

Friends of Mine / Mar. 17, 1998 / Hightone ✦✦✦

The Long Ride / Sep. 14, 1999 / Hightone ✦✦✦

Ballad of Ramblin' Jack / Jul. 25, 2000 / Vanguard ✦✦✦✦
This soundtrack to the 2000 documentary film about Elliott (directed by his daughter) also serves as a pretty good career retrospective. The 20 cuts are taken from an assortment of live, studio, television, radio, and film performances from 1953 to 1998. The chief flaw of Elliott's output is that he was not an innovator. He wrote little of his own music (only one of the songs on this release is original), and his competent, homespun brand of folk was similar to, but not nearly as good as, Woody Guthrie's or early Bob Dylan's. The strength of Elliott's music, on the other hand, is that he sounded the same pretty much whenever he sang or recorded. If you liked traditional American folk at any time during the last half of the 20th century, Elliott was the old reliable, there to provide it for international audiences. So it's no surprise that this soundtrack is a consistent listen of engaging, if unremarkable, roots American folk music. Elliott sounds a lot better, of course, when he's performing duets with greater talents, and there are a number of such duets on this compilation, including performances on Johnny Cash's television show in the late '60s and early '70s; a 1953 studio cut with his mentor, Guthrie (also including Sonny Terry on harmonica and vocals); and a song apiece with Odetta and Derroll Adams. There's also a live 1961 radio airshot of a duet with a then labelless Bob Dylan on the silly, and not terribly witty, early rock & roll parody & "Acne." —*Richie Unterberger*

Best of the Vanguard Years / Oct. 31, 2000 / Vanguard ✦✦✦✦

John Fahey

b. Feb. 28, 1939, Takoma Park, MD, **d.** Feb. 22, 2001, Salem, OR
Guitar, Guitar (Acoustic), Producer / Progressive Folk, Folk-Blues, Folk-Jazz, New Acoustic, World Fusion, Traditional Folk, Acoustic Blues

One of acoustic music's true innovators and eccentrics, John Fahey has been crucial in expanding the boundaries of the acoustic guitar over the last few decades. His music is so eclectic that it's arguable whether he should be defined as a "folk" artist. In a career that has seen him issue several dozen albums, he's drawn from blues, Native American music, Indian ragas, experimental dissonance, and pop. His good friend Dr. Demento has noted that Fahey "was the first to demonstrate that the finger-picking techniques of traditional country and blues steel-string guitar could be used to express a world of nontraditional musical ideas—harmonies and melodies you'd associate with Bartok, Charles Ives, or maybe the music of India." The more meditative aspects of his work foreshadowed new age music, yet Fahey plays with a fierce imagination and versatility that outshines any of the guitarists in that category. His idiosyncrasy may have limited him to a cult following, but it also ensured that his work continues to sound fresh. —*Richie Unterberger*

Blind Joe Death / 1964 / Takoma ✦✦✦✦
For his first Takoma release, Fahey essentially presented an altered version of his extremely limited-edition (less than 100 copies), self-pressed 1959 debut. All but one of the songs from that legendary 1959 effort are here, but some of them are 1964 re-recordings, as Fahey felt (correctly) that his technique had improved so much that they would benefit from being recut. The album's mystique probably owes more to the 1959 record's rarity (and utter oddity in the context of its era) than the music, in which Fahey's experimental blues-folk acoustic fusion is just beginning to take shape. It remains a very interesting record from a historical perspective, however, as few if any other guitarists were attempting to interpret blues and folk idioms in such an idiosyncratic fashion in the late '50s and early '60s. No need to look for the rare original 1964 album; all the cuts have been reissued on the CD compilation *The Legend of Blind Joe Death,* which also includes the entirety of the version of *Blind Joe Death* that he re-recorded yet again for Takoma in 1967. —*Richie Unterberger*

★ **The Transfiguration of Blind Joe Death** / 1965 / Takoma ✦✦✦✦✦
A strange man, John Fahey, with an unusual set of guitar styles. This album, originally released on Riverboat Records and later reissued by Fahey's own Takoma label, has a lot of rough edges in terms of the recording but a tremendous amount of power when it comes to the music. Fahey was at the top of his game, alternately playful and dark, so there's never a dull moment. There is always something new to be heard on each playing. —*Steven McDonald*

Vol. 3: Dance of Death & Other Plantation Favorites / 1965 / Takoma ✦✦✦
One of Fahey's less eccentric early efforts, featuring relatively straightforward instrumentals showcasing his deft finger work and occasional keening slide. Blues, ragtime, and Appalachian influences come to the fore on this even-toned collection, with occasional excursions into dark and somber territory, as on the closing track "Dance of Death." Also includes an adaptation of "Poor Boy, " taken from Bukka White, whom Fahey rediscovered with Ed Denson in the early '60s. The 1999 CD reissue on Takoma (with the "Vol. 3" taken out of the title) adds historical liner notes and four previously unreleased bonus tracks from the session, which are somewhat on the briefer and more traditional side than the other cuts on the disc. —*Richie Unterberger*

Vol. 4: The Great San Bernardino Birthday Party / 1966 / Takoma ✦✦✦✦✦
This hodgepodge of tracks from 1962-66 was among the last of Fahey's early Takoma albums to make it onto CD (which it did in 2000). Perhaps that's because Fahey himself has a low estimation of the record. Nevertheless, it stands as his most, well, far-out work, and one of his most innovative. Edited together from several pieces, the 19-minute "The Great San Bernardino Birthday Party" anticipated elements of psychedelia with its nervy improvisations and odd guitar tunings. The six briefer pieces that comprised the rest of the record also broke ground with their unsettling moods and dissonances: "Knott's Berry Farm Molly" suddenly moving from a characteristically placid instrumental to backwards tapes that Fahey assembled on a tape recorder, and the lo-fi "Will the Circle Be Unbroken" putting some aggressive picking against a mysterious church organ played by Flea. The beautiful "900 Miles" also had unexpected instrumental accompaniment, by Nancy McLean on flute, while future Canned Heat member Al Wilson played "veena" (sitar) on "Sail Away Ladies." Despite Fahey's curmudgeonly dismissal of the record several decades later, it's an important, if uneven, effort that ultimately endures as one of the highlights of his discography. —*Richie Unterberger*

Vol. 1: Blind Joe Death / 1967 / Takoma ✦✦✦
In 1967, Takoma decided to re-record Fahey's *Blind Joe Death* for the stereo market. Thus, although the songs here were first recorded by Fahey for his rare, self-pressed edition of *Blind Joe Death* from 1959, this actually marks the *third* version of the record, each of which had presented different performances of the same material. To make matters more confusing, it was issued with the same catalog number as the 1964 release that had mixed cuts from the 1959 *Blind Joe Death* LP with 1964 remakes of *Blind Joe Death* material. The important thing for consumers to note is that the 1967 version of Takoma 1002, though featuring the same songs as the 1964 version of Takoma 1002, has entirely different performances. The fidelity is notably clearer and the technique more polished, although it really doesn't make a significant difference in the quality of the final product. Now, however, you don't have to worry about making a choice between the different Takoma 1002s, because they're both available, in their entirety, on the CD reissue *The Legend of Blind Joe Death.* —*Richie Unterberger*

Voice of the Turtle / 1968 / Takoma ✦✦✦✦✦
Like some of Fahey's other projects in the '60s, this was actually recorded/assembled over a few years, primarily composed of duets with various other artists (including overdubs with his own pseudonym, Blind Joe Death). One of his more obscure early efforts, it's both listenable and wildly eclectic, going from scratchy emulations of early blues 78s and country fiddle tunes to haunting guitar-flute combinations and eerie ragas. "A Raga Called Pat, Part III & IV" is a particularly ambitious piece, its disquieting swooping slide and brief bits of electronic white noise reverb veering into experimental psychedelia. Most of this is pretty traditional/acoustic in tone, however, though it has the undercurrent of dark, uneasy tension that gives much of Fahey's '60s material its intriguing combination of meditation and restlessness. —*Richie Unterberger*

America / 1971 / Takoma ✦✦✦
In some respects this was Fahey at his most ambitious; two of the four songs ("Mark 1:15"

and "Voice of the Turtle") clock in at around the 15-minute mark, and one of the others is entitled "The Waltz That Carried Us Away and Then a Mosquito Came and Ate Up My Sweetheart." It's actually typical of his work of the period, however: inventive acoustic guitar instrumentals that draw from folk and blues, with a sedate presentation that has a relaxing effect. The CD reissue, however, transforms it into an entirely different work. *America* was originally envisioned as a double LP, but around half of the material remained unreleased when it was cut down to a single disc; the CD restores the other nine songs that would have been included on the original program, pushing the length of the album to 79 minutes. The additional tracks are pretty similar in feel to the ones chosen for the original release, though perhaps more eclectic, including a Skip James cover, the third movement of Dvorak's "Eighth Symphony," and "Amazing Grace." The song "America" (oddly omitted from the original *America* album) is a rare example of Fahey on the 12-string, and includes some pleasing passages of muted notes. *—Richie Unterberger*

The Best of John Fahey 1959-1977 / 1977 / Takoma ✦✦✦✦✦
One of the finest and most underrated blues acoustic guitarists to come out of California, John Fahey was a master of fingerpicking and modal blues and gospel explorations. He also had the ability to reinterpret Elizabethan ballads and other English folk material. All of this talent is represented in this excellent anthology. On cuts such as "Poor Boy a Long Way From Home" and "St. Louis Blues," Fahey is virtually a reincarnation of Son House and Mississippi John Hurt. Medieval-oriented tracks like "Revolt of the Dyke Brigade" show Fahey's incredible mastery of modal tunings and complex chord structures, all of which come out sounding deceptively simpler than they really are. A real guitar player's record, this is excellent to learn by, and even more fun to listen to. *—Matthew Greenwald*

Yes! Jesus Loves Me / 1980 / Takoma ✦✦✦

Old Girlfriends & Other / 1992 / Varrick ✦✦✦

★ **Return of the Repressed: Anthology** / 1994 / Rhino ✦✦✦✦✦
Back in the 1960s, when fingerpicking folk guitarists were a dime a dozen, John Fahey stood out for several reasons. For one thing, his sense of humor was sophisticated and unfashionably cynical for the period (this is the guy, remember, who simultaneously celebrated the blues tradition and ridiculed his own blues pretensions by adopting the nom de plume of Blind Joe Death). But most of all, he possessed absolutely astounding chops, and made no attempt to hide his superior guitar skills despite a pop music climate which was much kinder to earnest amateurism than to hard-earned virtuosity. Since that period, though, his profile has stayed pretty low. While he remains a revered cult figure among guitarists and a segment of the aging boomer population, the current music market is less amenable than ever to his particular brand of sly, hard-edged acoustic music. So this two-disc retrospective, culled from numerous Fahey LPs, is a rare and valuable overview, one which has met with significant critical approval. That said, it is certainly true that Fahey's music won't please everyone, and not just because of its complexity. Fahey's technique, while impressive, is sometimes a bit ham-fisted, especially on the early material. Songs like "Desperate Man Blues," "Sligo River Blues" and "Night Train to Valhalla" (you've just gotta love his song titles) are too loud at any volume—you wish he'd vary the attack just a bit from phrase to phrase. But the stylistic juxtapositions he executes—going from blues to flamenco and back, sometimes within the same chorus—are awe-inspiring, as is his melodic inventiveness. Later material benefits from better production and the participation of guest musicians. Overall, this set is recommended, but the faint-hearted should try to listen before buying. *—Rick Anderson*

The Legend of Blind Joe Death / 1996 / Takoma ✦✦✦✦✦
The saga of *Blind Joe Death* is an extremely confusing one, for those listeners who haven't been following Fahey's career from the beginning. In short: Fahey originally recorded *Blind Joe Death* in 1959, in an extremely rare, self-released edition of less than 100 copies. Though few heard it, his debut album was a groundbreaker on the acoustic folk scene in its unusually experimental approach to blues and folk styles, though its innovations sound relatively tame when compared to the best of Fahey's subsequent work. Fahey reissued the album in 1964 on Takoma, re-recording some of the cuts, and dropping one selection ("West Coast Blues"). In 1967, when the album was issued for the stereo market, Fahey re-recorded the entire album from scratch, resulting in performances of the exact same new material, but with improved fidelity and technique. This reissue does us all a mammoth favor by combining the 1964 and 1967 editions of the album (which, to make matters more confusing, bore the exact same catalog number, Takoma 1002) onto one 75-minute disc. A previously unreleased 1964 version of "West Coast Blues," a song which had been on the 1959 edition of *Blind Joe Death* but was left off subsequent configurations, is added as a bonus cut. Completists should note that this is not the final word in the *Blind Joe Death* saga. Several of the versions originally presented on the 1959 album that were re-recorded for both the 1964 and 1967 remakes are still absent, for space reasons and because the compilers themselves feel that the later renditions are notably superior. Still, it's a near-definitive package of the important *Blind Joe Death* material, with extensive historical liner notes explaining the circumstances that gave rise to its various incarnations. *—Richie Unterberger*

Death Chants, Breakdowns and Military Waltzes / 1998 / Takoma ✦✦✦✦✦
Fahey recorded two entirely different versions of this record: one issued in 1963 and one mostly of re-recordings in 1967. The CD reissue of *Death Chants, Breakdowns and Military Waltzes* does Fahey fans a massive favor by combining both versions onto one disc. Preceded only by the super-rare original version of *Blind Joe Death*, the 1963 LP of *Death Chants* was the first Fahey album to gain reasonably wide distribution. It's a work that beautifully displays both Fahey's virtuosity on folk and blues guitar and a distinct composing voice that draws much from folk and blues traditions, but is not quite part of either school. Fahey's gift for making music that's tranquil and evocative, but also with enough odd angularity and minor melody to give it depth and ambiguity, is evident right from the start, and heard to best advantage on "When the Springtime Comes Again," "Some Summer Day," and the epic "America." Even on the pieces with more straight blues connections, Fahey achieves a full and reverberant quality that sets it off not just from the average country blues revivalists of the period, but from vintage country blues itself. He takes a journey into the avant-garde with "The Downfall of the Adelphi Rolling Grist Mill," a creepy duet with flute player Nancy McLean. On the re-recorded versions that comprised most of the 1967 version of *Death Chants*, the fidelity is clearer, and having improved his technique Fahey probably felt more satisfied with these renditions. But as often happens on remakes, it must be said that the originals have an intangibly more affecting, more mysterious quality that does not come through as strongly on the more carefully executed rehauls. *—Richie Unterberger*

The Best of the Vanguard Years / Jul. 7, 1999 / Vanguard ✦✦✦✦

The Dance of Death & Other Plantation Favorites / Jul. 13, 1999 / Takoma ✦✦✦✦
The title *The Dance of Death and Other Plantation Favorites* might lead some to believe that this is a collection of public-domain items that go back to the Deep South of the 19th century. However, while this 1964 session does contain a song titled "Dance of Death," most of the material (including that tune) was written by Fahey himself in the early 1960s. So an intriguing title is simply that: an intriguing title. Nonetheless, Fahey's music does have strong southern roots. Unaccompanied, the acoustic guitarist/instrumentalist demonstrates his love of African-American blues as well as the Anglo-American country, folk, and hillbilly music of Appalachia. This is essentially a folk album, but a folk album with strong country and blues leanings; in fact, numbers like "Worried Blues" and "Revelation on the Banks of the Pawtuxent" incorporate the slide guitar technique that came from Mississippi Delta blues. Not that Fahey limits himself to American influences—Appalachian music is a descendent of British, Scottish, and Irish music, and Fahey is hardly unaware of its European heritage. Further, Indian raga is an influence on the Fahey piece "On the Banks of the Owchita." Reissued on CD in 1999 with four bonus tracks (including an interpretation of "Steel Guitar Rag"), this album makes it clear that even back in 1964 Fahey was quite original. *—Alex Henderson*

Mimi Fariña

b. Apr. 30, 1945, California, **d.** Jul. 18, 2001
Vocals, Guitar / Folk Revival, Traditional Folk
Mimi Farina, Joan Baez's younger sister, first got into performing professionally in partnership with her husband, novelist and songwriter Richard Farina, whom she married in 1963. Singing harmony, the couple released two remarkable albums on Vanguard, *Celebrations for a Grey Day* in 1965 and *Reflections in a Crystal Wind* (1966), before Richard was killed in a motorcycle accident. Mimi Farina was 21.

She subsequently released an album of the duo's outtakes, *Memories*. (The two albums made during Richard's lifetime were reissued as a best-of two-fer.) In the late '60s, Farina, based in California, worked with a satiric improvisational acting group and began to write her own songs. She re-emerged on record in 1971 on *Take Heart*, a duo album with Tom Jans that included her tribute song to Janis Joplin, "In the Quiet Morning." (This and other songs of hers were also recorded by her sister.)

In the '70s, Farina founded Bread & Roses, a charity organization devoted to putting on musical performances in hospitals and prisons. Several of the organization's annual benefit concerts, featuring some of the biggest names in folk and popular music, have been recorded and released. In 1985, Farina finally released a solo album, appropriately entitled *Solo*, and undertook a national tour. *—William Ruhlmann*

● **Solo** / 1985 / Philo ✦✦✦✦

Richard & Mimi Fariña

f. 1964, **db.** 1966
Group / Folk Revival, Folk-Rock, Singer/Songwriter, Traditional Folk
Richard Farina was a noted counterculture author and folksinger in the early '60s. Married for a time to folksinger Carolyn Hester, he was an early intimate of Bob Dylan, and in fact recorded a collectable album with Dylan (playing under the pseudonym "Blind Boy Grunt") and Ric Von Schmidt in 1963. After marrying Joan Baez's sister Mimi, he formed a folk-rock duo that released two acclaimed albums in the mid-sixties. Unlike folk-rock figureheads like The Byrds, the Farinas were far more firmly rooted in folk than rock.

Their recordings effectively flavored their material (mostly written by Richard) with jangling electric guitars and a rhythm section, ably assisted by such session players as guitarist Bruce Langhorne (who also played on Dylan's first electric recordings), bassist Felix Pappalardi, and harmonica player John Hammond. The Farinas themselves also played guitar, autoharp, and dulcimer. Least successful with blues, they recorded some effective Appalachian-flavored material, and several excellent bonafide midtempo folk-rockers and ballads. Their best songs effectively balanced world-wise, sardonic observations with good-natured, melodic optimism.

The Farinas' promising career ended prematurely with the death of Richard in a motorcycle accident on his birthday in 1966. His novel of the same year, *Been Down So Long It Looks Like Up To Me*, became a cult favorite. Since Richard's death, Mimi Farina has sporadically recorded and performed as a solo act. *—Richie Unterberger*

Celebrations for a Grey Day / 1965 / Vanguard ✦✦✦
The duo's debut effectively laid out their approach: Appalachian-like instrumentals that put the dulcimer to the fore alternate with strong contemporary folk compositions, which are by turns mournful and high-spirited. The world-weary "Reno Nevada" (a part of Fairport Convention's repertoire in their early days) is the duo's best song. *—Richie Unterberger*

Reflections in a Crystal Wind / 1965 / Vanguard ✦✦✦
Basically a continuation of the first album with a slightly more electric feel, finding Richard developing deeper insight and a subtler touch. *—Richie Unterberger*

Memories / 1968 / Vanguard ✦✦✦
A posthumous collection of odds and ends, this actually holds considerable appeal for anyone who likes their pair of fully realized albums. The twelve songs include a few studio outtakes, a few solo turns by Mimi on compositions written by Richard but incompletely recorded at the time of his death, a couple performances from the 1965 Newport Folk Festival, and a couple of Joan Baez tracks from sessions for an aborted album Richard was pro-

ducing with her. These leftovers are generally up to the standard of the two "real" albums, especially "The Quiet Joys Of Brotherhood" (covered by Fairport Convention) and "Morgan The Pirate" (a farewell to Bob Dylan, according to the sketchy liner notes). The two cuts by Baez (which Richard wrote or co-wrote), especially the compellingly melancholy "All The World Has Gone By," are excellent, leading one to wonder if the projected album they came from would have been one of Baez's best if it had been completed. These may be leftovers, but it's a worthwhile collection nonetheless. *— Richie Unterberger*

The Best of Mimi and Richard Farina / 1971 / Vanguard ✦✦✦✦✦
While a 26-song double album is not ordinarily recommended as the best introduction to such a short-lived act, the Farinas' work was so consistent that it makes sense to pick up this compilation, which combines *Celebrations for a Grey Day* and *Reflections in a Crystal Wind* into one package. *— Richie Unterberger*

★ **Pack up Your Sorrows: Best of Vanguard Years** / Sep. 28, 1999 / Vanguard ✦✦✦✦✦
When Vanguard Records issued its double album *The Best of Mimi & Richard Fariña* in 1971, five years after the motorcycle crash that claimed Richard Fariña's life, the label simply repackaged the duo's two regular album releases, *Celebrations for a Grey Day* (1965) and *Reflections in a Crystal Wind* (1966). In 1988, when it reissued the package on CD, Vanguard cut six tracks to fit *The Best Of* on a single disc, leaving 20. Eighteen of those tracks are repeated on *Pack Up Your Sorrows: Best of the Vanguard Years,* which restores one of the cut songs and adds two tracks from the 1968 outtakes album *Memories,* plus one previously unreleased instrumental, "Tuileries." All of that makes the new compilation a slight improvement in terms of selection, while the CD remastering improves the sound. (Ed Ward's enthusiastic but ill-informed liner notes—he confuses *the Big Sur Folk Festival* with *the Newport Folk Festival* and makes other errors—are not a plus.) As a lyricist, Fariña matched the elliptical style of mid-'60s Bob Dylan image for image, and tracks such as "Hard Loving Loser" are stylistically identical to the folk-rock of Dylan's *Bringing It All Back Home,* partly because they employ some of the same sidemen. But Fariña and his wife Mimi gave his words a sweet-and-sour harmony style, and their most distinctive music was made when they duetted on autoharp and dulcimer, as on the instrumentals that make up a good part of the song list. Richard Fariña's early death robbed the music world of an important singer/songwriter (not to mention robbing literature of a promising novelist), but the work he left behind ranks with the best folk-rock of the 1960s. *— William Ruhlmann*

Sally Fingerett

b. Dec. 25, 1955
Vocals, Piano, Guitar / Contemporary Singer/Songwriter, Contemporary Folk
Sally Fingerett is best known as a member of the Bitchin' Babes, an all-female folk-pop group founded by humorous singer/songwriter Christine Lavin in 1990. A craftsmanlike songwriter and possessor of a emotion-tinged soprano voice, Fingerett has been nearly as effective on her own—her solo albums have showcased her warm vocal style and heartfelt lyricism. Inspired by Steve Goodman and John Prine, she wrote her first song, "Rock-a-Line Caroline," at the age of 23. Her debut solo album, *Enclosed,* was released in 1983. In 1990, Fingerett won the prestigious New Folk award at the Kerrville Folk Festival. Fingerett's second solo album, *Unraveled,* was released in 1992; *Ghost Town Girl,* was released the following year. *— Craig Harris*

● **Unraveled** / 1990 / Amerisound ✦✦✦✦✦

My Good Company / Aug. 18, 1998 / Shanachie ✦✦✦

Fotheringay

f. 1970
Group / British Folk-Rock, British Folk
A short-lived offshoot of Fairport Convention, featuring key member and leader Sandy Denny. A second album was planned but never completed; tracks from it turn up on the triple-CD Denny anthology *Who Knows Where the Time Goes.* This is far more interesting and beguiling than their work with Fairport Convention, especially the Bob Dylan songs, but it lacks Fairport's precision and focus. *— Bruce Eder & William Ruhlmann*

● **Fotheringay** / 1970 / Hannibal ✦✦✦✦✦
Also featured are Trevor Lucas and Jerry Donahue, both of whom eventually joined Fairport when Denny rejoined. The album is a close relative of Denny's other solo and group work and features several of her flowing ballads, showcasing her lovely voice. A footnote, but a pleasing one. *— Bruce Eder & William Ruhlmann*

4 Bitchin' Babes

f. 1990
Group / Contemporary Singer/Songwriter, Contemporary Folk, Novelty
The Four Bitchin' Babes began as a musical revue by humorous singer/songwriter Christine Lavin. But since Lavin's departure in September 1997, the group has shown that it's taken on a life of its own. The Four Bitchin' Babes was one of several projects founded by Lavin ("folk music's cheerleader") in the early 1990s; while her other projects, including *On a Winter's Night,* featured both men and women, the Babes showcased only female artists. The original quartet featured Lavin, Sally Fingerett, Megon McDonough and Patty Larkin. When Larkin left to concentrate on her solo career following the release of the group's debut album, *Buy Me, Bring Me, Take Me: Don't Mess with My Hair...,* singer/songwriter Julie Gold ("From a Distance") replaced her, singing with the group on their second album, *Buy Me, Bring Me, Take Me: Don't Mess with My Hair... Volume 2.* Vocalist Debi Smith, who replaced Gold, has remained with the Four Bitchin' Babes through two albums. Lavin retained much of the group's spotlight until leaving in 1997 and being replaced by Camille West. *— Craig Harris*

● **Life According to 4 Bitchin' Babes** / 1992 / Philo ✦✦✦✦✦

Fax It! Charge It! / Nov. 1995 / Shanachie ✦✦✦

Gabby Road / Oct. 21, 1997 / Shanachie ✦✦✦

Beyond Bitchin' / May 9, 2000 / Shanachie ✦✦✦
Beyond Bitchin' finds the four employing a common musical background provided primarily by producer/keyboardist Jeff Bova and T-Bone Wolk, who plays a variety of acoustic instruments, giving the overall sound a distinct country-pop feel. But it remains the work of four different performers who do nothing more than sing backup vocals on each other's songs. In fact, the album has a strict form, its 12 tracks carefully divided into three groups of four songs in which Debi Smith, Sally Fingerett, Megon McDonough, and Camille West, in turn, take the lead, always in the same order. The first quartet of songs consists of philosophical and abstract songs, the highlights being Smith ruminating over "Little Stars" in the sky and Fingerett celebrating a "Little Mistake." The second quartet consists of love songs of one sort or another: Smith praises "My Kinda Man," a man who can cook; while West tells the lusty story of a chemical truck spill in "Viagra in the Waters." The final set of songs concern family and topical matters with Smith belaboring a metaphor about travel to bring up autism in "Italy and France," Fingerett attacking tabloid journalism in "I Don't Wanna Know," McDonough speculating on what she would do "If I Were Brave," and West commiserating with a teenage child in "Hold on to My Love." Some songs are better than others, and $4 Bitchin' Babes remain four individual performers traveling under a flag of convenience, but the album as a whole treats a variety of issues and situations with humor and affection, which seems to have been the group's purpose from the beginning. *— William Ruhlmann*

Jackson C. Frank

Vocals, Guitar / Folk Revival, Traditional Folk
One of the most interesting and enigmatic cult figures of 1960s folk, Jackson Frank's reputation rests almost solely upon one hard-to-find album from the mid-'60s. A stronger composer than a singer, he nonetheless had an appreciable influence on many more famous performers of the decade, including Paul Simon, Sandy Denny, and Nick Drake. Trauma and misfortune have dogged Frank throughout his life. An elementary-school fire left him with burns over most of his body, though he later traveled to England thanks to a large insurance settlement. After sharing a flat with Paul Simon and Art Garfunkel, Simon produced Frank's self-titled debut album. While his voice was tremulously earnest, the quality of the compositions was often impressive, with a reflective, melancholic air that most likely influenced Simon, Al Stewart and Nick Drake. Unable to come up with a similar quality of material, Frank returned to the States in 1969 without releasing another album. By the mid-'70s, problems with depression and family had resulted in homelessness. For most of the next two decades, Frank lived on the streets or hospitals, too discouraged to contact old friends and family, especially after a shooting incident that left him legally blind in his left eye. He resumed songwriting and performing occasionally during the mid-'90s, while Frank's legendary vintage recordings were finally issued on CD in 1996. *— Richie Unterberger*

● **Blues Run the Game** / 1996 / Mooncrest ✦✦✦✦✦
Ten songs from Frank's legendary (and rare) self-titled mid-'60s album, including "Blues Run the Game," "Here Come the Blues," "Milk and Honey," and "You Never Wanted Me," as well as five previously unreleased tracks from 1975. The '60s tracks are perhaps not as stunning as some have been led to believe, sounding a bit naive and dated, but at their best have an appealingly moody, troubadour feel. The songs from the '70s, also performed solo on acoustic guitar, are surprisingly worthwhile; similar in quality to the ones from the previous decade, they're very much of a piece with his '60s work. *— Richie Unterberger*

Kinky Friedman (Richard Friedman)

b. Oct. 31, 1944, Rio Duckworth, Palestine, TX
Vocals / Outlaw Country, Country Comedy
Outrageous and irreverent but nearly always thought-provoking, Kinky Friedman wrote and performed satirical country songs during the 1970s and has been hailed the Frank Zappa of country music. In 1971 he founded the Texas Jewboys; in keeping with the group's satirical nature, each member had deliberately un-PC names such as Little Jewford, Big Nig, Panama Red, Rainbow Colors and Snakebite Jacobs. Friedman got his break in 1973 thanks to Commander Cody, who contacted Vanguard Music on behalf of the acerbic young performer. That was the year he and his group made their debut album, *Sold American.* In the mid-'70s, Friedman and his band began touring with Bob Dylan's Rolling Thunder Revue. In 1976 he made his third album, *Lasso from El Paso,* featuring Dylan and Eric Clapton. The Texas Jewboys disbanded three years later and Friedman moved to New York where he played at the Lone Star Cafe. In 1983, he released *Under the Double Ego* for Sunrise Records. It was his last recording to date and since then Friedman has turned toward writing with a series of mystery tales such as *Greenwich Killing Time, A Case of Lone Star* and *Frequent Flyer,* all of which feature "The Kinkster," a Jewish country-singer turned Greenwich Village private-eye. *— Sandra Brennan*

Sold American / 1973 / Vanguard ✦✦✦✦✦
A renegade figure who often stresses the outrageous. The title song is a gem. Part of the '70s country/folk/rock wave. *— Hank Davis*

● **Lasso from El Paso** / 1976 / Varese ✦✦✦✦✦
Of the many albums that grew out of Bob Dylan's *Rolling Thunder Revue,* this must be the strangest. Friedman has a husky voice and an off-kilter sense of humor best captured on the live-from-the-revue track, "Sold American." Also notable for a version of the Bob Dylan outtake, "Catfish." *— William Ruhlmann*

Old Testaments & New Revelations / 1992 / Fruit of the Tune ✦✦✦
Kinky Friedman, backed by his faithful combo The Texas Jewboys, bring old-time swing to Hollywood with plenty of satire on *Old Testaments and New Revelations.* Social satire from a Jewish perspective is Friedman's forte, and this generous live recording blends classics like "We Refuse the Right To Refuse Service To You" with a whole new set of barbed hooks. *— Roch Parisien*

Alice Gerrard

Singer, Vocals, Guitar, Fiddle, Banjo / Appalachian Folk, Contemporary Folk, String Bands, Old-Timey

The daughter of trained classical musicians, Alice Gerrard didn't grow up with bluegrass or folk music. Her earliest musical memories are of singing along with family members and friends around the living room piano. Gerrard's albums with West Virginia-born folksinger Hazel Dickens, however, rank among the most influential recordings in folk music history.

Gerrard's first exposure to folk music came while she was attending Antioch College in Ohio. Inspired by the folksongs played by dorm-mates, Gerrard abandoned the piano and became absorbed with the more rural sounds that she heard on such albums as *The Anthology Of American Folk Music.*

Moving to Washington, D.C. to complete her college co-op experience, Gerrard encountered a thriving bluegrass scene. Hanging out in her spare time at the Famous Restaurant in Washington, D.C., Gerrard met numerous bluegrass and old timey musicians including Mike Seeger of The New Lost City Ramblers who introduced her to Dickens. With their mutual love of traditional American music, Gerrard and Dickens became close friends. Developing a unique harmony style that combined the alto-below-lead of The Carter Family and the tenor-above-lead of Bill Monroe, the two vocalists soon became frequent performers in the folk clubs and coffeehouse of the Capitol region. Their repertoire continued to expand as they studied sheet music at the Library of congress and taped old-timey musicians at folk festivals.

Gerrard and Dicken's debut album, *Who's That Knocking* released in 1965, was recorded for $75 at the First Unitarian Church in Washington and featured accompaniment by David Grisman (mandolin), Lamar Grier (banjo) and Chubby Wise and Billy Baker (fiddles). Although their second album, *Won't You Come And Sing?,* featuring the same musicians, was recorded the same year, it wasn't released until 1973. Gerrard and Dickens' first two albums were later combined and released as *Pioneering Women Of Bluegrass* in 1996. The twenty-six tunes on the reissued album includes six Carter Family songs, five Bill Monroe tunes, three original songs by Dickens and Gerrard's hard-hitting satire of sexist attitudes towards women, *Custom Made Woman Blues.*

Gerrard and Dickens' most recent album, *Get Acquainted Waltz,* was released in 1975 and featured accompaniment by Seeger, who was at the time Gerrard's husband, and his New Lost City Ramblers band-mate Tracy Schwartz.

Gerrard subsequently recorded two albums with Seeger—*Mike And Alice Seeger In Concert* in 1970 and *Mike Seeger And Alice Gerrard* in 1980—and one solo collection, *Pieces of My Heart* in 1994. Since 1987, Gerrard has published *The Old Time Herald,* a quarterly magazine devoted to the preservation of old timey music. *—Craig Harris*

● **Pioneering Women of Bluegrass** / 1996 / Smithsonian/Folkways ✦✦✦✦✦
Dickens and Gerrard recorded a couple of albums in the mid-1960s that are now acknowledged as groundbreakers in demonstrating that women could play and record quality bluegrass. This collection remasters and resequences 26 tracks from the sessions, as well as adding lengthy historical liner notes, much of them contributed by the performers themselves. Historical significance aside, it's pretty good bluegrass, the two singers and instrumentals supported by other good musicians, including a young David Grisman. Their set leaned heavily on covers of tunes by the Carter Family and Bill Monroe (who specifically gave "I Hear a Sweet Voice Calling" to the duo), with additional items by the Delmore Brothers, the Stanley Brothers, and the like. Alice Gerrard's low vocals give this a greater gravity than much bluegrass. A special highlight is the cover of the magnificently mournful "The One I Love Is Gone," another tune that Monroe donated to the pair. Inverting the usual bluegrass cliche, one might call it an example of the low and lonesome sound. *—Richie Unterberger*

Bob Gibson

b. Nov. 16, 1931, New York, NY, **d.** Sep. 28, 1996, Portland, OR

Vocals, Guitar, Banjo / Folksongs, Traditional Folk

While Bob Gibson's recordings may sound like run-of-the-mill white-boy folk to modern listeners, he played an important role in popularizing folk music to American audiences in the 1950s at the very beginning of the folk boom. His 12-string guitar style influenced performers like Gordon Lightfoot and Harry Chapin; he was a mainstay at one of the first established folk clubs in the U.S., the Gate of Horn in Chicago; and he wrote songs with Shel Silverstein and Phil Ochs, as well as performing in a duo with Hamilton Camp. Most of all, he was one of the first folkies on the scene—when he began performing and recording in the mid-'50s, there was hardly anyone else playing guitar-based folk music for an educated, relatively affluent audience. *—Richie Unterberger*

Bob Gibson & Bob Camp at the Gate of Horn / Jul. 1961 / Elektra ✦✦✦
In 2000, Roger McGuinn selected this as his pick in the "Last Night a Record Changed My Life" section of *MOJO* magazine. McGuinn was actually in the audience, as a 19-year-old, during the week in which this LP was recorded, and in his appreciation praises their harmonies and Gibson's 12-string guitar. No doubt it was a big influence, but that doesn't change the fact that it's really just an average 1960s folk album, and not as exciting as you might hope given *MOJO*'s note that "Gibson's 12-string virtuosity and strong vocals and Camp's wild harmonizing not only defined this area but broke new ground." Accompanied by Herb Brown on bass, the duo run through a set dominated by trad folk tunes given new words and arrangements, the best of these being the perennial "Wayfaring Stranger." The pair's vocals are stagey, the comedy between (and sometimes during) tunes not that funny, and the whole thing has that corny, dated air common to many folk LPs of the early 1960s, with more strident wholeheartedness than imagination or soul. It's hipper than the Kingston Trio, yes, but not by much, and not that dissimilar. This doesn't mean that Roger McGuinn and the Byrds were any less great than they were, but if this was indeed a key inspiration for McGuinn, one must say he certainly exceeded his role models by vast distances. Incidentally, Bob Camp changed his name to Hamilton Camp and became a solo folkie of some note, famous for writing "Pride of Man" (covered by Quicksilver Messenger Service); even Camp's 1964 solo debut, *Paths of Victory* (also on Elektra), is far more forceful and moving than this. *—Richie Unterberger*

Homemade Music / 1978 / Mountain Railroad ✦✦✦✦✦

The Perfect High / 1980 / Drive Archive ✦✦✦

Uptown Saturday Night / 1984 / Hogeye ✦✦✦✦
After his prolific initial period of recording, 1956 to 1964, when he made a series of albums for Riverside and Elektra Records, Bob Gibson entered the recording studio infrequently during the remaining 30 years of his career.

Uptown Saturday Night was on a small label, Hogeye Records, which he had founded with fellow folksinger Tom Paxton. It was a consistent collection of craftsmanlike original material that displayed the singer's talents well. His love songs, notably "Rest of the Night" and "Lookin' for the You," were tender and wistful, and they were offset by the comic material, which he rendered equally well. "Tequila Sheila," written by longtime associate Shel Silverstein and Mac Davis (and the only non-original on the album), provided a twist on the South of the Border theme, and the album-closing "Bein' on the Road" took successful pop musicians to task for their complaints about touring, which no doubt rang false to a performer who had traveled for decades in much less comfortable circumstances. Such songs as the title track and "Baby, If You Don't Know by Now" had a country-blues edge, but Gibson's renditions of the material were always restrained and considered.

Now in his early 50s, he was already an elder statesman of folk music, and this tempered album confirmed that place without breaking new ground. *—William Ruhlmann*

Joy Joy! the Young and Wonderful Bob Gibson / 1996 / Riverside ✦✦✦✦✦

● **Stops Along the Way** / Jul. 7, 1997 / Folk Era ✦✦✦✦✦
On his 60th birthday, Bob Gibson recorded this live album in a Chicago recording studio before a small invited audience. Gibson sought to sum up his career, and he succeeded. Gibson always occupied a middle position in postwar folk music, taking it up in the mid-'50s after a business career. By the early '60s, Gibson, like other folksingers, was turning to more topical concerns, though he was bypassed by the quickly changing trends in folk and folk-rock in the mid-'60s. After virtually a decade-long lost weekend, he returned to action in the mid-'70s to find the folk boom less than an echo. The last few songs in the concert displayed the results, from the anthemic "I Hear America Singing" to the rueful biography-in-song "Living Legend" and the more philosophical "Stops Along the Way." It is a convention to suggest that Bob Gibson is little more than a footnote to the folk revival of the late '50s and early '60s, but listening to this album one hears his unmistakable influence on a generation of folk-pop singers including Steve Goodman, John Prine, John Denver, and Harry Chapin. The influence is apparent in the very timbre of his voice as well as in the humor and hopefulness of his approach to music. That approach remained much the same, even if Gibson was a little wistful, at this concert. Though his friends helped him put together a country-oriented final album (*Makin' a Mess: Bob Gibson Plays Shel Silverstein*) in 1994, this concert is really Gibson's last performance in the style he forged over 40 years of shows. It gives an excellent impression of a long underrated singer and songwriter and, despite being a valedictory, provides the best introduction to his work. *—William Ruhlmann*

Steve Goodman

b. Jul. 25, 1948, Chicago, IL, **d.** Sep. 20, 1984, Seattle, WA

Vocals, Guitar / Contemporary Singer/Songwriter, Contemporary Folk, Singer/Songwriter

Growing up in what he called "a Midwestern middle-class Jewish family," Steve Goodman began playing the guitar as a teenager. He was influenced by the folk revival of the early '60s and by country performers such as Jimmie Rodgers and Hank Williams. Ater attending college in the mid-'60s, he turned to playing in Chicago clubs by night and writing commercial jingles by day. In 1971, he opened for Kris Kristofferson and was seen by Paul Anka, who financed demo recordings that led to a contract with Buddah Records and the release of *Steve Goodman,* which featured his train song "The City of New Orleans," a Top 40 hit for Arlo Guthrie in 1972 and now a folk standard. Goodman made a second album for Buddah, *Somebody Else's Troubles* (1973), then broke with the label, which went on to issue an outtakes record, *The Essential Steve Goodman* (1975). Goodman moved to the singer/songwriter-oriented West Coast label Asylum for his first charting album *Jessie's Jig & Other Favorites* in 1975, the same year that "outlaw" country singer David Allen Coe made the Top Ten of the Country charts with a cover of his "You Never Even Called Me by My Name" from the *Steve Goodman* album. Goodman's subsequent Asylum albums were *Words We Can Dance To* (Apr. 1976) (featuring "Banana Republics," popularized by Jimmy Buffett), *Say It in Private* (Oct. 1977), *High and Outside* (Feb. 1979), and *Hot Spot* (1980). None became a major commercial success, but Goodman established himself on the national club and festival circuits, frequently appearing with mandolin player Jethro Burns, formerly of the country duo Homer & Jethro. Goodman turned record producer for his friend and fellow Chicagoan John Prine on Prine's 1978 album *Bruised Orange.* In 1983, Goodman followed Prine in establishing his own independent label, Red Pajamas, which released the live *Artistic Hair* and *Affordable Art* (1984). Goodman died of leukemia after battling the disease for many years. Red Pajamas released *Santa Ana Winds* (1984) posthumously, as well as a double-disc LP drawn from a concert in his memory, *A Tribute to Steve Goodman,* which featured John Prine, Bonnie Raitt, and others. After a second posthumous release, *Unfinished Business,* Red Pajamas licensed the Asylum material and put out two *Best of the Asylum Years* compilations. *— William Ruhlmann*

Gathering at the Earl of Old Town / 1970 / Drive Archive ✦✦✦
Steve Goodman's first album, *Gathering at the Earol of Old Town,* was recorded live at the popular Chicago folk venue. The record has the feeling of a hootenanny, with a number of different artists—including Jim Post, Ed Holstein, Fred Holstein, Ginni Clemens and Aliotta Haynes & Jeremiah—stopping in to play on the record. While it's a little rough around the edges, the album is utterly charming, featuring the first versions of such seminal Goodman

songs as "City of New Orleans" and "Eight Ball," as well as "Chicago Bust Rag," which the singer-songwriter never performed again. *—Thom Owens*

★ **Steve Goodman** / 1972 / Buddha ♦♦♦♦♦
Steve Goodman's 1971 self-titled album marked the debut of a great new songwriter. "City of New Orleans, " which was (then) soon to be a hit for Arlo Guthrie, is the obvious standout, and "You Never Even Call Me by My Name, " later a country hit by David Allan Coe in a revised version, is also impressive, but "I Don't Know Where I'm Goin', but I'm Goin' Nowhere in a Hurry Blues" and "Would You Like to Learn Dance—" also show off different sides of this versatile talent. Versatility is the key here, as Goodman broke well out of the "folkie" tag to embrace pop, country, and arcane jazz, including not only his own compositions but also covers of songs by Hank Williams, Johnny Otis, and pal John Prine while utilizing a who's who of Nashville session musicians. Beyond the musical eclecticism, there was also a variety in tone, with gentle evocations of tenderness and humor alternating so that you didn't always know whether Goodman was serious or kidding. At a time when sensitive singer/songwriters were all the rage (a trend that probably earned Goodman his record contract), this was one guy who was at least as interested in picking an old country song as he was in baring his soul. [The 1999 reissue added two bonus tracks, "Election Year Rag," previously unissued in the U.S. and featuring Bob Dylan on piano, and the previously unreleased "Georgia Rag."] *—William Ruhlmann*

Somebody Else's Troubles / 1973 / Buddha ♦♦♦

Jessie's Jig & Other Favorites / 1975 / Red Pajamas ♦♦♦

Words We Can Dance To / 1976 / Red Pajamas ♦♦♦♦
A typical Steve Goodman mix of eclectic stylings and clever wordplay, *Words We Can Dance To* roams far and wide. The music ranges from a cover of the rock & roll classic, "Tossin' and Turnin'" to the Western swing of "Between the Lines," and from the country shuffle of "Death of a Salesman" to the solo acoustic blues guitar pickin' on the standard, "The Glory of Love." Within this broad musical spectrum, Goodman delivers his original lyrics, both humorous and heartfelt. "Banana Republics" became a staple of Jimmy Buffett's repertoire after its inclusion on *Changes in Latitudes.* In "Old Fashioned," Goodman tells of being "out of date and born too late" as he seeks the love of an "old fashioned girl," but in fact the lines probably described his music as well. Both "Between the Lines" and "That's What Friends Are For" offer compelling, personal looks at the elusiveness of love, while on "Death of a Salesman," Goodman goes for the laughs in a retelling of the old travelling salesman story. *—Jim Newsom*

Say It in Private / 1977 / Red Pajamas ♦♦♦♦♦
A full-blown studio affair with chestnuts like "Is It True What They Say About Dixie—" and wonderful originals; "The Twentieth Century Is Almost Over." *—Richard Meyer*

High and Outside / 1979 / Red Pajamas ♦♦♦♦

Hot Spot / 1980 / Red Pajamas ♦♦♦

Artistic Hair / 1983 / Red Pajamas ♦♦♦♦♦
Goodman achieved artistic control with this album, featuring his "City of New Orleans" and other classics. *—William Ruhlmann*

Unfinished Business / 1987 / Red Pajamas ♦♦♦
Released posthumously after Goodman's death from leukemia, it contains "A Fool Such as I," "My Funny Valentine" and "The Whispering Man." A sweet, more subdued collection. *—Richard Meyer*

The Best of the Asylum Years, Vol. 1 / 1988 / Red Pajamas ♦♦♦♦♦

The Best of the Asylum Years, Vol. 2 / 1989 / Red Pajamas ♦♦♦

☆ **No Big Surprise: Anthology** / 1994 / Red Pajamas ♦♦♦♦♦

Live Wire / Jul. 25, 2000 / Red Pajamas ♦♦♦♦♦

John Gorka

Vocals, Guitar / Contemporary Singer/Songwriter, Contemporary Folk
A singer-songwriter famed for his rich, expressive baritone, New Jersey native John Gorka was one of the leading lights of the New Folk movement. Gorka began his career while attending college in Pennsylvania in the early 1980s, appearing at open mike nights at a local coffeehouse before eventually forming his own group, the Razzy Dazzy Spasm Band. Soon he hit the road, performing up and down the Eastern seaboard before finally settling in Texas and winning the Kerrville Folk Festival's prestigious New Folk Award in 1984.

In 1987 Gorka cut his debut album, *I Know,* for the Red House label, winning acclaim for his songs' subtle wit and acute character observations. After a move to Windham Hill, he issued 1990's *Land of the Bottom Line,* followed two years later by *Jack's Crows.* With 1993's *Temporary Road,* Gorka garnered significant airplay from country outlets with the single and video "When She Kisses Me," resulting in tours supporting Mary-Chapin Carpenter and Nanci Griffith. For 1994's *Out of the Valley,* Gorka travelled to Nashville to team with producer John Jennings, who recruited guests including Carpenter, Kathy Mattea, guitarist Leo Kottke and Fairport Convention drummer Dave Mattacks; *Between Five and Seven* followed in 1996, and two years later he returned with *After Yesterday. Company You Keep,* which followed in early 2001, featured guest spots from

Mary Chapin Carpenter, Patty Larkin, Lucy Kaplansky, and others. *—Jason Ankeny*

● **I Know** / 1987 / Red House ♦♦♦♦♦
By the time he recorded his debut album *I Know,* John Gorka was already a seasoned veteran and it showed. With excellent harmony vocals from Shawn Colvin and Lucy Kaplansky, who also cut their teeth on the New York City folk circuit, John Gorka recorded an album of original songs that had been road-tested and audience approved. The chorus of nearly every song is instantly memorable, and the simple, acoustic arrangements help bring out his powerful voice. The most impressive feature of this debut is the ability of Gorka to move easily from light-hearted humorous songs ("Winter Cows," "Like My Watch") to serious songs about the complexities of relationships ("Love Is Our Cross to Bear"). The versatility in his songwriting and the expressiveness of his warm baritone would become his trademarks, and John Gorka has become a leader of the genre dubbed "contemporary folk." This stunning debut also established Gorka songs in the folk canon, as his inspirational song "Branching Out" is often sung in elementary schools. *—Vik Iyengar*

Land of the Bottom Line / Jun. 8, 1992 / Windham Hill ♦♦♦♦♦
This is a long record filled with a full range of Gorka's romantic and story songs. He states his case as an outsider forced to meet the mainstream with the title cut and confronts his demons on "Raven in the Storm." More sentimental tracks are "The One That Got Away" and "Love Is Our Cross to Bear." "Mean Streak" is gritty and shows that Gorka can howl when he wants to. *—Richard Meyer*

Jack's Crows / Dec. 8, 1992 / High Street ♦♦♦
The songwriting is particularly strong on this album. His ballad of the Marines and his father demonstrates how he can handle the most sentimental subjects well. "Silence, " the first cut, is a crystalline beauty and "Where the Bottles Break" is a rockin' song about personal convictions and the real-estate business. *—Richard Meyer*

Temporary Road / Dec. 8, 1992 / High Street ♦♦♦
John Gorka is widely regarded as one of the leading male voices of the "new folk" movement. Gorka has a warm, world-weary baritone that draws the listener equally into the emotionally naked "The Gypsy Life" (great background vocals from Nanci Griffith) and the more objective narrative of "Vinny Charles is Free." He keeps one foot in the atmospheric Windham Hill camp, and one in protest-folk coffeehouses, emerging with the best of both influences on his strongest material. *—Roch Parisien*

Out of the Valley / May 10, 1994 / High Street ♦♦♦

Between Five and Seven / Aug. 1996 / High Street ♦♦♦
On *Between Five and Seven,* John Gorka opens up his sound somewhat, touching on contemporary pop and rock without losing his confessional folk foundation. The result can be frustrating at times—occasionally, the production obsucres the simple beauty of his melodies—but overall, the album is another winner from Gorka, one of the finest songwriters of the '90s. *—Thom Owens*

After Yesterday / Oct. 20, 1998 / Red House ♦♦♦♦

Davey Graham

b. Nov. 22, 1940, Leicester, England
Vocals, Guitar / British Folk-Rock, Progressive Folk, British Folk
One of the most eclectic guitarists of the 1960s, Graham's mixture of folk, blues, jazz, Middle Eastern sounds, and Indian ragas was an important catalyst of the British folk scene. Like Sandy Bull and John Fahey—two folk-based guitarists with a similar taste for genre-bending experimentation—Graham could not be said to be a rock musician. But like Bull and Fahey, he shared the eagerness of the '60s psychedelic rockers to stretch out and incorporate unpredictable influences into his music. While he wasn't much of a singer, Graham's taste in material was broad and shrewd, encompassing blues, ragas, Joni Mitchell, Charles Mingus, and the famous instrumental "Anji," which Graham recorded in 1962, way before the more famous versions by Bert Jansch and Simon & Garfunkel. Besides cutting several albums of his own work in the 1960s with sympathetic, low-key rhythm sections, he also recorded with traditional folk singer Shirley Collins and British blues father Alexis Korner. Graham recorded only sporadically after the 1960s, although he performed with the renowned acoustic guitar wizards Stefan Grossman and Duck Baker. *—Richie Unterberger*

The Guitar Player . . . Plus / 1963 / See For Miles ♦♦♦♦♦
Graham established himself as one of the most innovative players in acoustic music with his 1963 debut, *The Guitar Player.* With this album, he became one of the first folk guitarists to fuse traditional virtuosity with cross-currents from contemporary jazz and blues. Accompanied by drummer Bobby Graham (a top British sessionman who played on many British Invasion rock records, including several by The Kinks), Davey invigorates pop and traditional standards, as well as compositions by Sonny Rollins, the Adderleys, and Ray Charles. Neither jazz nor folk, Graham displays eclectic bounce that was quite visionary for its time, and remains fresh today; in his subsequent 1960s recordings, he would branch out into Middle Eastern and psychedelic sounds as a natural extension of his experimental bent. As a significant bonus, the 1992 CD reissue of this album includes the three tracks from his rare 1962 EP, *3/4 A.D.* One of these is the original version of "Anji," which was reworked by Simon & Garfunkel on one of their early albums; another features British blues-rock godfather Alexis Korner on second guitar. *—Richie Unterberger*

Folk Blues & Beyond / 1964 / Decca ♦♦♦♦♦
This was Graham's most groundbreaking and consistent album. More than his solo debut *The Guitar Player* (which was pretty jazzy) or his previous collaboration with folk singer Shirley Collins, *Folk Roots, New Routes,* this established his mixture of folk, jazz, blues, and Middle Eastern music, the use of a bassist and drummer also hinting at (though not quite reaching) folk-rock. "Leavin' Blues," "Skillet (Good'n'Greasy)," and "Moanin'" are all among his very best folk-blues-rock performances, while on "Maajun" he goes full-bore into Middle Eastern music on one of his most haunting and memorable pieces. Covers of traditional folk standards like "Black Is the Colour of My True Love's Hair" and "Seven Gypsies" combine with interpretations of compositions by Bob Dylan ("Don't Think Twice, It's Alright"), Willie Dixon ("My Babe"), Charles Mingus ("Better Git in Your Soul"), and Reverend Gary Davis ("Cocaine") for an eclecticism of repertoire that wasn't matched by many musicians of any sort in the mid-1960s. If there is one aspect of the recording to criticize, it is, as was usually the case with Graham, the thin, colorless vocals. The guitar playing is the main attraction, though; it's so stellar that it makes the less impressive singing easy to overlook. Ten of the 16 songs were included on the compilation *Folk Blues and All Points in Between,* but Graham fans should get this anyway, as the level of material and musicianship is pretty high throughout most of the disc. *—Richie Unterberger*

Folk Roots, New Routes / 1964 / Decca ✦✦✦✦✦
This pairing of one of British folk's finest voices (Shirley Collins) with one of the country's finest acoustic guitarists (Davey Graham) had a notable influence on the U.K. folk scene, although it eluded wide acclaim at the time. Collins' rich, melancholy vocals were most likely an influence on Sandy Denny, Maddy Prior, and Jacqui McShee. Graham helped redefine the nature of folk accompaniment with his imaginative, rhythmic backing, which drew from jazz, blues, and a bit of Middle Eastern music as well as mainline British Isles folk. Performed with tasteful restraint and selected with imaginative eclecticism, it also includes an instrumental showcase for Graham in "Rif Mountain," which acts as evidence of his clear influence on guitarists such as Bert Jansch and John Renbourn, and the acoustic style of Jimmy Page. *—Richie Unterberger*

Midnight Man / 1966 / Decca ✦✦✦✦✦
Graham went into a somewhat harder-rocking bluesy groove on this record, though a strong jazz feel was always present in the rhythm especially. More than any other Graham LP, this offers proof that the guitarist would have established himself as a major star on the folk circuit in the '60s—if only his singing was better. As a guitarist, he's simply wonderful, combining folk, jazz, and blues styles into an invigorating, idiosyncratic style that can both swing and attain a delicate sadness. As an interpreter, he's relentlessly imaginative, breathing new vigor into overdone R&B standards, or devising fresh folk arrangements for Beatles and Paul Simon tunes. But as a vocalist, he's adequate at best; if he had even possessed the modest expressiveness of a Bert Jansch, the material would be that much more striking. Almost none of these tracks are available on Graham compilations, and this rare LP is definitely worth seeking by those who are familiar with some of his other '60s work. Especially excellent are the jazzy "Hummingbird" and the instrumental cover of Lalo Schifrin's "The Fakir," which blends the rhythmic drive of Charles Mingus with hypnotic raga-esque riffs. *—Richie Unterberger*

Large as Life & Twice as Natural / 1968 / London ✦✦✦✦✦
With the exception of 1965's *Folk Blues & All Points in Between,* this is Graham's finest non-compilation album. It's also his most fully arranged and rock-influenced effort, with backing by a meaty ensemble featuring Danny Thompson (of Pentangle) on bass and British blues stalwarts Jon Hiseman and Dick Heckstall-Smith (Graham Bond, Colosseum) on drums and sax respectively. Even Davey's singing sounds better than usual. Graham offers some decent blues, but more interesting are his frequent excursions into raga folk-rock of sorts, especially on "Blue Raga" (learned from Ravi Shankar and Ali Akbar Khan). The raga-jazz interpretation of Joni Mitchell's "Both Sides Now," which moves from meditative opening drones into a freewheeling explosion of modal folk-rock, is one of the highlights of Graham's career on record and one of the best expressions of his ability to make a standard his own. *—Richie Unterberger*

Hat / 1969 / Decca ✦✦✦

Godington Boundary / 1970 / See for Miles ✦✦✦

Holly Kaleidoscope / 1970 / Decca ✦✦✦

The Complete Guitarist / 1980 / Kicking Mule ✦✦✦✦

● **Folk Blues and All Points in Between** / 1985 / See For Miles ✦✦✦✦✦
Side one includes ten songs from his 1964 album *Folk, Blues and Beyond;* Side two features seven tracks from three of his late-'60s LPs. The 1964 record was probably his most accomplished, as Graham handled blues, jazz, and Northern African music with aplomb. His other '60s recordings were more erratic, but the highlights gathered here matched his mid-1960s work, peaking with the original "No Preacher Blues," his folk-jazz cover of Joni Mitchell's "Both Sides Now," and the Indian-influenced "Blue Raga." *—Richie Unterberger*

After Hours at Hull University / 1997 / Rollercoaster ✦✦✦

Clive Gregson

b. Jan. 4, 1955
Vocals, Guitar / Contemporary Folk, Adult Alternative Pop/Rock, Folk-Rock, Singer/Songwriter
Clive Gregson and Christine Collister were the most moving and memorable U.K. folk-rock duo to emerge since Richard and Linda Thompson. Gregson's wry tales of the ins and outs of love, sung in Collister's heartbreaking voice have earned the duo (and subsequent solo work) respect and a devoted following though commercial success and mainstream recognition have eluded them.

Gregson (b.Jan 4, 1955) was the founder of Any Trouble, a pub-rock/new wave quartet, in Manchester in 1975. The band's sound, and Gregson's songwriting and singing, reminded some of Elvis Costello, and Any Trouble was signed by Stiff, Costello's label. The band made several well-remembered but poor-selling albums, then split up in 1984.

In 1984, Gregson discovered Collister singing in a folk club and, impressed by her talents, he offered to work with her on future projects. Gregson had already begun an association with Richard Thompson, initially singing back-up on the classic *Shoot Out the Lights* album in 1982. While working on Thompson's *Hand of Kindness,* Gregson suggested using Collister for additional backup vocal duties. The formula worked and the two continued for years as integral parts of the Richard Thompson touring band—arguably the finest live band he's assembled. In 1985, Gregson made a solo album, *Strange Persuasions,* with Collister singing backup on a few tracks. The two began performing as a duo on the folk club circuit shortly thereafter. The duo's first release was a homemade tape sold at gigs, later released as *Home and Away.* It was followed by their first formal album, *Mischief,* in 1988, and by a *Change in the Weather* in 1990. *Love is a Strange Hotel,* released later the same year, was an album of cover versions of Gregson And Collister's favorite songs.

By 1992, the stress of constant touring and working together with out substantial success finally took its toll on them. The two decided to go their seperate ways after one parting shot, *The Last Word,* and on final tour. They both continued on as solo acts. Gregson eventually relocated to Nashville and has been the more active of the two, releasing the live "official bootleg" *Carousel of Noise* on his own label in 1994, *People & Places* in 1995, and *I Love This Town* in 1996 for Compass Records in addition to various production work and side collaborations with Boo Hewardine. Christine Collister continued to play the folk circuit, releasing a live album, *Live,* in 1995 and a new studio album, *Blue Aconite* in 1997. In 1998, after a brief stint in the group Plainsong, Gregson returned with *Happy Hour.* *—Chris Woodstra and William Ruhlmann*

Strange Persuasions / 1985 / Compass ✦✦✦
Strange Persuasions came out in England in 1985, but it wasn't released in North America until 1995. After leaving his group, Any Trouble, Gregson made a name for himself in the States as a member of Richard Thompson's band and later as half of the Gregson And Collister duo. *Strange Persuasions* provides a missing link between his pub/pop days with Any Trouble and the more subtle, folkier tendencies of his later work. Some tracks sound like big L.A. pop productions with a dash of Squeeze thrown in, while others, "Jewel in Your Crown," for example, offer his sophisticated ballad writing. Perhaps this is what Ralph McTell would have sounded like had he chosen a more produced musical road; the melodies are often rooted firmly in the late-'60s and '70s folk singer/songwriter genre with enough pop sense to things interesting. While there is nothing revelatory here—Gregson would perfect the formula later—*Strange Persuations* is a good album. *—Chris Woodstra and Richard Meyer*

Home & Away / 1986 / Flying Fish ✦✦✦✦
Home & Away is a collection of songs recorded during an early acoustic tour in 1986—originally a cassette only release to be sold at gigs, reportedly it cost under $60 to make. Despite the low budget and seemingly disposable nature of a release like this, the album has become a favorite among fans for its faithfull representation of the duo's charming acoustic shows. The duo run through new originals, some songs from Gregson's Any Trouble days, and a few well-chosen covers in a warm, intimate setting. *—Chris Woodstra*

Mischief / 1987 / Rhino ✦✦✦✦
Clive Gregson's songs treat romance with ironic charm: "We're Not Over Yet" is a compendium of reasons why they ought to be over, and "Everybody Cheats on You" is about more than just romantic infidelity. Christine Collister gives the songs a depth that often keeps them from being a bit too glib and clever, as do the folk-pop arrangements. *—William Ruhlmann*

● **A Change in the Weather** / 1989 / Rhino ✦✦✦✦✦
The self-insight continues in Gregson's lyrics, but the concerns are expanded. Collister does a fine job covering "Tryin' to Get to You." *—William Ruhlmann*

Welcome to the Workhouse / 1990 / Special Delivery ✦✦✦✦✦
Welcome to the Workhouse is a collection of Gregson's home demos and outtakes and while most albums of this sort appeal only to the diehard fans, this one stands out as one of his finest recorded moments, working surprisingly well as an album. The recordings span 1980 to 1985 and provide a good bridge between his work with Any Trouble and his partnership with Christine Collister. *—Chris Woodstra*

Love Is a Strange Hotel / Nov. 1990 / Rhino ✦✦✦

The Last Word / Mar. 24, 1992 / Rhino ✦✦✦✦
By 1992, the Gregson & Collister team had fallen apart, and the two had decided to record one more album before calling it quits. *Last Word* gives all the intimate details of a dissolving relationship, packed with real emotion and a dignified, stylish execution. In many ways, the duo tied things up with the high point of their career—their extraordinary harmonies and cool mix of folk, jazz, country and blues have never sounded better. And though the subject matter doesn't stray far from Gregson's usual themes, knowing the circumstances of the recording brings a new dimension to the songs, making the statements all the more powerful and touching. *—Chris Woodstra*

Carousel of Noise / 1995 / Gregsongs ✦✦✦

People & Places / Apr. 25, 1995 / Compass ✦✦✦

I Love This Town / Aug. 20, 1996 / Compass ✦✦✦✦

Happy Hour / Mar. 23, 1999 / Compass ✦✦✦
Recorded at his home studio in Nashville, *Happy Hour* is a do-it-yourself collection of 13 new originals produced and performed by Clive Gregson. The arrangements are kept sparse and simple, built around guitar or piano accompaniment with light touches of bass, keyboards, guitar, percussion, harmonica and on the opener, "I Get What I Deserve," banjo. Anything but happy, *Happy Hour* is a dark, somber, yet intelligent and honest look at love, life and longing, beautifully wrapped in Gregson's fetching melodies. It's to his credit that he's able to sustain this mood without becoming tiresome or falling into confessional self-pity. Because of the dour themes and stark, laid back sound, some of the songs may take a few listenings to distinguish themselves, though a little time spent will reward you with a number of small gems. *—Brett Hartenbach*

Stefan Grossman

b. Apr. 16, 1945, Brooklyn, NY
Guitar / Folk-Blues, Acoustic Blues
Guitarist, educator and historian Steffan Grossman was a student of acoustic blues and gospel singer/guitarist Rev. Gary Davis. After studying with Davis for eight years in high school and college, he learned and studied with other country blues guitarists: Mississippi John Hurt, Son House, Skip James, Mance Lipscomb and Fred McDowell. In the early 1960s, Grossman formed the Even Dozen Jug Band and worked with the political rock band the Fugs before moving to Great Britain. In 1968, he co-founded Kicking Mule Records with Ed Denson, a label that showcased idiosyncratic acoustic blues and folk guitar styles. From 1967 to the early 1980s, Grossman lived in Great Britain, where he carved a reputation on the European blues and folk festival circuit, playing with British-raised acoustic guitarists like John Renbourn and John Fahey. Grossman's solo discography goes all the back to 1966, when he recorded *How to Play Blues Guitar* for Elektra. Since the early 1980s, when Grossman be-

gan a long relationship with Shanachie Records, he has toured infrequently, but recorded extensively. *—Richard Skelly*

• **Yazoo Basin Boogie** / 1970 / Shanachie ♦♦♦♦♦
Grossman has spent so many years producing videos and how to books on acoustic guitar, it's hard to think of him as a guitarist himself, which is why albums like this are so valuable and reassuring. Grossman can back up everything he says and believes musically, with an encyclopedic knowledge and feel for country-blues, rags, and fiddle tunes as demonstrated here. He runs through a gaggle of fine-sounding instruments, alternating between slide, 12-string, and fingerpicked six-strings in a plethora of tunings, and never fails to deliver top-notch playing on every track. A must-have for folk-blues guitar enthusiasts. *—Cub Koda*

Black Melodies on a Clear Afternoon / 1972-1975 / Shanachie ♦♦♦
This disc, packed to the gills, captures a very wide selection of early Black American music arranged for fingerstyle guitar. As always, Grossman plays with taste and precision, negotiating blues, rags, and piano tunes in a variety of tunings and approaches, which makes every second of this collection a totally pleasurable experience. Taken from five different Kicking Mule vinyl albums, these 34 tracks are a veritable cornucopia of fingerstyle guitar played by an absolute master of the form. *—Cub Koda*

Under the Volcano / 1980 / Kicking Mule ♦♦♦♦
An excellent collaboration between this pair of folk guitar virtuosos, *Under the Volcano* includes seven guitar duets and a solo piece by each of the principals. Although the guitar picking is primarily acoustic, the duo occasionally uses understated electric guitar for accents and tonal color. The material is a mix of traditional and original, the playing superb. Grossman and Renbourn combine their talents and mix of styles here to produce appealing instrumental music of rare beauty and taste. *—Jim Newsom*

Shining Shadows / 1988 / Shanachie ♦♦♦♦♦
Shining Shadows offers another solid collection of Grossman's stirring guitar instrumentals. *—William Ruhlmann*

Guitar Landscapes / 1990 / Shanachie ♦♦♦
Guitar Landscapes offers a diverse collection of blues, jazz, country, and folk. Grossman's skill is evident on every track—he weaves subtle, inventive phrases throughout the album. If he can be faulted for anything, it's that the songs are occasionally *too* subtle, drifting into the background. Nevertheless, there is plenty of wonderfully evocative music on *Guitar Landscapes,* making it a necessary listen for his fans. *—Thom Owens*

Shake That Thing: Fingerpicking Country Blues / Apr. 21, 1998 / Shanachie ♦♦♦♦♦
Drawing on over 30 years of experience playing the country-blues, complete with tutorials from some of the undisputed masters, it comes as no surprise that Stefan Grossman can so consistently conjure up the authentic spirit of the music with each successive release. His original compositions show Grossman to be the most confident of guitarists in his genre, effortlessly borrowing from the stylings of Mississippi John Hurt, Reverend Gary Davis, and Blind Willie McTell among various others. While his playing isn't overly flashy, it need not be. The precision and craftsmanship injected into the fluid, rolling original "Yazoo Strut," the harder blues groove of "Spider Web Blues," and a powerful rendition of Reverend Gary Davis' "Candy Man" are country blues at its very best. Grossman might not possess the most versatile singing voice, combining the nasal qualities of Doc Watson's vocals with Mississippi John Hurt's hushed phrasing, but he can more than do justice to tracks like "Death Come Creeping" and the classic "All My Friends Are Gone." While much of *Shake That Thing* might be said to have something of a similar quality, Grossman demonstrates more than enough distinctive country-blues styles to hold the attention of any serious fan and prove that he is one of the genre's most masterful ambassadors. *—Matt Fink*

Dave Guard

b. Nov. 19, 1934, San Francisco, CA, **d.** Mar. 22, 1991
Vocals, Guitar, Banjo / Folk Revival, Contemporary Folk, Folk-Pop
Dave Guard was an important figure in the late '50s and early '60s folk boom, principally as a member of the Kingston Trio, and for a brief time as the central attraction in Dave Guard's Whiskeyhill Singers. Guard, with Nick Reynolds and Bob Shane, was an original member of the Kingston Trio and did his share of songwriting in that group, co-writing their 1959 hit "A Worried Man." In 1961, however, Guard left the still-thriving act (to be replaced by John Stewart), upset about some problems with the handling of their finances and wanting to pursue different musical directions. This he did with Dave Guard & the Whiskeyhill Singers, who made but one album for Capitol in 1962, also including future noted folk and rock singer Judy Henske, Cyrus Faryar (later of the Modern Folk Quartet and then a solo singer-songwriter), and David Wheat (who had worked with the Kingston Trio as an accompanist on bass). The album wasn't that much different from what the Kingston Trio had played, with the notable exception of the inclusion of a female vocalist, and didn't do much commercially.

Dave Guard & the Whiskeyhill Singers made a second, unreleased album before breaking up in 1963. After that, Guard kept a low profile musically, although he somehow showed up on Tim Buckley's 1967 album *Goodbye and Hello,* playing kalimba and tambourine; that album was produced by Jerry Yester, then the husband of Guard's ex-bandmate Judy Henske. Guard died of lymphatic cancer in 1991. Incidentally, a couple of previously unreleased 1957 demos by Guard's pre-Kingston Trio group, Dave Guard & the Calypsonians, appear on the Kingston Trio box set *The Capitol Years,* which also has one song by Dave Guard & the Whiskeyhill Singers. *—Richie Unterberger*

Dave Guard & The Whiskeyhill Singers / 1962 / Capitol ♦♦♦
The sole album by Guard's sole post-Kingston Trio recording project isn't anything special. It's par-for-the-course, clean-cut, early-1960s folk, not too different from what he'd done with the Kingston Trio. Perhaps it was more diverse in repertoire, and the female harmony (and sometimes lead) vocals by Judy Henske were an element missing in his former group. Of course, as it turns out Henske steals the show from the ostensible leader perhaps more often than was intended; her trademark husky, powerful vibrato vocals featuring strongly throughout, and coming to the fore on the cover of Bessie Smith's "Nobody Knows You When You're Down and Out" especially. When she does take the lead, things get a little more interesting, with a bluesy bent that would have been downright foreign to the Kingston Trio. The group's earnest interpretation of Woody Guthrie's "Plane Wreck at Los Gatos (Deportees)" is one of the stronger tracks, but the dumb, dated humor of "We're the World's Last Authentic Playboys" is a decided lowlight, and the other detours into comedy-tinted tunes are corny too. Really, the only reason to search for this would be if you're a big Judy Henske or Kingston Trio fan. Even then, it's not nearly as good as the best things Henske did as a soloist or part of other groups, as she grew into folk-rock and even psychedelia throughout the rest of the 1960s. *—Richie Unterberger*

Arlo Guthrie

b. Jul. 10, 1947, Coney Island, NY
Vocals, Guitar / Contemporary Folk, Folk-Rock, Singer/Songwriter
Like his father Woody Guthrie, Arlo Guthrie has carved out a career as a folksinger and songwriter with a social conscience who leavens political messages with humor. Though Woody Guthrie was hospitalized for much of Arlo's youth, the youngster nevertheless grew up in a musical community that included Pete Seeger, Leadbelly, and Cisco Houston. He learned to play the guitar at age six and was performing in coffeehouses by his late teens.

Guthrie's early fame was based on his anti-Establishment shaggy-dog story in song, "Alice's Restaurant," actually a comic monolog about the singer's troubles with the police and the draft board that was extremely timely when it appeared on record in 1967. The *Alice's Restaurant* album became Guthrie's only gold record, but he made a series of folk-rock records through the '70s, filling them with his own songs and those of his contemporaries, notably Steve Goodman's "The City of New Orleans," which became Guthrie's sole hit single in 1972.

Guthrie's commercial fortunes, like those of most folkies, declined by the end of the '70s, and he made his last album for Warner Bros. in 1981. Since then, he has launched his own label, Rising Son, which has reissued his Warner albums and released his new recordings. He continues to tour extensively and to work for such causes as environmentalism, issuing *Mystic Journey* in 1998. *—William Ruhlmann*

☆ **Alice's Restaurant** / 1967 / Reprise ♦♦♦♦♦
In 1967 when this album came out it was totally radical, directly political and so deliciously funny that it deflated a great deal of the seriousness of the growing anti-war movement. In this one stroke Guthrie established himself as more than the son of the famous man and major star. Aside from the title cut, people often forget about the "Motorcycle Song" and "Chillin' of the Evening" which were on side two. *—Richard Meyer*

Arlo / 1968 / Rising Son ♦♦♦
Arlo Guthrie was still prone to long story-songs and occasional humorous introductory monologues on his second outing. Three of the seven tracks last for longer than five minutes, though none remotely approach "Alice's Restaurant" in epic length. Recorded live at *the Bitter End,* it shows Guthrie starting to adapt more wholeheartedly to folk-rock instrumentation, with a full if subdued band including drums and keyboards. The songs are nothing major, and the jokes aren't as funny as they were in the late 1960s, but it's an agreeable, pleasant, intelligent album. "The Motorcycle Song" should please those looking for more comic narratives, as should "The Pause of Mr. Claus," most of which is actually a spoken monologue that does finally lead up to fairly funny punchlines. In a more purely musical vein, he touched (mildly) upon raga-rock on "Meditation (Wave Upon Wave)," with tabla by Ed Shaughnessy. It may not have been a great record, but Arlo Guthrie was managing to establish himself as a folk-rock talent with an identity quite distinct from his famous father, not an easy feat. *—Richie Unterberger*

Running Down the Road / 1969 / Koch International ♦♦♦

Washington County / 1970 / Koch International ♦♦♦
This album is more homey and roots flavored, with cuts like "Valley to Pray" with Doc Watson, and "Lay Down Little Doggies." It's a good relaxed effort. *—Richard Meyer*

Hobo's Lullaby / 1972 / Koch International ♦♦♦♦
A typical Arlo Guthrie mix of contemporary folk songs and unexpected material from the past, with a little Bob Dylan and dad Woody Guthrie added for good measure. Arlo's cover of Dylan's "When the Ship Comes In" is superb, as is his slide guitar take on Hoyt Axton's "Lightning Bar Blues." Also worth noting are renditions of Woody's sad ballad, "1913 Massacre," Axton's "Somebody Turned on the Light," and Arlo's own "Days Are Short." And then there is his definitive cover of "The City of New Orleans," Steve Goodman's ode to the vanishing railroads of middle America. "New Orleans" was Arlo's only real hit single, and its "Good morning, America, how are ya—" chorus echoed from AM radios throughout the land, making the song a folk music standard. *—Jim Newsom*

The Last of the Brooklyn Cowboys / 1973 / Koch International ♦♦♦♦
In the midst of the singer/songwriter era, Arlo Guthrie chose to become his generation's true folk singer, closer in spirit to Pete Seeger than to James Taylor, more an interpreter than a prolific songwriter. In this role, he kept songs alive that may have been forgotten or were never known, and recorded songs from the pens of his contemporary peers. *Last of the Brooklyn Cowboys* follows a formula similar to its predecessor, *Hobo's Lullaby,* with one exception—there is no hit single *a la* "City of New Orleans." However, this release has some very strong material woven into its mix. Arlo gives his father's "Gypsy Davy" a bouncy Caribbean feel, breathing new life into this tale of wanderlust in a way probably not envisioned by Woody Guthrie. Arlo also pays tribute to Hank Williams with a yodeling rendition of "Lovesick Blues," and delivers his customary Dylan song. This time it's "Gates of Eden," featuring the fingerpicked electric guitars of Clarence White and the bottleneck slide of Ry Cooder. The album also contains two of Arlo's finest original songs, "Last Train" and "Cooper's Lament." *—Jim Newsom*

Together in Concert / 1975 / Reprise ♦♦♦♦♦
Separately and together, Arlo Guthrie and Pete Seeger delight in a live setting. *—William Ruhlmann*

● **Amigo** / 1976 / Koch International ✦✦✦✦✦
With *Amigo*, Arlo Guthrie's ninth album, he cemented his place as an important artist in his own right. Like Woody, Arlo has always tempered his sense of tradition and what's important, with a playfulness and sense of humor. The opener, "Guabi, Guabi," a traditional African tune, is as quirky and lighthearted as it is straightforward, whereas & "Grocery Blues" is a typical, if humorous and effective Guthrie novelty song. On the other hand, what places *Amigo* a slight notch above his previous work is the strength of his original material. & "Massachusetts" is a gorgeous paean to his home state, while & "Darkest Hour," an evocative tale of love, lust, power and intrigue, is folk storytelling at its finest. However, it's at the end of the first half of the record that Arlo does the memory of his father most proud. & "Victor Jara," the story of the martyred Chilean folk-singer and activist, is one of the best and most moving topical songs of the decade, while "Patriot's Dream" is a stirring call-to-arms to the fading protest movement of the '60's. While side two may lack the sheer power of the first, it possesses a certain charm of its own. & "My Love" and & "Ocean Crossing" are tender love songs, "Manzanillo Bay" is a lovely, south-of-the-border travelogue and there's even a respectable cover of the the Rolling Stones' & "Connection" to close the album. His last studio recording for three years, *Amigo* is a passionate, touching and funny collection of songs, and remains the pinnacle of Arlo Guthrie's career, as well as a perfect illustration of his many sides and strengths. *—Brett Hartenbach*

The Best of Arlo Guthrie / 1977 / Reprise ✦✦✦✦✦
This includes "Alice's Restaurant, " and the equally comic "Motorcycle Song, " "Coming into Los Angeles, " and "City of New Orleans." *— William Ruhlmann*

Outlasting the Blues / 1979 / Rising Son ✦✦✦✦

Precious Friend / 1982 / Reprise ✦✦✦✦✦

Mystic Journey / Feb. 1996 / Koch International ✦✦✦

Woody Guthrie

b. Jul. 14, 1912, Okemah, OK, **d.** Oct. 3, 1967, Queens, NY
Vocals, Harmonica, Guitar / Field Recordings, Political Folk, Traditional Folk
Woody Guthrie was the most important American folk music artist of the first half of the 20th century. By the time he gained recognition in the '40s, Guthrie had written hundreds of songs, many of which remain folk standards to this day. When he was interviewed by Alan Lomax for the Library of Congress in March 1940, Guthrie punctuated his reminiscences by singing "So Long, It's Been Good to Know You," "Dust Bowl Blues," "Do-Re-Mi," "Pretty Boy Floyd," "I Ain't Got No Home," and other songs. He later wrote "Pastures of Plenty," "The Grand Coulee Dam," and his masterpiece, "This Land Is Your Land." He was also an author (*Bound for Glory*) and a newspaper columnist. Guthrie made some recordings for RCA in 1940, but much of his work was issued on the small Folkways label. Meanwhile, in the late '40s and early '50s, versions of his songs became hits for such artists as The Weavers. By then, Guthrie himself was in physical decline, suffering from Huntington's chorea, a hereditary neurological disorder. But during his long illness, Guthrie's influence spread to the next generation, fostering the folk boom of the late '50s and early '60s. Not only is Bob Dylan unimaginable without him, but large segments of popular music are permanently affected by his concerns as a songwriter and his approach to the form. *— William Ruhlmann*

The Science of Sound / 1933 / Smithsonian/Folkways ✦✦✦

Woody Guthrie Sings Folk Songs / 1962 / Smithsonian/Folkways ✦✦✦✦✦
Guthrie sings traditional material here, with Leadbelly and others. *— William Ruhlmann*

★ **Dust Bowl Ballads** / 1964 / Buddha ✦✦✦✦✦
Woody Guthrie's powerful, evocative, insightful narratives about the life and trials of Southwestern migrant workers battling the Dust Bowl were initially issued on two six-song albums in 1940. Later, the entire 14-song session was released on a 1964 album. This LP was reissued on CD in 1988. It includes some of Guthrie's finest, most memorable prose, coupled with poignant vocals and sparse, effective harmonica accompaniment. The resiliency, spirit, and memories of both his early life and people he'd known are presented on such cuts as "I Ain't Got No Home," "Dust Pneumonia Blues," and "Dust Bowl Blues." Guthrie was a master storyteller, and his semi-autobiographical accounts remain among American music's most striking some 54 years after their original issue. The 2000 reissue CD on Buddha adds an alternate version of "Talking Dust Bowl Blues" and the original liner notes written by Guthrie himself. *—Ron Wynn*

☆ **Library of Congress Recordings, Vols. 1-3** / 1964 / Rounder ✦✦✦✦✦
Not so much an album as a historical aural document, this nearly three-hour, three-CD set chronicles three days of interviews and songs featuring a 27-year-old Woody Guthrie on March 21, 22 and 27, 1940. Alan Lomax and his wife, Elizbeth, take Guthrie through his autobiography and his reflections on the Dust Bowl, and he proves a witty, rustic raconteur who is even more impressive when he picks up the guitar and performs such original songs as "So Long, It's Been Good to Know You," "Talking Dust Bowl Blues," "Do-Re-Mi," and "Pretty Boy Floyd," as well as traditional material. Guthrie did not make his first studio recordings until later in 1940, but his repertoire and performance style were clearly long-established by this time. It is easy to hear why he was such a revelation to the folk world of the '40s, especially because his influence has been so pervasive: much of the next 20 years in folk music derives from these sessions, even though they were not commercially released until 1964, as a box set on Elektra Records. Rounder reissued the album on LP in the 1988 and on CD in the 1997. *— William Ruhlmann*

Struggle / 1976 / Smithsonian/Folkways ✦✦✦✦✦
This album features Woody Guthrie, Cisco Houston and Pete Seeger playing political songs including "The Dying Miner," "Ludlow Massacre," and "Union Burying Ground." It's an energetic album. *—Richard Meyer*

Columbia River Collection / 1988 / Rounder ✦✦✦
An intelligent reconstruction of Guthrie's Columbia River songs, including "Grand Coulee Dam" and "Pastures of Plenty." *— William Ruhlmann*

Early Masters / Apr. 1996 / Rykodisc/Tradition ✦✦✦
The 12 tracks on this mid-priced reissue were recorded by Moses Asch of Folkways Records in 1944, but issued several times by Stinson Records, notably on the album *Woody Guthrie* (SLP 44). Accompanied by Cisco Houston and Sonny Terry, Guthrie performs a series of traditional folk songs in his own adaptations, which went on to become folk and pop standards, including such songs as "Worried Man Blues," "Going Down the Road," and "Pretty Boy Floyd." Despite sonic cleansing, the recordings are sometimes of marginal sound quality, but the historic nature of the work overcomes such limitations. This is not as impressive a collection as some of the Smithsonian Folkways reissues of material from the same sessions, but it is also less expensive. *— William Ruhlmann*

★ **This Land Is Your Land: The Asch Recordings, Vol. 1** / Feb. 18, 1997 / Smithsonian/Folkways ✦✦✦✦✦
You'd think the last word in Woody Guthrie reissues would have appeared before this. After all, the legendary folk singer recorded most of his best work nearly 60 years ago, and the bulk of it has been regularly reissued in fine collections on Folkways, Rounder, and other labels. So this CD is as surprising as it is welcome. What makes it probably the single best Guthrie disc you can own— For one thing, the compilers had total access to the archives of Folkways Records founder Moses Asch, for whom the singer made the lion's share of his most important recordings. And they picked for this package 27 songs that showcase the incredible range of his writing and performing talent—everything from children's ditties ("Car Song") to social commentary ("Do-Re-Mi") to historical tales ("End of the Line"). Then there's the title track—Woody's most famous tune—which was only sporadically available until this CD. It's here in two versions, including one that features the famous yet previously unreleased "private property" verses.

The sound quality is as notable as the program. The compilers went back to the master recordings and did a magnificent job of cleaning things up without altering what Guthrie waxed. The result sounds pure and intimate—as if the singer were right there in the room with you. Finally, there's a superb 36-page book, with all sorts of fascinating detail on Asch, Guthrie, and every track. The best news: This is only the first volume in a four-CD series. — *Jeff Burger*

Muleskinner Blues: The Asch Recordings, Vol. 2 / Sep. 16, 1997 / Smithsonian/Folkways ✦✦✦✦✦
Nearly 60 years after Woody Guthrie recorded most of his best work comes a series that finally does it total justice. The music all issues from the master tapes of Folkways Records founder Moses Asch, for whom Guthrie made his most important recordings. Sound quality is uniformly pristine, the liner notes are extensive and exceptional, and the gritty, direct, idiosyncratic performances leave no doubt why Guthrie is considered a giant of American folk. This second in a series of four CDs focuses on 25 examples of Woody's interpretive work—classic folk and country songs, most of which he learned on the road in Oklahoma, Texas, and California. The uninitiated should start with volume one, which contains mostly original compositions, but the present set proves that Woody was almost as interesting a performer as he was a writer. And he had great taste in material. Among the many highlights, some of which feature accompaniment by Cisco Houston, Sonny Terry, and Pete Seeger: Jimmie Rodgers' "Muleskinner Blues," and traditional numbers like "Stackolee" and "Danville Girl," and A.P. Carter's "Worried Man Blues." *—Jeff Burger*

☆ **Hard Travelin': The Asch Recordings, Vol. 3** / May 19, 1998 / Smithsonian/Folkways ✦✦✦✦✦
This 27-song collection focuses on Guthrie's topical songs, though not all of the topics are political; there is, for instance, a "Hanukkah Dance" and an excerpt from his variation on the "Rubaiyat of Omar Khayyam," the children's song "Howdjadoo," and the gospel number "I Ain't Got No Home in This World Anymore." Progressives will find plenty to cheer along with here, though, whether it's a labor anthem like "Farmer-Labor Train" or "Ladies Auxiliary"; there are also a few tunes specifically directed toward the anti-fascism war effort in World War II. Despite the nominal topical anthology theme, this is really just a decent sampling of Guthrie's 1940s recordings (most done for Moe Asch), some of it socially conscious, some not. Some of these are among his better-known songs ("1913 Massacre," "Hard Travelin'," "So Long It's Been Good to Know You"); major folkys like Cisco Houston, Sonny Terry, and Pete Seeger help out occasionally, though it's usually just Guthrie alone with his guitar. The sound quality is good (especially considering that some of these have been transferred from fragile acetates), and the quality of the material and performance is strong; a few of the performances were previously unreleased. *—Richie Unterberger*

Buffalo Skinners: The Asch Recordings, Vol. 4 / Apr. 20, 1999 / Smithsonian/Folkways ✦✦✦✦✦
This fourth and final volume of recordings Woody Guthrie made for Folkways and other small independent labels is just as remarkable as its predecessors. This time around, the focus is primarily on cowboy/Western music, and Guthrie—who is accompanied by Cisco Houston on many of the 26 tracks—proves himself a master of the genre. The program mixes well-known traditional material ("Go Tell Aunt Rhody, "Whoopie Ti Yi Yo, Get Along Little Doggies," "Red River Valley," and "Chisholm Trail") with equally strong Guthrie originals such as "Little Darling (At My Window Sad and Lonely)," "Ranger's Command," and "Dead or Alive (Poor Lazarus)." About a third of the tracks have never previously been released, among them the charming "Return of Rocky Mountain Slim and Desert Rat Shorty," a home recording on which Woody and Cisco make fun of radio ads for music songbooks. The sound quality is first rate, particularly considering the acetate-disc sources of this material. Also excellent is the 36-page accompanying booklet, which completes the biographical sketch started on volumes one through three and includes extensive notes on each track. *—Jeff Burger*

The Asch Recordings, Vol. 1-4 / Aug. 17, 1999 / Smithsonian/Folkways ✦✦✦✦✦
Woody Guthrie's *Asch Recordings, Vol. 1-4* is another shining example of Smithsonian/Folkways' ability to create a historically important document that is both fun and enriching. Combining four separate compilations (*This Land Is Your Land: The Asch Recordings, Vol. 1,*

Muleskinner Blues: The Asch Recordings, Vol. 2, Hard Travelin': The Asch Recordings, Vol. 3, and *Buffalo Skinners: The Asch Recordings, Vol. 4*) into one box, Smithsonian/Folkways presents a fairly complete overview of Guthrie's career. The collection features deep forays into his union songs, political and social issue songs, cowboy and outlaw songs, and early country and frontier ballads, with each CD separated into specific themes. The liner notes are intelligently written but never dry, going through track by track, bringing to light Guthrie's warm contributions to American folksongs. In listening to the set as a whole, the only question left is "where is Guthrie's comedy album—" His biting humor on songs like "Talking Hard Work," "Ladies Auxiliary," "Howdjadoo," and "Mean Talking Blues" tell of a wry and witty side of the activist that would fit alongside his topical children's albums nicely. Each of these CDs are available individually, but purchasing the box set gives the listener a more well-rounded experience and makes more sense economically. *—Zac Johnson*

☆ **Songs to Grow on for Mother and Child** / Smithsonian/Folkways ✦✦✦✦✦
Some of the last songs written and recorded by Woody Guthrie were his children's songs. Their strength, shown in *Songs to Grow on for Mother and Child*, is an unusually strong identification with actually being a child, in all its simplicity and charm, along with the ability to win over listeners. Good examples on here are "Rattle My Rattle" and "I Want My Milk." Guthrie is an acquired sonic taste worth acquiring. Ages 3-5. *—William Ruhlmann & Bob Hinkle*

Butch Hancock

b. Jul. 12, 1945, Lubbock, TX
Vocals, Harmonica, Guitar / Contemporary Singer/Songwriter, Americana, Alternative Country, Country-Folk, Singer/Songwriter, Progressive Country
Country music's ballad tradition is fused with the visionary poetry of contemporary folk music by Butch Hancock. In addition to being featured on his solo albums, Hancock's songs have been covered by the Texas Tornadoes ("She Never Spoke Spanish to Me"), Emmylou Harris ("If You Were a Bluebird") and his former bandmates in the short-lived but influential Flatlanders, Joe Ely and Jimmie Dale Gilmore. Hancock released his self-titled debut solo album in 1978. Selections from his first six solo albums were featured on the 1989 album *Own and Own.* In 1992, Hancock and Gilmore collaborated on a live album, *Two Roads.—Craig Harris*

Firewater / 1981 / Rainlight ✦✦✦✦✦
Off-the-cuff versions of Butch's classics are here, including "The Wind's Dominion," and "If You Were a Bluebird." The band includes Jimmy Dale Gilmore. *—Richard Meyer*

Yella Rose with Marce Lacoutre / 1985 / Rainlight ✦✦✦
This album has a rather big band with occasional horns, congas, accordian, and Marce Lacouture songs on the title cut. A good one. *—Richard Meyer*

● **Own & Own** / 1989 / Sugar Hill ✦✦✦✦✦
This compilation is culled from Hancock's many albums on his own Rainlight label from 1978 to 1987 (plus four tracks from 1989). *—William Ruhlmann*

Live in Australia / 1990 / Virgin ✦✦✦
An energetic live album of duets by Hancock and Gilmore, it was recorded in Sydney in 1990. The Flatlander "hit" "Dallas" is here and other ragged but right cuts from these musical pals. *—Richard Meyer*

Two Roads / Jul. 3, 1992 / Caroline ✦✦✦
Gilmore and Hancock take turns singing and accompanying each other on this live album recorded during an Australian tour. *—Kurt Wolff*

Eats Away the Night / 1995 / Sugar Hill ✦✦✦✦✦
After about 20 years, Butch Hancock has released his first produced studio album for a national label not compiled from his previously released Rainlight Records LPs. In many ways, Hancock set his style down with his very first self-produced album, *West Texas Waltz.* All the elements from that period remain—the Dylanesque vocal sound, his love of wordplay, and a deep feeling for the stories that make up an individual's life. The warm sound of this album makes it easier for newcomers to get past his dry voice, and the inclusion of his hit "If You Were a Bluebird" will help a new audience locate him properly in the contemporary Texas songwriting scene. The band is tight and steps back enough to let Hancock's stories and personality shine through. *—Richard Meyer*

Jack Hardy

b. 1948
Vocals, Guitar / Contemporary Singer/Songwriter, Contemporary Folk
Jack Hardy has been a central figure in folk music since his arrival in Greenwich Village in 1978. Instrumental in founding The Songwriter's Exchange, The SpeakEasy Musician's co-op, and *The Fast Folk Musical Magazine,* Hardy has released nine albums domestically on his Great Divide label. Considered a writer's writer, he is known for politics in his songs, Americanized Irish influences, and a preoccupation with mythological imagery, mixed up with standard New York folk & roll. *—Richard Meyer*

● **White Shoes** / 1982 / Great Divide ✦✦✦✦✦
A brilliant collection of songs by this husky-voiced founder of New York's "Fast Folk" movement. *—William Ruhlmann*

Collected Works, Vol. 1: 1965-1983 / Mar. 3, 1998 / 1-800-Prime ✦✦✦✦✦
On this first five-CD volume, Hardy has included his second through fifth albums, but not his debut LP, 1971's *Jack Hardy.* In place of that is *Early and Rare,* a 20-track disc containing seven of the 11 tracks from the LP, as well as unreleased demos and one teenage home recording. Especially as compared to Hardy's later work, this is embryonic juvenilia. The Jack Hardy of the early 1970s is something of a country singer; in contrast, the Jack Hardy of his second album, *The Mirror of My Madness* (1976), is a fully formed folk-rocker lyrically influenced by Dylan. Though cobbled together from various sessions held over a period of years, the album has a consistent sound. On 1978's *The Nameless One,* Hardy has grown much more interested in story-songs, often on centuries-old topics. This academic strain continues on the somewhat elegiac *Landmark* (1982), which is distinguished from its predecessor due to lead guitarist Frank Christian, who can suggest Mark Knopfler or Dylan associates Bruce Langhorne and Robbie Robertson. *White Shoes* (1982) finds Hardy surprisingly returning to romance as a subject, as well as biting political satire and history lessons in song. Taken together, Hardy's first 16 years of recording are a triumph of craftsmanship over commercial considerations. Perhaps his most telling song in this sense is *Landmark*'s "Wheelbarrow Johnny," in which the title character takes off for the gold rush, only to make his fortune building wheelbarrows for other forty-niners. Hardy has made a point of shunning the commercial trappings of the music industry, instead putting out albums as he liked on his own record label. If he hasn't grown rich in the process of building wheelbarrows, his *Collected Works* stand as sturdy musical tools. *—William Ruhlmann*

Collected Works, Vol. 2: 1984-1995 / Oct. 6, 1998 / 1-800-Prime ✦✦✦✦✦
This second five-CD set presented a mature artist plying his craft on five albums originally released on his own label from 1984-1994. While the albums differed somewhat in approach and instrumentation, in effect any of Hardy's songs could have appeared on any of them. Throughout, the husky-voiced singer picked his acoustic guitar sharply, discoursing on a variety of arcane subjects in songs that often could have been mistaken for traditional ballads of the Middle Ages or the Renaissance. He applied a highly poetic, allusive sense of language to his subject matter, doing so with more interest in the sound of words than clarity of meaning, so that it was easy to listen to several successive songs without having any idea what they were about. Free of any commercial considerations, Hardy could be a demanding writer, not so much in need of a reviewer as of a graduate student's doctoral thesis. Nevertheless, a close listener would find much to appreciate in these folk-rock efforts; Hardy sang feelingly and suggestively, pausing over words and then biting them off, chuckling, or caressing the lyrics in ways that gave them meaning the mere words did not convey. If he was ultimately a poet who wrote his poems for himself with only limited concern for being understood, he was also a singer who put them across effectively. If that meant that, in effect, a lot was liable to get lost in the translation, Hardy's material was still a rich listening experience that often rewarded the effort needed to appreciate it. *—William Ruhlmann*

Omens / Apr. 11, 2000 / 1-800-Prime ✦✦✦✦
Though he sounds nothing like him, Jack Hardy shares a particular set of strengths and weaknesses with Elvis Costello: namely, a seemingly effortless ability to turn a phrase, a great knack for melodies, and a terrible voice. That's not to say he's a bad singer—it's just that he doesn't have much of an instrument to work with. If anything, he sounds like a young Tom Waits. Luckily, good songs can make up for an awful lot of vocal limitation, and Hardy has those in spades, beginning with the wry and tuneful "I Ought to Know" and ending with the sweetly despairing "A Change of Heart." In between, there are such lighthearted moments as "The Boney Bailiff" (one of a number of Irish tunes on a program otherwise dominated by more typical singer/songwriter fare) and "Síar ón nDaingean (West of Dingle)," as well as some songs about yellow birds and raven-haired girls. Hardy is backed by a strong but restrained folk-rock ensemble, and because the album was recorded live in the studio, it has a nice, loose-limbed feel about it. *—Rick Anderson*

Richie Havens

b. Jan. 21, 1941, Brooklyn, NY
Vocals, Sitar, Guitar / Folk-Rock, Singer/Songwriter
Born in the Bedford-Stuyvesant section of Brooklyn, Richie Havens moved to Greenwich Village in 1961 in time to get in on the folk boom then taking place. He had a distinctive style as a folksinger, appearing in such clubs as the Cafe Wha— His guitar set to an opening tuning, he would strum it while barring chords with his thumb, using it essentially as percussion while singing rhythmically in a gruff voice for a mesmerizing effect. Havens was signed to Douglas Records in 1965 and recorded two albums that gained him a local following. In 1967, the Verve division of MGM Records formed a folk section (Verve Forecast) and signed Havens and other folk-based performers. The result was Havens's third album, *Mixed Bag.* It wasn't until 1968 and the *Something Else Again* album, however, that he began to hit the charts. In 1969 came the double album *Richard P. Havens 1983.* Havens's career benefited enormously from his appearance at the Woodstock festival in 1969. His first album after that exposure, *Alarm Clock,* made the Top 30 and produced a Top 20 single in "Here Comes the Sun." These recordings were Havens's commercial high-water mark, but by this time he had become an international touring success. *—William Ruhlmann*

Mixed Bag / 1967 / Verve ✦✦✦✦✦
Richie Havens' finest recording, *Mixed Bag* captures the essence of his music and presents it in an attractive package that has held up well. A close listen to lyrics like "I Can't Make It Anymore" and "Morning, Morning" reveals sadness and loneliness, yet the music is so appealingly positive that a listener actually comes away feeling uplifted. In fact, on most of the songs on this album, it's the sound of Havens' distinctive voice coupled with his unusual open-E guitar tuning, rather than the specific lyrical content of the songs, that pulls the listener in. The six-and-a-half minute "Follow" is structured like a Dylan composition in the "Hard Rain" mode, with its memorable verse-ending refrain, "Don't mind me 'cause I ain't nothin' but a dream." Both "Sandy" and "San Francisco Bay Blues" have a jazzy feel, while the aforementioned "I Can't Make It Anymore" would not have been out of place in a movie soundtrack or pop radio playlist of the time. "Handsome Johnny," one of Havens' best known songs as a result of the *Woodstock* film, is a classic anti-war ballad, stoked by the singer's unmistakable thumb-chorded guitar strumming. *Mixed Bag* winds up with a soulful cover of Dylan's "Just Like a Woman" and an electric piano-propelled take on the Lennon-McCartney classic, "Eleanor Rigby." *—Jim Newsom*

Electric Havens / 1968 / Douglas ✦✦✦
This was one of two albums (the other being *The Richie Havens Record*) comprised of overdubbed solo demos, probably from sometime between 1963-1965, that Havens had done prior to recording for Verve and making his official recording debut. In the late '60s, as

Havens rose to stardom, producer Alan Douglas took the original solo demos and overdubbed them with electric instruments. The albums were pulled from circulation and are hard to find today. One would understand why Havens might have disapproved of their release, but *Electric Havens* really isn't bad. The eight-song set is oriented toward the kind of traditional material that he was likely doing in clubs around that time, such as "Oxford Town," "C.C. Rider," and "900 Miles From Home," as well as an early Dylan cover, "Boots & Spanish Leather." Havens sings with his usual spontaneous conviction, and although the electric backing sounds a bit awkward—and, unsurprisingly considering the circumstances, wavering in time keeping—it's not overdone, or completed in such a fashion that it's difficult to enjoy the performances. Different years of release have appeared in discographies for both this and *The Richie Havens Record*, incidentally; it's almost certain that both came out in the late '60s, with 1968 serving as the best-guess year in both cases. *—Richie Unterberger*

The Richie Havens Record / 1968 / Douglas ♦♦♦

Somethin' Else Again / 1968 / Verve ♦♦♦♦
The sound here is more keyboard-heavy than its predecessor *Mixed Bag*, but Richie Havens continues in a similar vein with his distinctive smoky voice and thumb-fretted open-tuned guitar. "No Opportunity Necessary, No Experience Needed" and "Don't Listen to Me" are propelled by Warren Bernhardt's percussive electric piano, while "Inside of Him" and "Sugarplums" are pretty ballads featuring the flute of Jeremy Steig. "The Klan" and "Run Shaker Life" are cut from the same mold as "Handsome Johnny," the Woodstock show-stopper from *Mixed Bag*. The melody of "New City" has attractive, expansive intervals, and "From the Prison" is an intense piece of balladry built around a riff on the guitar's bass strings. Finally, the title track is seven-and-a-half minutes of sitar, flute, tamboura, and tabla, very much of its time, when George Harrison's interest in Ravi Shankar led many musicians to experiment with Indian instruments, rhythms, and melodies. This cut could be the soundtrack to a flower-power dance in the park or an incense-laced gathering around a hookah beneath posters and black lights. *—Jim Newsom*

Collection / 1987 / Rykodisc ♦♦♦

Sings Beatles & Dylan / 1990 / Rykodisc ♦♦♦♦
Richie Havens is probably the only '60s icon who could get away with an album like this without apology. But for the presence of the electric keyboards, synth bass, and '80s-style drums, these performances by Havens could easily have appeared 18 years earlier. His performances of "Here Comes the Sun," "If Not for You," "Strawberry Fields Forever," "Lay Lady Lay," etc. all display a satisfying intimacy, and "Rocky Raccoon" is just plain fun, but his cover of "The Long and Winding Road" is probably the best version of this song ever done, with "Let It Be" not far behind. Overall, they're more sophisticated than some of Havens' earlier work, a mix of soul and folk traditions with an overlay of rock, that any longtime fan will appreciate. *—Bruce Eder*

● **Resume: The Best of Richie Havens** / Apr. 6, 1993 / Rhino ♦♦♦♦♦
Havens' output has been so extensive that picking tunes for a single-disc anthology would be a difficult task for any label. Rhino has done a respectable job in compiling 17 selections, although there was no material from the LPs *Stonehenge* or *1984*, and while he certainly performed them his way, neither Ray Charles' "Drown In My Own Tears" nor Billie Holiday's "God Bless The Child" were among Havens' best songs. By comparison, "Handsome Johnny," "Freedom," "Here Comes The Sun," "The Klan" and "Just Like A Woman" had a strength and power that came partly from being ideally suited for Havens' style. This isn't the comprehensive or qualitative anthology Havens deserves; just a decent hits collection. *—Ron Wynn*

Cuts to the Chase / 1994 / Forward ♦♦♦

20th Century Masters—*The Millennium Collection: The Best of Richie Havens* / *Feb. 29, 2000 / Polygram* ♦♦♦♦
Another excellent entry in MCA's *Millennium Collection*, this features 12 of the singer/songwriter's best-known tunes. Havens' unique style moves effortlessly from standards like "San Francisco Bay Blues" to the bleakness of "The Klan" to very interesting covers of "Lady Madonna" and "Strawberry Fields Forever." A great little introductory set of Havens' best work. *—Cub Koda*

Judy Henske

b. Chippewa Falls, WI
Vocals / Folk Revival, Folk-Rock, Pop
Success is a matter of luck as well as talent. Given different circumstances, Judy Henske could have certainly been a much bigger star than she was. Instead she's a hazily remembered figure, known if at all for some recordings that faintly prefigured folk-rock, and tangential associations with more famous performers. Her strong, bold, and versatile delivery would have been well-suited for the folk-rock era; her timing was just a bit off. *High Flying Bird* is the best of her Elektra efforts, anticipating folk-rock with full arrangements that featured drums, guitars, and bass. A stay at Mercury later in the '60s presented her as an all-around entertainer, capable of folk, pop, blues, and Broadway, all backed by middle-of-the-road production. Henske wasn't bad at this, but one got the feeling that her truest talents were being under-utilized. She finally got her chance to blossom on the 1969 LP *Farewell Aldebaren*, a collaborative effort with Jerry Yester that appeared on Frank Zappa's Straight! label. The album was a wildly eclectic, impressive effort that showcased an astonishing range of vocal delivery on Henske's part, and owed more to psychedelic music than folk. That proved to be a one-shot, and aside from an effort as a member of the band Rosebud, Henske has not been heard from since. *—Richie Unterberger*

Judy Henske / 1963 / Elektra ♦♦♦
On this live LP, Henske, as she would throughout most of her career, eludes easy categorization. There's barrelhouse blues with a touch of Broadway belting, there's Dixielandish jazz, there are folk standards, and there's plenty of standup comedy between the songs. The husky, almost raunchy voice makes most of this worth hearing; one is tempted to describe her as one of the great White blues singers, except that there's a theatrical quality to much of her delivery that originates from pop traditions. She's at her best when she eschews the jivey jazz for a more straight folk-blues approach (on "Wade in the Water," "I Know You Rider," and "Love Henry"). *—Richie Unterberger*

● **High Flying Bird** / 1964 / Elektra ♦♦♦♦
Henske sings with a full-throated, bluesy style reminiscent of Mama Cass on her best album, which was one of the first contemporary folk records to use a rhythm section (including Earl Palmer on drums). Highlighted by the title track, a moody, soaring ballad that was covered by Jefferson Airplane. *—Richie Unterberger*

The Death Defying Judy Henske / 1965 / Reprise ♦♦♦
Jack Nitzsche, famed for his work with Phil Spector in the 1960s, arranged and conducted this live record (although some of the tracks sound like they may have been done in the studio). Henske's solo albums all suffered to some degree from too much versatility and too little direction. This is no exception: there's an attempt at White soul ("I've Been Loving You Too Long"), pop/rock numbers with light orchestration, a self-mocking gospel spiritual ("Saved"), a version of "Danny Boy," and semi-standup comedy routines. Henske's got a great down and dirty voice, even on L.A. pop tunes like "Nobody Knows" and the ballad "Sing a Rainbow" (both of which are among the best tracks here). But she really wouldn't find the optimum material for her considerable talents until she teamed up with then-husband Jerry Yester for their minor psychedelic pop masterpiece, *Farewell Aldebaran*. *—Richie Unterberger*

Little Bit of Sunshine . . . Little Bit of Rain / 1965 / Mercury ♦♦♦
Henske seemed to be trying to be all things to all people on this mid-'60s release. In the manner of a white Nina Simone, she tackles soul ("Any Day Now"), showtunes, the Gershwins, and brassy blues with gusto, as if to prove her versatility. Her rich vibrato is genuinely first-rate, but it would have been a better idea to stick with more contemporary soul and folk-rock all the way than play the all-around entertainer; this is the material from the album that holds up reasonably well today, while the more "adult" stuff is gratingly dated. The record was notable for her interpretation of two Fred Neil songs (the title track and "The Other Side of This Life") when the cult singer/songwriter was just emerging as a performer. A frustratingly spotty effort from a talented artist who never fully came into her own. *—Richie Unterberger*

Carolyn Hester

b. 1937, Waco, TX
Vocals, Guitar / Folk Revival, Folk-Rock, Psychedelic, Singer/Songwriter, Traditional Folk
Although Carolyn Hester's talent was tenuous, she was an important, if marginal, figure of the early '60s folk revival, singing traditional material with a high voice in the manner of Joan Baez and Judy Collins (though with less command). Some of her early and mid-1960s work points, if only ever so slightly, in directions that would lead to folk-rock. Hester herself was unable to make it as a folk-rocker despite a brief try, and unpredictably went into psychedelic music for a couple of albums before largely drifting out of the business in the 1970s and 1980s. In the '80s, she was a mentor for budding talent Nanci Griffith.

Born in Texas, Hester moved to New York in 1955 to get into music and acting. Her first album, *Scarlet Ribbons*, was produced by Norman Petty in 1957, and found release on Coral Records. In the early 1960s she was briefly married to author and folk singer-songwriter Richard Farina, who became friendly with Bob Dylan shortly after Dylan's arrival in New York. While recording her third album for Columbia and producer John Hammond in September 1961, she invited Dylan, then almost unknown, to play harmonica on a few cuts. His work on the album helped bring him to the attention of Hammond, who signed Dylan to Columbia as a solo artist shortly afterwards.

While other performers of the early-1960s folk revival made great strides forward in sales and influence—including Dylan, Baez, and Collins—Hester remained relatively obscure. She turned down a chance to form a folk trio with Peter Yarrow and Paul Stookey, offered by manager Albert Grossman; that position went to Mary Travers, and the trio found stardom as Peter, Paul & Mary.

In the late 1960s, Hester made the unexpected move to psychedelic music as part of the Carolyn Hester Coalition and throughout the next decades did some recording for Decca, RCA, and Capitol, and formed the Outpost label with her husband, jazz pianist/producer/songwriter David Blume. With Blume, she ran an ethnic dance club in Los Angeles, and she continues to record and tour occasionally. *—Richie Unterberger*

Carolyn Hester [Tradition] / 1961 / Tradition ♦♦♦
Except for one self-penned number, Hester's second album consisted entirely of traditional folk covers, accompanied only by her own guitar. In some respects, the selection was forward-looking for its time; she was among the first performers of the 1960s folk revival, for instance, to record "House of the Rising Sun," "She Moves Through the Fair," and "If I Had a Ribbon Bow," all included here. Still, in comparison to Judy Collins and Joan Baez—the two most convenient reference points for her high and clear vocals—it sounds twee and precious. Hester was friendly with Dylan at the outset of his career, and one wonders if Dylan got the idea to open "It Ain't Me Babe" with the title lyric of "Go Way From My Window," one of the traditional songs on this LP. *—Richie Unterberger*

Carolyn Hester [Columbia] / 1962 / Columbia/Legacy ♦♦♦♦♦
An album, in retrospect, more important for the accompanying musicians than Hester herself. Hester delivered a solid, somewhat precious set of traditional material in the early-'60s Greenwich Village folk mode. One of the first LPs of the scene to use a full band, it also featured guitar by future Dylan accompanist Bruce Langhorne, bassist Bill Lee (who also played on many other folk albums of the era by Ian & Sylvia and others), and Dylan himself, who contributed harmonica to a few tracks shortly before he made his own Columbia debut. The CD reissue adds a couple of bonus alternate takes. *—Richie Unterberger*

This Life I'm Living / 1963 / Columbia ♦♦♦
Hester's second Columbia album was similar to her first, but has gotten far less attention by historians, probably for the unfair but simple reason that Bob Dylan played on a few tracks on the first Columbia LP, but is not on the second. Again she played an assortment of tradi-

tional folk numbers, her vocals and guitar backed by light accompaniment from bass, another guitarist (Bruce Langhorne, famous for his work on early Dylan electric folk-rock sessions), and even an itsy bitsy bit of percussion. Actually, it has an edge on the first Columbia album because Hester favors moodier material that's usually heavy on the minor melodies. "East Virginia" (which she would re-record in the late 1960s in a folk-rock-psychedelic arrangement with the Carolyn Hester Coalition) and "Coo-Coo" are the only instantly familiar standards here; she also gets into something of a Latin/world music vein with "Pera Stous" and "Tumbando Cana." The entire album, along with unreleased outtakes of two songs left off the LP ("Summertime" and Buddy Holly's "Lonesome Tears"), is available as part of Bear Family's two-CD *Dear Companion* anthology. *—Richie Unterberger*

That's My Song / 1964 / Dot ✦✦✦

★ **At Town Hall** / 1990 / Bear Family ✦✦✦✦✦
This recording is probably the best existing representation of Hester's work, capturing her voice in all of its natural vibrancy, in a setting where spontaneity matters more than control. The repertory may also explain—along with Hester's southern/Texas twang—why she never quite caught on with folk audiences nationwide. By 1965, Hester was already falling behind the times—she does some topical songs like Phil Ochs' "What's That I Hear," and Gil Turner's "Carry It On," and her own haunting and ominous "Three Young Men," a tribute to murdered civil rights workers Goodman, Schwerner and Chaney; her choice of a Dylan song, "Playboys and Playgirls," however, and her Kennedy tribute "Captain, My Captain" (an old poem set to her own music, which works beautifully) were both just archaic enough by 1965 standards to show more thoughtfulness than the burgeoning, ever-angrier and more political folk/protest audience of the mid-to-late-'60s was looking for. And the presence of a lot of traditional songs such as "Water Is Wide" (beautifully sung) would've been ideal a year or two earlier, but by 1965 represented a period of the folksong revival that was already losing its edge with audiences and passing into history. Joan Baez and Judy Collins were more engaged politically, though one surprise for rock fans is Billy Ed Wheeler's "High Flying Bird," a song associated with the Jefferson Airplane of this approximate era. This disc not only contains the unedited tape of the Town Hall concert, in which Hester is backed up by fellow guitarist George Tomsco, but four additional songs from another concert. Her voice here not only evokes images of Nanci Griffith, but also a young Emmylou Harris. *—Bruce Eder*

● **Dear Companion** / 1995 / Bear Family ✦✦✦✦✦
Two-CD, 60-song compilation of 1960s recordings including both of her Columbia albums, her 1965 Dot album *That's My Song*, a couple of 1962 cuts ("My Love Is a Rider" and "Gregorio Cortez") whose initial release is unhelpfully unidentified in the liner notes, her two 1966-67 folk-rock Columbia singles, and no less than 18 Columbia outtakes and alternates spanning 1961-67. Although this doesn't have her mid-1960s live *Town Hall* albums (available on Bear Family's *At Town Hall* CD), her pre-Columbia album for Tradition, or her psychedelic late-'60s albums as leader of the Carolyn Hester Coalition, it's the best anthology of her 1960s material. Particularly interesting is the rare 1966-67 folk-rock stuff, produced by John Simon with mixed results. "Early Morning" was a single and is the best of these numbers, with its period pop-folk-rock feel; there are also covers of Jackson Frank's "Blues Run the Game, " Tim Hardin's "Reason to Believe," and, believe it or not, Cat Stevens' "I Love My Dog." On the other hand, the attempt at "Penny Lane" is pretty ghastly, and the 1966 rendition of Ravi Shankar's "Majhires," with Eric Weisberg on mandolin, is a noble but failed experiment. Going back a little further, highlights of the early-1960s Columbia outtakes include "Summertime" and an intriguing take of Buddy Holly's "Lonesome Tears" with light drums that oh-so-slightly prefigure folk-rock. *—Richie Unterberger*

From These Hills / Oct. 25, 1996 / Road Goes On Forever ✦✦✦

The Highwaymen

f. 1958, **db.** 1964
Group / Folk Revival, Folk-Pop
The Highwaymen stand alongside the Kingston Trio, the New Christie Minstrels, and the Brothers Four on the losing side of the early-'60s battle between the folk-pop acts and the more confrontational and politically oriented species of folk singer represented by Bob Dylan and Phil Ochs. Although history's view of folk music in the latter half of the 20th century has focused on social change and protest, the Highwaymen did have a major impact on the folk scene of the early 1960s. Apart from a couple of major hit singles, and appearances on *The Ed Sullivan Show*, they contributed a couple of future standards to the folk repertory ("Big Rock Candy Mountain," "All My Trials"), played a key role in the unearthing of a major, overlooked Leadbelly song, and also made the first American recordings of seminally important songs by Buffy St. Marie and Ewan McColl.

In the fall of 1958, Connecticut's Wesleyan University students Dave Fisher, Steve Butts, Bob Burnett, and Chan Daniels met through a performance at a college fraternity show, and guitarist Steve Trott came aboard during their rehearsals. An early B-side, "Michael, Row The Boat Ashore," recorded for United Artists slowly became popular across the northeast and broke out nationally in 1961, rising to the No. 1 spot that summer. After graduation, the Highwaymen began living in Greenwich Village in late 1962 and started an extended engagement at *the Gaslight Cafe*. The Highwaymen might've bridged the gap separating the folk-pop outfits from the harder, more topical political singers of the era, but for the fact that three of its members, Burnett, Daniels, and Butts, had never intended to dedicate their whole lives to music. Rather, the music was fun, and, as it turned out, a means to an end, in the form of relative financial security. They'd never planned on doing it for more than two years, and by 1964 were already passing that time limit. Various members reunited over the next few years in different configurations, and the group has continued perform a few weekends out of every year throughout the 1990s. *—Bruce Eder*

● **Michael, Row the Boat Ashore: The Best of the Highwaymen** / 1992 / Capitol ✦✦✦✦✦
Among the first successful folk groups, The Highwaymen emerged as leaders of the "hootenanny" movement of the '60s. Included is the immensely popular title song and 23 others. *—Roundup newsletter*

The Highway Men/Standing Room Only / Sep. 12, 2000 / Collectors' Choice Music ✦✦✦
The Highwaymen exhibit an enthusiastic optimism that can seem overly sugarcoated in the post-Vietnam, post-Watergate world. How many groups today would attempt to sing a song like "Big Rock Candy Mountain" without a heavy dose of irony— But the Highwaymen were young when they started performing and made their first two albums, *The Highwaymen* and *Standing Room Only!*, in 1960 and 1961. Songs like "Santiano" and "Michael" have the same tight harmony and joyous presentation as the early material of the Kingston Trio or the New Christy Minstrels. Their version of "Cotton Fields" has little in common with Leadbelly's, but few people listening at the time would have been aware of the original version. Neither would these listeners have thought it odd that five clean-cut college boys were singing about being in "cold iron and shackles" in "Take This Hammer." The Highwaymen must be understood and appreciated for what they attempted to be: popular interpreters of folk songs. Just about everything on their first album, *The Highwaymen*, sounds fresh and energetic, and the arrangements are simple and straightforward. *Standing Room Only!* varies this formula with less success. This album sounds "more produced" and the song choice less inspired. The guitar lead on a dulcimer-driven "Wildwood Flower" almost sounds electric. (And this is at least four years before folk-rock!) Musically, listeners will also notice that many of the tracks on both albums have drums. All nitpicking aside, these are fun albums that will transport the listener back to the heights of the folk revival when it was still "cool" to sing songs filled with hope. *—Ronnie Lankford, Jr.*

Anne Hills

Vocals, Autoharp, Guitar, Banjo / Contemporary Singer/Songwriter, Contemporary Folk
A stunning soprano tone has made Anne Hills one of contemporary folk music's premier vocalists. But her affinity for choosing unforgettable material and her knack for writing heartfelt original songs have brought her to the upper echelon of her craft. In addition to recording three memorable solo albums, Hills has recorded two duo albums with Cindy Mangsen and three trio albums with Mangsen and Priscilla Herdman. A veteran of the Chicago folk scene of the 1980s, she helped to found Hogeye Music, a folklore center and recording label. Her first three recordings—*The Panic Is On*, recorded with Jan Burda, in 1982; 1984's *Don't Explain*, and a multi-artist Christmas album, *On This Day Earth Shall Sing*, in 1984—were released on the label. Hills' next two solo albums, *Woman of a Calm Heart* and *October Child*, showcased the songwriting of others; with 1995's *Angle of the Light* though, she stepped forward as a songwriter as well as performer. She also recorded several albums as a trio with Cindy Mangsen and Priscilla Herdman. Hills reached her creative apex in 1997, when she released her first children's book, *Dreamcatcher*, adapted from an original song and featuring the song on an included cassette. She also contributed to Pete Seeger and Phil Ochs tribute albums, and was named Outstanding Female Vocalist for 1997 by the Kerrville Music Foundation. *—Craig Harris*

October Child / 1993 / Flying Fish ✦✦✦✦
"October Child" is a collection of fellow-Chicagoan Michael Smith's songs. Peter Erskine's arrangements are respectful of song's carefully crafted lyrics. One of the great benefits of this CD is the chance to hear some of Smith's less well-known songs, "Disappearing Heart" for example. *—Richard Meyer*

● **Angle of the Light** / 1995 / Flying Fish ✦✦✦✦
Anne Hills has finally made an album that lives up to her promise. Her voice has gotten progressively stronger and more flexible, and her writing has grown more detailed and evocative. On this release, she comes across as a thoughtful romantic with a mature compassionate view of how each of us must work to fit in the world. Her abstract "Follow That Road" directs how to find her, but more listeners will find some of their own past in her direction. Hills has come to terms with some part of herself when she sings " Today let me eat, Today let me breathe, Today let me speak with a friend, Today let the sun shine down on my head, Til moon light shines on me again, Its enough to live." *—Richard Meyer*

Tish Hinojosa

b. Dec. 6, 1955, San Antonio, TX
Vocals, Piano, Guitar / Contemporary Singer/Songwriter, Contemporary Folk
Tish Hinojosa has fashioned her blend of Mexican and American cultures into a compelling voice in music. Typically a Tish Hinojosa album or concert moves effortlessly from songs of loves forgotten and family struggles remembered, of eloquent cries against injustice and playful evocations of sawdust dance floors, of the rolling endless highways of the Southwest to the lonely struggles of the disenfranchised. Born Leticia Hinojosa in San Antonio to a large blended family, the budding musician listened to the songs of her parents as well as the Beatles, and began her musical career doing jingles and recording for a small Tejano label. She recorded in Taos, New Mexico, and in Nashville briefly, but found an eager audience in Austin, Texas. She rapidly became an integral part of the vibrant Austin musical scene by making many club appearances but also standing tall for her social concerns by being a willing participant in benefits for migrant farm workers. Over the years she has gone on to record a number of critically acclaimed albums for Warner Bros., Watermelon, and Rounder Records. Hinojosa also has a loyal following overseas and her touring itinerary often includes stops in Amsterdam and Scandinavia as well as the more familiar confines of clubs in Houston, Cambridge and Taos. *—Alonso Jasso & Michael Erlewine*

Homeland / 1989 / A&M ✦✦✦✦✦
This is her first album and a clear harbinger of what is to come. With most songs written by Hinojosa herself, already she has her own sound and style. Good songwriters are rare. Outstanding songs are "The Border Trilogy," "Voice of the Big Guitar," "Who Showed You the Way to My Heart," "Let Me Remember," and "Amanecer." *—Michael Erlewine*

● **Culture Swing** / Aug. 27, 1990 / Rounder ✦✦✦✦✦
If Joan Baez or Tracy Chapman were influenced by the Mexican-American music of Texas, they might sound something like Tish Hinojosa—a charming singer/acoustic guitarist who sings mostly in English but can be equally convincing in Spanish. Categorizing this expres-

sive vocalist isn't easy. While "By the Rio Grande," "The Window," and "San Antonio Romeo" bring Tex-Mex touches to the Anglo-American folk and singer/songwriter traditions, "Corazon Viajero (Wandering Heart)" and "Chanate, El Vaquero" are Spanish-language gems that would please Mexican traditionalists. "Drifter's Wind" and "Louisiana Road Song" essentially fall into the country category, while "San Antonio Romeo" pays homage to the Western swing sound defined by Bob Wills. Unpredictable as well as moving, Hinojosa showed considerable promise on this enriching CD. *—Alex Henderson*

Aquella Noche / 1991 / Watermelon ✦✦✦
A largely Spanish album, it balances traditional Mexican songs with her own romantic, clear-eyed originals. This was recorded live at Austin's Waterloo Icehouse the week of Cinco de Mayo 1991. *—Michael McCall*

Memorabilia Navidenia / 1991 / Watermelon ✦✦✦

Taos to Tennessee / 1992 / Watermelon ✦✦✦✦✦
Tish Hinojosa is an established Mexican-American singer with recent releases on A&M and Electra. Her Watermelon debut *Taos To Tennessee* features country material in English; 14 original and classic songs make up *Aquella Noche,* and *Memorabilia Navidena* is a Christmas album that combines both languages and old and new seasonal songs. *—Roch Parisien*

Destiny's Gate / 1994 / Warner Brothers ✦✦✦

Frontejas / 1995 / Rounder ✦✦✦
Not your standard album release, but a theme recording. This is a collection of border songs in sung in Spanish, some written by Hinojosa, some by others. The inspiration for this collection was her apprenticeship with Don Americo Paredes, the anthropologist, border historian, and professor emeritus at the University of Texas at Austin. Hinojosa writes "In a series of sessions in which I listened and enriched my soul with "corridos" (ballads that tell stories, news or history), love songs, and anecdotes of the borderland where he was raised and where my family's roots lie deeply embedded. These sessions continue still and the knowledge I receive is a precious resource from which I'll always draw." A number of these songs involve assistance from the likes of Flaco Jimenez, Ray Benson, Peter Rowan, and others. This makes for enjoyable listening, but is not the creative and fiery Hinojosa on an album like *Culture Swing.* *—Michael Erlewine*

Cada Nino (Every Child) / 1996 / Rounder ✦✦

Dreaming from the Labyrinth (Soñar del Laberinto) / May 1996 / Warner Brothers ✦✦✦
Tish Hinojosa's album, *Dreaming from the Labyrinth* (her second for Warner Bros.), is more what comes to mind with the word "traditional." Hinojosa was born in Texas to Mexican immigrant parents, and her multicultural upbringing is a defining characteristic of her acoustic folk music (she sings in both Spanish and English, for example), as is her association with the current folk and country scene in Austin. Hinojosa's music, however, is often so sweet and nice around the edges that it becomes a turnoff. The songs on *Labyrinth* are as pretty as Hinojosa's voice, but there's no dirt under the fingernails, which is exactly what makes the music of Lucinda Williams, for instance (another Austin-based artist), so vibrant and alive. *—Kurt Wolff*

Sonar Del Laberinto / May 5, 1997 / Warner Brothers ✦✦✦
Sonar del laberinto is the Spanish language version of Tish Hinojosa's fine *Dreaming from the Labryinth* and her lovely, folky songs are just as affecting in Spanish as they are in English. *—Thom Owens*

Sign of Truth / May 23, 2000 / Rounder ✦✦✦

The Holy Modal Rounders

f. 1963, **db.** 1979
Group / Folk-Rock
The Holy Modal Rounders were almost the very definition of a cult act. This isn't a case of a group that would be described by such cliches as "if only they got more exposure, they would certainly reach a much wider audience." Their audience was small because their music was too strange, idiosyncratic, and at times downright dissonant for mainstream listeners to abide. What makes the Rounders unusual in this regard is that they owed primary allegiance to the world of acoustic folk—not one that generates many difficult, arty, and abrasive performers. Not so much a group as a changing aggregation (centered around principals Peter Stampfel and Steve Weber), the Rounders began recording in the mid-'60s as an acoustic duo for Prestige. Although clearly accomplished musicians, and well-versed in folk traditions, they were determined to subvert these with off-kilter execution and strange lyrics that could be surreal, whimsical, or just silly. Stampfel and Weber added other musicians for 1967's *Indian War Whoop* and 1969's *Moray Eels Eat the Holy Modal Rounders;* the latter featured their most famous song, "If You Wanna Be a Bird" (which was used on the *Easy Rider* soundtrack). After a temporary separation during the early '70s, Stampfel and Weber eventually released three more albums (the last was billed to Stampfel & Weber), after which Stampfel became quite a visible presence as a solo recording artist. *—Richie Unterberger*

Indian War Whoop / 1967 / ESP ✦✦✦✦✦
Peter Stampfel and Steve Weber obviously loved American folk music as much as any of the kids who had their head turned around by Harry Smith's *Anthology of American Folk Music* in the 1950s, but unlike the many musicians who paid tribute to America's musical past by trying to re-create it as closely as possible, as The Holy Modal Rounders Stampfel and Weber opted to drag the music into the present, shrieking and giggling all the way. Even by the standards of The Holy Modal Rounders' first two albums, 1967's *Indian War Whoop* is a thoroughly bizarre listening experience; loosely structured around the between-song adventures of two seedy vagabonds named Jimmy and Crash, side one veers back and forth between neo-psychedelic fiddle-and-guitar freakouts and free-form (and often radically altered) interpretations of traditional folk tunes such as "Soldier's Joy" and & "Sweet Apple Cider," while side two is devoted to like minded originals (including a couple songs from their friend Michael Hurley, who would later join the group). Most certainly a product of its time, *Indian War Whoop* sounds rather dated today, but its buoyant good humor and chemically-altered enthusiasm remains effective, even when the Rounders' reckless pursuit of inner space sounds like it was more fun to create than to observe on record. The Calibre CD reissue features expanded liner notes, and while no bonus tracks have been added, the digital remastering sounds terrific. *—Mark Deming*

The Moray Eels Eat the Holy Modal Rounders / 1969 / Elektra ✦✦✦✦✦
Like a psychedelic folkie fusion of The Fugs and the Mothers of Invention, this ranks as one of the best "acid folk" albums. This sprawling, demented LP includes "Bird Song," which was featured on the *Easy Rider* soundtrack. *—Richie Unterberger*

Good Taste Is Timeless / 1971 / Metromedia ✦✦✦
Peter Stampfel himself has gone on record with his dissatisfaction with this LP, which he found too stiff and slick. Recorded in Nashville with ex-Elvis Presley guitarist Scotty Moore engineering, and Pete Drake and D.J. Fontana helping out occasionally, it's certainly more professionally produced than anything the Rounders did in the '60s. That doesn't necessarily mean it's bad; a lot of it's mildly bent countrified folk-rock. The zaniness of previous Rounders releases is toned down considerably, but on the other hand it's a lot more listenable than, say, *Indian War Whoop.* "Boobs a Lot," which the Fugs had recorded back in the mid-'60s, would become the most widely known Rounders track, with the exception of "Bird Song." *—Richie Unterberger*

Alleged in Their Own Time / 1975 / Rounder ✦✦

Last Round / 1978 / Adelphi ✦✦✦✦
Unless, like the Holy Modal Rounders, you've spent a lot of time listening to Harry Smith's *Anthology of American Folk Music* while ingesting recreational drugs, their music might sound a bit odd to you. Actually, given the ramshackle performances, it sounds a bit odd in any case, but as with any humorously intended work, appreciation of it depends on one's sympathy with the artists. For initiates, this seventh (and, so it seemed at the time of its release, final) album was one of the Rounders' better ones, with Peter Stampfel, Chris Weber, and especially Robin Remaily turning out characteristic new work and covers of old songs like "Euphoria" and "If You Want to Be a Bird" backed by a rhythm section. "August, 1967 (Hippies Call It STP)," borrows its tune from "Fishin' Blues," while head Rounders Peter Stampfel and Steve Weber sing a paean to psychedelic drug use that breaks down into odd references such as this allusion to Amos & Andy: " 'Splain dat to me, Kingfish, it ain't too clear/King it to me, 'splainfsh, said the engineer." The CD reissue released on June 27, 2000, added three bonus tracks. "TV Song" is a tribute to the addictive power of television; "Year of Jubilo" revives a Civil War victory celebration; and "Snappin' Pussy" is an appropriately bawdy follow-up to an earlier Rounders favorite, "Boobs a Lot." *—William Ruhlmann*

Too Much Fun / Jul. 13, 1999 / Rounder ✦✦✦✦
The Holy Modal Rounders once again breathe life into American folk music with *Too Much Fun.* This offbeat collection is more than enough fun, with "Tea Song, " "Year of Jublio" and "New John the Revelator" among the standouts. As they've done since 1963, the Rounders bring songs from several generations together for a whimsical tour of American music history. *—Mark Morgenstein*

● **Holy Modal Rounders, Vols. 1 & 2** / Aug. 17, 1999 / Fantasy ✦✦✦✦✦
Both of the Rounders' first two Prestige albums are combined onto one disc on this CD reissue, with the addition of new historical liner notes by Larry Kelp. Even if you already have the records, this might be of interest for the inclusion of two previously unreleased 1964 outtakes, "Sugar in the Gourd" and "Soldier's Joy." Also, the second album has been resequenced by Stampfel, who was always dissatisfied with how the tracks were sequenced on the LP, to conform to running order that the band originally had in mind. Altogether, this is the prime document of the Rounders in their early folk days, simultaneously paying homage to and sending up traditional folk with guitar, fiddle, banjo, and slightly zany vocals. *—Richie Unterberger*

Cisco Houston

b. Aug. 18, 1918, Wilmington, DE, **d.** Apr. 21, 1961, San Bernardino, CA
Vocals, Guitar / Singer/Songwriter, Traditional Folk
Cisco Houston is best remembered as a traveling companion and harmony vocalist for Woody Guthrie. But he was equally influential as a folk singer in his own right. With his acoustic guitar accompanying his unadorned baritone vocals, Houston provided a musical voice for America's downtrodden—the cowboys, miners, union activists, railroad workers and hobos—that resonated in the songs of the urban folk revival of the 1950s and '60s. In 1938, Houston and actor friend Will Geer heard a radio show on KFVD in Hollywood featuring Guthrie. Inspired by the performance, the two, struggling, decided to visit the young folk singer. When they did, it sparked a longtime friendship. Not long after meeting Guthrie, Houston began appearing on the radio show, singing tenor harmonies to Guthrie's lead vocals. The two subsequently began performing at migrant camps, and when Guthrie traveled to New York in 1939, he persuaded Houston to join him. After Guthrie signed a recording contract with Folkways, Houston sang high-tenor vocals on his recordings. He also made his debut solo recordings for the label. He also had his first success as a songwriter when his tune "Crazy Heart," co-written with Lewis Allen, became a minor hit for Jackie Paris. Just when it seemed that Houston's career was taking off, he was diagnosed with cancer. His death in the spring of 1961 was mourned throughout the folk community, and memorials were written and recorded by Tom Paxton ("Fare Thee Well, Cisco"), Peter LaFarge ("Cisco Houston Passed This Way") and Tom McGrath ("Blues for Cisco Houston"). *—Craig Harris*

● **900 Miles and Other Railroad Ballads** / 195 / Smithsonian/Folkways ✦✦✦✦✦

Cisco Houston Sings Woody Guthrie / 1963 / Vanguard ✦✦✦

Sings Songs of the Open Road / 1968 / Smithsonian/Folkways ✦✦✦✦✦
This Woody Guthrie sidekick sings Guthrie's songs and traditional tunes. *—William Ruhlmann*

The Folkways Years 1944-1961 / 1994 / Smithsonian/Folkways ✦✦✦✦✦
Except for a few tracks done for Decca between 1951 and 1952, and a lengthy session for

Vanguard in 1960, Cisco Houston did all of his recording for Moses Asch's record labels, primarily for Folkways. This comprehensive compilation packs 29 performances (eight of them previously unreleased) into just over 70 minutes, revealing Houston to be an unusually smooth-voiced folksinger with a straightforward professionalism that earned him criticism for not sounding "authentic" enough. Actually, Houston was so versatile that it's sometimes hard to believe all of these recordings are by the same vocalist, especially when he is fulfilling his best-known function of serving as a high-voiced harmony singer behind his friend Woody Guthrie (for example on "A Picture From Life's Other Side"). Houston's baritone, however, which he usually employs when singing alone, proves a clear interpretive device for his collection of folk songs, cowboy songs, and topical material. Sound quality varies; the earliest tracks from the 1940s are crude recordings, while the later ones are better. Throughout the album Houston remains a strong interpretive singer. Compiler Guy Logsdon's liner notes are based on Houston's papers on file at *the Smithsonian* along with other sources, and they paint one of the most complete portraits yet of Houson's life and career, helping to make this album the definitive survey of his work. *—William Ruhlmann*

Best of the Vanguard Years / Oct. 31, 2000 / Vanguard ✦✦✦✦
Of the singers who brought folk into the modern era around World War II, Cisco Houston seems to have less name recognition than either Woody Guthrie or Leadbelly. Not a songwriter himself, Houston did a great deal to promote the songs and legacy of Guthrie during the mid- to late-'50s, and a number of songs on this recording come from *Cisco Houston Sings the Songs of Woody Guthrie*. Houston also brings his smooth baritone to bear on a number of traditional songs, many of them with a political bent harking back to the Depression years. "Big Rock Candy Mountain" is a hobo song, a fantasy about a place where a bum can have everything that he or she desires. "Talking Dust Bowl" is a fun, apocalyptic little song about leaving one's home in a broken-down car, driving down a crooked mountain, and having an accident that "scatters wives and children all over the side [of] that mountain." He offers an amusing version of "Badman Ballad," a song similar in structure and content to "Cocaine Blues." Unlike "Cocaine Blues," though, Houston's narrator shoots and kills a deputy sheriff (not his woman) because he was feeling mean (not because he was on cocaine), and the overall tone is kept light and humorous. Most of these songs feature pretty straightforward arrangements, either with Houston on guitar or accompanied by a few friends. There are several tracks that have not been released before, including a fine version of "John Hardy." This collection of Houston material will be welcomed by old fans and is a good place to start for those wishing to learn more about the legendary folksinger. *—Ronnie Lankford Jr.*

Ian & Sylvia

f. 1960, **db.** 1973
Group / Folk Revival, Folk-Rock, Folk-Pop
One of the most popular acts of the early-'60s folk revival, Canadian duo of Ian and Sylvia Tyson made several fine albums that spotlighted their stirring harmonies on a mixture of traditional and contemporary material. While these recordings can seem a tad earnest and dated today, they were overlooked influences upon early folk-rockers such as the Jefferson Airplane, the Mamas and the Papas, and Fairport Convention, all of whom utilized similar blends of male/female lead/harmony vocals. They were also inspirations to fellow Canadian singer-songwriters such as Neil Young, Joni Mitchell, and Gordon Lightfoot. After moving from Toronto to New York in 1960, the duo released a self-titled debut (1962) that began a successful series of recordings for Vanguard, on which they helped expand the range of folk by adding bass. Ian & Sylvia were among the first to cover songs by Dylan, Lightfoot, Joni Mitchell, and Phil Ochs, and also began writing material of their own. By 1966, they began to use electric instruments, though their folk-rock generally lacked the focus and consistency of their acoustic recordings. In the late '60s, they would take stabs at country-rock and straight country music. The quality of their records, and the size of their audience, declined steadily after they ended their association with Vanguard in 1967. Both have since pursued separate solo careers. *—Richie Unterberger*

Ian & Sylvia / 1962 / Vanguard ✦✦✦
Ian & Sylvia's debut album is their most standard affair, and indeed a fairly typical folk recording for the era, with such traditional warhorses as "Rocks And Gravel" (also recorded, but not released, by Dylan during this time), "C.C. Rider," and "Handsome Molly." What made the pair immediately distinctive was their superb vocal dueting, which was definitely a case of the sum being greater than its parts. Blended together, they canceled each other's weaknesses and gave the material great freshness and vigor. Ian's guitar and Sylvia's autoharp are backed by stellar playing from guitarist John Herald and string bassists Bill Lee (director Spike Lee's father) and Art Davis. *—Richie Unterberger*

Four Strong Winds / 1964 / Vanguard ✦✦✦✦✦
Ian & Sylvia hit their stride on their second LP, which features the first in a line of talented second guitarists (John Herald) they would use to augment their original guitar-autoharp-bass lineup. The album featured an assortment of largely traditional material that was unsurpassed in its time, encompassing bluegrass, spirituals, gospel, hillbilly, the French-Canadian standard "V'La L'bon Vent," a British prison song, and two tunes from the Cecil Sharp collection of Southern mountain folk songs of British origin. Two of the most impressive cuts, however, were contemporary compositions. One was their version of Bob Dylan's "Tomorrow Is a Long Time," one of the first obscure Dylan tunes to be committed to vinyl. The title cut, an Ian Tyson original, would prove to be the duo's first song to influence rock musicians, as The Searchers covered it shortly afterwards with a reverent version that was quite close to the original; Neil Young revived it in the late '70s. *—Richie Unterberger*

Northern Journey / 1964 / Vanguard ✦✦✦
The duo continue to fill out their sound on another collection of mostly traditional material, with John Herald (guitar), Monte Dunn (mandolin and guitar), and Eric Weissberg and Russ Savakus (bass) backing Ian & Sylvia's own guitar and autoharp. The few originals stand out much more than the traditional updates on this LP; Tyson's "Four Rode By" and "Some Day Soon" clearly point toward his future CW/cowboy direction, and Fricker's "You Were on My Mind" remains their best (and best-known) song. *—Richie Unterberger*

Early Morning Rain / 1965 / Vanguard ✦✦✦
Side One of the original LP version of their fourth album continues in the eclectic folkie style of their earlier albums, containing only one original (Tyson's "Marlborough Street Blues"). The other cuts include the fine Gordon Lightfoot title track, a Johnny Cash cover ("Come in Stranger") that heralded their increasing interest in country and western music, one of their finest interpretations of a bonafide traditional warhorse ("Nancy Whiskey"), and "Darcy Farrow," a fine obscure composition that could pass for a traditional standard (written for the duo by an unknown Californian singer/songwriter pair). Side Two, however, with the exception of one traditional tune and another Lightfoot cover, is composed entirely of originals. The most notable of these is Tyson's "Song For Canada" (written with Pete Gzowski). A bittersweet plea for greater communication between French- and English-speaking Canadians, it could just as well be heard as a comment on any sort of deteriorating relationship. *—Richie Unterberger*

Ian & Sylvia Play One More / 1966 / Vanguard ✦✦✦
Ian & Sylvia rely mostly on original material for the first time on this erratic record. For the first time, they employ full modern arrangements on four of the tracks, which sometimes works (their cover of Bacharach-David's "24 Hours From Tulsa") and sometimes doesn't (unfortunately for them, on one of their best compositions, "The French Girl"). They also cover songs by Phil Ochs and Scott McKenzie, and their own tunes range from solid numbers in their proven contemporary folk style ("Short Grass") to mediocre. Future Cream producer Felix Pappalardi plays bass. *—Richie Unterberger*

So Much for Dreaming / 1967 / Vanguard ✦✦✦
Ian & Sylvia's adjustment to folk-rock was sometimes fine, sometimes awkward, and this was another inconsistent, though generally worthwhile, effort. Highlights include "Circle Game," one of the very first recorded covers of a Joni Mitchell composition. Tyson's "Wild Geese" and "Child Apart" count as some of their better unheralded tunes, and the occasional muted orchestration worked well on "Circle Game" and the melancholy title track. On the other hand, the attempts at blues were abominable, the traditional ballads anachronistic, and some of the material (especially Fricker's) undistinguished. *—Richie Unterberger*

The Best of Ian & Sylvia / 1968 / Vanguard ✦✦✦
Best-of collections are not the best way to experience album-oriented artists like Ian & Sylvia. And this 12-song anthology of their '60s Vanguard work is not the most extensive retrospective of that era; *Greatest Hits* is considerably lengthier. It does include several of their best and most famous originals ("You Were On My Mind" and "Four String Winds") and covers ("24 Hours From Tulsa," "Early Morning Rain," "Changes"). *—Richie Unterberger*

● **Greatest Hits** / 1987 / Vanguard ✦✦✦✦✦
This compilation (CVSD 5/6) captures much of their best work. Do not confuse it with the identically titled Vanguard album 73114, which includes only half the material found on this set. *—William Ruhlmann*

Long Long Time / Oct. 25, 1994 / Vanguard ✦✦✦
After leaving Vanguard in 1967, Ian & Sylvia spent the next few years recording in a much more countrified style for MGM, Ampex (as figureheads of the band Great Speckled Bird), and Columbia. This compilation—ironically on Vanguard—draws from five albums they released between 1967 and 1971. While the duo's ambitions to expand their artistic horizons were admirable, the fact is that they were much more effective as eclectic folkies than country-pop-folk-rockers. The harmonies remained intact, but the material (mostly original) is often humdrum, the arrangements sometimes lackadaisical. A few cuts, like "Salmon in the Sea" and "Last Lonely Eagle," are reasonably strong; the higlights are the 1967 versions of "Hang on to a Dream" and "Reason to Believe," which were among the first Tim Hardin covers ever recorded. *—Richie Unterberger*

Live at Newport / Jun. 18, 1996 / Vanguard ✦✦✦

The Best of the Vanguard Years / Aug. 11, 1998 / Vanguard ✦✦✦✦

The Incredible String Band

f. 1965, **db.** 1974
Group / British Folk-Rock, British Folk, Folk-Rock, Psychedelic
The Incredible String Band were one of the most engaging groups to emerge from the esoteric '60s. Comprising the duo of Mike Heron and Robin Williamson, its sound was haunting Celtic folk melodies augmented by a variety of Middle Eastern and Asian instruments. After signing to the British wing of Elektra Records, the group's 1966 eponymous debut featured mostly original numbers enthusiastically played in American and Celtic folk styles. For the String Band's second album, *The 5000 Spirits or the Layers of the Onion*, exotic touches such as the Middle Eastern oud or Indian sitars and tambouras began to permeate the Incredibles' sound. Their next album *The Hangman's Beautiful Daughter* was the band's brief flirtation with stardom. Although the music was less commercial than its predecessor, it reached the Top Ten in the British album charts and was also the group's highest *Billboard* chart placing in America, reaching #161. An electrically amplified lineup performed at the Woodstock Festival in 1969, though the group began to lose its momentum in the early '70s. The band made the transition to electric rock & roll in 1972, but broke up in 1974, following the album *Hard Rope and Silken Twine*. Both founding members later began prolific solo careers, Heron's taking him in a rock direction, while Williamson explored his Celtic roots. *—Jim Powers*

● **Hangman's Beautiful Daughter** / 1968 / Hannibal ✦✦✦✦✦
The ISB's most ambitious album, with Williamson and Heron employing an arsenal of unusual instruments (sitar, gimbri, pan pipe, oud, chahanai, and more), and Dolly Collins adding a couple of the more dignified arrangements. It's usually considered their most important effort by critics, but there were also traces of the sprawling, occasionally grating lack of focus that would increasingly come to characterize their work. *—Richie Unterberger*

Relics of the Incredible String Band / 1970 / Elektra ✦✦✦✦✦
The ISB's prolific output makes a compilation a virtual necessity, and this two-record set selects wisely from the seven albums the group released in the US between 1967 and 1970. From Robin Williamson's "First Girl I Loved" (covered by Judy Collins) and "Way Back in the 1960s" (recorded in 1967), to Mike Heron's "Air," and "This Moment," The ISB's eclectic, fanciful acoustic style is well portrayed. *—William Ruhlmann*

No Ruinous Feud / 1973 / Edsel ✦✦✦
The ISB began to change its approach in 1971, cutting back on its sometimes open-ended song structures and adding a rock rhythm section to selected tracks. But it wasn't until this album that everything came together, resulting in a delightful collection of songs that range from reggae to light pop, along with the traditional folk styles that had always been the group's strong suit. *—William Ruhlmann*

Wee Tam/The Big Huge / Oct. 18, 1994 / Hannibal ✦✦✦✦
Mixing English and American folk with what we now call "world music," the multi-instrumental Scottish duo of Robin Williamson and Mike Heron achieve a whimsical, delicate style that has never been duplicated. It reaches a peak here with such songs as "You Get Brighter." (*Wee Tam* is sometimes packaged with the simultaneously released *The Big Huge,* which is also recommended.) *—William Ruhlmann*

Chelsea Sessions 1967 / Oct. 7, 1997 / Resurgent ✦✦✦
These 13 demos were recorded in early 1967 shortly before the making of the ISB's second album, *The 5000 Spirits or the Layers of the Onion* (though the liner notes speculate that "God Dog" might date from later than the other tracks). Only six of these actually showed up on *5000 Spirits,* albeit in different, more produced versions; in fact, most of Robin Williamson's compositions on this release are performed solo by the writer. This gives fans a chance to hear the tracks (including their most famous song, "The First Girl I Loved") in acoustic, folkier incarnations, with slightly different lyrics on a couple of tunes. Of the remaining songs, "Lover Man" was recorded by Al Stewart on his debut album, "God Dog" by Shirley Collins in 1969, and "The Iron Stone" by ISB themselves on 1968's *Wee Tam and the Big Huge* album, while the others are unique to this disc. This unused material (the fidelity throughout is good, by the way) is both stylistically consistent and aesthetically up to par with what the ISB were recording on their early albums, and thus recommended to fans of the group. *—Richie Unterberger*

Burl Ives

b. Jun. 14, 1909, Huntington Township, Jaspar County, IL, **d.** Apr. 13, 1995
Vocals, Guitar / Sea Shanties, Cast Recordings, Folk-Pop, Traditional Folk
With his grandfatherly image, Burl Ives parlayed his talent as a folksinger into a wide-ranging career as a radio personality and stage and screen actor. He appeared in several Broadway shows and performed on his own radio show before making his recording debut for Stinson. Marginally successful with a single on Decca, Ives suddenly had a flurry of LP releases on Stinson, Decca and Columbia after the advent of the long-playing record. In 1951, he hit the Top Ten with "On Top of Old Smoky." By the '60s, Ives oriented himself toward country music, resulting in the hits "A Little Bitty Tear" and "Funny Way of Laughin'," both of which made the Top Ten in both the pop and country charts. He turned his attention primarily to movie work from 1963 on, especially with the Walt Disney studio. At the end of the '60s, Ives returned to Columbia Records for *The Times They Are A-Changin'* and *Softly and Tenderly.* He gave up popular recording, but returned in 1973 with the country album *Payin' My Dues Again.* He also continued to record children's music and also released several religious albums on Word Records. After turning 70 in 1979, he became less active and finally retired to Washington State. *—William Ruhlmann*

★ **The Wayfaring Stranger** / 1959 / Collectables ✦✦✦✦✦
The Wayfaring Stranger was the name of the CBS radio program on which Burl Ives first achieved lasting fame in broadcast circles and the name of Ives' autobiography as well, so it was also a natural for his Columbia Records debut. Ives' definitive Columbia album, *The Wayfaring Stranger* was also one of the bright spots in the very early folk revival of the mid-'50s, serving (every bit as much as the work of the Weavers) as the unofficial songbook for a generation of would-be folksingers who followed. Indeed, while the Weavers subsequently achieved much greater recognition and respect, their work up to this point in 1955 was decidedly more pop oriented, thanks to the presence of Gordon Jenkins' arrangements and accompaniments. In contrast, Ives' presentation on *The Wayfaring Stranger* was more basic and authentic, consisting of only his voice and acoustic guitar for all but one of the 26 songs. His singing is suited to the wide variety of material here, including folk ballads ("Darlin' Cory," "I Know Where I'm Going"), western songs ("Cowboy's Lament," better known as "The Streets of Laredo"), and tall tales ("The Divil and the Farmer"), among numerous other categories. Along with the work of the Easy Riders, this album has been one of the more undeservedly overlooked contributions that Columbia Records made to the folk boom that followed—listening to this record, it's clear that more than a couple of young folkies picked up a song or two or three from Ives. In November 2000, Collectables reissued *The Wayfaring Stranger* on CD (COL 6474) with three bonus tracks thrown in, bringing the album to nearly an hour's running time. *—Bruce Eder*

A Little Bitty Tear / 1994 / MCA Special Products ✦✦✦
A Little Bitty Tear is an engaging collection of Burl Ives' country-pop hits of the early 1960s—outside of the smash title track, other highlights include "Funny Way of Laughin'" and "Call Me Mr. In-Between." *—Hank Small*

Greatest Hits / 1996 / MCA ✦✦✦✦✦

Kate Jacobs

b. Jan. 11, 1959, Virginia
Vocals / Contemporary Singer/Songwriter, Contemporary Folk
Guitarist, singer and songwriter Kate Jacobs has an angelic voice and a unique gift for inventing characters and telling stories within the format of the four-minute song. Jacobs was born in Virginia but lived around the world in her youth, as her father worked as a diplomat. At the Unitarian Church in Virginia, Jacobs and her sisters learned civil rights marching songs, many of which were variations on old gospel traditionals. Jacobs cites such early influences as Elizabeth Cotten and Pete Seeger, both of whom visited her neighborhood Unitarian Church.

Jacobs' first album, *The Calm Comes After,* was a collection of songs with a band that skirted the borders between country and folk music. She followed up her independently released debut (on her own Small Pond Music) with a second album for Hoboken-based Bar/None Records, *What About Regret* (1995). Her first album, released in 1993, was later reissued on Bar/None.

Her music has been featured in the documentary film *Delivered Vacant,* and she's also written a book for children, *A Sister* (Hyperion Press), based on her song of the same name. But, of course, Jacobs' soprano voice is as attention-grabbing and captivating as her ballads and other song forms. She returned in 1998 with *Hydrangea.* *—Richard Skelly*

The Calm Come After / 1993 / Bar/None ✦✦✦✦✦
Originally an independent artist, Jacobs recorded *The Calm Comes After,* which was picked up by Bar None Records with three new cuts. The charm of this album is in Jacobs's friendly, almost naive, delivery. Her lyrics have a deeply knowing womanly innocence that really says she sees more than she says and acts on it. Think of this artist as a less-religious urban Iris Dement. Kate is supported by a sparse country-sounding band. *—Richard Meyer*

Bert Jansch

b. Nov. 3, 1943, Scotland
Vocals, Piano, Guitar, Guitar (Acoustic) / British Folk-Rock, British Folk, Folk-Rock
One of the most important figures in contemporary British folk, Bert Jansch brought an unsurpassed combination of virtuosity and eclecticism to the acoustic guitar, both as a solo act and a key member of Pentangle. Also a talented songwriter and affecting (if gruff) vocalist, he wrote dark and sparse material that recalled the folky side of Donovan, though he was much less pop-oriented than the psychedelic pop troubadour. Incorporating elements of blues, American folk, and British Isles traditional music into his playing, his influence was not only immense in the British folk scene. It also extended to the rock world—Neil Young and Jimmy Page, two electric guitar gonzos who often turn to acoustic picking as well, have acknowledged Jansch as a major influence. Young went as far as to tell *Guitar Player* that Jansch did for the acoustic guitar what Jimi Hendrix did for the electric. A revered elder statesperson in the UK, he has escaped widespread notice in the States. He has all the prerequisites for a large cult following, on the order of Nick Drake—another musician whose work contains definite echoes of Jansch. His first decade of recording attracts the lion's share of interest from listeners. But he's continued to record until the present day, his instrumental skills intact, although his best compositions date from the early part of his career. He also played for several years in reformed versions of Pentangle in the 1980s and '90s. *—Richie Unterberger*

Bert Jansch / 1965 / Transatlantic/Demon ✦✦✦✦✦
Recorded with a portable tape player on a borrowed guitar in the kitchen of his London flat, the impact of Jansch's debut has been somewhat blunted by time, but it was a vastly influential work. His masterful acoustic picking, which blended elements of traditional British folk, blues, and jazz, inspired not just other folk players, but rockers who frequently used acoustic guitars. Specifically, Jimmy Page and Neil Young have gone on record as noting their heavy debts to Jansch's early material. He was also a talented songwriter, and all but one of the 15 tracks on his debut was an original composition (the set closes with his version of the instrumental "Angi," originally performed by fellow British folk guitarist Davy Graham, and popularized by Paul Simon). The artist sounds quite close to early Donovan with his Scottish inflections, though he is darker and less pop-oriented; indeed, Donovan recorded a couple of early Jansch tunes, and wrote a couple of songs directly inspired by the artist ("Bert's Blues" and "House of Jansch"). Jansch reflects a rambling, beatnik sort of lifestyle with his compositions on this album, which includes one of his most famous tunes, the somber "Needle of Death" (about the heroin-induced death of one of his friends). In 1993, this LP and the artist's third album (*Jack Orion*) were combined onto one CD reissue. *—Richie Unterberger*

It Don't Bother Me / 1965 / Transatlantic/Demon ✦✦✦
Basically an extension of his 1965 debut, Jansch's second album is perhaps a bit lighter in mood and doesn't boast quite as strong material, although it's nearly in the same league. Includes one of his most explicitly political songs ("Anti-Apartheid"), his first recording with John Renbourn ("Lucky Thirteen," a Renbourn original), and his first use of banjo on record ("900 Miles"). The Demon reissue of this album adds four bonus tracks: a couple of songs cut around this time that only appeared on the obscure *Transatlantic LP Box Of Love: The Bert Jansch Sampler Volume 2* in 1972, and the two vocal tracks from Jansch's mostly instrumental 1966 album with John Renbourn, Bert And John. *—Richie Unterberger*

Jack Orion / 1966 / Vanguard ✦✦✦
After presenting almost all-original sets on his first two albums (albeit originals that sometimes borrowed heavily from traditional folk themes), Jansch opted to devote all of his third LP to traditional folk numbers. His future Pentangle partner John Renbourn joins him on four of the eight songs. Highlights include the ten-minute title track (whose length was a real oddity on contemporary folk albums of the time) and a cover of "Nottamun Town" (whose melody Dylan lifted for "Masters of War"). Not as original as the artist's first two LPs, the guitar and vocal work on these adaptations were still as influential to the '60s folk world as anything else in Jansch's catalog. *—Richie Unterberger*

Nicola / 1967 / Demon ✦✦✦

Birthday Blues / 1969 / Demon ✦✦✦✦✦
It's no accident that Jansch's 1969 album sounds like a modified version of the Pentangle. He was a member of the great British folk-rock group at the time of this album's release, which was produced by Shel Talmy (who also worked with the Pentangle). And he's backed by the group's sterling rhythm section of Danny Thompson (bass) and Terry Cox (drums), with oc-

casional touches of harmonica (played by British blues singer Duffy Power), alto sax, and flute. The effect is akin to hearing an unbalanced Pentangle, with no John Renbourn on dueling guitar or Jacqui McShee on vocals. That's not at all a bad thing—Jansch was one of the group's main motors, and can still be a compelling writer and performer on his own. All of the cuts on this LP are originals, showing the artist leaning a little more toward bluesy styles than usual, though the mood is predominantly British folk. It's a pleasant effort, but not his best work, either as a solo performer or within a group context. *Birthday Blues* and Jansch's 1967 release *Nicola* have been combined onto one CD on a 1993 reissue. *—Richie Unterberger*

Rosemary Lane / 1971 / Reprise ✦✦✦

The Best of Bert Jansch / 1980 / Shanachie ✦✦✦✦✦

Thirteen Down / 1980 / Kicking Mule ✦✦✦✦

Young Man Blues: Live in Glasgow 1962-1964 / Dec. 15, 1998 / Big Beat ✦✦✦
Taken from tapes recorded on non-professional equipment at three separate concerts in 1962, 1963, and 1964, this important archival release gives us a good idea of how Jansch sounded prior to his official recording debut (which was released in 1965). The surprise, perhaps, is that Jansch already sounds much like he would when he began recording professionally in the mid-1960s. His folk-blues guitar is already excellent, and his vocals confident. The 30 songs include seven numbers that would appear on his debut LP, as well as several that would show up on other Jansch recordings; there's even a version of "Train Song," the show-stopping track on Pentangle's *Basket of Light* album. More obscure selections include Davey Graham's "Angi," "Something's Coming" (from *West Side Story*), Jackson Frank's "Blues Run the Game," several blues on which Jansch keeps time with a stomping foot, and interesting Jansch originals like "One Day Old" and the instrumental "Joint Control." The sound isn't great, but it's listenable, and with 74 minutes of music and extensive historical liner notes, the packaging is excellent. *—Richie Unterberger*

• **The Gardener: Essential 1965-1971** / Transatlantic ✦✦✦✦✦

Victor Jara

d. Sep. 14, 1973
Vocals / Chilean Folk, Contemporary Folk, Latin Folk, Political Folk, Singer/Songwriter
Singer and activist Victor Jara grew up in severe poverty in rural Chile, and by the age of six or seven, he was already accompanying his father to work in the fields. Throughout his rough adolescence, Jara struggled through school, attempted to enter the priesthood, joined the Chilean Army, and studied theater. A turning point in his musical career came when he met Violeta Parra, a traditional folk singer and artist and the owner of a small cafe in Santiago. Taken under Parra's wing, Jara began to sing in the cafe, and, in 1966, released his debut self-titled album. From the beginning, Jara used his songwriting skills to supply a voice for Chile's working class and peasantry. Under the leadership of Dr. Salvador Allende (Chile's Socialist president), the Popular Unity Coalition planned to strengthen educational support, increase low-income housing and furnish free socialized medical care. Jara's dreams began to crumble, on September 11, 1973, when a military junta overthrew Allende and launched a brutal coup. Arrested in the aftermath, Jara was one of many political prisoners sent to the National Football Stadium where many were tortured, beaten and executed. Although his hands were broken, or as many have claimed, amputated, Jara continued to sing a song supporting the ousted Popular Unity Party. After receiving many brutal blows, Jara stopped singing only when a machine gun fired by a military officer took his life. In the decades since, Jara's songs and spirit have been celebrated by numerous politically-minded folksingers including Pete Seeger and Tom Paxton. Arlo Guthrie recorded the ballad "Victor Jara" on his album, *Amigo*. *—Craig Harris*

• **Unfinished Song** / 1990 / Redwood ✦✦✦✦✦
Jara's expressive, vibrant singing shows why he was the leading light of the South American New Song movement as well as a significant political figure. This compilation includes not only original political songs but also traditional Chilean folksongs and even an adaptation of Malvina Reynolds's "Little Boxes." The album's 23 tracks, taken from various sources, provide a thorough view of Jara's broad talent. (Also recommended: Monitor Records' four-volume series of Jara recordings.) *—William Ruhlmann*

Victor Jara Complete / Mar. 31, 1998 / Pläne ✦✦✦✦✦

Michael Jerling

Vocals, Guitar / Contemporary Folk
Acoustic guitarist, singer, and songwriter Michael Jerling plays an artful mix of blues, traditional and contemporary folk songs, jazz-flavored folk and country-folk. Unlike many other dyed-in-the-wool folkies, Jerling considers blues and early rock & roll to be forms of folk music. Also unlike so many other folk singers, Jerling also admits that the musical approach of a solo singer-songwriter with a guitar bores him. Jerling takes his guitar playing and singing cues from musicians as diverse as Robert Johnson, Hank Williams and Chuck Berry. After he moved from Illinois to New York City, he quickly established himself in the early 1980s folk/coffeehouse scene in Greenwich Village and was part of the "Fast Folk" folk music cooperative. After being part of the "New Voices, New Visions" folk music tour in 1992, he won the "New Folk" songwriting competition at Kerrville Folk Festival in Texas, joining an elite crop of singer-songwriters who have won that award in the past (Nanci Griffith, Shawn Colvin, and Lyle Lovett). Jerling's Shanachie releases showcase his exceptional talents as a guitarist and his mastery of a number of indigenous musical forms, including blues. *—Richard Skelly*

• **My Evil Twin** / 1992 / Shanachie ✦✦✦✦
Jerling has a way with words that can paint a picture in your mind's eye. "Take Me to Juarez" is a classic tale; also worthwhile are "Breakdown," and the title cut. "Before the Country Moved to Town" features Robin And Linda Williams singing nice background vocals. All in all, this is a good label-debut album, with great songs and great production. *—Chip Renner*

New Suit of Clothes / 1994 / Shanachie ✦✦✦
This collection has more bluesy-based ballads than Jerling's previous CD. The playing, including guest appearances by John Sebastian and Peter Ostroushko, is clean and unobtrusive allowing Jerling's warm baritone to serve his sophisticated lyrics well. *—Richard Meyer*

Flaco Jimenez

b. Mar. 11, 1939, San Antonio, TX
Vocals, Accordion / Tejano, Norteño, Conjunto, Tex-Mex
Flaco Jimenez is the best known of the talented Jimenez family of Tex-Mex accordionists. He has always been popular in the border region, and came to the attention of the wider pop-music-buying public with the help of roots-music enthusiast Ry Cooder. Since then Jimenez has toured internationally, made guest appearances on a number of recordings, teamed up with Doug Sahm and Freddy Fender in The Texas Tornados, and continued to record on small labels for the Texas Norteno community. *—Myles Boisen*

Flaco Jimenez & His Conjunto / 1978 / Arhoolie ✦✦✦

Ay Te Dejo en San Antonio y Mas! / 1986 / Arhoolie ✦✦✦✦✦

Arriba El Norte / 1988 / Rounder ✦✦✦✦
Another in a series of Rounder anthologies featuring Flaco Jimenez. These were all done for the DBL label in San Antonio, and are short, predominantly polka and ranchero tunes. They're mostly rousing, celebratory party songs, sung with passion and played exuberantly by Jimenez. Unlike some other performers, Jimenez's approach and appeal are quite insular; he doesn't attempt to do anything flamboyant, unusual or non-traditional, opting to sing and play the material in vintage conjunto style. As a result, while it's often quite delightful, the differences in song structure over the 14 numbers will seem minimal to those who aren't fans of the idiom. *—Ron Wynn*

Flaco's Amigos / 1988 / Arhoolie ✦✦✦

Entre Humo Y Botellas / 1989 / Rounder ✦✦✦

San Antonio Soul / 1991 / Rounder ✦✦✦
Flaco Jimenez has recorded dozens of conjunto songs and albums and done material for both the American and Latino markets. This 14-cut Rounder anthology featured material recorded for the Mexican-American audience, and includes tunes that address such issues as immigration and the lifestyle of the border community. There are three rollicking instrumentals that showcase Jimenez's ability and flashy style on accordion. Other songs include romantic fare and traditional polkas and rancheros. His vocals and instrumental abilities are quite impressive, and provide solid examples of classic ethnic music seldom heard outside its target area. *—Ron Wynn*

Partners / 1992 / Warner Brothers ✦✦✦

Un Mojado Sin Licencia / 1993 / Arhoolie ✦✦✦✦✦

Flaco's First! / 1995 / Arhoolie ✦✦✦✦✦

• **The Best of Flaco Jimenez** / 1999 / Arhoolie ✦✦✦✦✦
Drawn from his Arhoolie recordings (there is also a live recording from the soundtrack of the Chulas Fronteras documentary), this is a satisfactory 16-track compilation with tracks spanning the '50s to the '80s, although, unfortunately, exact dates are not given in the liner notes. The different sources for the material allow for a greater range of sounds than is frequently heard on conjunto records. Although Flaco sings throughout, he also duets with Fred Ojeda, Toby Torres and Henry Zimmerle. Purists may frown on the inclusion of an instrumental, "Poquita Fe," with slide guitar by high-profile guest Ry Cooder, but frankly, for those who don't specialize in conjunto, it makes for a nice change of pace. Another Anglo, Peter Rowan, takes a guest vocal on his composition, "The Free Mexican Airforce." *—Richie Unterberger*

Sleepytown / Aug. 29, 2000 / Narada ✦✦✦
Flaco Jimenez once again shows off his classic Texas style in *Sleepytown*. His rollicking band is a great backup for his catchy songs that feature performances from great musicians like Dwight Yoakam, Doug Sahm, and Buck Owens. The latter is featured on a cover of the Beatles' "Love Me Do," which is only one of this album's gems. Steeped in fun throughout, this album will remind fans why they love Jimenez. *—Stacia Proefrock*

Nic Jones

Vocals, Violin, Guitar / Contemporary Folk, British Folk, Singer/Songwriter
Singer Nic Jones was among the most acclaimed artists to emerge from the British folk revival, winning praise for his moving vocals as well as his prowess on guitar and fiddle. Greatly influenced by Martin Carthy, whose percussive guitar style Jones adopted for his own, he first surfaced during the late 1960s as a member of the group the Halliard, mounting a solo career in 1970 with his debut album *Ballads and Songs*. A collection of traditional tunes distinguished by Jones' outstanding instrumental work, the record also established his mastery of the long ballad; a self-titled effort followed in 1971, but was his last album for six years—the follow-up, *Noah's Ark Trap* finally appeared in 1977, with *From the Devil a Stranger* appearing a year later. Around that same time Jones also joined the short-lived group Bandoggs, releasing an eponymous LP in 1978; other projects included appearances on albums from artists including Richard Thompson and June Tabor. 1980's *Penguin Eggs*—named "Folk Album of the Year" by *Melody Maker*—was his final new recording; in 1982 he was critically injured in an auto accident and forced to retire from performing. *In Search of Nic Jones*—a compilation of archival material including home recordings and BBC sessions—was released in 1998. A year later, singer/songwriter John Wesley Harding issued *Trad Arr Jones*, a collection of traditional folk numbers directly inspired by Jones' arrangements. *—Jason Ankeny*

Ballads and Songs / 1970 / Trailer ✦✦✦✦
This debut album established him as one of the best. *—Steve Winick*

Nic Jones / 1971 / Trailer ✦✦✦

The Noah's Ark Trap / 1977 / Shanachie ♦♦♦
A few guests join him to fill out the arrangements. *—Steve Winick*

● **Penguin Eggs** / 1980 / Shanachie ♦♦♦♦♦
Even better than *The Noah's Ark Trap,* many critics consider this his best. *—Steve Winick*

Lucy Kaplansky

b. Feb. 2, 1960
Vocals / Alternative Folk, Contemporary Folk
When Lucy Kaplansky was 18 years old, she shocked her neighbors in the Hyde Park area near the University of Chicago when, instead of going to college, she went to New York City with her boyfriend to become a folk singer. Fifteen years later, having become a clinical psychologist as well as a sought-after duet and harmony singer, she made another surprising decision: she gave up her private practice and her position at a New York hospital to pursue a full-time singing career.

Drawn to Greenwich Village in the late 1970s by the resurgence of the folk scene, she became a regular at Gerde's Folk City. By 1982, she was a member of the CooP (later Fast Folk) and was featured on nine of the group's "musical magazines," along with Suzanne Vega, Shawn Colvin, John Gorka, Richard Shindell, and others. By 1983, however, Kaplansky had enrolled in New York University with the aim of becoming a psychologist. Well known on the folk scene for her crystalline harmonies, Kaplansky sang harmony vocals on Nanci Griffith's *Lone Star State of Mind* and *Little Love Affairs* albums and performed in New York clubs as a duo with Colvin while earning her Ph.D. from Yeshiva University. But when she and Colvin attracted attention from record companies, Kaplansky declined, becoming a staff psychologist at a New York hospital and establishing a private practice while Colvin recorded her first three albums for Columbia Records.

As a record of what Lucy had accomplished on the folk scene, and to give Colvin a chance to try her hand at production, the two collaborated on Kaplansky's first album, *The Tide,* comprising three of Kaplansky's own compositions and a collection of well-worn covers, including songs by Richard Thompson, Sting, and Robin Batteau. By 1994, when *The Tide* was released by Red House Records, Kaplansky decided to shift gears again and become a full-time touring folk singer. She spent much of the next few years playing the folk circuit of coffeehouses, church halls, and festivals, accompanying herself on guitar, and performing in concert with Shindell and Gorka. In 1996, Red House Records released her second album, *Flesh and Bone,* produced by Anton Sanko (Vega's *Solitude Standing* and *Days of Open Hand*). It includes eight original songs (co-written with Kaplansky's husband, filmmaker Richard Litvin), as well as duets with Shindell and Gorka. *Ten Year Night* followed in 1999. *—Claire Keaveney*

Tide / 1994 / Red House ♦♦♦
After over a decade off and on, Lucy Kaplansky, one of the primary support singer and interpreters of New York's Greenwich Village scene, has released her debut album. It contains three of her own songs and other classics from contemporary songwriters. Highlights are Tom Russell/Greg Trooper's "The Heart," and Bill Morrissey's "Texas Blues," and Robin Batteau's "Guinevere." She also makes classics her own with Sting's "Secret Journey" and Richard Thompson's "When I Get to the Border." Produced by Shawn Colvin, this is a warm, relaxed-sounding set that allows Kaplansky's individual and great singing to cut through. Kaplansky is a terrific interpreter blessed with a great voice, unlike anyone else. *—Richard Meyer*

● **Flesh and Bone** / Oct. 15, 1996 / Red House ♦♦♦♦
Produced by Anton Sanko, Lucy Kaplansky's second album showcases her songwriting, with strong ballads such as "If You Could See" and "Still Life," a moving character sketch that has been the centerpiece of her live performances. Her unique voice, steely and supple, moves easily from irony to aching sincerity, a feat not often accomplished since the early recordings of Judy Collins. Other highlights are a rollicking bluegrass version of Nick Lowe's "(What's So Funny 'Bout) Peace, Love and Understanding" and a duet with John Gorka on Gram Parsons' legendary "Return of the Grievous Angel." Reverse before the first track for a hidden version of the Beatles' "I've Just Seen a Face." *—Claire Keaveney*

Ten Year Night / Mar. 23, 1999 / Red House ♦♦♦

Robert Earl Keen, Jr.

Vocals, Guitar / Americana, Contemporary Folk, Alternative Country, Country-Folk, Singer/Songwriter, Progressive Country
Singer/songwriter Robert Earl Keen, a native of Bandera, Texas, began playing the guitar as a diversion from journalism classes at Texas AM. To fend off boredom, he and neighbor Lyle Lovett jammed together and, on Sunday mornings, serenaded churchgoers across the street from Keen's house sitting on the front porch in their underwear. As Keen's songwriting talent blossomed and he began to make a name for himself in Austin, Lovett recorded one of his songs, as did Nanci Griffith, Joe Ely, and Kelly Willis. This provided a springboard for a solo career, which culminated with the simultaneous release of his fifth and most accomplished album, 1994's *Gringo Honeymoon,* and the birth of his daughter. His sixth album, *Number 2 Live Dinner,* was released in March of 1996; *Picnic* followed the next year, and in 1998 Keen returned with *Walking Distance.* *—Steve Huey*

No. 2 Live Dinner / Mar. 19, 1996 / Sugar Hill ♦♦♦
Robert Earl Keen Jr. is a Texan who did not take the express lane to the radio airwaves. Instead, he spent more than a decade seasoning his talent while entertaining folks in the—yep, you guessed it—friendly honky tonks of Texas, where music fans tend to like individualists with plenty of personality. *No. 2 Live Dinner* finished off a consistently powerful string of albums recorded for Sugar Hill Records. Taped in front of rowdy, beer-swilling crowds in two Texas towns, Keen bears his good-natured raspiness into songs of desperation, danger and raucous humor. A contemporary of Steve Earle, Lyle Lovett and Nanci Griffith, Keen's work has been as consistent and occasionally as strong as that of his friends. It's taken him longer to gain a national profile, but it's coming at a deserving time. For those unfamiliar with him, this live album will convey how well he's loved in his home state. Listen closely, and the songs will explain why, too. *—Michael McCall*

● **No Kinda Dancer** / 1984 / Sugar Hill ♦♦♦♦♦
A well-crafted debut, not one bad song. "Armadillo Jackal & This Old Porch," co-written by Lyle Lovett, features Lovett and Nanci Griffith singing harmony. *—Chip Renner*

The Live Album / 1988 / Sugar Hill ♦♦♦♦♦
Good sound, new material, good stories, plus audience interaction make this worthwhile. Featuring great mandolin and fiddle by Johnathan Yudkin and a nice cut of "I Would Change My Life." *—Chip Renner*

West Textures / 1989 / Sugar Hill ♦♦♦

A Bigger Piece of Sky / 1993 / Sugar Hill ♦♦♦
This album contains the radio hit "Tangled up in Blue," asound-alike song "Jesse with the Long Hair," as well as more of Keen's rough and tumble story-songs. *—Richard Meyer*

Gringo Honeymoon / 1994 / Sugar Hill ♦♦♦

Picnic / Apr. 29, 1997 / Arista ♦♦♦♦

Walking Distance / Oct. 27, 1998 / Arista ♦♦♦♦
Sometimes a disc comes along without any expectations and hits one right out of the ballpark. Such is the case with Robert Earl Keen's *Walking Distance.* Although much less of an alt-country affair than his earlier work, *Walking Distance* comes across warm and friendly. Keen's humor crops up on "That Bucking Song," which he says is all about riding a horse, while "Down That Dusty Trail" is full of childhood memories. "Feelin' Good Again" shows that for all the bad times, it is the good times that make us feel, and then some. Perhaps that's the message that Keen is trying to convey this time out, and if it is, then sit back and feel good about feeling good. We get the next installment of Keen's twisted take on an original Christmas song in "Happy Holidays, Y'all." Once you hear it, you won't be able to help yourself from singing along to a tale that nearly everyone who's spent the holidays with the family can identify with. No matter what, Keen's *Walking Distance* is just around the next bend from wherever you might be. *—James Chrispell*

Jennifer Kimball

Vocals (Background), Vocals / Contemporary Singer/Songwriter, Contemporary Folk
Singer/songwriter Jennifer Kimball first emerged during the early 1980s as one half of the Story, a folk-pop duo she co-founded with Jonatha Brooke while both were students at Boston's Amherst College. Signed to Elektra in 1991, the Story issued a pair of major label LPs, *Grace in Gravity* and *Angel in the House,* before disbanding in 1993; Kimball then continued on as a solo performer, issuing her debut *Veering from the Wave* in mid-1998. *—Jason Ankeny*

Veering from the Wave / Aug. 18, 1998 / Imaginary Road ♦♦♦
Although it suffers from uneven material, Jennifer Kimball's *Veering from the Wave* is an engaging debut that suggests she is an adult contemporary vocalist of considerable potential. The best moments on the album are elegant, almost soulful, thanks to her rich vocals, which can even make the weaker moments palatable. Overall, only a handful of tunes are memorable, but Kimball's talents leave a lasting impression. One to watch. *—Rodney Batdorf*

Kingston Trio

f. 1956, Palo Alto, CA, **db.** 1967
Group / Folk Revival, Folk-Pop, Traditional Folk
In the history of popular music, there are a handful of performers who have redefined the content of the music at critical points in history: Blind Lemon Jefferson, Benny Goodman and his orchestra, the Beatles, Bob Dylan, Led Zeppelin—people whose music left the landscape, and definition of popular music, altered completely with its arrival. The Kingston Trio were one such group, transforming folk music into a hot commodity and creating a demand—where none had existed before—for young men (sometimes with women) strumming acoustic guitars and banjos and singing folksongs and folk-like novelty songs in harmony, of which the Trio themselves were the defining ensemble for the next five years. On a purely commercial level, from 1957 until 1963, the Kingston Trio were the most vital and popular folk group in the world. Their record was incontestable, one of the most popular acts in the history of Capitol Records and the American record industry, making them the most popular folk group in history, surpassing the Weavers' earlier success. Equally important, the trio—Dave Guard, Nick Reynolds, and Bob Shane—made folk music immensely popular among many millions of listeners who previously had ignored it. The group's success transcended their actual sales. Without the enviable record of popularity and sales, it is unlikely that Columbia Records would ever have had any impetus to sign an unknown singer/guitarist named Bob Dylan, or to put Weavers co-founder Pete Seeger under contract; for Warner Bros. to record the Greenwich Village-based trio Peter, Paul and Mary; or Vanguard Records to do as many albums as they actually ended up recording with the reformed Weavers in the late '50s and early '60s. *—Bruce Eder*

The Kingston Trio / 1958 / Capitol ♦♦♦
It's easy to rate the group's debut album too low, since its two best-known songs ("Tom Dooley," "Scotch and Soda") have had no shortage of appearances elsewhere in the decades since, and the group went on to cut more than 20 additional albums in their prime years. A little less polished and accomplished than, say, the music that Terry Gilkyson and the Easy Riders were cutting at Columbia around this time, it makes up for those shortcomings with youthful spring, exuberance, freshness, and a number of song choices that spoke of a new generation of folk singing —- not only their hits but the first version of the comedic piece "Coplas" and "Sloop John B," which would become a rock standard in the hands of the trio's fellow stripe-shirted labelmates the Beach Boys. Dave Guard was the most influential member of the group here, in terms of song selections and arrangements, but the entire trio is well represented. Additionally, producer Voyle Gilmore made their singing on "Bay of Mexico" and "Fast Freight" into something slightly larger than life. "Sara Jane," which the group learned

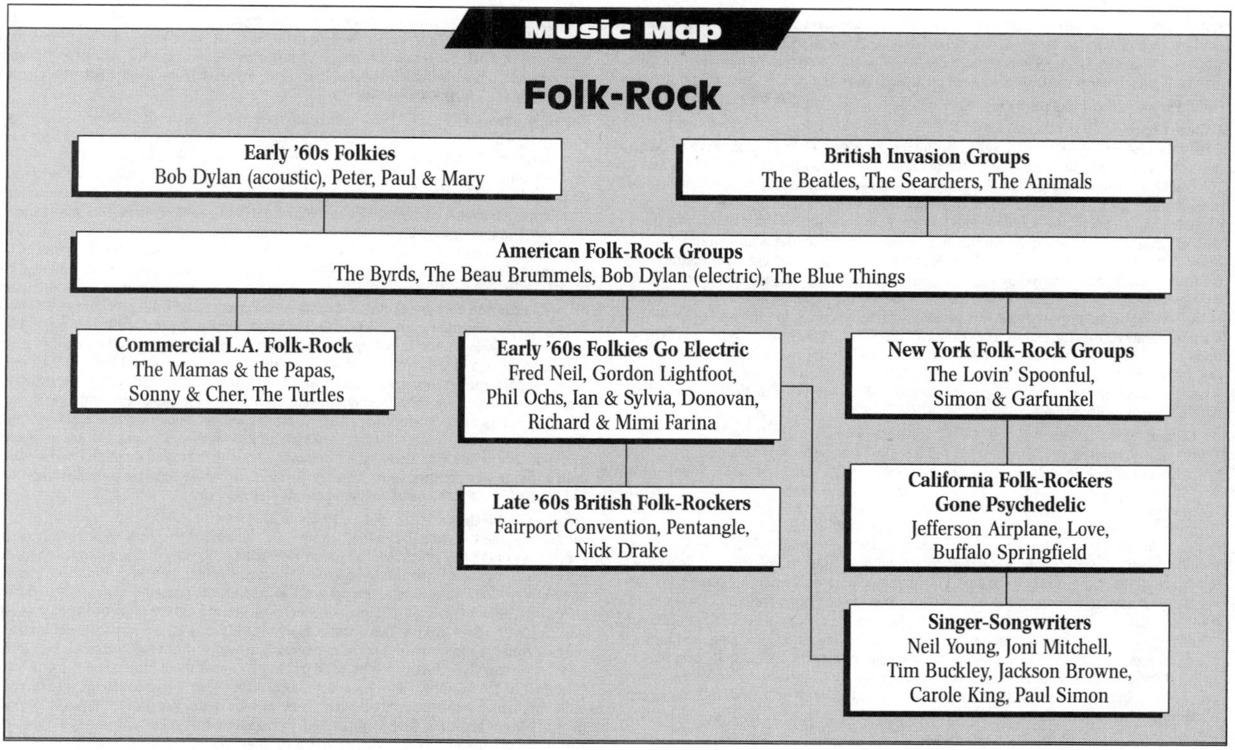

from Louis Gottlieb of the Gateway Singers and, later, the Limeliters, who also arranged it, isn't far behind, a potential hit single in the same league with "Wimoweh." Listening to this album, one also gets a sense of just how strong the trio was musically right out of the starting gate—*The Kingston Trio* was essentially an idealized version of the group's stage show of the era, recorded over three days in the studio, and a fine, bracing body of music. *—Bruce Eder*

Here We Go Again! / 1959 / Capitol ♦♦♦♦
Released in 1959, *Here We Go Again!* would be the last time the original Kingston Trio lineup (Bob Shane, Dave Guard, and Nick Reynolds) would have a hit single. The traditional chain gang tune "A Worried Man" made the Top 20, driving sales of the album to over 900,000 copies and perching the group on the number one chart position for eight weeks. By December of that year, the Kingston Trio would have four albums in the *Billboard* Top Ten. Spirited versions of "Haul Away" and "Molly Dee," as well as the gospel-ish "Round About the Mountain" are standout tracks among the 13 included. "The Unfortunate Miss Bailey" (which brings to mind the Clancey Brothers) and the stark "San Miguel" help make *Here We Go Again* a very well-rounded album. *—Matt Fink*

The Kingston Trio at Large / 1959 / Capitol ♦♦♦
The Kingston Trio's first stereo album was also the first LP on which they adopted the more sophisticated recording techniques that would characterize their subsequent records, including multiple overdubs and separate recordings of the different players of vocals and instrumentation. It shows in the far more complex sound achieved by the trio throughout this album, with voices and instruments more closely interwoven than on their earlier studio recordings and achieving control over their volume that, even today, seems astonishing. The group also sounds very energized here, whether doing Calypso-style numbers like Bob Shane's "I Bawled," soaring bluegrass-style harmony numbers such as "Corey, Corey," or the gossamer-textured "All My Sorrows." The hits "M.T.A." and "Scarlet Ribbons" helped propel *Kingston Trio at Large* to the number one LP spot, but it was the rest of the album—including "Early in the Mornin'" (a skillful adaptation of the song best known to most of us by its opening line, "What do you do with a drunken sailor") and "The Seine," which anticipates the later trio's classic "Take Her Out of Pity"—that helped keep it at the top spot for 15 weeks, an amazing feat for a folk album. Dave Guard's banjo playing, in particular, shines throughout this album, and it was beginning here that Guard was to exert a separate influence on a whole generation of aspiring folk musicians and even one rock star (Lindsay Buckingham) with his banjo. *—Bruce Eder*

Sold Out / 1960 / Capitol ♦♦♦
Though the packaging might seem to imply that this is a live album, the 12 tracks are definitely studio cuts—meaning that, as always, the very slick and studied Kingston Trio sound is intact. The majority of those songs are spirited and uptempo, such as the classic "El Matador" and the banjo-driven "Don't Cry Katie," though the collection does boast some fine balladry on "The Mountains O'Mourne" and "Raspberries, Strawberries," which is included in its second version, and is notable for its slower tempo and slightly different lyrics. Most of the tracks haven't turned up on too many compilations over the years, though nearly all of them can be found on the massive ten-CD *The Guard Years*. Overall, *Sold Out* is solid, pleasant listening, though not particularly challenging in any sense. *—Matt Fink*

String Along / 1960 / Capitol ♦♦♦♦♦
String Along has the most unusual sound of any Kingston Trio album, mostly by virtue of the crisp mixing and voicing of the instruments—guitars and banjo all appear in very high relief, matching the attention usually reserved for the voices on the Kingston Trio's records. The result is a somewhat quieter record, without much presence of the familiar unified group sound, as the individual members are relied upon more than the ensemble singing on many of the songs. One of the few exceptions is "Buddy Better Got On Down the Line," which has the sound that one associates with past trio recordings. But it's a true exception on an album that has other highlights such as oddities like the trio's surprisingly strong rendition of Ray Charles' "Leave My Woman Alone." Though no one could have realized it at the time, *String Along* was very close to the tail end of the original Kingston Trio's history—Dave Guard was losing interest in arguing over the direction of the group; and although their albums were still selling well and steadily, *String Along* (which hit number one) would yield the original group's last two charting singles. "Bad Man's Blunder," which also opens this album, became the original Kingston Trio's final Top 40 single; it was cut by the trio and issued as a single as a favor to composer Cisco Houston who was in the hospital and terminally ill. Other songs were done for more mundane reasons—according to Benjamin Blake, Jack Rubek, and Allan Shaw in their book *The Kingston Trio on Record*, the English folk-style "The Escape of Old John Webb" was featured on the album in the hope of helping to persuade EMI Records in England to promote the trio's albums more vigorously. *—Bruce Eder*

Close Up / 1961 / Capitol ♦♦♦♦♦
The Kingston Trio entered the '60s proper under seemingly less than ideal circumstances; founding member Dave Guard had announced his intention to leave the group early in the year, formally exiting in August, and not one single by the trio charted during all of 1961. They were hardly to be counted out, however, as demonstrated by the *Close Up* album, released just a month after Guard's exit. With new member John Stewart in place, the album showed the trio to be in solid musical shape, harmonizing beautifully, and with a new songwriting talent in their midst in the guise of Stewart, whose haunting, slightly bluesy ballad "When My Love Was Here" was the highlight of the record. *Close Up*, although not as groundbreaking as the trio's self-titled debut three years earlier, showed a surprisingly undiminished group and is a good representation of where popular folk music was in late 1961; the mix of traditional songs, well-known standards (most notably a rousing version of Woody Guthrie's "Reuben James"), gospel, humor, and pleasing folk-like originals was popular enough, rising to number three on the LP charts. The audience for folk music, especially among college students, was to shift dramatically, and into a more radical stance, in a couple of years, but this melodic and aesthetically pleasing album was perfect for its time and

still evokes that relatively innocent and calm period in our past. The group was also learning how to use stereo to great effect, even as an acoustic outfit; Nick Reynolds' percussion workout on "O Ken Karanga" was some of the best binaural stereo of this period in Capitol's history. It was reissued in 2000 and paired off with *College Concert.* —*Bruce Eder*

Goin' Places / 1961 / Capitol ♦♦♦

College Concert / 1962 / Capitol ♦♦♦♦♦
One of the best-selling LPs ever recorded by the Kingston Trio, *College Concert* is also the album by the trio that holds up best in the decades since—recorded on December 6 and 7, 1961, at UCLA, it contains several of their best-known songs, including "M.T.A.," in versions that are more spirited than their studio originals. There's also an unintentionally telling part of the trio's rap leading into "Chilly Winds," when someone says, "for those of you who think we steal songs..."—in fact, while on the tour ahead of the recording of this album, the trio heard Peter, Paul & Mary do a version of a Pete Seeger song called "Where Have All the Flowers Gone," which was parlayed by the Kingston Trio into a huge hit single. The presence of a live version of "Where Have All the Flowers Gone" on the album, which was released just as the studio version on the single was peaking, didn't hurt sales, but the overall quality of the performance, from the exquisitely arranged "500 Miles" to the rousing version of "Young Roddy M'Corley," was the album's most alluring overall feature. The only flaw that prevents this from getting an even higher rating is the thin-to-non-existent bass in the recording, which detracts from some of the impact of the music. It was reissued in 2000 and paired off with *Close-Up.* —*Bruce Eder*

An Evening with the Kingston Trio / 1962 / Folk Era ♦♦♦
There's no exact date or venue mentioned, but this 1962 concert recording, featuring the Nick Reynolds/Bob Shane/John Stewart version of the trio, is a lively account of the group's work. The 15 numbers here, including "Where Have All the Flowers Gone," "Tom Dooley," "Wimoweh," "Scotch and Soda," "Reuben James," "The Merry Minuet," "MTA," and "The Wagoner Lad," involve a lot of jokey asides (including a still-funny contemporary reference to Jack Paar during "MTA"), shouting, and mugging for the microphone that worked better visually. It's all in good fun, however, and the material is sung and played with lots of enthusiasm, which proves fairly infectious. This disc has more excitement than the trio's earlier Newport appearance, and a more interesting array of songs than Folk Era's Dave Guard-trio *Stereo Concert Plus* CD, though they aren't always quite as careful in their performance. "The Wagoner Lad" is the highlight of the concert: a low-key, exquisitely sung and harmonized number that ought to be a part of any collection of the trio. It's fascinating to realize, as this disc demonstrates, that the group was doing Woody Guthrie and Pete Seeger songs, yet ended up being regarded as too conservative and out of touch by serious folk audiences, who seemed to resent the trio's popularity. —*Bruce Eder*

The Kingston Trio #16 / 1963 / Capitol ♦♦♦

New Frontier / 1963 / Capitol ♦♦♦

Sunny Side! / 1963 / Capitol ♦♦

Time to Think / 1963 / Capitol ♦♦♦♦♦
The Kingston Trio got serious on this, their attempt to compete in the new era of topical folk songs. The opening track, "The Patriot Game," is a dead giveaway, introducing songs about the lot of coal miners ("Coal Tattoo"), the less fortunate among us ("Hobo's Lullaby"), Woody Guthrie's "Deportee," social justice ("Last Night I Had the Strangest Dream"), and the deceased John F. Kennedy ("Song For a Friend"). The group's sound works even in this setting, though their approaches to some of the songs do seem odd together—their twangy, upbeat version of Rod McKuen's "Seasons in the Sun" feels inappropriate next to more reflective versions (including the hit by Terry Jacks) that have appeared since. It was reissued on CD and paired off with *The New Frontier* in April of 2000. —*Bruce Eder*

The Kingston Trio (Nick-Bob-John) / 1965 / Folk Era ♦♦♦♦♦

Stay Awhile / 1965 / Folk Era ♦♦♦♦

Children in the Morning / 1966 / Decca ♦♦♦

★ **Capitol Collectors Series** / 1990 / Capitol ♦♦♦♦♦
The first serious compilation of the Kingston Trio's work is broader than any of the various "best of" albums that ever showed up on LP, although it also lacks some important tracks that were on those 12" discs ("Take Her Out of Pity" is especially missed). The Dave Guard era is especially well represented and at the time of this disc's release, the sound was better than anything heard from the group up to that time. However, the emphasis on singles—albeit all hits—limits the range of the music represented, and also creates an impression of the group that is somewhat skewed from most fans' memories. After 1960, the Kingston Trio was one of the relatively few pop acts of the period (Frank Sinatra was another, curiously also on Capitol) who sold albums more easily than singles, and this became more true as the John Stewart years progressed. As a result, Kingston Trio fans (and one assumes that those are the people who would buy this collection) often took in the group's songs 12 at a time rather than one or two at a time. It's for that reason that the four-CD set *The Capitol Years* can be recommended more highly to those who really want to understand the group's appeal and music, or just to remember the stuff they heard back when. This disc is a good introduction to one side of the Kingston Trio's work, but it shouldn't be the last compilation that one buys on the group. —*Bruce Eder*

The Capitol Years / 1995 / Capitol ♦♦♦♦♦
A mammoth four-CD, 107-song box set of their most famous and commercially successful work, recorded for Capitol between the late 1950s and mid-'60s. All of the big hits are here, as well as key album cuts and a whopping 33 previously unreleased studio and live tracks. Collectors will appreciate the inclusion of rarities by related groups like Dave Guard and the Calypsonians (a pre-Kingston Trio outfit), Dave Guard and the Whiskeyhill Singers (Guard's *post*-Kingston outfit, also featuring Judy Henske), and the Cumberland Three (John Stewart's pre-Kingston group), as well as the awesomely detailed 48-page insert. But this is *way* too much for anyone but the fanatic. It's interesting to hear the Kingstons' now-obscure versions of songs that would become hits many years later by other artists, like "Sloop John B," "The First Time (Ever I Saw Your Face)," "Seasons in the Sun," "It Was a Very Good Year," and (most incredibly) "Let's Get Together." But for all its historical significance, the execution is usually far too sterile and whitebread to appeal to contemporary listeners, unless it's on purely nostalgic grounds. —*Richie Unterberger*

The Guard Years / Aug. 19, 1997 / Bear Family ♦♦♦♦♦
For anyone who thought the four-disc *The Capitol Years* was overkill, along comes Bear Family with this superb ten-CD set (with a 108-page hardcover book). The fact that nine of these ten discs contain material intended for release over a period of just four years is an indicator of the demand for their music—the Kingston Trio was the first popular act whose albums outsold their singles, and the result was 200 songs cut in just four years. That may be more Kingston Trio than most fans feel they need, but not more than can stand the test of listening. Running from early 1958 to early 1961, *The Guard Years* gives a fuller picture of the group's development than *The Capitol Years,* although the latter covers more territory. The trio's approach evolved from relatively unsophisticated enthusiasm into a close-knit ensemble, with exquisite harmonies and an overall sound constructed from careful layers of overdubs. With the advent of multi-track recording in late 1958 and early 1959, their sound blossoms, a phenomenon that is vividly presented on this set—the trio was the first folk group to take advantage of the recording studio's ability to capture vocal and instrumental proficiency, and their music became infinitely more sophisticated in the process. Showing off the range of their repertory, they draw on influences from blues to Broadway, with detours into the work of Ray Charles and Uncle Dave Macon, as well as Woody Guthrie and Lee Hayes. There are 17 previously unissued live tracks from 1958-59, spread among four dozen concert numbers concluding with their 1959 *Newport* show, with corrected dates and performance orders. The box is daunting in its scope, as is the book, whose separate song histories are a welcome addition to the usual sessionography. —*Bruce Eder*

The Best of the Decca Years / Jun. 2, 1998 / MCA ♦♦♦♦
By the time the Kingston Trio ended up on Decca in early 1964, they were already established stars of the folk music set. But as a commercial entity, they had arguably peaked, losing original member Dave Guard and replacing him with John Stewart. But the group soldiered on for four more studio albums and the best of it is collected here on this 16-track collection. Although painted as a quaint coffeehouse group from the hootenanny days of folk music's history, the Kingston Trio actually had pretty big ears for a wide variety of material, ranging from pop to obscure Broadway material, to songs from up-and-coming folk artists they had originally influenced. John Stewart clocks in with three originals ("Hit And Run," "Children of the Morning" and "Gonna Go Down the River"), and contributes to the only other original on here, the group-penned "Stay Awhile." With plenty of great tunes from the pens of Mason Williams, Rod McKuen and Tom Paxton, this collection shines a light on a part of the group's history usually ignored, and shows that much good music emerged during their final days. —*Cub Koda*

The Stewart Years / Apr. 25, 2000 / Bear Family ♦♦♦♦♦

John Kirkpatrick

Button Accordion, Anglo Concertina, Melodion, Vocals, Concertina, Accordion / British Folk
With a thorough understanding of folk traditions and a virtuosic mastery as an instrumentalist, John Kirkpatrick has risen to the top echelon of British folk music. A master of the button accordion, anglo concertina and melodeon, Kirkpatrick has balanced solo work, collaborations with ex-wife and hammer dulcimer/oboe player Sue Harris in the 1980s, and session work with a lengthy and diverse list of artists including Richard Thompson, Pere Ubu, Steeleye Span, Tarika Sammy, Gerry Rafferty, and Loudon Wainwright III. Kirkpatrick has combined time-honored folk music with modern sensabilities, and according to Richard Thompson, is "a traditional musician who is incredibly quick at understanding other genres and forms."

Kirkpatrick's interest in traditional music was sparked when he joined a morris team sponsored by a local Church youth group. Initially playing the melodeon, he moved to the button accordion within fifteen months. After building a solid reputation with semi-pro bands, he made his recording debut as a sideman for Tony Rose's 1970 album, *Young Hunting.* After recording his first solo album, *Jump At The Sun,* in 1972, he gained worldwide recognition in 1974; recording his first duo album with Sue Harris, *The Rose Of Britain's Isle* (named album of the year by *Folk Review*), and performing on Richard and Linda Thompson's *I Want To See The Bright Lights Tonight.* The years following have found Kirkpatrick performing as a touring member of Steeleye Span, in his own group Brass Monkey (which he founded with British guitar wiz Martin Carthy), as well as hosting a program on BBC radio, and leading the John Kirkpatrick Band. —*Craig Harris*

★ **Plain Capers: Morris Dance Tunes from the Cotswolds** / 1976 / Topic ♦♦♦♦♦
Focusing on Morris as practiced in the Cotswolds, John Kirkpatrick has here crafted an album of traditional Morris music without recourse to electrification (the ultimate curse of The Albion Band.) Energetic, entertaining and sometimes highly amusing, one of the best results of the 1970s Morris boom in the U.K. Martin Carthy is among the supporting cast. —*Steven McDonald*

Shreds and Patches / 1977 / Topic ♦♦♦

Going Spare / 1978 / Free Reed ♦♦♦♦♦
Of these all-original songs and tunes, some are weird and hilarious. —*Steve Winick*

Force of Habit / 1996 / Omnium ♦♦♦♦
Fans of traditional British dance music will get a huge kick out of this album. John Kirkpatrick is one of England's finest button accordion and concertina players, and the band that he leads on this collection of live tracks is also first-rate: it includes drummer Michael Gregory, guitarist Graeme Taylor (of the Albion Band), fiddler/recorder player Paul Burgess, and bassist Dave Berry. What's both surprising and impressive about this album, apart from the lively and virtuosic playing, is how many of these very traditional-sounding numbers are ac-

tually Kirkpatrick originals; "Pepper in the Brandy" and the 7/8 romp "The Seven Coloured Linnet," which open the program as a medley, are both his own, as are the songs "George's Son" (which Kirkpatrick sings capably if not beautifully) and the blues-based (!) "Blue Balloon." The traditional numbers are well chosen, too, and include an affecting rendition of "The Oakham Poachers" and the gently rollicking "Princess Royal." Highly recommended to fans of Fairport Convention, the Oyster Band, and the Albion Band. *—Rick Anderson*

"Spider" John Koerner

b. Aug. 31, 1938, Rochester, NY

Vocals, Harmonica, Guitar / Folk Revival, Folk-Blues, Acoustic Blues

Korner was a major force in the '60s folk community around Minneapolis. His Vanguard album *Running, Jumping, Standing Still,* recorded with Willie Murphy, was a seminal album of American folk and blues played by urban players. *—Richard Meyer*

• **Nobody Knows the Trouble I've Been** / 1970 / Red House ✦✦✦✦✦

Nobody Knows the Trouble I've Been contains classics from the American songbag like "Cotton Eyed Joe," "The Leatherwing Bat," "Froggy Went A-Courting" and "Shenandoah." Koerner sings and plays (12-string guitar) with a knowing but commanding casual authority that brings this material to life brilliantly. The music jumps out of the speaker so effortlessly you can appreciate the fun and dark side of these old songs. *Nobody Knows the Trouble I've Been* is an excellent example of contemporary interpretations that don't treat the songs like academic artifacts. "The Leatherwing Bat," for example, is a courting song that sounds cute and innocent in most interpretations. Koerner brings out, and seems to delight in, the licentious innuendo as each verse leads to the advice that for a girl to catch the boy she should keep him up both day and night. Blood, love and murder are at the heart of many songs so familiar that we have forgotten to even listen anymore while we sing along. A record like this is a wake-up call to all interpreters. The fact that it was impeccably recorded live to 2 track in one day with killer musicians only adds to its reputation. *—Richard Meyer*

Raised by Humans / 1992 / Red House ✦✦✦✦

Produced in the same style as *Troubles,* this includes some Koerner originals as well as driving jubilant versions of "The Titanic," and "The Fox and the Boll Weevil." *—Richard Meyer*

Stargeezer / May 21, 1996 / Red House ✦✦✦

Stargeezer is the standard brew of endearingly clever originals and energetic covers that fans have come to expect from Spider John Koerner. There aren't any standout songs, but the entire album has a relaxed, welcoming vibe that makes it quite a pleasant listen. *—Thom Owens*

Leo Kottke

b. Sep. 11, 1945, Athens, GA

Slide Guitar, Vocals, Guitar, Guitar (Acoustic) / Progressive Folk, Contemporary Folk

Raised in 12 different states, innovative acoustic-guitar virtuoso Leo Kottke absorbed a variety of musical influences as a child, flirting with both violin and trombone before trying his hand at the guitar. After developing a love for the country-blues of Mississippi John Hurt, Kottke became a fixture on the Twin Cities' folk club circuit and issued his debut LP *Twelve String Blues* in 1969. He earned a contract with Capitol for 1971's *Mudlark,* though the label positioned him in the singer/songwriter vein despite his wishes to remain an instrumental performer. Despite battles with label heads, Kottke flourished during his tenure on Capitol, branching out with guest musicians and unusual song covers drawing on folk, rock, jazz and bluegrass, all the while honing his propulsive finger-picking mastery. During the mid-'70s, he moved to Chrysalis and gained an international cult following thanks to his performances at folk festivals. After 1983's *Time Step,* Kottke's contract with Chrysalis ended, and he moved over to the independent Private Music label. After his powerful technique resulted in a lingering pain in his hands, Kottke was forced to shift his technique closer to classical guitar performance. Though he recorded six albums for Private Music between 1986 and 1991, his release schedule slowed significantly by the end of the decade. *—Jason Ankeny*

6 & 12 String Guitar / 1971 / Rhino ✦✦✦✦✦

Kottke's debut came about after he sent a cassette to John Fahey's Takoma label. Not surprisingly, it recalls Fahey's work in a number of respects: the synthesis of numerous influences from blues, pop, classical, and folk styles, the weirdly titled instrumentals, even the tongue-in-cheek liner notes. Kottke's brand of virtuosity, however, is more soothing and easy on the ear than Fahey's. It's far from sappy, though, the rich and resonant picking intimating some underlying restlessness, like peaceful open fields after a storm. Establishing much of the territory Kottke was to explore throughout his career, this release was also one of his most popular, eventually selling over 500,000 copies. *—Richie Unterberger*

My Feet Are Smiling / 1973 / One Way ✦✦✦✦✦

The prodigious technique, deadpan sense of humor, and infamous singing are all evident less than a minute into the opening tune. Performing solo and playing more slide guitar than usual, Kottke wows a supportive hometown audience in Minneapolis with some of the finest playing of his career. That's saying a lot. Sensational one moment and sentimental the next, he presents a varied, well-paced set that's worth adding to your collection if you can find it. The well-traveled "Louise" is only one highlight, although it's Leo's playing that will drop your jaw, not his singing. *—Mark Allan*

Ice Water / 1974 / One Way ✦✦✦

Kottke adds vocals, drums, bass, dobro, and steel guitar for a unique Kottke sound. *—Chip Renner*

Chewing Pine / 1975 / One Way ✦✦✦

Besides his eight originals, this unpredictable musician ranges far afield for his material. He plucks songs for this album from Procol Harum and Marty Robbins, as well as covering the lightweight country instrumental standard "Wheels." Although he made his reputation by playing solo, Kottke sounds fine here with a band. The piano especially helps to distract listeners from his earnest but flat singing. *—Mark Allan*

Burnt Lips / 1978 / BGO ✦✦✦

The subjects of death and betrayal permeate this understandably dark album. Opening with the Nick Lowe chestnut "Endless Sleep" as a slow acoustic blues, this unpredictable guitar un-star also sings about "Sonora's Death Row" and offers the opinion that "Everybody Lies." His always problematic singing assumes a prominent role, which might not be the best strategy. He showcases his string wizardry on "A Dull Thud" and several other instrumentals. *—Mark Allan*

Balance / 1979 / BGO ✦✦✦

Good guitar work, featuring "Embryonic Journey" and Buddy Holly's "Learning the Game." *—Chip Renner*

Guitar Music / 1981 / Chrysalis ✦✦✦

My Father's Face / 1989 / Private Music ✦✦✦

Funky songs and staccato picking make this a very good album. *—Mark A. Humphrey*

Great Big Boy / 1991 / Private Music ✦✦✦✦✦

Kottke sings on this record to good effect. Features Lyle Lovett and Margo Timmons. *—Chip Renner*

Peculiaroso / 1991 / Private Music ✦✦✦

In terms of musical mastery, few instruments deserve more attention and respect than the twelve-string guitar, and few masters of that instrument deserve that same attention and respect more than Leo Kottke. From his lyrics ("Room at the Top of the Stairs") to his playing ("Wonderland by Night"), this 1994 Private Music release, well produced by Rickie Lee Jones, is at turns humorous, haunting, and highly enjoyable. *—Jeff Crooke*

Standing in My Shoes / 1997 / Private Music ✦✦✦

Working with former Prince sideman David Z, Leo Kottke comes up with one of his most unusual records with *Standing in My Shoes.* David Z doesn't necessarily bring Kottke toward funk, but the spare rhythm section gives the guitarist a stronger sense of groove than ever before, and Kottke really shines in such a setting. His solos are loose and swinging, and even his trio of vocal numbers have a charming, carefree quality. *Standing in My Shoes* does bog down occasionally, particularly when the execution is more compelling than the material, but on the whole, it is one of his more fascinating records of the '90s. *—Stephen Thomas Erlewine*

• **Leo Kottke Anthology** / May 5, 1997 / Rhino ✦✦✦✦✦

Two-CD, 37-track retrospective of the first 15 years of Kottke's recording career, drawing from over a dozen albums recorded between 1969 and 1983. This has a higher proportion of Kottke's vocals than some might expect, which may mildly disappoint fans who value his guitar virtuosity more than any of his other attributes. It's still a good, well-chosen compilation, leaning most heavily on his first three albums from the late '60s and early '70s, although this comprises less than half the set. It's also a good representation of both his original material and his wide-ranging abilities as an interpreter, with a diverse assortment of covers from the Byrds, Beau Brummels, John Fahey, Paul Siebel, Jorma Kaukonen, Buddy Holly, Santo & Johnny, Tom T. Hall, and John McLaughlin. The liners include detailed comments on each track by Kottke himself. *—Richie Unterberger*

One Guitar, No Vocals / Jun. 29, 1999 / Private Music ✦✦✦

Leo Kottke has always been known primarily as a guitarist, yet it has been a number of years since he's released a solo guitar record, which is what makes *One Guitar, No Vocals* welcome. Kottke is at his most impressive at his most intimate, turning out alternately gentle and intense solo guitar pieces. No matter how complex the music is—and it is, at minimum, moderately complex—Kottke pulls it off with grace, making it all seem easy. And that's the curious thing about *One Guitar, No Vocals:* The music is calm enough to function as background music, yet it reveals much more when examined closely. Of course, that's the key to all of Kottke's best work, and while this album isn't as exciting or revelatory as his earliest records, it's still a joy to hear a master at the top of his form. *—Stephen Thomas Erlewine*

Jim Kweskin

b. Jul. 18, 1940, New England, MA

Vocals, Guitar / Jug Band, Folk Revival, Traditional Folk, Old-Timey

The fun side of folk music was explored by the Jim Kweskin Jug Band. During the five years they were together, the group successfully transformed the sounds of pre-World War II rural music into a springboard for their good-humored performances. Kweskin had been involved in the folk scene around Boston and Cambridge during the late '50s; after being invited to record for Vanguard in the early '60s, he hooked up with a band including Geoff Muldaur and began recording a series of well-received albums for the label. Later additions included fiddler/vocalist Maria D'Amato (better-known as Maria Muldaur after her marriage to Geoff) and banjoist Bill Keith. The Kweskin Jug Band continued to bring their unique style of folk music to a national audience until the early '70s, when, just at the brink of commercial success, Kweskin broke up the band. He continued to work as a soloist, forming the U & I Band in the mid-'80s. Geoff and Maria Muldaur recorded several memorable duo albums before their marriage dissolved in the 1970s. *—Craig Harris*

Side by Side / 1979 / Drive Archive ✦✦✦

Side By Side is an entertaining collection of ragtime songs from Jim Kweskin, finding the folk singer running through familiar songs by Benny Goodman, Johnny Mercer, the Sons of the Pioneers, Fats Waller and Somethin' Smith & the Redheads. There's an endearing sense of good humor to Kweskin's versions that makes the record a charming delight. *—Thom Owens*

• **Greatest Hits** / 1990 / Vanguard ✦✦✦✦✦

Washboards, kazoos, novelty songs, and general hilarity combine to make some of the most delightful, foolish music of the 60s. The jug-band craze was small and short-lived, but Kweskin and his band, which included Maria D'Amato, soon to marry bandmember Geoff Muldaur, were its premier act, and this double-disc set captures much of their whimsical style. *—William Ruhlmann*

Peter LaFarge

b. 1931, Fountain, Colorado, **d.** 1965
Vocals / Traditional Folk
To the uninitiated, he seems like little more than a footnote in the biography of Bob Dylan and the recordings of Johnny Cash, but during the early and middle 1960s, Peter La Farge occupied a special niche in contemporary folk music as the first politically aware Native American to attract serious attention. He was dead before the age of 34, but La Farge managed to make an a vital and unique contribution to the early-1960s folk revival. Finding his way to the folk music community in Greenwich Village, the young La Farge spent time with the likes of the young Bob Dylan, Ramblin' Jack Elliot, Dave Van Ronk, and veteran political minstrel Pete Seeger. He was unusual, as a Native American in the beat Mecca of lower Manhattan, and his songs were welcomed for the power of his words and his message. Additionally, he had a far more mature outlook on the decadence that surrounded him—at one point, according to some accounts, he was something of an unofficial guardian to the young Dylan, keeping him from finding his way into too much trouble, especially where drugs were concerned. He was signed to Columbia around the same time that Dylan was making his way as a sessionman on Carolyn Hester's albums, but his relationship with Columbia was short-lived, lasting for one commercially unsuccessful album. His performances in Greenwich Village, however, convinced Moses Asch, the founder of Folkways Records, that La Farge had something to offer, and he immediately offered to record the singer/songwriter. The result was a series of five albums recorded between 1962 and 1965 devoted to Native American themes. *—Bruce Eder*

As Long As the Grass Shall Grow / 1968 / Smithsonian/Folkways ✦✦✦✦✦
Surprisingly, this collection of songs about what we now call Native Americans does not include LaFarge's best-known song, "The Ballad of Ira Hayes." But the singer/songwriter, who was a Native American himself, still manages to turn in one of the most thorough and moving examinations of the sorry history of White deception and aggression ever recorded. He gives his songs a dramatic, near-spoken delivery, making the messages all the more convincing. *—William Ruhlmann*

● **On the Warpath/As Long As The Grass Shall Grow** / 1992 / Bear Family ✦✦✦✦✦
Peter La Farge's two best-realized albums, 26 songs with a final spoken invocation, on one CD. The best material here is from *On the Warpath*, La Farge's last album, including "The Ballad of Ira Hayes" and the chilling "Crimson Parson" (about Col. Chivington and the Sand Creek massacre), are most effective, but the material off of the other record, including the wider-ranging "Alaska" and "Tecumseh," is well worth hearing. La Farge's spare approach to his music can make these 26 songs somewhat difficult to take in one sitting, but it is a perspective on topical songwriting that few people presented and is worth hearing on that basis alone, to see what even some of the hardcore folkies found too rich for their blood. *—Bruce Eder*

Song of the Cowboys/Iron Mountain & Other Songs / 1992 / Bear Family ✦✦✦
These two albums, originally released by Folkways, fit well together as collections of cowboy songs and more personal songs of the West. Unfortunately, *Songs of the Cowboys*, which makes up the majority of the material here, isn't nearly as interesting as his two albums devoted to Native American-focused material, *As Long As the Grass Shall Grow* or *On the Warpath* (both issued together on a separate CD already). The familiarity of the songs (apart from notable exceptions like "Sirey Peaks") makes the stuff less "special," and his attempt to create an authentic sound runs into the reality that we are hearing it today—we'd never "hear" it the same way as audiences, say, around 1920, before the advent of attempts to make cowboys songs into popular music. La Farge makes no concessions to popular music in his singing, accompanied by nothing but his own guitar, and these could almost pass for authentic field recordings of the late 1920s. The *Iron Mountain* songs are much more personal (including the biographical title track) and are also more interesting, most notably due to the inclusion of songs such as the very funny "Marijuana Blues," as well as several other, similar numbers ("Snowbird Blues") that show off other sides of La Farge's playing and singing, and allow him to stretch out in ways unique to his recording career. *—Bruce Eder*

Patty Larkin

Vocals, Guitar / Contemporary Singer/Songwriter, Contemporary Folk
Boston-based folk artist Patty Larkin is a talented singer/songwriter and guitarist with a large New England following. She considers herself a musical adventurer and desires to write songs designed to invite audiences to share her journeys. She began recording in the mid-'80s for Philo Records and each successive album reflects her growth as an artist. Her compositions are known for their depth, sensuality and introspection. Proficient on acoustic, electric and slide guitar, her playing style has been compared to Bonnie Raitt's. Since 1991, Larkin has been recording acclaimed albums for HighStreet Records and though her strongest following remains in New England, she remains a favorite on folk circuits throughout the U.S. *—Sandra Brennan*

Step into the Light / 1985 / Philo ✦✦✦✦✦

I'm Fine / 1987 / Philo ✦✦✦✦✦

In the Square: Live / 1990 / Philo ✦✦✦

Tango / 1991 / High Street ✦✦✦✦
Most polished of her releases—backed by John Gorka and Darol Anger. Very mature. *—Chip Renner*

Angels Running / Sep. 14, 1993 / High Street ✦✦✦✦
As she churns out quality albums and engaging performances like clockwork, you have to wonder why Patty Larkin is one of the most overlooked, underrated singer/songwriters around. Perhaps she is destined to lead the "underground" folk movement alongside Ellis Paul, John Gorka, and Dar Williams, rather than break through to the masses à la Shawn Colvin. Either way, with 1993's *Angels Running*, Larkin continues the good fight, penning some fantastic tunes and delivering them with a fine blend of class and humor. In songs such as "Who Holds Your Hand" and "I Told Him That My Dog Wouldn't Run," she both questions and embraces faith, in whatever form it takes. The latter piece details an encounter with an old flame who has been distanced emotionally, physically, and spiritually. The character struggles with his demons by reading *the Bible* every day, searching for his salvation, having lost who he once was. With her added harmonies, Mary-Chapin Carpenter is the perfect grounding point in this poignant tale. It's the kind of song you'll listen to many times as you dig through the layers of emotion. Never to bog things down for too long, Larkin counteracts the sentimental stuff with her unfailing sense of humor in "Might As Well Dance" and her keen observations in "Pundits & Poets." If you have ever seen her perform live, you might remember her talent for impressions that has thusly been recorded in "Channeling Marlene," as in Dietrich. *Angels Running* is pure Patty Larkin from "Banish Misfortune/Open Hand," an instrumental showcase, to "Helen," a story lifted from New England's coastal heritage. Every ounce of this record reflects a piece of who she is. It didn't top any charts, but being a cult hero isn't necessarily a *bad* thing. *—Kelly McCartney*

Strangers World / 1995 / High Street ✦✦✦✦
Continuing her examination of the various aspects and structures of faith, Patty Larkin expands her realm somewhat on *Strangers World*. This time around she chooses to include family, friends, and lovers in her exploration of what and who is worthy enough to believe in. (Apparently, the train was, but Johnny wasn't.) Producer John Leventhal, presumably *not* a pyro, brings his signature sound and steady musical sidekicks to Larkin's world, creating a spacious, yet cozy atmosphere through which her material soars. Drummer Shawn Pelton and bassist Zev Katz provide a solid foundation, while guest vocalists Bruce Cockburn, Shawn Colvin, Jonatha Brooke, and Jennifer Kimball work their individual heavenly magic. The combined result is both haunting and delightful. As for the songs, Larkin is in fine form. "Johnny Was a Pyro," "Don't," "When the Heavens Light Up," "Mary Magdalene," "Open Arms (Don't Explain)"—just pick one and it will be great. Larkin is a cherished treasure to her fans and colleagues. *Strangers World* is a wonderful example of why. *—Kelly McCartney*

Perishable Fruit / Aug. 26, 1997 / High Street ✦✦✦

● **A Gogo: Live on Tour** / Sep. 28, 1999 / Vanguard ✦✦✦✦
After recording for Philo/Rounder and High Street, Patty Larkin moved to Vanguard with *A Gogo: Live on Tour*. Vanguard has been synonymous with folk since the 1950s, so it was a logical place for the Boston-based singer/songwriter. A collection of live performances from Larkin's 1997 tour of the U.S., *A Gogo* wasn't her first live album—Philo had put out *Live in the Square* in 1990. She favors an intimate, stripped-down setting on these acoustic-oriented performances, and that works to the folk-rocker's advantage on gems that range from "Do Not Disturb" and "Good Thing" to "The Book I'm Not Reading," "Tango," and the bluesy "Dear Diary." Because Larkin is such a strong storyteller, going the unplugged route was an excellent idea—the spare approach really makes her lyrics stand out, whether she's being humorous on "Wolf at the Door" or poignant on "Mary Magdalene" and the Bruce Springsteen-ish "Me and That Train." This excellent CD is easily recommended to both casual listeners and Larkin's diehard fans. *—Alex Henderson*

Regrooving the Dream / Jul. 25, 2000 / Vanguard ✦✦✦✦
Patty Larkin digs deep into her bag of influences for a barrier-bending collection of songs that are nonetheless rooted in acoustic traditions. Her rich, everywoman voice suits her evocative guitar style effortlessly as she matches mood to sound. The effect of mixing it up makes "Only One" convincingly spooky as it merges folk blues with whispery, Astrid Gilberto vocalizing; "Anyway the Main Thing Is" goes East with its winding vocal riff. But "Mink Coats" is the centerpiece: With its old-as-time rock chords and its image sharp lyrics, Larkin may have crafted her finest hour. Guitarists John Leventhal (Shawn Colvin) and Marc Shulman (Suzanne Vega, Jewel) color the basic multi-instrumental tracks that Larkin laid down with co-producer Bette Warner. Within folk boundaries, the instrumental bridges linking songs and adventurous guitar sounds might be tippling on the edge of experimentation, but that would be overstating the case of stylistic departure. The "new direction" won't upset anyone accustomed to Larkin's already mature and fluid song style. *—Denise Sullivan*

Sam Larner

b. 1878, **d.** 1965
Vocals / Sea Shanties, British Folk, Traditional Folk
Sam Larner was the living embodiment of the folk tradition. A herring fisherman from the age of twelve, he built an extremely huge repertoire of folk songs and sea chantys that he sang while asea. Larner's reputation as a folk singer spread until his tale was taken up by folksingers Ewan MacColl, Peggy Seeger and Charles Parker who used him as an inspiration for their radio ballad, "Singing The Fishing," in 1960. Broadcast by *the BBC*, the story of Larner's life and the songs he collected made him a folk hero in England. The radio ballad became the basis for two albums—*Now Is The Time For Fishing*, released in 1961 and reissued in 1994, and *Singing The Fishing*. An album of songs recorded by Larner between 1959 and 1960 was issued as *A Garland For Sam*. *—Craig Harris*

● **Now is the Time for Fishing** / 1961 / Topic ✦✦✦✦✦
This classic comes from perhaps the finest of all English source singers. Larner (1878-1965) was at sea much of his life, but his repertoire was extremely varied. These recordings from 1959 and 1960 are a wonderful mix of songs both famous and less known, with reminiscence, rhymes and sea lore (once a Folkways LP of the same title). *—John Storm Roberts, Original Music*

Christine Lavin

Vocals, Guitar / Contemporary Singer/Songwriter, Contemporary Folk
Christine Lavin emerged out of the crowded New York City songwriter scene of the '80s with a style that distinguished her from her peers. First, her songs were overwhelmingly concerned with contemporary romantic mores (that scary, uncertain world of "relationships," "commitments" and "biological clocks"). Second, while her takes on this subject could sometimes be sentimental or even maudlin, more often they were humorous. "If You Need Space,

Go to Utah" was the first track on her second recording, a 1983 EP called *Husbands and Wives.* (Her first album, 1982's *Absolutely Live,* was out of print until 2000, when it was reissued on CD.) In 1984, Lavin self-released her first full-length studio album, *Future Fossils,* which included both her serious and comic numbers, notably "Damaged Goods" (what people start to feel like after enough failed relationships) and "Don't Ever Call Your Sweetheart by His Name" (how difficult it is to remember people's names after enough failed relationships). In 1986, she signed to Rounder's Philo label, which issued *Beau Woes (And Other Problems of Modern Life), Another Manís Woman* (a 1987 reissue of *Husbands and Wives*), *Good Thing He Canít Read My Mind* (1988), *Attainable Love* (1990), *Compass* (1991), and *Live at the Cactus Café: What Was I Thinking?* (1993). She moved to Shanachie Records in 1995, releasing *Please Donít Make Me Too Happy* and *Shining My Flashlight on the Moon* (1997). Then she set up her own record company, named after her web site, christinelavin.com, and released *One Wild Night in Concert* (1998) and *Getting in Touch with My Inner Bitch* (2000) herself; that year, Rounder also released *The Bellevue Years* collection. Lavin has also made a particular point of promoting the work of her contemporaries, notably on such collections as *When October Goes,* and with 1991's *Buy Me, Bring Me, Take Me, Don't Mess My Hair!!! (Life According to Four Bitchin' Babes),* she launched the part-time group Four Bitchin' Babes. *—William Ruhlmann*

Future Fossils / 1984 / Philo ♦♦♦♦♦
A bright, wry, and earthy collection of her early songs. A great introduction. *—Bruce Eder*

● **Beau Woes (and Other Problems of Modern Life)** / 1986 / Philo ♦♦♦♦♦

Good Thing He Can't Read My Mind / 1988 / Philo ♦♦♦♦♦

Attainable Love / 1990 / Philo ♦♦♦

Buy Me, Bring Me, Take Me: Don't Mess My Hair!!! Life According to Four Bitchin' Babes / 1991 / Philo ♦♦♦♦♦
Buy Me, Bring Me, Take Me: Don't Mess My Hair is more than just a best-of sampler of four of the best contemporary folksinger/songwriters. This live album presents a cohesive group as well as soloists performing material that ranges in subject matter from romance to vacation troubles, and in mood from heartbreaking to sidesplitting. It will make you want to hear each of the singers on her own, but it will also make you hope they tour together more often. *—William Ruhlmann*

Compass / 1991 / Philo ♦♦♦
From Tracy Chapman, Sarah McLachlan and Michelle Shocked to Suzanne Vega and Shawn Colvin, most of the female singer/songwriters who emerged in the 1980s and 1990s favored an ultra-serious tone. But with Christine Lavin, you could generally count on getting a healthy dose of wit and humor. True to form, Lavin makes sure that her humorous outlook is what defines *Compass.* Lavin's take on male/female relationships isn't necessarily optimistic—tunes like "Blind Dating Fun" and "Rushcutter's Bay" don't paint a very rosy picture of relationships in the 1990s. But the songs manage to laugh just the same. "Prisoners of Their Hairdos" has at good laugh at the expense of people famous for their hair (including Crystal Gayle and Don King), while "You Think You've Got Problems" takes a pointed jab at chronic whiners, hypochondriacs and complainers who go out of their way to be miserable and make everyone around them miserable. One frequent complaint about Lavin is that she can be overly maudlin on occasion—and, to be sure, "Replaced" and "Until Now" are on the maudlin side. But the New York resident doesn't inundate us with such songs—so it's OK for her to include a few maudlin numbers on her albums as long as humor continues to be dominant. Lavin's fans will want this album. *—Alex Henderson*

Shining My Flashlight on the Moon / Feb. 18, 1997 / Shanachie ♦♦♦

One Wild Night in Concert / Sep. 1, 1998 / christinelavin.com ♦♦♦♦
After stints on Philo and Shanachie, Christine Lavin returned to making her own records with this, her second live album, recorded November 22, 1997, at *the Blue Moon Coffeehouse* on the campus of Illinois Wesleyan University in Bloomington. Though she had no idea the show would be recorded until she was introduced, Lavin made an excellent decision to issue the result. Her mixture of comic novelties and sentimental ballads is best heard before an audience, complete with her entertaining introductions. Possessed of the same bubbly insouciance that makes Rosie O'Donnell a successful talk show host, Lavin is immensely likable onstage, which helps put across the novelty songs that examine small domestic concerns—losing your glasses, trying to kill a bug—and intriguing fantasies such as being replaced by a clone ("They Look Alike, They Talk Alike…" and "National Apology Day"). The serious songs are useful as changes of pace, but are less impressive, the major exception here being the lengthy "The Wild Blue," a factual description of kamikaze pilots based on a documentary that is one of the best songs Lavin has ever written and should prove a breakthrough for her. *—William Ruhlmann*

Getting in Touch with My Inner Bitch / 2000 / christinelavin.com ♦♦♦
Getting in Touch With My Inner Bitch, is a live release, assembled from five different shows in the spring and summer of 1999. It's a mixture of half new and half old songs, and Lavin might have been better advised to wait until she had a whole new album's worth of new material, but the product demands of having your own label may have precluded that. The result, however, is that *Getting in Touch With My Inner Bitch* is something of a hodgepodge, none of its new songs really standing up to the best of the old. Only "Harrison Ford," which the singer herself describes as a four-minute song about a one-second encounter, sounds like a keeper; the title song is really a spoken word comedy routine with a musical chorus. The other side of the humor is sadness, explored in such songs as "Plateau," which describes an unhappy, long-term marriage, and "Adjust Your Dreams," in which people deal with disappointment. While she always includes such songs on her albums and in her shows, Lavin never seems to do more than sketch a serious scene and then move on to the next bit of comic shtick, which tends to render that material closer to bathos than pathos. *—William Ruhlmann*

The Bellvue Years / Jun. 13, 2000 / Rounder ♦♦♦♦
Lavin's lost EP *Husbands and Wives* and *Another Woman's Man* are compiled with previously unreleased live radio interviews and songs recorded at the sessions for what's essentially an '80s career retrospective (it was also a period when Lavin had a day job at New York's Bellevue Hospital and, thus, the title). You can't beat Lavin for sarcasm, humor, and heartbreak and it's all here, from the sharp "If You Need Space, Go to Utah" to the tearjerker "The Vacation of Their Lives." Lavin fingerpicks her way through the pure folk, but comedy (of the long lost Steve Goodman variety) may be her strong suite; the self-explanatory "Cold Pizza For Breakfast," the anti-nature "Camping," and the ode to marital aids "Artificial Means" are gut-busters. *—Denise Sullivan*

Leadbelly (Huddie William Ledbetter)

b. Jan. 20, 1888, Mooringsport, LA, **d.** Dec. 6, 1949, New York, NY
Vocals, Accordion, Piano, Guitar / Field Recordings, Folksongs, Folk Revival, Folk-Blues, Country Blues, Acoustic Blues

Leadbelly was the first blues musician to achieve fame among White audiences. For this reason alone, and more for the sheer novelty of his career as an ex-convict-turned-singer than for any recognition of his abilities, he was the first bluesman to be treated as a major media figure in the mainstream press. By the time Huddie Ledbetter was 14, he was known for his ability with the guitar and his way with a song; he later switched from the six-string to the 12-string guitar, a pivotal decision in the development of his own career. He was already performing songs of his own and adapting others during the 1890s, and his abilities in this area grew with his experience. He first picked up a song known as "Irene" sometime in the first decade of the 20th century and as "Goodnight, Irene" it became one of Leadbelly's best-known songs. While serving a prison term in 1933, he first met John Lomax, an ambitious researcher for the Library of Congress, who was traveling through the South with his son Alan, collecting blues and any other authentic American music that they could find. They found in Leadbelly a talent and a resource beyond anything they could have hoped for—the man was not only a gifted player who exuded a musical charisma that transcended the prison setting, but he was a veritable human jukebox, in the range of songs that he knew. Leadbelly dazzled the Lomaxes with his singing, playing, songwriting, and Lomax recognized in his new discovery a talent that was very different from the makers of the commercial "race" records of the period. Leadbelly's style and repertory were unaffected by the currents running through commercial blues and country music, but a talent that was worth trying to develop commercially, into a valid and successful brand of Black American folk music. Leadbelly's place in blues history is a peculiar one; unassailable as a source for much of the country-blues repertory as it has been passed down to us, and a major contributor to the folk music revival of the 1950s, but virtually non-existent in terms of his effect upon the commercial blues market in his own lifetime or since. *—Bruce Eder*

Congress Blues / 194 / Aldabra ♦♦♦♦♦
Congress Blues collects a batch of folk songs that Leadbelly recorded in the early '40s. There is wonderful music here, to be sure, but it is available on better collections from Folkways and Rounder. *—Thom Owens*

☆ **Library of Congress Recordings** / 1966 / Elektra ♦♦♦♦♦
These powerful performances date from 1939-43 when Ledbetter had moved to New York City after his years in prison. He was a fluid performer and his command of his trademark 12-string guitar is evident. Recorded by John and Alan Lomax, these sessions include "Boll-Weevil," "The Titanic," "Tight like That" and "Henry Ford Blues." *—Richard Meyer*

Good Mornin' Blues (1936-1940) / 1969 / Indigo ♦♦♦♦♦
Wonderful mid-'30s and early-'40s material from Leadbelly, including some of his finest and most colorful blues tunes and good folk numbers as well. *—Ron Wynn*

Sings Folk Songs / 1990 / Smithsonian/Folkways ♦♦♦♦♦
Included are '40s Folkways recordings with Woody Guthrie, Cisco Houston, and Sonny Terry. *—Mark A. Humphrey*

☆ **Gwine Dig a Hole to Put the Devil In** / 1991 / Rounder ♦♦♦♦♦
An excellent sampling of material from Leadbelly's early Library of Congress sessions, including versions of some of the first songs he ever learned, "Green Corn" and "Po' Howard," his song to Governor Neff that helped secure his release from a Texas prison in 1925, his first recorded version of "If It Wasn't for Dickie" (later transformed into "Kisses Sweeter than Wine")—the master of which is, alas, somewhat damaged—and "C. C. Rider." *—Bruce Eder*

☆ **Midnight Special** / 1991 / Rounder ♦♦♦♦♦
In early July of 1933, Alan and John Lomax visited Angola Penitentiary in Louisiana with the intention of recording the music of the inmates who lived there. That day, Huddie Ledbetter, aka Leadbelly, cut his first recorded version of what became known as "Goodnight Irene" and 11 other songs, opening a career that would keep his name alive more than a half-century after his death, carried far beyond the boundaries of Louisiana and the United States. Those sides are not on this CD but the sides that he cut on their next visit, a year later, are here. The runs, fills, fingerpicking, and strumming heard on this disc are at a virtuoso level to match the work of just about any bluesman playing in 1934.

On "Ella Speed," which clocks in at nearly six minutes, Leadbelly doesn't even keep a particularly quick tempo, yet he generates a range of sound suggesting that more than his lone guitar is accompanying him. "Red River" is just as startling, with Leadbelly shouting out the lyrics like a field holler as his guitar chimes and surges, alternating the lyrical and sweet with the emphatic and powerful. There are a number of classics-to-be on this disc, including the title track, "Irene," "Take a Whiff on Me," and "Roberta," making this an essential piece of Leadbelly's output. The CD transfer is clean enough to pull out some of the ambient sound behind the performance, giving a vague sense of the space and place. There were earlier blues recordings, to be sure, and Leadbelly recorded hundreds of songs in the 15 years that followed, but the impact of these early recordings cannot be underestimated. *—Bruce Eder*

Leadbelly's Last Sessions / 1994 / Smithsonian/Folkways ♦♦♦
Four CDs containing the best part of Leadbelly's only recordings on magnetic recording tape, which allowed him to stretch his songs to their usual length for the first time on record. The

clarity of the recording, the presence of the between-song comments, and the selection of material makes this a seminal part of any serious collection. *—Bruce Eder*

Leadbelly in Concert / 1996 / Magnum ♦♦♦♦♦
Leadbelly's final concert from June 15, 1949, reissued on CD at last. The sound is very clean, the fidelity excellent, and the recording indispensable. *—Bruce Eder*

Where Did You Sleep Last Night— Lead Belly Legacy, Vol. 1 / Feb. 20, 1996 / Smithsonian/Folkways ♦♦♦♦♦
The bulk of the best performances by Leadbelly—whose influence on the folk revival of the 1950s and '60s cannot be overstated—were recorded during the 1940s for Folkways Records founder Moses Asch. Inferior copies and rerecordings of these tunes have appeared over the years, but the original masters have sat in the vaults of Folkways. The three-volume "Leadbelly Legacy" collection shows what we've been missing: The compilers dug out the best-available versions of Leadbelly's finest songs and carefully transferred them from the original acetate masters. As the liner notes promise, "these recordings can again be heard the way they sounded in the early 1940s, for in the original masters you can still hear the ringing of the guitar and thumping of the bass." This 34-song first volume is a must for anyone interested in the roots of American folk. It opens with "Irene," which (as "Goodnight Irene") became a national hit for the Weavers less than a year after Leadbelly died on welfare; it includes many more of his most-famous tunes, among them "Rock Island Line," "Cotton Fields," and "Good Morning Blues." *—Jeff Burger*

Bourgeois Blues: Lead Belly Legacy, Vol. 2 / Mar. 18, 1997 / Smithsonian/Folkways ♦♦♦♦♦
Volume two in a three-volume series of the recordings Leadbelly made for Folkways founder Moses Asch is as indispensable as the first. The 28 songs have been beautifully remastered, and the liner notes—including a 1946 tribute by Woody Guthrie—are extensive and revealing. This second CD focuses mostly on best-available versions of songs that first appeared on Folkways' *Easy Rider: Leadbelly's Legacy, Vol. 4* and *Midnight Special.* Among the standout tracks: Leadbelly's own "Bourgeois Blues" and such folk standards as "Careless Love," "John Henry" and "Midnight Special." *—Jeff Burger*

Shout On: Lead Belly Legacy, Vol. 3 / Mar. 17, 1998 / Smithsonian/Folkways ♦♦♦♦
Although the original Leadbelly LP bearing this name (Folkways 31030) was drawn from October 1948 sessions, the CD reissue adds 17 tracks, some recorded as early as 1941, and so should be now considered an anthology of 1940s work. This does not rate among the best Leadbelly collections: due to illness, his guitar skills had diminished by the 1948 sessions that comprise much of the disc, and there are better versions of some of the songs elsewhere. It's still plenty worthwhile, though, particularly when Leadbelly is boosted by Sonny Terry's vocal and harmonica on several numbers, including Leroy Carr's blues "How Long, How Long." The CD is divided into thematic sections that, other than the '48 recordings, feature three patriotic tunes about U.S. efforts in World War II; five numbers recorded with Woody Guthrie and Cisco Houston in 1946, including the perennial favorite "Midnight Special"; and seven children-oriented selections. *—Richie Unterberger*

Sings for Children / Mar. 23, 1999 / Smithsonian/Folkways ♦♦♦♦♦
A dozen of these 28 songs were first issued on the 1960 Folkways album *Negro Folk Songs for Young People.* But this is not so much a CD expansion of that album as a lengthy compilation of children-friendly performances from the 1940s that uses *Negro Folk Songs for Young People* as its core. The additional tracks were recorded by Moe Asch of Folkways in 1941-1948, and include five of the six songs released on the 1941 album *Play Parties in Song and Dance as Sung by Lead Belly,* and a previously unreleased radio broadcast of "Take this Hammer." While many of these are simple tunes that can easily be picked up by young kids for singing along to, like "Skip to My Lou" and "Blue-Tailed Fly (Jimmy Crack Corn)," a bunch of these are classic folk songs of equal appeal to all age groups. Some of them are particularly identified with Leadbelly's interpretations, such as "Rock Island Line," "John Henry," "Cotton Fields," "Midnight Special," "Pick a Bale of Cotton" and "Take this Hammer"; other familiar standards like "Swing Low, Sweet Chariot" and "Sally Walker" are also aboard. As the liner notes explain, Leadbelly didn't limit the repertoire of his performances for children solely to simple tunes, also putting in blues and folk songs that you wouldn't think of as kids' tunes, like "Good Morning Blues." The result is a disc that is simply a good Leadbelly album, whether listened to by kids or others. *—Richie Unterberger*

★ **King of the 12-String Guitar** / 199 / Columbia/Legacy ♦♦♦♦♦
Although Huddie Ledbetter had recorded for the Library of Congress while still in jail in 1933, this CD contains some of the music from his earliest commercial recording date, only five months after getting out of prison for the second (and final) time. The majority of the material (other than the first four numbers) consists of alternate takes and previously unissued performances, although some of the numbers were formerly out on LPs by Folkways or Biograph. The music (ranging from blues to folk music) is highly recommended both to veteran collectors (who otherwise probably do not have most of these cuts) and to those just discovering the legendary and unique musician. Forty-six at the time, Leadbelly's powerful voice and his work on 12-string guitar are consistently memorable. *—Scott Yanow*

Gordon Lightfoot

b. Nov. 17, 1938, Orillia, Ontario, Canada
Vocals, Piano, Guitar / Folk-Rock, Soft Rock, Singer/Songwriter
Canadian Gordon Lightfoot first began to gain recognition in the mid-'60s as a songwriter when his compositions "For Lovin' Me" and "Early Morning Rain" became hits for Peter, Paul & Mary, and Marty Robbins topped the country charts with "Ribbon of Darkness." Lightfoot's own style was understated, his tasteful folk arrangements topped by a gentle burr of a voice. His albums began to appear in 1966, but it was not until the start of the '70s that he became a big success as a performer, scoring in 1970 with *Sit Down Young Stranger,* which contained his hit "If You Could Read My Mind," a song with a typically flowing melodic line and gently poetic lyrics.

Thereafter, the first half of the '70s were his. Lightfoot hit a peak in 1974 with *Sundown,* which went to number one, as did the title song when released on a single. Though he had developed a timeless style, Lightfoot was caught by the popular decline of folk-based music in the latter half of the 1970s, and has performed and recorded less frequently since, sometimes trying to conform to perceived commercial trends without success. But concert appearances in the early '90s confirmed that he remains an engaging performer and that his catalog of original songs is hard to match. *Painter Passing Through* followed in 1998. *—William Ruhlmann*

Lightfoot! / Mar. 1966 / United Artists ♦♦♦♦♦
Lightfoot was already 27 at the time of his solo debut, which might have accounted in part for the unusually fully developed maturity and confidence on this recording, in both his songwriting and vocals. Contains some of his best compositions, including "Early Mornin' Rain," "I'm Not Sayin'," "The Way I Feel," "Lovin' Me," and "Ribbon of Darkness." At this point, Lightfoot was still including some covers in his repertoire, and he handles numbers by Phil Ochs ("Changes"), Ewan McColl ("The First Time Ever I Saw Your Face"), and Hamilton Camp ("Pride of Man") well. The whole album is included on *The United Artists Collection. —Richie Unterberger*

The Way I Feel / Apr. 1967 / United Artists ♦♦♦♦♦
Lightfoot had used additional guitar and bass on his debut, but for his second LP he went for a fuller band sound, using a couple of the noted Nashville sessionmen (Charlie McCoy and Ken Buttrey) who had played on Bob Dylan's *Blonde on Blonde.* The result was a brighter and more accessible sound, with the country elements more to the fore. The songs weren't quite as impressive as his first batch, but they were still very good, highlighted by the epic "Canadian Railroad Trilogy" and an electrified remake of "The Way I Feel." The whole album is included on *The United Artists Collection. —Richie Unterberger*

Did She Mention My Name / Jan. 1968 / United Artists ♦♦♦♦♦
Every '60s singer-songwriter of note expanded their instrumental approach as time went on, and Lightfoot was no exception. For his third album, he worked with John Simon (who would handle the Band and Big Brother), and occasionally used low-key orchestration. Though a tad more erratic than his earlier efforts, his songwriting remained remarkably consistent. His characteristically bright, uplifting outlook became more diverse as well, allowing for the chilling "Black Day in July" (written in response to the 1967 Detroit riots), the odd "Pussywillows, Cat-Tails" (an unusual and successful detour into baroque orchestral pop), and the ambiguous sobriety of "Does Your Mother Know." The whole album is included on *The United Artists Collection. —Richie Unterberger*

Back Here on Earth / Nov. 1968 / United Artists ♦♦♦
After the mild experimentation of *Did She Mention My Name?, Back Here on Earth* was a retrenchment of sorts, recorded in Nashville with a three-piece acoustic lineup and a more countrified approach. It's not quite as outstanding as his first three albums, lacking highlights on the order of "Early Mornin' Rain" or "Black Day in July." Lightfoot never offered weak material on his United Artists efforts, however, and *Back Here on Earth* is still a very solid set, certainly worth acquiring if you like his other LPs for this label. And all of the studio LPs for United Artists, of course, are available on the two-disc *The United Artists Collection. —Richie Unterberger*

Sunday Concert / 1969 / Capitol/EMI ♦♦♦
Recorded at a March 1969 concert in Toronto, this holds more interest than the usual live album because about half of the songs are Lightfoot compositions that had not been previously recorded in the studio. Accompanied by Red Shea on lead guitar and Rick Haynes on bass, he also mixed old favorites like "I'm Not Sayin'" and "Canadian Railroad Trilogy" with the new material on this set, which has good (though not outstanding) sound. These then-new songs aren't among his classics, but are up to the general high standard of his '60s work, with the socially conscious "The Lost Children" and the poetic "Leaves of Grass" standing out as lyrical highlights. This is the only one of Lightfoot's '60s United Artists albums that is not included on *The United Artists Collection;* EMI reissued it on CD in 1996. *—Richie Unterberger*

Summer Side of Life / 1971 / Reprise ♦♦♦
This extraordinary release doesn't have big hits on it but contains some of his finest songwriting, from the political song "Miguel, " to the wistful songs about divorce, "Same Old Loverman" and "Talking in Your Sleep, " to the joyous "Cotton Jenny." This is highly recommended. *—Richard Meyer*

Don Quixote / 1972 / Reprise ♦♦♦
Perhaps one of his most Canadian releases, *Don Quixote* is a very pleasant folk sounding album. From "Alberta Bound" to "Christian Island" to "Ode to Big Blue," Lightfoot pays tribute to the many and varied places that make up his homeland. Also of note are such love songs as "Beautiful" and the lovely "Looking at the Rain." All in all, there's not a bad cut here. It's well worth your time. *—James Chrispell*

Sundown / 1974 / Reprise ♦♦♦♦♦
Lightfoot's commercial peak came with this album, which topped the US charts, containing both the *1 title song and the Top 10 hit &"Carefree Highway."* But songs like "Somewhere U.S.A." and "High and Dry" are textured, catchy folk/rock on a par with the better known tunes. *—William Ruhlmann*

Cold on the Shoulder / 1975 / Reprise ♦♦♦
Once you find a formula that works, why not try it again— That is just what Gordon Lightfoot does on "Cold On The Shoulder." He doesn't vary from his success of the "Sundown" album by much, although some of these new tunes are little more upbeat. Highlights include the hit "Rainy Day People" and the title track. Not another watermark, as it's sort of a holding pattern, but nothing bad about it either. *—James Chrispell*

Gord's Gold / 1975 / Reprise ♦♦♦
Following the success of *Sundown,* Gordon Lightfoot continued his success by releasing a greatest-hits compilation. A double album (now a single CD), it contained his most popular songs from his Warner Bros. years on disc two and he re-recorded many of his early songs

for side one of record one. Although not as good, perhaps, than the originals, this did bring them up to date with his current sound-style. Just about all the favorites are here. A good overview of a strong talent. *—James Chrispell*

Early Morning Rain / 1976 / Sunset ♦♦♦
Early Morning Rain is a budget-line, 12-track sampler of Lightfoot's early recordings, featuring versions of "Early Morning Rain," "The Last Time I Saw Her," "I Want to Hear It from You," "The First Time Ever I Saw Your Face," "Did She Mention My Name," "The Way I Feel" and "Does Your Mother Know." There are better collections of this material, but this is still a fine selection. *—Stephen Thomas Erlewine*

Summertime Dream / 1976 / Reprise ♦♦♦♦♦
With *Summertime Dream,* Gordon Lightfoot produced one of his finest albums, and wrapped up a six-year period of popularity that he would not recapture. Propelled by his second biggest hit, "The Wreck of the Edmund Fitzgerald," *Summertime Dream* summed up the sound that had served Lightfoot so well in his post-"If You Could Read My Mind" days. This distinctive sound featured Lightfoot's strummed six- or 12-string guitar complemented by Terry Clements' electric guitar lines and Pee Wee Charles' pedal steel guitar accents. The material here is excellent, and the singer's voice is at its strongest. Mixing upbeat songs like "Race Among the Ruins," "I'd Do It Again" and the title track with beautiful ballads such as "I'm Not Supposed to Care" and "Spanish Moss," Lightfoot and his band deliver a tasty smorgasbord of intelligent, grown-up music. As for "Edmund Fitzgerald," its continued popularity more than 20 years after its release attests to the power of a well-told tale and a tasty guitar lick. *—Jim Newsom*

Endless Wire / 1978 / Warner Brothers ♦♦

Shadows / 1982 / Warner Brothers ♦♦♦♦
A surprisingly strong collection from Gordon Lightfoot six years after the hits had stopped, *Shadows* finds him shedding his folk-singer image for that of an adult contemporary singer. There are keyboard textures here where previously there had been all stringed instruments. The change obviously reflected the performer's attempt to remain contemporary, and though *Shadows* found no radio airplay and little sales, the music on this disc is very good, mature and melodic. Songs like "In My Fashion" and "Heaven Help the Devil" sound like classic Lightfoot, built around folk song structures but more heavily orchestrated than in the '60s and '70s. "14 Karat Gold" sounds like a hit, while the title track and "All I'm After" are reminiscent of classic Lightfoot ballads like "Beautiful," with the acoustic guitar mixed upfront but augmented with tasteful keyboard colors. "She's Not the Same" borrows its introductory licks from "Down in the Boondocks," while "Triangle" hearkens back to the singer's lyrical story tales of old. Throughout this fine disc, Lightfoot's attractive baritone voice sounds great. *Shadows* is a little-known recording well worth checking out. *—Jim Newsom*

If You Could Read My Mind / Mar. 2, 1987 / Reprise ♦♦♦♦♦
Originally released as *Sit Down Young Stranger* in the summer of 1970, this album was reissued under this name a few months later, as the song "If You Could Read My Mind" began its climb up the pop chart. The single peaked at number five, while the album reached number 12. It seemed as though "If You Could Read My Mind" was everywhere in the early months of 1971. Its appeal crossed genres and age groups, and its simplicity and acoustic arrangement fit in nicely with the burgeoning singer/songwriter scene then storming the airwaves and record stores. "If You Could Read My Mind" was not the first track released as a single from this album; Lightfoot's recording of Kris Kristofferson's soon-to-be-classic "Me and Bobby McGee," the only non-original in this collection, preceded it but barely dented the charts. The entire album is rich in the simple beauty of its folky melodies and personal lyrics. Lightfoot is accompanied here by his regular band of the time, Red Shea on guitar and Rick Haynes on bass. This trio is expanded on several cuts with Warner/Reprise labelmates Ry Cooder on bottleneck guitar and mandolin, John Sebastian on autoharp, harmonica and electric guitar, and Van Dyke Parks on harmonium. In addition, there are subtle string arrangements by Randy Newman on two tracks, Nick DeCaro on three. There are no drums to be found anywhere on this disc. This album fits in very well with the acoustic-based music being made at the turn of the '70s. Even so, the music here is timeless, still feeling and sounding great many years after its release. *—Jim Newsom*

★ **The United Artists Collection** / Oct. 5, 1993 / EMI ♦♦♦♦♦
This double CD contains all four of the Toronto singer/songwriter's '60s studio albums (the live LP *Sunday Concert,* not included here, was also released in the '60s). On these records, his resonant vocals, lyrical ambition, and melodic strengths produced as close a rival to Bob Dylan as Canada ever fashioned during that decade, and foreshadowed work by other major Canadian singer/songwriters of the late '60s, such as Joni Mitchell, Neil Young, and Leonard Cohen. "Early Mornin' Rain" (covered by fellow Canadian folkies Ian & Sylvia), the folk-rock protest number "Black Day in July," the epic "Canadian Railroad Trilogy," and his cover of Ewan McColl's "The First Time Ever I Saw Your Face" are all present, and are among the most popular tracks Lightfoot has issued during his long career. Featuring both acoustic and folk-rock recordings, this neatly bundles Lightfoot's early work into a listenable and fairly inexpensive package. *—Richie Unterberger*

A Painter Passing Through / May 12, 1998 / Warner Brothers ♦♦♦

Songbook / Jun. 15, 1999 / Rhino ♦♦♦♦♦
Career-spanning four-CD, 88-song box set, with a pretty chronologically even balance of material from the mid-'60s through 1998. It also has 15 previously unreleased cuts, as well as his 1962 debut single, "(Remember Me) I'm the One"/"It's Too Late, He Wins" (which is lame MOR Nashville country). One could quibble with the song selection ("Black Day in July" is missing, for instance) and the relatively light attention to his 1960s work (which is limited to disc one); an opportunity was also missed to include a rarity by excluding his mid-'60s single of Bob Dylan's "Just Like Tom Thumb Blues." But generally it's a representative sampling of his most meaningful, or commercially successful, recordings. As for the previously unreleased songs, it's a tribute to Lightfoot's consistency that these don't sound out of step with the rest of the program, but also true that none of these are particularly exceptional or interesting. The following is true of so many box sets of this type that it feels like a cliché to point this out once again, but by giving equal space to various phases of his career, the music starts to go downhill steeply at around the middle of disc three, marking Lightfoot's descent (more graceful than some) into adult contemporary office music. There are extensive liner notes in the enclosed hardbound book, along with comments on each song by Lightfoot himself. Unless you're a Lightfoot obsessive, though, *The United Artists Collection* (with the bulk of his 1960s recordings) and *Gord's Gold* will cover just about everything you would want. *—Richie Unterberger*

The Limeliters

f. 1959, Hollywood, CA, **db.** 1965
Group / Folk Revival, Folk-Pop, Traditional Folk
Along with the Kingston Trio, the Limeliters were one of the most successful folk groups of the early '60s, a time when the folk music revival was in itself a sort of backlash against the anti-establishment rock & roll generation. Formed by Glenn Yarbrough, Lou Gottlieb and Alex Hassilev, the group began harmonizing in 1959, and a successful stint at San Francisco's hungry i led to their recording debut for Elektra and then a series of best sellers for RCA Victor. Between 1961 and 1963, the Limeliters were one of the hottest acts in show business. They made appearances on television, sang on commercials, and embarked on an exhaustive touring schedule. After Yarbrough embarked on a solo career in 1963, the group disbanded two years later. In 1973, the original Limeliters reunited and began touring, though Yarbrough quit again in 1981. The group continued to perform at small venues throughout the '80s and '90s, building up a loyal following consisting mostly of fans from their glory years. Gottlieb's death in 1996 threatened to put an end to the group's existence, but Hassilev has since kept the flame alive. *—Cary Ginell*

● **Tonight in Person** / 1961 / RCA ♦♦♦♦♦
The Limeliters' debut album for RCA Victor was not only one of their finest, but was also a smash hit on the *Billboard* album charts, reaching the number five position and staying on for over a year. The success of the album propelled the folk trio "perilously close to solvency," as group wit Lou Gottlieb often observed. Recorded live at the Ash Grove in Hollywood on July 29, 1960, the album showed the tremendous poise and versatility the group only hinted at on their first album for Elektra, which was just getting on the market at the time. From their rousing traditional concert opener, "There's a Meetin' Here Tonight," to the Bahaman adapted singalong "Hey Li Lee Li Lee," this album is a winner all the way and one of the shining examples of the best of the urban folk revival of the early '60s. Each Limeliter was given a chance to shine: Glenn Yarbrough's shimmering tenor and whistling on "The Far Side of the Hill," Alex Hassilev's linguistic polish on "The Monks of St. Bernard," and Gottlieb's lascivious humor and hamminess on the Flanders & Swann tale of debauchery after dark, "Madeira, M'Dear." When the group sings the Russian song of farewell, "Proshchai," it makes one wish the record wouldn't end. *—Cary Ginell*

Through Children's Eyes / 1962 / Folk Era ♦♦♦♦♦
Each of the original Limeliters, surprisingly enough, chose this album as their most satisfying. In the midst of their hectic rise to the top of their profession, the group decided to record a children's album, live (in the best hootenanny tradition), featuring a chorus of 70 elementary school children from Berkeley, California. The result is what the folk process is all about: children learning songs from the "town troubadours." As a youngster in the early '60s, I myself sang along with this record and learned such classics as "The Riddle Song," "This Train," and "The Lollipop Tree." Singalongs like "Join Into the Game" and "B-A Bay" made long car trips shorter for our family. Also included are country music's Carter Family's "Stay on the Sunny Side" and a moving medley of "America the Beautiful" and Woody Guthrie's "This Land is Your Land," sung at a time when the song could still mean something for youngsters. This album is still available on cassette, and copies were sold by the Limeliters during their concert appearances in the '80s and '90s. Hassilev and Gottlieb were amazed by the middle-aged former kid fans who eagerly asked them to autograph their worn-out, tattered LPs. It's still a great album. Get it for your kids. *—Cary Ginell*

Our Men in San Francisco / 1963 / Collectors' Choice Music ♦♦♦♦
The Limeliters were catapulted to fame in the city by the bay, and so it was only natural for their next album to be recorded at the site of their initial success, *the hungry i.* The album was part of RCA's series of releases for 1963 with the "Our Man In..." theme. By this time, folk audiences were hip to Lou Gottlieb's deliberately pompous introductions; and one can hear snickering in anticipation of the next "Lou-ism." The result is the usually (for the Limeliters) entertaining blend of humor, poignancy, and instrumental virtuosity. The extended "Civil War Medley" does not include the usual well-worn tunes on the order of "Battle Hymn of the Republic," but some newer songs by folk singer Bob Gibson and cartoonist-cum-songwriter Shel Silverstein. Traditional songs ("The Jam on Jerry's Rock" and "Wabash Cannonball") were "written" by the group's mythical arranger-in-residence, "Cal Bagby." Although their albums were being produced and released at a manic pace, comparable to the group's equally hectic touring schedule, it remains amazing that their act remained as fresh as it did. It's a tribute to the ingenuity, drive, and imagination of Hassilev, Gottlieb, and Yarbrough. *—Cary Ginell*

Two Classic Albums from the Limeliters / 1996 / Collectors' Choice Music ♦♦♦♦
Two of their most popular early '60s albums, *The Slightly Fabulous* (which was live) and *Sing Out!,* are combined onto one disc on this reissue, which offers a good representation of their commercial, mildly satirical brand of pop-folk. *—Richie Unterberger*

The Complete RCA Singles Collection / Mar. 21, 2000 / Taragon ♦♦♦♦
With all the tracks in true stereo—most of them for the first time since their original release—this collection of Limeliters material highlights the height of the folk-music revival of the early '60s. It's a brace of show tunes, folks staples, and oddball stabs at pop, sometimes at odds with the detached irony that the group usually brought to their songs. The Limeliters were never really a singles band the way the Kingston Trio and other acts were, and these are some of the rarest and least reissued sides in their discography. *—Cub Koda*

Alan Lomax

b. Jan. 15, 1915, Austin, TX

Compilation, Engineer, Producer / Italian Folk, Field Recordings, Work Songs, Traditional Folk

Few figures deserve greater credit for the preservation of America's folk music traditions than Alan Lomax. Scouring the backroads, honky tonks and work camps of the Deep South, he unearthed a treasure trove of songs and singers, documenting the music of the common man for future generations to discover; through Lomax's pioneering efforts, cultural traditions ranging from the Delta blues to Appalachian folk to field hollers continue to live on, with his invaluable recordings offering a compelling portrait of times and cultures otherwise long gone. The son of noted folklorist John A. Lomax, the nation's preeminent collector of cowboy songs, from childhood on he followed in his father's footsteps, assisting in song-gathering missions whenever possible. In 1932, John was contracted to assemble a book of folk songs, and soon he and Alan set out with a crude recording machine paid for by the Library of Congress; covering some 16,000 miles of the southeastern U.S. in just four months, they collected a wealth of African-American work songs, many of them recorded at various penitentiaries. Among the musicians the Lomaxes encountered during their travels that summer was a Louisiana prisoner named Huddie Ledbetter; they helped obtain his release, employing him as a chauffeur and making his first recordings. Ledbetter went on to fame under the name Leadbelly, and remains one of the true legends of American folk and blues. *—Jason Ankeny*

Black Appalachia: String Bands Songsters Hoedowns / Mar. 9, 1999 / Rounder ✦✦✦✦
Another sub-series in Rounder's Alan Lomax collection, these are field recordings documenting African-American life in the Appalachia chain, from the Blue Ridge mountains to the hill country of Northeast Mississippi. It's music that spans from string bands to blues solos and hoedowns to songsters. Performers aboard this collection (recordings made by Lomax between 1933 and 1946) include Leadbelly, Jimmie Strothers, Sid Hemphill, the Nashville Washboard Band and Brownie McGhee and Sonny Terry. Highlights include "Cripple Creek," "Skillet Good and Greasy," "The Red Cross Store," "How Long" and a five-minute-plus rendition of "Arkansas Traveler." Like other volumes in the series, this sheds some serious light on a chunk of American history not often documented. *—Cub Koda*

Black Appalachia: String Bands Songsters Hoedowns / Mar. 9, 1999 / Rounder ✦✦✦✦
Another sub-series in Rounder's Alan Lomax collection, these are field recordings documenting African-American life in the Appalachia chain, from the Blue Ridge mountains to the hill country of Northeast Mississippi. It's music that spans from string bands to blues solos and hoedowns to songsters. Performers aboard this collection (recordings made by Lomax between 1933 and 1946) include Leadbelly, Jimmie Strothers, Sid Hemphill, the Nashville Washboard Band and Brownie McGhee and Sonny Terry. Highlights include "Cripple Creek," "Skillet Good and Greasy," "The Red Cross Store," "How Long" and a five-minute-plus rendition of "Arkansas Traveler." Like other volumes in the series, this sheds some serious light on a chunk of American history not often documented. *—Cub Koda*

World Library of Folk & Primitive Music, Vol. 2: Ireland / Jul. 14, 1998 / Rounder ✦✦✦✦

World Library of Folk & Primitive Music, Vol. 3: Scotland / Jul. 14, 1998 / Rounder ✦✦✦✦✦

Caribbean Voyage: Caribbean Sampler / Jan. 12, 1999 / Rounder ✦✦✦✦✦
This is the first entry in a multi-volume set exploring the Caribbean side of recordings made by Alan Lomax on his explorations for songs the world over, this batch emanating from 1962. When Lomax went song collecting in the Lesser Antilles—the chain of small islands that form the southeastern edge of the Caribbean Sea—these islands were all just gaining their independence. Lomax's job was to find a commonality to the songs and dances of these intertwined islands. These recordings went into University of the West Indies for social study work, but it has taken until now for the general public to be able to hear them as Lomax originally intended. In this initial volume sampler, we're treated to pass-play and work songs, children's nursery rhymes, calypso, East Indian chaupai, and steel band music. Selections from the islands of Dominicia, Grenada, Guadeloupe, Martinique, Carriacou, St. Lucia, St. Barthelemy, Anguilla, Nevis, and Trinidad complete the collection. It's a marvelous blend, reflecting the Central and West African, English, Celtic, French, East Indian and Spanish contributions to Caribbean culture and, as such, a marvelous introduction. *—Cub Koda*

Songs of Seduction / Jan. 25, 2000 / Rounder ✦✦✦✦
Songs of Seduction is a wonderful compilation of historic and humorously ribald tones from Ireland, Scotland, Wales, and England. Most of the songs are solo, a cappella renditions of centuries-old sexually charged tales—some cleverly wrapped in metaphor, and some completely forthright. Alan Lomax and others traveled to document these chapters in oral tradition between 1951 and 1956. Many of the recordings took place at local pubs, and on these tunes, the crowd joins in on the chorus. Multiple versions of a few songs—including "the Jolly Tinker" and "the Cuckoo's Nest"—are heard back to back; first sung, then as an instrumental reel played on fiddle, uilleann pipes, or tin whistle. With 33 tracks and informative liner notes, *Songs of Seduction* is a priceless addition to the collections of roots music fans. *—Joslyn Layne*

John Martyn

b. Sep. 11, 1948, Glasgow, Scotland

Vocals, Keyboards, Harmonica, Guitar / British Folk-Rock, British Folk, Folk-Rock, Singer/Songwriter

Scottish born singer-songwriter/guitarist John Martyn began his innovative and expansive career at the age of 17 with a style influenced by American blues artists such as Robert Johnson and Skip James, the traditional music of his homeland, and the eclectic folk of Davey Graham. He eventually caught the attention of Island Records founder Chris Blackwell, who made him the first solo white act to join the roster of his reggae-based label. The subsequent album, *London Conversation* (Feb. 1968), only hinted at what was to come in Martyn's career. Although it contained touches of blues along with Martyn's rhythmic playing and distinctive voice, it was for the most part a fairly straightforward British folk record. With his follow-up later that same year, the Al Stewart-produced *The Tumbler,* Martyn began to slowly test other waters, employing backup musicians such as jazz reedman Harold McNair, to flesh out his sound. His voice also started to take on a jazzier quality as he began to experiment musically. The following years saw Martyn continuing to expand on his unique blend of folk music, drawing on folk, blues, rock and jazz as well as music from the Middle East, South America and Jamaica. His voice continued to transform with each album while his playing became more aggressive, yet without losing its gentler side. *—Brett Hartenbach*

The Road to Ruin / 1970 / Island ✦✦✦
Much more of a collaboration here than on their previous effort, John & Beverly Martyn continue on their way through the British folk/jazz of the seventies. Flowing with a subtle improvisation that incorporated a greater ethnic feeling, *Road to Ruin* makes for enjoyable listening indeed. The track, "Give Us a Ring," was written for Nick Drake. Good singing and playing make this a great album to sit back and reflect upon. *—James Chrispell*

Bless the Weather / 1971 / Island ✦✦✦✦✦
Bless the Weather, the first release following two records with his wife Beverley, is a transitional effort for John Martyn. The Glasgow-born singer-songwriter's third solo album emphasizes a darker, smokier sound built around his increasingly jazzy vocals, plus sometimes aggressive, sometimes gentle acoustic guitar work, and Danny Thompson's double bass, which skirts in and out around Martyn's voice and guitar. It also contains the extended instrumental "Glistening Glyndebourne," which highlights his early experimentation with the Echoplex, a sound that would become a major part of his work in the coming years. *Bless the Weather,* with songs such as the title cut and "Head and Heart," stands as a fine representation of Martyn's early work. *—Brett Hartenbach*

Inside Out / 1973 / Island ✦✦✦
Probably his most experimental effort, *Inside Out* saw John Martyn's work with the Echoplex become a linchpin in his overall sound. His voice, which was transforming with each recording, also became more of an instrument, developing at times a rough, bluesy quality and slipping further and further into a jazz-like slur. The album, which features Steve Winwood and Chris Wood of Traffic, as well as long time cohort Danny Thompson, balances smoldering tunes like "Ways to Cry" and "Fine Lines" with fiery, hypnotic excursions with the Echoplex, such as "Make No Mistake" and "Look In." Some of his fan base may have felt alienated by the strange flights of *Inside Out,* but it's proven to be an important record in Martyn's oeuvre. *—Brett Hartenbach*

Solid Air / 1973 / Island ✦✦✦

Sunday's Child / 1974 / Island ✦✦✦✦
John Martyn's follow-up to 1973's *Inside Out* is a much more song-oriented, less experimental effort which concentrates on the joys of home and family. *Sunday's Child* skillfully blends the sensual ("You Can Discover") with the sweet ("My Baby Girl"), the modern ("Root Love") with the traditional ("Spencer the Rover"), and the tormented ("Sunday's Child") with the satisfied ("Satisfied Mind," "Call Me Crazy") while retaining its cohesiveness. The record, his sixth on his own, shows the many facets of Martyn's playing, from his effects-driven electric guitar to his signature acoustic work, which can be both aggressive ("The Message") and gentle ("Lay It All Down"). This album contains a collection of strong original songs, as well as a pair of wonderful covers: the traditional British ballad "Spencer the Rover" and the country standard "Satisfied Mind." His last recording of new material for three years, *Sunday's Child* is a fine farewell to this period of John Martyn's ever-changing career. *—Brett Hartenbach*

One World / 1977 / Island ✦✦✦✦✦
Mining the same loose-ended jazz improvisations that Steve Winwood was exploring at the same time, *One World* sounds fuzzy and a touch out of focus. A great record for late-night listening, it includes the minor hit "Couldn't Love You More." "Small Hours" captures that time just before dawn. *—James Chrispell*

Grace & Danger / 1980 / Island ✦✦✦✦✦
Following a short layoff, John Martyn returned with his 12th record (including two with wife Beverley and a best-of collection), *Grace & Danger.* The album, which finds Martyn fronting a tight quartet featuring Phil Collins on drums and backing vocals, paints a stark, painful portrait of Martyn and Beverley's crumbling marriage. Close friend and Island Records president Chris Blackwell reportedly found the songs so personal and unsettling that he delayed its release for a year. Martyn sets a somber feel right from the start with the seductive opener "Some People Are Crazy" and carries it, for the most part, throughout the record. The hushed, tormented blues of "Hurt In Your Heart," the beautiful "Sweet Little Mystery," and the heartbreaking closer "Our Love" are a few of the highlights. With some of his clearest, strongest singing in years and a collection of terse, honest originals, as well as a cover of the Slickers' reggae classic "Johnny Too Bad," *Grace & Danger* shows John Martyn at the top of his game. *—Brett Hartenbach*

Philentropy / 1983 / Blueprint ✦✦✦✦
John Martyn's second live release, *Philentropy,* is an interesting look back at his career from his transitional period in the early 1970s through 1982's *Well Kept Secret.* Built largely around electric guitar and synthesizers without even a trace of acoustic instruments, he continues to move even further away from the folk sound of his early days. Along with a tight three-, sometimes four-piece band, Martyn takes this opportunity to use years of experience perfecting his sound to attempt to update these selections from his back catalog. Songs such as "Sunday's Child," "Smiling Stranger" and "Root Love" seem to reach fruition in this setting and soar above their previous incarnations, while "I Don't Wanna Know" and "Make No Mistake" retain the passion of the original recordings. *Philentropy,* which may put off fans of his earlier work, isn't just a typical rehashing of past work in a live setting, but more a completion of a journey. *—Brett Hartenbach*

No Little Boy / 1993 / Mesa ✦✦✦✦
A wonderful collection of songs that deserve to be heard, *No Little Boy* serves as a sort of

greatest-hits package for John Martyn, and also makes an excellent introduction to the music of this unique performer. This album is made up of newly re-recorded versions of some of Martyn's finest material from throughout his career. With assistance from longtime fan and friend Phil Collins, and contributions from an all-star cast including vocalist Levon Helm of the Band, Pink Floyd guitarist David Gilmour, saxman Andy Sheppard and others, Martyn delivers definitive takes on his catalog of folk- and jazz-flavored material, recorded with pristine clarity and crispness. His trademark vocal slur is in evidence here, but the enunciation is more decipherable than on earlier recordings. This is beautiful, haunting, densely atmospheric, at times funky music. *—Jim Newsom*

● **Sweet Little Mysteries: The Island Anthology** / 1995 / Island ✦✦✦✦✦
Sweet Little Mysteries is Island's anthology of John Martyn's career. All of his most famous cuts are here, along with many overlooked treasures. Touching on most phases of Martyn's career, only his earliest works and his stuff on Atlantic are not included here. A very well-put-together overview of one of Britain's finest exports of the folk/jazz/rock mold. *—James Chrispell*

The Church with One Bell / May 1998 / Thirsty Ear ✦✦✦

David Massengill

Vocals, Guitar, Dulcimer / Contemporary Singer/Songwriter, Contemporary Folk
New York-based David Massengill has been involved in folk music, particularly the New York Fast Folk community, for over two decades. Renowned as a brilliant writer of songs noted for their universally applicable themes and their faithfulness to American folk traditions, he has also earned a reputation as an excellent guitarist and mountain dulcimer player, in addition to being a top-notch storyteller. Massengill released two independent cassettes—*Great American Bootleg Tape* in 1987 and *Kitchen Tape* in 1987—both received rave reviews throughout the folk community. He has since signed to Flying Fish Records, releasing *Coming Up for Air* in 1992 and *Return* in late 1995.*—Sandra Brennan*

★ **Great American Bootleg Tape** / 1986 / Bowser Wowser ✦✦✦✦✦
Massengill assembled this tape himself, using tracks recorded for the Stash Records *Cornelia Street* collection, *The Fast Folk Musical Magazine,* and the video of the Folk City 25th-Anniversary concert. The result is the single most impressive folk-based song collection of the decade. Massengill's lyrical facility is the most astounding to appear since that of Elvis Costello—he can be wickedly funny and deeply touching in the same line, and his imagination seems unlimited. By rights, this should be on all lists of the best albums of the 80s. (Write to David Massengill, 179 E. 3rd St., Apt. 20, NY, NY 10009.) *—William Ruhlmann*

Coming up for Air / 1992 / Flying Fish ✦✦✦✦✦
Massengill's first studio album. He does a great job on several old songs like "Fairfax," "My Name Joe," and some new material. Producer Steve Addabbo, who has produced Suzanne Vega, manages to bring out the best in the music. Long overdue, but well worth it! *—Chip Renner*

The Return / Oct. 31, 1995 / Plump ✦✦✦
David Massengill's second commercial release contains a good selection of the classic songs that have earned him his national reputation ("The Great American Dream," "Sightseer," "Jesus, the Fugitive Prince") and others equally good, though perhaps not as immediately forceful. Steve Addabbo's production sustains Massengill's dulcimer-based arrangements with a modern setting. The traditional sounding melodies are here in abundance, but in the end, it is the lyrical nature of Massengill's songs that keep the listener's attention. "Rider on an Orphan Train" is a poignant beginning to this record's journey through America's present age. The loss of place in this song reflects the fragile innocence in our country that was beginning around the time the orphan trains crossed the continent. "The Great American Dream" is understated, blunt in its restating of the nation's promise. Other highlights are "Perfect Love" and the wrenching "What's Wrong with the Man Upstairs." *—Richard Meyer*

Ian Matthews

b. Jun. 1946, Lincolnshire, England
Vocals, Guitar, Guitar (Acoustic) / British Folk-Rock, British Folk, Folk-Rock, Singer/Songwriter
Ian Matthews (now spelled Iain to reflect his Celtic roots) has had a widely varied and complex recording career. He began as the lead singer for Fairport Convention, but during their 1969 *Unhalfbricking* sessions, he decided to leave due to growing musical differences with the band. After making his first solo album, *Matthews Southern Comfort,* he released two albums with a band of the same name. They had a hit with a version of "Woodstock." Matthews left in 1971 for a second chance at a solo career, releasing two fine folk-rock albums for Vertigo. He then formed Plainsong while finishing the contractual obligation album, *Journey from Gospel Oak*—one of his finest recorded moments despite the conditions. Plainsong released one critically acclaimed album on Elektra and then disbanded while recording the second. His stay at Elektra ended after two more acclaimed yet overlooked country-folk albums— *Valley Hi* (1973) and *Some Days You Eat the Bear Some Days the Bear Eats You* (1974). He began experimenting in different styles for the rest of the '70s, often with uninspired and unsuccessful results. He did, however, have a U.S. Top Ten hit in 1978 with "Shake It" from the *Stealin Home* album. The '90s have found him reviving his solo career, signing to Watermelon Records and returning to his folk-rock roots. *—Chris Woodstra*

Matthews Southern Comfort / 1969 / Decca ✦✦✦
This is a transitional album for Matthews. Having recently exited Fairport Convention, this record pays tribute to that period of his career in both material ("A Castle Far") and in the choice of musicians who back him (many of them from Fairport Convention). At the same time, songs like "A Commercial Proposition" indicate where Matthews is headed on 1971's *Later that Same Year.* *—Jim Worbois*

Second Spring / 1969 / Line ✦✦✦
With this album, Matthews' Southern Comfort is a real band and, in addition to Matthews, also includes Roger Swallow (ex-Marmalade) and Marc Griffiths (ex-Spooky Tooth). Though there is really nothing that makes this a memorable record, it's still quite a nice record overall. If you already know his work on Elektra, Mooncrest, or even *Later that Same Year,* it would be well worth your while to search this record out. *—Jim Worbois*

Later That Same Year / Dec. 1970 / Line ✦✦✦
Best known for the hit "Woodstock," this is really the album on which Matthews first finds his direction. A nice mix of covers and originals, this record has held up nicely over the years. *—Jim Worbois*

If You Saw Thro' My Eyes/Tigers Will Survive / Vertigo ✦✦✦✦✦
Vertigo combined Ian Matthews' two 1971 albums, *If You Saw Thro' My Eyes* and *Tigers Will Survive,* on one CD. After leaving Southern Comfort, Matthews reunited with Fairport Convention members Richard Thompson and Sandy Denny and made one of his finest albums with *If You Saw Thro' My Eyes.* Though the material and playing is superior to his previous work, it was unfortunately overlooked at the time. Recorded during two different periods of time broken up by a U.S. tour, *Tigers Will Survive,* his follow-up to *If You Saw Through My Eyes,* lacks the focus of its predecessor. Still worthwhile if only for "Morning Star," one of Matthews' most beautiful originals. *—Chris Woodstra*

Journeys from Gospel Oak / 1972 / Mooncrest ✦✦✦✦✦
Billed as a contractual obligation record by the artist, *Journeys from Gospel Oak* is easily as good as Matthews' best work. It is most assuredly a companion piece to Plainsong's *In Search of Amelia Earhart* (an album loosely based on the disappearance of Amelia Earhart), this time loosely based around the night Hank Williams died. This album includes such solid tracks as Gene Clark's "Polly," "Bride 1945" by Paul Siebel, and the haunting Jimmy Webb tune, "Met Her on a Plane." A strong (but often overlooked record) and well worth the effort it takes to find a copy. *—Jim Worbois*

Valley Hi / 1973 / Elektra ✦✦✦✦✦
Often regarded his best solo album, *Valley Hi* finds Matthews combining his folk-rock expertise with producer Mike Nesmith's country leanings. Highlights include the Nesmith penned "Propinquity" and Jackson Browne's "These Days." *—Chris Woodstra*

Some Days You Eat the Bear Some Days the Bear Eats You / 1974 / Elektra ✦✦✦
His final LP recorded for Elektra continues in the country spirit of *Valley Hi* with a stronger pop sensibility. Includes a brilliant rendition of Tom Waits' "Old 55" and the touching tribute to Hank Williams, "A Wailing Goodbye." *—Chris Woodstra*

Go for Broke / 1975 / Columbia ✦

Hit and Run / 1976 / Columbia ✦✦

Stealin' Home / 1978 / Line ✦✦

Siamese Friends / 1979 / Line ✦✦

Discreet Repeat / 197 / Rockburgh ✦✦✦

Spot of Interference / 1980 / Rockburgh ✦✦✦

Moods for Mallards / 1983 / Shanghai ✦✦

Walking a Changing Line / 1988 / Windham Hill ✦✦✦

Pure & Crooked / Aug. 1990 / Watermelon ✦✦✦

● **The Best of Matthews' Southern Comfort** / Mar. 10, 1992 / MCA ✦✦✦✦✦
A fine 16-track collection drawing from Matthews' first solo effort and the two Matthews' Southern Comfort albums. Includes the band's hit version of "Woodstock." *—Chris Woodstra*

Orphans & Outcasts, Vol. 1 / 1993 / Dirty Linen ✦✦✦
An exceptional collection of demos, rarities and outtakes from Matthews' '70s period, *Orphans & Outcasts* is essential for fans. *—Chris Woodstra*

● **The Soul of Many Places** / May 11, 1993 / Elektra ✦✦✦✦✦
The Soul of Many Places compiles the best moments from Matthews' recording high point for Elektra (1972-1974). Featuring selections from *Valley Hi, Some Days You Eat the Bear…* , and Plainsong's *The Search for Amelia Earhart,* this is the best introduction to Matthews' finest work. The inclusion of non-LP tracks makes this essential for fans as well. *—Chris Woodstra*

Skeleton Keys / May 18, 1993 / Rhino ✦✦✦
Matthews emerges from his experimental '80s period with a return to his classic acoustic country-folk sound. With his first album comprised solely of originals, he shows more focus than he has in nearly two decades. *—Chris Woodstra*

Orphans & Outcasts, Vol. 2 / 1994 / Dirty Linen ✦✦✦
Volume 2 of the series, essentially a demos collection of the late '70s/early '80s material, is more interesting than the actual albums of the time. Fans of Matthews' folky early-'70s albums who couldn't connect with this somewhat misdirected phase of his career should find this much more enjoyable. *—Chris Woodstra*

Dark Ride / Jun. 7, 1994 / Watermelon ✦✦✦

Seattle Years 1978-1984 / Oct. 8, 1996 / Varese ✦✦✦✦
Between 1978 and 1984, Ian Matthews relocated to Seattle, shed the acoustic folkiness and introspection he had become known for in favor of a more contemporary, commercial sound; *The Seattle Years* collects the highlights from the four solo albums he recorded during this period—*Stealin' Home, Siamese Friends, Spot of Interference,* and *Shook* (unfortunately, the one album he did with Hi-Fi in the same period is sadly unrepresented). Though Matthews is best remembered for his work just prior to this period, the collection presents the high points into a highly listenable fashion and, in retrospect, his take on ultra-slick soft-rock stands up against the best of the genre. Included is his biggest hit, "Shake It," as well as lesser-known but well-executed album tracks like a new wave/power-pop reading of the Left Banke classic "She May Call You Up Tonight" and Jona Lewie's "The Baby She's On the Street." *—Chris Woodstra*

Nights in Manhattan (and Points West) / Aug. 5, 1997 / DCC ✦✦✦

Orphans & Outcasts, Vol. 3 / 1999 / Perfect Pitch ✦✦✦
With *Orphans & Outcasts, Vol. 3,* Iain Matthews once again digs into his seemingly endless vault of unreleased recordings for another collection of oddments from his 30-plus year career. *Vol. 3* runs the gamut from his first recorded lead vocal (a scratchy 1965 recording by Pyramid) to the live, previously unreleased "Sing Sister Sing," a song scheduled to appear on his next solo record. In between, we get outtakes, live recordings, radio broadcasts, and an assortment of demos (ranging from a 1969 recording of "Woodstock" to "Jaques and Tambo" from 1996). Unlike the first two collections, not much here is necessarily essential, though a number of cuts would fit nicely on the corresponding Iain Matthews album and should be of interest to fans. Highlights include three tracks ("Hearts," "Home," and "Never Ending") from a 1970 BBC broadcast featuring backing by Andy Roberts and Richard Thompson, Plainsong's beautiful a capella arrangement of "I'll Fly Away," and the demos for Jules Shear's "This Fabrication" and "Except for a Tear," sans synthesizers. *—Brett Hartenbach*

Mary McCaslin

b. Dec. 22, 1946, Indianapolis, IN
Vocals, Guitar, Banjo / Contemporary Folk, Country-Folk, Singer/Songwriter
As a singer/songwriter who wrote story-songs combining elements of country, folk, and pop, Mary McCaslin was one of the most appealing contemporary folk performers of the 1970s. As a country-folk singer working totally outside of the Nashville sphere, singing of prairies and Old West images in almost mythic terms, her audience was confined to the folk circuit (though within that boundary, it was very wide). Yet her ability to appeal to rock and pop listeners helped pave the way for country-folk-pop stars like Nanci Griffith and Mary-Chapin Carpenter, although her influence in this area has remained relatively unacknowledged. *Way out West* was the first of three albums that she made for Philo in the 1970s, featuring her finely wrought songs, strong upper-register vocals, and sympathetic, fully arranged accompaniment. Her Philo era is recognized as her artistic peak, although she maintained her presence on the folk scene with albums for Mercury (*Sunny California,* 1979) and Flying Fish (*A Life and a Time,* 1981). 1994's *Broken Promises* was her first album in 13 years. *—Richie Unterberger*

Way Out West / 1974 / Philo ✦✦✦✦✦
This was the album that established McCaslin as a major folk performer. Her interpretive skills are in evidence on covers of "Let It Be" and Randy Newman's "Living Without You," but most of the set was devoted to original material, showing her to be an impressive songwriter (if not quite as impressive a singer). The title track and "San Bernardino Waltz" are standouts, the latter being probably her most famous song. *—Richie Unterberger*

Old Friends / 1977 / Philo ✦✦✦
McCaslin wrote only one of the ten songs (the title track) on her fourth album. The remainder of the program stressed her abilities as one of folk music's most eclectic interpretive artists, as in addition to folk-country tunes, there were two Lennon-McCartney compositions ("Things We Said Today" and "Blackbird," both among her best-known tracks); the Who's "Pinball Wizard"; the Supremes' "My World Is Empty Without You"; Cole Porter's "Don't Fence Me In"; and the huge 1950s pop hit "The Wayward Wind." At a glance, the breadth of repertoire seems outlandish. But McCaslin's vocals are consistently strong, and she does make all of these work as folk songs (with occasional light rhythm section), without sounding like a dilettante. Perhaps "Pinball Wizard" would have been better, though, with just McCaslin's voice and banjo and without the rhythm section. *—Richie Unterberger*

● **The Best of Mary McCaslin** / 1990 / Philo ✦✦✦✦
The best of her 1970s material, taken from her first three solo albums. Many strong originals, and two excellent Beatle covers ("Things We Said Today" and "Blackbird") that remain among the best folk interpretations of Lennon/McCartney compositions. *—Richie Unterberger*

Things We Said Today: The Best of Mary McCaslin / 1992 / Philo ✦✦✦✦
This collection features the dusty vocals and wide-open country/folk sound of Mary McCaslin. Her fascination with the West comes through on a number of songs, specifically on her own "Prairie in the Sky" and a version of "Ghost Riders in the Sky." She also covers "My World Is Empty Without You" and The Beatles' "Blackbird" and "Things We Said Today," but the bulk of the tunes are originals. Culled from four previous Philo releases, it includes some of her best-loved compositions, such as "The Bramble and the Rose" and "Way out West." McCaslin is backed by her own guitar and banjo as well as a number of other musicians. *—Roundup newsletter*

Country Joe McDonald

b. Jan. 1, 1942, El Monte, CA
Vocals, Harmonica, Guitar / Folk-Rock, Political Folk, Singer/Songwriter
Political and ecological issues were set to musical accompaniment by Country Joe McDonald, who co-founded and led the psychedelic folk-rock band Country Joe and the Fish, the leading left-wing band of the 1960s. Since the group's breakup in 1971, McDonald has continued to musically espouse his political views through his original, folk-tinged songs.

McDonald grew up in El Monte, California, and following his discharge from the U.S. Navy, he attended Berkeley College. In school he was distracted by his love of music and spent most of his time playing in bands like the Berkeley String Quartet and the Instant Action Jug Band. Finding an interest in politics in the mid-1960s, McDonald published a left-wing magazine, *Rag Baby.* One "issue" was a record featuring his "I Feel Like I'm Fixing To Die Rag," a Dixieland-like indictment of the Vietnam War, credited to "Country Joe and the Fish." Following the completion of the project, McDonald and guitarist Barry Melton agreed to form a more serious rock band.

With McDonald's political lyrics set to a dynamic rock beat, Country Joe and the Fish became popular in the San Francisco Bay area, performing frequently at the Jabberwocky coffeehouse in Berkeley and the Avalon and Fillmore Auditorium in San Francisco. In addition to performing with the group at Woodstock in August 1969, McDonald performed a solo set that was capped by his obscene altering of the "Fish Cheer" intro to "I Feel Like I'm Fixin' to Die." Featured in the movie of the festival, the intro brought McDonald to international attention. In the aftermath of the festival, McDonald was arrested in Worcester, Massachusetts for inciting an audience to lewd behavior, while Melton was arrested for possession of marijuana, and Country Joe and the Fish disbanded in 1971.

McDonald soon became active in the growing anti-war movement, and his political activism continued through the 70s. In 1982, McDonald became involved with furthering the cause of Vietnam veterans and worked with the Vietnam Veterans of America, as well as recording a number of albums for Vanguard, Fantasy and One Way Records. *—Craig Harris*

Thinking of Woody Guthrie / 1969 / Vanguard ✦✦✦✦✦
McDonald proves to be an adept Guthrie interpreter on his debut solo album, recorded with the cream of Nashville session men. *—William Ruhlmann*

● **The Vanguard Years (1969-1975)** / 1990 / Vanguard ✦✦✦✦✦
McDonald worked with Vanguard on this 18-track solo career overview, which effectively demonstrates the range of his singing and writing talent. *—William Ruhlmann*

Superstitious Blues / 1991 / Rykodisc ✦✦✦
This excellent comeback album finds McDonald in acoustic mode, accompanied by Jerry Garcia for some strong picking on a thoughtful collection of songs. *—William Ruhlmann*

Something Borrowed, Something New / May 19, 1998 / Big Beat ✦✦✦✦
This compilation of material McDonald released on his Rag Baby label throughout the '70s and '90s (plus the previously unissued track "Thinking of John Fahey") is a must for any fan of the San Francisco rock iconoclast. Titles alone are enough to make one smile—"Entertainment Is My Business," "Kiss My Ass" and "Starship Ride"—but the real gems are the performances, like the flawless take of the anti-conscription rag "Free at Last." Perhaps one of folk's most underrated voices, the collection showcases McDonald's unique jugband sound; his voice veers with ease from the mocking tone on the signature sarcastic tracks, to eerie on the beautiful "Who Am I—" *—Denise Sullivan*

Kate and Anna McGarrigle

f. 1974
Group / Contemporary Folk, Singer/Songwriter
Kate (b.1946) and Anna (b.1944) McGarrigle are Canadian songwriting sisters whose work first came to international recognition in 1974 when Linda Ronstadt recorded Anna's "Heart Like a Wheel" as the title song to one of her albums. The sisters were signed to Warner Brothers and recorded *Kate & Anna McGarrigle,* an album of deeply felt (sometimes deeply funny) songs with a homey, eclectic folk backing and tart, striking vocals. It was widely hailed. Its two follow-ups seemed rushed, though they contained some good songs. In 1981, the sisters (having left Warner) recorded *French Record* for Joe Boyd's Hannibal label, and it showed considerable charm. *Love Over and Over,* in 1982, marked a move toward rock that cheered fans but also turned out to be their last album for almost a decade.

In the meantime, they raised families and ventured out every now and then to play a few rapturously received dates, especially in the Northeast. At one of these in the late '80s, they said they'd been working on a musical with producer Roma Baran. That project never came to fruition, but in 1990 they finally returned to the record racks with *Heartbeats Accelerating. The McGarrigle Hour* followed in 1998. *—William Ruhlmann*

★ **Kate & Anna McGarrigle** / 1975 / Hannibal ✦✦✦✦✦
This album was *Melody Maker*'s pick for Best Record of 1975, and it's hard to argue with that choice when you listen to the tart harmonies and solo singing on one of the best songwriting collections ever. From Anna's famous "Heart Like a Wheel" to Kate's bouncy "Kiss and Say Goodbye," the songs paint a deeply felt, highly detailed portrait of life and romance. A revelation when it was released and a classic today. *—William Ruhlmann*

Dancer with Bruised Knees / 1977 / Hannibal ✦✦✦

French Record / 1980 / Hannibal ✦✦✦
Many McGarrigle fans cite this as their favorite, even if they don't speak French. The Canadian-based sisters are expressively at home in the country's other language, and this may be the most musical of their albums. *—William Ruhlmann*

Love Over and Over / 1983 / Hannibal ✦✦✦
The first English-language record the sisters had done in several years found them rocking harder (Mark Knopfler of Dire Straits was a prominent guest star), but the layoff had also given them time to write a strong set of songs that found new things to say about love and motherhood. *—William Ruhlmann*

Heartbeats Accelerating / 1990 / Private Music ✦✦✦
Eight years later, The McGarrigles have adopted a more new-age sound, with extensive synthesizer programming. The sound may be lush and modern, but the sentiments are still deeply felt and the observations remain laser-sharp. *—William Ruhlmann*

Matapedia / Sep. 3, 1996 / Hannibal ✦✦✦

The McGarrigle Hour / Oct. 13, 1998 / Hannibal ✦✦✦✦
An interesting idea, given the talented family tree of the McGarrigle Sisters: gather the family together (including Kate's ex-husband, Loudon Wainwright), and record a CD as they play the family piano and sing traditional folk tunes, originals, and old pop standards. Add in some friends (Emmylou Harris turning in a stirring vocal on "Skip Rope Song"), Linda Ronstadt, and Chaim Tannenbaum, and the end result is a pleasant yet somewhat mediocre CD. But even a mediocre release from this family has several redeeming qualities. Kate and Anna's harmonies have never sounded tighter, and the choice of using Joe Boyd as producer (he produced their first two albums) was a good one, as he seems able to highlight their vocals and harmonies. There are some truly amazing songs as well, especially when they tackle pure, traditional folk tunes. Loudon Wainwright's "Schooldays," the opening track, is an early highlight, featuring great vocals and a great tune. The traditional folk song "Dig My Grave,"

featuring Chaim Tannenbaum, is chilling, and Anna's version of her own "Cool River" is incredibly moving—all beautiful songs. The problem with this album is that there are no new songs, which is a real shame since this is the follow-up to 1996's brilliant *Matapedia.* This may be a small complaint, as the songs all mean something to the family, as evidenced in the notes in the package. Overall, however, a good album, but not the best release from the McGarrigles. *—Aaron Badgley*

Ralph McTell

b. Dec. 3, 1944

Vocals, Harmonica, Guitar / British Folk-Rock, British Folk, Singer/Songwriter

Although he's best known for his classic folk song "Streets of London," Ralph McTell is a multi-dimensional guitarist and singer/songwriter who's influenced hundreds of folk singers around the world. McTell was raised in post-WWII London and began to show musical talent when he was seven, playing harmonica. When skiffle bands became all the rage, McTell formed his first band; at first playing ukulele, and soon moving to guitar. At the College Jazz Club in London, McTell first heard Ramblin' Jack Elliott whose performance proved to be a revelatory experience for the impressionable guitarist.

After graduation, McTell began a long tenure at Les Cousins in the Soho section of London where he began to make a name for himself. A music publisher was so impressed by McTell's early songs that he secured a recording deal for him. The third song he ever wrote, "Streets of London," was something he deliberately left off his debut album, but at a producer's insistence, it was included on *Spiral Staircase* in 1969. The song has since been recorded more than 200 times by artists as diverse as Bruce Springsteen, Aretha Franklin, and even the punk group Anti-Nowhere League, and is still McTell's most requested song. By May 1970, McTell completely sold out the Royal Festival Hall and was booked to play the Isle of Wight Festival alongside Jimi Hendrix and Bob Dylan. He made his first U.S. tour in 1972 and returned to London to sell out the Royal Albert Hall in 1974. The pressures of worldwide success temporarily became too much for the reserved McTell, and in the spring of 1975 he announced his intention to withdraw from the music business for a while.

He continued recording for Warner Bros. in the 1970s, and for most of the 1980s, he spent his time touring and working on a children's television show called *Alphabet Zoo.* With a gentle voice, superb guitar playing skills, and a level of modesty that showed through on stage, McTell demonstrates his commitment to his craft as a songwriter. Though many of his albums are hard to locate, they're well worth seeking out. *—Richard Skelly*

★ **You Well-Meaning Brought Me Here** / 1971 / ABC ✦✦✦✦✦

You Well-Meaning Brought Me Here is generally considered Ralph McTell's finest album; it is also one of the best albums of the singer/songwriter movement of the early 1970s. Gus Dudgeon (Elton John) was enlisted as producer, and he brought in guitarist Caleb Quaye, as well as Roger Pope and, on mandolin, Davey Johnston. The sessions also featured soon-to-be-famous keyboardist Rick Wakeman and arranger/conductor (and future David Bowie producer) Tony Visconti, among others. Like Dudgeon's early Elton John records, *You Well-Meaning Brought Me Here* had a restrained production in which the added instrumentation and string arrangements were only used to support McTell's vocals and acoustic guitar. The songs made for a loose concept album that began with creation ("Genesis I Verse 20"); continued with primitive man ("First and Last Man"); and, while taking in love ("In Some Way I Loved You"), drinking, and celebration ("Lay Your Money Down"), man's best friend ("Old Brown Dog"), and war ("Pick Up a Gun"), merged into the singer's own autobiography. The second half of the album revolves around character and story songs, but the whole album reflects McTell's broad experience, especially of some of the seamier sides of life. In that sense, the substitution on the American version of the album of his most famous song, "Streets of London," for "Chalkdust," which appeared on the British version, was an appropriate one, since it fit with the sympathetic depictions of other poor people on the record. McTell's calm singing and the discreet touches of Dudgeon's production gave these portraits even greater depth, making this a singularly impressive work. *—William Ruhlmann*

Not Till Tomorrow / 1973 / Reprise ✦✦✦✦✦

In signing Ralph McTell, already known for his song "Streets of London" and his critically acclaimed fourth album, *You Well-Meaning Brought Me Here,* Reprise/Warner Bros. probably was hoping for a rival to Cat Stevens—a British folk-rock artist who could cross over to America—as well as a complement to homegrown superstar James Taylor. And there were moments on McTell's Reprise label debut *Not Till Tomorrow* when he sounded a little like each of them, especially on "First Song." But the album revealed an artist uncomfortable with his growing renown, unlikely to spend much time in the States, and more interested in local concerns. Pulling back from the string settings that had characterized the ambitious *You Well-Meaning Brought Me Here,* producer Tony Visconti (who had contributed some of those string charts) recorded McTell alone with his acoustic guitar or piano, adding only occasional instrumental colorings. And McTell, who had turned *You Well-Meaning Brought Me Here* into a concept album with big subjects, turned inward and wrote about much smaller matters, many of them pastoral English topics like "Nettle Wine" and the childhood reminiscence "Barges." All in all, his American record company would have been justified in concluding that he was too English to have stateside appeal and not likely to want to go after it anyway. *Not Till Tomorrow* was McTell's first album to chart in the U.K., presaging a commercial rise that would culminate with the singles success of a re-recorded "Streets of London" in late 1974. In the U.S., the album passed unnoticed, and though McTell remained contracted to Warner Bros. until the end of the 1970s, the label never again released one of his albums in America, an injustice both to the artist and his potential audience. *—William Ruhlmann*

Slide Away the Screen / 1979 / Road Goes On Forever ✦✦✦

Slide Away the Screen, originally released in 1979, represents one of McTell's finest recorded moments with backing by several friends from Fairport Convention. The CD reissues restores the full title (*Slide Away the Screen & Other Stories*) and rounds out the album by including five additional tracks from the recording sessions. *—Chris Woodstra*

Sand in Your Shoes / Jan. 1996 / Transatlantic ✦✦✦

From Clare to Here: The Songs of Ralph McTell / May 21, 1996 / Red House ✦✦✦✦

Folk fans owe a debt of gratitude to Minnesota independent label Red House for putting a thorough Ralph McTell compilation into print in the U.S. This collection, copyright 1991, contains 16 tracks at a running time of nearly 71 minutes. One song is new and three others are re-recordings, but none of that matters very much. New listeners are liable to be reminded of McTell's contemporary Al Stewart, who has a similarly becalmed British delivery and musical arrangements keyed to his delicate fingerpicking. (Various members of Fairport Convention, past and present, frequently accompany McTell, with lead guitarists Jerry Donahue's and Richard Thompson's playing sometimes suggesting Mark Knopfler, although since McTell preceded Dire Straits by a decade, maybe it should be the other way around.) Other soundalikes would include James Taylor and Chris DeBurgh, though McTell has none of the pop sensibility of the former or the melodramatic tone of the latter. Rather, he delivers his songs in an unhurried manner that corresponds to the wistfulness and regret of his lyrics, which are reflections on working-class life, full of aspirations and disappointments. His story songs have a fable-like quality, not so much in the sense of being grandiose as in the sense of being distanced—the emotion has been distilled by time so that they always seem to be works of memory. Even "Streets of London" (presented here in its third, "hit" recording), which has a point to make, does so in such a prosaic way that there's no sting. It may be that the reason it has been McTell's only hit is that he's essentially a formalist, less interested in the opportunities folk music presents for expressiveness than in the ties it maintains to tradition. *—William Ruhlmann*

Spiral Staircase: Classic Songs / 1997 / Snapper ✦✦✦✦✦

Spiral Staircase: Classic Songs collects Ralph McTell's early recordings for the Transatlantic label from 1967 to 1970, including, of course, his most famous song, "Streets of London." Although this material has been endlessly reissued over the years in one form or another, this is the final statement on this period, offering extensive liner notes and essentially everyting he recorded during his stint with the label. Until a cross-licensing miracle allows for the definative package chronicling his 30+-year career (including the brilliant *You Well-Meaning Brought Me Here,* which unfortunately remains out of print), this is the best introduction to McTell's work. *—Chris Woodstra*

Best of Ralph McTell: Street of London / Apr. 11, 2000 / Castle ✦✦✦✦

Bill Miller (Fush-Ya Heay Aka)

b. Jan. 23, 1955

Vocals, Piano, Guitar, Flute / Contemporary Singer/Songwriter, Americana, Contemporary Folk

The strength of the Native American people and the hardships of their lives are captured through the folk-like balladry of Nashville-based singer/songwriter Bill Miller. Miller's best-known tune, "Tumbleweed," co-written with Peter Rowan and included on Rowan's 1990 album *Dust Bowl Children,* reflects on a memorable Native American character; *Trail of Freedom,* however, focuses on alcoholism among Native Americans. Miller moved to Nashville in 1984, to pursue a career as a singer/songwriter. His biggest break came when Tori Amos asked him to be her opening act on her "Under the Pink" tour of the United States. Although he mostly accompanies his baritone vocals on acoustic guitar, Miller has mastered the Native American flute. His 1991 album *Loon, Mountain and Moon* was a showcase of traditional Native American flute songs. *—Craig Harris*

Raven in the Snow / Oct. 1995 / Reprise ✦✦✦✦✦

Native American artist Bill Miller released his second album, *Raven in the Snow,* in 1995. Any preconceived notion that this might be new age or traditional music is put to rest immediately with the opening track, "River of Time." The song is a harmonica-driven, midtempo rocker that compares favorably with the music of artists like Peter Himmelman. The song contains a heavy spiritual vibe that runs through the entire record, from the powerful lyric of "Listen to Me" to the fire-and-brimstone tone of "The Final Word." The proceedings, however, never fail to be highly melodic. There are several instrumentals that take a more traditional Native American bent; these don't really add to the record, but they don't detract from it either. *—Tom Demalon*

● **Ghostdance** / May 18, 1999 / Vanguard ✦✦✦✦✦

Combine Native American touches with a healthy appreciation of storytellers like Bruce Springsteen, Neil Young, and Leonard Cohen and you have Bill Miller, a distinctive singer/songwriter who shows how compelling he can be on *Ghostdance.* This superb CD is essentially folk-rock, but it's folk-rock with Native American elements. Not only has Native American culture influenced him musically, but his reflective lyrics are also greatly influenced by the history and culture of Native Americans. Like Springsteen, Miller realizes that great singer/songwriters often draw on their own backgrounds and experiences. The Boss' frame of reference is working-class New Jersey—he sings so convincingly about blue-collar life that you know he has been there—whereas Miller's is the Native American experience. And his insights as a Mohican help to enrich "There Is You," "Every Mountain I Climb," and other pearls on *Ghostdance.* But you don't have to have a Native American background to be moved by this album any more than you have to be from New Jersey to savor Springsteen's *Born to Run.* The Boss might be writing about people in Asbury Park, NJ, but listeners in Melbourne, Australia, or Dublin, Ireland, can easily relate to his stories; and similarly, *Ghostdance* offers insights that people from a variety of backgrounds will appreciate. *—Alex Henderson*

Chad Mitchell

b. 1939, Spokane, WA

Vocals / Folk Revival, Folk-Pop, Traditional Folk

Back in the early '60s, the Chad Mitchell Trio was one of the top singing attractions on the campus and club folk circuit, rivaling for a time their somewhat more well established competitors the Kingston Trio and '60's newcomers Peter, Paul and Mary. And but for a mistake in judgment by their record label, they might have been one of the most enduring '60s folk trios. Although the Chad Mitchell Trio was closely associated during their best years with New York City, where they recorded three live albums in as many years, they actually hailed from the other end of the United States. Chad Mitchell was a student at Gonzaga University in Spokane, WA when he met Mike Kobluk, and together with a third student, Mike Pugh, they formed a trio in 1958. Part of the secret of their success, both on stage and on their albums, was that they presented a careful mix of topical songs and humor, and some of the latter, although also at times topical (their recording of "The John Birch Society" remains a very funny song, as well as the probable inspiration for Bob Dylan's formerly banned "Talking John Birch Society Blues"), was also sometimes just goofy. They were perceived properly as funny and irreverent, but not "dangerous," and sensible rather than radical, attributes that may have helped get them picked as part of a cultural exchange program sponsored by the Kennedy White House and sent on a tour of South America, where more politically oriented folk groups were passed over. Of course, this same "irreverence" made the trio anathema to the more radical political elements that soon overtook folk music and later folk-rock as well. But in 1962, it worked very well, and no one questioned their relevance or that of their records. *—Bruce Eder*

The Chad Mitchell Trio Arrives / 1960 / Collectors' Choice Music ✦✦✦

Mighty Day on Campus / 1961 / Folk Era ✦✦✦

The At the Bitter End / 1962 / Folk Era ✦✦✦✦✦
This album shows the Chad Mitchell Trio at their best—an informal, irreverent, totally entertaining concert recorded at Greenwich Village's Bitter End on March 19, 1962. Discarding their suits from earlier album covers, the trio now performed in comfortable sweaters along with their accompanists, future Byrd Jim McGuinn, former Weaver Fred Hellerman and bassist Bill Lee. The audience was more intimate as well, the coffeehouse audience responding more reverently than the raucous, huge crowd on the *Mighty Day on Campus* album. The trio's choice of material is solid, mixing traditional folk songs arranged by Milt Okun with more contemporary songs written by the likes of Bob Gibson ("You Can Tell the World," "Blues Around My Head") and Tom Paxton ("Come Along Home"). The album starts off with a bang with the ingeniusly wicked "The John Birch Society" ("if Mommy is a Commie, then you've gotta turn her in"). Woody Guthrie's "Great Historical Bum" is preceded by some humorous bragging by the group members about their respective hometowns. The trio also performs the humorous one-hundred-year-old ballad, "The Unfortunate Man," which was brought out of obscurity by folklorist J. Barre Toelken and Arkansas country singer Jimmie Driftwood. The subject deals with a man marrying for looks only to discover that beauty is not even skin deep. When the audience started singing along with Ed McCurdy's pacifist anthem, "Last Night I Had the Strangest Dream," it resulted in one of the most moving moments of the urban folk revival. The song so impressed Simon and Garfunkel that they recorded it on their debut album, *Wednesday Morning, 3 AM* several years later. Despite an average age of 22, Mitchell, Joe Frazier, and Mike Kobluk show tremendous poise and folk sensibilities on this marvelous album. *—Cary Ginell*

Blowin' in the Wind / 1962 / Folk Era ✦✦✦

The Very Best of Chad Mitchell / Aug. 20, 1996 / Vanguard ✦✦✦
Apparently lacking enough tracks to make up a full-fledged *Live at Newport* album on the Chad Mitchell Trio from its archives as it has with other artists recently, Vanguard opted to license four tracks from the Trio's early years and five from their later years to go with the five tracks they have from Newport. The result doesn't quite live up to the somewhat misleading title. True, this collection includes such Trio favorites as "Lizzie Borden" and "The John Birch Society," but the Newport material, while entertaining, hardly fits into the "very best of" category. And the rest of the disc consists of songs that, while familiar ("Four Strong Winds," "Get Together," "Last Thing On My Mind"), are not known for the Trio's versions. Some of them, by the way, are not technically by the Chad Mitchell Trio, since they date from after the point when Chad Mitchell left the group and was replaced by John Denver in what was called "The Mitchell Trio." No reason for anyone to complain about Denver's performances, of course, but that's another example of the truth-in-packaging problems presented here. *—William Ruhlmann*

The Chad Mitchell Trio Collection: Original Kapp Recordings / Feb. 11, 1997 / Varese ✦✦✦✦

● **The Best of the Chad Mitchell Trio: The Mercury Years** / Mar. 17, 1998 / Chronicles/Mercury ✦✦✦✦✦
The Chad Mitchell Trio signed to Mercury Records in 1963 after achieving initial success on Kapp Records. The group made four charting albums for the label, the second two under the more democratic name of the Mitchell Trio, after which Chad Mitchell quit and was replaced by a young John Denver.

Two non-charting albums followed before they left Mercury in 1966. This is a good compilation of that material, featuring songs written by such folk luminaries as Tom Paxton (including "The Marvelous Toy," the trio's biggest hit), Ian Tyson, and Phil Ochs. Those cheery harmonies, often expressing topically satiric sentiments in such songs as "Alma Mater" (about college integration struggles), "Barry's Boys" (about Barry Goldwater), and "The Draft Dodger Rag," still sound fresh and funny, if inevitably dated. The seven tracks featuring Denver have historical interest, especially since three of them are his compositions, including a 1965 version of "For Bobbi." Of course, to be really comprehensive, a compilation would have to contain material from both the Kapp and Mercury catalogs, but this disc tells the second half of the trio's story well. *—William Ruhlmann*

Katy Moffatt

b. Nov. 19, 1950, Fort Worth, TX
Vocals, Guitar / Americana, Country-Folk, Contemporary Country, Progressive Country
Though mainstream success has eluded Katy Moffatt, her blend of country, rock, blues and folk has gathered a devoted following of fans and colleagues just the same. While singing on a Denver radio station beginning in 1973, she became locally popular and signed to Columbia by 1975. Columbia released her rock-oriented debut *Katy* as a country album, but one of the singles, "I Can Almost See Houston from Here," still became a low-level country hit. Changing its promotional direction yet again, Columbia released her second LP *Kissin' in the California Sun* (1977) as a pop album. Permian Records president Chuck Robinson valued her distinctive style and set her up with producer Jerry Crutchfield, a partnership that spawned three impressive singles, including "This Ain't Tennessee and He Ain't You" (1984). In the mid-'80s, the Permian label folded and she moved to Philo/Rounder, where her albums gained wider exposure. With her brother Hugh, she recorded the 1991 duet album, *Dance Me Outside*, and has also done duet work with Tom Russell, Mary Flower and Rosie Flores. *—Sandra Brennan*

Walkin' on the Moon / 1976 / Philo ✦✦✦✦✦
Katy Moffatt's *Walkin' On the Moon* is not over-produced. It features her on vocals and acoustic guitar and Andrew Harden on vocals and guitar. Moffatt co-wrote with Tom Russell and covers three of her brother Hugh Moffatt's songs. Nice job on "Walkin' on the Moon." *—Chip Renner*

Kissin' in the California Sun / 1978 / Columbia ✦✦✦
A nice album. Features Dickie Betts, Chuck Leavell (Sea Level), the Allman Brothers rhythm section, and The Muscle Shoals horn section. *—Chip Renner*

Child Bride / 1990 / Philo ✦✦✦

★ **The Evangeline Hotel** / 1993 / Philo ✦✦✦✦✦
The first thing to be aware of is that this album was briefly released with a different cover and title—*The Greatest Show on Earth*. Be assured, it is the same album and a great one it is too. Many of the tracks were co-written with Tom Russell who produced the CD. Andy Hardin plays great parts as usual and it's all held together by some of the most open and honest-sounding vocals among contemporary songwriters. *—Richard Meyer*

☆ **The Greatest Show on Earth** / 1993 / Philo ✦✦✦✦✦

Hearts Gone Wild / 1994 / Watermelon ✦✦

Angel Town / Aug. 25, 1998 / HMG ✦✦✦✦✦
Katy Moffatt is all perfection and substance, an endearing figure in the music business whose talent is just as admirable. Sturdy and enduring, Katy Moffatt's beauty belies the great strength of character with which she operates. Both in the studio and on stage, Moffatt is a power to be reckoned with. Subtle and soft, she reaches out to her audience and takes them by the heart. As both an interpreter of the work of other songwriters as well as a marvelous voice for her own compositions, Moffatt sparkles. This time around she covers Chris Smither's gigantic blues hit "Love Me Like a Man" with aplomb and grace, while retaining all the baser animal instincts Smither so delicately wove into his song. Just as good is Cole Porter's "Miss Otis Regrets," an out-of-time tidbit that comes to life in an different time and place. Steve Goodman's "I Just Keep Falling in Love" is brilliant. As for herself, Moffatt presents several wonderful tunes which she wrote with longtime friend Tom Russell. "Jigsaw Love Affair," "The Game" and "Mother of Pearl" are reflective of the high caliber of talent both Moffatt and Russell possess. Magnificent is the only word one can use to describe this steely yet gossamer-like project. Katy never sounded better. *—Jana Pendragon*

Bill Morrissey

Vocals, Harmonica, Guitar / Contemporary Singer/Songwriter, Progressive Folk, Contemporary Folk
Since 1984, Bill Morrissey has released four albums of original songs that have startled and delighted the following he's built up in touring around the Northeast. By the second one, *North*, he'd been picked up by the Philo division of Rounder. Morrissey sings in a surprisingly flexible deep voice (somewhat reminiscent of Leon Redbone's croak, but more supple). His songs are full of humor and pathos, expressed in keenly observed details. This is small-town life, sometimes desperate, sometimes hopeful, but always presented in new, unexpected ways on releases including 1989's *Standing Eight*, 1992's *Friend of Mine* and 1996's *You'll Never Get to Heaven*. *—William Ruhlmann*

Bill Morrissey / 1984 / Philo ✦✦

North / 1986 / Philo ✦✦✦✦✦
Morrissey's New England country accent and self-deprecating humor make it easy to miss the bite in many of his songs, which have a Hemingwayesque understatement both in their sly, sidelong observations and their matter-of-fact presentation. In fact, Morrissey is a taste well worth acquiring for anyone seeking perceptive songwriting and the occasional dry laugh. *—William Ruhlmann*

★ **Standing Eight** / 1989 / Philo ✦✦✦✦✦
His third release may just be his best yet. If there's anything about Morrissey that becomes wearing, it may be his croak of a voice which might be more than many can take. Still, he has a wryness and toughness of character that makes his tales of hard-won love seem so fresh and devoid of cliche and excess melodrama. *Standing Eight* may also be seen as Morrissey's super session. But this is clearly Morrissey's show from start to finish, and he's wise enough to give his famous pals the slack they need to contribute some tight, winning performances (Shawn Colvin's especially good on "She's That Kind of Mystery"). *—John Dougan*

Inside / 1992 / Philo ✦✦✦
Like jazzman Chet Baker (whom he sounds nothing like), folk-pop artist Bill Morrissey is a perfect example of a singer who manages to be quite expressive and charismatic despite the fact that he doesn't have much of a voice or much of a range. Morrissey's thin, fragile, cracking vocals can take some getting used to, but for those who have acquired a taste for them, *Inside* shows us just how poigant a storyteller he can be. The obscure singer/acoustic guitarist isn't one to run away from his vulnerability, and he wears it on his sleeve on such tales of disillusionment as "Long Gone" and "Everybody Warned Me." The thoughtful "Robert Johnson" is a ode to the Delta blues legend, while the title song (a tearjerker that employs Suzanne Vega on background vocals) finds a blue-collar man lamenting his inability to give

his wife the comfortable life he'd hoped to. Not perfect but consistently enjoyable, *Inside* showed that Morrisey deserved to be better known. *—Alex Henderson*

Friend of Mine / 1993 / Philo ✦✦✦✦
Bill Morrissey and Greg Brown's paths had been crossing on the folk circuit when, in 1993, they formed an acoustic duet in a Massachusetts studio for *Friend of Mine*. Brown clearly has more of a range than Morrissey, but when it comes to singing with plenty of warmth, humanity and feeling, neither are lacking. And the singers/guitarists clearly enjoy a solid rapport on this intimate collection of folk, folk-rock, country-folk and folk-blues. Their main focus is familiar material, and they pleasantly surprise by bringing everything from Chuck Berry's "Memphis, Tennessee" and the Rolling Stones' "You Can't Always Get What You Want" to Hank Williams' "I'll Never Get Out of This World Alive" into an acoustic-oriented setting. Popularized by Howlin' Wolf, Willie Dixon's "Little Red Rooster" is generally associated with roaring, high-volume electric Chicago blues, but Morrissey and Brown give the classic an unplugged, back-porch, Mississippi Delta-type flavor. *Friend of Mine* is an unpretentious date that followers of both artists will appreciate. *—Alex Henderson*

Night Train / 1994 / Philo ✦✦✦✦✦
His style has really matured and this album contains another solid thoughtful set of story songs. The sound on this album is more stripped down, as basic as a Lou Reed record and just as effective. *—Richard Meyer*

You'll Never Get to Heaven / Apr. 1996 / Philo ✦✦✦

Songs of Mississippi John Hurt / Feb. 2, 1999 / Philo ✦✦✦

Fred Neil

b. 1937, St. Petersburg, FL **d.** Jul 7, 2001
Vocals, Guitar / Folk-Rock, Singer/Songwriter
Moody, bluesy, and melodic, Fred Neil was one of the most compelling folk-rockers to emerge from Greenwich Village in the mid-'60s. His albums showcased his extraordinarily low, rich voice on intensely personal and reflective compositions, sounding like a cross between Tim Buckley and Tim Hardin. His influence was subtle but significant; before forming the Lovin' Spoonful, John Sebastian played harmonica on Neil's first album, which also featured guitarist Felix Pappalardi, who went on to produce Cream. The Jefferson Airplane featured Neil's "Other Side of This Life" prominently in their concerts, and dedicated a couple of songs ("Ballad of You and Me and Pooneil" and "House at Pooneil Corner") to him. On the B-side of "Crying" is Neil's "Candy Man," one of Roy Orbison's bluesiest efforts. Stephen Stills has mentioned Neil as an influence on his guitar playing. Most famously, Nilsson took Fred's "Everybody's Talkin'" into the Top Ten as the theme to the movie *Midnight Cowboy*. For all his tangential influence, Neil himself has remained an enigmatic, mysterious figure. His recorded output was formidable but sparse. Always a recluse, he retreated to his home in Coconut Grove, FL, after achieving cult success, and hasn't released anything since a live album in 1971. *—Richie Unterberger*

Bleecker & MacDougal / 1964 / Elektra ✦✦✦✦✦
Neil's Greenwich village coffeehouse roots are in strongest evidence on this album (later retitled *Little Bit of Rain*). The drummerless (but not entirely acoustic) album is also his bluesiest recording. The uniformly strong tracks include "Other Side of This Life" and "Candy Man." *—Richie Unterberger*

Hootenanny Live at the Bitter End / 1964 / FM ✦✦

Tear Down the Walls / 1965 / Elektra ✦✦✦
Before establishing himself as a solo singer/songwriter, Neil briefly played and recorded as a duo with Vince Martin in the mid-1960s, resulting in one rare Elektra LP, *Tear Down the Walls*. Far more based in early-'60s troubadour/coffeehouse folk than Neil's solo efforts, this is divided pretty evenly between the artist's originals and trad folk covers, although there is one Martin original. Neil's earthy, bluesy vocal style is already fully formed, but somewhat compromised by the higher, sweeter, and more conventional tones of Martin, who duets with Neil on most of the tunes. Neil's bluesy, laconic persona does come to the fore on "Weary Blues," "Baby" (which has a tinge of Indian raga), and especially "Wild Child in a World of Trouble," which Neil sings by himself. Even the more standard-style numbers are at the least pleasant, including a good version of "Morning Dew." *—Richie Unterberger*

Everybody's Talkin' / 1966 / Capitol ✦✦✦✦✦
Originally released in early 1967 as simply *Fred Neil* and re-released as *Everybody's Talkin'* in 1969 after Harry Nilsson had a huge international hit from the soundtrack of "Midnight Cowboy," this album is one of the greatest progressive folk albums to date. At the time of its recording, Neil was a well-known figure in the folk world, and an influential hero to such up-and-coming, future legends as David Crosby, Tim Buckley, John Sebastian, Stephen Stills, and many others. The reasons for this are all on this record. Every track on this superb album is marked by Neil's wholly original approach, combining folk, blues, gospel, and jazz (among other things) to create a synthesis that is beguiling to both the ear and the heart. Neil's baritone reaches its lowest, honey-soaked depths on cuts like "Faretheewell," "That's the Bag I'm In," the title track, and many more. Folk music (and music in general) doesn't get much better than this. *—Matthew Greenwald*

Fred Neil / 1967 / Capitol ✦✦✦✦✦
Neil's second album was his best, fully completing his transition to electric folk-rock. "Everybody's Talkin'," "The Dolphins," and "That's The Bag I'm In" are all among his best (and most frequently covered) compositions. Currently hard to find, all of its tracks reappeared on the British mid-'80s *The Very Best of Fred Neil* compilation, although that LP is itself hard to locate these days. *—Richie Unterberger*

Sessions / 1967 / Capitol ✦✦✦
Sessions was a peculiar record that seemed to find Neil losing his focus to some degree, even as he increased his appetite for experimentation with arrangements and songwriting. The loose, informal feel of most of the cuts suggested that the performances were rehearsals or jams, rather than finely honed finished products; indeed, the take number of each track was appended onto the songs' actual titles. This meant that the virtues of compositions like "Fools Are a Long Time Coming," which would have been quite good if edited down, were a bit obscured by the swirling layers of guitars and casual execution. Others, like "Merry Go Round," "Roll On Rosie," and the interminable "Look Over Yonder," meandered for minutes on end in search of a definite groove or tempo, dallying with raga-type improvisations at times. Neil's vocal genius, however, remained intact, and the best two cuts were the most straight-ahead: "Felicity" is a nice oblique meditation-cum-love song, and the cover of Percy Mayfield's "Please Send Me Somebody to Love" is effective. *—Richie Unterberger*

Other Side of this Life / 1971 / Capitol ✦✦✦
Neil's final album was an odd, stitched-together affair matching one LP side of live, acoustic material with a side of studio leftovers. The live half (on which Neil is assisted by second guitarist Monte Dunn) does not provide any revelations when compared to the studio prototypes, but he does deliver decent versions of several of his best songs, including "The Dolphins," "Everybody's Talkin'," and "Other Side of This Life." Side two has OK, but not remarkably interesting, alternates of "Badi-Da" and "Felicity," as well as a fair version of the soul standard "You Don't Miss Your Water" and a traditional blues, "Come Back Baby," with Les McCann on piano. *—Richie Unterberger*

The Very Best of Fred Neil / 1986 / See For Miles ✦✦✦✦✦
It doesn't include any of his Elektra tracks, but this is a good compilation of his Capitol work, including all of the 1967 album *Fred Neil* (which featured Stephen Stills) and four tracks from his follow-up LP *Sessions*. Contains "Everybody's Talkin'," "Green Rocky Road," and the beautiful "The Dolphins." *—Richie Unterberger*

★ **The Many Sides of Fred Neil** / 1998 / Collectors' Choice Music ✦✦✦✦✦
For many, the name Fred Neil will be familiar only as that belonging to the songwriter of the modern classic "Everybody's Talkin'," or perhaps "Candyman," "The Dolphins" or "Other Side of This Life," songs that Roy Orbison, Tim Buckley and Jefferson Airplane, respectively, recorded. However, Neil's influence extends much farther. John Sebastian, David Crosby, Stephen Stills and Bob Dylan all claimed him as an influence, since he blended traditional and contemporary folk, blues, rock, gospel, Indian and pop influences into a distinctive, idosyncratic style. His music was not only influential, it was quite rich on its own terms, some of the best music of its era. Unfortunately, since Neil chose a life of seclusion in 1971, disappearing from both recording and performing, his work was neglected. Remedying the situation, *The Many Sides* bypasses his Elektra material, instead offering a complete summary of his Capitol recordings, including his three albums for the label (*Fred Neil, Sessions, Other Side of This Life*), both sides of a non-LP single with the Nashville Street Singers and six unreleased cuts. It's a long overdue compilation and one that certainly stands as a definitive portrait of an influential and criminally underappreciated folk-rock figure. After listening to *The Many Sides of Fred Neil*, it makes sense that Neil turned into a recluse—this is moody, haunting music, unlike much of the work of his contemporaries. In particular, his eponymous album boasts challenging, innovative arrangments that remain fresh and startling to this day. The rest of his work may be a little uneven in comparison, but it's frequently compelling and often matches its heights. Most importantly, *The Many Sides of Fred Neil* grants Neil his proper place in folk-rock history, confirming his unique vision and talent. *—Stephen Thomas Erlewine*

The New Christy Minstrels

f. 1962, New York, NY, **db.** 1971
Group / Folk Revival, Folk-Pop
When the definitive popular history of post-World War II folk music is written, the chances are excellent that the Kingston Trio will be mentioned prominently along with Peter, Paul & Mary. Less clear will be the fate of the New Christy Minstrels. The group received little respect in folk circles in their own time, despite the fact that—to a significant number of casual listeners—the Christys were the most familiar folk group in America.

The story of the New Christy Minstrels began at the beginning of the 60s with Randy Sparks, a young singer/guitarist. Sparks saw the possibility of putting together an ensemble of 10 voices, big enough generate a huge sound together but also able to retain the more personal, rough hewn, basic sound of a folk trio. He accomplished this task by breaking the group's performances down into smaller units. Sparks controlled the group's repertory and recording agenda, and he knew exactly what he wanted—rousing, memorable, broadly sung, generally upbeat songs, in the same spirit as Mitch Miller & the Gang. It had been Sparks' goal to use this 10-person ensemble roughly as the professional equivalent of a school chorus, whence he would find his most promising soloists, duos, trios, and quartets, which would take on a life of their own and be the real focus of his work.

Smiling, fresh-faced young people with a generally upbeat and rousing approach to their repertory, the New Christy Minstrels used folk music as a means of entertaining audiences rather than raising their respective consciousness. Ironically, their very lack of controversy made them controversial, especially in folk music circles, where they were deeply resented and frequently derided. The group was active throughout the 60s and sporadically through the 70s and had many hits over the years including "Green, Green," "This Land Is Your Land," "Saturday Night" , and the Disney song "Chim Chim Cher-ee." More impressive however is the group's ever-changing roster, which served as a springboard for the careers of Barry McGuire, Art Podell, Gene Clark, Kenny Rogers, Kim Carnes, Karen Black and many others. *—Bruce Eder*

☆ **Presenting: The New Christy Minstrels** / 1962 / Columbia ✦✦✦✦✦
Presenting: The New Christy Minstrels, The Christys' first album, was also the closest founder Randy Sparks came to his conception of a modern folk chorus singing such American standards as "Nine Hundred Miles" and "That Big Rock Candy Mountain." The original group contained some excellent solo and ensemble singers, and the overall impact is of full, warm harmony with an unabashedly sunny outlook. *—William Ruhlmann*

☆ **Ramblin' Featuring Green, Green** / 1963 / Columbia ✦✦✦✦✦
The Christys scored their biggest seller with their fourth album, which also contained their

biggest hit single, Barry McGuire's "Green, Green." The album was also their artistic high-water mark. Their arrangements were never more stirring and their singing never lustier, as Barry Kane and McGuire made their marks as soloists. *—William Ruhlmann*

The New Christy Minstrels' Greatest Hits / 1966 / Columbia ✦✦✦✦✦
Decent folk-pop like "Green, Green" (sung by Barry McGuire), grouped with pure-pop choir versions of "Downtown." An honest anthology. *—Bruce Eder*

● **The Very Best of the New Christy Minstrels** / 1996 / Vanguard ✦✦✦✦✦
An admirably succinct, 12-song distillation of their most popular cuts, including the massive hit "Green, Green," and the modest chart singles "Saturday Night," "Today," "This Land Is Your Land," and "Silly Ol' Summertime." The rest is mostly whiter-than-White cover versions of folk/pop staples like "Wimoweh," "Flowers on the Wall," and "Kisses Sweeter than Wine" that make the hit versions (by the Tokens, Statler Brothers, and Jimmie Rodgers respectively) sound authentically raucous in comparison. *—Richie Unterberger*

★ **Definitive New Christy Minstrels** / Sep. 15, 1998 / Collectors' Choice Music ✦✦✦✦✦
This two-disc set, containing 45 tracks with a running time of two hours, is the most thorough retrospective of the New Christy Minstrels. In assembling it, the compilers have looked beyond the group's two Top 20 hits, "Green, Green" and "Today," to all six of their chart singles, including a couple, "Saturday Night" and "Silly Ol' Summertime," that didn't get onto their albums. Also included are four non-album B-sides, a couple of foreign singles sung in French and Italian, and the previously unreleased track "Elijah Rock." Of course, the bulk of the material comes from ten of the 11 albums the group released between 1962 and 1965 (there's nothing from *Merry Christmas*), including six tracks each from their debut album *The New Christy Minstrels,* the gold-selling *Ramblin',* and *Land of Giants. Today,* their only Top Ten LP, is underrepresented, and *In Person,* their live album, deserved more than three excerpts, but otherwise there is a good balance, and the selections are reasonable. Since Tom Pickles' liner notes painstakingly detail the many personnel changes in the nine- or ten-member group, it's odd that the compilers have not presented the selections chronologically to make it easier for the listener to delineate the resulting alterations in the Christys' sound, opting instead to mix up the tracks. Maybe that's because, as Pickles acknowledges, the group declined over time, and that would have been more apparent in such a sequencing. As it is, however, *The Definitive New Christy Minstrels* lives up to its name. *—William Ruhlmann*

Live at Ledbetters / Apr. 11, 2000 / DRG ✦✦✦✦✦
This live recording by the New Christy Minstrels was lost in Columbia Records' vaults for 35 years, forgotten by the participants and neglected by the record company, which regarded its acoustic folk and blues-based material as too much of a departure from the pop-folk material for which the group was known. That it may have been, but this is a very fine and also, at times, a very funny record. Art Podell, in particular, engages successfully in a lot of humorous banter (parodying folk-song analysis) during an otherwise very straight and satisfying rendition of "Waltzing Matilda." Karen Gunderson turns in a stunning jazz vocal performance on "Listen, I'll Sing You the Blues" while Barry Kane provides a Flamenco showcase on "Tani," and Ann White's voice is hauntingly beautiful and lyrical on "Jamie." The entire CD reveals the prodigious individual talents hidden beneath the group's collective sound, without neglecting the group's wider audience, which can take pleasure in rousing versions of "Glory, Glory" and "Saturday Night," among other songs. The sound is very crisp, with full bodied harmonies and just the right balance on the instruments, except for weakness in the upright bass. The producers have also included a handful of bonus tracks, among them the previously "Oh, Miss Mary," and "All The Pretty Horses" by Art Podell and Paul Potash (Art & Paul), from four years before they were teamed again in the Christies. Reassembled under the guidance of Christies founder Randy Sparks by producer Doug Wygal and engineer Ken Robertson—from songs where most of the applause cut off instantly on the master, and the order was indeterminate—it's a masterful excavation and reconstruction job for fans of the group and early-'60s folk enthusiasts in general. *—Bruce Eder*

The New Lost City Ramblers

f. 1958, **db.** 1975
Group / Folk Revival, String Bands, Traditional Folk, Old-Timey
During the folk boom of the late '50s and early '60s, the New Lost City Ramblers introduced the authentic string-band sound of the 1920s and 1930s, in the process educating a generation that had never heard this uniquely American sound of old-time music. While maintaining music with a social conscience, they added guts and reality to the folk movement, performing with humor and obvious reverence for the music. Mike Seeger, John Cohen, and Tom Paley in 1958 modeled their band after groups like The Skillet Lickers, the Fruit Jar Drinkers, and the Aristocratic Pigs, choosing a name in keeping with the past. When Tracy Schwarz replaced Paley in 1962, The Ramblers added solo songs from the Appalachian folk repertoire, religious and secular, educating a large segment of the American population about traditional music. Folkways recorded The NLCR on five albums in the early 60s, making The Ramblers famous and leading to TV appearances, successful tours, and appearances at the Newport Folk Festival. The NLCR served at least three important purposes: They brought real folk music to a huge audience, they entertained us well with their highly entertaining acts, and they led us to rediscover the original music on which they had based their band. *—David Vinopal*

★ **The Early Years (1958-1962)** / 1991 / Smithsonian/Folkways ✦✦✦✦✦
These influential revivalists of old-time string-band music played it straight, but with spirit and a keen ear for the music's inherent humor. *—Mark A. Humphrey*

New Lost City Ramblers Vol. 2, 1963-1973, Outstanding in Their Field / 1993 / Smithsonian/Folkways ✦✦✦✦
This 72-minute companion piece to *The Early Years (1958-1962)* is drawn from the seven Folkways albums that the New Lost City Ramblers recorded between 1963 and 1973, following the entry of Tracy Schwartz and the departure of Tom Paley, and it's every bit as essential as the first volume. Continuing their emphasis on careful replication of many difficult regional and popular folk forms, one is continually amazed by the versatility of Schwartz, John Cohen, and Mike Seeger, as they bounce from lively fiddle tunes, to instrumental waltzes, from more traditional bluegrass songs to Cajun influences. No doubt, this was a productive period for the NLCR, as many of the 27 tracks should be required listening for fans of traditional string-band music. Excellent liner notes and commentary by Jon Pankake also make this a quality collection. *—Matt Fink*

☆ **There Ain't No Way Out** / May 20, 1997 / Smithsonian/Folkways ✦✦✦✦✦
More than 20 years after their last studio recordings, Mike Seeger, John Cohen, and Tracy Schwarz have gotten back together for this 26-track celebration of old-time music, including bluegrass, yodel blues, spirituals, Cajun, and what is usually referred to generically as "folk" music. They haven't lost much of their edge, even if—by their own admission—there are younger, sharper players out there in the wake of the path they opened. Highlights include a sweetly sung "God's Gonna Ease My Troublin' Mind," A.P. Carter's "Anchored In Love Divine," the Dixon Brothers' "Weave Room Blues" (which has a Jimmy Rodgers sound to it), "Cumberland Gap," "Shady Grove," "Skip to My Lou," and "Crapshooters Hop." They still harmonize beautifully, their instruments sing even sweeter, and the advantages of modern recording aren't lost on this sharp body of music. The notes, featuring contributions by all three players, are exceptionally detailed and informative about their history, as well as that of the songs. *—Bruce Eder*

Penny Nichols

b. Dec. 26, 1947
Vocals, Guitar / Contemporary Folk
Penny Nichols, with a background as a composer and vocal arranger, has worked as a backup singer for a wide variety of R&B and rock acts, including Jimmy Buffett, Arlo Guthrie, Art Garfunkel, Susie Quatro, and Donna Summer. She received a platinum record with Jimmy Buffett and a Grammy nomination. Nichols is one of the new lights in the modern folk scene and her songs are living proof that all the great folk songs were not written 60 years ago. "Pioneer Woman" and "New Moon Refugees" are on their way to becoming modern folk classics. You can catch her live at any number of folk festivals, and her most recent album, *All Life Is One,* is mandatory listening for all folk-music fans. *—Michael Erlewine*

● **All Life Is One** / 1990 / Penny Nichols' Music ✦✦✦✦✦
Includes "Pioneer Woman" and "New Moon Refugees." *—Michael Erlewine*

Phil Ochs

b. Dec. 19, 1940, El Paso, TX, **d.** Apr. 9, 1976, Far Rockaway, NY
Vocals, Guitar / Folk-Rock, Singer/Songwriter
Singer/songwriter Phil Ochs was a self-coined "singing journalist" when he began performing in New York in the early '60s. Like Bob Dylan, the rival who always outpaced him, Ochs made his reputation singing topical protest songs. He stayed with them much longer than Dylan (and indeed would never really abandon them), but eventually he too would follow Dylan into electric music and more personal, abstract, and romantic compositions. Ochs came off as a perennial second-best to critics during his heyday. It was only after his tragic tailspin and eventual death that he was properly appreciated as one of the most sincere and humane songwriters of his day, whether detailing political atrocities or more poetic concerns. More melodic than Dylan (if not as lyrically innovative), his music's strident accusations were tempered by a warm delivery and underlying compassion, addressing all manner of anti-war, civil rights, labor, and social justice issues. *—Richie Unterberger*

All the News That's Fit to Sing / 1964 / Hannibal ✦✦✦

I Ain't Marching Anymore / 1965 / Hannibal ✦✦✦✦✦

Phil Ochs in Concert / 1966 / Elektra ✦✦✦✦✦
It's since been revealed that some or all of these tracks were not "in concert" at all, but recorded in the studio, with audience noise dubbed on afterwards. Nevertheless, this is Ochs' finest acoustic album. As a lyricist, he was moving from the singing journalist mode to more abstract symbolism, but still attacked U.S. imperialism, knock-kneed bleeding hearts, and even organized religion with an uncompromising sensitivity. Some haunting, wistful ballads transcended topical concerns entirely, including the beautiful love song "Changes" and "There But for Fortune" (a British hit for Joan Baez). *—Richie Unterberger*

★ **Pleasures of the Harbor** / 1967 / A&M ✦✦✦✦✦
Going into the studio after Dylan's move into rock accompaniment and *Sgt. Pepper*'s vast expansion of pop music, Ochs wanted to make a record that reflected all these trends, and he hired producer Larry Marks, arranger Ian Freebairn-Smith, and pianist Lincoln Mayorga—all of whom had classical backgrounds—to help him realize his vision. The result was *Pleasures of the Harbor,* his most musically varied and ambitious album, one routinely cited as his greatest accomplishment. Though the lyrics were usually not directly political, they continued to reflect his established points of view. His social criticisms here were complex, and they went largely unnoticed on a long album full of long songs, many of which did not support the literal interpretations they nevertheless received. The album was consistently imbued with images of mortality, and it all came together on the abstract, electronic-tinged final track, "The Crucifixion." Usually taken to be about John F. Kennedy, it concerns the emergence of a hero in a corrupt world and his inevitable downfall through betrayal. Ochs offers no satisfying resolution; the goals cannot be compromised, and they will not be fulfilled. It was anything but easy listening, but it was an effective conclusion to a brilliant album that anticipated the devastating and tragic turn of the late '60s, as well as its maker's own eventual decline and demise. *—William Ruhlmann*

Tape From California / Jul. 1968 / A&M ✦✦✦
On his fourth album, *Pleasures of the Harbor,* Phil Ochs broke from both his topical songwriting style and his acoustic folk music approach for an album of long, poetic songs set to elaborate, eclectic arrangements. For its follow-up, *Tape From California,* he combined his earlier and more recent styles, addressing such issues as war and union organizing along

with more discursive efforts, and including a few more complicated arrangements mixed in with simple guitar accompaniments. There were some directly political efforts, but in the more poetic songs, Ochs seemed to be painting a portrait of a desperate, debased society and his own sense of personal decline. For example, the marathon "When in Rome" conflated images from slavery, the Nuremberg trials, and ancient Rome to compile a compendium of evil and decadence through the centuries, clearly implying that the present day was another such era. Ochs imbued his lyrics with his characteristic sense of irony, and the arrangements by producer Larry Marks, Bob Thompson, and Ian Freebairn-Smith complemented the songs wittily. But released in the middle of 1968, the most tumultuous year of the tumultuous '60s, *Tape from California* was often hard to listen to, because it was such a frighteningly accurate portrait of its times, eerily mirroring the point at which passionate argument over the direction of the country spilled over into violence and a widespread sense of absurdity. *— William Ruhlmann*

Rehearsals for Retirement / 1969 / A&M ✦✦✦

Gunfight at Carnegie Hall / 1975 / A&M ✦✦✦✦✦
On the cover of *Greatest Hits,* Phil Ochs had appeared in a gold lamé suit like the one Elvis Presley wore on the cover of the 1959 album *50,000,000 Elvis Fans Can't Be Wrong: Elvis' Gold Records, Vol. 2.* On the back cover was the legend, "50 Phil Ochs fans can't be wrong!" The suit and the *Greatest Hits* title were part of a concept Ochs, who had recently seen Presley perform in Las Vegas, was pursuing at the time. Always a student of popular culture, he harked back to the rebellious tone of 1950s rock & roll and wedded it to the revolutionary fervor of the late '60s—or at least that was the idea for *Gunfight at Carnegie Hall.* Beginning a tour the month that *Greatest Hits* was released, he wore the suit onstage and for the first time used a backing band, mixing his own new and old songs with medleys of songs associated with Presley and Buddy Holly, as well as a version of "Mona Lisa," and even Merle Haggard's recent anti-hippie anthem "Okie From Muskogee." His two *Carnegie Hall* shows on the nights of March 27th and 28th, 1970, were marred by various incidents recounted on the back cover of the album. *Gunfight at Carnegie Hall,* containing 46-and-a-half minutes of the reported three-hour second show, focuses on the singer's attempt to explain his concept to a skeptical audience, which he does with a certain cockeyed wit, if without complete success, at least in front of these listeners. Ochs lobbied long for *AM* to release an album drawn from the embattled show, which the label belatedly did, but only briefly and in Canada. *Gunfight at Carnegie Hall* was eventually reissued as part of a Collector's Choice two-fer, paired with *Rehearsals for Retirement. — William Ruhlmann*

A Toast to Those Who Are Gone / 1987 / Rhino ✦✦✦

The War Is Over: The Best of Phil Ochs / 1988 / A&M ✦✦✦
This single disc compilation was never the "best of" that it claimed to be, and wasn't even a reasonably definitive representation of Ochs's music for very long (the Vancouver live album showed up two years later and took that honor away). Now, with the release of Rhino's triple-CD *Farewells & Fantasies* and the European A&M double disc *American Troubadour,* this disc's indifferent sound and huge holes in its song line-up render it useless even for the casual fan. Indeed, it may even be harmful to Ochs's reputation, missing pieces like "Crucifixion" (which is like leaving "Imagine" or "Mother" off of a John Lennon portrait). Save up your money if you have to, but go with the Rhino set or the A&M import, or both. *— Bruce Eder*

The Broadside Tapes 1 / 1989 / Smithsonian/Folkways ✦✦✦

There But for Fortune / 1989 / Elektra ✦✦✦✦✦
The best of his early sides, covering his first three albums, though weighted heavily toward the third, *Phil Ochs in Concert,* probably because it's the only one not reissued by Hannibal-Cathage. *— Bruce Eder & William Ruhlmann*

There and Now: Live in Vancouver / 1990 / Rhino ✦✦✦✦✦
This is the definitive Phil Ochs live album, found in a search of tape vaults 21 years after the fact. A "lost" 1968 concert, with poet Allen Ginsberg playing the bells on (you guessed it!) "The Bells," and featuring the best parts of his concert repertory, old and new, from "The Highwayman" through "William Butler Yeats Visits Lincoln Park And Escapes Unscathed," with stops along the way for "Outside of a Small Circle of Friends" and other underground calls-to-arms and reality checks. *— Bruce Eder*

Live at Newport / Mar. 12, 1996 / Vanguard ✦✦✦✦

Farewells & Fantasies / Aug. 19, 1997 / Rhino ✦✦✦✦✦
For anyone with the cash, this 53-song triple-CD set is the most comprehensive collection of Ochs' career we're likely to see. This set largely supplants Ochs' Elektra discs. The 21-song first disc, steeped in the defiant, leftist politics of the early 1960s—sort of a political time capsule—sums up his early career as a singing activist/journalist, filled with a mixture of seething outrage and youthful optimism, and sparked by the more than occasional turn of phrase and inventive topical allusion. In addition to expected tracks like "I Ain't Marchin' Anymore," "The Bells," "The Power and the Glory," "Bound for Glory," and "The Highwayman" (from the Vancouver show), we get a pair of previously unreleased tracks, including "Morning," one of the very first songs Ochs wrote in New York. The second disc takes a more poetic turn and show the first signs of maturation, as well the deepening despair and resignation that would ultimately destroy Ochs. Its 16 songs merge his later *AM* material with the transitional songs present on his 1966 Elektra "live" album, along with a pair of 1964-vintage demos. And the third disc sums up Ochs in his most daring musical guise, holding audiences spellbound with live performances of "Crucifixion" and his other epic compositions; venturing successfully into "art-rock" with "Pleasures of the Harbor"; parodying his own style as he satirizes the country's foibles ("Outside of a Small Circle of Friends"); performing obituaries to his life ("Chords of Fame") and its purpose ("No More Songs"); and generally challenging even those who thought they knew and understood him. The 98-page booklet is richly annotated and impressively illustrated, and the sound is uniformly excellent. *— Bruce Eder*

The Early Years / Jun. 20, 2000 / Vanguard ✦✦✦✦
This is actually an expanded version of the Vanguard CD *Live at Newport,* although it isn't billed as such. It includes all 13 songs from that album, prefacing them with seven studio tracks that Ochs did for the 1964 Vanguard compilation LP *The Original New Folks, Vol. 2.* Even if you think you own everything by Ochs, you'll need this if you're a completist, because only five of those Vanguard studio tracks actually made it onto *The Original New Folks, Vol. 2.* The other two, "How Long" and "Davey Moore," were recorded at the same sessions, but were previously unreleased. Although these seven studio cuts still find Ochs a ways from hitting his mid-1960s peak, they're worth hearing as good, if sometimes didactic, topical/protest tunes. The version of "There But for Fortune," one of his most famous compositions, has much more of a hasty troubadour gallop than the more renowned take on *Phil Ochs in Concert.* In addition, the songs "Talking Airplane Disaster," "How Long," and "Davey Moore" (yes, about the same fatal boxing incident that inspired the similarly obscure Bob Dylan song "Who Killed Davey Moore?") are not available in any other versions. The live material was taken from Ochs' performances at the 1963, 1964, and 1966 *Newport Folk Festivals.* While all of the tunes are available in studio versions, these are worthwhile supplements, particularly the five 1966 songs, as four of them would appear in far more elaborately produced arrangements on his *Pleasures of the Harbor* and *Tape from California* albums. These solo acoustic performances are interesting contrasts, putting the voice and the lyrics at the forefront, in the best unplugged tradition. *— Richie Unterberger*

Maura O'Connell

Vocals / Contemporary Folk, Singer/Songwriter, Progressive Bluegrass
Maura O'Connell embodies many paradoxes: lead singer for De Danaan, she was not a traditional Celtic singer; resident of Nashville, she is not American; collaborator with New Grass Revival, she is not a bluegrass performer. Nevertheless, O'Connell has made a name for herself on two continents as a superb singer.

O'Connell was born and raised in County Clare, Ireland, where she began singing at an early age. Involvement in the folk club scene led to an invitation from celtic traditionalists, De Dannon, to join their ranks. Her involvement with De Dannon resulted in the recording of *Star Spangled Mollie,* a clear indication of interest in trans-Atlantic culture. O'Connell then began to collabrate with members of New Grass Revival, and in particular with Bela Fleck who produced several of her tracks. Together with Fleck and others, she recorded *Just in Time* and made the decision to settle in Nashville, Tennessee. Since then, she has released *Helpless Heart, Blue is the Colour of Hope,* and *Real Life Story,* each album registering a move toward a pop synthesis. *Stories* followed in 1995, with *Wandering Home* appearing two years later. *— Leon Jackson*

Just in Time / 1988 / Philo ✦✦✦
This album, produced by Bela Fleck with string arrangements by Edgar Meyer, is one of O'Connell's cleanest and most uncluttered releases. Her voice sounds beautifully free; while some of her recordings sound forced, this one is relaxed and natural. This album demonstrates why she is often compared with Mary Black. The album's band is an all-star affair with Jerry Douglas, Bela Fleck, Mark O'Conner and Nanci Griffith contributing, among others. Maura O'Connell can be given credit here for picking up Paul McCartney's "I Will" seven years before Alison Krauss. *— Richard Meyer*

● **Helpless Heart** / 1989 / Warner Brothers ✦✦✦✦✦
Irish interpretive singer O'Connell has suffered from the inability of her record company to figure out whether she's a folkie, a country singer, or a pop artist. Meanwhile, she keeps singing her heart out, cherrypicking the work of such writers as Paul Brady, Nanci Griffith, Linda Thompson, and others. If you already own the albums those writers have made, maybe she's redundant. However, great songs still benefit greatly from being performed by great singers, and if you're looking for a sympathetic sampler of the best of today's songwriters, here it is. *— William Ruhlmann*

A Real Life Story / 1991 / Warner Brothers ✦✦✦

Blue Is the Colour of Hope / 1992 / Warner Brothers ✦✦✦
This charmingly eclectic album may be O'Connell's best. Working with producer Jerry Douglas, O'Connell finds sympathetic accompaniment on all these songs, whether its the piano and arco bass on the gently painful "So Soft Your Goodbye," the small-combo swing on "Love to Learn," or the full-band acoustic pop on "Still Hurts Sometimes." Though O'Connell records songs by Nashville stalwarts like Pat McLaughlin and Tom Kimmel, her ear for a wider range of material makes *Blue Is the Color of Hope* such a joy. "Bad News at the Best of Times," by rockers Paul Carrack and John Wesley Harding, is a real find, and O'Connell's cover of Mary-Chapin Carpenter's "It Don't Bring You" is simply gorgeous. *— Brian Mansfield*

Stories / Oct. 1995 / Hannibal ✦✦✦✦

Wandering Home / Jun. 10, 1997 / Hannibal ✦✦✦✦

Odetta (Odetta Gordon)

b. Dec. 31, 1930, Birmingham, AL
Vocals, Guitar / Folksongs, Folk Revival, Folk-Blues, Country Blues
Odetta was born on New Year's Eve, 1930, in Birmingham, Alabama. By the time she was six years old, she'd moved with her younger sister and mother to Los Angeles. She showed a keen interest in music from the time she was a child, and when she was about 10 years old, somewhere between church and school, her singing voice was discovered. Odetta's mother began saving money to pay for voice lessons for her, but was advised to wait until her daughter was 13 years old and well into puberty.

Thanks to her mother, Odetta did begin voice lessons when she was 13. She received a classical training, which was interrupted when her mother could no longer afford to pay for the lessons. The puppeteer Harry Burnette interceded and paid for Odetta to continue her voice training.

When she was 19 years old, Odetta landed a role in the Los Angeles production of *Finian's Rainbow,* which was staged in the summer of 1949 at the *Greek Theatre* in Los Angeles. It was during the run of this show that she first heard the blues harmonica master Sonny Terry. The following summer, Odetta was again performing in summer stock in California.

This time it was a production of *Guys and Dolls*, staged in San Francisco. Hanging out in North Beach during her days off, Odetta had her first experience with the growing local folk music scene. Following her summer in San Francisco, Odetta returned to Los Angeles, where she worked as a live-in housekeeper. During this time she performed on a show bill with Paul Robeson.

In 1953, Odetta took some time off from her housecleaning chores to travel to New York City and appear at the famed *Blue Angel* folk club. Pete Seeger and Harry Belafonte had both taken an interest in her career by this time, and her debut album, *The Tin Angel*, was released in 1954. From this time forward, Odetta worked to expand her repertoire and make full use of what she has always termed her "instrument." When she began singing, she was considered a coloratura soprano. As she matured, she became more of a mezzo-soprano. Her experience singing folk music led her to discover a vocal range that runs from coloratura to baritone.

Odetta's most productive decade as a recording artist came in the 1960s, when she released 16 albums, including *Odetta at Carnegie Hall, Christmas Spirituals, Odetta and the Blues, It's a Mighty World* and *Odetta Sings Dylan*. In 1999 she released her first studio album in 14 years, *Blues Everywhere I Go*. Vanguard Records has released two excellent Odetta compilations: *The Essential Odetta* (1989) and *Odetta: Best of the Vanguard Years* (1999).

On September 29, 1999, President Bill Clinton presented Odetta with the National Endowment for the Arts' Medal of the Arts, a fitting tribute to one of the great treasures of American music. *—Philip Van Vleck*

Sings Ballads and Blues / 1956 / Rykodisc/Tradition ✦✦✦✦✦
Odetta's debut album was a strong, confident effort featuring just her and her guitar on 16 tracks, most of which were traditional in origin. In its day, it was quite an influential recording; Bob Dylan, in fact, once cited this record in particular as the one that made him decide to trade in his electric guitar and amplifier for an acoustic guitar. Several of the songs would find their ways into the repertoires of subsequent folkies, and even some folk-rock bands. There's no way of knowing whether they heard the tunes first on this release, but it's entirely possible, as it was one of the first strong traditional folk LPs. It's now been reissued on CD, and retains a lot of its original appeal in the power and emotional depth of the performances. *—Richie Unterberger*

Christmas Spirituals / 1960 / Alcazar ✦✦✦✦✦
Odetta's husky voice is often stunning, both in her a cappella performances and her songs with accompaniment. She says these songs are traditional spirituals, neither purely African nor American, but songs that emerged from the sufferings of slavery. Powerful stuff. *—Dennis MacDonald*

At Town Hall / 1962 / Vanguard ✦✦✦
This is similar to a prior concert album that Odetta made for Vanguard in the early 1960s, *At Carnegie Hall;* both sets even have the same accompanist (Bill Lee, on bass). The repertoire is entirely different on each, however. *At Town Hall* has somewhat lesser-known tunes than the ones on *Carnegie Hall*, although "He's Got the Whole World In His Hands," "Take This Hammer," and "Another Man Done Gone" should certainly be familiar to many. The album is also available in its entirety, paired with the *Carnegie Hall* recording, on Vanguard's double-LP *Essential Odetta*, although the CD version of that release omits a few songs from each disc. *—Richie Unterberger*

● **The Essential Odetta** / 1989 / Vanguard ✦✦✦✦✦
Although the title leads one to believe this is a best-of of sorts, in fact it's a straight pairing of two live concerts from the early 1960s that were originally released as *Odetta At Carnegie Hall* and *At Town Hall*. It's still a worthy representation of Odetta in good form, accompanied throughout by Bill Lee on bass, and covering a variety of traditional folk songs, spirituals, and later compositions such as "If I Had a Hammer." Be aware that the CD reissue of this title omits a few tracks from each LP, although the double-LP version has everything. *—Richie Unterberger*

To Ella / Oct. 6, 1998 / Silverwolf ✦✦✦✦
Although *To Ella* is dedicated to Ella Fitzgerald (who died in 1996), it isn't actually a tribute to the influential jazz singer. Nor does it find Odetta moving into jazz territory. Rather, this excellent CD is an example of Odetta doing what she does best: acoustic, storytelling folk that is influenced by African-American spirituals as well as rural blues. Odetta had been recording for over 40 years when *To Ella* was recorded at the Kerryville Folk Festival in the late 1990s, and the veteran folk artist sings with as much conviction as ever on such moving performances as "Black Woman," "Ol' Lady Sally" and "900 Miles" (which is part of a 27-minute suite that also includes "Red Clay Country," "Shenendoah" and several other songs). Those who have been following Odetta for decades will be glad to hear how well her voice has held up over the years—without a doubt, her range was still as impressive as ever. *—Alex Henderson*

Blues Everywhere I Go / Sep. 28, 1999 / M.C. ✦✦✦✦✦

Livin' with the Blues / Apr. 18, 2000 / Vanguard ✦✦✦✦

Absolutely the Best / Sep. 19, 2000 / Fuel 2000 ✦✦✦

Oysterband

Group / Celtic Rock, Contemporary Folk, British Folk

The British folk-rock band Oysterband formed in the late '80s and mixed contemporary dance rhythms (played by a rock rhythm section) and political lyrics with a traditional English folk flavor. Members are John Jones (melodeon, accordion), Ian Telfer (fiddle, viola, concertina), Alan Prosser (guitar, mandolin), Chopper (bass), and Russell Lax (drums). They debuted with 1986's *Step Outside*, while the following year's *Wide Blue Yonder* featured a Billy Bragg cover as well as Northumbrian pipes. The group ended the decade with *Ride* and *From Little Rock to Leipzig*, a mostly live collection. After touring and collaborating with June Tabor, Oysterband issued 1992's *Deserters*, which introduced a harder-edged sound from the band. The following year's *Holy Bandits* was even more influenced by the group's modern rock influence than its predecessor, which won them favor with the UK's early-'90s' "Crusty" scene. Two years later, Oysterband returned with a retrospective, *Trawler*, and a new album, *Shouting End of Life*, their most political work to date; surprisingly, 1997's *Deep Dark Ocean*—released during an election year—ignored politics in favor of eclectic folk-pop. The following year, their longtime label Cooking Vinyl released *Pearls From the Oyster*, a retrospective of their early work; in 1999 the group returned with a new album *Here I Stand*, on the Omnium imprint. 2000 saw the release of another retrospective, *Granite Years: Best of 1986–1997 Era*. *—William Ruhlmann*

Step Outside / 1987 / Cooking Vinyl ✦✦✦
While commercial—even slick—traditional English music seems oxymoronic, it's somehow an apt description for the Oyster Band's *Step Outside;* after all, the record kicks off with a rock version of the traditional "Hal-an-Tow." But despite the gloss, the majority of the album stays true to the traditional spirit, and the contemporary production brings a modern vantage to the music's age-old themes. *—Jason Ankeny*

● **Ride** / 1989 / Cooking Vinyl/Polydor ✦✦✦
The Oyster Band's second album suffers somewhat from weird, slightly claustrophobic production and a curious bloodlessness due less to a lack of energy than to a scarcity of solid melodies. These aren't completely missing: the traditional "New York Girls" and the rollicking end-of-empire anthem "Too Late Now" are both irresistible singalongs, and "Tincans" draws charmingly on English country dance music in a manner both tuneful and rhythmically propulsive. But too many other tunes, notably the meandering "Gamblers (We Do Not Do That Anymore)," the reggae-inflected but tedious "My Dog (Knows Where the Bones Are Hid)," and an inexplicable cover version of New Order's "Love Vigilantes," give the impression of a band distracted by other concerns. The best material on this program would appear later in better versions on the live album *From Little Rock to Leipzig*, which is a must-own for fans of British folk-rock. *—Rick Anderson*

Trawler / 1995 / Cooking Vinyl ✦✦

Here I Stand / Aug. 3, 1999 / Omnium ✦✦✦

Ellis Paul

Vocals, Keyboards, Violin / Contemporary Singer/Songwriter, Contemporary Folk

A troubadour, a singer/songwriter, a folkie, and a storyteller—all fair labels, but they do not quite suffice. However, the tattoo of Woody Guthrie worn proudly on his arm is a good starting place from which to grasp Ellis Paul, for it is from the Woody Guthrie tradition that he hails, and Maine, as well. Joni Mitchell, Bob Dylan, and James Taylor are also listed among his influences, and their spirits seem to occasionally grace his work. With an acoustic guitar in hand, he weaves intimate, provocative, and romantic tales of lives that were obviously witnessed by a most talented voyeur. Based in Massachusetts, Paul has been called the quintessential Boston songwriter more than a few times and has garnered the recognition and awards to back up that claim, including a shelf full of Boston Music Awards. Since coming onto the scene in 1993 with his independent debut *Say Something*, Paul hasn't slowed or weakened as a performer or a writer. Spending two-thirds of most years on the road has helped him perfect both crafts, with lots of practice on stage and lots of people whose stories he retells in song. In fact, his 1994 album, *Stories*, proved enchanting enough to secure him a deal with Rounder Records and a national following of dedicated fans. Over the years and albums, his songs have gotten more personal. He purposely turned the looking glass onto his own life for 1998's aptly titled *Translucent Soul* as he publicly worked through the pain of his divorce. Following hot on the heels of 1999's double-CD *Live*, the new millennium saw Paul's song "The World Ain't Slowing Down" featured in *Me, Myself and Irene* starring Jim Carrey. *—Kelly McCartney*

● **Stories** / 1994 / Philo ✦✦✦✦✦
Ellis Paul probably gets compared a lot to Bob Dylan for the sound of his voice and the tone of his songs, but the comparisons really should cease there—Paul takes his sound off in his own direction more often than not, and the songs have characters of their own that are far from Dylan. Paul's commentaries are much to do with the ills of the world and the twisted nature of society—"Autobiography of a Pistol" is a trenchant little piece about a gun gone astray, and how this happened, while "Who Killed John Lennon" starts out pointing the finger at the media and winds up seemingly lost for an answer. Ellis Paul is a fine songwriter, a fair singer; *Stories* is an excellent album that ranges nicely from the hard-edged to the sad and soft. *—Steven McDonald*

Translucent Soul / Sep. 15, 1998 / Philo ✦✦✦✦✦
American East Coast singer-songwriter Ellis Paul has always been successful at coming up with songs that seem to mirror the everyday foibles of small-town, working-class America. Here he turns the lens on himself and the dissolution of his marriage, the centerpiece of this very intimate, close-to-the-bone album. Strong playing out of producer Jerry Marotta and guest players Bill Dillon and Tony Levin frame the tunes in a highly supportive way. Highlights include "Did I Ever Know You?," "She Loves a Girl," "Seven," "Take Me Down," "The World Ain't Slowin' Down," "Angel In Manhattan" and the title track. An album full of sound textures and emotions big and bigger. *—Cub Koda*

Tom Paxton

b. Oct. 31, 1937, Chicago, IL

Vocals, Guitar / Folk Revival, Singer/Songwriter

Though he has never achieved widespread popular success, Tom Paxton has proven to be one of the most talented and certainly the funniest of the topical folksinger/songwriters who emerged in the '60s. His first national release was *Ramblin' Boy* on Elektra in 1965. In addition to his own renditions, his songs were recorded by a variety of fellow performers, including Peter, Paul & Mary and Judy Collins. Paxton recorded seven albums for Elektra through 1971, two of which, *The Things I Notice Now* and *Tom Paxton 6*, sold well enough to reach the charts. He then switched to Reprise Records for three albums, two of which, *How Come the Sun* and *Peace Will Come*, also made the charts. Paxton continued to write satiric

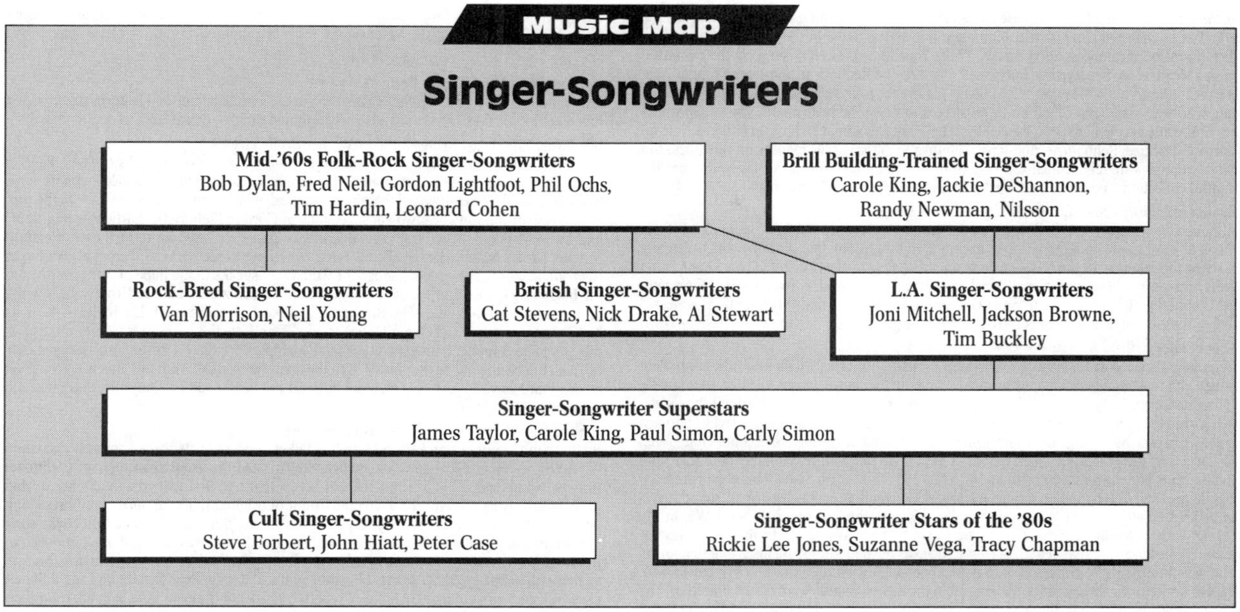

topical material over the years, from "I'm Changing My Name to Chrysler" (an attack on the government bailout of the auto giant) to "Little Bitty Gun," which mocked Nancy Reagan. But his songs can also be scathingly serious, such as his account of "The Death of Stephen Biko," and romantically touching, such as "The Last Thing on My Mind." Paxton recorded more children's music and penned books for children as well. *—William Ruhlmann*

Ain't That News / 1965 / Elektra ♦♦♦

Morning Again / 1968 / Elektra ♦♦♦
Paxton's fourth album occasioned his first, albeit quite tentative, ventures into tracks employing some full band backing and orchestration. Among the session musicians were some notable players, including David Grisman on mandocello, Paul Harris on keyboards, and Herb Brown on bass. His songwriting, too, was becoming more diverse, from character sketches ("Victoria Dines Alone," about a lonely elderly woman) to comedy ("The Hooker") to languid introspection ("So Much for Winning," which ran almost seven minutes). The expected political commentary was present in "Talking Vietnam Pot Luck Blues," and as much as U.S. involvement in Vietnam cried out for protest, this was a card that Paxton had arguably overplayed by this time. Unfortunately the best song, the odd "Mr. Blue" (whose protagonist is something of a Kafkaesque figure), isn't served too well by the almost tuneless arrangement and under-emoted vocals. The psychedelic cover by Clear Light (which actually preceded the release of Paxton's own version) absolutely tears it to pieces, and Judy Collins' interpretation (heard on a 1967 TV special, although not included on her albums) was also considerably superior. "Now That I've Taken My Life" rates as a highlight for its mordantly lighthearted and slightly surreal suicide note, complemented by mock-jaunty brass and orchestral fanfares. Another modest album, with modest updates on his original format, by a 1960s singer/songwriter whose very musical persona was defined, too much really, by modesty. Only one of these songs was selected for the CD anthology *The Best of Tom Paxton*, so if you're hungry for more from his Elektra era, this is one of the more desirable places to begin. *—Richie Unterberger*

Tom Paxton 6 / 1970 / Elektra ♦♦♦♦♦
The best of Paxton's Elektra albums came toward the end of his tenure with the label and featured an above-average collection of trenchant originals. "Whose Garden Was This" remains a masterpiece on ecology, while "Forest Lawn" is one of Paxton's funniest songs ever. *—William Ruhlmann*

Heroes / 1978 / Vanguard ♦♦♦♦♦

Up and Up / 1979 / Drive Archive ♦♦♦

The Paxton Report / 1980 / Mountain Railroad ♦♦♦
An unusually high quotient of comic/political material makes this one of his most scathing collections. "I Am Changing My Name to Chrysler" nails its subject perfectly. *—William Ruhlmann*

Even a Gray Day / 1983 / Flying Fish ♦♦♦♦♦

One Million Lawyers & Other Disasters / 1985 / Flying Fish ♦♦♦

A Paxton Primer / 1986 / Pax ♦♦♦♦♦
One of the frustrating things about Tom Paxton is his tendency to scatter his best material across his many albums, a couple of gems per record. This makes him a prime candidate for a "Best of," and though these are re-recordings, they are the artist's own choices, issued on his own label. This is the compilation that covers the most ground and therefore the one to look for. (74 East Park Place, East Hampton, NY 11937) *—William Ruhlmann*

It Ain't Easy / 1991 / Flying Fish ♦♦

● **I Can't Help Wonder Where I'm Bound: The Elektra Years** / Jan. 19, 1999 / Rhino ♦♦♦♦♦
The recordings Paxton made at the beginning of his career for Elektra Records in the 1960s and early 1970s are inarguably his most important and influential. Those Elektra albums have been out of print for quite some time, and this 26-track survey of his 1964-71 recordings for the label is an overdue compilation of his most significant work. The original versions of all of his most famous songs are here: "Ramblin' Boy," "The Last Thing on My Mind," "Bottle of Wine," "Lyndon Johnson Told the Nation," "I Can't Help But Wonder Where I'm Bound," and "Goin' to the Zoo," just for starters. His acoustic mid-1960s period is more heavily represented than his mild, later electric folk-rock material—there are seven songs alone from his 1964 debut LP, *Ramblin' Boy*—but that's an appropriate decision, as Paxton's most durable songs were produced when he was recording acoustically. In addition to zeroing in on Paxton's best music, the track selection also ably illustrates several facets of his gentle and warm (if not always brilliantly melodic or compellingly sung) repertoire: anti-war protest ("Lyndon Johnson Told the Nation"), love songs ("The Last Thing on My Mind"), original compositions that sound like folk standards ("Ramblin' Boy"), comic satire ("Forest Lawn"), and kids' songs ("Goin' to the Zoo"). *—Richie Unterberger*

Best of the Vanguard Years / Jun. 20, 2000 / Vanguard ♦♦♦

Pentangle

f. 1968
Group / British Folk-Rock, British Folk, Folk-Rock
Were Pentangle a folk group, a folk-rock group, or something that resists classification—They could hardly be called a rock & roll act; they didn't use electric instruments often, and were built around two virtuoso guitarists, Bert Jansch and John Renbourn, who were already well-established on the folk circuit before the group formed. Yet their hunger for eclectic experimentation fit into the milieu of late-'60s progressive rock and psychedelia well, and much of their audience came from the rock and pop worlds, rather than the folk crowd. With Jacqui McShee on vocals and a rhythm section of Danny Thompson (bass) and Terry Cox (drums), the group mastered a breathtaking repertoire that encompassed traditional ballads, blues, jazz, pop, and reworkings of rock oldies, often blending different genres in the same piece. At least in England, Pentangle were very popular for a time; their third LP *Basket of Light* made number five, and "Light Flight" was a small hit single. They introduced some electric guitars on their early-'70s albums, which generally suffered from weaker material and a less unified group effort. After the original lineup broke up in 1973, Jansch and Renbourn recorded often as soloists and remained top attractions on the folk circuit. The original group reunited in 1985 for *Open the Door*, and other versions of the group recorded and toured throughout the '80s and '90s. *—Richie Unterberger*

The Pentangle / 1968 / Reprise ♦♦♦
A thrilling debut, which saw five virtuosos creating a progressive folk album that added up to more than the sum of its parts. Divided between traditional and original material, highlights included their arrangement of "Bruton Town" and the seven-minute instrumental laden "Pentangling." *—Richie Unterberger*

Sweet Child / 1968 / Reprise ♦♦♦
This album, released in 1968, at the peak of the Pentangle's career, is probably the most representative of their work. A sprawling two-record set, half recorded in the studio and half live

at *the Royal Festival Hall,* showcases just how versatile the Pentangle were in their unique brand of English folk, jazz, Celtic, blues, and pop styles. Some of the live covers are easily their finest performances. Furry Lewis' "Turn Your Money Green," sung by the delightful Jacqui McShee, swings sweetly, buttressed of course by Renbourne and Jansch's guitar tapestry. Charlie Mingus' "Haitian Flight Song" features a great solo by bassist Danny Thompson, who was easily one of the finest musicians to grace the instrument. The studio tracks are uniformly excellent as well, especially "The Time Has Come," which turns waltz time inside out. McShee, Renbourne, and Jansch all turn in career performances on this track. But these examples merely scratch the surface of the Pentangle's peak. An awesome and delightful collection, and probably their finest hour. *—Matthew Greenwald*

Basket of Light / 1969 / Castle Music America ✦✦✦✦✦
Although *Sweet Child* is usually cited as the group's high-water mark, *Basket of Light* finds them at their most progressive and exciting. Highlights of this album—which actually reached the Top Five in the U.K.—include the buzzing jazz dynamics of "Light Flight, " and their moving rendition of the traditional folk song "Once I Had A Sweetheart, " their reinvention of the girl-group smash "Sally Go Round The Roses, " and "Springtime Promises, " one of their finest original tunes. *—Richie Unterberger*

Cruel Sister / 1970 / Reprise ✦✦✦✦✦
Originally released in 1970, this was the fourth release from the British folk-rock group Pentangle and may qualify as their swan song. With only five songs, Jacqui McShee, Bert Jansch, John Renbourn, Terry Cox, and Danny Thompson create a dense, layered sound that is woven within the fabric of each song like a tapestry. Although known for their eclectic approach and love of jazz, here the group concentrates on traditional material like "A Maid That's Deep in Love" and the 18-minute "Jack Orion." A Pentangle fan will immediately note that John Renbourn is playing an electric guitar on "A Maid That's Deep in Love." This departure from purely acoustic doesn't create a bigger Fairport Convention or Steeleye Span sound but is imbedded quietly into the song. What really sets both this song and "When I Was in My Prime" apart is McShee's clear, vibrant vocals. On "When I Was in My Prime," she sings unaccompanied, proving that her talent runs as deep as the better-known Jansch and Renbourn. The seven-minute title cut also features McShee singing an absolutely lovely ballad with darker undertones. Jansch sings the enjoyable though straightforward "Lord Franklin." The crowning jewel of this masterpiece is the epic "Jack Orion," though one has difficulty imagining what possessed Pentangle to record a folk song that took up an entire side of an album. Jansch shares vocals with McShee on this multiple part song, and generous time is left for Renbourn to turn in a bluesy, then jazzy, electric solo. *Cruel Sister* shows Pentangle at their artistic height, combining all of their skill and inspiration to create a vital and enduring album. *—Ronnie Lankford, Jr.*

● **Early Classics** / 1992 / Shanachie ✦✦✦✦
A 14-song, 63-minute collection (originally a double LP) comprising many of the highlights (but no "Light Flight") of the original group's history from 1968 through 1972. The notes are minimal, and there are no original release dates or any identification of the albums (*The Pentangle, Sweet Child, Basket of Light, Cruel Sister,* etc.) whence this material originated. The latter are the only flaws in what is otherwise a fine if not completely comprehensive cross-section of the group's work, showcasing their many and varied sides—Bert Jansch's, Danny Thompson's, and Terry Cox's jazz leanings in "Train Song," John Renbourn's more traditional approach in "Let No Man Steal Your Thyme," their forays into medieval music ("Lyke-Wake Dirge") and progressive folk ("House Carpenter," "Bruton Town") etc., much of it projected by Jacqui McShee's clear, soaring vocals. The CD also highlights their early records' effective use of stereo as a format for their contrasting technique, especially among the guitars and the rhythm section. *—Bruce Eder*

Peter, Paul & Mary

f. 1961, New York, NY, **db.** 1970
Group / Children's Folk, Folk Revival, Contemporary Folk, Folk-Pop, Traditional Folk
The trio of Peter, Paul & Mary was the most popular singing group in the U.S. just before the Beatles arrived, using their three-part harmony arrangements to introduce the work of some of the 1960s' best songwriters. More than 30 years later, they were still performing and recording regularly. Their manager, Albert Grossman, assembled the group using the earnest singer/songwriter Peter Yarrow, former Broadway singer and Song Swappers member Mary Travers and singer/comedian Noel "Paul" Stookey in 1961 to capitalize on the folk boom and the success of such performers as the Kingston Trio. But PP*M* immediately harked back to the early-'50s heyday of the Weavers, especially given the prominence of Travers, reminiscent of Ronnie Gilbert in the earlier group, and the left-wing political commitment both groups shared. Signed to Warner Bros. Records, they released their debut album, 1962's *Peter, Paul & Mary,* which was a massive hit, reaching number one, selling two million copies, and spawning the hit singles "Lemon Tree" (which made the Top 40) and the Weavers song "If I Had a Hammer" (which reached the Top Ten and won Grammy Awards for Best Performance by a Vocal Group and Best Folk Recording). *(Moving)* (Jan. 1963) was another enormous hit, reaching the Top Ten, going gold, and featuring the Top Ten hit "Puff, The Magic Dragon," co-written by Yarrow and now a children's standard. The group's next single, released in June 1963, was "Blowin' in the Wind," written by the then-little-known folk singer Bob Dylan. PP*M* changed that by taking his song to number one, earning two more Grammys in the process. *— William Ruhlmann*

Peter, Paul & Mary / 1962 / Warner Brothers ✦✦✦

In the Wind / 1963 / Warner Brothers ✦✦✦
Their third recording was one of the group's stronger outings, even if it confirms their status as folk popularizers rather than musical innovators. In particular, this record was essential to boosting the profile of Bob Dylan, including their huge hit cover of "Blowin' in the Wind," their Top Ten version of "Don't Think Twice, It's All Right," and the bluesy "Quit Your Low-down Ways," which Dylan himself would not release in the '60s (although his version finally came out on *The Bootleg Series*). "Stewball," "All My Trials," and "Tell It on the Mountain" were other highlights of their early repertoire, and the dramatic, strident, but inspirational "Very Last Day" is one of the best original tunes the group ever did. *—Richie Unterberger*

Moving / 1963 / Warner Brothers ✦✦✦

In Concert / 1964 / Warner Brothers ✦✦✦✦✦
This definitive collection highlights Paul Stookey's comedic talents and features the expected hits plus "Single Girl," a surprisingly early feminist song. *—Bruce Eder*

See What Tomorrow Brings / 1965 / Warner Brothers ✦✦✦
See What Tomorrow Brings is a strong album that plays to the strengths of Peter, Paul, & Mary. There is a good variety of material within their folk format, and a nice *esprit de corps* that pervades the recording. All members sing lead, which brings a good balance to the proceedings. Worth noting are two early versions of Gordon Lightfoot's "Early Morning Rain" and Ewan MacColl's "The First Time Ever I Saw Your Face." Although there isn't one number that shouts instant classic, all cuts have something to recommend them. Lest we forget the trio's idealism, the opening song "If I Were Free" speaks to the hope of wars ending and the beginning of peaceful times. "Jane, Jane" and "Because All Men Are Brothers" show the group's gospel roots, while "The Rising of the Moon," an intense cut, has Irish music as its base. "Tryin' to Win" and "On a Desert Island" manifests the humorous side of the trio as they sing about real and imagined love relationships. Throughout the album, arrangements are tasteful, clean, and never obtrusive to the songs presented. All in all, this is a very good album that has variety, strong material, tasteful production, and a fine spirit that gives it a winning edge. *—Michael Offord*

A Song Will Rise / 1965 / Warner Brothers ✦✦✦
By their fifth album, Peter, Paul & Mary had fallen into a consistency of approach that could be viewed as either dependable or predictable. This had the usual assortment of traditional songs ("Motherless Child," "The Cuckoo"), songs that had first gained an audience during prior folk revivals ("Wasn't That a Time"), a bit of original material, mediocre blues ("San Francisco Bay Blues" and Paul Stookey's "Talkin' Candy Bar Blues"), and a Bob Dylan song ("When the Ship Comes In"). The biggest find, material-wise, was the Gordon Lightfoot composition "For Lovin' Me" (a *30 hit single), which gave the Canadian songwriter (who had yet to release his first @United Artists* LP) some of his first wide exposure in the United States. Overall, the trio's sound and balance of repertoire had still changed little, if at all, from their debut. They were at their best on folk tunes with sad melodies and harmonies, as on "Jimmy Whalen" and "Ballad of Spring Hill." *—Richie Unterberger*

The Peter, Paul & Mary Album / 1966 / Warner Brothers ✦✦✦
With this record the trio were, in their halting fashion, making some concessions to or trying to keep up with the times. This was the first Peter, Paul & Mary album to include significant additional instrumentation other than the usual acoustic guitars. It wasn't exactly folk-rock, as there were drums on just three tracks. It was more folk-rockish folk, particularly as the rotating cast of backup players included musicians who had played with Bob Dylan (Mike Bloomfield, Kenneth Buttrey, Charlie McCoy, Bobby Gregg, Al Kooper) and Ian & Sylvia (bassists Bill Lee and Ross Savakus). The group was also leaning more toward contemporary songwriters, and made some astute choices in that regard by covering Laura Nyro's "And When I Die" (when that singer was barely known), Fred Neil's "The Other Side of This Life," and Richard Farina's "Pack Up Your Sorrows." For those who wanted the "classic" PPM sound, there were a few cuts in that mold, such as "Kisses Sweeter Than Wine." On the couple of occasions on which they actually tried to play rock music, they sounded, well, uncomfortable, as on the overlong "The King of Names" (with several members of the Paul Butterfield Blues Band) and Paul Stookey's odd "Norman Normal," an apparent psychedelic parody of "Secret Agent Man" on which he played all of the instruments and multi-tracked all of the vocals. They would have been better off just being themselves (and Mary Travers' absence from both of those cuts seemed to indicate that she wasn't totally into that direction herself). What the group couldn't control, however, was the unavoidable fact that the times were starting to pass them by. *—Richie Unterberger*

Album 1700 / 1967 / Warner Brothers ✦✦✦

Late Again / 1968 / Warner Brothers ✦✦✦

Peter, Paul and Mommy / 1969 / Warner Brothers ✦✦✦
This particular reissue gets a lower audio rating because of a general music mix that comes across as far too busy, between the usual guitars (picked with folky enthusiasm), the vocal arrangements (often with children incorporated), and the addition of not only acoustic bass (heard before on the group's albums), but banjo, autoharp, hammer dulcimer, etc. The tape hiss is more evident on this album, too. Peter, Paul and Mary had the essential appeal of seeming like a family—Peter Yarrow and Noel Paul Stookey looked as though they could have been brothers, and it really wasn't a stretch to see Mary as their sister. It's this picture that informs *Peter, Paul and Mommy,* an album of songs for children (as played by people accommodating to adults) and prevents it from becoming a lump of sugar. As a result you get Tom Paxton's "The Marvelous Toy" with its charming imagery, Yarrow's "Day Is Done," a melancholy paean to the truth of passing the flame to a new generation, and the outright goofiness of Shel Silverstein's "Boa Constrictor." As a fillip you also get "Puff (The Magic Dragon)." While short at 35 minutes (it would have been nice to have as a two-fer) it's a charming, well-done album that's as delightful for grown-ups as for kids—and as vital for kids as it ever was. If you have children, you can sit with them and enjoy this album. *—Steven McDonald*

● **Ten Years Together: The Best of Peter, Paul & Mary** / 1970 / Warner Brothers ✦✦✦✦✦
Even decades after its initial release, *Ten Years Together: The Best of Peter, Paul & Mary* remains the best single-disc retrospective of the trio's work, offering a baker's dozen of their most popular and enduring tunes; highlights include "Puff (The Magic Dragon), " "Leavin' on a Jet Plane, " "Blowin' in the Wind" and "If I Had a Hammer." *—Chuck Donkers*

Reunion / 1978 / Warner Brothers ✦✦✦
Much underrated, with a hauntingly beautiful version of Bob Dylan's "Forever Young." *— Bruce Eder*

A Holiday Celebration / 1988 / Warner Brothers ✦✦✦✦✦

Flowers and Stones / Aug. 25, 1992 / Warner Brothers ✦✦✦

Peter, Paul & Mommy, Too / 1993 / Warner Brothers ✦✦✦✦

Around the Campfire / Apr. 28, 1998 / Warner Brothers ✦✦✦✦✦
Including four new tracks, the two-disc set *Around the Campfire* is an excellent overview of Peter, Paul and Mary's career as it nears the four-decade mark. As indicated by the title, the focus of the collection is to shine a spotlight on songs which express ideals of community, tunes commonly sung in schools and churches as well as at more intimate gatherings; toward that aim, the trio offer newly recorded renditions of such perennials as "Kumbaya," "Michael Row Your Boat Ashore," "Down by the Riverside" and "Goodnight, Irene." The inclusion of such longtime favorites as "Puff, the Magic Dragon," "If I Had a Hammer," "Blowin' in the Wind" and "Leaving on a Jet Plane" solidifies *Around the Campfire* as a superior retrospective of Peter, Paul and Mary's music, one particularly ideal for younger listeners. *—Jason Ankeny*

Songs of Conscience & Concern / Mar. 23, 1999 / Warner Brothers ✦✦✦✦

Pierce Pettis

Vocals, Guitar / Contemporary Singer/Songwriter, Contemporary Folk, Country-Folk
You know you've got a shot when Joan Baez covers one of your songs. That's what sparked the career of Alabama singer-songwriter Pierce Pettis in 1979 when Baez chose to include "Song at the End of the Movie" on her *Honest Lullaby*. From there, Pettis was involved with the Fast Folk movement in New York in the 1980s alongside artists such as Shawn Colvin and Suzanne Vega. He continued to write songs and eventually embarked on his solo career in 1987 with the independent release of *Moments*, an album which some still consider his finest. Following that, Pettis made his way onto High Street Records, issuing four releases between 1991 and 1996. *Tinseltown, While the Serpent Lies Sleeping, Chase the Buffalo,* and *Making Light of It* all garnered much critical praise, but failed to find a widespread audience. What Pettis did find were fans in other artists who began adding his original tunes to their own repertoires. Dar Williams snagged "Family" for her *Mortal City* disc, while Garth Brooks tapped "You Move Me" for his hit *Sevens*. Maintaining his status as a songwriter has always been a focus for Pettis, from his time at Muscle Shoals Sound Studios to his work as a staff writer for PolyGram Publishing in Nashville. Making his name as an artist is another matter, and one that Pettis continues to pursue. In 1998, he aimed himself in a slightly different direction, signed on with Compass Records, and released *Everything Matters*. A fine collection of poignant character sketches, *Everything Matters* has a more refined, mature sound than previous efforts, perhaps due to the production of Grammy winner Gordon Kennedy who is best known for his work on Eric Clapton's "Change the World." *—Kelly McCartney*

Moments / 1987 / Small World ✦✦✦✦✦
Containing the title cut, "Grandmother's Song, " and "St. Paul's Song, " this is his first album, and still his best. *—Richard Meyer*

• **While the Serpent Lies Sleeping** / Jan. 15, 1992 / Windham Hill ✦✦✦✦✦
While the Serpent Lies Sleeping. The keen observations in Pettis' songwriting gain force from the caught-in-the-throat emotionalism of his singing. As befits this record label, the instrumental settings are somewhat busy in a new-age way. But where the drum and keyboard programming leave off, a strong contemporary folk album remains, especially on "Legacy," in which Pettis confronts the conflicts of his Southern heritage. *— William Ruhlmann*

Chase the Buffalo / 1993 / High Street ✦✦✦
On Pierce Pettis's fourth album, *Chase the Buffalo*, he shows a great deal of growth as a writer and studio performer. Pettis's other releases have had some high points, but on this CD, Pettis's politics and Southern gothic folk style are integrated better. His writing is more consistent and stands up to his mature and controlled vocals. The production by David Miner is also more focused on Pierce's style than before. This is an album worth tracking down. *—Richard Meyer*

Everything Matters / Jun. 16, 1998 / Compass ✦✦✦✦✦
Pierce Pettis is an engaging vocalist and an excellent guitarist, but he's primarily one of the pre-eminent songwriters of our time. Any disc of his is an event, and this one is no exception. His fifth album and second for Compass, *Everything Matters* is a series of self-portraits capturing the passion, longing, faith, release, compassion and humanity that is Pierce Pettis. He wraps his baritone voice lovingly around clever phrases and rich, everyday language which results in a fine disc by an artist of exceptional ability. *—Sigmund Finman*

Utah Phillips

b. 1935
Vocals, Guitar / Political Folk, Singer/Songwriter, Traditional Folk
"The golden voice of the great American Southwest," Bruce "U. Utah" Phillips is not one to take retirement sitting down. "Officially" retired from touring since 1996, the politically-conscious, Nevada City, California-based, singer and storyteller has maintained a constant flow of new recordings and reissues. Phillips' political awareness was inherited from his parents who were union organizers in the 1930s. After cutting his early musical teeth on a baritone ukelele on which he learned to play from Ukelele Ike songbooks, Phillips' musical direction was altered after he left home and traveled to Yellowstone Park to work on a road crew. As a soldier during the Korean conflict, Phillips continued to find refuge in music and helped to form a band, the Rice Paddy Ramblers. On the way to a demonstration at a Hiroshima Peace Memorial, Phillips was encouraged to write his first song, "The Enola Gay." Phillips continued to balance his love of music with his political involvement. In the early-1960s, he was involved with Fair Play for Cuba and the struggle for open housing laws in Utah. In 1968, he was nominated and campaigned for the U.S. Senate on the Peace and Freedom ticket. Phillips moved to the East Coast in 1969. Temporarily stopping in New York's Greenwich Village, Phillips settled, for several years, in Sarasota Springs, NY, where he became a regular performer at Cafe Lena. *—Craig Harris*

Good Though / 1973 / Philo ✦✦✦✦✦
This 1973 Philo album includes a mix of Phillips originals with traditional tunes like "Cannonball Blues," the notorious "Moose Turd Pie" (from whence comes the album's title), and "Wabash Cannonball." *—Roundup Newsletter*

• **I've Got to Know** / 1991 / Alcazar ✦✦✦✦✦

Past Didn't Go Anywhere / Oct. 15, 1996 / Righteous Babe ✦✦✦
Singer-songwriters Ani DiFranco and Utah Phillips team for *The Past Didn't Go Anywhere,* a collection of modern folk songs including "Bridges," "Nevada City," "California," "Anarchy" and "Mess with People." *—Jason Ankeny*

Loafer's Glory / Apr. 22, 1997 / Red House ✦✦✦✦
Utah Phillips returned to recording with Ani DiFranco's encouragement for their duet album, *The Past Didn't Go Anywhere.* Evidently, the collaboration inspired Phillips, because he delivered *Loafer's Glory* just months after *The Past,* which was released six years after his last album. *Loafer's Glory* captures him at the top of his form, running through songs and stories with glee, especially when he's subverting traditional American mores. Anyone who learned of Phillips through DiFranco couldn't ask for a better introduction to his style than *Loafer's Glory. — Stephen Thomas Erlewine*

Moscow Hold / Aug. 17, 1999 / Red House ✦✦✦✦
Utah Phillips, hot off his collaborations with Ani Difranco, returns to his primary vocation: that of teller of tall and hysterical tales. At times his one-liners verge on the vaudevillian, but he is always irreverent. Culled from performances between 1977-99 (the bulk of the material here was recorded in the late '80s and mid-'90s) Phillips takes on new agers and political correctness: It's his prerogative as a Northern California lefty. A master of the put-down (he even zings the untouchable Leonard Cohen), Phillips makes the perfect traveling companion—the kind of guy you want in the seat next to you on a never ending road trip, spinning yarns the whole way home. *—Denise Sullivan*

Phranc

b. 1957
Vocals, Guitar / Alternative Folk, Anti-Folk, Contemporary Folk, Singer/Songwriter
Bursting onto the L.A. punk scene in 1985 like the proverbial breath of fresh air, self-proclaimed Jewish lesbian folksinger Phranc has one of the most beautiful vocal instruments in the business. Born Susan Gottlieb in Los Angeles in 1957, Phranc began as a folksinger in the '70s before becoming a member of L.A. hardcore bands Catholic Discipline and Nervous Gender. Tiring of the genre's sexist and fascist leanings, she picked up her acoustic guitar again and debuted with *Folksinger* in 1985—a spare affair that tackled such topical and taboo subjects of the time like lesbianism, L.A. coroner Thomas Noguchi and "Female Mudwrestling." Delivered in Phranc's unique, forthright punk/folk style, the album received critical endorsement but never led to wider acceptance. Signed to Island by 1989, she enlisted the services of a band to play on the more fleshed-out *I Enjoy Being a Girl,* which included one of her trademark odes to a female sports figure in "Martina" (as in Navratilova). She followed it with 1991's *Positively Phranc,* a return to the spare style with which she made her mark. For the 1995 EP *Goofyfoot,* she paired up with Team Dresch's Donna Dresch and other Olympia, WA underground female musicians for a collection of novelty songs. During the four-year period she didn't record, Phranc occasionally performed in drag as Neil Diamond. Though not extremely prolific, Phranc was and is an icon among alternative and lesbian musicians, as well as folksingers everywhere. *—Denise Sullivan*

• **Folksinger** / 1985 / Island ✦✦✦✦
Jewish lesbian folksinger Phranc took the punk world by surprise when she released her militant folk record in 1985. A former punk rocker herself, Phranc set topical songs like "Noguchi" and "Everywhere I Go (I Hear the Go Go's)," the anti-suicide "Lifelover," and the sing-along "Female Mudwrestling" beside her strict cover of Dylan's "The Lonesome Death of Hattie Carroll" to great effect. Acoustic folk music had yet to be embraced by the punk/new wave underground, making *Folksinger* a watershed album. *—Denise Sullivan*

I Enjoy Being a Girl / May 1989 / Island ✦✦✦✦✦
Folksinger Phranc attempted to bust out of the solo acoustic mode for this record, produced by Violent Femme Victor DeLorenzo. Though some of the songs, like "Folksinger," "Take Off Your Swastika" and "Martina," work beautifully, others suffer from kitsch overkill (like her cover of "I Enjoy Being a Girl") and are not her strongest efforts. However, "Myriam and Esther," a traditional folk ballad with a distinctly female perspective, is the type of earnest song that only Phranc seems able to pull off in post-modern times. *—Denise Sullivan*

Positively Phranc / Mar. 19, 1991 / Island ✦✦✦
Phranc returned to form on this record of some of her strongest songs since her debut. "I Like You" and "Outta Here" are spare acoustic guitar standouts, as is her adaptation of Jonathan Richman's "Pablo Picasso," retitled "Gertrude Stein." *—Denise Sullivan*

Goofyfoot EP / Aug. 18, 1995 / Kill Rock Stars ✦✦✦
After a few years off, Phranc returned to record this EP with Olympia, WA musicians, including Donna Dresch from Team Dresch. Largely a collection of novelty songs, the EP includes covers of "Mrs. Brown You've Got a Lovely Daughter" and "Ode to Billie Joe," along with her "Bulldagger Swagger," a popular live favorite during her recording hiatus. It's a vital piece of the Phranc catalog after her long absence. *—Denise Sullivan*

Milkman / Nov. 3, 1998 / Phancy ✦✦✦
After a seven-year hiatus from performing and recording her own material in full-length form, this "comeback" has all of the essential Phranc elements in proper alignment: there's humor on "Yer the One" and "Cuffs"; grief is addressed during "Gary" and the gently strident "Where Were You?" And then there are the songs that make you laugh and cry, like "Ozzie and Harriet." She delivers the line "Where's my Harriet?" in her perfect voice, filled simultaneously with the dueling emotions of hope and despair that unless you're dead, chances are it will touch some part of you. L.A. cats (and kitten) Steven McDonald, Tal Bergman, Phil

Parlapiano and Anna Waronker step in to fill the spaces on bass, drums, accordion and vocals respectively. *—Denise Sullivan*

Plainsong

f. 1972, **db.** 1974
Group / Folk-Rock
A quartet formed by Ian Matthews in 1972 with Andy Roberts, Bob Ronga and Dave Richards. They released the brilliant *In Search of Amelia Earhart* the same year to critical praise but little commercial success. While working on their follow-up, the more country oriented *Plainsong III,* Ronga quit and Matthews and Richards were unable to agree on the direction the band would take musically. They disbanded before the album's completion. In 1993, a revived interest in the band inspired a new studio album, *Dark Side of the Room* as well as a BBC recording of a promotional tour from 1972. In 1994, the band released *Voices Electric. Sister Flute* followed in 1996. In 1997, Clive Gregson (ex-Any Trouble, Gregson & Collister) joined the band, with *New Place Now* appearing two years later. *—Chris Woodstra*

• **In Search of Amelia Earhart** / 1972 / Elektra ✦✦✦✦✦
The theme of this album is loosely based on the disappearance of Amelia Earhart and features four tunes penned by Matthews including the spooky "For the Second Time" and "Call the Tune." Matthews also shows his ability to pick top-notch material by covering Paul Siebel's "Louise," The Jim & Jesse classic "Diesel on My Tail" and Rick Cunha's "Yo Yo Man" (a song Cunha attempted to chart with a year later). *—Jim Worbois*

The Pozo-Seco Singers

f. 1965, Texas, **db.** 1970
Group / Folk-Pop
Although they are most remembered for including Don Williams in their lineup prior to his ascension to solo country stardom, the Pozo-Seco Singers were much more oriented toward pop/folk than country music. The Texas threesome formed in Corpus Christi, Texas, where Williams and Lofton Kline had a duo called the Strangers Two; with the addition of Susan Taylor, they became the Pozo-Seco Singers. Playing cleanly executed, coffeehouse-style folk, the trio could sound like a far more commercial, pop-conscious version of Ian & Sylvia with their conscientious blend of male and female lead vocals and harmonies. Not as hip as Ian & Sylvia or Peter, Paul & Mary, and not as blatantly commercial as, say, the Seekers, the group had a few small pop hits in the mid-'60s, "I Can Make It with You" and "Look What You've Done" both entering the Top 40. After a few albums for Columbia in the last half of the 1960s, the act broke up, leaving Williams to pursue a solo career in the country field. *—Richie Unterberger*

• **Time/I Can Make It with You** / 1996 / Collectors' Choice Music ✦✦✦✦✦
Their first two Columbia LPs are combined onto one CD on this reissue, with the addition of a couple of bonus tracks, the low-charting singles "I Believed It All" and "Louisiana Man." Including half a dozen minor hits in all, the disc in effect functions as a best-of for this slight but pleasant folk-pop trio. Their dated approach may work better as live background music at a beachfront cafe than it does on a CD re-release, but it's not a bad guilty pleasure all the same. *—Richie Unterberger*

Blind Alfred Reed

b. 1880, Floyd, VA, **d.** Jan. 17, 1956
Vocals, Fiddle / Traditional Folk, Traditional Country, Old-Timey
This West Virginia singer/songwriter and fiddler was one of Ralph Peer's discoveries on the legendary 1927 Bristol field trip that unearthed the Carter Family and Jimmie Rodgers. Reed was one of those uniquely Southern contradictions, both reactionary and progressive in his songs. "How Can a Poor Man Stand Such Times and Live?" echoed the sentiments of the rural poor, who tasted none of the Roaring Twenties prosperity (a myth for all but a privileged few). "Why Do You Bob Your Hair, Girls?" invoked Biblical sanctions against flappers. Topical commentary of this sort was rare in early hillbilly recordings: Reed's contemporaries usually pruned a branch from the folk tree or swiped a page from Mom's Victorian songbook. Incongruously, Reed was a protest singer/songwriter out of time and place. Ry Cooder revived a couple of his songs in the '70s, the decade of Rounder's reissue of several Reed performances, *How Can a Poor Man Stand Such Times and Live? —Mark A. Humphrey*

• **How Can a Poor Man . . .** / 1920 / Rounder ✦✦✦✦✦
How Can a Poor Man Stand Such Times and Live is '20s hillbilly social commentary, both reactionary ("Why Do You Bob Your Hair, Girls?") and progressive ("How Can a Poor Man Stand Such Times and Live?") from this West Virginia singer and fiddler. It's austere and engaging. *—Mark A. Humphrey*

Complete Recorded Works / Mar. 2, 1998 / Document ✦✦✦✦

John Renbourn

Vocals, Guitar, Guitar (Acoustic) / British Folk-Rock, Classical Guitar, Folk-Blues, British Folk
Guitarist John Renbourn is one of the fathers of contemporary British folk music and is one of the finest fingerstyle players in the world. A founder of the seminal group Pentangle, Renbourn's music fuses British and Celtic folk with blues, jazz, British early music, classic guitar and Eastern styles. Born and raised in Torquay, England, Renbourn began playing guitar as a teen. By 1966 he was playing folk music in Soho where he met many other musicians, including Paul Simon, Davey Graham and most importantly, Bert Jansch, a guitar player whom Renbourn greatly admired. Renbourn performed on Jansch's second album and afterward they teamed up formally to record *Bert and John.* In 1967 the two founded Pentangle and remained together through 1978. Renbourn, as with the other group members, continued to release such solo albums as *The Hermit* and *The Black Balloon.* He formed the John Renbourn Group in the '80s and began adding an East Indian percussion and jazz woodwinds to his music. *—Sandra Brennan*

There You Go / 1965 / Columbia ✦✦✦✦✦
This was the first album to feature Renbourn's name prominently in the billing, although it was not a solo LP but a collaboration with vocalist Dorris Henderson, with Renbourn providing the guitar accompaniment. Henderson and Renbourn focused on traditional folk material like "Cotton Eyed Joe," "Ribbon Bow" and "The Water Is Wide" on this album, which also had a few songs by Renbourn, Bob Dylan's "Mr. Tambourine Man," Ewan MacColl's "The Lag's Song" and Willie Johnson's much-covered "You'll Need Somebody on Your Bond." Although a tad restrained in execution, Henderson's vocals are assured and moving, like a link between the strict interpretive folk singers of the 1950s and the looser ones of the 1960s. Renbourn's guitar playing is already brilliant, and the recording (the tracks were largely done in one take) has a sparse and spontaneous feel, in the kind of setup where you can hear a slight echo on the vocals. The CD reissue on Big Beat adds the non-LP 1965 single "Hangman"/"Leaves that Are Green" (the latter an early Paul Simon composition), with the echo turned up high enough that it sounds as if it might have been recorded in an actual freight train—not to the detriment of the tracks, it actually enhances the atmosphere. *—Richie Unterberger*

Sir John Alot of Merrie Englandes Musyk Thyng & ye Grene Knyghte / 1968 / Shanachie ✦✦✦✦
An instrumental album (originally called *Sir John Alot of Merrie England*) featuring Renbourn with his Pentangle bandmate Terry Cox on percussion and Ray Warleigh on flute. Originally released in England in 1968, the same year that Pentangle started to record, *Sir John Alot* was steeped largely in English folk music. Highlights include "The Trees They Do Grow High" (aka "Long A-Growing"), solo guitar miniatures such as "Lady Goes to Church," the epic "Morgana," with its sharply nuanced tempo and timbre changes, and the sprightly "My Dear Boy." Some parts of this album are surprisingly contemporary-sounding, such as the bluesy "Transformation," which sounds like "What'd I Say" transposed for acoustic guitar and African drums; "White Fishes," which veers dangerously close to quoting George Gershwin's "It Ain't Necessarily So" and Rodgers & Hammerstein's "My Favorite Things"; and "Sweet Potato," which sounds like a folk-rock song without words, even as Renbourn quotes "Satisfaction" at one point. *—Bruce Eder*

The Hermit / 1976 / Shanachie ✦✦✦

A Maid in Bedlam / 1977 / Shanachie ✦✦✦✦✦

The Enchanted Garden / 1980 / Shanachie ✦✦✦

Live in America / 1981 / Flying Fish ✦✦✦✦
Originally a two-LP set, this 70-minute concert CD recorded on April 16, 1981 in San Francisco features the core of the band that appeared on *The Enchanted Garden*—Jacqui McShee on vocals, Tony Roberts on flute, krumhorn, and pipes, John Molineaux on dulcimer, violin, and mandolin, and Keshav Sathe playing the tabla. The repertory is rooted, of course, in English folk music, including "The Trees They Grow High," a beautiful a cappella number ("Ye Mariners All"), and "John Barleycorn Is Dead." Renbourn's playing is showcased throughout, most notably on "English Dance," a dazzling 3-minute guitar solo; "Breton Dance," by contrast, is a vehicle for the entire band. McShee's crystalline vocals hold much of the spotlight, and the disc is worth owning just for her performance, her presence making this as valuable as any Pentangle release. *—Bruce Eder*

Ship of Fools / 1988 / Flying Fish ✦✦✦

• **The Essential: The Best of John Renbourn** / 1994 / Transatlantic ✦✦✦✦✦
This 22-song anthology lives up to its name, covering Renbourn's career from his first solo album, *John Renbourn* from 1965, up through *The Hermit* in 1973. The selection is very generous, not only in number but range, running the gamut from basic folk-blues to the more diverse stylings of his Pentangle work. The early tracks, especially a quartet of numbers from 1965, show just how much Renbourn was influenced early in his career by the pioneering blues work of Alexis Korner and Cyril Davies, and also how far he'd moved from their basic, traditional approach in just a couple of years, stretching the blues out in some surprising directions—he could easily have crossed swords successfully with Jimmy Page during this period. When he gets back to the blues in the early 1970s, Renbourn sounds more like himself, without trying to imitate an American sound—on "White House Blues," he reinvents his approach to the music in his own image, and the results are quietly spectacular. The playing and singing cover a multitude of styles, embracing the full range of Renbourn's work during those eight years, with Pentangle (understandably) slightly underrepresented and the blues perhaps emphasized more than is usual. Even longtime fans will want to own this collection for those early blues tracks that aren't so easy to find, while anyone who wants to start learning about Renbourn should also consider this compilation. The notes are very extensive, too. *—Bruce Eder*

Wheel of Fortune / 1994 / Flying Fish ✦✦✦✦✦
This live album, recorded in partnership with Robin Williamson (who plays Celtic harp, rhythm guitar, and whistle) at the Old Town School of Folk Music, is the most beguiling of Renbourn's albums, not a bad achievement 30 years into his recording career. The sound is excellent, the repertory consists almost entirely of traditional folk songs (there are two modern originals by Archie Fisher and Randy Weston) arranged by Renbourn and/or Williamson, and it's all fresh and bracing. Williamson takes the lead vocals on four songs, Renbourn on three, and the other four are instrumentals, with one dazzling piece of storytelling ("Finn and the Old Man's House") to musical accompaniment. Renbourn's contribution is slightly understated in these surroundings, although when he sings, his voice achieves great expressiveness and power. This is also a good showcase for his playing, and the running time, at more than an hour, is generous. *—Bruce Eder*

Keeper of the Vine: Best of John Renbourn and Stefan Grossman / Nov. 16, 1999 / Shanachie ✦✦✦✦
Keeper of the Vine presents a collection of songs from the fertile collaboration of John Renbourn and Stefan Grossman in the late '70s and '80s. Renbourn is known for playing medieval, early classical, traditional blues, rock, and contemporary jazz. Grossman is more

known for ragtime, Delta blues, boogie, and American folk styles; the remarkable thing is how well they mesh together, aided by their love for the acoustic guitar. This is a fine album that manages to educate and enthrall the listener while conveying the history of a great partnership. *—Stacia Proefrock*

Malvina Reynolds

b. 1900, **d.** 1978

Vocals / Contemporary Folk, Political Folk, Singer/Songwriter

A topical songwriter who came to prominence in the '60s when she was at an age at which most people retire, Malvina Reynolds is best known as the author of the satirical song "Little Boxes," which was Pete Seeger's only pop singles hit in 1964. She also wrote "What Have They Done to the Rain," a hit for the Searchers in 1965. Her songs also have been covered by Joan Baez, Judy Collins, and others. Reynolds herself recorded for Columbia (*Malvina Reynolds Sings the Truth*), Folkways (*Another Country Heard From*), and her own Cassandra label. She also wrote children's songs and material for the TV show *Sesame Street*. *—William Ruhlmann*

• **Malvina** / 1972 / Cassandra ✦✦✦✦✦

Reynolds is best known for Pete Seeger's versions of her compositions, songs like "Little Boxes" and "What Have They Done to the Rain." The first is included on this collection, along with 11 other uncompromisingly political songs that mark Reynolds as one of the great topical songwriters of the 60s. She has other excellent albums (including a long out-of-print Columbia LP), but this is a good place to start. *—William Ruhlmann*

Ear to the Ground / May 23, 2000 / Smithsonian/Folkways ✦✦✦

Although the scope of this anthology is wide, it shouldn't be mistaken for a definitive best-of retrospective. All of the selections are taken from albums released on Reynolds' own Cassandra label between 1970 and 1980, with the addition of a couple of spoken-word introductions from Susan Wengraf's film on the singer, *Love It Like a Fool*. That means that there's nothing from her prior recordings on Folkways and Columbia in the '60s, and that the versions of her most well-known songs—"Little Boxes" and "What Have They Done to the Rain?"—are not the originals. At any rate, the music is interesting if quite uneven, and not always as well sung and performed as it is well-written. While Reynolds is known as a folk singer, her Cassandra recordings usually used a full electric band, and are actually more properly classified as folk-rock. With topical songs that take such a progressive and good-hearted position, one is almost reluctant to point out that Reynolds' straining, wavering vocals are not wholly up to the material. That's a shame, because although some of this stuff is sanctimonious, some of it is also quite good: not just "Little Boxes" and "What Have They Done to the Rain?," but others as well. Those who think of her as a protest folk singer might be surprised to find some pretty good, melodic folk-rockers here. The melancholic "The World's Gone Beautiful," as unlikely as it might seem, could have easily fit into the repertoire of a Jefferson Airplane-type group in the late '60s. It might be heresy to suggest this, but it could be that Reynolds' songs would have been better served by strong interpreters than by the singer herself. Still, this collection has its merits, including comprehensive, affectionate notes by friend and fellow folk singer Rosalie Sorrels. *—Richie Unterberger*

Jean Ritchie

b. Dec. 8, 1922, Viper, KY

Vocals, Dulcimer / Folk Revival, Singer/Songwriter, Traditional Folk

Singer, songwriter, song collector, dulcimer player, and author. Jean Ritchie, who was born in the heart of the Cumberland Mountains of Kentucky, was raised in the folk music of that area. She has been active in preserving and performing traditional mountain ballads and songs. She eventually moved to the New York City area and achieved a national reputation throughout the '50s and '60 singing solo voice, or with the mountain dulcimer. A number of Ritchie albums are still available from Smithsonian/Folkways recordings. *—Michael Erlewine*

Jean Ritchie & Doc Watson at Folk City / 1990 / Smithsonian/Folkways ✦✦✦✦

According to reissue annotator Joe Wilson, Doc Watson and Jean Ritchie had never heard of each other before they got together for a concert at Folk City in 1963, which says something about the 40-year-old Watson's obscurity at the time and about his limited knowledge of other performers, since 39-year-old Ritchie had been recording for more than a decade. The two had a lot in common, however, the North Carolina-born guitarist and banjo player sharing a repertoire of traditional material with the Kentucky-born dulcimer player. During their set (actually featuring only six songs performed together, with seven solos by Watson and four by Ritchie), they mixed murder ballads with spirituals and dance tunes. The titles included many songs that were familiar to country fans, and that would become familiar to folk fans as well: "Pretty Polly," "Wabash Cannonball," and "Amazing Grace." Especially interesting were "Go Dig My Grave," "Hiram Hubbard," and "House Carpenter," on which Watson played banjo and Ritchie sang. This was very much a joint appearance rather than a real duo outing, but the performers were sufficiently strong and complementary enough to make it work. (The 1990 Smithsonian/Folkways reissue added three tracks—"East Virginia," "Blue Ridge Mountain Blues," and "Pretty Saro"—to the original 1963 release.) *—William Ruhlmann*

• **The Most Dulcimer** / Greenhays ✦✦✦✦✦

The Roches

f. 1978, **db.** 1997

Group / Contemporary Folk, Singer/Songwriter

Noted for their lush harmonies, quirky songs and impressive stylistic range, the three Roche sisters—Maggie, Terre and Suzzy—were among contemporary folk music's most endearing artists. Maggie and Terre began touring professionally in the late '60s, sang backup on Paul Simon's *There Goes Rhymin' Simon* and recorded their debut LP, 1975's *Seductive Reasoning*. Restored to a trio by the late '70s, the Roches became a staple of the Greenwich Village folk circuit and signed to Warner Bros. for a 1979 self-titled LP produced by Robert Fripp, which earned acclaim for their exquisite harmonies (equal parts Terre's ethereal upper register, Maggie's near-baritone low notes and Suzzy's midrange acrobatics). For 1980's *Nurds*, they changed direction and augmented their basic folk sound with a rock rhythm section. Fripp returned to produce a largely acoustic effort, 1982's *Keep On Doing;* when neither it nor its follow-up, 1985's *Another World*, was a commercial success, the trio left Warner to return to touring. The Roches eventually signed to MCA for 1989's *Speak* though after 1992's *A Dove*, the trio left MCA as well, to record a children's album. For 1995's *Can We Go Home Now?*, they signed to Rykodisc. In 1997, the Roches announced they were going their separate ways; both Terre and Suzzy released solo work. *—Jason Ankeny*

• **The Roches** / 1979 / Warner Brothers ✦✦✦✦✦

An extraordinary debut record with ringing, soaring harmonies rubbing up against a beautiful and spare instrumental sound. A powerful piece of work. *—Bruce Eder*

Nurds / 1980 / Warner Brothers ✦✦✦

Keep on Doing / 1982 / Warner Brothers ✦✦✦

This is a comeback after the bizarre misstep of their second album. *—Bruce Eder*

We Three Kings / 1990 / Rykodisc ✦✦✦✦✦

Well, why not a Roches Christmas album— It's actually perfect, if you stop and think about it—there's always been something cute and childlike about their tone, and when they put their formidable vocal chops to work on tunes as potentially complex as "Angels We Have Heard on High" and "The Holly and the Ivy," the results can be as gorgeous as they are unique. Their Brooklynese versions of "Frosty the Snowman" ("Why, I oughta...") and "Winter Wonderland" ("Gone away is da blueboid") are a hoot, and the a cappella "Star of Wonder" is a fascinating obscurity. There are a couple of missteps—the pseudo-Latin rhythm and soprano sax don't contribute much to "We Three Kings," nor does the synth really enhance "Angels We Have Heard on High." But overall, this album will make an utterly charming addition to anyone's holiday playlist. *—Rick Anderson*

A Dove / 1992 / MCA ✦✦✦✦✦

An update from the singing sisters finds them living in the urban jungle and overcoming romantic expectations in favor of self-reliance, though not without regret and not, thank God, without moments of humor and absurdity. For the most part, the trio's folkie past has given way to a rock-pop approach on this album. *—William Ruhlmann*

Can We Go Home Now— / 1995 / Rykodisc ✦✦✦

The Roche sisters have been called oddballs more than once, and with good reason—though their approach has generally been a sweetly appealing folk-rock fusion, there's always been something distinctly off-kilter about their sound. It could be the almost eerie blend of their three voices, or maybe it's their collective tone, which is often reedy to the point of girlishness; sometimes the way they're singing makes you wonder if you're missing a joke somewhere. And chance are pretty good that you are, though the humor is too often self-referential and slightly smug. This album largely avoids those pitfalls, though not entirely. "Move" and "You (Make My Life Come True)" are both perfect love songs with charms as straightforward as the plainspoken singing that delivers them. Ditto for the quirky but endearing "I'm Someone Who Loves You." But "Home Away from Home" deals in distressingly broad political stereotypes, and "When You're Ready" wallows in artsy self-indulgence. The low points are worth enduring for the high points on this album, but it's kind of a close call. *—Rick Anderson*

Stan Rogers

b. 1949, Hamilton, Ontario, Canada, **d.** Jun. 2, 1983

Vocals, Guitar, Bass / Contemporary Folk

Stan Rogers came from Hamilton, Ontario, a six-foot-four poet who started out as a rock bassist before turning to folk music. With his rich voice, he used his music to call to life all of the wonder and mysticism of his native Canada. His singing is occasionally mistaken for that of Gordon Lightfoot, but it's huskier and earthier than Lightfoot's, and his repertoire—made up of song cycles drawn from throughout Canada—is also more tradition-oriented and more mystical. Rogers died in a fire aboard an Air Canada flight in Cincinnati, OH, in June 1983, leaving behind a half-dozen albums. *—Bruce Eder*

• **Fogarty's Cove** / 1976 / Fogartys Cove ✦✦✦✦✦

A dozen songs of and about Nova Scotia, mostly about the sea and all but one written by Rogers. They successfully capture not only a people but their sense of time and beauty, with the Rogers baritone tastefully and effectively moving through the spaces and ages of his subject, and with traditional acoustic backing (guitar, violin, flute, etc.) *—Bruce Eder*

Northwest Passage / 1981 / Fogartys Cove ✦✦✦

Precisely what its title indicates—a collection of material from and about the vast western expanse of Canada, all filled with robust singing and melodies that are practically part of the landscape. *—Bruce Eder*

From Fresh Water / 1984 / Fogartys Cove ✦✦✦

The final Stan Rogers album, mixed and mastered after his death, is a dazzling array of songs devoted to the Great Lakes region and the rest of inland Canada. Some of the environmental sensibilities are bitter, and the politics, as with all his work, are defiantly Canadian. *—Bruce Eder*

For the Family / Feb. 20, 1996 / Gadfly ✦✦✦✦

This album was originally released on the Folk Tradition label in 1983, shortly before$ Rogers' tragic death in an airplane crash; it was reissued on CD by the small but very cool Gadfly label in 1996. Rogers had a deep, rich singing voice and an amazing melodic talent; his original songs are of legendary quality. But this album consists of songs by other writers and a few traditional numbers from his native Canada, many of them remembered from his childhood. Accompanied by his brother Garnet on fiddle and bassist Jim Morrison, Rogers performs several tunes by his uncle Lee Bushell, including the amusing "Strings and Dory Plug," a Calgary cowboy song "Two-Bit Cayuse" and, most affectingly of all, the aching "Cape

St. Mary's" and the 19th century Scots song "Scarborough Settler's Lament." *—Rick Anderson*

From Coffee House To Concert Hall / Jan. 25, 2000 / Fogartys Cove ♦♦♦

Rooftop Singers

f. 1962, **db.** 1967

Group / Folk Revival, Folk-Pop, Traditional Folk

The Rooftop Singers were the most successful of the folk revival's one-hit wonders—their single major chart entry, "Walk Right In," was a number one record and also the biggest-selling single in the history of their label, Vanguard Records. The group, formed by former Weaver Erik Darling specifically to record the song, also included vocalist Bill Svanoe and jazz singer Lynne Taylor. The trio cut "Walk Right In" for Vanguard in 1963, in a version with updated lyrics and a new arrangement featuring paired 12-string acoustic guitars, which reached the number one spot later that year and yielded an album of the same title. The group differed markedly from the Weavers and most of the popular folk trios of the era, being far more influenced by blues and ragtime, as well as less profoundly earnest in its political sensibilities. Taylor's singing showed more of a jazz influence than was usual, while Darling and Svanoe's guitar playing showed higher-than-average dexterity. The Rooftop Singers made it to the Newport Folk Festival in 1963 (and there was a resulting live album), but their popularity only lasted about a year. The trio released further singles and a pair of albums before splitting up in 1967. *—Bruce Eder*

Walk Right In! / 1963 / Vanguard ♦♦♦

● **The Best of Rooftop Singers** / 1992 / Vanguard ♦♦♦♦♦

Sixteen songs drawn from all three of the group's albums, featuring, of course, "Walk Right In," and along with a good cross-section of their best music. Other highlights include their upbeat version of Jesse Fuller's "San Francisco Bay Blues," a sultry, folky rendition of Duke Ellington's "It Don't Mean a Thing," the traditional songs "Old Joe Clark," "R.C. Frog," and "Ha Ha Thisaway" (the latter two featuring extraordinarily wry and sensitive performances by Taylor), and Jimmie Rodgers' "Peach Pickin' Time Down In Georgia." The original trio was especially good at harmonizing old-style blues. Taylor's solos were always filled with surprising nuance and expressiveness, while the second lineup with Mindy Stuart was more conventional and didn't have as much of a feel for blues, though they do try hard on "That Ain't Love." Their "Rainy River" is rather sweet, but Lynne Taylor's sides outclass the later stuff. *—Bruce Eder*

Tom Rush

b. Feb. 8, 1941, Portsmouth, NH

Vocals, Guitar / Singer/Songwriter

Tom Rush came up in the Cambridge folk scene of the early '60s, playing folk-blues on a series of albums for Prestige Records, then moved to Elektra, and by the late '60s was interpreting the work of such upcoming writers as Joni Mitchell and James Taylor. By the early '70s, he was mixing his own songs on albums for Columbia. In recent years, Rush has become something of a folk packager, putting together road shows that include some of the newer folk performers. *— William Ruhlmann*

Got A Mind To Ramble / 1963 / Prestige/Folklore ♦♦♦

An acoustic 1963 session, from Rush's Cambridge folk/blues days. Much of this is White acoustic revival blues, but there are detours on selections like Merle Travis's "Nine Pound Hammer," and Rush's own "Duncan and Brady," and the instrumental "Mole's Moan," which was written by Maria Muldaur. The album has been combined with another 1963 LP, *Blues, Songs and Ballads*, on Fantasy's expanded CD reissue of *Blues, Songs and Ballads*. *—Richie Unterberger*

Tom Rush [Elektra] / 1965 / Elektra ♦♦♦♦♦

Signing with then-fledgling Elektra records proved a wise move for Tom Rush in the mid-'60s, as this self-titled album attests. Full of urban blues and folk songs, Rush delivers the goods and then some. Helped out with the bare minimum of musicians and delivered with love, *Tom Rush* is a must. *—James Chrispell*

Take a Little Walk with Me / 1966 / Elektra ♦♦♦

The Circle Game / 1968 / Elektra ♦♦♦♦♦

Always best known as an interpreter of other people's songs, Tom Rush struck gold here by covering the likes of then-unknowns James Taylor, Joni Mitchell and Jackson Browne. *The Circle Game* is great from start to finish, including Joni's "Urge for Going" and the title cut, James' "Something in the Way She Moves" and "Sunshine Sunshine," and Jackson's "Shadow Dream Song," alongside his own "No Regrets." *—James Chrispell*

Tom Rush [Columbia] / 1970 / Columbia/Legacy ♦♦♦

Wrong End of the Rainbow / 1970 / Columbia ♦♦♦♦♦

Adding four original compositions to the mix helped Tom Rush gather even more acclaim with *Wrong End of the Rainbow*. But it was his covers of "Sweet Baby James" and Jesse Winchester's "Biloxi" that made listeners sigh. More country-rock than previous efforts, nothing here should be forsaken because all cuts merit listening. Again, Tom Rush found the right mix of material and released another solid effort. *—James Chrispell*

Merrimack County / 1972 / Columbia ♦♦♦

Ladies Love Outlaws / 1974 / Columbia ♦♦♦

Returning to covering other people's tunes, Tom Rush's main strength, *Ladies Love Outlaws* plunges the listener full-tilt into the country-rock sound which so many were finding in the mid-'70s. Included here are Guy Clark's "Desperados Waiting for a Train," Lee Clayton's title track, and a stunning redo of Rush's own "No Regrets" helped along by the likes of the Eagles and Carly Simon on backup. But the best is saved for last, where Rush covers Bruce Cockburn's "One Day I Walk," showing that he hadn't lost his touch. A bit rough in places, but well done for the most part. *—James Chrispell*

Blues, Songs and Ballads / 1989 / Fantasy ♦♦♦

A 23-song collection combining two albums that Rush recorded in 1963 (*Got a Mind to Ramble* and *Blues, Songs and Ballads*) onto a single CD. Rush plays acoustic guitar, accompanied only by Fritz Richmond on washtub bass, on a selection of almost exclusively traditional material; the only track penned by Rush himself is the opener, "Duncan and Brady." This anthology is definitive early-'60s Cambridge coffeehouse music, which means that it's a bit quaintly dated, but also that it's Sunday-morning listening in the good sense of the term. Rush plays accomplished acoustic guitar and sings with calm authority, though he's no one's ideal bluesman (or even ideal White bluesman). The traditional blues covers, which dominated the original *Blues, Songs and Ballads* LP (now the second part of this CD), can sound pretty callow; the folkier ones work better, one highlight being the instrumental "Mole's Moan," penned by a young Maria Muldaur. *—Richie Unterberger*

● **The Very Best of Tom Rush: No Regrets** / Oct. 5, 1999 / Columbia/Legacy ♦♦♦♦♦

Columbia/Legacy's *The Very Best of Tom Rush: No Regrets* is the first comprehensive overview ever assembled on Rush, one of the finest interpretive singers and singer/songwriters of the folk revival. The disc begins with "San Francisco Bay Blues," from his 1962 debut, *Tom Rush at the Unicorn*, and concludes with "River Song," a previously unreleased song recorded for the compilation in November 1998. Between those two tunes are 15 songs that touch on each of his albums. Since it's only a single-disc, 17-track compilation, there are inevitably some fan favorites missing, but what's most impressive about *No Regrets* is that it nevertheless conveys the scope of his career and accomplishments. Almost all of his major moments are here—"On the Road Again," "Galveston Flood," "Joshua Gone Barbados," "No Regrets," "Lost My Driving Wheel"—and while they're not sequenced in straight chronological order, they nevertheless capture the spirit of Rush and his music. The end result is a terrific compilation—a perfect introduction for neophytes and a welcome reminder of Rush's talents for longtime fans. *—Stephen Thomas Erlewine*

Buffy Sainte-Marie

b. Feb. 20, 1941, Piapot Reserve, Saskatchewan, Canada

Vocals, Guitar / Contemporary Folk, Folk-Rock, Singer/Songwriter, Folk-Pop, Country-Pop

Buffy Sainte-Marie enjoyed a long career that has seen her rise to stardom on the folk circuit and try her hand at country, rock, soundtrack themes, acting, activism, and children's television. For most listeners, she remains identified with the material she wrote and sang for Vanguard in the mid-'60s. Her songs that addressed the plight of the Native American, particularly "Now That the Buffalo's Gone" and "My Country 'Tis of Thy People You're Dying," were the ones that generated the most controversy. Yet she was also skilled at addressing broader themes of war and justice ("Universal Soldier") and romance ("Until It's Time for You to Go"). She was also a capable interpreter of outside material, although her idiosyncratic vibrato made large-scale commercial success out of the question. *—Richie Unterberger*

☆ **It's My Way!** / 1964 / Vanguard ♦♦♦♦♦

This is one of the most scathing topical folk albums ever made. Sainte-Marie sings in an emotional, vibrato-laden voice of war ("The Universal Soldier," later a hit for Donovan), drugs ("Cod'ine"), sex ("The Incest Song"), and most telling, the mistreatment of Native Americans, of which Sainte-Marie is one ("Now That the Buffalo's Gone"). Even decades later, the album's power is moving and disturbing. *— William Ruhlmann*

Many a Mile / 1965 / Fontana ♦♦♦

Sainte-Marie's second LP was most notable for the original version of her most famous composition, "Until It's Time for You to Go," which is her most melodic and memorable track. The rest of the album is more traditional and rough-hewn than some would expect, including a Child ballad with a "Greensleeves"-like melody ("Must I Go Bound"), the Bukka White blues "Fixin' to Die," the oft-done ballad "Lazarus," an Irish-American murder ballad, and a traditional tune accompanied only by mouthbow ("Groundhog"). Of more interest are Sainte-Marie's own compositions, including "Los Pescadores" (which has some of her most uncompromising vibrato) and "Welcome Welcome Emigrante." *—Richie Unterberger*

Little Wheel Spin & Spin / 1966 / Vanguard ♦♦♦♦♦

Sainte-Marie took some tentative steps toward a more contemporary sound here, with contributions from supporting musicians such as Bruce Langhorne, Patrick Sky, Eric Weissberg, and Felix Pappalardi, all of whom were noted New York folk and folk-rock players. It's an average collection of songs, not among either her best or worst work, including some covers of traditional ballads among a mostly original program. It was one of those originals, "My Country 'sTis of Thy People You're Dying," that caught the most attention and remains her most protest-oriented composition. *—Richie Unterberger*

Fire & Fleet & Candlelight / 1967 / Vanguard ♦♦♦♦

Recorded in 1967, the 1999 re-release of *Fire & Fleet & Candlelight* marks its first appearance on CD. Buffy Sainte-Marie's reputation as a fine folk singer/songwriter is accentuated by the reissue of this classic album, which contains songs steeped in her Native American heritage and social consciousness. "Mayoo Sto Hoon," "Now That the Buffalo's Gone" and "Universal Soldier" reflect the lyrical and emotional tenor of *Fire & Fleet & Candlelight*, a work that remains fresh and challenging years after its creation. *—Heather Phares*

I'm Gonna Be a Country Girl Again / 1968 / Vanguard ♦♦

● **The Best of Buffy Sainte-Marie** / 1970 / Vanguard ♦♦♦♦♦

Sainte-Marie pursued a variety of musical styles, from folk to country to experimental rock, and all are represented on this wide-ranging double-record compilation. It doesn't all work, but there are some terrific songs, among them the Native American lament "My Country 'Tis of Thy People You're Dying," and the romantic "Until It's Time for You to Go," and a musical adaptation of a passage from a Leonard Cohen novel, "God Is Alive, Magic Is Afoot." (Beware of the abbreviated version, Vanguard 73113.) *— William Ruhlmann*

Illuminations / 1970 / Vanguard ♦♦♦

The Best of Buffy Sainte-Marie, Vol. 2 / 1971 / Vanguard ♦♦♦

Sainte-Marie's best-known and best songs were used on Vanguard's *Best of Buffy Sainte-*

Marie Vol. 1. This 24-song set features mostly original material, along with some traditional tunes and the odd cover, like Joni Mitchell's "Song to a Seagull." While not all of the songs are good, it does illustrate the considerable range of her early recordings—from traditional folk accompanied only by mouthbow to country and western, a truly odd version of "Lyke Wake Dirge," a psychedelic rock cover of Richie Havens' "Adam," a French-pop remake of "Until It's Time for You to Go," and more. There was a lot more to Sainte-Marie than the early acoustic folk recordings, although those are what she's most famous for (and justly so). Like several of Vanguard's anthologies, however, this is sequenced poorly, jumping all over the place chronologically. It makes for a far more uneven experience than would be the case if the sides were arranged more or less in the order in which they were recorded. *—Richie Unterberger*

She Used to Wanna Be a Ballerina / 1971 / Vanguard ♦♦♦

Quiet Places / 1973 / Vanguard ♦♦

Coincidence & Likely Stories / 1992 / Chrysalis ♦♦♦
Native American activist and singer/songwriter Buffy Sainte-Marie makes an incredible comeback on this recording after 16 years away from the studio. Busting all myths about dippy folkies, Sainte-Marie takes on the still-hot topic of Indian oppression while exploring sonic ground that is completely unexpected: programmed keyboards with Laurie Anderson-style voice-over ("The Priests of the Golden Bull"). The entire work is a hard-hitting condemnation of corporate greed and dirty politics, masked in new-agey sounds—about as subversive as it gets. *—Denise Sullivan*

Mike Seeger

b. Aug. 15, 1933, New York, NY
Vocals, Autoharp, Mandolin, Guitar, Fiddle, Banjo / String Bands, Folklore, Traditional Folk, Traditional Country, Old-Timey
Mike Seeger is the greatest musician in traditional folk music. He has done more to preserve and to perpetuate old-time music than any other person. Mike has "discovered" more traditional musicians than anyone else. He has brought many traditional musicians to the world, with out ever attempting to exploit them. He has mastered every old-time musical instrument. As performer, collector, teacher, lecturer, producer and friend to so many, Mike has earned the admiration and respect of all of us. He is an intense perfectionist, with himself. Ever gentle with those he has helped, he is a relentless taskmaster to himself. Every recording—every performance—of his is something to treasure. There are not enough adjectives, nor space to do him justice in this review. Take every opportunity to see and hear him. We will not see another like him in our lifetimes. *—Don Stevens*

Solo: Old Time Music / 1962 / Rounder ♦♦♦♦♦
Old-Time Country Music is an excellent 1991 recording of traditional mountain music and old timey string band material. All of Seeger's interpretations on the album are faithful without being dull, meaning that *Old-Time Country Music* is one of the best contemporary collections of traditional material to be recorded in the '90s. In fact, it's not a bad introduction to the rich variety of string bands, in general. *—Thom Owens*

American Folk Songs for Christmas / 1989 / Rounder ♦♦♦♦♦
This set is based on the famous Ruth Crawford Seeger book of the same name. Among the 53 (!) songs are "Bright Morning Stars Are Rising," "Look Away to Bethlehem," "Go Tell It on the Mountain," "Sing Hallelu," and "Breaking up Christmas." Mike Seeger, Penny Seeger, Peggy Seeger, Sonya Cohen, Calum MacColl, Ewan MacColl, Kitty MacColl and Kim Seeger accompany their own vocals on traditional acoustic instruments. Liner notes explain the traditions behind these lesser-known Christmas songs, and the cover is decorated with wonderful woodcuts. *—Roundup newsletter*

Southern Banjo Sounds / Sep. 15, 1998 / Smithsonian/Folkways ♦♦♦
With this collection, Seeger's intention is to illustrate the wide variety of banjo sounds heard in the rural South before 1950. Each of the 26 tracks employs a different style, using a range of techniques, many in the clawhammer, two-finger, and three-finger style; "Come My Little Pink," for instance, specifically emulates Earl Scruggs' playing. The repertoire of the songs chosen covers a similarly wide range, from blues and bluegrass to 19th-century African-American banjo and traditional folk. As icing on the cake, no less than 23 separate banjos were used in the recording (photos of each model are in the liner notes). As you might gather from such a carefully assembled disc, the presentation tends toward the academic and preservationist, rather than the original and artistic; Seeger is a fine and versatile player, though only adequate as a singer. It's of most use to banjo players and scholarly types looking for a handy reference to Southern banjo styles, and it's a successful project when judged by those standards, embellished by lengthy and readable liner notes from Seeger, including a brief history of the American banjo and details about each track. The most unusual item is "Down South Blues" (which Seeger learned from Dock Boggs), on which he achieves a slide banjo-like effect. *—Richie Unterberger*

American Folk Songs for Children / Rounder ♦♦♦♦♦

● **Music from the True Vine** / Mercury ♦♦♦♦♦

Peggy Seeger

b. Jun. 17, 1935, New York, NY
Vocals, Guitar, Banjo, Dulcimer / Folksongs, Folk Revival, Singer/Songwriter, Traditional Folk
The half-sister of Pete Seeger and the widow of Ewan MacColl, singer/songwriter Peggy Seeger continued her family's long history of championing and preserving traditional music, most notably emerging as a seminal figure in the British folksong revival of the 1960s. Peggy began playing the piano at the age of seven, and soon added a half-dozen other instruments to her repertoire. She began performing professionally while at college, and issued a Folkways ten-inch in 1955. Four years later, she settled in London, where she became involved with MacColl, the famed British musician and playwright. In the decades which followed prior to MacColl's 1989 death, the couple toured the world singing, lecturing and preaching the importance of the British folk song tradition, typically emphasizing the connections between roots music and sociopolitical activism. From the mid-'50s onward, Seeger recorded regularly, cutting both original material and traditional compositions as a solo artist and in collaboration with MacColl as well as artists including her siblings Mike and Penny. After MacColl's death, she began working with the traditional Irish singer Irene Scott under the name No Spring Chickens, and in 1995, she completed work on the collections *The Peggy Seeger Songbook, Warts and All* and *The Essential Ewan MacColl Songbook*. *—Jason Ankeny*

At the Present Moment / 1973 / Rounder ♦♦♦♦♦
This album collects some of Seeger's best topical material, some of which she sings with her husband, Ewan MacColl. The most striking song remains "I'm Gonna Be an Engineer," which encapsulates most of what the women's movement has been saying for the past 20 years. *—William Ruhlmann*

● **Folkways Years, 1955-1992: Songs of Love and Politics** / 1992 / Smithsonian/Folkways ♦♦♦♦♦
As a title, *The Folkways Years* is something of a misnomer for this compilation album because it is a broader collection, in which recordings made by Peggy Seeger for Folkways Records constitute less than half of the 21 selections, along with eight previously unreleased, mostly live recordings made in the 1980s, three tracks licensed from Rounder Records, and a sample from Seeger's upcoming new album. Taken together, the recordings constitute a musical autobiography that traces her interest in traditional folk music: her original, feminist songs such as "Lady, What Do You Do All Day—" and "Gonna Be an Engineer," songs associated with her husband Ewan MacColl, including "First Time Ever I Saw Your Face," which he wrote for her, and songs she wrote for each of her children. In her self-deprecating liner notes, Seeger confesses that for most of her life she has been unable to bear the sound of her recordings, which may explain why she has drawn so little from her large body of work with Folkways. Her thin voice can be an acquired taste, though her talent for songwriting overcomes the limitations of her performing ability. *—William Ruhlmann*

Period Pieces: Women's Songs for Men & Women / Aug. 25, 1998 / Tradition ♦♦♦♦♦
Billed as a compilation of Peggy Seeger's feminist compositions, *Period Pieces*, whose songs were written between 1963 and 1994, and recorded between 1979 and 1998, is actually a compendium of the singer's various topical concerns, with 11 of the 17 tracks newly recorded. Early on, the songs concern specifically feminist and women's issues, such as equal pay ("I'm Gonna Be an Engineer"), contraception and abortion rights ("Nine-Month Blues"), mother-daughter relations ("Different Tunes"), domestic violence ("Winnie and Sam"), and rape ("Reclaim the Night"). But as of the seventh song, "Missing," which is about a "disappeared" Chilean activist, Seeger expands her subject matter to broader political issues including unionism ("Union Woman II"), apartheid ("I Support the Boycott"), work-related injury ("R.S.I.," which stands for repetitive strain injury), the rights of the disabled ("Woman on Wheels") and nuclear disarmament ("Carry Greenham Home"), though she always places them in the context of women's viewpoints. As the album title suggests, some of these subjects are now historical rather than topical. The result is a thorough survey of left-wing views over the past 40 years that is sometimes doctrinaire ("Marriage is a feudal custom," she sings in "Winnie and Sam," "Women are one of the props"; while in "R.S.I." she declares, "The world's not big enough for conscience and the profit motive"), but always impassioned and, occasionally, not without humor. Seeger is more of a proselytizer than a singer, but her pinched voice, backed by various acoustic instruments and voices (including those of her family members) serves the material well. *—William Ruhlmann*

Familiar Faces / Redwood ♦♦♦♦♦

Peggy Seeger / Riverside ♦♦♦
This is a beautiful collection of old songs and ballads performed solo. Part of what makes this 30-year-old LP so great is the youthful sound of Seeger's voice and her much more knowing understanding of the material, much of which has the dark overtones that make so many traditional songs haunting, such as the "Waggoner's Lad." *—Richard Meyer*

Pete Seeger

b. May 3, 1919, New York, NY
Vocals, Guitar, Banjo / Children's Folk, Folksongs, Folk Revival, Political Folk, Traditional Folk
Pete Seeger probably has had a greater influence on the development of modern folk music than any other single individual. The son of musicologist Charles Seeger, he hooked up with Woody Guthrie in the late '30s, and the two formed the politically oriented Almanac Singers with several other folksingers to promote unions and condemn fascism. He was a cofounder of such organizations as People's Songs and People's Artists. In 1948 he formed the folk group The Weavers, which scored massive hits with "Tzena, Tzena, Tzena," Leadbelly's "Goodnight Irene," and "On Top of Old Smokey" before losing its record contract and bookings during the Communist witchhunts of the '50s. In 1961, he signed to Columbia Records, staying with the label until the end of the decade. Seeger was a major force at the Newport Folk Festivals and a promoter of upcoming talent. His marathon-length concerts included Spanish songs, African songs, Negro worksongs, new protest songs, and old folk songs, sometimes with rewritten lyrics. Seeger's own songs, sometimes adaptations from other sources, became hits for others: "If I Had a Hammer" for Trini Lopez and Peter, Paul, & Mary; "Turn! Turn! Turn!" for The Byrds—but he was also known for his hit version of Malvina Reynolds's "Little Boxes," for "We Shall Overcome," for "Guantanamera," and for dozens more. *—William Ruhlmann*

American Industrial Ballads / 1957 / Smithsonian/Folkways ♦♦♦♦♦
This collection demonstrates Seeger's interest in and respect for workers of all stripes. It's a wonderful record. *—Richard Meyer*

Broadsides / 1964 / Folkways ♦♦♦♦♦
Pete Seeger's fearless, clearly articulated voice and spare, accurate guitar and banjo playing

are presented here in the service of a collection of songs published in early editions of *Broadside,* the topical song magazine, among them Malvina Reynolds's "From Way Up Here" and the civil rights anthem "We Shall Overcome." *—William Ruhlmann*

Dangerous Songs!— / Feb. 7, 1966-Feb. 8, 1966 / Columbia ✦✦✦✦
In 1966, when the topical song movement had gained national attention through the newly written material of Bob Dylan and such compatriots as Tom Paxton and Phil Ochs, Pete Seeger set out to demonstrate that "protest" songs were not a new thing by putting together an album largely made up of traditional material that had its roots in long-since-forgotten political issues, everything from the nursery rhyme "Little Jack Horner" to the Civil War march "John Brown's Body." Further, Seeger suggested that everything is political, whether it's the apparently comic children's song "Beans in My Ears" or that piece of Irish advice "Never Wed an Old Man." ("In the long run, the most truly dangerous songs of all may prove to be love songs and lullabies," he wrote in the liner notes.) And then there were songs that all would agree are political (though humorous), such as "The Pill" and Ochs' "Draft Dodger Rag." The resulting collection is one of Seeger's funniest, and at the same time most pointed albums. It took Columbia Records 32 years to reissue it on CD, with three bonus tracks from the sessions. *—William Ruhlmann*

☆ **Abiyoyo (& Other Songs & Stories)** / 1967 / Smithsonian/Folkways ✦✦✦✦✦
What can one say about the father of it all— He has been a staple in this music for a long, long time. His voice and banjo—and his life—stand for positive values for people in general, especially on this album. For ages three to seven. *—Bob Hinkle*

★ **The World of Pete Seeger** / 1973 / Columbia ✦✦✦✦✦
An excellent two-disc compilation of Seeger's Columbia years, this album contains 20 songs, most of which will be familiar to Seeger fans and folk enthusiasts in general. There's far more valuable Seeger on Columbia, but it's good to have "Turn! Turn! Turn!" as sung by its adapter and "If I Had a Hammer" as sung by its coauthor, not to mention such Seeger concert staples as "Guantanamera" and "Last Night I Had the Strangest Dream." *—William Ruhlmann*

Singalong Demonstration Concert / 1980 / Smithsonian/Folkways ✦✦✦✦✦
Having reached his 60s, Seeger asked Folkways to document a typical concert "before my voice, memory, and sense of rhythm and pitch were too far gone." What they got is this 25-track, two-record boxed set containing the amazing variety and depth of Seeger's repertoire, from the traditional "John Henry" to the African lullaby/story "Abiyoyo" to Charlie King's anti-nuke tune "Acres of Clams." But what most impresses is Seeger's rapport with an audience that is willing and able to sing along on every song. *—William Ruhlmann*

We Shall Overcome: The Complete Carnegie Hall Concert / 1989 / Columbia ✦✦✦✦

Waist Deep in the Big Muddy / 1993 / Columbia ✦✦✦✦

Pete / Apr. 16, 1996 / Living Music ✦✦✦
Having long since decided to give up recording, Pete Seeger was coaxed into making a new album (his first in 17 years) by Paul Winter, who co-produced this 18-track, nearly 64-minute collection and recorded it at his studio. Winter's approach was to have Seeger sing his usual repertoire, accompanied on most of the tracks by one of three choruses: the 30-member Gaudeamus, the Union Baptist Church Singers, or the Cathedral Singers. The result is like a Pete Seeger concert in which the audience sings along with much better harmony, but in a much more formal manner than usual. There are three songs previously unrecorded by the artist, including a tribute to Lead Belly, but the other 15 are familiar songs such as "Kisses Sweeter Than Wine" and "The Water Is Wide." "Singing an old song is an act of reaffirmation," he writes in the CD booklet. But recording a bunch of them makes this album more a coda to Seeger's recording career than another milestone. *—William Ruhlmann*

Link in the Chain / Sep. 3, 1996 / Columbia ✦✦✦✦✦
While the neophyte might be better advised to start with the 20-track 1972 Columbia compilation *The World Of Pete Seeger,* this collection would make a good second purchase to hear the highlights of Seeger's major-label sojourn. Eschewing such favorites as "Little Boxes" (Seeger's sole chart single) and "If I Had A Hammer" (which Seeger co-wrote), but including many other familiar performances (among them "Turn! Turn! Turn!" and "Where Have All The Flowers Gone?," the set is thematically organized into story songs, political songs, biographical songs, and children's songs. This separation sometimes seems arbitrary—"Waist Deep In The Big Muddy" and "Harry Sims" (about a mine workers union organizer) would seem to fit better in the political column than as stories or biographies—and in concert, where much of this material was recorded, Seeger deliberately mixes his songs up while drawing on at least a few other categories. But for the most part, the grouping works on disc, and along with classics like "We Shall Overcome" and "This Land Is Your Land," there are some pleasant discoveries, such as the story of "Aimee Semple McPherson" from Seeger's debut Columbia album *Story Songs,* and Woody Guthrie's "Belle Star," a duet with Ramblin' Jack Elliott, from *The Badmen.* At a running time well under two hours, the album could have been more comprehensive, and the liner notes, spread among seven writers, amount to little more than superficial tribute. So, this is not the kind of retrospective Seeger deserves. But it gives a good sense of the range of his talent, and it is full of enlightening, entertaining songs and performances. *—William Ruhlmann*

God Bless the Grass / 1998 / Columbia ✦✦✦

☆ **Birds, Beasts, Bugs & Fishes** / Feb. 17, 1998 / Smithsonian/Folkways ✦✦✦✦✦
Previously available on two separate 1955 Folkways LPs (*Birds, Beasts, Bugs and Little Fishes* and *Birds, Beasts, Bugs and Bigger Fishes*), this CD combines both of these children's records onto one disc, complete lyrics included in the accompanying booklet. As the titles make plain, the songs were devoted to animals of all sorts; *Birds, Beasts, Bugs and Little Fishes* were aimed toward younger kids, and *Birds, Beasts, Bugs and Bigger Fishes* for older ones. It'll still do the job today, although it can get a bit much for over-tens to take when Seeger does animal noises, and even if you're just leaving your little one in a corner to enjoy the CD, 28 songs might be too much for both you and your kid to endure all at once. *—Richie Unterberger*

If I Had a Hammer: Songs of Hope & Struggle / May 19, 1998 / Smithsonian/Folkways ✦✦✦✦✦
Seeger's repertoire was not limited to songs with specific sociopolitical goals, and the most familiar versions of his most popular tunes were done for Columbia. Still, it's hard to imagine doing better than this compilation of Folkways recordings (most from the late 1950s and 1960s) if you want evidence of Seeger's importance and skills as a spokesperson for worthy causes. Dividing into segments addressing "unions and labor," "peace," "civil rights" and "hope," this has the original 1956 versions of "If I Had a Hammer" and "Where Have All the Flowers Gone," along with other tunes identified with Seeger like "We Shall Overcome" and "Turn, Turn, Turn" (the last from an unreleased tape of unspecified vintage). The liner notes explain the origins of each song, as well as how their structures have evolved over the years; a couple of 1998 tracks show his spirit intact, but his voice (as he himself admits) losing strength. *—Richie Unterberger*

Headlines & Footnotes: Collection of Topical Songs / May 18, 1999 / Smithsonian/Folkways ✦✦✦✦✦
Like the prior compilation *If I Had a Hammer,* this focuses a little loosely on topical songs, concentrating on (but not limited to) ones that deal with specific events. At a glance this might seem like a less essential anthology, since *If I Had a Hammer* contained major songs identified with Seeger like "If I Had a Hammer," "Turn, Turn, Turn," "We Shall Overcome" and "Where Have All the Flowers Gone." It's actually on the same musical and lyrical level, however, and again has versions of some of the most famous tunes written or popularized by Seeger: "Waist Deep in the Big Muddy," "Wimoweh," "Guantanamera," "Wasn't that a Time," Malvina Reynolds' "Little Boxes," "I Come and Stand at Every Door" and "The Bells of Rhymney" (the last two of which were covered by the Byrds in the mid-1960s). About half of these are taken from Folkways Recordings, but about half are previously unreleased live versions or studio outtakes, so from a collector's point of view this disc is pretty interesting as well. Of course with a Seeger recording, the educational and inspirational values are about as important as the musical ones, and the lesser-known songs usually also have something to make one think, whether it's a narrative of the Titanic disaster or the anti-racist "Listen Mr. Bilbo." Almost all performances were recorded in the 1950s and 1960s; three songs recorded between 1994 and 1999 find Seeger's voice fading and shaky, though his heart's intact. *—Richie Unterberger*

American Folk, Game and Activity Songs for Children / Jan. 25, 2000 / Smithsonian/Folkways ✦✦✦
This hour-long CD combines the entirety of two children's-oriented Seeger LPs, 1953's *American Folk Songs for Children* and 1962's *American Game and Activity Songs for Children,* onto one disc. The eleven songs on *American Folk Songs for Children* were specifically selected from an identically titled book anthology of folk songs for children collected by Seeger's stepmother, Ruth Crawford Seeger. Pete Seeger renders them plainly and simply, singing and playing and banjo, on a program designed especially (but not solely) for children between three and seven years of age. "Jim Crack Corn," "Frog Went A-Courting," and "She'll Be Coming 'Round the Mountain" are some of the better-known tunes on the record, but not all of them are as overly familiar. *American Game and Activity Songs for Children* focuses especially on songs associated with activities and dancing, sometimes sung a cappella, sometimes sung with accompaniment from Seeger's banjo. "Skip to My Lou," "Ring Around the Rosy," "Here We Go Round the Mulberry Bush," and "Yankee Doodle" are some of the more well-known songs here—at this point, they're probably more over-familiar than they were when the album was first released—but there are less overdone ones here too, including the spiritual "Liza Jane." *—Richie Unterberger*

Brother John Sellers

b. May 27, 1924, Clarksdale, MS
Vocals, Guitar / Folk Revival, Folk-Blues
Somewhat in the mold of Josh White and (to a lesser degree) Leadbelly, Brother John Sellers was an African-American all-around folk entertainer, singing blues, folk, gospel, and bits of jazz. Born in Clarksdale, MS, he joined the mass migration to Chicago at the age of 11. In the mid-'50s, he recorded one of the earlier long-playing albums aimed at the folk audience, which included accompaniment by Sonny Terry and the original Count Basie rhythm section. *—Richie Unterberger*

● **Sings Blues & Folk Songs** / 1954 / Vanguard ✦✦✦✦
A bit tame even by the standards of the folk revival, this showcased Sellers as a smooth and accomplished presenter of folk, blues, and a bit of jazz. The singer mixed original compositions with standards like "John Henry," "Down By the Riverside," and "Nobody Knows the Trouble I Have Seen" on a set that seemed conscientiously programmed to demonstrate his versatility. The blues and folk numbers were graced by harmonica from Sonny Terry; the less successful jazzy efforts had accompaniment from a combo featuring the original Count Basie rhythm section. *—Richie Unterberger*

Martin Sexton

Singer, Vocals / Alternative Folk, Contemporary Singer/Songwriter, Contemporary Folk
Martin Sexton is one of the most talked-about recent arrivals to the "new folk" acoustic music scene. The guitarist, singer and songwriter has an amazing vocal range and makes effective use of it in his live shows and on his debut for the Massachusetts-based Eastern Front label. Unlike so many other contemporary singer-songwriters, his vocal style can best be described as soulful, combining the best qualities of singers like Van Morrison, Al Green, Aaron Neville and Otis Redding. He began playing his brand of soul-filled folk music around Boston's open mike nights and street corners in 1989. In 1991, he released his own record in cassette format, *In the Journey,* and much of the material on this and *Black Sheep,* his 1996 debut for Eastern Front Records, is autobiographical in nature, concerning his life on the road. Incredibly, Sexton sold 15,000 copies of his cassette-only album through the strength of his live shows and grueling tours around the U.S. He now has a deal with Atlantic Records, releasing *The American* in 1998. *—Richard Skelly*

● **In the Journey** / 1990 / Koch ✦✦✦✦✦
Martin Sexton recorded *In the Journey* in a friend's attic in 1990, while he was making his living busking on the streets of Boston. He sold cassette copies out of his suitcase in remarkable volumes for a demo tape (half a decade later the album was finally released on CD, distributed in part by Sexton's new label, Eastern Front). The cassette's success should be no surprise to anyone who has heard him sing. The chief purpose of a demo tape is to show off the artist's talent, and Sexton enthusiastically embraces any opportunity to show off. Splitting the nine songs evenly between Bostonian contemporary folk and mostly acoustic blues and jazz, Sexton displays a vocal elasticity which would be amazing even if he weren't only 23 years old. On "Things to Come," he gives his rangy Steve Wonder baritone a splash of reggae spice. On the title track (a freshly produced Toad the Wet Sprocket-like folk-pop tune) he starts off in a restrained impersonation of mumbly '90s rockers, then belts out the chorus with R&B bravado. On "Hard Times," he interrupts his soulful blues performance to do a dead-on impersonation of a wah-wah trumpet. On "13 Step Reprise" he becomes the whole band, imitating not only a Motown background chorus but also a full brass section. He even does character voices, playing a froggy-voiced old man on the well-written folk narrative "The Way I Am." Sexton seems to be able to make his voice do anything he pleases without effort. The album is also very well produced by Sexton, despite the slightly schizophrenic division between the folk and the jazz. He mixes musical elements with creative assurance, incorporating mandolins, guitars, flutes, accordions, a variety of shuffling rhythms, and a plethora of vocal tracks. *—Darryl Cater*

Black Sheep / 1996 / Koch International ✦✦✦✦✦
Martin Sexton's acoustic singer/songwriter routine is just one of many flavors here; along with Motown-style R&B, sweeping pop ballads, gypsy fiddling, blues and jazz, there's even a little rapping. The genre-jumping works surprisingly well. Producer Crit Harmon sequences the switches with sensitivity and class, and gives the set a consistant sound—warm, spontaneous, grounded in acoustics, deeply soulful.

Vocally, Sexton handles the stylistic gymnastics with extravagant ease. He'll belt out a tune with all the velvet bombast of Wonder, retreat to a Billie Holiday warble, ascend to an Aaron Neville falsetto, then swagger his way home like Ray Charles or Johnny Popper. There is, however, a cost for his expanded palette: originality. Such soulful singing is rarely set against a sparse folk background (which is often associated with off-key eccentrics like Bob Dylan and Neil Young). As his band imitates the soul masters who influenced his vocals, his act seems less fresh, and stands against somewhat stiffer vocal competition. Sexton has told interviewers that folk music tends to speak only to his head ("like a thick novel"), while simpler pop music hits him in the gut. His songwriting seems to reflect that as he edges away from the urban poetry of his Bostonian peers, toward plain old pop, and it's not bad—his lyrics previously seemed a little overreaching—but it does make some of the songs on *Black Sheep* a little less interesting than the ones on his1991 demo tape, *In the Journey.* All of the diversity, though, does make the solo acoustic moments all the more gratifying, spot-lighting not only Sexton's sensational singing but also his warm, bass-heavy, rythmically slick acoustic guitar playing. *—Darryl Cater*

The American / Oct. 6, 1998 / Atlantic ✦✦✦✦✦
Martin Sexton's aptly titled major label debut finds the ostentatiously talented singer on a spirited, cross-country tour of nearly every genre the nation has ever produced. Folk, roots rock, grunge, country, soul, R&B, blues, and jazz—Sexton pulls it all off with a voice that exhibits all the rangy flexibility of a ballet dancer. *The American* is a little more consistent than its indie label predecessor, *Black Sheep,* although it comes dangerously close to ruining the best song from the first record by re-imagining "Glory Bound" as a fiery rock anthem. In contrast, "Candy" is actually improved by the acid grunge treatment it gets here, acquiring a gritty bite that it lacked on *Black Sheep.* He also revisits two songs from the demo recording *In the Journey* ("Way I Am," "Love Keep Us Together"). But there's plenty of sharp new material here as well, such as the jazzy "Diggin' Me" and the country western-flavored title track. Throughout all the genre hopping, Sexton's indefatigable vocal chords provide a constant. "My Maria" once again demonstrates the singer's preternatural ability to create astonishing simulations of musical instruments—wailing electric guitar solo winds seemlessly into a wailing Sexton falsetto, leaving the listener to puzzle over what was live and what was Memorex. These are the kind of infectiously exuberant moments that populate Sexton's recordings, capturing an American virtuoso in love with American music. *—Evan Cater*

Wonder Bar / Oct. 10, 2000 / Atlantic ✦✦✦✦
Singer/songwriter Martin Sexton blends passion similar to Bruce Springsteen with the raucous excitement of Jeff Buckley and the abrasive wordplay of Jackson Browne and Living Colour's Corey Glover. On his sophomore effort, 2000's *Wonder Bar,* the Boston-bred falsetto cues up his thick, gruff vocals for a soul-slicker that is quite genuine. Again, Sexton plays with genre-specific hums of roots rock, folk, country, blues, and R&B, and the initial sound on *Wonder Bar* is solid. The 11-track song list soars with humorous emotions; songs such as "Hallelujah" and "Things You Do to Me" showcase such free-spirited rock & roll. Sexton, however, is a love sucker. Like his crooning counterparts (Ryan Adams, David Gray), Sexton plays into the heart of things, reaching for the deepest mystery and sweetest piece. Songs such as "Elephant's Memory" and "She Cries and Sings" reveal his once broken heart and the mending process. Part of Sexton's appeal is his natural blending of moods and *Wonder Bar* shines throughout many shades of feeling. It's unpretentious and the album's namesake indicates Sexton's appreciation for the simple things; most of the record's songs were written in a pizza parlor of the same name in Worcester, MA. It's as basic as that, for Sexton is one earnest individual and *Wonder Bar* illustrates his playful use of traditional sides of American music. *—MacKenzie Wilson*

Richard Shindell

b. Lakehurst, NJ
Vocals, Guitar / Contemporary Singer/Songwriter, Contemporary Folk
An enigmatic singer/songwriter whose work veered from the bitterly comic to the profoundly spiritual, Richard Shindell gained his first notoriety via the *Fast Folk Musical Magazine* series (which previously launched then-unknowns like Lyle Lovett and Nanci Griffith as well). A native of Lakehurst, New Jersey, Shindell was a former seminary student whose first musical exposure came while playing guitar in the Razzy Dazzy Spasm Band alongside the young John Gorka; he began composing songs during the late 1980s, quickly earning a word-of-mouth cult following. After a featured appearance on Christine Lavin's 1991 compilation *When October Goes,* a year later he recorded his Shanachie label debut, *Sparrow's Point; Blue Divide* followed in 1994, and in 1997 Shindell resurfaced with *Reunion Hill.* He next teamed with Dar Williams and Lucy Kaplansky in the group Cry, Cry, Cry, issuing a self-titled LP in 1998; the solo *Somewhere Near Paterson* followed in early 2000. *—Jason Ankeny*

● **Sparrows Point** / 1992 / Shanachie ✦✦✦✦✦
A strong debut release "Ö la Eric Andersen." Shindell's songwriting is intense at times ("Sparrows Point," "The Courier," "On the Sea of Fleur de Lis"). His "Kenworth of My Dreams" is the classic blue-collar truck-driver song, and the title song should not be missed, either. "Are You Happy Now" is the most commercial song—very strong. This is an up-and-coming artist you should check out. *—Chip Renner & Richard Meyer*

Blue Divide / 1994 / Shanachie ✦✦✦
While not as startlingly original as *Sparrow's Point,* Shindell's second CD is still far better than the work of his many contemporaries. His political songs, "Arrowhead" and "Fishing," make their points as affecting stories well told rather than by posturing. Never one to shy away from difficult subjects, the "Ballad of Mary Magdalene" is a masterful casting of one of religion's pivotal relationships; that by implication says a great deal about the confused state of human affairs. The playing and singing are all first-rate. *—Richard Meyer*

Reunion Hill / Aug. 19, 1997 / Shanachie ✦✦✦

Somewhere Near Paterson / Feb. 8, 2000 / Signature ✦✦✦

Paul Siebel

Vocals, Guitar / Contemporary Folk, Country-Folk, Folk-Rock, Singer/Songwriter, Country-Rock
Despite the undeniably high quality of his songs—which have been covered by the likes of Linda Ronstadt, Bonnie Raitt, Ian Matthews, and Waylon Jennings—Paul Siebel is far from being a household name. Within folk circles and among songwriters however, his two albums—1969's *Woodsmoke and Oranges* and 1971's *Jack-Knife Gypsy*—are legendary.

Paul Siebel was born in 1937 in Buffalo, NY. Inspired by Hank Williams and Hank Snow, he taught himself to play guitar while in his teens. By the early '60s, after serving in the military, he began playing playing folk clubs, eventually moving to Greenwich Village where he found support in the coffeehouse circuit. In 1969, a collections of demos he made with David Bromberg caught the attention of Elektra Records owner, Jac Holzman, who offered a him a modest recording deal (reportedly he was only given enough money to finance four three hour recording sessions). The resulting album, *Woodsmoke and Oranges,* was met with critical praise from the media including *Rolling Stone* magazine. Despite the attention, the album and its equally praised follow-up, *Jack-Knife Gypsy,* sold disappointingly little. Aside from a live album released in 1981, *Live at McCabes,* Siebel hasn't released an album since. *—Chris Woodstra*

☆ **Wood Smoke and Oranges** / 1970 / Elektra ✦✦✦✦✦
Fans of Linda Ronstadt, Bonnie Raitt, or Ian Matthews records from the '70s will know some of these tunes already. Let their interpretations stand only as your introduction to this fine songwriter. While his style may not be as polished or commercial as any of the people who covered him, this is a fine batch of songs and deserve to be heard. *—Jim Worbois*

Jack Knife Gypsy / 1971 / Line ✦✦✦
The first record may have drawn listeners for the opportunity to hear Siebel originals of songs they knew from elsewhere. This record does not have that same kind of pull but is every bit as good. His strong sense of melody and storytelling style paved the way for such current songwriters as Butch Hancock and Robert Earl Keen. *—Jim Worbois*

★ **Paul Siebel** / Oct. 31, 1995 / Philo ✦✦✦✦✦
Though known mainly through others' interpretations of his songs (Ian Matthews, Linda Ronstadt, Bonnie Raitt), Paul Siebel's first two albums for Elektra are prime examples of the New York folk scene of the early '70s and easily among the scene's finest moments. While these albums were sadly overlooked at the time by all but his singer/songwriter peers and critics, they have since reached near-legendary status. *Paul Siebel* is a long-overdue collection of the high points of both albums, featuring *Woodsmoke and Oranges* in its entirety and five tracks from the follow-up, *Jack-Knife Gypsy.* *—Chris Woodstra*

Shel Silverstein

b. 1932, Chicago, IL
Vocals, Guitar / Children's Folk, Folksongs, Folk Revival, Musical Comedy, Contemporary Folk, Novelty
Silverstein originally gained fame as a cartoonist and satirist for *Playboy* magazine. His satirical songs first found a national audience with Johnny Cash's "A Boy Named Sue," Loretta Lynn's "One's on the Way," and Doctor Hook's interpretations of several of Silverstein's best, including "Sylvia's Mother" and "Cover of the Rolling Stone." Silverstein's own recordings have earned him a deserved cult following. *—Cub Koda*

● **Inside Folk Songs** / 1962 / Atlantic ✦✦✦✦✦
A hilarious collection of folk songs by the gravel-voiced humorist. *—David Szatmary*

Freakers Ball / 1972 / Columbia ✦✦✦

Where the Sidewalk Ends / 1976 / Sony Kids' Music ✦✦✦
If the Shel Silverstein book *Where the Sidewalk Ends* isn't already in every child's hands, it should be; it's as poignant and whimsical as the day it was written. The album version is another matter. Silverstein already had plenty of experience in the recording studio, and his musical delivery of his poems is certainly unique. He sounds a little like Emo Phillips reading verse, which is about as unsettling as one might imagine. Children may enjoy this, but

the adults who have to listen to it over and over with them will just be spooked. Still, this album is sure to have fans who treasure it for its disquietingly offbeat delivery. *—Paul Collins*

The Great Conch Train Robbery / 1979 / Flying Fish ✦✦✦✦✦
Silverstein is joined by Sam Bush, Josh Graves, John Hartford, Roy Husky, Benny Martin, Pig Robbins, Joe Stuart, and Amos Garrett. A great, funny album. *—Chip Renner*

Fred Small

b. Nov. 6, 1952
Vocals, Guitar / Contemporary Singer/Songwriter, Contemporary Folk, Political Folk
The political insight and human compassion that inspired Cambridge, Massachusetts-based Fred Small to seek a law degree continues to be expressed in his folk-rooted songs. Over the past two decades, Small has musically addressed everything from homosexuality in the military and the unnecessary difficulties of the disabled to radioactive frogs and a moose's infatuation with a cow. Pete Seeger, Rosalie Sorrels, The Flirtations, Steve Gillette and Priscilla Herdman are only some of the many musicians who have covered Small's songs. Small's tune, "Everything Possible" was used for the finale of the AIDS benefit musical, *Heart Strings*, in 1992.

The grandnephew of famed painter Thomas Hart Benton, Small was primed for intellectual pursuits. After graduating Phi Beta Kappa from Yale University, he went on to study for a law degree and a masters degree in natural resources policy from the University of Michigan. Although he grew up listening to his parent's record collection, which included several Kingston Trio albums, Small didn't become serious about music until his early-twenties. He composed his first song a few hours before taking his first law school exam.

After finishing school, Small accepted a staff attorney position for the Conservation Law Foundation in Boston. Although it appeared his future was secure, Small became increasingly absorbed by his songwriting. Appearing in local folk music clubs and coffeehouses, he soon attracted acclaim for his witty, politically-tinged, tunes. Small's views made him a popular performer at political and anti-nuclear demonstrations including the nationally-broadcast M.U.S.E. Concert at New York's Battery Park in 1978. The enthusiastic response he received inspired Small to resign from his law position and seek his fame as a singer-songwriter. Small's debut album, *Love Will Carry Us*, was released in 1981. Although the album centered around his acoustic guitar and vocals, Small's subsequent recordings have been increasingly produced with instrumental and vocal support by New England's best folk performers. Accompanied by fiddler Johnny Cunningham, guitar and mandolin player John Curtis (The Pousette-Dart Band) and background vocalist Catherine David, Small recorded a live album, *Everything Possible: Fred Small In Concert*, at the Old Cambridge Baptist Church on March 26, 1993. *—Craig Harris*

● **The Heart of the Appaloosa** / 1984 / Rounder ✦✦✦✦✦

I Will Stand Fast / 1988 / Flying Fish ✦✦✦

Everything Possible: Fred Small in Concert / Mar. 1993 / Flying Fish ✦✦✦✦✦
A concert recording of Fred Small with a small group including Johnny Cunningham, it features a set of well-played story-songs that are always carefully politically correct. *—Richard Meyer*

Springfields

f. 1960, London, England, **db.** Oct. 1963
Group / Folk Revival, Folk-Pop, Traditional Folk
British folk-rock performers The Springfields were the group that first introduced Dusty Springfield to the public, and served as the template upon which Dusty's brother Tom molded his role as producer/songwriter for the Australian-formed folk-pop group the Seekers. The Springfields came along just as the same folk boom that had begun sweeping America in the late '50s hit England, highlighted by Dusty's powerful vocal delivery and a group sound that vaguely recalled the Weavers.

They hit the Top 20 in England with "Bambino" in early 1962, and were named "Best Vocal Group" in *New Musical Express* and "Top Vocal/Instrumental Group" in *Melody Maker.* Their next single, a hyperactive and cacophonous cover of Leadbelly's "Goodnight Irene" was a commercial flop, but its follow-up, "Silver Threads and Golden Needles," got to the Top 20 in America, the first single by a British group ever to achieve that level of success in the United States. Driven by Dusty's full-throated vocals and a robust guitar sound, it was a precursor to the kind of folk-rock sound that the Byrds would codify in 1965. The group was never able to duplicate this success in America, but late in 1962 they had the biggest hit of their career in England, "Island of Dreams," which rode the British charts for six months, rising to number five along the way. Its success, however, also helped to sow the dissent that would destroy the group. The pressure to replicate this success brought to the fore the musical differences between Dusty and Tom. She was far more interested in American-style R&B than folk music, and was also a talented musician, which she later revealed by effectively producing her own sessions when she went solo.

Their Nashville-produced second album, *Folk Songs From the Hills* released in mid-1963, collided with the changing musical taste in England, where the Beatles had inaugurated the British beat boom. The British sound, with its increasing emphasis on R&B source material, beckoned to Dusty, and the personal differences between her and her brother remained unresolved. The trio played their last concert in London in October of 1963. *—Bruce Eder*

● **The Very Best of the Springfields** / Oct. 20, 1998 / Taragon ✦✦✦✦✦
Dusty Springfield's original pose was not as a British soul chanteuse but as a peppy British folkie as a member of the Springfields, Britain's answer to Peter, Paul and Mary. They were the hottest group in Brit music circles for a period of three years in the pre-Beatle days of the early '60s, breaking up in the summer of 1963 at the height of their success with Dusty going on to even greater fame as a solo artist. In their short time in the spotlight, their music grew more complex while never really straying far away from the folk roots, as witnessed on later tracks like "No Sad Songs for Me" and the alternate take of "Allentown Jail" included here. Of course, their big hit "Silver Threads and Golden Needles" is here in both original English and German language versions along with folkie staples like "Cottonfields," "Goodnight Irene," and "Dear John." Half of the album's 20 tracks are items seeing their very first United States issue including the beautiful "Come on Home," "Far Away Places," and "Star of Hope." An interesting view back at the beginnings of Britain's finest pop singer and the group she was a part of. *—Cub Koda*

Stampfel & Weber

Group / Folk Revival, Contemporary Folk, Folk-Rock
Peter Stampfel and Steve Weber are the founding members of the Holy Modal Rounders. Some of their albums together have been billed as "Stampfel & Weber," however, perhaps for contractual reasons, perhaps to distinguish them from the Rounders albums that featured a larger band. *—William Ruhlmann*

Going Nowhere Fast / 1981 / Rounder ✦✦✦✦✦
Properly speaking, this is a reunion album by The Holy Modal Rounders, which is the name Peter Stampfel and Steve Weber used for their folk duo when they formed it in the early 60s. The group eventually expanded and went electric, then disbanded. This album is a return to form in more ways than one, restricted to Weber's guitar and Stampfel's banjo and fiddle, plus their squeaky, enthusiastic vocals. It blends folk standards and novelty tunes as the early Rounder albums did and, like them, is an off-the-wall gem. *—William Ruhlmann*

Peter Stampfel

b. Oct. 29, 1938
Vocals, Banjo / Folk Revival, Folk-Rock, Singer/Songwriter
Peter Stampfel was born in Wauwautosa, Wisconsin in 1938. He dropped out of The University of Wisconsin after attending for two years, and began supporting himself by playing music, living in New York, Florida, Chicago, and several cities in California. In 1963, Stampfel formed the folk pop unit Holy Modal Rounders with his collaborator Steve Weber. Stampfel also played in the bands Bottle Caps (who released albums in 1986 & 1989) and the Fugs. In 1994, he and guitarist Gary Lucas began a duo, the Du-Tels, to play originals, and covers of Charlie Patton, the Stanley Brothers and other such personal heroes. By 1999, Stampfel lived in lower Manhattan, active in the Du-Tels, working as a science fiction editor, and occasionally collaborating with Chicago's the Dysfunctionells. *—Joslyn Layne*

Peter Stampfel & the Bottle Caps / 1986 / Rounder ✦✦✦
Peter Stampfel remains a folkie eccentric, and the main difference between his 80s band and his 60s one (the Holy Modal Rounders) is that the later one rocks harder and that more of the material is original. But much of the act still consists of novelties ("Surfer Angel" and "Funny the First Time," to name only two), and it's never quite clear whether Stampfel is celebrating or parodying his sources. Not that it matters. *—William Ruhlmann*

● **People's Republic of Rock 'n' Roll** / 1989 / Homestead ✦✦✦✦✦
Stampfel hasn't quite turned pro on this album, but the band is a lot tighter than usual, which only makes the result funnier in songs such as "Bridge and Tunnel Girls" and "Bigfoot Stole My Wife." *—William Ruhlmann*

You Must Remember This . . . / 1995 / Gert Town ✦✦✦
The king of goofball roots music devotes almost all of this album to cover material, concentrating mostly on songs from the pre-rock era. Few folk-based performers are as skilled at reviving old songs with as much reckless imagination. His vocals, simultaneously affectionate and wildly irreverent, will not be to everyone's taste. But certainly many listeners whose sense of humor extends beyond the boundaries of *Saturday Night Live* will find Stampfel's joyfully twisted singing putting grins on their faces. The arrangements adroitly tap country, Tin Pan Alley, New Orleans, and even a bit of rock influence; the blazing covers of "Goldfinger" and "Cry of the Wild Goose" are highlights. *—Richie Unterberger*

Steeleye Span

f. 1970
Group / British Folk-Rock, British Folk, Folk-Rock
Aside from Fairport Convention, Steeleye Span were the most successful and enduring British folk-rock band. The parallels between the band are numerous: both updated traditional British folk material with rock arrangements, both featured an excellent female lead singer (Sandy Denny for Fairport, Maddy Prior for Steeleye Span), both frequently employed multi-part harmonies, and both mixed original and traditional songs. Although Fairport were more innovative in their early days, Steeleye Span were arguably the more interesting band after 1970, when personnel changes had gutted the original Fairport lineup. Steeleye Span, too, would undergo numerous personnel changes even at their peak. Prior was the constant factor that gave the group something of a recognizable identity at all phases of their journey. One thing that differentiated Steeleye Span from their counterparts was that Fairport came to traditional folk from a rock background, whereas Steeleye traveled in the opposite direction. While Steeleye Span played folk music, they had no aversion to playing it loud, and proved that it was possible to create an energetic ruckus without a drummer. *—Richie Unterberger*

Hark the Village Wait / 1970 / Shanachie ✦✦✦

Please to See the King / 1971 / Shanachie ✦✦✦

Ten Man Mop / 1971 / Shanachie ✦✦✦
The third Steeleye Span album opens with possibly the most beautifully sung number of their entire history, "Gower Wassail," and which also makes a very strong case for the use of electric guitars in a traditional folk setting. "Paddy Clancy's Jig/Four Nights Drunk" was the group's first great electric adaptation of traditional dance, None of the rest is quite that good, highlighted by Maddy Prior's haunting performance on "When I Was on Horseback" (although the song drones on a little too long at six-and-a-half minutes), the delightful "Marrowbones," the riveting "Stewball," and the rousing reels "Dowd's Favourite," "£10 Float," and "The Morning Dew." *—Bruce Eder*

Below the Salt / 1972 / Shanachie ✦✦✦✦✦
The most successful of all Steeleye Span lineups, with Bob Johnson and Rick Kemp in place of Martin Carthy and Ashley Hutchings, makes its debut on what could be their best album. There's not a weak note here, and all of its has a harder, more muscular sound courtesy of Kemp and Johnson, matched to impeccable vocals and uniformly excellent material. Kemp's bass playing makes it possible to overlook the absence of a drummer, while the match-up of Johnson and Hart made them one of the best electric guitar teams in English folk-rock (and helps explain Steeleye's successful eclipsing of the post-Richard Thompson Fairport Convention). Prior's voice was never better than on this album, and while Carthy's backing vocals are missed, the group's singing is still up to a very high standard, with "Rosebud in June" perhaps the best a cappella number in their repertory and "Royal Forester" their most charmingly lusty performance. "John Barleycorn"—which every Traffic fan should hear—is in a class by itself, and the dazzling "Gaudette" actually made the British charts and got Steeleye Span onto *Top of the Pops*. *—Bruce Eder*

Parcel of Rogues / 1973 / Shanachie ✦✦✦✦✦
The group's first real rock album, with a sound clearly rooted in modern sensibilities, with the guitars are turned up very loud for the first time. The singing is still modeled on traditional patterns, and is quite beautiful (especially "One Misty Moisty Morning" and "Allison Gross"), but the resonances and undertones of electric guitars are everywhere—the result is a record that, in some ways, recalls Fairport Convention's *Liege and Lief* (the record that led indirectly to the spawning of Steeleye Span in the first place), with some very flashy playing by Johnson on some of the breaks. The rousing "Ups and Downs" is played on acoustic instruments, and the atmospheric "Weaver and the Factory Maid" could've come off of any of the earlier albums, while "The Bold Poachers" is more traditional sounding, starting out on acoustic instruments before the amplified guitars chime in—it sets the tone for the album, as wah-wah pedals punch up instrumentals such as "Robbery with Violins" and "The Wee Wee Man" (which includes drums). A lot of the time it works—the ominous and dazzling "Cam Ye O'er Frae France" would not have succeeded half as well without amplification, and every fan of the group should hear this track at least once. *—Bruce Eder*

Now We Are Six / 1974 / Shanachie ✦✦✦✦

All Around My Hat / 1975 / Shanachie ✦✦✦

Commoner's Crown / 1975 / BGO ✦✦✦✦✦
From the opening bars of "Little Sir Hugh"—an extraordinarily brisk and upbeat sounding treatment of an incredibly grim song—the band playing on *Commoners Crown* scarcely sounds like the same group on *Now We Are Six* or *Parcel of Rogues*. Now a full-fledged rock group, competing with the likes of Jethro Tull and pumping out higher amperage than Fairport Convention, Steeleye engages in heavy riffing, savage attacks on their instruments, and generally kicks out the jams on this album. But they're also fairly clever, interweaving Bach with traditional Irish music—actually, Bach-meets-the-Mooncoin-Jig from their previous record—on "Bach Goes to Limerick." There's not a bad song here, and even if it is more rock than folk, it's all very substantial and vibrant music-making, and maybe the classic Steeleye Span's most engaging album. *—Bruce Eder*

Rocket Cottage / 1976 / BGO ✦✦✦✦✦
The second of Steeleye Span's Mike Batt-produced albums was released at a time (1976) when the acceptance of British folk-rock was on a rapid downhill slide. That was unfortunate because *Rocket Cottage* remains one of the strongest yet most unappreciated of Steeleye's catalog. Their knack for adapting English folk songs to rock & roll has never been more adeptly executed than on this record. Rob Johnson's electric guitar work became more consistently aggressive as did Nigel Pegrum's drumming and Rick Kemp's bass playing. Tracks like "The Brown Girl," "The Twelve Witches," and the instrumental "Sligo Maid" are indicative of this more muscular Batt treatment. While several tracks from Steeleye Span's past repertoire are frequently labeled as definitive (like "Alison Gross" and "All Around My Hat") when describing their unique style of folk-rock, none surpasses the anthemic "Sir James the Rose." It combines their trademark macabre lyrical content with a forceful rock arrangement, innocent sounding vocal harmonies, and a timely Peter Knight violin interlude to remind the listener that this song actually has traditional roots. So while this album was greeted with overwhelming indifference in 1976, it has stood the test of time as well as any "classic" '70s album. *—Dave Sleger*

Original Masters / 1977 / BGO ✦✦✦✦✦

Live at Last / 1978 / BGO ✦✦✦
Steeleye's only live album, recorded at their farewell concert, features Martin Carthy and John Kirkpatrick. *—Steve Winick*

Back in Line / 1986 / Shanachie ✦✦✦

Tempted & Tried / 1989 / Shanachie ✦✦✦
The reformed group's most recent work. An impressive return, complete with videos; their best album since reforming in the mid '80s. *—Bruce Eder & Stephen Winick*

Tonight's the Night, Live! / 1992 / Shanachie ✦✦✦
Steeleye Span's live album, recorded on their 1991 tour, is a surprisingly fulfilling work, covering new territory ("Ca the Ewes") and songs familiar from other hands ("Tam Lin," long a Fairport Convention standard), as well as a rousing version of "All Around My Hat" that is superior to the studio original. It's well-made, though it would've been nice to have included a list of the dates from which the performance derived. *—Bruce Eder*

● **Spanning the Years** / 1995 / Chrysalis ✦✦✦✦
A 35-song, two-CD best-of, moving from their earliest 1970 recordings through the early 1990s. The emphasis is properly on their 1970s work, and accordingly the first disc is more essential, though the second part also has merit. With lengthy liner notes by Maddy Prior, it's an excellent survey of the group, and may serve the essential needs of most listeners who aren't devoted fans. *—Richie Unterberger*

Horkstow Grange / May 11, 1999 / Park ✦✦✦

Bedlam Born / Oct. 24, 2000 / Park ✦✦✦✦

John Stewart

b. Sep. 5, 1939, San Diego, CA
Vocals, Guitar / Contemporary Folk, Folk-Rock, Soft Rock, Adult Contemporary, Singer/Songwriter
John Stewart first gained recognition as a songwriter when his songs were recorded by the Kingston Trio. In 1960, he formed the Cumberland Three, which recorded three albums for Roulette. The following year, he joined the Kingston Trio, replacing Dave Guard, and stayed with them until 1967. His song "Daydream Believer" was a *1 hit for $the Monkees* at the end of that year. Stewart traveled with Senator Robert Kennedy on his 1968 Presidential campaign, an experience that affected him deeply. In 1969, he released his classic album *California Bloodlines*, the first of seven solo albums to reach the charts through 1980. Stewart found his biggest commercial success with the Top Ten album *Bombs Away Dream Babies* and its single "Gold" in 1979. He released several of his albums and albums by others on his own Homecoming label starting in the 1980s. *—William Ruhlmann*

California Bloodlines/Willard (minus 2) / 1969-1970 / Bear Family ✦✦✦✦✦
This German import contains some of Stewart's most powerful work. *California Bloodlines* offers 12 original tunes backed by Nashville's finest studio musicians. *Willard Minus 2*, though not so powerful as *Bloodlines*, still features many great snogs (two tracks missing from the original) and a good cast of musicians. Highly recommended. *—Chip Renner*

Lonesome Picker Rides Again / 1971 / Warner Brothers ✦✦✦

Cannons in the Rain/Wingless Angels / 1973-1975 / One Way ✦✦✦✦
In this two-fer (*Cannons in the Rain/ Wingless Angels*) the *Wingless Angels* release is the stronger collection of music, featuring Robert "Waddy" Wachtel on guitar and a guest appearance by John Denver. *Cannons…* is a nice collection of ballads and folk-rock. *—Chip Renner*

Bombs Away Dream Babies / 1979 / Razor & Tie ✦✦✦✦✦
After departing the Kingston Trio and struggling for more than a decade to find success with his critically acclaimed folk albums, John Stewart finally reached his commercial peak with 1979's *Bombs Away Dream Babies*. It hit the Top Ten and temporarily turned him into a "new" pop star at age 40. Stewart's folk leanings are evident on this album, but it's mostly a straightforward pop/rock affair. The guest performances by Fleetwood Mac's Lindsey Buckingham on guitar and Stevie Nicks on background vocals certainly helped, especially since they were still riding high on the success of *Rumours*. "Gold" was a thinly veiled criticism of the music business set to a smooth shuffle beat. Ironically, it became a Top Five hit. The bittersweet "Lost Her in the Sun" and the darkly dramatic "Midnight Wind" also hit the Top 40. *—Bret Adams*

Dream Babies Go Hollywood / 1980 / RSO ✦✦✦✦
After folk-based Kingston Trio veteran John Stewart had a Top Five single with "Gold" from the Top Ten album *Bombs Away Dream Babies* in 1979, he largely repeated the pop/rock formula the next year with *Dream Babies Go Hollywood*. This time, Stewart didn't have the assistance of Fleetwood Mac's Lindsey Buckingham and Stevie Nicks (who were likely concentrating on *Tusk* hubbub). However, Linda Ronstadt and Nicolette Larson helped out and sang background vocals on most *Dream Babies Go Hollywood* cuts. "Hollywood Dreams" is a bright, easygoing pop tune. "Wind on the River," a dreamy, folk-pop ballad, is enriched by Stewart's warm, supple vocals. "Wheels of Thunder" is a pleasant surprise here because it's a straightforward rock & roll song; heavily distorted electric guitar licks cut through the warm keyboards, the crisp acoustic guitar, and the fast rhythm section. "Odin (Spirit of the Water)" is boldly dark and brooding; Stewart's lead vocals and the background vocals are fiercely energetic. "The Raven" is another highlight thanks to Stewart's ethereal, urgently whispered vocals and the female harmony vocals in the chorus. *Dream Babies Go Hollywood* marks Stewart's last sliver of solo mainstream success to date—a shame because his music is criminally underrated. Fortunately, a diehard core of Stewart cultists have kept his name alive by packing his club and theater concerts and buying the albums he released on smaller independent labels as well as on his own Homecoming imprint. *—Bret Adams*

Punch the Big Guy / 1987 / Shanachie ✦✦✦✦✦
If there were justice in the music world, *Punch the Big Guy* would have been a huge commercial success. John Stewart took his songwriting prowess to its zenith, brought in a stellar cast of musical compatriots, and put together his finest three-quarters of an hour. His lyrics here are fired with anger, righteous indignation, political awareness, compassion, and ultimately, love. The arrangements, built around Stewart's finger-picked electric guitar, are mesmerizing, and his muscular baritone provides the perfect delivery van for sharing these observations, memories, questions and vows. One cannot come away from this music unaffected. On "Midnight of the World," Stewart asks, "Will you always be my girl?" while simultaneously pondering the last days of the world. "Runaway Train" later became a number one country hit for Rosanne Cash, who contributes eerie vocal harmonies to "Price of the Fire" and "Angels with Guns." Throughout, however, Stewart expresses the sense of faith and hope outlined in "Ticket to the Stars": "There are forces to guide you/spirits beside you/Rivers to ride you home to the stars."

John Stewart achieves a genuine merger of the personal, the spiritual and the political on *Punch the Big Guy*, and wraps it all up in a darkly colored but accessible package. The mix of ballads and upbeat rockers holds the attention of even a casual listener, but for those who invest a little of themselves in the depth of its songs, this album offers a chest full of rare musical treasure. *—Jim Newsom*

Deep in the Neon: Live at McCabe's / Jun. 1991 / Homecoming ✦✦✦

Airdream Believer / 1995 / Shanachie ✦✦✦✦
This recording started out as a career retrospective and reconsideration by John Stewart, devoted to his own songs plus a few he really dug (like Johnny Cash's "Get Rhythm" and Billy Ed Wheeler's "The Reverend Mr. Black"), before it turned into something more. The music dates back, in some cases, to his days with the Kingston Trio, performed with Johnny Cash, Roseanne Cash, Nanci Griffith, Sara Hickman, and his former Kingston Trio bandmates Nick

Reynolds and Bob Shane. Stewart is in excellent voice throughout, a husky baritone closer in spirit to Bruce Springsteen than to the Kingston Trio; the mix of songs is quirky enough, and the reconsiderations of the songs fresh enough, to prevent this from being a mere exercise in nostalgia—"Lost Her in the Sun," "Midnight Wind" (with Roseanne Cash on the harmonies), and a moody "Daydream Believer" (with Nanci Griffith) are major highlights, but the entire recording is worthwhile, and the presence of the guest artists is not just a gimmick. *—Bruce Eder*

• **Turning Music Into Gold: The Best of John Stewart** / 1995 / Polydor ♦♦♦♦♦
The title of 1995's *The Best of John Stewart: Turning Music Into Gold* is actually a misnomer. This German release is actually two complete albums—1979's *Bombs Away Dream Babies* and 1980's *Dream Babies Go Hollywood*—and two previously unreleased bonus tracks collected on one CD. *Bombs Away Dream Babies* has been the biggest commercial success of Stewart's critically acclaimed solo career. This Top Ten effort included the Top Five hit "Gold" and two other Top 40 singles, "Midnight Wind" and "Lost Her in the Sun." Fleetwood Mac's Lindsey Buckingham and Stevie Nicks were featured prominently on the album. *Dream Babies Go Hollywood* was the less successful follow-up. It duplicated the pop/rock leanings of its predecessor and its notable tracks include "Hollywood Dreams," "Wind on the River," "Odin (Spirit of the Water)," and "Lady of Fame." "Hard Time Town" and "Children of the Morning" are the acoustic guitar-based bonus cuts. The former is driven by bright strumming while the latter, written by Stewart's wife Buffy Ford, is based on sweet fingerpicking. The liner notes were assembled by Peter O'Brien, who compiled insightful Stewart quotes from various interviews conducted between 1977 and 1984. *The Best of John Stewart: Turning Music Into Gold* is invaluable for die-hard fans because *Dream Babies Go Hollywood* was still not available individually on CD as of mid-2000. *—Bret Adams*

American Journey / 1996 / Delta ♦♦♦
A cut-price box set may seem like a contradiction in terms, but this triple-disc John Stewart compilation answers to that description. It contains three separate albums, which are also available separately. *The Last Campaign* is Stewart's 1985 theme album on the America of Robert Kennedy, a lovely, reflective set that echoes Kennedy more in spirit than in narrative. *The Trio Years* presents Stewart's re-recordings of songs he wrote for the Kingston Trio between 1959 and 1966, on which he is joined by surviving Trio member Nick Reynolds. (The credits may leave the impression that these are the original recordings; don't be fooled.) *An American Folk Song Anthology* contains performances of 12 mostly traditional folk songs. Stewart betrays some evidence of vocal deterioration on these recent recordings, but remains an effective interpreter. The overall effect is more miscellaneous than comprehensive, and at a total running time well under two hours, this is a fairly short three-disc set. At the discount price typical of Laser Light product, it's not a bargain, but may be reasonable value for money. *—William Ruhlmann*

Rough Sketches / Apr. 22, 1997 / Folk Era ♦♦♦♦♦

Gold: Best of John Stewart / Apr. 18, 2000 / Wrasse ♦♦♦♦♦
John Stewart's *Gold* is a spectacular two CD, 41 song best of compilation. It is perfect for the casual fan... if there is such a thing. Stewart has a diehard cult of fans who probably have every LP or CD they can get their hands on anyway, and that's quite a task considering the bulk of the former Kingston Trio member's early solo output is shamefully either out of print or only available as expensive imports. *Gold* collects everything from Stewart's singer/songwriter acoustic work to his rock-oriented songs, including his only three Top 40 hits, all from 1979's *Bombs Away Dream Babies:* "Gold," "Lost Her in the Sun," and "Midnight Wind." The 1969 critical favorite *California Bloodlines* is represented by five remarkable songs including the title track, "Mother Country," and "July You're a Woman." "Durango," "All Time Woman," and "Cannons in the Rain" are other fine examples of early Stewart, but "Armstrong/Spirit" is the best illustration. This poignant song about Neil Armstrong's moon landing and its unifying effect on problem-filled Earth is resonant in its dignified simplicity. "Hung on the Heart" and "Runaway Train" are highlights of disc two, but of particular note are "Sweet Dreams Will Come and "I Remember America." The former is a joyous bluegrass/folk/rockabilly duet with Nanci Griffith while the latter, although a tad curmudgeonly, recalls America's pre-JFK-assassination promise and laments modern society's breakdown. *Gold* includes an essay by John Tobler, but it lacks musician credits, which would document the caliber of "anonymous" session aces—particularly those in Nashville—and high-profile stars who have worked with Stewart over the years. *—Bret Adams*

The Story

f. 1981, **db.** 1994
Group / Contemporary Singer/Songwriter, Contemporary Folk
The folk-pop duo the Story comprised singers/songwriters Jonatha Brooke and Jennifer Kimball, who first teamed in 1981 while freshmen at Amherst College. Originally appearing under the name Jonatha and Jennifer, they performed regularly throughout the Boston area until graduation, at which time Brooke joined a dance company and Kimball joined a publishing firm. The occasional gig followed, however; in 1989, the duo finally recorded a demo, dubbed *Over Oceans,* and were quickly signed by the Green Linnet label. Changing their name to the Story, their debut LP *Grace in Gravity* appeared in 1991; Elektra then snapped up the band, reissuing the album a year later. *Angel in the House* followed in 1993, but a year later the Story dissolved; both Brooke and Kimball continued on as solo performers. *—Jason Ankeny*

Grace in Gravity / 1991 / Elektra ♦♦♦♦

• **The Angel in the House** / 1993 / Elektra ♦♦♦♦
From the recorders and whistles that open "So Much Mine," to the latin rhythms of "Fatso," *The Angel in the House* is a fiercely and unapologetically feminist album that addresses, among other themes, maternity, anorexia and the underlying horrors of domestic life. Both in her spirit and in her narrative manner Jonatha Brooke, who wrote almost the entire album, is a descendant of Virginia Woolf, and these songs, each one a beautifully arranged and well orchestrated tale of longing, love and/or loss, are some of her best. A well crafted and thought provoking album, arguably her best to date. *—Peter Stepek*

Linda Thompson

b. 1948
Singer, Vocals / British Folk-Rock, British Folk, Folk-Rock, Singer/Songwriter
Born Linda Pettifer, Linda Thompson, then known as Linda Peters, made an inauspicious debut as half of Paul and Linda in 1968. In 1972, following a couple of years of session work, singing commercial jingles and working the folk clubs around London, she teamed with friend Sandy Denny and other assorted members of the British folk-rock scene to record *Rock On,* a collection of early rock & roll favorites, under the name of the Bunch.

Peters met Fairport Convention guitarist and songwriter, Richard Thompson in 1969, but did not work with him until 1972. That same year, Richard and Linda were married, and in 1974, with the now classic *I Want to See the Bright Lights Tonight,* began a musical partnership that would span nearly ten years and six critically-acclaimed, yet commercially unsuccessful albums. During this time Linda would also make her mark as one of the finest female voices in pop music. The Thompsons' musical, as well as personal, relationship came to an end just as they were gaining some long overdue notoriety, especially in the U.S., with their brilliant and moving 1982 release, *Shoot Out the Lights.* The record, recorded on a shoestring budget for tiny Hannibal Records, has been widely heralded as one of the true masterpieces of the rock *roll era, and garnered $Linda Thompson* honors as female vocalist of the year in many year-end critics polls. 1982 also saw the couple embark on their first and only U.S. tour.

Following the breakup, Linda signed with Warner Bros. Records in 1985. The subsequent record, *One Clear Moment,* turned out to be her only post-Richard album. Hysterical dysphonia, a psychological inability to produce speech sounds which had plagued Thompson on and off throughout her career, eventually ended it. *—Brett Hartenbach*

• **Dreams Fly Away** / Jul. 2, 1996 / Hannibal ♦♦♦♦♦
Dreams Fly Away, a retrospective of the career of Linda Thompson, is a terrific introduction to one of the great female voices in popular music. A healthy dose of rare and unreleased tracks, along with previously available material from her career with Richard Thompson and solo, make this a must for fans and novitiates alike. Some of the unreleased gems include a haunting, live "The Great Valerio," what may be the definitive version of Sandy Denny's "I'm a Dreamer" from the Gerry Rafferty-produced *Shoot Out the Lights* sessions, and "Pavanne," recorded live in Hamburg, Germany. *—Brett Hartenbach*

One Clear Moment / Warner Brothers ♦♦♦♦
Linda Thompson's solo debut following her breakup with husband Richard is a slightly more polished effort than one might expect from the former folk-rock diva. With help from keyboardist, vocalist, and songwriting collaborator Betsy Cook and Cook's husband, producer Hugh Murphy, Thompson creates a slick-sounding pop record replete with big drums and electronic keyboards. The material lifts the album above the somewhat glossy production, although Cook's arrangements on "Can't Stop the Girl" and Ravel's "Les Trois Beaux Oiseaux de Paradis," along with the stark and affecting "Only a Boy," are superb. Thompson's lyrics, along with titles such as "Telling Me Lies" and "Hell, High Water and Heartache," tell you this is the voice of a woman scorned without being overly vindictive. *—Brett Hartenbach*

Artie Traum

b. 1943
Vocals, Guitar, Banjo / Singer/Songwriter
Artie Traum is a singer/songwriter based in Woodstock, NY. Born in the Bronx, he followed his brother Happy into folk music in the early '60s in the New York area, taking guitar lessons from jazz artists. He and his brother formed the folk-rock group the Children of Paradise in the mid-'60s and, after Happy's departure, they changed their name to Bear and recorded an album for Verve/Forecast. Traum moved to Woodstock in 1967 and has worked as a record producer and written film soundtracks. He has also recorded albums with his brother and with the Woodstock Mountain Revue; among his solo releases were 1986's *Cayenne,* 1993's *Letters From Joubee* and 1996's *View From Here. —William Ruhlmann*

• **Life on Earth** / 1974 / Rounder ♦♦♦♦♦
A fine album with Pat Alger, featuring "Is There Life on Earth," "Girls of Montreal," and "Riptide." *—Chip Renner*

From the Heart / 1980 / Rounder ♦♦♦♦♦
Traum and Pat Alger are two guys who were meant to play together. Highlights include "Gambling Man," "City Lights," and "Screwin' It Up." *—Chip Renner*

Cayenne / 1986 / Rounder ♦♦♦♦♦
Artie Traum is a fine acoustic guitarist, but this release was more of a showcase for his technical skills than a thoughtful or gripping effort. The 12 numbers were so short (none longer than four minutes) that frequently all Traum could do was present an opening melody, improvise briefly, and complete the track. In addition, they were mostly on the light/impressionistic side, creating an atmosphere that came perilously close to background caliber. Traum is too fine a player to be forgettable, but he was relegated more to coloration and establishing moods than to presenting accomplished, memorable songs. *—Ron Wynn*

Letters from Joubee / 1993 / Shanachie ♦♦♦

The View from Here / Feb. 20, 1996 / Shanachie ♦♦♦

Meetings with Remarkable Friends / Feb. 23, 1999 / Narada ♦♦♦

Happy Traum

b. 1939
Vocals, Guitar, Banjo / Singer/Songwriter, Folk-Pop
Happy Traum is a singer/songwriter based in Woodstock, New York who served as editor of *Sing Out!* magazine for three years and currently runs Homespun Tapes, a company that sells

instructional tapes narrated by well-known folk and rock musicians for aspiring musicians. Born in the Bronx, Traum attended the High School of Music and Art, where he took up music and was drawn into the folk music boom of the late '50s in the New York area. He was a member of the New World Singers and formed a folk-rock band in the mid-'60s called the Children of Paradise with his brother Artie, Eric Kaz, and others. He moved to Woodstock in 1967. Traum conducted one of the first interviews Bob Dylan granted after the 1966 motorcycle accident and, in October 1971, he recorded several tracks with Dylan that appeared on *Bob Dylan's Greatest Hits, Volume II*. He has made solo albums, records with his brother, and recordings with the Woodstock Mountain Revue. *—William Ruhlmann*

Doubleback / 1971 / Capitol ♦♦♦
A nice album featuring Artie Traum, Bill Keith, Amos Garrett, Eric Kaz, Billy Sanford, and Buddy Spicher. *—Chip Renner*

Hard Times in the Country / 1975 / Rounder ♦♦♦♦♦
Artie Traum, Paul Butterfield, Roly Salley, Arlen Roth, Pat Alger, and Jim Rooney blend nicely. Great covers of "Blow Your Whistle," "Freight Train," and "Penny's Farm." *—Chip Renner*

● **Bright Morning Stars** / 1980 / Greenhays ♦♦♦♦♦
A fine collection of music and friends make this a special album. With Pat Alger, Merle Watson, John Sebastian, Richard Manuel, Maria Muldaur, and Artie Traum. *—Chip Renner*

Bucket of Songs / 1983 / Shanachie ♦♦♦♦♦
This pleasing collection of covers and instrumentals was performed along with some of the Mud Acres Gang, Andy Robinson, Pat Alger and Rolly Sally. This is a compilation up to earlier Kicking Mule LPs. The album has an enjoyable feel to it. *—Richard Meyer*

Ian Tyson

b. Sep. 25, 1933, Victoria, British Columbia, Canada
Vocals, Guitar / Americana, Contemporary Folk, Cowboy
Half of the early-'60s folk group Ian & Sylvia, Ian Tyson retreated from performing and recording after the duo disbanded in the mid-'70s to become a rancher in the foothills of Southern Alberta, Canada. He quietly returned to music-making in the 1980s, releasing a series of albums that focused on detailed songs about the concerns of the working cowboy.

Tyson was born in Victoria, British Columbia. As a child he was involved in rodeo, not music—he didn't learn to play the guitar until he was recovering from rodeo-related injuries. In the late '50s, he began performing as a folk singer. In 1961, he met singer/songwriter Sylvia Fricker and the two musicians began performing together; they also married three years later. Ian & Sylvia and their band, Great Speckled Bird, became popular on the folk scene and released their self-titled debut album in 1962. In 1963, they released *Four Strong Winds;* the title track, written by Tyson, became a folk standard. Ian & Sylvia successfully recorded together through the mid-'70s. The duo also began hosting a television show, *Nashville North*, which became the *Ian Tyson Show* when the couple split up in the middle of the decade.

After Ian & Sylvia's break-up, Tyson recorded *Ol'Eon*. He temporarily retired from recording in 1979 to work his ranch, but returned with *Old Corrals and Sagebrush* in 1983. In 1984, he toured with Ricky Skaggs and also released an eponymous album. Tyson released a third album, *Cowboyography*, two years later, and in 1991, he released another popular Canadian album, *And Stood There Amazed*, which contained the hits "Springtime in Alberta" and "Black Nights." Subsequent releases include 1994's *Eighteen Inches of Rain*, 1996's *All the Good 'Uns* and 1999's *Lost Herd*. *—Sandra Brennan and Michael McCall*

Cowboyography / 1987 / Vanguard ♦♦♦
One of the few Ian Tyson albums to be released in the United Sttaes, *Cowboyography* is also one of his best records, demonstrating his skill for melding traditional western musical and lyrical themes with contemporary arrangements, productions and sensibilities. *—Thom Owens*

I Outgrew the Wagon / 1989 / Stony Plain ♦♦♦♦♦
This is the best of his series of homegrown album on what he calls "cowboy culture." Included are simple, unadorned songs affectionately yet unromantically examining rural life on the Canadian plains, as well as a couple of philosophical offerings. *—Michael McCall*

Eighteen Inches of Rain / 1994 / Vanguard ♦♦♦♦♦
He's been absent from the U.S. of A. for a while since the dissolution of Ian & Sylvia, but he certainly hasn't been idle—Tyson is quite a success in Canada, and Vanguard, a label he's been associated with previously, is taking a chance on repeating that success here. *Eighteen Inches of Rain* is the latest in Tyson's "Cowboy Culture" series (Vanguard is also reissuing *Cowboyography*), and it's a damn fine collection of songs about contemporary cowboys, ranchers and just plain folks, beautifully performed and sung, elegantly designed, and equipped with excellent lyrics. Many cuts are above the run of country music—songs like "Horsethief Moon" and "Rodeo Road" are songs that transcend boundaries. *—Steven McDonald*

All the Good 'uns / 1996 / Stony Plain ♦♦♦♦♦
Ian Tyson is the undisputed master of traditional cowboy culture music and *All the Good 'uns*, drawn from his five *Cowboyography* releases, removes any possible excuse for those who even casually appreciate roots music from being converted. Nineteen distinctive narratives of wide-eyed wonder, love of the land, and sagebrush wisdom conveyed through good, honest songs performed with integral simplicity. *—Roch Parisien*

Lost Herd / Mar. 23, 1999 / Vanguard ♦♦♦♦
Ian Tyson's *Lost Herd* paints nine musical portraits of life in the West. Recorded in Toronto, Calgary and Nashville with those cities' finest musicians, the album captures the loneliness of the plains, long days of summer, and dreams of the Canadian landscape. Songs like "La Primera" and "Brahmas & Mustangs" represent true cowboy culture, while Tyson's cover of "Somewhere Over the Rainbow" adds a rustic dreaminess to the classic tune. *Lost Herd* is a welcome blend of cowboy traditions from yesterday and today. *—Heather Phares*

● **Greatest Hits, Vol. 1** / Vanguard ♦♦♦♦♦

Dave Van Ronk

b. Jun. 30, 1936, Brooklyn, NY
Vocals, Guitar / Singer/Songwriter
Guitarist, singer and songwriter Dave Van Ronk has inspired, aided and promoted the careers of numerous singer/songwriters who came up in the folk/blues tradition. Most notable of the many musicians he's helped over the years is Bob Dylan, whom Van Ronk got to know shortly after Dylan moved to New York in 1961 to pursue a life as a folk singer. Van Ronk's recorded output over the years is healthy, but he's never been as prolific a songwriter as some of his friends from that era, like Dylan or Tom Paxton. Instead, the genius of what Van Ronk does lies in his flawless execution and rearranging of classic acoustic blues tunes. His recording career began with *Ballads, Blues and a Spiritual*, a 1959 LP for Folkways. Often regarded as the grand uncle of the Greenwich Village coffeehouse scene, he gained additional respect with his Prestige albums of the early '60s. Different recordings of Van Ronk's serve different purposes: to check out Van Ronk the songwriter, pick up *Going Back to Brooklyn*, which was his first all-originals album; for students of his complex guitar technique, pick up *Dave Van Ronk*, a reissue of two earlier Prestige albums. Van Ronk continued to record and perform at folk festivals around the world throughout the '90s. *—Richard Skelly*

& The Ragtime Jug Stompers / 1960 / Mercury ♦♦♦

With the Red Onion Jazz Band / 1963 / Prestige ♦♦♦♦
Most people think of Van Ronk as a folk singer, and that is the community he has been most a part of, but he has always thought of himself as a jazz singer. On this album from his early career he shows why. Van Ronk offers up exuberant performances of "Cake Walkin Babies from Home" and "Ace in the Hole." There are some solo guitar songs such as Son House's "Death Letter Blues," and even a Bob Dylan tune, "If I Had to Do It All over Again, I'd Do It All over You." These days this record, as well as his others which have not made the jump to CD, is hard to find; but well worth picking up if found in some unsuspecting record bin. *—Richard Meyer*

● **Inside Dave Van Ronk** / 1969 / Fantasy ♦♦♦♦♦
Somewhat confusingly titled, this CD reissue includes both the 1962 album of the same name and the *Folksinger* LP (recorded around the same time), encompassing 25 tracks in all. Anyway, this is certainly Van Ronk's most enduring work, and indeed one of the few relics of the early-'60s traditional folk boom that holds up well today. With the possible exception of Bob Dylan (whom Van Ronk and his wife helped immensely when Dylan was a struggling unknown in New York), Dave was the finest interpreter of traditional folk tunes of that time, with a big bear of a voice that was both anguished and tender. One of the few white folkies who could sing acoustic blues without embarrassment, Van Ronk was also an accomplished acoustic guitar picker; instrumentally and vocally, he brought an intensity to his covers that made the songs his own. Of the two albums brought together on this CD, *Inside* has the edge because of its more varied instrumentation, including 12-string guitar, dulcimer, and autoharp (*Folksinger* only has Dave's vocals and guitar). Dominated by classics like "Motherless Child," "Silver Dagger," "Poor Lazarus," and "Fixin' To Die," this also has an arrangement of "He Was A Friend Of Mine" that Van Ronk learned from Dylan, who apparently claimed the traditional song as his own at the time. *—Richie Unterberger*

Sunday Street / 1976 / Philo ♦♦♦♦♦
This album, originally released in 1976, may or may not be, as annotator (and former Dave Van Ronk guitar student) Elijah Wald claims, "Dave's greatest single album" (frankly, Van Ronk has made so many albums for so many fly-by-night labels that it is hard to endorse so sweeping a statement), but it is certainly a very good one. Van Ronk had made various efforts in recent years to accommodate pop and rock music on his albums, but this one was a return to his usual repertoire of folk-blues tunes and jazz and ragtime transcriptions for guitar, with one Joni Mitchell song ("That Song About the Midway") and an original, the title song, thrown in. And it was a solo album on which Van Ronk sang and accompanied himself on acoustic guitar. Thus, it approximated what a good set in a club by this artist would sound like, minus the singer's witticisms, of course. Van Ronk never hid his influences, but he never sounded exactly like them, either, and on this album he was very much himself. Maybe it is his greatest single album; it is certainly one of his most representative. *—William Ruhlmann*

☆ **Folkways Years (1959-1961)** / 1991 / Smithsonian/Folkways ♦♦♦♦♦
Van Ronk sums up this album well with his own notes; "I never really thought of myself as a 'folksinger' at all. Still don't. What I did was to combine traditional fingerpicking guitar with a repertoire of old jazz tunes." This then is the first recorded statement, not of a folk musician, but of a kind of jazz manqué. On this album Van Ronk covers folk and blues songs such as "Hesitation Blues," "Twelve Gates to the City," and Spike Dreiver's "Moan." *—Richard Meyer*

To All My Friends in Far-Flung Places / Dec. 6, 1994 / Gazell ♦♦♦♦

Townes Van Zandt

b. Mar. 7, 1944, Fort Worth, TX, **d.** Jan. 1, 1997
Vocals, Guitar / Americana, Contemporary Folk, Singer/Songwriter, Country-Rock, Progressive Country
Townes Van Zandt's music doesn't jump up and down, wear fancy clothes, or beat around the bush. Whether he's singing a quiet, introspective country-folk song or a driving, hungry blues, Van Zandt's lyrics and melodies are filled with the kind of haunting truth and beauty that seems instinctive. His music comes straight from his soul by way of a kind heart, an honest mind, and a keen ear for the gentle blend of words and melody. The magic of his songs is that they never leave the listener alone.

Van Zandt was a Texan by birth and, after a wandering adolescence, eventually settled in Houston. Another Texas songwriter, Mickey Newbury, saw Van Zandt performing in Houston one night and soon had him set up with a recording gig in Nashville (with Jack Clement producing). The sessions became Van Zandt's debut album, *For the Sake of the Song,* released in 1968. The next five years were the most prolific of his career, writing and recording the songs "For the Sake of the Song," "To Live's to Fly," "Tecumseh Valley," "Pancho and Lefty," and many more that have made him a legend in American and European songwriting circles. After several decades of sporatic touring and recording, Townes Van Zandt died unexpectedly on January 1, 1997; he was 52 years old.

Despite his warm, dusty-sweet voice, as a singer Townes has never had anything resembling a hit in his nearly 30-year recording career—he's had a hard enough time simply keeping his records in print. Nonetheless he's widely respected and admired as one of the greatest country and folk artists of this generation. The long list of singers who've covered his songs includes Merle Haggard and Willie Nelson (who had a number one country hit with "Pancho and Lefty" in 1983), Emmylou Harris, Jimmie Dale Gilmore, Nanci Griffith, Hoyt Axton, Bobby Bare, the Tindersticks, and the Cowboy Junkies. *—Kurt Wolff*

For the Sake of the Song: First Album / 1968 / Rhino ✦✦✦
Produced by Jack Clement, Townes' debut is unfortunately marred by inappropriate arrangements. Includes the first recordings of the title song and "Tecumseh Valley" along with obscure songs like "The Velvet Voices" and "Talkin' Karate Blues." Re-released by Rhino in 1993 as *First Album. —Kurt Wolff*

Our Mother the Mountain / 1969 / Tomato ✦✦✦✦✦
Weirdly heavy on the strings behind Townes' sweet and smooth—but eternally haunted—voice, though in this case the arrangements work. Songs like "Kathleen," "St. John the Gambler," and the title track will last forever. *—Kurt Wolff*

Townes Van Zandt / 1969 / Tomato ✦✦✦✦
On his third album, Townes Van Zandt recut three crucial tracks from his debut album, "For The Sake Of The Song," "Waiting Around To Die," and "I'll Be Here In The Morning." It was some indication of the obscurity in which he remained enveloped, but no indication of the quality of his work. (Actually, Van Zandt rerecorded songs from his first album on his later ones because he disliked the earlier recordings.) As usual, his closely observed lyrics touched on desperate themes, notably in tbe mining ballad "Lungs," but they were still highly poetic, especially the album-closing "None But The Rain," which reflected on a failed relationship. Van Zandt's finger-picking was augmented by spare arrangements, usually featuring one added instrument for color, such as a fiddle or flute. (Originally released by Poppy Records in 1969, *Townes Van Zandt* was reissued by Tomato Records in 1989.) *—William Ruhlmann*

Delta Momma Blues / 1971 / Tomato ✦✦✦
Townes Van Zandt's dour viewpoint found more expression on his fourth album, its most characteristic song being "Come Tomorrow," on which he looked forward to how lonely life would be when his lover left. Even "Brand New Companion," which hailed the arrival of a lover, was done as a blues. "Here's to feeling good," he sang in "Only Him Or Me," then added, "Here's to feeling bad." But, as usual, what made Van Zandt so compelling was that, in songs like "Rake" and "Nothin'," the painted despair so vividly. (Originally released by Poppy Records in 1970, *Delta Momma Blues* was reissued by Tomato Records in 1989.) *—William Ruhlmann*

High, Low and In Between / 1972 / Rhino ✦✦✦✦✦
Townes Van Zandt's fifth album was different from his first four starting with the first few notes. Lead-off track "Two Hands" was an uptempo gospel number featuring piano and backup vocals. Van Zandt returned to religion in the country waltz "When He Offers His Hand," sang rock 'n' roll with a harmony vocal on "Standin'," tried a martial beat worthy of Johnny Cash on the gambling story song "Mr. Gold And Mr. Mudd," and even turned to comedy in "No Deal." The musical variety made *High, Low And In Between* a more interesting listen than Van Zandt's previous work, but what made it his best album since his debut was the quality of the songs, especially "You Are Not Needed Now" and "To Live Is To Fly." (Originally released by Poppy Records in 1971, *High Low And In Between* was reissued by Tomato Records in 1989.) *—William Ruhlmann*

The Late Great Townes Van Zandt / 1972 / Tomato ✦✦✦✦✦
On his sixth album in five years, Townes Van Zandt seemed to be getting less prolific, but his songwriting craft only improved. Van Zandt rerecorded yet another track from his debut album, "Sad Cinderella," and did three cover tunes, including one by main influence Hank Williams. But among the remaining seven new originals were "Pancho and Lefty," a sly Western story song about two outlaws, and "If I Needed You," among his most telling romantic statements. The two songs would become valuable copyrights for Van Zandt, and they made this oddly titled album one of his best, which was good since, as it happened, it would be his last release for five years. (Originally released by Poppy Records in 1972, *The Late, Great Townes Van Zandt* was reissued by Tomato Records in 1989.) *—William Ruhlmann*

★ **Live at the Old Quarter (Houston, Texas)** / 1977 / Tomato ✦✦✦✦✦
Townes Van Zandt is one of the most impressive songwriters to emerge in the 70s, and his extensive catalog is sufficiently consistent to be recommended in its entirety, once the listener has acquired a taste for his spare, dry delivery and gallows humor. The place to get that taste is on this live disc (originally a two-LP set), which features the best of Van Zandt's early songs, including "If I Needed You" and "Pancho and Lefty." *—William Ruhlmann*

Flyin' Shoes / 1978 / Rhino ✦✦✦

At My Window / 1987 / Sugar Hill ✦✦✦✦✦
Van Zandt's first album after a long layoff found him in a more accessible musical setting, courtesy of producers Jack Clement and Jim Rooney, with his striking lyrical observations intact. Van Zandt's qualities are sometimes subtle, and this is an album that gets better every time it's listened to. *—William Ruhlmann*

Live & Obscure / 1989 / Sugar Hill ✦✦✦

The Nashville Sessions / 1993 / Tomato ✦✦✦

Rear View Mirror / 1993 / Sundown ✦✦✦

Roadsongs / 1994 / Sugar Hill ✦✦✦
An album of nothing but covers, recorded off the soundboards at various live dates. Includes "Ira Hayes," "Racing in the Streets," two Dylan songs, and four by Lightnin' Hopkins. *—Kurt Wolff*

No Deeper Blue / 1995 / Sugar Hill ✦✦✦

Rain on a Conga Drum: Live in Berlin / Nov. 7, 1995 / MMS ✦✦✦✦

High, Low and In Between/Late Great Townes Van Zandt / Oct. 1, 1996 / Capitol ✦✦✦✦
High, Low and In Between and *The Late Great Townes Van Zandt,* Townes Van Zandt's two classic records from 1972, were reissued on a single CD from Capitol in 1996. *High, Low and In Between,* Van Zandt's fifth album, was different from his first four starting with the first few notes. The lead-off track "Two Hands" was an uptempo gospel number featuring piano and backup vocals. Van Zandt returned to religion in the country waltz "When He Offers His Hand," sang rock & roll with a harmony vocal on "Standin'," tried a martial beat worthy of Johnny Cash on the gambling story song "Mr. Gold and Mr. Mudd," and even turned to comedy in "No Deal." The musical variety made *High, Low and In Between* a more interesting listen than Van Zandt's previous work, but what made it his best album since his debut was the quality of the songs, especially "You Are Not Needed Now" and "To Live Is To Fly." By *The Late Great Townes Van Zandt,* his sixth album in five years, Van Zandt seemed to be getting less prolific, but his songwriting craft only improved. Van Zandt re-recorded yet another track from his debut album, "Sad Cinderella," and did three cover tunes, including one by main influence Hank Williams. But among the remaining seven new originals were "Pancho and Lefty," a sly Western story-song about two outlaws, and "If I Needed You," among his most telling romantic statements. The two songs would become valuable copyrights for Van Zandt, and they made this oddly titled album one of his best—which was good, since, as it happened, it would be his last release for five years. *—William Ruhlmann*

Loudon Wainwright III

b. Sep. 5, 1947, Chapel Hill, NC
Vocals, Guitar / Contemporary Folk, Singer/Songwriter
Loudon Wainwright III became a folk singer/songwriter in the late '60s, singing humorous and nakedly honest autobiographical songs. Signed to Atlantic Records, he recorded *Album I* (1970) and *Album II* (1971), accompanying himself on acoustic guitar, before switching to Columbia Records, for which he made the folk-rock *Album III* (1972), which featured the Top 40 novelty hit "Dead Skunk." *Attempted Mustache* (1973) and the half-live *Unrequited* (Feb. 1975) did not continue that commercial success, though Wainwright's humor and engaging stage persona made him a cult figure and a concert favorite. Meanwhile, his songs were recorded by others, notably Kate (his wife, since divorced) and Anna McGarrigle, and Wainwright appeared in the off-Broadway show *Pump Boys and Dinettes* and played a featured role on the successful *M*A*S*H* television series. Wainwright began to gain more notice in England than in the U.S., and he moved to London in 1985. *I'm Alright* (1985) and *More Love Songs* (1986) were co-produced by British singer/guitarist Richard Thompson. *Therapy* (1989) found Wainwright on the major label-distributed Silvertone imprint and back living in the U.S., and he signed to Virgin Records' Charisma subsidiary for *History. —William Ruhlmann*

Album 1 / 1970 / Atlantic ✦✦

Album 2 / 1971 / Atlantic ✦✦✦

Album III / 1972 / Columbia/Legacy ✦✦✦
Wainwright's directly autobiographical songs are both brutally honest and extremely funny. Usually he plays alone, but here he gets a full folk/rock backup, which brings out the pop implications of his music. His fluke hit "Dead Skunk" is here, and so is "Red Guitar," about the destruction of one. *—William Ruhlmann*

Attempted Moustache / 1973 / Columbia ✦✦✦✦
Following on the heels of the fluke success of Loudon Wainwright III's only hit single, "Dead Skunk," and *Attempted Mustache* is an excellent encapsulation of all things Loudon. Even so, sales were disappointing, and Wainwright's audience did not expand beyond that of a small, loyal cult. The LP kicks off with "The Swimming Song," a tongue-in-cheek celebration full of clever lines, banjo pickin' and a touch of Doug Kershaw's Cajun fiddle. "A.M. World" reflects on life with a hit single, obviously written while "Dead Skunk" was climbing the charts. "Liza" is an a cappella folk song about childhood friend and classmate Liza Minnelli, who had recently won an Oscar for *Cabaret.* "I Am the Way" recasts Woody Guthrie's talking blues "New York Town," with Jesus Christ hanging out in Jerusalem proclaiming, "Every Son of God gets a little hard luck some time," and confessing, "Don't tell nobody but I kissed Magdalene." "Dilated to Meet You" is a welcome-to-the-world greeting card for a soon-to-be-born child, but on "Lullaby," the singer pleads with his son Rufus to "shut up and go to bed," complaining "you're a late night faucet that's got a drip." This album also includes the Wainwright classic "The Man Who Couldn't Cry," a lengthy short story set to music about a character who suffers all manner of tragedy and abuse, but is still incapable of showing emotion. Throughout *Attempted Mustache,* Loudon Wainwright III's droll, dry sense of humor is conveyed by his world-weary everyman's voice, capturing small vignettes of life through a skewed, slightly left-of-center lens. *—Jim Newsom*

Unrequited / 1975 / Columbia ✦✦✦✦
The first half of *Unrequited* is made up of studio recordings with various accompaniments, while side two was recorded live at the Bottom Line in New York City. This duality effectively showcases the strengths and weaknesses of Loudon Wainwright III's music, for he has always been much more potent when less orchestration is added to his simple folk songs. The album kicks off with a heavily rocked-up "Sweet Nothings," aperhaps the least interesting track on the disc. It is followed by "The Lowly Tourist," which moves to a reggae beat with a sound that borrows blatantly from Paul Simon's "Mother and Child Reunion." The album picks up after this, as the instrumentation becomes less obtrusive and the lyrics come more to the forefront. "Crime of Passion" features an understated arrangement with a nice touch from Richard Greene's violin. Side two presents Wainwright in his natural element, alone with a guitar on the stage of a small Greenwich Village club. Here, one can hear the lyrical

craftsman at work, taking the audience along on an entertaining ride. "On the Rocks" begins, "You say you got domestic problems, well you should get a load of mine." "Mr. Guilty" is a classic Wainwright performance piece, with the title character feeling anything but. The album wraps up with "Rufus is a Tit Man," about Loudon's boy Rufus being fed by his mom: "You can tell by the way the boy burps that it's gotta taste fine." *—Jim Newsom*

T Shirt / 1976 / Arista ✦✦

A Live One / 1979 / Rounder ✦✦✦✦✦
Wainwright is well served by this collection of samples of his live work, which also doubles as the best of his 70s material, with songs like "Whatever Happened to Us," "Nocturnal Stumblebutt," and "Clockwork Chartreuse." *— William Ruhlmann*

Fame and Wealth / 1983 / Rounder ✦✦✦

I'm Alright / 1984 / Rounder ✦✦✦

More Love Songs / 1986 / Rounder ✦✦✦✦✦

Therapy / 1989 / Silvertone ✦✦✦✦

● **History** / 1992 / Charisma ✦✦✦✦✦
The best album of Loudon Wainwright III's career, *History* features a mix of the humorous and the serious, the autobiographical and the observational, the rockin' and the balladic, all wrapped up in some classy arrangements. There is a mood of personal reflection hanging over the entire proceeding, inspired by the death of Wainwright's father, a noted American writer and editor.

"People in Love" kicks the whole thing off with one of Wainwright's trademark observations on the perils of love. On "Men," the singer quietly discusses the whys and wherefores of male behavior, while "The Picture" is a musical reflection on a picture of Loudon and his sister taken forty years earlier (and reproduced inside the CD booklet). The album then continues with a clever classic of the satirical talking folk-blues genre, "Talking New Bob Dylan," in which Wainwright, once considered one of the many "new Dylans," salutes the original on his fiftieth birthday. The last three songs on the album form a powerful triumvirate, with "A Father and a Son" written by a man who is both, and "Sometimes I Forget" an extremely personal ballad about the loss of his own dad. The final track, "A Handful of Dust" was actually written by Loudon Wainwright, Jr., in 1952, and adapted by his son for this recording.

For those familiar with Loudon Wainwright III only through his novelty hit, "Dead Skunk," or who don't know his work at all, *History* will come as a revelation. For the small cult of Wainwright fans, its power and poignancy may also come as a wonderful surprise, for it's the album his previous work hinted might be within him. It is his masterpiece. *—Jim Newsom*

Career Moves / Jan. 8, 1993 / Virgin ✦✦✦✦✦
Following on the heels of *History, Career Moves* gave Loudon Wainwright III two of his best albums back to back. *Career Moves* captures Wainwright live at the Bottom Line in New York City, performing a sort of greatest-hits set and throwing in a few new songs as well. He goes through most of the concert alone with his guitar, bringing out multi-instrumentalists Chaim Tannenbaum and David Mansfield for a few numbers midway through the concert. The material here is universally strong, mixing satire and silliness with serious looks at Wainwright's personal life, his kids, his ex-wives, and his own life experiences. "Your Mother and I" is one of his greatest songs on one of his favorite topics, marital dissolution and its effect on children. "Tip That Waitress" should be in the repertoire of every struggling barroom musician. "The Acid Song" takes him over the top, and there is much laughter provided by songs like "Suddenly It's Christmas," "He Said She Said," and "T.S.M.N.W.A.," on which he bemoans the many ways his name has been misspelled through the years. There are also several examples of Wainwright's poignant, bittersweet autobiographical balladeering, and reprises of twenty-year-old classics like "The Swimming Song" and "The Man Who Couldn't Cry." The between-song patter and asides show Wainwright to be an entertaining standup comic, and the whole album provides lively evidence of his skills as a songsmith and live entertainer working an audience. *—Jim Newsom*

Grown Man / Oct. 1995 / Virgin ✦✦✦

Little Ship / Feb. 24, 1998 / Virgin ✦✦✦

BBC Sessions / Nov. 3, 1998 / Varese ✦✦✦

Social Studies / 1999 / Hannibal ✦✦✦✦✦

The Atlantic Recordings / 2000 / Rhino Handmade ✦✦✦✦
Internet mail-order firm Rhino Handmade's *The Atlantic Recordings* reissues Loudon Wainwright III's first two LPs—1970's *Loudon Wainwright III* (sometimes called *Album I*) and 1971's *Album II*—on a single CD for the first time. These are stark folk recordings on which Wainwright accompanies himself on acoustic guitar, often straining to reach the high notes with his limited, slightly hysterical tenor. Even at this young age, Wainwright had already embarked upon his lifelong musical autobiography, a painfully honest, highly detailed account of his experiences, including his personal failings. You'd better be taken with the literate, self-conscious sad sack depicted in his lyrics, because there is precious little melodic invention or melodic variation to engage you. But it's hard not to love a young man who sounds like he's spent enough time on a psychiatrist's couch to have lost any inhibitions; he discusses everything from lust and suicidal feelings to his delight at sightseeing and the minute details of an airplane trip. He can show a childlike enthusiasm, but he also often seems old beyond his years. When these albums were first released, with performers like James Taylor and Joni Mitchell defining the confessional singer/songwriter trend, Wainwright seemed like its logical extreme, but at the same time, he punctured the seriousness of his peers, poking fun at their solemn introspection. These songs are the opening statements in his ongoing autobiography-in-song, one that has been by turns hilarious, embarrassing, and moving, but always striking in its willingness to uncover real feelings. These uneven albums might have benefited from being compressed into a less-lengthy compilation, but this is a limited edition for fans, who are actually more likely to wish this was a two-CD set that contained several documented, unissued outtakes. (www.rhinohandmade.com) *— William Ruhlmann*

Norma Waterson

Vocals / British Folk
Since the mid-'60s, Norma Waterson, along with brother Mike, sister Lal and others, have performed together as the Watersons to make some of the most beautiful records in British traditional music. While performing one evening with her family at McCabe's in Santa Monica, California, club booker and producer John Chelew inquired if Waterson had ever considered recording a solo album. The subsequent record, entitled *Norma Waterson,* was recorded in Los Angeles in late 1995 with the help of friends and family. The recording, which was produced by Chelew, featured a veritable who's-who of the British folk world, with husband Martin Carthy (Steeleye Span, the Watersons) and Richard Thompson (Fairport Convention) on guitars, Danny Thompson (Pentangle) on double bass, Roger Swallow (Albion Country Band) on drums, and daughter Eliza Carthy (the Watersons) on vocals and violin. The final product, which was recorded in a mere five days, was released by Hannibal Records in 1996. *Bright Shiny Morning* followed five years later. *—Brett Hartenbach*

● **Norma Waterson** / 1996 / Hannibal ✦✦✦✦
It may have taken nearly 30 years for someone to suggest a Norma Waterson solo project, but the outcome was well worth the wait. Waterson's eponymous titled debut, with the exception of "There is a Fountain in Christ's Blood," isn't the traditional collection some would expect, but is filled with material from contemporary writers which makes it much closer in sound to the folk-rock of an artist like Richard Thompson. The record kicks off with a beautiful reading of Jerry Garcia and Robert Hunter's "Black Muddy River" and rolls through a range of songs by the likes of Thompson, Billy Bragg, Elvis Costello, Ben Harper and Norma's sister Lal. The backing is sympathetic throughout, mixing Martin Carthy's intricate acoustic guitar with Richard Thompson's lyrical electric work, Danny Thompson's bass, Roger Swallow's drums and bits of violin from Eliza Carthy. It would be easy for such an all-star band to outshine a lesser talent, but it's Norma Waterson's world-weary alto that instills the songs with a timelessness and gives them real life. *—Brett Hartenbach*

Bright Shiny Morning / Oct. 16, 2000 / Topic ✦✦✦✦✦
Although Norma Waterson has been a fixture of the English folk scene for 35 years, *Bright Shiny Morning* is only her second solo album (her first, *Norma Waterson,* was released in 1996). She has remained a fixture due to her resonant voice and the depth of her interpretations of traditional English songs. From "The Chaps of Cockaigny" to "My Flower, My Companion & Me" Waterson's voice stands front and center, filled with romantic trills and often expressing a deep sadness. The individual arrangements add spice to this material, from the piano accordion on "Three Maids A-Milking" to the brass of "Barbary Allen." "Game of All Fours" is sung without accompaniment, recalling other traditional singers like Anne Briggs. Waterson writes, "All these songs, one way or another, are love songs," but love doesn't always go as one would like it to. Indeed, "One April Morning" carries the unhappy refrain, "Young men are false/young men they are deceitful." "Green Grows the Laurel" finds the narrator sadly parted from her lover, turned out of her home, and left to ramble with her baby. The artist receives a great deal of support from Eliza Carthy, Martin Carthy, and harp player Mary Macmaster, each tastefully adding touches that serve the voice of the singer. Eliza Carthy also receives credit for the fine production of *Bright Shiny Morning,* which has a crisp, vivid sound-brighter perhaps than one might expect for strict traditional music, but it works perfectly. Waterson has created a lasting artistic statement, and fans can only hope that she doesn't wait quite as long for her next effort. *—Ronnie Lankford, Jr.*

The Watersons

Group / British Folk
A singing family from Yorkshire, England, the Watersons have been performing and recording unaccompanied harmony singing for years. Martin Carthy married into the family, and appears on many of their recordings. If you like a cappella, four part harmony singing of folk material, you can't do better than this group. *—Steve Winick*

Watersons / 1966 / Topic ✦✦✦
The Watersons was a strong follow-up to *Frost and Fire,* featuring a greater variety of songs. *—Steve Winick*

Yorkshire Garland / 1966 / Topic ✦✦✦
Again, this has variety of songs, but all of them come from Yorkshire. *—Steve Winick*

Bright Phoebus / 1972 / Trailer ✦✦✦

● **For Pence & Spicey Ale** / 1975 / Shanachie ✦✦✦✦✦
This lovely album, almost entirely acappella, was first released by The Watersons in 1975. It is considered by many to be their finest recording and includes the participation of Martin Carty in addition to family members. This reissue also includes some later solo Waterson recordings which feature others helping out. This record sounds like the back room of an old pub in its charming immediacy. You really get a sense of the fun it is to sing these old songs with affection and respect. *—Richard Meyer*

Mike Waterson / 1977 / Topic ✦✦✦
Mike Waterson's solo recording features big ballads and other wonderful traditional songs. *—Steve Winick*

Sound, Sound Your Instruments of Joy / 1977 / Topic ✦✦✦
On this one, they return to one of their first loves: hymns and carols. *—Steve Winick*

True Hearted Girl / 1977 / Topic ✦✦✦
Lal and Norma Waterson, known unofficially as "the Waterdaughters," perform traditional songs solo and in harmony. *—Steve Winick*

Frost and Fire / 1995 / Topic ✦✦✦✦✦
The original LP, a recording of seasonal songs, remains one of their greatest accomplish-

ments. The CD re-release, featuring tracks from Sound, Sound Your Instruments of Joy, is indispensible. *—Steve Winick*

Doc Watson (Arthel Watson)

b. Mar. 2, 1923, Deep Gap, NC

Vocals, Harmonica, Guitar, Banjo, Guitar (Acoustic) / Traditional Folk, Traditional Country, Old-Timey

In this half of our century there have been three preeminently influential guitar players: Merle Travis, Chet Atkins, and Arthel "Doc" Watson, a flat-picking genius from Deep Gap, North Carolina. Unlike the other two, Watson was in middle age before gaining any attention. Since 1960, though, when Watson was recorded with his family and friends in Folkways' *Old Time Music at Clarence Ashley's*, people have remained in awe of this gentle blind man who sings and picks with a pure and emotional authenticity. The present generation, folkies and country pickers alike, including Ricky Skaggs, Vince Gill, the late Clarence White, Emmylou Harris, and literally hundreds of others, acknowledge their great debt to Watson. Watson has provided a further service to country/folk by his encyclopedic knowledge of many American traditional songs. While Merle Travis and Chet Atkins started on acoustic guitars and moved to electric, before Watson's "discovery" during the folk revival in the early '60s, he played electric in a local all-purpose band that played current rock, swing, country, and of course folk music. He gained recognition gradually, first from the *Clarence Ashley* album, which led to a rave performance at the Newport Folk Festival in 1963. Folkways soon recorded an album of Watson, followed in 1964 by a series of albums by Vanguard, nearly one a year through the decade. No sooner had interest in folk music waned than Watson was back in great demand because of the three-disc *Will the Circle Be Unbroken*, a watershed album in 1972 that was created by the Nitty Gritty Dirt Band. It featured Watson, Travis, Roy Acuff, and a Who's Who of country greats. Merle, Watson's son and a talent in his own right, began appearing with his father regularly. The result was good enough for them to win two Grammys for traditional music, in 1973 and 1974. Father and son played beautiful music together for over fifteen years, until Merle died tragically on the family farm in 1985. Following his son's death, Doc Watson continued with his appearances, showcasing his beautiful voice, his great instrumental talent, and his mastery of traditional material. He is an American treasure. *—David Vinopal*

★ **Doc Watson** / 1964 / Vanguard ✦✦✦✦✦

His first Vanguard album, ca. 1964, features warm vocals, influential guitar, harmonica, and old-time banjo. *—Mark A. Humphrey*

Treasures Untold / 1964 / Vanguard ✦✦✦✦✦

Treasures Untold is comprised of unreleased performances recorded at the 1964 Newport Folk Festival. At the concert, Doc Watson and his family were in fine form, breathing life into a number of old timey songs, ranging from ballads to folk songs to gospel. It's an exciting, affectionate performance, highlighted by four duets by Clarence White. *—Thom Owens*

Home Again / 1966 / Vanguard ✦✦✦

Watson's fourth Vanguard album is his most affecting folk-style record, with unexpectedly warm vocals matched to the quiet virtuosity of his playing. With only a couple of instrumentals on this 14-song collection, the rest features Watson performing lively, achingly beautiful renditions of popular folk standards ("Katie Morey," "Georgie," "Froggie Went A-Courtin'," "Matty Groves"). There isn't a weak number here, although highlights include the haunting "Winter's Night," and "The F.F.V.," the latter a grim but lively song in memory of a train wreck and a dead engineer. All are played with very imposing dexterity by Watson, joined by his son Merle and Russ Savakus on upright bass. This album was a great showcase for Watson's voice—vaguely similar to but rougher-hewn than Burl Ives—which is often overlooked in the aura of his playing. *—Bruce Eder*

☆ **Southbound** / 1966 / Vanguard ✦✦✦✦✦

Southbound was a pivotal record for Doc Watson. Upon its 1966 release, it demonstrated that Watson was capable of more than just dazzling interpretations of folk songs, but that he could also write excellent original material and rework new country songs in a fascinating manner. *Southbound* also marked the recorded debut of Merle Watson, Doc's astonishingly talented son. *—Thom Owens*

Ballads from Deep Gap / 1967 / Vanguard ✦✦✦

Doc Watson on Stage (Featuring Merle Watson) / 1971 / Vanguard ✦✦✦✦

One of Doc Watson's finest later records, *On Stage* is a virtual travelogue of his entire career in one record, almost a greatest hits record, live. Assisted by Merle Watson, the program flows from lightning fast hoedowns such as "Brown's Ferry Blues," where Watson picks lightning fast with a dexterity that is almost unbelievable. His feel and command of the instrument is truly incredible. "Open Up Them Pearly Gates for Me" has a similar effect. There are also numerous stories and patter (mostly about the songs) in between the cuts, and it guides you through the performance. Watson also shines on this album as well, especially his exquisite fingerpicking on "Banks of the Ohio." A timeless slice from one of the fathers of modern country music. *—Matthew Greenwald*

The Elementary Doc Watson / 1972 / Flying Fish ✦✦✦

Long before the term "Unplugged" became en vogue, Doc Watson made some of the finest accoustic albums around. A nice blend of standards and some more contemporary songs, Doc and band perform each with a warmth and affection that few others can emulate. *—Jim Worbois*

Memories / 1975 / Sugar Hill ✦✦✦✦✦

22 songs originally recorded by Watson (with Merle Watson producing in association with Chuck Cochran) for Capitol-EMI in the mid-1970s, a life-retrospective including traditional numbers like "Shady Grove," and A.P. Carter's "Wabash Cannonball," Jimmie Rodgers' "In the Jailhouse," and the old jug band standard "Mama Don't Allow No Music," among others. Apart from the fact that some of the songs were apparently overdubbed (Watson plays more than one instrument on certain numbers) and the presence of a more or less full country/bluegrass band (with unobtrusive electric piano and bass on a few tracks), there's nothing here to distinguish these recordings from Watson's Vanguard and Folkways stuff of the mid-1960s—not only is Watson's playing as fine as, or better than, on the earlier records, but the voice is still there, so much that maybe the best track on this record is the a cappella "Wake Up, Little Maggie," maybe the most beautiful song Watson has ever recorded. Notes might have been nice, but the recording credits and song histories are thorough, and the sound is superb, right down to the exquisite harmonies on numbers like "Keep On the Sunny Side." *—Bruce Eder*

Down South / 1984 / Rykodisc ✦✦✦

Riding the Midnight Train / 1984 / Sugar Hill ✦✦✦

This bluegrass album has Nashville super-pickers Sam Bush, Mark O'Connor, and Bela Fleck. These are the last recordings of Merle Watson. *—Mark A. Humphrey*

Pickin' the Blues / 1985 / Flying Fish ✦✦✦✦✦

As the title says, *Pickin' the Blues* featuress Doc Watson playing the blues with his son, Merle. The two guitarists are backed by a small band, which gives the two musicians the opportunity to stretch out.. By the time of the album's 1984 release, Merle had already demonstrated that he was an exceptional blue guitarist, which makes the real revelation of the album Doc's hard, gritty playing. Rarely, if ever, had Doc ever sounded so gritty and tough, and that alone makes *Pickin' the Blues* a true delight. *—Thom Owens*

☆ **The Essential Doc Watson** / 1986 / Vanguard ✦✦✦✦✦

It's a measure of how succinct Doc Watson's interpretations of traditional music are that this 26-song collection is one of the few Vanguard double-LP compilations to make it onto CD completely intact, with no songs eliminated, and it still clocks in at under 70 minutes. It's also one of the better sounding of the Welk Music Group's mid-'80s CD reissues from the Vanguard catalog, and one only wishes that the label could have included a set of liner notes about the performer. The first half of this disc (and the first LP of the original double album) is made up of studio recordings that feature Watson working solo, in a small-group setting, and also accompanied by a full band of top Nashville session musicians, including Grady Martin, Tommy Jackson, and Buddy Spicher; tracks 13-26 were recorded live at the *Newport Folk Festival* in 1964 and 1965, and feature a relaxed, outgoing Watson accompanied by no more than a pair of musicians. As for the music itself, it's about as wide and varied a body as one could wish for—from Watson's very stylized versions of "Tom Dooley," "Shady Grove," and "Rising Sun Blues" (his rendition of "House of the Rising Sun") to gospel numbers, all of it beguiling in its musicianship as well as its content. Watson's singing and playing are sweeter on the studio sides, but the live tracks show him in a relaxed, outgoing mood. Although it's not as thorough an account of his musicianship as the four-CD *Vanguard Years* compilation, this disc does give any neophyte a good look at what he's about, and the music is excellent on its own terms. *—Bruce Eder*

The Doc Watson Family / 1990 / Smithsonian/Folkways ✦✦✦✦✦

Featuring musical support from such family members as fiddler Gaither Carlton, Doc Watson's debut album, *The Doc Watson Family*, boasts the most traditional performances of Watson—this is as authentic as country music gets. *—Mark A. Humphrey & David Vinopal*

Remembering Merle / Jun. 1992 / Sugar Hill ✦✦✦✦✦

Remembering Merle is an affectionate tribute to Doc Watson's deceased son, featuring several songs—which were all recorded live between 1970 and 1976—that showcased his work. Doc and Merle touch on a number of different genres, from folk and blue to rockabilly, all the while demonstrating the younger Watson's considerable talent. *—Thom Owens*

Vanguard Years / Nov. 14, 1995 / Vanguard ✦✦✦✦✦

Four-CD, 64-song collection drawn principally from Doc's Vanguard releases of the 1960s and early 1970s (tapped his solo LPs and performances at the 1963 and 1964 Newport Folk Festival). This was Doc's best period recording-wise, and certainly you couldn't hope for a better document of his virtuosity, as the guitarist covers all manner of American folk and blues styles over the course of the set. It's too much, however, for listeners who aren't big fans; Vanguard's *Essential Doc Watson* is a more economical survey. If you *are* a big fan, though, you'll be especially interested in the 16 previously unreleased performances. Comprising the whole of disc four, these are mostly taken from live duets with Merle Travis or Doc's son, Merle Watson. *—Richie Unterberger*

The Best of Doc Watson: 1964-1968 / Apr. 20, 1999 / Vanguard ✦✦✦✦✦

Boasting 23 tracks (three unreleased) culled from six of Watson's classic Vanguard albums, *The Best of Doc Watson 1964-1968* is a great summing up of the music he made during that period and a perfect testament to his standing as a true American musical treasure. Showcasing the amazing depth of ability that Watson has made his trademark, this collection covers all the bases, including outstanding examples of his virtuosic flat-picking guitar work in great instrumentals like "Dill Pickle Rag," "Windy and Warm" and the amazingly dexterous "Beaumont Rag." A perfect synthesis of country, blues and folk, Watson bounces from haunting murder ballads like "Omie Wise" and the solemn "Tom Dooley" to lighthearted numbers like "Muskrat" and "Intoxicated Rat." Faithful covers of Jimmie Rodgers' "My Rough and Rowdy Ways" and the Carter Family's "The Cyclone of Ryecov" show the reverence with which Watson tackles the work of the masters who have inspired his music. No fan of flat-top guitar picking should be without this one in their collection. *—Matt Fink*

Third Generation Blues / Apr. 20, 1999 / Sugar Hill ✦✦✦✦

Watson Family Tradition / Rounder ✦✦✦

Doc Watson's playing is put into the context of his extended musical family on *Tradition*. Featuring several cuts with Gaither Carlton, who is Watson's father-in-law, the record features a wealth of old-timey music, filled with fiddles and flat-picked guitar. *—Thom Owens*

The Weavers

f. 1948, New York, NY

Group / Folk Revival, Political Folk, Traditional Folk

Pete Seeger, Lee Hays, Fred Hellerman, and Ronnie Gilbert formed the Weavers in 1948 to sing folk music in harmony. The group got its big break at a two-week gig at the Village Vanguard in New York City at Christmas, 1949; the gig lasted six months. The Weavers were signed to Decca and scored a double-sided hit in the summer of 1950 with "Tzena, Tzena, Tzena," which went to #2, and "Goodnight Irene," which topped the charts for 13 weeks, one of the biggest hits of the first half of the century. More hits followed through 1952, but then the Weavers fell afoul of the Communist Red scare of that decade, and their career declined precipitously. They came back, however, at a Carnegie Hall concert in 1955 that is remembered as the birth of the late-'50s/early-'60s folk boom. They then toured and recorded (for Vanguard) more successfully. Seeger left in 1958, replaced by a succession of good musicians: Frank Hamilton, Bernie Krause, and Erik Darling. In 1963, the Weavers (with Seeger and his replacements onstage) staged a reunion and farewell at Carnegie Hall. There was a final reunion and farewell of the original four at the hall in 1980. In addition to their considerable musical accomplishments, the Weavers are remembered as popularizers of folk music and as the inspiration for a whole generation of folk performers. *—William Ruhlmann*

☆ **The Weavers at Carnegie Hall** / Dec. 1956 / Vanguard ✦✦✦✦✦
The Weavers made a dramatic comeback from the McCarthy era at their 1955 Christmas Eve Carnegie Hall concert, immortalized here. Many of the songs were the same ones from the pop-star days—"Kisses Sweeter than Wine," "Goodnight Irene"—but backed only by guitar and banjo, they were fresh and stirring. *—William Ruhlmann*

Greatest Hits / 1957 / Vanguard ✦✦✦✦✦
This is an excellent double-disc compilation of this group's more directly folk-related work from the mid 50s to the mid 60s. Note, however, that these are not the original Weavers recordings of their hits. *—William Ruhlmann*

The Weavers at Carnegie Hall, Vol. 2 / 1960 / Vanguard ✦✦✦✦✦
By April 1, 1960, when they recorded their fifth Vanguard album (which was their third live disc and second to be recorded at *Carnegie Hall*), the Weavers had overcome the loss of Pete Seeger and fully integrated his replacement, Erik Darling, who proved a banjo virtuoso and exuberant humorist (listen to his kazoo solo on "Bill Bailey Come Home"). They had an excellent act, mixing old favorites dating back to the days of the Almanac Singers ("The Sinking of the Reuben James") and newer songs that would become standards of the folk boom ("Last Night I Had the Strangest Dream"). And, at least at this point, they seemed to be riding the crest of that boom, which they had inspired with their 1955 Carnegie Hall show, recorded for their first Vanguard album, *The Weavers at Carnegie Hall* (1957), which belatedly jumped into the album charts a couple of months after this album became their chart debut at the start of 1961. In retrospect, however, the cannily titled *Vol. 2* (you'd think it was more from the first concert, wouldn't you—) represented the peak of the Weavers' comeback; in '60s terms, with their bow ties and tuxedos, they seemed like something from an earlier time compared to the collegiate earnestness of the Kingston Trio and the political seriousness of Peter, Paul and Mary (who debuted the following year)—and, of course, they were. But with *The Weavers at Carnegie Hall, Vol. 2* however briefly, they finally exorcised the ghost of Seeger and demonstrated that they were a valid and popular act on their own. *—William Ruhlmann*

The Almanac / 1963 / Vanguard ✦✦✦
Given that the Weavers evolved out of the politically oriented Almanac Singers, and that this album was released during a period when Peter, Paul & Mary and other folk groups were reviving their songs with commercial success, calling it *The Weavers' Almanac* evoked their past in a newly fashionable present. Having reached the best-seller charts twice the previous year, the group seemed on the verge of regaining their popularity, and this album must have been intended to foster that comeback. But though the performances were as effective as ever, this collection of songs, among them such stirring and topical works as the Depression-era standard "Brother Can You Spare a Dime," "Fight On" and "Which Side Are You On," failed to return the Weavers to their old prominence. Erik Darling left the group, which carried on with Frank Hamilton, but, by late 1963, following a last-gasp reunion concert, they were on their last legs. In retrospect, this is an enjoyable album (if brief in the CD era), though it lacks the fervor of the Weavers' younger competitors of the day. *—William Ruhlmann*

The Reunion at Carnegie Hall, 1963 / 1963 / Vanguard ✦✦✦
"So this is the final Weavers record," writes Vanguard Records head, Maynard Solomon, in his liner notes to the second album (mostly) culled from the group's May 2-3, 1963, stand at Carnegie Hall, performances at which Ronnie Gilbert, Lee Hays and Fred Hellerman were joined by all four occupants of the tenor position: original member, Pete Seeger; his replacement, Erik Darling; then-current member, Frank Hamilton; and his replacement, Bernie Krause. The album doesn't spell out who's singing when, but it's not hard to tell that Seeger is present on old favorites like "Frozen Logger," "Kisses Sweeter Than Wine," and "Rock Island Line." The Weavers made a lot of live albums, a lot of them at Carnegie Hall (this was the fourth), so they can be difficult to tell apart, even when you're listening to one. Happily, they all share the qualities of humor, passion and good singing. And though the Weavers broke up more than a year before this album was released, it wasn't their final record, not even their final record to be recorded live at Carnegie Hall. *—William Ruhlmann*

☆ **Wasn't That a Time** / Sep. 1993 / Vanguard ✦✦✦✦✦
Wasn't That a Time! is a treasure for serious Weavers fans. Featuring 87 songs on its four discs, including several unreleased numbers, the box set is designed for devoted fans; the liner notes are filled with anecdotes and photos that provide a good portrait of the group. For some casual fans, it might be a bit too much, but *Wasn't That a Time!* is a fitting tribute to the seminal folk group. *—Stephen Thomas Erlewine*

Kisses Sweeter Than Wine / 1994 / Vanguard/Omega ✦✦✦✦✦
This two-disc live set is drawn from vintage concerts by the original Weavers from the early to mid-'50s. It captures them at the height of their fame and during the chilly era of McCarthyism. It's a good example of how the political leanings (perceived or real) of the performances color essentially neutral material. The performances themselves sound immediate and not at all dated. It's great to hear the vocal blend and commitment to a world of songwriting rarely equaled since the Weavers broke up. Ford Hellerman, who compiled this album from a variety of previously unreleased sources including concerts at Town Hall, has left in many of the song's introductions and comments among the group. We really get to feel their enthusiam and "History in the Making." The hits are here in new versions that stand up well to the "standard" versions. There are 11 songs never released in any form on Weavers records. As an added bonus and not mentioned on the package anywhere is the inclusion of a third CD of previously unreleased material by Leadbelly recorded in 1947. He performs a dozen driving blues songs including "Howard Hughs," "Hangman's Blues" and "Black Betty," and it sounds great. *—Richard Meyer*

★ **The Best of the Decca Years** / Oct. 22, 1996 / MCA ✦✦✦✦✦
The Best of the Decca Years is a thorough overview of the Weavers' peak hit-making years, containing all of their biggest '50s hit, including the chart-topping single "Goodnight Irene." Many of these recordings boast light orchestra and choral arrangements, which mean they may sound fairly dated to contemporary listeners, yet these were historically important singles, bringing folk music to a larger audience. Though *Best of the Decca Years* isn't quite as thorough as 1987's *The Best of the Weavers*, it nevertheless remains an excellent retrospective of the most popular and controversial folk group of the '50s, as well as an excellent introduction to their work. *—Thom Owens*

Gospel / May 27, 1997 / Vanguard ✦✦✦✦
Given their reputation for being, well, godless Communists, the concept of a gospel album by the Weavers is curious on its face. In fact, however, much of the group's repertoire derived from folk and spiritual sources, sometimes with specifically religious subject matter, sometimes just with church-based origins. In these tracks, compiled from their 1955-63 recordings, the Weavers address such familiar inspirational material as "When the Saints Go Marching In," "Sinner Man," and "True Religion," as well as gospel-influenced folk songs like "Follow the Drinking Gourd," which concerns the Underground Railroad that helped slaves to freedom, and their own politically charged "If I Had a Hammer (The Hammer Song)," which bridged religious fervor and social activism. Combining the Pete Seeger and Erik Darling eras of the group, this is an excellent thematic arrangement of Weavers music, the only serious criticism of it being that, at under 38 minutes, it could have been longer. *—William Ruhlmann*

Best of the Weavers / Sep. 30, 1997 / Vanguard ✦✦✦✦
Vanguard's *Best of the Weavers* is a solid, if brief, collection featuring many of the group's best-known songs—"Goodnight Irene, " "This Land Is Your Land, " "On Top of Old Smoky, " "Michael Row Your Boat Ashore, " "Kisses Sweeter Than Wine"—thereby offering a serviceable, affordable introduction to the groundbreaking folk group. *—Stephen Thomas Erlewine*

☆ **Goodnight Irene: The Weavers 1949-1953** / Apr. 25, 2000 / Bear Family ✦✦✦✦✦
In 2000, Bear Family Records boxed the Decca recordings and other early tracks on *Goodnight Irene: The Weavers 1949-1953*, a four-CD set with an additional 15-minute DVD containing five television performances (also heard elsewhere in the set). The Decca material takes up the second and third CDs: 54 tracks originally released between 1950 and 1960, plus four alternate takes and two previously unreleased Christmas songs. The group's earliest studio recordings include some very topical songs, but by the time they were starting to attract national attention in the winter of 1949-50, they had toned down the political material, as shown by a previously unreleased 19-song demo tape that takes up much of the first disc. The demo also reveals that the Weavers already sounded like they would for the rest of their career, and that songs like "Rock Island Line," "Goodnight Irene," "Tzena, Tzena, Tzena," and "Wimoweh" were already in their repertoire in finalized form, regardless of later orchestral accompaniment. The group's interest in adapting traditional folk songs, tunes by Woody Guthrie and Leadbelly, and a broad range of international material on their subsequent Decca recordings may not have been overtly political, but it suggested an open sense of culture at a time when the U.S. was in a repressive phase. The set finishes with a fourth disc devoted to some interesting odds and ends, including several great examples of the commercial compromises that allowed the Weavers to infiltrate popular music in the early '50s and ultimately to influence it profoundly. The 50-page hardcover book contains Samuelson's notes, a couple of sidebars by Ronald D. Cohen, a discography, and extensive illustrations including reproductions of record covers and numerous photographs. *—William Ruhlmann*

Best of the Vanguard Years / Jan. 23, 2001 / Vanguard ✦✦✦✦
The Weavers' stint at Vanguard, it should be noted, took place after they had their big pop hits in the early 1950s. That might be construed as either an advantage or disadvantage, depending on your perspective. These are not the biggest-selling original versions of the staples of their repertoire, but they also feature only the group and their acoustic instruments, without the added orchestration that some felt diluted their early studio recordings. In any case, this has 24 songs drawn from live and studio performances in 1955 and 1963, almost all of them including Pete Seeger in the lineup (there are also two previously unreleased tracks from the 1960 *Newport Folk Festival*). Listening to these, one is struck by the sheer number of folk standards that the Weavers were instrumental in popularizing: "Kisses Sweeter Than Wine," "Tzena Tzena," "Goodnight Irene," "Wimoweh," "On Top of Old Smoky," "Guantanamera," "Rock Island Line," "The House of the Rising Sun," "Michael Row the Boat Ashore," "If I Had a Hammer," and "Midnight Special." It's also undeniable that their interpretations can smack of tame quaintness so far removed, time-wise, from their original setting. It's a serviceable overview of their post-blacklist output, though fans might prefer the less patchwork flow of the original albums, especially the ones recorded just after the group reformed in 1955. *—Richie Unterberger*

Gillian Welch

b. 1968
Vocals, Guitar / Americana, Alternative Country, Singer/Songwriter
A young singer/songwriter armed with a voice and sensibility far beyond her years, Gillian Welch drew widespread acclaim for her deft, evocative resurrection of the musical styles most commonly associated with the rural Appalachia of the early 20th century. Welch was born in 1968 in California and grew up in West Los Angeles, where her parents scored the

music for the comedy program *The Carol Burnett Show.* It was as a child that she became fascinated by bluegrass and early country music, in particular the work of the Stanley Brothers, the Delmore Brothers and the Carter Family.

In the early 1990s, Welch attended the Berklee School of Music in Boston, Massachusetts, where she began performing her own material, as well as traditional country and bluegrass songs, as part of a duo with fellow student David Rawlings. After honing their skills in local open mike showcases, the duo began performing regularly throughout the country. While opening for Peter Rowan in Nashville, they were spotted by musician and producer T-Bone Burnett, who helped Welch and Rawlings land a record deal. With Burnett producing, they cut 1996's starkly beautiful *Revival,* an album split between bare-bones duo performances—some even recorded in mono to capture a bygone sound—and more full-bodied cuts featuring legendary session men like guitarist James Burton, upright bassist Roy Huskey, Jr., and drummers Buddy Harmon and Jim Keltner. *Hell Among the Yearlings* followed in 1998. *—Jason Ankeny*

• **Revival** / Apr. 1996 / Almo Sounds ♦♦♦♦♦
Gillian Welch's debut album, *Revival,* is one of the strongest artistic introductions of the year. Produced by T Bone Burnett, *Revival* could be lifted from some long lost Depression Era folk recording. Welch sings with a focused austerity, bypassing any modern conceits to concentrate on songs about the rudiments of life: survival, heartbreak, struggle, honesty, natural beauty. The closest thing to decadence comes when a dying man asks that his still be burned down, turning to ash the bane of his life. The closest thing to optimism comes in a song about a fragile mountain flower's ability to endure the elements.

Welch may be accused of losing herself in the styles of the past; her music evokes the primitive yet aesthetically timeless work of the Carter Family and the Stanley Brothers. But such an argument becomes empty when hearing the deep passion, and compassion, of Welch's songs. From the astringent quality of her voice to the bare beauty of her melodies to the resourceful moodiness of guitarist David Rawlings, Welch comes on like a rare and precious talent with a vision so set and strong that it can't be denied. *—Michael McCall*

Hell Among the Yearlings / Jul. 28, 1998 / Almo Sounds ♦♦♦♦
Lacking some of the focus that made her debut album so stunning, *Hell Among the Yearlings* is nevertheless a thoroughly satisfying second album from Gillian Welch. Instead of backing away from the rustic folkiness of *Revival,* Welch deepens her bleak, clear-eyed worldview, which makes her spare, old-timey arrangements all the more powerful. On occasion, the performances and songs are a bit too studied to be truly effective, but those moments are fleeting—*Hell Among the Yearlings* offers ample proof that Welch is a talented, individual songwriter and that her debut was no fluke. *—Thom Owens*

Cheryl Wheeler

b. Jul. 10, 1951, Timonium, MD
Vocals, Guitar / Contemporary Singer/Songwriter, Contemporary Folk, Country-Folk
Known for her comic as well as her emotionally intense songs, folk singer/songwriter Cheryl Wheeler was raised in Timonium, Maryland, and began playing the guitar and ukulele as a child. She first performed professionally at a local restaurant, but soon graduated to clubs in the Baltimore and Washington, D.C., areas. In 1976, she moved to Rhode Island, where she began a protégé of country-folk singer/songwriter Jonathan Edwards, for whom she initially served as bass player. Her first recording, a four-song EP called Newport Songs, was released in 1983. Edwards produced her first full-length album, Cheryl Wheeler, released on North Star Records in 1986. One of the songs on the album, "Addicted," was covered by Dan Seals and became a #1 country hit in September 1988. North Star licensed her second album, Half A Book (1988), to the short-lived Cypress imprint of A&M Records. She then signed to the Nashville division of Capitol Records and released Circles And Arrows in 1990; Suzy Bogguss's cover of "Aces" from that album was a Top Ten Country hit in 1992. (Subsequently, her songs were covered by Bette Midler, Juice Newton, Maura O'Connell, Linda Thompson, and others.) In 1993, Wheeler moved to the Philo imprint of the independent Rounder label for her fourth album, Driving Home (Rounder reissued Circles And Arrows in 1994). She followed it with Mrs. Pinocci's Guitar (1995) and Sylvia Hotel (1999).*— William Ruhlmann and Jason Ankeny*

• **Cheryl Wheeler** / 1986 / North Star ♦♦♦♦♦
Her debut album features her hit "Addicted, " and is more rock & roll than her other albums. If you like the rest, you should add this to the collection. *—Chip Renner*

Circles & Arrows / 1990 / Philo ♦♦♦♦
Wheeler shines on this CD. Guests include Mark O'Connor, Jerry Douglas, Jonathan Edwards, and Billy Joe Walker. Every song is a winner, especially "Northern Girl," "Aces," and "I Know This Town." *—Chip Renner*

Half a Book / 1991 / Cypress ♦♦♦

Driving Home / 1993 / Philo ♦♦♦
On *Driving Home* Cheryl Wheeler has finally got the natural sounding production that her material needs. Her melodies are highly ornamented and shine through. The distinctive nature of her voice is never overshadowed by synthesized sound as on previous albums. As in the past the material is often humorous, as in "Don't Forget the Guns," commercially romantic; "Silver Lining" and heart-warmingly beautiful; "Arrow." This is an excellent album. *—Richard Meyer*

Mrs. Pinocci's Guitar / Oct. 17, 1995 / Philo ♦♦♦

Sylvia Hotel / Jan. 26, 1999 / Philo ♦♦♦

Erica Wheeler

Vocals, Guitar / Contemporary Singer/Songwriter, Contemporary Folk
The literary sensitivity of New England is combined with the spiritual vision of the American West by Massachusetts-based singer/songwriter Erica Wheeler. Her original songs inspired the *New England Folk Almanac* to observe that "...one of (Wheeler's) greatest strengths is her ability to temper love, light and goodness with darkness and wistfulness."

A self-taught guitarist, Wheeler grew up listening to folk-pop vocalists such as Judy Collins and Joan Baez. After seeing the documentary film *Harlan County U.S.A.*, Wheeler was so inspired by folk singer Hazel Dickens that she bought a songbook, *1001 Folk Songs,* and began to take music more seriously. She subsequently taught herself to play songs from the repertoire of Cat Stevens. After writing a few original songs in high school, Wheeler focused on songwriting in college. Although she enrolled in Massachusetts' Hampshire College in hopes of becoming a wildlife biologist, her studies convinced her that she had more to say as a writer.

Wheeler's skills as a performer were sharpened by her appearances at the Iron Horse in Northampton, MA. As a frequent opening act, Wheeler not only gained exposure, but she learned showmanship by watching headliners like Bill Morrissey, Patty Larkin and Shawn Colvin. In 1989, Wheeler released a ten-song cassette titled *Strong Heart.* Her first full-length recording, *From that Far,* was released in 1992 and produced by Darlene Wilson. It included stellar musicians such as Johnny Cunningham (fiddle), Doug Plavin (percussion), Peter Calo (acoustic slide and electric guitars), and Diane Ziegler and Cosy Sheridan (harmony vocals).

Shortly after placing first in the troubadour contest at the *Rocky Mountain Folk Festival* in 1995, Wheeler recorded her second CD, *The Harvest.* Produced by bluegrass fiddler and bandleader Laurie Lewis, the album featured top-notch instrumentalists including Darol Anger, Barbara Higbie and Todd Phillips. Wheeler's third CD marks her first collaboration with producer Steve Miller (no relation to the musician), who previously produced two CDs by Dar Williams. *—Craig Harris*

Strong Heart / 1989 / Blue Pie ♦♦♦

• **From That Far** / 1992 / Blue Pie ♦♦♦♦♦

The Harvest / 1996 / Signature ♦♦♦♦♦
Thanks to better distribution and her own continued artistic growth, *The Harvest* proved to be Erica Wheeler's breakthrough to a wider national audience. Wheeler's music has been categorized as contemporary folk, progressive bluegrass, "new country," and Americana; the truth probably lies somewhere in the middle. Nanci Griffith is still a dominant influence, but Wheeler has her own voice. *—Steve Huey*

Three Wishes / Apr. 20, 1999 / Signature ♦♦♦♦
Erica Wheeler's fourth album, 1999's *Three Wishes,* was produced by Steven Miller, who has also worked with Dar Williams on *The End of Summer* as well as producing Wheeler's previous album, *The Harvest.* As with her previous albums, *Three Wishes* showcases Wheeler's literate, sensitive, rootsy folk. Tracks include "January Wind," "Frozen River," "Angels" and "Saturday," all of which display her fine songwriting and down-to-earth voice. *—Heather Phares*

Jim White

Vocals, Guitar / Contemporary Singer/Songwriter, Alternative Country, Lo-Fi
Southern Gothic singer/songwriter Jim White grew up in Pensacola, Florida, enamored with the sounds of the white gospel music he heard on the *Gospel Jubilee* television series. After spending his formative years on the outskirts of a deeply Pentecostal community, he entertained a career as a professional surfer, followed by a stint in Milan as a fashion model. A band-saw accident which resulted in a maimed left hand seemed to end White's hopes as a musician, but after writing a collection of simple songs on his guitar, a friend convinced him to record a demo which ultimately made its way to the offices of David Byrne's Luaka Bop label. After re-recording the songs, White issued his debut *Wrong-Eyed Jesus!*—a collection of atmospheric, oddly spiritual country-folk performances—in 1997. *No Such Place* was issued in early 2001. *—Jason Ankeny*

• **Wrong-Eyed Jesus (Mysterious Tale of How I Shouted)** / Apr. 22, 1997 / Warner Brothers ♦♦♦♦
Jim White's debut album is a cinematic collection of Appalachia-inspired country-folk rendered with a Gothic sensibility and junkyard atmospherics (the inclusion of Tom Waits collaborator Ralph Carney on several tracks lends the record a distinctly Waitsian veneer). Drawing on his bizarre life experiences and troubled Pentecostal upbringing, White's narratives are surreal and crazed, shot through with disturbing spiritual imagery and backwoods dementia; a strangely beautiful record, *Wrong-Eyed Jesus!* is a fine introduction to a uniquely twisted talent. *—Jason Ankeny*

Josh White

b. Feb. 11, 1908, Greenville, MS, **d.** Sep. 5, 1969, Manhasset, NY
Vocals, Guitar / Prewar Gospel Blues, Blues Revival, Folk Revival, Folk-Blues, Piedmont Blues
Most blues enthusiasts think of Josh White as a folk revival artist. It's true that the second half of his music career found him based in New York playing to the coffeehouse and cabaret set and hanging out with Burl Ives, Woody Guthrie, and fellow transplanted blues artists Sonny Terry and Brownie McGhee. He was a show business personality—a star renowned for his sexual magnetism and his dramatic vocal presentations. What many people don't know is that Josh White was a major figure in the Piedmont blues tradition. The first part of his career saw him as apprentice and lead boy to some of the greatest blues and religious artists ever, including Willie Walker, Blind Blake, Blind Joe Taggart (with whom he recorded), and allegedly even Blind Lemon Jefferson. On his own, he recorded both blues and religious songs, including a classic version of "Blood Red River." A fine guitar technician with an appealing voice, he became progressively more sophisticated in his presentation. Like many other Carolinians and Virginians who moved north to urban areas, he took up city ways, remaining a fine musician if no longer a down-home artist. *—Barry Lee Pearson*

★ **The Legendary Josh White** / 1996 / Collector's Edition ♦♦♦♦♦
This release highlights 18 songs cut by Josh White during the early 1960s. Accompanied by his solo acoustic guitar and a string bass, he goes through a range of songs, from his concert favorite "One Meat Ball" to more generic traditional numbers such as the guitar virtuoso showcase "Prison Bound." White also performs contemporary pieces with which he is asso-

ciated, including the Earl Robinson and Allen Lewis song "House I Live In" (which became much more famous in the hands of Frank Sinatra), jazz pieces like "Miss Otis Regrets," and even his version of "Waltzing Matilda," which in its tempo and accents is perhaps the most stylized rendition ever heard. The material shows off White's range to exceptionally good advantage, and this is as fine a representation of the music that made him famous in the 1960s as any single CD collection currently available. *—Bruce Eder*

● **Blues Singer 1932-1936** / Feb. 6, 1996 / Sony/Legacy ✦✦✦✦✦
The suave and debonair blues sex symbol in his earliest and purest period, when the Piedmont influence was at its peak in his playing. This is strong stuff, eons away from the collegiate crowd-pleasing folkie stuff he engaged in during the '60s: "Milk Cow Blues," "Lazy Black Snake Blues," and "Silicosis Is Killin' Me" are acoustic solo blues of a consistently high quality, and there are a few religious tunes thrown in to spotlight the other side of White's early recording activities. *—Bill Dahl*

Free & Equal Blues / Mar. 17, 1998 / Smithsonian/Folkways ✦✦✦✦✦
Fine 26-song compilation of material recorded by folklorist Moe Asch in the 1940s, at a time when White was beginning to reach an urban, educated audience with his mixture of blues, folk, and pop styles. What comes across particularly strong in this set is his versatility and all-around appeal; he handles topical songs about discrimination and war, spirituals, covers of blues by Leroy Carr and Victoria Spivey, folk ballads, and theatrical pieces, even extending to a cover of Cole Porter's "Miss Otis Regrets." "One Meat Ball" provided some of the musical inspiration for the classic Merle Travis tune "Sixteen Tons"; "Freedom Road" had lyrics by poet Langston Hughes. Because he was less earthy and not as Southern-sounding as Leadbelly and Big Bill Broonzy, White has been accorded less critical respect, but this anthology shows him to be one of the unquestioned linchpins of the first stirrings of the folk revival. Includes copious notes by White biographer Elijah Wald. *—Richie Unterberger*

Josh White Jr.

b. Nov. 30, 1940, New York, NY
Vocals, Guitar / Blues Revival, Folk Revival, Folk-Blues, Country Blues, Singer/Songwriter, Traditional Folk
Folksinger and actor Josh White, Jr. proudly upheld the musical tradition begun by his father, the legendary bluesman and social activist Josh White. Born November 30, 1940 in New York City, he made his performing debut at the age of four, appearing alongside his dad at the Big Apple nightclub Café Society; for close to two decades, father and son regularly shared the stage, frequently co-starring together on Broadway as well—for 1949's *How Long Til Summer?*, the younger White even earned a special Tony Award as "Best Child Actor." He made his solo debut in 1956 with the Decca release "See Saw," co-written by Marvin Hamlisch (White's classmate at the Professional Children's School along with Elliott Gould, Sandra Dee, Leslie Uggams and Christopher Walken); as the folk revival blossomed, he increasingly turned his energies from acting to music, mounting a full-fledged solo career with the minor 1962 hit "Do You Close Your Eyes." A popular attraction on the campus circuit, White toured regularly throughout the years to follow, recording albums including 1967's *The Josh White, Jr. Album*, 1968's *One Step Further*, and a 1978 self-titled effort for Vanguard. In 1979, he headlined the PBS concert special *Ramblin' with Josh White, Jr*, and in 1983 starred in theatrical biography of his father, *JOSH: The Man and His Music*. White, Jr. again celebrated White, Sr.'s music with 1987's Grammy-nominated instrumental album *Jazz, Ballads and Blues*. A children's album, *My Favorite Toy*, followed in 1994, and five years later, he returned with *In Tribute to Josh White: House of the Rising Son*. *Cortelia Clark* was issued in fall 2000. *—Jason Ankeny*

Jazz, Ballads & Blues / 1986 / Rykodisc ✦✦✦
Josh White Jr., son of the distinguished folksinger, displays an eclectic nature and stylistic adaptability on this 1986 set. The ten selections range from folk tunes like "Frankie and Johnny" to pre-rock standards like "You'd Be So Nice to Come Home To" and "House of the Rising Sun," written by White's father, who also supplied the original arrangements. He doesn't have his father's sheer power or personality, but sings and plays in a resolute, affable manner. Well supported by violinist Robin Batteau and bassist Jerry Burnham, the trio does a nice job of showing the links between the three forms covered in the session's title. *—Ron Wynn*

In Tribute to Josh White: House of Rising Son / Oct. 12, 1999 / Silverwolf ✦✦✦✦
All things considered, it's somewhat surprising that Josh White Jr. hadn't recorded a full-fledged tribute album for his father earlier, but however long overdue the collection is, it more than makes up for the delay with the quality of the collection. Creating a truly fitting tribute, he displays the wonderfully rich guitar playing and singing that made his father a legend on classics like "Gonna Live the Life," "Jesus Gonna Make Up My Dying Bed," and a smoldering "House of the Rising Sun." A strongly spiritual quality shines through White Jr.'s expressive folk blues, and though he doesn't outshine his father, he definitely more than does the material justice. *—Matt Fink*

David Wilcox

Vocals, Guitar / Contemporary Singer/Songwriter, Contemporary Folk
A warm, baritone vocal tone and poetic lyricism are combined with a unique guitar style that blends soft jazz and folk sensibilities and an intimate stage persona by singer/songwriter David Wilcox. Often compared to James Taylor and John Martyn, Wilcox has built a solid fan base for his well-crafted folk-pop tunes. Although he took four lessons with a classical guitarist, Wilcox developed most of his playing technique on his own. In addition to being inspired by Joni Mitchell to play in a variety of tunings, he designed a capo that produced an unusual sound by leaving one or more strings unaltered. His debut album, *The Nightshift Watchman*, was released in 1987 on his own label, Song of the Woods; it featured scaled-down arrangements and launched Wilcox's career as a touring musician. He signed with A&M in 1989. His first release on the label, *How Did You Meet Me Here*, sold over 100,000 copies by word of mouth. His 1997 album, *Turning Point*, recorded in the log cabin studio in the woods behind his home, represented a shift to a more controlled approach to music, while his February 1999 release, *Underneath*, continued to focus on his vocals and guitar playing despite the additional instrumentation of electric guitars, keyboards and rhythm section. *—Craig Harris*

Nightshift Watchman / 1987 / Song of the Wood ✦✦✦

How Did You Find Me Here / 1989 / A&M ✦✦✦✦
Nice songs that, although sometimes sad, are all solid on this sophomore release. *—Chip Renner*

Home Again / 1991 / A&M ✦✦✦✦
David Wilcox's second major-label release finds him exploring the complexities of relationships, whether they are among family members ("Covert War") or between lovers ("Farther to Fall"). However, the overall mood of the album is decidedly upbeat as he takes a positive spin and focuses on how a fresh perspective can lead to greater understanding. The sincerity in his voice prevents his uplifting songs from sounding preachy and his romantic songs from sounding hollow. Although the production is more glossy with fuller acoustic instrumentation on this album, his exquisite guitar work (and use of open tunings) makes the music more interesting than the average set of adult easy listening songs. Still, Wilcox is at his best under the minimalist setting of voice and guitar, as on the opener "Burgundy Heart-Shaped Medallion" and "Last Chance Waltz." The latter song, about attending his ten-year high school reunion, perfectly conveys the apprehension and excitement of facing old fears and getting reacquainted with one's past. If you enjoyed his previous album *How Did You Find Me Here*, this album will be a welcome addition to your collection. *—Vik Iyengar*

Big Horizon / Feb. 8, 1994 / A&M ✦✦✦

● **East Asheville Hardware** / Feb. 20, 1996 / Koch ✦✦✦✦✦
For all the recordings they may do, folkies earn their living on the road, and David Wilcox has been doing that long enough to have developed a repertoire of crowd-pleasers that are not the sort of thing he likes to put on his more sober, earnest studio albums. Comic, bawdy, whimsical, sentimental, touching, these songs are in essence novelty material, and it is one of the characteristics of novelty songs that, like jokes, they are at their best the first time you bear them. But now that David Wilcox has been dumped by A*M after failing to go platinum with three albums, he's back to living off the land, and so, here are his previously unrecorded live favorites (a few of them written by other people), from $Chuck Brodsky's* "Blow 'Em Away," and a justification for (or maybe just a celebration of) drive-by shootings, to "Mango," perhaps the most straight-spoken song of romantic disappointment since Nilsson's "You're Breakin' My Heart." Physical characteristics ("Top of My Head," "Boob Job"), current events ("Barbie"), and religion ("Carpenter Story") all make appearances, along with a pleasant if aimless nine-minute story song called "Johnny's Camaro," and then there's "Levi Blues," which is about what happens when you put a new pair of jeans in the washing machine with your other clothes. The funny thing is, this album of throwaways may be David Wilcox's best album. It's certainly his most immediately enjoyable. *—William Ruhlmann*

Turning Point / May 20, 1997 / Koch ✦✦✦

Underneath / Feb. 23, 1999 / Vanguard ✦✦✦

What You Whispered / 2000 / Vanguard ✦✦✦

Dar Williams

Vocals, Guitar / Alternative Folk, Adult Alternative Pop/Rock, Singer/Songwriter
Dar Williams has become a major force on the New England folk scene. An idiosyncratic songwriter who writes folk songs from a unique, often insightful perspective, Williams takes pains to avoid the coy, and the quirky; her songwriting and performing style has been compared to that of Joni Mitchell and Joan Baez but with a few acidic and, at times, hilarious twists. Williams claims to draw much inspiration from her home community. Her love of the folk scene stems from her admiration of its integrity toward honesty and real emotion, and a creative freedom not found in more popular music genres. She loves trying to use traditional methods to express the realities and foibles of contemporary life. After several self-released cassettes, Williams made her proper debut in 1993 with the independent *Honesty Room* to considerable critical acclaim for both her beautiful soprano voice and her lovely, intriguing songs. Her second album, *Mortal City* (1995) has been similarly praised, and was followed by 1997's *End of the Summer*. Williams often performs on the college and coffeehouse circuit and has also won rave reviews for festival appearances. She issued *Cry, Cry, Cry* in 1998. *—Sandra Brennan*

The Honesty Room / 1993 / Razor & Tie ✦✦✦
This, Dar Williams' first full-length album, was originally released on her own private label and was then picked up by the tiny but prestigious indie-folk label Waterbug Records. In its Razor & Tie incarnation, *The Honesty Room* is a bit more rocked-up, which, frankly, has generally proven to be a good thing for the music of Dar Williams. Although she is a lyricist of striking originality and endearing humor, and although she can craft a hooky tune with the best of them, there's still a certain preciousness that creeps in when she's not being careful—she has always sung with the light, fluttery consonants and flattened vowels that make so many of today's female singer/songwriters sound like 13-year-olds, and when that vocal approach combines with an unaccompanied acoustic guitar and lines like "Once upon a time there was a nuclear family," well, it's hard not to let your eyes roll. But on the other hand, when an all-out rock song combines a gorgeous singalong melody with lyrical references to Ronald Reagan and Sid Vicious in the very first line, you know you've stumbled across something very special and you tend not to notice the quirks of delivery so much. And then there's "The Babysitter's Here," a song that manages to deal simultaneously with early childhood and incipient adulthood, that will make you bawl every time you hear it. *—Rick Anderson*

● **Mortal City** / Jan. 23, 1996 / Razor & Tie ✦✦✦✦
On the first track of her second album, Dar Williams makes clear her intention to break out of the acoustic singer-songwriter ghetto: "As Cool As I Am" is full-out rock & roll with funky drums and a chorus built on massed choo-choo harmonicas. She doesn't stay in rock mode

for long, but the more aggressive approach continues to inform her sound even when she retreats into a more typical acoustic setting. It's interesting to note that as her music gets more consistent, so do her lyrics. Over a spare guitar-and-cello accompaniment, she muses on the various ways that February can symbolize stages in a relationship ("And when we got home, we just started chopping wood/Because you never know how next year will be"). Elsewhere she finds her boyfriend "in the arms of a Student Against the Treacherous Use of Fur" and wishes she hadn't called a certain friend to help her move out. Funny? Oh, yes—"The Christians and the Pagans" is hysterical, and so is "The Pointless, Yet Poignant, Crisis of a Co-Ed" (believe it or not). And it's the humor gone before that makes a song as naked as "Family" or as conceptually risky as "Pompeii" come across not just well, but with enormous power. The really exciting thing is that her next album is even better. *—Rick Anderson*

End of the Summer / Jul. 15, 1997 / Razor & Tie ♦♦♦♦♦
This could be Dar Williams' best effort yet. Her friends and fans from back in the day might well disagree, since it's also her slickest and most rocking, and old fans tend to get all disgusted when songwriters stop sounding as raw as they did before they learned how to make records. But just listen; where she was clearly working hard to achieve hooks on *The Honesty Room*, they flow effortlessly here. The eerie radio ode "Are You Out There," a slightly defensive paean to therapy called "What Do You Hear in These Sounds," the gentle and moving "My Friends"—all of them stick in the mind for days and reveal more with each listen. Yes, it's slick; there are drum loops and timbales and lots of electric guitars, and a huge cast of guest musicians. But slick is only bad when it means soulless, and her soul is in fine shape. *—Rick Anderson*

The Green World / Aug. 22, 2000 / Razor & Tie ♦♦♦♦
Dar Williams has succeeded in crafting a number of great songs for her fourth album, *The Green World*, and the album works on a number of levels. The melodies are memorable, the arrangements are evenly balanced, and the lyrics are well written. Williams kicks things off with "Playing to the Firmament," an uplifting song full of jingly guitars and soaring vocals. The lyric playfully invites one to lose oneself, like a child playing games, in order to get beyond the seriousness of everyday life. "After All" is a beautiful, fragile song of self-searching with the wonderful line, "Go ahead/Push your luck/Find out how much love the world can hold." The song builds with quiet intensity, with an organ offering a spare background for Williams' lyrics. The narrator of "I Won't Be Your Yoko Ono" playfully wonders if Ono ever thought it would've been better to stay solo. The narrator informs her own lover, "I won't be your Yoko Ono if you're not good enough for me." A number of excellent musicians, including guitarist/organist Steuart Smith, bassist Graham Maby, and drummer Steve Holley, join Williams. The band can be front and center on songs like "What Do You Love More Than Love" or quietly fade into the background on "It Happens Every Day." A Hammond organ is used on a number of cuts to great effect, and Williams is in good voice throughout, delivering her lyrics with relaxed confidence. The album ends with the happy "Another Mystery," an upbeat tune with lively banjo accompaniment. *The Green World* is a lovely album, and should be warmly appreciated by Williams' fans, old and new. *—Ronnie Lankford Jr.*

Lucinda Williams

b. Jan. 26, 1953, Lake Charles, LA
Vocals, Guitar / Alternative Folk, Heartland Rock, Americana, Contemporary Folk, Alternative Country-Rock, Singer/Songwriter
Lucinda Williams isn't the kind of artist who caves in easily. Faced with label executives and producers who want to shape her music into clean-cut, radio-friendly rock or country numbers, Williams has time and again proven herself to be as stubborn as she is talented. She's released a mere four albums (and one EP) since her debut partly because she's had such a hard time finding a label whose demands don't get in the way of the music as she hears it. Her 1979 debut for Folkways, *Ramblin' on My Mind*, was followed by *Happy Woman Blues* on Smithsonian/Folkways, though it was another eight years before Williams' eponymous third album appeared on the indie-rock label Rough Trade. It immediately stood out for its integration of traditional folk, country, and blues influences into a rock and roll format. An ill-fated association with RCA followed, and her next album, 1992's *Sweet Old World*, was released on another indie label, Chameleon. Since then Williams has switched labels again, this time to American Recordings, where after a brief stay she landed at Mercury, which in 1998 finally released her long-delayed *Car Wheels on a Gravel Road*. *—Kurt Wolff*

Ramblin' / 1979 / Smithsonian/Folkways ♦♦

Happy Woman Blues / 1980 / Folkways ♦♦♦♦
Williams' first collection of original material—recorded with a full band—is stunning for its mixture of blues, folk, and country traditions with her captivating, complex, and visceral approach to writing and singing. Songs like "Lafayette," "King of Hearts," and "Sharp Cutting Wings" are classics: structurally solid and emotionally intense. A gutsy, refreshingly rootsy album. Re-released by Smithsonian/Folkways in 1990. *—Kurt Wolff*

Lucinda Williams / 1988 / Rough Trade ♦♦♦♦♦
Lucinda Williams took eight years to write and record her second album of original songs. While some producers and record executives have said that she is difficult to work with, one can never argue with the finished product. She crafts each song meticulously and deftly blends country, blues, and folk to create a unique sound that cannot be pigeonholed into any particular format. Her voice contains a heartache comparable to Emmylou Harris, but she has a darker side and a toughness that allows her to live inside the blues or rock with abandon. Re-released with bonus tracks after receiving long overdue commercial acclaim for *Car Wheels on a Gravel Road*, *Lucinda Williams* is an album that has been long been recognized as a classic. It has been mined for hit songs over the years by such artists as Mary Chapin Carpenter, who turned "Passionate Kisses" into a country hit, and Tom Petty, who included "Changed the Locks" on his soundtrack album *She's the One*. In addition to writing strong melodies, Lucinda Williams is an amazing songwriter with a knack at writing a lyric that acknowledges the complicated nature of relationships while cutting right to the heart of the matter. Every song packs an emotional punch line and rewards the listener each time with something new. The bonus tracks mostly feature Williams accompanied only by her guitar, and it adds emotional weight to the album's highlight, "Side of the Road," which expresses the delicate balance of giving up oneself in a relationship without losing one's own identity. A must-own for country and blues fans that appreciate great songwriting. *—Vik Iyengar*

● **Sweet Old World** / Aug. 25, 1992 / Chameleon ♦♦♦♦♦
After seemingly coming out of nowhere to be hailed as a major songwriter and roots music stylist, it took Lucinda Williams four years to prepare the follow-up to her masterful 1988 eponymous album. When it finally arrived, *Sweet Old World* proved to be every bit the equal of its predecessor, if not even better. Although *Sweet Old World* isn't really a concept album, it often feels like one. Its first half is dominated by the title track and "Pineola," two stunning meditations on suicide. Their sense of tragedy is reinforced with the closing cover of Nick Drake's "Which Will," and their shadow hangs heavy over the rest of the album. Several character portraits ponder where and why their subjects' lives went wrong; in this context, the dead-end situations seem that much more tragic and final. Moreover, when Williams offers an emotionally complex love ballad or a sexy blues strut, it's hard to take them as truly celebratory; here, the singer sounds as though she wants to appreciate who she has while she still can. That's also why "Little Angel, Little Brother" doesn't come off as remotely sentimental; the affectionate tribute works so well that, sandwiched between "Sweet Old World" and "Pineola," Williams' brother sounds like the suicide victim (it was actually a family friend). Williams' voice glows with the same warmth, for although it's limited in range, it's also a gorgeous instrument that WIlliams has learned to manipulate for maximum impact. Stylistically, *Sweet Old World* is similar to *Lucinda Williams*, juggling both the sounds and instruments of country, folk, blues, and rock & roll. It might not explode with confidence in the manner of *Lucinda Williams*, but *Sweet Old World* is no less vital; it's a gorgeous, elegiac record that not only consolidates but expands Williams' ample talents. *—Steve Huey*

Car Wheels on a Gravel Road / Jun. 30, 1998 / Mercury ♦♦♦♦♦
It isn't surprising that Lucinda Williams' level of craft takes time to assemble, but the six-year wait between *Sweet Old World* and its 1998 follow-up, *Car Wheels on a Gravel Road*, still raised eyebrows. The delay stemmed both from label difficulties and Williams' meticulous perfectionism, the latter reportedly over a too-produced sound and her own vocals. Listening to the record, one can understand why both might have concerned Williams. *Car Wheels* is far and away her most produced album to date, which is something of a mixed blessing. Its surfaces are clean and contemporary, with something in the timbres of the instruments (especially the drums) sounding extremely typical of a late-'90s major-label roots-rock album. While that might subtly alter the timeless qualities of Williams' writing, there's also no denying that her sound is punchier and livelier. The production also throws Williams' idiosyncratic voice into sharp relief, to the point where it's noticeably separate from the band. As a result, every inflection and slight tonal alteration is captured, and it would hardly be surprising if Williams did obsess over those small details. But whether or not you miss the earthiness of *Car Wheels*' predecessors, it's ultimately the material that matters, and Williams' songwriting is as captivating as ever. Intentionally or not, the album's common thread seems to be its strongly grounded sense of place—specifically, the Deep South, conveyed through images and numerous references to specific towns. Many songs are set, in some way, in the middle or aftermath of not-quite-resolved love affairs, as Williams meditates on the complexities of human passion. Even her simplest songs have more going on under the surface than their poetic structures might indicate. In the end, *Car Wheels on a Gravel Road* is Williams' third straight winner; although she might not be the most prolific songwriter of the '90s, she's certainly one of the most brilliant. *—Steve Huey*

Robin and Linda Williams

f. 1973
Group / Americana, Contemporary Folk, Country-Folk, Singer/Songwriter, Progressive Bluegrass
The sounds of rural America are explored through the warm vocal harmonies and acoustic guitar-driven arrangements of Virginia-based husband and wife duo Robin and Linda Williams. Accompanied by the appropriately named Their Fine Group, the Williamses blend a mixture of bluegrass, folk and acoustic country music. As semiregular performers on Garrison Keillor's nationally-broadcast radio show, A Prairie Home Companion, the duo and their band have developed a solid international following. In addition to being featured on the duo's 12 albums, the Williams' songs have been covered by many artists including Tom T. Hall, Mary Chapin Carpenter, Emmylou Harris, Tim and Mollie O'Brien and the Seldom Scene. *—Craig Harris*

Harmony / 1981 / June Appal ♦♦♦♦
Very hard to find, but it should be in your collection. *—Chip Renner*

● **Close As We Can Get** / 1984 / Flying Fish ♦♦♦♦♦
Perfect in all ways. "The Leaving Train" is one of their best songs. As good as *All Broken Hearts*. *—Chip Renner*

Nine 'Til Midnight / 1985 / Flying Fish ♦♦♦
A very good live album featuring gospel, traditional country, and contemporary songs. *—Chip Renner*

All Broken Hearts Are the Same / 1988 / Sugar Hill ♦♦♦♦♦
With top-notch songwriting and smooth vocals, this features Jerry Douglas, Stuart Duncan, and T. Michael Coleman. *—Chip Renner*

Rhythm of Love / 1990 / Sugar Hill ♦♦♦

Turn Toward Tomorrow / 1993 / Sugar Hill ♦♦♦
Produced by John Jennings, this collection of primarily Robin And Linda songs is held together by great economical band arrangements. Weepers like "When the Last Tear Falls" and "Chain of Pain" are given an uptempo treatment so we don't have to get to torn up about life's hardships. "Lying to the Moon" brings the CD to a peaceul close. *—Richard Meyer*

Robin & Linda Williams & Their Fine Group Live / 1994 / Sugar Hill ♦♦♦

In the Company of Strangers / Jan. 25, 2000 / Sugar Hill ✦✦✦
Whenever they perform on *A Prairie Home Companion,* this husband-and-wife team is always the best element on the program—with their powerful, sinewy voices (both grew up on gospel music) and instrumental chops (she's a great clawhammer banjo player, he's a very fine guitarist) they take every song they perform firmly by the throat and squeeze every drop of emotion from it, and they always do so in a way that manages to direct your attention to the song itself, rather than to their performance of it. They have a vocal blend as perfect in its way as that of the Stanley Brothers; when Linda's singing lead and Robin's belting out a low harmony it will raise the hairs on the back of your neck. But somehow their albums are often a disappointment. It's tempting to blame it on the studio environment or some other metaphysical factor, but the painful fact may simply be that the songs they write aren't as good as the ones they often sing onstage, which are likely to be old gospel or other traditional material. Lyrically, this stuff is all great; there just aren't many memorable tunes. It's telling that on *In the Company of Strangers* the only really memorable original song is the title track (which is outstanding) and the best song of the program is a Hank Williams number. Their version of "Cold, Cold Heart" rivals Williams', frankly. If only they could write like he did. *—Rick Anderson*

Victoria Williams

b. Dec. 23, 1958, Shreveport, LA
Vocals, Guitar / Alternative Folk, Contemporary Folk, Adult Alternative Pop/Rock, Alternative Country-Rock, Folk-Rock, Singer/Songwriter
Despite a successful career as a idiosyncratic country-folk performer, Victoria Williams was perhaps best known as a songwriter—thanks, ironically enough, to a tribute album recorded in her honor. Williams made her solo recording debut in 1987 with *Happy Come Home,* a collection showcasing her vivid songcraft as well as her off-kilter, squeaky vocal style; a follow-up record, *Swing the Statue!,* appeared in 1990. Two years later, while opening for Neil Young, Williams was diagnosed with the degenerative neurological disorder multiple sclerosis. The medical bills quickly piled up, and like many musicians, she was not covered by health insurance. In response, her manager began assembling friends and fans to record Williams' songs for a benefit album; the result, 1993 *Sweet Relief: A Benefit for Victoria Williams,* featured the likes of Pearl Jam, Lou Reed and Soul Asylum, whose rendition of "Summer of Drugs" was the record's first single. Due to its all-star line-up, *Sweet Relief* far outsold any of Williams' own efforts. In 1994 Williams issued *Loose,* a varied collection featuring duets with Soul Asylum's Dave Pirner and the Jayhawks' Mark Olson, Williams' second husband. *—Jason Ankeny*

Happy Come Home / 1987 / Geffen ✦✦✦
This debut album by Victoria Williams is as wonderful as it is eclectic. Van Dyke Parks's arrangements give the collection a carnival feel, while Anton Fier's pop productions never let this become anything close to an ordinary singer/songwriter album. But how could it, with Williams's elastic vocals and trippy lyrics— This is a great record to play when anyone says that all L.A. pop albums are slick and sanitized. *—Richard Meyer*

● **Swing the Statue** / 1990 / Mammoth ✦✦✦✦✦
Victoria Williams' second album was her most accomplished set of folk-rock, featuring the remarkable "Summer of Drugs." *—Stephen Thomas Erlewine*

Loose / 1994 / Mammoth ✦✦✦✦✦
What a great collection. Victoria Williams has put together a fine-tuned tight but loose band, as expressed in the title. Her folk-rock Carol Channing voice is perfectly suited to the arrangements, some of which were written by Van Dyke Parks, and include players such as Greg Cohen, Peter Buck, and Don Heffinton. Her originals are quirky and beautiful. WIlliams's choice of covers is also refreshing. She does a heartbreaking take on "What a Wonderful World" and revives the psychedelic chestnut "Nature's Way," making it her own. *Loose* is a wonderful album, full of life. *—Richard Meyer*

This Moment: Live in Toronto / Nov. 7, 1995 / Atlantic ✦✦✦
Recorded on the *Loose* tour, Victoria Williams's live album *This Moment: Live in Toronto* demonstrates the depths of her songwriting talents. Performing with a sympathetic folk-rock supporting band, Williams runs through her catalog, playing nearly all of her fans' favorite songs. She is in fine voice, turning an impassioned performance but the best thing about the record is how all of the songs play off each other. Unlike her other records, there is no filler on *This Moment,* which makes the album a perfect introduction to her rich talents. *—Stephen Thomas Erlewine*

Musings of a Creek Dipper / Jan. 13, 1998 / Atlantic ✦✦✦

Water to Drink / Aug. 15, 2000 / Atlantic ✦✦✦✦

Robin Williamson

b. Nov. 24, 1943
Vocals, Keyboards, Violin, Guitar / British Folk-Rock, British Folk, Folk-Rock
Between 1966 and 1974, Robin Williamson was one half of the Incredible String Band, but his career did not founder after ISB's demise, although it might be said to have taken a few quirky turns, including collaboration on a spy novel and the publication of a bizarre semi-autobiography. Away from these literary avocations, Williamson formed the Far Cry Ceilidh Band with Stan Schnier and Mark Simos, but never made it to the recording studio. In 1976, Williamson met with harpist Sylvia Wood, and together with Chris Caswell and Jerry McMillian, they formed Robin Williamson and His Merry Band. Between 1977 and 1979, they released three albums: the highly traditional *Journey's Edge* in 1977, *American Stonehenge* in 1978, and *A Glint at the Kindling* in 1979, which featured the epic historical cycle, "Five Denials on Merlin's Grave." After the breakup of the Merry Band, Williamson started to tour solo, offering highly ambient sets dominated by traditional stories set to song. Releases of this period include *Songs of Love and Parting* and the dedicated folklorist's *Legacy of the Scotish Harpers.* Williamson's concern with the British bardic tradition also manifested itself in several books and tapes containing spoken renditions of traditional tales. Subsequent projects have seen the the prolific Williamson recording tapes and discs of music for children and pouring his energies into environmental projects for the Scottish Wildlife Trust. *—Leon Jackson*

Journey's Edge / 1977 / Edsel ✦✦✦
This album features an unusual blend of baroque, traditional, and contemporary music played by Robin Williamson, one of the founders of The Incredible String Band, and his then-current band. *—AMG*

● **American Stonehenge** / 1978 / Edsel ✦✦✦✦✦
This album is perhaps Williamson's most generally accessible, featuring his late-70s touring band on a variety of humorous and pastoral Williamson originals. *—William Ruhlmann*

Music for the Mabinogi / 1984 / Flying Fish ✦✦✦

Kate Wolf (Kathryn Louise Allen)

b. Jan. 27, 1942, San Francisco, CA, **d.** Dec. 10, 1986
Vocals, Piano, Guitar / Contemporary Singer/Songwriter, Contemporary Folk
Although she was a significant presence on the folk scene between the late '70s and mid-'80s, it's difficult to categorize Kate Wolf as a folk performer (though that is ultimately the broad category that suits her best). Although she largely employed acoustic instrumentation, she really owed more to the contemporary singer-songwriting movement than folk-based traditions. While it's easy to imagine her music appealing to fans of, say, Joni Mitchell, she never made the slightest impact on the rock audience, and barely drew from rock elements at all in her own work. Her music also had a strong country flavor, though not of the Nashville variety. Her fusion of country, folk, and singer-songwriter influences helped point the way for later country-folk-pop performers such as Nanci Griffith and Mary-Chapin Carpenter. The appeal of Wolf's music is broad—folk, pop, and rootsy country fans can all find something to like—yet elusive. Her songs describe family, romance, and the rural life of her native Northern California with fine (though not studious) detail, projecting a sort of reserved sensitivity with her lower-than-average vocals. Hers is a voice of wisdom, comfort, and independence. If those aren't the most exciting things around, there are few other performers who convey such consistent warmth and dignity, making listeners she never met personally feel as if they were hearing letters from a friend. *—Richie Unterberger*

Back Roads / 1976 / Rhino ✦✦✦✦✦
Wolf's debut album introduced an approach that would, in most essential respects, vary little over the next decade: gentle, slightly mournful country/folk songs with a strong narrative voice, and a semi-rural Callifornian ambience with the frequent evocation of golden, natural landscapes. Even at this stage, Wolf stood out from the pack with her restrained, tasteful vocals, sincere compositions that avoided maudlin clichés, and careful, almost diligent arrangements. *—Richie Unterberger*

Lines on The Paper / 1977 / Rhino ✦✦✦
Wolf's second album indicated that there weren't going to be any significant changes in her style. At the same time, it also gave notice that she was an extraordinarily consistent performer with a deep catalog of original compositions. More reflective song-stories about family and life passages, sensitively but not sappily performed. *—Richie Unterberger*

Safe at Anchor / 1979 / Rhino ✦✦✦
While at this point you knew what to expect from a Kate Wolf album, it would be inaccurate to call her work formulaic. Her musical arrangements didn't vary all that much, but each of her compositions was carefully constructed and performed with commitment. That's true of all of the songs here, with occasional tracks (such as "Early Morning Melody") emerging as true standouts. *—Richie Unterberger*

Close to You / 1981 / Rhino ✦✦✦
Wolf's arrangements got a little more complex on this album, with occasional string arrangements and drum tracks. "Leggett Serenade" especially sounds like (the probably inevitable) attempt to craft a track with more pop/adult contemporary appeal. Largely, though, it's the same dependable sparsely arranged, strong material, with support from noted musicians Nina Gerber, Tony Rice, Norton Buffalo, and Darol Anger. *—Richie Unterberger*

Give Yourself To Love (Live In Concert) / 1983 / Rhino ✦✦✦✦✦
A worthy live supplement to her studio albums, as many of the songs were previously unrecorded. Taken from shows in 1982 and 1983, it features both Wolf compositions and covers of songs by Sandy Denny, John Stewart, Jim Ringer-Mary McCaslin, Robin Williamson, and others. This is identical to the initial Kaleidocope release of *Give Yourself to Love,* though the Rhino CD adds an unnecessarily confusing "Vol. 1 & 2" to the title. *—Richie Unterberger*

Poet's Heart / 1985 / Rhino ✦✦✦✦✦
Wolf's final studio album found her continuing to capably explore pretty much the same musical territory she always had, perhaps with a slightly heavier heart and somewhat more acute lyricism. She was still looking for new ways to modify her core approach, making imaginative use of dobro and steel guitar player Mike Auldridge, and Celtic harpist Kim Robertson. *—Richie Unterberger*

● **Gold in California** / 1986 / Rhino ✦✦✦✦✦
Featuring 20 songs from 1975 to 1985, this is the definitive Kate Wolf retrospective, compiled by the singer herself shortly before her death. For most listeners, it will serve as *the* Kate Wolf album to own, assembling the best of her somewhat similar albums in one place (and for those who want more, Rhino has reissued her entire catalog). Every one of these titles was previously released, with the exception of a version of Alice Stuart's "Full Time Woman." This is identical to the initial Kaleidocope release of *Gold in California,* though the Rhino CD adds an unnecessarily confusing "Vol. 1 & 2" to the title. *—Richie Unterberger*

The Wind Blows Wild / 1988 / Rhino ✦✦✦

Evening in Austin / 1989 / Rhino ✦✦✦

Looking Back at You / 1994 / Rhino ✦✦✦

Breezes / 1995 / Gadfly ✦✦✦

● **Weaver of Visions: The Kate Wolf Anthology** / Apr. 4, 2000 / Rhino ✦✦✦✦✦
Rhino's *Weaver Of Visions: The Kate Wolf Anthology* features a slightly different track listing than their 1986 collection of Wolf's work, 1986's *California Gold*, and adds a few live and previously unreleased songs. Like the earlier set, *Weaver of Visions* is a double-disc package that provides a good overview of her quiet confessional style, particularly with songs like "Back Roads," "The Lilac & the Apple," "Early Morning Melody," and "Here in California." But live versions of "Cornflower Blue," "Give Yourself to Love," "Eyes of a Painter," and the previously unreleased songs "Shadow of a Life" and "Minstrel," add another dimension to this updated retrospective. *—Heather Phares*

Glenn Yarbrough

b. Jan. 12, 1930, Milwaukee, WI
Vocals / Folk Revival, Pop, Folk-Pop, Traditional Folk
From his days as the singing mainstay of "The Limeliters" through a long solo career that's seen its share of hits, Glenn Yarbrough has been a respected interpreter of folk and popular music. He's had a top hit in "Baby, The Rain Must Fall" and his interpretation of "Seven Daffodils" is the benchmark against which love songs are measured. From his days in a boys choir through today, Glenn's powerful voice has rung with lusty conviction about all that he cares about. Listen to Glenn Yarbrough. He's what singing should be. *—Allan Shaw*

● **Baby The Rain Must Fall/It's Gonna Be Fine** / Jul. 27, 1999 / Collectables ✦✦✦✦

The Bramble & The Rose / Folk Era ✦✦✦✦
With Holly Yarbrough and fingerpicking guitar champion Muriel Anderson. *—Allan Shaw*

Various Artists

40th Anniversary Collection 1960-2000: The Journey of Chris Strachwitz / Sep. 26, 2000 / Arhoolie ✦✦✦✦✦
Combine a great ear for music with a firm commitment to recording only what you personally like and you've got the formula that has fueled Arhoolie Records for 40 years. Founder Chris Strachwitz—a German immigrant and former schoolteacher—may have seemed an unlikely candidate to become one of the great compilers of regional American popular music, but that's sure what he turned out to be. This five-disc, 95-artist label retrospective is truly monumental. On disc one, which begins before Arhoolie's launch and covers 1954-1965, blues dominate. By the the time you've worked your way through all six hours of this collection, though, you'll understand why Strachwitz could never make it as a DJ even on a blues radio station; not only does he eschew mainstream commercial music, he couldn't possibly live within any format. Just when you think you've got Arhoolie pegged as a blues label, on comes a folk number. You settle into a zydeco groove, and the set shifts into gospel. Or Tex-Mex. There's also some bluegrass here. And jazz. Incredibly, all of this music makes some sort of sense together and the quality never flags throughout. Though the bulk of the package's greatest treats come from virtual unknowns (more than a few recorded in their own homes), you may already be familiar with some of these artists, including Jesse Fuller, K.C. Douglas, Mance Lipscomb, Clifton Chenier, and Flaco Jimenez. The accompanying 68-page, 41,000-word color "booklet" is more like a book. Co-producer Elijah Wald limited selections to recordings that Strachwitz himself made or supervised—keeping the box from mushrooming beyond five discs—but this meant the elimination of other great material. That will have to wait for the next box. *—Jeff Burger*

40th Anniversary Collection 1960-2000: The Journey of Chris Strachwitz / Sep. 26, 2000 / Arhoolie ✦✦✦✦✦
Combine a great ear for music with a firm commitment to recording only what you personally like and you've got the formula that has fueled Arhoolie Records for 40 years. Founder Chris Strachwitz—a German immigrant and former schoolteacher—may have seemed an unlikely candidate to become one of the great compilers of regional American popular music, but that's sure what he turned out to be. This five-disc, 95-artist label retrospective is truly monumental. On disc one, which begins before Arhoolie's launch and covers 1954-1965, blues dominate. By the the time you've worked your way through all six hours of this collection, though, you'll understand why Strachwitz could never make it as a DJ even on a blues radio station; not only does he eschew mainstream commercial music, he couldn't possibly live within any format. Just when you think you've got Arhoolie pegged as a blues label, on comes a folk number. You settle into a \zydeco groove, and the set shifts into \gospel. Or \Tex-Mex. There's also some bluegrass here. And jazz. Incredibly, all of this music makes some sort of sense together and the quality never flags throughout. Though the bulk of the package's greatest treats come from virtual unknowns (more than a few recorded in their own homes), you may already be familiar with some of these artists, including Jesse Fuller, K.C. Douglas, Mance Lipscomb, Clifton Chenier, and Flaco Jimenez. The accompanying 68-page, 41,000-word color "booklet" is more like a book. Co-producer Elijah Wald limited selections to recordings that Strachwitz himself made or supervised—keeping the box from mushrooming beyond five discs—but this meant the elimination of other great material. That will have to wait for the next box. *—Jeff Burger*

● **Alan Lomax Collection Sampler** / Apr. 22, 1997 / Rounder ✦✦✦✦✦
An outstanding promotional sampler for Rounder's extensive and ongoing Alan Lomax series. This set draws selections from all over the world, and comes with a very nice booklet that delves into the background of the series. Worth finding. *—Steven McDonald*

Anglo-American Ballads, Vol. 1 / Feb. 9, 1999 / Rounder ✦✦✦✦✦
This was the first of six albums of field recordings issued in 1942 by the Archive of Folk Song in the Library of Congress, and it has subsequently appeared in LP form before this CD. Edited by Alan Lomax, this first volume was recorded between 1936 and 1941. It presents folk songs that were often derived from ballads of Anglo origin, and were largely performed by Southern singers. Most of the selections are a cappella solo vocals, although sometimes there's guitar or banjo accompaniment. Several well-known folk standards are on board: "Barbara Allen," "Pretty Polly" (two versions), "The House Carpenter" and "The Gypsy Davy," the last of which is rendered by Woody Guthrie, the only famous performer on the set. Some other singers might be recognized by those with a deep folk schooling (Mrs. Texas Gladden, E.C. Ball), but by and large the artists will be unfamiliar to almost all listeners. This is important American source music, delivered with serious sincerity and piety. Just as notably, the performances are better and more enjoyable to listen to than on many such folkloric compilations, including some others that were assembled by Lomax and/or the Library of Congress. *—Richie Unterberger*

☆ **Anthology of American Folk Music, Vol. 1-3** / Aug. 19, 1997 / Smithsonian/Folkways ✦✦✦✦✦
Originally released in 1952 as a quasi-legal set of three double LPs and reissued several times since (with varying cover art), *Anthology of American Folk Music* could well be the most influential document of the '50s folk revival. Many of the recordings that appeared on it had languished in obscurity for 20 years, and it proved a revelation to a new group of folkies, from Pete Seeger to John Fahey to Bob Dylan. The man that made the *Anthology* possible was Harry Smith, a notoriously eccentric musicologist who compiled 84 of his favorite hillbilly, gospel, blues, and Cajun performances from the late '20s and early '30s, dividing each into one of three categories: Ballads, Social Music, and Songs. Smith sequenced the three volumes with a great amount of care, placing songs on the Ballads volume in historical order (not to be confused with chronological order) so as to create an LP that traces the folk tradition, beginning with some of the earliest Childe ballads of the British Isles and ending with several story songs of the early 20th century. The cast of artists includes pioneers in several fields, from the Carter Family and Uncle Dave Macon to Blind Lemon Jefferson, Mississippi John Hurt, and the Alabama Sacred Harp Singers. Many of the most interesting selections on the *Anthology,* however, are taken from artists even more obscure, such as Clarence Ashley, Bascom Lamar Lunsford, and Buell Kazee. After the *Anthology* had been out of print for more than a decade, Smithsonian/Folkways reissued the set in a six-disc boxed set, with the original notes of Harry Smith, as well as a separate book of new reminiscences by artists influenced by the original and a wealth of material for use in CD-ROM drives. *—John Bush*

☆ **Anthology of American Folk Music, Vol. 4** / May 23, 2000 / Revenant ✦✦✦✦✦
The Harry Smith-compiled three-volume *Anthology of American Folk Music* set, originally released in the 1950s and reissued to much brouhaha in 1997, was one of the most important records in launching the folk revival. It was not well known, though, that Smith compiled a fourth volume that was unissued. Revenant finally put it out in 2000, and like its three predecessors, it contains classic pre-World War II American country, blues, and folk music, with some gospel and Cajun too. It does differ from the first three volumes in its focus on a slightly later period, with all the tracks culled from the years 1928-1940. Leadbelly, Robert Johnson, Joe Williams, Bukka White, Memphis Minnie, and John Estes are all major blues artists; the Monroe Brothers, the Carter Family, Uncle Dave Macon, and the Blue Sky Boys all giant country/bluegrass pioneers; and the Hackberry Ramblers are one of the pre-eminent Cajun groups. A few of these songs are archetypes that have burned their way into the American collective musical consciousness: John Estes' "Milk Cow Blues," the Carter Family's "No Depression in Heaven," Joe Williams' "Baby Please Don't Go," and the Monroe Brothers' "Nine Pound Hammer Is Too Heavy." Other less famous performances are quite intriguing, like Sister Clara Hudmon's "Stand By Me" (believed by some to be Bessie Smith recording under a pseudonym) and Jesse James' raw and rollicking piano blues "Southern Casey Jones." At 28 songs spread over two CDs, it's a little shorter than might be expected for a box set, though as compensation, it's enclosed in a pretty incredible 96-page liner-note-sized hardcover book with writing by Dick Spottswood and John Fahey. *—Richie Unterberger*

Banjo Jamboree / 1996 / Tradition ✦✦✦✦✦
If a diverse anthology of banjo-driven folk music is what you're after, this is an excellent choice. Besides folkies like Eric Weissberg, Marshall Brickman, and Mike Seeger, it has contributions by a few unexpected names like Roger McGuinn (who offers a "Banjo Cantata"), David Lindley, hot country and rock sessionman Joe Maphis, and Mason ("Classical Gas") Williams. Selections by less celebrated names like Jim Helms and Dick Weissman round out the collection, the major strike against it being the near-total lack of source information in the liner notes, which don't give any of the original session dates. *—Richie Unterberger*

Best of Broadside 1962-1988 / Aug. 22, 2000 / Smithsonian/Folkways ✦✦✦✦✦
From the early '60s to the late '80s, *Broadside* magazine printed numerous topical songs by contemporary writers, in addition to articles and commentary. By far the most influential years of its life span were the earliest ones, in the early to mid-'60s, when it helped steer the folk movement toward original material that directly addressed modern society and social injustice. This five-CD box set is an important document of Broadside's contribution to 20th century American popular music. The *Broadside* LPs included material by emerging songwriters that didn't show up on those performers' own albums, and undoubtedly this box will get its most attention for featuring some of those items by Bob Dylan, Phil Ochs, Tom Paxton, Janis Ian, and Eric Andersen. If you're a committed 1960s folk collector, there are a number of such goodies for cherry-picking here. From a wider perspective, however, this anthology is an important record of how social consciousness as a whole grew within American popular music, especially in the 1960s. Don't get the idea this is all great stuff; there are too many obscure strident singer/songwriters, in the mold of Dylan and others, singing dry, didactic, unmelodic tunes with unimaginative plain arrangements. *Broadside* also missed the boat almost entirely as far as folk-rock and socially conscious rock was concerned, with rare exceptions. When the Fugs' "Kill for Peace" blasts off, it's such a refreshing change to hear an all-out rocker you can move to, though that's definitely not the rule on this anthology. Nevertheless, there's much good music here, and certainly as a whole it's an incredible history lesson, with more than 150 pages of liner notes detailing the magazine, its founders, the performers, and each of the songs. *—Richie Unterberger*

Choose Your Partners!: Contra Dance & Square Dance Music of New Hampshire / Jun. 22, 1999 / Smithsonian/Folkways ✦✦✦
New Hampshire is one of the American locales in which square dancing is most popular,

both in contra dances (in which two lines of partners face each other) and square dances (in which four couples arrange themselves in a square formation). This 67-minute disc has 16 tunes suitable for the purpose, recorded in early 1999 by half a dozen bands active in the New Hampshire square dancing community. It's heaviest, as you might expect, on the fiddle, also including some dulcimer, mandolin, flute, and other instrumentation. The repertoire concentrates on music derived from British Isles and Celtic folk, including reels, jigs, and a couple of slower waltzes that break up the pace nicely; some of the songs include dance callers. It's more fun to dance to than listen to, but it's well recorded and annotated, and indeed probably good fodder for practicing these styles of folk dancing. *—Richie Unterberger*

Close to Home: Old Time Music From Mike Seeger's Collection (1952-1967) / Jun. 17, 1997 / Smithsonian/Folkways ♦♦♦
Collected by Mike Seeger from 1952 to 1967 as he roamed around the Appalachian Mountains, *Close to Home* is one of the better detailed sets of authentic old-time Southern American music to be found. Though mostly recorded at the musician's home on a single, handheld microphone, the warmth and charm of the performances captured make up for any supposed lack of recording quality, as Seeger no doubt took great pains to document these archaic stylings before they died with their performers. Of the 38 tracks featured, some legends like Sara and Maybelle Carter of the Carter Family fame, Elizabeth Cotten, and fiddler Eck Robertson appear, though the majority are simply local legends or unknowns. As such, it might come as some surprise to hear the level of accomplishment reached by these common folks, as a few were even said to have been badly out of practice when recorded. A majority of the tracks are lively fiddle or banjo instrumentals, though a few harmonica workouts, gorgeous autoharp and dulcimer tunes, and a cappella tracks appear, as well. This is very honest music, without a hint of pretension, and one can only wonder how many similar talents lived and died without ever having shared their talents outside of their local community. Excellent liner notes composed by Seeger himself give a wonderfully detailed commentary on how he came about to record the featured artists, and also place the performers within their historical context. There might be more complete collections on the market, but for the single-disc price and the amount of quality music here, *Close to Home* is highly recommended. *—Matt Fink*

Folk, Gospel & Blues: Will the Circle Be Unbroken / Oct. 12, 1999 / Columbia/Legacy ♦♦♦♦
The scope of the 45-track *Folk, Gospel & Blues: Will the Circle Be Unbroken,* culled from the gargantuan 26-disc box set *Sony Music 100 Years: Soundtrack for a Century,* is impressive. Columbia was one of the biggest labels in the early days of the record industry, as is evident from the beginning of this collection, which features cuts by Bessie Smith, Mississippi John Hurt, Blind Willie Johnson, the Mississippi Sheiks, and Thomas A. Dorsey. As a matter of fact, Columbia and its various offshoots stayed strong throughout pre-war blues and folk; the first disc alone also features Blind Willie McTell, Leadbelly, Robert Johnson, Big Bill Broonzy, Josh White, Burl Ives, Memphis Minnie, Paul Robeson, Big Joe Williams, the Dixie Hummingbirds, Mahalia Jackson, and a pre-electric Muddy Waters. After the war, Columbia stumbled somewhat in this genre. The label recorded no blues or folk until the early '60s, when the folk and blues revivals brought these musical styles to new audiences. Consequently, a major portion of the genre's history is missing from this collection—the only volume in the *Sony Music 100 Years* series to suffer such a gap. But the second disc presents a good history of post-revival folk and blues, picking up with Bob Dylan, Pete Seeger, Simon & Garfunkel, and Son House. Some may argue that Dan Fogelberg and Steve Forbert are more singer/songwriters than folk artists, or that Stevie Ray Vaughan rocks too hard to be blues, but this merely signifies what happened to the individual genres during the '60s, '70s, and '80s. So, even if there is a big gap on the compilation, the set is excellent overall. Its two discs offer a thorough history of folk and blues, and it's an incredible, impressive, entertaining history. *—Stephen Thomas Erlewine*

Folk Classics / 1989 / Columbia ♦♦♦♦♦
Though one thinks of Elektra and Vanguard as the main record labels of the folk revival, the giant Columbia Records also made some inroads into the field, signing up not only Bob Dylan but also a wide range of folkies, from Pete Seeger to The New Christy Minstrels. This 15-track compilation delves deeper into the Columbia vault for tracks by Leadbelly and Burl Ives, but its focus is on 60s performers—The Brothers Four, Carolyn Hester, Malvina Reynolds. Many of them, like Dylan, are John Hammond signings. The focus of the album is scattered, but the selection is excellent, and Columbia was long overdue to examine its folk archives. *— William Ruhlmann*

From the Heart of Studio A: The Folkscene Collection / Apr. 21, 1998 / Red House ♦♦♦♦♦
If you like folk music and have ever lived in Los Angeles, chances are you know the names Roz and Howard Larman. Their *FolkScene* radio show on KPFK has been an L.A. institution since 1970, and one of its highlights has been visits to the studio by just about everybody you can think of from the world of folk. There have been more than 1, 500 such guest appearances over the history of the show, so this 13-track CD of *FolkScene* performances from the 1990s barely scratches the surface. Still, it's a start, and a fine one. The sound quality is amazingly good, especially considering that the disc contains unvarnished live recordings, with no overdubbing or "fixing in the mix" later on. Noteworthy performances include Bruce Cockburn's "Pacing the Cage," Kate and Anna McGarrigle's "Goin' Back to Harlan," Richard Thompson's "Waltzing's for Dreamers" and Mary Black's "Columbus." The best track, though, is Iris Dement's "Our Town," a self-penned ode to a dying hometown with an aching, heartfelt vocal that will stay with you after the singing has ended. *—Jeff Burger*

☆ **Greatest Folksingers of '60s** / 1972 / Vanguard ♦♦♦♦♦
Not only was Maynard Solomon's Vanguard Records one of the major folk labels of the 60s (having the prescience to pick up Joan Baez early on, and then recording the cream of the singer/songwriters thereafter), but it also had the rights to record and release material from the Newport Folk Festival, giving it access to several artists who were not signed to the label. As a result, this double-packet compilation features songs by nearly every major folk figure of the decade, from The Weavers to José Feliciano, with Vanguard artists such as Buffy Sainte-Marie, Eric Andersen, and Odetta sharing space with Elektra's Phil Ochs and Judy Collins and Columbia's Bob Dylan. Listen to this one record and you'll know what the 60s folk revival sounded like. *—William Ruhlmann*

Hawaiian Slack Key Guitar Masters / 1995 / Dancing Cat ♦♦♦
The Dancing Cat label has been the chief vehicle for exposure of Hawaiian roots music on the mainland, particularly of the slack-key guitar style, a virtuosic finger-picking genre that nonetheless is far more tranquil than frenetic. This acts as a label sampler, with cuts from eleven different albums in the *Hawaiian Slack Key Guitar Masters* series. With songs by the leading slack-key performers—including Cyril Pahinui, Keola Beamer, Ray Kane, and Sonny Chillingworth—it's a good introduction to the style, or a good collection for those who just want one representation of the form. It's surprisingly homogenous for a sampler, but then its serene washes of strings are very characteristic of the slack-key sound. *—Richie Unterberger*

Mademoiselle, Voulez-Vous Danser / May 18, 1999 / Smithsonian/Folkways ♦♦♦♦
Mademoiselle, Voulez-Vous Danser? collects 22 Franco-American folk songs from the New England borderlands. French, French-Canadian and American influences blend on songs like "Devil's Dream," "Entre Moi" and "Valse Des Pasteraux." Performers like Chanterelle, Les Franco-Americains and Paul Baril also reflect the cultural intermingling of the borderlands, providing a distinctive, diverse musical treat. As with other Smithsonian Folkways releases, *Mademoiselle, Voulez-Vous Danser?* features the label's attention to detail in its track listing and informative liner notes, written by Clare Pinkert and Theodore Levin. *—Heather Phares*

Masters of the Banjo / 1994 / Arhoolie ♦♦♦♦
Collecting live performances from the *Masters of the Banjo* tour from the early 1990s, an impressive audio history of the banjo is provided by way of 26 performances by 11 different artists. Everything from Seleshe Damessae's performances on African krar, an ancient precursor to the modern banjo, to Ralph Stanley's bluegrass workouts is represented, with a large number of the samples coming from a Celtic tradition, as well. Kirk Sutphin, from the legendary Sutphin family, provides fine examples of early American banjo tradition, using claw hammer style in "John Brown's Dream" and a rollicking string band tune in "Let Me Fall." Multi-talented Tony Ellis contributes four of his amazingly intricate original compositions, representing the progression of the instrument from primarily being dance accompaniment to something altogether more pensive. Irish tenor banjo workouts by Seamus Egan show a strong influence of Irish uilleann pipes, as he embraces both traditional and contemporary styles. Carroll Best's unique three-finger style and Will Keys' two-finger up-picking style are extraordinary examples of how differently the instrument has developed even from region to region in the southern United States. All in all, you have a concise, though certainly not complete, history of the progression of the banjo that does a fine job showing the past, present, and future of the instrument. *—Matt Fink*

The Music Never Stopped: Roots of the Grateful Dead / Nov. 1995 / Shanachie ♦♦♦
An interesting concept: a compilation of the original versions of 17 songs frequently covered by The Grateful Dead in concert. Thoughtfully assembled, it showcases several aspects of their eclectic roots, encompassing jugband folk, country & western, Appalachian mountain music, country blues, '50s Chicago electric blues, R&B, Dylan, Guthrie, Holly, Berry, and more. Some of the recordings are very famous (Dylan's "It's All over Now, Baby Blue," Holly's "Not Fade Away"); others are downright obscure (Obray Ramsey's "Rain and Snow," the rare original version of "Morning Dew" by little-known Canadian folkie Bonnie Dobson). If you're a Dead fan, this is a valuable, very listenable collection of some of their key influences. It may seem churlish to point this out to Deadheads, but if you're *not* a Dead fan, you'll find this to be a first-rate collection of roots music that's much more enjoyable than hearing The Dead's interpretations of the same tunes. *—Richie Unterberger*

The Music of Kentucky: Early American Rural Classics 1927-1937, Vol. 1-2 / 1995 / Yazoo ♦♦♦♦♦
Many rural fiddlers, guitarists, and banjo players from the state of Kentucky were taped while the recording industry was in its infancy. This interesting and valuable two-volume set, numbering 53 songs in all, presents a wide-ranging set of old-timey folk styles, by artists who are known only to scholars in the field. Much of the material is taken from the famed Bristol sessions of the late '20s, and late-'30s field recordings by renowned folklorist Alan Lomax. The roots of much modern country, folk, and even blues can be heard in these heartfelt, occasionally stirring performances of great conviction, religious or otherwise. It's not just a history lesson, and is a lot more accessible to modern-day listeners than many would assume. *—Richie Unterberger*

North Carolina Banjo Collection / Mar. 10, 1998 / Rounder ♦♦♦♦♦
An outstanding primer and introduction to a set of regional styles that give credence to the banjo as a virtuoso instrument. Much of the music on these two discs comes from field recordings made with the aid of local players who are semi-professional musicians at best, but that consideration does not affect the overall quality of the performances. The banjo has often been held up to ridicule (as often as not by way of referencing #Deliverance); this collection does a lot to redress that. *—Steven McDonald*

Northumberland Rant: Traditional Music from the Edge of England / Sep. 21, 1999 / Smithsonian/Folkways ♦♦♦♦♦
Northumbrian folk music is often characterized by instrumental music played on smallpipes, which differ from other bagpipes in that their chanters (or melody pipes) are chromatic and closed at the bottom end, which enables them to produce shorter, more staccato notes. Smallpipe instrumentals are the main, but not exclusive, fare on this collection, consisting of performances recorded in the field and studio between 1954 and 1998 (mostly from the latter portion of that time frame). The fiddle also features strongly on some of the selections, either alone or in tandem with the Northumbrian pipes and other instruments. The contrast between the types of instrumentation alone provides more variety than many a British Isles folk compilation. But the Northumbrian pipes are the main attractions, as they have a tonal clarity and economy not associated with much bagpipe music. The 1954 field recording by Jack Armstrong & the Barnstormers has that slightly wobbly feel beloved by those who like

their folk with a faint patina of moldy mystery, but for the most part the tracks are of very modern fidelity. *—Richie Unterberger*

Prison Songs, Vol. 1: Murderous Home / Aug. 5, 1997 / Rounder ✦✦✦✦✦
In the late 1940s, ethnomusicologist Alan Lomax went to Parchman Farm in Mississippi to record African-American prisoners. This penitentiary was renowned for its anachronistically harsh conditions, and it's something of a miracle that Lomax was allowed in to document the music in the first place. Most of the material was recorded while the men were actually at work, and reflect the rhythms of chopping trees, splitting fireweed, chopping weeds, and other such tasks. The liner notes make much of how the subjugation and misery of the community is reflected in the music. While the dreariness of their lives was no doubt genuine, the music itself—mainly gospelish work songs and chants geared toward getting the men through their daily grinds, usually sung a cappella, often by groups—is not depressing to hear. True, it's hard to call it uplifting knowing what the prisoners were enduring, but there's an enormous pride and spiritual strength. It's as convincing as any gospel, and a number of these made their way into pop and rock repertoires in adapted forms, such as "Rosie," "Early in the Mornin'," and "Stackerlee." (This record was originally issued on LP in 1957 as Negro Prison Songs, on Tradition 1020; the Rounder CD has a new title and different, historically slanted liner notes.) *—Richie Unterberger*

Prison Songs, Vol. 2: Don'tcha Hear Poor Mother Calling / Aug. 5, 1997 / Rounder ✦✦✦
These were recorded during the same field trips to Parchman Farm that yielded the material heard on Rounder's Prison Songs Vol. 1. Unlike that set, everything here is previously unreleased; what's more, most of the singers on this collection were not heard on the other volume. It's quite similar to Vol. 1, however, in that most of the material is a cappella, much of it recorded while the men were at work. Perhaps it's a bit starker and rawer, although exactly what made some selections suitable for release while others remain unissued is not obvious, other than the intrinsic lack of commercial potential for several discs' worth of projects of this nature. These performances, like those on the previous volume, project great spiritual fortitude, with a dignity and force that evokes more admiration than pity. *—Richie Unterberger*

River of Song: A Musical Journey Down the Mississippi / Nov. 17, 1998 / Smithsonian/Folkways ✦✦✦
A companion double-CD set to a four-part 1999 PBS television series of the various styles of music found along the Mississippi River, from northern Minnesota to the river's mouth in Louisiana. This has 36 complete performances that the documentary makers recorded as part of the project, encompassing Delta blues (Robert Lockwood, Jr.), Native American powwows, Cajun (D.L. Menard) and zydeco (Geno Delafose), New Orleans soul (Irma Thomas), rockabilly (Sonny Burgess), singer-songwriter folk (Greg Brown), bluegrass, gospel, polka, jazz, and less expected things like traditional Swedish, Laotian, and norteno music. There's even alternative rock, via Babes in Toyland (whose selection is frankly ill-fitting), Soul Asylum, and the Bottle Rockets. This might be better seen on film than heard all at once: it covers a full smorgasbord of American music in one go, and although in concept that might be appealing, remember that when you actually eat at smorgasbords, you don't try and sample every last damn dish in the course of one meal. The most unusual items are the Skal Club Spelmanslag's "Red-Headed Swede," with its eerie musical saw; Sonny Burgess' "T for Texas," on which he sounds far more like a genuine soul man than a cult rockabilly singer; and the Memphis Horns and Ann Peebles' "St. Louis Blues," done without a rhythm section. Little Milton, Henry Butler, Levon Helm, James Cotton, Fontella Bass, and John Hartford are some of the other recognizable names contributing to the album. If you're interested, the project also generated a book with the same title as the CD, written by Elijah Wald and John Junkerman, and published by St. Martin's Press. *—Richie Unterberger*

Song of the Hills: Instrumental Impressions of America's Heartland / Jan. 19, 1999 / Shanachie ✦✦✦✦
Featuring an all-star cast of traditional folk musicians including Eric Weisberg, Jay Ungar, Molly Mason, Tony Trischka, Norman Blake, and John Doan, *Song of the Hills* is composed of light and airy interpretations of old-time American music. Fiddle, flatpicked guitar, Dobro, and subtle orchestration run through most songs, giving a rich full sound on compositions ranging from spirituals to barn dances. Although the performances are clean and flawless, it is almost a shame to see such brilliant musicians slowed to a rather bland pace. While not for the most die-hard bluegrass and old-timey aficionados, the album is a gentle walk through pleasant versions of these comfortable tunes. *—Zac Johnson*

★ **Songs for Political Action: Folk Music, Topical Songs and the American Lef** / 1996 / Bear Family ✦✦✦✦✦
Leave it to Bear Family Records to release a ten-disc collection of Communist and leftist-activist songs that only a dyed-in-the-wool Republican can afford! However, there's a lot of stuff on these discs—songs about lynchings, anti-union murders and riots, and other injustices, including wretched working conditions permitted by earlier governments, et cetera. There's folk material, of course, but also cowboy songs, country songs, blues and country-blues. These ten CDs also tear down the stereotype of the dry and doctrinaire political song.

Highlights include Disc One ("The Roots of the Folk Revival,") which is primarily given over to the oldest union songs and farm-related protest songs. Disc Three is given over to the Almanac Singers; this body of work was recorded when the official Communist Party line (to which they adhered) was non-aggression against Nazi Germany. Some of the music on Disc Four ("Fighting the Fascists") was surprisingly complex, given the spartan conditions under which a lot of it was done. Disc Seven ("Pete Seeger: 1946-48") is mostly made up of Seeger's masterpieces Roll the Union On and *Songs for Political Action.* Disc Nine ("Campaign Songs: 1944-1949") represents the last significant cohesive body of topical political songs to come from the American left. By the time of Disc Ten ("An Era Closes"), the Left couldn't do more than snipe at the reactionaries setting the agenda and the passive moderates who stood by. The sound quality on most of the material in this set is astonishingly good and the ten discs are accompanied by an over-200-page hardcover book featuring historical and musical essays, photographs, session information and lyrics—one of the finest documents of the relationship between music and politics of the period that has ever been published. *—Bruce Eder*

☆ **Southern Journey, Vol. 1: Voices from the American South** / Apr. 22, 1997 / Rounder ✦✦✦✦✦
In 1959 and 1960, folklorist Alan Lomax made now-celebrated field trips through the South that resulted in a literal mountain (80 hours) of recordings of all kinds of American traditional music. These tapes led to the eventual release of 19 albums. Seven of them formed the series known as Sounds of the South on Atlantic (now available as a four-CD box set). The other 12 were issued as volumes of a Prestige series entitled Southern Journey. Rounder has now made the *Southern Journey* recordings available on CD in a 13-volume set that also includes some previously unreleased material. Lomax's recordings have been justly hailed as a foundation of American musical scholarship. He was not only among the first to conscientiously document living American musical traditions with links to centuries past; he was also the first to record them with sonic clarity that enables contemporary listeners to appreciate them as living art forms, rather than dusty museum relics. The sheer quantity of work that Lomax recorded during this period is daunting, so for those who just want to dip their toes into the water, this first volume is a suggested starting point. Most of the Southern Journey CDs are arranged thematically; *Vol. 1,* however, draws from all forms of Southern folk music, including blues, spirituals, sea chanteys, work songs, ballads, and more. What surprises the modern-day listener is that, apart from the immense academic interest of the recordings, the performances themselves are emotional, moving, and often downright enjoyable. There are actually a couple of well-known musicians on this disc (bluesman Fred McDowell, early country artist J.E. Mainer), but almost all the other artists perform at a similar level. Nine of the 24 tracks (including the one by McDowell) were previously unissued. *—Richie Unterberger*

Southern Journey, Vol. 2: Ballads and Breakdown / Apr. 22, 1997 / Rounder ✦✦✦✦✦
Lomax's first stop for his *Southern Journey* series was the Blue Ridge Mountains of southeastern Virginia, where he recorded the 26 tracks (six previously unreleased) that comprise this collection. The music of this region relied heavily upon guitars, fiddles, and banjos, with a repertoire influenced by the British, Irish, and Scottish ancestry of the Americans who settled the region. Understandably, to contemporary listeners it sounds like the roots of bluegrass; several of the artists (Texas Gladden, Wade Ward, and Hobart Smith) had already made recordings for Lomax in the 1930s and '40s. This may have somewhat less appeal than other volumes of the set, simply because of its specialized focus—if you don't have a taste for bluegrass-like sounds, you may find the sharp fiddles and occasionally shrill vocals to be too unhoned. If you *do* like bluegrass or old-time folk, it upholds the consistently fine standards of the *Southern Journey* series, combining education and entertaining, with diverse approaches (as in Gladden's a cappella songs) within the traditional framework. *—Richie Unterberger*

Southern Journey, Vol. 3: 61 Highway Mississippi / Apr. 22, 1997 / Rounder ✦✦✦✦✦
Twenty-four tracks from Alan Lomax's 1959 blues recordings in Mississippi, five previously unreleased. Fred McDowell (who has five songs) is the "star," you might say, of these sessions; he would go on to establish a successful performing and recording career, and is the only name recognizable to most listeners. This is an effective document, however, of the different strands of country blues and their roots. It includes not just rural Delta guitar blues, but also field hollers, spirituals, prison songs, fife-and-drum tunes, and Sid Hemphill's quills. Lomax would later note that when he revisited the area 20 years later, most of these forms had all but disappeared from view. This disc is a good reminder of how blues developed from several African-American Southern folk traditions whose influence has sometimes been underestimated. *—Richie Unterberger*

Southern Journey, Vol. 4: Brethren, We Meet Again / Apr. 22, 1997 / Rounder ✦✦✦✦✦
This volume of the *Southern Journey* series focuses on Southern White spirituals recorded in 1959, including hymns, gospel, Sacred Harp singing, and some spoken testimony. If that sounds daunting to listeners who do not engage in fervent religious observance, Protestant and otherwise, be aware that the emotional qualities of the singing outweigh any reticence one might have regarding the lyrical focus. As in all the *Southern Journey* volumes, care is taken to present a diverse, well-programmed set that offers gospel congregations, harmony singers, and guitar-accompanied ballads that sound more at home on the front porch than the pulpit. It's about as accessible to the general listener, in fact, as any such collection could be, with some cuts (like Ruby Vass' "The Old Gospel Ship" and Almeda Riddle's "I Am a Poor Wayfaring Stranger") sounding like clear antecedents of the folk revival of 1950s and '60s. *—Richie Unterberger*

Southern Journey, Vol. 5: Bad Man Ballads / Apr. 22, 1997 / Rounder ✦✦✦✦✦
Seventeen "songs of outlaws and desperadoes," recorded by Lomax with a wide variety of Southern performers, Black and White. The themes of murder, violence, and running from the law have been perennial themes in the folk music of all cultures. This collection has versions of a few fairly well-known songs in this vein ("John Henry," "Pretty Polly," "Po' Lazarus"), though most are more obscure. The artists range from Black Mississippi prisoners and a cappella mountain singers to string bands and harmonizing quartets. As is often the way in this sub-branch of folk music, the music isn't nearly as upsetting or depressing as the lyrics; indeed, it's often uplifting, if not downright celebratory. *—Richie Unterberger*

Southern Journey, Vol. 6: Sheep, Sheep Don'tcha Know the Road / Apr. 22, 1997 / Rounder ✦✦✦✦✦
"Southern music, sacred and sinful" is what this volume is subtitled, gathering 16 songs that either extol the holy (the sacred) or warn against/describe evil temptations (the sinful). This has some of the more renowned performers of the *Southern Journey* series, such as Fred McDowell, Almeda Riddle, Estil Ball, Hobart Smith, and Neil Morris, though they don't necessarily overshadow the other performers. As always, the diversity is the most attractive element of the package, encompassing Georgian Sea Island groups, fiddlers, Delta blues, and church congregations. Willie Jones' down-home "You Got Dimples in Your Jaws," the same song as John Lee Hooker's "Dimples" (one of the blues great's most famous early recordings), seems a bit uptown in the *Southern Journey* context, though its inclusion is

hardly upsetting. Estil Ball and Lacey Richardson's "Tribulations" is a close-harmony highlight that will appeal to anyone who likes the Louvin Brothers or the Delmore Brothers. —*Richie Unterberger*

Southern Journey, Vol. 7: Ozark Frontier / Sep. 9, 1997 / Rounder ✦✦✦✦
Ballads and old-time music from the Arkansas hills, recorded in 1959. Includes tunes on fiddle, guitar, and banjo, as well as a cappella selections by Ollie Gilbert and Almeda Riddle. Some of the songs have roots in the English ballad repertoire, while others are relatively topical and modern ("The Titanic"); "Buffalo Gals" (performed on banjo by Bookmiller Shannon) is a tune not solely known to folklorists. As is the case with all Alan Lomax productions, the music is of considerable ethnomusicological interest, with performances that illustrate diverse aspects of the region's tradition. For general-listening purposes, however, it's of more limited value than some of the other titles in the *Southern Journey* series, due to its stark, almost dry presentation (particularly on the unaccompanied vocal numbers) and material that is somewhat further removed from the popular consciousness than many other Lomax projects. Five of the 25 tracks are previously unreleased. —*Richie Unterberger*

Southern Journey, Vol. 8: Velvet Voices / Sep. 9, 1997 / Rounder ✦✦✦✦✦
Recorded mostly in Virginia in 1960 (two recordings were made in St. Simon's Island, Georgia), this documents African-American folk musics of the region, focusing mostly on gospel quartets, although there are also some fife-and-banjo tunes. This has to count as one of the more accessible installments in the *Southern Journey* series; the singing is up to the level of what you'd expect from most gospel acts with record deals, but the execution is less slick and calculated. The Peerless Four even use electric guitar, piano, and drums, sounding less like folkloric discoveries and more like contemporary (circa 1960, that is) R&B-influenced gospel; the Bright Light Quartet feature light, rhythmically propulsive guitar accompaniment that fleshes out the sound in an ingratiating fashion. The result is more buoyant, jubilant gospel than you're likely to find on more commercially minded spiritual recordings, from that or any other period. Six of the 20 tracks are previously unreleased. Of the unreleased items, Charles Barnett's "Run to Jesus for Refuge, Run Right Along," on which the 84-year-old creates African-like rhythms by accompanying himself on an overturned metal washtub, is a real standout. —*Richie Unterberger*

Southern Journey, Vol. 9: Harp of a Thousand Strings / Jan. 13, 1998 / Rounder ✦✦✦✦
Recorded by Alan Lomax in 1959 at the United Sacred Harp Musical Convention in Fyffe, Alabama, *Southern Journey, Vol. 9: Harp of a Thousand Strings* assembles old-time Southern "shape-note" vocal performances. Another worthy addition to the Lomax collection. —*Jason Ankeny*

Steel Rails: Classic Railroad Songs, Vol. 1 / 1997 / Rounder ✦✦✦✦
As long as railroads have existed, there have been songs sung about them, whether to praise their wonders, tell stories, or condemn them as tools of evil. *Steel Rails* and its companion volume, *Mystery Train*, set out to sample this particular vein of American song, offering up versions of "Wabash Cannonball" and "The Orange Blossom Special" (an amusing live version from the Johnson Mountain Boys) alongside twelve other songs that might not be quite as familiar as those two. A mixture of well-known artists and fairly new names is also a plus for the package—Kieran Kane, slipped in between Jimmie Rodgers and Alison Krauss, holds his own with a moody take on Hank Williams' "Ramblin' Man." Meanwhile, it's no accident that much of the music here is country, western or bluegrass—by the time rock & roll came along, fast cars were the order of the day, not cannonballing trains. —*Steven McDonald*

The Story That The Crow Told Me, Vol. 1: Early American Rural Children's, Songs Classic / Mar. 14, 2000 / Yazoo ✦✦✦
The Story That the Crow Told Me, Vol. 1 compiles a fun selection of rural folk songs for children. Included among these recordings of the 1920s and '30s are songs about cows, rabbits, birds, the barnyard, and classics like "Animals Coming In" ("...who built the ark— Noah, Noah...") and "King Kong Kitchie Kitchie Ki-Me-O" ("froggy went a-courtin' and he did ride..."). Some of the performers, such as Bo Carter, will be familiar to fans of the Yazoo label, while other performers may be known to listeners of early rurai recordings in general, such as Bradley Kincaid, Uncle Eck Dunford, and Clayton McMichen. Obviously, this album is not about presenting big names, nor is its focus excellent sound quality, since it draws from historical recordings of the 1920s and '30s. This album succeeds in gathering upbeat bluegrass and folk tunes with whimsical lyrics that can be enjoyed by kids and adults alike. —*Joslyn Layne*

Taquachito Nights: Conjunto Music from South Texas / Jun. 22, 1999 / Smithsonian/Folkways ✦✦✦
Recorded live at the 1998 Conjunto Festival of the Narcisco Martinez Cultural Arts Center in San Benito, TX. This has 19 tracks, and 71 minutes, of conjunto, almost unvaryingly played by small combos with accordion, bajo sexto, bass, and drums. It's a good representation of the conjunto you'd hear live in South Texas in the 1990s, though as is the music's wont, it's not heavy on variety. When Ruben Vela drops just a hint of funk into his "Eo Coco Rayado" cumbia, that's enough to make it stand out in this crowd. The sound is good and the liner notes include a detailed eight-page overview of the evolution of conjunto as a whole. —*Richie Unterberger*

That's Why We're Marching: WWII and the American Folk Song Movement / Feb. 20, 1996 / Smithsonian/Folkways ✦✦✦✦✦
Fifteen of the 25 tracks on this 71-minute disc are previously unreleased and the rest are not easily available. That's no reflection on their quality, but it is a clue to their limited typicality: These are songs written and recorded in the first half of the 1940s in response to world events before and during World War II; after the war, they dated fast. In fact, some of them became obsolete even before the U.S. entered the war. The earliest songs are three tracks by the Almanac Singers (who included Woody Guthrie, Pete Seeger, and others) from the spring of 1941 decrying the actions of the Franklin Roosevelt Administration that inclined the country toward the war. When the songs were recorded, they expressed a commonly held sentiment. But only a couple of months later, when Germany invaded the Soviet Union, the singers themselves repudiated their sentiments, and another six months later, when the Japanese attacked Pearl Harbor, they seemed positively treasonous. The rest of the album's songs are patriotic, pro-war expressions of the need to overcome Hitler and win the war. But even amid such mainstream sentiments, the left-wing folksingers slip in lyrics in support of unions and civil rights, more long-standing views for them. They also find space to praise U.S. ally the Soviet Union in songs that became politically unacceptable after the war. Fifty years later, of course, all of this makes for a musical, historical curiosity, and a listener's primary interest is likely to be the opportunity to hear previously unissued music by Guthrie, Seeger, Lead Belly, Josh White, Burl Ives, Sonny Terry and Brownie McGee, and a host of other excellent folksingers. —*William Ruhlmann*

Times Ain't Like They Used to Be, Vol. 1 / Apr. 22, 1997 / Yazoo ✦✦✦✦✦
These are 23 rare 78s from the 1920s and 1930s, chosen to illustrate the wide range of "early American rural music" that made its way onto disc in the early days of the recording industry. This will not get nearly as much press as Harry Smith's *Anthology of American Folk Music* box, yet it's on par with that ballyhooed re-release as an overview of the roots of American roots music, so to speak. Styles vary from country blues and fiddle hoedowns to banjo music and jug bands. The Memphis Jug Band is the only name here that might be familiar to more than the most well-versed folk historians. Highlights include J.P. Nestor and Norman Edmonds' "Train on the Island," a frenetic string band gallop; the Four Wanderers' eerie gospel tune, "The Fault's in Me"; and Ken Maynard's "Fannie Moore," a direct predecessor of country music in its vocal phrasing. —*Richie Unterberger*

★ **Troubadours of British Folk, Vol. 1: Unearthing the Tradition** / Nov. 21, 1995 / Rhino ✦✦✦✦✦
Rhino's *Troubadours of British Folk* series, encompassing three volumes, four decades, 49 songs, and almost as many performers, is a model genre retrospective. For those who want a representative collection of the style's highlights, it covers virtually all of the major performers and innovators of British folk, represented by their best-known (and usually best) songs. For those who want an introduction/guide to the form, it's equally useful, serving as an excellent foundation to build upon if you're motivated to seek out more albums by these performers after an initial taste. *Volume One* covers the mid-'50s to the early '70s, encompassing skiffle (Lonnie Donegan), elder statespersons (Ewan MacColl), virtuoso guitarists (Davy Graham, Bert Jansch, Martin Carthy), traditional singers (Jean Redpath, Shirley & Dolly Collins), singer-songwriters (Donovan), and early efforts by the major players of British folk-rock (Fairport Convention, Pentangle, The Incredible String Band, Steeleye Span). Then there are names which are virtually unknown these days in the States, like the Young Tradition, Anne Briggs, and Wizz Jones. Along with some expected classics (Fairport's "Fotheringay," Donegan's "Rock Island Line," Jansch's "Needle of Death") are some rare coveted treasures, like MacColl's "Dirty Old Town" (eventually covered by The Pogues) and Graham's "Angi" (popularized by Simon & Garfunkel). The liner notes, with quotes from many of the artists and extensive commentary, are great, as they are for each volume of the series. —*Richie Unterberger*

★ **Troubadours of British Folk, Vol. 2: Folk into Rock** / Nov. 21, 1995 / Rhino ✦✦✦✦✦
All of the cuts on this volume hail from what is commonly considered the golden age of British folk-rock, 1969-75. Virtually all of the major players, including Fairport Convention, Nick Drake, Roy Harper, Ralph McTell, Steeleye Span, and Richard Thompson, are represented by some of their most famous tracks. Not as renowned, but of near-equal importance, are the contributions by Shirley Collins, Fotheringay, Amazing Blondel, Lindisfarne, Mr. Fox (by far the most obscure name on the set), and the surprise inclusion of Traffic, represented by "John Barleycorn." It may be that big British folk-rock fans are already familiar with most or all of this. But you can't fault the content: this is the cream of the crop of a vital strain of both folk and rock, though it wasn't nearly as popular in the States as the U.K. —*Richie Unterberger*

★ **Troubadours of British Folk, Vol. 3: an Evolving Tradition** / Nov. 21, 1995 / Rhino ✦✦✦✦✦
The final volume of the series covers the mid-'70s to the mid-'90s, emphasizing traditional acts who pepped things up with a bit of electricity and eclecticism (Silly Wizard, Mouth Music), acoustic guitarists (Nic Jones, Dick Gaughan, Martin Simpson), "rogue" folkies who merged traditional sounds with influences from modern rock, world music, and punk (Billy Bragg, Oyster Band), and esteemed veteran singers (Richard Thompson, June Tabor, Maddy Prior). If this collection doesn't seem as essential to many listeners as the first two volumes, that may be because these artists (mostly still in their primes at the time of this reissue) are still forging their place in history. But few would deny that they are certainly some of the most significant British folk performers of recent times. Those wishing to catch up on the evolution of British roots music in the '80s and '90s will find this a handy primer, especially as that scene is for the most part little known in the U.S. —*Richie Unterberger*

● **Troubadours of the Folk Era, Vol. 1** / Apr. 21, 1992 / Rhino ✦✦✦✦✦

★ **Troubadours of the Folk Era, Vol. 2** / Apr. 21, 1992 / Rhino ✦✦✦✦✦
Here are some of the performers and their signature songs on which the '60s folk revival were based. Pete Seeger's rendition of "Turn, Turn, Turn" and Tim Hardin's "Reason to Believe" remind the listener that contemporary performances have a vital history. Other strong cuts are "There but for Fortune;" Phil Ochs, "Who Knows Where the Time Goes," by Judy Collins. —*Richard Meyer*

★ **Troubadours of the Folk Era, Vol. 3: The Groups** / Apr. 21, 1992 / Rhino ✦✦✦✦✦
These group performances represent some of the more commercial releases of the folk revival. Beginning with Leadbelly's "Goodnight Irene" performed by The Weavers and the hit "Tom Dooley" by The Kingston Trio continuing through to recordings by Jim Kweskin's Jug Band, this collection demonstrates how more "authentic" and "traditional" folk songs were sanitized and popularized for mass consumption. It's an interesting reminder of how essentially neutral material can take on political weight due to the actions of the performers themselves, as in the case of The Weavers. —*Richard Meyer*

Vanguard Collector's Edition / Aug. 19, 1997 / Vanguard ✦✦✦✦
This four-CD set isn't quite as comprehensive as it might have been. All of the major bases are covered, from Paul Robeson, the Weavers, and Count Basie to Alison Brown and John McEuen, and even Circus Maximus ("Oops—I Can Dance") is here, with cuts by the Frost ("Sweet Lady Love") and the Third Power ("Gettin' Together"). But there's no Sandy Bull, and there are other holes—where is Bruce Langhorne? On the other hand, the label has included tracks off of its recent Newport Folk Festival archival releases, and six previously unissued cuts by Leon Bibb, Buffy Sainte-Marie, the Greenbriar Boys, and the Siegel-Schwall Band. The booklet gives a good overview of the company's history, with detailed histories of each artist present, and the sound is generally extremely high quality. *—Bruce Eder*

What's That I Hear?: The Songs of Phil Ochs / Mar. 10, 1998 / Sliced Bread ✦✦✦✦✦
Twenty-eight songs by Phil Ochs, covered by several generations of musicians, from Tom Paxton ("Draft Dodger Rag"), Peter Yarrow ("There But for Fortune"), Dave Van Ronk ("Outside of a Small Circle of Friends"), Eric Andersen ("When I'm Gone"), and Iain Matthews ("Flower Lady") to the Roches ("The Bells," which offers the best singing here), Agnelli-Rave and the Charmers ("Chords of Fame"), and Sid Griffin & Billy Bragg ("Sailors and Soldiers"). The quality of the performances is uniformly first-rate, and it's astonishing to discover the full range of admirers that Ochs' songs attract, as well as the sheer selection of songs, some of which Ochs never got to record officially—few key bases are left untouched in the two-hour-plus collection, although it would have been nice if someone had covered released obscurities such as "Basket in the Pool." The notes are very thorough, personal, and affecting. *—Bruce Eder*

Celtic

There is in me (faint memory of a smile)
The soul of a shivery old cat—
Let the wood-grey body be wounded, beaten,
Whatever be at it, it will live.

These words, written in the 14th century by the Welsh bard Dafydd ap Gwylim, express the unquashable endurance of the Celtic cultures of Europe. Through centuries of oppression, of systematic attempts by foreign occupiers to destroy Celtic cultural identity, their expressive arts have continued to develop and to spawn new and emergent forms. It is a supreme and fitting irony that we consider English folk music under the rubric of "Celtic and British Isles" music.

The term "Celtic" in its most rigid sense refers to languages: to Irish, Manx, and Scots Gaelic, and to Welsh, Cornish, and Breton Brythonic. However, what we think of as Celtic music is performed by both Celtic speakers and speakers of English and French, in the Celtic homelands in the British Isles, Ireland, Brittany and the diaspora that spans the globe from Australia to America. It is defined here as music that has sprung from the ancient, ever-developing musical tradition of the Celtic homelands.

There are various levels of "professionalism" and "traditionality" among performers of this music. The tradition continues of amateur musicians and singers who watch and listen to their elders, gradually learning to express themselves within the medium of traditional musical performance. On the other hand, a renewed interest in traditional music since the '60s has created an international demand for newer groups influenced by classical, folk, jazz, and pop music. The result is a musical system with many genres and styles, ranging from unaccompanied singing or solo playing to highly structured arrangements of folk ensembles and to rock 'n' roll bands belting out jigs and reels with a vicious backbeat.

The standard of musicianship in this music is extraordinarily high. This is due partly to the important role of music in the cultural and national identities of the countries and ethnic groups in question, partly to vigorous systems of musical competition leading to national championships for each instrument. The high standard of performance, combined with the multifarious genres and styles considered in this section, lead to a problem of sorts: there are a huge number of good records to buy and limited space for us to guide you to them. This section concentrates somewhat on the newer, revival acts, which have a broader appeal than strictly traditional approaches. Many of these groups list their traditional sources in the notes to their albums, giving the interested listener leads for further listening.

This, then, is but a tip of the old cat's tail, a vantage point from which to begin your own explorations of the rich realms of Celtic and English folk music. *—Steve Winick*

Artist Reviews

The Albion Dance Band

f. 1972

Group / British Folk-Rock, British Folk, Folk-Rock

Originally used as a name to credit the musicians hired to accompany Shirley Collins in 1971, The Albion Band later became a group in their own right. Bass player Ashley Hutchings, who had previously founded and left both Fairport Convention and Steeleye Span, is the driving force behind this group. The members use acoustic and electric instruments to create a folk-rock sound something like Fairport Convention's, but usually more typically English in character. They have existed as the Albion Band, the Albion Country Band, and the Albion Dance Band. *—Steve Winick*

Battle of the Field / 1976 / BGO ✦✦✦✦✦

Rise Up Like the Sun / 1978 / Hannibal ✦✦✦

Less of the Morris dancing, a little less of the ancient instruments approach (though Phil Pickett is certainly not wasted on this album) and a deal more of the updated rock approach to things. This excellent reissue is well worth adding to a folk-rock collection, mind you, with selections that range from the gruffly rough ("Poor Old Horse") to the thoughtful ("Gresford Disaster") and sometimes all the way to the downright jolly—keeping in mind that outfits such as the Albion Band paved the way for the more worldly malarkey of bands such as 3 Mustaphas 3, Cordelia's Dad and Boiled in Lead. *—Steven McDonald*

● **Songs from the Shows** / 1990 / Road Goes on Forever ✦✦✦✦✦

The Acoustic Years 1993-1997 / 1997 / HTD ✦✦✦

Significant changes occurred leading up to the Albion Band's mid-'90s resurgence. Tracks from their studio albums from this period are revisited here. The addition of Chris While and Julie Matthews, who both contribute immeasurably in the songwriting and vocal departments, yields a vastly different sound—acoustic, contemporary folk—as opposed to the British folk-rock sound which has become synonymous with Albion and their various manifestations. The absence of a drummer allows Ashley Hutching's acoustic bass to be noticed and appreciated as never before, and the three fiddlers utilized during this period create a freshness and individuality with each respective recording: Ashley Reed on *Acousticity* (1993), Chris Leslie on *Demi Paradise* (1996), and Joe Broughton, who played on the previously unreleased tracks from the 1997 lineup. Acoustic guitarist and vocalist Simon Nicol has become an Albion staple, having performed with them regularly since the mid-'70s. He appears with them on all but the most recent Broughton lineup of 1997. *—Dave Sleger*

Demi Paradise / Nov. 23, 1999 / Castle Music America ✦✦✦

Altan

f. 1983

Group / Celtic New Age, Traditional Celtic, Celtic Fusion

With its northern Ireland-style twin fiddling and accordion melodies accented by acoustic guitar and bouzouki, Altan has grown into one of the top traditional bands in Ireland. *The Boston Globe* called them, "one of the hottest groups in the Celtic realm these days," while, *The Wall Street Journal* referred to them as "the preeminent Irish band in the world today." *The New York Times* praised them for their "clarity and coordination of its textures." The inspiration for Altan was sparked when Donegal-born fiddler and vocalist Mairead Ni Mhaonaigh met Belfast-born flute player Frankie Kennedy. Ni Mhaonaigh had learned the traditional style of fiddling from her father, Francie, who had learned it from his mother, Roise. Influential Irish fiddler Dinny McLaughlin, who frequented her childhood home, added to her knowledge of the instrument. Kennedy, who studied flute as a youngster, was extremely interested in Irish music and made several trips to Ireland during school vacations. Meeting during an informal jam sessions, Ni Mhaonaigh and Kennedy began to play together at every opportunity. Although they both took jobs as trainee teachers at St. Patrick's College in Dublin, music remained their shared passion. In 1979, the two musicians made their recording debut as accompanists for Gaelic singer Albert Fry on his self-titled debut album. Two years later, Ni Mhaonaigh and Kennedy graduated from college and were married. Together with bouzouki player Donal O'Hanlan and Mairead's brother, Gearoid O'Maoinaigh, who played guitar, the Ni Maoinaigh and Kennedy formed a band, Ragaime. Although they recorded for RTE, the group disbanded by the time that Gael-Linn released Ni Maoinaigh and Kennedy's debut album, *Ceol Adualigh* in December 1983. One track on the album, "An Clar Bog Dell," featured Enya, then known as Eithne Ni Bhraonain, on Prophet Five synthesizer. In 1987, Ni Mhaoinaigh and Kennedy recorded their second album as a duo, *Altan,* named after a lake in northwest Donegal. Produced by Donal Lunny, the album featured accompaniment by Ciaron Curran on bouzouki, Mark Kelly on guitar, and Mairead's sister, Anna Ni Mhaoinaigh, then a member of the all-woman group, Macella. Shortly after the completion of the album, the musicians agreed to continuing working together. During the summer of 1988, Altan began work on their first album as a band, which now included Paul O'Shaugnessy on twin fiddle. Produced by Phil Cunningham and released in 1989, the album, *Horse With A Heart,* featured a more dynamic sound than its predecessors. As the band's touring schedule expanded, O'Shaughnessy and Kelly were forced, by their day jobs, to restrict their activity with Altan to recording and performances close to home. During the band's U.S. tours, their places were taken by Daithi Sproule on guitar and Ciaran Tourish on fiddle. Altan reached their top-form with their 1990 album, *Red Crow,* which recieved a NAIRD award as "best Celtic traditional album." Their next album, *Harvest Storm,* released in 1992, received the award as well. All news was not good for the band, however. In 1991, Kennedy was diagnosed with cancer. Although he was hospitalized the following year, he recovered sufficiently to rejoin the band's tour. On September 19, 1994, he succumbed to his illness and passed away. Altan has continued to bring their music to the international stage. Accordion player Dermot Byrne, who had played on *Red Crow* and on Altan's 1993 album, *Island Angel,* joined the group formally in 1994. 1996's *Blackwater* and 1997's *Runaway Sunday* were released on the Virgin label before the group jumped to Narada for 2000's *Another Sky.* *—Craig Harris*

Ceol Aduaidh / 1983 / Green Linnet ✦✦✦

Like Altan, this album is by Mairead Ni Mhaonaigh (fiddle and vocals) and Frankie Kennedy (flute). It also includes Ciaran Curran, still an Altan member, on cittern. Synthesizers are added by Eithne Ni Bhraonain, who would later become a pop sensation as Enya. Like all recordings by these spectacular musicians, this one is an excellent piece of work. *—Steve Winick*

Altan / 1987 / Green Linnet ✦✦✦

This album is technically credited to Mairead Ni Mhaonaigh and Frankie Kennedy, but it's clearly the first step in Altan's development into a tight band. It's full of beautiful, fiery music, a little less dense and powerful than the later recordings. *—Steve Winick*

Horse With a Heart / 1989 / Green Linnet ♦♦♦
This album was evidence that Altan would become the best Irish traditional band in the world. *—Steve Winick*

The Red Crow / 1990 / Green Linnet ♦♦♦

Harvest Storm / 1992 / Green Linnet ♦♦♦♦♦
Harvest Storm represents one of the group's best—a true necessity. *—Steve Winick*

☆ **Island Angel** / Jul. 1993 / Green Linnet ♦♦♦♦♦
Another magnificent performance, it's a worthy successor to *Harvest Storm*. *—Steve Winick*

● **The First Ten Years: 1986-1995** / 1995 / Green Linnet ♦♦♦♦♦

Blackwater / 1996 / Virgin ♦♦♦

Runaway Sunday / 1997 / Virgin ♦♦♦

The Best of Altan / Jan. 21, 1997 / Green Linnet ♦♦♦♦♦
If you don't count The Chieftains, Altan is probably the most popular traditional Irish group in the world right now. And they continue to find favor among hardcore folkies where The Chieftains don't, since they resist the temptation to record albums with the likes of Roger Daltrey and Van Morrison. The band originally formed around the husband-and-wife nucleus of flutist Frankie Kennedy and fiddler/singer Mairead Ni Mhaonaigh, who recorded their first duo album in 1983. Other members accreted to the group over time, until it gradually hardened into the five-piece ensemble that is responsible for most of the music on this timely retrospective, which draws on the five Altan discs that have appeared on the Green Linnet label. All have been distinguished by exceptional energy and musicianship, and while some listeners will disagree with one or two programming choices, the selections here are all excellent; Ni Mhaonaigh's sweet singing is always a special highlight. Best of all, the first pressings include a bonus disc of live recordings—a poignant addendum, given the tragic death of Frankie Kennedy from cancer in 1996. Very highly recommended. *—Rick Anderson*

Another Sky / Feb. 29, 2000 / Narada ♦♦♦♦

Once Again (1987-1993) / Nov. 28, 2000 / Recall ♦♦♦

Dan Ar Bras

Vocals, Guitar / Celtic Folk, Contemporary Celtic
One of the most melodic guitarists in Celtic music, Dan Ar Braz has recorded as a soloist and with innovative Celtic harp, bagpipe and flute player Alan Stivell. A pioneer of electric folk in the early 1970s, Ar Braz has continued to explore the textural possibilities of electric and acoustic guitar.

Ar Braz hooked up with Stivell in 1967, shortly after moving to Brittany, a region in western France. He remained an essential element of Stivell's sound for more than a decade and made important contributions to nine of Stivell's albums, including the influential *Renaissance of the Celtic Harp* in 1972, and the reunion album *Again* in 1994. After Stivell broke up the band in 1976, Ar Braz spent six months as a member of Fairport Convention, leaving before recording with the group. Although he assembled his own tradition-rooted band, they were equally skilled at electric music and recorded a rock version of Lennon and McCartney's "Rain." Ar Braz switched to a Celtic style of playing acoustic guitar in the mid-1980s and recorded a heavily atmospheric album, *Music for Silences to Come*, in 1985. In the 1990s, Ar Braz assembled a 50-piece band, L'Heritage Des Celtes. A self-titled studio album was released in 1994 with a live recording, *En Concert*, following a year later.

Ar Braz continues to be involved with Fairport Convention, recording in Dave Pegg's Wormwood studios in London and performing regularly at Fairport's annual festival in Cropedy. *—Craig Harris*

● **Allez Dire a La Ville** / 1978 / Hexagone ♦♦♦♦♦
A well-crafted pop album with Celtic leanings, this foregrounds Ar Braz's electric guitar and voice, as well as several songs written by poet Xavier Grall. *—Steve Winick*

Finisterres / Jan. 12, 1999 / Sony International ♦♦♦
Perhaps Brittany's most well-known Celtic artist, guitarist Dan Ar Braz completes the trilogy of his ambitious mid-'90s undertakings. *Finisterres* is another gathering of the most talented Celtic musicians performing today: Donal Lunny, John McSherry, Sharon Shannon, Noel Bridgeman, and Carlos Nunez, with vocals from Karen Matheson (Capercaillie) and Elaine Morgan (Rose Among Thorns). This recording brings together the traditional music of Ireland and Brittany in a contemporary framework in which no instrument is overlooked; harp, pipes, accordion, fiddle, and guitar are all given their due. The two additional Ar Braz albums on Columbia France, *Heritage des Celtes* and *En Concert*, run along similar lines. *—Dave Sleger*

Arcady

Group / Irish Folk
The traditional music of Ireland combined with virtuosic musicianship and warm vocal harmonies have made Arcady one of the most respected traditional bands in Ireland. According to *Pulse* magazine, Arcady "is poised to emerge as the strongest act in the current wave of Irish folk revivalism. *Dirty Linen* described Arcady as "a band with its own vital identity ensured of a place among the first rank of Irish traditional groups." Arcady was formed by bodhran, bones and percussion player Johnny "Ringo" McDonagh shortly after leaving De Danaan in 1989. Initially an eight piece group, Arcady has gone through numerous personnel changes. Among its most illustrious alumni are Sharon Shannon, Frances Black, Sean Keane and McDonagh's De Danaan bandmate, Jackie Daly. The group made its debut in a big way, performing at Ireland's largest hall, Point Depot, in a show that was filmed for a television show, *The Sessions*. After recording a still un-released album, Arcady released their debut album, *After The Ball*, in 1991. Recorded with a six piece band, the album took a pan-Celtic approach with songs from Ireland, Scotland, Wales, Canada, Brittany and the United States. Their second album, *Many Happy Returns*, was released four years later. The album, which featured the lead vocals of Niamh (pronounced: Neeve) Parsons, who replaced Frances Black, and the accordion playing of County Clare native of Colin Keane, who replaced Jackie Daly, stuck closer to home and emphasized songs that would not sound out of place in an Irish pub. The present line-up of Arcady features flute, whistle and guitar player and vocalist Nicolas Quemenar from Brittany, keyboardist Patsy Broderick and fiddler Brendan Larrissey, along with McDonagh, Parsons and Keane. *—Craig Harris*

● **After the Ball** / 1991 / Shanachie ♦♦♦♦♦
This features traditional Irish tunes, sentimental ditties, and one French song from Brittany. *—Steve Winick*

Ar Log

Group / Traditional Celtic, Contemporary Celtic
Ar Log formed in 1976, more or less at the drop of a hat, to represent Wales at a Celtic Music festival after the original Welsh entry withdrew at the eleventh hour. Less a band than an accident, they referred to themselves as the band-for-hire, and so came by their Welsh name Ar Log (literally, on hire). The band caught the wave of celtic revivalism, while adding their own distinctively Welsh sound to the scene, most notably through their adoption of the Welsh triple harp. The band has been through innumerable membership changes since Dvid Burns (mandolin, guitar, bodhran, vocals), Iolo Jones (fiddle, recorder), Dafydd Roberts (triple harp, flute), and Gwyndaf Roberts (knee harp, Clarsach) came together. Since the 1980s, the band (greatly expanded) has gone into semi-retirement, preferring to confine its touring activities to Wales, but continues to record albums. *—Leon Jackson*

Ar Log / 1978 / Dingles ♦♦♦
This debut is full of great singing and playing, if still a little rough. *—Steve Winick*

● **Ar Log II** / 1981 / Dingles ♦♦♦♦♦
Smooth vocal harmonies and powerful virtuoso playing make this their best. *—Steve Winick*

Ar Log III / 1982 / Dingles ♦♦♦
Very similar in style, presenation and quality to *Ar Log II*, it featured gentle electric bass accompaniment. *—Steve Winick*

Meillionen / 1982 / Dingles ♦♦♦
This all-instrumental release of tunes for dancing features Ar Log's classically-tinged arrangements, as well as new sounds like accordion and keyboards. Ar Log did not consider *Meillionen* a regular Ar Log album, but rather a special project. *—Steve Winick*

Pedawar / 1985 / Ar Log ♦♦♦
Pedwar is Welsh for four; this fourth Ar Log release (not counting the *Meillionen* project) is very much like its predecessors, highly orchestrated but still sprightly. *—Steve Winick*

Arlog V / 1988 / Sain ♦♦♦

Frankie Armstrong

b. Jan. 13, 1941, Workington, Cumbria (UK)
Vocals / British Folk
Whether singing a cappella or with minimal accompaniment, Frankie Armstrong uses her powerful soprano vocals to breathe new life into centuries-old British balladry. Best known for her rendition of Peggy Seeger's feminist anthem, "I'm Gonna Be an Engineer," Armstrong has been an influential presence in England since 1962.

A longtime member of the late Ewan MacColl's Critic's Group, Armstrong has been a frequent performer at folk festivals throughout Great Britain and the United States.

While Armstrong's early albums focused on traditional ballads, she's branched out in recent years. In 1989, she collaborated with Greenwich Village-based folk singer Dave Van Ronk for an duo album, *Let No One Deceive You*, featuring songs by Bertolt Brecht. Armstrong's most prolific year came in 1997. In addition to reissuing a live concert recording, *Ways of Seeing*, she released an album of child ballads, *Till the Grass O'ergrown the Corn*, and a solo album, *The Fair Moon Rejoices*, which includes original songs, Leon Rosselson compositions and a series of William Blake poems set to the saxophone and bagpipe playing of Peter Stacey. *—Craig Harris*

Birds in the Bush / 1966 / Topic ♦♦♦♦♦

Out of Love, Hope and Suffering / 1974 / Bay ♦♦♦
Serious, humorous, and bawdy songs and ballads are featured. *—Steve Winick*

● **And the Music Plays So Grand** / 1981 / Briar ♦♦♦♦♦
A live performance of traditional and contemporary songs, held in Sweden in 1978, is captured on this wonderful album. *—Steve Winick*

Margaret Barry

Vocals, Banjo / Traditional Irish Folk, Traditional Celtic, Folksongs
The traditional folk songs and ballads of Ireland were preserved by the 1950s recordings of Margaret Barry. Accompanying her powerful, but untrained, vocals with rustic banjo picking, Barry was a musical influence for such trad-rock groups as Fairport Convention, Pentangle and Steeleye Span. Her recording of "I Sang Through The Fair," inspired numerous interpretations and transformed the song into a classic of Celtic music. Starting her career as a street busker in Dublin, Barry attracted international attention when she was recorded in 1953 by folklorist Alan Lomax. She subsequently moved to London where she worked for Lomax as a housekeeper and cook. For many years, Barry was accompanied by Michael Gorman, a folk musicians she had met while performing on a BBC television program of traditional music hosted by Lomax in 1953. In addition to her repertoire of Irish songs, Barry performed many English art songs and ballads. *—Craig Harris*

● **Her Mantle So Green** / 1994 / Topic ♦♦♦♦♦
Cork streetsinger Barry and Sligo fiddler Gorman were among the aristocracy of the 1950s London-Irish music scene. Gorman was superb, but Barry was the queen of the come-all-ye's, whether in "The Wild Colonial Boy" or the title-song, or comic songs like "The Bicycle Race."

This CD has their classic Topic recordings, including an EP with Seamus Ennis, and it's one degree more than essential. *—John Storm Roberts, Original Music*

I Sang Through the Fairs / Sep. 15, 1998 / Rounder ♦♦♦

Folk Songs (Ireland) / Smithsonian/Folkways ♦♦♦♦♦
Barry sang some of her best material on this album. *—Steve Winick*

The Battlefield Band

f. 1970
Group / Scottish Folk, Folk Revival
The Glasgow-based Battlefield Band is one of Scotland's foremost folk-revival bands. Their older albums are quite traditional in style and content, but their later ones are tinged with pop. Along the way, they were among the first bands to incorporate the sounds of electric keyboards and the great Highland bagpipe into a folk-pop setting. *—Steve Winick*

Battlefield Band: Scottish Folk / 1976 / Arfolk ♦♦♦
Battlefield Band's first recording features Alan Reid, Brian McNeill and Ricky Starr. They sing and play pretty arrangements of tunes and songs from the Scottish tradition. *—Steve Winick*

Battlefield Band 2 / 1977 / Arfolk ♦♦♦
This third album had the same year and lineup as their second, and a very similar title. However, it features different material and was released on a different label. It also features three guests who add three different types of bagpipes to Battlefield's sound. Buy it if you can find it. *—Steve Winick*

At the Front / 1978 / Topic ♦♦♦♦♦
A brilliant older album, it features the singing of Jamie McMenamy (later of Kornog) and Pat Kilbride. *—Steve Winick*

Home Is Where the Van Is / 1980 / Temple Music ♦♦♦♦♦
Their first U.S. release, this excellent album introduces Ged Foley, later of The House Band. It is also the first to feature Brian McNeill's excellent songwriting, and achieves a very nice balance between their traditional roots and their modern sensibilities. *—Steve Winick*

The Story So Far / 1982 / Temple ♦♦♦
A compilation of some of their older material, it includes rare tracks. *—Steve Winick*

There's a Buzz / 1982 / Temple Music ♦♦♦
The same line-up as *Home Is Where the Van Is* gives a less compelling performance. *—Steve Winick*

Anthem for the Common Man / 1984 / Temple Music ♦♦♦
Alistair Russell replaces Foley, Dougie Pincock replaces MacGillivray. They begin to experiment more with electronics and with new sounds and rhythms. *—Steve Winick*

On the Rise / 1986 / Temple Music ♦♦
There's still more experimentation on this eighth collection of new material; this one even features a cover of "Bad Moon Rising." *—Steve Winick*

☆ **After Hours** / 1987 / Temple Music ♦♦♦♦♦
This compilation of material from Battlefield's Temple Records releases is probably the place to start listening. *—Steve Winick*

Celtic Hotel / 1987 / Temple Music ♦♦♦
The last and best trip to the studio for the band's longest-lived lineup, this album is one of their best. It features almost exclusively original material based on Scottish traditions. *—Steve Winick*

Home Ground Live / 1989 / Temple Music ♦♦♦
Captured live in the highlands, the band perform old favorites and new. *—Steve Winick*

New Spring / 1991 / Temple Music ♦♦♦

Quiet Days / 1992 / Temple Music ♦♦♦

★ **Opening Moves** / 1993 / Topic ♦♦♦♦♦
This CD combines most of the material from *At the Front* with extra tracks taken from *Battlefield Band* and *Stand Easy*. It's the essential compilation of Battlefield's Topic period. *—Steve Winick*

Rain, Hail or Shine / Apr. 7, 1998 / Temple ♦♦♦♦♦

Leaving Friday Harbor / Sep. 28, 1999 / Temple ♦♦♦

Derek Bell

b. 1935, Belfast, Northern Ireland
Oboe, Harp, Piano / Traditional Celtic, Contemporary Celtic, Irish Folk, Classical
Although best known as the harpist with the Chieftains, Derek Bell's career includes a raft of musical achievements and credits extending into the worlds of both classical and folk music—and he didn't begin playing the harp until he was in his 30s. A major figure in music education as well as music performance, Bell is perhaps the leading Irish harpist in the world, and has done more to elevate the instrument to a level of international respectability before a wider audience than any other musician today. Bell took up the harp in his early 30s, and joined the Chieftains in 1972; his presence on harp, oboe, and dulcimer greatly extended the range of the group, which had acquired a large following in England and, during the mid-'70s, became an international phenomenon. His interest in Irish folk music has led to his writing numerous arrangements of traditional Irish folksongs for different size ensembles. He has also composed many classical works, and arranged others derived from various ethnic sources, including Hungarian and Peruvian dances; the Tocatta Burlesca (a recording of which, with Bell playing eight instruments, has been made), two symphonies, and suite entitled *The Violet Flame*, many works for solo harp and orchestra. Bell's work with the Irish harp, in repertory ranging across many centuries, has helped elevate it from near-extinction to one of the most beloved of folk instruments. *—Bruce Eder*

Musical Instruments of England and the Celtic Countries

BAGPIPES—Bagpipes are found all over the world. In its simplest form, a bagpipe consists of an air reservoir (or bag), a chanter (a pipe fitted with a double reed), and an inflation device for the bag. It may also be fitted with one or more drones (pipes that sound a single continuous note). Scottish Highland pipes, called "warpipes" in Ireland, have a mouth pipe to inflate the bag, three drones, and a nine-note fingered chanter. In the lowlands of Scotland and the north of England, mellow-toned, bellows-blown smallpipes are the norm. In Ireland, the Uillean pipe, the world's most complex bagpipe, reigns supreme. It consists of a bellows, a bag, a two-octave chanter, three drones, and three regulators (keyed drones controlled by the player's wrist) that can play short rhythmic bursts of any of a number of chords as accompaniment to the chanter.

FREE REEDS—Named after their metal reeds, which are free to vibrate on three sides, these instruments include the harmonica and various squeezeboxes. The harmonica (or "moothie" in Scotland) is popular all over Britain and Ireland, owing to its affordability and small size. The melodeon (or diatonic accordion) is a squeezebox with one, two, or three rows of buttons tuned to different diatonic scales. The accordion can be the familiar piano-keyed instrument or a melodeon whose rows are tuned a half-step apart, creating a chromatic instrument. In general, chromatic-button accordions are the most popular in Ireland, melodeons are the most popular in England, and piano accordions are the most popular in Scotland, but all forms are played in all countries. The concertina is a squeezebox of hexagonal cross-section, whose buttons are spread over both ends.

WOODWINDS—The whistle is a metal tube with either a wooden fipple or a plastic mouthpiece, with fingerholes like a recorder. The flute, either wooden or metal, was popular originally in Ireland but is beginning to find popularity elsewhere as well. The bombarde, a high, piercing oboe, is one of the national instruments of Brittany.

STRINGS—The fiddle, or violin, is popular everywhere in Europe. The harp is a very important instrument, historically speaking, to the Celtic countries; it is still the national symbol of Ireland. Celtic harps are smaller and have fewer strings than the familiar concert harp, and have no pedals. Fretted, plucked, and strummed strings like guitars, banjos, and mandolins have become important to the folk revival, both as accompaniment to singing and as solo instruments. The bouzouki, a Greek instrument imported to Irish music, and the cittern, a revived Renaissance instrument, as well as mandolas and mandocellos, also grace the music frequently.

PERCUSSION—Anything handy may be knocked together as percussion, but the most common are spoons and bones, which can become amazingly precise, rhythmically speaking, in the right person's hands. In Ireland, the bodhran, a goatskin on a wooden frame, is the drum of choice, and this has spread all over the Celtic lands. In Scotland, side drums and snare drums are used, mostly in military music. *—Steve Winick*

Derek Bell's Musical Ireland / 1987 / Shanachie ♦♦♦♦♦
These 13 tracks represent personal and cultural touchstones for Derek Bell. Some songs ("She Moved Through the Fair," "The Boys of Bluehill," "Hillsborough Castle," and "The Greencastle Hornpipe") present Bell as a solo harpist (and occasionally on oboe, English horn, or gong), some include backing by the New Irish Chamber Orchestra, and others feature Chieftains alumni Sean Potts on tin whistle and Peadar Mercier playing bodhran and bones. All the songs are in their most basic forms, with few of the embellishments that one would get from, say, a Chieftains record, and the entire record has a beguiling gentle lyricism that is quite poignant ("Down by the Sally Gardens" and "Eibhlín a R'in," in particular). "The Gartan Mother's Lullaby" alone is worth the price of the disc, and anyone seeking an instrumental version of "She Moved Through the Fair"—which has been done by the likes of Davey Graham, Jimmy Page (ripping off Graham's arrangement note for note under the title "White Summer"), and Marianne Faithfull—couldn't do better than Bell's exquisitely lilting harp version. *—Bruce Eder*

● **Carolan's Favorite** / 1988 / Shanachie ♦♦♦♦♦
Probably Bell's best and most mystical album, a subdued and varied account of Turlough Carolan's music. *—Bruce Eder*

Ancient Music for the Irish Harp / 1992 / Claddagh ♦♦

Carolan's Receipt: The Music of Carolan, Vol. 1 / 1992 / Shanachie ♦♦♦
Irish harpist Derek Bell's solo album of compositions by the great bard Turlough O'Carolan is one of the more important documents of traditional Celtic music. Now that the venerable Claddagh label has been taken under Atlantic's wing, there's been a steady stream of reissues, none more welcome than this one. Many of these tunes will be familiar to lovers of Irish music; "Sheebeg and Shemore," "Carolan's Receipt," and "Planxty George Brabazon" are all standards. Interestingly, Bell plays a steel-string harp on most of the tracks—though gut-string harps are more commonly used in Celtic music today, this particular instrument was specifically constructed to resemble the kind used by Carolan himself. On several tracks Bell is accompanied by other members of the Chieftains. *—Rick Anderson*

The Mystic Harp / 1996 / Clarity Sound & Light ♦♦♦♦
Famed Celtic harpist Derek Bell (of the Chieftains) is featured on 19 lovely Celtic-style com-

positions by J. Donald Walters, with most melodies originally from his work *A Celtic Suite.* Walters' dreamy synthesizer arrangements set off Bell's harp with lush synthesizer strings played by David Miller. Bell also plays concert harp, oboe, oboe d'amore, and English horn—all of which add stately nobility and an Irish sense of longing to the pieces. Seagulls and surf on "Maura's Lament" add an atmospheric touch, while snare drums beat home "Parade." One of the most magical tracks is "Ancient Memories," a breathtaking track whose feet hardly touch the ground. "Deirdre's Sorrows" is one of the few fast-paced pieces; the liner notes reveal a woman's distraught musings before she stabs herself and falls on her lover's grave (ah, the Irish!). Walters sings the final song, "Emerald Isle," with a human warmth and innocence. Also featured on "New Dawn" is violinist Alasdair Fraser. The duet between Bell and Fraser is like new sweethearts holding hands for the first time. *The Mystic Harp* radiates the delicate and loving side of the Celtic tradition. *—Carol Wright*

Mystic Harp, Vol. 2 / Mar. 9, 1999 / Clarity Sound & Light ♦♦♦

Peter Bellamy

b. Sep. 8, 1944, Bournemouth, Dorset, England, **d.** Sep. 24, 1991
Vocals / Folk Revival, British Folk
Peter Bellamy was one of the English folk revival's greatest voices. In the early days of 1965 he moved to London, where he met up with Royston Wood and Heather Wood, and the three got a regular gig at a club whose name they would eventually adopt—The Young Tradition. In flamboyant costumes, with witty presentation, and with the startling power of Bellamy's voice backed by his companions, they recorded a pair of albums, gained a reputation for excellence, and were still unable to make a living as performers. So, in 1969, they broke up. As Bellamy would later point out, they became important and influential, even legendary, after they had ceased to exist. In 1970 the idea first struck Bellamy to set the poems of Kipling to music. This fascination with Kipling continued until Bellamy's death, resulting in no fewer than five albums of Kipling songs. Also in the '70s, Bellamy composed *The Transports,* a ballad opera in the mold of Ewan MacColl's work. Often he expressed regret that interest in traditional song was simply on the wane, not only with audiences, but with performers as well. He always acknowledged that his own unwillingness or perhaps his inability to compromise had led to the demise of The Young Tradition. Perhaps, some 22 years later, it helped lead to his own; in September 1991, Peter Bellamy took his own life. *—Steve Winick*

Peter Bellamy Sings the Barrack-Room Ballads of Rudyard Kipling / 1974 / Green Linnet ♦♦♦

Tell It Like It Was / 1975 / Trailer ♦♦♦
Over the ten years previous to this release, Bellamy had been writing tunes to traditional words and words to traditional tunes. This release showcased some of the results. *—Steve Winick*

☆ **The Transports** / 1977 / Topic ♦♦♦♦♦
Bellamy's masterpiece ballad opera starred himself and other influential folk singers. *—Steve Winick*

★ **Both Sides Then** / 1979 / Topic ♦♦♦♦♦
Traditional songs of England, Ireland and America, sung in Bellamy's amazing voice and accompanied by guests such as Louis Killen and Dave Swarbrick, are simply beautiful. *—Steve Winick*

Songs An' Rummy Conjurin' Tricks / 1991 / Fellside ♦♦♦♦
Recorded live a scant nine months before his death, this album is an excellent example of Bellamy's charm as a live performer. *—Steve Winick*

The Black Family

f. 1965
Group / Contemporary Celtic, Celtic Pop
The Black Family is one of the most important musical clans in Ireland. While sisters Mary and Frances rank among the best-selling folk artists in the world, the three albums that they recorded with their brothers-Shay, Michael and Martin-document the strength of this family collaboration. The three brothers and two sisters inherited their love of music from their parents. Their father, who hailed from Rathlin Island, played fiddle, while, their mother sang traditional and music hall songs. Although the five siblings performed together in Dublin pubs in the mid-1970s, Mary left the group in 1977 to sing with General Humbert and DeDanaan and as a soloist. The Black Family continued to perform as a trio, releasing their self-titled debut album in 1986. Three years later, Mary returned to tour and record an album, "Time For Touching Home" with her brothers and younger sister Frances. Soon afterwards, she resumed her solo career with Frances, Shay, Michael and Martin continuing as a quartet. Before long, however, Frances left the group to sing with Arcady and on her own. BMary and Frances returned to sing harmony on their brothers' 1995 album, "What A Time," which also included the singing of their mother, Patty, on an old music hall tune. Although Shay and Michael emigated to San Francisco in the mid-1990s, the Black Family continues to periodically come together to sing. In 1997, they reunited at Milwaukee's Irish Festival for a benefit concert to raise funds to restore their father's birthplace on Rathlin Island. *—Craig Harris*

★ **The Black Family** / Celtic Corner ♦♦♦♦♦
One of the best albums of Irish singing you'll find, this features old ballads, sea shanties, and contemporary numbers all together. *—Steve Winick*

Frances Black

Vocals / Celtic Folk, Contemporary Celtic
A pure vocal tone and an energetic, pop-minded delivery has made Frances Black one of Ireland's top vocalists. In 1995 and 1997, Black was named by the Irish Record Industry Awards (IRMA) as Ireland's Best Female Artist. She also received the Most Popular Artist award at the National Awards ceremony.

A former member of Arcady and The Black Family, in 1993 Black made her solo debut with two tracks on the million-selling, multi-artist compilation *Woman's Heart.* An album-related tour with Maura O'Connell, Dolores Keane, Sharon Shannon, Sinead Lohan and her sister, Mary Black, broke all of Ireland's box office records. While$ Black's debut solo album, *Talk to Me* (released in 1994), sold over 100,000 copies and spent eight weeks at the top of Ireland's music charts, her releases *The Sky Road* (1995), *The Smile on Your Face* (1996) and *Don't Get Me Wrong* (1998) further established her as an internationally known performer. Black has proven as effective interpreting the songs of American singer/songwriters as she is with Irish music. *Talk to Me* featured four songs by Nanci Griffith ("On Grafton Street," "Talk to Me While I'm Listening," "Always Will" and "Time of Inconvenience." Among Black's most successful singles are re-recordings of Acker Bilk's "Stranger on the Shore" in October 1996 and the Yvonne Elliman-popularized tune "Love Me, Please" in August 1997.

Black made her professional debut in 1986 with The Black Family, a group that also featured her three brothers (Michael, Shay and Martin) and her sister (Mary). In addition to singing on the group's two albums (*The Black Family* in 1986 and *Time for Touching Home* in 1988)—Black sang on her brothers' album, *What a Time.* Shortly after recording *Time for Touching Home,* Black joined Irish trad-folk band Arcady, which also featured accordion players Shannon and Jackie Daly and bouzouki player Johnny Moynihan. Black remained with the band until 1994, when she formed a duo with Irish singer/songwriter Kieran Goss. In 1994, Black performed a benefit concert and recorded an EP, *Fear Is the Enemy of Love and Children,* for the Aoibhneas Women's Refuge that featured her children, Eoghan and Aoife, singing background vocals. *—Craig Harris*

● **Talk to Me** / 1995 / Celtic Heartbeat ♦♦♦

Sky Road / Aug. 12, 1997 / Uptown/Universal ♦♦♦

Mary Black

b. May 22, 1955, Ireland
Vocals / Traditional Irish Folk, Celtic Folk, Contemporary Celtic, Irish Folk, Contemporary Folk
Mary Black is a performer equally at home singing traditional Irish folk tunes and contemporary music including blues, rock, jazz, country and soul. She started out professionally with her brother and sister in Dublin nightclubs and then performed with the folk group General Humbert until 1982, when she released her eponymous solo debut. The album made it to the Top Five on the Irish album charts and won the Irish Independent Arts Award for Music. At the invitation of Alec Finn, Black then joined the band De Danaan, remaining with them for three years. She was still performing with De Danaan when she launched the solo album *Without the Fanfare.* Many of the tracks went gold and for both 1987 and 1988 she was named Best Female Artist in the Irish Rock Music Awards Poll. Black's music crossed the Atlantic in 1990 when her album *No Frontiers* debuted in the U.S. and climbed to the Top 20 of the New Adult Contemporary charts. *—Sandra Brennan*

Mary Black / 1983 / Gifthorse ♦♦♦

Without the Fanfare / 1985 / Gifthorse ♦♦♦

By the Time It Gets Dark / 1987 / Gifthorse ♦♦♦♦

● **Collected** / 1988 / Gifthorse ♦♦♦♦♦
She's a pop icon in her native Ireland who evokes barely a ripple of recognition in the U.S., mainly because she's spent most of her career gradually moving away from traditional Irish music (which still has a relatively small listening constituency in the States) and into the sort of Broadway-esque demi-pop that thrills Europeans and befuddles Americans. You can agree or disagree with her choice of musical direction, but there's no disputing the heartbreaking beauty of her voice. This album compiles recordings from the early 1980s, when her repertoire still consisted mainly of chestnuts like "Song for Ireland," "She Moves Through the Fair" and "Both Sides the Tweed," all of which are included here. Chestnuts they may be, but her crystalline voice and her affecting delivery are enough to invest them all with new life. Highlights include the simple and perfect "Mo Ghile Mear" and a nicely nuanced rendition of Archie Fisher's acerbic "Men of Worth." *—Rick Anderson*

No Frontiers / 1989 / Gifthorse ♦♦♦

Babes in the Wood / 1991 / Gifthorse ♦♦♦♦♦
Babes in the Wood is Mary Black's finest, most consistently pleasing album. There is no filler here, and her song selection, culled from new songwriters such as Noel Brazil and classic folkies such as Richard Thompson, is impeccable. The acoustic arrangements (including guitar, piano, mandolin, Dobro, and accordion) are carried out by her longtime backing musicians, although the music has a decidedly more pop than Celtic flavor on this album. As with most of her releases, there are many romantic ballads sung with a subtly that adds emotional weight to every song. The main difference on this album is an omnipresent religious tone, whether it's overt in the gospel opener "Still Believing" or just below the surface in songs such as "The Golden Mile." Even a few of the love songs refer to having faith that love will come around again after heartbreak ("Just Around the Corner"). However, the album is peppered with playful, upbeat tunes that propel the album forward to the final song, a wonderful cover of Joni Mitchell's "Urge for Going." A great introduction to the music of Mary Black, and a must-own for fans. *—Vik Iyengar*

The Holy Ground / Apr. 1993 / Gifthorse ♦♦♦

Shine / Mar. 18, 1997 / Curb ♦♦♦♦
Mary Black abandons her usual sound and production on *Shine,* an album of songs recorded in Los Angeles with local session musicians. At the production helm is studio veteran Larry Klein (who has worked with Peter Gabriel and Joni Mitchell), and he aided in selecting songs from a new crop of songwriters. Most notably, Mary Black sings five songs by David Gray, a gifted songwriter who would later break into the mainstream with 1999's *White Ladder.* The first half of *Shine* is a strong collection of songs that rank among her best work, with the uplifting title track and "Almost Gone" as the highlights. The second half is a bit uneven as slow ballads are sandwiched between harder-edged tracks. Despite the fuller sound and the presence of electric guitar, most of the songs work and it is refreshing to hear Mary Black try

something new. However, she often stretches her voice and, therefore, loses some of the subtleties that are her trademark. The hidden track "Dancers in the Dark" shows that she has not abandoned spare acoustic arrangements, and it appears that this was a one-album experiment. Fans will definitely want to get this album, but casual listeners should start elsewhere. *— Vik Iyengar*

Song for Ireland / Mar. 16, 1999 / Gifthorse ♦♦♦

Speaking with the Angel / Mar. 7, 2000 / Atlantic ♦♦♦♦
Ironically, traditional folk vocalist Mary Black's first American release (*Shine*) buried her traditional Irish roots in glossy pop production, obscuring the very quality that interested the labels in the first place. *Speaking with the Angel* corrects the errors of its predecessor by bringing Black back to her folky origins. The result is not only more marketable, it's also more genuine, more innovative and more listenable. Though production duties are split between Donal Lunny, a ubiquitous presence in Celtic circles, Steve Cooney and Black herself, the sound of the record is remarkably consistent and cohesive. The electronic keyboards that have played a leading role in many of Black's recent efforts are reduced here to tasteful cameos, replaced by the mellow warmth of acoustic guitar, bouzouki, accordion, piano, fiddle, harp and flute. Some of Black's other regrettable tendencies—oversinging, sentimentality are present, though in palatable doses. And there are two excruciatingly perky pop songs ("Message of Love," "Big Trip to Portland") that shouldn't have made the final cut. But for the most part, Black is very successful at finding the heart of the songs she's chosen and expressing them with honesty and reserve. Which is especially gratifying since she's chosen some excellent songs. Among the artists covered in this collection are Dougie McLean, John Gorka, Ron Sexsmith, and Neil Finn. She does justice to all of them and even improves on Sting's "Fields of Gold" with a soft, lilting version that features a graceful harmonica solo by Brendan Power. *—Evan Cater*

The Bothy Band

f. 1975, Ireland, **db.** 1979
Group / Celtic Folk, Irish Folk
In the three years the Bothy Band were together, they emerged as one of the exciting bands in Celtic history. Although much of their repertoire was rooted in the traditional music of Ireland, their enthusiasm and musical virtuosity set off ripples that continue to be felt. Despite their great legacy, the Bothy Band only recorded three studio albums—*The Bothy Band, Old Hag You Have Killed Me* and *Out of the Wind Into the Sun*. A live album, *After Hours*, released in 1979, was recorded at the Palace Des Arts in Paris. In 1995, a second live album, *Live In Concert*, was released that included tracks recorded in London by the BBC at the Pares Theater in July 1976 and the Kilburn National Theater in July 1978. *—Craig Harris*

1975: The First Album / 1975 / Green Linnet ♦♦♦♦♦

☆ **Old Hag You Have Killed Me** / 1976 / Green Linnet ♦♦♦♦♦
An electrifying set, *Old Hag* features some of Bothy Band's strongest material and best performances. It marks the debut of Kevin Burke as a member. *—Steve Winick*

Out of the Wind into the Sun / 1977 / Green Linnet ♦♦♦
Perhaps their weakest album, this is still very much worth hearing. It features more synthesizer and electric piano than before, and marked an era when the band was uncertain of its future. *—Steve Winick*

After Hours (Live in Paris) / 1979 / Green Linnet ♦♦♦
The Bothy Band are back at their peak on this live farewell album. Some of their greatest hits are reprised, and some new material is introduced in a concert context. *—Steve Winick*

★ **The Best of the Bothy Band** / 1988 / Green Linnet ♦♦♦♦♦
Intricate arrangements, lovely singing, and powerful rhythms make this an absolute must. *—Steve Winick*

Robin Huw Bowen

Harp / British Folk
The eighteenth century Welsh triple, a fully chromatic instrument with three rows of strings, has been transformed into instrument of beauty by Liverpool-born and Wales-based harper Robin Huw Bowen. A former member of traditional Welsh band, Mabsant, Bowen has continued to weave his multi-stringed melodies as a soloist and with the duo, Cusan Tan, featuring Ann Morgan Jones (vocals, flute) and Sue Jones (harmony vocals). Bowen is the youngest of three triple harp-playing brothers. His older brothers, Dafydd and Gwandaf Roberts, played the instrument with the traditional group, Ar Log. In addition to what he learned from his brothers, Bowen studied with influential gypsy harp player Nansi Richard. His first opportunity to show what he had learned came in 1986 when he joined the traditional band, Mabsant. Bowen remained with the group for two years, recording one album, *Trwy'r Weiar*, in 1987. Much of Bowen's repertoire was collected while he was supplementing his income as a musician by working at the Welsh National Library. After discovering a treasure-trove of ancient Welsh tunes, he opened a press, Gwasg Teires (Triple Harp Press) to publish them. A collection of two hundred hornpipes was published as *Tro Llaw*. *—Craig Harris*

Cyfarch Y Delyn (Greet the Harp) / 1988 / Sain ♦♦♦
A collection of beautiful airs and dances is played by Bowen on solo harp. *—Steve Winick*

● **Telyn Berseiniol Fy Ngwlad (The Sweet Harp of My Land)** / 1991 / Flying Fish ♦♦♦♦♦
More of the same, this CD features two tracks from Cyfarch Y Delyn as bonus tracks. *—Steve Winick*

The Boys of the Lough

Uilleann Pipes, Accordion, Guitar, Banjo / Traditional Celtic
A fun-loving approach to Celtic music has made the Boys of the Lough one of folk music's most influential groups. In the three decades since they were formed, the Ireland-based band has been instrumental in the evolution of traditional Irish music. The Boys of the Lough initially came together in 1967 as a trio featuring Cathal McConnell (who had won the all-Ireland championship in flute and tin whistle in 1962), Tommy Gunn, and Robin Morton. When Gunn left two years later, McConnell and Morton recorded their first album, *An Irish Jubilee*, as a duo.The group continued to experience numerous personnel changes, culminating in the addition of cittern, banjo and mandolin player Dave Richardson. Among the six albums recorded by this lineup were two live albums—*Live at Passim's*, recorded at the Cambridge, Massachusetts coffeehouse, and *Wish You Were Here*, recorded while touring the Scottish Highlands. In 1979, original member Robin Morton left the band and was replaced by Richardson's brother, Tish, on guitar. Tish Richardson remained with the group until 1983, when he died in an auto accident, and was replaced by British guitarist Chris Newman.—*Craig Harris*

● **The Boys of the Lough** / 1973 / Shanachie ♦♦♦♦♦
This debut album is particularly brilliant because of Robin Morton and Dick Gaughan's contributions. *—Steve Winick*

Live at Passim / 1975 / Philo ♦♦♦♦
The Boys of the Lough influenced countless other traditional Irish groups in the early '70s, and the reissue of their classic live album (recorded in 1974 at the legendary Passim club in Harvard Square) is cause for rejoicing. At that time, the quartet consisted of mandolinist Dave Richardson, flutist Cathal McDonnell, the legendary fiddler Aly Bain and Robin Morton on bodhran and concertina. Apart from the raw-edged but sprightly jigs and reels that one would expect, the set also includes a couple of hilarious songs and an interesting number called "The Hound and the Hare," a tone poem complete with baying dogs and the rabbit's screaming death. One wonders whether there might not have been some outtakes available to lengthen the CD program (this is a 20-year-old recording, after all, being reissued at full price), but it's still a wise investment. Highly recommended. *—Rick Anderson*

Good Friends-Good Music / 1977 / Philo ♦♦♦♦♦
During the course of 1977, the Boys of the Lough cut tracks in a variety of locations ranging from Dublin, Ireland to Ferrisburg, Vermont, these widespread recording dates being determined by the desire to create an album featuring both a variety of guests and a broad variety of Celtic-influenced music. The result has a musical range that reaches from Irish country pubs to Acadia and Louisiana. The 1997 reissue provides the album with a clarity that is highly beneficial to its entertainment value. *—Steven McDonald*

To Welcome Paddy Home / 1986 / Shanachie ♦♦♦

Farewell and Remember Me / 1987 / Shanachie ♦♦♦

Sweet Rural Shade / 1988 / Shanachie ♦♦♦

Midwinter Night's Dream / Sep. 3, 1996 / Blix Street ♦♦♦

Live at Carnegie Hall / Sage Arts ♦♦♦

Brass Monkey

Group / British Folk
Brass Monkey were a most unusual and appealing English folk group. Composed of Martin Carthy (guitar, mandolin, vocals), John Kirkpatrick (squeezeboxes, vocals), Howard Evans (trumpet, flugelhorn, vocals), Martin Brinsford (saxophone, mouth-organ, percussion) and, depending on the date, either Roger Williams or Richard Cheetham (trombone), they were a powerful and commanding group. Unfortunately, these very busy musicians were unable to find enough time for the band to continue. *—Steve Winick*

Brass Monkey / 1971 / Rare Earth ♦♦♦♦♦
This was the band's majestic debut album, featuring Carthy and Kirkpatrick's singing backed by the innovative combination of instruments. *—Steve Winick*

See How It Runs / 1986 / Topic ♦♦♦
A worthy successor, this features more bold and brassy arrangements of traditional songs. *—Steve Winick*

★ **Complete Brass Monkey** / 1993 / Topic ♦♦♦♦♦
A CD re-release of all the Brass Monkey material, it's thoroughly indispensible and is the one to buy. *—Steve Winick*

Sound & Rumour / Mar. 9, 1999 / Topic ♦♦♦♦
The legendary English folk group reunited for *Sound & Rumour*, an inspirational album featuring the talents of Martin Carthy, Richard Cheetham, John Kirkpatrick, Howard Evans and Martin Brinsford. *—Jenna Woolford*

Maire Brennan (Máire Ní Bhraonáin)

b. Aug. 4, 1952
Vocals, Harp / Celtic New Age, Contemporary Celtic, Celtic Fusion, British Folk
For many years, Maire Brennan has been the lead singer of the Celtic new age group Clannad. In 1992, she released her first solo album, *Maire*, on Atlantic Records. Three years later, she released *Misty Eyed Adventures* on BGM. For 1998's *Perfect Time*, she switched labels and signed with Word/Epic; *Whisper to the Wild Water* followed a year later. *—Stephen Thomas Erlewine*

Maire / 1992 / Atlantic ♦♦♦♦

Misty Eyed Adventures / Jun. 6, 1995 / Atlantic ♦♦♦

● **Perfect Time** / Mar. 10, 1998 / Word/Epic ♦♦♦♦

Whisper to the Wild Water / Oct. 19, 1999 / Epic ♦♦♦♦
Máire Brennan sets a series of prayers in English and Gaelic to music on her second album for the religious label Word. The musical style is informed by Celtic music and hymns, but also uses elements of rock, as Brennan sings with considerable echo, sometimes suggesting the round tones of Judy Collins. The massed backup vocals with their ethereal sound often recall the work of Brennan's sister Enya, though her songs are more focused. The tone of generalized religious devotion in the lyrics and Brennan's angelic singing sometimes make the

music sound like it comes from centuries ago, despite the occasional electric instrumentation and 1990s production values. *— William Ruhlmann*

Anne Briggs

b. Sep. 29, 1944, Toton, Nottinghamshire, England
Vocals, Guitar, Bouzouki / British Folk
In the annals of pop and folk music, there are few sagas stranger than that of Anne Briggs. An awesomely talented singer of traditional English folk music, possessing of as pure and breathtakingly beautiful a voice as one could hope to have, she was the single most important influence on a group of female British folk singers that includes Sandy Denny, Maddy Prior, June Tabor, and Linda Thompson. What makes this story so odd is that Anne Briggs' entire recorded output consists of about 30 songs. She stopped singing at the age of 27, supposedly because she hated the sound of her recorded voice. As folk music became electrified and increasingly popular and bands such as Fairport Convention and Pentangle were reinventing the British folk tradition, and more and more women (Sandy Denny et al) were singing in a style started by Anne Briggs, her legend flourished, yet she still refused (and continues to refuse) to sing. Discovered by British folk legend Ewan MacColl, Briggs recorded her debut EP *Hazards of Love* with a co-architect of the British folk music revival, Bert Lloyd. But Briggs hated the way she sounded, so much so that she retired from music, already touted as the greatest legend in English folk music. She still lives semi-reclusively in England and is still not recording or singing in public, but her influence remains powerful. *— John Dougan*

★ **Classic Anne Briggs** / 1990 / Fellside ✦✦✦✦✦
A great compact disc that contains much of Anne Briggs' recorded output, with the exception of her second and final solo record, *The Time Has Come.* This wonderful collection is a must for any fan of English folk music and will prove beyond a doubt that all of the accolades heaped upon Briggs were well-deserved; she is a remarkable singer. Much of the music here is rendered a cappella, and her crystal clear soprano is riveting on songs like "The Doffing Mistress" and "Polly Vaughn." She has gobs of technique, but never oversings or gets too flashy; her control and execution are amazing, and you can easily understand why she remains as influential as she has for all these years. Much more than simply a great collection of folk music, *Classic Anne Briggs* is also a textbook on how to sing English folk music, and it's a venerable volume that has lost none of its immediacy, power, and importance. *— John Dougan*

Robin Bullock

Mandolin, Guitar, Fiddle / Celtic Fusion, Irish Folk, Progressive Bluegrass
Imaginative flatpicking and an expertise in the musical traditions of Scotland, Ireland and Brittany are combined through the virtuosic playing of Washington, D.C. multi-instrumentalist Robin Bullock. Balancing a solo career with work with the John Whelan Band, three trios—Helicon, Greenfire and Travellers—and a percussive dance ensemble, Footworks, Bullock has showed a mastery of a lengthy list of stringed instruments. The *Baltimore City Paper* referred to Bullock as "one of those guys who can play just about anything with strings disgustingly well," while, *Classical Guitar* magazine called him, "a musician whose technical skill and stylistic expertise are second to none..

Inspired by the playing of Doc and Merle Watson, Bullock began playing guitar at the age of seven. Although he studied piano and learned basic music theory and harmony, his limited sight-reading skills led him to focus on stringed instruments. While he played with bluegrass bands, after graduating from high school, he became frustrated by his lack of commercial success and temporarily left music to become a veterinarian assistant. A turning point in Bullock's musical career came in 1986 when he met wooden flute player Chris Norman and hammer dulcimer player Ken Kolodner at the Deer Creek Fiddler's Convention in Westminster, Maryland. Norman and Kolodner, who had released a Celtic-influenced duo album, *Daybreak,* were so impressed by Bullock's playing and enthusiasm that they agreed to continue as a trio, Helicon.

On his debut solo album, *Green Fields,* released in 1993, Bullock explored the traditional music of Ireland and Scotland, playing all instruments on the album by himself. The album led to Bullock receiving a major solo artist grant from the Maryland State Arts Council. Bullock's second solo outing, *Midnight Howl,* released in 1996, was nominated for a Grammy award as "Best traditional folk album of the year" and resulted in his receiving a Washington Area Music Award (WAMMIE) as "Folk/Traditional Instrumentalist of the year." His third solo album, *Between Earth And Sky,* released in 1998, featured such guests as All Ireland champions Joanie Madden and John Whelan, dobro player Mike Auldridge, Bruce Hornsby's reedsman Bobby Read and West African percussionist Laryea Addy. The album earned Bullock his second WAMMIE award as "Folk/Traditional Recording of the year." A faculty member of the Swannanoah Gathering at Warren Wilson College in Asheville, North Carolina and Common Ground at Western Maryland College in Westminster, Maryland, Bullock writes a column, "Celtic And More" for *Acoustic Guitar* magazine. *—Craig Harris*

● **Green Fields: Celtic Music For Cittern & Guitar** / 1993 / Dorian Discovery ✦✦✦✦
The ancient melodies and rhythms of Celtic music are played here using the music's likely original instrumentation. With creativity and spark, the group combines tradition with contemporary elements, creating a nonpareil fusion. *Green Fields* will appeal to those who love the sounds of classical/traditional Celtic music as well as those who are more attuned to new age; the disc does not sacrifice the integrity that the best of musicians in both camps hold. Carrying its vision, the group has direction and a flowing force; soft though it may be at times, the music still moves and gathers energy. "The Knocknaboul" starts in a dreamy state and slowly wends its course, all the time drawing more direction and force until it reaches a full-blown and dynamic conclusion. The group takes full advantage of the fact that all the players are approaching frontiers in their musical careers. No single performer dominates, and all combine to form a special blend. This is an exceptional group that has raised a standard through both sheer technical expertise and the love they share for Celtic music, which together bring spontaneous creativity and music that is quite special. *— Bob Gottlieb*

Midnight Howl / 1995 / Maggie's Music ✦✦✦

Between Earth and Sky / Mar. 10, 1998 / Maggie's Music ✦✦✦✦

Kevin Burke

Fiddle / Irish Folk
Kevin Burke is a master of the highly ornamental Sligo style of Irish fiddling. A former member of the Bothy Band, Patrick Street and a duo he shared with Irish guitarist Michael O'Domhnaill, Burke has also performed as a soloist and with his own band, Open House. His music career began shortly after moving to Ireland in 1974, when he teamed up with singer-songwriter Christy Moore. who had just left the influential Irish trad-rock band Planxty. When the Bothy Band separated, Burke emigrated to Portland, OR, where he joined Bothy Band guitarist Michael O'Domhnaill for several tours and two albums—*Promenade* and *Portland*—as a duo. Recording a solo album, *Open House,* in 1992, Burke assembled the musicians—Mark Graham (harmonica, clarinet, vocals), Paul Kotopish (guitar, mandolin, cittern, bass) and Sandy Silva (percussion)—who became his current band. He also recorded three instruction tapes for Homespun Tapes and Videos—*Music Instruction: Fiddle, Twenty Irish Fiddle Tunes* and *Learn to Play Irish Fiddle.* *— Craig Harris*

If the Cap Fits / 1978 / Green Linnet ✦✦✦

Promenade / 1979 / Green Linnet ✦✦✦
With Michael O Dhomhnaill, it's not to be missed. *— Steve Winick*

● **Eavesdropper** / 1981 / Green Linnet ✦✦✦✦✦
Kevin and Jackie Daly show amazing empathy for one another's playing—a true musical union. *— Steve Winick*

Up Close / 1984 / Green Linnet ✦✦✦✦✦
A gem, it features guests like Matt Molloy, Joe Burke, and the Murphy family of harmonica players. *— Steve Winick*

No. 2 Patrick Street / 1988 / Green Linnet ✦✦✦

Open House / 1992 / Green Linnet ✦✦✦✦✦
An astounding disc comes from Burke and his band. *— Steve Winick*

Celtic Fiddle Festival / 1993 / Green Linnet ✦✦✦✦✦
This magnificent fiddle album also stars Johnny Cunningham and Christian LeMaitre of Kornog. *— Steve Winick*

In Concert / Apr. 27, 1999 / Green Linnet ✦✦✦✦
Maybe the prospect of listening to almost an hour's worth of solo Irish fiddle doesn't sound that exciting to you. That's understandable. Most non-fiddlers would probably feel the same way. Let's give Kevin Burke's live solo album a try, though: listen to the opening number, a modal slip jig called "The Butterfly" (which I believe is also known by the less diplomatic name "Skin the Peelers"); notice how he plays with the rhythm, hesitating in unexpected places while never losing the thread of the tune, spinning the whole thing out like some kind of mournful dance. Then hang on while the applause dies down, and listen to him swing into "Bonnie Kate," an utterly joyful and footloose reel. Hear him pounding out those backbeats—Don't you feel like you've just been forgiven of all your sins— Elsewhere he welcomes fellow fiddler Martin Hayes on stage for several duets and on a couple of tunes he's accompanied by guitarist Aidan Brennan. All of it is marvelous. *— Rick Anderson*

Ian Campbell

b. Jun. 10, 1933
Vocals, Drums / Folk Revival, British Folk
Ian Campbell & the Ian Campbell Folk Group were Britain's favorite folk performers, bar none, during the '60s. Based in Birmingham, they featured singers Ian and Lorna Campbell of Aberdeen as well as Dave Swarbrick and Dave Pegg, later of Fairport Convention. Their arrangements are somewhat dated today, but with their rousing guitar, banjo, and fiddle accompaniments, some songs still sound fresh, and Swarbrick in particular was ahead of his time. *— Steve Winick*

Across the Hills / 1964 / Castle ✦✦✦

● **Coaldust Ballads** / 1965 / Transatlantic ✦✦✦✦✦

The Singing Campbells / 1965 / Topic ✦✦✦
Ian and Lorna, plus their sister Winnie, their parents Dave and Betty, and their friend Bob Cooney play all unaccompanied traditional songs, including old ballads and modern street songs. *— Steve Winick*

Tam O'shanter / 1968 / Xtra ✦✦✦

Capercaillie

f. Scotland
Group / Celtic New Age, Contemporary Celtic, Celtic Pop
The musical traditions of Scotland are fused with the dynamic drive and electronic instrumentation of contemporary music by Capercaillie (pronounced: Kap-ir-kay-lee). While their initial repertoire focused on traditional tunes collected from Christine Primrose, Flora MacNeill and Na h'Oganaich, the group has increasingly incorporated modern influences. In a review of their 1999 album, *To The Moon,* Victor Arenas wrote, "It has been more than a decade of a constant evolution, of modelling their traditional past with those modern ingredients that have made of their music that for which no doubt they will be known in the future."

The inspiration for Capercaillie was sparked in the early-1980s by high schools friends Karen Matheson (grand-daughter of traditional Scottish vocalist Elizabeth MacNeill and a former member of a folk group, the Etives), and English-born/Scotland-raised keyboard player Donald Shaw. The original band included Canadian bodhran and whistle player Marc Duff (who had played in several bands with Shaw), fiddler and vocalist Joan MacLachlan, guitar and bouzouki player Shaun Craig, and bass and fiddle player Martin MacLeod. After building a reputation with local performances, the band recorded their debut album, *Cascade*, in a fast-paced, three day, recording session.

Capercaillie has gone through numerous personnel changes with only Matheson, Shaw and Duff remaining from the original group. Shortly after British fiddler Charlie MacNeill replaced Elizabeth MacNeill in 1991, the band recorded their second album, *Crosswinds*, and embarked on their first American tour. Their earliest success came in 1988 with their commissioned soundtrack for a television series about the history of Gaelic Scots, *The Blood Is Strong*. A soundtrack album, introducing Irvine, Scotland-born bassist John Saich, sold more than 100,000 copies in Scotland and was reissued on cd in 1995.

With the addition of influential Irish bouzouki and guitar player and vocalist Manus Lunny in 1989, Capercaillie became one of Celtic music's most repected ensembles. At the same time, they continued to reach to a much larger audience. With their fourth album, *Sidewaulk*, produced by Lunny's brother Donal, the band began to incorporate English-language lyrics. The group reached their creative peak with their fifth album, *Delirium*, in 1991. A ground-breaking fusion of traditional and modern influences, the album included "Coisich A Ruin," a four hundred year old song, that became the first Scots Gaelic song to reach the U.K. top 40 when it was used as the theme song for a British television show featuring Prince Charles, "A Prince Among Islands," and "Breisleach," which featured lyrics by Edinburgh-based poet Angus Dudb (Black Angus), and became the theme song of a Gaelic-language soap opera, "Machair."

In 1992, Capercaillie released *Get Out*, featuring live tracks and tunes from earlier albums, and a video, *Two Nights Of Delirium*, that captured the band's live performances. Although their albums, *Secret People*, released in 1993, and *Capercaillie*, released the following year, featuring new tunes and remixed versions of earlier material, were highly criticized for their overly-commercial sound. Capercaillie's soundtrack for the film, *Rob Roy* was released in 1995, and the group rebounded with the impressive albums, *To The Moon* in 1996 and *Beautiful Wasteland* in 1997; *Nadurra* followed in 2000. *—Craig Harris*

Crosswinds / 1987 / Green Linnet ✦✦✦✦
On the band's debut album, you can hear Capercaillie mapping out what would become its signature sound—a musical style built on a deep foundation of Celtic tradition but incorporating modern technology and dance-oriented rhythms. It's a fusion that makes purist folkies cringe, but Capercaillie has achieved significant succes with it. *Crosswinds* is more traditional than the band's later efforts; although synthesized keyboards and distinctly non-Celtic percussion are used throughout, the album is dominated by sets of traditional dance tunes and songs like "My Lagan Love." If there's a complaint to be made at all, it's that the lustrous voice of Karen Matheson is too rarely placed front and center. She opens the album with a lovely piece of puirt a beul (a rhythmic singing style used in Scotland to accompany dancing), and practically steals the show with her rendition of the gorgeous "Soraidh Bhuam Gu Barraidh." The instrumentals are also excellent, but not quite as distinctive as her singing—strangely, the funk basslines that play such an important part in Capercaillie's musical strategy are kept far back in the mix. *—Rick Anderson*

Sidewaulk / 1989 / Green Linnet ✦✦✦✦✦
Donal Lunny's production and the band's skill make this collection of driving, syncopated tunes and songs very exciting indeed. *—Steve Winick*

Secret People / 1995 / Green Linnet ✦✦✦

To the Moon / Jan. 1996 / Green Linnet ✦✦✦✦✦
Following in the footsteps of *Secret People* and *Delirium*, this album offers mainly original compositions with the inclusion of the occasional Gaelic song and instrumental. Karen Matheson's voice is the featured instrument, and she is again accompanied adeptly by Charlie McKeron on fiddle, Manus Lunny on bouzouki and guitar, John Saich on bass, and Donald Shaw on keyboards. A new accent was added to the mix with the introduction of piper Fred Morrison, who plays the Highland small pipes on four cuts. Davy Spillane (Uilleann pipes) makes a guest appearance on "Ailein Duinn," which was originally performed by Capercaillie in the film *Rob Roy*. Although the objections from old-school Capercaillie fans are growing more faint with each release, muffled cries of "sellout" can still be heard in reference to songs like "Why Won't You Touch Me" and "Claire in Heaven," slick pop/rock pieces that the dissenters claim merely include traditional instruments in order to uphold a "false" integrity. The group, however, attributes their ongoing tendency toward fuller production and contemporary instrumentation to "natural musical progression." *—Dave Sleger*

Get Out / Jul. 1996 / Green Linnet ✦✦✦✦

Beautiful Wasteland / 1997 / Rykodisc ✦✦✦

● **Dusk Till Dawn: The Best of Capercaillie** / Aug. 15, 2000 / Valley ✦✦✦✦
Capercaillie was responsible for some of the more forward-thinking Scottish/Celtic sounds of the '90s. Although the Scots were well aware of their country's rich musical traditions, they refused to be enslaved by them. For Capercaillie, it made perfect sense to fuse Scottish/Celtic music with rock and pop. And the band's risk-taking often paid off handsomely. Released in 2000, *Dusk 'Till Dawn: The Best of Capercaillie* is a 17-song collection that paints an attractive picture of the explorers' 1991-1998 work. By Survival's own admission, this CD isn't the last word on Capercaillie; the label laments the fact that it was unable to include anything from 1989's *Sidewaulk* due to licensing restrictions. Nonetheless, Survival had access to a lot of first-rate material, and selections from albums like 1991's *Delirium*, 1992's *Get Out*, 1993's *Secret People*, and 1997's *Beautiful Wasteland* leave the listener with a very favorable impression of Capercaillie and its expressive, charming lead vocalist Karen Matheson. For those who are seeking an introductory overview of Capercaillie in the '90s, this generally excellent CD would be the logical choice. *—Alex Henderson*

Nadurra / Sep. 26, 2000 / Valley ✦✦✦✦
To a Celtic purist, Scottish/Celtic music isn't something you combine with rock and pop; you treat it like a museum piece and don't do anything to alter it. Thankfully, Capercaillie doesn't see things that way. Bringing a healthy appreciation of rock and pop to the table, Capercaillie favored an expansive approach to Scottish/Celtic music in the '90s, and the Scottish band doesn't lose any of its freshness on 2000's *Nàdurra*. Like their previous releases, this CD ranges from instrumental jigs to contemplative vocal numbers that feature Karen Matheson, a jewel of a storyteller who is as expressive in English as she is in Gaelic. Most of the people who acquire *Nàdurra* won't understand the Gaelic lyrics of "Tighinn Air A'mhuir Am Fear A Phosas Mi," but one doesn't have to understand the words to feel the warmth and emotion Matheson brings to them. And on the instrumental tracks that don't feature her, Capercaillie reminds us that they never has a problem finding their way around a traditional jig. Anyone who savored the Scots' '90s recordings will also find a great deal to admire about this solid 2000 release. *—Alex Henderson*

Danny Carnahan

Vocals, Mandolin, Guitar, Fiddle / Contemporary Celtic
Danny Carnahan and Robin Petrie have enjoyed a fruitful partnership since the 1970s, when they first began to perform folk and experiment with a widening variety of world musical styles. Carnahan and Petrie met while students at the University of California at Irvine and soon began to play together, he on guitar and subsequently fiddle; she on recorder and later the hammered dulcimer. While Petrie gave up on music to become a potter, Carnahan embraced Irish and Scottish music, teaming up with Chris Caswell and recording two albums. Then, in 1980, Petrie rejoined Carnahan, and the two of them began to play a music that was at once very celtic and very American; the results were heard on 1984's *Two for the Road*. There followed *Journeys of the Heart* also released in 1984 and *Continental Drift*, released in 1987. In 1988 the band decided to change emphasis away from the celtic fringe and toward a more synthetic sound: one less derivative, more coherent. Their release, in 1989, of *No Regrets* was welcomed as a refreshing departure and a new chapter in the annals of the band. *—Leon Jackson*

● **Journeys of the Heart** / 1984 / Celtoid ✦✦✦✦✦
One of the best recordings of traditional and original Irish and Scottish material from an American act, this features Carnahan's voice and instruments backed by Petrie on a few tracks. *—Steve Winick*

No Regrets / DNA ✦✦✦✦✦
Mostly contemporary folk-style material with a Celtic flavor, this is a new direction for the duo. It works well. *—Steve Winick*

Two for the Road / Flying Fish ✦✦✦
Another great set of tunes and songs, this features more participation by Petrie. *—Steve Winick*

Martin Carthy

b. May 21, 1940, Hatfield, Hertfordshire, England
Vocals, Guitar / Folk Revival, British Folk
If the English folk revival of the 1960s had a single "father" and guiding spirit, then Martin Carthy was it. Carthy's influence transcends his abilities, formidable though those are—apart from being one of the most talented acoustic guitarists, mandolinists, and general multi-instrumentalists working the folk clubs in the 1960s, he was also a powerful singer with no pretentions or affectations, and was an even more prodigious arranger and editor, with an excellent ear for traditional compositions. In particular, he was as much a scholar as a performer, and frequently went back to the notes and notebooks of folksong collectors such as Percy Grainger, scouring them for fragments that could be made whole in performance—no second hander, he used the earliest known transcriptions and recordings of many of the oldest folksongs known in England as his source, and worked from there. By 1966, at the time he was cutting his first two albums, Carthy was already an influence on Bob Dylan and Paul Simon, and by the end of the 1960s was de facto mentor to virtually every serious aspiring folk musician in England. At least three major English folk-rock bands, Fairport Convention, Steeleye Span, and the Albion Band, were formed either directly or indirectly with his help and influence. *—Bruce Eder*

Martin Carthy / 1965 / Topic ✦✦✦✦✦
Carthy's debut album rates a place alongside the album by Bob Dylan, as the debut work of a man who ultimately revolutionized folk music performance in England (Carthy is mentioned as an influence on the notes to Dylan's *Freewheelin'* album). This is Carthy's purest and simplest folk effort, an all-acoustic recording done in barely an afternoon that includes his version of "Scarborough Fair," awhich Paul Simon learned from Carthy (including the chords and changes from Carthy's arrangement) and transformed into a hit of his own. Also here is "Two Magicians," a song that later entered the repertory Steeleye Span, and "Lovely Joan," a folk song that is most familiar to classical listeners as the source of the counter-melody to Ralph Vaughan Williams' "Fantasia on Greensleeves." The playing and the interpretations are somewhat less ambitious and rather rougher than subsequent efforts, with Dave Swarbrick guesting on fiddle on about half the tracks, and Carthy's guitar covering all but the acapella tracks. *—Bruce Eder*

Second Album / 1966 / Topic ✦✦✦✦
This record stands in British music history and Carthy's career roughly where *Another Side of Bob Dylan* does in American music—the more florrid tracks here, recorded with violinist Dave Swarbrick, show the path to the bridge between Carthy's traditional singer/scholar background and the folk-rock played by bands such as Fairport Convention and Steeleye Span. "Lord Franklin" is a narrative tour-de-force (from which Bob Dylan got the melody for "Bob Dylan's Dream" on *Freewheelin'*), "Ramblin' Sailor" is boisterous cautionary tale about the company the title character keeps ashore, and there's also an acoustic recording of "Sailor's Life," a song that Fairport Convention would transmute into an epic electric version, and "Lowlands of Holland," which Steeleye Span later recorded. *—Bruce Eder*

Byker Hill / 1967 / Topic ✦✦✦✦✦
Byker Hill was the first album on which Carthy and Swarbrick had more than two or three hours' studio time, and, as a result, which was actually rehearsed and programmed weeks in advance. The results are less spontaneous than their earlier work, but also show a level of

professionalism that few folk albums of the era ever demonstrated. The differences lie in the careful nuances, and the sophistication of the paired voice and instruments, which are much more studied than anything previously heard. The music is glorious in its own unassuming way—Carthy's acapella performance on the haunting "Brigg Fair" (a Lincolnshire tune originally collected by Percy Grainger, and which was the basis for a classical piece by Frederick Delius), the interweaving of Carthy's voice and Swarbrick's violin on "The Bloody Gardener," the dazzling title track, and maybe the best version of "John Barleycorn" ever recorded, are among 14 of the most prized songs in their careers. *—Bruce Eder*

But Two Came By / 1968 / Topic ♦♦♦♦
Fans of Fairport Convention or Steeleye Span will find the clean, stripped down, spirited performances here a revelation: The beautiful, original "Lord of the Dance" (which transforms the Shaker hymn "Simple Gifts" into something wonderful in its own right), a delightfully ominous reading of "The White Hare," a lively "Banks of Sweet Primroses" (which, in various forms, became part of the repertories of numerous folk-rock revival bands), and, most impressive of all, a dazzling rendition of "Jack Orion." Carthy's voice (featured acapella on the beautiful "Creeping Jane" and the ominous "Lord Lankin") is a very fine instrument, he gets a surprisingly rich sound from his single guitar, and Swarbrick's violin is all the support he really needs. And lest anyone doubt that this record was done during England's flower-power era, check out the acoustic psychedelic-folk version of Leon Rosselson's "Brass Band Music." *—Bruce Eder*

Prince Heathen / 1969 / Topic ♦♦♦♦
An astonishingly good album coming toward the end of Carthy's original partnership with Dave Swarbrick (they were to join the lineups of Fairport Convention and Steeleye Span, repectively, within a year). The singing is, as always, first rate, nowhere better than on the haunting acapella songs "Salisbury Plain" and the nine-minute "Little Musgrave and Lady Barnard." Carthy's playing by this time had become less self-consciously complex and more confident, allowing him to accomplish more with less on his guitar. The resulting sound is spare but powerful, particularly on "Arthur McBride and the Sergeant" and "Polly on the Shore"—his notes seem to chime like little bells on the latter. His playing on "Seven Yellow Gypsies" seems like the work of more than one guitar, and gives one a reason to listen to the song several times, taking in the playing and singing separately. Even more remarkable is the fact that the title track is another of Carthy's cut-and-paste jobs, assembled from fragments and melodies of several incomplete traditional songs. *—Bruce Eder*

Because It's There / 1971 / Topic ♦♦♦

Crown of Horn / 1971 / Topic ♦♦♦

Out of the Cut / 1971 / Topic ♦♦♦♦♦
The trio of Carthy, Kirkpatrick, and Evans are back for this album, one of Carthy's very best. *—Steve Winick*

Sweet Wivelsfield / 1971 / Topic ♦♦♦

Shearwater / 1972 / Mooncrest ♦♦♦♦♦

Right of Passage / 1988 / Topic ♦♦♦

Life and Limb / 1991 / Green Linnet ♦♦♦♦

Skin & Bone / May 1992 / Green Linnet ♦♦♦♦♦
Martin Carthy joined by Dave Swarbrick again, for one of the best of their many collaborations. The touch on the acoustic guitars and fiddle is uncommonly nimble and lyrical, even for this duo, while the singing is rich and robust. From "The Sheep Stealer" to the Turlough O'Carolan-derived "Mrs. Bermingham," this collection carries the listener across myriad sounds, sources, and traditions, all distilled from acoustic guitar and fiddle. Other highlights include "The Skewbald" (which was adapted into dozens of American variations), the bracing "Carthy's Reel/The Return to Camden Town," and the rollicking "The Ride in the Creel." Swarbrick gets a workout on several tunes written for harp, and collector A.L. Lloyd's work is well represented, along with a handful of younger contemporaries. *—Bruce Eder*

★ **The Collection** / 1993 / Green Linnet ♦♦♦♦♦
For anyone who's ever been a fan of any of Carthy's music—solo or with Steeleye Span or anyone else—*The Collection* is probably superfluous. On the other hand, for someone who's only heard of him, this 20-song, 65-minute anthology, with songs chosen by Carthy himself from 28 years of recording, is a fair overview of his work. One can argue that the order might have been shuffled a bit, and the notes could have identified the albums off of which each of these songs were taken (you'd think the record label would insist upon it). On the other hand, the music is sufficiently diverse—from Rosselson back to Ralph Vaughan Williams and Cecil Sharp, the various trails of English folk music are represented—and the notes give enough history on each to leave the listener wanting lots more. Featured numbers include "Palaces of Gold," and the ubiquitous "Lord Randal," the epic "Cottage in the Wood," the concertina-driven "I Sowed Some Seeds," the haunting "Lovely Joan," the mysterious gypsy-originated "Eggs In Her Basket," and the dance "Swaggering Boney" (i.e. Napoleon). *—Bruce Eder*

The Chieftains

f. Ireland
Group / Traditional Irish Folk, Celtic Folk, Traditional Celtic, Contemporary Celtic, Irish Folk, British Folk
The original traditional Irish folk band, as far as anyone who came of age in the '70s is concerned, the Chieftains' sound is built principally around the sound of Paddy Moloney's pipes. It is an other-worldly sound, entirely instrumental, and the Chieftains have done more over the 20 years since they first emerged (several years after the recording of their debut album, *Chieftains 1*) to reintroduce the sound of pipes, bodhran, and whistle to the world outside of Ireland than any other group of musicians. Their breakthrough to an audience beyond the ranks of Irish music enthusiasts came with the group's appearance on the soundtrack to Stanley Kubrick's movie *Barry Lyndon* (their "Women of Ireland" became a radio hit, and led to extensive further film work). Since the late '70s, their albums have settled into an effective but less-than-fully-inspired mode of creativity as the group has sought to add new wrinkles to an old repertory without repeating itself. *—Bruce Eder*

The Chieftains 1 / 1965 / Shanachie ♦♦♦

The Chieftains 2 / 1969 / Shanachie ♦♦♦♦
This is the real stuff, the very best of the group's early albums and the best representation of the Chieftains' original sound. If anything, the group is more confident the second time out, and the material, consisting of traditional airs, jigs, and polkas, is stronger than on the first album. Opening with the gorgeous double jig "Banish Misfortune, Gillan's Apples," which goes back to the time of the 16th century fiddler Raftery of Connacht, the record simply gets better all the way through. Though more familiar as a harp piece, "Planxty George Brabazon" (written by the harper-composer Turlough O'Carolan) comes off stunningly here played on pipes, flutes, etc., without a plucked instrument in sight; "The Foxhunt" is a great showcase for Martin Fay and Seán Keane's fiddle skills; the mournful, somber, but beautiful "Am Mhaighdean Mhara" was the tune that Stanley Kubrick absorbed into his movie *Barry Lyndon*, and tells a magical story of torment and lost love. Production on the album is first-rate and, in particular, makes excellent use of stereo separation. *—Bruce Eder*

The Chieftains 3 / 1971 / Shanachie ♦♦♦

☆ **The Chieftains 4** / 1973 / Shanachie ♦♦♦♦♦
This record, made on the eve of the group's breakthrough in the United States, is where the modern Chieftains sound began. It is filled with too many instances of hauntingly beautiful music to name, from the gorgeous, reflective "Morgan Magan" to the rousing fiddle reel "The Bucks of Oranmore." Not only is all of the material absolutely first rate—and *all* of it holds up on repeated listening—but this was the first of the group's albums to include harpist Derek Bell. His presence has the curious effect of softening but deepening their sound, and adding a degree of lyricism that they'd previously lacked. There are moments on this album where the group sounds as much like a chamber orchestra as a folk ensemble, and it fulfills both roles exceptionally well (as listeners to the numerous albums that have appeared since can attest). The lineup here—Paddy Moloney (pipes, tin whistle), Sean Potts (tin whistle), Michael Tubridy (flute, concertina, tin whistle), Martin Fay (fiddle), Seán Keane (fiddle), Peader Mercier (bodhran, bones), Derek Bell (harp)—is generally considered the peak of the group's membership and history, and lasted until the end of the decade. *—Bruce Eder*

The Chieftains 5 / 1975 / Shanachie ♦♦♦

Bonaparte's Retreat / 1976 / Shanachie ♦♦♦

The Chieftains 7 / 1977 / Columbia ♦♦♦

Chieftains Live! / 1977 / Shanachie ♦♦♦

Chieftains 8 / 1978 / Columbia ♦♦♦♦
Sony Music didn't reissue this, the best of the Chieftains' three albums for Columbia Records, until nearly 20 years after its original release. What they were waiting for is anyone's guess, as it contains the best of their late-'70s work, most notably Derek Bell's arrangement of Carolan's "Dr. John Hart," and the haunting tone poem "Sea Image," the brooding "An Speic Seoigheach," as well as the exuberant "If I Had Maggie In The Wood." Some of it is on Sony's *Best of the Chieftains*, but not enough to justify passing this disc up. *—Bruce Eder*

Boil the Breakfast Early / 1980 / Columbia ♦♦♦

☆ **The Chieftains 10: Cotton-Eyed Joe** / 1981 / Shanachie ♦♦♦♦♦

Year of the French / 1982 / Shanachie ♦♦♦♦♦

Ballad of the Irish Horse / 1985 / Shanachie ♦♦♦
Quite a concept album—songs devoted to the Irish horse and its importance and role in legend and history. *—Bruce Eder*

The Chieftains in China / 1987 / Shanachie ♦♦♦♦♦
Here's one for multiculturalism: In 1987, the Chieftains ventured to Beijing and Shanghai, united with Chinese ensembles and successfully fused the type of traditional Irish music they're known for with Chinese music. It seems a most unlikely combination but, in fact, the two prove quite compatible on *The Chieftains in China*, a superb, mostly instrumental live album. As ambitious and risk-taking as they are, none of these performances sound the least bit pretentious, forced, or contrived. Chieftains leader Paddy Moloney insightfully shows us the parallels between Chinese and Irish forms and makes the fusion sound completely organic and natural. *—Alex Henderson*

Irish Heartbeat / 1988 / Polydor ♦♦♦
Van Morrison sings traditional Irish songs with The Chieftains. *—Steve Winick*

Chieftains Celebration / 1989 / RCA Victor ♦♦♦

Reel Music: The Film Scores / 1991 / RCA Victor ♦♦♦
The collected film tracks by the group, which constitute their most famous work to the public at large. A generous collection. *—Bruce Eder*

☆ **The Bells of Dublin** / Oct. 1991 / RCA Victor ♦♦♦♦♦
Joined by Nancy Griffith, the Irish group presents a superb concert, blending folk and country music. Well recorded and well photographed. *—Bruce Eder*

Another Country / 1992 / RCA Victor ♦♦♦♦

Irish Evening / 1992 / RCA Victor ♦♦♦

● **The Best of the Chieftains** / Jan. 14, 1992 / Columbia/Legacy ♦♦♦♦♦
Well, sort of—the 50 minutes of music here represents the best of the group's three albums (*Chieftains 7, Chieftains 8, Boil The Breakfast Early*) recorded for Columbia Records during 1977, 1978, and 1979. It's a good collection, and not a bad place to start for the new listener, though it won't offer any revelations for longtime fans, who'd tuned in long before this point in their history. The line-up during this era was Paddy Moloney (Uilleann pipes, tin whistle), Sean Keane (fiddle), Mick Tubridy (flute, tin whistle, concertina), Kevin Cunniffe (bodhran), Martin Fay (fiddle), Derek Bell (harp, timpan, oboe), and Sean Potts (tin whistle), with Matt Molloy (flute) replacing Mick Tubridy on *Boil The Breakfast Early*. The material, a good dis-

tillation of the best of those three albums, all sounds fine and represents the group's virtuoso sound from this period. *—Bruce Eder*

Long Black Veil / 1995 / RCA Victor ✦✦✦✦✦

Santiago / 1996 / RCA ✦✦✦✦

Here the Chieftains have embarked upon an exploration of the "lost Celtic Province" of Galicia (the northwest corner of Spain), and areas extending to Portugal, the Basque provinces, and Cuba. They have used the finest musicians from these areas to propel their music with a conviction that staggers the imagination. It catapults the listener into a musical excursion that seamlessly flows through the styles and music of these different lands, so that they can no more distinguish a beginning and an end then you can separated the waters of the Mississippi River from those rivers that flow into it on its journey from its heart to its mouth.

Attempting to find highlights of the album is virtually impossible due to the incredible musicianship displayed by the too numerous to mention guests that populate this work. The opening five-part suite, "Pilgrimage to Santiago;" with its use of ancient traditional instruments, such as the tralaparta (large wooden planks that are laid on baskets and maize leaves, and played with sticks), and the use, in a different section of the suite, of the Ulteria Choir. The other track is "Dueling Chanters," with "7th Chieftain," Carlos Nunez, a Galician gaita player, who has toured with the group for about 2 years. With Paddy Moloney on Uilleann pipes, and Carlos on gaita, trading dazzling licks. An absolute delight to hear these two, on their cousins to the bagpipes, playing off each other so beautifully. *—Bob Gottlieb*

Fire in the Kitchen / Jun. 16, 1998 / RCA ✦✦✦

Unbeknownst to some, a healthy Celtic music scene developed in Canada during the '80s and '90s and the Chieftains wisely chose to spotlight the region with *Fire in the Kitchen.* Every track was recorded with a different artist and, like the group's previous collaborations, the album brings out the best in both the Chieftains and their guests. To casual Celtic fans, Ashley MacIsaac may be the only familiar name here, but Natalie MacMaster, the Great Big Sea, Laura Smith, the Barra MacNeils, Rita MacNeil, La Bottine Souriante, Mary Jane Lamond, the Rankins, Leahy and the Ennis Sisters all give equally compelling performances, helping make *Fire in the Kitchen* yet another splendid entry in the Chieftains' canon. *—Stephen Thomas Erlewine*

Tears of Stone / Feb. 23, 1999 / RCA ✦✦✦

The Chieftains Collection: The Very Best of the Claddagh Years / Oct. 5, 1999 / Atlantic ✦✦✦✦

Before they signed to Columbia and became an international sensation (and long before they ever recorded a concert album in China or collaborated with Tom Jones or Luciano Pavarotti), the Chieftains recorded several albums for Ireland's respected Claddagh label. This compilation features 12 tracks from that period, and although the material is more strictly traditional and the playing a bit more conservative than it has become since, the group's taste for intricate arrangements is already apparent. Never satisfied to simply bash straight through a set of two or three reels in unison, on tunes like "Tadhair dom do Lamh" and "The Walls of Liscarroll" they essentially take turns soloing or playing in twos and threes before finishing up in exuberant ensemble. These were the days before Matt Molloy, so the flute playing was somewhat more restrained than it is now, and Peadar Mercier's bodhran is a bit ponderous. But for the most part the playing is exciting and expert and the recorded sound is very good. The only complaint might be with the disc's length—surely the band's first five albums could have yielded more than 40 minutes of worthwhile material. *—Rick Anderson*

The Claddagh Years / Oct. 19, 1999 / Atlantic ✦✦✦✦

As the title suggests, The Chieftains' *Claddagh Years* box set gathers together some of the best of their early recordings for the Claddagh label. The set's material comes primarily from the group's first four albums and gives a good representation of the group's roots as well as their wide repertoire of traditional jigs, airs, reels, polkas, mazurkas and other Celtic music forms. Tracks like "The Connemara Stocking, " "The Foxhunt, " "Carolan's Concerto, " "The Morning Dew" and "Carrickfergus" trace the roots of the Chieftains' fresh and expressive interpretations of Celtic music. *—Heather Phares*

Water from the Well / Feb. 22, 2000 / RCA Victor ✦✦✦✦

Chieftains Collection: The Very Best of the Claddagh Years, Vol. 2 / Oct. 24, 2000 / Atlantic ✦✦✦✦✦

When the powers-that-be get around to assembling the second volume of a greatest hits collection, only a few songs often remain to choose from and the rest must be left to filler. Not so with this album, which isn't surprising given the Chieftains' four-decade history of steady musical releases. Like the first volume, this album focuses on the classic era of the Chieftains prior to the noodling that made up albums like *Tears of Stone.* Two things shine through: superior musicianship and a sense of wit and joy. Some of the best songs include "Drowsy Maggie," "Cherish the Ladies," and "Round the House and Mind the Dresser." *—Stacia Proefrock*

The Clancy Brothers

f. Ireland

Group / Traditional Irish Folk, Folk Revival

The Clancy Brothers are a family of singing Irish expatriates who have been important figures in re-popularizing their native music in North America and are still among the most internationally renowned Irish folk bands. Some even credit the band as important figures in starting the folk revival of the '50s and '60s. The Clancys, along with friend Tommy Makem, chose to forego the stereotypical maudlin Irish ballads in favor of lusty party songs, traditional American and Irish folk songs and even protest tunes sung in close harmony and performed most theatrically. Early recordings include "The Rising of the Moon" and "Come Fill Your Glass with Me." By recording and touring often, the Clancys continued to become more and more popular in Eastern and Midwestern clubs, but it was their debut on the *Ed Sullivan Show* in 1961 that brought them national exposure. Originally scheduled to only play three minutes, they ended up playing for 16 minutes and became an instant national sensation, soon signing a major contract with Columbia Records. The Clancys continued recording and performing together through 1969. That year Makem left to pursue his solo career. *—Sandra Brennan*

The Rising of the Moon: Irish Songs of Rebellion / 1959 / Tradition ✦✦✦

Their first album, recorded in Kenneth S. Goldstein's kitchen with Tommy Makem, is free from some of the hokeyness of later efforts. *—Steve Winick*

● **Greatest Hits** / 1973 / Vanguard ✦✦✦✦

This set was recorded with Lou Killen, a famous singer of Northumberland folksongs and sea shanties. Killen and The Clancys make an interesting combination; it's a record worth getting and features more Scottish material than is common for The Clancys. *—Steve Winick*

Irish Drinking Songs / 1993 / Tradition ✦✦✦

Drawn from a variety of albums released by the Dubliners and the Clancy Brothers with and without Tommy Makem, this compilation celebrates the mix of the Irish and their booze in its various different guises. Wisely, the compilers selected the Dubliners' version of "Whisky In the Jar," opening the set effectively. The lion's share of the collection goes to the Clancy Brothers, however, with their upmarket and often jollied-up performances—the Dubliners, in comparison, are a rough and gruff lot. Entertaining, if your capacity for Irish drinking songs isn't limited. *—Steven McDonald*

The Clancy Brothers & Tommy Makem / Sep. 3, 1996 / Tradition ✦✦✦✦

The Clancy Brothers and Tommy Makem's third album for their own Tradition Records label was recorded and released in 1961 after they had already made their celebrated appearance on *The Ed Sullivan Show* and signed a non-exclusive recording contract with major label Columbia Records. Clearly, they were feeling confident in their musical approach, and this collection of traditional Irish folk songs is enthusiastically performed, with guitarist Bruce Langhorne and banjo player Erik Darling sitting in. One can hear the music's influence easily: "The Work of the Weavers" had helped give a name to a popular folk group years earlier; the tune of "Brennan on the Moor" was borrowed by Bob Dylan the following year for his "Rambling, Gambling Willie," which was slated for *Freewheelin' Bob Dylan* but not legitimately released until 1991; "The Maid of Fife-E-O" has been much covered (notably by the Grateful Dead) under the titles "Peggy-O" and "Fennario"; and other familiar songs included "The Jug of Punch" and "Johnny I Hardly Knew You." Varying from ballads to uptempo numbers, and from solo performances to group-sung drinking songs, the album demonstrates the diversity of Irish music. Incidentally, fans of Frank McCourt's best-selling memoir *Angela's Ashes* will enjoy the song "Roddy McCorley," which figures prominently in the book. (In 1996, Rykodisc refurbished the album and reissued it on its revived Tradition label at a midline price.) *—William Ruhlmann*

Best of the Vanguard Years / Jan. 25, 2000 / Vanguard ✦✦✦✦

The Clancy Brothers left a considerable recorded legacy at Vanguard during their tenure there, and this 28-track collection is a strong sampling of it. With four previously unreleased tracks added to the double dozen, this is the most solid single-disc collection available of the group's best, adorned with extensive notes from Liam Clancy and Marsha Sculatti. *—Cub Koda*

Clannad

f. 1970, Ireland

Group / Celtic New Age, Contemporary Celtic, Celtic Fusion, Celtic Pop, Ethnic Fusion

Clannad bridged the gap between traditional celtic music and pop. Usually, their results were an entrancing, enchanting form of pop that managed to fuse the disparate elements together rather seamlessly. Such fusions have earned the band an international cult of fans. Taking their name from the Gaelic word for "family," Clannad formed in 1970 when the Brennan family—Maire (vocals, harp), Ciaran (vocals, guitar, bass, keyboards), Pol (guitar, percussion, flute, vocals)—began playing at their father Leo's tavern with two of their uncles, Padraig Duggan (guitar, vocals, mandolin) and Noel Duggan (guitar, vocals). They released their self-titled first album in 1973, yet the band didn't earn any wide-spread success until they toured Germany in 1975. Maire's sister, Enya, joined the group in 1979, yet left in 1982, just as the group was beginning to come into some pop success in the U.K. Clannad recorded the theme song for the television program "Harry's Game"; the single hit number five on the charts. The band recorded the soundtrack to the television production "Robin of Sherwood" in 1984; it won a British Academy Award for best soundtrack the next year. Clannad's success continued in 1986, when U2's Bono was featured on the Top 20 hit "In A Lifetime." The band continued to release albums into the 1990s, building their pop following without losing their folk audience. —Stephen *Thomas Erlewine*

Clannad / 1973 / Philips ✦✦✦

From a latter-day vantage point, Clannad's first album is probably too pop-oriented for traditionalists, but too traditional in feel for those who were attracted to the group's later pop-oriented recordings. For those listeners without any particular preconceptions, it's an invigorating blend of Irish traditional folk with modern influences. More than any of Clannad's subsequent albums, this debut bears the influence of the eclectic, jazzy edge of Pentangle, particularly in the fat double bass lines; Maire Brennan's high, pristine vocals show an affinity with Pentangle's Jacqui McShee as well. Maire's harp and Paul Brennan's flute, however, give the music a strong Irish stamp. Sung mostly in Gaelic and occasionally in English, the material is quite varied in scope, and the arrangements and vocals are vastly pretty and melodic. The cover of Tim Rose's "Morning Dew" that concludes the album is one of the best versions ever of this oft-covered folk-rock tune. *—Richie Unterberger*

Clannad in Concert / 1978 / Shanachie ✦✦✦

Crann Ull / 1980 / Tara ✦✦✦

Fuaim / 1982 / Atlantic ✦✦✦✦

Combining traditional Irish folk with touches of contemporary pop, Clannad has acquired a small but loyal following with its distinctive music. One thing that makes *Fuaim* so effective is its use of simplicity. Whether interpreting Irish songs that go back centuries or embracing songs written in recent years, Clannad (whose members sing in both English and Gaelic) is a band that knows how to use subtlety and understatement to great artistic advantage. *Fuaim* offers a striking blend of acoustic and electric instruments. Synthesizers and electric guitar successfully interact with the harp, the flute and the mandola on this consistently enriching celebration of Irish culture. *—Alex Henderson*

Magical Ring / 1983 / RCA ✦✦✦

The Legend / 1984 / RCA ✦✦✦

Macalla / 1985 / RCA ✦✦✦✦✦

Sirius / 1987 / RCA ✦✦

Pastpresent / 1989 / RCA ✦✦✦✦✦

Anam / 1990 / Atlantic ✦✦✦✦✦

Banba / 1994 / Atlantic ✦✦✦

Clannad Themes / 1995 / Celtic Heartbeat ✦✦✦
There's only so much passion you can wring from a collection of film and TV theme songs. The cover of Joni Mitchell's "Both Sides Now" (from the Blake Edwards movie *Switch*), all cuddly synths and dewy vocals (Maire Brennan duetting with Paul Young), is very pleasant. Of marginally more substance is "Ancient Forest," from the British TV series *Robin of Sherwood*, and "Theme from Harry's Game," the first Gaelic song to become a Top Ten hit in the U.K. (1982). It also earned a *Billboard* World Music Award and a Grammy nomination and have kept Clannad in soundtrack gravy ever since. *—Roch Parisien*

Lore / Feb. 27, 1996 / Atlantic ✦✦✦✦
On its first album in three years, Clannad turns in another set that combines the group's Irish traditional background with elements of Western pop and world music. Five of the eleven songs contain at least some English lyrics, but the most contemporary-sounding track is "Seanchas," which, though its lyrics are in Gaelic, could pass for a Peter Gabriel track. Clannad's sound features many high-pitched sounds, from saxophone to tin whistle and Uilleann pipes, with lots of synthesized equivalents, all supporting the lush choral parts that surround singer Maire Brennan. Brennan's breathy soprano is a cross between Judy Collins and Agnetha Faltskog of AREA, and she suggests the latter especially when she is singing in English in a plaintive, but slightly distanced way, phrasing oddly as if she had learned the words phonetically. *Lore* doesn't contain any individual tracks as memorable as "Harry's Game" or "In a Lifetime" (which is what the group would need to consolidate its success in the U.S.), but it is more of the same from musicians who have established an identifiable sound as their own. *—William Ruhlmann*

● **Rogha: The Best of Clannad** / Jan. 28, 1997 / RCA ✦✦✦✦✦
The best of Clannad's 1982-1989 tenure on RCA is compiled on the 19-track compilation *Rogha*, which includes "Theme From 'Harry's Game'," "In a Lifetime" (the group's duet with U2's Bono), and a pair of collaborations with Bruce Hornsby, "Second Nature" and "Something to Believe In." *—Jason Ankeny*

Landmarks / Mar. 3, 1998 / Atlantic ✦✦✦✦

An Diolaim: Folk Roots of One of Ireland's Groups / Jun. 16, 1998 / Music Club ✦✦✦
The material on this discount-priced compilation is drawn from *Clannad 2* (1974) and *D'lamán* (1976), the two albums the band recorded for the Irish Gael-Linn label (both of which were subsequently released in the U.S. on Shanachie). On these early tracks, Clannad hews much closer to traditional Irish folk music than it would later. However, the potential broad appeal of the group is apparent in the already rich and varied arrangements of mostly acoustic instruments and the powerful and stirring vocals—both Máire Nì Bhraonáin's lead solos and choral parts—whether sung in Gaelic or English. International fans who came to Clannad with its later recordings will find the result bracing, and some may even prefer this to more eclectic later efforts. *—William Ruhlmann*

Greatest Hits / Jan. 25, 2000 / RCA ✦✦✦✦
It seems odd that RCA would release two different single-disc best-of compilations covering Clannad's 1982-1989 recordings, and odder still that there would be so little overlap between *Rogha: The Best of Clannad* and *Greatest Hits* (only about seven tracks out of 18-19). Perhaps it's that the newer *Greatest Hits* volume concentrates on their more popular successes, while the former collection attempted to present an idea of Clannad's diversity. In any case, there's more than enough quality material here to make *Greatest Hits* appealing even for those who already own *Rogha*, although that collection's greater variety still gives it a very slight edge as the better introduction. *—Steve Huey*

Michael Coleman

Fiddle / Irish Folk
Michael Coleman (1891-1945) of Killavil, Co. Sligo, is one of the seminal figures in Irish and Irish-American traditional music. He came to the United States in 1914, and became a successful performer of Irish music in Vaudeville and variety theaters across America. He settled in New York City, where Irish music was in great demand by the large Irish population. Between 1921 and 1944 he recorded many 78 RPM recordings of fiddle music that even today exert a great influence on players both here and in Ireland. Coleman's recorded material is one of the reasons why the Sligo fiddle style and tune repertoire predominates in much Irish and Irish-American fiddling. Many of Coleman's classic recordings have been re-released on albums. *—Steve Winick*

★ **Michael Coleman 1891-1945** / 1992 / Gael-Linn/Viva Voce ✦✦✦✦✦
This stunning double-CD release features 48 of Coleman's hugely influential sides, as well as a booklet over 100 pages long with fascinating accounts of Coleman and his music. It's the best Coleman compilation available. *—Steve Winick*

Shirley Collins

b. Jul. 5, 1935, Hastings, Sussex, England
Vocals, Guitar, Banjo / British Folk-Rock, Folk Revival, British Folk
Shirley Collins was an immensely important figure in Britain's early-'60s folk revival *and* the golden age of British folk-rock in the late '60s and early '70s. She is one of British folk's most golden-throated vocalists, and one of its most eclectic, handling traditional fare, Renaissance music, and folk-rock. Any discussion of her recordings must also note the important contributions of her non-singing sister, the late Dorothy Collins, who was co-billed with Shirley on several albums. Shirley actually made her first album way back in 1959 for Folkways. For a time she was a companion of noted folklorist Alan Lomax, whom she accompanied on trips through the American South that produced some of the most widely praised field recordings of traditional American folk music. In 1964, she helped point the way for a more eclectic approach to British folk music by recording with guitar wizard Davey Graham on the album *Folk Roots, New Routes*. Shirley made her true mark when she teamed with sister Dolly to offer several albums of medieval-based folk music. The most widely hailed effort in this direction was 1969's *Anthems in Eden*, a suite of sorts combining traditional material and original instrumental interludes. With husband Ashley Hutchings, she later sang in a couple of the mid-'70s' most traditionally-oriented British folk-rock outfits, the Albion Country Band and the Etchingham Steam Band. *—Richie Unterberger*

Folk Roots, New Routes / 1964 / Topic ✦✦✦✦✦
This pairing of one of British folk's finest voices (Shirley Collins) with one of the country's finest acoustic guitarists (Davey Graham) had a notable influence on the U.K. folk scene, although it eluded wide acclaim at the time. Collins' rich, melancholy vocals were most likely an influence on Sandy Denny, Maddy Prior, and Jacqui McShee. Graham helped redefine the nature of folk accompaniment with his imaginative, rhythmic backing, which drew from jazz, blues, and a bit of Middle Eastern music as well as mainline British Isles folk. Performed with tasteful restraint and selected with imaginative eclecticism, the album also includes an instrumental showcase for Graham in "Rif Mountain," which provides evidence of his clear influence on guitarists such as Bert Jansch and John Renbourn, and the acoustic style of Jimmy Page. *—Richie Unterberger*

The Sweet Primeroses / 1967 / Topic ✦✦✦
Her sister, Dolly Collins, adds portative pipe organ to Shirley's voice and banjo. *—Steve Winick*

Love Death & The Lady / 1970 / Harvest ✦✦✦✦✦
More outstanding arrangements of medieval fare, given emotional resonance by Shirley's outstanding interpretations and Dolly's dignified, haunting arrangements for an ensemble featuring Christopher Hogwood on harpsichord, Pentangle drummer Terry Cox on percussion, and Dolly herself on organ and piano. Just as impressive as *Anthems in Eden*, although not as widely discussed. *—Richie Unterberger*

No Roses / 1971 / Mooncrest ✦✦✦
This features a truly impressive folk-rock backing band, later to become The Albion Band. *—Steve Winick*

● **Anthems in Eden/Amaranth** / 1999 / BGO ✦✦✦✦✦
Considered a landmark recording in some circles, this was constructed as a concept album of sorts. The suite-like flow of Renaissance-period material (sung by Shirley) was linked by instrumental passages. Dolly Collins' intricate arrangements, executed with the help of David Murrow of the Early Music Consort, displayed her virtuosity on pipe organ. The duo's next album, *Love, Death & the Lady* (1970), was equally noteworthy; *Anthems in Eden* is only recommended as the first purchase because it is regarded by the folk community as a pivotal release. *—Richie Unterberger*

Arthur Cormack

Vocals / Contemporary Celtic
With a clear, pure, tone, Arthur Cormack was one of the most promising Gaelic-language vocalists of the 1980s. His debut album, *Nuair Bha Mi Og (When I Was Young)*, received a National Mod Gold award in 1983. Although he followed with *Ruith Na Gaoith: Old & New Songs Of The Scottish Gael*, in 1989, and toured as a member of Macmeanmna in the award-winning production, *Skye-The Island*, Cormack has devoted most of his attention to EISD, the music shop he opened in the mid-1980s. *—Craig Harris*

Nuair Bha Mi Og: Gaelic Songs by the Mod Gold . . . / 1984 / Temple Music ✦✦✦
Accompanied by members of The Battlefield Band and by Alison Kinnaird, Cormack uses his naturally strong voice to great effect. *—Steve Winick*

● **Ruith Na Gaoith** / 1989 / Temple Music ✦✦✦✦✦
Many of the same accompanists, plus some new ones, join Cormack for his second album. Like his first, this one is restrained and tasteful. The arrangements are a bit more contemporary in sound, making it just a bit more accessible. *—Steve Winick*

Phil Coulter

b. Feb. 1942, Derry, Northern Ireland
Vocals, Piano, Producer / Celtic New Age, Contemporary Celtic, Celtic Fusion
Composer, producer and performer Phil Coulter was the reigning king of contemporary Celtic music, becoming the best-selling Irish artist of his generation. Born in Derry, Northern Ireland in 1942, Coulter began his career while studying music at Belfast's Queens University, writing the Capitol Showband's 1963 hit "Foolin' Time" and later penning the ensemble's 1965 Eurovision Song Contest entry "Walking the Streets in the Rain." Other notable compositions of the era include Twinkle's 1964 smash "Terry" and Them's oft-covered garage-rock classic "I Can Only Give You Everything." Still, Coulter enjoyed his greatest success as a writer after teaming up with collaborator Bill Martin; together they authored some of the biggest pop hits of the period, including Sandie Shaw's Eurovision-winning "Puppet on a String" and Cliff Richard's "Congratulations." Despite his pop success, he remained drawn to the Irish folk of his youth, working with acts including the Dubliners, Planxty and the Furey Brothers while concurrently writing a series of hits for the Bay City Rollers. After his partnership with Martin ended during the late '70s, Coulter turned increasingly to performing, and in 1983 issued his solo debut *Classic Tranquility;* its meditative, lushly-orchestrated renditions of traditional Celtic favorites immediately scored with Irish audiences, and on the strength of subsequent efforts including 1984's *Sea of Tranquility* and

1985's *Phil Coulter's Ireland*, he emerged as the country's best-selling artist. Later material including 1990's *Words and Music*, 1993's *Recollections* and 2000's *Highland Cathedral* introduced Coulter to a growing international audience as well. The intimate *Songs I Love So Well* was issued on Shanachie in early 2001. *—Jason Ankeny*

● **Scottish Tranquility** / 1984 / Shanachie ✦✦✦✦✦

Peace and Tranquility / 1989 / Shanachie ✦✦✦

A Touch of Tranquility / 1992 / Shanachie ✦✦✦

Recollections / 1993 / Shanachie ✦✦✦

Highland Cathedral / Feb. 22, 2000 / RCA ✦✦✦
Phil Coulter's *Highland Cathedral* collects more of his lush Celtic fusion pieces, which blend traditional instruments such as Uilleann pipes, whistles, piano, accordion, and strings with contemporary-sounding synths. "Our Island Barque," "Going Home," and "The Enchanted Glen" define the album's lilting, relaxing feel, and Aoife's delicate vocals on "If These Stones Could Speak" and the title track add another soothing, ethereal dimension to *Highland Cathedral*, an album that will please Coulter fans as well as anyone fond of atmospheric, new age-inspired Celtic music. *—Heather Phares*

Cythara

Group / Contemporary Celtic
The Anglo-Scottish duo Cythara takes its name from the Latin word that means to play a stringed instrument, which was often used to decribe the harp and other similar instruments. Jennifer Crook (Celtic harp, penny whistle) was a graduate of Middlesex University, England, and is a trained multi-instrumentalist, with background in harp, piano, flute, voice, and guitar. MacLaine Colston (hammered dulcimer, guitar, bodhran) first took up the hammered dulcimer under the inspiration of an American virtuoso, Jim Couza, with whom he later toured and recorded an album. Crook and MacLaine began playing together as Cythara in 1992, and winning numerous folk competitions, before recording their debut album late that year. Their sound is all acoustic, and generally centers on playing the contrasting textures of the harp and the hammered dulcimer off against each other, and their repertory is built around traditional folk material, mostly English, Scottish, Irish, and Breton. *—Bruce Eder*

Cythara / 1992 / KRL-Lochshore ✦✦✦✦✦
About as pretty a debut recording as any folk group ever came up with. Some of the material here will sound familiar, despite being cast in unfamiliar forms, such as "Scarborough Fair" (which couldn't possibly sound less like the Simon & Garfunkel version) and, most beautiful of all, "Star of County Down," a variant of the old folk song "Dives and Lazarus" (or "The Unquiet Grave"), immortalized by Ralph Vaughan Williams. Other tracks (e.g., "Brittany") have an unearthly, ethereal quality to modern ears. The music never veers anywhere near new age emptiness, however, instead taking on elements of jauntiness ("Chanter"), ravishing lyricism ("Carolan's Concerto"), and baroque elegance (*Canon* by Johannes Pachelbel). The arrangements are clean and crisp and make amazingly little use of any artificial recording tricks, despite the obvious temptations to do so. Fans of Derek Bell or Alan Stivell will love this recording. *—Bruce Eder°*

De Danaan

Group / Contemporary Celtic, Irish Folk
De Danaan has played an influential role in the development of modern Irish music. Although they're remained rooted in Ireland's musical tradition, the band's virtuosic instrumental skills and expressive vocalizing has enabled them to reach out to a worldwide audience. According to Earle Hitchner, music writer for *The Wall Street Journal* and *The Irish Echo*, "any serious discussion of the evolution of Irish traditional music over the past quarter century must include the enormous contribution of De Danaan." The seeds that grew into De Danaan were planted during informal, Sunday morning, jam sessions at *Hughes Pub* in Spiddal, a small town in County Galway. Two participants of these sessions, Frankie Gavin, a firery fiddler, and Yorkshire-born Alec Finn, a bouzouki and guitar player who had previously played with Connemara, agreed to pool their resources. Joined by bohran and bones player Johnny "Ringo" McDonogh and banjo player Charlie Piggott, Gavin and Finn began to perform as De Danaan, taking their name from the legendary Irish prince, Tuartha De Danaan. Prior to recording their self-titled debut album in 1975, the group added vocalist Delores Keane. Over the past two decades, De Danaan has gone through numerous personnel changes with only Gavin and Finn remaining from the original group. Lead vocalists have included Mary Black, Maura O'Connell, Johnny Moynihan, Eleanor Shanley and their current singer, Tomie Fleming. Past instrumentalists include accordion aces Jackie Daly and Aidan Coffey. The band's present lineup features Cork-born bodhran player Colm Murphy and accordionist Derek Hickey. De Danaan has received "Best Celtic album" awards from *NAIRD* (National Association of Independent Record Distributors) for their albums, *Star Spangled Molly* in 1981, *Song For Ireland* in 1983, and *Ballroom* in 1987. Their 1996 album, *Hungarian Rhapsody*, was inspired by the late Freddie Mercury (1946–1991) of Queen with the title track based on Queen's hit, "Bohemian Rhapsody." *—Craig Harris*

De Danaan / 1976 / Decca ✦✦✦✦✦

Star-Spangled Molly / 1978 / Shanachie ✦✦✦
This time, the singer du jour is Maura O'Connell, and the theme is Irish-American music of the '20s. *—Steve Winick*

The Mist Covered Mountain / 1980 / Shanachie ✦✦✦✦✦
One of their strongest albums instrumentally, this release also features the singing of Tom Phaidin and Sean O Conaire. *—Steve Winick and Bruce Eder*

A Jacket of Batteries / 1983 / Green Linnet ✦✦✦
This album features many new members but achieves remarkable continuity of sound with De Danaan's previous albums. *—Steve Winick*

Song for Ireland / 1983 / Sugar Hill ✦✦✦✦✦
Mary Black contributes the stunning vocals that have made her famous, and the instrumentals have even more energy than usual. *—Steve Winick*

Ballroom / 1987 / Green Linnet ✦✦✦
Featured are music-hall songs sung by Dolores Keane, along with more great instrumentals. *—Steve Winick*

1/2 Set in Harlem / 1991 / Green Linnet ✦✦✦
They blend their traditional music with gospel, klezmer, and other styles. *—Steve Winick*

★ **The Best of De Danaan** / 1991 / Shanachie ✦✦✦✦✦
Probably as good a way as any to start off, with the most popular cuts from the group's albums. *—Bruce Eder*

Deanta

Group / Traditional Celtic, Contemporary Celtic
Deanta (pronounced: Jaunt-a) is one of the top traditional Celtic bands in Ireland. Formed in Northern Ireland's County Antriam, the group is known for its tight, ensemble, playing and the crystalline vocals of All-Ireland champion singer Mary Dillon. According to Irish Music Magazine, "Unlike some of the other guns currently making waves on both sides of the Atlantic, Deanta have not gone down the well worn route of 'give it a dose of rocket fuel, foot to the floor, out blast The Bothy Band and divil the pillion passenger." In his liner notes for Deanta's self-titled 1993 album, Jackie Dixon took a similar view, writing, "The old values inherent in traditional music are held intact and are never under threat from modern influences that the band judiciously introduce into their repertoire." The musical foundation of Deanta was furnished by Katie O'Brien, who played fiddle and viola, and her brother, Eoghan, who played guitar and harp. The original group also featured Paul Mullan (flute, whistles), Clodagh Warnock (bouzouki, fiddle, bodhran, percussion) and Mary Dillon (vocals, synthesizer, guitar, harp). By the time that they released their second album, *Ready for the Storm*, in 1994, Mullan had been replaced by Deidre Havlin and Rosie Mulholland (keyboards, fiddle) had been added. Although they were one of the best selling acts on the Green Linnet label, each musician maintained a day job and the group toured rarely. In early 1998, Deanta announced that they were disbanding. *—Craig Harris*

● **Deanta** / 1993 / Green Linnet ✦✦✦✦
A very energetic album full of great playing and singing, it's a bit marred by overproduction in places. *—Steve Winick*

Ready for the Storm / 1994 / Green Linnet ✦✦✦

Whisper of a Secret / Jun. 10, 1997 / Green Linnet ✦✦✦

Joe Derrane

b. Mar. 16, 1930
Button Accordion, Accordion / Traditional Celtic, Irish Folk
The Boston-born son of Irish immigrants, Joe Derrane is ranked among the finest button accordionists in the history of Celtic music. Although he recorded a series of Irish tunes on 78 rpm in the 1940s and '50s, he disappeared from the traditional music circuit until performing at the *Irish Folk Festival* at Wolf Trap Farm Park for Performing Arts in Vienna, Virginia in 1994. The performance followed the release of *Irish Accordion*, reprising 16 tracks that Derrane recorded as a teenager. Since his return, Derrane has recorded three albums—*Give Us Another*, in 1995, with accompaniment by Irish pianist Felix Dolan, and *Return to Inis Mor*, in 1996, which featured pianist Carl Hession of Moving Cloud and a string quartet. The title track, one of four original tunes on the album, referred to Derrane's ancestral home on an island in Galway Bay. *The Tie That Binds*, released in 1998, featured Derrane playing a new 23-key, two-row button accordion that he helped design, plus accompaniment by Frankie Gavin, Zan McLeod, Seamus Egan and Jerry O'Sullivan.

The oldest of three brothers, Derrane grew up in a musical home. His father played accordion and melodeon and his mother played violin. A daily listener of Irish radio station broadcasts in Boston, Derrane became so enchanted by the playing of Jerry O'Brien, a melodeonist who had played with Joe O'Leary's Irish Minstrels, that his parents sought O'Brien out to instruct their son. Derrane began lessons with O'Brien at the age of ten and continued to study under him for two years, playing the single-row accordion for five years. At the age of fifteen, Derrane studied piano accordion and learned to read music; he became a fanatic of Brooklyn-born diatonic acordionist John J. Kimmel, "The Irish Dutchman," and learned to play much of his repertoire.

During his senior year at Mission High School in Roxbury, Derrane recorded 16 solo tracks with pianist Johnny Connor. In 1948 and 1949, he recorded ten duets with O'Brien, his former teacher. Although he lived in New York for two years (1952 and 1953), he returned to Boston and became a regular performer on the ballroom dance circuit. During the late 1940s and early '50s, he performed with such bands as Johnny Powell's Irish Dance Band, the Stars of Erin, the Galway Bay Band, the Irish All-Stars and the All-Star Ceili Band.

After studying harmonics and arranging at the Schillinger House (later the Berklee College of Music) for six months, Derrane performed with numerous bands that specialized in Jewish and Italian music. *—Craig Harris*

● **Give Us Another** / 1995 / Green Linnet ✦✦✦✦

Tie That Binds / Jan. 20, 1998 / Shanachie ✦✦✦

Johnny Doran

Pipe / Traditional Irish Folk
Johnny Doran was one of the most influential of Ireland's great pipers. The grandson of travelling piper John Cash and his wife, Polly Connors, a stepdancer, Doran traveled by horse-drawn caravan to share his love of traditional Irish music and his virtuosity on the Uilleann pipes throughout the Emerald Isle. According to P. J. Curtis, author of *Notes from The Heart: A Celebration Of Traditional Irish Music*, "My own father saw Johnny play many times at

horse and cattle markets in north Clare and used to say it was the most amazing, magical music he had ever heard in his life. He said that Johnny used to make as much as thirty shillings a day busking at fairs at a time when a labourer earned two shillings a week." Only two years old when his grandfather died, Doran, nevertheless, inherited his skills as a piper. Launching his career as a traveling piper in the early-1920s, Doran remained active until a freak accident in 1948 when a brick wall fell on him and his spine was so damaged that he remained a cripple for the rest of his life. Although he continued to play the pipes, propped up on a mattress and pillows, he re-entered the hospital on October 27, 1949 and died January 19, 1950. Despite reports of additional recordings, the only recordings of Dolan known to be available are nine acetate discs that he recorded for the Irish Folklore Commission in 1947. These were remastered and released as *Bunch of Keys: The Complete recordings Of Johnny Dolan* in 1989. *— Craig Harris*

The Bunch of Keys / 1989 / Irish Folklore Commission ✦✦✦✦✦
This tape includes the handful of recordings he made for the Irish Folklore Commission in the mid-'40s. *— John Storm Roberts*

Dubliners

Group / Traditional Irish Folk, Irish Folk
Nearly three decades since they first came together during informal sessions at *O'-Donoghue's Pub* in Dublin, The Dubliners remain one of the most influential of Ireland's traditional folk bands. Unlike their counterparts, The Clancy Brothers, The Dubliners have never strayed from the raw looseness of the pub scene. According to *Dirty Linen*, "Whereas The Clancys were well-scrubbed returned Yanks from rural Tipperary, decked out in matching white Arab sweaters, The Dubliners were hard drinking backstreet Dublin scrappers with unkempt hair and bushy beards, whose gigs seemed to happen by accident in between fistfights."

Initially known as The Ronnie Drew Folk group, The Dubliners have gone through several personnel changes since they were formed in 1962. The original group featured Ronnie Drew on vocals and guitar, Luke Kelly on vocals and five string banjo, Barney McKenna on tenor banjo, mandolin, melodeon and vocals and Ciaren Bourke on vocals, guitar, tin whistle and harmonica.The first change occured in 1964 when Kelly left temporarily and Bobby Lynch (vocals and guitar) and John Sheahan (fiddle, tin whistle, mandolin, concertina, guitar and vocals) were added. The following year, Kelly returned and Lynch departed.

The Dubliners' earliest recordings included appearances on the multi-artists compilations, *The Hoot'nanny Show* and *Folk Festival—Festival Folk*, released in 1964, their first break came when they met Nathan Joseph, owner of Transatlantic Records, at the *Edinburgh Festival* in 1963. Signing with Joseph's label, the group released their debut full-length album, *The Dubliners*, later the same year.

In 1967, The Dubliners recorded their breakthrough single, "Seven Drunken Nights," based on Child Ballad number 273. Although its risque lyrics caused it to be banned from officially-sanctioned radio stations, it became a top five hit after being aired by pirate radio station, RTE. With the song's success, the band began touring throughout the world. In the early-1970s, The Dubliners toured in a production of Brendan Behan's "Cork Leg."

A second phase of personnel changes began in 1974 when Bourke suffered a brain hemorrhage during a show. Although he subsequently appeared to have recuperated and rejoined the group, he collapsed again on the stage and left for good. He died on May 10, 1988 at the age of fifty three. Following Bourke's first departure, Ronnie Drew left to pursue a solo career and was replaced by Jim McCann. With Drew's return, five years later, McCann departed. The group's problems, however, were not over. In the same year, Kelly collapsed from a brain tumor during a concert and was required to undergo several surgical operations. He died on January 30, 1984, at the age of forty-four.

In 1987, The Dubliners regained their earlier popularity when Eamonn Campbell, who had often been a guest musician on their albums, produced an album, "Celebration," featuring a collaboration with The Pogues on an updated version of the traditional folk song, "The Irish Rover." Released as a single, the tune reached number seven on the British music charts. Campbell subsequently joined the band as a regular member. In 1990, The Dubliners and The Pogues reunited for a single, "Jack's Heroes"/"Whiskey In The Jar," that celebrated Ireland's winning the world cup. Two years later, The Dubliners joined with Hot House Flowers to record a single, "The Rose," that reached number two on the British music charts. *30 Years A'Greying*, released the same year, featured collaborations with Rory Gallagher, Billy Connolly and De Danaan. In December 1995, Drew left the band for the second time and was replaced by Paddy Reilly. Despite the changes in the band's lineup, they continue to perform and record their gutsy style of Irish music. *— Craig Harris*

Live at the Albert Hall / 1969 / Starline ✦✦✦✦
An early live set shows what all the fuss was about. *— Steve Winick*

20 Original Greatest Hits / 1978 / Chyme ✦✦✦✦✦
You can't go wrong with this compilation; it spans about ten years of The Dubliners. *— Steve Winick*

● **Collection** / Jul. 1, 1992 / Castle ✦✦✦✦✦

The Best of the Dubliners / Feb. 13, 1996 / Passport ✦✦✦

A Parcel of Rogues / Arc ✦✦✦✦✦
Out of all The Dubliners' original albums, this one shines the brightest. *— Steve Winick*

Seamus Egan

b. 1970
Tin Whistle, Whistle (Instrument), Mandolin, Guitar, Flute, Banjo / Traditional Celtic, Contemporary Celtic, Irish Folk
Though he gained greatest success with his 1995 soundtrack to the film *The Brothers McMullen*, Seamus Egan has been an important presence on the Irish music scene for far longer. A four-time winner of the All-Ireland award (on an unprecedented four different instruments), Egan has been a member of an all-star congregate of Irish musicians and singers (Green Grass of America), an Irish trad-folk band (Solas), and a soloist. In addition, he has recorded Irish music with Eileen Ivers, John Doyles and African percussionist Kimati Dinizulu, and even hip-hop with Vernon Reid of Living Colour.

Raised in Ireland, Egan returned to the US as a teenager and recorded his debut solo album, *Traditional Music of Ireland*, in 1985. He released a live album four years later as part of Green Fields of America, a large group of America-based Irish musicians led by Mick Moloney (with whom Egan also recorded albums as a duet) and returned with his second solo album, *A Week in January*, in 1990.

Egan gained a great deal of recognition after *The Brothers McMullen* won a Grand Jury prize at the Sundance Film Festival and gained distribution through 20th Century Fox; his music was subsequently featured in the PBS documentary *Out of Ireland*. *When Juniper Sleeps*, Egan's third solo album, was released in 1996 and marked his debut as a nylon-string guitarist. He then formed a traditional band named Solas, that recorded the albums *Solas* in 1996 and *Sunny Spells & Scattered Showers* in 1997. *— Craig Harris*

Traditional Music of Ireland / 1985 / Shanachie ✦✦✦
Egan and his sisters, Siobhan and Rory Ann, rip through some fine tunes. *— Steve Winick*

● **Week in January** / 1990 / Shanachie ✦✦✦✦
Seamus Egan was only 20 years old when he recorded *A Week In January*, but at that young age, it was crystal clear that he had already mastered traditional Irish folk. Egan, an Irish-American from Philadelphia who spent seven years in Ireland, demonstrates his mastery of the flute and the banjo on this entirely instrumental CD. In contrast to contemporary musicians who fuse Irish folk with elements of American pop and often use electric instruments in the process, Egan's approach is traditional and consistently acoustic. From the brisk tempo of "The Congress Set" and "Fermoy Lasses" to the soft reflections of the title song, this fine release makes it clear that Egan's love of Irish culture runs deep. *— Alex Henderson*

When Juniper Sleeps / Feb. 20, 1996 / Shanachie ✦✦✦

John Faulkner

Vocals, Guitar, Bouzouki / Traditional Irish Folk, Celtic Folk, Irish Folk, Traditional Folk
Multi-instrumentalist John Faulkner has recorded and/or performed with Ewan MacColl's Critic's Group, De Danaan and his ex-wife, Dolores Keane, and as a soloist.His greatest success, however, has come as the composer of soundtracks for BBC documentary videos, the owner of a recording studio in County Galway and the producer of albums by Keane, John Beag, The Lonely Stranded Band and Alec Finn. Faulkner co-produced De Danaan's albums, *Ballroom* and *Hibernian Rhpsody*. In 1989, Faulkner's song, "Lion In A Cage," written for Nelson Mandela, remained at the top position of the Irish music charts for four weeks. *— Craig Harris*

● **Kind Providence** / 1986 / Green Linnet ✦✦✦✦✦
Faulkner plays every instrument, including guitar, bouzouki, fiddle, and hurdy-gurdy. He also sings many lovely songs on this excellent album. *— Steve Winick*

Fanaithe Nomads / Nov. 10, 1999 / Mariposa ✦✦✦✦

Figgy Duff

Group / British Folk-Rock, Contemporary Celtic
Playing traditional folk with elements of rock, Figgy Duff was founded in the mid-'70s by Noel Dinn, with Pamela Morgan, David Panting, Philip Dinn and Arthur Stoyles. The band's self-titled debut appeared on Phonodisc in 1981. Nine years later, their sophomore album, *Weather out the Storm*, was released. *After the Tempest* (1991) and *Downstream* (1993) followed, but Noel Dinn died of cancer in mid-1993. *— John Bush*

● **A Retrospective 1974-1993** / 1996 / Amber/EMI ✦✦✦✦✦
Nineteen tracks trace one of Newfoundland's finest from their early traditional recordings through the maturing songwriting of vocalist Pamela Morgan and late bandleader Noel Dinn. The group's inviting contemporary fusion turns on Morgan's smoky, evocative vocals and an atmosphere you can slice through like a thick Maritimes fog. Think of a Celtic Cowboy Junkies, or Clannad had they remained rooted to the soil. *— Roch Parisien*

The Fisher Family

Group / Traditional Celtic
Children of a Gaelic speaker and occasional singer from the isle of Barra and a Glasgow police inspector who sang choral music, opera, and music-hall songs, the Fishers have become respected traditional and contemporary folksingers. Archie Fisher sings the old songs, as well as writing his own, Ray sings the old ballads in a magnificent voice, and Cilla, with her husband Artie Tresize, performs both traditional and contemporary music as well as a large repertoire of children's music. The siblings occasionally unite for tours or special appearances, but most of their recorded material is separate. *— Steve Winick*

The Fisher Family / 1965 / Topic ✦✦✦✦✦
In 1965, when this was recorded, she was barely a teenager. Still, she makes valuable contributions along with Archie, Ray, and her other sisters Joyce, Audrey, and Cindy. The guitar accompaniments by Archie are little more than simple strumming, but the singing is all wonderful. This is a real collector's item. *— Steve Winick*

Archie Fisher

Vocals, Guitar / Scottish Folk, Celtic Folk
Singer/songwriter and guitarist Archie Fisher is a popular contemporary has created many Scottish folk standards such as "Will Ye Gang, Love," "Men O'Worth" and "Mally Lee." He is a member of the Fisher family, a group of highly respected folksingers who occasionally regroup for performances. Fisher's style has been compared to that of Martin Carthy and Dick Gaughan. *— Sandra Brennan*

Archie Fisher / 1968 / Celtic Music ✦✦✦
Released in 1968, this first album shows off Fisher's gentle voice and guitar accompaniments. *— Steve Winick*

- **The Man with a Rhyme** / 1976 / Folk Legacy ✦✦✦✦✦
More gentle singing and guitar make this his best. *—Steve Winick*

Off the Map / 1986 / Snow Goose ✦✦✦
Archie Fisher's singing and guitar are wedded to Garnet Rogers's fiddle and flute. *—Steve Winick*

Will Ye Gang, Love / 1993 / Green Linnet ✦✦✦✦
This album was originally released on the Topic label in 1976 and suffers occasionally from a rather hollow production quality, but the singing and the songs are more than strong enough to make up for any sonic limitations. Though Archie Fisher is an excellent and influential songwriter, here he focuses primarily on traditional Scots songs both familiar ("Mally Lee," "Will Ye Gang, Love") and obscure ("Looly, Looly," "The Flower of France and England, O"). But the album's emotional and musical high point is Fisher's own "Men o'-Worth," a starkly beautiful lamentation over the changes brought to the northeast of Scotland by the North Sea oil boom. *—Rick Anderson*

Sunsets I've Galloped Into / 1995 / Red House ✦✦✦

Finbar Furey

b. Sep. 28, 1946
Vocals, Pipes / Irish Folk
Finbar Furey has left his mark on the music of Ireland for more than four decades. As the lead singer and Uilleann pipes player for The Fureys, a group he shared with his brothers Eddie, Paul and George, Furey helped to guide the evolution of Ireland's traditional music. Since leaving the band to pursue a solo career in 1993, Furey has continued to attract attention with his gutsy approach to the music of the Emerald Isle.

A native of Dublin's Coombe district, Furey was raised, from the age of five, in Ballyfermot. From earliest memory, music played an essential role in the family home. His father, Ted, a horse dealer by profession, played fiddle and pipes and his mother played melodeon and five stringed banjo. By 1958, Finbar and Eddie were performing, along with their father, at informal jam sessions at *O'Donoghue's Bar.* Finbar quickly exhibited extraordinary skills as a musician. winning three all-Ireland championships on Uilleann pipes. In 1964, he placed first in the world championship. Together with Eddie, Finbar made a powerful impression at the *Tralee International Festival* in 1961, winning major awards in the main event, the pub event and the street event.

Emigrating to Scotland, in 1966, Finbar and Eddie were soon playing in folk music clubs, colleges and universities throughout Great Britain and Europe. Their greatest break came when they were invited to be the opening act for the Clancy Brothers' tour of the United States in 1969. The enthusiastic reponse they elicited resulted in them becoming headliners with Paul and George joining their older brothers.

In 1993, Furey left the group to launch a solo career. His debut solo album, *The Wind And The Rain,* released in 1997, was followed by *Traditional Irish Pipe Music* the following year. Another seasonal effort, *We Dreamed Our Dreams: A Celebration of St. Patrick's Day,* was issued in early 2001. *—Craig Harris*

- **Wind and the Rain** / Dec. 9, 1997 / Nora ✦✦✦✦
On this solo release, Finbar Furey delivers both original and tradtional Celtic music distinguished by his mastery of the Uilleann pipes. *—Jason Ankeny*

Traditional Irish Pipe Music / Oct. 13, 1998 / Wooded Hill ✦✦✦

Furey Finbar and Eddie

Pipe / Irish Folk
The sons of fiddler Ted Furey from Ireland, Finbar and Eddie rose to fame in the '60s. Finbar is a flamboyant and forceful Uillean piper who won his first all-Ireland championship at the age of fifteen, while Eddie is a singer and guitarist. They have been members of The Furey Brothers and Davey Arthur but their most charming recordings are the ones they did as a duo. *—Steve Winick*

Finbar & Eddie Furey / 1968 / Transatlantic ✦✦✦
A good set of tunes and songs, it includes Irish and Scottish songs and dance tunes. *—Steve Winick*

- **The Best of Finbar & Eddie Furey** / 1991 / Pickwick ✦✦✦✦✦
Here is one of the few currently available collections of early Finbar And Eddie. *—Steve Winick*

Collection / Jul. 1, 1992 / Castle ✦✦✦✦✦

Irish Pipes of Finbar Furey / Nonesuch ✦✦✦
A modern piper, sometimes with guitar or flute. *—David L. Mayers*

The Fureys

f. 1974
Group / Traditional Irish Folk, Irish Folk
The Fureys are one of Ireland's most influential traditional bands. Formed in 1974 by brothers Finbar, who sang lead and played Uillean pipes, and Eddie, the group, which also included younger brothers Paul and George, toured throughout the world. Their many hits included "When You Were Sweet Sixteen," "I Will Love You Every Time," "Leaving Nancy," "Tara Hill," "Red Rose Cafe," "Lonesome Boatman" and "Green Fields of France." According to Shaun Dale of *Cosmik.Com,* "(The Fureys) distinquish themselves from the hardcore trad groups with a willingness to attack an updated songbook that draws from British and American pop, as well as their own deep Irish roots."

Raised in Ballyfermot, the Fureys inherited their musical skills from their parents. Their father, Tom, a horse dealer by profession, played fiddle and Uillean pipes and their mother played melodeon and five stringed banjo.

The Fureys' were an outgrowth of a duo featuring Finbar and Eddie, who performed with their father during informal jam sessions at *O"Donoghue's Bar* in Dublin as early as 1958. In 1961, the two brothers dominated the *Rose of Tralee International Festival,* placing first in the main event, the pub event and the street event. Relocating to Scotland in 1966, the duo began appearing regularly in folk clubs, colleges and universities throughout Great Britain and Europe.

The group's first break came when they were invited to be the opening act for the Clancy Brothers' tour of the United States. Their performances were so well received that they subsequently became headliners of concerts in Canada, The United States, Germany, Sweden, Denmark, Holland, Belgium, France, Switzerland, Australia and New Zealand. *—Craig Harris*

- **The Best of the Fureys and Davey Arthur, Celtic Dreams** / 1996 / Music Club ✦✦✦✦✦

Finbar & Eddie Furey/Lonesome Boatman / Jun. 24, 1997 / Castle ✦✦✦✦
At a time when many aspiring musicians drew inspiration from the Beatles and the Rolling Stones, these brothers set sail for Scotland in the hopes of making a name for themselves in Edinburgh's burgeoning folk scene. Already accomplished performers, having won numerous competitions in Ireland, the Fureys weren't content at home. Their gamble quickly paid dividends as they caught the attention of the reputable folk label Transatlantic Records. In 1968, their eponymous debut of predominantly melancholy traditional songs (like "Come by the Hills" and "The Flowers in the Valley") coupled with lively tunes was released. The set was essentially a showcase for Finbar's commanding Uilleann pipe playing and Eddie's complementary (though unpolished) baritone voice. 1969's *The Lonesome Boatman* again favored the plaintive traditional compositions, but Eddie's guitar and occasional mandolin were featured more and Finbar's instrumentation was well-balanced between the pipes and his array of whistles. The bittersweet resonance of his Indian flute on the title track is particularly moving. *—Dave Sleger*

Dick Gaughan

b. May 17, 1948
Vocals, Guitar / Scottish Folk, Celtic Folk, Traditional Celtic, Irish Folk, Contemporary Folk, British Folk, Political Folk, Singer/Songwriter
Though primarily steeped in the traditions of folk and Celtic music, Scottish singer/songwriter Dick Gaughan enjoyed a lengthy and far-reaching career in a variety of creative pursuits. He issued his debut solo LP *No More Forever* in 1972, then signed on with the folk-rock group the Boys of the Lough, releasing a 1973 self-titled LP before returning to his solo career with 1976's *Kist o Gold.* However, he soon returned to the group format, forming a band named Five Hand Reel and issuing another eponymously titled effort that same year. In the late 1970s and early 1980s, he worked as a critic and columnist with *Folk Review* magazine, and also acted as a member of the 7:84 Theatre Company; after a three-year absence from the studio, Gaughan also returned to regular musical duty with the release of 1981's *Handful of Earth.* After 1988's *Call It Freedom,* Gaughan again retreated from view; much of his time was devoted to his increasing interest in computer technology, and he later earned notice for his skills as a programmer and web designer. Finally, he formed a new band, the short-lived Chan Alba, which disbanded after releasing their 1995 self-titled debut; the solo *Sail On* arrived the next year. *—Jason Ankeny*

☆ **No More Forever** / 1972 / Leader ✦✦✦✦✦

Copper and Brass / 1977 / Green Linnet ✦✦✦
Solo guitar arrangements of traditional Irish and Scots folk tunes will generally tend to appeal strictly to aficionados, and that's certainly the case with this album by acclaimed folksinger Dick Gaughan. He originally recorded it in 1976 and released it on the British label Topic in 1977. But even if the starkness of these arrangements virtually ensures that the disc remains in the Celtic music ghetto, those who love this type of music already will find much to enjoy. As well as being a top-flight singer, Gaughan shows himself here to be a very fine fingerstyle guitarist, delivering highly idiomatic arrangements of such tunes as "O'-Keefe's Reel," "Jack Broke the Prison Door," and the lovely "Planxty Johnson." His set of 6/8 marches ("Alan MacPherson of Mosspark/The Jig of Slurs") is self-accompanied with a dry and heavy open-string drone, but on other tracks he is accompanied by a piano (a poorly recorded one, unfortunately). Strongly recommended to Celtic music fans. *—Rick Anderson*

Gaughan / 1978 / Topic ✦✦✦✦✦
This CD re-release features all of the excellent 1978 album *Gaughan,* plus four sets from *Coppers and Brass* and two from his guest spots on The High Level Ranters album *Bonnie Pit Laddie.* *—Steve Winick*

- **Handful of Earth** / 1981 / Green Linnet ✦✦✦✦✦
Another fine album. "Song for Ireland" is a classic. Features Brian McNeill, Phil Cunningham, and Stewart Isbister. Voted Album of the Decade of the '80s by *Folk Roots* magazine, *A Handful of Earth* is Gaughan's best blend of traditional and contemporary songs. *—Chip Renner & Stephen Winick*

A Different Kind of Love Song / 1983 / Appleseed ✦✦✦

Redwood Cathedral / Oct. 20, 1998 / Appleseed ✦✦✦✦✦

Great Big Sea

Bodhran, Drums (Snare), Whistle (Instrument), Vocals, Accordion, Mandolin, Guitar, Fiddle, Bouzouki, Bass / Celtic Rock, Contemporary Celtic, Irish Folk
The sea chanty tradition of Newfoundland is fused with the spirit and energy of contemporary rock and popular music by Great Big Sea. Their hard-driving approach has not only made them popular in their homeland, where they've been nominated for four Juno awards, but, has brought them a growing recognition throughout North America and Europe. British music magazine, called them, "a high spirited and richly expressive acoustic quartet who reinvent traditional Newfoundland music, lending it a powerful and resonant contemporary charge." The inspiration for Great Big Sea was sparked during informal, kitchen party, jam sessions in the Newfoundland fishing village of Petty Harbor. In an interview with *the Toronto Star,* guitar, mandolin and bouzouki player Alan Doyle said, "We started out with a

simple goal of playing the old songs but picking them up, where need be, with modern tempos." Doyle, whose mother is a piano teacher, learned piano and drums as a youngster. His most natural musical voice, however, was expressed on the guitar. Having joined his uncle's rockabilly-meets-traditional Newfoundland music band, the New Standells, at the age of fifteen, he formed a duo, Staggering Home, with John Benton, while attending St. John's University. The other members of Great Big Sea—Sean McCann (tin whistle, bodhran), Bob Hallett (button accordion, fiddle and mandolin) and Darrell Power (bass)—initially played together in Celtic rock band, Rankin Street. Hallett and McCann had previously played in a traditional, politically-slanted, group, The Newfoundland Republican Army. Soon after releasing a self-titled, self-produced, album in 1992, Great Big Sea signed with Warner Brothers Canada, who reissued their debut album. Enthusiasm for the band's hard-driving sound and close-knit harmonies continued to spread. While their second album, *Up*, released in September 1995, took nearly a year to sell 100,000 copies in Canada and be certified platinum, their third album, *Play*, released in June 1997, was certified platinum within three months. By February 1998, *Play* had sold more than 200,000 copies. Releasing their first United States-distributed album, *Rant And Rave*, a compilation of tunes from their previous album, in 1998, Great Big Sea spent many months touring the U.S..The following year, the band released their fifth album, *Turn*, produced by Steve Berlin of Los Lobos and Tragically Hip fame. The album included a traditional French tune, "Trois Navires De Ble," recorded with the Chieftains. *Road Rage* was issued a year later. *—Craig Harris*

Great Big Sea / 1992 / NRA Productions ✦✦✦
While The Rankin Family may have spurred the interest in Celtic music in Canada, Great Big Sea were the ones to really take the style and run with it, bringing it to a younger audience that previously regarded it as a style more suitable for fishermen and grandparents. This self-titled album is the most traditional of the group's albums, both earnest and upbeat. While it might be tempting to fault the band for playing it too safe (versions of both "I'se the B'y" and "Drunken Sailor" are included here), it's nonetheless a good introduction to a band that would soon bring the traditional Newfoundland sound kicking and screaming onto the Canadian pop charts. *—Sean Carruthers*

Up / 1996 / Wea International ✦✦✦✦✦
Although Great Big Sea initially started out as a fairly traditional Newfoundland outfit, *Up* shows the band adding more rock muscle to the fiddles and accordions. It's still a pretty traditional sound by most standards, with jigs and reels galore, but it allows the band to do a revved-up cover of Slade's "Run Runaway" and make it appealing to both the traditionalist and the rock fan. There's everything you'd expect from a bunch of young Maritime musicians from Canada: a good dose of Celtic, songs about the sea and about drinking, a good dose of fun, but a healthy reverence for the musical tradition. "Mari-Mac," where the lyrics accelerate to a terrifying speed by the end, is worth the price of admission alone. *—Sean Carruthers*

● **Play** / May 20, 1997 / Wea International ✦✦✦✦
The pride of Newfoundland, Great Big Sea are a great big deal in Canada and as of 1997 have made inroads into pockets of Europe. With their third album, is the time is right to make their presence known elsewhere— *Play* has all the makings of a breakthrough album. It is superbly produced by Danny Greenspoon, who successfully combines the traditional maritime and Celtic music of Newfoundland with modern rock tendencies. It is chock full of catchy folk-rock anthems, and has major-label affiliation; plus, worldwide interest in Celtic rock has grown immensely throughout the '90s and into the new millennium. Some may scoff or roll their eyes at the notion, but GBS, with their strong lead vocals, calculated harmonies, and regional yet universally identifiable themes, musters up idle speculation as to how a modern-day Dubliners might manifest themselves. Great Big Sea proves that they are fully capable of creating intelligent hook-abundant songs like "Seagulls," "My Apology" and "Something I Should Know," but their forte definitely lies in the reworking and modernizing of Newfoundland folk songs. The rollicking "Night Pat Murphy Died" features some fine accordion playing by Bob Hallett and boisterous vocals by all. Those wonderful harmonies steal the show on "Donkey Riding," which tells of the unenviable task of manhandling winches, ropes and chains aboard sailing ships in all types of weather. The a cappella "General Taylor" contains a marvelous but uncredited bass vocal line, and "Jakey's Gin" is a roguish, Pogues-like ditty; all infectious as the dickens. Amid the exceptional selection of original and traditional songs, GBS found room to cover cuts by R.E.M. and Oysterband. Fans of the latter will love this album. *—Dave Sleger*

Rant and Roar / Jun. 2, 1998 / Sire ✦✦✦✦✦
Essentially a compilation for the U.S. market, where the first three albums were unreleased, *Rant and Roar* samples tracks from the more commercially oriented second and third albums. While some great tracks are missing (notably a few from the first album), the songs included on this collection nevertheless provide a pretty representative and enjoyable retrospective. *—Sean Carruthers*

Turn / Mar. 7, 2000 / Sire ✦✦✦

Road Rage / Oct. 31, 2000 / Rounder ✦✦✦

Martin Hayes

b. 1961
Fiddle / Traditional Irish Folk, Irish Folk
Ireland-born and Seattle-based Martin Hayes is a master of the slow, lyrical Clare style of fiddling. The son of P.J. Hayes, fiddler and leader of the 50-year-old Tulla Ceili Band, Hayes has continued to expand on his father's legacy.

Hayes comes from one of Ireland's most important musical families. In addition to his father's influence, Hayes inherited his musical skills from a grandmother who played concertina, and an uncle (by marriage), Paddy Canny, who was a national fiddle champion. A six-time winner of the All-Ireland fiddle championship, Hayes received his first fiddle as a Christmas gift at the age of seven; much of his youth was spent playing with his father's band. After college, Hayes emigrated to Chicago where he played with a rock band, Midnight Court.

Shortly after moving to Seattle, Hayes recorded his first solo album of traditional Irish music, *The Shores of Lough Graney*, released on cassette by Ice Nine. His subsequent albums—*Martin Hayes* and *Under the Moon*—have been released by Green Linnet. *Under the Moon*, which was recorded in County Clare, featured instrumental contributions by P.J. Hayes, guitarist Steve Cooney and Hayes' American band, the Randal Boys. In June 1997, Hayes recorded an album, *The Lonesome Touch*, with Irish accordion player Dennis Cahill. *Live in Seattle* followed two years later. *—Craig Harris*

Martin Hayes / Nov. 1992 / Green Linnet ✦✦✦✦
Martin Hayes was just coming to international prominence when this, his first solo album, was released. He plays fiddle in a style modeled on the playing of the older fiddlers in his home county of Clare in the west of Ireland; it's a gentle, understated approach, never very fast, with lots of slides and a subtle but very expressive use of dynamics. On this album, Hayes had not yet achieved the maturity of tone that would later manifest itself on his next effort (*Under the Moon*, GLCD 1155), nor is his intonation as effortlessly perfect as it would later become. But his basic conception is fully in place: his aching, midtempo delivery of "The Morning Star" (which is usually played much more briskly) is completely convincing, as is his intricate solo turn on "The Star of Munster" and the simple but gorgeous "The Britches." Guitarist Randal Bayes is a modest presence throughout, but pay attention to what he's doing and you'll find it's almost as impressive as Hayes' playing. *—Rick Anderson*

● **Under the Moon** / 1995 / Green Linnet ✦✦✦✦✦
Martin Hayes is a fiddler from County Clare whose sure but gentle touch and deep musical intelligence have combined to produce one of the most satisfying recordings of traditional music in a long time. Accompanied in most cases by only an understated guitar, and in duet on one lovely track with his father, Hayes performs a long set of tunes that range from the familiar ("Rakish Paddy," "The Cliffs of Moher") to the more obscure ("Kilnamona Barndance," "Farewell to Milltown"). What is special about this album isn't so much the material Hayes has chosen, though it's all lovely; instead, it's his unflagging focus on the tunes themselves rather than on his own virtuosity that makes "Under the Moon" both musically inspiring and emotionally rewarding. In a field dominated by fiery virtuosos, many of whom seeming intent on throwing every fleet-fingered ornament possible into every phrase they play, Hayes plays for the tune itself. He interprets and embellishes it, of course, but always in a way that reveals the music rather than obscuring it. There are no barnburners on this album; even the uptempo numbers are played with gentle assurance instead of headlong abandon. When he cuts a note, it is with the quietest, quickest tap of a finger; when he slides into another, it is with the slow, languorous grace of a lover's caress. Yet he never sounds overearnest or academic in his playing, either; he sounds conscientious, not self-conscious. The effect is one of an expatriate speaking after a long exile the native language that he loves, or of a father gently explaining an ancient craft to his child. Stunning. It nearly made me tear up. *—Rick Anderson*

Lonesome Touch / Jun. 10, 1997 / Green Linnet ✦✦✦✦

Live in Seattle / Sep. 14, 1999 / Green Linnet ✦✦✦✦✦
The live context often tends to exaggerate a musician's natural inclinations—punk bands play louder and faster, reggae bands crank up the bass an extra notch or two, Irish musicians thrown in wilder ornaments and wind the tempo up a bit. For fiddler Martin Hayes, whose natural tendency is to play in a stately, decorous style that shows off the tune to maximum advantage and minimizes "look at me!" pyrotechnics, the stage is a place to play even more gently and sweetly than he does in the studio. On the other hand, the relative looseness of the live context gives guitarist Dennis Cahill the chance to step out a bit more than he does with Hayes in the studio, and that works very nicely too. This program's centerpiece is an almost 30-minute set of reels and dances that includes the achingly beautiful "Kilnamona Barndance" (taken even more slowly here than on Hayes' debut album), the standard "Rakish Paddy," and a delightful adaptation of Pachelbel's *Canon in D minor*. Although you might expect fiddle and guitar to sound lonesome and stark without other instruments, Hayes plays with such a sweet tone and Cahill is such a skilled accompanist that the two of them manage to fill the room quite nicely. Highly recommended. *—Rick Anderson*

The House Band

f. 1984
Group / Scottish Folk, Traditional Celtic, Contemporary Celtic, Irish Folk, British Folk
A pan-Celtic approach is taken by the British group House Band; while their sound is rooted in traditional music, their repertoire includes tunes from Ireland, Scotland, Brittany, Bulgaria and even Africa. In addition to numerous folk songs and instrumentals, the House Band has interpreted songs by contemporary songwriters ranging from Archie Fisher and Richard Thompson to Elvis Costello and jazz pianist Dollar Brand. The House Band was formed as a quartet by Ged Foley, Chris Parkinson, Iain MacLeod and Jimmy Young. They were together for just over a year before recording their self-titled debut album. In 1986, MacLeod and Young left the group, and John Skelton joined along with vocalist Brian Brooks. When Brooks left the House Band after two years, the group temporarily continued as a trio. The band's newest member, Roger Wilson (guitar, fiddle, vocals), joined shortly before the recording of the House Band's seventh album, *Rockall*, in 1996. Tracks from the House Band's first two albums, *The House Band* and *Pacific*, were released in the United States as *Groundwork* in 1993. *—Craig Harris*

Word of Mouth / 1988 / Green Linnet ✦✦✦
Ged Foley's vocals are a bit dreary on this record, but the fresh and inspired instrumentals make it more than worth having. *—Steve Winick*

● **Stonetown** / 1991 / Green Linnet ✦✦✦✦✦
Same story, but the vocals pick up just a bit. The instrumentals are still the group's strength. *—Steve Winick*

Rockall / Jun. 18, 1996 / Green Linnet ✦✦✦✦
With *Rockall*, the House Band stays within the Celtic tradition and with acoustic instruments,

while maintaining a fresh and lively sound. All four group members are multi-intrumentalists, more dedicated to blending and interweaving than soloing. In particular, Roger Wilson uses fiddle and viola as a sympathetic background drone more than as a solo instrument. And Ged Foley's vocals have a matter-of-fact delivery that lets the storytelling tunes alternate effectively with the instrumental tracks.

The group pushes the envelope a little by including Tom Waits' "Shiver Me Timbers," but their delivery makes it sound like a Celtic ballad, a touch that is a good sign for the continuation of the genre. *—David Howell*

Groundwork / Green Linnet ✦✦✦
As on most House Band releases, *Groundwork* is highlighted by its lively Celtic instrumentals. *—Jason Ankeny*

Willie Hunter

Fiddle / Traditional Irish Folk, Traditional Scottish Folk
In the liner notes of his final album, *Leaving Lerwick Harbor,* recorded several weeks before his death in 1993, Shetland fiddler Willie Hunter was praised for his "unrivaled vitality and lyricisim." In his early-sixties when he died, Hunter was a major influence on such Scottish fiddlers as Aly Bain of The Boys of The Lough and Tom Anderson. According to *Musical Traditions,* Hunter "was a musician with a formidable technical arsenal". Hunter, who taught in Shetland schools, had an extremely large repertoire that included original pieces such as the now-classic, "The Cape Breton Fiddlers Welcome To Scotland" and many tunes by James Scott Skinner. Although his masterful fiddling remained at the heart of his recordings, his albums were strengthened by the piano playing of his longtime collaborator Violet Tulloch. *—Craig Harris*

Willie Hunter Sessions / Dec. 9, 1997 / Greentrax ✦✦✦✦
Hunter hand-picked these 18 tracks for release just prior to his 1994 death, and they serve as a fitting tribute to his fiddling skills; joined by pianist Violet Tulloch, he interprets traditional Scottish reels and other fiddle tunes with elegance and affection. *—Jason Ankeny*

Iona

Group / Contemporary Celtic, Celtic Fusion
Though Iona is included with Enya and Clannad in the list of contemporary Celtic artists, the Scottish band's influences—including jazz-fusion, prog-rock and ancient Christian themes—are more varied. Named for an island off Scotland's western coast, the group was formed in the late '80s by vocalist Joanne Hogg and multi-instrumentalists David Fitzgerald and Dave Bainbridge.

For Iona's 1990 self-titled debut album included further acquisitions: drummer Terl Bryant, bassist Nick Beggs (former vocalist of Kajagoogoo) and several studio musicians—Fiona Davidson (Celtic harp), Peter Whitfield (strings), Troy Donockley (Uilleann pipes) and Frank Van Essen (tuned percussion). The album received very little press, even in their home country, though a Dutch network compiled a documentary based on Iona, the band and the island.

Two years later, Iona returned with *Book of Kells,* and the album was praised by North American critics as well as those of the British Isles. David Fitzgerald left in 1992 to pursue a degree in music and, as a result, Iona lost much of its jazz influences by the following year's *Beyond These Shores.* The group made up for Fitzgerald's absence, however, by inviting Robert Fripp to guest on the album. A contract with England's Alliance Music led to 1995's *Journey into the Morn;* the album was released early the following year in the U.S. and Canada. Fitzgerald returned to active recording in 1995, when he released the solo album *Columcille. Journey into the Morn* followed in 1996. —John Bush

• **Iona Live: Heaven's Bright Sun** / Jul. 1, 1997 / Forefront ✦✦✦✦
For years Iona loyalists have been saying "but you must see them live" in defense of their lengthy, ambient-laden instrumentals and sometimes partially realized studio concepts. They have a point to an extent. A greater intensity and sense of purpose does exist in this two-disc live set, but invariably, whenever that dynamic reveals itself, Iona drifts further from anything inherently Celtic, and closer to '70s pop/prog like Camel, Renaissance and Genesis (which isn't a knock, because Iona doesn't place labels on themselves). An obvious exception is the previously unrecorded reel medley, "Mountain Road/Ivy Leaf/Hunter's Purse/Rip the Calico," which boasts a stunning seven-minute Uilleann pipes clinic by Troy Donockley. Now that's Celtic rock! "When I Survey," utilizing the traditional melody of "Waly Waly" and the lyrics of 17th-century English theologian/hymn writer Isaac Watts, is sure to please devotees of both the folk-rock and progressive camps. Lead vocalist Joanne Hogg displays tendencies that evoke comparisons to Karen Matheson and Annie Haslam. Evidently, guitarist Dave Bainbridge picked up a few tips from Robert Fripp (who appeared on their previous two studio albums), as his epic, impressionistic 12-minute guitar intro on "Survey" eventually gives way to a fiery solo which wouldn't sound out of place on an early-'70s King Crimson album. Throughout *Heaven's Bright Sun,* Mike Haughton's unsolicited wailing sax outbursts do little to solidify Iona's classification as either a progressive or folk-rock group. And Iona wouldn't have it any other way. *—Dave Sleger*

The Irish Rovers

f. 1964, Alberta, Canada
Group / Traditional Irish Folk
This quintet started out in the late '50s (curiously, by way of Canada) and by the mid-'60s were a popular folk ensemble on television on two continents. Although their work, exuberant and boisterous, with relatively little scholarship, and lacking a traditional sound, became less fashionable with the ascent of groups like the Chieftains, the Irish Rovers continue to have a devoted core following. *—Bruce Eder*

The Unicorn / 1971 / MCA ✦✦✦
The single most popular record that The Irish Rovers ever made, their cover of Shel Silverstein's slyly written "The Unicorn" stands apart from the more straightforward material on this album, which is devoted to good times, family, and religious differences, and other significant elements of Irish song. *—Bruce Eder*

• **Irish Rovers' Greatest Hits** / 1981 / MCA ✦✦✦✦✦
The record to start with to get to know The Irish Rovers even though it isn't representative of their full range of material. *—Bruce Eder*

The Best of Irish Rovers / Mar. 9, 1999 / MCA ✦✦✦✦
Somewhere between Bing Crosby's vocal novelties back in the '40s and the current popularity of dance troupes like Riverdance and Michael Flatley's Lord Of The Dance, the flag of Irish music was held aloft in North America during the '60s by the success of the Irish Rovers. Patterning themselves after the Clancy Brothers (another popular group during the folk boom of the late '50s and early '60s), the group scored their 15 minutes of fame with the children's novelty, "The Unicorn," included here. But the group was no children's novelty act, as witnessed by the preponderance of straight ahead Irish drinking songs that spice up this 16-track collection. Highlights include "The Irish Rover," "Whiskey on a Sunday," "Mrs. Crandall's Boarding House," Lucy Simon's "Winken, Blinken, and Nod," "Nancy Whiskey," "Goodbye Mick and Goodbye Pat" and Gordon Lightfoot's "Did She Mention My Name." Those who are only familiar with the group's one big hit will find much to love in this collection. Excellent notes from Todd Everett, too. *—Cub Koda*

Upon a Shamrock Shore: Songs of Ireland & the Irish / Feb. 1, 2000 / MCA ✦✦✦✦
On this compilation, Will Millar's singing is alternated with that of the more sober Jimmy Ferguson, who handles ballads. Even on this Irish-themed material, the Irish Rovers are original and of their late 1960s time. "Pat from Mullingar" celebrates a hero of the I.R.A., while "Pennywhistle Peddler" seems to describe a person and a milieu more reminiscent of the Haight-Ashbury hippie scene in which the group was living than an Irish village. Nevertheless, more traditional fare is heard in the bawdy "Up Among the Heather" and in a quartet of songs about the Irish diaspora to America in the 19th century and the immigrants' subsequent experiences. This is a varied collection by a distinctive group that took its heritage in sometimes surprising directions. ("The Rovers Street Song Medley" is previously unreleased, while "Pigs Can't Fly" has been stripped of overdubs.) *—William Ruhlmann*

The Irish Tradition

f. 1975
Button Accordion, Vocals, Guitar, Fiddle / Traditional Irish Folk, Traditional Celtic, Irish Folk
Centered around the virtuousic fiddling of Northampton, England-born and New York-raised Brendan Mulvihill and the emotional button accordion playing of Brooklyn, New York-born Billy McComiskey, the Irish Tradition is one of the most influential Irish bands in the United States. Their two albums on the Green Linnet label—*The Corner House,* released in 1978, and *Makin' The Rounds,* released in 1981—have been a major inspiration on the growing popularity of traditional Celtic music in North America. Mulvihill and McComiskey first came together as The Irish Tradition to perform during a week-long celebration of Irish music at Washington, D.C. pub, The Dubliner, in January 1975. They became a more permanent fixture when the one-week celebration led to a five night a week gig that lasted four years. The trio became so enthusiastic about playing together that they would host jam sessions at another Washington, D.C. pub, the Benbow, on their off-nights. The sessions spawned a number of other Irish-American bands including Celtic Thunder, the Hags and the Boiling Spuds. *—Craig Harris*

The Times We've Had / 1985 / Green Linnet ✦✦✦✦✦
A thoughtfully performed album, it varies in material but is consistent in quality. *—Steve Winick*

Andy Irvine

b. Jun. 14, 1942
Vocals, Mandolin, Harmonica, Bouzouki / Irish Folk, Bulgarian Folk
Andy Irvine has been a major influence on traditional Irish music for more than three decades. A former member of Sweeny's Men and Planxty, the London-born multi-instrumentalist and vocalist has continued to extend the musical traditions of the Emerald Isle as a soloist, a duet partner of Dick Gaughan and Paul Brady, and a founding member of Irish supergroup Patrick Street. After moving to Dublin in the early '60s, Irvine became involved with the city's folk circuit and helped form Sweeney's Men in 1964. Although they were together for only two years, the group sparked a revival in traditional Irish music and had two hits, "Waxies Dargle" and "Old Maid in the Garret." Following his participation in the recording of Christy Moore's 1972 album *Prosperous,* Irvine joined with Moore, Donal Lunny and Liam O'Flynn to form the trad-rock band Planxty. Despite numerous personnel changes, the band continued until 1983. Irvine then recorded his debut solo album, *Rainy Sundays.... Windy Dreams,* and a duo album with Dick Gaughan, *Parallel Lines.* With Kevin Burke and Jackie Daly of De Danaan plus Arty McGlynn, Irvine recorded three albums during the late '80s as Patrick Street. His second solo album, 1991's *Rude Awakening,* came after the group's breakup. In 1993, Irvine resumed his association with Patrick Street. *—Craig Harris*

• **Andy Irvine and Paul Brady** / 1976 / Green Linnet ✦✦✦✦✦
Irvine and Paul Brady (former Planxty members) team up for one of the greatest albums ever of traditional Irish songs. Their unique sound will stay with you long after the music has stopped. *—Steve Winick & Chip Renner*

Andy Irvine and Dick Gaughan / 1983 / Green Linnet ✦✦✦
On *Andy Irvine and Dick Gaughan: Parallel Lines,* Irvine and Gaughan make a formidable duo, performing both traditional and contemporary material, all nicely balanced. *—Steve Winick & Chip Renner*

Eileen Ivers

Fiddle / Traditional Irish Folk
Eileen Ivers has transformed the Irish fiddling tradition from a folk music staple into an internationally-acclaimed art. A former member of Cherish The Ladies, The Green Fields

Of America, Chanting House and the Hall & Oates Band and a session player on albums by Paula Cole, Hothouse Flowers and Patti Smith, Ivers has continued to expand the traditions on her own. In addition to maintaining a highly successful solo career, Ivers continues to perform as a cast member of Bill Whelan's production, *Riverdance.* While *The Washington Post* called Ivers, "the future of the Celtic fiddle," The L.A. Times said that Ivers' "originality and rhythmic swing may well provide the bridge Irish music needs to break through to a mainstream audience." An eight-time All-Ireland fiddle champion, Ivers hails from the Woodland Heights section of the Bronx. The roots of her music, however, were inherited from her parents, John and Annie, who emigrated from County Mayo, Ireland. Although she and her sister, Maureen, were sent for lessons in Irish dancing, she soon convinced her to send her for fiddle lessons instead. While she later claimed that her fascination for the fiddle was inspired by country music television show, *Hee Haw,* she remained tied to her Irish roots and studied with County Limerick-born fiddler Martin Mulvihill. Ivers' musical skills were evident from an early age. Traveling with her parents to Ireland, at the age of nine, she received an All-Ireland medal for her banjo playing. Ivers has subsequently received thirty-four additional All-Ireland awards—eight for solo fiddling, six for slow air playing and the remainder for duets, trios and banjo playing. Although she limited her involvement with music, while studying math at Iona University, Ivers turned her full-time attention to the fiddle after her graduation. Performances with Mick Moloney and Seamus Egan led to an invitation to join the Irish-American supergroup, Green Fields Of America. After working briefly with Luka Bloom, Ivers was recruited to join a year-long tour with the Hall And Oates Band. The tour introduced her virtuosic playing to stadium-sized audiences around the United States. Returning to New York, Ivers began playing with Irish emigrees with John Doyle, and Seamus Egan and African-American percussionist Kimitri Dinizulu. Together with Dinizulu, she performed as duo during weekly Monday night concerts at Paddy Reilly's Bar in Manhattan. Ivers later joined Paddy A Go Go, a band formed by Chris Byrne of Black 47. When Maire Bhreathnach announced she was leaving the cast of *Riverdance,* Ivers agreed to replace her. Ivers has continued to work with top-notch musicians. On her album, *Crossing The Bridge,* she was joined by Seamus Egan, Steve Gadd, Randy Brecker and Al DiMeola. Signing with Sony Classical in 1999, Ivers released *Back To Titanic,* which included original film music not used in the film, new versions of tunes from James Horner's score and original pieces based on the theme of the album. *—Craig Harris*

Eileen Ivers / 1992 / Green Linnet ♦♦♦

● **Traditional Irish Music** / 1994 / Green Linnet ♦♦♦♦♦
Tradition and innovation go hand in hand on Ivers's surprising, fresh, and impeccably played solo recording. *—Steve Winick*

So Far: The Collection 1979-1995 / Sep. 23, 1997 / Green Linnet ♦♦♦♦♦
Released after Eileen Ivers became known as the fiddler in *Riverdance, So Far: The Collection 1979-1995* is a good summation of her career, containing highlights from her entire career (including a couple of unreleased cuts) and wisely concentrating on her early-'90s records. *—Stephen Thomas Erlewine*

Dafydd Iwan

Vocals / Celtic Rock, British Folk-Rock, British Folk
Dafydd Iwan was one of the first successful musicians to come out of the Welsh rock scene. Although he claims, "There are no stars in Wales," citing small audiences and minimal financial rewards, Iwan has attracted attention despite his committment to singing in the Welsh language. Iwan's biggest hit, "Yma O'Hyd (Still Here)," released in 1981, has become an anthem in his homeland. Iwan has continued to make this presence felt, financing an independant recording studio, *Recordiu Sain.* *—Craig Harris*

● **Canueuon Gwerin** / 1993 / Sain ♦♦♦♦♦
Iwan's renditions of traditional songs are played with punchy, pop-tinged arrangements. *—Steve Winick*

Yma O Hyd / 1993 / Sain ♦♦♦
This CD features tracks from two albums Iwan recorded with the band Ar Log. It contains almost the entirety of *Rhwng Hwyl A Thaith* (1982) and *Yma O Hyd* (1983). It's stirring stuff, but it's mostly lost on non-Welsh speakers. *—Steve Winick*

The Johnstons

Group / Traditional Irish Folk, Celtic Folk
The Johnstons rose to prominence in Dublin in the late '60s. Formed by Luci, Adrienne and Michael Johnston, the group featured harmony singing with guitar accompaniment. Eventually, Michael left the group and was replaced by Mick Moloney (vocals, mandolin, banjo) and Paul Brady (vocals, guitar). This four-piece band became extremely popular in Ireland and toured the world, starting off the careers of both Moloney and Brady. Unfortunately, their albums are equally split between innovative treatments of traditional material and fairly derivative covers of American folk/pop. Look for the traditional stuff! *—Steve Winick*

● **Transatlantic Years** / 1992 / Transatlantic/Demon ♦♦♦♦♦
This anthology is about equally split between their traditional material and their arrangements of Joni Mitchell, Gordon Lightfoot, Leonard Cohen, etc. It's a great way to get a feel for the group. *—Steve Winick*

The Johnstons/The Barleycorn / 1996 / Castle ♦♦♦
The Johnstons' excellent self-titled 1968 debut is full of the good stuff, while more great ballads and songs are found on *Barleycorn.* *—Steve Winick*

Give A Damn/Bitter Green / Sep. 2, 1997 / Castle ♦♦♦♦♦
Two of the Johnstons' 1969 LPs, *Give a Damn* and *Bitter Green,* are included on this two-fer, released in 1997. *—Jason Ankeny*

Ron Kavana

Vocals, Mandolin, Guitar, Banjo / Celtic Rock, British Folk-Rock, Contemporary Celtic, British Blues
Ron Kavana has been on the cutting edge of contemporary Celtic and British pop music for more than two decades. His collaborations have brought him together with such influential musicians as Alexis Korner, Charlie Watts of the Rolling Stones, Jack Bruce, The Pogues, Donovan, The Chieftains, Elvis Costello, Clarence "Frogman" Henry, Doug Sahm, Richard Thompson and the late Sandy Denny. Performing with a lengthy list of bands, Kavana has blended the musical traditions of the British Isles with blues, Tex Mex, country, Cajun and rock influences. Called a "hard hitting, no nonsense, realist" by *The Village Voice,* Kavana has produced music that has been described, by *Music Week,* as "charming, disarming with a very dry sardonic wit." The son of an Irish father and an American mother, Kavana was born in the County Cork village of Fenmoy. After cutting his early musical teeth in a R&B band, The Wizards, Kavana helped to form a trad-rock group, Loudest Whisper. Although together for a very brief period, Loudest Whisper recorded one album, *The Children Of Lyre,* for the Polydor label. The album was re-recorded, in 1993, by a group that included Donovan, Liam Og O'Flynn, Philip Donnelly and the RTE Chamber Orchestra. Leaving Loudest Whisper in 1993, Kavana moved to London and became involved with the city's top folk, country and R&B musicians. As a member of Panama Red, an all-acoustic, harmony-emphasizing band, Kavana played nightly at the *Hope & Anchor* in Islington. Replacing Albert Lee in the Thunderbirds, Kavana began a long association with Chris Farlowe. Kavana continued to change bands as fast as a chamaleon changes colors. Together with Irish guitarist Ed Deane, he formed a duo, Identity Kit. With the addition of four top British session players, the duo evolved into a band, Juice On The Loose, which supplied musical accompaniment for touring American vocalists. In the late-1970s, Kavana veered from the Irish music on which he had built his reputation. Accepting a position as bandleader/producer for Ace Records, he spent seven years recording with many of England's best known performers. Joining the Alexis Korner Band, in the early-1980s, Kavana remained with the group through several incarnations including the Boogie Band, which featured Ian Stewart, Charlie Watts and Jack Bruce. Kavana left the group to join Bees Make Honey, one of the most influential of London's Irish pub-rock bands. By the mid-1980s, Kavana's reputation was strong enough that he decided to strike out on his own. Together with Miriam Kavana (fiddle), Rod Demick (bass), Andy Martin (accordion), and Les Morgan (drums), he formed the eclectic group, Alias Ron Kavana. The group was subsequently named "Best Live Act In The World" by *Folk Roots* in 1989, 1990, and 1991. A solo album, *Rollin' & Coasting,* was followed by the first of three tours as opening act for The Pogues. Although he was invited to join the Pogues, business difficulties prevented him from accepting. Joined by two members of the Pogues—Ron and Terry Woods—Kavana formed a twenty-nine piece ensemble and recorded an album, *For The Children,* to raise funds for LILT (London Irish Live Trust), a charity organization working for peace in northern Ireland. Kavana and Terry Woods have continued to work together. They recorded an album, *Home Fire,* released as Kavana's second solo effort, featuring Irish music performed in an unrehearsed, spontaneous, style. Together with Miriam Kavana and Rod Demick, Kavana and Woods formed a band, The Bucks, and recorded an album, *Dancing To The Ceili Band,* in 1995. Kavana has appeared in and/or composed music for the soundtracks of such films as *Sid And Nancy* and *Ryan's Daughter.* *—Craig Harris*

● **Home Fire** / 1991 / Green Linnet ♦♦♦♦♦
Angry, impassioned, gritty singing. Wild, boisterous, irreverent playing. Excellent musicianship, songwriting, and production. It adds up to one heck of an album. *—Steve Winick*

Dolores Keane

Vocals / Traditional Irish Folk, Contemporary Celtic, Irish Folk
A member of one of Ireland's most respected singing families, Dolores Keane is the possessor of some of the sweetest tones in Celtic music. The first vocalist for Irish band De Danaan, Keane has sung with the Chieftains and Planxty as well as with her husband, John Faulkner, and on her own. After joining De Danaan in the mid-'70s, Keane remained with the group for four years and was featured on their self-titled debut album. She emigrated to England in the late '70s, married John Faulkner, and began performing with him as well. Her debut album *There Was a Maid* was released in 1978. Her second album, *Brokenhearted I'll Wander,* was a collaborative effort with Faulkner. Keane briefly joined the Irish trad-rock band Planxty in 1983, but returned to De Danaan in the mid-'80s and made an appearance on the Chieftains' *Bonaparte's Retreat.* She and Faulkner collaborated on two additional albums: *Farewell to Eireann* in 1980 and *Sail Og Rua* in 1983. Keane also recorded solo albums for Celtic Corner and Shanachie. A greatest-hits collection, *The Best of Dolores Keane,* was released in 1997. On the 1998 tribute album to Pete Seeger, *Where Have All the Flowers Gone,* Keane collaborated with Tommy Sands and Vedran Smailovic for a unique rendition of Seeger's "Where Have All the Flowers Gone." *—Craig Harris*

There Was a Maid / 1978 / Atlantic ♦♦♦♦♦
Dolores Keane was already something of a household name in Celtic music circles when this, her solo debut, was originally released in 1978. By that point she had won several All-Ireland awards as a singer and served time as a member of De Danaan, in addition to her work with other world-class ensembles such as Planxty and the Chieftains. *There Was a Maid* finds her supported by a band called the Reel Union (whose members are not listed anywhere in the liner notes). On standout tunes like "The Bantry Girl's Lament" and "Johnny and Molly," that group's tastefully low-key accompaniment does a good job of keeping the spotlight on Keane's simple and lovely voice. Some of the finest performances on this album, though, are the unaccompanied songs, of which "There Was a Maid in Her Father's Garden" and "The Generous Lover" are especially noteworthy. The Reel Union breaks things up with an instrumental or two during the program, and while the theory behind that approach is sound, it's an unnecessary measure in this case; Keane's singing is not something from which most Celtic music lovers will feel that they need a break. *—Rick Anderson*

Brokenhearted I'll Wander / 1979 / Green Linnet ✦✦✦✦✦
Featured is Reel Union, a band including pipes and fiddle, as backup. A truly gorgeous album, this is Keane and Faulkner's best work. *—Steve Winick*

Sail "g Rua / 1983 / Green Linnet ✦✦✦
Dolores Keane and John Faulkner lead a traditional music session that includes talented guests Uilleann pipes player Éamonn Curran, vocalist (and Keane's aunt) Sarah Keane, button accordionists Jackie Daly and Martin O'Connor, and more. The music on *Sail "g Rua* rotates between a cappella Gaelic songs, instrumental numbers, and lovely traditional ballads. *—Joslyn Layne*

★ **Dolores Keane** / 1988 / Celtic Corner ✦✦✦✦✦

Best of Dolores Keane / Feb. 17, 1998 / Celtic Corner ✦✦✦✦✦
This is an essential collection chronicling the incomparable interpretive genius of Dolores Keane, spanning her solo career and also touching upon her early De Danaan contributions. Among the 13 cuts are several previously unreleased tracks, as well as familiar songs covering a host of styles, including contemporary ballads penned by Dougie McLean, Paul Brady and Van Morrison. Also covered are John Faulkner's tribal "Lion in a Cage" and the World War II staple "Lili Marlene." Keane's take on "Galway Bay" might understandably be the definitive rendition of that song. Some of the arrangements are sappy and overproduced, but it's Keane's natural and strong voice that demands all of the attention here. *—Dave Sleger*

Night Owl / Mar. 14, 2000 / Alula ✦✦✦✦✦
Like Ralph Stanley and June Tabor, Dolores Keane is one of those rare singers whose voices mellow and improve rather than weaken with age. Also like June Tabor (though not like Ralph Stanley), she has broadened her stylistic range and her performing repertoire in recent years, still focusing on the traditional music of her native Ireland but also exploring themes from other cultures and tunes by modern songwriters. *Night Owl* opens on a somber note, with a despairing song apparently about the Northern Irish Troubles, and the mood is scarcely lightened at any point thereafter; there is a gorgeous rendition of the mournful "Wind that Shakes the Barley," one lament, two back-to-back farewells, a lover's plea, a tale of mass martyrdom, and a song inspired by the street urchins of Sao Paolo. By all rights this should be a terribly depressing album. But Keane's singing is such a joy, and the instrumental accompaniment so well arranged and expertly played, that every moment is a pleasure, if a bittersweet one. This is one of those albums you'll find yourself giving to friends as gifts. *—Rick Anderson*

Seán Keane

b. 1946
Violin, Fiddle / Traditional Irish Folk, Traditional Celtic, Contemporary Celtic, Irish Folk
The brother of Dolores Keane, one of Ireland's finest singers, Sean Keane has consistently garnered acclaim for his own talents. A former member of Reel Union, which featured his sister, Mairtin O'Connor and Johnny Faulkner, and Arcady, which featured Johnny "Ringo" McDonagh, Sharon Shannon, Cathal Hayden and Frances Black, Keane has made his greatest mark as a soloist. His first solo album, *All Heart, No Roses*, released in 1994, was named "debut album of the year" by *Q Magazine*. Three years later, *Keane* was voted "performer of the year" by readers of *Irish Music Magazine*. Keane displayed musical talent at an early age. Although he tried his hand at the accordion and fiddle, he felt most comfortable as a vocalist. Singing from the age of seven, he soon placed first in a singing competition at the Connaught Fleadh. By his late-teens, he had received thirteen all-Ireland medals for his singing. Despite his involvement with music, Keane was initially drawn more to the theater. He starred in Druid's production of Merriman's poem, "The Midnight Court" and a production of Tom McIntyre's play, *Sheep's Milk On The Boil*, at the *Abbey Theater*. He did not fully committ himself to music until 1994. Throughout his musical career, Keane has balanced traditional music and modern compositions. *All Heart, No Roses* focused on traditional tunes, many of which Keane had learned from his grandmother. His second album, *Turn A Phrase*, released in April 1996, took a different approach and showcased contemporary songwriting. Keane's third album, *No Stranger*, released in July 1998, continued in a similar vein. Keane's current band features James Blennerhassett (bass, background vocals), Robbie Overson (guitar, background vocals) and Ted Ponsonby (guitar, background vocals). *Gusty's Frolicks* was issued in fall 2000. *—Craig Harris*

All Heart No Roses / 1993 / Shanachie ✦✦✦
A charming and expressive Irish folk singer, Seán Keane takes an approach that is steeped in tradition, even though he doesn't qualify as a purist. Indeed, it's hard to think of him as a purist when *All Heart No Roses* finds him interpreting a Bob Dylan classic, "Abandoned Love," with so much soul and conviction. One song that's especially revealing is the opener "Home Away From Home"; influenced by American country music yet very Irish-sounding, the song beautifully underscores the impact Irish and Scottish music had on American country music. But while American influences haven't escaped him, Keane isn't someone the Irish traditional market should ignore. In fact, "Erin's Lovely Home," "Bundlin," "Taglione," and "The County of Mayo" leave no doubt that his command of traditional Irish songs is as strong as his command of a Dylan gem. This is a CD to savor. *—Alex Henderson*

● **Turn a Phrase** / 1996 / Kells ✦✦✦✦

The Kennedys

Group / Contemporary Celtic, Contemporary Folk
The Kennedys, a D.C.-area husband-and-wife folk-pop team, have been tearing up the scene since their 1995 debut, the Celtic-tinged *River of Fallen Stars*. The jangly guitars, tight harmonies, positive energy and smart lyrics found on this album and its all-star follow-up, 1996's *Life Is Large*, garnered the couple many regional awards. Pete and Maura first worked together in Nanci Griffith's Blue Moon Orchestra, and began opening up for Griffith on a European tour. Signed to Green Linnet, they released *River of Fallen Stars* to much acclaim. The duo's second album, *Life is Large*, featured visits from a large variety of folks, including Roger McGuinn, Steve Earle, Kelly Willis, Nils Lofgren, the Dixie Hummingbirds, Peter Holsapple, Susan Cowsill and John Gorka, among others. The Kennedys took a different path in recording 1998's *Angel Fire*, their first for Rounder's Philo label. They recorded all of the new songs in their home studio, Maple Ridge House, within hours of actually writing the tunes. *—Mark Miller*

River of Fallen Stars / 1995 / Green Linnet ✦✦✦✦
Sure, this is standard-issue jangly American guitar pop, but the world could use more standard-issue jangly American guitar pop, especially when the melodies are this strong and the lyric writing this assured. While it's clear that nothing on this album is meant to change the face of modern music, this disc is still a solid contribution to an honorable rock & roll tradition. Sometimes the Kennedys' allegiance to that tradition is explicit, as on "Month of Hours," which is presented as a Byrds tribute and features the requisite haunting melody and chiming Rickenbackers. Their cover of "Wall of Death," a classic Richard & Linda Thompson number, is a gutsy move and one they pull off admirably; hats off to Pete Kennedy for daring to take a guitar solo on a Thompson tune, and for having the wisdom not to try to outgun him. Lyrically, they need to beware of overindulgence: "jangle poets," "jangle dreamers," "gospel horses," "pilgrim travelers," and a "midnight bridge" all show up in one stanza of the title track, and "Chelsea Embankment" comes off as an excuse for Anglophilic name-dropping. But when they keep it simple, the result can be magical: "Here in my heart/I've built a mansion for you," Maura sings on "Day In and Day Out," and that unadorned image is perfect in its evocation of doomed young love. This is an album filled with such beautiful moments from a duo that will bear close watching in the future. *—Rick Anderson*

Life is Large / May 7, 1996 / Green Linnet ✦✦✦✦
The sophomore effort from the Kennedys finds the husband-and-wife songwriters developing and refining the slightly raw jangle pop offered on their debut, *River of Fallen Stars*. This time out the production is a bit bigger and a bit fuller, harking back even more explicitly to the lush 1960s melodicism that is the duo's musical ideal. From the opening title track, their chiming guitars and Maura Kennedy's sweet singing voice invoke the days when paisley was cool and melody was king. "Velvet Glove" and "Life Is Large" both couch a mildly didactic theme in layers of shimmery pop bliss ("Be yourself and stand your ground/Don't let anybody turn you 'round"), but for the most part the Kennedys continue their practice of churning out thoroughly charming pop for pop's sake. "St. Mark's Square" is a tuneful ode to a nonexistent urban neighborhood, "Tribe" is a heartfelt (if kind of sappy) expression of marital solidarity, and "Blackberry Rain" is a wonderful and shameless Beatles ripoff. On this album the duo is joined by a truly amazing list of guest musicians, including obvious choices like Roger McGuinn (of Byrds fame) and Peter Holsapple (formerly of the dBs) and such less obvious ones as country-punk rocker Steve Earle and gospel legends the Dixie Hummingbirds. The lyrics get a bit soft in the middle sometimes ("Baby, look into my eyes/True love never dies/No matter what they say"), but Maura Kennedy is such a winning singer and the group's melodic sense is so solid that it's easy to overlook the occasional maudlin moment. *—Rick Anderson*

● **Angel Fire** / Sep. 15, 1998 / Philo ✦✦✦✦✦
The Kennedys' hopelessly romantic and literary aspirations as an acoustic duo come into much sharper focus with this album. After an exhausting tour behind their *Life Is Large* album (loaded with guest artists helping out), the Kennedys bought a small house in Reston, Virginia and turned it into their own 16-track studio. The respite from the road refueled their songwriting muse, and this intimate little album came as a result. The songwriting is stark, pulling from pop and folk-rock genres as well as contemporary folk traditions. There's a lot of ambience on this album, and highlights include "The Fire & The Rose," the starkness of "Angels Cry," "Bells & Loaves & Letters," the 12-string jangle of "Common Bond," "A Place of Time" and the sing-along coolness of "Just Like Henry David." The duo takes a major leap forward artistically with this album. *—Cub Koda*

Evolver / Jan. 11, 2000 / Zoe ✦✦✦
Edgy confection from the husband-wife team of Pete and Maura Kennedy, *Evolver* continues their tradition of presenting intelligent pop that hides its dark core under a fine coating of cotton-candy. "Keep the Place Clean" features a not uncreepy stalker who has been following a woman around while she runs her errands, fantasizing that he could lure her into staying with him and cleaning his house. "Never Learn" sounds like a love song, but ends ambiguously. The sweet, clear vocals of Maura Kennedy keep everything subversively happy and the band plays along as a well balanced, fluid unit reminiscent of other deceptively upbeat bands like Belly. While missing many of the literary references of their earlier work, The Kennedys still manages to bring a smarty-pants esthetic to an enjoyable listening experience. *—Stacia Proefrock*

Kila

Group / Celtic Pop
Celtic pop group Kila formed in Dublin in 1987, originally comprising vocalist/Bodhrán player Rónán Snodaigh, his multi-instrumentalist brother Rossa and Uilleann piper Eoin Dillon. The schoolmates soon welcomed another Snodaigh sibling, flautist Colm, and began busking throughout the Dublin area; a series of other members passed through Kila's ranks before the line-up finally solidified with the additions of fiddler Dee Armstrong, guitarist Lance Hogan and his bassist brother Brian. Debuting with *Mind the Gap*, the group returned in 1998 with *Tóg é go bog é*. *Lemonade and Buns* followed two years later. *—Jason Ankeny*

Tóg é Go Bog é / Mar. 10, 1998 / Private Ear ✦✦✦
In the tradition of Mouth Music, the Afro Celt Sound System, and, to some degree, Capercaillie, Kila blends Celtic folk music with Afro-European rhythms; the band has achieved huge success in Ireland, where this album achieved gold record status. And it's pretty easy to see why: the combination of Irish melodies and Afrobeat rhythms is a winning one, and Kila's approach is unique enough for the band to stand out in an increasingly crowded field. They're far more traditional in orientation than Mouth Music ever were; the electric guitars and exotic percussion are there to serve the tunes, not the other way around, and their

sound is much more down to earth than that of the famously slick Capercaillie. Singer Ronan O'Snodaigh has a truly unique voice, and he uses it to good effect on the lovely "Bi Ann" and the title track; there are also lots of great instrumentals, mostly taken at mid-tempo with fretless electric bass and African percussion percolating along underneath. If you're looking for something a bit different in traditional Irish music, this band is for you. *—Rick Anderson*

● **Lemonade & Buns** / Apr. 4, 2000 / Green Linnet ♦♦♦♦
Inevitably, any genre of music will have its traditionalists and its innovators. Irish/Celtic music is no different—there are still plenty of Irish artists who play traditional jigs, reels and airs the way their great grandparents played them, and there are others who are committed to forging ahead and pointing Irish/Celtic music in new directions. One such Celtic band is Kíla, whose *Lemonade and Buns* combines Irish/Celtic music with elements of African, Middle Eastern and East European music. While Kíla essentially comes from the Irish school of Celtic music (as opposed to the Scottish or Breton schools), this CD is hardly oblivious to the Celtic sounds of Scotland. And much to its credit, Kíla makes such experimentation sound organic and logical rather than unnatural or forced. There's a definite freshness to *Lemonade and Buns*, which won't appeal to Celtic purists but is enthusiastically recommended to anyone who is seeking something fresh and challenging from Celtic music. *—Alex Henderson*

Pat Kilbride

Cittern, Vocals, Guitar / Contemporary Celtic, Celtic Fusion
A virtuoso cittern and guitar player and an excellent singer and songwriter, Pat Kilbride is one of the most dynamic solo performers in Irish music. He was a member of The Battlefield Band for a brief time in the '70s, then moved to Belgium and eventually Brittany, where he performed in a more pop-oriented group. In the '90s, Kilbride's a New Yorker and plays music both solo and with The Kips Bay Ceili Band. *—Steve Winick*

Rock & More Roses / 1989 / Temple ♦♦♦♦♦
This extra-length CD and cassette includes the entirety of Kilbride's 1980 *Rock and Roses* album, along with six tracks of instrumental music recorded in 1986 and 1987. It's brilliant and a bargain to boot. *—Steve Winick*

Undocumented Dancing / 1992 / Green Linnet ♦♦♦
This album has everything that made *Rock and More Roses* great, plus Kilbride's original songs. *—Steve Winick*

● **Loose Cannon** / 1995 / Green Linnet ♦♦♦♦♦
Kilbride starts this set off with the muscular and funky "The Working Man." This is Celtic music with a more modern touch than is often heard. Musicians Denny McDermott, Mike Visceglian and Larry Campbell, who are one of New York's premier rhythm sections, put a bracing polish and tightness into these songs. Augmented by Lucy Kaplansky's vocals and Jerry Sullivan's Uilleann pipes, Kilbride has produced a great allbum that showcases the wide range of his writing and interpretive talent. *—Richard Meyer*

Kornog

Group / Scottish Folk, Traditional Folk
The music of Brittany was introduced to much of the world through the playing of Kornog. During the six years that they were initially together (1981 to 1987), the group toured nearly non-stop and released four memorable albums. More than a decade since they went their separate ways, the members of Kornog have reunited. Despite the lengthy sabbatical, the group's mixture of Scottish ballads and original instrumentals sound as exciting as ever.

Kornog represented the combined vision of four highly-talented musicians. The sole non-Breton member, Jamie McMenemy (vocals, bouzouki, mandolin, cittern) had played with several traditional folk bands while a student at Glasgow school of Art. Turning professional in 1976, he toured and recorded with the Battlefield Band until moving to Brittany in 1979. Two years later, he recorded a solo album, *The Road to Kerrigouarch*, and helped to from Kornog. Although he remained outside of music during the first six years following Kornog's breakup, he began to resurface in 1993. His many projects since include performances with Belgium-based Celtic band, Orion, a duo with Kornog fiddler Christian Lemaitre, and a trio, Taxi Mauve, that accompanied vocalist Gerard Delahaye.

Lamaitre began playing fiddle in his birthplace of Paris before moving to Brittany, his ancestral home. During the years that he first played with Kornog, he balanced his involvement with the band with performances with a Breton dance group, Pennou Skoulm and a string ensemble, Archetype. Following Kornog's breakup, Lemaitre remained active, performing with an ensemble of traditional music teachers, Tantad, and a fez-noz group, Storvan. In 1992, 1995 and 1999, he toured with fiddlers Kevin Burke and Johnny Cunningham as Celtic Fiddle Festival. Lemaitre resumed his collaboration with McMenemy in a duo in 1999. In addition to rejoining Kornog, he continues to work with Celtic vocalist Gilles Servat.

Wooden flute and bombarde player Jean-Michel Veillon was one of the first musicians to use the wooden flute to play Celtic music. Playing the bombarde from the age of fourteen, he taught himelf to play the wooden flute in 1977. Prior to becoming a founding member of Kornog, Veillon recorded two albums of Breton dance music with the band, Galorn. He continued to play Breton dance music, while touring and recording with Kornog, forming a band, Pennou Skoulm in 1985. After the breakup of Kornog, he explored non-traditional music with three bands—Den, Barbaz and the Alain Genty Group. Since 1993, Veillon has performed in a duo that he shares with Breton guitarist Yvon Riou. Veillon has also continued to record as a soloist. His 1993 album, *'E Koat Nizon*, was the first album devoted to Breton music played on the wooden transverse flute. A similar album, *Er Pasker*, followed in 1999.

The newest member of Kornog, Nicolas Quemener (guitar, flutes, vocals) has replaced original member Soig Siberil in the revived band. A master open-tuning guitarist, Quemener grew up in Angers, France and studied percussion in the National School of Music. Emigrating to Ireland in 1990, he joined Arcady, remaining with the group until 1994 when he joined the Belgian band, Orion. Relocating to Brittany in 1993, he co-founded the traditional Breton dance band, Skeduz. In 1997 and 1998, Quemener toured with Dan Ar Braz' fifty-piece group, Heritage Des Celtes. In addition to working with Kornog, he continues to play in a duo that he shares with Uilleann piper Ronan Le Bars, and, joined by Lemaitre, in a trio that backs Celtic vocalist Gilles Servat. *—Craig Harris*

Kornog [Escalibur] / 1983 / Escalibur ♦♦♦
The debut album overlaps in material with *Premiere*, but is still worth having. *—Steve Winick*

● **Première: Music from Brittany** / 1984 / Green Linnet ♦♦♦♦
Maybe you don't think of France as a hotbed of Celtic culture. And for the most part, you're right. But Brittany, a region in the west of France, is actually home to an entire Celtic subculture with its own very ancient language and a musical tradition that comes partly from eastern Europe and partly from the same sources as the Gaelic music of Ireland and Scotland. Kornog is a Breton group that was founded by a bouzouki-playing Scots emigre named Jamie McMenemy; the Breton members of the group play fiddle, guitar and flute. This album is taken from a concert the group played in Minneapolis in 1983, and it's a marvelous recording. Jean-Michel Veillon plays flute and Christian Lemaitre plays fiddle in a style that would fit perfectly in an Irish pub session, but the tunes they play—with names like "Gwerz Ar Marc'Hadourig Bihan" and "Dans Loudieg"—have a rhythmic intricacy and a modal edge that set them apart from the Gaelic traditions of Celtic music. "Dans An Dro" includes some lovely interplay between McMenemy's bouzouki and Soig Siberil's guitar; "Laride/An Dro" incorporates the bombarde, a reed instrument that plays a central role in Breton music. *—Rick Anderson*

Ar Seizh Avel (On Seven Winds) / 1985 / Green Linnet ♦♦♦♦
Kornog's second album features a broad range of material, from the lovely set of Breton gavottes that opens the program to the Bulgarian ratchenitza that ends it in a lightning-fast 7/16 dance meter. The combination of French and East European dance steps with a Celtic instrumentation (flute, guitar, fiddle, bouzouki) and playing style is part of what distinguishes the music of Brittany from other, more familiar Celtic traditions. The angular, modal melodies are also distinctive, as demonstrated on tunes like the almost medieval-sounding "Toniou Bale" and the stark and lovely "Dans Plinn." In a somewhat strange juxtaposition with the rest of the program, bandleader Jamie McMenemy sings "The Shuttle Rins," a 19th-century Scottish song written by Henry Syme "for the encouragement of the working classes." "Sweetly may the shuttle rin/That wins the bairnie's bread," goes part of the chorus, and the melancholy image of a young mother toiling at a loom to feed her baby contrasts heartbreakingly with the song's sweet and gentle melody. This is a lovely record. *—Rick Anderson*

Kornog [Green Linnet] / Sep. 26, 2000 / Green Linnet ♦♦♦♦♦
Like Galicia in Spain, Brittany (in northwest France) nurtures a Celtic culture that is far removed from the Gaelic peoples that most Americans think of as Celts. And like that of Galicia, the Celtic music of Brittany has developed into a style all its own. The Breton style hasn't had many famous exponents over the years; in the 1970s the harper Alan Stivell made himself a household name thanks to extensive international touring and a folk-rock playing style, and guitarists Gabriel Yacoub (of Malicorne) and Dan Ar Bras are still spoke of with reverence in folkie circles. The only other Breton band to make a splash on the international folk scene was Kornog, which was organized in 1981 by the Scots singer and bouzouki player Jamie McMenemy, with guitarist Soig Siberil and fiddler Christian Lemaitre (flute player Jean-Michel Veillon joined shortly thereafter). The group disbanded in 1987, which makes *Kornog* a reunion album of sorts, though Siberil was absent from the sessions due to scheduling conflicts. The band's music is as beautiful as ever, still an entrancing combination of familiar Gaelic elements and the strange, indefinably mysterious flavor of Breton music. "Child Noryce" staggers gracefully in and out of 7/8 time; "Ar Plac'h Diw Wech Eureujet" is a slow air played in an Irish style but with a melody that sounds almost Balkan; and the group's rendition of "Lassie Wi' the Yellow Coatie" is strangest of all—the music sounds as if it's being played at twice the speed of the sung melody, turning it into a sort of Celtic adaptation of drum'n'bass. This is a stunning album; it's great to have Kornog back again. *—Rick Anderson*

Leahy

Group / Contemporary Celtic, Celtic Pop, Contemporary Instrumental, Adult Alternative
Previously known as the Leahy Family, this Celtic-pop group hailing from Lakefield, Ontario comprised the nine Leahy siblings—from oldest to youngest, singer/songwriter Julie, bassist Siobheann, fiddler Donnell, guitarist Maria, drummer Frank, pianist Agnes, fiddler Doug, pianist Erin and fiddler Angus. The family, along with their parents Frank & Julie and two other siblings who declined to pursue music professionally, began performing during the 1970s, developing a distinctive style informed not only by Celtic traditions but also Canadian folk and French-Canadian step-dancing. The subject of the Academy Award-winning 1985 student film *The Leahy's: Music Most of All*, real-world concerns like school, careers and marriage eventually relegated the family's performances to special occasions, but by the mid-1990s, with all of the children grown, they decided to turn professional; dubbing themselves simply Leahy, they issued their eponymous debut LP on Narada in 1997. *—Jason Ankeny*

● **Leahy** / 1997 / Narada ♦♦♦♦♦
By combining traditional Celtic music with country and a spectacular live act, Canada's Leahy is drawing rave reviews, and their self-titled debut is the closest you can get to the excitement of a Leahy concert. The two best tracks are undoubtedly "The Call to Dance" and "B Minor," which both have accompanying videos as well. The former starts quiet and slow, eventually becoming a full-blown dance tune, while the latter is the album's leadoff track and serves as a fine introduction to Leahy (foot stomping rhythms, swirling fiddles, piano flourishes, etc.). Other highlights include "Czardas," a Hungarian dance tune that is a showcase for the talents of fiddler Donnell, and "Alabama," which creates a wonderful, festive atmosphere. Leahy's self-titled debut is a must-have for fans of expertly crafted—and played—world music. *—Greg Prato*

Ewan MacColl

b. 1915, **d.** 1989

Vocals / Folksongs, Folk Revival, British Folk

Ewan MacColl may well have been the most influential person in the current British folksong revival. From his early manhood until his death in 1989, he remained passionately committed to folksong, though not exclusively; he was also a poet, playwright, organizer, activist, songwriter, husband, and father. The most ambitious project he undertook was to record a representative sampling of Professor Francis James Child's English and Scottish popular ballads. While his early repertoire was mainly of street songs and traditional material, he has always also been an important songwriter. Most impressive was his competence in producing expressions that had appeal for all levels of society; his songs have been covered by performers as diverse as Dick Gaughan, the Pogues, Roberta Flack and Elvis Presley, and many have been collected in several versions from the oral tradition. MacColl was married to Peggy Seeger, herself a singer of folk songs (and half-sister to American icon Pete Seeger). Together MacColl and Seeger have recorded quite a few albums as well. All, like MacColl himself, are important factors in the history of the folk revival, to be cherished by all who encounter them. This great singer made many, many albums over many years. All of them are recommended for fans of great singing, though some may be a bit specialized (i.e., unaccompanied singing in broad Scots dialect) for some listeners. *—Steve Winick*

English/Scottish Popular Ballads / 1956 / Riverside ♦♦♦♦♦

This nine-album set, edited by Kenneth S. Goldstein and performed by MacColl and A.L. Lloyd, is the first systematic attempt to record a representative sampling of the Child canon of ballads in a traditional British singing style. It is important for academic reasons, but more so for those who simply love the English-language ballad. The disc features exquisite performances by MacColl and Lloyd. *—Steve Winick*

Classic Scots Ballads / 1961 / Tradition ♦♦♦♦

The recording is admittedly a bit rough around the edges, but the passion is definitely there in this duo collection. MacColl contributes the main part of the vocals, with able support from Seeger, whose guitar and banjo provide a sparse but solid backup. Amongst the fourteen offerings, you'll find excellent versions of "Aikendrum" and "The Banks of the Nile." *—Steven McDonald*

★ **Black and White** / 1990 / Green Linnet ♦♦♦♦♦

A compilation of 20 important tracks. The album works well as an introduction though it will undoubtedly lead you to further listening. *—Steve Winick*

Real Maccoll / 1993 / Topic ♦♦♦♦♦

A CD reissue of tracks recorded during the '50s and '60s, the arrangements are somewhat dated, but the singing is marvelous. *—Steve Winick*

Chorus From the Gallows / Mar. 9, 1999 / Topic ♦♦♦♦♦

A beautifully remastered CD edition of this bleak MacColl release, which opens with the tale of Craig and Derek Bentley and closes with "Go Down Ye Murderers," which relates the story of Timothy John Evans, convicted and executed for murders he did not commit, both true and awful stories from the annals of 20th century British justice. While MacColl, in collaboration with partner Peggy Seeger, visits a number of traditional ballads of criminal misfortune, the underlying theme here is one of protest against the vagaries of the justice system in both England and America. Despite the odd attempt of levity, the unremitting darkness of the material is likely to put some listeners off. For all that, this is a vital piece of work from the British folk movement of the 1950s-1960s. *—Steven McDonald*

Ashley MacIsaac

Vocals, Fiddle / Alternative Folk, Contemporary Celtic, Celtic Fusion, Adult Alternative Pop/Rock

Ashley MacIsaac is, in a sense, the musical representative of the pre-millenial generation of Eastern Canada. An ardent traditionalist (and cousin of international Celtic performer Natalie MacMaster) with a penchant, nevertheless, for experimentation, this 25-year-old Nova Scotian native has been taught to play the fiddle the working-class, pub-stomp Cape Breton way: fast, furious and with phenomenal precision. Alternately considered a rebel, taking the old fiddling conventions in newfangled directions they were never meant to go, or a champion, reforging and recreating Celtic music with an updated, mass-appeal quality, MacIsaac has unarguably put his own spin on the sounds he was brought up with. This headstrong approach has led to MacIsaac working with an impressive array of talent: David Byrne, the Chieftans, Mary Jane Lamond, and others. Already considered something of a local legend and prodigy by the time of his impressive 1992 debut *Close To The Floor*, MacIsaac was not really introduced to Canadian audiences at large until he released the genre-bending *Hi!, How Are You Today?* in 1995. Along with nation-wide radio play for the first single, "Sleepy Maggie," featuring the dream-like Gaelic vocals of Mary Jane Lamond, and a regular slot on Canadian video channel MuchMusic, MacIsaac was soon recognized coast-to-coast as something of a minor national icon. His ability to cross the boundaries of folk, punk, garage rock, and metal, all bound together by his astonishing fiddle-playing, branded him as an eccentric, an upstart, and in many cases, a pioneer. Additionally, his refusal to conform to a quick and easy "studio image" earned him a solid fanbase. In 1998, MacIsaac released his follow-up to *Hi!, How Are You Today?*, a more traditional return to form entitled *Fine!, Thank You Very Much.* In 2000, he again pushed the boundaries of stylistic conformity with the electronic- and ambient-tinged *Helter's Celtic*. *—Neufeld*

● **Hi How Are You Today?** / 1995 / A&M ♦♦♦♦

Like any crossover musician, this unconventional Canadian fiddler from the East Coast Maritime region risks not being accepted by traditionalists or rockers. If you can get past that, there's great music here. With the help of Big Sugar guitarist Gordie Johnson, the fleet-fingered fiddler comes off on some tracks like a Celtic Mahavishnu Orchestra. At other times, including "Sleepy Maggie" with the haunting Gaelic voice of Mary Jane Lamond, he's down-right traditional. A powerful and promising debut. *—Mark Allan*

Fine Thank You Very Much / Jun. 16, 1998 / RCA ♦♦♦

Collective eyebrows were raised with the release of 1995's *Hi, How Are You Today* and its subsequent tour. Fans and critics awaited the arrival of with eager anticipation and wariness, respectively. Although it clearly states "a traditional album" on the cover, suspicions weren't fully quelled until an actual listen took place. After all, MacIsaac could be pulling a fast one. Well, he did and he didn't. Yes, this is a traditional recording that few expected, and no, he didn't engage in false advertising despite some feeling duped over his abrupt change of direction. Equally sudden was MacIsaac's permutation from traditional fiddler on his debut *Close to the Floor* to alternative rocker on *Fine, Thank You Very Much.* This album begins with the three-minute slow air "Rosebud of Allenville," but after that, MacIsaac shows no signs of slowing down. It's midtempo to uptempo jigs, reels, hornpipes, and strathspeys for the remaining 50-plus minutes. With the exception of John Cameron's aggressive acoustic guitar on "Athole Cummers," this record is all MacIsaac. In addition to his exemplary fiddle playing, he accompanies himself on piano in the unique and oft-alluded to Cape Breton style. For those expecting more thumbing of the nose by MacIsaac, it should be noted that his eccentricities wouldn't have received nearly the attention they did if he hadn't first established himself as an excellent fiddle player. *—Dave Sleger*

Talitha MacKenzie

Vocals / Contemporary Celtic, Worldbeat

New York-born and Edinburgh-based vocalist Talitha MacKenzie has made her greatest impact since adopting the musical traditions of the Scot Gaels. Mouth Music, her short-lived collaboration with computer programmer Martin Swan, yielded a chart-topping album in 1988. Her solo album, *Solas*, reached the top three on the Euro World charts in 1994 and was followed by the equally-successful album, *Spiorad*, two years later. According to *the Manchester Guardian*, MacKenzie is "one of the most exciting vocalists on the folk/world stage."

Studying piano from the age of four, MacKenzie became fascinated with traditional Scottish music before her eighth birthday. Inspired by field recordings of Gaelic music, she taught herself to speak Gaelic as a teenager. She continued to strengthen her connection with the tradition while studying ethnomusicology at the New England Conservatory of Music. She worked as a team teacher at Harvard University from 1982 to 1983 and helped develop a course, "Structure and Form in Music and Movement." While living in the Boston area, MacKenzie was involved with a variety of musical projects. Working with several dance companies, she increased her understanding of the Russian, Baroque, Balkan and Celtic traditions. In addition to performing in a multicultural acapella duo with Anne Goodwin, she was a founding member of the worldbeat group, Sedenka. In 1985, she recorded an album with Celtic dance band, St. James Gate.

MacKenzie's debut album, *Shantyman*, released in 1986, showcased her eclectic tendencies. A collection of traditional maritime songs, the album reflected her experiences as a shantyman on square-rigged ships. The following year, MacKenzie emigrated to Scotland and enrolled in the Celtic department of Edinburgh University's School of Scottish Studies. She had made her first trip to the area in 1979 and had returned in 1984 to record singers from the Scottish west coast and islands. *—Craig Harris*

Solas / 1994 / Shanachie ♦♦♦

Starting from a multilayered treatment of a Hebridean waulking song nestled in electronics, this solo release by the Mouth Music alumnus keeps getting better—until the deadly halfway point, when the disc doesn't so much run out of steam as abandons its smarts. The best cuts show how the eccentricities and earthiness of Celtic music lend themselves to various traditional and avant-garde marriages, like "Sein O," which embeds a clipped-syllable *puirt-a-beul* lyric in a bogle rhythm introduced by a hair-raising sample of Huun Huur Tu's Tuvan throat singing. But the disastrous ode to positive thinking, "Owen's Boat," belongs in a TV movie, and "Chi mi na Morbheanan/JFK" uses St. Jack soundbites about fighting tyranny without a trace of irony—hallowing our descent into Southeast Asia. Decent songs follow, but try fighting your way back. *—Bob Tarte*

Spiorad / Sep. 24, 1996 / Shanachie ♦♦♦♦

Talitha MacKenzie's second solo album, *Spiorad*, is an invigorating update of traditional Celtic, Gaelic and Eastern European music. MacKenzie bases her songs on traditional folk melodies, sending ancient music into uncharted territory by performing them with the immediacy of pop and the freewheeling eclecticism of the best jazz. It's a wonderful result that reveals rich, hidden layers upon each repeated listen. *—Thom Owens*

● **Mouth Music** / Rykodisc ♦♦♦♦♦

Natalie MacMaster

b. 1973

Fiddle / Traditional Celtic, Irish Folk

The niece of influential Cape Breton fiddler Buddy MacMaster, Natalie MacMaster has turned the music of Cape Breton, an island off the east coast of Canada near Nova Scotia, into an international phenomenon. Whether performing with her band, featuring guitar, piano, bass, drums and percussion, or with a classical orchestra such as the Edinburgh Symphony, MacMaster has thrilled audiences with her exciting fiddling and dynamic stage persona. After releasing two self-produced cassette-only albums—*4 On the Floor* in 1989 and *Road to the Isle* in 1990—MacMaster expanded her following with her first release in the United States, *Fit as a Fiddle*, which received a East Coast Music Award as Best Roots/Traditional Album of 1992. MacMaster's first album released by Warner Brothers Canada, *No Boundaries*, established her as one of the top musicians in Canada. *—Craig Harris*

No Boundaries / Mar. 11, 1997 / Rounder ♦♦♦♦

In the '60s and '70s there was growing concern within Celtic music circles that the perceived lack of interest and participation could jeopardize the future of that tradition. With the arrival and subsequent success of artists like Altan, Seamus Egan, Eileen Ivers, and Ashley MacIsaac, those worries amount to nothing but a distant memory. The educational opportunities are now abundant, the development of talent is ongoing, and the fruits of these efforts are being harvested routinely. One of the 1990s' most exciting and gifted fiddlers is Natalie MacMaster from Cape Breton, the wonderfully Celtic-rich region of Nova Scotia. Although only 24 years of age at the time of its release, *No Boundaries* is her fourth recording, and as the title suggests, her most diverse. In addition to MacMaster's extremely fluid, precise technique and her devotion to the traditional Cape Breton fiddle tunes, there are a few surprises here, most notably the bluegrass and erstwhile Texas swing favorite "Beaumont Rag," performed in true swing fashion. The oft-interpreted "Reel Beatrice" receives a funky treatment with full band, and special guest Cookie Rankin provides Gaelic singing and "scatting" to the slow hip-hop beat of "The Drunken Piper." Acoustic guitarist Dave MacIsaac deserves mention for his accomplished work throughout and producer Chad Irschick (Rankin Family and Loreena McKennitt) ties together some seemingly disparate music forms with amazing ease and dexterity. *—Dave Sleger*

● **Compilation** / Feb. 10, 1998 / Rounder ✦✦✦✦✦
While it might be preferable to have both *Four on the Floor* and *Road to the Isle* as complete and separate CDs, this condensation works very nicely, showing off MacMaster's lively fiddle style and her ability to select tunes from a variety of traditional sources. A good place to start with her work. *—Steven McDonald*

In My Hands / Sep. 14, 1999 / Rounder ✦✦✦
The basic approach taken by Celtic fiddler Natalie MacMaster and her producer, arranger, and guitarist Gordie Sampson is to take a group of traditional tunes, for example, the march and three reels mixed together and called "The Farewell," and come up with a folk-rock arrangement that emphasizes MacMaster's lyrical playing as well as a sturdy backbeat. But the two feel the need to spice things up even more, and so there are several unusual tracks, starting with the lead-off title song, in which MacMaster recites a lyric in tribute to her instrument, and including "Space Ceilidh," which features some appropriately spacy "programming"; "Olympic Reel, " a rock workout with new age elements written by Mark O'Connor, who duels with MacMaster on his own fiddle; and "Get Me Through December," a ballad with Alison Krauss on vocals. The result is a hybrid album intended to appeal to a broader audience than the purist Celtic crowd, or perhaps to introduce them to some new sounds without putting them off. *—William Ruhlmann*

My Roots Are Showing / Apr. 11, 2000 / Rounder ✦✦✦✦✦
Since Natalie MacMaster is basically a traditional Cape Breton Island Celtic fiddler who sometimes adds more modern elements to her music, a traditional album is an ideal way to hear her in her most natural environment, and *My Roots Are Showing,* finally issued in the U.S. by Rounder in April 2000 after having been released by Warner Bros. in Canada in 1998, is that album. On most of the 13 cuts, MacMaster combines a series of either public domain pieces or originals by the old masters, including reels, marches, strathspeys, and jigs. For example, "Glad You Made It, Howie!," which probably owes its name to the arrival of pianist Howie MacDonald, who plays on the track, consists of the strathspeys "Mary Scott" (written by J. Scott Skinner), "The Ewie wi' the Crookit Horn," "Lord Kelly," and "Sir Harry's Welcome Home" (written by Peter Hardie), plus the reels "The Dismissal Reel" (written by Sandy MacLean), "Paddy on the Turnpike," and "The Yellow Tinker." The exceptions to these lively medleys are two slow, mournful airs, "The Shakin's o' the Pocky" and "A' Chuthag (The Cuckoo)." The best is saved for last, as "A Glencoe Dance Set," a performance "live at Glencoe" fades up, featuring MacMaster and her fiddler uncle Buddy MacMaster. Natalie MacMaster was only in her mid-twenties when she made *My Roots Are Showing,* but it proved her sense of the music went back long before her birth. *—William Ruhlmann*

Joanie Madden

Whistle (Instrument), Flute / Celtic New Age, Contemporary Instrumental, Ethnic Fusion
Born in the Woodlawn section of The Bronx, New York, Joanie Madden has found her musical inspiration in her ancestral home of Ireland. The first American to win the Senior All-Ireland championship on the tin whistle, Madden is the youngest member inducted into the Irish-American Musicians Hall of Fame. The founder and leader of Cherish the Ladies, a band comprised of first generation Irish-American musicians, Madden has been equally successful on her own. Her second album, *Song of the Irish Whistle,* released in 1996, is the top selling whistle album of all time. A second volume was released in 1999.

Madden inherited her musical skills from her parents. Her mother, Helen Meade, a native of County Clare, is a dancer of Clare sets. Her father, Joe Madden, who hails from County Galway, is an amateur accordion player. Although she took five lessons on the piano, Madden didn't discover her musical voice until a family friend introduced her to the tin whistle. With money earned by babysitting, she began studying with Jack Coen, an influential East Galway-born whistle player who lived around the corner, at the age of thirteen. Madden took to the instrument instantly. After learning two songs, she began performing with her father's band. Her skills were further sharpened during jam sessions with fiddler Eileen Ivers, who attended the same elementary school. Within five years, Madden had become so proficient on the instrument that she easily placed second for the first of two consecutive years in the All-Ireland competition. She received her first gold medal, in 1983, at the age of twenty-five, the same age that her father was when he won the competition as an accordionist.

Shortly after receiving the gold medal and returning to New York, Madden received a congratulatory phone call from Mick Moloney. During their conversation, Moloney explained that he was putting together a series of concerts that would showcase the leading female Irish-American musicians at the *Ethnic Folk Arts Center* in New York. The series, called "Cherish The Ladies" after a traditional jig, proved a success. An album compiled during the series was named one of the best folk albums of 1985 by the Library of Congress. The same year, an album, *Fathers and Daughters,* was released which featured each of the women performing a duet with their father.

A more formal band was organized in May 1987, sponsored by the *Ethnic Folk Arts Center* and the NEA. This group has continued to work together and has released five additional albums—*The Back Door* in 1992, *Out And About* in 1993, *New Day Dawning* in 1996, *Threads Of Time* in 1998 and *At Home* in 1999—as well as a "best of" compilation.

Madden has balanced her involvement in Cherish the Ladies with solo performances and recordings. Her debut solo album, *A Whistle On The Wind,* was released in 1994. Madden has performed half a dozen times with the Boston Pops and played on their Grammy-nominated album, *The Celtic Album.* Madden has also performed on albums by Sinead O'Connor, Pete Seeger, Andy Cooney, and Eileen Ivers. *—Craig Harris*

A Whistle on the Wind / 1994 / Green Linnet ✦✦✦✦

● **Song of the Irish Whistle** / 1996 / Hearts of Space ✦✦✦✦✦
This sweet-natured and soaring album shines a relaxed contemporary light on the old tin whistle. There's a grand lineup supporting her, too, with John Whelan, Paul Averginos, John Boswell, Eileen Ivers, Jerry O'Sullivan and John Doan mixed in. Not only thoughtful throughout, but fun too, as she proves handily on "The Otter's Nest/Richie Dwyer's," a tune that gives one an idea of how grunge whistle might sound (Madden is, in fact, playing an air whistle, an instrument that sounds like someone tuning an air brake). One of the best releases to date from Hearts of Space's Celtic subsidiary. *—Steven McDonald*

Tommy Makem

b. 1932, Keady, County Armagh, Ireland
Vocals, Banjo / Irish Folk
Folk singer Tommy Makem is one part storyteller, one part musician, one part singer, and one part actor, so his live shows are usually quite lively and engaging, especially since he has spent more than five decades in folk music. A typical Makem concert involves traditional and contemporary Irish tunes performed on banjo and tin whistle, with a bit of background on each song's history as well. Born and raised in Ireland, Makem moved to New York in the mid-'50s to become an actor and began singing professionally in the Greenwich Village folk scene. A few years later, he teamed up with Tom, Liam and Paddy (Patrick) Clancy to form the Clancy Brothers with Tommy Makem. Signed to Columbia by talent scout John Hammond in 1961, the group frequently shared festival bills with Seeger, Bob Dylan and other beacons of the acoustic movement—at the 1961 Newport Folk Festival, Makem and Joan Baez were chosen as the two most promising newcomers to the American folk music scene. After playing to sellout audiences at Carnegie Hall in the early '60s, the Clancy Brothers with Tommy Makem made television appearances throughout the decade and recorded many albums for Columbia and Vanguard. He often toured with Liam Clancy during the 1970s and '80s, and continued recording for Shanachie. Makem has also been involved in numerous television projects over the years, presenting Irish traditional music to the masses, mostly on public TV. *—Richard Skelly*

Songs of Tommy Makem / 1961 / Tradition ✦✦✦✦
A rare instance of Tommy Makem stepping out and away from the Clancy Brothers. This set had him collaborating with guitarist and banjo player Eric Weissberg to good effect, the sparse arrangements helping to bring out the qualities of the tunes themselves, with some of these traditional songs getting very dramatic readings. It remains a shame that Makem did not step out on his own more often. *—Steven McDonald*

● **Songbag** / 1990 / Shanachie ✦✦✦✦

Malicorne

Group / Contemporary Celtic, Neo-Traditional, Worldbeat
Malicorne founder Gabriel Yacoub, taking his inspiration from the French/Celtic explorations of Alan Stivell and Dan Ar Braz as well as the British folk/rock of Steeleye Span, led his crew in producing rich, haunting arrangements of the folk music of France, Brittany, and francophone Canada. The band's later recordings feature original compositions and more contemporary instrumentation while retaining a traditional flavor. *—Michael P. Dawson*

Malicorne / 1974 / Hexagone ✦✦✦
Their debut is more acoustic and folky than their later works, and just as terrific. *—Steve Winick*

Quintessence / 1977 / Antigon ✦✦✦
This is a compilation of tracks from Malicorne's early albums. *—Steve Winick*

En Public a Montreal / 1979 / Acousteak ✦✦✦✦✦
Malicorne's live album features material from their albums as well five new tracks. A set of French-Canadian reels drives the Montreal audience wild. *—Steve Winick*

● **Legende: Deuxiéme Epoque** / 1991 / Hannibal ✦✦✦✦✦
It's standard procedure to refer to Malicorne as "the French Fairport Convention," though the comparison isn't really that appropriate. While Fairport Convention took traditional British Isles folk music and put it through a rock & roll filter, Malicorne went clear back to renaissance France for its influences, and imposed less modernism on what it finds. The group was led by Gabriel Yacoub, a guitarist with an exceptional singing voice, and recorded and toured throughout the 1970s and into the 1980s before breaking up. Malicorne's albums are generally now available in the U.S. only as pricey and hard-to-find imports; this album remedies that regrettable situation somewhat by compiling the highlights from the group's last five albums. It opens with a 16th-century anti-war song, sung a cappella, then proceeds to demonstrate the band's remarkable stylistic range as it veers from adaptations of Renaissance dance tunes to modern folk-rock. The band's use of such ancient instruments as the hurdy-gurdy, krumhorn and rebec makes their sound unique, even when guitars and drums predominate. Highly recommended. *—Rick Anderson*

Andy McGann

Fiddle / Traditional Irish Folk, Traditional Folk
New York-based fiddler Andy McGann attracted international attention with his recording debut in November of 1965. A collaboration with button accordionist Joe Burke and pianist Felix Dolan, *A Tribute to Michael Coleman* celebrated the music of the influential Sligo fiddler (1891-1945) and became one of the all-time best-selling albums of traditional Irish music. McGann has continued to make his presence felt. In addition to releasing an impressive solo album, *Irish*

Fiddle and Guitar, in 1992, he's recorded duo albums with Paul Brady (*Traditional Music of Ireland*) and Paddy Reynolds (*Fiddle Duets* and It's a Hard Road to Travel). *—Craig Harris*

It's a Hard Road to Travel / 1995 / Shanachie ✦✦✦✦✦
This album makes it obvious why McGann was revered as the top fiddler of the Bronx. A robust, almost classical tone combines with an easy grace and fluttering ornaments for a distinctive and masterful sound. Paul Brady's guitar accompaniments bring out the best. *— Steve Winick*

Loreena McKennitt

b. 1957, Morden, Manitoba
Vocals, Harp / Celtic New Age, Celtic Fusion, Adult Alternative
The musical career of Loreena McKennitt came to a tragic end when her fiancé, Ronald Rees, died while on a sailing trip with his brother and a family friend in Georgian Bay in July 1998. Although she was one of contemporary folk music's most successful artists, having sold more than four million copies of her 1998 album, *The Book of Secrets,* she claimed her hiatus from music was permanent. As she told one interviewer, her songs remained tied to memories of her loss.

The daughter of a nurse mother and a livestock trader father, McKennitt studied classical piano and vocal training and learned to dance in the Highland style as a youngster. Her love of traditional music was strengthened in the folk clubs of Winnipeg, which she frequented during the brief period she studied veterinarian science at the University of Manitoba. Relocating to Stratford, Toronto, she continued to sharpen her skills as a composer and performer. In 1981, she auditioned for a role in the city's Shakespearean theater. Although she did not get the role, she remained inspired. After reading Diane Sward Rapaport's book *How to Make and Sell Your Own Record,* she formed her own label, Quinlan Road. After releasing two albums; a nine-song cassette, *Elemental,* in 1985; and a collection of Christmas tunes, *To Drive the Cold Winter Away,* in 1987, she had her first breakthrough with her 1989 album, *Parallel Dreams.* Distributed through a network of small, independent distributors, the album sold more than 40 thousand copies within four months. Its success was surpassed by McKennitt's fourth album, *The Visit.* Distributed by Warner Canada, the album sold more than 700 thousand copies and received a Juno (Canada's equivalent of the Grammy) award.

While her albums have featured soothing, ultra-melodic, arrangements, McKennitt's lyrics have reflected her interests in the poetry of W.B. Yeats, William Blake, and Alfred Lord Tennyson. Her unique musical approach was addressed by her lighting director, Tracey Ploss, who explained, "When you get used to pop artists, the songs are mainly verse-chorus-verse-chorus-solo. With McKennitt, it's prologue-bridge-verse. You've got all these segues at different parts of the song."

McKennitt's music has been heard on the soundtracks of numerous plays and films. In 1989, she was commissioned by the National Film Board of Canada to compose the music for a film series, *Woman and Spirituality.* Her subsequent commissions include such films as *Jade, Highlander III, Disney's the Santa Clause,* and TV shows, including *Northern Exposure, Due South,* and *EZ Streets.*

At the time of her fiancé's death, McKennitt was mixing a new album, *Live in Paris and Toronto,* at Peter Gabriel's Real World studios. Recorded in Salle Pleyel in Paris and Massey Hall in Toronto during the Spring of 1998, the album was released in 1999. All profits from the album have gone to the Cook-Rees Memorial Fund, which McKennitt set up to finance water safety and recovery equipment for the Ontario Provincial police. *—Craig Harris*

Elemental / 1985 / Quinlan Road ✦✦✦
McKennitt's first album features mostly traditional songs and light, open arrangements. This is her best album for folksong fans. *—Steve Winick*

Parallel Dreams / 1989 / Quinlan Road ✦✦✦
This album marks a shift for McKennitt away from traditional material and toward songs she wrote herself. Guitarist and co-producer Brian Hughes also makes his first appearance. *—Steve Winick*

● **The Visit** / 1992 / Warner Brothers ✦✦✦✦✦
McKennitt's breakthrough album, this one uses exotic and fascinating pop-world music fusion sounds. It's creeping even further away from Celtic roots, but in equally interesting directions. *—Steve Winick*

The Mask & Mirror / 1994 / Warner Brothers ✦✦✦✦✦
Exotic world music filtered through Celtic themes and McKennitt's ethereal vocals; the performances here are steeped in a palpable sense of history and spirituality. *—Roch Parisien*

A Winter Garden / Nov. 1995 / Quinlan Road/Warner Brothers ✦✦

Book of Secrets / Sep. 30, 1997 / Warner Brothers ✦✦✦
The follow-up to 1994's *The Mask and Mirror* (there was a Christmas EP released in 1995, *A Winter Garden*) finds McKennitt in the same musical vein, mixing Celtic, Spanish, Italian, and new age to create her own distinct sound. The only problem is that she did not seem to progress much during the time between releases. This is not necessarily a bad thing, since she still knows how to write incredible melodies and layer instruments to produce peaceful images. "Night Ride Across the Caucasus" and "Dante's Prayer" are just two prime examples of this. And she continues her practice of setting classic poetry to music (Alfred Noyes' "The Highwayman"). Expertly recorded at Peter Gabriel's Real World studios, this CD serves as a travelog of sorts for McKennitt, musically detailing her travels during 1995 and 1996. She provides the musical and lyrical inspirations from each location she visited, utilizing the instruments and sounds she encountered on her travels.

Although she may be referred to as the Canadian Enya, Loreena McKennitt is definitely her own person, producing music of beauty and warmth. *—Aaron Badgley*

Live in Paris and Toronto / May 20, 1999 / Quinlan Road ✦✦✦✦✦

To Drive the Cold Winter Away / Quinlan Road ✦✦✦
This one features old carols of Christmas. It was recorded in various churches, which gives it a somewhat cavernous sound. *—Steve Winick*

Susan McKeown

Vocals / Celtic Folk, Contemporary Celtic
The traditional vocal sounds of Ireland are fused with a modern urban sensitivity by Dublin-born and New York-based vocalist Susan McKeown (pronounced "mick-yone"). Accompanied by her band, the Chanting House, McKeown's alto vocals have inspired comparisons to June Tabor, Chrissie Hynde, Sarah McLachlan, Grace Slick and the late Sandy Denny. McKeown's musical approach was described by *Time* magazine as "the kind of music that will link Ireland's musical past with its future."

Since emigrating to the United States in 1990 with a scholarship to attend a New York performing arts school, McKeown has been attracting attention with her dynamic vocals and enthusiastic stage persona.

The Chanting House, which initially focused on an updated version of traditional Irish music when founded by McKeown, Eileen Ivers and Seamus Egan, has increasingly added elements of modern rock since the departure of Ivers and Egan in 1993.

Although they released a pair of self-produced cassettes, *Chanting House Live* and *Snakes,* in the early 1990s, McKeown and the Chanting House came into their own with the Prime CD-released *Bones* in 1996. Their second CD, *Bushes and Briars,* released in 1998, featured musical accompaniment by Celtic musicians Johnny Cunningham, Andy Irvine, Seamus Egan and Jerry O'Sullivan. McKeown and Chanting House bass/bass clarinet/tin whistle player Lindsey Horner collaborated on an album of seasonal songs, *Through the Bitter Frost and Snow,* in 1996.

McKeown was a featured vocalist in the Obie award-winning musical *Peter and Wendy,* singing Johnny Cunningham's score at the Geffen Theater in Los Angeles in December 1997 and on the soundtrack album released by Alula. The following year, McKeown released *Bushes & Briars* and *Mighty Rain Depth of Field.* In 1999, *Mother: Celebration of Mothers & Motherhood North Star) was issued with Lowlands* appearing in fall 2000. ~ *—Craig Harris*

● **Bones** / Sep. 17, 1996 / 1-800-Prime ✦✦✦✦
Susan McKeown has one of those voices that takes you by surprise- murmuring and indistinct one moment, then suddenly shuddering to a full-throated, quavering howl that manages always to teeter on the right side of pretty without ever letting you relax completely and get inattentive. McKeown's songs make terrible background music, which I suspect is exactly the way she likes it. That said, *Bones* is not her finest album. "Ce Leis E—," the opening track, is a heartfelt but melodically dry ode to an inaccessible man that leaves the listener loving the words but grasping for a tune worth holding on to. "Albatross" follows and improves things substantially-the melody is still subtle, but this time it rewards close attention and the modest hook in the chorus comes like a glass of cool water after a walk on a hot day. That's about it for highlights, though, apart from an intelligent and lovely rendition of the ancient English song "Western Wind" that updates the original without diluting it (take that, Thomas Tallis). She also rocks out on "Snakes/Mna na hEireann." The rest hints at great things to come. *—Rick Anderson*

Through the Bitter Frost and Snow / Oct. 14, 1997 / 1-800-Prime ✦✦✦✦
This thematic collection of songs about winter and Christmas finds McKeown beginning to realize the potential that peeked out at irregular intervals on her last full-length effort (*Bones,* Prime CD PCD-027). Now that the focus is primarily on her voice and on the muscular but sensitive bass playing of Lindsey Horner, things are a bit lighter and jazzier, especially on "Winter King" and the lovely "Bold Orion," which includes an out-of-place but strangely satisfying electric guitar solo. "Green Grow'th the Holly" is a 15th-century English Christmas song that McKeown delivers in gorgeous multi-tracked three-part harmony. But the album's centerpiece is the stark and beautiful voice-and-bass rendition of "Auld Lang Syne" that had NPR's phones ringing off the hook when McKeown and Horner performed it during a New Year's Eve broadcast. This is a perfect disc to play while sitting by the fire with a loved one on a frigid winter night-not because it's romantic, exactly, but because it lets you feel alternately the severity of winter and the warmth of the Christmas season's promise, all without leaving your living room. A remarkable album. *—Rick Anderson*

Lowlands / Sep. 26, 2000 / Green Linnet ✦✦✦✦✦
Susan McKeown is an Irish folk musician with an unusually diverse resume. She has made albums of original music and albums of traditional songs, including a stunning collection of seasonal tunes entitled *Through the Bitter Frost and Snow,* on which the primary instruments were McKeown's voice and Lindsey Horner's string bass. She has also collaborated with numerous musicians from traditions both within and without the Celtic the world, and her music has been used in TV commercials for products as diverse as facial cream and automobiles. At this point, the only really surprising thing she could have done would have been to make a primarily traditional Irish album, which is exactly what she's done with the beautiful *Lowlands.* Granted, the instrumentation is frequently unusual—on the haunting "Dark Horse on the Wind" she's accompanied by banjo and erhu (a Chinese bowed instrument), and on "Bonny Greenwoodside" she plays finger cymbals while others play the tabla and caxixis. But the songs are very definitely from the Irish tradition, and her delivery is as hair-raising as ever. Highlights include the slightly flamenco-flavored "Slan agus Beannacht (Goodbye and Farewell)" and the anguished, a capella "Dark Horse on the Wind". Highly recommended. *—Rick Anderson*

Matt Molloy

Flute / Celtic Folk, Irish Folk, Traditional Folk
A master of the Sligo tradition of flute and tin whistle playing, Matt Malloy has played a vital role in the evolution of Irish music. A charter member of the Bothy Band, Malloy has continued to bring a modern sensibility to Ireland's traditional music. In addition to recording four memorable solo albums, Malloy has applied the warm, airy tones of his flutes to the music of Paul Brady, Tommy Peoples, Michael O'Suillabhain, Donal Lunny, Planxty, and the Irish Chamber Orchestra. Malloy has been one of two non-Dubliners in the Chieftains since 1979.

A native of the small County Rosecommon village of Ballaghadereen, Malloy represents the third generation of flute players in his family. Starting to learn the instrument at the age of eight, he won the *All-Ireland Flute Championship* nine years later. An invitation to join the National Fleadh Cheoil And Oirechta followed shortly afterwards. Moving to Dublin in the early '70s, Malloy quickly established himself as one of the city's leading traditional musicians. When his busy schedule allows, Malloy can be found at the pub that he owns in Westport, County Mayo. *—Craig Harris*

Matt Molloy / 1984 / Green Linnet ♦♦♦♦
Matt Molloy's first solo album came after he'd had more than ten years' experience as a founding member of both Planxty and the Bothy Band. He subsequently took flutist Mick Turbridy's place in the Chieftains, where he has remained ever since while continuing to produce solo albums on a regular basis. This is one of his finest and most focused recordings; the minimal accompaniment from guitarist Donal Lunny keeps the spotlight on Molloy's finely crafted, virtuosic playing style. Apart from his remarkable dexterity and speed, two things set him apart from other Irish players: the very advanced degree to which he has integrated piping technique into his flute style, and his astounding breath control. The latter is particularly noticeable on "The Humours of Ballyloughlin," on which he produces more ornaments with his lungs than many flute players can execute with their fingers. A sharp, reedy tone in the low registers is another hallmark of Molloy's playing; the tonal definition he achieves on the gorgeous "Lament for Staker Wallace" and the midtempo reel "The Templehouse" is a wonder to hear. But no matter how important his playing is from a technical standpoint, you never get the feeling Molloy is showing off. There's such an unaffected, joyous quality to his virtuosity that it's impossible not to be swept along with his playing. *—Rick Anderson*

Contentment Is Wealth / 1985 / Green Linnet ♦♦♦♦
To an aspiring Irish flute player, the experience of hearing Matt Molloy is a thrilling one tinged with despair. How can anyone play like that— But for lovers of Celtic music who don't feel the need to compare themselves to the musician, the response is more straightforward: pleasurable awe. On this album, Molloy teams up with fiddler and fellow Chieftains member Sean Keane (and, on several tracks, Arty McGlynn on guitar) for a bracing set of traditional tunes both familiar and obscure. Keane is an outstanding fiddler, not as immediately recognizable as Molloy but no less skillful, and their blend is remarkable. They almost sound like one instrument on "The London Lasses" and on the midtempo reel "George White's Favorite." Other highlights include Molloy's solo turn on "Kitty in the Lane" (accompanied by a nice guitar pedal-point courtesy of McGlynn) and the lovely "Seamus Ennis' Jig." The production could have been a bit more consistent; the instruments sound closer on some cuts than on others. That's a quibble, though. *—Rick Anderson*

Heathery Breeze / 1988 / Shanachie ♦♦♦♦
Molloy's flute is once again backed only by Donal Lunny's guitar, bouzouki and synthesizer. *—Steve Winick*

● **Music at Matt Molloy's** / Jan. 22, 1993 / Real World ♦♦♦♦♦
Live music comes from the locals at Matt Molloy's pub in County Mayo, Ireland, in which Molloy himself plays flute. It's one of the better recordings of "live-in-the-pub" style Irish music anywhere. *—Steve Winick*

Shadows on Stone / 1996 / Venture ♦♦♦

Mick Moloney

Vocals, Mandolin, Guitar, Banjo / Traditional Irish Folk, Celtic Folk, Traditional Celtic, Irish Folk
Limerick-born and Philadelphia-based multi-instrumentalist and vocalist Mick Moloney is one of the most influential Irish musicians living in the U.S. In addition to recording as a soloist, Moloney has recorded duo albums with Eugene O'Donnell and trio albums with Robbie O'Connell and Jimmy Keane as well as with O'Donnell and Seamus Egan. As a session player, Moloney has contributed to albums by Martin Mulvihill, Brendan Mulvihill, James Keane, Robbie O'Connell, Seamus Connolly, and Jerry O'Sullivan. His recordings with trad-folk group the Johnstons in the late '60s and early '70s were instrumental in the evolution of modern Celtic music.

Playing guitar since childhood, Moloney was initially influenced by American folk musicians including Burl Ives, Pete Seeger, and the Weavers. While still a teenager, he played with a series of skiffle groups. Relocating to Dublin in 1964 to study economics at University College, Moloney regularly played at jam sessions in local pubs. Together with fellow student Donal Lunny, he formed a traditional folk group, the Emmett Folk Band. Although they failed to record, the group attracted a loyal following among Ireland's folk music aficionados. Following the band's breakup in 1967, Moloney became involved with a new folk club. Among the groups that he booked was a family act, the Johnstons, who invited him to become a member. Accepting the invitation, he remained with the group for five years and recorded five albums. Their interpretation of Ewan MacColl's song, "Travelling People," reached the top position on the Irish music charts.

Temporarily moving to London in 1972, Moloney took a job as a social worker for West Indian families. While in London, he met and began playing with Derry-born fiddler Eugene O'Donnell. The collaboration resulted in three duo albums—*Mick Moloney With Eugene O'Donnell, Slow Airs and Set Dances,* and *Uncommon Bonds*—and a trio album, *Three Way Street,* with Seamus Egan. In 1973, Moloney emigrated to the U.S. for graduate studies in the Folklore and Folklife Department of the University of Pennsylvania. The 650-page dissertation *Irish Music in America: Continuity and Change* that he researched and wrote for his Ph.D. was published by the university press; he received his Ph.D. in 1992. Accepting a position with the Smithsonian Festival of American Folklife, Moloney assembled a group, Green Fields of America, with top-notch Irish-American musicians. The ensemble made its debut during a special *Old Ways in the New World* program at the festival in 1976. A decade later, Moloney brought together a star-studded collection of Irish-American women musicians to perform as Cherish the Ladies.

Moloney has continued to play an important role in the development of Irish-American music. In addition to being named "best tenor banjo player" by *Frets,* he was named "traditionalist of the year" by the *Irish Echo* in 1999. The same year, he received a National Heritage Fellowship. A founder of the annual Irish music week at *the Augusta Center* in West Virginia, he continued to teach at Villanova University in Philadelphia. Moloney served as musical producer and consultant for the PBS documentary series *Out Of Ireland* in 1995. As a record producer, Moloney has overseen albums by Uilleann piper Joe Shannon, flute player Jack Coen, concertina player Father Charlie Coen, and fiddler Johnny McGreevy. *—Craig Harris*

We Have Met Together / 1973 / Green Linnet ♦♦♦
An interesting first solo album, it includes traditional and modern songs and tunes. *—Steve Winick*

With Eugene O'Donnell / 1978 / Green Linnet ♦♦♦♦♦
A beautiful album, it includes lovely songs and tune arrangements. Derry-born O'Donnell is king of slow airs and set dances on the fiddle. *—Steve Winick*

Strings Attached / 1980 / Green Linnet ♦♦♦♦
His only all-instrumental recording features his mastery of tenor banjo and mandolin as well as guitar and bouzouki accompaniments. *—Steve Winick*

Uncommon Bonds / 1984 / Green Linnet ♦♦♦

There Were Roses / 1986 / Green Linnet ♦♦♦
This also has a brilliant title track. Fiddler Liz Carroll guests. *—Steve Winick*

● **Kilkelly** / 1988 / Green Linnet ♦♦♦♦♦

Paddy Moloney

b. 1938, Dublin, Ireland
Uillean Pipes, Whistle (Instrument) / Traditional Irish Folk, Celtic Folk, Traditional Celtic, Irish Folk
The sweet melodies of tin whistle and uillean pipe player Paddy Moloney has been a vital element of the Chieftain's sound for nearly four decades. His distinctive playing and imaginative compositions have led the group to the upper echelon of tradition-rooted Celtic music. In addition to his work with the Chieftains, he's performed with a long list of folk and pop artists including Jackson Browne, Mick Jagger and Sting. His whistle playing was featured on *'Rain Clouds,* 'the flip side of Stevie Wonder and Paul McCartney's million-selling single, *'Ebony And Ivory'* His compositions have been featured on the soundtracks of such films as *Tristan And Isolde, The Year Of The French* and *Treasure Island* and the National Geographic television special, *The Ballad Of The Iron Horse.* A native of Donnycarney, a small village in Dublin, Moloney hails from a musical family. His grandfather played flute and an uncle performed with the Ballyfin Pipe Band. After playing a plastic tin whistle, as a youngster, he began studying the Uilleann pipes with influential piper Leo Rowsome at the age of eight. After finishing school, Moloney accepted a position as an accountant for a major building firm, Baxendales. Music remained an important part of his life, however, as he balanced his accounting career with collaborations with such stellar Irish musicians as Sean Potts, Michael Tubridy and Martin Fay. In the late-1950s, Moloney began playing with Sean O'Riada, who subsequently formed a band, Ceoltoiri Cualann. In 1963, Moloney assembled several of the band's musicians, including Sean Potts, Mick Tubridy, Martin Fay and Peadar Mercier to record an album entitled *The Chieftains.* Intended as a one-time project, the album was so well received that the musicians agreed to continue as a more-formal ensemble. Moloney continued to work at Baxendales until 1968 when he was hired to work for a new record label, Claddagh. During the five years that he worked for the label, he produced or co-produced more than four dozen albums by such Irish musicians as Paddy Taylor, Maire Ni Donnachadha and Denis Murphy.. In 1988, Moloney received an honorary doctorate in music from Trinity College in Dublin. *—Craig Harris*

Tin Whistles / 1993 / Atlantic ♦♦♦

● **Silent Night: A Christmas in Rome** / Sep. 15, 1998 / RCA ♦♦♦
Silent Night: A Christmas In Rome unites Paddy Moloney and the Chieftains with Maire Brennan, Montserrat Caballe, Carlos Nunez, Sissel, Zucchero, the Harlem Gospel Choir, the Vatican Choir, Voices of Bulgaria Angelite and the Glenstall Abbey Monks. Needless to say, this album is an epic holiday celebration, and tracks like "Silent Night" "Journey To Bethlehem, " "Gloria" and "The Shepherds" combine Christmas spirit with Celtic and choral splendor. *—Heather Phares*

Christy Moore

b. May 7, 1945
Bodhran, Vocals, Guitar / Traditional Irish Folk, Traditional Celtic, Contemporary Celtic, Celtic Pop, Singer/Songwriter
The older brother of Irish folk-pop singer-songwriter Luka Bloom, Christy Moore is one of contemporary Irish music's best singer-songwriters. The former lead vocalist and chief songwriter of Planxty and Moving Hearts, Moore helped to bring the musical traditions of Ireland up to modern standards. As a solo singer-songwriter, he has continued to add elements of rock and popular music to his well-crafted, tradition-based tunes and has been a major inspiration to such modern Irish artists as U2, Sinead O'Connor and the Pogues. Moore's debut solo album, *Paddy on the Road,* was released in 1969. While recording his third album, *Prosperous,* in 1972, he assembled a band that evolved into Planxty. The group's fusion of Celtic music and high-energy rock made them one of Ireland's most influential bands. Although he left Planxty in 1974, Moore returned when the band's original lineup reunited in 1979. He remained with Planxty until 1983, when it evolved into a new band, Moving Hearts, and served as their frontman until leaving to resume his solo career in 1985. *—Craig Harris*

Prosperous / 1972 / Tara ♦♦♦
Guests include Andy Irvine, Liam O'Flynn, Donal Lunny, and Kevin Conneff. It's a collector's item, mainly because it was the album that spawned Planxty. *—Steve Winick*

• **Christy Moore [Polydor]** / 1975 / Polydor ♦♦♦♦♦
This is a terrific album of traditional songs and ballads. *—Steve Winick*

The Christy Moore Folk Collection / 1978 / Tara ♦♦♦

The Iron Behind the Velvet / 1978 / Tara ♦♦♦
His band on this one includes Moore's brother Barry, aka Luka Bloom. *—Steve Winick*

Live in Dublin / 1978 / Tara ♦♦♦
Christy at his best on this better-than-average live album. *—Chip Renner*

Ride On / 1984 / Green Linnet ♦♦♦♦♦
A powerful CD featuring "Ride On," "City of Chicago," "Lisdoonvarna," and "Among the Wicklow Hills." This one is so good it can make his other good ones seem weak. *—Chip Renner*

Christy Moore [Atlantic] / 1988 / Atlantic ♦♦♦♦
This self-titled album, Christy Moore's first on Atlantic Records, seemed intended to introduce him to a wider audience, possibly including American listeners. The album cover includes quotes from Irish music celebrities like Elvis Costello, Shane McGowan and Bono, describing Moore as the "greatest living Irishman" and the Irish equivalent to Woody Guthrie. These endorsements are true enough, but the album they promote proceeds to water down Moore's greatness almost beyond recognition. On several tracks the predominant instrument is the synthesizer rather than the acoustic guitar. And where the guitar is used, it is often in a paper-thin remedial picking pattern that does nothing to demonstrate the artist's virtuosic abilities on the instrument. The album also does little to demonstrate Moore's songwriting talents, featuring only one original Christy Moore song, "Delirium Tremens." It is a clever and tuneful song about a man's hallucinations while trying to give up alcohol, but the twinkly keyboard arrangement it receives here (by producers Moore and Donal Lunny with assistance from new age icon Enya, who also provides background vocals) is inappropriately soft and lilting. But two of the brightest points on *Christy Moore* are not political at all: "City of Chicago," written by Christy's brother Barry (better known as Luka Bloom), and Jimmy McCarthy's "Lisdoonvarna," a witty song about a summer music festival in County Clare, Ireland. *Christy Moore* is not a bad album, but it makes a poor introduction to his music. Moore may well be "the most powerful Irish folk singer today," as Jackson Browne claims on the record jacket, but this album is not so much folk music as easy-listening '80s pop. *—Evan Cater*

Voyage / 1989 / Atlantic ♦♦♦

Live at the Point / 1994 / Grapevine ♦♦♦♦♦

Graffiti Tongue / 1996 / Grapevine ♦♦♦♦♦
With *Graffiti Tongue,* Christy Moore eschews the multi-instrument arrangements of recent albums in favor of a simple, man-and-his-guitar approach which allows an undiluted focus on his crisp and sparing songwriting. It is perhaps his most mature and finely crafted record, with an incisive lyrical focus on politics and morality that is both compassionate and unflinching. The opening "Yellow Triangle," dedicated to Holocaust victims, is a powerful reflection on the perils of apathetic and isolationist thinking: "When they took the Bible students, rounded up the homosexuals, then they gathered up the immigrants and gypsies, I did not speak. Eventually they came for me and there was no one left to speak." The equally passionate "North and South (of the River)," written with U2's Bono and The Edge, is a plea for reconciliation and healing in war-torn Ireland. "On the Mainland" expresses Moore's outrage upon hearing a BBC newscast that referred to the Nobel Prize winning Irishman Seamus Heaney as "a British poet." On "Riding the High Stool" the songwriter almost seems to apologize for his political outspokenness, warning that "knowin' it all is a lonely place to be." No apology is necessary; *Graffiti Tongue* is the finest studio effort in years by one of the finest writers in Irish folk. *—Evan Cater*

Traveller / 1999 / Columbia ♦♦♦♦♦
It is perhaps not coincidental that Christy Moore's last albums of the '90s, recorded as he struggled with the possibility that poor health would force him to retire from live performance, rank among the best of his career. *Traveller* is a lushly produced foray into the previously uncharted territory of U2-esque technopop. Many of the songs on *Traveller* are traditional Irish favorites that have appeared in more conservative arrangements on previous Moore albums. Producer/engineer/programmer/keyboardist Leo Pearson plays a significant role in crafting every track, gracefully blending his synthesizers, drum machines, and electric guitars (including some played by U2's The Edge) with healthy doses of Uilleann pipe, bouzouki, bowran, flute, and acoustic guitar. The results are occasionally strained, but always fascinating and often brilliant. "Last Cold Kiss" is a chillingly executed tragic ballad that allows Moore to sing a duet beyond the grave with a recording of his father, Andy Moore, who died in 1956. Another highlight is "The Sirens Voice," a powerful and startlingly original indictment of Irish callousness toward immigrant refugees from Somalia. Throughout the album, the cultural clash afforded by the juxtaposition of modern musical technology with time-honored folk tradition is used to profound effect; it underlines the emotional and spiritual alienation of contemporary life and adds weight to timeless questions of mortality and justice. If this album is the result of Moore's retirement from concert performance, then it hasn't been a total loss. *—Evan Cater*

Moving Cloud

f. 1989

Melodeon, Viola, Accordion, Flute, Fiddle / Traditional Irish Folk, Irish Folk

The traditional dance music of Ireland is played with fervor and excitement by the County Clare-based quintet Moving Cloud. Originally formed to provide the accompaniment for set dancing, Moving Cloud has evolved into a virtuosic concert band. Their self-titled debut album, released in 1994, was named Best Traditional Album by *The Irish Echo.* Their second album, *Foxglove,* released in 1998, further established the band as one of Ireland's leading instrumental ensembles. Moving Cloud, named after a classic Irish reel, made their debut appearance at the Old Cloud Hotel in Ennis, County Clare on May 18, 1989. The group brought together five musicians who had established themselves with other bands and solo recordings. Accordion player Paul Brock had recorded an album with De Danaan fiddler Frankie Gavin in 1986. His solo album, *Mo Chairdin,* was released in 1992. Galway-born composer, arranger and keyboardist Carl Hession had previously performed with Gavin, Joe Derrane, Matt Molloy and Joe Burke and had been a member of the Shaskeen Ceili Band. Hession has recorded four solo albums: *The Galway Suite* (1984), *Echoes of Ireland* (1987), *Ceol Inne/Ceol Innui* (1995) and *Tra* (1997). A native of Birmingham, England whose parents hail from West Clare, Kevin Crawford (flute and percussion) has lived in Ireland since 1988. In addition to recording with Joe Derrane, Crawford has performed with the septet Grianan and the trio Raise the Rafters. His debut solo album, *D'Flute Album,* was released in 1995. A major characteristic of Moving Cloud's sound is the twin fiddling of Sligo-born Manus McGuire and Galway-born Maeve Donnelly. McGuire previously toured and recorded three albums with Buttons and Bows, a quartet that also featured his brother Seamus, Jackie Daly and Garry O'Briain. The winner of several All-Ireland fiddle championships, Donnelly is a master of the East Galway fiddle style. *—Craig Harris*

Foxglove / May 19, 1998 / Green Linnet ♦♦♦
Moving Cloud is a quintet of Irish musicians who face something of a quandary: they want to be regarded as concert performers rather than a dance band, but while it's true that their chops are more than sufficient to hold an audience's attention, they play in a style that owes far more to the ceilidh than to the concert hall. For one thing, they tend to take tunes at a brisk but moderate tempo (unlike some of their more flamboyant contemporaries who play everything at speeds no one could dance to even if they wanted to), and for another, they've got Carl Hession banging out the off-beats on his piano in a way that just begs you to spin around the floor with your fair colleen. And then there are the tunes themselves: *Foxglove* consists almost entirely of dance sets (there is one slow air), and the program even includes a waltz. So Moving Cloud should probably just accept its fate and let the rest of us dance gratefully. Highlights include flutist Kevin Crawford's gorgeous playing on "Mooney's Mazurka" and the perfect ensemble blend on the sprightly and lovely song air "Suil Suil a Ghra." *—Rick Anderson*

Moving Hearts

f. Ireland

Group / Celtic Rock, Contemporary Celtic

Together for only four years, Moving Hearts had a profound effect on the development of modern Celtic music. One of the first Irish folk bands to use electric instruments, after Horslips, Moving Hearts took a high-energy approach to their tradition-rooted music. Recalling an early appearance by the band, *Q* magazine wrote, 'saw them in Dublin, must have been 1982, and they just blew me apart ' they're a sort of Celtic Little Feat'.

The original line-up of Moving Hearts united some of Ireland's best musicians. Multi-instrumentalist Donal Lunny and singer, guitarist and songwriter Christy Moore had previously played together in Planxty. Guitarist Declan Sinnott had produced and arranged material for such Celtic performers as Mary Black and Sinead Lohan. Dublin piper Davy Spillane had performed with Horslips. Within a few months, the band was joined by saxophonist Keith Donald, a veteran session player and a member of such jazz bands as Jim Doherty's Spon and Noel Kelehan's Quintet. Moving Hearts was rounded out by drummer Brian Calman and bassist Eoghan O'Neill.

Although the original band performed together for two years, the departure of Calman, over 'musical differences', signaled the first of several personnel changes. Following the release of the group's second album, , Moore left to pursue a solo career and was replaced by vocalist Mick Hanley. After recording one album with the band *'Live Hearts'* Hanley was replaced by female vocalist Flo McSweeney. The changes continued, however. By the time that they recorded their final album, Moving Hearts had become an all-instrumental unit.

Politics played an important role in Moving Hearts's repertoire. The struggles of hunger strikers and impoverished in Northern Ireland were addressed through such songs as "Landlord" and "On The Blanket", while, the proliferation of nuclear weaponry was reflected in such tunes as "Hiroshima Nagasaki Russian Roulette" and an emotional interpretation of Jackson Browne's "After The Deluge".

Moving Hearts was featured as the backup band on Van Morrison's 1985 album, *A Sense Of Wonder.*

In the aftermath of Moving Hearts's breakup, several members went on to perform in the cast of Bill Whelan's musical production, *Riverdance.* *—Craig Harris*

• **Moving Hearts** / 1981 / Green Linnet ♦♦♦♦
This compilation album features Hearts standards such as "Hiroshima, Nagasaki, Russian Roulette" and "McBrides," as well as a version of Jackson Browne's "Before the Deluge" that turns it into an Irish folk song. *—William Ruhlmann*

The Storm / 1985 / Tara ♦♦♦♦

Martin Mulvihill

Fiddle / Traditional Irish Folk

Martin Mulvihill, a fiddler who came from Limerick, Ireland, to the Bronx, had a major impact on Irish music in the eastern U.S. It was not so much his playing that influenced others, but his teaching; Mulvihill ran a highly successful Irish music school and even went on the road to other cities to teach Irish music to interested youth. Many of the good and great young players studied with Mulvihill. *—Steve Winick*

• **Traditional Irish Fiddling from County Limerick** / 1978 / Green Linnet ♦♦♦♦
There's nothing flashy or fancy here, just solid and spirited playing from Mulvihill and his accompanist, Mick Moloney. *—Steve Winick*

Mairead Ni Dhomhnaill

Vocals, Fiddle / Traditional Irish Folk, Traditional Celtic, Irish Folk

With the release of her long-overdue debut solo album No Dowry in 1999, the world was reminded of the power of Maighread Ni Dhomhnaill's vocals. Although she had hinted at her strengths as a member of Skara Brae, a Gaelic-language ensemble that she shared with her brother Michael O'Dhomhnaill, sister Triona Ni Dhomhnaill, and multi-instrumentalist Daithi Sproule, Ni Dhomhnaill had maintained a low profile since the group's demise in the early '80s.

A native of Rann na Feireste (Ranafast), County Donegal, Ni Dhomhnaill was raised in Kells, County Meath. Music played an essential role in her early family life. Her father, Aodh O'Domhnaill, and aunt, Neili Ni Dhomhnaill, were avid collectors of traditional Irish folksongs. *—Craig Harris*

Mairead Ni Dhomhnaill / 1976 / Gael Linn ✦✦✦
As fine as her sister's solo album, this features some excellent musicians backing Mairead (as she then spelled her name) on fiddle, concertina, guitar, whistle and keyboards. *—Steve Winick*

● **Gan Dha Phingin Spre (No Dowry)** / 1991 / Shanachie ✦✦✦✦
Maighread Ni Dhomhnaill's solo debut is an exquisitely crafted collection of traditional Irish songs of doomed love—tunes like "A Mhaithrin Dhileas," "An Cailin Gaelach" and "Martha, the Flower of Sweet Strabane" all depict tales of heartbreak, loss and unrequited romance, although Ni Dhomhnaill's luminous vocals ensure that the gloom never becomes too oppressive. *—Raymond McKinney*

Idir an Da Sholas (Between the Two Lights) / Oct. 10, 2000 / Green Linnet ✦✦✦✦
Triona Ni Dhomhnaill was a charter member of the Bothy Band in the 1970s and later played for Touchstone and Nightnoise. Her sister Maighread sings with Donal Lunny's band Coolfin, and Lunny contributes guitar, bouzouki, arrangements, and production on this album of traditional Irish songs. The result of this three-way collaboration is striking, if not surprising, in its loveliness; the songs are mostly of the sweetly despairing type so familiar to lovers of Irish music: "Liostail me le Sairsint" is the lament of a young conscriptee who, despite the luxuries of his new life overseas, yearns for the Old Sod; "Spanish Lady," with its mysterious numerical chorus, is a reflection on the treachery of fortune and the perfidy of womankind; "Foireann an Bhaid" is one more in a long line of laments for young fishermen lost at sea. On the brighter side are a whimsical ode to an especially yummy variety of whitefish and "The Banks of Claudy," in which a young swain returns from the war in disguise to test the fidelity of his lover; she passes the test and they live, presumably, happily ever after. Or not—there's probably a sadder song out there about whatever became of them afterwards. The arrangements of these songs are modern, but tastefully so, and the Ni Dhomhnaill sisters' voices are consistently beautiful whether solo or blended. Highly recommended. *—Rick Anderson*

Triona Ni Dhomhnaill

Clavinet, Vocals, Keyboards, Harpsichord, Piano, Synthesizer / British Folk-Rock, Traditional Irish Folk, Contemporary Celtic, Irish Folk
Triona Ni Dhomhnaill is one of the most influential female vocalists in the history of Irish music. In addition to a superb solo album, *Triona*, released in Ireland in 1975 and the United States in 1984, Ni Dhomhnaill's high-pitched vocals and keyboard playing has been an integral element of Skara Brae, the Bothy Band, Touchstone, Nightnoise and Relativity. She first attracted attention with a family folk group, Skara Brae, that specialized in songs sung in Gaelic. In 1975, Ni Dhomhnaill and her brother Michael helped form the Bothy Band with Donal Lunny. One of the first groups to bring the musical traditions of Ireland up to contemporary standards, the Bothy Band finally broke up in 1979, after which Ni Dhomhnaill moved to America and formed Touchstone. The band's two albums, 1982's *The New Land* and 1984's *Jealousy*, combined songs sung in Gaelic, original singer/songwriter tunes, and traditional folk songs from the United States and Nova Scotia. Back together with her brother in the mid-'80s, she formed the group Relativity. They also collaborated in a Celtic-tinged new age group, Nightnoise. *—Craig Harris*

Triona / 1975 / Green Linnet ✦✦✦✦
This solo album features some of her loveliest recorded songs, some in English and some in Gaelic, with accompaniment by some of Ireland's greatest players. *—Steve Winick*

Danny O'Flaherty

Vocals, / Contemporary Celtic
The ballad traditions of Ireland have been expanded through the efforts of Irish-American multi-instrumentalist, vocalist, radio announcer and songwriter, Danny O'Flaherty. In addition to performing concerts around the globe with his band, Celtic Folk, featuring his brother, Patrick, O'Flaherty has provided an outlet for Irish musicians at his Irish Channel Center in New Orleans.

While traditional ballads serve as the foundation of his repertoire, O' Flaherty has masterfully composed new tunes in the traditional styles. His original compositions include "The Ballad of the Yellow Ribbons," written for the American hostages in Iran, "Derby Day In Ireland" and "The Blushing Bride," which has increasingly been heard at wedding celebrations. As the founder and president of the non-profit Celtic Nations Heritage Foundation, O'Flaherty has hosted an annual festival of Irish music and art since the early-1990s. Initially held in Madisonville, Louisiana, the increasing attendance forced the festival to move to a larger site. Held at Marconi Meadows in New Orleans' city park, the event has averaged more than fifty thousand people annually since 1997. *—Craig Harris*

● **From the Heart** / Sep. 16, 1997 / Hy-Brasl ✦✦✦✦

Old Blind Dogs

f. 1990
Percussion, Guitar, Fiddle, Bass / Celtic Folk, Contemporary Celtic
In Britain and Ireland, as in America over the last 25 years or so, a number of folk music bands have sprung up that have combined strong elements and foundations of the traditional with a variety of influences from other cultures and styles. Steeleye Span, the Tannahill Weavers, Fairport Convention, the House Band, Wolfstone and others have all produced music that borrows as freely from reggae, African rhythms, and American folk and rock music, as from the ancient ballads and tunes of their own cultures. Among the most striking and interesting of these bands was Scotland's Old Blind Dogs, an Aberdeen based band that toured Europe and North America extensively throughout the '90s before dissolving in 1998. The genesis of Old Blind Dogs dates to 1990, when three veterans of the Aberdeen music scene came together after having played with each other in various other bands. Guitarist and lead singer Ian F. Benzie, the elder statesman of the band, had been involved with folk music since the glory days of the late '50s and early '60s. It was the realization that many of his favorite songs by American folk icons like Joan Baez were, in fact, songs from centuries past in his own culture that steered him toward the traditional side of the music, while becoming adept at writing his own powerful material. As a singer, Benzie has been compared to fellow Scotsmen Dick Gaughan and Archie Fisher, a master of phrasing and delivery, whether of his own songs or of classics like "The Cruel Sister." Joining Benzie in the original configuration of the Dogs were fellow Aberdeen natives Jonny Hardie on fiddle and Buzzby McMillan, a jack of all trades on bass, whistles, cittern and just about anything else with frets and strings. Though classically trained as a viola player, Hardie became enamored of the traditional fiddle tunes he heard while travelling throughout Britain. Meeting up again with McMillan after returning from music college, they began busking together on the streets and playing in a succession of bands before forming the Dogs with Benzie. By 1992, they had gained a reputation as a band adept at mixing traditional Scottish fare with more modern material, but it was the addition of percussionist Davy Cattanach in that year that gave the band a character unlike any other of their contemporary bands and allowed them to branch out in new directions. Cattanach had played drums in a number of reggae, rock and blues bands that McMillan had also been part of. After spending five years or so in London, Cattanach returned to Aberdeen, where he met up again with McMillan. He had never played or been involved with traditional music before, but was intrigued with the sound of the band his friend was playing in, and on being told they were looking to add a percussionist, immediately went out and got a set of congas. With the addition of the exotic rhythms Cattanach brought to the band, they were able to explore new ways of expressing their distinctive blend of old and new. For the next five years, they toured and recorded to rave reviews on both sides of the Atlantic, such as this one from the *Scottish Daily Record*: "From the exciting driving energy of traditional tunes to the haunting melody [they] will give you goosepimples on the back of your neck." In 1997, a fifth Dog was added in the person of piper and woodwind player Fraser Fifield, whose work was welcomed by the band's die-hard fans as an added dimension to the sound. In 1998, Cattanach departed the band and was replaced by long-time Wolfstone drummer and percussionist Graeme "Mop" Youngson. Following their 1998 U.S. tour, though, the years of being on the road induced Benzie to also quit the band, and as the clock wound down on the century, Old Blind Dogs was in hiatus. *—John Lupton*

Five / 1997 / Lochshore ✦✦✦
The fifth record from these Scottish folkies introduces new member Fraser Fifield on pipes, whistles, and sax. His presence is immediately felt on "Trip to Pakistan," a Scotland meets the Mideast instrumental seasoned by Fifield's border pipes and Davy Cattanach's hand drums. Cattanach opts for a similar percussive cadence on several selections; in fact, Old Blind Dogs seem committed to uniting diversified cultural and musical elements. Abandoning its customary dirge-like shroud, "Parcel of Rogues" adopts a surprising upbeat and almost cheerful arrangement creating an interesting instrumentation-to-lyric paradox. Similar (but not equivalent) to classical music's canon, Old Blind Dogs have the tendency of starting small, building on a theme, and ending with a flourish. Their core members are Johnie Hardie on fiddle and mandolin, Buzzby McMillan on cittern and bass, and lead vocalist Ian Benzie. Together they display an acute awareness of the celebrated path the Scottish musical tradition has traversed and the possibilities that lie ahead. They delight in creating just enough bumps and detours on that road to keep things fresh. *—Dave Sleger*

● **The World's Room** / Oct. 12, 1999 / Green Linnet ✦✦✦✦
With harmonica and conga drums in the mix, you know that Old Blind Dogs are not the kind of traditional Scots musicians who waste too much time worrying about authenticity. But their overall sound is one that will appeal greatly to fans of the Battlefield Band and, especially, the Tannahill Weavers, a group whose vocal approach is quite similar to that of Old Blind Dogs. This band's secret weapon is piper Rory Campbell, who composed a number of the tunes on this album and who also plays a mean low whistle. Singer and guitarist Jim Malcolm does himself proud on the rollicking "Forfar Sodger" (one of many tracks that benefit greatly from the percussion of Paul Jennings), and the group's ensemble singing is especially attractive on "To the Beggin' I Will Go," the album's lead track. The instrumentals are even better; "Roslin Castle," an ancient and melancholy air, is given a minimalist and almost spooky arrangement for fiddle, whistle, and guitar, while Campbell's "Soup of the Day" is underpinned by what sounds suspiciously like a drum loop. Excellent. *—Rick Anderson*

Sean O'Riada

b. Aug. 1, 1931, Cork, Ireland, **d.** Oct. 3, 1971, London, England
Composer / Traditional Irish Folk, Traditional Celtic, Irish Folk
Sean O'Riada was the founder of the modern school (which is to say, the authentic ancient-style of playing) Irish folk music and, equally important, a vital nationalistic voice in the orchestral music of Ireland. Best known today as a composer, he was also present at the recording of the first album by the Chieftains, and founded the folk chamber orchestra Ceoltoiri Cualann, Paddy Moloney's group before forming the Chieftains. Among his generation of Irish composers, O'Riada was the most deeply involved with traditional Irish music. Curiously, however, most of his works for the concert hall utilized no folk material, and some of it, most notably *Nomos No. 1*, is a contrapuntal piece that uses 12-tone ("serialist") technique. O'Riada also prepared numerous arrangements of traditional Irish songs, and in the late 1950's, he organized Ceoltoiri Cualann, a folk chamber orchestra whose membership consisted of the best traditional musicians in Ireland. O'Riada's group performed Irish folk mu-

sic stripped of all the pop inflections and sentimentality that usually afflicted their performance. *—Bruce Eder*

Mise Eire (I Am Ireland) / 1959 / Shanachie ♦♦♦
Along with the first Chieftains album, this is the most easily available example of Sean O'Riada's work, but it doesn't necessarily qualify as folk music, at least not directly, but that's where it is categorized because of its sources. In 1959, the movie *Mise Eire* was released, featuring a full orchestral score by O'Riada. It proved a landmark in movie music and Irish folk music, drawing upon sources as ancient as Ireland itself and casting it in an orchestral setting that proved viable on its own, separate from the film itself. This collection includes O'Riada's music for that movie and two others, *Saoirse!* (Freedom) (1960) and *An Tine Bheo* (The Living Fire) (1966), conducted by the composer. This is one of the most beautiful adaptations of Irish folk music in an orchestral setting that one is ever likely to find, and the comparisons with Sibelius, in particular, are apt (so would comparisons with Sir William Walton's Shakespearean film scores, and Sir Arnold Bax's music from *Oliver Twist*). Although he uses a full orchestra, much of what is here does cross paths with the work of the Chieftains, and no concert harp was ever used in so warm and intimate a way as it is here. *—Bruce Eder*

Ossian

Group / Scottish Folk, Traditional Scottish Folk
Formed in the mid '70s, Ossian became one of Scotland's best-loved folk revival bands. Members have included fiddler John Martin, highland bagpipe virtuoso Iain MacDonald, composer and multi-instrumentalist Billy Jackson, and singer and guitarist Tony Cuffe. The group broke up after Cuffe and Jackson moved to the U.S. The other members have remained prominent on the Scottish folk scene. *—Steve Winick*

St. Kilda Wedding / 1978 / Iona ♦♦♦
Featured is Billy Ross singing in English and Gaelic. *—Steve Winick*

Borders / 1984 / Iona ♦♦♦♦♦
Every tune and song is gorgeous on this masterpiece. *—Steve Winick*

● **The Best of Ossian** / 1995 / Iona ♦♦♦♦♦

Carrying Stream / Nov. 18, 1997 / Greentrax ♦♦♦

Jerry O'Sullivan

Uilleann Pipes, Pipe / Celtic New Age, Contemporary Celtic, Celtic Fusion, Pipe Bands, Neo-Traditional
Jerry O'Sullivan is one of the United States' finest Uilleann pipers. He won the all-Ireland piping championship in 1979, and since then has played at major Irish events up and down the east coast and spent several years in co. Clare honing his piping skills still further. He has appeared on several film soundtracks, including *Far and Away*. *—Steve Winick*

● **The Invasion** / 1987 / Green Linnet ♦♦♦
For him, music is a social force, a thing to be shared with friends. This is reflected on his solo album, which features several of his musical pals, including Joanie Madden (flute), Eileen Ivers (guitar) and Seamus Egan (flute, banjo, whistle). *—Steve Winick*

The Gift / Feb. 17, 1998 / Shanachie ♦♦♦
Uilleann pipe master Jerry O'Sullivan's album *The Gift* is an impressive trip through a variety of genres. Playing the war-pipes, low whistle, tin whistle, smallpipes and his trademark Uilleann pipes, O'Sullivan demonstrates with ease that the pipes are a versatile instrument which can adapt to many different types of music. From gospel ("Wayfaring Stranger") to baroque (a three-part selection from a Bach orchestral suite) to jazz (the piece "Clear Blue Sky" features O'Sullivan's merging of pipes with smoky jazz club piano), O'Sullivan expertly weaves a thread of intriguing musical versatility and pipe mastery throughout. *—Lisa Schwartzman*

Patrick Street

f. 1986
Group / British Folk-Rock, Traditional Irish Folk, Celtic Folk, Contemporary Celtic, Irish Folk
Patrick Street is comprised of some of Ireland's most accomplished musicians. Formed in Dublin in 1986, the current group includes fiddler Kevin Burke (the Bothy Band), bouzouki player and vocalist Andy Irvine (Sweeney's Men, Planxty), button accordionist Jackie Daly (DeDanaan) and guitarist Ged Foley (the Battlefield Band, The House Band). Previous members include guitarists Arty McGlynn (Van Morrison, Planxty) and Gerry O'Beirne and Uillean pipe and keyboard player Declan Masterson. Patrick Street's self-titled debut album was produced by multi-instrumentalist Donal Lunny (Planxty, the Bothy Band, Moving Hearts).

Burke, Irvine, Daly and O'Beirne first came together to tour the United States as "Legends Of Irish Music". The enthusiastic reception that they received encouraged them to make the band more permanent. Taking the name "Patrick Street," the four musicians recorded four albums and toured the United States five times between 1987 and 1993. In the Fall of 1994, O'Beirne was replaced by Foley and Patrick Street joined with French Canadian band, La Boutine Sorriente, for a tour of New England. While much of Patrick Street's repertoire is traditional Irish music, the group has recorded original tunes by Irvine, Daly and O'Beirne, as well as tunes by Si Kahn, Woody Guthrie, Andy Mitchell, Dave Richardson and Colum Sands.

The core quartet of Patrick Street has been augmented by additional musicians on several albums. Donal Lunny played keyboard and bodhran on the group's first album. Enda Walsh played keyboards on their second effort, *No. 2 Patrick Street*. Patrick Street's third album, *3 Irish Times 3*, featured the group's largest arrangements with the addition of Declan Masterson (Uillean pipes, low whistle, keyboards) and Bill Whelan (keyboards). The producer of Patrick Street's 1993 recording, *All In Good Time*, Whelan played keyboards and sang background vocals on the album. *—Craig Harris*

Patrick Street / 1986 / Green Linnet ♦♦♦
Much lighter, airier, and less intense than a lot of Irish music, it's a style that fits the artists well. *—Steve Winick*

● **3 Irish Times 3** / 1989 / Green Linnet ♦♦♦♦♦
The addition of pipes and another fiddle makes for a fuller sound on this, their best work. *—Steve Winick*

Cornerboys / Jan. 30, 1996 / Green Linnet ♦♦♦♦
In the '80s and '90s, artists ranging from Luka Bloom and Susan McKeown, to the Pogues, have done their part to keep Irish/Celtic music growing by combining it with rock and/or pop. But traditional Irish/Celtic music still has its place, and Patrick Street has been a solid and very consistent source of Celtic traditionalism. Street is to Bloom what Talip Ozkan is to Turkish pop—the band keeps alive the musical traditions that paved the way for what today's innovators are doing. *Corner Boys* underscores the group's reliable nature. Turning its attention to time-honored jigs, reels and folk ballads, Street lives up to its reputation for excellence. Singer/bouzouki player Andy Irvine is as expressive and charismatic as ever on traditional ballads like "Moorlough Shore" and "Sweet Lisbweemore," and Kevin Burke has many inspired moments on the fiddle. *Corner Boys* isn't innovative or experimental, but it's richly satisfying. *—Alex Henderson*

All In Good Time A / 1997 / Green Linnet ♦♦♦♦♦
The four original recording members are back as a cohesive band for another excellent outing. *—Steve Winick*

Made in Cork / Nov. 4, 1997 / Green Linnet ♦♦

Live from Patrick Street / Feb. 23, 1999 / Green Linnet ♦♦♦♦

Compendium: The Best of Patrick Street / Jan. 16, 2001 / Green Linnet ♦♦♦♦♦

Tommy Peoples

Viola, Fiddle / Traditional Celtic, Contemporary Celtic
An electrifying fiddler from Donegal, Tommy Peoples has converted more than one person to the religion of Irish traditional music. A member of The Bothy band in 1975, he was the propulsive fiddler that powered that group's landmark first album. He also has some magnificent solo work. *—Steve Winick*

High Part of the Road / 1977 / Shanachie ♦♦♦
Shortly after his stint with the Bothy Band, Peoples recorded this masterful solo album. Even on his slower tunes, his rolls are lightning flurries of notes. He's backed by Paul Brady, who was then Ireland's premiere guitar accompanist. *—Steve Winick*

● **The Iron Man** / 1995 / Shanachie ♦♦♦♦♦
This features extremely strong fiddling backed by Daithi Sproule's guitar. A set of Donegal strathspeys steals the show. *—Steve Winick*

Planxty

Group / British Folk-Rock, Contemporary Celtic
Along with groups like the Bothy Band, Planxty helped to usher in a new era for modern Celtic music. While their sound remained rooted to traditional music, the band's virtuosic musicianship and high-energy delivery reflected modern influences, while their unique vocal harmonies and instrumental counterpoint was unprecedented in Irish music.

The founding members of Planxty ñ Christy Moore, Donal Lunny, Liam Og O'Flynn and Andy Irvine—initially came together to provide instrumental accompaniment for Irish singer-songwriter Christy Moore's 1973 album, *Prosperous*. The sessions proved so inspiring that the musicians agreed to continue working together. With the release of their debut single, *Cliffs Of Dooneen*, the new band attracted international attention. An equally memorable, self-titled, album, affectionately known as the *Black Album*, followed shortly afterwards.

Despite its success, Planxty was plagued by a series of personnel changes. Following the release of the band's second album, *After The Break*, Lunny departed for the Bothy Band and was replaced by Johnny Moynihan, who had previously played with Irvine in the Sweeney Men. Moore followed, after the release of the band's third album, *Cold Blow And The Rainy Night*, to resume his solo career and was replaced by singer-songwriter Paul Brady. The loss of Moore and Lunny was devastating and, shortly after releasing their fourth album, *The Woman I Loved So Well*, Planxty disbanded in 1975.

The seeds for Planxty's resurrection were planted in late-1978. In addition to the original members, the reformed group featured ex-Bothy Band and future Chieftains flute player Matt Molloy and keyboardist and future *Riverdance* producer Bill Whelan. Fiddlers James Kelly and Noelle Casey were added for the first album by the reunited group, *Words And Music*.

The renewed energy petered out quickly. By 1983, Lunny and Moore had gone off to form a more-electric trad-rock group, Moving Hearts. *—Craig Harris*

★ **Planxty** / 1973 / Shanachie ♦♦♦♦♦
This stunning 1973 debut features arrangements of traditional songs and tunes with both punch and subtlety. *—Steve Winick*

The Well Below the Valley / 1973 / Shanachie ♦♦♦♦♦
Perhaps not quite as compelling as the debut album, it's still a treasure. *—Steve Winick*

Cold Blow and the Rainy Night / 1974 / Shanachie ♦♦♦♦♦
Lunny is replaced by Johnny Moynihan of Sweeny's Men and De Danaan fame. *—Steve Winick*

The Planxty Collection / 1976 / Shanachie ♦♦♦
Just a notch below *Well Below the Valley*. Well-produced. *—Chip Renner*

After the Break / 1979 / Tara ♦♦♦♦♦
With brilliant tunes and songs, it features Matt Molloy. *—Steve Winick*

The Woman I Loved So Well / 1980 / Tara ♦♦♦
Some of the fire is gone from their arrangements, but a few of the songs are their best ever. *—Steve Winick*

Words & Music / 1983 / Shanachie ♦♦
Various new members like fiddlers James Kelly and Nollaig Casey add fire to the tunes, but the songs sound lethargic. *—Steve Winick*

Poozies

Group / Traditional Celtic, Contemporary Celtic, Singalong, Educational

For over a decade, the British folk band the Poozies has combined innovative arrangements with a love of classic Celtic melodies. The group formed in 1989, when former Sileas members Mary Macmaster (metal-strung and electro harps, percussion, and vocals) and Patsy Seddon (gut and electro harps, percussion, vocals, and fiddle) shared their idea of an all-female folk group with guitarist/vocalist/percussionist Sally Barker. They connected with accordion player/vocalist Karen Tweed and fiddler Jenny Gardner. Though Gardner left shortly after their first few gigs—which included a performance at *the Shetland Folk Festival*—the Poozies continued as a quartet and released 1993's *Chantoozies* and 1995's *Dansoozies* with this lineup. Barker left the group in 1996 and was replaced briefly by up-and-coming vocalist Kate Rusby, who recorded the *Come Raise Your Head* EP and the *Infinite Blue* album with them before continuing her solo career. By the late '90s, vocalist/fiddler Eilidh Shaw joined the group, and the 2000 release *Raise Your Head: A Retrospective* celebrated the group's first ten years. *—Heather Phares*

Infinite Blue / Jan. 19, 1999 / Compass ✦✦✦

● **Raise Your Head: A Retrospective** / May 9, 2000 / Compass ✦✦✦✦

Maddy Prior

b. Aug. 14, 1947

Vocals / British Folk-Rock, Traditional Celtic, Contemporary Celtic, Contemporary Folk, British Folk

Singer Maddy Prior gained a following in England's folk clubs as a member of a duo with Tim Hart. In the late '60s, she recorded several albums with Hart (see Hart, Tim, and Maddy Prior). After meeting Ashley Hutchings at a folk festival, Prior and Hart joined Steeleye Span, the highly acclaimed electric folk group that Prior still fronts today. Along the way, she has been part of another duo with June Tabor, called "Silly Sisters." She has also recorded several albums solo and with her husband, Rick Kemp. Over the years, her various projects added up to a considerable number of albums. In 2000, after having sung for 35 years she released her 35th album, *Ravenchild*. *—Steve Winick*

● **Silly Sisters** / 1976 / Shanachie ✦✦✦✦✦

Maddy Prior and the then-little-known June Tabor teamed to keen a delightful lark of an album. An enduring minor piece with many, many of the English folk revival's best players, it's whimsical and spirited. *—Mark A. Humphrey*

Carols & Capers / 1991 / Park ✦✦✦

Admittedly, it would be a stretch to file this as a Celtic recording, but since Maddy Prior's connections to that revival of the '60s and '70s are well documented (her band Steeleye Span borrowed heavily, at times, from the Celtic tradition), prevailing interest in her music still exists in Celtic circles. This is her second Christmas recording with the Carnival Band, a musical troupe that specializes in early music forms, playing instruments like clarinet, recorders, shawm and lute as well as fiddle, tin whistle and bagpipes. *Capers and Carols* is an unlikely collection of secular and mostly sacred songs that range from the seldom-heard "Boar's Head Carol" and the Cajun forerunner "Monsieur Charpentier's Christmas Stomp" to instrumental interludes of "Turkey in the Straw" and "Old Joe Clark." The a cappella American spiritual "Poor Little Jesus" contains a moving four-part harmony backup by the Carnival Band. This album doesn't necessarily produce images of snowflakes, holly and St. Nick, but it does provide a welcome alternative to some of the overplayed ghosts of Christmas past. *—Dave Sleger*

Year / 1993 / Park ✦✦✦✦

Year features a few traditional songs, plus a suite of songs written by Prior about the passing of the year. *—Steve Winick*

Sing Lustily & with Good Cheer / 1994 / Saydisc ✦✦✦✦✦

Maddy Prior's second recording with the Carnival Band (the first being *A Tapestry of Carols*) is a celebration of hymns by such figures as John Bunyan (1628-1688), Charles Wesley (1707-1788), et al., dating from the year 1700, when they were still not fully legitimate within either the Anglican or nonconformist churches in England. This isn't the wild and woolly sound of Steeleye Span, but something much more studied, coming out of a serious music tradition. Prior's solo singing, as on "As Pants the Hart," is as good as any on her Steeleye Span albums, but a lot more restrained and purposeful; some of the ensemble vocals, as on "O for a Thousand Tongues to Sing," are very pretty. Most of the material here is still sung today, although the instrumentation—including lutes, mandolin, tabors, and 19th century bassoon—has changed in use. "Lo He Comes With Clouds Descending" is one of the prettier pieces here, and a few, like "How Firm a Foundation," dating from the late 18th century, recall counterparts from the American religious experience. *—Bruce Eder*

Flesh & Blood / May 26, 1998 / Park ✦✦✦✦✦

Not as derivative as some of her earlier recordings, this Maddy Prior album hinted at a direction change for the longtime British folk singer. If ever a voice begged for pipes and whistle backing, it's Prior's. She never received that type of support with Steeleye Span, so it was promising to discover that Troy Donockley would co-produce and play on *Flesh and Blood*. He's a multi-instrumentalist who specializes in Uilleann pipes and is a fine low whistler as well. Too bad that union didn't fully pan out here. Donockley had one pipe solo ("Finlandia") and played the intro and closing fade on "Heart of Stone," so unfortunately the two ne'er did meet. The best cuts are the traditional pieces, "Sheath and Knife" and "Bitter Withy"—the former dealing with such dubious predicaments as incest and murder, and the latter a tale describing the abuse of power wielded by a young, impish Jesus. The last seven selections, subtitled "Dramatis Personae," are melancholy and personal originals penned by Prior and Rick Kemp that favor the keyboards of the other co-producer, Nick Holland. *—Dave Sleger*

Ravenchild / May 16, 2000 / Park ✦✦✦

On *Ravenchild*, Maddy Prior teamed up again with keyboard player Nick Holland and multi-instrumentalist Troy Donockley, whose arsenal included Uilleann pipes and low whistle, as she had on her previous album, *Flesh & Blood*. The centerpiece of the album was a six song suite dubbed "In the Company of Ravens" (also the title of the first song), a series of Prior originals concerning the carrion birds who give the word "ravenous" its meaning. This was sometimes gritty stuff, as Prior described the birds' eating habits, though their mating habits were far more inspiring. The album also contained a three song suite, "With Napoleon in Russia," tracing that famous historical defeat. Then there was "Rigs of the Time," a condemnation of contemporary media culture set to a traditional melody, and the album concluded with what Prior herself described as the eerie traditional song "Great Silkie of Sules Skerry." The music and Prior's singing could be haunting, but *Ravenchild* was an album of disquieting material, whether the subject was aviary, historical, or contemporary. *—William Ruhlmann*

Summer Solstice / Shanachie ✦✦✦✦

This heralded British folk release by Prior and Hart led to the creation of Steeleye Span. It includes "Three Drunken Maidens," "Fly up My Cock," "Bring Us in Good Ale," "Sorry the Day I Was Married," and nine others. *—Roundup Newsletter*

The Rankin Family

f. Mabou, Cape Breton

Group / Contemporary Celtic, Contemporary Folk

The Rankin Family, from Cape Breton, Canada, began performing at family parties. John Morris Rankin (piano, fiddle) and vocalists Cookie, Heather, Jimmy and Raylene Rankin began playing various folk festivals in 1989. The group released two independent cassettes, a self-titled debut album in 1989 and *Fare Thee Well Love* the following year. EMI signed the Rankin Family in 1992, re-released their first two albums, and issued *North Country* in 1993. Returning three years later with *Endless Seasons*, the Rankins issued *Uprooted* in 1998 but called it quits in 1999. John Morris died in a car accident in Sydney, Nova Scotia on January 16, 2000; he was 40. *—John Bush*

● **Rankin Family Collection** / 1996 / Rounder ✦✦✦✦✦

As one of the key groups to set the Celtic music revolution rolling in Canada, the Rankin Family definitely has their place in the country's musical tapestry. As a compilation of the band's early years, the *Collection* contains pretty much all the hits, and a fairly good sampling of all the aspects of the band: pop/country, original/traditional, male/female vocals, acoustic/lush. To be fair, the compilation tends to lean away from the more overtly Celtic material that the band does and more toward the polished pop numbers. The CD also contains bonus multimedia material on an enhanced CD program. *—Sean Carruthers*

Uprooted / Jun. 1998 / Rounder ✦✦✦

Jean Redpath

b. Apr. 28, 1937, Edinburgh, Scotland

Vocals / Traditional Scottish Folk

Blessed with a sweet, but slightly roughened mezzo-soprano as gentle as mist and haunting as the highlands, Jean Redpath is one of the definitive interpreters of Scottish traditional songs. She is also a noted folk music ethnographer who has played an important role in the reconstruction of nearly forgotten Scottish songs. She emigrated to New York in 1961 where she began singing in Greenwich village coffeehouses. Redpath also gave formal concerts at events such as the Lincoln Center's Mostly Mozart Festival and soon became an extremely popular performer on the folk circuit. Not only did they love her unique, sensitive voice, audiences were also impressed by her knowledge about the over 400 songs in her repertoire and the fascinating insights about the music that Redpath offered during her concerts. After a stint with Elektra, where she recorded through 1975, she switched to the Vermont-based Philo label. With them she has become one of folk music's most prolific recording artists. *—Sandra Brennan*

The Jean Redpath Scottish Ballad Book / 1964 / Elektra ✦✦✦

Laddie Lie Near Me / 1967 / Elektra ✦✦✦

Laddie Lie Near Me features another solid batch of Scottish interpretations. *—Steve Winick*

★ **Frae My Ain Countrie** / 1973 / Folk Legacy ✦✦✦✦✦

First Flight / 1989 / Rounder ✦✦✦✦✦

The Songs of Robert Burns / 1996 / Philo ✦✦✦

The six LPs that are collected on this three-CD reissue (released in 1996 to commemorate the 200th anniversary of Robert Burns' death) were originally recorded between 1976 and 1984. Redpath sings in a voice the color of sunlight shining through a whiskey jar, and with an indisputable authority that comes from a combination of her Scottish heritage and years of hard work perfecting her craft. Such authority resides not at all with Serge Hovey, the arranger whose faux-classical settings for these songs reflect both his Los Angeles heritage and his years of study with Arnold Schoenberg and Hanns Eisler. Redpath's voice and Keith Jarrett's crystalline eloquence throughout volume five aside, this collection is a genuine disappointment. To hear Redpath at her best, check out just about any of her Folk-Legacy recordings, none of which feature tympani, Arp synthesizer or French horn. *—Rick Anderson*

Sue Richards

b. Muscle Shoals, AL

Harp / Scottish Folk, Celtic Folk, Traditional Celtic, Irish Folk

Sue Richards specializes in Scottish and Irish material on the Celtic harp. She is well-known to audiences in the D.C. area and beyond as a three-time American Scottish harp champion and as a member of the groups Ceoltoiri (Celtic music) and Ensemble Galilei (early music). *—Steve Winick*

Grey Eyed Morn / 1991 / Maggie's Music ✦✦✦

Richards plays mostly Scottish tunes, along with a few irish and Welsh pieces. Guests include Bonnie Rideout (Scottish fiddle) and members of Ceoltoiri. *—Steve Winick*

● **Morning Aire** / 1993 / Maggie's Music ♦♦♦♦♦
This one's split equally between Irish and Scottish material. Billy McComiskey (accordion, concertina) and Myron Bretholz (bodhran) add an Irish touch to arrangements. It's wonderfully played all-round. *— Steve Winick*

Hazel Grove / 1995 / Maggie's Music ♦♦♦♦

Bob Roberts

d. Jan. 21, 1930
Accordion, Guitar / Celtic Folk, Sea Shanties, British Folk
The accordion was an important British folk and popular instrument from the mid-19th century on, and also very much a sailors' instrument. Roberts, who worked on sailing cargo wherries much of his life, was a fine melodeon player and a singer with a very wide repertory: a hilarious epic about a North Sea oil rig; "The Grey Hawk," of Renaissance origin; "The Foggy Dew" in an eastern English version; shanties and more. *— John Storm Roberts*

Songs from the Sailing Barges / Topic ♦♦♦♦♦
The accordion, particularly the button melodeon, was an important British folk and popular instrument from the mid-19th century on. Accordions were also sailors' instruments. Roberts, who worked on sailing cargo wherries much of his life, was a fine melodeon player and a singer with a very varied repertory: a hilarious epic about a North Sea oilrig; "The Grey Hawk," of Renaissance origin; "The Foggy Dew" in an eastern English version; shanties and more. *— John Storm Roberts, Original Music*

Loeiz Ropars

Vocals / Traditional Celtic
Loeiz Ropars is one of the fathers of the Breton music revival. In the early '40s, he became interested in revitalizing the kan ha diskan, a special kind of call-and-response singing used to accompany dances. He made himself a part of the post-war reawakening of Breton cultural identity. His background of peasant life and his involvement in the the "Cercle Celtique" or Celtic cultural association, of Poullaouen led him to the idea of creating a new type of event for Breton music and dancing. It would be like the community based fest-noz, or night party, except that it would bring people together from different parts of Brittany. His idea, the "new-style" fest-noz, is the most important type of folk music event in Brittany today. *— Steve Winick*

● **Kan Ha Diskan** / 1992 / Keltia Musique ♦♦♦♦♦
This is an album of pure, unaccompanied vocals. It's melodically and rhythmically catchy, and sung with enthusiam by Ropars and his partners. Still, the inaccessibility of the language makes this a release for diehard fans of Breton music. For those diehard fans, it's a treasure. *— Steve Winick*

Leo Rowsome

d. 1970
Uilleann Pipes, Pipe / Irish Folk, Pipe Bands
Leo Rowsome was one of the most influential pipers of his generation, indeed of all time. He came from a long line of Wexford pipers but lived himself in Dublin, where he taught many of the current generation of pipers. He died in 1970. *— Steve Winick*

Classics of Irish Piping / Topic ♦♦♦♦♦
The Irish Uilleann pipes are less austere than the Scots—the pipes play chords as well as drone and melody, much like a concertina with a drone. This gives the songs a familiar structure to go with the entrancing sound, which is also warmer than in the Scots pipes. Rowsome was not only a master piper (he was a teacher at 16) but a master craftsman as well, and his own pipes were never equalled in his lifetime. This stunningly beautiful recording is a monument to a remarkable musician.*— Carl Hoyt, Original Music*

★ **The King of the Pipers** / Shanachie ♦♦♦♦♦
Originally released on Dublin's Claddagh label in the '60s, this classic is now available again on CD. Rowsome's open-piping style flows beautifully. *— Steve Winick*

Tommy Sands

Vocals, Guitar / Contemporary Celtic, Irish Folk, Political Folk, Singer/Songwriter
Not to be confused with the pop singer of the 1950s, Tommy Sands was the prime songwriter with the Sands Family, a group with his five siblings that became one of Ireland's most influential folk groups of the 1960s and '70s. Although the group has limited its touring in the past decade to an annual tour of Germany and Ireland, Sands has continued to pave new ground as a solo singer/songwriter and as the host of a popular radio show, *Country Ceili*, broadcast weekly via Belfast's Downtown Radio since 1976.

Sands grew up in a very musical family. His father and six uncles played the fiddle, while his mother played accordion. The family farm, in the foothills of the Mourne Mountains, was one of the few places that Protestants and Catholics joined together to listen to music and dance. Sands began writing songs shortly after learning to play the fiddle. Many of his songs reflect the political turmoil and sociological struggles of his homeland.

Although Sands attended college to study theology and philosophy, music proved too great a lure. Dropping out of the school, Sands began to walk the 120 miles home. He hadn't gotten far when a car with his siblings stopped to pick him up to perform a concert. Inspired by the Clancy Brothers, the Sands Family (Tommy, Eugene, Ben, Colum and Ann) became leaders of the Irish folk revival.

The Sands Family first came to the United States in 1970, after winning a concert trip to New York in a national ballad contest. After performing at *Carnegie Hall*, the group hooked up with a manager in Boston and remained in America for six months. Returning to Europe in 1971, the Sands Family found that they had acquired an enthusiastic following in Germany.

The Sands Family's string of success ended in 1975, when youngest brother Eugene was killed in an auto accident. In the aftermath of the tragedy, Ann Sands announced her retirement from the group. Subsequent tours have been limited to the three remaining brothers.

Tommy Sands' debut solo album, *Singing of the Times*, released in 1985, included his now-classic tunes "There Were Roses" and "Daughters and Sons." Sands' second album, *Down By Bendy's Lane: Irish Songs and Stories for Children*, followed three years later. On his third album, *Hedges of County Down*, released in 1989, Sands focused on traditional Irish material. He returned to original songs for his fourth effort, *Beyond the Shadows*, released in 1990. Sands' fifth album, *The Heart's A Wonder*, released in 1995, included a tune, "The Music of Healing," co-written with American folk singer Pete Seeger. The song was used as an anthem for a "Citizen's Assembly" that Sands organized in Belfast, in August 1986, which included many of Ulster County's top artists and literary figures. *The Heart's a Wonder* also marked the first time that Sands collaborated with Sarajevo cellist Vedran Smailovic. Sands and Smailovic joined with Irish songstress Dolores Keane on the 1997 title track of the multi-artist album *Where Have All the Flowers Gone: The Songs of Pete Seeger*. One of Sands' most ambitious projects is a stage musical, *The Shadow of O'Casey*, that he co-wrote with playwright Sean O'Casey's daughter, Shivaun. *— Craig Harris*

★ **Singing of the Times** / 1985 / Green Linnet ♦♦♦♦♦
Jam-packed with great songs and emotions, "There Were Roses" is a classic, dealing with the senseless killing in Northern Ireland. "I'm Going Back on the Bicycle" and "Don't Wake Me Early in the Morning" are fun songs. "Humpty Dumpty Was Pushed" questions us, and "Your Daughters & Your Sons" has been used as an anthem throughout the world. Highly, highly recommended! *— Chip Renner*

Down by Bendy's Lane: Irish Songs & Stories for Children / 1988 / Green Linnet ♦♦♦♦♦
A delightful children's album featuring songs and stories Sands has picked up since childhood. "The Boy with No Story" will have you on the edge of your seat. "Moya Is My Darling," about his daughter, is priceless. Even an adult can enjoy this one. *— Chip Renner*

Beyond the Shadows / 1990 / Green Linnet ♦♦♦♦♦
Tommy's "We Will Rise Again" and "1999" are songs of hope. "Red Wine" and "Make Me Want to Stay" are finely written love songs. "When the Boys Come Rolling Home" is an infectious, good-time song. This CD is my pick for Top Ten of 1992. Keep up the good work, Tommy! *— Chip Renner*

The Hearts' a Wonder / Oct. 31, 1995 / Green Linnet ♦♦♦

Sharon Shannon

Accordion, Fiddle / Celtic Rock, Contemporary Celtic, Celtic Folk
Sharon Shannon is a young, gifted accordion player from Galway. Her pared-down, speeded up and rocked-out approach to traditional music appeals to other artists as much as it does to her fans. It earned her a place in the Waterboys and in Christy Moore's band before she toured Europe and the U.S. with her own successful band. She issued her self-titled debut in 1989; *Out of the Gap* followed in 1995, *Each Little Thing* and *Spellbound: the Sharon Shannon Collection* both arrived on Green Linnet in 1997. The new millennium release, *Diamond Mountain Sessions* surfaced in early 2001. *— Steve Winick*

Sharon Shannon / Jul. 1, 1993 / Philo ♦♦♦♦♦
Shannon and band breeze through some great material with amazing virtuosity. This one'll keep your toes tapping for weeks. *— Steve Winick*

Out the Gap / 1995 / Green Linnet ♦♦♦♦
Although Irish/Celtic jigs and reels are Sharon Shannon's musical foundation, it would be wrong to call her a purist. The risk-taking accordion player and instrumentalist is far from that—her approach is quite expansive, and on *Out the Gap* she demonstrates that Irish/Celtic music can be fused with everything from calypso to French-Canadian Quebecois music to Scandinavian folk. In fact, many of the songs that Shannon interprets on this CD didn't come out of Ireland or Scotland. While "Butterflies" is a traditional Finnish folk song and "Reel Beatrice" is a French-Canadian Quebecois tune, "Sandy River Belle" is a number that experts on American folk will recognize. "Bjorn Again Polka" successfully incorporates polka, and "The Mighty Sparrow" (named after the famous calypso singer) has a strong Caribbean influence. For those seeking something fresh and adventurous from Celtic music, *Out the Gap* would be an excellent choice. *— Alex Henderson*

Each Little Thing / Sep. 23, 1997 / Green Linnet ♦♦♦♦
The follow-up to 1994's *Out the Gap, Each Little Thing* is full of pleasant surprises at every turn. After playing a predominently traditional Irish-based accordion with Arcady, the Waterboys and on her solo debut, Sharon Shannon displays her diverse and esoteric nature on several instances. "Kids" is a bouncy piece featuring fine playing by guitarist Steeve Cooney, which cleverly segues into Fleetwood Mac's "Never Going Back Again." Emanating from "Bonnie Mulligan" is an Aaron Copland vibe, where Winnie Horan (Solas) leads the hoedown with some commanding fiddle playing. The underlying electric guitar adds interesting layering. "The Bag of Cats" brandishes a heavy programmed rhythm by Oisin Lunny, and Shannon lays down her box in favor of the fiddle to duel it out with Mary Custy. Chanteuse Kirsty MacColl renders a seductive reading of "Libertango" as Shannon assumes the role of strolling French accordionist with aplomb and savoir faire. "El Mercado Testaccio" is a delightful Inti-Illimani tune that, despite the hammer dulcimer and bouzouki, sounds amazingly South American. Donal Lunny does an excellent job of piecing this album together, allowing the songs to flow gracefully. His bouzouki playing and Trevor Hutchinson's double bass provide a stable rhythm section capable of chauffeuring Shannon to whichever destination she fancies. *— Dave Sleger*

● **Spellbound: Best of Sharon Shannon** / Jan. 12, 1999 / Green Linnet ♦♦♦♦♦
All of the albums that Sharon Shannon recorded for Green Linnet in the '90s are worth owning, but if you've never experienced the pleasures of her neo-Celtic experiments, *Spellbound* would be the most logical starting point. This CD, which spans 1989-1998, isn't the last word on the experimental button accordionist, but it can still serve as an impressive introduction to her work. *Spellbound* paints an accurate picture of Shannon—an exploratory artist who

benefits from Irish/Celtic traditions without being enslaved by them. On this eclectic, entirely instrumental collection, one hears Shannon fusing her Celtic foundation with pop, French-Canadian music, calypso, ska, polka and other styles. Instruments typically associated with Celtic music—including fiddles, mandolins and hammer dulcimers—are prominent, but Shannon also employs saxophonists, organists and electric guitarists. There are many rewards on this CD, which illustrates how nicely Shannon's risk-taking has paid off. *—Alex Henderson*

Sileas

f. 1985

Group / Scottish Folk, Contemporary Celtic, Traditional Scottish Folk, Singer/Songwriter

More than a decade since Scottish harpers Patsy Seddon and Mary MacMaster's first collaborations, their duo, Sileas (pronounced: She-less) remains the only duo of its kind. While they remain rooted in traditional Scottish folk music, Sileas' combination of nylon-strung acoustic harp and brass-strung electro-harp creates a lively, exciting and contemporary sound. Although Seddon and MacMaster have recently focused their attention to The Poozies, the eclectic band that they share with accordionist Karen Tweed and guitarist Kate Rusby, their harp duo has been a regular feature of The Poozies' concerts. Named after a 17th century female poet who wrote in Gaelic, Sileas released their debut album, *Delighted With Harps*, in 1986. It showcased the two women's unique harp playing and their silken vocal harmonies with songs sung in both Gaelic and English. *—Craig Harris*

Delighted with Harps / 1986 / Green Linnet ✦✦✦
This is a pretty collection of traditional melodies and songs. Material includes dance music, airs, and songs in both Scots and Gaelic. *—Steve Winick*

Beating Harps / 1987 / Green Linnet ✦✦✦
More fine tracks include one original composition by Seddon. *—Steve Winick*

● **Harpbreakers** / 1990 / Lap Wing ✦✦✦✦✦
Sileas continue their trend of playing top-quality Scottish and Irish music on harps. They also keep up the lovely singing *—Steve Winick*

Play on Light / Nov. 19, 1996 / Green Linnet ✦✦✦✦

Silly Sisters

Group / Traditional Celtic, British Folk

Steeleye Span's Maddy Prior and folk diva June Tabor teamed up in 1976 for the first Silly Sisters album. It was more than a decade before they followed it up with a second, but both recordings feature a gorgeous melding of Prior's clear, brassy soprano with Tabor's darker tones. *—Michael P. Dawson*

No More to the Dance / 1988 / Shanachie ✦✦✦✦
The first time June Tabor and Maddie Prior made a duo recording, it was released under their names and was entitled *Silly Sisters*. On this, their second album, Silly Sisters is the name of the group. Officially, it still consists of just Tabor and Prior, but most tracks also feature Breton guitarist Dan Ar Braz, Welsh harper and keyboardist Huw Warren, and various other guests. As with their first album, the program is a winning mix of traditional and modern British folk music. An eerie and haunting arrangement of Andy Irvine's "Blood and Gold" is followed immediately by an almost African-sounding instrumental by Ar Braz; Tabor and Prior perform a brief a cappella "catch" by Henry Purcell entitled "Cakes and Ale"; and the traditional "Hedger and Ditcher" shows up in an arrangement that features both bagpipes and soprano saxophone. But interesting as things get instrumentally, Tabor and Prior's almost telepathic musicality and sharp, reedy voices are always at center stage, and the songs are always well served by the arrangements. *—Rick Anderson*

Silly Wizard

Group / Traditional Celtic, Contemporary Celtic, Celtic Fusion

Generally considered the world's finest performers of traditional and contemporary Scottish music—and with good reason. Silly Wizard's music is at once driving and sensitive, powerful and poignant, at times hypnotic, often humorous, with sensitive group interplay and virtuoso-level musicianship, particularly from brothers Phil (accordion, keyboards, whistles, guitar, vocals) and Johnny (fiddle) Cunningham. Their repertoire includes centuries-old instrumental dance music along with traditional and contemporary narrative ballads: tales of joy and woe, of men and women, of time and travel, of love and loss. Silly Wizard is not just another folk music group; they rank with the greatest creators and performers from any country from any time.

Several members of the group, particularly the Cunningham brothers and vocalist Andy Stewart, have made solo and duo recordings and have performed and recorded with other artists, primarily Scottish traditionalists. These recordings are also well worth investigating, but get the Silly Wizard stuff first. *—Niles J. Frantz*

Silly Wizard / 1976 / Xtra ✦✦
They're still sounding quite tentative on this, their first release. Freeland Barbour handles the accordion well, and Andy M. Stewart's voice is clearly something special, but arrangements and playing are a bit loose. *—Steve Winick*

Caledonia's Hardy Sons / 1978 / Shanachie ✦✦✦
Stewart's voice is sweeter and more innocent on this early album than on later works. *—Steve Winick*

So Many Partings / 1980 / Shanachie ✦✦✦

● **Wild & Beautiful** / 1981 / Shanachie ✦✦✦✦✦
Produced by renowned songwriter Archie Fisher ("The Witch of Westmoreland"), this album presents Silly Wizard doing contemporary songs built on traditional themes. The mixture of original songs and favorite jigs strung together is compelling throughout, and the contemporary songs all have the feel of having been written centuries ago. A gorgeous Andy M. Stewart arrangement of two different versions of the same song, "If I Was a Blackbird," opens the album, and the music only gets more beautiful from there. Phil Cunningham's "The Pearl," written to honor his parents' 30th anniversary, may be one of the prettiest instrumentals ever composed for a modern folk group. The production and recording also give a wonderfully up close image of each instrument's distinctive timbre, imparting the intimacy of a chamber music performance to the proceedings. *—Bruce Eder*

The Best of Silly Wizard / 1985 / Shanachie ✦✦✦
Really only the best of their Shanachie releases, it's still a great compilation. *—Steve Winick*

Glint of Silver / 1986 / Green Linnet ✦✦✦
Just because the Celtic roots-rock band Silly Wizard is actually Scottish—and just because they spice up their sound with bass and electronics—doesn't mean the group isn't reverent about the music. *Glint of Silver* opens with a dance medley, but it's smooth sailing from there on out, with the emphasis on delicate love songs and lush instrumentals. *—Jason Ankeny*

☆ **Live Wizardry** / 1988 / Green Linnet ✦✦✦✦✦
This two-for-one bargain captures the a brilliant live set in 1988, at the culmination of their career. *—Steve Winick*

Martin Simpson

b. May 5, 1953, Scunthorpe, South Humberside, England

Slide Guitar, Vocals, Guitar, Banjo / Contemporary Singer/Songwriter, Contemporary Celtic, Contemporary Folk, British Folk

Martin Simpson is one of the most visible examples of the relationship between the Celtic folk of the United Kingdom and American musics such as country and the blues, which branched away from their British sources as American immigrants grew distanced from their past countrymen. Simpson's life charts a similar journey—one of the most technically gifted guitarists alive today, he was born in South Humberside, England, but moved to the United States in the late '80s (after recording several solo albums and appearing with many major British folk-rock figures) to absorb Stateside forms of guitar playing, meanwhile recording both as himself and with his American wife, Jessica Radcliffe Simpson.

Born in the Humberside town of Scunthorpe in northern England, Simpson began playing guitar at the age of twelve, and just two years later was playing local pubs. Well-known on the regional circuit by the early '70s, he recorded his debut album, *Golden Vanity*, in 1976, for Bill Leader's Trailer Records. Instead of aligning itself with the new contemporary folk songs or their traditional precursors, *Golden Vanity* borrowed elements of both, with Dylan covers alongside ancient ballads. He toured with Steeleye Span and the Albion Band during the late '70s, and began a long relationship with June Tabor, working on her solo albums and earning a co-billing for 1981's *A Cut Above*. His next three albums, released from 1981 to 1986, were quite good, and though they generated little fanfare, Shanachie Records signed him just after his move to the U.S. in 1987. That same year, he released a duet album with his wife Jessica entitled *True Dare or Promise*. His first Shanachie release, 1989's *Leaves of Life*, signalled another period of artistic excellence, exemplified by its follow-ups *When I Was on Horseback*, *A Closer Walk with Thee* and *Red Roses*, again recorded with Jessica. During the mid-'90s, the Simpsons played with a group called the Band of Angels and recorded for such labels as Rhiannon, Red House and Waterlily Acoustic. Upon entering the new millennium, Simpson released *Sad or High Kicking* in 1999 and *True Dare or Promise* in 2000, both on the Fledg'ling label. *—John Bush*

Grinning in Your Face / 1983 / Topic ✦✦✦✦
Martin Simpson's 1983 album *Grinning in Your Face* may contain only two originals, but his unique imprint is apparent all over the record, from his instrumental arrangement of "The First Cut Is the Deepest" to his elastic vocals on Buddy Holly's "It Doesn't Matter Anymore." Those vocals might make Simpson an acquired taste for some, but his guitar playing is rich and warm, both on the acoustic and electric, which makes the album feel quite inviting. As a matter of fact, it works its charms quite subtly, opening with its most disarming cut ("It Doesn't Matter Anymore") and then quickly—almost imperceptibly—slipping into a groove, alternating between traditional folk songs and more contemporary covers (including "Masters of War" and "Your Cheatin' Heart"), and always taking a slightly different approach than expected. And that's what's nice about the record: It's rooted in, but not bound to, tradition. Simpson walks the fine line between traditional and contemporary folk, and he comes up with a winner this time. *—Stephen Thomas Erlewine*

● **The Collection** / Aug. 9, 1994 / Shanachie ✦✦✦✦✦
British guitarist Martin Simpson covered rock, country and urban blues, originals and traditional tunes, and even Irish, gospel, and country pieces. This disc's 17 cuts cover every base, from anti-war numbers to reels, duets with his wife Jessica, folk tunes on dobro, acoustic guitar, and jew's harp, and oldtime rural numbers that recall the voices of the Delta masters. Anyone unable to make quick leaps through genres need not approach Simpson's work; he not only makes radical shifts from song to song, but sometimes within individual songs. His vocals are pleasant and often engaging, while his playing is accomplished on acoustic, sometimes spectacular on electric, and never less than enjoyable on any instrument. *—Ron Wynn*

Cool & Unusual / Sep. 16, 1997 / Red House ✦✦✦

Sissel (Sissel Kyrkjebø)

b. Bergan, Norway

Vocals / Contemporary Celtic

Born in Bergen, Norway in 1969, Sissel had appeared on Norwegian television several times as a child, but came into the public eye with her stellar vocal performances at the 1994 Winter Olympics in Lillehammer. She sings in her native tongue, in addition to English and Latin, similar in style and substance as the Irish ethereal vocalist Enya. Two albums in the mid-'90s, *Innerst I Sjelen* and *Deep Within My Soul*, found a small but dedicated audience and led to a prominent place as the voice of James Horner's maritime muse in the smash 1997 film *Titanic*. 1997 also brought about a project with rapper Warren G on an unusual compilation of hip hop and classical recordings on Mercury/Def Jam, which became a hit in Europe.

Recording under her full name, Sissel Kyrkjebø, she recorded *Gift of Love* for Polygram in 1999. *—Michael Ofjord and Zac Johnson*

- **Innerst I Sjelen** / 1994 / Skandisk Inc. ✦✦✦
Innerst I Sjelen is a showcase for the crystal clear, pure sound of the voice of Sissel Kyrkjebø. Released in conjunction with her stellar performances at the 1994 Winter Olympics in Lillehammer, Norway, this recording features songs celebrating nature, love of homeland, and spiritual beliefs. The songs occupy the territory where folk, new age, and jazz meet, but all feature the angelic yet powerful sounds of Sissel. She sings in her native tongue, in addition to English and Latin. Keyboard flourishes and quiet guitars predominate, but rarely does the music overwhelm Sissel's voice. From a vocal standpoint, "Eg Veit I Himmerik Ei Borg" ("I Know There Is a Castle in Heaven") is both ethereal and stunningly beautiful. Showing clarity, power, and purity that is truly her own, Sissel overwhelms the listener with a performance that overshadows everything else on the album. The title cut and "Se Ilden Lyse" (another version is sung in English with Placido Domingo) are the closes things to "pop tunes" on the record. At times one wishes that the selections were more challenging or suited to the strengths of Sissel's voice, but even the most pedestrian melodies still have something to offer. *—Michael Ofjord*

Deep Within My Soul / 1995 / Mercury ✦✦✦

Davy Spillane

b. 1959

Low Whistle, Uilleann Pipes, Dulcimer (Hammer), Whistle (Instrument), Pipe / Celtic Folk, Traditional Celtic, Contemporary Celtic, Irish Folk

A founding member of progressive Celtic folk-rock band, Moving Hearts, Davy Spillane helped bring the music of the Emerald Isle up to modern standards. Since the band's breakup in 1986, Spillane has continued to forge a new musical direction while firmly grasping the traditions of the past.

Spillane launched his musical career while still in his early teens. Learning to play the tin whistle, as a youngster, Spillane switched to the Uilleann pipes at the age of thirteen or fourteen and began frequenting weekly seisuns (Irish music jam sessions) at local pubs. Spillane had a lead role as a piper in a gypsy band in the 1974 film, *Traveller.*

Moving to County Clare, Spillane became absorbed by the Doolin music scene. Approached by Donal Lunny and Christy Moore to join their experimental folk-rock band, Moving Hearts, Spillane accepted the invitation. Although Moving Hearts experienced numerous personnel changes, Spillane remained at the heart of the band's sound for the five years of its existence.

Shortly after Moving Hearts disbanded, Spillane recorded his debut solo album, *Atlantic Bridge.* Joined by American musicians including Bela Fleck, Jerry Douglas and Albert Lee, Spillane used the album to focus on the connections between Celtic music and bluegrass. Spillane has subsequently recorded two additional solo albums—*Shadow Hunter* and *Pipedreams*—and one album, *Out of the Air,* with the Davy Spillane Band. In 1991, Spillane collaborated with ex-Bothy Band guitarist and vocalist Andy Irvine to record the stunning, tradition-rooted, album, *East Wind.* Spillane's first release on a major record label, *Place Among the Stars,* released in 1998, featured guest vocals by Marie Brennan of Clannad and Steve Winwood.

A much-demanded session player, Spillane has performed and/or recorded with such artists as Kate Bush, Van Morrison, Elvis Costello and Emmylou Harris. In 1998, Spillane toured with Canadian rocker Bryan Adams. Spillane also opened his own recording facility, Burrenstone Studios, in Dublin. *—Craig Harris*

- **Atlantic Bridge** / 1987 / Tara ✦✦✦✦✦

Out of the Air / 1988 / Tara ✦✦✦✦

Shadow Hunter / 1990 / Tara ✦✦✦✦

Pipedreams / 1992 / Tara ✦✦✦

A Place Among the Stones / Mar. 26, 1996 / Relativity ✦✦✦✦

Sea of Dreams / Sep. 8, 1998 / Covert ✦✦✦

Andy M. Stewart

b. 1952

Vocals, Guitar, Bouzouki / Traditional Irish Folk, Scottish Folk, Traditional Celtic, Traditional Scottish Folk, Irish Folk

The musical traditions of Ireland and Scotland have been extended through the singing and tenor banjo playing of Andy B. Stewart. A former member of Silly Wizard, Stewart has continued his musical exploration through several solo albums and recordings with such influential Celtic players as Manus Lunny, Gerry O'Beirne and ex-Silly Wizard band-mates Phil Cunningham and Martin Hadden. In addition to interpreting the traditional ballads of Ireland and Scotland and the poetry of Robert Burns, Stewart has composed such original songs as "The Blackbird," "The Queen Of Argylle," "Golden, Golden," and "The Ramblin' Rover." *—Craig Harris*

By the Hush / 1982 / Green Linnet ✦✦✦✦
One of the finest Scots folksingers of his generation, Andy M. Stewart spent his early career with the hugely influential Silly Wizard before heading out on his own and producing a string of excellent solo albums. This one was *Melody Maker*'s Folk Album of the Year in 1983, and with good reason. Stewart has a warm tenor voice, a light touch, and exquisite taste in songs, and these simple, delicate arrangements set off his voice beautifully. On *By the Hush* he opens with the bittersweet "Haud Your Tongue Dear Sally," then romps through "The Ramblin' Rover" before coming to a skidding halt on "The Orphan's Wedding," a sad, creepy tale of an accidentally incestuous marriage. Then there's "The Parish of Dunkeld," a song about a town that gets tired of its minister and hangs him before going on a collective drunk. Yeesh. But he sings all of these songs with such tenderness and empathy that you find your sympathies becoming complicated. "By the Hush" is about escaping the privations of 19th century Ireland for America, only to be conscripted into the Civil War; "They Wounded Old Ireland" is, of course, a lament for the war-torn North. Okay, so this sounds like a pretty grim program, and maybe it is.

But it sure is pretty somehow. You just have to hear it. *—Rick Anderson*

Fire in the Glen / 1986 / Shanachie ✦✦✦
This album features Stewart along with Phil Cunningham and Manus Lunny. It's a fine piece of work. *—Steve Winick*

- **Dublin Lady** / 1987 / Green Linnet ✦✦✦✦✦
A masterpiece and a must for Celtic music fans, it includes Manus Lunny. *—Steve Winick*

At It Again / 1990 / Green Linnet ✦✦✦
With Manus Lunny, it's not as fantastic as *Dublin Lady,* but is still a fine record. *—Steve Winick*

Songs of Robert Burns / 1990 / Green Linnet ✦✦✦
Anybody with a fondness for Burns's poetry should hear this album. Andy's renditions are stirring and beautiful, even if the arrangements are a little weaker than Lunny's usual. *—Steve Winick*

Man in the Moon / 1994 / Green Linnet ✦✦✦
Credited to Stewart as a solo artist, this one features Gerry O'Beirne handling much of the accompaniment and production work. With some great songs, plus a few sappy ones, it's a beautiful album on balance. *—Steve Winick*

Donegal Rain / Nov. 4, 1997 / Green Linnet ✦✦✦

Alan Stivell (Alan Cochevelou)

b. 1944, Gourin, Brittany, France

Vocals, Pipe, Flute, Bagpipes / British Folk-Rock, Celtic Fusion, Ethnic Fusion

If there is a single savior of Celtic music, Alan Stivell is probably it. Since the end of the 1960s, he has done more to revive interest in the Celtic (specifically Breton) harp than anyone in the world and, in the process, almost singlehandedly made the world aware of native Breton Celtic music. Since 1971, he has been recording albums of extraordinary beauty and diversity, ranging from ancient Breton and Irish material to modern folk-rock and progressive rock. A major influence on a multitude of folk-rock musicians with his interweaving of electric and traditional instruments, Stivell's first major solo album, *Renaissance of the Celtic Harp* (1972), remains a favorite among fans of the stringed instrument, while his later albums also display his abilities with bagpipes and as a singer. For a time during the mid-'70s, his success placed traditional Breton and Celtic music on the English charts on a regular basis. Stivell's biggest accomplishment, however, involved the rebirth and rediscovery of an instrument and an entire cultural history. His career brought to fruition the revival of the Breton harp. His music captures the mystery and strangeness of Breton, Irish, Welsh, and Scottish landscapes that are both ageless and timeless. It is haunting, mysterious, and beautiful, with no equivalent in modern popular music and few peers in the realm of commercial folk music. *—Bruce Eder*

E Langonned / 1976 / Fontana ✦✦✦✦✦
Stivell's finest acoustic band performs traditional and original material. *—Steve Winick*

Journee a La Maison / 1978 / Rounder ✦✦✦
Stivell's arrangements here are tinged with jazz and pop, but it's still very Breton. *—Steve Winick*

Celtic Symphony / 1979 / Rounder ✦✦✦
Stivell's most advanced and ambitious work to date, the *Symphonie Celtique* is a long way from his solo harp excursions. In addition to various harps, pipes, and whistles played by Stivell, the instrumentation includes a rock band (guitars, bass, drums, keyboards), uilinn pipes, an orchestra of 40-plus players, and a choir directed by ex-Swingle Singer Christianne LeGrand. The music is sublime and profound, surging and droning at times with massed voices and instruments, at other times retreating to gentle, quietly lyrical passages. It is not traditional Breton, Irish, or Scottish music, but it is a modern, mixed-ensemble successor to those sources. To date, it is Stivell's magnum opus (originally a double album). *—Bruce Eder*

Legend / 1984 / Celtic Music ✦✦✦
Based on the ancient Irish invasion legends, this album is atmospheric and new age in feeling. *—Steve Winick*

The Mist of Avalon / 1991 / Dreyfus ✦✦✦✦
This album—which, at times, recalls parts of Kate Bush's *Hounds of Love*—is also reminiscent of Bo Hansson's *Lord of the Rings,* being a musical homage to Marion Zimmer Bradley's Arthurian novel *The Mists of Avalon,* much as Hanson's was a homage to Tolkien's trilogy. But Stivell's record is not instrumental—rather, it has lots of songs sung partly in Breton and partly in English. It is essentially a progressive rock album (it could even have charted had he done it in the early-1970's), complete with electronic keyboard-driven passages, and a full rock band sharing space with Stivell's harps, bagpipes and tin whistles. Stivell's voice is something of an acquired taste, but his vocals are supported by a trio of guest singers and a small female chorus. *—Bruce Eder*

- **Zoom 70-95** / Jul. 15, 1997 / Dreyfus ✦✦✦✦✦
Breton harpist Alan Stivell brought the Breton harp out of the pages of history and into reality. He's also been a groundbreaker, with his innovative interpretations of traditional Celtic music. His album *The Renaissance of the Celtic Harp* (a Grammy award winner in 1972), which included nature sounds, was revolutionary then, and sounds fresh even today. This two-album set is the definitive 25-year retrospective of the Breton harpist. The first disc offers his more meditative and mellow compositions, most drawn from traditional Celtic melodies: Irish, Scottish, Welsh, and Breton. The second disc showcases examples of Stivell's progressive interpretations of Celtic music, combining traditional instruments with electric guitars, trap set, and keyboards. The 1977 "Rouantelezh Vretzh (Breton Kingdom)" is a hard-driving song with very complex rhythm sequences. "An Nighean Dubh" (1972) is a dynamic

swirl of bagpipes, acrobatic tongue-twisting vocals, penny whistles, and harp. Whether belting out a protest song or whispering to a love, Stivell has a unique and expressive voice. There are 35 tracks in all here; the album ends with the epic "Lands of My Fathers." The ending chorus is sung by the 15,000 spectators singing a Breton and Welsh anthem at a rugby match, with Stivell singing a passionate descant overhead. Stivell, a champion of the cause of Breton identity, can really rally a crowd, and this track will really get your heart pounding. *Zoom* is quintessential Stivell. A must-have album. The only drawback to the album is that the liner notes are in French. *—Carol Wright*

Back to Breizh / May 23, 2000 / Dreyfus ♦♦♦
Back to Breizh from Breton Harp master Alan Stivell utilizes a wide variety of influences on this 12-song disc. Added to his Celtic melodies are bagpipes, hints of rock guitar, DJs' turntables, and folk-rock in the tradition of Fairport Convention. Acoustic guitarist Jean Charles Guigen formerly of the group Ar Re Yaoank along with 15 musicians who play traditional and modern instruments compliments Stivell. This is an interestingly eclectic release on Dreyfus records. *—Al Campbell*

Dave Swarbrick

b. Apr. 5, 1947
Vocals, Violin, Mandolin, Fiddle / British Folk-Rock, Traditional Celtic, British Folk
Dave Swarbrick is one of England's most influential fiddlers. As a member of Fairport Convention, between 1970 and 1979, Swarbrick was instrumental in the band's transformation from Byrds-style folk rock band to its focus on updating the jigs and reels on Great Britain. Although he's continued to perform at Fairport annual reunion festival in Cropedy, Swarbrick has successfully explored a variety of outside projects as a soloist, a duo partner of Martin Carthy, Simon Nicol, Alisdair Hulett and Pete Hawkes, and a member of tradition-rooted bands Whippersnapper and the Keith Hancock Band. *—Craig Harris*

● **Rags, Reels & Airs** / 1967 / Topic ♦♦♦♦♦

Lift the Lid & Listen / 1978 / Sonet ♦♦♦
This continues the trend started on his first two albums. *—Steve Winick*

Smiddyburn/Flittin' / 1996 / Raven ♦♦♦♦
Raven reissued two fine Dave Swarbrick albums from the early '80s, *Smiddyburn* and *Flittin',* on a single disc in 1995. *—Stephen Thomas Erlewine*

Swarbrick/Swarbrick II / Mar. 10, 1996 / Castle ♦♦♦
This is a compilation of Dave Swarbrick's first two Transatlantic Records albums *Swarbrick* and *Swarbrick 2.* They were released in 1976 and 1977, respectively, and are comprised of all traditional material with the exception of two pieces by the legendary Irish harpist Turlough O'Carolan, which are essentially traditional pieces with unknown authors. These are acoustic recordings that involve Swarbrick's bandmates from Fairport Convention: guitarist Simon Nicol, bassist Dave Pegg, and percussionist/producer Bruce Rowland, as well as several other musicians that have been influential to Swarbrick's career like Martin Carthy and his old ceilidh bandmembers Roger Marriott, Kate Graham, Alan Robertson, and Beryl Marriott. These recordings are indicative of Dave Swarbrick's dedication to the folk tradition and offer a unique contrast to his involvement on the two Fairport albums released during the same time period, *Gottle o' Geer* and *Bonny Bunch of Roses.* *—Dave Sleger*

SwarbAid / 1999 / Woodworm ♦♦♦
It's always a treat when fiddler Dave Swarbrick "rosins up the bow" with his old pals in Fairport Convention. The concert and CD proceeds were directly earmarked to benefit an ailing Swarbrick but you'd never guess that he was in questionable health based on this recording. Members of Fairport's 1999 lineup join Swarbrick on stage for "The Bonny Black Hare" (first recorded by Fairport and Swarb on 1971's *Angel Delight*) and two of the fiddler's original pieces, "My Heart's in New South Wales" and the ever-popular "Rosie." Culminating this EP is Bob Dylan's "When I Paint My Masterpiece." *—Dave Sleger*

June Tabor

b. Dec. 31, 1947, Warwick, England
Vocals / Contemporary Folk, British Folk, Folk-Rock
June Tabor is probably the finest female traditional British folk singer of the late 20th century—if not the best British folk singer of her time, period. What links her to Britain's past traditions are the chilling and emotional qualities of her voice. What links her to the British present is her fine taste in material, arrangements, and backing musicians, along with a willingness to try different things and interpret work by contemporary songwriters.

Tabor's first high-profile project was a duet album with Steeleye Span's Maddy Prior in the 1970s (the duo dubbed themselves the Silly Sisters for the occasion). An all-star cast of some of the leading lights of the British folk scene supported the singers, including Martin Carthy, Nic Jones, and Andy Irvine. For her own albums and tours she has worked with outstanding guitarists, most notably Jones and Martin Simpson. She's also tread into folk-rock waters with Fairport Convention (whom she's guested with onstage) and the Oyster Band (with whom she collaborated on a 1990 album). Her 1994 album, *Against the Stream,* found her still at her peak, interpreting both traditional tunes and efforts by modern-day composers, including Elvis Costello and Richard Thompson. Subsequent efforts include 1996's *Singing the Storm,* 1997's *Aleyn* and 2000's *Quiet Eye.* *—Richie Unterberger*

Airs & Graces A / 1976 / Shanachie ♦♦♦♦♦
Tabor's first solo record is an understated triumph full of good songs, great arrangements and a crack groups of backing musicians led by the guitar playing of Nic Jones. Much of the record is pure English folk, and Tabor has much fun with such ancient numbers as "While the Gamekeepers Lie Sleeping" and "Young Waters." The standout track, however, is her version of Eric Bogle's brilliant anti-war ode "The Band Played Waltzing Matilda." Sung a cappella, you can almost feel the bitterness in her voice, a breathtaking, stunning moment indicative of how amazing she can be. Reissued on compact disc by Shanachie. *—John Dougan*

Ashes and Diamonds / 1977 / Green Linnet ♦♦♦

A Cut Above / 1980 / Green Linnet ♦♦♦♦♦
This album was originally released on the Topic label in 1980, when June Tabor was just coming into her own as a solo artist. She had made two albums with Maddy Prior (of Steeleye Span) in the 1970s, both of which were fairly lighthearted collections of English folk songs. On *A Cut Above,* she is teamed up with uber-guitarist Martin Simpson and begins to show the darker colors that would typify her subsequent work. "Admiral Benbow" (a gorgeous sea song with a lovely choral tag at the end) and the cheerfully despairing "Flash Company" are light enough, but her hair-raising a cappella performance of "Number Two Top Seam," a song about a coal mine explosion, shows her at her best—stark, chilling and beautiful. She also manages to cut Linda Thompson with her rendition of "Strange Affair," possibly the saddest and most beautiful of all the sad and beautiful songs written by Linda's ex-husband Richard. Martin Simpson, who is the very soul of taste throughout this album, mars "Strange Affair" with an ill-advised slide guitar solo, but it's the only mistake anyone makes on this album. *—Rick Anderson*

Abyssinians / 1983 / Shanachie ♦♦♦

Some Other Time / 1989 / Hannibal ♦♦♦♦♦
No folk music here, as Tabor records an album of standards that includes Ellington's "Sophisticated Lady," and Monk's "'Round Midnight," Cole Porter's "I've Got You Under My Skin," and the Sammy Cahn/Jule Styne-authored title track. What's intriguing is that while many of these songs swing hard in their original versions, Tabor reinvents them as ballads, and for the most part is very successful. It seems counterintuitive, but in rearranging the songs to suit her ballad style, Tabor manages to uncover a dark heart in many of these songs, making this an audacious effort. Not recommended to those who want faithful renditions of these classics, but to those who want new ways of considering how this music can be interpreted. Extra kudos go to longtime Tabor pianist Huw Warren for his great arrangements. *—John Dougan*

Freedom and Rain / 1990 / Rykodisc ♦♦♦♦♦
Tabor teams up with one of Britain's leading folk-rock outfits, the Oyster Band, with fairly successful results, although it won't be the favorite of June's most traditionally-minded fans. She takes all the lead vocals on these fully electrified arrangements. The material is certainly varied, including both traditional numbers and covers of contemporary folk and rock tunes by Richard Thompson, Si Kahn, the Pogues, Billy Bragg, and the Velvet Underground. *—Richie Unterberger*

Angel Tiger / 1992 / Cooking Vinyl ♦♦♦♦♦
It is nearly impossible to qualitatively periodize Tabor's recorded output; all of it (with the exception of the record with the Oyster Band) is worth owning. It's not as if Tabor's early stuff is significantly better than her later work, it's a little different. In fact, I tend to play her later stuff as much, probably more than *Airs and Graces,* and I love that record. *Angel Tiger* is a perfect example of how well Tabor's voice has aged, becoming deeper and more luscious. On this disc, Elvis Costello gave her "All This Useless Beauty," and it's a stunning collaboration. She also brilliantly covers Billy Bragg's "Rumours of War," but the best track is a melancholy ballad entitled "Sudden Waves," which may be Tabor's greatest single moment on record. It's so rife with sadness, it's tough to listen to it without shedding a tear or two. *—John Dougan*

★ **Against the Streams** / 1994 / Green Linnet ♦♦♦♦♦
This addition to June Tabor's catalog reveals a woman exploring new aspects of her considerable talent while still feeding the roots of the folk tradition in which she grew up. A piano-and-concertina accompaniment provides a stark, dry background to Tabor's voice on "Shameless Love," the album's opening track, and on this song you hear her moving a little bit away from the traditionalism which has dominated so much of her work in the past. "I Want to Vanish," a song penned for Tabor by Elvis Costello, moves her even farther afield—it almost sounds like a turn-of-the-century parlor song. But the next three tracks find her on more familiar terrain: the traditional "False, False" and Richard Thompson's typically cynical and lovely "Pavanne" both sound like they were written for Tabor's rich alto voice, and "He Fades Away" is an emotionally devastating meditation in the voice of an Australian woman watching her husband die from the effects of asbestos mining—"He fades away," she says, "not like the leaves of autumn turning gold against the grey," but rather "like the bloodstains on his pillowcase that I wash every day." If you can remain unmoved through this song, then you need to have your pulse checked. "Beauty and the Beast: an Anniversary" is an awkward spoken-word interlude, but "Waiting for the Lark," the tender lullaby that closes the album, is a gorgeous counterweight to "He Fades Away." This is one of Tabor's finest efforts. *—Rick Anderson*

Aleyn / Aug. 26, 1997 / Green Linnet ♦♦♦

A Quiet Eye / Jan. 11, 2000 / Green Linnet ♦♦♦♦
As June Tabor ages her voice seems, paradoxically, to become clearer and sharper. She is also becoming increasingly interested in expanding her repertoire beyond the traditional British and Irish folk music on which her early career was built. There are no fiddles or guitars on this album; instead there are Huw Warren's piano and the Creative Jazz Orchestra, a big band complete with French horn and two trombones. So has she finally crossed the line that separates a mere singer from a chanteuse? Not yet, thankfully. While one of these songs does come from a musical, a plurality of them (including such standbys as "The Water Is Wide" and "I Will Put My Ship in Order") are traditional, and there are two Richard Thompson covers ("Waltzing's for Dreamers" and "Pharaoh") and a fine version of Ewan McColl's immortal "The First Time Ever I Saw Your Face." The big band arrangements are surprisingly effective, especially on the Maggie Holland composition "A Place Called England" and on the dour "Pharaoh." Not everyone will prefer this album to her earlier work, but Tabor herself has never sounded better. *—Rick Anderson*

The Tannahill Weavers

Group / Scottish Folk, Celtic Folk, Traditional Celtic, Traditional Scottish Folk
The Tannahill Weavers, who started as a band 20 years ago, occupy a unique position among the groups on the Scottish folk scene. Stalwarts Roy Gullane and Phil Smillie have sur-

rounded themselves wuith a rotating cast of great musicians. Their music, which uses the highland bagpipe, flute, and fiddle as its melodic core, is tighter, more intense, and harder-driven than the Battlefield Band, Silly Wizard, or other of their contemporaries. Despite their mostly acoustic sound, they're the closest thing to a rock and roll band in intensity and attitude that the Scottish traditional music scene has to offer. Green Linnet Records has been the major force in promoting the Weavers, releasing more than a dozen albums over three decades. In 2000, the label continued that trend into the next millenium by releasing *Alchemy.* — *Steve Winick*

Tannahill Weavers / 1979 / Green Linnet ♦♦♦♦♦
A classic album of Scottish folk music, it features fiddle, bagpipe, flute and more. — *Steve Winick*

Passage / 1984 / Green Linnet ♦♦♦
The weavers add electric guitarist Bill Bourne for an excursion into electric folk. — *Steve Winick*

Land of Light / 1986 / Green Linnet ♦♦♦
After a brief experiment with electric instruments, the Tannies returned to a primarily acoustic approach on this album. As always, it's the singing that sets them apart most decisively from the competition: songs like "The Scottish Settler's Lament," "The Rovin' Heilandman" and the album's title track practically shimmer with the band's dense harmonies. Enjoyment of the instrumentals will hinge mainly on one's appreciation for the highland pipes, which are generally the core of the sound, though Phil Smillie's flute and whistle playing are also frequently out in front. Bandleader Roy Gullane is a fine songwriter, and contributes both the title track and "Bustles and Bows," a song decrying the whaling industry. — *Rick Anderson*

Dancing Feet / 1987 / Green Linnet ♦♦♦♦♦
This album finds The Weavers as energetic as in the days of their classic early albums. — *Steve Winick*

★ **Best of 1979-1989** / 1989 / Garland ♦♦♦♦♦
A great compilation, this is the place to start. — *Steve Winick*

Cullen Bay / 1990 / Green Linnet ♦♦♦
Fiery and ferocious, they're up to their old ways once again. — *Steve Winick*

Mermaid Song / 1992 / Green Linnet ♦♦♦
Their arrangements are beginning to sound a little formulaic, but there's great material and fine performances here. — *Steve Winick*

Capernaum / 1994 / Green Linnet ♦♦♦♦♦
The Tannahill Weavers are the class of the modern Scottish folk bands—not only do they boast great singers and focus primarily on traditional material, but they also make tasteful use of the Highland bagpipes. Don't laugh—for many listeners, that's a serious issue; the Highland pipes have a sound that you either love or hate. The Tannies help you love it by putting great care into their arrangements. For example, the opening medley on this disc features no fewer than five traditional fiddle tunes (performed in under five minutes), and that approach is part of what makes those skirling pipes so easy on the ear; by the time you get tired of hearing one melody you've already heard two more. Then they throw themselves into the serious vocal work on the title track, and you think you've died and gone to Aberdeen—or Edinburgh, given the tune's subject matter. "Capernaum" is a setting of Lewis Spence's poetic lament over the bloody and repressive history of that city, and the melody is a bracing dirge sung with authority by the Weavers, who handle the dense, tight harmonies with passionate ease. The next track is a heartwrenching ballad called "The Plooboy Laddies," and from this high point on, the album's quality basically never falters. Instrumentals and songs are fairly evenly distributed; the liner notes include a handy glossary of Scots Gaelic terms used in the lyrics. — *Rick Anderson*

Tannahill Weavers Collection: Choice Cuts 1987-1996 / Aug. 26, 1997 / Green Linnet ♦♦♦♦
An excellent, if sometimes amorphous, collection that covers the latter-day incarnations of the Tannahill Weavers. This is a solid introduction to the range of Scottish music performed by the band, including their rousing take on "Wild Mountain Thyme" (always a concert centerpiece). — *Steven McDonald*

Epona / Sep. 15, 1998 / Green Linnet ♦♦♦♦
No great departure here from the Tannies' usual fare: lovely and expertly arranged sets of jigs and reels alternating with traditional Scottish songs, equally well-arranged and often featuring startlingly dense and tight vocal harmonies. *Epona* gets off to a rather slow start, with the weak and sludgy "Interceltic Set." But the gorgeous harmony singing on "When the Kye Come Hame" brings things back up to speed, and they stay there for the remainder of the program; the multi-tracked whistles on "Lord Drummond" are heartbreakingly lovely, as are (yet again) the sung harmonies on "The Braes o' Gleniffer." Guitarist Roy Gullane's own "The Great Ships" is one of the album's highlights, and with "Rich Man's Silver" provides a spot of astringent social commentary on the otherwise traditional program. There are also excellent arrangements of two Robert Burns songs, "Craigieburn Wood" and the ever-popular "Westlin' Winds." *Epona* doesn't stand head and shoulders above the rest of the Tannahill Weavers' catalog, but it is certainly up to the group's usual high standard. — *Rick Anderson*

Cyril Tawney

Vocals / Sea Shanties, British Folk
Cyril Tawney has been a mainstay of the English folk scene for many years. He is well known both as an interpreter of traditional material and as an excellent songwriter. His songs have been sung by many other folk revival performers, further enhancing his reputation. He is strongly associated with his native region of Devon and Cornwall, and has recorded much material from that part of southern England. The years he spent in the Royal Navy also make him a natural interpreter and writer of sea songs. — *Steve Winick*

In Port / 1972 / Argo ♦♦♦♦♦
Original Tawney songs focusing on the sea fill up this album. Many of his best-known songs appear on this album, including "Sally Free and Easy," "The Grey Funnel Line," and "The Ballad of Sammy's Bar." — *Steve Winick*

● **Sally Free & Easy** / 1990 / Neptune ♦♦♦♦♦
Included are fresh interpretations of some of the material from *In Port,* plus new songs. — *Steve Winick*

Seamen Bold / 1993 / Neptune ♦♦♦
Traditional and original songs of the sea are here. — *Steve Winick*

Steve Tilston

b. Mar. 6, 1950, Liverpool, England
Vocals, Mandolin, Guitar / Contemporary Celtic
Along with Maggie Boyle, his Irish wife, Steve Tilston is one of the most compelling artists in this genre of music. His songwriting, singing and guitar work are all excellent, and her singing of traditional songs and her instrumental work are likewise impressive. — *Steve Winick*

Swans at Coole / 1989 / Gold Castle ♦♦♦♦♦
An absolutely beautiful album of guitar music, this features traditional tunes played in a classical vein. — *Steve Winick*

★ **Of Moor & Mesa** / 1992 / Green Linnet ♦♦♦♦♦
An extremely well-balanced album, this features beautiful traditional songs sung by Boyle and equally lovely original songs written and sung by Tilston. Accompaniments on guitar, flute and other instruments help make this a joy to hear. — *Steve Winick*

All Under the Sun / 1996 / Flying Fish ♦♦♦♦

Tri Yann

Group / Celtic Rock, British Folk-Rock, Contemporary Celtic
This band is the most important exponent of urban folk-rock from Brittany. Over the years, their music has ranged from punchy acoustic arrangements of traditional songs to rock & roll based on the Breton and Gallo traditions. — *Steve Winick*

Suite Gallaise / 1974 / Marzelle ♦♦♦
Their best acoustic album is full of bouncy energy. — *Steve Winick*

La Decouverte Ou L'ignorance / 1976 / Marzelle ♦♦♦♦♦
An excellent album, this was their first to use electric guitars, drums and other rock instruments in a mostly folk setting. — *Steve Winick*

● **Si Mort a Mors** / 1982 / Philips ♦♦♦♦♦
This excellent double-album compilation covers the first ten years or so, without overlapping *Les Filles des Forges.* — *Steve Winick*

Belle Et Rebelle / 1990 / Marzelle ♦♦♦

Jean-Michel Veillon

Whistle (Instrument), Flute / Traditional Celtic
Jean-Michel Veillon was a child prodigy on the bombarde, that piercing woodwind characteristic of Breton music. Later in life, he became interested in Irish music, particularly the wooden flute, which was not played in Brittany. Through his exemplary work with groups like Galorn, Kornog, Barzaz, Den and Pennou Skoulm, Veillon has made the wooden flute an acceptable instrument in the Breton tradition. — *Steve Winick*

★ **E Koad Nizan** / 1993 / Coop Breizh ♦♦♦♦♦
Accompanied by the best musicians Brittany has to offer, Veillon plays the flute in a lovely, lilting style. This is the first album ever to focus on Breton music played on the wooden transverse flute, and it's a landmark for that reason. However, buy it simply because it's wonderful. — *Steve Winick*

John Whelan

Accordion / Irish Folk
A great button accordion player, Whelan has won the all-Ireland championship on the instrument six times, and the all-Britain seven. His playing is exciting and fresh, if not strictly traditional. Ivers is his match, having won the all-Ireland fiddle titles seven times herself. — *Steve Winick*

● **Fresh Takes** / 1987 / Green Linnet ♦♦♦♦♦
Accompanied by Mark Simos and Triona Ni Dhomhnaill, Whelan and Ivers tear into some wonderful tunes, using consistently fresh and newfangled arrangements to keep the album interesting. — *Steve Winick*

Celtic Crossroads / Feb. 25, 1997 / Narada ♦♦♦
To their credit, when Narada decided to dabble in Celtic music, they went with the "reel" thing, not an ethereal, synthesized version designed to appease an otherwise disinterested audience. Though willing to experiment and incorporate new elements into his music, accordionist John Whelan is not about compromise either. Yes, the production is slick, and yes, there's little spontaneity in these tracks, but Whelan's soulfulness and superb musicianship cannot be overlooked. Stars abound, including Jerry Douglas, Johnny Cunningham, Kathy Mattea, multi-instrumentalist Seamus Egan, and Whelan's Kips Bay cohort Pat Kilbride, who plays cittern and guitar. (Whelan declares Kilbride to be the best accompanist he's ever played with.) Kilbride, along with percussionist John Ballestero, creates an eerie and metronomic effect on "Mabel Ruddy's/Windy Gap." Whelan is perhaps without peer when it comes to delivering a melody on accordion; his style is generally of a cheerful and uptempo nature. On *Celtic Crossroads,* there are just enough doses of the sweet, sorrowful and haunting to yield an emotionally well-rounded listen. The combination of styles and textures is best ex-

emplified on the Tommy Sands classic "There Were Roses," clearly an Irish song although Douglas' dobro and Mattea's vocals give it an American flavor. The backdrop of fiddle and pipes bring the song safely back home again to Ireland. Such a pattern is reflective of Whelan's own experience as an Irishman living in the U.S., playing music influenced by his native homeland. *—Dave Sleger*

Flirting with the Edge / Feb. 24, 1998 / Narada ♦♦♦

Wolfstone

Group / Celtic Rock, Contemporary Celtic

If they did more vocal music, Wolfstone might almost qualify as Scotland's answer to Ireland's Horslips. The group, formed by Duncan Chisholm (fiddle) and David Foster (bass, drums, sequencer), with Roger Niven (lead guitars, acoustic guitar), Stuart Eaglesham (rhythm guitar, lead vocal), Struan Eaglesham (keyboards), and Iain MacDonald (pipes, whistle, flute), plays traditional Scottish music in a manner that recalls the most articulate recordings of Steeleye Span and the hardest-rocking sides of Horslips and the Pogues, as well as Planxty. *—Bruce Eder*

• **Unleashed** / 1991 / Green Linnet ♦♦♦♦♦
Wolfstone's first official album, featuring Duncan Chisholm (fiddle), Stuart Eaglesham (guitars), Struan Eaglesham (keyboards), Ivan Drever (acoustic guitar, vocals), Andrew Murray (lead guitar, vocals), and Allan Wilson (pipes, whistle, flute) sounds like a lost Steeleye Span session circa 1972 crossed with the best moments off the first Big Country album. The spirits are high, and the melodies flow freely—the mix of dances and balladry, mythic and contemporary references, and folk traditions is utterly compelling. "Song for Yesterday," and the dance instrumental "Cleveland Park," and the more traditionally based "Erin" are just a few of the highlights. *—Bruce Eder*

The Chase / 1992 / Green Linnet ♦♦♦♦
If Big Country had been more of an instrumental band with more of a commitment to folk music, they might have produced a record like this. Wolfstone's second album to date opens with a beautiful and riveting instrumental invocation (a salvage job, no less, from a failed attempt to write a signature tune for the BBC Radio Orkney), followed by a haunting (and hard-rocking) drinking song; it gets better from there, plunging into Scottish history ("The Prophet") and topical songwriting, all of it memorable and gorgeous. The lineup here is Chisholm (fiddle), Ivan Drever (vocals, guitar), Struan Eaglesham (keyboards), Stuart Eaglesham (vocals, guitars), and Andy Murray (electric guitar). Even when they try for a more contemporary sound, as on "The Appropriate Dipstick," the presence of Dougie Pincock's pipes (which start the break solo, and then join with Duncan Chisholm's fiddle) gives the music a challenging duality between the old and the new. The rhythm section—Neil Hay on bass and John Henderson on drums (who does a killer job on "The Prophet")—is better integrated into the group's sound, making for a solid piece of folk-rock. *—Bruce Eder*

Wolfstone / 1994 / Celtic Music ♦♦♦♦
Traditional tunes, mostly instrumental, dominate on this delightful 36-minute exploration of the Scottish folk heritage by way of electric instruments. The album never lets the listener go; much of it is dance-oriented, and even the most sedentary listeners may be pulled to their feet by the beat of "Banjo" or "Brolum," the latter a lovely fiddle tune that also features some sharp, crunchy electric guitar by Roger Niven. The acoustic playing by the two axemen on "How Long" is also fairly compelling. The two modern vocal numbers here, "Ready for the Storm" and "How Long," are highlighted by Stuart Eaglesham's charismatic lead vocals and a killer beat and attack, all recalling elements of the best work of U2 and the Pogues, filtered through Scotland rather than Belfast (though, of course, it's *all* Celtic). *—Bruce Eder*

Year of the Dog / 1994 / Green Linnet ♦♦♦

Half Tail / Aug. 1996 / Green Linnet ♦♦♦♦

Pick of the Litter: The Best of Wolfstone 1991-1996 / 1997 / Green Linnet ♦♦♦♦
An excellent place to start getting into Wolfstone's brand of rock 'n' reel. As with Horslips before them, Wolfstone's approach is to blend traditional Celtic themes with more contemporary rock instrumentation and songwriting, resulting in a raucous end result. Unlike Horslips, however, Wolfstone have no ambitions to crack the pop charts as such, so never lose sight of the Celtic and folk origins of their work. What does get lost on occasion is their drive—1996's *The Half Tail* was an unusually weak effort. *—Steven McDonald*

This Strange Place / Feb. 24, 1998 / Green Linnet ♦♦♦

Seven / May 18, 1999 / Green Linnet ♦♦♦♦
As rock & reel bands go, this Scots band is considerably more rock than reel. Wolfstone's approach is sort of an inversion of that taken by groups like the Oyster Band and the Pogues, whose music is based on traditional material infused with a rockish intensity. In Wolfstone's music there's plenty of Highland pipes and fiddle, but the predominant voices in the mix are overdriven electric guitars and drums; the overall impression is one of rock & roll infused with Celtic influences rather than the other way around. And if the singing sometimes comes off as a bit fey, it's fey in a heavy metal sort of way, high-pitched and modestly operatic. On "Brave Boys," which seems to be an antiwar tune, singer Stuart Eaglesham delivers a lovely melody over a churning Hammond organ and driving acoustic guitars, while a fiddle keens away in the distance; "Fingal's Cave" is an extract of poetry by Iain Chrichton Smith set to a traditional tune. Elsewhere there are several fine instrumentals, most of them originals. Fans of the band will not be disappointed. *—Rick Anderson*

Various Artists

Celtic Fingerstyle Guitar, Vol. 1: Ramble to Cashel / Jun. 9, 1998 / Rounder ♦♦♦♦♦
This disc is the first in a two-volume survey of modern fingerstyle (as opposed to flatpicking) guitarists who specialize in arrangements of traditional Irish and Scots tunes; for each disc, there is a companion videotape of the same title available separately. The videotape includes complete notation of all the arrangements in tabulature and traditional notation. Volume 1 is perhaps the more consistently satisfying of the two discs, but that may be an illusion based on the appearance at the very beginning of three unbelievably sumptuous performances by uber-guitarist Martin Simpson. His medley of "Believe Me If All These Endearing Young Charms" and "Waters of Tyne" is one of the loveliest things ever committed to tape. Steve Baughman, who takes a funkier approach on "Bony Crossing the Alps," isn't far behind him. The legendary French guitarist Pierre Bensusan has lots of fun with "Merrily Kiss the Quaker," but his style is a bit more clattery than the others. El McMeen should get a medal for making "Danny Boy" sound fresh. Aficionados will wonder at the omissions from these collections (where's Dick Gaughan— Bert Jansch— John Renbourn—), but they're still essential listening. *—Rick Anderson*

Celtic Folk Festival / 1996 / Munich ♦♦♦♦♦
Recorded at two Dutch folk festivals in the early 1980s, this has good performances by some of the biggest names in British Isles traditional folk/folk-rock, including Clannad, Andy Irvine, the Tannahill Weavers, Silly Wizard, and Battlefield Band. The program's rounded out by three lesser-known acts from Brittany (Kornog, Dan Ar Bras, and Sonerien Du). Material, sound, and performance are good, and while it may not be the first place you should stop to check out the artists, it's a good addition for those building a deep Celtic collection. Incidentally, the Clannad tracks were recorded during their first performances with then-14-year-old Enya in the lineup; the Silly Wizard cut is one of the few recordings of the group with Dougie McLean. *—Richie Unterberger*

The Celtic Lullaby / 1996 / Ellipsis Arts ♦♦♦♦
A sweet and beautiful low-key collection of lullabies performed by a variety of artists ranging from Jean Redpath to Alison Kinaird. The arrangements cover everything from multiple voices (with and without instrumentation) to solo performers singing a cappella. The common thread: all songs you can play to lull the children to sleep (and these recordings are perhaps equally as useful for lulling the grownups to sleep as well.) *—Steven McDonald*

The Drones and the Chanters: Irish Pipering / Apr. 25, 2000 / Atlantic ♦♦♦♦
If you are a #Riverdance fan in search of concordant Celtic tunes, then *The Drones and the Chanters* is definitely not the CD for you. Alternatively, if you have been frantically flipping through album after album looking for music that reflects more than just a TV friendly, commercial side of Irish culture, then the 21 tracks on this CD are for you. This all bag-piping release begins with the guttural wheezing, insect-like buzzing, and twitchy upbeat melody of Seamus Emis' excellent "Jenny's Welcome to Charlie." This particular song form, known as a reel, is widely thought of as being the "dance-form par excellence." The jig, examples of which are generously distributed about on this CD, is also revered as being among the lively repertoire of dance tunes for pipers. Another style brought to life by pipers are lullabies and airs of the ceol mall (slow music). A handy booklet that answers such time honored questions as "what are the parlour pipes" and "what is a chanter" accompanies the CD. Whatever the particular song form, the top-notch tunes from Seamus Ennis, Paddy Moloney, Tommy Reck, Willie Clancy, Peader Broe, and Dan Dowd ought to guarantee these lads honorary doctorates from bag-piping schools around the globe. And though *The Drones and the Chanters* may, for some, take a little time getting use to, its 21 gratifyingly dissonant songs are well worth the wait. *—John Vallier*

☆ **Flight of the Green Linnet** / 1988 / Rykodisc ♦♦♦♦♦
If you've seen +Riverdance or a Chieftains video and think you might be interested in Celtic music but aren't quite sure where to start, this sampler is just what you've been looking for. Frankly, if you're a longtime aficionado of Celtic music and are looking for a solid collection of great music by the world's greatest Irish and Scots performers, this album is for you, too. It's compiled from various releases on the Green Linnet label and includes artists ranging in orientation from strictly traditional (the Tannahill Weavers, Mick Moloney) to the more progressive (Silly Wizard, Relativity) and thus reflects the wide stylistic spectrum of Celtic folk music as it is currently interpreted. The tunes range from standard-issue sets of jigs and reels to synthesizer-tinged modern folk songs, and there's enough variety to maintain the interest of just about anyone. Highlights include Silly Wizard's medley of "The Secret Portrait" and "Wha'll Be King but Charlie—" and a lovely piece of puirt a beul by Capercaillie. *—Rick Anderson*

Heart of Scotland: Collection of Gaelic Songs / Jun. 16, 1998 / Music Club ♦♦♦♦
This 16-track collection makes a perfect introduction to the many moods of Scottish music, both in the traditional and more modern Gaelic styles. Collected up from holdings in the vaults from Scotland's Greentrax label—the Sun/Chess Records of Scottish music—this features acclaimed selections from Catherine-Ann MacPhee ("Puirt-A-Reel"), Peatbog Faeries ("The Manali Beetle"), Tony McManus ("A Tune for Frankie"), Deaf Shepherd ("Jean Carignan"), Mairi MacInnes ("Puriri-A-Beul"), Ceolbeg ("Galician Set"), Seelyhoo ("The Lost Job/The Old Copperplate/The Diesel Accordion") and others, totaling over an hour of the finest this genre has to offer. *—Cub Koda*

Heart of the Gaels / 1992 / Green Linnet ♦♦♦♦♦
This is one of several very good compilations drawn from the vaults of Green Linnet, the best Celtic music label in America. Like all the others, this one is generously packed with fine performances by a variety of Celtic artists from all over Europe—most of the artists are Irish or Scottish, but the Breton band Kornog makes an appearance (with a very nice set of gavottes), as does a Galician band called Milladoiro; their track is a jig called (get this) "Muineira de Chantada." And let's not forget the deeply rooted Celtic traditions of Quebec, which are represented here by Ad Vielle Que Pourra. Throw these all in with sprghtly performances by Altan, the Tannahill Weavers, Matt Molloy, Phil Cunningham and the rest of the usual suspects, and you've got a surprisingly diverse and tasty stew of ancient and modern Celtic folk music. *—Rick Anderson*

☆ **Iron Muse** / 1993 / Topic ♦♦♦♦♦
Based on a compilation album from 1956, this 1993 CD features extra tracks. The original

Iron Muse album was put together by A.L. Lloyd (author of Come All Ye Bold Miners and, later, Folk Song in England) to foreground an idea that he and other folksong scholars had only recently accepted: industrial folklore. The CD version is indespensable for anyone interested in the range of occupational songs in the industrial parts of England. *—Steve Winick*

Joyful Noise: Celtic Favorites from Green Linnet / Oct. 13, 1998 / Green Linnet ✦✦✦✦
Joyful Noise: Celtic Favorites from Green Linnet samples the label's catalog over the course of two discs, concentrating on the more upbeat side of contemporary Celtic music with dances, reels, and cheerily romantic ballads. Just a few of the many artists included on the infectious collection are Altan, Capercaillie, Seamus Egan, Tommy Sands, Dick Gaughan, the Tannahill Weavers, and Patrick Street. *—Steve Huey*

Song of the Green Linnet / Sep. 12, 2000 / Green Linnet ✦✦✦✦
No American label can boast a Celtic music catalog as rich and deep as Green Linnet's, and the company has demonstrated that over the years with a string of very fine compilations. This one focuses on vocal performances by such world-class solo artists as June Tabor, Niamh Parsons, and Andy M. Stewart, as well as ensembles as diverse as Celt-rockers Wolfstone, Scots harmony masters the Tannahill Weavers, and modern Scots supergroup Capercaillie. The highlights are many: Niamh Parsons is given two slots, which was a wise programming move, her renditions of "Bonny Woodhall" and "Kilnamartyra Exile" just about steal the show. The Green Fields of America deliver a rousing and hilarious ode to homemade whiskey, entitled "Stick to the Craythur," while June Tabor exhibits her growing tendency towards art song with an elaborately arranged medley consisting of "The Water is Wide," "St. Agnes," and "Jeannie and Jamie." Wolfstone turns in an uncharacteristically restrained performance on "Till I Sleep." There's hardly an item in the Green Linnet catalog that isn't worth picking up, and this compilation is a great place to start. *—Rick Anderson*

There Was a Lady: The Voice of Celtic Women / Feb. 25, 1997 / Celtophile ✦✦✦✦✦
A splendid compilation drawn from the Green Linnet catalog, focusing on solo artists and bands with female vocalists. The track listing is fairly eclectic, but entertaining throughout—uniformly good enough that nothing stands out from the entire collection. A good place to start looking for an example of the female voice in Celtic music. *—Steven McDonald*

● **Traditional Music from Cape Breton Island** / 1993 / Nimbus ✦✦✦✦
The 1993 Cork University traditional music festival was the first to feature non-Irish music. Specifically, it featured some of the best musicians from Cape Breton Island, Nova Scotia, Canada, whose style and repertoire is more closely related to Scottish than to Irish music. *—Steve Winick*

Cajun

Zydeco and Cajun are the premier cultural expressions of the spirited and hardy people of southwest Louisiana. While the two styles have some similarities, they are also quite different.

Cajun music as we know it today can be traced back to early Acadian, French, Creole, and Anglo-Saxon folk songs. These early ballads and lullabies—typically concerned with troubles and hard times—were often sung a cappella. For the most part, they were performed at home and passed down orally from generation to generation; however, the singers of these traditional songs were eventually accompanied by simple instrumentation.

Cajun music is of course meant for dancing—one-step, two-step, and waltzes. Traditionally, the Cajun dance ("Fais-do-do" in Cajun) was the major social function in Cajun society. The principal instrument in Cajun music is the diatonic accordion, preferably in the key of C. Although it is a German instrument, the Cajun people adopted it in the 1870s. To a lesser degree, the fiddle is also a favorite instrument in Cajun music. Early Cajun bands featured both of these instruments as well as a triangle to keep the rhythm. Acoustic guitars were added to the lineup by 1920, then, three decades later, steel, electric guitars, and sometimes drums. Although Cajun music has changed somewhat over the years and has been influenced by other styles of music—notably country and blues—it has remained a distinctive style.

The first Cajun record was Joe Falcon's "Allons à Lafayette" from 1928. Although the style was recorded only sporadically for several decades, Iry Le Jeune, Harry Choates, Nathan Abshire, Lawrence Walker, Leo Soileau, and Vin Bruce had become influential Cajun artists by the middle of the 20th century. While the music's popularity continued to grow within Louisiana, it didn't enter the spotlight nationally until the mid-'80s, riding on the coattails of the Cajun food explosion. Today several traditional and contemporary Cajun artists—including Dewey Balfa, Zachary Richard, and Beausoleil — tour nationally and internationally.

Compared to Cajun music, zydeco music has a much shorter history. Like Cajun music, the dominant instrument is the accordion, but unlike Cajun music, zydeco adds electric bass, horns, and sometimes keyboards. In a nutshell, zydeco is creole (Black) dance music of southwest Louisiana that blends Cajun music with R&B and soul. The word "zydeco" is actually a bastardization of an early zydeco song, "L'Haricots Sont Pas Salés" (The Snap Beans Aren't Salted). The first Black-French recordings were made in 1928 by Amadé Ardoin, an accordion player who played in the Cajun style. However, the music we know as zydeco today didn't begin to evolve—at least on record—until the mid-'50s, when Clifton Chenier and Boozoo Chavis made their initial recordings.

Like Cajun music, zydeco didn't achieve national popularity until 1980, buoyed somewhat by Rockin' Sidney's surprise hit "My Toot Toot." By the '90s, several zydeco artists were signed to major labels, including Terrance Simien, Boozoo Chavis, Buckwheat Zydeco, and Rockin' Dopsie. *—Jeff Hannusch*

Artist Reviews

Nathan Abshire

b. Jun. 23, 1913, Gueyden, LA, **d.** May 13, 1981, Basile, LA

Vocals, Accordion / Traditional Cajun, Swamp Blues, Louisiana Blues

Nathan Abshire helped bring the blues and honky tonk to Cajun music and re-popularized the accordion with his recordings during the '50s and '60s, but still never managed a living from his music. Born in Gueyden, LA, on June 23, 1913, Abshire began playing professionally in the 1920s, and he first recorded in the early '30s with Happy Fats & the Rainbow Ramblers. Abshire went to work at the Basile, LA town dump around that time, and he held the job for most of his working life.

His fortunes began looking bright by 1936, however, when the Rainbow Ramblers began backing him on sides for Bluebird. After serving in World War II, Abshire cut "Pine Grove Blues"—his most famous single and later his signature song—for D.T. Records. He recorded for Khoury/Lyric, Swallow and Kajun during the 1950s and '60s, meanwhile playing local dances and appearing on sessions by the Balfa Brothers. A renewal of interest in Cajun and folk music during the '70s gave Abshire a chance to play several festivals and colleges, and star in the 1975 PBS-TV Cajun documentary, *Good Times Are Killing Me.* The title proved prophetic, however, as Abshire fought alcoholism during his last years. Several sessions for Folkways and La Louisienne followed in the late '70s, but he died on May 13, 1981. *—John Bush*

Cajun Social Music / 1990 / Smithsonian/Folkways ✦✦✦✦✦

A summit meeting of Cajun stars yields outstanding renditions of classics and originals. *—Ron Wynn*

The Cajun Legend: Best of Nathan Abshire / 1991 / Swallow ✦✦✦✦✦

With "The Good Times Are Killing Me" emblazoned on his accordion case, Abshire embodied the Cajun musician's ethos. There are 20 two-steps and waltzes here, some with the Balfa Brothers—includes a remake of the great "Pine Grove Blues" and a heartfelt "Tramp Sur La Rue" with wailing vocals from Nathan. *—Mark A. Humphrey*

★ **French Blues** / 1993 / Arhoolie ✦✦✦✦✦

Recorded between 1949 and 1956, this is prime Cajun music. The fidelity is slightly better than the best Cajun discs of the 1930s, but the approach is still satisfyingly raw and spontaneous, with waltzes, boogies, and blues. A steel guitar is present to varying degrees on most of the tracks, giving the fiddle/accordion-dominated arrangements a bit more flavor. This has a great spontaneous feel that stops short (but not that short) of raggedness, highlighted by Abshire's joyous calls and asides. Includes his big "hit," "Pine Grove Blues," although a hit by the standards of this regional style only constituted about three thousand copies sold. With 28 tracks and 78 minutes running time, it's the usual excellent value for an Arhoolie reissue. *—Richie Unterberger*

Johnnie Allan

b. Mar. 10, 1938, Rayne, LA

Vocals, Guitar / Swamp Blues

Johnnie Allan's been a prominent Cajun performer since his teens, when joined accordionist Lawrence Walker's band as a steel guitarist. When the band split, Allan teamed with pianist/fiddler U.J. Meaux, producer Huey Meaux's cousin, in the Krazy Kats, a rock band. Allan continued singing rock and roll and R&B in the late '50s and early '60s. He alternated between music and education for a while, at one point even becoming principal of an elementary school. But his popularity soared when his Cajun-flavored cover of Chuck Berry's "Promised Land" became a hit. Allan's style mixes rock flamboyance with Cajun authenticity, and has been featured on many regional labels. *—Ron Wynn*

Johnnie Allan & Krazy Kats 1959-1960's / 1985 / Krazy Kat ✦✦✦✦✦

A collection highlighting Johnnie Allan's straight rock and R&B singles recorded in 1959 and 1960. The high point is the cover of Chuck Berry's "Lonely Days and Lonely Nights." *—Ron Wynn*

● **South to Louisiana** / 1985 / Ace ✦✦✦✦✦

A compilation featuring Allan doing both prime rocking and traditional Cajun material. *—Ron Wynn*

Alphonse "Bois Sec" Ardoin

b. Nov. 16, 1915, Duralde, LA

Accordion / Zydeco, Creole

Alphonse "Bois-Sec" Ardoin is one of Cajun's music influential players. His appearance at the Newport Folk Festival in 1966 helped to spread Cajun and Creole music past southwest Louisiana while his 1971 album *La Musique Creole,* recorded with five of his sons, the Ardoin Brothers, and blues-tinged Cajun fiddler Canray Fontenot, was a major influence on such modern Cajun bands as Beausoleil and File. Although Ardoin and Fontenot played together as youngsters, they didn't record their first album until the 1970s. They joined together in 1948 to perform as the Duralde Ramblers. In 1986, they received a National Heritage Fellowship from the National Endowment for the Arts. They continued to collaborate until Fontenot's death in July 1995. *—Craig Harris*

● **Musique Creole** / 1966 / Arhoolie ✦✦✦✦✦

The superb *La Musique Creole* is most notable for its inclusion of the rare 1966 Alphonse "Bois Sec" Ardoin and Canray Fontenot LP *Les Blues du Bayou,* the record cut in the wake of the duo's triumphant appearance at that year's *Newport Folk Festival.* Long renowned as among the finest Creole records ever made, its 16 tracks capture Ardoin and Fontenot at the peak of their powers; their interplay on cuts like "Les Blues du Voyager," "Duralde Ramble," and the bluesy instrumental "La Danse de la Misere" borders on the telepathic. The inclusion of eight tracks from a 1971 Arhoolie LP also titled *La Musique Creole,* as well the Ardoin Family Orchestra's previously unreleased "Ardoin Two-Step," is just the icing on the cake. A must for all Creole fans. *—Jason Ankeny*

Allons Danser / Jul. 14, 1998 / Rounder ✦✦✦✦✦

This is another in the long line (these musical families go back to the nineteenth century) of joinings of these two families. The Balfa family is from the Cajun tradition, while the Ardoins stem from the Creole tradition (they were playing back when it was called "French music"). The music on this disc evolved out of friendship and mutual admiration for the music that they share; it is a special album that not only has the latest band from the Balfa family group playing with the 82-year-old elder of the Ardoins, but it has Steve Riley playing the drums. This disc is about as close as you are going to get to the pure music of this region before it was "discovered," its children introduced to VH-1 and MTV, and the hybrids formed when the "French music" was mixed with rock & roll and R&B. Balfa Toujours have two very good discs out on Rounder and play around the country, but Bois Sec Ardoin is 82 years old and not traveling the club circuit any longer. He and his former partner, legendary fiddler Canray Fontenot, who died in 1995, earned several National Heritage Awards for their music. This is music that will inspire one to turn to one's partner and say, "Allons danser!" ("let's dance"). *—Bob Gottlieb*

Amédé Ardoin

b. Mar. 11, 1896, L'Anse Rougeau, LA, **d.** Nov. 9, 1941, Alexandria, LA
Vocals, Accordion / Zydeco, Creole
Amadé Ardoin is to zydeco music as Robert Johnson is to the blues and Buddy Bolden is to jazz. Like Johnson and Bolden, Ardoin not only died under still mysterious conditions, but also shares the potency of their musical influence, having laid the foundation for southwest Louisiana's zydeco music. The first Creole to be recorded, Ardoin is best remembered for his resonating, high-pitched vocals and sizzling-hot accordion playing. He began playing at local house parties, and first recorded in 1929 with fiddler Dennis McGee. He made subsequent recordings during the 1930s for Brunswick, Vocalion, Decca, Melotone and Bluebird labels. Ardoin's death remains shrouded in mystery. One report has him being brutally beaten after wiping his brow with a handkerchief handed to him by the daughter of a white farm owner. According to McGee, Ardoin was poisoned by a jealous fiddler. More recent studies have concluded that Ardoin died of venereal disease at the Pineville Mental Institution. *—Craig Harris*

★ **Louisiana Cajun Music, Vol. 6: Amade Ardoin—*His Original Recordings*** / *Mar. 1983 / Old Timey* ✦✦✦✦✦
Amadé Ardoin's *His Original Recordings, 1928-1938* is divided between seven songs Ardoin recorded with Dennis McGee and seven solo tracks. The duets with McGee are among the most legendary Cajun recordings; McGee's fiddle perfectly meshes with Ardoin's accordion and raw, bluesy voice. These are the recordings that laid the foundation on contemporary Cajun and Zydeco. Ardoin's solo recordings are nearly as influential and exciting, capturing him alone with his accordion. While these aren't quite as kinetic as the duets, they are nevertheless enjoyable. *—Thom Owens*

☆ **The Roots of Zydeco** / 1995 / Arhoolie ✦✦✦✦✦
Amadé Ardoin was arguably the founder of zydeco music, incorporating blues into French folk. The songs on this collection were recorded in 1930 and 1934. Though the sound might be a bit harsh for some—these were taken from 78s, after all—these are important recordings and they continue to sound fresh and vital. *—Thom Owens*

First Black Cajun Recording Artist / Arhoolie ✦✦✦✦
Violinist Dennis McGee is featured on this 14-track album, which contains recordings from 1929, 1930, and 1934. *—AMG*

Lawrence "Black" Ardoin

b. Nov. 17, 1946, Duralde, LA
Drums, Accordion / Zydeco, Creole
The son of Creole accordion legend Alphonse "Bois Sec" Ardoin, Lawrence "Black" Ardoin not only carried on the family's musical traditions, but he later passed on the torch to his own son Chris, one of the most acclaimed proponents of the nouvelle zydeco sound. Born in Duralde, Louisiana in 1946, Ardoin was the second of Bois Sec's sons, joining his father and siblings Morris and Gustave in the Ardoin Brothers Band; originally a drummer, he took over accordion duties when Gustave was killed in a 1974 auto accident, and upon his father's mid-1970s retirement assumed full leadership of the group. However, over time the confines of traditional Creole music stifled Ardoin, and in the early 1980s he formed a new combo, the French Zydeco Band, which also allowed him to pursue his interests in Cajun and swamp-pop sounds. In 1984, the group debuted with the LP *Lawrence "Black" Ardoin and His French Zydeco Band;* a long recording hiatus preceded the release of 1992's follow-up, *Hot and Spicy Zydeco.* Following its release, Ardoin formed a new group, Lagniappe, which included his son Chris on accordion; as the youngster continued his creative evolution, he began leading his own unit, Double Clutchin', which Lawrence also managed. *—Jason Ankeny*

● **Lawrence "Black" Ardoin & His French Band** / 1984 / Arhoolie ✦✦✦✦✦

Hot & Spicy Zydeco / 1992 / La Louisianne ✦✦✦✦
Although it doesn't match the heights of Lawrence "Black" Ardoin's 1984 album for Arhoolie, *Hot & Spicy Zydeco* nevertheless cooks, boasting some hot zydeco jams that carry the album through some uneven material. *—Leo Stanley*

The Balfa Brothers

f. 1967
Guitar, Fiddle / Traditional Cajun
The Balfa Brothers helped keep traditional Cajun music alive in the 1960s, when it was in danger of disappearing. Siblings Dewey, Rodney, Will, Harry and Burkeman began playing informally at family parties and local gatherings during the '40s, and achieved enough local popularity to play up to eight dances a week at local dance halls. The Balfas were later joined by neighbor Hadley Fontenot on accordion. They made their recording debut in 1951 with "La Valse de Bon Baurche" and "Le Two Step de Ville Platte," which were captured on a home recorder and released as a 78-rpm single. Fiddler Dewey then went on to a solo career playing with numerous Cajun artists and recording on such labels as Khoury, Kajun, and Swallow. In 1967, Dewey, Rodney, Will and his daughter Nelda, along with Fontenot, reformed the group and began spreading the Cajun sound throughout Europe and at folk festivals across the U.S. Although most of their musical focus was on tradition, the Balfas were not averse to trying more modernized Cajun songs with a nightclub orchestra. Things went well for the band until February 1979, when Rodney and Will were killed in a car wreck. Despite the tragedy, the Balfa Brothers continued (with a few personnel changes) even after Dewey's death in 1992. Through them, his rich and valuable legacy of Cajun music carries on. *—Sandra Brennan*

● **Play Trad. Cajun Music, Vols. 1 & 2** / 1987 / Swallow ✦✦✦✦✦
The Balfa Brothers Play Traditional Cajun Music, Vols. 1 & 2 combines both of the group's original *Play Traditional Cajun Music* albums onto one disc. The first volume was released on Swallow Records in 1965 and helped kick-start the Cajun revival of the '60s. It's an excellent album, featuring wonderful harmonies from Rodney, Will and Dwey, as well as stellar instrumental work. The second volume, recorded and released in 1974, isn't quite as strong as its predecessor, but it is still very good and is filled with terrific music. Both albums represent the Balfa Brothers at their peak. They may have a number of very good albums in their catalog, but *The Balfa Brothers Play Traditional Cajun Music, Vols. 1 & 2* effectively explains what they are all about. *—Thom Owens*

J'ai Vu Le Loup, Le Renard Et La Belette / 1988 / Rounder ✦✦✦✦
The Balfa Brothers' long heritage in traditional Cajun music has never been exemplified better than on this 13-cut CD recorded in 1975. There were mostly short songs (only one song longer than four minutes), which were predominantly uptempo dance numbers with some two-steps, waltzes and romantic pieces mixed in, as well as an interesting version of "Casey Jones." The session was produced and recorded by Gerard Dole and was originally issued on the Cezame label in France. True believers and purists couldn't find a better example of the vintage sound anywhere. *—Ron Wynn*

Balfa Toujours

Group / Zydeco
The legacy of late Cajun fiddler Dewey Balfa continues through the music of his daughters, Nelda and Christine, and their band, Balfa Toujours. Performing in the traditional acoustic style of Cajun music, the group combines the bayou sound with enthusiasm and front porch intimacy.

Although the Balfa sisters played guitar as youngsters and often jammed with their father and uncles, they didn't dream of a musical career until their father's death in 1992. In the aftermath of his passing, they began writing songs to express their sorrow. After they had written nine tunes, they recorded a tape to pass along to family members. The project proved so successful that they agreed to form a more permanent band. Their debut album, *Pop, Tu Me Parles Toujours,* was produced by Al Tharpe of Beausoleil and released in 1993.

Following the release of their second album, *A Vielle Terre Haute,* in 1994, Nelda Balfa left the group to focus on her career as a hairdresser. Although she occasionally plays local gigs with the band, she continues to limit her involvement since. *La Pointe* followed in 1998, and the live album *Live At Whiskey River Landing* arrived two years later. *—Craig Harris*

● **Pop, Tu Me Parles Toujours** / 1993 / Swallow ✦✦✦✦
There's no rock/pop flavor or sweetening in the music of Balfa Toujours. Their twin fiddle/accordion/guitar lineup and menu of French language tunes, two-steps and waltzes are aimed at the Cajun hardcore, and the CD serves as a wonderful tribute to Dewey Balfa's memory. The music is traditional, but has a modern sensibility and contemporary sound and is mostly performed in French, with Nelda and Christine Balfa handling vocals. *—Ron Wynn*

Deux Voyages / 1996 / Rounder ✦✦✦
For the non French speaker, Balfa Toujours, means Balfa forever; a reference to Christine Balfa's father Dewy Balfa, and her uncles Rodney, Will, and Burke. All were purveyors of traditional Cajun music, and the tradition that went along with it. Cajun music is music of the heart and the passions that go with affairs of the heart, and this fire is so integral to the music. When it is here on this disc it flares and you can't sit still, but sadly it is sometimes lacking. Please do not get me wrong, it is here, just not in the doses or with the consistency of some other fine performers of this tradition, such as Steve Riley and the Mamou Playboys (also available on Rounder). Give a listen to "Chicot Two Step" and also "Le Falcon Gris," both good example of the hard driving passion that should be there all the way through the disc, but lamentably appears in flashes. I think there is a tremendous promise in this group, the playing is always tight, and the songs they wrote are good examples of traditional music taken into present time. It may just be time and some more road miles will make this a group that can hold the fire the length of the disc. I would love to see this group as I have a sneaking suspicion that they truly show their fire in a live performance. I look forward to the next one. *—Bob Gottlieb*

La Pointe / Sep. 15, 1998 / Rounder ✦✦✦✦✦
Christine Balfa, daughter of Cajun pioneer Dewey Balfa, comes up with her third album in the company of Dirk Powell's beautiful accordion playing and Kevin Wimmer's spot on fiddle work. With the bass duties being swapped out between Mitchell Reed and Peter Schwarz (who also doubles up on fiddle on certain tracks) and family member Nelda Balfa on triangle, this is as down-home real as you can get. Recorded in Christine and Dirk's home in La Pointe, Louisiana, the music is comprised of new originals and old time material gathered from several sources. Balfa Brothers material is trotted out ("Nonc Charlot," "La Valse De Bayou La Fourche"), along with songs that tip the regional hat to local legends like Octa Clark ("Black Top Blues," "Freight Train Blues"), Dennis McGee ("Le Reel De Courville," "Pa Janvier") and the Fontenot family ("The Freeman Fontenot Medley," "Bernadette"). Balfa's rhythm guitar work is spotless and driving, Powell's multi-instrumental work on fiddle, guitar, accordion and banjo is diverse yet focused and both contribute authentic Cajun vocals in the native tongue that are full of wistful heartbreak and good times. Wimmer's fiddle workout on "Bernadette" once again reminds us that fiddle can be one bluesy instrument in the right hands. An amazingly simple, unaffected and beautiful album. *—Cub Koda*

Live at Whiskey River Landing / Aug. 15, 2000 / Rounder ✦✦✦✦
Angelle's Whiskey River Landing, a modest but regionally famous bar and dancehall on the levee of Louisiana's Atchafalaya Basin, almost deserves credit as a bandmember on this thrilling live album. *Angelle's* is Balfa Tourjours' favorite place to play, and you can hear it on every song; the band is completely relaxed, laying down a stomping, rolling rhythm under the constant ripple of fiddle and accordion and Christine Balfa's wailing vocals. The band members laugh and compliment the dancers between songs and lapse from English into French and back again apparently without thought. The tunes range from the soaring "La Chandelle Est Allume" to down-and-dirty stompers like "The Towing Truck Blues" and "Le Two-Step du Platin" without much variation in mood; this isn't a concert, it's a dance party,

so the music is there to serve a higher purpose. You might expect that fact to make the music less interesting, but it doesn't. Instead, what's consistently amazing is the sheer force of humor and goodwill that permeates every note. Highly recommended. *—Rick Anderson*

Dewey Balfa

b. Mar. 20, 1927, Big Mamou, LA, **d.** Jun. 17, 1992, Eunice, LA
Vocals, Fiddle / Traditional Cajun, Zydeco
A seminal figure in the revival of traditional Cajun music, fiddler Dewey Balfa was among his native culture's most impassioned ambassadors, helping introduce the Cajun sound to countless new fans across the globe and inspiring an entire generation of performers to explore their roots. His first recordings came in 1951 after he teamed with three siblings.. Acclaimed for his fluid, precise style, Balfa emerged as a fiddle virtuoso much sought after by other Cajun performers. In 1964, Balfa led a group of Cajun musicians during a landmark appearance at the Newport Folk Festival. With brothers Rodney and Will, daughter Nelda and accordionist Hadley Fontenot, Dewey officially formed the Balfa Brothers band one year later. Balfa's experiences at Newport galvanized him to become an advocate for traditional Cajun culture. At the same time, the Balfa Brothers continued recording and performing live on a regular basis, growing in popularity throughout the years to come. Even when both brothers, plus his wife and son, were killed within several years, Balfa soldiered on and reformed the Balfa Brothers with his daughter and nephew. After a long battle with cancer, Balfa died in 1992; his daughters soon formed Balfa Toujours—"Balfa Forever"—to continue promoting the Cajun tradition into the next century. *—Jason Ankeny*

Souvenirs / 1987 / Swallow ♦♦♦♦♦
A low-key but excellent effort comes from the late king of Cajun fiddle. *—Jeff Hannusch*

Cajun Legend / Swallow ♦♦♦
Featured are such artists as Tracy Schwartz, Robert Jardell, and other friends of Balfa on this album's 21 tracks. *—AMG*

• **Fait a La Main** / Swallow ♦♦♦♦♦
These 21 tracks compiled from two '80s Swallow albums offer a fine introduction to the fiddling of one of the architects of the Cajun music revival. Balfa sings four songs, but instrumentals carry the day here, most of them standards of the Cajun repertoire ("Grand Mamou," "La Jolie Blonde," "Les Flumes D'Enfer"). Balfa's lead fiddle is seconded (and thirded) by the father-son duo of Tracy and Peter Schwartz. A disciple of Nathan Abshire, Robert Jardell, holds down the accordion chair. Homespun and heartfelt, this set exudes the generosity of spirit of a rare man who has inspired many younger musicians to follow his example. *—Mark Humphrey, Roundup newsletter.*

Beausoleil

Group / Traditional Cajun, Zydeco, Creole
The formation of BeauSoleil, one of the best known and most highly respected cajun bands in the world is due to fiddler Michael Doucet's desire to keep the unique southern Louisiana culture and music from extinction. But while BeauSoleil originated to help preserve his cajun musical heritage, over the years it has been also known for its innovation. They are continually adding spice from other musical genres including jazz and Caribbean. In this way, BeauSoleil's keeps the music vital and contemporary.

Doucet was born and raised in Cajun country surrounded by the old French songs that comprise the basis of the music. But from the time of his birth to adulthood in the 1960s, Cajun culture began to disappear. Young Doucet, thinking Cajun music antiquated and passe, began his musical career playing rock with New Orleans influence. He began getting into folk rock towards the end of the '60s and even tried singing a few of his numbers in French. It was a song from the British folk group Fairport Convention and their song, "Cajun Woman," that resparked his interest in his native music. He went to France and England in 1973 just before he was to enter grad school in the U.S. He ended up staying many years studying with Scottish fiddle great Barry Dransfield, who eventually introduced him to his idol Richard Thompson. Later, Doucet credited Thompson for influencing his own compositions. The young fiddler's stay in France also had a profound influence. There he saw that the roots of Cajun were still very much alive. The old songs were still sung, and he heard their centuries-old influence in newer folk songs. It made him realize how modern Cajun music was in comparison. In the mid-'70s, Doucet joined Coteau, an improvisational folk-music based French group that was known as the Cajun equivalent to the Grateful Dead. After a time with them, he returned to the U.S., determined to immerse himself in Cajun musical history. A grant from the National Endowment for the Arts supported him as he located the nearly forgotten early composers and performers of Cajun music.

Armed with many traditional Cajun songs, Doucet formed BeauSoleil with some of the finest Cajun musicians, Dennis McGee, Dewey and Will Balfa, Varise Connor, Canray Fontenot, and Bessyl Duhon. Their band name literally means 'good sun' and is a reference to a fertile region in Nova Scotia. In the 17th century, French speaking Acadians lived in the Canadian province until conflicts with the French and British forced them to migrate down to Louisiana where they became called Cajuns. BeauSoleil cut its first record in 1976 and released it only in France. They made their American debut the following year with *The Spirit of Cajun Music.* It was an eclectic work illustrating the many musical styles from which Cajun music is derived. Between then and the early '90s, BeauSoleil released over a dozen albums. Some are traditional while others are more experimental. In 1988, Doucet received the first annual Clifton Chenier Award as the finest musician in French-speaking Louisiana. Since 1985, the band has been nominated for numerous Grammy's. They have played on movie soundtracks such as *The Big Easy, Passion Fish* and *Belizaire the Cajun.* They have played at jazz and folk festivals round the world and have also appeared on numerous television shows ranging from CNN's *Showbiz Today* to *Austin City Limits* to *Late Night with Conan O'Brien.* BeauSoleil also performs regularly on public radio, most notably on Garrison Keillor's *Prairie Home Companion.* Keillor has hailed them as the "best Cajun band in the world." They have performed with Mary Chapin Carpenter, and opened for the Grateful Dead.

As of the mid-'90s the line up for BeauSoleil includes Doucet's brother David on guitar, Acadian accordion player Jimmy Breaux, Al Tharp on bass/banjo and fiddle, percussionist Billy Ware and drummer Tommy Alesi. Doucet and other bandmembers periodically record solo albums such as Doucet's *Beau Solo. —Sandra Brennan*

Bayou Boogie / 1987 / Rounder ♦♦♦
A fine modern Cajun collection, it includes "Cajun Dead" at full tilt. *—Jeff Hannusch & Mark A. Humphrey*

Hot Chili Mama / 1988 / Arhoolie ♦♦♦♦♦
It's the perfect blend of Cajun, zydeco, and rock & roll. *—Jeff Hannusch*

Bayou Cadillac / 1989 / Rounder ♦♦♦
Those who define everything in strict, unflexible color terms consider all black South Louisiana sounds zydeco and all white sounds from that region Cajun. However, Beausoleil, an obviously white group, open this release with a signature zydeco tune, Clarence Garlow's "Bon Temps Roulet." Quite simply, they're unaware of this "rule," violating it repeatedly. They included entertaining remakes of "Bo Diddley" and "Iko Iko" in the title medley and also covered Big Joe Williams' "Baby Don't Go," doing them just as effectively as "Couchon de Lait" and "Flammes D'Enfer." While they sometimes ventured a bit afield, as with the concluding "Island Zydeco," much of Beausoleil's fare artfully crossed genres and successfully combined divergent influences and material. This disc should satisfy audiences regardless of idiomatic preference. *—Ron Wynn*

Live from the Left Coast / 1990 / Rounder ♦♦♦
This is an excellent example of this popular group's live sound. *—Jeff Hannusch*

Déjá Vu / 1991 / Swallow ♦♦♦

Cajun Conja / Sep. 1991 / Rhino ♦♦♦

Parlez-Nous á Boir & More / Oct. 1991 / Arhoolie ♦♦♦
Parlez-Nous A Boire and More is an all-acoustic album from Beausoleil, which means that it is among the group's most traditional albums. The band displays a remarkable empathy on the record, trading lines and solos with ease and joy. *—Thom Owens*

Vintage Beausoleil / 1995 / Music of the World ♦♦♦♦
It's hard to believe that this was the case, but Beausoleil were the first Cajun musicians to decide to go into performing and producing Cajun music on a full-time basis—no day job, no support, no net. The 1986 decision to be a full-time band of professional musicians paid off wonderfully for Michael Doucet and company, however, with a series of albums and a great deal of national attention. The attention garnered led to a series of New York concerts in 1986 and 1987, which have been excerpted for this album. For the band and its fans, this collection is a blast from the past—and what a blast it is! The performances are energetic and heartfelt, delightful and captivating; there are rough edges all around, but that's all part of the power of these tracks, and of this music. Don't believe for a second that this is just a collection of old stuff tossed onto the market to keep sales up—this is essential. *—Steven McDonald*

L'amour Ou La Folie / Jan. 14, 1997 / Rhino ♦♦♦
Guitar titan Richard Thompson and Tex-Mex star Augie Meyers guest on the latest raucous release from Beausoleil, which includes both original and traditional Cajun music, as well as a song performed in English by frontman Michael Doucet. *—Jason Ankeny*

• **The Best of Beausoleil** / Mar. 25, 1997 / Arhoolie ♦♦♦♦♦
This isn't as wide-ranging as Rhino's *Bayou Deluxe* compilation; it only draws from records the group recorded for Arhoolie during the 1980s. It's a decent collection in its own right, though, conveying the group's skill at arranging Cajun music with the right mix of musical chops and laidback charm. It also might find more favor with more traditional-minded Cajun fans than the band's more eclectic releases or compilations, with a high percentage of traditional French-language tunes. The booklet includes lyrics in both French and English. *—Richie Unterberger*

Arc de Triomphe Two-Step / Nov. 18, 1997 / Hemisphere ♦♦♦
The music that comprises *Arc de Triomphe Two-Step* was recorded in 1976 in Paris, but it sat unreleased for several years before it was finally released on CD in 1997. Although this was recorded early in his career, the album is surprisingly lively and accomplished. Michael Doucet's fiddling is vigorous, infectious and almost astonishing, breathing new life into this set of traditional tunes. For any longtime Beausoleil fan, this is a necessary listen, if only for the revelations it offers about his early career. *—Thom Owens*

Cajunization / Mar. 16, 1999 / Rhino ♦♦♦♦
Michael Doucet and Beausoleil come up with another interesting album in *Cajunization.* It has traditional sound, along with a variety of songs that have blues, jazz, and multiple genre influences. The musicians, guest artists, and band members, are of the highest caliber of talents in the Cajun genre. They put their heart and soul into every song and it comes out in the final products. These are songs that are worthy of becoming standards for future generations of the Cajun culture. The first cut on the album, "La Terre de mon Grandpére (My Grandfather's Land)," tells a story about how important the powerful spirit of the Cajun family is to the culture. The hot fiddle of Michael Doucet carries the melody, challenged only by Jimmy Breaux's electrifying accordion playing. Beausoleil follows the traditional style by using the Dennis McGee sound formula. One of the most intriguing tunes on the album is "Zarico Boogie"; it has a ZZ Top boogie beat blended with a jazz feel. This genre-blending song is a fabulous piece of original artistry. Whether your search is for traditional Cajun music, or for some music that has branched off from the well-traveled path, Beausoleil will deliver. True Cajun spirit is at the foundation, but Beausoleil is building skyscrapers with their expansions on the genre. The founding fathers of Cajun music must be very proud of their children and their disciples. *—Larry Belanger*

Looking Back: Beausoleil Live / Jan. 16, 2001 / Rhino ♦♦♦

Shirley Bergeron

b. Nov. 16, 1933, Point Noir, Church Point, LA, **d.** Nov. 18, 1995, Church Point, LA
Vocals / Traditional Cajun
Cajun singer and steel guitarist Shirley Bergeron (a man, not a woman) recorded, for the most part, standard Cajun music in the late 1950s with his accordionist father Alphee Bergeron and backup band the Veteran Playboys. Cajun music for the most part, that is, because there was one 1962 single, "French Rocking Boogie," that tried to get some action by fusing Cajun with rock'n'roll. Actually it was a pretty enjoyable, energetic track, and the one that Shirley Bergeron is most known for among collectors.

However, for the rest of his recording career Bergeron stuck to Cajun music of a much more typical sort, always accompanied by his father Alphee on accordion. Alphee Bergeron had done one 1949 single with the Veteran Playboys, but Shirley made his recording debut in 1957 with two songs at a radio session that eventually got issued on an LP. There were some recordings for Goldband in 1960, but Bergeron spent most of the 1960s doing singles for the small Lanor label, recording at the Crowley Studios run by Jay Miller, who did so much for Louisiana popular music of all kinds in the 1950s and 1960s by cutting bluesmen like Slim Harpo. Some of the Lanor recordings had drums, but Bergeron just used guitar, Alphee's accordion, violin, and triangle when he recorded the album *Cajun Style Music* at the music store of Marc Savoy in Eunice, LA in late 1969. A compilation of Bergeron's 1957-69 sides, *French Rocking Boogie*, came out on CD on Ace. *—Richie Unterberger*

Cajun Style Music / 1970 / Lanor ♦♦♦
Bergeron recorded this album in Marc Savoy's Eunice, LA music store because he thought his father, accordionist Alphee Bergeron (who plays on the LP), was getting old, and Shirley wanted to have a document for posterity. It was recorded by Lanor Records owner Lee Lavergne, who stood in the middle of the circle of musicians and held a mike, although the fidelity is alright. It's typical Cajun music, more traditional in feel than what Bergeron recorded on Lanor singles earlier in the 1960s, particularly since no drummer was used. All 12 of the tracks are on the Ace CD compilation *French Rocking Boogie*, which also has earlier material that Bergeron did for Lanor. *—Richie Unterberger*

● **French Rocking Boogie** / 1992 / Ace ♦♦♦♦
This compiles most of the singles Bergeron did for Lanor in the 1960s, along with two songs from a 1957 radio appearance and the entirety of the 1970 album *Cajun Style Music*. Although it's the kind of heretical remark that might get you thrown out of a Louisiana accordion shop, "French Rocking Boogie," the only song with a strong rock & roll flavor, is quite the standout in comparison with the routine Cajun fare that comprises the rest of the disc. The sides from 1960s Lanor singles are pretty basic in arrangement and execution, sometimes including a drum; bluesman Lazy Lester even plays cardboard box on a couple of 1960 sides. The most traditional-sounding selections (although all of the songs are credited to Bergeron and Lanor owner Lee Lavergne) are those done in Marc Savoy's music store in 1969; they're the only ones, in fact, that have triangle, played by Savoy himself. Bergeron does have an appealing crying quality to his vocals, as many Cajun singers do, but overall, this is ordinary Cajun music. *—Richie Unterberger*

Vin Bruce (Ervin Bruce)

b. Apr. 25, 1932, Cut Off, LA
Vocals, Guitar / Traditional Cajun, Swamp Blues, Zydeco
Known as the "King of Cajun Singers," this native of Cut Off, LA, born Ervin Bruce, first recorded for Columbia in 1951, where he found some success with the ballad "Dans La Louisianne." A decade later this singer/guitarist was recording for Floyd Soileau's Swallow label, where he scored a hit with "Jole Blon" (at least the third go-round for "the Cajun national anthem"). Bruce currently resides in Galliano, LA, and is widely respected in Louisiana for his country-tinged Cajun traditionalism. *—Jeff Hannusch & Mark A. Humphrey*

Cajun Country / 1979 / Swallow ♦♦♦
A good country-tinged album featuring Doc Guidry on fiddle, Harry Anselm on guitar, and Eldridge "Johnny" Comeaux on steel guitar. *—Chip Renner*

● **Greatest Hits** / 1979 / Swallow ♦♦♦♦♦
Recorded by one of the pioneers of Cajun music, these early-'60s sides are a mix of traditional songs and French interpretations of country hits. *—Jeff Hannusch*

Carousel for Two / Oct. 17, 2000 / Louisiana Red Hot ♦♦♦

Buckwheat Zydeco (Stanley Dural)

b. Nov. 14, 1947, Lafayette, LA
Keyboards, Accordion, Piano, Organ / Zydeco, Creole
Contemporary zydeco's most popular performer, accordionist Stanley "Buckwheat" Dural was the natural successor to the throne vacated by the death of his mentor Clifton Chenier; infusing his propulsive party music with strains of rock and R&B, his urbanized sound—complete with touches of synthesizer and trumpet—married traditional and contemporary zydeco with uncommon flair, in the process reaching a wider mainstream audience than any artist before him. Although often exposed to traditional zydeco as a child, he preferred R&B and began backing notables like Joe Tex and Clarence "Gatemouth" Brown on the piano. From 1971 to 1976, he led a 16-piece funk band but finally fell under zydeco's sway when recruited to back Chenier—a friend of his father—on tour. He picked up the accordion within two years, rechristened himself Buckwheat Zydeco and formed his own combo (the Ils Sont Partis Band) by 1979. The group recorded albums for Blues Unlimited and Rounder, including the Grammy-nominated *Turning Point* and *Waitin' for My Ya Ya*. In 1986, he became the first zydeco act ever signed to a major label (Island), and recorded three albums before moving to Charisma for 1992's *On Track*. The years to follow saw the band drifting from one label to another, including Warner and Atlantic. The group remains hugely popular as a live attraction, despite purists' charges of commercialism. *—Jason Ankeny*

★ **100% Fortified Zydeco** / 1983 / Black Top ♦♦♦♦♦
Currently the most visible zydeco artist nationally, this mid-'80s effort is his best, as the material recorded is more inventive. The sound is great and the song selection is superior. *—Jeff Hannusch*

Turning Point / 1983 / Rounder ♦♦♦

Waitin' for My Ya-Ya / 1985 / Rounder ♦♦♦
Buckwheat Zydeco came closest on this 1985 session to balancing his R&B and pop tendencies with a zydeco authenticity missing from his releases on other labels. The Ils Sont Partis Band, especially guitarist Jimmy Reed, rubboard man Elijah Cudges and trumpeter Calvin Landry put some spark and drive behind the arrangements on the covers of Fats Domino's "Walkin' to New Orleans" and Percy Sledge's "Warm and Tender Love," while Zydeco's singing on these and other numbers like "Lache Pas La Patate" and "Tee Nah Nah" was more focused, less gimmicky and more on target than at any time before or since. Although he never was as talented as some of his supporters claimed, Buckwheat Zydeco was closer to a serious zydeco performer than merely another copyist here. *—Ron Wynn*

On a Night Like This / 1987 / Island ♦♦♦
Not bad, it's still not as good as his Black Top or Rounder label work. *—Jeff Hannusch*

Menagerie: The Essential Zydeco Collection / 1993 / Mango ♦♦♦♦
Menagerie: The Essential Zydeco Collection collects highlights from Buckwheat Zydeco's three albums for Island Records between 1987 and 1990. There are a number of really good songs here ("Ma 'Tit Fille," "Hey Good Lookin'," "Where There's Smoke There's Fire"), and the compilation actually distills his uneven Island albums into a strong single-disc collection. However, if you're looking for Buckwheat at his best, stick to the Rounder and Black Top releases. *—Thom Owens*

Trouble / Apr. 29, 1997 / Atlantic ♦♦♦
Since 1979, Buckwheat Zydeco has been synonymous with good vibes, party music and zydeco itself. *Trouble* is far more than just an example of an artist of his reputation coasting on his laurels. This album was originally released in 1997 by Mesa/Atlantic. That release and Mesa's corporate structure were, to say the least, problematic, and it was good fortune that "Buckwheat" Dural was able to retain rights to the master, as it has now been properly released. From the smoking meltdown of "It's So Hard to Stop" to the title track (which is as good as a New Orleans R&B-based dance track as you'll ever hear), this album is easily one of Buckwheat Zydeco's finest efforts. This CD also includes a super-funky version of the Robert Johnson classic "Crossroads," which gives a great new spin on one of the greatest blues-rock warhorses of all time. This record is infectious, fun (like that's new for this band), and one of their most worthwhile discs. *—Matthew Greenwald*

● **Buckwheat Zydeco Story: A 20 Year Party** / Jul. 6, 1999 / Tomorrow Recordings ♦♦♦♦♦
The Buckwheat Zydeco Story: A 20-Year Party paints a nice portrait of Buckwheat Zydeco's rise from independent labels to stardom, following him from *Turning Point*, his first record for Rounder in 1983, to 1997's *Trouble*, the last record he cut for a major label. In the years separating those two albums, he recorded a wealth of great music, more than can fit on a 15-track collection, but *The Buckwheat Zydeco Story* is nevertheless a good, concise sampler that works as an excellent introduction for neophytes. Yes, longtime followers will probably have a few favorites missing, but they'll only need to turn here for the previously unreleased 1998 live recording of "Hey Baby," which is really good. Curious listeners, however, will find that this gives a nice feeling for the arc of Buckwheat Zydeco's career, and that it gives a good idea of where to turn to next—whether that would be the early Rounder material or the Island albums that made him a near-household name. That makes the compilation a good introduction to Buckwheat, even if it may not be definitive. *—Stephen Thomas Erlewine*

Ultimate Collection / Jul. 18, 2000 / Hip-O ♦♦♦♦♦

Chubby Carrier (Roy Carrier)

Vocals, Accordion / Contemporary Blues, Zydeco
Deadheads wouldn't normally be a group associated with a zydeco artist. But in the case of Chubby Carrier, you would have to make an exception. The Grateful Dead did a cover of Bobby Bland's "Turn on Your Love Light." Carrier later did the tune on one of his albums. The Deadhead kids would come up to him after the show and say 'cool, bro. Jerry's the man'. Which suited Carrier just fine because he looked at himself as a man on a mission. To bring zydeco to the world like it's never been brought before. A drummer who started out on accordion at the age of 12, Carrier's first big break came in 1987 when he began playing drums with Terrance Simien and the Mallet Playboys touring the country. He formed his own band two years later and cut his first album *Go Zydeco Go* that year. He moved up to Flying Fish for 1991's *Boogie Woogie Zydeco*, and Blind Pig for 1993's *Dance All Night*. With a strong reputation of high-energy performances, Carrier and his Bayou Swamp Band blaze a trail all over the US, Canada, Europe and North Africa of more than 275 dates a year. *—Ed Hogan*

★ **Boogie Woogie Zydeco** / 1991 / Flying Fish ♦♦♦♦♦
After building a resume in zydeco circles playing with Terrance Simien & the Mallot Playboys, singer/accordion player Chubby Carrier struck out on his own in 1990 and soon signed with the Chicago-based Flying Fish label as a solo artist. *Boogie Woogie Zydeco* may have been recorded in the Chicago suburb of Evanston, but sweaty, exuberant originals like "Allons Dancez," "Hey Barbariba" and "Bernadette" are pure Louisiana. Carrier slows down the tempo for the 1960s-type soul numbers "Be Fair to the People" and "Sherrie," both of which are so appealing that they make one wish he embraced slower tempos more often. On the whole, however, the Louisiana native favors zydeco that is unrelenting in its energy. Zydeco fans should make a point of hunting for this CD. *—Alex Henderson*

Who Stole the Hot Sauce— / 1996 / Blind Pig ♦♦♦♦♦

It's Party Time / 1999 / Right Click ♦♦♦
Chubby Carrier and the Bayou Swamp Band's album *It's Party Time!* offers a good amount of variety. The album opens up with "Bernadette," which is a traditional number with a classic Zydeco sound. This album celebrates the way that the Cajuns partied years back, gathering

friends and family for house parties. "They Wanna Party Now" adds a unique sound to the guitar work with the use of a voice box. It also uses a great bass riff on the uptempo beat of the tune. On "Funky BSB" the listener is treated to some of Chubby Carrier's signature swamp-funk sound. The listener is going to want to get up and cut a rug on this jazzy, boogie tune. The title track "It's Party Time" kicks off with a fantastic lead guitar intro, then moves into a Zydeco-flavored "Soul Train." As this tune builds an urge to shout, "Come on everybody climb aboard the Zydeco Train, It's Party Time! " might rise—a symptom of the Chubby Carrier and the Bayou Swamp Band fever. " I Don't Want to Leave You" is a harmonious, romantic number. Overall this is a great party album with funk and variety. It does stray from the traditional Cajun roots music, moving into the swamp-funk sound and beyond. Some may be surprised on how far from their roots the band has wandered while maintaining their quality party style. A search for traditional Cajun music should lead one to other sources, but for listeners looking for some refreshingly new music from Louisiana by musicians cranking out their own, original sound, then it would be safe to say *It's Party Time.* —*Larry Belanger*

Too Hot to Handle / Mar. 23, 1999 / Louisiana Red Hot ✦✦✦
This is a disc that shows great promise— this man and his band can stir it up and hit a groove that is incandescent. One problem, though, is that this live disc lacks the fire and energy of their live performances. Part of that missing energy is the sound, which seems dull —almost dead. When this band plays live, the sound is raw and alive, and everyone, including the lame and the dead, rise up and dance. As a band, they are tight and hold together well, each member is more than capable on his instrument and the sum is greater than the parts would seem to be capable of adding up to. They have one of the best bass players heard in a long time—he is not only good but incredibly inventive, ranking up there with players such as Victor Wooten and Ron Carter. On this disc he never really gets a chance to shine. Chubby has a way of picking songs that showcase the band's strengths; "Fire on the Mountain" is an extended dub version that outshines the other versions, which shows the versatility of this band in mixing up the tempos. Chubby is writing some good new songs he has three on this disc, and they fit right into the zydeco pattern, yet at the same time add some new wrinkles. Listen to and catch the time stops, horn arrangements and wah-wah guitar of "Wasting Time." This is truly a new level of "swamp funk" that is going to start rising from the mists of the bayous and taking the country by insidious invasion. Overall, the disc cooks and shows off a band that is definitely on the rise. Dancing is mandatory. —*Bob Gottlieb*

Boozoo Chavis

b. Oct. 23, 1930, Lake Charles, LA, **d.** May 5, 2001
Vocals, Accordion / Zydeco
Boozoo Chavis (born: Wilson Anthony Chavis) was one of the pioneers of Zydeco, the Cajun and blues hybrid originating in southwest Louisiana. Although his self-composed 1954 single, "Paper In My Shoes," was the first Zydeco hit, Chavis was distrustful of the music industry and refused to perform publicly or record again until 1984. In an interview featured in the 1990 book, *The New Folk Music,* Chavis explained, "I got gypped out of my record. I get frustrated, sometimes. I love to play, but, when I get to thinking about 1955.... ..They stole my record. They said that it only sold 150,000 copies. But, my cousin, who used to live in Boston, checked it out. It sold over a million copies. I was supposed to have a gold record."After leaving the music business, Chavis devoted his attention to raising champion racehorses in Shrevesport and Lafayette, Louisiana and Texas. Chavis waited until 1984 before returning to music. Signing a five year contract with the Maison De Soul label, he recorded four albums—*Louisiana Zydico Music, Boozoo Zydeco!, Zydeco Homebrew* and *Zydeco Trail Ride.* Chavis' 1997 album, *Hey, Do Right,* was produced by Terry Adams, keyboardist for NRBQ, who paid tribute to Chavis in their 1989 song, "Boozoo, That's Who."

Chavis' performances, with his band, The Majic Sounds, included much-heralded appearance at the *Newport Folk Festival* and the *New Orleans Jazz And Heritage Festival. The New York Times* wrote, "(Chavis is) chaos on two feet. A little bullet of a man, he runs around onstage, shouting and yelling.... (his) music can achieve a trancelike intensity." In a review of Chavis' performance at the *Southwest Louisiana Zydeco Music Festival,* Paul Scott wrote, "There are a lot of Boozoo prototypes coming out. They may be smoother than Boozoo but they try to get his hard accordion; that rough, raw, style; and his sore throat type of singing. And with that single-note and triple-note accordion, he's doing a lot to bring a return to basic zydeco".

The son of tenant farmers, Chavis acquired his nickname as a youngster. Chavis was raised by his mother who cleaned houses and sold barbecue at horseraces until raising enough money to buy a three acre tract of land where she and Chavis moved in 1944. Acquiring an accordion from his father and teaching himself to play, Chavis was soon playing at local barn dances and in the dance club, opened by his mother, where he often sat in with Morris Chenier and his sons, Clifton and Cleveland. In 1994, Chavis appeared in Robert Mugge's video documentary, *The Kingdom Of Zydeco.* He was inducted into the Zydeco Hall of Fame four years later. And continuing to release music into the new millennium, Chavis issued *Johnnie Billy Goat* in fall 2000. —*Craig Harris*

Louisiana Zydeco Music / 1986 / Maison de Soul ✦✦✦✦✦
This is a zydeco masterpiece and a down-home foot-stomper. —*Jeff Hannusch*

Paper in My Shoe / 1987 / Ace ✦✦✦✦✦
If it hadn't been for the fact that he quit playing for three decades, Boozoo Chavis might have been one of the great names of zydeco. His recent renaissance presumably prompted this reissue of the early sessions he made, in often chaotic conditions, for the small local Goldband label. This was the Black bayou sound unselfconscious, local and pure. It's still wonderful. —*John Storm Roberts, Original Music*

★ **Zydeco Trail Ride** / 1989 / Maison de Soul ✦✦✦✦✦
This collects his best sides from the Maison de Soul label. Whoop-ti-yo cover and bootin' sounds to match. —*Jeff Hannusch & Mark A. Humphrey*

Boozoo Chavis / 1990 / Elektra/Nonesuch ✦✦✦
Still bluesy and rockin' in the '90s, this was part of the celebrated *American Explorer* series. —*Mark A. Humphrey*

The Lake Charles Atomic Bomb / 1990 / Rounder ✦✦✦
Boozoo Chavis vaulted to fame in zydeco circles during the mid-'50s, when his gritty, anthemic "Paper In My Shoe" helped get the fledgling zydeco industry off the ground. The 14 tracks on this 1990 anthology showcase a younger, more vocally spry and dynamic Chavis, singing short, simple two-step tunes and zydeco/blues hybrids. There wasn't anything intricate or complicated about pieces like "Hamburgers and Popcorn," "Oh Ho She's Gone" and "Telephone Won't Ring." They were either anguished heartache songs, novelty tunes or wailing uptempo pieces, and Chavis didn't vary his approach, attack or treatment. But they were direct, honest and often memorable. It's good to have them available on one anthology. —*Ron Wynn*

Boozoo, That's Who! / 1993 / Rounder ✦✦✦
Boozoo Chavis was singing zydeco long before it got widespread exposure outside Louisiana. He's never bothered to try and tap into trends or vie for crossover dollars. The 14 cuts on this release are primarily vintage zydeco numbers, though he also does an occasional novelty song like "Billy Goat Number Three." These are sizzling two-step pieces, waltzes and driving zydeco numbers, with Chavis' aging but still effective vocals leading the way. —*Ron Wynn*

Live! at the Habibi Temple / 1994 / Rounder ✦✦✦✦
This 1994 recording captures Chavis and his band, the Magic Sounds, in full cry in front of a hometown crowd in Lake Charles, Louisiana. One song runs into another and the groove stays constant throughout, as if Boozoo gains strength from the dancers. This is as real as zydeco gets, and a better modern-day representative would be hard to find. Put your dancing shoes on. —*Cub Koda*

Hey Do Right / Jan. 14, 1997 / Discovery ✦✦✦
Hey Do Right collects more of Chavis' zydeco party tunes and Creole dances. —*Jason Ankeny*

Who Stole My Monkey / Mar. 2, 1999 / Rounder ✦✦✦
Chavis continued to roll on, pumping out joyous zydeco music, on this session recorded in September 1998. With a relaxed feel to everything on here, Chavis turns 16 classic examples of the form minus the commercial overlay found on most modern zydeco records. With his regular working band, the Magic Sounds, following every quirky move of his irregular time and meter, Boozoo lays down tunes just like he was working a dance in Louisiana rather than making a record in the sterile confines of a recording studio. As a result, the time gets constantly shifted on and off the beat on several tunes ("Bottle Up and Go" is a classic example of this, at times sounding like there's two different takes of the same song being played simultaneously), an odd by-product of what is, after all, dance music. But the overall feel is amazing, capturing the good-time feel that is at the heart of Chavis' music. Highlights include "Dance All Night," "I'm Going Away to Stay," "Lucille," "Baby, Please Don't Go," "Valse de Derniere Fois" and the title track. Rubboard player Charles Chavis taking the vocals on "Marksville Slide" and "Sock It to Me," and Boozoo finishes off the album with recut versions of both sides of his X-rated single, "Deacon Jones" and "Uncle Bud," two tracks not for the weak of heart or the prudish among you. —*Cub Koda*

C.J. Chenier

b. Sep. 28, 1957, Port Arthur, TX
Vocals, Sax (Alto), Accordion / Zydeco, Creole
C.J. Chenier may no longer be under his father Clifton's shadow, but he is certainly following in his illustrious footsteps as one of the hottest, most recognizable zydeco artists in the world. Like his father, Chenier is constantly perfecting zydeco, helping it to stay up with contemporary tastes infusing it with an unparalleled raucous energy that commands listeners to get up and dance. By the late '70s, Chenier was seriously considering a career in R&B or soul, but his father had other plans, calling his son in 1978 and asking him to join the Red Hot Louisiana Band as a replacement for sax player John Hart. Though C.J. knew none of the songs, he joined his father. It took over a year for Chenier to really understand the cajun beat. Around 1983, the ailing Clifton began teaching C.J. to play the accordion to prepare him to take over the band—during many performances, the elder Chenier was too ill to finish and his son began taking over. Clifton Chenier died in 1987, and it only seemed natural to C.J. that he play his father's music. A week after his father's burial, Chenier began accepting bookings for the band, and he continued to perform and record throughout the '90s. —*Sandra Brennan*

● **Hot Rod** / Oct. 30, 1990 / Slash ✦✦✦✦✦

The Big Squeeze / 1996 / Alligator ✦✦✦
C.J. Chenier carries on the blues-drenched zydeco tradition of his father Clifton Chenier, but this effort, while competent, is just not as fun to listen to as a zydeco record ought to be. The arrangements by Vasti Jackson seem overwrought at times, as though the players (and there is no shortage here of guitarists, horns, or percussionists) are trying too hard. Bright highs and thick lows dominate the sound; one longs for more mid-range. C.J.'s voice sounds gruff, perhaps showing signs of wear and tear from ten years fronting the band he inherited from his father. Still, there are some fine cuts, like "Cheatin' on the Man You're Cheatin' With," "Lion's Den," and his dad's "No Shoes Zydeco," and C.J. remains one of the top talents on the zydeco circuit. —*Steve Hoffman*

Clifton Chenier

b. Jun. 25, 1925, Opelousas, LA, **d.** Dec. 12, 1987, Lafayette, LA
Vocals, Accordion / Zydeco, Creole
Clifton Chenier was a master Louisiana musical chef of the highest order. On a good night with a crowd in high spirits, Chenier's musical gumbo had Cajun two-steps and waltzes sitting right next to slow blues or a scorching rendition of "Bon Ton Roulet," which was Clifton's version of Louis Jordan's "Let the Good Times Roll" sung in French. The musical hybrid that he helped to create—zydeco, or "zodico," its spelling variant and superior phonetic pronunciation—is as rich and as deep as the area from which it sprang. Chenier may not have invented the form—an accordion-driven, blues-inspired variant of Cajun music played for dancing—but he single handedly helped give it shape and define the form as we know it to-

day. In his own words, "What I did was to put a little rock & roll into the zydeco to mix it up a bit. You see, people been playing zydeco for a long time, old style, like French music. But I was the first one to put the pep to it." Chenier had taken a backwoods art form, mixed it up with rock & roll, country, R&B, and blues, put a heavier beat to it, and ended up bringing this spicy gumbo concoction to the world. Of course, it also helps that Clifton put this Creole hybrid over with personality to spare, singing and playing his squeeze box with a high energy approach that made the music damn near impossible to ignore. While the crown for the king of the blues sits uneasily on a number of heads, merely ask anyone in the South who was there during his reign and there's absolutely no doubt that Clifton *was* the King of Zydeco, and had the crown to prove it. *—Cub Koda*

Zodico Blues & Boogie / 1955 / Specialty ♦♦♦♦♦
Clifton Chenier's mid-'50s singles for Specialty were among his rawest and simplest; they were short ditties with rippling accordion and gritty vocals on top and driving rhythms and surging instrumental accompaniment underneath. That's the formula displayed on this 20-cut presentation of Chenier's early work, where he was often backed by guitarists Phillip Walker or Cornelius Green (Lonesome Sundown), with his brother Cleveland handling rubboard duties. This is Chenier in his stylistic infancy, building and nurturing what ultimately became a signature sound. *—Ron Wynn*

Bayou Blues / 1970 / Specialty ♦♦♦♦♦
Bayou Blues compiles a selection of 12 tracks Clifton Chenier cut for Specialty Records in 1955, including the original versions of "Boppin' the Rock," "Eh, Petite Fille," "I'm On My Way" and "Zodico Stomp." It may not be a definitive retrospective, but it's an entertaining and necessary sampler of Chenier at the beginning of his career. *—Thom Owens*

King of the Bayous / 1970 / Arhoolie ♦♦♦♦♦
After gaining initial notoriety in the '50s and '60s on Specialty Records and a variety of small Texas and Louisiana labels, Zydeco King Clifton Chenier brought the blues-fueled Cajun music he practically invented to Chris Strachwitz's roots label Arhoolie, subsequently recording a series of fine albums including 1970's *King of the Bayous*. Featuring brother and longtime partner Cleveland Chenier on rubboard, Robert St. Judy on drums, Joe Morris on bass and Antoine Victor on guitar, *King of the Bayous* includes Chenier's standard blend of zydeco two-step, waltzes and blues, and provides an excellent taste of what the band no doubt played on countless one-niters along the Louisiana-Texas Gulf Coast. Zydeco-brand blues predominates with Chenier originals "Hard to Love Someone," "Who Can Your Good Man Be" and "I Am Coming Home," in addition to a cover of the honky-tonk weeper "Release Me." Offering a contrast to the blues and something for the dancers, the band lays down a lively two-step beat on "Tu Le Ton Son Ton," "Josephine Par Se Ma Femme" and "Zodico Two Step." Throughout the varied set, Chenier's irrepressible vocals and accordion playing stand out. A nice sample of bayou zydeco by one of its finest and most original practitioners. *—Stephen Cook*

Out West / 1974 / Arhoolie ♦♦♦♦♦
Special guests Elvin Bishop and Steve Miller joined Chenier for an excellent outing blending blues and rock influences with zydeco. Chenier's vocals were tough and convincing, while Bishop and Miller, along with saxophonist Jon Hart, were outstanding. *—Ron Wynn*

And His Red Hot Louisiana Band in New Orleans / 1979 / GNP Crescendo ♦♦♦
In New Orleans was recorded in the late '70s with one of Clifton Chenier's classic bands, which featured his brother on washboard, saxophonist John Hart, and guitarist Paul Senegal, among others. The album is textbook Chenier—it rocks & rolls, wails and shouts. It's may be a typical record for the king of zydeco, but that means it's very, very enjoyable. *—Thom Owens*

Live! at the Long Beach & San Francisco Blues Festivals / 1985 / Arhoolie ♦♦♦
The 19 selections on this disc were done in the early '80s, when Chenier was past his romping prime but still keeping the zydeco engine running. He has done them all before on other releases, but keeps them entertaining and enjoyable through sheer will and personality. *—Ron Wynn*

Bogalusa Boogie / Jul. 1987 / Arhoolie ♦♦♦
Backed by a fuller band on this release, he sounds great. Here's the hottest of the red-hot Louisiana bands, and they're feelin' frisky. *—Jeff Hannusch & Mark A. Humphrey*

60 Minutes with the King of Zydeco / 1988 / Arhoolie ♦♦♦♦♦
Zydeco at its best, it compiles his greatest hits from the Arhoolie label. *—Jeff Hannusch*

Live at St. Mark's / 1988 / Arhoolie ♦♦♦
Live at St. Mark's captures a rollicking concert performed in Richmond, California. Chenier leads the band through a blend of zydeco and blues, singing with gusto and spice all along. Furthermore, he plays to the audience, telling jokes and stories, which give the album a special, intimate feel. With all the wonderful music and joy that *Live at St. Marks* radiates, there's little question that it is one of Chenier's finest live albums. *—Thom Owens*

★ **Zydeco Dynamite: The Clifton Chenier Anthology** / 1993 / Rhino ♦♦♦♦♦
Clifton Chenier was to zydeco what Elvis Presley was to rockabilly, only more so—the genre's founding father and tireless ambassador. Rhino has done an admirable job of collecting the accordionist's important work for this two-disc, 40-track set, harking back to a wonderfully chaotic "Louisiana Stomp" that he waxed in Lake Charles, Louisiana in 1954 for J.R. Fullbright's tiny Elko label. Whether you're in the market for one zydeco collection to summarize the entire genre or ready to delve deeply into the legacy of the idiom's pioneer, this is precisely where to begin. *—Bill Dahl*

Zydeco Sont Pas Sale / Apr. 22, 1997 / Arhoolie ♦♦♦♦♦
Clifton Chenier is the acknowledged Little Richard of zydeco. He is the grand architect of the real, Creole French, pseudo-Caribbean blend of blues and R&B. This mid-priced sampler culls all its cuts from seven other Arhoolie releases. Chenier continually updated his sound, while retaining the royal title King of Zydeco. While condensing his nearly four-decade career into 15 cuts can scarcely do it justice, this is an excellent starting point. You should be able to identify the periods of Chenier's career that merit further investigation. Or, you have an excellent po-boy party disc that has something to satisfy every zydeco opinion. *—Thomas Schulte*

Squeezebox Boogie / Jun. 22, 1999 / Just a Memory ♦♦♦♦
Squeezebox Boogie is among the late-'90s CDs that came from Just a Memory's *Collectors Classics* series, which also gave us blues titles by Muddy Waters, the Reverend Gary Davis, James Cotton, and the Sonny Terry/Brownie McGhee team. *Collectors Classics* is an appropriate name for the series, for it was aimed at serious collectors rather than casual listeners. *Squeezebox Boogie* isn't meant to serve as an introduction to the talents of Clifton Chenier, but seasoned fans will find a lot to admire about this rare recording made in August 1978 at the long gone *Rising Sun Club* in Montreal. True to form, the bilingual Louisiana singer excels as a bluesman on "I'm a Hog for You," "Bon Ton Roulet," and B.B. King's "Rock Me Baby," but is equally impressive as a zydeco artist on "Zydeco cha-cha" and his familiar "Joli Blonde." Also quite infectious is Chenier's blues/jazz/zydeco interpretation of the Glenn Miller smash "In the Mood." The sound quality is fine; those who complained about the sound quality and distorted vocals on Muddy Waters' *Hoochie Coochie Man* (another *Collectors Classics* title recorded at the *Rising Sun Club* in the late '70s) will find that the sound is much cleaner and sharper on this CD. Although not for novices, *Squeezebox Boogie* is easily recommended to seasoned Chenier fans. *—Alex Henderson*

Live at 1966 Berkeley Blues Festival / Jan. 25, 2000 / Arhoolie ♦♦♦♦
Recorded live on KAL radio in Berkeley, CA. on April 15, 1966, this presents roughly equal shares of material from Clifton Chenier, Mance Lipscomb, and Lightning Hopkins, performing at the 1966 *Berkeley Blues Festival*. The sound is not state-of-the-art, but decent considering the vintage. The material is not going to surprise anyone familiar with the artists: good news if you're in love with their music and want typical excerpts of their sets, bad if you think you might have enough of them and are considering whether to investigate further. Chenier's performance (lasting nine songs) might be of the greatest historical interest of the three on this disc, as it was his first appearance before a "a mostly young, white, relatively sophisticated concert audience," as Chris Strachwitz writes in the liner notes. It's just Chenier, his accordion, and drummer Francis Clay, mostly on original tunes, as well as zydeco arrangements of Slim Harpo's "Baby Scratch My Back" and Ray Charles' "What'd I Say—" Half of the material on this disc was previously available on Arhoolie LP 1030, but eleven of the 23 songs on the CD (and six of Chenier's nine contributions) were previously unreleased. *—Richie Unterberger*

Harry Choates

b. Dec. 26, 1922, Rayne, LA, **d.** Jul. 17, 1951, Austin, TX
Fiddle / Traditional Cajun, Western Swing
Harry Choates was not only one of the most influential musicians in the history of Cajun music but one of its most tragic figures. A wild, imaginitive, fiddler, Choates wrote such classic tunes as the cajun national anthem, "Jole Blon" and popularized such songs as "Allons A Lafayette." Recording for Gold Star, DeLuxe, D.O.T., Alklied, Cajun Classics, Macy's and Humming Bird, Choates introduced western swing, blues, jazz and country music to the two-steps and waltzes of southwest Louisiana's bayous, influencing nearly every Cajun musician who followed in his footsteps.

Like Hank Williams, Choates balanced his musical talents with painful struggle in his real life. An acute alcoholic, he sold the rights to "Jole Blon" for $100 and a bottle of whiskey. His habit of missing concerts led him to be blacklisted by the musicians union in San Antonio and resulted in his band breaking up. His death was equally tragic. Failing to make support payments of $20 a week for his son and daughter, following his divorce, he was jailed by a judge who found him in contempt of court. After three days of being forced to curtail his drinking habit, he began beating his head against the cell bars and fell into a coma. He died a few days later on July 17, 1951.

Born in either Rayne or New Iberia, Louisiana, Choates moved to Port Arthur, Texas, with his mother in the 1930s. Rather than going to school, Choates spent much of his childhood in bars and tavers, listening to honky tonk and blues records on the jukebox. By the age of twelve, Choates was playing fiddle in barbershops for tips.

Launching his professional music career in Cajun bands led by Leo Soileau and Leroy "Happy Fats" LeBlanc, Choates formed his own group, The Melody Boys, in 1946. The same year, he rewrote the classic Cajun tune, "Jolie Blone," for his daughter, Linda, and recorded it for the Gold Star label. Although the tune became a country hit when covered by Aubrey "Moon" Mulligan, Choates had given up all rights to the song and received no further compensation for his composition. Choates and The Melody Boys continued to record at a prolific rate, releasing more than two dozen songs for Gold Star in 1946 and 1947. Adapting the western swing of Bob Wills And His Texas Playboys to Cajun music, Choates became known as "the fiddle king of Cajun swing."

Although he performed with Jesse James And His Gang on radio station, KTBC, after the disbanding of the Melody Boys in 1951, Choates suffering ended a few months later. His grave was left unmarked until 1980 when money was raised for a gravestone with the bilingual inscription, "Purrain De La Musique Cajun—*The Godfather of Cajun Music*."

In the mid-1960s, Cajun musician Rufus Thibodeaux was one of the first to pay homage to Choates' influence when he recorded an album of Choates' songs, *A Tribute to Harry Choates*. *—Craig Harris*

Jole Blon / 1979 / D ♦♦♦♦♦
The title cut has become the "Cajun national anthem, " plus many other great fiddle-led Cajun tunes. *—Jeff Hannusch*

★ **Fiddle King of Cajun Swing** / 1982 / Arhoolie ♦♦♦♦♦
Fiddle King of Cajun Swing is a 26-track collection featuring most of Harry Choates' finest recordings. All of the material on this compilation was recorded for Gold Star Records between 1946 and 1950. Though his biggest hit, "Jole Blon," is inexplicably missing, the music on this disc demonstrates Choates talent for blurring the lines between Western Swing and

Cajun music. It's an excellent introduction to one of the finest Cajun fiddlers of the '40s and '50s. *—Thom Owens*

Five-Time Loser 1940-1951 / 1990 / Krazy Kat ✦✦✦
A followup to "Jole Blon" and thirteen other performances, it includes the Hank Williams-inspired "Cat 'n Around." It has a rough sound but great music, blending Cajun, swing, and honky tonk. *—Mark A. Humphrey*

His Original 1946-1949 Recordings / Arhoolie ✦✦✦✦
Sixteen performances by the man dubbed "The Godfather of Cajun Music, " include his swingin' takes on such standards as "Allons Ö Lafayette" and "Grand Mamou." *—Mark A. Humphrey*

Bruce Daigrepont

b. 1959
Vocals, Accordion / Zydeco
An admitted child of the Cajun revival, Daigrepont only began regarding Cajun music as something other than the music of his grandparents' generation when he heard such young Turks as Michael Doucet and Zachary Richard in the '70s. Ironically, this singer and accordionist developed a style somewhat more traditional than that of his mentors. Writing his own material and fronting a tight band, Daigrepont has earned both the approval of his elders and the respect of his peers. *—Mark A. Humphrey*

● **Stir up the Roux** / 1988 / Rounder ✦✦✦✦✦
While Daigrepont is aware of other sounds like rock and country, he integrates their edge and sensibility into his work without losing or deserting the basic Cajun mode. The 10 tunes on this release are predominantly driving, uptempo pieces with his frenetic accordion and infectious vocals setting the pace, backed by a sharp band that includes tremendous fiddler Waylon Thibodeaux. Daigrepont makes no lyrical concessions, but the color and flair of his singing should overcome any hesitancy non-French speakers might have about the material. It's certainly up-to-date, but also thoroughly steeped in the old ethic. *—Ron Wynn*

Coeur Des Cajuns / 1989 / Rounder ✦✦✦
Bruce Daigrepont's second album for Rounder was even more traditionally Cajun than his award-winning first effort. The title track and other works such as "Les Mains du Bon Dieu," "Acadie a la Louisiane" and "Laissez Moi Tranquille" presented tales of Cajun life and times ranging from struggles to triumphs, and were sung with power, earnestness and verve. His accordion playing was equally assertive. Artists such as Bruce Daigrepont indicate that the future is bright for Cajun music. *—Ron Wynn*

Petit Cadeau / May 2, 1994 / Rounder ✦✦✦

Paradis / Jul. 13, 1999 / Rounder ✦✦✦✦
Bruce Daigrepont is proud of his Cajun/French heritage and he translates this pride into what he does. He respects the traditions yet is not bound by them; rather, he uses his strength to build and expand existing parameters. His transitions on *Paradis* are seamless, without sounding artificially polished. He has done a stellar job not only as musician, but also as the producer turning out this disc. One of the highlights is the treatment he gives to the hauntingly beautiful "La Voix du Passé (The Voice of the Past)." This song has the potential to become a standard in Cajun music (as do a couple of others here). He also wrote nine of the 13 songs. Pick this one up. *—Bob Gottlieb*

Geno Delafose

b. 1972, Eunice, LA
Vocals, Drums / Zydeco
The son of the great accordionist John Delafose, Geno Delafose carried on the family name with his own distinctive sound spanning from traditional Creole and Cajun music to contemporary R&B. Born in Eunice, Louisiana in 1972, he began his career at the age of eight, playing rubboard and drums in his father's band the Eunice Playboys; he eventually adopted the accordion as well, and was among the few zydeco performers of his era to play both the button and piano models of the instrument. Over the years Delafose's prominence in the group grew, and he and his father often traded lead vocals; when John retired in the months prior to his 1994 death, Geno took over the band, and that same year he recorded his debut LP *French Rockin' Boogie; That's What I'm Talkin' About!* followed in 1996, and in 1998 he returned with *Chanson Perdue*. *—Jason Ankeny*

● **That's What I'm Talking About!** / Jun. 1996 / Rounder ✦✦✦✦✦
This will stand as one of the finest zydeco albums of the decade. Young Geno (age 24) plays in a more tuneful and traditional style than competitors on the 1990s South Louisiana zydeco circuit like Beau Jocque and Keith Frank, whose thumping dance-beats, one-chord riffs, and grunted lyrics constitute a sort of zydeco/hip-hop synthesis. Geno instead draws inspiration from the older Creole songs of his father, John Delafose. But he hasn't merely followed in his father's footsteps; he's outpaced him. His music has just the right combination of lilt and kick to it, thanks in large part to his cousin Jermaine Jack's drum work. *That's What I'm Talking About!* is like a zydeco carousel that whirls you delightedly round and round. Geno handles button and piano-accordion proficiently, and his voice, used to better advantage here than on his 1994 debut album *French Rockin' Boogie*, possesses that lovely "key of heartbreak" quality that characterizes the best South Louisiana music. *—Steve Hoffman*

La Chanson Perdue / Jun. 9, 1998 / Rounder ✦✦✦✦✦
Delafose's devotion and consuming interest in traditional Creole and Cajun material is brought to full fruition on this delightful platter. English translations are right alongside their French counterparts in the booklet, but the message comes through loud and clear in either language. With his regular working band French Rockin' Boogie, contributing trance-like grooves ("Bon soir Moreau"), Delafose digs deep for his roots on every track. He brings aboard Steve Riley for a couple numbers (his fiddle is particularly effective on "Joilie Basette/Quo faire"), then cuts a four-song acoustic session with Christine Balfa on acoustic guitar and fiddler Dirk Powell. The overall effect is an album that looks forward and backward for its inspiration and never disappoints for a second. *—Cub Koda*

John Delafose

b. Apr. 16, 1939, Duralde, LA, **d.** Sep. 17, 1994, Lawtell, LA
Vocals, Accordion / Zydeco
John Delafose and his band the Eunice Playboys bridged the gap between zydeco's roots and its contemporary sound with a mastery matched by few of their peers; despite an affinity for early Creole styles, French lyrics and two-step waltz rhythms, they played with all of the fiery intensity demanded by modern-day audiences, tapping into a wide array of sources—blues, Cajun, even country—to forge a propulsive traditionalist sound all their own. Delafose and the Eunice Playboys debuted in 1980 with the regional hit "Joe Pete Got Two Women," from the LP *Zydeco Man; Uncle Bud Zydeco* followed in 1982, and as interest in traditional Creole culture swelled, the group became one of the hottest attractions on the Gulf Coast circuit. 1993's *Blues Stay Away from Me* was his final album; failing health forced him to curtail his touring schedule soon after, and on September 17, 1994, Delafose died. Son Geno succeeded his father as bandleader. *—Jason Ankeny*

Heartaches & Hot Steps / 1984 / Maison de Soul ✦✦✦✦✦
Explosive arrangements, powerhouse vocals and accordion playing, and good band support make this a first-rate contemporary zydeco date. *—Ron Wynn*

● **Joe Pete Got Two Women** / 1988 / Arhoolie ✦✦✦✦✦
Delafose's best contains his popular saga of Joe Pete. Zydeco fundamentalism from this singer/accordionist, who's so down-home, his music clearly echoes African hypnotic grooves. *—Jeff Hannusch & Mark A. Humphrey*

Père Et Garçon Zydeco / 1992 / Rounder ✦✦✦
While zydeco and Cajun-influenced hybrids have been the norm in many circles during the 1980s and '90s, John Delafose & the Eunice Playboys have remained true to the classic style. This session featured predominantly hardcore material, emphasizing the two-steps, waltzes, and French lyrics at the heart of zydeco/Cajun. Delafose and his son Geno alternated lead vocals and accordion support, each singing and playing with vigor, conviction and authenticity. Meanwhile, the band backed them with equal electricity, and while such tunes as "Watch That Dog," "Morning Train" and "Go Back Where You Been" were lyrical departures, they were as fully in the zydeco framework as "Mon Coeur Fait Mal" or "Grand Mamou." *—Ron Wynn*

Bo Dollis

Vocals, Tambourine / Zydeco
Although perhaps more R&B than jazz, one of the most distinctive features of the New Orleans musical landscape is the ritual observance of Mardi Gras and St. Joseph's Day by the so-called Mardi Gras Indians. The tradition of African-Americans masqued in feathers has been traced back as far as the 18th century, but the organization of marching clubs following that practice probably dates from 1885, when the participation in Mardi Gras parades of native Americans in full regalia from Buffalo Bill's Wild West Show caused a sensation. The Mardi Gras Indians are thus not unlike the various marching clubs that parade annually in New Orleans, but their outfits and musical style are unique. Chanting a traditional repertoire sung in a patois that can be traced back to the Haitian origins of many black New Orleanians, the Indians use only percussion for musical accompaniment—drums, tambourines, cowbells, and rattles—as they play the streets of their designated neighborhoods. In the past, borderlines between these areas could be the scene of bloodshed. These are now replaced by staged mock-combat tableaus which show off the elaborate handmade costumes. An entourage of "spy boys" clears the way for the tribes, whose dancing, chanting, and outfits become the deciding factors in who "backs down." Although it has evolved into a friendly competition, the ritual is taken very seriously: individual members can spend upwards of a thousand dollars on their costumes, which take a full year's work to prepare.

The Wild Magnolias are one of many tribes, divided into "uptown" and "downtown" factions. Some of the other tribes are the Black Eagles, the Wild Tchoupitoulas, Gorden Star Hunters, Creole Wild West, Creole Osceolas, and the Golden Eagles, to name a few. Like the brass bands, the Indians attract a "second line" of dancers who become a part of the progression. The Wild Magnolias were the first to release a recording, "Handa Wanda," as early as 1970, but the street music played by the Indians does not follow the same instrumentation or interpretation heard on such recordings, which are specially made for the popular market. Even so, the music of The Wild Magnolias, whether on the street or on disc, defies the listener to keep still. As is the case with most New Orleans music, it is made for dancing. The spirit of the Mardi Gras Indians has influenced New Orleans musicians from Jelly Roll Morton through Professor Longhair and constitutes another of the enduring elements that has shaped this wonderfully distinctive and musical regional culture. *—Bruce Boyd Raeburn*

★ **I'm Back at Carnival Time** / 1990 / Rounder ✦✦✦✦✦
Bo Dollis, New Orleans' most popular "Indian" chief, has been heading the Wild Magnolias since 1964. His fiery, flamboyant, charismatic style is ideal for the backdrop of Mardi Gras. He's an exuberant vocalist, equally gifted at rousing chants, energetic up-tempo tunes, or even more traditional gospel-tinged soul. This session featured Dollis and the Wild Magnolias backed by a great set of session musicians and, at times, the Rebirth Brass Band. This links the Indian performing tradition with Crescent City blues, R&B, and vintage jazz sensibilities, resulting in several superb, roaring performances. The best in both Mardi Gras and contemporary/classic New Orleans fare. *—Ron Wynn*

David Doucet

b. 1957
Vocals, Guitar / Zydeco
The acoustic guitar has been transformed into an important voice of southwest Louisiana's Cajun music by David Doucet. The younger brother of Cajun fiddler Michael Doucet, Doucet has used his distinctive hybrid of folk-style fingerpicking and bluegrass-like flatpicking to

strengthen the performances of Beausoleil, the band he's shared with his brother for over 21 years. With the release of his debut solo album, *Quand J'ai Parti* in 1991, Doucet successfully stepped into the spotlight.

Doucet first played the guitar after recuperating from a broken arm sustained while practicing with his high school football team. Although he initially taught himself to play by using Bob Dylan and Paul Simon songbooks, Doucet became fascinated with flatpicking after listening to an album by Doc Watson.

Together with his brother and banjo player Raoul Breaux, Doucet played Cajun music in Louisiana clubs in 1975. When the project proved commercially unsuccessful, the band broke up with Doucet enrolling in college and his brother going on to form the Cajun rock band Coteau and the original lineup of Beausoleil. A turning point in Doucet's evolution as a guitarist came when he heard the playing of the late Clarence White on an album, *The Kentucky Colonels 1965-1967*, in 1980. Inspired by White's use of unusual chords and imaginative melodies, Doucet began to develop his own unique style.

Although Doucet did not play on Beausoleil's first recording session in Paris, he joined the group before the recording of their debut album, *The Spirit of Cajun Music*, in 1976.

Doucet moved to New Orleans, where he continues to reside, in 1980 to work at the World's Fair. In addition to his solo album and recordings with Beausoleil, Doucet was featured on albums by Chuck Guillory (*Grand Texas*), Octa Clark & Hector Duhon (*Ensemble Encore*) and Michael Doucet (*Dit BeauSoleil*).

Doucet was accompanied on *Quand J'ai Parti* by members of Beausoleil (Michael Doucet, Jimmy Breaux, Tommy Comeaux, Billy Ware and Tommy Alesi) and influential dobro player Josh Graves, whom he met during a—"Legends of Folk Violin" tour. *—Craig Harris*

Quand J'ai Parti / Jan. 1990 / Rounder ✦✦✦✦✦
David Doucet both expanded and narrowed his scope on this release. He decided to concentrate on guitar and incorporate it into a traditional Cajun setting; at the same time, he used wide-ranging band Beausoleil and recruited bluegrass great Josh Graves on dobro and bassist Josh Stewart. The results were gratifying; Doucet's guitar playing was unpredictable, edgy and crisp, while Beausoleil, Graves and Stewart made fine partners on 13 thoroughly Cajun tracks, right down to the French lyrics, waltz and two-step arrangements, and accordion/fiddle backing fortified by mandolin/dobro/bass. *—Ron Wynn*

Michael Doucet

b. Feb. 14, 1951, Scott, LA
Vocals, Fiddle / Zydeco, Creole
Since the mid '70s, Doucet has been one of the dominant figures of the Cajun music revival, respected for his scholarship and admired for his showmanship. On the one hand Doucet dredges up ancient Cajun tunes with medieval French roots, and on the other plays flamboyant fiddle with Beausoleil. Aside from Beausoleil, singer and fiddler Doucet has performed and recorded with the more purely traditional Savoy-Doucet Cajun Band. He is as passionate about Cajun tradition as he is eager to drop-kick it into the 21st century, and for that reason Doucet has earned the applause of both purists and plebians who just wanna boogie. *—Mark A. Humphrey*

Allons a Lafayette / 1988 / Arhoolie ✦✦✦
This is a more traditional sound as compared with the group's other albums. *—Jeff Hannusch*

And Cajun Brew / 1988 / Rounder ✦✦✦✦✦
Sometime Beausoleil member Michael Doucet heads a different type of ensemble in Cajun Brew. This band is a fusion/rock/pop group, and this release began with a reworking of "Wooly Bully" and included covers of "Hey, Good Looking" and "Louie Louie." The roster included flamboyant, stirring guitarist Sonny Landreth, whose blues-rock leanings were quite evident. As if aware that there might be questions about allegiances, the group's song roster contained such numbers as "Un Autre Soir Ennuyant" and "Like A Real Cajun" alongside the covers. While they sometimes blurred or hedged their focus, there was enough Cajun flavor in the arrangements, performances and instrumentation to keep purists from grumbling, while they aimed for a wider audience with their joyful rock/pop remakes. *—Ron Wynn*

Le Hoogie Boogie: Louisiana French Music for Children / 1992 / Rounder ✦✦✦✦
Ever wondered how to sing "The Hokey Pokey" in French— If not, maybe your kids have, and this disc is for them anyway. That's not all they'll learn, either: "L'Arc en Ciel" will help them with their colors, and "A, B, C et 1, 2, 3" will have them counting and chanting the alphabet with a French Lousiana twang before you know it. There are several songs about alligators, of course, as well as a charming ode to lost love entitled "Les Maringouins Ont Tout Mange Ma Belle" ("The Mosquitoes Ate My Sweetheart All Up"). The music itself is a spicey stew of Cajun fiddle tunes and folksong melodies, all of which are guaranteed to have you and your kids waltzing and stomping furiously around the room. Doucet's singing voice, as always, is less than inspiring, but c'mon, it's a kid's record. Very highly recommended. *—Rick Anderson*

● **Bayou Deluxe: The Best of Michael Doucet & . . .** / 1993 / Rhino ✦✦✦✦✦
Bayou Deluxe: The Best of Michael Doucet & Beausoleil collects 17 tracks from the group's 10 album, adding one previously unreleased cut. Wisely, the collection is sequenced as a live set would be, instead of being a slave to chronological order. The result is a lively, exciting romp through Doucet's past that entertains while it illuminates. In other words, it's not only an ideal retrospective, it is arguably Doucet and Beausoleil's finest album. *—Thom Owens*

Joseph Falcon

b. Sep. 28, 1900, Rayne, LA, **d.** Nov. 19, 1965, Crowley, LA
Vocals, Accordion / Traditional Cajun, Creole
One of the pioneers of Cajun music, Falcon made the first commercial Cajun recording, "Lafayette" ("AllonsÖLafayette") with his wife Cleoma in 1928. Cleoma's simple guitar and emotive singing, driven by Joe's crying accordion, was an instant hit in Cajun country, foisting a regional stardom on the team, who recorded for Columbia, Decca, Bluebird, and Okeh in the '30s. Cleoma's death in 1941 and changes in listeners' taste (the accordion was out, the fiddle in) led Falcon away from performing, though he and his second wife, Theresa, fronted a band in the years before his death. Falcon's early recordings are among the enduring classics of the Cajun genre. *—Mark A. Humphrey*

★ **Live at a Cajun Dance** / 1988 / Arhoolie ✦✦✦✦✦
Perhaps the best live Cajun album of all time, this was recorded near the end of Falcon's career in the early '60s. *—Jeff Hannusch*

Cajun Music Pioneer / Mar. 25, 1997 / Arhoolie ✦✦✦✦✦

Filé

f. 1983
Accordion / Swamp Pop, Zydeco, Creole
Southwest Louisiana's traditional Cajun music is played with exuberance and dance-inspiring energy by File. While accordion player/percussionist/lead vocalist Ward Lomand and bassist/acoustic guitarist/vocalist Kevin Shearin are the only original members, the group continues to maintain the high energy of its earliest performances.

Lomand and Shearin first played together in the Cajun band Cush-Cush in 1980. Raised in his father's bar in the French-speaking Louisiana town of Ossun, on the prairie northwest of Lafayette, Lomand has been singing and playing drums since childhood. A native of the Catskill Mountains region of New York, Shearin played bass for numerous bands before moving to Louisiana.

A veteran of bluegrass and country-rock bands in the Appalachian region in the 1970s, Peter Stevens (drums, washboard, spoons and bones), played with Lomand and Shearin on File's first album, *Live at Mulate's* in 1985. The most recent additions to the group, D'Jalma Garnier and David Egan, joined File in the early 1990s. St. Paul, Minnesota-born Garnier inherited his love of Cajun music from his Creole father. After studying composition, arranging and orchestration with Lyle "Spud" Murphy, Garnier (fiddle, guitar, tenor banjo, vocals) studied Creole fiddling under a Texas Folk Life Resources grant with influential Creole fiddler Canray Fontenot. Egan, a native of Shreveport, Louisiana, majored in music at North Texas State College. In addition to playing keyboards for the swamp R&B band, A-Train, he spent three years in Jo-El Sonnier's band prior to joining File in 1991.

Although they initially sought to recapture the traditional sounds of Cajun music, File has increasingly incorporated elements of R&B, Dixieland jazz, rock, zydeco and Creole lala. Their 1996 album *La Vie Marron* reached number 18 on the Gavin Americana chart. *—Craig Harris*

● **Cajun Dance Band** / Oct. 1987 / Flying Fish ✦✦✦✦✦
This is the debut album by one of the more popular contemporary Cajun bands. *—Jeff Hannusch*

Two Left Feet / 1990 / Flying Fish ✦✦✦✦✦

La Vie Marron: The Runaway Life / Sep. 3, 1996 / Green Linnet ✦✦✦✦
From the opening fiddle on "La Vie Marron" to the closing strains of "Boogaloo, " it is apparent you have entered the bayou country of Louisiana. This is Cajun music through and through, but this band puts a unique twist on the music with the addition of piano to the traditional mix of instruments and their own refreshing style, without losing any of the integrity of the Cajun tradition. It brings through on the disc all the sounds and smells of the back-in-the-woods, friendly neighborhood honky tonk. The band is tight and strong throughout, no matter what spins and whirls they take off on, and the disc contains no throwaways at all. Five of the eleven songs were written by the group; humorous highlights include "Fido Dixieland" and "Loup Garou Mange Pas Mes Enfants" ("werewolf don't eat my children"). Go out and get this one now. *—Bob Gottlieb*

Allen Fontenot

b. 1932, Grand Prairie, LA
Vocals, Fiddle / Zydeco
Allen Fontenot is one of the best-known fiddlers in Cajun music. Fontenot always loved the fiddle and made his own on several occasions out of such materials as a ukulele, cigar boxes, bow and arrow sets, and wire. At age 15, his grandfather, also a fiddler, bought him his first real one. After working for several years as a bill collector, Fontenot founded the five-piece Country Cajuns in the early '70s. The first members—concertina player Leroy Veilloa, guitarist Hudson Dauzat, drummer Darrel Brasseaux, and bass player John Scott—recorded a few singles and played at the Jazz and Heritage Festival. The Country Cajuns also appeared regularly on a Sunday morning radio show and made their feature film debut in 1975 in Charles Bronson's *Hard Times*. They also appeared on the television shows *Good Morning America* and *Austin City Limits*. When not playing with the band, Fontenot worked as a popular deejay in Slidell, Louisiana. In the late '70s, he opened the Cajun Bandstand in Kenner, Louisiana, which served authentic Cajun cuisine and showcased authentic Cajun music; he and his band frequently played there until he sold the club in 1982. Fontenot's work can be found on the Great Southern, Antilles and Delta labels. *—Sandra Brennan*

● **Jole Blon & Other Cajun Honky Tonk Songs** / Jan. 1980 / Great Southern ✦✦✦✦✦

Keith Frank

b. 1972, Louisiana
Vocals / Zydeco
One of the leading lights of the "nouveau zydeco" movement, accordionist Keith Frank—the son of zydeco great Preston Frank—fused the traditional sound of his father's generation with latter-day influences ranging from James Brown to Bob Marley to forge his own urbanized and infectiously danceable style. Born in Soileau, Louisiana in 1972, Frank began playing professionally at the age of four, sitting in on a variety of instruments with his father's combo the Family Zydeco Band; despite focusing on the accordion from the age of six onward, he initially loathed zydeco and the pressures of performing, but in high school finally gave in to the music's pull and formed his own group. As Preston Frank began to ease into retirement, Keith gradually assumed leadership duties of the family band, which now

also included his sister Jennifer on bass and brother Brad on drums; as he gained confidence, he began adding elements of rap to his music, a move which dismayed purists but met with wide approval from younger listeners. Frank issued his debut album *What's His Name?* in 1994 and remained a prolific force in the years to follow. *—Jason Ankeny*

Get on Boy / Jul. 25, 1996 / Zydeco Hound ✦✦✦✦

Live at Slim's Y-Ki-Ki / Apr. 20, 1999 / Shanachie ✦✦✦
One very hot live recording of Frank in full roar in the music's heartland. Frank puts a lot of sweat and high energy to his brand of zydeco and tracks like "Hey Pretty Baby (With Your Teeth So White)," "Sometimes We Make You Move Your Feet," and "Soileau Zydeco" are classic examples of it. A dynamite party record for any celebration. *—Cub Koda*

● **Ready or Not** / Mar. 14, 2000 / Shanachie ✦✦✦✦
Accordionist Keith Frank is one of the leading figures in the nouveau zydeco movement, incorporating influences like pop and rap with traditional zydeco instrumentation. *Ready or Not* features several rowdy originals along with covers of "I Got Loaded" by Lil' Bob and the Lollipops (also covered by Los Lobos) and Katrina and the Waves' 1983 hit "Walking on Sunshine." The Soileau Zydeco Band includes Frank's sister Jen on bass and brother Brad on drums along with James "Chocolate" Ned on scrubboard and Kent Pierre August on guitar. *—Al Campbell*

Wade Frugé

b. 1916
Accordion, Fiddle / Zydeco, Creole
Wade Frugé was one of the last of the great old timey Cajun fiddlers. Known for his delicate grace notes, piercing chords and powerful bowing, Frugé combined soulful playing with highly-skilled articulation. Although never a full-time musician, Frugé's love of music gave his playing a rarely-heard emotional depth. Much of Frugé's repertoire was inherited from his grandfather, Napoleon Fruge, and blues-tinged fiddler, Douglas Ballard, who also taught Canray Fontenot. The complete set of twenty five tracks that he recorded during his lifetime were compiled on the album, *Old Style Cajun Music*, featuring guest musicians Michael Doucet and Marc and Ann Savoy. *—Craig Harris*

Old-Style Cajun Music / Oct. 20, 1998 / Arhoolie ✦✦✦
Frugé fiddled in what he called a "yokedy-yokedy" style, described in the liner notes as one which "consists of delicate grace notes, piercing chords, and a rocking of the bow from treble to bass strings and back to treble." He plays traditional Cajun standards and some songs he picked up from Cajun Black fiddlers on this 1988 recording, which features some vocals from Vorance Barzas and Ann Savoy (the latter of whom also plays some guitar). Originally issued on LP as Arhoolie 5044, the 1998 CD reissue adds ten bonus cuts recorded in 1979, 1983, and 1989 at the home of renowned local musicians Ann & Marc Savoy; Marc Savoy and Michael Doucet add some guitar and fiddle on these. It's traditional Cajun fiddle music for diehard fans of that idiom. *—Richie Unterberger*

Chuck Guillory

b. Aug. 16, 1919
Fiddle, Vocals / Zydeco
Cajun fiddler Chuck Guillory was born August 16, 1919 in Mamou, Louisiana; as a child, he regularly performed alongside his father, playing fiddle duets at a local bar each Saturday afternoon. After appearing at his first country dance at age eight, two years later Guillory formed his first band, and was a popular local attraction throughout the pre-war era. After World War II, he made his first recordings alongside accordionist Milton Molitor, subsequently forming the popular Cajun band the Rhythm Boys; among its early members was a young singer from Beaumont, Texas named George Jones. Later featuring guitarist Jimmy Newman and steel player Julius "Papa Cairo" Lamperez, the group cut their earliest sides in 1949, among them a Papa Cairo original titled "Just Wait and See" which its author later claimed was the uncredited basis for onetime Rhythm Boy Marty Robbins' "Pretty Words."

Guillory and the Rhythm Boys scored their first regional hit around 1950 with "Big Texas; " as the track featured Papa Cairo handling vocal duties, he soon formed his own group to record a new rendition of the track under his own name. Guillory forged on for a number of years before retiring from the dancehall circuit in 1958 to run a grocery store; he continued playing the occasional party, however, and years later performed at a gathering recorded by folklorist Dr. Henry Oster. That evening's version of "Grand Texas" was released on the LP *Folksongs of the Louisiana Acadians*, becoming an underground hit; in the late 1980s Guillory also reformed the Rhythm Boys to play dances and record for the Arhoolie label, with his 1987 sessions for the company later collected on the 1998 release *Grand Texas*. *—Jason Ankeny*

Grand Texas / 1998 / Arhoolie ✦✦✦✦✦
Most of this 26-song compilation is devoted to two sessions from the 1980s. The first eleven tracks are from 1982, with a band including Michael and David Doucet. It's spirited Cajun music with a relaxed and happy feel, with guitarist Preston Manuel taking most of the vocals, and no, it's not the kind of stuff that will stop you in your tracks and compel you to bring out your wallet. It's just representative, well-played Cajun music, and get s more interesting on the eight selections from 1987, mostly because Papa Cairo's steel guitar (and occasional weathered vocal) adds texture and personality. The final six cuts date from 1949-50, and have a little more of a Western swing and honky-tonk feel than the modern material; Cairo's steel guitar soloing is outstanding on "Chere Petite." *—Richie Unterberger*

Hackberry Ramblers

f. 1933
Group / Traditional Cajun, String Bands
The most important Cajun band of the 1930s, the Hackberry Ramblers were formed in 1933 by fiddler Luderin Darbone. They soon became the best-known band around the area, and began recording for RCA Bluebird in 1935 with a lineup including vocalist Lennis Sonnier, guitarists Glen Croker, Lonnie Rainwater, Floyd Shreve and Joe Werner, bassist Johnnie Parket and occasional accordion player Edwin Duhon. The initial sides were recorded in French, but a partnership with Montgomery Ward to perform on KVOL-Lafayette, LA prompted the Ramblers to record in English as the Riverside Ramblers—after Ward's brand of tires. Joe Werner provided most of the English vocals, and 1936's "Wondering" became a modest hit, sparking his brief solo contract with Decca. The band broke up early in the World War II years, but re-formed in 1946, recording for Deluxe and establishing a Saturday-night residency at a Lake Charles club that lasted ten years. The part-time band recorded an album for Arhoolie in 1963 and a few titles for Old Gold, and is still together, playing the occasional festival or event. *—John Bush*

Early Recordings: 1935-1948 / 1988 / Old Timey ✦✦✦✦✦
The Hackberry Ramblers were arguably the most influential Cajun string band from Louisana, creating a raw fusion of western swing, old timey string bands, and Cajun. The Ramblers never used accordions—they were a pure string band, creating a distinctly New Orleans brand of country music. *Early Recordings, 1935-1948* collects highlights from the group's Bluebird and Deluxe material and offers a perfect distillation of why the Ramblers were important. *—Thom Owens*

● **Cajun Boogie** / Jun. 1992 / Flying Fish ✦✦✦✦✦
As they sing on the theme song that opens this CD, the Hackberry Ramblers "play you some music and try to make you smile" with their infectious brand of hoedown music. By and large the Hackberry, Louisiana band succeeds on this album, which features original members Glen Croker (guitar) and Luderin Darbone (fiddle). Since 1933, they've been blending Cajun, country, and Western swing music with touches of blues and pop. Croker and Darbone are now in their eighties, but haven't lost their manic energy and taste for get-down party sounds. Besides presenting several of their own compositions, they cover tunes by Bob Wills, Ray Price, and Howlin' Wolf. This CD features guest fiddle by zydeco star Michael Doucet on four tracks, as well as a guest vocal by country star Rodney Crowell on "Old Pipeliner." *—Richie Unterberger*

Jolie Blonde / 1993 / Arhoolie ✦✦✦✦
These 1960s recordings came about as a result of Chris Strachwitz tracking down fiddler Luderin Darbone in Louisiana in 1963. The Ramblers had not recorded for years, but assembled again for some sessions in both the Goldband Studio and Darbone's home. Two other Ramblers from the 1930s-era lineup, Edwin Duhon and Lennis Sonnier, were also on board, with the personnel filled out by some younger musicians. Old-timey purists will probably still prefer their 1930s and 1940s sides; this collection has the advantages of clearer fidelity and easier availability. The CD adds nine previously unreleased bonus cuts, most taken from their appearance at the 1995 UC-Berkeley Folk Festival. *—Richie Unterberger*

Deep Water / May 13, 1997 / Hot Biscuits ✦✦✦✦✦
The Hackberry Ramblers are among the very few popular musicians who seem to be reaching their peak well past Social Security age. Ramblers mainstay Luderin Darbone was in his early 80s when this was recorded, and the rest of the six-piece group (except for youthful drummer Ben Sandmel) doesn't look much younger, yet they continue to play with more exuberance than almost any act of any style or age. Buying this disc is not, as is often the case when buying recent efforts by old-time legends, an act of charity. It's a good set that encompasses Western swing, boogie, blues, French Cajun, and even a bit of rock (in the cover of "Proud Mary"), performed with a spontaneity that veers toward sloppiness without falling into carelessness. This stuff has diversity and eclecticism, two qualities which are often underemployed, even ignored, by Cajun musicians in the studio. There are guest shots by Jimmie Dale Gilmore, Rodney Crowell, Marcia Ball, and Michael Doucet, but they really don't add or subtract anything of note. The main show is the Ramblers themselves, playing with an utter lack of self-consciousness, as if they're performing at the neighborhood barbecue, not in front of studio mikes. *—Richie Unterberger*

Beau Jocque

b. 1957, Kinder, LA, **d.** Sep. 10, 1999, Kinder, LA
Vocals, Accordion / Zydeco, Creole
Easily the biggest new zydeco star of the 1990s, Beau Jocque heralded the rise of the genre's new, urbanized style; infusing his high-octane sound with elements of rock, soul, hip-hop and even reggae, he bridged the gap between traditional Creole culture and contemporary music to create a funky, bass-heavy hybrid calculated for maximum mainstream appeal. In 1987 he suffered a serious back injury which left him paralyzed from the waist down for over a year; during his recovery period he picked up his father's Cajun accordion, but always bored by traditional zydeco, he set about updating the music more to his own contemporary tastes. Jocque and his wife Michelle then spent the next five years painstakingly researching zydeco clubs, discovering which kinds of songs earned the greatest response from patrons. Finally, in 1991, he formed the Zydeco Hi-Rollers; the band was an immediate smash in the New Orleans circuit, drawing huge audiences—many of them new to the Creole dancehall scene—captivated by their hard-edged rhythms and Jocque's primal, cavernous vocals. In 1993, the Hi-Rollers debuted with *Beau Jocque Boogie*, one of the best-selling zydeco records of all time. *—Jason Ankeny*

Beau Jocque Boogie / 1993 / Rounder ✦✦✦
Beau Jocque and the Zydeco Hi-Rollers represent the genre's new school; hip-hop and rap are an element of their style, as well as blues and R&B. Beau Jocque's music has the requisite kick and edge, with his vocals and non-stop excitement spilling out through such songs as "Richard's Club" and "Beau Jocque Boogie." Where he may raise eyebrows is his embrace of sampling technology alongside standard instrumentation. Jocque also speaks fluent French and covers some traditional songs, but puts more emphasis on his own music. This debut disc includes nine originals out of 14 numbers, with Jocque providing arrangements of classic tunes like "Oh Bye Moreau" and "Chere Allien" and establishing this band as prime challengers for honors as the top zydeco ensemble in the 1990s. *—Ron Wynn*

● **Pick Up on This!** / Mar. 30, 1994 / Rounder ✦✦✦✦✦
Beau Jocque's first album for Rounder Records, *Pick Up on This!*, is arguably his best effort

to date. The key is in the groove—there might not be much variety on the album, but he keeps the zesty zydeco rhythms pumping throughout. Jocque isn't the only one who shines, however. Every member of the band keeps things cooking, doing their best to ensure that *Pick Up on This!* is a first-rate party album. And that's exactly what it is. —*Thom Owens*

Gonna Take You Downtown / 1996 / Rounder ✦✦✦✦

Check It Out, Lock It In, Crank It Up / Aug. 18, 1998 / Rounder ✦✦✦✦✦

Doug Kershaw

b. Jan. 24, 1936, Tiel Ridge, LA

Vocals, Guitar, Fiddle / Traditional Cajun, Traditional Country

Doug Kershaw has combined a pioneering style of Cajun fiddling with exciting live performances, which often include his Cajun standard "Louisiana Man"—covered by other artists over 800 times. Kershaw played in his first band at the age of nine, but began performing with brothers Pee Wee and Rusty in the group Pee Wee Kershaw & the Continental Playboys at the age of 12. Though the group initially sang only in French, a meeting with J.D. Miller—who owned the Feature label—convinced them to begin writing songs in English. As a duo, Rusty & Doug recorded "So Lovely, Baby" in 1955; Miller shopped the single around Nashville, and came up with a contract for Hickory Records. The single reached the Country Top 15 in August 1955. "Love Me to Pieces" also hit Top 15 in late 1957, and "Hey Sheriff" almost reached the Top 20. Doug wrote "Louisiana Man" soon after he returned home from the army; the song reached the Country Top Ten in February 1961. "Diggy Liggy Lo" made Top 15 later in 1961, but after a short stint on RCA Victor, the brothers split in 1963. Doug Kershaw began recording for Mercury and MGM, and though his live performances kept him quite popular with fans, chart success didn't necessarily follow. Kershaw averaged more than one album per year for Warner Bros. throughout the 1970s, but charted only three times; he moved to Scotti Bros. in 1981. That same year, "Hello Woman" became his biggest solo hit, reaching number 29. —*John Bush*

The Cajun Way / 1969 / Warner Brothers ✦✦✦

Louisiana Man / 1971 / Warner Brothers ✦✦✦

It contains the infamous title-track hit and several other goodies. —*Jeff Hannusch*

★ **The Best of Doug Kershaw** / Aug. 8, 1989 / Warner Brothers ✦✦✦✦✦

This compilation of Kershaw's '60s/'70s Warner Bros. sides features "Everly Brothers-on-the-bayou" vocal harmonies, Doug Kershaw's fiddle, and crisp Nashville production. —*Mark A. Humphrey*

The Best of Doug & Rusty Kershaw / 1991 / Curb ✦✦✦✦✦

The Best of Doug and Rusty Kershaw collects 12 of the Kershaw brothers' recordings for Hickory Records in the late '50s, including the hit singles "Louisiana Man" and "Diggy, Diggy Lo." During this time, the group sounded like a cross between a Cajun string band and the Everly Brothers, which resulted in one of the most unique sounds of the late '50s. They might not have had many hits and some of their material now sounds dated, but Doug and Rusty's musical interplay still sounds fresh. *The Best of* isn't a perfect collection—it's missing the hits "So Lovely, Baby," "Love Me to Pieces," and "Hey Sherrif"—but what is here is very good, making it an adequate retrospective. —*Thom Owens*

Diggy Diggy Lo / Mar. 16, 1999 / Ronn ✦✦✦✦

This 1999 album finds Kershaw at the top of his well seasoned game, playing and singing with both conviction and abandon. Kicking off with "Diggy Diggy Lo," Kershaw's fiddle has real bite and a downright nasty tone while his vocals are full of exuberance. Duets with Hank Williams, Jr. on "Cajun Baby" (a tune started by Hank Sr. and finished years later by his son) and Fats Domino on "My Toot Toot" are highlights, but every track on this album is an inspired performance, Kershaw pouring his blood and guts into each track on here. If you're looking for great Cajun fiddle music, you've hit paydirt with this one. —*Cub Koda*

Rusty Kershaw

b. Feb. 2, 1938, Tiel Ridge, LA

Vocals, Guitar / Traditional Cajun, Traditional Country

As a soloist, Rusty (Russell) Kershaw has yet to match the success that he had in the early-1960s when he shared a duo with older brother, Doug Kershaw. His albums, however, have been well-conceived samplings of Cajun two-steps and country ballads and have featured accompaniment by top-notch musicians. While *Cajun In Blues Country,* released in 1970, featured Charlie Daniels on fiddle, *Now & Then,* released in 1992, was a tour-de-force featuring Art Neville of The Neville Brothers on piano and Ben Keith on dobro, flute, piano, pedal steel and background vocals. Introduced to Cajun and country music by his multi-instrumentalist brother, Kershaw was only ten when he began performing with Doug and Peewee in the Continental Playboys. The enthusiastic response that the group received helped to sooth the pain he had felt since their father, an alligator hunter, committed suicide five years before. Following the departure of Peewee, in the early 1950s, Rusty and Doug continued to play together as a duo. Their debut single, "So Lovely, Baby," became a top five country hit in August, 1955. Soon afterwards, the two brothers were invited to become cast members of the "Louisiana Hayride," a popular country music radio show broadcast from Shrevesport. In 1957, they became members of the Grand Ole Opry. Simultaneously enlisting in the U.S. Army, in 1958, the Kershaws devoted their attention to the military for the next three years. Discharged in 1961, the brothers soon recorded their greatest hit, "Louisiana Man," an autobiographical tune written by Doug. Their followup single, "Diggy Diggy Lo," was nearly as successful. Although they released their debut album, *Rusty And Doug,* in July 1964, Rusty and Doug had already gone their seperate ways. While Doug went on to become an internationally-known superstar, Rusty has maintained a much lower key presence. —*Craig Harris*

● **Cajun in Blues Country** / 1970 / Cotillion ✦✦✦✦✦

Rusty's best Cajun LP as a leader includes both solid vocals and first-rate playing. —*Ron Wynn*

Sonny Landreth

b. Feb. 1, 1951, Caton, MS

Slide Guitar, Vocals, Guitar, Dobro / Swamp Blues, Louisiana Blues, Southern Rock, Modern Electric Blues

Southwest Louisiana-based guitarist, songwriter and singer Sonny Landreth is a musician's musician. The blues slide guitar playing found on his two Zoo Entertainment releases, *Outward Bound* (1992) and *South of I-10* (1995) is distinctive and unlike anything else you've ever heard. His unorthodox guitar style comes from the manner in which he simultaneously plays slide and makes fingering movements on the fret board. Landreth, who has an easy-going personality, can play it all, like any good recording-session musician. His distinctive guitar playing can be heard on recordings by John Hiatt, Leslie West and Mountain, and other rock & rollers.

Landreth was born February 1, 1951, in Canton, MS, and his family lived in Jackson, MS, for a few years before settling in Lafayette, LA. Landreth, who still lives in southwest Louisiana, began playing guitar after a long tenure with the trumpet. His earliest inspiration came from Scotty Moore, the guitarist from Elvis Presley's band, but as time went on, he learned from the recordings of musicians and groups like Chet Atkins and the Ventures. As a teen, Landreth began playing out with his friends in their parents' houses.

"They would ping-pong us from one house to another, and though we were all awful at first, as time went on we got pretty good. It's an evolutionary process, just like songwriting is," Landreth explained in an interview on his 44th birthday in 1995. After his first professional gig with accordionist Clifton Chenier in the 1970s (where he was the only White guy in the Red Beans and Rice Revue for awhile), Landreth struck out on his own, but not before he recorded two albums for the Blues Unlimited label out of Crowley, LA, *Blues Attack* in 1981 and *Way Down in Louisiana* in 1985. If anyone is living proof of the need to press on in spite of obstacles, it is Landreth.

The second of those two albums got him noticed by some record executives in Nashville, which in turn led to his recording and touring work with John Hiatt. That led to still more work with John Mayall, who recorded Landreth's radio-ready "Congo Square." More recently, he's worked with New Orleans bandleader and pianist Allen Toussaint (who guests on several tracks on *South of I-10,* as does Dire Straits guitarist Mark Knopfler).

On Landreth's brilliant albums for Zoo, the lyrics draw the listener in to the sights, sounds, smells and heat of southwest Louisiana, and a strong sense of place is evident in many of Landreth's songs. Although his style is completely his own and his singing is more than adequate, Landreth admits that writers like William Faulkner have had a big influence on his lyric writing. The fact that it's taken so long for academics at American universities to recognize the great body of poetry that blues is concerns Landreth as well. Robert Johnson is Landreth's big hero when it comes to guitar playing. "When I finally discovered Robert Johnson, it all came together for me," Landreth said, noting that he also closely studied the recordings of Skip James, Mississippi John Hurt and Charley Patton. —*Richard Skelly*

Outward Bound / 1992 / Zoo ✦✦

Down In Louisiana / Mar. 23, 1993 / Epic ✦✦✦

This is music from the Saturday night dances in Louisiana; the hot and sweaty have a good time dancing, drinking, and looking at all the people. Do not look for the *Royal Albert Hall* production on this CD, as on his stunning *South of I-10* with its myriad "guest artists." The feel for this music is shown by someone who grew up with it. Listen to the respect and feeling he gives to Clifton Chenier's "If I Ever Get Lucky." Try to keep your body and feet from bouncing to the beat of "Sugar Cane" or "Little Linda." Doesn't your eye start to look around for a dance partner, even though you're in your living room— There is solid playing throughout this CD even though the sound is a bit thin at times and the big-name guests are nowhere to be found. It is a solid effort that spans the musical boundaries of all of Louisiana. Cajun, zydeco, blues, and country are all blended together so they are no longer confining, but a homogenous mix. A solid effort. —*Bob Gottlieb*

South of I-10 / 1995 / Praxis/Zoo ✦✦✦✦✦

Sonny Landreth's screaming slide guitar plows right into you and carries you along on its feral journey. This CD opens going for your guts and never quits, though at times its touch is more caressing than careening, as in "Cajun Waltz." This CD got a lot of airplay yet never got tiresome, the true test of good music. A wide variety of slide guitar styles, backed by an extremely tight rhythm section and various other New Orleans musicians adds to the pleasure of the album. This music combines the best of zydeco, New Orleans R&B, Cajun, and rock & roll into one mood-elevating experience. Listen to "Mojo Boogie" next to "C'est Chaud," then go on to "Shootin' for the Moon"; there is no letdown, but there is great variety. A must-buy. —*Bob Gottlieb*

● **Crazy Cajun Recordings** / Jun. 22, 1999 / Edsel ✦✦✦✦✦

Prodigal Son: The Collection / Feb. 8, 2000 / Music Club ✦✦✦✦

This 15-track compilation brings together slide guitar master Sonny Landreth's earliest known recordings. The bulk of these sides were recorded in a single session in 1973 (when Landreth was 22), while the remaining tracks were cut in 1977. It's a youthful Landreth, playing more Southern than distinctly Louisianian, but this still holds some of the secrets of his signature style. A fascinating glimpse into this slide genius' beginnings. —*Cub Koda*

Levee Town / Oct. 17, 2000 / Sugar Hill ✦✦✦✦✦

There's something about the overall tone produced by guitarists like Mark Knopfler, Rory Gallagher, and Sonny Landreth: it isn't a matter purely of the guitar playing and the technical flash and wizardry, and it isn't down to a considered mix of guitar, amp, and pedals plus endless hours of practice. None of that connects to the bigger picture, which is the song, the album, the entirety of a live set. Landreth is one of those charmed performers who takes a brilliant and unique guitar style, a knack for songwriting, an OK voice, and a great choice of sidemen to create performances that grab hold and won't let go. Consider this: A large part of this album was produced or co-produced by Mike Post, hardly the name you might associate with gutbucket blues and wild slide guitar—for Landreth, Post is one more ingredient of the mix, and even when things develop that Mike Post kind of sound (as happens on "Angeline"), the show is still firmly Landreth's. An engaging and, in no uncertain terms, *funky* album. *—Steven E. McDonald*

LaTouché

Group / Traditional Cajun, Zydeco
La Touché is a five piece band that plays traditional style cajun music along with original progressive cajun music with a country and country-rock flavor. Wilson Touchet, the band leader and accordian player was raised in the cajun parish of St. Martin, LA, on a farm producing mostly cotton and cayenne pepper. His Dad was a sharecropper and they moved several times between Cypress Island and Breau Bridge, LA.. Wilson Touchet spoke only Cajun French until he started school and was taught English. He was raised listening to traditional Cajun music and brings this heritage to the music of La Touché. Chris Sharkey, the bass player, is a native of Boston, Mass.. He has a degree in music from Berkely School of Music in Massachusetts. Chris Sharkey shares lead vocals in La Touché. Calvin Gaudin, the drummer is from New Orleans, LA.. He has been with Wilson Touchet and La Touché the longest. Calvin Gaudin plays rub-board and triangle on La Touché's live acoustic gigs. Eddy Deloney, the guitar player is from New Orleans via Shreveport, LA.. He has written songs for three of La Touché recordings, as of 1999. He also is the appointed representative for the band. Eddy Deloney is the owner of Ralph Records the label that handles La Touché and Allen Fontenot as well as other artists. On the fiddle is, John Babin from Thibodaux, LA.. Some of the bands he has been with are, Gene Savoy and Evan Smith as well as others. John Babin also shares lead vocals for La Touché. Some of the venues La Touché has appeared at are, *the John Anson Ford Theater* in Hollywood, CA., on river boats in New Orleans, The University of Miami, Blossom Music Center in Akron, Ohio for MCA Records, Walker and Grand Portage, Minn., Michaul's Restaurant and Mulate's Restaurant in New Orleans, New Year's Eve Public Street Party in Mobile, Alabama, and the *International Celtic Festival* in Glasgow, Scotland. In 1999 La Touché had four albums available in the U.S. and one available in Europe. *—Larry Belanger*

LaTouché III: On the Bayou / 1994 / Ralph [2] ✦✦✦
La Touché have come up with another exciting formulated album on this 1994 release, *III—On the Bayou;* incorporating a number of instrumental numbers that are powerful as well as entertaining. A fine example is "Lover's Waltz," which contains some smooth licks from the fiddle and accordion. Strains of the Celtic, French, and Louisiana bayou influences shine bright throughout this instrumental. "Potbelly Polka," which was penned by the group's guitarist, Eddy Deloney, is another instrumental that really swings. A great sample of blending the traditional with a new Louisiana sound can be heard on "Zimmerman." The short but oh so sweet "Taz's Two-Step" is a boogie woogie instrumental with a Southern rock feel. "Ti Joe Bicycle" will fit the bill with some great Cajun French lyrics and a full sound complemented by Clyde Thompson's fiddle playing. "Valse du Cable Raide" gets a Cajun boost from Wilson Touchet's magic accordion playing and his marvelous Cajun French vocals. "Cane Pole Fishin'," with its swamp boogie beat, is certain to be a dance club favorite, and the accordion and fiddle duet on the close of the tune is a nice touch. "Long Way Home," with its high energy Southern rock flavor, is a tune that could very easily be mistaken for a Lynyrd Skynyrd or a Charlie Daniels number. There is some hot picking from the lead guitar, courtesy of Deloney, that can be heard throughout the song. La Touché covers the traditional and the modern Louisiana music with a finesse that very few are capable of achieving, making this album a very desirable piece of work. *—Larry Belanger*

● **LaTouché IV: Traditional Cajun Dancin' Music New Orleans, Louisiana** / Nov. 28, 1995 / Ralph [2] ✦✦✦✦
This release from La Touché contains some of the very best traditional Cajun music, written by Iry LeJeune, Link Davis, L. Walker, Sidney Simien, Harry Choates (the fiddler king of Cajun swing), Clyde Thompson, and Wilson Touchet. La Touché give a high-energy beat to a tight and beautifully mastered rendition of "Bosco Stomp," which features sizzling fiddle and accordion playing. Thompson is one of the '90s finest Cajun/zydeco fiddle players, having captured the essence and the beauty of the Cajun fiddle signature sound. Although his fine playing is found throughout the album, some of his hottest riffs happen on "Mardi Gras" and "Lawtell Two Step." Touchet, whose vocals are found on most of the songs here, can croon out lyrics in true Cajun French with the best of 'em. Though Touchet leads the band's vocal expositions his accordion playing is as much a part of the music as his vocals. Whether he's contributing accentuations or taking the lead solo, his playing is an intricate and very important part of the overall intensity of the arrangements. Some of his steamiest squeezebox licks can be heard on Walker's "Les Petits Yeux Noirs" and Simien's "Alligator Waltz." Eddy Deloney contributes stellar guitar throughout the album. His rhythm work is unrivaled, with expressive accentuations, tight chordal arrangements, and lead solos that are very articulate and melodic. The rhythm section extraordinaire of bassist Byo D Myo and drummer/rubboardist Calvin Gaudin lay down a very solid foundation. This album stands as one La Touché's greatest accomplishments, and is an absolute must for any Cajun music library. *—Larry Belanger*

Deux / Jul. 26, 1996 / Ralph [2] ✦✦✦✦
On *Deux,* La Touché is found incorporating "a touch of old" and "a touch of new." There is some fine traditional Cajun music herre, as in the opening number "Pouloon," with its Cajun French lyrics accented by classic fiddle and accordion. This is followed by a beautiful country rock style tune, "Marie's Waltz," which has some swamp pop qualities along with a very fresh sound. Beautifully written lyrics arranged around a captivating melody make this a very attractive song. The band has a terrific knack for being able to put across a traditional sound blended with a new generation drive, with some powerful, country-based vocals and instrumentations. They have a sound similar to greats like the Nitty Gritty Dirt Band, Charlie Daniels, the Band, and Kenny Rogers and the First Edition. One of the top songs on the album is the original tune "Touché 2-Step," which is an instrumental that features a solo by each band member. The various changes in the song sound complex, but the danceable boogie in the song is what makes it a star arrangement. For a touch of humor, La Touché has included "Cajun Rap" to the album. An a cappella number with vocal nuances for rhythm sounds, this tune shows that the band has a funny bone in its bag of tricks. For those in search of traditional Cajun tunes, "Evangeline," "Grandparent's Waltz," and "Linda's Waltz" are sure to conjure up some memories of the old French Cajun soirees. *—Larry Belanger*

LaTouché V: Louisiana / May 13, 1997 / Ralph [2] ✦✦✦✦
For 1997's *V,* La Touché have made some changes to their lineup. Nathanael Burkhamer adds some excellent fiddle to the proceedings, while Jeff Lifford shares lead and backup vocals and plays bass. Lifford wrote the first tune on the album, "Louisiana." The song strongly recalls the Outlaws' rendition of "Freeborn Man," but instead of using ferocious lead guitars as the driving force, as the Outlaws did, La Touché use fiddle, accordion, and Nolan Cormier's pedal steel guitar to power "Louisiana." On La Touché's previous albums, the music was tight and rock-steady, and nothing has changed for this record. Wilson Touchet, Eddy Deloney, and Calvin Gaudin have taken two new musicians into their camp, and they not only maintain the quality instrumental sound, but the vocal finesse as well. Burkhamer and Touchet play incredibly well together, complimenting each other repeatedly. This is clearly evident on "Cowboy" and "Johnny Can't Dance," but the finest example has to be "Valse de Grand Mamou." On "Les Haricots Sont Pas Sale's," the Clifton Chenier zydeco anthem, Gaudin shows just what he can do on the drum kit, astonishing and astounding with his expertise, while Lifford contributes some fanciful bass fret work. This classic number has never been more powerful. Aided by awesome guitar playing and the full string sound of the *AR Orchestra,* Deloney contributes one of the album's most beautiful melodies on "Thanks," a piece that is sure to gain him the recognition he deserves. *La Touché V* is simply an amazing album. Each of its 21 tracks is jam-packed with great Cajun music, done by the finest musicians in the business. Don't pass this one up. *—Larry Belanger*

Rosie Ledet

b. Oct. 25, 1971, Louisiana
Vocals / Zydeco
Accordionist, singer and songwriter Mary Roszela Bellard, "Rosie" Ledet (pronounced leddett), was raised on rock & roll music. During her teenage years in southwest Louisiana, she listened to classic rock & roll radio stations in nearby Eunice; her favorite groups included Santana and ZZ Top.

Like so many other French kids raised in rural southwest Louisiana, she paid no particular attention to all the zydeco music that was around her in her formative years; even though her parents had tried to raise her with a healthy respect for zydeco music, the music held little appeal for her as a kid. But one day, after attending a zydeco dance when she was 16, hearing Boozoo Chavis, and meeting Morris Ledet—who would later become her husband—she was smitten.

She married Morris, the bassist in her band, when she was 17, and while he was on the road touring regionally with a group he led, she stayed home and took care of her ailing mother-in-law. It was during this period of several years that Ledet worked on her accordion playing, honing her skills. At first, she would play along to the recordings of Boozoo Chavis and John Delafose. She began to learn songs intuitively, by ear, and one day surprised her husband by playing a complete Delafose song. Her husband encouraged young Rosie to continue in her efforts, and within a matter of months, she had recorded a demo of her own songs and secured a record deal with Maison de Soul, a zydeco label in nearby Ville Platte.

In a very short time, the prolific songwriter released three albums of her own material, with a backing band that included her husband and father-in-law on bass and rub board, respectively. Ledet's albums include *Sweet Brown Sugar* (1994), *Zydeco Sensation* (1997) and *It's a Groove Thing!* (2000), all for the Maison de Soul label of the Flat Town Music Co. in Ville Platte. All of Ledet's albums showcase superb songs, strong vocals and adequate accordion playing. She and her band began performing in 1994 throughout the Texas-Louisiana triangle, where they continue to concentrate their efforts, and gradually began to spread their touring base to include the rest of the U.S. Ledet and band have been on several European tours as well. *—Richard Skelly*

● **Sweet Brown Sugar** / 1994 / Maison de Soul ✦✦✦✦
Since there aren't many female zydeco singers, the very existence of Rosie Ledet would be noteworthy. Fortunately, her debut album, *Sweet Brown Sugar,* shows that there's a reason to be interested in her outside of sheer novelty. Ledet proves herself to be a strong songwriter and energetic accordionist on *Sweet Brown Sugar.* Her voice may be a little too restrained for some tastes, but she makes up for that with her propulsive, infectious instrumental work. Also, her songs suggest that she could develop into a distinctive lyrical voice in her own right. All in all, it's a fine debut. *—Thom Owens*

Zesty Zydeco / 1995 / Maison de Soul ✦✦

Zydeco Sensation / 1997 / Maison de Soul ✦✦✦
Rosie Ledet's playing is solid, and her singing is soulful, if untrained. But what she brings to this music is not your bayou-variety heat. "Roll It Over" and "My Joy Box" churn insistently while Ledet purrs and moans. "Sweetheart Style" shows that she can also be a tad more subtle, though for the most part the thrust (sorry) of *Zydeco Sensation* is sex. This is a good thing. The chugging rhythms work well with her choice of lyrics. The sound is sparse, and a tad underproduced, though this doesn't detract from this memorable music whatsoever. *—Brian Briscoe*

Eddie LeJeune

d. Jan. 9, 2001
Vocals, Accordion / Zydeco
The son of influential Cajun accordionist and songwriter Iry LeJeune, Eddie LeJuene was only five years old when his father was killed in a tragic automobile accident. Although most of his knowledge of his father's music came from old 78 rpm records, LeJeune has success-

fully continued his family' s great musical heritage. According to *Time Out* magazine, "It would be no exaggeration to say that Eddie LeJeune is the finest Cajun accordionist alive."

A native of Ardoin Cove, a small town near Lacassine, LA, LeJeune retains few memories of his father. In the liner notes to his 1998 album, *It 's In The Blood*, he recalls "sitting on his lap and doing a few things, like him riding his bicycle on a cloudy day." Much of what he's learned about his father came from his maternal grandmother, Adelina Blanchard, an accordion player who regaled him with stories as a youngster.

Picking up the accordion at the age of six, LeJeune felt a natural affinity for the instrument. Within two years, he was proficient enough to become a regular performer at family gatherings, barbecues and house dances.

LeJeune has continued to focus on the traditional styles of Cajun music. While his debut album included four original tunes, the remainder of the album was comprised of songs by Cajun originators Lawrence Walker, Joe Falcon and his father and faithful arrangements of traditional tunes.

LeJeune was accompanied on *It's In The Blood* by his band, The Morse Playboys featuring fiddler Lionel Leleux and guitarist Hubert Maitre. In 1992, LeJeune joined with Cajun guitarist/vocalist D.L. Menard and fiddler Ken Smith to record a trio album, *Le Trio Cadien*. *— Craig Harris*

• **Cajun Soul** / 1988 / Rounder ✦✦✦✦✦
Although he had been singing traditional, evocative Cajun music for many years, Eddie LeJeune didn't record an album for a general label until this 1988 date. He made the most of his opportunity, singing with abandon, fervor and intensity on 15 tunes. Some, such as "Jolie Blon" (a CD-only cut), were familiar efforts; others had some country flavor, but were Cajun through and through. The backing, which included assistance from the great D.L. Menard on guitar and LeJeune's own spicy accordion, never veered from its straight Cajun path and was quite invigorating. The lack of thematic and musical variety might have been a detriment to the session's appeal outside Cajun circles, but within them it was a winner. *— Ron Wynn*

It's in the Blood / 1991 / Rounder ✦✦✦
Eddie LeJeune's 1991 Rounder release, the second for the company, continued to build his reputation among those who hadn't heard his contributions to efforts by such greats as D.L. Menard. While LeJeune was a steady, occasionally intriguing vocalist, he's a super instrumentalist. His accordion solos and fills added extra bite to these songs, and while the 15 numbers were predominantly basic Cajun, he demonstrated on "The Happy Hop" the ability to do credible rock and pop if he desired. The close, tight backing of The Morse Playboys provided additional spark to the session. *— Ron Wynn*

Le Trio Cadien / Jul. 15, 1992 / Rounder ✦✦✦✦✦
When three Cajun music greats and virtuosos team, it seems inevitable that they would make a superb recording. *Le Trio Cadien* wasn't quite that magical, but it was certainly first-rate. D.L. Menard's vocals and guitar work were at their usual fervent peak, while Eddie LeJeune provided some swaying, rocking accordion and poignant, moving vocals during his numbers. Ken Smith was a superior instrumentalist, taking the spotlight on "Bayou Pon Pon" and "Blues de Port Arthur." There's very little wrong with this album, and plenty that's excellent. Only the air of casual intimacy rather than charged intensity kept this from being one of those unforgettable summit meetings. Instead, it's more like a wonderful get-together. *— Ron Wynn*

Iry LeJeune

b. Oct. 28, 1928, Point Noir, LA, **d.** Oct. 8, 1955, Eunice, LA
Accordion / Zydeco
Despite a tragically short career, during which he recorded less than three dozen tunes, Iry LeJeune (born: Ira LeJeune) was one of the most influential accordion players and songwriters in the history of Cajun music. His short list of compositions, including "The Love Bridge Waltz," "The Waltz Of The Mulberry Limb" and "The Church Point Breakdown," have been covered by such Cajun performers as the California Cajun Orchestra, Geno Delafose, The Magnolia Sisters, Steve Riley, Jo-el Sonnier and his son, Eddie LeJeune.

Born and raised on a small farm near Church Point, LA, LeJeune suffered from extremely poor eyesight and wore heavy, coke bottle-like, glasses throughout his life. Unable to work on the farm, he had little direction until an uncle, Angelos LeJeune, taught him to play the accordion. Music was in his blood. His father, Guston, was an amateur fiddler and his brother, Theobert, played accordion. LeJeune took to the squeezebox quickly and was soon hitchhiking to town, with his fiddle in a flour sack, to play for tips in local beer halls. In a late-50s interview, Angelos LeJeune remembered, "As a young boy of fifteen, (Iry) would come to my house almost every day to practice on my accordion." LeJeune's first accordion of his own was a gift from another uncle, Stephen LeJeune.

Although LeJeune recorded in Houston, in the mid-1940s, the record label lacked sufficient funds to adequately distribute the recording and it quickly went out of print. Frustrated by the experience, LeJeune returned home.

LeJeune didn't remain idle for long. Soon after hearing that Eddie Schuller, a deejay on Lake Charles radio station, KPLC, featured local musicians during a fifteen minute segment of his show, LeJeune made his radio debut. Although the appearance was a hit with the listening audience, the station manager had little fondness for Cajun music and banned LeJeune from an encore appearance. Schuller, however, was excited by LeJeune's playing and signed him to record for his independant record label, Goldband, using the KPLC studios late at night. LeJeune went on to record twenty-six tunes for the label over the next seven years.

Word about LeJeune's heavily-syncopated playing spread quickly. In addition to performing at dances with fiddler J.B. Fuselier, he sat in often with Alphee Bergeron And The Veteran Playboys at the Dixie Club in Eunice.

LeJeune's career and life came to a tragic ending on the night of October 8, 1954. Returning home from a dance, the car in which he was riding got a flat tire. While a band member prepared to change it, LeJeune stood by the side of the road. Within minutes, an intoxicated driver came speeding down the road and ran into LeJeune and two band members. LeJeune's body was thrown more than one hundred feet off the road into a swamp. He died instantly.

Nearly five decaces since his death, LeJeune's legacy has continued to influence Cajun musicians including his son, Eddie. *— Craig Harris*

• **Cajun's Greatest: The Definitive Collection** / Ace ✦✦✦✦✦
Cajun's Greatest: The Definitive Collection compiles Iry LeJeune's original '78s, which *do not* feature the overdubbed bass that was added in the '60s, onto one compact disc. All of LeJeune's best and most groundbreaking cuts are included here, making this the best compilation of his available. (Goldband's *The Legendary Iry LeJeune* features a similar track selection, but features the overdubbed bass on each song). *— Thom Owens*

Dennis McGee

b. Jan. 26, 1893, Bayou Marron, LA, **d.** Oct. 3, 1989, Mamou, LA
Vocals, Fiddle / Zydeco
Dennis McGee was one of Cajun music's most influential fiddlers. Although he only recorded for a brief five years (1929 to 1934), McGee remained an inspiration for Cajun musicians through his Acadienne festival performances and his large repertoire, which included hundreds of old Cajun songs.

McGee's first fiddle was a gift from a cousin. After spending two days in his room teaching himself to play, McGee had mastered two songs. Within six months, McGee was playing for house parties throughout southwest Louisiana.

McGee and second fiddler Sady Courville traveled to New Orleans in March and October 1929 to record a number of singles, including his original compositions "Madame Young Donnez Moi Votre (Madame Young, Give Me Your Sweetest)," "Mon Chere Bebe Creole (My Creole Sweet Mama)" and "The Happy One-Step." During subsequent recording sessions, McGee was accompanied by fiddlers Ernest Fruge and Amedee Ardoin.

Although he learned to play accordion and played the squeezebox during several early dances, the fiddle remained McGee's prime instrument. A highly rhythmic player, McGee was known for his use of seven different tunings and his mastery of a lengthy list of dance styles. *— Craig Harris*

• **Complete Recordings 1929-1930** / Sep. 25, 1994 / Yazoo ✦✦✦✦✦

Tommy McLain

Vocals / Swamp Blues, Swamp Pop, Rockabilly, Zydeco
With his gutsy blend of rockabilly and Cajun music, Tommy McLain helped to lay the foundation of Louisiana's swamp pop tradition. The writer of more than 150, McLain is best known as the writer of Freddy Fender's hit, "If You Don't Love Me (Leave Me Alone)," and the performer of a swamp pop version of "Sweet Dreams" that sold more than three million copies in 1966. In addition to being twice inducted into the Louisiana Hall of Fame, McLain was inducted into the rock & roll hall of fame in Sweden. McLain has had a career-long involvement with country singer Clint West. In the late '50s, they were both members of Red Smiley's Vel-Tones and moved together to the Boogie Kings in the mid-'60s. In 1965, McLain and West recorded a duet single, "Try to Find Another Man." A native of the small central Louisiana city of Jonesville, McLain began playing guitar at the age of five. He soon added piano, keyboards, drums, bass, fiddle, and bagpipe. A former DJ at KREH in Oakdale, LA, McLain toured with Dick Clark's *Caravan of Stars* and *Where the Action Is* in the 1960s. He also appeared in the film *The Drowning Man* starring Paul Newman. McLain continues to perform with his group, Tommy McLain and the Mule Train Band. *— Craig Harris*

• **The Cajun Rod Stewart: Crazy Cajun Recordings** / Jul. 27, 1999 / Edsel ✦✦✦✦
McClain, believe it or not, had the only version of "Sweet Dreams" to ever make the pop charts. This companion volume to Edsel's other McClain compilation features his entire faux live album from 1979, four sizzling duets with Freddy Fender on some old rock & roll classics, and some odds and ends that were left off the other package due to time constraints. Still active today and still a massive draw in his home state, this package makes a nice introduction to McClain and his brand of Cajun soul music. *— Cub Koda*

D.L. Menard (Doris Menard)

Vocals, Accordion, Guitar / Zydeco, Creole
Affectionately known as "the Cajun Hank Williams," D. L. Menard (born Doris Leon Menard) only met Williams one time– at the Teche Club in New Iberia in 1951—but, in the nearly five decades since, William's melancholy country songs have continued to be his major influence. Best known for his hit, "La Porte Dans Arrière (The Back Door)," which sold more than one half million copies in 1962, Menard remains one of Cajun music's strongest link to country music. He received a National Heritage fellowship award from the National Endowment for the Arts in 1994. Menard's earliest inspiration was furnished by his father who played harmonica and an uncle, who played in a Cajun band. Attending a rehearsal by the group, Menard became enchanted by his uncle's guitar playing. Convincing his uncle to teach him a few rudimentary chords, Menard took the instrument quickly. Six months after buying his first guitar, from a Sears And Roebuck catalog, he performed his first gigs. Shortly after joining Elias Badeaux's band, the Louisiana Aces, in 1952, Menard took over the band's leadership. He continued to balance his music career, however, with a variety of jobs. He composed "La Porte Dans Arrière" while working at a gas station. Menard has continued to supplement his income as a musician by building rocking chairs in the factory that he owns with his wife, Louella. In 1994, Menard received a National Heritage Fellowship from the National Endowment for the Arts. *— Craig Harris*

• **Cajun Saturday Night** / 1985 / Rounder ✦✦✦✦✦
Out of all of his albums, *Cajun Saturday Night* ranks as one of D.L. Menard's least Cajun-influenced. Throughout the album, Menard tears through Cajun-informed honky tonk numbers, singing entirely in English and playing with a crack band that includes Buck White, Ricky Skaggs, and Jerry Douglas. Menard re-records some of his Cajun songs in English, while he jacks up five Hank Williams songs with New Orleans instruments. It's an exciting,

intoxicating listen and, for country fans reluctant to explore Cajun, it's an easy introduction to the genre. *—Thom Owens*

No Matter Where You at There You Are / 1988 / Rounder ✦✦✦
Although most of the songs on this release were two-steps and/or waltzes, Menard also sang such country-flavored numbers as "The Little Black Eyes," "I Went To The Dance Last Night" and "The Heart Of The City." His voice rang with clarity, conviction and intensity, whether doing heartache tunes, bittersweet narratives or exuberant dance numbers. Menard's vocals got an additional boost on several tunes by the hot accordion of Eddie LeJeune, giving the songs a backing just slightly superior to what they received without him. *—Ron Wynn*

D.L. Menard Sings "The Back Door" and His Other Cajun Hits / Swallow ✦✦✦✦✦
To most, Cajun music is simply an archaic sound produced by the uncouth yokels of the Louisiana swamps. While stereotypes persist, the music's old time feel is actually part of its charm. As a result, hearing someone like D.L. Menard sing in Creole French is like hearing a moment frozen in time. With a voice easily comparable to Hank Williams, the accordion driven music will drive detractors insane. But, to fans of old fashioned Cajun sound, this album, which spans 15 years of Menard's career, is truly a gem. *—Curtis Zimmermann*

Nathan & the Zydeco Cha-Chas

f. 1988, St. Martinville, LA
Rubboard, Drums, Accordion, Guitar, Bass / Swamp Pop, Zydeco
The blues-inflected sounds of southwest Louisiana's zydeco are fused with the dance-inspiring drive of R&B by accordion player Nathan Williams and his band, the Zydeco Cha--Chas. Showing promise as a musician, Williams' older brother Sid arranged for him to take lessons from Buckwheat Zydeco (Stanley Dural). After forming the Zydeco Cha-Chas, named after a Clifton Chenier instrumental, Williams became a regular performer at his brother's dance club, El Sid O's, where they became known for their exciting four-hour shows. Nathan and the Zydeco Cha-Chas made their recording debut with a string of single released on the El Sid O's label, then released their first album-length recording, *Rock Steady,* in 1989. The reggae-tinged title track, written by R&B performer Paul Kelly, became a regional hit in Louisiana. The first hints of success outside their home state came when Nathan and the Zydeco Cha-Chas performed an eight-night stint at the New York hot spot Tramps. Recorded at Rock N' Bowl, a popular zydeco club in the Mid City Bowling Center in New Orleans, *I'm a Zydeco Hog,* their sixth album, released in 1997, captures the excitement of Nathan and the Zydeco Cha-Chas' concerts. *—Craig Harris*

Steady Rock / 1989 / Rounder ✦✦✦✦✦
Nathan Williams has emerged near the head of the class among contemporary zydeco artists. This release featured mostly zydeco-tinged versions of blues and R&B tracks, although the cuts "Zydeco Joe" and "Everything On The Floor" were closer in structure and arrangements to straight zydeco. But Williams' voice, flair and energy, coupled with his band's ability to keep the beat moving, helped him retain a sizable following among Louisiana music purists, yet also branch out and do material that could gain attention from less knowledgeable fans. It was fiery, enjoyable music, produced with a modern sensibility and performed in vintage fashion. *—Ron Wynn*

Your Mama Don't Know / Oct. 1990 / Rounder ✦✦✦
Nathan Williams continued his string of solid releases with this 1991 date. It included good pop and R&B tracks like "Outside People" and "Don't Burn No Bridges," plus vibrant traditional material such as "El Sid O's Zydeco Boogaloo" and "Mardi Gras Zydeco." Williams again sang with zest, drive and non-stop intensity, while the band showed once more why they're considered the tightest unit working in the genre. There weren't any surprises nor low points, just a consistently fine set spotlighting the best group in 1990s zydeco. *—Ron Wynn*

● **Follow Me Chicken** / 1993 / Rounder ✦✦✦✦✦
A rich product of the Creole-American culture in Louisiana, singer/accordion player Nathan Williams and his band the Zydeco Cha-Chas became one of the most popular zydeco dance bands of the late 1980s and early to late 1990s. *Follow Me Chicken* points to the fact that while Williams is very much an admirer of the great Clifton Chenier, he's also a fine artist in his own right. This CD is full of surprises—in addition to providing sweaty originals like "Hey Maman" and "Tout Partout Mon Passe," *Chicken* finds Williams interpreting bluesman Z.Z. Hill's "I Need Someone to Love Me" and translating Stevie Wonder's 1977 hit "Isn't She Lovely" into French Creole. Another high point of the risk-taking album is "Mama's Tired," which combines zydeco with both ska and 1960s-type soul. And African influences are incorporated on "Zydeco Road" and "Zydeco Is Alright," both of which employ guest Kenyatta Simon on the djembe (a West African instrument). *Follow Me Chicken* is a disc that zydeco enthusiasts should make a point of obtaining. *—Alex Henderson*

Creole Crossroads / Oct. 3, 1995 / Rounder ✦✦✦
Michael Doucet teams up with Nathan Williams for a power-filled set that constantly blurs the line between what is Cajun and what is zydeco. The set list is a nice blend of modern originals from both men (Williams' "Zydeco Hog" and Doucet's "La Nuit de Clifton Chenier") and traditional favorites like "Jolie Noir" and "I Want to Be Your Chauffeur," all of them suitably souped for the ocassion. A spirited session that makes you want to dance. *—Cub Koda*

I'm a Zydeco Hog: Live at the Rock 'N' Bowl, New Orleans / Aug. 5, 1997 / Rounder ✦✦✦

Let's Go / Feb. 8, 2000 / Rounder ✦✦✦✦
From "Let's Go," the first track on the album, be prepared to be rocked in the good old Louisiana fashion, because that's the way Nathan & the Zydeco Cha-chas do it. This song serves to showcase everybody in the band as they all have their own little solo, even the rub board player gets a chance to shine. If the search is for melodic tunes, this album certainly fits the bill. With 14 original tunes that have a familiar charm, it won't be long until one finds themselves singing along. It could also be the charismatic piano accordion playing from Nathan Williams that attracts many a listener. Or quite possibly it's the tight arrangements that fill the album that pull the listener's ear to the groove. Whatever it is that attracts the listener to Nathan & the Zydeco Cha-Chas, it's common opinion that they have found the perfect formula that keeps the party going and going all night long. This album is a prime example of what Nathan & the Zydeco Cha-Chas can do with playful lyrics and bouncing rhythms. They have captured the essence of vibrant and colorful Louisiana music at its finest, as one will find on "Zydeco Rumble" (which has been used on commercials for Louisiana tourism). The lyrics are provocative and entertaining, keeping the listener sitting on the edge of their seat with keen interest, as in the bluesy "Hard Times." This is far from being the typical Zydeco album, it is as original and fresh as one can hope to find within the genre. Nathan & the Zydeco Cha-Chas have bestowed Cajun/Zydeco fans with an extraordinary dance music album that will have everyone shouting, "Let's Go!" one more time. *—Larry Belanger*

Queen Ida

b. Jan. 15, 1929, Lake Charles, LA
Accordion / Zydeco
Queen Ida was the first female accordion player to lead a zydeco band. Favoring a 31-button accordion, she is noted for her melodic playing, and for focusing on the treble side of her instrument, which makes her style similar to Mexican playing styles. Though like many other zydeco artists of the '80s, her music was well grounded in Creole traditions, she also integrates Caribbean, Cajun, blues and other genres. She came to professional music rather late in life, in the early '70s. After performing at the Monterey Jazz and Blues Festival in 1976, she signed to GNP/Crescendo Records and released her first album in 1980. She continued recording and touring through the 1980s, recording most of her albums while on tour because she feels she and the band sound best live. During the late '80s, Queen Ida toured the world, visiting Japan, Africa and Australia. For many, Queen Ida is not only an excellent musician, she is also a fine example of how a determined middle-aged woman can still find success in a youth-obsessed culture. *—Sandra Brennan*

The Queen Ida Zydeco Band on Tour / 1982 / GNP Crescendo ✦✦✦✦✦

Caught in the Act / 1985 / GNP Crescendo ✦✦✦
Live from San Francisco, CA. It includes classics "Jole Blon," "Don't Mess with My Tu Tu," and Nick Lowe's "Half a Boy, Half a Man." Rollicking zydeco from The Queen. *—Michael G. Nastos*

In San Francisco / 1988 / GNP Crescendo ✦✦✦✦✦
A Grammy award-winning, live, and potent album, with Al Rapone on accordion. *—Michael G. Nastos*

★ **Cookin' with Queen Ida** / 1989 / GNP Crescendo ✦✦✦✦✦

Al Rapone

b. 1936, Lake Charles, Louisiana
Vocals, Accordion / Contemporary Blues, Zydeco
The brother of zydeco's renowned Queen Ida, accordionist and guitarist Al Rapone was not only a driving force behind the success of his sister but also a noted solo performer. Born Al Lewis in Lake Charles, Louisiana in 1936, he first picked up the accordion at age 13, and following the family's relocation to California he was regularly performing live throughout the West Coast by the early 1950s. Within a few years, Rapone also began playing guitar, quickly becoming a noted sideman on the San Francisco blues circuit, where he backed the likes of Big Mama Thornton, Clarence Gatemouth Brown and Jimmy Reed; while in college, he studied composing, producing and arranging, and after graduation formed a group with his sister. However, as Queen Ida soon settled down to raise a family, Rapone assembled a new unit, the Bon Ton Zydeco Band, and over time forged a unique sound combing his distinctive guitar leads with zydeco accordion and country music rhythms. Ida began sitting in with the group during the mid-1970s, and as her career blossomed, the Bon Ton Zydeco Band mutated to become her permanent backing band; Rapone served not only as his sister's ace sideman but also as her producer and arranger, helming her 1982 Grammy-winner *Queen Ida and the Bon Ton Zydeco Band on Tour,* as well as composing one of her best-loved songs, "Frisco Zydeco." Soon afterwards, Rapone left the group to again pursue a solo career, enjoying his greatest success in Germany, where he recorded efforts including 1982's *Cajun Creole Music* and 1984's *C'est La Vie;* upon returning Stateside, he settled in New Orleans, issuing *Zydeco to Go* in 1990. *—Jason Ankeny*

Zydeco to Go / Oct. 1990 / Blind Pig ✦✦✦✦
On his second album, *Zydeco to Go,* Al Rapone turns out an infectious, joyful record, filled with good spirits and great music. The album is firmly in the classic zydeco tradition, spiked with some blues, R&B and Cajun country, and Rapone shines on each of the tracks, as does his supple, sympathetic supporting band. His cousin, Roy L. Chantier, drops in to sing a couple of tracks, turning "Our Hearts Will Dance in Love Again" into a beautiful thing and making sure that "Good Ole Cajun Music" and "Yvette U.B. Dancin'" catch fire. Still, this is Rapone's show, and he keeps things cooking with his robust accordion and gleeful vocals. All in all, *Zydeco to Go* is a good-time record that delivers. *—Thom Owens*

● **Plays Tribute: A Tribute to Clifton Chenier** / May 6, 1997 / Atomic Theory ✦✦✦✦✦
It may be a salute to the master of zydeco, but Al Rapone's *A Tribute to Clifton Chenier* is a terrific testimonial to his own talents as well. Part of the reason the album works so well is that there isn't a weak song on the record—in fact, almost all of the 15 songs are acknowledged zydeco classics. These songs give Rapone a platform for his rambunctious, infectious accordion style. He plays these songs a little bluesier than Chenier, but it's great to hear them played in a different way, and the record itself is just a blast. *—Thom Owens*

Zachary Richard

b. Sep. 8, 1950
Vocals, Accordion, Guitar / Zydeco, Creole
Cajun rebel Zachary Richard has been offering his zesty, unique fusion of traditional cajun, zydeco, rock and New Orleans blues since the early '70s. Though not well-known outside of Louisiana, Canada and France, Richard, along with Michael Doucet and others has been a key figure in the revitalization of Cajun music. He has also been a long-time social activist

using his potent song lyrics to promote Cajun pride and solidarity in the face of long-standing injustice and prejudice. A full-blooded Cajun, Richard was signed to Elektra for a brief time in the early '70s, though no material was ever released. Tutored by Clifton Chenier, Richard began perfecting his accordion technique and formed the Bayou Drifter Band in 1974 with cousin Michael Doucet and Kenneth Richard to play a mixture of Cajun and rock that they called swamp rock. The new style didn't catch on in Louisiana, but proved extremely popular in French-speaking Canada and earned him several gold records. By the time he returned to Louisiana in the early '80s, Cajun culture and music had become a national fad that spurred new recording activity for Richard. He released a pair of albums for Rounder, then signed with A&M. He continued to tour and record both Cajun rock and more traditional music. *—Sandra Brennan*

Live / 1970 / Arzed ✦✦✦
An exciting live performer, he's at his best here. *—Jeff Hannusch*

☆ **Looking Back** / 1985 / Arzed ✦✦✦✦✦
These are the greatest hits from this important artist. *—Jeff Hannusch*

Mardi Gras Mambo / 1989 / Rounder ✦✦✦✦
Zachary Richard blended Cajun with classic R&B on this set, paying homage to the link between Louisiana's Mardi Gras heritage and its other musical styles. He did spirited and convincing versions of "Iko Iko," "Big Chief," and "Down On Second Street," while also including "Creole Lullaby" and scoring with "Moi Connais Pas" and "Ton Ton Gris-Gris." Richard had expert assistance from The Bon Ton Playboys, plus a guest vocal corps, and he handled production chores himself, ensuring the musical backdrops he wanted. This wasn't a crossover project but a unified one that demonstrated the intrinsic links between all Louisiana genres. *—Ron Wynn*

☆ **Women in the Room** / 1990 / A&M ✦✦✦✦✦
Zach's writing comes together on this release with his most powerful songs to date. "No French, No More" is a sad tale about how teachers denied the Cajun people the use of their language. "Who Stole My Monkey" is a knock-you-out fun song. A very diverse release. Highly recommended. *—Chip Renner*

Zack's Bon Ton / 1990 / Rounder ✦✦✦
Zachary Richard has been among Cajun music's finest performers during the 1980s and '90s, and this late-'80s session was one of his finest. The 12 tracks included hot versions of "Jolie Blonde," "La Valse de Grande Rivière" and "Ma Petite Fille Est Gone." Richard also demonstrated his country proficiency with a heady cover of Johnny Horton's "The Battle of New Orleans," as well as "Big River" and "Take Me Deep (Song For C)." The Bon Ton Playboys also include outstanding musicians in fiddler Rufus Thibodeaux, saxophonist Pat Breaux, keyboardist Craig Lege with Richard doubling on Acadian accordion, harmonica, and acoustic guitar in addition to doing leads. This was alternately spicy and reflective material, providing a good look at Cajun music's past, present and future. *—Ron Wynn*

Bayou des Mystées / 1991 / Arzed ✦✦✦

Snake Bite Love / Sep. 8, 1992 / A&M ✦✦✦✦
This CD stands up as an energetic *tour de force.* It carries a high head easily with some of the best song writing and singing to come out of the Louisiana scene that has included Sonny Landreth's *South of I-10,* and Richard's own *Women in the Room.* For this record he has culled some of the best people from the southern Louisiana music scene (Brian Stoltz, Doctor John, the Dirty Dozen Brass Band, and Daryl Johnson to name a few) to take part in this fine blending of zydeco, Cajun, rock, and country. We are the lucky recipients that have the pleasure of enjoying the ambiance and excitement of the dance hall in the comfort of our living rooms. The only bother with this CD is that you can't sit and listen to it, you are compelled to get up and do. Try and sit and contemplate while "Dancing at Double D's" is spinning. Bet you can't! (I am having trouble sitting at the keyboard to finish this). Listen to the heartfelt vocals and the exposed emotions of "Cote Blanche Bay" or "Sunset on Louisianne," feel the love and hurt from his voice come coursing through your body. *—Bob Gottlieb*

Cap Enragé / Jan. 13, 1997 / Aris ✦✦✦✦✦
This disc is quite possibly the best piece of work that Zachary Richard has done. This Louisiana Cajun musician went back to Canada to make this disc, but then again, that is where the Cajun people originally migrated from, and that is where Richard made his first recordings. The whole disc is done in the French language, but at the same time it is such a beautiful and heartfelt work that it is eminently accessible even if you don't speak French. Do not mistake me, I very much liked his music from his two albums on Rounder Records, *Mardi Gras Mambo* and *Zack's Bon Ton,* right on through *Women in the Room* and *Snake Bite Love.* The latter two were some of his best work, but this disc leaves the others squatting on their haunches at the starting gate. His voice is gaining a greater range of expressiveness with the experience and wear the years have piled onto it. He sings with a controlled fervor here, and the sparse arrangements and instrumentation are the perfect complements to his expressive singing, particularly on the slow to midtempo numbers. Richard wrote or co-wrote all but two songs on the disc, and you know these songs come from his heart, whether you understand the language or not. Do not be put off by the language—grab this one, because it's worth it. *—Bob Gottlieb*

★ **Silver Jubilee: Best of Zachary Richard 1973-1998** / Jan. 18, 2000 / Rhino ✦✦✦✦✦
Music fans who enjoy Cajun music in general, and the work of Zachary Richard in particular, will find that this retrospective is a very musical, quite effective summary of his career to date. Richard is without question one of the most distinctive and significant artists Acadien music has ever produced. The CD features 19 songs, all either Richard originals or his arrangements of traditional material like "Travailler C'est Trop Dur" and "Bon Temps Rouler." Richard can get down on that two-step boogie as proficiently as anyone—just listen to "Filé Gumbo," "Joe Pitre," "Crawfish," "Johnny Danser," and his definitive rendition of "Who Stole My Monkey" (a Richard original). His more pop-oriented persona—no doubt the result of his extended sojourns in Quebec—is well represented by "Cap Enragé" and "Dans la Nord Canadien," and his fancy for blues and R&B is typified by songs like "La Berçeuse Créole" and "Everytime." Richard is everything you'd expect from a Cajun artist, but he's also pursued music much further afield than any other Acadien musician of his generation. *Silver Jubilee* does an especially good job of showcasing the range of music Richard has performed in the past quarter century. *—Philip Van Vleck*

Travailler C'est Trop Dur: Anthologie, 1976-1999 / Arzed ✦✦✦✦✦
Compiled by Zachary Richard himself, this collection gathers many of the Cajun rebel's best recordings. There's a wonderful mix of songs here—most of them written or co-written by Richard—but it's on slow ballads like "Dear Darling," "Les Ailes des Hirondelles," and "La Berceuse Creole" that Richard's voice is shown to best effect. The collection also includes stompers like "Flammes D'Enfer," "Zack's Bon Ton," and "Snake Bit Love," as well as a few waltzes. Richard is backed by the best players in the biz, including Michael Doucet, Sonny Landreth, Bessyl Duhon, and Dana Breaux, among many others. Despite liner notes written entirely in French, this does a beautiful job of sampling Richard's best work thus far, and certainly deserves a place in any self-respecting Cajun/zydeco collection. *—Bob Gottlieb*

Steve Riley

b. 1970, Mamou, LA
Vocals, Triangle, Drums, Accordion, Fiddle / Zydeco, Creole
Steve Riley and his band, the Mamou Playboys, have quickly risen to the top of the Cajun music heap in recent years, and the band is now as well known on the festival and club circuit as Beausoleil. Clearly, the band's 1990s-styled Cajun rhythms and melodies have touched a nerve with crowds around the U.S., Canada and Europe. The band sings only in French, reflecting their serious attitude about maintaining the Cajun music tradition as practiced in southwest Louisiana. The band's early albums reflect their respect for tradition, as they do a lot of covers of well-known and obscure Cajun tunes; later albums, especially 1995's *La Toussaint,* reflect the band's growth as a touring and performing entity unto themselves, as there are more self-penned compositions. *—Richard Skelly*

● **Steve Riley & the Mamou Playboys** / 1990 / Rounder ✦✦✦✦✦
When accordion player/singer Steve Riley and his band the Mamou Playboys came out of Louisiana in the late 1980s, it came as a pleasant surprise to hear younger musicians embrace traditional Cajun music with so much enthusiasm. This rewarding CD doesn't contain zydeco or experimental Cajun music *a la* Wayne Toups & Zydecajun, but instead, is highly traditional in its approach. The band sticks to traditional Cajun songs such as "Ton Papa Et Ta Maman M'ont Jete Dehors," "Valse De La Belle" and "La Pointe Aux Pins," and most of the lyrics are sung in French. The band's supporters commented that its repertoire was something one would expect from older Cajuns, but thankfully, this CD gives us the chance to enjoy these classics with the digital sound quality of 1990. *—Alex Henderson*

'Tit Galop Pour Mamou / Mar. 1, 1992 / Rounder ✦✦✦
Singer/fiddler/accordionist Steve Riley and his Mamou Playboys are at the forefront of Cajun music's resurgence in popularity. The Cajun French Music Association voted the band's Rounder debut, *Steve Riley and the Mamou Playboys* (Rounder 6038, CD and cassette), best album, best group, and best new group, and Riley was also voted best accordion player. And this album is even better. In his liner notes for this release, Ben Sandmel cites the group's "clarity of vision, consistent finesse, and commitment to quality, classic Cajun music." The group exhibits "grass-roots integrity and toe-tapping appeal" on the 14 tracks included here. *—Roundup Newsletter*

Bayou Ruler / Jun. 9, 1998 / Rounder ✦✦✦✦
Steve Riley and the Mamou Playboys, purveyors of traditional Cajun music, range far out of the bayous to incorporate most all the musical styles of Southern Louisiana. Bringing in the traditional Zydeco of Clifton Chenier (this they have flirted with for a stretch), the 1950s country-swing influence, swamp rock, and plain, straight-ahead-down-the-road rock & roll. Those of you who are traditionalists should still be happy with this disc because it uses as its base the very secure foundation that the band has established in Cajun music as its launching pad into its musical forays into new territories. As with all the S.R. & the M.P.s efforts, it displays the same musical drive at perfection that we have come to expect from them. The guests that appear on this disc do nothing but enhance the efforts that are made; just listen to "King Zydeco," a Riley/C.C. Adcock-penned tune, with additional musicians supporting the style shift and helping to swing it across. Producers Adcock and Tarka Cordell deserve a nod, as they took this gamble and helped to turn it into a winning disc. There still is some ineffable spirit lost with this disc, for all its strong points, but maybe it is the strong step to again revitalize Cajun music. *—Bob Gottlieb*

Sherman Robertson

b. Oct. 27, 1948, Breaux Bridge, LA
Guitar / Swamp Blues, Contemporary Blues, Zydeco
Guitarist, singer and songwriter Sherman Robertson is a product of the region of the country that he grew up in: he's one part zydeco, one part swamp blues, one part electric blues and one part classic rhythm & blues. His guitar playing style is extremely rhythm-based, but at the same time, he plays some extraordinary slide guitar and in the course of one of his typical three hour shows, he'll play a lot of great solos. Robertson's rhythmic playing is no doubt an outgrowth of his several years on the road in the 1980s with the king of zydeco, Clifton Chenier. He also served tenures with Rockin' Dopsie and Terrance Simien & the Mallet Playboys before deciding he wanted to venture out with his own high energy blues style several years ago. Fortunately for Robertson, some folks at a major label, Atlantic/Code Blue, took notice.

Robertson recorded two albums for Atlantic/Code Blue, a label that shut down operations in 1996. Robertson's albums include his stunning debut, *I'm The Man* (1994) and *Here & Now* (1995).

"I focus on the good time, upbeat blues," says Robertson, born in Breaux Bridge, Louisiana but raised across the border in nearby Houston.

"Playing with zydeco bands all that time, everybody was always dancing. The guys I learned from were all playing dance music. When zydeco blues comes to town, you can't sit still. Yet people have this concept of blues as depressing. I say,'Forget your problems, I play dance music.'"

Robertson drew his first inspiration from a TV performance by Hank Williams, the country singer known in bayou country for his composition, "Jambalaya." He was 13 when he first saw Williams perform and that experience changed his life. Robertson heard the blues coming out of the country legend, and his interest in playing guitar was piqued. Robertson's father bought him an old Stella guitar for $12 and the younger Robertson began playing the songs of Freddie King and Floyd London, often playing until his hands bled and often falling asleep with the instrument nestled beside him.

Growing up in Houston, just down the street from Don Robey's famed Duke/Peacock Records studios, Robertson had the chance to befriend many of the great musicians who stopped in there to make records. By 17, he was honing his craft with a local blues band and playing in the bars in his Fifth Ward neighborhood in Houston.

In 1982, when Robertson's band was playing at the Crosstown Blues Festival, zydeco legend Chenier heard him play. Chenier told his bus driver to "get that guitar player," and a long alliance with Chenier's band was forged.

Robertson moved to Louisiana with Chenier's band and learned a lot from the accordionist about how to read an audience. Later, Robertson worked with singer-songwriter Paul Simon during recording sessions for his *Graceland* album, and also had the chance to sit in with all of his heroes, Albert Collins and B.B. King and Lightnin' Hopkins among them. In 1987 and 1988, after Chenier's passing, Robertson hooked up with accordionist Terrance Simien, and furthered his musical education, particularly with the overseas dates that band performed in Egypt and Africa. After all those years of playing zydeco, Robertson yearned to get back to more basic forms of blues, and in the early '90s, after two and a half years with the Mallet Playboys, he assembled his own band that would later take much of the blues festival circuit by storm. A few years and hundreds of shows later, critics were saying Robertson would inherit the seats left open by people like Albert King and Albert Collins.

Robertson's *I'm the Man* was the first release via Atlantic Record's alliance with Code Blue, and they couldn't have picked a stronger album. Every track is radio-ready and a winner. Robertson's follow-up, *Here & Now,* includes his cover of the Tracy Nelson song, the title track of the album. He described his second release as his blues opera.

The rest of the 1990s will show this to be the case, since there are few other musicians who combine great songs, fluid guitar playing and strong, powerful vocals so well. Robertson hasn't let the record company troubles bother him in the least, and he'll no doubt find a new home at a significant independent record company and continue to do what he's been doing so well. *—Richard Skelly*

Going Back Home / Sep. 15, 1998 / AudioQuest ✦✦✦
Looking for Robertson represented on a studio CD that matches the intensity of his live performances—Producer Joe Harley has done it. Harley lets Robertson rip loose, mixing his zydeco roots with his growing years breathing Texas fire. Joining him on the cattle drive are Little Feat's Richie Hayward and Bill Payne, Bob Glaub (John Fogerty), and fellow Texan Joe Sublett of the Texacali horns. *—Char Ham*

Rockin' Dopsie

b. Feb. 10, 1932, Carencro, LA, **d.** Aug. 26, 1993, Opelousas, LA
Vocals, Accordion / Zydeco
If Clifton Chenier was the king of zydeco music, Rockin' Dopsie—with his unequaled proficiency on the button accordion—was its crown prince. Like Chenier, Dopsie was devoted to preserving the old French songs that form the basis of zydeco. Through the '50s and '60s, Dopsie occasionally recorded with independent labels. He recorded his debut album with Sam Charters for Sweden's Sonet label. Over the next decade, Dopsie recorded five more albums for the label. Released in Europe, Dopsie soon became an extremely popular performer. He began touring Europe twice annually in 1979. It wasn't until well into the '80s that Dopsie's music began garnering attention back home. His U.S. career got a big boost in 1985 when he recorded "That Was Your Mother" with Paul Simon on the latter's landmark *Graceland* album. Later Dopsie would also record with other pop singers including Cyndi Lauper and Bob Dylan. He continued performing and recording through his death in 1993. *—Sandra Brennan*

Big Bad Zydeco / 1988 / GNP Crescendo ✦✦✦✦✦
Hot Louisiana R&B/zydeco from one of its most popular modern practitioners. *—Hank Davis*

Good Rockin' / 1988 / GNP Crescendo ✦✦✦

● **Louisiana Music** / 1991 / Atlantic ✦✦✦✦✦
The jumping Atlantic debut by Rockin' Dopsie and the Zydeco Twisters has a killer dance blend of rootsy zydeco full of grit, funk, and soul with pedal-to-the-metal rhythms. Tunes include "I'm in the Mood," "Keep a Knockin'," "The Things I Used to Do," "Zydeco Two Step," and six others. *—Roundup Newsletter*

Zydeco Man / Jun. 6, 2000 / Mardis Gras ✦✦✦

Rockin' Sidney

b. Apr. 9, 1938, Lebeau, LA, **d.** Feb. 25, 1998
Vocals, Accordion, Harmonica, Guitar, Organ / Swamp Blues, Zydeco
With his 1985 novelty smash "My Toot Toot," Rockin' Sidney scored zydeco's first true international hit. Born Sidney Semien on April 9, 1938 in Lebeau, Louisiana, he began playing harmonica and guitar professionally while in his teens, and made his first R&B-styled recordings on the Fame and Jin imprints during the late '50s; his first regional hit, "No Good Woman," appeared in 1962. Between the mid-'60s and the late '70s, Sidney cut well over 50 singles for the Louisiana-based Goldband label, working in a variety of contemporary blues, soul and R&B modes; none proved successful, however, and upon learning the accordion he began playing zydeco. He issued his first true zydeco record, *Give Me a Good Time Woman,* on the Maison de Soul label in 1982; two years later he cut *My Zydeco Shoes Got the Zydeco Blues,* which included the track "My Toot Toot." Although Sidney himself was reportedly unhappy with the song, it became a local jukebox hit, and soon regional radio stations began playing it regularly; in time, the single became a grass-roots smash, selling well over a million copies on its way to charting in the U.S. and the U.K. and even winning a Grammy Award. While Sidney never again reached the same commercial peaks, he remained one of zydeco's most notable artists, setting up his own label, Bally Hoo, and touring regularly until his death on February 25, 1998. *—Jason Ankeny*

● **My Toot Toot** / 1986 / Ace ✦✦✦✦✦
Rockin' Sidney had the biggest zydeco release of all time—"My Toot Toot"—and it has enjoyed many subsequent covers. Some of this release is unfortunately unacceptable, as it includes updated covers, but he rises above it most of the time. *—Jeff Hannusch*

Savoy-Doucet Cajun Band

Accordion, Guitar, Fiddle / Traditional Cajun
The Savoy-Doucet Cajun Band is a group with not one, but two missions: to play outstanding music, and to keep cajun free of external influences. With its peerless lineup, it succeeds well in both respects. Savoy is not only one of the nation's leading accordianists, he is also a master craftsman and makes the instruments he plays. Doucet, when not fronting for the popular group Beausoleil, plays fiddle, while Savoy's wife, Ann, plays guitar. Ann is author of the book *Cajun Music—A Reflection of People* which articulates the group's traditionalism. *—Leon Jackson*

Home Music with Spirits / 1981 / Arhoolie ✦✦✦✦✦
Home Music With Spirits compiles highlights from the Savoy-Doucet Cajun Band's first three albums, making it an excellent introduction to the husband/wife duo. *—Thom Owens*

Sam's Big Rooster / Mar. 28, 2000 / Arhoolie ✦✦✦
The Savoy-Doucet Band had played together, off and on, for more than 20 years by the time of this 2000 release. They're tight, featuring three of the most prominent figures in contemporary Cajun music. It would be unreasonable to go into this 73-minute disc expecting surprising departures, like synthesizers or covers of 2Pac songs. No, it's a tried and true approach to Cajun music, mixing originals (by Marc Savoy and Ann Savoy, writing separately or together; Doucet doesn't contribute any compositions) and traditional material. There's more variety here than on the usual Cajun release, as evidenced by the mix of male and female lead vocals, the alternation of fast and slow numbers, and the inclusion of some instrumentals and a couple of live cuts. Still, it's not *that* varied, and 73 minutes is going to be too long for those not enamored of the basic Cajun format. Some mildly unusual fare is offered by the title track, on which Marc Savoy takes a bird's-eye view of the rooster, and Ann Savoy's "C'Etait Dessus Un Triste Samedi," which was written about a 1957 hurricane and has a pious, funereal air. *—Richie Unterberger*

● **Live!** / Arhoolie ✦✦✦✦✦
Any album featuring Michael Doucet's fiddle playing is a treat. But here in the bare-bones company of Marc Savoy on accordion, Anne Savoy on acoustic guitar and vocals, and string bassist Billy Wilson on seven tracks performing live before enthusiastic dancers, we get a true slice of the real thing without the commerical studio overlay. Featuring 18 tracks that total over a 76-minute running time, this one's a delightful toe tapper every note of the way. *—Cub Koda*

Two Step D'Amadé / Arhoolie ✦✦✦✦
This is the kind of acoustic music you used to hear only at Cajun houseparties. Very spirited and a timepiece, it's a glorious tribute to Cajun-pioneer Amadé Ardoin. *—Jeff Hannusch*

Terrance Simien

b. Sep. 3, 1965, Eunice, LA
Vocals, Accordion / Zydeco
One of zydeco's most soulful vocalists and fieriest accordionists, Terrance Simien was also among the music's most pop-oriented artists, infusing his sound with elements of R&B, funk, gospel and reggae. Born September 3, 1965 in Eunice, Louisiana, he first heard zydeco at local dances as a boy, but did not show any real interest in the music until it began growing in popularity during the early 1980s. After learning the accordion and writing a handful of songs in collaboration with his brother Greg, Simien formed his first band; in the years to follow, he honed his chops in area zydeco clubs each weekend, working as a bricklayer during the day. His big break arrived in 1984, when an appearance at the New Orleans World's Fair launched him to the attention of Paul Simon, with whom Simien recorded a cover of Clifton Chenier's "You Used to Call Me." He also was tapped to appear in the feature film *The Big Easy,* writing and performing a song with star Dennis Quaid. With his band the Mallet Playboys, Simien made his full-length debut in 1990 with *Zydeco on the Bayou; There's Room for Us All* followed in 1993, and after a six-year recording hiatus he returned with *Positively Beadhead.* *—Jason Ankeny*

● **Zydeco on the Bayou** / 1990 / Restless ✦✦✦✦✦
A modern zydeco artist whose songs aren't yet in an essential category. More rock than zydeco, but lots of energy nonetheless. *—Ron Wynn & Jeff Hannusch*

There's Room for Us / Sep. 17, 1993 / Black Top ✦✦✦

Jam the Jazzfest [EP] / Apr. 7, 1998 / Tone-Cool ✦✦✦✦
Before the release of his third full-length album, Simien released this five-song EP. A tribute to his regular appearances at the New Orleans Jazz Fest, Terrance cooks up a potent groove on the title track. A medley of "Iko Iko/Brother John/Jambalaya" stretches out to almost seven minutes, followed by a great version of Dylan's "Baby Stop Crying." A great little zydeco instrumental, "Macque Choux," sets the stage for the closer, "May Your Music Live On," a tribute to John Delafose, one of Terrance's early influences. As always, the Mallet Playboys keep the groove steady and rocking throughout. As a stopping-off point between full length projects, this makes a wonderful appetizer. *—Cub Koda*

Positively Beadhead / May 4, 1999 / Tone-Cool ✦✦✦✦
A smooth and flowing disc that has many of the rough edges of his energy knocked off without diminishing that same energy. The passion is strong in his voice and there is a seasoned maturity that replaces the flaming rawness that reigned before. He is no longer the wild 20 something year old playing his accordion while doing black flips on stage, but he is presenting the songs (he wrote or co-wrote 8 of the 12) in a total and much tighter fashion. This band has been with him for years and they are tight and playing better than ever, providing the support that allows him to take the chances he does. There also seems to be a real dedication to the family, happiness, and getting a handle on all of the twists and turns that life presents. Many of his songs seem to be reflections along these lines. From his beautiful love song "All Her Lovin'" to the thoughts and revelations expressed in "Grandma's House," Terrance Simien has always been more associated with a burst of sheer energy than playing with the subtleties of a song. *Positively Beadhead* is one of the finest Zydeco discs to come down the pike in a long time and it represents a giant step toward the bright future for this fine musician. *—Bob Gottlieb*

Jo-El Sonnier

b. 1946, Rayne, LA
Vocals, Accordion, Guitar / Traditional Cajun, Americana, Progressive Country
In the late '80s, when Nashville realized that country consisted of more than the Tennessee-Texas axis, they started looking for new sounds. One of the best was that of Cajun accordionist Jo-El Sonnier, who had kicked around for a number of years, gaining a reputation as a "musician's musician." He recorded *Cajun Life* for Rounder in 1984 and that year garnered his first Grammy nomination. In 1987, he signed to RCA and though encouraged to continue recording pure Cajun material, began exploring country-, rock- and pop-influenced music. The result was *Come on Joe* (1988), an acclaimed album with several country Top 20 hits, including "Tear Stained Letter." He signed to Capitol-Nashville in the early '90s and though few would dispute his expertise and versatility on the accordion, Sonnier's career did not take off. *—Brian Mansfield and Sandra Brennan*

Cajun Life / 1975 / Rounder ✦✦✦
Jo-El Sonnier, like Jimmy C. Newman, has found a comfortable middle ground between traditional Cajun and contemporary country music, working both styles and achieving a measure of commercial and aesthetic success in each. This session accented the Cajun side, although it included competent pop/country material as well. Besides the autobiographical title track, Sonnier demonstrated his roots facilty on "Les Yeux Bleu," "Jolie Blon" and "Les Grands Bois." Sonnier has gone on to become a bigger name in country, but this earlier date will appeal to both lovers of vintage material and those unaware of his solid Cajun skills and background. *—Ron Wynn*

● **Come on Joe** / 1987 / RCA ✦✦✦✦✦
Sonnier's French-Cajun accent brings new life to songs by Randy Newman, Richard Thompson, Moon Martin, and Dave Alvin. Steve Winwood takes an organ solo on a cover of Slim Harpo's "Raining in My Heart." Cajun-tinged contemporary country with a rock edge and intelligent songs, it is the best of Sonnier's Nashville work. *—Brian Mansfield & Mark A. Humphrey*

Have a Little Faith / 1990 / RCA ✦✦✦
The emphasis here lies more heavily on ballads, as Sonnier discovers John Hiatt and delivers penetrating versions of his "Have a Little Faith" and "I'll Never Get over You." The album also includes a remake of Iry LeJeune's 1945 "Evangeline Special" and a straight-country single in "If Your Heart Should Ever Roll This Way Again." *—Brian Mansfield*

Tears of Joy / 1991 / Liberty ✦✦✦
It's in the Cajun/pop/country mold of his RCA albums. *—Mark A. Humphrey*

The Complete Mercury Sessions / 1992 / Mercury ✦✦✦✦✦
Fifteen fine '70s country songs are here, including the aching "Blue Is Not a Word." *—Mark A. Humphrey*

Cajun Young Blood / Jul. 29, 1996 / Ace ✦✦✦✦✦
Cool collection of 28 sides recorded at Goldband Studios in Lake Charles, Louisiana in the late sixties and early seventies. Sonnier is an accomplished traditional Cajun accordionist and singer, and some of the sides here are in the straight-ahead Cajun mold. But this was also a time at which outside influences were creeping into the region, and this stuff is most interesting when it absorbs odd traces of rock, blues, and country. "Jump Little Frog," for instance, has an organ that wouldn't sound out of place on a Sir Douglas Quintet record; "Rolling Pin (Special)" has a fuzzy rock guitar; "Monkey On My Back" is a classy honky-tonkish tune. He sure sounds like he's trying to replicate Norman Greenbaum's classic guitar riff from "Spirit in the Sky" on "Tasso Gumbo." That might sound too off-the-wall for Cajun purists, but for the general listeners that means that this is a far more diverse, and hence more enjoyable, Cajun anthology than most. *—Richie Unterberger*

Warren Storm

Vocals, Drums / Swamp Blues, Zydeco
Swamp-pop pioneer Warren Storm was born Warren Schexnider in Abbeville, LA on February 18, 1937; after beginning his professional career began at age 12 while filling in for his father, a drummer in the Cajun band Rayne-Bo Ramblers, three years later he signed on with the country group Larry Brasso's Rhythm-aires, followed by a stint with the Herb Landry Band. In addition to later fronting his own combo, the We-Wows, Storm became one of the top session drummers in southern Louisiana before making his solo debut in 1958 with the single "The Prisoner's Song"; the record went on to sell a quarter of a million copies, its fusion of R&B, country, Cajun and Creole sounds pointing the way for the emergence of the south Louisiana swamp-pop aesthetic. In 1962 Storm teamed with fellow regional legends Rod Bernard and Skip Stewart to form the Shondells, and in the decades to follow he released a series of singles for local labels like Nasco, Rocko and Zynn, among them "Lord I Need Somebody Bad Tonight" and "My House of Memories." With saxophonist Willie "Tee," he formed the group Cypress in 1980—although the band dissolved four years later, the duo continued collaborating until 1994. Storm's solo albums include 1977's *Boppin' Tonight*, 1992's *Night After Night*, and 1999's *Live and In the Studio*. *—Jason Ankeny*

King of the Dance Halls / Mar. 7, 2000 / Edsel ✦✦✦✦
Warren Storm has been singing or playing on Louisiana swamp pop, rock, and blues records since his 1950s tenure at Excello Records, but these sides come from his '70s tenure with Huey Meaux's Crazy Cajun label. Storm is still working in his Fats Domino bag on several of these tunes, but as a cross-section of what swamp pop was going though when the music's popularity was at a low ebb. Solid material makes this another important chapter cataloged in the history of the music. *—Cub Koda*

Jude Taylor

b. 1949, Grand Coteau, LA
Vocals, Accordion / Zydeco
A zydeco performer in the blues-based tradition of Clifton Chenier, Creole singer and accordionist Jude Taylor was born in Grand Coteau, Louisiana in 1949. After growing up singing in church and school choirs, he later fronted a number of blues combos before turning to zydeco after receiving an accordion as a gift from his brother-in-law; assembling a backing band dubbed the Burning Flames which included his sons "Curly" on drums and Errol on rubboard, Taylor debuted in 1994 with the LP *The Best of Zydeco*. *Zydeco Bayou!* followed in 1997. *—Jason Ankeny*

● **The Best of Zydeco** / Dec. 14, 1994 / Mardis Gras ✦✦✦✦✦
The title of *The Best of Zydeco* makes it sound like a greatest-hits collection, but the record is actully Jude Taylor's debut effort. The accordionist has assembled a great band—including his sons Curly (drums) and Errol (rubboard)—and leads them through rollicking zydeco and steamy slow blues. Occasionally, he flirts with soul and blues, such as on a cover of Clarence Carter's "Strokin'," but Taylor is at his best when he sticks to classic zydeco sounds. The inclusion of these storming, party-oriented tracks is how *The Best of Zydeco* nearly lives up to its name. *—Thom Owens*

Zydeco Bayou / Jun. 3, 1997 / Mardis Gras ✦✦✦

Waylon Thibodeaux

Vocals, Fiddle / Zydeco
Cajun fiddler Waylon Thibodeaux was born and raised in Louisiana's Bayou Country, where he began playing music at the age of eight. At 16, he was named the state's fiddle champion, his live performances going on to become an institution of New Orleans' Bourbon Street area. Thibodeaux earned his first wide exposure when he landed three tracks on the 1995 compilation *Margaritaville Café New Orleans—Late Night Gumbo;* for Mardi Gras Records. Other albums include 1993's *Cajun Festival* and 1995's *Like a Real Cajun*. Subsequent efforts include *In Jackson Square* and *Tu Me Fais Crier*. *—Jason Ankeny*

Dans La Louisiane / Jun. 3, 1996 / W.G. ✦✦✦✦✦
The amazing thing to me is that the gorgeous full sound captured on this disc is done a 4 track deck! This is Cajun dance music at its best, and it goes to show that you don't need a full band to get the dance floor hopping. The fullness of the sound is amazing, considering that this was recorded on a four-track, not a state-of-the-art 24-track recorder. The one thing missing here is a lot of the information about who does what and, very important to some, who wrote which songs. Waylon Thibodeaux does most of the leads here, and Gina is credited with the lead guitar work—as well as supplying the tasteful leads, she also supplies a lot of the underlying dance rhythms. The vocals are handled with more than usual grace by this duo. Both have a long pedigree, hers perhaps a bit more diverse, as she has a good name as a singer-songwriter on the folk circuit, but they just get down and have a grand old good time here; it will leave you with a smile on your face wishing to hear more. *—Bob Gottlieb*

Lawrence Walker

b. Sep. 1, 1907, Nr. Duson, LA, **d.** Aug. 15, 1968
Vocals, Accordion / Traditional Cajun, Zydeco
Lawrence Walker, the reigning king of accordion players during the 1950s, is still considered one of the all-time great Cajun performers. Born near Duson, Louisiana, Walker was the son of a prominent fiddler, who later moved the family to Orange, Texas. Lawrence and brother Elton, a fiddler, formed their first band in the early '20s and played Cajun and hillbilly songs. The Walker Brothers made their recording debut for Bluebird in 1929 with "La Breakdown la Louisiane" and "La Vie Malheureuse." Seven years later, he and his band won rave reviews and first place at the National Folk Festival in Dallas, Texas. Despite his notoriety as a musician, Walker made the bulk of his living as a rice farmer until after World War II, when he returned to Louisiana and played in clubs throughout southern Texas with his band the Wandering Aces. He next recorded in the early '50s and had success with such Cajun tunes as "Reno Waltz" and "Evangeline Waltz" for George Khoury's label. Walker had quite a following in his day, and was known as a perfectionist, running his band with an iron hand. Unlike other Cajun performers from his time, Walker wrote only original songs. He died of heart failure in 1968. *—Sandra Brennan*

A Legend at Last / Swallow ✦✦✦
The LP compilation *A Legend At Last* collects Lawrence Walker's finest singles for Khoury and Swallow Records, which were recorded in the '40s, '50s and '60s. It's an excellent, if brief, retrospective that shows why he was one of the most popular accordionists of his era. *—Thom Owens*

● **A Tribute to the Late Great** / La Louisianne ✦✦✦✦

Wild Tchoupitoulas

f. Louisiana
Group / New Orleans R&B, Zydeco, Creole
The Wild Tchoupitoulas—Spy Boy (Amos Landry), Trail Chief (Booker Washington), Big Chief Jolly (George Landry), Flag Boy (Carl Christmas), The Third Chief (Thomas Jackson),

and Second Chief (Norman Bell)—are a Mardi Gras ceremonial parade group and "Black Indian tribe" based in New Orleans. George Landry is an uncle to the Neville brothers. *The Wild Tchoupitoulas* is their only album. —*William Ruhlmann*

★ **The Wild Tchoupitoulas** / 1976 / Mango ✦✦✦✦✦
The Wild Tchoupitoulas—a group of Mardi Gras Indians headed by George "Big Chief Jolly" Landry—only released one album, but that one record caused a sensation upon its initial 1976 release. It was one of the first records of the album-rock generation that captured the heady gumbo of New Orleans R&B and funk. Landry may have fronted the Wild Tchoupitoulas, but the key to the record's success was his nephews, Charles and Cyril Neville, who headed the rhythm section. They drafted in their brothers, Art and Aaron, to harmonize, and thereby unwittingly gave birth to the band that became the Neville Brothers. Still, the fact that *The Wild Tchoupitoulas* ranks among the great New Orleans albums isn't because of the Nevillles themselves, but the way the Tchoupitoulas lock into an extraordinary hybrid that marries several indigenous New Orleans musics, with swampy, dirty funk taking its place in the forefront. There are only eight songs, and they are all strung together, as if they're variations on the same themes and rhythms. That's a compliment, by the way, since the organic, flowing groove is the key to the album's success. —*Stephen Thomas Erlewine*

Zydeco Force

f. Opelosuas, Louisiana
Group / Zydeco
Originally formed in the spirit of the rural, old-time zydeco style, over time the Opelousas, Louisiana-based group Zydeco Force began moving towards a funkier, more bass-driven sound reflecting a wide range of influences. Upon debuting in 1988, Zydeco Force comprised bandleader Bobby "Mann" Robinson, vocalist/accordionist Jeffery Broussard (the son of Lawtell Playboys frontman Delton Broussard), his brothers Hebert on rubboard and Shelton on guitar, and drummer Raymond Thomas. Quickly their propulsive sound caught on with dancehall audiences throughout Louisiana and East Texas, and in 1990 they released their self-titled debut LP, followed a year later by *The Sun's Going Down*. After issuing 1992's *Shaggy Dog Two-Step*, Zydeco Force returned in 1994 with *The Zydeco Push*, with the title track spawning a lambada-like dance craze among fans. *It's La-La Time* followed in 1995. —*Jason Ankeny*

● **Zydeco Push** / 1994 / Maison de Soul ✦✦✦✦
Zydeco Force are caught between trying to extend their popularity with pop covers and then verifying their credentials doing Clifton Chenier's "I'm On The Wonder" and Lightnin' Hopkins' "12-String Boogie." As a result, an air of confusion reigns, and they seldom sound either comfortable or creditable. —*Ron Wynn*

Zydeco Hounds

Group / Zydeco
Together since the early 90's, the Zydeco Hounds are always sought out when one is looking for some of the finest Cajun and Zydeco musical entertainment. Chris Belleau is a physiatrist (a specialist in physical therapy and rehabilitation) by day, at night you can find him cookin' up a storm with the Zydeco Hounds as their accordian player and lead vocalist. Some of the other instruments you might find him playing are the trombone, harmonica and piano. Another band member, Greg Ward, has the same occupation as a physiatrist. Greg Ward is the percussionist, playing the frottoir plus. Probably the band member that most people will be familiar with is the guest bass player, Joe Osborn. He is one of the most recorded bass players in the history of recorded music. He has played with America, The Carpenters, Neil Diamond, England Dan & John Ford Coley, The Fifth Dimension, Art Garfunkel, The Grass Roots, Mamas & Papas, Olivia Newton-John, Helen Reddy, Kenny Rogers, Simon & Garfunkel, Barbra Streisand and Three Dog Night. In 1999, being in semi-retirement, Joe Osborn had moved back to his hometown of Shreveport Louisiana. Two of his sons, David and Darren, appear on the 1997 release, *Shake It Don't Break It*. David Osborn plays the drums and Darren Osborn sits in on the piano and drums. Al Courouleau is the guitarist for the Zydeco Hounds. He was the staff guitarist at Studio in the Count in Bogalusa for many years. He has recorded with a lot of different artists including Gatemouth Brown, Luther Kent, and Johnny Winter. Richard Courtney is the drummer for the Zydeco Hounds. Some of the artists he has played drums for include Wayne Cochran, Z Z Hill, and John Connely. In their live shows and appearing on the album, *Shake It Don't Break It*, on the bass is Dave Ellis. He is a stockbroker by profession, but also considers being a musician a job because keeping a band tight is work. This is how the Zydeco Hounds describe their 1997 release, "This is a collection of Louisiana swamp music, La La, Zydeco and Cajun Rock and Roll, with a touch of New Orleans Rhythm and Blues. It is best appreciated while eating crawfish and sipping on your favorite festive beverage. Play it loud!" —*Larry Belanger*

Shake It Don't Break It / 1997 / Proud Dog ✦✦✦
The album features Joe Osborn on bass guitar, and what a feature it is. It all begins from the first track on the album, the title track and a cover of a Clifton Chennier tune; Joe uses some unconventional riffs that add a lot of depth to the tune. "Ya Ya" features Chris Belleau's trombone playing in action. "Bayou Pon Pon" a French Cajun classic with a beat that really rocks the house. Another song that has French lyrics and is sure to be a favorite, "Janine," is an original number that has a catchy melody with a very basic bass run that enhances the guitar work and vocals. "Lucille," another cover tune, showcases Richard Courtney's soulful lead vocals along with Al Coureleau's screaming lead guitar work and Chris Beleau's fantastic harmonica playing. "Bulldog" is a great bluesy, jazzed-up, rocking instrumental that features the entire Osborn entourage: Darren on piano, David on drums, and father Joe on guitar and bass. The horn work on this neat little gem is courtesy of Belleau, and it adds great color to the tune. The whole package wrapped up with a very tight strand makes for an interesting and entertaining audio adventure. With 16 tracks of mostly uptempo music, *Shake It Don't Break It* is sure to be a favorite album to throw down at the next party. Though not entirely a Cajun/zydeco compilation, it certainly deserves a spot in any Cajun lover's library and has enough variety to interest others, too. —*Larry Belanger*

Various Artists

☆ **Alligator Stomp, Vol. 1** / 1990 / Rhino ✦✦✦✦✦
Alligator Stomp is a stellar collection of zydeco, featuring stars and lesser-known musicians. The disc is filled with great, rollicking music—there simply isn't a weak moment on the disc and it provides an excellent introducion to one of America's most distinctive musics. —*Stephen Thomas Erlewine*

☆ **Alligator Stomp, Vol. 2** / 1991 / Rhino ✦✦✦✦✦
If you're exploring the pleasures of Louisiana's zydeco and Cajun music, one of the best starting points is Rhino's excellent Alligator Stomp series of the 1990s. Vol. 2's main flaw is its failure to list recording dates—even if Rhino couldn't find exact recording dates for all of its 18 songs, couldn't the label have at least given the years or approximate years— But the sound quality is fine, Mary Katherine Alden's liner notes are informative, and Rhino's selections are excellent. For high-energy zydeco, it's hard to go wrong with Queen Ida ("My Girl Josephine"), Buckwheat Zydeco ("Zydeco Boogaloo") or the late Clifton Chenier ("Choo Choo Ch-Boogie," "Mama Told Papa"). And for traditional Cajun music, listeners won't be disappointed by Iry LeJeune's "Evangeline Special," the Balfa Bros.' version of the familiar "Jolie Blond" or Jo-El Sonnier's hit remake of "Jambalaya," which was originally a hit for country legend Hank Williams, but has become a Cajun standard. Spanning the 1940s to the 1980s, this gem-laden CD shouldn't be missed. —*Alex Henderson*

☆ **Alligator Stomp, Vol. 3** / 1992 / Rhino ✦✦✦✦✦
The response to *Alligator Stomp*'s first two volumes was so favorable that in 1992, Rhino gave us Volume 3 of the fine series. Regrettably, the CD (which runs from the 1960s to the 1980s) doesn't list either exact or appropriate recording dates. But the sound quality, detailed essay by Chuck Taggart and choice of material aren't anything to complain about. The CD illustrates are the differences between zydeco and traditional Cajun music. While Eddie LeJeune's version of "La Valse de Pont D'Amour," the Savoy-Doucet Cajun Band's arrangement of "High Point Two-Step" and Lawrence "Black" Ardoin's interpretation of "You Used To Call Me" are examples of Cajun traditionalism, gems by Buckwheat Zydeco ("Hot Tamale Baby"), Clifton Chenier ("S'Mappel Fou") and his son C.J. Chenier ("My Baby Don't Wear No Shoes") show us exactly what zydeco is—Cajun music combined with R&B/soul, blues and Creole music. When French-speaking African-Americans with Creole heritage were influenced by French-speaking Cajun-Americans with Anglo-French heritage, the potent result was zydeco. And when one plays this disc, the richness of those cultures comes alive in a major way. —*Alex Henderson*

Arhoolie American Masters, Vol. 5: 15 Louisiana Zydeco Classics / Feb. 25, 1997 / Arhoolie ✦✦✦✦
This is a representative sampling from ten of Arhoolie's zydeco releases. The range is from upbeat, accordion party music to material that sounds very much like early R&B. Included are Clifton Chenier, Sam Brothers 5, John Delafose, Ambrose Sam, C.J. Chenier, Preston Frank, Canray Fontenot, Amede Ardoin, Lawrence "Black" Ardoin, Alphonse "Bois Sec" Ardoin, and Peter King and Lester Herbet . —*Tom Schulte*

Cajun & Zydeco Classics / Jun. 18, 1996 / Rhino ✦✦✦✦✦
Cajun & Zydeco Classics is an excellent budget-line sampler of some of the biggest names in contemporary cajun music, including Buckwheat Zydeco, Rockin' Sidney, Boozoo Chavis, Beausoleil, and Queen Ida. Although the disc is brief, there are no weak tracks on the compilation and it offers a terrific introduction to the musical genre. —*Stephen Thomas Erlewine*

Cajun Honky Tonk / 1995 / Arhoolie ✦✦✦✦
Drawn from the vaults of the Khoury's label and its Lyric Records subsidiary, the 26 sides here date from the late 1940's and early 1950's. This is some of the best documentation available of what was a thriving music scene, spawned by the absence of younger players during the mid-1940's (they were off fighting the war), leaving the field to older musicians, who played Cajun music and found an audience in local clubs and an outlet in these two labels. Nathan Abshire's 1949 hit "Pinegrove Blues" got the ball rolling, and all of the 26 sides here (including Abshire's "Crying Pinegrove Blues") were spawned from that beginning. The sides here, in addition to Abshire's "Crying Pinegrove Blues," include various waltzes, stomps and blues laments by the Texas Melody Boys, Harry Choates ("Valse de Lake Charles," "Jolie Blon's Gone"), Floyd LeBlanc, Elise Deshotel with Dewey Balfa (his first four records), Lawrence Walker (his five earliest sides), and Shuk Richard and Marie Falcon. The focus may be history, but sound is also astonishingly good, incidentally. —*Bruce Eder*

☆ **Cajun Music Anthology, Vol. 2: Raise Your Window** / Aug. 23, 1994 / Country Music Foundation ✦✦✦✦✦
All three of the Country Music Foundation's Cajun music anthologies are important, well-assembled overviews of early commercial recordings of the music, although the scope is limited to discs cut for Victor/Bluebird. *Vol. 2* has a few well-known names like the Falcon Trio, Hackberry Ramblers and Nathan Abshire, but is mostly devoted to efforts by artists that never became recognizable names outside of their region. This is mostly in the raw, accordion-dominated waltz-timed style typical of early Cajun recordings, but there are some surprising deviations along the way, like Arteleus Mistric's solo harmonica arrangement of "You Belong to Me" and Floyd Shreve's "Lonesome Blues" (which sounds closer to Jimmie Rodgers than early Cajun music). Happy Fats' "Joilie Schvr Rouge," as the latest of the tracks (from 1941), is graced by a steel guitar and looks forward to post-war country music. —*Richie Unterberger*

☆ **Cajun Music Anthology, Vol. 3: The Historic Victor Bluebird Sessions** / Aug. 23, 1994 / Country Music Foundation ✦✦✦✦✦
The third volume of the Country Music Foundation's anthologies of early Cajun music recorded for Victor and Bluebird focuses on string-band music from the late 1930s. The sides reflect a move within Cajun away from accordion-dominated arrangements into a more country-and-swing-influenced sound. For this reason it's probably more accessible and enjoyable to listeners with modern-day tastes than the earliest Cajun recordings are. The Hackberry Ramblers and Rayne-Bo Ramblers (sometimes led by Happy Fats) are especially well represented, snag-

ging six and eight cuts respectively; the influence of Bob Wills and other Texas bands is evident in the frequent whoops and cries, as well as the rhythms and fiddle riffs. *—Richie Unterberger*

Cajun Social Music / 1987 / Smithsonian/Folkways ✦✦✦✦✦
Recorded during the summer of 1975 at gumbos and fish fries throughout the southwestern Louisiana region, *Cajun Social Music* captures the traditional Cajun sound in its most natural setting; a kind of summit meeting between up-and-comers like Marc Savoy and Lurlin Lejeune and old masters Nathan Abshire and Allie Young, the 13-track collection contains stellar performances of both classic material and original songs, and is an ideal introduction for new listeners. *—Jason Ankeny*

Early American Cajun Music / Jan. 19, 1999 / Yazoo ✦✦✦✦
Featuring three Louisiana performers, Alcide "Blind Uncle" Gaspard, John Bertrand, and Delma Lachney, this Yazoo Records release digs deep into the Avoyelles County swamps and presents 24 shining examples of traditional Cajun folksongs. While excellent examples of field recordings, Early American Cajun Music is not for the faint of heart. These down-home, straight from the bayou songs are a far cry from the accordion driven party music now associated with zydeco, rather they creak and croak through the old bones of three French speaking vocalists and their brittle stringed instruments. The honesty and tradition imbued within each of the tracks is as deep as the Delta and the melodies wind around themselves hypnotically, even though their lazy vocal whine could rub some listeners the wrong way. *—Zac Johnson*

☆ **Louisiana Cajun, Vol. 2** / Rounder ✦✦✦✦✦
The second of two superb Cajun anthologies issued by Rounder in 1989 featured 13 more selections by vintage artists. Like its predecessor, the featured artists sang exclusively in French, performed waltzes, two-step tunes, quadrilles and traditional material with a country flavor, using primarily fiddle/accordion backing. The opening five cuts spotlighted vocalist and fiddler Canray Fontenot teaming with accordion player Alphonse "Bois Sec" Ardoin. The middle section blends a modern country flavoring and looser rhythmic style, with the final cuts by Adam and Cyprien Landreneau on vocals, fiddle and accordion are early indications of an evolving modernism and spirited Cajun sound emerging in the late '60s. All the songs on both anthologies were recorded by the Newport Folk Foundation during three field trips in the mid-'60s. *—Ron Wynn*

☆ **Louisiana Cajun Music From The Southwest Prairies, 1964-1967** / 1994 / Rounder ✦✦✦✦✦
This first of two 1989 Rounder anthologies spotlighting traditional Cajun music from the mid-'60s began with a great group, The Balfa Freres. This was among the finest and most intense of the founding Cajun bands, characterized by wonderful harmonizing, intense leads and great fiddle backing. Others on this anthology were Austin Pitre & The Evangeline Playboys, a hard-driving, upbeat unit, and the venerable Edius Nacquin, in his 70s when he cut the anthology's final four tracks and still an energetic, distinctive singer. The selections were recorded as part of several field sessions initiated by the Newport Folk Foundation from 1964 through 1967. *—Ron Wynn*

Zydeco Essentials / Aug. 24, 1999 / Hip-O ✦✦✦✦
The fittingly named *Zydeco Essentials* provides a good starting point for novices to this musical style, which fuses elements of creole—such as the accordion, harmonica and fiddle—with urban R&B. The collection includes songs from some of the most prominent zydeco artists, including Buckwheat Zydeco, Clifton Chenier, Zachary Richard, Beau Jocque, Boozoo Chavis and Queen Ida. *—Heather Phares*

The Zydeco: The Early Years / 1989 / Arhoolie ✦✦✦✦✦
This isn't necessarily the early years of zydeco itself, which had probably been around in several variations for decades prior to these tracks, which were mostly recorded in the early 1960s. This was still years before zydeco had anything like the level of international esteem it now enjoys, and Chris Strachwitz, who made most of the recordings, was among the first to recognize the form's importance. In comparison to the boisterous full sounds of zydeco stars of the '80s and '90s, this is fairly primitive-sounding; usually there's nothing more than accordion, vocals, and washboard, although drums are sometimes present. It could use more variety, frankly, but these are significant documents of how zydeco sounded when it was music for friends and house parties rather than records of House of Blues clubs, and the music—by artists including Albert Chevalier, Peter King, Willie Green, and Sidney Babineaux—does have a rough, unforced upbeat charm. As nice bonuses, there are also both sides of Clifton Chenier's 1954 debut single (which are far more R&B-influenced than the field recordings), and a 1949 jump blues-zydeco hybrid by Clarence Garlow, "Bon Ton Roulet." *—Richie Unterberger*

World Music

Any book with a single chapter on "world music" runs straight into a very basic problem. You can tell it like it really is, from the perspective of the proverbial "musical Martian," giving a balanced picture of styles (99% of which are totally unknown to Americans,) or you can wildly distort reality and produce something your public can relate to. The latter course is the only reasonable one in a book like this, but the result is a little like a supermarket with three shelves: "soup," "pretzels," and "everything else."

Even if you simply divide the world into The West and The Rest, ignoring the fact that a good deal of Western music ends up in the World category, we're looking at one chapter devoted to at least 85% of the world's music. Obscure stuff, of course—like Chinese music, which is relevant to a mere one-fifth of the world's population (a bit more than that, if you count the millions of overseas Chinese). Or Indian music, with not one but two major classical traditions, three "universal" religions, and many more regional ones. Latin America: 33 nations, two major languages, and styles that have transformed the whole rhythmic basis of popular music in the United States. And if international influence rather than numbers is the issue, there's Cuba: an island of 10.5 million people whose sounds beat the US out for enduring influence on other cultures.

Just as no chapter (and no book and no ten-volume series) can really offer more than a drop in the ocean of world music, there's no way I can pretend to sum things up in a few hundred words. Instead I've decided to point out a few hidden confusions and traps in the American (and therefore this chapter's) concept of the subject.

Much the most important of these is the very major difference between what I like to call "other people's music" and the intercultural experiments of Western musicians, whether it's Yehudi Menuhin playing with Ravi Shankar, Art Blakey playing with Solomon Ilori, or Annababoula mixing various Middle Eastern styles with various Western idioms. Though these mixes have recently come to be called "world beat," they're really Western styles with non-Western elements, just as willow-pattern Delft china was Dutch plates with Chinese motifs.

This would be a lot more obvious if almost every music in the world didn't stem from a mix of other music, very frequently from different cultures. There may be a couple of Amazonian nose-flute players and a didjeridu virtuoso in central Australia who was never influenced from outside, but that really isn't the way most music works, and the richest cultures are usually the most mixed (United States, Balkans, Latin America, India). On this level, pretty much all music is crossover music.

"Other people's music" is in fact most of the music that exists. This would be more obvious if the US weren't so large, so geographically isolated, and so musically deprived. I know somebody who did a survey of recordings on sale in an open-air market in Abidjan, the capital of Ivory Coast. There were local recordings. There were recordings from other African countries. There was soul. There was jazz. There was French pop. There were the Beatles. There was US country music (lots of it, though stressing Jim Reeves). There was New York salsa. There were several sorts of Cuban music. There was more, which I've forgotten. All of this in a stall next to a woman selling yams. I defy anybody to find an equivalent range of music in your average US mall.

We also tend to overestimate our influence on the rest of the world. So it comes as a bit of a surprise to learn that, while the rest of the world has consumed US music quite freely for the last half century, Cuba and Argentina have been overwhelmingly more influential internationally over the last 75 years or so. Over the long term, the powerhouse has been the Middle East, which gave both Asia and the West most of their musical instruments.

One reason for listening to "world music" is because it's most of the music there is. The second reason—and most important—is because it's enriching beyond belief. World beat can be nifty, but the real thing can strike like lightning—it can raise the hair on the nape of your neck. It wasn't some worldbeat recording (or Xavier Cugat) that really launched the Latin takeover in the US in 1930; it was a recording of "The Peanut Vendor" by a genuine Cuban band. And the same is true for individuals. I've known people whose entire lives have been changed by the revelation of Cuban or Indian music (or, in my case, calypso-and-blues-and-flamenco-and-Arabic music all at once).

So, welcome to "other people's music" in all its many-splendored glory. *—John Storm Roberts*

AFRICA

Angélique Kidjo

Vocals / Afro-Pop, Worldbeat, World Fusion

Afro-funk, reggae, samba, salsa, gospel, jazz, Zairean rumba, zouk and makossa are combined through the music of soulful, Benin-born and Paris-based, vocalist, Angelique Kidjo. Since the release of her self-produced, debut, solo album, *Pretty,* in 1988, Kidjo has been embraced by the international press. The *New York Times* hailed her for "growls and swoops that link African tradition to American soul music," while, *iMagazine* claimed, "There has rarely been an African diva of such wholesomeness and fertility to the power and intoxication of Angelique Kidjo."

Kidjo's albums have been strengthened by contributions from top-notch guest musicians and producers. *Parakou,* her first internationally-distributed album, featured jazz keyboardist Jasper Van't Hof, the leader of Pili Pili, a Holland-based Afro-jazz band with whom Kidjo had performed at the *Montreux Jazz Festival* in 1987. *Logozo,* recorded in Miami in 1991 and produced by Joe Galdo of the Miami Sound Machine, featured Branford Marsalis on saxophone. Marsalis later performed on Kidjo's album, *Oremi.* Released in, the album featrued Kidjo singing duets with Cassandra Wilson ("Never Know") and Kelly Price ("Open Your Eyes"). Kidjo's most ambitious album, *Fifa,* featured more than one hundred percussionists, flautists, cowbell and berimbau players, singers and dancers from Benin and one track featuring Carlos Santana. Kidjo's husband, Jean Hebrail, a French bass player and composer she met in 1987, has played a major role in the recording of her albums.

The daughter of an actress, dancer and theatrical producer, Kidjo was born in Quidah, a coastal city in the West African country of Benin. Inheriting her mother's love of performing, she made her stage debut with her mother's theatrical troupe.

Inspired by the rock, pop and soul music of Jimi Hendrix, Santana, Miriam Makeba, James Brown and Aretha Franklin, she was singing professional by her twentieth birthday. Although she recorded an album, *Pretty,* produced by Cameroun-based vocalist Ekambi Brilliant, that yielded a hit single, "Ninive," the oppressive political environment of Benin led her to relocate to Paris in 1980.

Although modern technology and electronics played an important role in the recording of her first four albums, *Kidjo* returned to her traditional roots with *Fifa.* Armed with eight track tape recorders and microphones, Kidjo and a team of engineers traveled to Benin to record traditional musicians, singers and dancers. The album was completed during recording sessions in Paris, London, Los Angeles and San Francisco.

With her next album, *Oremi,* Kidjo returned to her futuristic approach. Incorporating elements of hip hop and Afro-Celtic grooves, *Oremi* featured a reconstructed interpretation of Jimi Hendrix's "Voodoo Child (Slight Return)." Kidjo explained her refusal to be limited to her native music in an article featured in *World Music: The Rough Guide.* "I won't do my music different to please some people. I'm not going to play traditional drums and dress like bush people. I don't tell Americans to play country music."

Kidjo's enthusiastic presence was evident on the video of her international hit, "Agolo," from her album, *Aye.* Produced by Will Mowatt of Soul II Soul and long-time Prince collaborator David Z, the video was nominated for a Grammy award. Kidjo's songs have been featured on the soundtracks of such films as *My Favorite Season, Street Fighter* and *Ace Ventura: When Nature Calls. —Craig Harris*

● **Logozo** / 1991 / Mango ✦✦✦✦✦

State-of-the-art production and mainstreamed African dance beats are poised to propel this talented singer from Benin to international pop stardom. Branford Marsalis, Ray Lema, and Manu Dibango contribute. *—Bob Tarte*

Aye / 1994 / Mango ✦✦✦

Angelique Kidjo has alienated some musicians and fans who want her to do traditional African music rather than mix and match her slashing delivery with rock, R&B and pop elements and arrangements. But Kidjo doesn't want to do a strictly African date. She recorded five numbers at Paisley Park studios, and they reflect the punchy guitar and synth-dominated Minneapolis sound. The other five tunes were recorded in London, with both a dance-soul flavor and nice horn backing and arrangements. Kidjo hasn't done a sellout album, despite singing in English on some cuts (another move designed to anger some of the hardcore). Rather, she's trying to link all her interests and do a respectable pop effort with some African elements. *—Ron Wynn*

Zap Mama

f. 1990

Group / Acappella, Worldbeat, World Fusion

Zap Mama is an all-female a cappella quintet founded by Zaire native Marie Daulne. Daulne's father, a white Belgian, was killed during the revolution of 1960 while her mother was pregnant with her, so the remainder of the family fled to the forests and found refuge with a tribe of pygmies. Daulne was raised primarily in Europe, but when she heard a recording of traditional pygmy music at age 20, she decided to return to Africa to learn about her heritage. She was trained in pygmy onomatopoeic vocal techniques before returning to the West to found Zap Mama. Her group blends world music styles from all over the globe with little, if any, instrumental or percussive backup other than what group members can do with their voices and bodies. Their 1993 debut, *Adventures in Afropea I,* became the biggest-selling non-compilation album in the history of Luaka Bop Records, helped in part by an opening slot on that summer's 10, 000 Maniacs tour. A year later, they released a follow-up, *Sabsylma; 7* followed in 1997. *A Ma Zone* appeared in 1999. *—Steve Huey*

● **Adventures in Afropea, Vol. 1** / 1993 / Warner Brothers ♦♦♦♦♦
Warner Brothers presents this exciting, innovative, dynamic group of five women from Brussels. They are new to the States, but already extremely well-received in Europe. Led by Marie Daulne, they weave their polyphonic, polyrhythmic harmonies displaying the strength and brilliance of unaccompanied voices. The songs, inspired by traditional African and European melodies, celebrate the richness and diversity of these cultures. The album incorporates Central African Pygmy chants and their unique yodels and clicks, the ululating sounds of a Syrian harem, anti-apartheid chants, as well as songs from Zaire, Tanzania, France and Spain... *—MusD*

Sabsylma / 1994 / Luaka Bop ♦♦♦♦♦
On their second release, *Sabsylma,* the all-female band Zap Mama offers more of their original sound—a cappella vocals joined by exotic and worldly rhythms. Although they've been compared to Bobby McFerrin in the past, there is really no one out there today who sounds the way Zap Mama does. By bridging the tribal sounds of Africa with more conventional music, Zap Mama is ideal for music fans curious about giving world music a listen. The album kicks off with "Furahi," a group chant/sing-along, which eventually leads into gentle music and perfectly blended vocalizations. The title track shows how the quintet can (amazingly) use their voices as rhythmic/percussive instruments, with almost all the beats being sung rather than played. But the best and most interesting track has to be "India." The group follows a male Indian singer at the beginning in a call-and-chant setup, but it's not long before the group takes over the song themselves, proving that they can masterfully handle just about any style of foreign music. Recommended to fans of great vocal work, regardless of genre. *—Greg Prato*

7 / Feb. 25, 1997 / Warner Brothers ♦♦♦♦

A Ma Zone / Oct. 19, 1999 / Narada ♦♦♦♦
Zap Mama's last album was the first one to incorporate instrumental sounds into the group's six-voice a cappella mix; it was also the first to include male voices. On *A Ma Zone,* group leader Marie Daulne has expanded the exploration of American R&B and hip-hop that she began with *Seven.* Breakbeats, jazzy upright bass, and turntable manipulation are now a part of the mix—a mix that was already rich with European and West African influences. "Gissie" draws most deeply on Daulne's Central African Pygmy roots, with its call-and-response structure and her unearthly yodeling; "Rafiki," which opens the album, is a collaboration with Black Thought (of the Roots) that segues beautifully into "W'Happy Mama," on which Daulne shows off her own speed-rap flow (in French, of course). "'Allo 'Allo" and "Call Waiting" both hint at her ongoing obsession with the telephone, an instrument that she seems to find mildly repellent but can't seem to ignore. Everything on this album is both complex and immediately accessible, simultaneously deeply funky and sweetly gentle. Very highly recommended. *—Rick Anderson*

Africa Collection

Adventures in Afropea 3: Telling Stories to the Sea / Nov. 1995 / Luaka Bop ♦♦♦♦♦
Adventures In Afropea 3: Telling Stories to the Sea, is one of the first and most comprehensive anthologies of Afro-Portuguese out there. The music hails from Lisbon, Angola, São Tomé, and the Cape Verde islands, all fantastically represent here. Afropea may be the most soulful foreign music, as you can hear a variety of other heartfelt popular musical styles within its confines (blues, sambas, and rumbas, to name a few). Only the genre's very best artists are represented here, making it essential for newcomers. Bongo (aka Barceló de Carvalho) is possibly the most famous, and supplies the album's best track, "Mona Ki Ngi Xica." Originally released back in 1972, the track actually got Bongo arrested for its rebellious (for the time) lyrics, which is surprising since it's a lovely acoustic ballad. Another highlight is 60-year-old singer Césaria Évora, who contributes the song "Sobade." With a similar acoustic sound to Bongo's track, $Évora possesses a ravishing voice, singing in a sad tone. A superb compilation compiled by David Byrne himself. *—Greg Prato*

African Heartbeat: The Essential African Music Collection / Apr. 21, 1998 / Shanachie ♦♦♦♦

Anthology of World Music: Africa—*The Dan / Feb. 10, 1998 / Rounder* ♦♦♦♦♦
Another volume in Rounder's reissuance of Alain Danielou's vision, the Anthology of World Music: Africa—The Dan covers the music of a tribe that occupies territory in both the Cote d'Ivoire and Liberia. For the most part, the music is highly energetic, and the selections (originally recorded by ethnomusicology legend Hugo Zemp) show the way in which music is a part of every part of life for this tribe (and indeed for most of Africa). From sowing to harvesting, from music for chieftains to music for little girls, every aspect of life is enhanced by music for the people of the Dan. The festival musics are exceptional, and the demonstration of drum rhythms (with the lead drummer actually from a different tribe) would put other drummers to shame. Luckily, there is a short example of the sanza, that African-encompassing instrument. Other highlights include the trumpet orchestra, where six trumpeters use side-blown ivory trumpets, used for speech surrogation as well as music, and the mask race music, which is fuller of excitement than most rock concerts, with more complicated rhythms and interlocking vocals than you could shake a stick at. As is the case with most of the recordings from this Rounder set, the music is good both in an ethnographic studies sense as well as in a purely musical enjoyment sense. Buy it whether you like African music or not. *—Adam Greenberg*

☆ **Echoes of the Forest: Music of the Central African Pygmies** / 1995 / Ellipsis Arts ♦♦♦♦♦
Currently the definitive release of pygmy music, this CD brings together outstanding recordings by three men who have written most of what we know about the people of the forest: Colin Turnbull, Jean-Pierre Hallet, and Louis Sarno. By offering three distinct, intimate portraits of pygmy bands in northeast Zaire (Turnbull and Hallet) and the western Congo basin (Sarno), this album conveys the uniqueness and breadth of pygmy singing better than any other. Like other releases in Ellipsis Arts' *Musical Expeditions* series, it's packaged in a beautifully designed CD-sized 64-page clothbound book that includes high-quality photos and substantial commentary by the three ethnographers. Some of Turnbull's contributions are duplicated on the Lyrichord collection, but this is well-rounded sampling of his recordings of the Mbuti pygmies, including the extraordinary "Girl's Echo Song" in which entrancing fragments of dense harmony break off suddenly as the singers listen for an echo. Hallet's recordings, previously unreleased, include excellent examples of Efe violin, flute, and thumb piano playing. (A portion of the sale of each CD goes to his charitable foundation, The Pygmy Fund.) Sarno's tapes capture a darker, more intense side of pygmy life exemplified by mangissa and ejengi, secret BaBenzele rituals of exorcism and possession. For a straightforward introduction to pygmy music, culture, and life, there's no better option. *—Ted Greenwald*

The Rhythm Safari: The Best of World Music / 1991 / Rhythm Safari ♦♦♦
Rhythm Safari: The Best of World Music is a budget-priced, 11-track collection that concentrates on African music, but it does toss in some Mediterranean, Spanish and Indian music for good measure. It's a good sampler, especially since it is faithful to the PC tastes of collegiate worldbeat fans of the early '90s, containing numbers from such well-known artists as Johnny Clegg, Gipsy Kings, Ladysmith Black Mambazo, Bhundu Boys and Youssou N'Dour. *—Stephen Thomas Erlewine*

Safarini (In Transit): Music of African Immigrants / Nov. 25, 2000 / Smithsonian/Folkways ♦♦♦♦
This 12-song, 67-minute compilation is devoted to the music of African musicians who have immigrated from their homelands to the United States. Specifically, it's devoted to African musicians who have settled in Seattle, WA, and Portland, OR, with five acts—Wawali Bonane with Yoka Nzenze, Frank Ulwenya & Afrisound, Lora Chiorah-Dye & Sukutai, Kofi Anang, and Obo Addy (the best-known artist of the group)—contributing two or three songs apiece. Although the experience of African musicians establishing themselves in America is a nominal theme of this collection, there's little influence to be heard from American music. In fact, if you told people that these songs had been recorded in Africa by musicians who never left the continent, very few would be surprised. The musicians represent styles from various African regions: Zimbabwe, Kenya, the Republic of the Congo, and Ghana. The Afropop contributions of Bonane, Ulwenya, and Addy are competent and well recorded, though they don't really stand out—in terms of either style or quality—from typical, late 20th century Afropop. Care is taken, however, to represent some diversity within these performers' repertoires: One of Addy's tracks is a solo piece of voice and percussion, and one of Ulwenya's features only his voice and guitar. Chiorah-Dye & Sukutai play rhythmic music built around multiple marimba, mbira, and vocal parts, while Anang mixes xylophone and environmental sounds on "Ko (Forest)," and plays kalimba in collaboration with didgeridoo and flute players on "Hail." *—Richie Unterberger*

Sahara: Music of Gourara / Auvidis/UNESCO ♦♦♦
Gourara, an area of oases, was once prosperous and wealthy, and though some of its music is common to the whole Sahara, some of the most ancient reflects a strong cultural individuality. There's a wide range of music here, some religious, some secular, but mostly reflecting a classic sacred/secular unity-in-duality. The singing is mostly choral with a strong solo lead, and much of it is underpinned with percussion, but there's also some fine reed flute and spike fiddle. *—John Storm Roberts*

Secret Museum of Mankind: Music of North Africa, 1925-1948 / Feb. 18, 1997 / Yazoo ♦♦♦♦
Music of North Africa from *The Secret Museum of Mankind* is a compilation of 24 songs and instrumental pieces from the Maghreb (the region of North Africa that is west of Egypt). All of the tracks, originally recorded during the first half of the 20th century, were initially circulated on fragile wax cylinders or brittle 78s. These crackling recordings have since been mastered and transferred onto CD by the staff at the Secret Museum. Particular cultural regions represented on this CD include Tunisia, Morocco, Algeria, Libya, Sudan, and Timbuktu. If all you've ever heard from North Africa are Moroccan talents—such as Hassan Hakmoun and the Master Musicians of Jajouka—then check out this wonderfully eclectic and inspiring collection of North African "roots" music. *—John Vallier*

Secret Museum of Mankind: Music of East Africa, 1925-1948 / Apr. 21, 1998 / Yazoo ♦♦♦♦
If anyone is operating under the misconception that the all traditional African music is and has been characterized by drumming ensembles, they should listen to *Music of East Africa* from The Secret Museum of Mankind: Music of East Africa, 1925-1948. Though there are plenty of excellent drummers and percussionists grooving on this CD's 25 tracks, much of these songs emphasize solo and choral vocals, harmony, melody, and such stringed instruments as African lyres, harps, and lutes. Though the majority of the cuts are from Kenya, a number of cuts from such East African countries as Uganda, Sudan, Ethiopia, Somalia, and Mozambique are also presented. Extensive liner notes, complete with photographs and an illustration, help listeners navigate their way through the CD's diverse musical tracks. *—John Vallier*

Algeria

Cheb Khaled (Khaled Hadj Brahim)

b. 1960, Sidi-El-Houri, Algeria
Vocals / Rai, Africa, Algeria
Affectionately known as "the King Of Rai," Cheb Khaled (born: Khalidu Hajji Brahim) has been the guiding force in the evolution, the popular youth-oriented music of Algeria. Khaled (who dropped the "Cheb," translated as "kid," from his stage name in the mid-1990s) has continued to expand on the lyrically outspoken rai style of music despite the disapproval of militant Islamics and self-imposed exile in Paris.

Learning to play the guitar, bass, accordion and harmonica as a child, Khaled released his debut recording, *La Route De Lycee*, at the age of fourteen. Leaving home and forming a band, The Five Stars, he began performing at local parties, weddings and clubs.

After releasing several self-produced cassettes, Khaled became involved with pop-minded record producer, Rachid Baba Ahmed. Under Ahmed's influence, Khaled's recordings increasingly incorporated western influences and instruments including synthesizers and electric guitars.

Khaled experienced great resistance towards his music, which often incorporated anti-fundamentalist lyrics and spoke candidly about romance. Until 1983, his recordings were censored by the Algerian government. Khaled was not the only harrassed rai performer. Cheb Hasni, known as "The prince of rai" was one of several rai artists murdered. Fearing for his own life, Khaled moved to Paris in 1990.

Khaled's first Paris-recorded album became an international hit and yielded a hit single, "Didi." Although his next albums were less successful, he rebounded, in 1996, with a major hit, "Aicha," from his Don Was co-produced album, *Sahra*. *—Craig Harris*

● **Kutche** / 1989 / Stern's ✦✦✦✦✦
Though its heart-of-hearts is in the right place, even the best Algerian rai usually suffers from a less than state-of-the-art synthesizer sound. Not so here. Collaboration between Paris-based keyboard-whiz Safy Boutella and one of rai's most powerful voices sets tough standards for other discs. *—Bob Tarte*

N'ssi N'ssi / 1993 / Cohiba ✦✦✦

Kenza / Apr. 4, 2000 / Ark 21 ✦✦✦

Cheb Mami

Vocals, Keyboards, Accordion / Rai, Africa, Algeria
The traditional music of Algeria is combined with Spanish, Moroccan, French and Arabic influences to create the dance-inspiring sounds of "The Prince Of Rai," Cheb Mami (born: Khelifati Mohamed). Cheb Mami's music was described, in a press release from the ARK 21 record label, as "Arabic rock and roll retaining virtues of traditional music but infused with urban urgency." Reviewing his 1999 album, *Meli Meli*, *CMJ New Music Report* wrote, "As perhaps rai's most popular vocalist, Cheb Mami is one of the leaders of the pack, turning the genre into a futuristic dance/funk hybrid with the power to pack the dance floors of North Africa, Paris and New York."

A native of Saida, a small village in southwest Algeria, Cheb Mami has been attracting attention with his soulful singing since his early teens. In 1971, he placed second in a talent contest organized by Ihan Wa Chabab.

Despite recording several successful cassettes in the 1980s, he made little money from their sale. Frustrated by the music industry in his homeland, he soon began to consider alternatives. Although he served a stint in the Algerian military, he relocated to Paris, France following his discharge in 1975.

With the release of his first internationally-distributed album, *The Prince Of Rai*, in 1989, Cheb Mami reached the upper echelon of rai music. Cheb Mami has continued to take the rai tradition to new heights. *Meli Meli* featured a song, "Parisian Du Nord," performed with rap singer K-Mel of Alliance Ethnique and a remix of the title track, which featured help from Gordon Cyrus (Neneh Cherry, Massive Attack) and Soul II Soul's Simon Law. *—Craig Harris*

● **Let Me Rai** / 1990 / Rhythm Safari ✦✦✦✦✦
In the 1980s and '90s, much of Algeria's rai music made extensive use of electronic instrumentation and Western elements. Cheb Mami's *Let Me Rai* is especially pop influenced. This inviting CD was recorded in Los Angeles, not Algeria, and the singer's music has an even stronger pop orientation than that of other Algerian rai stars. While "Maandi" has an overtly Middle Eastern groove, cuts like "Douha Alia," "Yo Yo," and the reggae-influenced "Let Me Cry" are essentially pop music sung mostly or entirely in Arabic. Quite often, Mami's harmonic sense recalls American pop and pop/rock of the early '60s. The John Coltrane-influenced jazzman Ben Clatworthy is employed on sax, though he doesn't stretch out or improvise. *—Alex Henderson*

Meli Meli / Apr. 27, 1999 / Ark 21 ✦✦✦✦
One of the finest records of the wildly-heralded "rai" movement, *Meli Meli* is a true vocal lovers record. Mani's voice is one of the most versatile and powerful in world-pop music today. His three-octave range is truly something to behold, and his use of it on such songs as "H'Rabti" and "Parisien Du Nord" and others will leave you breathless. Originally released to platinum success in France, *Meli Meli* is an awesome document that shows why Mani is one of the most respected middle-Eastern artists in existence today. *—Matthew Greenwald*

Algeria Collection

100% Rai, Vol. 1 / Jan. 11, 2000 / Sony ✦✦✦
100% Rai, Vol. 1 is a pretty decent introduction to the rebellious Algerian popular music, featuring contributions from rai legends Cheb Mami and Khaled (aka Cheb Khaled), plus French vocalist Alabina, Cheb Sahraoui, Cheb Kader, Cheb Amrou, Cheb Nasro, Cheb Hasni, Chaba Zahouania, Kamal El Oujidi, and Noria. *—Steve Huey*

☆ **Rai Rebels** / Jun. 29, 1992 / Earthworks ✦✦✦✦✦
Virgin's collection goes beyond the obvious rai heavies, though it includes Fadela's "N'sel Fik" yet again. Here is the great Chaba Zahouania and a particularly fine newcomer, Houari Benchenet, who gets a great deal of mileage out of mixing the older harmonium sound with his electronics—plus, natch, Sahraoui, Khaled, and Hamid. Adequate sound and rather ragged editing on this wonderful music. *—John Storm Roberts*

Burundi Collection

Burundi: Traditional Music (Burundi: Musiques Traditionnelles) / Ocora ✦✦✦
Part of Ocora's extensive traditional music lines, this album of music from Burundi attempts to present some of the salient examples of musical traditions in the old Kingdom. Some of the music is really quite amazing in the way that it can be both incredibly simple, but at the same time almost mesmerizing. The works on the album are really more of the form for an ethnomusicologist, in that many are simply a minute or two and exist solely to demonstrate a given technique or instrument, but for those ethnomusicologists, it will be quite worthwhile. There are demonstrations of native inanga zithers, ubuhuha vocal techniques, drum troupes, whispered singing techniques, musical bows, and ritualized greetings. Most aspects of the musical culture are represented in some fashion in the course of the album. For those with the patience to endure it, this album is very noteworthy, at least in its musicological values, if not for its aesthetics. *—Adam Greenberg*

☆ **Calypso Breakaway** / 1990 / Rounder ✦✦✦✦✦
This disc centers on some of the best Decca calypsos of the late '30s. Here are the songs and singers that sparked the calypso boom in the United States. They include Beginner, Lion, Radio, Invader, Caresser, Tiger, and Atilla. The notes are not very informative, but the transcriptions are good. *—Don Hill*

Cameroon

Manu Dibango

b. Feb. 10, 1934, Africa, Cameroon
Vocals, Saxophone, Keyboards, Percussion / African Jazz, Worldbeat, World Fusion, Cameroon, Africa
Dibango is Cameroon's, and perhaps Africa's, best-known jazz saxophonist. Starting in the 1950s, he became a globe-trotting musician, living and performing in France, Belgium, Jamaica, Zaire, and Cote d'Ivoire, as well as in Cameroon. In 1960, Dibango was one of the founding members of the Zairean band African Jazz, with whom he spent five years. World attention came to Dibango with the release in 1972 of *Soul Makossa*, a work that actually had precious little of the makossa sound in it, and scored later hits with *Seventies* and *Ibida*. Dibango's output has been prodigious and multi-faceted. He has worked with musicians as diverse as Fela Kuti and Sly Dunbar and Robbie Shakespeare, Don Cherry and the Fania All-Stars. In addition to being one of the leading jazz saxophonists of his generation, Dibango has also run nightclubs, directed orchestras, and started one of the first African musical journals. A recent release, *Polysonik*, featuring English rapper MC Mello, Cameroonian singer Charlotte M'Bango leading a choral section, and sampled pygmy flutes, shows that Dibango is continuing to flourish and expand in challenging new directions. *—Leon Jackson*

★ **Soul Makossa** / 1972 / Accord ✦✦✦✦✦

Afrovision / 1978 / Island ✦✦✦✦
Dibango displays his virtuosity on vocals, saxophone, percussions, and keyboards in a set that attempts to pick up commercially where *Soul Makossa* ended. Most recording artists releasing albums in the late '70s included a disco tune, and Dibango is no exception; "Big Blow," a mighty slab of African funk, is his contribution to the style. "Aloka Party" and "Bayam Sell'am" have the same driving force that propelled "Soul Makossa" up the charts. A favorite is the instrumental "Dakar Street" which is African fusion-jazz at its finest. The title cut "Afrovision" is the most unusual cut; the rhythms are different, complex, and indigenous to Dibango's West African roots. *—Andrew Hamilton*

Wakafrika / 1994 / Giant ✦✦

Cape Verde

Césaria Evora

Vocals / Morna, Fado, Worldbeat, Africa, Cape Verde
A native of the island nation of Cape Verde, Cesaria Evora is known as the country's foremost practitioner of the morna style, which is strongly associated with the islands and combines West African percussion with Portuguese fados, Brazilian modhinas, and British sea-chanteys. Evora began singing morna at age 16 after meeting an attractive young guitarist. Her talent soon had her performing all over the islands, and in the late '60s, two of her radio tapes were released as albums in the Netherlands and Portugal, respectively. However, Evora never left her country, and gave up singing in the mid-'70s owing to lack of profit. In 1985, at the age of 45, she decided to return to music and traveled to Portugal to record two songs for an anthology of female Cape Verdean singers. This led to subsequent recording sessions in Paris, which resulted in four albums from 1988 to 1992. Her international fame grew, and she toured Europe, Africa, Brazil, and Canada, with stops in the United States to perform for Cape Verdean audiences. In the fall of 1995, she mounted her first large-scale American tour; subsequent recordings include 1997's *Cabo Verde* and 1999's *Mar Azul* and *Cafe Atlantico*. *—Steve Huey*

● **Miss Perfumado** / Jun. 1992 / Melodie ✦✦✦✦✦
Ravishing is the word that springs to the lips: one of those tiresome British understatements, but it'll have to do. Evora has the most glorious voice, the melodies are heartrendingly Portuguese, the guitar-runs have escaped from a fado recording. The classic piano and string group of *Miss Perfumada* help explain its near-bestselling status, the near-Brazilian rhythms add the zip that tops the whole thing off. *—John Storm Roberts, Original Music*

Cafe Atlantico / Aug. 10, 1999 / RCA ✦✦✦

Congo/Zaire

Doctor Nico

Guitar, Africa, Congo/Zaire
Dr. Nico (Born: Nicolas Kasanda) was one of the guitar heroes of the music emanating from the Democratic Republic of the Congo during the early-1960s. Accompanied by his band, L'Africa Fiesta Sukisa, Dr. Nico sparked dancing in the region's youth with his firery playing.

According to influential soukous guitarist Diblo Dibala, Dr. Nico was "the school of Zairean guitar."

Launching his career while still a youngster, Dr. Nico initially attracted attention as a member of Joseph "Le Grand Kalle" Kabasele's band. His reputation continued to grow after forming his own group. Although he fell into obscurity in the late-1960s and '70s, Dr. Nico recorded his final tracks shirtly before he died in a Brussels hospital in 1985. *— Craig Harris*

1966/1968 / 1966-1968 / African Music ✦✦✦✦✦
Whatever any Zairian guitarist does (and therefore almost an African guitarist from anywhere), he is in some way echoing something created 20 years ago by the late Docteur Nico. A constant experimenter, Nico did for the guitar what Rochereau (his colleague in both African jazz and African fiesta) did for Congo music vocals, blending and reworking the idiom's Cuban and local strains into something brilliantly new. All these recordings, therefore, are basic to any soukous collection. The second listing here dates from around 1969, when the kiri-kire was hip but the rhumba still ruled. *— John Storm Roberts*

Grand Kalle & l'African Jazz

f. 1930, **db.** 1983
Group / Afro-Cuban Jazz, Africa, Congo/Zaire
Considered the father of modern Congolese/Zairean pop as well as the first Grand Master of Zairean music, Kalle was an enormously influential musician. He began his career by founding the seminal Afro-Cuban band African Jazz, the most popular early band on the scene, whose personnel at various times included guitarist Dr. Nico and Rochereau. In 1960, he established his own label, Surboum African Jazz, which was home to superstars OK Jazz. Kalle was responsible for striking deals with European labels to ensure high quality recordings of his bands' music throughout the Francophone market. *— Steve Huey*

1958-1960, Vol. 1 / Mar. 8, 1994 / Sonodisc ✦✦✦✦

● **1967/1968/1970** / Sonodisc ✦✦✦✦✦
Founder of the great Orch. African Jazz, discoverer of Nico and Rochereau, Kalle tried unsuccessfully for a comeback with this band featuring Cuban flutist Gonzalo. These highly individual recordings, which tilted the Congo sound back toward Cuba and in particular toward the classic Cuban flute-and-fiddle charanga, proved too oblique to their times to sell much. But they were and remain wonderful. *— John Storm Roberts, Original Music*

Kanda Bongo Man

b. 1955, Inongo, Zaire
Vocals, Guitar / Soukous, World Fusion, Africa, Congo/Zaire
Soukous, the dance music of Zaire, was updated by Paris-based vocalist and bandleader, Konda Bongo Man. With his high tenor vocals alternating between lyrics in Lingala and French, Bongo Man and his band, which has included influential guitarists Diblo Dibala in the 1980s and Rigo Star in the 1990s, has sparked dancing in audiences around the globe. *The New York Times* wrote "Zairean soukous is a lilting, riplling, dance groove that seems to smile from every register, with melody and rhythm inseperable. Kanda Bongo Man himself sings melodies that curl through the patterns like vines on a trellis." *Option* magazine took a similar view, writing, "Kanda Bongo Man sure knows how to have fun. This is some of the most joyous music I've ever heard, heavy on both melody and rhythm."

While rooted in the soukous tradition, Bongo Man has incorporated an eclectic range of influences. M. Doughty of alt-rock band, Soul Coughing explained, "You can infer all sorts of stuff in that loping beat and those guitars soaked in digital delay: flamenco, surf music, the wacked-out chops of a master oud player, steel guitar of the Hawaiian and Nashvillian varieties. The combined effect feels something like a distillation of sunshine and spring's bloom.rhythm."

The son and grandson of drummer/percussionists, Bongo Man left school to perform with a Kinshasa band in 1973. Three years later, Orchestre Bella Mambo, one of Zaire's most popular dance bands.

Moving to Paris, in search of a larger audience, in 1979, Bongo Man worked in a window pane factory while building a solo career. His earliest success came with his album, *Iyole,* recorded with Orchestre Bella Mambo and Diblo in 1981.

Performing at *the WOMAD* in England in 1983, he reached the audience he had hoped to find. Releasing his first American-distributed album, *Kwassa Kwassa,* which combined tracks from two French releases—*Lela Lela* and *Sai*—in 1989, Bongo Man continued to expand his following with Zing Zang, dedicated to Soki Vangu and Soki Diazenza of Bella Bella, in 1991. Bongo Man's third U.S.-distributed album, *Soukous In Central Park,* released in 1993, captures the excitement of his live performances. With his 1998 album, *Welcome To South Africa Mr. Kanda Bongo Man,* Bongo Man emphasized the South African influences on his music. *— Craig Harris*

★ **Amour Fou** / 1988 / Hannibal ✦✦✦✦✦
In part because he believes in keeping his groups down to a reasonable sound, Kanda Bongo Man's recordings all have something of the feel of the great pre-soukous period of Zairian music. Fad-hounds will be interested, and many others relieved, to note further evidence that the disco-bomp that has recently shackled Zairian rhythm sections is on the way out. *— John Storm Roberts, Original Music*

Tabu Ley Rochereau (Tabu Pascal)

b. 1940, Bundundu, Zaire
Vocals / Soukous, Africa, Congo/Zaire
Tabu Ley Rochereau (born: Tabu Ley) is one of Africa's most influential vocalists and one of its most prolific songwriters. Since making his professional debut, in 1954, as a member of Joseph "Grand Kalle" Kabasele's band, African Jazz, Rochereau has written more than two thousand songs. Together with his band, Orchestre Afrisa International, which he formed in 1970, Rochereau has continued to play a major role in the shift from Congolese, Cuban and Caribbean rumba to faster-paced soukous. Describing the musical approach of Rochereau and Orchestre Afrisa International, Wired World.3: The Global Netcast (http://www.Hotwired.lycos.com wrote, the group's high-octane soukous continues to move audiences all over the world by weaving together elements of Zairean folk music such as the lokole (log drum), the soul and drive of R&B, Latin syncopation, digital percussion and synthesizers, silken harmonies and the crystalline guitar stylings of Tabu Ley's longtime collaborator Huit-Kilos Bimwela Nseka, into a sophisticatedly sensual, irresistibly danceable, true world music. While he received the honorary title of "Knight" from Senegal, Rochereau was named "Officer of the National Order" by the Republic of Chad. A member of the Bayanzi people of Zaire (Democratic Republic of the Congo), Rochereau first attracted attention when he won a singing contest at the Kinshasa Stadium. Recruited to sing lead for Africa Jazz, he remained with the group until 1963 when he, and guitarist Dr. Nico formed their own group, African Fiesta. Two years later, Rochereau and Dr. Nico split over artistic differences with Rochereau formring African Fiesta National also known as African Fiesta Flash. With Rochereau at the helm, the group became one of the most successful bands in African history, surpassing record sales of one million copies by 1970. Papa Wemba and Sam Mangwana were among the many influential African musicians that passed through the group. In the mid-1970s, African Fiesta National evolved into the larger group, Orchestre Afrisa International. Rochereau emigrated to the United States in the early-1990s. He continues to reside in southern California. *— Craig Harris*

Omana Wapi / 1976 / Shanachie ✦✦✦✦✦
Picked by the Village Voice's Robert Christgau as one of the greatest albums of the '80s, this historic collaboration teams Rochereau with Franco, Zaire's greatest singer and guitarist, for one of the few "super-sessions" worthy of the title. *— J. Poet*

● **Babeti Soukous** / 1989 / Plan 9/Caroline ✦✦✦✦✦
There is an infinity of projects more worthwhile than yet another recording by Zaire's most-recorded name. But this is a fine performance with touches probably never heard from Rochereau before, along with such felicities as his new focus on solo rather than ensemble horns. It's excellent, except for the silly DJ and "live recording" conceit. *— John Storm Roberts, Original Music*

Man from Kinshasa / 1991 / Shanachie ✦✦✦

Africa Worldwide: 35th Anniversary Album / 1996 / Rounder ✦✦✦✦✦

1964/5/6 / African Music ✦✦✦✦

Face ¿ Face / Out of Africa ✦✦✦✦✦
The remaining Old Lion of zoukous really has it down a little too pat at times, but there's still a lot of perhaps-too-mellow charm here, and Rochereau still sings like a butterfly, particularly in his duets with the beguiling Faya Tess. And lead guitarist Huit Kilos is one of the younger heavies-about-studio, which keeps things from blanding out. *— John Storm Roberts, Original Music*

Papa Wemba (Shungu Wembadia)

b. 1953, Kasai, Zaire
Vocals, Guitar / Soukous, Africa, Congo/Zaire
Stylish, suave, and singularly talented, Papa Wemba has become as much a fashion icon as a pop star. Wemba served his musical apprenticeship listening to Cuban dance music and, later on, to Otis Redding. He got his musical break with the ubiquitous ZLL before going on to pursue his own projects. Now based in Paris, Wemba looks toward Japan for both corporate support and clothes styles. An extremely articulate individual, Wemba eschews the soukous label, insisting that he is sui generis and simply performs to be danced to. In Wemba's music one finds no heavy funk/R&B overlays, no horns: at most some bluesy flashes in the scintillating guitar work. Just a sparkling, glittering interplay of guitars, drums and voices that doesn't let up. *— John Storm Roberts and Leon Jackson*

Le Voyageur / 1992 / Earthbeat! ✦✦✦✦✦
Since emerging in the 1970s, Papa Wemba has been a major figure in modern African pop. The Zairean native was never one to specialize in the traditional acoustic tribal music of Zaire—his lively and usually danceable music is definitely pop, and he has often incorporated elements of African-American soul, funk, and disco. One of the many Wemba albums worth owning, *Le Voyageur* illustrates his consistent nature and shows how charismatic and expressive a singer he can be. Listening to such inviting Afro-pop offerings as "Jamais Kolongo," "Ombella," and "Yoko," it's clear that Wemba's music was still very fresh sounding in the early '90s. R&B elements serve him especially well on "Matinda" and "Maria Valencia." Highly recommended. *— Alex Henderson*

Molokai / Jun. 2, 1998 / Caroline ✦✦✦✦

★ **L' Esclave** / Gitta ✦✦✦✦✦
This recording, a massive hit for a full six months when it first came out, testifies to a driving Zairian style that other big names have neglected in favor of more laidback sounds. *— John Storm Roberts*

Congo/Zaire Collection

Compact D'Afrique / 1986 / Globestyle ✦✦✦✦✦
If it's soukous that a listener is looking for, they need look no further than this album. The sheer amount of rippling guitar riffs on the album is astounding. There are actually songs from four pieces of Zaiko Langa Langa (one of the original Congolese new wave soukous bands): a collaboration of Papa Wemba and Mavuela on "Izia," ZLL offshoots the Choc Stars on "Lascar Pa Kapi," and original ZLL rhythm guitarist Teddy Sukami on "Le Bon Samaritain." The sound of the soukous new wave is a bit harder than the original soukous, and maybe a tiny bit edgier, but all of the songs on this album still smile from every note. The tiny quaver inherent to the guitar work of soukous fills every work from end to end, along with stunning vocals from the best in the genre—Papa Wemba, Kanda Bongo Man, and the more refined Aurlus Mabele. Though soukous can on occasion be an acquired taste, this al-

bum is the perfect starting point for those new to the genre, and a nice compilation for those that have known the style for years. *—Adam Greenberg*

Lightning over the River: The Congolese Soukous Guitar Sound / Apr. 20, 1999 / Music Club ✦✦✦
A joyful, irrepressible album, *Lightning Over the River* showcases the exuberant sounds of the Congolese soukous guitar. Many of the stars of this style are represented here, including Kanda Bongo Man on "Yesu Christo," Pepe Kalle and Popolipo with "Roger Milla" and Tabu Ley with "Ponce-Pilate." A fresh, spontaneous mix of swinging rhythms and expressive guitars, *Lightning Over the River* is filled with beautiful, danceable moments. *—Heather Phares*

Music of the Rain Forest Pygmies / 1961 / Lyrichord ✦✦✦✦✦
Although the bulk of Turnbull's pygmy recordings can be found on Smithsonian Folkways, the first half of this Lyrichord issue comprises his most musically satisfying material, which finds the Mbuti at a hypnotic peak. Like the original Folkways release, it's divided between pygmies and neighboring peoples. The non-pygmy cuts, unfortunately, are far less interesting—except for a rendition, by members of the Twa (not pygmies, but ancestrally related), of what is unmistakably "Clementine." Turnbull's liner notes indicate that this was sung in response to his request for "a really old song, one of the great religious songs of the past." *—Ted Greenwald*

On the Edge of the Ituri Forest: Northeastern Belgian Congo / Dec. 14, 1999 / Sharp Wood ✦✦✦✦✦
On the Edge of the Ituri Forest: Northeastern Belgian Congo, 26 selections from Hugh Tracey's numerous recordings of the Bundu, Mangbele, Nande, Mbuti, and Bira peoples are presented. Originally collected in 1952, these field recordings were made in villages located around the eastern and northeastern boundaries of the Congo, close to the edge of the immense Ituri rain forest. On this CD one can hear Pygmies playing on a variety instruments that were stored for them by the sedentary Nande, Budu musicians performing a party songs on conical drums covered with elephant ear drum heads, the sound of flute encased in a shriveled up pig's tail, and a Mangbele percussion ensemble's call for circumcision. Though Hugh Tracey's inclination to at times conduct the performers he was recording gives his work less ethnographic and ethnomusicological authority, his detailed documentation of the performances should win him commendation. The detailed booklet that accompanies the CD is liberally peppered with vivid descriptions, photos, and many names of the performers. Stunning performances of exceptional audio quality to be heard by many around the world. *—John Vallier*

Ethiopia

Mahmoud Ahmed

Vocals / World Fusion, Africa, Ethiopia
In Ethiopia the word is "eskeusta," which roughly translated means ecstasy, more specifically it is a shaking sensation that begins at one's shoulders, quivering down the spine and into the legs and feet. And of all of the great male vocalists that Ethiopia has produced (don't laugh, there have been quite a few) none are able to create eskeusta better than Mahmoud Ahmed.

For 30 years Mahmoud Ahmed has deftly combined the traditional Amharic music of Ethiopia (essentially a five-note scale that features jazz style singing offset by complex circular rhythm patters which gives the music a distinct Indian feel), with pop and jazz yielding some of the most adventurous, passionate, ear-opening, downright surrealistic sounds this side of the deepest, darkest, dub or the most out-there free jazz. In fact, until you've heard Ahmed's sweeping multi-octave voice in full workout, words hardly do it justice. As with the late great Nusrat Fateh Ali Khan, he simply has to be heard to be believed and appreciated.

Ahmed has been a star in Ethiopia almost since the day he began recording. His swooping vocals, complimented by the freewheeling jazziness of the Ibex Band (with whom he recorded his masterpiece *Ere Mela Mela*) is very different from what normally is lumped into the broad expression afro-pop. The rhythms are repetitive and intense, not too dissimilar from, say, Fela, just a little less hard. But it's Ahmed voice: swirling high notes that sound as if they're chasing one another, impeccable tone and phrasing that is the distinguishing element. By singing in this style Ahmed has attempted to fuse the past and present. He's not an elitist when it comes to singing older Ethiopian music but rather he hears the similarities in Ethiopian pop that have thrived over time and is keen to bring them together.

As the western critical attention to afro-pop centered on the music of sub-Saharan Africa, Ethiopian artists like Ahmed and Hirut Bekele, Ali Birra, and Alemayhu Eshete were less likely to receive coverage in the music press. Recently, younger performers such as Aster Aweke (who emigrated to the US in the mid-1980s), and Netsanet Mellesse have received more ink thus opening the doors for those so inclined to explore the music that influenced the. And for those so inclined that means becoming familiar with brilliant, demanding, but unknown artists such as Mahmoud Ahmed. *—John Dougan*

★ **Ere Mela Mela** / 1986 / Hannibal ✦✦✦✦✦
My pal and world music authority Will Hermes told me in no uncertain terms that I should purchase this record the moment I laid eyes on it. Trusting his judgment, I did just that, and it was one of the best buys I have ever made. Recorded over a three-year period from 1975-1978 (though much of it was recorded in 1975), this is Ahmed's crowning work, a record so sublime, passionate and demanding, that numerous plays only hint at its greatness. Despite the language barrier, it's hard to imagine that anyone with open ears can play this record and not get sucked into its glorious undertow of sound. The Ibex band (featuring the great sax duo of Fekade Amdemsekel and Theodorus Meteku) swings, wails, jumps, and jives, and Ahmed's voice is in excellent form. If you had to rate the best records to ever come out of Ethiopia, this would be on the short list, if not number one. *—John Dougan*

Ethiopiques, Vol. 6: Almaz / Aug. 10, 1999 / Buda Musique ✦✦✦

Ethiopiques, Vol. 7: Ere Mela Mela / Sep. 14, 1999 / Buda Musique ✦✦✦✦

African Music

There's no way to write coherently about the music of a continent covering 52 independent nations, between 800 and 1600 languages (depending on your definition), and at least five major cultural groupings. The confusions inherent in this kind of diversity are many, but a few stand out. Some of the confusion stems from the fact that African music has been both influential and influenced. The direct or indirect influence on new-world popular music has been varying, but all of it, "White," "Black," or "Latin," has at least a touch of Africa. And the compliment has been returned. African music has always been (and remains) essentially local, but African musicians have always drawn from elsewhere: for over a thousand years from Islam, for over a couple of hundred years from Europe, over half a century from the Americas, somewhat (and increasingly) from US African-American styles and reggae, greatly in the past from US country music, and enormously from Cuba and Latin New York.

More confusion results from the Western stereotype that associates drums with African traditional music. In reality, western Nigeria (for example) has a dozen or so 20th-century urban styles for voices and percussion alone, and at least one of these outshines in popularity all the Nigerian musicians known to the West.

There's another confusion of immediate importance to this listing of African recordings. Different circumstances have led to noticeably different levels of "Africanness" in contemporary pop styles. At the most "African" level, there's what happens when a whole culture falls in love with an overseas influence, as the Congolese did with Cuban music. Sophisticated individual bands sometimes develop styles with an abnormally high proportion of overseas influence (Fela Kuti, Manu Dibango). When expatriate musicians form bands to play the music of their homeland, as did Osibisa in London, they come under different influences and produce a different mix. Different yet again are groups combining expatriate African musicians with Europeans, like the Germano-Ghanaian "Burger-Highlife" bands in Germany. Lastly, famous musicians with a local or expatriate African audience (N'Dour, Ade, many others) have recently been trying to "cross over" internationally, with still different results.

All this tends to mislead newcomers to African music. At first, naturally enough, people tend to like music that's not too foreign, which means very American-influenced. So we latch onto individual musicians with a strong American element and assume, usually incorrectly, that Africans think as much of them as we do. The result is that Fela or Manu Dibango get described as "African superstar" when they are not by any means the superstars of their own countries and are pretty much unknown elsewhere in Africa. (In fact, the only musicians with a real pan-African appeal are the big names of soukous, and even they don't have any noticeable following in South Africa.)

All of which means that if you want to explore African music, albums by Fela or the recent big-label recordings of Youssou N'Dour make handy vehicles for starting the journey. But if that's as far as you go, you haven't even landed yet.

— John Storm Roberts

Alemayehu Eshete

b. 1947, **d.** 1969
Vocals, Africa, Ethiopia
Despite a 1948 Imperial edict banning the distribution of Ethiopian pop music, Amha Eshete launched a record label, Amha Records, and released 103 singles and a dozen albums by Ethiopian artists between 1969 and 1975. In addition to making Ethiopian music known throughout the world, Eshete helped to spark a modern period of creativity in his homeland. During an interview in the early-1990s, Eshete said, "I had a gut feeling that it was the right thing to do. I took the risk." The governmental resistance against Eshete's efforts proved ultimately insurmountable. By the mid-1990s, Eshete had emigrated to the United States. *—Craig Harris*

Addis Ababa / 1992 / Shanachie ✦✦✦✦

Ethiopia Collection

Ethiopia / 1994 / Topic ✦✦✦✦✦
Another outstanding regionally organized collection recorded by Jean Jenkins during the 1960s, drawn from three Tangent LPs covering the Central Highlands, the desert nomads and Eritrea respectively. In general terms, of course, it is somewhat similar to the Ocora set. In detail, the music is different, and arguably provides a better introduction if you're unfamiliar with Ethiopian traditional idioms. *—John Storm Roberts, Original Music*

Music from Ethiopia / Caprice ✦✦✦✦
A really nifty release, Caprice has combined two forms of urban music usually rigidly separated: professionally performed "traditional" music for krar, flute, voice, and Ethio-soul by electric groups that play the real local thing rather than the crossover material we're usually offered. The result is splendid: very varied and splendidly performed music and truth-in-classification. *—John Storm Roberts, Original Music*

Gambia

Foday Musa Suso

Kora, Kalimba, Vocals, Drums / Kora, Africa, Gambia
Foday Musa Suso is a master musician with one foot on the dance floor and one foot in the villages of Africa. Suso was born in Gambia to a distinguished family of griots (musician storytellers) that can trace their line back almost a thousand years. He has been tireless in his

efforts to spread African music and culture to all corners of the globe. On his solo recordings, and as a member of his Mandingo Griot Society, he plays traditional African folk music. On his Mandingo records he leads an electro funk fusion band that can rock the house with the best rap, funk, and house groups. He's played extensively with Herbie Hancock (that's his kora on "Rockit") and frequently collaborates with Bill Laswell on various Afro-fusion experiments. *—J. Poet*

The Dreamtime / 1969 / CMP ♦♦♦

• **Mandingo Griot Society** / Sep. 1979 / Flying Fish ♦♦♦♦♦
Musa Suso, a kora player from Gambia, joins a contemporary rhythm section for this African-flavored fusion music. *—AMG*

New World Power / 1981 / Axiom ♦♦♦♦♦
On this album Suso continues his Afro-funk experiments with Bill Laswell and other members of New York's Downtown Art-Rock Mafia. *—J. Poet*

Jali Kunda / Dec. 1996 / Ellipsis Arts ♦♦♦

Ghana

Obo Addy

b. 1936
Vocals, Drums, Percussion / Worldbeat, Africa, Ghana
The musical traditions of Ghana have been explored and extended by Ghana-born and Seattle-based drummer, composer and bandleader Obo Addy. Together with his world beat band, Kukrudu, and traditional quartet, Okropong, Addy continues to be one of Ghana's greatest musical ambassadors. A recipient of the prestigious national Heritage Fellowship Award by the National Endowment for the Arts, Addy has toured extensively through the United States, Europe, the Middle East and Australia. The son of a Wonche priest and medicine man, Addy was exposed, as a youngster, to the rituals and traditions of the Ga people of Ghana. This included the drumming, dancing and singing that accompanied his father's work. Addy has been playing music since earliest memory. Although he began by playing bells at village rituals, he soon switched to the drums. Joining Joe Kelly's Band, at the age of eighteen, Addy learned to play and sing western pop music in theaters, hotels and night clubs in the capitol city of Accra. A year later, he joined the Builder's Brigade Band. In 1961, Addy joined the Farmers Council of Ghana, an organization dedicated to educating farmers through drama, music and cinema. The same year, Addy was inspired to present concerts of traditional music. The show, Edzo, was debuted at Accra Stadium. In 1962, Addy became assistant leader of the Farmers Band and master drummer and leader of the group's traditional unit. He remained with the group until 1966. Leaving the Farmers Band, in 1966, Addy formed a band to perform popular music from around the globe at the Continental Hotel. Two years later, he accepted an invitation to join the Ghana Broadcasting Band. In 1969, Addy formed a band, Anasi Krumian Soundz, the group group to exclusively use traditional Ghanaian instruments including the giri (African xylophone), Atentenben (bamboo flute), Whi (whistle) and calabash (rattles). The group performed in clubs, theaters and embassies and worked for the American peace Corps and Canadian Voluntary Service. At the same time, Addy studied, taught and performed traditional music of the Ewe, Ashanti, Fanti, Dagomba, Nafana, Konkomba and Ga people at the Arts Council of Ghana. The experience provided an opportunity to begin fusing traditional and contemporary African music. After touring in Israel, in June, 1972, with other members of the Arts Council, Addy formed a band, Oboade ("Ancient"), with his brothers. Following a successful performance at the Olympic Games in Munich, Germany, Addy and Oboade began touring worldwide. The group made their U.S. debut in 1973 at the invitation of the Cultural Enrichment Program of Washington to perform in state schools and universities. Together with his brother, Yacub Addy, Addy moved to the United States in 1977 and formed a band, Ablade, with American musicians. Two years later, Addy began teaching private lessons and performed for six weeks in the Black Repertory Theater's production of "For Coloured Girls Who Have Considered Suicide When The Rainbow Is Enuf." Forming a new band, Kukrudu, in 1981, Addy and the band recorded two albums—"Obo" in 1983 and "Obo Addy/Kukrudu" in 1984. In 1986, Addy recorded a traditional solo album, "Born In The Tradition" and a contemporary album, "African-American." The traditional and contemporary sides of Addy's musical persona continued to be explored in 1987. While Kukrudu performed at the Saskatoon, Calgary and Edmonton jazz festivals, Addy also assembled a four-piece group, Okropong, to focus on traditional music and dance. In 1989, Addy developed a music and dance concert production that traced the history, culture and meaning of Highlife music in Ghana. Funded by the NEA, he toured with the production throughout California. Addy's composition, "Wawshisijay (Our Beginning)," was recorded by the Kronos Quartet and featured on their chart-topping 1992 album, *Pieces of Africa.* The same year, Addy's album, *Let Me Play My Drums,* which spent one month on the "Billboard World Music" chart. In 1994, Addy released a solo album, *The Rhythm Of Which A Chief walks Gracefully* and performed with the Charlestown Symphony String Quartet. The following year, he performed three new compositions with the Kronos String Quartet in Seattle. Addy has taught African song, dance and drumming in schools, including The Cornish Institute and Lewis And Clark College, and has done residencies at African-American Centers in North Carolina, the Sweetwater Art Center in Sewickley, Pennsylvania, Washington State University in Pullman, Washington and Williams College in Williamstown, Massachusetts. *—Craig Harris*

• **The Rhythm of Which a Chief Walks Gracefully** / 1994 / Earthbeat! ♦♦♦♦♦

Born in the Tradition / Earthbeat! ♦♦♦
With *Born in the Tradition,* master drummer Obo Addy serves up a tasty stew of traditional African music. Though a long-time resident of the United States, Addy was born into a family of drummers belonging to the Ga ethnic group of southern Ghana, and his versions of traditional Ga hand-drumming pieces like "Kpanlogo" and "Oge" are riveting. Most of the pieces featured on this album are really songs with drum accompaniment, and Addy carefully arranges each track so that the closely harmonized call-and-response vocals aren't drowned out by the powerful drumming that supports them. The material ranges quite widely, and includes several pieces that appear in traditional Ga religious ceremonies (like "Tigari," whose hypnotic rhythms are used to induce trance). Addy also presents strong renditions of several pieces that are more commonly associated with other ethnic groups in Ghana, thereby making this album a good introduction to traditional Ghanaian drumming in general. Most unusual, however, is the fact that Addy (through the magic of overdubbing) plays and sings just about every part heard on this recording. While this robs the album of the spontaneous energy that a group of strong individual players can generate in the heat of the moment, it does allow him to present nearly flawless versions of several core pieces in the repertoire. That sense of perfection slips only slightly on "Oshi," where Addy farms a flute solo out to a second player—and judging by the sound of things, he might have been better off handling that himself, too. *—Alexander Gelfand*

E.T. Mensah (Emmanuel Tetteh Mensah)

b. 1919, Ussher Town, Accra
Trumpet, Saxophone, Vocals / Highlife, Africa, Ghana
With the passing of trumpet player, saxophonist and vocalist Emmanuel Tettey 'E.T.' Mensah on July 19, 1996, at the age of 78, Ghana lost one of its most influential musicians. Respectfully known as 'the father of modern highlife,' Mensah played a vital role in the evolution of Ghana's music. In the early-1990s, Mensah recalled his revamping of highlife, explaining, "We urgently wanted an indigenous rhythm to replace the fading foreign music of waltz, rhumba, etc. We evolved a music type relying on basic African rhythms, a criss-cross African cultural sound."

A native of the small village of Ussher Town in Accra, Ghana, Mensah initially played fife in an elementary school band. Switching to trumpet and saxophone in his teens, he quickly attracted attention with his expressive playing. At the age of eighteen, he formed his first band, the Accra Rhythm Orchestra, a group comprised of five saxophones, guitar and African drums. Although he joined Scottish trumpet player Jack Leopard's band in 1940, he remained only a few months before accepting an invitation to become a charter member of a highlife band, the Tempos. He soon assumed leadership of the group. In contrast to early highlife groups, which were modeled after jazz big bands of the 1940s, the Tempos was one of the first to adapt highlife rhythms to a small ensemble approach. An essential element of the band's sound was Mensah's singing in a variety of indigenous Ghanaian languages.

Although the original line-up of Tempo disbanded in 1942, Mensah reorganized the group six years later. Mensah and the group toured successfully throughout Great Britain in 1953. Among their many hit singles were "Donkey Calypso," "School Girl" and "Sunday Mirror."

Trained as a pharmacist, Mensah occasionally worked in the field to supplement his income as a musician. Music, however, remained his prime focus. Mensah attracted global attention when he performed with Louis Armstrong during celebrations of Ghana's independence in 1957. Two years later, he composed a song to celebrate Queen Elizabeth's visit to Ghana.

Although he maintained a low profile in the early-1960s, Mensah began the first of several comebacks in 1969. Despite being confined to a wheelchair, he embarked on a world tour in 1986. In 1986, a biography of Mensah by musicologist John Collins, *E.T. Mensah: King Of Highlife* was published by *Off The Record Press* in London and *Ghana State Publishing Company* in Accra. *—Craig Harris*

• **All for You** / 1986 / Retroafric ♦♦♦♦♦
The first of two volumes of vintage E.T. Mensah material, *All for You* finds the master of Ghana's highlife music leading his Tempos Dance Band on 17 excellent cuts. The set include calypsos, sambas, and highlife numbers, culled from Mensah's most successful period during the '50s and '60s. Mensah doubles on trumpet and saxophone, leading his fine band of brass, saxophone, guitar, and percussion players through hits like "Donkey Calypso" and "Sunday Mirror" (this last number's reference to the London newspaper figures in with other imprints of British colonialism, namely the joys of drinking tea espoused on "Tea Samba"). While these and a few other cuts are sung in English, Mensah favors a variety of Ghanaian languages when at the microphone, including Twi, Fante, and Ga. Other song highlights include the topical "Inflation Calypso," breezy highlife cuts like "Odofo," the Caribbean traditional "John B. Calypso," and a handful of instrumentals; excellent saxophone and guitar solos abound, especially on the instrumentals. One of just a few Mensah compilations, *All for You* is essential listening for fans of West-African popular music. *—Stephen Cook*

Day By Day / 1987 / Retroafric ♦♦♦♦♦

Kenya Collection

☆ **Guitar Paradise of East Africa** / 1990 / Earthworks ♦♦♦♦♦
The "other" guitar sound of Africa is rootsier than soukous—with an emphasis on melody to match the propulsive rhythms—benga dance music from Kenya explodes in a sweet, energy-laden combination of fraternal vocal harmonies and chiming electric guitars. *—Bob Tarte*

Kenya & Tanzania: Witchcraft & Ritual Music / 1991 / Elektra/Nonesuch ♦♦♦
This album, an early portion of the Nonesuch Explorer Series, makes use of music from East Africa, primarily Kenya, with one track from Tanzania as well. Despite the title saying that witchcraft and ritual music is the focus here, there is little that would now be considered witchcraft-based, and for that manner, many of the pieces are of daily life and simple instrumental playing, without ritual involvement. Nonetheless, for its date, this is a relatively good recording, with a few tracks dealing with witch doctors attempting to heal patients (with accompaniment by drummers, dancers, and singers), a few wedding, funeral, and circumcision ceremonial songs, and various pieces of simple musical works—marimba playing (but of course, in the East African style that is so similar to mbira playing), bung'o (horn) playing, harp-accompanied vocal pieces, and the like. The quality of the music is relatively good, though there are now more authentic pieces on the market, of course. Still, despite tiny bits of forgivable cultural ignorance, the album is a worthwhile soundbite into Kenyan traditional music. *—Adam Greenberg*

The Nairobi Beat: Kenyan Pop Music Today / 1989 / Rounder ✦✦✦✦✦
This 10-song anthology showcases modern African music made in Kenya, but not dominated by local artists. Instead, Kenya served as a center for new and emerging acts in the 1980s who were merging Western musical influences with traditional African sounds, creating some exciting blends in the process. There's a bit of everything here, from flowing, mid-tempo works to rhumbas, rock-tinged pieces, rhythmically intricate offerings, jazz-based numbers, pop and lots of guitar-dominated tunes. One more in an impressive series of valuable ethnic music collections issued by Rounder. *—Ron Wynn*

Madagascar

Tarika Sammy

f. 1983
Group / International Folk, Worldbeat, Africa, Madagascar
Probably the most notable contemporary Malagasy group to achieve international exposure in the 1990s, Tarika Sammy update traditional and regional sounds of their country in invigorating ways. Dressed up in full-bodied arrangements without sounding slick, the group employ zithers and hand-drums in addition to more modern instruments. The songs also deal with contemporary concerns like drought, cattle rustlers with automatic weapons, and even Madagascar's national transportation system. For most listeners, the most appealing elements of the group's sound are the mellifluous vocals of the two sisters who sing much of Tarika Sammy's material.

Tarika Sammy was formed by Samoela Andriamalalaharijaona in 1983 in Antananarivo, the capital of Madagascar. The group had a floating lineup (tracks by some versions appear on compilation albums) until 1991, when Tina Norosoa Raharimalala and her sister Hanitra joined as singers. This arrangement was recommended by Ian Anderson, a longtime figurehead of the British folk and roots music scene (as editor of *Folk Roots* and a BBC DJ) who married Hanitra. After some well-received recordings, Tarika Sammy changed into Tarika in the mid-'90s with the departure of Samoela Andriamalalaharijaona. *—Richie Unterberger*

Fanafody / 1992 / Green Linnet ✦✦✦

● **Balance** / 1994 / Green Linnet ✦✦✦✦✦
More oriented toward contemporary, original material than their debut (*Fanafody*), though still sung entirely in Malagasy. Characterized by effervescent vocals and arrangements, it strikes a rare, even balance between traditional and contemporary regional African music without sounding strained. *—Richie Unterberger*

Madagascar Collection

Madagasikara One / 1986 / Globestyle ✦✦✦✦✦
Madagasikara One: Current Traditional Music of Madagascar features the rapid, tumbling accordion styles and the sound of the valiha box-harp that typify the airy music of the Malgasy Republic. It also contains selections by master flutist Rakotofrah and the out-of-place military-band troupe Tsimialona Volambita. *—Bob Tarte*

☆ **Madagasikara Two** / 1986 / Globestyle ✦✦✦✦✦
Island-accented township jive, Trio FA's irresistible accordion jam, and a pair of African outreach cuts by rising star Rossy testify to the richness of island culture. The diversity of material here (and its uniqueness) is impressive. *—Bob Tarte*

The Music of Madagascar: Classical Traditional Recordings of the 1930's / 1995 / Yazoo ✦✦✦✦✦
Poised in the Indian Ocean off the southeast coast of Africa is the island of Madagascar. Home to about 14 million people, the island's two official languages, Malagasy and French, speak to the island nation's diverse cultural heritage. Malagasy belongs to the Malayo-Polynesian linguistic family. Though it is strikingly similar to certain languages found in South Central Borneo, it has developed connections with Arabic, Bantu, and some French linguistic elements.

Like the variously influenced make up of the Malagasy language, the music of Madagascar is at once unique and an amalgam of sounds from disparate cultural traditions. The Music of Madagascar release from Yazoo admirably showcases this singular diversity by presenting 20 tracks of music from the country that was originally recorded during the 1930s in both Paris and Madagascar. As far as one can gather from the sometimes confusing prolixity of the liner notes, this CD is a compilation of works by Hiran'ny Tanoran'ay Ntao Lo, Hiran-d Razafimahefa, and other native artists. The fiddle, an instrument introduced to the island by French missionaries, is featured on "Hadalana, Hadisoana" and "Indrisy Mantsy Zareo Mpilalo Tsy Manan Tiana," while an indigenous tube zither known as the valiha can be heard on many of the CD's 20 tracks. All in all, this is a beautiful collection of older music form Madagascar that is as exquisite as it is unique. *—John Vallier*

Malawi

Donald Kachamba

Rhumba, Africa, Malawi
Donald Kachamba has been attracting attention with his musical virtuosity since his early teens when he was called "the Malawian Mozart." Together with his brother, Daniel (1947–1987), he brought the urban dance music of southern Africa to the global stage as the Kachamba Brothers. Since his brother's death, Kachamba has continued to thrill audiences with his mixture of kwela, sinjonjo, saba-saba, huayani and simanje-manje. Kachamba has toured throughout the world, performing in thirty-three countries in Africa, Europe and the Americas. In addition to performing concerts, he's participated in symposiums and colloquiums on African music. Kachamba will be an artist-in-residence at UCLA's Department of Ethnomusicology from November 1999 until July 2000. *—Craig Harris*

● **Concert Kwela** / 1994 / Le Chant du Monde ✦✦✦✦✦
Donald Kachamba was part of The Kachamba Brothers' Band, recorded by Austrian ethnomusicologist Gerhard Kubik way back, on one of the world's most obscure LPs. Kubik plays clarinet and guitar here in a group that does swinging pennywhistle kwela the way it used to be played three decades ago. Weird notes by another ethnomusicologist don't even mention South Africa. *—John Storm Roberts, Original Music*

Mali

Toumani Diabate

b. 1965
Kora / Kora, Africa, Mali
A master of the kora (21 string West African harp), Diabate has brought the traditional music of his native Mali to the attention of an international audience with a series of well received solo albums, and some unlikely, but acclaimed, collaborations. Although he came from a family of musicians, Diabate (born August 10, 1965) taught himself to play the kora from an early age, as his father, who also played the instrument, was often away, touring. He developed a style of playing which, whilst being strongly rooted in the Malian tradition, is also open to a wide range of other influences, such as jazz and flamenco. He has subsequently sought out other musicians from around the world who are willing to experiment with him, even performing a concert in Amsterdam with a classical harpist. His 1989 debut, *Kaira*, made history as the first ever solo kora album to be released. Stark, haunting, and full of breath-taking improvisational flourishes, it made him a star in his home land and an in demand performer internationally. In the same year Songhai, a highly acclaimed collaboration between Diabate, the Spanish flamenco group Ketama, and British jazz-folk bassist Danny Thompson, also released their acclaimed debut. Over the next six years Diabate performed at festivals and concerts all over the globe, doing much to broaden the appeal of the music of Mali, in general, and the kora, in particular. In 1995, a second Songhai album was released, as well as *Djelika*, on which he led a group of musicians featuring Keletigui Diabate, (a veteran master of the xylophone-like balafon and no relation to Toumani) and ngoni (a miniature guitar-like stringed instrument) player Basekou Kouyate. He concentrated on performing in Mali over the next few years, before releasing *New Ancient Strings*, his 1999 collaboration with fellow new generation kora master Ballake Sissoko. The album was a tribute to their fathers who, nearly 30 years earlier, had released an album of kora duets called Ancient Strings. In the same year, the very highly acclaimed *Kulanjan* was released. This featured Diabate, Sissoko, and other fellow Malians, including singer Kasse Mady Diabate in a 'West Africa meets the blues' collaboration with US guitarist Taj Mahal. To promote the album, these musicians toured internationally at the end of 1999. In 2000, Diabate performed and recorded with Blur frontman Damon Albarn, when the latter visited Mali as part of an OXFAM project. *—Jamie Renton*

Kaira / 1988 / Hannibal ✦✦✦

● **Djelika** / Oct. 1995 / Hannibal ✦✦✦✦✦
The African kora, which is like a cross between a lute and a harp, is one of the world's most beautiful instruments. It isn't as sweet as a harp and, with some of the quick action of a lute or guitar, it is as much a "classical" instrument as it is a "folk" one. On *Djelika*, Diabate is accompanied by Keletigui Diabate on balafon, an instrument like the xylophone which usually acts as a rhythm section, and Basekou Kouyate on the ngoni, a small instrument thought to be the ancestor of the banjo whose sharp timbre provides a contrast with the kora. The songs are simply beautiful. The title cut is a jazzy piece that slyly quotes the soundtrack "The Good, the Bad, and the Ugly." Keletogui sits out on "Cheick Oumar Bah," a traditional song in honor of one of Mali's spiritual leaders. It is thoughtful and dignified. "Kandjoura," on the other hand, is just fun, fast, and whimsical. It sounds like it's based on an Afro-pop song. The three musicians, each a virtuoso on his instrument, do a wonderful job providing sonic variety to keep the ear intrigued. *Djelika* is true African art music and should be sought out not only by fans of "world music," but also by aficionados of jazz and Western classical music. *—Kurt Keefner*

Salif Keita

b. Djoliba
Vocals / Afro-Pop, Fusion, Africa, Mali
Salif Keita gave up a lot to pursue his dreams of a career in music. Born to royal lineage, with ancestral roots going back to Soundjata Keita, the founder of the Malian Empire in 1240, Keita was disowned by his father after announcing his plans to play music. Keita's dreams, however, were too strong to be shattered. Moving to the capitol city of Bamako, in 1967, he was soon playing in nightclubs with one of his brothers. Within two years, he was invited to join the Rail Band. A popular, government-sponsored, group that played regularly at *the Buffet Hotel De La Gare*, the Rail Band featured influential Malian guitar player Kante Manfila. Keita's soulful singing soon brought the band to a much higher plateau. In 1973, Keita and several members of the Rail Band relocated to Abidjian, the capitol of Cote D'Ivoire (The Ivory Coast). Renamed Les Ambassadeurs Internationaux, the group continued to attract attention with their lively fusion of Cuban, Zairean and Malian influences. In 1977, Keita received the prestigious National Order of Guinea from President Ahmed Sekou Toure. Encouraged to pursue a solo career, Keita moved to Paris in 1984. Settling in the city's Montreuil section, he found a thriving community of more than 15,000 transplanted Malians. Predictions of success proved true with the release of Keita's debut solo album, *Soro*, in 1987. Produced by Ibrahim Sylla, the album combined African, jazz, funk, Europop and R&B influences. In a review of the album, *Rolling Stone*, wrote, "Keita's voice is remarkable in itself. Its' high, bracing purity is heightened by a unique phrasing that combines full-tilt warrior strength, the sensual lilt of the Brazilian samba and Islamic prayer calls." *—Craig Harris*

Amen / 1991 / Mango ✦✦✦✦✦
Produced by Joe Zawinul (Weather Report), this set is more international in scope, with guest shots by Carlos Santana and Wayne Shorter adding to its commercial appeal. *—J. Poet*

● **The Mansa of Mali . . . A Retrospective** / 1994 / Mango ✦✦✦✦✦
The ten cuts on this anthology range from the late-'70s "Mandjou," with its stinging guitar

riffs, throbbing organ and gorgeous sax backing, to the spectacular "Souareba," in which Keita's vibrant vocals are backed by electric drums and synthesizers, plus "Tenin," from the LP *Ko-Yan.* This was produced by Joe Zawinul and included his contributions on keyboards, assistance from the great Antillean bassist Etienne M'Bappe, and appearances by many other African music superstars. The anthology covers Keita's three Mango releases, plus the LP *L'Enfant Lion.* While it's not a substitute for the complete LPs, those unaware of Keita's vocal prowess and mastery will hopefully be persuaded to get the complete package by this fine sampler. *—Ron Wynn*

Folon / Oct. 1995 / Mango ✦✦✦✦

Papa / Jul. 13, 1999 / Blue Note ✦✦✦

Morocco

Ahlam

Group / Worldbeat, Africa, Morocco

The second of the Moroccan electro-trad bands to have their music distributed by the Barbarity label in Switzerland (Aisha Kandisha's Jarring Effects were the first). By the standards of world music, Ahlam is unusual, employing traditional instruments such as djembe and mandolin, and rai-type vocals, against some electric guitar, bass, and electronic sampling. By the standards of Moroccan music, they're downright radical, not only in their mix'n'match of indigenous music with modern Western rock, dance, and dub, but in their lyrical attitude. The liner notes to their first album, for instance, advocate a "non-violent intifada"; one of the tracks is meant to be a "call for peace between Araba & Jews." That debut record, *Revolt Against Reason,* was a smorgasbord of Moroccan pop and left-field sound effects and electronics. Bill Laswell co-produced the second album, *Messages from Arabs,* which has a more club-friendly feel (especially in the programming and sampling), but loses some of the unpredictable inspiration of the previous recording. *—Richie Unterberger*

● **Revolt Against Reason** / 1992 / Barbarity ✦✦✦✦✦
There's a general rule when evaluating the Moroccan pop recordings handled by the Barraka El Farnatshi Productions/Barbarity axis in Switzerland: The further back in time you go, the better the music is. This was, after Aisha Kandisha's landmark *El Buya* release, the first recording to be distributed through that organization. There's more Western consciousness in the electronic dance rhythms especially, but there's still a lot of resonant verve to the string instruments, some wonderfully emotional singing, and a bit of an anything-goes attitude to the insertion of samples and electronic effects. One gets the feeling that the group is still trying to wrestle, both physically and conceptually, with modern equipment and dubbing/editing techniques. In cultural collisions such as these, that's a *good* thing, not a bad one, lending the whole project a degree of frontier-stretching spontaneity. *—Richie Unterberger*

Acting Salam / 1995 / Barbarity ✦✦✦

Les Riam / 1996 / Barbarity ✦✦✦

Aisha Kandisha's Jarring Effects

Group / Traditional Middle Eastern Folk, Worldbeat, World Fusion

Starting in the late '80s as a traditional Shabee dance band, this Moroccan quintet became one of the few North African acts to successfully merge traditional and modern sounds and technology on their electrifying 1990 debut. In addition to haunting violins, mandolins, guitars, and mesmerizing Arabic vocals and chanting, the album utilized electronic tinkering and turntable DJing, aided by the post-production work of the Swiss producer Pat Jabbar. Their 1992 followup, *Shabeesation,* was produced by Bill Laswell (who also contributed bass), and featured appearances by Omar Ben Hassen of the Last Poets and Parliament-Funkadelic keyboardist Bernie Worrell. For all that, it was a disappointment, relying much more heavily on thumping modern electronic dance rhythms. *—Richie Unterberger*

● **Aisha Kandisha's Jarring Effects** / 1990 / Farnatshi ✦✦✦✦
One of the most exciting blends of traditional North African music with up-to-the-minute influences like dub reggae and hip-hop scratching. Sounding like a traditional Moroccan jam that has been somehow trapped in an arty, rattling echo chamber, this is one of few contemporary African pop albums that uses state-of-the-art production techniques to augment indigenous music instead of subsume it. *—Richie Unterberger*

Shabeesation / 1993 / Ryko ✦✦✦✦

Master Musicians of Joujouka

Group / Worldbeat, Africa, Morocco

An album, produced by the Rolling Stones' Brian Jones a month before his drowning death in 1969, *Brian Jones Presents The Master Musicians Of Jajouka,* introduced the unique sound of the Master Musicians of Jajouka to much of the western world. At the time, the group had been performing their unique, drone-heavy, music for several thousand years. The band, comprised of sons of sons of musicians, has subsequently recorded several unforgettable albums on their own and have been featured on albums by Ornette Coleman, The Rolling Stones, Randy Weston, Maceo Parker and Jimmy Page & Robert Plant. An album released by the group in 1992, *Apocalypse,* was produced by Bill Laswell. Proclaimed "one of the most musically inspiring groups in the world" by Mick Jagger, the Master Musicians of Jajouka perform a hypnotic style of music that *The African Music Encyclopedia* described as "a strange (at least to western ears) combination of high-pitched, nasal, buzzing, sounds (imagine a swarm of bees) with surging waves of rhythm which can induce an ecstatic trance state." An all male group, the Master Musicians Of Jajouka features fifteen rhaita (a double-reed, oboe-like, instrument) players and five drummers. Only a son of a master musician can become a master musician. Members of the group, who speak Arabic, adopt the surname "Attar," which translates as "the perfume maker." The band continues to reside in Jajouka, a small village in the foothills of the Rif Mountains.

Unknown to the western world for most of their history, the Master Musicians Of Jajouka were "discovered" in the 1950s by beat novelist William Burroughs and Paul Bowles, who recorded the band for the Library Of Congress. Brian Jones was introduced to the group by painter, writer and metaphysician Brion Gysin.

In the early-1990s, the Master Musicians Of Jajouka were led by Bachir Attar, whose father had led the group in the late-1960s. Attar, who lives half the year in New York, has subsequently left the band to pursue a solo career.

The Master Musicians Of Jajouka's first tour of the United States, in 1997, included a reenactment of the week-long lunar feast of Aid El Kabir. In 1999, the group was visited bv Sonic Youth guitarist Lee Renaldo. By the end of the '90s, the electronica world embraced the group as well; Talvin Singh produced their 2000 album *Master Musicians Of Jajouka Featuring Bachir Attar.* *—Craig Harris*

Master Musicians of Jajouka / Aug. 29, 2000 / Polygram ✦✦✦
Talvin Singh was reportedly pleased and amazed to win the Technics Mercury Prize in the U.K. in 1999, a highly commendable trade achievement, for his eclectic CD *OK.* His instant reaction to receiving the award was to disappear off the European club and concert circuit to jam for months with the famed Master Musicians of Jajouka, heroes of the Rif mountains in a less than easily accessible region of Morocco. Beat author William Burroughs once described the Master Musicians as "the World's Only 4,000-year-old band," and Brian Jones recorded a tremendous album with them in 1969 shortly before he died. The outfit of long, strange, and wonderful renown achieves something heretofore unexplored in the company of Singh. Here the guest introduces a hallucinogenic, soulfully high-tech texture to the primordial rhythms and riffs of the masters, creating one of those rare syntheses of past and present, a gorgeous (of loosely hooked) carpet of colors and shapes. There is a whiff of the controlled jam here, not as fresh or far from the studio as one might expect from the high Rif, but this may be due to the production hand of Singh himself in the elaborate remix. A heartfelt and utterly noncommercial collaboration, probably meaning that winning the Mercury doesn't mean that everything, stylistically, must be cast in stone. *—Becky Byrkit*

● **Brian Jones Presents: The Pipes of Pan at Jajouka** / 1971 / Rolling Stones ✦✦✦✦✦
In 1968 Brian Jones of the Rolling Stones traveled to Morocco and taped parts of music at the *Rites of Pan Festival.* It's uncertain whether this should be considered a Brian Jones album, or an album by the Pipes of Pan at Joujouka, or an album by the Master Musicians of Joujouka, as the performers on this recording are most commonly known in the West. The important thing to know is that it's a document of Moroccan traditional music that achieves trance-like effects through its hypnotic, insistent percussion, eerie vocal chanting, and pipes. Originally divided into two untitled, unbroken LP sides (although these are broken down and officially titled on the CD reissue), it should be kept in mind that these are merely edited excerpts of performances which can last for hours, and thus they offer only a taste of the live event. Although the first part in particular builds and builds in relentless energy to whirling climaxes, there are discrete and different performances here, some featuring female chants, others less intense male vocals, and others passages of unaccompanied instruments which sound like flutes (credits and details on the original release are sparse). While this music had been performed in this fashion for a long time before Jones documented it, this was among the first of such recordings to receive reasonably wide exposure (although it was released after Jones' death) in Europe and North America. Thus this recording anticipated the wider popularity of trance-like music among both electronic rock and progressive African musicians later in the 20th century. *—Richie Unterberger*

Apocalypse Across the Sky / 1992 / Axiom ✦✦✦✦✦
The Master Musicians of Jajouka are an ensemble of full-time Moroccan musicians who live in the small rural village of Jajouka, which is in the Jibala hills south of Tangier. For them, music isn't a part-time interest or a mere hobby; it's an integral part of their day-to-day lives. Their passionate music was documented in 1991, when *Apocalypse Across the Sky* was recorded using a digital 12-track recorder. Some of the songs on this CD favor chanting vocals and use of the call-and-response technique, while the instrumentals make extensive use of percussion and the ghaita, an African wind instrument with a high pitch and an oboe-ish quality. The ghaita has been heard as a solo instrument on many African recordings, but on *Sky* (for which ghaita player/singer Bachir Attar serves as leader), listeners are given the chance to hear several ghaitas in unison. This is enriching music that shouldn't be overlooked. *—Alex Henderson*

☆ **Master Musicians of Jajouka** / 1972 / Adelphi ✦✦✦✦✦
Recorded in 1972, this album is something of a follow-up to *Brian Jones Presents the Pipes of Pan at Joujouka, the album recorded by the Rolling Stones* guitarist in 1968 that was released on Rolling Stones Records in 1971. In fact, there is even a track called "Brian Jones." There is such an encrustation of myth and purple prose attending the Jajouka musicians that daring to review an album of their music seems almost heretical, but here goes. The music is quite varied, from the high-pitched reed instruments (rhaitas) that wail through "Sidi Hamid Sherk" to the stringed instruments (gimbris) found on some of the more soothing tracks and the ululations of the women singing "Teasing Bonjeloud." But while enjoyable, it is difficult to appreciate from a mere recording the claims made by adherents who have made a pilgrimage to the musicians' village and perhaps imbibed some of the local stimulants along with the atmosphere. *— William Ruhlmann*

Morocco Collection

Anthology of World Music: Music of Islam and Sufism in Morocco / Jan. 26, 1999 / Rounder ✦✦✦

Moroccan Street Music / Lyrichord ✦✦✦✦✦
This is a very fine recording of the kind of music played by entertainers in the market squares. Most tracks are for voice and ud, or ud and percussion, and the material ranges from urban chaabi to more rural songs. There's also a street performer's pitch, in which he tries to draw and hold an audience, and one song to bendir frame drum. Plain-man-splendid performances, remarkable recording quality. *—John Storm Roberts, Original Music*

Mozambique Collection

Mozambique 1 / 1995 / Globestyle ✦✦✦✦✦
Recorded in 1989 but issued only last year, this is a really splendid collection of music ranging from traditional musical bow through large voices-and-percussion groups and wonderful Makua fiddle via Shangaan rural guitar and accordion to an a cappella group performing a form of mbube brought back from South Africa by migrant workers. *—John Storm Roberts, Original Music*

Nigeria

King Sunny Ade (Sunday Adeniyi)

b. 1946, Oshogbo, Nigeria
Vocals, Drums, Guitar / Afro-Beat, Juju, Worldbeat, Africa, Nigeria
King Sunny Ade is the undisputed king of juju music, the dance-inspiring hybrid of western pop and traditional African music with roots in the guitar tradition of Nigeria. Although he's yet to equal the success that he enjoyed with his early-1980s albums and American tours, Ade and his band, His African Beats, continue to weave an infectious blend of electric guitars, synthesizers and multi-layered percussion. Born to a family of Nigerian royalty, Ade left school to pursue a career in music. In the mid-1960s, he performed with a Highlife band, Moses Olaiya's Federal Rhythm Dandies. Ade formed his own band, The Green Spots, in 1967. Frustrated by the exploitation of the record industry, Ade launched his own record label in 1974. In the two and a half decades since, the label has released more than one hundred of Ade's recordings in Nigeria. Ade began to attract attention in the western world when three of his albums—*Juju Music, Synchro System* and *Aura*—were released in the early-1980s on the Mango label, a subsidiary of Island Records. Ade and His African Beats made their debut American performances to enthusiastic crowds in 1983. Although *Juju Music* and *Synchro System* showed signs that Ade was going up to live up to billing as "the African Bob Marley," *Aura* was a commercial disappointment and the group was dropped by Island Records. While they released an album, *Authority*, in 1990, it too failed to stir much commercial interest. *E Dide (Get Up)*, released in 1995, offered hints that the best days of Ade and His African Beats are yet to come. The group followed it with *Odu*, a collection of ancient Nigerian songs, in 1998; the album was nominated for a Grammy. Its follow-up, *Seven Degrees North*, appeared in 2000. Ade has remained a powerful force in Nigeria. Money received from his early albums has been used to launch an oil firm, a mining company, a nightclub, film and video production company, a PR firm and a record label specializing in recordings by African artists. It's been estimated than more than seven hundred people are employed by Ade's companies. In the mid-1990s, Ade founded the King Sunny Ade Foundation, an organization that includes a performing arts center, state of the art recording studio and housing for young musicians and performers on a five acre tract donated by the Lagos state government. Ade currently serves as chairperson of the Musical Copyright Society of Nigeria. In 1996, Ade formed a "supergroup," The Way Forward, featuring top-notch Nigerian musicians. Ade and His African Beats have been featured in three films—*Juju Music* in 1988, *Live At Montreux* in 1990 and *Roots of Rhythm* in 1997. *—Craig Harris*

● **Juju Music** / 1982 / Mango ✦✦✦✦✦
The first of Ade's international releases on Mango, this is the classic record that made North American and British fans aware of the richness of African music. *—J. Poet*

Synchro System / 1983 / Mango ✦✦✦✦✦

Live Live Ju Ju / 1988 / Rykodisc ✦✦✦✦

Odu / Mar. 17, 1998 / Mesa/Atlantic ✦✦✦✦

Seven Degrees North / Jun. 20, 2000 / V2 ✦✦✦✦✦
As King Sunny Ade embodies good humor and unflagging desire to realize a brighter future for Nigeria and its people, the music from his 23 piece band overflows with a buoyant optimism that is indelibly energetic and celebratory. Songs that praise the sacred ("Appreciation" and "Merciful God") and honor the ancient Yoruban King Sijuade Olubuse Okunande ("Sijuade") are interspersed with songs that ask for ("Solution") and offer guidance on such things as finding your path in life or making sure that the string on a dancer's bikini doesn't break ("Ogidan O Ni Se Barber" and "Samba," respectively). The most nimbly played track on the CD, "Ariya," begins with a series of synchronized punctuations, smoothly darts forward at an impressive pace, and then—about half way through—breaks down into an even more accelerated percussion jam that highlights a talking drum solo. Signaling the end of the tune with a trail of notes from his guitar, Ade comes back in with the other instruments of the band moments before the tune fades out. Other notable characteristics on the CD include the polished harmonies on such songs as "Appreciation," the tasty guitar melodies on songs like "Solution," and the elastic steel guitar lines by Biodun Fatoke. *Seven Degrees North*—which refers the relative equatorial position of Lagos, Nigeria—is the third Mesa release by the royal Yoruban. Though it has been almost 40 years since he began playing highlife and 30 years since he debuted his sounds for large American audiences, King Sunny Ade's *Seven Degrees North* does not drag. On the contrary, he and his band crank out good humored, upbeat, intelligent, and smartly constructed tunes that make one want to dance in celebration of Nigeria's determination and future. *—John Vallier*

I.K. Dairo (Isaiah Kehinde Dairo)

b. 1930, Offa, Nigeria, **d.** Feb. 7, 1996
Vocals, Drums, Accordion, Guitar / Juju, Worldbeat, Africa, Nigeria
Considered by many to be the "father of juju" for his many innovations, Isaiah Kehinde Dairo was born in Kwara State, Nigeria, in 1931. One story has it that his lifelong love of music stemmed from a drum that his father, a carpenter, made for him in his youth and that accompanied him wherever he went. In early adulthood, Dairo tried earning a living as a barber, a construction worker, and a cloth merchant, among other jobs. Dairo sat in with early juju bands at night, led by musical pioneers Ojoge Daniel and Oladele Oro. In the mid-'50s he formed his own group, the ten-member Morning Star Orchestra, which gained fame later as the Blue Spots.

Though highlife was the most popular form of band music in West Africa at the time, Dairo and his band released a long succession of influential singles that, by the end of the Nigerian Civil War in 1970, helped establish juju as the premier Nigerian sound. Dairo changed the tenor of juju by introducing the accordion and talking drums to the orchestra and singing in a variety of regional dialects, which widened the rural appeal of the music. When his appeal began to wane at the end of the 70s, he gave up performing, turning first to managing clubs and a hotel in Lagos, then to a ministry in the Cherubim and Seraphim church movement. In 1990 he recorded his first album in 15 years with a re-formed Blue Spots band. *—Bob Tarte*

The Glory Years / 1991 / Original Music ✦✦✦✦✦

★ **Definitive Dairo** / Nov. 5, 1996 / Xenophile ✦✦✦✦✦
So influential and beloved was juju godfather I. K. Dairo in his home country of Nigeria, that in observance of the four-day wake following his February 1996 death, the government-run Nigerian broadcasting network played only songs by Dairo, and professional musicians agreed not to perform in public. This disc partly explains the reasons why in an unusual collection of shorter Dairo pieces clocking in at under 8:00, which is a mere eye-blink by juju standards. The radio-friendly lengths reveal lots of hooks, strong melodies, and catchy vocal parts along with arrangements that pack the maximum amount of variations into a limited space. It's A+ juju from start to finish from one of the greatest innovators in African music. *—Bob Tarte*

Fela Kuti

b. 1938, Abeokuta, Nigeria, **d.** Aug. 2, 1997, Lagos, Nigeria
Vocals, Sax (Alto), Saxophone, Keyboards, Horn, Piano, Guitar / Highlife, Afro-Beat, Africa, Nigeria
It's almost impossible to overstate the impact and importance of Fela Anikulapo (Ransome) Kuti (or just Fela as he's more commonly known) to the global musical village: producer, arranger, musician, political radical, outlaw. He was all that, as well as showman *par excellence*, inventor of Afro-beat, an unredeemable sexist, and a moody megalomaniac. His death on August 3, 1997 of complications from AIDS deeply affected musicians and fans internationally, as a musical and sociopolitical voice on a par with Bob Marley was silenced. A press release from the United Democratic Front of Nigeria on the occasion of Fela's death noted: "Those who knew you well were insistent that you could never compromise with the evil you had fought all your life. Even though made weak by time and fate, you remained strong in will and never abandoned your goal of a free, democratic, socialist Africa." This is as succinct a summation of Fela's political agenda as one is likely to find.

Born in Abeokuta, Nigeria, north of Lagos in 1938, Fela's family was firmly middle class as well as politically active. His father was a pastor (and talented pianist), his mother active in the anti-colonial, anti-military, Nigerian home rule movement. So at an early age, Fela experienced politics and music in a seamless combination. His parents, however, were less interested in his becoming a musician and more interested in his becoming a doctor, so they packed him off to London in 1958 for what they assumed would be a medical education; instead, Fela registered at Trinity College's school of music. Tired of studying European composers, Fela formed his first band, Koola Lobitos, in 1961, and quickly became a fixture on the London club scene. He returned to Nigeria in 1963 and started another version of Koola Lobitos that was more influenced by the James Brown-style singing of Geraldo Pina from Sierra Leone. Combining this with elements of traditional highlife and jazz, Fela dubbed this intensely rhythmic hybrid "Afro-beat," partly as critique of African performers whom he felt had turned their backs on their African musical roots in order to emulate current American pop music trends.

In 1969, Fela brought Koola Lobitos to the Los Angeles to tour and record. They toured America for about eight months using Los Angeles as a home base. It was while in L.A. that Fela hooked up with a friend, Sandra Isidore, who introduced him to the writings and politics of Malcolm X, Eldridge Cleaver (and by extension the Black Panthers), and other proponents of Black nationalism and Afrocentrism. Impressed at what he read, Fela was politically revivified and decided that some changes were in order: first, the name of the band, as Koola Lobitos became Nigeria 70; second, the music would become more politically explicit and critical of the oppression of the powerless worldwide. After a disagreement with an unscrupulos promoter who turned them in to the Immigration and Naturalization Services, Fela and band were charged with working without work permits. Realizing that time was short before they were sent back to Nigeria, they were able to scrape together some money to record some new songs in L.A. What came to be known as the *'69 Los Angeles Sessions* were remarkable, an indication of a maturing sound and of the raucous, propulsive music that was to mark Fela's career. Afrobeat's combination of blaring horn sections, antiphonal vocals, Fela's quasi-rapping pidgin English, and percolating guitars, all wrapped up in a smoldering groove (in the early days driven by the band's brilliant drummer Tony Allen) that could last nearly an hour, was an intoxicating sound. Once hooked, it was impossible to get enough.

Upon returning to Nigeria, Fela founded a communal compound-cum-recording studio and rehearsal space he called the Kalakuta Republic, and a nightclub, the Shrine. It was during this time that he dropped his given middle name of Ransome, which he said was a slave name, and took the name Anikulapo (meaning "he who carries death in his pouch") . Playing constantly and recording at a ferocious pace, Fela and band (who were now called Africa 70) became huge stars in West Africa. His biggest fan base, however, was Nigeria's poor. Because his music addressed issues important to the Nigerian underclass (specifically a military government that profited from political exploitation and disenfranchisement), Fela was more than a simply a pop star; like Bob Marley in Jamiaca, he was the voice of Nigeria's have-nots, a cultural rebel. This was something Nigeria's military junta tried to nip in the bud, and from almost the moment he came back to Nigeria up until his death, Fela was hounded, jailed, harassed, and nearly killed by a government determined to silence him. In one of the most egregious acts of violence committed against him, 1,000 Nigerian soldiers attacked his Kalakuta compound in 1977 (the second government-sanctioned attack). Fela suffered a fractured skull as well as other broken bones; his 82-year old mother was thrown from an upstairs window, inflicting injuries that would later prove fatal. The soldiers set fire to the compound and prevented fire fighters from reaching the area. Fela's recording studio, all his master tapes and musical instruments were destroyed.

After the Kalakuta tragedy, Fela briefly lived in exile in Ghana, returning to Nigeria in 1978. In 1979 he formed his own political party, MOP (Movement of the People), and at the start of the new decade renamed his band Egypt 80. From 1980-1983, Nigeria was under civilian rule, and it was a relatively peaceful period for Fela, who recorded and toured non-stop. Military rule returned in 1983, and in 1984 Fela was sentenced to ten years in prison on charges of currency smuggling. With help from Amnesty International, he was freed in 1985.

As the '80s ended, Fela recorded blistering attacks against Nigeria's corrupt military government, as well as broadsides aimed at Margaret Thatcher and Ronald Reagan (most abrasively on the album *Beasts of No Nation*). Never what you would call progressive when it came to relationships with women or patriarchy in general (the fact was that he was sexist in the extreme, which is ironic when you consider that his mother was one of Nigeria's early feminists), he was coming around to the struggles faced by African women, but only just barely. Stylistically speaking, Fela's music didn't change much during this time, and much of what he recorded, while good, was not as blistering as some of the amazing music he made in the '70s. Still, when a Fela record appeared, it was always worth a listen. He was unusually quiet in the '90s, which may have had something to do with how ill he was; very little new music appeared, but in as great a series of reissues as the planet has ever seen, the London-based Stern's Africa label re-released some of his long unavailable records (including *The '69 Los Angeles Sessions*), and the seminal works of this remarkable musician were again filling up CD bins. He never broke big in the U.S. market, and it's hard to imagine him having the same kind of posthumous profile that Marley does, but Fela's 50-something releases offer up plenty of remarkable music, and a musical legacy that lives on in the person of his talented son Femi. Around the turn of the millennium, Universal began remastering and reissuing a goodly portion of Fela's many recordings, finally making some of his most important work widely available to American listeners. *—John Dougan*

Open and Close / 1971 / Stern's Africa ✦✦✦✦✦
Another long-thought-lost gem from the Fela Anikulapo Kuti archives, *Open & Close* was originally released in 1975 and, in the manner of *He Miss Road* and *Fela's London Scene*, is a total groove-fest loaded to the gills with raucous horn blowing, ferocious percussion (once again, Tony Allen take a bow), and song lengths over ten minutes. By this point, Fela could do no wrong when it came to recording; Afro-beat dissenters will claim that there is a trance-inducing similarity to much of Fela's '70s recorded output, that the grooves aren't enough to make the songs distinctive enough on their own. That's true of some of his later recordings (like in the mid- to late '80s), but at this point he was still breathing fire and the band was in top form. Perhaps the distinguishing factors of records like *Open & Close* and some of Fela's other '70s releases are that as much as he liked to ride a groove, he also liked to disrupt it, twist it and turn it, reshape it, only to bring it back to its original shape. There was less of that later in his career. *—John Dougan*

Shakara / 1972 / EMI ✦✦✦✦✦
Fela Kuti was often described as "the James Brown of Africa," but one could also argue that he was Africa's equivalent of Miles Davis or John Coltrane. Truth be told, either description is valid. Kuti was highly eclectic, and his innovative, visionary music contained elements of funk/soul, jazz, and blues, as well as African music. That eclectic spirit proves to be a major asset on *Shakara*, which consists of two 13-minute performances by Kuti's Africa 70 band: "Lady" and "Shakara (Oloje)." Performed in English, "Lady" finds Kuti criticizing modern African women in a humorous way for becoming what he sees as overly westernized and embracing a western view of feminism. You might agree or disagree with the song's viewpoint, but the groove and the beat are irresistible. Equally addictive—and equally sarcastic—is "Shakara (Oloje)," which is sung in both Yoruba and English and makes fun of the type of pompous, loud-mouthed braggarts who can never make good on their empty boasts. When *Shakara* first came out in 1972, it was a vinyl LP with "Lady" on one side and "Shakara (Oloje)" on the other. But in 2000, MCA reissued *Shakara* on the same CD as *Fela's London Scene*. *—Alex Henderson*

Afrodisiac / 1973 / Regal Zonophone ✦✦✦

☆ **Gentleman** / 1973 / Creole ✦✦✦✦✦
Gentleman is both an Africa 70 and Afro-beat masterpiece. High marks go to the scathing commentary that Fela Anikulapo Kuti lets loose but also to the instrumentation and the overall arrangements, as they prove to be some of the most interesting and innovative of Fela's '70s material. When the great tenor saxophone player Igo Chico left the Africa 70 organization in 1973, Fela Kuti declared **he** would be the replacement. So in addition to bandleader, soothsayer, and organ player, Fela picked up the horn and learned to play it quite quickly—even developing a certain personal voice with it. To show off that fact, "Gentleman" gets rolling with a loose improvisatory solo saxophone performance that Tony Allen eventually pats along with before the entire band drops in with classic Afro-beat magnificence. "Gentleman" is also a great example of Fela's directed wit at the post-colonial West African sociopolitical state of affairs. His focus is on the Africans that still had a colonial mentality after the Brits were gone and then parallels that life with his own. He wonders why his fellow Africans would wear so much clothing in the African heat: "I know what to wear but my friend don't know" and also points out that "I am not a gentleman like that!/I be Africa man original." To support "Gentleman," the B-side features equally hot jazzy numbers, "Fefe Naa Efe" and "Igbe," making this an absolute must-have release. [In 2000, MCA released *Confusion* and *Gentleman* as a two-fer.] *—Jack LV Isles*

He Miss Road / 1974 / Sterns African Classics ✦✦✦✦

☆ **Confusion** / 1975 / Polydor ✦✦✦✦✦
Fela Kuti's 1975 *Confusion* shows him and Africa 70 at the heights of instrumental prowess and ambiguous jibes (the stabs are about to get a bit more direct and heated with 1977's *Zombie*). "Confusion" begins with an unusual free jazz interplay between Fela on organ and drummer Tony Allen that has the presence of *2001: A Space Odyssey* in its omnipresent drama. Then the group falls into a lengthily mid-tempo Afro funk that plays with a sureness that only comes from skilled musicians and a dictator-like leader; here is the formula that had made Fela a genius: Once he has the listener (or the crowd—as all of his songs were originally meant to entertain and educate his audiences at the Shrine) entranced in his complex (and at the same time, deceptively simple) arrangements of danceable grooves, he hits them with what he wants to say. "Confusion" is a comment on the general condition of urban Nigeria (Lagos, in particular). Fela uses traffic jams, no fewer than three dialects, and a multitude of currencies that make trading difficult to complete the allusion to the general post-colonial confusion of a Nigeria lacking in infrastructure and proper leadership. *Confusion* is a highly recommended 25-minute Afro-beat epic. [In 2000, MCA released *Confusion* and *Gentleman* as a two-fer.] *—Jack LV Isles*

Expensive Shit / 1975 / Editions Makossa ✦✦✦✦✦
The Lagos authorities were frequently raiding Fela Anikulapo Kuti's rapidly growing Kalakuta Republic in 1974. Soon after Fela beat a marijuana possession charge, the police arrived at the compound with a search warrant and a joint they planned to plant on him. Apparently, Fela's reflexes were as fast as his wit, as he snatched the joint and swallowed it. The police promptly placed him in custody and would wait to examine his feces. With help from fellow inmates, the police wound up examining evidence that contained no trace of the drug and released Fela. The 1974 record *Expensive Shit* was Fela's response. Musically, "Expensive Shit" is the classic Afro-beat groove. The vibe is up-tempo and concise. As a keyboard chord progression and chorus line repeat to the outro and the choir finishes their rant, the pace slides on in an almost psychedelic fashion. The content of this song is quite funny and is one of his best scatological works. The B-side, "Water Get No Enemy," is a flowing interaction between the musicians that is at once organic and contrived. On this track, Fela speaks a bit more metaphorically than its flip side, using water as the symbol of a respected power (the opposite of the powers that stood in Nigeria). "Even if water kills your child, you still use water." The smallest collection of Fela Kuti CDs should contain *Expensive Shit*. [MCA released *Expensive Shit* and *He Miss Road* as a two-fer in 2000.] *—Jack L.V. Isles*

Yellow Fever / 1976 / Polydor ✦✦✦

No Agreement / 1977 / Terrascape ✦✦✦✦✦
Recorded in 1977, *No Agreement* follows the Afro-beat template to a masterful level: amazingly catchy guitar lines that replicate a bass guitar in their construction, a second guitarist to add some JB's funk power, driving horn section proclamations, intricate saxophone, trumpet and organ improv solos, and then Fela Anikulopo Kuti's wit and message for the people. Even though Fela had vowed to speak his mind, he turns in a song where he proclaims to keep his mouth shut if it means that he will harm his brothers and sisters in the population (not that he actually does, as some of his most scathing songs have yet to come). "No Agreement" is decidedly some of the most interesting instrumentation that he had turned in. With help from Art Ensemble of Chicago trumpeter extradordinare Lester Bowie (Bowie turned in a tenure of about a year with Fela), the solos are magically inspired and the rhythm section rolls on with the power of a steamroller. "Dog Days," the instrumental B-side, sounds more like "No Agreement" part two; it does, however, carry its own weight—again with the help from Bowie. [In 2000, MCA released *No Agreement* with *Shuffering and Shmiling* as a two-fer.] *—Jack LV Isles*

Opposite People / 1977 / Polydor ✦✦✦✦✦

☆ **Shuffering and Shmiling** / 1977 / Celluloid ✦✦✦✦✦
After the 1977 police attack on Fela's Kalakuta Republic, where his mother and about 80 members of his entourage and band were injured and arrested, he set out to light a fire underneath the authority figures and his various other enemies that were causing him and, in his eyes, the people of Nigeria to suffer in the form of harassment, oppression, and economic devastation. *Shuffering and Shmiling* is one of those comments. While continuing along in his tradition of savvy instrumental innovation, "Shuffering and Shmiling" plays out with the same intensity and voracious soloing that mark other great Africa 70 performances like *Confusion, Gentleman,* and *No Agreement;* but the point of departure here is the outward remarks he makes on a touchy topic: religion. Fela had become increasingly concerned about the growing influence of non-traditional religions fracturing African countries. He believed that these divisions had created a population unable to unify and stand up for themselves and instead had them living in conditions that forced "them go pack themselves in like sardine (into a bus): Suffering and smiling," and without trying to change things he says they "Suffer suffer for world/Enjoy for heaven." *Shuffering and Shmiling* is another highly recommended Fela Kuti and Africa 70 release. [In 2000, MCA released *Shuffering and Shmiling* and *No Agreement* as a two-fer.] *—Jack LV Isles*

Stalemate / 1977 / Polydor ✦✦✦✦

Zombie / 1977 / M.I.L. Multimedia ✦✦✦✦✦
Zombie was the most popular and impacting record that Fela Anikulopo Kuti and Africa 70 would record—it ignited the nation to follow Fela's lead and antagonize the military zombies that had the population by the throat. Fela is direct and humorous in his attack as he barks out commands to the soldiers like: "Attention! Double up! Fall In! Fall out! Fall down! Get ready!" Meanwhile, his choir responds with "Zombie!" in between each statement. Since the groove was so absolutely contagious, it took the nation by storm: People in the street would put on a blank stare and walk with hands affront proclaiming "Zombie!" whenever they would see soldiers. If "Zombie" caught the attention of the populous it also cought the attention of the authority figures—this would cause devastating personal and professional effects as the Nigerian government came down on him with absolute brute force not long after the release of this record. Also included are "Monkey Banana," a laid-back groove that showcases drummer Tony Allen's mastery of the Afro-beat, and "Everything Scatter," a standard mid-tempo romp. Both songs are forgetful in relation to "Zombie," but this is still an es-

sential disc to own for the title track alone. [*Zombie* was passed up on the run of domestic two-fers put out by MCA, but the track is available on *The Best of Fela Kuti*.] *—Jack LV Isles*

Sorrow Tears and Blood / Jan. 1, 1977 / Kalakuta ✦✦✦

Authority Stealing / Jan. 1, 1980 / International ✦✦✦

I.T.T. / Jan. 1, 1980 / Polygram ✦✦✦✦✦
Fela Kuti's records in the early and middle 1980s contain some of the most directly scathing remarks ever put to disc (notably, *Original Suffer Head*, *Coffin for Head of State*, and *Authority Stealing*). Sure, Ice-T, NWA, and Eminem have since been more pointedly offensive, but Fela deploys a smarter, slyer, and wittier approach to satire than anyone else. In *I.T.T.* (a play on the telecommunications company, International Telephone and Telegraph), he attacks two central characters that Fela calls out as thieves by name: President of Nigeria, Olusegun Obasanjo, and Chairman of ITT and President of Decca Records, M.K.O. Abiola. Fela gets the jabbing started by describing how the British used to employ their African subjects to carry trailers full of excrement throughout the cities for disposal then transposes the attack to Obasanjo and Abiola as they have forced their African subjects to carry their metaphorical shit of oppression, inflation, and corruption. He says, "We don't tire to carry anymore of them shit" while a rousing call to arms chorus backs him up; Fela continues, "We go fight them well now." His methods were very dangerous as his enemies were extremely powerful and his audience very receptive. For his actions, Fela would continue to be beaten and jailed throughout his life. Musically, *I.T.T.* is an average instrumental attack; however, average for Fela and Africa 70 is still quite above the watermark. [In 2000, MCA released *I.T.T.* as a two-fer with *Original Suffer Head*.] *—Jack LV Isles*

Black President / 1981 / Capitol ✦✦✦✦✦
It was during the early '80s that Fela Anikulapo Kuti's profile was high enough to warrant releasing his records in the U.S. So for the first time, one did not have to scour the import bins or pay import prices to get a dose of Afro-beat. On *Black President*, the politics are at the forefront as Fela rails against colonialism and the military government growing rich at the expense of Nigeria's poor. The grooves are dense and supple and in many ways this is classic Fela, it just doesn't kick quite as hard as *Expensive Shit* or *He Miss Road*. *—John Dougan*

Teacher Don't Teach Me Nonsense / 1987 / Mercury ✦✦✦

Odoo (Overtake Don Overtake Overtake) / 1989 / Shanachie ✦✦✦

V.I.P. (Vagabonds in Power) / May 25, 1999 / Polydor ✦✦✦✦

★ **The Best Best of Fela Kuti** / Nov. 1, 1999 / Universal ✦✦✦✦✦
More than two years after his death, the first coordinated reissue campaign of Fela Kuti material began with this collection, a double-disc set including 13 of his best-known jams. Beginning with three tracks from 1972 (the second disc also has a track from that year), *The Best Best of Fela Kuti* ranges through his entire career, though the focus is appropriately on the '70s. Kuti's infectious combo of high-stepping soul revival and African township jazz has never been equaled. And his band was chocked with excellent musicians, starting with the keyboards and saxophone of its leader but also including propulsive drummer Tony Allen, baritone saxophonist Lekan Animashaun, trumpeter Tunde Williams, and bassist Franco Aboddy. As good as the music is, *The Best Best of Fela Kuti* really shines when it comes to the songwriting. It's an excellent primer on Kuti's various protest targets—the oppressive Nigerian government and military, the increasing Westernization of Africa, unnecessary violence, hypocrisy, and pride—and wisely includes explanatory notes for each track. The editing and compilation work are also done very well. Though many of the tracks had to be modified down to the ten-minute range, the flow is natural and very smooth. The one caveat is the detrimental effect of diminishing returns; Kuti's style was practically trademarked, and after over 150 minutes of jams, the tracks tend to blend together and obscure their individual significance. Overall though, this is an incredibly important work; it's the first truly historical item on Kuti and should finally bring the magic of Fela Kuti to Western audiences. *—John Bush*

Femi Anikulapo Kuti

b. Jun. 16, 1962, Lagos, Nigeria
Producer / Afro-Beat, Afro-Pop, Africa, Nigeria
The son of influential Nigerian bandleader Fela Anikulapo Kuti, Femi Anikulapo Kuti has successfully inherited his father's legacy. Backed by his heavily-percussive, horn-driven, band, Kuti creates dance-inspiring sound with his dynamic saxophone playing and soulful vocals. While he shares his father's passion for politically-infused lyrics, Kuti continues to place the emphasis on groove-laden rhythms and spirited performances. According to *The Boston Globe*, "Kuti's 26 year old body is part of his show. He conducts his horn section, background singers and dancers (two of them his sisters) and rhythm section with it. He opens up holes in the universe and throws it through, taking the audience with him."

A member of his father's Egypt 80 band since the early-1980s, Kuti assumed leadership of the group when his father was imprisoned by the Nigerian government in 1985. Following his father's release from jail, two years later, he formed his own band, Positive Force.

Signing with Motown in 1994, Kuti released one album, *Femi Kuti*, and a few singles, including "Wonder Wonder," for the label. In late-1999, Kuti signed with Polygram International's Barclay subsidiary. His first album for the label, *Shoki Shoki*, was followed by *Shoki Remixed*, featuring remixed versions of his songs done by Chateau Flight, Kenny Chandler and The Roots. *—Craig Harris*

● **Femi Kuti** / 1995 / Tabu ✦✦✦✦
This debut album was an extremely popular record in Africa and Europe; it introduced Kuti's cleaner, more succinct take on his father Fela Kuti's legendary Afro beat sound. Packed with contagious rhythms born of African, jazz, and funk melodies, *Femi Kuti* represents an important offering to world music. Standout tracks include "Wonder," which is full of funky grooves and pointed lyrics about African unity, and "Survival," with its swinging, hip-rolling percussion. *—Rosalind Cummings-Yeates*

Shoki Shoki / Feb. 15, 1999 / Barclay ✦✦✦
Now that he's assumed the mantle of Afro-beat superstardom from his father, Femi Kuti seems much more assured on his third album, *Shoki Shoki*. Femi is just as focused on political and social situations as Fela Kuti, as displayed on several tracks here ("Blackman Know Yourself," "What Will Tomorrow Bring," "Victim of Life," "Look Around"). Also like his father, he never lets the lyrically conscious material get in the way of pushing irresistible grooves. From the openers "Truth Don Die" and "Beng Beng Beng"—both of which were passed off to dance remixers including Masters at Work and Black Science Orchestra—to later tracks like "Sorry Sorry," Femi is a strict bandleader who knows how to get the most out of his charges. In fact, the only real stylistic difference between father and son is the fact that songs by Femi are shorter and poppier than those by Fela. *—John Bush*

Prince Nico Mbarga (Nicholas Mbarga)

b. 1950, Abakaliki, Nigeria
Vocals, Guitar / Highlife, Africa, Nigeria
The death of vocalist and guitarist Prince Nico Mbarga, following a motorcycle accident on June 24, 1997, marked the passing of one of Africa's most influential performers. Although he only recorded one significant hit, "Sweet Mother," in 1976, which sold more than 13 million copies, Mbarga played an important role in the evolution of African music. The son of a Nigerian mother and a Cameroonian father, Mbarga embraced the musical traditions of both cultures. With his soulful vocals set to the light melodies of his acoustic guitar, Mbarga created a unique hybrid of Ibo and Zairean guitar playing and uplifting highlife rhythms. Mbarga's musical approach was inspired by the five years he spent in Cameroon during the Nigerian Civil War of the late '60s. Sharpening his instrumental skills while playing xylophone, conga, drums, and electric guitar in school bands, he made his professional debut as a member of a hotel band, the Melody Orchestra, in 1970. Returning to Nigeria two years later, he formed his own group, Rocafil Jazz, to perform regularly at the Naza Hotel in the eastern Nigerian city of Onitsa. After releasing a disappointing single in 1973, Mbarga and Rocafil Jazz had their first success with their second single, "I No Go Marry My Papa," which became a regional hit. The band's inability to break past their local following, however, resulted in their recording contract being dropped by EMI. The label's decision proved ill-fortuned when the band signed with the Onitsa label and recorded "Sweet Mother." Sung in Pidgin English, the song became one of the top sellers in the history of Nigerian music. In the six years that Mbarga and Recotal Jazz remained with Onitsa, 1975 to 1981, they recorded nine albums. Temporarily relocating to England in 1982, Mbarga became known for his flamboyant, '70s glam rock-inspired performances. While he continued to appear with Rocafil Jazz, Mbargar also performed with London-based highlife band the Ivory Coasters and Cameroonian vocalist Louisiana Tilda. Despite launching his own Polydor-distributed record label, upon returning to Nigeria, Mbarga and the original members of Rocafil Jazz separated after several Cameroon-born members were deported. Although he later formed the New Rocafil Jazz Band, Mbarga failed to match his early success. Leaving music, he turned his attention to managing the two hotels that he owned, Hotel Calbar and the Sweet Mother Hotel. *—Craig Harris*

● **Aki Special** / 1987 / Rounder ✦✦✦✦✦
Mbarga plays panco, a style from East Nigeria that borrows from reggae, funk, soukous, highlife, and more. This CD collects most of the tracks from Mbarga's two Rounder albums, *Sweet Mother* and *Free Education*. *—J. Poet*

Ebenezer Obey

b. 1942, Idogo, Western Region, Nigeria
Vocals, Drums, Guitar / Juju, World Fusion, Africa, Nigeria
Since the 1960s, Ebenezer Obey has been one of the most popular, prolific, and influential musicians in Nigeria, releasing over fifty albums, developing juju style, and conducting an informal and highly creative campaign against his competitors in the musical world. Obey's first band, the International Brothers, was formed in 1964, and played a slow and music composed of layered guitars and Yoruban percussion sounds. Always a cultural and religious traditionalist, Obey worked within the praise song mold, vaunting both Christianity and the various heads of state for whom he played. But while his lyrics were traditional, his musical direction was highly innovative. In an effort to rise above his competition, Obey began to develop new musical "systems," adding as many as 20 new musicians to his ensemble at a time, extending the length of his album tracks, and pumping out hit after hit. A stylish and bluesy guitarist whose music had been contagious in Nigeria for years, Obey finally enjoyed international success in 1980 with *Current Affairs*. *—Leon Jackson*

★ **Juju Jubilee** / 1985 / Shanachie ✦✦✦✦✦
Obey and Sunny Ade are the kings of juju, and for 20 years each has tried to top the other by adding more guitars, more singers, pedal steel licks, and so forth. This compilation, Obey's first U.S. release, collects Obey's best-selling singles and album tracks from the early '80s. *—J. Poet*

Get Yer Jujus Out / 1989 / Rykodisc ✦✦✦

Juju Jubilation / May 19, 1998 / Hemispere ✦✦✦✦✦
Juju Jubilation is a terrific disc that collects recordings Chief Ebenezer Obey made between the mid-'70s and early '90s. Obey was at the peak of his career at that point in time, and the music here remains vital, exciting and terrific. *—Stephen Thomas Erlewine*

Babatunde Olatunji

Vocals, Percussion, Traditional Drumming / Worldbeat, World Fusion, Africa, Nigeria
Babatunde Olatunji was a virtuoso drummer who became a sensation in the '60s with his albums of traditional Nigerian drumming and chanting. If Olatunji debuted in today's environment, he would be subjected to much tougher scrutiny and evaluation regarding "authenticity" than he received in the '60s. His heralded albums, particularly *Drums of Passion*, weren't quite the innovative event some claimed. They were fine LPs, but also contained a

heavy dose of show business and sanitized playing that would be duly noted today, particularly in the specialist press. Still, his albums reportedly were very influential on John Coltrane. They were among the few international releases to not just make the charts, but remain on them for years. Olatunji didn't make many albums in his prime. From 1964 until 1967 he had four hit LPs. He'd originally come to America in the early '60s to study medicine. Olatunji formed a band of African expatriates mainly as an exercise and way to help each other avoid being homesick. The ensemble scored a hit record and he became a musician. The popularity of *Drums Of Passion* and *More Drums Of Passion* predated the '60s black nationalist movement and Afrocentricity of the '80s and '90s. They also had some impact in jazz circles, though they weren't as significant as the Afro-Latin revolution initiated by Mario Bauza, Machito and Chano Pozo. Olatunji resurfaced in the late '80s on the Blue Heron label with *The Beat Of My Drum*, a release featuring a 17-piece band that included Carlos Santana and Airto Moreira. He subsequently recorded more sessions for Rykodisc, including a digital remix of "Drums of Passion." A few of his albums are available on CD. —*Ron Wynn and J. Poet*

★ **Drums of Passion** / 1959 / Columbia ✦✦✦✦✦
Having come to the U.S. from his native Nigeria to study medicine, percussionist Babatunde Olatunji eventually became one of the first African music stars in the States. He also soon counted jazz heavyweights like John Coltrane ("Tunji") and Dizzy Gillespie among his admirers (Gillespie had, a decade earlier, also courted many Cuban music stars via his trailblazing Latin jazz recordings). And, in spite of it being viewed by some as a symbol of African chic, *Drums of Passion* is still a substantial record thanks to Olatunji's complex and raw drumming. Along with a cadre of backup singers and two other percussionists, Olatunji works through eight traditional drum and chorus cuts originally used to celebrate a variety of things in Nigeria: "Akiwowo" and "Shango" are chants to a train conductor and the God of Thunder, respectively, while "Baba Jinde" is a celebration of the dance of flirtation and "Odun De! Odun De!" serves as a New Year's greeting. The choruses do sound a bit overwrought and even too slick at times (partly due to the fact that most of the singers are not African), but thankfully the drumming is never less than engaging. The many curious world music fans who are likely to check this album out should also be sure to look into even better African drumming by native groups like the Drummers of Burundi and the percussion outfits featured on various field recordings. —*Stephen Cook*

☆ **Drums of Passion: The Invocation** / 1988 / Rykodisc ✦✦✦✦✦
The first in a pair of releases that featured percussionist Olatunji showcasing his celebrated multi-rhythmic style in a fresh context. Olatunji was adding African beats to jazz and R&B dates back in the '60s, and does roughly the same thing on this date, fueling careening, expansive tracks that are long enough to incorporate everything from singers to numerous drummers playing traps, congas, shakers, and all manner of drums. It's infectious and among the best blends of traditional and contemporary African and American elements. —*Ron Wynn*

Drums of Passion: The Beat / 1989 / Rykodisc ✦✦✦✦✦
Percussionist Olatunji was championing African music long before anyone devised the worldbeat marketing strategy. His 1989 recording *Drums of Passion: The Beat* updated his classic *Drums of Passion* concept, adding rock and pop energy and instrumentalists to the wall of multiple rhythms. The idea clicks, and Olatunji's African beats are contrasted by Airto Moreira's Latin percussion, Mickey Hart's bombastic presence, and such special guests as Carlos Santana and Bobby Vega. —*Ron Wynn*

Drums of Passion: Celebrate Freedom, Justice & Peace / 1993 / ✦✦✦✦

Senegal

Etoile de Dakar

Group / Mbalax, Africa, Senegal
Etoile De Dakar was one of the most influential bands to come out of Senegal. Best known for its work with vocalist Yassour N'Dour, a member from 1975 to 1978, the group created a Latin-tinged style of African pop that influenced such western artists as Peter Gabriel, Paul Simon and David Byrne.

The roots of the Etoile De Dakar were planted in 1960 when Ibra Kasse, owner of the Miami Club in Dakar, assembled members of two bands—Guinea Band De Dakar and Star Band De Senui—and created a supergroup, known initially as The Star Band. Although it reached its apex with the arrival of N'Dour in 1975, The Star Band splintered three years later when several members left with N'Dour to form Etoile De Dakar. Relocating to Paris in 1983, the group changed its name to Super Etoile. —*Craig Harris*

Etoile de Dakar, Vol. 2: Thiapathioly / 1994 / Sterns ✦✦✦
Youssou N'dour and friends, vintage 1980, show just how to update African music with non-African elements for modern audience without stripping it of any of its essential Africanness. The rhythm is a beefy Cuban-derived slink, with juicy dynamic changes and gorgeous solos which provide a perfect accompaniment to N'dour's voice. —*Carl Hoyt, Original Music*

Baaba Maal

Vocals, Guitar / Afro-Pop, Africa, Senegal
A superstar in his native Senegal, spiritual pop singer Baaba Maal was not even born to be a performer—in West African culture, tradition dictates that the ancient griot caste must produce the singers and storytellers, and Maal was born in the city of Podor in 1953 into the fisherman's caste. Despite his parents' insistence that he become a lawyer, he grew up surrounded by music, absorbing both the traditional sounds of the region as well as American R&B and soul, later discovering jazz and blues. As a teen Maal moved to Dakar, joining the 70-piece orchestra Asly Fouta and teaming with his guitarist friend Mansour Seck to form the group Lasli Fouta; during the early 1980s, the duo also spent several years in Paris, where they recorded the 1984 album *Djam Leelii*. Upon returning to Senegal, Maal formed the group Daande Lenol—literally, "The Voice of the Race"—and began honing a highly distinctive sound fusing traditional African music with elements of pop and reggae; in 1988 he issued the LP *Wango*, the first in a series of highly successful albums which also included 1991's *Baayo*, 1992's *Lam Toro* and 1994's *Firin' in Fouta*. In 1998, Maal released *Nomad Soul*—the first recording on Chris Blackwell's new Palm Pictures label, it featured cameos by Brian Eno, Howie B. and others. *Jombaajo* followed in the spring of 2000. —*Jason Ankeny*

★ **Baaba Maal, Mansour Seck & Djam Leelii** / 1989 / Mango ✦✦✦✦✦
Baaba Maal and Mansour (Thione) Seck, two of Senegal's biggest pop stars, return to their roots (and the roots of the blues, from the sound of it) on this beautifully hypnotic picking session, which also features Djam Leelii. Two guitars, accented by a bit of African percussion and some tasty electric fills by Aziz Dieng, produce pure magic. —*J. Poet*

Firin' in Fouta / 1994 / Mango ✦✦✦
Senegalese pop legend-to-be Baaba Maal released *Firiní in Fouta* in 1994. The album starts with a tribute to his bass player (and his family lineage of griots). Following is a tribute to African women that has more than a tinge of Latin thrown in. "Swing Yela" is a piece infused with more than his usual amount of pop, including a small dose of rap. Following songs range in topic from the Muslim faith to the world market to children's games. The thing that makes Baaba Maal appealing, especially on the Western market, is the way in which he combines seemingly traditional vocal techniques with up to date instrumentation. The keyboards and, more importantly, the drum loops give the songs a deep European club feel along with a strong push in the way of the vocals. Overall, its not a bad album in any way, though it could be attacked by fundamentalists on either side of the range of the album. African traditional music fanatics as well as Parisian clubbers. Conversely, it could easily be embraced by both. For a look into the brightest form of new music in the worldbeat tradition (traditional + western *worldbeat),* Firiní in Fouta *might be a pretty good shot.* —Adam Greenberg

Live at the Royal Festival Hall / Mar. 16, 1999 / Palm ✦✦✦✦

Youssou N'Dour

b. 1959, Dakar, Senegal
Vocals, Drums / Mbalax, Worldbeat, Africa, Senegal
Some of the most exciting sounds to come out of Africa in the late-1980s and 1990s have been produced by Senegal-born vocalist Youssou N'Dour. Although rooted in the traditional music of his homeland, N'Dour has consistently sought new means of expression. In addition to recording as a soloist, N'Dour has collaborated with a lengthy list of influential artists including Paul Simon, Peter Gabriel, Neneh Cherry and Branford Marsalis. According to *Rolling Stone*, "If any third world performer has a real shot at the sort of universal popularity last enjoyed by Bob Marley, it's Youssou, a singer with a voice so extraordinary that the history of Africa seems locked inside it."

A native of the impoverished Media section of Dakar, N'Dour inherited his musical skills from his mother, a griot (oral historian) who taught him to sing as a child. A seasoned performer before his teens, N'Dour joined the popular group, the Star Band Of Dakar at the age of nineteen. Within two years, he had assumed leadership of the group, which he renamed Super E'toile De Dakar. With the band accompanying his four or five octave vocals, N'Dour helped to pioneer mbalax, an uptempo blend of African, Caribbean and pop rhythms. Performing for the first time in Europe in 1984, N'Dour and Super E'toile De Dakar made their North American debut the following year.

N'Dour's talents soon attracted the support of top-rated musicians. In 1986, his vocals were featured on Paul Simon's *Graceland* and Peter Gabriel's *So.* He subsequently toured around the world as opening act for Gabriel. His greatest exposure came when he agreed to be a co-headliner, along with Gabriel, Bruce Springsteen, Sting and Tracy Chapman, on the Amnesty International *Human Rights Now!* tour in 1988. The same year, he performed at the much-publicized birthday concert for South African activist (and now president) Nelson Mandela at Wembley Stadium in London.

N'Dour cemented his reputation, in 1989, when he released his first internationally-distributed album, *Set*, which included a tune, "Shaking The Tree", that he co-wrote with Gabriel.

Signing with Spike Lee's Columbia-distributed 40 Acres & A Mule label, in 1991, N'Dour scored a Grammy nomination with his first effort for the label, *Eye's Open.* He continued to seek new outlets for his creativity including an African opera that premiered at the Paris Opera in July 1993.

Recorded in Senegal, N'Dour's album, *The Guide*, released in 1994, included his hit duet with Swedish-born vocalist, Neneh Cherry, *'Seven Seconds'.* —*Craig Harris*

Immigrés / 1988 / Earthworks ✦✦✦
Though he was already one of the biggest names in Sahelian pop when it was made back in the 1980s, this album was a good part of what put him on the international map. On their way away from their earlier Cuban sound, N'Dour and Super Etoile did a nice job of marrying Sahel and soul, despite some rather pointless synthesizer. And, of course, by now this one is part of recent musical history—almost a classic, in fact. And yes, it's disgracefully short. —*John Storm Roberts, Original Music*

The Lion / 1989 / Virgin ✦✦✦

★ **Set** / 1990 / Virgin ✦✦✦✦✦
The title tune became the anthem of Senegalese youth in 1990. This is the first album N'Dour hasn't re-recorded for the international market. It's very African and his best recorded work to date. —*J. Poet*

Eyes Open / 1992 / 40 Acres & A Mule ✦✦✦

Guide (Wommat) / 1994 / Chaos ✦✦✦
Youssou N'Dour is a Senegalese singer who documents the intersection of the past and the present, so it is no surprise that there is a parable in every song on *Wommat (The Guide).* The record is propelled by talking drums, a horn section and guitar and bass polyrhythms that will sound familiar to fans of South African township music (or Paul Simon's masterpiece *Graceland*), and N'Dour's distinctive voice (in Wolof and French, with a smattering of English) is captivating. Unfortunately, *The Guide* is overproduced and seldom lives up to the

promise of "7 Seconds," the vaguely menacing duet with Neneh Cherry. Buy it to hear N'-Dour's voice soar through the history and lessons of *The Guide.* —*Peter Stepek*

● **Hey You: The Essential Collection 1988-1990** / Jul. 21, 1998 / Nascente ✦✦✦✦✦

Touré Kunda

Group / Djabdong, Africa, Senegal

Toure Kunda was formed in Senegal by Amadou Tilo Toure to provide singing and drumming accompaniment to the djabadong ceremonies of their native region. To some, djabadong sounds much like reggae, so when Amadou Tilo and his three brothers moved to Paris in the 70s, it seemed natural for them to experiment with a djabadong/reggae fusion. As their popularity increased, the brothers Toure added electric guitars, keys, and more percussion, finally hiring more musicians from Africa and the French Caribbean. After the death of Amadou Tilo the band reorganized and went on to become one of the top commercial attractions in France with their winning mix of reggae, rock, funk, and traditional Senegalese rhythms. —*J. Poet*

Live / 1984 / Celluloid ✦✦✦✦

Les Freres Griots (E'mma Africa) / 1985 / Charly ✦✦✦✦✦
The first hit album from the brothers Toure includes "E'mma," one of the most irresistible of African pop tunes. —*J. Poet*

Karadindi / 1988 / Celluloid ✦✦✦
There are lots of catchy, danceable hits on this good African pop release, with growing rock and funk influences. —*J. Poet*

Salam / 1990 / Trama ✦✦✦✦
The brothers Toure still use traditional material, but there's more funk and a more commercial edge to the production in evidence; this import recording (on the French label Trama) is very user-friendly to non-African ears. —*J. Poet*

● **The Best of Toure Kunda** / Oct. 14, 1998 / Charly ✦✦✦✦

Senegal

Ali Farka Toure

b. 1939
Vocals, Guitar / World Fusion, Africa, Senegal

One of the most internationally successful West African musicians of the last decade, Ali Farka Toure has been described as "the African John Lee Hooker" so many times that it's probably beginning to grate on both Toure's and Hooker's nerves. There is a lot of truth to the comparison, however, and it isn't exactly an insult. The guitarist, who also plays other instruments such as calabash and bongos, shares with Hooker (and similar American bluesmen like Lightnin' Hopkins) a predilection for low-pitched vocals and mid-tempo, foot-stomping rhythms, often playing with minimal accompaniment.

Toure's delivery is less abrasive than Hooker's, and the general tone of his material somewhat sweeter. Widespread success on the order of Hooker will probably not be in the offing, though, as Toure sings in several languages, and only occasionally in English. As he once told *Option*, his are songs "about education, work, love, and society." If he and Hooker sound quite similar, it's probably not by conscious design, but due to the fact that both draw inspiration from African rhythmic and musical traditions that extend back many generations.

Toure was approaching the age of 50 when he came to the attention of the burgeoning world music community in the West via a self-titled album in the late '80s. Since then he's toured often in North America and Europe, and recorded frequently, sometimes with contributions from Taj Mahal and members of the Chieftains. 1994's *Talking Timbuktu*, on which he was joined by Ry Cooder, was his most well-received effort to date. It was also proof that not all Third World-First World collaborations have to dilute their non-Western elements to achieve wide acceptance. However, Toure didn't release a record on American shores for five years afterwards; he finally broke the silence in 1999 with *Niafunke*, which discarded the collaborative approach in favor of a return to his musical roots. —*Richie Unterberger*

★ **Ali Farka Toure** / 1988 / Mango ✦✦✦✦✦
At first blush you think you're hearing American Delta blues—then the Malian-language vocals kick in. This starkly beautiful acoustic guitar has tasty calabash and bongo percussion. —*Bob Tarte*

The River / Jan. 1990 / Mango ✦✦✦✦✦
Toure's second release expands his adventuresome blues-based approach, with a harmonica, sax, and native violin beefing up the sound on several cuts. —*Bob Tarte*

African Blues / Feb. 1990 / Shanachie ✦✦✦✦

The Source / Nov. 1991 / World Circuit ✦✦✦✦✦
African guitarist Ali Farka Toure's previous releases were wonderful mixes of traditional language and rhythms being supported by contemporary concerns, instrumentalists, and producers. His most recent session features his working band backing Toure in a series of impassioned, animated tunes that are done in both his native tongue and English. The similarity between Toure's sparse playing and percussive writing and early blues songs has been noted. What also deserves mention is the cohesive qualities his band have and the way his electric and acoustic playing, with its light, frilly air, fills in the spaces underneath his vocals easily. —*Ron Wynn*

Talking Timbuktu / 1994 / World Circuit ✦✦✦
Guitarist Ali Farka Toure has repeatedly bridged the gap between traditional African and contemporary American vernacular music, and this release continues that tradition. The CD features him singing in 11 languages and playing acoustic and electric guitar, six-string banjo, njarka, and percussion, while teaming smartly with an all-star cast that includes superstar fusion bassist John Patitucci, session drummer Jim Keltner, longtime roots music great Ry Cooder (who doubled as producer), venerable guitarist Gatemouth Brown, and such African percussionists and musicians as Hamma Sankare on calabash and Oumar Toure on congas. —*Ron Wynn*

Radio Mali / 1996 / World Circuit ✦✦✦✦✦

Niafunké / Jun. 22, 1999 / Hannibal ✦✦✦✦
Malian guitarist Ali Farka Toure's music has always managed global travel with ease and musical grace, shrinking the miles between Western Africa and the Mississippi Delta and seemingly visiting every city in between. Toure has received his share of accolades for blurring the lines between his contemporary/traditional finger-picking style and "country blues." Toure has routinely collaborated with musicians from other cultures and musical genres, most notably the prolific and internationally influenced Ry Cooder, on their widely acclaimed 1994 album *Talking Timbuktu*. He establishes a firm aesthetic residence on *Niafunke*, his first and most welcome CD in five years. *Niafunke* was recorded using a state-of-the-art portable studio in Toure's home village of Niafunke, which clearly lends a decisive authentic flavor and sense of musical place to the disc. Each tune is a lithe and resonant labyrinth of call-and-response patterns: a finger-picked guitar speaks to a one-stringed njarka fiddle, calabash pummelings weave into those of the conga drums and a lively small chorus answers Toure's authoritative lead vocals. A couple of the best cuts include "Ali's Here" and "Saukare," as the marriage of present-day musical technologies and long-explored African musical tapestries. A beautifully rendered and intoxicating record. —*Becky Byrkit*

Senegal Collection

A Land of Drummers / Nov. 19, 1996 / Village Pulse ✦✦✦✦
A Land of Drummers is actually a compilation of songs from six other albums on the Village Pulse label: Mapathe Diop's Sabar Wolof: Dance Drumming of Senegal, Boubacar Diagne's Tabala Wolof: Sufi Drumming of Senegal, Mamadou Ly's Mandinka Drum Master, Malang Mane's Balanta Balo: Talking Wood of Casamance, Amadu Bamba's Drums of the Firdu Fula, and Saikouba Badjie's Bougarabou: Solo Drumming of Casamance. Two songs from each are represented on this album, and good choices were made as to the presence of each track. The best works from each album were definitely chosen. Mapathe Diop shows amazing skill on his two tracks, especially "Thie Bou Dienne," which utilizes heavily opposing rhythms. Mamadou Ly carries some amazing speed on "Chingo." Malang Mane and his accompanying friend Oumar Sadio work side by side on an unusually large balofon for a medley of griot works. The Firdu Fula drumming utilizes the same set of drums as the Mandinka drummers, but at a slightly slower pace. Both of the tracks by Saikouba Badjie are praise songs, one of the chief of his village, the other of the chief's wife. Overall, the album is a worthwhile effort to procure, though those that find the drumming good should definitely dig up the six albums that spawned this compilation, as they are quite superior on each of their respective styles to the measly two songs taken from each. Still a good compilation though. —*Adam Greenberg*

South Africa

Johnny Clegg

b. Jul. 13, 1953, Rochdale, Lancashire, England
Vocals, Guitar / Mbaqanga, Worldbeat, Ethnic Fusion, Africa, South Africa

The white, English-speaking, society and Black, African, culture of South Africa was brought together by Johnny Clegg. Together with Sipho Mchunu, a Zulu musician who came to Johannesburg in search of work, Clegg formed South Africa's first multi-racial band, Jujuka. In the seven years that they were initally together, the band recorded two platinum and five gold albums and became an international success. Following the group's disbanding in 1986, Clegg continued to blend African music with European pop influences with the band, Savuka. Reunited with Mchunu in the mid-1990s, Clegg reformed Jujuka and toured throughout the world as opening act for King Sunny Ade. A native of Lancashire, England, Clegg moved to Africa as a youngster. Although he temporarily lived in Zimbabwe and Zambia, he eventually settled, with his family, in South Africa. Starting guitar at the age of fourteen, Clegg was introduced to South African music when he heard a street musician, Mntonganazo Mzila. Enchanted by what he heard, Clegg apprenticed himself to Mzila for two years, learning the basics of Zulu music and Inhlangwini dancing. Soon after meeting Sipho Mchunu and forming Jujuka, Clegg recorded his debut single, "Waza Friday." Although racial prejudice in South Africa prevented their first album, *Universal Man*, from attaining radio airplay, the album became a word of mouth hit. Their second album, *African Litany*, released in 1981, included the South African hit, "Impi." Two years later, Jujuka attracted international acclaim for their album, *Scatterling*. The political climate of South Africa began to take its tollon the group in the mid-1980s. By 1985, Clegg and Mchunu seperated with Mchunu returning to his homeland to work on his farm. Clegg's second band, Savuka, which took its name from the Zulu word meaning "we have risen" or "we have awakened," took a more pop-minded approach to African music. The group's debut album, *Third World Child*, sold more than two million copies. Following their second album, *Shadow Man*, the band embarked on a world tour, opening shows for Steve Winwood in the United States and George Michael in Canada. Savuka reached its peak with its fourth album, *Heat, Dust And Dreams*, which was nominated for a Grammy in the "best world music" category and received a *Billboard* music award as "Best World Music Album." —*Craig Harris*

African Litany / 1982 / Rhythm Safari ✦✦✦
Juluka's second release with Johnny Clegg, the first album by an integrated rock band in South Africa, went gold in three months. This first single, "Impi," was based on a Zulu war chant and was considered a call to revolution by people in the know. —*J. Poet*

Ubuhle Bemvelo / Jan. 1982 / Rhythm Safari ✦✦✦

Scatterlings / Oct. 1982 / Warner Brothers ✦✦✦
A supergroup that defied racial barriers in their South African homeland, Juluka's album *Scatterlings* was the first introduction to the band for many Americans. Led by lead singer

Johnny Clegg, *Scatterlings* featured Juluka's blend of African and Western rhythms, melodies, and instrumentation. Clegg delivered his self-penned lyrics in a warm voice singing in both English and Zulu. The title track is a jaunty romp that managed to receive a bit of airplay. The rest of the album ranges from the galloping "Shake My Way" to the martial drumming on "Simple Things" to the pop-tinged "Digging for Some Words." *Scatterlings* failed to break the band to a wider audience, but remains a rewarding listen and a solid introduction to this groundbreaking act. *—Tom Demalon*

Stand Your Ground / 1985 / Warner Brothers ✦✦✦

Third World Child / 1987 / Capitol ✦✦✦✦✦
"Asimbonanga (Mandela)" is an anthem already adopted by Joan Baez and others, while the title tune devastatingly discusses what it's like to be asked to "walk in the dreams of the foreigner." *—William Ruhlmann*

Cruel, Crazy, Beautiful World / 1989 / Capitol ✦✦✦✦

Shadow Man / Aug. 1989 / Capitol ✦✦✦

★ **The Best of Juluka** / 1991 / Rhythm Safari ✦✦✦✦✦
This is a good summary of Clegg's work with Juluka. *—Scott Bultman*

Universal Men / 1992 / Rhythm Safari ✦✦✦✦
Universal Men, Juluka's 1979 debut album (belatedly released in the U.S. in 1992), was a remarkable document for its time. Johnny Clegg and Sipho Mchunu achieved a canny mixture of Western folk-rock and Zulu chant, creating a pop hybrid like nothing that had been heard before, even if the flute and sax solos of Robbie Jansen, playing against the acoustic guitars and Clegg's reedy voice, sometimes suggested Jethro Tull. And Clegg, Mchunu, and company were just as ambitious lyrically, constructing a concept record about the life of a South African migrant worker that played into the band's social consciousness and pan-African nationalism, notably in the song "Africa," which became one of their signature tunes. In retrospect, *Universal Men* is not as impressive as later Juluka albums that expanded upon its basic formula, but it retains historical importance as a major document in African popular music and thus an influence on world popular music, leading to the development of mbaqanga. And those Zulu choruses are catchy, too. *—William Ruhlmann*

Heat, Dust and Dreams / 1993 / Capitol ✦✦✦

Johnny Clegg & Juluka Collection / 1996 / Putumayo ✦✦✦✦

Ladysmith Black Mambazo

Vocals / Mbube, Mbaqanga, Worldbeat, Africa, South Africa
Ladysmith Black Mambazo was founded by Joseph Shabalala in 1974. They've cut well over 30 albums since, but the group did not become well known outside of South Africa until Paul Simon asked them to perform on *Graceland*.

Shabalala was born into a poor family that lived on a White man's farm near the town of Ladysmith. There were eight children in the Shabalala family, and, as the oldest boy, it was Joseph's duty to take care of the family after his father died.

Shabalala's first musical experience, save for a bit of fooling around on the guitar, came with a choral group called the Blacks. Shabalala eventually took over leadership of the group and became its main composer. The Blacks won most of the local vocal competitions and became the most popular Zulu vocal group, but Shabalala felt that something was missing. "I had been hearing a voice inside me," Shabalala said. "I didn't know it, but it was the voice of God." When the voice told him to fast, Shabalala obeyed, and on his fast, he had a vision of a new kind of vocal music. Shortly thereafter he became a Christian. Taking the choral music he heard in the Christian church, he combined it with the Zulu tradition to create his own style.

When the Blacks refused to take part in Shabalala's experiments, he formed Ladysmith Black Mambazo. The group consists of seven bass voices, an alto, a tenor, and Shabalala singing lead. Even if you don't speak Zulu, when they hit a low rumbling note, you can literally feel the power of their voices in your body.

"In Zulu singing there are three major sounds," Shabalala explains. "A high keening ululation; a grunting, puffing sound that we make when we stomp our feet; and a certain way of singing melody. Before Black Mambazo you didn't hear these three sounds in the same songs. So it is new to combine them, although it is still done in a traditional style. We are just asking God to allow us to polish it, to help keep our voices in order so we can praise Him and uplift the people." *—J. Poet*

Induku Kethu / 1984 / Shanachie ✦✦✦

Ulwandle Oluncgwele / 1985 / Shanachie ✦✦✦✦✦
A relatively early release by the supergroup from South Africa, *Ulwandle Oluncgwele* makes use of the same style of Zulu mbube that Shabalala's group has always used. It is a stirring sort of sound that emerges from the doubled techniques of call and response along with the synchronized vocals that have made the group famous. It is quite a good album, though mildly slow in points (at least for those that don't speak the Zulu language and, thus, have nothing semantic to process); the style is such a stunning display of virtuosity in its own way that one can hardly help but to enjoy the album, at least at some level. *—Adam Greenberg*

Inala / 1986 / Shanachie ✦✦✦

Shaka Zulu / 1987 / Warner Brothers ✦✦✦✦✦
In the wake of their participation on his *Graceland* album, Paul Simon produced this Ladysmith album, their most accessible work for Western ears, which is pristinely recorded and sung partially in English. *—William Ruhlmann*

● **Classic Tracks** / 1990 / Shanachie ✦✦✦✦✦
This is a selection of tunes from Ladysmith's many South African albums. *—J. Poet*

Two Worlds One Heart / 1991 / Warner Brothers ✦✦✦
Few artists specializing in a cappella performances have enjoyed the commercial success of Ladysmith Black Mambazo, one of the most respected groups in South Africa. Singing to instruments for a change, Ladysmith gave its followers quite a surprise with the eclectic *Two Worlds, One Heart*, one of the most ambitious and eclectic albums it has ever done. The songs employing instruments range from the vibrant "Township Jive" to "Scatter the Fire" (a blend of synth-funk and African chanting that group leader Joseph Shabalala produced with American funkster George Clinton) to the doo wop-influenced "Love Your Neighbor." More typical of Ladysmith, songs like "Ofana Naye," "Cothoza Mfana" and "Emhlabeni" contain a cappella singing that blends South African sensibilities with the fervor of an African-American church choir. This is one of the most ambitious albums Ladysmith has ever done, and its risk-taking pays off handsomely. *—Alex Henderson*

The Best of Ladysmith Black Mambazo / 1992 / Shanachie ✦✦✦✦✦

Gift of the Tortoise / 1994 / Warner Brothers ✦✦✦

Liph' Iqiniso / 1994 / Shanachie ✦✦✦
The seventh Shanachie release by the premier South African a cappella group Ladysmith Black Mambazo is both short (36 minutes) and decisive. The ten selections feature their trademark layered vocals, shimmering harmonies and producer/lead vocalist Joseph Shabbala's transcendent singing rising over the backgrounds. The tracks don't feature any spotlight numbers, but each has sections with memorable exchanges and appealing leads. If anything, the group's customary excellence has led fans to take them for granted. These aren't their finest cuts, but they're not far from them. *—Ron Wynn*

The Best of Ladysmith Black Mambazo, Vol. 2 / Oct. 20, 1998 / Shanachie ✦✦✦✦
Soaring with with grace and beauty, the a cappella harmonies of South African supergroup Ladysmith Black Mambazo were selected from over 40 albums for this excellent collection of spiritual songs. As the most famous ambassadors of Zulu iscathamiya, a musical style characterized by high-voiced lead singing layered against four-part harmonies, Ladysmith Black Mambazo released the first African album to achieve gold status (sales of 25,000) with 1973's *Amabutho*. Since then, they have continued their popularity, selling as much or more worldwide. *The Best Of, Vol. 2*, sung entirely in Zulu, illustrates the group's ability to reach beyond language and cultural barriers, capturing the pure spirit of music. *—Rosalind Cummings-Yeates*

Live at the Royal Albert Hall / 1999 / Shanachie ✦✦✦✦
Although they've been performing together for over 30 years and have made more than 40 records, Ladysmith Black Mambazo have never made a live album until this performance. Before a sold-out crowd at *the Royal Albert Hall* in London, this show recording finds the group (and particularly leader Joseph Shabalala) at the peak of their powers. Running through a program consisting of eleven Shabalala compositions that will be familiar to fans, the group sings on themes of love ("Hello My Baby," "Ngamthola"), spirituality ("King of Kings," "Ngothandaza NJalo (I Will Keep on Praying)"), the weather ("Rain Rain Beautiful Rain") and even Christmas ("Inkanyezi Nezazi (Star and the Wiseman)"). There's the requisite declaration of the group's musical superiority over competitors ("Vulani Amasango") and the even more requisite rendition of "Homeless," a song that Shabalala co-wrote with Paul Simon and that Ladysmith Black Mambazo performed with him on the *Graceland* album. Highly recommended. *—Rick Anderson*

● **The Warner Brothers Collection** / Oct. 17, 2000 / Rhino ✦✦✦✦✦
The Warner Brothers Collection covers the first three albums Ladysmith Black Mambazo recorded for the American major label in the wake of their mass exposure on Paul Simon's *Graceland*. There's nothing from the 1994 children's album *Gift of the Tortoise*, nor (naturally) is there anything from the group's smaller-scale recordings, which in the U.S. are covered by albums and compilations on Shanachie. But, given the title, you wouldn't expect that in the first place. Instead, this is a valuable look at some of Ladysmith's most accessible (if not quite rootsiest) material, with full English translations of all the lyrics. *The Warner Brothers Collection* also includes two tracks with Paul Simon ("Homeless" and "Amazing Grace") and a collaboration with gospel's Winans ("Leaning on the Everlasting Arm"). All in all, it's an effective distillation for the casual fan. *—Steve Huey*

Sipho Mabuse

Vocals / Mbaqanga, Africa, South Africa
With his massive 1984 hit, "Jive Soweto," Sipho Mabuse helped to make the Township pop music of South Africa an international phenomenon. Mabuse has continued to combine South African musical traditions with exciting dance rhythms.

Mabuse launched his musical career as a drummer for R&B group, The Beaters, in the mid-1970s. Heavily influenced by American and British pop music, the group changed its name to Harari following a tour of Zimbabwe in 1981. Mabuse remained with the band until leaving to embark on a solo career in 1984. Success came quickly as "Jive Soweto," recorded with saxophonist West Nkosi, became an unofficial anthem of the anti-apartheid movement. Mabuse continued his involved with the struggle against apartheid. A leading force in the political group, South African Musicians Against Apartheid, in 1986, Mabuse currently works with the South African Musician's Alliance. *—Craig Harris*

Burn Out / 1985 / CBS ✦✦✦
This EP introduced Europe and America to Mabuse. The title track is an African dance-pop classic and worldwide hit. CBS sold several thousand copies of this one to American dance clubs in 1985, but they were unable to get it to cross over to the pop market. *—J. Poet*

● **Sipho Mabuse** / 1987 / Virgin ✦✦✦✦✦
One of the first African pop records to get wide U.S. distribution, it contains "Burn Out" and several other tracks from the South African album of the same name; again, the market wasn't ready. *—J. Poet*

Mahotella Queens

Group / Jive, Mbaqanga, Africa, South Africa
The Queens, often heard in concert and on record with deep-voiced "groaner" Simon Mahlathini, represent the South African township style with absolute perfection. Established

in 1964 as a session harmony group, they came to prominence in the '70s with their tough vocal style and rock-solid mbaqanga backing band. Some of the original Queens have toured the States with Mahlathini recently, displaying their sprightly dancing and gutsy harmonies to appreciative Western audiences. They are also heard to great effect on the collection album *Soweto Never Sleeps—Classic Female Zulu Jive* (Shanachie 43041) with other sister groups. *—Myles Boisen*

Phezulu Eghudeni / 1984 / Hannibal ✦✦✦✦
The Mahotella Queens' *Putting on the Light* is a terrific 12-track collection that pulls together a variety of tracks the group recorded in various incarnations, from group efforts by the Queens and Mthunzini Girls to solo efforts by Mahlathini and Indodaumahlathini. *—Stephen Thomas Erlewine*

★ **Izibani Zomgqashiyo** / 1986 / Shanachie ✦✦✦✦✦

Marriage Is a Problem / Jun. 1991 / Shanachie ✦✦✦

Miriam Makeba

b. Mar. 4, 1932, Johannesburg, South Africa
Vocals / Political Folk, Ethnic Fusion, Africa, South Africa
Following a three decade long exile, Miriam Makeba's return to South Africa was celebrated as though a queen was restoring her monarchy. The response was fitting as Makeba remains the most important female vocalist to emerge out of South Africa. Hailed as The Empress of African Song, and Mama Africa, Makeba helped bring African music to a global audience in the 1960s. Nearly five decades after her debut with the Manhattan Brothers, she continues to play an important role in the growth of African music.

Makeba's life has been consistently marked by struggle. As the daughter of a sangoma, a mystical traditional healer of the Xhosa tribe, she spent six months of her birth year in jail with her mother. Gifted with a dynamic vocal tone, Makeba recorded her debut single, "Lakutshona Llange," as a member of the Manhattan Brothers in 1953. Although she left to form an all-female group named the Skylarks in 1958, she reunited with members of the Manhattan Brothers when she accepted the lead female role in a musical version of *King Kong*, which told the tragic tale of Black African boxer, Ezekiel "King Kong" Dlamani, in 1959. The same year, she began an 18 month tour of South Africa with Alf Herbert's musical extravaganza, *African Jazz And Variety*, and made an appearance in a documentary film, *Come Back Africa*. These successes led to invitations to perform in Europe and the United States.

Makeba was embraced by the African-American community. "Pata Pata," Makeba's signature tune was written by Dorothy Masuka and recorded in South Africa in 1956 before eventually becoming a major hit in the U.S. in 1967. In late-1959, she performed for four weeks at *the Village Vanguard* in New York. She later made a guest appearance during Harry Belafonte's ground-breaking concerts at *Carnegie Hall*. A double-album of the event, released in 1960, received a Grammy award. Makeba has continued to periodically renew her collaboration with Belafonte, releasing an album in 1972 titled *Miriam Makeba and Harry Belafonte*. Makeba then made a special guest appearance at the Harry Belafonte Tribute at *Madison Square Garden* in 1997.

Makeba's successes as a vocalist were also balanced by her outspoken views about apartheid. In 1960, the government of South Africa revoked her citizenship. For the next thirty years, she was forced to be a 'citizen of the world.' In 1964 and 1975, she addressed the General Assembly of the United Nations on the horrors of apartheid. Makeba received the Dag Hammerskjold Peace Prize in 1968. After marrying radical Black activist Stokely Carmichael, many of her concerts were cancelled, and her recording contract with RCA was dropped, resulting in even more problems for the artist. She eventually relocated to Guinea at the invitation of president Sekou Toure, but remained a harsh critic of apartheid. Agreeing to serve as Guinea' s delegate to the United Nations, she twice addressed the General Assembly of the United Nations.

Makeba remained active as a musician over the years. In 1975, she recorded an album, *A Promise*, with Joe Sample, Stix Hooper, Arthur Adams, and David T. Walker of the Crusaders. Makeba joined Paul Simon and South Africa 's Ladysmith Black Mambazo during their world-wide Graceland tour in 1987 and 1988. Two years later, she joined Odetta and Nina Simone for the One Nation tour.

Makeba published her autobiography, *Miriam: My Story*, in English in 1988 and had it subsequently translated and published in German, French, Dutch, Italian, Spanish and Japanese. Following Nelson Mandela's release from prison, Makeba returned to South Africa in December 1990. She performed her first concert in her homeland in thirty years in April 1991. Makeba appeared in South African award-winning musical, *Sarafina*, in the role of Sarafina's mother in 1992. Two years later, she reunited with her first husband, trumpeter Hugh Masakela, for the Tour Of Hope tour. In 1995, Makeba formed a charity organization to raise funds to help protect the women of South Africa. The same year, she performed at the Vatican's *Nevi Hall* during a world-wide broadcasted show, *Christmas In The Vatican*. Makeba's first studio album in a decade, *Homeland*, was released in 2000. *—Craig Harris*

Pata Pata / 1983 / Sonodisc ✦✦✦✦✦

Sangoma / 1988 / Warner Brothers ✦✦✦✦✦
Makeba's comeback album, her first U.S. release in almost a decade, is a beautiful collection of traditional South African songs with spare production values that highlight the power of Makeba's vocals. This is an excellent set of Xhosa folk songs she learned as a child. *—J. Poet & Bil Carpenter*

Eyes on Tomorrow / Jun. 11, 1991 / Polydor ✦✦✦

★ **The Best of Miriam Makeba [Castle]** / Oct. 24, 1994 / Castle ✦✦✦✦✦
There are classics and there are Classics. The Skylarks recordings were and are Classics, the setting in which Makeba's unparalleled voice shone most brightly (aided, let's remember, by the almost equally fine Dorothy Masuka). This stuff is pure heaven, with or without Spokes Mashiyane sitting in on penny-whistle: the greatest moments of the greatest women's sound in Africa. *—John Storm Roberts, Original Music*

Live from Paris and Conakry / 1996 / DRG ✦✦✦
This compilation of songs performed live by Miriam Makeba, one of the original international divas (with, perhaps, Susana Baca among others), was released roughly two decades after the recording dates. The songs are from two live concerts, one in Paris in 1977 and the other in Conakry in 1970. On the album are both political songs of various sorts ("Malcolm X," "U. Shaka") as well as songs meant more for dance and fun ("Pata Pata" being the most recognizable). Realistically, Makeba may have other albums of a higher recording quality out there, but the inclusion of crowd noises, monologues with the audience, and some acoustic irregularities (inherent in any live recording) make the album seem more worthy as a document of a live performance, giving the listener a feel for what a live concert by the great singer would be like. Any fan of Makeba's music should be overjoyed upon hearing this compilation, and those who haven't particularly heard of her would find this to be a good starting point. *—Adam Greenberg*

Best of Miriam Makeba & the Skylarks / 1998 / Camden ✦✦✦✦✦
The Best of Miriam Makeba & the Skylarks is a good overview of Makeba's '50s recordings with the Skylarks. These are seminal South African recordings, and while they are available on a better, more comprehensive collection, this nevertheless is a good affordable overview of her music that functions as a nice introduction for the curious. *—Stephen Thomas Erlewine*

Homeland / Apr. 25, 2000 / Putumayo ✦✦✦

Dudu Pukwana

b. Jul. 18, 1938, Port Elizabeth, South Africa, **d.** Jun. 28, 1990, London, England
Sax (Alto) / African Jazz, Avant-Garde Jazz, Africa, South Africa
A fiery, inspirational alto saxophonist, Dudu Pukwana's wailing leads and indomitable spirit brillantly fused township jive, free music and honking R&B. Pukwana actually began on piano, taking lessons from his father at age ten. He joined Tete Mbambisa's Four Yanks as a teen in the late '50s after the family moved from Port Elizabeth to Cape Town, South Africa. He also started learning saxophone from Nick Moyake, and listening to imported American jazz and R&B records. Chris McGregor invited Pukwana to join the Blue Notes, an integrated band in the early '60s. He'd eventually depart his homeland with the rest of the band, settling temporarily in Switzerland, then later in London. Pukwana stayed with McGregor's groups until 1969, when he joined Hugh Masekela's Union of South Africa in America. After they disbanded in 1970, Pukwana returned to England and formed his own band. They were initially Spear, and later Assegai. Pukwana also worked with Keith Tippett's Centipede, Jonas Gwangwa, Traffic, the Incredible String Band, Gwigwi Mrwebi, Sebothane Bahula's Jabula, Harry Miller's Isipingo, and the Louis Moholo Unit. Pukwana recorded with Mrwebi in 1970, and made two albums with Assegai before founding a new edition of Spear in 1972. He also played that year on Masekela's *Home Is Where The Music Is* Chisa session. The new Spear, which included Mongezi Feza, Moholo and Miller, plus Bixo Mngqikana, made some excellent albums, among them *In The Townships* and *Flute Music*, before they disbanded in 1978. Pukwana formed the big band Zila, recorded with them, and continued heading the group until his death of liver failure in 1990. Sadly, none of Pukwana's sessions are available in America on CD. *—Ron Wynn*

● **Diamond Express** / 1975 / Freedom ✦✦✦✦✦
An early-'70s recording of this saxophonist, with the late trumpeter Mongezi Feza, in their last meeting before Feza died of pneumonia. Squeaky sax and ensemble in an unabashed mood. South African free jazz. *—Michael G. Nastos*

Zila / 1981 / JIKA ✦✦✦✦
A live date at the 100 Club in London, with a larger ensemble and great soloists. *—Michael G. Nastos*

South Africa Collection

★ **Indestructible Beat of Soweto** / 1986 / Shanachie ✦✦✦✦✦
This anthology of South African artists surprised everyone by becoming a best-seller. It introduced worldbeatniks to Ladysmith Black Mambazo, Mahlathini, and Moses Mchunu and paved the way for Paul Simon's *Graceland*. Winner of The Village Voice's Jazz and Pop Poll for Best Record of 1987, it's an essential sampler of modern African styling, a revelation and a joy. *—J. Poet & Hank Davis*

Indestructible Beat of Soweto, Vol. 4: Jive Soweto / Dec. 1, 1995 / Earthworks ✦✦✦✦
"Jive" is the generic term used to refer to South African pop music, and is often modified by reference to the featured instrument—hence sax jive and pennywhistle jive. The term "township jive" generally means mbaqanga, a unique fusion of rural and urban music characterized by prominent electric bass, tightly arranged horns, and cascading guitar lines. The fourth volume in the Earthworks label's excellent Indestructible Beat of Soweto series focuses on early-'90s hits by the Soul Brothers, one of South Africa's finest mbaqanga groups, but it also includes tracks by such other eminent combos as Mahlathini & the Mahotella Queens and Steve Kekana. The program opens with a hair-raisingly beautiful Soul Brothers number entitled "Hluphekile" but bogs down a bit after that; mbaqanga, while structured, is not the world's most linear musical form, and it can get a bit tedious if you're not dancing to it, and Sipho Mabuse's "Jive Soweto" and Ihashi Elimhophe's "Uqanduqandu," for example, both meander a bit too aimlessly. But the gems on this program, which also include Steve Kekana's stunning "Ngayivuye" and "Angithandi Ukulwa," are enough to make the album a must-own for fans of the genre. *—Rick Anderson*

● **The Kings and Queens of Township Jive: Modern Roots of the Indestructible Beat** / 1991 / Earthworks ✦✦✦✦✦
Those who were introduced to the percolating rhythms and cascading guitars of township jive (or *mbaqanga*) by Paul Simon's Graceland album and fell in love with it in that context are sure to get a kick out of this collection of early township jive by the original artists. Recorded in the late 1960s and 1970s, these singles feature such legendary performers as

Mahlathini & the Mahotella Queens, whose combination of growling lead voice and sweet female backing vocals continued to be extremely popular through the 1990s, the Soul Brothers, and saxophone legends West Nkosi and Lulu Masilela. The program alternates between examples of "sax jive" (instrumental saxophone showcases built on brief, jazzy, repeated riffs) and vocal performances, which are often accompanied by harder-edged and more complex instrumental parts. Highlights include Masilela's "Six Mabone" (an instrumental ode to the elaborately-appointed American cars that were popular at the time) and "Jive Makgona" by Mahlathini & the Mahotella Queens, on which bassist Joseph Makwela makes astonishing use of tightly controlled feedback. Considering the vintage of these recordings, the sound quality and production values are very high throughout. Highly recommended. *—Rick Anderson*

No Easy Walk to Freedom: 14 Classics / Jun. 16, 1998 / Music Club ✦✦✦✦
Subtitled 'classics from the shebeens of South Africa, ' this compilation brings together 14 tracks that were big hits in the last days of apartheid and the early times of the new, restructured South Africa. All of the music is very uplifting in spirit, but of particular note are "Trouble in the Night Vigil" by Chico, "I'm in Love with a Rastaman" by Mahlathini & the Mahotella Queens, "Khoma, Khoma" by Splash, "Kangivumanga" by Ladysmith Black Mambazo, "Take It to Jah" by Lucky Dube, "Shebeleza" by Joe Mafela and "Don't Ask Why" by Stimela. The shebeens (drinking clubs) provided the forum and this music provided the soundtrack of the times it so clearly mirrors on this wonderful collection. *—Cub Koda*

☆ **Noise Khanyile: The Art of Noise** / Globestyle ✦✦✦✦✦
Dynamite Zulu fiddling, with township bands and more rural groups, by a man who played with most of the big names of the time. This has to rank as one of the best reissues of downhome '70s sounds so far—one not to be missed. The notes are better than most, too, despite the misuse of the word traditional—an irritating inaccuracy that seems to be spreading. *—John Storm Roberts*

Putumayo Presents: South African Legends / Apr. 25, 2000 / Putumayo ✦✦✦
Putumayo Presents: South African Legends is an excellent basic introduction to the rich, varied music of South Africa, featuring tracks from many of the country's most important, internationally famed artists—Hugh Masekela, Mahlathini and the Mahotella Queens, Ladysmith Black Mambazo, Miriam Makeba, Johnny Clegg and Juluka, and Lucky Dube, among others. If the collection has a shortcoming, it's the relatively short playing time (only ten tracks), but what is here is terrific and will only whet the listener's appetite for more. *—Steve Huey*

Singing in an Open Space / 1990 / Rounder ✦✦✦✦✦
This set of Zulu semirural music from 1962 to 1982 is perhaps the best South African release in the current glut. None of it is traditional (as the above-average notes rightly point out, the word is routinely misused). All of it—voices, guitars, fiddles, harmonicas—is far more intense than the usual city sounds. *—John Storm Roberts*

Sudan

Hamza el Din

Oud, Vocals, Lute / Neo-Traditional, World Fusion, Africa, Sudan

One of the first African musicians to gain widespread international recognition, Hamza El Din is a Sudanese master of the oud, or the fretless lute. Western listeners are as likely as not to have been exposed to his work via the Grateful Dead, who have played with him onstage occasionally. (El Din also helped arrange the Dead's tour of Egypt.) He has played an integral role in modernizing Nubian music, using his work to both evoke and tell stories of Nubian life.

El Din was originally trained to be an engineer, but changed direction and enrolled in the Middle Eastern School of Music, where he began to compose his own songs. On a fellowship to study Western classical music in Rome, he met American Gino Foreman, who exposed Hamza's work to Joan Baez and Bob Dylan. This resulted in a contract with Vanguard. His mid-'60s debut, *Al Oud—Instrumental and Vocal Music From Nubia,* was one of the first "world" music recordings to achieve wide exposure in the West.

In the second half of the 1960s, El Din spent much of his time in America, living in guitarist Sandy Bull's apartment for a while. Taking a series of teaching positions in various American locations, he also found time to record a Nonesuch album in 1968, *Escalay,* that is considered one of the best documents of Nubian music. *Eclipse* is his most notable post-*Escalay* record, raising his profile in the U.S. when it was issued on CD by Rykodisc. *—Richie Unterberger*

Al Oud / 1965 / Vanguard ✦✦✦✦✦

★ **Escalay: The Water Wheel** / 1968 / Nonesuch ✦✦✦✦✦
Extensive selections of a unique style of music personally developed by the soloist-vocalist on oud and tar. *Escalay: The Water Wheel—Oud Music of Nubia* is the recording that brought El Din's Nubian traditions to the attention of many in the West—an ethnomusicological classic. *—Myles Boisen & David L. Mayers*

A Song of the Nile / Aug. 17, 1982-Aug. 18, 1998 / JVC ✦✦✦✦

Muwashshah / 1996 / JVC ✦✦✦✦✦
One of the many excellent albums he's recorded, *Muwashshah* offers abundant proof that when it comes to Middle Eastern and North African music, Hamza El Din is as impressive a musician as he is a singer. El Din's soulful vocals are something to treasure, but even if he did no singing whatsoever, his oud playing on hypnotic gems like "Assaramessuga," "Gala 2000" and "Bint Baladna" would make the CD worth the price of admission. The oud is a very recognizable lute that has been prominent in traditional Arabic music for centuries—anyone who has spent time listening to traditional Middle Eastern music has more than likely been exposed to the oud at some point—and El Din's mastery of it is undeniable. Thankfully, one doesn't have to choose between El Din's singing and his oud playing; both do their part to make *Muwashshah* the triumph that it is. *—Alex Henderson*

Abdel Karim el Kabli

Oud, Vocals / African Folk, Africa, Sudan

The musical traditions of the Sudan have been preserved by oud, shetern and pennywhistle player, vocalist and folklorist Abdel Karim el-Kabli (sometimes spelled "Kably"). Gifted with a finely-pitched audio memory, which allows him to learn songs after hearing them only a few times, el-Kabli has built a repertoire of hundreds of traditional Sudanese songs. His album, *Sudan,* recorded between 1963 to 1967, remains one of the most important anthologies of Sudanese folk music. Born in Port Sudan, along the Red Sea coast, El-Kabli was inspired by the itinerant folk musicians he heard as a child. Teaching himself to play pennywhistle, and, then, the oud (lute) and shetern (small drum), he studied their methods of tuning and playing their instruments. Moving to Khartoum, at the age of sixteen, to attend the Khartoum Commercial Secondary School, he went on to study Sudanese folk music and Arabic poetry at the University of Khartoum. Although he took a position as a courts inspector for the clerical division of the Sudanese judiciary, following his graduation, he continued to be fascinated by music. Although he moved temporarily to Saudia Arabia in the late-1970s, he subsequently returned to his homeland. *—Craig Harris*

Abdel Karim El Kabli, Vol. 3 / Sudanphone ✦✦✦✦✦
One can only be both a- and be-mused by the British record labels' competing claims that their Sudanese is the only truly national star. Whether Karim el-Kabli is "the only truly," he's certainly "a major": deep, bluesy voice, organ, strings, traditional rhythms and themes. *—John Storm Roberts, Original Music*

Togo Collection

Togo: Music From West Africa / 1991 / Rounder ✦✦✦✦✦
Just released for the first time on CD, this compilation offers an exceptionally diversified sampling of traditional Togolese music. It is also a glimpse of the rich culture of this region of West Africa once termed the "slave coast" by slave traders. The folk songs included here convey popular concerns and reveal, at least in part, the profound spirit of these people. *Togo: Music from West Africa* was originally released in 1978. *—Roundup Newsletter*

West Africa Collection

Juju Artists: 1930s to '50s / 1930-1950 / Rounder ✦✦✦✦✦
The earliest juju music evolved from the West African palmwine guitar style and went through many changes before emerging as a potent world music phenomenon in the hands of Sunny Ade. This is a superb "roots" collection, as well as one of a very few non-import compilations of African 78 rpm recordings. The scholarly notes are a plus. *—Myles Boisen*

Zimbabwe

The Bhundu Boys

f. Zimbabwe
Group / Jit, Africa, Zimbabwe

The Bhundus built up a national following in Zimbabwe by taking the more traditional guitar styles of chimurenga (made popular by Thomas Mapfumo), adding some English/American-style finger-picking and a heavy disco-like bass drum beat, and playing with a lilting, rhythmic swing that's part highlife and part soukous. They call their hybrid "jit." In 1986 the Bhundu Boys put out their first record; when Scottish booker Gordon Muir heard it, he called Zimbabwe and flew the Bhundu Boys to England for a tour that became a year-long residence. With music industry heavies like Elvis Costello and Madonna touting them to the press, the Bhundus were soon under contract to Warner Brothers International (Island in the US). Influenced by the Rolling Stones and soukous as well as the traditional music of their native Zimbabwe, the Bhundu Boys are one of Africa's most ass-kicking guitar bands. *—J. Poet*

★ **Shabini** / 1986 / Disque Afrique ✦✦✦✦✦
An earlier album with a relatively under-produced sound, this exciting music from Zimbabwe features guitars, bass, keyboard, and percussion. *—Hank Davis*

Tsvimbodzemoto / 1987 / Disque Afrique ✦✦✦
Their second album is another great recording that mines the roots of Zimbabwe and serves them up with plenty of dazzling rock guitar. *—J. Poet*

True Jit / 1988 / Mango ✦✦✦✦✦

Thomas Mapfumo

b. 1945, Marondera, Zimbabwe
Vocals, Guitar / Chimurenga, Africa, Zimbabwe

Thomas Mapfumo made revolutionary changes in Zimbabwe's pop-music scene by recording a song for which he'd written his own music. Before Mapfumo, songs in the traditional style were always based on tunes that had been handed down for generations. Mapfumo's music, chimurenga ("music of struggle"), became popular during the civil war against White minority rule, but his popularity made the government unhappy. In 1977 he was sent to a prison camp for subversion. To obtain his release, Mapfumo agreed to perform for the ruling party, but at the concert he sang only his most revolutionary songs. "I told them that since I'd been in detention, I didn't have time to write new ones." Mapfumo grew up in the country, went to a British colonial school, and worked as a herd boy, watching over the cattle. After hearing the Beatles and Wilson Pickett in the early 60s, Mapfumo taught himself guitar and started a band that played pop music from African countries as well as Beatles, Rolling Stones, funk, and soul. Mapfumo left Western music behind to form the Acid Band. Their first album, *Hokoyo* ("Beware"), contained the songs that led to Mapfumpo's detention. After Zimbabwe's liberation in 1978, Mapfumo formed Blacks Unlimited and released *Gwindingwe Rine Shumba* ("Lion in the Bush"), a joyous celebration of his country's independence.

Jumbo Van Renen, the president of Earthworks Records, arranged to put out Mapfumo's music in England; when Van Renen later became CEO of Island Records in the UK, he signed Mapfumo again, this time to an international recording contract. *—J. Poet*

★ **Chimurenga Singles** / 1984 / Shanachie ♦♦♦♦♦
The early hit singles by Mapfumo and Blacks Unlimited, these classic sides were recorded during the long civil war; their musical and lyrical content completely revamped the face of pop music in Zimbabwe. *—J. Poet*

Corruption / 1989 / Mango ♦♦♦

Shumba / 1990 / Earthworks ♦♦♦♦♦
Mapfumo is one of the greatest talents of African music. This is another smashing recording by a man whose mix of Zimbabwean tradition with African and non-African contemporary influences is masterly. (This is, incidentally, a new recording—not the *Shumba* issued in Zimbabwe some years back.) *—John Storm Roberts, Original Music*

Vanhu Vatema / 1994 / Zimbob ♦♦♦

Chimurenga: African Spirit Music / 1997 / World Circuit ♦♦♦
Chimurenga: African Spirit Music captures Thomas Mapfumo and the Blacks Unlimited at their most accessible. For those that don't understand Shona, the political message to the music is lost, since the music itself is so melodic and rhythmic, it's easy to get caught in its sway. Nevertheless, that's the primary charm of the music, since its percolating rhythms and joyous melodies speak the universal language of music. *—Leo Stanley*

Chimurenga Explosion / Sep. 4, 2000 / Anonym ♦♦♦♦♦
While the two discs on Anonymous Web prior to *Chimurenga Explosion* have been substandard in Mapfumo's discography, *Chimurenga Explosion* is a return to form, reminiscent of the extraordinary depth and reflectiveness of releases like *Hondo* and *Chamunorwa*. The recording was roughly split between a studio in Oregon and one in Harare, but the American setting doesn't seem to hamper Mapfumo in any way, and his band is in top form, relaxed and upbeat. In fact, this disc exudes a general good-natured optimism that hasn't been present in Mapfumo's music since *Vanhu Vatema*, and *Chimurenga Explosion* may in fact be one of his happiest. From the very first notes of "Musanyepere," you know you're in good hands. "Mamvemne" begins with the classic Mapfumo formula of a short introduction pausing to let the mbiras introduce the main groove. And Mapfumo's falsetto singing in the chorus of "Nherera" is simply heavenly, worth the entire album by itself. Besides the band as a whole, guitarist Joshua Dube stands out as a star of this recording. He truly captures the spirit of both Jonah Sithole and Eprhaim Karimaura, who both buoyed the Blacks Unlimited over long periods of time. Dube's sparkling yet mellow tone and instinctive sense of the appropriate thing to play set him apart and elevate the music to its status as one in a long line of classic Mapfumo releases. The other amazing strength of *Chimurenga Explosion* is its strong vocal forces, demonstrated best on "Zvichapera," where the call and response could be taken from any of Mapfumo's many great recordings of the '70s and '80s. *—Tom Chandler*

ASIA

Armenia

Djivan Gasparyan

Duduk / World Fusion, Armenia, Asia
The acknowledged master of the Armenian reed instrument known as the duduk, Djivan Gasparayan was born just outside of the nation's capital city of Yerevan, first picking up the instrument at age six. After joining the Tatool Altounian National Song and Dance Ensemble in 1948, his first professional engagement was as a soloist with the Yerevan Philharmonic Orchestra; Gasparyan later went on tour extensively throughout Europe, Asia, the Middle East, and the United States, and in 1973 was the first musician given the honorary title of People's Artist of Armenia by the nation's government. Gasparayan's commercial breakthrough followed in 1989 when he was featured on Peter Gabriel's soundtrack to the Martin Scorsese film *The Last Temptation of Christ;* he subsequently contributed to the soundtracks of *The Russia House* and the cable TV production *Storm and Sorrow*, additionally performing with the Kronos Quartet and the Los Angeles Philharmonic Orchestra. His debut solo album, *I Will Not Be Sad in This World*, appeared on the Opal label in 1989; recordings including *Ask Me No Questions, Apricots from Eden* and *Moon Shines at Night* followed. In 1998, Gasparayan teamed with virtuoso guitarist Michael Brook for *Black Rock; Armenian Fantasies* followed two years later. *—Jason Ankeny*

★ **I Will Not Be Sad in This World** / 1989 / Opal ♦♦♦♦♦
These singularly beautiful pieces backed by a second duduk acting as a drone are, so to speak, meditations on folk themes rather than traditional performances. *—John Storm Roberts*

Ask Me No Questions / 1994 / Traditional Crossroads ♦♦♦♦

Black Rock / Oct. 20, 1998 / Real World ♦♦♦♦

Moon Shines at Night / Gyroscope ♦♦♦♦♦
Armenian duduk player Gasparyan hits the deepest emotional resonance in an atmosphere of dead calm unperturbed by peaks or valleys, just modulations of the flavors of grief. Not exactly party music, but Gasparyan's mastery of the vernacular oboe is dazzling, separating a warm shade of grey into an array of pastel colors. He's got the physics of his instrument down cold, pushing the limits of form and geometry in pursuit of wringing out the last nuance of meaning, so that the sound of wood and the shape of the instrument are constantly palpable. *—Bob Tarte*

Armenia Collection

The Music of Armenia / Mar. 25, 1997 / Celestial Harmonies ♦♦♦♦
This seven-CD collection is truly beautiful and truly eye-opening. Through Christianity, Armenia shares a common musical origin with Europe, especially in choral works. Due to geography, culture, and the pre-Medieval split of the Armenia Church from the Roman Catholic, Armenia is foreign and nearly Eastern. The musical result is a treasure, at times an unearthed gem of familiarity and then siren calls of exotic charm. The Music of Armenia, *Vol. 1: Sacred Music* sounds right out of Gregorian songbook. The similarity cannot be denied. The exquisite production invites back to a Middle Ages monophone recital; powerful and moving. *Vol. 2: Medieval Chant* follows in the same vein. Here the Sharakan Early Music Ensemble backs a cavalcade of Armenian guest artists. *Vol. 3: Duduk* feels distinctly Armenian. (The duduk is a double-reed wind instrument.) The next in the series is *Vol. 4: Kanon* (A kanon is a zither-like folk instrument). With both CDs it was apparent the featured instruments were offering melodies ripe for vocalization. Indeed, each recording is composed entirely of transcriptions of vocal works. The results are addictive and lyrical, giving each track life and strength. *Vol. 1: Sacred Music* and *Vol. 3: Duduk* are the most touching—very human and emotional in delivery—warm documents of a people rich in art. *Vol. 5* is a double CD. One disc features The Shoghaken Folk Ensemble and the other The Sasun Folk Group. Here are songs for dancing and remembering—an evocative collection from a time when history was passed on lyrically. *Vol. 6: Nagorno-Karabakh* represents the contemporary form of Armenian folk music. These are mostly songs of grief. Nagorno-Karabakh is the region most torn by war and strife. The entire set is instantly open to the Western ear. A rewarding and singular musical experience. *—Tom Schulte*

Bali Collection

Between Heaven & Earth / Sep. 21, 1999 / Music Club ♦♦♦
This compilation of Balinese gamelan music demonstrates the diversity of sounds possible in the percussive style, since each gamelan ensemble consists of different homemade instruments. Three of the six tracks are by Gamelan Jegog Werdi Sentana, and these are clearly wooden instruments with short, warm notes and rapid playing. Variations in pitch, speed, and volume maintain interest over tracks that run as long as 25 minutes. Gamelan Semar Pegulingan Saih Pitu features more chimelike sounds and even what sound like wind instruments in the course of the ensemble's ten-minute track, and Gender Wayang Pemarwan employs even more ringing tones in its two relatively brief tracks. The performances are sequenced in such a way that the sound changes periodically, but these remain long, repetitive instrumental recordings that have a trancelike effect. *—William Ruhlmann*

Cambodia Collection

Music of Cambodia / Mar. 1, 1994 / Celestial Harmonies ♦♦♦
Celestial Harmonies' *Music of Cambodia* box set collects three volumes of traditional Cambodian songs as performed by indigenous orchestras and musicians. The Pinpeat Orchestra's "Sathouka," the Trot Orchestra's "Somplov," Taam Ming's "Klang Chanat," and the Mahori Orchestra's "Trorpean Piey" are some of the collection's highlights, all capturing the mysterious, hypnotic sounds of Cambodia. *—Heather Phares*

Music of the Royal Palace / 1994 / Ocora ♦♦♦
This court music was recorded in 1966 and 1970, the last flowering of Khmer court musicianship before Cambodia's national cataclysm. Represented are two orchestral styles and one choral one: pinpheat marimba and gong orchestra and mohori marimba and string group, and rare examples of the ritual sakrava choir style. These good recordings have notes that read a trifle flowery in English. *—John Storm Roberts, Original Music*

China

Wu Man

Pipa / Traditional Chinese, China, Eastern Asia
Wu Man is a virtuoso of the pipa, a Chinese lute. She is of the Pudong school of playing and was a pupil of Lin Shicheng. Wu Man received the first Master's degree in the pipa, won the first National Academic Competition for Chinese Instruments, and received the City of Toronto Glenn Gould Protege Prize. She was chosen for this award by prize recipient Yo-Yo Ma, with whom she performed at the White House for Chinese and U.S. leaders. She has collaborated with the Kronos Quartet and the New York New Music Consort, and has given first performances of works by new Chinese composers. At the close of the '90s, Wu Man was residing in the U.S. She has performed on recordings for a number of labels, including Axiom, Tzadik, Columbia, Water Lily Acoustics, and Ellipsis. She has also led her own releases for Nimbus Records. *—Joslyn Layne*

● **Chinese Music for the Pipa** / Mar. 1993 / Nimbus ♦♦♦♦

Music for Chinese Pipa and Chinese Traditional Contemporary Music / Jan. 11, 2000 / Nimbus ♦♦♦♦

China Collection

Anthology of World Music: China / Feb. 10, 1998 / Rounder ♦♦♦♦♦
As part of Alain Danielou's 50th album vision, Rounder has released the volume China for its Anthology of World Music. Luckily enough, Rounder has held true to Danielou's ideas, and kept the album to classical pieces, as opposed to the newer classical works created under Chairman Mao. There are works here for the zheng, a 16-string zither, as well as the qin, a seven- string zither. Also are works for the pipa, a lute, and the xiao, a bamboo flute. The virtuosity of the musicians on the album is astounding. Li Tingsong, with only four strings, can evoke a full-scale ambush and the ensuing battle in "Shimian Maifu" (the great ambuscade). The qin pieces as well hold the beauty necessary for any great classical work for qin.

"Liushui" tells the tale of a pair of friends, one a qin player and the other a woodcutter, and "Ao'ai" is based on a poem of a fisherman from the eighth century. "Meihua San Nong" is a touchingly soft duet between the qin and the xiao, and "Pingha Luo Yan" is a beautiful work of virtuosity on the zheng, with notes running rapidly enough to make Charlie Parker envious. The album ends with the long, and almost North Indian sounding qin piece "Guangling San" (the Song of Guangling), which brings the compilation to a stately close. Without delving into the earlier Barenreiter Musicaphon versions of the recordings, or Danielou's original field recordings, there is hardly a better version of Chinese classical music out there to be found than this Rounder compilation, unless it's the "silk and bamboo" music that one is looking for. Anyone with an inclination for Chinese music should definitely find this recording and listen thoroughly. *–Adam Greenberg*

☆ **Spring Night on a Moonlit River** / Nonesuch ✦✦✦✦✦
Spring Night on a Moonlit River—Music of the Chinese offers beautiful Chinese classical music, featuring the soulful sounds of the seven-string ch'in. *–Myles Boisen*

India

Alaap

Group / Bhangra, India, Southern Asia
Alaap provides a practical demonstration of bhangra's progress. Founded in 1977 in Southall, their debut album, originally on their own label, focused on traditional Punjabi folk music. Under the influence of producer Deepak Khazanchi and the hi-energy of disco and rock, Alaap's music went electric and employed drum machines. Later albums took religious themes (Shabe Ghat Ram Bole) or paired them with guests such as Asha Bhosie (Chham Chham Machdi Phiran) and Anuradha Paudwal (Na Dil Mang Ve). *–Ken Hunt*

Remixx Extra Hot 4 / 1994 / Multitone ✦✦✦

● **The Best of Alaap** / Multitone ✦✦✦✦
Alaap, one of the top groups, is relatively laidback and rather traditional, but overall quite eclectic. *–John Storm Roberts*

Nikhil Banerjee

Sitar / Indian Classical, Raga, India, Southern Asia
When Nikhil Banerjee died in 1985, India didn't just lose one of its greatest sitar but one of its most influential classical musicians. A former child prodigy, who won the All-Bengal sitar competition at the age of nine, Banerjee grew up to earn international acclaim as a highly-skilled musician. According to *The San Francisco Chronicle*, Banerjee's "technique is a phenomenon, faster than cheetahs, more secure than the dollar." "Music And Musicians" observed that "his improvisations always sound completely natural and spontaneous." In an obituary published after his death, "The New York Times" wrote "the extraordinary fluidity and assurance of his rhythmic ideas and phrasing set a standard that would have left the more international 'stars' of Indian music behind."

The son of an amateur musician, Banerjee was fascinated by his father's playing. Although he wanted to try his hand at an instrument as early as the age of four, he was discouraged by his father and grandfather. At the age of five, however, they relented and he acquired a small sitar. Banerjee took to the instrument immediately. In addition to winning the All-India sitar competition, he became the youngest musician employed by All-India radio at the age of nine. He remained a featured radio performer for five years. One of fifteen children, Banerjee was great influenced by Ustad Amir Khan, who would come to his family home to teach his older sister. Banerjee also studied with Mustaq Ali Khan for three months and Jnan Prakesh Ghosh, who taught him to play tabla. HIs greatest teacher, however, was Baba (Allaudin Khan), with whom he apprenticed, along with Ravi Shankar, from 1947 until 1952. Following Khan's death, Banerjee went on to study with Khan's son, Ali Akbar Khan, for an additional five years. Banerjee subsequently performed an estimated thousand concerts in India as Khan's accompanist. Banerjee performed his first concerts outside of India in 1955 as a member of a cultural delegation sent by the Indian government to Poland, Russia and China. He made his United States debut in 1967. For many years, Banerjee spent three months each summer teaching, performing and lcturing-demonstrating at U. C. Berkeley.

In 1968, Banerjee was awarded the honorary title, Padma Shri. The same year, he was named India's "outstanding musician of the year" by the Sangeet Nagat (music and dance) Academy. *–Craig Harris*

The Hundred-Minute Raga: Purabi Kalyan / 1982 / Raga ✦✦✦

Live: Berkeley 1982 / 1982 / Raga ✦✦✦

● **Immortal Sitar of Pandit Nikhil Banerjee, Ragas: Purabi Kalyan, Zila-Kafi, Kirwa** / 1986 / Chhanda Dhara ✦✦✦✦✦
This is one of the best and unfortunately last recordings of Banerjee, the incomparable sitarist. His beautiful rendering of "Purabi Kalyan," a combined raga, expresses with restraint the peaceful and devout mood of this twilight raga through an original melody. Another combined raga ("Zila-Kafi") is next, played with liberal development of the romantic mood. The concluding South Indian raga, "Kirwani," begins in a mood of devotion and develops into a fast Jhala. *– "Blue" Gene Tyranny*

Pandit Nikhil Banerjee / 1999 / Amigo Musik ✦✦✦✦

Sheila Chandra

b. Mar. 14, 1965
Vocals / Indian Pop, India, Southern Asia
One of the most unusual and successful singers of the '80s and '90s that has attempted to fuse the music of non-Western cultures with Western pop, Sheila Chandra began recording as a teenager in Monsoon. Of Indian ancestry, but born and raised in Britain, Chandra took lead vocals in the band, which pursued a sort of new wave-tinged raga-rock along the lines of George Harrison's explorations on Beatles tracks like "Love You To." The combination yielded an album and an unexpected British hit single, "Ever So Lonely," in the early '80s. Chandra, however, felt limited by the label's pressures for more commercial product, and signed to a small indie label, Indipop, which she felt would offer more freedom for her explorations as a solo artist.

In the mid-'80s, Chandra was astonishingly prolific, releasing five solo albums over a period of about two or three years that drifted away from the Asian dance-pop of Monsoon into a more personal sort of world fusion. Chandra also began to write much of her own material, usually in collaboration with producer and husband Steve Coe; Coe had also helped produce, write, and perform the music in Monsoon with Martin Smith, who also assisted on Chandra's early solo records. Indian instruments were still usually employed, and electronic rhythm tracks still sometimes used to guarantee some measure of danceability and pop-rock appeal. But with increasing frequency, Chandra was pushing herself beyond the parameters of pop-rock with wordless pieces of both melismatic singing and percussive mouth noises, ambitious song cycles, interwoven overdubbed vocal tracks, and a 27-minute track based around a raga. (Her mid-'80s Indipop albums have been reissued in the U.S. by Caroline.)

Chandra truly matured as an artist, however, with her '90s albums for Peter Gabriel's Real World label (distributed in the U.S., again, by Caroline). As proof that adulthood doesn't have to mean tamer and more mainstream product, these found Chandra achieving a true world fusion that drew from Indian ragas, elements of British folk, Middle Eastern chants, sophisticated studio overdubs, and more vocal percussion compositions, the last of which bordered on the downright experimental.

Chandra and Coe were now almost solely responsible for the music (Martin Smith no longer being an active participant), constructing drone-like instrumental textures to suitably complement Chandra's oft-wordless singing. Pop and rock were hardly factors anymore; Chandra was primarily interested in extending the limits of vocal expression, whether applied to Indian, Spanish, or Islamic forms, or the kind of material that could find a suitable home in the repertoire of June Tabor or Laurie Anderson. These recent works have firmly established Chandra as one of the principal boundary jumpers of contemporary music, but she's not a dilettante, and she imbues her music with a haunting, spiritual grace. *–Richie Unterberger*

Quiet / 1984 / Narada ✦✦✦✦✦
This was truly the album where Chandra broke away from the pop structures underlying much of Monsoon's work. Beginning to write much of her material (in collaboration with Martin Smith and producer Steve Coe), the dance rhythms of her debut were virtually eliminated, although the emphasis on Indian instrumentation remained intact. The music simultaneously incorporated elements that were both more traditional and more free-form than her previous work. Traditional in the sense that she drew upon Indian vocal styles such as spoken bols; free-form in that there were no lyrics, just wordless vocalizations, often overdubbed numerous times. Divided into ten tracks with a single title ("Quiet 1," "Quiet 2," etc.), the suite-like piece remained cognizant of modern technology and outside musical influences, without being overwhelmed by them. In most crucial respects, the album outlined the approach she has taken to her idiosyncratic brand of world music ever since. *–Richie Unterberger*

Nada Brahma / 1985 / Narada ✦✦✦

The Struggle / 1985 / Caroline ✦✦✦

★ **Silk 1983-1990** / 1991 / Shanachie ✦✦✦✦✦
A career retrospective of one of the innovators of the British Indi-pop style, this album contains moody and danceable hits collected from various '80s releases. *Silk* combines classical Indian music and Western pop into exotic club/dance music. *–Bob Tarte & Myles Boisen*

Weaving My Ancestors' Voices / 1992 / Real World ✦✦✦✦✦
Although Chandra had been recording for over a decade when this was released, this may be the album where she truly found her creative voice. Most vestiges of the pop/dance/rock rhythms of Monsoon, and some of her early albums, are absent. Chandra is now a virtuoso of the voice, offering almost avant-garde presentations of vocal gymnastics on "Speaking in Tongues." More often, though, she presents explorations of various musical cultures: India, of course, but also Irish folk, a Spanish lullaby, and Islamic singing. The spiritual quality of the material is enhanced by the drone-like textures of much of the music, devised by Chandra and her writing/production partner, Steve Coe. *–Richie Unterberger*

Zen Kiss / 1994 / Real World ✦✦✦✦✦

● **Moonsung** / Apr. 6, 1999 / Real World ✦✦✦✦✦
World music pioneer Shelia Chandra's diverse, groundbreaking works for the Real World label are collected on the 1999 retrospective *Moonsung*. The album explores Chandra's spectrum as a vocalist; she combines influences from Ireland, India, Andalucia and the Arabic world in a timeless, distinctive style. Creative and spiritual, *Moonsung* provides the perfect introduction—or reacquaintance—to Chandra's global artistic vision. *–Heather Phares*

Hariprasad Chaurasia

Wind Instruments, Bansuri, Flute / Indian Classical, India, Southern Asia
With his virtuousic blowing technique, Hariprasad Chaurasia has turned the Bansuri (bamboo) flute into an instrument of beauty. Blending the musical traditions of India with imagination and innovation, Chaurasia has reached beyond classical music to create a sound of his own. Presented with the national award of the Sangeet Natak Academy in 1984, Chaurasia received the Gaurav Puraskar from the state government of Maharashtra, India in 1990, the Padma Bhushan and the Konarak Samman in 1992 and the Yash Bharati Samman in 1994. In addition to recording as a soloist, Chaurasia has collaborated with such jazz musicians as John McLaughlin and Jan Garbarek. His compositions have been heard in several Indian films including *Silsila*, which he co-wrote with Pandit Shiv Kumar Sharma.

Although he began his musical studies as a vocalist, Chaurasia switched to the flute after hearing a performance by Pandit Bholanath a year later. Inspired by what he heard, Chaurasia spent the next eight years studying with Bholanath. He later studied with surbahar player Shrinimati Annapurna Devi, the daughter of Ustad Allaudin Khan and the siter of Ali Akbar Khan. In 1957, Chaurasia began playing and composing material for All India Radio in Calcutta. Ten years later, he collaborated with Shivkumar Sharma and Brijbhushan Kabra on a much-celebrated raga suite, "Call Of The Valley." *—Craig Harris*

Rag Bhimpalasi / 1987 / Nimbus ✦✦✦

• **Rag Kaunsi Kanhra** / 1989 / Nimbus ✦✦✦✦✦
This sensuous evening raga for the bamboo bansuri flute was recorded with tabla by Sabir Khan. *—Myles Boisen*

Rag Lalit / 1989 / Nimbus ✦✦✦✦✦

Venu / Apr. 1990 / Rykodisc ✦✦✦

Hariprasad Chaurasia / Nimbus ✦✦✦✦
Together with tabla-player Ustad Zakir Hussain, India's best-known flutist expands at length on the popular night melody, "Raag Chandrakauns," following it with a briefer pastoral dhun, "Dadra Dhun." The 90-minute performance of "Chandrakauns," far more than earlier recordings, reveals the enrichment of Chaurasia's style of the heterogeneous flute traditions he has studied, a model of integration without pastiche. As the performance nears its climax, the interplay between Chaurasia and Zakir Hussain becomes particularly powerful. *—John Storm Roberts*

Zakir Hussain

b. Mar. 9, 1951
Tabla, Drums, Concertina, Percussion / Indian Classical, World Fusion, India, Southern Asia
The tradition of Indian percussion has been revolutionalized by tabla player Zakir Hussain. The son of Ustad Allah Rakha, the long time collaborator of Ravi Shankar, Hussain has inherited his father's quest for bringing the music of India to the international stage. His recording credits include albums with George Harrison, Joe Henderson, Van Morrison, Jack Bruce, Tito Puente, Pharoah Saunders, Billy Cobham, the Hong Kong Symphony and the New Orleans Symphony. His work with Mickey Hart of The Grateful Dead have included performances and albums with the Diga Rhythm Band and Planet Drum. Hussain joined with British guitarist John McLaughlin and Indian violinist L. Shankar to form the east-meets-west supergroup, Shakti, in 1975. Although the group disbanded in 1978, they reunited to tour as Remember Shakti in 1998. Hussain has been equally successful as a bandleader. During the 1980s, he toured with Zakir Hussain's Rhythm Experience. His debut solo album, *Making Music*, released in 1987, was called "one of the most inspired East-West fusion albums ever recorded." In 1992, Hussain launched a record label, Monument Records, that focused on Indian music. A lengthy list of awards have been bestowed upon Hussain throughout his career. In 1988, he became the youngest percussionist to be awarded the title "Padma Shri" by the Indian government. Two years later, he recieved the Indo-Ameican award in tribute to his contributions to furthering relations between the United States and India. *Planet Drum*, an album co-produced with Hart in 1992, received a Grammy for "best world music album," a NARM Indie Best Seller award and won the *Downbeat* Critics Poll for "Best world music album." Still a youngster when he began to attract attention with his virtuosic playing, Hussain began his musical career at the age of seven and was touring by the age of twelve. In 1970, he made his American debut as accompanist for Ravi Shankar. Three years later, he became the leader of the Tal Vadya Rhythm Band. The group subsequently evolved into the Diga Rhythm Band. In 1976, the band collaborated on a self-titled album with Mickey Hart. Hussain has performed on the soundtracks of numerous films including *Apocalypse Now!*, *In Custody* and *Little Buddha*. At *the 1983 Cannes Film Festival*, he was nominated for an award as composer and music director of the film, *Heat And Dust*. *—Craig Harris*

• **Tabla Duet** / 1988 / Chhanda Dhara ✦✦✦✦
This release reversed the usual order placing son before father in the billing. A riveting performance with Sultan Khan accompanying on sarangi. Exemplary musicianship all round. *—Ken Hunt*

Zakir Hussain & The Rhythm Experience / Nov. 1991 / Moment ✦✦✦

Ali Akbar Khan

b. 1922, Shivpur, Bangladesh
Sarod, Sitar / Indian Folk, Indian Classical, Ethnic Fusion, India, Southern Asia
The son of influential Hindustani musician, Allaudin Khan, Ali Akbar Khan is one of the eastern world's greatest musicians. A master of the sarod, a twenty-five stringed, lute-like, Indian instrument, Khan has brought the Northern Indian classical music to the international stage. A five time Grammy nominee, Khan was called, by Yehudi Menuhin, "an absolute genius, the greatest musician in the world." Tracing his ancestral roots to Mian Tansen, a sixteenth century musician in the court of Emperor Akbar, Khan began studying music at the age of three. Initially studying vocal music with his father, he studied drums with his uncle, Fakir Aftabuddin. Although he tried playing a wide variety of instruments, he felt most comfortable on the sarod. Training and practicing eighteen hours a day, he slowly mastered the instrument. In 1936, he made his public debut during a concert in Allahabad. In the early-1940s, Khan became a court musician for the Maharaja of Judhpur. He soon acquired the title, "Ustad" (master musician). In 1955, Khan accepted an invitation from Menuhin to perform in the United States. In addition to performing at *the Museum of Modern Art* in New York, he recorded the first western album of Indian classical music and became the first Indian music on an American television when he appeared on Alistair Cooke's *Omnibus*. In 1971, Khan performed with his brother-in-law, Ravi Shankar, during George Harrison's Concert For Bangladesh at *Madison Square Garden*. Khan has received numerous awards including the President of India award in 1963, the Padma Vibhusan in 1988, the Bill Graham Lifetime Achievment award in 1993 and the Asian Paints–Shiromani Hall of Fame award in 1997. He received the Kalidas Sanman from the Madya Pradesh Academy of Music And Fine Arts and became the first Indian musician to be awarded a MacArthur Foundation. "Genius Grant" in 1991. Khan received a National Heritage Fellowship from the National Endowment of the Arts in 1997. In 1956, Khan founded the Ali Akbar Khan College of Music in Calcutta. Teaching in the United States, since 1965, he opened the Ali Akbar College of Music in Berkeley, California two years later. In 1968, the school moved to its present site in San Rafael. Khan currently teaches six classes a week for nine months a year. In the early-1990s, the school opened branches in Fremont, California and Basel, Switzerland. The lengthy list of films featuring Khan's music includes Chetan Anand's *Aandhiyan*, Satyajit Ray's *Devi* and Bernardo Bertolucci's *Little Buddha*. He received a "best musician of the year" award for his soundtrack for the film, *Khudita Pashan*. *—Craig Harris*

The Artistic Sound of Sarod / 1985 / Chhanda Dhara ✦✦✦

Journey / Aug. 1990 / Triloka ✦✦✦
At 67, veteran Indian music master Ali Akbar Khan successfully blends tradition and technology on *Journey*, a moving CD produced by his protege and student Jai Uttal. *Journey*, however, isn't modern secular Indian pop, but rather is best described as traditional Indian spiritual and devotional music using high-tech elements. Under Uttal's direction, Khan's sarod and other acoustic Indian instruments like the sitar, the tabla and the dholak successfully interact with electronic synthesizers (none of which sound forced or mechanical). Uttal had learned a lot from Khan, and showed his appreciation by seeing to it that technology was used soulfully throughout this album. *—Alex Henderson*

Signature Series, Vol. 1-2 / 1990 / AMMP ✦✦✦✦✦
His long-unavailable 1967 recordings for the Connoisseur Society were the gateway to raga for many Americans. More than that, they are examples of one of the great schools of Hindustani classical music. Among the first of the Connoisseur series to be reissued, these and all his recordings are essential. *Volume 1* has ragas "Chandranandan," "Gauri Manjari," "Jogiya Kalingra"; *Volume 2*, ragas "Medhavi," "Khammaj," "Bhairavi Bhatiyar w. Ragmala." *—John Storm Roberts*

Plays Alap a Sarod Solo / May 5, 1992-May 6, 1992 / Alam Madia ✦✦✦✦

Rag Manj Khammaj & Rag Misra Mand / 1994 / AMMP ✦✦✦✦✦
When Ali Akbar Khan was still young he would help Nikhil Banerjee prepare for the arduous study regime of Allauddin Khan, who was Ali Akbar Khan's father as well as Nikhil Banerjee's guru. Years later Ali Akbar Khan would play with the sitarist some nine years his junior and this sarod-sitar jugalbandi is an example of the heights they could achieve as this unexpected unearthing proves. It has a rare, essential beauty. Evidently his clandestine visits paid off handsomely. *—Ken Hunt*

Traditional Music of India / Apr. 17, 1995 / Prestige ✦✦✦✦

★ **Duet** / RSM ✦✦✦✦✦
A near-perfect example of the classical duet, this superb live concert features star violinist L. Subramaniam and tabla drummer Zakir Hussein. *—Myles Boisen*

Ustad Vilayat Khan

Surbahar, Sitar / Indian Classical, Raga, India, Southern Asia
Vilayat Khan, one of the greatest Hindustani musicians of the century, was born in Gouripur in East Bengal (later Bangladesh) in August 1922. (Various other dates are strewn throughout the literature but that is the date that he confirmed in 1993.) His grandfather, Imdad Khan (1848-1920) and his father Enayat Khan (1894-1938)—Vilayat Khan gives the spelling Inayat Khan—were famed musicians in their lifetimes and Vilayat and his younger brother Imrat Khan inherited their musicality. Their gharana is known as the Imdadkhani gharana after their grandfather.

He studied initially with his father. On his father's death in 1938 his training became the

The Music of India

The music of India has enjoyed a worldwide explosion since coming into vogue in the psychedelic '60s. Most Indian musicians come from musical families and begin study from an early age at the knee of a father or uncle. In the classical tradition (the majority of recordings available in the US are by North Indian classical musicians), music is a prestigious, lifelong pursuit where sustained solo expression figures prominently. Centuries-old scales called ragas serve as the basis for extended improvisation in small groups, typically involving a tabla drummer and tambura player, whose ethereal drone reinforces the mood of the raga for the lead instrumentalist.

Popular lead instruments in the North Indian school are the multi-stringed sitar, sarod, sarangi, and santour, and woodwinds—bamboo flute and shehnai. A double-reed oboe is sometimes heard in larger ensembles. The voice is also featured in both North and South Indian classical forms—in the South the dominant art music is the Carnatic style, which emphasizes highly ornamented improvisation based on long melodies of folk, sacred, and classical origin. Common instruments in the South are the stringed vina and violin, often used in larger groups with singers and a variety of percussion—the double-headed mridangam, clay-pot drum, and tambourine. In recent years, Western instruments—mandolin, guitar, clarinet, piano, and even the saxophone—have been embraced by younger innovators and incorporated into the classical tradition (though not without protest).

India also has a rich legacy of regional folk music; religious songs of various sects; theatrical epics involving mythology, dance, and music; pop forms; and of course an extremely prolific film-music industry, just beginning to be appreciated abroad. Recordings offered by American companies are just the tip of the iceberg—go to an Indian market in a major city and you will find a bewildering array of national styles, most on inexpensive cassettes.

— *Myles Boisen*

responsibility of his mother, Bashiran Begum, his grandmother, Bande Hussain Khan, and his maternal uncle, Wahid Khan. Around the same period Vilayat Khan began recording 78s. Peculiarly it is reported that he had to cope with odious comparisons with his father. Gradually he developed a style which, while acknowledging his kinsfolk's contribution, spoke with his own distinctive voice. His most outstanding contribution to his gharana's tradition is the evolution of what is known as a vocal style or gayaki ang on sitar. To some degree this is a term of convenience. Other contemporary musicians were striving to develop instrumental styles which more closely resembled the human voice—it was after all the goal of all instrumentalists to mimic as far as possible the human voice—and Vilayat Khan did not have a monopoly in this endeavor whatever some commentators claimed. That is not to detract from his achievement which was considerable and caused a sensation.

Vilayat Khan's strides in compensating for the sitar's shortcomings were immense. His career has been marked by a regally consistent musical quality. An outspoken critic of low standards, he has maintained levels of personal integrity that on occasion have earned him the disfavor of the establishment. Little of his work has been in any context other than the strictly classical one although he worked with Satyajit Ray on the soundtrack to the film *Jalsaghar* and the Ismail Merchant/James Ivory film *The Guru*. He might be summed up as a keeper—not a quencher—of the flame. —*Ken Hunt*

• **Raga Bhairavi** / 1991 / India Archive Music ♦♦♦♦♦
There is something particularly captivating about Vilayat Khan's sitar voicings. His alluringly playful style is thick with deep and subtle variations. His rendering of the much recorded late-morning raga Bhairavi combines the tranquil depth of classical interpretations with the lighter sentimentality of the semi-classical thumri. Hidayat Khan is on tanpura. —*Raissa St. Pierre, Original Music*

Night at the Taj / 1994 / EMI India ♦♦♦♦

Sitar / 1994 / Navras ♦♦♦

Raga Jaijaivanti / Mar. 11, 1994 / India Archive Music ♦♦♦♦
If you wish to inaugurate a new label with an auspicious event there can be little better way than having Vilayat Khan. "Raga Bhairavi" is a studio interpretation from April 1989 performed solo. A landmark performance, it sends shivers up the spine. It would be an auspicious place to begin a lifetime's love of the man's music. —*Ken Hunt*

Lata Mangeshkar

b. Sep. 28, 1929, Indore, India
Vocals / Indian Pop, Indian Classical, India, Southern Asia
Any account of Indian playback music must start with Lata Mangeshkar. While it is not possible to more than list the most important playback singers, one, because of her supreme stature, merits detailed attention. Born September 28, 1929 in Indore, India, Lata Mangeshkar has been active in all walks of Indian popular and light classical music having sung ghazals, bhajans and pop. She is the supreme voice of popular Indian music, an Indian institution. Her importance rests not solely with her prodigious output. Many of her performances are considered timeless and undatable, although her voice has changed and matured over the years. In effect she sang the soundtrack for millions of Indians' lives. Until the 1991 edition, when her entry disappeared, the *Guinness Book of Records* listed her as the most recorded artist in the world with not less than 30,000 solo, duet and chorus-backed songs recorded in 20 Indian languages between 1948 and 1987. By 1990 she supposedly had worked on over 2000 film soundtracks as a playback singer—meaning she pre-recorded the songs to which the films' leading ladies lip-synched.

Dinanath Mangeshkar, her father, owned a theatrical company and was a classical singer, a disciple of the Gwalior school, and gave her singing lessons from around the age of five. She also studied with Aman Ali Khan Sahib and later Amanat Khan. Her God-given musical gifts meant that she could master the vocal exercises effortlessly on first pass and from early on she was recognized as being highly gifted musically. Also in the family were brother Hridaynath, a music director, and sisters Meena, Asha (the famed Asha Bhosle), and Usha. Hridaynath's soundtrack work included *Lekin...* (EMI India CD PMLP 5206) released in 1990 which, keeping it a family affair, placed Lata Mangeshkar well to the fore. Usha also became a playback singer. Only Asha Bhosle's career can compare in any way with her sister's award-strewn output although by 1994 reports were appearing to the effect that Asha Bhosle had overtaken her big sister's output.

Lata Mangeshkar began work as playback singer in the 1940s and grew to become the most famous playback singer of the century. She received her first proper named credit under her own name in actor/director Raj Kapoor's 1949 film *Barsaat* (the soundtrack from which forms a third of the *Barsaat/Aah/Aag* album on EMI India CD PMLP 5188). She would sing for every major actress, including Geeta Bali, Nanda, Nargis, Nimmi, Nutan, Padmini, Sadhana and Meena Shorey. The sheer scale of recording activity makes any examination of her life and works impossible in such a confined space. —*Ken Hunt*

• **Hits in the 80's** / 1990 / EMI India ♦♦♦♦♦
Subtitled "Duets by Lata Mangeshkar," this anthology includes work with S.P. Balasubramanyam (the title track from "Maine Pyar Kiya" and "Tere Mere Beech Mein" from *Ek Duuje Ke Liye*), Nitan Mukesh and Kishore Kumar. A good representative collection of songs but left waif-like, like most Hindi film collections, to fend for themselves since sleeve notes would be a frivolous luxury. —*Ken Hunt*

Memorable Duets / 1994 / EMI India ♦♦♦

Sabri Brothers

Group / Qawwali, India, Southern Asia
The Sabri Brothers, Haji Ghulam Farid (or Fareed) Sabri (1930-1994) and Haji Maqbool Ahmed Sabri (also born in Kalyana in East Punjab, on October 12, 1945), they were taught music by their father, Ustad Haji Inayat Sen Sabri. The family claims descent from Mian Tansen, one of the greatest and most legendary Hindustani musicians of all time. The musically gifted Tansen was a musician in the court of Akbar and is credited with miraculous powers of musicianship. Maqbool Ahmed Sabri formed his first party of qawwals at the age of 11; soon afterwards in 1956 his elder brother (who had been singing with Kallan Khan's qawwal and party) joined him and the Sabri Brothers proper came about. Their career was marked by brotherly squabbles followed by periods of each doing solo work. The duo created a body of recorded work, consistent in quality, but rather more traditional than Nusrat Fateh Ali Khan's recorded work. Ghulam Farid Sabri's funeral in Karachi was attended by an estimated 40,000 mourners. Haji Maqbool Ahmed Sabri continues to carry the torch. —*Ken Hunt*

Ya Habib / 1990 / Plan 9/Caroline ♦♦♦♦♦
Quawwali, the music of Islam's Sufi sect, can be found in Middle Eastern countries ranging from India to Saudi Arabia to Turkey. How prevalent it is in a particular country depends on how friendly that country is to Sufis (who, like Hindus, believe music to be a sacred and necessary element of religious life). For centuries, Quawwali was prevalent in Iran, but when the Ayatollah Khomehni outlawed all music in that country in 1979, Persian Sufis faced tremendous danger. One of the finest Quawwali groups in Pakistan is the Sabri Brothers. In contrast to secular Pakistani pop music, *Ya Habib* concerns itself only with spiritual matters. Whether singing or playing the harmonium, Haji Ghulam Farid Sabri and Haji Maqbool Ahmed Sabri spare no passion on the extended pieces heard on this enriching CD. Highly recommended. —*Alex Henderson*

★ **Qawwali Masterworks** / 1993 / Piranha ♦♦♦♦♦
A trawl through the archives of EMI Pakistan, the label which released their domestic product for decades, produced this double-CD set of vintage Sabri material. The concluding piece, a 14-minute rendition of two Sufi themes titled "Posida Posida" ("Discreetly, Discreetly"), demonstrates the power of their poetic vision. —*Ken Hunt*

Ya Mustapha / 1996 / Xenophile ♦♦♦♦♦
Pakistan's Sabri Brothers command tremendous respect among enthusiasts of Quawwali music, and the two live up their much deserved rep on the soulful and consistently moving *Ya Mustafa*. Sufis believe that music can and should induce a state of ecstacy and bring one closer to God (Allah in Arabic)—in fact, spirituality is the only concern of this outstanding CD. While a lot of great Middle Eastern music is secular, lengthy offerings like "Khwaja ka Diwana," the 21-minute "La Illaha" and the 26-minute "Tajdar-e-Haram" are strictly devotional. Because Quawwali material tends to be go on quite a while, the CD format has served as an excellent means of documenting such artists as the Sabri Brothers. Thankfully, Xenophile provides an English-language translation of their lyrics. —*Alex Henderson*

• **Greatest Hits** / May 20, 1997 / Shanachie ♦♦♦♦♦

Bally Sagoo

DJ / Club/Dance, Bhangra, India, Southern Asia
The New Delhi-born Bally Sagoo grew up in Britain where he established a reputation as one of the more happening purveyors of dance music. His music incorporates all manner of bhangra, hip-hop and ragga. His old Indian film music background has also influenced his art, made tangible around the time of 1995's *Bollywood Flashback* but also in an underlying sense since film music has created a series of conventions for presenting itself. The kitchen-sink approach so beloved of non-Indian commentators was a tradition that Bally Sagoo could take to heart. Bally Sagoo and Devissaro contributed the music to new dance works by Daksha Sheth and Roger Sinha performed by Yuva (a young South Asian dance company) under the collective title of *Tongues Untied* in September as part of the annual Vivarta Festival in London. In 1994 it was announced that he had signed a major deal with Columbia/Sony. It was evidence of his versatility and their belief in his potential. *Rising from the East* followed in 1996, and *Sountracks: For Your Life* was released in 1999. —*Ken Hunt*

• **Bally Sagoo on the Mix: The Story So Far** / 1993 / Star ♦♦♦♦♦
Aimed at a ragga and bhangra audience this album draws on previous releases. Of the people remixing past recordings Bally Sagoo's approach is the most likely to succeed. Where Bally Sagoo scores is that his treatments combine respect and an innate feel for qawwali and other forms with a pinch of good humor. Featured guinea pigs include Malkit Singh Golden Star (U.K.), Nusrat Fateh Ali Khan, Rama and A.S. Kang. —*Ken Hunt*

Rising from the East / 1996 / Columbia ♦♦♦

Anoushka Shankar

Sitar / Indian Classical, India, Southern Asia
The daughter of sitar legend Ravi Shankar, Anoushka Shankar began studying under her father at age nine, making her performing debut four years later. Appearing alongside her father as he toured the world, she appeared at Carnegie Hall while still in her teens, and also performed with Peter Gabriel's WOMAD festival; the youngest and only female recepient of the House of Commons Shield awarded by British Parliament "in recognition of her artistry and musicianship—as a pre-eminent musician of the Asian Arts," Shankar made her solo debut with 1998's *Anoushka*, released when she was still just 17 years old. *Anourag* followed two years later. —*Jason Ankeny*

• **Anoushka** / Oct. 20, 1998 / Angel ♦♦♦♦
While the sitar is usually taught master to student in a male to male tradition, this beautiful daughter to renowned sitar master Ravi Shankar has been given access to the art. Debuting in 1994 and touring with Ravi since, this album of five compositions, four of which are Ravi Shankar's, is a fitting recording debut. The pieces begin with a slow introduction of fluid rhythm (*alap* or *aochar*) and build in crescendo to a spirited display of virtuosity with tabla accompaniment. It appears Anoushka, who appears on the J card in stunning traditional garb but in the booklet in more Western clothes, including white, feathery boas, has chosen compositions that build to multi-note runs. These "sitar leads" are less like the traditional, serene raga collection usually heard from traditional Indian masters and more like the effect gotten by rock guitarists employing sitar for timbre difference. Perhaps it is that she is just choosing a faster tempo on this material, as speed is up to the player in this music tradition. Of

course, whatever Anoushka's stylistic direction, she is overtly masterful on the 20-string instrument. Poetic texts, in English, are provided for the instrumental tracks. A detailed glossary and track-by-track notes further elucidate the musical science behind these fascinating, exotic sounds. *—Tom Schulte*

Anourag / Angel ✦✦✦

Lakshminarayana Shankar

b. Apr. 26, 1950, Madras, India
Violin / Fusion, World Fusion, India, Southern Asia
This violinist has found a comfortable style that melds and combines classical Indian influences and jazz devices. He moved to America in 1969, eventually earned a doctorate in ethnomusicology at Wesleyan, where he began meeting jazz musicians like Ornette Coleman, Jimmy Garrison, and John McLaughlin while working as a teaching assistant and concert master of the university chamber orchestra. He studied with McLaughlin in 1973, and two years later, they cofounded the group Shakti, which was active until 1978. During the '80s and beyond, Shankar has recorded periodically as a leader, doing both jazz-based material and Indian classical music. He's also worked with rockers Peter Gabriel, Phil Collins, and Frank Zappa. *—Ron Wynn*

● **Who's to Know** / Nov. 1980 / ECM ✦✦✦✦✦
Having already established himself as member of John Mclaughlin's jazz and Indian music ensemble Shakti, violinist L. Shankar set himself up as a virtuoso leader in contexts ranging from /Indian classical music to modern hybrids featuring synthesizers and drum machines. Through it all, he brought the unique sound of his 10-string double violin (from an original design) to dates featuring the likes of Zakir Hussein, Frank Zappa, Peter Gabriel, and Steve Vai. For this 1980 session, the violinist focuses on the traditional ragas of his native India, with two extended pieces. Joined by Hussein on tabla, Umayalpuram K. Sivaraman on mridangam, and conductor V. Lakshminarayana, Shankar produces a wealth of solo climaxes while weaving myriad thematic improvisations. On the first raga (both pieces here are reconfigurations of traditional ragas), he moves from a meditative solo stretch to some frenetic interplay with Hussein, eventually ending the piece with an incredible, lightening-fast display of technique. The group opt for a more even-keeled pace on the second raga. Shankar is impressive again, while Hussein makes the best of some lengthy solo spots. An essential disc for L. Shankar fans. *—Stephen Cook*

Vision / Apr. 1983 / ECM ✦✦✦

Song for Everyone / Sep. 1984 / ECM ✦✦✦✦
Song For Everyone heralds the return of the groove in Shankar's East-West-minded music, with former Shakti colleague Zakir Hussain on tabla, Trilok Gurtu on percussion, and Shankar's own manipulation of a drum machine tending to the rhythms. The result is a brighter, more outgoing record than its predecessor *Vision,* veering between Western acoustic and electric grooves and the complex beats churned out by the tabla. Jan Garbarek again shines beams of light on soprano and tenor, engaging Shankar's 10-string double-necked electric violin in some complex interplay on the title track. Some tracks are driven entirely or partially by the drum machine; "Paper Nut" has a particularly infectious revolving pattern. But sometimes Shankar overdoes it; the lengthy "Watching You" has an overly mechanized feeling that can be either mesmerizing or infuriating, depending upon your mood. On another track, "I Know," the Western percussion is gradually swallowed up by the Indian tabla. Fascinating, free-thinking music, beautifully recorded as usual by ECM. *—Richard S. Ginell*

Pancha Nadai Pallavi / Jul. 1989 / ECM ✦✦✦✦✦
As if playing one violin within the Western art music tradition wasn't difficult enough, the virtuoso L. Shankar has made it his trade to both sing and play a customized double violin within the contexts of Hindustani, Carnatic, Western, and experimental musical sensibilities. On this 1990 ECM release, *Pancha Nadai Pallavi,* he lays down two tracks, the first without percussion and the second in collaboration with Zakir Hussain on tabla and Vikku Vinayakram on ghatam. Caroline also accompanies the L. Shankar with the drone setting sruthi (a small one-note hand-pumped reed organ) and talam (a pair of small hand cymbals). With the first track L. Shankar performs the ragam "Sankarabharanam" (a ragam is the Carnatic equivalent to the Hindustani raga). For nearly 30 minutes he elegantly articulates an innumerable series of variations on traditional forms, melodies, and rhythms. The double violin allows him to imitate the sounds of a multi-octave string ensemble. On the CD's second cut a serpentine nine and one-half beat rhythmic cycle, the Mahalakshmi Tala, provides the temporal framework for the performance. An original creation by L. Shankar himself, this tala is realized by tabla superstar Zakir Hussain and the celebrated ghatam (clay water pot) player Vikku Vinayakram. Both of these percussive masters draw a myriad of tones and conjure up a fortified stew of rhythmic cadences from their respective instruments. In sum, Shankar's *Pancha Nadai Pallavi* is a smashing CD that represents virtuosic creativity and experimentation at work in both solo and collaborative contexts. *—John Vallier*

Nobody Told Me / 1990 / ECM ✦✦✦

Songs of Devotion / 1990 / Auvidis/Ethnic ✦✦✦

Ravi Shankar

b. Apr. 7, 1920, India
Surbahar, Sarod, Sitar / Indian Classical, Raga, World Fusion, India, Southern Asia
Born on April 7, 1920, at Varanasi near Benares in West Bengal into an orthodox, well-off Brahmin family, Rabindra Shankar Chowdery's father, ShyΔm Shankar, was employed as a diwan (minister) by the Maharajah of Jhalawar. By the age of 13, Ravi Shankar was going along on every tour of his brother Uday Shankar's Compaigne de Danse et Musique Hindou (Company of Hindu Dance and Music). At the All-Bengali Music Conference in December 1934 he met the multi-instrumentalist Allauddin Khan. Precisely when Allauddin Khan was born is uncertain. People hazard dates in the 1860s around 1862 but in later years he himself gave his age haphazardly. He would transform many musicians' lives but he had an incalculable effect on Ali Akbar (his son), Annapurna Devi (his daughter) and Ravi Shankar himself.

Allauddin Khan joined Uday's troupe as its principal soloist around 1935-36. In 1938 Ravi Shankar gave up a potential career as a dancer and went to study with Allauddin Khan in Maihar. In 1939 he began giving public recitals and came out of training at the end of 1944. Until 1948 he based himself in Bombay and gave programmes all over India. He toured and wrote for films and ballet. Around this time he began his recording career with a small session for HMV (India). Work for All India Radio followed—as music director from February 1949 to January 1956 in New Delhi. Concurrently, his international star was on the rise. In 1954 he performed in the Soviet Union. In 1956 he played his debut solo concerts in Western Europe and the U.S. Within a decade he would be the most famous Indian musician on the planet. Within two decades he would become probably the most famous Indian alive. His English-language autobiography, *My Music, My Life* (1969) is still one of the best general introductions to Hindustani music.

Ravi Shankar is not one-dimensional. Apart from pursuing a career as a classical performer, he has also experimented outside this field. For this reason he has attracted criticism from purists. Some of this, especially during the Beatles era, undoubtedly had an element of jealousy to it: some was certainly warranted, because Ravi Shankar did take many chances. In fact, that was one of the things that kept his music exciting. To use a cricketing image—baseball would be wholly inappropriate—Ravi Shankar's batting average has remained high throughout a long and illustrious career. *—Ken Hunt*

☆ **Three Ragas** / 1967 / Angel ✦✦✦✦✦
Perhaps Ravi Shankar's finest post-World Pacific record, *Three Ragas* is not only a fantastic artistic statement, but also an excellent introduction to the medium of Indian music itself. Performed by Shankar and a very simple trio, the pieces on this record show the true heart of Indian music at its most intimate. The second side, "Raga Jog," will take your breath away. A showcase in Indian ensemble performing as well as in Shankar's own endurance and grace, this side truly shows why he has been called (by David Crosby, no less) the finest musician on the planet. This record was put together at a time when Shankar and Indian music were reaching mass audiences via the Beatles and others (hence the Capitol Records connection), but there is no cheapening of the art here. An excellent record by a true master. *—Matthew Greenwald*

In Concert 1972 / 1972 / Apple ✦✦✦✦

★ **Ragas** / 1973 / Fantasy ✦✦✦✦✦
A less-than-perfect recording, this double-album is still an impeccable document of inspired raga duets by the masters Ravi Shankar and Ali Akbar Khan. *—Myles Boisen*

Sitar Concerto No. 2 / 1981 / Angel ✦✦✦✦
Dedicated to Ravi Shankar's collaborator Zubin Mehta, *Sitar Concerto No. 2* (or *Raga-Mala*), commissioned in 1981 by the New York Philharmonic, combines a rich base of Indian classical forms with Western classical conventions. *—Jenna Woolford*

Tana Mana / 1987 / Private Music ✦✦✦✦
On his first release for Private Music, Ravi Shankar combined the traditional instruments of Indian music (sitar, sarod, tabla, etc.) with synthesizers and heavy sampling keyboard usage. Surprisingly enough, the combination works out for the best on the majority of the tracks. The reverberant quality of the sitar combines rather well with the chosen electronic accompaniments to form a set of coherent songs, unlike many other such attempted combinations of traditional instruments and technology. The sitar playing is, as usual, superb—who would expect anything else to come from the legend himself (and/or his associate Shubho Shankar). With an extra sarod thrown in, a small front line of synthesizers, and Shankar's friend George Harrison assisting on the autoharp, the pile of musicality that forms allows an unexpectedly coherent, clear, and relatively focused piece of music to emerge. There are no specific highlights to speak of on this album, as all of the tracks are equal, and the level at which they are equal is rather high. The only real gripe to be had with the album is the lack of straight Indian classical playing by Shankar, though with his multitude of other albums, that can be forgiven. *—Adam Greenberg*

Farewell, My Friend / 1992 / EMI India ✦✦✦

Ravi Shankar / 1993 / Deutsche Grammaphon ✦✦✦✦✦
Released around 1993, this limited-edition triple CD reinstated to catalog three of the most interesting releases in Ravi Shankar's career. The first source is *East Greets East,* a trailblazing collaboration between Indian and Japanese musicians dating from 1978. Straddling it and the second CD is the album *Ragas Hameer & Gara* from 1979. The middle CD completes that album and adds *Raga Jogeshwari* from 1980. These last two albums are also available individually as Music India CDNF 010 and 009, respectively. Completing the trilogy is one of Ravi Shankar's finest ever studio albums, *Homage to Mahatma Gandhi & Baba Allauddin* from 1981, also available as Music India CDNF 119. The only thing weakening this compilation is its German-only text, a curiosity in some senses since the original Deutsche Grammophon/Polydor releases carried English (and French) texts. *—Ken Hunt*

Ravi Shankar in San Francisco / 1995 / One Way ✦✦✦✦
On Ravi Shankar's World Pacific sides, the longer ragas were usually the highlight. These contained the true essence of Indian music: long, undulating ragas that slowly evolved and built in intensity. Unfortunately, there was usually only room for one on each album (if that); however, *Live in San Francisco* contains three extended pieces and is perhaps his best World Pacific album. Accompanied by Alla Rakha on tabla, Shankar shows his rhythmic grace and sheer stamina on these performances to a live audience's delight. Recorded at *the San Francisco Civic Auditorium* at a time (about 1967) when consciousness in Indian music was growing at an incredible rate, *Live in San Francisco* is an awesome performance and an amazing historical document as well. *—Matthew Greenwald*

Portrait of Genius / Oct. 20, 1998 / Angel ✦✦✦✦
Ravi Shankar has been described as one of the greatest musicians on the planet. This record,

one of his classic World Pacific albums, clearly lends credence to that statement. But the thing that makes this record interesting is the fact that it contains a unique fusion of Shankar and his group performing with respected jazz flutist Paul Horn. It's an extremely gratifying combination, and Horn plays with a true jazzman's restraint on the five short selections that open the record. The second half is devoted to one long (20-minute) traditional raga, "Raga Multani," in which Shankar's awesome ability and stamina is matched only by that of his ensemble, especially Alla Rakha on tabla. Essential for any fan of Shankar or Indian music. Awesome. *—Matthew Greenwald*

West Meets East: The Historic Shankar/Menuhin Sessions / Nov. 2, 1999 / Angel ♦♦♦♦
West Meets East: The Historic Shankar/Menuhin Sessions collects the best from Ravi Shankar and Yehudi Menhuin's three *West Meets East* albums. This compilation features "Prabhati" and "Swara-Kakali" from the first album, "Raga Piloo" and "Dhun" from the second, and "Tenderness" and "Twilight Mood" from the third. All of the tracks feature the hypnotic interplay of Menuhin's violin and Shankar's sitar that made the individual albums critically and commercially popular when they were first released. *—Heather Phares*

★ **The Sounds of India** / Columbia ♦♦♦♦♦
A CD reissue of an important introduction to Indian music, this release is one of the few recordings featuring Chatur Lal on tabla and N.C. Mullick on tanpura. Notes are by the American composer Alan Hovhaness. *—Ken Hunt*

Shivkumar Sharma

b. Jan. ??, 1938
Santur, Dulcimer / Indian Classical, India, Southern Asia
Shivkumar Sharma is one of the truly great visionaries in the Hindustani classical music firmament. His popularity has created a knotty problem for his admirers. Popularity has led to a demand for recordings by him, to a degree that having a Shivkumar Sharma album acts like a kind of validation for a label. Consequently the market is flooded with his recordings. His playing is consummate, therefore he is unlikely to produce a piece of work that is below par, which makes selecting a shortlist even more difficult.

Sharma's story is one of dedication. He was born in January 1938 in Jammu Kashmir. His father Uma Dutt Sharma asked him to pursue the development of the Kashmiri santoor. Being a dutiful son he obeyed and persevered despite private reservations. Though its Persian relative, the santur, had associations with Persian and Iranian classical music, elevating the Indian instrument to the classical concert platform was widely viewed as folly in conservative quarters. But Shivkumar Sharma persisted, experimented, restrung and reconfigured his instrument. His first major santoor recital took place in Bombay in February 1955, but it took, he reckons, until the 1970s to finally silence the querulous, "the die-hard connoisseurs of the music, musicologists and purists." Parallel with his development of the santoor he worked as a tabla player (he accompanied acts as diverse as the renowned Punjabi folksinger Surinder Kaur and sitar maestro Ravi Shankar), and his understanding of tabla playing and rhythm has immeasurably enhanced his performance style and stagecraft. *—Ken Hunt*

★ **Rag Madhuvanti & Rag Misra Tilang** / 1987 / Nimbus ♦♦♦♦♦
Shivkumar Sharma is accompanied on this album by Zakir Hussain. Nimbus's importance as the first CD pressing plant in Britain meant that its recording wing had developed a keen and early appreciation of the technology and potential of CD production. A beautiful, sensitively played pairing. *—Ken Hunt*

Hypnotic Santoor / 1988 / Chhanda Dhara ♦♦♦♦♦
An unusual repertoire item, "Raga Gorakh Kalyan," opens this album and, acting as an acknowledgment of Shivkumar Sharma's cultural and folk roots, the album closes with "Dogri Folklore." (Dogri is his first language.) It is a semiclassical piece set in a folk "Raga Mishra Pahadi" to a six-beat metrical cycle. Shafaat Ahmed Khan accompanies on tabla. *—Ken Hunt*

Raga Yaman / 1990 / Chhanda Dhara ♦♦♦♦♦
Shivkumar Sharma, accompanied by Zakir Hussain on tabla, is captured on this recording at one of Stuttgart's *Indian Nights* concerts in 1988. This particular raga is a popular beginner's piece. This is not to belittle it. It is commonly chosen for that purpose because it offers a range of options for interpreting its shape and color that can absorb the mind for a lifetime. Shivkumar Sharma's rendition—subtitled 'A Concerto in Raga Yaman'—is proof of its nourishing qualities. *—Ken Hunt*

Santoor / 1991 / Music Today ♦♦♦♦♦

Raga Purya Kalyan / 1996 / World Network ♦♦♦

The Valley Recalls, Vol. 1 / Sep. 15, 2000 / Navras ♦♦♦♦
Pandit Shivkumar Sharma and Pandit Hariprasad Chaurasia reunite some 30 years later for a follow-up to their beautiful and groundbreaking *Call of the Valley*. Sharma (santoor) and Chaurasia (flute) were highly regarded on their instruments back then, and are now acknowledged as living masters. Although Brij Bhushan Kabra has been replaced on Indian acoustic slide guitar by Jayanti Shah, the overall mood is just as lovely and contemplative, even though the role of the guitar has been diminished. *The Valley Recalls* is beautiful, gentle work, and a worthy successor to *Call of the Valley*. *—Sean Westergaard*

Call of the Valley / EMI India ♦♦♦♦♦

L. Subramaniam

b. Jul. 23, 1947, Madras, India
Violin / World Fusion, India, Southern Asia
A gifted South Indian counterpart of Jean-Luc Ponty on the electric violin and endlessly curious about all kinds of music, Subramaniam has been a pioneer in exploring intelligent fusions between European classical music, American jazz, rock and South Indian music. His father, a master Indian violinist, and mother, who played the Indian vina, were his first musical influences, and after abandoning a career in medicine, he formed a violin trio with his two brothers while still in India. He toured America and Europe with Ravi Shankar and ex-Beatle George Harrison in 1974, made his first fusion album in Copenhagen Garland and wrote material for Stu Goldberg and Larry Coryell in 1978. He settled in the Los Angeles area in the late '70s in order to earn a doctorate in Western music at California Institute of the Arts, where he also taught South Indian music. He led a group with Coryell, George Duke and Tom Scott in the 1980s and recorded several fascinating LPs for Milestone—including an LP with Stephane Grappelli—that fused classical music, electric and acoustic jazz, and South Indian music. Subramaniam has also written works for classical orchestras; his *Violin Concerto* juxtaposes naive Hollywood-ish Romantic music with South Indian instruments and structures. His debut for the Erato Detour label, *Global Fusion*, followed in 1999. *—Richard S. Ginell*

Music of the Ramayana, Vol. 1 / 1970 / Ocora ♦♦♦
This wonderful idea is, like so many wonderful ideas, quite a simple one. This series shows the ways in which three musical cultures have treated a central Hindu legend. Most of the 71-minute Indian CD is devoted to a 1979 recording of The Kalakendra dance drama, "Ramlila," a Maharashtra song from the tournament episode, and a Carnatic kriti hymn by the great M.S. Subbulakshmi. *—John Storm Roberts*

Blossom / 1981 / MCA ♦♦♦

Spanish Wave / 1983 / Milestone ♦♦♦♦
The first of violinist L. Subramaniam's string of Milestone recordings (and one of the ones that have been reissued on CD), this fusion-oriented set has strong doses of world music. In addition to the leader, the key players include Tom Scott on lyricon, soprano and flute, and guitarists Jorge Strunz and Larry Coryell; other guests include keyboardist George Duke and bassist Stanley Clarke. The music is atmospheric, challenging and often quite accessible, certainly falling into a unique niche. *—Scott Yanow*

● **Conversations** / 1984 / Milestone ♦♦♦♦♦
Although fellow violinist Stephane Grappelli is billed as co-leader, this is very much L. Subramaniam's date. All eight compositions (except for Grappelli's solo piano rendition of his "Tribute to Mani") are by Subramaniam, and the music (which utilizes electronics, modern rhythms and the influence of Mani's Indian heritage) is quite unusual for a Grappelli session. Altoist Frank Morgan helps out on "Memories," and other sidemen include such notables as keyboardist Joe Sample and guitarist Jorge Strunz. The contrast between the two surprisingly complementary violinists is a strong reason to acquire this CD. *—Scott Yanow*

L. Subramaniam en Concert / 1985 / Ocora ♦♦♦♦

Mani and Co. / 1986 / Milestone ♦♦♦♦
As with the best jazz musicians, violinist L. Subramaniam has carved out his own unique area of music. Originally an Indian classical musician, Subramaniam developed into an expert improviser who combined together several jazz styles (including fusion and straight-ahead) with the strong influence of his homeland's heritage. On his fourth and thusfar final Milestone recording, Subramaniam plays seven originals, varying the personnel on each number. Among his guests are trumpeter Maynard Ferguson, Bud Shank on alto and flute, guitarist Larry Coryell, keyboardist Mark Massey and drummer Tony Williams. *—Scott Yanow*

Global Fusion / Jul. 6, 1999 / Elektra ♦♦♦♦

India Collection

★ **Anthology of South Indian Classical Music** / 1990 / Ocora ♦♦♦♦♦
The best general primer for the vocal and instrumental music of South India. Compiled by Dr. L. Subramaniam, this four-volume set has excellent booklet notes explaining the wonders of Carnatic music and boasts contributions from many of the genre's greatest exponents illustrating vocal genres or instrumental techniques or instruments. Contributing vocalists include M.S. Subbulakshmi, Trivandrum R.S. Mani, Alathur Srinivasalyer and T. Mukti. All the major instruments traditionally found in Carnatic music are illustrated—among others, violin (L. Subramaniam, V.V. Subrahmanyam—Subramaniam in the text), vina (Raajeshwari Padmanabhan), gottuvadyam (N. Ravikiran), flute (T.R. Mahalingam), morsing or Jew's harp (T.H. Subashchandran), kanjira, that is, a type of small drum (V. Nagarajan), ghatam or clay pot drum (T.H. Vinayakram), jalatarangam or tuned liquid-filled porcelain cups (Seeta Doraiswamy) and clarionet or clarinet (A.K.C. Natarajan). An anthology of great vision, essential for any general appreciation of Carnatic music. *—Ken Hunt*

● **Dancing to the Flute: Music & Dance in Indian Art** / Jul. 1, 1997 / Celestial Harmonies ♦♦♦♦♦
Recorded in Varanasi (better known to westerners as Benares), a holy city on the banks of the River Ganges, this album serves the practical purpose of providing background music for an art exhibition at the Art Gallery of New South Wales. Instruments were rigidly tuned to avoid harmonic clashes as patrons moved between sections of the exhibition, while some pieces were recorded with percussion and others without to avoid rhythmic incompatibilities. A strong, fascinating album featuring some exquisite playing. *—Steven McDonald*

Doob Doob O'Rama: Filmsongs of Bollywood / 1999 / Normal ♦♦♦
So some of the songs sound like they were recorded with a hand-held setup in front of a TV, but what the heck— It's all part of Indian cinema's charm—a little of this, a little of that—it's not always perfect but it's always frenetic and a jumble of genres. The songs collected are made by some of Bollywood's finest dubbing voices and singers (Asha Bosle, Mohaamed Rafi) and make for a perfect introduction to Indian film music. The grunts, squeaks, and general mayhem from the movie scores remain—disconcertingly so—though it all sounds fairly sensible next to the rest of the millennial multicultural offerings floating in the sonic environment. *—Denise Sullivan*

☆ **Fabulous Years 1946-1956** / 1991 / EMI India ♦♦♦♦♦
Excellent anthology of one of the golden periods of Indian film music in EMI's *Playback the Melodious Years* series. The era's greatest playback singers, music directors and films are all represented. Vocalists include Mohd. Rafi, Lata Mangeshkar, Shamshad Begum, Mukesh, Asha Bhosle, Talat Mahmood, Uma Devi and Hemant Kumar. Music directors include C.

Ramchandra, Naushad, S.D. Burman and, of interest in the light of his later classical career, A.R. Quereshi, better known subsequently as the tabla maestro Alla Rakha in the guise of music composer for the 1952 film *Bewafa*. —*Ken Hunt*

★ **Golden Voices from the Silver Screen, Vol. 1** / Globestyle ✦✦✦✦✦
Western compilations have tended to focus on film songs with quirky and gimmicky arrangements. GlobeStyle's three volumes have their fair share of those but as a primer for western audiences the trilogy remains unbeatable. After all, once the ears are attuned to the nuances and variation available in the quirky and the straight an appreciation of filmi can develop. Matchless compilations with extensive notes which explain the context of this music. —*Ken Hunt*

☆ **Indian Classical Music** / Hyperion ✦✦✦✦✦
This standout set of two LPs covers several different approaches to both of the major classical traditions. Young sitarist Debu Chaudhuri takes a strongly traditional approach. So does S. Balachander, the greatest Carnatic vina player of the older generation. Bhimsen Joshi, too, sings khayal and thumri with more austerity than vocalists like Parveen Sultana. Lastly, flutist Hariprasad Chaurasia and santurist Shivkumar Sharma play Vivaldi and Bach in performances that are airy and playful, while in no way less serious. —*John Storm Roberts*

Musical Traditions of the Gond / VDE-Gallo ✦✦✦✦✦
The Gond of Central India are an aboriginal people whose music earlier figured on an LP called *Tribal Music of India: The Muria and Maria Gonds of Madhya Pradesh* (Folkways 4028), one of the more lucid titles in Folkways' catalog (which during its founder Moses Asch's lifetime and while run by him was renowned for its ability to confuse and lose). Here the Gond are captured in a variety of ceremonial and social music, vocal and instrumental, including wedding and harvest songs, love songs and a rain dance. —*Ken Hunt*

Musicians and Poets of Rajasthan / Long Distance ✦✦✦✦
This fine collection of vocal and instrumental music offers the material of the Langas and Manganiyars. The volume presents an interesting and varied assortment of musical styles. The final track by Suwa Devi, a member of the nomadic Kalbelya tribe, blends a high soaring voice and pungi, described in the notes as a double clarinet. The undated recording sounds as if it is of recent origin. —*Ken Hunt*

North India: Vocal Music / Aug. 11, 1998 / Unesco ✦✦✦✦✦
North India Vocal Music is a two-piece collection of North Indian classical vocal music. The CD contains a prime example of dhrupad from the premier singers the Dagar Brothers (Aminuddin and Moinuddin, not to be confused with their elder or younger relatives) on Raga Kamboji. It also has a decent example of khyal from Robin Kumar Chatterjee on "Raga Malkosh." It should be noted that the recordings were originally released in 1971 by Alain Danielou, so the recording equipment of the day was occasionally overpowered by the Dagars' amazing voices, which causes a small amount of feedback in a normal stereo and a small amount of head trauma in a high-end one. Aside from the recording quality, the pieces are wonderful examples, as most of the original Danielou recordings are. The prime gripe with this album is that the ragas used in it are labeled as "Alap and Dhrupad" or "Alap and Khyal," which is a heavy incident of misnomer, as an alap is actually the introduction portion of a North Indian piece, and dhrupad and khyal are simply the styles of classical vocal music employed by the artists. As recordings of this pair of Dagar Brothers are rare, the album is a good buy, if only for the ability to hear the masters of the form, though other recordings, such as the out of print Raga Asavari by the brothers may be better works, they are incredibly difficult to find, and this one album has had some considerable release and is attainable. Buy it to hear the Dagar Brothers, and dig harder for their other recordings if this one interests you. —*Adam Greenberg*

North Indian Folk Music / Auvidis/UNESCO ✦✦✦✦✦
This is a really fine glimpse into an enormously rich musical culture. Aside from their very great instrinsic merits, many of these recordings—among them a bhajan by a wandering monk, a shahnai solo, an episode from the Ramayana—give a feeling for the popular equivalents of music more familiar in their classical aspect in the West. (50:30) —*John Storm Roberts*

The Rough Guide to Bhangra / Aug. 29, 2000 / World Music Network ✦✦✦✦
A 13-track release that starts out with an example of traditional bhangra, dips a toe into the beginnings of its cross-cultural metamorphosis, and then dives headfirst into some examples of bhangra as sound system devotees know it best, with walloping beats, reggae riddims, and rap amongst the elements swirled into the folk elements. This Rough Guide sampler provides a very limited look at the style and its practitioners, unfortunately, and there is a sense that they needed to produce a rather more extensive release to give potential fans a better idea of what bhangra represents, and just how many countries and communities it connects with. That said, this is a record that is both listenable and danceable, and a lot of fun to boot. Also, most will learn something from the liner notes. —*Steven McDonald*

Thumri / India Archive Music ✦✦✦✦
Thumri is a short, sweet genre of love song. These tracks by a wide range of artists—Halim Jaffer Khan, vocal and sitar; Vidyadhar Vyas, vocal; Dhruba Ghosh, sarangi; Rajeev Taranath, sarod; Ajoy Chakrabarty, vocal and Debashish Bhattacharya, guitar—show equally varied aspects of its flowering. From the scintillating Mand of Vyas, to the incredible filigree of Chakrabarty, to the melting charm of the instrumentalists, these are snapshots of Indian music at its most appealing. —*Original Music*

● **Vintage Music from India** / 1993 / Rounder ✦✦✦✦✦
Not exclusively a Hindustani compilation since seven of its 24 tracks are Carnatic but a remarkable collection of Hindustani music nevertheless. Writer Peter Manuel's selection of material whets the appetite for more. It captures a time before records and radio set in train a homogenization of India's musical styles. *Vintage Music from India* features selections from the courtesan-singer or tawaif Janki Bai from Allahabad dated circa 1906-08, two qawwali acts called Pearu Qawwal and Kaloo Qawwal recorded in the late '20s, the exceptional tawaif Gauhar Jan from Calcutta from around 1912, thumri and khyal from Narayanrao Vyas from the late '20s. The Carnatic selections include the nagaswaram player V. Kandaswany, the flautist Nagaraja Rao and a character mysteriously called Venu (flute). For its historical insights and the musicality of Gauhar Jan alone this volume is worth seeking out—an old critical cliche but accurate nevertheless in the case of *Vintage Music from India*. —*Ken Hunt*

Women's Songs from India / Apr. 25, 2000 / Rounder ✦✦✦✦
Rounder's *Women's Songs From India* collects hymns, wedding songs, and other ritual songs traditionally sung by Maithili- and Bhojpuri-speaking Indian women. Parati's "Morning Hymn," Sindurdan's "Application of Vermilion," Gosauni's "Mother Goddess Hymn," Kanyadan's "Gift of the Virgin," and Parachan's "Song for Blessing the Bride" are some of the highlights of this authentic collection of women's songs from India. —*Heather Phares*

Indonesia Collection

☆ **Discover Indonesia** / Jul. 25, 2000 / Smithsonian/Folkways ✦✦✦✦✦
This is a great sampler of Smithsonian Folkways' Music of Indonesia series, which is 20 volumes large. Adding the entire set to your music library will seem more reasonable—and necessary—after hearing this and realizing what an astonishing variety of music comes from Indonesia, which consists of over 13,000 islands. At the very least, this sampler will let you know which volumes to start with. This release offers a sampling of the country's diversity with music from the forests of Sumatra's mainland (Volume 7, here represented by the xylophone duet, "Tetigo") to West Kalimantan (Volume 17, and here, "Kalimantan," a ritual senggayung piece, played on seven bamboo) to Flores (Volumes 8 & 9, here represented by the a cappella choral festival piece, "Teke Song") to Maluku (Volume 19, heard here on "Mares," a surprisingly celtic-reminiscent string and drums dance number) to South Sulawesi (Volumes 15 & 18 focus on music from Sulawesi, but the folk guitar and singing heard on "Kemayoran" comes from the Indonesian guitar compilation, Volume 20). And, of course, there are also selections of music by gong and gamelan ensembles (Volumes 12 and 14, among others). Two gong ensemble selections appear on the sampler, "Tabuh Kenilu Sawik," an upbeat, wedding piece and "Tabung," which is played only at funerals, and one gamelan track from West Java, "Welasan." Through Indonesia's own internal variety, as well as the unexpected similarities to (and influences of) other cultures' music, you begin to hear unguessed-at links between different cultures' music. There is a wealth of music and musical history to be heard in this series. —*Joslyn Layne*

Music of Indonesia / Smithsonian/Folkways ✦✦✦✦✦
Smithsonian Folkways spent the last decade of the 20th century exploring the Indonesian archipelago and recording music there for its 20-volume Music of Indonesia series. The music in this series simply overwhelms with its scope and diversity. Much of it enchants and seduces the listener with the romance of a tropical paradise. Some of it challenges the ear with starkly alien sounds—cragged, old voices and dissonant tuning systems—or inexplicable associations, like the West Flores vocal tradition that bears an uncanny resemblance to the famed female choirs of Bulgaria.

This is serious musicology, and sometimes the music is not easily accessible to the casual listener. Series architect Phillip Yampolsky has taken pains to avoid the familiar and break new ground with every volume of the series. So in all these hours of music, there is none of the Javanese and Balinese court gamelan music that has been almost exclusively the content of prior Indonesian music releases.

The series is well organized, and the fact that each volume is sold separately lets each listener find the appropriate path through the Indonesian musical maze, as well as the appropriate pace. The more time spent with the Music of Indonesia series, the more the listener will likely find to appreciate in it. —*Banning Eyre*

The Rough Guide to the Music of Indonesia / Oct. 17, 2000 / World Music Network ✦✦✦✦
The Rough Guide to the Music of Indonesia won't make the listener an expert on Indonesian music, but what it will do is give novices a pleasing taste of some of the many styles that Indonesia's islands have to offer. From urban Jakarta to the villages of Bali and Java, Indonesian music includes traditional acoustic sounds as well as modern electric Indonesian pop. The Indonesian pop singers on this CD range from Elvy Sukaesih and Rhoma Irama (both of whom favor the music known as dangdut) to Detty Kurnia, who commands a loyal following in Sunda (the western part of Java). For traditional Indonesian styles that don't have a strong western influence, some of the artists to check out are CBMW and Gentra Pasundan, whose "Kucap-Kucup" is an example of the type of hypnotic *gamelan* music that has existed in Sunda for centuries. Indonesia is heavily Muslim, and listeners will notice a strong Middle Eastern influence on Nasida Raia's "Boleh Bersuka Ria" and on "Ceurik Rhwana," a track by the male/female duo of Imas Permas and Asep Kosasih. Depending on the artist and the area, Indonesian music can be Middle Eastern-minded or more Asian-sounding. This collection spans the early '70s through the '90s; unfortunately, World Music Network fails to list either recording dates or release dates. So in many cases, listeners won't have any idea when a particular track was recorded. But despite that regrettable flaw, this collection has a lot going for it. The CD's diversity is commendable, and novices are left with a very favorable impression of Indonesian music, both traditional and modern. —*Alex Henderson*

Japan

Kodo

Japanese Drum, Taiko Drums / Asian Folk, Traditional Japanese, Worldbeat, Japan, Eastern Asia

Kodo is a Japanese group that has become an international phenomenon, based on the island of Sado, that has taken the world by storm with their new stylings on semi-traditional taiko drumming. Founded in 1981, the group's name, Kodo, has a dual meaning, according to the group translating both to "heartbeat—the primal source of all rhythm," and "children of the drum, a reflection of Kodo's desire to play their drums simply, with the heart of a child." The group spends 1/3 of an average year touring in Japan, 1/3 touring the rest of the world, and 1/3 in rigorous workouts in their village on Sado. They have toured in all continents except Antarctica in their attempts to spread world peace via the messenger of music. Among their projects, aside from straightforward taiko performances, are a collaboration with new age synthesizer genius Isao Tomita, on *Nasca Fantasy,* instructing the uber-eclectic Cirque du Soleil in taiko for their own performances, the soundtrack for *The Hunted,* and a yearly "Earth Celebration" festival on Sado, for percussionists from around the world to attend. They are ambassadors of peace through music, and the current top bearers of the living art form of taiko drumming. *—Adam Greenberg*

Heartbeat Drummers of Japan / 1985 / Sheffield Lab ♦♦♦

● **The Best of Kodo** / 1994 / Tristar ♦♦♦♦♦
To the uninitiated, all songs on a given Kodo album sound the same. To the initiated, though, subtle differences, as well as broad ones, can be noted. On *Best of Kodo,* the band cuts loose on a journey through their own history, piecing together a compilation of some of the best tracks in current Japanese music, further still, music in general. The album starts with "Lion," a fast-paced round of drumming and grunting, then moves on, past the flutes of "Irodori," to rest on "Yumi-Ga-Hama," which sounds nearly like something from the Edo period. "Zoku" has a throbbing beat and a quick call-and-response vocal section. "Kazauta" is another of the heartbeat-paced pounding songs, and "Monochrome" is a complicated polyphony of lighter drums. "Yu-Karak II" is almost a conga rhythm, and the album ends on "Yatai Bayashi," which is basically a jam session of Taiko drummers. This album is a perfect place for those new to Taiko to begin, as it gives the full variety of sounds possible under such percussionists. For those that are already fans, it is also a prime pick, as can it hold all of the beauty of an Edo flute song, combining it with every ounce of perfection in rhythm that is the trademark of Kodo's work. Given a good enough stereo system, this album could almost serve as the anthem for a block party, among open-minded citizens, anyway. *—Adam Greenberg*

Nasca Fantasy / 1994 / TriStar Music ♦♦♦♦♦

Ibuki / Jan. 28, 1997 / Tristar ♦♦♦♦♦
On *Ibuki,* Kodo worked with Bill Laswell to pump out an album of intense Taiko drumming, as usual. This time around, they reworked a few pieces that had been done on previous albums, including a piece from the soundtrack to *The Hunted* and "Zoku" by Leonard Eto, which shows up here and there in the Kodo collection. The driving force behind Kodo is the perfection and precision of all of the drumming taking place. This is what separates the drum troupe from your average hippie drum circle. Usually, with this many percussion instruments collected together, any piece of music quickly transforms itself into a sloppy, roundabout loop of mushed patterns. With Kodo, however, every stroke on every drum and every vocal or handclap that takes place is carefully planned out and executed crisply. The end result is what you can hear on *Ibuki:* pure ecstatic drumming. The beats can easily move a person to move themselves, through the sheer energy driven through the speakers (even better is seeing Kodo live). Any aficionado of world music or percussion should already have the full Kodo album lineup in their collection, but those outside the loop could consider *Ibuki* a decent opening foray into the style. *—Adam Greenberg*

Japan Collection

Jammin' in the Bronx: A Live Concert Tribute to Machito / Dec. 3, 1996 / Rmm ♦♦♦♦
In October 1995, the employees of the Bronx-Lebanon Medical Center sponsored an all-star concert at the Hostos Center for the Arts and Culture. The resultant CD, besides being a fundraiser (for hospital equipment), documents a well-programmed concert of the highest quality Latin jazz. High-energy big-band salsa is interspersed with an elegant Chucho Valdes ballad, an intriguing Dave Valenti solo flute piece, and a wonderfully controlled conga solo by Carlos "Patato" Valdez that plays with time, timbre, and the audience's expectations. The Machito Orchestra is as big, bold and brassy as ever; an unexpected delight is the smaller, very tight ensemble playing of the Papo Vasquez Latin Jazz Group. *—Janet Rosen*

Japanese Masterpieces of the Shakuhachi / Lyrichord ♦♦♦♦♦
One of a long series of albums put out by Lyrichord dealing with traditional musics from around the world, *Japanese Masterpieces of the Shakuhachi* reprises the major schools of playing for the traditional Japanese bamboo flute. The liner notes, though leaving the performers uncredited, are quite detailed on the history of the flute and of the playing styles used. As many "world music" aficionados know, the shakuhachi lends itself well to making beautiful, earthy tones that Coleman Hawkins could only have dreamed about. The album starts with "Koku," a 12th century piece written by a priest for relaxation. "Sekihiki No Fu" is an accompaniment for a sung Chinese poem. "Matsukaze" represents a pine tree, which itself represents man; the work makes use of komibuki, a panting technique, used here to symbolize the wild breath of a samurai. "Ajikan" is a beautiful meditation on nothingness, and "Oshusanaya" is a pastoral piece. "Sagariha" uses a choppy rhythm that implies waves, though the translation is "drooping leaves." Finally, "Kyushi Reibo" is a piece written in memoriam of the Buddha's death by a pilgrim who was impressed by the strong spirit *(reibo)* of the Buddha on the island of Kyushu. Throughout, the album shows some noteworthy playing by the musicians of this mysterious sounding flute, and beauty in all aspects of the playing. The sound is perfect for tranquil relaxation, regardless of the century or the continent. *—Adam Greenberg*

Japan: Music of the Koto / Apr. 18, 1995 / JVC ♦♦♦
Although the koto was actually created in China, it has enjoyed its greatest prominence in Japan; in fact, it is the most famous string instrument in traditional Japanese music. The very recognizable koto is one of the first instruments one thinks of when the subject of Japanese music comes up, and it was the instrument that jazz great McCoy Tyner chose to play when he combined jazz with Japanese music on his 1972 recording *Valley of Life.* This enjoyable CD, recorded in Tokyo, consists of traditional koto music (which is called *sokyoku* in Japan) and turns the spotlight on six different koto players: Kin'ichi Nakanoshima, Fumikatsu Yonekawa, Fumiko Yonekawa, Koji Inogawa, Masayasu Mishina, and Kiyoko Miyagi. The performances include koto duets as well as unaccompanied solo performances, and on "Haru No Umi" (a piece that was written in 1929), Miyagi performs a memorable duet with *shakuhachi* player Reibo Aoki. Recommended. *—Alex Henderson*

Rough Guide to the Music of Japan / Apr. 20, 1999 / World Music Network ♦♦♦♦
If you conducted a really exhaustive study of Japanese musicians, you'd hear everything from religious Buddhist chanting and traditional shakuhachi and koto music to heavy metal, alternative rock and rap. Hip-hop, in fact, became huge in Japan in the 1980s. There is no metal or rap on *The Rough Guide to the Music of Japan,* but it does provide an interesting and eclectic survey of Japanese artists in the 1990s. This CD isn't for purists—much of it consists of modern Japanese pop—but it isn't without its share of traditional acoustic sounds. The compilation ranges from the contemporary pop of the Ayame Band's "Hiyami Kachi Bushi" and Kawachiya Kikusuimaru's reggae-influenced "Kakin Ondo" to more traditional work by singer Yasuko Yoshida, shakuhachi player Shozan Tanabe, vocalist Tetsuhiro Daiku and biwa player Yukihiro Goto. The album's most unorthodox instrumentals come from Cicala Mvta (who combines the Japanese brass band music known as "chindon" with klezmer on the frantic "Shi Chome") and Kenji Yano, whose quirky take on the "James Bond Theme" successfully fuses Okinawan elements with surf rock. Like other Rough Guide compilations, *The Rough Guide to the Music of Japan* keeps us guessing and provides a variety of rewarding music along the way. *—Alex Henderson*

Java Collection

Java: Sundanese Folk Music / 1994 / Auvidis/UNESCO ♦♦♦
This is a reissue of a particularly fine old UNESCO recording. The music here is all for small groups: angklung buhun (bamboo "gongs"); recak (angklung with oboe lead); kacapi suling (two differing zithers, bamboo flute, two-string fiddle); ketuk tilu (drums and gongs); tarangswa fiddle with kacapi zither; and wrestling music for oboe and drums. Charming and highly accessible music, it's backed by solid notes. *—John Storm Roberts, Original Music*

Javanese Court Gamelan . . . / Nonesuch ♦♦♦♦♦
Javanese Court Gamelan from the Pura Paku Aleman, Jogjakarta offers some extended stately and beautiful pieces by a very traditional Central Javanese gamelan. *—David L. Mayers & Myles Boisen*

☆ **Street Music of Java** / 1989 / Original Music ♦♦♦♦♦
Featured are three major street-popular idioms. Kroncong, a seductive music for fiddle, ukulele, and guitar, is thought to have originated under Portuguese influence as far back as the 17th century. Dangdut is a newer style, with strong Muslim influences (including Egyptian film music). The street versions here are based on the percussion that gives it its name. Langgan Jawa is a regional form of kroncong with stronger musical links to other local styles. Also included is some village ronggeng and a guitar-backed style called melayu that crosses local, Latin, and Indian influences. *—John Storm Roberts*

Korea Collection

★ **P'ansori: Korea's Epic Vocal Art & Instrumental . . .** / 1988 / Elektra/Nonesuch ♦♦♦♦♦

Mongolia Collection

Mongolia: Living Music of the Steppes / May 27, 1997 / Multicultural Media ♦♦♦♦♦
Multicultural Media has been releasing relatively exceptional albums of international traditional musics in recent years, and this installment for Mongolia is no exception. The album covers the ensemble music and song of Mongolia, with various bogino duus (short songs) as well as urtin duus (long songs) showcasing the pastoral style of music enjoyed by the Mongolians. Also included are shorter bits showcasing both the traditional instruments in solo works, as well as the fabled khoomi singing, or as more Westernized groups such as Huun Huur Tu have popularized, "throat singing," where the formant of the sound spectrum is shifted to a higher overtone of the fundamental to effectively create a dual tone from the voice. Finally, songs from and/or about Mongols in China are included. Highlights on this album are mainly the shorter bits of instrumental soloing, particularly Nergui's morin khuur solo on "Jonon Qara's Run," Dandram's solo on the shudraga for "Copper and Steel," and the two khoomi pieces by Tserendawah. One last highlight is the long song by Gereltu about Dugureng Zaan, a folk hero wrestler murdered by the Han because he defeated one of their wrestlers. Overall, the album is an exceptional reprise, if a short one, of Mongolian music, and should be checked out by anyone with a leaning towards the Central Asian sound, though it can range from overly complex to drab for the uninitiated. *—Adam Greenberg*

Vocal and Instrumental Music of Mongolia / 1994 / Tangent ♦♦♦♦♦
This amalgam of two classic Tangent LPs recorded by the late Jean Jenkins provides a little chronological depth to a recently "discovered" musical tradition. They include the richly ornamented "long songs," the simpler, more direct "short songs," milking songs, games, an extraordinary form of mouth music, flutes and stringed instruments (including two-stringed horse's-head fiddle), mostly solo. *—John Storm Roberts, Original Music*

Pakistan

Nusrat Fateh Ali Khan

d. Aug. 16, 1997
Vocals / Qawwali, Pakistan, Southern Asia
Without doubt the most important qawwal is Nusrat Fateh Ali Khan & Party—Party is a generic term for a qawwali ensemble but is also used in Sikhism and to describe some classical music ensembles, for example, shehnai maestro Bismillah Khan and Party. Dubbed Shahen-Shah-e-Qawwali (the *Brightest Star* in Qawwali), he was born on October 13, 1948, in Lyallpur in the Punjab Province of Pakistan. He made his first recording in 1973 in Pakistan and a number of early EMI (Pakistan) albums jointly billed him with his uncle Mubarak Ali Khan. Since these mainly cassette albums were invariably undated and nu-

merous, it is difficult to place them in any more accurate chronological sequence than catalogue number order. Between 1973 and 1993 his recorded output could only be described as prodigious, with more than 50 album releases to his name on numerous Pakistani, British, American, European and Japanese labels. Heavily over-recorded, blighted with a rash of poppy remix albums or albums with Westernized instrumentation or arrangements, his recorded work is a mire to suck in the uninitiated and their money. Converts, however, do not escape scot-free. Although some releases hint at their nature with coded titles such as *Volume 4 Punjabi* (Oriental Star CD SR013) from 1990 or *Ghazals Urdu* (Oriental Star CD SR055) from 1992, the chosen language and style is frequently a matter of conjecture or uncertainty. While the Western market is saturated with his work, the Indian market is supersaturated, and his recorded output is in danger of overwhelming any sense of taste.

Real World was the label largely responsible for Khan's breakthrough into a non-Indian audience. It was their marketing skills and the platform provided by the WOMAD organization which introduced him to Westerners. *Musst Musst* (Real World CD RW 15) released in 1990 was a deliberate attempt to target the White market with its non-traditional arrangements, yet it seems positively cherubic beside later abominations. "All these albums are experiments," he told me in 1993. "There are some people who do not understand at all but just like my voice. I add new lyrics and modern instruments to attract the audience. This has been very successful." Success, however, bred indifference to the virtues and values of the original music. Many find the remix albums, the Western and youth-market releases a source of despair: buyer beware remains the watchword. When singing his traditional work he remains peerless. Many, including myself, regret the dilution of his talent that has occurred with his 'experiments.' However, in 1994, reportedly tired of unauthorized releases, he took greater control of both his business affairs and his concert and recording activities. With his international renown at an all-time peak, Khan died on August 16, 1997; a seemingly endless procession of posthumous releases appeared in the years to follow. *—Ken Hunt*

Mustt Mustt / 1990 / Real World ✦✦✦✦✦
When the *Ayatollah* Ruhollah Khomehni banned all music in Iran and declared it to be sacrilegious, his views by no means reflected the outlook of all Muslims. In fact, Islam's Sufi sect believes music to be a sacred and necessary element of spiritual life. Like Hindus, the Sufis passionately encourage meditation, dancing and chanting. Nusrat Fateh Ali Khan is a master of traditional Qawwali, the music of the Sufis. Soulful and hypnotic, Khan's passionate singing on these songs of praise underscores the richness and vitality of Sufi culture. While Qawwali music goes back centuries, the use of synthesizers adds a modern edge to the highly absorbing *Mustt Mustt*. *—Alex Henderson*

Day, Night, Dawn, Dusk / 1991 / Shanachie ✦✦✦✦

☆ **Shahbaaz** / 1991 / Real World ✦✦✦✦✦
Two years after the groundbreaking *Shahen Shah,* Nusrat returned to Peter Gabriel's Real World studio to record this set of four powerhouse pieces. Canadian guitarist and producer Michael Brook had collaborated with Nusrat on the 1990 crossover project *Mustt Mustt,* which created a sensation in Nusrat's native Pakistan. Brooke returns here to preside over a straight traditional recording of Nusrat's party. The notes make the point that Nusrat's immense popularity stemmed from his ability to merge separate traditions—secular and classical, Muslim and Hindu. This set of pieces all come out of Sufi philosophic and religious tradition. But from start to finish, this session has rock & roll intensity about it. The tempos are feverishly fast, and the vocal arrangements quickly rise to vivid emotional crescendos. The improvisational passages are extended and adventurous. The lead track, "Beh Haadh Ramza Dhasdha," tells the story of a controversial Persian martyr of the tenth century, crucified for proclaiming, "I am the truth." This and the lengthy final piece revolve around a catchy refrain that anchors long, wandering forms. In contrast, the other two pieces unfold through successive permutations, ever striving into new spiritual territory. Nusrat can draw upon six centuries of musical tradition just within his own family. But here, on the qawwali star's most electrifying international release, it's clear even to the naïve listener that he's stretching the boundaries of that tradition, embracing his own present even as he honors his ancestors' past. *—Banning Eyre*

Shahen-Shah / 1988 / Real World ✦✦✦✦
This 1988 recording helped to launch Peter Gabriel's Real World label. It also introduced Nusrat Fateh Ali Khan to the non-Pakistani world, presenting him as a kind of world music rock star. Nusrat and his nine-man "party" perform their trademark qawwali here without alterations for the Western market. They sing in Urdu, using religious and romantic texts drawn from the poetry of Sufiism, the mystical sect of Islam. And yet, all the elements that would make Nusrat a world pop sensation are here, above all his enormous voice, husky and trenchant, powerful as a hurricane, severe and foreboding on the darkest tracks, but always bursting with the ecstatic joy of revelation, as on the classic, "Shamas-Ud-Doha, Badar-Ud-Doha." The relentless hand clapping and tabla drum accompaniment convey an aggressive tranciness that combines the contemplative serenity of Indian classical music with the headbanging frenzy of punk rock. Droning harmonium melodies introduce each of these six, ten-minute-plus tracks, and then wind through the escalating vocal fireworks. Singers repeat lines with building intensity, each repetition squeezing more emotional juice from the words. Nusrat's scat-like improvisations are always a high point, often leading to swelling unison chant melodies sung by the entire party. This release effectively rallied a host of samplers, re-mixers, and film scorers who would keep Nusrat busy for the remaining decade of his life. But in retrospect, nothing they created surpasses this, Nusrat's first session at Real World. *Shahen Shah* means the "brightest star," and though qawwali music now has other international stars, Nusrat still merits his title. *—Banning Eyre*

★ **Devotional Songs** / 1992 / Real World ✦✦✦✦✦
The first thing you notice is the chunking guitar and mandolin that Majawar Abbas adds to Nusrat's classic blend of male vocals, harmonium, and tabla here. The strings add a folksy element to these six religious songs, making this 1988 session about as warm and cuddly as Nusrat's spiritually charged qawwali music gets. Shorter selections with more nods to pop music arranging give the music a different character than that found on more traditional records, while remaining well short of the reinventions found on Nusrat's famous crossover collaborations with Canadian guitarist Michael Brook and others. This set begins with a friendly rendition of "Allah Hoo Allah Hoo," which was always a crowd-pleaser in Nusrat's legendary live shows. "Haq Ali Ali Haq" begins like a flamenco song full of lyrical melancholy, but as its praise for Hazrat Ali, the fourth Caliph, gathers steam, the tempo rises, and the mood shifts to righteous resolve and the blooming ecstasy that is qawwali's trademark. A love song, called a ghazal, opens with strumming guitar work that seems to promise Celtic music, but before long, you're back in familiar qawwali territory. This tends to be the pattern, colorful intros that morph into traditional qawwali. The final track, "Ni Main Jogi De Naal," starts out sounding like Greek bouzouki music. Some tracks fade out in order to stay in or around eight minutes. This tends to keep the energy several notches below that found in the full-blown, ten-plus minute selections featured on other releases. Call this back porch Nusrat, something you can enjoy without being whisked straight to heaven. *—Banning Eyre*

Love Songs / 1992 / Real World ✦✦✦✦✦
The companion CD to Nusrat's set of *Devotional Songs*—both recorded in 1988—features the ghazal, a kind of love song. The name ghazal derives from the Arabic for "to converse with women." Originally, ghazals were sung in the language of Persia, Urdu, but the form has become a staple throughout much of Asia and the Middle East and is now sung in many languages. Love songs in this part of the world can often be seen as thinly disguised religious songs, but some of the lyrics here are unabashedly secular: "She is boldly unveiling in front of everyone and I am cowardly concealing." Musically, too, the feeling here is lighter. The melodies are lyrical, the improvisation relatively restrained. As in the devotional song session, the musical backing expands beyond the standard harmonium and tablas to include plucked strings, acoustic guitar, and mandolin. These provide occasional melodies, but more often fall back into the meld of tones and textures that support what is first and foremost vocal music. Despite the short song lengths—all under eight minutes—and the romantic moods, this set does still pack the trademark Nusrat punch. "Bibi Sada Dil Morr De," a contemporary composition, is dark and moody. "Sanson Ki Mala Pey," a Pujabi song, begins gently like a waltz, but Nusrat quickly moves to spitfire scat singing ratcheting up the spiritual energy before easing into languid, flowing melodies. In love as in religion, Nusrat proves a heavyweight. *—Banning Eyre*

Traditional Sufi Qawwalis, Vols. 1 & 2 / 1993 / Navras ✦✦✦✦✦
Recorded live in London in December 1989, this four-volume series available separately is an exemplary illustration of the sort of repertoire the listener would hear at a qawwali concert where the audience is made up largely of Muslims of Asian descent or Indians of other religions. (Khan tends to adjust his repertoire and performance style to take account of the style of venue, the devotional situation—for example, his presence at a Sufi shrine—or the composition of his audience.) *—Ken Hunt*

Devotional and Love Songs / Feb. 12, 1993 / Real World ✦✦✦✦✦
Nusrat Fateh Ali Khan opens this album as he often opened his live shows, by calling upon God in the form of Allah to come and bless the gathering with His presence. For that is the sole purpose of the qawwal: to reach God through music, through his voice. And this collection of *Devotional and Love Songs* is set forth with that in mind. Unlike some of Khan's more Western-influenced releases, such as *Mustt Mustt* and *Night Song,* the songs are presented here with minimal instrumentation (mostly harmonium and tabla) in the traditional call and response form, with Khan singing a line that is echoed by the party of musicians that shares the stage with him. Surprisingly accessible and captivating, you need not be a Muslim or a seeker of any kind to recognize the power of this music. Just try to *not* sway and clap in rhythm. Bet you can't. With the repetition of certain phrases and syllables, qawwali music is designed to bring both the musicians and audience to a heightened plane of reality, an almost trance-like state of existence. For when Khan's voice soars up to the heavens and then swoops back down to bring you along for the ride, you are swept away without a second thought. That is why, prior to his death in 1997, Khan was considered the brightest star in qawwali, the master of this art form. *—Kelly McCartney*

The Last Prophet / 1994 / Real World ✦✦✦

Night Song / Feb. 20, 1996 / Real World ✦✦✦✦✦
Canadian guitarist Michael Brook worked with Nusrat to create the 1990 crossover hit *Mustt Mustt,* and the release was hailed internationally and credited with leading Pakistani youth to discover Sufi religious music, qawwali. This follow-up project helped establish something of a tradition for Real World crossover projects. The genre features dreamy, atmospheric keyboards and guitars, simple, mid-tempo rhythms, and a kind of low-key understatement that, depending on your point of view, sounds either profoundly mystical or else tedious and bland. With West African kora and electronic backing and Nusrat singing in a relaxed mid-range voice, the opener "My Heart, My Life" sounds almost like a Salif Keita ballad as it works up to its energized closing chant. "My Comfort Remains" and "Crest" are essentially pop numbers with catchy melodies, the former bouncy but static, the latter building towards a revelatory crescendo. Not until the fifth of eight tracks, "Longing," do we hear Nusrat's signature scat singing and his singular wail, unmistakable even when lavished with effects. "Sweet Pain" might be the strongest track, beginning deep in dream space with a wandering bass line and a simple backbeat, and then heating up to powerful close with Nusrat delivering spitfire scat. Wherever you stand on Real World's arty aesthetics, you have to admire the qawwali star's sense of adventure here. You also have to recognize that no crossover project, including Nusrat's far more fun collaboration with London DJ Bally Sagoo, approaches the power of his standard fare qawwali. *—Banning Eyre*

Intoxicated Spirit / May 21, 1996 / Shanachie ✦✦✦

Rapture: An Essential Selection / Mar. 18, 1997 / Music Club ✦✦✦✦

● **Greatest Hits of Nusrat Fateh Ali Kha** / May 20, 1997 / Shanachie ✦✦✦✦✦
The idea of a religious singer whose ecstasy-inducing opuses commonly run over 20 minutes having "greatest hits" borders on the hilarious. But when you consider the fanatical following the Pakistani qawwali star has gained around the world, the top-of-the-charts concept

becomes less far-fetched. Upon hearing the great qawwal in person, Pakistanis in foreign cities were known to bang their heads against the stage until they bled. This set of four pieces was released in 1997, the year Nusrat died. By the time the world discovered Nusrat in the late '80s, he had produced literally hundreds of recordings, so whether you consider these archival selections "hits" or not, they are significant and worthwhile additions to his catalog. "Haq Ali Ali" is the only one of these to appear on any of Nusrat's nine Real World releases, but the short version on *Devotional Songs* is only a warm-up for this expansive, 25-minute rendition. Nusrat's sound remained fairly constant throughout his career. He changed his instrumental backing some before settling on harmonium as his backing instrument of choice, and his voice gathered some ragged edges in the '90s, but other than that, there was no overarching progression in his music, only side trips. None of those side trips are represented here (although 1990's *Mustt Mustt* really *was* a hit, electrifying Pakistani youth with its crossover sound). Still, there are some unusual sonic textures among the older tracks here. "Data Ke Ghulamon Ko" begins like a processional hymn, the harmonium hanging on long, organ-like chords. And "Mangte Hail Karim" uses the qanun (a hammer dulcimer) and a clarinet-like reed instrument to set up its 3/4 feel. *—Banning Eyre*

Peace / Feb. 23, 1999 / Omni Park ✦✦✦✦

Passion / May 11, 1999 / NYC Music ✦✦✦✦

At the time of his death in 1997, Nusrat Fateh Ali Khan was not only the greatest living exponent of qawwali (the Sufi devotional music of Pakistan), but also its most successful popularizer, an international star known for the power of his live performances. And in addition to bringing the music to large audiences both inside and outside of Pakistan, Khan was also responsible for bringing it into the 20th century, collaborating with Western musicians and producers to create a fascinating qawwali-techno hybrid. *Passion* is comprised of recordings he made for a television documentary shortly before his death; the tracks were laid down live in the studio with the help of Indian and Pakistani DJs as well as his usual backing musicians. Along with his reedy, acrobatic voice and the tabla accompaniment that one would expect, there is the occasional sax solo, acoustic guitar, or overdubbed female backing vocals. The result is lovely, especially on the yearning "I Remember Her" and the gently regretful "The Magic Touch." Production values could have been a bit higher, but the music itself is excellent. *—Rick Anderson*

Dust to Gold / Jun. 20, 2000 / Real World ✦✦✦

Three years after the qawwali star's death in 1997, Real World began releasing material "discovered" in Nusrat's hometown, Lahore, Pakistan. These four pieces were evidently recorded there just months before he died, but they sound closer to the pristine Real World Studios sessions than to the earlier Pakistani material available on reissue releases. Here and there, one detects a little more rasp than usual in that fabulous voice, but the music is fresh and the tempos are, if anything, super energized, almost as if the party sensed it didn't have much time. The lead track, "Khawaja Tum Hi Ho" *("Master It Is Only You")*, strikes with ferocity and doesn't let up for over 15 minutes. This and the second selection are as intense as the music on *Shahbaaz* (Real World 1991), perhaps the qawwal's fieriest studio session. The third selection, with it's Zen-like title "Koi Hai Na Ho Ga" ("There Was No One, There Will Not Be Anyone") unfolds over a clopping rhythm. Nusrat's voice rips and lashes its way through a moody refrain and the soaring counter melodies of vocal soloist Mujahed Mubarak Ali Khan. The closer "Noor-E-Khuda Hai Husn-E-Sarapa Rasool" ("The Light of God Is the Embodiment of the Prophet") is cooler. Like the final track on many Nusrat releases, it unfolds in a cantering triplet rhythm, letting the listener down gently from the spiritual heights of the earlier material. If there are more recordings of this quality in the vault, the world needs to hear them. *—Banning Eyre*

Pakistan Collection

☆ **Treasures of Pakistan** / Playasound ✦✦✦✦✦

Excellent examples of music for sarinda and sarangi fiddles as well as the rabab lute, extremely well recorded on location. As a nice touch, the producer is Kudzi Erguner, a Turkish musician, rather than the usual Western ethnomusicologist (not the first—Deben Bhattacharya's recordings are remembered with nostalgia—but still too rare). Brief but cogent notes are included. (69 minutes) *—John Storm Roberts*

South Korea Collection

Ritual Songs from the Island of Chindo / 1994 / VDE-Gallo ✦✦✦✦✦

Chindo possesses three "intangible national treasures": a form of women's ritual songs and the two women who lead the choruses on this CD, probably the only one devoted to Chindo tradition. They perform ritual, rice-planting and funeral songs with groups they have trained as part of their duties, in a "sorrowful voice" style whose striking rubato is known as "twisted rhythm." *—John Storm Roberts, Original Music*

Tibet Collection

Ritual of the Drugpa Order from Thimpu, Vol. 1 / Lyrichord ✦✦✦✦

This welcome CD reissue of a classic John Levy recording was made in Bhutan in 1971. As a guest of the then king of Bhutan, Levy got all possible facilities in recording a wide range of music of the Tibetan monastic orders in Bhutan. This cooperation, together with his own expertise, made the resulting four volumes a remarkably thorough document of Tibetan ritual and ceremonial music. This remastered reissue of the first recordings comes with expanded liner notes by Levy. *—John Storm Roberts, Original Music*

Tibet: The Heart of Dharma / Aug. 13, 1996 / Ellipsis Arts ✦✦✦

For pop music centrists like myself who have been daunted by the sobriety and pacing of sacred Tibetan chants, this attractive book/CD combo may be the ticket to enlightened listening. Monks from two great Tibetan monasteries (Khampagar and Loseling) perform their extended chants alone, with focus on the extraordinary voices, and in combination with traditional trumpets, cymbals, and percussion. The 64-page book chock full of pictures and bite-size essays helps the entry into the music, but the music itself is so compelling and beautifully recorded that anyone who makes the effort to abandon the usual search for hooks, refrains, and other instant gratification will be rewarded with an impressive experience. *—Bob Tarte*

Tibet: Musiques Sacrées / 1989 / Ocora ✦✦✦✦✦

This album was recorded in Nepal at Tibetan Buddhist monasteries of the Gelugpa and Nyingmapa sects. Most of the cuts are Gelugpa, including part of the Chîd—a cleansing ritual. Other sections include the assembly call (with conch horns), prayer wheel, prostration rites, and more. A second group of tracks includes a ritual to Vajrayogini—a major female deity in Tibetan Buddhist practice. Various ritual instruments (thigh-bone trumpets, hand drums, cymbals, oboes, etc.) are heard. *—Michael Erlewine*

Tibetan Ritual Music / Lyrichord ✦✦✦✦✦

A rare recording of an entire Tibetan ritual from The Nyingmapa monastery of Dehra Dun. Divided into three parts, each of which has both chanting and music for metal horns and trumpets as well as oboes and drums. Nominally an invocation to the goddess Yeshiki Mamo, though the notes overstate the shamanistic elements involved. *—Carl Hoyt, Original Music*

Tuva

Huun-Huur-Tu

Group / Tuvan Throat Singing, Tuva, Asia

The remote region of Tuva, one of the new countries formed with the dissolution of the U.S.S.R., has produced one of the world's most unusual vocal groups, Huun-Huur-Tu. Masters of the throat singing style of xoomei, in which a vocalist produces two or three notes simultaneously, the group has been warmly by an international following. According to *Jazz Times*, "a rustic joyousness and unadulterated expresiveness come out of these musicians." Analyzing Huun-Huur-Tu's music, *The Chicago Tribune*, wrote, 'it is unfamiliar yet very accessible, an other-worldly but deeply spiritual music that is rooted in the sound of nature." *Dirty Linen* took a similar view, claiming, "this music is both very spiritual and down to earth, grounded in a strong sense of place, yet its appeal is universal." In addition to recording their own albums, the members of Huun-Huur-Tu have contributed their unique vocals to albums and/or performances by Frank Zappa, The Chieftains, Johnny "Guitar" Watson, The Kronos Quartet and L. Shankar and Ry Cooder's soundtrack of the film, *Geronimo*. Their on-going collaboration with Angelite, the Bulgarian Woman's Choir under the direction of Mikhail Alperin, has yielded two memorable albums—*Fly, Fly My Sadness* in 1994 and *Mountain Tale* in 1998. Although its name translates literally as "sun propeller," Huun-Huur-Tu represents much more. In a 1994 interview, founding percussionist Alexander Bapa explained, "(the name of the band refers to) the vertical seperation of light rays that are often seen on the grasslands just after sunrise or just before sunset." Initially named "Kungurtuk," Huun-Huur-Tu came together, in 1992, to play "the old and forgotten songs." Founding members Sasha and Sayan Bapa and Kaigalool Khovalyg had previously performed a state-sanctioned ensemble during the Soviet regime. Although Tuvan music had traditionally been performed by a solo singer or instrumentalist, the group sound of Huun-Huur-Tu set them apart. Huun-Huur-Tu has experienced several personnel changes. Original member Anatoli Kuular left to form a new band, Yat-Kha, in late 1993, and was replaced by Anatoli Kuular, a master of the borbangnadyr style of singing and a virtuosic player of the mouth harp (xomuz) and byzanchi. Percussionist Alexander Bapa left, in 1995, to become a producer in Moscow, and was replaced by Alexander Siraglar, a sygyt singer, string player and percussionist. *—Craig Harris*

The Orphan's Lament / Nov. 23, 1994 / Shanachie ✦✦✦✦✦

From the first track, their second album, *Orphan's Lament* grabs your attention with "Prayer"—the deep, unearthly, sounds of Tibetan Lamaist chant. Next they move to khoomei singing. Known in the West as "throat singing," the performer produces two or more high- and low-pitched tones simultaneously. The resulting sound—somewhat eerie, somewhat haunting—is a combination somewhere between the sounds of a long whistle and a Jew's harp.

But Huun Huur Tu also adds new elements to the traditional sounds of Tuvan music. In addition to the igil, a two-stringed horsehead fiddle played with a bow, and the khomuz, a Jew's harp, (both traditional instruments) the group has incorporated percussion—not a usual device in Tuvan music. Their use of a large goat-skin drum, generally reserved for shamanistic rituals, gives a rhythm to their music, making it very appealing to a Western ear. Similarly, their use of pouch rattle (made from a bull's scrotum filled with sheep knucklebones) adds a beat.

The fact Huun Huur Tu plays together, as a group, is itself unusual. Not content to blindly follow traditional Central Asian folk music, Huun Huur Tu's four, sometimes five, performers create an ensemble that offers a complex, fascinating, and harmonious mixture. *—Robert Walker*

Tuva Collection

Deep in the Heart of Tuva: Cowboy Music from the Wild East / 1996 / Ellipsis Arts ✦✦✦✦✦

They're not likely to be found singing "Tumbling Tumbleweeds," even though that plant hails from their country, but the Tuvans are having an impact on the rest of the world when it comes to their music. Tuvan throat-singing, a fascinating style in which a single vocalist can produce a haunting four-part harmony, has turned up on Ry Cooder's film soundtracks and as part of the style of bluesman Paul "Earthquake" Pena, while concerts by groups such as Huun-Huur-Tu continue to be extremely popular. This compilation, produced and annotated by Ralph Leighton, brings together traditional and contemporary Tuvan music, opening with a demonstrative medley from Kongar-Ool Ondar and closing with a duet between Ondar and Pena. The text, meanwhile, provides a glimpse into the history and culture of Tannu Tuva, with translations of Tuvan stories and poetry as an added bonus. To cap things off, this is all presented as a miniature hardcover book with attractive coffee-table design—a typically excellent Ellipsis Arts presentation. *—Steven McDonald*

☆ **Tuva: Voices from the Center of Asia** / 1990 / Smithsonian/Folkways ♦♦♦♦♦
Not only are there 33 examples here of some of the most impressive vocal techniques in the world (including chordal throat-singing), with some almost equally remarkable instrumental work, but the notes, though cheaply produced, are extremely thorough. *—John Storm Roberts & Myles Boisen*

Vietnam Collection

Anthology of World Music: Music of Vietnam / Mar. 23, 1999 / Rounder ♦♦♦♦

CARIBBEAN

Belize Collection

Paranda: Africa in Central America / Sep. 14, 1999 / Elektra ♦♦♦
Paranda is a musical tradition of the Garifuna, whose ancestry can be traced to West Africans (Ibo, Yoruba, and Ashanti tribes) and the Arawak Indians of the island of St. Vincent in the Caribbean. Today the Garifuna live in Belize, where they established communities in 1802 after being first exiled to Honduras from their native St. Vincent, then fleeing Honduras to escape a civil war. Paranda combines Spanish, Arawak, and West African influences to make a lively, acoustic music that is heavy on percussion. Nearly all Paranda features large wooden drums called primero and secundo, as well as shakers and smaller drums made from turtle shells. This collection, titled simply Paranda, brings together some of Belize's few remaining Paranderos to document this fascinating musical genre. *—Stacia Proefrock*

Caribbean Collection

Caribe! Caribe! / Jun. 22, 1999 / Putumayo ♦♦♦♦
When many Americans hear the term "Caribbean music," they tend to think of calypso, soca, and steel drums. But technically, music of the Caribbean also includes everything from Afro-Cuban salsa, Dominican merengue, and Puerto Rican plena to Jamaican ska and reggae. If any label can be counted on to have an eclectic, broad-minded approach to Caribbean music, it's Putumayo; and sure enough, Putumayo's compilation *Caribe! Caribe!* takes you all over the Caribbean. Not one to be predictable, Putumayo keeps the listener guessing by providing everything from the Black Uhuru-ish reggae of Don Carlos and Gold's "Movin' to the Top" to energetic, infectious sounds from St. Thomas (Osha's "Come Again"), Martinique (Kali's reggae-influenced "La Biguine des Enfants du Bon Dieu"), Belize (Andy Palacio's "Nabi"), and Barbados (Krosfyah's "In Mi System"). Nothing from Cuba, Puerto Rico, or the Dominican Republic is included, but one can hear a strong salsa influence on Haitian singer Beethova Obas' "Lina" and Curacao group La Perfecta's "Bai Drecha Bo Bin." Especially infectious is Aruban band E.Q.Q.'s exuberant "Promo Bia," which is sung in Papiamento, a language that is an unlikely combination of romance and African languages and Dutch. Like many other Putumayo compilations, *Caribe! Caribe!* boasts comprehensive, informative liner notes and treats the music with the respect it deserves. *—Alex Henderson*

☆ **Caribbean Island Music** / Nonesuch ♦♦♦♦♦
I recorded this material on my first field trip in 1971. Many of these recordings are still unique: Jamaican country mento, digging songs, and nine-night songs; a Haitian acoustic merengue group; Dominican merengues, salves, tonadas, drum groups, and the English-language Mummies later featured in the British Repercussions TV/video series. *—John Storm Roberts*

Dominican Republic

Juan Luis Guerra

Vocals, Guitar / Tropical, Merengue, Bachata-Merengue, Salsa, Caribbean, Dominican Republic
In his native Dominican Republic, merengue superstar Juan Luis Guerra is considered a poet and musician of the people. He and his band 440 are much loved throughout the Latino world and he has become one of the new wave of artists responsible for revitalizing the tropical music that had been languishing during the late '80s from overplay and lack of innovation.

Guerra is the son of a professional baseball player and grew up next to the National Music Gallery. As a teen, he was influenced by the Beatles and by the music of the U.S. hippies. Initially, he taught himself the basics of guitar playing, but after winning a contest, attended the National Conservatory on a scholarship. One of his instructors then helped Guerra get into the prestigious Berklee College of Music in Massachusetts and the many genres of jazz. In time, he found he missed his native Dominican Republic and so returned to experiment with blending local African-influenced music, folk songs and jazz with his group 440. The band takes its name from the universal tuning pattern of the A note, 440 Hertz. The name was chosen by Guerra's brother José Gilberto who used to sit and watch them rehearse. One day he commented that they seemed so obsessed with staying in perfect tune that they should call themselves that.

Their debut album, *Soplando,* made little impact. For their next efforts, *Mudanza y Acarreo* and *Mientras Más Lo Pienso Tu,* Guerra and 440 began adding merengue and lightning-quick riffs of "perico ripiao," and suddenly found success with a young crowd tired from hearing the same old thing. The new music, called "bachata-merengue," soon won considerable acclaim in the Dominican Republic. The group was selected by their government to represent the country in the International Music Festival of OTI, the Oraganization of Iberoamerican Television. In 1988, Guerra and 440 had one of their biggest hits, *Ojalá Que Llueva Café,* which became the third best-selling album in Latin America. That year he lost his lead vocalist, Maridalia Hernández, who left to pursue her solo career in Europe, leaving Guerra to become the new lead singer. In 1991, he released *Bachata Rose* which became a smash hit throughout the Americas and won Guerra his first Grammy in the U.S. The album was particularly popular in Los Angeles and soon Guerra and his band were touring. His next album, *Areito,* caused controversy in the Dominican Republic for speaking out against social injustice that the desperately poor felt Guerra had never personally experienced. Still, he must be given credit for his sincerity and interest in improving things in his oft-troubled homeland. Musically, Guerra changed directions again for his 1995 effort *Fogaraté.* This album incorporated more of the increasingly popular African soukous music. It became quite popular. His 1998 release *Ni Es Lo Mismo Ni Es Igual* garnered Guerra three Grammys for Best Merengue Performance, Best Tropical Song for "El Niagara En Bicicleta," and for Best Engineered Album at the first annual Latin Grammy Awards in fall 2000. *—Sandra Brennan*

Bachata Rosa / 1990 / RCA ♦♦♦
Bachata was originally rural and guitar-backed, above all bolero-type songs. It began moving to town a few years back, and has reached the bigtime with this big-deal production. The basics (guitar ensemble, simple percussion, sentimental lyrics, rural associations) have gotten kind of generalized, but it's really fine of its kind, which includes a touch of mbube. *—John Storm Roberts, Original Music*

Areito / 1992 / RCA ♦♦♦

Ojalá Que Llueva Café / 1995 / RCA ♦♦♦

● **Ni Es Lo Mismo Ni Es Igual** / Dec. 15, 1998 / Karen ♦♦♦♦

Toño Rosario

Vocals / Merenhouse, Tropical, Merengue, Caribbean, Dominican Republic
The one-time leader of the merengue band Los Hermanos Rosario, Toño Rosario began a successful solo career in 1990. A native of the Dominican Republic, he formed the band in 1978 with his brother; despite the group's success during the 1980s, Rosario moved to Puerto Rico and began his solo career with 1991's *Atado A Ti.* Four of his solo albums went gold (two made it to platinum as well), and he became one of the island's biggest singing stars. *Exclusivo* followed in 1998, and a year later Rosario returned with *Magia de el Cuco. —John Bush*

● **Historia Musical Rosario** / May 26, 1998 / WEA International ♦♦♦♦
Historia Musical Rosario is an excellent overview of Toño Rosario's recordings for WEA International that makes for a fine introduction to his music. *—Terry Jenkins*

Sergio Vargas

Vocals (Background) / Tropical, Merengue, Caribbean, Dominican Republic
Talented Sergio Vargas is primarily a merengue singer, but has also earned acclaim for his ability to sing other forms of Tropical music, including ballads. He was born in the Dominican Republic and got his start singing with the local group La Banda Brava. In 1980, he sang a version of José José's "Amor, Amor" and won second place in a talent contest. Two years later he had begun working with one of the country's most popular merengue artists, Dionis Fernández. Vargas founded his band, Los Hijos del Rey, in 1986 and by 1988 had become a major star throughout Latin America where he began touring. Later that year, Vargas signed to CBS Records in the U.S. and his debut album eventually went gold. By 1991, he was recording with Sony and remains one of his country's top artists. *—Sandra Brennan*

Juntos / May 19, 1998 / RCA International ♦♦♦
Juntos is a typically classy and entertaining collection of merengue and ballads from Sergio Vargas. *—Terry Jenkins*

● **A Tiempo** / Jan. 12, 1999 / RCA International ♦♦♦♦
On *A Tiempo,* Vargas' combination of his distinctive romantic tropical style with contemporary dance rhythms really jells—tracks like "Espera un Poco Mas," "Aquello Que Me Diste" and "Fantasma" all strike an ideal balance. *—Jason Ankeny*

Wilfrido Vargas

Vocals / Tropical, Merengue, Tropicalia, Salsa, Caribbean, Dominican Republic
Wilfrido Vargas (b. Wilfrido Radamés Vargas Martínez, April 24, 1949, Altamira, Puerto Plata, Dominican Republic), was a bandleader, trumpeter, vocalist, arranger, composer and producer who was instrumental in making the merengue style a worldwide phenomena. He began his musical studies early, attending the Municipal Academy of Music beginning at age 10. Before he was 12, he was the trumpet soloist and director of a small local band. It was in his twenties, however, that he begun to have commercial and critical successes. His band, Los Beduinos, produced their first album, *Wilfrido Vargas y sus Beduinos,* on the Karen label in 1974. It was the first of 17 albums that Vargas would record with Karen, all the while acting as mentor to a new generation of merengue musicians. Half of that first album was written by pianist and composer Sonny Ovalle, who helped develop Los Beduinos' sound and who would later make a major contribution to Vargas' hit albums in the '80s.

Vargas' first hit came with his fourth album, *Punto y Aparte!,* which was issued by Karen in 1978. It produced a hit single, "El Barbarazoí," and helped touch off a worldwide merengue craze, providing exposure for scores of Dominican artists. Vargas had a series of hit albums in the '80s, beginning with his duet with Los Beduinos vocalist Sandy Reyes, *Wilfrido Vargas y Sandy Reyes,* which was issued in 1982. In 1987 he switched to the Sonotone label and produced five albums with them, including *Animation,* which received a 1989 Grammy nomination. From 1991 on he was with the Rodven label, and while he remained a major name in merengue, he would never again achieve the prominence that he had known in the '80s. Outside of the merengue genre, Vargas also made a major contribution to the Fania All-Stars, joining them for their historic performances in Cuba in 1979 and contributing to the recording of the All Stars' *Habana Jam* album, recorded March 3 of that year at a concert in Havana. *—Stacia Proefrock*

Itinerario / Feb. 1993 / TH-Rodven ♦♦♦

Años Dorados / 1995 / Karen ✦✦✦✦✦
For once an extravagant album title is justified! The power behind the throne in the recent merengue renaissance flexes his muscles. If you've been following merengue, you've heard these songs covered time and again. Wilfrido is special because his roots as a merenguero are buried deep in Latin American and Caribbean culture in general—not just in the Dominican Republic, so some of his best efforts come in songs by Calixto Ochoa (Columbian cumbia maestro), Tabou Combo (Haitian mini-jazz heavies) and Kassav'! He is that rarity, an originator and a synthesizer. Though there are no dates here, I would say this collection runs from the mid-'70s. *—Carl Hoyt, Original Music*

● **Oro Merenguero: 20 Exitos** / Jan. 23, 1996 / T.H. Rodven ✦✦✦✦

El Jardinero / Karen ✦✦✦✦✦
If this is your first Vargas experience, you'll promptly fall for the inspired lunacy of "El Jardinero"'s merengue-rap. But lunacy, however inspired, was only part of why this album carried Vargas to the top of the New York Latin hit parade. The rest was the revelation of a new salsa-merengue heavy with the lightest of touches. *—John Storm Roberts, Original Music*

Wilfrido 86 / 1986 / Karen ✦✦✦✦✦
Vargas was the most creative head of '80s merengue, and in fact pretty much masterminded the entire merengue renaissance of the period. Virtually every Dominican band or singer of the '80s either started out with him or was encouraged by him. He had hit after hit, and used his popularity as license for experiments. A list of the external novelties—harmonica, highly original guitar licks, what sounds like harp (though none's credited), ditto harpsichord—no way does justice to the general air of jovially manic creativity. *—John Storm Roberts*

Johnny Ventura

Arranger / Tropical, Merengue, Caribbean, Dominican Republic
Johnny Ventura is the man who almost singlehandedly developed and modernized the contemporary merengue sound, beginning with his first recordings in the early '60s. He was influenced by the original wave of rock & roll, and quickly imported the energy as well as some dance routines inspired by Elvis. He continued to record into the 1990s, though other merengue singers such as Wilfrido Vargas and Juan Luís Guerra had usurped much of his popularity. *—John Bush*

● **40 Aniversario: En Vivo** / May 26, 1998 / WEA International ✦✦✦✦✦

Dominican Republic Collection

Putumayo Presents: Republica Dominicana / Feb. 22, 2000 / Putumayo ✦✦✦
@Putumayo's compilations are known for making unlikely choices; so when the label released a collection of Dominican music in 2000, it was safe to assume that the CD wouldn't emphasize the really big names in neo-merengue. And sure enough, *Putumayo Presents: Republica Dominicana* is hardly a collection of recordings by Olga Tanon (the top young female merengue star of the 1990s). This album isn't the place to go in search of the type of slick, high-tech neo-merengue that was incredibly popular among young Dominicans in the 1990s. Instead, Putumayo surprises us by emphasizing the Dominican Republic's earthier, less-produced bachata sounds. Though this CD contains a few examples of merengue (including the late Alberto Beltrán's "Caña Brava"), it pays a lot more attention to the bachata or bachata-son of such artists as Bolívar Peralta, Raulín Rodriguez, Juan Manuel, Juan Bautista, and Luis Vargas. "Los Bodegueros" is a 1999 bachata that finds veteran merengue singer Joseito Mateo joining forces with fellow Dominican legend Luis Kalaff and exalting owners of bodegas (small Latin corner groceries) as working-class heroes. The only piece on the CD that was recorded long before the 1990s is "Caña Brava" by Beltrán (b. 1923, d. 1997), who Cuban salsa lovers know for his work with La Sonora Matancera in the 1950s. If you've lived in an area with a large Dominican population and have spent any time listening to Latin stations that play a lot of tropical music, chances are you've heard the slicker, more electronic sounds of modern neo-merengue. However, if those airwaves haven't exposed you to a lot of bachata, *Republica Dominicana* can be a very nice revelation. *—Alex Henderson*

French Antilles

Kassav'

Vocals, Keyboards, Drums, Guitar / Afro-Pop, Zouk, Caribbean, French Antilles
The zouk scene evolved from a studio project by Guadeloupian Pierre-Edouard Decimus, who had moved to Paris in the late 70s following an extremely successful career as co-leader of the legendary cadence band Les Vikings de la Guadeloupe. Enlisting the services of his brother Georges and Paris studio wizard Jacob Desvarieux, himself a Guadeloupian, Decimus began to forge a new sound that treated Antilles musical traditions to the state of the art recording technology available in Paris. By 1984 the three had settled on a stable lineup of musicians and singers (now representing both Guadeloupe and Martinique), had made their first live performance (in Guadeloupe), and had achieved their first massive radio success with "Banzawa" from a Desvarieux solo album.

Parties in the Antilles are called "zouks," and since Kassav's new records were the music of choice at the zouks, their music came to be called "zouk music." By 1985 nearly every Antilles musician was jumping on the zoukwagon and a whole new style of music was born.

Supported by a horn section, two dancers, extra keyboard, drummer, and percussion, the core of Kassav' is Jocelyne Beroard, Jacob Desvarieux, Jean-Philippe Marthely, Patrick St. Eloi, Jean-Claude Naimro, and until recently, Georges Decimus (who recently quit the band to pursue a career with a new group; Pierre-Edouard comes and goes at whim, never performing live but often resurfacing as a songwriter). Through the release of *Majestik Zouk,* the band has released ten studio albums and one live album. Each bonafide member of the band has also released solo albums that include support by the entire band. In fact, since 1987, all re-pressings of the back catalog of solo releases has had the name Kassav' added to the cover in bold letters. Add various carnival projects under the pseudonyms Soukoue Ko Ou and Turbo II, and the total number of Kassav'-related albums approaches 30.

The early releases were certainly experimental in nature as Desvarieux And The Decimus brothers searched for the right mix of musicians and musical elements. The best of the solo and carnival efforts can be found under the discography entries for the particular band member or carnival project. It's indisputable that much of the most dramatic groundbreaking occurred on the early- to mid-80s solo releases. Of the official Kassav' albums, all are interesting in that they provide a view into the development of what became the zouk sound. The formula from which the whole Antilles zouk scene evolved had kicked in by the sixth release, so from there on specific preferences are merely a matter of personal taste. *—Gene Scaramuzzo*

Passeport / 1983 / Sonodisc ✦✦✦

An-Ba-Chen'n La / 1985 / Georges DEBS ✦✦✦✦✦
Kassav's output has always intriguingly tended to veer before the roots and funk sides of their mix. *An-Ba,* the one that cemented the band's position as the biggest deal pretty much anywhere on the Afro-French circuit, returned to the individual approach and general hang-loose joviality of the earlier salsa-based style at its best. It was also a very highly worked album: "thanks also to..." brass, string and synthesizer types outnumbered the basic band. *—John Storm Roberts, Original Music*

Live Au Zenith / 1986 / SONY/Tristar ✦✦✦

● **Zouk Is the Only Medicine We Have** / 1988 / Greensleeves ✦✦✦✦✦
A superb greatest-hits collection comes from the top band. *—Robert Leaver*

Caribbean Music Styles

BIGUINE—Throughout the long history of the biguine, the dominant sound has been that of the clarinet and trombone, both solo and as a duet, and, while the phrasing often recalls New Orleans jazz, the overall sound is unmistakably Caribbean. The signature sound of the biguine is the interplay between the clarinet and trombone, which can still be heard today throughout the Antilles musical milieu, from the most traditional music to the music of the cadence era or the pop sounds of today's zouk. Any contemporary music that uses biguine as its base, even that which ventures as far off as contemporary jazz, is considered "biguine moderne." The classic music of carnival in the Antilles is an uptempo version of the biguine rhythm, called "biguine vide."

CADENCE—A constantly changing style that evolved primarily among the islands of Guadeloupe, Martinique, Dominica, and Haiti. The cadence era was exciting and extremely fertile, requiring musicians of only the highest calibre, who could master not only Antilles pop styles like biguine and Creole mazurka but also those of Haiti and the other neighboring islands. The cadence years saw the evolution of the pop influences that embellish the rootsier foundation of today's Antilles musicians, allowing for expression in an internationally familiar musical language: electric instruments, riffing horn sections, trapset drums, topical lyrics, and specific stylings of rock music, reggae, soca, American Black music, and more. In addition to Les Aiglons, this was the heyday of big bands like La Perfecta, Typical Combo, La Selecta, Les Maxels, Les Léopards, Les Vikings de la Guadeloupe (whose co-leader, Pierre-Edouard Decimus, went on to create Kassav' at the end of the decade), and Gordon Henderson's Exile One of Dominique. Recordings from this era, while fascinating and enjoyable, often suffer from out-of-tune instruments and sub-par recording quality. Cadence led directly into the early '80s and the rise of zouk, and it was the musicians schooled in cadence who were the first zouk stars. The major catalyst behind the emergence of zouk was the desire to produce a new Caribbean music that treated the multifaceted music of the Antilles to the state-of-the-art recording technology of the Paris studios.

CHOUVAL BWA—A rural Martiniquan style of music that evolved as accompaniment to the "manege" (or carousel). Originally featuring a large drum like a bass drum, hand drums, and ti bwa, chouv' was led by melodic instruments like accordion, bamboo flute, and wax-paper/comb-type kazoos. One young artist, Claude Germany, is attempting to carry on the traditional form of chouval bwa, while others have updated it minimally (by the addition of electric bass) or dramatically (as in the case of zouk chouv', which features an array of electric instruments, including synthesizer). Chouval bwa is Creole for the French term "cheval bois," meaning "wooden horse."

COMPAS—Haitian dance music, started by Nemours Jean-Baptiste in the '50s, known first as compas-direct.

GWO KA—The various indigenous rhythms of Guadeloupe are played on a two-drum family of hand drums called gwo ka. Gwo ka music is rhythm-driven by the two drums and is often accompanied by a mounted stick or bamboo log hit with sticks called a ti bwa. The drummers lead the way for dancers, and usually there is singing accompaniment. Gwo ka has been an underlying element of zouk from day one, and, in fact, Kassav's first album was entitled Love and Ka Dance. Anzala and Ti Celeste (or Ti Seles) are two gwo ka artists still recording today, the latter sticking to the roots while the former has electrified his sounds.

ROAD MARCH—Chosen at the carnival in Trinidad, this is the most popular song of the year.
—Gene Scaramuzzo

French Antilles Collection

☆ **Dance! Cadence!** / 1985 / Globestyle ♦♦♦♦♦
This classic is a wonderful look at cadence, biguine moderne, ti kannot, (kalenda), and early zouk by the likes of Eugene Mona, Georges Decimus, and Michel Godzom. *—Gene Scaramuzzo*

☆ **Hurricane Zouk** / Jun. 29, 1992 / Earthworks ♦♦♦♦♦
Classic high energy mid-'80s zouk, it includes some collaboration with African musicians in Paris. *—Robert Leaver*

☆ **Zouk Attack** / 1992 / Rounder ♦♦♦♦♦
This zouk anthology features such outstanding zouk groups as Pier' Rosier and Gazoline, Love Stars, Typical, Tatiana and Zouti, but sounds just a bit smooth in many places. It's a reminder that zouk was and is a roots-oriented pop sound, and as such has a soft center as well as frenetic edges. *—Ron Wynn*

Haiti

Boukman Eksperyans

Group / Afro-Pop, Caribbean, Haiti
Boukman Eksperyans announce their radicalism in their name, an allusion to Boukman the slave who initiated the island's 1804 independence uprising. Always aware that freedom and culture go hand in hand, this ten-member band sing in the sporadically outlawed creole tongue and blend African religious motifs and street slang into a wild, syncretic celebration of Haitian voodoo culture. To sing out so boldly in Haiti, however, is to invite repression; although the band's "Wet Chenn" (Remove the Chains) won first place in a 1989 musical contest, their 1992 entry was banned. In an environment torn apart with military unrest and governmental crackdowns, Boukman Eksperyans are regarded as a radical threat. Thus, their 1990 song, "Kem Pa Sote" was banned from Haitian airwaves. 1991's *Vodou Adjae* was the first Boukman Eksperyans album released in the U.S.; subsequent offerings include 1992's *Kalfou Dangare*, 1995's *Libete/Freedom (Let's Take It!)* and 1999's *Live at Red Rocks*. *Kanaval Rasin-Vodou Adja* followed in mid-2000. *—Leon Jackson*

● **Vodou Adjae** / 1991 / Mango ♦♦♦♦♦
This is an exciting blend of traditional drum rhythms and modern Caribbean pop attack. *—Bob Tarte*

Revolution / Jul. 14, 1998 / Lightyear ♦♦♦

Live at Red Rocks / Jul. 20, 1999 / Lightyear ♦♦♦♦

Haiti Collection

Angels in the Mirror: Vodou Music of Haiti / Nov. 4, 1997 / Ellipsis Arts ♦♦♦♦

Panama

Nando Boom

Vocals / Tropical, Caribbean, Panama
The traditional music of Panama is combined with reggae and soca rhythms to create the Tropical sounds of Nando Boom. Formed by Fernando Brown, a vocalist who had sung at dances since the age of ten, the group was successful from their inception in 1985. Their first single, "My Woman Thus Speaks" b/w "The Drum To Me" shattered previous sales records in Panama. Since emigrating to the United States, with the onslaught of political difficulties in Panama, Brown and Nando Boom have continued to make their presence felt. In 1992, the band received the Caracol of the Caribbean award from Colombia. Two years latre, they received a Stefano award in Miami. *—Craig Harris*

● **Nando Boom & The Explotion Band** / 1992 / Ariola ♦♦♦♦♦
A very satisfying recording in the Spanish-reggae vein—the music is straightahead dancehall with no surprises, but Nando has a fabulous voice and knows exactly how to work it. He reminds me a lot of the English toasters in style, especially Smiley Culture, and he even does a Spanish-English translation rap like Smiley's "Cockney Translation." A special bonus is a Spanish reggae version of then-Cat Stevens's "Wild World"—also a fine soca. *—Carl Hoyt, Original Music*

Trinidad and Tobago

Lord Invader (Rupert Westmore Grant)

d. Oct. 15, 1961, New York, NY
Vocals / Caribbean Folk, Calypso, Caribbean, Trinidad and Tobago
Most famous as the composer of "Rum and Coca-Cola," Lord Invader was a popular calypso performer in both his native Trinidad and New York, recording from the late '30s through the early '60s. Born Rupert Westmore Grant, he made his recording debut for RCA Bluebird in Port-of-Spain, Trinidad in 1937, with a song about boxer Joe Louis, and continued to record (for both RCA and Decca) and place in the upper reaches of Trinidadian calypso competitions through the early '40s, when he also began to perform and make recordings in New York City. In Trinidad in September 1943, visiting American comedian Morey Amsterdam heard Lord Invader's "Rum and Coca-Cola" and made it known back in the US, where the Andrews Sisters had a huge hit with the song. Lord Invader sued for plagiarism, the case eventually getting decided in his favor in 1947, although he didn't receive money from the defendants for seven years.

"Rum and Coca-Cola," however, was but one of many songs that the singer performed and recorded. As with many other calypso singers of that and other eras, Lord Invader was skilled at devising songs with social and political commentary, as well as singing more conventional lyrics based on romantic situations, or based upon traditional folk songs. From the mid-'40s through the early '60s, he recorded off and on for Moe Asch of Folkways Records, and during that period he was performing and recording in New York, London, and Europe. A compilation of 26 tracks Lord Invader did for Asch—some with his Calypso Group, some with full and somewhat jazzy bands—was issued by Smithsonian Folkways in 2000. *—Richie Unterberger*

● **Calypso in New York** / Sep. 26, 2000 / Smithsonian/Folkways ♦♦♦♦♦
All of the material on this 26-song, 73-minute CD was recorded for Moe Asch of Folkways Records between 1946 and 1961; half of the tracks were previously unreleased. It may be that many of the arrangements he used were more accessible to American ears than those used by some of his calypso peers, or just that the fidelity on many of these numbers (particularly those from the later 1950s and early 1960s) is superior to that heard on many vintage calypso recordings. But Lord Invader does seem more comfortable with full-band, slightly jazzed-up calypso arrangements than some other calypso performers, without compromising the verve and bite of his lyrics and vocal delivery. Occasionally these recordings have minimal backing, as on "Ten Thousand to Bar Me One," on which he's accompanied only by drum, bottle, spoon, and chorus; sometimes the songs are traditional, such as the arguably overdone "Brown Girl in the Ring," on which again he's backed only by percussion and chorus. More often he combines calypso with instrumentation reminiscent of pre-war jazz, especially on the cuts on which he's accompanied by Felix and His Internationals, featuring Gregory Felix on clarinet. The topicality of his songs actually isn't too overt, but it's there to hear on songs about taking the New York subway, his experiences in Chicago, and "Yankee Dollar" (about his frustration question for compensation in his "Rum and Coca-Cola" plagiarism suit). "God Made Us All," prefaced by a speech from the ubiquitous Pete Seeger (a staple of Smithsonian Folkways releases), is a gentle anti-racism admonition. Whatever he's singing about, however, Lord Invader conveys easygoing nobody's-fool charm, in a manner that's less strident than some other calypsoites of the time. *—Richie Unterberger*

Lord Kitchener

b. Apr. 18, 1922, Arima, St. George, Trinidad, **d.** Feb. 11, 2000, Port of Spain, Trinidad
Vocals / Calypso, Caribbean, Trinidad and Tobago
Lord Kitchener (born Aldwyn Roberts) shares with Mighty Sparrow the title of the world's best known Calypso singer. He began his career in Trinidad and won his first Road March award for singing in 1946. In 1948, Kitch emigrated to England in the company of singer Lord Beginner and newsreel footage of the time shows him singing "London Is the Place for Me." In less than two years, he and Beginner were recording for EMI. Kitch enjoyed massive popularity in England, winning the support and affection of England's Princess Margaret. In the 1950s, he toured West Africa and enjoyed a big hit there with his single, "Nora." Like many calypsonians, Kitch drifted toward soca and in 1978 hit the charts with "Sugar Bum Bum." Additonally noted for his hit single, "Give Me the Ting," he died February 12, 2000 at the age of 77. *—Leon Jackson*

Kitchener Goes Soca / 1981 / Charlie's ♦♦♦

★ **Roots of Soca** / 1984 / Charlie's ♦♦♦♦♦
This album doesn't have a single second-rate song on it and was one of the high points of Carnival 1984. *—Gene Scaramuzzo*

A Musical Excursion / 1990 / JW ♦♦♦

Klassic Kitchener / Ice ♦♦♦
A several-volume set, it includes high-quality versions of the original hit songs by Kitchener from the beginning of his career to the onset of the soca era in the late '70s. *—Gene Scaramuzzo*

Mighty Sparrow

b. Jul. 9, 1935, Grandroy Bay, Grenada
Vocals / Caribbean Folk, Calypso, Soca, Caribbean, Trinidad and Tobago
With his ultra-sweet vocals and lyrics that speak of romance and topical politics, Mighty Sparrow (born Slinger Francisco) has risen to the upper echelon of Trinidadian calypso. Best known for his hits "Jean And Dinah" in 1956 and "Carnaval Boycott" in 1957, Sparrow is an 11-time winner of the calypso monarchy and an eight-time winner of Trinidad and Tobago's Carnaval Road March competition. Born to a poor working class family in Gran Roi, a small fishing village in Grenada, Sparrow moved to Trinidad at the age of one. Learning to sing in the boy's choir of St. Patrick's Catholic Church, he became the head choirboy. At the age of 14, he formed a steel band to perform at the Carnaval, sparking his interest in calypso. Teaching himself to play guitar, Sparrow began to write his own songs. Winning the Carnaval competition with "Jean And Dinah," he received a grand prize of 40 dollars. In protest, he wrote a scorching indictment of the Trinidadian music industry, "Carnaval Boycott." Despite his refusal to compete in the Carnaval contests for the next three years, Sparrow became one of the Caribbean's most successful artists. *—Craig Harris*

★ **King of the World** / 1984 / B's ♦♦♦♦♦
Included is the classic "Doh Back Back," a hopelessly infectious soca that brought Sparrow the *Road March* title. *—Gene Scaramuzzo*

A Touch of Class / 1986 / B's ♦♦♦♦♦
Another classic, it includes "Coke Is Not It," "Ah Fraid De AIDS" and "Invade South Africa," all performed to killer soca beats. This is one of the most topical of Sparrow's '80s releases. *—Gene Scaramuzzo*

Hot Like Fire / 1992 / BLS ♦♦♦

Roaring Lion (Raphael de Leon)

b. 1910
Vocals / Calypso, Soca, Caribbean, Trinidad and Tobago
One of the major figures of early calypso music, Roaring Lion recorded copiously between

the 1930s and 1950s, and was instrumental in spreading the international popularity of calypso. His vintage sides are what many listeners think of as calypso at its best—infectious rhumba rhythms, lighthearted (sometimes nonsensical) lyrics, and a combination of Trinidadian musical elements with Anglo pop sensibilities.

Roaring Lion was born as Hubert Raphael Charles around 1910, although he later changed his name to Raphael de Leon. Already a writer of poetry as a boy, he launched his career as a singer in 1927, when—much to his surprise—he won a calypso competition. The event also occasioned his nickname of Roaring Lion, inspired by his style of vocal delivery (although if he was indeed a roaring lion, he was a pretty gentle and charming one).

In the 1930s, Roaring Lion (with help from partner Attila The Hun) was crucial to the development of calypso, devising the calypso duet and calypso drama, and introducing new melodies to a style that originally had very few. Between 1934 and 1941 he was the most prolific calypso recording artist, cutting nearly 100 singles, including some of the music's most popular standards, such as "Mary Ann," "Netty Netty," and "Six Feet High." One of his most famous compositions, "Ugly Woman" (originally recorded in 1933), formed much of the basis for Jimmy Soul's 1963 #1 hit "If You Wanna Be Happy."

Roaring Lion performed and recorded in the United States occasionally during the 1930s and 1940s. In fact, he spent much of 1945 singing in New York clubs, including the Village Vanguard, where he was replaced by a young Harry Belafonte. Roaring Lion has claimed that Belafonte subsequently performed and recorded some of Lion's songs without crediting or compensating the originator.

In 1951, Roaring Lion relocated to Great Britain for 15 years, performing, recording, and running both a cosmetics company and a bureau that helped immigrants find jobs and places to live. After his British jaunt he returned to Trinidad to assume his position as an elder statesman. He is also the author of a treatise devoted to his theory that calypso's roots can be traced back to 13th-century France, *Calyspo from France to Trinidad: 800 Years of History*. In 1993, he issued an album of re-recordings of a dozen of his hits, with Eddy Grant producing, and guest appearances by Grant and David Rudder. Ice also issued many of his classic originals on CD with *Sacred 78's*. *—Richie Unterberger*

★ **Sacred 78's** / 1994 / Ice ✦✦✦✦✦
More than 70 years after beginning his singing career in 1927 at the age of 18, the venerable calypsonian Rafael de Leon is still roaring, performing shows in Miami and in his native Trinidad. *Sacred 78's* is a collection of 25 singles recorded between the early 1930s and late 1960s, when he was at the peak of his powers. The sound quality is a bit dodgy, as you might expect, but it's surprisingly clear—the better to catch all of the double entendres, political propaganda, social commentary, and romantic chest-pounding that characterizes calypso in general and the Roaring Lion's singing in particular. "Cheek to Cheek" (which borrows subtly from the melody of the Irving Berlin standard, but is otherwise unrelated) expresses puzzlement over a lady friend's preference for other ladies when it comes to, um, dancing. In "Weather Man" he criticizes the inaccuracy of weather reporting. "Advantage Mussolini" (one of the least sonically attractive selections) takes Fascism to task. Perhaps more to the point, though, he counsels his friend Melda to wash her hands and clean her nails and faults several other ladies for their ugliness. Delicate it's not, but this stuff is a lot of fun. *—Rick Anderson*

Shadow

Bass / Social Commentary, Party Soca, Soca, Caribbean, Trinidad and Tobago
There are many calypso lovers who await Shadow's annual release more than that of any other calypsonian. Like Stalin and just a handful of others, Shadow is a totally unique calypsonian; there is no other like Shadow. Since 1974 and his landmark composition "De Bassman," he has never failed to deliver some of the toughest basslines, most infectious grooves, and most original compositions of anyone in the Caribbean. On top of all this, he has a low, authoritative voice that lends an air of truth and finality to all he sings. His social and political commentaries are delivered in such a clever way (and propelled as they are by his unique soca beat) that the messages often sink in subliminally, a testimony to his unique lyrical skills. With this in mind, how does one narrow down his nearly 20 records to a handful of recommendations *—Gene Scaramuzzo*

If I Coulda I Woulda I Shoulda / 1979 / Charlie's ✦✦✦

★ **Columbus Lied** / 1991 / Shanachie ✦✦✦✦✦
Shadow is one of the few calypsonians who has been anthologized on an American label. This recent release presents eight of the best of his songs from 1988 through 1990, a landmark period in his career. *—Gene Scaramuzzo*

Winston Bailey Is the Shadow / 1992 / Kisskidee ✦✦✦
There is a decidedly different approach on this album. Only one song, "Hard Head," twas Road March bound. Neither "Soucouyant," the superb commentary on AIDS, nor the late-bloomer "Music" (aka "Dingolay") were typical uptempo grooves, showing that Shadow can hit no matter how far he strays from formula. *—Gene Scaramuzzo*

Trinidad and Tobago Collection

Calypso Calaloo / 1994 / Rounder ✦✦✦✦✦
This most recent in Rounder's continuing anthology series spotlighting vintage Caribbean music features 16 cuts by calypso artists from the early 1900s to the '50s outlining carnival music's evolution. The earliest material was recorded in 1914, when songs were seldom more than Caribbean updates of current American hits, to the 1950s, when a distinct style and form had emerged that reflected Trinidad, yet also contained African, Afro-Latin and African-American musical elements. The anthology also covers related styles like steel band (pan). It's a nicely sequenced, expertly notated collection. *—Ron Wynn*

Calypso Pioneers: 1912-1937 / 1989 / Rounder ✦✦✦✦✦
Companion CD to a prior Rounder anthology devoted to classic calypso, these 16 cuts present formative songs from 1912-1937. The music is still emerging from a confluence of American dance band sounds, African and Afro-Latin rhythms, plus Caribbean social situations and influences. As carnival became an entrenched celebration within the Caribbean community, the songs composed to be performed during that time came to be known as calypso. The anthology includes early performances by such calypso heroes as Atilla The Hun, Wilmouth Houdini, Phil Madison, Julian Whiterose and Sam Manning. Vocal styles, instrumental backing, lyrics, arrangements and production are quite unsophisticated and uneven on the early cuts, but a sound and unified approach began to appear in the middle section and is quite evident by the final numbers. *—Ron Wynn*

★ **Fall of Man: Calypsos on the Human Condition 1935-1941** / Feb. 9, 1999 / Rounder ✦✦✦✦✦
Classic Trinidadian calypso, from the point at which it began to achieve international popularity. Indeed, most of these 25 tracks were actually recorded in New York City, although a few actually were cut in Trinidad. Atilla the Hun (aka Raymond Quevedo) is featured especially heavily, performing or co-performing on ten selections; other notable figures including Neville Marcano (aka the Tiger) and the Lion. The liner notes perhaps make too much of lyrical analysis, with little detail about the music or the individual tracks. Certainly the lyrics (mostly about romantic and sexual deception) have their interesting aspects, but above all this is fun music, sung with a lighthearted poesy. It's also played and arranged with an inventive bounce that owes much to early jazz as well as Trinidadian music. The sound, remastered for compact disc, is very good considering the age of the source material. And for those who do get off on lyrical analysis, full librettos are provided in the liner notes, along with a glossary explaining some of the words employed and terms referred to in the songs. *—Richie Unterberger*

Zouk

When zouk music from the French Antilles islands of Guadeloupe and Martinique exploded onto the international music scene in the mid-'80s, attention was again focused on a part of the Caribbean that hadn't been heard from musically since the popularity of the biguine in the early 20th century. Created in the late '70s by a small clique of Guadeloupian musicians residing in Paris, zouk presented a mélange of global influences that touched millions in the French-speaking African diaspora, subsequently acting as a catalyst for an exciting mid-'80s period of musical experimentation.

With the Paris recording studios as a common meeting ground, francophone musicians from Africa and the Caribbean gathered to exchange ideas and "zoukify" their respective pop music forms, placing an indelible mark on the soukous of Zaire/Congo, the makossa of Cameroon, and a host of others. Haitian musicians, themselves a major influence on the French Antilles music scene, were in turn deeply affected by zouk, as were eventually (to a much lesser degree) English-speaking Caribbean artists from the Virgin Islands to Montserrat to Antigua.

Zouk truly draws its power from the rich musical heritage of Africa and the Caribbean. In its bubbly, light, loping beat can be heard elements from Guadeloupe, Martinique, Dominica, and Haiti, with dashes thrown in from Paris, Zaire, Antigua, Trinidad, Cuba, Puerto Rico, and the Dominican Republic. With so many influences, it's not surprising that popular zouk can range from highly percussive, driving dance music to slow ballads that hover dangerously close to French disco and cabaret singing.

Since the late '80s, zouk has become somewhat locked into a restrictive formula not unlike soca, and from an international viewpoint, its popularity has waned. Ironically, this has obscured from view the fact that today the French Antilles are bubbling with exciting musical experimentations involving many classic types of Antilles music like the biguine, chouval bwa, bele (belair), and ti kannot (kalenda). Inspired by a renewed sense of identity (and a dramatically increased knowledge of recording technology) afforded by the success of zouk, older Antilles musicians are returning to the musical riches of their islands. Now in the '90s, the overall musical output of the Antilles is bursting with rhythmically propulsive, melodic sounds like zouk, zouk chouv', biguine moderne, biguine vide, and more.

With zouk (and to a lesser extent the modernized forms of classic music), the Antilles music scene revolves around the studio rather than live performance. Only a dozen or so self-contained bands exist that actually tour outside of Paris and the islands. Like many forms of Caribbean music, the majority of Antilles recordings reflect studio projects involving certain cliques of musicians, and it's not unfair to say that looking at the musicians' names on the record jacket will give a fair idea of the music within, before the shrink wrap is even peeled off. As for the lyrics, aside from a few rare exceptions, all projects are in Creole and avoid anything "angaje" (political or social commentary).

Records come out twice a year in the Antilles, timed either for summer vacation or for the Christmas holidays leading into carnival. Most recordings are done in Paris, with Henri Debs' studio in Guadeloupe running second, and J-P Mauriello's Hibiscus Studio in Martinique running a far-distant third. Excluding sure sellers like Kassav' and occasional huge successes, most releases are treated to only one pressing by Antilles record producers. This means records quickly become hard to find after their initial appearance.

Fortunately, compilations featuring collections of hits are becoming increasingly available and often represent the only means of hearing the music. Of even more interest is the recent appearance of a few anthologies of artists, like the superb Hibiscus Records releases of early music by Eugene Mona and other classic music from the defunct 3A label.

—Gene Scaramuzzo

Heat in De Place: Soca from Trinidad / 1990 / Rounder ✦✦✦✦✦
Outstanding numbers by seven contemporary calypsonians were spotlighted on this 1990 disc, one of two Rounder issued that year featuring various soca stars. Shadow took honors with a pair of selections, one the roaring "Tension," athe other more humorous "Garden Want Water." Another sizzling tune was Singing Francine's "Soca Do That," as well as Johnny King's "Wet Me Down" and Bally's "Shaka Shaka," which now sounds lyrically dated, but retains a potent musical punch. *—Ron Wynn*

Rough Guide to Calypso & Soca / Sep. 28, 1999 / World Music Network ✦✦✦

Say What— Double Entendre Soca / Rounder ✦✦✦✦✦
Soca rivals "slack" dancehall reggae and vintage "hokum" blues for great risque material. That's the theme linking the seven songs featured on this anthology. The CD includes sassy, suggestive hits from Shadow, Poser and particularly Bally, whose "Gimme Piece" leaves absolutely nothing to the imagination. Each tune features catchy melodies and throbbing arrangements, showing soca's musical punch and hypnotic grooves. There aren't any weak links, and only limited distribution and publicity prevents soca from rivaling reggae as the prime Caribbean musical import. *—Ron Wynn*

Steelbands of Trinidad & Tobago / 1994 / Delos ✦✦✦✦✦
Trinidad and Tobago is the country which originated the steel pan, an oil drum whose head has been flattened to produce a wide range of pitches when pounded by mallets. The steel pan is the predominant instrument found in this collection of large percussion orchestras perfoming arrangements of classical pieces, including Tchaikovsky's *Fourth Symphony*, Mendelssohn's *Hebrides*, and Offenbach's *Orpheus in the Underworld*, in addition to original compositions. *—Jason Ankeny*

Trinidad (1912-1941) / 1992 / Harlequin ✦✦✦✦✦
This is a mixed bag of enchanting music and cuts only a collector could love. Pretty much all—and all the best—material is instrumental, with gems ranging from charming Venezuelan-influenced string-band to a superb piano solo by George Cabral. The preceding spate of reissues has swept up most of the treasures already, though The Lion is on form. *—John Storm Roberts, Original Music*

West Indies Collection

Musical Traditions of St. Lucia, West Indies: Dances and Songs from a Caribbean Island / Smithsonian Folkways ✦✦✦✦
These recordings were made between 1975 and 1987. This is the best of all the albums of traditional Antillean music, and the notes are absolutely first-rate. It includes play-song dances, beach party and game seasonal music, work songs, religious (kete), wake songs, quadrille music, and St. Lucian (La Rose) society songs. *—Don Hill*

EUROPE

Albania Collection

Folk Music of Albania / Topic ✦✦✦
Sandwiched between Yugoslavia and Greece, part Christian and part Muslim, Albania is a tiny land with a rich and ancient musical culture. These are fine recordings by A.L. Lloyd of songs, dances, and instrumentals, among them bagpipe, flutes, and lutes. Given the country's beleaguered history, the vocals include many epic ballads, old and new. *—John Storm Roberts*

Bulgaria

Le Mystère Des Voix Bulgares

Group / Bulgarian Folk, Bulgaria, Europe
The Mysterious Voices of Bulgaria belong to The National Radio And Television Chorus, the premier women's choir popularized worldwide through the efforts of ethnomusicologist Marcel Cellier. His recordings, issued on various import labels before appearing on Nonesuch, made a big splash in western Europe and the US, cultivating vast new audiences for the group's dramatic adaptations of folk singing styles. Their spine-chilling harmonies, punctuated by whoops and quavers, are presented in full choral arrangements and smaller groups—duos and trios—with and without instrumental backing. *—Myles Boisen*

From Bulgaria with Love: The Pop Album / 1993 / Mesa Blue Moon ✦✦✦✦✦
Newly renamed for chart success, Bulgaria's premier, normally solemn choir cuts up with a babbling Italian rapster on a disc of computer-crazy house mixes. Equal parts horrible and marvellous, it's the *Foucault's Pendulum* of world music or an episode of *Mystery Science Theatre 3000* with sampling standing in for robot commentary. In fact, the flesh-and-blood choir has little real-time interaction with instrumentalists on this disc. It's mainly digital sleight of hand, with phrases and fragments of a few Le Mystere standards stuttering atop gothic machinations. No need to listen to the disc twice. Every bit of its undeniable pleasures can be harvested at the first and only hearing—a truly audacious concept. Think of the hours to be saved if every new CD could be mainlined, savored, then discarded. *—Bob Tarte*

★ **Le Mystere des Voix Bulgares** / Nonesuch ✦✦✦✦✦
The record that started the boom, this is an excellent introduction to the thrilling Bulgarian women's choir. *—Myles Boisen*

Ivo Papasov

Clarinet / World Fusion, Bulgaria, Europe
A towering figure of the contemporary Bulgarian wedding music movement, clarinetist Ivo Papasov earned international success on the strength of his influential jazz-folk style. Born in 1952 of Turkish Rom (Gypsy) ancestry, in 1974 he founded the group Trakiya, quickly emerging as the unrivaled king of wedding music ("Stambolovo"), the most popular Bulgarian style; Papasov's distinctive sound—an improvisational, energetic aesthetic heavily influenced by diverse sources including traditional folk, film scores and cartoon music—found its most fervent following among younger listeners, the attraction undoubtedly the music's similarites to the kinetic spirit of Western rock. Papasov's success did not come without a price, however, and in 1982 he was imprisoned on charges of spreading anti-Communist propaganda; after three weeks of incarceration he was scheduled to be sent to a labor camp, finally earning a last-minute reprieve. In Bulgaria's new democratic society of the 1990s, his music thrived, with long-awaited official recordings seeing the light of day not only at home, but also in the U.S. *—Jason Ankeny*

Orpheus Ascending / 1989 / Hannibal ✦✦✦

● **Balkanology** / 1991 / Hannibal ✦✦✦✦
One of the most revered musicians in Bulgaria, clarinetist Ivo Papasov is a master of Bulgarian wedding music. The superb and largely instrumental *Balkanology* draws not only on Bulgarian elements, but also the music of Greece, Turkey and Romania. Listening to this heartfelt music (much of it quite fast), one can hear the parallels between Middle Eastern, Mediterranean and East European forms. Papasov is quite the improviser, and in fact, American jazz has had a significant impact on his loose and very spontaneous modal playing. (Modal or "scalar" improvisation has been a significant part of jazz since the late 1950s.) Of course, Western influence in wedding music is something Bulgaria's old Leninist regime took a dim view of, but with the fall of communism in that country in 1989, the form seemed destined to grow even more popular. *—Alex Henderson*

Bulgaria Collection

Folk Music of Bulgaria / 1966 / Topic ✦✦✦
Like the other Topic re-releases, this has the double strength of outstanding music (even by the high standards of the late A.L. Lloyd, who recorded it) and a chronological perspective given by the fact that it is more or less four decades old. It's a magnificent overview, from vocal solos and duets through fiddles, flutes, bagpipes and the rest, fine though these are. *—John Storm Roberts, Original Music*

England Collection

Christmas Carols from English Pubs / Oct. 12, 1999 / Smithsonian/Folkways ✦✦✦
A bright collection of warm field recordings, these traditional carols are presented with the style that Smithsonian Folkways has become known for: clear documentation, informative liner notes, and a real sense of living history. Primarily a cappella or with sparse organ accompaniment, the carolers themselves will never be mistaken for professional singers, but their genuine passion for singing and sense of community is evident and pervasive. The performances themselves are reminiscent of the boisterous joy of sacred harp or "shape note" singing and really bring the feel of a crowded English pub on a brisk December eve. *—Zac Johnson*

The Rough Guide to English Roots Music / Aug. 25, 1998 / World Music Network ✦✦✦✦✦
Every decade or so, it seems that English folk and roots music develops the impetus to revisit and reinvent, taking familiar elements and bending them into new shapes that have the twin appeals of familiarity and newness. Such sudden reinventions have provided listeners with the work of artists as diverse and closely linked as Ewan MacColl, Fairport Convention, Steeleye Span, June Tabor, and Phillip Pickett; the music may hail from the present or from 600 years ago, and instrumentation may involved electric guitars, trap drums, concertina, and someone blasting away with a crumhorn (a combination likely to reveal the presence of Ashley Hutchings, with the Albion Band or without). *The Rough Guide to English Roots Music* pulls together 18 likely suspects, with an accent on the closing years of the 20th century, which means selections from Eliza Carthy & the Kings of Calicutt and Billy Bragg alongside such expected icons as Martin Carthy and the Watersons. There are some excellent choices to be found in this set, but it functions all too well as an appetizer—indulging in this collection could lead to rash actions later, such as carting off boxes of albums of English roots artists, or purchasing one each of everything in the Topic Records back catalog; the most hopeless cases will never again be able to imagine having led a life without Ashley Hutchings. *—Steven McDonald*

Finland

Värttinä

Vocals / Finnish Folk, Scandinavian Folk, Worldbeat, Folk-Pop, Finland, Europe
One of the most internationally successful acts to emerge from the contemporary Finland music scene, Värttinä revitalized the nation's folk traditions with an aggressive and ultra-modern style which eschewed not only the costumes of their ancestors but also the long-accepted cultural notion that women should sing unaccompanied. A product of the the folk music department at Helsinki's Sibelius Academy, Värttinä formed in the early 1980s, its 21 original members all previously associated with an area youth group; over time their ranks gradually slimmed down, and by the early 1990s the group primarily consisted of vocalists Sari Kaarinen, Mari Kaasinen, Kirsi Kahkonen and Sirpa Reiman, backed by an ever-revolving lineup of backing musicians. Their records, beginning with 1994's *Oi Dai*, revived the unique polyphonic music of the Finno-Ugric people of Karelia, a region of eastern Finland extending into Russia; subsequent albums including 1995's *Aitara* and the following year's *Kokko* launched Värttinä to European superstardom, cementing their reputation among the most important and innovative Finnish performers of their generation. *—Jason Ankeny*

Oi Dai / 1990 / NorthSide ✦✦✦✦✦
Once a 15-member chorus with pipes and girth to rival the Bulgarian women's choirs, this

formerly traditionalist Finnish chorale slimmed to a four-woman brat-pack to deliver a bracing disc of speed-folk. Reportedly, one in every hundred people in Finland bought a copy when it was released in 1990. The nightmarish joy of bright, unison singing, and merry-go-round tempos pays off in surprising Finno-Ugric lyrics. Who would guess that the cheerful chipmunks of "Marilaulu" darkly fantasize, "The old hags nag with their jaws clanking. I should cut out their tongues and fill up their mouths with hot tin"— *—Bob Tarte*

Seleniko / 1992 / NorthSide ♦♦♦

Aitara / 1994 / Xenophile ♦♦♦♦
It must be admitted that Värttinä is not for everyone. The quartet of high-pitched, rapidly singing Finnish women who front the group would be a migraine-sufferer's worst nightmare. But if you like vocal enthusiasm and precision, this album is for you.

sAitara prominently displays the band's secret weapon: its instrumentalists. These four men and one woman coax a big, rich, and varied song out of bouzouki, accordion, sax, Hammond organ, violin, drums, and Finland's traditional instrument, the kantele, a kind of zither. If the low, reedy sounds of the accordion and baritone sax on "Mie Tahon Tanssia" ("I Want to Dance") were not there to offset the ladies, then they would be pretty hard to take, even for a fan. On "Outona Omilla Mailla" ("Stranger in My Own Land"), the instruments set an almost gothic mood of alienation. At first, the singers reinforce this mood but then reverse it with one of those quick shifts at which they are experts.

The album consists mostly of original melodies and lyrics derived from and including some traditional material as well. For anyone interested in contemporary Scandinavian music, this album cannot be too highly recommended. *—Kurt Keefner*

★ **Kokko** / Oct. 1996 / Elektra ♦♦♦♦♦
After four previous American releases, the short, sharp and focused *Kokko* hones the girl-group midnight sunners to a laser beam of pop-music strengths in the service of ditties largely derived from the country's Karelian tradition. The male-dominated instrumental side finally holds its own with the massed female vocalists on this release, even earning a fiery cut of its own. Bright and constantly evolving arrangements keep the listener's attention shifting between the vocal maelstrom and assorted accordions, fiddles, keyboards, reeds, guitars, percussion, and drum loops. Of all the immaculate conceptions here, the most inspiring may be "Halla" with its dervish riff, hey-yeah goose herding calls, klezmer and EZ jazz sax figures, and a funky horn caesura which stops everything in its tracks. *—Bob Tarte*

Former Soviet Union Collection

☆ **Musics of the Soviet Union** / 1989 / Smithsonian/Folkways ♦♦♦♦♦
This superb sampler of traditional regional styles covers many of the significant republics. The uniformly genuine quality makes this highly commendable. It's a fine overview with good non-academic notes. *—Myles Boisen & David L. Mayers*

France

Manu Chao

Vocals, Guitar / French Rock, France, Europe
The former leader of the French rock band Mano Negra, singer Manu Chao made his solo debut in 1998 with *Clandestino. —Jason Ankeny*

● **Clandestino** / 1998 / Virgin ♦♦♦♦
The first solo album released by the former frontman of Mano Negra, *Clandestino* is an enchanting trip through Latin-flavored worldbeat rock, reliant on a potpourri of musical styles from traditional Latin and salsa to dub to rock & roll to French pop to experimental rock to techno. Chao's voice tends to be a bit nasally, but the best songs ("Mentira," "Mama Call," and the silly novelty "Bongo Bong") here benefit from his infectious, freewheeling delivery which incorporates balladry, chorus vocals, rapping, and tossed-off spoken-word passages. Just about every track has odd sampled bits from what sound like pirate radio-station broadcasts (a possible link to the title). There are so many great ideas on this record that it's difficult to digest in one listen, but multiple plays reveal the great depth of Manu Chao's artistry. *—John Bush*

Mano Negra

Group / Rock en Español, France, Europe
Named in honor of an Andalucian anarchist group, Mano Negra emerged from the same Parisian artists' scene which also gave rise to the like-minded Les Negresses Vertes, drawing equal influence from the punk ethos of the Clash and the multitude of sounds and rhythms endemic to the global music community. Formed in 1986 from the remnants of the neo-rockabilly unit the Hot Pants, Mano Negra essentially consisted of vocalist Manu Chao, his trumpeter brother Tonio and drummer cousin Santiago Casiriego, Spanish natives who fused rock, rap, flamenco and rai to create a heady brew they dubbed "Patchanka," a name derived from a Spanish pejorative for dancehall music. Mano Negra's debut LP, also titled *Patchanka,* appeared in 1988, scoring the French indie hit "Mala Vida."

The record's success led to a contract with Virgin, which in 1989 issued the group's sophomore effort *Puta's Fever* (Dominican slang for a sexually-transmitted disease caught from a prostitute), increasing the band's visibility abroad as well as establishing them as France's most popular alternative act. While 1991's *King of Bongo* attempted to broaden their Anglo fanbase via the inclusion of several English-language tracks, but their focus quickly turned to South America when in 1992 they embarked on the "Cargo Tour," travelling to a series of port cities to perform on a stage built into their ship's hold. Mano Negra returned the following year, this time journeying by rail from Colombia's Caribbean coast to the capital city of Bogotá, giving free concerts at stations en route. Latin influences dominated 1994's *Casa Babylon,* which proved to be the group's final record; Manu Chao later resurfaced in Radio Bemba, and released his first solo album (*Clandestino*) in 1998. *—Jason Ankeny*

● **The Best of Mano Negra** / May 11, 1999 / Ark 21 ♦♦♦♦
The Best of Mano Negra showcases the eclectic style that made the band an influential cult favorite among political punks. Mano Negra's combination of Arab, African and punk styles and a socially conscious outlook inspired like-minded artists such as Rage Against the Machine, and this 24-track collection spotlights their incendiary, energetic sound. Tracks include "Mala Vida," "Rock Island Line," "Peligro" and "Mad Man's Dead." *—Heather Phares*

Georgia (Republic)

Tsinandali Choir

Group, Georgia (Russia), Asia
This all-male Eastern Georgian ensemble specializes in "table songs"—not songs about tables, but sung *at* tables at holidays, feasts, marriages, births, deaths, and other special events. With their beautiful polyphonic vocals and strong harmonies, they evoke comparisons to the work of another all-male Georgian ensemble, the Rustavi Choir. Their polyphonic arrangements will appeal to fans of the *Le Mystere Des Voix Bulgares* series in its similar devotional tone and expert vocal interplay, though Western listeners tend to find this branch of Georgian music smoother and less striking than the famous female Bulgarian choirs. *—Richie Unterberger*

Table Songs of Georgia / 1993 / Real World ♦♦♦♦♦
Impassioned and lovely performances of traditional Georgian table/folk songs, performed without instrumentation. Originally released on Melodiya Records in Georgia in 1988, it was licensed for wide availability in the West by Peter Gabriel's RealWorld label five years later. *—Richie Unterberger*

Georgia (Republic) Collection

Georgia: The Resounding Polyphony of the Caucausus / May 27, 1997 / Multicultural Media ♦♦♦♦
Part of a relatively well put together series, Music of the Earth, Multicultural Media put out one volume dealing with the Russian state of Georgia, with its resplendent polyphonies that fill every song. In all truth, much of the music sounds like a cross between Western Christian hymns and Muslim prayers. Georgians use three-part singing in almost every work (and occasionally four parts). By the listings of the songs on the well-done liner notes, there are roughly four types of song utilized in Georgia: drinking songs, working songs, lullabies, and Westernized Christian hymns. Roughly half of the songs on the album are drinking songs, though they still utilize the somber polyphony that all of the works have. There is definitely a state of melancholy in the music, mostly due to the tempo and the three-part singing combined. The performances are well executed in all cases, though they can get a bit dreary for any listener. While some may have an ear for this type of music, others will most likely become tired of it. Only those that know what they're getting into should dig up these recordings, for their own safety. *—Adam Greenberg*

Greece

Mikis Theodorakis

b. Jul. 29, 1925, Chios, Greece
Composer, Greece, Europe
Mikis Theodorakis is a renowned Greek troubadour and one of his country's greatest composers. He wrote many symphonies, cantatas, several ballets and operas, plus popular songs including "Zorba the Greek," famous from Herb Alpert's instrumental hit. Born in 1925 on the Greek island of Chios, Theodorakis began writing songs quite early. He formed his own choir and gave his first performance at the age of 17. An active resistance fighter during World War II, he studied at the conservatories in both Athens and Paris (the latter with Oliver Messiaen). Theodorakis wrote several symphonies during the late '50s, but later returned to Greece to apply his musical knowledge to the traditional Greek music he'd grown up with. After several years of film scoring, in 1964 he composed the music for the film adaptation of the Nikos Kazantzakis novel *Zorba the Greek.* When 1967 brought a fascist government into control of the country, Theodorakis went underground and formed a revolutionary group to combat abuses—including a ban on playing or even listening to his music. He was later arrested, exiled, and sent to an internment camp, though the work of a global solidarity movement—led by Leonard Bernstein, Dmitri Shostakovich, Arthur Miller, and Harry Belafonte—helped secure his release in 1970. Still exiled from his country, Theodorakis served as the greatest ambassador of Greek music during the 1970s, playing thousands of concerts across the world. After the government toppled, he served as a member of the new parliament, also working as General Musical Director of the Symphony Orchestra and Chorus of the Hellenic Radio and Television. *—John Bush*

The Best of Mikis Theodorakis / Sep. 15, 1994 / Koch ♦♦♦♦

Poetica / Feb. 1996-May 1996 / Peregrina ♦♦♦♦
In the '90s, Mikis Theodorakis had a major asset in singer Maria Farantouri, who handles all of the vocals on *Poetica.* Blessed with a gorgeous voice and a fantastic range, Farantouri brings a great deal of charisma and humanity to such Theodorakis melodies as "With Half a Moon," "Color of Love" and "Sobbing Angels." Theodorakis is a superb composer—one of the true poets of Greek pop, to be sure—and Farantouri has the sensitivity and depth needed for his songs. Interestingly, *Poetica* wasn't recorded in Greece, but was recorded for the German Peregrina label at a studio in Ludwigsburg, Germany. In fact, the band that Theodorakis leads on this CD, is comprised of German musicians. Highly recommended. *—Alex Henderson*

Aemata / Feb. 9, 1999 / Peregrina ♦♦♦

- **Very Best of Theodorakis** / May 18, 1999 / Koch ♦♦♦♦

Greece Collection

★ **The Dance of Heaven's Ghosts** / 1997 / Metro Blue/EMI Hemisphere ♦♦♦♦♦

☆ **Folk Music of Greece** / Topic ♦♦♦♦♦
Rural Greek music is commonly divided into the Mountains and the Islands. This collection opens with a variety of mainland music, including some splendid clarinet as well as the usual impassioned and highly decorated vocals. The second side focuses on the very different styles of the Aegean Isles, stressing fiddle and lute as well as the ancient Balkan bagpipe. *—John Storm Roberts*

Greek Folk Dances / Monitor ♦♦♦
A series of recordings of various Greek dance ensembles, it has superb variety throughout the series. *—Myles Boisen*

☆ **Greek-Oriental Rembetika** / Folk Lyric ♦♦♦♦♦
This is a wonderful introduction to one of the great 20th-century urban musics. Not only does it include both famous names (Papasideris and Abatsi, who are widely reissued elsewhere) and names otherwise entirely obscure, but it has excellent notes in English. It's even more important now that the Greek EMI recordings have become so hard to find. *—John Storm Roberts*

Mourmourika: Songs of Greek Underworld / Jan. 26, 1999 / Rounder ♦♦♦♦

☆ **Rembetica** / Rounder ♦♦♦♦♦
This is a welcome collection. There are some musical and conceptual cavils, but each is more than balanced by a strength. Some of the cuts are far from their singers' best, and the Papaioannis piece is plain unworthy. But there's a great deal of fine music from unfamiliar as well as familiar artists (including the first recorded bousouki solo—check out the "Moonlight Sonata" piano!). *—John Storm Roberts*

Songs of la Belle Époque: Tangos of the Thirties / Apr. 22, 1997 / FM ♦♦♦♦
Songs of la Belle Époque: Tangos of the Thirties is a collection of 22 tangos written and recorded by Greek artists. Unavoidable, due to the era of the recording, is the record crackle and hiss, which is quite pronounced on some tracks. Regardless, this is a gem for fans of early Greek singers, and early world music recordings in general. Some of the vocalists who sing these romantic tangos are Sofia Vembo, Dimitris Philipopoulos, Danae, Eleni de Rose, Angela Lykiardopoulou, and P. Epitropakis. Rare, old 78s by these artists and more are cleaned up and lovingly compiled into this installment of FM Records' Greek Archives series. The accompanying booklet includes all of the song lyrics in Greek, with excerpts translated into English. *—Joslyn Layne*

Gypsy Collection

Gypsy Road / Jan. 12, 1999 / Ethnic ♦♦♦♦
Few compilations of Gypsy music are as broad-minded as *Gypsy Road.* Other collections have focused specifically on the folk of Russian Gypsies or the flamenco of Spanish Gypsies in Madrid. But, with *Gypsy Road,* Alula spotlights Gypsy artists from all over Europe as well as parts of the Middle East. The Gypsies who enrich this CD come from India (Musafir) and Turkey (Kemani Cemal) as well as Spain (Gerardo Nunez, Casta), Italy (Acquaragia Drom) and France (Energypsy). Gypsy culture has, of course, been a part of Eastern Europe for centuries—so it's only right that several tunes on this album would be recorded in that part of the world. The Eastern European Gypsies heard on *Gypsy Road* come from Bulgaria (Yuri Yunakov), Hungary (Ando Drom, Kalyi Jag), Romania (Taraf de Haidouks) and naturally, Russia (Loyko, Kolpakov Trio). Many different languages are heard on *Gypsy Road,* and the instruments vary from one country to another. But as diverse as this CD is, one can hear the parallels between these artists. Most of them use what is called "modal" or "scalar" playing—even if you don't understand the technical meaning, you can recognize modality when you hear it. (Modal playing is also used in everything from Jewish klezmer to Indian raga and Algerian rai). *Gypsy Road* is a fine collection that world music enthusiasts should make a point of acquiring. *—Alex Henderson*

Rough Guide to the Music of the Gypsies / Sep. 28, 1999 / World Music Network ♦♦♦♦
The Rough Guide To The Music Of The Gypsies traces the origins of gypsy music from India, Turkey, Greece, Italy, the Balkan States, the UK and Finland. The wide geographical and musical territory the gypsies covered is reflected in the album's 16 tracks, which include Kostas Pavlidis' "Jastar Amenge Dur," Pata Negra's "Yo Me Quedo En Sevilla," Musafir's "Anghuti," Jasper & Levi Smith's "Cock O' The North" and "Flowers of Edinburgh" and Kalman Balogh's "Cigany Szinek." *—Heather Phares*

Ireland Collection

Irish Drinking Songs / Jan. 26, 1993 / Columbia/Legacy ♦♦♦♦♦
The Irish tradition of drinking songs is not one that dwells on the problems of overindulgence, as the liner notes point out. This compilation presents 16 mostly exuberant 1960s tracks by two of the most famous Celtic folk bands, the Dubliners and the Clancy Brothers. Although "Whiskey in the Jar," the tale of a bold highwayman (known these days largely thanks to Thin Lizzy and Metallica!), isn't exactly a drinking song, the rest of the songs capture the informal, lively essence of Irish pub music. Drink is celebrated for bringing out swaggering braggadocio, teary-eyed farewells (at closing time, doubtless), and not least humor. There's much good-natured fun in these charming tunes with their evocative lyrics and catchy choruses made even more pleasant by the artists' superb musicianship and arranging skills. "Whiskey you're the divil," proclaims one song, but then adds, "Whiskey you're my darling drunk or sober." That about sums up the party atmosphere. *—Nick Leggatt*

Legends of Ireland / Mar. 3, 1998 / Rhino ♦♦♦♦♦
Legends of Ireland traces the evolution of contemporary Irish and Celtic music through the course of 18 tracks. Beginning in the early '60s with the Clancy Brothers' "Holy Ground," the disc runs through a number of folk songs before moving into the modern era with Christy Moore's "Ride On" and the Pogues' "A Pair of Brown Eyes." Granted, those have more in common with the folk roots of Celtic than the ethereal, atmospheric work of Clannad, Eleanor McEvoy, Altan and Solas, who dominate the last third of this record. By juxtaposing those two periods, the disc does a good job of tracing the evolution of contemporary Celtic music and its rise in popularity. There are some major groups, including the Chieftains, missing from this collection, but in general, it offers a nice one-stop introduction to the genre. *—Stephen Thomas Erlewine*

Magic & Mystery: Majestic Music From Scotland and Ireland / Feb. 11, 1997 / Temple ♦♦♦♦
A very nice selection from Temple's ever-growing collection of recordings, mixing traditional performances with a handful of more contemporary outings from such performers as the Battlefield Band and Alison Kinnaird. The selections are congenial, the atmosphere is gentle and while it's unlikely to set entire pubs ablaze in the Shetlands, the collection's good entertainment. *—Steven McDonald*

Compas

Haitian bandleader Nemours Jean-Baptiste coined the phrase "compas direct" in the '50s to refer to his style of music. Compas means "musical measure" in Spanish, and direct refers to the absence of a third chord. Although similar to merengue, compas has a more driving rhythm; its moderate tempo is paced by a steady bass, which anchors the drum and cowbell percussion.

The instrumentation changed from a big band with a full horn section to the smaller "mini-jazz" combos of the later '60s and '70s, who introduced electric guitars and trap drums while retaining the solo saxophone (most typically, the alto sax) and sometimes the accordion. Compas now had a less direct meaning and became a generic term to refer to the Haitian style or, more specifically, rhythm. New York City became home to the top compas bands as the immigrant community grew. Compas spread to Miami, Montreal, Paris, and throughout the Caribbean, especially Guadeloupe and Martinique.

In exile, compas has been influenced by soul and funk and more recently by zouk, a popular dance music inspired by Haitian compas.

—Robert Leaver

Italy

Zucchero

f. Sep. 25, 1955, Roncocesi, Italy
Group / Italian Pop, Political Folk, Modern Electric Blues, Italy, Europe
Italian blues artist Zucchero "Sugar" Fornaciari began his recording career in the mid-'80s, with the release of *Zucchero & the Randy Jackson Band* in 1985. He released three more albums during the '80s, and issued his in-concert *Live at the Kremlin* album in 1991. Two additional albums followed, and in 1996, Zucchero released the compilation LP *The Best of Zucchero. Overdose D'Amore* followed two years later. *—John Bush*

Spirito DiVino / Jan. 30, 1996 / A&M ♦♦♦

- **The Best of Zucchero: Sugar Fornaciari's Greatest Hits** / Apr. 22, 1997 / Polygram ♦♦♦♦♦
Best of Zucchero: Sugar Fornaciari's Greatest Hits is an excellent sampler of the Italian star's best material, featuring all of his biggest hits, plus three previously unreleased tracks as good as any of the other songs, making the disc an excellent encapsulation of his career and a fine introduction. *—Rodney Batdorf*

Overdose d'Amore (The Ballads) / Sep. 28, 1999 / Ark 21 ♦♦♦
Italian singer Zucchero made his name in his homeland largely working with blues-inflected material, but *Overdose d'Amore: The Ballads* showcases a rather different side. Zucchero demonstrates on this compilation of previously released material that he can also hold his own as an emotional, adult contemporary-style pop balladeer, taking on duet partners like Sting, Sheryl Crow, and even Luciano Pavarotti. It may not be quite as distinctive as his more typical sound, but *Overdose d'Amore* may serve to highlight a side that's more accessible to some listeners. *—Steve Huey*

Italy Collection

Italian String Virtuosi / 1995 / Rounder ♦♦♦
Though "virtuosi" is overstating the case, this very pleasant recording also documents a pretty much totally forgotten branch of hyphenated-American music. The 1920s and '30s mandolin, banjo and guitar players here come from a fairly polished professional urban-popular background and with the exception of one splendid family group they mostly play the repertoire (which includes ragtime-influenced numbers, at least one tango and even "Keyboard Kapers") with more skill than dash. *—John Storm Roberts, Original Music*

Poland Collection

Polish Village Music / 1995 / Arhoolie ♦♦♦♦
This is in fact first-generation Polish-American music from recordings made in Chicago and New York between 1927 and 1933, and very nice too. Very varied also, with plenty of vocal material as well as early examples of polka as it prepared to metamorphose into an Ameri-

can ethnic (and to some extent regional) style. Included is nifty, forgotten music, remarkable recording quality, excellent notes. *—John Storm Roberts, Original Music*

Portugal

Amália Rodrigues

b. 1920, **d.** Oct. 6, 1999

Vocals / Fado, Portugal, Europe

The unrivaled queen of the Portuguese fado, singer Amália Rodrigues was born in Lisbon's Alfama district in 1920; one of ten children, she was abandoned by her mother at the age of one and raised by her grandmother, spending her formative years selling produce on the streets and working as a seamstress. Against the wishes of her family, as a teen Rodrigues performed as a tango dancer, and at 19 she made her professional singing debut alongside her sister Celeste at the fashionable Lisbon nightspot Retiro da Severa. Within a year she was a star, selling out clubs every night; in 1944, she traveled to Brazil, drawing huge crowds during her stay at the Copacabana Casino and later returning to Rio de Janeiero to make her first recordings. Rodrigues not only popularized the fado throughout South America, she reinvented it—brilliantly fusing the urban and rural styles of Lisbon and Coimbra, she also sought out material which moved far beyond the traditional tales of failed romance to instead explore the deepest crises of the soul and spirit, delivering performances unmatched in their fatalistic power and haunting beauty.

Because Rodrigues' manager José de Melo believed her native fans would stop attending her live appearances if they could buy her recordings, she did not enter a Portuguese studio until 1951, issuing a handful of sides on the Melodia label before moving to the Valentim de Carvalho imprint the following year. In the wake of World War II she began touring outside of South America, and scored an international hit in 1955 with "Coimbra," recorded live at Paris' Olympia Theater. In all, Rodrigues recorded upwards of 170 albums and even appeared in a number of feature films, retaining her drawing power even after the popularity of fado itself began to dissipate during the 1960s. She continued touring well past her 70th birthday, entering retirement only after undergoing surgery; she spent the final years of her life as a recluse, making her final public appearance at the opening of Lisbon's Expo 1998. Rodrigues died October 6, 1999 at the age of 79; upon receiving news of her passing, Portuguese Prime Minister Antonio Guterres ordered three days of national mourning, declaring her "the voice of Portugal." *—Jason Ankeny*

★ **Fados e Guitarradas** / 1989 / Festival ♦♦♦♦♦

Almost all of Amalia Rodrigues's greatest recordings were made during the 78-rpm era when she was a purely national treasure. Many have disappeared, but some of the best are available on a French release with gorgeous packaging but no notes beyond the titles, lengths, and composers. The CD version consists of only one of the LPs in the vinyl set. Still, here are some of the great moments in 20th-century urban popular music. *—John Storm Roberts*

Fado / 1990 / Celluloid ♦♦♦♦

Raizes / 1994 / Planet ♦♦♦

Here is more evidence that fado is one of the great urban sounds, and Amalia herself, at her best, one of the finest singers this century has produced. No frills here, just enchantment backed by the equally classic duo of guitars, Portuguese (Jaime Santos) and six-stringed (Domingos Camarinha or Santos Moreira). Three cuts are in Spanish. The rest are pure Lisbon saudade. *—John Storm Roberts, Original Music*

Portugal Collection

Fados from Portugal, Vol. 1: Fado De Lisboa 1928-36 / Heritage ♦♦♦♦♦

The singers here represent a simpler, less-stylized style than the very high-octane technique of Amalia Rodriguez and her successors. Rodriguez at her best sounded like some force of nature. Most of the singers here sound like people, though some of them do have something of the cosmic yowl. As usual for the genre the men, though fine, are heavily outgunned by the women—notably the splendid Maria Silva. *—John Storm Roberts, Original Music*

★ **The Story of Fado** / 1997 / Metro Blue/EMI Hemisphere ♦♦♦♦♦

Russia

Terem Quartet

Domra, Balalaika, Accordion / World Fusion, Russia, Asia

The Terem Quartet was formed by four graduates of the Leningrad Conservatory by four young men on accordion, balalaika, and (two) domras. They play both traditional folk as well as their own material, and their hallmark is a lively and irreverent eclecticism. They have toured several times with WOMAD. *—Leon Jackson*

● **Terem** / 1992 / Virgin ♦♦♦♦♦

Quotes from Tchaikovsky share equal space with Gypsy melodies in this highly literate set of compositions by an ensemble of Russian folk instruments. The Quartet's eccentric approach transforms everything it touches into shades of humor and delight. *—Bob Tarte*

Classical / 1995 / Real World ♦♦♦

This immensely talented quartet interprets a variety of classical themes on this release. While their choice of material is questionable in some instances, the overall performance is delightful. Admirers of Mozart's "Eine Kleine Nacht Musik" and Schubert's "Ave Maria" will be thrilled at hearing these standards in an entirely new light. Further, the original "Flea Waltz" is perhaps the most representative piece the quartet have yet performed, equally illustrating their virtuoso talent and sense of humor. *—Steve McMullen*

Scandinavia Collection

Nordic Roots: Northside Sampler / May 19, 1998 / NorthSide ♦♦♦♦

This is great way to get hip to all the great end-o-millennium music coming out of Scandinavia. The 20 tracks running in length from two-plus to six-plus minutes get right to the heart of a healthy traditional music scene as well as modern compositions. This is a wide spectrum of eclectic voices and instrumentation covering all of NorthSide's artists. This material is as good as and goes beyond the *Riverdance* rave. These are unadorned, brazen, frolic-in-the-tundra tunes, alive with centuries of history and inspiration from fjord to frigid highlands. Listeners are treated to the majestic magic vocals of Garmana, the fiery fiddle of Hege Rimestad, the ribald Horslip-ian folk-rock/world fusion of Hoven Droven, and many more. You can feel the hearty warmth in the "Arctic Circle club" style of music. "Come on in, the water's just above freezing but what a rush!" An enjoyable and recommended sampler. *—John Patterson*

Nordic Roots, Vol. 2: Northside Sampler / Oct. 12, 1999 / NorthSide ♦♦♦

These 22 tracks culled from the Northside catalog represent artists such as Hoven Droven, Boot, Hedningarna, Garmarna, and Wimme. Altogether it is an excellent second introduction to the gems found on the Northside label, which has done a terrific job of bringing Scandinavian artists to wider attention in the United States. The musical styles range from serious folk to energetic contemporary offerings involving the use of large amounts of electricity. *—Steven McDonald*

Scandanavian Valley Music / 1993 / Ocora ♦♦♦♦♦

An anthology of 31 short, pristinely recorded traditional tunes from the valleys of Sweden and Norway. Material ranges from ancient shepherds' songs, medieval ballads, and various dance and work songs to intriguing miniatures called stav or stev that immortalize quick snapshots of the daily grind. Most compositions are not unexpectedly stately and measured, including a delicate, staccato bagpipe performance by Per Gudmonson, who helped rescue this Norwegian instrument from historical obscurity. Best of all are songs in the vein of "Gyris Anders Svit," whose wild 2+4+3 rhythm scheme and eccentric quarter-tone modalities bring pagan overtones closer to the surface than most other Western European musics. *—Bob Tarte*

Spain

El Camaron de la Isla (Jose Monge Cruz)

b. 1951, **d.** Jul. 2, 1992

Vocals / Flamenco, Spain, Europe

El Camaron de la Isla (born Jose Monge Cruz) was the acknowledged king of flamenco for almost 30 years. He was born in the early '50s to a family of gypsy blacksmiths, and, by the end of the '60s, he was electrifing audiences across Spain with his exquisitely agonized singing. Camaron—his name means "The Shrimp of the Island," a reference to his diminutive stature—enjoyed fruitful collaboations with guitarists Paco and Pepe de Lucia and Tomatito and is said to have thoroughly re-energized the flamenco world with his powerfully emotional voice. Lamentably, Camaron's songs of pain were not a pretense, but testaments of a tortured soul. Turning increasingly to drugs to cope with inner demons, he died a tragically early and meaningless death on July 2, 1992, at the age of only 41. *—Leon Jackson*

● **Mejor de Camaron de la Isla: Una Leyenda Flamenca, Vol. 1** / Sep. 24, 1993 / Philips ♦♦♦♦♦

Paco de Lucia aside, nobody in Nuevo Flamenco comes near Camaron de la Isla, who died recently in his early 40s. Cubanisms, jazz-fusion, flamenco-with-strings, like de Lucia he did it all; like De Lucia too (and no other New Flamenco artists) he built on an ability to perform the classic forms superbly, with freshness and relevance. This retrospective shows him in both classic and eclectic vein. *—John Storm Roberts, Original Music*

Paco de Lucía

Guitar / Contemporary Flamenco, Post-Bop, Flamenco, World Fusion

One of the leading flamenco guitarists of the late 20th century, Paco de Lucia was born in Algeciras, began to study guitar at the age of 12, and at 14 won first prize in a major flamenco competition. He achieved national status with the release of his *Entre Dos Aguas* in 1974. De Lucia was greatly inspired by a trip to Brazil and upon his return began a series of innovative developments in flamenco guitar style, based on new rhythms derived from the bossa nova. In addition to leading his own sextet, de Lucia enjoyed a long and creative partnership with leading flamenco singer, El Camaron de la Isla. Other musicians with whom he has worked include Chick Corea, John McLaughlin, Al DiMeola, and, in 1989, tenor Placido Domingo. 1999's *Luzia* heralded de Lucia's return to traditional flamenco. *—Leon Jackson*

★ **Sirocco** / 1987 / Verve ♦♦♦♦♦

At times, flamenco phenomenon De Lucia has branched out into jazz, bossa nova, and Cuban mixes. Here, however, he plays essentially solo compositions based on pure flamenco, though with a virtuosity and reach that belong in a concert hall rather than in the traditional settings. *—John Storm Roberts*

Guitar Trio: Paco de Lucia/John McLaughlin/Al Di Meola / Oct. 15, 1996 / Polygram ♦♦♦♦

Guitar Trio is an excellent collaborative effort from three of the finest jazz guitarists of the post-rock & roll era—Paco de Lucia, John McLaughlin, and Al DiMeola. Throughout the record, the trio doesn't just showcase their instrumental skills, they demonstrate their musicality. This is sympathetic, emotional musicianship, where each musician compliments each other instead of trying to out-do the other. For jazz guitar fans, it rarely gets more exciting than *Guitar Trio*. *—Leo Stanley*

Gipsy Kings

f. 1979

Group / Flamenco, Ethnic Fusion, Spain, Europe

The Gipsy Kings are largely responsible for bringing the joyful sounds of progressive pop-oriented flamenco, called *Sevillana* in Spain, to the world. The band started out in Arles, a village in southern France during the '70s when brothers Nicolas and Andre Reyes, the sons of renowned flamenco artist Jose Reyes, teamed up with their cousins Jacques, Maurice and Tonino Baliardo, whose father is Manitas de Plata. They originally called themselves Los Reyes and started out as a gypsy band traveling about playing weddings, festivals, and in the streets. Because they lived so much like gypsies, the band adopted the name the Gipsy Kings. Later, they were hired to add color to posh parties in St. Tropez. Popularity did not come to Los Reyes right away and their first two albums attracted little notice. At this point the Gipsies played traditional, albeit passionate flamenco music punctuated by Tonino's precise guitar playing and Nicolas' exceptional voice. Though they had devoted fans, they still had yet to gain wider recognition until 1986 when they hooked up with visionary producer Claude Martinez who could see that the Kings had the makings of a world-class band.

Thanks to Martinez, the Kings began to relax a bit and take on a more contemporary edge, combining their traditional songs with sounds from the Middle East, Latin America, North Africa, a hint of rock, and their inimitable joy. It was, in a music industry filled with flamenco purists who resisted any kind of change, a very daring move, and many felt the Gipsy Kings would fall flat and disappear. But the nay-sayers were wrong. In 1987, they released "Djobi Djoba" and "Bamboleo," on an independent label and scored two smash hits in France. Their success led them to sign with Sony Music and release their eponymous debut album later that year. Again, they had tremendous sales in France and then found their album was appearing on the Top Ten album charts in 12 European countries including England, which is traditionally unreceptive to international music. In the late '80s, the Gipsy Kings, debuted in the U.S. at a New York New Music Seminar. This led them to sign to Sony in America. In 1989, they were invited to perform at the inaugural ball for George Bush, but they chose to return home to rest and be with their families. Later that year, they held an SRO concert at the Royal Albert Hall, where the Gipsy Kings hobnobbed with some of the world's biggest pop stars including Elton John and Eric Clapton. To top off their great year, the Kings' debut album spent 40 weeks on the U.S. charts and went gold, becoming one of the few all Spanish albums to do so. *—Sandra Brennan*

★ **Gipsy Kings** / Feb. 1988 / Elektra ✦✦✦✦✦
Their US debut is an especially dynamic introduction to the sound of the Spanish Gypsy ensemble. *—Myles Boisen*

Allegria / Jul. 1989 / Elektra ✦✦✦

Luna de Fuego / Aug. 1989 / Fania ✦✦✦
Both sides of this album run continuously as though in a live performance, but there is no audience apparent. What background noise there is sounds like group interaction and is not intrusive, rather it adds to the feeling of excitement and fiery authenticity. It is recommended for all those who like to dig a little deeper into "overnight successes," and for those who have any interest in flamenco and/or gypsy music. *—Roots & Rhythm*

Mosaique / Nov. 1989 / Elektra ✦✦✦

Este Mundo / Jul. 1991 / Elektra ✦✦✦

Live! / 1992 / Elektra ✦✦✦✦✦
As captivating as the Gipsy Kings are on their studio albums, it's hard to imagine how a recording mixed by a studio engineer could compete for sheer impressiveness with the spectacle of six acoustic guitars ablaze simultaneously in the same room. Particularly when the guitars are managed with the flamboyant virtuosity of the Reyes and Baliardo brothers. *Gipsy Kings Live*, recorded during the band's 1991 *Este Mundo* tour, captures some of that concert magic and features several of their most memorable songs. There are fiery renditions of "Bem Bem Maria," "Bamboleo," and "Djobi Djoba," as well as several dynamic instrumentals. One of those instrumentals, "Galaxia," and the rousing "La Dona" were later included on the band's popular *Greatest Hits* compilation. And with good reason: Both capture the enthusiastic bravura that makes the Gipsy Kings such potent performers. *Gipsy Kings Live* might even rival *Greatest Hits* as the definitive Gipsy Kings CD were it not for the disappointing quality of the recordings. The sound mix, by Francois Delabriere, has a tendency to overemphasize the vocals and the gaudy keyboards that have regrettably become a staple of Gipsy Kings recordings—with the result that the marvelously resonant tone of the guitars sometimes gets watered down. Unfortunately, the only way to really experience the power of a Gipsy Kings performance is to buy a ticket to one of their concerts. *—Evan Cater*

Love & Liberte / 1994 / Elektra/Nonesuch ✦✦✦

Tierra Gitana / Feb. 27, 1996 / Nonesuch ✦✦✦

Compas / Aug. 12, 1997 / Elektra/Asylum ✦✦✦✦
The Gipsy Kings' main strength is their consistency. Throughout their career, they have managed to craft an accessible, pop-oriented version of flameco and gypsy music that also pushes boundaries. During it all, they recorded classy, satisfying albums like *Compas*. There's not much different about *Compas*, but since the album is so well-made and enchanting, that isn't a curse; it's a blessing. *—Thom Owens*

Cantos de Amor / Aug. 4, 1998 / Elektra ✦✦✦✦
Cantos de Amor is a lovely collection of love ballads, both original and traditional, as performed by the Gipsy Kings. Even though they have performed love songs throughout the years (in fact, they have been collected on a love song compilation), the band has never before devoted themselves to simply love songs—they've barely done a concept album, actually—and the results are terrific. It's a focused, consistent album that is warm, seductive and romantic, delivering everything that long-time followers could want from a record called *Cantos de Amor*. *—Thom Owens*

Love Kings / Mar. 23, 1999 / Sony International ✦✦✦

● **Volare!: The Very Best of the Gipsy Kings** / Sep. 5, 2000 / Elektra ✦✦✦✦✦
Although this compilation contains many of the songs featured on their 1995 release *Best of the Gipsy Kings*, this expanded two-CD set features many stellar tracks recorded since then. Featuring their unique style of pop-influenced flamenco, *The Very Best of the Gipsy Kings* is a passionate and uplifting collection featuring familiar, but not exhausted, Spanish-language songs. *—Zac Johnson*

European Music

As the small list here suggests (even allowing for the fact that Great Britain and Ireland are taken care of in the Celtic and British Isles section), the reaction against Euro-centrism can go too far. True, Eastern Europe has recently been "discovered," with much harrumphing from the marketing departments, but even here the proportion of derivative to authentic is notably out of whack. But the traditional music of western Europe is not only extraordinarily varied (perhaps most startlingly so in the case of Italy), much of it comprises the other major root of New World styles of all kinds. Spain isn't so badly off, though the focus is exclusively on flamenco. Portugal is beginning to surface. Greece is beginning to take an interest in its roots. But the rest is—almost everywhere—silence. While there are plenty of revivalists, less than a dozen recordings of true traditional French singers ever existed and all but two are now deleted. Germany is not so badly off, thanks only to an active regional commercial industry: German ethnomusicologists no sooner hatch than they fly south to Africa and beyond, like so many geese in winter.
—John Storm Roberts

Carmen Linares

Vocals / Flamenco, Spain, Europe
Carmen Linares is one of the world's greatest flamenco singers. A master of the "jondo" style of singing, Linares has set her vocals to the classical-oriented accompaniment of symphonic and chamber orchestras for nearly two decades. Linares was the first flamenco singer to perform with the Philharmonic Orchestra of New York. Linares has been equally forceful performing with the classic flamenco accompaniment of sole acoustic guitar. While *The New York Times* praised her for her "extraordinary and expressive power," *Al Mundo* claimed "she possesses three invaluable virtues: power of communication, purity without purism and all-around competence."

Linares has been honored with numerous awards including the Prize Icaro of the Music and the Prize of the Culture Ministry in 1988, the French Academy Prize in 1992, and the Silver Medal of the Junta De Andalucia in 1997. *—Craig Harris*

● **La Luna en el Rio** / 1991 / Auvidis/Ethnic ✦✦✦✦✦
This is an example of "new flamenco." Linares, an important figure in the field, works with young new wave flamenco musicians to mix fairly traditional singing with contemporary approaches to playing style, and at times lyrics from major poets living and dead. *—John Storm Roberts*

Cantaora / Riverboat ✦✦✦✦

Spain Collection

Flamenco: Fire and Grace / 1996 / Narada ✦✦✦✦✦
This Narada collection brings together eight phenomenal flamenco artists. The players here are a who's who of modern day flamenco, including guitarist Rafael Riqueni and renowned flamenco singer Enrique Morente. This collection emphasizes amazing flamenco guitar work and instrumentals like the fierce opening track "Mori Sonando" by Miguel de la Bastide. The album is split about fifty-fifty between fiery dance numbers and lamenting ballads. Three tracks feature vocals: two scorching songs by Enrique Morente and a medium-tempo ballad by Diego Carrasco. Flamenco is the lively dance music of the poorest neighborhoods and bars of southern Spain, infused with sorrow, struggle, and celebration. It is the intense expression of these emotions that makes this compilation a must-have for both flamenco fans and those just starting to explore the genre. *—Susan Cruickshank*

The Story of Flamenco / Jul. 29, 1997 / Capitol ✦✦✦✦

☆ **The Young Flamencos** / Nov. 22, 1991 / Hannibal ✦✦✦✦✦
In Spain, the nuevo flamenco movement of the 1970s, 1980s and 1990s has inspired the type of heated debates that surrounded jazz-rock fusion in the U.S. Just as older, hardline jazz purists detested fusion and argued that Miles Davis should have stuck to bebop, older flamenco purists have had no kind words for younger nuevo flamenco artists. Combining flamenco guitar with rock, salsa, merengue or pop, nuevo flamenco is considered musical heresy by purists; meanwhile, its supporters counter that it has kept flamenco fresh and healthy. They're absolutely right; the experimental, risk-taking nature of nuevo flamenco has made for some incredibly exciting listening and kept Spain on the cutting edge of Latin music. One of the many compilations illustrating the genre's vitality is *The Young Flamencos*, which spans 1983-1990 and boasts first-class material by such nuevo flamenco greats as Jorge Pardo ("Que de Flauta!"), Ketama ("La Barbaria Del Sur," "Me Llama") and the especially rock-minded Pata Negra ("Yo Me Que Quedro En Sevilla" and "Blues De La Frontera"). "Besos De Caramelo" is a passionate, salsa-influenced gem by female singer Aurora, who some have argued is to Madrid's nuevo flamenco scene what Olga Tanon is to 1990s merengue. Boasting informative liner notes and excellent sound quality, this is a CD that those exploring contemporary flamenco should make a point of obtaining. *—Alex Henderson*

Ukraine Collection

Unblocked: The Music of Eastern Europe / Oct. 14, 1997 / Ellipsis Arts ✦✦✦✦✦
If you were captivated by The Mystery of Bulgarian Voices, you will be spellbound by this amazing collection of music. While three CDs may sound like overkill, the variety and beauty of this music makes this collection a treasure without a bit of excess. It's not just the variety, but the tasteful programming of the tracks that makes this set so rewarding. The first disc opens with Belarusian chant and a few tracks later offers the jazzy guitar of Ukrainian En-

ver Ismailov without a moment of culture shock. The detailed booklet gives you everything you need to know about the artists, and the cultural backgound of a varied and wondrous chunk of the globe. *— Tim Sheridan*

LATIN CONTINUUM

Argentina

Los Fabulosos Cadillacs

Group / Rock en Español, Worldbeat, Argentina, Latin Continuum

The internationally renowned and versatile Argentine band Los Fabulosos Cadillacs have been thrilling audiences with their eclectic mixture of rock, rap, ska, reggae, and traditional South American sounds for over ten years. The nine piece band began in 1985 and chose the name Los Fabulosos Cadillacs only because they thought it sounded good. Then as with now, the band is run democratically and there is no one leader; they play whatever style most appeals to them at the moment and each of their ten albums is different from the last. In 1995, they recorded the album *Rey Azucar* for S.D.I./Sony and featured guest appearances from Debbie Harry and from Mick Jones, the ex-guitarist from the Clash. According to the band members, working with Jones was a dream come true. One of their biggest commercial hits in South America is "Matador" which, with it's uptempo samba-reggae inspired beat, appeared as a bonus track on their 1995 greatest hits album *Vasos Vacíos.* The Cadillacs have extensively toured Latin America and in 1995, appeared in Anaheim, CA, where they knocked 'em dead with their lively performance. Though the band was in kind of a slump during the early '90s, their greatest hits album revitalized their career. *Marcha del Golazo Solitario* followed in 1999 and two live albums, *Hola* and *Chau,* were issued in early 2001. *— Sandra Brennan*

● **20 Grandes Exitos** / Apr. 28, 1998 / Sony International ✦✦✦✦✦
20 Grandes Exitos is an excellent collection of newly-recorded versions of Los Fabulosos Cadillacs' best and best-known songs that should serve as a good introduction for the curious. *— Stephen Thomas Erlewine*

Carlos Gardel

d. Jun. 24, 1935

Vocals / Tango, Argentina, Latin Continuum

Carlos Gardel was one of the biggest stars of the Argentine tango in its classic period between the wars. He was a handsome, passionate singer backed by the leading "orquestras t°picas," and also enjoyed considerable fame in Paris when tango and other Latin American music was all the rage. His most popular songs are issued on RCA International, and a comprehensive reissue series has come out on the import El Bandoneon label; among the collections of his work were 1985's *Classic Gardel* and 2000's *Canciones de Carlos Gardel. — Myles Boisen*

Classic Gardel / 1985 / Original Music ✦✦✦✦

El Rey del Tango: Gold Collection / Sep. 1, 1998 / Fine Tune ✦✦✦

● **The King of Tango, Vol. 1: 1927-1930** / Jan. 26, 1999 / Nimbus ✦✦✦✦✦
Tango's greatest singer, Carlos Gardel is represented on this 29-track collection featuring recordings from 1927-1930. Gardel is considered the bridge that transformed the tango, initially considered vulgar, into a cultural treasure. When he died in a plane crash in 1935, the loss created mass hysteria in Argentina, not experienced since. This set provides a respectable overview from this later phase in the career of the songbird of Buenos Aires. *— Al Campbell*

Miguel Mateos

Vocals, Piano, Guitar / Rock en Español, Argentina, Latin Continuum

Singer/songwriter from Argentina Miguel Mateos started getting involved in the local music scene when leading a band called Cristal. Along with his brother Alejandro Mateos and musician Jorge Infusino, the talented artist formed a band called Zas in 1979. The group was presented live while opening for British rock act Queen in February of 1981. A self titled debut album was released in 1982 followed by *Huevos* in 1983. By that time bassist Ra´l Chevalier and guitarist Eduardo Sanz joined the band. After issuing *Tengo Que Parar* in 1984 Miguel Mateos y Zas hit local charts with a song called "Tira Para Arriba,." Soon after a live recording was made at Argentinian Coliseo Theater, later released as *Rockas Vivas.* The success of that record allowed Miguel Mateos to perform four acclaimed shows at Buenos Aires' Luna Park, one of the most important local venues. The following year the group moved to the U.S., this time having guitarist Carlos García and bass player Cachorro López. The result of that reunion was *Solos En America,* a Latin rock marterpiece. During the 1990s Miguel Mateos settled down in Miami, where the artist made four solo records. In 1998 keyboardist Mario Maselli and bassist Ariel Pozzo joined the new band's line-up recording *Bar Imperio. — Drago Bonacich*

Bar Imperio / Apr. 6, 1999 / Universal Latino ✦✦✦✦
Miguel Mateos fuses today's rock and pop with the passionate musical traditions of his native Argentina. With *Bar Imperio,* Mateo continues to blend yesterday and today, adding rock and funk to his sound. Songs like "Encuentra Un Lugar" and "Desamor" showcase his unique Latin rock sound. *— Heather Phares*

Astor Piazzolla

b. 1921, **d.** Jul. 5, 1992

Accordion / Latin Jazz, Tango, Latin Pop, Argentina, Latin Continuum

Often referred to as the originator of the "nuevo tango," Piazzolla was an Argentine visionary who endured the wrath of many of his countrymen for adapting their national dance to his own modern ends. A soulful and accomplished performer on the accordion-like bandoneon, Piazzolla's many recordings placed him as a leading international composer. Besides his own hand-picked groups, he recorded with a mix of jazz and classical players in the US. *— Myles Boisen*

Astor Piazzolla: The Central Park Concert / Sep. 1987 / Chesky ✦✦✦✦
This powerful concert was recorded live in New York City on September 6, 1987. Piazzolla was playing with his best ensemble: a quintet consisting of himself on the bandoneon (the oversized German accordion used in Argentinian tango), Pablo Ziegler on piano, Fernando Suarez Paz on violin, Horacio Malvicino on electric guitar, and Hector Console on bass. Piazzolla plays some of his finest material—about half of *Tango: Zero Hour* surfaces, for example. Two of the most paradigmatic Piazzolla pieces show up too: "La Camorra" with its alternating moments of tense dance-rhythms and creepy atmosphere, and "Verano Porteño," with its dancing bear rhythms. The concert closes with "Concierto para Quinteto," one of those long pieces that Piazzolla favored which visits many styles and moods—almost many eras. It would be very easy to lose the thread on such an epic composition in live performance, but the quintet keeps it together admirably. The recording is surprisingly good for live; there is an appropriate echo and the balance is nearly perfect. The audience is completely unobtrusive—inaudible except when they applaud. And the instruments are very clear, especially when the musicians coax those "zings" and "pops" out of them that Piazzolla loved. For someone new to his work, the "special effects" on this recording can be a revelation. There is also a wonderful spoken track by Piazzolla where he tells us about himself, tango, and the mysterious bandoneon. This album is a wonderful place to start—or finish—with this charismatic composer of New Tango music. *— Kurt Keefner*

★ **Tango: Zero Hour** / Apr. 23, 1992 / Pangaea ✦✦✦✦✦
Astor says it's his best—he's right. This is the perfect haunting, passionate recording from the master of the new tango, with his best group. *— Myles Boisen*

The Vienna Concert / Aug. 7, 1992 / Messidor ✦✦✦

The Late Masterpieces / 1993 / American Clave ✦✦✦✦✦

Live at the BBC 1989 / Mar. 3, 1998 / Intuition ✦✦✦✦✦
Sadly, the 1989 performance heard on this CD turned out to be among Astor Piazzolla's last live performances. The Argentinian tango revolutionary would subsequently suffer a major stroke that left him severely disabled and ended his musical career. But there is no evidence of Piazzolla's health failing on this outstanding release, which finds him leading his New Tango Sextet and being joined by pianist Gerardo Gandini, guitarist Horacio Manvicino, fellow bandoneon player Daniel Binelli, cellist Jose Bragato and bassist Hector Console. Piazzolla gave 100% on stage, and he is in excellent form on such celebrated pieces as "Michelangelo," "Milonga del Angel," "Tango Zero Hour" and "Tanguedia III." This isn't optimistic music—there is a great deal of sadness in Piazzolla's playing as well as a lot of passion, depth and beauty. Piazzolla had long since found the courage to be himself, and that courage continued to be artistically rewarding during the twilight of his long career. *— Alex Henderson*

Soda Stereo

f. 1982, **db.** 1997

Group / Rock en Español, Latin Pop, Argentina, Latin Continuum

Soda Stereo was one of the most important Argentinean pop/rock band of the '80s and early '90s. Their success and influence was spread to the rest of Latin America. Created as a trio in 1982 and dissolved in 1997, the band was formed by guitarist/vocalist Gustavo Cerati, bass player Zeta Bosio, and drummer Charly Alberti. In the beginning they were deeply influenced by new wave and bands such as the Police, Television and Talking Heads. Musically, they had an ever-changing style based on pop that avoid their own formulas, pursuing new sound territories exploration. They were a pop band that took elements from different styles such as new wave, ska, reggae, dark, soul, noise rock and electronica in different times in their career.

The group reached national success with their self-titled debut, released in 1984. *Signos,* released in 1986, was one of the best albums of their career. The musical arrangements and the lyrics reached a subtlety never heard before from the band's production, and led the press to take them seriously. Thanks to the help of Argentinean techno-pop pioneer Daniel Melero, 1990's *Cancion Animal* represented a sudden and successful movement for the band. Melero's influence waned, however, with their next studio work, *Dynamo,* a controversial, low-selling album. In 1995, Soda Stereo returned with their calmest and most relaxed work, *Sueño Stereo.* Personal problems between the members and 15 years of coexistence led the band to announce their end in 1997. *— Iván Adaime*

Signos / 1986 / Sony International ✦✦✦✦✦
This album represents a landmark in Soda Stereo's career basically in two aspects: artistically and commercially. Despite the fact that with their first two albums they achieved national success, the band was pegged as frivolous entertainers, related with other Argentinean bands such as Virus or Los Twist; with this album, the press and the audience began to take them seriously. Commercially it represented the breakthrough from Argentina to the rest of Latin America. After the release of the album, they started touring Latin America, achieving a success that no Argentinean pop/rock band had achieved before in countries such as Chile, Peru, and Venezuela. The result of the extensive tour can be heard in the live album *Ruido Blanco.* Although it's not a concept album, the eight songs on it have coherence and consistency. Maybe it's the band's darkest and obscure album, but strangely it didn't conspire with the audience acceptance, and many hits came out. Songs such as "Signos," "Persiana Americana," and "Profugos" gave the band the possibility of conquering wider audiences and, at the same time, allowed them to explore new musical directions. The general feeling of the album could be resumed in the song that concludes it: "Final Caja Negra." A masterpiece. *— Iván Adaime*

Doble Vida / 1988 / Sony International ✦✦✦✦
When Soda Stereo released this album they were the most important pop/rock Latin Amer-

ican band. The album confirmed it. Recorded and mixed in New York, the album was produced by David Bowie's guitarist Carlos Alomar. He gave them a sound that brought the album near but timidly to soul music. Alomar even rapped in "En el Borde." A horn section was included in many songs and that gave a flavor that the band never had before and would not in the future, except in the forthcoming EP *Languis.* Although the album contains some of the most beautiful songs from the band, such as "En la Ciudad de la Furia" and "Corazón Delator," the album lacks the consistency of the previous studio album *Signos.* —*Iván Adaime*

● **Cancion Animal** / 1990 / Sony ♦♦♦♦
With this release Soda Stereo reinvented themselves. Lyrically and musically the band acquired an elegant fury never shown before. Although the album supposed a big change to the fan's expectations, it didn't disturb the band's popularity. The songs are among the band's strongest and most popular. Included is the instant hit "Musica Ligera," the one chosen by the band to play as their last song in their last show in 1997. "Entre Caníbales" and "Un Millón de Años Luz" reveal almost sexually explicit but delicate lyrics, while the exquisite "Té para Tres" was inspired by Cerati's father's agony. The strong concept and consistency of the album is due in part to Daniel Melero, a former member of Los Encargados. Althought Soda Stereo had played one of Melero's songs in their debut album *Soda Stereo,* they didn't really work together until this recording, on which he plays keyboards and is also credited as "concept contributor." Along with *Signos, Canción Animal* is the most consistent work of the band. —*Iván Adaime*

Dynamo / Jan. 26, 1993 / Sony ♦♦♦♦

Sueño Stereo / Aug. 15, 1995 / RCA ♦♦♦♦
This was Soda Stereo's last studio album. Released at the end of June 1995, it helped the band regain public attention after *Dynamo*'s commercial failure and the three-year gap between those two albums. Three hits came from the record: "Ella Uso Mi Cabeza Como un Revolver," "Paseando por Roma," and especially "Zoom." The album was the band's most melancholic, and included the beautiful "Efecto Doppler," which contained drum samples from Echo & the Bunnymen's "All My Colours." —*Iván Adaime*

Mercedes Sosa

Vocals / Latin Folk, Argentina, Latin Continuum
The driving force behind the nueva canción movement, singer Mercedes Sosa was born and raised in Tucamán, Argentina, beginning her performing career at age 15 after taking top honors in a radio station amateur competition. A rich, expressive vocalist and a gifted interpreter, Sosa was dubbed "the voice of the silent majority" for her choice of overtly political material, and alongside artists including Violetta Parra and Atahualpa Yupanqui she spearheaded the rise of the so-called "nueva canción" movement, which heralded the emergence of protest music across Argentina and Chile during the 1960s. The movement was crippled in 1973 by the CIA-sponsored coup which ousted democratically-elected Chilean President Salvador Allende; with her repertoire of songs championing human rights and democracy, Sosa was viewed as a serious threat by the military regime which assumed power, and in 1975 she was arrested during a live performance which also resulted in the incarceration of many audience members. Death threats forced her to leave Argentina in 1979, and she remained in exile for three years, finally returning with a triumphant comeback performance in February 1982. Sosa recorded prolifically in the years to follow. In fall 2000. Sosa won a Grammy for Best Folk Album for *Misa Criolla* at the first annual Latin Grammy Awards. —*Jason Ankeny*

● **Amigos Mios 15 Exitos** / 1989 / Polydor ♦♦♦♦♦
The enormously influential queen of Argentinean nueva trova solo and in duets with various like-minded artists, local and from other countries, among them Nascimento and Carvalho from Brazil and Cuba's Milanes. Sosa's influence has been so widespread within and outside Latin America that one ironically tends to forget what a groundbreaker she originally was. —*John Storm Roberts, Original Music*

Argentina Collection

Argentina Bailemos Tango: A Century of Tango on the Dance Floor / Jun. 20, 2000 / Rhino ♦♦♦♦♦
Featuring 19 tracks spanning the years 1920-1990, *Bailemos Tango!: A Century of Tango on the Dance Floor* is as comprehensive a single-disc overview of Argentina's greatest musical form as you're likely to find; Rhino's compilers took great pains to cover as much of tango's history as they could, and the result is a vibrantly eclectic sampler that makes a terrific introduction to tango for the newcomer, and a historical document that will fascinate many aficionados as well (thanks in part to its extremely detailed and informative liner notes). Listeners can compare the differences between various tango styles (valze, milonga, canyengue, etc.) and piece together some of the foreign influences (African and Spanish music, as well as indigenous South American forms) that eventually cohered into something uniquely Argentinian. Artists present include Astor Piazzolla, Osvaldo Pugliese, Carlos Gardel, Trio Hugo Diaz, and many more. —*Steve Huey*

The Rough Guide to Tango / May 25, 1999 / World Music Network ♦♦♦♦
Jazz producer Orrin Keepnews once argued that when you get down to it, there are two main types of jazz: before Charlie Parker and after Charlie Parker; similarly, one could argue that there are only two types of tango: before and after Astor Piazzolla. Just as Parker introduced a whole new way of playing jazz, Piazzolla radically altered the tango by bringing in jazz influence, playing it with different chords and making it darker. Piazzolla certainly wasn't without opposition—he was hailed as a visionary by many, but his opponents saw his breakthroughs as musical heresy and an insult to Argentinean culture. In Buenos Aires, the bandoneon player was even beaten and threatened! A diverse collection that came out in 1999, *The Rough Guide to Tango* shows us how tango sounded before and after Piazzolla. Hearing such Piazzolla recordings as "Melancolico Buenos Aires" and "Tres Minutos Con la Realidad" on the same CD as pre-Piazzolla, 78-era pearls like Carlos Gardel's "Caminito" (Gardel died in 1935) and Juan D'Arienzo's "La Cumparsita" (recorded in 1937), one is reminded just how tremendous Piazzolla's contributions to tango were. It's impossible to miss Piazzolla's influence on selections by such modern tango artists as bandoneon player Carlos Buono ("Retrato de Nana"), singer Adriana Varela ("Cada Vez Que Me Recuerdes") and violinist Antonio Agri ("200 Anos"). If you were to assemble a comparable jazz collection, you'd have to include Louis Armstrong, Duke Ellington and Benny Goodman along with Charlie Parker, Dizzy Gillespie, Miles Davis, John Coltrane and Joe Henderson—that's how far-reaching this CD is. The frustrating thing about *The Rough Guide to Tango* is its lack of recording dates—the World Music Network should have known better. But except for that flaw, this compilation is nicely put together. —*Alex Henderson*

The Story of Tango / Jul. 29, 1997 / Capitol ♦♦♦♦

Brazil

Badi Assad

b. 1966
Vocals, Percussion, Guitar / Classical Guitar, Brazilian Jazz, Brazilian Pop, Bossa Nova, Brazil, Latin Continuum
Badi Assad (pronounced bah-jee Ah-Sahj) is one of Brazil's most talented performers. A heartfelt vocalist who sings in English and Portuguese and is known for her Bobby McFerrin-like improvisations, Assad is also one of the country's truly accomplished guitar players. In 1995, Assad was voted Best Acoustic Fingerstyle Guitarist by editors of *Guitar Player,* while readers of the magazine named her album *Rhythms* the Best Classical Album of the Year. Although her earlier albums focused on unique interpretations of songs by songwriters such as Egberto Gizmonte, Milton Nascimento, Ralph Towner and George Harrison, Assad displayed her songwriting talents on her 1998 album, *Chameleon,* co-writing nine of the album's 12 tracks.

The younger sister of famed guitarists Sergio and Odair of the duo Assad, Assad, who grew up in Rio de Janeiro, studied piano at age eight. By age 14, however, she had switched to the guitar and was accompanying her father who played chorinhos or Brazilian music on the bandolim. Sharpening her skills at the University Conservatory in Rio de Janeiro, Assad placed first in a Young Instrumentalist Contest in 1984. Assad's professional debut came as a member of the Guitar Orchestra of Rio de Janiero, conducted by Turbio Santos, in 1986. The same year, she sang and acted in a musical, *Mulheres de Hollanda,* written by Tatiana Cobbett and based on works by Chico Buarque de Hallanda.

Assad returned to music in 1987, performing throughout Israel, Europe and Brazil, along with guitarist Francoise-Emmanuel Denis as Duo Romantique. In 1988, she wrote and starred in a solo performance piece, "Antagonism, " in which she played guitar, sang, acted and danced.

Danca Dos Tons, Assad's debut album, was released in Brazil only in 1989 and limited to 2,000 copies. Her first worldwide release, *Solo,* was recorded in April 1993 at St. Stephens of Hungary Church in New York. —*Craig Harris*

● **Solo** / 1994 / Chesky Jazz ♦♦♦♦
This young, dazzlingly virtuosic Brazilian guitarist performs entirely solo on this album, even though sometimes she seems to be doing the work of three or more musicians simultaneously. Borrowing sonic ideas from the innovative Brazilian group Uakti, she simulates various percussion instruments and sings and scats in clear, vibrant Portuguese while playing rapid-fire, technically impeccable acoustic guitar. She also chooses merely to play guitar alone on several tracks in an often rhythmically complex or delicate manner. The material she plays ranges all over her nation's spectrum from the music of her brother Sergio (half of the famous Assad classical guitar duo), Edu Lobo, Chico Buarque de Hollanda, Heitor Villa-Lobos, Egberto Gismonti and non-Brazilian Ralph Towner. The combination of classical technique, a Brazilian jazz sensibility and the unique touches of percussion and voice are exquisitely captured by Chesky's purist audiophile equipment. —*Richard S. Ginell*

Rhythms / Jun. 26, 1995-Jun. 29, 1995 / Chesky ♦♦♦♦

Echoes of Brazil / Apr. 15, 1997 / Chesky ♦♦♦♦

Maria Bethania (Maria Bethania Vianna Telles Velloso)

b. 1946, Santo Amaro da Purificacao
Vocals / Brazilian Pop, MPB, Tropicalia, Brazil, Latin Continuum
Maria Bethânia, sister of Caetano Veloso, is a renowned singer on her own. Her scenic, dramatic abilities, in a profoundly Brazilian tradition, make her performances quite personal, which has brought her a massive and faithful audience over the decades.

She first worked as an actress, and appeared in a show called *Nós, Por Exemplo* that brought her together with Veloso, Gilberto Gil, Gal Costa, and later Tom Zé In 1965, she substituted for Nara Leão in the highly successful show *Opinião,* recording her first single and LP soon after. In 1968, she released *Recital Na Boite Barroco.* In 1969 and 1970 respectively, released the LPs *Maria Bethânia* and *Maria Bethânia Ao Vivo.* In 1971, she recorded *A Tua Presença* and wrote the lyrics for Caetano's song "Trampolim," released in her album *Drama.* In 1976, she toured Brazil with Caetano Veloso, Gilberto Gil, and Gal Costa as part of the show *Os Doces Bárbaros,* which yielded a double album as well. In 1977, her show *Pássaro da Manhã* was released as an LP and brought her second golden record. One year later, *ilibi* became a gold record before hitting the streets, the first album released by a Brazilian female singer to reach 1 million sold copies. In 1986, she signed with RCA for the release of three albums: *Dezembros, Maria,* and *Memória da Pele.* Her 1993 album *As Canções Que Você Fez Para Mim* was the best-selling record of that year. For the label EMI Odeon recorded the album *-mbar,* also a show which was recorded live and released in 1997 as *Imitação da vida.* —*Alvaro Neder*

Mel / 1979 / Verve ♦♦♦
This is the CD reissue of the LP recorded in 1979, one year after *ilibi,* which had sold one million copies and inaugurated Maria Bethânia's popular phase, after her cult beginning in the

Salsa

In 1974 salsa became a household word in the Hispanic communities. It was first heard when Cuba's Ignacio Pineiro's Sexteto Nacional introduced his tune "Echale Salsita" at the 1932 Chicago World's Fair. Salsa, the Spanish word for spicy sauce, was uttered when dancers urged bandleaders to swing the music. The word lay dormant until 1962, when Seeco Records released Joe Cuba's *Stepping Out* album, which was vocalist Jimmy Sabater's tune "Salsa y Bembe." Salsa's boost to national recognition occurred after Cal Tjader's 1964 recording of "Soul Sauce" (Salsa del Alma), which received airplay on jazz, R&B, and Latin-music programs across the United States. It achieved international acceptance after the fiery music of the Fania All-Stars and the bands of Larry Harlow, Johnny Pacheco, Ray Barretto, Eddie Palmieri, Orchestra Broadway, La Sonora Poncena, Willie Rosario, El Gran Combo, the Willie Colon/Ruben Blades combination, and Tito Puente modernized the Afro-Cuban sound in the '70s.

The roots of salsa sprouted with the Cuban son, a rhythm created in Santiago De Cuba by Theodora Ginez. El son began its rhythmic change in 1791 after hundreds of White Frenchmen and Haitians fled the revolution and relocated in Cuba. During the 18th century, the Cuban government forbade the playing of el son, because its lyrics protested the inhuman slavery conditions, causing riots. Soldiers from as far away as Havana were sent to Oriente. Those who were musicians returned home with the new rhythm, and it soon made its way throughout Cuba.

In 1920, during a carnival in Havana, Guillermo Castillo's Grupo Tipica, Oriental played el son. After the carnival, the group became El Sexteto Habañero, and the era of the trumpet conjunto and the popular el son rhythm began.

In April 1930, the Cuban orchestra of Don Aspiazu started the New York salsa era when it overwhelmed its audiences with its version of "The Peanut Vendor." From the RKO Palace in midtown Manhattan, the tune's infectious melodies filtered to all of New York. RCA Victor recorded it on May 13, 1930, and released it five months later. "El Manisero" was the background music for the 1931 movie *Cuban Love Song.* By the mid-'30s, every Latin music aggregation included el son in its repertoire. The most popular groups were those of Vicente Sigler, Nilo Melendez, Alberto Socarras, Rafael Hernandez's Grupo Victoria, Augusto Coen, Xavier Cugat, Montecino's Happy Boys, and Alberto Iznaga's La Siboney. In Cuba during the late '30s, Afro-Cuban rhythms were demonstrating further innovations. Orestes Lopez, a revered musician of Antonio Arcano's charanga (a piano, flute, strings, and rhythm section), invented the danzon mambo rhythm in 1938. The mambo became the standard third part of the danzon, adding an overwhelming excitement that has not yet been improved upon. During the '40s, the Cuban guaracha rhythm joined el son in popularity; the best recordings were by Miguelito Valdes, Machito and the Afro-Cubans, Anselmo Sacassas, Noro Morales, José Curbelo, and Marcelino Guerra.

The next innovation occurred in 1943 at La Conga Club in midtown Manhattan. On Sunday evening, May 28, 1943, the Machito orchestra finished playing a tune. While the next number was being searched for, pianist Luis Varona began to play the introduction to the tune "El Bottellero" (The Bottlemaker). All of a sudden, bassist Julio Andino joined in, plucking the same notes. At a rehearsal the following evening, Mario Bauza (trumpeter and Machito's musical director) told Varona and Andino to play the same introduction while he sang out the broken chords he wanted saxophonists and trumpeters to repeat. Bauza then wrote a melody for the band to play on top of the broken chords. Thus the tune "Tanga" was conceived, and Afro-Cuban jazz (now Latin jazz) was created.

In 1949, Perez Prado's "Mambo #5" became a monstrous hit and officially kicked off the mambo era. Among the then-new bandleaders who revised Prado's sound for New York dancers were Tito Puente and Tito Rodriguez, whose orchestrations were the model for the Palladium mambo. In addition to the two Titos, the most popular bands of the '50s included Machito, Miguelito Valdes, Pupi Campo, Joe Loco Quintet, Alfredito, La Playa Sextet, Cal Tjader, and Noro Morales, along with the Cuban bands of Arsenio Rodriguez, Orquesta Aragon, Enrique Jorrin, Felix Chappotin, Jose Fajardo, Roberto Faz, Bebo Valdes, Cachao y Su Descargo, and Beny More.

The pop dance bands of the '60s were Johnny Pacheco, Charlie Palmieri, Eddie Palmieri, Joe Quijano, Orlando Marin, Joe Cuba Sextet, Ricardo Ray, Pete Rodriguez, and Lou Perez, along with the boogaloo bands of Johnny Colon, King Nando, Joey Pastrana, the Le Bron Brothers, and Joe Bataan. The '70s was an exciting decade because of Gerald Masucci, president of Fania Records. Mr. Masucci spent thousands of dollars in the '60s and '70s promoting unknown musicians who today are superstars earning great sums of money. Masucci bought three hours of air time in every large Hispanic-populated city, including San Juan, Puerto Rico. He flew artists all over the world until they became well known. Eddie Palmieri was the superstar of the '70s. Ray Barretto's tune "Cocinando" was the best of the '70s. The most popular bands were those of Larry Harlow, Johnny Pacheco, Ray Barretto, Bobby Valentine, Willie Colon, Willie Rosario, Tipica Novel, Bobby Rodriguez y La Compania, Angel Canales, La Sonora Poncena, El Gran Combo, Mongo Santamaria, and the sizzling Orchestra Broadway, which never failed to pack ballrooms.

The '80s saw the comeback of Tito Puente among the top bands, with great Concord Jazz label recordings. Joining Puente were Orchestra Broadway, Oscar DeLeon, Louis Ramirez, Willie Rosario, Ray Barretto, Eddie Palmieri, Luis "Perico" Ortiz, Roberto Torres, Papaito Munoz, Charanga America, Conjunto Candela, Grupo Fascinación, Santiago Ceron, Wayne Gorbea, Libre, and the red-hot Conjunto Clásico. So far the '90s have included Poncho Sanchez, Bongologic, Shades of Jade, José Alberto, Tito Nieves, Columbia's Joe Acosta, Santo Domingo's Cuco Valoy, and Japan's Orquesta de la Luz. Salsa would have never achieved its heights of popularity without music arrangers, the music-makers who create hit records—for example, Marty Sheller, Louie Ramirez, Papo Lucca, Oscar Hernandez, Isidro Infante, Alfredito Valdes, Jr., Hector Rivera, Rene Hernandez, Lou Perez, Israel "Cachao" Lopez, Arturo "Chico" O'Farrill, Ray Santos, Joe Loco, and Tito Puente. *—Max Salazar*

Teatro Vila Velha (Salvador BA) continued in the political show *Opinião.* This album had her biggest hit with "Grito de Alerta," the first of many written by Gonzaguinha and interpreted by Bethânia. "Mel" (Caetano Veloso/Wally Salomão) also became successful, while Bethânia's usual wisdom in recording older composers is concretized in "Loucura" (Lupicínio Rodrigues). Not a remarkable album, this is a good choice for fans of this expressive singer. *—Alvaro Neder*

The Art of Maria Bethania / Jun. 11, 1992 / Verve ✦✦

As Cancoes Que Voce Fez Pra Mim / Feb. 22, 1994 / Philips ✦✦✦✦
At first, this seems like an implausible meeting. Maria Bethania, sister of Caetano Veloso, member of the iconoclast movement Tropicália since its inception, dedicated this album to the duo of songwriters Roberto Carlos/Erasmo Carlos, long since associated with a heavily romantic repertoire that makes the delights of their middle-aged feminine fan base. But, in fact, the songs by Roberto and Erasmo are quite poetic and well resolved in formal terms. If Roberto (and others) decided to profit on their jewels through condescending arrangements/renditions, it can't be assumed that their material isn't worth it, and Bethânia shows why. Deeply romantic, yes—but extremely tasteful. The album sold 1.5 million copies. *—Alvaro Neder*

Imitação da Vida / 1998 / ✦✦✦✦✦

● **Brazilian Collection** / Apr. 14, 1998 / Polygram ✦✦✦✦✦

Luiz Bonfá

b. Oct. 17, 1922, Rio de Janeiro, Brazil, **d.** Jan. 12, 2001, Rio de Janeiro, Brazil
Guitar, Composer / Brazilian Jazz, Bossa Nova, Brazil, Latin Continuum
Although overshadowed by the towering figure of Antonio Carlos Jobim and to a lesser extent by Joao Gilberto, Luiz Bonfa was right there at the birth of bossa nova as well. In fact, at least two of his songs, the haunting "Manha de Carnaval" and equally evocative "Samba de Orpheus," swept the world at least three years before Jobim's songs began to make a global impact, paving the way for the first Brazilian wave. In addition, Bonfa cultivated a delicate, precise classical guitar style, though more attuned to the traditional samba rhythm than the Gilberto/Jobim bossa nova lilt. Born near the bay of Guanabara in Rio—his father was an Italian immigrant—Bonfa took up the guitar at eleven and studied classical guitar with the Uruguayan master Isaias Savio. He began to work Rio's clubs as a singer with the Quitandinha Serenaders, and by 1946, he was appearing on Brazil's Radio Nacional. By 1957, Bonfa was beginning to split his time between New York City and Rio, touring the U.S. with singer Mary Martin, as well as writing and recording Brazilian film scores. The turning point in his career came in 1959 when film director Marcel Camus asked Bonfa to contribute some songs to his film version of the play *Orfeo do Carnaval* (to be renamed *Black Orpheus* on the screen). The director originally rejected "Manha de Carnaval" as the film's main theme, but after coming up with what he felt was an inferior second effort, Bonfa fought for his first tune and got his way, and "Manha de Carnaval" became a global pop/jazz/folk standard. In the late 1950s and 1960s, Bonfa began recording several albums for the American market on EMI Odeon (Capitol), Dot, Atlantic, Cook, Philips, Epic and Verve, and he and his songs appeared prominently on the *Jazz Samba Encore* album with Jobim and Stan Getz. His songwriting skills were in demand in the most unpredictable places; for example, he wrote the schmaltzy "Almost In Love" for Elvis Presley (included in the forgettable 1968 film *Live a Little, Love a Little*). Bonfa's profile in America virtually disappeared after the 1960s, although he continued to tour and write, eventually cutting over 50 albums. But he resurfaced in U.S. CD shops after a 15-year gap in 1989 with *Non-Stop to Brazil* for Chesky, followed by the ravishing *The Bonfa Magic* in 1991 (released domestically on Milestone) and 1993's *Moods* on GSP. Also, the original soundtrack for *Black Orpheus* is available on a Verve CD, a firsthand snapshot of Bonfa and Jobim lighting the fuse for the worldwide Brazilian music explosion. On January 12, 2001, Luiz Bonfa died of cancer in Rio de Janeiro. *—Richard S. Ginell*

● **Non-Stop to Brazil** / Apr. 17, 1989-Apr. 18, 1989 / Chesky ✦✦✦✦✦
Ever since his songs "Manha de Carnaval" and "Samba de Orfeu" were included in the 1959 film *Black Orpheus,* Luiz Bonfa has been one of the most celebrated figures in Brazilian music. In fact, the composer/acoustic guitarist's work commands the type of reverence enjoyed by such all-time greats as Antonio Carlos Jobim, Laurindo Almeida and Joao Gilberto. The entirely instrumental *Non-Stop to Brazil* marked the first time Bonfa (a master of samba and bossa nova) had set foot in an American recording studio in 15 years. Under the direction of jazz guitarist and Chesky Records President David Chesky, Bonfa (who is joined only by percussionist Cafe and, on three pieces, fellow guitarist Gene Bertoncini) revisits many of his best-known works. Anyone with even a basic knowledge of Brazilian music will recognize "Manha de Carnaval" and "Samba de Orfeu," and songs like "Sambolero," "Gentle Rain" and "Danca India" (an ode to South American Indians) are also highly regarded. Longtime Bonfa aficionados won't be disappointed by these intimate and introspective performances. *—Alex Henderson*

Joao Bosco

b. 1946, Minas Gerais
Vocals, Guitar / Brazilian Pop, Latin Jazz, MPB, World Fusion, Brazil, Latin Continuum
Since no others leap to mind, I would have to say that Joao Bosco is the greatest civil engineer turned singer/songwriter in the history of Brazilian popular music. He graduated with

his degree in 1972 but since then has been concentrating on becoming one of Brazil's most formidable songwriters. For most of his early career he supplied Elis Regina with some of her best material, indeed it could be said that each one made the other's career, but since her death, Bosco has stepped into the performance limelight with a great degree of authority and has been one of the more compelling figures in Brazilian music for the last 25 years.

Born in Ponte Nova in 1946, Bosco cut his musical teeth in family in which music was as important as eating and sleeping. His mother is an accomplished violinist, his father a singer of samba, his sister a concert pianist, and his brother a composer. While attending Ouro Preto University he became steeped in American jazz (Miles Davis in particular), and the bossa nova sound of Joao Gilberto and Antonio Carlos Jobim, it was also at university that he met lyricist Vinicius de Morais who contributed his elegant, poetic lyrics to Bosco's music. It was not long after that record companies began offering Bosco and de Morais their services. Later in the 70s Bosco became involved musically with Aldir Blanc a psychiatrist who decided to give up his practice to become a lyricist. Witty, surreal, at times pretentious, but more often than not extremely clever, Blanc became the perfect foil for Bosco and the two would work together, quite successfully, until the mid-1980s.

Bosco's career rise coincided roughly with Brazil's military dictatorship which lasted from 1964-1985 and his work, even the most innocuous love song, was frequently censored. As he noted in an interview in the early 90s, "Anything you composed or sang was censored. And there were no guidelines as to what you could or couldn't do. Every piece of music I wrote meant spending hours in the censorship bureau, debating with them, sometimes over one word." In 1977 Bosco wrote what was (and is) his most personal protest song, "O Bebaido e a Equilibrista" (The Drunkard and the Tightrope Walker), which became the theme song of Amnesty International. Despite his fame in Brazil, Bosco wasn't known to Americans until he made a guest appearance with jazz guitarist Lee Ritenour on the latter's 1988 record Festival. The guest spot wasn't enough to make Bosco an international superstar, but he did begin attracting more interest in the US. It wasn't until the early 90s that Bosco mounted a major tour of the US, but since then he has become increasingly popular internationally regularly performing at the prestigious Montreux Jazz Festival which over its history has frequently featured Brazilian performers.

Despite his growing popularity outside of his homeland, Bosco remains rooted in Brazil to the point of never leaving it for extended periods. So, while he remains somewhat obscure to American audiences, his music, rooted in Brazil's classic samba and bossa nova traditions, combines rock and roll, jazz and other ethnic styles in an eclectic brew that is a inventive and challenging as is he. *—John Dougan*

● **Comissão De Frente** / 1982 / Polygram ✦✦✦✦✦
The last of the albums shared by João Bosco with lyricist Aldir Blanc has all-time hits like "Nação," "Coisa Feita," "Comissão de Frente," "A Nível De . . . ," and others. With swinging sambas as the main vehicle, and humorous bolero supporting readings of suburban life ("Querido Diário"), the duo is in sharp form on this must-have release. *—Alvaro Neder*

Bosco: João Bosco / 1989 / CBS ✦✦✦✦
After several public and critical successes, João Bosco was enjoying a phase of great self-confidence in 1989, and this album wholly composed by himself (with the exception of "El Manisero") marks a departure point from where he would try different languages with no purism. Funk sounds, jazz-inspired sax solos, and even atonalism in small fade-out sections are experimented with here, with the song "Jade" being the highlight in terms of melody/harmony. Caribbean rhythms are heard in his heavily rhythmic version with his trademark in the improvised vocals for "El Manisero," and interesting Bahian folklore research is evident in "Sassaô." *—Alvaro Neder*

Personalidade / 1990 / Polygram ✦✦✦

Millennium: Joao Bosco / Apr. 13, 1999 / Mercury ✦✦✦✦

Carlinhos Brown

Percussion / Brazilian Jazz, Brazilian Pop, Brazil, Latin Continuum
Percussionist/composer Carlinhos Brown's name ranks up there with such brasileiran legends as Gilberto Gil, Sergio Mendes, and Caetano Veloso. He is the father of the Timbalada and known for his genius, musical daring and unflinching tendency to criticize the music of his peers while figuratively tooting his own horn. Brown is ever the innovator, always taking his music to new, different levels though which direction he will take at any given moment remains an enigma that he jealously guards. Brown takes his drumming very seriously. He considers it a form of education and is well-versed in the different forms of Brazilian percussion, its rich history and possibilities for the future. When composing music and recording it, Brown likes to be in charge of every aspect and produces his own work. As he describes it, he hears the completely orchestrated sound in his head and then seeks to reproduce it in the recording studio; he believes he has hundreds such records in his head. He sees Timbalada music as a collective genre, a means for others to express themselves artistically rather than a strictly commercial venture. To him music is constantly evolving and does not want to be limited to only one type. Recordings include 1997's *Alfagamabetizado* and 1999's *Omelete Man*. *—Sandra Brennan*

● **Carlinhos Brown** / 1996 / EMI ✦✦✦✦
Since Carmen Miranda, the image of an exotic, tropical, stereotyped Brazil has been explored worldwide. Well, the Brazilian soul is much more complex than that. The trend of "world" music has delighted producers in Brazil, who continue to sell this bizarre, exotic package. This album follows that line. Bringing all trendy artifices and mixing them with genuine Brazilian rhythms, Carlinhos Brown, an excellent percussionist who sings his songs with a small, juvenile voice, believes he's expanding the Brazilian musical tradition. He isn't. Brazilian music is strong enough to stand for itself without any tricks. Therefore, this is a world pop album—not a Brazilian music album. It may appeal to many people, as it delivers fully danceable pop music with the surprising flavor of an impossible land. There are some catchy melodies, and all songs are performed with professional competence, ranging from tranquil violão moments to wild Bahian percussion in a careful production. But please be aware—the real thing is aloof. *—Alvaro Neder*

Omelete Man / May 4, 1999 / Blue Note ✦✦✦

Chico Buarque

b. 1944
Vocals, Composer / Bossa Nova, Latin Pop, Brazil, Latin Continuum
Of the early stars of MPB (musica popular brasileira), Chico Buarque was one of the first to become a certifiable pop star. With his warm, nasally croon, elegant phrasing, and considerable skill at lyric writing, Buarque became extremely popular with women, who loved his understated sensuality. However, Buarque was uncomfortable playing the role of pop star, preferring to be seen as a serious artist. Throughout his career he's managed to have the best of both worlds, but not without some significant bumps along the way. Still, he remains a towering figure in Brazilian pop music, one of the country's greatest singer-songwriters and interpreters of the samba.

After studying architecture during the early '60s, it wasn't long before Buarque was hanging out with Sao Paulo's bossa nova cognoscenti. His career took off in 1965, with his own single "Pedro Pedreiro" plus three popular compositions for the queen of bossa nova, Nara Leao. Despite charges of aesthetic conservatism leveled against him by Brazil's radical tropicalista movement, Buarque took a huge career chance in 1968 writing a bleak, existential play entitled *Roda Viva* that was critical of obsessive fan culture. With a military dictatorship in power this was considered extremely controversial stuff and soldiers were sent out to disrupt performances of *Roda Viva*, and Buarque himself was jailed briefly.

In 1971 he recorded the album *Construction* which was decided break from his earlier bossa nova records. Though much of his '70s material was rejected by government censors, in the '80s Buarque was given compositional leeway and recorded some stunning music. Always challenging, always conscious of cultural history, he remains a towering figure in Brazilian music. *—John Dougan*

● **Construcao** / 1971 / Philips ✦✦✦✦✦
This is the CD reissue of the fifth album by Buarque for Philips (1971). It is a classic album, where all songs became hits. In an acoustic setting, almost completely aloof to the Tropicália movement (the courageous orchestration of "Construção" is too much reminiscent of the influential work by Rogério Duprat), which was being joined by almost every other artist, Buarque delved in the Brazilian tradition of sambas and romantic or doleful songs, coming up with "Deus Lhe Pague" and "Construção," both having strong lyrics subliminally criticizing the military dictatorship; "Cotidiano," existentially thematic, revolving around the man-woman relationship routine; "Olha Maria" (written with Tom Jobim and Vinícius de Moraes), a sad separation farewell; "Samba de Orly," a reference to the French airport and city that became paradigms of the exiled Brazilians; "Valsinha," a beautiful love story; and other immortal songs in which the genius of the composer meets sensitively and reverently the heart of the Brazilian feel. *—Alvaro Neder*

Chico Buarque & Maria Bethania / 1975 / Philips ✦✦✦✦✦

Vida / 1980 / Polygram Brazil ✦✦✦✦✦
Reissue in CD format of the LP released in 1980. Chico Buarque remains an extremely sensitive poet, telling sagas of women's lost lives in scattered beds ("Vida"), describing an improbable love affair between sea and moon ("Mar E Lua"), trying to convince the former lover of the end of the passion ("Já Passou"), and detailing an artist after the performance ("Bastidores"). But also remains an exciting sambista, counseling a jealous guy in "Deixe A Menina," opening the doors of imagination ("Fantasia"), or celebrating the dark charms of the "Morena de Angola." The album also has two soundtrack themes: "Eu Te Amo" (written with Tom Jobim) and "Bye Bye Brasil," both themes of the same-named films. Another of Buarque's classic, must-have albums. *—Alvaro Neder*

Caetano E Chico Juntos E Ao Vivo / 1993 / Polygram ✦✦✦✦✦

Chico Buarque en Español / May 2, 1997 / Polygram Brazil ✦✦✦✦✦
Chico Buarque brings many of his greatest hits for this album dedicated to the Spanish-speaking audiences. Together with Milton Nascimento, he delivers a version of "O Que Será—à Flor da Terra." The other covered hits are "Mar e Lua," "Geni e o Zepelim," "Apesar de Você," "Meu Caro amigo," "Construção," "Eu te Amo" (with Telma Costa), "Cotidiano," "Acalanto," and "Mambembe." All are versions by Daniel Viglietti. This is a CD reissue from an album from 1982, a typical Chico Buarque high-standard production in terms of Brazilian musicality. *—Alvaro Neder*

Dori Caymmi (Dorival Tostes Caymmi)

b. 1943
Vocals, Guitar, Composer / Latin Jazz, Bossa Nova, MPB, World Fusion, Brazil, Latin Continuum
Dori Caymmi is an internationally celebrated composer and singer, having an expressive production recorded by many important artists worldwide, along with a prominent career as arranger and producer, having also been writing music for soundtracks.

Son of the composer Dorival Caymmi and the former singer Stella Maris (Adelaide Tostes Caymmi), Dori began very early to study music, taking the piano at eight, with L`cia Branco, and later with Nise Poggi Obino. Attending the Conservatório Lorenzo Fernandez for musical theory classes, he also studied harmony with Paulo Silva and Moacir Santos. In 1959 debuted at the stage, accompanying his sister Nana. In 1960 he joined the Grupo dos Sete, writing music for televised plays. In December 1964, the important play *Opinião* (performed in the theater with the same name, in Rio), which buried bossa nova and generated the MPB, as a movement derived from the protest songs, had his musical direction and violão playing. In 1966 directed the music for the also important play *Arena conta Zumbi*, in its Carioca season. From 1964 to 1966 he produced the recordings of such artists as Edu Lobo, Eumir Deodato and Nara Leão for the Philips label. In 1965 he performed in the historic *Beco das Garrafas*, Rio's 52nd street, at the *Bottle's* nightclub, together with Francis Hime. Next year he presented himself, together with Francis Hime, Wanda Sá and Vinícius de Moraes at the *Teatro de Bolso*, Rio. With Nelson Motta, he composed several songs presented in Brazil's historic festivals, being classified several times. In 1966, their song "Saveiros," interpreted by Nana Caymmi, got the first place in the national competition and the second place at the international, at the *I FIC* (International Song Festival) from TV Rio. Next year, with "Cantiga," performed by the MPB-4, they got the 9th. place at the *II FIC* from TV Globo, Rio. One of the biggest hits of the duo, "O cantador" ("Like a lover"), recorded by many artists such as Flora Purim, Nathalie Cole and Sarah Vaughn, was also classified at TV Record's *III FMPB* (Festival of Brazilian Popular Music). The duo also wrote "De onde vens," recorded by Elis Regina and Nara Leão, and "Festa," recorded by Jair Rodrigues, Elis Regina and Sérgio Mendes. Joining Paul Winter's sextet as arranger and violonista (acoustic guitar player), he toured with them U.S.A. and Canadá. The first Lps by Caetano Veloso and Gal Costa, *Domingo*, and by Gilberto Gil, *Louvação*, had his musical direction and (non-credited) arrangements. Knowing the baianos since Salvador, he was the one who, together with Roberto Menescal and Edu Lobo, convinced João Ara˙jo, the Philips director, to record Caetano and Gal, both novice artists then. Together with Menescal and Francis Hime, he wrote the arrangements for that album. Caetano acknowledged Dori as the best Brazilian violonista after João Gilberto. Dori was on the vortex of the Tropicalista movement, being present at the historic reunion at Sérgio Ricardo's home, where Gil and Caetano tried to convince him, Edu Lobo, Sidney Miller, Chico Buarque, Francis Hime, Paulinho da Viola, Torquato Neto and Capinam to join the movement. Dori hadn't accepted— he couldn't take The Beatles or any pop music for that matter. Among the several soundtracks he's written for movies, deserve mention a partnership with Tom Jobim in Paulo César Sarraceni's *Crônica da casa assassinada* (1971); a partnership with Paulo César Pinheiro in Bruno Barreto's *Tati, a garota* (1973); and Paulo Tiago's *O duelo* (1974). For TV Globo, wrote the soundtrack for the TV soap opera Gabriela (1975), and the Sítio do Picapau Amarelo, televised from 1977 to 1984, among others. Since 1989 living in Los Angeles, due to the lacking of Brazilian identity in the mass production of easy listening hits, in his own words, in 1994 he participated of Dionne Warwick's album *Aquarela do Brasil*. In the same year performed at the *Montreux Festival*, Switzerland, with Toots Thielemans, Oscar Castro-Neves, Eliane Elias and Ricardo Silveira, Toots' Brazil Project. The Project also toured though USA and Europe. Next year he participated, together with Gilberto Gil, Branford Marsalis, Herbie Mann, Paula Robinson, Eliane Elias, Joyce, Paulo and Daniel Jobim, Ottmar Liebert, Ma˙cha Adnet and Orpheus Chamber Orchestra in the tribute for Tom Jobim, one year after his decease, held at the *Carnegie Hall* in New York. He would be also present in the two subsequent shows in tribute to Tom, always in the same hall. In that year also appeared in Edu Lobo's album *Meia-noite*, in the *Songbook Edu Lobo* (Lumiar) and wrote the arrangements for Spike Lee's film *Clockers*. In 1996 played in Brazil's *Heineken Concerts*, also performed shows accompanied by the Orquestra Jazz Sinfônica and appeared in the *Tom Jobim Songbook* (Lumiar). He spent some time in Rio in 1997 for writing, orchestrate and record Fábio Barreto's movie *Bela Donna*. Also in that year, he worked in the album *'Sketches of James Taylor*, a jazz project over the compositions of the American writer, together with Flora Purim and Airto Moreira. Also took part in Djavan's *Songbook* (Lumiar), released his Cd *Toma conta do meu filho, que eu também já fui do mar...*, and conducted the Orquestra Philarmonia Brasileira. Dori's Cd *Romantic vision* was nominated to the Grammy Award as Best Arranger for Henry Mancini's "Pink Panther." In the same year he performed at the *Blue Note*, in New York. *—Alvaro Neder*

● **Brazilian Serenata** / 1988 / Qwest ✦✦✦✦✦
Like his late father Dorival Caymmi, Dori Caymmi is someone who knows the value of subtlety. Caymmi's gently introspective pop and pop-jazz is never a shout, but an articulate, highly effective whisper. The Brazilian singer/acoustic guitarist/composer joined Quincy Jones' Qwest roster with *Brazilian Serenata*, a seductive, caressing gem illustrating just how charismatic he can be. Caymmi isn't a bossa nova artist per se, but like Joao Gilberto and other bossa icons, he is someone who has obviously learned a lot from American jazz as well as the rich history of the Brazilian samba. "Flower of Bahia," "Historia Antigua," "The Colors of Joy" and other offerings leave no doubt that he has long since mastered the samba rhythm completely. Whether singing in English or Portuguese, Caymmi never fails to command attention on this magnificent CD. *—Alex Henderson*

Dorival Caymmi

b. 1914
Vocals, Composer / Samba, Brazil, Latin Continuum
If one were to look for a geographical region in Brazil that resembles the Mississippi delta in terms of producing a lion's share of influential performers, a good case could be made for the region of Bahia in Brazil's northeast. The list of Bahian performers is formidable: Caetano Veloso, Gilberto Gil, Gal Costa, Maria Bethania, etc. What links all of these people is the influence of Dorival Caymmi perhaps the single most important composer to come from this region.

Born in 1914, Cammyi composed popular songs that echoed the nation's indigenous songforms: sambas, toadas (melancholy romantic tunes), modinhas (sentimental songs), songs and chants from fishermen, and singing from the Afro-Brazilian religion of candomble (practiced most widely in Bahia). In many ways Caymmi is a very conservative songwriter in that he relies on simple, beautiful melodies and sharply imagistic lyrics, the latter generally about the people and place, life and love in Bahia. Most importantly, Caymmi is a great storyteller in a folkloric tradition, a tradition that Americans might associate, with, say, Woody Guthrie. This is not to say that Caymmi resembles Guthrie—he doesn't compositionally (although his writing is frequently poetic) or vocally—but there is a similarity in the way he creates a sense of place and fills that place with mostly common, working folk, characters who are richly drawn and sensitively portrayed (a good example would be his songs that detail the hard life of fisherman). It is unsurprising to find that Caymmi's songs have become so beloved in that everyone is familiar with his music as if it were in the air they breathe—perhaps it is.

Caymmi is also well-known as the man who composed hit songs for the legendary Carmen Miranda, but it was during the heady days of tropicalia in the late '60s when performers such as Veloso, Gil, Elis Regina and other began recording Caymmi's songs as a tribute to their Bahian heritage as a way to preserve (and in some cases update) Brazilian musical tradition. Believe it or not even a schlocky pop singer like Andy Williams recorded a Caymmi song. A true legend, Caymmi's influence lives on with his extraordinarily talented children, Nana, Danilo, and Dori all of whom have achieved great success in Brazil. *—John Dougan*

● **Caymmi Visita Tom** / 1964 / Elenco ✦✦✦✦✦
It was renowned producer Aluísio de Oliveira's idea to record, in 1963, a meeting attended by Tom Jobim, recently returned from the U.S., Dorival Caymmi, and Caymmi's family: sons Dori and Danilo, daughter Nana, and wife Stela (who wasn't supposed to sing, but she surrendered to de Oliveira's insistence, fortunately, and recorded one track, "Canção Da Noiva," taken from Caymmi's "Suíte Dos Pescadores"). Additionally, on this recording there are some Brazilian musicians who got international acclamation: bassist Sérgio Barroso and drummers Dom Um Romão and Edison Machado, arguably the best Brazilian drummer of all times.

The album, formerly an LP later released in CD format through Polygram, contains two until then unpublished songs that became instant hits, later true classics: Caymmi's "Das Rosas" and "Só Tinha Que Ser Com Você" (Tom Jobim/Aluísio de Oliveira). It also gave the two composers the opportunity to interpret material from other writers, on an album with more instrumental soloing than their previous releases. It was because of this album that Nana, until then married and living in Venezuela, decided to break with her domestic life and depart for a solo career as a singer. Also was important as a professional affirmation for Danilo, whose somewhat naïve though relaxed flute soloing betrayed his 15 years of age at that time. Caymmi has a strong grasp on the melodies, as usual, and Jobim is singing better than on his later albums. This historic album certainly appeals to every Jobim and Caymmi fan. *—Alvaro Neder*

Caymmi's Grandes Amigos / 1986 / EMI ✦✦✦✦✦

Gal Costa (Maria da Graça Costa Pena Burgos)

b. 1946
Vocals / Brazilian Pop, Bossa Nova, MPB, Tropicalia, Latin Pop, Brazil, Latin Continuum
Gal Costa is an awarded singer with an extensive solo discography and international experience. A fundamental presence in the Tropicália movement, she has been in Brazil's leading team of singers for the last 33 years.

Since very young involved with music as a singer and violão player, when her mother's business broke she became a record shop attendant, where he spent long hours listening to music, especially João Gilberto. She became acquainted with Caetano Veloso in 1963, and friendly disputed him as boyfriend with her girl friend Dedé, who would later be Caetano's wife. In 1964, Caetano was invited to organize a Brazilian popular music show at the opening of Salvador's *Teatro Vila Velha*. The show, called *Nós, por exemplo*, brought Caetano, his sister Maria Bethânia, Gilberto Gil and Gal (still under her name Maria da Graça). The show was a success and was reenacted two weeks later, with the addition of Tom Zé (still presented as Antônio José). The success was even bigger, and the group (without Tom) soon presented another show, *Nova Bossa Velha, Velha Bossa Nova*. In September 26, 1965, the group opened the show *Arena canta Bahia*, at São Paulo's *Teatro de Arena*. In the end of that year, she was taken to the presence of her idol João Gilberto, who asked her to sing while he accompanied; after listening to her in several songs, he declared "Girl, you sing beautifully. Someday I will return only to record an album only with you." Also in that year she appeared in Bethânia's first album, singing "Sol Negro" (Caetano Veloso). In 1966 she recorded a single for RCA (completely unperceived by the general audiences) and interpreted "Minha senhora" (Gilberto Gil/Torquato Neto) at TV Rio's *I FIC;* also took the name Gal Costa by suggestion of the impresario Guilherme Ara˙jo. In 1967 Gal recorded her first Lp, together with Caetano (also his first Lp) in *Domingo*. In 1968 recorded two tracks in the Lp-manifesto *Tropicália, ou Panis et circensis* which became her first hits, "Mamãe coragem" and "Baby." Also in 1968 she achieved great popularity at TV Record's *IV FMPB* (São Paulo), when she got the first place for "Divino maravilhoso" (Gilberto Gil/Caetano Veloso). In the next year she recorded for Philips her first individual Lp. She then began a busy schedule of performances throughout Brazil and recorded for Philips the Lp *Meu nome é Gal*. In 1970 performed in England, and returning next year to Brazil, recorded the Lp *Legal*. In 1971 she got success in the show Deixa sangrar, presented in several capitals. In 1971 joined João Gilberto and Caetano in a live TV Tupi performance. In 1972 her show Gal a todo vapor was recorded live in a double album, and she performed with Gil and Caetano in several venues. In 1973 performed at the *MIDEM* in Cannes, France, and recorded the Lp *Õndia*, after the show by the same name. In 1976 recorded the album *Os doces bárbaros* with Caetano, Gil and Bethânia, also performing a series of shows with them under the same name, and recorded the solo album *Gal canta Caymmi*. She recorded four more albums in the 70's. In the 80's, she gained international exposure with the albums *Aquarela do Brasil* (1980), *Gal Costa* (1981), *Gal* (1983) and *Bem bom* (1985), also touring through Japan, France, Israel, Argentina, U.S.A., Portugal, Italy and others. In 1984 she performed in the show O sorriso do gato de Alice (her 20th. album), which was awarded by APCA and received the Shell Prize. In 1997 commemorated 30 years of career with the Cd and video *Ac˙stico MTV* (BMG), with many important special guests. In 1998 Polygram released *30 anos de barato*, a three-Cd box set. *—Alvaro Neder*

☆ **Gal Canta Caymmi** / 1975 / Verve ✦✦✦✦✦
In this 1975 release, Costa sings ten of Dorival Caymmi's musical vignettes of life in Salvador, Bahia, about which she knows a great deal (it's her hometown). *—Terri Hinte*

Fantasia / 1981 / Philips ✦✦✦
A huge record for Costa in 1981, it contains songs by Ivan Lins ("Roda Baiana"), Caetano Veloso ("Meu Bem, Meu Mal"), and Djavan ("Faltando um Pedaco"). *—Terri Hinte*

Plural / 1983 / RCA ✦✦✦

● **Meu Nome E Gal (My Name Is Gal)** / 1990 / Verve ✦✦✦✦✦
Although she has released dozens of recordings in her three-decade long career, this anthol-

ogy is the best place to be introduced to one of the great voices in pop music. Covering a period from the start of tropicalia in the late '60s up to post-military dictatorship years of the '80s, this is as strong a collection of Costa's material as one is likely to find. The cream of the Brazilian songwriting crop is well represented here, especially Caetano Veloso with seven tracks; Chico Buarque's "Foltheim (A New Leaf)" and Dorival Caymmi's "So Louco (Just Crazy)" are also noteworthy. But it's when Costa sings Veloso that the record takes off. Many of the Veloso songs included in this collection were songs he wrote while in exile in London, when the only way to hear his music was through recordings by Gal Costa. All of the songs are excellent, but it is the bluesy and melancholy "Luz do Sol (Sunlight)" that's transcendent, easily one of Costa's greatest moments on record. —*John Dougan*

Gal Canta Tom Jobim / 1999 / BMG ✦✦✦✦

Vinícius DeMoraes (Marcus Vinícius da Cruz de Melo Morais)

b. 1913, **d.** 1980

Vocals / Brazilian Pop, Latin Jazz, Bossa Nova, MPB, Samba, Brazil, Latin Continuum

Vinícius de Moraes was a fundamental figure in Brazilian music. As a poet, he wrote lyrics for a great number of songs which became all-time bossa nova and samba classics. As a composer, he wrote some good music, and as an interpreter, he left several important albums. He began writing poetry and songs from an early age, and composed lyrics for ten recorded songs while at law school in the early '30s. After school, he wrote several books while working in Brazil's diplomatic service. His first samba (with Antônio Maria) was "Quando Tu Passas por Mim" from 1953. Three years later, he staged *Orfeu da Conceição,* later filmed by the French writer Marcel Camus and given a score by a then-unknown pianist, Antonion Carlos (Tom) Jobim. In 1958, Elizete Cardoso released an album with five compositions by Tom and Vinícius, which marked the beginning of bossa nova.

The careers of all of them had a great impetus after that record, and the songs written by Tom & Vinícius became indisputed by singers. In 1962, together with Tom Jobim, João Gilberto and Os Cariocas, he opened the show *Encontro* with the first airing of the classic songs "Garota de Ipanema," "Insensatez," "Ela é Carioca," and "Só Danço Samba." In 1969, he became the partner of Toquinho, his most frequent partner and biggest friend (they would evntually record 20 LPs together). In 1971, an LP with his compositions (with Toquinho) "Tarde em Itapoã" and "Como Dizia o Poeta" was released with great success. It brought a great number of invitations for touring in Brazil and abroad. —*Alvaro Neder*

Vinicius & Odette Lara / 1963 / Elenco ✦✦✦✦

Como Dizia O Poeta . . . Musica Nova / 1971 / RGE ✦✦✦✦✦

This historic album reuniting three great values of Brazilian music was recorded in Argentina in January, 1971. Bringing some of Vinícius biggest hits with several partners (Toquinho, Baden Powell, Tom Jobim), along with Gilberto Gil's "Viramundo" and a theme by Albinoni, the album shows singer Maria Bethânia interpreting his brother Caetano's "É de Manhã" and "Apelo," "O Que Tinha de Ser," and "Viramundo." The Argentinean musicians here are quite passable as samba players, and the worst in the album is a minor recording problem, as Toquinho's voice seems to be caught only by a far away mike. In all, this is an excellent album. —*Alvaro Neder*

● **São Demais Os Perigos Desta Vida . . .** / 1977 / RGE ✦✦✦✦✦

In this CD reissue from an album previously released in 1977, the great poet/singer/composer Vinícius de Moraes and his longtime partner, violonista (acoustic guitar player)/singer/composer Toquinho, deliver several of their biggest hits, like "Cotidiano No. 2," "Tatamirô," "São Demais Os Perigos Desta Vida," "Valsa Para Uma Menininha," "Pra Viver Um Grande Amor," and "Regra Três." The other songs are also masterpieces. In delicate renditions that range from mid-tempo sambas (in their stylized middle-class version, very different from the traditional samba do morro style) to tender lullabies, the duo also exhibits their appreciation for the genuine Afro-Brazilian tradition, exploring pontos de macumba (music for the Afro-Brazilian religion macumba). The wonderful poetry of Vinícius is declaimed by himself in some moments, such as the famous interlude in "Pra Viver Um Grande Amor." A must-have where, as always is the case of Vinícius, the key is tenderness and love. —*Alvaro Neder*

Djavan

b. 1950

Vocals / Latin Dance, Brazilian Pop, MPB, Samba, Brazil, Latin Continuum

Djavan is a Brazilian composer and singer, owner of a respectable discography. His international success has taking him to the highest-ranking venues worldwide, and his songs have been recorded by dozens of major artists. A singer for soap-opera soundtracks during the early '70s, Djavan also worked at several nightclubs before his breakthrough as a composer. He took second place in a songwriting contest with "Abertura," and his first single came four months later. In 1976, he recorded his first LP, *A Voz, O Violão e a Arte de Djavan,* and "Flor de Lis" became a big hit. After signing with CBS in 1982, he recorded *Luz* in America with help from Stevie Wonder.

He recorded many successful albums during the '80s, including *Brazilian Knights and a Lady, Meu Lado,* and *Bird of Paradise.* In 1989, *Djavan* was accompanied by flamenco guitar player Paco de Lucia in the track "Oceano," included in a major soap opera. Followed *Puzzle of Hearts* (1990), *Coisa de Acender* (1991, with a partnership with Caetano Veloso in "Linha do Equador"), and *Novena* (1994). In 1996, he recorded *Malásia,* which had Tom Jobim's "Correnteza," included in a prime-time soap opera, and, in 1998, *Bicho Solto—O 13O.* In 1999, he recorded *Ao Vivo,* in two volumes, which sold one million copies. —*Alvaro Neder*

★ **Seduzir** / 1981 / World Pacific ✦✦✦✦✦

By the time he recorded his third album, *Seduzir,* Djavan was a superstar in Brazil, and was attracting attention in American jazz, R&B and pop circles as well. Though his style inspires comparisons to fellow Brazilian great Milton Nascimento, Djavan is a distinctive vocalist whose inspirations range from Northeastern Brazil's tropiscalismo school to jazz to the Beatles and Stevie Wonder. Having absorbed so wide a variety of music, Djavan (a native of the state of Alagoas in Northeastern Brazil) has no problem making *Seduzir* a very diverse listen. Though all of the players on this five-star date (reissued on CD in 1990) are Brazilian and Djavan's lyrics are entirely in Portuguese, it's hard to miss the impact American artists have had on him. From the impressionistic "Morena de Endoidecer" and the complex, jazz-oriented "Jogral" to the enchanting "Faltando Um Pecado" and the Wonder-ish title song, Djavan keeps listeners guessing. —*Alex Henderson*

Bird of Paradise / 1988 / Epic ✦✦✦✦✦

Bird of Paradise came roosting around the time the second Brazilian wave began to crest in North America, following Djavan's extensive contributions to the Manhattan Transfer's *Brasil* album. And this album's a beaut—full of strong, haunting, lusciously melodic songs often backed by that gently jumping, uplifting rhythm that runs through much of his material. Unusual among Brazilian singers, Djavan's English is excellent, and whether singing in English or Portuguese, his dark, virile vocals are crystal-clear in enunciation, and his range of subjects and moods is virtually as wide as that of countryman Milton Nascimento. Standout tunes here include "Carnival in Rio," "Madness (Doidice)," "Stephen's Kingdom" (presumably dedicated to South African martyr Stephen Biko), and "Take Me (Me Leve)." The backup sounds, gathered under the polished production of Ronnie Foster, are usually made by an American crew of L.A. session vets who nevertheless capture the feeling and rhythm of Djavan's material with uncanny sympathy. —*Richard S. Ginell*

Oceano / 1989 / Columbia ✦✦✦✦

A Voz e o Violão / 1976 / Gala ✦✦✦✦✦

This is a reissue of Djavan' first recorded LP. In 1975, he was awarded with the second place at TV Globo's *Festival Abertura* for his song "Fato Consumado." The following year he recorded this album, which contained one of his biggest hits, "Flor de Lis," along with his previous award winning song. The highlights are the wonderful melodies, the musical sonority of his lyrics (it even doesn't matter if you understand them, as his focus is on its musicality), the smart violão of Djavan, and the rich rhythmic interplay between voice and violão. All of the compositions are great, exploring from samba to baião, and, more importantly, it's mostly an acoustic band album, with cool touches of a Rhodes. It may appeal to those who have a hard time swallowing the massive electronics on his latest albums. —*Alvaro Neder*

Gilberto Gil (Gilberto Passos Gil Moreira)

b. Jun. 29, 1942, Salvador, Bahia, Brazil

Vocals, Guitar / Brazilian Pop, MPB, Tropicalia, Brazil, Latin Continuum

Multi-instrumentalist, singer/songwriter Gilberto Gil began learning to play and sing the bossa nova after hearing singer and guitarist Joao Gilberto on the radio, and was so impressed that he immediately bought a guitar and learning to play and sing the bossa nova. In 1965, he had his first hit when singer Elis Regina recorded his song "Louvacao." Gil began to establish himself as a singer of protest songs, and became very popular with Brazilians involved in the Tropicalia movement, which opened up native Brazilian folk music to other kinds of influences. His own first hit came in 1969, with "Aquele Abraco."

After three years exiled in England by the repressive Brazilian government, Gil returned to Brazil in 1972 and recorded *Expresso 2222,* which spurred the hit singles "Back in Bahia" and "Oriente." In 1975, he recorded with Jorge Ben for the album *Gil and Jorge.* For most of the 1970s, he recorded for a variety of Brazilian record companies until signing an international deal with the WEA group of labels in 1977. He toured U.S. colleges in 1978 and firmly established his place in the international jazz world with his albums *Nightingale* (1978) and *Realce* (1979) . In 1980, Gil teamed up with reggae musician Jimmy Cliff. The pair toured Brazil, and Gil's cover of Bob Marley's "No Woman, No Cry" climbed to number one, selling 700,000 copies. Gil followed up in 1981 with *Gente Precisa Ver O Luar,* one of his most acclaimed recordings. He followed up with *Um Banda Um* (1982), *Extra* (1983), and *Raca Humana* (1984).

The early '90s saw Gil continuing his involvement in social and political causes in his native country, finding widespread support for his political stances, and he was elected to office in the port city of Salvador. Because Gil fused samba, salsa and bossa nova with rock and folk music, he's recognized today as one of the pioneers in world music. —*Richard Skelly*

Louvação / 1967 / Philips ✦✦✦

☆ **Gilberto Gil [1968]** / 1968 / Mercury ✦✦✦✦✦

Gilberto Gil's second album is packed with some of the best songs of his career—jubilant pop extravaganzas like "Domingo No Parque," "Pega a Voga, Cabeludo," and "Frevo Rasgado" that were equally inspired by the irresistible, brassy bombast of Carnaval and intelligent rock & roll from America and Britain. Even more than the other Tropicalistas, though, Gil blends his rock and native influences seamlessly, resulting in songs like "Ele Falava Nisso Todo Dia," which chart an intriguing fusion of Brazilian and British Invasion (before he breaks into Portuguese for the first verse, the intro sounds exactly like a few early Rolling Stones productions). Gil's occasional backing band, the teenage Tropicalia breakouts known as Os Mutantes, join in on the feel-good Brazilian pop anthem "Domingou." Enjoyable and never as experimental as his work would soon become, *Gilberto Gil 1968* is one of the best Tropicalia albums ever released. —*John Bush*

Gilberto Gil [1969] / 1969 / Philips ✦✦✦✦✦

It's not only ironic that the record with Gilberto Gil's first major hit ("Aquele Abraço") is also his most experimental album; it also speaks to the diversity of Brazil's emerging pop superstar. Beginning with the loose-jointed groove-pop of "Cérebro Eletrónico" (the album's subtitle), this second of three straight self-titled LPs includes a few Carnival-styled pop songs, as on his previous album. Most of the experimentation comes at the end of side two with "2001" and "Objeto Semi-Identificado," both of which are filled with odd tape-music portions, spoken-word elements, and a reliance on studio trickery rarely seen on any Western pop albums. Even the pop songs are produced with an eye toward noise; the tropicalia anthem "Volks Volkswagen Blue" features a few psychedelic guitar lines breaking into distortion, and a small but devastatingly brassy horn section punctuating the melody. It's a very disjointed album, not quite as consistently entertaining as last year's entry, but definitely a masterpiece of forward-looking pop. *—John Bush*

Gilberto Gil [1971] / 1971 / Paramount ✦✦✦
As on Caetano Veloso's album from the same year, Gilberto Gil does not sound happy away from his homeland. Recorded in London, the eight songs on his final self-titled album are mostly blues and introspective, downbeat pop songs. Stevie Winwood's "Can't Find My Way Home" is an inspired choice, delivered with a crushing sentimentality rarely found in other versions. Gil also reprises "Volkswagen Blues" from his 1969 LP. The effect isn't quite as doom-laden as Veloso's work, but Gil is definitely homesick, as the touching "Nega Photograph Blues" shows. *—John Bush*

★ **Gil & Jorge (Ogum Xangô)** / 1975 / Verve ✦✦✦✦✦
Recorded with little rehearsal and only two acoustic guitars (plus a percussionist) for accompaniment, Gil & Jorge focuses squarely on the individual talents of Gilberto Gil and Jorge Ben as musicians, vocalists, performers, and improvisers. Of course, they prove up to the task. The nine lengthy tracks on the album (it was originally configured as a double LP) feature Gil and Ben interacting to a high degree, trading lines and often repeating them several times. The best tracks here—"Nega," "Taj Mahal," and "Meu Glorioso Sao Cristovao"—are highly rhythmic and have the heft of ancient Brazilian folksongs. Unfortunately, there isn't another record in Gil's discography even remotely close to it. *—John Bush*

Refazenda / 1975 / WEA Latina ✦✦✦✦✦
Recorded the same year as *Gil & Jorge (Ogum Xangô),* his brilliant collaboration with Jorge Ben, *Refazenda* keeps up the pace, but in a completely different way. Instead of the acoustic Brazilian folk of *Gil & Jorge,* Gil focuses on breezy pop. "Jeca Total," " , Povo, ," "Tenho Sede," and the title track are dominated by flute, accordion, horns, and gentle strings. Gil is in excellent voice, whether he's delivering a driving song like "Essa É Pra Tocar No Rádio" or more intimate ballads like the last two tracks, "Lamento Sertanejo" and "Meditação." Though "Pai e Mãe" and a few other tracks are slightly reminiscent of the *Gil & Jorge* LP, Gil reasserts himself here as the pop star whom all of Brazil had expected him to be. *—John Bush*

Refestança / 1978 / Philips ✦✦✦

☆ **Realce** / 1979 / WEA Latina ✦✦✦✦✦
A good example of how Gil mixes it all up: recorded in Los Angeles with a Brazilian/American cast, this 1978 session combines Gil's unique samba-rock-funk fare with a Portuguese version of Bob Marley's "No Woman, No Cry." *—Terri Hinte*

Um Banda Um / 1981 / WEA Latina ✦✦✦

Extra / 1983 / WEA Latina ✦✦✦✦
Reflecting the then recent association with Jimmy Cliff, this Gilberto Gil album opens with the reggae "Extra," in which he exorcises the powers of political obscurantism invoking the liberating forces of mysticism. "E Lá Poeira" anticipated the crossover pop/Northeastern music made successful in the world music of the '90s. "Mar de Copacabana" has the old Gil, composer of melodies full of a refreshing feeling but at the same time with the two feet rooted in the samba tradition. "A Linha E O Linho" could be a minor pop ballad if it weren't for the sensitive and indigenous lyrics solution, where he used the metaphor of sewing to talk about two people united by a deep love. "Preciso de Você" is a pop dance tune sung by his daughter Nara. "Punk Da Periferia" was a hit, talking about the violent world of the punks of São Paulo's periphery. "Funk-se Quem Puder" is a funk where the biggest interest is to provide a danceable sound. "O Veado," a curious experience that mixes samba and pop music, had its lyrics responsible for the importance of this song; "Veado" can be alternatively a deer or a gay person, in Brazilian Portuguese. Gil keeps the ambiguity in the text, which compares the veado to Greta Garbo. In spite of the frenetic graphic artwork of the cover, the album is not the most pop based in Gil's discography, having sensitive and reflexive moments as well as simple entertainment. *—Alvaro Neder*

Dia Dorim Noite Neon / 1985 / WEA Latina ✦✦✦✦

Gilberto Gil em Concerto / 1987 / Westwind ✦✦✦✦

Parabolic / 1991 / WEA Latina ✦✦✦
As one of the leaders of the tropicalismo style created in Northeastern Brazil in the 1960s (along with Caetano Veloso), Gilberto Gil proved to be as important to Brazilian pop as bossa nova hero Joao Gilberto (one of his influences). Revered by everyone from Djavan to Flora Purim to Marisa Monte, the singer/acoustic guitarist has occupied an enviable niche in Brazilian culture. *Parabolic,* a welcome addition to his huge catalog, is state-of-the-art Gil: seductive, richly melodic Brazilian pop. "Neve Na Bahia," "Buda Nago," and "Parabolicamara" are gems that his fanatic admirers shouldn't miss. On the funk-influenced "Quero Ser Teu Funk," he shows us some delightful parallels between the Afro-Brazilian and Afro-American cultures. Tropical Storm thoughtfully provides English translations of these songs, all of them sung in Portuguese. *—Alex Henderson*

Acoustic / 1994 / Atlantic ✦✦✦✦

Luar / Dec. 11, 1996 / WEA Latina ✦✦✦✦
After the hard years dominated by social convulsion in Brazil, in which it was demanded that every artist explicate his political views, the end of dictatorship in the '80s brought an uncommitted inebriating feel of liberty that was translated in music by Caetano Veloso's "Odara" (where all the composer wanted to do was to dance) to the horror of political activists. This is the Gilberto Gil version of those days. One of his most danceable albums, most songs make it clear that no further considerations are taken into account, just plain Saturday night entertainment. Songs like "Luar," "Palco," "Sonho Molhado" (whose biggest virtue is the use of accordion and other northeastern touches), "Lente do Amor" (with a subtle reference to sexual freedom, which also coincides with Fernando Gabeira's loincloth, from around the same period), "Morena," "Cara Cara" (a frevo by Caetano Veloso interpreted as dance music), the beautiful "Cores Vivas," and "Axé Babá" (with its heavy Afro-Bahian percussion) all have in common the desire for pleasure and the avoidance of deeper questions. The last two songs break this uniformity, though: "Flora" is a delicate bossa with a beautiful melody in Gil's style, in which a melodic sequence is transposed in ascendant manner, and "Se Eu Quiser Falar Com Deus" (If I Want to Talk With God), a deeply heartfelt slow song where Gil dialogues with his own relationship with religion. The album had several hits ("Palco," "Lente do Amor"—which was included in a TV series—"Axé Babá," and "Se Eu Quiser Falar Com Deus"), representing a document of a period, and having at least two melodically/lyrically highly expressive songs. *—Alvaro Neder*

O Sol de Oslo / Oct. 13, 1998 / Blue Jackel ✦✦✦✦✦
In his extensive discography, Gilberto Gil has explored almost every possible shade of pop music. In this album, produced by the independent label Pau Brasil (Gil is a WEA artist), he felt safe to shamelessly go back to earlier days, where his wonderful melodies were free of the artist's anxiety for fame and success. This album is a delicate collection of acoustic grooves (with a couple of electric renditions), with several different world references, ranging from folkloric chants (the researcher/singer Marlui Miranda is instrumental here), northeastern coco (the folkloric "Tatá Engenho Novo" is hot, swinging, and thrilling), cantigas ("Mana," folklore), xote-ska ("Xote"), new age ("Kaô"), modern ciranda ("Ciranda," beautiful, dissonant melody by Moacir Santos), rap ("Rep," excellent deconstruction of that style by the smart percussion of Trilok Gurtu), xaxado ("Onde O Xaxado Tá," faithful acoustic rendition), and the hot Olodum rhythm ("Oslodum"). There is even a traditional coco, "17 Na Corrente," which may be a hit in the dance clubs in its funk rendition with drum machines and brass attacks. Pay attention to the beautiful jazz-baião solo in "Eu Te Dei Meu Ané." Joined by excellent musicians Marlui Miranda, Bugge Wesseltoft, Trilok Gurtu, and Toninho Ferragutti, Gilberto Gil makes justice to his name with *Sol de Oslo,* which stands several notches above the average pop record. *—Alvaro Neder*

Caribbean Music Styles

BIGUINE—Throughout the long history of the biguine, the dominant sound has been that of the clarinet and trombone, both solo and as a duet, and, while the phrasing often recalls New Orleans jazz, the overall sound is unmistakably Caribbean. The signature sound of the biguine is the interplay between the clarinet and trombone, which can still be heard today throughout the Antilles musical milieu, from the most traditional music to the music of the cadence era or the pop sounds of today's zouk. Any contemporary music that uses biguine as its base, even that which ventures as far off as contemporary jazz, is considered "biguine moderne." The classic music of carnival in the Antilles is an uptempo version of the biguine rhythm, called "biguine vide."

CADENCE—A constantly changing style that evolved primarily among the islands of Guadeloupe, Martinique, Dominica, and Haiti. The cadence era was exciting and extremely fertile, requiring musicians of only the highest calibre, who could master not only Antilles pop styles like biguine and Creole mazurka but also those of Haiti and the other neighboring islands. The cadence years saw the evolution of the pop influences that embellish the rootsier foundation of today's Antilles musicians, allowing for expression in an internationally familiar musical language: electric instruments, riffing horn sections, trapset drums, topical lyrics, and specific stylings of rock music, reggae, soca, American Black music, and more. In addition to Les Aiglons, this was the heyday of big bands like La Perfecta, Typical Combo, La Selecta, Les Maxels, Les Léopards, Les Vikings de la Guadeloupe (whose co-leader, Pierre-Edouard Decimus, went on to create Kassav' at the end of the decade), and Gordon Henderson's Exile One of Dominique. Recordings from this era, while fascinating and enjoyable, often suffer from out-of-tune instruments and sub-par recording quality. Cadence led directly into the early '80s and the rise of zouk, and it was the musicians schooled in cadence who were the first zouk stars. The major catalyst behind the emergence of zouk was the desire to produce a new Caribbean music that treated the multifaceted music of the Antilles to the state-of-the-art recording technology of the Paris studios.

CHOUVAL BWA—A rural Martiniquan style of music that evolved as accompaniment to the "manege" (or carousel). Originally featuring a large drum like a bass drum, hand drums, and ti bwa, chouv' was led by melodic instruments like accordion, bamboo flute, and wax-paper/comb-type kazoos. One young artist, Claude Germany, is attempting to carry on the traditional form of chouval bwa, while others have updated it minimally (by the addition of electric bass) or dramatically (as in the case of zouk chouv', which features an array of electric instruments, including synthesizer). Chouval bwa is Creole for the French term "cheval bois," meaning "wooden horse."

COMPAS—Haitian dance music, started by Nemours Jean-Baptiste in the '50s, known first as compas-direct.

GWO KA—The various indigenous rhythms of Guadeloupe are played on a two-drum family of hand drums called gwo ka. Gwo ka music is rhythm-driven by the two drums and is often accompanied by a mounted stick or bamboo log hit with sticks called a ti bwa. The drummers lead the way for dancers, and usually there is singing accompaniment. Gwo ka has been an underlying element of zouk from day one, and, in fact, Kassav's first album was entitled Love and Ka Dance. Anzala and Ti Celeste (or Ti Seles) are two gwo ka artists still recording today, the latter sticking to the roots while the former has electrified his sounds.

ROAD MARCH—Chosen at the carnival in Trinidad, this is the most popular song of the year.

—Gene Scaramuzzo

Antonio Carlos Jobim

b. Jan. 25, 1927, Rio de Janeiro, Brazil, **d.** Dec. 8, 1994, New York, NY
Vocals, Piano, Guitar, Composer / Brazilian Jazz, Latin Folk, Latin Jazz, Bossa Nova, World Fusion, Brazil, Latin Continuum

It has been said that Antonio Carlos Brasileiro de Almeida Jobim was the George Gershwin of Brazil—and there is a solid ring of truth in that, for both contributed large bodies of songs to the jazz repertoire, both expanded their reach into the concert hall, and both tend to symbolize their countries in the eyes of the rest of the world. With their gracefully urbane, sensuously aching melodies and harmonies, Jobim's songs gave jazz musicians in the 1960s a quiet, strikingly original alternative to their traditional Tin Pan Alley source.

Jobim's roots were always planted firmly in jazz; the records of Gerry Mulligan, Chet Baker, Barney Kessel and other West Coast jazz musicians made an enormous impact upon him in the 1950s. But he also claimed that the French impressionist composer Claude Debussy had a decisive influence upon his harmonies, and the Brazilian samba gave his music a uniquely exotic rhythmic underpinning. As a pianist, he usually kept things simple and melodically to the point with a touch that reminds some of Claude Thornhill, but some of his records show that he could also stretch out when given room. His guitar was limited mostly to gentle strumming of the syncopated rhythms, and he sang in a modest, slightly hoarse yet often hauntingly emotional manner.

Born in the Tijuca neighborhood of Rio, Jobim originally was headed for a career as an architect. Yet by the time he turned 20, the lure of music was too powerful, and so he started playing piano in nightclubs and working in recording studios. He made his first record in 1954 backing singer Bill Farr as the leader of "Tom and His Band" (Tom was Jobim's lifelong nickname), and he first found fame in 1956 when he teamed up with poet Vinícius de Moraes to provide part of the score for a play called *Orfeo do Carnaval* (later made into the famous film *Black Orpheus*). In 1958, the then-unknown Brazilian singer Joao Gilberto recorded some of Jobim's songs, which had the effect of launching the phenomenon known as bossa nova. Jobim's breakthrough outside Brazil occured in 1962 when Stan Getz and Charlie Byrd scored a surprise hit with his tune "Desafinado"—and later that year, he and several other Brazilian musicians were invited to participate in a Carnegie Hall showcase. Fueled by Jobim's songs, the bossa nova became an international fad, and jazz musicians jumped on the bandwagon recording album after album of bossa novas until the trend ran out of commercial steam in the late '60s.

Jobim himself preferred the recording studios to touring, making several lovely albums of his music as a pianist, guitarist and singer for Verve, Warner Bros., Discovery, AM, CTI and MCA in the '60s and '70s, and Verve again in the last decade of his life. Early on, he started collaborating with arranger/conductor Claus Ogerman, whose subtle, caressing, occasionally moody charts gave his records a haunting ambience. When Brazilian music was in its American eclipse after the '60s, a victim of overexposure and the burgeoning rock revolution, Jobim retreated more into the background, concentrating much energy upon film and TV scores in Brazil. But by 1985, as the idea of world music and a second Brazilian wave gathered steam, Jobim started touring again with a group containing his second wife Ana Lontra, his son Paulo, daughter Elizabeth and various musician friends. At the time of his final concerts in Brazil in September 1993 and at Carnegie Hall in April 1994 (both available on Verve), Jobim at last was receiving the universal recognition he deserved, and a plethora of tribute albums and concerts followed in the wake of his sudden death in New York City of heart failure. Jobim's reputation as one of the great songwriters of the century is now secure, nowhere more so than on the jazz scene where every other set seems to contain at least one bossa nova. *—Richard S. Ginell*

The Composer Plays / May 9, 1963-May 10, 1963 / Verve ♦♦♦♦♦
In his first American album, Jobim presents a dozen of his songs, each one destined to become a standard—an astounding batting average. Jobim, who claimed to have been out of practice at the time of the session, merely plays single notes on the piano with one hand, punctuated by chords now and then, sticking to his long, undulating melodies with a few passages of jazz improvisation now and then. Yet it is a lovely idea, not a gesture is wasted. Arranger Claus Ogerman unveils many of the trademarks that would define his Creed Taylor-produced albums with Jobim—the soaring, dying solo flute and spare, brooding unison string lines widening into lush harmony; flutes doubling on top of Jobim's piano chords—again with an exquisitely spare touch. The songs include "Desafinado," "Corcovado," "Chega de Saudade" (No More Blues), "The Girl From Ipanema," "Meditation," "One Note Samba" and half-a-dozen others (every one of which is included on *The Man from Ipanema.* set) *—Richard S. Ginell*

★ **The Man from Ipanema** / 1963-1994 / Verve ♦♦♦♦♦
Issued nearly a year after Jobim's death, this three-CD set is ground zero, the place to start if you don't have any Jobim in your collection or for anyone who wants a single package of his multifaceted art. The set encompasses not only Jobim's own sporadic work for Verve from 1963 until his final 1994 *Carnegie Hall* concert and the two *AM* albums of 1967 and 1970, but also sessions led by Stan Getz, Joao, and Astrud Gilberto in which Jobim appeared as a sideman. Guitarist Oscar Castro-Neves, who selected the music for this set, follows a unique game plan, devoting disc one to vocal renditions of Jobim's songs, disc two to instrumental versions, and disc three to multiple comparisons of a few Jobim standards by different performers. The selections are often adventurous, and the programming digs deeply into Jobim's PolyGram catalog for such overlooked gems as the bossa waltz "Mojave," the sly "Captain Bacardi," and the self-mocking "Chansong." For casual listening, discs one and two flow beautifully, and even disc three works, for despite the repetition of tunes, the approaches are varied enough to keep one's attention. Jobim collectors probably have almost everything on the set anyway, as there are no unreleased tracks other than a humorous uncredited rehearsal of "Aguas de Marco" tacked onto the end of "Vivo Sonhando." But they are certain to be attracted by the unique packaging—a double-spiraled fold-out book containing lots of fascinating interviews and essays, and three discs wrapped in paper cutouts environmentally designed to look like fish, flowers, and leaves. The CD era's most imaginative graphics department has done it again. *—Richard S. Ginell*

Composer / Sep. 1965-1968 / Warner Brothers ♦♦♦

★ **Wave** / May 22, 1967-May 24, 1967 / A&M ♦♦♦♦♦
When Creed Taylor left Verve/MGM for his own label under the auspices of *AM,* he quickly signed Jobim and they picked up right where they left off with this stunningly seductive record, possibly Jobim's best. Jobim contributes his sparely rhythmic acoustic guitar, simple melodic piano style, a guest turn at the harpsichord, and even a vocal on "Lamento," while Claus Ogerman is on board lending a romantically brooding hand with the charts. A pair of instant standards are introduced ("Wave," "Triste") but what makes this album so cherishable are the absolutely first rate tunes—actually miniature tone poems—that escaped overexposure and thus sound fresh today. The most beautiful sleeper is "Batidinha," where the intuitive Jobim/Ogerman collaboration reaches its peak. One only wishes that this album were longer; 31:45 is not enough. *—Richard S. Ginell*

Stone Flower / Mar. 16, 1970-May 22, 1970 / Epic/CTI ♦♦♦♦♦
Recorded during the same period as *Tide* with the same producer (Creed Taylor), arranger (Eumir Deodato), and musicians, *Stone Flower* is a stronger record, leading one to speculate that *Tide* may have been released to fulfill Taylor's and Jobim's *AM* contracts just as Taylor was forming his own CTI label. Jobim is in a more expansive mood, displaying a swinging samba touch at some length on electric piano in the only non-Jobim song, "Brazil," and Deodato's charts are more subtle and atmospheric. Also Jobim draws from superior material, pulling away from the bossa nova in the direction of the emerging CTI sound, with excursions into darker Brazilian interiors. Most striking are the exotically-shaped title track (soon to be covered by Latin rock group Santana), the haunting "Children's Games" (better known as "Double Rainbow"), and the frightening "God and The Devil in the Land of the Sun." CD buyers get an extra take of "Brazil" as a bonus. *—Richard S. Ginell*

Tide / May 1970 / Polygram Brazil ♦♦♦
On Jobim's second *AM* album, Eumir Deodato takes over the chart-making tasks, and the difference between him and Claus Ogerman is quite apparent in the remake of "The Girl From Ipanema": the charts are heavier, more dramatic, and structured. Sometimes the arrangements roll back so one can hear, say, the dancing multi-phonic flute of wildman Hermeto Pascoal on "Tema Jazz," and the rhythms often veer away from the familiar ticking of the bossa nova. Jobim is his usual understated self, adding very subtle electric piano to his arsenal of acoustic piano and guitar, but the material sometimes falls short of Jobim's tip-top level (dead giveaway: "Tide" is a clever rewrite on the chord changes of "Wave"). Still, it's beautifully made and very musical at all times. *—Richard S. Ginell*

Jobim / Dec. 11, 1972-Dec. 13, 1972 / Verve ♦♦♦

Elis & Tom / Feb. 22, 1974-Mar. 9, 1974 / Verve ♦♦♦♦♦
Elis Regina, a cool, feminine Brazilian singer who died tragically of cocaine/alcohol poisoning at age 36, made this often deeply affecting album with Jobim in Los Angeles for the Brazilian market only; it was not released in the U.S. until 1989. While there is plenty of bossa nova here, the arrangements at times reflect the more cinematic, more inward directions that Jobim's music was taking, and the lyrics often speak even more harrowingly of heartbreak than ever. Yet this pair can also celebrate Jobim's music, as they do in a rendition of "Aguas de Marco" that nearly collapses in unself-conscious laughter. Throughout, Regina is in the spotlight, with Jobim a supporting, sometimes invisible, always pervasive presence. *—Richard S. Ginell*

Urubu / Nov. 1976 / Warner Archives ♦♦♦♦♦
Urubu is the album that MCA's *Jobim* probably aspired to be, a total break away from the bossa nova past that is both ambitious and strikingly original. The shock of dissonant strings, percussive and wind sounds from the Brazilian interior greet us on the first track "Bôto," the first of four songs in which a defiant Jobim throws structural complexities at us and sings in Portuguese only. The second four tracks are an even more radical departure; all are classical orchestral pieces, melancholy and even anguished in tone, owing little or nothing to anyone, streaked with imaginative, even avant-garde orchestral touches from Claus Ogerman. Clearly we are not on the Ipanema beach anymore, and although this may be rough going for jazz-minded Jobim fans, the payoff is a glimpse into the depths of Jobim's soul. *—Richard S. Ginell*

Terra Brasilis / 1980 / Warner Archives ♦♦♦♦

Passarim / 1987 / Verve ♦♦♦♦♦
Passarim is Jobim's major statement of the '80s, emerging during a time when Jobim's concerns were turning increasingly toward Planet Earth issues. The title song is one of Jobim's most haunting creations, a cry of pain about the the destruction of the Brazilian rainforest that resonates in the memory for hours. Also, by this time Jobim had resumed touring with a large group containing friends and family, and they carry a great deal of the load here, with lots of airy female backup vocals, two worthy songs by Jobim's multi-talented son Paulo and another by flutist/singer Danilo Caymmi. Recorded entirely in Rio, the record's overall sound is very different from Jobim's '60s and '70s work—denser, hazier, still grounded in the samba yet rougher in texture (as is Jobim's voice). Though not as immediately winning as the Creed Taylor-produced albums, this music repays repeated listening—particularly the extended suite from Jobim's score for the film *Gabriela*—and there are samples of Jobim's wry humor in "Chansong" and the bossa nova reworking of "Fascinatin' Rhythm" *—Richard S. Ginell*

Antonio Carlos Jobim and Friends / Sep. 27, 1993 / Verve ♦♦♦♦♦

Antonio Brasilero / 1995 / Sony International ♦♦♦♦

Girl from Ipanema: The Antonio Carlos Jobim Songbook / Feb. 13, 1962-Nov. 16, 1988 / Verve ♦♦♦♦♦
The first of several tribute albums issued just after Jobim's death, this one generally sticks to Jobim's most famous songs as interpreted by several Brazilian and American artists from PolyGram's archives. Jobim himself appears on such obvious choices as the best-selling Stan Getz/Joao and Astrud Gilberto hit "The Girl From Ipanema," and with Astrud on "Agua De Beber" and "Dindi," and again with the late Elis Regina on an "Aguas de Marco" that nearly

breaks up with laughter. The American contributions are a mixed bag; Sarah Vaughan's "Corcovado," for example, is rather inappropriately overwrought but Wes Montgomery's "How Insensitive" is a beautiful recording, with Jobim's favored arranger Claus Ogerman in top wistful form. The other jazzers on the CD are Billy Eckstine, Ella Fitzgerald, Oscar Peterson, Shirley Horn and Dizzy Gillespie, proving that Jobim's timelessly aching music attracted quite a diverse cross-section of admirers. *—Richard S. Ginell*

Wave: Antonio Carlos Jobim Songbook / Feb. 13, 1962-Nov. 6, 1994 / Verve ✦✦✦✦✦
The sequel to the popular *The Girl from Ipanema* anthology basically reshuffles the deck, duplicating nine of the earlier CD's songs and adding six new ones, using mostly the same performers with a few additions. The new wrinkle is that the artists perform different tunes, a game that one imagines could be continued indefinitely on future issues. Among the highlights: Ella Fitzgerald has a marvelous time bouncing to the rhythms of "So Danco Samba," Wes Montgomery the consummate musician scores again with a lovely "Amor Em Paz," Oscar Peterson is a surreal speed demon on "Triste." Lowlight: Sarah Vaughan's awkwardly mannered "The Boy For Ipanema." Again, there is plenty of Stan Getz—along with his tenor sax successor in matters Jobim, Joe Henderson—plus Astrud and Joao Gilberto, Dizzy Gillespie, Toots Thielemans, Charlie Byrd, Herbie Hancock, Chick Corea, Pat Metheny, and Jobim himself. As a jazz buff's introduction to Jobim, either *Songbook* will do, but Verve's *The Man From Ipanema* triple album is the best, most comprehensively idiomatic choice overall. *—Richard S. Ginell*

Rita Lee

Vocals / Brazilian Pop, MPB, Tropicalia, Dance-Pop, Brazil, Latin Continuum
Rita Lee is a central figure in Brazilian rock. A former member of the seminal rock band Os Mutantes, she eventually departed from that group and began an extremely successful solo career in the rock and dance styles which has been spanning for more than 30 years.

Rita formed her first band with two other friends, but later formed the seminal Os Mutantes with brothers Arnaldo and Sérgio Dias Baptista. The band recorded several albums in the late '60s before Rita recorded her first solo album, 1970's *Build Up*. After one more solo album, 1972's *Hoje é o Primeiro Dia do Resto de Sua Vida*, she departed from the group and began writing the material which would make her famous as a solo artist, hits like "Ovelha Negra," "Agora só Falta Você," and "Esse Tal de Roque Enrow." Though 1979's "Mania de Você" became her biggest hit, Rita fired her band and became a true solo singer. With "Lança Perfume" she achieved international recognition, and in the early '80s she made great success recording "Joujou e Balangandãs" together with João Gilberto.

While her albums, openly danceable and fully committed to a commercial result, were breaking all selling records, she began having health problems, though she bounced back to release several more albums during the '80s. In 1990, she performed in her show *Bossa n' Roll*, which had the greatest audience in that year. After an album recorded with her early companion L´cia Turnbull, she toured with *A Marca da Zorra*. In the following year, she became the first woman and first pop icon to be awarded with the Prêmio Shell de MPB. *—Alvaro Neder*

● **Fruto Proibido** / 1975 / EMI ✦✦✦✦✦
Rita Lee, a former member of the seminal rock band Os Mutantes, always had lots to say about Brazilian rock, but she spent most of her post-Mutantes career on innocuous dance grooves. On this CD reissue of the album recorded in 1975, she is a truthful rock artist. Backed by the strong grip of her rock band Tutti Frutti, she delivers some of her biggest hits here: "Agora Só Falta Você," "Esse Tal de Roque Enrow" (composed with mega-selling esoteric writer Paulo Coelho, when he was an alternative rock composer [he was the main partner of the late rocker Raul Seixas]), and the eternal "Ovelha Negra," the anthem of the rebellious youngsters in Brazil. Lee can be a singer as competent in wild rock as in softer ballads when she acquires a girlish, tender quality. The album is a document of a time when she could be truthful about her ideals. *—Alvaro Neder*

Babilonia / 1978 / EMI ✦✦✦
This is the CD reissue of the LP recorded in 1978, the last with Rita Lee's band Tutti Frutti. It revealed the direction she would take in her subsequent releases: less rock & roll and more dance orientated. The album is extremely different from *Fruto Proibido*, released three years before. It played well, which confirmed her commercial approach. Several tracks became hits: "Miss Brasil 2000," "Disco Voador," "Agora é Moda," "Jardins da Babilônia," "O Futuro Me Absolve," and "Eu E Meu Gato" (theme of a broadly popular soap opera). *—Alvaro Neder*

Rita Lee Em Bossa 'n Roll / 1992 / Som Livre ✦✦✦✦

Acustico (Portuguese) / Nov. 24, 1998 / Polygram ✦✦✦✦✦
In this acoustic production for MTV Brasil, Rita Lee competently revisits her old successes with important guests: Cássia Eller, Osvaldinho do Acordeon, Armandinho, Paula Toller, Milton Nascimento, Titãs, and her old guitarist (from the Tutti-Frutti band) Lee Marcucci. Rogério Duprat is still a vigorous and dissonant orchestral rock arranger, as shown by the strings and brasses in "O Gosto Do Azedo." The album focuses on tight acoustic rock/ballad performances for her old hits, like "Agora Só Falta Você," "Mania de Você," "Jardins Da Babilônia," "Doce Vampiro," "Luz Del Fuego," the Raul Seixas classic "Gitâ," and 12 other songs. *—Alvaro Neder*

3001 / 2000 / Polygram ✦✦✦✦

Ivan Lins

b. 1945
Vocals, Piano / Brazilian Pop, MPB, Samba, Brazil, Latin Continuum
Renowned as a carioca songwriter, vocalist, and pianist, Ivan Lins recorded several albums for EMI Brasil and Reprise as well as writing Brazilian standards. Born in 1945, Lin came to fame in Brazil in 1970 when Elis Regina recorded his song "Magdalena" for a hit. His worldwide debut, *A Noite*, appeared in 1979. Ivan Lins' most famous composition, "Love Dance" ("Lembrança"), has been recorded by dozens of jazz artists including Kenny Burrell, Sarah Vaughan, Betty Carter, Nancy Wilson, Mark Murphy, George Benson, Diane Schuur, and James Blood Ulmer. Other noted songs by Lins ("The Island," "Comecar de Novo," "Dona Palmeira," "Nocturna") have been recorded by artists including Airto Moreira, Herbie Mann, and Terence Blanchard. *—John Bush*

A Noite / 1979 / Odeon ✦✦✦✦✦
This album contains impassioned performances of some of Lins's best-known songs—"Antes Que SejaTarde," "Comecar de Novo" ("The Island"), and "Velas" (a Grammy winner as recorded by Quincy Jones). *—Terri Hinte*

Awa Yio / 1990 / Reprise ✦✦✦✦
This album reflects the seven-year international experience of Ivan Lins, with the careful production by Stewart Levine and Larry Williams. The thoughtful balance between Brazilian elements turned more palatable to international audiences through pop touches made it a big hit, the patriotic "Meu País." All lyrics in this album are from Vítor Martins (with a bit of Aldir Blanc), his longtime musical partner, and his business partner since the previous year when the label that released this and other Lins' albums, Velas. Lins' lyrics are all the way Brazilian, using regional expressions and praising the country's beauties. Most songs are quite rhythmic, using Caribbean grooves ("Ai Ai Ai Ai Ai"), samba ("Leva E Traz," a tribute to the unforgettable Elis Regina, with the valuable Brazilian seven-string violão by the great late Rafael Rabello), ballads ("Que Quer de Mim," "Meu País"), and Afro-pop ("Clareou," with a bright trumpet solo by South African Hugh Masekela). *—Alvaro Neder*

Meus Momentos / 1994 / EMI ✦✦✦✦

Vivanoel / 1997 / Velas ✦✦✦✦✦
Ivan Lins has been a distinguished Brazilian interpreter/composer for some decades. On this two-album project, he pays tribute to one of the best Brazilian composers of all time: Noel Rosa. The music of Rosa is quite frankly eternal, but is always endangered by the excessive greed of the recording business, which insists in piling up too much trash over it. In this album, Lins does a faithful interpretation of Rosa's work, but didn't limit himself to a traditionalistic approach. The true Rosa spirit is there, but the interpretation is modern—and purely Brazilian and Carioca. The musicians, all experienced professionals among the best in Brazil, deliver with competence and sensitivity a subtle contemporary samba. And Lins, even if he lacks the true, hot swing of the hills, is respectful enough of the tradition to provide a satisfactory interpretation for Rosa's classics. He has also several welcomed guests, important sambistas Nelson Sargento, Nei Lopes, Zeca Pagodinho, Arlindo Cruz, Sombrinha, Época de Ouro, along with Chico Buarque, and several others. This is one of the best tributes to Rosa so far, until the complete compilation of his works by Omar Jubran comes out. *—Alvaro Neder*

Anjo de Mim / Nov. 10, 1998 / Import ✦✦✦✦

A Cor Do Pôr-do-sol / 2000 / Abril ✦✦✦✦

● **A Love Affair: The Music of Ivan Lins** / Sep. 26, 2000 / Telarc ✦✦✦✦✦
Bring together an all-star lineup of singers and musicians, match them with accessibly romantic melodies and radio-friendly arrangements, and the results will either be lightweight pabulum or superb high-quality pop music. In the case of producer Jason Miles' *A Love Affair*, it's unquestionably the latter. Even after 30 years on the world music scene, Brazilian musician/composer Ivan Lins may not have had a high profile. However, as this tribute recording demonstrates, his music is as fine as anything that has come out of his native country since the bossa nova heyday of the early '60s. Taken individually, each of these songs is a piece of joyous musical exuberance. Taken as a whole, this recording is better than an hour with any radio station you're going to find on the dial or online. *A Love Affair* opens with the never before recorded "She Walks This Earth," a performance by Sting that is as good as anything he's recorded as a solo artist. Vanessa Williams has never sounded better than on the sultry "Love Dance," and "So Crazy for This Love" is a piece of funk featuring a multi-tracked Chaka Khan purring a deceptively complex, original, and memorable melody that also has "hit" written all over it. Grover Washington Jr. defines smooth jazz with his ride through "Camaleao," while Freddy Cole recalls a smokier version of his brother Nat in his reading of the beautiful ballad "I'm Not Alone." Lins himself plays piano on several tracks and closes the album with a vocal of his own on "Somos Todos Iquais Nesta Noite." Kudos go to producer Miles for bringing this remarkable assemblage together, and a special mention is due to guitarist Romero Lubambo and percussionist Cyro Baptista, whose work throughout the recording is exemplary. Don't miss this CD. *—Jim Newsom*

Ed´ Lobo

b. 1943
Vocals, Guitar / Brazilian Pop, Latin Jazz, Bossa Nova, MPB, Brazil, Latin Continuum
A driving force behind the rise of the MPB (Musica Popular Brasileira) sound, singer/composer Ed´ Lobo was born in Rio de Janeiro in 1943; at 18 he formed his first trio with Dori Caymmi and the great Marcus Valle, and in 1962 forged a long-term writing partnership with renowned lyricist Vinicius de Moraes. Drawing influence from bossa nova masters including Antonio Carlos Jobim, João Gilberto and Baden Powell, Lobo released his debut LP *A Musica de Ed´ Lobo por Ed´ Lobo* in 1963; that same year he also authored the music for Oduvaldo Vianna Filho's play *Os Azerados Mais Os Benvidos*, the first of many stage collaborations. The album *Cinco Na Bossa*, recorded with Nara Leão and the Tamba Trio, followed in 1965, the same year Lobo took top honors at the First Annual Brazilian Popular Musical Festival with his composition "Arrastão," a major hit for singer Elis Regina. (In 1967, he repeated the feat with "Ponteio.")

Albums including 1968's *Ed´* followed before Lobo met Sergio Mendes in 1969, resulting in a contract with A&M Records for *From the Hot Afternoon*, which featured saxophonist Paul Desmond; by now a resident of Los Angeles, he toured with Mendes and Brasil 66 before resurfacing in 1971 with *Sergio Mendes Presents Lobo*, followed later that same year by *Cantiga de Longe*. Upon returning to Brazil, Lobo focused his energies on composing for films before returning to the studio for 1973's *Missa Breve;* he then spent the mid-1970s writing music for Globo, the world's fourth-largest television network, including work on the hit series *Caso Especial.* 1976 saw the release of the LP *Limite Das Aguas,* with the widely-acclaimed *Camaleão* appearing two years later; in 1979, Lobo's score to the feature *Barra Pesada* earned "Best Soundtrack" honors at the Gramado Film Festival.

Lobo inaugurated the 1980s with a flurry of activity, following the LP *Tempo Presente* with the 1981 soundtrack *Jogos de Danca* (a work composed for the Ballet Guaira) as well as *Tom e Edu,* a collaboration with Antonio Carlos Jobim. In the wake of two more ballet scores, *O Grande Circo Mistico* and *Gabriela,* Lobo worked on a series of stage musicals—*Vargas, O Corsario do Rei* and *Danca da Meia-Lua*—before finally returning to the studio in 1990 for the LP *Serie Personalidade. Corrupião* followed in 1993, and two years later he returned with *Meia Noite.* The score to the 1997 film *Guerra de Canudos* preceded Lobo's next project, a planned adaptation of Jo Soares' book *A Samba for Sherlock.* —Jason Ankeny

★ **Sergio Mendes Presents Lobo** / 1969-1971 / A&M ✦✦✦✦✦
Edu Lobo is one of the least-celebrated of the major songwriting lions of the first Brazilian wave, and a talented performer in his own right—which his first North American album makes stunningly clear. Painstakingly produced by one of Lobo's most persistent advocates, Sergio Mendes, the album overflows with cunningly-devised, first-class tunes like "Ponteio," "To Say Goodbye," the marathon "Crystal Illusions," "Casa Forte," and the irresistible "Jangada." Some have Portuguese lyrics, some are in English, but others simply use sharp scatted syllables, an art at which the low-key but nimble-tongued Lobo excels.

The material is so strong that one wonders why the Beatles' "Hey Jude" had to be added to the lineup (presumably to attract a wider audience for the record, which it didn't). The backings strip down the base of Sergio Mendes' Brasil '66 sound to its rhythm section, fortified by the playful and enigmatic electric piano and flute multiphonics of Hermeto Pascoal (who also had a big hand in the arrangements), Airto Moreira's multifaceted percussion talents, and an occasional cello quartet. Collectors of Brazilian jazz should seek this one out wherever the search may take them. *—Richard S. Ginell*

Cantiga De Longe / 1971 / Polygram ✦✦✦✦✦
This is the CD reissue of a 1970 LP. With a few more instrumental solos than the regular Lobo albums, this one takes advantage of the genius of the arranger/instrumentalist Hermeto Pascoal. The album has other stars, including percussionist Airto Moreira and drummer Cláudio Slom. There are several important songs on this album: "Casa Forte" (which would be recorded later by Flora Purim), "Mariana, Mariana," "Cantiga de Longe," "Zanzibar," and others. Not Lobo's biggest hits, but beautiful melodies/lyrics on an album with stronger instrumental support. *—Alvaro Neder*

Tempo Presente / 1980 / Philips ✦✦✦✦

Minha Historia / 1987 / Philips/Polygram ✦✦✦

Marisa Monte

Vocals / Brazilian Pop, MPB, Brazil, Latin Continuum

Of the more recent crop of Brazilian singers, easily one of the most stunning is Marisa Monte. Born in Rio de Janiero in 1967, Monte began studying music at the age of 14. Under the influence of the great samba, bossa nova, and tropicalia performers of the '60s and '70s (e.g., Joao and Astrud Gilberto, Caetano Veloso, Gilberto Gil, and Antonio Carlos Jobim), Monte saw herself as a part of the next generation of Brazilian singers that would continue this uniquely Brazilian sound while interpolating elements of international jazz and pop singers. As with most young women growing up in Brazil in the '70s, Monte was greatly influenced by Elis Regina; she didn't try to sing exactly like Regina (her voice simply isn't as big), but she did adopt the latter's supple phrasing and emotionally charged delivery.

In the late '80s, Monte spent some time studying European classical singing in Rome, returning to Brazil on a mission to combine the knowledge she had gleaned abroad with the music of her native country. The result was an extraordinary pop music that was as adventurous as it was tuneful. It was her second record, *Mais,* that brought Monte to the attention of a global pop audience. A huge hit in Brazil (where it went platinum), *Mais* was notable for its use of Arto Lindsay (the Brazilian-bred noise rocker of DNA) as producer, as well as the contributions of such eclectic sidemen as Nana Vasconcelos, Ryuichi Sakamoto, and John Zorn. The success of *Mais* led to Monte touring internationally, including her first gigs in America and Europe and a triumphant performance at the Montreux Jazz Festival. Despite the worldwide acclaim, Monte remains devoted to Brazil in that her popularity there is more important to her than establishing worldwide superstardom (which, if she were willing to be more Madonna-like, could happen almost overnight; thankfully, she has chosen a different route to stardom).

Since *Mais,* Monte has released two more excellent records, 1994's *Rose and Charcoal,* and arguably her best effort, 1996's *A Great Noise,* both produced by Arto Lindsay. Both releases show off her growing maturity, savvy songwriting, and good choice of cover songs, but more importantly, they reveal a maturing voice and performance style that is among the best to have emerged from Brazil in the last 20 years. In mid-2000 *Memories, Chronicles and Declarations of Love* was released. *—John Dougan*

Mais / Jun. 10, 1991 / World Pacific ✦✦✦
Marisa Monte, a very warm, charismatic and vulnerable artist, turned out to be one of Brazil's top female vocalists of the 1990s. *Mais* proves that her popularity is well deserved. Most of the songs on this CD, which did a lot to establish her success, are quite memorable—including the humorous "Diaramente," the charming "Rosa" and Caetano Veloso's playful "De Noite Na Cama." Drawing on both Brazilian and American influences, Monte is someone who, with the right exposure, could easily become as prominent in the U.S. as she is in Brazil. The thing that's kept this from happening is the assumption that English-speaking audiences won't be receptive to Portuguese lyrics. But whether or not one understands the lyrics, this is an album to savor. *—Alex Henderson*

● **Rose & Charcoal (Verde Anil Amarelo Cor de Rosa e Carvão)** / 1994 / Blue Note ✦✦✦✦✦
Marisa Monte is one of the best figures of today's Brazilian pop (a category that does not comprise pure samba, choro, canção, baião, and other Brazilian popular musics). While most new bands and interpreters center their work on futile material and focus on easy formulas and clichés, she is concerned in really adding something to the superb tradition of MPB, which is quite a challenging task. This is her third album, where, with special guests Philip Glass, Laurie Anderson, Gilberto Gil, Paulinho da Viola, Velha Guarda da Portela, Época de Ouro, Naná Vasconcelos, Carlinhos Brown, and others, she delivers some of her hits: "Maria de Verdade," "Na Estrada," "Segue O Seco," "Dança Da Solidão," "De Mais Ninguém," "Bem Leve," and "Balança Pema." One of the best pop albums from the '90s, she makes clear that she is after a new language in which the respect for the rich musical tradition of Brazil is evident. *—Alvaro Neder*

Barulhinho Bom / 1996 / EMI ✦✦✦✦✦
In the 21st century mainstream pop scene of Brazil, Marisa Monte is one of the few young successful artists concerned with delivering music based in the rich culture of that country, which has yielded her an unwanted "cult" tag. While most pop productions overflow with electronic drum machines and keyboards, taken from the beginning to the end by American grooves, this album evidences a search for a personal synthesis of the required elements for a successful commercial career together with a respectful treatment to the Brazilian music richness. One of the discs of this double-album release was recorded live during her Northeastern tour *Cor-de-rosa E Carvão* from 1994; it is no surprise that she included several Northeastern instruments (like accordion and percussion) and grooves, which add to the album's interest. The songs cover two hits from the Tropicália times, "Panis Et Circensis" (Caetano Veloso/Gilberto Gil) and "Cérebro Eletrônico" by Gilberto Gil (her vocal delivery here is clearly inspired by Gal Costa's). Also deserving mention is a beautiful samba by the authentic composer Paulinho da Viola, "A Dança da Solidão," which was again a big hit in her interpretation. The rest of the 16 songs are divided between Monte's originals, hits by the latest generation of Brazilian pop composers, and other hits, including George Harrison's "Give Me Love" (the only foreign composition). *—Alvaro Neder*

A Great Noise / Jan. 14, 1997 / Capitol ✦✦✦

Memories, Chronicles and Declarations of Love / Aug. 15, 2000 / Blue Note ✦✦✦✦
On this album, the always correct Marisa Monte preferred to stick to pop grooves, instead of the strong adherence to Brazilian rhythms heard in some of her previous albums. There are exceptions, though. "Abololô" is an exquisite rendition for a beautiful melody in a typical Northeastern modal scale (Lydian b7), which sounds pretty exotic, haunting in a sad piano backing, shocking with the expectation of a full-steam percussive regional, representing a welcomed expansion of the tradition. Also in the same line, "Para Ver As Meninas," a wonderful samba by Paulinho da Viola, receives a treatment where typical cavaquinhos and cuícas coexis with Jaques Morelembaum's cello and a stylized percussion. Nelson Cavaquinho/Guilherme de Brito's "Gotas de Luar" got a straightforward samba rendition where her sensitive voice is backed simply by a traditional samba violão and jazzy guitar counterchants. In an album dedicated to love, accordingly, one can find the romantic ballads "Amor I Love You," which has an excerpt of *Primo Basílio* (Eça de Queiroz) read by the former Titãs Arnaldo Antunes, "O Que Me Importa," and her "Gentileza." Also, the romantic song "Perdão Você" and the romantic Olodum (is there such a thing—) "Tema de Amor." The rest of the 13 songs are in medium tempo funk/soul or Olodum-like (maracatu). *—Alvaro Neder*

Os Mutantes

f. 1965, São Paulo, Brazil

Group / Obscuro, Foreign Language Rock, Brazilian Pop, MPB, Tropicalia, Brazil, Latin Continuum

A seminal rock band in Brazil, Os Mutantes used their solid musical background to take major pop/rock contributions from the Beatles and American bands and mix everything with deep electronics knowledge, Brazilian music, '60s psychedelia and irreverent attitude, creating a result which can be discerned in today's Brazilian pop.

Brothers Arnaldo and Sérgio Dias Baptista formed Mutantes with Rita Lee Jones in 1965. The bizarre outfit was backed by competence and inventiveness, such as insecticide cans which were perfect to simulate cymbals—and were used effectively in recording sessions. It was evident that their path was linked to tropicália—which had the same ideals proposed by Os Mutantes, in its salad of philosophy, cultural industry, and pop culture. Gilberto Gil was immediately attracted by their anarchic attitude, and invited them to back him and record their single "O Relógio." In 1968, they performed in the album-manifesto *Tropicália ou Panis et Circensis,* with Gil, Caetano Veloso, Gal Costa and Tom Zé. Soon after, they recorded their first LP (*Os Mutantes*), an unexpected translation of *Sgt. Pepper's* to the Brazilian idiom. In 1969, they recorded their second album, also self-titled. Among the band's own hits, they shamelessly included in that album the jingle "Algo Mais," which they had written for Shell Combustibles. The LP *A Divina Comédia* appeared in 1970, and *O Jardim Elétrico* the next.

Though Rita departed from the group not long after, the duo continued to play together, and advanced a progressive rock direction with *A E o Z.* In 1975, Os Mutantes recorded *Tudo Foi Feito Pelo Sol.* In the '90s, David Byrne began promoting their old recordings, which provoked a revival movement with plenty of reissuing of their albums. *—Alvaro Neder*

Os Mutantes / 1968 / Omplatten ✦✦✦✦✦
The band's debut album, *Os Mutantes,* is far and away their best—a wildly inventive trip that assimilates orchestral-pop, whimsical psychedelia, *musique concrète,* and found-sound environments—and that's just the first song! Elsewhere there are nods to Carnaval, albeit with distinct hippie sensibilities incorporating fuzz-tone guitars and go-go basslines. Two tracks, "O Relogio" and "Le Premier Bonheur du Jour," work through pastoral French pop, sounding closer to the Swingle Singers than Gilberto Gil. Though not all of the experimentation succeeds (the languid Brazilian blues of "Baby" is rather cumbersome), and pop/rock listeners may have a hard time finding the hooks, Os Mutantes' first album is an astonishing listen—far more experimental than any of the albums produced by the era's first-rate psychedelic bands of Britain or America. *—John Bush*

Mutantes / 1969 / Omplatten ✦✦✦✦
One album into their career in 1969, *Mutantes* showed few signs of musical burnout after turning in one of the oddest LPs released in the '60s. Similar to its predecessor, *Mutantes* is reliant on an atmosphere of experimentation and continual musical collisions that walk a fine line between innovation and pointless genre exercises. The lead track "Dom Quixote" has the same focus on stylistic cut-and-paste as their debut LP's first track "Panis et Circenses." Among contemporary music, *Mutantes*' tracks sound similar only to songs like the Who's miniature suite "A Quick One While He's Away"—though done in three minutes instead of nine, and much more confusing given the language barrier. The album highlights "Nao Va Se Perder por Ai" and "Dois Mil e Um" come with what sounds like a typically twisted take on roots music (both Brazilian and American), complete with banjo, accordion, and twangy vocals. Though there are several other enjoyable tracks, including "Magica" and a slap-happy stomp called "Rita Lee," there's a palpable sense that the experimentation here isn't serving much more than its own ends. If the first album's relentless eclecticism did in fact occasionally resulted in dry passages, it's especially true here. *—John Bush*

Divina Comedia Ou Ando Meio Desligado / 1970 / Omplatten ✦✦✦

E Seus Cometas No Pais Do Baurets / 1972 / Polydor ✦✦✦✦✦

● **Everything Is Possible: The Best of Os Mutantes** / Jun. 8, 1999 / Luaka Bop ✦✦✦✦✦
The first major-label release of Mutantes material was this 1999 compilation, put together by longtime Brazilian fan David Byrne through his Luaka Bop label. Including tracks from the band's late-'60s and early-'70s LPs (available separately through Omplatten), *Everything Is Possible* is a solid collection that only includes 14 tracks but does spotlight Mutantes' tremendous diversity. From the birth of tropicalia on their first album from 1968 (wildly experimental pop songs like "Panis Et Circenses" and "Bat Macumba") plus their later, more straight-ahead incarnations, the album gives beginners a solid place to start. The inclusion of both versions of the rather tiresome Janis Joplin retread "Baby" is a bit regrettable, but all around, *Everything Is Possible* gets it right better than could be hoped from a domestic compilation. *—John Bush*

Milton Nascimento

b. 1942, Rio de Janeiro, Brazil
Vocals, Piano, Guitar / Brazilian Pop, MPB, Samba, Brazil, Latin Continuum
International singing superstar and songwriter Milton Nascimento may have his roots in Brazil, but his songs have touched audiences all over the world.

Born in Rio, Nascimento's adoptive parents, both white, brought him to Tres Pontas, a small town in the state of Minas Gerais, when he was two. His mother sang in a choir and at local music festivals, often accompanied by Milton. Nascimento's father was an electronics tinkerer, math teacher and at one point ran a local radio station, where a young Milton occasionally worked as a DJ. He began singing as a teenager. When he was 19, Nascimento moved to the capital Belo Horizonte and began singing wherever and whenever he could. Finally he caught a break when the pop singer Elis Regina recorded one of his songs, "Cancao do Sal" in 1966. Regina got him a showcase on a popular Brazilian TV program, and after performing at Brazil's International Song Festival the following year, his career was launched.

In 1972 he collaborated with fellow lyricists Marcio Borges, Fernando Brant, Ronaldo Bastos and other friends to record *Clube Da Esquina*, a double album that spurred three hit singles, including "Cais (Dock)" and "Cravo e Canela (Clove and Cinnamon)." The singles are still being recorded and have become standards in Brazil over the years. Since he began recording with his self-titled debut in 1967 for the Codil label, Nascimento has written and recorded 28 albums.

Nascimento's many achievements include Grammy nominations for his *O Planeta Blue Na Estrada Do Sol* in 1992, and in 1995 for his Warner Bros. debut, *Angelus*. Nascimento is also winner of the 1992 *Down Beat* International Critics' Poll and the 1991 *Down Beat* Readers' Poll. Nascimento has toured throughout the U.S., Europe, Japan and Latin America.

His lengthy discography includes *Courage*, a 1969 album for A&M and *Milton Nascimento* that same year for EMI-Odeon; *Milton*, also for the EMI-Odeon label, recorded in 1970, and then four more albums for the label EMI-Odeon: *Clube Da Esquina* (1972), *Milagre Dos Peixes* (1973) *Milagre Dos Peixes (Ao Vivo)* (1973), and *Minas* (1975).

His other titles include *Native Dancer*, (CBS, 1976), *Geraes* (EMI-Odeon, 1976), *Milton* (A&M, 1977), *Clube Da Esquina 2* (EMI-Odeon, 1978), *A Brazilian Love Affair*, a collaboration with George Duke (1980, CBS Records), *Journey to Dawn* (1979, A&M Records), and a series of five albums for Ariola: *Sentinela* (1980); *Cacador De Mim* (1981); *Missa Dos Quilombos* (1982); *Anima* (1982), and *Milton Nascimento Ao Vivo*, (1983).

His output through the rest of the 1980s and '90s has been steady and reliable, though never musically predictable. Like any true jazz and pop veteran, Nascimento has a deep need to keep challenging himself, vocally, lyrically and stylistically. Nascimento's other releases include *Encontros E Despedidas* for Barclay in 1985, *Corazon Americano* for PolyGram in 1986, *A Barca Dos Amantes* for Barclay in 1986, *Milton/RPM* for Epic/CBS in 1987, *Yauarete* for CBS in 1987, *Miltons* in 1988 for CBS, *Txai* for the same label in 1990 and *O Planeta Blue Na Estrada Do Sol* for CBS in 1991.

In the mid-'90s, Nascimento switched to Warner Bros. He released two excellent, readily available albums for the label, *Angelus*, his 27th recording, in 1995 and *Amigo*, his 28th, in 1996.

This charismatic Brazilian superstar just won't slow down any time soon, and whether he's packing a stadium in Brazil or singing at a club in New York, his experienced stage persona allows everyone in the audience to feel as if they're in his living room. On *Angelus*, he's joined by saxophonist Wayne Shorter, who pays tribute to Nascimento's 1975 *Native Dancer* LP, the high point of which was the synthesis between Nascimento's voice and Shorter's saxophone. That album helped to solidify Nascimento's place on the international jazz and pop scene in the 1970s. Whatever he writes and sings about, be it the planet, our ways of living and loving and dieing, his music has always carried an eternally optimistic spirit. As he entered the millennium, Nascimento won a Grammy for Best Contemporary Pop Album for 1999's *Crooner* at the first annual Latin Grammy Awards in fall 2000. *—Richard Skelly*

Personalidade: The Best of Brazil / 1990 / Verve ✦✦✦
One of Brazilian PolyGram's anthologies of homegrown music, this volume offers a cross-section of Milton Nascimento's Brazilian output from 1980 to 1985, with a sidetrip way back to the unforgettable tune that launched him in 1967, "Travessia." From North American rock/funk—a live rendition of a tune dedicated to the Beatles, "Para Lennon e McCartney"—to smooth-textured pop, lush electronic backdrops, a mournful Villa-Lobos melody ("Cantiga"), and various Brazilian backgrounds, this CD reflects the multiplicity of influences that the Brazilian superstar had been pulling in. Alas, with tiny exceptions like the presence of Hubert Laws' bright flute on "Encontros e Despedidas," the emphasis on Brazilian popular music slights Nascimento's associations with jazz. Still, since most of this material was not released in North America, this sampler—not too hard to find in big cities—will give you the basic idea. *—Richard S. Ginell*

★ **Courage** / Dec. 19, 1968-Feb. 27, 1969 / A&M ✦✦✦✦✦
Milton Nascimento's first album for North American ears, recorded at *Van Gelder Studios* in New Jersey under the watchful eye and discerning ear of Creed Taylor, is a masterpiece, a gorgeously executed tour through his early songs. Backed beautifully by Eumir Deodato's lush orchestrations and a clutch of sidemen from the Taylor stable (including Herbie Hancock, Airto Moreira and Hubert Laws), Nascimento unveils one first-class tune after another, many of which would ignite a rush of cover versions. Among the songs North Americans heard for the first time were "Vera Cruz," "Tres Pontas," "Morro Velho," the scatted "Catavento," and the intensely moving "*Bridges* (*Travessia*)"—the latter which launched Nascimento's name on the world music scene. Singing in English, Portuguese and often, no words at all, Nascimento's odd yet masculine and expressive baritone stands out like a moaning foghorn from the smooth *AM*/Taylor sonic formula, a haunting combination. This was Nascimento before tropicalismo, when he latched onto the tail end of the bossa nova movement and quickly became one of its most inspired performers and songwriters. To some admirers, *Courage* remains his best record, period. *—Richard S. Ginell*

★ **Clube Da Esquina** / 1972 / EMI Hemisphere ✦✦✦✦✦
This is the CD reissue of a classic double LP recorded in 1972 by Milton Nascimento and Lô Borges. The album had orchestrations of Eumir Deodato and Wagner Tiso under the conduction of the renowned clarinetist/composer/orchestrator Paulo Moura. The title *Clube da Esquina* is related to the gang of mineiros (people from the Minas Gerais state) that populate this release, either singing compositions or vocal/instrumental performances, like Nascimento and Borges themselves: Wagner Tiso, Beto Guedes, Milton Guedes, Tavito, Toninho Horta, Márcio Borges, Ronaldo Bastos, and Fernando Brant, among others. The album covers a great number of Clube da Esquina hits, like "Tudo Que Você Podia Ser," "Cais," "O Trem Azul," "Caravo E Canela," "Um Girassol da Cor do Seu Cabelo," "San Vicente," "Clube da Esquina No. 2," and so many others, with the competent backing of some of the best musicians in Brazil, including bassist Luiz Alves and percussionist Robertinho Silva. A must-have. *—Alvaro Neder*

Milagre Dos Peixes / 1973 / Intuition ✦✦✦✦✦
One of Milton Nascimento's most experimental albums, *Milagre Dos Peixes* was originally released in 1974. Accompanied by the Som Imaginário, Nascimento presented this album in a theater show in Rio and São Paulo, with orchestra, and the result live recorded and released on a double album called *Milagre Dos Peixes Ao Vivo*. In one of the worst periods of military dictatorship, all lyrics were systematically censored, the reason why the album is instrumental. Not entirely, to be sure. He can be heard crying "Eu Tô Cansado" (I Am Tired), and he also sings the lyrics of "Sacramento," having the boy Nico Borges delivering "Pablo" with that mixture, so dear to Nascimento, of a poor boy's ingenuity filled with a religious aura. It can be said that this album was especially suited for the talents of Naná Vasconcelos, who adds so much life to it. A must-have classic. *—Alvaro Neder*

Geraes / 1976 / Odeon ✦✦✦✦✦
This is the CD reissue of an album recorded in 1976. At this point, Nascimento had an experience with fusion in the Som Imaginário, and with jazzers such as Herbie Hancock (who had recorded with him in the previous year's *Milton*) or Wayne Shorter (*Native Dancer*). In this album, Nascimento experiments economically with orchestra, trying to recover his roots, the culture of the Minas Gerais state, whose already strong civilization made possible an expressive Baroque and sacred music in the 17th century. Therefore, the atmosphere here is not as swinging, but it reaches deeper emotional dimensions in some hits like the bucolic "Fazenda," the religious folkloric "Calix Bento," the Latin "Volver a los 17," the fundamental "O Cio da Terra," and others. The album also has special guest Chico Buarque on his "O Que Será (¿ Flor da Pele)." *—Alvaro Neder*

Journey to Dawn / Aug. 1979 / A&M ✦✦✦✦

Anima / 1982 / Polydor ✦✦✦✦✦
This is a striking example of the essential Milton Nascimento that has made him a beloved figure in Brazil—a lush, eloquent, unified concept album that cries for universal happiness and personal fulfillment, lashes out briefly at hypocrisy, and haunts the memory with its often stirring tunes. The record opens boldly with a tone poem accurately entitled "Evocation of the Mountains," and a gorgeous lengthy opening vocalese with a plush string backdrop, and it ends simply with the unadorned voice of Nascimento urging us not to analyze things if we want to be happy. As powerful a stylistic antenna as ever, Nascimento utilizes the Brazilian folk instrumental group Uakti on the title track and "Coracao Brasileiro" and even inserts the low drone of a sitar very effectively on the latter. Caetano Veloso duets with Nascimento on "The Various Points of a Star," a ghostly Elis Regina closes "What Was Done for Real," and other well-known Nascimento sidekicks like keyboardist Wagner Tiso, rock-tinged guitarist Ricardo Silveira and drummer Robertinho Silva help out on several tracks. Nascimento's fans needn't be told twice to snap this one up. *—Richard S. Ginell*

Encontros E Despedidas / 1985 / Polydor ✦✦✦

Yauaretê (Black Panther) / 1987 / Columbia ✦✦✦
As the second Brazilian wave neared its crest, Milton Nascimento signed with CBS and brought forth a typically eclectic offering, with contributions from familiar collaborators Wagner Tiso, Robertinho Silva, Uakti, and some stellar North American admirers. The key coup of the record was Nascimento's duet with Paul Simon on the reflective "Dream Merchant" (he would later return the favor by appearing on Simon's brilliant Brazilian/African *The Rhythm of the Saints* album), with Herbie Hancock on electronic layered keyboards. Keyboardist Don Grusin, guitarist Eric Gale and drummer Alex Acuna turn up now and then, and Hancock and old collaborator Wayne Shorter almost—but not quite—take over "Mountain." The lovely "Heart Is My Master" is almost a lush throwback to his breakthrough in the bossa nova era—and indeed, he revisits one of his early standards, "Morro Velho," in an affectingly lush production supervised by Nascimento aficionado Quincy Jones. "Letter to the Republic" is a measured, post-military-government, state-of-the-state address by Nascimento to the Brazilian people, and the concluding "Songs and Moments" finds Milton Nascimento again addressing his fans directly, explaining why he does what he does. *—Richard S. Ginell*

Milton's / 1989 / Columbia ✦✦✦✦
Here Nascimento strips his normally expansive resources way down and basically uses just his own voice and guitar, Herbie Hancock's acoustic piano and synthesized bass, and Nana Vasconcelos' percussion, with occasional self-overdubs and choral interjections. For strict jazz fans, then, this release has an unusually high quota of interest; Hancock—who is in inspired, affectionate form throughout—gets lots of solo space, and we hear more of Nascimento's own driving, idiosyncratic guitar than usual. The songs, in collaboration with Nascimento's perennial lyricist Fernando Brant and others, overflow with Nascimento's unquenchable life force, having never abandoned the peace-and-love core of the 1960s. For openers, Nascimento delivers a touching note to actor River Phoenix well before the latter's tragically early death. There is also a hypnotic, revolving, vocalise version of "La Bamba" and he revisits earlier tunes like "San Vicente" and "Sock Ball, Marbles." This is unusually intimate Nascimento, but no less full and rich in impact. *—Richard S. Ginell*

Txai / 1990 / Columbia ✦✦✦
"Txai" is described as a term of respect for those who are allies of the forest—and such is the focus of this concept album, the end result of a fact-finding voyage through part of the northern Brazilian watershed. Utilizing forces ranging from a simple dialogue between Nascimento's baritone and percussion to a large orchestra and chorus (often arranged by Wagner Tiso), Nascimento shares his thoughts about the rivers and nature, ultimately warning us not to let the forces of capitalism destroy the Amazon rain forest (reinforced by a spoken passage written and narrated by actor River Phoenix). The songs are separated by wild-sounding interludes of folk music from the peoples of the region, and there is a fascinating vocal/percussion arrangement of Villa-Lobos' "Nozani Na." As much as one applauds the sentiments and sincerity of Nascimento—and as much as one wants to enjoy this record—one is still forced to admit that despite the unity of conception, Nascimento's own material isn't as strong as it could have been. But the record's ambition and the continued allure of Nascimento's voice will commend it to the dedicated fan. *—Richard S. Ginell*

Angelus / 1993-1994 / Warner Brothers ✦✦✦

Amigo / Sep. 22, 1994 / Warner Brothers ✦✦✦✦✦

Nascimento / 1997 / Warner Brothers ✦✦✦✦✦
This is Milton Nascimento's most deeply Brazilian-sounding album in a long time, also the most downcast, but none the worse in its emotional impact. He adopts the battering, heavy percussion rhythms of the folia boxes (popularized by OLODUM) on several tracks, which frame the main portion of the album and give it enormous vitality. There isn't a bumper crop of new songs here (only half of the 12 tracks), but what there is represents the most interesting material he has recorded in some time, including the beautiful "Rouxinol" with its haunting accordion, flute and a gently hypnotic rhythm, and the arresting "Louva-A-Deus," pitting Nascimento's voice against the huge drums. Particularly affecting is Leo Masliah's "Guardanapos De Papel," sung in Portuguese at first and reprised in Spanish at the album's close, which has an almost despairing Nascimento singing about prophetic yet impoverished poets with tasteful piano/keyboard textures. He offers a touching vocalese on his friend Wayne Shorter's "Ana Maria" from their collaboration *Native Dancer* as a memorial to Shorter's late wife (lost on the TWA plane that crashed into the Atlantic in 1996), with soprano saxophonist Nivaldo Ornelas offering a different take on Shorter's lead. Just about everyone seems to take on "Ol' Man River" sooner or later, but Nascimento does it as a vocalese with large choir—and it works. So far, this CD represents his best work of the 1990s and even a good part of the '80s, a genuine renaissance for the Brazilian icon. *—Richard S. Ginell*

Crooner / Nov. 23, 1999 / Warner Brothers ✦✦✦
Surely one of the world's most distinctive crooners, Milton Nascimento prepared an album of pop songs he's known for years, performed early in his career when he played innumerable Brazilian clubs, including the first song he ever wrote, "Barulho de Trem," as well as a range of pop classics from Brazil and America. Nascimento also looks back to his early years with his collaborators, including Bebeto from Tamba Trio on the chestnut "Mas Que Nada," his *Clube da Esquina* companion Lô Borges on "Resposta," and the bossa nova collective Os Cariocas on "Rosa Maria" and "Lamento No Morro." The arrangements by longtime friend Wagner Tiso are very sympathetic, and Nascimento's voice is just as full of power and grace as it was 20 years ago. The cover of Michael Jackson's "Beat It" may have been a mistake, but the rest of *Crooner* is a tribute to Nascimento's brilliant range of material and his singing style. *—John Bush*

Clara Nunes

b. 1943, **d.** 1983
Vocals / Brazilian Pop, Bossa Nova, MPB, Samba, Brazil, Latin Continuum
If you had to list the best female samba singers of all time the name that might well top that list would be Clara Nunes. Although she died at a very young age (39), she is still revered as one of Brazil's preeminent and popular female vocalists. Born in 1943, Nunes' breakout recording was released when she was 21, that record, *Alvorecer* became the first record by a female singer to hit 500,000 in sales. From that point on Nunes became the signature female voice of samba. And with good reason. She was a dynamic singer with impeccable phrasing and range that effortlessly and skillfully negotiated the genre's subtle rhythmic twists and turns. She could also envelop a song with the fullness of her voice, despite the fact that she was not a screamer or shouter. Much of Nunes material explores the intriguing world of candomble (the Afro-Brazilian religion) and it is somewhat surprising that such subject matter became the fodder for so many pop hits. Thus proving that along with possessing a great voice, Nunes never underestimated the cultural concerns of her audience. An international star after the release of *Alvorecer,* Nunes tragic death in 1983 was a huge blow for Brazilian pop, but her spirit lives on in the work of female samba sisters such as Beth Carvalho and Alcione. *—John Dougan*

Comvida / 1995 / Hemispere ✦✦

Clara Nunes / 1999 / EMI ✦✦✦✦✦
Clara Nunes was a great samba singer, owner of a powerful voice and a generous swing. In this compilation some of her hits were reunited, all pure samba, both Bahian (samba-de-roda) and Carioca with the samba do morro (samba of the Carioca hills) playing an expressive role, with the sole exception of "Nação," a more mid-class view of samba by João Bosco but not less respectful to the truest spirit of the Brazilian genre. The overall arrangements are based in the purest morro instrumentation (cavaquinho, violão sete cordas, percussion) with the addition of some studio instrumentation such as the drum set. *—Alvaro Neder*

★ **2 in 1 Series** / ✦✦✦✦✦

Baden Powell (Roberto Baden Powell de Aquino)

b. Aug. 6, 1937, Rio de Janeiro, Brazil, **d.** Sep. 26, 2000, Rio de Janeiro, Brazil
Guitar, Choro / Latin Jazz, Bossa Nova, Samba, World Fusion, Brazil, Latin Continuum
Baden Powell is a Brazilian musician with a solid international reputation. A gifted instrumentalist and composer, he was a key figure in the bossa nova movement nad bridged the gap between classical artistry and popular warmth. Thanks to his father, Powell studied the violão for several years. After finishing high-school, he joined the cast of Rádio Nacional as an accompanist and also played jazz at the *Plaza* nightclub. He also began to compose songs including his first big hit, 1956's "Samba Triste." In 1962, he met his future partner Vinícius de Moraes, and their first song "Canção de Ninar Meu Bem" became a great success. In 1963, Baden Powell recorded his first LP, *Um Violão Na Madrugada.* One year later, he wrote the popular samba "Berimbau," with lyrics by Vinícius. Powell recorded many more LPs, and played during the late '60s in America (with Stan Getz) and France. His 1968 LP *Baden Powell* included the famous "Manhã de Carnaval" by Luís Bonfá and Antônio Maria. Powell lived in Germany for several years, but returned to Brazil in 1994. Two years later, he toured in France with Brazilian accordionist Sivuca and recorded *Baden Powell Live at the Rio Jazz Club.* After spending several weeks in the hospital, Baden Powell died on September 26, 2000 at the age of 63. *—Alvaro Neder*

● **Solitude on Guitar** / Dec. 10, 1971-Dec. 11, 1971 / Columbia ✦✦✦✦✦

The Frankfurt Opera Concert 1975 / 1975 / Tropical Music ✦✦✦

Melancolie / 1985 / Accord ✦✦✦
Baden Powell is among the greatest of the many guitarists who bridge samba and bossa nova and jazz. Alas, his finest recordings were on unobtainable small Brazilian labels. But even on these French recordings, with a mix of Brazilian and European musicians, he's outstanding. *Melancolie* contains a mix of familiar and less-known tunes, but mostly the latter. The overall sound is hotter than bossa nova (or most U.S. jazz-bossa), more mellow than most street-samba-based idioms. It also comes with strings, which are no improvement but are par for the course: most Brazilian musicians, even the most avant-garde, seem happy with string arrangements that would give you diabetes). *—John Storm Roberts, Original Music*

Seresta Brasileira / 1988 / Milestone ✦✦✦✦
An excellent Brazilian guitarist, Baden Powell has played with his share of American jazz greats (including Herbie Mann and the late Stan Getz). But there's no jazz to be found on *Seresta Brasiliera,* which was recorded for the Brazilian Caju Music label in 1988 and released in the U.S. on Milestone/Fantasy in 1994. The title *Seresta Brasiliera* translates to "Brazilian serenade," and an unaccompanied Powell embraces the Brazilian serenade style on personal, introspective versions of Pixinguinha's "Rosa," as well as songs he wrote with his frequent partner, the late Vinicius De Moraes (including "Velho Amigo," "Cancao Do Amor Ausente" and "Serenata Do Adeus"). A melancholy mood defines much of the CD, and Powell's playing is often as beautiful as it is sad and remorseful. *Seresta Brasiliera* is an album with little optimism and plenty of soul. *—Alex Henderson*

Baden Powell: Millennium Series / 1994 / EMI ✦✦✦✦✦
This compilation has some of Baden Powell's biggest instrumental hits, like "Canto de Ossanha" (from the Afro-sambas phase, fruit of his research of genuine Afro folklore in Bahia), "Berimbau," "Tempo Feliz," the unusual melodic solutions in "O Astronauta," and "Samba Triste." Sometimes backed by a rhythm section (non-credited in the poor inlay), sometimes alone at the violão, he also pays tribute to Pixinguinha (through his classics "Lamento" and "Carinhoso"), Tom Jobim ("Garota de Ipanema"), Vinícius de Moraes ("Eurídice"), and Sílvio Caldas (in the romantic seresta classic "Chão de Estrelas"). This constitutes a good introduction to the master's instrumental work and improvisations. It is more interesting than the *Minha História* series (the millennium series was devised to neutralize that one), which contains "Deve Ser Amor" and "Tempo Feliz," not included here, but it doesn't bring "Samba Do Avião," "A Lenda Do Abaeté," "Consolação," "Samba de Uma Nota Só" (with the American drummer Jimmy Pratt), "...Das Rosas," "Na Baixa Do Sapateiro," "Viagem," or "Saudades da Bahia." *—Alvaro Neder*

Elis Regina (Elis Regina Carvalho Costa)

b. 1945, Porto Alegre, Brazil, **d.** Jan. 19, 1982
Vocals / Brazilian Jazz, Latin Folk, Brazilian Pop, Latin Jazz, Bossa Nova, World Fusion, Brazil, Latin Continuum

Temperamental and moody, capable of fits of extreme generosity that could quickly turn into moments of rage-filled paranoia, Elis Regina was one of the most ferociously talented singers to emerge from Brazil. A perfectionist who was frequently dissatisfied, Regina drove herself and members of her band relentlessly, leading to her being dubbed "hurricane" and "little pepper" by musicians and music journalists. Her tempestuous nature aside, she commanded the respect of Brazil's leading songwriters, who lined up for the chance to have her record one of their songs, and for much of her short life was the country's most popular female vocalist.

A teenage star, she moved to Rio in 1963 at the age of 18, and became a fixture on Brazilian variety shows. Although the cool, supple, jazzy, bossa nova sound was in vogue at the time, Regina preferred more raucous rhythms and full-throated singing. In 1965, Regina sang the controversial song "Arrastao" at Rio's first big popular music festival, posing in Christ-like crucifixion in a performance that may well have been the defining moment of her career. From that moment on her popularity rocketed, and she became most popular and highest-paid singer in the country—at the age of 21.

Although not as overtly political as other singer/songwriters of her generation, Regina was not shy about criticizing Brazil's military rule and her career showed no signs of slowing as the 1970s came to a close. Some of her best records were recorded during this time, and one album simply called *Elis & Tom* (recorded with Antonio Carlos Jobim) has been called one of the greatest Brazilian pop records ever made. However, while her career was in full swing, her personal life was in disarray, and she was found dead of alcohol and cocaine intoxication in 1982. *—John Dougan*

Dois Na Bossa, No. 3 / 1967 / Polygram Brazil ✦✦✦✦✦
In May 1965, Elis Regina and Jair Rodrigues began hosting a weekly show at TV Record (São Paulo), *O Fino Da Bossa*. At the same time, they opened a show at *the Teatro Paramount*, in the same city, which was recorded live. The LP *Dois Na Bossa* (Philips) was a national best-seller. They would repeat the dose in 1966 (*Dois Na Bossa No. 2*) and in 1967, with this album. The atmosphere was clearly dominated by a polarization conduced by the fact that Brazil was under a severe military dictatorship—Regina' passionate address to the audiences and her choice of repertoire ("Marcha Da Quarta-feira de Cinzas" can be read in this context even if it was written before 1964) contrasts with Rodrigues' silence in that respect. As in all three albums, together they cover a medley of sambas along with solo performances. The album is not a typical bossa album, despite what the title indicates. It is more of a samba release, with strong influences of bossa in harmonies and arrangements, but with the stronger, hotter grip of the samba groove. The section dedicated to bossa is a romantic medley shared by both artists. *—Alvaro Neder*

Elis Especial [1968] / 1968 / Polygram Brazil ✦✦✦✦
Classic early material is accompanied by an uncredited, relentlessly swinging piano trio. The sound quality could be better (it was recorded in 1968), but by the end of the first song you won't care anymore—you'll be blissfully tapping your foot. *—David Rumpler*

Elis / 1974 / Philips ✦✦✦✦
Elis Regina had discovered the duo João Bosco/Aldir Blanc two years later, and they contributed with four songs for this album, the same as Gilberto Gil, leaving only two tracks to be filled by old guard hits ("Folhas Secas," a beautiful samba classic by Nelson Cavaquinho/Guilherme de Brito, and "É Com Esse Que Eu Vou" by Pedro Caetano). The fusion-sounding album with arrangements/execution by César Camargo Mariano opens with the slow pace of the mysterious "Oriente," "O Caçador de Esmeraldas," and "Doente Morena" until "Agnus Sei" is introduced with its suggestive percussion; the dynamics continue to grow with the swinging samba "Meio de Campo" but recede with the romantic introduction of the tango "Cabaré," which develops until its marked tango beat. Another swinging samba follows, "Ladeira da Preguiça"; "Folhas Secas" receives a cool bossa rendition; "Comadre" is a mid-samba; and "É Com Esse Que Eu Vou" is another bossa interpretation. *—Alvaro Neder*

A Arte de Elis Regina / 1975 / Verve ✦✦✦
This 1975 best-of is a well-rounded portrayal of Regina's rich artistry, including hits like "Madalena" and "Arrastao" and her definitive performances of songs by many of Brazil's most important composers. *—Terri Hinte*

Falso Brilhante / 1976 / Verve ✦✦✦✦✦

Transversal Do Tempo / 1978 / Philips ✦✦✦✦✦
Released after Regina's successful show *Transversal Do Tempo*, the album's concept was to portray the perplexity in the face of Brazil's complexity. Its biggest hit was Milton Nascimento's "Morro Velho," but "Fascinação," "Sinal Fechado," "Deus Lhe Pague," "O Rancho Da Goiabada," "Saudosa Maloca," "Querelas Do Brasil," and "Cartomante" also were successful. Arrangements/piano by César Camargo Mariano. *—Alvaro Neder*

Elis Espial [1979] / 1979 / Philips ✦✦✦✦
Released originally in 1979, this was one of the last albums recorded by the great Brazilian singer Elis Regina. The sound is quite bad, with predominance of the middle harmonics in the fusion arrangements. Her exciting swing can be heard in "Noves Fora," "Ou Bola Ou B'lica," and "Dinorah, Dinorah," while deep sorrow is conveyed in "Violeta de Belford Roxo," the curious mix of valsa and marcha-rancho "Valsa Rancho," and "Bodas de Prata." The album also has bossa nova, in "Entrudo" and "Bonita" (with lyrics in English), and the typical Milton Nascimento 6/8 grooves in "Credo." "Deixa O Mundo E O Sol Entrar" had such a kitschy interpretation/arrangement that the tune shouldn't be included, but the French atmosphere of "Joana Francesa" is part of the identity of the song and helps to establish a nostalgic feel. The album is a document of her generosity in recording contemporary composers: Fagner, Belchior, João Bosco, Aldir Blanc, Milton Nascimento, Fernando Brant, Ivan Lins, Vitor Martins all owe a lot to her. *—Alvaro Neder*

Saudade Do Brasil / 1980 / WEA Latina ✦✦✦✦

● **Nada Sera Como Antes (Elis Interpreta Milton Nascimento)** / Nov. 7, 1990 / Verve ✦✦✦✦✦
On this album dedicated to the wonderful compositions by Milton Nascimento with lyricists Ronaldo Bastos, Fernando Brant, or Márcio Borges, Regina covers in great shape, with all her sensitivity, classic tunes such as "Nada Será Como Antes," "Morro Velho," "Cais," "Travessia," and many others. The atmosphere ranges from the calm, poetic, longing, meditative, to mid-tempo 6/8 grooves that are preferred by Nascimento and the mineiros, but nothing about those fierce, hot, swinging sambas that are Regina's trademark. This is the CD reissue of a compilation album recorded between 1966 and 1978 by Polygram (Fontana Special). *—Alvaro Neder*

Elis Por Ela / 1993 / WEA Latina ✦✦✦✦✦

Millennium: Elis Regina / Apr. 13, 1999 / Polygram International ✦✦✦✦
This compilation has 20 hits by the excellent, late singer. Her swinging samba renditions can be recalled through "O Bêbado E A Equilibrista," "Madalena," "O Mestre-sala Dos Mares," and "Canto de Ossanha" (with Toots Thielemans, in a jazzy rendition). Bossa nova can be found in "Aquarela do Brasil," "Nega do Cabelo Duro," and "iguas de Março" (with Tom Jobim, from the album *Elis & Tom*). Flower power nostalgia is the raw material for "Como Nossos Pais," "Casa No Campo" has bucolic intentions, just like "Romaria," while "Fascinação" is a somewhat kitschy old romantic valse taken from the seresta repertoire with all its grandiose images, while the option for kitsch was conscious in the boleros "Dois Pra lá, Dois Pra Cá" and "Me Deixas Louca." The festival years are recalled by the energetic "Louvação" (in a live 1966 recording, with Jair Rodrigues). The distinctive sound of Milton Nascimento's lively compositions is found in "Caxangá" and "Nada Será Como Antes." Finally, her extreme dramatic sensibility is brought by "Atrás da Porta." One of the best Regina compilations. *—Alvaro Neder*

Robertinho Silva (Roberto da Silva)

b. Jun. 1, 1941, Rio de Janeiro, Brazil
Drums, Percussion / Brazilian Jazz, Brazil, Latin Continuum

Reputed Brazilian drummer and percussionist, Robertinho Silva has played and recorded with great names. His international experience includes performances at the *MIDEM* (Cannes, France, 1973) and the *Montreux Jazz Festival* (Switzerland, 1974).

Began to teach himself the drums, becoming a professional at 15, when joined dance bands like the Conjunto Flamingo. At 17, began his two-year apprenticeship with Albano Mesquita and Joaquim Neagle. In 1964 recorded for the first time, accompanying Caubi Peixoto. In 1969 became acquainted with Milton Nascimento, being since then his regular accompanist. In 1970, joined the Som Imaginário, remaining with them until 1974, having participated in the two *Som Imaginário* albums (1970/1971). Was sideman for João Donato, Marcos Valle, Gilberto Gil, Taiguara, Toninho Horta, Roberto Carlos, Gal Costa, João Bosco, Paulo Moura and many others. Moved to the U.S. in 1974 (where stayed for four years), backing Airto Moreira, Moacyr Santos, Ron Carter, Wayne Shorter, Shelly Manne, Peggy Lee, Cal Tjader, Sarah Vaughan, George Duke, Flora Purim, Egberto Gismonti and other musicians. In 1981 released the first solo album in the *M sica Popular Brasileira Contemporânea* series (Polygram), with special guests Raul de Souza and Egberto Gismonti. In 1984 recorded *Bateria*, followed by *Bodas de Prata* (1989), *Speak No Evil* (1991) and *Shot on goal* (1995), released internationally. In 1985, recorded, together with pianist Luiz Eça and bassist Luiz Alves the album *Triângulo*. In 1997 opened the Centro de Percussão Alternativo Robertinho Silva, at Rio de Janeiro, having a busy schedule with its drums/percussion workshops. Released *Jaquedu* in 2000. *—Alvaro Neder*

● **Shot on Goal** / Oct. 1991 / Milestone ✦✦✦✦
On his fourth album as a leader, Silva puts together a highly percussive (naturally) series of sessions mixing American jazz standards and jazz-rock idioms with Brazilian instruments and material. The results sometimes resemble fellow percussionist Airto Moreira's fascinating electric Brazilian jazz recordings of the '70s, though Silva's tracks are more disciplined in structure. A solo flute or saxophone, mostly in the capable hands of Mauro Senise, rises above the ensemble a la Wayne Shorter, and seven different keyboardists, including Silva himself on "Festa De Terreiro," sprinkle notes or lay down electronic textures. Aided by Silva's sons Ronaldo and Vanderlei on percussion, "Ceco Aderaldo" has a dense, rapidly fibrillating underbrush of Brazilian percussion sounds propelling the music, and Silva puts forth a thundering, hypnotic 7/4-meter display on the tom-toms in "Barra 200." In the American material, "Bemsha Swing" receives a quasi-samba treatment while also emphasizing the tune's strong roots in the blues, and "Nefertiti" rarely departs from the usual Miles Davis-oriented approach. Indeed, in the latter tune, the versatile Silva does a pretty good, meter-shifting Tony Williams impersonation. *—Richard S. Ginell*

Speak No Evil / Jul. 30, 1994 / Milestone ✦✦✦
On Robertinho Silva's first U.S. release as a leader, he distilled the varied influences of some 25 years as a major player on the Brazilian scene. Tunes from a number of composers, including Milton Nascimento and Wayne Shorter, both honor his associates and allow Silva to demonstrate his facility in diverse genres. A large supporting cast of musicians, including Nascimento, Egberto Gismonti, and José Bertrami show up to augment the basic band from track to track. Not as sure-footed or cohesive as the follow-up, *Shot on Goal*, this is nonetheless an impressive debut, well worth a listen. *—Janet Rosen*

Marcos Valle

b. Sep. 14, 1943, Rio de Janeiro, Brazil
Vocals, Guitar / Obscuro, Brazilian Pop, Bossa Nova, MPB, Brazil, Latin Continuum

Marcos Valle was the Renaissance man of Brazilian pop, a singer/songwriter/producer who straddled the country's music world from the early days of the bossa-nova craze well into the fusion-soaked sound of '80s MPB. Though his reputation in America never quite compared to contemporaries like Caetano Veloso, Milton Nascimento, Gilberto Gil, or even Tom Zé, Valle is one of the most important and popular performers in the history of Brazilian pop.

Born in Rio de Janeiro in 1943, Marcos Valle studied classical music as a child but listened to much music in his native Brazil. He began writing songs with his brother Paulo Sérgio—Marcos was the tune-writer, Paulo the lyricist—in the early '60s, and was named Brazil's Leading Composer of the Year at the age of 19. An album contract soon folowed, and in 1964 he released his first album, *Samba Demais*, for EMI Brazil. A tour with Sergio Mendes & Brasil '65 the following year brought his first show-business connections in America (via Merv Griffin), and in 1966 Walter Wanderley took Valle's song "So Nice (Summer Samba)" into the US Top 40. Valle soon earned his own American contract, and in 1967 Warner Brothers released the instrumentals album *Braziliance!*. One year later, his Verve debut *Samba '68* became a Brazilian classic thanks to simple, infectious pop songs like "Batucada," "Chup, Chup, I Got Away," and "Crickets Sing for Anamaria" (all of which featured spot-on harmony vocals by his wife Anamaria).

Despite the incredible promise revealed by Samba '68, it was his last American album to date. That same year, the Brazilian-only Viola Enluarada became a big hit in South America, thanks in part to the title track (with vocals by a young Milton Nascimento). The rock & roll era that had already influenced tropicalistas like Os Mutantes, Caetano Veloso, and Gilberto Gil soon began inspiring Valle as well. With albums like the irresistible 1971 classic Garra, he moved away from native Brazilian forms like the bossa nova or samba and into a rock-influenced sound that played up groove-heavy bass and smooth funk even while courting his amazing melodic sense. He continued recording for EMI until he moved to America in 1975. There, he wrote and arranged tracks for Eumir Deodato, Airto Moreira, and Chicago. He continued to record solo albums during the early '80s, adding electronics and an smooth production techniques to the mix with surprisingly solid results, but also moved into writing music (often with Paulo) for film and novellas, including the theme to Brazil's version of *Sesame Street*.

During the late '80s, the rare-groove craze centered in London resurrected and relentlessly compiled dozens of crucial, overlooked tracks from the 1960s and '70s, including Valle's "Crickets Sing for Anamaria." In 1995, the British label Mr. Bongo released a two-volume series *(The Essential Marcos Valle)* dedicated to his work. One year later, Valle appeared on the jam-session compilation *Friends from Rio*, and in 1998 he returned with a new album, *Nova Bossa Nova*. That same year, the Lumiar label released *The Marcos Valle Songbook, Vols. 1-2*, including new versions of Valle standards by Gal Costa, Caetano Veloso, Maria Bethania, Edu Lobo, Joyce, Chico Buarqe, Joao Bosco, and Azymuth, among others. *—John Bush*

O Compositor E O Cantor / 1965 / Odeon/EMI ♦♦♦

• **Samba '68** / 1968 / Verve ♦♦♦♦♦
Samba '68 is a vibrant set of Brazilian pop, indebted to bossa nova and samba but undeniably Americanized for a domestic audience. The result is a joyous album throughout that wears its dated sound quite well. Valle interprets eleven of his own songs, including Brazilian standards like "Chup Chup, I Got Away," "Batucada" and "So Nice (Summer Samba)," as well as new tracks like "Crickets Sing for Anamaria" and "The Answer." The vocal harmonies of his wife (the Anamaria of the song title) provide a beautiful counterpoint to Valle's voice on several tracks, making *Samba '68* one of the best Brazilian crossovers of the 1960s. *—John Bush*

The Essential Marcos Valle, Vol. 2 / 1996 / Mr. Bongo ♦♦♦♦♦
The second volume in Mr. Bongo's *Essential* wrap-up of Brazilian wunderkind Marcos Valle focuses more on his easy listening and quasi-instrumental output, a set of suitably light productions that are far, far beyond the likes of Sergio Mendes and his breezy Brazilian contemporaries. The disc leads off with a darker, brassy rendition of "Os Grilos" (his breakout hit, known best to English-speaking audiences as "Crickets Sing for Anamaria" from *Samba '68*) and proceeds through 15 more of the best-produced songs in the Brazilian repertoire. For fans digging deeper than the widely available *Samba '68*, Mr. Bongo also includes several excellent Portuguese re-recordings of familiar songs; besides "Os Grilos," there are versions of "The One I Love" ("Seu Encanto") and "Chup Chup, I Got Away" ("Gente"). Also included are a few songs from 1971's outstanding *Garra*—"Wanda Vidal" and "Com Mais de 30." *—John Bush*

Nova Bossa Nova / Jun. 16, 1998 / Far Out ♦♦♦

Caetano Veloso

b. 1942
Vocals, Guitar / Brazilian Pop, MPB, Tropicalia, Brazil, Latin Continuum
A true heavyweight, perhaps one of the greatest figures in international pop music, Caetano Veloso is a pop musician/poet/filmmaker/political activist whose stature in the pantheon of international pop musicians is on a par with that of Bob Dylan, Bob Marley, and Lennon/McCartney. Following his sister Maria Bethania (a very successful singer in her own right) to Rio in the early '60s, Veloso won a lyricwriting contest and was quickly signed to Phillips.

It wasn't long before Veloso represented the new wave of MPB (i.e. musica popular brasileira), the all-purpose term used by Brazilians to describe their pop music. Bright, ambitious, creative, and given to an unapologetically leftist political outlook, Veloso would soon become a controversial figure in Brazilian pop. Along with Gilberto Gil, he helped create a new form of pop music, dubbed tropicalismo. Arty and eclectic, tropicalismo retained a bossa nova influence, adding bits and pieces of folk-rock and art-rock to a stew of loud electric guitars, poetic spoken-word sections, and jazz-like dissonance. Such radical music made by such radical musicians faced almost immediate censorship from the Brazilian government (a military dictatorship), and both Veloso and Gil spent time in prison, as well as four years of exile in London from 1968 to 1972.

Although his commitment to politicized art never wavered, Veloso, over the next 20 years, went from being a very popular Brazilian singer/songwriter to becoming the center of Brazilian pop. He kept up a grueling pace—recording, producing, performing, even writing—and in the '80s, Veloso became increasingly better known outside of Brazil by touring in Africa, Paris, Israel, and America. Still, his work over the years remained challenging and intriguing without being modified for American tastes. After his 1989 recording *Estrangeiro* (produced by Ambitious Lovers Arto Lindsay and Peter Scherer) became his first non-import release in America, Veloso's stateside profile reached its highest point with 1993's *Tropicalia 2*, recorded with Gilberto Gil. He embarked on his largest American tour in 1997, and was acclaimed worldwide for his 1998 album *Livro*. *—John Dougan*

Caetano Veloso [1967] / 1967 / Philips ♦♦♦♦
The first Caetano Veloso solo album was recorded in 1967. Soon after *the III FMPB*, where Veloso took fourth place with "Alegria, Alegria," he and his group (which would soon constitute the tropicália movement) were news, dividing opinions concerning the group's interest in fusing Brazilian music with international pop culture, lysergic psychedelia, generalized irreverence, and whatever crossed their minds. The arrangements were done by three classically trained composers, fully committed to the most adventurous experiments in modern music: J'lio Medaglia, Damiano Cozzella, and Sandino Hohagen. Veloso's concept was that the album should surpass the Beatles' *Sgt. Pepper's*, being also very Brazilian and, at the same time, international. The record has immortal classics, such as "Clarice," "Soy Loco Por Ti América" (Gilberto Gil/Capinam), composed under the effect of the recent death of Che Guevara, "Superbacana," "Tropicália," and "Alegria, Alegria." The rest of the album has had less success but consists of excellent tracks that remain modern until today. "Tropicália," the title track, was an unnamed song when its recording began. By suggestion of the then photographer Luís Carlos Barreto, Veloso used the same name of an installation by the visual artist Hélio Oiticica, which was composed by a labyrinth made with plants and birds conducing to a television set. The suggestion was accepted—and the tropicália was born. *—Alvaro Neder*

Caetano Veloso [1969] / 1969 / Philips ♦♦♦
This second Caetano Veloso solo LP was recorded in June 1969, when Veloso and Gilberto Gil were behind the bars of the military dictatorship. The albums (Gil also recorded his own) were devised in part to provide them with a connection to the outside world through which authorities would be discouraged of attempting some violence against them. The voices were unsophisticatedly recorded with the sole backing of their own violões and a metronome, and the arrangements added later in the studio, which was an indigenous and competent subversion of the basics of production, especially if you take into consideration the available technology at that time. The general tone of this album is coherent with the depressing moment Veloso and the rest of the country were going through. The English lyrics of his "The Empty Boat" have several strong images of desperation and sadness, and "Irene" has been largely misunderstood—especially the verse "quero ver Irene rir" (I want to see Irene laughing). "Irene" was the "name" of a machine gun owned by Tenório Cavalcanti (a robber somewhat celebrated by leftists at the time). His fado "Os Argonautas" represents implicitly the aspiration that, as Portugal had got ridden of Salazar (in the precedent year by a stroke), Brazil could also got rid of its dictatorship. The superbly modern arrangements of Rogério Duprat and the songs "Não Identificado," "Acrilírico," and "Marcianita," on the other hand, contribute to the anarchic, chaotic, and psychedelic setting of tropicália in which make part the rustic fuzzed-out guitars. But maybe the most important thing here is the evident artistic sincerity felt throughout the album: it is when the listener feels himself as a voyeur, peeping through the artist's deepest emotions. *—Alvaro Neder*

Caetano Veloso [1971] / 1971 / Philips ♦♦♦♦♦
Another year, another self-titled album. I know little about this recording other than that it was recorded while Veloso was in exile in London, and it was his first album recorded entirely in English. It was during this period that Veloso was sending many of his newest songs to Brazilian tropicalistas such as Gal Costa, Elis Regina, Erasmo Carlos, and his sister Maria Bethania. This album was followed by his first European tour, some dates shared with one of his biggest supporters, Sergio Mendes. *—John Dougan*

Transa / 1972 / Polygram Brazil ♦♦♦♦♦
This is the CD reissue of the first LP recorded by Veloso upon his return of the exile in London, England (1972). The sound of '70s electric rock predominates, fused with Brazilian rhythms and percussion, berimbau sounds, and his own violão playing. Several lyrics in English, and also in Portuguese, carefully avoid direct reference to politics, which may be found disguised in all songs, especially in the melancholic and depressed images of the poem by Gregório de Mattos, "Triste Bahia," for which Veloso wrote the music. "It's A Long Way" also makes ciphered references to the political situation and was broadly played in the '70s. The broad use of *pontos de capoeira* (music used for accompaniment of capoeira, a martial art developed by Brazilian slaves as a resistance against the whites) can also be understood in that sense. The album also has "Mora Na Filosofia," a classic and beautiful samba by Monsueto that scandalized people with its rock rendition. *—Alvaro Neder*

Doces Barbaros / 1976 / Philips ♦♦♦♦

Bicho / 1977 / Polygram Brazil ♦♦♦♦♦
Just prior to the recording of *Bicho*, Veloso was invited to take part in the Negro Festival of Art and Culture in Lagos, Nigeria. Veloso was so knocked out by the music he heard that he scrapped his original plans for the album to record something more redolent of his experiences in Lagos. Veloso himself refers to *Bicho* as "sweet melodies on a hot rhythm," and he's absolutely right. A marvelous record. For the record, "bicho" is the Portuguese word for beast. *—John Dougan*

Cinema Transcendental / 1979 / Verve ♦♦♦♦♦
One of Veloso's last quasi-acoustic albums, this one is dedicated to Brazilian grooves (with the exception of a couple of reggae tracks). The album has been very well spun, and several tracks were hits: "Lua de São Jorge," "Oração Ao Tempo," "Badauê" (Bahian grooves), "Cajuína" (Northeastern xote), "Menino do Rio" (pop ballad), "Elegia" (bolero), "Trilhos Urbanos" (reggae), "Louco Por Você" (Carioca samba). There are also other tracks whose experimental character prevented them from being hits, but they still constitute excellent material. Delicate and also swinging arrangements, these are excellent compositions by an artist still in full-steam creative impetus. *—Alvaro Neder*

Outras Palavaras / 1981 / Philips ♦♦♦

Cores, Nomes / 1982 / Verve ♦♦♦♦

Uns / 1983 / Verve ♦♦♦♦
Uns opens with the swinging title track, with its rhythmic poetry based in the word that means "some people," opening endless possibilities: "Musical" is a melancholic and delicate melody, delivered with simplicity; "Eclipse Oculto" was the big hit of the album with its hybrid reggae rhythm and his lyrics that are a monologue directed to a former lover; "Peter Gast" is the best melody/arrangement of the album, a sophisticated ballad; "Quero Ir Aa Cuba" has swinging Caribbean rhythms; "Coisa Mais Linda" (Carlos Lyra/Vinícius de Moraes), a bossa classic, is delivered in the purest bossa style; "Você É Linda," which also was a hit, is a ballad whose lyrics describe in detail the charms of a certain Bahian girl; "Bobagens, Meu Filho, Bobagens" (Marina Lima/Antônio Cícero) is a minor pop ballad; "A Outra Banda Da Terra," a reggae song, talks about territorialism with redneck accent; the samba-funk "Salva Vida," with special guest Maria Betânia, provokes conservatives with references to masculine beauty; and the classic, beautiful samba-enredo "É Hoje" (Didi/Mestrinho) closes the album. *—Alvaro Neder*

Caetano / 1988 / Verve ♦♦♦
On this album, Veloso dedicated almost all the tracks to talk about himself. It is not surprising that it went unnoticed. Eu ("I") is the most frequent sound heard in the album, obsessively repeated in the reggae "Eu Sou Neguinha?" "Noite de Hotel" can sincerely translate the existential void of an artist incarcerated in a hotel room after a performance, but also brings some pathetic, egotistic overtones: what is the urgency of the theme— The beautiful "Valsa de Uma Cidade" (Ismael Netto/Antônio Maria) is a poetic moment of self-description. The merengue "Vamo Comer" opens with social concerns until everything is channeled to "me," even if it is a "me" citizen. Through the other songs, he follows his self-centered approach talking about jealousy and separation. The only song in which he allows himself to look at the other had its public execution vetoed by censorship: "Giulietta Masina" (a tribute to the late actress, wife of Federico Fellini), which includes the word puta (a profane expression for whore). Musically, the album has its best moments in the nostalgic "O Ci¨me," in the percussive approach for "Lá Omin Bum," "Depois Que O Ilê Passar," and in the "Valsa de Uma Cidade." *—Alvaro Neder*

Estrangeiro / 1989 / Elektra ♦♦♦
Produced by Peter Scherer and Arto Lindsay, with a band that features significant contributions from Bill Frisell, Nana Vasconcelos, and Marc Ribot, *Estrangeiro* (in English it means foreigner) was Veloso's first American release. Adventurous, idiosyncratic, and frequently beautiful, it in many ways is Veloso at his most topical and artfully lyrical. The title track makes references to Paul Gauguin and anthropologist Claude Levi-Strauss (two figures not normally associated with pop music), Veloso composes some stream-of-consciousness dialogue recited by Lindsay, and the excellent band swings from bossa nova to rock to jazz without missing a beat. In many ways, *Estrangeiro* is the embodiment of what Veloso, Gil and others were trying to get at with tropicalismo, the removal of genre barriers and the wondrous results possible when all forms of pop were conflated into one artful, stylistic melange. A lyric fragment from the song "Branquinha (Little White One)" says it best: "I go against the grain/sing against the melody/swim against the tide." He does all this, and the results are extraordinary. *—John Dougan*

Caetano Veloso [1990] / 1990 / Elektra ♦♦♦

★ **Sem Lenco, Sem Documento** / 1990 / Verve ♦♦♦♦♦
As anyone who has read this up to this point would guess, I recommend that if you have developed an interest in Caetano Veloso that goes beyond nominal, you really should own every record of his you can find. However, for the benighted who only want a taste, this is the best place to start. Translated, the title means "without handkerchief without passport," and while I cannot tell you what relevance that has, I can tell you that you will not find a better single-disc overview of Veloso's prodigious output, that is up until 1984. Opening with the most famous song from his early period (1968's "Alegria, Alegria"—with fuzztone psychedelic guitars!!), this disc covers the best music from his long relationship with Phillips including "Soy Loco Por Ti, America" (written by Gilberto Gil), "Voce e Linda," "Lua de Sao Jorge," and 15 more. Although he's recorded much great music after 1984, this is the best place to start. Originally available only as a Brazilian import, the disc has since been released in American with more comprehensive English liner notes. *—John Dougan*

Fina Estampa / 1994 / Polygram ♦♦♦♦♦
In his 26th album, devoted to the Hispanic market that quickly reached the Latin Top Ten at Tower, Veloso sings great classics and new songs in Spanish, several recalled from his childhood; among them are boleros, rumbas, guarânias, and canções of Cuba ("Rumba Azul," "Contigo en la Distancia," "Maria la O," "Mi Cocodrilo Verde"), Argentina ("Un Vestido y un Amor," "Vete de Mi," Piazzolla's "Vuelvo Al Sur," and "Pecado," the latter two in bossa style), Mexico ("Maria Bonita," "La Golondrina"), Paraguay ("Recuerdos de Ypacarai"), Peru ("Fina Estampa"), Puerto Rico ("Capullito de Aleli," "Lamento Borincano"), and Venezuela ("Tonada de Luna Llena"). A sensitive, delicate acoustic release in which Veloso's precious vocal interpretations (without vibrato) are backed by string, wood, cello, and rhythmic sections. The instrumental arrangements (by Jaques Morelembaum) are based less in the fundamental orchestrations of the '40s and are more erudite. This studio album was so successful in terms of critics and selling that it yielded a live show from which was recorded a live album, *Fina Estampa Ao Vivo*. *—Alvaro Neder*

Tropicália 2 / 1994 / Elektra/Nonesuch ♦♦♦♦
Between harsh criticism (due to the retro opportunistic use of Tropicália), and sectarian defense, *Tropicália 2* yielded a Caetano Veloso/Gilberto Gil tour through E.U.A. and Europe one year after this release. The reference to Tropicália was used as a safe-conduct for the duo's incursions in electronics, axé music (the contemporary and pragmatic sound of Bahia) and other commercial exploitation—since under Tropicália everything goes (or used to go, some 30 years ago). The album opens with "Haiti," a dry percussive electronic pattern over which Caetano and Gil speak verses dealing with racism; "Cinema Novo" is a beautiful samba, whose lyrics "explain" and greet the Brazilian cinema movement which gained the world. "Nossa Gente" brings the percussive sounds of axé music together with funk brass attacks. "Rap Popconcreto" is a musical concrete poem which echoes as a synthesis of the old concept of Tropicália—utilizing samplers in an improbable atmosphere, piling several old recordings from various artists singing the word "Quem?" ("Who?"). The Jimi Hendrix song "Wait Until Tomorrow" receives a Brazilian percussion treatment, and "Cada Macaco No Seu Galho" is a Novos Baianos hit which received an old baião groove treatment in the drum-machine programming, mixed with modern Bahian percussion. "Baião Atemporal" is a beautiful baião with a very modern and haunting melody and arrangement. The album, in philosophical terms, expresses fragile concepts. Poetically and musically, represents good entertainment, and, in its best moments, good Art. *—Alvaro Neder*

O Quatrilho / Oct. 15, 1996 / Blue Jackel ♦♦♦

Livros / Nov. 10, 1998 / Elektra/Asylum ♦♦♦♦♦
Caetano Veloso continues his free-thinking explorations of tropicalismo on this ambitiously arranged, elaborately packaged suite of songs devoted to whatever happens to cross his mind. Veloso says that he was listening a lot to the collaborations of Miles Davis and Gil Evans around this time, and Jaques Morelenbaum's charts often reflect their darkly urbane ethos. Yet for Morelenbaum's yin there is also the yang of the battering Bahian percussion that dominates many of the rhythm tracks. "Livros" in Portuguese means "books," so Veloso gives you a sample of his book *Verdade Tropical* in the booklet notes and pays eloquent tribute to them on the title track: "Books are transcendental things/But we can love them with our hands." He is alternately awestruck and appalled by the ambiguities of New York City on "Manhata"; here, the arrangement definitely contains haunting echoes of Evans. He can venture into atonality on "Doideca" (12-tone, but pointedly translated in the booklet as "loony"), recite the horrors of a slave ship voyage, tell someone off ("Nao Enche," which means "Piss Off"), or simply sing "How beautiful could a being be" over and over, presumably to a child, in falsetto to a hot groove. One of the most amazing songs is an epic about the life of Alexander the Great; it comes off like a great saga song. Finally, he runs down a long list of all his favorite Brazilian singers, seemingly leaving out no one, only to close with "Better than this there's only silence/And better than silence, only Joao." Can't add anything to that, except don't miss this CD if you love Brazilian music. *—Richard S. Ginell*

Prenda Minha / Apr. 13, 1999 / Polygram ♦♦♦♦
In this uneven album, Caetano Veloso used cool jazz and Gil Evans' orchestrations as the raw material for his synthesis with contemporary Bahian rhythms—"Terra," from 1978, is an epic description in which *Sketches of Spain* influences dialogue with their rhythmic similarity with Bahian grooves. The track is the best of the album, which brings no news other than the interpretation of "Prenda Minha," from the ga¨cho folklore, and the ridiculous yet highly rewarding financially track "Sozinho" (which may be the best reason for a Veloso album reaching the cipher of 1,200,000 sold copies for the first time), which propelled the selling of the album and its presence in the top radio charts. "Jorge de Capadócia" (Jorge Ben, 1975) is an emotional and beautiful delivery of the important song, but included in this repertory after Racionais MC's recorded it, it sounds a bit opportunistic—the visceral phrase "eu estou vestido com as roupas e as armas de Jorge" (I am dressed with the clothes and weapons of Jorge's," a reference to the religious syncretism that unifies Saint Georges and Oxum in a Negro entity of protection, resistance, and survival) sounds incongruous when delivered by this elegant gentleman in an expensive suit. Musically, the excellent cool jazz orchestral arrangements for "Esse Cara," "Prenda Minha," "Terra," "Meditação" (a bossa classic propelled by a Bahian percussion), the also splendid Latin jazz arrangements for "Mel" (recorded by sister Maria Bethânia, here sung in Spanish in a convenient Mercosul version), and the delicate, straight voice/violão renditions for "Bem Devagar," "Drão," "Saudosismo," and the beautiful Chico Buarque song "Carolina" make the album worthwhile—even if listeners must endure the shameless plug for Veloso's book, the pretentious *Verdade Tropical*. *—Alvaro Neder*

Tom Ze (Antônio José Santana Martins)

Vocals / Brazilian Pop, MPB, Tropicalia, Brazil, Latin Continuum
Brazilian artist Tom Zé began his career as a street performer in his hometown of Irara, later becoming a Tropicalista renowned for his sharply satiric songs. By the mid-'70s he had again switched gears, creating highly experimental music by means of blenders, floor polishers, radios, typewriters and prepared acoustic guitars; the evolution left Zé something of a musical exile in his homeland, however, and he struggled well into the late '80s, at which time he was contacted by David Byrne, who'd come into possession of one of his old LPs. Byrne agreed to begin issuing Zé's music on his Luaka Bop label, resulting in a series of collections including 1990's *Brazil Classics 4: Best of Tom Zé—Massive Hits*, 1992's *The Hips of Tradition* and 1998's *Com Defecto de Fabricacao (Fabrication Defect)*. *Postmodern Platos Remixes* was released in 1999. *—Jason Ankeny*

● **Brazil Classics, Vol. 4: The Best of Tom Ze—*Massive Hits*** */ 1990 / Luaka Bop* ♦♦♦♦♦
A cofounder of the tropicalista movement with Veloso, Gil, Bethania, et al., Zé has faded into obscurity as his music becomes more and more experimental and eccentric. This is by far the best Brazilian recording I've ever heard (caveat emptor!), partly because of the gentleness of Zé's weirdness and partly because he sounds so Brazilian even as the other tropicalistas come to associate "avant-garde" with increasingly Pan American pop-soup. *—Carl Hoyt, Original Music*

Brazil Classics, Vol. 5: The Hips of Tradition / 1992 / Luaka Bop ♦♦♦♦♦

Com Defecto de Fabricacao (Fabrication Defect) / 1998 / Luaka Bop ♦♦♦♦♦

Brazil Collection

Afro Brazil / 1988 / Philips ♦♦♦♦♦
Verve's international division issued a four-disc anthology series of Brazilian music covering selections mostly from the 1970s and '80s, plus a few things done in 1990. The 18 tracks compiled for Afro Brasil spotlight the rhythms and sounds from Bahia, the most African section

of Brazil. The influence of the Candomble and Macumba religions, coupled with the sounds of samba, reggae, and the afoxes and bloco afros genres, are displayed by such artists as Caetano Veloso, Nana Vasconcelos, the Bushdancers and the lush vocals of Margareth Menezes and Beth Carvalho. This is the modern Afro-Brazilian sound, captured in stark, digital glory. *—Ron Wynn*

Batucada Brazileira / Parrot ✦✦✦✦✦
Rio carnival aside, Brazil is full of African-derived percussion. Batucada descends directly from the social dances permitted slaves once a week; batucada is a dynamite percussion music. This release focuses on batucadas for drums leavened by the whistles beloved also of African drum choirs, passages of fine cavaquinho (a small guitar) and manic, squeaky-squeak cuica friction drum. Maddeningly generic packaging, but this really is the best Brazilian percussion release I've met these many years, with technical quality as sparkling as the drumming. *—John Storm Roberts*

Blue Brazil, Vol. 1 / Nov. 10, 1998 / Blue Note ✦✦✦
Culled from EMI and Blue Note's impressive archives, *Blue Brazil* is another of the universally stellar releases in the *Blue* compilation series. Featuring some of the greatest Brazilian muscians of all time, the album contains vibrant boogie music and smooth tropical harmonies from artists like Luiz Arruda Paez, Marcos Valle, Mandrake Som, Bossa 3, Quarteto Novo, and others. *—Stacia Proefrock*

Blue Brazil, Vol. 2 / Nov. 10, 1998 / EMI ✦✦✦✦✦
Featuring some artists heard on the equally fine first volume, Blue Brazil, Vol. 2 spotlights the country's fertile musical output from 1964-1975. The majority of tracks here are vocal bossa nova or samba numbers, many framed in top-drawer jazz arrangements. Plenty of tasty horn charts, electric piano, and percussion crop up on infectious cuts by Milton Banana ("Ladeira Da Preguice"), Silvio Cezar & Meirelles ("Sambo Do Carioca"), and Leny Andrade ("Estamos Al"). Standout vocal performances are turned in by Elza Soares, including her stellar version of the Jorge Ben classic "Mas Que Nada," while fine instrumentals are contributed by Quinteto Villa Lobos and Som Tres. The relatively modern style of '70s tropicalismo (a rock meets bossa nova and beyond hybrid forged by Milton Nasciemento and Caetano Veloso) is taken up in fine fashion by Quarteto Em Cy and Di Melo, with the more experimental side of the genre (Tom Ze, Os Mutantes) being represented by Edu Lobo's Ligetiesque, choral bossa nova "Libera Nos." Add the dancefloor extravagance of a Bahian rhythms and synthesizer workout of Richard Strauss' "Also Sprach Zarathustra" (sure to be on Meco's Disco Brazil Classics) and the prevalence of Sergio Mendes & Brasil '66-inspired vocal harmonies, and you have an excellent collection. One of the best and most unique compilations of Brazilian music available. *—Stephen Cook*

Brasileiro / May 25, 1999 / Putumayo ✦✦✦✦
The great thing about Putumayo's world music compilations of the '90s was the label's tendency to make such unlikely choices. If a Putumayo compilation focused on Celtic music, many of the artists wouldn't be Irish or Scottish—and if the focus was salsa, Putumayo wasn't about to limit itself to big stars out of Cuba and Puerto Rico. A collection of Brazilian pop that spans 1974-1999, *Brasileiro* isn't as much of a musical rollercoaster as some might expect from Putumayo—you would have expected the collection to aim for maximum diversity and jump from forro, lambada and tropicalismo to bossa nova and serteneja before spotlighting a rap group from Bahia. But while *Brasileiro* isn't as far-reaching as it could have been, it's enjoyable and satisfying. Anyone who's seriously into Brazilian pop should be familiar with Beth Carvalho, Joao Bosco, Jorge Ben, Chico Buarque and the late Clara Nunes, but Putumayo also turns its attention to some artists who weren't huge names in Brazil when the compilation came out, including Zeca Baleiro, Chico Cesar (whose "Mama Africa" combines Afro-Brazilian music with reggae) and Rosa Passos, who embraces the Portuguese lyrics to the Jobim standard, "Waters of March." *—Alex Henderson*

☆ **Brazil Classics, Vol. 1: Beleza Tropical** / Oct. 1989 / Luaka Bop ✦✦✦✦✦
Brazil Classics, Beleza Tropical is the first in a series compiled by Talking Heads singer David Byrne that preceded the big wave of interest in Tropicalia during the late '90s by almost a decade. Performers include such influential Brazilian figures as Gilberto Gil, Caetano Veloso, and Jorge Ben, with several songs from each. The selected recordings span the 1970s and '80s, also including tracks from Milton Nascimento, Nazare Pereira, and more. The liner notes feature the original lyrics as well as their English translations. *—Joslyn Layne*

Brazil Classics, Vol. 2: O Samba / Jan. 1990 / Luaka Bop ✦✦✦✦✦
Compiler David Byrne has better taste than most U.S. concocters of Brazilian compilations. I prefer *O Samba* over the previous *Beliza Tropical* because I have a strong preference for the samba-based artists over the more eclectic types (e.g. Gil and Nascimento) on Beleza. But a few small cavils aside, Byrne's choices of cuts are all excellent. *—John Storm Roberts*

Brazil Classics, Vol. 3: Forró, Etc. / 1991 / Luaka Bop ✦✦✦✦✦
When David Byrne first visited the Salvador/Bahia region in 1986, a new musical form that he never heard before amazed him. Dubbed forro, this dance-sound originally hailed from Northeastern Brazil, described as "a mixture of ska with polka" by Byrne himself. All of the album's tracks radiate a strong, positive energy, created in the most part by reggae-ish acoustic guitars, melodic accordions, and never-ending contagious rhythms. And although this musical style could be compared to America's zydeco sound, forro is intended mainly for parties. *Brazil Classics 3* was compiled by Byrne himself and features the very best artists and compositions that the genre has to offer. Highlights include Luiz Gonzaga's excellent opener, "O Fole Roncou" (bordering on funk), Dominguinhos' laidback "Querubim," as well as the hyperenergetic "Festa do Interior" by Gal Costa. A superb introduction to the exotic style of forro, and highly recommended. *—Greg Prato*

Historia del Carnaval de Brasil 1902-1952, Vol. 1 / 1994 / Ubtugui ✦✦✦✦✦
1960s bossa nova aside, these might be the only historical reissues of any of Brazil's wonderful musical traditions. Not everything here is original—some gaps were filled by re-recording around 1950. But the real stuff starts in 1902 and keeps right on coming. The sheer joy and variety of the music aside, it's fascinating to hear the influences and sounds change over time (a lot of jazz from the 1920s on, of course). Volume 1 runs from 1872 to 1933. *—John Storm Roberts, Original Music*

Musique du Nordeste, Vol. 1: 1916-1945 / Feb. 9, 1999 / Buda Musique ✦✦✦✦
A wide variety of Brazilian-oriented compilations came out in the '90s, when labels turned their attention to everything from Rio bossa nova to the tropicalismo, Afro-Bahian music and accordion-driven forro of Northeastern Brazil. Spanning 1916-1945, *Musique du Nordeste, Vol. 1* is a French release focusing on music that was recorded in Northeastern Brazil during the 78 Era. This compilation is as fascinating as it is diverse, and the label spotlights frevo, choro, embolada and other styles with consistently appealing results. The singers and instrumentalists heard on *Musique du Nordeste* are some of the most important of their time and place, including Luis Gonzaga (a seminal figure who is considered the grandfather of forro), Luperce Miranda, Adelmar Tavares, guitarist Joao Pernambuco, Jararaca & Ratinho and band leaders Nelson and Levino Ferreira. The oldest recording in the collection, Armando and Alfredo Gama's "Os Que Sofrem," goes all the way back to 1916, while the most recent is Gonzaga's infectious "O Xamengo da Guiomar," from 1945. Highly unpredictable, *Musique du Nordeste* ranges from fast, exuberant numbers like Miranda's "Pinao," Jararaca & Ratinho's "Accende a Luz" and Joao Frazao's "Bataiao Nava," to dramatic ballads such as Capiba's "Maria Betania" and Tavares' "Historia Triste de uma Praieira." Overall, Buda's digital remastering is impressive; the Paris-based label has done a lot to clean up these classic recordings and make them much less scratchy and noisy than they could have been. If you've enjoyed Brazilian sounds of recent decades but haven't heard anything recorded in Brazil before the '50s, check out this compilation—it's quite a revelation. *—Alex Henderson*

Musique du Nordeste, Vol. 2: 1928-1946 / Mar. 9, 1999 / Buda Musique ✦✦✦✦✦
Like Vol. 1 of Buda Musique's *Musique du Nordeste* series, this equally superb CD examines some of the music that came out of Northeastern Brazil during the 20th century's first half. Buda once again turns its attention to such styles as choro, frevo and embolada, and many of the greats heard on Vol. 1 are also heard on *Vol. 2*, including Joao Pernambuco, Nelson Ferreira, Alfredo Gama, Minona Carneiro and accordion dynamo Luiz Gonzaga (who was the father of the late Brazilian pop star, Gonzaguinha, and is considered the godfather of forro and baiao). Variety is the rule on this CD, which ranges from the exuberance of Gonzaga's "Sanfonando" (1942), Carneiro's "Meu Girasol" (1928) and Capiba's "Julia" (1938) to the dramatic ballad singing of Alfredo Gama's "Saudades" (1928) and Valdemar de Oliveira's "Adeus Oh! Terra Onde Nasci" (1928). And here's a fact that's really ironic—as much ground as this collection covers, it doesn't even get into the Afro-Brazilian music of Bahia, one of the states in Northeastern Brazil. Had Buda (which provides informative liner notes in both French and English) decided to get into Bahian sounds of that era, a two-CD set would been in order! Of course, many of the non-Black artists on this compilation were influenced by Afro-Brazilian culture and rhythms of Bahia. Neither volume of *Musique du Nordeste* is meant to tell the entire story of Northeastern Brazil prior to the '50s—this collection simply scratches the surface, and does so with enriching results. *—Alex Henderson*

Rough Guide to the Music of Brazil / May 5, 1998 / World Music Network ✦✦✦✦✦
So much great music has come out of Brazil that when a label decides to assemble a Brazilian compilation, it has to decide whether it's going to focus on one particular area of Brazilian music or go for variety. With this excellent 19-song CD, the World Music Network opted for variety and decided to take listeners to various parts of that very large country. *The Rough Guide to the Music of Brazil* ranges from funky Afro-Brazilian music of Bahia like Ze Paulo's "Batom Vermelho" and Muzenza's rap-minded "Charles Anjo 45" to breezy, jazz-influenced samba from Rio de Janeiro such as Ivan Lins' "Provei," Rosa Passos' "E Luxo E" and Leny Andrade's bossa nova offering "Voce Vai Ver." Dominguinhos' exuberant "A Lolta Da Asa Branca" is an example of forro, an accordion-dominated style that has been called "Brazilian zydeco," while Pena Branca & Xavantinho's "Santos Reis" falls under the heading of sertaneja, which is considered Brazil's equivalent of country & western and can also be compared to Mexican mariachi. Far from one-dimensional, this was one of the more ambitious Brazilian collections to come out in the late 1990s. *—Alex Henderson*

Tropicalia Essentials / Sep. 21, 1999 / Polygram ✦✦✦✦✦
Tropicalia Essentials capitalizes on the rising popularity and influence of tropicalia, a politically-charged Brazilian musical movement from the late '60s and early '70s that combined indigenous styles with rock, blues, jazz, folk and psychedelic elements. Hip-O's collection of tropicalia classics includes songs from some of the movement's finest songwriters, including Caetano Veloso and Gilberto Gil. *—Heather Phares*

Chile

Inti Illimani

Group / Andean Folk, Latin Folk, Chile, Latin Continuum
The musical traditions of Latin America and the Andes Mountains have been preserved for more than three decades by Inti-Illimani. Performing on more than thirty instruments, the group has brought a fresh vitality and excitement to their traditional repertoire. Through non-stop touring, Inti-Illimani has exposed audiences around the globe to their musical roots. In addition to performing on their own, the group has shared stages with Pete Seeger, Mikis Theodorakis, Mercedes Sosa and John Williams. During the Amnesty International Tour in 1988, Inti-Illimani performed with Sting, Bruce Springsteen, Peter Gabriel and Tracy Chapman. Initially an eight piece group, Inti-Illimani was formed, in 1967, by engineering students at the Santiago Technical University. Forsaking their studies, the group was soon touring throughout Latin America. On tour when Chilean president Salvador Allended was deposed in 1973, the band found themselves exiled from their homeland. For the next fourteen years, their base of operations was in Rome, Italy. They were allowed to return to Chile in 1988. *—Craig Harris*

El Vuelo del Condor / 1982 / BBC ✦✦✦✦

● **Imaginacion** / 1984 / Redwood ✦✦✦✦✦
Andean folkloric instrumental music; 14 tracks with the emphasis on joy and light. *—Michael G. Nastos*

Andadas / Aug. 1992 / Green Linnet ♦♦♦♦

Amar de Nuevo / Jul. 13, 1999 / Xenophile ♦♦♦♦

When *Amar de Nuevo* was recorded in Santiago, Chile, in 1998, Inti-Illimani had been together for 31 years. But the Chilean band was showing no signs of losing its freshness. After all those years, Inti-Illimani was still taking chances and continued to experiment with a variety of Latin styles. The music of South American Indians—Chilean and Peruvian as well as Bolivian—was still Inti-Illimani's foundation, and the band was still uniting that foundation with styles from all over Latin America. On this CD, South American music is successfully fused with everything from Afro-Cuban salsa ("Negra Presuntuosa," "La Fiesta Eres Tu") to Mexican ranchero ("Corrido de la Soberbia"). On the instrumental "Entre Amor," the Chileans combine Andean music with elements of tango. Those who have admired the band's previous releases will find Amar de Nuevo to be equally rewarding. *—Alex Henderson*

Colombia

Joe Arroyo

b. Nov. 1, 1955, Cartagena, Colombia

Vocals / Tropical, Salsa, Colombia, Latin Continuum

A diverse sampling of Caribbean music styles, including salsa, compas, merengue, reggae and soca, is fused into the dance-inspiring sounds of Colombia-born vocalist Joe Arroyo (born: Alvaro Jose Arroyo Gonzalez). A former member of leading salsa band, Fruko Y Sus Tesos, Arroyo has continued to blend musical influences with his own group, La Verdad (The Truth), since 1981.

Arroyo began his musical career at the young age of eight when he sang in a strip joint in his hometown of Cartagena. His first break came after he signed with record label, Discos Fuentes, in 1971, and was overheard by bass player, singer, composer and producer Ernesto Estrada, better known as Frugo, who recruited him for his band. Arroyo continued to work with Frugo for the next decade. Although he nearly died from a drug overdose in the early-1980s, Arroyo recovered and began to attract attention with his own group, La Verdad. *—Craig Harris*

● **Fuego** / 1993 / Sonotone Latino ♦♦♦♦♦

Arroyo had become a major favorite among European salsa buffs, and a considerable success on the Latin concert circuit. Novelty aside, the reason is that while he hews to a tight but pretty standard salsa sound, he uses all sorts of Colombian rhythms (including cumbia), thus giving his universality strong local roots. *—John Storm Roberts*

30 Pegaditas de Oro / Nov. 25, 1997 / Discos Fuentes ♦♦♦♦♦

Colombia Collection

☆ **Cumbia Cumbia** / 1989 / World Circuit ♦♦♦♦♦

Running from the 50s to the 80s, these cuts perfectly showcase the most charming of Latin American music—a kind of musical equivalent to the poetry of Edward Lear. *—Carl Hoyt, Original Music*

Greatest Salsa Classics of Colombia / Apr. 1, 1997 / Discos Fuentes ♦♦♦

The Rough Guide to Cumbia / May 2, 2000 / World Music Network ♦♦♦♦

Cumbia is to Columbia what samba is to Brazil, tango is to Argentina, and merengue is to the Dominican Republic—it isn't the country's only style of music, but it is definitely its most famous and popular. Numerous cumbia compilations have come out in the U.S., Europe, and Latin America; one of them is *The Rough Guide to Cumbia*. This collection, released in 2000, spans the 1950s-1990s, although it tends to favor classic cumbia over contemporary cumbia. Regrettably, World Music Network fails to provide recording dates; if the company didn't want to go to that trouble, it could have at least listed the years in which the CD's 22 tracks were released. But to the Network's credit, the sound quality is good and its choices are usually first-rate. Listeners are exposed to some of cumbia's true heavyweights thanks to classics by Lucho Bermudez ("Columbia Tierra Querida," "Danza Negra"), Alfredo Gutiérrez ("La Banda Borracha"), Leonor González Mina ("Yo Me Llamo Cumbia"), and Jaime Llano González ("Cumbia en Azul"). Meanwhile, Lisandro Meza's "Salsipuedes" from 1991 is among the collection's more modern recordings. One thing the compilation doesn't get into is the cumbia of Mexico and the southwestern U.S., where Mexican artists have been playing their own interpretations of cumbia; this disc is Columbian all the way. *The Rough Guide to Cumbia* is hardly the last word on cumbia, but it's generally rewarding and can serve as a fine introduction to the style, although it would have been nice if the World Music Network had listed recording dates. *—Alex Henderson*

Cuba

Afro-Cuban All Stars

Group / Afro-Cuban Jazz, Latin Jazz, Cuba, Latin Continuum

The loose confederation of performers working under the Afro-Cuban All Stars umbrella included, among others, pianist Ruben Gonzalez, guitarist Eliades Ochoa, trumpeter Manuel Mirabal Vasquez, bassist Orlando Lopez Vergara, laudista player Barbaro Alberto Torres Delgado, flautist Richard Egues, percussionist Julienne Oviedo Sanchez and singers Ibrahim Ferrer, Omara Portuondo, Manuel Licea, Raul Planas, Felix Vanoy, Jose Antonio Rodriguez and Pio Leyva—indeed, a who's who of 20th century Cuban music. Their debut LP *A Toda Cuba Le Gusta* appeared in 1997; *Distinto Diferente* followed two years later. *—Jason Ankeny*

● **A Toda Cuba Le Gusta** / Sep. 16, 1997 / Elektra/Asylum ♦♦♦♦

The first of a stream of albums highlighting the elder statesmen of Cuban music, *A Toda Cuba le Gusta* is a true ensemble piece with brilliant contributions from a variety of artists. Perhaps the most stunning is pianist Ruben Gonzales, who lends both depth and brightness to a sound that manages to be joyful and melancholy at the same time. Ibrahim Ferrer also lends a clear and powerful voice to the project, but this is really a triumph of the total ensemble. *—Stacia Proefrock*

Distinto Diferente / Oct. 26, 1999 / Elektra ♦♦♦

Adalberto Alvarez

Vocals / Cuban Jazz, Son, Tropical, Salsa, Latin Pop, Cuba, Latin Continuum

Adalberto Alvarez has been a leading force in the revival of Son, the Cuban dance music that reached its peak in popularity in the 1950s. The former leader of Son 14, Alvarez has continued to pay homage, as well as expand, the Son tradition with Y Su Son, the band that he formed in 1984. While his music signals a return to the traditional sounds, Alvarez has successfully incorporated more modern musical influences. According to "The New York Times," "(Adalberto Alvarez Y Su Son) is one of Cuba's great bands, one that has had an enormous influence on Salsa; it's modern and unstoppable and it doesn't sound like the Havana-based dance music called timba. Instead, it sounds a bit more traditional, closer to New York and Puerto Rican salsa, smooth and elegant for a moment, until the volcano loses the top." Alvarez studied musical directing and composition at the national Arts School in his hometown of Camaguey. Following his graduation, he was asked to form an orchestra in Santiage de Cuba. That group became Son 14, one of the pioneer ensembles of modern Son. In 1984, Alvarez formed a new band, Adalberto Alvarez Y Su Son, in Santiago De Las Vegas, a suburb of Havana. Although they use the traditional Son instruments, including the Cuban tres, a guitar with triple sets of double strings, and plucked bass, the group's sound is enhanced by electronic keyboards, timbales, trombones and other brass instruments. Jorge Luis Rojas (Rojitas), the band's original vocalist left to join Jesus Alemany's band, ¡Cubanismo!, and was replaced by Aramis Galindo. While many of Adalberto Alvarez Y Su Son's songs reflect on the usual Son themes of everyday life, several tunes deal with Santeria, the religion in which Alvarez is a babalao or priest. *—Craig Harris*

● **Jugando con Candela (Playing with Fire)** / Apr. 20, 1999 / Atlantic ♦♦♦♦

Cuban composer/musician Adalberto Alvarez blends past and present musical influences, including son and salsa, into his stylish and sensual works. On his fifth album *Jugando Con Condela* ("playing with fire") he lives up to his own musical tradition as well as that of his homeland, leading his orchestra through intense and graceful works like "Estas Como Villegas" and "Una Mulata en la Habana." Alvarez's musical territory balances past and present, and promises a beautiful future for Cuban music. *—Heather Phares*

Adalberto Alvarez Y Su Son / 1990 / Egrem/Artex ♦♦♦♦

It's good to be reminded by this 1990 recording that Cuba still produces bands that can hew to the classic forms (and they don't come more classic than the son). Alvarez's powerful vocals are backed by a macho sound that shares a lot of the power and weight of the New York version but with plenty of individual quirks. Check the samba-son "El Regreso de Maria," from the piano intro on in. Plus (for Spanish-speakers) the lyrics have the classic son/calypso/plena topicality: "What Happened to Me on the Bus" or "I Got Married Drunk." *—John Storm Roberts, Original Music*

Desi Arnaz

b. Mar. 2, 1917, Santiago, Cuba, **d.** Nov. 2, 1986

Vocals, Bandleader / Tropical, Latin Pop, Cuba, Latin Continuum

To most of the public, Desi Arnaz is known as the lovable, temperamental Ricky Ricardo, husband of Lucille Ball in the 1950s (in real life and on screen) on one of the most successful television series of all time, *I Love Lucy*. Within the industry, he's known as one of the forces behind Desilu Productions. Yet before he became an international star, he was known primarily as a musician, not an actor or executive. It was Arnaz who may have done more to popularize the conga in the United States than any other figure, leading an orchestra that mixed Latin-Cuban music with big-band pop, and putting it over to the masses with his irresistibly good-natured, melodramatic vocals. He's attracted far less critical acclaim than more ambitious Latin-American hybrids like Machito, the Dizzy Gillespie Orchestra of the late '40s, or his one-time mentor Xavier Cugat, but his recordings contain a surprising amount of shake-em-loose verve.

Born in Santiago, Cuba, Arnaz moved to Miami in his teens, and began to work as a conga player, singer, and guitarist. For six months, he apprenticed with Xavier Cugat's orchestra, and then split to form a band of his own. He made his first sides as a bandleader around 1940 with his La Congra Orchestra, and his New York shows created enough of a buzz to get him a stage role in a musical by Richard Rodgers and Lorenz Hart, *Too Many Girls*, in 1939. He repeated his *Too Many Girls* role on screen, leading to a Hollywood career and his marriage to comedienne Lucille Ball.

After serving in the Army during World War II, Arnaz focused on music for the rest of the 1940s, cutting quite a few infectious sides for Victor between 1946 and 1949. Certainly some of his accented routines could be corny, but he and his orchestra could also whip up a storm on tracks like "Babalu" and "El Cumbanchero," achieving his avowed goal of combining the rhythm of Machito with the melody of Andre Kostelanetz. After recording his last session for Victor in 1949, Arnaz refocused his attention on Hollywood, putting his musical career on permanent back burner after becoming one of television's first superstars with *I Love Lucy*. *—Richie Unterberger*

● **Babalu** / 1996 / RCA ♦♦♦♦♦

Twenty tracks from his 1946-49 prime, mostly paced by Arnaz himself on vocals, with some instrumentals and occasional pieces for female singers Jane Harvey, Elsa Miranda, and Amanda Lane. Sure, this is sometimes corny, but more often it's invigorating Latin big-band pop, Arnaz' conga and quasi-operatic vocals to the forefront. Those who dismiss this as Cuban rhythms watered down for American consumption are missing the essential point: it's *fun* stuff that's usually overflowing with joie de vivre, as a listen to "Babalu," "Carnival in Rio," "Quizas, Quizas, Quizas," "Guadalajara," and "El Cumbanchero" will confirm. *—Richie Unterberger*

Buena Vista Social Club

Group / Cuban Jazz, Modern Son, Afro-Cuban Jazz, Latin Jazz, Cuba, Latin Continuum
Less a band than an assemblage of some of Cuba's most renowned musical forces, Buena Vista Social Club's origins lie with noted American guitarist Ry Cooder, who in 1996 traveled to Havana to seek out a number of legendary local musicians whose performing careers largely ended decades earlier with the rise of Fidel Castro. Recruiting the long-forgotten likes of singer Ibrahim Ferrer, guitarists/singers Compay Segundo and Eliades Ochoa, and pianist Rubén González, Cooder entered Havana's Egrem Studios to record the album *Buena Vista Social Club;* the project was an unexpected commercial and critical smash, earning a Grammy and becoming the best-selling release of Cooder's long career. In 1998 he returned to Havana with percussionist son Joaquim to record a solo LP with Ferrar; the sessions were captured on film by director Wim Wenders, who also documented sell-out Buena Vista Social Club live performances in Amsterdam and New York City. (Wenders' film, also titled simply *Buena Vista Social Club,* earned an Academy Award nomination in 2000.) The public's continued interest in Cuban music subsequently generated solo efforts from Segundo and González as well as a series of international live performances promoted under the Buena Vista Social Club aegis. *—Jason Ankeny*

★ **Buena Vista Social Club** / Sep. 16, 1997 / Classic Compact Disc ✦✦✦✦✦
This album is named after a members-only club that was opened in Havana in pre-%Castro times, a period of unbelievable musical activity in Cuba. While bandleader Desi Arnaz became a huge hit in the States, several equally talented musicians never saw success outside their native country, and have had nothing but their music to sustain them during the Castro reign. Ry Cooder went to Cuba to record a musical documentary of these performers. Many of the musicians on this album have been playing for more than a half century, and they sing and play with an obvious love for the material. Cooder could have recorded these songs without paying the musicians a cent; one can imagine them jumping up and grabbing for their instruments at the slightest opportunity, just to play. Most of the songs are a real treasure, traversing a lot of ground in Cuba's musical history. There's the opening tune, "Chan Chan," a composition by 89-year-old Compay Segundo, who was a bandleader in the '50s; the cover of the early '50s tune "De Camino a La Verada," sung by the 72-year-old composer Ibrahim Ferrer, who interrupted his daily walk through Havana just long enough to record; or the amazing piano playing on "Pablo Nuevo" by 77-year-old Ruben Gonzalez, who has a unique style that blends jazz, mambo and a certain amount of playfulness. All of these songs were recorded live—some of them in the musicians' small apartments—and the sound is incredibly deep and rich, something that would have been lost in digital recording and overdubbing. Cooder brought just the right amount of reverence to this material, and it shows in his production, playing and detailed liner notes. If you get one album of Cuban music, this should be the one. *—Steve McMullen*

Cachao (Israel Lopez)

b. Sep. 14, 1918, Havana, Cuba
Bass, Composer / Big Band Latino, Son, Tropical, Afro-Cuban Jazz, Mambo, Latin Jazz, Salsa, Latin Pop, Cuba, Latin Continuum
Cuban bassist Cachao is credited as the man who created mambo music. He spent most of his 76 years living in Cuba where he was a prominent jazz sideman who specialized in Afro-Cuban dance music. He eventually made it to the US and lived in Miami almost nine years with little or no recognition, due in part to his extreme modesty. He was first introduced to the world by actor/ filmmaker Andy Garcia, who was born in Cuba but raised in Miami, via his 1993 documentary *Cachao . . . Como Su Rítmo No Hay Dos.* The film earned glowing reviews, especially for the music. On January 16, 1993, Cachao played a sold-out Radio City Music Hall in New York to considrable acclaim. In March of 1995, Cachao earned a Grammy for his album *Master Sessions, Vol. 1. —Sandra Brennan*

Cachao Y Su Descarga '77, Vol. 1 / May 1978 / Sony ✦✦✦
One of the greatest Cuban bassists (and the bass is what pegs all that superb rhythmic interplay), Cachao has played with all the greatest names in his time. Alas, the personnel of this superlative '60s recording isn't given, but greatness is everywhere present. And not just greatness in the splendid tres playing, the brilliant trumpet and singing and on and on, but richness and variety. The numbers range from extremely Afro-centric pieces to classic son ("Tres Lindas Cubanas," and the delights along the way include a rare-as-hen's-teeth clarinet solo of enormous charm. Quintessential about sums it up . . .). *—John Storm Roberts, Original Music*

● **Master Sessions, Vol. 1** / 1994 / Crescent Moon/Epic ✦✦✦✦✦
Too often when historical forms (think danzón, son, rumba) are given note-for-note renderings, they end up museum pieces. Doesn't happen here, though. Of course, it doesn't hurt at all that Cachao has had a hand in the development of almost every significant modern Latin style (think mambo, chachachá, descarga). *—Original Music*

Compay Segundo (Máximo Francisco Repilado Muñoz)

Vocals / Afro-Cuban Jazz, Latin Jazz, Cuba, Latin Continuum
Legendary Cuban guitarist Compay Segundo was born in 1907; collaborating with the likes of Sindo Garay, Miguel Matamoros and Benny Moré, he emerged as one of the most respected musicians of the pre-revolution era, and in the late 1920s invented the armónico, a guitar customized with a double third string to fuse the tonal qualities of the traditional Cuban tres guitar and its Spanish counterpart. Following Fidel Castro's rise to power, Segundo worked as a cigar roller before returning to music during the late 1980s; now in his early nineties, he attracted worldwide attention in 1998 for his contributions to Ry Cooder's wildly successful *Buena Vista Social Club* album, issuing the solo *Calle Salud* the following year. *Buena Vista Connection* was issued in fall 2000. *Flores de la Vida* followed a year later; *Trova Cubana* surfaced in early 2001. *—Jason Ankeny*

Calle Salud / Nov. 2, 1999 / Elektra ✦✦✦✦✦
Compay Segundo is one of the legends of Cuban music. When he started playing the clarinet in the municipal band of Santiago de Cuba as a teenager, the world was just recovering from World War I. Segundo is one of the musicians who shaped the Cuban son style. More recently, he was a major contributor to 1999's surprise hit *Buena Vista Social Club.* Segundo is a well-respected clarinetist and guitarist, and he's probably been even more widely celebrated in Cuba for his bass vocal harmonies. *Calle Salud* treats listeners to a truly old-world sound. Segundo and his collaborators reprise tunes in the son, bolero-son, merengue, son-afro, and cha cha styles. Within this incredibly mellow and unfailingly romantic music, the listener will notice the dominance of the clarinet and guitars and the absence of brass, which is typical of pre-1940s son, giving the music a gentle, lyrical feel, yet maintaining a beat that's every bit as rhythmic as modern salsa or samba. For the most part, Segundo's music is for slow dancers, though a son number like "Viejos Sones de Santiago" is as rumba-friendly as timba, the currently-happening Cuban dance music. *—Philip Van Vleck*

Celia Cruz

b. Oct. 21, 1924, Havana, Cuba
Vocals / Son, Tropical, Mambo, Latin Jazz, Salsa, Latin Pop, Cuba, Latin Continuum
Celia Cruz is one of Latin music's most respected vocalists. A ten-time Grammy nominee, Cruz, who sings only in her native Spanish language, has received a Smithsonian Lifetime Achievement award, a National Medal Of the Arts and honorary doctorates from Yale University and the University of Miami. A street in Miami has been renamed in her honor. Cruz' trademark orange, red and white polka dot dress and shoes have been placed in ther permanent collection of the Smithsonian Institute of Technology. The Hollywood Wax Museum includes a statue of the Cuba-born songstress. According to "The European Jazz Network," Cruz "commands her realm with a down-to-earth dignity unmistakeably vibrant in her wide smile and striking pose." One of fourteen children, born in the small village of Barrio Santra Suarez, Havana, Cruz was drawn to music from an early age. Her first pair of shoes was a gift from a tourist for whom she sang. In addition to spending many evenings singing her younger siblings to sleep, Cruz sang in school productions and community gatherings. Taken to cabarets and nightclubs by an aunt, she was introduced to the world of professional music. At the encouragement of a cousin, Cruz began to enter and win local talent shows. Although her father attempted to guide her towards a career as a teacher, Cruz continued to be lured by music. In a 1997 interview, she said, "I have fulfilled my father's wish to be a teacher as, through my music, I teach generations of people about my culture and the happiness that is found in just living life. As a performer, I want people to feel their hearts sing and their spirits soar." Enrolling in Cuba's Conservatory of Music in 1947, Cruz found her earliest inspiration in the singing of Afro-Cuban vocalist Paulina Alvarez. Her first break came when she was invited to join the band led by Sonora Matancera in 1950. The group was revered as the Latin equivalent of the Duke Ellington Orchestra. Cruz remained with the group for fifteen years, touring throughout the world. She married the band's trumpet player Pedro Knight on July 14, 1962. With Fidel Castro's assuming control of Cuba in 1960, Cruz and Knight refused to return to their homeland and became citizens of the United States. Although they initially signed to perform with the orchestra of the Hollywood Palladium, Cruz and Knight eventually settled in New York. Knight became Cruz' manager in 1965, a position he held until the mid-1990s when he began to devote his attention to serving as her musical director and conductor of her band. Leaving Sonora Matancera's band in 1965, Cruz launched her solo career with a band formed for her by Tito Puente. Despite releasing eight albums together, the collaboration failed to achieve commercial success. Cruz and Puente resumed their partnership with a special appearance at the Grammy award ceremonies in 1987. Signed by Vaya, the sister label of Fania, Cruz recorded with Oscar D'Leon, Cheo Feliciano and Hector Rodriquez in the mid- to late-1960s. Cruz's first success since leaving Sonora Matancera came in 1974 when she recorded a duo album, *Celia And Johnny,* with Johnny Pacheco, trombone player and the owner of Fania. She subsequently began appearing with the Fania All Stars. Cruz' popularity reached its highest level when she appeared in the 1992 film, *The Mambo Kings.* Cruz also appeared in the film, *The Perez Family.* She sang a duet version of "Loco De Amor," with David Byrne, in the Jonathan Demme movie, *Something Wild.* In 1998, Cruz released *Duets,* an album featuring her singing with Willie Colon, Angela Carrasco, Oscar D'Leon, Jose Alberto "El Canario" and La India. *—Craig Harris*

Celia & Willie / 1994 / Vaya ✦✦✦✦✦

Irrepetible / 1994 / Sony International ✦✦✦

● **100% Azucar: The Best of Celia Cruz & La Sonora Matancera** / Sep. 16, 1997 / Rhino ✦✦✦✦✦
Female singers are abundant in Latin pop, but for whatever reason, salsa has remained a male-dominated idiom. From the 1950s to the mid-'90s, salsa's most prominent female vocalist has been Celia Cruz, a pearl of a singer rightly exalted as "The Queen of Salsa." This excellent CD focuses largely on the recordings she made with La Sonora Mantancera in her native Havana, Cuba in the 1950s. La Sonora was already one of Cuba's top dance bands when Cruz was hired to replace singer Myrta Silva in 1950, and her passionate performances on such classics as "Ritmo, Tambo y Flores" (1951), "Burundanga" (1953) and "Melao De Cana" (1953) made it clear that she was the right choice. For even casual salseros, "Mi Sonito" (1955), "Me Voy a Pinar Del Rio" (1956), "Chango Ta Veni" (1958) and other gems on *100% Azucar!* are essential listening. *Azucar!* also contains a handful of recordings made in the early to mid-1960s in New York, including an excellent version of Ignacio Pineiro's "Suavecito" (1962). With Cuba under communism, Cruz and her husband, Sonora trumpeter Pedro Knight, made a permanent move to the U.S. in 1961. *100% Azucar!* isn't quite the last word on early Cruz—where are "Cao Cao Mani Picao" (1951) and "Tumba La Cana, Jibarito" (1960)— Nonetheless, it can serve as a fine introduction to her legacy. *—Alex Henderson*

¡Cubanismo!

Group / Cuban Jazz, Modern Son, Cuba, Latin Continuum
¡Cubanismo! certainly has good timing. Releasing their first album just before the seminal

world music success of *Buena Vista Social Club,* they were poised to make a real impact with their melodic Cuban music, that kept its roots strong, but also reached outward with a rhythmic kick and a sense of adventure. The band was formed by trumpeter Jes's Alemañy, who been a Cuban child prodigy, gliding through Havana's Conservatorio Amadeo Roldan, then joining Sierra Maestra, the group that helped rejuvenate Cuban *son,* when he was just 16. The solid grounding in Cuban musical traditions stood him in good stead when he was finally ready to go it alone after more than a decade. He moved to London in 1992, playing and learning, and networking with fellow Cubans—including percussion Patato Valdez, for whom he helped organize a *descarga,* or jam session, in Paris in 1994. Among those invited was record producer, and head of Hannibal Records, Joe Boyd. He liked what he heard and suggested that Alemañy return to Cuba and organize another *descargo,* this one to be recorded. It took a little while, but in 1995, a group of musicians assembled at Egrem Studios in Havana, including veteran pianist Alfredo Rodríguez, and 10 year-old bongo player Julian Oveido—a wide cross-section of ages, but all extremely talented. They laid down some classic Cuban material, with sizzling solos and percussion, and the result was the first, self-titled ¡Cubanismo! record, released in 1996. Extensive touring, and frequent lie-up changes followed, meaning that *Malembe,* the band's 1997 follow-up, had noticeably different personnel. But, if anything, the music was hotter and jazzier than before, with the emphasis remaining on Cuban classics, although some original material crept into the mix. Arriving as it did when *Buena Vista Social Club* started opening American ears to Cuban sounds, it helped ¡Cubanismo! tap into the Zeitgeist for the music and become known as they continued to tour the world ceaselessly. Certainly, by 1998 they were firing on all cylinders, as *Reencarnacion* showed, with the rhythm on fire, and the trumpet solos louder and higher than ever, as the rest of the band—with many different faces once more—seemed to burn hard and bright. However, it was really beginning to seem that they'd gone as far as they could down that particular street, unless they began repeating themselves. What followed was a two-year gap between records, which ended with the 2000 release of *Mardi Gras Mambo,* a record that connected the dots between the musics of Havana and the Crescent City. And they certainly seemed to have a lot in common, and second-line rhythms, New Orleans R&B, and even a little rap mixed with son and mambo. A bunch of Louisiana guests, including veteran singer John Boutté, lent their talents to tunes like the traditional *Iko Iko* and Huey P. Smith's *It Do Me Good,* as well as some originals, to create a gumbo with plenty of Cuban spice, and a ¡Cubanismo! that sounded reinvigorated. A successful U.S. tour followed the record's release. *—Chris Nickson*

Malembe / Apr. 29, 1997 / Hannibal ✦✦✦✦

● **Reencarnacion** / Sep. 15, 1998 / Hannibal ✦✦✦✦✦
As the title suggests, ¡Cubanismo!'s third album is a reincarnation of sorts, with several new band members and an even greater variety of musical stylings explored. One thing that hasn't changed is the almost tangible intensity and excitement that Jesus Alemany and company bring to every song, whether a traditional Cuban number originally performed a half century ago or a new composition. This album is slightly more subdued than the previous two, but is excellent nonetheless. While *Malembe* is recommended as the best starting point for neophytes, one really can't go wrong with any of this group's first three albums. *—Steve McMullen*

Ibrahim Ferrer

Vocals / Cuban Jazz, Latin Jazz, Cuba, Latin Continuum
Cuban singer Ibrahim Ferrer was born in the city of Santiago in 1927, beginning his performing career at age 14; by the 1950s he was fronting Pacho Alonso's Havana-based orchestra, remaining with the group for over two decades. Ferrer also guested with Cuban legends like the Orquesta de Chepin and Beny Moré, but by the 1980s he was out of music, shining shoes and living on a tiny monthly pension; finally, in 1997 he was lured out of retirement to make his recorded debut on the Afro-Cuban All Stars' debut *Toda Cuba Le Gusta,* followed that same year by an appearance on Ry Cooder's *Buena Vista Social Club* LP. In 1999, he released his solo debut, *Buena Vista Social Club Presents Ibrahim Ferrer.* His critical acclaim was not disregarded, for Ferrer won a Grammy for Best New Artist at the first annual Latin Grammy Awards in fall 2000. *—Jason Ankeny*

● **Buena Vista Social Club Presents Ibrahim Ferrer** / Jun. 8, 1999 / Elektra/Nonesuch ✦✦✦✦✦
When the *Buena Vista Social Club* album was released to great acclaim in 1997, it revived the careers of quite a few incredibly talented aging Cuban musicians. Like Ibrahim Ferrer, most of those musicians (who had been legendary in the '40s through the '70s) hadn't been performing professionally in decades. With the success of the Buena Vista Social Club, everything changed; they toured the globe, and plans for follow-up albums followed. Ibrahim Ferrer's was the second of what became a line of Buena Vista releases, all hoping to cash in on the success of the first. Ferrer's album is pleasant, the kind of album you could put on during brunch on a sunny morning. The album features many classic Cuban compositions. Original arrangers, musicians, and bandleaders were involved whenever possible. One standout is "Mami Me Gusto," a rolling upbeat tune by the legendary Cuban composer/bandleader Arsenio Rodriguez. On that tune Ferrer is lively and loose, and he is joined by Rodriguez's original pianist, the masterful Ruben Gonzales. The rest of the album is nice, but rarely as inspired or joyous as the original Buena Vista release. This is a much more romantic sounding album and on the right tunes, like "Aquellos Ojos Verdes," they really hit the mark; Ferrer shines and Gonzales sends glistening piano lines cascading down the keys. At age 63-plus, Ferrer was long overdue for a debut album, and as a result the disc communicates a feel of easy satisfaction. If you're looking for classy cocktail party music that will hold the attention of music fans, and won't bother the uninterested, look no further. *—David Lavin*

Ruben Gonzalez

b. 1920
Piano / Cuban Jazz, Son, Rhumba, Latin Jazz, Cuba, Latin Continuum
Ruben Gonzalez is one of the last of Cuba's great Afro-Cuban piano players. Although he had played and recorded with the band led by Enrique Jorrin, the creator of the cha-cha, for a quarter of a century, he had retired from music by the mid-'80s. Things began to change when Gonzalez recorded with the Afro-Cuban All-Stars in 1996. The album, *A Todo Cuba Le Gusta,* released the following year, helped to inspire an international fascination for Afro-Cuban music and brought Gonzalez to the attention of a global audience. His performance on the Ry Cooder-produced album, *Buena Vista Social Club,* made him an international phenomenon. Signing a contract with Cooder's label, World Circuit, Gonzalez released his debut solo album, *Introducing Ruben Gonzalez,* at the age of seventy-eight. He's subsequently released three additional solo albums, *Indestructible,* released on the Egrem label in 1998, *Estrellas De Arieto,* released on the Eden Ways label in 1999 and *Chanchullo,* released on Nonesuch in 2000. Showing great promise, as a pianist, from an early age, Gonzalez graduated from the Cienfuego Conservatoire in 1934. Although he briefly attended medical school, hoping to become a doctor, the lure of music proved unsurmountable. Leaving school, Gonzalez moved to Havana to become a full-time musician in 1941. After recording with influential multi-instrumentalist Arsenio Rodriquez, Gonzalez joined Orquestra de Los Hermanos, a group featuring Cuban percussionist Mango Santamaria. Following an extended period in Panama and Argentina, during which he worked with tango musicians, he returned to Havana and played with a series of cabaret bands. In the early '60s, Gonzalez joined Enrique Jorrin's band, remaining with the group until Jorrin's death. Although he assumed leadership of the band, Gonzalez was forced, by arthritis, to announce his retirement. He maintained a low-key presence until 1996. Since his return, however, Gonzalez has enjoyed the fame that has been long overdue, releasing two albums in the U.S, including 2000's *Chanchullo* and R. Gonzalez & R. Planas con la Orquestra. *—Craig Harris*

● **Introducing . . . Ruben Gonzalez** / Sep. 16, 1997 / Elektra/Asylum ✦✦✦✦
Elegant piano playing with impeccable timing is the hallmark of septuagenarian Cuban maestro Rubén González. He explores all the rhythms on this, his first recording in 50 years, done live in the studio. With a highly responsive small ensemble backing him, the result is a pleasant listen. However, although Ry Cooder calls him "the greatest piano soloist I've ever heard," this is not the "best" Afro-Cuban piano on record, nor is it in the same league as Ellington, Monk or Tatum. *—Janet Rosen*

Chanchullo / Sep. 19, 2000 / Elektra ✦✦✦

Irakere

f. 1973
Group / Cuban Jazz, Afro-Cuban Jazz, Latin Folk, Latin Jazz, Cuba, Latin Continuum
Many of the top Cuban jazz musicians have played in Irakere during the past 30 years including altoist Paquito D'Rivera and trumpeter Arturo Sandoval (before both individually defected). Pianist Chucho Valdes has been the orchestra's longtime leader and its music ranges from Latin-jazz and bop to Cuban folk melodies with an emphasis on infectious rhythms and advanced improvisations. Several of Irakere's records have been made available domestically (including sets for Columbia and more recently Jazz House) but the exciting band was not able to visit the United States until 1996. The album *Toda Cuba Baila con Irakere* followed two years later. *—Scott Yanow*

● **The Best of Irakere** / Jun. 28, 1978-Apr. 1979 / Columbia/Legacy ✦✦✦✦✦
For today's Latin jazz fans, this is a succinct and nearly complete roundup of Irakere's two North American albums, a brief peek through Cuba's door before politics slammed it shut again for another generation. *Irakere* is represented by four tracks, including the lengthy, uncut "Black Mass," and *Irakere II* by six tracks. The live *Irakere* was an exciting breakthrough, a real advance in the alliance between Afro-Cuban and American jazz that took into account the electronic developments in music since politics isolated Cuba from the U.S. *Irakere II,* a studio product, is not nearly as startling; the sound and arrangements are slicker, there are strings and voices on some cuts, supertrumpeter Arturo Sandoval was encouraged to show off his pretty tone as well as his fire, and the Cubans even tried to churn out a disco beat on some tracks, negating all of those wild, wonderful Afro-Cuban cross-rhythms. Still, there are passages where the more commercially motivated grooves take off, as in the central section of "Ciento Anos De Juventud," and "Xiomara" is a killer in the old Cuban tradition. Interestingly, when Irakere made their belated American comeback at the *Playboy Jazz Festival* at Hollywood Bowl in 1996, some of their innovative edge was gone, replaced by overt attempts to get the crowd up on its collective feet. All the more reason to cherish this CD—which has become the only option one has to sample this Cuban band at, and nearly at, its peak. *—Richard S. Ginell*

Irakere / May 1979 / CBS ✦✦✦✦✦
North American Latin jazz audiences were knocked out when this LP came out, for it was the first idea many of us had of the explosive power of this Cuban jazz/rock band, which had been let briefly out of Cuba to tour. Columbia taped them live at New York's *Newport Festival* and Switzerland's *Montreux Jazz Festival,* and the result was a noisy, ambitious, frenzied, tremendously exciting mixture of everything but the kitchen sink. Co-founder, keyboardist and arranger Chucho Valdes was as thoroughly attuned to the thumping electric bass, the careening buzz of a synthesizer and bell-like electric piano as he was to his homeland's complex rhythms and his own classical training—and despite the cultural embargo, the 11-piece group was in touch with then-current developments in American jazz/rock. "Juana Mil Ciento," curiously the only track not available on CD, comes roaring out of the box with an incendiary mix of battering Cuban drumming, Arturo Sandoval's wild trumpet and Paquito D'Rivera's wailing alto. Paquito also contributes a free-floating, sometimes slapstick fantasy on themes of Mozart. The most audacious number is the 17 1/2-minute "Black Mass," which unleashes Valdes' staggering classical piano technique, knockabout rock guitar, Cuban chanting, high-wire brass, and lots of drums without somehow losing its train of thought. All but one of these tracks were reissued on CD as part of *The Best of Irakere;* admittedly, the LP's raucous sound is a bit more exciting than the cleaned-up CD. *—Richard S. Ginell*

El Coco / Aug. 3, 1980+Aug. 5, 1980 / Milestone ✦✦✦

Live at Ronnie Scott's / Sep. 1991 / World Pacific ✦✦✦✦✦

In Irakere's earlier days, this premiere Cuban group often had to disguise the fact that they were playing imperalistic music from the West (i.e. jazz). Maybe now the masquerade is no longer necessary for the music on this definitive CD would never be mistaken for anything else. Heavily influenced both by Dizzy Gillespie and the rhythms of Cuba and South America, the 11-piece group is in top form interpreting the compositions of its pianist/leader Chuco Valdes (who has a memorable workout on "Mr. Bruce"). Five of the six selections are primaily features for individual players. Throughout this memorable set, the ensemble work is clean and loose, the percussionists keep the proceedings fiery and the soloists are excellent. *—Scott Yanow*

Misa Negra / Aug. 7, 1992 / Rounder ✦✦✦✦✦

Yemaya / Jan. 26, 1999 / Blue Note ✦✦✦✦

The sudden breakout of Chucho Valdés as a solo artist in North America in 1998 was no doubt the leverage behind the new billing of his band, "Irakere featuring Chucho Valdés," and the large amount of exposure that his piano fireworks get here. The band sometimes doesn't sound all that electrified by the prospect, though ultimately they do take us on a wide-ranging tour of acoustic and electric Latin jazz idioms and grooves. "Mister Bruce" most emphatically features the leader, a *tour de force* for Valdes who unleashes a torrent of notes (not always coherently) over percussion, bass and drums. "Santa Amalia" is straight ahead Latin jazz with lots of Valdes, hot horn solos and a flourish of vocals at the close, yet for all of its 13 minutes, it doesn't totally ignite. "La Explosión," with quotes from "Love for Sale" near the end, presents a multi-sectioned serpent of funk, bop and mambo—nothing really fused since the grooves appear in sections—while "San Francisco" is a fine, barely updated Latin boogaloo. "Son Montuno," which also appears on Valdes' *Bele Bele en la Habana* solo album, is blown open by some rough rock guitar, the old freewheeling Irakere spirit at work. Though *Yemayá* has its big moments, Valdés seems to have saved his most heated inspirations of the late '90s for his own solo work. *—Richard S. Ginell*

Ernesto Lecuona

b. Aug. 6, 1895, Havana, Cuba, **d.** Nov. 29, 1963, Tenerife, Canary Islands

Piano / Latin Pop, Cuba, Latin Continuum

Arguably the most important Latin musical figure of the early 20th century, Ernesto Lecuona wrote hundreds of works during the era, including popular standards ("Malagueña," "Andalucia" aka "The Breeze and I," "Siempre en Mi Corazon," "Comparsa," "Noche Azul") as well as operettas, ballets, and an opera. Born in the Guanabacoa section of Havana in 1896, Lecuona earned fame first as a concert pianist. Taught piano by a sister (all three of his siblings were musicians), he studied at the National Conservatory in Havana and later, with Maurice Ravel in Paris. He debuted in New York at the age of 21, and soon became a concert sensation (his piano recordings run into five volumes). Lecuona had been composing songs even while studying piano however, and he copyrighted two of the most famed songs in the Latin repertoire—"Malagueña" and "Andalucia"—during the late '20s. His group, the Palau Brothers Cuban Orchestra (later renamed the Lecuona Cuban Boys), toured America during the 1930s and became a huge success. Lecuona composed the scores for four MGM films during the early '30s, and earned an Academy Award nomination for the title song to 1942's *Always in My Heart.* Lecuona, named the cultural attaché to the Cuban embassy in Washington, D.C. in 1943, rarely performed after World War II, preferring instead to cultivate his Cuban farm. He left his native country in 1960 however, denouncing Castro's revolution and vowing never to play again until Cuba was free of communism. Apparently, he never did perform professionally again, and he died in 1963 while on vacation in the Canary Islands. *—John Bush*

● **Cuban Originals** / Sep. 28, 1999 / RCA ✦✦✦✦✦

This volume of RCA's *Cuban Originals* series spotlights Ernesto Lecuona, and includes original recordings of classic songs like "Malaguena, " "Siempre En Mi Corazon, " "Noche Azul, " "En Tres Por Quatro, " "Estudiantina" and "Maria La O, " all of which focus on Lecuona's pioneering writing and arranging abilities. *—Heather Phares*

Pablo Milanés

Vocals / Nueva Cancion, Tropical, Nueva Trova, Cuba, Latin Continuum

Along with Silvio Rodriguez, Pablo Milanes was one of the crucial figures in Cuba's nueva trova popular-song movement of the late '60s; sponsored by Fidel Castro's government, the collective of nueva trova musicians were essentially supposed to reconfigure and update traditional Cuban folk musics for the nation's new, modern, post-revolutionary society. Milanes gained renown for his highly poetic lyrics and smooth yet emotional singing, becoming one of the most popular and respected Cuban musicians and songwriters of the late 20th century, and releasing a hefty number of records. He is a controversial figure to some—exiles despise his staunch support of Castro, while others criticize his musical forays into sentimental, orchestrated jazz-pop—but his status as one of the most important links between traditional and contemporary Cuban music has remained virtually unassailable into the new millennium. *—Steve Huey*

● **Ao Vivo No Brasil** / 1984 / Polygram ✦✦✦✦

The important Caribbean musical tradition has in Pablo Milanés one of its noted composers/performers. The natural bonds of musical identification and fraternity with Brazil are celebrated in this intense album recorded live in this country with the participation of Chico Buarque. "Yo Pisare las Calles Nuevamente" (in a voice/violão rendition), the nostalgic "Años" (with his band), the energetic "Creeme" and "Yo No Te Pido," the lyrical "Para Vivir" (backed only by the piano of Jorge Aragón), and "Acto de Fé" opened the show, which in the second part began with Chico Buarque's dramatic "Pedaço de Mim" (together with Buarque). Buarque also joins Milanes in the lachrymose "Yolanda" and in "Homenaje." The highly emotional impact of meeting, enhanced by Buarque and Milanes's natural sound affinity, can be verified by the audience's response and in the thrilled address by Elba Ramalho and Caetano Veloso. The musical aspect is subordinated to the lyrical content, with no improvisation or other signals of instrumental independence. *—Alvaro Neder*

Beny Moré (Bartolome Maximilliano)

b. Aug. 24, 1919, Santa Isabel de las Lajas, Cuba, **d.** Feb. 19, 1963, Havana, Cuba

Vocals / Big Band Latino, Son, Bolero, Tropical, Rhumba, Sonero, Mambo, Cuba, Latin Continuum

Beny Moré is the greatest singer of popular music Cuba has ever produced. Think Frank Sinatra or Nat "King" Cole and you'll get an idea of how he's perceived in Cuba, and how he should be regarded elsewhere. In the 40 years since his death, no Cuban vocalist has emerged to fill his shoes, and he remains as close as ever to the hearts of the Cuban people. Few singers in this hemisphere have consistently matched his interpretive gifts, vocal virtuosity, and comfort with a range of styles.

Moré's genius lay in his synthesis of two of the major currents of Cuban song—Afro-Cuban son and the Spanish-derived guajiro music of the Cuban countryside. He owed at least some of his singing style to a series of soneros who preceded him: Antonio Machin, Miguelito Valdes, and Orlando "Cascarita" Guerra. Moré's intimacy with both the African and European elements in Cuban music allowed him to be comfortable in all different styles. He was equally successful with boleros as with mambos and rumbas. Most important is what he conveyed with his singing: a tenderness and direct emotional appeal in his boleros, a hip-shaking exuberance in his mambos. Though he could not read music, Moré composed two of his smash hits, "Bonito Y Sabroso" and "Que Bueno Baila Usted." He also doubled as a bandleader and assembled a powerful big band comprised of talented musicians like trumpeters Alejandro "El Negro" Vivar and Alfredo "Chocolate" Armenteros, and trombonist and arranger Generoso "El Tojo" Jimenez. His was the quintessential Afro-Cuban big band sound of the 1950s: brash, multi-textured, dynamic. But unlike New York bands like Machito and his Afro-Cubans, Moré was not pushing the boundaries of Latin jazz. His music was more "pop" than Machito's, but it was anything but formulaic. *—Spencer Harrington*

Magia Antillana / 1949-1953 / RCA ✦✦✦✦✦

Mata Siguaraya / 1949-1951 / RCA Victor ✦✦✦✦✦

★ **The Most from Beny More** / 1976 / RCA ✦✦✦✦✦

Even though this reissue lacks documentation except for titles, his biggest '50s hits are a basic item for your collection. Worth every cent and more. *—Ned Sublette & John Storm Roberts*

El Barbaro del Ritmo (1948-50) / Mar. 21, 1995 / Tumbao ✦✦✦✦✦

Beny More's famous RCA/Tropical albums include only some of the recordings made by the singer in the late '40s with Perez Prado's Orchestra. Fortunately, the fine Tumbao Cuban Classics label has chronicled the complete More/Prado catalog on El Barbaro del Ritmo, bringing into focus the incredible partnership of one of the Latin world's most accomplished singers and one of its most innovative band leaders. If you are looking for the "Mambo without a Migraine" experience, though, you'll need to stick to More's later RCA recordings which include a selection of his subdued bolero numbers. On *El Barbaro del Ritmo* the emphasis is on high-energy mambos including More's big hit "Pachito E Che" as well as "Mamboletas" and "Toncineta," which feature fine examples of Prado's menacing and convoluted brass arrangements. Luckily, with More's assured and smooth delivery, and the relatively subdued reed charts keeping fast and complex brass playing in check, the numbers here are not so intense as to cause the dance floor to vacate. The group perfect the blend on the album's standout track "RaboY Oreja" as More's vigorous yet smooth vocals mirror the give and take of the band's swirling brass and purring reeds. Prado further echoes the contrast in a solo that sandwiches crashing chords between furtively played notes and romantic flourishes. More's RCA discs are certainly worth owning, but for a close look at of one of his most charged outings one shouldn't miss *El Barbaro del Ritmo.* *—Stephen Cook*

Voz y Obra / Oct. 1, 1996 / Milan ✦✦✦✦✦

Encantado de la Vida / 1997 / International ✦✦✦✦

Latin labels have put out quite a few Beny More compilations over the years. Released in 1997 by the Latin Musica Del Sol label, *Encantado De Mi Vida* focuses mainly on the Cuban band leader's classic son, mambo and boleros of the 1950s. The liner notes are far from ideal; while the CD booklet contains a short essay summarizing More's history, neither recording dates nor personnel are listed. Even if exact recording dates of these 12 songs weren't available, the company could have at least given the years in which they were recorded. But the songs themselves are certainly first rate. No salsero should be deprived of the exhilarating joys of such classics as "Mi Chiquita," "Cinturita," "Locas Por El Mambo" or "A Media Noche." Though much of *Encantado* is upbeat and danceable, More's magnificent way with dramatic boleros (Latin ballads) is illustrated by "Corazon Rebelde," "Oh Vida" and "Te Quedaras." Make no mistake—everything on this disc is a gem. *—Alex Henderson*

NG La Banda

Group / Tropical, Afro-Cuban Jazz, Latin Jazz, Cuba, Latin Continuum

Probably the best and most exciting Cuban dance group of the 1990s, NG La Banda formed in 1988 and has been led by flute player José Luis Cortés ever since. Including many brilliant musicians who had formerly played with Irakere and Los Van Van, the group is known for placing emphasis on tight rhythms and their aggressive brass section, nicknamed the Terror Brass. NG La Banda has recorded for RCA, Milan, Artex and QBA. *—John Bush*

● **The Best of NG La Banda** / Feb. 1, 2000 / Blue Note ✦✦✦✦

En la Calle / QBA ✦✦✦✦✦

The horn section used to be Irakere's; the leader, Jose Cortes, was in both Irakere and Los Van Van. The album, compiled from two Cuban LPs, includes "La Expresiva," athe number one hit of Havana 1990, and "Los Sitios Entero," a smoking guaguanco. It's about an hour long and not a weak cut. *—Ned Sublette*

Eliades Ochoa

Vocals, Guitar / Modern Son, Son, Tropical, Cuba, Latin Continuum

Cuban vocalist and guitarist Eliades Ochoa worked with many groups during his career, including the Septetos Cubanos, Casa De La Troya and Cuarteto Patria, with which he recorded two albums, 1993's *A Una Coqueta* and 1998's *Cubafrica*. His work on Ry Cooder's *Buena Vista Social Club* raised his mainstream prominence; on his second solo album, 1999's *Sublime Illusion*, Ochoa collaborated with Cooder and Cuarteto Patria once again. Other releases include *Son de Santiago* and *Cuarteto Patria*. Fall 2000 saw the release of *Eliades Ochoa Y el Cuarteto Patria*. *Cuidadito Compay Gallo* was issued a year later. *—Heather Phares*

Sublime Illusion / Jun. 29, 1999 / Higher Octave ✦✦✦✦✦

• **Tribute to the Cuarteto Patria** / Sep. 12, 2000 / Higher Octave ✦✦✦✦✦
One of the most talented members of the Buena Vista Social Club project, Eliades Ochoa was slower to gain recognition in the United States after the project than Ibrahim Ferrer or Ruben Gonzalez, which is a shame because while his *campesino* style may not be as polished as some of the more urban traditions of his contemporaries, his guitar playing is infused with fire and passion that make his music a sheer delight to listen to. This album, which possesses superior songwriting to his previous solo release *Sublime Illusion*, pays tribute to the band that Ochoa has played with for years, as well as to the musical traditions, the Cuban landscapes, and the clubs that helped nurture his love for song. Ochoa displays a passionate voice which is a good partner for his expert guitar playing, and overall this is a nearly flawless portrait of great Cuban music. *—Stacia Proefrock*

Orquesta Aragon

f. 1939
Vocals, Violin, Percussion, Guitar / Bolero, Tropical, Charanga, Cuba, Latin Continuum
Orquesta Aragon are a popular charanga band hailing from Cuba. Their distinctive sound is based on traditional son with its African rhythm section and Spanish melodies, over which they added three violins. Orquesta Aragon were not only popular as interpreters of son, but are also credited with inspiring New York mambo. They can be heard performing on *That Cuban Cha-Cha-Cha* and in collaboration with Beny More and Perez Prado on *Riverside Years*. *—Leon Jackson*

• **Cha Cha Charanga** / Jul. 14, 1997 / Candela ✦✦✦✦✦
Aragon are the premier active charanga band to come from Cuba, and they prove their mettle on this incredible disc of bubbling dance rhythms, soaring strings, and great singing. Violinist Lazaro Gonzalez Sibore and cellist Alejandro Tomas Valdes are the principals who provide the distinct string sound prevalent in charanga, with lead vocalist Juan Carlos Villegas leading a multi-vocal charge through these ten precious tunes. An interactive ensemble sounding larger than they are, Aragon puts out sheets of sound from vocal, percussive, and string sections while flutes dart in and out of the pieces. This is the essence of the charanga, and this grand combo plays it to the hilt. American audiences will immediately pick up on the "Guantanamera"-like strains of "Son de la Loma," very much following the tone and style of the most famous of all Afro-Cuban tunes. The band can cook in steamy-hot fashion, as they do during "Me Quede con la Gorde," but they specialize in a steady, consistent slow burn that's best typified by the beautiful dance of "Dale Contracandela." If the style and stance of Aragon aren't compellingly infectious, you have yet to catch the fever. Included in the liner notes are helpful tips on how to dance to these tunes. Time and time again they lead the way for this type of music, and though there are some parallel bands, none do it like Aragon. Highly recommended, especially as an entry point to new listeners of Latin-jazz and Afro-Cuban expressionism. *—Michael G. Nastos*

Cuban Originals / Sep. 28, 1999 / RCA ✦✦✦✦✦

Arsenio Rodriguez

b. Aug. 30, 1911, Guira de Macurijes, Matanzas, Cuba, **d.** Dec. 31, 1971, Los Angeles, CA
Vocals, Guitar / Son, Tropical, Cuba, Latin Continuum
Arsenio Rodriguez, one of the most important figures in the history of Cuban music, was a prolific composer (he penned close to 200 songs), tresero, percussionist, and bandleader whose innovations changed the face of Latin dance music and paved the way for what would eventually become known as salsa. He is considered the father of the instrumental format known as the conjunto, and his many standards frequently emphasized Afro-Cuban elements in their subject matter.

Blinded as a child by a horse's kick, he soon played a variety of instruments, including Afro-Cuban drums and percussion, bass, and tres, a Cuban six-string guitar that would become his primary instrument. He began composing in his teens and formed his own band by the late '30s. Though the standard format for playing son was the septeto, this would all change around 1940 when Rodriguez added conga, piano, and a second trumpet to the typical son ensemble, giving birth to the conjunto. Rodriguez also introduced the son montuno (featuring improvised vocals by the lead singer over a repeated chorus) and adaptated the Afro-Cuban style known as the guaguancó to the dance band/conjunto format. These further "Afro-Cubanizations" of the son were among Rodriguez' most important and lasting contributions.

The 1940s were a classic period in Rodriguez' career and the history of the son. He recorded many famous compositions, including "A Belen le Toca Ahora," "Juventud Amaliana," and the bolero "La Vida es un Sueño." Rodriguez left his conjunto in Cuba after moving to New York, though his popularity in America, while strong, would never match what it had been in Cuba. In his final years he continued to experiment, developing a style he called "swing son" before dying of pneumonia in 1970. *—Nick Herman*

• **Cuban Counterpoint: History of the Son Montuno** / 1992 / Rounder ✦✦✦✦✦
The son montuño, a somewhat more Afro-Cuban subset of the Afro-European creole son, is a basic rhythm (the most compelling of all) in all forms of Cuban music and salsa. This is a mega-must overview, ranging from field recordings of rural guitar-and-percussion to Celia Cruz, Arsenio Rodriguez, and just about every great name in one of the world's great musics. *—John Storm Roberts, Original Music*

A Todos Los Barrios / Jun. 1992 / RCA ✦✦✦✦

Tocoloro / Nov. 15, 1999 / Musica Latina ✦✦✦✦✦
Recorded several years before he moved to New York, *Tocoloro* consists of 19 songs, all but one recorded at either of two sessions from 1946 and 1948. The jubilant conjunto includes fabulous playing by trumpeter Rafael Corbacho, pianist Luis Lili Martinez, conga player Felix Alonso, and lead vocalist René Scull. Its leader, on tres guitar, contributes much to the collection's highlight, "Dame un Cachito Pa'Huele." *Tocoloro* also includes several classic Rodriguez compositions, among them "Juventad Amaliana," "La Vida Es un Sueño," and "A Belen Le Toca Ahora." Though the sound quality is definitely of mid-'40s vintage, the quality of playing is unparalleled in Cuban music of the time. *—John Bush*

Sexteto Habañero

Vocals, Percussion, Guitar, Bass / Son, Tropical, Sonero, Cuba, Latin Continuum
At the beginning of the 20th century, three Cuban musicians formed Trio Oriental to perform the folk music that hailed from the west of the island. The trio later added members, changed their name to Sexteto Habanero, and became the first and most influential performers of son, a vivid Afro-Spanish fusion of musical styles. Son consists of two stylistic levels. The first level (African in origin) is a rumba rhythm over which a variety of percussionists improvise. The second level (deriving from Spain) is provided by a combination of three string guitars known as tres and a makeshift bass. Spanish lyrics are sung over the instruments in traditional decima form with rhymed octosyllabic lines. During the 1920s, Sexteto Habanero were the definitive son band of cuba. Their music is featured on two compilations: *Cuban Counterpoint: History of the San Montuno* and *Cuba—El son es la mas sublime* as well as *The Roots of Salsa*. *—Leon Jackson*

Son Cubano, Vol. 1 / Tumbao ✦✦✦
The perfect tart is a balance of strawberries, cream and short pastry. The perfect small-music group is a balance of voices, trumpet, guitars and percussion—in short, an Afro-Cuban sexteto or septeto performing sones of the great inter-war years. The Sexteto Habanero was one of the two or three greatest of all, and these 1924-1927 recordings caught them in their early prime. This is what they play in Heaven when the Andeans and the Burmese put down their harps. *—John Storm Roberts, Original Music*

Chucho Valdés

b. Oct. 9, 1941, Quivican, Cuba
Piano / Cuban Jazz, Afro-Cuban Jazz, Latin Jazz, Cuba, Latin Continuum
The son of the noted musician Bebo Valdes, Chucho began playing piano when he was three and by the time he was 16 he was leading his own group. In 1960 his father defected from Cuba but Chucho stayed behind. In 1967 he formed the Orquesta Cubana de Musica Moderna and in 1973 he founded Irakere, the top Cuban jazz orchestra; among its original members were Arturo Sandoval and Paquito D'Rivera. Valdes has been Irakere's musical director almost from the start and has recorded with the full band, in small groups and as an impressive solo pianist. He remains one of the top jazz musicians living in Cuba. *—Scott Yanow*

• **Solo Piano** / Sep. 1991 / World Pacific ✦✦✦✦✦
The leader and founder of Irakere, Chucho Valdes is also a brilliant pianist who may be on the same level of Gonzalo Rubalcaba. He has a very impressive classical technique and is able to hint at such players as McCoy Tyner, Lennie Tristano and Cecil Taylor without watering down his Cuban heritage. This dazzling set covers a lot of ground with highlights including "Blue Yes" (which is based on the chords of Charlie Parker's "Confirmation"), a sensitive Bill Evans tribute and several nearly free explosions. Despite the CD's title, the final two of the ten selections add bass, drums and percussion and feature Valdes closely interacting with and pushing his sidemen. Highly recommended. *—Scott Yanow*

Bele Bele en La Habana / Jan. 12, 1998-Jan. 13, 1998 / Blue Note ✦✦✦✦✦
Issued just after his landmark two-week June 1998 gig at the *Village Vanguard* and subsequent U.S./Canada tour, Chucho Valdés' first album for Blue Note bears out a lot of the hype surrounding this hugely gifted Cuban pianist. Unlike many of today's younger Cuban keyboard hotshots, Valdés not only has great technical chops and musical erudition, he manages to stay closely tied to his Cuban rhythmic roots. Thus, he employs a Cuban percussionist Roberto Vizcaino Guillot along with the standard bass (Alain Pérez Rodriguez) and drums (Ra'l Pineda Roque), which dramatically increases the possibilities for rhythmic experiments. Valdés more often than not is all over the keyboard, comfortable with everything from Ravelian classical complexity to Bill Evans' introspection to Cecil Taylor-like crunches. But there are surprisingly few wasted motions; all of the notes fit. He creates tremendous excitement on "Con Poco Loco" (which ends with a sly steal from "Giant Steps"), and suddenly breaks into a cornucopia of European stream-of-consciousness fireworks before returning to Cuba on "Son Montuno." However, the best moments come when Valdés hooks his fire-eating technique into the groove and doesn't let go. "El Cumbanchero" contains some sudden rhythmic shifts that will have you leaping out of your chair, and "Tres Lindas Cubanas" gradually builds a great head of steam. This CD will give you a much better idea of Valdes' pianistic capabilities than any of his records with Irakere. On a political level, it is interesting and disheartening to note that Valdés recorded this album in Toronto under the auspices of EMI Music Canada; a direct signing with Blue Note would have exposed the American company to charges of trading with the enemy. Obviously, as of 1998, the Cold War was not completely over. *—Richard S. Ginell*

Babalu Ayé / Feb. 16, 1999 / Bembe ✦✦✦✦

Live at the Village Vanguard / Apr. 11, 2000 / Blue Note ✦✦✦✦
If Blue Note's alert microphones were present at Chucho Valdés's historic 1998 debut at the hallowed Village Vanguard, the results haven't officially landed in our CD machines yet. But the mikes were there, alright, the following year—and they caught some virulent Cuban tempests (as the announcer warns, accurately, "There's a hurricane approaching from the Caribbean"). Yet the heat was turned up so much on Valdés's previous studio albums that the presence of a live audience only increases the temperature slightly here. Once again, Valdés's command of the keyboard is so technically staggering as to be stupefying, and he liberally

throws in quotes from just about everything he ever absorbed—from Chopin and Debussy to the Gershwins, Cecil Taylor and avant-garde strumming of the piano strings. He has so powerful an individual identity that "To Bud Powell" is more about Chucho than the late bop pianist. Yet the best, most fun track on the CD, "Punto Cubano," gives credence to the old saw about less being more. Built mostly around a simple tonic-dominant vamp; it has a Jarrett-like directness of melody and irresistible swing, though Chucho still isn't loath to turn on the big guns when desired. The long-running rhythm section of Francisco Rubio Pampin (bass), Ra'l Pineda Roque (drums), and Roberto Vizcaino Guillót (congas), keeps Chucho all stoked up and steaming throughout the set. Also Valdés's sister, Mayra Caridad, lends a husky Miriam Makeba-sized voice to the not-so-peaceful lullaby "Drume Negrita." This is yet another excellent addition to the distinguished line of eventful *Village Vanguard* live sessions, brought to you through the politically neutral resources of EMI Music Canada. —*Richard S. Ginell*

Los Van Van

Group / Tropical, Charanga, Salsa, Cuba, Latin Continuum

Led by Juan Formell, Los Van Van have beome one of the most successful son groups in the world. To the Afro-Spanish sound of traditional Cuban music, Los Van Van have added a strong jazz emphasis. It is this fusion that has led to their popularity outside of Cuba and to a series of foreign record deals. They can be heard on *Songo, Sandunguera,* and *Dancing Wet.* The group released *Azucar* on the Xenophile label in 1995; *La Habana Si* followed a year later, and Los Van Van remained a prolific presence throughout the decade, releasing albums including 1997's *Con la Salsa Formell* and 1999's Llego Van Van. —*Leon Jackson*

Songo / 1988 / Mango ✦✦✦

Van Van is the unchallenged number one dance band in Cuba, formed in 1969 and going full blast today. The mix is a little cold on this album, but it gets played a lot. A high-tech rerecording, in Paris, of some of their '80s tunes—it includes their biggest hit, "Muevete," and an irresistible "Que Palo Es Ese." It's a great record, really, but the band has an even greater one in them. —*Ned Sublette*

Dancing Wet (Bailando Mojao) / Apr. 20, 1993 / World Pacific ✦✦✦✦✦

Because of an embargo imposed by the U.S. government, very little of the Cuban-rooted music enjoyed by predominantly Latino audienes in the U.S. is actually recorded in Cuba. Most of the salsa hits heard in the U.S. are recorded in New York, San Juan or Miami. It isn't that there's ever been a shortage of high-quality salsa artists in Cuba, where such styles as son, mambo and cha-cha were born; it's that their albums don't make it to American shores. Hands down, Cuba's most successful salsa band of the 1980s and '90s has been Los Van Van. A compilation boasting some of Van Van's strongest material, *Dancing Wet* is essential listening for salseros. "Yo No Me Explico Lo Que Tiene," "Bailando Mojao," "Aqui El Que Baila Gana" and other gems remind us that were it not for the embargo, this band would be as popular in the U.S. as El Gran Combo or El Conjunto Classico. This CD leaves no doubt that Van Van's tremendous popularity in Cuba is well deserved. —*Alex Henderson*

Azucar / 1994 / Xenophile ✦✦✦✦

Con La Salsa Formell / 1997 / Cubacan ✦✦✦✦

● **The Legendary Los Van Van: 30 Years of Cuba's Greatest Dance Group** / Nov. 9, 1999 / Ashe ✦✦✦✦✦

The Legendary Van Van is a two-disc compilation collecting 24 of Los Van Van's favorite numbers, spanning their career from the late '60s all the way into the '90s. As excellent as the track selection and remastering are, the packaging wins additional points: included with the CD is not only a complete history of the group—tracing Los Van Van's development from a regional band into Cuba's mightiest orchestra—but lyrics for each song and many photos. It's one of the best Los Van Van compilations released to date, up to the level of 1993's *Dancing Wet.* —*Earl Simmons*

Cuba Collection

Afro Cuban Roots, Vol. 1: 50 Years of Cuban Music / May 19, 1998 / Max Music ✦✦✦

Afro Cuban Roots, Vol. 1: 50 Years of Cuban Music is a good 14-track sampler of Cuban music and Afro-Cuban jazz. It may not be definitive, but it's a nice introduction for the curious. —*Thom Owens*

Afro Cuban Roots, Vol. 2: Cuban Feelings—*Bolero Era* */ May 19, 1998 / Max Music* ✦✦✦

Like its predecessor, *Afro Cuban Roots, Vol. 2: Cuban Feelings—Bolero Era* is a good sampler of Cuban music designed for neophytes. This time, the disc has a specific theme—the bolero. While this is by no means a definitive overview, it nevertheless is a good introduction for curious listeners. —*Thom Owens*

Casa De La Trova / May 18, 1999 / Elektra ✦✦✦

Titled after the community centers where Cuban *trovadores* (troubadours) gather to sing poetic serenades, the *Casa de la Trova* collection gathers 14 such serenades by important Cuban songwriters from throughout the 20th century, performed by an all-star group of current practitioners of the form. Musical contributors present include Daniel Castillo, Zaida Reyte, Manuel Napoles, Pablo Rodriguez, Roberto Sotolongo, Lusson Bueno, Alfredo Alonso Martinez, Lucia Lago, Cascarita, the Ferrin Sisters, the Faez Sisters, and the Miraflores Trio. —*Steve Huey*

Cuba / May 25, 1999 / Putumayo ✦✦✦✦✦

Cuba wasn't the first Afro-Cuban compilation that Putumayo released in the '90s. Latino! Latino! had focused on Afro-Cuban sounds from artists in locations ranging from Africa to South America, while Afro-Latino examined the parallels between African and Latino artists. On Cuba, Putumayo's main focus is on salseros who were active in Cuba in the '70s, '80s and '90s. Some of the groups included on *Cuba* go back much further than that—the Septeto Ignacio Pinero was formed in 1927, while Orquesta Sublime (a charanga band) was formed in the '50s and los Guaracheros de Oriente go back to 1940. Cuba favors more recent lineups by these groups, which have gone through their share of personnel changes over the years. (Most, or all, of $Pinero's original members are dead). But this CD doesn't focus exclusively on veteran acts—Mi Son (heard on "Mecanica de Amor"), for example, was formed in 1992. Irakere, the salsa/Latin jazz explorers heard on "Boliviana," came out of the '70s and gave us such improvisers as Paquito D'Rivera and Arturo Sandoval (both of whom defected from Cuba and became U.S. citizens). "Boliviana" is an ode to a Bolivian woman, and the song fuses Afro-Cuban and South American elements in a most appealing way. Boasting comprehensive liner notes and enjoyable performances, Cuba is among the many compilations that Putumayo can be proud of. —*Alex Henderson*

Cuba Classics 1: Canciones Urgentes / Warner Brothers ✦✦✦✦✦

This anthology, compiled by David Byrne, consists of various tracks by Silvio Rodriquez, one of the leaders of Cuba's nueva trova (new song) movement. —*Ned Sublette*

Cuba Classics 2: Dancing with the Enemy / 1988 / Luaka Bop ✦✦✦✦✦

Peter Watrous at The New York Times gave this one the number-two spot on his Ten Best of 1991 list. These are obscure recordings mostly, the majority from the '60s and '70s. —*Ned Sublette*

Cuba—Dances of the Gods / Oct. 1988 / Ocora ✦✦✦✦✦

Here's something crucial for percussion buffs: field recordings covering all the major religious traditions (lucumi, arara, palo monte, tambor yuka, abakwa, transplanted Haitian), along with a couple of street rumbas (guaguanco and columbia). More of the latter would have been nice, and the notes are a bit confused on relationships between denominations. But this is still essential stuff. —*John Storm Roberts*

Cuba Grandes Compositores / Jan. 26, 1999 / Orfeon ✦✦✦✦✦

The fourth volume in Orfeon's series of two-disc Cuban greatest-hits collections, *Cuba Grandes Compositores* focuses on *the* seminal composer of the early 20th century, Ernesto Lecuona, with versions of his classics like "Malagueña" (by Alfredo Munar), "Comparsa" (by Ruth Fernandez), "Siempre en Mi Corazon" (by Munar), "Juventud" (by Zoraida Marrero), and "Andalucia" (by Munar). In addition to the 22 Lecuona tracks are five by Oswaldo Farrès and three by Luis Marquetti. —*Earl Simmons*

Cuba: I Am Time / Jul. 1, 1997 / Blue Jackel ✦✦✦✦

For such a small island, Cuba has had an enormous musical impact both inside and outside of Latin America. Salsa is the music of choice among Cubans and Puerto Ricans, and Afro-Cuban music has influenced everyone from American jazz players to Dominican merengue artists to Spanish "nuevo flamenco" stars. A four-CD box set, *Cuba: I Am Time* spotlights Cuban artists past and present. Ranging from tribal-type chanting inspired by Santeria and the Yoruba faith to dance bands to modern Afro-Cuban jazz, this package shows us what a wealth of music the island has provided. Disc One focuses largely on traditional sounds that are closely related to African tribal music, and material by Pancho Quinto, El Clave y Guaguanco and others consists of only percussion and vocals. Meanwhile, large and small bands playing son, mambo, guaguanco and other styles that make up salsa are the focus of Discs Two and Three, which boast classics by such greats as Beny More, Miguelito Cuni, Merceditas Valdes and Tito Gomes. And finally, Disc Four illustrates the ways in which Mario Bauza, Cachao, Irakere, Chico O'Farrill and others have successfully fused improvisatory jazz with Afro-Cuban music. Regrettably, the set's 111-page booklet fails to list recording dates, though it does boast an extremely informative essay. This set would be too much for casual listeners, but those with a deeper interest in Afro-Cuban music will find it a gold mine. —*Alex Henderson*

☆ **Cuban Counterpoint: History of the Son Montuno** / 1992 / Rounder ✦✦✦✦✦

This 22-track anthology issued by Rounder in 1992 covered the wide-ranging son montuno idiom and its diverse, yet related forms. It included segments from the 1920s to the 1970s; there were Spanish vocal arrangements and ensembles, polyrhythmic African percussion, linguistic elements of each, and material that sometimes sounded like the songs heard in saloons and cantinas on the Mexican border and other times like the bustling jam sessions heard in East Coast clubs. The songs were mostly short (none longer than three and a half minutes) and included several contributions from the great bandleader Arsenio Rodriguez as well as cuts by Sexteto Habanero, Beny More and the Cachao All Stars featuring El Nino Rivera. It was exhaustively annotated as well. —*Ron Wynn*

Cuban Danzón / Feb. 16, 1999 / Arhoolie ✦✦✦

This Arhoolie Records compilation is a fascinating look at the early Cuban danzón, which evolved in the 1870s from the contradanza, becoming a distinctive creole blend of African rhythms with melodic elements drawn from the European country dance, or "contradance." The first track, "Patti Negra" by Orquesta Pablo Valenzuela, is transferred from a rare early wax cylinder, while the others are taken from historic 78 rpm records. The CD also contains a twelve-page booklet with notes about the history of the Cuban danzón, the musicians, and the selections. As is to be expected, there is considerable surface noise on many of the tracks, but this slight imperfection almost adds to the historical interest of the recordings. —*Zac Johnson*

Cuba Si: Pure Cuban Flavor / May 18, 1999 / Rhino ✦✦✦✦

Puerto Ricans have made many outstanding contributions to salsa; even the more casual salsero should be hip to Tito Puente, Ray Barretto, Manny Oquendo y Libre, El Gran Combo and El Conjunto Clasico. But it's important to stress that son, cha-cha, guaguanco, mambo and other styles that fall under the heading of salsa didn't originate in Puerto Rico or New York—they were created in Cuba. This excellent collection spotlights some of the salsa that has come from Cuban artists in the 1980s and 1990s. Some of the artists were still living in Cuba when Rhino released this compilation in 1999—including Los Van Van, Son 14, Sierra Maestra and NG La Banda—while others were residents of Miami (Cachao, Albita Rodriguez) and even San Francisco (Conjunto Cespedes). The CD is full of "salsa tipica"—that is, salsa that is very traditional, such as Jesus Alemany's "Descarga de Hoy" (a jazz-influenced, Cachao-type descarga or Latin jam) and Conjunto Cespedes' infectious son montuno "Umelina." But on more experimental offerings like Los Van Van's "Esto Te Pone la Cabeza Mal" and NG La Banda's "El Tragico," you can hear salsa being mixed with pop and/or hip-hop. Albita Rodriguez's exuberant "Ta' Bueno Ya," meanwhile, fuses Afro-Cuban elements with the Puerto Rican bomba. Boasting comprehensive liner notes by the L.A.-based disc jockey Nina Lenart, *Cuba Si* is one of the more thoughtfully assembled salsa packages of 1999. *—Alex Henderson*

Mambo Mania!: The Kings & Queens of Mambo / 1995 / Rhino ♦♦♦♦♦
Mambo Mania! may not be the last word on the Afro-Cuban music of the 1950s and '60s, but for beginners, it's a darn nice place to start. Rhino can usually be counted on to do its homework when assembling compilations, and this superb 18-song CD is no exception. Serious fans of what came to be called salsa will be more than familiar with such classics as Celia Cruz's "Tumba La Cana, Jibarito," Beny More's "Me Gusta Mas El Son" and Tito Puente's "Guaguanco Margarito"—all of which are essential listening for even the most casual salseros. Recorded in 1949, the oldest song here is the infectious "Un Poquito De Tu Amor" by Desi Arnaz, who became well known for his role on the television comedy "I Love Lucy." From Tito Rodriguez, Cachao and the ultra-influential Machito to master percussionists/band leaders Ray Barretto and Mongo Santamaria, many of salsa's all-time greats are well represented by this outstanding collection. *—Alex Henderson*

Music of Cuba: 1909-1951 / Jul. 4, 2000 / Columbia/Legacy ♦♦♦♦♦
It seems reasonable to presume that without the unexpected success of the Buena Vista Social Club at the end of the 1990s, Columbia would not have been interested in digging through its vaults for vintage Cuban pop recordings. Whatever it takes to unlock a flood of ethnic music, however, should be welcomed. And you certainly get a wealth of it on this disc, which assembles 25 tracks from 1909-1951, although all but three are from 1926-1942. It's lighthearted, for the most part, danceable popular music (although Sexteto Nacional's "Siboney" has a nice melancholy aura), roaming among the various branches of the Cuban sound, including danzon, son, bolero, rumba, and conga. Considering the age of the recordings, the remastering is exceptional, although there's still a lot of noise on some of the cuts, probably unavoidably so. There's certainly a lot of variety, with men and women singers, cuts with barely any instrumental accompaniment, full orchestras, an unaccompanied choral song (save for a brief bit of bagpipe near the beginning), numbers with clear American pop and jazz influences, and more. There's even one name that will be known to most of the general public—Desi Arnaz—heard doing congas with his orchestra on two tracks, done in 1939 and 1940, respectively. Includes detailed liner notes by Dick Spottswood in both English and a Spanish translation. *—Richie Unterberger*

The Rough Guide to Cuban Son / May 2, 2000 / World Music Network ♦♦♦
Some of the greats of classic Cuban music are featured on this compilation, which focuses on the son style—the predecessor and heart of salsa music. Ranging from rustic bands to urban big band styles, this collection features some of Cuba's finest musicians. *—Stacia Proefrock*

Dominican Republic Collection

Salsa Clasica / Oct. 19, 1999 / Music Club ♦♦♦♦♦
The discount label Music Club put this salsa collection together, and similar to their retrospectives of everyone from Horace Andy to Beny Moré, it's a knockout. Focusing mostly on the Dominican branch of salsa and its main domestic proponent, Miami's Kubaney Records, *Salsa Clasica* does indeed include a brace of classic salsa cuts from excellent artists including Cuco Valoy ("Juliana," "Mariana Engracia"), Johnny Ventura ("Salsa Conmigo," "Guajira"), Miguel Cruz ("Noche de Rumberos"), Luis Varona (the irresistible "Ven Pa' La Loma"), and many others. Though the classic salsa names from Fania and Tico are missing, *Salsa Clasica* is a great, inexpensive way to collect some excellent salsa. *—John Bush*

Stripping the Parrots: Essential Merengue / 1995 / Corason ♦♦♦
It's hard to beat the loony rural merengue of the Dominican Republic, which may or may not add a splendidly manic solo sax style bouncing off the accordion. This is a great introduction from five bands, four of them accordion-centered (one with sax), the fifth a bachata guitar group. All have that real rural sound, jaunty, repetitive and exhilaratingly unpretentious. (The title comes from the Spanish name of the style—it's all in the notes. *—John Storm Roberts*

Guatemala Collection

Music from Guatemala, Vol. 1 / Mar. 14, 2000 / Caprice ♦♦♦

Latin Collection

Latino! Latino! / Jun. 24, 1997 / Putumayo ♦♦♦♦
A New Yorker dedicated to promoting multiculturalism, Dan Storper opened the small Latin-oriented craft and clothing store Putumayo in Manhattan's Soho section before going on to found and head his label Putumayo World Music. Putumayo had released over 22 albums (everything from reggae to Celtic music to African pop) by the time it turned the spotlight on salsa and Afro-Cuban music with *Latino! Latino!*. This isn't a typical salsa compilation offering only major hits—rather, Putumayo approaches salsa in a very eclectic fashion and avoids stressing the obvious. The exciting CD does include material by some of salsa's big names, including Willie Colon ("Asia") and Oscar D'Leon ("Volver a Verte"). But Putumayo also includes recordings by everyone from Zaire native Richard Lemvo (who adds a bit of soukous to the Cuban standard "Yiri Yiri Bon") to Spanish group Manzanita (which combines salsa and flamenco on "Arranca") and Colombian singer Toto La Momposina (whose "Carmelina" is a departure from the type of cumbia she's best known for). Salsa CDs don't get much more diverse than *Latino! Latino!*. *—Alex Henderson*

Mambo Mania: Talkin' Verve / Jun. 23, 1998 / Verve ♦♦♦
Mambomania: Talkin' Verve collects 16 hot Latin jazz tracks from the Verve vaults. Much of this is by artists who specialize in Latin jazz, such as Cal Tjader and Chico O'Farrill, but there are also cuts from the likes of Wes Montgomery and Lalo Schifrin, who only occasionally played Latin jazz. That may seem like a minor distinction, but the blend of specialists and dabblers makes Mambomania a varied, entertaining listen. *—Stephen Thomas Erlewine*

Que RykoLatino! / Feb. 1, 2000 / Rykolatino ♦♦♦♦
Que RykoLatino! is a sampler of the Rykodisc label's roster of Latin-music acts who mix modern sensibilities with firm groundings in tradition. Artists present include ¡Cubanismo!, Plena Libre, José Alberto, Jimmy Bosch, and Truco; it's an excellent introduction to an exciting assortment of musicians. *—Steve Huey*

Reconquista!: The Latin Rock Invasion / Apr. 15, 1997 / Rhino ♦♦♦♦♦
American pop has been a strong influence on Latin artists for decades, but with the rise of the "rock en espanol" movement in the 1980s, numerous artists from all over Latin America as well as the U.S. and Spain started offering an impressively wide variety of hard-edged, guitar-powered rock with Spanish lyrics. "Rock en espanol" is every bit as diverse as English-language rock, and has given us everything from Pat Benatar-loving hard rockers and Clash-inspired punks to Ministry-ish industrial noisemakers. *Reconquista* spotlights some of the leaders of the movement, including Argentina's Los Fabulosos Cadillacs and Mexico's Maldita Vecinidad Y Los Hijos del Quinto Patio, both of whom incorporate reggae, ska and rap; and the U2-influenced Mexican band Caifanes. While Cuca goes for a Van Halen-ish gloss on "El Son de Dolor" and Negu Gorriak combines salsa and dissonant "alternative" rock on "Ipurbegia," Dividios draws on everything from blues-rock and reggae to Middle Eastern music. For those who haven't yet explored "rock en espanol," this anything-but-predictable CD can be a splendid introduction. *—Alex Henderson*

Red Hot + Latin: Silencio " Muerte / Apr. 22, 1997 / Hola ♦♦♦
Red Hot & Latin: Silencio Equals Muerte is another installment in the Red Hot series of charity albums designed to promote AIDS awareness. "Latin" doesn't necessarily mean that the music falls into the traditional boundaries of Latin music—after all, there's no way the Brazilian metal band Sepultura could sound anything other than brutally heavy—and many of the tracks are Latin songs performed by the likes of David Byrne, Laurie Anderson, Fishbone, Cibo Matto and Hurricane G. Musically, the record spans everything from Latin jazz and Latin dance to rock, reggae and folk. It's an intriguing blend, for the most part, and while some of the tracks fall flat, most succeed, and the record is certainly a charity event worth checking out. *—Stephen Thomas Erlewine*

Red Hot + Rio / 1996 / Antilles/Verve ♦♦♦

RMM 10th Anniversary Concert / Dec. 2, 1997 / Rmm ♦♦♦
The 22nd New York Salsa Festival: RMM 10th Anniversary Concert is an excellent, double-disc set that finds the entire RMM roster—including Tito Puente, Marc Anthony, India, Celia Cruz, Oscar D'Leon, Tony Vega, Manny Manuel, Jose Alberto, Hilton Ruiz, Grupo Heavy and Jesus Enriquez—singing live versions of current and past hits. For fans of any of these artists, or modern Latin music and salsa in general, this collection is fun and entertaining, even if it offers nothing unexpected. *—Stephen Thomas Erlewine*

Rough Guide to Salsa / Nov. 18, 1997 / World Music Network ♦♦♦♦♦
The Rough Guide to Salsa is a superb introduction to the spicy sound of this popular Latin American music—newcomers to the genre will particularly find much to savor here. Highlights include Joe Arroyo's "Pal Bailador," Jes´s Alemañy & ¡Cubanismo!'s "Mulence," and Alfredo Rodriguez's "Tumbao a Peruchin." *—Raymond McKinney*

Mexico Collection

La Trova Tradicional de Yucatan: 1928-1932 / Jan. 25, 2000 / Lirio Azul ♦♦♦♦♦
Under the rubric of "Mexican music" there exists a heterogeneous constellation of genres, styles, and sounds. Though many North Americans have a tendency to oversimplify and equate all Mexican music with Mariachi, such distinctive genres and regional styles as Norteno, Banda, Cumbia, Son Huesteco, and Son Jarocho—to name but a few—flourish in and outside of Mexico. On La Trova Tradicional de Yucatan: 1928-1932 23 vintage 78 rpm recordings of one distinctive Mexican song form known as Yucatecan Trova have been brought together. This particular Trova, or popular music genre, flourished in the Yucatan city of Merida between the 1900s and the 1940s. Now all but forgotten, the Yucatecan Trova was sung by serenaders and played on a variety of guitars, vihuelas, guitarrones, and other stringed instruments. It was heavily influenced by Cuban rhythms and, thanks in great measure to an energetic literary scene in early 20th century Merida, the lyrical content of the songs were infused with rich, poetic texts. Each of the songs on *La Trova Tradicional de Yucatan: 1928-1932* comes across as being performed with sincere, heartfelt, and amorous sentiments. The ensembles responsible for these emotive performances include Quinteto Merida, Duo MediaSalas, Los Peninsualres, and Cancioneros Yucatecos. Equally attractive to both the tragic romantic and the rigid music researcher, this album is a must have for anyone interested in exploring Mexico's incredible musical diversity. *—John Vallier*

Peru Collection

☆ **Afro-Peruvian Classics: The Soul of Black Peru** / 1995 / Luaka Bop ♦♦♦♦♦
The Afro-Peruvian style heard on *The Soul of Black Peru* compilation originated hundreds of years ago from the Spanish slave trade. The music is a mix of African, Spanish, and Andean traditions, due to the fact that the slaves who came to Peru were not from one specific region, so they did not have a common language to communicate with. It's easy to break the music down and see which culture contributed what—the lyrics are all sung in Spanish (Spain), have a slight melancholy approach (similar to the Yaravi form from the Andes), and boast interesting rhythms (Africa). The musical form is just starting to catch on in other parts of the world, and deservedly so. And since this is heartfelt, emotional music, fans outside of the world music circle can easily grasp and appreciate it. Ranging from Manuel Donayre's "Yo No Soy Jaqui" to Chabuca Granda's "Lando" (Luaka Bop Records head David Byrne even contributes a track, "Maria Lando"), Afro-Peruvian Classics, The Soul of Black Peru is a true musical treasure. *—Greg Prato*

★ **Huayno Music of Peru, Vol. 1** / 1989 / Arhoolie ✦✦✦✦✦
The popular huaynos of Peru go back hundreds of years and come in all sorts of forms, from village square to (relatively) bigtime pop. Part Spanish, part Indian, they are almost nothing like the better-known Latin forms in feeling or rhythm. As this superlative collection shows, the truly popular versions are almost hypnotically beguiling. *—David L. Mayers*

Mountain Music of Peru, Vol. 1 / 1986 / Smithsonian/Folkways ✦✦✦✦✦
What makes a satisfactory national compilation is obviously to some extent a question of ideology. This one is superb as an overview and introduction. It ranges from shepherd pipe, solo voice, and carnival music, to popular huaynos from the towns. Unlike the plethora of middle-class groups with a political agenda that beclutter the field, this one does music that is real and superb, as are John Cohen's notes. Parts were released in 1966, but 15 minutes' worth has been added for this re-release. (68:17) *—John Storm Roberts*

Traditional Music of Peru 1: Festivals of Cusco / Nov. 21, 1995 / Smithsonian/Folkways ✦✦✦
Volume one of this series, produced by the Lima, Peru-based Archives of Traditional Andean Music, investigates the music of religious festivals, which remains one of the most crucial kinds of artistic expression in the Andes. These 1989 recordings draw on the festival music of the Cusco region, typified by flute and drum, harp and violin, brass band, accordion and vocal performances. *—Jason Ankeny*

Traditional Music of Peru 2: from the Mantaro Valley / Nov. 21, 1995 / Smithsonian/Folkways ✦✦✦
While Peru's Mantaro Valley is most renowned for its clarinet and saxophone ensembles (sampled here), Vol. 2 illustrates the sheer diversity of the indigenious music of the region. Drawn from a batch of 1985 archival recordings, the collection hops from work songs to funeral dirges to instrumental dance music performed with saxophones, clarinets, harps, violins and drums that recalls American jazz and Klezmer music, albeit with a distinctly Andean flavor. *—Jason Ankeny*

Puerto Rico Collection

Music of Puerto Rico 1929-1947 / 1992 / Harlequin ✦✦✦✦✦
This is a very fine set of recordings, mostly string groups, mostly from the mid-'30s. Many of them are by New York-Puerto Rican groups in the fashionable Cuban idioms of the time—boleros, sones, and so forth—by major composers like Pedro Berrios and Rafael Hernandez. These have a lot of charm, but the gems are a handful of truly Puerto Rican forms: seises, aguinaldos, and plenas. A major bonus is a two clarinet-lead danza. The only bummer: The greatest of all early pleneros, Canario, appears just once, playing a commercial bolero. *—John Storm Roberts*

LATIN POP

Latin Continuum

Maria Conchita Alonso

Vocals / Latin Pop, Latin Continuum
Maria Conchita Alonso has it all—beauty, talent and a personality that has allowed her to become a star of films and Broadway and a Grammy-nominated singer. Miss Teenager of the World in 1971 and Miss Venezuela in 1975, Alonso was named "Hispanic Woman of the Year" by the Mexican American Opportunity Foundation in 1990. Alonso's phenomenal career began shortly after winning the Miss Teenager of the World award. She became an internationally-known actress in the 1984 film, "Moscow On The Hudson," featuring Robin Williams. Alonso's subsequent films have included "Touch And Go," with Michael Keaton, and "A Fine Mess," with Ted Danson and Howie Mandel, in 1986; "Running Man," with Arnold Schwarzenegger, and "Extreme Prejudice," with Nick Nolte, in 1987; "Colors," with Robert Duval and Sean Penn, in 1988; and "Vampire's Kiss', with Nicholas Cage, in 1989. In 1992, Alonso co-starred in the HBO film, "Teamster Boss: The Jackie Presser Story." Two years later, she co-starred with Kenny Rogers in the NBC Movie of the week, "McShayne." In April 1995, Alonso appeared in the four hour mini-series, "Texas." Alonso had the lead role in the NBC situation comedy, "One Of The Boys." Alonso's first Grammy nomination came in 1985 when she was nominated as "Best Latin artists" for her self-titled album. Her second album, "Otra Mentira Mas," released in 1988, was nominated for a Grammy as "Best Latin Pop performance." Alonso's 1992 album, "Imaginame," which she co-produced with K.C. Porter and Mari Spiro, was nominated for a Grammy as "Best Latin Pop album." Alonso co-wrote seven of the album's eleven tunes. Alonso has remained one of the biggest stars in Latin America. She hosted a weekly, Spanish-language, variety show, "Picante," from January 1992 to January 1993. In February 1994, Alonso starred in "Alejandra," based on Dela Fiallo's novella. The show was broadcast in forty Spanish speaking countries and attracted an audience of more than three million people. An album of romantic ballads was recorded in conjunction with the show. On March 20, 1995, Alonso became the first Latin-born actress to star in a Broadway show when she appeared in "Kiss Of The Spider Woman." *—Craig Harris*

● **Lo Mejor de Maria Chonchita Alonso** / A&M ✦✦✦✦
Lo Mejor de Maria Conchita Alonso collects some of her biggest hits for AM, including "Sueltame," "Tomame O Dejame," "Noche de Copas," and "Dueno de Me Cuerpo." An enjoyable, adequate collection of Latin pop from the Grammy-nominated singer and actress. *—Heather Phares*

Marc Anthony

Vocals / Cuban Pop, Rock en Español, Latin Dance, Tropical, Club/Dance, Merengue, Mambo, New York Salsa, Adult Contemporary, Latin Pop, Cuba, Latin Continuum
Marc Anthony is one of the hottest salseros around. He started out in salsa in 1993 when he released *Otra Nota* on Soho Latin. The album produced such hits as "Palabras de Alma," and "El Ultimo Beso." His career really took off when he and La India recorded "Vivir Lo Nuestro," during a live performance at Madison Square Garden. He next album took two years to make and is therefore appropriately named *Todo a Su Tiempo*. It too has become quite popular. He was born Marco Antonio Muñiz to Puerto Rican parents in New York City. As a child he used to sing with his father, a composer and musician who played bachata, and Latin folk music for his friends and family. It is from his father, that Anthony learned about music and singing. Although he came from a traditional Latino home, Anthony had little professional interest in Hispanic music and started out writing songs for house, dance and club music performers such as the Sapphires, the Latin Rascals, and Menudo. This led him to get involved with arranging additional vocal parts for songs and occasionally singing back-up vocals. He signed to Atlantic in 1990 and began working with Little Louie Vega on a dance compilation album comprised of different artists. Vega suggested that Anthony sing one of the songs and was so impressed that he immediately had the young singer do all of them. The result was the album *When the Night is Over*, and featured the work of Tito Puente, Eddie Palmieri and Luis Perico Ortiz. It was about this time that Anthony began to get interested in Latin music and its origins. After the album came out, Puente invited him to be his opening act at Madison Square Garden for his 100th Album Celebration Party. Anthony began immersing himself in the music and thanks to his manager, met and became friends with salsa king Ruben Blades. He began recording and touring with Blades, who encouraged Anthony; after becoming a major star among Latin listeners, he made his English-language debut with his eponymous 1999 album, launching the pop hit "I Need to Know." In fall 2000, Anthony won a Grammy for Song of the Year for his song "Dimelo (I Need to Know)" at the first-ever Latin Grammy Awards. *—Sandra Brennan*

● **Todo a Su Tiempo** / 1995 / Soho Latino ✦✦✦✦✦

Contra la Corriente / Oct. 21, 1997 / Sony International ✦✦✦✦✦

Marc Anthony / Sep. 14, 1999 / Columbia ✦✦✦
Marc Anthony was a salsa superstar throughout the '90s, long before the Latin pop explosion of the 1999. Once Ricky Martin ushered in a new era of crossovers that spring with "Livin' la Vida Loca," there was a rush of crossover acts, almost enough to make it seem like Anthony was left behind. After all, his bid for mainstream success as the starring role in Paul Simon's broadway musical +The Capeman was undone as it became one of the Great White Way's most notorious failures. Still, Anthony had his own English-language album in the works. Titled *Marc Anthony*, the record appeared in the fall of 1999, guaranteeing it a shot at a mass audience, which is exactly what it was designed to do. As a matter of fact, it's almost a bit too calculated, opening with two interchangeable ballads that set the tone for a pleasant, subdued set of Latin-tinged adult contemporary pop. Anthony sings beautifully throughout, but he's never given the opportunity to be truly electric, the way he can be with hot salsa numbers. The liveliest the album gets is the catchy mid-tempo single "I Need to Know," which is gently danceable, or the mild salsa of "That's Okay" and the Latin dance-pop of "She's Been Good to Me." The rest is almost all pop ballads, perfectly produced and gamely sung by Anthony. Some of these work very well, others simply fade into the slipstream. That's particularly frustrating because Anthony is such a talented singer that it's evident that he's capable of much more than this. *Marc Anthony* isn't bad for what it is, and a few of its singles are quite good, but it's not at the level of his earlier records, or Martin's crossover bid of 1999, either. *—Stephen Thomas Erlewine*

Enrique Iglesias

Vocals, Violin / Latin Pop, Latin Continuum
Following in his father's footsteps as a sensual Latin vocalist, Enrique Iglesias became the most popular Latin singles artist during 1996, with five immense hits—"Por Amarte," "Si Tu Te Vas," "No Llores por Mi," "Experiencia Religiosa" and "Trapecista"—from his self-titled debut album, released in late 1995. The LP sold over one million copies. The Spanish star resurfaced in 1997 with *Vivir;* two years later, he scored an international smash with the single "Bailamos," followed by the release of *Enrique*. *—John Bush*

● **Vivir** / 1997 / Fonovisa ✦✦✦✦
Enrique Iglesias' *Vivir* is a wonderful collection of contemporary Latin pop, dance-pop and adult love ballads, all graced with his rich, alluring vocals. *—Terry Jenkins*

Enrique / Nov. 23, 1999 / Interscope ✦✦✦✦
Enrique Iglesias' Interscope debut *Enrique* was designed to be a massive crossover success, breaking him to the pop audience that devoured Ricky Martin and "Livin' la Vida Loca." So, the Latin roots were pushed to the background and the record leaned heavily on mainstream dance-pop and adult contemporary ballads. Iglesias and Andres Restrepo served as executive producers, overseeing a number of producers whose work all sound fairly cohesive. That may be because each specialized in a certain area: dancefloor numbers or slow-burners. It's all impeccably crafted and appealing, the way a big-budget record like this should be. Song wise, there are a couple of stretches that are a little rote but not unappealing, and for the most part, the tunes are endearing; as a matter of fact, the first breakthrough hit, "Bailamos," pales in comparison with much of the first half of the album, including "Rhythm Divine," "I Have Always Loved You," and "Oyeme." If *Enrique* doesn't pack a knock-out punch, it's because it wasn't structured that way. It was made to be a sturdy and satisfying mainstream crossover effort, and that's exactly what it is. *—Stephen Thomas Erlewine*

Menudo

f. 1977
Group / Latin Pop, Latin Continuum
Formed around a cast of lovable teenage Puerto Ricans (each of whom were forced out once they reached the age of 16), Menudo was the first Latin group to gain success around the world. The initial lineup formed in 1977 around brothers Carlos, Oscar and Ricky Melendez plus Nefty and Fernando Sallaberry, but the first replacements were installed before the end of the 1970s. Menudo made a medium-sized splash in America during the mid-'80s—though

all of the original members had long since passed—with the 1984 LP *Reaching Out,* which included English-language versions of their biggest hits.

Though Menudo's brand of disposable synthesizer-pop dated and faded quickly in America, the group continued to rule much of Central and South America, and ousted member Ricky Martin made a successful solo career. By the late '90s, there were over thirty ex-members of Menudo, and the then-current version of the group—known as MDO and including Alexis Grullon, Abel Talamántez, Didier Hernández, Anthony Galindo and Daniel Weider—included no native Puerto Ricans and none under the age of 16. *—John Bush*

El Reencuentro: 15 Años Despues / 1992 / Fonovisa ♦♦♦♦
Since Menudo was designed to be a group of perennial teenagers, it's not surprising that the original members wanted to reunite—perhaps to take care of some unfinished business, perhaps just to cash in on their good name. And so *Reencuentro: 15 Anos Despues* was born—and, surprise surprise, it's actually pretty good. The key is that the group has grown up. There's no teeny-pop posturing that could make their early albums insufferable. Instead, it's filled with dance-pop, adult contemporary ballads and Latin Pop that make the group sound their age. It's an entertaining record, a successful reunion and possibly their best album yet. *—Stephen Thomas Erlewine*

Luis Miguel

Vocals / Bolero, Tejano, Latin Pop, Latin Continuum
Mexican performer Luis Miguel is an international star who is loved for both his well-produced albums and his strong live performances. Since 1990, he has been the most popular performer in Latin America. In the United States, he has become the only Latino artist to have two Spanish language albums, *Romance* and *Segundo Romance* go platinum. Both are comprised of tender South American romantic songs. In the U.S., Miguel has earned three Grammys. *Segundo Romance* won him one of them. It also earned Miguel a total of 34 platinum records throughout South and Central America in 1995. Follow-up releases included *Musipistas* and 1996's *Nada Es Igual;* in 1998, he co-starred in the film *Fiebre de Amor,* and also appeared on its soundtrack. *Amarte Es un Place* followed a year later. Miguel's international stardom was heavily recognized in fall 2000— he won two Grammys (Male Pop Vocal Performance and Best Pop Album) for *Amarte Es un Place* at the first annual Latin Grammy Awards. *—Sandra Brennan*

Romance / 1991 / WEA Latina ♦♦♦
The usual smooth, well-crafted pop ear candy from Luis Miguel, earnestly sung over strings and polite Latin rhythms. This may be a concept CD: each tune title is preceded by a year, which one assumes refers to its year of composition or original release. There are printed lyrics, albeit in a totally different song order, and no liner notes explain what we are to make of this presentation. Ultimately, it doesn't matter… the title of the release says it all. *—Janet Rosen*

Romantico Desde Siempre / Nov. 29, 1994 / EMI International ♦♦♦

● **15 Hits: Pistas Favoritas** / Oct. 7, 1995 / Spartacus Discos ♦♦♦♦♦

Romances / Aug. 12, 1997 / WEA Latina ♦♦♦♦
Luis Miguel's *Romances* is part of his series of records of classic Boleros. This time around, he hired Bebu Silvetti as musical director and arranger and Armando Manzanero as artistic director. Those two musicians wrote two new songs to augment the 13 classic love ballads from Argentina, Brazil and Mexico, and their impeccable taste, along with Miguel's seductive vocals, make *Romances* a sensuous, enchanting album. *—Terry Jenkins*

Eros Ramazzotti

Vocals / Latin Pop, Latin Continuum
As a Latin-pop singer, Eros Ramazzotti became especially popular in Germany, Mexico and Argentina (as well as his native Italy) during the '90s, and he has sold over 20 million records worldwide, though his success in America has been limited. He was born in the Rome suburb of Cinecitta during the mid-'60s, and moved to Milan to make a career of music as a teenager. Beginning with 1991's *In Ogni Senso,* Ramazzotti recorded three albums for Arista during the first half of the '90s. With a new BMG deal which included his RadioRama production company, Eros moved from pop-oriented music to more straightahead rock, even recruiting a rock band for the 1995 Rock over Europe festival. *Eros Live* followed in 1998. *—John Bush*

In Ogni Senso / 1991 / Arista ♦♦♦

Donde Hay Musica / Jun. 1996 / Arista ♦♦♦♦
Eros Ramazzotti stretches his wings and covers a wider variety of styles on his 1996 album *Donde Hay Musica.* This outing is much less rock-oriented than the previous *Todo Historias.* The album opens with the pop feel of the title track, and never really ventures into the guitar-laden territory that dominated his previous effort. Standout cuts include the ballads *Yo Amare* and the beautiful *Casi Amor,* as well as the album's closer *Buena Vida.* Other high-points include *Este Inmenso Show,* which is upbeat, bears a hip-hop influence and ends as a soaring, gospel-tinged number complete with a saxophone. *Yo Sin Ti* finds Eros exploring more Latin sounds, and the result is a pleasant, sunny and breezy offering. *La Aurora* is also a good song, finding Eros sounding somewhat like Phil Collins. The only problem with *La Aurora,* however, is that it sounds a tad too similar (especially in the chorus) to his earlier hit *A Medio Camino* (from the *Todo Historias* album). If it worked once, it will work again, correct— Not entirely, because this album is, first and foremost, a departure from his earlier sounds and makes for quite a pleasant listening experience. *—Jose Promis*

Eros / Jan. 27, 1998 / RCA International ♦♦♦
A sampler of Eros Ramazzotti's extensive back catalog, the Italian version of *Eros* (not to be confused with the Spanish edition issued the previous year) compiles five remastered tracks, nine re-recorded cuts and two brand new songs. Fans of Ramazotti's Latin recordings will no doubt be pleased to hear him perform in his native tongue, especially on highlights including "Cose Della Vita/Can't Stop Thinking of You," a duet with Tina Turner. *—Jason Ankeny*

Selena (Selena Quintanilla Perez)

b. Apr. 16, 1971, Lake Jackson, TX, **d.** Mar. 31, 1995, Corpus Christi, TX
Vocals / Tejano, Adult Contemporary, Latin Pop, Dance-Pop, Latin Continuum
The tragic shooting death of Tejano singer Selena spawned a reaction within the Latino community that can be compared to the reactions to the deaths of Elvis Presley and John Lennon. An enormously popular singer in Latino communities across North America, her music crossed cultural boundaries to touch the lives of young and old alike. A flamboyant, sexy stage performer, sometimes hailed as the Latina Madonna, Selena was nonetheless considered a role model for off-stage she was family oriented, active in anti-drug campaigns and AIDS awareness programs. In 1990, she and backing band Los Dinos released their eponymous debut album. Later that year she issued *Ven Conmigo;* the title track became the first Tejano record to go gold. In 1995, Selena began preparing to make her breakthrough into the American pop mainstream; *Dreaming of You,* her final album, was released posthumously in 1995. It became the first Tejano album to reach number one in America and was double platinum by the end of the year. *—Sandra Brennan*

Selena / 1989 / EMI Latin ♦♦♦
Selena—The Original Motion Picture Soundtrack isn't quite a greatest-hits collection, but it's not really a rarities compilation, either. Instead, the record comprises selected Tejano hits, live medleys and cuts by the Vidal Brothers, Emilio, and the Barrio Boyz, among others. The end result is an enjoyable sampler, even if it isn't the best place to become acquainted with the tragically departed Tejano icon. *—Stephen Thomas Erlewine*

Entre a Mi Mundo / 1992 / EMI Latin ♦♦♦

Live / May 4, 1993 / EMI Latin ♦♦♦♦♦

★ **Amor Prohibido** / Mar. 13, 1994 / Capitol/EMI Latin ♦♦♦♦♦
Amor Prohibido was Selena's biggest album before her crossover attempt, *Dreaming of You.* While the album is slightly uneven, she was a dynamic, charismatic singer and is able to pull across the weaker material. Indeed, the record is her strongest album and shows why she was the biggest tejano star of the '90s. *—Stephen Thomas Erlewine*

★ **Dreaming of You** / 1995 / EMI Latin ♦♦♦♦♦
Most of America first learned of Selena because of her tragic murder; accordingly, the posthumous *Dreaming of You* was the first record they ever heard. While it isn't her best—*Amor Prohibido* is a more consistent release—it was an effective introduction, and showed why she was so beloved among tejano fans. The English tracks on the album are no different than her Spanish songs. Selena was essentially a singer much like her idol Madonna. She was able to sing ballads and dance-pop convincingly. *Dreaming of You* would have been a stronger album if she had lived, but it still stands as a powerful—and touching—testament to her talents. *—Stephen Thomas Erlewine*

Anthology / Mar. 31, 1998 / EMI International ♦♦♦♦

Los Temerarios

f. 1983
Group / Onda Grupera, Tejano, Latin Pop, Latin Continuum
Los Temerarios' bubblegum ranchera has been the romantic soundtrack of millions of Mexican and Mexican-American youths' lives during the '90s. Combining elements of traditional Mexican ranchera music with keyboards, electric bass and stately percussion, they created a sound whose appeal frequently took them to the top tier of the Latin charts. Formed by brothers Adolfo and Gustavo ingel, the group's early-'80s output comprised organ-driven ballads, rancheras, good-time cumbias and even corridos. However, Los Temerarios failed to make a major impact until the late '80s. By then, Gustavo's voice had developed into a sugary cross between Art Garfunkel and George Michael, and Adolfo's songwriting skills were advancing. Sentimental ballads "Tu Infame Engaño," "Ven Porque Te Necesito," and "Sí Quiero Volver" solidified their reputation for dramatic melodies and pleading, if naïve, lyrics.

The 1991 release *Mi Vida Eres T* (*My Life Is You*) propelled the group to superstardom. The unique sound of the title track, which backed mariachi instrumentation with electric bass and a dramatic crash on each bar's second beat, became a standard and spawned legions of imitators. Critics considered the lyrics banal, but young fans identified with the themes of romantic loss and heartbreak, influenced by the songwriting of Juan Gabriel and José Alfredo Jimenez. The group added a calliope-like keyboard sound to its 1993 release *Tu /ltima Cancion,* and 1995's *Camino del Amor* continued in the same vein. "Por Qué Te Conocí," the first single from their 1998 album *Cómo Te Recuerdo,* became the group's second number one hit in the span of a year. The group also ventured into movies, appearing in *Sueño y Realidad* in 1993. *—Douglas Shannon*

★ **Mi Vida Eres T˙** / 1992 / Angel ♦♦♦♦♦
Los Temerarios achieved superstardom with Gustavo ingel's ethereal vocals drifting across tales of heartbreak and deceit. "Mi Vida Eres T˙" became the group's calling card, as Gustavo cried out over a soundscape combining mariachi instrumentation with electric bass and percussion. The album also moved the group closer to pop turf, containing eight ballads and two cumbias, a formula the group would follow throughout the nineties. Despite the abundance of ballads, they managed to sound distinct thanks to keyboardist Adolfo Angel's melodies, which excelled at creating tension and building to a memorable climax. *—Douglas Shannon*

15 Exitos en su Punto / Aug. 3, 1993 / Sony International ♦♦♦

Camino del Amor / Nov. 21, 1995 / AFG Sigma ♦♦♦♦
While the group doesn't show any signs of challenging itself, it plies its trade well, delivering tales of romantic loss via Gustavo ingel's beautiful tenor. The group sticks to pop power ballads, cumbias, and the mariachi-pop it's been associated with since 1991. Keyboardist and chief composer Adolfo ingel duets with brother Gustavo on first single "La Mujer de los Dos," (The Woman of Both) but despite his techincally correct performance, he doesn't deliver the passion that his brother does. Ego sounds like it's creeping in on "Mi Alma Reclama," (My Soul Asks) in which the singer feels self-pity because although he's had a thousand lovers,

he's lonely tonight. The songs are also beginning to lengthen a la Juan Gabriel, though the melodies are still strong enough to keep them interesting. *—Douglas Shannon*

Como Te Recuerdo / Jan. 27, 1998 / Fonovisa ✦✦

Charlie Zaa

Vocals / Bolero, Latin Continuum

Colombian pop star Charlie Zaa began recording in 1996, and soon became one of his country's best-selling artists, with the album *Sentimientos*. With 1998's *Segundo Sentimiento*, Zaa's influence expanded into Mexico and the rest of Central America; an album of *Remixes* followed a year later, and in early 2000 he returned with *Ciego de Amor*. *—John Bush*

● **Sentimientos** / Nov. 19, 1996 / Sonolux ✦✦✦✦✦
Charlie Zaa's *Sentimientos* is a terrific romantic ballad effort, thanks to his seductive vocals, the impeccable production and an ace set of songs that effortlessly showcase his ample gifts. *—Terry Jenkins*

Segundo Sentimiento / May 26, 1998 / Sonolux ✦✦✦✦
Charlie Zaa's second album *Segundo Sentimiento* is—like the title suggests—strikingly similar to his debut album, *Sentimientos*. That's not a bad thing, since Zaa excels at romantic ballads, but it does suggests his limits. Still, it's pretty entertaining. *—Terry Jenkins*

Ciego de Amor / Feb. 1, 2000 / Sonolux ✦✦✦

Mexico

Cafe Tacuba

Group / Rock en Español, Mexico, Latin Continuum

Latin rockers Café Tacuba took its name from a small restaurant in their native Mexico City. Comprised of singer Cosme, guitarist Joselo Rangel, bassist Enrique Rangel and keyboardist Emanuel del Real, the group issued their self-titled debut album in 1992. Two years later Café Tacuba resurfaced with their creative breakthrough *Re*, a sprawling, genre-hopping landmark which encompassed not only the breadth of contemporary Latin sounds but also touched base with everything from samba to punk. *Avalancha de Exitos* followed in 1996, and three years on Café Tacuba issued *Reves/Yo Soy*.

The following year, *Reves/Yo Soy* won an award for Best Rock Album at the first annual Latin Grammy Awards. *—Jason Ankeny*

Cafe Tacuba / 1992 / WEA Latina ✦✦✦✦
Cafe Tacuba is a product of a movement of the '80s and '90s known as "rock en espanol"—rock with lyrics in Spanish. From Mexico to Spain to Argentina, "rock en espanol" became absolutely huge among Hispanic youths and presented an aggressive, hard-edged alternative to softer Latin pop. It was Mexico that gave us Cafe Tacuba, which goes for a punkish snarl on this excellent CD. But while the snarl and aggression are hard to miss, Tacuba is undeniably musical and far from predictable. Punk rock is a strong influence, but so is everything from Jamaican ska to Mexican tejano and banda music. Melody is important to this band, which might have reached English-speaking rockers with this self-titled release were it not for the language barrier and the fact that Latin rock is usually promoted only in Latino circles. *—Alex Henderson*

Re / Jul. 22, 1994 / WEA Latina ✦✦✦✦

Avalancha de Exitos / Nov. 5, 1996 / WEA International ✦✦✦✦

● **Reves/Yosoy** / Jul. 20, 1999 / Warner Brothers ✦✦✦✦✦
On *Reves/Yosoy*, the critically acclaimed Café Tacuba prove why they are among the pioneers of the "Rock en Espanol" movement. This double album includes the group's traditional and experimental sides, devoting a disc to each. Over the course of *Yosoy* (the more song-based of the albums), the group weaves harp, piano, vibes and accordion into 15 diversely textured pop songs. Zippy tracks like "La Locomotora" and "Bicicleta" keep company with languid, sunny songs like "El Rio" and "Arboles Frutales," while "Guerra" and "Dos Ninos" shift between those extremes. The more experimental *Reves* includes collaborations with the Kronos Quartet, ambient electronica and musique concrete pieces. Though *Reves Yosoy* covers an extensive amount of musical territory, the album's depth is as impressive as its reach, and showcases Cafe Tacuba's inventive, engaging talent. *—Heather Phares*

Alejandro Fernandez

Vocals / Tejano, Mexico, Latin Continuum

One of Mexico's most famous performers of romantic songs, ballads and traditional mariachi favorites, Alejandro Fernandez has played New York's Madison Square Garden and routinely sells out Mexico City's Auditorio Nacional (once for 12 dates within three weeks). He debuted with a self-titled 1992 album on Sony Discos and continued to sell millions of records for CBS/Sony over the course of half a dozen albums in as many years. His album roster includes 1993's *Piel de Nina*, 1995's *Que Seas Muy Feliz*, and 1997's *Muy Dentro de Mi Corazon* and *Me Estoy Enamorando*. *Mi Verdad* followed in 1999 and *Entre Tus Brazos* was released a year later. At the first annual Latin Grammy Awards in fall 2000, *Mi Verdad* won Best Regional Song. *—John Bush*

● **Me Estoy Enamorando** / Sep. 23, 1997 / Sony International ✦✦✦✦✦
Me Estoy Enamorando is a fine romantic record from Alejandro Fernandez, highlighted by "Yo Naci Para Amarte," "No Se Olvidar," "Como El Sol Y El Trigo," "Noche Triste," "Promesa" and "En El Jardin," a duet with Gloria Estefan. *—Terry Jenkins*

Mi Verdad / May 11, 1999 / Sony International ✦✦✦

Entre Tus Brazos / Apr. 25, 2000 / Sony International ✦✦✦
After re-examining his ranchera roots on *Mi Verdad*, Alejandro Fernandez returned to concentrating on the romantic ballad style for which he's best known on *Entre Tus Brazos*. Fernandez wraps his rich baritone around the ballads and rancheras here, mixing pop savvy with mariachi-flavored instrumentation. In terms of his standing in contemporary Mexican music, fans believe Fernandez deserves to be placed in the upper echelon alongside Luis Miguel, and the performances here only strengthen that case. *—Steve Huey*

Jaguares

Group / Rock en Español, Mexico, Latin Continuum

In 1995, Jaguares was formed out of the skeleton of Califanes, a Mexico City rock group. The name change was due to a dream had by lead singer Saul Hernandez, who dreamed that he was playing inside a Jaguar's mouth. Shortly after the name change, Jaguares took off in popularity, becoming one of Mexico's most loved rock bands—their first album, *El Equilibrio de los Jaguares*, released in 1996 by RCA International, built a solid fan base in a time when it was difficult for Mexican rock bands to get airplay or venues to play in—the genre was frowned upon because of violence during the late '60s at *Woodstock*-like events. Their second release in 1999, a double album called *Bajo de Azul de Tu Misterio*, was put together by band members Hernandez, Sabo Romo on bass, Cesar Lopez on guitar, Jarris Margalli on guitar and Alfonso Andre on drums, as well as a number of supporting musicians, including a string section. The album enjoyed remarkable commercial success and helped them fill stadium-sized venues in both Mexico and the U.S.. An EP, *Saul Hernandez, Compositor* arrived in 2000. *—Stacia Proefrock*

● **Bajo el Azul de Tu Misterio** / Aug. 24, 1999 / RCA International ✦✦✦✦✦
At the time of its release, *Bajo el Azul de Tu Misterio* was the highest debuting alternative rock album on the *Billboard* Latin charts, an accomplishment that is given more weight by the fact that it is a double album. Jaguares, playing upon their rapidly expanding popularity in Mexico, recorded this mixture of live and studio tracks with an almost orchestra-sized group of supporting players, resulting in an incredibly ambitious album. Their greatest Mexican influences seem to come from their Spanish lyrics, largely written by Saul Hernandez, that often deal with the issues of social justice and culture—otherwise, this album sounds like a mixture of Metallica, Def Leppard, and early U2. Overall, though, the mix works and the legion of supporting producers and players have made a slick, professional album that should please fans on both sides of the border. *—Stacia Proefrock*

Grupo Ladron

Group / Onda Grupera, Norteño, Mexico, Latin Continuum

Riding to fame by staying close to the pop side of onda grupera, Ladrón (in English, Thief) has found itself admired throughout central Mexico and the Midwestern U.S., while ironically keeping a low profile in its native Monterrey, where norteño reigns supreme.

Group director and guitarist Sergio Villarreal (b. 1968), who writes nearly all the group's songs, began penning tunes at age 14 and has written at a prolific pace ever since, averaging 75 compositions per year. Determined to have another career to fall back on, he graduated engineering degree and briefly taught math and physics at the Universidad Autónoma de Nuevo León with a mechanical Regiomontana. At Universidad Regiomontana, Villarreal and three students formed the rock group Gatos Con Botas (Cats With Boots). The group quickly decided it felt more comfortable with the softer onda grupera style, and became Ladrón in 1991. Simplicity and softness characterize their output, which consists almost entirely of cumbias and adult contemporary ballads. Villarreal also incorporated harmonies in the clean-cut tradition of the Association. With keyboard player Omar García (b. 1969), bass player Edgar "Gary" García (b. 1970), and drummer William Mejía (b. 1971), the four-man group was the smallest in a style known for six- to eight-man ensembles.

Signed by Discos Sabinas that same year, the group found an influential patron in the legendary Mexican composer Armando Manzanero, who produced its first album, *Corazón Desvalido* (*Broken Heart*). International success arrived in 1992 with *No Tengo Lágrimas* (*I Don't Have Tears*), which produced five hit singles, a rare feat in a genre whose artists average one album per year.

Villarreal's arranging and songwriting talents weren't lost on his colleagues; he has worked as arranger for albums by groups whose style is much different from Ladrón's, including Banda Móvil, Cardenales de Nuevo León and Banda R-15. In addition, he has written songs for Liberación, Flash, and Sonido Mazter, among others, saying someday he would like to be a full-time producer and songwriter.

Ladrón added two mariachi songs to 1994's *Culpable De Tu Amor* (*Guilty of Your Love*) and recorded some rapid-fire quebraditas for its 1998 CD *Enamórate De Un Ladrón* (*Fall In Love With a Thief*), but never strayed far from its trademark romantic sound, which includes frequent references to its earlier songs. The 1996 greatest-hits CD *15 Super Temas* is the only U.S. release to include songs from *Corazón Desvalido*. *Tu Me Quieres Lastimar* followed in 1998.; *Misma Historia* appeared three years later. *—Douglas Shannon*

● **No Tengo Lágrimas** / 1992 / Fonovisa ✦✦✦✦✦
The group's second CD was its major breakthrough. The Sergio Villarreal-led group developed a grupera-lite style that featured echoing keyboards and Villarreal's delicate tenor. He composed all of the album's songs, showing a knack for melody on the disc's four cumbias and six ballads. Ballads "Mi Castigo" ("My Punishment"), "Tarde O Temprano" ("Sooner or Later"), and the title track won fans with simple but effective hooks that stuck in the brain. Villarreal sounds just a little too sensitive on the hit "T' Me Quieres Lastimar" ("You Want to Hurt Me"), in which he whines for three minutes about his girlfriend not showing up at his birthday party. *—Douglas Shannon*

Culpable de Tu Amor / 1994 / Disa Dimusa ✦✦✦

Enamorate de un Ladron / Feb. 10, 1998 / EMI International ✦✦✦
The inclusion of four quebraditas (curiously referred to as cumbias on the track listing) helped Ladron recover its pulse from the sleepy 1996 effort *Piden Tu Mano*. Vocalist and composer Sergio Villarreal, known for his languid songs, sounds positively energetic on the first single, "Celos Por Tí." ("Jealousy For You") And no, the group didn't go banda—it conserved its grupera-lite sound for the fast-paced tunes. The group also showed more creativ-

ity on the real cumbias, adding a touch of vallenato to "Tu Recuerdo" ("Your Memory") and harp to the standout "La Luna Me Engañó" ("The Moon Fooled Me"). The ballads don't fare as well; despite decent harmonies, "Lastima" is nothing more than a rewrite of "No Tengo Lágrimas," and "Qué Vas A Hacer" ("What Are You Going to Do") wastes a good melody on arrangements which make it sound like a leftover from the *No Tengo Lágrimas* sessions. —*Douglas Shannon*

Marco Antonio Solis

b. Ario de Rosales, Michoacan, Mexico
Vocals / Tejano, Norteño, Mexico, Latin Continuum
Marco Antonio Solis is without question one of the most important figures in the rise of Mexican and Latin music to world prominence during the last two decades of the 20th century. Born in Michoacan, Mexico, Solis was only twelve when he formed his first group, Los Hermanitos Solis, with brother Joel. He was still a teenager when he formed Los Bukis in the early '70s. Over the course of the next two decades, Los Bukis came to profoundly influence the norteño and Tejano music of Mexico and the southwestern United States. Though Solis continued to work closely with Los Bukis, he also initiated a solo career which resulted in platinum certifications for mid-'90s LPs such as *Quiereme, Inalcanzable* and *Por Amor A Mi Pueblo. Trozos de Mi Alma* followed in 1999. —*John Bush*

● **Marco** / Sep. 30, 1997 / Fonovisa ♦♦♦♦
Marco is Marco Antonio Solis' best effort to date, an exciting and melodic collection of contemporary Latin pop. Solis wrote all of the songs on the album, and they demonstrate that he's a skilled commercial songwriter in addition to being a fine singer, and this is the first time he's pulled all of his skills together in a consistently, rousingly enetertaining package. [There's also an unlisted bonus track on *Marco* that he didn't write.] —*Terry Jenkins*

Chavela Vargas (Isabel Vargas Lizano)

b. Apr. 17, 1919, Guerrero, Mexico
Vocals / Ranchera, Mexico, Latin Continuum
The best and longest preserved of the Mexican *cancion ranchera* singers, Chavela Vargas began singing rather late in life—past the age of thirty—but continued well into old age, charming audiences until she was well into her 70s. Born in Guerrero, Mexico in 1919, she first sang on a professional level in the early '50s, and toured with the legendary José Alfredo Jiménez. Her first recordings appeared in 1961, and she became quite popular during the 1960s and '70s, both in her native land as well as across the ocean in Spain and Europe. Although she retired in 1979, a victim of alcoholism, Vargas returned in 1990 after accepting a role in the Werner Herzog film *A Cry of Stone*. One year later, she contributed a song to the soundtrack of *Tacones Lejanos*, and in 1993 she entered a recording studio for the first time in decades. —*John Bush*

Chavela Vargas / May 26, 1998 / WEA International ♦♦♦
WEA International's *Chavela Vargas* is another fine installment in her '90s comeback. Vargas may be past her prime, but she nevertheless can sing, as she proves on this album. There are a few weak spots, to be sure, but it's simply a joy to hear her sing. —*Terry Jenkins*

Mexico Collection

15 Early Tejano Classics / Jan. 20, 1998 / Arhoolie ♦♦♦♦♦
Tracks from 15 of the Tejano albums in the Arhoolie catalog on this budget-priced sampler; Freddie Fender and (to a lesser degree) Lydia Mendoza are the only artists who might enjoy a reasonably wide degree of name recognition among the general public. An advantage of a sampler such as this, which at a glance draws helter-skelter from a bunch of unrelated artists, is that there's more diversity than there is on typical Tejano music anthologies, most of which draw from a certain style or era. Actually, a lot of this does date back a few decades (or even more). There are some good orquestas with a near big-band feel to the arrangements, a raw (almost garage) sentimental Spanish rocker from Fender, a melancholy bolero from Chelo Silva, and good harmonies by Carmen y Laura. It's a good intro compilation to the style whether you're on a budget or not, although because it's in a budget series, there are hardly any liner notes. —*Richie Unterberger*

☆ **Polkas de Oro** / 1993 / Rounder ♦♦♦♦♦
This most recent Rounder conjunto anthology covers polkas, a sound and dance style most commonly linked with Poland, but which is also a major component of both contunjo and Cajun/zydeco fare. In this sampler, the 14 instrumentals show how the polka beat is diffused and incorporated into conjunto settings like the redova and huapango. Such groups as Los Vaqueros, Los Terribles, Los Dos Gilbertos and Los Hermanos Farias, as well as individual performers like Tony De La Rosa, adapt polkas and waltzes using the 10-button accordion, 12-string bajo sexto (Mexican guitar) and traditional arrangements. It's an instructive example of how styles are linked across ethnic lines. —*Ron Wynn*

Puerto Rico

Ismael Rivera (El Sonero Mayor)

b. Oct. 5, 1931, Santurce, Puerto Rico, **d.** May 13, 1987, Santurce, Puerto Rico
Salsa, Puerto Rico, Latin Continuum
Ismael Rivera, El Sonero Mayor "Maelo" was born in Santurce, Puerto Rico on October 5, 1931. It all started on the very same street Ismael was born and raised on—Calle Calma. There he was instilled with the sounds and rhythms of Puerto Rico—the bomba and plena. At a young age, Rivera was exposed to the influences that would set him on his musical destiny. First his mother Margarita bore in him a love for singing. And next, his boyhood friend, Rafael Cortijo, provided Rivera with the impulse and drive as well as a more structured musical forum for him to unleash his unique vocal style. Their relationship would take the sound of calle Calma, and all of Puerto Rico, around the world and immortalize their names and music in the evolution of Latin music and salsa.

In 1954, Ismael Rivera and Cortijo recorded their first hit, "El Bombon de Elena." From the mid- to late '50s, Cortijo y su Combo, with Ismael Rivera as singer, took the Carribean by storm. At the turn of the decade, they travelled to New York for the first time, and it didn't take long for Cortijo and Rivera to solidify their position in the growing Latin music scene of Manhattan. Their popularity was largely due to their rhythmic sound and the band's ability to simultaneously play great music and entertain through rapid choreographed dance routines. However, the one element that separated Cortijo y su Combo from all the other Latin song-and-dance bands was the voice of Ismael Rivera. A key ingredient to the bomba and plena sound of Puerto Rico is vocals, and Maelo's voice is the single most defining aspect of his music. With a booming, precisely rhythmic, yet equally spontaneous voice, Ismael Rivera was a master of the Cuban son.

He earned the title "El Sonero Mayor" from none other than Beny Moré, the legendary Cuban singer. The title not only emphasized Maelo's great talent but showed how Latin music at the time was beginning to mix and blend together all the distinctive musical traditions of America into one sound—salsa. Ismael Rivera embodied a mix of the traditional folk Puerto Rican bomba and plena with the Cuban son vocal singing style. After his successful trip to the USA, though, Cortijo lost his "voice" when Rivera began a five-year prison sentence in 1962 on drug charges. Maelo later sang about his experience on a track titled "Las Tumbas (The Tombs)," named after the Kentucky prison which had several floors below ground.

After serving four years, Rivera was eager to get back to singing with Cortijo, but clubs would not book dates for the Latin musician whose past they could not forgive. Cortijo and Rivera found themselves in a changed Latin music scene that would force them to go separate ways. "El Sonero Mayor" however, would go on to record some of his best work with his own band, the Cachimbos, showcasing his unequalled talent better than ever. In the 1970s, Rivera was looked upon as a legend from another era, and he helped a number of young musicians get their start in the New York salsa scene, including Ismael Miranda and Ruben Blades. —*Roberto Ledesma*

● **Sonero Numero 1** / 1990 / Mpl ♦♦♦♦♦
Of his musical generation—roughly the '60s and '70s—*Puerto Rico's Rivera was the finest non-Cuban singer of all, and perhaps the finest without restriction. His improvising brilliance was enhanced by a deep, heavy voice of a type rare in Latin singing. He and percussionist/bandleader Cortijo were major influences in NYC proto-salsa through their superb recordings of Puerto Rican bombas and plenas. Unfortunately an extended sabbatical at the federal government's expense interrupted his career at a critical moment, but those who know, know just how good he was.* —John Storm Roberts, Original Music

Los Dos Granes de Siempre / Aug. 2, 1993 / AF Productions ♦♦♦♦

Frankie Ruiz

Vocals / Tropical, Salsa, Puerto Rico, Latin Continuum
One of the driving forces behind the salsa romantica movement of the 1980s, Frankie Ruiz was born in Paterson, New Jersey on March 10, 1958; after relocating to Mayaguez, Puerto Rico at age seven, he began singing professionally on the local nightclub circuit while still in his teens, joining the band La Solucion. A few years later Ruiz enlisted with the Tommy Olivencia Orchestra, leaving in 1980 to mount a solo career. "La Rueda," his first big hit, was inspired by the death of his mother; in total, his debut LP *Solista... pero no Solo* launched three salsa chart-toppers. Renowned for his provocative lyrics and pulsing rhythms, Ruiz was also known for his signature sung phrase "Vaya, mi China!" (roughly, "Go, baby!"); his seven studio LPs generated numerous hits, among them "La Cura," "Desnudate Mujer" and "Mi Libertad." Tragically, he was also infamous for the often tawdry details of his personal life, battling drugs and alcohol throughout much of his career until his death from cirrhosis of the liver on August 9, 1998. Ruiz's final recordings were collected posthumously on 1998's *Nacimiento y Recuerdos*. A hits collection, *Leyenda*, followed a year later and *Juntos Por Primera Vez: Salsa de Primera Clase* was issued in fall 2000. —*Jason Ankeny*

● **Mas Grande Que Nunca** / Thl ♦♦♦♦♦
For quite some time now, Ruiz has been battling Eddie Santiago for top of the salsa charts. Both are salsa romantica bloods, with all that implies: love songs set to driving rhythms and arrangements. Santiago as a singer is preferable to Ruiz by a whisker, but Ruiz has a very heavy band in the tough New-York-salsa vein. Otherwise, if you know him you know what you think of him, and like the style or not, it's a large part of what's happening in salsa these days. —*John Storm Roberts, Original Music*

Voy Pa Encima / TH/Rodven ♦♦♦♦♦
This is the now-classic, though still fairly new, salsa romantica sound: basic salsa backing (trumpets and trombones) for love-song lyrics. Ruiz has been a perennial Latin-chart-topper lately. —*John Storm Roberts, Original Music*

La Sonora Poncena

f. 1954
Group / Tropical, Salsa, Puerto Rico, Latin Continuum
One of Puerto Rico's most popular orchestras, which was founded by Quique Lucca in 1954 in Ponce, Puerto Rico. La Ponceea is directed by Lucca's son, the brilliant composer, arranger, and keyboardist, Papo, born in 1950. Papo Lucca's career started in 1964 when he became the band's pianist. At the moment, La Poncena is among the top five salsa and Latin jazz bands in Latin music. —*Max Salazar*

● **On the Right Track** / 1988 / Inca ♦♦♦♦♦
Sonora Ponce§a is one of the best bands around—and not just in Puerto Rico, though that's where it's based. With the possible exception of pianist Papo Lucca, these aren't names—just a very tight, fresh group with the ability to make a tradition-based sound brand new. Listen to the sudden trumpet duet in "Odiame" and rejoice. —*John Storm Roberts*

Into the 90's / Inca ✦✦✦✦✦
Sonora Ponce§a, always a tight, fresh avant-mainstream group, has arguably become one of the great bands. With this recent release they're adding things around the edges—an effective touch of soul, an entirely out-of-idiom piano intro, a gravely beautiful bowed-bass break, and all sorts of other unexpected doings. All of which makes the title a little more substantial than such slogans usually are. *—John Storm Roberts*

United States

Eddie Palmieri

b. Dec. 15, 1936, New York, NY
Piano / Cuban Jazz, Afro-Cuban Jazz, Charanga, Latin Jazz, New York Salsa, Salsa, United States, Latin Continuum
Eddie Palmieri is one of the foremost Latin jazz pianists of the last half of the century, blessed with a technique that fuses such ubiquitous jazz influences as the styles of Herbie Hancock, Thelonious Monk and McCoy Tyner into a Latin context. No purist, he has also shown a welcome willingness to experiment with fusions of Latin and non-Latin music. However, despite a number of stints with major labels and numerous industry awards and nominations, he has yet to break into the American record scene in a big way. He made his professional debut with Johnny Sequi's orchestra in 1955 and eventually joined Tito Rodriguez's popular band in 1958-60. In 1961, Palmieri formed his highly influential band La Perfecta, whose flute and twin- or triple-trombone front line made American jazz musicians like Herbie Mann take notice; he also scored heavily in an excellent 1966 collaboration with Cal Tjader, *El Sonido Nuevo* (Verve). While recording for the Latin Coco label in the mid-1970s, Palmieri started to mix salsa with R&B, pop, rock, Spanish vocals and jazz improvisation. *—Richard S. Ginell*

Echando Pa'lante (Straight Ahead) / 1964 / Tico ✦✦✦✦✦

La Perfecta / 66 / Alegre ✦✦✦✦✦
One of the best albums released by one of Palmieri's best bands, *La Perfecta* features 12 crisp, uptempo songs ranging from guajiras to pachangas to sones montuno—with a cha-cha-cha thrown in for good measure. Palmieri sounds inspired on piano, vocalist Ismael Quintana leads the group well, and the stinging brass section includes major players like Joao Donato on trombone and Willie Matos on trumpet. *La Perfecta* is an excellent example of early Latin dance before Western fusion became the name of the game. *—John Bush*

Mambo con Conga Is Mozambique / 1966 / Tico ✦✦✦✦✦

Sentido / 1973 / Mpl ✦✦✦✦
Sentido may offer a better portrait of Eddie Palmieri than any of the compilations. "Puerto Rico" is typical of his anthemic, crowd-rousing capability. "No Pienses Asi" is an affecting ballad that rivals those of musicians considered more as singers than Palmieri. "Condiciones Que Existen" is just funky enough to sound like an outtake from the great *Harlem River Drive* album. "Adoracion" begins spacily but soon becomes, over the course of nine delicious minutes, a hefty jam. "Cosas del Alma" is another ballad. It may be only a half hour of music, but no one will miss the filler. The liners credit Palmieri's fasting as an ingredient in his success; clearly he understands the importance of "leaving them hungry for more." *—Tony Wilds*

★ **The Sun of Latin Music** / 1973 / Mpl ✦✦✦✦✦
This album almost perfectly combines Palmieri's experimentalism with the devastating swing that kept him ahead on the street. The "Un Dia Bonito" suite got most attention, but "Una Rosa Española," a one-cut mini-history of salsa, is enchanting. *—John Storm Roberts*

Unfinished Masterpiece / 1974 / Mpl ✦✦✦✦✦
The late-'70s *Unfinished Masterpiece* caused a huge quarrel because he couldn't or wouldn't get it done to his own satisfaction (Coco finally put it out anyway, thus the title). Unfinished or no, it's classic Palmieri from his late Golden Age and long unavailable. *—John Storm Roberts*

Palmas / 1994 / Elektra ✦✦✦✦

Arete / 1995 / RMM ✦✦✦✦✦
Pianist/composer Eddie Palmieri has long been a giant of Afro-Cuban (or Latin) jazz. While some recordings in this idiom lean too far in one direction—not enough jazz improvising, or in other cases, a percussion section that sounds as if it were added on as an afterthought—Palmieri has struck a perfect balance. In trumpeter Brian Lynch, trombonist Conrad Herwig and altoist Donald Harrison, he has three strong soloists who match well with the trio of percussionists. In addition to Palmieri, bassist John Benitez and drummer Adam Cruz (the latter is on just four of the eight Palmieri originals) are flexible enough to play both swing and Latin. A strong plus to this date are the compositions/arrangements of Palmieri, which pay close attention to varying moods, instrumental colors and grooves. Consistently complex and unpredictable, the music is still always quite accessible and enjoyable, thanks to the percussionists. *—Scott Yanow*

Live / Jun. 15, 1999 / Rmm ✦✦✦✦✦
Backed by a superb, largish Latin jazz ensemble, Eddie Palmieri went into the *Hostos Center for the Arts and Culture* in the Bronx to record this benefit album for the Bronx Lebanon Hospital Center. The elaborate piano/string synthesizer intros by the erudite pianist/leader are deceptive, for they soon give way to some heated yet paradoxically poised Afro-Cuban vamps, executed with breathtaking clarity and—under the circumstances—recorded quite well. Everything burns, but not blatantly; best of all is the easygoing yet sexy guajira, "Slow Visor." The soloists are all fine jazzmen, with Juancito Torres Vélez and Barry Danielen, alto saxophonist Héctor Veneros, trombonist Juan Pablo Torres, and bassist Hugo Duran getting some choice spots—and Anthony Carillo takes a long, unaccompanied bongo solo on "Camagueyanos y Habaneros." You don't have to know that this album is going for a good cause in order to pick it up. *—Richard S. Ginell*

Ray Barretto

b. Apr. 29, 1929, Brooklyn, NY
Conga, Percussion / Boogaloo, Afro-Cuban Jazz, Latin Jazz, New York Salsa, Salsa, Latin Pop, United States, Latin Continuum
While Ray Barretto's congas have graced more recording sessions than virtually any other conguero of his time, he has also led some refreshingly progressive Latin jazz bands over the decades. His records often have a more tense, more adventurously eclectic edge than those of most conventional salsa groups, unafraid to use electronics and novel instrumental or structural combinations, driven hard by his rock-steady, endlessly flexible percussion work. This no doubt reflects Barretto's wide range of musical interests and also the fact that he came to Latin music from jazz, rather than the usual vice-versa route for Latin-descended musicians. Indeed, he has said that he learned how to play swing-style before he came to master Latin grooves. Puerto Rican by extraction, Barretto took up the congas while stationed in Germany during an Army hitch. He began working with American jazz musicians upon his return to New York, eventually replacing Mongo Santamaria in the Tito Puente band for four years, beginning in the late 1950s. Barretto made his debut as a leader for Riverside in 1962 and scored a crossover hit (No. 17 on the pop charts) the following year on Tico with "El Watusi" (in tandem with a dance craze of the time). He tried to modernize the charanga sound with injections of brass, covering rock and pop tunes of the time as several Latin artists did then. However, Barretto made his main mark in the '60s as a super session player, playing on albums by Gene Ammons, Cannonball Adderley, Kenny Burrell, Lou Donaldson, Red Garland, Dizzy Gillespie, Freddie Hubbard, Wes Montgomery, Cal Tjader and several other jazz and pop albums. In moving over to the Fania label in 1967, Barretto began to achieve recognition as one of the leading Latin jazz artists of the day, eventually becoming music director of the Fania All-Stars. In the '70s, he was incorporating rock and funk influences into his music—with only limited success—while recording for Atlantic, and in 1981, he made a highly-regarded album for CTI La Cuna, with Puente, Joe Farrell and Charlie Palmieri as guest players. He became music director of the "Bravisimo" television program and took part in the multi-idiom, all-star, anti-apartheid *Sun City* recording and video in 1985. In 1992, he unveiled a new Latin jazz sextet New World Spirit, which made some absorbingly unpredictable albums for Concord Picante. *—Richard S. Ginell*

Charanga Moderna / 1962 / Tico ✦✦✦

Viva Watusi! / 1965 / Polydor ✦✦✦

● **Acid** / 1968 / Fania ✦✦✦✦✦
Barretto's Latin/soul crossover record of 1968, *Acid* includes a few tracks of his ebullient, instrumental salsa, but also plays off the boogaloo craze of the past few years with a few Latin soul numbers. The crossovers "A Deeper Shade of Soul," "The Soul Drummers," and "Teacher of Love" (all written by Barretto himself) are a lot of fun, but the (relatively) straight-ahead salsa of "El Nuevo Barretto" and the title track easily edge out the competition. It's nowhere near as psychedelic as the title would indicate, but *Acid* holds up nevertheless as a great document of the late-'60s confluence of Latin, funk, and soul. *—John Bush*

Hard Hands / 1968 / Fania ✦✦✦✦
A 1968 album with Barretto in midst of his most productive period. He had made inroads into pop and jazz markets and was a dominant figure on the Latin jazz and salsa circuit. The album not only provided the great conga player and percussionist with a nickname, it yielded hit single "Abidjan" and also brought personnel changes. Joseph Roman replaced Rene Lopez on trumpet (he'd been drafted), and Tony Fuentes joined the group on bongos. *—Ron Wynn*

La Cuna / Aug. 1979 / CTI ✦✦

Handprints / Mar. 1991 / Concord Picante ✦✦✦✦

Contact! / Apr. 3, 1997-Apr. 9, 1997 / Blue Note ✦✦✦
Internationally renowned bandleader, conguero and percussionist, Ray Baretto and his ensemble, New World Spirit, continue their tradition of jazz excellence on *Contact!* Released in 1997 on Blue Note/EMI, their fifth CD is a conscious break from the dance-oriented Ray Barretto Orchestra many of his fans may remember, in that *Contact!* explores the deeply personal musical relationships throughout the phases of Baretto's career. Songs are masterfully syncretized and utilizing Baretto's unique musical vocabulary, including call-and-response, cubop rhythms and 4/4 swing—the ten-track CD ignites a sensual fire on "Dance of Denial," a melodic, midtempo piece that showcases brilliant solos by Michael Philip Mossman on trumpet, Adam Kolker on saxophone and John Di Martino on piano. The incomparable Baretto adds finality to the piece with a polyrhythmic statement that represents the conguero at his finest. As deep and enjoyable as each piece is, what gives the CD its impact is the vehement delivery by Baretto which portrays the profound impressions left by his musical mentors and his revolutionary development as a result of their influence. He introduces a facet of this influence on "La Bendicion" and "Liberated Spirit," both original compositions by Baretto that focus the listener on the dynamic forces surrounding his imagination. Jazz definitely receives the respect it deserves at the hands of this jazz linguist. Let there be no doubt that Ray Baretto is a master that fully comprehends his craft and is strongly deserving of the critical and popular acclaim he is receiving throughout the world. *—Paula Edelstein*

Rubén Blades

b. Jul. 16, 1948, Panama City, Panama
Vocals, Guitar / Tropical, Latin Jazz, Latin Soul, New York Salsa, Salsa, Latin Pop, United States, Latin Continuum
Ruben Blades is one of the most successful vocalists in the history of Panamanian music. A former member of bands led by Ray Baretto and Willie Colon, Blades has continued to influence salsa music with his highly-literate, politically-tinged lyrics and his modern-minded arrangements which substitute the usual horn and Latin percussion sections with synthesizers and drum sets. Often referred to as "the Latin Bruce Springsteen," Blades has provided a musical voice for the middle class of Central America.

Raised in Panama City, Blades began singing pop and rock songs in his early teens. After the university he was studying law at was temporarily closed by the Panamanian government, Blades made his first trip to America and *From Panama to Nueva York* with Pete Rodriguez. He later completed his studies, but returned to the United States and began working in the mailroom at Fania Records. A year later, he became the featured vocalist in Ray Barretto's band and later took over as bandleader for the group (renamed Guarare). In 1975, Blades composed and sang lead on Willie Colon's *The Good, The Bad, The Ugly* and worked with the Fania All Stars. Their collaboration reached its apex with the massive album *Siembra.* He formed his own band, Los Seis del Solar, in 1982 and began performing an exciting fusion of Latin, rock, reggae and Caribbean music. Their debut album, *Buscando America,* was released in 1983.

Since the early '80s, Blades has balanced his musical career with acting and writing songs for films such as *The Last Fight, The Milagro Beanfield War, Color of Night,* and Paul Simon's Broadway musical, *The Capeman.* Blades also remained active with politics, placing as the runner-up for the president of Panama in 1994. *—Craig Harris*

Bohemio y Poeta / 1979 / Fania ♦♦♦
This release was a transition between Blades's post-Willie Colon sound and the '80s Seis del Solar. The salsa sounds predominate much of the time, and there's a Cuban classic in among his own compositions. But keyboards and vibes (presumably from Louie Ramirez, who did some of the arranging) point to a new dispensation in the offing, with their (here, at least, very successful) fusion edge. *—John Storm Roberts*

Buscando América / 1984 / Elektra ♦♦♦♦♦
A masterful concept album (the title means "searching for America"), it spins hard-hitting tales of Latino strife and American injustice. This album includes some of his most gorgeous ballads. *—John Floyd*

Escenas / 1985 / Elektra ♦♦♦

Antecedente / 1988 / Elektra ♦♦♦

★ **Ruben Blades y Son del Solar . . . Live!** / Mar. 20, 1990 / Elektra ♦♦♦♦♦
A smoldering set, it was recorded live with his 11-piece band, Son del Solar, who romp and stomp for over an hour. Perfect for parties. *—John Floyd*

Tiempos / Jul. 13, 1999 / Sony International ♦♦♦♦♦
Afro-Cuban purists would have loved it if Rubén Blades had stuck with the type of straight-ahead salsa that put him on the map. But in the 1980s, Blades felt the need to branch out and start experimenting with other Latin styles—a move that disappointed salsa purists while earning him a reputation as one of Latin music's major risk-takers. Even though Blades was still considered a salsa vocalist in the late '90s, 1999's *Tiempos* is far from a pure salsa album. Rather, it's an adventurous, probing Latin pop effort that incorporates salsa along with Brazilian, Spanish, and Central American elements. On *Tiempos,* Blades is joined by the Costa Rican band Editus, whose members fit in perfectly and help the Panamanian singer provide an unpredictable, eclectic album. And *Tiempos* is as compelling lyrically as it is musically. Often sociopolitical, Blades' lyrics reflect on such topics as poverty in Latin America and corruption on the part of some governments in that part of the world. Though much of *Tiempos* is melancholy, it isn't without optimism or hope for the future—Blades sees a lot of suffering and hardship in Latin America, but he also has hopes for a brighter tomorrow. Of course, those who don't speak Spanish won't understand Blades' lyrics; they'll have to settle for savoring the album's musical richness. *—Alex Henderson*

Willie Bobo (William Correa)

b. Feb. 28, 1934, New York, NY [Spanish Harlem], **d.** Sep. 15, 1983, Los Angeles, CA
Timbales, Percussion / Boogaloo, Latin Folk, Latin Jazz, Salsa, United States, Latin Continuum
Willie Bobo was one of the great Latin percussionists of his time, a relentless swinger on the congas and timbales, a flamboyant showman onstage, and an engaging if modestly endowed singer. He also made serious inroads into the pop, R&B and straight jazz worlds. Bobo began on the bongos at age 14, only to find himself performing with Perez Prado a year later, studying with Mongo Santamaria while serving as his translator, and joining Tito Puente for a four-year stint at age 19. He stepped forward in 1963 with his first recording as a leader; recording for Verve in the mid-'60s, Bobo achieved his highest solo visibility with albums that enlivened pop hits of the day with Latin rhythms, spelled by sauntering originals like "Spanish Grease" and "Fried Neck Bones and Some Home Fries." In addition, Bobo played on innumerable sessions in New York, recording with artists like Miles Davis, Cannonball Adderley, Herbie Hancock, Wes Montgomery, Chico Hamilton and Sonny Stitt. In 1969, he moved to Los Angeles where he led jazz and Latin jazz combos, appeared on Bill Cosby's first comedy series (1969-1971) and short-lived 1976 variety show, and recorded on his own for Sussex, Blue Note and Columbia. *—Richard S. Ginell*

Spanish Grease / Aug. 20, 1965-Sep. 8, 1965 / Verve ♦♦♦♦

● **Uno, Dos, Tres/Spanish Grease** / Oct. 8, 1965-Apr. 26, 1966 / Verve ♦♦♦♦♦
Willie Bobo's 1965 LP *Spanish Grease* has been combined with the 1966 LP *Uno Dos Tres 1-2-3* on one CD reissue. One pass through the title cut of *Spanish Grease,* and you know that Carlos Santana was listening. The easy R&B/Latin-jazz shuffle on this Bobo original, with its mix of Spanish and English vocals, is an obvious touchstone of cuts like "Evil Ways" on Santana's first two albums. What a shame, then, that the rest of the record is primarily comprised of covers of pop hits of the day like "It's Not Unusual" (a vocal AND an instrumental version!) and "Our Day Will Come." The timbales player and his band lay down respectable grooves, but "Spanish Grease" is the only original on the album, and by far the most rewarding number. As with his previous album *Spanish Grease,* the toughest and most memorable track is the one Bobo original, *"Fried Neck Bones and Some Home Fries."* Its creeping Latin soul groove was, like "Spanish Grease," an obvious inspiration for Carlos Santana. But on most of the rest of the recording, Bobo coasts through interpretations of period hits like "Michelle," "Goin' Out of My Head," and Jay & The Americans' (!) "Come a Little Bit Closer," with some jazz and pop standards as well. *—Richie Unterberger*

Talkin' Verve / 1965-1968 / Verve ♦♦♦♦
Whatever the meaning of the word "talkin," this is still a most valuable release because it succinctly sums up Willie Bobo's Verve recordings, most of which have yet to see the light of the laser. By this time, Bobo had followed Mongo Santamaria into the marketplace as an energetic exponent of the Latin boogaloo, even scoring a minor hit with "Spanish Grease." But Bobo went even further than Mongo toward an accommodation with the '60s scene, adding the R&B-oriented electric rhythm guitar of Sonny Henry, dropping the piano, incorporating strings and even an occasional graceful vocal now and then. While there are a few covers of '60s standards here, like "The Look of Love" and "Grazing in the Grass"—and he had the great sense to seek out and record a hip-shaking version of Eddie Harris' "Sham Time"—Bobo's biggest contribution on these tracks was in providing the inspiration for the Latin rock boom to come. "Evil Ways" is almost an exact blueprint for Carlos Santana's career-launching hit version; "Spanish Grease" reappeared uncredited six years later as Santana's "No One to Depend On," and Santana also played Bobo's lowdown "Fried Neck Bones and Some Homefries" in the band's early days. With Bobo's galvanic congas and timbales swinging at all times, few CDs by a single artist capture the ambience of late-'60s jazz radio in the evening as well as this one. *—Richard S. Ginell*

Juicy / Jan. 12, 1967-Feb. 2, 1967 / Verve ♦♦♦

Willie Colón (William Anthony Colón)

b. Apr. 28, 1950, New York, NY [The Bronx]
Vocals, Trombone / Boogaloo, Tropical, Latin Jazz, Latin Soul, New York Salsa, Salsa, United States, Latin Continuum
Trombone player, composer and bandleader, Willie Colon was one of the pioneers of Latin-American music. Despite initial criticism, Colon's album *El Malo* has become known as one of the first albums to feature the "New York Sound" that sparked a renewed interest in Latin music during the 1970s. Inspired by the music of various cultures, Colon has recorded with such musicians as Panamanian cuatro player Yomo Toro and David Byrne. In addition to eleven Grammy nominations and one Grammy award, Colon has received a CHUBB fellowship from Yale University, the most prestigious award given by the Ivy League school.

Colon switched from trumpet to trombone at the age of 14, and made his recording debut in 1967. One year later, he signed to the Fania label and recorded *El Malo,* his first LP with vocalist Hector Lavoe. Lavoe remained a vital member of Colon's band until the mid-'70s when an increased drug addiction caused him to miss or show up late for several gigs. Although Colon and Ruben Blades met backstage before a concert in Panama in 1969, the pair didn't begin collaborating until five years later, on the album classic *The Good—The Bad—The Ugly.*

The session was so satisfying that Blades became a full-time member of Colon's band following the departure of Lavoe, and their 1978 album *Siembra* became the top-selling album in Fania's catalog. Although Colon recorded two solo albums—*Baguine de Angelitos Negros* in 1977 and *Solo* in 1979—and Blades recorded a solo album in 1980, their solo work failed to match the commercial success of their joint efforts. The two quarreled foten, though they also collaborated on the Grammy-winning album, *Canciones del Solar de Los Aburridos.* Following a reunion concert at the *Hollywood Bowl* in 1997, Colon and Blades performed a series of concerts together. In the late '80s, Colon formed a new band, Legal Aliens, with younger musicians. Signing with Sony, Colon and the band recorded *American Color* in 1990 and *Honra Y Cultura* in 1991. Since leaving Sony, over a lack of promotional support, Colon has continued to remain active. *—Craig Harris*

El Malo / 1968 / Fania ♦♦♦

Guisando / 1969 / Fania ♦♦♦
His third album has, for trivia buffs, his second-favorite cover. Colon was 20 at the time, and this is still the funky, riotous, sometimes mildly ragged and chaotic sound of his early days. The hallmarks are exuberance, humor, innovation, lots of Colon compositions and, as a bonus, the fine piano of the band's African-American pianist, Mark Diamond. *—John Storm Roberts*

Asalto Navideno / 1972 / Fania ♦♦♦
A groundbreaking early-'70s recording, *Asalto Navideño* was a Christmas album, and Christmas is the time when the old jibaro mountain sound comes briefly into its own. Colon hired cuatro player Yomo Toro and gave him a leading role, launching him on a new career. A major album, it includes one of Colon's finest Panamanian-flavored early hits, "La Murga." *—John Storm Roberts*

★ **The Good-The Bad-The Ugly** / 1975 / Fania ♦♦♦♦♦
This classic recording is by one of the most creative heads in New York salsa. In 1975 *The Good . . . ,* a New Directions release after Colon got fed up with the two-trombone sound, was the evidence that he could reach beyond his youthful sound into an idiom both wider and deeper. It was also the last album with Hector Lavoe, who had decided to stay a teen idol. *The Big Break, Asalto Navideño,* and this album in their different ways were pinnacles of early- to mid-'70s salsa. *—John Storm Roberts*

Metiendo Mano / Oct. 1977 / Fania ♦♦♦♦♦
Salsa history in the making: the album in which Willie Colon introduced Ruben Blades to the wider world. An obvious classic, given Blades's subsequent history, but it's also a gorgeous album with Yomo Toro on two tracks (one playing guitar), the great pianist Sonny Bravo on two cuts, and ace percussion with Milton Cardona and Nicky Marrero. *—John Storm Roberts*

Tiempo Para Matar / 1984 / Fania ♦♦♦

Criollo / Aug. 1984 / RCA ♦♦♦

Color Americano / 1990 / Discos CBS International ♦♦♦

Honra y Cultura / 1991 / Discos CBS International ✦✦✦
Though the adulation given Colon's early recordings is fully justified, it has the unfortunate side-effect of blinding people to his equally fine recent recordings. Yet aside from the fact that he'd turned himself into an excellent and very individual singer, the recordings he made just before his political ambitions took over are by any measure outstanding. The 1991 *Honra y Cultura* reverted to Colon's historic passion for Puerto Rican music, featuring cuatro player Yomo Toro in two compositions by the great jíbaro singer Ramito. But as always, the references—not just jíbaro, but touches of both rap and toasting, jazz, on and on—were unified by an overall vision combining passion and humor. *—John Storm Roberts, Original Music*

Joe Cuba (Gilberto Calderon)

b. Apr. 22, 1931, New York, NY
Conga / Boogaloo, Tropical, Latin Jazz, New York Salsa, Salsa, Latin Pop, United States, Latin Continuum
Joe Cuba's music career started with La Alfarona X in 1950. In 1955 the Joe Cuba Sextet came into being and his vibraharp sound caught on. In 1962, when the group recorded "To Be with You" for Seeco Records, the band began to soar to popularity because of Nick Jimenez's arrangements and the vocals of Cheo Feliciano and Jimmy Sabater. When the boogaloo era arrived, the majority of the popular New York bands were put out of work. The Cuba sound changed with its recordings of "El Pito" and "Bang Bang"; it not only sold millions but enabled The Cuba sextet to enjoy the *1 spot in the Latin music world along with the Eddie Palmieri Orchestra.* —Max Salazar

Steppin' Out / Jul. 1963 / Seeco Tropical ✦✦✦

• **We Must Be Doing Something Right** / 1965 / Tico ✦✦✦✦✦
The '50s and '60s cusp saw a last flowering of the bilingual, Cubop-inflected, often vibraphone-led quintet sound. Puente was one of its heavies, but in New York at least, the tradition was maintained into the pachanga and even boogalu era of the '60s by Joe Cuba. Jaunty mambo, soupy English-lyric boleros, Latin-jazz or neo-t°pico; this was an archetypal Latin New York sound. *—John Storm Roberts*

Wanted Dead or Alive (Bang! Bang! Push Push Push) / 1966 / Tico ✦✦✦

Fania All-Stars

Group / Tropical, Latin Jazz, New York Salsa, Salsa, Latin Pop, United States, Latin Continuum
The flagship act for Fania Records, the Fania All-Stars popularized New York salsa during the 1970s by organizing concerts at larger and larger venues (from the *Red Garter* in Greenwich Village all the way to Yankee Stadium in the Bronx) that spotlighted not only the label's, but the salsa world's biggest stars—Ray Barretto, Willie Colon, Johnny Pacheco, Ruben Blades, Hector Lavoe, and dozens of others. LPs by the collective were usually recorded live, and featured long jams with plenty of space for solos for each of the salsa heroes onstage at the time.

The Fania label, formed by Johnny Pacheco and lawyer Jerry Masucci, began promoting jam-session concerts in the late '60s, and the Fania All-Stars' first two LPs, *Live at the Red Garter, Vols. 1-2,* were recorded in similar fashion. Another pair of live LPs *(Live at the Cheetah)* followed in 1971, and the group played sell-out shows from Puerto Rico and Panama to Chicago. The salsa wave crested with the group's 1973 performance at New York's Yankee Stadium in front of 44,000 fans, and another appearance at Yankee Stadium in 1975 was recorded and released as a pair of albums.

That same year, the Fania All-Stars made their studio debut with *A Tribute to Tito Rodriguez.* During the late '70s, the group recorded four LPs for Columbia, sacrificing the loose improvisational feel of their early work for a slick, studio-bound effect that placed emphasis on producers and engineers. Though albums like 1977's *Rhythm Machine* did well with audiences not used to buying salsa, they ultimately failed to connect. Fania Records' fortunes began to decline by the beginning of the '80s, though the Fania All-Stars recorded a total of eight studio albums during the 1980s and gradually moved to a more organic Latin jazz. *—John Bush*

Live at the Cheetah, Vol. 1 / 1971 / Fania ✦✦✦✦
Recorded live at New York's premier discotheque with the usual, stellar All-Stars lineup, the groove is incessant, the mood exultant, and the players palpably happy with the audience and themselves as they exchange licks. The tunes are a bit long—"Quitate Tu," the closer, is a 16-minute jam session in which the band members one by one contribute lyrics, to the delight of the audience. Ray Barretto's "Descarga Fania" features a lovely piano break and some inspiredly raucous horn playing (a nice contrast to the tightly arranged horn charts one usually hears), and Cheo Feliciano's lead vocal on "Anacaona" soars. 24 years later, still the first salsa recording to reach for; ultimate party music played by the masters. *—Janet Rosen*

• **Live at Yankee Stadium, Vol. 1** / 1976 / Fania ✦✦✦✦✦
In the '70s, Fania Records was often called "the Motown of salsa," and in fact, Fania was every bit as important to salsa as Motown was to soul. Fania's '70s roster boasted some of the decade's biggest names in Afro-Cuban music; so when Fania assembled a band called the Fania All-Stars, you knew that some major-league salseros would be on board. The list of musicians and singers on this live LP, which came out in 1975 and was recorded at *Yankee Stadium* in New York and *Roberto Clemente Coliseum* in San Juan, Puerto Rico, reads like a who's who of '70s salsa—Ray Barretto, Larry Harlow, Willie Colon, Johnny Pacheco, and Bobby Valentin are among the musicians, and the featured vocalists include Santos Colon on "Soy Guajiro," Ismael Miranda on "Que Rica Suena Mi Tambor," and Pete "El Conde" Rodriguez on "Pueblo Latino." Meanwhile, Hector Lavoe has some joyful moments on his mega-hit "Mi Gente," and Celia Cruz is in fine form on "Diosa del Ritmo." *Live at Yankee Stadium, Vol. 1* documents some historic moments in Afro-Cuban music and is highly recommended to salseros. *—Alex Henderson*

Rhythm Machine / 1977 / Columbia ✦✦✦✦
As part of Bob James' Tappan Zee Records agenda, house producer Jay Chattaway was handed the Fania All-Stars, no doubt with instructions to make a hit record with them as he did with Maynard ("Rocky") Ferguson that year. So he did—with a little help from James on electric piano, other New York studio experts like Eric Gale, Randy Brecker, John Tropea, Joe Farrell, and Jon Faddis, and, as an integral part of the All-Stars, Mongo Santamaria. The results are not at all bad, nor irredeemably diluted. Sometimes the crisp outboard brass section, voices and strings intrude on the action, and the disc was made in layers, as opposed to herding the band into the studio for a day and letting them wail. But in most instances, the Latin rhythm section of Mongo, Nicky Marrero and Roberto Poena is permitted to dictate the direction and feel of the sessions—and that gives this CD the vitality that Mongo's own album with Chattaway two years later (*Red Hot*) lacked. *—Richard S. Ginell*

Cheo Feliciano (Jose Luis Feliciano)

b. Jul. 3, 1935, Ponce, Puerto Rico
Vocals / Tropical, Charanga, Salsa, United States, Latin Continuum
Romantic salsa vocalist José Cheo Feliciano began pursuing a career in music at an early age, dropping out of high school at 17 to study the best salsa orchestras in New York. His devoted interest in the city's Latin music scene led to a stint as a valet for one of New York's best-known salsa singers, Tito Rodríguez. This connection provided the opportunity to audition as a singer for bandleader Joe Cuba, and Feliciano soon became the vocalist for Cuba's sextet. Feliciano recorded 17 albums with them during the '50s and '60s on the Seeco and Tico labels. By 1965 Feliciano was a soloist with many of New York's finest salsa groups and Latin music artists, including Eddie Palmieri.

After a short retirement, Feliciano returned in 1972 as a part of Fania Records' All-Stars ensemble, and also recorded as a solo artist for the label for a decade. Feliciano's career experienced another rebirth in 1990, when he was signed to RMM Records. As with his previous projects, his records for the label spotlight his sensual, passionate vocal style. *—Heather Phares*

Cantando / 1991 / Sony Discos ✦✦
For Cheo Feliciano's first outing under his own name, he presumably had the pleasure and responsibility of selecting the material and the musicians. Given that he has generally worked with top-notch musicians anyway, and that he has chosen to stay with salsa rather than take the opportunity to experiment with other forms, this breaks no new ground. It is a solidly mainstream, well-presented salsa session. *—Janet Rosen*

La Mafia

f. 1986
Group / Bolero, Tejano, Latin Pop, United States, Latin Continuum
La Mafia is among the most versatile Latino bands. Hailing from Houston, they are largely responsible for the resurgence of the "norteño sound," which has some basis in country and western music. The group was founded by Oscar and Leonard Gonzalez, both of whom were raised in the north end of Houston. The other group members are drummer Michael Aguilar, bass player Rudy Martinez, and keyboard players Armando Lichtenberger, Jr. (he also plays accordion) and David de la Garza. La Mafia released their eponymous debut album in 1986 for Sony. Extensive touring of the U.S. and Mexico brought them renown. Their second album, *Estas Tocando Fuego,* came out in 1991 and sold nearly 1 million copies. Their 1993 album *Ahora y Siempre* went triple platinum. La Mafia has also won numerous awards including an award for Top Regional Mexican Album and Song of 1992; other releases included 1993's *International,* 1995's *Exitos en Vivo* and 1996's *Un Millon de Rosas.* *—Sandra Brennan*

Un Millon de Rosas / 1996 / Sony Discos ✦✦✦✦✦
With *Un Millon de Rosas,* lead vocalist Oscar Gonzalez changed his name to Oscar De La Rosa and made it part of the group's name—hence, the band was now officially called Oscar De La Rosa & La Mafia. Underneath those surface changes, the music of La Mafia remains the same. Based in conjunto and cumbia, the group's music is a slick, pop-oriented fusion that relies as much on producer Mando Lichtenberger Jr.'s studio savvy as it does on De La Rosa's soulful vocals. Whether the band is tackling mariachi or tear-jerking ballads ("Mejores Que Ella," recorded with Marc Anthony), La Mafia pulls it off with grace, style, and professionalism, making *Un Millon De Rosas* an essential purchase for Latin fans. *—Stephen Thomas Erlewine*

• **14 Super Exitos** / Nov. 18, 1997 / EMI International ✦✦✦✦✦
14 Super Exitos contains La Mafia's most popular romantic ballads, including "Alas de Papel," "Si Tu Supieras," "Un Million de Besos," "You Quiero Ser," "Con Tanto Amor," "Tu, Tu y Solo Tu," "Loca Pasion," "Devolucion" and "Amor Chiquito." *—Stephen Thomas Erlewine*

Hector Lavoe (Hector Juan Perez)

b. Sep. 30, 1946, Ponce, Puerto Rico
Vocals / Tropical, Salsa, United States, Latin Continuum
Hector Lavoe was born to sing—as Latin Music evolved from the "boogaloo" of the late sixties to the "salsa" boom of the seventies Hector Lavoe was at its forefront and "El Cantante(The Singer)" of some of its most representative songs. Born Hector Juan Perez in Ponce, Puerto Rico on 9/30/46, Hector was influenced by the Latin singers he heard on the radio—Daniel Santos and Chuito el de Bayamon just to name a couple. As he grew more involved in music he drew his inspiration from Puerto Rico's great sonero Ismael Rivera, as well as Cheo Feliciano. These influences are obvious in Lavoe's singing style: he attacks the son and montuno like the masters Ismael Rivera and Beny More but Lavoe's natural talent for improvosation made him unique and very popular with salsa fans.

At the age of 17 Hector decided to quit music school in Ponce and set his sights on a singing career in New York City. By 1966 he found himself fronting Willie Colon's orquestra. Hector and Willie formed a partnership that would go on to include 14 albums—nearly all of which are gems in the world of Latin music. In 1973 Willie left Hector in charge of his orquestra, pushing Hector into his solo career. Without Willie, Hectors solo efforts only reconfirm his singing ability and his inevitable rise to stardom. The pressures of being a huge salsa star were apparently too great for Hector. He had a difficult time handling his success and suffered a number of personal setbacks along the way. But Hectors fans never forgot about him and he always came back singing. In 1987 his final album *"Strikes Back"* was nominated for a Grammy.

With all the excess, fame, fortune and tragedy from such humble beginnings—Hector Lavoe's life has gone on to symbolize the salsa era of the seventies. With Willie Colon, Hector helped shape the salsa sound of the seventies. As a solo artists he defined the salsa sound of the seventies. And as one of the lead singers of the Fania All Stars—Hector Lavoe was the star among stars… "El Cantante de los Cantantes." *—Roberto Ledesma*

Strikes Back / Fania ✦✦✦✦✦
LaVoe and Willie Colon came blazing out of the bugalu era and wrote a new script for New York salsa during the late '60s and early '70s: a script that included Puerto Rican and Panamanian graftings on the basic Cuban scion, and a tough lyricism that spoke of "barrio" problems to a "barrio audience." Then the pair split, and eventually Ruben Blades filled LaVoe's place in the Colon band's developing persona. Now—for this album at least—LaVoe and Colon are back together with that fat, macho trombone sound and the old width of reference (including a splendid plena, "En el Fiando.") *—John Storm Roberts, Original Music*

Manny Oquendo

b. Jan. 1, 1931, New York, NY
Timbales, Bongos, Percussion / Tropical, Afro-Cuban Jazz, Latin Jazz, Salsa, United States, Latin Continuum
Manny Oquendo began percussion studes in 1945 and gained drumming experience with the bands of Carlos Valero, Luis del Campo, Juan "El Boy" Torres, Jose Budet, Juanito Sanabria, Marcelino Guerra, Jose Curbelo and Pupi Campo before becoming Tito Puente's bongo player in 1950. Four years later Oquendo was with Tito Rodriquez and with Vicentico Valdes in 1955. For the following six years, Oquendo freelanced and recorded for New York's top bands. In 1962 he settled with the Eddie Palmieri orchestra. Before 1974 ended, Oquendo's Conjunto Libre came into being. Oquendo gained world-wide recognition in 1983 with his recording of "Little Sunflower," considered one of the best recordings of the year. *—Max Salazar*

• **Mejor Que Nunca (Better Than Ever)** / 1994 / Milestone ✦✦✦✦✦
Conjunto Libre was a lineal descendant of Grupo Folklorico, the hip salsa group of the 1970s; but conceptually brilliant though it was, its early albums were a tad careful. No longer. Their first album for Milestone combines mainstream mellow and drive with all sorts of elegances, from a nifty version of the plena "Las Ingratitudes" to a witty, jazz-flavored danzón. *—John Storm Roberts, Original Music*

On the Move! (°Muevete!) / May 24, 1996 / Milestone ✦✦

Ahora / Apr. 13, 1999 / Milestone ✦✦✦✦
Although *Ahora* was recorded in 1993, Milestone/Fantasy didn't release this excellent CD until 1999. While Manny Oquendo & Libre's other '90s releases, *Mejor que Nunca* and *On the Move*, contain both salsa and Latin jazz, *Ahora* offers no instrumentals and no outright Latin jazz. However, it does unite Libre with some guest jazz musicians (including trombonist Steve Turre and vibist Joe Locke) and isn't without jazz elements. For this album, Oquendo wrote three songs: "Concierto de Oquendo" (an exuberant, 11-minute descarga or Latin jam), the exuberant "El Son" and the anti-drug commentary, "Drogas Fatal." Equally strong are the songs that Oquendo didn't write, which include "Asia Minor" (a tribute to the great Machito/Mario Bauza team) and Pedro Flores' gorgeous bolero, "Sabor a Mi." A bilingual gem, "Sabor a Mi" finds Libre pianist, Willie Rodriguez, handling the English lyrics while Libre's main singer, Herman Olivera provides the Spanish part. Those who have enjoyed other Oquendo projects will also find *Ahora* to be quite rewarding. *—Alex Henderson*

Johnny Pacheco

b. Mar. 25, 1935, Santiago de los Caballeros, Dominican Republic
Saxophone, Percussion, Flute / Tropical, Charanga, New York Salsa, Salsa, United States, Latin Continuum
Relocated to New York during the late '40s, Johnny Pacheco learned to play sax, percussion and flute in high school. In September 1959, he left Charlie Palmieri's flute and strings orchestra to organize his own. With his first recording, *Pacheco y su Charanga*, released by Alegre Records in 1961, Pacheco changed the sound of music throughout Latin America and ushered in the "Pachanga" (a strenous dance) era which faded out in 1964. Pacheco and attorney Gerald Masucci founde the Fania label in 1964 and with its first album, LP 325 (Pacheco's birthdate) kicked off the yet unborn salsa era in New York City. *—Max Salazar*

Que Suene la Flauta / 1962 / Alegre ✦✦✦✦✦
Pacheco's first avatar was as a flutist, first with Charlie Palmieri's groundbreaking 1959 charanga, then—until he switched to conjunto in 1964—with his own flute-and-fiddles group. Though the band followed Cuban models (far too closely, some Cuban musicians grumbled), his own style was very distinctive, tougher and less flowing than his Cuban rivals, and his wildly successful band benefited also from a very fine singer in Elliot Romero. "Alto Songo," from this album, was one of his personal classics. *—John Storm Roberts, Original Music*

• **Lo Mejor de Pacheco** / 1974 / Alegre ✦✦✦✦✦

Los Compadres / 1970 / Fania ✦✦✦

Charlie Palmieri

b. 1927, New York, NY, **d.** 1988, New York, NY
Piano / Latin Jazz, Salsa, Latin Pop, United States, Latin Continuum
The older brother of Eddie Palmieri, Charlie Palmieri was every bit as gifted a pianist as his sibling, very percussive and responsive to rhythm while also flashing florid passages that were clearly the product of a classical education. His piano studies began at seven, and he attended the Juilliard School of Music, turning pro at 16. He started the group "El Conjunto Pin Pin" in 1948, and then played in a series of ensembles—including those of Tito Puente, Tito Rodriguez and Pupi Campo—before forming his own Charanga Dubonney group in 1958. As music director of the Alegre All Stars while recording for the Alegre label in the 1960s, Palmieri stimulated competition among Latin labels like Tico and Fania, which formed their own all-star bands in response. Like many Latin jazz artists of the time, Palmieri flirted with the popular Latin boogaloo style in the 1960s and made some records for major labels like RCA Victor and Atlantic. He endured a mental near-breakdown in 1969, but rebounded to work again for Puente on his *El Mambo De Tito Puente* television program, and he also found a second career as a historian and teacher of Latin music and history at various New York colleges in the 1970s. Palmieri moved briefly to Puerto Rico from 1980 to 1983, and after suffering a severe heart attack and stroke upon his return to New York, he recovered to lead various Latin combos, including Combo Gigante. One of his last recordings was a galvanizing cameo appearance on Mongo Santamaria's "Mayeya" in 1987 (now on Mongo's *Afro Blue: The Picante Collection* [Concord Picante]), and he appeared in England for the first time in 1988 shortly before his death. Almost all of Palmieri's work is hard to find through domestic channels, but Messidor's *A Giant Step* is available on CD. *—Richard S. Ginell*

Let's Dance the Charanga! / 1960 / United Artists ✦✦✦

Latin Bugalu / 1968 / Atlantic ✦✦✦✦
Latin Bugalu suffers from the usual affliction of New York Latin albums. By the time the recording is made, times have changed and the artist has moved on to something new. The boogaloos here are better than average, and even first-rate in the case of Frank Ross' "Bugalu." But the star tracks, at least at a distance safe from the boogaloo fad, are the several Latin jazz instrumentals. The best of these all-out jams are mambos played at a frenetic pace. It is a top album, even by Palmieri and Ramirez standards, but one wishes there had been separate issues for both the boogaloos and the jams. "A Night to Remember," a vocal ballad, really does not fit. But these are eight impressive tracks, and Charlie Palmieri is about as loose as he gets. *—Tony Wilds*

Vuelve el Gigante / 1973 / Alegre ✦✦✦✦

• **Impulsos** / 1975 / Mpl ✦✦✦✦✦
The late Charlie P. was a greater pianist than his brother, as deeply musical, as universally loved, and with far more sense. He picked musicians by talent not fame, and they blew their hearts out for him. This mid-'70s session has the swing, as hot as EPs but more benign; the jazz solos and tipico ensembles. *—John Storm Roberts*

A Giant Step / 1984 / Tropical Budda ✦✦✦✦✦
The late Charlie Palmieri always wanted to do a piano-plus-rhythm album, and in 1984 he got, and royally profited from, the chance. Tracks range from the classic danza "Bajo las Sombras de un Pino" through Puente's "Tito a la King" through Irving Berlin's "Be Careful, It's My Heart." The sidemen are two generations of heavy, and Palmieri's own playing runs from magnificent to superb. *—John Storm Roberts, Original Music*

Pucho & His Latin Soul Brothers

f. 1959, **db.** 1973
Drums, Percussion / Boogaloo, Hard Bop, Latin Jazz, Latin Soul, Soul-Jazz, Salsa, United States, Latin Continuum
In the 1960s, no one combined more or less equal elements of jazz, Latin music, soul, and funk as well as Henry "Pucho" Brown (b. Nov. 1, 1938). A somewhat forgotten figure until quite recently, Pucho never achieved the wide recognition of some other Latin-jazz performers exploring similar territory, such as Mongo Santamaria, Willie Bobo, and Cal Tjader. The timbales player and bandleader also may have been too eclectic, and too open to outside influences, to achieve much recognition within the jazz community.

What's a weakness in one circle's view, however, is a strength for other listeners. As a result, Pucho has a wider appeal than many straight jazz performers. Fans of R&B, rock, and Latin music can immediately connect with him, especially as he's always made sure to play music that's hot and danceable. His accessibility, however, has by no means compromised the quality of his material or his Latin Soul Brothers bands, which have featured fine and versatile players.

Contrary to the assumptions of many listeners, Pucho himself is not Latino, but African-American. As a Harlem teenager, he cultivated loves for jazz, rhythm & blues, and mambo. In the late '50s, he served for several years in the band of pianist Joe Panama. When the group broke up in 1959, Pucho formed a band of his own, recruiting several alumni from Panama's outfit. Even before he'd cemented his reputation on record, Pucho's band attracted notice from top Latin jazzmen. Willie Bobo took several musicians from Pucho's band for his own group, as did Mongo Santamaria. One of the musicians that Santamaria lured away, in fact, was a young Chick Corea.

Pucho began recording in 1963, and really hit his stride between 1966 and 1970, when he cut over half a dozen albums for Prestige. On these he helped pioneer a style termed Latin boogaloo, which mixed jazz, New York-style Latin music, R&B/soul, and the sort of funk that was just emerging from James Brown and other performers. Pucho wasn't afraid to mix up his material on his LPs, which placed originals by Brown and the Latin Soul Brothers next to covers of tunes by Herbie Hancock, the Temptations, the Beatles, Duke Ellington, and John Barry.

This ensured a certain erratic flavor, but the groove was almost always on the money. The Latin Soul Brothers were at their best when they went for the hottest and funkiest grooves, as on their fine version of "Canteloupe Island," or eccentrically titled originals like "Soul Yamie" and "Vietnam Mambo." Once in a while, he even used engagingly raw soul vocals, as on the infectiously good-natured "Shuckin' and Jivin'," which could have been an R&B hit. The Latin Soul Brothers certainly couldn't have been accused of predictability, incorporating straight modern jazz chops, psychedelic flourishes, and soul-jazz organ grooves into their repertoire when the mood suited them. The constant factor was the active Latin percussion section, featuring conga, bongos, and Pucho's own timbales.

When his brand of Latin-soul-jazz fusion started to fall from commercial grace in the early '70s, Pucho disbanded the Latin Soul Brothers. For the next 20 years, he made his livelihood by performing conventional Latin music in the Catskill Mountain resorts of New York State. In the early '90s, however, Pucho's back catalog began to generate interest in Britain, where he was a hit with the acid-jazz crowd, and where several albums were reissued by the Ace label. Happily, he made a return to Latin-soul-jazz-funk with his 1995 comeback effort, *Rip a Dip,* which found his skills intact. *How'm I Doing* followed in mid-2000. *—Richie Unterberger*

Tough! / Feb. 15, 1966-Nov. 10, 1966 / Prestige ✦✦

Saffron Soul / Nov. 8, 1966+Nov. 10, 1966 / Prestige ✦✦✦
As he did on his other '66 session (*Tough!*), Pucho mixed pop and soul hits with the stronger stuff. That means the best and funkiest pieces—"Aye Ma Ma," "Soul Yamie," and a typically irreverent cover of "Caravan"—are mixed with the likes of "Reach Out I'll Be There" and "Alfie." The entire album has been added to the CD reissue of *Tough!,* so you should look for that disc instead of an original copy of the LP. *—Richie Unterberger*

Legends of Acid Jazz: The Best of Pucho & His Latin Soul Brothers / Aug. 9, 1967-Jan. 12, 1970 / Prestige ✦✦✦✦✦
This is an entirely different set than the British import compilation on Ace called *The Best of Pucho & the Latin Soul Brothers;* only six tracks are found on both CDs. Which one you prefer totally depends upon your individual taste. Soul and rock fans will be far better off with the Ace collection, which concentrates far more heavily on his soul-jazz, R&B, and psychedelic-influenced numbers. The Prestige set focuses on his more sedate, straight jazz side, with tracks taken from his 1967-1970 albums (there's nothing from his first two Prestige records, which have been combined onto one CD on the *Tough!* reissue). This is nicely atmospheric stuff with a Latin lilt, but not Pucho at his funkiest and most adventurous. It's also wholly instrumental, with none of the un-honed but energetic vocals that occasionally adorned his material on cuts like "Shuckin' and Jivin'." *—Richie Unterberger*

★ **The Best of Pucho & the Latin Soul Brothers** / 1993 / Ace ✦✦✦✦✦
Not only the best overview of Pucho's work, but one of the best Latin jazz recordings available, and certainly one of the best in the nowadays-obscure sub-genre of Latin-jazz-soul. Contains 17 tracks from his 1966-70 heyday, intelligently weighted toward his most dance groove-oriented original material and covers, and eliminating the routine pop covers that filled out some of his LPs. "Canteloupe Island," "Soul Yamie," "Shuckin' and Jivin'," "Maiden Voyage," and "Strange Thing Mambo" are all among his very best cuts. With a running time of 76 minutes, it's a good deal even at import prices. *—Richie Unterberger*

Rip a Dip / Jun. 1995 / Milestone ✦✦✦

Tito Rodriguez

b. Jan. 4, 1923, San Juan, Puerto Rico, **d.** Feb. 28, 1972, New York, NY
Vibraphone, Vocals, Guitar / Cuban Jazz, Bolero, Tropical, Charanga, New York Salsa, United States, Latin Continuum
Multi-instrumentalist Tito Rodriguez played an important role in New York's thriving Latin dance scene of the 1950s and '60s. His expressive playing was an important factor in the success of his brother Johnny Rodriguez's band. A native of San Juan, Puerto Rico, Rodriguez displayed his talents at a very young age. Accomplished on a variety of instruments, he could interpret popular tunes while still in his childhood. He secured his first contract as a musician at the age of 13. Although he made his first trip to the United States as a member of Cuarteto Caney, his tenure with the band was short-lived. After coming late to an important gig, he was fired by bandleader Noro Morales. He quickly found employment with the band led by Enrique Madriguera. Following his brother to New York in 1939, Rodriguez accepted a position with the Johnny Rodriguez Orchestra. Although he was tempted by offers to join Xavier Cugart's group, he remained faithful to his brother's group. While in New York, he sharpened his skills as a student of Professor Moe Goldenberg. In 1952, he received a mention of honor award from the Century Conservatory of Music of New York. During the early rock era, Rodriguez played for a while with Leroy Holmes' orchestra and produced albums by El Cuarteto Los Hispanos, Los Montemar, and Teddy Trinidad. In the mid-'60s, Rodriguez returned to Puerto Rico. In addition to performing frequently in San Juan hotels, he hosted popular television show *El Show de Tito Rodriguez.* Rodrigues died from leukemia on February 28, 1972. *—Craig Harris*

Three Loves Have I / 1957 / RCA ✦✦✦✦

Señor Tito Rodriguez / 1958 / Tico ✦✦✦

Tito Rodriguez at the Palladium / 1960 / United Artists ✦✦✦✦✦
"The thrilling experience of a 'live' performance has been permanently captured on this recording to be enjoyed whenever you choose." The thrill is that somehow there is all the spontaneity and airiness of a live recording, without any crowd noise. The sound quality is superior to most studio recordings. The *Palladium* was, of course, the premier showcase for Latin-American music in New York, if not America, and the favorite place to play for Titos Puente and Rodriguez. With fresh material and plenty of room for solos, *At the Palladium* is America's top Latin band at its peak. *—Tony Wilds*

Back Home in Puerto Rico / 1962 / United Artists ✦✦✦

Dancing with Tito (Bailando con Tito) / 1968 / United Artists ✦✦✦
Dancing with Tito is at least partly a reissue, some of which material was at least six years old in 1968. For effort and uniqueness, it is among his better albums. For instance, "Meditacao" and "So Em Teus Bracos" are from *Let's Do the Bossa Nova.* And "Se Te Acabo El Jamon" is from *Back Home in Puerto Rico.* As a compilation, it's only fair, and not as good as the original albums. *—Tony Wilds*

Rondo Musical Sudamericana / 1973 / US Latino ✦✦✦

The Best of Tito Rodriguez & His Orquesta / Nov. 1992 / RCA ✦✦✦✦
"Me lo Dijo Adela" comes from 1955's *Mambos* album. The rest of *Best Of* must be similar high-fidelity but pre-stereo recordings, from 1950-57. Curiously, there is nothing here from *Three Loves Have I,* although the two have much in common. The sound is superb and cohesion high for a compilation. While the material is not his absolute best, it is very authentic and progressive for Latin-dance-band music of the time. "Los Marcianos" must have inspired Al Castellanos' "Martian Cha Cha Cha" on *Mardi Gras.* *—Tony Wilds*

Mambo Gee Gee (1950-1951) / Mar. 21, 1995 / Tumbao ✦✦✦✦✦
Along with Tito Puente, Tito Rodriguez helped perfect the big-band mambo creations of Machito and Perez Prado. Rodriguez had a slightly smoother sound than Puente, showing more of an affinity for jazz via many swinging horn charts; it was a winning musical blend that brought Rodriguez fame from mambo's epicenter in the '50s, New York's *Palladium,* to cities throughout the U.S. and Latin America. The fine reissue compilation *Mambo Gee Gee* includes 20 tracks from the early part of the bandleader's successful run, covering the years 1950-1951. With a four-trumpet front line, piano, and Afro-Cuban rhythm setup of timbales, congas, and bongos, Rodriguez works through a program of mostly mambos, while including a few bolero numbers for variety (these "Latin ballads" would figure more prominently into his set during the late '50s and early '60s). Highlights include signature, smooth-groove mambos like "Ya Soy Feliz" and "Chen-Cher-En-Guma," more charged, percussion features such as "Mania, Go!," and the melancholic bolero "Ardent Night" (this last cut was penned by pianist Gilberto Lopez, who contributes most of the album's excellent charts). The ensemble is augmented with trombones and saxes for four highly engaging numbers by bandleader Billy May and revered Latin jazz composer Chico O'Farrill (reflecting a trend in New York mambo outfits, Rodriguez here enlists the talents of jazz soloists Eddie Bert and Billy Byers). An excellent Rodriguez title that would serve as a fine introduction to the mambo maestro's extensive catalog. *—Stephen Cook*

Mambo Mona (1949-1951) / Mar. 21, 1995 / Tumbao ✦✦✦✦✦
After valuable stints in New York with Quarteto Caney, Xavier Cugat (replacing singer Miguelito Valdes), and Noro Morales, Puerto Rican-born singer and percussionist Tito Rodriguez went out on his own to form a group in the late '40s. Inspired by the incredible success of Perez Prado's "Mambo No. 5" and the subsequent mambo craze, Rodriguez and his band Los Lobos del Mambo (originally the Mambo Devils) began preaching their own tight and swinging brand of mambo music. Featuring four trumpets, piano, and an array of Afro-Cuban percussion, the group steadily rose to fame during 1949-1953, eventually gaining widespread fame and selling out shows in Miami, Las Vegas, and all over Latin America. This impressive Tumbao collection covers Rodriguez's early years, featuring 18 choice cuts from 1949-1951. The mostly up-tempo collection is a mix of engaging instrumentals with loads of percussion and biting horn charts ("Esto Es Felicidad," "Desert Dance") and smoothly swinging vocal cuts featuring Rodriguez's fine pipes ("Ay Que Mambito," "Joe Lustig Mambo"). Other highlights include the original version of Rodriquez's classic "Mama Guela" (here titled "Mama Mona") and two equally classic Chano Pozo numbers, "Blen, Blen, Blen" and "Boco Boco" (Rodriguez worked with the Cuban star and future Dizzy Gillespie collaborator during a brief stay in Machito's band in 1947). Benefiting greatly from subtly complex horn charts, astounding solos by pianist Tom Garcia, and an impassioned percussion base, these highly enjoyable Rodriguez selections make *Mambo Mona* a stellar collection. *—Stephen Cook*

● **Un Retrato De . . .** / TR ✦✦✦✦✦
The great TR was, of course, part of the New York mambo troika of which Puente and Machito were the other members. A fine singer of both mambo and romantic material, he ran a band as fiery as any. Here are "Mama Guela" and "Yambu" in the former vein, and the monster hit "Cuando Cuando" in the latter, as well as much more. This is a major re-release. *—John Storm Roberts*

Los Tigres del Norte

Group / Tejano, Norteño, Latin Pop, United States, Latin Continuum
Since the late '60s, Los Tigres del Norte have been bringing their distinctive norteña music to audiences and continue to set the standards by which other norteña bands must aspire. Their founding members are the three Hernández brothers, Jorge, Ra'l, and Hernán, and Oscar Lara, their cousin. All four are still with the band. Many of their songs are tinged with a wry humor as they sing about life for Mexican Americans in Texas; among their many releases were 1994's *Dos Plebes,* 1996's *Unidos Para Siempre,* 1997's *Asi Como Tu,* and 1999's *Herencia de Familia.*

The following year, the band won a Grammy for Best Norteno Performance for *Herencia de Familia* at first annual Latin Grammy Awards. *—Sandra Brennan*

● **Mi Buena Suerte** / 1989 / Fonovisa ✦✦✦✦✦
Los Tigres, Mexico-born but based in San Jose, are the hottest of all accordion conjuntos. *Mi Buena Suerte* is typical of their gutsy style, with a crisp accordion, a kicking rhythm with more bass and less bajo sexto than most groups, and a hokey sax on some numbers. Two good corridos are here—one on "Cesar Chavez"—but unusually, no song about la migra. *—John Storm Roberts, Original Music*

La Tropa F

Group / Tejano, Tex-Mex, United States, Latin Continuum
The Tejano group La Tropa F comprised members of the musical Farias family—Joe (bajo sexto and vocals) David (lead vocals and accordion), Juan (drums), Jaime (keyboards), Jesse (bass) and Jesse Jr. (percussion). Already with several recordings under their collective belt, they signed to the Manny Music label in 1990, scoring their breakthrough hit with the chart-topping "Mil Noches." In 1992, La Tropa F won the "Best Local Conjunto" award at the first annual "Pura Vida" Hispanic Music Awards; a year later, they also won the committee's "Best Conjunto" award, that same year taking home "Conjunto of the Year" honors at the 13th Annual Tejano Music Awards. Their many recordings include 1994's *Culturas,* 1995's *Hermanos*

Hasta El Fin, 1996's *A Un Nuevo Nivel,* 1997's *Musica Sin Frontera* and 1998's *Desde el Corazon de Texas.* —*Jason Ankeny*

Hermanos Hasta El Fin / 1995 / Manny/WEA Latina ✦✦

Live in Combat / Nov. 4, 1997 / EMI International ✦✦✦

● **Mejor de la Tropa F** / Nov. 18, 1997 / EMI International ✦✦✦✦✦
Lo Mejor De La Tropa F is a 10-track compilation culled from the group's early recordings. All songs are arranged in the Norteno Tejano style, including two English cuts, "Just When I Needed You Most" and "Mechanical Cowboy." While the tape is far from perfect, it's a nice sampling of the group's early work. —*Stephen Thomas Erlewine*

Desde el Corazon de Texas / Mar. 10, 1998 / EMI International ✦✦✦✦
On *Desde el Corazon de Texas,* La Tropa F shakes up their conjunto-based sound slightly by recording a country song ("I'll Just Keep Your Picture"), a medley of "Tejano Polkas" and a medley of Spanish standards, "Canciones Alegres." These three diversions are welcome departures from the band's trademark, but their signature conjunto and progressive Tejano does sound particularly good this time around, as the Farias brothers have written five solid new songs (the country and polka cuts are also original compositions). The result is one of the group's finest studio albums. —*Stephen Thomas Erlewine*

United States Collection

Sabroso: The Afro-Latin Groove / Mar. 17, 1998 / Rhino ✦✦✦
Sabroso! The Afro-Latin Groove is a terrific 18-track collection of Latin jazz recorded between 1954 and 1972. Many of the songs here are making their debut appearence on CD, and several of the artists here—including major artists like Willie Bobo—are underrepresented on disc, so this is a helpful way to round up cool, groove-oriented cuts by the likes of Bobo, Willie Rosario, Tito Rodriguez, Jue Cuba Sextette, Mongo Santamaria, Cal Tjader, Ocho, Machito, Tito Puente, Charlie Palmieri, Kako and Ray Barretto. It's not a perfect collection, especially since it leans a little too heavily toward the groove, but it has an abundance of hot music and makes for a good introduction to the genre. —*Stephen Thomas Erlewine*

Salsa, Sweat & Soul: The Best of New York's Latin Scene Today / Aug. 8, 2000 / Shanachie ✦✦✦✦
A bright collection of Latin soul and Afro-Cuban jazz, *Salsa, Sweat and Soul* is a good overview of contemporary salsa stylings by a broad range of performers. A fiery instrumental version of James Brown's "Sex Machine" performed by Pucho and his Latin Soul Brothers and "Cogele El Gusto" by Wayne Gorbea & Salsa Picante stand out as instant party numbers, while the breathy "Belleza" (courtesy of Xiomara Laugart) represents the mellower side of the genre. Altogether, *Salsa, Sweat and Soul* is a worthwhile introduction to some of the bigger names in salsa. —*Zac Johnson*

Tejano Roots: The Women (1946-1970) / 1991 / Arhoolie ✦✦✦✦✦
Recorded for the Ideal label in Texas between 1946 and 1970, this gathers about an hour's worth of female-sung Tejano music, from a time in which the form was ignored by companies outside of the region. Most (but not all) of the 22 tracks are duets, sometimes between sister teams, and are often punched up with conjunto and orquesta accompaniment; the liner notes speculate that this was because the growing Tejano middle class disapproved of the accordion sound and its proletarian associations. From a sociological point of view, this music was interesting in that it offered Tejano women creative outlets in a musical and social environment in which females were discouraged from taking place in activities outside of the home. Anthropological considerations aside, it's a decent collection of ranchera, bolero, and cancion variants of the Tex-Mex sound, with occasional solo artists (including Lydia Mendoza) amidst the duets; Chelo Silva's dignified bolero "Si Acaso Vuelves" is a standout. —*Richie Unterberger*

Venezuela

Los Amigos Invisibles

Group / Worldbeat, Venezuela, Latin Continuum
A performance-oriented Latin dance band from Venezuela heavily indebted to funk and disco (with a dash of acid jazz), Los Amigos Invisibles made a big splash in their homeland in 1995 with their debut album, *A Typical and Autoctonal Venezuelan Dance Band,* which featured odd Japanese *animé*-style artwork. Band members Julio Briceño (vocals), José Luis Pardo (guitar, songwriting), Armando Figueredo (keyboards), Mauricio Arcas (raps), José Rafael Torres (bass), and Juan Manuel Roura (drums) supported their growing reputation with a series of underground dance parties at the mostly deserted clubs of Caracas. However, financial difficulties led the group to move to New York in 1997. They signed with David Byrne's Luaka Bop imprint and released their American debut, *The New Sound of the Venezuelan Gozadera,* in 1998. *Arepa 3000: A Venezuelan Journey into Space* was release two years later. —*Steve Huey*

Arepa 3000: A Venezuelan Journey Into Space / Sep. 12, 2000 / Luaka Bop ✦✦✦✦✦
Perhaps even better than their debut American release *The New Sound of the Venezuelan Gozadera, Arepa 3000* proves that Los Amigos Invisibles have an unlimited number of musical rabbits to pull out of their hats. This band from Venezuela manages to infuse all of their songs with a funky Latin flavor while tromping through swanky lounges, disco halls, and the occasional horse race. Named after a common Venezuelan food, this band serves up a tasty buffet of sound. It is no wonder that they have found themselves on David Byrne's prestigious world label Luaka Bop, which seems to find the best music, regardless of ethnic markings, from around the world. —*Stacia Proefrock*

Oscar d'Leon

Vocals, Bass / Tropical, Salsa, Venezuela, Latin Continuum
A skill at improvisation is combined with a highly-textured vocal tone by Venezuela-born Oscar D'Leon. A top-ranked performer in his homeland, D'Leon has continued to solidify his following throughout the world. A joy for entertaining has been a constant thread throughout D'Leon's career. In a 1996 interview with *The Chicago Tribune,* D'Leon said, "My message is not about ecology or politics, but, it's simply that people have a good time and remember me as someone who loves them." Born in the Caracas neighborhood of Etamin, D'Leon was influenced by Cuban musicians including Beny More and La Sonora Mantacera and by New York-based Latin performers including Eddie Palmieri and Willie Colon. He taught himself to play bass by listening and playing along to records. "I am not a maestro like they say, " he explained. "I try to make my instrument sound coherent." D'Leon balanced his early career as a vocalist with full-time employment as a taxi driver and factory worker. Forming a band, La Dimension Latina, in 1973, he recorded his first hit, "Pensando En Ti," shortly afterwards. Three years later, he formed a second group, Salsa Mayer. D'Leon, who's known affectionately as "El Leon De La Salsa (The Lion Of Salsa)," has toured with very large groups. In addition to touring and recording with a nineteen piece band featuring five saxophones, four trombones and four trumpets, D'Leon toured with a fifteen piece group in 1996. And after a slew of releases in the late nineties, D'Leon returned in the new millennium with *Doble Play.* —*Craig Harris*

Riquitiqui / 1996 / Thl ✦✦✦
D'Leon's last recording spent an awful long time in the New York salsa charts, and it's easy to hear why. The base is international salsa, the sound on many tracks a splendidly fat, rich big-band one, but above all (like the Dominican bands) these fellows are high-energy. Could Venezuela be brewing the next Big Thing— Odd though it sounds, don't discount the possibility. —*John Storm Roberts, Original Music*

La Formula Original / Aug. 24, 1999 / RMM ✦✦✦✦✦
Veteran bassist D'Leon's larger band signifies the mambo, clave and danzon rhythms of the Caribbean isles with infectious percussion, multiple horn backdrops, and layered vocal coro behind his own singing and that of Jose Mangual Jr., Johnny Silva, Humberto Becerra, Samuel Seijas, Raul Agras or Milton Cardona. Oscar Reyes lays down solid piano montuno, and though there isn't much soloing, the collective happiness of the band comes shining through. D'Leon either wrote or arranged all but two of the ten cuts—the sharp horns and sharper vocals of Moises "Yumuri" Valle's "Mi Mujer Es Una Bomba," and the only slower number for the date, a wistfully flavored look at old folks; "Mi Viejo" has harp, strings and synth tacked onto a near-tango-metered lament. The rest of the program is upbeat, exciting party music, much of it danceable. They don't let up, starting with the "Bomba," leading to the love paean to "Michelle" (with "William Tell" horse romp quotes), the popping staccato group vocals of "Deja Que Te Quiera," a rave-up about a female's spectacular hair-do on "Monta Al Pelo," the proclamatory, more "ah-oh" vocally poppish "El Pregonero," and the interactive "Prestame Tu Piel" with its conversational lead vocal and chorus. Jazz fans will relate to "Esperando Por Ella/Waiting for Ella," and the closer, "No Hay Mujer Mala," quotes "Fascinating Rhythm" several times. The musicianship is consistently solid, hugely conceived and played with puffy-chested pride. After listening to this timeless Latin-jazz amalgam, you definitely want to hear it again and again. —*Michael G. Nastos*

En Vivo! / Sep. 12, 2000 / RMM ✦✦✦

● **12 Exitos de Oscar D'Leon** / Sony International ✦✦✦✦✦

Venezuela Collection

Music of Venezuela / Zu-Zazz ✦✦✦✦✦
A very fine set of recent recordings by amateur and semi-professional groups, with a focus on stringed instruments—violin as well as members of the huge family of Latin guitars and mandolins. Many of the styles included are available on commercial recordings, but not on the whole in such grassroots idioms, nor with such excellent notes. This album is also available in the U.S. on the High Water label. —*John Storm Roberts & Myles Boisen*

Latin Pop Collection

Best Latin Party Album in the World . . . Ever / Apr. 6, 1999 / Virgin ✦✦✦✦
The name pretty much says it all here. *The Best Latin Party Album in the World . . . Ever!* features every aspect of Latin party music, from classics like Jose Feliciano's "Light My Fire" and Milton Nascimento's "Cravo E Canela (Clove and Cinnamon)" to trendy chart-toppers like Los Umbrellos' "No Tengo Dinero," Kaoma's "Lambada" and Los Del Rio's mega-hit "Macarena." Rock and pop acts with a Latin flair are represented here too, from the Ritchie Valens classic "La Bamba" to the Gypsy Kings' "Bamboleo" to Beck's "Burro." Jazzy cuts like Mongo Santamaria's "Watermelon Man" and Quincy Jones' "Soul Bossa Nova" combine with the rest of the mix for a diverse and fun album of Latin and Latin-influenced party music. —*Heather Phares*

Billboard Hot Latin Hits: The 80's, Vol. 1 / Mar. 17, 1998 / Rhino ✦✦✦
Hot Latin Hits: The '80s, Vol. 1 contains ten of the most popular uptempo Latin-pop hits from the '80s, featuring such songs as Marisela's "Tu Dama de Hierro," Lucia Mendez's "Castigame," Lorenzao Antonio's "Doce Rosas," Amanda Miguel's "El Pecado," Los Bukis' "Tu Carcel," Ana Gabriel's "Ay Amor," Jose Feliciano's "No Hay Mal Que Por Bien No Venga" and Yuri's "Que te Pasa." —Stephen Thomas Erlewine

Billboard Hot Latin Hits: The 80's, Vol. 2 / Mar. 17, 1998 / Rhino ✦✦✦
Hot Latin Hits: The '80s, Vol. 2 contains ten of the most popular Latin-pop ballads from the '80s, featuring such songs as Marisela's "Ya No," Mijares' "Uno Entre Mil," Isabel Pantoja's "Asi Fue," Lucerito's "Cuentame," Myriam Hernandez's "El Hombre que Yo Amo," Kaoma's "Lambada," Ana Gabriel's "Quien Como Tu" and Alvaro Torres' "Ni Tu Ni Ella." —*Stephen Thomas Erlewine*

Billboard Hot Latin Hits: The 90's / Aug. 18, 1998 / Rhino ✦✦✦
Billboard Hot Latin Hits: The '90s contains ten charting Latin hits from the early '90s, ranging from uptempo dance tracks to love ballads. It's a good sampling of the era and introduction to '90s Latin pop. Among the highlights are Mijares' "Para Amarnos Mas," Daniela

Romo's "Todo, Todo, Todo," Sergio Dalma's "Bailar Pegados," Pandora's "No Lastimes Mas," Julian's "Si Ella Superia," Cristian's "Nunca Voy a Olvidarte" and Selena's "Como La Flor." —*Terry Jenkins*

MIDDLE EAST

Afghanistan Collection

Afghanistan: On Marco Polo's Road / May 27, 1997 / Multicultural Media ✦✦✦✦✦
Part of the Music of the Earth series, this album of Afghan music is surprisingly pleasant. It starts out with a piece on the ghichak (related to the Iranian kamantcha), which sounds like something one might hear in the midst of a bazaar, minus the background noise. Following is a similar piece, but at a softer level, with a slower tempo. The third piece is actually a small medley of two songs, in the same genre as the first two—love songs. The fourth piece is a splendid work following in the genre, but with only two instruments, played by a father and son team (the son is nine years old). After this is a solo improvisation on the zirbaghali drum by the nine-year-old son of the previous song's performer. The rest of the tunes are folk songs from various areas of Afghanistan. Overall, the quality of the musical works is amazing. The songs hold the same humanistic quality that much of the middle eastern music is based on—to be on a par with humanity while remaining only simple musical instruments is something special. The highlights are almost every track of music, whether the listener is accustomed to these styles of music or not. —*Adam Greenberg*

Arabic Collection

Archives of Arabic Music, Vol. 1 / Ocora ✦✦✦✦✦
Archives de la Musique Arabe, Vol. 1 is the Arabic equivalent of the earliest Yazoo recordings (i.e., taken from old 78s dating from the first quarter of the century; in this case, 1908-1920). Consequently, the sound quality is often quite rough, and there is never a lack of surface noise. However, this is amazing music of great historical importance, so many listeners will not have a problem overlooking the record noise. The Ocora label, in conjunction with the Institut du Monde Arabe, presents historic early recordings of such influential and famous musicians as Egypt's Yusuf al-Manyalawi and Abduh al-Hamuli. Among the artists' repertoire are qasidas (improvisation on classical poems), a dawr (chant with improvisation and refrain), a bashraf (instrumental overture), and a taqsim (instrumental improvisation). —*Joslyn Layne*

The Music of Arab-Americans: A Retrospective Collection / Oct. 21, 1997 / Rounder ✦✦✦✦
In the first half of the 20th century, Arab-Americans recorded for a small audience in the Arab-American community, often on 78s for tiny labels. This is a collection of 14 of those rare performances from 1916 through the early 1950s. The material covered is diverse enough to elude easy generalizations about the sound, although it's fair to say that it holds up well against the recordings of such music that were made in the countries from which these immigrants hailed. If there's any distinguishing mark to these recordings, it's that the bands are usually smaller (three- to six-member) groups than they would have been in their homelands, as the pool of available musicians was much smaller. The oud and violin are often (though not always) prominent in the arrangements, and the melodies often have a satisfying mix of sadness and sweetness. There's an unexpected appearance by a star on "Arabic Folk Songs," sung by comedian Danny Thomas. Certainly the weirdest of the lot is Kahraman's "Only You," which alternates English lyrics (basically, the title) with Egyptian ones, and cranks the reverb to 11 to produce some eerie quasi-psychedelic effects in the middle section. —*Richie Unterberger*

Egypt

Farid Al Atrache

b. 1915, **d.** 1974
Vocals, Egypt, Middle East
Singer/instrumentalist/composer al-Abash was notable for a deep voice with an evocative quality of poignancy, the fact that within the pop field he sang in styles regarded as "authentic" in both Egypt and the Levant, and above all for his extensive use of the ud. He was born in Syria, but moved to Egypt with his mother, when he was around nine years old. Atrash was part of a musical family: His mother, "Aliyah," supported the family by singing, and his sister, Asmahan, appeared with him in many movies. Aside from his singing prowess, Atrash was a virtuoso ud player: he studied the instrument at Cairo's Institute of Arab Music and in fact began his professional career accompanying and older singer. Atrash revived the dying use in concert of improvised instrumental solos (tagasim) as part of a longer piece, by lengthening the instrumental introductions to his songs and building tagasim into them. Through recordings of his concerts he thus became the most famous ud player in the Arab world and earned the nickname "King of the Ud." —*John Storm Roberts*

● **Addi Errabi** / Voice of Lebanon ✦✦✦✦✦
This 1973 live recording is thought by many to be his finest, and is certainly a splendid example of his way of building ud taqasim into his performances. It is certainly typical of his concerts in its progression from solo ud to Atrache's tenderly stark vocals, all punctuated by an equally typical passionate audience response. —*John Storm Roberts*

Farid Al Atrache / Voice of Lebanon ✦✦✦✦✦

Les Années 30 / Club du Disque Arabe ✦✦✦✦✦

Abdel Halim Hafez

b. 1929, **d.** 1977
Vocals, Egypt, Middle East
Despite a fairly short career, singer/movie-actor Hafez was one of the most influential Egyptian stars of the 1950s and '60s. His mellow, resonant voice, subtle vocal style and notably clean intonation marked him out, along with a liking for long, seemingly endless musical phrases. When Mohamed Abdel Wahhaab switched from singing to composition, he pretty much stepped into his shoes. Born in 1929, Abdel Halim studied at Cairo's Institute of Arabic Music and the Higher Institute for Theatre Music, and began his career teaching and playing oboe before taking aim at vocal stardom. His first hit came in 1951, and he soon signed a contract with Abdel Wahhaab to sing his songs and appear in his films. During the 1960s, he started to sing colloquial poetry more colorful and meaningful and nearer to popular folk song than ordinary pop songs, and his work on these lines had a significant influence on popular song in general. He cofounded a film company and the Saut el-Fann record label in the early '60s, and remained a major star until he died in 1977 of Bilharzia, which he had caught as a child and which had begun to affect him intermittently from 1955 onward. —*John Storm Roberts*

Mawood / 1994 / Soutelphan ✦✦✦

● **Ala Hasb Weddad** / Soutelphan ✦✦✦✦✦
A concert recording by a major star of the post-World War II generation. Like Lebanon's Fairuz, Hafez fronts settings that range from the now-traditional chorus and strings-and-percussion orchestra to various groups with heavy overseas influences. But his own style and the melodies he sings are both quintessentially Egyptian. —*John Storm Roberts*

Umm Kulthum

b. 1904, **d.** 1975
Vocals / Ballads, Operettas, Egypt, Middle East
Without question the best-known 20th-century Middle Eastern singer, Umm Kulthum went from performing in the villages of the Egyptian delta to international stardom as great as virtually any Western pop artist. She first sang in public as a child with her father, an imam who performed religious songs at local celebrations, and was so popular that in 1922 the family moved to Cairo so she could try for commercial success. Though her style struck Cairenes as overly rural, her first recordings in 1924 and 1925 did well because her years singing in small villages and towns had built her a larger audience outside Cairo itself than most singers. By 1928 she was the most popular singer in Egypt, and during the 1930s her work on radio and in films brought her international fame. From 1937 until shortly before her death she gave a live broadcast concert on the first Thursday of every month heard by millions of listeners.

Umm Kulthum started out with a repertoire of traditional and mostly religious songs she had learned as a child. During the late '20s and the '30s she moved to new and more virtuoso romantic material, and in the 1940s and '50s she adopted her best-known repertoire, a mix of colloquial, populist material and neo-classical compositions. But her style was always marked by her early involvement with religious material: clarity of diction and stress on syntax and meaning were at its core, and the varied renderings of individual lines for which she was famous were designed to increase understanding of her texts as well as to give musical pleasure. During the 1960s and '70s Umm Kulthum became an important public figure, a symbol of authentic Egyptian and Arab culture, member of commissions on the arts and president of the musicians' union. After Egypt's defeat in the 1967 war with Israel she gave benefit concerts throughout the Arab world to earn money for the depleted Egyptian treasury. —*John Storm Roberts*

★ **El Atlaal** / Sono Cairo ✦✦✦✦✦
El Atlaal is typical of Kulthum at her prime, shortly after the LP form allowed her to record songs the way she sang them live—at length and in depth. —*John Storm Roberts*

Hakam Alena Al-Hawa / Sono Cairo ✦✦✦✦✦
The last recordings by one of the greatest singers of our century, anywhere. Kulthum was rooted in the Egyptian earth, but she touched millions throughout the entire Muslim world for 30 years and more. Towards the end her arrangements became a little less starkly classic (in this case with some fine organ-playing). But she herself never changed and never faltered. —*John Storm Roberts*

Rubayeat el-Khayyam / Sono Cairo ✦✦✦

Shams Al-Aseel / Sono Cairo ✦✦✦✦✦
This well-known song with a deceptively simple melodic setting was written by Zakariya Ahmad on a colloquial poem by Bayram al-Tunisi. "Shams al-Aseel" was one of Umm Kulthum's favorites among her own recordings. —*Original Music*

Egypt Collection

Egypt: Echoes of the Nile / May 27, 1997 / Multicultural Media ✦✦✦✦✦
One of the nicest things about Multicultural Media's *Music of the Earth* series is that they attempt to piece together a full sound environment, vaguely in the tradition of Steven Feld (and others). This album of Egyptian music is no exception to this noble goal. Small bits of sound from mere church bells, Coptic wedding ceremonies that the recording engineer happened to pass by, and tiny demonstrations of simple percussion instruments—all are included, along with more complicated works of folk songs, biblical (both Christian and Muslim) recitations, and popular songs. Quite possibly the most beautiful work on the album is the impassioned call to prayer (though officially not music, according to those making the calls) by a mu'adhdin in Cairo. The simplicity and power inherent in a good azan is hardly to be rivaled by another vocal form on earth (save perhaps Dorzdhagva's Mongolian shilen boor works). —*Adam Greenberg*

☆ **Hitlist Egypt** / 1990 / Mango ✦✦✦✦✦
A hard-hitting overview of a variety of gritty, hardworking Egyptian pop, it mixes elements of bazaar culture with Eurodisco technocraft. The disc is divided equally between uptown

and street styles. It contains "Elli Shatr Enhaa Tgannen, " the naughty newlywed rap that had Cairo's elders blushing. *—Bob Tarte & Myles Boisen*

Islam Collection

The Music of Islam / Apr. 14, 1998 / Celestial Harmonies ✦✦✦✦
Inimitable world music producer Eckart Rahn again brings listeners a collection of recordings that is as moving as it is obscure as it is technically perfect. This sampler selects from a 15-volume set documenting the state of Islamic music from Turkey south to Yemen and Morocco east to Indonesia. The sampler is available for sale, separate from the perhaps imposing set. Detailed documentation discusses Islamic music cursorily and technically. Instrumentation, the role of religion in the music, and Islam and its history are also covered. Unfortunately, there is not much track-by-track text other than the source of each cut. The sampler begins very strongly, with an unaccompanied feat of vocal acrobatics in a Koran recitation recorded in Istanbul, followed by a rich arrangement of Iranian strings and percussion. From Marrakesh, Morocco, comes a sonorous example of deep-pitched drums backing group song. After this example of Gnawa music is an Egyptian flute, string, and percussion melody that clearly brings pyramids and oases to mind. Returning to Istanbul, listeners hear a surprisingly sedate male chorus backed by flute and tambourines from Music of Islam, Vol. 9: Mawlawiyah Music of the Whirling Dervishes. (Perhaps even dervishes need to relax.) Coming from Yemen is a very intricate and hypnotic melody from a plucked string instrument. The compilers chose to represent Pakistan with a near seven-minute raga. A clear, bright, Oriental female voice defines an Indonesian ensemble. Having heard from lower Egypt, listeners make a visit to upper Egypt where the leader of a Nubian troupe initiates each verse answered by the chorus, all to a lively drum beat. More exotic, moving, and densely structured music is heard from Qatar, Egypt, Morocco, Turkey, Tunisia, and Morocco. *—Thomas Schulte*

Music in the World of Islam, Vol. 2: Stings, Flutes & Trumpets / 1994 / Topic ✦✦✦✦✦
This is a super-welcome return in CD form of a classic (as in magnificent) collection of recordings covering almost the entire sweep of the Islamic musical world, from Algeria to Malaysia by way of the Gulf, Ethiopia, you name it. Volume 2 deals in shawms and flutes in all their forms as well as non-lute strings, including saroz, quanun, rabab, sarangi and others. *—John Storm Roberts, Original Music*

Music in the World of Islam, Vol. 3: Reeds & Bagpipes / 1994 / Topic ✦✦✦✦✦
This is a super-welcome return in CD form of a classic (as in magnificent) collection of recordings covering almost the entire sweep of the Islamic musical world, from Algeria to Malaysia by way of the Gulf, Ethiopia, you name it. Volume 3 is for the oboes and bagpipes (far more of these than you might expect), and drums and other percussion, including tabla, dholak, zarb and bendir. *—John Storm Roberts, Original Music*

Israel

Ofra Haza

b. Nov. 19, 1957, Hatikva, Tel-Aviv, Israel, **d.** Feb. 23, 2000, Tel Aviv, Israel
Vocals / Worldbeat, Ethnic Fusion, World Fusion, Ethnic, Disco, Israel, Middle East
Long one of Israel's most popular singers, Ofra Haza broke through to international recognition during the mid-1980s when her traditional music found favor on the U.K. club circuit, its success leading to a series of unlikely pop projects. Born in Tel Aviv on November 19, 1959, Haza was the daughter of Yemenite parents forced to flee from their native country's Muslim regime; at the age of 12 she joined the renowned Hatikva theatrical troupe, and with the group cut a number of award-winning records before serving a compulsory two-year tour of duty in the Israeli army. Upon her discharge, in 1979 she mounted a solo career, becoming a star not only at home but also in neigboring Arab nations; in 1983, her recording of "Hi!" placed second in the annual Eurovision Song Contest.

Inspired by the ancient melodies taught to her by her mother, in 1985 Haza recorded *Yemenite Songs*, which featured traditional instruments as well as lyrics drawn from the 16th century poetry of Shalom Shabazi; not only a major hit at home, the album was also a worldbeat smash in England as well. With 1988's *Shaday*, she turned away from traditional sounds to pursue more dance-flavored material, and the single "Im Nin'al" even reached the Top 20 on the U.K. pop charts, additionally becoming a club favorite in the U.S. Haza's music was also sampled on the Eric B. and Rakim rap classic "Paid in Full," and her vocals later found their way into M.A.R.R.S.' seminal "Pump Up the Volume" as well.

1989's *Desert Wind* was sung largely in English, and its release corresponded with Haza's first American tour. For 1992's Grammy-nominated *Kirya*, she teamed with producer Don Was, and welcomed guests Iggy Pop and Lou Reed; that same year, Haza also recorded the single "Temple of Love" with British goth-rockers the Sisters of Mercy. Despite her success, however, she was silent throughout the middle of the decade, finally resurfacing in 1997 with a self-titled LP issued on her new label BMG Ariola. Haza died unexpectedly of AIDS-related complications on February 23, 2000. *—Jason Ankeny*

Fifty Gates of Wisdom: Yemenite Songs / 1984 / Shanachie ✦✦✦✦
Like the Berber songs of Algeria's Markunda Aures, Haza's contemporary versions of Yemeni Jewish songs feature tradition-based singing with pop backings. Her gorgeous voice carries all before it, but the arrangements are over-slick at times. Still, this was Haza as kibbutz popstar, unlike her later worldbeat wanderings. *—John Storm Roberts*

Shaday / 1988 / Sire ✦✦✦✦✦
This CD made Haza a household name throughout Europe because it was her first to sell millions of copies there, earning her the nickname "the Israeli Madonna." She combines Hebrew, Yemenite, and English in prayers and original compositions with a driving European dance beat. Included is the international hits "Im Nin Alu" and "Galbi" (later made famous after rap stars Eric B. & Rakim sampled it for one of their hits). It's also available domestically on Sire with bonus remixes of the above tracks. *—Phil Fink*

● **Desert Wind** / 1989 / Sire ✦✦✦✦✦

Kirya / 1992 / Shanachie ✦✦✦
Kirya heralds a return to the style of her *50 Gates of Wisdom* album (and her return to the Shanachie label). Guided by producer Don Was (the B-52's, Bonnie Raitt, Bob Dylan), the album offers a unique contemporary groove and Haza's striking vocals (here in Aramaic, Hebrew, and English). Guests include Lou Reed. *—AMG*

Simon Shaheen

b. 1955, Tarshiha, Galilee
Violin, Israel, Middle East
Simon Shaheen has established himself as a virtuoso on not one, but two instruments—the violin and the oud, a Middle Eastern precursor of the lute. In addition to being a master player, he's also a renowned composer of Arabic and Western music and a teacher who has done a great deal to foster Arabic music in the West. Born in 1955 in Tarshiha, Galilee, music surrounded him from the start, as his father Hikmet Shaheen taught and composed Arabic music as well as played the oud. At the age of five, Shaheen began learning the oud, and a year later picked up the violin. "I just picked up on the instruments and they felt like an extension of me," he recalled. "With the oud I watched my father, I grew musically with him. That was the greatest school for me. Not necessarily that he taught me lessons, just living and playing with him." Enrolled at the Conservatory for Western Classical Music, he began what would turn out to be many years of study. He moved on to the Academy of Music in Jerusalem, graduating from there in 1987 at the age of 23. The institution appointed him an instructor of Arabic Music, but Shaheen wanted to travel—and there was no shortage of offers, as schools around the world wanted him for graduate studies. He settled on New York, where he had a choice of two places—Juilliard or the Manhattan School of Music. He picked the latter, then finished up his graduate work in music education and musicology at Columbia. In 1982, having seen that the prevailing image of Arabic and Middle Eastern music in America was that of the belly dancing stereotype, he formed the Near Eastern Music Ensemble, a group dedicated to performing traditional Arabic music, and which performed in concerts and workshops ranging from elementary schools to such prestigious universities as Harvard and M.I.T. Shaheen's career as a solo artist also blossomed, seeing him perform at major venues around the world from Carnegie Hall to Le Palais des Arts in Brussels. However, it wasn't until the '90s that he began recording, although he had scored music for films *The Sheltering Sky* and *Malcolm X*. His first disc, *Taqasim*, was a Middle East-fest, where Shaheen exercised his fleet fingers in extended improvisations with Lebanese buzuq player Ali Jihad Racy. He collaborated with producer Bill Laswell on the album *Hallucination Engine* by fusion project Material, although he wasn't happy with the outcome. However, he and Laswell did work together on other records, including *The Music of Mohamed Abdel Wahab*, where Shaheen interpreted compositions by the famed Egyptian, and *Turath*, where Shaheen's remarkable oud skills got a workout. The more meditative *Saltanah* found him working with Indian player Vishwa Mohan Bhatt on a series of Shaheen compositions that offered examples of the range of his writing, which had moved far beyond the Arab world to include Western classical and jazz. But he'd already received compositional grants from the National Endowment for the Arts and a number of foundations. In 1994, Shaheen began the Annual Arab Festival of the Arts in New York, intended to showcase the top Arabic musical talent, and three years later he founded the Annual Arabic Music Retreat, held at Mount Holyoke College, a week-long series of lectures, workshops, and performances. He began the band Qantara in 1995. The group, whose name translates as "arch," was intended to be his vehicle to explore the fusion of musics, from Arabic to jazz to classical in a free and open place. Their first recording came when they contributed two tracks to *The Two Tenors* album, recorded live in Las Vegas. Shaheen also acted as musical director for the orchestras accompanying singers Wadi Al-Safi and Sabah Fakhri. In 2000 Shaheen became the one of the first Arabs to appear on the Grammy Awards, conducting the orchestra while Sting and Algerian Cheb Mami duetted on their hit "Desert Rose." Late in 2000 Qantara began recording their debut disc, set for release in 2001, and Shaheen started work on a commission to compose a Western classical piece for the Philadelphia Symphony Orchestra. *—Chris Nickson*

The Music of Mohamed Abdel Wahab / 1990 / Axiom ✦✦✦
Cairo was once a major movie-making capital, and Wahab invented the soundtrack sound that still influences how we think about Egyptian music. 'Ud dervish Simon Shaheen, backed by an energetic orchestra and chorus, interprets some of the composer's most intoxicating pieces. *—Bob Tarte*

● **Turath (Heritage): Masterworks of the Middle East** / 1992 / CMP ✦✦✦✦✦
This rarity is a very welcome one: a really outstanding classical recording by a quartet of young musicians. Shaheen, an excellent oud-player and violinist, is joined by fine nay quanun and percussion in a recital of classic and contemporary works in the linked Arabic and Ottoman-Turkish tradition. *—John Storm Roberts*

Iran Collection

Anthology of World Music: Iran / Feb. 10, 1998 / Rounder ✦✦✦
These are taken from the fifty albums compiled by Alain Danielou for the *Anthology of World Music* series, but apart from noting that this series was originally issued between 1968 and 1987, there is nothing to indicate when the material on this double-disc anthology of Iranian traditional music was recorded. Anyway, the ten lengthy tracks on this double CD (some around 20 minutes in duration) offer a respectable, well-recorded cross-section of Iranian music, performed on stringed instruments such as the bowed kamantche, the lute-like sehtar, or the nai flute; there is also a piece for solo dombak (the Iranian single-skin drum) and sung poems. It's mostly very somber in tone, without enough melodic variation to appeal to Western ears; the most interesting selections are Teherani's dombak solo, and Zabihi's quavering, unaccompanied rendition of a mystic poem of Araqi, in which he gets some amazing vibrating vocal tones. *—Richie Unterberger*

☆ **Classical Music of Iran . . .** / 1991 / Smithsonian/Folkways ♦♦♦♦♦
The *Classical Music of Iran: The Dastgah Systems* collection of classical Iranian music performances was recorded before the 1979 Iranian revolution drove many accomplished players into exile. Extensive liner notes add to the appeal of this historic document. *—Linda Kohanov*

Musique Persane/Persian Music / Ocora ♦♦♦♦♦
Music from the culture at the root of both Arabic and Indian classical music. This re-release of a deleted 1971 recording consists of two contrasting suites (so to say), one in Dastgah Mahu, the other in Dastgah Segah, for a group consisting of ud, santur, tar, kamantche, nay and tumbak. (The seven Dastgah are the basic modal structures of Iranian music). *—John Storm Roberts*

Jewish Collection

A Jewish Odyssey / Sep. 26, 2000 / Putumayo ♦♦♦
This collection of music from across the Jewish Diaspora shows the diverse influences that Jewish culture has absorbed over the years. From Arabic-influenced Sephardic sounds to the jazzy styles of modern kezmer to the Middle Eastern dance-pop of Ofra Haza, this collection goes around the world and back to present the sound of a people. This compilation hangs together better than most of the comprehensive offerings from Putumayo and contains some real winners like Haza's "Rachamin" and "Di Goldene Pave" from the Klezmatics featuring Chava Albertstein. *—Stacia Proefrock*

The Rough Guide to Klezmer / Jul. 25, 2000 / World Music Network ♦♦♦♦
The editors at the *Rough Guide* seem almost uniquely able to glean the best of a particular genre for their compilations—gathering the classic and the visionary, the famous and the undiscovered gems—and making every song count. This collection is no exception. From Naftule Brandwein, the clarinet legend in New York in the '20s and '30s who left behind a few dozen 78s for the inspiration of future generations, to the downtown avant-garde mania of Naftule's Dream, who hit their stride seven decades later, the compilation is a swinging pendulum of musical and cultural history. Several tracks show the evolution of klezmer as it progressed through the history of the Jewish diaspora and picked up local elements, whether folk instruments of Eastern Europe or funk-jazz riffs of New York City. Some of the most fascinating facets of the klezmer tradition are shown through performers like Alicia Svigals, with her ethereal melodic lines, and the passionate, exuberant performances of many others, including Budowitz, Brave Old World, and the Flying Bulgar Klezmer Band. *—Stacia Proefrock*

Sufi Collection

Land of the Sufis: Soul Music from the Indus Valley / Feb. 16, 1999 / Shanachie ♦♦♦♦
The music of the Sufi culture is one of worldbeat's most stirring but under-recognized treasures—although the qawwali sound has captured considerable attention internationally, other dimensions of Sufi culture have gone sadly unnoticed, a situation that this excellent and expertly compiled compilation from Shanachie goes far in rectifying. The 11 tracks that comprise *Land of the Sufis: Soul Music from the Indus Valley* possess a beauty and spiritual power that is remarkable, spotlighting the many facets of Sufi expression in their purest and most compelling forms. *—Raymond McKinney*

Turkey Collection

Archives of Turkish Music / Ocora ♦♦♦♦
Here are sounds from the living past: a lively and very local style as fresh now as it was when these early-1900s 78s were made. Faster than Turkish music of the past (and today, for that matter), and played without drums, it has a invigorating and far from archival feeling—from crisp songs for voice and ud to small ensembles with a joie de vivre sometimes lacking in more modern Turkish recordings.*—Carl Hoyt, Original Music*

Folk Music of Turkey / 1994 / Topic ♦♦♦
This collection of field recordings was made in rural Anatolia from 1968 to 1976 by Wulf Dietrich. The sound quality is nearly as good as in a modern studio. The music is fascinating, too. Dietrich made a decision to stay away from the big cities like Istanbul and Ankara, where the music has become westernized. He sought instead to catch Turkish music as it has existed for the last 500 years.

Not that he was averse to innovation. One track features an instrument called a cumbus, which is strung and played more or less like an oud but with the body of a banjo, with its round, screw-tightened resonating membrane. This instrument was only developed between the world wars, and is a real treat to listen to. As one might expect, there is an enormous variety of instruments and voices. The voices are unremarkable, but the occasional instrument opens the eyes. An example would be the jangly lute known as the saz, played by Hansan Durkun. Of course, even the Western violin takes on a new timbre in Turkish hands. The Turkish bagpipe, on the other hand, can be hard to take, although it's amusing to listen to its efforts to emit a secret message in its own private Morse code of beeps and squeaks. This is not necessarily an album for specialists. It has enough material of interest on it to justify a purchase by an advanced world music listener who want to learn more about folk music of the region. The liner notes are informative and well-written. *—Kurt Keefner*

Masters of Turkish Music / 1996 / Rounder ♦♦♦♦♦
23 tracks of Turkish classical music, taken from 78s recorded between 1906 and 1949. This has much wider appeal than the typical archival world music release. The taksim (improvisations) and gazels (vocal improvisations) are extremely emotional and moving, and there is a good deal of variety in the 75-minute program, in both content and instrumentation. The "classical" term shouldn't scare off those who are not approaching this music from a scholarly viewpoint; it draws heavily on folk traditions, and is as passionate as any middle eastern music you're likely to encounter. Especially entrancing are the full-throttle gazel improvisations of Hamiyet Yuceses. On the more instrumentally-oriented pieces, the ud and tanbur playing is a clear source point for modern musicians working in the style. It certainly seems as though Sandy Bull, for instance, may have been exposed to this music, either directly or indirectly. Despite the age of the recordings, the sound is very good—even on the performances dating back to the early 20th century, the transfers seem to be clear as technology will allow. *—Richie Unterberger*

Masters of Turkish Music, Vol. 2 / Aug. 20, 1996 / Rounder ♦♦♦
Masters of Turkish Music, Vol. 2 is an excellent continuation of the first set of Turkish music. Instead of concentrating on indvidual artists, it focuses on the attributes of the region's music, which makes for a more listenable and instruction compilation. Like the first volume of *Masters of Turkish Music, Vol. 2* functions as a good introduction to the music of Turkey. *—Thom Owens*

My Only Consolation: Classic Pierotic Rembetica 1932-1946 / Feb. 9, 1999 / Rounder ♦♦♦♦♦
Rembetica is the style of popular music that developed in the 19th century in port cities of Western Asia minor, particularly in Turkey. It usually featured a male vocalist, and accompaniment by bouzouki and guitar. Rembetica was popular in the Greek city of Piraeus, where many Turkish refugees had moved to after the Greco-Turkish War of 1922, and was often performed in the most disreputable sectors of society: hashish dens, prisons and shanty towns. It was recorded frequently between 1932 and 1937, which is when the bulk of the 22 recordings on this compilation were made; after 1937 a dictatorship imposed censorship upon such material, although some other such tracks dribbled out in the 1940s. The performances are plaintive and earnest, stressing minor melodies, occasional harmonies and skilled bouzouki picking. If you're the kind who can only handle bouzouki in limited doses, you should give this anthology a wide berth: the instrument's at the forefront almost all the time, and while the music is moving and emotionally delivered, the melodies and arrangements aren't too diverse. The lyrics (translations are included in the sleeve notes) were often shockingly grim and realistic, sometimes with explicit violence and drug references. On "The Junkie's Pain," An. Dhelias (who would die of a drug overdose in the street) sings, "First I started snorting dope, then I began the needle/And my body did begin slowly to waste away . . . Since heroin, it has caused me to die out here on the street." Lou Reed, eat your heart out. The sound, remastered from old 78s, is surprisingly good given the obscure sources. *—Richie Unterberger*

Yemen Collection

Samar: Music From Yemen Arabia / Oct. 26, 1999 / Rounder ♦♦♦
Music of Yemen Arabia: Samar is a reissue of a recording originally released by Lyrichord in 1975. The album remains an interesting collection of small-group music from the tribal areas of North Yemen. Samar is the name for the time in the evening when friends gather to drink coffee, chew the narcotic, quat, and play music—with the exception of the last track, a wedding song, this collection represents the music of Samar, featuring the oudh, male vocalists and various drums. The music is largely hopeful and upbeat, with lyrics that combine religious influences with tales of passion and lovesickness that echo the beauty of Arabic devotional poetry. One of the only flaws of this album is its brevity—there are only four tracks and even though the wedding song at the end is over 20 minutes long, the listener is left with the impression that only the surface has been scratched in the exploration of this music. *—Stacia Proefrock*

NORTH AMERICA

Canada Collection

Sounds of Nova Scotia, Vol. 1 / Sep. 28, 1999 / Stephen Mcdonald ♦♦♦♦
The Sounds of Nova Scotia, Vol. 1 celebrates the Celtic and folk heritage of the Atlantic Canadian province with performances from some of Nova Scotia's best-known artists, including the Rankin Family and the Barra MacNeils. Howie MacDonald's "Skye Boat Song," John Gracie's "Sea Bird's Cry," the Garrison Brothers' "Song for the Mira," and Les Tymeux de la Baie's "Bienvenue en Clare" are some of the many highlights from this entertaining, authentic collection of Atlantic Canadian singer/songwriters. *—Heather Phares*

Native American

Douglas Spotted Eagle

Percussion, Flute / Meditation, Ethnic Fusion
Douglas Spotted Eagle is a Native American flute virtuoso and composer who, in addition to recording his own albums, has been involved in a variety of film and television projects. Raised in Valley Junction, Iowa, Spotted Eagle began playing the Native American flute at age 12, constructing his own; when his family moved to Salt Lake City, he formed a rock band that had a chance to open for ZZ Top. Having put aside music to raise his family, he began making home recordings featuring flute and synthesizer in 1988, which eventually got him a contract with Sound of America; by the '90s, he was appearing on Native American musical projects and contributing to television shows like *The Tracey Ullman Show, Millennium,* and *The X-Files,* as well as the PBS documentary *The Way West, 500 Nations,* and Robbie Robertson's score for *The Native Americans. —Steve Huey*

Canyonspeak / 1992 / Sound of America ♦♦♦♦

Sacred Feelings / 1992 / Sound of America ♦♦♦

Stand at the Center / 1993 / Natural Visions ♦♦♦

● **Ultimate Collection** / 1994 / Natural Visions ♦♦♦♦

Voices / Aug. 24, 1999 / Higher Octave ♦♦♦
Native American music has its share of purists who play traditional acoustic Lakota, Sioux,

Navajo, or Cherokee music the way their families have played it for generations. But there are also plenty of artists who have a more contemporary take on Native American music; one of them is flute player/guitarist Douglas Spotted Eagle, whose *Voices* combines Native American music with ambient, new age, and pop-jazz/NAC elements. While Eagle's haunting solos demonstrate that he knows a lot about traditional Native American flute playing, no one would mistake *Voices* for the work of a purist. Most of the selections are instrumental, although *Voices* detours into pop/rock-adult contemporary territory when vocalist Samantha Ward is featured on "We Are Still Here." On the whole, the material isn't remarkable—interesting and enjoyable, but not remarkable. However, Eagle takes some chances here and there, and he deserves credit for doing his part to carry Native American music forward. *—Alex Henderson*

Native American Collection

• **Creation's Journey: Native American Music** / 1994 / Smithsonian/Folkways ✦✦✦✦✦

Rough Guide to Native American Music / Oct. 27, 1998 / World Music Network ✦✦✦✦
After providing Rough Guides for everything from reggae, salsa and flamenco to the music of South Africa, Eastern Europe and Brazil, the World Music Network's excellent *Rough Guide* series turned its attention to Native American music with this 18-song CD. Assembled in 1998, *The Rough Guide to Native American Music* isn't meant to be the last word on Native American culture, but does offer an interesting, exciting variety of music by Native Americans. "Variety" is definitely the key word for this compilation, which ranges from the traditional to the contemporary. Some of the disc's more traditional offerings include R. Carlos' Nakay's "Cleft in the Sky," Primeaux and Mike's "Healing Song," The Garcia Brothers' "Basket Dance" and the late Ed Lee Natay's "Sacred Mask Dance" (which was recorded in 1951). On other selections, you'll find Native Americans embracing everything from folk-pop (Joanne Shenandoah's "Tekanatsyaslitha" and Sharon Burch's "Sacred Wind") and Mexican ranchero music (Southern Scratch's "Cuatro Vidas Polka") to hardcore rap (WithOut Rezervation's "Are You Ready for W.O.R.?"). The latter is quite compelling: bringing to mind the searing political commentary of Public Enemy, "Are You Ready for W.O.R.?" finds Oakland rappers WithOut Rezervation pulling no punches as they rail against the oppression that Native Americans have suffered. Again, this collection isn't meant to be the last word on Native American music (for example, it contains nothing by Kevin Locke, an adventurous flute player from North Dakota). The collection only scratches the surface, and that surface is a very inviting one. *—Alex Henderson*

Songs of Earth, Water, Fire & Sky / 1991 / New World ✦✦✦✦✦
Featured are nine ceremonial dances from various tribes of the American Southwest, plus East and West Coast tribes. Clear and vibrant field recordings from 1975. *—Myles Boisen*

• **Songs of the Spirit** / Jul. 2, 1996 / Triloka ✦✦✦✦✦
A very nice collection of music by Native American performers, with styles that range from somewhere close to ambient to just a hair short of serious folk-rock. Little Wolf has a good showing with two tracks (including the somewhat overexposed "Coyote Dance"), but there really isn't a dud anywhere in this album. A nice introduction to several Native American artists. *—Steven McDonald*

United States Collection

Music of New Mexico: Hispanic Traditions / 1992 / Smithsonian/Folkways ✦✦✦✦✦
Recorded between 1973 and 1992, this documents several forms of folk music that remain vital in Hispanic New Mexico: narrative ballads, Catholic Mass hymns (which are, incidentally, delivered with far greater exuberance and humility than they are by many other cultures), polka, religious dances, and serenades. Guitars, violin, and sometimes accordion are integral to the arrangements, as are buoyant harmonies. It's a good sampler of the folk styles that persist in the area after several hundred years. But more than that, it's actually something you would consider playing for pleasure once in a while, which is not something you can say about quite a few folkloric projects of this sort, whether by the Smithsonian and other labels. The lilting harmony-laden guitar ballads are highlights, but there's a lot of diversity on the 73-minute disc, from a cappella and solo flute to full-band dance tunes. The tracks with modern arrangements, by the way, don't sound nearly as generic as ones that you'll find on some Southwest compilations by indie labels with higher commercial profiles than the Smithsonian has. *—Richie Unterberger*

Native American Odyssey / Nov. 10, 1998 / Putumayo ✦✦✦
This ambitious collection aims to include a diverse roster of contemporary North and South American Native musicians. The album begins with music by Canadian Inuit and Montagnais Indians, and spans America with tracks from Apache, Mohican, and Ute musicians. South American Zapotec, Amazon, and Andean musicians round out the album. In addition to the mournful flutes and driving drums you might expect to hear, there are violins, guitars, and keyboards present in some songs. These musicians express their traditional Native values mixed with pop music influences. Tracks like "Wind River" by Andrew Varquez of the Apache are more traditional and contain only melodic flute and express a longing for the days when "gas stations, supermarkets, waffle houses" were not present in the Indian world, and there were no official boundaries or fences restricting their people. Right alongside the traditional pieces are songs like "Ghost Dance" by Bill Miller. This is a pop song with Native influences, sung in English, about a warrior's spirit coming home. The eclectic mix of what listeners tend to think of as traditional Native American instruments and modern songs makes the music accessible to all people, even those who think they might not be interested in Native American music. *—Susan Cruickshank*

Navajo Songs / 1992 / Smithsonian/Folkways ✦✦✦✦✦

Nu Yorica Roots! / 1999 / Soul Jazz ✦✦✦✦✦
One of the best collections of Latin American music ever assembled, *Nu Yorica Roots!* compiles some of the funkiest Latin soul and, occasionally, traditional music recorded in the Big Apple during the 1960s and '70s. The disc definitely concentrates on groove tracks, with standout inclusions by Joe Cuba ("El Pito"), Ray Barretto ("Acid," "Together"), and Tito Puente ("Oye Como Va," "Tito on Timbales"). But *Nu Yorica Roots!* also salutes the more tribal, drum-centered facets of Latin music during the era, with Mongo Santamaria ("Druma Kuyi"), Eddie Palmieri ("My Spiritual Indian"), and Sabu Martinez ("The Oracle") paying homage to their Afro-Cuban roots with flair. Harvey Averne's swinging cover of "The Word" by the Beatles and Orchestra Harlow's dance novelty "Horsin' Up" are a bit silly (even if they're good representations of the Latin soul scene), but without exception, this compilation nails the late-'60s convergence of amazing Latin instrumentalists and more groove-centered black music around El Barrio in East Harlem. Though it's saying quite a bit, *Nu Yorica Roots!* is the finest compilation produced by the inestimably valuable reissue label Soul Jazz Records. *—John Bush*

PACIFICA

Australia

Yothu Yindi

Didjeridu, Keyboards, Drums, Guitar / Aboriginal Rock, Worldbeat, Ambient
Yothu Yindi is the most successful and internationally recognized of Australia's aboriginal bands. Their importance lies in their fusion of traditional music and performance with contemporary rock.

The name of the band translates as "mother and child" and is essentially a kinship term used by the Yolngu people of the Northern Territory's Arnham Land. The group's central figure Mandawuy Yunupingu and clansman Witiyana Marika were originally part of the rock band the Swamp Jockeys with non-aboriginals Cal Williams and Stuart Kellaway. They gathered other aboriginal musicians and dancers to become Yothu Yindi, a troupe initially created to perform at cultural events both in Australia and internationally.

A late 1988 tour supporting Midnight Oil both in Australia and Northern America brought the band to Sydney where they spent a day recording a demo tape. Mushroom Records released the demo as it was as Yothu Yindi's first album, *Homeland Movement*. One side comprised Midnight Oil-like politicized rock. The other side of the album concentrated on traditionally based songs like "Djapana (Sunset Dreaming)" written by former teacher Mandawuy Yunupingu.

Mandawuy's family has a long and proud tradition in the struggle for aboriginal land rights and at the beginning of the 1990s there was political talk of the possibility of a symbolic treaty between black and white Australians. In an attempt to keep the idea on the political landscape, Midnight Oil's Peter Garrett and Paul Kelly collaborated with Mandawuy on a song called "Treaty." When it was initially released the song hardly created a ripple, treated as the political statement it was. Melbourne dance remixers Filthy Lucre decided to work their magic on the song, favoring the musical message over the political one. "Treaty"s success spread to Yothu Yindi's second album, *Tribal Voice*, which took the band around the world and eventually saw Mandawuy Yunupingu named as 1992 Australian of The Year.

Initially, Mandawuy used his music profile to further the cause of his "other" job, as headmaster of a culturally mixed school in Arnham Land, but he ended up being forced to apply for leave to concentrate on his music career.

Ever since "Treaty," Yothu Yindi has straddled its two music words, traditional and commercial, with varying success. *—Ed Nimmervoll*

Tribal Voice / 1992 / Hollywood ✦✦✦✦
The release of *Tribal Voice* marked an important step in the development of Australian music. It was the first time that an Aboriginal recording artist had received serious public recognition, to the extent that a song from this album, "Treaty," became an Australian hit. Yothu Yindi's music is a strange mixture of influences, ranging from the haunting traditional instruments and singing on tracks like "Gapu," to the modern rock of "Treaty" and "Tribal Voice." This range of styles serves to encompass all facets of the Aboriginal experience: reminders of the Aboriginal heritage, pleas to young Aborigines to maintain their links with their culture, and political protest over the controversial question of land rights (as previously tackled by Midnight Oil on *Diesel and Dust*). This album proved successful thanks to the release of a remixed version of "Treaty" (also included here), but it also provided the impetus for other Aboriginal performers—Archie Roach, Kev Carmody and Ruby Hunter, to name a few —to receive serious media attention. There are criticisms of *Tribal Voice*, though. The traditional songs are stunning, and Mandawuy Yunupingu's voice is suited perfectly to these, but it is the rock tracks that are the weak links in this disc. Yunupingu is not a particularly good pop singer, and the music is sometimes insipid; it seems unlikely that "Treaty" would have become a successful single in its original form. Despite this, *Tribal Voice* is a fine example of both traditional and modern Aboriginal music. *—Jonathan Lewis*

• **Freedom** / 1994 / Hollywood ✦✦✦✦✦

Australia Collection

Rough Guide to Australian Aboriginal Music / Apr. 20, 1999 / World Music Network ✦✦✦✦
When the World Music Network assembled a collection of recordings by Australian Aboriginal artists, it could have taken a purist approach and focused exclusively on acoustic tribal music. But instead, the Network opted for diversity, and the label keeps things unpredictable by spotlighting the most traditional Aboriginal artists as well as the most modern. This collection of 1980s and 1990s recordings ranges from the Aborignal pop of Christine Anu's haunting "Sik O" and Archie Roach's "Native Born" to raw, highly rhythmic traditional recordings by Arnhem Land ("Nyindi-Yindi"), Rimijmara ("Wongga Initiation Song"), Budal Lardil ("Buthamar") and the late Alan Maralung ("Bushfire"). Many of the CD's tribal offerings employ the very recognizable didgeridoo, which is known for its ultra-deep sound and

is the best-known wind instrument invented by Aborigines. The didgeridoo has one of the deepest sounds you'll hear in music—in terms of deepness, it even rivals some of the sounds that Catholic monks of Europe have provided during Gregorian chants. Those who have appreciated other Aboriginal collections will find a lot to admire about this one. *—Alex Henderson*

Hawaii

Cyril Pahinui

b. Apr. 21, 1950, Waimanalo, HI
Vocals, Guitar, Hawaii, Pacifica
Hawaiian slack key guitarist Cyril Pahinui was born on April 21, 1950, and raised on the island of Oahu; his father, Pops Gabby Pahinui, was a famed slack key guitarist as well, with the family's home a frequent gathering place for local musicians. Influenced by his father as well as family friends like Atta Isaacs and Sonny Chillingworth, Pahinui took up the guitar at age seven, quickly gaining entry to the endless jam sessions going on in his home; he began playing professionally about five years later, and at age 15 he and his brother Bla started a rock band dubbed the Characters. In 1968 Pahinui joined the group Sunday Manoa; a two-year Army stint followed, and upon his return from duty, he joined his father on a series of classic LPs cut for the Panini label. During the mid-1970s he formed the Sandwich Isle Band, one of the first young groups to revive the traditional steel guitar and perform the jazz-inspired material of the pre-World War II era; in 1979, Pahuini also joined the Peter Moon Band. After a series of solo records as well as a collaboration with siblings Bla and Martin, he signed to the Dancing Cat label in 1994 to cut the acclaimed *6 & 12 String Slack Key*, winner of the Na Hoku Hanohano Award for Instrumental Album of the Year; the follow-up, *Po Mahina*, appeared in 1997. Two years later Pahuini teamed with Bob Brozman to cut the duets collection *Four Hands Sweet & Hot*. *—Jason Ankeny*

6 & 12 String Slack Key / 1994 / Windham Hill ✦✦✦✦

● **Night Moon: Po Mahina** / Aug. 25, 1998 / Windham Hill ✦✦✦✦✦
One of the "younger" generation slack key guitar masters, Cyril Pahinui is the son of the great Philip "Gabby" Pahinui, quite possibly the best-known Hawaiian slack key master. Cyril learned from his father, as well as his father's friends and co-masters Sonny Chillingworth and Atta Isaacs. Every bit of their virtuosity seems to have been passed along by the time of this album. Cyril is able to play both the six- and 12-string guitars, combining them in five of the works with stunningly gentle vocal work that could lull even the heaviest of metal listeners to sleep. His attitude toward the music is almost stereotypically Hawaiian in its simplicity, but the beauty of the works, by some of the great composers in the history of Hawaiian music (Gabby Pahinui, Queen Liliuokalani, Leonard Kwan) is astounding. Everything on the album is its own highlight in the beauty aspect, and the technical aspects aren't left wanting either. Those that are already familiar with slack key probably already know of Cyril, and should pick up the album. Those that aren't familiar should consider giving this album a listen to start their journey. *—Adam Greenberg*

Gabby Pahinui

d. Oct. 13, 1980, Honolulu, HI
Vocals / Ethnic, Hawaii, Pacifica
Gabby Pahinui helped to lay the foundation for Hawaiian slack key guitar playing. Although he recorded only one internationally-released album, *Gabby Pahinui Hawaiian Band, Volume 1,* his influence continues to be reflected in the playing of Hawaiian slack key players and American guitarists including John Fahey, Leo Kottke and Ry Cooder. During an early-1990s interview, Pahinui's son, James 'Bla' Pahinui, also a skilled slack key guitarist, recalled, 'My dad got away with a lot of stuff because it worked. He touched so many people because he shared what was in his heart in such an honest and direct way.'

Pahinui recorded the first slack key recordings in 1946. He continued to lead his own band, the Sons of Hawai'I, until the early 1970s when he formed a new group with his sons, Charles, Cyril and James. Their first steps towards international fame came when Ry Cooder traveled to Hawaii to record, *Gabby Pahinui Hawaiian Band, volume 1,* during a two week-long session at Pahinui's home in Kona in 1975 The home had been the site for nightly jam sessions for many years. The same year, Pahinui made a guest appearance on Cooder's album, Chicken Skin. *—Craig Harris*

Gabby / Panini ✦✦✦✦✦
When the newly founded Panini label approached Gabby Pahinui in 1971 to record a new album with family and friends, the innovator of the slack-key guitar lately jumped on the opportunity. What evolved was one of the most celebrated recordings in Pahinui's career. *Gabby* (also known as "the Brown Album" due to the brown hues of the album cover) was released in 1972 with open arms from the Hawaiian community, and helping him on this project were his sons Bla, Phillip, Cyril, and Martin, along with longtime friends Manuel "Joe Gang" Kupahu and Leland "Atta" Issacs. The music itself was full of Pahinui's wonderful guitar playing and his unique, soulful voice. Includes "Ka Makani Ka'ili Aloha," "Royal Hawaiian Hotel," "Hula 0 Makee," "Aloha O'e," and his trademark song "Hililawe." All contemporary Hawaiian groups owe a great debt to him and this album. *—John Book*

Hawaii Collection

Hawaiian Steel Guitar Classics / 1927-1938 / Arhoolie ✦✦✦✦✦
Similarities between Hawaiian steel players and blues, country, and jazz artists abound on *Hawaiian Steel Guitar Classics*, a new anthology that contains 26 songs recorded over an 11-year period in the '20s and '30s. A song like Sol K. Bright's "La Rosita" has a marked similarity to both "St. James Infirmary" and "The Yellow Rose of Texas," while Sol Hoopi was a master player whose speed, facility, and range are impressive today, and were unparalleled in his genre at this time. Hoopi is the most dazzling player, but others who deserve examination include Bright, King Nawahi, the duo Jim And Bob, and The Kaai Serenaders. These selections have been transferred from vinyl 78s to digital tape and sound remarkable. *—Ron Wynn*

Slidin' on the Frets: the Hawaiian Steel Guitar Phenomenon / Jun. 13, 2000 / Yazoo ✦✦✦✦✦
While not exactly luau music, Slidin' on the Frets: The Hawaiian Steel Guitar Phenomenon is steeped in island tradition. Made up of historical recordings highlighting the Hawaiian music craze of the early part of the 20th century, these 23 songs range in origin from Trinidad, Argentina, France, Greece, and more and feature a style quite removed from Don Ho's "Hawaiian Wedding Song." These gritty recordings have an earthy, bluesy feel to them much more akin to a Delta blues or pedal steel guitar sound, but at times have a wacky vaudeville/ragtime feel. Quite eclectic and never the same sound twice, Slidin' on the Frets is an interesting listen as well as an historical document. *—Zac Johnson*

Vintage Hawaiian Music, Vol. 1: Steel Guitar Masters / 1989 / Rounder ✦✦✦✦✦
In the 1880s, Hawaiian native Joseph Kekeku invented the Hawaiian slide guitar style by moving a metal bar (Kekeku originally used a metal comb) up and down the neck of the guitar and raising the action of the strings. By 1920, the sound became embodied in the thousands of National guitars which flooded the market. Between invention and mass marketing, many top Hawaiian players brought their unique music to the States and throughout the world. The world, in turn, went hula crazy, and the effects can be heard in the bottleneck playing on many country-blues sides and the dominance of pedal-steel guitars in country music. This rounder companion to a Hawaiian singer's showcase collects prime 78s cut between 1928-1934, a period considered to be the golden age of Hawaiian music. Standout players include master guitarist Sol Hoopii and the svelte playing George Ku; while Hoopii goes in for some jazz on "Lady Be Good," Ku sticks to the traditional hula on "Na Ali'i." This song variety gets reflected in the gamut of bands on the collection, including a Mexican trio and a German salon orchestra (apparently, Teutonic countries especially took to the music). The recordings were made all around the world too (U.S., Japan, etc.) and take in a mix of hula rhythms, jazz, sweet dance band music, and south of the border love songs. Highlights include one of the earliest known recordings of "My Little Grass Shack" and Jim & Bob, the Genial Hawaiians' smooth and lowdown "Hula Blues." A perfect introduction to the music. *—Stephen Cook*

Vintage Hawaiian Music, Vol. 2: The Great Singers (1928-34) / 1989 / Rounder ✦✦✦✦
In 1989 Rounder released this compilation of early recordings of Hawaiian singers, with other volumes released to represent other genres of Hawaiian music. While the sound quality is less than exceptional on many of the tracks (all of the recordings were made before 1934, and many have only a few known copies in existence—one can't be too picky), the musical quality is rather good. There are no less than four recordings of Mme. Riviere's Hawaiians, featuring Rose and Tau Moe for the vocals, showcasing the use of yodeling in Hawaiian music, probably introduced by immigrants in the early 19th century. Also included are a couple of tracks from the steel guitar legend Sol Hoopii (also the only native to ever record "Aloha'oi," though that song isn't included in the compilation). Aside from those major highlights, the main components of the album (and post-missionary, post-immigration Hawaiian music in general) are the use of falsetto singing and yodeling, by both genres, probably originating from Mexican and Portuguese cowboys, the "paniolos," who also introduced the second major feature of the music: the guitar. The addition of a steel (similar to bottlenecks) on a guitar by the locals made a music distinctively Hawaiian. Both of these features are well showcased on the album, as are most aspects of music that is stereotypically Hawaiian (though the pre-missionary form of hula chanting is almost entirely absent). If a listener were interested in early music of this type, this might not be a bad place to start. *—Adam Greenberg*

Solomon Islands Collection

Music of Guadalcanal / Apr. 5, 1994 / Ocora ✦✦✦✦✦
The sound on these 1970 field recordings, brought to us by Ocora, is just fine. With liner notes in French, English, and German, *Music of Guadalcanal* is an educational listen, affecting in the culture it documents. The opening ten selections are of a coastal population of the Ghaobata region (named for a large clan) of Northern Guadalcanal. First come three women's rope dances, which feature two women soloists whose voices intertwine while the rest of the group hum a drone that drops a few notes at the end of each phrase. Throughout, the rhythm is marked by handclaps and shells that rattle with each step. The two loloele songs are a cappella, sung by 17 women, two of whom solo in parts while the rest reply in chorus. The loloele is the type of song and dance traditionally performed by the women in connection with the now-defunct female coming-of-age ritual of ornamental scarification of the face. During the festivities—which would begin the night before to tire the girl so she would feel less pain—the men would sing the silaru, festive songs, such as the next two tracks on this disc. The eighth and ninth tracks capture a ballet performed by 12 costumed men, with two lead parts backed by a wordless chorus. The last of the recordings documenting the coastal population is of the ancient Aeolian organ, which is made of bamboo canes and played by the wind. The second part of this release documents music from the Bahomea region at the center of the island. The recordings from two villages of the mountain-dwelling population include the hypnotizing instrumentals of the Panpipe Ensemble (tracks 11-18) and a cappella women's chorus singing funeral chants. *—Joslyn Layne*

Papua New Guinea Collection

Voices of the Rainforest / Apr. 5, 1991 / Rykodisc ✦✦✦
This recording deserves a place of its own. Steve Feld's new recordings from Kaluli territory set it in a sonic context reflecting the reality that the rainforest is a "dense, layered aural tapestry to which the Kaluli lend their voices." The arrangement is that of a day in the life of the

Kaluli and the rainforest. Its powerful effect is enhanced by outstanding recording technique and admirable notes. *—David L. Mayers*

Tanzania Collection

Taarab, Vol. 3: Music of Zanzibar / Dec. 13, 1995 / Globestyle ✦✦✦✦✦
This is one of four volumes of taarab music recorded on location in Zanzibar in February 1988 by Ace Records (the others are single-artist releases by Ikhwani Safaa Club, Culture Musical Club, and Seif Salim Saleh with Abdulla Mussa Ahmed). Taarab music is a beguiling combination of African, Indian, and Arab musical influences, usually delivered by a small, quasi-orchestral ensemble and melismatic vocals. This volume differs from its companions not just in that it's a various-artists compilation, but also in its focus on smaller taarab groups (although Ikhwani Safaa Musical Club do have a couple of tracks), who are also more apt to include women as singers. In truth, to casual listeners there isn't much difference between these combos and the more famous (in Zanzibar, anyway) and bigger groups, aka "clubs." There sometimes isn't as much instrumentation, perhaps, but the sound is still pretty full and rhythmic. According to the liner notes, the songs (largely composed and played by men and sung by women, although as of 1988 some women were getting involved in the songwriting and playing) are often arguments of sorts between clubs, which you wouldn't necessarily guess from the ebullient tone of the singing. Aside from (and more important than) its interesting social dimensions, this is good, emotional music, recommended to listeners looking for a satisfying blend of continents and a combination of traditional and modern forms. *—Richie Unterberger*

Tonga Collection

Ifi Palasa: Tongan Brass / 1994 / Pan ✦✦✦✦✦
The tongans took with gusto brass bands partly because they already played various wind instruments including conch-shell shawms. This charming recording gives several examples of traditional horns, as well as the brass ensembles themselves. These are nearer to their Western models than many Asian bands, but there are local developments, including the habit of mixing choirs and brass bands. *—John Storm Roberts, Original Music*

Malie! Beautiful!: Dance Music of Tonga / 1994 / Pan ✦✦✦✦✦
This is a wild, woolly and wonderful collection, not so much because the music is such (it's jovial, but reasonably restrained) but for its enormous variety. Here are traditional dances; traditional-style Christian dances; the "national dance," lakalaka, with great choirs accompanied by deep drums; even a cousin of the steeldrum made from galvanized roofing. *—John Storm Roberts, Original Music*

WORLDBEAT

The Afro-Celt Sound System

f. 1995
Group / Alternative Pop/Rock, Ethnic Fusion, International, Worldbeat
The traditional music of Western Africa and Ireland is fused into a seamless blend by the Afro-Celt Sound System. The band's exciting performances have become a popular attraction at the WOMAD festival in Reading, England since 1995, while their 1996 debut album, *Volume 1,* remains one of the most successful examples of cultural exchange.

The Afro-Celt Sound System brings together top-ranked musicians including traditional Irish vocalist Iarla O'Lionard, uilleann pipers Davy Spillane (Moving Hearts) and Ronan Browne, whistle player James McNally (the Pogues), Kenyan nyatiti player Ayub Ogada and Baaba Maal band members Kauwding Cissakho and Massamba Diop. Jo Bruce, the son of British bassist/vocalist Jack Bruce (Cream), rounds out the group on keyboards and electronic programming. Several tracks on the band's debut album, produced by Grammy-nominated producer Simon Emmerson, featured members of Shooglenifty on mandolin, bongos, banjo, guitar and fiddle. Released initially on the EMD/Real World label, *Volume 1* was issued in the U.S. by Caroline Records. The Afro-Celt Sound System made their U.S. concert debut in July 1997. Their second album, *Volume 2: Release,* was finally issued in 1999 by Real World. *—Craig Harris*

● **Sound Magic, Vol. 1** / 1996 / Real World ✦✦✦✦

Volume 2: Release / Jan. 25, 1999 / Real World ✦✦✦

Agricantus

Group / Worldbeat
The Palermo, Italy-based worldbeat group Agricantus took their name from the Latin expression for "song of the wheat fields"; their membership includes Giuseppe Panzeca (vocals, mandolins, sitar, other stringed instruments), Tonj Acquaviva (keyboards, samples/programming, vocals, and a huge array of percussion instruments) Rosie Wiederkehr (guitar, vocals, samples/programming), Mario Rivera (bass, keyboards, vocals, samples/programming), and Antonjo Corrado (guitar, keyboards). Agricantus' music combines a dizzying array of traditional world music forms from across the globe not only with each other, but with club-ready electronic dance grooves, producing a compelling juxtaposition between old and new. Their first U.S. release was the 1999 compilation *The Best of Agricantus.* *—Steve Huey*

● **The Best of Agricantus** / Jun. 22, 1999 / World Class ✦✦✦✦
Palermo, Italy's Agricantus blends traditional and contemporary instruments into an electro-acoustic sound that tributes and departs from southern Italy's musical heritage. The group's name means "song of the wheat fields" and their U.S. debut *Best of Agricantus* collects some of their finest moments, including "Com' U Ventu," "Disiu," and "Sy E Duar." *—Heather Phares*

Alabina

Vocals / Rai, Worldbeat, Flamenco, Ethnic Fusion
World peace and intercultural relationships provide the theme for the songs of the Paris-based group Alabina, led by vocalist Ishtar. Combining the musical traditions of the Middle East with the virtuosic rhythms of Flamenco, Alabina's albums have been a cultural exchange involving Ishtar and her band, Los Niños de Sara, a group of four gypsy musicians from the south of France who previously accompanied Manitas de Plata and Paco de Lucia.

The daughter of an Egyptian mother and a Maroccan father of Spanish extraction, Ishtar was raised in Israel. Inheriting her love of music from her grandmother, a popular Egyptian singer, she began her musical career as a teen. By age 17, she was already singing in Israeli nightclubs and acting in theatrical productions. The following year, she enlisted in the Israeli army and became one of the country's first female jet fighter airplane mechanics.

Leaving Israel at age 24, Ishtar performed for a brief period in Austrian nightclubs before settling in Paris. In 1996, Jewish-French record producer Charles Ivgi asked her to perform a updated version of a Mideastern song, "Yallbina." Her recording of the song, which was renamed "Alabina, " became an international dance hit. *—Craig Harris*

Alabina / Feb. 4, 1997 / Astor Place ✦✦✦

● **Sahara** / Mar. 23, 1999 / Atoll ✦✦✦✦
Inspired by the North African desert, this Parisian fusion vocalist conjures visions of restless, whirling sand with a surprisingly supple backing by her band, Los Niños de Sara. Highlights include "Me Encuento en Tu Desierto" and the near cover "(Lolole) Don't Let Me Be Misunderstood." *—Keith Farley*

Baka Beyond

f. 1992
Group / Worldbeat, Ethnic Fusion
Baka Beyond reflects the multicultural vision of ex-Outback guitar, mandolin and bouzouki player Martin Cradick and his wife, Su Hart. A fusion of Celtic and West African musical traditions, the band represents a collaboration of musicians from northern Europe and West Africa.

Cradick and Hart conceived Baka Beyond shortly after the breakup of Outback in 1992. Traveling to the rain forest of Cameroon, the couple lived with Baka pygmies and recorded their music. A field recording, *Heart of the Forest: The Music of the Baka Forest People of Southeast Cameroon,* was released the following year. Joined by Breton fiddler Paddy LeMercier, Cradick and Hart recorded two albums with musicians from the Baka tribe: *Spirit of the Forest,* released in 1994; and *The Meeting Pool,* released in October 1995. The group continued to evolve into a touring ensemble with the addition of Senegalese percussionist Sagar N'Gom, an ex-member of Outback; keyboardist Tom Green, formerly of the Orb; drummer Sam Pope; bassist Marcus Pinto; and vocalist Kate (Budd) Hardy. Baka Beyond's 1998 album, *Journey Beyond,* was a heavier produced project featuring guests including percussionists from the Ghanaian band Kakasitsi. Although most of the album was recorded in England, African vocals for two songs—"Migrations" and "Konti"—were recorded while Cradick, Hart and their son traveled through Senegal. *—Craig Harris*

● **Spirit of the Forest** / 1994 / Hannibal ✦✦✦✦✦
Guitarist Martin Cradick's stay with the Baka Pygmy people resulted in songs co-written in Cameroun with the villagers. Others constructed later in London set guitar, violin and other instruments to rhythmic ideas from the pygmies, creating a non-derivative style that avoids trying to either duplicate or dilute the songs of the Baka, while still capturing their highly charged lightness of being. "Ngombi," for example, pipes the birdlike call of a forest flute above Cradick's compelling acoustic guitar, while fellow Outback alumnus Paddy Le Mercier goes for the emotional jugular with a romantic, Gypsy-flavored violin. A spirited Baka rhythm ties the instruments together. *—Bob Tarte*

The Meeting Pool / Oct. 1995 / Hannibal ✦✦✦

Journey Between / Apr. 28, 1998 / Hannibal ✦✦✦✦

Boiled in Lead

Group / Experimental, Klezmer, Worldbeat, Avant-Garde
Arbiters of a style that's been variously called celtopunk and rock & reel, Boiled in Lead originally consisted of Drew Miller (bass), Jane Dauphin (guitar, vocals), fiddler Brian Fox, and a drum machine known as Amos Box. This lineup played a handful of gigs around the Minneapolis area. As of St. Patrick's Day 1983, the band had expanded to include drummer Mitch Griffin and fiddler David Stenshoel. This lineup recorded the 1985 *bOiLeD iN lEaD,* an energetic self-produced, self-released LP that hit the Celtic folk market like a rocket. BiL might well have played traditional music as part of their repertoire, but the format and delivery was anything but traditional.

Second guitarist Todd Menton joined the band in 1985 after an encounter with Miller at an Irish session led him to sit in with the band for a few gigs. It also led to a change of instrument for Menton, who had been playing saxophone up to that point. The expanded lineup set to recording their second album, *Hotheads,* in the summer of 1986, but by the time the album was released in early 1987, both Griffin and Dauphin had left the band. *Hotheads* received a Minnesota Music Award for Best Celtic/Bluegrass/Folk Album of the Year. *Old Lead* compiles both albums onto a single CD.

Griffin was replaced by drummer Robin "Adnan" Anders, whose style took in everything from straight-ahead rock to complex Middle Eastern structures that helped influence the direction of the band. BiL spent much of 1987 touring, heading into the studio at the end of the year to record *From the Ladle to the Grave,* which moved away from the loud Celtic approach to add Eastern European, Russian and even African material to the band's repertoire. Cooking Vinyl then signed BiL for European distribution. The album was released in April 1989, and proceeded to win another Minnesota Music Award, this time for Album/CD of the Year.

The band was back in the studio in early 1990 to record *Orb,* working with Hijaz "Hank"

Mustapha from the fairly like-minded 3 Mustaphas 3 (who signed to BiL's Omnium Records label for the *Friends, Fiends & Fronds* album). Fiddler Stenshoel had officially exited the band at this point, but did have a guest spot on the album. Once again, BiL displayed some stylistic movement, this time towards a more acoustic tone, although things could be quite loud and electric, as "Tape Decks All Over Hell" proved handily. For live shows through the end of 1991, Stenshoel's place was filled by Michael Ravaz on fiddle and bouzouki.

Josef Kessler took over the fiddle spot as of 1992, with his first recorded appearances occurring on the limited-release live cassette, *Boiled Alive '92*. The band made limited live appearances through 1992, and in November of that year Todd Menton left, to be replaced by Adam Stemple, formerly of Cats Laughing, a Minnesota band with strong ties to the science fiction fandom community, a connection that would have a distinct bearing on later work.

Stemple's first recorded work came with the thunderous *Antler Dance*, recorded in the summer of 1993 with Frank London in the producer's chair. The album reintroduced hard rock elements with a vengeance, with a cover of Bruce Springsteen's "State Trooper" getting a gruff treatment that would warm the cockles of Neil Young's heart. An assortment of other material kept up the Celtic and world music sides, even as a riotous cover of Boney M's "Rasputin" aimed straight for the heart of audience appeal. BiL also released a single, the no-airplay-guaranteed "Fück the Circus," backed with "Raca (Bunny Hop)."

This accomplished, the band hit the road for two years' worth of electric, acoustic, and house concerts, taping shows here and there. 1995 yielded a collaboration with Steven Brust on *Songs From the Gypsy*, an album of songs by Miller and Brust based on the Steven Brust & Megan Lindholm novel, *The Gypsy*, the text of which was incorporated into a CD-ROM section on the disc. Once again, the band shifted directions somewhat, with the biggest influence on the music being Hungarian, though the overall feel was a mixture of hard rock and heavy folk, more in keeping with Brust's own style. The connections with Minnesota's strong science fiction community had come full turn.

Since 1995, BiL have kept up a reasonable touring schedule, though band members have been involved with other projects—Drew Miller is working for Eastside Digital, heading up Northside Records' attempts to gain a U.S. foothold for Scandinavian music (following Omnium's release of Garmana's *Vittrad*), while Robin Anders has released solo recordings and instructional percussion videos.

1998 brought about the release of a BiL compilation, *Alloy*, that once again firmly demonstrates the Boiled in Lead directive of never being boring in direction. While it includes several cuts taken directly from the released albums, it consists in the main of alternate mixes, demos, outtakes and live cuts (including Brust's ode to Scottish overindulgence, "Puking in the Heather"). It's a sometimes raw, sometimes rude, sometimes smooth and glossy look at a band that never rests on either its laurels or a body of traditional music. A second compilation, *Alloy 2*, is a two-CD set available only through the fan club.

It seems very likely that Boiled in Lead may someday be seen as one of the more interesting and important bridges between world music and rock, with an influence that stretches far beyond its actual record sales. *—Steven McDonald*

From the Ladle to the Grave / 1989 / Omnium ✦✦✦
The group's first album with Anders on guitar proved to be the catalyst for turning what was already a strong, multifaceted group into a flat-out amazing one. Bringing not merely generally good fretboard skills but an encyclopedic knowledge of many world music traditions to the group, he helps fire the quartet up on a series of brilliant performances. The opening track "The Pinch of Snuff" might initially have raised warning signals, with a steady hard rock punch seemingly the furthest thing from BiL's folk roots. However, the electric mandolin soon changes that impression, and by the time everything speeds up, tin whistle and fiddle played like the devil, it's clear BiL are in full effect and out to slay the house once again. Melton's lightly but not stereotypically Celtic-inflected vocals add to the show, but *Ladle's* many instrumental performances do the business just fine. Perhaps the most striking thing about BiL is how its many fusions never feel forced, a quality shown in spades throughout the album. Combinations range from "Cuz Mapfumo," at once a tribute to East African musician Thomas Mapfumo and Celtic-American performer Cuz Teahen, to "Stop! Stop! Stop!," a giddily entertaining romp through the old Hollies hit mixed with a traditional Egyptian song. Perhaps appropriately, the band weaves its political and social commentary roots as skillfully into its songs as its musical inspirations, never sounding preachy at the expense of entertainment. "My Son John" makes for a fierce ending, dedicated to an anti-military protestor horrifically injured in the course of his work, while "The Microorganism" is a catchy yet still affecting caution regarding AIDS. *—Ned Raggett*

Orb / 1990 / Omnium ✦✦✦✦✦

Old Lead / 1991 / Omnium ✦✦✦

● **Alloy** / Mar. 17, 1998 / Omnium ✦✦✦✦✦
A fun, 70-minute collection of some of BiL's best moments over its career, *Alloy* works as both something for the hardcore Leadhead (as the band's fans are known) and the neophyte. The chronological ordering of the collection demonstrates how BiL became more involved and just plain great over time, as new members like Anders and Kessler joined to take the overall abilities of the band even higher. At least one track from each of the five previous albums or collections surfaces on *Alloy*, sometimes in an alternate mix or take, but plenty more rarities, live tracks, and other obscurities help show the group's full range. Early member Dauphin gets a vocal spotlight via a hitherto unreleased version of the folk standard "The Dreadnaught"—she's in fine voice, though admittedly the arrangement by the band is more straightforward than might be expected. The shift from Menton's slightly cleaner lead vocals to Stemple's touch more emotive and rougher singing is nicely illustrated by a version of "All the Little Horses" recorded for *Antler Dance* but never released. Kessler's fiddle is quite fine as well, while his notoriously rude contribution to the BiL archives, the goofy heavy-metal pisstake "Fuck the Circus," appears here on CD for the first time. The various live and radio sessions really showcase the performing abilities of the group and then some, mostly focusing on the later Stemple/Kessler/Miller/Anders lineup. Two fine instrumentals from a 1994 radio visit, Miller's original "Drowning" and Kessler's arrangement of "Pontiaka," are alternately bewitchingly beautiful and kick-up-your-heels fun. BiL's hilarious, raucous cover of "Rasputin" surfaces as part of a 1997 live set in which the group's collaborations with writer Steven Brust are saluted with a wickedly great version of his drinking-gone-wrong song "Puking in the Heather." *—Ned Raggett*

Mickey Hart

b. Sep. 11, 1943
Drums, Percussion / Worldbeat, Ethnic Fusion
Mickey Hart is a drummer, an ethnomusicologist, and an author. He joined the Grateful Dead as its second percussionist in 1967. In 1970, Hart left the Dead and cut the solo album *Rolling Thunder* in 1972, featuring various members of the Dead. Hart returned to the band in 1974.

Hart's musical activities outside the Dead have been extensive. In 1976, the Dead's Round Records label released *Diga* by the Diga Rhythm Band, an early experiment in worldbeat fusion put together by Hart. His interaction with drummers from around the world sparked an abiding interest in the role of the drum in other cultures—and a steadily expanding curiosity about non-Western musics. 1979 and 1980 saw the release of two albums of music from the film *Apocalypse Now*, much of it contributed by Hart. In 1983, Hart released albums under the heading *The World*. These began with a reissue of *Diga Rhythm Band* (an album by Babatunde Olatunji produced by Hart). Then came a series of albums of music Hart had recorded around the world. In 1989 Hart released *Music to Be Born By*, an album based on the heartbeat of his son in the womb, and 1990 saw the simultaneous release of Hart's first book, *Drumming at the Edge of Magic*, and an album, *At the Edge*. In 1991, another book and disc, both called *Planet Drum*, appeared. Both albums made the upper reaches of the new age and world-music charts. *Supralingua* followed in 1998, and two years later Hart returned with *Spirit into Sound*. *—William Ruhlmann & Bob Tarte*

Rolling Thunder / 1972 / Grateful Dead ✦✦✦

Däfos / 1983 / Rykodisc ✦✦✦✦
An established audiophile classic for its thrilling, nearly overpowering sonics, this percussion-based journey to a mythical country features Brazilian percussionist Airto Moreira and vocalist Flora Purim. *—Bob Tarte*

Yamantaka / 1983 / Celestial Harmonies ✦✦✦

Music to Be Born By / 1989 / Rykodisc ✦✦✦

At the Edge / 1990 / Rykodisc ✦✦✦

Planet Drum / Dec. 1991 / Rykodisc ✦✦✦

● **Mickey Hart's Mystery Box** / Jun. 1996 / Rykodisc ✦✦✦✦✦
With *Mickey Hart's Mystery Box*, the former Grateful Dead drummer no longer makes worldbeat that is academic and theoretical in its approach. Instead, he shapes his rhythms and drones into actual pop songs, complete with identifiable hooks and melodies. It manages to not alienate world music while it appeals to a whole new set of listeners, which is quite a difficult trick to pull off, indeed. *—Thom Owens*

Supralingua / Aug. 4, 1998 / Rykodisc ✦✦✦
Ever since the early '90s, when he released the acclaimed *Drumming at the Edge of Magic* book and the book/record set *Planet Drum*, Mickey Hart was nearly as well-known as a world-music aficionado as he was a member of the Grateful Dead. World music was an obsession of his for many years, but those two projects thrust both his interests and himself into the national spotlight, making him a figurehead for the genre. Once the Dead disbanded in the mid-'90s, he was able to devote more time to his world music projects, resulting in first the fine *Mystery Box*, then *Supralingua*. Basically, *Supralingua* is a continuation of the direction he began with *Planet Drum*, boasting a similar selection of polyrhythmic, multicultural pieces. There aren't really any songs on the record—just extended grooves, where even the vocals fit into the gigantic, everlasting drum beats. To some, this can be quite monotonous, to others utterly mesmerizing—there's no middle ground, really, and it all depends on whether the strength of the grooves and their inherent mysticism outweigh the formless compositions. Still, it's hard to argue that *Supralingua* isn't a successful extension of the ideas Hart began with *Planet Drum*, even if it isn't as compelling as *Mystery Box*. *—Stephen Thomas Erlewine*

Spirit into Sound / Jan. 25, 2000 / Arista ✦✦✦
Though *Spirit into Sound* does not break much new ground creatively for Mickey Hart, it does feature some nice elements. Hart's new age sort of blend of melodic elements and percussion are here again, centering around a very spiritual sound with heavy South American and African tribal influences. Rebeca Mauleon provides lush vocals which are reminiscent of Zap Mama's Marie Daulne. Zakir Hussein provides percussion with his trademark complexity, making use of a world full of instruments. Bob Weir provides fine acoustic guitar, and Hart is in full force, giving the whole project a backbone of drums and other percussive lines. While Hart fans are not likely to be disappointed, some of his recent material on Ryko shines more brightly. *—Stacia Proefrock*

3 Mustaphas 3

f. 1986
Group / Worldbeat, World Fusion
The 3 Mustaphas 3 pratfell onto the burgeoning worldbeat scene from out of nowhere in 1986—or from Szegerely, somewhere in the Balkans, if you believe their press releases. According to Mustapha mythology, The Balkan Beat Boys first sharpened their musical teeth at the Crazy Loquat Club under the guidance of Uncle Patrel Mustapha Bin Mustapha. Then, seeking broader horizons, they stole away one night, accompanied by their favorite refrigeration equipment, to seek world success from a UK base.

The Mustapha's humor has been a double-edged scimitar, however. In the beginning it allowed them to introduce difficult music to unsuspecting audiences new to the worldbeat sound. But the burlesque that initially forwarded their agenda also worked against them by threatening to consign the group to the purgatory of novelty act. An increasing emphasis on solid musicianship, plus their collaboration with revered African performers like Stella Chiweshe, have begun to win the band the critical respect they deserve. And no one else makes a crash course in world music so much fun. *—Bob Tarte*

Shopping / 1987 / Shanachie ✦✦✦

Heart of Uncle / 1989 / Rykodisc ✦✦✦✦✦
"Conventional" is the last word one will use to describe the music of 3 Mustaphas 3, whose *Heart of Uncle* looks to locations ranging from Istanbul to Dublin for inspiration. Though a variety of Middle Eastern and Mediterranean styles make up its foundation (including Arabic, Greek, Turkish, Indian, and Jewish music), the quirky, wildly experimental British group doesn't hesitate to surprise listeners by throwing in influences from Ireland ("Sitna Lisa") and Latin America. "Trois Fois Trois (City Version)" is a merengue song that is sung in French as well as Spanish, while "Trois Fois Trois (Country Version)" has more of a quasi-ambiance but is sung only in French. Meanwhile, "Kem Kem" and "Yeni Yol" show that Scottish/Celtic and Mid-Eastern elements can, in fact, be quite compatible. A musical roller coaster from start to finish, the album is one only the most adventurous listeners should acquire. *—Alex Henderson*

★ **Soup of the Century** / 1990 / Rykodisc ✦✦✦✦✦
When was the last time you heard country music sung in Japanese— Something that outlandish could only be attempted by the ever adventurous 3 Mustaphas 3. Every bit as daring and fun as its predecessor, *Soup of the Century* finds the risk-taking Britons singing in languages ranging from Hindi to Spanish to Albanian and playing everything from Hawaiian guitar to Scottish/Celtic bagpipes to Greek bouzoukis. Middle Eastern music remains their foundation, and like before, these eccentric players don't hesitate to draw on influences from all over the globe. "Soba Song" is essentially country music, but with mostly Japanese lyrics (and touches of Jewish klezmer thrown in), while "This City Is Very Exciting!" may be the only time Mexican ranchero music has been sung in Hindi. And on "Lipovacko Kolo," the Mexican polka beat is united with both Celtic music and klezmer. *—Alex Henderson*

Friends, Fiends & Fronds / 1991 / Omnium ✦✦✦✦✦
A collection of mostly singles (both "A" and "B" sides) and remixes, *Friends, Fiends and Fronds* is yet another example of 3 Mustaphas 3's unpredictable and risk-taking nature. A generous dose of Middle Eastern and Mediterranean styles can be found, and true to form, the group successfully incorporates everything from Afro-Cuban salsa to Scottish/Celtic music. Some of the material, although enjoyable, isn't essential, and in general, this CD isn't in a class with *Heart of Uncle* or *Soup of the Century*. Nonetheless, there's a lot to admire here—including "Linda Linda" (which brings together Afro-Cuban and Middle Eastern elements) and the Greek-oriented "Anapse to Cigaro." This is a CD that can make you think you're in Ankara one minute and Havana the next. *—Alex Henderson*

Worldbeat Collection

Around the World for a Song / Oct. 22, 1991 / Rykodisc ✦✦✦✦
The early 1990s found Grateful Dead drummer Mickey Hart producing Rykodisc's world music series *The World*. One of the compilations that came out of that series was *Around the World for a Song*, which includes African, Middle Eastern and East European sounds, as well as some offerings by Hart himself. This wasn't one of the better world-music releases of 1991, but it has its moments, including the Golden Gate Gypsy Orchestra's "Tov L'Hodot," and a fine example of Russian Gypsy music; Hamza El-Din's version of the traditional Islamic song "Mwashah," and Ustad Sultan Khan's tranquil Indian raga offering "Raga: Bageshree." But Hart's own material isn't nearly as exciting—"Udu Chant," for example, fuses new age and African music with weak results. Despite the inclusion of a few gems, listeners would be better off passing on this CD and investing in a more consistent world music compilation. *—Alex Henderson*

The Big Bang: In the Beginning Was a Drum / 1994 / Ellipsis Arts ✦✦✦✦
Whatever your feelings about Grateful Dead drummer and prolific ethnopercussionist Mickey Hart, most can agree on one thing: he makes the point he wants to make about the world and its fabulous drums. *The Big Bang* is a wildly eclectic compilation featuring instruments possibly previously unheard, from countries previously unheard-of, by the average listener. Hart emphasizes that the beat is as universal as it is diverse by presenting, among 200-plus drumming artists and groups, the spirited Tumuenua Dance Group of the Cook Islands, as well as some slick, sax-laden licks by Greg Lake with his famous studio pals Keith Emerson and Carl Palmer ("Karl Evil 9"). Hart tours far from Western shores, standing out with the reverberating "Water Drums" by the Baka Forest People, and the startling "Fuenyang Drum" by the Orchestra of Chinese Central Music College. Versatile keyboard maestro Bernie Krause (whose discography includes early stints with Link Wray and Van Morrison) begins and ends each of the the four discs with much whooping and sticks in "Amazon Days/Amazon Nights." CD proceeds trendily but admirably benefit the besieged rainforest (Rainforest Alliance), where the worldbeat clearly fuses on. *—Becky Byrkit*

Big Noise, Vol. 2: Another Mambo Inn / Sep. 23, 1997 / Hannibal ✦✦✦✦✦
The Mambo Inn was a London club that seems to have achieved, perhaps uniquely, all the promise of worldbeat fusion. By taking African jazz, Brazilian tropicalismo, Jamaican reggae and every other exotic beat-based music within reach and treating them as nothing more than branches on the tree of universal dance music, the Mambo Inn's legendary DJs turned a whole generation of Londoners into something like a United Nations delegation with rhythm. Though the club itself only lasted nine years, its legacy lives on in two *Mambo Inn* compilations on the Hannibal label. This one features dance grooves both organic and remixed, from artists as familiar as Caetano Veloso and the ubiquitous Baaba Maal and as obscure as Hamid Baroudi (formerly of Dissidenten) and the Haitian-American Jephte Guillaume. Highlights include Veloso and Gal Costa singing the timeless "Que Pena" and a great deejay turn from ragamuffin extraordinaire Macka B on Baaba Maal's "Hamady Boiro." This one is guaranteed to nice up any party in any country. *—Rick Anderson*

New World Party / Nov. 9, 1999 / Putumayo ✦✦✦✦
The Putumayo label has sometimes been guilty of a certain overweening multicultural earnestness in its presentation of various ethnic music traditions. On this winning compilation, though, it's all about the groove. Leading off with a cool, beat-heavy remake of Miriam Makeba's "Pata Pata" and proceeding through examples of, among other things, Senegalese funk ("Xel" by Aby N'Dour), reggae-inflected Haitian creole hip-hop (Wyclef Jean's exceptionally fine "Sang Fezi"), and bouncy South Asia-influenced pop (Dissidenten's "Lobster Song"), *New World Party* delivers a pretty flawless combination of cultural edification and booty shakification.Los Mocosos, a San Francisco-based Latin band, contribute a sort of salsa-reggae fusion on "La Boa"; Algeria's Hamid Baroudi delivers straight-ahead funk that George Clinton could be proud of (albeit with a quavering Arabic vocal accompaniment); Daude combines downtempo hip-hop with Brazilian soul on the lovely "Vamos Fugir." The album title says it all. *—Rick Anderson*

GENERAL

General Collection

Africa in America: Music from 19 Countries / Nov. 1993 / Corason ✦✦✦✦✦
Featured is African-influenced or -derived music from all over the Americas. Besides the usual santeria, vaudou, merengue, son, punta, cadence, plena and so on are some unexpected charmers: an Antiguan pan soca band that cooks like few steel drum group ever heard, a Dominican reggae about Mozambique, but no Jamaican reggae. There is no trimming of long songs AND there's some of the most hard to find stuff, like Surinamese winti and Afro-Mexican music. Also included are blues, jazz and zydeco—and they fit right in. Absolutely stunning, this album is a must.*—Carl Hoyt, Original Music*

Dancing with the Dead / Feb. 23, 1999 / Ellipsis Arts ✦✦✦✦✦

An Eternal Chant: Anthology of Classic Gregorian Chants / Atlantic ✦✦✦✦✦
An absolutely splendid three-disc box set drawn from the archives of Studio SM, a French label that began recording plainsong in 1946 and now has thousands of hours available in the vaults. During the time Studio SM has been recording chant, they have made and applied a number of technical developments to provide for the best recordings possible. The attention to recording quality shows in this set, which provides a deep, clear soundstage for each of the recordings. Studio SM and Atlantic have chosen pieces from a large variety of performers, grouping them into three discs. The first, An Overview of Gregorian Chant, provides as broad a range as possible of styles and songs, from lamentations to offertory and onwards, with performances ranging from full choral enterprises all the way down to a solo performer. The second disc strives to provide A Monk's Day in Chant, beginning and ending with bells, following the different types of plainsong that a monk would perform between dawn and dusk. The third disc is devoted to material that would be performed around Christmas and Advent. There is a beautiful solemnity to all three discs, reverberant and fascinating, and this set presents plainsong magnificently. The enclosed booklet has a brief overview of the development of Gregorian chant, and of the historical context for it, along with information about the recordings and transcriptions of many of the songs. Both the serious and casual listener will draw a great deal from this set. *—Steven McDonald*

Global Meditation / 1992 / Ellipsis Arts ✦✦✦✦✦
On this four-disc, three-hours-plus anthology of "spiritual, ritual and meditative music," the traditions of more than 40 different ethnic groups are sampled. Because the musical selections are determined more by aesthetics than by geography, the four discs (broken down into songs/chants, ensembles, percussion and melody instruments) move from continent to continent, resulting in fascinating juxtapositions from nations as diverse as Burkina Faso, Tibet and Java. *—Jason Ankeny*

A Mediterranean Odyssey: Athens to Andalucia / 1999 / Putumayo ✦✦✦✦
Putumayo's world music compilations of the 1990s were musical rollercoasters—when a theme was chosen, listeners expected the label to be as broad-minded and eclectic as possible. Released in early 1999, *A Mediterranean Odyssey: Athens to Andalucia* was no exception. The theme of this collection is 1990s music from the Mediterranean countries of southwestern Europe (including Spain, Italy and Greece), but you won't find any one particular style on the CD. Anything but predictable, *A Mediterranean Odyssey* ranges from the Greek pop and rembetiko sounds of George Dalaras' "Pame Gi Allou," Glykeria's "Pare Me Apopse Pare Me" and Anemos' "Miazis Me Fotia" to Spanish singer Maria Salgado's haunting ballad "Solo Por Miedo" and Sardinian group Calic's evocative "Un Poeta." On "Saudade," France's Barrio Chino offers an intriguing mixture of Middle Eastern and Latin elements. There are some parallels between the CD's rembetiko offerings and "Bebiendo al Alba" by Madrid oud player Luis Delgado. The very recognizable oud (an Arabic lute) has been a part of traditional Arabic music for centuries, and Delgado is someone whose music celebrates the Moorish influence in Spanish music. A person could nitpick and wonder why there aren't any artists from Portugal on this compilation—some Portuguese fado music would have been appropriate—but instead of nitpicking, it's best to grab a copy of this compilation and savor it. *—Alex Henderson*

Music of the World's Peoples, Vols. 1-5 / Folkways ✦✦✦
The prototypical collection of traditional music from around the world (and possibly the best), Folkways' five volumes of *Music of the World's Peoples* were compiled and annotated by avant-garde composer and amateur ethnomusicologist Henry Cowell in the early '50s. There's no attempt at geographic or any other kind of coherence—just a hodgepodge of charming, sometimes baffling, often gorgeous music. Cowell's keen ear makes for extraordinary diversity of conception and style as well as topnotch performances all around. By and

large, these field recordings were made before the influence of recorded popular music seeped into local traditions in even remote regions of the globe. Thus, most of the music found here is thoroughly exotic, and the lo-fi presentation only serves to enhance the impression that these sounds come from some distant, unrecoverable past. Unlike its closest analog—Ellipsis Arts' multi-CD international compilations—the *Music of the World's Peoples* series presents performances that, for the most part, show little sign of having been cut short. Most of the pieces form a coherent whole, albeit frequently all too brief. Like the individual cuts, many of these volumes (originally pressed on two LPs per box, currently available on cassette or on CD by mail order only) clock in a bit short. Nonetheless, their scope is nothing short of universal, a catalog of human imagination matched by few if any other releases. Cowell's introductory essay is a quick summary of the folk process as it applies to the contemporary world, followed by helpful analytical remarks and a thumbnail description of each cut. —*Ted Greenwald*

Onda Sonora: Red Hot & Lisbon / Jul. 20, 1999 / Bar/None ✦✦✦✦
The 12th album in the Red Hot Organization's compilation series, *Onda Sonora: Red Hot & Lisbon* is a musical travelogue of Portugal, Angola, Mozambique, Cape Verde, Goa, and Brazil. The album brings some of the finest musicians from those countries together with acts from the U.S. and the U.K., and features David Byrne and Caetano Veloso's collaboration "Dreamworld: Marco de Canaveses," k.d. lang's "Fado Hilario," and Antonio Chaino's "Variacoes Em Mi Menor," along with tracks by Madredeus, Arto Lindsay, and Durutti Column. As with the other albums in the *Red Hot* series, *Onda Sonora: Red Hot & Lisbon*'s proceeds go toward the Red Hot Organization's worldwide AIDS education and prevention efforts. —*Heather Phares*

☆ **Passion Sources** / Jan. 29, 1993 / Real World ✦✦✦✦✦
A superb sampler of passionate world music on Peter Gabriel's Real World label concentrates on Asia and Africa. —*Myles Boisen*

Putumayo Presents Romantica: Great Love Songs from Around the World / Jan. 13, 1998 / Putumayo ✦✦✦✦✦
If most labels decided to assemble a collection of romantic world music, they would tend to make obvious choices like Latin ballad singers Julio Iglesias and Jose Jose. But Putumayo has never been a label that inundates listeners with obvious choices, which is why its compilations are such an adventure. While everything on *Romantica* can be described as "romantic world music," the 11-song CD is hardly one-dimensional. Looking to Europe, Africa and Latin America, Putumayo provides everything from Greek music (Nikos Kypourgos' "The Gypsy Girl") and Scottish music (Dougie MacLean's "She Will Find Me") to caressing sounds from Brazil (Bella Velloso's "Toda Sexta-Feira"). If you need an example of how diverse African music is, just compare Ugandan singer Samite's pastoral, folk-influenced "Ngwino Rukundo" next to Sudanese vocalist Rasha's sexy and jazz-minded "Azara Alhai." Another real gem comes from Brazilian singer Fortuna, whose "Ay, Madre!" draws on Spanish and Middle Eastern music instead of modern Brazilian pop or samba. Boasting one surprise after another, *Romantica* is one of the many reasons why Putumayo is a name that all world music enthusiasts should be familiar with. —*Alex Henderson*

Putumayo Presents the Best of World, Vol. 1: World Vocal / 1993 / Rhino ✦✦✦✦
A compilation from Putumayo dealing primarily with vocal works, although much of the work is very instrumental as well. Appearing here are multiple stars of different traditions. The great Jorge Ben (famous in the U.S. primarily for "Mas Que Nada," popularized by Sergio Mendes) shows up to sing a song praising soccer great Pele. Miriam Makeba's "Pata Pata" is also present, a happy song about a dance. Johnny Clegg and Juluka (Savuka before the departure of Sipho Mchunu) contribute a wonderfully clear vocal work on "Walima 'Mbele," a warning against inter-tribal fighting during droughts in South Africa. The wonderful Samite of Uganda shows off his prowess on the kalimba in "Munomuno." Even the incredibly old Jolly Boys resurfaces from the tourist hotels of Jamaica to contribute a nice piece of mento (Jamaican calypso of sorts). To finish off the album, Costa Rican Jorge Strunz and Iranian Ardeshir Farah combine for a vaguely flamenco sound on "Americas," a song exhorting the masses to respect the native traditions of North and South America; and a love song from King Sunny Ade's former bass player Ken Okulolo and Kotoja. Overall, a surprising clear and well worked album from Putumayo, seeming to deal less with the mainstream Starbucks sound they tend to fall into from time to time. While it's labeled as a vocal album, the instrumental virtuosos here are really the highlight. Pick it up for an amazing run of guitars, kalimbas, and more. —*Adam Greenberg*

Rough Guide to World Music / Oct. 25, 1994 / World Music Network ✦✦✦✦✦
The Rough Guide to World Music is a sampler of sounds from across the globe—for newcomers to the complexities of worldbeat, it's an ideal way to taste-test the endless flavors the genre has to offer. Highlights include Buckwheat Zydeco's "Hot Tamale Baby," Oumou Sangare's "Dugu Kamelenba" and Etoile de Dakar's "Zaiko Wa Wa." —*Raymond McKinney*

Rough Guide to World Roots / Sep. 28, 1999 / World Music Network ✦✦✦✦
The Rough Guide to World Roots is a concise primer of many different types of world music, including African, Latin American and Eastern European styles. Some of the biggest names in world music are included in this compilation, including Natacha Atlas, whose "Marifnaash" showcases her North African/Arabian-inspired singing, Senegalese vocalist Baaba Maal, Hungarian vocalist Marta Sebestyen, Nusrat Fateh Ali Khan and the Afro-Cuban All Stars. Over the course of 14 tracks, *The Rough Guide To World Roots* delivers what its title promises: a solid grounding in some of the most popular and influential styles of contemporary world music. —*Heather Phares*

Secret Museum of Mankind: Ethnic Music Classics, Vol. 1 / 1995 / Yazoo ✦✦✦✦✦
World music recorded during the first half of the 20th century, once etched onto wax cylinders and brittle 78s, has been diligently rescued and revived for presentation on this, the first volume from *The Secret Museum of Mankind.* This CD opens with a late '30s recording of an alluring yet laid back performance by a Nigerian choral, organ, and drum ensemble. An impressive Sardinian launeddas (triple read pipe) solo rendered by an experienced player comes next. Circular breathing and lightning fast chops highlight the Herculean nature of this master musician's effort. Other noteworthy tracks on this CD include a rare '20s recording of Japan's serene Imperial Household Orchestra, a performance by Hindustani musicians that feature melodic clusters of suspended bells, a 1924 recording of a trombonist's "Jewish Jazz" band, and a Vietnamese string and vocal ensemble's graceful rendition of "Worthy Gem." The superb musicianship and creative approaches displayed on these varied recordings makes this CD a must-have for any real "world music" fan. —*John Vallier*

Secret Museum of Mankind: Ethnic Music Classics, Vol. 2 / Oct. 1995 / Yazoo ✦✦✦✦✦
Volume Two of *The Secret Museum of Mankind: Ethnic Music Classics, 1925-48* is a diverse collection of old and rare international musical recordings. Opening with an all male choral bellow from a 1930s New Caledonian group, this CD jumps to a Bulgarian rachinitza, a lyrical Puerto Rican aguinaldo that's usually associated with Christmas festivities, and a Hindustani vocal display by a jamming scholar. The rest of the CD continues along in a similarly adventurous way, presenting early 20th century recordings from Turkish, Sri Lankan, Ukranian, Algerian, and Tibetan cultures, to name but a few. Of particular note is a recording of a Sundanese group. The wailing sounds of the Javanese rebab (a single stringed spiked fiddle) and the suling (bamboo flute) provide a wafting backdrop for the ether-like vocals of the group's singer, Miss Narem. From another island nation, Trinidad, comes the CD's upbeat ninth track, "Old Time Cat-O'-Nine." Backed up by his band The Tiger, Lord Invader attempts to persuade his fellow citizens to send the country's hooligans off to another island, Carrera Prison. In short, *Volume Two* is yet another interesting and great sounding contribution to *The Secret Museum's* set of old real "world music" recordings. —John Vallier

The Secret Museum of Mankind: Ethnic Music Classics, Vol. 3 / 1996 / Yazoo ✦✦✦✦
Volume Three is another eclectic sampling of vintage "ethnic" recordings taken from the storerooms at *The Secret Museum of Mankind.* A Rhodesian hymn of praise precedes a 1948 recording of an Uzbeki diva, while the serpentine melodic lines of a Greek clarinetist follows the contemplative resonance of a 1939 solo performance on the Chinese qin or chin (a plucked zither). Though one may think that the enormous musical breath of the CD might make listening to it a scattered and unsatisfactory experience, this is not the case. The historical context within these works presented—worldwide recordings made between 1925 and 1948—give this and the other Secret Museum works a cohesion that allows for disparate musical examples to be placed side by side. All in all, this CD gives the listener a window into another time, when recording technology was young and Western popular music had not invaded every corner of the globe. —*John Vallier*

Secret Museum of Mankind: Ethnic Music Classics, Vol. 4 / Feb. 18, 1997 / Yazoo ✦✦✦✦
This fourth volume is yet another solid contribution from *The Secret Museum of Mankind.* Once again, long forgotten 78s have been salvaged from oblivion, dusted off, and digitally remastered onto CDs by the museum's industrious staff. This release, not unlike the others in this series, is comprised of selections that span a vast spectrum of musical and cultural genres. The first track features a Swedish herder calling her flock with a high-pitched croon that must have penetrated the deep Scandinavian forests with ease. A track from Pakistan displays a mesmerizing fusion of the Scottish war-pipes, a North Indian melodic sensibility, and Hindustani percussion. Captivating examples of Brazilian, Egyptian, Bolivian, Italian, Turkish, Hungarian, Albanian, Serbian, Kuwaiti, and Balinese music help round out the remaining 22 cuts. All in all, this CD brings together variance and difference in a format that allows any listener (not just an ethnomusicologist) the chance to appreciate nearly forgotten world musics. —*John Vallier*

Squeeze Play: A World Accordion Anthology / Jan. 1997 / Rounder ✦✦✦✦✦
Archivist Dick Spottswood does his usually excellent job unearthing vintage world music nuggets on this collection of accordion tunes from around the world. Highlights include a couple of klezmer pieces from 1920, two plaintive Romanian tunes from 1927, San Antonio's Trio Huracan on 1938's "Corrido de los Caminoeros" (Song of the Bus Drivers), and the legendary conjunto star Santiago Jimenez, Sr. doing the lively polka "La Piedrera." Spottswood also lincludes tracks that, in effect, downplay the accordion, such as a Polish goralski highlander ensemble recording of "Kumotersko," where accordionist Joe Pat is just audible under violins and string bass, and Joseph Dingaan's "Nonyembezi," a South African piece from 1954 which features a harmonica playing in accordion style. You'll also find rare Acadian French and Scottish sessions on this wonderful collection. —*Bob Tarte*

Trance 1 / 1995 / Ellipsis Arts ✦✦✦
In intensive exploration of the methods and meanings of the trance state, this superb CD/book package begins with an extraordinary 27-minute Sufi dervish invocation, Sadreddin Ozcimi's vertiginous ney (flute) solo over a deliberate, repetitive accompaniment of frame drums and oud that modulates into ever higher realms—until, inexplicably, it simply fades out. So much for the trance! Not to worry. Next comes 25 minutes of Tibetan Buddhist chanting from the Shartse Dratsang Garden Monestary in India. This is a recording to savor at high volume; when the bronze trumpets and shawms suddenly roll in, the effect is more apocalyptic than trance-inducing. Leave it to 24 minutes of dhrupad, an ancient vocal style of Indian devotional music, finally to put you under. Against a backdrop of sweetly droning tanpura, Ustad N. Zahiruddin Dagar and F. Wasifuddin Dagar probe the selected raga with supreme authority. The 64-page book's topflight text, illustrations, and design are the hallmark of the Musical Expeditions series. —*Ted Greenwald*

Trance 2 / 1995 / Ellipsis Arts ✦✦✦
Less musically consistent than *Trance 1,* this set extends its predecessor's focus to rituals of healing and possession. Naqshbandi sufis of Turkestan, distantly miked in a dead hall, make for something less than mystical communion. A women's healing ceremony by the Halima Chedli Ensemble, unflaggingly propelled by a typically kinetic Moroccan beat, fares better but can't quite sustain 12 minutes of play. Things pick up with a substantially more varied African song performed in Marrakesh by the Abdenbi Binizi Ensemble. The concluding Balinese selection, a montage of gamelan percussion orchestra and chant, is

fascinating in its restless gathering and dispersal of energy, particularly during the middle vocal section; one wishes producer David Lewiston had stuck with a single striking piece of music rather than crossfading from one to the next. The text, which dutifully emphasizes the spiritual goals of trance before diving breathlessly into outlandish practices such as "self stabbing," is bound in a sumptuous 64-page book-cum-CD jacket. —*Ted Greenwald*

Unwired: The Rough Guide to Acoustic Music from Around the World / May 25, 1999 / World Music Network ♦♦♦♦

Although its focus is acoustic-oriented world music, *Unwired* doesn't limit itself to traditional sounds—in fact, much of the compilation consists of contemporary, even cutting-edge pop from various continents. Covering a lot of territory, this excellent CD take us to various parts of Africa with selections by Toumani Diabate and Baaba Maal, as well as to Spain with Duquende's "Lo Bueno y lo Malo" (an appealing example of the type of nuevo flamenco that has been the rage in Spain since the 1970s), and to Latin America with Argentinean tango vocalist Adriana Varela's dramatic "La Casita de Mis Viejos" and Colombian vallenato artist Maximo Jimenez's "Vuelo en Libelula." (Quite different from cumbia, vallenato is an exuberant, accordion-based style that comes from Colombia's Atlantic coast.) India is represented by Shivkumar Sharma and Hariprasad Chaurasia's "Love," while instrumental Finnish folk is represented by the all-female quintet Niekku's "Yski Ruusu." One of the best songs on the album is Sudanese singer Rasha's "Azara Al Hay," a haunting, jazz-influenced gem. Not the least bit predictable, *Unwired* is well worth obtaining. —*Alex Henderson*

Voices of Forgotten Worlds: Traditional Music of Indigenous Peoples / 1993 / Ellipsis Arts ♦♦♦♦♦

Concentrating on vocal traditions, the two-disc set Voices of Forgotten Worlds delivers cut after cut of wonderful music, frequently in stunning high-fidelity recordings. Producer Brook Wentz' sensitive sequencing minimizes the inevitable discontinuity from one cut to the next. The only flaws would seem to be unavoidable with such a diverse and wide-ranging collection: Individual pieces are too short, and they bear no real relation to one another. Things get off to a rousing start with a Tuvan (south Siberian) song in which the singers form a melody of whistling overtones that careens above their voices. From there the set skips through Japanese, South American, Northern European, Chinese, South Seas, and Australian examples before settling into an insistent Afghan ghazal and a glorious instrumental Newar celebration from Nepal. Performances from Greenland, Mexico, and Azerbaijan give way to the surprising choral singing of the Maori of New Zealand, which seems to bend local tradition with harmonies learned from church hymns. Among the more familiar patterned bells of the Balinese gamelan and otherworldly chanting of Tibetan monks, unique highlights include a hypnotic pan pipe ensemble from the Solomon Islands; a surprisingly gentle chant from the Kayapo (notoriously warlike denizens of the Amazon jungle); a compelling rapid-fire pulse of drums, bells, and a double reed from the Batak people of Sumatra; and a Wodaabe chorus from Niger, whose sinuous, irregular vocal phrases suddenly take form with the addition of hand claps. Rather than displaying various traditions as artifacts to be studied, Ellipsis Arts presents them as music to be enjoyed, an approach that has borne fruit in several of the label's top-notch collections. —*Ted Greenwald*

REGGAE

"Reggae music is boring; it all sounds the same."

Those are fighting words in the torpid back alleys of Kingston, because nowhere on the face of the earth is there more recorded output per capita than on this Isle of Springs, where literally hundreds of 7-inch singles are released each week, in a staggering variety of styles. It started as the '60s dawned, when steamy-hot and ripe-for-revolution JA was about to oust its British master, and the music (ska) drove the engine of change—double-time, frenetic, and as unyielding as a fully loaded cane truck on a hairpin turn. Ska turned to the half-time lope of rock-steady for a couple of years, producing some of the most lyrical and lasting musical mementos of the century, songs of freedom that will be chanted by sufferers I-ternally. Then reggae burst on the scene in 1968, and the world has never stopped listening.

Reggae is as close to a universal music as this receding century has—with superstars like Bob Marley, Peter Tosh, Jimmy Cliff, Toots and the Maytals, and other touring pioneers; with the cult classic movie "The Harder They Come" and a soundtrack that has never stopped selling; with the success of the annual Sunsplash extravaganzas in Montego Bay and their touring counterparts from Japan, Europe, and North America; and with major American labels turning gold and platinum with artists such as Ziggy Marley and Shabba Ranks.

Check it! Maori, Tongan, and Fiji Islanders put aside age-old battles to form a reggae band called Herbs; a Japanese boy toasts (raps) in the rattle-blasted patter of a Kingston speed-rapper; Havasupai Indians at the foot of the Grand Canyon regard Marley as a prophet and display his picture in their homes; Poland's top ethnic fiddler joins a Twinkle Brother for a Polski hoedown/dub showdown, while at the shipyards in Gdansk, 10,000 people (most in red, gold, and green clothing) cheer an eight-hour reggae festival; and Aboriginals form a protest group whose chosen rhythm of resistance is reggae, calling themselves No Fixed Address. Reggae is triumphant, the irresistible heartbeat call to consciousness, the call of the LA rioters—"No Justice, No Peace!"

It is a call that can be as deep and spooky as a bad dream; as lopey and leering as Red Foxx after hours; ethereal and eternal—the true new Psalms; as understated as a pause and as robust as a rocket. This is the music of the Movement of Jah People, future folk who know God is a living man and paradise is right here right now. It is Jah love made manifest, not fe de weakheart, and definitely not boring. *—Roger M. Steffens*

Artist Reviews

The Abyssinians

Group / Roots Reggae, Dub

The Abyssinians recorded their first single, *Satta Massa Gana* at Clement Dodd's Studio One in 1969, though by 1971 they had their own label, Clinch. The trio of vocalists, brothers Lynford and Donald Manning and Bernard Collins were a defining force in the roots reggae close harmony singing style. To make this move, they veered away from the American soul music origins and added a more stately, religious aspect to the sound. Their debut album in 1976, *Forward On To Zion* reprised a few of their earlier cuts for various studios. The group only released a few albums before leaving the fold of "small axes" and broke into two separate groups of Abyssinians—one led by Bernard Collins, and one led by the Manning Brothers, which is the current state of the group(s). *—Adam Greenberg*

● **Forward** / 1982 / Alligator ✦✦✦✦✦

"Satta" and other hymns for the hearticle are included. *—Roger Steffens*

Satta Massagana / 1993 / Heartbeat ✦✦✦

This is one of those legendary reggae albums that's easier to admire than enjoy. There's no doubt of its importance: if you had to pick the five most influential Rasta anthems of the 1970s (and Jah knows there have been few if any since then), the title track of this album would be one of them. So, most likely, would "Declaration of Rights," which has been remade in countless different versions. And the Abyssinians themselves are a fine vocal trio. If they're not as sweet-sounding as the Mighty Diamonds, and not as tight and compelling as the Heptones, they do have a fierce and intense spirituality that is pretty compelling in its own right. But all that said, this is an album that takes some time and adjustment to enjoy. For one thing, every single song is taken at exactly the same tempo. Reggae is a music that is built on subtle differentiation (or, as philistines and Babylonians might say, it all tends to sound the same), and that means that it's important to sow a little variety wherever you can. It's also true that the group's spiritual intensity sometimes leads the harmonies to, shall we say, wander in the wilderness a bit. But the deep religious conviction of the songs and singers, as well as that unchanging, loping, serene groove, will begin to draw you in after a few listens. *—Rick Anderson*

Declaration of Dub / 1998 / Heartbeat ✦✦✦✦

The long-awaited *Declaration of Dub* is the dubwise companion to the Abyssinians' classic album *Satta Massagana*, an archetypal roots-reggae document featuring nothing but the deepest, darkest and dreadest riddims churning beneath the supernal trio harmonies of Bernard Collins, Donald Manning and Lynford Manning; the lyrics are all standard Rastafarian fare, dealing with African repatriation, sociopolitical observations and the goodness of Jah. The dub version focuses on the instrumental grooves, while the group's vocals float wispily in and out of the mix. Though the title track is presented here in an unnecessarily slick-sounding "New Version," most of the tracks benefit greatly from the attention of Karl Pitterson and Bunny Tom Tom, who strip the instrumental tracks down to their essential elements, isolating and fortifying the groove. This is an outstanding dub album and should be considered an essential part of any roots reggae collection. *—Rick Anderson*

Laurel Aitken (Lorenzo Aitken)

b. 1927

Vocals / Roots Reggae, Mento, Calypso, Lovers Rock, Ska

Though born in Cuba, Laurel Aitken played a pivotal role in helping break Jamaican music internationally. He moved to Jamaica from Cuba in the '50s, then came to England in the '60s. Aitken's recording "Boogie in My Bones" was the first Jamaican single issued in England in 1958. Aitken's debut Bluebeat label release "Boogey Rock" was released two years later. More importantly, his evolution from an imitative R&B vocalist to a premier ska and reggae singer influenced many ska, bluebeat and reggae vocalists. Aitken recorded hundreds of singles, ranging from incendiary protest to sentimental romance and crass sexual innuendo. He continued performing with his band The Full Circle well into the '80s. *—Ron Wynn*

● **Rasta Man Power** / 1992 / ROIR ✦✦✦✦✦

Blue Beat Years / Jan. 30, 1996 / Moon ✦✦✦✦

Laurel Aitken was born in Cuba, raised in Jamaica, and emigrated to England in the 1960s, where he helped fuel the first British ska craze. His recordings on the Blue Beat label spawned an entire ska subgenre, and this new album finds him revisiting the music of his youth without a hint of age or fatigue in his voice. The material is old but the performances are new—backed by the cream of London's third-wave ska musicians, Aitken delivers the goods with remakes of the songs that made him famous back in the '60s, as well as several from the early '80s; there are such bluebeat classics as "Little Sheila" and "Boogie in My Bones," as well as the classic rudeboy anthem "Rudi Wedding." The band crackles and pops, and Aitken sings with the energy of a 20-year-old. This album is a solid winner from a ska master. *—Rick Anderson*

The Pioneer of Jamaican Music, Vol.1 / Jul. 24, 2000 / Reggae Retro ✦✦✦✦✦

This Laurel Aitken disc provides something of an audio tour of early Jamaican music history. Covering the years 1957-1966, the selections take in the island's popular musical styles of the period, including calypso, mento (Jamaican folk music with calypso strains), Jamaican R&B, and ska. A mix of calypso and mento numbers kicks things off, some including hand drums and proto-Rastafarian lyrics inspired by Jamaica's popular gospel revival churches ("Mas Charlie (Prisoner Song)," "Nebuchadnezzar"). The topical bent of calypso is well represented too, with songs covering both politics ("Ghana Independence (They Got It)") and sports ("West Indian Cricket Test"). Aitken indulges in several Jamaican R&B numbers in the middle of the disc, showing how island musicians turned the U.S. R&B beat inside out; standout tracks in this style include "Going Back to Kansas City" and "Mash Potato Boogie." Also in the R&B vein are gospel tunes like "Judgement Day" and "I Believe," the latter featuring an infectious New Orleans shuffle-blues beat. The last third of the program is dedicated to some excellent ska, including such standouts as "We Shall Overcome," the joyously manic "Green Banana," and "Bachelor Life" ("A life without a wife is like a kitchen without a knife"). Contributing to the fine musical backing heard throughout are tenor saxophonists Val Bennett and Stanley Ribbs, guitarist Ernest Ranglin, and trombonist Rico Rodriguez. This is a great title for students and fans of early Jamaican music. For listeners expecting a program of just ska and/or rocksteady, though, the good number of calypso and R&B tunes here might be a turn off. *—Stephen Cook*

Dennis Alcapone

b. Aug. 6, 1947, Clarendon, Jamaica

Vocals, DJ / Ska

Dennis Smith (aka Dennis Alcapone) became a dominant toaster/DJ during the early '70s, using a similiar style to U-Roy, though not as fast nor as clever. Alcapone worked with such top producers including Prince Tony and Keith Hudson. Alcapone also recorded for many labels including Studio One and Treasure Isle. Alcapone's popularity began to dip when toasters praising Jah and decrying political, social and moral injustices began winning the audience's hearts and minds rather than those doing comedic and novelty tunes. Alcapone moved to England, but also found the going there tough. Despite teaming with Bunny Lee on such records as "Investigator Rock" and "Six Million Dollar Man," Alcapone was a non-factor by the end of the '70s. *—Ron Wynn*

● **Universal Rockers** / 1992 / RAS ✦✦✦✦
Toaster/DJ Dennis Alcapone was at his humorous, barbed and bizarre best on this collection of 1970s material. His style was often a near mirror imitation of Big Youth's, but he was also at his performing peak during this period. *—Ron Wynn*

My Voice Is Insured for Half a Million Dollars / 2000 / Trojan ✦✦✦✦
Consisting of tracks recorded between 1970 and 1973, when the young DJ was at the peak of his popularity, this album remains the single best summation of Dennis Alcapone's art. It's true that his style owed a deep debt to U Roy, but he managed to improve on his lyricism and melodic interest; although Alcapone was primarily a "chatter" in the established tradition, he frequently lapsed into singing and was also known for his strange whoops and yelps. *My Voice* has been reissued by Trojan before, but this issue ups the ante considerably by adding ten bonus tracks to the original program. Highlights are numerous and include the spectacular "Musical Alphabet," "Joe Frazier Round 2" (which continues a popular topic for DJs of the period), and most of all, his brilliant DJ cuts on the Ethiopians' classic "Selah" (titled "Rocking to Ethiopia") and Augustus Pablo's deathless instrumental "Java" ("Mava"). Of course, he's helped considerably by the consistently high quality of the rhythm tracks, which came to him courtesy of such top producers as Duke Reid, Winston "Niney" Holness, and Bunny Lee. This album should be considered an essential part of any serious reggae collection. *—Rick Anderson*

Roland Alphonso

b. Jan. 12, 1931, Havana, Cuba, **d.** Nov. 20, 1998
Sax (Tenor), Flute / Roots Reggae, Calypso, Rocksteady, Ska
Saxophonist Roland Alphonso was one of the major figures of early ska and reggae on several fronts: his recordings as a soloist and bandleader, his work as a member of the Skatalites, his prolific log of session appearances on 1960s Jamaican recordings, and his role as arranger for Studio One. Although his roots were in the jazz he played as a teenager and young man, he adapted to the emerging Jamaican popular music so well that he became one of its defining innovators. Certainly he was one of reggae's most accomplished instrumentalists; while many horns on ska and rock steady discs of the 1960s are off-key or whiny, Alphonso's tone was in a league with American jazzmen and R&B players, and his versatility allowed for a wide scope of recorded material. In the early '60s, Alphonso pioneered the ska sound on instrumentals that matched R&B and boogie influences from the States with the clipped, quick rhythms of Jamaica. Around the end of 1963, he teamed with several other top Jamaican musicians to form the Skatalites, the most important ska instrumental band. The Skatalites broke up in August 1965, but Alphonso continued to play and record, either as a part of prominent bands or under his own name. In the early '70s, he suffered a stroke at the age of 41; he was able to recover pretty quickly, however, moving to the United States at the end of 1972 and soon returning to performing and recording. The Skatalites re-formed for the first time in 1983, and in the '80s and '90s received far more international acclaim than they had in their mid-'60s heyday. Alphonso suffered a burst blood vessel in his head during a Skatalites show in Hollywood in November 1998 and died after another burst vessel a few weeks later. *—Richie Unterberger*

★ **Something Special: Ska Hot Shots** / Jul. 18, 2000 / Heartbeat ✦✦✦✦✦
No single compilation could fairly represent the breadth of Alphonso's career—so often did he record as a solo artist, bandleader, band member, and session musician. This, however, is an excellent 20-song retrospective of vintage sides from 1958-68 released largely under his own name; if they weren't, they were by groups in which Alphonso was the leader or principal player. Actually, he recorded in a staggering variety of guises, and this anthology includes cuts that were billed to Roland Alphonso & the Alley Cats, Roland Alphonso & the Studio One Orchestra, Roland Alphonso & the Soul Brothers, just the Soul Brothers, Rolando & His Group, Soul Vendors, Clue J & His Blues Blasters, Rolando & the Sharks, and so on... you get the picture. The important thing is that these are exciting, seminal ska and reggae instrumentals, with styles traversing ska roots to rock steady and soul-influenced reggae. There's more variety to be heard here than with almost any other single-artist ska compilation—from ska takes on spy movie themes and witty novelties like "Rollie Pollie" to the cooking "Do It Good" (which is as close to early American funk-soul as it is to reggae). Alphonso plays imaginative, jazzy sax throughout, and unlike many of the ska brassmen, was not prone to a wobbly or out-of-tune squeak. Among the dozens of other musicians heard on this collection are numerous major ska-reggae figures: Tommy McCook, Rico Rodriquez, Ernest Ranglin, Rita Marley, Clement Dodd, Jackie Mittoo, and even Lee Perry. The liner notes, recording and release dates, and session personnel are amazingly comprehensive for an early reggae reissue. Three of the songs were previously unreleased. *—Richie Unterberger*

Reggae Sax / Rohit ✦✦✦
Tasty jazz-tinged sax solos and smart, aggressive playing highlight this collection spotlighting one of Jamaica's premier studio musicians. *—Ron Wynn*

Bob Andy

Vocals / Rocksteady, Ska
Bob Andy (born: Keith Anderson) is one of reggae's most influential songwriters. His late-60s hits, including "Going Home", "Unchained", "Feeling Soul", "My Time", "The Ghetto Stays In The Mind" and "Feel The Feeling", and his 1992 hit, "Fire Burning", have become reggae standards and have been covered numerous times. Andy first attracted attention as the lead vocalist of mid-'60s reggae band, The Paragons. His apex as a solo artist came in the late-60s when he recorded a string of singles for Coxsone Dodd's Studio One. In 1988, these singles were compiled on an album, "*The Bob Andy Songbook*". During the early-'70s, Andy teamed with Marcia Griffiths to record several tunes, including the U.K. hits, "Young, Gifted And Black" and "Pied Piper". as a duo, Bob and Marcia. In 1978, Andy took a five year long sabbatical from music to concentrate on his career as an actor. Andy's 1988 album, *Freely*, recorded in London and Jamaica, was re-issued in 1997. The same year, he released an all-new album, *Hangin' Tough*, produced by Willie Lindo. *—Craig Harris*

● **Retrospective** / 1986 / Heartbeat ✦✦✦✦✦
A fine overview of a sorely overlooked reggae vocalist, composer, arranger, and session singer. *—Ron Wynn*

Song Book / 1988 / Studio One ✦✦✦✦✦
These are among Coxsone Dodd's most important albums ever, with virtually every cut a classic. *—Roger Steffens*

Horace Andy (Horace Hinds)

b. Feb. 19, 1951, Kingston, Jamaica
Vocals / Smooth Reggae, Roots Reggae, Dub, Lovers Rock
Although he has one of the most distinctive voices in reggae music, Horace Andy, despite considerable exposure in the early '90s as a guest vocalist with British trip-hoppers Massive Attack, is venerated primarily by hardcore reggae aficionados. Andy came on the reggae scene as part of the second generation of great singers, following in the footsteps of seminal reggae vocalists such as Ken Boothe, John Holt, and Delroy Wilson. What separated him from that group and virtually all Jamaican male vocalists of the early '70s was his clear, powerful, high tenor voice. With the ability to shift from sultry croon to full-throated wail (not unlike, say, Al Green), as well as his delicately impeccable phrasing, Andy could be positively stunning. In the early '70s he was one of the most in-demand vocalists on the island, recording great sides for Bunny Lee. Given the latitude needed to craft his own records by subsequent producer Everton DaSilva, Andy recorded his signature work, *In the Light*, in 1977. He continued recording throughout the '80s, but remained an obscure figure until he was asked in 1990 to contribute vocals to Massive Attack's brilliant debut *Blue Lines*. Ecstatic with the results, the group asked him back for two subsequent albums. Andy continued to make solo records as well, including a tribute LP to Bob Marley. *—John Dougan*

● **In the Light/In the Light Dub** / 1995 / Blood & Fire ✦✦✦✦✦
The difference between an essential reggae reissue and a craven ripoff usually comes down to two things: sound and packaging. This two-for-one reissue of Horace Andy's *In the Light* album (which includes dub mixes of all the original album's songs) is a classic example of the Blood & Fire label's loving devotion to both sonic and cosmetic detail. The sound is phenomenal; modern ears jaded by years of direct-from-vinyl remastering will be stunned by the clarity, definition, and sonic depth of these recordings. Andy himself is at the top of his form through most of the album, though not on all tracks; he'd have done better to leave the lover's rock stuff for someone else, and "Do You Love My Music" and "Fever" are far from essential. But he's at his best on such cultural roots excursions as "Leave Rasta" and "In the Light," and in that genre he has few peers. His all-star backing band includes Leroy Sibbles, Horsemouth Wallace, and even Augustus Pablo on keyboards. Solidly recommended overall, with minor reservations. *—Rick Anderson*

Skylarking / Mar. 25, 1997 / Caroline ✦✦✦✦✦

Good Vibes (1975-1979) / Jul. 1, 1997 / Blood & Fire ✦✦✦✦
Horace Andy, an enormously popular reggae singer in the 1970s, enjoyed a resurgence of popularity in the late '90s, due in part to his extensive work with the British band Massive Attack. This has led, thankfully, to massive reissues of his earlier work, of which this is one of the better examples. Each of the ten tracks is presented in "discomix" style: The normal, vocal version comes first, and then segues seamlessly into the dub version. Those who have found his recent solo work under the aegis of Mad Professor to be a bit bloodless and overproduced will find this collection of 1970s singles refreshing. It starts out slow, with a disappointing piece of meta-reggae—reggae songs about how wonderful reggae is are rarely revelatory—but things pick up quickly with "Serious Thing" and the inevitable "Skylarking," and the momentum stays strong up to the end. Andy's high, almost girlish voice and weird vibrato may be an acquired taste for some, but he's worth the effort. *—Rick Anderson*

Living in the Flood / Feb. 29, 2000 / Astralwerks ✦✦✦✦

Wicked Dem a Burn: Best of Horace Andy / Jan. 23, 2001 / Varese ✦✦✦✦✦

Aswad

f. 1975, United Kingdom
Group / Roots Reggae
Despite a series of dramatic fluctuations in popularity, the reggae trio Aswad is one of Britain's most enduring and many say, greatest roots band. The group had a unique sound comprised of jazz/funk, soul, and fusion layered over a rock steady reggae beat. Over the latter part of the '70s through the '80s, Aswad underwent many stylistic changes. The group had great early success with such tunes as "Back to Africa," "Three Babylon" and "Warrior Child." Their first eponymous album was far more jazz-oriented than their second album, *Hulet*. Critics were not thrilled by the group, considering them pale imitations of real reggae music, despite the fact that they still had a large devoted fan base. By the early '80s, they had signed to CBS and released *New Chapter* (1982). The following year's *New Chapter on Dub*, released on the independent Mango label, sold even more copies than the original. With no commercial breakthrough in sight, they reverted to their original style and returned to their old haunts, recording such early dancehall tunes as "Bubblin'" and "Kool Noh." The strategy eventually worked and gave Aswad a number one hit in 1988 with "Don't Turn Around." Though they have yet to re-enter the British Top Ten, they continue to perform and record. In 1994 they released the self-produced *Rise and Shine*. *—Sandra Brennan*

Aswad / 1976 / Mango ✦✦✦

New Chapter / 1981 / Columbia ✦✦✦✦✦
Aswad made its debut on Columbia's British division with this release. It marked a musical shift as keyboardist Tony Gad (also known as Tony Robinson) moved to bass, replacing the

departed George Oban. The songs were well produced and exuberantly performed, while there was a good mix between fiery uptempo tunes and passionate love songs. *—Ron Wynn*

Live and Direct / 1983 / Mango ♦♦♦

Crucial Tracks: The Best of Aswad / 1989 / Mango ♦♦♦♦♦

● **Roots Rocking: The Island Anthology** / Mar. 11, 1997 / Island ♦♦♦♦♦
Aswad is a rarity among reggae groups—one that started out relatively weak and got better as it incorporated more pop and soul influences into its sound. The band's albums of the '70s were primarily roots reggae of the blandest sort: two-chord vamps loping along beneath negligible melodies and by-the-numbers Rastafarian lyrics. By contrast, Aswad's chart-topping version of "Don't Turn Around," released in 1989 after the band had hardened and slicked up its sound, remains the group's biggest hit and arguably the best single it ever produced. This retrospective collection presents a nice two-disc précis of the band's work from its earliest albums until it jumped labels around 1990. Disc One is certainly not bad—while there is little exceptional material to be found (and the worst of it, such as the embarrassingly atonal "Rainbow Culture," should clearly have stayed out of print), there are moments of real musical and spiritual uplift, including a live version of "Not Satisfied" and the dubwise excursions on "Three Babylon" and "It's Not Our Wish." But Disc Two is the payoff. The band's sound is tough, lean and modern, though still well grounded in Rasta roots and culture. "Don't Turn Around" shows up in a 12″ version, as do such other gems as "Don't Get Weary," "Gimme the Dub" and a surprisingly attractive version of the '70s soft-rock potboiler "On and On." This set is very nice overall, and probably represents everything most people need to hear from Aswad's earlier years. *—Rick Anderson*

Roots Revival / Jun. 29, 1999 / Ark 21 ♦♦♦♦
Roots Revival is an apt title for this album, since Aswad's greatest successes have been as a pop-reggae crossover band, most notably with the huge 1988 hit "Don't Turn Around." On this one the group returns to its roots with a vengeance. The sound is still pretty slick, but the material includes a remake of Ken Boothe's rocksteady classic "Freedom Street," two seldom-covered Bob Marley tunes ("Caution" and "Thank You Lord"), a decent cover of the Police's "Invisible Sun" (featuring Sting in a guest appearance), and a bunch of relatively roots-wise new originals. The only remaining members of the band, Drummie Zeb and Tony Gad still have a great melodic sense, as evidenced on the smooth and silky "Follow '99" and the churning "Breakout." But the rhythms are deep and compelling as well, resulting in a sound that will move them in the dancehall even as it pleases more roots-oriented fans. *—Rick Anderson*

Badawai

DJ / Dub
Badawai was born Raz Mesinai in 1973 in Jerusalem. By spending a lot of time with Bedouins in the Sinai desert as a youngster, he picked up on their unique musical style. When he reached the age of seven, he was taken under the wing of dervish sheik Murshid Hassan (of the Palestinian refugee camp of Balata), who taught the youngster all about exotic Middle Eastern drumming. Soon he had mastered such percussive instruments as the bendir, zarb, and darbukka. He also discovered spirituality along the way, following the Hasidic rabbi and folk musician Harav Shlomo Carlebach. After moving to New York City, he found himself emerced in the burgeoning NYC Academy of Underground DJs (which included DJ Spooky and a host of others), and changed his name to Badawai (which means "desert dweller," or simply "Bedouin"). By utilizing home recording technology, he recorded his debut for ROIR, *Presents Bedouin Sound Clash*, which was released in 1996. A year later, the more experimental (but just as good) *Jerusalem Under Fire* surfaced, which confirmed him as one of the best dub/reggae DJs of the late '90s. *—Greg Prato*

● **Presents Bedouin Sound Clash** / 1996 / ROIR ♦♦♦♦♦
Recorded entirely in a basement studio on a four-track recorder with a multivox echo chamber, percussionist/dub master Badawi creates quite a stir on his ROIR debut, *Presents Bedouin Sound Clash*. Unlike his future release, 1997's *Jerusalem Under Fire*, this is not an instrumental affair, due to the aid of vocalist/lyricist Honeychild. But it does share the same approach, which is to create an original and irresistible new musical style with its combination of reggae rhythms and exotic percussion from the Middle East. This consistent collection of originals would sound perfect in a cavernous dance hall, with bass-heavy rhythms that instantly bring to mind dub legends such as Lee "Scratch" Perry and the Mad Professor. *—Greg Prato*

Jerusalem Under Fire / Sep. 16, 1997 / ROIR ♦♦♦♦♦
Due to releases like *Jerusalem Under Fire*, Israeli percussionist Badawai (real name Raz Mesinai) has become one of the world's most renowned Middle Eastern percussionists. He's become an influential figure for the New York City trip-hop (or illbient) style of underground dancehall/dub music, a scene that has spawned the likes of DJ Spooky, DJ Olive, and a host of others. Amazingly, almost all the sounds you hear on *Jerusalem Under Fire* are played by Badawai himself, who handles percussion, flute, and effects duties, as well as supplying the string arrangements and remixing and rearranging the songs. Two other musicians (violinist Simi Sernaker and tabla player Karsh Kale) help fill out the already rich sound, while all of the compositions are entirely instrumental. Highlights are many, but the very best would have to be the constant violin swirl of "Soldier of Midian," and the percussion-driven opening track "Critical Combustion," and the traditional reggae sounds of "Kill the Messenger." *—Greg Prato*

Buju Banton

b. 1973, Jamaica
Vocals / Roots Reggae, Dancehall
During the early '90s young dancehall deejay Buju Banton exemplified almost everything that many critics hated about ragga music. Perhaps realizing that his negative music would not find a great market outside the Jamaican context, or perhaps just having matured, he has undergone a gradual but tremendous transformation since his early releases. After becoming a Rastafarian, his music developed a new social consciousness and was more about love rather than sex. He began performing as a sound-system deejay at age 13, began recording soon after, and released his first album in 1992. Though his harsh, sexually explicit lyrics seemed to encourage nihilism and violence, Banton became one of Jamaica's biggest dancehall acts with several chart toppers that included such singles as "Bogle" and "Love Me Browning/Love Black Woman." In 1995, a new Banton released the album *'til Shiloh* and changed the face of dancehall music, bringing back a studio band complete with horns. "Murderer," released as a single in 1994, was a powerful condemnation of exploitational sex, gun culture and violence in dancehall music. *Inna Heights* followed in 1997. *—Sandra Brennan*

Mr. Mention / 1993 / Penthouse ♦♦♦
This set concentrates on love and romance, with Banton's ideas falling into the arch-traditional vein on such songs as "Love Black Woman," "Love How The Gal Dem Flex" and "Love Me Brownin." While he avoids the easy vulgarity that plagues several of his comrades, Banton's heavy-voiced quips lack the flexibility, speed, tonal color or creativity of several top toasters, and he seldom discusses anything other than his sexual desires or abilities, except his proficiency on the microphone. Within that limited universe, a couple of the CD's cuts are interesting. But thus far, it's hard to understand why he's so popular based on the content of his recordings. *—Ron Wynn*

Voice of Jamaica / 1993 / Mercury ♦♦♦
Growling, gravelly-voiced toaster Buju Banton's recent Mercury release contains entertaining slack material, such as "Good Body" and "Willy (Don't Be Silly)," and respectable social commentary with "Deportees (Things Change)" and "No Respect." But Banton is not that creative or imaginative a wordsmith, and once the delivery wears thin, the lightness of his sentiments becomes acute. The single "A Little More Time" features a great, soulful vocal from the criminally underrated Beres Hammond. For the most part, this is competently produced and performed major-label dancehall. *—Ron Wynn*

● **'til Shiloh** / 1995 / Loos Cannon ♦♦♦♦♦
'Til Shiloh displays a more mature songwriter than that of its predecessor, *Voice of Jamaica*. On *'Til Shiloh*, Banton explores a variety of subjects, ranging from social commentary and Rastafarian culture to love songs. Similarly, the music is diverse, taking in dancehall, ska, and reggae, as well as an acoustic number, "Untold Stories," that strongly suggests Bob Marley's "Redemption Song." Throughout the record, Buju Banton justifies his position as one of the leading reggae stars of the mid-'90s. *—Stephen Thomas Erlewine*

Inna Heights / Nov. 18, 1997 / VP ♦♦♦♦
Buju Banton continues to grow on *Inna Heights*, adding depth, tradition and true feeling to the occasionally shallow genre of dancehall reggae. Occasionally he falls prey to ragga conventions, but on the whole, the album has a laidback, organic groove that is considerably appealing. And when Toots Hibbert appears for a storming version of his classic "54-46 Was My Number," it becomes clear that Banton has more heart, depth and grit than most of his peers. *—Leo Stanley*

Unchained Spirit / Aug. 22, 2000 / Epitaph ♦♦♦♦♦

Pato Banton

Vocals, Producer / Ragga
Birmingham, England reggae singer/toaster Pato Banton (born Patrick Murray) made his debut on the English Beat's third album, 1982's *Special Beat Service*, helping out Ranking Roger on the track "Pato and Roger a Go Talk." Five years later, Banton returned with his debut solo release, *Never Give In*, which featured backing by Birmingham's Studio Two house band and a guest appearance by Paul Shaffer; the album was enlivened by Banton's comic vocal characterizations. An EP featuring several versions of the *Never Give In* track "Pato and Roger Come Again" (another duet with Ranking Roger) appeared in 1988, followed the next year by the full-length *Visions of the World*, which found Banton moving towards a poppier soul/reggae approach. 1990's *Wize Up! (No Compromize)* contained Banton's first American college radio hit, a cover of the Police's "Spirits in the Material World," as well as a duet with Steel Pulse's David Hinds on the title track. After a dub collaboration with the Mad Professor (*Mad Professor Recaptures Pato Banton*) and a live album (*Live and Kickin' All Over America*), Banton recorded *Universal Love* in 1992. It took him a while to come up with brand new material afterwards; he finally resurfaced in 1994 with a version of Eddy Grant's "Baby Come Back" performed with Robin and Ali Campbell of UB40, which hit the British charts and prompted the best-of *Collections*. Banton finally delivered a full album of new material in 1996 with *Stay Positive*. *Life Is a Miracle* followed in the spring of 2000. *—Steve Huey*

● **Wize Up! (No Compromize)** / 1990 / IRS ♦♦♦♦♦

Universal Love / Jul. 1992 / IRS ♦♦♦
A seriously infectious outing from Pato Banton, one of Birmingham, England's crowd of reggae performers. Most of the music here was performed by Banton with very few others involved—the "friends" part of it comes in the vocal area, which sees him working with David Largie, Ranking Roger, Ray Watts, Macca B and Yasmin Alexander. The album is full of good songs and good rhythms, not to mention a great attitude—even the obligatory rap track is interesting. Altogether, a very positive and enjoyable release with some excellent songs. *—Steven McDonald*

Life Is a Miracle / Apr. 4, 2000 / Hollywood ♦♦♦
Once again, it's time to party with Pato. "Sweet Reggae Music" is the soundtrack song for his life. Banton says "Life Is a Miracle," fueled by the endangered "Mama Nature" and her beloved herb. "Legalize It!" and "United We Stand!" yells the artist. Banton's heart is in the right place, but we've heard these exact messages over and over since the Wailers brought reggae to the masses outside of Jamaica. The lyrics may inspire you, but creative they're not. If you just want to dance, then Pato has done his job. *—Mark Morgenstein*

Beenie Man (Moses Davis)

b. 1972, Kingston, Jamaica
Vocals, DJ / Ragga, Dancehall
Ragga deejay Beenie Man has been burning up dancehalls and the Jamaican singles charts since he was seven years old. As a singer, he is known for his unusually flexible voice, which over the years has developed just the right amount of rawness without losing the qualities that made it musical. He was just about nine when he had his first number one Jamaican single ("Too Fancy"), though his career stalled during his teenage years until his songs took a more radical turn. About this time he and fellow deejay Bounty Killer began a well-publicized rivalry, with each accusing the other of stealing his style. He really hit the big time in 1995 with the monster international hit "Slam." Since then, Beenie Man, always a prolific recording artist, has continued his ride at the top. In concert, he and his Blaze Band are known for interacting directly with the audience. By 1997, Beenie Man was ready to release his fourth album, *Many Moods of Moses; Rough & Tough* followed a year later, and he returned in 1999 with *Ruff 'n' Tuff*. *—Sandra Brennan*

● **Blessed** / 1995 / Island Jamaica ✦✦✦✦✦
Beenie Man's first international album *Blessed* proves that why the young reggae star is one of the most popular ambassadors of dancehall in the world. Featuring hit singles like "World Dance" and "Blessed," the album is an infectious, danceable collection that never makes any deep lyrical statements—even though Beenie Man does make a couple of stabs at philosophical and political insights on a couple of songs—but is carried by a set of deep bass grooves and Beenie Man's dynamic charisma. *—Stephen Thomas Erlewine*

Maestro / Dec. 10, 1996 / VP ✦✦✦✦
Reggae DJ Beenie Man recruits producers Sly & Robbie, Aiden Jones and the Shocking Vibes Crew for *Maestro,* which includes duets with Lady Saw ("Long Longi Lala"), Silver Cat ("Oh Jah Jah") and Little Kirk ("Nuh Lock"). *—Jason Ankeny*

Many Moods of Moses / Dec. 9, 1997 / VP ✦✦✦
Since *Many Moods of Moses* contains a high proportion of singles, it's predictably quite a strong outing for Beenie Man, featuring Jamaican hits like "Oysters and Conch," "Bad Man," "Foundation," and "Who Am I." Beenie Man also duets with the likes of Lady Saw, Little Kirk, and Buju Banton. *—Steve Huey*

Ruff 'N' Tuff / Apr. 6, 1999 / Varese ✦✦✦✦

Doctor / May 18, 1999 / VP ✦✦✦

Y2K / Sep. 14, 1999 / Artists Only ✦✦✦
Produced by King Jammy's, Beenie Man's salute to Y2K doesn't really include any tracks dealing with the millennium bug. Instead, the dancehall veteran takes on social causes ("Illiterate Girl, " "AIDS Veteran") with his irresistible delivery and chants. Leroy Sibbles guests on one of the highlights, "Feel Good." *—Keith Farley*

Art & Life / Jul. 11, 2000 / Virgin ✦✦✦

Big Youth

b. Apr. 19, 1949, Jamaica
Vocals, Percussion, DJ / Contemporary Reggae, DJ
Though most would call long-time toaster Big Youth a DJ, he prefers to think of himself as an "inspirator," one who calls his audiences towards a higher Jah consciousness of love, clean living, and commitment to building society up rather than tearing it down with slackness and violence. During the early '70s, he was the most popular toaster in Jamaica. He got his start working with the Mightyness Emperor Lord Tippertone sound system located on Princess Street in Kingston at night while working by day as a porter. He then worked for a time with Gregory Isaacs and Jimmy Rodway and first gained notice singing on Errol Dunkley's "Movie Star" and "The Black Cinderella" during the early '70s. Producer Keith Hudson gave Big Youth his first two hits including a tribute to the current fad for Honda S. 90 motorcycles, "S.90 Skank." With Hudson, Big Youth recorded a number of successful songs. At one point he had seven simultaneous chart entries with five of them in the Top Ten. His style and uplifting message inspired many subsequent artists, including Bob Marley, who in turn called Big Youth his favorite toaster. *—Sandra Brennan*

Screaming Target / 1973 / Trojan ✦✦✦✦✦
Excellent toasts and fine instrumental versions of reggae classics by Dennis Brown, Gregory Isaacs, and others. *—Ron Wynn*

★ **Natty Cultural Dread** / 1976 / Trojan ✦✦✦✦✦
A definitive early-period album from this reggae toaster. A must for every reggae lover. *—Michael G. Nastos*

Everyday Skank: The Best of Big Youth / 1980 / Trojan ✦✦✦✦✦
A tremendous anthology containing early, out-of-print singles and album cuts. *—Ron Wynn*

Live at Reggae Sunsplash / 1984 / Sunsplash ✦✦✦
High-energy live performances of Big Youth's greatest hits are backed by The Soul Syndicate. *—Roger Steffens*

Black Uhuru

f. 1974, Jamaica
Group / Roots Reggae, Dub
By 1992, Black Uhuru (Black Sounds of Freedom) had gone through six distinct incarnations, the only common factor being Duckie Simpson, their dreadly serious harmonist and sometime composer. Founded in the mid-'70s, the group hit its key period in the early '80s with a charismatically scowling lead singer named Michael Rose, who remade his classic "Dreadlocks Coming . . ." as "Guess Who's Coming to Dinner." A fearsome prowler onstage with a Far East style of roots warbling, Rose was often touted as the "next Bob Marley," an observation that has ruined the career of many a lesser performer. The militancy of the group was enhanced by an African-American woman with a Master's degree from Columbia University, Puma Jones, whose wavy-armed dancing and high, chromatic harmonies echoed the communal gatherings she had witnessed while working in Mama Africa. Add to this the essential underpinnings of rhythm twins Sly & Robbie, who were considered equal members of the group while Rose was aboard, and you have the quintessential reggae lineup of the post-Marley era and reggae's first-ever Grammy winners. *—Roger Steffens*

☆ **Sinsemilla** / 1980 / Mango ✦✦✦✦✦
An outstanding set that helped break them in the States. *—Ron Wynn*

Black Sounds of Freedom / 1981 / Shanachie ✦✦✦✦
Formed in 1974, Black Uhuru had been recording singles exclusively when the trio joined forces with the highly regarded reggae producer Prince Jammy for its debut album, *Black Sounds Of Freedom* (originally titled *Love Crisis*). Although not quite in a class with subsequent treasures like 1981's *Red* and 1982's *Chill Out,* this engaging date (which Shanachie reissued on CD in 1990) is has all of Uhuru's trademarks—haunting themes, addictive grooves and deeply spiritual lyrics based on the Rastafarian faith. Longtime followers of the group (whose 1977 lineup included Michael Rose, Errol Nelson and original member Duckie Simpson) will be more than familiar with such heartfelt classics as "I Love King Selassie," "African Love" and "Satan Army Band." These songs point to the fact that in 1977, Uhuru was well on its way to becoming the reggae powerhouse it would be in the '80s. *—Alex Henderson*

Guess Who's Coming to Dinner / 1981 / Heartbeat ✦✦✦
Generally acknowledged to be Black Uhuru's masterpiece as well as one of the defining documents of roots reggae, *Guess Who's Coming to Dinner* (originally released on the Taxi label under the title *Showcase*) was the first album to feature singer Puma Jones as a member of the group's vocal trio lineup, and it was also their first with Sly Dunbar and Robbie Shakespeare. These additions gave the group a tremendous lift: Jones' keening, almost North African-inflected voice became an instantly identifiable part of Black Uhuru's sound, and the chugging rhythms supplied by Dunbar and Shakespeare were the perfect instrumental accompaniment. True to its original title, this collection of singles and new tracks is presented in "showcase" style; each track is followed without pause by a dub version. "Leaving to Zion" and "General Penitentiary" are typical of Black Uhuru's lyrical concerns, and lead singer Michael Rose's sharp tenor voice and wordless ululations convey a sense of dark foreboding; on "Guess Who's Coming to Dinner" he sounds like a muezzin calling the faithful to prayer and repentance. Highly recommended. *—Rick Anderson*

★ **Red** / 1981 / Mango ✦✦✦✦✦
The sophomore release from the third and most successful incarnation of Black Uhuru (singers Don Carlos, Erroll "Jay" Wilson, and Rudolph "Garth" Dennis had come before), *Red* spotlights the singing talents of then rising star Michael Rose, American-born Sandra "Puma" Jones, and original member Derrick "Duckie" Simpson. Backed by the tight and dancehall-era defining Sly & Robbie band, the trio reels off eight high-quality reggae cuts here, including classics like "Youth of Eglington" and "Sponji Reggae." Filled with Rose's astute lyrics, the album provides an engaging blend of steppers rhythms and social commentary. Sly & Robbie's ingenious mix of sophisticated roots reggae and a variety of modern touches (synthesizers, electronic drums) not only brought Black Uhuru widespread fame but, along with Henry "Junjo" Lawes and Prince Jammy's contemporary productions, also helped define the slicked-up last stand of roots rhythms in the first half of the '80s, while foreshadowing reggae's coming digital age. A very enjoyable listen, recommended along with other fine offerings by the band like *Chill Out* and the Grammy-winning *Anthem*. *—Stephen Cook*

Chill Out / Dec. 1982 / Mango ✦✦✦✦✦
Superb Sly & Robbie backing—dark, haunting, and bare. *—Roger Steffens*

Anthem / 1983 / Mango ✦✦✦

Brutal / 1986 / RAS ✦✦✦
Black Uhuru's late-'80s trio didn't garner as much crossover attention or publicity as earlier editions, but were equally outstanding from a content and performance standpoint. While Sly Dunbar and Robbie Shakespeare's production embraced the computerized mode, Junior Reid's lead vocals were as dynamic and explosive as those of former lead singer Michael Rose, and the occasional leads and sparkling harmonies of Puma Jones and Ducky Simpson were expertly incorporated into the mix. *Brutal* included strong message tracks, good love/romantic fare and a fine spiritual number, "Dread In the Mountain." *—Ron Wynn*

Brutal Dub / 1986 / RAS ✦✦✦

Now / 1990 / Mesa Blue Moon ✦✦✦

Iron Storm / 1991 / Mesa Blue Moon ✦✦✦

★ **Liberation: The Island Anthology** / Sep. 21, 1993 / Mango ✦✦✦✦✦
During the band's heyday in the late 1970s and early 1980s, Black Uhuru was one of the most unique and influential reggae bands in the world. This was partly due to their distinctive vocal sound—which was dominated by the keening wail of Michael Rose and the haunting harmonies of American expatriate Puma Jones—but in large part it was also due to their backing band, which was led by the legendary drum-and-bass duo of Sly Dunbar and Robbie Shakespeare and was one of the few that could challenge the Wailers in terms of telepathic tightness and sheer rhythmic wallop. *Liberation* goes one better than most retrospective compilations: instead of simply collecting two discs' worth of previously released singles and selected album tracks, it takes familiar songs (such as the anthemic "I Love King Selassie" and the apocalyptic "Guess Who's Coming to Dinner") and presents them in live versions, early mixes, 12" "showcase" versions (wherein the dub mix follows without a break on the heels of the vocal mix), etc. Little of this material is actually rare, and a good chunk of it actually does consist of standard singles and album tracks. But the rarities are plentiful enough to please fans, while the two-disc program is comprehensive enough to serve as a fine overview for beginners. Highlights abound, but they particularly include the showcase version of "Darkness" and the 12" mix of "Sponji Reggae." Excellent. *—Rick Anderson*

Ras Portraits / Jun. 24, 1997 / RAS ✦✦✦✦

Ultimate Collection / Mar. 14, 2000 / Hip-O ✦✦✦✦✦
This generous compilation isn't really a career retrospective, since it focuses almost exclusively on Black Uhuru's years on the Island label. However, it does take several tracks from the group's Greensleeves and RAS catalog and a Joe Gibbs single version of "Rent Man." What it all boils down to is an overview of the trio when it consisted of Michael Rose, Derrick Simpson, and Puma Jones, which is generally considered to be the classic Black Uhuru lineup (Rose is replaced by Junior Reid on two tracks). Fans will have most of this material already, of course, but for the uninitiated this is a good an overview as one could imagine—all of the most important songs are here, from the inevitable "I Love King Selassie" to "Youth of Eglington" (paired with its dub version from the *Dub Factor* collection). "Guess Who's Coming to Dinner" is mixed in showcase style, but with a dubwise appendix that differs significantly from the one on Heartbeat's *Showcase* album. "What Is Life—" and "Try It" are both presented in their original Jamaican mixes. No track is less than worthwhile, and some of them are among the finest reggae ever recorded. *—Rick Anderson*

Alpha Blondy

b. Jan. 1, 1953, Dimbokora, Cote d'Ivoire
Vocals / Contemporary Reggae, Reggae-Pop, World Fusion
Hailing from the Cote d'Ivoire, Alpha Blondy is among the world's most popular reggae artists. With his 12-piece band Solar System, Blondy offers a reggae beat with a distinctive African cast. Calling himself an African Rasta, Blondy creates Jah-centered anthems promoting morality, love, peace and social consciousness. With a range that moves from sensitivity to rage over injustice, much of Blondy's music empathizes with the impoverished and those on society's fringe. Blondy is also a staunch supporter of African unity and to this end, he sings to Moslem audiencess in Hebrew and sings in Arabic to Israelis. Blondy got his big break from friend Fulgence Kass, an employee of Ivory Coast Television who helped him land a spot on the *Premiere Chance* talent show. Singing three of his own tunes plus Burning Spear's "Christopher Columbus," the young artist was a hit with the audience. Blondy then hooked up with producer G. Benson who recorded his eight-song debut album *Jah Love* in a single day. The most popular song, "Brigadier Sabari," was an account of Blondy's run-in with an Abidjan police street raid in which he was nearly beaten to death. It was the first time a West African artist had dared to mention random police brutality in public. After releasing the album, he and the newly formed Solar System band signed to EMI. They recorded his second album *Cocody Rock* in Paris in 1984. By the release of his 1987 album *Revolution,* Blondy had established himself as an international artist.. *—Sandra Brennan*

Cocody Rock!!! / 1984 / Shanachie ✦✦✦
Alpha Blondy's 1983 first album, a smash hit featuring an all-local band the Natty Rebels, had all the accessibility and directness that made him an international star. Two cuts are agreeable reggae in English; the rest is Afro-reggae and a lot more interesting for that. In some ways Blondy's music is typical of the Ivory Coast: light, accomplished, and geared to a regional rather than local audience. Though the notes don't tell you so, *Cocody Rock* is a re-release of Blondy's 1984 second album, recorded in Paris and Kingston with a mix of African and Jamaican musicians (plus Kassav's Jocelyne Beroard on backup vocals). Pre-superstar Blondy, it has the freshness you'd expect from somebody pretty much just starting out. He sure believes in touching all the bases. Besides its so-so title song, *Cocody Rock* has something for both Muslims and Christians as well as a hilarious cut claiming Ivory Coast's ultra-conservative president as a Rasta. *—John Storm Roberts*

Jah Glory / 1985 / Moya ✦✦✦✦✦
A dynamic early 80s album with Blondy establishing his sound and style. It hasn't yet been released on a US label. *—Ron Wynn*

Apartheid Is Nazism / 1987 / Shanachie ✦✦✦✦✦
While it might be sacrilege in reggae circles to say that any artist could challenge Bob Marley's mastery of the genre, Alpha Blondy fires a dead-on shot literally heard around the world with *Apartheid Is Nazism.* Furthermore, this work proves that great reggae does not have to come from Jamaica. "Afriki" opens the album with a nod to Jamaica, but while the music is classic, offbeat reggae, there is a strong African feel here, especially in the backing vocals. On every track, the carefully arranged and smartly played music of Blondy's band, the Solar System, tickles the ears with muscular polyrhythms and a variety of stealthily intoxicating percussion. Maneuvering skillfully on top of all of this is Blondy's uniquely plaintive voice. Blondy, like many reggae stars before him, tackles political issues with a dagger wit and thundering bass lines. The title track, one of only two songs sung predominantly in English, pleads for America to "break the neck of this apartheid." Like the patois in which Blondy makes his incantations, his religious message is more mixed than the standard reggae paeans to Jah Rastafari. With tracks like "Come Back Jesus" and "Jah Houphouet" on the same album, it's clear that Blondy is attempting to strike a universal theme in the same way Marley did. While Blondy's career can't measure up to Marley when taken as a whole, *Apartheid Is Nazism* can stand up to most Marley releases. *—Matthew Hilburn*

Revolution / 1987 / Shanachie ✦✦

The Prophets / 1989 / Capitol ✦✦✦✦✦
Blondy's first international release under a new worldwide contract with EMI is as soulful and militant as past efforts, with an added gloss to the production that may win new listeners. *—J. Poet*

● **The Best of Alpha Blondy** / 1990 / Shanachie ✦✦✦✦✦
This disc lives up to its title with hits like "Jerusalem, " "Cocody Rock, " and "Apartheid Is Nazism." *—J. Poet*

Yitzhak Rabin / Aug. 18, 1998 / Lightyear ✦✦✦✦✦
Alpha Blondy storms back with his best release since *Apartheid Is Nazism.* Nothing much has changed stylistically for Blondy, as he is still able to pound out throbbing, international reggae laced with sharp messages of peace, love, and universality. Perhaps in an attempt to avoid some of the experimental failures which plagued other albums, *Yitzhak Rabin* was recorded at the Tuff Gong studios in Kingston, Jamaica and accompanying vocals were provided by I-Three. "Saraka" is an immediate standout complete with characteristically majestic horns, a feral flute hook, and, of course, Blondy and the I-Threes' mellifluous vocals. These same elements combine seamlessly throughout the entire album and leave great music in their wake. "Bakoroni" and "Les Imbeciles" are other great examples of Blondy at his best. Even the weak ballad "Les Armes de Therese" is saved by Blondy's gritty vocals. While *Yitzhak Rabin* can't be considered a step forward for Blondy, it is a graceful step back to what made him an international star. *—Matthew Hilburn*

Ken Boothe

b. 1948, Kingston, Jamaica
Vocals / Roots Reggae, Rocksteady
Legendary producer Coxsone Dodd dubbed Ken Boothe "Mr. Rock Steady" in the mid-'60s and this hard-belting crooner had some of that genre's biggest hits. His career has spanned the past 30 years, in a style rooted in the Jamaican fundamentalism called "pocomania" and mixed with a touch of Otis Redding. His cover of Bread's "Everything I Own" hit number one on the U.K. pop charts in the mid-'70s. He got his start at age 15 when Dodd paired him up with Stranger Cole to form the ska-beat duo Stranger and Ken. They had some success, most notably the songs "World's Fair" and "All Your Friends." It was when rock-steady music evolved that Boothe really found his niche. Still working with Dodd, he had major local hits with "Just Another Girl," and "Moving Away." In the early '70s, he hooked up with producer Lloyd Charmers and became popular in both Jamaica and the U.K. With a smooth, at times sentimental style (it has also been compared to that of Wilson Pickett) that appealed to a wide audience ranging from young teens, to the more conservative, older middle-class Jamaicans, Boothe is credited with helping reggae music gain acceptance as a valid style. *—Roger Steffans & Sandra Brennan*

Everything I Own / 1974 / Trojan ✦✦✦✦✦

● **Live Good** / 1978 / United Artists ✦✦✦✦✦
Coxsone sessions include the hits "Moving Away, " "Live Good, " and "Thinking." *—Roger Steffens*

A Man and His Hits / Aug. 10, 1999 / Heartbeat ✦✦✦✦
Ken Boothe's *The Man and His Hits* features chart-topping reggae songs like "You're No Good," "Thinking," "Without Love" and "The Train Is Coming," which he recorded with the Wailers. This collection also includes many classic sides for the Studio One label that make their debut on CD here. *—Heather Phares*

Born Jamericans

Group / Ragga, Club/Dance, Dancehall, Hip-Hop
Fusing hip-hop and dancehall reggae, Born Jamericans earned a cult following with their pair of mid-'90s albums. The duo was comprised of Mr. Notch, who favored smooth vocals, and Edley Shine, who delivered rough ragga raps. Born Jamericans' debut album, *Kids From Foreign,* became a reggae hit upon its 1994 release, and they became a favorite of the reggae circuit, opening for Buju Banton, Shabba Ranks, Zhane and Shai, among many others. Mad Lion, Shinehead and Johnny Osbourne all were featured on the group's second album *Yardcore,* which was released in the spring of 1995. *—Stephen Thomas Erlewine*

● **Kids from Foreign** / 1994 / Delicious Vinyl ✦✦✦✦
Although the duo occasionally falls prey to style over substance, Born Jamericans' debut, *Kids from Foreign,* is an impressive collection of street-oriented hip-hop and dancehall reggae, highlighted by the singles "Boom Shak-A-Tack" and "Cease & Seckle." *—Leo Stanley*

Yardcore / May 27, 1997 / Delicious Vinyl ✦✦✦
While most hip-hop/reggae hybrids feature endless streams of lyrics indistinguishable to those not familiar with the dialect, Born Jamericans slow up the beat and infuse the style with lover's rock. The result is a rather seductive album of mellow grooves and sensual lyrics that leans much closer to the sounds of Jimmy Cliff than that of Buju Banton. High points include "State of Shock," which features Johnny Osbourne, and the cover of Frankie Avalon's "Venus." Even though the style gets a bit long winded and the tracks tend to blur, there is still enough strong material on this album to make it worth listening to, and perhaps slow dancing to as well. *—Curtis Zimmermann*

Bounty Killer

b. Jun. 12, 1972
Vocals / Contemporary Reggae, Ragga, Dancehall
By the mid-'90s, much of the guntalk and slackness that characterized dancehall had been toned down (some of it forcibly by Kingston police authorized in 1994 to shut down sound systems continuing to promote guntalk) in favor of more upbeat socially conscious messages, but not for deejay Bounty Killer who continues to unapologetically fires off his white hot while rapid-fire gun rap and stands firm against those critics trying to shoot his music down. Born Rodney Price in Kingston, Bounty Killer began toasting with Trenchtown sound systems at age nine. Price took his original stage name, Bounty Hunter, in the early '90s around the time he recorded his first single at the King Jammy studio where he used to hang out. The single caught fire and soon they called him Bounty *Killer.* His career has closely paralleled that of his musical nemesis Beenie Man with whom he has had a notorious, well-publicized rivalry. Beenie swears that Bounty Killer has stolen his act, while B.K. asserts that Beenie is the real thief. True, both artists affect an uncannily similar style and choice of music, but whether any of the accusations have any merit remains unclear. Though still best known for songs promoting violence, it would be unfair to judge Bounty Killer solely on those terms, for in performance and even on his records, he demonstrates that he is capable of doing much more and actually sings about a variety of subjects, some of the slack and some earnestly socially conscious. Though not generally known, he is a strong defender of the poor (he himself grew up in poverty in the Seaview Gardens ghetto) and with little fanfare frequently donates large amounts of money to help rapidly decaying schools around

Kingston. As a singer, he is noted for his booming voice and extremely energetic performances. He crossed over to hip-hop territory in 1995 with his hit "Cellular Phone." Many of his earlier hits have since been re-mixed to hip-hop rhythms and rereleased. He has truly become one of Jamaica's hottest dancehall artists. In the mid '90s he was awarded an honorary doctorate by the students of the University of the West Indies. In 1996, he founded a production company, Scare Dem Productions, and his own label Pricele$$ Records. *The Next Millennium* followed in 1998, and a year later Bounty Killer returned with *The 5th Element*. *—Sandra Brennan*

● **My Xperience** / Sep. 17, 1996 / VP ✦✦✦✦✦
In the 1990s, Bounty Killer became one of the top figures in dancehall reggae, a form also associated with such Jamaican stars as Lt. Stitchie, Shabba Ranks and Ninjaman. In contrast to the melodic nature of mainstream reggae, *My Xperience* is an abrasive, rhythmic disc that has little use for melody. Those who aren't big dancehall fans may find the hip-hop-influenced CD hard to get into; those who are heavily into it will find a lot to admire on *My Xperience*, which contains major dancehall hits like "Living Dangerously" and "Virgin Island." A variety of guests join Bounty—everyone from the Fugees on "Hip-Hopera" to reggae singer Barrington Levy on "Living Dangerously" to hardcore rapper Jeru the Damaja on "Suicide Or Murder." Granted, dancehall has its limitations and can wear thin after awhile, but even so, *My Xperience* makes for an exhilarating listen. *—Alex Henderson*

Next Millennium / Nov. 3, 1998 / TVT ✦✦✦
In the 1990s, Bounty Killer was a prime example of someone who illustrated reggae's generation gap. Many 35-and-over Jamaicans expressed their disdain for his controversial gun talk and wondered why their kids didn't embrace "real" reggae like Desmond Dekker or Jimmy Cliff (just as many African-American baby boomers didn't understand why their kids would choose Ice Cube and Snoop Doggy Dogg over Smokey Robinson). But among younger Jamaicans (as well as post-baby boomers in the U.S. and Europe), he became an icon. Not as consistently hardcore as some of Bounty's previous releases, *Next Millennium* finds him liberally incorporating urban contemporary elements while continuing to bring a passion for hip-hop to his dancehall reggae foundation. Slick, urban contemporary-flavored tunes like "Reggae Party" (which features Third World and Shaggy), "It's a Party" and "A Love That's Real" are fairly commercial by Bounty's standards, but grittier, more hardcore offerings such as "Scare Dem Way," "Can't Believe Mi Eyes" and "Deadly Zone" (which features Queens rappers Mobb Deep) should dispel any notions that Bounty was trying to become a pop star. A varied and decent CD, *Millennium* allows Bounty to branch out without forgetting his dancehall roots. *—Alex Henderson*

The Best of Bounty Killer / Jan. 26, 1999 / Artists Only ✦✦✦✦

Brigadier Jerry

Vocals, DJ / Dub
Brigadier "Briggy" Jerry (Born: Robert Russell) is one of Jamaica's top dee-jays. Despite releasing only three albums in the two decades since he first attracted attention as a dee-jay for the U Roy-owned King Sturgav Hi Fi sound system, his live performances have made him one of Jamaica's most recognized performers. Brigadier Jerry, who joined the Twelve Tribes of Israel sound system in 1978, released his first single, "Love & Harmony," as a twelve inch disc the same year. His debut album, *Jamaica Jamaica*, released in 1985, featured a powerful rendition of the Bunny Wailer-penned tunes, "Armagideon" and "Everyman A Mi Breadren." Together with his family, Brigadier Jerry resided in New York from 1988 until 1991. His second album, *On The Road*, recorded with instrumental accompaniment by the Roots Radics and released in 1990, included the hits, "Jah Creation" and "Born To Love Jah." Brigadier Jerry's third album, *Hail Him*, released in 1993, included two hits—"Bangarang" and "Raggamuffin." In 1993, he performed with Charlie Chaplin and Sister Carol at *Club Quattro* in Tokyo, Japan. *—Craig Harris*

● **Jamaica Jamaica** / 1985 / RAS ✦✦✦✦✦
Toaster/DJ Brigadier Jerry moves from praise to political and dancehall tunes. The eight tracks include the lightweight throwaway "Three Blind Mice," more substantial "Kushunpeng" and "Armadiddeon Style," reverent "Jah Jah Move" and "Give Thanks And Praise" and the powerful "Everyman A Me Brethren." Jerry is a no-nonsense toaster who seldom does novelty numbers or emphasizes speed and verbal facility at the expense of his message. Only the set's brevity (less than 40 minutes) works against it, as it ends just when Brigadier Jerry has generated some momentum. *—Ron Wynn*

On the Road / 1990 / RAS ✦✦✦
Backed by the Roots Radics, longtime reggae DJ Brigadier Jerry grabs the microphone himself for *On the Road*. Mixing toasting and singing, Jerry tips his hat to Bob Marley, Nelson Mandela and Jah; his voice isn't startling, but it's enough to make this worth a listen. *—Jason Ankeny*

Dennis Brown

b. Feb. 1, 1957, Kingston, Jamaica, **d.** Jul. 1, 1999
Vocals / Smooth Reggae, Ragga, Dancehall, Lovers Rock
Dennis Brown had a long career as one of the top reggae singers in Jamaica. Bob Marley often cited his smooth voice as being one of his favorites. His partnership with producer Niney the Observer and rhythm wizards Sly and Robbie is captured on the budget priced Reggae Savers series from the Heartbeat label. "Can't Take Another Day," "My Heart Is an Open Book," "If I Gave My Love," and "Groovin" are only a small sampling from a vocalist with the ability to encapsulate dancehall or reggae with ease. *—Al Campbell*

Visions / 1977 / Shanachie ✦✦✦✦✦

Brown Sugar / 1986 / RAS ✦✦✦

Hold Tight / 1986 / Live & Learn ✦✦✦

Inseparable / 1988 / VP ✦✦✦✦✦

Unchallenged / 1990 / VP ✦✦✦✦✦

★ **Love & Hate: The Best of Dennis Brown** / Jul. 1996 / VP ✦✦✦✦✦
Love Hate: The Best of Dennis Brown is an adequate but incomplete retrospective of Brown's length career. Although it gives a fair representation of Brown's sound, it only includes a handful of hits like "Money in My Pocket" and omits a number of other important tracks. Nevertheless, the collection is useful as a starting point, even if it doesn't provide a definitive retrospective. *—Leo Stanley*

Ras Portraits / Jun. 24, 1997 / RAS ✦✦✦✦

The Prime of Dennis Brown / Oct. 20, 1998 / Music Club ✦✦✦✦
The ubiquitous Dennis Brown, one of reggae's most enduringly popular singers, is here represented by sixteen cuts from the Trojan Records vaults. The program is divided more or less evenly between his highly influential work in the early and mid-'70s and performances from the mid-1990s. His soft, mellow voice has changed little over the last twenty years, so what distinguishes the two periods is primarily the production quality of the backing tracks and the playing styles of the session musicians. Listen to the difference between this album's lead track, "The Closer I Get to You," with its digital keyboards and slick production, and the second track, the classic "Money in My Pocket," presented in a rougher mix with scrappy live instrumentation. Most of these tracks are classics, though there are a couple of poor choices, including a truly awful rendition of Bob Marley's "I'm Still Waiting." But the disc's midline price is more than enough to make up for the occasional clunker. *—Rick Anderson*

Tribulation / Jan. 12, 1999 / Heartbeat ✦✦✦✦
In the 1970s, the teenaged Dennis Brown was one of the most popular singers in Jamaica, a reggae artist generally referred to in the same breath as Gregory Isaacs (with whom, in fact, he collaborated from time to time) and Bob Marley. Dubbed the "Crown Prince of Reggae," Brown seems to be ageless; although his voice has mellowed somewhat with time, his more recent work has the same emotive power as his vintage recordings from reggae's golden age, and he continues to effortlessly combine cultural and religious themes with romantic pleas. *Tribulation* finds him teamed up with some of the top reggae session players around (notably the redoubtable Roots Radics, who sound at the top of their form here) on 16 new songs, all of them presented in the rootsy but contemporary style that has typified Brown's work since the 1980s. Highlights include the aching "Go On Now Girl," which is supported by a very fine computer bassline; the old-school throb of "Rougher Yet," and the more electronic "This Love of Mine." Alvin Ranglin's production is top-notch throughout. *—Rick Allen*

Stone Cold World / Sep. 21, 1999 / VP ✦✦✦✦✦
Stone Cold World stands as reggae legend Dennis Brown's last work before his death, and this in itself is enough to recommend this disc. Filled with Brown's slightly scratchy, emotional crooning, the 13 tracks showcase flawless examples of the classic reggae sound. As much a part of the foundation of reggae music as Bob Marley and producer Coxsone Dodd, he helped create the laid-back, uplifting style categorized as lovers rock and *Stone Cold World* shows why even after his death, few can top his widely imitated talent. The title tune serves up a good illustration of what made him so popular. The mid-tempo rhythm is complemented perfectly by Brown's strong, yet mellow vocals advising listeners, "it's a stone cold world/your freedom lies within." "Let's Start Something Serious Tonight" provides a rolling beat and sweet harmonies, and "This Morning" highlights the singer's flowing style. This is a fittingly solid last offering for a highly influential artist. *—Rosalind Cummings-Yeates*

Ultimate Collection / Mar. 7, 2000 / Hip-O ✦✦✦✦✦
The Ultimate Collection features 18 of Dennis Brown's greatest recordings, blending well-known hits with top-notch songs never before released in the United States. If the collection has a flaw, it's that it doesn't quite contain every one of the *most* essential Dennis Brown items ("The Promised Land" is one notable omission). But what is here makes for a fantastic testament to Brown's talents, as well as a fine introduction for newcomers. *—Steve Huey*

The Golden Years, 1974-1976 / Jul. 4, 2000 / Cleopatra ✦✦✦✦✦

Burning Spear

b. 1969
Vocals / Political Reggae, Dub
Winston Rodney took his stage name from Jomo Kenyatta, hero of Kenyan independence. The Spear, as he is called, first recorded in 1969 for Coxsone Dodd. Those productions, collected six years later on a pair of Studio One albums, were lean, mysterious, and way ahead of their time: a similar sound would sweep Jamaica in the late 70s and be dubbed the "Rockers" style. Eventually he returned in 1975 as part of a self-named trio for producer Jack Ruby. This time the world woke up, and Spear was recognized as a major figure. After two albums Spear dismissed his backing trio, journeyed to London, and cut one of the most astonishing live reggae sets ever for Island, for whom he recorded until 1980. Spear is one of those artists whose style is so immediately recognizable that those who like him from the start seem to have followed his every move with joy. He is similar to a trance singer, especially in his horn-lofted live performances, whirling around the stage with arms outstretched, a dreadlocked dervish chanting of dark carnal nights of captivity and imminent deliverance. Without question, Spear is one of reggae's greats. *—Roger Steffens*

★ **Marcus Garvey** / 1975 / Mango ✦✦✦✦✦
A reggae cornerstone, this is the most focused and musically exhilarating tribute to Marcus Garvey, a recurring theme in his music. *—John Floyd*

Man in the Hills / 1976 / Mango ✦✦✦✦✦
This nearly repeats the success of his debut, through a wide-ranging array of topics and a sturdy groove. *—John Floyd*

☆ **Live** / 1977 / Mango ✦✦✦✦✦
Aswad backs Spear's solo debut, one of reggae's greatest live sets ever. *—Roger Steffens*

Social Living / 1978 / Stop ✦✦✦✦

☆ **Harder Than the Best** / 1979 / Mango ✦✦✦✦✦
A magnificent career overview, it includes every highlight from Spear's canon, the best songs from otherwise turgid albums. *—John Floyd*

Hail H.I.M. / 1980 / Heartbeat ✦✦✦

Mek We Dweet / 1990 / Mango ✦✦✦✦
One of the finest and best-selling reggae singers of the 1970s, Burning Spear (aka Winston Rodney) successfully entered the 90s with *Mek We Dweet.* Though not quite on a par with such '70s gems as *Marcus Garvey* and *Man In The Hills, Dweet* proved that Spear could still deliver a thoroughly satisfying album. In contrast to reggae singers who, in 1990, were incorporating heavy doses of dancehall, Spear wisely sticks with the type of earthy, simple reggae that earned him so devoted a following in the '70s. Cuts like "Elephant," "Garvey" (one of his many odes to Marcus Garvey) and "My Roots" aren't much different from what Spear was doing 15 years earlier and leave no doubt that he was intent on remaining true to himself. *—Alex Henderson*

★ **Chant Down Babylon: The Island Anthology** / Jun. 18, 1996 / Island ✦✦✦✦✦
Spanning two compact discs and over 30 songs that cove his entire career at Island Records, *Chant Down Babylon: The Island Anthology* is the definitive Burning Spear collection, featuring all of his classic songs, plus a bevy of essential rarities, including 12-inch mixes and dub versions. While the original singles and album tracks are classics, the rare dub and 12-inch mixes are nearly as essential, since Burning Spear's dub mixes were as influential, if not more so, than the original versions. Since *Chant Down Babylon* showcases both sides of his talents, it is the definitive retrospective—it's a necessary item for any reggae library. *—Leo Stanley*

Calling Rastafari / Aug. 24, 1999 / Heartbeat ✦✦✦✦

Junior Byles

Vocals / Dub
Although not mentioned in the same breath with some of the other great voices in reggae (e.g., Winston "Burning Spear" Rodney, Toots Hibbert, and Culture's Joseph Hill), Junior Byles, whose best music was recorded over two decades ago, belongs in such lofty company. Sadly, what he is perhaps best remembered for is his unpredictable, bizarre behavior, the result of chronic depression—depression so severe that it saw his career go from the top of the Jamaican charts in the mid-'70s, to living on the streets, scavenging in dumpsters for food in the late '80s. Born Kerrie Byles, Jr. in Kingston, Jamaica in 1948, Byles grew up in a ghetto section of the city known as Jonestown. As a youth he began singing in the church, as well as imitating the vocal styles of his favorite reggae singers (the Maytals, the Wailers, and the Techniques) and American performers such as Ray Charles, Nat King Cole, and Johnny Cash. In the late '60s, Byles put together his own vocal group (based on the Maytals) called the Versatiles. While auditioning for a spot in the Kingston-based Festival Song Competition, the band came into contact with Lee "Scratch" Perry, who was looking for acts for his new label Amalgamated, owned by reggae legend Joe Gibbs. Impressed, Perry produced their first session, but soon left Amalgamated after an acrimonious split with Gibbs. After a year working with Gibbs, Byles and the other Versatiles were unhappy with the financial arrangements and sought out Perry. The group split up in 1970, and Byles embarked on a furiously creative period with Perry at the controls.

It was during this time with Perry at his Black Ark Studios that Byles recorded his signature song, "Curly Locks," as well as other Jamaican hits such as "Beat Down Babylon" and "Place Called Africa." The success for these records meant considerable profits for both Byles and Perry, and along with the early Perry-produced Bob Marley & the Wailers sides, solidified Black Ark's status as the hippest recording studio on the island. However, it was not long before Byles, as well as Perry, became more unpredictable in their behavior; Byles, especially, slipped into deep funks for extended periods, and was virtually incommunicado with friends and other musicians.

In 1975 Byles attempted suicide upon hearing of the death of Ethiopian emperor Haile Selassie (the earthly God of Rastafarians), and was hospitalized for mental illness. Although plagued by depression, he continued to record into the '80s, even after he was homeless and penniless. Song royalties never seemed to make their way to Byles, but did manage to line the pockets of unscrupulous producers and record label owners (Lee Perry is not in either category). And if living in abject poverty wasn't bad enough, in rapid succession Byles endured the death of his mother and the emigration of his wife and children to America. He released his last album, *Rasta No Pickpocket* in 1982; by the end of the 1980s it was not uncommon to see him begging for food in the streets of Kingston.

Although he hasn't released an album in over 15 years, Byles has recorded tracks with Winston "Niney the Observer" Holness. If there is anything remotely approaching a happy ending to this story, it is that Rounder Records, through its reggae label Heartbeat, released an anthology entitled *Curly Locks,* 22 tracks of Byles' best work, produced by Lee Perry. *—John Dougan*

● **Curly Locks: The Best of Junior Byles** / Feb. 11, 1997 / Heartbeat ✦✦✦✦✦
Not the complete recordings of Junior Byles by a long shot, but the best collection of his solo material currently on the market. All of the solo hits are here as well as a good amount of previously unreleased material and outtakes. The revelatory tracks include "A Place Called Africa" and "Informer Man" both of which show off the richness of Byles' voice and the astute and sympathetic production offered by Lee "Scratch" Perry. Roots/riddim singing in a fine style, this is where to go to get your first sampling of this vastly underrated reggae singer. *—John Dougan*

129 Beat Street: Ja-Man Special 1975-1978 / Sep. 15, 1998 / Blood & Fire ✦✦✦✦
A collection of four Junior Byles tracks from his post-Lee "Scratch" Perry era and seven tracks from lesser-known artists like Rupert Reid, Pablo Moses and others, *129 Beat Street* highlights some of the best cuts from the little-known House of Music studio operated by Dudley "Manzie" Swaby and Leroy "Bunny" Hollett. In addition to that unifying theme, all the classic roots tracks are held together by thumping bass, exquisite singing and strongly conscious Rastafarian messages. While most of the reggae from the same era came from such big name studios as Black Ark and Studio One, this compilation demonstrates that the supply of talent in Jamaica was extremely pervasive, as is clearly evident on standout tracks like "Chant Down Babylon," "See the Dread Deh" and "Remember Me." *—Matthew Hilburn*

Cornell Campbell

b. Jamaica
Vocals / Rocksteady, Ska, Soul
Perhaps best known for the series of "Gorgon rock" records he cut with legendary producer Bunny Lee, reggae singer Cornell Campbell was born in Jamaica in 1948. As a teen he recorded his first material for Studio One, cutting a series of ska sides both as a solo artist and as one half of a duo with Alan Martin; from 1964 to 1967, Campbell seemingly disappeared from the music business, however, finally resurfacing as a member of the short-lived rocksteady harmony trio the Uniques. As the decade ended, he helmed the Eternals, scoring a number of Studio One-generated hits including "Queen of the Minstrels" and "Stars," but in 1971 again went solo after teaming with Lee, a pairing which spotlighted Campbell's distinctive falsetto to stunning effect. Despite earning acclaim for a self-titled LP issued on Trojan two years later, in 1975 he shifted from the lovers rock sensibility of recent efforts toward the more explicitly rastafarian approach of records like "Natty Dread in a Greenwich Farm" and "Natural Fact," both of which emerged among his biggest hits to date. Later that year Campbell and Lee also launched "The Gorgon," a boastful smash which yielded a series of hit sequels. While 1977's "The Investigator" heralded a successful return to lovers rock, Campbell's commercial clout waned in the years to come, and in 1980 he and Lee parted ways; subsequent pairings with producers including Winston Riley, Niney the Observer and King Tubby failed to recreate the excitement of past sessions, however, and during the mid-1980s he slipped into retirement. *—Jason Ankeny*

I Shall Not Remove: 1975-1980 / Jan. 25, 2000 / Blood & Fire ✦✦✦✦
Most Blood & Fire releases should be considered essential purchases for any fan of golden-era reggae, but this one is even better than most. Cornell Campbell is one of the best reggae singers ever recorded—a sweet-toned falsettist with effortless intonation and a cool, assured delivery that is incredibly easy on the ear. The centerpiece of this collection is the three-part "Gorgon" series of singles produced by the legendary Bunny "Striker" Lee, all featuring the "flying cymbals" style of drumming popular at the time. "The Gorgon" having been a huge hit, it was followed quickly by "The Gorgon Speaks" and "The Conquering Gorgon," all three of which are presented here (the first two in extended versions, the second in its original version and then again in a Rastafarian variation titled "Lion of Judah"). Almost equally important, though, are "Natty Dread in a Greenwich Town" (an answer record to Bob Marley's "Natty Dread") and "Dance in a Greenwich Town," the latter in a megamix format that incorporates a deejay version by Dr. Alimantado and a dub version mixed by King Tubby. But really, just about every track reaches the same standard—there is not a single weak cut or boring moment on this spectacular album. *—Rick Anderson*

Capleton (Clifton Bailey)

b. Apr. 13, 1967
Vocals / Smooth Reggae, Contemporary Reggae, Roots Reggae, Reggae-Pop, Ragga, Club/Dance, Dancehall, Rocksteady
Jamaica's dancehall tradition was veered back towards its musical and Rastafarian roots by Peter Tosh-like vocalist Capleton (born: Clifton Bailey). A phenomenon at the 1990 Reggae Sunsplash, Capleton has gone on to become one of reggae's most successful vocalists with such dancehall hits as "No. 1 On the Look Good Chart," "Woman Mi Lotion" and the risque "Bumbo Red." Capleton's debut album, *Prophesy,* released in 1995, included the Caribbean Music Awards' single of the year, "Taxi."

Born in the small, farming, village of Islington in St. Mary, Capleton balanced his Rastafarian politics and spiritual commitment to Jah with his love of music from earliest memory. By the age of twelve, he was a veteran at sneaking into dances. Within six years, he moved to Kingston, seeking to make his mark as a vocalist. His first break came when he passed an audition for the cast of the Toronto cast of Stewart Brown's musical production, *African Star.* The show was such a success that, soon after returning to Jamaica, he was signed by reggae producer, Philip "Faddis" Burrell. Despite being banned from radio airplay for its suggestive lyrics, Capleton's first single, "Bumbo Red," became a dancehall hit and established him as an important new voice. *—Craig Harris*

Prophecy / Nov. 1995 / Def Jam ✦✦✦

I-Testament / Sep. 9, 1997 / Def Jam ✦✦✦

● **More Fire** / May 23, 2000 / VP ✦✦✦✦
From the very beginning, Capleton issued in a new era of conscious dancehall with his caustic, status quo-challenging lyrics, stirring up flames of controversy with every bellow of his thunderous vocals. *More Fire* continues the assault on Babylon with a tight package of sizzling beats and thought-provoking poetry. From the scorching riddims on "Danger Zone" to the wicked groove of "Who Dem?," this album guarantees non-stop dancing, as well as spiritual counsel, with tunes such as the anti-violence anthem "Jah Jah City" and "Good in Her Clothes," which offers praise for feminine modesty. On the opening track, "Fire Chant," Capleton explains, "Well, the fire is for purification and how can you fight fire?" If *More Fire* is any indication, listeners will have to admit defeat. *—Rosalind Cummings-Yeates*

Don Carlos

Vocals / Roots Reggae, Lovers Rock
Sweet-voiced vocalist and composer, Don Carlos (born: Euvin Spencer) has had his greatest success singing with Black Uhuru, the reggae trio he formed in 1974 with two friends—Rudolph Dennis and Derrick "Duckie" Simpson—from the "Waterhouse" district in Kingston. Carlos recorded only one single with the group, leaving to pursue a solo career and to perform with a band, Don Carlos And Gold. Sixteen years later he returned and joined

with Dennis and Simpson to resurrect the original trio. Their first album together, *Now,* released in 1990, helped Black Uhuru to recapture the popularity they enjoyed in the 1970s and '80s. Carlos involvement with the trio was brief. Shortly after helping Dennis and Simpson to record a second trio album, *Iron Storm,* Carlos resumed his solo career. While he's recorded some impressive albums, including his 1997 solo outing, *Seven Days A Week,* Carlos has yet to match the success he had with Black Uhuru. *—Craig Harris*

● **Just a Passing Glance** / 1972 / RAS ✦✦✦✦✦
One of reggae's finest "sweet" vocalists, Don Carlos's earnestness and sincerity overcome occasionally overwrought and sentimental material. He was more forceful on the message cuts. *—Ron Wynn*

Laser Beam / Jan. 25, 1995 / Culture Press ✦✦✦✦✦

Groove with Me / Apr. 27, 1999 / Orange Street ✦✦✦✦
One of the founding members of Black Uhuru, Don Carlos left to pursue a solo career in 1978, achieving significant success during the dancehall craze of the early 1980s. His singing style and lyrical focus, though, have always been somewhat at odds with the dancehall ethos—he's a roots singer at heart, and has always sounded most comfortable singing about justice and Rastafari. This collection consists of tracks Carlos recorded with producer Bunny Lee in the 1980s, using such stellar backing bands as the Aggrovators and Sly & Robbie's Revolutionaries. "Laser Beam" and "Spread Out" will be familiar to anyone who purchases reggae anthologies on a regular basis, but the stentorian "Johnnie Big Mouth" is less frequently heard, and the title track is always worth hearing again. There's also "Ababa John I," which is based on the timeless "Real Rock" rhythm. At 32 minutes the program is a bit skimpy, but what's here is all killer, no filler. *—Rick Anderson*

Day to Day Living / Greensleeves ✦✦✦✦✦
Featuring the excellent backing of the Roots Radics band, Don Carlos' *Day to Day Living* includes ten self-penned, sophisticated roots-reggae cuts. With his slightly hoarse yet sweet vocals, Carlos takes on his usual topical mix of spiritual/Rastafarian themes, ghetto life, and dancehall culture, showing the kind of lovers rock and roots lyric blend also favored by contemporaries like Gregory Isaacs and Dennis Brown. Musically, Carlos alternates between the dimly lit, minimalist drum'n'bass backdrops on "Street Life" and "Hog and Goat," and sunnier, bubbly organ and horn-driven cuts like "Hey Mr. Babylon" and "English Woman," with the updated rock-steady cut "I'm Not Crazy" standing out in particular. While producer Henry "Junjo" Lawes (Barrington Levy, Eek-A-Mouse) supplies the album's rugged but slick backdrop, Scientist delivers a spacious, dub-tinged mix. Special mention should also be made of Winston Wright's tasty organ work throughout the set, and "Flabba" Holt and "Style" Scott's rock-solid rhythmic support. As is the case with his *Harvest Time* record, *Day to Day Living* includes some of the best music Carlos released in the '80s. *—Stephen Cook*

Johnny Clarke

b. Jan. 1955, Jamaica
Vocals / Roots Reggae, Reggae-Pop
A contemporary of the great Horace Andy, Johnny Clarke, despite his relative obscurity, was at one time one of the most popular vocalists in Jamaica. In fact, in the mid-70s, while working with producer Bunny Lee, Clarke was considered to be the main act in Lee's stable of talent—more important than even Andy—although Clarke has not benefitted from the kind of career renaissance that Andy has. It was under Lee that Clarke recorded some of his best work usually at a fast and furious pace (such was the style of Lee and many other producers at the time). Clarke quickly became Lee's bread and butter act, no small feat considering that along with Clarke and Andy, Lee was also supervising the careers of Cornel Campbell, Derrick Morgan, and Linval Thompson. In the mid-70s, Clarke recorded some of his best work including songs such as "Cold I Up," the anti-violence ode "Too Much War," and a very funky cover of Little Anthony's "Tears on My Pillow." Into the 80s, still working with Lee, Clarke was still making the charts, usually the British charts, but his voice had lost none of its grace and suppleness. *—John Dougan*

Enter into His Gates / 1975 / Attack ✦✦✦✦✦
These mid-'70s tracks were mixed by virtuoso King Tubby. *—Roger Steffens*

● **20 Massive Hits** / 1985 / Striker Lee ✦✦✦✦✦
A superb and soulful vocalist, Johnny Clarke never sounds less than inspired on this anthology. The cuts range from evocative to commonplace, the lyrics from enlightening to cliched, humorous to vulgar. *—Ron Wynn*

Don't Trouble Trouble / 1989 / Attack ✦✦✦✦✦
For a peak into Johnny Clarke's best 1970s output with the Aggrovators, this is the release to covet. With Bunny Lee calling the shots, this has his most urgent material that ranges from pure pop ("Rock with Me Baby") to the more socially conscious ("Rebel Soldering" and "Too Much War"). Although it's a collection, the playing is so uniformly great that its consistency will make you think it's a single session. Two cover versions are noteworthy: "Tears on My Pillow," for starters, and even better is Clarke's take on Ivory Joe Hunter's "Since I Fell for You." A wonderful record. *—John Dougan*

Authorised Rockers / Jul. 26, 1991 / Frontline ✦✦✦✦✦
Johnny Clarke is one of the greatest of the roots reggae singers, a sweet-voiced crooner who delivers messages of cultural awareness, prophetic warning, and romantic devotion with equal aplomb. *Authorised Rockers* actually compiles two of his finest albums, *Rockers Time Now* and *Authorised Version.* Both were recorded at Channel One and feature backing by the Revolutionaries; the former was mixed by King Tubby, and the latter by Bunny Lee. The combination of Clarke's exalted voice, the fierce, stripped-down rhythms of the Revolutionaries, and the production wizardry of Bunny and Tubby makes for one of the most consistently rewarding reggae discs available. Clarke moves from strength to strength, from the gently imploring "Be Holy My Brothers and Sisters" to the stern "Declaration of Rights," from the chilling "Marcus Garvey" to the romantic "I Wish It Would Go on Forever." Most of these songs were made famous by other singers—you'll recognize tracks originally recorded by Bob Marley, Culture, the Mighty Diamonds, and others—but in no case do Clarke's versions seem redundant. This is a must-own disc. *—Rick Anderson*

Jimmy Cliff (James Chambers)

b. 1948, St. Catherine, Jamaica
Vocals / Reggae-Pop, Soul
The first artist in Lesley Kong's groundbreaking Beverly's label stable in 1962, Jimmy Cliff has been a figure of major influence in the internationalization of Jamaican music for thirty years. Despite a number of ska hits and an Island Records contract in 1967, it wasn't until he was recruited to act in Perry Henzell's rollickingly hypnotic film *The Harder They Come* that Cliff achieved true stardom. He sang a number of his own compositions in the movie, including "Many Rivers to Cross," "Sitting in Limbo," and the title track, three standards that helped make the soundtrack album one of the biggest sellers in reggae history. The followup albums, however, were generally unfocused, their spotty material spoiling Cliff's bid to become reggae's main exponent, a gap rushed into and filled brilliantly by Bob Marley. By 1976, Cliff had regrouped and enlisted Wailers tutor Joe Higgs to be his bandleader. A yearly stream of albums followed, with songs as good as anything he ever recorded ("Beyond the Boundaries," "Bongo Man"); and Cliff became a mainstay on the international festival and touring circuit, achieving huge fame in places like Nigeria, where he keeps a second home. Cliff's style is a high, almost gospel plaint, with a keen rhythmic sense that echoes Africa as well as R&B. *—Roger Steffens*

Wonderful World, Beautiful People / 1970 / A&M ✦✦✦✦✦

★ **The Harder They Come** / 1972 / Mango ✦✦✦✦✦
In 1973, when the movie *The Harder They Come* was released, reggae was not on the radar screen of American pop culture. The soundtrack went a ways toward changing that situation. It is a collection of consistently excellent early reggae songs by artists who went on to thrive with reggae's increased popularity and others for whom this is the most well-known vehicle.

Jimmy Cliff is both the star of the movie and the headliner on the soundtrack. He contributes three excellent songs: the hymnal "Many Rivers to Cross," "You Can Get It If You Really Want," and "The Harder They Come" (the latter two are repeated at the end of the album, but you probably wanted to hear them again anyway). Interestingly, the better production values of his songs actually seems to detract from them when compared to the rougher, but less sanitized, mixes of the other tracks.

All the songs on this collection are excellent, but some truly stand out. Toots and the Maytals deliver two high-energy songs with "Sweet and Dandy" and "Pressure Drop" (covered by the Clash and Izzy Stradlin, among others). Scotty develops a mellow, loping groove on "Stop That Train" (not the same as the Wailers' song by the same name) and the Slickers prove on "Johnny Too Bad" that you don't have to spout profanity or graphic violence to convey dange

The Harder They Come is strongly recommended both for the casual listener interested in getting a sense of reggae music and the more serious enthusiast. Collections don't come much better than this. *—Toby Ball*

Struggling Man / 1973 / Mango ✦✦✦✦✦
Although not as well regarded nor as vocally spectacular as *The Harder They Come,* this was nevertheless some outstanding early Jimmy Cliff material. The title cut was especially strong, and there were also some good ballads. *—Ron Wynn*

Reggae Greats / 1991 / Mango ✦✦✦

★ **Ultimate Collection** / Nov. 23, 1999 / Uptown/Universal ✦✦✦✦✦
It seems somewhat odd that there has never been a really good best-of compilation devoted to Jimmy Cliff, one of reggae's seminal figures and a major force in popularizing the music in America and beyond. Hip-O's *Ultimate Collection* is probably the best one assembled to date, collecting Cliff's legendary hits from *The Harder They Come,* high-quality material from his early years (including the hard-hitting protest song "Viet Nam"), and a selection of highlights from his major-label recordings over the remainder of the '70s. Some songs have never before been available on CD in the U.S., an added enticement for Cliff fans. *The Harder They Come* is still a tour de force, but as this collection proves, there's more to Cliff that needs to be heard. *—Steve Huey*

Dave and Ansell Collins

f. Jamaica
Group / Rocksteady
An enjoyable trivia question of reggae history, Dave & Ansel Collins had one of the first international reggae hits in 1971 with "Double Barrel." Kicking off with unforgettable, heavily reverbed, basically incomprehensible boasting ("I am the magnificent!" being the only readily discernible phrase), the track then locked into a tight rocksteady groove highlighting rinky-tink piano lines and swelling organ. More echoing, infectiously silly boasts and exhortations to "work!" pushed the cut along, with a brief digression into a chord sequence nicked from Bob Dylan's "Lay Lady Lay." That's a tough act to follow, and Dave & Ansel Collins were destined to be a one-shot in the U.S., although they did make the British Top Ten one more time with the less remarkable "Monkey Spanner." Winston Riley played a strong hand in the duo's recordings, producing and writing all of their material. *—Richie Unterberger*

● **Double Barrel: Original Yard Classics** / 1995 / RAS ✦✦✦✦✦
This 1995 reissue, not to be confused with another album released under the title *Double Barrel* back in the 1970s, features 12 songs from the early '70s, more often than not instrumentals, but also including some straight vocal numbers. Nothing's nearly as impressive as "Double Barrel," unfortunately. For the most part these are good-natured but tame and simplistic ditties, with the cheesy piano and organ parts highlighted in the mix. Includes their other big hit (at least in the U.K.) "Monkey Spanner," though the actual high point (other than "Double Barrel") is a rendition of Gene Chandler's soul-pop hit "Groovy Situation," there retitled "That Girl." *—Richie Unterberger*

The Congos

f. Jamaica

Group / Dub

A duo comprised of Cedric Myton and Roydel "Ashanti" Johnson, the Congos are known primarily known for one record, *Heart of the Congos,* released in 1977. The album, which was produced by Lee Perry, has earned a place alongside other great reggae recordings like Bob Marley and the Wailers' *Natty Dread,* Burning Spear's *Marcus Garvey,* and the Mighty Diamonds' *Right Time.*

Cedric Myton grew up in St. Catherine, Jamaica and began his singing career as a member of the Tartans in the late '60s. Roy Johnson, a native of Hanover, Jamaica, grew up singing spirituals at home and cut his teeth as a member of Ras Michael and the Sons of Negus. A chance meeting led to Myton and Johnson working under the name the Congos and hooking up with such major musical talents as Sly Dunbar, Ernest Ranglin, and "Sticky" Thompson. And while the music that backed the Congos was undeniably great, their most distinctive feature was their vocals: Johnson's strong, clear tenor and Myton's breathtaking falsetto. What Lee Perry brought to this mix was his usual anarchic presence, but also his technique of using primitive (even for its time) four-track recording technology that emphasized a cluttered, dense, but hot live sound.

Great as it was, *Heart of the Congos* sold only reasonably well in Jamaica, and became a hotly sought-after collectible in America and Britain by a cult of reggae aficionados. Not long after the record was released, Myton and Johnson went their separate ways but continued to use the name the Congos or Congo as a means of identification. Myton continued to record with other singers as the Congos, and Johnson now identifies himself as Congo Ashanti Roy, working as a solo act and as a member of some of Adrian Sherwood's experimental dub/funk aggregations. *—John Dougan*

★ **Heart of the Congos** / 1977 / Blood & Fire ✦✦✦✦✦

Not simply one of the best reggae reissues of all time, *Heart of the Congos* is one of the great reissues of all time. Digitally remastered from the original Black Ark master tapes (which in itself is remarkable, as Lee Perry was not the most efficient and organized producer in the world; plus, he burned Black Ark to the ground in 1980), the entire record is remastered as are a handful of remixes that survived. One listen to Cedric Myton's soaring falsetto on the lead track "Fisherman," and you'll have an indication of how great this record is. Intense, relentlessly rhythmic, and recorded and produced in a manner that would be impossible with today's enhanced technology, *Heart of the Congos* is easily one of the ten greatest reggae records ever made, a meeting of body and spirit so moving it will take your breath away. No reggae collection can be considered complete (or taken seriously) without this release a part of it. *—John Dougan*

Creation Rebel

Group / Dub

The product of the fertile and prolific British producer, mixmaster and dub genius Adrian Sherwood, Creation Rebel was one of Sherwood's first endeavors as a producer. Originally the backing group for the late reggae great Prince Far-I, Creation Rebel worked with Sherwood from 1977-1980, recording some of the best reggae dub music this side of Lee Perry during the early English punk era. Languorous, funky, spacy and totally intoxicating, it's exciting to hear the awesome production/mixing talents of Sherwood in their early days. Similarly, the band (drummers Style Scott and Fish Clarke, bassist Clinton Jack, keyboardist Bigga Morrison, guitarist Crucial Tony, and percussionist Slicker) play with a grace, effortlessness and power that most studio bands would kill to achieve. With the band's talents so wonderfully used by Sherwood, this is without a doubt some of the best and most important non-rock music to be made in England in the late '70s. *—John Dougan*

● **Historic Moments, Vol. 1** / 1994 / On-U Sound ✦✦✦✦✦

Long out of print, nearly all the crucial recordings of Creation Rebel are now readily available thanks to CD technology. Both volumes (with another one in the offing) are absolutely essential dub records, seductive and compelling play after play after play. Sherwood's avant-garde tendencies were in the early stages of development here, and he adds a daring bravado to the insistent, undeniable groove that Creation Rebel lays down. *Volume 1* is a little more song-oriented; *Volume 2* is a bit more adventurous (and slightly better). Both of these are essential for any reggae fan's library. However, those interested in experimentation will walk away from this experience with their lives changed for the better. *—John Dougan*

Culture

f. 1976

Group / Political Reggae, Roots Reggae

This outstanding vocal trio has been hailed as prophetic visionaries and since their inception in the mid-'70s, Culture has been an influential group, calling Jamaica's poor to rise up in peace and fight against oppression. At the center of Culture is chief songwriter and leader Joseph Hill, who is the fiery one, energetic and charismatic while cousins Albert Walker and Roy "Kenneth" Dayes are ice cool and steady. They came together in 1976, originally as the African Disciples and recording for producer Joe Gibbs. After leaving Gibbs, they recorded their first album, *Two Sevens Clash,* in 1978. Released during a time when reggae music was at a crossroads, the album is credited for having helped to guide the genre towards new directions and for Culture that direction was to spread a more aggressive political message. An excellent example of their political bent can be heard on the title track of their 1982 Heartbeat album, *Lion Rock,* a powerful call to African Jamaicans to throw of the cultural chains placed upon them by the Anglo colonialists. As chief songwriter, Hill is inspired by many things from current political events to the sounds of nature when he is out in the country meditating. Throughout their long, distinguished careers, Culture has gone on to influence and work with many of reggae's greats. *—Sandra Brennan*

★ **Two Sevens Clash** / 1978 / Shanachie ✦✦✦✦✦

The landmark debut, with gorgeous vocals, concise rhythms, and tough and properly impassioned heart, makes this a cornerstone of any reggae collection. *—John Floyd*

Cumbolo / 1979 / Shanachie ✦✦✦✦✦

A classic, almost on par with *Two Sevens,* it utilizes similar themes and is sung with similar amounts of passion. *—John Floyd*

International Herb / 1979 / Shanachie ✦✦✦✦✦

● **Strictly Culture: The Best of Culture 1977-1979** / 1995 / Music Club ✦✦✦✦✦

Desmond Dekker (Desmond Dacres)

b. 1943, Kingston, Jamaica

Vocals / Bluebeat, Rocksteady, Ska

Born Desmond Dacres in Kingston, Desmond Dekker scored a stunning international hit with with an unlikely ode to a small Christian/Rastafarian cult in 1969. Propelled by obscure lyrics and a quirky, galloping beat, Dekker's "Israelites" brought Jamaican rock-steady music to the Top Ten in America and Europe largely on the strength of an incredible, soaring tenor rarely heard in pop. But back home Dekker was already a mainstay with a succession of drop-dead beautiful singles beginning with "Honor Your Mother and Your Father" in 1963 and including 1967's rude boy anthem "007 (Shanty Town)" featured in the film "The Harder They Come." As rock-steady made way for reggae, Dekker faded from the scene. Despite a pair of solid albums for Stiff Records in 1980 and 1981 (both out of print but worth seeking) and the use of "Israelites" in two recent movie soundtracks, he hasn't made the comeback other rock-steady-era pioneers like Lee Perry, Johnny Clarke, or Toots Hibbert have achieved. The purity of his voice and his witty approach to songwriting are sorely missed. Gift us again, Desmond. *—Bob Tarte*

Black & Dekker / 1980 / Stiff ✦✦✦✦✦

A fierce ska version of "Israelites" sets the tone and tempo for this release that came at the crest of the U.K. 2-Tone revival, initiated by such bands as The English Beat and the Specials. Not meant to take the place of the originals, these punk-intense versions of a half-dozen of Dekker's biggest hits are cleverly arranged, meticulously (albeit loosely) performed, and shed not a single nostalgic tear, not when the music remains this fresh. *—Bob Tarte*

Compass Point / 1981 / Stiff ✦✦✦

Proof positive that Dekker had a potentially vital future along with his accomplished past, this Robert Palmer-produced release brings state-of-the-art studio craft and a global sensibility to a set of strong new Dekker tunes. Rich, varied, and mature, this should have had more impact, but it came a few crucial years too early for the world music boom. *—Bob Tarte*

★ **Rockin' Steady: The Best of Desmond Dekker** / 1992 / Rhino ✦✦✦✦✦

His unmistakable voice is irrevocably tied to the rocksteady era—not a question of limitation but the versatility the times demanded. Dekker could be light as a sigh in the strangely portentuos "Fu Manchu," wax comic in "Licking Stick" or summon enough raucousness to blow down a picket fence ("Warlock"). At his most righteous he never succumbed to preachy, shifting instead into an otherworldy eccentricity that shaped an outstandingly memorable body of work, including one of the most transcendent records in anybody's canon, the still-jarring "Israelites." *—Bob Tarte*

The Original Rude Boy / May 20, 1997 / Music Club ✦✦✦✦✦

Desmond Dekker only had one hit in America, 1969's rocksteady smash "Israelites." But Dekker's career as an early exponent of ska has been a long-lasting one, beginning in 1963 with his debut disc, "Honour Your Father and Mother" and reaching into the 1990s paired with his disciples, 2-Tone group the Specials, for a remake of 1964's "King of Ska." Both versions, plus 1993's cover of "Carry Go Bring Come," are aboard, along with 13 prime cuts ranging from the ethereal drift of 1996's "Big Head" to the rude boy sounds of "Get Up Edina," "007 (Shanty Town)," "Mother's Young Girl" and "You Can Get It If Really Want." As a wide, sweeping compilation, this hits all the high spots of Dekker's career and makes an essential first purchase in assembling a Jamaican music collection. *—Cub Koda*

Dillinger

Vocals, DJ / Dancehall

Lester Bullocks AKA Dillinger was a seminal stylist in DJ/toaster circles during the '70s. His blazing, witty and irreverent style, sometimes comedic, sometimes tragic or poignant, was featured on many singles as he moved from simply recyling Big Youth and U-Roy's style and developed his own gripping approach. Dillinger began as a disc jockey on Prince Jackie and El Brasso's sound systems' during the early '70s. He enjoyed his first hit with "Freshly" in 1974, cutting it for Yabby U. Later came singles for Augustus Pablo, Joe Joe Hookim and Coxsone Dodd. Dodd Issued the LP *Ready Natty Dreadie* in '75 and '76, establishing Dillinger as a star, while Kim issued the second album containing the classics "Cocaine In My Brain" and "Crank Face," a superb duet with Trinity. Dillinger tried to repeat the formula with "Marijuana In My Brand," which did reasonably well. But as audience interests shifted during the '80s, Dillinger's fortunes plummeted. He eventually left music, but returned with "Say No to Drugs" in 1990. *—Ron Wynn*

● **Cocaine** / 1983 / Charly ✦✦✦✦✦

Dillinger's "Cocaine" remains an all-time anthem. It's without question the high point on an otherwise erratic album, one whose rambling qualities accurately reflect Dillinger's entire career. The songs are great one moment and utterly forgettable the next. *—Ron Wynn*

Phyllis Dillon

Vocals / Rocksteady

Phyllis Dillon recorded in rough, tough Kingston, Jamaica at Duke Reid's Treasure Isle studio, but lived in Linton, St. Catherine—considered the country—in the middle of Jamaica. She began her singing career with a band called the Vulcans. A gig with that band in

Kingston brought her to the Reid's attention. She signed with him in 1965 and never recorded for another Jamaican producer. Her first single, the beautiful ballad "Don't Stay Away" came out in 1966 and was an instant local success. A succession of engaging singles further enhanced her legend and she became the uncrowned Queen of Rock Steady. She also recorded popular duets with Alton Ellis and Hopeton Lewis.

Her solo hits include "Perfidia," the self written "Rock Steady," "One Life To Live," "Tomato," "Nice Time," "We Belong Together," and many others. Despite this string of hits, she never got much money from her records and continued to live in Linton with her parents until 1967. That year, she left Jamaica for New York City, eventually finding work in a bank and returning occasionally to Jamaica to produce new recordings. *—Andrew Hamilton*

Midnight Confessions: Classic Rock Steady & Reggae 1967-71 / May 16, 2000 / West Side ♦♦♦♦♦

Unquestionably the Queen of rocksteady, you only need a few takes of Dillon to fall in love with her infectious soprano. This compilation features rock steady renditions of pop/soul hits and enough originals to please traditionalists. She possesses an exciting, pretty voice that massages lyrics for the sole purpose of melting your heart. Remakes of Bettye Swann's "Make Me Yours," Kitty Lesters' "Love Letters," and "Woman of the Ghetto," rate with the originals. Her first recording "Don't Stay Away," and the sassy "Perfidia," are two early hits. One glaring omission,"One Life to Live," makes you believe more Dillon compilations are coming. She duets with Hopeton Lewis, and Alton Ellis on a few tracks as well. An essential artist who left the business too quick to be all she could be musically. *—Andrew Hamilton*

Clement "Coxsone" Dodd

Producer / Roots Reggae, Rocksteady, Ska

One of the most important producers in the history of reggae music, Clement "Coxsone" Dodd was a vital figure in the journey of Jamaican popular music from ska through rocksteady and early reggae, on par with Duke Reid and Lee Perry. Dodd got his start in the Jamiacan scene by operating sound systems in the '50s, beginning to record discs at the end of the decade, and opening the first black-owned Jamaica studio in 1963. Exact details of who he produced, and when, in the 1960s are sketchy, as they are for most vintage reggae music, but it's agreed that there very few early reggae performers of consequence who did NOT record for Dodd at one point. While he has worked with stars like Burning Spear, Sugar Minott, Frankie Paul, Brigadier Jerry, and Niney The Observer, his best work is considered to have been laid down during the rocksteady era; many of the tracks he produced during this time have been "versioned" ever since. *—Richie Unterberger*

● **Musical Fever 1967-1968** / 1989 / Trojan [UK] ♦♦♦♦♦

A double CD of 28 rock-steady tracks produced by Dodd during the late '60s. Most of these were very obscure; the only well-known names are organist Jackie Mittoo and a young Niney The Observer, recording as Winston Holness. A few of the cuts are little more than basic instrumental grooves, but mostly this is top-notch, and fairly diverse, rock-steady. The best attributes of the style are captured in the easy, shuffling grooves, ethereal organs, and dreamy horn lines that anchor nearly all of the songs. The tracks featuring vocal harmony groups make the connection between early reggae and American soul music explicit. *—Richie Unterberger*

Mikey Dread

Vocals / Punk, World Fusion, Hip-Hop

Some of the most innovative sounds of the late-1970s, 1980s and early-90s were produced by Mikey Dread (Born: Michael Campbell). In addition to a lengthy list of dub albums, including seven that reached the top slot on the international and reggae charts, Dread produced such groundbreaking singles as UB-40's "Red, Red, Wine" and The Clash's "Bankrobber" and albums including The Clash's *Sandanista* and *Live: From Here To Eternity* and the debut solo effort by Guns And Roses guitarist, Izzy Stradlin, *Izzy Stradlin & The Ju Ju Hounds*.

Dread's earliest reputation was earned as the host of a weekly, four hour, radio show, "Dread At The Controls", broadcast by the Jamaican Broadcasting Company in the late-1970s. Although his wild personality led to the show being cancelled, Dread had already begun to be known for his unique production work. When his work with UB40 on their 1983 single, "Red, Red, Wine", resulted in a number one hit, Dread's future was secured. The success of the single was more than duplicated when the Dread-produced single for The Clash, "Bankrobber", sold more than ten million copies. Although his first full-length collaboration with The Clash, *Sandanista*, failed to sell as many as the band's preceeding album, *London Calling*, it became known for its eclectic, punk-spirited, approach.

During the 1990s, Dread has continued to make his presence and unique vision felt. In addition to furnishing the narration for a video history of reggae, *Deep Roots Music*, he produced a ten part series, *Rockers International*, for the Youth Music program on British television. *—Craig Harris*

Dread at the Controls / 1979 / Trojan ♦♦♦

Beyond World War 3 / 1981 / Heartbeat ♦♦♦♦

● **Best Sellers** / May 24, 1991 / Rykodisc ♦♦♦♦♦

In rock circles, Mikey Dread is best known for his work on the Clash's *Sandinista* and *Black Market Clash* albums of the late 1970s. And in reggae, the distinctive and slightly quirky singer has been one of the top artists of the '80s and '90s. Spanning 12 years of his career, *Best Sellers* boasts many songs that were major hits in the reggae markets of Jamaica and Britain—including early material like 1980's "Jah Jah Love" and the number one U.K. singles "Barber Saloon Haircut" (1979) and "Warrior Stylee" (1981). Dread, a Rastafarian, expresses his faith on those treasures, as well as 1989's previously unreleased "Choose Me" (a number based on Barbara Lynn's early-'60s soul classic "You'll Lose a Good Thing"). Another cut with a delightfully retro flavor is 1982's "S.W.A.L.K.," which is obviously influenced by the northern soul of the early to mid-1960s. For casual listeners who are purchasing their first Dread CD, *Best Sellers* is the logical choice. *—Alex Henderson*

Come to Mikey Dread's Dub Party / 1995 / ROIR ♦♦♦♦

Mikey Dread came to international prominence as a producer for the Clash in the early '80s, after his "Dread at the Control" radio show made him a star in Jamaica. Mikey is one of the more heavy-handed dub producers, and his solo albums are typically laden with ten-ton bass and dripping echo. His singing voice is something of an acquired taste, but for those with adventurous tastes, his work is some of the most exciting in reggae. "Dub Party" finds him working in a style similar to that of the *African Anthem* albums he made for RAS a while back (and recycling a few of the same tracks, as well). The musicians vary and a few tracks are synthesized; several of the numbers feature Mikey's rather nasal singing voice. All are at least pretty good, and many are excellent. Not quite as essential as the Niney the Observer album that ROIR released at around the same time, but much better than average. *—Rick Anderson*

Don Drummond

d. Apr. 21, 1971

Trombone / Rocksteady, Ska

Trombone master Don Drummond was among the seminal figures behind the evolution of ska—a founding member of the legendary Skatalites, he was the genre's most prolific composer, with well over 300 songs to his name before his brief career ended in tragedy. Beginning his studio career in 1956, he composed and arranged hundreds of classic ska recordings for both Studio One and Treasure Island, under the direction of producer Coxsone Dodd. When Studio One musical director Jackie Mittoo set about assembling the Skatalites in 1964, he did not hesitate to bring Drummond aboard, and he quickly emerged among the group's creative and spiritual leaders. The quintessential ska band of their time, the Skatalites' influence was incalculable—their 1964 debut *Ska Authentic* ruled Jamaican airwaves throughout the year and even hit the British Top Ten with the single "Man in the Street." The group disbanded soon after though, brought on by the beginning of Drummond's own tragic downfall; in 1965, he was arrested for the murder of his girlfriend. Deemed legally insane, Drummond was committed. He died in hospital four years later, reportedly a suicide though there was no official autopsy and rumors about his death continued to swirl. In any case, his death was the true end of an era, but his influence lives on. *—Jason Ankeny*

● **Greatest Hits** / 1989 / Treasure Isle ♦♦♦♦♦

It's not clear from the scant liner notes whether some or all of these may have in fact been Skatalites tracks, though it is known that the Skatalites (including Roland Alfonso and Tommy McCook) are featured on some or all of this LP. As there aren't any domestic compilations of this important ska trombonist, this Jamaican anthology, which does pop up from time to time at specialist stores in the U.S., is the best collection of his work. Snappy ska instrumentals, with a couple of vocal tracks featuring "Margarita" and "Dotty & Bonnie." *—Richie Unterberger*

Lucky Dube

Vocals / Contemporary Reggae

Lucky Dube, with his trademark military beret, sings powerful songs calling for social reform, freedom and God's love.With his on-stage charisma, broad vocal range, exuberant Zulu-inspired dancing and lively rapport with his audience, Dube's concerts are an unforgettable experience. In his native South Africa, Dube had one of his country's biggest selling albums, *Slave*, and he has been the first South African reggae artist to have international success. He was also the first Black performer to have a song, "Together As One," to get airplay on the segregated South African White radio stations, eventually making it on to the White record charts. Regardless of his lack of formal training in politics, Dube's songs are infused with awareness that cries out for interracial unity and strongly protests injustice, false prophets, and self-righteousness as can be heard in such numbers as "War and Crime," the first track on his *Prisoner* album. *—Sandra Brennan*

Slave / 1990 / Shanachie ♦♦♦

Prisoner / 1991 / Shanachie ♦♦♦♦♦

This is one of the best efforts from the South African reggae superstar, whose vocal style owes much to Peter Tosh. Dube is one of the finest post-Marley singer/songwriters in the reggae field. *—J. Poet*

House of Exile / 1992 / Shanachie ♦♦♦♦♦

● **Serious Reggae** / Oct. 29, 1996 / Shanachie ♦♦♦♦♦

Serious Reggae collects Lucky Dube's biggest hits along with new recordings and alternate takes, including his cover of the Foreigner hit "I Want to Know What Love Is." The enhanced CD also includes video and interview footage. *—Jason Ankeny*

Taxman / Jun. 17, 1997 / Shanachie ♦♦♦♦

During his career, Lucky Dube has witnessed major political changes in his native South Africa. When he first earned recognition in the 1980s, the country's apartheid system was still in place. But when the Peter Tosh-influenced reggae hero recorded his eighth album, *Taxman*, in 1997, apartheid had been outlawed for several years, and the once-imprisoned Nelson Mandela held the position of prime minister. One of his strongest albums ever, *Taxman* deals largely with the struggles of the new South Africa. The title song asks the same question many Americans ask—where are all our tax dollars going?—while "Is This the Way" and "Well Fed Slave/Hungry Free Man" poignantly address the poverty that was still very much a problem in Dube's country. Dube's songs may have been inspired by events and problems of South Africa, but their appeal is universal—one doesn't have to be from Johannesburg or Cape Town to appreciate Dube's reflections on the struggles of the poor, the unemployed and the homeless. Whether you live in Philadelphia, London or Kingston, Dube writes songs that hit home. *—Alex Henderson*

The Way It Is / Aug. 17, 1999 / Shanachie ♦♦♦♦

Lucky Dube is widely considered to be Africa's "King of Reggae" and *The Way It Is* brilliantly continues his reign. Brandishing one of the most haunting voices in modern reggae, Dube tackles social and political issues with the style and sincerity of Bob Marley, coupled with the ferocity of his biggest influence, Peter Tosh. Opening with melancholy vocals on the sublime "Crying Game," capturing a touch of his South African Mbaqanga roots on "Let the Band Play On," and dabbling in a little classical chamber music for "Till You Lose It All," the singer manages to deliver hardcore roots reggae with a fresh perspective. This album showcases reggae at its best by one of the best. *—Rosalind Cummings-Yeates*

Clancy Eccles

Vocals / Rocksteady, Ska

Though not nearly as well known as Duke Reid or Coxsone Dodd, producer and sometimes vocalist Eccles made a lot of rock steady in the late '60s and early '70s, much of it on his Clandisc label. As a singer, Eccles had started recording back in the late '50s, when he cut some ska for Dodd. After bouncing around the ska and early reggae scene for a while, he became more active in the studio in the late '60s, overseeing tracks by Alton Ellis, Joe Higgs, Beres Hammond, and several less famed artists. Not as distinctive as the works of Reid or Dodd, Eccles' oeuvre nonetheless included some solid and enjoyable material that contributed to the peak of the rock steady movement. His greatest achievement took place outside of the studio: in the early '70s, he organized a traveling stage show to contribute to the successful campaign of Jamaican socialist politician Michael Manley. *—Richie Unterberger*

● **Presents His Reggae Review** / 1990 / Heartbeat ♦♦♦♦♦
A 16-track survey of Eccles productions by Alton Ellis, Beres Hammond, Eccles himself, and several other artists, recorded at West Indies Records in the late '60s and early '70s. It's not the most top-rank rock-steady compilation, and some of the cuts are fairly generic. But it's solid, highlighted by the floating silkiness of Ellis' "Feeling Inside" and Eccles' own "The Revenge," with its enchanting wordless female harmonies. *—Richie Unterberger*

Fatty Fatty: 1967-1970 / Jan. 21, 1998 / Trojan ♦♦♦♦♦
Although viewed by some as more of an overseer than a hands-on producer, Clancy Eccles did feature a groove-heavy mix of stomping beats and vaporous organ accompaniment on the majority of his recordings (most likely a collaborative effort with his house band the Dynamites, later to become the Crystalites under producer Derrick Harriott). On *Fatty Fatty*, the group works through Eccles' eclectic mix of soulful vocal numbers, early DJ cuts, proto-dub, and plenty of the kind of early, up-tempo reggae the producer was instrumental in bringing forth. Eccles is at the mic for the rocksteady-into-reggae cuts "Bag a Boo" and "Fatty Fatty" (a U.K. hit upon its release), while Eric "Monty" Morris takes over on "My Lonely Days" and what became the Eccles' first hit, "Say What You're Saying." Other vocal highlights include Larry Marshall's "Please Stay," and Cynthia Richards' incredible "Foolish Fool," with fine instrumentals coming from the Dynamites and Drumbago. Rounding out the set are vocal harmony numbers by the Silvertones and Barrington Sadler's calypso-inspired "Rub It Down" and "Jamaican Countryside," as well as the blend of flute and bongos on "Soul Power." Topped off with excellent contributions from Dynamite members Winston Wright on organ and Ernest Ranglin on guitar, *Fatty Fatty* qualifies as one of best records of rocksteady and early reggae. Along with Heartbeat Records' excellent *Clancy Eccles Presents His Reggae Revue*, it also, unfortunately, is one of just a few collections of the producer's trailblazing work. *—Stephen Cook*

Eek-A-Mouse

Vocals / Ragga, Dancehall

Born Ripton Hylton, this "six-foot-six above sea level" toaster was named after a race horse. The Mouse's Far Eastern "bong-gong-giddy-mem-giddy-hoy" style set the pace for many early-80s imitators. His sing-jay lyrics run the gamut from wildly funny to terrifying and touching. A master of stagecraft, his witty costumes range from Mexican caballero to Samurai warrior and help keep him touring successfully into the 90s. *—Roger Steffens*

Wa-Do-Dem / 1982 / Shanachie ♦♦♦♦♦
The classic innovative title track and autobiographical material make this a major debut. *—Roger Steffens*

Mouseketeer / 1984 / Shanachie ♦♦♦♦♦
Definitive toasting from Eek-A-Mouse. This LP included the definitive "Star, Daily News Or Gleaner," in which he examined the bitter rivalry between Jamaica's newspapers, and the entertaining "How I Got Me Name," for all those interested in his origins. *—Ron Wynn*

● **The Best of Eek-A-Mouse** / 1987 / Greensleeves ♦♦♦♦♦
A strong anthology collecting Eek-A-Mouse's most clever and popular cuts from the early '80s. *—Ron Wynn*

Eek a Nomics / 1988 / RAS ♦♦♦
This includes good songs in "Calamity," "Lies" and "Rich And Famous," plus more conventional dancehall offerings "The Freak" (with both the regular and a dance version) and "Oh Me Oh My." Eek-A-Mouse's yells, upper register squeals and other trademarks are evident on other cuts like "Do Me" and "Goon-A-Goon." While not breaking new ground, Eek-A-Mouse offered his fans a good group of dance and love numbers, with an occasional lyric insight available as well. *—Ron Wynn*

U-Neek / 1991 / Island ♦♦♦
In the 1980s, Eek-A-Mouse (a quirky, eccentric toaster/singer) made significant contributions to dubwise, which evolved into the more abrasive dancehall style associated with Shabba Ranks, Nardo Ranks and Lt. Stitchie. Essentially, toasters like Mouse are reggae's equivalent of rappers, although dub was around long before hip-hop emerged in the late '70s. *U-Neek* finds the distinctive Mouse incorporating hip-hop touches here and there without becoming as forceful as the dancehall artists he influenced. Most of this CD—which ranges "Gangster Chronicles" (a number that finds him adding lyrics to the theme from *The Godfather*) and the troubling "Rude Boys a Foreign" to a cover of Led Zeppelin's "Dyer Maker"—is fairly melodic. Despite the presence of rappers Daddy-O and D-Nice, *U-Neek* isn't a radical departure from the Jamaican's earlier recordings. Highly recommended. *—Alex Henderson*

Alton Ellis

Vocals / Rocksteady, Ska

One of Jamaica's first singers, the silken-smooth Alton Ellis made his first hit "Muriel" in 1959 as part of a duo with Eddie Perkins. Producer Coxsone Dodd oversaw a string of subsequent successes. Eventually Ellis, seeing little financial remuneration, left for Coxsone's archrival Duke Reid and his Treasure Isle label. Tunes like "Dance Crasher," "Cry Tough," and "Girl, I've Got a Date" gave Reid his first chance to pass Dodd in the popular mind as Jamaica's heaviest studio and sound system. By 1966 the red-hot double-time ska beat had given birth virtually overnight to a much slower, hiccupping rhythm dubbed "rock-steady," and it was Alton who was to be its midwife. Coxsone lured Alton back, and by 1968 Alton was the undisputed King of Rock-Steady with shots like "Willow Tree," "I'm Just a Guy," and "Sitting in the Park," often highlighted with his trademark yelp of "Looka here now!" Again, the money failed to follow the hits, and somewhat disillusioned, Alton spent several years in the U.S. and Canada before pulling up stakes and moving permanently to England in 1973. Scores of songs were issued steadily, cementing his reputation as one of the most consistent reggae artists around. *—Roger Steffens*

Alton and Hortense / 1990 / Heartbeat ♦♦♦
The brother/sister duo of Alton and Hortense Ellis were among Jamaica's more intriguing combinations. This outstanding CD collected several rare singles by each singer, with only one duet number, their marvelous rendition of "Breaking Up Is Hard to Do." Hortense Ellis was best on soul covers; she turned Billy Stewart's "Sitting in the Park" and Tyrone Davis' "Can I Change My Mind" inside out, using the role reversal ploy to recast them as statements of female anguish rather than male uncertainty. Alton Ellis moves from the spiritual tone of "Lord Deliver Us" to the heartache of "When I'm Down" and "Can't Get Used to Loving You," then becomes emphatic on "Wide World" and closes on a reflective note with "The Picture Was You." An extremely attractive set of classic rockers and lover's rock reggae. *—Ron Wynn*

Legendary Alton Ellis / 1990 / Alltone ♦♦♦♦♦
Ska, rocksteady, and early reggae singles include the essential "Cry Tough" and "Dance Crasher." *—Roger Steffens*

★ **Cry Tough** / 1993 / Heartbeat ♦♦♦♦♦
This 20-track collection features the finest moments from one of Jamaica's great vocalists. Concentrating mainly on his strong mid-'60's rocksteady material, this serves as the best introduction for newcomers. Longtime fans will also be pleased with the inclusion of rare takes from the long lost Treasure Isle Sessions. Essential for any lover of Reggae or rocksteady. *—Chris Woodstra*

Sunday Coming / 1995 / Heartbeat ♦♦♦♦♦
Alton Ellis is one of the best Jamaican vocalists to have emerged during the ska and rocksteady periods in the '60s. His singing prowess remained intact through the reggae, dancehall, and ragga years as well, proving that his uniquely soulful delivery and impeccable phrasing could transcend reggae's many changes. Recording with his preferred producer Clement Dodd, Ellis cut *Sunday Coming* around 1969-1970 at Dodd's legendary Brentford Road studio. Most likely backed by the producer's Sound Dimension band (featuring the great Jackie Mittoo as arranger and organist), Ellis offers up a typical set of originals and choice covers from the day's charts. On the handful of tracks Ellis co-wrote with Dodd, breezy medium-tempo cuts like "It's True" and "The Picture Was You" particularly stand out; the buoyant soul-based rocksteady beats, occasional jazz chords, and sweet harmonies all seem to be part of a musical setting in which Ellis thrived. The point is substantiated by great Ellis performances on similarly disposed covers like the Guess Who's "These Eyes," Blood, Sweat & Tears' "You Make Me So Very Happy," and the "Junior Walker hit "What Does It Take (To Win Your Love)." Ellis also shows some musical flexibility with his funky James Brown-inspired jam "Alton's Groove" and the fine roots reggae track "Reason in the Sky"; he even proves his contemporary relevance on two impressive tracks from 1994, including the updated rocksteady cut "Joy in the Morning" and a digitally enhanced number entitled "The Winner." This disc is one of Ellis' best and comes highly recommended to newcomers and reggae enthusiasts alike. *—Stephen Cook*

The Ethiopians

f. 1966, db. 1977

Group / Rocksteady, Ska

The Ethiopians were an important group in the evolution of reggae music. Founded in 1966, they were a tough act combining rudeness with righteousness and performed an early, exciting version of rocksteady. Comprised of Leonard "Sparrow" Dillon and Stephen Taylor, the group's distinctive sound is characterized by sweet, at times mournful harmonies that speak of the social injustice and racism that has plagued the island's Africans since colonial times. Following their first recording session, the two were out of music for awhile but returned with a breakthrough hit, "Train to Skaville." Among their most famous songs are the reggae standard "The Whip" and their 1968 career single "Everything Crash." After the group went bankrupt and Taylor was killed in a car accident, Dillon retired from music for awhile but later revived the Ethiopians with Aston Morris and continued recording and performing through the '70s. Afterward, they continued to release new versions of some of their greatest hits as can be heard on such albums as 1994's *Owner fe de Yard*. *—Sandra Brennan*

Engine '54: Let's Ska and Rock Steady / 1968 / Jamaican Gold [West Indies] ♦♦♦♦♦
Their debut album, far more rocksteady than ska, recorded with Tommy McCook and the Supersonics. It's excellent, consistent stuff from the prime of rock steady, with seductively cooing harmonies and falsettos; few if any other acts brought '60s soul and Jamaican rhythms together with such entrancing results. The CD reissue adds a Lee Perry production ("Love and Respect") and an updated version of "Train to Ska-Ville." *—Richie Unterberger*

Slave Call / 1977 / Heartbeat ♦♦♦♦♦

★ **All the Hits** / 1986 / Trojan ♦♦♦♦♦
The Ethiopians were one of the best of the many vocal groups to come up during Jamaica's

rocksteady period. What set them apart from a good number of their contemporaries, though, were their percussion-heavy mixes and spiritually focused lyrical elements that presaged the expanded sonic-scape and religiousness (Rastafarianism) of the coming reggae sound. Trojan's *All the Hits* includes some of the Ethiopians trailblazing work from 1966-1972: a cross section of styles including the late-ska cut "Free Man," breakthrough rocksteady numbers like "Train to Skaville" and "Everything Crash," and the early reggae tracks "The Pirate" and "The Word Is Love." The subject matter of the lyrics reflect the music's variety, taking in biblical themes, civil liberties, and (in a lighter mode) the island's beauty. This Ethiopians collection is the best and most representative available and even offers a bit of a crash-course history of Jamaican music (kudos to Steve Barrow for his fine liner notes on this and many other Trojan reissues). *—Stephen Cook*

Owner Fe De Yard / 1994 / Heartbeat ✦✦✦✦✦
For lovers of the classic reggae sound, nothing will ever match the music that came out of Coxsone Dodd's Studio One in the 1960s, '70s and '80s. The 15 tracks on this superb anthology spotlight The Ethiopians, one of Jamaica's most consistent vocal groups, thanks largely to the tremendous leads of Leonard Dillon. Whether singing love tunes, protest songs, soul covers or in patois, Dillon turned each number into a shimmering, radiant masterpiece. Dodd's production lacked the multi-track sophistication, computerized synth-backing and other colorations that are now routine. Instead, he relied on the brilliance of individual musicians. *—Ron Wynn*

Tuffer Than Stone / Oct. 19, 1999 / Warriors ✦✦✦✦✦
The Ethiopians first came on the scene before there was such a thing as reggae—like their contemporaries the Maytals and the Wailers, they started out in the mid-1960s, singing political and religious message songs in tight harmony over the ska and rocksteady rhythms that would soon slow and thicken into that familiar one-drop reggae beat. It's pretty amazing that the Ethiopians (in the person of lead singer Leonard Dillon) are still recording; even more impressive is the continued quality of the music. The latest offering from Dillon features 16 tracks of outstanding modern roots reggae. Instead of the traditional male harmony trio, Dillon is here supported by two female backing singers, and the music is provided by a crack team of Jamaican session players that includes a full complement of Nyabinghi drummers. Dillon's voice has mellowed somewhat with age, but his technique is still impeccable. Highlight tracks include the churning title song, "Throne of Justice," and the horn-driven "Africa Is Our Home." Excellent. *—Rick Anderson*

The Gaylads

f. 1963, **db.** 1973
Group / Rocksteady
Renowned rocksteady harmony trio the Gaylads was formed in 1963 by Harris "B.B." Seaton and Winston Delano Stewart, who as the duo of Winston & Bibby previously enjoyed a series of hits. With the addition of local singer Maurice Roberts, the newly-formed Gaylads cut their first songs. Changing their style from ska to the slower rocksteady rhythm brought with it a huge shift in the Gaylads' approach—no longer restrained by the demands of uptempo material, they were free to attempt more complex and sophisticated harmonies, resulting a number of 1967 hits which were all later included on the trio's debut LP, *The Soul Beat*). After the follow-up, *Sunshine Is Golden*, was released, Stewart left the trio to mount a solo career; Seaton and Roberts forged ahead as a duo, collaborating with a number of producers during 1969 (most notably Lee "Scratch" Perry).

As the decade drew to its close, the Gaylads signed with producer Leslie Kong. Under Kong, the group enjoyed one of their most fruitful periods until August, 1971 when Kong suffered a fatal heart attack. The devastated Gaylads tapped producer Rupie Edwards to helm their next smash, "*Can't Hide the Feeling.*" After recording a few final songs, Seaton left the group.

Roberts, the lone remaining original member, selected brothers Randell and Hopeton Thaxter to carry on the Gaylads name; the new lineup never matched the success of its predecessor, however, and after releasing the album *Love and Understanding* as the Gayladds, Roberts rechristened the trio the Psalms, landing as backing vocalists for Bunny Wailer. The founding duo of Seaton and Stewart reformed for the first time in over two decades for an appearance at the 1991 Studio One concert, and two years later Roberts joined them for a performance at the *Rocksteady Reunion* in Kingston. *—Jason Ankeny*

Over the Rainbow's End: The Best of the Gaylads / 1995 / Trojan ✦✦✦

Gladiators

f. 1967
Group / Rocksteady, Ska
The dynamic combination of founding member Albert Griiffith's gutsy, baritone, lead vocals and the harmonies of Clinton Fearon and falsetto singer Galimore Sutherland have made the Gladiators one of reggae's most influential acts. Over the past three decades, the group has continued to extend the Rockers tradition. Born to poor, Christian, farmers, in the parish of St. Elizabeth's, Griffith was fascinated wih Church music from an early age. Taught his first guitar chords by an uncle, he added to his knowledge of the instrument through the lessons he got from local guitarists in exchange for carrying their instruments to gigs. Coming to Kingston, in 1960, in search of work, his pursuits were so unsuccessful that he decided to focus on his music instead. This dream was no more successful, however, as he continued to be discouraged by local record producers. A turning point came when he found employment as a mason. A fellow worker, Leonard Dillon, who later formed the Ethiopians, shared his passion for music and the two agreed to pool their resources. Convincing their employer to finance a recording session, Griffith recorded his debut single, "You Are the Girl". Released in 1966 and credited to Al & the Ethiopians, the tune was the flipside of the Ethiopian's major hit, "Train to Skaville". In 1967, Griffith recruited David Webber and Errol Grandison and formed the Gladiators. Their first single as a group, "The Train Is Coming Back", became a modest hit. Although the group recorded for Duke Reid and Lloyd Daley, they scored their first major hit in 1968 with the Coxsone Dodd-produced, "Hello Carol". They continued to record for Dodd in the 1970s, .in addition to recording several singles for Lee Perry and Randy's Studio 17. In the mid-'70s, the group began a long association with Tony Robinson who released their albums on the Groovemaster label in Jamaica and the Virgin label in the U.K.In the early '80s, the Gladiators swiched to the Nighthawk label for three albums—*Symbol of Reality, Serious Thing* and *Full Time*—and one album, *Dread Prophesy*, recorded in collaboration with Leonard Dillon. The group recorded five albums in the late '80s and early '90s for the Heartbeat label. The Gladiators experienced personnel changes in 1969 and 1973. Webber was replaced by Clinton Fearon in 1969 and Grandison by Galimore Sutherland in 1973. In the mid-'80s, the Glaiators toured with Yabby You and the Ethiopians. *—Craig Harris*

Trench Town Mix Up / 1978 / Virgin ✦✦✦✦

Live at Reggae Sunsplash 1982 With Israel Vibration / Aug. 1982 / Genes ✦✦✦✦

Full Time / Apr. 16, 1995 / Nighthawk ✦✦✦✦
The Mighty Diamonds and Culture may be more famous, but when it comes to reggae harmony groups, the Gladiators can give the best of them a run for their money. Figure in the fact that lead singer Albert Griffiths is also a fine songwriter and that all three singers play instruments as well (unusual for a harmony group in this genre), and all of a sudden you start wondering why the Gladiators haven't gotten all the press. Not that they've been ignored—their two Groovemaster LPs (*Trenchtown Mix Up* and *Proverbial Reggae*, both later picked up by Virgin and reissued together on one CD in the early 1990s) are generally regarded as classics. In the early 1980s they recorded several albums for the American Nighthawk label, and *Full Time* is a collection of tracks left over from those album sessions, filled out with a generous handful of dub versions. These don't really sound like outtakes — "Boy in Long Pants," "Run Them," and "Reggae Jamboree" all rank with the best of the group's previous work, and Griffiths is in fine voice. The production, by Griffiths, Leroy Pierson, and Nighthawk label head Bob Schoenfeld, is excellent. *—Rick Anderson*

● **Bongo Red** / 1998 / Heartbeat ✦✦✦✦
This superb collection, which consists primarily of rare tracks previously unreleased on CD, shows Albert Griffiths and his band at the height of their powers in the early to mid-1970s. The core of the album is fifteen tracks recorded at Clement Dodd's Studio One, and there's a surprising variety of sound in evidence, from the drum machine-driven version of "Roots Natty" to the dark and reverb-drenched setting of "Bongo Red." While the Gladiators were a harmony trio along the same general lines as the Mighty Diamonds and Culture, they distinguished themselves from their peers by being accomplished instrumentalists as well; they play with a tight assurance that underscores their vocals nicely. As a special bonus, this album is appended by two songs ("Time" and "Ungrateful Girl") recorded with Lee Perry at his legendary Black Ark studio. "Ungrateful Girl," in particular, shows a powerful synergy between the Gladiators and the Upsetter; the singing is top-rate and Perry achieves a guitar sound that is both perfect and slightly bizarre. This is an unusual but essential reggae document. *—Rick Anderson*

Eddy Grant (Edmond Montague Grant)

b. Mar. 5, 1948, Plaisance, Guyana
Vocals, Guitar, Synthesizer, Producer / Contemporary Reggae, Reggae-Pop
Eddy Grant was a member of the London group the Equals during the '60s; after they broke up, he established Coach House Studios in London in 1973 and founded the Ice Records label in 1974. He made records throughout the late '70s, gaining a following in the U.K. In 1982, he hit big with "Electric Avenue" in the U.S. While Grant has not been able to repeat the success of "Electric Avenue" in the U.S., he remains popular in other countries. *—Stephen Thomas Erlewine*

Walking on Sunshine / 1979 / Ice ✦✦✦
The title cut was a monster hit, while "Living on the Frontline" and "The Frontline Symphony" were also gems. *—Ron Wynn*

★ **Killer on the Rampage** / 1982 / Portrait ✦✦✦✦✦
In his Barbados recording studio, Eddy Grant doesn't play reggae music so much as dance-oriented music with thoughtful lyrics. His big U.S. hit, "Electric Avenue," had a new-wave beat and a message about poverty. The rest of his album is also toe-tapping and timely. *—William Ruhlmann*

Born Tuff / 1984 / Portrait ✦✦✦

● **Walking on Sunshine: The Best of Eddy Grant** / 1989 / Parlophone ✦✦✦✦✦

Albert Griffiths

b. Jan. 1, 1946
Vocals, Guitar / Rocksteady, Ska
Reggae legend Albert Griffiths was born in St. Elizabeth, Jamaica on January 1, 1946, relocating to Kingston 14 years later. After a series of unsuccessful recording auditions, he accepted a job as a mason; among his co-workers was Leonard Dillon, the frontman of the Ethopians, and together, the two singers convinced their employer Leebert Robinson to fund a recording session at the famed Studio One, with the resulting sessions yielding Griffiths' debut "You Are the Girl, " released as the flipside to the Ethiopians' 1966 smash "Train to Skaville." Griffiths then enlisted David Weber and Errol Grandison to form the Gladiators, scoring a minor hit in 1967 with "The Train Is Coming Back"; singles including "Live Wire, " "Freedom Train" and "Hello Carol" followed before Weber exited in 1969, replaced soon after by Clinton Fearon. Sessions with the inimitable Lee 'Scratch' Perry followed before the trio recorded their first LP, *Presenting the Gladiators;* Gallimore Sutherland replaced Grandison in 1973, and under producer Tony Robinson the group cut several classic albums of the period, including *Trenchtown Mix Up* and *Proverbial Reggae.* Early 1980s efforts including *Symbol of Reality* and *Serious Thing* preceded the Gladiators' first U.S. tour in 1983; despite regular line-up changes Griffiths remained a staple of the group, navigating his way through a series of well-received releases on Heartbeat. *—Jason Ankeny*

- **Trenchtown Mixup** / 197 / Virgin ♦♦♦♦♦
Captured at their peak with some of their most representative compositions, this includes "Hello Carol" and "Thief in the Night." *—Roger Steffens*

On the Right Track / 1989 / Heartbeat ♦♦♦

Marcia Griffiths

Vocals / Dancehall
Jamaica's longest-running and perhaps biggest female vocalist ever. Griffiths began as a teenager in Coxsone's Studio One, racking up hit after hit, then joined with paramour Bob Andy as Bob & Marcia for the Top Five U.K. pop hit "Young, Gifted and Black." She formed The I Threes to back Bob Marley's international tours and recordings from 1974-1980 and scored a massive international hit with "Electric Boogie" in the '80s. Despite a few '70s Rasta tunes like "Stepping out of Babylon," she is known primarily for her strong, smooth-as-mousse love songs and captivating live performances. *—Roger Steffens*

- **Naturally** / 1978 / Shanachie ♦♦♦♦♦
This is one of two exceptional albums Marcia Griffiths recorded in the late 1970s for producer Sonia Pottinger's High Note label. Her singing voice (known to many now from the years she spent as part of Bob Marley's backing trio, the I-Threes) is a thing of wonder, almost classical in its nuanced sweetness and perfect control. Opening with "Dreamland," a Bunny Wailer composition and one of the undisputed classics of mystical roots reggae, Griffiths takes the listener on a guided nostalgia tour of her time at Studio One in the early days of reggae. Old hits like "Melody Life" and the Bob Andy compositions "Truly" and "Tell Me Now" are given new performances in what was then the more current "rockers" style, courtesy of the Revolutionaries. With *Steppin',* this album is an essential piece of reggae history. *—Rick Anderson*

Steppin' / 1979 / Shanachie ♦♦♦♦♦
Steppin' is the companion album to *Naturally,* which was also recorded for the High Note label under celebrated producer Sonia Pottinger just a year earlier. Marcia Griffiths delivers a program consisting primarily of love songs, including "Why There Is No Love" (based, strangely enough, on the chord progression to "People Get Ready") and Bob Marley's "I'm Hurting Inside." But the album's focal point is the title track, a stirring repatriation theme that stands out as both the only political number and the strongest singalong tune. "Give and You Get" is curiously Beatlesque; "It's Impossible" updates a rocksteady classic. The Revolutionaries provide solid professional backing but know better than to try to upstage Griffiths, who is at her finest on this album. *—Rick Anderson*

Marcia / 1988 / RAS ♦♦♦
This session wasn't a strict reggae effort; Griffiths did a straight soul version of "Don't Let Me Down" and a quasi-jazz/pop turn on "Blue Skies." But when Griffith turned to reggae, she was as captivating as ever. Her duet with Bunny Clark, "It's Not Funny," was beautifully performed on both sides, while "Trenchtown Rock" and "I'm Leaving" were the type of unadorned, from-the-heart singing that's sorely lacking in contemporary reggae and a lot of urban music. *—Ron Wynn*

Put a Little Love in Your Heart: The Best of Marcia Griffiths 1969-1974 / Dec. 5, 1995 / Trojan ♦♦♦♦♦

Truly / Jan. 12, 1999 / Heartbeat ♦♦♦♦

Certified / Jul. 27, 1999 / VP ♦♦♦
Marcia Griffith's debut for VP Records, *Certified,* features 16 romantic tunes like "Then Came You," "I Got to Cry," and "Just Try Me," as well as the title track. Famed reggae producer Willie Lindo of Heavybeat Records gives the album his smooth, stylish sound, which spotlights Griffith's legendary pipes. *—Heather Phares*

Beres Hammond

Vocals / Dancehall, Soul
Beres Hammond is one of reggae's great soul singers though for much of his twenty years he has only been known for the most part in his native Jamaica. His style harkens back to the Rastafarian sounds of the '70s that center on a strong melody coupled with socially conscious lyrics and intricate harmonies. Hammond got his own start between 1972 and 1973 during auditions for a Merritone Amateur show, resulting in recording a soul version, in the style of Alton Ellis, of "Wanderer." Hammond became the lead singer of Zap Pow in late 1975; his first solo album *Soul Reggae* was released a year later, while the ballad "One Step Ahead" stayed at No. 1 for over 14 weeks. In 1978, Joe Gibbs produced Hammond's second single, "I'm in Love," and it too became a chart topper. Though he had two chart hits and a top-selling album by then, Hammond saw very little money from the sales. He decided to curtail his solo work concentrating instead on more profitable session work. He soon demonstrated a knack for singing and arranging harmony parts. Hammond then decided to start his own label, Harmony House; his debut single "Groovy Little Thing," was a substantial hit. His next single, "What One Dance Can Do," became one of his biggest hits not only in Jamaica, but also abroad. In 1995, Hammond recorded *In Control* on Elektra, an excellent blend of ballads, and socially conscious reggae targeted toward an international audience. *—Sandra Brennan*

- **Live & Learn Presents: Beres Hammond & Barrington Levy** / 1991 / Live & Learn ♦♦♦♦♦
Beres Hammond and Barrington Levy rank among reggae's greatest pure vocalists, and this eight-track CD presents five Levy numbers. Hammond is more soulful, while Levy is more vocally flexible and spirited. Levy does playful fare such as "Some Girls Are Trouble" and political/topical material like "Juggling Soldier," although the emphasis is clearly on entertainment rather than relevance. "Sho-Be-Do-Sho" showcases Levy's verbal facility, and "Strictly Rocker" features his classic reggae sound. Hammond's "Never Let Go" and "I Will Follow You" are gloriously sung, powerful performances, while "When The Grass Is Green" falters lyrically, but Hammond's evocative singing elevates it. *—Ron Wynn*

Putting Up Resistance / Aug. 1996 / RAS ♦♦♦♦
Beres Hammond's *Putting Up Resistance* is a more consistent effort than several of his mid-'90s releases. There are still problems with the album—a few of the songs are filler, RAS provides no information about the sessions and the recording quality is occasionally substandard—but Hammond's wonderful vocals more than make up for these shortcomings. *—Stephen Thomas Erlewine*

Day in the Life / Oct. 27, 1998 / VP ♦♦♦♦
As the king of lover's-rock reggae, Beres Hammond consistently delivers rich and mellow ballads, spreading his sensual vocals over a song like a velvet blanket. *A Day In the Life* is no exception to this rule; the crooner packs the album with smooth sounds from beginning to end. "All I Need" and "Nothing's Gonna Change" represent Hammond's strong, if unnecessary, efforts to capture the American R&B market. As a bombastic anthem, the former displays his ability to lend sincerity to even the corniest lyrics, and the latter melds hot R&B beats with reggae inflections for a satisfying mix. *—Rosalind Cummings-Yeates*

Reggae Max Tracklisting / Jan. 25, 2000 / Jet Star ♦♦♦

Music Is Life / Feb. 6, 2001 / VP ♦♦♦♦

Hepcat

f. 1989
Group / Third Wave Ska Revival, Rocksteady
Hepcat was among the most celebrated bands to emerge from the Southern California ska revival scene of the 1990s, winning fans with their infectious Caribbean melodies, soulful harmonies and swinging rhythms, all informed by elements of reggae, rock steady, R&B and jazz. Comprising vocalists Greg Lee and Alex Desert, keyboardist Deston Berry, guitarist Aaron Owens, bassist Dave Fuentes, saxophonists Efren Santana and Raul Talavera, trumpeter Kincaid Smith and drummer Scott Abels, Hepcat was formed in 1989; word quickly spread, and in 1993 they issued their debut LP, *Out of Nowhere.* After 1996's *Scientific,* they signed to Epitaph, touring as a featured artist on the following year's Warped Tour before releasing their third LP, *Right on Time,* in 1998 and *Push N' Shove* followed in summer 2000. *—Jason Ankeny*

- **Right on Time** / Jan. 20, 1998 / Epitaph ♦♦♦♦
Hepcat's third album, *Right on Time,* was released at the peak of ska-core's popularity. Consequently, it received more attention than their previous albums, but it would have deserved that attention anyway, since it's their best record to date. Unlike their ska-core peers, Hepcat keeps fairly close to the sound of original ska, spiking it with some reggae, soul, rocksteady and jazz. It's an energetic, welcoming sound that's quite entertaining, even if the group occasionally has trouble writing distinctive material. That doesn't matter, because the group keeps the good times going throughout the entire album, which is easily their most consistent and best to date. *—Stephen Thomas Erlewine*

The Heptones

f. 1965
Group / Roots Reggae, Rocksteady
The legendary lead vocals of Leroy Sibbles and the close harmonies of Earl Morgan and Barry Llewellyn are what made the Heptones one of the finest, most important reggae harmony trios of the '60s and '70s. During the '60s, the Heptones played a key role in the transition between ska and rocksteady. They first began recording at Caltone with a very strange adaptation of "The William Tell Overture." The next year Coxsone Dodd signed them to his Studio One. Under his guidance, they honed their harmonies and Sibbles began to improve his naturally formidable songwriting skills. They had their first real hit in 1966 with "Fattie Fattie." The Heptones remained at Studio One through 1971; following a bitter split between Sibbles and Dodd, they signed on with astute producer Joe Gibbs. It was a good move, and they began gaining an even bigger following. They worked with other producers such as Pablo and Rupie Edwards until 1973 when they teamed up with Lee "Scratch" Perry, the one producer with the skills to update their sound without losing touch with the rootsiness that made them so popular. *—Sandra Brennan*

Party Time / 1973 / Mango ♦♦♦♦♦
Sizzling. One of the first reggae vocal groups to hook Americans. *—Ron Wynn*

Night Food / 1976 / Mango ♦♦♦♦♦
Night Food features the Heptones' trademark wonderful harmonies and some of their finest material. *—Ron Wynn*

Sea of Love / Mar. 21, 1995 / Heartbeat ♦♦♦♦♦
Sixteen tracks recorded under the direction of C.S. Dodd at Studio One, probably from the late '60s and early '70s. (The liner notes, as is par for the course on reggae reissues, seem to avoid even general estimates of the actual dates as if these were sensitive state secrets.) Studio One maintained an extremely consistent track record during this era, and the Heptones, though not the very best Jamaican harmonizers, were certainly in the top league. So it comes as no surprise to find this a fine collection of rock-steady cuts, including quality originals and soulful covers of hits by Curtis Mayfield, Aretha Franklin, and the Righteous Brothers. Especially sweet is the version of "I Shall Be Released," one of the finest overlooked Bob Dylan covers. *—Richie Unterberger*

Heptones & Friends, Vol. 1-2 / Oct. 1995 / Trojan ♦♦♦♦♦

★ **The Meaning of Life: Best of the Heptones 1966-1976** / Jul. 14, 1999 / Trojan ♦♦♦♦♦
Although the earliest recordings compiled here are rather fuzzy, and even the later recordings don't have terrific sound quality, the relaxed, rock steady warmth of the Heptones overcomes any thoughts of low fidelity. Starting with their earlier recordings in 1966, through some of their last sides of 1976 (right before lead singer Leroy Sibbles left the group), this collection presents an interesting mix of material that ranges from lovelorn cries ("I Am Lonely," "I'm Crying") to matter-of-fact warnings ("Hypocrite," "Babylon Falling")). Also included are gentle and pleasantly straightforward renditions of "I'm in the Mood for Love" and "You've Lost That Loving Feeling." Reggae's sunny and upbeat musical side is paired with the Heptones' particularly soulful vocals for a relaxed and soothing overall sound, even

during essentially melancholy songs like "Suffering So" and "Meaning of Life." This is simply a wonderful compilation of Heptones material—even if it is missing their first big hit, "Fatty Fatty" (1966), it includes their first recording, "Gunmen Coming to Town," with Tommy McCook & the Supersonics present as backing band. *—Joslyn Layne*

Joe Higgs

d. Dec. 18, 1999

Vocals, Percussion / Roots Reggae

One would be hard pressed to find a more significant and unheralded figure in reggae than Joe Higgs; while he may not be the proverbial household name when it comes to roots reggae, his fingerprints are on nearly every important recording and band that emerged from Jamaica in the 1960s and 70s. Higgs' career began as a songwriter for seminal reggae acts such as Toots and the Maytals and Delroy Wilson. While establishing himself as an in-demand songwriter, Higgs was also developing a solo vocal career as well as working as a high school music teacher. The role of teacher suited Higgs and he was soon working regularly as a vocal arranger and coach as well as guitar instructor. The most famous of his pupils was Bob Marley. As a solo performer Higgs' success was intermittent at best and his work appreciated mainly by hardcore reggae afficiandos. It wasn't until 1976 that he released his first solo album, *Life of Contradiction,* a title that accurately summarized Higgs' career up to that point. It wasn't until 1985 when Alligator records, a label best known for blues music, released Higgs' masterpiece, *Triumph.* Since then he has kept a low profile, issuing a record every now and then, his work revered by reggae fans around the world. Sadly, Joe Higgs remains the greatest reggae artist you've never heard of. *—John Dougan*

Life of Contradiction / 1975 / Vulcan ✦✦✦✦

Remakes of big '60s hits include "There's a Reward" and "Song My Enemy Sings." *—Roger Steffens*

● **Triumph** / 1985 / Alligator ✦✦✦✦✦

The title says it all. This is an incredible record that contains some of Higgs' finest songs and a rock-steady roots band that features "Family Man" Barret, Augustus Pablo, Junior Marvin, and "Chinna" Smith. Smith's vocals are graceful and sinuous, and the arrangements (done by Higgs and "Chinna" Smith) are mesmerizing. This was the record that everyone familiar with Joe Higgs' legend knew he had in him, and there isn't a duff moment on the record. *—John Dougan*

Family / 1988 / Shanachie ✦✦✦

A bit of a letdown after the greatness of Higgs' *Triumph, Family* is a more laid-back record. It's also a bit off-putting; with its bright pastel colors and Higgs' beaming countenance on the cover, you might think that this is a reggae LP for the *Sesame Street* crowd. But with songs like "Free Africa" and "There's a Reward," you'll quickly realize that more mature listeners are who he had in mind. Higgs' vocals are strong, but the backing band doesn't have the punch of the "Chinna" Smith-led band of *Triumph.* Still, *Family* is a fine, if low-key, record. *—John Dougan*

Blackman Know Yourself / 1990 / Shanachie ✦✦✦✦

One of the founding fathers of reggae, Joe Higgs was a major influence on Bob Marley, Peter Tosh, Jimmy Cliff, Desmond Dekker and countless others. In that genre, Higgs commands the type of reverence that Marvin Gaye and Sam Cooke enjoyed in soul. Entering the 1990s with *Blackman Know Yourself,* the prolific Jamaican singer/composer hadn't changed his style much. When other reggae artists were going for high-tech productions and incorporating hip-hop or urban contemporary elements, Higgs stuck with the type of simplicity that had characterized him since the 1960s. Joined by the Wailers, Higgs is highly convincing on such gems as "Wave of War," "Small Axe" and "Sons of Garvey." Another one of this CD's high points is a remake of "Stepping Razor," a major hit for Tosh. While Higgs' recordings of the 1960s and '70s would be a better introduction to his legacy, *Blackman* is a most welcome addition to his catalogue. *—Alex Henderson*

Justin Hinds

Vocals / Rocksteady, Ska

Throughout the crucial period which bore witness to the emergence of ska and its later mutations into rock steady and finally reggae, Justin Hinds was among the most successful recording artists on the Jamaican music scene, his sweet tenor spotlighted on hundreds of Duke Reid-produced singles cut between 1963 and 1972. Hinds' greatest music was created in the company of his backing vocalists the Dominoes, a duo comprising Dennis Sinclair and Junior Dixon; they first recorded at Reid's Treasure Isle studios in late 1963, their debut session yielding the hit "Carry Go Bring Come" in just one take. Between 1964 and 1966, Hinds was Reid's most popular artist, and during this period alone he recorded some 70 singles backed by session aces Tommy McCook and the Supersonics; among his biggest ska hits were "King Samuel," "Jump Out of the Frying Pan," "The Ark" and "Rub Up Push Up." Around 1966, Hinds made the transformation to rock steady, and the hits kept coming—over the next several years, he released smash after smash, including "The Higher the Monkey Climbs," "No Good Rudy," "On a Saturday Night," "Here I Stand" and "Save a Bread." *—Jason Ankeny*

Jezebel / 1976 / Mango ✦✦✦

● **Just in Time** / 1979 / Mango ✦✦✦✦✦

Travel with Love / 1984 / Nighthawk ✦✦✦

John Holt

Vocals / Smooth Reggae, Reggae-Pop, Lovers Rock

John Holt's career began as a member of the 1960s Jamaican vocal group the Paragons whose biggest hit was the sultry, "The Tide Is High," a song that would be made internationally famous by Blondie in the '80s. Holt left the Paragons amid money squabbles in the late '60s recording solo material with Paragons mentor and head of Treasure Isle records Duke Reid. Under Reid's guidance Holt cut such successful records as *Let's Build Our Dreams* but it wasn't long before he became restless working with Reid, eventually branching out to record songs with Coxsone Dodd and Prince Buster. Holt's style was more pop friendly than most reggae singers, he certainly didn't project the dread vibe of roots-heavy reggae of the Bob Marley era, but Holt's material, even when not the most scintillating, was usually helped by his soaring vocals and elegant phrasing.

Holt's career peaked in the 70s with, of all things, a cover of Kris Kristofferson's "Help Me Make It Through The Night." He continued to have numerous hits throughout the decade only to have his sales slow down as reggae music was being re-shaped by people like Marley, King Tubby, and Lee Perry. And while John Holt is perhaps not the first name one thinks of when reciting a list of great reggae vocalists, his influence upon singers such as Gregory Isaac and Frankie Paul is evident. *—John Dougan*

● **A Love I Can Feel** / 1970 / Bamboo ✦✦✦✦✦

Fine Coxsone productions from the early '70s are here. *—Roger Steffens*

2000 Volts of Holt/3000 Volts of Holt / May 27, 1997 / Trojan ✦✦✦✦

Many of John Holt's best performances are scattered throughout *2000 Volts of Holt* and its *3000 Volts* follow-up, both included on this two-fer. *—Jason Ankeny*

Reggae Max / Mar. 28, 2000 / Jet Star ✦✦✦✦

Like the other installments in Jet Star's compilation series, John Holt's *Reggae Max* features a blend of singles, album tracks, and rarities, all gathered from his recordings circa the turn of the millennium. It isn't the best introduction to his work, although some of the more collectible tracks may entice devotees, while those wanting a simple mid-priced sampling may be satisfied as well. *—Steve Huey*

Keith Hudson

b. 1946, Kingston, Jamaica

Drums, Producer / Dub

Ominously known as "The Dark Prince of Reggae," Keith Hudson was born into a musical family in Kingston, Jamaica in 1946. His musical education began as Hudson worked as a sort of roadie for Skatalite and Jamaican trombone king Don Drummond. By age 21, Hudson, who had been trained as a dentist, sunk his earnings into his own record label, Inbidimts, and had a hit with Ken Boothe's recording of "Old Fashioned Way." Not long after this chart success, the suddenly hot Hudson was producing some of the biggest names (and soon-to-be biggest names) in reggae—John Holt, Delroy Wilson, Alton Ellis, and the great toasters U-Roy and Dennis Alcapone, all of whom benefited from what would be Hudson's trademark production style: groove-centered, bass/drum-dominated, lean and mean stripped-down riddims. By the mid-'70s, Hudson began releasing more solo work, hitting paydirt from the start with his 1974 debut, *Entering the Dragon* and his intense second record, *Flesh of My Skin,* an ominous, dark record that earned Hudson his title as reggae's "Dark Prince." In 1976, Hudson relocated to New York City and worked pretty much nonstop, producing as well as recording solo records up until 1982. He succumbed to lung cancer in 1984, at age 38, robbing reggae of one its greatest, most adventurous, and unhearalded producers and performers. *—John Dougan*

★ **Pick a Dub** / 1974 / Blood & Fire ✦✦✦✦✦

In his excellent book *England's Dreaming,* Jon Savage refers to *Pick a Dub* as "the greatest dub album ever, twelve cuts, all fantastic." It's easy to concur with Savage's assesment, with the lone caveat that there are some Lee Perry and King Tubby sides that might be as good. That caveat notwithstanding, *Pick a Dub* is sensational, arguably the crowning achievement of Hudson's career. In fact, coming as early as it did in the development of dub—it was originally released in 1974—*Pick a Dub* is seminal work, a landmark in progressive remixing on a par with early King Tubby, Augustus Pablo, and Rupie Edwards. What makes this record so scintillating is the intensity of the bass and drums, as well as Hudson's relatively naked production. There are not a lot of goofy sound effects and studio screwing around, just buckets of blood and sweat all rolled into a seductive slab of percussive heaviness that will rattle every filling in your head. Once a forgotten obscurity, *Pick a Dub* was rescued by the folks at Blood and Fire, who re-released it in 1994. Go buy it today. *—John Dougan*

Flesh of My Skin / 1988 / Atra ✦✦✦✦✦

The record that "demonized" Keith Hudson, a doom-and-gloom bass-heavy retreat into the dark recesses of one's psyche. Loaded with intense, at times violent imagery, this is an intense record with oppression and racism as its main subject matter. Interestingly, according to reggae scribe Steve Barker, the original master tapes have disappeared. As a result, the album only exists in a remixed version, not by Hudson but by his engineer Sid Bucknor, and was re-released in 1988. Still, I haven't heard any complaints about Bucknor's remix; after all, he was the engineer on the original session. *—John Dougan*

Studio Kinda Cloudy / 1988 / Trojan ✦✦✦✦✦

An excellent, borderline indispensable collection of Hudson's best production work featuring songs by Alton Ellis, Dennis Alcapone, John Holt, and Delory Wilson. Although it's easy to focus on Keith Hudson the solo performer, his talents in the studio behind a mixing board were as good as any of the big-name producers in Jamaica. What is even more amazing is how young Hudson was (early 20s) when he worked on much of this material. An important piece of reggae history. *—John Dougan*

I-Roy (Roy Reid)

b. 1949, Spanish Town, Jamaica

Vocals, DJ / Ragga, Dancehall

In order to get to the origins of contemporary rap and hip-hop, one must pay attention to the permutation of reggae known as toasting. Popularized in Jamaica in the late '60s by the deejays that ran mobile sound system parties, toasting was, conceptually speaking, very simple: an existing song (preferably a popular one) was remixed, the vocal track removed and the "deejay" (a word that eventually became the all-purpose description for toasters) would improvise spoken word segments over the backing tracks. If well executed the deejay version could become as popular (sometimes more popular) than the original vocal track. The deejay often credited with inventing toasting is the great U-Roy. However, the deejay seen as his equal is the remarkable Roy Reid, a.k.a. I-Roy. Under the spell of U-Roy, I-Roy (whose taken name was a tribute to the great originator of toasting) became a major figure in toasting in the early 70s along with such estimable deejays as Dennis Alcapone. *—John Dougan*

Truth & Rights / 1975 / Grounation ♦♦♦♦♦
Horns, organ, and a rhythm section by Sly & Robbie. Top-drawer toasting. *—Michael G. Nastos*

Musical Shark Attack / 1976 / Virgin ♦♦♦♦♦
This album features "Semi-Classical Natty Dread" and "Tribute to Marcus Garvey." *—Michael G. Nastos*

● **Don't Check Me with No Lightweight Stuff: 1972-1975)** / Feb. 25, 1997 / Blood & Fire ♦♦♦♦♦
This is an extraordinary collection of 16 tracks of prime I-Roy. His rich, dramatic voice is perfect for the material and his semi-improvised verbal pyrotechnics are alternately funny and frightening. The opening track "Sidewalk Killer," recorded in 1972, displays a kind of macho brashness that sounds almost like a parody, while his version of Bob Marley's "Talking Blues" (here called "Straight to the Heathen Land") is part homage, part radical reinvention. A stunning record that should be a part of any reggae collection, especially anyone under the spell of U-Roy or other toasters of the period. These are crucial riddims impossible to ignore. *—John Dougan*

Impact All-Stars

Group / Contemporary Reggae
Between 1968 and 1977, Randy's Studio 17 was the site for some of all-time greatest reggae recordings including seminal albums by The Wailers and Burning Spear. Owned by Vincent "Randy" Chin, the studio sparkled with the visionary engineering of Errol "E.T." Thompson and his successors, George Philpott and Karl Pitterson. In addition to scores of early reggae hits, Randy's Studio 17 helped to pioneer the stripped-down, bass and drums, sounds of dub. Unlike the dub style of influential producer King Tubby, Chin's approach lacked echo, reverberation, delay and sound effects. In 1975, Impact released a ten track album of dub tunes that had been recorded at Randy's Studio 17 over the preceding three years. Credited to the Impact All-Stars, the album featured such influential musicians as Aston Barrett (bass), Carlton Barrett and Sly Dunbar (drums), Tyrone Downie, Earl Lindo and Augustus Pablo (keyboards) and Tommy McCook (tenor saxophone). With the addition of five previously-unreleased tracks, the album was reissued in 1998 by the British reggae label, Blood And Fire. *—Craig Harris*

Forward the Bass: Dub from Randy's, 1972-1975 / Jun. 9, 1998 / Blood & Fire ♦♦♦♦♦
Though Randy's Studio 17 doesn't enjoy the same instant name recognition as other legendary Kingston studios of the early 1970s—Lee Perry's Black Ark or Coxsone Dodd's Studio One, for example—its influence on the development of reggae music was arguably just as great. When Lee Perry was first recording the fledgling Wailers and when Niney Holness was producing hits with the young Dennis Brown, they did so at Randy's. Burning Spear's *Marcus Garvey* album was recorded there, which fact alone is enough to secure Randy's an honored place in reggae history. The studio was owned by Vincent "Randy" Chin and featured the mixing prowess of a young engineer named Errol "E.T." Thompson, who would later go on to work with the legendary producer Joe Gibbs.

While Thompson was at Randy's, though, he helped create one of the first dub albums, a ten-cut set entitled *Randy's Dub,* of which fewer than 200 copies were pressed. Forward the Bass reissues those original ten with five additional tracks, all of which are sweet, dark and lovely examples of the somewhat restrained but still innovative dub that was coming out of Randy's at the studio's peak. Highlights include "Shining Dub," a version of an early Wailers track entitled "Sun Won't Shine for Me" (pity there weren't any leftover vocals on this version) and "Ordinary Version Chapter 3," in which E.T. pretends to give a lesson to an aspiring engineer. Dub can get wilder than this, but it doesn't get much better. *—Rick Anderson*

Inner Circle

f. 1968, Jamaica
Group / Contemporary Reggae, Reggae-Pop
Inner Circle has been playing their own brand of rock/pop-influenced reggae since the early '70s. While lacking much of the raw, rough edges that make their rootsier Rasta-brothers great and sometimes inaccessible to mainstream audiences, the music of Inner Circle could be classified as 'reggae lite,' still rocking steady and focused on typical reggae issues such as Jah-love, social consiciousness and the healthful qualities of the collie weed, but done in a way to invite mass appeal. Reggae purists may have turned up noses at Inner Circle's music, but international audiences loved it and they became quite popular, especially in the U.S. During the mid-'70s, Inner Circle recorded a bit with the American disco band KC and the Sunshine Band. In 1980, Inner Circle came apart, but eventually reformed; they came back even more strongly with the song "Bad Boys," which became a major hit after Fox Television selected it as the title of their new reality-series *Cops.* *—Sandra Brennan*

● **The Best of Inner Circle: The Capitol Years 1976-1977** / Aug. 24, 1993 / The Right Stuff ♦♦♦♦♦
Before they were fluke pop stars, Inner Circle recorded a series of solid reggae singles in the 1970s; the best of these are compiled on this 14-track collection, which draws from their two Capitol albums. Anyone who was turned on to the group through "Bad Boys" should continue their exploration here. *—Stephen Thomas Erlewine*

Gregory Isaacs

Vocals / Reggae-Pop, Lovers Rock, Soul
Nobody sings a love song quite like Gregory Isaacs, reggae music's "Cool Ruler." His voice is languidness personified, insinuating itself around snatches of rhythm like a duppy through a canefield. There's no insistence here, more an intimation. His is the voice of lullabies and laments and loneliness, of indignation and sufferation, of soothing and seething. Few singers in Jamaica have had as many hits as he, few his impressive durability. Recording initially in the late 60s as part of The Concordes, he cut his first solo disc, "Another Heartache," for WIRL, the label founded by onetime Jamaican prime minister Edward Seaga. Almost immediately, Gregory decided to establish his own labels, Cash and Carry and African Museum, and produce himself. On his third album, *Extra Classics,* he found his own voice on such laidback laments as "Mr. Cop" and "Rasta Business," and most especially "Loving Pauper." His streak of classics culminated in 1983's *Night Nurse,* one of his all-time best-sellers. Throughout the '80s, Gregory released more music than any other artist of the time, sometimes offering six singles in the space of a week. Many of them were critically and commercially successful, such as "Rumours" and "Private Beach Party." *—Roger Steffens*

Extra Classic / 1981 / Rohit ♦♦♦♦♦

★ **Night Nurse** / 1982 / Mango ♦♦♦♦♦
One of Isaacs' most popular and enjoyable releases, 1982's *Night Nurse* sports the kind of slicked-up roots sound that emerged in the early days of dancehall-era reggae. In addition to effortlessly delivering the same smooth, "lonely lover" vocals that graced his many successful sides from the '70s, Isaacs, along with bassist "Flabba" Holt, also produced the eight high-quality tracks here. Showing his secular, dancehall-minded hand, Isaacs works magic on the classic lovers rock titles "Night Nurse," "Objection Overruled," and "Cool Down the Pace." The singer is in his best and most vulnerable lovers mode, though, on outsider themes like "Stranger in Town" and "Sad to Know (You're Leaving)." And as was his way—and many other of his contemporaries for that matter (Dennis Brown, Frankie Paul, etc.)—Isaacs mixes his concerns with the flesh with those of a more spiritual nature, coming up here with two of his finest Rasta-cultural themes in "Material Man" and "Hot Stepper." Isaacs once again utilizes the incredible talents of the Roots Radics band (the favored early-'80s Jamaican studio outfit), which includes Holt on bass, Eric "Bingy Bunny" Lamont on rhythm guitar, "Style" Scott on drums, and Wycliffe "Steelie" Johnson on keyboards. With a crossover hit in their sights, Mango also brought in funk synthesizer player Wally Badarou to liven things up. Along with other fine Isaacs titles like *Cool Ruler* and *More Gregory, Night Nurse* is essential listening for reggae fans. *—Stephen Cook*

Sly & Robbie Present Gregory Isaacs / 1988 / RAS ♦♦♦♦♦
Gregory Isaacs has recorded so often and for so many labels, it's both difficult and almost impossible to label anything other than individual compositions as his finest work. But this early-'70s session for Sly And Robbie's Taxi label certainly ranks among his finest full LPs. There were no flimsy soul or pop covers, and Isaacs sang with clarity, depth, verve, and confidence, whether covering "Slave Driver," ripping through "Soon Forward" and "Going Downtown," or embellishing "Motherless Children." There were no unnecesssary or exaggerated mannerisms, and his voice and range were at their peak. The CD includes both vocals and versions, and also has a bonus track in the 1987 single "I'm Coming Home." *—Ron Wynn*

Call Me Collect / 1990 / RAS ♦♦♦

Cool Ruler/Soon Forward Select / 1990 / Frontline ♦♦♦♦♦

☆ **Love Is Overdue** / 1991 / Heartbeat ♦♦♦♦♦
Love Is Overdue was originally a 1974 recording that was remixed in 1990 and now reissued on Heartbeat Records. This recording contains Isaacs' first career hit "Love Is Overdue" that elevated him to Reggae popularity. Much of this album exemplifies Isaacs' career that has balanced between love ballads and politically conscious themes; taking the position of the "sufferer's lot," this recording conveys the tribulations of love and documents the social injustices in his native land. Recorded early in his singing career, one can hear the youth and urgency of emotion in his vocal expressions. Collaboration with DJ U-Roy on the title track and "Financial Endorsement" highlights his prominence as Jamaica's premier DJ. Tommy McCook, Earl 'Chinna' Smith, the Soul Syndicate Band and production by Alvin Ranglin supplement this early work, creating a fuller roots dimension. For Isaac fans, this reissue will be well received. *—Cliff Samaniego*

Pardon Me! / 1992 / RAS ♦♦♦♦♦
Few of Isaacs' recent recordings have proven more satisfying than this 10-track release issued in 1992. *Pardon Me* not only had the classic guitar/horn section underpinning, but featured Isaacs singing with the care, confidence and earnestness that marked his finest early work for Mango. Other than an occasional tendency to crunch his words, Isaacs was soulful on the love songs, defiant on the protest numbers and totally in command throughout. The finest songs included "Mister Cop," and with a good toast from Macka B, "Pride And Dignity," "Judge And Jury," and the title cut. There was also an entertaining remake of Leadbelly's "House Of The Rising Sun." *—Ron Wynn*

Looking Back / Jun. 18, 1996 / RAS ♦♦♦

● **Prime of Gregory Isaacs** / Aug. 18, 1998 / Music Club ♦♦♦♦♦
Gregory Isaacs is not a reggae superstar because of his singing, which is rather unlovely and often only approximately on pitch. His genius is in the perfect realization of a unique and frequently self-contradictory persona: Gregory the "Loving Pauper" who is always dressed in snappy suits and expensive hats; the crooner with a thin, weedy voice; the "Lonely Lover" who can barely keep track of his numerous conquests. Reggae music is full of interesting characters, but Gregory's persona is in a league of its own. That said, his singing really is worth listening to, even if he's no Dennis Brown, and he's made some immortal music during his long and prolific career. Like all Music Club compilations, this one features some of the artist's best-known work as well as a few obscurities; you'll find such usual suspects as "Lonely Lover" and "Loving Pauper" along with the excellent "Bad Da" and "My Time," the latter featured in "showcase" style with a dub version appended. One of the album's highlights is the deeply weird mix of "Hard Road to Travel" that closes the set. As is also true of all Music Club compilations, this disc lists for $9.98, which clinches it as an essential purchase. *—Rick Anderson*

Israel Vibration

f. 1977

Group / Contemporary Reggae

Israel Vibration consists of three young men who met in a polio rehab center. Their voices are among the holiest of Jamaican trinities. Dr. Dread of RAS Records arranged their reunion following a mid-'80s period of breakup, and reggae fans have been thanking him ever since. Ever soulful, ever sure, their voices are so close to the roots you can hear the earth itself in their blending. After debuting in 1978 with *Same Song,* Israel Vibration recorded steadily throughout the 1980s and 1990s, issuing three sets—*Feelin' Irie!, Israel Dub* and *Free to Move*—in 1996 alone. —*Roger Steffens*

● **Forever** / 1991 / RAS ✦✦✦✦✦
The flowing "Reggae on the River" celebrates some of America's most famous reggae locales; a satisfying and sultry collection. —*Roger Steffens*

Why You So Craven / 1991 / RAS ✦✦✦
Containing "Highway Robbery" and a great title track, this formative album was produced by Junjo and engineered by Scientist. —*Roger Steffens*

Free to Move / Aug. 1996 / RAS ✦✦✦
Free to Move continues Israel Vibration's streak of winning albums, offering another collection of soulful, socially aware reggae. Occasionally, the album sounds a bit too similar to its predecessor, *On the Rock,* but since that sound is so fine, it doesn't really matter. The record is an intoxicating listen on its own terms, filled with spiritual messages and deep grooves. —*Leo Stanley*

The Itals

Group / Political Reggae, Roots Reggae

Since the mid-'70s, the Itals have been dedicated to keeping roots-reggae alive. They are a harmony trio noted for their strong voices, close harmonies, and sharp Rasta lyrics that stress cultural consciousness; even their few love songs are written from that perspective. Frontmen Keith Porter and Ronnie Davis had recorded together and separately before forming the Itals during the mid-'70s. The group recorded for many different labels, and some of their best, including "Time Will Tell," "Don't Wake the Lion" and "Temptation," were released on Spiderman. The taut backing of the Roots Radics can be heard on several of these tracks, many of which have been gathered by their primary label Nighthawk and released as *Early Recordings 1971-1979.* Shortly after the release of their 1983 album *Give Me Power,* the Itals embarked upon their first U.S. tour. In 1987, the Itals released their *Rasta Philosophy,* and again proved to be a consistently strong group with such tracks as "Don't Blame It on Me," and "No Call Dread Name." —*Sandra Brennan*

● **Brutal Out Deh** / 1982 / Nighthawk ✦✦✦✦✦
The powerhouse reggae trio is in fine form on this, their debut outing. —*Ron Wynn*

Give Me Power! / 1983 / Nighthawk ✦✦✦

Cool & Dread / 1984 / Nighthawk ✦✦✦✦✦

Early Recordings 1971-1979 / 1984 / Nighthawk ✦✦✦✦✦
Groundbreaking records that brought this trio initial recognition. —*Ron Wynn*

Modern Age / Apr. 21, 1998 / RAS ✦✦✦✦✦

Linton Kwesi Johnson

Vocals / Political Reggae, Dub Poetry

A towering figure in reggae music, Linton Kwesi Johnson invented dub poetry, a type of toasting descended from the deejay stylings of U-Roy and I-Roy. But whereas toasting tended to be hyperkinetic and given to fits of braggadocio, Johnson's poetry was more scripted and delivered in a languid, slangy, streetwise style. His grim realism and tales of racism in an England governed by Tories was scathingly critical. For one so outspoken in his politics, Johnson's recorded work, while politically explicit, is not simply a series of slogans or tuneful/danceable jeremiads. Although he never intended to, Johnson became a star in England and in 1980, he decided to turn his back on a lucrative contract from Island in order to concentrate on poetry readings, organizing activities and greater involvement with political organizations. He finally returned to pop music in 1984 with perhaps his best record, *Making History.* Unfortunately, it wasn't until 1991 that his next record, *Tings an' Times,* was released. Another period of recording silence was broken by the release of a music-less poetry album named *LKJ A Cappella Live* and in 1999, he released *Music Time.* —*John Dougan*

Dread Beat An' Blood / 1977 / Frontline ✦✦✦✦
The title pretty much says it all. This is a stunning debut and an indication of the great things that were to come. Johnson's debut is longer on spoken-word pieces than it is on poetry and music, but Dennis Bovell's influence can be felt in these eight tracks. Songs such as "It Dread Inna Inglan," which describes the death of George Lindo at the hands of racists, or "Five Nights of Bleeding," which recounts tales of British police's capricious use of violence against London's West Indian population, are moving and confrontational mini-masterpieces of anger and a man searching for justice in a country that seems all to willing to deny it to him and other Afro-Brits. A powerful and compelling record. —*John Dougan*

Forces of Victory / 1979 / Mango ✦✦✦✦✦
If *Dread Beat An' Blood* brought Johnson and initial flush of notoriety, then *Forces of Victory* was the record that cemented his growing reputation as a major talent. Bovell and the Dub Band swing hard on this set, especially on the album's opening track "Want Fi Goh Rave." This contains some of Johnson's most memorable songs/poems, such as the heartfelt prison saga "Sonny's Lettah" and the confrontational "Fite Dem Back," which he delivers in his trademark sing-song Jamaican patois. Dramatic and intense to the point of claustrophobia, *Forces of Victory* is not simply one of the most important reggae records of its time, it's one of the most important reggae records ever recorded. —*John Dougan*

Bass Culture / 1980 / Mango ✦✦✦
I remember at the time of its release that many reviewers considered *Bass Culture* a slight disappointment because it didn't reach the highs of *Forces of Victory.* Granted, following up a record as great as *Forces of Victory* is no easy task, but all these years later I wonder what were people thinking. *Bass Culture* is tremendous, another successful collaboration between Johnson and Bovell with songs that are, at times, even more confrontational (e.g., "Inglan is a Bitch") than anything he had previously recorded. I will admit that the Dub Band sounds better on *Forces of Victory,* but Johnson is hitting his stride at the time of this release and experimenting with song structure and lyrics a little more (i.e., not everything is explicitly political here). Still, I defy anyone to come up with a reason to not own this record. An extra added bonus is John Kpiaye's great guitar playing. —*John Dougan*

Lkj in Dub / 1980 / Mango ✦✦✦✦✦
Probably the least essential of Linton Kwesi Johnson's recordings. It is what it says it is, an album of dub versions of songs from *Forces of Victory* and *Bass Culture.* As dub goes it's very good; Bovell acquits himself nicely as mixer and producer. This would be the last LKJ release for four years. —*John Dougan*

Making History / Oct. 1984 / Mango ✦✦✦✦✦
On the days I don't think *Forces of Victory* is LKJ's best album, I think it's *Making History.* It was as if the four-year break (despite his arduous schedule) re-energized him and Bovell, and the result was this masterpiece of swinging reggae. Johnson's poetry, still delivered in his semi-tuneful sing-song voice, takes on greater musical force on this record, blending in almost seamlessly with the band. Bovell has also taken some chances on this record, namely in the arrangements. There's a lot of busy horn work here, and the rhythms pop and roll more vigorously than ever before, but this doesn't detract from Johnson's intensely lyrical writing, which has rarely sounded more determined. OK, I'll fess up, this is the LKJ album to own if you only intend to buy one. But why you would limit yourself to only one is beyond comprehension. —*John Dougan*

★ **Independant Intavenshan: The Island Anthology** / Oct. 27, 1998 / Island ✦✦✦✦✦
If Bob Marley was the high priest of reggae, then Linton Kwesi Johnson is its dub poet laureate. LKJ teamed up with the renowned reggae producer and bandleader Dennis Bovell to record three albums for the Island label between 1979 and 1984, and Bovell compiled an album of dub tracks based on selections from each of them. The entirety of those four albums is included on this two-disc compilation, and the compilers had the good sense to shuffle the tracks around so that the dub versions come after the vocal versions. In addition, several of the vocal versions are presented here in extended 12" remixes, a nice plus. As always, a good portion of this music's attraction lies in Bovell's masterful production and the always rock-solid grooves laid down by the musicians. Two-and-a-half hours of LKJ may be a bit too much for all but devoted fans, but Island has done the world a favor by gathering all of these essential recordings together in one package. —*Rick Anderson*

More Time / Feb. 23, 1999 / LKJ ✦✦✦✦
Linton Kwesi Johnson, one of the founding fathers of the reggae subgenre known as "dub poetry," doesn't always get all the respect he deserves. Purists point out that his patois is something of a put-on—he writes songs (or poems, as he prefers) with titles like "If I Waz a Tap Natch Poet" and "New Word Hawdah," but he can turn it on and off at will and has written in standard English for scholarly journals. But despite his tweedy, bespectacled image, his politics are anything but objective or disengaged—he writes about social injustice in general and racism in particular with a quiettly seething sense of outrage and an incisive wit. His latest effort finds him exploring familiar territory—racist violence ("Reggae fi Bernard"), police oppression ("Liesense fi Kill"—"liesense," get it—)—but also getting a bit more introspective as he ponders poetry itself ("If I Waz a Tap Natch Poet") and domestic bliss ("Seasons of the Heart"). As always, the music is provided by Dennis Bovell's top-notch Dub Band, whose springy, sometimes swinging groove provides an interesting counterbalance to Johnson's often dour poetic insights. —*Rick Anderson*

Judge Dread

d. Mar. 12, 1998

Vocals / Ska Revival

A mutant hybrid of toaster and stand-up comic, Judge Dread drew equal influence from ska and musichall to become one of the most popular reggae artists of the 1970s; only Bob Marley and the Wailers charted more genre hits throughout the decade, an accomplishment made all the more remarkable given that Dread was in fact a white Englishman whose raunchy lyrics made radio airplay an impossibility. Born Alex Hughes in Kent, he fell in love with Jamaican music at the age of 16, lodging at a West Indian house in the Brixton area. An enormous man, Dread's size seemingly dictated all of his early career choices, which included stints as a debt collector, a stripclub bouncer and a security guard—he was even briefly employed as a minder for the Rolling Stones.

Inspired by London DJ appearances by legendary producers including Duke Reid and Coxsone Dodd, Dread adopted his stage name, set up his own sound system, and even began speaking in a Jamaican patois; to keep one step ahead of his rivals, he also traveled once a month to meet the banana boats as they docked, buying the latest reggae records long before they reached British retail outlets. In 1972 he cut his debut record "Big Six," a response to Buster's obscene hit "Big 5;" despite a ban from the BBC and *Top of the Pops* prompted by Dread's own lascivious lyrics, the record—produced at a cost of only £6—was an underground smash, ultimately rising to number 13 on the British pop charts. Each of his increasingly lewd follow-ups, including "Big Seven" and "Big Eight," performed more successfully than the record before it; finally, after "Big Ten," he retired the theme once and for all.

Dread's next hit was a reggae cover of Serge Gainsbourg's infamous "Je T'aime... Moi Non Plus," which like the original was banned by the BBC. "Up with the Cock" and "Y Viva Suspenders" followed, but by 1976—after a string of a dozen hits—the harder-edged roots reggae sound began surging in popularity, leaving Dread's novelty appeal in the dust. While the chart hits dried up, he continued performing on a regular basis, and for a time worked as a newspaper columnist in the village of Snoodland. After a long absence from the spotight, in 1995 Dread made headlines when he attempted to sue producers of the Sylvester Stallone vehicle *Judge Dredd*, claiming that audience confusion over the picture was destroying his reputation. While performing with his backing band the Originals in Canterbury on Friday, March 13, 1998, Dread suffered a fatal heart attack onstage; he was 53. *—Jason Ankeny*

● **Collection** / Mar. 17, 1998 / Cleopatra ♦♦♦
The Collection may not quite be a definitive overview of Judge Dread's career, but it is a decent one-stop sampler, featuring such comic, risqué British underground hits as "Big Six," "Je T'Aime," and "Up With the Cock." *—Steve Huey*

Ini Kamoze

Vocals / Contemporary Reggae, Ragga, Club/Dance
For Ini Kamoze, the road to success has been arduous and he has undergone many substantial changes musically and physically since he burst onto the music scene in 1983 with his highly successful eponymous debut album for Island. Known as "The Hotstepper," Kamoze advocates change through what he calls "intelligent and constructive militancy" rather than random acts of violence. Kamoze made his recording debut in the early '80s with a 12" single "Trouble You a Trouble Me" on Taxi and found immediate success. During this time, he was 6' tall, reed thin and appeared too frail to contain his powerful stage presence. After several hit singles recorded on his Slekta label, by 1988 Kamoze's successes became intermittent and his career erratic. He returned with a new, more aggressive image in 1994, signing to Sony and exploded back into the charts with "Here Comes the Hotstepper," which spent two weeks at the top of *Billboard*'s Hot Singles Chart. Kamoze made a video for the song and with his beefy, well-muscled physique and long dreadlocks, no longer fit the description of the liner notes on his 1983 debut album that characterized him as a "pencil thin.... disentangled.... six-foot vegetarian." With the success of his new single, Kamoze was now a gangster and began a series of promotional tours in LA. At this point, Kamoze refuses to categorize his music and remains open to singing a variety of songs from different sources. *—Sandra Brennan*

★ **Ini Kamoze** / 1984 / Island ♦♦♦♦♦
Essential to the understanding of early-'80s roots, it's simply brilliant. *—Roger Steffens*

Shocking Out / 1988 / RAS ♦♦♦
Before Ini Kamoze made his name in America with his more hip-hop influenced work (including the number one hit "Hot Stepper" in 1995) he produced a small number of highly influential digital dancehall albums in Jamaica with some of the island's top producers of the late 1980s. *Shocking Out* finds him teamed up with the Steelie and Clevie production team for a fine set of fairly typical late-'80s dancehall reggae, distinguished by the excellent backing band and Kamoze's unique delivery. Highlights include "Come Now" (which is dedicated, perhaps unfortunately in light of later events, to boxer Mike Tyson) and the political anthem "Cool It Off." "Revolution" includes a cameo appearance from radical dub poet Mutabaruka; "Clown Talking" provides perhaps the only example of a digital rock-steady rhythm. Nothing here will change the way you listen to reggae, but neither is any track less than very good. Recommended. *—Rick Anderson*

Here Comes the Hotstepper / 1995 / Columbia ♦♦♦♦♦
The title track of *Here Comes the Hotstepper* was Ini Kamoze's big pop crossover hit. Also featured on the soundtrack to *Ready to Wear*, the song lifts a line from "Land of 1000 Dances" and places it on an infectious dancehall beat—it's a great single that deserved to be a huge hit. The rest of the album isn't as strong, but there enough first-rate tracks to make it enjoyable for most fans of the single. *—Stephen Thomas Erlewine*

King Tubby (Osbourne Ruddock)

b. 1941, Kingston, Jamaica, **d.** Feb. 1989, St. Andrews, Jamaica
Engineer, Producer / Dub
Dub music had to come from somewhere, and the consensus is that it came from the mind and four-track mixing board of Osbourne Ruddock, known far and wide as King Tubby. Born in Kingston, Jamaica in 1941, Tubby began his career in the mid-'50s repairing radios and DJ sound systems. Near the end of the decade, Tubby went to work cutting and mixing records for Jamaican impresario and Treasure Isle label honcho Duke Reid, recording hit singles by popular singers such as the Melodians and Phyllis Dillon. It was while working with Reid that Tubby began what seemed to be a deceptively simple bit of experimentation: he would remix songs starting by dropping the vocal track, boosting parts of the instrumental track (e.g., suddenly there would be nothing but bass or rhythm guitar), and add subtle effects like echo or delay to the instruments he had isolated. The immediate impact of this process of dub mixes was that songs became hits twice. Tubby was remixing recognizable tracks like the Melodians' "You Don't Care," and played for the crowds who gathered to dance to the mobile sound systems, the effect was mesmerizing. Reggae historian Steve Barrow, writing about the crowd reaction to Tubby's first public airing of his dub mixes, notes "the crowd did a quick double take and then went wild, pushing down the fence until it was flattened and then rushed in, knocking the speaker boxes flying." Tubby had clearly stumbled on to something very powerful with dub.

Soon Tubby, relying on extremely primitive four-track recording and mixing equipment, was the mixer in demand for most of Jamaica's big-name producers such as Reid, Vivian Jackson (aka Yabby You), and Winston "Niney" Holness. However, his most prodigious period of creativity was during the mid-'70s, when Tubby worked with Bunny Lee. Lee relied on Tubby's brilliance for mixing dub tracks of Lee's studio band the Aggrovators. Virtually every record released on Lee's labels (Jackpot, Justice, and Attack) featured a dub mix done by or supervised by Tubby (the mixers he supervised were none other than Prince Jammy and Philip Smart, aka "Prince" Philip). This prolific output and the success of many of the records had cemented Tubby's reputation as the King of Dub. Tubby eventually opened his own studio and continued to engineer and produce records for Lee, and was also a crucial part of a series of roots-heavy releases on Carlton Patterson's Black and White label.

By the start of the '80s, Tubby was on top of his game, running his studio, training a new generation of mixers, picking and choosing artists he wanted to work with, and in general becoming comfortable with being a reggae icon. This ended abruptly and brutally in February 1989, when Tubby was shot and killed during a robbery outside of his home in St. Andrew, Jamaica. Violence has claimed many great reggae musicians and producers, and the loss of King Tubby was especially significant due to his groundbreaking technique and his role as a teacher who passed the word and science of dub down to succeeding generations who took Tubby's trip even farther out than he had. *—John Dougan*

☆ **King Tubby & Friends: The Rod of Correction Showcase** / 1974-1979 / Abraham/Clockwise ♦♦♦♦♦
King Tubby & Friends: Rod of Correction Showcase features tracks recorded from 1974 to 1979. What makes this collection of songs significant is the fact that all the tracks bear the seal of King Tubby. Not only did Tubby engineer all these songs, but he mixed them as well. Also, he and the Aggrovators provided much of the instrumental backing. Despite the presence of many reggae heavyweights, including Augustus Pablo, Touter, Scully, Brad Osbourne, Tommy McCook, Bobby Ellis, Chinna Smith, and Ronald Robinson, it's the Aggrovators that really stand out here. Consisting of Carlton Barrett, Sly Dunbar, Carlton "Santa" Davis, Robbie Shakespeare, Aston Barrett, and Tony Chin, the Aggrovators maintained melodically interesting rhythms that were frighteningly steady. Unlike many groups playing Jamaican music at the time, the bands featured on this collection were not influenced by American and British pop music. More often than not, the tempos were higher—closer to the danceable side of things. A testament to the power and might of the Rastafarian god, "Jah Jah the Conqueror" is a rhythmic juggernaut, featuring the vocals of Linval Thompson and the instrumental support of the Aggrovators. Other standout tracks on this compilation are "Dub of Rights" and "Brother Marcus Dub," which treat the listener to the silken vocals of Johnny Clarke. One of the least inspiring tracks is Pablo's "Forever"; although a fairly bouncy tune, it has an excessive lightness to it that makes it less compelling. Overall, though, this is an excellent collection of songs, and a shining example of King Tubby's golden touch. *—Qa'id Jacobs*

● **King Tubby Special 1973-1976** / 1989 / Trojan ♦♦♦♦♦
This two-disc set brings together some of the finest dub mixes ever produced by the legendary King Tubby. The first disc compiles 13 tracks played by the Observer Allstars and originally produced by Winston "Niney" Holness; the second consists of 17 cuts by the Aggrovators (produced by Bunny Lee) and includes the collection's title track, a DJ talkover featuring the great U Roy. King Tubby's approach to dub was always distinctive; his mixes are distinguished by a touch that is sweet sounding and endlessly creative, balancing innovation with respect for the original even during the most drastic deconstruction of a song. And unlike some other dub producers, Tubby generally left swatches of the vocal line in place, dropping it in and out of the mix and applying dirty analog echo, sometimes subtly changing the lyrical focus. This collection's unusually helpful liner notes will assist interested listeners in finding original versions of many of the tracks. A truly essential dub collection. *—Rick Anderson*

If Deejay Was Your Trade / 1994 / Blood & Fire ♦♦♦♦
Another in a seemingly endless series of excellent reissue by the Blood and Fire label. This features some superb Tubby mixes from 1975-79. Fat bass and drums create a Spectorish wall of sound that envelops the other players, as Tubby's savvy behind a mixing board is frequently awesome. Not much overlap with the two-LP set *King Tubby's Special*, it deserves a place in your CD bin if you've caught the dense Tubby vibe and are hungry for more. *—John Dougan*

Dub Gone Crazy: The Evolution of Dub at King Tubby's '75-'77 / 1995 / Blood & Fire ♦♦♦♦♦

Dub Gone 2 Crazy / Jul. 22, 1996 / Blood & Fire ♦♦♦♦♦
An excellent second collection of dub mixed by Tubby and Lloyd "Prince Jammy" James. Many of the tracks were taken from recordings by Johnnie Clarke, and feature Tubby and Jammy cutting loose with their trademark echo explosions combined with machine gun fire and outer space blips and boinks, all rolled together with the sinewy rocksteady beat provided by the Aggrovators. Although the remixes of the Clarke tracks are stellar, it's the dub version of the Jah Stitch and Dr. Alimantado track "The Barber Feel It" (here called "The Poor Barber") that gets the blood pumping. A little wilder than the first Blood and Fire collection of Tubby dub, this is the first time these tracks (all of which were released as singles) have been anthologized in this manner. A real treat. *—John Dougan*

Dangerous Dub / Nov. 12, 1996 / Greensleeves ♦♦♦♦♦

Megawatt Dub / Oct. 21, 1997 / Shanachie ♦♦♦

The Best of King Tubby: King Dub / Oct. 24, 2000 / Music Club ♦♦♦♦♦
Whittling King Tubby's prolific output down to a 15-track best-of that covers just four years of his career (1973-1977) ensures that the title *The Best of King Tubby* is a highly debatable proposition among serious reggae fans. Whether or not this is his best, or what most fans would choose as his best, it's a good collection of work from the period that most would agree represented his prime. These are among the first and best recordings that innovated the traits of dub that are now taken for granted: the wildly careening repeated echoes, ghostly organs, irregular insertion of ethereal lead vocals and wordless vocal harmonies, deep deep bass, sorrowful horns, trance-like rhythms, and odd electronic effects (the burst of computer-like sounds that kick off "Dub From the Roots" would be at home on a 1990s electronica record). It often adds up to a peculiar alternate-universe, just-out-of-step-with-reality dreamlike feel, never more so than on "King Tubby's Talkative Dub," based on the 1960s Mitty Collier soul gem "I Had a Talk With My Man," though utilizing the voice of reggae vocalist John Holt. Among the artists whose source material is plundered and embellished here are Ronnie Davis, the Heptones, Clarence Reid, Horace Andy, Johnny Clarke, and Bob Marley. Dub music is not the easiest genre to collect in a stepping-stone fashion, and although those familiar with King Tubby's work might find this album on the perfunctory side, those not yet immersed in dub discs will almost certainly find it a decent introduction or sampler. *—Richie Unterberger*

Lady Saw (Marion Hall)

b. 1972, St. Mary's, Jamaica
Vocals, Producer / Ragga, Dancehall
The First Lady of Dancehall, Lady Saw is a Jamaican bad girl with loads more attitude and sex appeal than hip-hop mistresses like Lil' Kim or Foxy Brown, plus one of the most distinguishing images in reggae. Born in 1972 in the small Jamaican village of St. Mary's, Marion Hall signed to the Jamaican grassroots label VP Records and debuted in 1994 with *Lover Girl.* Lady Saw soon proved she was up to the challenge of Jamaica's rudest bwoys by teaming up with Shabba Ranks on the single "Want It Tonight."

Her second album, *Give Me the Reason,* was followed by 1997's *Passion,* which featured her X-rated vocal swaggering on duets with Shaggy ("Mr. Lover Lover") and Beenie Man ("Healing"). The album was her most popular, prompting the 1998 release of two greatest-hits packages, *Collection* and *Raw: The Best of Lady Saw.* —*John Bush*

Collection / Jan. 13, 1998 / Diamond Rush ✦✦✦✦✦
A strong introduction to Lady Saw's unique brand of dancehall, *The Collection* offers 20 hits spanning from 1991 to 1997, and features duets with performers including Frankie Paul, Dennis Brown and Ghost. —*Jason Ankeny*

● **Raw: The Best of Lady Saw** / Feb. 10, 1998 / VP ✦✦✦✦✦
The scandalous Jamaican MC shouts out 19 shockers on this best-of compilation. Lady Saw nee Marion Hall is sultry and seductive; she's the island's answer to Lil Kim or Foxy Brown. A multitude of producers make these tracks possible. Therefore, there are subtle differences among the tracks; the many "cooks" keep the CD from becoming boring and stagnant. The best include "Hardcore," "Find a Good Man," "No Long Talking," and "Give Me a Reason." If you didn't purchase Lady Saw's previous releases, this is a good introduction to her provocative, dancehall world. —*Andrew Hamilton*

Byron Lee

Vocals, Producer / Tropical, Party Soca, Dancehall, Ska, Soca
In the years before reggae or even ska was known outside of the Caribean, Byron Lee was the first band leader to achieve an international following playing Jamaican music, and played a vital role in popularizing it around the world. And when Bob Marley was a struggling young musician and of the little-known Wailers, Byron Lee was probably the most well known Jamaican band leader in the world.

Lee was 20 years old when he formed his band the Dragonaires in 1956. They began making a name for themselves almost immediate, as a kind of big-band equivalent to the solo Calypso singing that Harry Belafonte (and Sir Lancelot before him) brought to enormous popularity in the late 1950's. Touring behind Belafonte, they became internationally famous, and justifiably so-they played Calypso and the ska, but their musicianship was impeccable in any idiom, with a trumpet and sax section that could've passed muster with any big band, and Lee's bass playing itself was extraordinarily distinctive. With Lee leading and manager Ronnie Nasralla co-producing and handling the business arrangements, the Dragonaires made all of the right moves.

They were also lucky enough to be signed to Edward Seaga's WIRL (West Indies Recording Limited) label, which was not only a new and powerful label, but notably honest in paying its artists. Lee had a hit in 1959 with his WIRL debut, "Dumplings," which also became the first release of the British-based Bluebeat label.

One of their other shrewd moves was getting featured in the debut James Bond movie, *Dr. No* (1962). Largely shot in and around Kingston, the film was filled with local Jamaican color, right down to the Calypso number that closed the credits and opened the action, but Lee and the Dragonaires had the choicest spot of all as a musical showcase, playing the song "Jump Up" in the scene at Pussfeller's club where Bond and his allies discuss the mystery before them, and confront an agent of the opposition wielding a lively camera. Millions of people saw the movie, either in its initial release or on its re-release to theaters in 1964, after the success of *Goldfinger,* and they saw and heard Byron Lee and the Dragonaires, who were also all over the Dr. No soundtrack from United Artists, which sold in the hundreds of thousands. (The scene in which Lee and his band appear is doubly interesting from the standpoint of cultural happenstance; among the extras dancing to the band's music is a white Jamaican named Chris Blackwell, who formed Island Records about a year later-in that one scene are two of the biggest and most important entrepreneurs in Jamaican music crossing paths).

One of the first ska bands, the Dragonaires-a 14-piece outfit whose line-up was always changing (and sometimes worked under the name the Ska Kings)—toured throughout the Caribbean and into North America, spreading the ska sound. Lee opened a concert booking and promotion agency in the early 1960's, Lee Enterprises Limited, as well as his own label, Dragon's Breath. He brought American acts like the Drifters, Chuck Berry, Sam Cooke, and Fats Domino into Jamaica, booking them into the Carib and Regal Theaters, with local Jamaican acts opening for them.

Lee's big year was 1964, when he and the Dragonaires played the New York *World's Fair,* in their own set and backing Prince Buster, Eric Morris, and Peter Tosh. They were all a sensation at the fair, and even managed to work in some major gigs at some of Manhattan's best nightclubs. It spread their names into the gossip columns (there weren't any music columns as we know them today) and newspaper entertainment sections, and did wonders to boost Jamaica's tourism to even higher levels.

That same year, Lee made his biggest business move, buying WIRL from Edward Seaga (now a government minister, in fact the very one who had booked Lee into the *World's Fair*) and renaming it Dynamic Sounds Recording, Inc. He also began establishing a relationship with Ahmet Ertegun at Atlantic Records, which resulted in his first release on an American label, the multi-artist compilation *Jamaican Ska,* and a follow-up, *Jump Up,* that was all Lee and his band, and gave him the distribution rights to Atlantic's r&b releases in the Carribean.

Amid all of those business activities, Lee maintained a full performing and recording schedule, cutting singles regularly and albums at least once a year after the mid-1960's. In addition to his own singles, these frequently contained covers of other artists' ska hits of the period.

Lee was eminently successful, although in later years, he would incur the editorial wrath of writers who regarded his dance band as a pale, watered down version of ska, compared to outfits like the Skatalites, the Maytals, or the Wailers. Lee and his band, however, did more to popularize ska and Jamaican music than any performer of the 1960's. Coupled with the success in 1964 of Millie Small's Island Records single "My Boy Lollipop," which sold upwards of six million copies worldwide, it was the opening of a booming musical era for Jamaican music.

By 1969, Lee was owner of the best recording studio in Kingston, and Dynamic Sounds became the most popular recording venue in the entire Caribean. By the early 1970's, the biggest American and English rock stars had discovered its appeal, including the Rolling Stones, Paul Simon and Eric Clapton. Paul Simon's "Mother And Child Reunion," in particular, became a showcase for Lee's studio. Meanwhile, he continued making his own music, having evolved from ska to reggae and, by the late 1970s, to the soca style. For all of their supposed watered-down nature, Lee and the Dragonaires have maintained a following right into the end of the twentieth century, their Jamaican dancehall-influenced sound delighting crowds at the annual Carnival celebration. Lee and his band also cut annual collections of covers of the year's most popular Carnival hits, an extension of his early- and mid-1960's covers of ska hits. —*Bruce Eder*

Tiney Winey / 1985 / Dynamic Sounds ✦✦✦✦✦
The first recording of "Tiney Winey," a song written by Arrow but set aside as second-rate, it was one of the huge hits of the Caribbean in 1985. Arrow went on to record the song in 1988. —*Gene Scaramuzzo*

Soft Lee, Vol. 6 / Jan. 6, 1998 / VP ✦✦✦
Byron Lee and the Dragonaires' *Soft Lee Vol. VI* concentrates mostly on the soca star's balladeering skills, featuring pop covers like "Wind Beneath My Wings" and "Candle In the Wind," as well as "My Last Date With You." But Lee doesn't forget to include danceable, uptempo material, as the Latin-flavored "Amor Amor Amor" and "Come Closer to Me" prove. —*Steve Huey*

Soca Frenzy / Apr. 14, 1998 / Dynamic Sounds ✦✦✦

● **Ska Reggae Soca Style 1964-1996** / Jan. 18, 1999 / Music Club ✦✦✦✦✦

Soca Bacchanal / Dynamic Sounds ✦✦✦✦✦
Hot tunes and fine leads make *Soca Bacchanal* one Lee's finest recorded moments. —*Ron Wynn*

Barrington Levy

b. Apr. 30, 1964
Vocals / Dancehall
Though veteran performer Barrington Levy is closely associated with dancehall music, he considers himself a straight reggae man committed to using his powerful lyrics and music to promote Rastafari's message of universal love and peace. Instead of drawing his inspiration from anger, frustration and lust like many 90's style dancehall performers, Levy bases his songs on his observations of the daily lives and travails of ordinary people. His first single was "A Ya We Deh," but his first major hit was "Collie Weed" produced by Junjo Laws for Jah Guidance. This was followed up by such successes as "Twenty-One Girls Salute" and "Mind Your Mouth." In 1983, Levy made a big splash in Great Britain with "Under Mi Sensi," a tune that spent 12 weeks topping their charts. In the early 1990s, Levy scored a major recording contract with the U.S. label MCA and has since been gaining an international following. —*Sandra Brennan*

Englishman / 1979 / Nyam Up ✦✦✦✦

Teach Me Culture / 1983 / Live & Learn ✦✦✦
Barrington Levy's earlier material doesn't have the sophisticated production of his recent releases, but was more lyrically varied and intense. This nine-track set presents Levy doing the rich, powerful, traditional reggae that made him a legend in the 1970s and early '80s. The menu includes the anguished "To Love Someone" and "Lonely Man," the prophetic title cut and the poignant "Jah Is With Me." While these songs often invoke a melancholy note or bittersweet mood, there's nothing dispirited or solemn about Levy's soaring vocals and vigorous delivery. —*Ron Wynn*

Barrington Levy / 1984 / Clock Tower ✦✦✦✦✦
Barrington Levy, one of reggae's golden voices, straddles the fence between dancehall and roots material on his major label debut. Levy is better suited to love tunes and traditional material than the busy, hip-hop-influenced contemporary dancehall sound, but he still manages to sound interested when doing songs like "Work," "Vice Versa Love," and "Go There." But those aware of Levy's glorious, swirling style and incandescent voice will be more pleased by his remake of the classic "Under Me Sensi," the powerful "Murderer," and "Nothing's Changed," tunes that showcase his vocal might rather than his ability to incorporate it into a sea of production gimmicks. —*Ron Wynn*

● **Broader than Broadway: The Best of Barrington Levy** / 1990 / Profile ✦✦✦✦✦
This is a fine collection of his best hits of the '80s. —*Roger Steffens*

Prison Oval Rock / 1991 / VP ✦✦✦
Reggae fans knew about Levy's vocal brilliance early in his career, especially his dynamic roots material and equally fervent love ballads and romantic tunes. The 10 tracks on this Ras set are from that period, when he was among the great crooners and pleaders in reggae. If you want anger and venom, there's the slashing fury of "Robber Man" and the title cut; those who prefer sensuality and suggestiveness will devour "Good Loving" and "Mary Long Tongue," while the religious zealots can delight in "Please Jah Jah." —*Ron Wynn*

Divine / 1994 / RAS ✦✦✦
While Barrington Levy continues to soak up the publicity riches from his recent MCA set,

Ras reminds everyone of his greatness in more conventional reggae settings with several discs showcasing him away from trendy dancehall productions. This 10-track set has some nods to the present, notably an inspired remake of Del Shannon's "Runaway," although it's credited to someone called "S. Crook." The real gems are his brilliant covers of Ken Boothe's "Silver Words" and John Holt's "Darling I Need Your Loving." This is the kind of urgent, convincing material on which Levy made his reputation. *—Ron Wynn*

Duets / 1995 / RAS ✦✦✦
The great reggae vocalist Barrington Levy engages a number of other singers—including Beenie Man, Cutty Ranks, Bounty Killer, and Spragga Benz—on a series of duets on the appropriately-titled *Duets*. Unfortunately, the material isn't always as strong as the singers, but there are several killer cuts on the record. *—Stephen Thomas Erlewine*

Ras Portraits / Jul. 8, 1997 / RAS ✦✦✦✦
Ras designed *Ras Portraits* as a concise introduction to a particular artist's recordings for the label. Since the information behind Ras releases is always shady, it's difficult to discern the origin of tracks on *Ras Portraits*, but the disc is one of the better collections of Barrington Levy material that Ras has released, and listeners curious about his albums for the label should start here. It should not, however, be seen as a definitive introduction to his music in general. Among the featured tracks on Levy's *Ras Portrait* are "Do the Dance," "Prison Oval Rock," "Robber Man," "Living Dangerously," "Little Children Cry," "Hypocrites," "Her I Come," "Please Jah Jah" and "Mary Long Tongue." *—Stephen Thomas Erlewine*

J.C. Lodge

Vocals / Reggae-Pop, Dancehall
With her classic girlish pop voice, J.C. Lodge helped bankrupt producer Joe Gibbs when he failed to pay songwriter's royalties to Charley Pride for J.C.'s million-selling cover of "Someone Loves You, Honey." In the late '80s, her "Telephone Love" became a massive, long-lasting international hit penetrating the dancehalls as well as radio stations. Among her prolific output were the albums *Home Is Where the Hurt Is* (1991), *Activate Me* (1993) and *Love for All Seasons* (1996). *—Roger Steffens*

• **Revealed** / 1985 / RAS ✦✦✦✦✦
J.C. Lodge's teasing, lithe sound has made her one of the 1990s' top female reggae singers; her coy, suggestive leads have proven quite potent commercially. This nine-track session was recorded before she became a star, and while there's a preponderance of synthesizers and electronic backing, it's less busy and heavily produced than her recent material. Lodge is mostly creditable, although the cover of "You Can't Hurry Love" is disposable, and "You Can Dance" and her version of The Bee Gees' "To Love Somebody" strictly generic. But "Stick By Me," "Stalemates" and "You Make Me Shine" demonstrate the potential other producers have since tapped. *—Ron Wynn*

Tropic of Love / 1992 / Tommy Boy ✦✦✦
J.C. Lodge is the type of artist reggae purists have no use for. As they see it, blending reggae with elements of pop, urban contemporary and dance music in so sleek a fashion only serves to water reggae down. But then, Lodge never claimed to be a purist, and in fact, *Tropic of Love* is fairly decent. The expressive Lodge has an alluring, sexy quality to her voice that works to her advantage on such sleek pop-reggae offerings as "The Prey," "Why" and the hit "Telephone Love." Most of the material is very 1990s-sounding, but "Come Again" is a pleasant number that, except for some dancehall-minded toasting, recalls the reggae of the '60s (when Jamaican artists were paying very close attention to what the American soulsters of Motown were up to). Also noteworthy is Lodge's cover of Sylvia Robinson's seductive 1973 hit "Pillow Talk." *Tropic* isn't breathtaking, but it's definitely more soulful and enjoyable than reggae's purists claim. *—Alex Henderson*

To the Max / 1993 / RAS ✦✦✦✦
Since her "Telephone Love" hit, reggae songstress J.C. Lodge has been repeatedly playing the mid-tempo romantic seductress game; this disc continues that pattern. Lodge also tries her hand at social commentary with the original "I Am Someone," a tune about interracial marriages and what happens to the couple's children. It is a well-meaning number, but Lodge sounds more hurt than angry when singing lyrics meant to register protest and outrage. She is much better on the remake of Minnie Riperton's "Lovin' You," striking the right note of tribute and romance while wisely trying not to emulate Riperton. This is uneven, but about as good as can be expected in current reggae circles. It's not completely slack or totally roots, but somewhere uncomfortably in-between. *—Ron Wynn*

Love for All Seasons / Aug. 1996 / RAS ✦✦✦
Recorded with Mad Professor, *Love for Seasons* captures the more experimental tendencies of J.C. Lodge. Throughout the record, Lodge and the Mad Professor delve deeply into dub reggae, occasionally surfacing for relatively straightforward reggae numbers. In the process, the team creates a hypnotic, trance-like groove that exemplifies nearly all the best qualities of dub-influenced reggae. *—Leo Stanley*

Luciano (Jepther McClymont)

b. 1994
DJ / Dancehall, Roots Reggae
A superstar in his native Jamaica, Luciano combines his love of God and beauty into a soulful, spiritual blend of rock and R&B-tinged reggae. Born Jepther McClymont in Davey Town, he began his musical career singing in church and moved to Kingston to pursue music professionally.

After working with prominent reggae producers like Herman Chin-Loy and labels like Aquarius and Sky High, Homer Harris of Blue Mountain changed McClymont's name to Luciano. He then released singles for labels like Big Ship, New Name Muzik and Sky High, and began working with longtime producer Phillip "Fattis" Burrell. However, the pressures of constant recording and performing caused him to leave the music scene in 1993 to regroup and reconsider his life.

His return, the 1995's *Where There is Life* reflected Luciano's sabbatical with its spiritual, contemplative style, and found critical acclaim for its artistic integrity and stylistic diversity. Luciano's sacred approach to life and music fills his other albums, including 1996's *After All*, 1997's *Messenger* and 1999's *Champions in Action*. *Great Controversy* was issued two years later, as was *A New Day*. *—Heather Phares*

Where There is Life / Nov. 1995 / Island Jamaica ✦✦✦
Luciano's debut, *Where There Is Life* shows the strong spiritual influence on his music. Comprised of some of his greatest island hits and new material produced by Philip "Fatis" Burrell, *Where There Is Life* showcases Luciano's strong voice and rock and R&B-inflected reggae. Hopeful messages like *Lord Give Me Strength* and *He Is My Friend* abound on the album, making it a strong artistic and philosophical statement from this Jamaican superstar. *—Heather Phares*

After All / Nov. 7, 1995 / VP ✦✦✦
Luciano downplays the spiritual aspects of his music on this album, focusing instead on love and relationships. The beautiful vocal arrangements on tracks like "Hold Me In Your Arms" and "True Love" stand out, while "Took Me for Granted" and "Shake It Up Tonight" deliver a modern reggae sound. Though not as musically diverse or lyrically cohesive as his later works, *After All* is a solid release with moments like "After All" and "Hold on to Your Dreams" that suggest Luciano's future direction. *—Heather Phares*

Jet Star Reggae Max: Luciano / 1997 / Jet Star ✦✦✦
Luciano's *Reggae Max* collects some of his biggest hits and most memorable singles, including "Nature Boy," "Ragga Muffin," "That's the Way Life Goes," "Show You How," and "One Way Ticket." While it's not the deepest collection of his work, the album does cover most of Luciano's hits plus a few lesser-known album tracks. *—Heather Phares*

Messenger / Apr. 14, 1997 / VP ✦✦✦
Luciano's second album to feature a positive message, *Messenger* continues his musical quest for a meaningful life. The title track, "Mama," and "Never Give Up My Pride" deliver Luciano's message of love and strength, while "Friend in Need" and "How Can You" question the status quo of relationships. Musically, *Messenger* sounds lush and diverse, with different tempos and arrangements expanding on Luciano's reggae foundation. "Life's" Latin guitar and piano touches, the brass flourishes of "Over the Hills" and the vocal arrangement on the title track give Luciano's songs an added resonance. *—Heather Phares*

• **Sweep over My Soul** / Feb. 9, 1999 / VP ✦✦✦✦
As one of the forerunners in the "conscious" dancehall movement, Luciano has consistently produced positive, well-crafted and beautifully sung hits since 1995. The singer continues this pattern with *Sweep Over My Soul*, his third album. Overflowing with soothing vocals and affirming lyrics, this album provides the highest quality reggae, with easygoing beats, catchy choruses and Luciano's melt-your-heart singing. Several of the albums tunes were already hits in 1998, such as the gospel-driven title track and the swerving melody of "Ulterior Motive," but most of the other songs are just as strong, especially "Can't Stop Jah Works," with its spoken word lyrics and gorgeous melody and "Talking' Bout," with Morgan Heritage. *—Rosalind Cummings-Yeates*

Macka-B

Vocals / Dancehall
Macka B, the originator of the Exodus Dancehall Sound System, describes his style as "dancehall with plenty of one-drop grooves." His lyrics attack racism, sexual abuse, alcoholism and apartheid. The winner of a Best British DJ award, he saw his "Squeeze Me" single reach number one in Hawaii in mid-1994. His *Discrimination* album on Ras Records, released in February 1995, featured production from Mad Professor. *—John Bush*

Buppie Culture / 1984 / RAS ✦✦✦
Another of four Macka-B Ariwa/Ras sessions issued in 1990, this one took vicious swipes at upper and upper-middle-class blacks worldwide, although much of what he bemoans in the title track would probably would apply more to African-Americans than any other group. His rhetoric gets incendiary at times, skirting the lines of racism (or at least anti-white venom) on "Hole In The Atmosphere." But he also includes universal themes in "Human Rights," "Respect Our Mothers," and "We Love The Children." He's more strident and forceful on these nine tracks, and although still not the most exciting DJ, Macka-B was an effective protest voice on this release. *—Ron Wynn*

We've Had Enough / 1984 / Ariwa ✦✦✦
Macka-B was one of the busier toaster/DJs on Ariwa's roster in 1990, issuing at least four sessions that found their way to these shores. This six-cut outing started curiously with "Indian Girl." It was unclear whether Macka-B was advocating or attacking interracial romance, immigration practices and political/cultural preferences, as he mixed and blurred his metaphors and message. Other songs, notably "False Preacher," "Apartheid" and the title track, were much clearer, while "Big Mack" was the disc's lone silly song/novelty tune. Macka-B has an easily understandable style, but isn't that compelling a toaster. *—Ron Wynn*

• **Sign of the Times** / 1986 / Ariwa ✦✦✦✦
Sign of the Times was one of the landmark reggae records of the mid-'80s, mainly because Macka B's powerful, political vocals were given an ambitious, stunning musical backdrop by Mad Professor. It pushed song-oriented reggae into the world of dub, helping create a new musical language along the way. And that music is given force by Macka B's toasting, which is never simplistic or dull. Truly a wonderful, provoking record that has stood the test of time. *—Leo Stanley*

Looks Are Deceiving / 1990 / RAS ✦✦✦

Natural Suntan / 1990 / RAS ✦✦✦

Peace Cup / 1991 / RAS ✦✦✦
DJ/toaster Macka B dropped the slash from his name on this session, and picked up two part-time partners in Sister Audrey (the title track) and John McLean ("Gone Home"), but otherwise continued performing the same potent protest, cultural and roots material that high-

lighted his previous releases. Macka B dispels the notion that only contemporary dancehall matters anymore with "Roots Ragga," prophesies the coming apocalypse on "Revelation Time," and otherwise keeps the fiery messages coming. Some cuts, especially "Going Home," had a breezy, vintage sensibility punctuated by tight horn lines. It was another good, occasionally evocative session by the prolific Macka B. *—Ron Wynn*

Mad Cobra (Ewart Everton Brown)

b. Mar. 31, 1968, Kingston, Jamaica
Vocals / Ragga, Dancehall
Ragga dee-jay Mad Cobra was only 26 years old when he became the first reggae artist to score a number one hit on the US. Billboard pop charts. He was the first dancehall artist to do so and only the second in all of reggae to have that distinction. Born Ewart Everton Brown in Kingston, he was raised in St. Mary's Parish until returning to Kingston in his teens. His nickname came a character in the G.I. Joe comic books and was given to him by a schoolteacher who noticed young Brown's tendency to doodle fearsome snakes all over his notebooks. He got his start with such sound systems as Mighty Ruler, Inner City and Climax. It was his uncle Delroy "Spiderman" Thompson, an engineer at Tuff Gong who produced his debut single "Respect Woman" in 1989. More local hits followed and Cobra was then produced by Banton Nelson and Captain Sinbad. In emulation of Ninjaman's dancehall success with gun talk, they steered Cobra towards such titles as "Shoot to Kill" and "Merciless Bad Boy." They soon garnered him a devoted following on the dancehall circuit and led him to sign to Donovan Germain's Penthouse studio where he had even more hits with such Dave Kelly produced singles as "Yush" and "Gunderlero." He teamed up with Beres Hammond to record "Feeling Lonely" and in 1991 had a major hit with the album *Bad Boy Talk.* During this time, the dancehall market was nearly flooded with Mad Cobra singles. He was a hardcore dee-jay at that time and was controversial for promoting gay-bashing in such songs as "Crucifixion" long before Buju Banton and Shabba Ranks gained similar notoriety. Homophobic lyrics on the albums *Spotlight* and *Exclusive* led to their being pulled from the shelves in the US. By 1991, Cobra's popularity had spread to the UK and in one year he had five number one hits on the country's reggae charts and at one time had nine Top 20 hits on the British charts. Cobra has frequently worked with other artists including Bee Cat, Mafia & Fluxy and Fashion. But though known for his hard-core lyrics, Cobra didn't have his big US success until he softened up and recorded the buttery smooth "Flex," which he recorded over a Jamaican version of the Temptations' '60s hit "Just My Imagination." The song's success led him to sign with the US label Columbia. His next single, "Legacy" (both songs appear on his Columbia album *Hard to Wet, Easy to Dry*) did little on the charts and he soon went back to the Jamaican dancehalls, laying low until 1993, when he returned to energetic ragga music with such songs as "Mek Noise" and "Matie Haffi Move." *—Sandra Brennan*

• **Goldmine** / 1993 / RAS ✦✦✦✦✦

Mister Pleasure / May 20, 1994 / VP ✦✦✦

Exclusive Decision / Jun. 1996 / VP ✦✦✦
Though it occasionally dips into political rhetoric, Mad Cobra's *Exclusive Decision* is more or less a party album, driven by his infectious toasting. Since it is a party album that means, of course, that there is a fair amount of chaff with the wheat, but the best tracks make the effort worthwhile. *—Leo Stanley*

Sexperience / Jul. 29, 1996 / Critique ✦✦✦✦
This slick dancehall reggae outing from Mad Cobra features the single "Wish You Were Here" as well as remakes of the club hits "Never Gonna Give You Up" and "Dirty Cash." *—Jason Ankeny*

Milkman / Sep. 17, 1996 / Capitol ✦✦✦
Joined by producers Salaam Remi, Tiny Dofat, Clifton "Specialist" Dillon and Dave Kelley, Mad Cobra continues in the explicit vein of his hit "Flex (Time to Have Sex)" on this banal light reggae outing, which includes "Big Long John" and "Sting Night," recorded with Ninja-Man. *—Jason Ankeny*

Mad Lion

Group / Club/Dance, Fusion, Dancehall, Hip-Hop
Weaving a seamless blend of reggae and hip hop, Mad Lion (born: Oswald Priest) created one of the most influential sounds of the past two decades. The recipient of the 1994 "Source" award as "Reggae artist of the year", Mad Lion has inspired similar-sounding recordings by such artists as Ini Kamozi, Cappleton and Rayvon.

A native of London, England, Mad Lion was raised in Jamaica. Shortly after moving to Brooklyn, New York, he met reggae performer, Super Cat, at Super Power Records. At Super Cat's suggestion, he adopted his professional name, an acronym for Musical Assassin Delivering Lyrical Intelligence Over Nations.. Mad Lion's earliest success came in the mid-1980s when he applied his hip hop rhythms to Shabba Rank's hit single, "Jam". He later appeared, along with Queen Latifah, on Salt'n'Pepper's 1997 album, *Brand New.*

Launching his own label, Spinners Choice, Mad Lion was working on his debut album when he met and convinced producer KRS-One to work with him. The collaboration proved fruitful as Mad Lion's single, "Shoot To Kill", sold more than one hundred thousand copies. His next single, "Take It Easy", did even better, exceeding the three hundred thousand sale mark.

After releasing an album, *Real Ting,* in 1993, Mad Lion made countless guest appearances on such albums as *the New Jersey Drive* and *D&D All Stars* compilations and produced a tune for Born Jamaicans. His second album, *Ghetto Gold Platinum Respect,* was released in 1997.Three years later his third album *Predatah Or Prey,* which also included an interactive game, arrived. *—Craig Harris*

Real Ting / 1995 / Weeded ✦✦✦
KRS-One's production gives the beats on this album a precision that contrasts with Mad Lion's gravelly ragga vocals. The lyrics are typical dancehall material. *—John Bush*

Mad Professor (Neal Fraser)

b. Guyana, West Indies
Vocals, Drums, Percussion, Producer / Dub
A mastery of electronic gadgetry has been expressed through the imaginative recordings produced by Mad Professor (born: Neil Fraser). Working from his own studios, Mad Professor has overseen more than one hundred albums including ground-breaking remixes for Massive Attack, Sade and Pato Banton. A native of Guyana, Mad Professor earned his professional name for his childhood fascination for electronics. At the age of nine or ten, he built a radio from scratch. Moving to London, at the age of thirteen, Mad Professor continued to experiment with electronics. Although he bought a semi-professional reel to reel tape recorder in 1975, he was unable to record in sync. This prompted him to purchase more and more equipment. By the following year, he had begun experimenting with dubbing. Over the years, Mad Professor's studio, which he named "Ariwa", after the Nigerian word for sound, has continued to evolve. Opened in a south London house in 1979, it moved to a much larger space in the Peckham ghetto the following year. During the four years that the studio remained at the site, Mad Professor found that the seemingly unsafe location cost him much of his clientele. After a brief return to the original house, the studio relocated to its present site in Whitehorse Lane. *—Craig Harris*

Beyond the Realms of Dub: Dub Me Crazy Pt. 2 / 1982 / Ariwa ✦✦✦
On this, the second installment in the *Dub Me Crazy* series, Mad Professor opens simply by saying, "Tune into *Dub Me Crazy Pt. 2*," just before plunging headlong into ten tracks of space age dub that are sure to twist your brain up nice and tight. After all, that's the goal here, right— At times, some of the tracks sound a bit too much like a '70s video game with low batteries and seem too crammed with extraneous electronic noises. Sometimes it works, like on "Elastic Plastic," and at other times it doesn't, like on "Africa 1983 Dub." Indeed, on tracks like the steel drum-laced "English Connection," simpler is better. Despite the few weak tracks, true Mad Professor fans will find satisfaction in his characteristic deep space piano chords that seem to reverberate forever, bass lines that will nail you to a wall, and just the right amount of quirkiness thrown in for good measure. *—Matthew Hilburn*

Dub Me Crazy: Dub Me Crazy Pt. 1 / 1982 / Ariwa ✦✦✦
On his own small British Label lurks the most sonically (and electronically) creative producer of the age. The Mad Professor's own albums, while still clearly reggoid, mix in a vision like George Clinton on astrodust and an approach to sampling, synth and so on that makes other electron-maniacs sound like nice little old ladies playing hymns. Macka is a little more conservative, though still pretty ionospheric, what with the synth balafon and Martian belly-drums. *—John Storm Roberts, Original Music*

The African Connection: Dub Me Crazy Pt. 3 / 1983 / Ariwa ✦✦✦✦✦
One of the best of Mad Professor's many *Dub Me Crazy* releases, *The African Connection* spotlights the engineer's bubbly and spacious dub conception. Foregoing the denser, more claustrophobic sound of pioneers like King Tubby and Augustus Pablo, this successful English producer (by way of Guyana) fills each track with an ongoing parade of vocals, brass, reeds, percussion, and synthesizers. Even though many dub techniques are used -≠ echo, flanger effects, etc. - Mad Professor (born Neil Fraser) produces a more hyperactive and funky sound than heard on Tubby's methodical sound deconstructions; the Jamaican influence in Fraser's work probably stems more from the slicker and sound effects-riddled style of Tubby protégés Scientist and Prince Jammy. Highlights include the rockers' cut "Bengali Skank," the alto saxophone vehicle "Natural Vegetation," and the trombone-in-dub side "Lion Dance." Working with some fine tracks by his Ariwa Band (featuring the vocals of '70s Jamaican star Johnny Clarke, among others), Mad Professor produces a consistently enjoyable and engaging dub set. Highly recommended. *—Stephen Cook*

Escape to the Asylum of Dub: Dub Me Crazy Pt. 4 / 1983 / RAS ✦✦✦
These 1983 sessions are his most traditional dub, but they point the way to the craziness to come. Many female vocalists are heard here. *—Myles Boisen*

Feast of Yellow Dub / 1984 / RAS ✦✦✦✦
It's fashionable to slag British producer Mad Professor these days. And it's true that his sound, a digitally clean yet sonically adventurous combination of Lee Perry-style quirkiness and roots-wise rhythm, is distinctive enough and his output prolific enough that he does open himself up to charges of repetition. It might be fair to call him the Vivaldi of reggae; he borrows from himself shamelessly, and you can generally identify a Mad Professor production within about four bars. But really, that's not necessarily a bad thing. And when you team him up with a personality as strong as that of Yellowman—Jamaica's famous Afro-albino toaster—the results can be outstanding, as they are here. Actually, Yellowman's contributions are pretty passive; this is a collection of Yellowman singles in dub versions by the Professor, and Yellowman's voice only pops into the mix occasionally. Even then, it's often digitally manipulated past recognition; fans who pay close attention may recognize "A Dose of Diseases" as the dub version of "AIDS" and "Some Wild Western Peppers" as the dub of "Wild Wild West." The Roots Radics provide the instrumental raw material for this crazy dub concoction and, as usual, their performances are impeccable. *—Rick Anderson*

Who Knows the Secret of the Master Tape—: Dub Me Crazy Pt. 5 / 1985 / RAS ✦✦✦✦

Captures Pato Banton / 1988 / RAS ✦✦✦✦✦
This collaboration with Jamaican singer Pato Banton is typically mind-expanding, with more pop intent and extending vocal tracks. *—Myles Boisen*

Science & the Witchdoctor: Dub Me Crazy Pt. 9 / May 1989 / RAS ✦✦✦
The professor's treatment of reggae backing-tracks is most inspired on side two. Wild keyboards abound. *—Myles Boisen*

Recaptures Pato Banton / Jul. 1989 / RAS ✦✦✦✦✦
This collaboration with Jamaican singer Pato Banton is typically mind-expanding, with more pop intent and extending vocal tracks. *—Myles Boisen*

Psychedelic Dub: Dub Me Crazy Pt. 10 / 1990 / RAS ✦✦✦
More craziness, with guest appearances by singer Macka B and the legendary trombonist Rico. *—Myles Boisen*

Hijacked to Jamaica: Dub Me Crazy Pt. 11 / 1991 / RAS ✦✦✦
Part 11 of the *Dub Me Crazy* series was actually done in Jamaica, rather than in The Professor's England home. *—Myles Boisen*

It's a Mad, Mad, Mad, Mad Professor / 1995 / RAS ✦✦✦✦
Mad Professor is a British reggae producer whose incredibly prolific output rivals that of Jamaica's legendary sound factories of the late '60s and early '70s in both quantity and quality. His particular genius is an ability to produce music that is completely modern in sound and technique but that nevertheless draws heavily on the "roots and culture" tradition of golden-era Jamaican reggae. His collaborations with Pato Banton, Macka B, and the legendary Lee Perry (whose influence is felt heavily in Mad Professor's work) have brought him fame in the broader reggae community, while the *Dub Me Crazy* series on his Ariwa label (distributed by RAS in the U.S.) has earned him the adoration of dub fans around the world. This sampler is the place for a neophyte to begin. It includes rarities and tracks from his earlier albums, all recorded in "Dubarama." That means that instruments and voices fly in and out of the mix, echoing crazily and careening off into the darkness only to return when you least expect them. Mad Professor doesn't do the introspective, mystical dub of so many of his predecessors; there's always an intense energy and a mischievous sense of humor at work, even on his more political material. *—Rick Anderson*

● **Ras Portraits** / Jul. 8, 1997 / RAS ✦✦✦✦✦
Ras designed *Ras Portraits* as a concise introduction to a particular artist's recordings for the label. Since the information behind Ras releases is always shady, it's difficult to discern the origin of tracks on *Ras Portraits*, but this disc is one of the better collections of Mad Professor material that Ras has released, and listeners curious about his albums for the label should start here. It should not, however, be seen as a definitive introduction to his music in general. Among the featured tracks on the Professor's *Ras Portraits* edition are "Dub Science," "Beyond the Realms of Dub," "Zion," "Holokoko Dub," "Sistren Version," "Buccaneer's Cove," "Hi-Jacked to Jamaica," "Fire on Mt. Sinai," "Black Skin, White Minds," "Anti-Racist Braodcast," and "Harder Than Babylon." *—Stephen Thomas Erlewine*

Bob Marley (Robert Nesta Marley)

b. Feb. 6, 1945, St. Ann, Jamaica, **d.** May 11, 1981, Miami, FL
Vocals, Guitar / Political Reggae, Roots Reggae, Rocksteady, Ska
Born of a middle-age white father and a teenage Black mother, Robert Nesta Marley transcended the humility of his rural beginnings to become not only a million-selling artist and stadium-filling entertainer but—more importantly—a nearly religious figure whose pleas for brotherhood and justice achieved universal anthemic status.

He began singing professionally at 16 with his self-penned "Judge Not!" It and its follow-up were not successful, and he returned to his ghetto neighborhood of Trenchtown to be tutored by Joe Higgs, a recording artist who coached promising youngsters like Marley, Bunny Livingstone, and Peter Tosh (who would become The Wailers). Signed in 1963 to Coxsone Dodd's influential, pace-setting Studio One, The Wailers saw their first release, "Simmer Down," become an instant #1. During the next two-and-a-half years, the group recorded over a hundred songs, and at one point in 1965 held five of the top ten slots on the Jamaican charts.

Forming their own label, Wail 'n Soul 'm, in 1966, The Wailers continued a series of local hits, with little financial remuneration. Following an album with Leslie Kong (*Best of the Wailers*), they hooked up with the seminal oddball producer, Lee Perry, and produced an amazing series of singles that are collected under a variety of names and remain their finest hour.

In 1972, Island Records prez Chris Blackwell signed The Wailers, but after two albums the group broke up, leaving Marley at the head of the band, to which he added a female backing trio, The I Threes. By 1975, Marley had gone clear as a revolutionary standard bearer, the inheritor of the 60s activist energy and hippie ganja enlightenment. Almost assassinated in 1976 in Kingston, Marley was given the UN Peace Medal on behalf of 500 million Africans in 1978 for his humanitarian achievements. He headlined a Peace Concert that same year in Jamaica, uniting the warring factions in the Kingston slums. But his greatest honor came when he was invited to headline the Zimbabwe Independence Celebrations in 1980. He outdrew the Pope in Milan, fathered eleven children by seven women, sold tens of millions of records worldwide, left a $30 million estate, wrote "the new Psalms," and died at 36 of melanoma. *—Roger Steffens*

Soul Rebels / 1970 / Trojan ✦✦✦✦✦

☆ **African Herbsman** / 1973 / Trojan ✦✦✦✦✦
To Bob Marley's emotionally charged music and lyrics, add the tight riddims and harmonies of the Wailers and then put all of that talent into the ceaselessly creative hands of production wizard Lee "Scratch" Perry. What you get is a 16-track reggae masterpiece capturing what is perhaps some of the best music Bob Marley and the Wailers ever committed to tape. The songs range from beautiful love songs like "Don't Rock the Boat" to cathartic political anthems like "Brain Washing," but even with the broad scope, no tracks miss the mark. They all cut straight to the heart and burn with an urgency rarely felt in music of any genre. So defining are the tracks that Marley himself was to return to the same themes later in his career, reviving such classics as "Lively Up Yourself" on *Natty Dread*, "Trench Town Rock" on *Live!* and "Kaya" on *Kaya*, among others. While this is a Bob Marley and the Wailers album, Perry's unique production almost steals the show. Perry's bare-bones, heavy sound provides an interesting contrast to the slicker approach taken on *Catch a Fire*, produced by Bob Marley and the Wailers and Chris Blackwell and also made in 1973. *Catch a Fire* has an almost rock edge to it, but on *African Herbsman*, one can hear Perry's swirling mix madness lurking just beneath the surface of each Trench-Town-tough track. *—Matthew Hilburn*

☆ **Burnin'** / 1973 / Tuff Gong ✦✦✦✦✦
Another extraordinary collection of songs with The Wailers, strongly featuring the vocal blend of Marley, Peter Tosh, and Bunny Livingstone on such songs as "Get Up, Stand Up," "I Shot the Sheriff," and "Burnin' and Lootin'." The last album to feature the original group. *—William Ruhlmann*

☆ **Catch a Fire** / 1973 / Tuff Gong ✦✦✦✦✦
Catch a Fire was the major label debut for Bob Marley and the Wailers, and it was an international success upon its release in 1973. Although Bob Marley may have been the main voice, every member of the Wailers made valuable contributions and they were never more united in their vision and sound. All the songs were originals, and the instrumentation was minimalistic in order to bring out the passionate, often politically charged lyrics. Much of the appeal of the album lies in its sincerity and sense of purpose—these are streetwise yet disarmingly idealistic young men who look around themselves and believe they might help change the world through music. Marley sings about the current state of urban poverty ("Concrete Jungle") and connects the present to past injustices ("Slave Driver"), but he is a not a one-trick pony. He is a versatile songwriter who also excels at singing love songs such as his classic "Stir It Up." Peter Tosh sings the lead vocal on two of his own compositions—his powerful presence and immense talent hint that he would eventually leave for his own successful solo career. More than anything else, however, this marks the emergence of Bob Marley and the international debut of reggae music. Marley would continue to achieve great critical and commercial success during the 1970s, but *Catch a Fire* is one of the finest reggae albums ever. This album is essential for any music collection. *—Vik Iyengar*

☆ **Natty Dread** / 1974 / Tuff Gong ✦✦✦✦✦
Natty Dread is Bob Marley's finest album, the ultimate reggae recording of all time. This was Marley's first album without former bandmates Peter Tosh and Bunny Livingstone, and the first released as Bob Marley and the Wailers. The Wailers' rhythm section of bassist Aston "Family Man" Barrett and drummer Carlton "Carly" Barrett remained in place and even contributed to the songwriting, while Marley added a female vocal trio, the I-Threes (which included his wife Rita Marley), and additional instrumentation to flesh out the sound.

The material presented here defines what reggae was originally all about, with political and social commentary mixed with religious paens to Jah. The celebratory "Lively Up Yourself" falls in the same vein as "Get Up, Stand Up" from *Burnin'*. "No Woman No Cry" is one of the band's best-known ballads. "Them Belly Full (But We Hungry)" is a powerful warning that "a hungry mob is a angry mob." "Rebel Music (3 O'Clock Roadblock)" and "Revolution" continue in that spirit, as Marley assumes the mantle of prophet abandoned by '60s forebears like Bob Dylan. In addition to the lyrical strengths, the music itself is full of emotion and playfulness, with the players locked into a solid groove on each number.

Considering that popular rock music was entering the somnambulant disco era as *Natty Dread* was released, the lyrical and musical potency is especially striking. Marley was taking on discrimination, greed, poverty and hopelessness while simultaneously rallying the troops as no other musical performer was attempting to do in the mid-'70s. *—Jim Newsom*

Rasta Revolution / 1974 / Trojan ✦✦✦✦✦

Live / 1975 / Tuff Gong ✦✦✦✦✦
"One good thing about music—when it hits, you feel no pain." So proclaims Bob Marley in the opening line of this concert recording, and he and his band proceed to brutalize the crowd with the finest reggae then being produced. *Live!* can be taken on either of two levels: First, as one of the greatest live albums of all time, and second, for the uninitiated, as an excellent introduction to the music Marley & the Wailers were making in the early to mid '70s. It is, in a very real sense, Marley's "greatest hits" collection of the 1973-75 era. *—Jim Newsom*

Rastaman Vibration / 1976 / Tuff Gong ✦✦✦✦✦
Marley's breakthrough American album finds him discovering new polyrhythms while continuing to turn out powerful new songs, among them the title tune, "Who the Cap Fit," and "War." *—William Ruhlmann*

Birth of a Legend / 1977 / Epic ✦✦✦✦✦

Exodus / 1977 / Tuff Gong ✦✦✦✦✦
Recorded in London following an attempt on his life, *Exodus* shows Marley mellowing a bit. Despite some powerful political tracks, Marley adopts a less fiery, more reflective approach than his previous outings. Still, it's hard to find reggae as good as this. *Exodus* has all one would expect from a Bob Marley album; rumbling statements like "Exodus" and "The Heath" as well as poetic love songs like "Turn Your Lights Down Low." Considering how good these tracks are, *Exodus* does not stop here. Marley also unleashed the huge international hits "Jamming," "Waiting In Vain" and "One Love/People Get Ready." These inspired tracks, perhaps more than any others, came to define Marley around the world. They are irresistible no matter how many times they are played. Never one to dodge innovation, "Exodus" hints that Marley was taking cues from the emerging dub scene. *Exodus*, even though it contains some of Marley's best work, has an underlying nostalgic feel to it hinting that Marley was getting a little formulaic. *—Matthew Hilburn*

Kaya / Jan. 1978 / Tuff Gong ✦✦✦
Here are laidback ganja meditations, love songs, plus "Running Away, " which tells the critics he hasn't gone soft. *—Roger Steffens*

☆ **Babylon by Bus** / Feb. 1978 / Tuff Gong ✦✦✦✦✦
Arguably the most powerful live album in reggae's history, it was recorded with The Wailers at various international stops over a three-year period and demonstrates how Marley remade his music constantly, especially in performance. *—Roger Steffens*

Survival / 1979 / Tuff Gong ✦✦✦
Perhaps Marley's most militant statement, its bare-boned production put many off at first, but it returned him to the political realm in powerful fashion. "One Drop," "So Much Trouble," and "Babylon System" are among his best. *—Roger Steffens*

Uprising / 1980 / Tuff Gong ✦✦✦✦✦
The last album Marley released in his lifetime, this collection is one of his most impassioned, especially the acoustic folk song that closes it, "Redemption Song." *—William Ruhlmann*

Confrontation / Sep. 1983 / Tuff Gong ✦✦✦
This posthumous collection of singles and newly created tracks was based on work Marley left behind. It includes "Buffalo Soldier." *—Roger Steffens*

★ **Legend** / 1984 / Tuff Gong ✦✦✦✦✦
The classic Marley album, the one that any fair-weather reggae fan owns, *Legend* contains 14 of his greatest songs, running the gamut from "I Shot the Sheriff" to the meditative "Redemption Song" and the irrepressible "Three Little Birds." Some may argue that the compilation shortchanges his groundbreaking early ska work or his status as a political commentator, but this isn't meant to be definitive, it's meant to be an introduction, sampling the very best of his work. And it does that remarkably well, offering all of his genre-defying greats and an illustration of his excellence, warmth, and humanity. In a way, it is perfect since it gives a doubter or casual fan anything they could want. Let's face it, the beauty and simplicity of Marley's music was as important as his message, and that's captured particularly well here. *—Stephen Thomas Erlewine*

One Love / 1991 / Heartbeat ✦✦✦✦✦
Bob Marley and the Wailers' early ska sides, recorded from 1963-1966, are a too-often overlooked part of the group's oeuvre, and the best place to hear them is on *One Love at Studio One*, a two-disc, 40-track anthology that strikes a nice balance between the Wailers' massively popular Jamaican hit singles and long-lost rarities, alternate takes, and outtakes. What impresses most is the sheer range of the music; Marley, Livingston, and Tosh are influenced not just by indigenous Jamaican music, but also doo wop, late-'50s/early-'60s American R&B, gospel (these sides were recorded before the group converted to Rastafarianism), and even rock & roll (present are covers of the Beatles' "And I Love Her" and Bob Dylan's "Like a Rolling Stone"). Tender love ballads and spirituals alternate with raucous odes to Kingston rude boy culture, including the classics "Simmer Down" (their first single) and "Hooligans," arguably the first songs which made their rude-boy subject matter explicit. But, as the original version of "One Love" (here with a skipping ska beat, as opposed to the more familiar, slowed-down version on *Legend*) makes clear, Marley was able to speak to his fan base while at the same time expressing himself in universal, anthemic terms. The Wailers made some of the most infectious, soulful ska of the era, and in spite of the occasionally uneven sound quality, it's hard to imagine a better distillation of the 100-plus tracks the group recorded for Studio One than *One Love*. *—Steve Huey*

Songs of Freedom / Oct. 6, 1992 / Tuff Gong ✦✦✦✦
Originally released as a limited-edition box set in 1992, *Songs of Freedom* presents an alternate history of Bob Marley's career, tracing his progression with outtakes, rare singles, alternate mixes, live tracks, and album tracks instead of the songs that formed the bulk of his legacy, as it were. The question is, is this a reasonable track to take— For the most part, yes it is, even if it tends to be a little misleading. That problem isn't too great, since *Songs of Freedom* isn't targeted at the audience that would want just the basics—*Legend* already exists for them, and that sums up everything they need to know about Marley, the ambassador of reggae. The remainder of Marley's audience realizes this box exists just to get rarities to the diehards, and they're thrilled that it exists for that purpose. Because of its nature, *Songs of Freedom* isn't especially compelling to anyone that isn't a hardcore fan—although the first disc of ska and rocksteady material will be delightful to anyone that likes early reggae and isn't thrilled by Marley's rock-star posturing in the '70s—but for those very fans, it's a valuable addition to their collection, since it rounds up rarities with ease and purpose. What *Songs of Freedom* should not be seen as is a definitive overview of Marley's career—it's just for collectors and hardcore fans, the kind of listener who has memorized the original studio albums. For those listeners, it's hard to resist *Songs of Freedom*, but everybody else will be able to safely pass it by. *—Stephen Thomas Erlewine*

Natural Mystic: The Legend Lives On / May 23, 1995 / Island ✦✦✦✦✦
Where *Legend* concentrated on singles, its sequel *Natural Mystic: The Legend Lives On* is a collection of album tracks. Consequently, it isn't cohesive as *Legend* most of these songs work better in their original context, since Bob Marley created albums that were carefully constructed and sequenced. Since it contains a fair share of gems, *Natural Mystic* will be a reasonable way to supplement the greatest hits collection for casual Marley fans, but it doesn't quite convey the depth of his talents the way the original albums did— or *Legend* itself, for that matter. *—Stephen Thomas Erlewine*

Destiny: Rare Ska Sides from Studio One / Jun. 8, 1999 / Heartbeat ✦✦✦✦✦
The billing of this CD is slightly inaccurate. Although Marley does appear on the majority of the tracks, these 1963-1966 cuts were released under the name of the Wailers, not Bob Marley & the Wailers, and some of the later selections were recorded without Marley (who moved to the U.S. for a while in 1966). Which isn't to say this isn't quality ska (moving towards the rocksteady sound on the later songs) that also sheds light on the roots of the music of Bob Marley and fellow Wailers Peter Tosh and Bunny Wailer. Although some of these songs have been reissued before, most of them were previously unavailable on CD, or are alternative takes or versions that were not overdubbed. The 19 tracks are quite varied and entertaining: sweet soul-influenced rockaballads ("Wages of Love"), solid straight-ahead ska ("Do You Feel the Same Way Too," "Dance With Me," "Do It Right"), the gospel cover "Let the Lord Be Seen in You," and one of the first Wailers songs to reflect Rastafarian beliefs, "I Stand Predominant" (written by Bunny Wailer and producer Coxsone Dodd). There are even versions of "White Christmas" and "What's New Pussycat?" Although it's not quite as essential as the two other most easily available early Marley/Wailers comps (*One Love* and *The Birth of a Legend*), it's almost as worthy, and sure to be of interest to anyone who enjoys those other two collections. The liner notes are extremely detailed, with track-by-track comments that even include many dates and quotes from Bunny Wailer—a rarity in vintage reggae reissues, and a trend to be encouraged. *—Richie Unterberger*

The Complete Upsetter Collection / Mar. 7, 2000 / Trojan ✦✦✦✦✦
The singles that Bob Marley and the Wailers cut for Lee Perry's Upsetter label in the late 1960s and early 1970s are among some of the most historically significant in reggae. They mark Marley's break with the ska and rock-steady styles of the mid-1960s and the beginning of his mature reggae sound. Of course, historical significance doesn't always translate into musical enjoyment, but in this case it definitely does. The band, which had formed the core of Perry's mighty Upsetters studio group, gives up slow, churning grooves that move with a tremendous, ponderous energy, like an elephant charging. Marley, Peter Tosh, and Bunny Wailer sing harmonies that are rarely smooth and never exactly pleasant, but always somehow beautiful.

This six-disc box set includes every track known to have been recorded by the Wailers for the Upsetter label, and the resulting program may be a bit daunting for all but the most dedicated fans. The song list includes such immortal material as "Small Axe," "Put It On," "African Herbsman," and "Soul Rebel" (not to mention relative obscurities like "Riding High" and "Who Colt the Game"), but when dub versions, alternate takes, alternate mixes, and deejay versions are taken into account, there are as many as five versions each of many of these songs on the program; it's also worth noting that at this point in Perry's development as a producer, his "dub versions" were little more than unadorned instrumental tracks. For Marley completists and reggae scholars, however, this box is a treasure trove, and anyone can appreciate the impeccable sound quality, not to mention the sheer musical solidity of these performances. It would be an exaggeration to say that every reggae fan must own this box, but anyone with a serious interest in reggae history should certainly consider it. *—Rick Anderson*

Rita Marley

Vocals / Roots Reggae
Rita Anderson was the leader of The Soulettes, a Studio One trio in 1964, when she met her husband-to-be Bob Marley. She recorded with two separate lineups of her group in the 60s, backed several early Wailers recordings, then became a solo artist before helping form The I Threes in 1974 (along with Marcia Griffith and Judy Mowatt) to back Bob on his world-spanning tours through 1980. Following her husband's passing in 1981, she had the biggest hit of her career, a frothy pro-ganja delight called "One Draw." She devoted the 80s to guiding her children's careers in The Melody Makers, and now that The Marley estate's legal battles have been mostly settled, she continues to showcase her teenage-high voice again. *—Roger Steffens*

● **Who Feels It Knows It** / 1981 / Shanachie ✦✦✦✦
Fueled by the controversial single, "One Draw," *Who Feels It Knows It* was the album that truly put Rita Marley on the map as a solo artist. "One Draw," a hilarious ode to sinsemilla, was a big seller in England and Jamaica despite its problems at radio—like Peter Tosh's "Legalize It" several years earlier, "One Draw" was banned from airplay on British radio by the BBC. The most controversial part of the song comes when a Rastawoman school teacher educates her class of students on the "proper" way to smoke sinsemilla. It's hysterically funny and disturbing at the same time—the very thought of a school teacher doing such a thing is appalling. Meanwhile, the other gems on the album are also quite soulful. Lovers of pre-urban contemporary R&B can't miss the parallels between Rastafarian oriented tunes like "Jah Jah Don't Want," "Good Morning, Jah" and "Thank You," and the great soul music of the '60s and '70s. Of course, there were some reggae lovers who bought the album simply because Rita Marley was the wife of Bob Marley, who had died in 1981. But the fact is that she would have been a talented singer if she hadn't been married to the King of Reggae. *Who Feels It Knows It* made it clear that Rita Marley was a fine singer in her own right. *—Alex Henderson*

We Must Carry on / 1988 / Shanachie ✦✦✦✦
From doo wop to funk and disco, American R&B has long had a major impact on reggae. But reggae and R&B differ radically when it comes to women. While women have always played a key role in R&B, reggae has been very male-dominated. One of reggae's more visible female vocalists has been Rita Marley, wife of the late King of Reggae Bob Marley. As a member of the Wailers' backing singers, the I-Threes, she was relegated to the background for many years, but successfully launched a solo career in 1983. Earthy and unpretentious, *We Must Carry On* is very close in spirit to the American soul music of the 1960s and early '70s. Both her own songs and Bob Marley compositions like "Who Colt The Game" and "So Much Things To Say" beautifully demonstrate just how effective simplicity can be. Though *Who Feels It, Knows It* remains her best album, this fine release is a more than welcome addition to Rita Marley's catalog. *—Alex Henderson*

Ziggy Marley

b. Oct. 17, 1968
Vocals, Guitar / Contemporary Reggae, Reggae-Pop
The oldest son of reggae legend Bob Marley and his wife Rita, Ziggy Marley was the natural heir to the throne left vacant by his father's untimely 1981 death; along with backing band the Melody Makers, a unit comprised of his brothers and sisters, he successfully carried on the tradition of communicating the music's message to a growing global audience, in the process even scoring a US Top 40 single—a claim neither of his parents could make. Marley was not even 17 when he and the Melody Makers (his sister Cedelia, brother Stephen and half-sister Sharon) issued their EMI debut LP, 1985's *Play the Game Right*. The burdens of becoming a second-generation star weighed heavily on the youth—who looked and sounded almost eerily like his father—and he allowed the record and its 1986 follow-up *Hey World!* to veer closely towards pop music, resulting in derision from reggae purists. After jumping to Virgin, the group recorded their masterpiece, 1988's *Conscious Party*, a critical and commercial smash sparked by the number 39 single "Tomorrow People." After three more albums for Virgin, Marley and the Melody Makers moved to Elektra for 1995's *Free Like We Want 2 B*. In addition to the four siblings in the Melody Makers, three other Marley children also pursued careers in music. *—Jason Ankeny*

Play the Game Right / 1985 / Capitol ♦♦♦

Hey World! / 1986 / EMI ♦♦♦

The Time Has Come: The Best of Ziggy Marley & the Melody Makers / 1988 / EMI Manhattan ♦♦♦
A compilation of his formative material. Not his finest period but interesting nonetheless. —*Ron Wynn*

One Bright Day / 1989 / Virgin ♦♦♦
An excellent followup album that helped cement Ziggy's popularity. —*Ron Wynn*

Conscious Party / Aug. 1989 / Virgin ♦♦♦♦♦

Jahmekya / 1991 / Virgin America ♦♦♦♦♦
Possibly his best overall release, it didn't enjoy the same impact as other material. —*Ron Wynn*

• **The Best of Ziggy Marley & the Melody Makers (1988-1993)** / Apr. 8, 1997 / Virgin ♦♦♦♦♦
The Best of Ziggy Marley and the Melody Makers (1988-1993) is an excellent 17-track compilation of Marley's most popular work, featuring all of his best and best-known songs from the peak of his career. During the late '80s, Ziggy was among the most pop-oriented of all reggae artists, and as his career progressed, he toughened his music up by exploring worldbeat to a fuller extent. Although *The Best of* is not arranged chronologically, it's possible to hear this progression, and it therefore makes a strong introduction to his work. More importantly for casual fans, it's an infectious listen, containing all of the songs that you need. —*Stephen Thomas Erlewine*

Fallen Is Babylon / Jul. 15, 1997 / Elektra ♦♦♦♦
Fallen Is Babylon is a rebirth of sorts for Ziggy Marley, as he re-injects soul and pop influences into his slinky reggae. The result is a tuneful, engaging record that is just as impassioned, yet more enjoyable, than many of his mid-'90s releases; it demonstrates that he is one of the more reliable and entertaining mainstream reggae artists of the '90s. —*Leo Stanley*

Ziggy Marley & the Melody Makers Live, Vol. 1 / Nov. 7, 2000 / Elektra ♦♦♦

Larry Marshall

Vocals, Keyboards, Organ / Contemporary Reggae, Roots Reggae
Despite being an energetic, convincing and very soulful vocalist, Larry Marshall's not well known except among the reggae faithful. He's both a superb romantic balladeer and excellent message and roots vocalist. Marshall's single "Nanny Goat" was among the early transitional tunes signaling the music's evolution from rock steady to reggae. He cut his first single at Studio One in the mid-'60s; it was later remade by Clancy Eccles. Later came sessions for the Prince Buster and Top Deck labels, then a return to Studio One where he attained stardom. He eventually became an engineer as well as vocalist at the label. He's since recorded for various companies, among them Heartbeat and King's Music. —*Ron Wynn*

I Admire You / 1975 / Heartbeat ♦♦♦
Although he's almost completely unknown outside of reggae circles, singer/songwriter Larry Marshall had a huge influence on reggae music during its formative years. His warm, romantic delivery and rich baritone voice made his singles favorites at the Kingston sound system dances in the late 1960s and early 1970s. He cut the majority of his most important sides with Clement "Coxsone" Dodd at Studio One (the best of them compiled on another Heartbeat release, *Presenting Larry Marshall*), but he maintained a very high standard of quality after leaving Dodd to produce his own material at Harry J's, Randy's, and Joe Gibbs' studios. Originally released in 1975, *I Admire You* is remarkably consistent—although "Captivity" drags a bit, there are virtually no clunkers on this album. A few tracks stand out, including the epochal sufferer's anthem "Heavy Heavy Load" and the aching love ballad "Oh Girl" in particular. (Perhaps recognizing the superb quality of these two tracks, the producers of the CD reissue have provided them in extended mixes.) Yet "My Foreparent" and "Thelma" are equally fine, and the title track comes very close. Highly recommended. —*Rick Anderson*

• **Presenting Larry Marshall** / Jan. 15, 1992 / Heartbeat ♦♦♦♦♦
A fine ballad stylist and effective uptempo singer, Larry Marshall is an obscurity to all except the reggae faithful. This is a nice album featuring more recent material. —*Ron Wynn*

Tommy McCook

b. 1932, **d.** May 5, 1998, Atlanta, GA
Sax (Tenor), Horn / Ska
The leader of the legendary Skatalites, tenor saxophonist Tommy McCook was among the most innovative and influential Jamaican musicians of his generation, a prime catalyst behind the evolution and international popularity of ska and reggae. Born in 1932, McCook learned to play sax while attending Kingston's Alpha Cottage School, an institution for wayward boys; upon exiting the school at the age of 14, he toured with the dance bands of Eric Deans and Roy Coburn, emerging as a highly skilled jazz player. Between the late 1940s and early 1950s, he also frequently collaborated with the famed Count Ossie, lending his talents alongside those of the Rastafarian hand-drummers and chanting vocalists who comprised Ossie's group. In 1954 McCook relocated to the Bahamas to join a dance band there, and in the years to follow his mastery of jazz became increasingly pronounced.

McCook did not return return to Jamaica on a permanent basis until 1962, arriving in time to help push the developing ska sound to the next level. In 1963, he was approached by Studio One musical director Jackie Mittoo to lead a new group he was forming dubbed the Skatalites; McCook initially declined the offer, but by mid-1964 he accepted the role of bandleader, drawing on his extensive knowledge of jazz and R&B to add distinctive new dimensions to their sound. Though existing only 14 months, the Skatalites were the quintessential ska band of their time, backing every major vocalist and producing an astounding amount of prime instrumental material. In the wake of the group's demise, McCook founded the Supersonics, who were soon installed as the house band at Duke Reid's Treasure Isle studio; the most sought-after studio unit of the rock steady era, they appeared on classic hits from artists including Alton Ellis, Justin Hinds and the Techniques.

McCook remained a fixture of the Jamaican session circuit throughout the years which followed, and he also issued a number of solo albums for producer Bunny Lee, among them 1974's *Cookin'*, 1975's *Brass Rockers* and 1977's *Hot Lava*. For Glen Brown, in 1976 McCook also issued a blank-labelled LP generally referred to as *Horny Dub*, and two years later he teamed with trumpeter Bobby Ellis for *Blazing Horns*. In 1983 he reformed the Skatalites nearly two decades after their initial break-up, relocating the group to the U.S. in 1985 just months after the release of their comeback album *Return of the Big Guns*. A series of new releases from the group followed in the years to come, and they even notched a pair of Grammy nominations; in 1994 the Skatalites mounted their first world tour, which included appearances as part of the Skavoovee U.S.A. tour, a package which included their descendants the Specials, the Selecter and the Toasters. McCook died at his home in Atlanta, Georgia on May 5, 1998. —*Jason Ankeny*

Down on Bond Street / Jul. 9, 1997 / Trojan ♦♦♦♦♦
Like Roland Alphonso did while leading Clement Dodd's own Soul Vendors outfit (with organist Jackie Mittoo), McCook and the Supersonics cut several instrumental sides, focusing on groove-heavy beats and tasty horn and organ solos. Trojan's *Down on Bond Street* brings together 20 of these gems, ranging from late ska cuts like "A Yellow Basket (A Tisket a Tasket)" to early reggae sides such as "Second Fiddle." Focusing primarily on rocksteady material, McCook also delves into some updated Jamaican R&B ("Heatwave (Moving)"), several choice covers ("Ode to Billie Joe"), and a few breezy originals ("Real Cool"). Showing off his considerable jazz chops, McCook is ever present with his vaporously tart and sinewy tenor lines (he turns in impressive flute work on a handful of cuts as well). Also part of that select crew of Jamaican jazz musicians, many being fellow Skatalite alums as well, the Supersonics featured alto saxophonist Lester Sterling, trumpeter Johnny "Dizzy" Moore, trombonist Vin "Don Drummond Jr." Gordon, guitarist Lynn Taitt (whose Jets found work with producer Joe Gibbs), and organist Winston Wright. While Heartbeat's fine *Tribute to Tommy* and a few albums with the Aggrovators cover ska and reggae ground respectively, this McCook title is one of the few, if not the only wide-ranging collection of the saxophonist's instrumental output during the '60s. Highly recommended. —*Stephen Cook*

The Authentic Ska Sound of Tommy McCook / Jan. 27, 1998 / Moon ♦♦♦♦
Authentic Ska Sound of Tommy McCook finds the lead tenor saxophonist surrounded by other ska legends including other members of the Skatalites (keyboardist Bill Smith, bassist Lloyd Brevett, trombonist Will Clark) and early Jamaican studio musicians (drummer Aston Henry), but the group also includes third-wave ska musicians such as Toasters trumpeter Brian Sledge. This album was recorded during the summer of 1997, one year before McCook's death, and released by Moon Ska the following year. In addition to the traditionals, "Secret Love" and "Loving Princess Diana," are decent renditions. Also included are McCook's own "Yelling King Bravo" and a cover of Wynonie Harris' "Bloodshot Eyes," here titled "Blood Clad Eyes." Most of the songs feature vocals by either Lord Tanamo (who also wrote a couple of songs on this album) or King Bravo. —*Joslyn Layne*

Top Secret / Jan. 26, 1999 / Beatville ♦♦♦♦♦
This reissue is being marketed as a ska classic, which is understandable since Tommy McCook was a charter member of the Skatalites and, therefore, one of the primary architects of the ska sound. However, *Top Secret* is actually more of a document of the rocksteady period, when the galloping tempos of ska were slowing and the rhythm was congealing into the elastic groove that would slow even further over the next couple of years, until it settled into the one-drop beat that characterized early reggae. Accompanied by such top-flight musicians as drummer Lloyd Knibbs, guitarist Jah Jerry, bassist Lloyd Brevett, and organist Jackie Mittoo, McCook recorded these brilliant sides at Duke Reid's Treasure Isle studio in 1969; the album has been out of print for years and is here reissued with four previously unreleased bonus tracks. The sound quality is better than you'd have any right to expect, and the musical quality is so consistently high that it's a little bit difficult to pick out highlight tracks—though the proto-reggae strut of "Jungle Skank" is particularly nice, as are the twin saxophone harmonies on "Hot Shot." Highly recommended. —*Rick Anderson*

• **Tribute to Tommy: The Best of Tommy McCook and the Skatalites** / Aug. 10, 1999 / Heartbeat ♦♦♦♦♦
Subtitled *The Best of Tommy McCook and the Skatalites*—this is *not* a tribute album, it is the real deal—this has 18 tracks from 1962-1965, when McCook and his accompanists were in their ska prime. Tommy McCook & the Skatalites recorded prolifically during this time, and it's hard for the modern American listener—without access to McCook's entire discography—to judge whether this is the optimum selection. It certainly sounds good, though, in respect to both McCook's playing and the infectious ska groove of his band, which included luminaries in their own right like saxophonist Roland Alphonso, pianist Jackie Mittoo, and trombonist Don Drummond. The instrumental riffs do have a certain sameness over a full-length disc, which makes some of the more unusual covers ("Exodus," a wacky "Goldfinger") and minor-key melodies ("Freedom Sounds," "Ska Ba") standouts. "Wheel and Turn" has an irresistibly smoky lilt, enhanced by strange, barely audible strains of what sounds like violin in the background. There are also a couple of atypical cuts showing that McCook's versatility covered more than ska; "Jazz Walking" has a jazz-soul arrangement with organ, and the seven-minute "The Answer" is pretty straight-ahead jazz. —*Richie Unterberger*

Freddie McGregor

Vocals, Keyboards, Bass / Roots Reggae, Dub, Dancehall, Lovers Rock
"Little Freddie" joined the Clarendonians at the age of seven in 1963 and hasn't stopped singing since, first for Coxsone Dodd's Studio One, through the Soul Syndicate in the late '70s, then as his own producer in the '80s. *Bobby Bobylon* became one of the finest productions in Dodd's history, compiling a decade's worth of unreleased tracks into Freddie's masterpiece. Equally at home in lovers rock or Rasta roots, composer/singer McGregor is con-

sistently satisfying; his releases include 1984's *Come on Over,* 1988's *Big Ship,* and 1995's *Forever My Love.* —*Roger Steffens*

Across the Border / 1984 / RAS ✦✦✦
Freddie McGregor's wondrous, soulful voice and engaging delivery are sometimes wasted on this mid-'80s album, issued on CD in 1992. The title track, as well as the hard-hitting message cuts "War Mongers," "Freedom, Justice & Equality" and the lyrically naive "Love Will Solve The Problems" address issues and offer McGregor a worthy forum for his glorious singing. But he's sorely tested by the cover of "Guantanamera," which was a silly pop hit and sounds even sillier in a reggae version. "Freddie" and "Work To Do Today" have awkward arrangements and vapid lyrics, forcing McGregor to waste energy and intensity trying to make them palatable. This wasn't one of his most consistent releases, but McGregor never coasts or plods on a session, even on tepid tunes. —*Ron Wynn*

Big Ship / 1988 / Shanachie ✦✦✦✦✦

☆ **Jamaican Classics** / 1991 / VP ✦✦✦✦✦
Excellent vintage tracks brilliantly sung by one of reggae's all-time greats. —*Ron Wynn*

Jamaican Classics, Vol. 3 / Jun. 24, 1996 / VP ✦✦✦✦✦
Jamaican Classics, Vol. 3 offers an entertaining but frustratingly incomplete overview of Freddie McGregor's career, including songs like "Everything Crash" and "Danger in Your Eyes," but missing a number of other hits. Still, this disc is a good sampler of McGregor's sound. —*Leo Stanley*

★ **Anthology** / Oct. 5, 1999 / VP ✦✦✦✦✦
Like Bob Marley and the Wailers, Freddie McGregor started his career as part of the legendary Studio One cadre of Jamaican crooners. Golden-voiced and subtly charismatic, he has been a consistently popular singer since the '60s. *The Anthology* presents a brilliant overview of Freddie McGregor's deep impact on Jamaican music. Opening with his best-known hits, the '80s classics "Big Ship" and "Stop Loving You," McGregor's soulful talent is unquestionable, but it's on the rare Studio One tracks that a glimpse of his skilled ability to translate emotion is really evident. From the haunting melody on "Africa Here I Come" to his caressing delivery on "Bobby Babylon" to the flawless harmonies on "Bandulu," he paints landscapes of feeling and longing. *The Anthology* is an essential addition to all reggae collections. —*Rosalind Cummings-Yeates*

Signature / Feb. 22, 2000 / VP ✦✦✦✦✦
Like the Jamaican sun, Freddie McGreggor's rich, warm voice affects everyone it touches, constantly drawing admirers for its soothing brightness. A beloved roots singer for 25 years, he manages to stay on the forefront of reggae music by melding his conscious lyrics with cutting-edge riddims and melodies. *Signature* boasts a strong collection of tunes that do just this, as well as portraying the brilliant textures of his vocals. From the upbeat, catchy rhythm on "If You Wanna Go" to the uplifting, sincere lyrics of "Key to the City" to the spiritual lessons offered in "Inna De Fire," this album spotlights all the best that reggae music offers. —*Rosalind Cummings-Yeates*

☆ **Bobby Bobylon** / Heartbeat ✦✦✦✦✦
His overall best, the product of a decade's work, is sung over nothing but classic Coxsone rhythms. —*Roger Steffens*

Freddie McKay

Vocals / Rocksteady, Ska
Rocksteady singer Freddie McKay had a few hits in the '60s (one of which was miscredited to someone else!), recorded with the Soul Defenders, among other studio groups, and worked with Jamaica's top reggae producers Duke Reid, Coxsone Dodd, and Prince Buster.

Purportedly born in the late '40s in St. Catherine, Freddie McKay went on to record for the Studio One and Treasure Isle labels, working with studio bands the Revolutionaires, the G.G. Allstars, and the Soul Defenders, with whom McKay cut "Picture on the Wall" (his biggest hit), "High School Dance," and other enjoyable, but non-charting, songs including "Old and Gray." According to the compilation *Wake Up Jamaica,* another one of McKay's hits, "Love Is a Treasure," was initially released in the late '60s as a Treasure Isle Boys single. The song's reissue in the early '70s got the performer wrong again, this time listing Tommy McCook's All Stars. Eventually, the record was set straight and a few of Freddie McKay's singles remained perennial favorites on ska and rocksteady compilations decades later. —*Joslyn Layne*

● **Doin' It Right** / Jul. 1, 1999 / Charly ✦✦✦✦✦

The Meditations

f. 1975
Group / Roots Reggae
The Meditations have been in and out of reggae music since the 1970s spreading their Rastafarian message of unity and love for all humankind regardless of race. Despite the many social and political changes in the world since their inception, the group has stayed true to their message and continue to play largely roots music. Like many other bands of their era, the Meditations were heavily influenced by American R&B; in 1976, they recorded their debut album, *Message from the Meditations.* The album was successful in both Jamaica and the U.S. with such classic tracks as "Woman Is like a Shadow," "Tricked," and "Running from Jamaica." In late 1978, following their second album, *Wake Up!,* the group hooked up with Lee "Scratch" Perry who had been very impressed with the harmonies on "Running from Jamaica." In early 1979, they began doing back-up work for Bob Marley. They produced a few singles during this time, including "Miracles" on Marley's Tuff Gong. As back-up singers, the Meditations worked with such artists as Jimmy Cliff, Gregory Isaacs, and the Congos. —*Sandra Brennan*

● **Greatest Hits** / 1984 / Shanachie ✦✦✦✦✦
Just as it says, here are two sides of pleasing meditations. —*Roger Steffens*

Deeper Roots: The Best of the Meditations / Mar. 30, 1994 / Heartbeat ✦✦✦✦
The Meditations have long been a premier reggae trio, equally spectacular on urgent protest tunes, danceable uptempo tunes, love songs or novelty cuts. This 20-track collection features excellent 1970s and '80s cuts, notably the emphatic "Wake Up," "What A Bam Bam" and "No Peace," plus the sensual "Quiet Woman" and "Woman Like A Shadow." Their sound is neither aggressive nor passive, and retains its appeal regardless of tempo. Those unaware of reggae's long harmony trio tradition should start with The Meditations; they've had few equals. —*Ron Wynn*

Reggae Crazy: Anthology, 1971-1979 / Sep. 30, 1997 / Nighthawk ✦✦✦✦
The Meditations were one of the earliest vocal trios to follow reggae's trend towards a darker, "dreader" sound in the early '70s; although their first album was released in 1977, they had recorded numerous singles up to that point, and some of the best of those songs are compiled on this album (along with some tracks recorded later). The piercing falsetto singing on "Must Be a First" is reminiscent of the Congos at their best (perhaps owing in part to the distinctive sound of Lee Perry's Black Ark studio, where this song was recorded), and there's an echo of the Mighty Diamonds in the sophisticated harmonies on "Get Left." But "Woman Piabba" draws on calypso traditions to a degree unusual in reggae, while "Play I" employs a drum arrangement (courtesy of Sly Dunbar) that prefigures some of the innovations that would later be heard in U.K. reggae. The album's title track, a tiresome one-chord vamp, is the only clunker on this album. Everything else is strictly killer. —*Rick Anderson*

The Melodians

f. 1963
Group / Rocksteady
The Melodians are among the rocksteady greats and have provided reggae music with some of its most enduring hits including "Swing and Dine," "Too Young to Fall in Love," and their monster hit "Rivers of Babylon." At producer Duke Reid's Treasure Isle studio, their career took off with three fast hits including "Expo 67." They had steady success with Treasure Isle, but left after a monetary dispute and moved to the High Note label. Another steady stream of hits including their classic "Little Nut Tree," emerged. With their mellow tones, and sweet harmonies, the Melodians became one of the chief proponents of lover's rock. After a brief attempt at producing themselves, they teamed up with producer Leslie Kong and his Beverly label in 1969. "Sweet Sensation" was one of their biggest hits from this period. Following Kong's death in 1971, the Melodians performed for almost every major studio in Jamaica. They did, however stay far away from Studio One. Unfortunately things had changed and the Melodians, while not unsuccessful, were unable to rekindle the fire of their earlier careers and so went their separate ways in the mid-'70s. —*Sandra Brennan*

Sweet Sensation / 1976 / Mango ✦✦✦✦✦
Sweet Sensation is the finest collection of the trio's soulful rocksteady. This showcases the period of 1969-1971, when The Melodians found their greatest success, thanks in part to Leslie Kong's brilliant production. Includes the anthemic "Rivers of Babylon," their international hit. —*Chris Woodstra*

Pre-Meditation / 1986 / Sky Note ✦✦✦✦✦
"Swing and Dine" and "Don't Get Weary" make this an exemplary collection of the rocksteady style. —*Roger Steffens*

☆ **Irie Feeling** / 1990 / RAS ✦✦✦✦✦
The Melodians were a superb rock steady vocal group, and they smoothly made the transition to reggae on this session. Despite the faster pace and different rhythmic patterns, The Melodians' harmonies and vocals were just as smooth and convincing, whether they were doing party cuts, love songs or message tracks. The most passionate tunes were the title cut, "You Don't Need Me," and "Hold On Tight," while they stoked the spiritual fires on "Down Here In Babylon" and "Jah Reggae" and had a good time with "Get Up and Dance" and "Push A Little Harder." One of the best discs in Ras's entire reggae collection. —*Ron Wynn*

Swing & Dine / 1992 / Heartbeat ✦✦✦✦✦
Rather than the customary single lead contrasted by twin harmonies, The Melodians divided lead duties between Tony Brevette and Brent Dowe, with Trevor McNaughton harmonizing with the singer who wasn't featured on a particular track. This outstanding 16-track collection includes their biggest hits for Treasure Isle. The threesome glided along atop skipping, light rhythms provided by such bands as the Gaytones, Lyn Taitt and the Jets, the Soul Syndicate, and Tommy McCook and the Supersonics. The Melodians primarily did poignant love tunes, although they could also handle evangelical or political material. The set features such classics as "Little Nut Tree," "Hey Girl," "You Don't Need Me," and "Love Is A Doggone Good Thing." It's also thoroughly annotated and superbly mastered. —*Ron Wynn*

★ **Rivers of Babylon: The Best of the Melodians 1967-1973** / Sep. 23, 1997 / Trojan ✦✦✦✦✦
Rivers of Babylon: The Best of the Melodians 1967-1973 is an extraordinary 26-track collection that contains all of the group's hits and singles, from "Sweet Sensation" and "I'll Get Along without You" to the classic "Rivers of Babylon." It may be a little too much music for neophytes, but there's little question that this is the definitive overview of their peak years. —*Stephen Thomas Erlewine*

Michigan & Smiley

DJ / Dancehall
Papa Michigan (born Anthony Fairclough) and General Smiley (born Erroll Bennett) were among the first dual-toasters on the Jamaican scene. Beginning in the late '70s while still in school, the humorous duo (Smiley got his name because he never smiles) scored immediately with "Rub a Dub Style" and "Nice up the Dance," two ubiquitous songs on the dancehall circuit. "One Love Jam Down" became a popular anthem, and 1982's "Diseases" established them as major stars, especially at the annual Sunsplash festivals. They broke up in the late '80s, although occasional attempts at reunions have been made recently. —*Roger Steffens*

Sugar Daddy / 1986 / RAS ✦✦✦
Michigan & Smiley are reggae's best toaster duo. Their voices are similar enough to make their unison lines flow, yet there is enough difference to make their separate verbal improvisations effective. There are some strident social and message tracks among the 10 on this album, including "Pass It To The Church," "The System," "Blackness Awareness" and "Give The Children A Helping Hand." "Here We Go Again" mixes political, comedic, and religious themes, while the title track, "A Who—" and "Queen Of The Minstrel" aren't quite as specific in their targeting, but are prime examples of their wordplay and slick blending of sung and spoken lines. *—Ron Wynn*

● **Rub-A-Dub Style** / 1992 / Heartbeat ✦✦✦✦✦
General Smiley & Papa Michigan helped to pioneer the DJ duo format in reggae. Trading rhymes over versions of crucial roots-reggae songs, they've created ripples of excitement in Jamaican dance halls. Their talent for wordplay energizes tracks like "Rub a Dub Style" and "Nice up the Dance," both of which were massive hits on the island. Find out why with this welcome reissue, produced by Clement "Coxsone" Dodd. *—Roundup newsletter*

The Mighty Diamonds

f. 1976
Group / Roots Reggae
The Mighty Diamonds were one of Jamaica's top vocal trios in the 1970s. More than two decades after the release of their groundbreaking debut album, *Right Time,* in 1977, the trio remains what CMJ-NMR called 'simply one of the best practicing vocal harmony groups in the world'. Formed by harmony singer and disc jockey Pat 'Lloyd' Ferguson, with lead singer Donald 'Tabby' Shaw and background vocalist Bunny Simpson, the Mighty Diamonds celebrated their thirtieth anniversary in 2000 with a fourteen track compilation, *Everlasting,* that included such hits as, "Tour Of The World", "Jah Bless The Rastaman", "Natural Rasta" and "Ghetto Living".

Ferguson has also recorded under such alias as Jah Lloyd, Jah Lion and Jah Ali. *—Craig Harris*

★ **Right Time** / 1976 / Shanachie ✦✦✦✦✦
The right album at the right time, it has the right musicians, the right mix, and the right things to say. *—Roger Steffens*

The Roots Is There / 1982 / Shanachie ✦✦✦✦
Try to ignore the unbelievably cheesy cover photo (good heavens, did we all dress like that in the '70s—). This is yet another fine collection of Channel One recordings from the late '70s and early '80s by the sweetest-voiced harmony trio in reggae history. As usual, the Mighty Diamonds are backed by Sly & Robbie's crack Revolutionaries band, and the propulsive, almost martial rockers' rhythms that Sly Dunbar churns out contrast nicely with the silky voice of lead singer Donald "Tabby" Shaw. There's an interesting remake of the Abyssinians' classic "Declaration of Rights" (complete with not quite tasteful synthesizer in the bridge), the typically dread "Heads of Government" and even a reggae version of the Stevie Wonder/Paul McCartney composition "Ebony and Ivory." Danged if that last one doesn't top the original, too. *—Rick Anderson*

Struggling / 1985 / RAS ✦✦✦
Although it says 1985 on the back of this CD, it might as well be the early '70s, for The Mighty Diamonds stick to the principles that guided vintage reggae. They're still singing devout praise songs, defiant protest tunes, and infrequent but moving love ballads. The Diamonds wrote seven of the 10 tracks, and also cover three fine Al Campbell originals, including the dynamic "Reggae-Lution." The production blends contemporary and classic touches. If you've had problems in determining where the hip-hop and pop ends and the reggae begins in current material, you'll have no such problems with The Mighty Diamonds. *—Ron Wynn*

Reggae Street / 1987 / Shanachie ✦✦✦✦

Deeper Roots & Dub / Jul. 15, 1997 / Caroline ✦✦✦✦
Deeper Roots was originally released on Virgin's Front Line imprint in 1979; this long-overdue CD reissue sweetens the deal by adding dub versions of all the original album tracks. It's too bad that the dub versions had to be mastered from vinyl rather than tape (and pretty crappy vinyl, too, in a couple of instances), and it's also a pity that the label didn't see fit to alternate the dubs with the vocal versions, instead choosing to run the vocals and dubs in separate sequences. But scratchy dub versions are certainly better than none at all, and you can always program your CD player. There's no arguing with the material—"Dreadlocks Time" is as good as roots reggae gets, and "One Brother Short" isn't far behind. "Diamonds and Pearls" features a great cheesy analog synthesizer; all of the tracks shimmer with lead singer Donald Shaw's incredibly sweet-toned vocals. Joe Hookim's dub versions are all excellent and shine easily through the surface noise. Highly recommended. *—Rick Anderson*

Jacob Miller

d. Mar. 23, 1980
Vocals, Bass / Roots Reggae
One of reggae's brightest lights, Miller was abruptly snuffed out in a car crash in 1980, at which time he had become more popular than Marley among the in-crowd. Huge, bubbling, and boyish, Jacob blew spliff smoke in the face of authority (literally) and demanded that "we jam all night until daylight." His songs are timeless testaments to Jah and the healing power of herb. His loss is immense. *—Roger Steffens*

Jacob "Killer" Miller / 1978 / RAS ✦✦✦
"Shaky Girl" and "Forward Ever," backed by The Fatman riddim section of The Lewis Brothers, peg Jacob's stuttering style for all time. *—Roger Steffens*

● **Reggae Greats** / 1984 / Mango ✦✦✦✦✦

Collector's Classics / 1988 / RAS ✦✦✦✦✦
Although they've enjoyed pop success in the post-Jacob Miller era, Inner Circle has never been the same since his death. This is a comprehensive anthology featuring Miller's powerful, captivating voice at its finest. *—Ron Wynn*

Sugar Minott

b. May 25, 1956, Kingston, Jamaica
Vocals, Drums / Ragga, Dancehall
One of reggae's enduring cult artists, Lincoln "Sugar" Minott was also among the music's most prominent producers, nurturing a steady stream of young talent via his Youth Promotion collective. Minott first emerged during the mid-1970s as a member of the group the African Brothers. After a series of hits, including "Torturing" and "Party Night," he was recruited by the staff at the famed Studio One, where he not only lent his dulcet backing vocals to a variety of sessions; more impressive still was his gift for writing new songs over existing rhythms, often surpassing the original compositions. Although Minott scored a number of hits for Studio One, he was less well known at home than in Britain, where his self-produced 1979 effort "Hard Time Pressure" was an underground smash. Minott founded Youth Promotion/Black Roots to nurture aspiring musical talent from the Kingston ghettos, and ultimately his uncompromising devotion to the company threatened his own career, as he refused all deals which did not make accomodations for the Youth Promotion crew. Minott's idealism seemingly threatened his own creativity, and as the decade wore on his releases were increasingly hampered by lifeless dancehall rehashing. *—Jason Ankeny*

● **Slice of the Cake** / 1984 / Heartbeat ✦✦✦✦✦
Including "Buy out the Bar," " "Level Vibes, " "No Vacancy, " this is all killer, no filler. *—Roger Steffens*

Showcase / May 15, 1992 / Heartbeat ✦✦✦✦✦
Singer/songwriter Sugar Minott has carved out an impressive niche for himself in the reggae world, gaining more and more fans all over the world with each release and tour. This reissue of an earlier Studio One album, produced by Clement "Coxsone" Dodd, features extended mixes of popular Minott songs like "Oh Mr. D.C." and "Vanity." Backing musicians include drummer Leroy "Horsemouth" Wallace, bassist Earl "Bagga" Walker, and keyboardist Jackie Mittoo. *—Roundup newsletter*

Dancehall Business / Jul. 18, 2000 / Heartbeat ✦✦✦✦
Sugar Minott's sweet vocals and songwriting ability have translated to just about every aspect associated with Jamaican music. Early in his career he was known as a reggae artist, but ended up becoming one of the spearhead figures in the development of dancehall and the U.K. based lovers rock. *Dancehall Business* is a budget *Reggae Savers* compilation from Heartbeat, showcasing Minott's versatility from the smooth lovers rock on "Lover's Race," the politically militant "Hard Time Pressure," and the dance hit "Dancehall Business." *—Al Campbell*

Jackie Mittoo (Donat Roy Mittoo)

b. Mar. 3, 1948, Browns Town, Jamaica, **d.** Dec. 16, 1990
Vocals, Keyboards, Piano, Organ / Reggae-Pop, Pop, Rocksteady, Ska
Keyboard virtuoso Jackie Mittoo was among the true legends of reggae—a founding member of the Skatalites and an extraordinarily prolific songwriter, he was perhaps most influential as a mentor to countless younger performers, primarily through his work as the musical director at the famed Studio One. He frequently skipped school to play with the house band at nearby Federal Studios, and it was there that he met producer Coxsone Dodd, who recruited Mittoo for recording sessions when the scheduled pianist failed to appear on time. While attending Kingston College, he began jamming with fellow students Augustus Pablo and Tyrone Downie, and they eventually formed a trio—the Jackie Mitree—which performed his orignal compositions. When Dodd opened Studio One in Kingston in 1963, he tapped Mittoo to serve as musical director; in the years to follow he played on virtually every disc the studio produced, arranging much of the material and helping develop new songs until they were sufficiently polished to meet standards. By the early months of 1964, he set about forming a new band with other Studio One session regulars; dubbing themselves the Skatalites, they were to become the quintessential ska band of the period, and although the group lasted just 14 months—from June 1964 to August 1965— their influence on music worldwide remains incalculable. After the Skatalites split, Mittoo began a solo career. At the same time, he continued his relentless pace at Studio One—according to the terms of his basic arrangment with Dodd, he received payment upon delivering five new rhythms a week, which over the years resulted in literally thousands of compositions which he both produced and arranged. *—Jason Ankeny*

● **Tribute to Jackie Mittoo** / 1995 / Heartbeat ✦✦✦✦✦
Featuring 31 songs, *Tribute* is a wonderful selection of organist Jackie Mittoo's work. The music on the album illustrates his diversity, as he switches between reggae, soul-jazz, and Memphis-style R&B. *—Stephen Thomas Erlewine*

Derrick Morgan

b. Mar. 1940
Vocals / Rocksteady, Ska
A member of the classic first wave of Jamaican ska artists, Derrick Morgan was among the genre's founding fathers, emerging alongside pioneers including the Skatalites, Laurel Aitken, Prince Buster and Desmond Dekker. Born in March, 1940, Morgan was raised in the Kingston area, exposed to a variety of musical sources spanning from New Orleans R&B to the choral music of the nearby church where his father served as deacon. At the age of 17, he took top honors at the annual Vere John's Opportunity talent show, delivering blistering renditions of Little Richard's "Long Tall Sally" and "Jenny Jenny," and in 1959 teamed with producer Duke Reid to record his debut single "Lover Boy." Morgan's follow-up, "Fat Man," was a smash throughout Jamaica, and he later scored with recordings of "Leave Earth" and "Wigger Wee Shuffle," both cut with the legendary Clement "Coxsone" Dodd.

By 1960, Morgan was the unrivaled King of Ska—at the peak of his popularity, he was the first and only Jamaican artist to date to hold down the top seven slots on the national pop singles chart during the same week, generating a string of smashes including "Be Still," "In My Heart," "Don't Call Me Daddy," "Moon Hop" and "Meekly Wait and Murmur Not." In 1961, he recorded his biggest hit ever, "Housewives' Choice," and a year later—in celebration of Jamaica's emancipation—recorded the first independence song, "Forward March." Morgan and Prince Buster, arguably the two biggest ska performers of the era, became embroiled in a fierce musical feud which quickly spilled over among their respective fans, and as of 1963 disputes between the two camps became so heated that leaders of the newly formed Jamaican government were forced to intervene, calling a cease-fire and bringing the two performers together for publicity photos to bury the hatchet.

In 1966, Morgan issued "Tougher Than Tough," widely credited as the first record in the rock steady genre. He continued to innovate in the years to follow—among his most enduring contributions were "Went to the Hop" (the first Jamaican song with an electric bass guitar), "Blazing Fire" (the first song to employ an electric piano), "Love Not to Brag" (the first duet with a female artist, Millicent Patsy Todd) and "Seven Letters" (the first reggae song, produced in collaboration with brother-in-law Bunny Lee). Morgan also produced many of the era's most notable up-and-comers, among them Bob Marley, Jimmy Cliff and Garnet Silk. Although he lived in Britain from 1963 onward, Morgan remained a towering figure in Jamaica throughout the remainder of the decade; even after his fame began to slip in the 1970s, he continued recording regularly in the years to follow. —*Jason Ankeny*

Ska Man Classics / Oct. 31, 1995 / Heartbeat ✦✦✦✦✦
And here you thought the 2-Tone label was a trip down memory lane. Derrick Morgan takes the Interstate to the past in a convoy that includes English performers Mafia, Fluxie, the Allstonians and Steady Ernest, rolling out 18 cuts that take in a remarkable number of ska and rocksteady favorites. These sorts of cover sets run a risk of sounding dopey or pointless, but this one has the benefit of excellent performances, respect for the originals, and an energetic vocal performance from Morgan, who sounds like he was having a ball recording these tunes. Mixed into the track list: "007", in a terrific version; "Israelites," which gets a decent updating; a nice "Simmer Down," a take on "Train to Skaville," and even a successful run at "Easy Snapping." The album comes equipped with informative sleeve notes, by the way, so you get a double shot of history in one package, making this doubly worth buying. —*Steven McDonald*

• **Time Marches On: Derrick Morgan Sings Ska, Rock Steady and** / 1997 / Heartbeat ✦✦✦✦✦
Time Marches On is a superbly assembled, career-capping Derrick Morgan compilation spanning from his first recording, 1959's "Lover Boy," to a fierce reading of his classic "Moon Hop" taped live in San Francisco in 1996. In the decades separating the two, Morgan essentially created the framework for ska, rocksteady, and reggae; over the course of seminal tracks like "Fatman," "Love Not to Brag," "Conquering Ruler," and "Tougher Than Tough," it's possible to trace the evolution of Jamaican music, with history made on almost each and every cut. Although regrettable omissions like "Housewives' Choice," "Tougher Than Tough," and "Don't Call Me Daddy" prevent *Time Marches On* from staking a claim as the definitive Morgan collection, it's still an ideal introduction for new fans, and the abundance of unreleased and rare material makes it essential for long-timers as well. —*Jason Ankeny*

I Am the Ruler / Trojan ✦✦✦
Derrick Morgan was one of the earliest and biggest stars in Jamaica. His low-key vocal style, fun-loving and boastful lyrics, and strong partnerships with the island's best producers (Clement Dodd, Duke Reid, Prince Buster, and, especially, Leslie Kong) kept him at the top throughout the '60s. The fruits of Morgan's talent and savvy production can be heard on the fine Trojan collection *I Am the Ruler.* Included are early ska hits like "The Hop" and the whimsical duet "Housewives Choice" (the first of many with female vocalists), as well as rocksteady gems like "Got You on My Mind" and "I Am the Ruler." Early reggae tracks like "Gimme Back" and the Little Anthony cover "Tears on My Pillow" round out the package. Another highlight is the musical bragging rights number "Conquering Ruler" (done in the talk/sing style of Morgan's rudeboy hit "Tougher Than Tough" and reminiscent of another fine rivalry song, Clancy Eccles' "The Revenge"). With many excellent cuts and very good sound quality, *I Am yhe Ruler* is a great buy for the fan of early Jamaican music. —*Stephen Cook*

Pablo Moses

Vocals / Contemporary Reggae, Roots Reggae
Pablo Moses burst onto the reggae scene in 1975 with the puzzling song "I Man a Grasshopper" from his debut album *Revolutionary Dream.* The song was a hit in both Jamaica and England, but Moses himself remained fairly unknown. Moses got his start performing with informal school bands. He and chum Don Prendes eventually formed the Canaries, which remained his back-up group, and began performing at talent shows. Following the success of "Grasshopper," Moses released a few more singles, including "We Should Be in Angola," but for some reason, they did better in England than they did in Jamaica. The song "Give I Fe I Name" was an exception. In 1980, he returned to reggae with *A Song,* an innovative album produced by Moses and Geoffery Chung that was recorded in Jamaica using the island's finest session players and the remixed in London. The result was a multi-layered blend of roots and sophisticated international reggae that many consider Moses' masterpiece. —*Sandra Brennan*

★ **A Song** / 1980 / Mango ✦✦✦✦✦
This is a masterpiece of forward-looking sophistication from a roots perspective. —*Roger Steffens*

In the Future / 1983 / Alligator ✦✦✦

Reggae Greats / 1984 / Mango ✦✦✦

Tension / 1985 / Alligator ✦✦✦
This second album on Alligator Records tops the first. —*Ron Wynn*

Live to Love / 1988 / Rohit ✦✦✦

We Refuse / Nov. 1990 / Profile ✦✦✦
A Jamaican reggae singer/composer whose influences include Bob Marley and Burning Spear, Pablo Moses isn't one for a lot of gimmicks. Even when his albums became more high-tech in the 1980s, the Rastafarian remained artistically successful because of his simplicity. The consistently sociopolitical *We Refuse* was Moses' first album of the 1990s and boasts some of his strongest material so far, including "Under Your Spell" (an attack on colonialism), "What's the Problem" and the poignant "South Africa." On the haunting "Charlie," Moses addresses a one-time childhood friend who has turned to violent crime and sees him as a potential victim. For those who enjoyed Moses' '80s albums, *We Refuse* is also a CD to savor. —*Alex Henderson*

Judy Mowatt

Vocals / Roots Reggae
Starting as lead singer for The Gaylettes in the mid-'60s, Judy Mowatt has been one of reggae's leading female vocalists for a quarter century with no signs of diminishment. Originally planning to become a preacher, Mowatt posesses one of the most sweetly powerful voices in Jamaica, an instrument she places in the service of Rastafarian and feminist causes above all else. After a series of local hits for her group or under the temporary pseudonym of Juliann, Mowatt became an international celebrity by helping form The I Threes, Bob Marley's backup singers, in 1974. When Marley built Tuff Gong, his own studio in Kingston, in 1977, Mowatt's seminal album *Black Woman* was the first to be recorded there. Considered by many critics to be the finest female album ever made in Jamaica, Mowatt wrote nearly all its tracks (Freddie McGregor and Bob Marley wrote the others). The title track and "Sisters Chant" are two ethereally beautiful cuts that encapsulate women's concerns everywhere and have achieved the status of anthems. Following Bob Marley's death, Mowatt has carved out a successful solo career, releasing a series of carefully crafted albums of canny originals and clever covers ("Grooving" and "Sing Our Own Song") that have solidified her forefront position in reggae's pantheon. —*Roger Steffens*

★ **Black Woman** / 1980 / Shanachie ✦✦✦✦✦
Judy Mowatt was one of the I-Threes, the vocal trio who served for years as Bob Marley's backup. While Marcia Griffiths was a legendary singer before the I-Threes were established, and Rita Marley has retained her status as a reggae icon (due in part to her marriage to Bob), Mowatt has been unjustly overlooked by the general public. Her voice may not be quite as refined as Griffiths', but it's a rich, earthy instrument with strong gospel overtones. Gospel traditions also deeply inform her lyrics, which are generally concerned with spiritual issues. That said, *Black Woman* is something of a mixed bag. It includes three fine versions of Bob Marley compositions ("Concrete Jungle," "Put It On" and the rare and lovely "Down in the Valley"), as well as Freddie McGregor's "Zion Chant" and six Mowatt originals. Mowatt's songs vary rather drastically in quality: "Slave Queen," for example, is flat both lyrically and melodically, but "Many Are Called" is a masterpiece. The proceedings are not livened by a rather lackluster mix. —*Rick Anderson*

Only a Woman / 1982 / Shanachie ✦✦✦✦
This is one of Judy Mowatt's better solo albums. An alumna of the Wailers (for whom she sang backup with Marcia Griffiths and Rita Marley), she brings gospel phrasing and a rich alto voice to her repertoire, which consists here of three covers (one a Curtis Mayfield song) and seven originals. Her version of "Big Woman" sounds a little out of place on this program of cultural and spiritual message songs, but it's still very charming. Mowatt's all-star studio band provides her with propulsive grooves and her own production is excellent; note in particular the midtempo skank of "You Don't Care," and the Nyahbinghi drumming on "King of Kings." "You're My People" is upbeat and inspiring, as is much of the rest of the program. Highly recommended. —*Rick Anderson*

Hugh Mundell

b. Jun. 14, 1962, **d.** 1983
Vocals / Roots Reggae, Political Folk
With the tragic murder of Hugh Mundell, who was shot and killed while sitting in a car with Junior Reid, in 1983, reggae lost one of its most promising young performers. Mundell's 1975 debut album, *Africa Must Be Free By 1983,* produced by Augustus Pablo remains a classic roots reggae recording. In a review of the album, *http:www.reggaeexpress.com* wrote '(Mundell's) singing style and soothing voice will lull you into tranquility if you let it.'

Mundell was still a teenager when he teamed with influential producer Joe Gibbs to record a still-unreleased single, "Where Is Natty Dread". His first break came when he was hired as a deejay for Augustus Pablo's Rockers sound system. His debut single, "Africa Must Be Free," was released in early-1975. Mundell also recorded several twelve-inch singles as Jah Levi.

Beginning in 1979, Mundell took over the production of his own recordings. He also produced the debut album, *Speak The Truth,* by 'Little' Junior Reid, on Pablo's label, Rocker. A dub version of *Africa Must Be Free By 1983* was released in 1989. —*Craig Harris*

• **Africa Must Be Free by 1983** / 1975 / RAS ✦✦✦✦
The teenaged Hugh Mundell cut this album under the tutelage of the legendary producer Augustus Pablo in the mid-1970s, and had a Jamaican hit with the title track. Mundell's artlessly fervent singing is attractive far out of proportion to his technical skill. It's the sincerity and devotion in his voice that make successes of songs like "Let's All Unite" and "My Mind"—that and the rock-solid instrumental backing of Pablo's studio band, which at this time included bassist and trombonist Leroy "Horsemouth" Wallace and guitarists Earl "Chinna" Smith and Jeffrey Chung. The CD issue of this album includes dub versions of six of the original album's eight tracks as well as several other miscellaneous dub tracks. Like too many of Jamaica's best reggae musicians, Mundell died young—in an almost creepy irony (given the title of his hit song), he was shot and killed in 1983 at the age of 21. —*Rick Anderson*

Junior Murvin

Vocals, Guitar / Roots Reggae

Junior Murvin has yet to match the success of his chart-topping 1976 hit, "Police & Thieves". Produced by Lee Perry, the song became the anthem of the Notting Hill Carnaval in 1977, and, was subsequently covered by The Clash and Boy George. Although he recorded a number of other reggae hits, including "Cool Out Son", "Miss Kushie", "Bad Man Posse" and "Muggers In The Street", none have achieved the sales of "Police & Thieves".

A native of Port Antonio, Jamaica, Murvin was gifted with a uniquely high falsetto. In a review of a late-1970s concert, a writer for *www.reggaeexpress.com* wrote, "I was mesmerized by his voice and you could have knocked me over with an eyelash".

Murvin's musical career began at a very slow pace. Having established his reputation, in the late-1960s, with his soulful interpretations of Curtis Mayfield songs, he teamed with producers Sonia Pottinger and Derrick Harriott to record Mayfield's tunes, "People Get Ready" and "Closer Together, under the moniker Junior Soul. Although his 1972 rendition of the traditional Jamaican air, "Solomon", was a local hit, he became disappointed when it failed to reach an international audience. Retreating to his home in the Jamaican hills, he taught himself to play guitar and worked on improving his songwriting skills. Reemerging in 1976, Murvin hooked up with Lee Perry and began recording at Perry's Black Ark studio in Kingston. It took only weeks before "Police & Thieves" had provided with the hit that he sought. The recording, however, was Murvin's last collaboration with Perry, who was on the verge of a nervous breakdown. Although he continued to work with such producers as Joe Gibbs, Mikey Dread, Henry "Junjo" Lawes and Prince Jammy, it appears that Murvin's fifteen minutes of fame had passed. *—Craig Harris*

★ **Police and Thieves** / 1977 / Mango ♦♦♦♦♦
This is one of those albums that winds up on just about every list of essential reggae recordings, and with good reason. Like Max Romeo's *War Ina Babylon* (which is equally essential, and can be considered a companion to this one), it was recorded under the auspices of Lee "Scratch" Perry at his legendary Black Ark studio, and is saturated with Perry's trademark dense, murky sound. Murvin sings in a fierce and beautiful falsetto, a voice which lends a unique weight to such dark masterpieces as "Lucifer," "Roots Train" and the title track (which was later recorded by the Clash). Perry surrounds Murvin's voice with great washes of echo and reverb and keeps the tempos slow and intense, giving the album an almost Biblical feel. Ignore the goofy album art on the CD reissue—there is nothing lighthearted about any of these songs, nor is there a single wrong note or misplaced effect. There may be eight or ten perfect reggae albums in existence, and this is certainly one of them. *—Rick Anderson*

Mutabaruka

Vocals / Political Reggae, Dub Poetry

A devotion to Rastafarianism and a militantly radical stance are expressed through the dub poetry of Jamaica-born Mutabaruka (born: Allen Hope). While his early albums, including *Check It* in 1983, *Outcry* in 1984, *Black Wi Blak'k'k* in 1991 and *Melanin Man* in 1994, marked him as a logical successor to dub poet Linton Kwesi Johnson, he's made his recent mark as the organizer and leader of the Roots All Stars. Their debut album, *Gathering Of The Spirits*, was released in 1998. *—Craig Harris*

Any Which Way . . . Freedom / 1989 / Shanachie ♦♦♦
His first release in three years was as potent, abrasive, and defiant as any of the prior dates. *—Ron Wynn*

Blakk Wi Blak . . . K . . . K . . . / 1991 / Shanachie ♦♦♦

Melanin Man / 1994 / Shanachie ♦♦♦♦
Mutabaruka was among the earliest "dub" poets, a firebrand who repeatedly attacked the injustices and hypocrisy he saw both in Jamaica and the Western world at large. If anything, he sounds more strident and angry on this latest set of poems. The title track, with its embrace of the controversial melanin theory, will probably dismay those who find the link between genetics, color and behavior a tenuous one at best. The other numbers continue his tradition of unrelenting, pro-Jamaican, pan-African political fare. He does take a different tack on the last work, however; "Dance" is reminiscent of The Last Poets or Gil Scott-Heron, and for just a little while shows that he can talk about something besides cultural conflict and racial oppression. *—Ron Wynn*

● **The Ultimate Collection** / 1996 / Shanachie ♦♦♦♦
In 1996, Shanachie looked back on Mutabaruka's Shanachie output with *The Ultimate Collection*. The title is an exaggeration, and the CD is hardly the last word on Muta's work at Shanachie. In fact, some essential gems are missing—including "Blacks in America," "Angola Invasion" and *Outcry's* title song—so when these absences are taken into consideration, you realize just how lofty a title *The Ultimate Collection* is. All that said, this collection has a lot going for it. Drawing on *Melanin Man, Any Which Way Freedom, The Mystery Unfolds* and other albums, *The Ultimate Collection* contains such familiar gems as "Bun Dung Babylon," "Walking on Gravel" and "Witeman Country." But instead of offering the well-known studio version of "Witeman Country," Shanachie provides an exciting live version from 1989. *The Ultimate Collection* doesn't tell the whole story where Muta is concerned, but even so, it paints a compelling picture of the angrily socio-political dub poet. *—Alex Henderson*

Gathering of the Spirits / Jun. 16, 1998 / Shanachie ♦♦♦

Johnny Nash

b. Aug. 19, 1940, Houston, TX

Vocals / Pop-Soul, Reggae-Pop, Soul

Though by no means an artistic innovator on par with contemporaries such as Bob Marley or Jimmy Cliff, singer Johnny Nash nevertheless proved a pivotal force behind the mainstream acceptance of reggae with the international success of his 1972 chart-topper "I Can See Clearly Now." Born in Houston, TX on August 19, 1940, Nash honed his vocal skills singing in his Baptist church's choir and by 13 was a regular on the local television series *Matinee*, performing covers of current R&B hits; in 1956 he was discovered by Arthur Godfrey, appearing on his radio and TV broadcasts for the next seven years. Nash signed to ABC-Paramount to release his 1957 debut single "A Teenager Sings the Blues," scoring his first chart hit early the following year with a rendition of Doris Day's "A Very Special Love"; in late 1958, he also teamed with Paul Anka and George Hamilton IV for the inspirational "The Teen Commandments." Marketed as a rival to Johnny Mathis, he even began a film career with 1959's *Take a Giant Step*, also appearing in 1960's *Key Witness* before his career flagged with a series of little-noticed singles for Warner Bros., Groove, and Argo.

Nash returned to prominence in 1965 when the ballad "Let's Move and Groove Together" reached the R&B Top Five; more imporantly, the record became a major hit in Jamaica, where he traveled in 1967 on a promotional tour. During a return trip, he cut the ska-influenced single "Hold Me Tight" at Byron Lee's Federal Studios—a Top Five pop hit on both sides of the Atlantic, the record was issued on his own JAD label, which in early 1970 scored a Top 40 hit with a reggaefied rendition of Sam Cooke's "Cupid" as well. The following year Nash scored a major British hit with his reading of the Bob Marley perennial "Stir It Up"; while living in Britain, he signed to Epic, which in 1972 released his biggest hit, "I Can See Clearly Now," which sat atop the American pop charts for four weeks. Although his popularity at home again dimmed, Nash returned to the UK charts in 1975 with his number one cover of the Little Anthony classic "Tears on My Pillow," followed a year later by another Sam Cooke cover, "(What a) Wonderful World." He gradually retired from performing during the coming years, although Jimmy Cliff successfully covered "I Can See Clearly Now" in 1994. *—Jason Ankeny*

I Can See Clearly Now / 1972 / Epic ♦♦♦♦
Singer/songwriter/producer Johnny Nash's million-seller "I Can See Clearly Now" did more to bring the reggae music sound into the mainstream than any other single record up to that point. To be sure, there were previous reggae hits (Millie Small's "My Boy Lollipop," Desmond Dekker & the Aces's 1969 hit "Israelites"), but Nash's buoyant, breezy, optimistic classic proved to be a phenomenal record holding the number one pop position for four weeks and going to number one adult contemporary on *Billboard's* charts in fall 1972. Houston,TX, native Nash had been recording in Jamaica for some years before having his biggest hit. On the *I Can See Clearly Now* album, Nash used members of Bob Marley and the Wailers and recorded several Marley songs: "Stir It Up," the follow-up single, "Comma Comma," the smooth "Guava Jelly," and the Nash/Marley co-written ballad, "You Poured Sugar on Me." The tender album track "(It Was) So Nice While It Lasted" received radio play. Other standouts are the punchy horns-flavored "Ooh Baby You've Been Good to Me" and the lullaby-ish ballad "There Are More Questions Than Answers." It's tribute to its high quality that *I Can See Clearly Now* was in print almost three decades after its original release. *—Ed Hogan*

● **The Reggae Collection** / Sep. 21, 1993 / Epic ♦♦♦♦
Nash was the first American singer to incorporate reggae rhythms, and as such deserves a lot of credit for paving the way for the acceptance of bonafide Jamaican performers. His own pop-soul-reggae concoctions, though, were often rather watery in comparison to the real thing. This brings together 20 of the reggae-style tracks he cut between 1968 and the mid-'70s, including his hits "Hold Me Tight," "Cupid," and "Stir It Up"; the version of "I Can See Clearly Now" is an alternate take. This leans too heavily on his 1972-75 Epic material without enough of his late-'60s work; the small hit "You Got Soul" is missing, and the delightfully light and soaring "Hold Me Tight" towers over most everything else here. Almost half the tracks were previously unreleased or previously unavailable in the U.S. *—Richie Unterberger*

Sonny Okosun

b. 1947, Benin City, Nigeria

Vocals, Guitar / Contemporary Reggae

With 16 African album releases to his credit—many of them gold—Nigeria's Sonny Okosuns is one of the continent's most enduringly popular performers. Okosuns initially caught the pop music bug via Elvis and the Beatles, forming his first band, The Postmen, in 1964. In the early '70s, he helped usher in a back-to-African-roots trend with a stylistic mix of Western pop and local highlife he called "ozzidi." He later broadened it to include the rapidly spreading gospel of reggae. His diversity has kept him from being pigeonholed. He was featured in *Black Star Liner*, a 1983 anthology of African reggae, and more recently appeared on the anti-apartheid Sun City EP produced by Steve Van Zandt. His albums typically feature vocals in English as well as the Nigerian Ishan language. *—Bob Tarte*

3rd World / 1981 / OTI ♦♦♦♦

Liberation / 1984 / Shanachie ♦♦♦
Afro-reggae Okosun sometimes tends to Top 40 glibness, but at his best he's a significant member of the Nigerian new wave, with its pan-Africanism and its constant feedback between the New World and electronic juju. *—John Storm Roberts, Original Music*

African Soldiers / 1991 / Profile ♦♦♦♦
A superstar on the African Continent, Sonny Okosuns commands the type of reverence in African music that Bob Marley enjoyed in reggae and Stevie Wonder commands in R&B. Okosuns has recorded some five-star reggae over the years, although African pop is his main focus. And the fact that Okosuns sings in English much of the time certainly hasn't hurt his popularity among reggae audiences. A welcome addition to his catalog, *African Soldiers* is among the many superb albums he's delivered. Okosuns favors African dialects on some of the material and embraces English on such exuberant, uplifting Afro-pop as "Woman" and the title song. "Babylon," "Happy Days" and "King of Kings" illustrate his excellence in the reggae department, but it must be stressed that Okosuns brings a distinctly African flavor to a style associated primarily with Jamaica. *African Soldiers* never fails to impress. *—Alex Henderson*

● **The Ultimate Collection** / Mar. 14, 2000 / Ivory Music ♦♦♦♦

Count Ossie

d. 1976

Vocals, Horn, Drums, Percussion / Ska

The foundations of reggae and its association with Rastafarianism were established by drummer, percussionist and vocalist Count Ossie (born: Oswald Williams). Together with his band, The Mystic Revelation Of Rastafari, Count Ossie combined African-influenced music with the European hymnal tradition to create a unique sound that inspired everyone from Ras Michael And The Sons of Negus and The Skatalites to Bob Marley And The Wailers and Toots And The Maytals.

Count Ossie's earliest inspiration came from rasta elder Brother Job, who introduced him to the philosophies of Rastafarianism. A Nyabinghi drummer from the hills of Jamaica, Count Ossie cut his first singles, including "O'Carolina" and "Chubby", for Prince Buster at the studios of RJR radio. Beginning in 1959, Count Ossie recorded for Sir Coxsone Dodd at Studio One.

Together with music director, tenor saxophone, flute and clarinet player Cedric "I-m" Brooks, Count Ossie formed the Mystic Revelation Of Rastafari. Heavily percussive, the group featured philosopher orator Samuel Clayton, double bass player, poet and vocalist Ras Jose, Ras Jose, Little Bop and Count Ossie's son, Time, on fundae drum, bass drummer and percussionist King Rayo, percussionist and vocalist Bunny, percussionist Moses, baritone saxophone and clarinet player Ras Sam II and trombonist Nambo.

There has been some debate as to the cause of Count Ossie's death in 1976. While some sources claim that he was in an auto accident, others say that he was trampled to death when a crowd panicked at the *National Arena*. *—Craig Harris*

Grounation: The Indomitable Spirit of Rastafari / 1988 / Dynamic Sounds ♦♦♦♦

As the back cover says, Grounation is "a Rastafarian gathering at which nyahbingi music, usually relentless drumming accompanied by chanting, is played." Of all Jamaican music, nyahbingi is the closest in feel to African music. When recorded by its leading practitioners, Count Ossie and Ras Michael, it makes for intriguing sounds related to, but not exactly the same as, standard reggae. As there is not a ton of nyahbingi recordings out there, it's a good idea to have a compilation of them, and this disc does have a couple of offerings apiece from Ossie and Michael. Still, this isn't really a collection of nyahbingi music; it's more like a collection of nyahbingi music and various reggae cuts that have some nyahbingi influence. More disturbing, however, is the liner notes' total lack of original release dates, and the paucity of information about most of the artists represented. Chronologically, the cuts seem to cover the 1960s onward, but in the absence of documentation, the context of their presence is murky; some seem to have been selected because of the Rasta philosophy of the lyrics, rather than for Grounation/nyahbingi elements in the music. Such concerns aside, this does have some good reggae and/or nyahbingi, like Negril's "Rasta," with its swelling soul-funk organ and African beats; Nora Dean's wacky "Ay Ay Ay," with its hypnotic chanted vocals and birdcall-like effects; Michael's "In Zion (Dub Version)," with a riff based on "On Broadway"; Margarita and Don Drummond's ska cut "Woman-A-Come" (the Grounation connection seems tenuous here, other than in the cadence of the vocals); and Ossie's drum'n'chant-based performances, which are far starker than anything else here. *—Richie Unterberger*

Augustus Pablo (Horace Swaby)

b. 1954, St. Andrews, Jamaica, **d.** May 18, 1999

Melodica, Keyboards, Piano, Synthesizer, Organ, Producer / Dub

The name never gained the international recognition of Bob Marley's, but Augustus Pablo is one of reggae's legitimate legends, a pioneer who flipped the genre completely upside down. Along with producer King Tubby, Pablo almost singlehandedly invented dub, wherein reggae's fat bass and popping drums are twisted and contorted until they crack like bullwhips and rumble like syncopated earthquakes. This is instrumental music: voices will emerge from the supple rhythms only to trickle into an echo-shrouded void, forsaking their contribution to the bedrock grooves. And Pablo's haunting splashes of melodica (which at times conjure images of Ennio Morricone's Sergio Leone soundtracks) gave his music a sound that is immediately identifiable and as singular as anything Marley managed. Though Pablo's later work only occasionally matched the breathtaking innovation of his prime material., 1981's *East of the River Nile* equaled his early triumphs—the results weren't always great but they were always interesting. *—John Floyd & Roger Steffens*

Rebel Rock Reggae: This Is Augustus Pablo / 1973 / Heartbeat ♦♦♦

Augustus Pablo formed his mysterious dub style on these early sessions, with Lee Perry producing and the best reggae session players backing. *—Myles Boisen*

King Tubbys Meets Rockers Uptown / 1976 / Shanachie ♦♦♦♦♦

A compilation of the best King Tubby/Augustus Pablo collaborational sides available, *King Tubbys Meets Rockers Uptown* was released in 1976 to capitalize on the popularity of the title track, one of the seminal dub sides of all time. (It was so popular that Island flipped the original, "Baby I Love You So" by Jacob Miller, onto the B-side of the single for the first time.) The other 11 tracks are all variations on the same superb form, super tuff rhythms and echoplexed melodica lines, with the rock-solid contributions of bassist Robbie Shakespeare and members of Bob Marley's band. *—John Bush*

☆ **East of the River Nile** / 1977 / Message ♦♦♦♦♦

The best of the pure instrumental albums in Pablo's catalog, *East of the River Nile* finds the melodica master stretching out on various keyboards and strings as well on earthy, meditative tracks like "Chant to King Selassie I," "Jah Light" and "Natural Way." Though this is explicitly a non-dub occasion, "Natural Way" does get its own version with "Nature Dub." *—John Bush*

Original Rockers / 1979 / Greensleeves ♦♦♦♦

Original Rockers is a solid introduction to Pablo's haunting melodica playing, and includes brief flashes of his dub inspiration as well on "Tubby's Dub Song" and "Rockers Dub." As usual, the lineup is superb—Robbie Shakespeare, Aston and Carlton Barrett, Earl Chinna Smith and Bobby Ellis, among others. Though much of the album is instrumental, Dillinger guests on "Brace a Boy." *—John Bush*

Earth's Rightful Ruler / 1983 / Shanachie ♦♦♦♦♦

This is one of the more satisfying Augustus Pablo albums, for several reasons. For one thing—and this must be said—his sound is remarkably, er, consistent, even by reggae standards. Most of his records are completely instrumental, and all tend to focus on his melodica playing; while all of his albums reward any attention you pay to them, their more natural effect is soothing, not to say soporific. Not that there's anything wrong with that, but that general tendency in Pablo's solo work just makes *Earth's Rightful Ruler* stand out that much more from the rest. It opens with the title track, which features an unidentified singer (who sounds a lot like Hugh Mundell, but don't quote me) and a great, rootsy groove. Typical instrumentals follow, but there's some nice chatting on "Rastafari Liveth" and on "Java," the album's high point, which also features haunting background vocals and some very nice interplay between guitarist Earl "Chinna" Smith and Pablo's melodica. *—Rick Anderson*

Eastman Dub / 1988 / RAS ♦♦♦

Pablo extends his musical arsenal to include xylophone and various keyboards in addition to his trademark melodica. *—Myles Boisen*

Blowing With the Wind / Jun. 1991 / Shanachie ♦♦♦♦

A rare example of a reggae instrumentalist, Augustus Pablo has enjoyed a small cult following in Jamaican circles. The melodica player/keyboardist was never as well known as Peter Tosh, Dennis Brown or Burning Spear, but is well respected among the more knowledgeable reggae devotees. Like many reggae artists, he is heavily influenced by American soul and R&B, but he also shows an awareness of African, Asian and Middle Eastern music. After recording many memorable albums in previous decades, Pablo leaped into the 1990s with the solid *Blowing In The Wind.* From the haunting qualities of "Eastern Code," "Blowing In The Wind" and "Ancient Harmonies" to the pleasant optimism of "Twinkling Stars" and "Creation Blues," this is one of many CDs he can be proud of. *—Alex Henderson*

★ **Classic Rockers** / 1995 / Island Jamaica ♦♦♦♦♦

This generous collection of classic, rare, and previously unissued tracks is part of an outstanding reissue series from Island Jamaica (Island Records' reggae-specific imprint). The Augustus Pablo album may be the best of the bunch; it opens with the classic Jacob Miller song "Baby I Love You So," which is immediately followed by the dub version of that track ("King Tubby Meets the Rockers Uptown," perhaps the single best dub cut ever recorded). Instrumentals and vocal tracks by Pablo-produced artists follow, including a couple of previously hard to find Delroy Wilson tracks with their dub versions, and two classic performances by Junior Delgado and the late Hugh Mundell. Run, don't walk, to your nearest music store to get this one. *—Rick Anderson*

The Paragons

Group / Dub, Rocksteady

If you're familiar with the song "The Tide Is High" you probably know it as a huge hit for Blondie, but before Deborah Harry and company got a hold of it, it was a 1960s hit in for the Paragons.The early Paragons sound is heavily influence by American soul music and the singing is in the familiar tight, interlocking harmony style of Jamaican vocal trios and quartets of the early '60s. In 1964, the group caught the attention of legendary producer Coxsone Dodd who immediately brought the group to the famous Studio One and under the watchful eyes and ears of Duke Reid (who became the group's mentor) cut a succession of popular singles such as "Love At Last" and "Good Luck and Goodbye" for Reid's label Treasure Isle. Not long after, leader John Holt decided that the group should soften their soulful sound and go for a more root-heavy rock steady approach. It turned out to be a good idea as the Paragons became the most popular rock-steady vocal act in Jamaica and in Britain. But money problems, specifically issues over why the group wasn't rich after more than a dozen number one Jamaican hits, led to the band's breakup. *—John Dougan*

On the Beach with the Paragons / 1967 / Jet ♦♦♦♦

In 1998, the French Jet Set label reissued this classic 1967 album on CD. The original art work was included along with informative new liner notes and write-ups on both the Paragons and Duke "the Trojan" Reid (founder of the Kingston-based Treasure Isle Records and an important figure in Jamaican music). Originally a Treasure Isle LP, *On the Beach with the Paragons* sold well in Jamaica and also became a hit in England (where reggae and ska have been huge since the '60s). One of reggae's finest vocal harmony groups of the '60s, the Paragons were the reggae equivalent of soulsters like the Four Tops, the Delfonics and the Miracles—and it's impossible to miss the northern soul influence on such gems as "Island in the Sun," "Happy-Go-Lucky Girl," "Only a Smile" and their most famous hit, "The Tide Is High" (which Blondie covered with splendid results in 1980). The Paragons' charismatic lead singer, John Holt, has inspired comparisons to Bob Marley—to be sure, there was some similarity, but Holt was certainly his own man. Not only is *On the Beach* essential listening for reggae enthusiasts, it's also a CD that lovers of vocal-group soul can appreciate. *—Alex Henderson*

● **My Girl Wears My Crown (Rock Steady 1966-1968)** / Oct. 21, 1994 / Trojan ♦♦♦♦♦

Frankie Paul

b. 1965

Vocals / Dancehall, Soul

Since making his recording debut at the age of 15, "African Princess," in 1980, soulful Frankie Paul is one of the more prolific and among the most reliable dancehall artists around. Born the son of a singer, Paul was born blind, but later an operation provided him with very limited eyesight. As a young adult, he went to a New York eye specialist where he was given special glasses to allow him to see even more. Paul started singing while attending a Salvation Army School for the blind. Stevie Wonder came by to visit and the two sang a duet. Wonder was impressed and encouraged Paul to pursue music. While in school he learned the piano and then taught himself to play drums and guitar. He played these instruments and sang both leads and backups on two "Showdown" LPs in 1983 for Channel One. The first was with Sugar Minott and the second was with Little John. Paul went on to record with several major producers including Junjo Lawes, Prince Jammy and George Phang. In 1984, Paul had a number one hit with the Lawes produced "Pass the Tu Sheng Peng." During the '80s, Paul recorded over 100 cds. *—Sandra Brennan*

● **Pass the Ku-Sheng-Peng** / 1985 / Nyam Up ✦✦✦✦✦
Frankie goes to the dance and lives to sing about it. *—Roger Steffens*

Get Closer / 1990 / Profile ✦✦✦✦✦
Since the 1970s, reggae has been associated with angrily socio-political lyrics and odes to the Rastafarian faith, but in fact, quite a bit of apolitical lover's rock has also been recorded. Reggae greats ranging from Dennis Brown to Gregory Issacs to the late Bob Marley have excelled in the "lover's rock" field, often recording gems that weren't much different from the songs by classic African-American groups like the Delfonics, the Mad Lads and the Chi-Lites. Drawing on '60s and '70s sweet soul as well as urban contemporary, Frankie Paul embraces lover's rock exclusively on *Get Closer.* Though Paul is a likable singer with an impressive voice, most of this material is unremarkable and contrived. Paul, who has a fairly memorable offering in the moody "No Rest," is capable of a lot more. *—Alex Henderson*

Lee "Scratch" Perry

b. 1936, St. Mary's, Jamaica
Vocals, Percussion, Producer / Political Reggae, Roots Reggae, Dub, Rocksteady
Some call him a genius, others claim he's certifiably insane, a madman. Truth is, he's both, but more importantly, Lee Perry is a towering figure in reggae—a producer, mixologist, and songwriter that, along with King Tubby, helped shape the sound of dub, and made reggae music such a powerful part of the pop music world. Along with producing some of the most influential acts (Bob Marley and the Wailers and the Congos to name but two) in reggae history, Perry's approach to production and dub mixing was breathtakingly innovative and audacious—no one else sounds like him—and while many claim that King Tubby invented dub, there are just as many who would argue (myself included) that no one experimented with it or took it further than did Lee Perry. A word or two about Perry's discography: it's massive, unwieldy, and although there are plenty of great records, there's almost as much crap. The lack of quality control has little to do with Perry, but rather with sleazebags trying to rip off his legacy. After King Tubby's murder in 1989, his studio was looted, and many of Perry's tapes were stolen. Some of these recordings have shown up on poorly mastered, and expensive, anthologies. Releases on Trojan, Rounder's reggae subsidiary label Heartbeat, and Island (and its subsidiary label Mango) are generally excellent and are the best place to start building your Perry collection. Also, as with King Tubby recordings, purchasing a Perry release means you might be buying a record he produced, but not necessarily performs on. That said, happy hunting and listening. *—John Dougan*

Revolution Dub / 1975 / Orange Street ✦✦✦✦
In terms of value for money, this 30-minute collection isn't exactly world-class. But in terms of musical quality, you couldn't do much better—it's just about as good an encapsulation of the art of super-producer Lee "Scratch" Perry and his studio band, the Upsetters, as you'll find. Originally issued in the mid '70s on the Creole label (and reissued at least twice since, on Crocodisc and Lagoon), this album finds Perry at the peak of his somewhat creepy powers, taking such classic songs as Junior Byles' "The Long Way" and Ricky & Bunny's "Bush Weed Corn Trash" and subjecting them to the deconstructionist rigors of dub—the sound careening wildly between the left and right channels, bass and drums dropping out suddenly, leaving only guitar and snippets of sung vocals, while Perry adds his own apocalyptic imprecations and off-the-wall witticisms on top. What makes these tracks so powerful is the juxtaposition of Perry's insane production approach with the Upsetters' utterly rock-solid grooves, grooves which not even the chief Upsetter himself can dislodge. Essential. *—Rick Anderson*

Roast Fish Collie Weed & Corn Bread / 1976 / VP ✦✦✦✦✦
This is a classic chunk of early Perry that in its day was difficult to get even as an import. Now the French label Lagoon has reissued it (albeit with a cheap reproduction of the original cover that looks like a blurry photocopy), and it's somewhat easier to get a hold of (VP discs are not available at every record store). This is prime early Scratch, with tracks like "Roast Fish and Corn Bread" and "Soul Fire" pushing the mixological experimentation of Perry's earlier releases to another level, or planet as the case may be. *—John Dougan*

Super Ape / 1976 / Island ✦✦✦✦✦
As it says on the cover, "Dub it up, blacker than dread," and that bit of rastaspeak accurately describes the vibe of this great record. The Upsetters are in reeling and rollicking good form, and Perry's mastery of the mixing board is made manifest on tracks like "Zion's Blood" and "Dread Lion." The accent is bass heavy, which in reggae is no surprise, but here Boris Gardener's bass is so propulsive and commanding, and Perry mixes it so far up front, that it will shake your foundations. This is one of the few early Perry releases where his personality is less dominant than that of the band, but it only takes a few spins for Scratch's blood and fire to become evident. *—John Dougan*

Scratch on the Wire / 1979 / Island ✦✦✦✦
An early greatest-hits collection featuring some of Perry's best known early recordings and production work with the Upsetters. Best track is Junior Murvin's "Police and Thieves," a reggae classic. Not a bad collection, but don't spend a lot of time seeking it out; it's better to save your money for the more recent, three-CD *Arkology* collection, which includes all of these tracks and plenty more remixed versions. Still, if it's a concise sampler of Perry's best-known '70s material you want, this is a good place to start. *—John Dougan*

The Return of Pipecock Jackxon / 1980 / Black Art ✦✦✦✦✦
Recorded in Amsterdam while Perry was allegedly gobbling acid by the handful, *Return* is a truly spacy, meandering, borderline incoherent, but frequently amazing recording. As if Perry needed chemical stimulation to be far out, this record is a stunning glimpse of how far he was planning to push the production envelope. Must be heard to be believed. *—John Dougan*

Mystic Miracle Star / 1982 / Heartbeat ✦✦✦
Some folks love this record. I'm not one of them, but I do like it and recommend it. There is something restrained about the playing by the backing band the Majestics, specifically the rhythm section of bassist Jim Schwartz and Louis LaVilla, who don't seem to groove hard enough. Side one, which is only three tracks long, is better than side two, which tends to fall apart halfway through. Scratch, however, is in fine fettle, and his stream-of-consciousness toasting more than makes up for lackluster riddims. *—John Dougan*

Megaton Dub, Vol. 1-2 / 1983 / Seven Leaves ✦✦✦✦
Opinions (mine included) run hot and cold over this hard-to-find two volume set of Scratch dub. I don't think it is as excellent and crucial as many of its supporters claim, nor do I think it's as awful as its detractors insist. File it under odd and occasionally wonderful (but, ultimately not essential), especially if you like your Perry mix so loaded with echo it sounds as if it was recorded in a canyon. Extremely difficult to find. *—John Dougan*

History, Mystery and Prophesy / 1984 / Mango ✦✦✦
Perry's weakest Island/Mango release. All the rough edges are gone, and Perry's berserk charm is in short supply. Still, because it's Perry, there are tracks to recommend ("Heads of Government" being the most notable), but there are plenty better Perry records to be had. *—John Dougan*

● **Reggae Greats** / 1984 / Mango ✦✦✦✦✦
Almost the same track listing as 1979's *Scratch on the Wire,* but far less expensive and easier to find. My caveat with Mango's *Reggae Greats* series is they don't offer a lot of liner information and use unimaginative graphics. But you will get "Police and Thieves," and no reggae collection is complete without it. *—John Dougan*

Scratch Attack! / 1988 / Clock Tower ✦✦✦
Although it suffers a bit from shoddy packaging, ugly graphics, and no liner information to speak of, *Scratch Attack* is reissue of two excellent and long-unavailable Perry LPs, *Chapter One* and *Blackboard Jungle Dub.* The material is weirdly wonderful and represents some of Perry's earliest and most unrestrained efforts at dub madness. Issued on one disc, they ebb and flow seamlessly (set your CD player on "shuffle play" for proof), with tracks like "Jah the Dub Organizer" and "Dub From Africa" especially delicious. This is a great way to dig deep into Perry's unique mindset without spending a ton of money. *—John Dougan*

Chicken Scratch / 1989 / Heartbeat ✦✦✦
Of all the reissues from Lee Perry's early career, this is the most illuminating, because it captures the youthful Perry (in his early 20s) singing ska music. Backed by the phenomenal Skatalites, featuring trombonist Don Drummond, saxophonists Tommy McCook and Roland Alphonso, and keyboardist Jackie Mittoo, Perry belts out such Studio One ska/pop classics as "Please Don't Go," "Man to Man" (featuring backing vocals by the very youthful trio of Bob Marley, Bunny Wailer, and Peter Tosh), and "Solid as a Rock." The songs skitter along, filled to the brim with exuberance, and the Skatalites (as usual) are a joy to hear, banging out double-time rhythms with reckless abandon. Adding to the fun are female backing vocalists the Soulettes and the Dynamites, the former featuring Bob Marley's wife Rita. This is rarely heard Perry music and, considering how far from this music he is today, it's almost hard to imagine him recording it. If you are building a Lee Perry library, absolutely, positively make this one of your purchases. *—John Dougan*

Build the Ark / 1990 / Trojan ✦✦✦✦
The last of Trojan's three-record (two-CD) collections of Perry's crucial Black Ark production work of the '70s. And, as was the case with the previous collections (*The Upsetter Box* and *Open the Gate*), there's absolutely no good reason not to own this collection too. If you're thinking that three double-CD sets of Lee Perry starts to sound like overkill, look at it this way—that's like saying you've breathed enough air, and now you don't need any more. As with recordings of Sun Ra, there's always a reason (like amazing music, for a start) to add more Lee Perry to your collection. And with this release you will be able to get your hands on Junior Murvin's amazing "Cross Over" (nearly as good as "Police and Thieves"), Winston Heywood's "Long, Long Time," and Eric Donaldson's "Freedom Street." This is the sound of Black Ark at its most exciting and prolific, and remains a testament to Perry's genius as a producer, mixer, and arranger. A heavy groove indeed. *—John Dougan*

Meets Bullwackie in Satan's Dub / 1990 / ROIR ✦✦✦✦✦
The full title of this release is the rather unwieldy *Lee "Scratch" Perry Meets Bullwackie in Satan's Dub.* This is essentially a dub version of the 1988 recording *Satan Kicked the Bucket,* which Perry recorded at Bullwackie's studio in New Jersey. The dub version, which features contributions from the Chosen Brothers, is deep and dark and funky, with plenty of surreal verbal excursions and off sound effects. The groove established by the Upsetters is fine, and Bullwackie, to his credit, lets the groove go more often than he manipulates the sound. The result is a finely crafted chunk of dub that is surprisingly minimalist in its approach and is much better than the non-dub version of *Satan Kicked the Bucket,* which is a fairly lackluster affair. *—John Dougan*

Black Ark in Dub / Oct. 4, 1993 / Culture Press ✦✦✦✦✦
A fine collection of early Perry dub packaged in what seems to be a semi-legit, bootleg way. This label seems to be tied in with the French label Lagoon, which has released the Perry-produced Bob Marley session (two CDs, both of them essential). This is a good selection; Perry remixes are typically audacious and crazy, but there's little enclosed information telling you when the tracks were cut. Lack of information is an ongoing problem with Perry releases, since his entire output defies any kind of authoritative historical treatment. Still, this is worthy of your time, even if it doesn't provide the big buzz of some of Perry's other, more far-out experiments. *—John Dougan*

★ **Arkology** / 1997 / Island Jamaica ✦✦✦✦✦
Purportedly the definitive Lee "Scratch" Perry compilation, the three-CD set *Arkology* is

loaded with good intentions and is carefully constructed, but with a back catalog like Perry's—where it's nearly impossible to find out what's what—definitive in this case is a dream. Still, the compilers have done a fine job of providing an overview of Perry's career that makes sense musically, historically, and culturally. For those who want to jump headlong into Perry's world, this is the way to go. (Otherwise, buying two to three individual releases would be recommended.) *Arkology's* foundation is the 1979 anthology *Scratch on the Wire;* the compilers took those tracks and added a significant number of remixes and a few previously unreleased dub tracks to give it some weight. And that is perhaps the set's biggest drawback; it doesn't cover quite enough of Perry's career. Remixes are nice, but a representative sampling of the early, mid-, and late periods at Black Ark would have been better, as well as a few of the early-'60s ska tracks that didn't make it onto Heartbeat's excellent *Chicken Scratch* compilation. There are also some irritating audio considerations here; sometimes reggae reissues lose that warm, extremely loud bass sound that is crucial to the riddims. That's not always the case on this release, but there are some moments when you wish there was just a little more blood coming from the speakers. So, all that said, is *Arkology* worth it? Absolutely. Don't think that this large purchase will give you all the crucial Lee "Scratch" Perry recordings; it provides a good overview and is an excellent introduction, but consider it the start, rather than the completion, of your journey with Scratch and the Upsetters. *—John Dougan*

Ethiopia / Apr. 27, 1999 / Orange Street ♦♦♦♦
Just when you think you've probably heard all of the material recorded by Lee Perry at his legendary Black Ark studio, another collection pops up with tracks you haven't heard by artists you've never heard of. This one includes a few frequently collected classics (Perry's own "Stay Red," the Upsetters' "Thanks We Get"), but most of the program is less familiar—future Third World vocalist Bunny Ruggs covers "I Am I Said," and there's the repatriation anthem "Ethiopia," just to name two obscurities. Actually, one or two of these tracks could have remained buried and it wouldn't have hurt anyone—the Silvertones' excruciatingly polytonal rendition of "How Deep Is Your Love," for example—but most of this material is priceless. Other highlights include Leo Graham's classic "News Flash" (listed here as "News Splash") and the Upsetters' creepy horticultural anthem "Bless the Weed." Everything partakes of the signature Black Ark ambience: the splashy echo, the eerie, slightly distant vocal mix, and that slight edge of utter madness that characterizes every session over which the mighty Upsetter presides. *—Rick Anderson*

The Upsetter Shop, Vol. 2: 1969-1973 / May 4, 1999 / Heartbeat ♦♦♦♦
Although credited to Lee Perry & the Upsetters, this is in fact a various-artists compilation assembling 20 of Perry's productions from 1968-1973; only one cut is by Lee Perry, and only a couple are ascribed to the Upsetters. It's a solid, if not stunning, overview of some of Perry's early work, much of which is pretty obscure even to reggae fans. This includes quite a few vocal groups, like the Mellotones, the Blecchers, and the Inspirations, as well as soloists like Dillinger. It's pretty respectable rocksteady, and sounds better than many similar anthologies since it was taken from the master tapes. However, there's not much of the weirdness that Perry is most renowned for; at this point he was still a producer serving the artist and the song, not casting as dominant a figure over proceedings as he would in the future. There are some eccentric moments, though, like the Mellotones' "Uncle Charlie," with its squeaky hook and coughing and retching during the instrumental break, and Pat Satchmo, who sounds like a reggae Louis Armstrong on "Can't Take It Anymore." The Upsetters' own "Creation" is an atypical outing that finds them getting into Booker T. & the MGs-style instrumental soul, with a reggae tinge to the beat. Perry's influence seems entirely absent from the rehearsal tape of the Silvertones covering "Sweets for My Sweet." This charming relic has acoustic guitar and light percussion, the lack of accompaniment allowing reggae vocal harmonies to stand in bold relief. *—Richie Unterberger*

Chapter Two of Words / Sep. 28, 1999 / Trojan ♦♦♦♦

Lost Treasures of the Ark / Feb. 1, 2000 / Orchard ♦♦♦♦
Those who can't get enough of Lee "Scratch" Perry's particular brand of inspired mayhem have had plenty to celebrate at the end of the millennium, with one or two new box sets (many of them mining his celebrated Black Ark period) emerging each year. This one is a good, if not spectacular, collection of material that will appeal primarily to die-hard fans. What looks like a bargain isn't quite the great deal it appears to be at first glance, since the 150 minutes of music on these three discs would have fit easily on two. In addition, the packaging is cheesy and garish, and the liner notes are sloppily edited and not entirely accurate. Ultimately, though, what matters is the music, and much of it on this set is excellent. Interestingly, it's the work of the relative unknowns that really stands out: "Stand by Me" and "You Know What I Mean" by the Inspirations are two of the most affecting songs on the program, followed closely by Brent Dowe's exquisite "Down Here in Babylon." There are also a few superb performances by Bob Marley, including the slightly eerie "Who Colt the Game" and three versions of "Shocks Almighty." Perry's production is typical of the Black Ark period: cramped, splashy, and utterly idiosyncratic. His dub versions are also typical of the period, meaning that they're nowhere near as interesting as one might expect. But his touch on the standard versions is like magic, and the music he supervises almost always transcends the primitive quality of his equipment and his own borderline psychosis. *—Rick Anderson*

The Ultimate Collection / Feb. 29, 2000 / Hip-O ♦♦♦♦♦
There are so many Lee Perry compilations out there, and some of them are so good, that it's hard to take seriously any one that claims to be the "ultimate." And to be completely fair, it probably isn't possible to compile the ultimate Perry collection on a single disc; there's simply too much material out there, and too much of it is too good. But as single-disc distillations go, this one gets top honors. Partly because it does more than just round up the usual suspects —in addition to no-brainer selections like Max Romeo's "War Ina Babylon" and early Wailers songs "Duppy Conqueror" and "Small Axe," there are equally fine obscurities like "Dread Lion" (from the classic Upsetters album *Super Ape*) and two (count 'em) tracks by the Congos. And even on the obvious selections, the label was cool enough to use extended disco mixes in several cases (such as the Congos' "Neckodeemus" and the Heptones' "Mr. President"). The result is a richly diverse and thoroughly enjoyable collection of music produced by one of the most strange and wonderful figures in reggae history. *—Rick Anderson*

Maxi Priest (Max Elliot)

b. 1962, London, England
Vocals / Smooth Reggae, Contemporary Reggae, Reggae-Pop, Dancehall, Lovers Rock, Urban
Born in Max Elliot in Manchester, England in 1962, Maxi Priest changed his name when he converted to Rastafarianism. He stumbled into a career in reggae when he was discovered while building sound systems. Since then, Maxi Priest has become one of the '80s great crossover success stories, making chart-toppers on both sides of the Atlantic. A pleasant, easygoing vocal manner coupled with a sexy stage presence have yielded consistent hits—including a cover of "Some Guys Have All the Luck" in 1987, Cat Stevens' "Wild World" in 1988. Though he initially sang straight, ultra-slick lovers rock, the '90s have found him dabbling in dancehall with impressive results. In 1990, he scored a number one pop hit in the U.S. with "I Just Want to Be Close to You" and a Top 10 with "Set the Night to Music," a duet with Roberta Flack. *Man With the Fun,* released in 1996, contained another hit, "That Girl," featuring Shaggy. *So What If It Rains* was issued in 1999, followed by *CombiNation* later that year. *—Roger Steffens*

Intentions / 1986 / EMI-Capitol Special Markets ♦♦♦

Maxi Priest / 1988 / Virgin ♦♦♦♦
This bends the reggae/pop equation back toward the crossover side. *—Ron Wynn*

Bonafide / Jun. 1990 / Charisma ♦♦

● **The Best of Me** / 1991 / Charisma ♦♦♦♦♦

Man with the Fun / 1996 / Virgin ♦♦♦
Man With the Fun showcases Maxi Priest's talent for shaping reggae, dancehall and soul into a distinctly pop-oriented and commercial amalgam. *Man with the Fun* happens to be one of Priest's better efforts, simply because the quality of the production and songwriting is uniformly first-rate throughout the record. Of course, there are quite a few mediocre tracks, but the smooth sounds of Priest's voice and the seamless production holds your interest until the album arrives at highpoints like Maxi's duet with Shaggy, "That Girl." *—Leo Stanley*

CombiNation / Jul. 13, 1999 / Virgin ♦♦♦♦
Few artists have explored the possibilities of pop-reggae fusion as successfully as Maxi Priest, who is enormously popular in his native Britain and has achieved a level of stateside success that other reggae artists (with the exception of UB40) can only wish for. His smooth voice and his comfort with soul and hip-hop have only increased his marketability; purists may scoff, but there's no denying his talent. *CombiNation* finds him working in an explicitly soul-influenced style—"What a Woman Needs" and "Wasn't Meant to Be" are seductive smooth groove ballads that have no noticeable connection to any reggae tradition—with frequent detours into muscular hip-hop and dancehall grooves. "Mary's Got a Baby" is a monstrously funky collaboration with Beenie Man (a stripped-down remix ends the album); "Tell Your Man to Take a Walk" takes a similar approach, this time in partnership with the DJ Red Rat. Slow love songs predominate, although they don't provide most of the album's highlights. Recommended. *—Rick Anderson*

Prince Buster (Cecil Bustamente Campbell)

b. May 24, 1938, Kingston, Jamaica
Vocals / Bluebeat, Rocksteady, Ska
Cecil Bustamanate Campbell AKA Prince Buster was among Jamaica's first international stars. His singles were outrageous, sexist, hilarious, widely influential and inspirational. A onetime boxer, Prince Buster began working as a combination sound engineer and bouncer for Coxsone Dodd. His claims to be ska's inventor make him a Jamaican equivalent of Jelly Roll Morton for exaggerated importance, but Buster certainly helped popularize it. After parting company with Dodd, Buster established his own sound system, label and record store. His first recording session yielded the anthemic original "Oh Carolina" by the Folks Brothers. Buster soon had multiple labels operating, Wild Bells, Voice of the People and Buster's Record Shack. His singles were distributed on the Blue Beat label in England, and Buster's fame rose while such hits as "Al Capone" and "Madness" exploded. His talking/toasting records, filled with lewd imagery and vivid language, proved enormously popular. Buster doubled as a prolific performer and busy recording executive in the '70s, cutting sessions with Dennis Brown, Big Youth, John Holt and Alton Ellis among others. He reissued his old records, churned out compilations, bought record stores and built a huge empire. Buster stopped performing in the late '70s, then returned to the stage in the late '80s. He was still cutting fresh tracks as recently as '92. *—Ron Wynn*

★ **Greatest Hits: the Fabulous Prince Buster** / Oct. 25, 1994 / Sequel ♦♦♦♦♦

Prince Far I (Michael Williams)

Vocals, Percussion, DJ / Dub, DJ
The gun shot that took the life of Prince Far-I (born: Michael James Williams on September 15, 1983, cut short the career of one of roots reggae's greatest DJs. Although he recorded for less than a decade, Prince Far-I left a legacy that includes, at least, two groundbreaking albums—*Psalms for I* and *Under Heavy Manners.*

Hailing from Kingston's Waterhouse section, Prince Far-I launched his career as a DJ for Sir Mike the Musical Dragon Sound System, calling himself "King Cry Cry." After recording his debut single, "The Great Wooga Booga" for Bunny Lee, he went on to record for Sir Coxsone Dodd and Enos McLeod, who renamed him "Prince Far-I." His earliest success came when he recorded the album *Under Heavy Manners* with producer Joe Gibbs. The album included the hit single, "Heavy Manner."

In the mid-1970s, Prince Far-I assumed the production of his own albums, forming a record company Cry Tuff in 1976. *—Craig Harris*

Voice of Thunder / 1981 / Trojan ♦♦♦

★ **Black Man Land** / 1990 / Frontline ✦✦✦✦✦
The legendary gravel-voiced deejay is commemorated nicely on this generous collection, which combines the entirety of his 1981 album *Livity* with seven tracks from his earlier *Message From the King.* The Arabs provide a strong, supple instrumental backing for Far I's declamatory chanting—song titles like "Armageddon," "King of Kings" and "Moses, Moses" will give you an idea of the general mood and lyrical thrust. Everywhere on this album, the mood is slow, smoky and serious, and aficionados of this particular brand of roots reggae will love every minute of it. This disc also makes an excellent introduction for newcomers. *—Rick Anderson*

Dubwise / 1991 / Frontline ✦✦✦
The second Prince Far I collection in Front Line's reissue series brings to light four obscure singles along with their dub versions, as well as the entirety of the all-instrumental *Cry Tuff Dub Encounter Part 2.* The instrumental dub tracks are pretty much like those that make up the other volumes in the *Cry Tuff* series—perfectly fine, but not particularly distinctive, examples of the genre. But the singles show Prince Far I at his best. In his inimitable gravel-pit of a voice, he exhorts the ghetto youth to "fling away your gun and mek we have some fun," and implores his listeners in stentorian tones to remember Jah and to renounce war. Though not as consistently compelling as *Black Man Land,* this is a thoroughly worthwhile collection. *—Rick Anderson*

The Golden Years: 1977-1983 / May 4, 1999 / Cult ✦✦✦✦✦
For the small but devoted international cult that worships the gravel-voiced reggae DJ Prince Far I, this compilation is occasion for both rejoicing and gnashing of teeth. Since the five albums represented here are all impossible to find in the U.S. (*Voice of Thunder* being the sole exception), getting several tracks from each of them on this program is bittersweet. It's relatively easy to take the glass-is-half-full attitude, though, with music this great. The program includes such well-established classics as "Heavy Manners" ("Discipline what the world needs today/And etiquette, you know—") and "I and I Are the Chosen One" as well as more obscure but equally worthy numbers like "Deck of Life" and the super-stentorian "Ten Commandments," on which Far I sternly intones the commandments with minimal elaboration over a spare, bracing one-drop beat courtesy of his studio band, the Arabs. There are also several instrumental dub tracks, but while these are very good, they're not driven by quite the same spirit that is presentn whenever Prince Far I opens his mouth and holds forth on matters both spiritual and political in that deep, dark pit of a voice. Generally speaking, though, this excellent overview should bring in a whole new generation of converts. *—Rick Anderson*

Under Heavy Manners / Jul. 25, 2000 / T.P. ✦✦✦✦✦

Cutty Ranks (Philip Thomas)

Producer / Ragga, Dancehall
Cutty Ranks (born Philip Thomas) is a former butcher that became one of the first to pose an actual challenge to the dominance in the ragga world to Shabba Ranks. A representative of the sound system genre in the early '80s, he joined with Donovan Germain's Penthouse label in 1990, with a stone voice sound, much like Shabba's, running over the "gun talk and slackness" common to this era of ragga. Ranks also makes use of relatively lesser used beats, to set himself apart from the other deejays on the scene. The two major albums to look for are *The Stopper* (Fashion) and *Lethal Weapon* (Penthouse), both of which showcase his skills decently. *—Adam Greenberg*

● **Stopper** / 1991 / Profile ✦✦✦
Not to be confused with fellow "rude boy" Shabba Ranks, Cutty Ranks is a popular dancehall artist who has fared well in both reggae and hip-hop circles. *The Stopper* is typical of Ranks' work and illustrates the fact that he likes his dancehall tough, hard and amelodic. There isn't a lot of variety on this CD, which underscores dancehall's limitations. The complaint that Ranks' music "all sounds alike" really isn't off base, but be that as it may, cuts like "Pon Pause," "Hand Grenade" and "The Stopper" are lively, fun and exhilarating. As redundant and one-dimensional as Ranks tends to be, one really doesn't need more than one or two of his CDs. And if you have a taste for dancehall, this decent but limited album is worth a listen. *—Alex Henderson*

Shabba Ranks (Rexton Rawlston Fernando Gordon)

b. Jan. 17, 1966, Sturgetown, Jamaica
Rap, Vocals / Ragga, Club/Dance, Dancehall
During the '90s, Shabba Ranks was the reigning king of reggae-rap, a combination of Jamaican dancehall and New York hip-hop filled with X-rated slack lyrics. As a performer, Shabba is known for his high energy hypersexual shows. With unabashed ambition to become a trendsetter, sex symbol and innovator of Jamaican music, Shabba Ranks does not shy away from blatant commercialism in his music, and is more interested in providing listeners with a good-time than raising their consciousness. Shabba did not begin to make a real name for himself until the mid-'80s after he began working with some of Jamaica's biggest producers. His unpredictable energy on and off stage made him a hit on the dancehall circuit and soon Shabba was in demand all over the West Indies. Soon he even eclipsed Yellowman, Ninjaman, and Johnny P as the biggest DJ around with such hits as "Roots and Culture," Live Blanket" and his smash single "Wicked in Bed." *—Sandra Brennan*

Rappin' With the Ladies / 1988 / VP ✦✦✦✦
Shabba Ranks' career has focused on singles, including several on which he collaborated with other male DJs. *Rappin' With the Ladies,* in contrast, is a full album of songs by J.C. Lodge, Deborah Glasgow, and others reconceived as showcases for Shabba. The first track is "Telephone Love Deh Pon Mi Mind," a sequel to Lodge's "Telephone Love" constructed from the original. While this new version features studio remixing, the other new tracks rely on Shabba's presence alone to create a fresh sound. He comes through on "Mr. Loverman," a version of Glasgow's "Champion Lover." When Glasgow implores her lover "don't ease up tonight," Shabba answers her in a pulsating vocal delivery that heightens the power of the rhythm track. "Hardcore Loving" also makes good use of his presence to fill out the sound of Lodge's "Selfish Lover," and the remaining tracks follow this pattern. Shabba's sexual ability is the usual theme, of course, but the duet format forces a lyrical emphasis on intimacy and collaboration that is not typical in his solo work. That makes for a winning display of Shabba's talent, and with full-sounding production courtesy of Music Works, this disc offers consistent pleasures for dancehall fans throughout its generous length. *—John Gonsalves*

● **As Raw As Ever** / 1991 / Epic ✦✦✦✦✦
When dubwise (often described as reggae's equivalent of rap) evolved into dancehall in the 1980s, Shabba Ranks became one of the style's leaders. Most dancehall has come out on small independent labels, but in the early '90s, Epic saw how popular it had become and signed Ranks. Hard-edged, abrasive and tough, *As Raw as Ever* thrives on rhythm for its own sake. Listening to such cuts as "Gun Pon Me" and "Fist-A-Ris," one can hear the impact that classic dubwise artists like I-Roy, U-Roy, King Tubby and Big Youth had on dancehall. But while those greats could be very melodic, Ranks usually has little or no use for melody or harmony. Ranks is joined by artists ranging from rapper KRS-1 to reggae/pop singer Maxi Priest on this generally enjoyable, although limited, disc. *—Alex Henderson*

Rough & Ready, Vol. 1 / Jul. 14, 1992 / Epic ✦✦✦✦✦
Shabba Ranks kept the slack dancehall coming with this follow-up to *As Raw As Ever.* His thick, patois-laced delivery scored a pop hit with "Mr. Loverman," and a song that basically defined the CD. If you didn't get it the first time around, you sure understood it after hearing "Bad & Wicked," "Ca'an Dun," and "Gal Yuh' Good," among others. *—Ron Wynn*

X-tra Naked / Oct. 6, 1992 / Epic ✦✦✦✦✦
Shabba Ranks landed another pop hit on his third album to hit the charts over a two-year span. "Slow And Sexy" peaked at 33, providing ample momentum for another collection of sex cuts and come-ons. Ranks did include "Rude Boy" and "Two Breddrens," but otherwise, the focus stayed completely in the bedroom. *—Ron Wynn*

No Competition / 1993 / Critique ✦✦✦
DJ/toaster Shabba Ranks enrages reggae traditionalists and delights contemporary dancehall audiences with his fast-paced, sexually explicit commentary and quips. This 14-song set included not only Ranks but several other equally sassy dancehall stars such as Cocoa Tea, Laddy G, Deborah Glasgow, Cutty Ranks, Snagga, Krystal, E.T. and less suggestive veterans J.C. Lodge and the great Freddie McGregor. Ranks teamed with different performers on most cuts. Other than Cutty Ranks' hard-hitting "Wealth," there wasn't much socio-political material on this session. Instead, it was a showcase for dancehall, offering fans a primer of styles, sounds and themes. *—Ron Wynn*

Rough & Ready, Vol. 2 / 1993 / Epic ✦✦✦
Yet another sex-heavy dancehall collection from Shabba Ranks, whose super-lewd material rivals the pedantic ramblings of X Clan and other Islamic/Afrocentric rappers in its utter lack of thematic variety. Not only were almost all the songs alike, but Ranks seemed like he was recycling the raps and beats as well. *—Ron Wynn*

A Mi Shabba / 1995 / Epic ✦✦✦✦✦

Ras Michael

Vocals / Nyahbinghi
Negus is a title of Ethiopian Emperor Haile Selassie, the Almighty God of the Rastafarian movement, and none pays him more eloquent homage than Ras Michael and his group, the Sons of Negus. This is the beat of the heart, based on the original "instrument of ten strings," the hand-beaten drum. On *Dadawah* in 1975, Michael took a religious ceremonial gathering as the basis for an album of elegant poetry and raw, visceral power. Later, eschewing minimalism, such works as *Promised Land Sounds* added electronics and produced a primeval psychedelia without compare in Jamaican history. This is the sound of the Roots Church in the 21st century, highly charged hymns for humanity's future survival. *—Roger Steffens*

Promised Land Sounds / 1980 / Lions Gate ✦✦✦
Four extended Nyabinghi jams sound like the Grateful Dread meeting *2001.* *—Roger Steffens*

Rally Round / 1985 / Shanachie ✦✦✦
Here are more Rasta standards from their primary musical spokesman. *—Roger Steffens*

● **Dadawah** / Trojan ✦✦✦✦✦
The best Rasta testament from the '70s, spin it and become a "Man in the Hills." *—Roger Steffens*

Tony Rebel

Vocals / Ragga, Dancehall
Tony Rebel sings a peaceful, roots-oriented form of dancehall music designed to inspire his audience to take a more positive approach to life and social change. Born Patrick Barrett, Rebel is a Rastafarian, but rather than simply creating serious, philosophical tunes, he infuses his music with a lighthearted, liberal-leaning dose of humor. Prior to becoming a recording artist in the 1990s, he spent 14 years playing the local dancehall circuit. Examples of his uplifting approach to dancehall can be heard on his 1993 album *Vibes of Time;* other releases include 1998's *If Jah.* *—Sandra Brennan*

● **Rebellious** / 1992 / RAS ✦✦✦✦✦
Tony Rebel's recent Stateside release on Columbia/Chaos doesn't match the quality or depth of this earlier session recorded in Jamaica. Although there's still plenty of trendy "computerized" underpinning, Rebel's toasts aren't quite as fast, nor as obsessed with sex. Indeed, such songs as "Working Man" and "Rainbow People," with guest appearances from Ken Bob and Half Pint, respectively, are moving, strongly performed message pieces. "God Of Abraham" takes the melody of an old R&B song and recasts it as the foundation for expressive praises to Jah. Even the love tunes are romantic rather than lustful. *—Ron Wynn*

Vibes of the Time / 1993 / Chaos ♦♦♦♦
A landmark album on every level, *Vibes of the Times* announced the arrival of "conscious" dancehall and Tony Rebel, along with Garnett Silk, as its leading proponent. Armed with songs produced by legendary reggae producers Sly Dunbar, Steely & Clevie and Donovan Germaine, which shone with Biblical references and hopeful messages, this album lifted the genre up from the dominant muck of gun and sex lyrics and pointed it in a more positive direction. Using his pioneering "sing-jay" style, Rebel showcased his DJ and crooning skills on the classics "Chatty Chatty," "One Day" and "Sweet Jamaica." Guest appearances by Diana King and Garnett Silk add to the record's melodic sound. Released in 1993, when dancehall was still relatively new and spewing with arrogance, *Vibes of the Times* stands as an important symbol of what dancehall can aspire to. *—Rosalind Cummings-Yeates*

Junior Reid

Vocals / Roots Reggae, Lovers Rock
Junior Reid found himself in a difficult spot when he joined Black Uhuru in 1986. He replaced Michael Rose, who'd become quite popular as a longtime Uhuru contributor. Though essentially a good vocalist, Reid's style was so close to Rose's he didn't establish his own identity. The group also suffered compositional difficulties and personal crisis during Reid's tenure. Puma Jones left and was replaced by Olafunke. They also didn't always get quality material or support from Sly And Robbie during this period as well. Reid departed in '90, and has since been struggling as a solo artist to fulfill his considerable potential with releases like 1991's *Long Road*, 1993's *Big Timer* and 1996's *Listen to the Voices*. *—Ron Wynn*

One Blood / 1990 / Big Life/Mercury ♦♦♦
When Michael Rose left Black Uhuru in the mid-1980s, it was obvious that he would be a tough act to follow. But replacement Junior Reid, a similar vocalist, had no problem jumping right in and proving himself a worthy successor. By the early 1990s, the reggae trio had undergone even more personnel changes, and Reid was pursuing a solo career. Though not quite on a par with Reid's work with Uhuru, *One Blood* is a generally impressive effort showing how captivating he can be as both a singer and a composer. Indeed, Reid's thoughtfulness comes through loud and clear on everything from "Married Life" (a commentary on the misery that can result from marrying for all the wrong reasons) to the melancholy "When It Snows" to the poignant "Who Done It." And on a surprising cover of "Eleanor Rigby," Reid demonstrates that a Beatles classic and a reggae beat are most compatible. *—Alex Henderson*

● **Long Road** / 1991 / Cohiba ♦♦♦♦♦
Junior Reid has been unable to attain consistent stardom, despite being among reggae's better vocalists. This was his finest LP, marked by tremendous singing and both strong romantic and effective roots/message material. *—Ron Wynn*

Listen to the Voices / 1996 / RAS ♦♦♦
Junior Reid's *Listen to the Voices* is a typical collection of his genre-expanding dancehall, but it is too inconsistent to warrent the attention of anyone but his fans. *—David Jehnzen*

Ras Portraits / Jun. 10, 1997 / RAS ♦♦♦
Ras designed *Ras Portraits* as a concise introduction to a particular artist's recordings for the label. Since the information behind Ras releases is always shady, it's difficult to discern the origin of tracks on *Ras Portraits*, but the disc is one of the better collections of Junior Reid material that Ras has released, and listeners curious about his albums for the label should start here. It should not, however, be seen as a definitive introduction to his music in general. Among the featured tracks on Reid's *Ras Portrait* are "All Fruits Ripe," "Grammy," "Rasta World Dance," "Listen to the Voices," "Dance Na Keep Again," "Gun Court" and "Not a One Man Thing." *—Stephen Thomas Erlewine*

Max Romeo (Maxwell Smith)

b. Kingston, Jamaica
Vocals / Roots Reggae, Dub
Max Romeo was a performer who managed to rise above the rudest of beginnings (recording-wise) to become one of the first Rastaman singers to record a series of deeply spiritual and socially conscious roots songs. He was born Maxwell Smith in Kingston and first became famous for his raunchy early '60s hit "Wet Dream," containing suspiciously suggestive lyrics concerning a man in bed with his woman. The song was a runaway hit in Great Britain until older people began listening to it closely and banned it. Though Romeo publicly claimed the song was about a leaky roof, the ban remained. With that success under his belt (as it were) Romeo released a few more similarly themed "novelty" tunes such as "Wine Her Goosie" and "Pussy Watch Man" with only modest success. As the '70s progressed, Romeo underwent a few profound spiritual changes. By the time he teamed up with production wizard Lee Perry in the mid-'70s, he had become a committed Rastaman and was singing visionary songs praising Jah and calling the sufferahs to social consciousness and culture. With Perry, Romeo recorded his magnum opus, *War Ina Babylon* (1976).*—Sandra Brennan*

● **War Ina Babylon** / 1976 / Mango ♦♦♦♦♦
Like the epochal *Police and Thieves* by Junior Murvin, which also originated at Lee "Scratch" Perry's Black Ark Studio and thus shares with this album Perry's trademark dark, swampy ambience, this record is something of a mountain on the reggae landscape. But what makes it so remarkable is not just the consistently high quality of the music—indeed, by 1976 one had come to expect nothing but the finest and heaviest grooves from Perry and his studio band, the Upsetters—rather, it's the fact that Max Romeo had proved to be such a convincing singer of cultural (or "conscious") reggae after several years of raking it in as a purveyor of the most abject slackness. (His "Wet Dream" had been a huge hit in England several years earlier, and had been followed by such other delicacies as "Wine Her Goosie" and "Pussy Watch Man.") But there's no denying the authority of his admonishing voice here, and the title track (which describes the violent mood during Jamaica's 1972 general election) has remained a standard for over 20 years. Other highlights include "One Step Forward" and "Smile Out a Style." Essential to any reggae collection. *—Rick Anderson*

Open the Iron Gates / 1978 / United Artists ♦♦♦♦♦
Though Max Romeo got his start singing smutty novelty tunes (his first big Jamaican hit was titled "Wet Dream"), he later turned to serious political and religious themes, and while he always had some trouble gaining the respect he deserved as a singer, the recordings he made in the mid-'70s at the Harry J Studio, at Randy's, and especially at Lee Perry's Black Ark are some of the most powerful of that period, when much timeless music was being made in those studios. This marvelous collection brings together some of the best singles of the period, most of them in tandem with their dub versions. Romeo's sweet tenor voice and effortless delivery belie the lyrical content of these songs, which is invariably dread, dread, dread. The pleasant melody and gently loping rhythm on the classic "Warning, Warning" will lull you into blissful complacency until the lyrics wake you up with a jolt: "And now you rich people, listen to me/Weep and wail over the miseries/That are coming/Coming upon you." (By the way, this guy grew up in rural Jamaica, so when he addresses "rich people," he's talking to you, bud.) Elsewhere, he prays that he might always be found "in opposition, where I can fulfill thy works, oh Jah" and opines that "liars and thieves should not be cops." On a more religious theme, there's the rather, um, intolerant "Fire fe the Vatican," set to the deathless "War ina Babylon" rhythm. The backing musicians are mostly variations on the Upsetters' lineup, and much of the production bears the unmistakable Lee Perry imprint (though all of it is credited to Romeo on the reissue). This is an essential document of reggae's classic period. *—Rick Anderson*

Reconstruction / 1978 / Mango ♦♦♦♦
Several stirring vocal performances, even on otherwise shaky numbers, made this an above-average vehicle for Max Romeo. *—Ron Wynn*

Pray for Me: The Best of Max Romeo 1967-1973 / Sep. 26, 2000 / Trojan ♦♦♦♦♦
Max Romeo's transformation from crooning rocksteady loverman (whose early hits included songs like "Put Me in the Mood," "Great Lover," and the notorious "Wet Dream") to conscious reggae role model (a phase of his career that culminated in the epochal Black Ark production *"War in a Babylon"*) is now the stuff of reggae legend. On this generous compilation you get to see him in both modes, and the results are revealing. It turns out that in his more secular period he was a good, but not particularly outstanding, purveyor of standard-issue rocksteady; "Wet Dream," which Romeo often defended (wholly unconvincingly) as a song about sleeping under a leaky roof, is a fun but not really distinguished example of early reggae slackness, while several collaborations with the Emotions are a bit more interesting. But when he gets religion, the music takes a decided turn for the better. His sweet voice (reminiscent at times of Johnnie Clarke) is a perfect fit with yearning Rasta anthems like "Let the Power Fall on I" and "Don't You Weep," while it lends a bittersweet aspect to such dread pronouncements as "Babylon Burning" and "No Joshua No." At his best, Romeo was among the finest of reggae singers, and several of the tracks on this album show him at the peak of his form. *—Rick Anderson*

Roots Radics

Group / Dub
Roots Radics are the premier session band in Jamaica. In addition to touring and recording as Gregory Isaac's backup band, the group has collaborated with a lengthy list of artists including Bunny Wailer, Israel Vibration, Sugar Minot, the Wailing Souls, On-U-Sounds, Creation Rebel and Prince Far-I. The group toured the United Kingdom, with Prince Far-I, as the Arabs The genesis of Roots Radics traces back to Morris *Blacker* Wellington's band, the Marvells, a group that featured future Roots Radics members, Errol *Flabba* Holt on bass and Eric *Bingi Bunny* Lamont on guitar. Together with the Marvells, Holt and Lamont recorded such mid-1970s hits as *Swing And Dine, They Hold US Down* and *Kingston IS Tuffy*. Lamont had previously worked with bongo player Bongo Herman, with whom he recorded the 1971 hit, *Know Far-I*, and had produced an album for Pete Boggs. On his own, Holt had earlier recorded such hits as *A You Lick Me First, Gimme Gimme* and *Who Have Eyes To See*. Initially teaming together as members of Channel One session group, the Revolutionaries, which also featured the rhythm section of bassist Sly Shakespeare and drummer Robbie Dunbar. When Shakespeare and Dunbar left to launch their own label Taxi Records, the Revolutionaries evolved into Roots Radics. Roots Radics first hit on their own, *Bounty Hunter*, was produced by Henry *Junjo* Lawes and released in 1979. They soon became spearheads of the dancehall style that dominated reggae music in the early-1980s. Their status was lessened by the rise of the digital/ragga style in the mid-80s. Their final hit, *HhH Hot We Hot*, featuring the lead vocals of Dwight *Brother Dee* Pinkney, was released in 1989. The band's future became uncertain following Lamont's death, from prostate cancer, in January 1994. *—Craig Harris*

Forwards Ever Backwards Never / 1990 / Heartbeat ♦♦♦♦
Though best known as one of the pre-eminent backing bands in all of reggae, the Roots Radics have also cut a number of their own records; *Forward Ever* is a compilation of songs from those albums. Produced by songwriters/guitarists Dwight Pinkney and Bingy Bunny, the Radics' own material tends to suffer in comparison to their backing work simply because their vocals can't compare to those of Culture or Bunny Wailer; still, the musicianship is top-notch. *—Jason Ankeny*

● **World Peace III** / 1992 / Heartbeat ♦♦♦♦♦
Lots of singing is here, with a great Garvey song, "International Hero." It's the culmination of two decades' work in the studios. *—Roger Steffens*

Scientist (Overton Brown)

b. 1960, Kingston, Jamaica
Vocals, Producer / Dub, Ambient
Adolescent dub whiz the Scientist (born Overton Brown) learned basic electronics from his TV repairman father, skills that made him very popular with the mobile DJs and their not-always-functioning sound systems. Soon the Scientist was an employee of the legendary dub producer/mixer King Tubby, fixing transformers and televisions, when one day, after an an-

imated conversation about mixing records, Tubby challenged the Scientist to take a shot at remixing a record. Brimming with adolescent bravado, Scientist took the challenge, and that led to an extended apprenticeship in dub experimentation under Tubby's guidance. It was while at Tubby's that the Scientist developed his idiosyncratic dub style, playful and very psychedelic, loaded with echo explosions and blasts of feedback. At the end of the '70s, Scientist (now also referred to as "The Dub Chemist") left Tubby's to become the main engineer at Channel One Studios, and working with Henry "Junjo" Lawes, cut some best-selling dub LPs, only to leave for the greener pastures of Tuff Gong in 1982. *—John Dougan*

Scientist Rids the World of the Evil Curse of the Vampires / 1981 / Greensleeves ♦♦♦♦♦

Heavyweight Dub Champion / 1980 / Greensleeves ♦♦♦♦♦
At the ripe old age of 20, Scientist was working with "Junjo" Lawes, and came up with this stunner, a sinuous groove party with cartoonlike special effects (lots of bongs and boings like pans hitting one another, blips and squeals that sound like a Pac-Man game). All the "song" titles are references to boxing (a motif that Scientist was obviously mining for all it was worth), and all are great individual bits of dub sound that cohere into a meaningful whole. As it says on the LP jacket, "This ya a youthful sound fe come mash y'down." I couldn't agree more. *—John Dougan*

Scientist Vs. Prince Jammy / 1980 / Greensleeves ♦♦♦♦
Fat explosions of sound running headlong into echo delays that seem to go on forever, this is a great chunk of psychedelic dub mixing with Scientist and Jammy trading jabs like boxers (which is how the LP is set up). Neither one gets the upper hand, but both acquit themselves quite nicely. *—John Dougan*

Scientist Meets the Space Invaders / 1981 / Greensleeves ♦♦♦♦♦

Scientist Wins the World Cup / 1981 / Greensleeves ♦♦♦
Hey, why not a soccer motif; after all, it's popular in both England and Jamaica. More mixing tomfoolery with moments of true spaciness and avant-garde styling. Not an essential Scientist recording, but fine indeed. *—John Dougan*

Scientist Encounters Pac-Man / 1982 / Greensleeves ♦♦♦

★ **Tribute to King Tubby Dub** / 1990 / ROIR ♦♦♦♦♦
Dub whiz kid Scientist (Hopetown Brown) was a shoe-in for doing a King Tubby tribute disc. The prodigy engineer cut his teeth as Tubby's protégé in the '70s, going on to build up his own impressive catalog of solo dub discs during the early '80s. His primitively synthetic, effects-riddled style gets massively updated here on this 1990 Tubby memorial (the dub originator was killed by a robber a year earlier), taking on the digital garb of the ragga hits of the day with drum machine beats, computer soundscapes, and some vocal snippets here and there for good measure. Where his earlier space-age sonics were nicely balanced out by acoustic rhythm tracks, here Scientist gets lost in the mire of the wholly modern production. Inventive moments crop up on "King Pharoah" and the rub-a-dub Caribbean workout "Chant Down Babylon," but unfortunately the album is so immersed in a robotic sheen that dub experimentation is rare. Maybe the digital reggae world of Buju Banton is not the optimal environment for dub; the modern sound born out of producer Prince Jammy's ragga innovation "Under Me Sleng Teng" seems much better suited to dancehall hits than the more introverted and creative style King Tubby helped create. *—Stephen Cook*

Dub in the Roots Tradition / 1996 / Blood & Fire ♦♦♦♦♦
Leave it to the people at Blood and Fire to find the long-thought-lost recordings Scientist made in the mid- to late '70s under the supervision of Don Mais. Some of these recordings were mixed by Scientist when he was 16 and offer proof of his audaciously creative mind. Helping his mixology along is that the music was supplied by two of the most formidable session bands in Jamaica, the Soul Syndicate (featuring guitarist Chinna Smith), and the Roots Radics band (featuring the grumbling bass of Earl "Flabba" Holt). But it's the Scientist and his reverb and echo delays that turns this into a dancehall party, a trip that is long, strange and unforgettable. *—John Dougan*

Shaggy

Vocals, / Contemporary Reggae, Ragga, Club/Dance, Dancehall
Shaggy is a good example of how a single song can quickly take a relatively unknown performer straight to the top. For him, the song was a cover of the mid-'60s early reggae smash "Oh Carolina." Making full use of the production expertise of New York recording wizard Sting, and some excellent back-up musicians, including Latino percussionist Jimmy Delgado, and samples from the original recording and an underlying theme taken from "Peter Gunn," Shaggy added his own special "dog-a-muffin" (his name for his style) touch to the tune and found himself with a runaway international hit that was particularly popular in Britain, where his song shared the number one spot with a Michael Jackson tune in 1993. After "Oh Carolina" sold 600,000 copies in England, he signed to Virgin Records for a record-breaking 1.2 million British pounds, and they launched a successful promotion of the song in Sweden, Holland and Germany. They eventually released the song in North America, where it also made a strong showing, particularly in Canada. One thing Shaggy avoids is the temptation to make even more money by recording subsequent songs that sound just like "Oh Carolina." Musical diversity is his thing and Shaggy's dog-a-muffin sound incorporates elements of jazz and raggamuffin. *—Sandra Brennan*

Pure Pleasure / Aug. 24, 1993 / Virgin ♦♦♦

★ **Boombastic** / 1995 / Virgin ♦♦♦♦♦
Boombastic confirmed Shaggy's status as one of the most popular dancehall acts of the '90s, and for good reason—the record is a infectiously entertaining collection of deep, funky grooves that celebrate good times. Featuring the major hit title track, the album also sports a great guest appearance by Grand Puba on "Why You Treat Me So Bad," as well as a hot duet with singer "Wayne Wonder" on "Something Different." Despite a silly cover of "Day O," *Boombastic* keeps the funky reggae coming and is Shaggy's best album to date. *—Stephen Thomas Erlewine*

Midnite Lover / Aug. 26, 1997 / Virgin ♦♦♦♦
Midnite Lover, the followup to Shaggy's career-making *Boombastic,* doesn't have anything as memorable as that album's title track or his dancehall reworking of "Oh Carolina," but that hardly makes the album a failure. It's a consistently entertaining collection of ragga from one of the leaders of the genre. There is a bit too much sexism for some, but even "Sexy Body Girls" has one of the best beats on the record, and the title cut has a supremely funky hip-hop rhythm. It's hard to excuse the ridiculous cover of Janis Joplin's "Piece of My Heart," but his version of Bob Marley's "Thank You Lord" (featuring vocals by Ky-Mani Marley) shows that there's more to Shaggy than bumping and grinding. *—Leo Stanley*

Hot Shot / Aug. 8, 2000 / MCA ♦♦♦♦
Shaggy's fourth album is a classic hybrid of reggae, R&B, and pop. Following duets with Maxi Priest ("That Girl") and Janet Jackson ("Luv Me, Luv Me"), the Jamaica native teams up with master producers Jimmy Jam and Terry Lewis and a myriad of talented guest vocalists who complement his personality on each track. Coming with the minor hit "Hope" from 1999's *For Love of the Game* soundtrack, the first couple of singles, "Dance and Shout" (featuring a Michael Jackson sample) and "It Wasn't Me", show the strengths of this album—they are smart, warm, and playful. Shaggy's persona is hard to not like. On "It Wasn't Me," a friend laments being caught by his girl with another woman; Shaggy continually advises him to flatly deny it. To be able to use that sentiment and still seem likable is a gift. There are such heavy samples, some of the tracks almost sound like remakes at points, but there is such originality and gifted wordplay that the combination works as opposed to seeming unoriginal—something most rappers can't seem to accomplish. Each song on *Hot Shot* from the opening title track on is different, inviting, and infectious. *—Bryan Buss*

Garnett Silk

d. Dec. 16, 1996
Vocals / Roots Reggae, Ragga, Dancehall
Singer Garnett Silk was regarded as the next successor to Bob Marley and indeed, his meteoric rise to stardom spoke of much promise. Unfortunately, a freak accident on December 16, 1996, abruptly ended the life of the developing young performer. Though not yet as adept at singing and songwriting as Marley, Silk's passionate, socially conscious reggae, with its basis in R&B and rock, was a cry for peace and love in a genre increasingly filled with references to guns and violence. A versatile singer, he was equally at home with roots music, lover's rock, classic reggae, and even soul hits from the '70s. Silk's big break came in 1992 with a large string of hits recorded on various labels. These hits included "Seeing Zion" (on Black Scorpio) and "Fill Us Up with Your Mercy" (on Penthouse). Performing and recording so much—in 1994, he had released dozens of 7" singles in Jamaica—took its toll on Silk and rumors that he was using drugs and suffering from physical exhaustion abounded. In light of his pacifistic songs, it is ironic that a gun caused his death. According to the Jamaican press, he had borrowed two guns from his attorney after his home had been robbed. Someone was showing Silk how to use the gun when it accidentally went off and the bullet struck a small gas tank which instantly exploded, killing Silk, his mother, and severely burning two of his brothers. *—Sandra Brennan*

● **Tony Rebel Meets Garnett Silk in a Dancehall Conference** / 1994 / Heartbeat ♦♦♦♦♦
Two scorching hot dancehall artists are presented both solo and in tandem on this 19-cut anthology, which offers the latest in the idiom's conventions. Garnett Silk has a booming, yet engaging and soulful voice, which he can also lower effectively. Tony Rebel is in the harsh, attacking, booming class alongside Buju Banton. While they're similar in their abilities to dominate an arrangement, there's enough disparity to make their duets delightful, particularly the memorable "Help The Poor and Needy." The anthology also contains seven decent-to-fine dub tracks, the best being "Prisoner's Dub" and "Killer Dub." *—Ron Wynn*

Kilamanjaro Remembers Garnett Silk / Sep. 28, 1999 / Jam Down ♦♦♦♦
The late Garnett Silk was one of the most promising of the "cultural" dancehall singers of the early '90s, a period when "slackness" was in the ascendant and few of Jamaica's top-flight talents were still bothering to deliver the lyrical messages of spiritual and political uplift that had been reggae's stock in trade for so long. Silk spent some time with the Killamanjaro sound system, singing over new and vintage reggae rhythms, sometimes in collaboration with other singers and deejays. This collection brings together 21 such tracks, most characterized by the slightly rough, improvised feel that often attends sound system performances. Silk's talent, though, was such that even when getting lost in the chord progression of "Marley Medley" or grinding to a ragged halt on "Jaro Ruling," his voice still has the power to captivate. Notable team-ups on this album include a duet with Dennis Brown on "Sing With Me" and "Rule Dem" with Luciano. Recommended. *—Rick Anderson*

Sister Carol

Vocals / Ragga, Dancehall
The music of rastawoman Sister Carol carries a potent message to younger listeners, urging them to take the high road and work for lasting, peaceful change. Since the early '80s, she has also been a driving feminist force in a genre still dominated by male performers. By 1982 she had waxed her first two singles, "Black Cinderella" and "Jamaica Little Africa." Her first album *Liberation for Africa* had a limited release through Serious Gold. Her career got a real boost when she appeared in a couple of Jonathan Demme films, *Something Wild* (in which she sang "Wild Thing" during the closing credits) and *Married to the Mob.* Sister Carol's music carries strong messages about changing sexism, avoiding violence and the non-spiritual/medicinal use of drugs, and of encouraging self-respect and spirituality but with a wider variety of styles designed to appeal more directly to the younger audiences while still appealing to her long-time fans. Though many differentiate between dancehall and reggae, to Sister Carol it is all part of the same force. *—Sandra Brennan*

Call Mi Sister Carol / 1994 / Heartbeat ♦♦♦♦
This may be the best album yet from deejay Carol East. Not only does she get to show off her facility with standard bouncy dancehall grooves, as on "Jamaican People" and the title

track, but she also chats in a more rootswise context—"Ital Jacuzzi," which appears to be a charming ode to the pleasures of skinny-dipping, floats along on a booty-stirring one-drop groove. "I Am What I Am" is built on a solid rhythmic foundation of hip-hop/one-drop fusion, and "Mr. Moneyman" seems to share a melody with the Kenny Rogers hit "The Gambler," which is a nicely subtle touch, given the song's lyrical content. Elsewhere, Carol turns the Wailers' classic rock steady number "Lick Samba" into a Spanish lesson titled "Reggae Samba," and "Solomon and Sheba" mixes dancehall with a typically Rastafarian romantic theme. (Strangely, the remixed "long version" of the title track is shorter than the regular version.) *—Rick Anderson*

Lyrically Potent / Jun. 18, 1996 / Heartbeat ♦♦♦♦
As one of the few female reggae DJs who have been able to build a solid career without resorting to pop pandering or sexpot posturing, Sister Carol has always been an inspiration. And amazingly, she just keeps moving from strength to strength; each of her releases has been better than the last, and it's hard to imagine how she'll top this one. She's always been more of a sing-jay than a straight toaster, and she's always put as much emphasis on the groove as on her strict but joyous religious messages. Thus the plainly didactic cooking lesson of "Strong and Fit" is still sure to nice up any dance at which it's played, and even hohum pronouncements like "No matter how hard they try, they cannot stop reggae" are made compelling by the sheer exuberance of her delivery. Stylistically, she's an innovator (note the dancehall/rocksteady hybrid riddim in effect on "Dread Natty Congo"), but she's also comfortable working in a classic dancehall DJ tradition on cuts like "Red Eye" and "Strong and Fit." Sugar Minott stops in to pay his respects, and there's even a touch of version for dubhounds. Is it a perfect reggae album? Maybe so. *—Rick Anderson*

Isis: The Original Womb-Man / Jul. 6, 1999 / Lightyear ♦♦♦
Another typically skilled effort from Sister Carol, *Isis: The Original Womb-Man* showcases her tough and tender sides, with clever lyrics all around. *—Steve Huey*

● **Jah Disciple** / RAS ♦♦♦♦
Sister Carol emphasized truth and rights over sex and love on this session issued by Ras in 1989. She had harsh words for outer space exploration, internal African problems and rude boys who disrupt social affairs, while recalling an earlier, more enjoyable time on "Remember When" and calling for respect and dignity from an ignorant male on "A No Me Name Peggy." Her toasts were slower and paced differently than the rapid-fire dancehall mode; the arrangements and backing combined electronic and acoustic instrumentation, and there was more than a trace of vintage reggae in her style and sound. *—Ron Wynn*

Sizzla

Vocals / Roots Reggae, Dancehall
One of the leaders in the mid-'90s resurgence of roots-reggae as an inspiration for the aggressive dancehall sound, Sizzla and his producer Phillip "Fatis" Burrell debuted with 1995's *Burning Up*, released on RAS Records. He's also recorded for VP and Exterminator, releasing *Good Ways* in 1998. *Be I Strong* followed a year later, and in early 2000 Sizzla returned with *Liberate Yourself*. *—John Bush*

● **Praise Ye Jah** / Oct. 21, 1997 / Exterminator ♦♦♦♦♦

Freedom Cry / Nov. 17, 1998 / VP ♦♦♦♦
Since his debut in 1996, Sizzla's positive lyrics and strong delivery have earned him a place alongside the handful of best-selling conscious DJs—Tony Rebel, Cocoa Tea and Buju Banton. *Freedom Cry*, his sophomore effort, reaffirms his position with booming vocals and bass-heavy rhythms that combine a hip-rolling dancehall style with soothing roots melodies. "Real," the opening track, introduces catchy lyrics and beats that flow throughout the album, from the bounciness of "Rain Shower" to the smooth harmonies of "Saturated" and the title song. This album definitely indicates that great things are bound to come from Sizzla. *—Rosalind Cummings-Yeates*

Liberate Yourself / 1999 / Kariang ♦♦♦♦
This two-disc set makes an interesting package: disc one is a new album from Sizzla, currently one of the top deejays on the conscious dancehall scene; disc two is a compilation of similarly oriented artists from the Kariang label, all of them delivering cultural roots lyrics in a dancehall style. The Sizzla disc is rather uneven in quality. Its opening track, "Inna Africa," is bloody awful—Sizzla alternates chatting and singing what sound like purely improvised lyrics over an arrhythmic instrumental track, often straying off-key and rarely saying anything worth listening to. He gets things under control subsequently, though, delivering an earth-shaking sing-jay performance on "Takes Only Time" and tearing things up masterfully on "From Long Time." Yet he keeps veering off-course. On "Fire fi Burn" his chatting again seems strangely divorced from the music. Disc two is more varied in approach and more musically interesting. Though the best track is probably Garnet Silk's exquisite "Sayonara," other highlights include Doniki's very nice soca-influenced "I've Been There," Bushman's "Somewhere," and the supremely paranoid but kicking "Micro Chip" by Prezident Brown. Modern reggae doesn't get much better than this. *—Rick Anderson*

Be I Strong / Nov. 2, 1999 / VP ♦♦♦♦
Sizzla continues to shake things up with his third release, *Be I Strong*. This offering erupts with the DJ's volcanic delivery and scorching political lyrics. The hard-driving opening track, "Men and People," sets the tone by proclaiming, "Babylon your judgement a come right away". His powerful presence is such that you dare not question this or any of the other keen observations on this album. Backed by reggae legends such as Sly Dunbar on drums and Earl "Chinna" Smith on guitar, Sizzla's aim is near-perfect. *—Rosalind Cummings-Yeates*

Words of Truth / Sep. 5, 2000 / VP ♦♦♦
The fourth album by stridently conscious dancehall DJ Sizzla, *Words of Truth* reveals a lot about his performance style. Since the album is packaged with a bonus CD of a live show at *Brixton Academy* in the U.K., listeners can compare the recording with his live show, and it's not a completely flattering comparison. The first CD shows how Sizzla's overzealous delivery mars most of the tunes. Except for the slamming riddim on "Attack" and the hip-winding melody of "Love Ah Di Way," the tunes are mediocre at best, overshadowed by the performer's hard, rushed vocals and preachy lyrics. The second disc benefits greatly from melodic backup singers, live instrumentation, and a more measured delivery by Sizzla. From the languid rhythm of "Dem Ah Wonder" to the inspiring nyabingi drumming on "Make Dem Secure," this is a far more enjoyable CD. *Words of Truth* would be a lot stronger if the first CD contained the same level of enjoyment. *—Rosalind Cummings-Yeates*

The Skatalites

f. 1963, **db.** 1965
Group / Rocksteady, Ska
Ska was Jamaica's first indigenous creation, a compelling mix of fast R&B, Rastafarian African rhythms, and Afro-Cuban percussion highlight. This double-time delight ruled Jamaica from 1962 to 1966, and none played it more convincingly than its creators, The Skatalites. Led by a mentally disturbed world-class trombonist named Don Drummond, the Skatalites were composed of the top instrumentalists on the island at the time: Tommy McCook, Roland Alphonso, and "Ska" Campbell on tenor sax; Lester Stering on alto; Karl Bryan on baritone; "Dizzy Johnny" Moore and Baba Brooks on trumpet; Lloyd Brevett on bass; Lloyd Knibbs on drums; Jackie Mittoo on piano; and Lyn Tait and Jah Jerry on guitar. This is a roster of Jamaica's musical gods, the foundation of all that would come out of this tiny land of two million people to influence the entire world of music for the next 30 years. Rock-steady, reggae, rockers, dub—all are merely tempo reworkings of the skipping ska beat. It is remarkable, then, to note that The Skatalites existed for a mere 14 months. *—Roger Steffens*

Ska Authentic / 1967 / Studio One ♦♦♦♦♦
Early '60s ravers include "Lee Oswald" and "Bridge View" (any Studio One Skatalites collection is worth owning). *—Roger Steffens*

Heroes of Reggae Dub / 1975 / Triple X ♦♦♦♦♦
Actually, the Skatalites are heroes of ska; the existence of an all-reggae album by these guys comes as something of a surprise. But it really is great stuff, and the fact that the program consists of dub mixes by the legendary King Tubby makes it that much better—though it could have been improved even more by the inclusion of the original vocal versions, which are hinted at tantalizingly by the occasional scraps of vocals that peek through the mix. There certainly is plenty of room for those to have been included on this 33-minute program. But even without those versions, this disc should be considered an essential purchase for any reggae fan. "Close to Jah" and "Zion I Dub" are archetypal roots reggae, while "Herb Man Dub" (with its funky drumming, jazzy guitar and equally jazzy flute) sound more like the Skatalites that ska fans know and worship. The mixes are vintage King Tubby—swirling kaleidoscopes of sound, with crazily flanged drums and infinitely echoed guitars floating and swooping in and out of earshot. But it's the playing, especially by saxophonist Tommy McCook and bassist Lloyd Brevett, that really bears repeated listening. *—Rick Anderson*

Stretching Out / 1987 / ROIR ♦♦♦♦♦
In 1983, reggae founders/legends the Skatalites regrouped for a one-off concert at the Jamaica Sunsplash. Skatalites manager Herbie Miller (also Peter Tosh's manager at the time) flew in the band's original lineup from all parts of the world, sans member Don Drummond, who had unfortunately passed away. And even though they'd split up nearly 20 years before (they were together for a total of two years, 1963-1965), it's as if they'd been jamming together all along, as the newly re-formed group gels and excels in this live setting. The performances are taken from an intimate club gig that the band played to warm up for their upcoming festival gig, recorded at Miller's Blue Monk Jazz Gallery. Originally released in 1986 as a double cassette, the 1998 double-CD re-release adds five bonus cuts that didn't appear on the original version. It's clear that the band is having a good time stretching out musically, as evidenced on such outstanding cuts as "Ska Ba," "Man in the Street," "Lee Harvey Oswald," and "Tear Up." Also included in the reissue are up-to-date liner notes by Herbie Miller himself. *—Greg Prato*

Hog in a Cocoa / Nov. 18, 1993 / Orange Street ♦♦♦♦
This is a great collection of classic ska performed by the Skatalites (generally considered the greatest of the first-wave ska bands) with various vocalists and recorded at Duke Reid's Treasure Isle studio in the mid '60s. There are original versions of much-covered classics ("Housewife's Choice" by Derrick & Patsy, "Penny Reel" by Eric Morris and Baba Brooks) as well as obscure tracks by artists who would later gain worldwide fame ("The Higher the Monkey Climb," by Justin Hinds & the Dominoes, "When I Call Your Name," by Stranger & Patsy). Then there are the obscure tracks by artists who have remained obscure, sometimes deservedly (as in the case of the hapless and out-of-tune Marguerita). Throughout the album, the Skatalites provide a relentlessly high-energy and almost supernaturally tight groove; even when the tempose are relatively slow, there's a tensile power to the band's sound that makes each track special. Highly recommended. *—Rick Anderson*

Hi-Bop Ska / 1994 / Shanachie ♦♦♦♦
Over the years, the Skatalites went through their share of personnel changes. In the 1990s, their lineup ranged from newcomers to survivors of the band's classic 1960s lineup, including saxmen Tommy McCook and Roland Alphonso, bassist Lloyd Brevett, and drummer Lloyd Knibbs. But the 1990s personnel were quite faithful to the spirit of the 1960s band, and *Hi-Bop Ska* bears that out. Recorded 30 years after the breakup of the original Skatalites, *Hi-Bop Ska* finds the band's blend of R&B, jazz, and Afro-Caribbean music continuing to sound healthy and exuberant. On this project, the Skatalites are joined by distinguished guests who range from Jamaican icons Toots Hibbert (of Toots & the Maytals fame) and Prince Buster to such jazz improvisers as trumpeter Lester Bowie, saxman David Murray, pianist Monty Alexander, and trombonist Steve Turre. Bowie and Murray were best known for avant-garde jazz, but you won't find any dissonant, quirky outside playing on this album; from Alexander's "Renewal" and Murray's "Flowers for Albert" (dedicated to free jazz explorer Albert Ayler) to remakes of "Man in the Street" and "Guns of Navarone," the music on this mostly instrumental CD is quite accessible. The jazz guests get room to blow, but they are aware of the fact that *Hi-Bop Ska* is a ska project first and foremost. *—Alex Henderson*

Greetings from Skamania / 1996 / Shanachie ♦♦♦♦

★ **Foundation Ska** / Jan. 4, 1996 / Heartbeat ♦♦♦♦♦
Given the Skatalites' universal recognition as the best instrumental ska group, it's been surprisingly difficult to acquire top-flight anthologies of their classic mid-'60s material. This overdue two-CD, 32-track set instantly rectifies that situation. Everything here was recorded in the mid-'60s, mostly for legendary producer Coxsone Dodd. It's ska at its apogee: energetic, squeaky horns, irresistible shuffle beats, some brilliantly quirky arrangements ("Hanging Tree" is Dave "The Happy Organ" Cortez as Jamaican garage), and charming ska instrumental covers of the Beatles' "This Boy" and "I Should Have Known Better." The compilation also has few cuts on which they backed vocalists Jackie Opel, Margarita, Stranger Cole, Ken Boothe, and the Wailers (whose early classic "Simmer Down" is featured). As far as exact releases dates for this material, forget it, but the liner notes, in a refreshing change from the reggae reissue norm, at least make a valiant effort to reconstruct some of the history of the Skatalites' first incarnation. *—Richie Unterberger*

Ball of Fire / Jan. 27, 1998 / Island ♦♦♦♦

Ska Voovee / Shanachie ♦♦♦

Sly & Robbie

f. 1978, Kingston, Jamaica
Producer / Roots Reggae, Dub, Dancehall
Reggae's preeminent rhythm battery, the duo of drummer Sly Dunbar and bassist Robbie Shakespeare remained one of Jamaican music's most inventive and influential forces for decades; pioneers in the use of electronics and production effects, the aftershocks of their trademark Taxi sound are still being felt. The two first performed together in 1975, backing Peter Tosh. One year later, the duo formed the Revolutionaries, one of the era's leading dub bands. In 1978, Sly and Robbie founded their own label, Taxi Productions, which released work by Black Uhuru, Gregory Isaacs and Prince Far-I. A marriage of Robbie's bone-rattling bass and Sly's groundbreaking synthesized drum sound, the Taxi aesthetic remained at all times on the cutting edge of technology, proving that reggae could move forward without compromising the music's integrity. In 1980, Sly and Robbie signed a worldwide distribution deal with Island Records, resulting in a series of compilations of Taxi material. As their global notoriety grew they were invited to record with performers including Bob Dylan, Mick Jagger, Joe Cocker, Grace Jones and Robert Palmer. Sly and Robbie also recorded under their own names, and in the mid-'80s teamed with producer Bill Laswell for *Language Barrier* and the acclaimed *Rhythm Killers.* 1989 saw the release of *Silent Assassin,* an innovative fusion of dub and hip-hop. In 1999, the duo teamed with producer Howie B. for *Drum & Bass Strip to the Bone.* *—Jason Ankeny*

A Dub Experience: Reggae Greats / 1985 / Mango ♦♦♦
The Sly & Robbie installment in Mango's *Reggae Greats* series is a skimpy and not terribly exciting collection of dub versions culled from their work with various reggae singers. The raw material is beyond reproach—"Destination Unknown," for example, is a remix of Black Uhuru's "Chill Out," "Assault on Station 5" is based on "Revolution" by the great Dennis Brown, and "Jailbreak" is a version of Junior Delgado's "Fort Augustus." Perhaps the most effective of these tracks is "Skull & Crossbones," an excellent dub version of "Danger Zone" by Flabba Holt. In all cases, the trademark Sly & Robbie sound—the rock-solid, minimalist basslines and the snare drum that sounds like a bullet hitting concrete—is in full effect. However, most of these dub mixes sound tame, almost enervated, as if they were put together by someone with a hangover. All of them are pleasant enough, but few of them say anything new or especially interesting about a reggae subgenre that should always, at a minimum, be interesting. *—Rick Anderson*

● **Taxi Fare** / 1986 / Heartbeat ♦♦♦♦♦

Rhythm Killers / 1987 / Island ♦♦♦
Another session with Bill Laswell. The all-star guest lineup includes Bootsy Collins, Bernie Worrell, Bernard Fowler, Henry Threadgill, Nicky Skopelitis, Shinehead, and Pat Thrall. It features a killer version of the Ohio Players hit "Fire," with funky Bootsy Collins grooves throughout the album. *—Scott Bultman*

Drum & Bass Strip to the Bone by Howie B / Jan. 12, 1999 / Palm ♦♦♦
This isn't drum'n'bass in the currently understood sense, it's drum & bass in the original (that is to say, the reggae) sense. On this album, drummer Sly Dunbar and bassist Robbie Shakespeare, two of the most widely recorded musicians in the world and two of the architects of modern reggae, join forces with noted techno producer Howie B and step off into the dark nether region of dub-inflected electronic dance music that they helped to discover, and began to map, over 20 years ago. If the music is only mildly compelling, it's not for lack of attractive textures and watertight rhythms. It's because Sly & Robbie have always made their best contributions when they've been working behind great singers; when they step to the fore, the results are always mixed. Here they vary from highly effective (as on the fairly straightforward rocker's reggae of "Ballistic Squeeze") to long-winded and boring ("Exodub Implosion"). Howie B does do a great job with the sound throughout, however. This disc is definitely worth owning, but don't trade in any of your vintage Channel One collections for it. *—Rick Anderson*

Dub Fire / Jun. 13, 2000 / NYC Music ♦♦♦

Millie Small

b. Oct. 6, 1946, Jamaica
Vocals / Bluebeat, Ska, R&B
Jamaican teenager Millie Small stunned the music business by reaching number two in the U.S. and number one in the U.K. with "My Boy Lollipop" in 1964. Born Millicent Small in Clarendon, she was the daughter of an overseer on a sugar plantation (her reported date of birth varies from 1942 to 1948), and she was one of the very few female singers in the early Ska era in Clarendon. She was already recording in her teens for Sir Coxone Dodd's Studio One label with Roy Panton (as Roy & Millie), with a hit behind her in that capacity ("We'll Meet"), when Chris Blackwell discovered her and brought her to England in late 1963. Her fourth recording, "My Boy Lollipop," cut in London by a group of session musicians that included guitarist Ernest Ranglin (and, according to some accounts, Rod Stewart on harmonica) and featuring her childlike, extremely high-pitched vocals, was the first (and indeed, one of the few) international ska hits. It remains one of the biggest-selling reggae or ska discs of all time with more than seven million sales.

Millie, who was known as "the Blue Beat Girl" on her album, was perceived as a one-shot novelty artist from the start because of her unusual, almost screeching vocals (which actually owed a lot to Shirley Goodman of the '50s New Orleans R&B duo Shirley & Lee), and she only made the Top 40 one more time, with the "My Boy Lollipop" soundalike "Sweet William." She did cut an entire album around the two hits (and video clips exist of Millie miming to "My Boy Lollipop" and another single, "Henry"), which also includes the first of several of her covers of Fats Domino material ("I'm in Love Again") with whom she later recorded an entire album. *—Richie Unterberger & Bruce Eder*

● **My Boy Lollipop** / 1964 / Combo ♦♦♦♦
Besides the megasmash title track, this compilation of uncertain origin includes 17 other mid-'60s recordings, including her only other hit of any size, "Sweet William." Arranged by respected early reggae musician Ernest Ranglin, Millie's immediately identifiable high-pitched voice paces some fairly hot ska numbers, as well as quite a few New Orleans R&B classics given the ska treatment. *—Richie Unterberger*

Leroy Smart

Vocals / Ragga, Dancehall
A master at love songs and roots material, Leroy Smart's been on the reggae scene since the early '70s. He was raised in Kingston's Alpha Catholic Boys Home, and began recording in the early '70s. Smart worked with such producers as Gussie Clarke, Joe Joe Hookin and Bunny Lee while gaining fame for a flamboyant performance style and exceptionally anguished delivery and penetrating vocal manner. Smart's smashing voice often seemed about to collapse from anxiety and earnestness in mid-song. He's maintained his popularity through the '70s,'80s and '90s, never scoring any crossover or international hits, but retaining his pull with the notoriously fickle Jamaican audience. *—Ron Wynn*

● **Dread Hot in Africa** / 1988 / Burning Sounds ♦♦♦♦♦
Piercing, poignant and topical fare from a legitimate reggae great. Leroy Smart's cutting delivery and wailing leads are as moving and hypnotic as those of Dennis Brown, Gregory Isaacs, Freddie McGregor or any other better-known superstar. *—Ron Wynn*

Slim Smith

Vocals / Ska
In the '60s, Slim Smith was one of the lead singers of the seminal Techniques, then went on to form (with Jimmy Riley) The Uniques. Often compared to Curtis Mayfield (his major influence), Smith never achieved the financial rewards his extensive, big-selling output deserved. He died tragically in the early '70s when he punched his fist through a glass door in frustration and bled to death before he could summon help. One of Jamaica's most venerated and gifted interpreters, virtually everything he cut is worth owning, particularly if your tastes run to Impressions-style harmonics. *—Roger Steffens*

● **Born to Love** / 1979 / Heartbeat ♦♦♦♦♦
It includes the eternal "You Don't Care" and the oft-versioned "Rougher Yet." *—Roger Steffens*

Rain from the Skies / Jul. 9, 1997 / Trojan ♦♦♦♦♦
Showing the influence of Curtis Mayfield and Sam Cooke, singer Slim Smith's work spanned the ska, rock steady and early reggae eras in Jamaica, where he recorded with producer Bunny Lee both as a solo act and with the harmony group the Uniques. The excellent Trojan compilation *Rain from the Skies* includes selections from the years just prior to his premature death in 1973, and ably showcases Smith's expressively agile voice. Deftly moving between falsetto and low vibrato, Smith conveys a variety of moods on the Delroy Wilson covers "Money Love" and "Travel On"; studied cool turns into brash bravado, which then dissolves into anguish. Then on "Sitting in the Park," his aloof yet lonesome vocal performance perfectly distills the bittersweet taste of unrequited love. Smith's penchant for vocal variety influenced his choice of material as well. Covers of Mayfield's "It's Alright" and Cooke's "Send Me Some Loving" blend in well with pop material like Little Anthony and the Imperials' "Take Me Back" and Carole King's "Will You Love Me Tomorrow," in addition to the classic Smith originals "Sunny Side of the Sea" and "Stand Up and Fight." Backed by Jamaican studio luminaries such as bassist Aston "Family Man" Barrett, pianist Gladstone Anderson and tenor saxophonist Val Bennett, Smith delivers a generously varied selection of solid rock steady numbers on *Rain from the Skies.* Check this one out to get a nice slice of Jamaican soul before Rasta appeared on the scene. *—Stephen Cook*

Steel Pulse

f. 1975, Birmingham, England
Group / Contemporary Reggae, Roots Reggae, Reggae-Pop
One of Bob Marley's favorite bands, Steel Pulse became one of reggae's most successful bands in the late '70s and early '80s. The original members of Steel Pulse, David Hinds on keyboards, bassist Ronald "Stepper" McQueen, guitarist Basil Gabbidon, and Selwyn Brown, all hailed from the Birmingham ghettos of Handsworth, England. Their families were immigrants from the West Indies. Growing up in poverty, they were victimized by colonialist-racist attitudes that kept them from being accepted in the highly stratified British society. They found some solace and considerable cultural pride in the island music they grew up with, including calypso, mento, ska, bluebeat, and eventually reggae during their boyhood in the '60s. One of the biggest influences back then was Burning Spear (Winston Rodney), considered the father of the Rastafari music movement in Britain, from whom they heard

the radical messages and philosophies that later shaped their own music. After releasing their debut album, *Handsworth Revolution* (1978, Mango), and its successors, *Tribute to the Martyrs* and *True Democracy* (both for Elektra) in the early '80s, with their innovative blend of straight-ahead reggae, flamenco and Euro-pop containing potent pleas for social reform, critics and fans alike hailed them as Marley's successors. By the late '80s, Steel Pulse was making a blatant bid towards a commercial sound and lost its unique edge. However, 1992 live album from a Paris performance, *Rastafari Centennial: Live in Paris, Elysee, Montmarte,* was a turning point for Steel Pulse. The fans' positive response to the band's older material helped remind them of their original vision and set them back on course. They recorded *Vex* in 1994, which was the first album of new material to reflect this new vision. *Rage and Fury* followed three years later, and in 1999 the group returned with the live *Living Legacy.* — *Sandra Brennan*

Handsworth Revolution / 1978 / Mango ✦✦✦
Another among several unforgettable numbers penned and performed by Steel Pulse during their tenure on Island. The album as a whole was just a shade below *Babylon The Bandit.* — *Ron Wynn*

True Democracy / 1982 / Elektra ✦✦✦
Although the group's first three albums are generally considered their finest, there is a very strong case to be made for including Steel Pulse's Elektra debut in the core collection as well. Where *Reggae Fever* had found the band moving from hardcore Rasta politics into lover's rock and party anthems, *True Democracy* marks a return to more ideological subject matter; the cover art, which shows singer David Hinds reading the Bible to his rapt bandmates, is a dead giveaway. Their sound might be a little bit slicker than before, but it's also harder and the lyrics less compromising—"Leggo Beast" denounces adultery over a stripped-down one-drop beat; "Man No Sober" inveighs against drunkenness; "A Who Responsible?" uses a dour trombone line to call down judgment on Babylon. But the mood is lightened somewhat by "Your House," a gorgeous love song, and by the exalted "Chant a Psalm." This is one of Steel Pulse's most satisfying and fully realized albums. — *Rick Anderson*

Babylon the Bandit / 1986 / Elektra ✦✦✦✦✦
Biting, frequently riveting protest material from Steel Pulse. The title track is one of several anthemic numbers punctuated by the remarkable David Hinds. Only Aswad compares to them among British reggae bands, and they've never produced any roots or political tracks superior to routine Steel Pulse material. — *Ron Wynn*

Rastanthology / 1996 / Wise Man Doctrine ✦✦✦✦✦
While the two-disc *Sound System: The Island Anthology* remains the best introduction to Steel Pulse's early music, the single-disc *Rastanthology* is a good alternative for the budget-conscious, a handsomely packaged 18-track collection which assembles material from throughout the band's career. — *Jason Ankeny*

● **Sound System: The Island Anthology** / 1997 / Island ✦✦✦✦✦
The first three Steel Pulse albums, all recorded for the Mango label, were easily the best they ever made. This two-disc set compiles the entirety of those three albums (*Handsworth Revolution, Tribute to the Martyrs* and *Caught You,* the last of which was titled *Reggae Fever* for U.S. release) along with a handful of B-sides and live versions. The familiar pleasures are all here—the dry, heavy skank of "Bun Dem" and "Soldiers," the strangely dreamy outrage of "Tribute to the Martyrs," the lighter grooves that buoy "Shining" and "Rumours (Not True)." The extra tracks aren't much to write home about; frankly, the two B-sides and two live tracks sound like filler. But the 12" version of the majestic "Babylon Makes the Rules" feels like divine revelation, as does the dubwise extension of "Heart of Stone" that was hinted at so tantalizingly in its original album version. For all of his jazzy excesses, David Hinds remains one of the finest reggae singers around, and there has never been a rhythm section to match this one for brick-wall solidity. An essential collection of top-flight British reggae. — *Rick Anderson*

Ultimate Collection / May 9, 2000 / Hip-O ✦✦✦✦✦
Assembled chronologically and drawing its material from all the labels Steel Pulse recorded for (but rightly concentrating heavily on their early Island years), *The Ultimate Collection* may be the best single-disc anthology of the band's work thus far. In addition to collecting the cream of their first three albums (by far their best work), the compilation also includes the rare "Revolution Dub, Pt. 1," an extended, spliced-together version of "Back to My Roots/Dub to My Roots," and the latter-day trip-hop track "Evermore." It's the perfect introduction to the group for casual fans who don't want to spring for the two-disc *Sound System,* which contains most (but not all) of these songs. — *Steve Huey*

Steely & Clevie

f. 1986
Group / Roots Reggae, Dancehall
The rhythm battery of keyboardist Wycliffe "Steely" Johnson and drummer Cleveland "Clevie" Browne emerged as the dominant production team of the contemporary dancehall reggae era, lending their skills to records from acts including Shabba Ranks, Maxi Priest and Gregory Isaacs. Steely and Clevie first played together at Lee "Scratch" Perry's legendary Black Ark Studios during the late 1970s, and the two men immediately clicked, frequently teaming in the years to follow. By 1986 Steely and Clevie were established as the house band at King Jammy's Studio; by now the concept of electronic production was beginning to catch on among other artists, and the duo, whose experiments with computer technology went back several years, was well ahead of the pack. King Jammy's became the hub of the reggae scene in the latter half of the 1980s, and Steely and Clevie maintained a relentless pace, cutting upwards of ten sides a week. In 1988 they formed their own label, named simply Steely and Clevie, and soon scored major hits with singles from Foxy Brown, Tiger, Johnny P and Dillinger; the duo also issued a string of their own "one rhythm" records. — *Jason Ankeny*

● **21st Century Sound Clash** / 1988 / V75 ✦✦✦✦✦

Ghetto Man Skank / 1990 / ROIR ✦✦✦
A fairly straightforward dub album, with the accent on the computer stylee most often preferred by this duo. Sometimes too often bent toward the cool edge of musical precision, once in a while interesting. — *Steven McDonald*

Super Cat

Vocals / Ragga, Club/Dance, Dancehall
A major figure in the positive-consciousness dancehall movement, Jamaican DJ/toaster Super Cat was born William Maragh in a ghetto section of Kingston known as Cockburn Pen or Seivright Gardens (the same area that produced DJ stars like U-Roy and Prince Jazzbo). Interested in music from a very young age, Maragh was touring Jamaica with various sound system organizations by the time he was a teenager. His first DJ name, Cat-a-Rock, was eventually switched to Super Cat due to the former's resemblance to the word "cataract"; he also earned a secondary nickname, the Wild Apache. Super Cat made his recording debut in 1981 with the single "Mr. Walker," recorded for the Techniques label and produced by Winston Riley. A succession of singles for various labels followed, as did his debut album *Si Boops Deh,* which appeared on Techniques in 1985. Settling for a short time on the Skengdon label, Super Cat recorded another album, *Boops,* but soon grew dissatisfied enough with the business aspect of recording to start his own label, Wild Apache Productions. The self-produced album *Sweets for My Sweet* followed in 1988, as did a number of singles produced for other artists on the Wild Apache imprint; Super Cat also teamed up with Nicodemus and Junior Demus for the first triple-team DJ album in dancehall history, *Cabin Stabbin'.*

Emboldened by success, Super Cat decided to move to New York City and attempt to crack the American market. He secured a major-label deal with Columbia and landed the track "Nuff Man a Dead" on their compilation *Dancehall Reggaespanol;* in 1992, he issued one of the first major-label dancehall albums, the acclaimed *Don Dada.* Several high-profile TV and concert-festival appearances followed, and *Source* magazine named Super Cat their Dancehall Artist of the Year for 1993. The following year, he reunited with Nicodemus and Junior Demus, adding Junior Cat to make the resulting album *The Good, the Bad, the Ugly, and the Crazy* a four-way collaboration. Super Cat's own fusion of dancehall, roots reggae, hip-hop, and R&B was next showcased on the proper follow-up to *Don Dada,* 1995's *The Struggle Continues.* While the album was another success, Super Cat really raised his profile in the pop mainstream with his guest shot on Sugar Ray's 1997 smash "Fly," which prominently featured his toasting skills. Columbia capitalized on the resulting exposure in 1998 with the singles compilation *The Good, the Better, the Best of Super Cat.* — *Steve Huey*

● **The Good, the Better, the Best of Super Cat** / Mar. 31, 1998 / Columbia ✦✦✦✦✦
The Good, The Better, The Best of Super Cat is an excellent collection of Super Cat's greatest hits, containing 16 tracks, many of which are single versions and remixes that have previously been unavailable on CD. Most of these singles are the definitive versions, since dancehall reggae is about grooves and rhythms, and these extended versions keep the groove going longer than the album versions. Collectors will want these singles versions, but they also serve as a fine introduction to Super Cat's career for neophytes, making *The Good, The Better, The Best of Super Cat* the one definitive disc in his catalog. — *Stephen Thomas Erlewine*

Third World

f. 1973, Kingston, Jamaica
Group / Contemporary Reggae, Reggae-Pop
Third World is a band that some reggae purists disdain because they dare to deliberately cross-over to other genres to popularize their music for international mainstream audiences. Despite the critics, Third World remains one of most enduring and popular Jamaican bands in the world. Unlike many Jamaican reggae bands, comprised of hungry street kids with raw talent, no formal musical training and only their passion and drive to spur them to the top, the members of Third World come from the Kingston middle class. They made their debut at the 1973 Jamaican Independence Celebration; a year later, Third World went to London, released their debut single "Railroad Track" and signed to Island Records. Their first album came out in 1975. Though the title track of their second album, *96 Degrees in the Shade* (1977), has become a reggae classic, the second album only sold moderately, yet it is considered to be one of their finest albums. Their third album, *Journey to Addis,* finally broke through to a bigger audience thanks to the R&B staple "Now That We Found Love," that Third World sang with a sophisticated blend of pop, funk and reggae riddims. In response to critics, Third World justifies its forays into different genres as a means to keep the genre from stagnating. In making it accessible to wider audiences, they are also thereby making new inroads for their messages and making it music for the common people the world over. They are credited for being the first reggae act to add funk and to use a synthesizer. They were also instrumental in popularizing dub poetry, which in turn became the basis for dancehall. — *Sandra Brennan*

96 Degrees in the Shade / 1977 / Mango ✦✦✦✦✦
The album that cemented their stateside popularity. — *Ron Wynn*

Journey to Addis / 1978 / Island ✦✦✦✦✦
Probably the first and best fusion of reggae and soul music by a reggae group. Third World was looking to sell records worldwide and not just in Jamaica and England, and while the band's fusion of these genres may have infuriated the die-hard Rasta man, it helped the music reach a larger base. After the opening "One Cold Vibe," a melodic reggae bouncer, a tepid "Cold Sweat" (not the James Brown tune) has floating rhythms that soften the harsh lyrics. Falsetto vocals propel "Cool Meditation," which has a faster beat then most of these tracks, but it's the remake of the O'Jays' "Now That We Found Love" that established them as international stars. The title track "Journey to Addis" is an amalgamation of practically everything, and it works; though traditionalists will dismiss it and these other tracks, there's nothing superficial about this winning album that is now available on CD. — *Andrew Hamilton*

Rock the World / 1981 / Columbia ✦✦✦
One of Third World's best albums, *Rock The World* was also one of the reggae band's better

efforts at bringing reggae into the mainstream. Upbeat cuts like "Dancing on the Floor (Hooked on Love)," "Spritual Revolution," "With a Little Bit of Love," and the instrumental "Hug It Up" are nicely balanced by the mellow "There's No Need to Question Why" and the peppy "Shine Like a Blazing Fire." [Some of the LP's tracks can be found on the Sony Legacy CD *Super Hits*.] *—Ed Hogan*

Reggae Greats / Mar. 1985 / Mango ✦✦✦
A decent place to start on reggae's longest-lasting pop ensemble. *—Ron Wynn*

You've Got the Power / 1989 / Columbia ✦✦✦

● **Reggae Ambassadors: 20th Anniversary Collection** / Oct. 5, 1993 / Mercury ✦✦✦✦✦
While they didn't make groundbreaking albums, this pop-reggae outfit found a great deal of success with their ultra-smooth, mainstream singles. This two disc anthology may be too much for the casual listener but the more ambitious will want to start here. All of the essential tracks are here combined with some fine live performances. *—Chris Woodstra*

Tiger

b. 1960
Vocals / Calypso, Dancehall
After several obscure recordings during the late '70s and early '80s, Tiger burst onto Jamaica's early dancehall scene in 1985; for the next four years he produced a steady stream of popular songs, including his first hit "*No Wanga Gut*." He was born Norman Jackson and claims that it was his fans who nicknamed him Tiger. A rather eccentric character, Tiger's lyrics are noted for their witty off-beat attitude that he punctuates with his trademark growl and other strange vocalizations. In the late '80s, Tiger became involved in drugs and he seemed to have hit a creative lull. He dropped out of music for a while, but returned to performing and recording in the early '90s, signed to Chaos, and has since begun to reclaim the popularity that was once his. *—Sandra Brennan*

● **Me Name Tiger** / 1987 / RAS ✦✦✦✦✦
"No Wanga Gut" and "Puppy Love" anchor his U.S. debut. *—Roger Steffens*

Bam Bam / 1988 / RAS ✦✦✦✦
Peripathetic toaster/DJ Tiger first began attracting attention on the international circuit with this 1988 release. It featured frenetic verbal thrusts, quips and commentary, performed over a skeletal musical framework with authentic drums rather than rhythm machines, both acoustic and electric keyboards and occasional guitar/bass support. Harold "Papa Biggs" McLarty and Doctor Dread stripped down the backgrounds and let Tiger's verbal acrobatics carry the day on such tracks as "Carbon Copy," "Bam Bam," "Nominee" and "Presto." *—Ron Wynn*

New Brand Style / Jul. 18, 1995 / RAS ✦✦✦
Produced by "Papa Biggs" McCarty, this album by Tiger continues in his trademark style. While nothing on the album quite measures up to his 1986 hit "No Wanga Gut," *Brand New Style* shows Tiger as one of the standout artists in '90s reggae. *—Jonathan Ball*

Toots & the Maytals

f. 1966
Group / Rocksteady, Ska
Led by Frederick "Toots" Hibbert, the Maytals were key figures in reggae music, their reputation based on strong, well-blended voices and a seldom rivaled passion for their music (Hibbert's soulful style often led him to be compared to Otis Redding). They were popular from the start, but after recording a few sides with Studio One, they left producer producer Clement "Coxsone" Dodd in favor of Prince Buster. With him, they soon gained a bigger Jamaican following and also became popular in Great Britain. The Maytals were reaching the height of their popularity towards the end of 1966 when Hibbert was arrested for possession of marijuana and sent to prison for 18 months.When Hibbert was released, the band started working with legendary producer Leslie Kong; their first Kong single "54-46 That's My Number," a reference to Hibbert's prison number, became a huge hit in both Jamaica and England and has since become a rocksteady standard. One of their all time great hits, "Pressure Drop," came from the soundtrack of the definitive reggae film *The Harder They Come*. By 1971, a contract with Island had made them international stars, though the death of Leslie Kong curtailed the hits. Hibbert broke up the group in 1981 to pursue a solo career with producers Sly & Robbie. In the early '90s, he created a new Maytals and continues touring the world with them. *—Sandra Brennan*

★ **Funky Kingston** / 1973 / Mango ✦✦✦✦✦
This is the album that brought Toots's soul-infused testifying to American audiences. Forget about this being a great reggae album; this set transcends categorization. *—John Floyd*

Reggae Got Soul / 1976 / Mango ✦✦✦✦✦
Among his landmark releases, this album wasn't quite as magnificent as *Funky Kingston*, but still contained plenty of explosive numbers and Otis Redding-influenced leads from Toots Hibbert. *—Ron Wynn*

In the Dark / Jan. 1976 / Trojan ✦✦✦✦✦

Live / 1980 / Mango ✦✦✦✦✦
Anyone who had the pleasure of catching Toots and the Maytals live in the '70s or '80s will attest to the fact that they didn't hesitate to go that extra mile on stage. Without question, they had one of reggae and ska's finest live shows—in fact, you could say that singer/leader Toots Hibbert was as tireless a showman as James Brown or George Clinton. The band's vitality is beautifully captured by this superb album, which came out in 1980 and documents a show at *the Hammersmith Palais*. True to form, Hibbert spares no passion on performances of hits that range from "Funky Kingston," "Pressure Drop," and "Monkey Man," to "Get Up, Stand Up" (not to be confused with Bob Marley's song), "54-46, That's My Number," and "Time Tough." Thankfully, this album isn't the only documentation of a Toots and the Maytals show—the Genes CD *An Hour Live* (which was recorded live at *the Reggae Sunsplash Festival* in 1982) is also a gem. *—Alex Henderson*

Knock Out! / 1981 / Mango ✦✦✦✦

Hour Live / Aug. 1982 / Genes ✦✦✦✦✦
One band that never forgot reggae's ska roots was Toots & the Maytals, whose music has maintained the robustness associated with ska recordings of the 1950s and early '60s. The sweetness found in some Detroit, Chicago and Philadelphia R&B never had much of an impact on Toots Hibbert, who was more influenced by the urgency and rawness of southern soul and forms of rock. Recorded live at the 1982 Reggae Sunsplash Festival in Montego Bay, Jamaica, this album is essential listening for Toots devotees. Hard-hitting performances of "Funky Kingston," "Get Up, Stand Up" (not to be confused with the Bob Marley classic), "Monkey Man" and other major hits (in Jamaica and England) leave no doubt that Toots & the Maytals had one of the most exciting live shows in the history of reggae. *—Alex Henderson*

☆ **Time Tough: The Anthology** / Jun. 18, 1996 / Island ✦✦✦✦✦
Featuring over 40 songs and spanning the entire length of the group's career, the double-disc set *Time Tough: Anthology* contains every essential song Toots & the Maytals, from early ska material to reggae classics like "Pressure Drop" and "Funky Kingston." Not only are all of their best-known singles included in the collection, but so are prime album tracks, rare singles and three unreleased tracks which hold their own with nearly everything else on the collection. *Time Tough* is not only the perfect introduction to Toots & the Maytals' groundbreaking career, it is the only compilation to put their career in focus and feature all of their best songs. It's an essential item for any reggae collection. *—Stephen Thomas Erlewine*

☆ **The Very Best of Toots & the Maytals [Music Club]** / Aug. 19, 1997 / Music Club ✦✦✦✦✦
Toots Hibbert is generally credited with giving reggae music its name with his 1968 song "Do the Reggay." That was only one of a string of hugely influential hits, all of which drew heavily on American R&B styles and combined them with the rock steady and reggae sounds that were tearing up the charts in late-'60s Jamaica to create a unique hybrid that no one else has since tried to emulate. Songs like "Funky Kingston" and "54-46 Was My Number" owe as much to James Brown as to any Jamaican influence, and Toots even had the guts to cover John Denver (with "Take Me Home Country Roads"); luckily, he also had enough raw talent to make it work. But unique as it is, his sound fits squarely into the category of rock steady, a bouncy, elastic beat that shimmered and bopped at the nexus between ska's galloping up-up-up and reggae's slower, smokier groove. And the Toots influence has continued to be felt: "Pressure Drop" was covered by the Clash on their debut album, and "Monkey Man" became one of the signature songs of the Two-Tone ska revival in turn-of-the-'80s England. All of the classics are here on this compilation, including the glorious "Pomps and Pride" and his ill-advised (but, again, amazingly effective) cover of "Louie, Louie." These songs are an essential part of any reggae collection. *—Rick Anderson*

Never Grow Old / Oct. 7, 1997 / Heartbeat ✦✦✦✦✦
A reissue of the Maytals' debut album, recorded in 1962 and 1963, with four bonus cuts from the same era. Like all of the major Jamaican bands of the time, the Maytals were performing ska during this era, and doing a pretty good job of it, although the more distinctive stylings of their reggae prime are only hinted at here. Produced by C.S. Dodd (who co-wrote most of the songs with Toots Hibbert), and featuring the Skatalites on backup, it's respectable early ska, though not as good as the ska laid down by the Wailers in the mid-'60s. One of the bonus tracks, a cover of "I'm Gonna Sit Right Down and Cry (Over You)," is the highlight, with its infectiously bouncy verve. *—Richie Unterberger*

★ **Very Best of Toots & the Maytals [Polygram]** / Apr. 25, 2000 / Island ✦✦✦✦✦
Toots & the Maytals' *The Very Best Of* collects the highlights of their three-decade career, including '60s songs like "Broadway Jungle," "54-46 Was My Number," "Do the Reggay," and "Pressure Drop"; '70s tracks like "Funky Kingston" and "Reggae Got Soul"; and '80s solo work from Toots Hibbert, including "(I've Got) Dreams to Remember" and "Peace, Perfect Peace." Though it isn't the most comprehensive anthology of the Maytals available, this 19-track compilation provides a decent overview of some of the group's most important moments. *—Heather Phares*

Andrew Tosh

Vocals / Contemporary Reggae
Eldest son of the late Wailer Peter Tosh, Andrew made his debut at his father's funeral in 1987, wowing the mourners with his physical and vocal similarities to Peter. Two promising albums later, Andrew is looked upon as one of conscious reggae's greatest hopes. A tour with the Wailers in 1991 solidified his live reputation. With strong material, he could fill his famous father's shoes in a manner similar to that of Ziggy Marley. He released two albums at the close of the eighties (Original Man and *Make Place for Youth*, resurfacing a decade later with *Message From Jah*. *—Roger Steffens*

● **Make Place for the Youth** / 1989 / Tomato ✦✦✦✦✦

Peter Tosh

b. Oct. 9, 1944, Westmoreland, Jamaica, **d.** Sep. 11, 1987, Kingston, Jamaica
Melodica, Vocals, Guitar, Organ / Political Reggae, Roots Reggae
In the early Wailers lineup, Peter Tosh stood apart from the other members not only because of his six-foot-plus height but because of his boasty-boy attitude. Known as the "stepping razor," he actually had a soft, extremely humorous side as well, as evidenced in his frequent political wordplay. After more than ten years playing with the Wailers, Tosh felt the need to pursue a solo career and debuted with 1976's *Legalize It*, remaking many of his earlier Jamaican recordings and giving the marijuana movement its most potent anthem in the title track. A firm opponent of the hypocritical "shitstem," Tosh was a favorite target of Babylon's legal forces. Police in Jamaica beat him nearly to death on at least three occasions, and he bore the scars till his death. The Rolling Stones, impressed by Tosh's ferocious and unflinching posture, signed him to their fledgling label and released *Bush Doctor* in 1978, another series of hymns and harrangues. *Mystic Man* (1979) and *Wanted: Dread & Alive* (1981) kept a militant attitude while trying to cross over to the mainstream that Marley had conquered.

After a long hiatus following 1983's *Mama Africa*, Tosh released *No Nuclear War* in 1987, then was assassinated soon after at his home in Kingston. Like Marley, Tosh left at least ten children and no will. *—Roger Steffens*

★ **Legalize It** / 1976 / Columbia ♦♦♦♦♦
After years of being overshadowed by Bob Marley, Peter Tosh left the Wailers to pursue a solo career. Released in 1976, *Legalize It* is a bold statement that Peter Tosh had arrived and was a creative force in his own right. Although he explores some issues of spirituality, this is Tosh's most lightweight album in the sense that it is his least political. This is not meant as a criticism—in fact, Tosh's playfulness and joy ("Ketchy Shuby") only add to the album's charm. He does make political statements (the title track celebrates and promotes the use of marijuana), but they are done with a sense of humor and a melodic infectiousness that belie his sincere concern for the issues. Tosh incorporates many instruments and mixes slower ballads with upbeat grooving tunes. The album's highlight is "Why Must I Cry," a multi-layered song (co-written with Bob Marley) that conveys a sense of personal failure when fighting an uphill battle, whether it be against injustices of the world or within the confines of a relationship. *Legalize It* cemented Tosh's position as a giant in reggae, and the album is one of the best albums of the genre. *—Vik Iyengar*

Equal Rights / 1977 / Columbia ♦♦♦♦
Equal Rights was to be the album that propelled Peter Tosh to the top of the reggae world—the rival to onetime fellow Wailer Bob Marley. Time has shown that this lofty aspiration was not borne out, but *Equal Rights* remains among the handful of best, and most influential, reggae albums ever recorded. Tosh was always the most militant of the original Wailers and this album reflects that outlook. Whether it is preaching about the unity of the African diaspora ("African"), protesting conditions in South Africa ("Apartheid"), or giving a more general call to arms ("Get up Stand Up"), *Equal Rights* is a political album. This is at times crippling, as some tracks are more effective as political statements than they are as songs. This, in fact, is a primary difference between Tosh and Marley—Marley's political statements never overwhelmed his songs. Unfortunately, this is not always the case with Tosh. That being said, "Downpresser Man" (based on a folk standard), "Stepping Razor," and his definitive version of "Get up Stand Up" are as good a trio of songs as you will find on any album, reggae or not. Tosh's singing is angry and forceful and the music is intricate and distinctive. On these three tracks you can see why people thought that Tosh could become a transcendent international star. The rest of the album, however, shows why he never quite lived up to that potential. *—Toby Ball*

Bush Doctor / 1978 / Trojan ♦♦♦
"Creation" is Genesis set to music; "Moses" continues the story; "Don't Look Back" teams Tosh with Jagger. This is an appealing collection. *—Roger Steffens*

Wanted Dread & Alive / 1981 / EMI America ♦♦♦
Great Binghi roots-rave on "Rastafari Is, " plus the gorgeous ballad "Fools Die" and other mixed pleasures. *—Roger Steffens*

Mama Africa / 1983 / EMI America ♦♦♦♦♦
A strong collection, it has the hit "Johnny B. Goode" and remakes of "Maga Dog" and "Stop That Train." *—Roger Steffens*

The Toughest / 1988 / Heartbeat ♦♦♦♦♦
Tosh's roots were intertwined with Bob Marley's, and like Marley, his very earliest efforts had much more to do with ska than the reggae popularized by the Wailers. That doesn't mean that Tosh's earliest work wasn't very enjoyable and accomplished, although the spiritual and political concerns had yet to surface. This is a near-complete, 19-song retrospective of his Studio One recordings, two-thirds of which were produced by Coxsone Dodd in the mid-'60s, the remainder by Lee Perry at some later point. Exact source documentation is vague: some if not all of the Dodd tracks were certainly Wailers discs, not Tosh solo outings (some appear on compilations of Bob Marley & the Wailers' '60s material). At any rate, the Dodd sides are good cuts in the ska vein, with some flashes of developing diversity and sophistication: the rock-influenced "Can't You See," "Rasta Shook Them Up" (the first Wailers tune to refer to Rastafarianism), and a cover of the Temptations' "Don't Look Back" (which Tosh would record as a duet with Mick Jagger in 1978). The Lee Perry material, from an uncertain vintage, is much more identifiable as reggae entering its prime. "Rightful Ruler" has an early appearance by U Roy, and a reverb-soaked version of "Downpresser," which Tosh would re-cut on his *Equal Rights* album, is the highlight of the disc. *—Richie Unterberger*

The Best of Peter Tosh: Dread Don't Die / Apr. 1996 / EMI ♦♦♦♦♦
The title is inaccurate: this draws almost exclusively from his 1980s recordings for EMI. If you only want one or two late-period Tosh albums, this is a decent enough starting (and stopping) point, heaviest on 1981's *Wanted Dread or Alive* (five cuts are included), and also included a couple of concert remakes of classic material from his 1984 *Captured Live* record. It also licenses his 1978 duet with Mick Jagger, "(You Got to Walk and) Don't Look Back." It's got the feel, however, of a compilation that is far from exemplary, either in terms of eras spanned or depth of content. *—Richie Unterberger*

☆ **Honorary Citizen** / Sep. 1997 / Columbia/Legacy ♦♦♦♦♦
Although it runs a little too long for the average listener, the three-disc box set *Honorary Citizen* draws a superb portrait of Peter Tosh, capturing his musical mastery and his incendiary political rhetoric. All of the expected songs are here, from "Legalize It" to his hit duet with Mick Jagger, "(You Got to Walk and) Don't Looke Back," but what makes *Honorary Citizen* essential is that it compiles rare early singles and neglected album tracks. By including such obscurities with the familiar items, the set presents a full, rounded picture of Tosh's talents, making a thoroughly convincing argument that he was one of reggae's true greats. *—Leo Stanley*

★ **Scrolls of the Prophet: The Best of Peter Tosh** / Jul. 6, 1999 / Columbia/Legacy ♦♦♦♦♦
Scrolls of the Prophet is the first single-disc Tosh best-of to contain tracks from his Columbia, Rolling Stones, and EMI albums. Since the set originates with Columbia, the material from the other two labels is limited; there are five tracks from *Equal Rights* and four from *Legalize It*, with two from *Bush Doctor* and one from *Wanted Dread & Alive*, plus three rare or previously unreleased tracks. But the bulk of Tosh's most memorable tracks appeared on those first two Columbia albums, including his solo remake of the Wailers song "Get Up, Stand Up" and "Stepping Razor," "Equal Rights," and "Legalize It." Tosh was intense and directed, but not prolific. His tunes are sometimes borrowed; "Downpressor Man" is a rewrite of the folk-gospel tune "Oh Sinner Man." His themes are also repetitive, as the sequencing here—which follows "Legalize It," his ode to the legalization of marijuana extolling the drug's medicinal qualities, with "Bush Doctor," a song that bears much the same message—tends to emphasize. Nevertheless, he managed a surprising variety within the sometimes constricted reggae form, speeding things up on his hit remake of the Temptations' "Walk and Don't Look Back" (a duet with Mick Jagger) and slowing them down for the ballad "Fools Die," which has a haunting flute line. *—William Ruhlmann*

Twinkle Brothers

Group / Dub Poetry
It seems as though the Twinkle Brothers have been around since the beginning of time, or at least the beginning of reggae. Led by Norman Grant, the Twinkles began in the early '60s as a trio featuring Grant and his two brothers singing in the slick trio style similar to that of the Melodians and the Mighty Diamonds. It was in the early 70s when the group hooked up with influential producer and arranger Bunny Lee a union that produced a number of reggae hits including "We Can Do It Too," and "Miss Laba Laba." In 1975 the Twinkles released their best and most widely known record, *Rasta Pon Top*, a rasta-infused, roots-heavy demi-masterpiece that included soul and gospel vocal stylings within the deep grooves. Although hardcore reggae audiences were the principal fans of the Twinkle Brothers, Grant and company were consistently releasing chart-topping records. As much as this brought great success to the band it also created a significant amount of friction as Grant began seeing himself more as a solo act and less as a member of a trio. This culminated in Grant's pursuit of a solo career as more of a MOR soul singer. It wasn't an awful decision by any stretch of the imagination, but his solo work wasn't nearly as good as what the Twinkles had been doing. *—John Dougan*

Live at Reggae Sunsplash: Since I Throw / 1984 / Sunsplash ♦♦♦♦♦

★ **Free Africa** / 1990 / Frontline ♦♦♦♦♦
The Twinkle Brothers have been in existence since the 1960s, and although bandleader Norman Grant continues to record under the Twinkle Brothers name, the three Frontline LPs from 1979 and 1980 probably mark the high point of their work. Those albums (*Love, Praise Jah*, and *Countrymen*) are selectively represented on this 16-track compilation, which swings back and forth between songs that show a heavy gospel influence (the almost hymnlike "Solid as a Rock" and "Free Us") and others that betray a clear debt to vintage American R&B ("Shu Be Dup" and "Since I Threw the Comb Away"). Grant plays drums and sings from deep in his chest in a clear, resonant baritone voice, while various other band members contribute tight, soaring harmonies. During this period, the Twinkle Brothers had one of the few truly unique ensemble sounds in reggae music, and this collection is an excellent introduction to their art. *—Rick Anderson*

U-Roy (Ewart Beckford)

Vocals, DJ / Contemporary Reggae, Roots Reggae, Dub
In the late '60s, Ewart Beckford (U-Roy) almost single-handedly invented the modern DJ rap style in Jamaica by toasting on the sound system of pioneer King Tubby, who was the first engineer to mix reverb and echo effects on deconstructed rhythm tracks. This led directly to the Jamaican peculiarity of having only one song per 7-inch single (the A-side being the vocal, the B-side being the "dub version" or rhythm bed that any local toaster could "skank" over with the events of the day). But U-Roy remains the most trickily tasteful exemplar of the style, due largely to his uncanny choice in tracks over which to toast, creating ad hoc dialogs with the singer, commenting on and responding to the lyrics in such classics of the form as "On the Beach," "Wear You to the Ball," and "Tide Is High," not to mention the royalty-ridiculing '70s scat "Chalice in the Palace," on which he invites the Queen herself to suck on the ganja pipe (chalice). Still active, living in Los Angeles, he is now referred to respectfully as Daddy U-Roy. *—Roger Steffens*

● **Dread in a Babylon** / 1975 / Frontline ♦♦♦♦♦
It's this veteran rapper's best album, comparable to any in this idiom. *—Michael G. Nastos*

Rock with I / 1992 / RAS ♦♦♦
While not quite as fluid or able to maintain the rapid-fire verbal pace of past sessions, legendary DJ/toaster U-Roy can still spin a powerful, hypnotic yarn. He hasn't lost his fire, religious zeal or political and cultural convictions, and there are several strong message cuts and/or spiritual laments. But not everything is so heavy; there are also fun tracks where U-Roy demonstrates the flair, inflections, screams and style that made him a DJ innovator. The sound, arrangements and production are vintage reggae, with cymbals clashing, thudding bass lines, flickering guitars and the echo and fades that characterized 1970s reggae and dub. He's a venerable warrior, but U-Roy still has plenty to say. *—Ron Wynn*

Super Boss / Oct. 18, 1994 / Culture Press ♦♦♦♦

The Upsetters

Group / Roots Reggae, Dub
Producer Lee "Scratch" Perry's longtime house band, the Upsetters appeared on some of the most legendary records in reggae history, including the early hits of the Wailers. The group was named after Perry's 1968 smash "The Upsetter," and the Upsetter tag was also applied to his record label; although the line-up was mercurial—essentially the roster consisted of whoever was in the studio the minute the tape began to roll—among the key Jamaican musicians who passed through the Upsetters' ranks were siblings Aston and Carlton Barrett, Sly Dunbar, Glen Adams, Winston Wright and Boris Gardiner. Despite scoring a handful of their own hits, including 1969's "Return of Django," the unit was best known as a support act, en-

joying their greatest influence through the records they made during the late 1960s and early 1970s with the Wailers, including the seminal "Duppy Conqueror," "Small Axe" and "Soul Rebel." —*Jason Ankeny*

Blackboard Jungle Dub / 1980 / Clock Tower ✦✦✦✦
On *Blackboard Jungle Dub,* Lee Perry and the Upsetters produce another fine example of their subversive brand of dub with a unique blend of murky rhythm tracks, warbling guitar effects and distant-sounding horns. Although it does not quite match the quality of the classic Upsetters album *Super Ape, Blackboard* nevertheless impresses with both the brevity of "strictly" drum and bass cuts such as "Dreamland Dub" and "Kasha Macka Dub," and expansive touches like the animated DJ toasting on "Cloak A Dagger (Ver. 3)." Living up to the "Upsetter" moniker, Perry wreaks his inimitable brand of mayhem during "Fever Grass Dub" with a half-baked MC intro, lion roars and air raid siren imitations; effects which blend in well with other eccentric features like the spastic trombone solo on "BlackBoard ver. 2" and reverb-heavy percussion on "Cloak a Dagger." Just standard technique for Perry really, and part of the sound which made his productions instantly recognizable amongst many '70s and '80s dub releases. *Blackboard Jungle* contains classic dub taken to the outer limits and is one of the highlights of the Lee Perry catalog. —*Stephen Cook*

Upsetters a Go Go / Oct. 31, 1995 / Heartbeat ✦✦✦
Much has been written about the ever-stranger Lee "Scratch" Perry, master of the Black Ark and now off doing it dubwise in Switzerland or somesuch, but the Upsetters themselves have been glossed over to a surprising degree. This is really a shame, because two Upsetters members ended up as the rhythm core of the Wailers, and the legacy of this studio band is a grand one, with some of the best Jamaican music credited to it. This 16-cut collection, assembled from tapes kept by keyboardist Glen Adams, is primarily instrumental, with a few vocal incursions from Glen Adams, Lee Perry and Dave Barker, with the focus being on the Upsetters—without any of Perry's studio twistiness. This is mostly light, entertaining body-rhythm stuff, some of which will sound familiar ("Lock It Up" is a version of "Lockjaw"). The sounds and styles are a trip down memory lane, but that's where the best reggae is sometimes found. Cheerfully unessential, which is why you should get it. —*Steven McDonald*

● **Upsetting The Nation: 1969-1970** / Dec. 5, 1995 / Trojan ✦✦✦✦

Bunny Wailer

b. Apr. 10, 1947, Kingston, Jamaica
Vocals, Percussion / Roots Reggae
Born Neville O'Reilly Livingstone and dubbed Bunny Wailer, this crucial Jamaican singer and songwriter was raised as Bob Marley's brother from the age of nine. As co-founder of The Wailers (along with Peter Tosh), Bunny gave high chromatic shadings to some of the most exhilarating harmonies ever pressed on wax. His "Pass It On" was one of the standout tracks on the final album The Wailers did together as a trio, 1973's *Burning.* Three years later, Bunny released his first solo project, one of reggae's most majestic achievements, the roots classic *Blackheart Man,* which included hymnlike chants with titles like "Dreamland," "Bide Up," and "Rastaman." Bunny's baritone has been showcased in as many as three albums a year, most notably *Struggle* (1980); *Bunny Wailer Sings the Wailers* (1980's collection of covers); *Rock & Groove* (1981 dancehall classics); *Live* (recorded at his first solo concert in Kingston in December 1982); and *Liberation* (1988's consciousness-raiser that is the acknowledged peer of his spectacular debut. —*Roger Steffens*

★ **Black Heart Man** / 1976 / Mango ✦✦✦✦✦

Struggle / 1980 / Solomonic ✦✦✦✦
The title cut is anthemic; everything else is superb. —*Ron Wynn*

Roots Radics Rockers Reggae / 1987 / Shanachie ✦✦✦✦✦
The members of the original Wailers all had distinct personas: Bob Marley was the mystic, always looking off into the middle distance and frequently speaking in abstractions; Peter Tosh was the angry young man, with a sharp eye and sharper tongue; and Bunny Wailer was the gentle prophet, perhaps the most religious of the three and possessed of a calm, deliberate demeanor. Maybe it should come as no surprise that he is the only one of the three left alive; the world is a hard place for mystics and uppity cynics. Bunny's solo work has generally followed the same trajectory he established early on. His brand of reggae is thick, hot, and dark, like a more melodic Burning Spear, and his lyrical themes are generally in the mode of gentle admonishment or spiritual invitation. This exceptional album features a celebration of reggae itself (in the title track), a half-speed remake of his rocksteady classic "Let Him Go," and the stirring "Love Fire," among other gems. Though many critics put this album somewhere behind the classic *Blackheart Man,* it definitely belongs in the first rank of modern reggae recordings. —*Rick Anderson*

Crucial! Roots Classics / 1994 / Shanachie ✦✦✦
This 14-track collection covers 1979-1982; the major themes are Jamaica's wretched political wars and the necessity for radical change. Although Wailer doesn't always specifically address individuals or situations, it's clear from the force and vocal authority that he's discussing the inequities in his homeland. Other than "Baldheaded Woman," these are uplifting, searing tunes demanding that the citzenry stop ignoring evils and unite for change. His voice is clear, urgent and decisive, never more so than on "Free Jah Jah Children." —*Ron Wynn*

The Wailers

f. 1963
Group / Rocksteady
Following leader Bob Marley's death from cancer on May 11, 1981, the Wailers Band struggled nearly a decade for direction, hampered from releasing their own music by a Gordian knot of legal entanglements. Anchored by world-class bassist Family Man Barrett and his drummer brother Carlton (who was murdered by gunmen hired by his wife in April 1987), the Wailers Band performed well-received international tours almost constantly through the '80s. Lead guitarist Junior Murvin bravely handled most of the vocal chores, and keyboard stalwart Wya Lindo and percussionist Seeco Patterson (who brought the original Wailers to their first audition in 1963) added credibility, but as the '90s progressed, despite the title of their first solo offering, they were still struggling to establish their own identity on records like 1994's *Never Ending Wailers* and 1996's *Jah Message.* —*Roger Steffens*

Majestic Warriors / 1991 / Tabu ✦✦✦
Long after Bob Marley's death from cancer in 1981 and Peter Tosh's murder in 1988, members of Marley's band continued to record under the name the Wailers Band. On 1991's *Majestic Warriors,* some of the key players include lead singer/guitarist Junior Marvin and bassist Aston "Family Man" Barrett. Marley fans couldn't help but wonder if *Majestic Warriors* would sound anything like his classic albums of the '60s and '70s but, in fact, enjoyable selections like "Sweet Cry Freedom," "Bad Mind People," and "Trip" are notably slicker and more produced than anything you'll find on *Natty Dread, Catch a Fire,* or *Exodus.* Though one of its highlights is a likable cover of Marley's 1980 hit "Could You Be Loved," the CD on the whole isn't as Marley-sounding as one might expect. This decent but rather uneven album does have its moments, but those expecting something as extraordinary as *Rastaman Vibration* are bound to be disappointed. —*Alex Henderson*

Wailing Souls

Group / Dub
The Wailing Souls have been making their unique brand of reggae music since the early '60s, but it was during the '70s that they made their mark with their many recordings on the Channel One label. What made them unique back then was that they were a vocal quartet rather than a trio. Also, lead singer Winston "Pipe" Matthews has a style and voice quality remarkably similar to their contemporary Bob Marley. In 1976, they had their first big break through with a remake of "Back Out With It" for the newly established Channel One label. It climbed to No. 1 on Jamaican charts and they followed it up with "Jah Jah Give Us Life to Live." A long string of chart-topping 45s came afterward as well a few successful 12" singles including a remake of "Fire Coal Man" also brought tremendous success as well as the powerful "War." Following 1979's *Wild Suspense,* the Souls hooked up with Sly and Robbie's Taxi label where, with producer Junjo Laws they recorded some of their all-out best tracks including "Kingdom Rise Kingdom Fall." —*Sandra Brennan*

★ **Wild Suspense** / 1979 / Mango ✦✦✦✦✦
These brilliant quartet triumphs echo the harmonic heights of the early Wailers. It's virtually their greatest hits, backed by Sly And Robbie. —*Roger Steffens*

Firehouse Rock / 1980 / Shanachie ✦✦✦✦✦
Talk about a triple threat: first you have the (by this point well-established and effortlessly professional) Wailing Souls, one of the greatest of the cultural harmony groups; then you have the Roots Radics, the studio band that almost singlehandedly defined the new dancehall reggae sound in the early '80s; and to make everything perfect, you have the unassailable team of producer Henry "Junjo" Lawes (who can claim equal status with the Roots Radics as a dancehall pioneer) and engineer Hopeton "Scientist" Brown. The result is one of the finest reggae albums of all time, one which combines the Wailing Souls' top-notch songwriting and harmony singing with the absolute best in studio accompaniment-there may never be another reggae band with a sound as rock-ribbed as that of the Roots Radics. Each track is a highlight in its own way, but pay particular attention to the title track, the gently rolling "Who Lives It" and the smoky, apocalyptic "Kingdom Rise Kingdom Fall." —*Rick Anderson*

Kingston 14 / 1987 / RAS ✦✦✦
The Wailing Souls belong in any short list of great reggae vocal groups, especially in terms of harmonies and songwriting. The compositions on this '87 set are uniformly gripping, finely writtten and exquisitely performed, despite the fact Winston Matthews, Lloyd McDonald and Devon Bedford are all complementary singers rather than spectacular leads. But their trading of the spotlight and those shimmering harmonies are so superbly done that this slight defect is totally obscured. The Wailing Souls show those unaware of their skills that they're in the pantheon of great reggae trios. —*Ron Wynn*

Reggae Legends, Vol. 1 / Jun. 22, 1999 / Artists Only ✦✦✦
A specially priced best-of compilation covering the first half of the legendary reggae group's career. —*Heather Phares*

Josey Wales

DJ / Ragga
A dancehall DJ responsible for several hits in his native Jamaica, "the Outlaw" Josey Wales joined the Roots Unlimited Sound System in 1977. Five years later, he joined Junjo Lawes's Volcano Sound System. His first hit was 1983's "Leggo Mi Hand"; "Drug Abusing" (from his second album, *No Way No Better than Yard*) was also popular. Joining with King Jammy in 1985, Wales recorded "Na Lef Jamaica," "Hi Fi Say So" and "Right Moves." *Stone Love Vol. 2,* a live recording from Birmingham, England, appeared in 1991. After time on duet projects (with Super Cat and Beres Hammond), he released two albums, *Cowboy Style* and *The Outlaw.* —*John Bush*

● **Two Giants Clash** / 1984 / Greensleeves ✦✦✦✦✦

Rules / 1986 / Black Solidarity ✦✦✦✦
Wales, who surfaced in 1981, straddles late deejay and early dance hall. His most recent work hasn't quite matched this 1986 album, which combines the magisterial minimalism of the best deejay with moments of a highly oblique and original melodic sense. —*John Storm Roberts, Original Music*

Delroy Wilson

b. Oct. 5, 1948, Kingston, Jamaica, **d.** Mar. 6, 1995, Kingston, Jamaica
Vocals / Smooth Reggae, Roots Reggae, Reggae-Pop, Lovers Rock, Ska
A great veteran of the Jamaican vocal scene, Delroy Wilson's been performing and recording since he was 11 years old. His song "Better Must Come" became the theme song for

Michael Manley during the 1972 election for Jamaica's prime minister. Wilson's recorded for Studio One, CCAS, Empire, BP, Pioneer, Top Rank and Vista among others. He has a vibrant, extremely soulful sound and can also easily handle roots material. *—Ron Wynn*

● **The Best of Delroy Wilson** / 1991 / Heartbeat ✦✦✦✦✦
Delroy Wilson was one of Jamaica's biggest singing stars during the heyday of ska and rocksteady, maintaining his popularity well into the reggae era. Wilson's seductively soulful, slightly hoarse-sounding voice graced sides by the island's top producers Clement "Coxsone" Dodd, Sonia Pottinger, and Bunny Lee, leaving an impression on the young Bob Marley in the process. This fine collection brings together many of the rocksteady hits he recorded at Dodd's Studio One in the late '60s, including proto-lover's rock smashes like "Riding for a Fall" and "Run Run." The kind of medium-to-slow grooves Wilson excelled at are plentiful too, with his minor-mood version of the Temptations' hit "Get Ready" standing out in particular; the brash side of this in-the-pocket brilliance is aired on the sarcastic, "sound-clash" number "Conquer Me" (likely a response to singer Derrick Morgan's "Conquering Ruler," another in a line of boasting songs popular among Jamaican singers). More up-tempo material rounds out the set, including another dancehall favorite, "Ungrateful Baby," a fine cover of the Little Milton hit "We're Gonna Make It," and the collection's sole ska cut, "Impossible." Wilson gets solid backing from Coxsone's studio band of the time, the Soul Vendors, with the fine work of organist/arranger Jackie Mittoo, guitarist Eric Frater, and the horn section of tenor saxophonist Roland Alphonso, alto saxophonist Lester Sterling, and trombonist Vin Gordon deserving special mention. An essential collection for fans of rocksteady music. *—Stephen Cook*

Special / 1993 / RAS ✦✦✦
This set included a remake of Wilson's first major hit, "Time Hard," which became the theme song for Michael Manley's first triumphant campaign for Prime Minister in the 1970s. While the production has the requisite contemporary touches, it also gives Wilson's full, gritty voice prominence and doesn't overwhelm it with electronic or synthesized studio backdrop. Those unfamiliar with Wilson's early songs will be brought up to speed by the "Medley of Hits," which cleverly incorporates snatches of several early reggae gems. *—Ron Wynn*

Yabby You (Vivian Jackson)

Vocals / Roots Reggae

Yabby You was born Vivian Jackson in a Kingston ghetto. Taking his cues from divine inspiration that he feels comes from the sounds of nature around him, with the help of friends founded a harmony trio, the Prophets, in 1972. They made their single debut with "Conquering Lion," a classically styled reggae song with a deeply personal message. They made a few more singles and eventually they all appeared on Jackson's debut album, *Conquering Lion.* Throughout the decade, he recorded frequently on his Prophets labels. He was closely affiliated with King Tubby, whose dubs often appeared on the B-sides of Jackson's singles. When not recording his own material, Yabby You launched the careers of other new singers including Michael Prophet, Wayne Wade, and Tony Tuff. He also began producing the early recordings of such performers as Willie Williams, Ras I-buna and Half Pint. A Yabby You-produced recording usually features a distinctive bass line combined with organs, horns and soaring harmonies that he uses to create a meditative, spiritual atmosphere. *—Sandra Brennan*

Conquering Lion / 1975 / Prophet ✦✦✦

Deliver Me from My Enemies / 1977 / Prophet ✦✦✦✦✦

One Love, One Heart / 1983 / Shanachie ✦✦✦✦✦
When this retrospective collection was released in 1992, it was the definitive document of one of the most powerful roots reggae artists of the 1970s. Despite its skimpy 30-minute length, it contains many of the songs with which Yabby You helped define the classic roots sound—the stern "Anti Christ," the dark and brooding "Run Come Rally," the didactic but sweetly tuneful "Carnal Mind"—all recorded at the Channel One studio with the cream of reggae's session musicians and mixed by dubmaster King Tubby. While this remarkable collection has lost none of its power, it was somewhat overshadowed in 1997 by *Jesus Dread,* an exhaustive two-disc collection on the Blood & Fire label which contains most of the selections on *One Love, One Heart* in multiple versions. Strangely, though, the Blood & Fire set does not include "One Love, One Heart," nor does it include the archetypal "Babylon Gone Down" or "Judgement Time" ("Fire, Fire" is repeated on the Blood & Fire set under the title "Fire in a Kingston"). So if you don't feel the need to spend a little extra for almost three hours of Yabby You songs in multiple versions, this single-disc overview is still a wise purchase. *—Rick Anderson*

★ **Jesus Dread (1972-1977)** / 1997 / Blood & Fire ✦✦✦✦✦
The title of this two-disc set comes from the fact that Yabby You (born Vivian Jackson; his nickname comes from the chorus to his song "Conquering Lion") is a devout Christian Rastafarian. The depth of his religious faith informs every note on this remarkable album, which contains some of the darkest, dreadest reggae ever made. The medium-slow tempos, the minor chords, the song titles ("Love Thy Neighbor," "Carnal Mind," "Warn the Nation," etc.) all reflect an intent that goes beyond mere music-making. And yet the music itself is spectacular. Most of the songs featured on the album are presented in several versions—an original vocal mix, a dub version, a deejay version (with toasting performed by such deejays as Dillinger and Big Youth over the dub cuts), and, often, an instrumental version featuring saxophonist Tommy McCook. The McCook tracks tend to sound like filler, but the album is still utterly essential. It's hard to imagine a better example of golden-era reggae at its finest. *—Rick Anderson*

Yellowman (Winston Foster)

Vocals / Ragga, Dancehall

Yellowman was one of the hottest toasters in Jamaican dancehalls during the 1980s and though his career slowed down towards the decade's end, he has began to come back in the early '90s with a mellower, slightly less controversial style. It was his rude style filled with lyrics many consider homophobic and explicitly sexist that inspired the word "slackness" as a descriptor for some types of dancehall music. But he has always been more than merely vulgar and careful listening to his lyrics reveals a wicked sense of humor and even a genuine consciousness. He was born Winston Foster and is an albino, something that made life difficult growing up as albino's are considered outcasts in Jamaica. Rather than be consumed by this, he became charismatic and outgoing, marketing himself as Jamaica's newest sex symbol. With his witty, blindingly rapid-fire, erotic rap explicitly describing his bedroom prowess, he had little trouble convincing his audiences of the early '80s. He soon proved himself able to out slack the rudest toasters in town. This has earned him considerable criticism from those who find much of Yellowman's bawdy repartee irresponsible and damaging even though it is often spoken with tongue firmly in cheek. *—Sandra Brennan*

The Negril Chill / 1987 / Relativity ✦✦✦✦✦
A riotous live album with Yellowman and Charlie Chaplin going up against each other in an energetic clash of DJ styles, with Chaplin doing his best to overcome Yellowman's slackness. It's a good-natured contest balanced against an excellent live band and an audience that grows more and more enthusiastic throughout. Rude, often sexist, and sometimes screamingly funny, it may not be a landmark reggae release, but it *is* a great album. *—Steven McDonald*

● **One in a Million** / 1989 / Shanachie ✦✦✦✦✦
One of the few non-slack albums in his career, this boasts Yellowman's signature rap "Mad over Me" and serious scenarios of guns and fire. *—Roger Steffens*

Live at Maritime Hall / Sep. 1, 1998 / Artists Only ✦✦✦✦
You'd expect an aging reggae sex symbol recovering from cancer to perhaps have slowed down a bit, but not so. While it's true that Yellowman has mellowed somewhat in terms of subject matter—he no longer spends all of his time boasting in explicit terms about his sexual prowess—this live album finds him singing and toasting with all the inventiveness and energy he demonstrated at the peak of his career. Backed by the outstanding Sagittarius Band, he moves through a program of that consists primarily of predictable oldies: sweaty, uptempo versions of "Nobody Move Nobody Get Hurt" and "Two to Six, Supermix," a churning arrangement of "Oh Carolina" that segues nicely into "Holy Mount Zion" and "Poco Jump," etc. His interplay with the crowd and with the band is sharp and intuitive and keeps the energy level high throughout. This live album ranks with the best of his early studio work. *—Rick Anderson*

Life in the Ghetto / Tassa ✦✦✦✦
Before dancehall's ascension in the mid- to late 1980s, dubwise reigned supreme as reggae's dominant style of toasting. Since the '70s, one of the finest and most popular dub artists has been Winston Foster, aka Yellowman. In contrast to dancehall's abrasive tendencies, Yellowman is fairly relaxed, smooth and easygoing. The dub master is well respected in reggae circles, and lives up to his fine reputation on the captivating *Life In the Ghetto.* On such numbers as "Honour Your Mother," "Stand Up For Your Rights" and "Jack Sprat," Yellow toasts over groovin' tracks that recall the soul music of the '60s. Those new to reggae may find *Life,* with its emphasis on the Jamaican patois dialect, difficult to absorb; but for the more seasoned reggae fan, this CD is joyous listening. *—Alex Henderson*

Various Artists

Battle Axe / 1996 / Trojan FFFF
You won't see Lee Perry's name anywhere on this album unless you look very hard for the producer credit, which is in tiny print on the back. And it's probably true that he doesn't perform on any of these tracks, many of which are instrumentals by the Upsetters, and others that feature such well-known singers as Junior Byles, Delroy Wilson, and Little Roy (as half of a duo called Mark & Luke). But his production style is unmistakable, and the Upsetters' sound is one that he shaped. This collection of Jamaican hit singles was originally released in 1971, and it includes such deathless material as Junior Byles' "Place Called Africa," the Upsetters' instrumental version of "Blue Moon" (billed here as "Dark Moon"), and the title track, an instrumental version of Bob Marley & the Wailers' "Small Axe." The two Delroy Wilson songs, "I'm Yours" and "Cool Operator," are also excellent. Highly recommended. *—Rick Anderson*

★ **The Best of Studio One, Vol. 1** / Heartbeat ✦✦✦✦✦
Clement "Coxsone" Dodd ran Studio One, one of the best and most influential Jamaican recording studios in the 1960s and 1970s. From its production booth he essentially presided over the transition from rock steady to reggae, and artists as famous as Bob Marley, Burning Spear, and Dennis Brown recorded some of their earliest work under his supervision. This excellent collection of singles makes a solid case for Dodd's primacy among reggae producers of the period: "Melody Life" by Marcia Griffiths and "Party Time" by the Heptones remain two of the reggae's most loved standards; other highlights on this album include Larry Marshall's immortal "Throw Me Corn," "Row Fisherman Row" by the Wailing Souls (presented here in an extended version), and Dennis Brown's excellent version of "Impossible." Best of all may be the Termites' slightly eerie take on the aching "My Last Love." *—Rick Anderson*

Big Blunts / 1994 / Tommy Boy ✦✦✦✦

Black Foundation in Dub / Mar. 21, 1995 / Heartbeat ✦✦✦
All of these tracks were originally produced by Jack Ruby for Burning Spear, Justin Hinds & the Dominoes, the Heptones, and other groups. This disc is compilation of dub versions of the tunes, the dubs mixed by Errol Thompson, King Tubby, Sylvan Morris, and Chris Wilson. Now, it would be nice if there was any indication in the liner notes as to who did the original version that provided the base track for each selection, who did the dub mix of each track, and when the dub mixes (and for that matter the original tracks) were done. There are none such things, nor even any liner notes giving a general indication of the date range and where, if anywhere, this stuff originally appeared. Yes, that's not an uncommon situation in reggae

reissues (assuming this *is* a reissue of vintage material), but gosh darn it that doesn't make it right, does it— The best guess on the part of such uninformed chumps, then, is that the base tracks were done in the 1970s, and the dub mixes done relatively shortly afterward. As for the music, it's decent but not mind-blowing dub, retaining some of the lead and harmony vocals, and going rather mild on the effects relative to how radically dub remixes can reinvent the material in many cases. It's solid 1970s reggae with a dub spin, the most famous original track being Burning Spear's "Slavery Days." Who did that dub— Can't tell ya. —*Richie Unterberger*

Burning Up / Dec. 5, 1995 / Trojan ✦✦✦✦✦
Spanning a period from the late '60s to the early '80s, this Trojan compilation makes for a fine introduction to reggae's golden years. It's also filled with enough obscure material to appeal to even the most involved fan. The emphasis in the mix is not so much on dense, Rasta-themed cuts as it's on buoyant, dancehall-flavored material. Bubbly standouts include Delroy Wilson's "We're Gonna Work It Out" and Janet Kay's very agreeable cover of the Minnie Ripperton hit "Lovin' You." More secular nuggets come from a star-studded cast comprised of Don Carlos, Gregory Isaacs, Barrington Levy, Alton Ellis, the Heptones, and Pat Kelly. Special mention should also be made of Tony Jay's original version of "Telephone Line" and Dennis Brown's very soulful cover of "Black Magic Woman." On the more cultural-minded front, there's fine tracks like the Mighty Maytones' "Madness" and Little Roy's "Touch Not My Locks." Top things off with contributions from the seldom heard Fred Locks and the Morwells, and *Burning Up* qualifies as a very good bet for reggae lovers. —*Stephen Cook*

- **Celebration: 25 Years of Trojan Records** / 1992 / Trojan ✦✦✦✦✦
- **Clancy Eccles Presents His Reggae Revue** / 1990 / Heartbeat ✦✦✦✦✦

Dance All Night / Trojan ✦✦✦✦✦
Bringing together some quality rocksteady singles, Trojan's *Dance All Night* features a wealth of Jamaica's in-the-pocket grooves from 1966-1968. Although the liner notes don't list any credits, these 16 cuts probably come from a variety of producers, including Duke Reid, Clement Dodd, Joe Gibbs, and others, and Tommy McCook's Supersonics and the Studio One house band the Soul Vendors (with Roland Alphonso and Jackie Mittoo) more than likely provide the backing. While a few recognizable numbers like Justin Hinds and the Dominoes' "Save a Bread" are included, the cream of this collection comes from its many rare sides: among them, excellent vocal numbers like the Federals' trio harmony side "Shocking Love," Noel Brown's minor-mood solo spot "Heartbreak Girl," and Clancy (Eccles) and Cynthia's duet "Two of a Kind." More fine harmonies are provided by unsung groups like the Natives, the Federals, and the Tartans, while the Rulers' rude-boy cut "Wrong Emboyo" (covered by the Clash on their *London Calling* album) and Alfred Brown's version of John Lee Hooker's "One Scotch, One Bourbon, One Beer" provide some nice variety. And there's the added collector's bonus of "Silent River" by the Gaylets, one of the very few female vocal trios from the rocksteady era. So, turn down the lights, get in the mood, and don't be rude—this is top rocksteady for dancers and pundits alike. —*Stephen Cook*

Dancehall 101, Vol. 2 / 2000 / VP ✦✦✦✦
The second volume in the Dancehall 101 series is a bit more consistent than the first, though both succeed overall at presenting a good overview of the Jamaican dancehall reggae scene of the 1980s and early '90s. *Volume 2 presents a higher ratio of superstars to unknowns; Johnny Osbourne* (one of the first great dancehall singers), Pinchers, Foxy Brown (who would later make a name for herself with her cover version of Tracy Chapman's "Fast Car"), Sanchez, and Beres Hammond all put in appearances, though the album's best track may be by its most obscure artist, El General, who delivers an exquisite piece of Spanish toasting on "Pun Tun Tun." Other highlights include the great singer-DJ combo track "Love Him Haffi Get" by Beres Hammond and Cutty Ranks, and Sister Nancy's ruling take on the very popular "Bam Bam" rhythm. (Both volumes of Dancehall 101 include a bonus disc on which the album's tracks are mixed in live dancehall style: Volume 1 is mixed by the Adonai sound, Volume 2 by Road International.) —*Rick Anderson*

Duke Reid's Treasure Chest / 1992 / Heartbeat ✦✦✦✦✦
In addition to spotlighting the career of one of Jamaica's most productive and illustrious producers, Duke Reid's *Treasure Chest* is also a great overview of the rocksteady period of the mid-to-late '60s. Using trumpet star Tommy McCook and the Supersonics as his house band, Duke Reid recorded everything from vocal numbers, to instrumentals, to DJ pieces at his Treasure Isle Studios, and in the process he scored numerous hits which all bore his polished, heavy, drum'n'bass sound. The first of the two discs here features vocal numbers and reflects the prevalent influence of stateside soul artists such as the Impressions, Sam Cooke, and Smokey Robinson on Jamaican music. The connection gets explicit with Impressions covers by Alton Ellis ("La La Means I Love You") and the Techniques ("Queen Majesty") as well as the Silvertone's straight cover and U-Roy's treatment of Wilson Pickett's "In the Midnight Hour." Other highlights include harmony numbers by the Sensations and Melodians, Alton Ellis and Lloyd William's Sam and Dave workout on "I Can't Stand It," and Dobby Daubson's early lover's rock gem "Loving Pauper." The second disc fans out from the rocksteady/soul sound with Justin Hind and the Dominoes' outlaw ska classic "No Good Rudie," Winston Wright's early dub number "Holiday Version," and Ernest Ranglin and Tommy McCook's incredible ska instrumental "Ranglin' on Bond Street." Fortunately there are also more strong vocal numbers like Alton Ellis' "Girl I've Got a Date" and Phyliss Dillon's cover of "Perfidia." Whether it's the incredible roster of artists, distinct production values, or just the fact that the songs were staples at Kingston parties of the time, Duke Reid's *Treasure Chest* provides one of the best documents of Jamaica's golden rocksteady era. —*Stephen Cook*

Go Ska Go / Oct. 17, 1995 / Heartbeat ✦✦✦✦✦

- **In the Red Zone: The Essential Collection of Classic Dub** / Sep. 16, 1997 / Shanachie ✦✦✦✦✦

The single-disc, 14-track dub compilation *In the Red Zone: The Essential Collection of Classic Dub* makes for the perfect introduction to the genre, featuring classic cuts from the biggest names in dub: Augustus Pablo (the legendary "King Tubby Meets the Rockers Uptown"), Lee "Scratch" Perry, King Tubby, Prince Far I, Scientist, the Mad Professor, and Black Uhuru, plus slightly less well-known but equally talented artists like Keith Hudson, Yabby You, Tappa Zukie, and the Rockers Almighty. Further enhancing the package's value as an introductory sampler, the brief yet informative liner notes list the original albums from which all tracks were taken, providing starting points for deeper exploration. One could quibble that artists aren't always represented by signature cuts, and that there's much more necessary listening than what's included here, but *In the Red Zone* doesn't aim to be a definitive overview of dub; rather, it's one of the best introductory dub samplers yet assembled. It's everything a beginner could ask for, and even already-converted aficionados will likely be pleased with the uniform strength of the material, although some may long for a more thorough retrospective with more detailed annotation. —*Steve Huey*

Joe Gibbs Mood: The Amalgamated Label, 1968-1971 / Apr. 22, 1998 / Trojan ✦✦✦✦✦
Between 1968-1971, Jamaican producer Joe Gibbs released over 150 rocksteady and early reggae sides on his Amalgamated label. The 26 tracks collected on *Joe Gibbs Mood* might only skim the surface, but the selections are all top-notch and provide a very good introduction to Gibbs' work. Like many of his contemporaries, Gibbs deserves credit more for his excellent taste in musicians, singers, engineers (Erroll Thompson), and, of course, producers, than for his actual contributions behind the board (Lee Perry and later Winston "Niney" Holness oversaw most of the recordings). The fruits heard on this Trojan release represent the typical stylistic gamut of Gibbs' releases, ranging from a soulful vocal cut by Nicky Thomas ("Danzella") to the stratospheric musings of Jamaican DJ innovator Count Matchuki ("It Is I [Count Matchiki's Cooking]"). Along with three fine Pioneer cuts, including a nice cover of the Don Gibson hit "Sweet Dreams," there are plenty of vocal harmony tracks by the Royals, the Slickers, and the Reggay Boys. Other highlights include the Lee Perry vocal "Thank You," the Soul Sisters' salacious "Wreck a Buddy," singer Errol Dunkley's sly, minor-mood cut "The Scorcher," and the album's many fine instrumentals, in particular the Cobbs' tasty, Jamaican jazz cut "One Love." Drummer Aston "Family Man" Barrett and bassist Carlton Barrett, anchor the excellent band of Jamaican studio luminaries, including organist Glen Adams, trumpeter Dizzy Moore, and tenor saxophonist Carl "Cannonball" Bryan. For lovers of rocksteady and early reggae, it doesn't get much better than this fine collection of tracks from the Joe Gibbs catalog. —*Stephen Cook*

Kings and Queens of Rocksteady / Feb. 8, 2000 / Music Club ✦✦✦✦✦
On this decent compilation of vintage rock steady music, no dates are given for the tracks, as is the custom on reggae reissues. It's obvious, though, that most or all of these date from about 1966-70, and it's known that all were recorded by Duke Reid at Treasure Isle. Kicking off the disc is perhaps the best-known rocksteady classic of all, the Paragons' "The Tide Is High" (covered for a *1 hit by Blondie*), which has been reissued elsewhere, but certainly can't be faulted as an inclusion. The emphasis is on harmonizing groups, including the Melodians, the Jamaicans, the Ethiopians, and the Sensations, but there are also outstanding solo vocals from Alton Ellis and Phyllis Dillon, as well as an instrumental from Tommy McCook. Overall, it's reggae music at its most likable, the tempos dreamy but not sluggish, the melodies soul-influenced, and the harmonies often sumptuous. Other than "The Tide Is High," the best cut is Phyllis Dillon's "Perfidia," a great illustration of how to make a pre-rock pop standard a seductive rock steady cut. For a portent of future directions in reggae, there's an early cut by U Roy ("Everybody Bawling"), whom Reid produced rhyming over old rock steady backing tracks. —*Richie Unterberger*

Kingston Town: 18 Reggae Hits / Apr. 1, 1993 / Heartbeat ✦✦✦✦
Another of Heartbeat's fine compilations of classic reggae singles, this one consisting of songs produced by Clancy Eccles. Most titles and artists will be unfamiliar to all but the most devoted reggae fans—don't feel dumb if the names Tito Simon and Eric "Monty" Morris mean nothing to you—but the King Stitt instrumental "Vigorton Two" is an undeniable classic, as is Lord Creator's sweetly melancholy "Kingston Town" (covered in the late 1980s by UB40). Obscurities include Lee Perry's charmingly atonal "I Was Meant for You," "I Don't Care" by the Dingle Brothers, and the stirring "Come Together" by an American singer named Exuma. Heartbeat's production team has shown its usual loving care in remastering these tracks from the original master tapes, but it's not enough to overcome the limited quality of those original sources, and some tracks are sonically cleaner than others. The album is solid and enjoyable overall, however. —*Rick Anderson*

Love All Nite: 15 Lovers Rock Grooves / Apr. 20, 1999 / Music Club ✦✦✦✦
The reggae subgenre known as "lovers rock" came into existence in England in the late 1970s, in part as a reaction to the heavy political and religious messages that had come to dominate the music by that point. By focusing on lighter, more romantic themes, lovers rock actually returned reggae to its roots-in its earlier incarnations as ska and rock steady, Rastafarianism and politics had been largely absent. This compilation mines the vaults of Fashion Records, one of the best and most influential British reggae labels. American fans, whose exposure to lovers rock has probably been mainly limited to the work of Mad Professor on his Ariwa label, may not recognize names like Barry Boom, Vivian Jones and Neville Morrison. But those who can appreciate the romantic potential of the reggae groove will be sure to respond to the super-smooth horn lines, sweet harmonies and swooning lyrical sentiments that are present here in every track. Highlights include Nerious Joseph's "Guidance," Philip Leo's "I Want to Be Loved" and the ska-inflected "Rebel Woman" by Vivian Jones. —*Rick Anderson*

☆ **Mojo Rock Steady** / 1994 / Heartbeat ✦✦✦✦✦
Jamaican music fans still fondly remember the rock steady era, particularly those who love soulful, evocative ballads and romantic tunes. This 16-cut anthology culled from Coxsone Dodd's seminal Studio One vaults includes magnificent group numbers by The Clarendonians, Gaylads, Bassies and Minstrels, plus equally impressive solo outings from Hugh Godfrey, Denise Darlington and Hortense Ellis. There are also strong instrumentals by Roland Alphonso and the Soul Brothers and King Stitt, and Alton Ellis demonstrates his classic soul approach on "Whipping The Prince," aided by The Soul Vendors. Sublime, gorgeous singing from a prime period in Jamaica's rich musical history. —*Ron Wynn*

More Hottest Hits / May 28, 1994 / Heartbeat ✦✦✦✦✦
As a follow up to its incredible *Treasure Chest* collection, the Heartbeat label has put out this

second batch of Duke Reid produced rocksteady and early reggae tracks. While not as representative as the prior two-disc set, this new release does contain a solid selection of solo and harmony vocal numbers. Well-known cuts like the Paragons' "On the Beach" and the Jamaicans' "Dedicated to You" are included along with fine marginalia such as the early Gladiators number "Live Wire," Leroy and Junior's cover of the Stylistics hit "Break Up to Make Up," and an intriguing studio conversation between Reid and U-Roy. And in addition to U-Roy's DJ send-up of the Melodians' "Rock Away," organist Winston Wright's mod instrumental "Tonight" and Dave Barker's James Brown-inspired workout "Funky Funky Reggae" complement the collection's many smooth vocal cuts. Also worth mentioning are strong performances by Paragon singer Tyrone Evans, future roots reggae star Freddie McKay, and the lovely and underrated Phyllis Dillon. With superb sound (Heartbeat gets all its material from original master tapes) and faultless track selection, *More Hottest Hits* qualifies as an essential disc for lovers of rocksteady and early reggae. *—Stephen Cook*

Original Labour of Love Collection: 25 Trojan Reggae Classics / Jan. 25, 2000 / Trojan ♦♦♦♦
The title of The Original Labour of Love Collection: 25 Trojan Reggae Classics might lead reggae fans familiar with UB40's all-covers *Labour of Love* albums to believe that this set collects similar material. While it does contain versions of Motown classics, Neil Diamond tunes, and so on, this isn't exclusively a covers compilation; the "labour of love" in the title simply refers to the label's work in releasing ska, rock-steady, and reggae records over the years. And it is a very good collection, drawing material from throughout reggae's history and making up for its sometimes incoherent stylistic juxtapositions by choosing high-quality songs. Artists present include Ken Boothe, the Melodians, Bob Marley & the Wailers, U-Roy, John Holt, Jimmy Cliff, and more. *—Steve Huey*

Ragga Essentials: In a Dancehall Style / May 23, 2000 / Hip-O ♦♦♦♦♦
This compilation collects 18 tracks, some from extremely difficult to find singles, which register highlights of the ragga sound as it has mutated from 1985 through 1997. Kicking off with Half Pint's "Greetings" whose chorus of "Greetings I bring from Jah, to all Raggamuffin" is generally accepted as giving the genre its name, the album skips around chronologically, with the sequencing following musical, not historical, guidelines. Americans will be most familiar with Apache Indian's funky, singalong "Boom Shack-A-Lak from 1990 or JC Lodge's hypnotically romantic, sweetly melodic "Telephone Love," one of the few tunes on this disc to have actually charted on *Billboard*. But as the detailed, scholarly liner notes explain, the popularity of this predominantly club music can't be effectively gauged by sales or radio play. Ragga music is also unusual in that the same backing rhythm track is often used for a variety of lead singers and toasting DJ's to add their vocals on top of. If this all sounds too confusing, suffice it to say the 14 page booklet does a wonderful job of placing the genre in perspective with a track by track explanation of the music, and detailed information on the origination of each song's basic rhythm and production. In addition to the aforementioned artists, Luciano, Buju Banton, Junior Reid and ex-Black Uhuru lead singer Mykal Rose will likely be familiar to reggae fans, but rarities from Tenor Saw, Anthony Red Rose, and Tenor Fly, none easily available on CD before now, make this anthology an indispensable first purchase for anyone interested in this fascinating and often obscure offshoot of reggae. *—Hal Horowitz*

Raw Roots, Vol. 1 / Mar. 9, 1999 / Jet ♦♦♦♦
In '70s reggae, producer/arranger Phil Pratt occupied a place comparable to that of someone like Bobby Eli in Philadelphia soul. Though Eli wasn't as famous as Gamble & Huff or Thom Bell, he had an impressive track record. Similarly, Pratt wasn't as celebrated as Lee "Scratch" Perry, but he was respected in reggae circles and attracted his share of first-class talent. *Raw Roots, Vol. 1,* which the French Jet Set label put out in 1998, spotlights Pratt's 1971-75 work with selections by artists ranging from the Heptones (one of reggae's finest vocal groups) to solo singers like Dennis Brown, Pat Kelly and John Holt, and dubwise toasters such as U-Roy, Big Youth and Dennis Alcapone. On this compilation, original versions of songs are often followed by dubwise and instrumental versions. After you hear Kelly's Impressions-like "Talk About Love," Holt's haunting "Strange Thing" or Brown's remake of Santana's "Black Magic Woman," you'll also hear what happened when someone toasted over the track and how that track sounded without any vocals at all. Because it contains so many dubs and instrumental tracks, casual listeners might find *Raw Roots* a bit too esoteric. But hardcore reggae fans will find it to be a thoughtfully assembled, pleasing survey of Pratt's classic work. *—Alex Henderson*

Reggae Around the World / Jul. 14, 1998 / Putumayo ♦♦♦♦♦
This isn't the first compilation to feature reggae musicians from around the world, but it's probably the best so far. You've got the usual suspects, including the South African superstar Lucky Dube and Majek Fashek from Nigeria, but there are little-known Sudanese, Australian and Brazilian artists as well, not to mention Peter Rowan, an American bluegrass singer whose version of "No Woman, No Cry" is nowhere near as bad as you'd have every right to expect. Lucky Dube's "We Love It" is utterly typical—a gently rolling one-drop beat and a big, emotional melody that cuts right to the catharsis. No other reggae singer has so successfully written one song over and over; good thing it's such a great song. Blekbala Mujik is an aboriginal reggae band from Australia who play in a fairly aggressive but highly refined style and sing winningly in broken English. Jamaica is represented twice, once by the unsung guitar hero Ernest Ranglin and once by Burning Spear, whose "Jordan River" seems like an awfully obvious choice. Zeca Baleiro delivers brilliant Brazilian reggae, and there are similar delights to be found all over this fine collection. No track is less than acceptable, and a few are perfect. *—Rick Anderson*

☆ **Reggae Jamaica Stylee** / Sep. 28, 1999 / Dressed to Kill ♦♦♦♦♦
Try to ignore the cheesy packaging and the even cheesier compilation title. This six-disc set, which lists at around $20, is not only a world-class bargain, but it's also one of the better surveys of roots and early dancehall reggae ever put together. Usually these super-bargain reggae box sets are filled with second-rate cover versions by unknown artists or hackwork from tour-guide darlings like Byron Lee and the Dragonaires, but on this one, the quality is surprisingly consistent. There are a few unknown mediocrities like Dreadline and the Blackstones on the 108-song program, but the vast bulk of the artists represented are top-notch: Johnny Clarke, Alton Ellis, Marcia Griffiths, the Heptones, Dennis Brown, and even criminally under-anthologized performers like George Faith and the Paragons make appearances—most of them appear five or six times. Griffiths delivers the Bunny Wailer classic "Dreamland"; John Holt does a credible version of "In the Midnight Hour"; and Bob Marley weighs in with "Soul Rebel." There are lots of reggae version of 1960s and '70s pop hits ("Unchained Melody," "Release Me," etc.), which are always lots of fun. Highly recommended. *—Rick Anderson*

Reggae Train / Jan. 16, 1996 / Heartbeat ♦♦♦♦♦
Reggae is and has always been a man's world, but although she was never quite as well known as superstar producers like Duke Reid, Coxsone Dodd and the infamous Lee Perry, Sonia Pottinger is responsible for some of the finest rock-steady and reggae recordings to come from Jamaica during the early '70s. The revolving stable of talent at her High-Tone label included, at various times, such top-flight performers as Ken Boothe, Culture, Marcia Griffiths, and Justin Hinds and the Dominoes, but her secret weapon was engineer Errol Brown, who helped pioneer the use of eight-track recording techniques in the Jamaican studios and learned quickly how to put that technology to maximum use. This collection starts out with an extra-long mix of Culture's reggae adaptation of "This Train Is Bound for Glory," which sets a high standard for the rest of the album. The other artists rarely, if ever, fail to reach that standard: Marcia Griffith's "Dreamland" is a pure classic, and is followed by a Bojangles deejay version that almost does justice to the original. The Chantells' "How Can I Get Over" is so poignantly lovely that the listener is left amazed that that band didn't have greater success and frustrated that there isn't a more extensive record of their work. Delroy Denton's "Sufferer's Choice" is another classic, this one in the "woe-is-me" tradition that was so popular at the time. The sound is excellent, and there are really no duds on the whole album. *—Rick Anderson*

Respect to Studio One / 1994 / Heartbeat ♦♦♦♦♦
This is really more of a label sampler than a thematic compilation, as all of the 33 tracks have appeared on Heartbeat releases. What is for sure is that all of the rock-steady, ska, and dancehall numbers were recorded at the legendary Studio One recording studio, with the equally legendary Coxsone Dodd producing. There's little in the way of liner notes, and nothing in the way of dates (even as approximations); that could, after all, be setting a dangerous precedent in the hazy world of reggae reisues, where mysterious vagueness about the source material seems to be a prerequisite of sorts in order to gain official re-release. One could reasonably deduce that much of this is from the '60s and early '70s, and it's very tasty stuff indeed, both by major players (Lee Perry, Alton Ellis, The Skatalites, Marcia Griffiths, Sugar Minott, the Heptones, Burning Spear, Horace Andy, Don Drummond) and minor/unknown ones (Jackie Mittoo, the Termites, Ken Boothe, the Cables). Major reggae fans will most likely prefer to find most or all of the Heartbeat releases from which these tracks were plucked. But for those who want a big portion of relatively unknown vintage reggae, and are not concerned with building a comprehensive library, this is a solid investment. *—Richie Unterberger*

● **Revolutionary Sounds: The Essential Collection of Classic Roots Reggae, 1973-1981** / Aug. 18, 1998 / Shanachie ♦♦♦♦♦
Specially priced box sets of golden-era reggae are always hard to resist, and this one is no exception. It contains four discs previously released by Shanachie, all in their original configurations: By the Rivers of Babylon: Timeless Rasta Hymns (a great collection of strictly religious material), *The Power of the Trinity: Great Reggae Harmony* (which focuses on vocal trios like the Mighty Diamonds and Israel Vibration), Revolutionary Sounds: Essential Rockers Reggae (a compilation of reggae songs in a sociopolitical vein) and a dub collection entitled *In the Red Zone: Ultimate Dub Classics.* All four discs are excellent, and although any serious reggae fan will already own some of the material, this box is a worthwhile purchase for anyone who wants an extended overview of reggae's classic period. Particular highlights include the Joe Higgs classic "Blackman Know Yourself," Black Uhuru's take on "Natural Mystic" and almost every track on the dub compilation. *—Rick Anderson*

Roots of Reggae, Vol. 1: Ska / Aug. 20, 1996 / Rhino ♦♦♦♦♦
The small print inside reveals that "due to licensing restrictions, this collection does not include selections controlled by Island Records or Coxsone/Studio One." Hmm... when you're assembling a ska collection that makes any pretensions toward being definitive, that's more than a minor problem. On the other hand, it also means that Rhino, by necessity, plumbed for 17 early ska cuts (from 1959-67) that aren't overexposed on other compilations. It's pretty heavy on the Prince Buster (who's involved with half a dozen of the selections), but on the whole it's a pretty solid mix of prime ska, mixing some well-known names (Laurel Aitken, Joe Higgs) with ones that may not even be familiar to big reggae fans (Carlos Malcolm, Stranger Cole). The 1959 tracks by Aitken and Derrick Morgan are among the very earliest ska or reggae precursors ever recorded; Prince Buster's 1962 single "Madness" gave the 2-Tone band their name; and the Ska Kings' "Oil in My Lamp" is ska at its most R&B-influenced. One of the most interesting cuts is the most unusual: Bunny & Skitter's "Chubby" (from 1961) has backing by the Rastafarian percussive group Count Ossie & His Wareikas, and according to reggae scholar Roger Steffens' liner notes, is the first time that Rastafarian music could be heard with a pop lyric. *—Richie Unterberger*

Roots of Reggae, Vol. 2: Rock Steady / Aug. 20, 1996 / Rhino ♦♦♦♦♦
Like volume one of the *Roots of Reggae* series, cuts from the Island and Coxsone/Studio One companies were unavailable for licensing reasons. But unless you already have a deep reggae collection, the quality of the material is such that you wouldn't suspect that the pool was limited. It's a very good cross-section of the slow and soulful rocksteady sound as it was heard from 1966 to 1970, again mixing famous names (Tommy McCook, the Melodians, Prince Buster, Alton Ellis) with ones that will be unfamiliar to most listeners (Hopeton Lewis, Honey Boy Martin, Keith & Tex, Ken Boothe, the Gaylettes). The rhythms are slow and sexy, the vocals and harmonies are often gorgeous; this is reggae at its most emotional and romantic. All of the selections were big Jamaican hits, with the exception of Tommy McCook's "Soul Style,"

twhich was previously unreleased. The most famous song (and deservedly so) is the Paragons' "Tide Is High," taken to the top of the charts over a decade later via Blondie's cover version. *—Richie Unterberger*

Run Rhythm Run / 1996 / Heartbeat ✦✦✦✦✦
Vintage reggae reissues are notorious for a lack of concrete information in the liner notes, but this is even skimpier than most. All that's known is that these rock-steady instrumentals were produced by Duke Reid during the 1960s at Treasure Isle, and that the musicians included Tommy McCook & the Supersonics and the Duke Reid Group. That means that although this is a various artists compilation, there are no actual "groups" credited with the individual tracks; it's almost as if they were "found" riddim tracks. A little mystique isn't always a bad thing, though. What's important is that this is very good instrumental rock-steady, with lots of neat organ licks, squeaky violin, throbbing beats, and the occasional gripping guitar line. The more soul-inspired cuts sound something like a Jamaica-fied Booker T. & the M.G.s. Despite the anonymity of the actual contributions, it's one of the better rock-steady compilations floating around, with decent sound considering the standards of the era. *—Richie Unterberger*

Sir Lee's Rock Steady Party, Vol. 1: At Buckingham Palace / Mar. 15, 2000 / Jamaican Gold ✦✦✦✦✦
One of three excellent Bunny Lee collections from the Dutch label Jamaican Gold, Sir Lee's Rock Steady Party, Vol. 1: At Buckingham Palace includes the kind of infectious mix of vocal and instrumental rocksteady that brought the producer initial success during 1967-1968. Over the 20 tracks here, the famed Jamaican bands Lynn Taitt & the Jets and Bobby Aitken & the Carib Beats lay down Lee's signature mix of buoyant rhythm tracks and lithe guitar and horn parts. Selections include soulful vocal cuts by Roy Shirley, Ken Parker, Glen Adams, and Alva Lewis, whose "Revelation" represents a rare vocal outing for the session guitarist and is one of the highlights of the collection. Other standout tracks include the Uniques' (featuring Slim Smith and Roy Shirley) "Lesson of Love" and their rendition of the Curtis Mayfield and the Impressions' hit "Gypsy Woman." Fine Jamaican jazz instrumentals by saxophonists Val Bennett and Lester Sterling round out the set. Unlike a good number of ska and rocksteady releases, the majority of tracks here and on most of the Jamaican Gold releases are from original master tapes, making for a very clean and full sound mix. Along with Trojan's excellent Lee collection Jumping With Mr. Lee, Sir Lee's Rock Steady Party, Vol. 1: At Buckingham Palace makes for essential rocksteady listening. *—Stephen Cook*

★ **Ska Bonanza: The Studio One Ska Years** / 1991 / Heartbeat ✦✦✦✦✦
41-song, double-CD compilation of '60s ska, produced by Clement S. Dodd, largely (if not totally; the documentation is vague) at Studio One. Most of the big names of ska's vintage era are represented: Bob Marley & the Wailers, the Skatalites, Lee Perry, Don Drummond, Toots & the Maytals, Alton Ellis. Considering that ska's sometimes thought of as a homogenous style, the range of actual sounds and variants is impressive. There's New Orleans R&B-derivations, doo-wop-influenced ska, Motownish uptempo struts, soulful slower tunes, and instrumentals. The cuts by the unknowns include pleasurable surprises that match or exceed the ones by the stars; Frank Anderson's tropical instrumental "Wheel And Turn," for instance, or the goofy modern doo-wop jive of Chuck Josephs' "Du Du Wap." It isn't necessarily the best ska compilation that could have been concocted; Scandal Ska, to name just one, is on the whole a more exciting anthology. It is, however, one of the best of the relatively few available, and thus for the time being merits the highest rating. It's since been divided into two separate compilations, Streets of Ska and Go Ska Go. But get the original two-disc version if you can, as it's more convenient to have all the tracks and liner notes in one place. *—Richie Unterberger*

Ska-ntastic: Vintage Jamaican Ska 1963-66 / Nov. 23, 1999 / Richmond ✦✦✦✦
Ska-ntastic: Vintage Jamaican Ska 1963-66 is a terrific compilation of classic rock-steady ska from the mid-'60s. It includes better-known artists such as the Skatalites (with six songs, including "Love in the Afternoon" and the band's take on Duke Ellington's "Caravan" entitled "Ska-Ra-Van"); vocalist Jackie Opel (with the soulful "Pictures of Smoke") and trumpeter Baba Brooks (here with the Trenton Spence Orchestra on "Five O'Clock Whistle"); and virtually unknown but strong performing groups like the Jetts ("Someone"), Bibby and the Astronauts ("Please Beverley", and the Angelic Brothers ("Ten Virgins"). The sound quality is not the clearest, but there is no hiss, and the slight muddiness resulting from the age of the tapes does not detract from this excellent music. *—Joslyn Layne*

Soca Xplosion '99 / 1999 / Jamdown ✦✦✦✦
For those who think all reggae sounds the same, soca offers a sobering contrast: compared to soca, reggae is a kaleidoscope of rhythmic diversity. That's not to say that there's anything the matter with soca; it's just that most listeners might not be able to handle more than a few tracks at a time. The basic rhythm is a bit like house music, with a steady one-two-three-four pulse in the bass drum, but its distinctive feature is an accent on the "and" of the second beat, a highly unusual syncopation that makes you start to wiggle and twitch almost against your will. This fine collection of modern soca avoids tedium by varying the tempo and mood—for every two or three up-tempo ravers like "Whip Wine" by Super Fabulous or Ghetto Flex's "De Official Bum Bum Song," there's a midtempo offering like "Jamaican Lover" by Tanya Stephens and Ghetto Flex or the lovely "Harmony" by H2O Phlo. That last one draws heavily on the calypso vocal tradition; since "soca" comes from the term "soul-calypso," that's no big surprise. Overall, this disc makes a fine overview of the modern soca scene (not to mention a great party record). *—Rick Anderson*

Solid Gold from the Vaults, Vol. 1 / 1983 / Trojan ✦✦✦✦✦
This is a fine first installment to Trojan's "showcase (of) rare classic singles of the golden era of Jamaican music, from the sixties to the early seventies." Selected by London DJ Sir Tropical Downbeat, the set features version numbers as well as rock steady vocals and instrumentals. Dave Barker's treble-heavy, yelping DJ exclamations on "Shocks 71" start things off in an uproarious manner, with Winston Williams following suit on "DJ's Choice" and "People's Choice." Stratospheric organ solos and dark trombone rumblings figure prominently on instrumentals like Herman's "New Love" and the Rhythm Ruler's "Proud Feeling," while the Bleechers lay down some airy harmonies on "Ease Up." Hints of reggae show up on Stranger Cole's "Help Wanted" and Carl Bryan's "Red Ash." The sound is a bit rough, but that's what one would expect with a collection of rare sides. Of great appeal for the fan of the early years of Jamaican music, but probably not a good call for anyone new to the music. *—Stephen Cook*

Sound of Channel One: The King Tubby Connection / Aug. 3, 1999 / Triple X ✦✦✦✦✦
This two-disc set could almost be marketed as a roots reggae textbook, with its program of excellent examples of both secular and religious reggae recorded at the legendary Channel One studio by two of the finest engineers in reggae history (JoJo Hookim and Phillip Smart) under the direction of reggae's greatest producer (King Tubby), who also provides dub versions of all tracks. Although not all of the singers are big names—reggae fans will know Delroy Wilson and Larry Marshall, but few are likely to have heard of either Prince Pompidou or Badoo—the quality of the music itself is remarkably consistent. Prince Pompidou's "70 Times 7" is a classic of didactic deejay Rastafarianism, Calvin Stuart delivers the equally stern "Babylon a Turn Dem Back" and Desmond Irie contributes the very dread "Babylon You Must Go Down." The big names keep things a bit more secular: Wilson does trademark love songs like "You Have My Heart" and "Stop Look What You're Doin'" and Marshall performs "Nanny Goat." Although it's Wilson and Marshall that contribute the best singing (Stuart's is especially weak), not even amateurish vocals can drag down these powerful grooves. Highly recommended. *—Rick Anderson*

★ **The Story of Jamaican Music: Tougher Than Tough** / Mango ✦✦✦✦✦
Island Records was the Jamaican music lifeline for curious Americans in the 1960s, bringing us the music of Bob Marley and the Wailers, Toots and the Maytals, Justin Hines, Gregory Isaacs. This marvelous anthology's four discs are chronologically arranged, with the first covering the amalgam of American genres that were absorbed into Jamaican culture: bebop and swing, New Orleans R&B, Chicago and Memphis soul, country, and film soundtracks. The second volume cements reggae's emergence as an evocative love music and voice of the nationalistic/militant Rasta generation. Volumes three and four chronicle reggae's final maturation into a hit form and shows the inevitable production uniformities that arise when any style must produce hits for a large audience. This does not claim to be the definitive reggae anthology, so take it for what it is—Island's portrait of reggae's beginnings, growth, and flowering into a prime international style. *—Ron Wynn*

Studio One Showcase, Vol. 1 / Feb. 2, 1999 / Heartbeat ✦✦✦✦✦
About an hour's worth of 12-inch mixes of popular reggae songs, done (apparently—there are only a few sentences' worth of liner notes) in the 1970s. These are cuts by artists of moderate renown (the Heptones, Alton Ellis) or more obscure reputation (the Bassies, the Tonettes), extended or changed via dub effects and editing into tracks lasting from five to eight minutes. It's probably of equal appeal whether you're more interested in vintage vocal reggae or early dub and dance mix sounds. Because they're constructed around vocal cuts, though, they'll hold the attention of fans who like *songs* better than dub or dance-mix reggae will. The tunes are lilting and soulful, particularly those by the Heptones. The 1999 CD release has three bonus tracks of mixes of cuts by the Tonettes, Cornel Campbell and Johnnie Osbourne not on the original LP. *—Richie Unterberger*

This Is Ska: 16 Original Ska Classics / May 20, 1997 / Music Club ✦✦✦✦✦
Old-school ska compilations are appearing on all sides in the wake of huge hits by groups like No Doubt and the Mighty Mighty Bosstones. And that's a good thing; albums like this one can act as a necessary corrective to those who think that ska is a post-punk innovation. *This Is Ska* features a nice blend of hands-down classics-such genre-defining tracks as Desmond Dekker's "007 (Shanty Town)" and the Pioneers' "Longshot Kick de Bucket," for example—and songs that will be familiar to aficionados but probably not to those who are more casually acquainted with the music, such as Dave and Ansel Collins' "Double Barrel" or Derrick & Patsy's "Housewife's Choice." There's even a ska version of "Watermelon Man." If the 43-minute playing time strikes you as a little skimpy, bear in mind that these Music Club discs retail at $10.98. It's a steal, and this is definitely one of the better introductions to the wonderful world of classic ska that you're likely to find anywhere. *—Rick Anderson*

Tougher Than Tough: Rude Boy Ska Rock Steady & Reggae / Jan. 1, 1992 / Trojan ✦✦✦✦✦
The title of this compilation makes clear that the rude boy phenomenon influenced many Jamaican music styles, of course peaking with Jimmy Cliff's 1973 soundtrack to The Harder They Come, biopic of original rude boy and fugitive Vincent "Ivanhoe" Martin. Some of the tracks within demonstrate Jamaican musicians' respect for the island's criminal set: Desmond Dekker & the Aces immortalize rudies on the easy-swinging ska vehicle "Rudy Got Soul," and Honey Boy Martin defers to the ruthless outlaws on "Dreader Than Dread." The majority of acts represented here, though, point a collective finger at the gangster fringe: reform is recommended by Dandy on "Rudy A Message to You," while Derrick Morgan takes things to trial on "Court Dismiss"—Morgan seems to split the difference of opinion, in fact, with his contrasting praise on "Tougher Than Tough." Whether pro or con, the 18 high-quality selections here offer up a fine overview of the rich first decade of Jamaican music, including well-known songs like Desmond Dekker's "007 (Shanty Town)" and the Slicker's "Johnny Too Bad," as well as obscure gems like Boris Gardiner's organ-driven rock steady instrumental "Scarface." Another plus is the overall high-quality sound, which is not always the case with Trojan reissues. If your musical tastes run to the topical and you feel the need for a good introduction to the beginnings of reggae, then this is the disc to get. To be more democratic, the high-quality selections here make this a must for both the casual and serious fan of Jamaican music. *—Stephen Cook*

Trojan Box Set: Dub, Vol. 2 / May 23, 2000 / Trojan ✦✦✦✦✦
From the seemingly bottomless vaults of Trojan Records comes this very fine collection of dub from the '70s: reggae's classical period and the high point of dub as a producer's art form. One in a series of limited-edition box sets, this set features 50 tracks on three discs at three-for-two pricing with attractive, no-frills packaging. The bands featured include such eminencies as the Upsetters, Soul Syndicate, the Aggrovators, and the Revolutionaries, all of them at various times the house bands for the best studios in Jamaica. The producers re-

sponsible for the dub mixes presented here are primarily the grand masters of the genre: King Tubby, Scientist, Prince Jammy, and Lee "Scratch" Perry. Highlight tracks include the seriously twisted "Casanova Dub" (by the Observer All Stars), "Strictly Dub" (one of many versions of Rupie Edwards' hugely popular "Everyday Wandering" rhythm), and King Tubby's bracingly minimalist "Dancing Version." If you only feel you need one dub collection, this one should be it. *—Rick Anderson*

☆ **Trojan Box Set: Rock Steady** / May 11, 1999 / Trojan ♦♦♦♦♦
This 50-song, three-CD set is about as good as it gets as a compilation. The box delights, teases, and fascinates from its opening number, "Rock Steady" by Alton Ellis—practically the first record ever to use that term. Ellis and well-known acts like Desmond Dekker, the Maytals, the Paragons, Justin Hinds & the Dominoes, and the Melodians share space with lesser-known acts such as the Versatiles, the Federals, Derrick Harriott, and the Uniques. The majority of the acts emphasize vocals, and a great degree of soulful lyricism, whereas the Maytals display a sound and a quality of musicianship closer in content and spirit to the best folk-rock acts of the period. Not all of it is exactly groundbreaking; the pedestrian "You You" by the Natives becomes generic background music very quickly. The expected names, such as the Gaylads ("It's Hard to Confess") and Lyn Taitt & the Jets (a rare instrumental version of "To Sir With Love"), do tend to dominate the proceedings. Derrick Morgan's big rocksteady hit "Greedy Gal" isn't here, but in its place is "Conquering Ruler," another worthy showcase of his talents as a singer and songwriter. Also present is the Michael Jackson of the rocksteady boom, Errol Dunkley ("You're Gonna Need Me"), who cut a string of hits in his mid-teens. Juxtaposed with heavier numbers like "Dreader Than Dread" by Honey Boy Martin, this mix of songs is a good cross-section of this short-lived but dazzlingly creative period in Jamaican (and British) music. The sound quality is generally excellent, although a few of the tracks sound like they're not from first-generation sources. The only glaring flaw is the virtual absence of serious liner notes. *—Bruce Eder*

SOUNDTRACKS

The motion picture soundtrack as we know it today dates from the early '40s, although film music itself goes back much farther than synchronized sound. Piano and organ accompaniments were played live in theaters from the beginning of the century, and it was during 1916 that Victor Schertzinger wrote the first full orchestral and choral score for a motion picture.

During the '30s, it became customary for record companies to release official recorded versions of songs heard in musical films. Hence, much of the musical history of Fred Astaire's RKO work, in films such as *Top Hat* and *Swing Time*, was captured simultaneously on the Brunswick label (now reissued by Columbia Records). And certain orchestral scores by recognized composers, such as Arthur Bliss's music for Alexander Korda's 1936 science-fiction epic *Things to Come*, found a separate life in the concert hall.

But it wasn't until 1942 that a record company fixed on the notion of recording and releasing the major parts of a full orchestra score. The film was *The Jungle Book*, produced by Alexander Korda and scored by Miklos Rozsa. One piece of Rozsa's, the waltz from his score for the 1942 film *Lydia*, had previously been recorded on a single 78 RPM disc by RCA Records with some success. Shortly after *The Jungle Book*'s release, RCA brought Rozsa to New York to record a suite of the key movements from his new score with the NBC Symphony Orchestra, with a narration of the story provided by Sabu, the star of the film. This set of 78 RPM records, which has since been issued many times, marked the start of the movie soundtrack as a record genre.

The next major development took place in 1945, when MGM established its record label, MGM Records. The studio had originally planned to start the label in 1941, with Tommy Dorsey heading it, but the war intervened with a five-year delay. The first "musical biography" was *Till the Clouds Roll By*, inspired by the life and songs of Jerome Kern. It seemed logical to release eight of the musical highlights from the film in a set of four 78 RPM records, which was precisely what was done, with some modifications to make the songs suitable for release on record. These included the removal of lengthy instrumental breaks and sound effects that were germane to the screen presentation but not to the record.

Till the Clouds Roll By was a success, if not a raging best-seller, but it established the pattern for musical soundtracks. Its release ahead of the film secured radio play for the songs, thus promoting the film, and also made the record-buying public aware of the release of the movie in a way that print advertising alone would not have. Subsequently, with the advent of the long-playing record two years later, studios would release their musicals in reasonably complete form, either on their own labels or under contract to other record companies.

Looking at this history more than 40 years later, one must bear in mind just how important the soundtrack album was to the public. In the days before home video (and the boom in movie memorabilia shops), the soundtrack album was the only piece of a movie a fan could actually own, take home, and enjoy at will, without having to depend on the movie studio or the local theater or, in later years, the television station. Additionally, the early soundtrack albums appeared in the era of radio, before the visual medium completely overwhelmed popular culture, and their impact and importance were that much greater at the time.

For the film studios, the soundtrack album (whether devoted to dramatic film scores or musicals) became a major marketing tool, promoting the film by its release weeks ahead of the opening date, securing radio play for the major songs, and promoting the studio's own music-publishing interests. This often led to peculiarities in song and musical lineups. Most movie musical albums, for example, failed to include dance numbers, incidental music, and choral pieces, since these were not hooked to specific singing personalities. Additionally, the running-time restrictions on 78s and early long-playing records required the cutting of extended instrumental breaks, however pleasant.

Finally, there were the peculiarities of the music and movie businesses themselves: Frank Sinatra, who was under contract to MGM Studios for a period of five years and turned in at least one major musical performance on screen during that time (On the Town), never appeared on an MGM soundtrack album because he was under exclusive contract to Columbia Records in the '40s. However, the soundtrack album to MGM's 1956 *High Society*, featuring Sinatra, Bing Crosby, and Louis Armstrong, did appear on Capitol Records, where Sinatra was recording in the '50s.

The soundtrack business went along as an adjunct to the movie business until the '60s, when changes began occurring, most notably a splintering of the market. Swept up by the boom in pop and rock music and a decline in traditional entertainment and subjects, studios stopped making musicals (except for major, multi-million-dollar blockbusters) and began demanding a lighter touch in the scoring of their dramatic films. At the same time, two generations of listeners and fans—one that had grown up when the older films were originally in the theaters, and one that had grown up with them on television—began expressing an interest in the music that had filled their lives.

The business of reissuing soundtracks had existed, particularly where musicals were concerned, since the switch from 78s to long-playing records. But in the early '60s, various labels (most notably Capitol, Decca/London, and Warner Bros.) began commissioning new recordings that made use of the dramatic improvements that had been made in record fidelity and stereo sound. *Gone with the Wind* by Max Steiner, *Ben Hur*, *El Cid*, and *King of Kings* by Miklos Rozsa, and the *Adventures of Robin Hood* by Erich Wolfgang Korngold were just a few of the scores represented in new recordings, often done under the supervision of their original composers.

By the beginning of the '70s, with the recognition of film's cultural importance (it even became a field of academic study), re-recordings had become common. Producers Peter Munves and George Korngold and conductor Charles Gerhardt brought the first successful extended series of such efforts to RCA Records in the form of the *Classic Film Scores* series, with each volume devoted to a specific composer (e.g., *The Classic Film Scores of Alfred Newman*). The Gerhardt series was ideal for the serious listener and the novice just getting started.

Careful attention was paid to the details and nuances of the music itself, and the material was assembled in suites of easily absorbed length.

Meanwhile, on a more intensive level, Elmer Bernstein (himself a major movie composer) had begun a concerted effort to preserve scores and secure rights for the original composers and their estates. As an adjunct to this effort, he made a monumental series of re-recordings in England of vintage film scores in their entirety, through his Film Music Society label.

The '70s and '80s saw a veritable explosion in the field of film music, as a second generation of major screen composers—Elmer Bernstein, Jerry Goldsmith, Leonard Rosenman, Ennio Morricone (whose music for the Clint Eastwood/Sergio Leone "man with no name" Westerns virtually revolutionized that genre)—achieved wide recognition and major composer status. Along with new soundtrack albums, which now seem to accompany virtually every film release, even of the lowest-budgeted picture, re-recordings became still more common using various European orchestras, which work under far less restrictive union rules and for far less money than their American counterparts.

The '80s also saw the establishment of a new kind of soundtrack album, which actually had its roots in the '70s: the rock & roll soundtrack. Films built around rock groups and personalities had been common from the '50s onward (most notably the relatively well-made early films showing the young, lean Elvis Presley; the early British films of Cliff Richard and the Shadows; and the one great work in the genre, the Beatles in *A Hard Day's Night*), but the '70s saw the emergence of the rock soundtrack as a separate screen entity. It began with George Lucas's *American Graffiti*, the soundtrack which, filled with a superbly selected body of rock oldies, was nearly as prominent in the film as any of the actors. The accompanying double album also became a massive seller.

Francis Ford Coppola's *Apocalypse Now*, with its use of '60s hits, moved the formula up a decade and a notch in dramatic intensity, even if its most famous scene involved Wagner's "Ride of the Valkyries" and a helicopter attack. But it was *Fast Times at Ridgemont High*, another film about adolescent life, that brought the formula first used in *American Graffiti* into a contemporary time frame, with an enviable assembly of catchy singles and FM-style hits by contemporary rock artists. From there on, the die was cast: producers saw the path to success with otherwise flawed and conceptually weak movies was simply to license the right rock tracks, and many movies of the '80s and '90s acquired the feel of a jukebox in operation. With varying degrees of success, the specific music involved everything from post-new-wave (*I Was a Teenage Zombie*) to such vintage music-and-myth-mixing efforts as Oliver Stone's *The Doors*, where the songs structured the film and occasionally the soundtracks outperformed and outlasted the movies themselves. —*Bruce Eder*

Artist Reviews

John Barry (Jonathan Barry Prendergrast)

b. Nov. 3, 1933, York, England

Conductor, Composer / Spy Music, Original Score, Film Music, Soundtracks, Pop, Cool

John Barry is one of the best known composers of soundtrack music of the late twentieth and early twenty-first centuries, but his career has carried him through a multitude of music genres and styles. He is best known in film in connection with his work on the James Bond pictures, but Barry is also the holder of five Academy Awards, none of them for the Bond movies. Additionally, from 1957 until the early '60s, as leader of the John Barry Seven, Barry was one of the best known figures in popular music and early rock 'n roll in England.

Born in York, England on Nov. 3, 1933, Barry grew up around his father's movie theater business. After a short stint in the Army, Barry started his own band, John Barry and the Seven, later known as the John Barry Seven. He moved the group to London in 1957 and eventually band made it onto the British television show, *The Six-Five Special*. The group became immensely popular from their appearances on the program, and Barry was its star, not only playing trumpet but also handling the vocal chores.

It was out of their appearances on the program that they were signed to EMI's Parlophone Records label. The group's next big gig was as one of the resident house bands for *Oh Boy!*, which was a showcase for many of the most dynamic young rock 'n' roll singers coming up in England. It was from there that Barry moved on to become music director for *Drum Beat*, a dramatic program starring a young singer-actor named Adam Faith. He and Faith were an unbeatable combination, both on screen and in the recording studio, for three years, from 1959 until 1962, releasing a string of major British hits through the Parlophone label.

In 1960, Barry was also invited to write his first film score, for the juvenile delinquency drama *Beat Girl* starring *Adam Faith*. The results were an impressive mix of brass, heavy electric guitar and orchestra. Barry also later devised an entire album, *Stringbeat*, in which he juxtaposed the group's sound with that of a string orchestra. Barry was involved with numerous projects of all kinds during this period. Most notably, Barry was engaged by the producers of a film called *Dr. No*, to write and arrange a finished score from work begun by composer Monty Norman. The film itself was a hit, and Barry's work earned him a gig writing the full score for the next movie, and for more than two decades' worth of subsequent James Bond movies, up through 1985's *A View To A Kill*.

It was with *Born Free*, however, that he moved into the front ranks of popular film composers, with the score and the Oscar-winning title song. From then on, he scored some of the biggest and most daring films being made in England or Hollywood, ranging from the hour-long experimental film *Dutchman* to high profile dramas like *The Lion In Winter* (for which he won his third Oscar). In the midst of his burgeoning film work, Barry found time to make albums of his own on occasion, usually featuring re-recordings of his best movie-related music. In 1999, he also released one album of his classical instrumental style compositions, *The Beyondness of Things*. Barry suffered a life-threatening injury at the end of the '80s from which his recovery seemed problematic. He survived with help from a very good physician, and one of the first results of this new lease on life was Barry's music to *Dances With Wolves*, which was one of his most ambitious soundtrack creations ever, filled with complex orchestral parts and sweeping, almost Mahler-like melodic arcs and textures, earning his fifth Oscar in the process. In 1992, he was nominated for his sixth Oscar for his music for *Chaplin*. *—Bruce Eder*

☆ **A Lion in Winter** / 1967 / Columbia/Legacy ♦♦♦♦♦
While many of the traditional Barry phrases and sonic textures can be heard throughout this score, there is no hint that the composer was resting on his laurels and doing a journeyman job. Rather, he chose to reach for new textures, inspired by plainchant and driven by the need to match the subtext in the film that involved the influence of the Catholic church on the lives and choices of the characters. Consequently, Barry's score shifts in the most fascinating way between regal fanfares and haunting chant, resulting in this score being possibly the best work Barry has ever done. The Legacy remastering does not add anything new, but the sound is considerably improved. *—Steven McDonald*

Diamonds Are Forever / Jan. 1972 / EMI America ♦♦♦♦♦
John Barry made his reputation with highly enjoyable and sophisticated soundtracks for early James Bond pictures, including *From Russian With Love*, *Thunderball*, and 1971's *Diamonds Are Forever*. Like many Bond soundtracks, *Diamonds Are Forever* features a dynamic mix of brass-heavy orchestral numbers, reconfigurations of the original Bond theme, dreamy ballads, and a celebrity vocal performance of the title track. Following up her "Goldfinger" hit, singer Shirley Bassey returns here with another bravura performance on the "Diamonds Are Forever" theme; although not as memorable as Bassey's earlier classic, the song still impresses with a catchy mix of rock elements (wah-wah guitar, electric bass, 4/4 beat) and full orchestration. And as is the fashion with soundtracks, this main title is recycled more than once—in this instance, as both a flute-and-vibes lounge cut and as part of a darkly lush string arrangement. Along with easy listening, Henry Mancini-inspired cuts like "Tiffany Case," and "Q's Trick," Barry also gives a nod to Max Steiner's clamorous soundtracks with suspense and action backdrops like "Bond Smells a Rat" and "To Hell With Blofield." And the Bond theme gets its due on the noir-ish, cat burglar motif "Bond Meets Bambi and Thumper." With equally stunning pieces like the romantic waltz "Circus, Circus" topping things off, *Diamonds Are Forever* qualifies as one of Barry's most gratifying Bond soundtracks. *—Stephen Cook*

Dances with Wolves / Aug. 1990 / Epic ♦♦♦♦♦
This majestic John Barry score is slightly under-recorded but very rewarding despite its occasional overreliance on material all too familiar from the *James Bond* movies. *—Bruce Eder*

Elmer Bernstein

b. 1922, New York, NY
Conductor, Composer / Beat Poetry, Original Score, Film Music, Musicals, Pop, Instrumental Pop, Classical
If Elmer Bernstein had realized his childhood hopes, he might have been a successful concert pianist in the decades from the '40s thru the '60s. Instead, thanks to his ability as a composer, and the timely intervention of World War II, he has for more than five decades been a major force in popular music and film music, and a major influence on American popular culture.

Born in New York City, Bernstein was a natural prodigy. When he was 13, his music teacher arranged for the boy to audition for Aaron Copland, who was sufficiently impressed to arrange for him to study with one of his own students. He subsequently enrolled at The Julliard School in New York, where he continued as a piano student and also took up composition.

World War II interrupted Bernstein's career as a performer. Luckily, he was assigned to work with Glenn Miller and the United States Army Air Force Band, later writing the music for Armed Forces Radio programs. By the time he returned to civilian life, Bernstein had written the music for more than 80 broadcasts and wanted to pursue a career as a composer.

In 1949 further radio work led to an offer to work in movies. He spent the early '50s moving between the smaller major studios like RKO and Columbia and independent companies such as Astor Films. It was at Astor that Bernstein scored two of his stranger film vehicles, the notoriously bad *Robot Monster* and *Cat Women Of the Moon*.

Gradually, however, he moved up to doing films at the majors. Bernstein's professional breakthrough took place in 1955 with *The Man With The Golden Arm*. He produced a groundbreaking soundtrack that became the first of Bernstein's film music to get a commercial release—it also received an Oscar nomination, the first of many for the composer.

That same year, Bernstein was assigned to Cecil B. DeMille's *The Ten Commandments*. The movie was a monumental hit, and Bernstein's big orchestral score achieved great popularity—the composer's name was suddenly known and recognized among casual filmgoers in the same manner as his much older contemporaries Max Steiner and Franz Waxman.

In 1958, Bernstein moved into television, signing with Revue Productions, For the next few years, he turned up as a composer of the main title music of series such as the detective thriller series *Johnny Staccato* and *Riverboat*, among other shows. He also cut a pair of light pop-jazz albums in 1956 and 1960, respectively.

The next major milestone in Bernstein's career came in 1960, when he was engaged to score John Sturges' *The Magnificent Seven*. After *The Magnificent Seven*, Bernstein's career was made, although he took great pains to see to it that he got other projects besides more westerns. Bernstein's work during the 1960's ranged from delicate, sensitive dramas like *To Kill A Mockingbird* to such rousing adventure yarns as *The Great Escape*. His work as music director on *Thoroughly Modern Millie*won Bernstein his only Oscar to date.

At the beginning of the '70s, he formed his own record label, Filmusic Collection, and used it to release a series of recordings of scores that weren't otherwise available, including Miklos Rozsa's music for *The Thief of Baghdad* and Bernard Herrmann's unused score for *Torn Curtain*.

In 1977, he was asked by director John Landis to score the comedy *Animal House*. *Animal House* was a huge success and opened up a whole new class and variety of film to Bernstein's talents; over the next few years, he wrote the music for such comedies as *Airplane*, *Stripes*, *Ghostbusters*, and *The Three Amigos*.

At the same time, his status as the dean of living soundtrack composers opened up serious dramas and the works of major filmmakers to him in ways that they hadn't been since the '60s. He was chosen by Martin Scorsese to score his remake of the 1960 thriller *Cape Fear*, for which he did a rescoring of Bernard Herrmann's original music; he also wrote new music for Scorsese's *The Age Of Innocence*.

At the outset of the twenty-first century, Elmer Bernstein remains very busy as a composer, conductor and arranger, and he continues to devote his energy to the restoration of old film scores, making new commercial recordings of his own early works and those of other composers. *—Bruce Eder*

★ **Great Escape** / Feb. 24, 1998 / Rykodisc ♦♦♦♦♦
Rykodisc's CD reissue of Elmer Bernstein's score to the 1963 WWII drama *The Great Escape* is a welcome rediscovery—Bernstein's score is expressive and powerful, its sweep epic but never overly melodramatic. *—Jason Ankeny*

Danny Elfman

b. May 29, 1953
Vocals, Guitar, Producer, Composer / Original Score, Film Music, Soundtracks
Best known for his work in collaboration with director Tim Burton, composer Danny Elfman created one of the most distinctive bodies of work in contemporary film music, bringing his talents to a dark fantasy world populated by superheroes, monsters and freaks. The son of novelist Blossom Elfman, he was born May 29, 1953 in Amarillo, Texas; raised in Los Angeles, he and brother Richard relocated to France in 1971, where he joined a theatrical group. Elfman subsequently moved on to Africa, returning to the U.S. only after battling a bout with malaria; he then reunited with Richard, who had directed the 1980 film *The Forbidden Zone* and asked Danny to compose the score. Assembling a band dubbed the Mystic Knights of Oingo Boingo, Elfman recorded the movie's soundtrack; abbreviated to simply Oingo Boingo, the group remained a going concern following the project's completion, later earning a significant cult following during the New Wave era.

In 1985 Elfman met fledgling filmmaker Burton; after collaborating on the score to the hit *Pee-Wee's Big Adventure*, they reunited frequently in the years to come, with Elfman composing the music to later Burton projects including *Beetlejuice*, *Edward Scissorhands*, *Mars Attacks!* and the Grammy-winning *Batman*. In 1993 Elfman also scored the Burton-produced *Nightmare Before Christmas*, dubbing the vocals of the animated musical's lead character Jack Skellington. Outside of Burton's sphere of influence, Elfman also scored a number of other features, most of them strange fables such as *Darkman*, *Dick Tracy*, *Army of Darkness* and *The Frighteners;* in 1997, he composed the music for *Men in Black*, the summer's biggest hit. Among his television work: the theme song to *The Simpsons*. *—Jason Ankeny*

Pee Wee's Big Adventure/Back to School / 1988 / Varese Sarabande ♦♦♦♦♦
A nicely matched pair of scores, with the first having some charmingly goofy elements to its credit. Elfman hit the ground running with his score for *Pee Wee's Big Adventure*, serving the film well. *Back to School* is somewhat less distinctive, but it's still fun to listen to. No Elfman collection should be missing this one. *—Steven McDonald*

★ **Music for a Darkened Theater, Vol. 2: Film & Television Music** / Dec. 3, 1996 / MCA ♦♦♦♦♦
This two-disc set offers a superb overview of Elfman's innovative and evocative film music. In addition to compositions for *Edward Scissorhands*, *Tim Burton's The Nightmare Before Christmas*, *Batman Returns*, *Pee-Wee's Playhouse* and *Black Beauty*, the collection also includes seven unissued tracks. *—Jason Ankeny*

Ernest Gold

b. Jul. 13, 1921, Vienna, Austria, **d.** 1999
Composer / Television Music, Original Score, Film Music, Soundtracks
Ernest Gold was best remembered as one of Hollywood's most successful film composers. If things had been different in the world of the '30s, however, Ernest Gold might've been one

of the last of the post-romantic composers on the European continent. Hitler's rise to power made that impossible, and sent Gold to the United States. So Ernst Gold (as he was born and raised in Austria) came to Hollywood as Ernest Gold, and became one of the last European romantic music figures to carve a name for himself in film music.

Gold was born on July 13, 1921, to a Viennese family with long connections to music. He started playing the piano and violin at age six, and by the time he was eight he'd begun composing songs. He might've been a younger rival to Erich Wolfgang Korngold, writing a full-length opera when he was 13, but the Vienna of the '30s was too chaotic a place for a boy of any talent—especially from a Jewish family—to make too much of an impression.

Gold attended the State Academy of Music in Vienna until the beginning of 1938, when he and his family fled Europe. They arrived in New York where the 17 year old resumed his music career by presenting a piano concerto that received a performance that same year at Carnegie Hall.

Gold ultimately moved to Hollywood, arriving in 1945 and landing several jobs as an arranger and orchestrator, mostly in B-movies and low-budget genre films. For Lippert Pictures he scored the sci-fi adventure *Unknown World*, but most of Gold's first 10 years in Hollywood were a struggle to make worthwhile music while making a living and setting the stage for a real career.

By 1958, Gold had gotten his first major film composition assignment in the form of *The Defiant Ones*, which received multiple Academy Award nominations and represented a huge step up for Gold from the B-movies he had been scoring. For his next film, *On The Beach* Gold was able to come up with an expressive score despite the edict imposed on him by producer Stanley Kramer that the Australian anthem "Waltzing Matilda" was to be used as often as possible in the background music. Gold became Kramer's preferred composer for the next 20 years, working on every major picture that the producer made.

The big break for Gold as a popular composer came in 1960 with his music for Otto Preminger's production of *Exodus*, yielding his first (and only) enduring popular music hit. The film was a box office monster, but even more successful was Gold's main theme, a rousing, memorable, almost-Straussian piece that was later covered by hundreds of artists in arrangements for everything from full orchestra to electric guitar.

Gold's film work for the remainder of the '60s was focused on such high-profile Kramer productions as *A Child Is Waiting, It's A Mad, Mad, Mad, Mad World, Ship of Fools*, and *The Secret Of Santa Vittoria*. He wrote the score for the Broadway musical *I'm Solomon*, and after Kramer's theatrical film output slackened with the dawn of the '70s, he turned increasingly to writing for television. Made-for-TV features such as the excellent *Footsteps* and *Tom Horn* were sandwiched around occasional theatrical features such as *Cross of Iron* and *Fun With Dick and Jane*. During the late '70s, as Gold's career was beginning to wind down, his son Andrew Gold emerged as a successful pop recording artist with the songs "Lonely Boy" and "Thank You for Being a Friend." Gold kept himself busy when he wasn't writing film scores with the Santa Barbara Symphony Orchestra and the Los Angeles Senior Citizen's Orchestra, which he founded in the 1980s. He died in 1999, 11 years after writing his final score, for the television adaptation of *Gore Vidal's Lincoln*. *—Bruce Eder*

Jerry Goldsmith

b. 1929, Los Angeles, CA

Conductor, Composer / Spy Music, Original Score, Film Music, Soundtracks

For over four decades, Jerry Goldsmith ranked among the film and television industry's most highly-regarded and prolific composers; at the peak of his activity during the 1960s, he was estimated to have scored an average of about six films annually. Born in Los Angeles on February 10, 1929, Goldsmith studied music at the University of South Carolina, and after accepting a job as an office clerk at CBS television later graduated to the network's music department in 1950. There he composed themes for series including *Gunsmoke, Perry Mason, Have Gun Will Travel, The Twilight Zone* and *The Man From U.N.C.L.E.* before turning to film in 1957, debuting with the score to *Black Patch*. Under the tutelage of the great Alfred Newman, Goldsmith rose to prominence with 1962's *Lonely Are the Brave*, and subsequently emerged as one of Hollywood's most prolific composers. Among his credits were such diverse offerings as *Patton, Planet of the Apes, Seconds, Chinatown, Poltergeist* and *Rambo: First Blood Part II;* while nominated for over a dozen Academy Awards, Goldsmith won only one, for 1976's *The Omen*. Additionally, he regularly toured concert halls, performing his music and conducting the likes of the San Diego Symphony and Britain's Royal Philharmonic. *—Jason Ankeny*

Marvin Hamlisch

b. Jun. 2, 1944, New York, NY

Piano, Guitar, Composer / Musical Theater, Film Music, Soft Rock, Instrumental Pop, Show Tunes

Since he first emerged in the mid-'70s, Marvin Hamlisch has been one of the top composers in film, theater, and popular music, earning numerous awards and achieving commercial success.

Born in New York in 1944, Marvin Hamlisch auditioned for the Julliard School of Music at age seven by transcribing the then current hit "Goodnight Irene" into different keys spontaneously, on demand from the panel judging him. He was accepted, becoming the youngest student in Julliard's history; he later graduated from Queens College in New York.

In his teens, Hamlisch's performing talent was sidelined by terrible performance anxiety. He turned instead to composition, earning his first hit when he was 21 years old with Lesley Gore's recording of his song "Sunshine, Lollipops, and Rainbows", which rode the Billboard charts for 11 weeks in 1965, peaking at No. 13.

Liza Minnelli helped Hamlisch land a spot as the arranger on the Broadway productions of *Funny Girl* and *Fade In Fade Out*. On *Henry, Sweet Henry* and later on *Golden Ranbow*, he arranged the dance music, beginning a career in the theater.

Hamlisch broke into the movie business as a result of a party he attended where he overheard producer Sam Speigel saying that he needed music for a film adaptation of John Cheever's story "The Swimmer". Hamlisch went to work on his own and presented the producer with a main theme and was engaged to do the score for the move. He subseqeuntly composed the music for WoodyAllen's debut film, *Take The Money And Run*, and his second movie, *Bananas*. Hamlisch's other early films included *The April Fools, Save The Tiger* and *Fat City*. He also remained active in theater, writing the incidental music and dance arrangements for *Minnie's Boys*, a feature based on the early careers of the Marx Brothers. Later he was chosen by Groucho Marx to be his pianist and straight man in his stage act, performing at night clubs and college campuses.

In 1973, Hamlisch was engaged to score *The Way We Were*, starring Barbra Streisand and Robert Redford. The title song became one of the singer's biggest chart hits, and not only did the song win the Oscar, but so did Hamlisch's entire score.

Hamlisch pulled off an even more prodigious feat the next year with his score for *The Sting*. Built on the music of Scott Joplin, the music from *The Sting* helped spearhead a whole revival of interest in Joplin's work, resulting not only in a hit album for Hamlisch (*The Entertainer*) but also his second Oscar.

Hamlisch also wrote theme music for two television series in 1975, *Beacon Hill* and *The Hot L Baltimore*. Neither lasted, but Hamlisch made a more significant contribution to the small screen in 1976 when he wrote the music for the NBC adaptation of John Osborne's *The Entertainer*, starring Jack Lemmon.

That same year, Hamlisch scored perhaps the biggest hit of his career with *A Chorus Line*. Opening on Broadway in May of 1975, it became the most successful musical of the decade, winning multiple awards and running well into the '90s. In between his performing career and his writing for the stage and screen, Hamlisch managed to work in appearances on albums by such diverse figures as Aretha Franklin, the Carpenters, and Peter Allen, among many others. Hamlisch scored another hit as a composer with *They're Playing Our Song*, co-written with his wife Carole Bayer Sager. The couple also won an Oscar nomination for the song "Nobody Does It Better", written for the James Bond movie *The Spy Who Loved Me"* (1977) and a Top Five hit single for vocalist Carly Simon. The early '80s saw Hamlisch as busy as ever, writing the music to the Neil Simon comedies, *Chapter Two, Seems Like Old Times*, and *I Ought To Be In Pictures*. His music for the films *Sophie's Choice, The Champ Same Time Next Year* and *Shirley Valentine* was also nominated for Academy Awards. Hamlisch has been somewhat less visible as a composer since the early 1980's, but has been a producer and arranger for recordings by John Williams and the Boston Pops Orchestra, Liza Minnelli, and Barbra Streisand in the '90s. *—Bruce Eder*

Irving Berlin

Irving Berlin (1888-1989) was the most successful songwriter of the 20th century. Though, like his contemporaries, he spent the better part of his career writing songs (usually both words and music) to be used in Broadway musicals, he is better remembered for the songs themselves than for the shows (and sometimes films) in which they were introduced. This is because Berlin was a master at the kind of music that flourished from the turn of the century until World War II, shows that were really just collections of production numbers, scenes, and novelty acts (organized vaudeville presentations, really) rather than the story musicals that became prevalent starting with Rodgers and Hammerstein's *Oklahoma!* in 1943. It is also because Berlin, who did not read music and could play the piano in only one key and only on the black notes (he used a special piano with a lever that changed keys for him and employed a musical secretary to notate his compositions), wrote songs, not scores.

But what songs! Out of more than a thousand, a short list would include "Alexander's Ragtime Band" (his first major hit, in 1911), "God Bless America," "A Pretty Girl Is Like a Melody," "Always," "Blue Skies," "Puttin' on the Ritz," "How Deep Is the Ocean?," "Cheek to Cheek," "Let's Face the Music and Dance," "White Christmas," "There's No Business Like Show Business," "I Love a Piano," "What'll I Do?," "Easter Parade," and "Oh, How I Hate to Get Up in the Morning." The last came from one of the two shows Berlin organized and performed in during the two world wars (he can be seen in the film version of the second one, *This Is the Army*).

Berlin became his own song publisher and built and owned a Broadway theater, the Music Box, to house his shows. Perhaps his greatest and his last hit came with the musical *Annie Get Your Gun* in 1946, though he did write three more before retiring in 1962.

—William Ruhlmann

Bernard Herrmann

b. Jun. 29, 1911, **d.** Dec. 24, 1975

Composer / Original Score, Film Music, Soundtracks, Television Soundtracks

The dean of film composers, Bernard Herrmann was probably the most gifted musician ever to work in movies, with barely a note of music to his credit that is not worthwhile. A classically trained composer, Herrmann worked for Orson Welles' Mercury Theatre and the CBS radio network before going to Hollywood with Welles in 1940. His first two film scores, *Citizen Kane* and *The Devil and Daniel Webster*, were both nominated for Oscars in the same year (*Webster* won), and he was established from then on. Herrmann worked principally for 20th Century-Fox from the mid '40s until the end of the '50s, and did brilliant work on such movies as *The Ghost and Mrs. Muir, The Day the Earth Stood Still, Beneath the 12-Mile Reef*, and *Journey to the Center of the Earth;* in the '50s and '60s, Herrmann also contributed notably to the success of Alfred Hitchcock's films, and wrote inspired scores for early films by Brian De Palma and Martin Scorsese. He died the night he finished work on *Taxi Driver*. *—William Ruhlmann*

Taxi Driver / 1976 / Varese Sarabande ♦♦♦♦

The original 1976 record and initial CD versions contain half a magnificent film score, half

Danny Elfman

Since 1980 Danny Elfman has enjoyed modest success as frontman for the eccentric alternative band Oingo Boingo, but an opportunity to score Tim Burton's 1985 film *Pee Wee's Big Adventure* opened up a lucrative career as a composer of TV and film soundtracks. Since then, his credits have included *Batman, Dick Tracy, The Simpsons, Edward Scissorhands, Scrooged, Beetlejuice, Big Top Pee Wee,* and too many more to mention.
—Rick Clark

jazz-lite cover versions of the same music. Bernard Herrmann's soundtrack, full of dark, brooding brass, menacing percussion and a bittersweet dash of jazz saxophone, greatly enhance this big city tale of obsession, paranoia and violence. Robert DeNiro's chilling narration of "Diary of a Taxi Driver"—including the famous "You talking to me—" monologue—served as one of the models for the anger and isolation inherent in much of punk music. For some strange reason, the entire first side of the album is devoted to bland covers of Herrmann's music by arranger Dave Blume. Thankfully, Blume's arrangements are unnoticeable in the film itself, but their inclusion here distracts from a powerful soundtrack. Blume's arrangements are firmly rooted in L.A. mid-'70s fuzak, while Herrmann's score is one for the ages. *—Rick Watrous*

★ **Music from the Great Hitchcock Movie Thrillers** / 1996 / London ✦✦✦✦✦
Bernard Herrmann—Music from the Great Hitchcock Movie Thrillers is a well-programmed and well-performed overview of Herrmann's work in association with Hitchcock. None of the scores is anywhere near complete, but all of the famous movie selections from *Psycho, North by Northwest, Vertigo,* and *The Trouble with Harry* are represented. *—Bruce Eder*

☆ **Citizen Kane: The Classic Film Scores of Bernard Herrmann** / Jun. 1974 / RCA ✦✦✦✦✦
Citizen Kane: The Classic Film Scores of Bernard Herrmann is probably the best of the entire series by conductor Charles Gerhardt and the National Philharmonic Orchestra. Every track is worthwhile and memorably played, especially *Beneath the 12-Mile Reef* and the suite from *Citizen Kane,* the latter highlighted by Kiri Te Kanawa's performance of the Strauss-like aria from *Salammbo.* *—Bruce Eder*

Maurice Jarre (Maurice Alexis Jarre)

b. Sep. 13, 1924
Composer / Original Score, Film Music, Soundtracks
Film music composer Maurice Jarre attended the University of Lyons, then went to Paris, where he studied engineering at the Sorbonne before entering the Paris Conservatoire to study composition and percussion. He became musical director of the Théâtre National Populaire and composed his first film score for the short *Hôtel des Invalides* in 1951. He worked mostly on short films through the mid-'50s before graduating to mostly full-length features in the late '50s. By the early '60s, he had begun to attract international attention, getting assignments from British and American directors, and with that he embarked on a remarkably prolific career that found him scoring an average of over three films per year during the 40-year period 1960-1999.

Jarre's first major international success came with British director David Lean's 1962 epic *Lawrence of Arabia.* The soundtrack album containing the composer's appropriately lush and exotic music just missed topping the American LP charts, and when the film swept the Academy Awards, Jarre received his first Oscar for best original score. The following year, he was nominated for the award for best adapted score for the French film *Sundays and Cybèle.* He repeated his success with *Lawrence of Arabia* by scoring Lean's next mammoth production, *Doctor Zhivago* (1965). Again, he won the best original score Oscar, and the soundtrack album, stimulated by Ray Conniff's Top Ten vocal recording of "Lara's Theme" under the title "Somewhere, My Love," topped the charts and went gold. It was one of only a handful of all-instrumental recordings of movie scores ever to hit number one.

Jarre had his third soundtrack album in the charts in March 1967 with *Grand Prix,* the music for director John Frankenheimer's 1966 racing film, which spent more than six months among the LP best-sellers, and though the disappointing critical response to David Lean's 1970 effort *Ryan's Daughter* probably robbed Jarre of another Oscar, the soundtrack album of his music did get into the charts. The motion picture academy bestowed nominations on Jarre for *The Life and Times of Judge Roy Bean* in 1977 and *Mohammad, Messenger of God* in 1977, and he finally won a third Oscar for his music to David Lean's return to filmmaking and final work, *A Passage to India,* in 1984.

The 1980s were even busier for Jarre than the '70s had been, and he adapted himself to the expanded opportunities offered by technological innovations, composing and performing electronic music for such scores as the one for Peter Weir's *The Year of Living Dangerously* (1983) and *Witness* (1985). The latter earned an Oscar nomination, while Jarre's music for *Mad Max Beyond Thunderdome* produced a soundtrack album that reached the Top 40. There were further Academy Award nominations for *Gorillas in the Mist* in 1988 and *Ghost* in 1990. The composer slowed his busy pace after turning 70 in 1994, but he entered the new century still working, with *I Dreamed of Africa* released in 2000. (Jarre's son, Jean-Michel Jarre, is also a composer.) *—William Ruhlmann*

Andrew Lloyd Webber

b. 1948, London, England
Producer, Composer / Musicals, Show Tunes
Andrew Lloyd Webber (b. 1948) is the most successful composer of musicals of his generation and also a breaker of molds for the type. His predecessors were for the most part American: New York-based songwriters steeped in Broadway tradition. Lloyd Webber saw his share of shows as a child, too, but he was born in London, the son of William Lloyd Webber, Director of the London College of Music, and was trained at the Royal Academy of Music, hardly the sort of place where you'd be likely to hear *Oklahoma!*

Nevertheless, Lloyd Webber hooked up with lyricist Tim Rice, and the two began work on what would be a typical project for them, a musical based on the Biblical story of Joseph and his coat of many colors. Titled *Joseph and the Amazing Technicolor Dreamcoat,* it brought in a strong rock & roll influence. After writing a second unproduced musical, the two hit on the idea of writing a musical based on the life of Jesus Christ from the point of view of Judas (not the sort of idea likely to occur to a Broadway composer) and, again, imbued with rock. Unable to finance a stage version, Lloyd Webber and Rice did manage to record their show, and *Jesus Christ Superstar* went on to sales in the millions all over the world. The hit musical version followed.

Lloyd Webber and Rice then split, with the composer writing film scores and working on an abortive musical with playwright Alan Ayckbourne (*Jeeves*), after which Rice returned with another audacious idea: a musical based on the life of Argentine dictator (or dictator's wife, depending on how you look at it) Eva Peron. *Evita* (1976) repeated the pattern of *Jesus Christ Superstar,* with its hit record album followed by a successful theatrical run in the West End and then on Broadway.

The Lloyd Webber-Rice partnership, having proved itself again, was severed (Rice went on to write *Chess*), and Lloyd Webber next wrote a musical revue based on T.S. Eliot's whimsical poems about *Cats* (1981). This time the show came before the album, and it's still running. By this time, Lloyd Webber had largely abandoned the rock elements of his work in favor of what critics found a pastiche style that borrowed from classical and opera sources. He had also become a brand name (and a corporation, the Really Useful Company) that assured at least a modest success for subsequent shows, though critics were often unimpressed with his efforts.

Downgrading the status of his lyricists, Lloyd Webber went on to a series of successful shows (*Song and Dance, Starlight Express*) before scoring another long- (and still-) running hit in 1987 (1988 in New York) with a musical adaptation of *The Phantom of the Opera. Aspects of Love* (1989-1990) was less successful, however. Lloyd Webber debuted a musical adaptation of the Billy Wilder film *Sunset Boulevard* in the early '90s and it proved to be one of his rare disappointments, failing to earn either good reviews or healthy ticket sales. In 1996, Alan Parker adapted *Evita* for the screen; Webber and Tim Rice contributed a new song, "You Must Love Me," to the production, which starred Madonna. "You Must Love Me" won the Best Original Song award at the 1997 Academy Awards. *—William Ruhlmann*

George Gershwin

In a career tragically cut short in mid-stride by a brain tumor, George Gershwin (1898-1937) proved himself to be not only one of the great songwriters of his extremely rich era, but also a gifted "serious" composer who might bridge the worlds of classical and popular music. The latter is all the more striking, given that, of his contemporaries, Gershwin was the most influenced by such styles as jazz and blues.

Gershwin's first major hit, interpolated into the show *Sinbad* in 1919, was "Swanee," sung by Al Jolson. Gershwin wrote both complete scores and songs for such variety shows as George White's *Scandals* (whose annual editions thus were able to introduce such songs as "I'll Build a Stairway to Paradise" and "Somebody Loves Me").

After 1924, Gershwin worked primarily with his brother Ira as his lyricist. The two scored a series of Broadway hits in the '20s and early '30s, starting with *Lady Be Good* (1924), which included the song "Fascinatin' Rhythm." 1924 was also the year Gershwin composed his first classical piece, "Rhapsody in Blue," and he would continue to work in the classical field until his death.

By the '30s, the Gershwins had turned to political topics and satire in response to the onset of the Depression, and their *Of Thee I Sing* became the first musical to win a Pulitzer Prize. In the mid-'30s, Gershwin ambitiously worked to meld his show music and classical leanings in the creation of the folk opera *Porgy and Bess,* with lyrics by Ira and by Dubose Heyward. The Gershwins had moved to Hollywood and were engaged in several movie projects at the time of George Gershwin's death.
—William Ruhlmann

Jerry Goldsmith

Jerry Goldsmith (born in Los Angeles in 1929) is the leading figure in film music of his generation. After starting out in radio, he moved into television and motion pictures in the early '60s, where his instrumental inventiveness and superb melodic sense quickly moved him to the top of his profession. His scores are seldom less than inspired and are always absorbing, whether they are written for thrillers (*The Prize,* "The Twilight Zone" TV series), science fiction (*Logan's Run*), military subjects (*Patton, The Blue Max*), or serious drama (*A Patch of Blue*).
—William Ruhlmann

Ennio Morricone

b. Oct. 11, 1928, Rome, Italy
Conductor, Composer, Arranger / Original Score, Film Music, Soundtracks
Ennio Morricone is probably the most famous film composer of the 20th century. He is also one of the most prolific composers working in any medium. No exact figure is available, but

Bernard Herrmann

The dean of film composers, Bernard Herrmann was probably the most gifted musician ever to work in films, with barely a note of music to his credit that is not worthwhile. A classically trained composer, Herrmann worked for Orson Welles' Mercury Theatre and the CBS radio network before he went to Hollywood with Welles in 1940. His first two film scores, *Citizen Kane* and *The Devil and Daniel Webster,* were both nominated for Oscars in the same year (Webster won), and he was established from then on. Herrmann worked principally for 20th Century-Fox from the mid-'40s until the end of the '50s, and did brilliant work on such films as *The Ghost and Mrs. Muir, The Day the Earth Stood Still, Beneath the 12-Mile Reef,* and *Journey to the Center of the Earth.* In the '50s and '60s, Herrmann also contributed notably to the success of Alfred Hitchcock's films and wrote inspired scores for early films by Brian De Palma and Martin Scorsese. He died the night he finished work on *Taxi Driver.*
— William Ruhlmann

he's scored several hundred films over the past few decades, perhaps as many as 500. While these have been in almost every imaginable musical style (and for almost every imaginable kind of movie), he is most identified with the "spaghetti Western" style of soundtracks, which he pioneered when providing the musical backdrop for the films of director Sergio Leone. Morricone's palette is extraordinarily diverse, drawing from classical, jazz, pop, rock, electronic, avant-garde, and Italian music, among other styles. Esteemed by such important figures in modern music as John Zorn (not to mention contemporary directors like Martin Scorsese), he is increasingly placed among not just the finest soundtrack composers, but the most important contemporary composers of any sort.

Morricone began studying music at Rome's Conservatory of Santa Cecilia at the age of 12. Urged to concentrate on composition by his instructors, he supported himself by playing trumpet in jazz bands, and then worked for Italy's national radio network after graduating from the conservatory. He didn't begin scoring films until the early '60s, and didn't begin attracting international notice until he began collaborating with Leone, starting with *A Fistful of Dollars* in the mid-'60s. (Morricone had previously worked on other Italian Westerns with other directors.)

The spaghetti Westerns only comprised a phase of Morricone's career, but for many his work in this field remains his best and most innovative. Morricone amplified the film's plots and drama through ingenious use of diverse arrangements and instrumentation. Jew's harps, dissonant harmonicas, dancing piccolos, bombastic church organs, eerie whistling, thundering trumpets, oddly sung gunfighter ballads, and ghostly vocal choruses—all became trademarks of the Morricone-Leone productions, then of the spaghetti Western genre as a whole. The influence of rock & roll was felt in the low, ominous twanging guitars, which reflected (intentionally or unintentionally) the sound of contemporary recordings by the Ventures, Duane Eddy, the Shadows, and John Barry. Morricone's most famous composition, the theme to *The Good, the Bad and the Ugly,* made number two in the U.S. when it was covered by Hugo Montenegro.

Even while he was busy with collaborations with Leone, Morricone found time for various other film projects, such as the agitprop classic *Battle of Algiers* and *Burn!* By the 1970s, Morricone was winding down his involvement with both Leone and the spaghetti Western, working with numerous other directors all over the world. Grand orchestration and memorable motifs were commonplace in Morricone's work; Warren Beatty, for instance, once told the *Los Angeles Times* that "there's nobody better than Ennio to create a haunting theme." His scores also began to utilize more contemporary electronic influences, with mixed results.

Age has not slowed Morricone in the least. In fact, the 1980s and '90s saw his commercial success and widespread recognition at an all-time peak. He garnered several Academy Award nominations for *The Mission* in 1986. Since then he's worked for such top directors as Pedro Almodovar, Brian DePalma, Roman Polanski, Mike Nichols, and Barry Levinson. *Cinema Paradiso* is probably the most renowned of his recent scores.

With such an abundance of recordings, collecting Morricone remains a daunting proposition. It's doubtful that anyone will collect all of his soundtracks under one roof; after all, the composer himself doesn't even remember how many films he's worked on. RCA's *The Legendary Italian Westerns,* Virgin's two *Film Music* volumes, and Rhino's *Anthology* are useful collections, and the DRG label has begun reissuing other noteworthy compilations of his work. *—Richie Unterberger*

★ **The Ennio Morricone Anthology** / 1995 / Rhino ✦✦✦✦✦
Whittling the output of a composer with approximately 500 soundtracks to his credit down to two CDs rules out the possibility of a truly definitive career retrospective. Still, with 45 tracks spanning the mid-'60s to the early '90s, this is the best Morricone compilation of its sort available, though *Film Music Vol. 1 & 2* certainly have a lot of worthwhile material. Disc one is dominated by highlights from the '60s soundtracks, particularly the spaghetti Westerns, that remain his most famous; disc two is more eclectic, with a greater concentration of both his orchestral works and compositions utilizing a greater variety of electronic instruments, although the hints of electro-pop and Europop on some of the tracks can be aggravating. Comes with an excellent 36-page booklet of biographical liner notes. *—Richie Unterberger*

Alfred Newman

b. 1901 **d.** 1970
Composer / Original Score, Film Music
Alfred Newman (1901-1970) was, for much of his career, the most influential and respected composer and music director in Hollywood. His 44 Oscar nominations and nine Academy Awards are both records that are unlikely ever to be broken. The first-born of ten children to an impoverished produce seller in New Haven, Connecticut, Newman manifested his musical interests very early, and by the age of eight was well known locally as a piano prodigy. He played for virtuoso Jan Ignace Paderewski, who arranged a New York recital for the boy, and a performing career seemed in the offing, until he was forced to begin earning a living for his family. Newman worked his way up from vaudeville to the orchestra pit of the Broadway theaters, and eventually became an established conductor and arranger known and respected by all of the best composers, including Irving Berlin. When Berlin was brought to Hollywood at the dawn of the sound era, he arranged for Newman to come with him. There he was taken on by movie mogul Samuel Goldwyn and United Artists, and established himself as one of the movie capital's two undisputed masters of music (the other was Max Steiner). Soon, he also began working for 20th Century-Fox.

Newman spent the 1930s scoring some of the most prestigious movies of the decade, including *Street Scene, Dodsworth, Stella Dallas, Dead End, The Prisoner of Zenda, Gunga Din,* and *Young Mr. Lincoln,* among many others. Even when he wasn't working on a particular movie, he was often approached by studio production heads in need of advice when the scoring of a movie ran into trouble. Following his installation as Fox's music director in 1940, Newman worked on *How Green Was My Valley, Heaven Can Wait, Song of Bernadette, The Razor's Edge, Captain from Castille, The Robe,* and *Love Is a Many Splendored Thing,* among numerous other films; and, equally telling in his capacity as head of the studio's music department, he assigned the scoring of *Laura* to David Raksin, who wrote an immortal piece of movie music, and *Jane Eyre, Hangover Square,* and *The Day the Earth Stood Still* to Bernard Herrmann. In 1959, he left Fox for a career as an independent artist, and in 1961 conducted the Oscar-nominated score to *Flower Drum Song.* The next year, he wrote what may be his most familiar film score, *How the West Was Won,* with lyricist Ken Darby.

Ironically, for all of his accumulated honors, Newman remains viewed as a far greater arranger and conductor than composer. He could assimilate folk tunes or pseudo-folk tunes, as in *How Green Was My Valley* and *How the West Was Won,* and transform them into orchestral/choral works of tremendous power, and take a good original melody or two and turn them into something haunting and memorable, as in *The Razor's Edge* or *The Robe.* His compositions, however, lacked the boldness or adventurousness of Bernard Herrmann or Miklos Rozsa's most inspired work—his was tonal and accessible music that didn't demand too much of the viewer. But it was the palatable nature of Newman's music, coupled with his diplomatic skills, that helped him achieve his success. His scores were accessible without being trite, original in execution as film music without being jarring or troubling, and his affable nature, in contrast the the volatile, neurotic Herrmann or the seemingly aloof Rozsa, made him a favorite of studio executives. And all of that made his word about music the law in Hollywood for close to 30 years. He died in 1970, and his final soundtrack, for George Seaton's mega-hit *Airport,* became the last of Newman's 44 Oscar nominations. *—Bruce Eder*

Jerome Kern

Jerome Kern (1885-1945) is arguably the father of the modern American musical theater. Born in New York of German heritage, he attended the New York College of Music and began to break into Broadway theater during the first decade of the century by having songs of his interpolated into shows. An Anglophile and friend of P.G. Wodehouse, Kern scored his first success with songs inserted into *The Girl From Utah,* a British import, in 1914, including the ballad "They Didn't Believe Me." Breaking away from the European model of waltz music, Kern proved adept at adapting contemporary dance music into his songs as well as producing subtle, inventive ballads. He collaborated with Guy Bolton and, later, Wodehouse on a series of shows presented at the Princess Theater in the middle of the decade, notably *Very Good Eddie,* and continued to score successes into the '20s.

But Kern really entered the history books with *Show Boat* (1927), the first truly modern American musical, with an integrated story and such memorable songs as "Ol' Man River" and "Can't Help Lovin' Dat Man." Like many of his contemporaries, Kern divided his time between Broadway and Hollywood in the '30s, after sound came to the movies, and his movie hits included the Fred Astaire-Ginger Rogers film *Swing Time,* with such songs as "A Fine Romance" and "The Way You Look Tonight" (with lyrics by Dorothy Fields). Kern worked steadily—he wrote or contributed to 37 shows during his career—and was beginning work on *Annie Get Your Gun* when he died suddenly in 1945. He left behind one of the richest catalogs of show music in history.
— William Ruhlmann

Michael Nyman

b. Mar. 23, 1944, London, England
Piano, Composer / Original Score, Avant-Garde, Minimalism
Celebrated for his modular, repetitive style, minimalist composer Michael Nyman was among experimental music's most high-profile proponents, best known in connection with his film scores for director Peter Greenaway. Born in London on March 23, 1944, he studied at the Royal Academy of Music and King's College, London under communist composer Alan Bush and Thurston Dart, a musicologist specializing in the English Baroque. Under Dart's tutelage, Nyman was introduced to 16th- and 17th-century English rounds and canons, their repetitive, contrapuntal lines highly influencing his own later work; Dart also encouraged him to travel to Romania in the interest of seeking out the country's native folk music traditions. Upon graduating during the mid-'60s, Nyman found himself disconnected from both the pop music of the times and the school of modern composition heralded by Stockhausen; as a result, from 1964 to 1976, he worked not as a composer but as a music critic, writing

Erich Wolfgang Korngold

A composer and performer prodigy from an early age, Erich Wolfgang Korngold (born in 1897) was already an established and respected author of operatic and orchestral works by his twenties. He bid fair to be a successor to Richard Strauss when a chance offer to go to Hollywood to supervise the scoring of *A Midsummer Night's Dream* brought him to America. He stayed for over a decade, bringing his skills to bear on some of the most celebrated movies of that period. Beginning with *Captain Blood* in 1935, he was inextricably associated with the intense and rousing music for Errol Flynn's swashbucklers, but he also wrote the landmark dramatic scores to such serious films as *Kings Row* and *Between Two Worlds*. He returned to Europe during the period after WWII and attempted to resume his career in serious music, but he found that tastes and styles had altered too radically and that his work was regarded as archaic. He died in 1957.
— William Ruhlmann

for publications including *The Listener, New Statesman* and *The Spectator.* In a review of British composer Cornelius Cardew, he first introduced the word "minimalism" as a means of musical description.

During this same period, Nyman did continue performing, appearing with artists ranging from the Scratch Orchestra and Portsmouth Sinfonia to Steve Reich and the Flying Lizards. In 1974, he wrote the influential book *Experimental Music—Cage and Beyond,* an exploration of the influence of John Cage on a generation of composers and performers. Perhaps its most profound impact was on Nyman himself, who through writing the book seemed to discover his own muse; in 1976 he accepted an invitation from Harrison Birtwistle, Director of Music at the National Theatre, to arrange a number of 18th-century Venetian popular songs for a production of Goldoni's *Il Campiello.* Nyman's arrangements consisted of medieval instruments—rebecs, sackbuts and shawms, bass drums, soprano saxophones and the like—designed for maximum loudness to produce a distinctive instrumental color; when the production ended, he began composing original music merely to keep the same group of musicians together. Originally an acoustic unit, when rechristened the Michael Nyman Band in the early '80s, amplification became essential to their aesthetic.

Nyman's first major success came in 1982 with the score to the Greenaway film *The Draughtsman's Contract;* his subsequent collaborations with Greenaway on pictures including 1988's *Drowning By Numbers,* 1989's *The Cook, the Thief, His Wife and Her Lover* and 1991's *Prospero's Books* remain among his most high-profile works, their notoriety coming at the risk of overshadowing his forays into opera, chamber music, vocal music and dance scores. The signatures of Nyman's work include not only his use of propulsive repetition, but also a palette of idiosyncratic instrumental touches—thumping keyboards, "rude" bass clarinets and baritone saxophones, and extreme high and low octave doublings. Mozart was a central influence in much of his work, including 1976's *In Re Don Giovanni* and 1983's *I'll Stake My Cremona to a Jew's Trump;* Schumann, meanwhile, was the major inspiration behind the acclaimed 1986 chamber opera *The Man Who Mistook His Wife for a Hat,* while Bartok shades 1988's *String Quartet No. 2,* commissioned for the Indian dancer and choreographer Shobana Jeyasingh.

In 1990, Nyman composed *Six Celan Songs,* a work based on the poems of Paul Celan, for the German cabaret singer Ute Lemper, with whom he first worked on the score for *Prospero's Books.* His most emotional compositions to date, they served as the clear impetus for his score to Jane Campion's 1992 film *The Piano,* easily Nyman's best-known work; like so many of his compositions, he obsessively reworked the music to *The Piano* time and time again, the haunting melodies reappearing arranged for standard piano concerto, for two pianos, for chamber ensemble, for soprano saxophone and strings (*Lost and Found*) and for soprano and string quartet (*The Piano Sings*). While 1992's *The Upside-Down Violin* reflected Nyman's continuing fascination with traditional ethnic musics, 1993's *MGV,* or *Musique a Grande Vitesse,* returned to the propulsive sounds of the Michael Nyman Band. Other major works include 1992's *Time Will Pronounce,* 1993's *Yamamoto Perpetuo* (a composition for unaccompanied violin written for Alexander Balanescu), 1994's solo harpsichord work *Tango for Tim,* and 1995's *String Quartet No. 4.* Among Nyman's film scores: 1995's *Carrington* and 1997's *Gattaca.* *—Jason Ankeny*

Lerner and Loewe

Alan Jay Lerner (1918-1986) and Frederick Loewe (1901-1988) wrote some of the most stylish, sophisticated theater music of the 20th century. The collaboration didn't come until relatively late in the career of each. New York-born, Harvard-educated Lerner wrote material for radio and for individual performers in the '30s. Loewe, born in Berlin, came to the US in 1924 and gradually worked his way into theater music. The two were introduced in 1942. They scored their first hit, the fantasy *Brigadoon,* in 1947.

The Lerner-Loewe formula was to combine Loewe's lush, melodic music, redolent of Viennese waltz, with Lerner's witty, literate lyrics. This they did in some of the most popular and best-remembered musicals of the '40s, '50s, and '60s, notably *Paint Your Wagon, My Fair Lady,* and *Camelot* (plus the film musical *Gigi*). After Loewe's retirement, Lerner wrote with other composers, most successfully with Burton Lane (*On a Clear Day You Can See Forever*).
— William Ruhlmann

Andrew Lloyd Webber

Andrew Lloyd Webber (b. 1948) is the most successful composer of musicals of his generation and also a breaker of molds for the type. His predecessors were for the most part American: New York-based songwriters steeped in Broadway tradition. Lloyd Webber saw his share of shows as a child, too, but he was born in London, the son of William Lloyd Webber, director of the London College of Music, and was trained at the Royal Academy of Music, hardly the sort of place where you'd be likely to hear *Oklahoma!*

Nevertheless, Lloyd Webber hooked up with lyricist Tim Rice, and the two began work on what would be a typical project for them, a musical based on the biblical story of Joseph and his coat of many colors. Titled *Joseph and the Amazing Technicolor Dreamcoat,* it brought in a strong rock & roll influence. After writing a second unproduced musical, the two hit on the idea of writing a musical based on the life of Jesus Christ from the point of view of Judas (not the sort of idea likely to occur to a Broadway composer) and, again, imbued with rock. Unable to finance a stage version, Lloyd Webber and Rice did manage to record their show, and *Jesus Christ Superstar* went on to sales in the millions all over the world. The hit musical version followed.

Lloyd Webber and Rice then split, with the composer writing film scores and working on an abortive musical with playwright Alan Ayckbourne (Jeeves), after which Rice returned with another audacious idea: a musical based on the life of Argentine dictator (or dictator's wife, depending on how you look at it) Eva Peron. *Evita* (1976) repeated the pattern of *Jesus Christ Superstar,* with its hit record album followed by a successful theatrical run in the West End and then on Broadway.

The Lloyd Webber-Rice partnership having proved itself again, it was severed (Rice went on to write *Chess*), and Lloyd Webber next wrote a musical revue based on T.S. Eliot's whimsical poems about felines (*Cats,* 1981). This time the show came before the album, and it's still running. By this time, Lloyd Webber had largely abandoned the rock elements of his work in favor of what critics called a pastiche style largely borrowed from classical and opera sources. He had also become a brand name (and a corporation, the Really Useful Company) that assured at least a modest success for subsequent shows, though critics were often unimpressed with his efforts.

Downgrading the status of his lyricists, Lloyd Webber went on to a series of successful shows (*Song and Dance, Starlight Express*) before scoring another long- (and still-) running hit in 1987 (1988 in New York) with a musical adaptation of *The Phantom of the Opera. Aspects of Love* (1989-1990) was less successful, however. Lloyd Webber recently completed work on a musical based on the Billy Wilder film *Sunset Boulevard.*
— William Ruhlmann

Nino Rota

b. Dec. 3, 1911, **d.** Apr. 10, 1979
Composer / Original Score, Film Music, Soundtracks, 20th Century Classical/Modern Composition

Famed for his inspired work with director Federico Fellini, Nino Rota was one of the most prolific and acclaimed film composers of his era, with a list of soundtrack credits ranging from *La Dolce Vita* to Franco Zeffirelli's *Romeo and Juliet* to Francis Ford Coppola's *The Godfather.* Born December 3, 1911 in Milan. Italy, Rota was a child prodigy who had already written an opera and an oratorio prior to his fifteenth birthday; he subsequently studied at the Curtis Institute in Philadelphia as well as the Liceo Musicale in Bari, where from 1950 to 1978 he served as director. In 1933 Rota first entered the Italian film industry, scoring the "white telephone" romances and musicals prevalent during the era; before 1950, he composed the music for some 30 features, as well as the operas *Torquemada* and *The Florentine Straw Hat.*

With the 1952 release *Lo Sceicco Bianco,* Rota teamed for the first time with Fellini; their 30 year collaboration was one of the most fruitful director-composer pairings in film history, resuting in world classics including 1954's *La Strada* (later adapted by Rota into a ballet), 1963's *8 1/2,* 1974's *Amarcord* and, perhaps most famously, 1960's *La Dolce Vita.* Launched to international prominence through his work with Fellini, Rota also began composing material for other major filmmakers including Luchino Visconti (1960's *Rocco E I Suoi Fratelli*), King Vidor (1956's *War and Peace*) and Mario Monicelli (1959's *La Grande Guerra*). In 1968 he scored Zeffirelli's *Romeo and Juliet,* and its love theme became among his most recognized compositions; even more distinctive was his theme for Coppola's 1972 classic *The Godfather.* For 1974's *The Godfather Part II,* Rota won an Academy Award; he died on April 10, 1979. *—Jason Ankeny*

★ **The Godfather** / 1972 / MCA ✦✦✦✦✦

★ **Music for Film** / Jan. 13, 1998 / Sony Classical ✦✦✦✦✦
Music for Film contains selections from seven Rota scores— *The Godfather, The Godfather, Pt. 2, 8 1/2, The Orchestral Rehearsal, La Dolce Vita, Rocco and His Brothers, The Leopard*— as performed by Riccardo Muti and the Filarmonica della Scala. Muti has researched Rota's scores and notes, finding the composer's original ideas for the scores and basing his interpretations on those. The results are uniformly stunning, bringing the scores to vivid life and revealing new subtlties within the music itself. It's essential for any fan of Rota, Muti or film music. *—Stephen Thomas Erlewine*

Ennio Morricone

Morricone (an Italian composer born in 1928) came out of a mixed jazz and classical background and first started scoring low-budget action/adventure films in the early '60s. His music for Sergio Leone's three Clint Eastwood "man with no name" Westerns brought him to the attention of moviegoers around the world, who appreciated his mix of refined, elaborate scoring (often with chorus as well as full orchestra) and witty, clever humor—all rather like serious comic opera, and eminently listenable. In addition to his work with Leone, Morricone is famous for his music for such films as *The Mission* and has, by his own estimate, scored 600 or more films. *—William Ruhlmann*

Miklos Rozsa

b. Apr. 18, 1907, **d.** 1995

Composer / Original Score, Film Music

A Hungarian-born composer, most famous for his film scores, but also responsible for a significant body of chamber pieces, concertos, and orchestral music for the concert hall, Miklos Rozsa's music was steeped in post-Romanticism, with stylistic roots in the folk music of his native Hungary and some slight influences from those two giants of 20th-century Hungarian music, Bela Bartok and Zoltan Kodaly.

Born in Budapest to a wealthy industrialist and landowner, Rozsa began playing the violin at age five, and later studied the viola and the piano, and made his public performing debut at age seven. In 1925, he enrolled at the University of Leipzig as a chemistry major, to satisfy his father's wishes, but he switched to music after his first year. During his undergraduate years, Rozsa wrote his first formal composition, the *Trio-Serenade for Strings*, and followed this with the *Piano Quintet in F Minor*, the *Rhapsody for Cello and Orchestra*, and his *Variations on a Hungarian Peasant Song*. His *Serenade* received a performance in Budapest where it was heard by Richard Strauss, who strongly encouraged the young composer to continue writing music. His major breakthrough took place in 1934, with the premiere of his *Theme, Variations and Finale*, which was quickly taken up into the repertories of such renowned conductors as Charles Munch, Karl Bohm, and Carl Schuricht, and, later, Eugene Ormandy, Bruno Walter, and Leonard Bernstein.

In 1937 Rozsa was invited to write the score for the romantic espionage thriller *Knight Without Armour*, starring Marlene Dietrich and Robert Donat, which became an international hit. Soon after he was asked to join the staff of a production company founded by his fellow Hungarian expatriate Alexander Korda—and during the next three years, he scored such classic movies as *The Four Feathers* and *The Thief of Baghdad*. When Korda was forced to move the latter film's production from London to Hollywood in 1940, Rozsa was among the staff members who made the journey.

Having reached the filmmaking capital of the world, Rozsa made his way as a freelance composer for several years, primarily in the employ of Paramount Pictures in the films of Billy Wilder, David O. Selznick for Alfred Hitchcock (*Spellbound*), and the occasional Kordaproduction. Following his winning of Oscars for *Spellbound* (1945) and *A Double Life* (1948), Rozsa joined the staff of Metro-Goldwyn-Mayer, where he worked for the next 15 years, doing the music for such classic films as *Ben-Hur*, for which he won his third Oscar. During this period, he did not foresake his concert music, writing such pieces as his *Lullaby and Madrigal for Spring, Kaleidoscope, To Everything There Is a Season*, and his *First String Quartet*.

In 1953, the famed violinist Jascha Heifetz, having seen some of Rozsa's sketches for a proposed violin concerto, commissioned the piece from Rozsa—it was premiered in 1956 and recorded the same year on RCA. The *Violin Concerto* proved an enduringly popular work, and its success led to the 1961 joint commission from Heifetz and cellist Gregor Piatigorsky, for a piece utilizing violin and cello, the *Sinfonia Concertante*. The 1960s saw Rozsa compose such large-scale orchestral pieces as the *Notturno Ungherese*, a *Piano Concerto* for the virtuoso Leonard Pennario, and a *Cello Concerto* written for Janos Starker. His 1970s output saw Rozsa turn toward such solo works as the *Valse Crepusculaire* for piano, although he also completed a *Viola Concerto* for Pinchas Zuckerman, which was premiered in 1984.

Rozsa remained active as a composer in the mid-'80s, earning another Oscar nomination for his score for Nicholas Meyer's *Time After Time*, and continued publishing new works into the end of the decade.

Despite the onset of advancing age and a debilitating stroke, which combined to end his career in the concert hall, Rozsa retained an active interest in all of his music into the 1990s. He assisted in the recordings of new versions of his orchestral works by conductor James Sedares on the Koch International label in the 1990s, and even resurrected such works as the *Symphony in Three Movements*, which he withdrew from publication in 1930, adding to his already extensive catalog. *—Bruce Eder*

★ **The Epic Film Music of Miklos Rozsa** / Sep. 24, 1996 / Silva ✦✦✦✦✦

The Epic Film Music of Miklos Rozsa is an expanded version of the kind of soundtrack compilations that were available in the 1960s. Allowing for the fact that most of the Rozsa scores represented would stand up well on their own, this is a good survey of his work in the genre, especially for neophyte listeners. It is questionable, however, whether *The Golden Voyage of Sinbad, Beau Brummell*, and *All the Brothers Were Valiant* really are epics; the core of the hour's worth of music on this album is derived from such epics as *Quo Vadis, Ben-Hur, El Cid, King of Kings*, and *Madame Bovary*, and the material from the other films and their scores really fits more easily into other genres. Kenneth Alwyn does a decent job of conducting, and the music is well represented—the scope and majesty, as well as the complex expressiveness and stylistic density of Rozsa's music, come through. The only drawback is that much of the music represented here is now available on individual full-length recordings. *—Bruce Eder*

☆ **At Metro Goldwyn Mayer** / Oct. 19, 1999 / Rhino ✦✦✦✦✦

This is a dazzling two-CD set, representing 13 of the nearly 40 scores that Miklos Rozsa (1907-1996) composed in 14 years at MGM. Some of these movies are not among the best remembered that Rozsa worked on, but they all hold up well musically, in well-edited suites derived from the original 35mm film recordings for the movies themselves. Part of Rozsa's success was rooted in his ability to write in a wide variety of musical idioms, albeit largely centered and all shaped by the Romantic tradition in which his musical vocabulary was born. The 17-minute suite from *Madame Bovary* that opens the collection, and the producers have selected a generous portion of its highlights, including the ravishing waltz and the darker, more passionately dramatic passages. It is followed by one of Rozsa's most rousing action film scores, *Ivanhoe. Knights of the Round Table, Beau Brummell, Valley of the Kings*, and *Moonfleet* fill out the first disc, in a dazzling display of orchestral color. Disc two is devoted to *Green Fire, The King's Thief, Tribute to a Ban Man* (a rare example of Rozsa dealing with a western subject), *Diane, The World, The Flesh and the Devil* (one of two Rozsa forays into science fiction), *Lust For Life*, and *King of Kings*. Producer George Feltenstein has done a decent job of distilling the essentials of each score, all but one of which are represented by suites running at least ten minutes, and often double that. The content of the 13 scores here is so rich in musical ideas, and the latter range so widely, that even the listener who is less than wholeheartedly devoted to movie music will find plenty to enjoy and replay, for weeks at a time, on this set. *—Bruce Eder*

Carl Stalling

b. 1888, Lexington, MO, **d.** 1974

Composer, Arranger / Cartoon Music, Film Music, Soundtracks

Composer and arranger Carl Stalling was the visionary behind the kaleidoscopic music beating at the heart of the classic cartoons produced under the aegis of Warner Bros. Studios during the middle of the 20th century. Frenzied and impassioned, his work broke new ground by following the visual trajectory of the on-screen action instead of the accepted rules of composition; the result was unprecedented in its extremism, as melody, style and form crashed together in a glorious pile-up of sound and image. A maverick whose reach extended from pop to jazz to classical and beyond, Stalling's revolutionary cut-and-paste compositions remain a clear forerunner of the experimental music created in his wake—in fact, it could easily be argued that he succeeded in introducing entire generations of young cartoon fanatics to the music of the avant-garde.

Stalling was born in Lexington, Missouri in 1888; his musical education began in his infancy, as he spent hours upon end playing made-up songs on a broken toy piano. At the age of five, he saw Edwin S. Porter's early film landmark *The Great Train Robbery*, and an all-consuming passion for the cinema was born; by the 1920s was conducting his own orchestra and improvising music to accompany silent movies at the Isis Theater in Kansas City. There Stalling met Walt Disney, resulting in an invitation to score a pair of Mickey Mouse animated shorts; on cartoons like "Skeleton Dance," Stalling's soundtracks brought a new dimension to the Disney aesthetic —- his involvement in Disney's work ultimately grew so extensive that once, Stalling even dubbed Mickey Mouse's voice.

In 1930 Stalling left Disney to work under animator Ub Iwerks on the Flip the Frog series; six years later he landed at Warner Bros., remaining the animation department's musical director for over two decades.

At Warners, Stalling scored some 600 cartoons in all; in addition to creating their distinctive opening sound effect—a "boinnngggg!" achieved via an electric guitar chord—he also established their distinctive theme songs, using "Merrily We Roll Along" for the *Merrie Melodies* series and "The Merry-Go-Round Broke Down" for *Silly Symphonies*. Working with Warner's 50-piece orchestra under the direction of conductor Milt Franklyn, Stalling scored each cartoon in about three hours at a staggering rate of at least one a week, absorbing the influences of current pop hits, classical symphonies and the like and then quoting whatever seemed to fit; over time, motifs began developing in his work—drunken characters commonly stumbled about to the strains of "How Dry I Am," Bugs Bunny's frequent appearances in drag were heralded by "The Lady in Red," and bouts of hunger were accompanied by the obscure Billy Rose number "A Cup of Coffee, a Sandwich and You."

No discussion of Stalling's work is complete without making mention of composer and bandleader Raymond Scott, whose visionary recordings of the late 1930s, while never intended for use in conjunction with animation, remain the cornerstone of cartoon music. Stalling borrowed much from Scott, using his mechanized "Powerhouse" in the short "Mousemerized Cat" and, as a consequence, introducing a piece of music that would later resurface in *Ren and Stimpy* and other programs; other Scott creations popularized through Warner cartoons included "Dinner Music for a Pack of Hungry Cannibals." Nevertheless, Stalling himself surmised that as much as 80 or 90 percent of each score was entirely his own creation, as every composition needed to be perfectly synchronized to each moment on-screen; in his own compositions, bassoons, sliding trombones, odd viola effects and violin glissandos all achieved roles of great prominence, at times even replacing the myriad sound effects produced by the great Treg Brown. After scoring 1958's "To Itch His Own," Stalling retired; he died in 1974. *—Jason Ankeny*

☆ **The Carl Stalling Project: Music from Warner Bros. Cartoons 1936-1958** / 1990 / Warner Brothers ✦✦✦✦✦

The first volume in *The Carl Stalling Project* series is a revelation; more than just an essential part of a Warner Bros. staff that generated some of the finest and most inspired productions in the history of animation, Stalling was a visionary whose work deserves consideration among the finest American avant-garde music ever recorded. As these 15 selections from WB cartoons dating between 1936 and 1958 attest, his cut and paste style—a singular collision between jazz, classical, pop, and virtually everything else in between—was unprecedented in its utter disregard for notions of time, rhythm, and compositional development; Stalling didn't just break the rules, he made them irrelevant. That in the process he created music beloved by succeeding generations of children is more impressive still—perhaps even unwittingly, Stalling introduced the avant-garde into the mainstream, and as popular music

Cole Porter

Cole Porter (1891-1964) has been described as the greatest songwriter of the century; he was unquestionably the wittiest. A child of enormous wealth, Porter did not turn his complete attention to songwriting until the '20s, but from then until the end of the '40s, he turned out nearly a show a year, and he even managed three more in the '50s, not to mention a fair amount of work for motion pictures. Porter, who wrote both words and music, had a flair for melody, but his gift for lyrics was unparalleled. Like Irving Berlin, his work of the '30s is better remembered for individual song hits than complete scores, and those songs included "Let's Do It," "You Do Something to Me," "What Is This Thing Called Love?," "Night and Day," "Begin the Beguine," and "Just One of Those Things." An exception to this rule was *Anything Goes* (1934), which, in addition to the title song, included "You're the Top" and "I Get a Kick Out of You." The entire score is brilliant, and the show has been revived on stage and in films frequently.

Porter was severely injured in a riding accident in 1937 and lived in pain for the rest of his life. His work, however, continued largely without interruption. His greatest success came with an adaptation of Shakespeare's *Taming of the Shrew* called *Kiss Me, Kate* in 1948, after which he worked less frequently, though *Can-Can* (1953) and *Silk Stockings* (1955) were notable later hits.
— William Ruhlmann

continues to diversify and hybridize, his stature as a pioneer rightfully continues to grow. *— Jason Ankeny*

John Williams (John B. Williams, Jr.)

b. Feb. 8, 1932, New York, NY

Piano, Bass, Conductor, Composer, Arranger / Classical Crossover, TV Soundtrack, Movie Themes, Original Score, Film Music, Soundtracks, Orchestral Pop

The most popular film composer of the modern era, John Williams created music for some of the most successful motion pictures in Hollywood history—*Star Wars, E.T. the Extra Terrestrial* and *Jurassic Park* are just three of the credits in his extensive oeuvre. Born February 8, 1932 in Long Island, New York, he was himself the son of a movie studio musician, and he followed in his father's footsteps by studying music at UCLA and Julliard; initially, he pursued a career as a jazz pianist, later working with Henry Mancini to compose the score for the hit television series *Peter Gunn.* Williams then went solo to pen a number of TV soundtracks for series including *Playhouse 90, Wagon Train* and *Bachelor Father;* in 1959 he ventured into film with *Daddy-O,* and spent the majority of the 1960s alternating between the silver screen (*The Killers, The Plainsman*) and its smaller counterpart (*Gilligan's Island, Lost in Space*).

In 1968 Williams earned his first Academy Award nomination for his work in *Valley of the Dolls;* in 1970, he garnered nods for both *The Reivers* and *Goodbye, Mr. Chips,* and two years later finally won for *Fiddler on the Roof.* A slew of Oscar nominations followed, for features including *The Poseidon Adventure, Images, Tom Sawyer* and *The Towering Inferno.* In 1974 he first teamed with a young filmmaker named Steven Spielberg on a movie titled *The Sugarland Express;* the two frequently reteamed over the years to come, with often stunning results—*Jaws, Close Encounters of the Third Kind, Raiders of the Lost Ark, E.T., Jurassic Park,* and *Schindler's List* were just a few of the Spielberg/Williams pairings, with *Jaws, E.T.* and *Schindler's List* all winning the composer Academy Awards.

Williams' other most frequent collaborator was George Lucas; beginning with 1977's *Star Wars*—yet another Williams Oscar winner—they later teamed for 1980's *The Empire Strikes Back* and 1983's *Return of the Jedi,* with the composer agreeing to score Lucas' subsequent *Star Wars* films as they went into production in 1997. Other scores of note included 1979's *Superman,* 1987's *The Witches of Eastwick,* 1988's *The Accidental Tourist,* 1991's *JFK* and 1995's *Nixon.* In 1980, Williams also took over for the late Arthur Fiedler as the conductor of the Boston Pops. *—Jason Ankeny*

☆ **Jaws [Original Soundtrack]** / 1975 / MCA ♦♦♦♦♦

John Williams' first film score to capture the imagination of the public, and the first hit movie score of the 1970s not to involve a love theme (à la *Love Story*), *Jaws* has been on CD for more than a decade, but this is the first release that really does it justice. The centerpiece of the music is the bump-bump-bump-bump theme associated with the movements (usually unseen) of the shark, which became so well known that it was used as an essential part of various comedy sketches in a multitude of media at the time (Williams himself quoted it comically in his scoring for Steven Spielberg's *1941*). It does reappear in numerous forms (many of them veiled) throughout the score, along with a handful of additional memorable musical phrases associated with Williams' score, many involving the hunt for the shark. The anniversary edition of the score not only features the familiar portions of the original album, which didn't amount to 40 minutes of music, but 15 minutes or more of Williams' score from the actual film, and also music that was written and recorded for the movie but dropped from it. Little is totally unfamiliar, but the 24-bit remastering off of the original tapes adds fresh luster to the recording and the music. It's doubly interesting, hearing the music uncut and remastered, to realize anew just how many of the effects that turn up at key points in this score Williams reused in his music for *Close Encounters of the Third Kind* and other scores of his. This was not only where Williams' career as a superstar soundtrack composer began but also where he first started using the musical attributes that would identify that phase of his career. *—Bruce Eder*

★ **Star Wars Trilogy** / Jul. 1, 1991 / Columbia ♦♦♦♦♦

The original intent behind the release of the three Special Edition soundtracks was to place *all* of the available *Star Wars* music on the market and in the hands of fans. Though this collection includes new music from the Special Edition of the film—previously unreleased music, a concert suite, and an alternate version of the music for the assault on Jabba the Hutt's sail barge—it unfortunately doesn't include the original Sy Snootles track or the original Ewok celebration track. The music for *Return of the Jedi* is presented chronologically, with source music and alternate cues tucked away at the end of each disc, making those particular cuts easier to ignore (highly recommended in the case of the overbearing "Jedi Rocks," a new song composed for the Special Edition). Alas, ignoring John Williams' insipid, Yanni-like new addition to the score, "Victory Celebration," is only possible if you also manage to ignore the end title music. While the original celebration music, with its chorus line of demented Ewok voices, was no great joy, at least it had some interesting musical qualities. Despite its uninformative sleeve notes, this collection has a lot going for it. Musically, it sounds gorgeous; Williams turned in a score incorporating layer upon layer of thematic elements, risking a tendency toward composing music that was too ornate. Frills and trills abound, but Williams avoided allowing the score to be buried in them. Having the music assembled as a continuous master provides the listener with a more organic flow and a better listening experience overall, while the remixing and remastering have improved the sound and dynamic range enormously. Despite the missing music, this is definitely the version to have. *— Steven McDonald*

★ **Close Encounters of the Third Kind: The Collector's Edition Soundtrack** / Apr. 28, 1998 / Arista ♦♦♦♦♦

The *CE3K* score was a masterful mixture of eerie suspense and tremendous emotive bombast, complete with hair-raising moments and the great big playful musical conversation between the mothership and the humans. The album, alas, was a fairly pitiful affair, poorly mixed, sequenced lamely, and missing most of the conversation. This splendid CD edition has been designed to remedy the mistakes just after the twentieth anniversary. Most of the music from the film is included on the disc, along with an alternate cue and some music edited out of the film (much of which has found its way back into the special editions). Happily, the complete musical conversation is here, too, delightful and magnificent. The remixing and remastering has resulted in tremendous sound improvement, making this CD an essential acquisition. *— Steven McDonald*

Miklos Rozsa

Born in Hungary in 1907, Miklos Rozsa is the last surviving veteran of moviemaking's "golden age," having scored his first film in 1936 and his latest in 1984. His early success as a serious composer, working in an idiom inspired by the work of Bartók and Kodaly, gave Rozsa the foundation for his dual career in motion pictures. A post-romantic who never accepted atonalism, his best work—and there is much of it—is derived from the texture of native Hungarian folk songs. He began collecting these as a child, giving him a unique command of orchestral timbre and the most distinctive approach of any composer of his generation.

After working for Alexander Korda's London Films, where he provided the memorable and brilliant scores for *The Four Feathers, The Thief of Baghdad,* and *The Jungle Book,* Rozsa took up residence in Hollywood in the early '40s, and by mid-decade had made his mark in the area of film noir. The rhythmic nature of his music and his facility with dark melodic lines gave a brooding savagery to films like *The Killers* and *The Naked City.* In the '50s he became the master of the religious epic. His sweeping scores for *Quo Vadis, Ben Hur, King of Kings,* and *El Cid* found favor among serious choral groups as well as the public, who devoured his albums (originally on the MGM Records label) including two complete albums of music from *Ben-Hur.*

The end of the studio system, the increasing demand for pop tunes in movie soundtracks, and the general coarsening of film subjects in the '60s didn't serve Rozsa well, and his activity in films declined steeply after 1963. Fortunately, he had his career as a serious classical composer to keep him occupied, and by the '70s, filmmakers such as Alain Resnais (*Providence*), Nicholas Meyer (*Time after Time*), and Carl Reiner (*Dead Men Don't Wear Plaid*) gave him a chance for a satisfying "Indian summer" prior to his retirement in the mid-'80s.
— William Ruhlmann

Various Artists

● **Best of Andrew Lloyd Webber: Broadway** / Sep. 24, 1996 / Polydor ♦♦♦♦♦

Barbra Streisand, Glenn Close, Mandy Patinkin and Michael Crawford are a few of the stars on this collection of Lloyd Webber favorites, which includes material from *Cats, Evita, The Phantom of the Opera* and *Jesus Christ Superstar.* *—Jason Ankeny*

The Best of James Bond: 30th Anniversary / 1992 / EMI ♦♦♦

The Best of James Bond: 30th Anniversary is a limited-edition double-disc set that collects the hit versions of all the James Bond themes, as well as adding an extra disc of unreleased material, featuring commericals and incidental music composed by John Barry. Bond collectors will delight with the rarities, but many listerners will settle for the single-disc version, which just contains the theme songs, including "Goldfinger," "Diamonds Are Forever," "Live and Let Die," "A View to A Kill," and "For Your Eyes Only." *— Stephen Thomas Erlewine*

☆ **Black Orpheus** / 1959 / Fontana ♦♦♦♦♦

The prodigious talents of Antonio Carlos Jobim and Vin°cius de Moraes ("Felicidade") and Luiz Bonfa ("Manha de Carnaval") were introduced to the world on this unforgettable soundtrack. *— Terri Hinte*

Stephen Sondheim

According to most critics and theater historians, Stephen Sondheim (b. 1930) stands among Broadway show composers and lyricists not only as the greatest of his generation but as the only great one of his generation. There may be many reasons why Broadway has failed to produce consistently great writers to follow the Rodgers and Hammersteins and Lerner and Loewes of the '40s and '50s, but the fact remains that, though he operates without serious competition, Sondheim clearly ranks with such masters, as well as with the Jerome Kerns and Irving Berlins of an even earlier generation.

Sondheim became a mentor of Hammerstein's after befriending the lyricist's son in school, but he got his first big break when he was hired to write lyrics to Leonard Bernstein's score for *West Side Story* (1957), which turned out to be one of the biggest hits and most memorable works of its time. This led to a lot of lyric-writing work, though Sondheim always wanted to write music as well. Nevertheless, he worked with Jule Styne on *Gypsy* (1959), another enormous hit, and would later agree to do the same with Richard Rodgers for the unsuccessful *Do I Hear a Waltz?* (1965).

Before that, however, Sondheim scored his first success as composer and lyricist with *A Funny Thing Happened on the Way to the Forum* (1962). It was his last hit until *Company* (1970), a show about contemporary life and mores that did much to revolutionize the Broadway musical and, as Hammerstein's '50s shows had, move it more toward serious and exotic subjects. Since that time, Sondheim's shows have been amazingly daring in terms of subject matter, with unusual musical ideas and stunningly original lyrics. But they have not always been big hits and have marked a time in the theater when Broadway show music became a marginalized art form in terms of popular culture.

Nevertheless, Sondheim's shows of the '70s and '80s are benchmarks of the genre: *Follies* (1971) brought together aging follies girls for a look at middle-aged American life; *A Little Night Music* (1973) was based on Ingmar Bergman's film *Smiles of a Summer Night* and contains Sondheim's sole hit song, "Send in the Clowns"; *Pacific Overtures* (1976) ambitiously took on the subject of Japanese-American relations; *Sweeney Todd* (1979) was an operetta based on the British grand guignol tale of a murderous barber; *Sunday in the Park with George* (1984) was a biography of impressionist painter Georges Seurat; *Into the Woods* (1987) wove together children's fairy tales with the theories of psychologist Bruno Bettelheim, and *Assassins* (1991), a short piece about presidential killers. In recent years, Sondheim has turned toward films; he wrote a score for Stavinsky in the '70s, and wrote songs for Madonna in *Dick Tracy* in 1990.

— William Ruhlmann

Civil War: The Complete Work / Jan. 5, 1999 / Atlantic ♦♦♦♦
The Civil War offers the complete recorded adaptation of Frank Wildhorn's acclaimed stage musical; spread across two discs, the assembled roster spans not only the musical spectrum (everyone from Hootie and the Blowfish to Patti LaBelle to Deana Carter) but also the worlds of drama (Danny Glover, James Garner and Ellen Burstyn) and even literature (Dr. Maya Angelou). The results are often fascinating—both the personal and political drama of the war between the states resonate throughout these songs, and the performances achieve an intriguing balance between period texture and contemporary energy. *—Jason Ankeny*

Hollywood Years / Apr. 4, 2000 / Hallmark ♦♦♦
Taken from various movie soundtracks, this brings together 20 classic duets from the silver screen. Kicking off with Fred Astaire and Ginger Rogers' "A Fine Romance," the set also features standards from Nelson Eddy and Jeanette McDonald, Bing Crosby and the Andrews Sisters, Judy Garland and Gene Kelly, Bob Hope and Shirley Ross (the definitive version of his theme, "Thanks for the Memory"), and Frank Sinatra and Connie Haines. Although a bit reverb-heavy in the remastering, the sound quality is pretty astounding, considering the age and condition of the source material. *— Cub Koda*

The King & I [Soundtrack] / Jun. 11, 1956 / Capitol ♦♦♦♦
The 1956 film soundtrack to Walter Lang's *The King and I* is distinguished from the Broadway cast album chiefly by Alfred Newman's expanded orchestrations and by the presence of Marni Nixon in the role of Anna Leonowens. On film, the part was played by Deborah Kerr, but Nixon, one of the best invisible voices in Hollywood (she also ghosted Audrey Hepburn in *My Fair Lady*) is the wonderful singer of songs like "I Whistle a Happy Tune" and "Getting to Know You," sung onstage by Gertrude Lawrence, who died before the film was made. Yul Brynner repeats his performance as the king, and Rita Moreno gets to play Tuptim and sing "We Kiss in a Shadow." This is a Hollywood adaptation done right—bigger and more dramatic than Broadway can be, with a show that benefits from the frills—and makes you wonder why they didn't always do as well. *— William Ruhlmann*

The King & I [Original Broadway Cast] / May 28, 1951 / MCA ♦♦♦♦♦
Richard Rodgers and Oscar Hammerstein II's fifth musical, +The King and I, was their first to be designed as a star vehicle—written at the behest of British stage star Gertrude Lawrence to mark her return to the New York musical stage after ten years in 1951. Rodgers and Hammerstein were somewhat hamstrung by the principal cast members. Neither Lawrence nor Yul Brynner, a television director hired to play the part of the king, had much of a singing voice. The songwriters solved this problem by giving the rangy songs–"We Kiss in a Shadow," "Something Wonderful," and "I Have Dreamed"—to the secondary characters. As the star, Lawrence had to have several numbers, but Rodgers and Hammerstein played upon her role as a teacher to give her two simple tunes to be sung to children—"I Whistle a Happy Tune" and "Getting to Know You"—as well as a patter song expressing her anger with the king, "Shall I Tell You What I Think of You?" Even "Hello, Young Lovers" and her duet with Brynner, "Shall We Dance—," were pleasant ditties rather than demanding theater songs. And yet, the musical restrictions made for a highly enjoyable, pop-oriented score with slight Oriental touches. "Hello, Young Lovers" and "We Kiss in a Shadow" became minor hits, but the most memorable songs over time ended up being "I Whistle a Happy Tune" and "Getting to Know You," which became children's standards. The original Broadway cast album just missed topping the bestseller charts and remained listed there for over a year. It has remained in print through various reissues over the years, including a 50th-anniversary edition in 1993 and a 24-bit remastering in 2000. *— William Ruhlmann*

Kiss Me, Kate [Original Broadway Cast] / 1949 / Columbia ♦♦♦♦
The original cast album of *Kiss Me, Kate* has been reissued before, on a late 1980s CD, but the 1998 20-bit remastering can be taken as definitive, and not just because of the improved sound. (Actually, sound is still something of a weak link in this release; the audio is rather dry and the voices often seem somewhat distant and always compressed.) This is the best representation we likely will ever see of this cast—Alfred Drake, Patricia Morison, Lisa Kirk and Harold Lang—in these roles; further, it is the cheapest and easiest way for listeners to discover songs like "Tom, Dick or Harry" and, especially, "Too Darn Hot" (definitely not a featured number for a girl singer, as it appears on the movie soundtrack), in their original, intended form. The richly detailed liner notes are a delight to read and, with the accompanying photos, make this a very compelling purchase. In addition, the producers have restored the play's original overture (left off of the original recording), from a recording of the piece made a decade later. (Unfortunately, its presence is also a reminder of the fidelity, warmth, and crispness that is lacking in the original cast material.) *— Bruce Eder*

The Rocky Horror Picture Show 15th Anniversary / 1990 / Rhino ♦♦♦♦
Ode Records marked the 15th anniversary of The Rocky Horror Picture Show in 1990 with this commemorative four-CD/cassette box set, which contains the cast album from the 1974 Los Angeles stage production; the film soundtrack album; Rocky Horror International, a compilation of the songs performed by various casts; and Songs From the Vaults: A Collection of Rocky Horror Rarities, featuring recordings by performers who appeared in the movie, commercials for the movie, and other material. A satiric amalgam of glam rock and 1950s horror movies, The Rocky Horror Show was a minor sensation on the fringes of London musical theater in 1973. Veteran record executive and producer Lou Adler brought the show's star, Tim Curry, to L.A. and built a production around him; Adler also produced a cast album using the cream of the L.A. session scene. In these musicians' hands, the music became much slicker and more mainstream. Nevertheless, the recording was a far more professional effort than its British predecessor. The Rocky Horror Show ran for nine months in Los Angeles, after which a film version, The Rocky Horror Picture Show, was shot. Barry Bostwick and Susan Sarandon proved to be the best Brad and Janet ever; the original cast members, especially Curry, reveled in the opportunity to immortalize their portrayals; and *Rocky Horror*'s potential as a witty parody of cheap movies, rock & roll, and sexual mores was fully realized. The songs "Planet Shmanet Janet" and "The Sword of Damocles" were heard in the film but left off the soundtrack; those tracks, plus Bostwick's deleted performance of "Once in a While," have been included on the Rocky Horror International disc, along with songs from the original London cast album and performances by casts from Mexico, New Zealand, Norway, and Australia. The Songs from the Vaults disc is a mixed bag that will appeal to completists. *— William Ruhlmann*

☆ **The Rocky Horror Picture Show [Original Soundtrack]** / 1975 / Rhino ♦♦♦♦♦
For the 1975 film version of *The Rocky Horror Picture Show*, American producer Lou Adler wisely mixed the best of the London and Los Angeles stage versions, shooting the movie in England with Tim Curry and several of the other original cast members, plus Meatloaf (years before *Bat Out of Hell*), and Americans Barry Bostwick and Susan Sarandon as the innocent couple Brad and Janet. Adler also brought back original London stage musicians in place of the slick studio musicians who had marred the L.A. cast album. The film version resequenced the songs and reassigned some of the vocals, with Brad's song "Once in a While" dropped. But it all worked out fine. The strings that were added to ballads like "Science Fiction/Double Feature" only improved them; the rockers rocked out; Bostwick and Sarandon proved to be the best Brad and Janet ever; the original cast members, especially Curry, reveled in the opportunity to immortalize their portrayals; and Rocky Horror's potential as a witty parody of cheap movies, rock & roll, and sexual mores was fully realized. The film soundtrack album became the definitive version of the score, despite lacking the songs "Planet Shmanet Janet" and "The Sword of Damocles." The Rocky Horror Picture Show was not successful in its initial theatrical run, but then a strange thing happened. In 1976, the Waverly Theater in New York's Greenwich Village began showing the film at midnight on Fridays and Saturdays. Soon, a cult of repeat viewers began turning up every week; they began to dress like the characters, call out their own comments at strategic moments, sing along, and add their own theatrical effects. The phenomenon spread across the U.S., with fans rivaling Trekkies and Deadheads for loyalty and eccentricity, and The Rocky Horror Picture Show took on a life Richard O'Brien never could have anticipated. *— William Ruhlmann*

☆ **The Sound of Music [Original Soundtrack]** / 1965 / RCA ♦♦♦♦♦
This RCA release of *The Sound of Music* features the classic performances by the definitive original cast, led by Julie Andrews and Christopher Plummer. Its enduring popularity decades later is a testament to the extremely high quality of the material. Absolutely indispensable for even the most casual fan of musicals. *— Steve Huey*

Television's Greatest Hits, Vol. 1 / 1986 / TVT ♦♦♦♦♦
This is the disc (originally a double-LP) that started it all, 65 themes from television shows ranging from the mid-'50s until the late '60s, from, say, *Rin-Tin-Tin* through *Mannix* and *Mission Impossible*. The sound quality is variable—some of this stuff was taken off of film elements—and some of it is clever re-records, but it's all very familiar and, in some cases, rather enlightening. Not that there are revelations to be found in much of this, but fans of the late Joe Meek might be interested to know just how much of his production technique and signature sound found its way into the theme music from, say, *Fireball XL-5*. The producers have included opening and closing themes linked together where that latter add significantly to the material. Pop-

Cast Recordings

The truth is that the Broadway musical does not travel well. Conceived as a combination of comedy, drama, song, and dance for one of those thousand-seat theaters that sit on a handful of streets in midtown Manhattan, the Broadway musical, if it is successful, immediately gets translated into a variety of forms into which it doesn't really fit. A road version may travel the country, playing before abbreviated sets in much larger theaters. A film version may appear that, even if it doesn't alter the work in other ways, somehow looks less impressive on film than it does when you're in the theater. Why is it easy to accept that a person onstage may just burst into song, when it looks silly on celluloid? Maybe the stages are the real dream factories—in movies, things are just too realistic. And then, of course, there are the cast albums, which, in a sense, are the farthest-removed translations of Broadway musicals. Here are a few songs, but no story, no dance. The volatile chemistry of opposing art forms that gives birth to the musical simply isn't present. A cast album is a souvenir, but no more to be confused with the real thing than a three-inch model of the Statue of Liberty you can buy at Battery Park.

And yet Broadway musicals have been the spawning ground for some of the most important popular music of the 20th century. In the first few decades of this century, when most people heard new songs by obtaining the sheet music and playing them themselves, Broadway introduced America to most of its new music. Musicals then were often what we would now call revues, developed out of vaudeville and really just collections of individual scenes and songs. But the country's best songwriters—George M. Cohan, Irving Berlin, George Gershwin—were devoting their efforts to the Broadway stage. Despite this dominance, only occasionally was anything resembling an "original Broadway cast" recording made. Recordings had limited popularity, especially after the start of the Depression, when record sales fell precipitously, and while Broadway served as a source for pop songs, usually they were recorded by other singers. One reason for this, of course, was that the record industry's main format—the 78 rpm single—allowed for two songs, each no more than about three minutes in length. "Albums" (bound collections of several 78s) were rarities, though *Show Boat*, for example, appeared in this form a year after it hit Broadway in 1927. But *Show Boat* was different in many ways. For one thing, it told a single, unified story, and the songs were mostly integrated into the plot.

By the '40s, the style set by *Show Boat* became the norm for most shows, especially after *Oklahoma*. At the same time, CBS developed the 33 1/3 rpm, long-playing record, and CBS president Goddard Lieberson recognized the Broadway cast album to be ideal for the new medium. As a result, cast albums frequently became big hits. From 1945 to 1965, *Song of Norway* (1945), *Carousel* (1945), *Kiss Me, Kate* (1949), *South Pacific* (1949), *Three Little Words* (1950), *Guys and Dolls* (1951), *The Music Man* (1958), *My Fair Lady* (1958), *Flower Drum Song* (1959), *The Sound of Music* (1959), *Camelot* (1961), *Carnival* (1961), and *Hello Dolly!* (1964) all hit No. 1 on the Billboard album charts. The peak of popularity came in the late '50s and early '60s. Then came the rock & roll era, and Broadway show music (like many other pre-rock styles) was swept into a marginalized pop category. Only *Hair* (1968), a rock pastiche, got to the top of the charts, and most cast albums sold modestly.

Stephen Sondheim, the acknowledged master of the Broadway musical in the '70s and '80s, has enjoyed no genuinely successful cast albums, though his song "Send in the Clowns (from *A Little Night Music*) has become a standard. Andrew Lloyd Webber, on the other hand, has largely bucked the trend, starting with his *Jesus Christ Superstar*, of which the pre-stage studio version went to No. 1 in 1970. Webber has gone on to enjoy million-selling hit cast albums for *Evita*, *Cats*, and *Phantom of the Opera*. Alain Boublil and Claude-Michel Shonberg have also sold a respectable number of copies of *Les Miserables*. These are the exceptions, however. For the most part, not only is the Broadway cast album no longer a commercial sure shot, it may not even get made. It used to be that the week after a show opened and good reviews indicated a hit, the cast would be in a recording studio to get the album out fast. Today, it may be six months before a cast album appears. Recent cases in point include *The Will Rogers Follies* and *The Secret Garden*, both of which opened in the spring of 1991, with their cast albums not available until December. And *Grand Hotel* was at the conclusion of its two-year run before a cast album appeared, by which time it was impossible to append the word "original," since one of the principal actors had died. If this is what happens with big hits, you can imagine how things are for less successful shows.

In spite of all this, there is probably more recording of show music going on now than at any time in the past. Archivists such as John McGlinn, John Mauceri, and Thomas Z. Shepard are hard at work restoring full scores of vintage shows and presenting them in new studio recordings with classically trained singers, further blurring a line between musical and opera already grown fuzzy enough as opera companies have incorporated musicals like *Sweeney Todd* and *South Pacific* into their repertoires. In addition, a plethora of small labels—First Night, Bay Cities, DRG—have taken up the task of recording shows with limited popular appeal, while the majors are digging into their vaults and reissuing long-out-of-print cast albums on compact disc. And then, of course, people keep writing musicals, and audiences keep going to them. How much worry can we have for the musical when we look to the 1992-1993 Broadway season and see on the horizon a version of *Jekyll and Hyde* that already has a cast album out, as well as a new Lloyd Webber musical, *Sunset Boulevard*? Even if the original Broadway cast album is the souvenir of a great evening (as it's always been) and no longer the blockbuster seller it was 30 years ago, it's still the repository of some of the best music of yesterday and today.

—William Ruhlmann

ular choices here include *The Munsters, The Addams Family, Top Cat, The Flintstones, The Jetsons, Dobie Gillis, My Three Sons, Superman, Bonanza, Branded, Daniel Boone, The Rifleman, Perry Mason, Ironside, Dragnet, 77 Sunset Strip, The Mod Squad*, etc. *—Bruce Eder*

TV Land Crime Stoppers: TV's Greatest Cop Themes / Sep. 19, 2000 / Rhino ♦♦♦
Released in conjunction with Nickelodeon's TV Land cable channel (devoted to reruns of vintage programs), Rhino's *TV Land Crime Stoppers: TV's Greatest Cop Themes* gathers theme songs from cop shows. Classic themes from shows like *Dragnet, CHiPs, Hill Street Blues, Hawaii Five-O, Cagney and Lacey, Kojak, Miami Vice* (which was actually a number one pop single), and even *Cop Rock* are present, with composers including Randy Newman, Quincy Jones, Jan Hammer, Bill Conti, Elmer Bernstein, and Mike Post, among many others. A companion volume is devoted to P.I. shows, and as you might expect, there isn't much difference in musical style. *—Steve Huey*

TV Land Crime Stoppers: TV's Greatest P.I. Themes / Sep. 19, 2000 / Rhino ♦♦♦
Released as a promotional tie-in with Nickelodeon's TV Land cable channel, Rhino Records' *TV Land Crime Stoppers: TV's Greatest P.I. Themes* is exactly what the title says. Memorable opening theme music from shows like *The Rockford Files, Magnum P.I., Charlie's Angels, Peter Gunn, Hart to Hart, Remington Steele, and 77 Sunset Strip* highlights the collection, which features composers like Mike Post, Henry Mancini, Lalo Schifrin, and Mack David. A companion volume is devoted to cop shows, and as you might expect, there isn't a huge difference in style. *—Steve Huey*

Vocal Music

A broad term with a suitably large scope, vocal music gathers all sorts of nominally jazz-based singers of the past hundred years, from Al Jolson to Dick Haymes to Betty Carter to Nana Mouskouri. What the vast majority of vocal artists have in common is a commitment to classic popular song, a largely American style of songwriting that flourished in and around New York City's Broadway and Tin Pan Alley during the first few decades of the 20th century. Since the vocal tradition relies on songs and broad techniques many decades old, singers excel either by superiority of voice or by sheer strength of interpretation (the latter including their ability to express emotion and spirit through song). Frank Sinatra and Ella Fitzgerald rank at the top of the vocal field because of their uncommon mastery of both technique and interpretation, while figures like Barbra Streisand fall slightly lower—in the eyes of most—because of a lack of balance. Though the success of vocal music was superseded by rock & roll during the 1960s, many cultural critics look at the music's prime period as home to the best vocalists (Sinatra, Fitzgerald, Bing Crosby) and songwriters (Irving Berlin, Cole Porter, George Gershwin) of the entire century.

What we know as vocal music or traditional pop has deep roots in both American and European music, with both singers, songs, and arrangements calling on a variety of turn-of-the-century forms—jazz first and foremost, but also ragtime and minstrel songs, the blues, brass bands, and even opera. The rise of vocal music as a discernible style dovetails with the rise of an organized music industry. Even before the widespread sale of records, vocalists were necessary as song-pluggers—persons able to perform, at the drop of a hat, songs for prospective publishers (later to be sold as sheet music). Though classical vocalists and opera singers had already gained an audience for their scattered releases (records were far too expensive for the lower classes anyway), most jazz-based vocalists were shunted to the side, often singing just a short vocal refrain near the end of orchestra recordings. Broadway and vaudeville entertainers like Al Jolson and Eddie Cantor had a certain degree of star potential on their own, but the notion of recording stars in jazz-based vocal music was a rare thing until well into the '30s. The advent of serious vocal music came with the late-'20s ascendancy of Bing Crosby and Louis Armstrong, a pair of wildly successful and influential figures who paved the way for much to come. While Crosby's gentle croon and relaxed style was nearly ubiquitous during the pre-war era, Armstrong grew to become the singer's singer, a figure especially influential simply because his songs carried their weight despite his gruff, raspy voice.

Vocal music really hit its stride in the '40s, with vocalists like Frank Sinatra, Ella Fitzgerald, Billie Holiday, Peggy Lee, Doris Day, and Dick Haymes breaking away from the big bands and recording hits on their own. The '50s were the glory days; Sinatra, Fitzgerald, Mel Tormé, Nat "King" Cole, and others not only ruled the charts and airwaves, but recorded excellent full-length LPs as well. But just as jazz eventually splintered into rivaling factions, vocal music also reached a crossroads of sorts, which divided pop singers (Perry Como, Rosemary Clooney) and younger artists (Lambert, Hendricks & Ross, Nina Simone) who revealed influences from more recent jazz movements like bop and cool jazz.

Both jazz and pop vocalists found the going much more difficult during the '60s. They coped with the rock revolution as well as they could, occasionally covering newer material and crossing over (to an extent), but mostly catering to their core audiences whenever it was still lucrative. The sheer power of American popular song helped carry vocal music during the '70s and '80s, and the continued power of dozens of solid jazz singers kept the style strong and vital into the '90s. *—John Bush*

Artist Reviews

The Ames Brothers

f. 1948, Malden, MA, **db.** 1959

Group / Traditional Pop

A close-harmony vocal quartet with few equals during the 1950s, the Ames Brothers hit number one in 1950 with "Sentimental Me" and found their biggest hit three years later with "You You You." Though they were indeed a family group, the Ames Brothers' surname was actually Urick. Joe, Gene, Vic and Ed Urick were all born within four short years of each other in Malden, Massachusetts. After winning a few talent contests in their hometown, the group moved to Boston and began performing in nightclubs. They soon made the leap to New York and even Los Angeles, and signed to the Coral label in late 1958. After a few moderate hits, the Ames Brothers hit big in early 1950 with a double-sided number one hit, "Rag Mop"/"Sentimental Me." The B-side eventually triumphed over its flip, and the group hit again later in 1951 with "Undecided." The biggest hit of the Ames Brothers' career was 1953's "You You You," and their continued success during 1954 with "The Naughty Lady of Shady Land" bore fruit in the form of their own television program.

Though the quartet continued to record throughout the '50s, the dawn of the rock era definitely damaged their career; the group managed two Top Ten hits in 1957 ("Tammy," "Melodie D'Amour") but then folded in 1959. Ed, the youngest Ames brother, continued a performing career and appeared as an Indian named Mingo on the *Daniel Boone* TV series before hitting the Top Ten as a solo act with 1967's "My Cup Runneth Over." He also appeared on Broadway. *—John Bush*

★ **The Best of the Ames Brothers: Sentimental Me** / 1995 / Varese ✦✦✦✦✦

Featuring 18 songs recorded while the group was signed to Coral and Decca, *Best of the Ames Brothers: Sentimental Me* compiles some of their earliest hits, including "I'm Looking Over a Four-Leaf Clover, " "Sentimental Me, " and "Rag Mop." *—Stephen Thomas Erlewine*

The Very Best of the Ames Brothers / Jun. 30, 1998 / Taragon ✦✦✦✦✦

While modern-day audiences will perhaps have a tough time equating their old-time singing style with their massive success, this collection does a pretty fine job of putting it all in perspective. The Ames Brothers were the purveyors of strong, smooth vocal harmonies that soared, soothed and came to national prominence, largely prospering in the pre-rock & roll times of the '50s. Drawn entirely from their hit-making days at RCA Victor (it omits their 1950 original of "Rag Mop," the group's first hit on Coral), this straight-from-the-master-tapes compilation runs chronologically from the Ames' 1953 signing with the label to their last charting record, '60's "China Doll." With 17 of the 20 tracks aboard being chart entries (and ten of *those* landing in the Top 20), this is a most hit-laden package, their one M.I.A. hit notwithstanding. There's a strong theory among musicologists that sibling harmony is the best vocal harmony there is, and here's a bunch of good reasons why that theory holds water. There's some great empathetic singing on here, and pop music fans will love the way they put a song over. Great liner notes by Colin Escott complete the package. *—Cub Koda*

The Andrews Sisters

f. Minneapolis, MN, **db.** 1953

Vocals / Harmony Vocal Group, Traditional Pop, Vocal Pop

Building on the rhythmic harmonies of their forebears the Boswell Sisters, the Andrews Sisters became the most popular female act of the pre-rock era. The trio's incredibly close harmony, nimble delivery, and effervescent smiles defined the jitterbugging and boogie-woogie crazes of the '40s. With Bing Crosby, the Andrews Sisters also became one of the most popular recording artists of the war years, and provided hours of entertainment on USO tours.

The sisters, LaVerne, Maxene and Patty Andrews were all born in Mound, Minnesota. After performing around the region, the group finally hit New York in the mid-'30s. They signed to Decca soon after, and hit big early with the number one hit "Bei Mir Bist Du Schoen." Though it took several years to trump the success of their chart debut, the Andrews Sisters remained popular during the late '30s with their second Hit Parade chart-topper, "Ferryboat Serenade." The group hit Hollywood in 1940, appearing in a few small roles and introducing a new hit for 1941, "Boogie Woogie Bugle Boy," in an Abbott & Costello war movie. By the middle of World War II, the Andrews Sisters had hit their peak with year-defining singles like 1943's "Shoo-Shoo Baby" and "Pistol Packin' Mama," the following year's "Hot Time in the Town of Berlin" and "Don't Fence Me In," and 1945's "Ac-Cent-Tchu-Ate the Positive" and "Rum and Coca-Cola"—many of which featured duets with Bing Crosby.

The immediate post-war years found the trio falling a bit from the highs of 1943-45. After Patty recorded two number one hits ("I Can Dream, Can't I?," "I Wanna Be Loved") as a solo act, she left the group in 1953. Still, only one moderate hit resulted on either side after the split, and the records that did appear often featured all three sisters. A miniature revival kicked off by Bette Midler's 1973 rendition of "Boogie Woogie Bugle Boy" sparked interest in the Andrews Sisters once more, and remaining members Patty and Maxene teamed up for a WWII-themed Broadway musical named *Over Here*. *—John Bush*

● **The 50th Anniversary, Vol. 1** / 1990 / MCA ✦✦✦✦✦

The first of a very good two-volume collection of some of the Andrews Sisters' best work, this 16-song CD was more than essential at the time of its release, mostly due to the presence of several numbers that hadn't been heard in decades: "Pagan Love Song," "Shoo Shoo Baby," "Bounce Me Brother With a Solid Four," "Gimme Some Skin My Friend," their rendition of "Tuxedo Junction," and their Danny Kaye and Al Jolson collaborations, "Civilization" and "Way Down Yonder In New Orleans." Apart from the Jolson number, which was in release in 1956, none of the others had been available since the 1940s, and all were worth hearing. Among the previously "lost" tracks, "Pagan Love Song" as a boogie-woogie style number is worth the price of the disc by itself, and "Tuxedo Junction" isn't far behind, Patty Andrews luxuriating in the lead while her sisters wrap their voices around hers like a second skin and Vic Schoen's arrangement provides playful accompaniment by the trumpets and saxes. "Gimme Some Skin My Friend" and "Bounce Me Brother With a Solid Four" are unique Andrews Sisters creations, authored by Don Raye (of "Boogie Woogie Bugle Boy" fame) and nearly as successful in their use of early-'40s slang. "Corns for My Country" is a delightful period song about the Hollywood Canteen (from the movie of the same title) that shows off Patty Andrews' comical mugging for the microphone. Danny Kaye makes a better lead singer than one would expect, and not just in a comic vein, and Al Jolson sounds infinitely better than one would expect on a song cut in the year of his death. The notes are also a treat, featuring reminiscences by Patty Andrews and Maxene Andrews and arranger Vic Schoen. The only drawback to this collection is that it was done in 1987, and there are now better mastering techniques and technology available. Those just discovering the trio's work, however, should also be warned that this disc doesn't stand by itself—there are any number of key songs that only made it onto the second volume, and there are other anthologies that embrace still other parts of their vast catalog, but this and its companion volume are a nice place to start. *—Bruce Eder*

The 50th Anniversary, Vol. 2 / 1990 / MCA ✦✦✦✦✦

Capitol Collectors Series / 1991 / Capitol ✦✦✦✦✦
Twenty-five Andrews Sisters tracks dating mostly from October 1956, after the trio reformed following Patty Andrews' attempt at a solo career. On signing them, Capitol Records got the trio to do new versions of their classic Decca hits for the LP *The Andrews Sisters in Hi-Fi*. The effort was a worthy one, as the trio still sang splendidly, and with all of the verve they'd displayed 20 years earlier, and Vic Schoen, who'd done all of their band arrangements back when, was present for these sessions as well. In view of the easy availability of their hits for Decca Records, the material on this CD may seem superfluous, but the performances have much of the same easy, swinging charm that their late-'30s and '40s classics displayed, with better recording to go with it, and the trio's maturity—the sisters were in their forties rather than their twenties—works in their favor, allowing them to add a few fresh nuances and articulate the lyrics anew, giving listeners a pleasing look back at the old with just a smidgen of new thrown in. Additionally, at the time of its release, the sound on this disc was superior to that of any of MCA's CDs of the original hits, although they have since improved those masters. *—Bruce Eder*

All Time Greatest Hits / Oct. 11, 1994 / MCA ✦✦✦✦✦
In some ways, this 46-song double CD compilation is a brilliantly conceived and executed overview of the Andrews Sisters' career on Decca Records from 1939 until 1950—remastered in superb sound, with surprising presence and vivid detail, the material is priceless, and only a 20-bit digital treatment is likely to make it any better. And if the trio sounds good, along with Bing Crosby, who's featured on several songs, then Vic Shoen's orchestra also never had it as good as they do here. Plus, there are a few songs, such as "Aurora," that aren't on any other Andrews Sisters CDs. On the other hand, the producers have left off some numbers (such as "Bounce Me Brother With a Solid Four" and "House of Blue Lights") that appear on one or the other of their best-of compilations on Decca; add to that the fact that some numbers by the trio, such as "You're a Lucky Fellow Mr. Smith" (from *Buck Privates*), have never shown up on CD (and possibly not on LP either), and one gets a glimpse of some of the holes that are evident on this disc. It can be argued that some of the numbers mentioned weren't hits, but there are enough B-sides here ("Well All Right" is the most impressive of them, real killer, with extraordinary interplay between the three sisters), that this excuse hardly suffices. One would wish that MCA or, more likely, Bear Family would do a completely comprehensive reissue—the Andrews Sisters were good enough that it would be worthwhile. In the meantime, it's necessary to own this and two other single discs from Decca. *—Bruce Eder*

Greatest Hits: The 60th Anniversary Collection / Feb. 10, 1998 / MCA ✦✦✦✦✦

Julie Andrews

b. Oct. 1, 1935, Walton-On-Thames, England
Vocals / Traditional Pop, Musicals, Vocal Pop, Show Tunes
During her five decades in show business, on the stage, radio and in cinema versions of *The Sound of Music* and *Mary Poppins*, Julie Andrews perfected the image of the classic Englishwoman: refined, elegant and more than just a bit eccentric. Born in 1935, she began her career as part of her parents' variety show when she was just ten years old. Two years later, Andrews made her stage debut in *Starlight Roof*, and began working as a radio actor for the BBC not long after. On Broadway for *The Boy Friend* in 1954, she became available for Lerner & Loewe's *My Fair Lady*, and accepted the spot opposite Rex Harrison. Reprising her role in London, Andrews then returned to New York to star with Richard Burton in *Camelot*. Disappointed that she was passed over for the film versions of both (for Audrey Hepburn and Vanessa Redgrave, respectively), Andrews nevertheless gained an Oscar for her 1964 performance in *Mary Poppins*, with Dick Van Dyke. (The duo also reached number 66 on the pop charts with "Super-Cali-Fragil-Istic-Expi-Ali-Docious.") Her later film musicals include *Thoroughly Modern Millie*, *Victor/Victoria* and *Star!*, though none were as successful as *The Sound of Music* (1965). Soundtracks of all of the above are available, as well as several Christmas albums and a live appearance at the Lincoln Center with Carol Burnett. Andrews has also appeared in standard film roles, in *10* and *S.O.B.* *—John Bush*

A Little Bit of Broadway / 1977 / Columbia ✦✦✦✦✦
In effect, this compilation is "The Best of Julie Andrews on Columbia Records, 1957-1962." It is drawn from five albums released during that period: the television soundtrack to *Cinderella* (1957); the original London (not Broadway, as the liner notes mistakenly say) cast album for *My Fair Lady* (1959); the original Broadway cast album for *Camelot* (1960); and two Julie Andrews solo albums, *Broadway's Fair Julie* (1962) and *Don't Go in the Lion's Cage Tonight* (1962). (There is also a previously unreleased recording of Noël Coward's "I'll Follow My Secret Heart" made during the sessions for Broadway's *Fair Julie*.) The conceit here is that this is all material from Broadway musicals, but that isn't actually true, since the solo recordings include revivals of such independent songs as "By the Light of the Silvery Moon," "Alexander's Ragtime Band," and "Burlington Bertie From Bow" (the last later performed by Andrews in the 1968 film *Star!*). Never mind that, though. Andrews's stage appearances ended for decades after *Camelot*, and this set affords the listener a chance to hear what she might have been like in, for example, Leonard Bernstein's *West Side Story* ("I Feel Pretty") and *Wonderful Town* ("A Little Bit in Love"), even if it's hard to imagine her ever being cast in such shows. Naturally, she brings her precise phrasing and clear voice to every performance, enthusiastically trying on such diverse material as Lane and Harburg's "How Are Things in Glocca Morra?" (from *Finianís Rainbow*) and Rodgers and Hart's "I Didn't Know What Time It Was" (from *Too Many Girls*). Of course, her familiar performances from the shows with which she is associated remain stellar, though listeners would have preferred the Broadway cast versions of the songs from *My Fair Lady* (even if they are in mono). *—William Ruhlmann*

★ **The Best of Julie Andrews: Thoroughly Modern Julie** / Mar. 26, 1996 / Rhino ✦✦✦✦✦
While Rhino promoted this as a career overview of Andrews' vocal work, the unfortunate truth is that licensing restrictions did not permit them to include anything after 1967 and *Thoroughly Modern Millie*, thus leaving the latter part of her career unrepresented. The good news is that the album includes 19 selections, with several coming from Andrews' solo albums (which met with limited success at the time of their original release.) Many of the familiar numbers are here, too, of course, including "Super-Cali-Fragil-Istic-Expi-Ali-Docious" (though "A Spoonful of Sugar" is missing) and "My Favourite Things." For the average Julie Andrews fan, there's nothing here to disagree with, and a lot to be delighted about, in lieu of a series of catalog releases on compact disc. Another typically excellent mastering job from Rhino, of course (almost a boring report), along with interesting liner notes and scads of pictures. *—Steven McDonald*

Fred Astaire (Frederick Austerlitz)

b. May 10, 1899, Omaha, NE, **d.** Jun. 22, 1987, Los Angeles, CA
Vocals, Dancer / Traditional Pop, Standards, Show Tunes
Without question, one of the greatest all-around performers in motion picture history, though his vocal skills were among the least of his talents. Indeed, to overstate Fred Astaire's average musical ability only serves to demean his genius as a dancer. The extreme athleticism and rhythmic sophistication of his dance was masked by an air of off-handed suaveness that emphasized an utter control of his medium. That same delivery, transposed to song, revealed a genial, somewhat rhythmically astute, but ultimately unexceptional vocalist, whose limitations could not be hidden by strong material and/or a winning personality. Astaire's warbling mezzo tenor was little more than a slightly melodicized extension of his speaking voice—charming, perhaps, and certainly effective given the relatively low artistic standards of the run-of-the-mill Hollywood film, yet no more profound than one of their typically threadbare plots. In the '30s Astaire and Ginger Rogers co-starred in a series of superficial but often quite witty musical comedies, such as *Roberta*, *Top Hat*, and *Shall We Dance?* The most important songwriters of the '30s and '40s wrote songs especially for him—Irving Berlin, Johnny Mercer, Cole Porter, and George Gershwin among them. He was often the first to sing songs that would become standards—Berlin purportedly preferred Astaire's renditions of his tunes to those of any other vocalist. *—Chris Kelsey*

Fred Astaire at MGM / Oct. 16, 1933-Feb. 15, 1957 / Rhino ✦✦✦✦✦
Fred Astaire appeared in 30 movie musicals between 1933 and 1957, 11 each for the RKO and MGM studios. Most of the RKO pictures were made in the 1930s and co-starred Ginger Rogers; they are Astaire's best-known film work. But the MGM films, most of them made between 1944 and 1957, were often lavish, color spectaculars, and some of them, notably *Easter Parade* and *The Barkleys of Broadway* (a reunion with Rogers), were big box office hits. Astaire made few studio recordings during the period, and in those days soundtracks were only beginning to be released on record. So, this two-CD set, a compilation of 39 of Astaire's soundtrack performances at MGM running over two and a half hours, is a valuable document. One must imagine Astaire and his various partners (among them Joan Crawford, Judy Garland, and Jane Powell) dancing during the extended musical interludes, and the elaborate arrangements for large orchestra and chorus sometimes swamp the sterling efforts of such songwriters as Irving Berlin, Howard Dietz, George and Ira Gershwin, Burton Lane, Alan Jay Lerner, Johnny Mercer, Cole Porter, Arthur Schwartz, and Harry Warren. It must be noted, too, that with a handful of exceptions ("Steppin' Out With My Baby," "Easter Parade," "They Can't Take That Away From Me," "That's Entertainment," "I Guess I'll Have to Change My Plan"), the compositions are not among the songwriters' best and far inferior to the material Astaire had to work with at RKO. Still, these are some of the best performances of the last part of Fred Astaire's career as a musical entertainer. *—William Ruhlmann*

● **Starring Fred Astaire** / Jun. 26, 1935-Sep. 22, 1940 / Columbia ✦✦✦✦✦
This 36-track album traces Fred Astaire's recordings from June 1935 to September 1940, including his number one hits with "Cheek to Cheek," "I'm Putting All My Eggs in One Basket," "The Way You Look Tonight," "A Fine Romance," "They Can't Take That Away From Me," "Nice Work If You Can Get It," and "Change Partners." In addition to his movie stardom, Astaire was a major recording success in the second half of the '30s, introducing songs that would become standards by some of the great songwriters of the era—Irving Berlin, Jerome Kern, and Dorothy Fields, and the Gershwins, especially. These recordings, which are studio efforts, not identical to the same songs in the movies, show Astaire to be as effortless a singer as he is a dancer (and you get to hear the tapping of those famous feet now and then, too). *—William Ruhlmann*

★ **Fred Astaire & Ginger Rogers at RKO** / 1998 / Rhino ✦✦✦✦✦
Fred Astaire & Ginger Rogers is a stunning double-disc set featuring 35 tracks (including ten previously unreleased songs) culled from 11 musicals the pair made for RKO between 1933 and 1943, including *The Gay Divorcee*, *Swing Time*, *Flying Down to Rio*, *Top Hat* and *The Sky's the Limit*. The duo were at the height of their popularity and creativity during this era, and many of the songs that appeared in these films became standards including "A Needle in a Haystack," "Night and Day," "The Continental," "Top Hat, White Tie and Tails," "Cheek to Cheek," "Let's Begin," "I'll Be Hard to Handle," "I'm Putting All My Eggs in One Basket," "Let's Face the Music and Dance," "Pick Yourself Up," "The Way You Look Tonight," "A Fine Romance," "A Foggy Day," "Nice Work If You Can Get It," "Let's Call the Whole Thing Off," "They Can't Take That Away From Me" and "One for My Baby (And One More for the Road)."

These are the versions that became popular through their appearences in movies, and while Astaire was limited as a singer, his voice was charming and helped make these songs the standards they are. And there is no better way to get his best, original versions than *Fred Astaire & Ginger Rogers at RKO*. *—Stephen Thomas Erlewine*

The Complete London Sessions / 1999 / EMI ✦✦✦✦✦

Charles Aznavour (Chahnour Varinag Aznavourian)

b. May 22, 1924, Paris, France
Vocals / Vocal Pop
Singing from his own experiences of love and sorrow, Charles Aznavour was an international singing sensation in the 1950s and '60s. Being married three times, Charles Aznavour sings of unrequited and frustrating love. He is credited as being a singer, songwriter and actor performing in *Shoot the Piano Player, Candy* and *The Tin Drum*.

Charles Aznavour was born Chahnour Varinag Aznavourian in the Latin Quarter in 1924. His father was an Armenian cook while his mother was an actress and a seamstress. With encouragement from his parents, Charles Aznavour made his theatrical debut as a dancer at the age of nine. After performing with Jean Daste's dramatic troupe, he formed a nightclub act in 1944 with singer, composer Pierre Roche. During this partnership, Charles Aznavour wrote lyrics and began to be internationally known. This duet was short-lived. With encouragement from Mistinguette, Maurice Chevalier and Edith Piaf, he began performing on his own. His career began slowly but grew to include film, stage and theater.

Unfortunately for Aznavour, his songs were banned from French radio because they were too risque. His songs were drawn from his own life and love experiences, revolving around the philosophy of "Live now—tomorrow, who knows?" His fame as a singer and songwriter came only after his acting debut.

He made his Paris debut at the Cinema Alhambra. He appeared in Andre Cayatte's *Tomorrow Is My Turn*, earning himself the best-acting award at the 1960 Cannes Film Festival for his performance. He also played a pathetic neighborhood piano player in Francois Truffant's *Shoot the Piano Player*. His credits also include composing the title song for the 1970 film *Love Story*. It was a combination of appearing in stellar films and his melancholy songwriting that made Charles Aznavour a star in the entertainment industry. In his quest for truth in love and sorrow he overcame the obstacle of being banned from the airwaves to become a '50s and '60s musical genius. His raspy style of singing made his love songs even more believable and touching.

Aside from his acting, singing and songwriting, Charles Aznavour has three children and a passion for racing sports cars. He married his third wife, Ulla Thorsell, in Las Vegas in 1967. He is known as being a teetotaler and a milk drinker. His life philosophy is "I can relax eternally when I'm dead—*Life has to be lived*." —Kim Summers

Aznavour Live: Palais des Congres / 1999 / Angel ✦✦✦✦✦
The double-disc set *Aznavour Live: Palais des Congres* was ostensibly recorded during 1997-98, though the first song is a duet between Aznavour and Edith Piaf (who died in 1963). That irregularity aside, Aznavour is in excellent voice, and the backing orchestra is able to translate the moods of many different kinds of material, from playful songs like Pierre Roche's "Le Feutre Taupé" to tender ballads like "Plus Bleu Que Tes Yeux." The sound quality is amazingly vivid too, and this *Palais des Congres* concert is one of the highlights of Aznavour's long career. *—John Bush*

Mildred Bailey (Mildred Rinker)

b. 1901, Tekoa, WA, **d.** Dec. 12, 1951, Poughkeepsie, WA
Vocals / Traditional Pop, Standards, Swing, Classic Female Blues
An early jazz singer with a sweet voice that belied her plump physique, Mildred Bailey balanced a good deal of popular success with a hot jazz-slanted career that saw her billed as Mrs. Swing (her husband, Red Norvo, was Mr. Swing). Born Mildred Rinker in Washington state in 1907, Bailey began performing at an early age, playing piano and singing in movie theaters during the early '20s. By 1925, she was the headlining act at a club in Hollywood, doing a mixture of pop, early jazz tunes, and vaudeville standards. Influenced by Ethel Waters, Bessie Smith and Connie Boswell, she developed a soft, swinging delivery that pleased all kinds of nightclub audiences in the area. After sending a demonstration disc in to Paul Whiteman in 1929, she gained a spot with one of the most popular dance orchestras of the day.

The added exposure with Whiteman soon gave Bailey her own radio program. She had already debuted on a recording date with guitarist Eddie Lang in 1929, but in 1932 she gained fame by recording what became her signature song "Rockin' Chair"—written especially for her by Hoagie Carmichael—with a Whiteman small group. Recording for Vocalion during the '30s, Bailey often utilized her husband, xylophonist Red Norvo. She also appeared on his recordings of the late '30s, and the arrangements of Eddie Sauter proved a perfect accompaniment to her vocals.

Though she and Norvo later divorced, Bailey continued to perform and record during the 1940s. She appeared on Benny Goodman's *Camel Caravan* radio program, and gained her own series again during the mid-'40s. Hampered by health problems during the late '40s, she spent time in the hospital suffering from diabetes and died of a heart attack in 1951. *—John Bush*

★ **Her Greatest Performances (1929-1946)** / 1929-1946 / Columbia ✦✦✦✦✦
This three-LP box set (which deserves to be reissued on CD) lives up to its name. Bailey was one of the top singers of the '30s and this package, which features highlights from her career (mostly dating from 1933-1939), shows why. She holds her own with a variety of all-star groups which include such classic players as trumpeters Bunny Berigan, Buck Clayton, Charlie Shavers, and Roy Eldridge (the latter is great on "I'm Nobody's Baby"), trombonist Tommy Dorsey, clarinetist Benny Goodman, altoist Johnny Hodges, tenors Coleman Hawkins and Chu Berry, pianists Teddy Wilson and Mary Lou Williams, and her husband, xylophonist Red Norvo. There are lots of gems on this definitive set. *—Scott Yanow*

Pearl Bailey

b. Mar. 29, 1918, Newport News, VA, **d.** Aug. 17, 1990, Philadelphia, PA
Vocals / Traditional Pop
An unhibited vocalist who gave more to her performances than any other singers around, Pearl Bailey gained fame for her work in Broadway, cabaret, and Hollywood. Bailey's sultry, slurred delivery livened up many a stale standard, including "Baby It's Cold Outside" and her only hit, "Takes Two to Tango."

The daughter of a preacher, Bailey began singing at the age of three (her brother, Bill Bailey, also taught her a few dance steps). She was performing professionally by her early teenage years and after touring as a dancer for several years, she featured both as a singer and dancer with jazz bands led by Noble Sissle, Cootie Williams and Edgar Hayes. She began performing as a solo act in 1944, and wooed nightclub audiences with her relaxed stage-presence and humorous asides. After briefly replacing Sister Rosetta Tharpe in Cab Calloway's Orchestra during the mid-'40s, she debuted on Broadway during 1946 in the musical *St. Louis Woman*. Bailey earned an award for most promising newcomer, and made her first film, *Variety Girl*, in 1947.

Though it wasn't a hit, her version of "Tired" (from *Variety Girl*) increased her standing in the jazz community. She recorded for several different labels, including Columbia, during the '40s and finally found a hit in 1952 after signing to Coral. Her version of "Takes Two to Tango," backed by Don Redman's Orchestra, hit the Top Ten. That same year, she married drummer Louie Bellson, and he left his position with Duke Ellington to become her musical director. Bailey recorded several albums for Coral during the early '50s, and starred as a fortune-teller in the 1954 film *Carmen Jones*. More starring roles followed, in the W.C. Handy biopic *St. Louis Blues* as well as the first filmed version of Gershwin's classic operetta *Porgy and Bess*.

In 1959, a new recording contract (with Roulette) resulted in a change of direction. After her double-entendre LP *For Adults Only* was banned from radio play, it became a big seller and occasioned a string of similar albums during the early '60s. She continued to perform on Broadway, and won a Tony award in 1970 for her title role in *Hello, Dolly!*. She led her own television variety show in 1971, but retired from active performance several years later. She was named to the American delegation to the United Nations in 1975, and awarded the Medal of Freedom in 1988. *—John Bush*

Pearl Bailey Sings for Adults Only / 1959 / Roulette ✦✦✦✦✦
Delightfully wicked set of standards done up in the inimitable Pearl Bailey manner, with immaculately swinging support from husband/drummer/bandleader Louis Bellson. *—Cub Koda*

Porgy and Bess / Apr. 30, 1959 / Columbia ✦✦✦

● **16 Most Requested Songs** / 1991 / Columbia/Legacy ✦✦✦✦✦

Josephine Baker (Freda Carson)

b. Jun. 3, 1906, St. Louis, MO, **d.** Apr. 12, 1975, Paris, France
Vocals / Traditional Pop, Cabaret
Born into poverty in St. Louis, dancer and singer Josephine Baker progressed from vaudeville to New York theater to the Parisian cabaret scene and became the toast of Europe before the age of 21. Though her later career wasn't quite able to handle such an early peak, Baker spent much of her life working tirelessly against prejudice, during World War II in Europe and the civil-rights era in America. She's still one of the most famous expatriates in American history, perfectly epitomizing the hedonistic abandon of the Jazz Age in Paris.

Born in 1906, Baker spent a hardscrabble childhood in St. Louis. She began working in vaudeville, and caught her big break in 1921 while dancing in the chorus for the all-black revue *Shuffle Along*. A frenetic dancer and relentless onstage clown, she quickly attracted notice, and 1924's *Chocolate Dandies* made her a star in New York. One year later, she became the toast of Paris, her exotic dancing, uninhibited sexuality, and negligible attire suiting the continent much more than America. She starred in several movies and also made her first studio recordings during the early '30s; after a brief return to America however, she became a naturalized French citizen with her marriage to a sugar magnate.

Baker worked tirelessly for the French Resistance during World War II, though her return to active entertainment in the late '40s was a bit of a struggle; she worked the cabaret circuit in Paris for several years before returning to America yet again. During the early '50s, Baker's fight to spread the gospel of civil rights made headlines. Though Baker spent much of the '60s raising her many adopted children, she also participated in the 1963 civil-rights march on Washington and gave several concerts to raise funds for the cause. After suffering a heart attack in 1964, her performance career practically ended, except for a brief comeback just before her death from a stroke in 1975. *—John Bush*

● **Josephine Baker** / Dec. 1926-Nov. 1936 / Sandstone ✦✦✦✦✦
Josephine Baker was much more famous as a cabaret performer, dancer and personality than as a jazz singer but, as she shows on some of these early recordings, she could swing and improvise when she wanted to. The two-CD set gives one a well-rounded picture of Baker's prime period and a surprising percentage of the songs are jazz standards such as "Dinah," "I Found a New Baby," "Bye Bye Blackbird," "Blue Skies," "You're Driving Me Crazy," etc. The musicianship of the French bands, which is rather streaky on part of the first disc, greatly improves by the later tracks and Baker is heard at her best throughout. It's a perfect introduction to her singing talents. *—Scott Yanow*

Complete Recorded Works: 1926-27 / Oct. 12, 1999 / Document ✦✦✦
This finds Josephine Baker at the dawn of her music career, recording in France with various backing groups. While some of the later cuts emphasize the over-emoting chanteuse she eventually became, the early sides come closer to real jazz, even if the backing groups lack rhythmic pizzazz. The most interesting tracks here are her version of "Dinah" and her solo efforts (on which she accompanies herself on ukulele). If you're only used to hearing Baker singing in French and doing bombastic show tunes, this set will come as a revelation. *—Cub Koda*

Brigitte Bardot

Vocals / Celebrity, Obscuro, French Pop

The archetypal sex kitten, Brigitte Bardot was the first foreign-language star ever to attain a level of international success comparable to America's most popular homegrown talents. While the vast majority of her motion pictures failed to rank even remotely close to the best of her native France's prodigious New Wave-era output, they proved a major breakthrough in establishing a market for foreign films in English-speaking countries; indeed, for all of the acclaim deservedly heaped on the more gifted actors and directors of her day, perhaps no other factor was more crucial to the far-reaching success of world cinema than Bardot's sultry allure. After over a decade of modeling and acting in over a score of movies (notably *Le Trou Normand, Cette Sacree Gamine, La Verite*) Bardot released her first album with 1960's *Inside Brigitte Bardot.* Several other LPs, including 1963's *Brigitte Bardot Sings* and 1968's *Special Bardot,* were to follow, and she scored a number of hit singles in tandem with the infamous singer/songwriter Serge Gainsbourg. When several mid-'60s films failed to live up to international box-office expectations, few of Bardot's subsequent films were screened outside of France. By 1974, Bardot announced plans for retirement; apart from a handful of television appearances, she consistently refused all offers to return to the screen. In later years she became something of a recluse, but continued to make occasional headlines through her ardent support of animal rights causes. *—Jason Ankeny*

● **Best of BB** / Oct. 15, 1996 / Polydor ✦✦✦✦✦

Shirley Bassey

b. Jan. 8, 1937, Tiger Bay, Cardiff, Wales

Vocals / Traditional Pop, Show Tunes

Known to Americans most for her belting rendition of the theme to *Goldfinger,* the 1964 edition in the James Bond series (as well as 1971's *Diamonds Are Forever* and 1979's *Moonraker*), Shirley Bassey was one of the most popular female vocalists in Britain during the last half of the 20th century. Her early career in touring shows and cabaret brought her a recording contract with Philips by the late '50s. After reaching the top of the British singles charts twice around the turn of the '60s, a 1962 pairing with arranger Nelson Riddle increased her prestige in America, and a vaunted live show gained her headlining spots in both New York and Las Vegas. Tapped to swing the theme song to the third James Bond vehicle, her brassy, sexy version of "Goldfinger" conveyed the James Bond myth perfectly and became a big hit in America. Though later chart placings in the US were few, she continued to hit the British Top Ten during the mid-'70s, and gained her own highly rated BBC-TV show later that decade. Semi-retired by 1981, she nevertheless emerged quite frequently, spurred by the recording of several television specials and LPs. *—John Bush*

● **Goldsinger: The Best of Shirley Bassey** / 1995 / EMI ✦✦✦✦✦

Welsh/Nigerian belter Shirley Bassey's 1995 collection *Goldsinger: The Best of Shirley Bassey* is a near-perfect way for the novice American listener to be introduced to one of the international music community's most famous vocalists. Amazingly, she only scored one major hit in the United States, ("Goldfinger"), for which she is best remembered. Her overseas catalog of hits, however, is huge. This collection does a fine job assembling the best of her overseas hits, some of the biggest being "As Long as He Needs Me" from *Oliver!,* "Climb Ev'ry Mountain" from Broadway's "The Sound of Music," and "Reach for the Stars." That last song, as Joseph Laredo's excellent liner notes point out, peaked at number 120 on American charts, to give an idea of the disparity between her stateside and European careers. This collection includes some fine rarities (and gems in their own right) previously unavailable in the United States. Among those are "Ave Maria," her version of *West Side Story's* "Tonight," and her stirring early recording "With These Hands." To round the collection out, as expected, are the James Bond themes "Diamonds Are Forever" and "Moonraker," as well as two versions of the title track. For the uninitiated as well as the fan, this collection provides a fine summary of some of this legendary vocalist's best work. Kudos to the production team who made this album happen. *—Jose Promis*

Harry Belafonte

b. Mar. 1, 1927, Harlem, New York City, NY

Vocals / Caribbean Folk, Traditional Pop, Calypso, Traditional Folk

An actor, humanitarian and the acknowledged "King of Calypso," Harry Belafonte ranked among the most seminal performers of the postwar era. One of the most successful African-American pop stars in history, Belafonte's staggering talent, good looks and masterful assimilation of folk, jazz and worldbeat rhythms allowed him to achieve a level of mainstream eminence and crossover popularity virtually unparalleled in the days before the advent of the civil rights movement—a cultural uprising which he himself helped spearhead. Initially, he put his clear, silky voice to work as a straight pop singer, launching his recording career on the Jubilee label in 1949; however, at the dawn of the 1950s he discovered folk music, learning material through the Library of Congress' American folk songs archives while also discovering West Indian music. With his lead role in Otto Preminger's film adapation of Oscar Hammerstein's *Carmen Jones,* Belafonte shot to stardom; after signing to the RCA label, he issued *"Mark Twain" and Other Folk Favorites,* which reached the number three slot on the *Billboard* charts in the early weeks of 1956. His next effort, titled simply *Belafonte,* reached number one, kickstarting a national craze for calypso music; *Calypso,* also issued in 1956, topped the charts for a staggering 31 weeks on the strength of hits like "Jamaica Farewell" and the immortal "Banana Boat (Day-O)." As the Beatles and other stars of the British Invasion began to dominate the pop charts, Belafonte's impact as a commercial force diminished; after 1970's *Homeward Bound,* he retired from recording for the next several years, and his primary focus remained his work as a civil rights activist. *—Jason Ankeny*

★ **Calypso** / 1956 / RCA ✦✦✦✦✦

This is the album that made Harry Belafonte's career. Up to this point, calypso had only been a part of Belafonte's focus in his recordings of folk music styles. But with this landmark album, calypso not only became tattooed to Belafonte permanently, it had a revolutionary effect on folk music in the 1950s and 60s. The album consists of songs from Trinidad, mostly written by West Indian songwriter Irving Burgie (aka "Lord Burgess"). Burgie's two most successful songs are included: "Day O" and "Jamaica Farewell" (which were both hit singles for Belafonte), as are the evocative ballads "I Do Adore Her" and "Come Back Liza" and what could be the first feminist folk song, "Man Smart (Woman Smarter)." *Calypso* became the first million-selling album by a single artist, spending an incredible 31 weeks at the top of the *Billboard* album charts, remaining on the charts for 99 weeks. It triggered a veritable tidal wave of imitators, parodists, and artists wishing to capitalize on its success. Years later, it remains a record of inestimable influence, inspiring many folk singers and groups to perform, most notably the Kingston Trio, which was named for the Jamaican capital. For a decade, just about every folk singer and folk group featured in their repertoire at least one song that was of West Indian origin or one that had a calypso beat. They all can be attributed to this one remarkable album.

Despite the success of *Calypso,* Harry Belafonte refused to be typecast. Resisting the impulse to record an immediate follow-up album, Belafonte instead spaced his calypso albums apart, releasing them at five-year intervals in 1961, 1966, and 1971. *—Cary Ginell*

Belafonte Sings the Blues / 1958 / RCA Victor ✦✦✦

★ **Belafonte at Carnegie Hall** / 1959 / RCA Victor ✦✦✦✦✦

The granddaddy of all live albums, this double-LP set captures the excitement of a Harry Belafonte concert at the height of his popularity. Sampled from two consecutive performances of identical material, *Belafonte at Carnegie Hall* was an anomaly at a time when only comedy albums were recorded outside of the studio environment. It wasn't the first live album ever made, but it was certainly the first to be a major financial and artistic success. It stayed on the best-selling album charts for over three years, and remained in print until RCA discontinued pressing LPs.

From the opening trumpet fanfare and brief orchestral overture to the epic 12-minute version of "Matilda" (which set a standard for audience participation), the album never lets up. It is exciting, poignant, thrilling, intimate, and at times, spontaneously hilarious. Belafonte's mastery in front of an audience was never better displayed than here, a mastery that has resulted in him becoming one of the most popular concert draws in history. Producer Bob Bollard and orchestra leader Bob Corman deftly integrated the 47-piece orchestra into the performance but knew when to lay back to let Belafonte sing, accompanied by a small combo of two guitars, bass, and percussion. The concert is divided in three sections: "Moods of the American Negro," "In the Caribbean," and "Around the World." All the hits are here: "Day O," "Jamaica Farewell," "Mama Look A Boo Boo," and others, plus calypso, folk songs, chain gang songs, spirituals, and songs from other lands, representing a veritable best-of package of his first decade with RCA Victor. For sheer scope and genius of performance, this is the quintessential Belafonte package. *—Cary Ginell*

An Evening With Harry Belafonte & Friends / Aug. 26, 1997 / Polygram ✦✦✦✦✦

An Evening With Harry Belafonte & Friends is an album to accompany the live performance of the same shown on PBS television stations in 1997. It is a remarkable album, especially considering Belafonte's longevity. The album contains multiple songs dealing with oppression and freedom, as it is one of Belafonte's major endeavors. There are some beautiful pieces written by guitarist Richard Bona, of Cameroon, such as "Eyala" and "Eyando." Also, Jake Holmes provides numerous compositions that seem surely made solely for the soul of Belafonte. Of course, a Harry Belafonte album wouldn't be complete without Lord Burgess' "Jamaica Farewell" or "Day-O," so they are included as well. The main highlight on the album, though, is "Matilda," which is something of a calypso standard in itself. Belafonte turns the piece into a full-fledged, ten-minute *tour de force,* pulling out every stop that calypso can afford to make, in all its beauty. The video is a worthwhile piece by itself, but the album is also a worthy pick. *—Adam Greenberg*

☆ **Greatest Hits** / Jul. 25, 2000 / RCA ✦✦✦✦✦

Digitally remastered in 2000, RCA's triple-disc package *Greatest Hits* is a stellar overview of Harry Belafonte's career, covering 53 tracks spanning the years 1952-1972. While Belafonte is, of course, best known for popularizing calypso music, *Greatest Hits* doesn't place a disproportionate emphasis on that aspect of his career; instead, the collection is a testament to Belafonte's eclecticism and versatility. His voice may have been tailor-made for straight-ahead pop, but Belafonte was most at home on folk material, and his sources ranged far and wide. Not only from standard American folk repertory and his beloved Caribbean, but jazz, blues, Appalachian folk, British folk, and slave spirituals and work songs, not to mention the wealth of material rediscovered during the 1960s folk revival. *Greatest Hits* isn't the ultimate word on Belafonte—some of his individual albums remain important, essential works in their own right, particularly *Calypso*—but as a thorough encapsulation of his career, it's richly rewarding and virtually flawless. *—Steve Huey*

Tony Bennett (Anthony Dominick Benedetto)

b. Aug. 3, 1926, Queens, NY

Vocals / Vocal Jazz, Traditional Pop, Vocal Pop, Ballads, Show Tunes

Any discussion of Tony Bennett within the context of a book on jazz ought to start with the disclaimer that he is not, never was, and doesn't claim to be, a "jazz singer" per se. However, there isn't any question that Bennett has always felt a kinship with jazz musicians and has collaborated with them several times in his long career, often with delightful results. Though not an improviser, Bennett could always follow the contours of a jazz rhythm section with confidently jazzy inflections; indeed, he sounds absolutely ebullient whenever he records with jazzers. Bennett's pianist and musical director since the 1950s, Ralph Sharon, is a solid, dependable jazzman in his own right, and has occasionally steered his boss away from the all-American easy-listening ballad into a more jazz-oriented setting. Bennett counts among his influences Art Tatum, from whom he drew ideas on phrasing and breathing, Mildred Bailey for her relaxed delivery, and of course, the inevitable Billie Holiday and Frank Sinatra, who once proclaimed Bennett to be the best singer in the business. Indeed, as Sinatra's voice aged, Bennett found himself in the position of being the leading purveyor of American popular songs by 1990. *—Richard S. Ginell*

☆ **40 Years: The Artistry of Tony Bennett** / 1950-1972 / Columbia/Legacy ✦✦✦✦✦
When this impressive box set was released in 1991, it put the capstone upon Tony Bennett's remarkable return to prominence by looking back at a legacy that had been overshadowed by that of the colossus Sinatra. The collection methodically traces his career from his first Columbia record, "Boulevard of Broken Dreams," in 1950, through the hit singles and key or capriciously selected album tracks up until 1972. Then, after borrowing three tracks from Fantasy's 1975 Tony Bennett/Bill Evans project (including an exquisite "Some Other Time" with a "Peace Piece" introduction from Evans), the box leaps eleven years ahead to contemplate Bennett's unlikely resurrection as an icon of the cynical young. Bennett's early records are almost operatic in feeling, a honey-smooth Italian tenor building toward histrionic climaxes, but the voice eventually busts loose into an outgoing, life-celebrating baritone, and by the 1980s, re-emerges as a darker, softer, even somewhat raspy replica of itself. There isn't much for the jazz listener here other than an occasional session with Count Basie (dig their ebullient "Lullaby of Broadway" together), a few cameos by jazz names, the Evans tracks, or some upbeat charts by Ralph Sharon, Ralph Burns and a few others. Ultimately, the most striking difference between Bennett's records and Sinatra's is the sheer, unbeatably high quality of arrangements that Sinatra was able to get. Yet despite the abundance of period MOR treacle, many of these records are more interesting than memory recalls; for example, it's difficult to resist such a naively joyous track as Frank DeVol's rendering of "Put On a Happy Face" that has the Mitch Miller era written all over it. There is no better Tony Bennett retrospective at any price, although jazz specialists might be better served by the *Jazz* compilation. *—Richard S. Ginell*

All-Time Greatest Hits / 1950 / Columbia ✦✦✦✦✦
Tony Bennett's departure from Columbia Records after 22 years in 1972 inspired the label to put together a one-volume hits compilation (originally released on two LPs) of 20 songs covering his entire Columbia output, from "Boulevard Of Broken Dreams" and the early hits like "Because Of You" and "Rags To Riches," through the early-to-mid-'60s hit period of "I Left My Heart In San Francisco" and "I Wanna Be Around," to the more problematic late '60s and early '70s of "Something" and "Love Story." The selection sacrifices quality to achieve breadth; it represents all phases of Bennett's career up to this point, but doesn't really include his 20 best performances or even his 20 biggest hits. Nevertheless, it's a good place for the complete novice to start. (Note, however, that several selections are in fake stereo and several are re-recorded versions, not the original recordings.) *— William Ruhlmann*

★ **Jazz** / 1954-1967 / Columbia ✦✦✦✦✦
What a wonderful idea. This is a compilation album ranging across Tony Bennett's early career, from 1954 to 1967, highlighting some of his more adventurous sessions with jazz musicians, including Count Basie, Herbie Hancock, Herbie Mann, Art Blakey, Stan Getz, and others, and featuring jazz standards like "Green Dolphin Street," along with a healthy dose of Duke Ellington compositions. Bennett not only holds his own, he sounds delighted on every track. The ironic thing, of course, is that Columbia frowned on these kinds of side excursions from his pop career in the '50s. Now, all is forgiven, and this proves an unusually imaginative repackaging that illuminates an important part of Bennett's talent and further contributes to his '80s renaissance. (The album contains a previously unreleased 1964 performance of "Danny Boy" featuring Stan Getz. Originally released as a two-LP set, *Jazz* was compressed to a 68-minute CD by excising two tracks.) *— William Ruhlmann*

The Beat of My Heart / 1957 / Columbia ✦✦✦✦✦
On only his third full-length, 12-inch LP, Tony Bennett comes up with a concept album, singing against novel percussion arrangements, backed by drummers like Art Blakey, Jo Jones, Chico Hamilton, Billy Exiner, Candido, and Sabu. Several songs feature only drums and flutes. Over this unusual instrumentation, Bennett sings beautifully, giving his usual full-voiced emotion to songs like "Lullaby Of Broadway," "Let's Face The Music And Dance," and "Just One Of Those Things." This was the first album to give notice that Bennett was more than just another near-operatic, melodramatic pop singer of the early 1950s. Here was a man who had jazz chops, musical imagination, and a sense of swing. He was practically a hipster! *— William Ruhlmann*

Chicago / 1959 / DCC ✦✦✦

★ **Tony's Greatest Hits, Vol. 3** / 1960 / Columbia ✦✦✦✦✦
Tony Bennett's third hits collection isn't only the best of his best-ofs, it's a classic "classic pop" album. Bennett's career hit its second and highest artistic peak in the first half of the 1960s, starting with "I Left My Heart In San Francisco" and continuing through a series of magnificent ballad hits—"I Wanna Be Around," "The Good Life," "This Is All I Ask," "When Joanna Loved Me," "Who Can I Turn To," "If I Ruled the World"—all of which are here, along with such equally impressive album tracks as "Once Upon a Time" and "The Best Is Yet to Come." As a result, this album became Bennett's second gold seller, and it remains the definitive statement of a major pop singer at his zenith. A complete understanding of his work requires a listen to his 1991 box set, *Forty Years: The Artistry of Tony Bennett.* But this 12-song set, covering the years 1962-1965, remains the brightest jewel in his crown. *— William Ruhlmann*

☆ **I Left My Heart in San Francisco** / 1962 / Columbia ✦✦✦✦✦
Along with his producer, Ernest Altschuler, and his arranger/pianist Ralph Sharon, Tony Bennett had been searching for a repertoire and a musical approach beyond his long-gone pop work with Mitch Miller of the early '50s and his artistically pleasing but commercially dicey jazz work of the mid-to-late '50s. It seemed to be a combination of Broadway songs and other contemporary material, carefully selected and arranged to show off Bennett's now-burnished vocals, which, as he approached the end of his thirties, were starting to to be located in a more comfortable range closer to a baritone than a tenor. With this album, they found the key, not only by happening across a signature song in the title track, but also in the approach to songs like "Once Upon A Time," a gem from the flop musical *All American,* and Cy Coleman and Carolyn Leigh's "The Best Is Yet To Come," which Bennett helped make a standard. (Frank Sinatra didn't do it until two years later.) From here on until the world changed again toward the late '60s, Bennett would not have to feel that he had to compromise his art for popularity, making uptempo singles in an attempt to meet the marketplace while longing to do ballads and swing material instead. *I Left My Heart In San Francisco,* a gold-selling Top 10 hit that stayed in the charts almost three years, demonstrated that he could have it all. (Tony Bennett won two 1962 Grammy Awards for the title song: Record of the Year and Best Solo Vocal Performance, Male.) *— William Ruhlmann*

At Carnegie Hall / Jun. 9, 1962 / Sony Special Products ✦✦✦✦✦
Recorded on June 9, 1962, one week before the release of the *I Left My Heart in San Francisco* album that would catapult Tony Bennett's career into the stratosphere, this concert album effectively sums up his accomplishments so far. Some of the hits—"Stranger in Paradise," "Rags to Riches," "Because of You"—are still on the set list (although drastically rearranged), but clearly he has found his true repertoire in reinventions of older material like "All the Things You Are" (the version here is exquisite) and good choices of new songs—he champions the team of Cy Coleman and Carolyn Leigh, and introduces "San Francisco," which some in the audience already know. (Released as a single in advance of the *San Francisco* album, it was in the charts already.) And on the album's original four LP sides, Bennett managed to find time for such experiments as an up-tempo "Ol' Man River" featuring percussionist Candido, a throwback to his innovative *Beat of My Heart* album. More than his greatest-hits collections of the '50s and early '60s, it gives a broad sense of Bennett's work, and it does so in the format with which he's most comfortable—live in concert. *— William Ruhlmann*

I Wanna Be Around / 1963 / Columbia ✦✦✦✦✦

Who Can I Turn To / 1964 / Columbia ✦✦✦

If I Ruled the World: Songs for the Jet Set / 1965 / Columbia ✦✦✦

Movie Song Album / 1966 / Columbia ✦✦✦

The Tony Bennett Bill Evans Album / 1975 / Columbia ✦✦✦

Together Again / 1976 / DRG ✦✦✦

Art of Excellence / 1986 / Columbia ✦✦✦✦✦
This album marked Tony Bennett's return to recording after half a dozen years, his return to Columbia Records after 14 years, and the beginning of the third stage in his career. Back with the Ralph Sharon Trio and backed by The U.K. Orchestra, Bennett demonstrated that he had spent his time off from recording gathering a bunch of good songs and refining his singing. The older material, such as "A Rainy Day" and "I Got Lost In Her Arms," were better than the new discoveries, like "How Do You Keep The Music Playing?" and "Everybody Has The Blues," but the new ones weren't bad, and with this album Bennett joined and helped to lead the swelling trend toward classic pop. It became his best-selling album in 15 years. *— William Ruhlmann*

Bennett/Berlin / 1987 / Columbia ✦✦✦

Astoria: Portrait of the Artist / 1990 / Columbia ✦✦✦✦✦
Like *The Art Of Excellence,* the album that marked Tony Bennett's return to recording in 1986, *Astoria: A Portrait Of The Artist* was a non-thematic collection of new and old songs on which Bennett was backed both by his regular trio, led by pianist Ralph Sharon, and the U.K. Orchestra. Bennett's new songwriting discovery was Charles DeForest, three of whose songs—"When Do The Bells Ring For Me," "Where Do You Go From Love," and "I've Come Home Again"—were included, along with songs by the Gershwins and Jerome Kern, standards like "Body And Soul," and even a re-recording of Bennett's initial Columbia recording, "The Boulevard Of Broken Dreams." That recording had come in 1950, and the point of *Astoria* (which featured a cover photo of the young Bennett in the old neighborhood, with Bennett today standing in the same spot on the back) was to celebrate that 40-year anniversary while looking into both the past and the future, a task it accomplished admirably. *— William Ruhlmann*

Perfectly Frank / 1992 / Columbia ✦✦✦✦✦

MTV Unplugged / 1994 / Columbia ✦✦✦

Here's to the Ladies / 1995 / Columbia ✦✦✦

Bennett Sings Ellington: Hot & Cool / Sep. 28, 1999 / Columbia ✦✦✦

★ **The Ultimate Tony** / Oct. 3, 2000 / Columbia/Legacy ✦✦✦✦✦
The 20 tracks on this anthology cover Bennett's entire career at Columbia, from his 1951 number one single "Because of You" to "Mood Indigo" from 1999's *Hot and Cool: Bennett Sings Ellington.* Note, however, that "entire career at Columbia" is not synonymous with Bennett's entire career, as there's nothing representing the span between the mid-'60s and the mid-'80s. Since the best Bennett is from the 1950s and early '60s, anyway, that doesn't signify any great loss, particularly as the track selection is considerably weighted toward that era, with 15 of the 20 songs dating from 1951-1965. A 20-song compilation isn't an adequate overview of a singer who has recorded so much material, even in commercial terms; not one of his eight Top 40 singles from 1956 is here, for instance. For those who really want to dig deep into his repertoire, some other compilations, such as the box set *40 Years: The Artistry of Tony Bennett* and *Jazz,* might serve some fans better. For the casual fan, though, this might be the best choice, as it does include the songs listeners are most likely to be familiar with: "I Left My Heart in San Francisco," "Because of You," "Rags to Riches," "I Wanna Be Around," and well-selected non-hits like "The Boulevard of Broken Dreams (Gigolo and Gigolette)" and "Put on a Happy Face." *—Richie Unterberger*

Irving Berlin (Israel Baline)

b. May 11, 1888, Tumen, Russia, **d.** Sep. 22, 1989, New York, NY
Composer / Tin Pan Alley Pop, Traditional Pop, Show Tunes
Irvin Berlin was the most successful songwriter of the 20th century. Though, like his contemporaries, he spent the better part of his career writing songs (usually both words and music) to be used in Broadway musicals, he is better remembered for the songs themselves than

for the shows (and sometimes films) in which they were introduced. This is because Berlin was a master at the kind of music that flourished from the turn of the century until World War II, shows that were really just collections of production numbers, scenes, and novelty acts (organized vaudeville presentations, really) rather than the story musicals that became prevalent starting with Rodgers and Hammerstein's *Oklahoma!* in 1943. It is also because Berlin wrote songs, not scores. But what songs! Out of more than a thousand, a short list would include "Alexander's Ragtime Band" (his first major hit, in 1911), "God Bless America," "A Pretty Girl Is like a Melody," "Always," "Blues Skies," "Puttin' on the Ritz," "How Deep Is the Ocean?," "Cheek to Cheek," "Let's Face the Music and Dance," "White Christmas," "There's No Business like Show Business," "I Love a Piano," "What'll I Do?" "Easter Parade," and "Oh, How I Hate to Get Up in the Morning." Perhaps his greatest and his last hit came with the musical *Annie Get Your Gun* in 1946, though he did write three more before retiring in 1962. *—William Ruhlmann*

Irving Berlin in Hollywood / Feb. 16, 1999 / Rhino ✦✦✦✦✦
This 25-track compilation of Irving Berlin songs from Hollywood musicals was taken from the original soundtrack performances, spanning the dawn of talkies ("Blue Skies," sung by Al Jolson from *The Jazz Singer*) to the mid-1950s (Marilyn Monroe's "After You Get What You Want, You Don't Want It"). Several well-known classics are on board, like "There's No Business Like Show Business," "The Hostess with the Mostess" (sung by Ethel Merman), "Anything You Can Do" (by Judy Garland and Howard Keel), "Top Hat, White Tie and Tails" (by Fred Astaire), and Clark Gable's famous non-virtuosic performance of "Puttin' on the Ritz." Merman, Garland and Astaire perform a bunch of the selections, along with lesser-known actors and singers. Five tracks—notably "Mandy" by Eddie Cantor, Merman and others, and Merman's "Heat Wave"—were previously unreleased. The anthology's enhanced by detailed liner notes from vintage popular music authority Ian Whitcomb. *—Richie Unterberger*

Pat Boone (Charles Eugene Patrick Boone)

b. Jun. 1, 1934, Jacksonville, FL
Vocals / Teen Idol, Pop
In the years immediately prior to the British Invasion, only one performer rivaled the chart dominance of Elvis Presley, and that was Pat Boone. With his trademark white buck shoes, perfectly combed hair and gleaming smile, Boone was the very essence of wholesome American values, and at a time when the rise of rock & roll was viewed as a sign of the apocalypse, he made the music appear safe and non-threatening, earning some 38 Top 40 hits in the process. It's fitting that his achievements rank closest to those of Presley; after all, both claimed the sound of the black R&B culture for their own, in the process straddling both sides of the color line and popularizing a form of music which otherwise might never have gained widespread acceptance. Of course, while Elvis—with his flashy suits, swiveling hips and suggestive leer—remained persona non grata throughout many corners of mainstream America, Boone was embraced by teens and parents alike; his music polished rock's rough edges away, making songs like "Tutti Frutti" and "Ain't That a Shame" palatable to white audiences raised on the soothing pop traditions of a vanishing era. *—Jason Ankeny*

● **Pat Boone's Greatest Hits** / Aug. 1962 / MCA ✦✦✦✦✦
Including 18 of his highest charting hits for the Dot label in the '50s and early '60s, this is easily the best basic Boone collection. It doesn't include his hit covers of "At My Front Door" and Little Richard's "Long Tall Sally" and "Tutti Frutti," which is perhaps just as well for all concerned. *—Richie Unterberger*

More Greatest Hits / Oct. 25, 1994 / Varese Sarabande ✦✦✦
Contains 17 of Pat Boone's later and lesser chart hits. *—William Ruhlmann*

Fifties: Complete / Aug. 5, 1997 / Bear Family ✦✦✦✦✦

The Boswell Sisters

f. 1925, USA, **db.** 1936
Vocals / Vocal Jazz, Tin Pan Alley Pop, Traditional Pop, Classic Jazz, Swing
The Boswell Sisters were the greatest jazz vocal group prior to Lambert, Hendricks and Ross 30 years later. Consisting of Connee, Martha and Helvetia, the trio featured hard-swinging choruses and group scatting with numerous key and tempo changes. Connee received all of the solos but Martha and Helvetia both had very appealing voices too. They recorded "Nights When I'm Lonely" in 1925 and soon were appearing regularly on Los Angeles radio. The group really got going in 1930 with four recordings for Okeh. They were soon signed to Brunswick where they recorded regularly during 1931-35. Their records usually featured top jazz soloists (including Bunny Berigan, the Dorsey Brothers and Joe Venuti) and were often quite exciting. During this period the Boswell Sisters appeared in several films and were a popular radio attraction. They recorded four numbers for Decca in 1936, but by that year all three sisters were married. Martha and Helvetia retired and Connee Boswell (who had been recording solo sides on an occasional basis for several years) went out on her own. A high-point was her recordings with Bob Crosby but otherwise Connee's career (although reasonably satisfying) did not live up to its potential. Ella Fitzgerald always stated that Connee Boswell was her main influence. *—Scott Yanow*

★ **The Boswell Sisters Collection, Vol. 1: 1931-1932** / Mar. 19, 1931-Apr. 9, 1932 / Collector's Classics ✦✦✦✦✦
Most vocal groups that attempt to sing jazz instead end up in the genre of middle-of-road pop music. The Boswell Sisters (comprised of Connee, Vet, and Martha) were a strong exception, always swinging and, by changing tempos and keys frequently while including some other surprises, performing creative jazz of the early '30s. This Collector's Classics CD unfortunately skips their first seven recordings, but then reissues complete and in chronological order 24 of the Boswells finest performances. With a supporting cast frequently including trumpeters Bunny Berigan and Manny Klein, trombonist Tommy Dorsey, and clarinetist Jimmy Dorsey (all of whom receive a generous amount of solo space), the sisters are heard at their best throughout this consistently exciting set. Highlights include "Roll on Mississippi, Roll On," "Shine on, Harvest Moon," "Heebies Jeebies," "River Stay 'Way From My Door," "Put That Sun Back in the Sky," and "There'll Be Some Changes Made." This is an essential acquisition. *—Scott Yanow*

Okay, America!: Alternate Takes and Rarities / May 25, 1931-Jul. 19, 1935 / Vintage Jazz ✦✦✦✦

That's How Rhythm Was Born / 1931-1934 / Columbia/Legacy ✦✦✦✦✦
This 1995 CD has a sampling of the Boswell Sisters' recordings, 20 titles from the premier jazz vocal group's prime period. A few of the tunes are rarities (particularly "Song of Surrender," "Coffee In the Morning" and "Trav'lin All Alone"), while some others have been reissued numerous times ("Shuffle Off to Buffalo," a classic "Sentimental Gentleman From Georgia" and "Minnie the Moocher's Wedding Day"). Although one hopes that all of the Boswells' recordings will be reissued in chronological order someday (this collection skips around a bit), the CD acts as a strong introduction to the music of this magical and innovative group. The Dorsey Brothers Orchestra (with trumpeter Bunny Berigan) provides accompaniment on many of the titles. *—Scott Yanow*

Al Bowlly

b. Jan. 7, 1899, Mozambique, **d.** Apr. 17, 1941, London, England
Vocals, Guitar / Traditional Pop, Music Hall, Swing
The most popular vocalist in Britain during the 1930s, Al Bowlly showcased a range of material unsurpassed by any contemporary other than Bing Crosby. He was also a true international recording artist: born in Mozambique to Greek and Lebanese parents, he was raised in Johannesburg, but gained his musical experience singing for a dance band led by Jimmy Liquime in India and Singapore during the mid-'20s. Just one year after his 1927 debut recording date in Berlin, Bowlly arrived in London for the first time, as part of Fred Elizalde's orchestra. That year, "If I Had You" became one of the first popular songs by an English jazz band to become renowned in America as well, and Bowlly had gone out on his own by the dawn of the '30s. During the next three years, he recorded over 500 songs and appeared with orchestras led by Ray Noble and Lew Stone. A visit to New York in 1934 with Noble resulted in more success; he appeared at the head of an orchestra hand-picked for him and Noble by Glenn Miller (the band included Claude Thornhill, Charlie Spivak and Bud Freeman, among others).

During the mid-'30s, such songs as "Blue Moon," "Easy to Love," "I've Got You Under My Skin" and "My Melancholy Baby" were sizable American successes—so much so that Bowlly gained his own radio series on NBC and traveled to Hollywood to film *The Big Broadcast of 1936,* which also starred one of his biggest competitors, Bing Crosby. He was back in England that same year, appearing with his own band, the Radio City Rhythm Makers, as well as the orchestras of Sydney Lipton, Geraldo and Ken Johnson. Partnered with Jimmy Messini, Bowlly also branched out onto the London stage during the early '40s with an act called Radio Stars with Two Guitars. It was his last venture before his death in 1941, the victim of a German bomb exploded outside his apartment. Fifty years after his death, a British musical named *Melancholy Baby* toured the country with much success. *—John Bush*

● **Just a Bowl of Cherries** / 1993 / Pearl Flapper ✦✦✦✦✦

Jacques Brel

b. Apr. 8, 1929, Brussels, Belgium, **d.** Oct. 9, 1978
Vocals / French Pop, Cabaret, Vocal Pop
Singer/songwriter Jacques Brel created and performed a catalog of literate, thoughtful, and theatrical songs which brought him a large, devoted following in France that eventually extended internationally, making him a major influence on English-speaking writers and performers including Leonard Cohen and David Bowie, while translations of his songs were recorded by a wide range of performers from the Kingston Trio to Frank Sinatra. After relocating from Belgium to Paris to pursue a musical career, Brel played his first professional engagement in 1953. Within a few years, he had achieved prominence in France, and he even earned a U.S. record release with *American Debut* in 1957.

In the early '60s, poet Rod McKuen began writing English lyrics to Brel's songs, and the Kingston Trio recorded "Seasons in the Sun," McKuen's version of a song Brel had written. Brel himself debuted in America at Carnegie Hall in December 1965. In 1966, Damita Jo recorded "If You Go Away," McKuen's version of the Brel composition "Ne Me Quitte Pas," and it reached the charts. The wistful song, with its alternating happy and sad lyrics and lush melody, became a pop standard recorded by dozens of singers including Tom Jones, Frank Sinatra, and Neil Diamond.

In 1967, Brel signed to Reprise Records and undertook a U.S. concert tour, but back in France he abruptly announced his retirement from performing at a concert at the Olympia in Paris, though the following year he starred in a stage production of *Man of La Mancha.* Opening in early 1968, an Off-Broadway revue of his songs named *Jacques Brel Is Alive and Well and Living in Paris* ran nearly 2,000 performances, becoming one of the longest running Off-Broadway shows in history. Columbia Records released a double-LP box set of the complete show as an original cast album. In the mid-'70s, Brel moved to the Marquesas Islands, returning to France only to record *Brel,* his first album in ten years and a massive seller. Terminally ill with lung cancer, Brel again returned to France in July 1978 and died three months later. *—William Ruhlmann*

Brel en Public Olympia 1961 / 1961 / Polydor ✦✦✦✦
Backed by a small orchestra, Brel runs through 15 of his better-known early works with considerable energy and enthusiasm. The sound is good, and the rushes and fades of applause are so sudden that the listener can't be entirely sure whether or not the crowd noises have been dubbed rather than recorded live. For those only casually familiar with the Brel oeuvre, "Ne Me Quitte Pas" and "Marieke" will probably be the most familiar numbers; for those who know more about his repertoire, "Les Flamandes," "Les Biches," and "Les Bourgeois" also count among his more widely known compositions. Some might find this disc on the overwrought and over-the-top side, particular on several performances when the tempo winds itself into a whirlwind, ever-accelerating climax. Much of Brel's public, however, would

view such flamboyant devices and on-the-sleeve emotionalism as assets, not drawbacks. —*Richie Unterberger*

Quinze Ans d'Amour / Nov. 11, 1992 / Musicrama ✦✦✦✦
This 20-track collection from PolyGram compiles every one of Jacques Brel's most popular songs, all in their most famous versions. From his first hit "Quand On N'a Que l'Amour" to early peaks like "La Valse à Mille Temps," "Les Vieux," and "Mathilde," *Quinze Ans d'Amour* picks the best of his early material, with only one song recorded after 1968. —*John Bush*

• **Quand On N'a Que l'Amour** / 1996 / Polydor ✦✦✦✦✦
A massive undertaking, *Quand On N'a Que l'Amour* reissues in roughly chronological order, on ten compact discs, all of the material recorded by Jacques Brel for Barclay and PolyGram between 1955 and 1972—basically his entire career, except for the album recorded one year before his death. From Brel's earliest recordings—including his first hit, the title track—on volume one (subtitled "Grand Jacques"), the box moves into his peak period, the late '50s and early '60s, with famous songs like "Ne Me Quitte Pas," "La Valse à Mille Temps," "Les Vieux," "Jef," "Mathilde," and "La Chanson de Jacky." A pair of highlights are the two live albums Brel recorded at *the Olympia, Paris,* one in 1961 and another in 1964; both are masterpieces of dramatic yet often ironic French pop. In sum, though this enormous box set is obviously no place to begin for neophytes, the collection does indeed offer more experienced fans a *lot* of room to grow into Jacques Brel's music. And though Brel's charms are difficult to understand, especially for those with a language barrier to cope with, his dynamic singing and playful arrangements make a difficult task much easier. —*John Bush*

Teresa Brewer

b. May 7, 1931, Toledo, OH
Vocals / Traditional Pop, Swing
Teresa Brewer started out as a spunky novelty vocalist in the 1950s and weathered the rise of rock to emerge as an exuberant jazz singer in the 1970s. Though some find it disconcerting to hear her cutesy, slightly nasal, *Your Hit Parade*-style delivery in a jazz context, at her best she can swing with a loose and easy fervor, aided greatly by the distinguished company she often keeps on her records. Brewer started singing on *Major Bowes' Amateur Hour* at the age of five and scored her first big hit as a teenager in 1950 with the diabolically catchy "Music! Music! Music!" That ditty found its way onto almost every jukebox in the land and launched a series of hit singles on Coral stretching all the way to 1961. Her marriage to record producer Bob Thiele in 1972 led to her re-emergence via a long string of albums for Thiele's labels (Doctor Jazz, Signature, Red Baron), often in tandem with such luminaries as Count Basie, Benny Carter, Duke and Mercer Ellington, Stephane Grappelli, Earl Hines and Clark Terry. —*Richard S. Ginell*

American Music Box, Vol. 2 / Sep. 7, 1993-Sep. 8, 1993 / Red Baron ✦✦

• **The Music! Music! Music!: The Best of Teresa Brewer** / 1995 / Varese ✦✦✦✦✦
The highlights from Teresa Brewer's time on Coral Records are included on *Best of Teresa Brewer: Music! Music! Music!,* as well as her hit version of the title song, recorded for London. —*Stephen Thomas Erlewine*

Cab Calloway (Cabell Calloway)

b. Dec. 25, 1907, Rochester, NY, **d.** Nov. 18, 1994, Delaware
Vocals / Vocal Jazz, Jive, Swing
One of the great entertainers, Cab Calloway was a household name by 1932 and never really declined in fame. A talented jazz singer and a superior scatter, his gyrations and showmanship on stage at the Cotton Club sometimes overshadowed the quality of his always-excellent bands. Calloway worked in the 1929 revue "Hot Chocolates," started recording in 1930 and in 1931 hit it big with both "Minnie the Moocher" and his regular engagement at the Cotton Club. He was soon (along with Bill Robinson, Ethel Waters, Louis Armstrong and Duke Ellington) the best-known Black entertainer of the era. He appeared in quite a few movies (including 1943's *Stormy Weather*) and "Minnie the Moocher" was followed by such recordings as "Kicking the Gong Around," "Reefer Man," "Minnie the Moocher's Wedding Day," "You Gotta Hi-De-Ho," "The Hi-De-Ho Miracle Man" and even "Mister Paganini, Swing for Minnie." With the end of the big-band era, Calloway had to reluctantly break up his orchestra in 1948 although he continued to perform with his Cab Jivers. —*Scott Yanow*

1930-1931 / Jul. 24, 1930-Jun. 17, 1931 / Classics ✦✦✦✦✦
Cab Calloway is long overdue for a reappraisal. Long put down by some writers as a mere entertainer, he was actually a superior jazz-influenced singer whose vocal abilities were often overshadowed by his showmanship. The ideal way to acquire his best recordings are to get the 12 CDs in Classics' *Complete* series. Not only do these reissues include his hits, but also some jazz instrumentals and enjoyable obscurities that give one a more well-rounded picture of the "Hi-De-Ho Man." This particular Classics CD has his first 24 recordings; from the start, his colorful style was already fully formed. It is particularly interesting to hear Calloway performing some material associated with others, especially "Happy Feet" (Paul Whiteman), "The Viper's Drag" and "I'm Crazy 'Bout My Baby" (the latter two with Fats Waller), and several Duke Ellington hits. One of the better Harlem orchestras, Calloway's early band had formerly been known as the Missourians and included several fine soloists, particularly trumpeter Lammar Wright and Walter Thomas on tenor and baritone. Highlights include "St. Louis Blues," "Some of These Days," a classic rendition of "St. James Infirmary," "Nobody's Sweetheart" and the original version of "Minnie the Moocher." —*Scott Yanow*

1931-1932 / Jul. 9, 1931-Jun. 7, 1932 / Classics ✦✦✦✦
The second of 12 Classics CDs that reissue all of Cab Calloway's recordings from 1930-42 has 23 performances that trace the singer's success during an 11-month period. He shows what he learned from his older sister Blanche on some of the songs, but on "You Rascal You," "Aw You Dawg" and "Kickin' the Gong Around," the singer could be mistaken for no one else but himself. There is a bit of surface noise on some of the tracks (sometimes sounding like a light rain) and even a skip on "Without Rhythm" but the wonderful music far outvalues the minor technical faults. Due to the solos of trumpeter Lammar Wright, clarinetist Arville Harris and the tenor of Walter Thomas, the tight ensembles and Calloway's exuberant (in the case of "Basin Street Blues," rather silly) singing, there are many memorable selections on this set. Highlights include "Bugle Call Rag," "Stardust," "Trickeration," "Kickin' the Gong Around," "Corrine Corinna," "The Scat Song" and "Dinah." This is very enjoyable and often-classic music that lets one know immediately why Cab Calloway was so popular during the 1930s. —*Scott Yanow*

★ **Are You Hep to the Jive—** / 1935-1945 / Columbia/Legacy ✦✦✦✦✦
An excellent one-disc overview of Calloway's 1940s Okeh, Columbia, and Vocalion recordings. Beyond the showmanship and humor, Calloway had an amazingly swinging big band that was home to emerging jazz stars like Jonah Jones, Chu Berry, Cozy Cole and (briefly) Dizzy Gillespie. Calloway's riotous vocals and scatting are always a delight, and were an important precursor to bebop. The poet laureate of hip. —*Joel Roberts*

Hoagy Carmichael

b. Nov. 11, 1899, Bloomington, IN, **d.** Dec. 27, 1981, Palm Springs, CA
Vocals, Piano, Composer / Tin Pan Alley Pop, Traditional Pop, Standards, Classic Jazz, Show Tunes
One of the great composers of the American popular song, Hoagy Carmichael differed from most of the others (with the obvious exception of Duke Ellington) in that he was also a fine performer. Such Carmichael songs as "Stardust," "Georgia on My Mind," "Up the Lazy River," "Rockin' Chair," "The Nearness of You," "Heart and Soul," "In the Cool, Cool, Cool of the Evening," "Skylark" and "New Orleans" have long been standards, each flexible enough to receive definitive treatment numerous times. His first composition "Riverboat Shuffle" was recorded by Bix Beiderbecke and the Wolverines in 1924 and became a Dixieland standard. Carmichael led a few jazz sessions of his own in the late '20s (including one that interpreted "Stardust" as an uptempo stomp!) but became more popular as a skilled songwriter. In the 1940s he recorded some trio versions of his hits and in 1956 he cut a full set of vocals while backed by a modern jazz group that included Art Pepper. After that he drifted into semi-retirement, dissatisfied with how the music business had changed. —*Scott Yanow*

• **Stardust & Much More** / Nov. 18, 1927-Mar. 1, 1960 / Bluebird/RCA ✦✦✦✦✦
This is the definitive Hoagy Carmichael CD, documenting his most significant recordings of the 1927-34 period when he evolved from a little-known jazz pianist-vocalist to being widely recognized as a major composer. The 21-song CD starts and ends with previously unreleased solo versions of "Stardust" featuring Carmichael in 1960. also on the release is Hoagy's recording of his "Washboard Blues" with Paul Whiteman's Orchestra, "So Tired" with Jean Goldkette, dates led by Carmichael (including four songs in 1930 that have solos from cornetist Bix Beiderbecke), a guest spot singing "Come Easy, Go Easy Love" with Sunny Clapp's Band O'Sunshine and five solo piano/vocal numbrs from 1933-34 (including "Stardust"). Highly recommended. —*Scott Yanow*

Ole Buttermilk Sky / 1998 / Collectors' Choice Music ✦✦✦✦✦
Hoagy Carmichael recorded a few isolated singles on Decca Records in the late 1930s and early 1940s, then had an exclusive five-year relationship with the label from 1946 to 1951. Later in the '50s, he briefly recorded for Kapp Records, former Decca executive Dave Kapp's independent label. This long-overdue CD compilation draws upon that catalog for 24 tracks that trace Carmichael's career as a popular recording artist. Carmichael is best known as a songwriter, secondarily as a jazz musician and character actor, but these recordings recall Carmichael the recording star, who scored a No. 1 hit with "Huggin' and Chalkin'" in 1947. As in the case of that novelty song, many of Carmichael's records featured songs he had not written himself and on which he was accompanied by an orchestra. Still, he does have writing credits on 13 tracks here, among them such favorites as "Star Dust," "Hong Kong Blues," "Doctor, Lawyer, Indian Chief," "Rockin' Chair," "Georgia on My Mind," "My Resistance Is Low," and "Lazy River," often in arrangements featuring Carmichael and his piano backed just by a rhythm section. Of course, those are the most impressive recordings here, but the comic Carmichael who duets with Cass Daley on "The Aba Daba Honeymoon" is also a droll delight, and the disc provides a more well-round portrait of Carmichael than just a compilation of his own songs would. —*William Ruhlmann*

Betty Carter (Lorraine Carter)

b. May 16, 1930, Flint, MI, **d.** Sep. 26, 1998, Brooklyn, NY
Vocals / Vocal Jazz, Bop
A long period of struggling and near-complete obscurity preceded Betty Carter's surprising rise to fame; through it all she never compromised her musical vision. Although she never cared much for avant-garde jazz, her own interpretations of standards and originals are still so radical (with tonal distortions, a very wide range of tempos and many unexpected changes of direction) that there is simply no other term to describe her unique music. During 1948-51 she toured with Lionel Hampton (where she was nicknamed Betty "Bebop" Carter). After that association ended she settled in New York, gradually developed her style and recorded with Gigi Gryce in 1956. Although she recorded a 1961 duet album with Ray Charles that received some attention, it would be quite awhile before she gained much recognition. In 1969 she formed a trio and in 1971 organized her own record label Bet-Car. Gradually Carter's innovative singing began to be recognized and after she signed with Verve in the early '80s, she finally became a household name (and a consistent pollwinner) in the jazz world. Carter's singing was not to everyone's taste but her willingness to take chances was quite admirable and her ability as a talent scout (her pianists have included John Hicks, Mulgrew Miller, Benny Green, Stephen Scott and Cyrus Chestnut) is beyond criticism. —*Scott Yanow*

Meet Betty Carter / May 13, 1955-Mar. 25, 1956 / Columbia/Legacy ✦✦✦

Meet Betty Carter and Ray Bryant / May 13, 1955-Apr. 25, 1956 / Columbia/Legacy ✦✦✦✦

• **I Can't Help It** / Feb. 1958 / GRP ✦✦✦✦✦
This single-CD reissues the second batch of Betty Carter recordings, her Peacock and ABC-Paramount dates which followed her Epic/Columbia titles by two years. Formerly available

as a two-LP set (*What a Little Moonlight Can Do*), the 24 selections find the already-distinctive vocalist carving out her own sound from the bebop tradition; her more innovative work was in the future. Quite a few of the renditions are memorable including "I Can't Help It" (which is somewhat autobiographical), "You're Driving Me Crazy," "What a Little Moonlight Can Do," "Jazz (Ain't Nothin' but Soul)" and "Don't Weep for the Lady." While the second half of the CD has Carter accompnied by an orchestra arranged by Richard Wess, the first 12 numbers feature such top players as trumpeters Ray Copeland and Kenny Dorham, either Jerome Richardson or Benny Golson on tenor and pianist Wynton Kelly. Highly recommended. *—Scott Yanow*

Inside Betty Carter / Apr. 1964-May 26, 1965 / Capitol ♦♦♦

Finally / Dec. 6, 1969 / Roulette ♦♦♦

The Audience with Betty Carter / Dec. 6, 1979-Dec. 8, 1979 / Verve ♦♦♦♦

Look What I Got / 1988 / Verve ♦♦♦♦
This well-rounded set gives listeners a good look at the adventurous music of Betty Carter. For this CD, she is joined by one of two rhythm sections (with either Benny Green or Stephen Scott on piano) and, on four of the nine songs, tenor saxophonist Don Braden. Carter twists and turns some familiar songs (such as "The Man I Love," "Imagination" and "The Good Life") along with a variety of lesser-known material including two songs of her own. Consistently unpredictable (whether scatting or stretching out ballads) Betty Carter's recordings are always quite stimulating. *—Scott Yanow*

I'm Yours, You're Mine / Jan. 14, 1996-Jan. 25, 1996 / Verve ♦♦♦♦

Maurice Chevalier

b. Sep. 12, 1888, Menilmontant, France, **d.** Jan. 1, 1972, Paris, France
Vocals, Actor / French Pop, Traditional Pop, Cabaret, Vocal Pop, Show Tunes, Nostalgia
Dubbed "the French Al Jolson," Maurice Chevalier was among the most beloved song-and-dance men of the pre-war era. He began singing in Parisian cafes and music halls; although his voice lacked power, he compensated with his fine comedic skills, and before long was among the most popular performers in France. He appeared in several silent films before joining the French forces fighting in World War I (he was held as a POW by the Germans for two years). After his release, Chevalier returned to the cinema, as well as the cabaret circuit. Clad in his trademark straw boater and bow tie, in 1925 he introduced "Valentine," one of the songs with which he remained identified for the duration of his career. Chevalier relocated to Hollywood in 1928, and made his American debut a year later in *Innocents of Paris*, which popularized his song "Louise." He next appeared in the hit *The Love Parade*, and earned an Academy Award nomination for Best Actor.

With his happy-go-lucky charm and suave sophistication, Chevalier became a romantic superstar, but he abruptly left Hollywood in 1935, returning to Europe a triumphant global success. In the late '50s, after years away from the Hollywood spotlight, Chevalier appeared in Billy Wilder's *Love in the Afternoon* and *Gigi*, the latter film's Lerner & Loewe score providing him with the signature songs "Thank Heaven for Little Girls" and "I Remember It Well." In 1960, he co-starred with Frank Sinatra and Louis Jourdan in *Can-Can*, but he began appearing in smaller roles, typically cast as a patriarchal figure. Chevalier retired from the screen in 1967, and his vocal rendition of the title song to the 1970 animated Disney feature *The Aristocats* was his last work in Hollywood; he died at home in Paris in 1972. *—Jason Ankeny*

● **Valentine** / Jul. 1, 1997 / Arkadia Chansons ♦♦♦♦
Maurice Chevalier wasn't simply a cabaret singer; he was also a first-class *entertainer*, and someone who took great pride in being a showman. Like Edith Piaf, he was among the most famous French singers of the 20th century, but that's where the similarity ends. In contrast to Piaf's many deeply introspective and emotionally intense performances, Chevalier favored fun, happy entertainment. Spanning 1928-1942, *Valentine* boasts many of the essential recordings he was famous for. Chevalier's charm and charisma are hard to miss on such exuberant classics as "Paris Sera Toujours Paris," "Fleur De Paris" and "Donnez-moi La Main, Mama'Zelle" (not to mention "La Coupetta" and the title song). While Piaf's singing could bring tears to your eyes, Chevalier knew how to inspire laughter. Even if you don't speak a single word of French, it will be obvious that *Valentine* is a collection that is defined by good spirits. *—Alex Henderson*

The Chordettes

f. 1946, Sheboygan, WI, **db.** 1961
Group / Girl Group, Vocal Pop, Doo Wop, Pop
The Chordettes were one of the longest-lived vocal groups with roots in the mainstream pop and vocal harmonies of the 1940s and early '50s. First establishing themselves with the huge (and non-rock) pop hit "Mr. Sandman" in 1954, they continued to chart in the late '50s and early '60s, often with covers of rock and R&B songs like the number two hit "Lollipop". Although the group sound (at least in retrospect) among the Whitest and squarest of rock artists, they introduced enough rock into their repertoire and production to sound more contemporary than they had on discs such as "Mr. Sandman."

Leader Jinny Osborn first formed an a cappella quartet with three college friends, and they became regulars on Arthur Godfrey's television show. After recording for Columbia, the group moved to Cadence and began recording with musical backing, though the barbershop elements were still well to the fore on "Mr. Sandman," a bouncy, novelty-oriented tune that made number one for seven weeks. As early rock & roll began its successful threat to take over the mainstream audience, the Chordettes covered a song by Ronald & Ruby, "Lollipop," in their characteristic full round-like arrangement, complete with popping sounds. This was their best rock, or at least rock-ish, tune, though they had continued to record straight pop songs too, and had substantial hits with singles like "Born to Be with You" and "Just Between You and Me." After "Lollipop" there were a few more hits: "Zorro," "No Other Arms, No Other Lips," and "Never on Sunday." They disbanded shortly after "Never on Sunday" made the Top Twenty in 1961, however, when Jinny Osborn left and the group couldn't find a replacement. *—Richie Unterberger*

Mainly Rock & Roll / 1990 / Ace ♦♦♦

● **25 All-Time Greatest Recordings** / Feb. 8, 2000 / Varese ♦♦♦♦
The Chordettes are barber shop quartet singing filtered through four females. This rounds up all the hits and rarities you'll ever need on these gals, including their smash hits "Lollipop," "Mister Sandman," and "Zorro." For having a sound so obviously dated, these sides hold up remarkably well; the women harmonize like angels. The other side of the rock & roll explosion in the 1950s. *—Cub Koda*

June Christy (Shirley Luster)

b. Nov. 20, 1925, Springfield, IL, **d.** Jun. 21, 1990, Los Angeles, CA
Vocals / Vocal Jazz, Traditional Pop, Cool, Show Tunes
Though she was the epitomy of the vocal cool movement of the 1950s, June Christy was a warm, chipper vocalist able to stretch out her impressive voice on bouncy swing tunes and set herself apart from other vocalists with her deceptively simple enunciation. From her time in Stan Kenton's Orchestra, she inherited a focus on brassy swing from arranger friends like Pete Rugolo. Rugolo would become a consistent companion far into her solo days too, arranging most of her LPs and balancing her gymnastic vocal abilities with a series of attentive charts.

After singing professionally even during high school, Christy moved to Chicago in the early '40s and got her big break as the replacement for Anita O'Day in Stan Kenton's Orchestra. Despite an early resemblance (physically and vocally) to O'Day, the singer soon found her own style and enlivened Kenton's crossover novelties ("Shoo Fly Pie and Apple Pan Dowdy," the million-selling "Tampico") as well as intricately arranged standards ("How High the Moon"). After the Kenton orchestra broke up in 1948, Christy worked the nightclub circuit for awhile before reuniting with Kenton for his 1950 Innovations in Modern Music Orchestra. She had already debuted as a solo act the year before, recording for Capitol with a group led by her husband, Kenton tenor-saxophonist Bob Cooper. Christy's debut LP for Capitol, 1954's *Something Cool*, launched the vocal cool movement and hit the Top 20 album charts in America. She reprised her earlier big-band days with 1959's *June Christy Recalls Those Kenton Days*, and recorded a raft of concept LPs before retiring in 1965. Christy returned to the studio only once, for 1977's *Impromptu* on Musicraft. *—John Bush*

★ **Something Cool** / 1953 / Blue Note ♦♦♦♦♦
June Christy's classic *Something Cool* has been expanded from 11 songs to 24 on this essential CD with two unreleased cuts and six songs only previously out as singles. Christy's attractive "cool" tone was a trademark of jazz in the 1950s, her version of "Something Cool" remains a classic and many of the other numbers are nearly as memorable. Accompanied by Pete Rugolo's Orchestra, Christy is heard at her best on such numbers as "Whee Baby," "You're Making Me Crazy," "Midnight Sun," "A Stranger Called the Blues," "Softly as in a Morning Sunrise," "This Time the Dream's on Me" and "The Night We Called It a Day." *—Scott Yanow*

Duet / May 5, 1955-May 9, 1955 / Blue Note ♦♦♦♦
This set of duets between singer June Christy and pianist Stan Kenton is often quite emotional. Christy's cool sound and careful diction hint at darker feelings than appear on the surface during these ballads while Kenton provides sparse but effective piano. Emotions and melody are much more significant in this setting than mere chord changes and this haunting music is surprisingly memorable. *—Scott Yanow*

The Misty Miss Christy / Jul. 26, 1955-May 23, 1956 / Blue Note ♦♦♦♦
Singer June Christy is heard in prime form on this set. The reissue CD adds two numbers ("You Took Advantage of Me" and "Intrigue") to the original LP program. Backed by orchestras filled with West Coast jazz all-stars and arranged by Pete Rugolo, Christy is particularly memorable on "I Didn't Know About You," "Day Dream," "Dearly Beloved" and "There's No You." This is one of her finest all-round recordings. *—Scott Yanow*

Gone for the Day / Jun. 18, 1957-Jul. 15, 1957 / Blue Note ♦♦♦

The Song Is June! / 1959 / Blue Note ♦♦♦

Spotlight on June Christy / May 30, 1995 / Capitol ♦♦♦♦♦
Spotlight on June Christy contains 18 highlights from her work for Capitol Records, concentrating on her '50s recordings. It may not result in a definitive compilation, but it is a representative and enjoyable one, containing numerous highlights including "How High the Moon?," "I Remember You," "They Can't Take That Away from Me," "Bewitched," "The Song Is You," "Don't Get Around Much Anymore" and "How Long Has This Been Going On?" It's an ideal sampler for casual fans. *—Stephen Thomas Erlewine*

Rosemary Clooney

b. May 23, 1928, Maysville, KY
Vocals / Vocal Jazz, Traditional Pop, Film Music, Standards, Swing, Ballads, Show Tunes
Vocalist Rosemary Clooney's rise to fame in the '50s came on the strength of songs that in many instances were without question novelty tunes; she's not a vocal improviser like Carmen McRae, Betty Carter or Sarah Vaughan. She is an excellent lyric interpreter, has fine timing, phrases skillfully and intelligently, and performs with the dramatic quality evident among all great singers. Her background and foundation are jazz, even if her technique doesn't always adhere to rigid jazz scrutiny. She joined the Columbia roster in 1950, and made several hits for them, among them "You're Just In Love," "Beautiful Brown Eyes," "Half as Much," "Hey There," the number one hit "Come On-A My House" and "If Teardrops Were Pennies." Clooney had 13 Top 40 hits in the early '50s, among them duets with Guy Mitchell and Marlene Dietrich. The rock revolution and a decision to spend more time with her family resulted in Clooney going into semi-retirement. She returned in the late '70s, singing with renewed power and confidence while making swing-influenced dates and combo sessions for Concord. She's maintained that relationship through the '80s and '90s, doing standards,

repetory albums and demonstrating a resiliency and energy that validates her position among the fine jazz-based vocalists in American music. *—Ron Wynn and Bill Dahl*

Blue Rose / Jan. 23, 1956–Jan. 27, 1956 / Columbia ✦✦✦✦✦
Rosemary Clooney may have seemed to be a surprising choice to be featured with Duke Ellington & His Orchestra, but this collaboration is extremely successful in spite of the fact that Clooney was unable to join the band in the studio due to complications of a very difficult pregnancy. The solution was for the band to record the music (after Billy Strayhorn made the first of several trips to Los Angeles to consult with her). The results are stunning and not in the least bit canned, due to the professionalism of all parties involved and a stellar engineering of the separately recorded tracks. Clooney swings throughout "Me and You" and "It Don't Mean a Thing" without excess, her wordless vocal on "Blue Rose," and a captivating "Mood Indigo" are among the many highlights. The sound on this Legacy series reissue is greatly improved over the earlier Mobile Fidelity CD, plus there are two tracks added, the obscure but appealing "If You Were in My Place (What Would You Do?)" and "Just a-Sittin' and a-Rockin'," that were only issued as a single and omitted from the original release. It's a pity that the collaboration of Rosemary Clooney and Duke Ellington was only a one-shot deal, as she easily ranks as one of the greatest vocalists to appear on record with the maestro. *—Ken Dryden*

● **16 Most Requested Songs** / 1991 / Columbia/Legacy ✦✦✦✦✦
16 Most Requested Songs doesn't necessarily contain Rosemary Clooney's biggest hits—"Hey There," "This Ole House" and "Mambo Italiano" are here, but "Memories of You," "Mangos" and several others are missing. However, it has enough of her best material to make it worthwhile for budget-minded curious fans. *—Stephen Thomas Erlewine*

Everything's Coming Up Rosie / Jul. 7, 1977 / Concord Jazz ✦✦✦✦
Rosemary Clooney's first album for the Concord label set the standard for her work of the next 20 years. Long associated with middle-of-the-road pop music, Clooney really excelled in the jazz-oriented settings with The Concord All-Stars. Although she does not really improvise, her very pleasing voice and subtle phrasing should appeal to most jazz followers. On her Concord debut, Clooney is joined by trumpeter Bill Berry, tenor saxaphonist Scott Hamilton, pianist Nat Pierce, bassist Monty Budwig and drummer Jake Hanna. She lets the band run loose on two instrumentals and then really digs into her eight vocals, finding fresh things to say on eight familiar standards. *—Scott Yanow*

Here's to My Lady / Sep. 1978 / Concord Jazz ✦✦✦✦✦

Songs from the Girl Singer: A Musical Biography / Oct. 26, 1999 / Concord Jazz ✦✦✦✦✦
Rather than rely solely upon its back catalog as usual, Concord has gone the extra mile to make this Clooney career survey a must-buy, raiding the archives of various labels and the singer's own collection for a really valuable two-CD retrospective. Virtually all of the early stuff, where she emerges as a major pop hitmaker from Mitch Miller's Columbia stable, is on the first disc, while the second wraps up her latter-day resurrection as a jazz-tinged diva. Obviously, disc one carries the most fascination; besides being loaded with naive mid-century charm, it shows just how big Clooney was in the 1950s. There are duets with Bing Crosby, Bob Hope, and Frank Sinatra, and appearances with the orchestras of Duke Ellington (singing a vocalise on "Blue Rose"), Nelson Riddle, and Percy Faith. Yes, there is also the totally atypical 1951 "Come on-a My House" set against Stan Freeman's jangly harpsichord that broke Clooney into stardom. Concord picks up the thread in 1977-1980, surrounding her with jazz musicians; her voice gets a bit richer, losing some of the hard brassiness of youth, picking up some jazz inflections, yet she never quite becomes a "jazz" singer per se. When the set leaps into the '90s (skipping the '80s almost entirely), her timbre darkens more and develops an affecting quaver. The choice of material from this period, though, has strong autobiographical content (the set was released in conjunction with her 1999 autobiography); hence, the probable reason for giving short shrift to the '80s—the material may not have been there. And after hearing a final, affectionately sung capsule of philosophy, "Secret of Life," at the end of disc two, you realize you've been through a remarkable emotional journey. *—Richard S. Ginell*

Perry Como

b. May 18, 1912, Canonsburg, PA, **d.** May 12, 2001
Vocals / Traditional Pop, Vocal Pop
One of the most popular vocalists between the end of World War II and the rise of rock & roll in the mid-'50s, Perry Como perfected the post-big band approach to pop music by lending his own irresistible laidback singing—influenced by Bing Crosby and Mario Lanza—to the popular hits of the day on radio, TV, and LP. Both his early traditional crooning style plus his later relaxed manner and focus on novelty material were heavily indebted to Bing Crosby, though Como's appeal during the early '50s was virtually unrivalled. His big break came in 1945 with a song from the film *A Song to Remember.* His rendition of "Till the End of Time" spent ten weeks at the top of the charts and became the biggest hit of the year. In 1948, Como began crossing over to the emerging medium of television and eventually earned four Emmy Awards for his various programs. In the mid-'50s, Como began to indulge in light novelty fare, the titles often comprising nonsense words—"Bibbidi-Bobbidi-Doo," "Hoop-Dee-Doo," "Pa-Paya Mama" and "Hot Diggity (Dog Ziggity Boom)." Predictably, his appeal began to wane towards the end of the 1950s, and his last number one hit, "Catch a Falling Star," came in 1958. Como continued to record LPs and occasional television specials while making scattered appearances during the 1970s and '80s. *—John Bush*

☆ **We Get Letters** / 1957 / RCA Victor ✦✦✦✦✦
The most distinctive LP of Perry Como's career (and also the best), *We Get Letters* is ostensibly an album of requests, including songs Como sang on his television show for audience members. Instead of the usual large orchestra with strings and vocal chorus for accompaniment though, only a small section of Mitchell Ayres' Orchestra appears (usually just a four-piece of piano, drums, bass, and guitar with occasional trumpet solos). Como's relaxed manner and gentle crooning mesh perfectly with the small group's intimacy, and the number of standards—"It's Easy to Remember," "They Can't Take That Away from Me," "S'posin," "Deed I Do," "I Had the Craziest Dream"—makes *We Get Letters* a near-perfect vocal collection. Perry Como had numerous single successes throughout his career, but he never recorded a better full-length than this. *—John Bush*

Yesterday & Today: A Celebration in Song / Oct. 26, 1993 / RCA ✦✦✦✦✦
RCA's three-disc Perry Como box is an excellent summation of the career of one of the best adult-pop singers of the 1950s and '60s. It's the best compilation of hits available, and includes the best songs of his early career ("Till the End of Time," "Prisoner of Love," "Temptation") as well as those from his later easy-listening period ("Papa Loves Mambo," "Juke Box Baby," "Tina Marie"). Even the final disc is entertaining, as Como turns in excellent MOR versions of songs like the Beatles' "Something," "How Insensitive (Insensatez)" and "Bridge Over Troubled Water." It may be a bit too much material for neophytes, but the lack of quality compilations on the market makes this one of the best available. *—John Bush*

Greatest Hits / Sep. 28, 1999 / RCA ✦✦✦✦✦
An excellent halfway step for fans who are unwilling to purchase the three-disc Perry Como box set but who still want more than the scant 12-track best-ofs, *Greatest Hits* includes over 50 of his best-loved songs, mostly arranged in chronological order from 1945's "Prisoner of Love" all the way to 1973's "For the Good Times." The focus is on his late-'40s ballad peak, courtesy of hits like "It's Impossible," "Temptation," "Prisoner of Love," "Till the End of Time." Disc two includes many of his vocal-pop favorites ("Hoop-Dee-Doo," "Papa Loves Mambo," "Hot Diggity,") but leaves off *all* of his '60s material, assuredly not the best period of his career but still a time of beautiful MOR covers of "Yesterday" and "The Shadow of Your Smile," among others. Still, for those who need a bit more Perry Como than any single-disc collection can provide, *Greatest Hits* is a perfect addition. *—John Bush*

★ **Very Best of Perry Como** / Jul. 25, 2000 / RCA ✦✦✦✦✦
RCA's *The Very Best of Perry Como* delivers 21 of his best-loved songs, including number ones like "Catch a Falling Star," "Hot Diggity (Dog Ziggity Boom)," "No Other Love," "Some Enchanted Evening," and "Surrender." "Till the End of Time," "Papa Loves Mambo," "Don't Let the Stars Get in Your Eyes," "Because," and other million-selling singles have been digitally remastered and restored. Since most Como collections are either multi-disc collections or skimpy single discs, *The Very Best of Perry Como* is a welcome compromise, offering a good selection of Como hits for newcomers as well as fans who want his best on one disc. *—Heather Phares*

Harry Connick, Jr.

b. Sep. 11, 1967, New Orleans, LA
Vocals, Piano / Traditional Pop, Swing
With very few exceptions, the career of Harry Connick, Jr. can be divided in half—his first two albums encompassed straightahead New Orleans jazz and stride piano while his later career (which paralleled his rising celebrity status) alternated between more contemporary New Orleans music and pop vocals with a debt to Frank Sinatra. He first recorded with a local jazz band at the age of ten and studied with Ellis Marsalis before moving to New York to attend college. He gained a contract with Columbia, and released his eponymous debut—a set of mostly unaccompanied standards—in 1987. Jazz critics praised Connick's maturity and engaging style as well as his extended stays at New York hotspots during the year. His second album was the first to feature him on vocals. Connick really entered the American consciousness in 1989 with his prominent appearance on the double-platinum soundtrack to *When Harry Met Sally.* In 1990, he released separate vocal and instrumental albums simultaneously; the vocal album performed very well on the pop charts. Though his celebrity decreased slightly during the mid-'90s, In 1996, he had a brief role in *Independence Day,* the year's biggest blockbuster, but his album *Star Turtle* failed to connect with pop audiences. *Come by Me,* a return to big band sounds, followed in 1999. *—John Bush*

11 / Nov. 4, 1978–Nov. 11, 1978 / Columbia ✦✦

Harry Connick, Jr. / 1987 / Columbia ✦✦✦

20 / May 4, 1988-Jun. 29, 1988 / Columbia ✦✦✦✦
On a set of mostly unaccompanied piano solos and vocals, Harry Connick, Jr. shows a great deal of potential. His renditions of eleven standards are highlighted by collaborations with singer-organist Dr. John on "Do You Know What It Means to Miss New Orleans" and especially a memorable vocal duet with Carmen McRae on "Please Don't Talk About Me When I'm Gone." In addition, bassist Bob Hurst helps out on "Do Nothin' Till You Hear from Me." Years later, this still remains one of Harry Connick, Jr.'s finest recordings. *—Scott Yanow*

● **When Harry Met Sally** / Jun. 1989 / Columbia ✦✦✦✦✦
Harry Connick, Jr.'s vocals perfectly fit the moods throughout the 1989 Billy Crystal film *When Harry Met Sally.* This soundtrack album (which stands apart from the movie) was a big hit and a major step forward for the young pianist-vocalist although, from the vantage point of the late '90s, it appears to have been the highpoint of his career. Connick warmly sings such numbers as "It Had to Be You," "Our Love Is Here to Stay," "But Not for Me" and "Let's Call the Whole Thing Off" while usually accompanied by bassist Benjamin Wolfe, drummer Jeff "Tain" Watts and a big band; Frank Wess' warm tenor makes a brief appearance on "Our Love Is Here to Stay." In addition, there are a few melodic instrumentals including some solo Connick piano on "Winter Wonderland" and "Autumn in New York." Highly recommended. *—Scott Yanow*

We Are in Love / 1990 / Columbia ✦✦✦
At one point in 1990, two Harry Connick, Jr. albums were released almost simultaneously, an instrumental outing with his trio (*Lofty's Roach Souffle*) and this vocal-oriented album. Oddly enough *We Are in Love* is the more successful of the two. Connick's vocals, while limited, are personable, guitarist Russell Malone gets in some short solos and Branford Marsalis makes two strong guest appearances (one apiece on tenor and soprano). Most selections utilize an orchestra and, although Connick is heard on piano, the emphasis is on his voice. He contributed most of the tunes but the highpoints are the two standards "A Nightingale Sang in Berkeley Square" and "It's Alright with Me." *—Scott Yanow*

Lofty's Roach Souffle / Apr. 4, 1990-Apr. 22, 1990 / Columbia ✦✦✦

Blue Light, Red Light / Jun. 27, 1991-Jul. 14, 1991 / Columbia ✦✦

25 / Oct. 2, 1992-Oct. 9, 1992 / Columbia ✦✦✦

Star Turtle / Dec. 1995 / Columbia ✦✦

To See You / Nov. 11, 1997 / Columbia ✦✦✦✦
Harry Connick is heard in three roles on this CD. As a jazz pianist, he makes some cameo appearances and shows that his playing had evolved a bit from his earlier years. Connick had matured as a vocalist, and he sounds fine backed by a string orchestra and his quartet, never stretching himself. All ten selections (ballads dealing with love) are his originals, and Connick displays some talent as a composer/lyricist/arranger, although it is doubtful that any of these numbers will become standards in the future. A more interesting set overall than his preceding pop date, this CD was a step in the right direction for Harry Connick, Jr., also featuring brief, warm tenor solos from Charles Goold. *—Scott Yanow*

Come by Me / Jun. 1, 1999 / Columbia ✦✦✦✦

Noel Coward

b. Dec. 16, 1899, Teddington, Middlesex, England, **d.** Mar. 26, 1973, Jamaica
Vocals, Writer / Traditional Pop, Music Hall, Cabaret, Nostalgia
Noel Coward was among the most innovative and influential figures to emerge from the theatrical world during the 20th century; a playwright, director and actor as well as a songwriter, filmmaker and novelist, his witty, urbane stage productions forever altered the perceptions long inherent in theatre dialogue by shifting away from declamatory tones to a more natural, conversational approach, making them ideal for later film adaptations. He began his professional career as a child actor, and in 1913, while travelling with a production of *Hannele*, he met a girl named Gertrude Lawrence who would continue to exert a profound influence over his life and career, becoming both the inspiration behind and the star of many of his greatest works. Coward soon began writing plays and eventually turned to songwriting; in 1923, his "Parisian Pierrot" was performed by Lawrence in the revue *London Calling!*, becoming his first hit, and a year later his drug-addiction drama *The Vortex* was a controversial smash before moving to Broadway. Within a year Coward had another revue, *On With the Dance*, running in London simultaneously with a pair of comedies, *Hay Fever* and *Fallen Angels;* his record of three concurrent productions was not broken until half a century later by Andrew Lloyd Webber. In 1929 Coward mounted his most mature production yet with *Bitter Sweet*, a quasi-Viennese operetta which launched the song "I'll See You Again." 1930's *Private Lives*, a romantic comedy written in honor of Lawrence, further established his newfound mastery, and with the 1931 historical epic *Cavalcade* and its song "Twentieth Century Blues" his position as a talent of international renown was assured. *—Jason Ankeny*

● **Together with Music** / Oct. 1955 / DRG ✦✦✦✦✦
Mary Martin and Noël Coward were still-prominent veteran entertainers when they joined together in October 1955 to appear on the live, 90-minute television special that is aurally reproduced here. The 41-year-old Martin was fresh from her Broadway and TV triumph in *Peter Pan*, only the latest in a series of stage musicals with which she filled her career. The 55-year-old Coward, whose work as a playwright was in decline, had recently begun a new phase of his career as a nightclub performer in Las Vegas. The two had been working together since the problematic Coward-written, Martin-starring musical *Pacific 1860* in 1946. On TV, they largely worked separately, after opening with the show's specially written title song. Coward shows audiences what was wowing them in Las Vegas: his rapid-fire recitatives of his own comic songs like "Mad Dogs and Englishmen" and a medley of some of his more sentimental material. Martin shines on a medley of songs from her stage triumph, *South Pacific*, and a reprise of Cole Porter's "My Heart Belongs to Daddy," her Broadway debut. Together at the end, they do a lengthy and somewhat chaotic medley of old favorites. While the visual element is lost on record and the sound quality is TV-tinny, the exuberance of the show comes across. Unfortunately, the original two-LP set, which contained the entire show, was condensed to 56 minutes for CD reissue. *—William Ruhlmann*

The Masters Voice: Noel Coward, Vols. 1-4 / 1992 / EMI ✦✦✦✦✦

Michael Crawford (Michael Patrick Dumble-Smith)

b. Jan. 19, 1942, Salisbury, Wiltshire, England
Vocals / Show Tunes
Most popular to theatre audiences from his title role in Andrew Lloyd Webber's version of *The Phantom of the Opera*, Michael Crawford was in fact a star of the British stage and screen for almost two decades before. After first stepping on the London stage in the early '60s, Crawford's first regular television series was the BBC's 1960s show *Not So Much a Programme, More a Way of Life;* he appeared in several films as well before moving to New York in 1967, where Gene Kelly recruited him to star in the fim version of *Hello, Dolly!*, with Barbra Streisand. Other films proved less successful, and Crawford returned to England in the early '70s, winning an award for his role in the sitcom *Some Mothers Do 'Ave 'Em*. Alternating between television series and award-winning roles in theatre during the '70s, Crawford broke out with his title role in the musical *Barnum*, which earned him several awards and proved a smash hit. He toured with the show during the early '80s, and its popularity was the decisive factor in Webber's casting of him opposite Sarah Brightman in *The Phantom of the Opera* in 1986. The musical earned him immense critical praise, a Tony Award, and a hit single, "The Music of the Night," which reached the British Top Ten. In 1995 he mounted *EFX*, a $40 million production set at the MGM Grand Hotel in Las Vegas, featuring Crawford playing five different parts. *—John Bush*

Songs from the Stage & Screen / 1988 / Atlantic ✦✦

● **With Love** / 1989 / Atlantic ✦✦✦✦
Filled with familiar numbers, this collection is a better showing for Michael Crawford than *Songs from the Stage and Screen*. The LSO is balanced out better, the performances seem far less rushed, and Crawford is in far better shape vocally. The big surprise: Art of Noise keyboardist Anne Dudley turns in an arranging and conducting job on "When I Fall in Love" that would make Nelson Riddle nod appreciatively. *—Steven McDonald*

In Concert / Oct. 27, 1998 / Atlantic ✦✦✦✦

Bing Crosby (Harry Lillis Crosby)

b. May 3, 1903, Tacoma, WA, **d.** Oct. 14, 1977, Madrid, Spain
Vocals / Traditional Pop, Standards, Vocal Pop, Swing
Bing Crosby was, without doubt, the most popular and influential media star of the first half of the 20th century. The undisputed best-selling artist until well into the rock era, the most popular radio star of all time, and the biggest box-office draw of the '40s, Crosby dominated the entertainment world from the Depression until the mid-'50s, and proved just as influential as he was popular. Unlike the many vocal artists before him, Crosby grew up with radio, and his intimate bedside manner was a style perfectly suited to emphasize the strengths of a medium transmitted directly into the home; and in contrast to earlier vocalists, who were forced to strain their voices into upper registers to make an impression onto mechanically recorded tracks, Crosby's warm, manly baritone crooned to its heart's content without a thought of excess. Not to be forgotten in charting Crosby's influence is the music itself. His song knowledge and sense of laidback swing was learned from early jazz music, far less formal than the European-influenced classical and popular music used for inspiration by the vocalists of the '10s and '20s. Jazz was by no means his main concentration, though, especially after the '30s; Crosby instead blended contemporary pop hits with the best songs from a wide range of material. His wide repertoire covered showtunes, film music, country & western songs, patriotic standards, religious hymns, holiday favorites, and ethnic ballads. The breadth of material wasn't threatening to audiences because Crosby put his own indelible stamp on each song he recorded, appealing to many different audiences while still not endangering his own fanbase. Crosby was among the first to actually read songs, making them his own by interpreting the lyrics and emphasizing words or phrases to emphasize what he thought best. His influence and importance in terms of vocal ability and knowledge of American popular music is immense, but what made Crosby more than anything else was his persona—whether it was an artificial creation or something utterly natural to his own personality. He represented the American everyman—strong and stern to a point yet easygoing and affable, tolerant of other viewpoints but quick to defend God and the American way—during the hard times of the Depression and World War II, when Americans most needed a symbol of what their country was all about. *—John Bush*

1926-1932 / Dec. 22, 1926-Feb. 11, 1932 / Timeless ✦✦✦✦

☆ **Bing! His Legendary Years, 1931 to 1957** / Nov. 23, 1931-Dec. 27, 1957 / MCA ✦✦✦✦✦
This four-CD set does a superb job of summing up Bing Crosby's years with Decca. After nine titles from 1931 (which were acquired by Decca later on), the program concentrates on the 1934-57 period and, in addition to the expected hits, all aspects of his career are covered. Despite a few Dixieland-flavored selections, Crosby had largely abandoned jazz by the late '30s but his phrasing (which was influenced by Louis Armstrong) and appealing voice should be of interest to jazz listeners. In later years his ballads grew in stature while the uptempo performances tended to be less memorable novelties. Although it should be augmented by collections that focus on his recordings of the 1920s and early '30s, this is the definitive Bing Crosby set. *—Scott Yanow*

And Some Jazz Friends / Aug. 8, 1934-May 27, 1942 / GRP ✦✦✦✦

Bing Crosby & the Andrews Sisters: Their Complete Recordings Together / Sep. 20, 1939-Feb. 21, 1952 / MCA ✦✦✦✦✦
Just what the title says: a double-CD of 53 tracks from 1939-52 that includes all their official releases (many of which were substantial hits), as well as rarities that have only been available on bootlegs and some outtakes. There are also Christmas songs and a couple of tunes that also feature vocalist Dick Haymes, letting you know that this package is firmly targeted toward the serious '40s vocals fan. It's not the first (or second) preferred purchase for fans of either Crosby or the Andrews Sisters. On the other hand, if your interest in either Crosby or the Andrews is serious enough to warrant more than a greatest-hits CD, you'll likely enjoy this reissue. *—Richie Unterberger*

Bing Sings Whilst Bregman Swings / Jun. 11, 1956-Jun. 12, 1956 / Verve ✦✦✦✦✦
Joined by a big band arranged and conducted by Buddy Bregman, Crosby is in prime voice on a dozen standards which (according to the breezy liner notes) he had never recorded before. The concise performances (all between two and four minutes) are straightforward and generally swinging. Highlights include "'Deed I Do," "Heat Wave," "The Blue Room" and "Jeepers Creepers." [An audiophile CD reissue appeared on Mobile Fidelity in 1996.] *—Scott Yanow*

☆ **Bing with a Beat** / 1957 / RCA Victor ✦✦✦✦✦
The best LP of Bing Crosby's career, *Bing with a Beat* is a loose, freewheeling recording date that comprised 12 near-standards and was recorded with the New Orleans jazz backing of Bob Scobey's nine-piece Frisco Jazz Band. Though Crosby was in better voice earlier in his career, his later mastery of phrasing comes through loud and clear on this record. In true throwback fashion, Bing leaves plenty of room for solos and often calls out to Scobey. Most of the songs are familiar, and include nuggets such as "Let a Smile Be Your Umbrella," "I'm Going to Sit Right Down and Write Myself a Letter," "Dream a Little Dream of Me," and "Tell Me," among others. Throughout his career, Crosby always sounded relaxed, but on *Bing with a Beat* he really sounds like he's enjoying himself, reflecting on a lifetime of great music. *—John Bush*

The Complete United Artists Sessions / 1974-1977 / EMI ✦✦✦

★ **Bing Crosby's Greatest Hits** / 1977 / MCA ✦✦✦✦✦
According to chart researcher Joel Whitburn, Bing Crosby hit the singles charts 361 times between 1931 and 1965, including 40 number one hits—by far the most successful recording career of all time. Most of those hits were recorded for Decca Records, subsequently owned by MCA Records. In 1977 (the year of Crosby's death), when MCA came to compile an album

called *Bing Crosby's Greatest Hits,* it began by limiting its choices to the most successful decade of Crosby's career, from the late '30s to the late '40s. But even within that limitation, the label did not stick to the biggest hits. Some of them were here, to be sure: "Swinging on a Star" from the film *Going My Way* and the Andrews Sisters duet "Don't Fence Me In," both long-running chart-toppers and gold records; the 1947 rerecording of "White Christmas," which scored in the holiday season almost annually through 1962; and such big hits as "Ac-Cent-Tchu-Ate the Positive" and "Pistol Packin' Mama" (both also featuring the Andrews Sisters). But beyond these, the selections become more idiosyncratic and seem intended to display Crosby's versatility and the breadth of his career, rather than actually compiling his greatest hits. These include a 1939 recording of "I Surrender, Dear"; a 1945 recording of "Where the Blue of the Night Meets the Gold of the Day," which he used as his radio theme song; "Too-Ra-Loo-Ra-Loo-Ral (That's an Irish Lullaby)," the gold-selling 1944 hit that showed off his Irish heritage; and "Deep in the Heart of Texas," which features accompaniment by Woody Herman and His Woodchoppers. It's a varied collection, but it does not by any reasonable measure contain his "greatest hits." *—William Ruhlmann*

16 Most Requested Songs / Aug. 25, 1992 / Columbia/Legacy ✦✦✦

Top O' the Morning: His Irish Collection / Feb. 27, 1996 / MCA ✦✦✦✦✦

★ **Bing Crosby's Gold Records** / Nov. 4, 1997 / MCA ✦✦✦✦✦
Bing's Gold Records is a splendid collection of all of Crosby's 21 gold singles for Decca Records. Each song is represented in its original version, including "White Christmas," which is not often heard in its 1942 Academy Award-winning version. Among other highlights are "New San Antonio Rose," "Pistol Packin' Mama," "Jingle Bells," "Swinging On a Star," "Too-Ra-Loo-Ra-Loo-Ral (That's an Irish Lullaby)," "Don't Fence Me In," "Galway Bay," "Play a Simple Melody" and "Silent Night, Holy Night," which has never been available on CD prior to this collection. It's a concise, thorough overview of Bing's peak years, functioning as a nice introduction for the curious. *—Stephen Thomas Erlewine*

Vic Damone

b. Jun. 12, 1928, Brooklyn, NY
Vocals / Traditional Pop, Vocal Pop, Ballads, Show Tunes
In the late '40s and the first half of the '50s, Vic Damone had a great deal of success with an approach that owed a great deal to Frank Sinatra, although his delivery was stiffer, and his material about as middle of the road as you could get with a tape measure. Backed by the orchestras of Glenn Osser, George Siravo, George Bassman, Richard Heyman, and others, Damone had well over a dozen big hits for Mercury. A*R man Mitch Miller* helped Vic select some of the material, which sometimes delved into Italian folk songs or novelties. Damone left Mercury in the mid-'50s for Columbia, where he continued working with Miller and scored one of his biggest hits, "On the Street Where You Live" (from the *My Fair Lady* musical), in 1956. Only one Top 20 hit awaited him in the future, but by the late '50s Damone was making the transition to the adult-oriented album market. Recording throughout the ensuing decades with limited success, Damone could always rely on a healthy living on the club-and-casino circuit, where his principal constituency now resides. *—Richie Unterberger*

16 Most Requested Songs / Aug. 25, 1992 / Columbia/Legacy ✦✦✦✦✦
16 Most Requested Songs is a midline-priced collection that spotlights many of Vic Damone's best-known and most popular performances for Columbia Records, including "On the Street Where You Live," "War and Peace," "Smoke Gets in Your Eyes," "An Affair to Remember," "You're Breaking My Heart," "Gigi," "Separate Tables" and "In the Blue of the Evening." Although it's far from a perfect retrospective of his career, it's still a nice sampler of familiar items, and it may satisfy the needs of some casual fans who only want the hits. *—Stephen Thomas Erlewine*

● **The Best of Vic Damone: The Mercury Years** / Aug. 20, 1996 / Mercury ✦✦✦✦✦
The Best of the Mercury Years contains 25 tracks from Vic Damone's tenure at Mercury Records. Over the course of the compilation, the majority of the vocalist's hits for the label—including the number one "Breaking My Heart," "Por Favor," "Ebb Tide," and "My Heart Cries For You"—are included, as well as terrific lesser-known numbers which help make this album the definitive retrospective of Damone's stint with Mercury. *—Stephen Thomas Erlewine*

Dorothy Dandridge

Vocals / Traditional Pop, Show Tunes
Actress/singer Dorothy Dandridge was Hollywood's first African-American superstar, becoming the first black performer ever nominated for a Best Actress Oscar. Born November 9, 1923 in Cleveland, she was the daughter of actress Ruby Dandridge, and with sister Vivian teamed in the song-and-dance duo the Wonder Children. The family relocated to Los Angeles during the mid-1930s, and in 1937 Dandridge briefly made her film debut in the Marx Brothers classic *A Day at the Races.* Concurrently she continued her singing career, and with Vivian performed as the Dandridge Sisters, sharing stages with the likes of Jimmie Lunceford and Cab Calloway as well as recording with Louis Armstrong. During the early 1940s Dorothy appeared in a series of musical film shorts, and as the decade progressed she became a sensation on the nightclub circuit. Dandridge's mainstream breakthrough was her title role in Otto Preminger's 1954 screen musical *Carmen Jones,* a performance which earned her an Academy Award nomination and made her a star; nevertheless, she did not reappear onscreen until 1957's *Island in the Sun,* and despite winning a Golden Globe for her work in 1959's *Porgy and Bess* she was offered virtually no future film roles, returning to nightclubs by the early 1960s. Plagued by years of personal hardships as well as professional hurdles, Dandridge was found dead of an overdose of anti-depressants on September 8, 1965. Three decades later her career enjoyed a kind of renaissance with an acclaimed 1997 biography by film historian Donald Bogle in addition to *Introducing Dorothy Dandridge,* a 1999 HBO telefilm starring Halle Berry. *Smooth Operator,* a long-unreleased recording date from 1958 featuring the Oscar Peterson trio, was finally issued in 1999 as well. *—Jason Ankeny*

Smooth Operator / Jul. 20, 1999 / Verve ✦✦✦✦
Smooth Operator explores a little-known aspect of the beautiful, troubled African-American actress Dorothy Dandridge: her vocal abilities. Most of this album comes from a 1958 recording session featuring Dandridge's lovely interpretations of "When Your Lover Has Gone, " "Body & Soul" and the title track. That her backing band is an augmented version of the Oscar Peterson Trio makes her album even more special, and a must for jazz fans and film buffs. *—Heather Phares*

Sammy Davis, Jr.

b. Dec. 8, 1925, New York, NY, **d.** May 16, 1990, Beverly Hills, CA
Vocals / Vocal Jazz, Traditional Pop, Vocal Pop, Pop, Show Tunes
Recognized throughout much of his career as "the world's greatest living entertainer," Sammy Davis, Jr. was a remarkably popular and versatile performer equally adept at acting, singing, dancing and impersonations—in short, a variety artist in the classic tradition. A member of the famed Rat Pack, he was among the very first African-American talents to find favor with audiences on both sides of the color barrier, and remains a perennial icon of cool. Davis made his stage debut at the age of three performing with Holiday in Dixieland, a black vaudeville troupe featuring his father and helmed by his de facto uncle, Will Mastin; dubbed "Silent Sam, the Dancing Midget," he proved phenomenally popular with audiences and the act was soon renamed Will Mastin's Gang Featuring Little Sammy. Later rechristened the Will Mastin Trio, in 1946 they opened for Mickey Rooney, who encouraged Davis to begin including his many impersonations in the Trio's act; where previously they had exclusively performed music, the addition of comedy brought new life to the group, and by the beginning of the next decade they were headlining venues including New York's Capitol club and Ciro's in Hollywood. In 1954 Davis signed to Decca, topping the charts with his debut LP *Starring Sammy Davis Jr,* followed by a series of hit singles including "Something's Gotta Give," "Love Me or Leave Me" and "That Old Black Magic." In 1972 Davis topped the pop charts with "The Candy Man," from the film *Willy Wonka and the Chocolate Factory. —Jason Ankeny*

Decca Years / 1990 / MCA ✦✦✦
Long before he became a kitsch Vegas cliché, Sammy Davis, Jr. was simply the finest all-around entertainer in show business. That talent is on open display in this delightful collection of the best of Sammy's Decca sides. Running from 1954's breakthrough hit, "Hey There," to 1959's "Change Partners," Davis finally found a groove to sell his immense talent on disc after a dismal start at Capitol Records in the late 1940s. While everything is in a brassy over-the-top Broadway style, his take on "Because of You" is straight out of his nightclub act, complete with star-turn impressions. If you've only heard the Nehru-jacket-and-beads Sammy Davis, Jr., then this set is well worth investigating. *—Cub Koda*

★ **I've Gotta Be Me: The Best of Sammy Davis, Jr. on Reprise** / Oct. 8, 1996 / Reprise ✦✦✦✦✦
I've Gotta Be Me: The Best of Sammy Davis Jr. on Reprise is a thorough 15-track retrospective of Davis' '60s recordings for Reprise, featuring the bulk of his hit singles—including "What Kind of Fool Am I," "As Long as She Needs Me," "The Shelter of Your Arms," and "I've Gotta Be Me"—plus album tracks that illustrates Davis' depth as a singer. The album is assembled as an argument for Davis' skills as a vocalist and entertainer, shunning many of his lighter numbers for show tunes and interpretations of '60s professional songwriters. The gambit works, since *I've Gotta Be Me* not only showcases Davis' immense vocal talent, but also the variety of his '60s recordings. Though these sometimes exhibit a glossy Vegas sheen, they are more varied and intriguing than his later work, while they demonstrate a versatility that his earlier Decca work only hinted at. In short, *I've Gotta Be Me* captures much of the essence of Sammy Davis, Jr. *—Stephen Thomas Erlewine*

★ **Yes I Can! The Sammy Davis Jr. Story** / Nov. 9, 1999 / Rhino ✦✦✦✦✦
It's hard to believe that a Sammy Davis Jr. box set retrospective was not released until 1999. One simple reason for the delay is that Davis' discography is a licensing nightmare, so the initial triumph of Warner Archives/Reprise/Rhino's four-disc *Yes I Can! The Sammy Davis Jr. Story* is that it brings together material controlled by Time Warner, EMI-Capitol, Universal, and the Davis estate. But another reason why a Sammy Davis Jr. box set may not have been an immediate priority is that recording was never his primary medium. Davis was first and foremost a live performer with an act that included singing, dancing, and impressions; everything else—Broadway shows, films, television, record-making—was secondary. Despite being possessed of a clear, powerful baritone and precise diction, Davis was always more a performer than a singer. His repertoire as presented here is dominated by songs written for stage and movie musicals by the cream of the interwar pop songwriters. Davis renders this material well, but the lyrics rarely mean much to him beyond being vehicles for his own self-expression (vocal effects, comic interjections, etc.). When this began to change in 1961, it was because a highly self-referential performer found a songwriter, Leslie Bricusse, whose subject was self-absorption. Writing for musicals, Bricusse secondarily provides Davis with material he sings with unprecedented conviction, because it allows him to explore his own dreams and doubts. The claims for Sammy Davis Jr.'s importance as an all-around entertainer cannot be disputed by anyone who has seen him perform in any medium, and strictly as a recording artist, much of that appeal comes across. *Yes I Can! The Sammy Davis Jr. Story* is more the statement of a magnetic personality than it is a collection of meaningfully sung songs, but it is no less impressive for that. *—William Ruhlmann*

☆ **Sammy and Friends** / Jan. 18, 2000 / Rhino ✦✦✦✦✦
Rhino's *Sammy & Friends* isn't a greatest-hits compilation, but for many casual fans this 20-track collection may be definitive, since it concentrates on his early-'60s recordings—all cut when the Rat Pack was at the height of its powers. Like many of Frank Sinatra's friends, Davis signed with Frank's new label, Reprise, as soon as he could, and once he was there, his arrangements became brassier and jazzier, and his records had many celebrity duets, usually with friends who were also signed to Reprise. Apart from standards, Sammy was never given the prime material during his time at Reprise, but he worked with great arrangers and bands, including Billy May, Nelson Riddle, Marty Paich, Benny Carter, Buddy Rich, and Morty

Stevens. Still, what mattered most was his personality and the intoxicating intoxication of the Rat Pack. No other collection captures their charm better than *Sammy & Friends*. Almost all of the songs were recorded for Reprise between 1962 and 1964, with a stray selection from 1969 ("The Goin's Great"), a couple of 1965/1966 selections, and, most importantly, three tunes from the Rat Pack's greatest accomplishment, the heist flick *Ocean's 11*, including "Eee-O-Eleven," which makes its CD debut here. That certainly makes this single disc attractive to collectors, but for anyone who isn't a dedicated fan, *Sammy & Friends* is still the disc to own. Yes, it's missing his early Decca hits and such latter-day smashes as "I've Gotta Be Me" and "The Candy Man." Yes, there are some silly throwaways scattered throughout this collection, and, rather inexplicably, Dean Martin's *Ocean's 11* version of "Ain't That a Kick in the Head" is included (apparently, that falls under the "& Friends" category). But that's all nitpicking, since *Sammy & Friends* delivers the swinging, sophisticated, funny, and stylish showman that was Sammy Davis, Jr. *— Stephen Thomas Erlewine*

Doris Day (Doris Mary Anne von Kapelhoff)

b. Apr. 3, 1922, Cincinnati, OH
Vocals / Traditional Pop, Vocal Pop
Doris Day has packed four careers into one lifetime, two each in music and movies. The pity is that all most of us remember are her movies from *Teacher's Pet* (1957) onward, as the quintessential All-American Girl, the perpetually virginal screen heroine, cast opposite such icons of masculinity as Clark Gable and, rather ironically, Rock Hudson. She also transposed this following to television at the end of the 1960s with a situation comedy that lasted into the early 1970s. If most people remember her as a singer, it's usually for such pop hits as "Secret Love" and her Oscar-winning "Que Sera, Sera (Whatever Will Be, Will Be)," which became her signature tune. But before all of that, from 1939 until the end of of the 1940s, Doris Day was one of the hottest, sultriest swing band vocalists in music. That body of work—which contains at least one unabashed classic early-1940s recording, "Sentimental Journey"—is one of the most impressive in the fields of swing and popular jazz, and deserves to be heard far more than it is. Moreover, before those late-'50s comedies, Day had a film career that included adaptations of Broadway musicals (*The Pajama Game*), classic thrillers (*The Man Who Knew Too Much*), and searing social drama (*Storm Warning*). *— Bruce Eder*

- **A Day at the Movies** / 1978 / Columbia ✦✦✦✦✦
This exceptionally well-programmed compilation album is a triple threat. First, it assembles, in chronological order, notable songs that Doris Day sang in her films during her first decade as a movie star; second, with titles like "It's Magic," "Secret Love," and "Whatever Will Be, Will Be (Que Sera, Sera)," it functions as a hits collection; and, perhaps surprisingly, third, it arguably is a rarities album as well. Annotator Max O. Preeo, writing with the benefit of an interview with his subject, notes that the version of "It's Magic" included here is the actual original hit version recorded in 1947; apparently all subsequent reissues of the title song have been of a re-recording Day did in 1952. Several other songs, including the title tunes from her second and third films, *My Dream Is Yours* and *It's a Great Feeling*, are given their first release since they came out initially, and the version of "I Love The Way You Say Goodnight" from *Lullaby of Broadway* is released commercially for the first time. While making a series of musicals for Warner Bros. pictures in the late 1940s and early 1950s, Day benefited from the opportunity to sing old and new songs by such classic pop writers as Sammy Cahn, Vernon Duke, Ray Evans, Sammy Fain, E.Y. Harburg, Lorenz Hart, Gus Kahn, Jay Livingston, Richard Rodgers, Jule Styne, Harry Warren, and Vincent Youmans, and to perform (on these, mostly non-soundtrack studio versions) backed by such bandleaders as Frank DeVol, Percy Faith, Ray Heindorf, Harry James, Axel Stordahl, and Paul Weston. She made the most of those connections, using her band-singer background and warm tone to create performances that were the highpoints of the often flimsy films in which they appeared. The results are here to enjoy. *— William Ruhlmann*

- **16 Most Requested Songs** / Aug. 25, 1992 / Columbia/Legacy ✦✦✦✦✦
16 Most Requested Songs contains some, but not all, of Doris Day's biggest hits. Consequently, it's more of a sampler for casual fans than a definitive retrospective, but it still highlights some of her very best performances, including "A Bushel and A Peck," "You Won't Be Satisfied," "Till the End of Time," "In Love In Vain," and "Black Hills of Dakota." *— Stephen Thomas Erlewine*

16 Most Requested Songs, Encore! / 1996 / Columbia/Legacy ✦✦✦✦

☆ **Complete Doris Day with Les Brown** / Apr. 21, 1998 / Collectors' Choice Music ✦✦✦✦✦
Forty-two songs cut between November 1940 and August 1946, and the perfect companion to Bear Family's *It's Magic* box set—anyone who's been even tempted to own that will have to get this more modestly priced precursor to that material. Day's period singing with Les Brown is, today, regarded with a degree of love and affection reserved for Ella Fitzgerald's era with Chick Webb, or Frank Sinatra's work with Harry James and Tommy Dorsey. Yet Sony Music's own releases devoted to Doris Day and Les Brown spread the music around to several different CDs, and suffered from sound that, today, seems substandard. These newly remastered tracks, offered in chronological order, including one previously unissued song ("Are You Still in Love with Me"), not only display a far richer, warmer sound, but have been presented with the kind of care that is normally reserved for the best parts of a label's catalog—which these sides definitely are. Day's voice during this period (she was 16 when she cut her first sides with Brown) was an astonishingly expressive instrument. Anyone who thinks that 42 songs is more than they want simply hasn't heard her darkly emotive rendition of "When the Music Plays On," or the playful "Three at a Table with You," her jaunty "Broomstreet," or her gossamer enunciation (highlighted by some lovely high notes) on "Between Friends"—the arrangements and the performances have the texture of the most finely spun silk. The hits are here, of course, but there's hardly a song on hand that doesn't deserve a hearing 50-odd years later. The notes by Joseph Laredo are also lively and informative. *— Bruce Eder*

Golden Girl: Columbia Recordings 1944-1966 / Jun. 1, 1999 / Columbia/Legacy ✦✦✦✦✦
Released as a celebration of Doris Day's three decades with Columbia Records, *Golden Girl: Columbia Recordings 1944-1966* is a definitive portrait of Day at the peak of her career. Over the course of two discs and 48 songs, all of her big hits—including "Sentimental Journey" and "Whatever Will Be, Will Be (Que Sera, Sera)"—are featured, along with selected album tracks, duets, and five previously unreleased tracks. This may be a little too comprehensive for the average fan just looking for the hits, but for any serious fan, this is essential. *— Stephen Thomas Erlewine*

Blossom Dearie

b. Apr. 28, 1926, East Durham, NY
Vocals, Piano / Vocal Jazz, Standards, Bop
A distinctive, girlish voice, crisp, impeccable delivery, and an irrepressible sense of playful swing made Blossom Dearie one of the most enjoyable singers of the vocal era. Her warmth and sparkle ensured that she'd never treat standards as the well-worn songs they often appeared in less capable hands. And though her reputation was made on record with a string of excellent albums for Verve during the '50s, she remained a draw with Manhattan cabaret audiences long into the '80s.

Actually born with the name Blossom Dearie in the New York Catskills, she studied classical music and jazz while at high school. After graduation, she moved to New York and began appearing with vocal groups. She spent time in Paris during the early '50s as the head of her own group, the Blue Stars of France, but returned to America after signing to Verve in 1956. Her eponymous debut was the template for much of her later career, with nods to her cabaret background and a focus on intimate readings of standards ("Deed I Do," "Thou Swell") amidst a relaxed trio setting (with bassist Ray Brown and drummer Jo Jones). Dearie performed in solo settings at supper clubs all over New York, and also appeared on the more cultured of the late-'50s New York-based talk shows. She recorded just one LP during the '60s, but later formed her own Daffodil Records label to release her own work, including 1974's *Blossom Dearie Sings*. Blossom Dearie continued to perform and record during the 1980s, centered mostly in New York but also a regular attraction in London as well. *— John Bush*

- **Blossom Dearie** / Sep. 11, 1956-Apr. 9, 1959 / Verve ✦✦✦✦✦
Other than a pair of sessions for the French Barclay label during 1955-56, this set (which has been reissued on CD) has pianist-vocalist Blossom Dearie's first recordings as a leader. Teamed up with bassist Ray Brown and drummer Jo Jones, Dearie is heard in her early prime. Although her voice has always been an acquired taste, its sincerity and sense of swing wins one over after a few songs and Dearie's piano playing is first class. In addition to the 14 original selections (mostly swing-era standards plus a couple of French songs), there are three previously unreleased numbers including "Blossom's Blues" which dates from 1959. This CD is the perfect introduction for listeners to the unique sound of Blossom Dearie. *— Scott Yanow*

Give Him the Ooh-La-La / Sep. 12, 1957–Sep. 13, 1957 / Verve ✦✦✦✦✦
Of the six recordings Blossom Dearie did for the Verve label in the '50s, *Give Him the Ooh-La-La* is the third one to be released on CD. Three titles still remain in the vaults including a Betty Comden and Johnny Green tribute as well as a *Broadway Hits* collection. It's a shame because Dearie's girlishly dynamic voice, subtle piano playing, and rarified choice of contemporary material made her recordings unique among '50s jazz vocal outings. *Give Him the Ooh-La-La* is no exception, with stellar backing by regular bassist Ray Brown, drummer Jo Jones and guitarist Herb Ellis, and Dearie's taut arrangements of a set of glowing ballads and brisk swingers. Included are a few well-worn standards like "Just One of Those Things" and "Between the Devil and the Deep Blue Sea." More intriguing, however, are Dearie's inclusion of obscure titles like Cy Coleman's "The Riviera," a tongue and cheek portrait of Europe's playground, as well as his "I Walk a Little Faster." Additionally, there's the gently executed and innocuous self-help number "Try Your Wings," a bouncy "The Middle of Love," and a nod to her club stint in Paris with the French tune "Plus Je T'Embrasse." As usual, both Dearie's piano and voice are instilled with impeccable playfulness on mischievous numbers like the title track and in the tender pathos of ballads such as "Like Someone in Love." Like Dearie's two other available titles *Blossom Dearie* and *Once Upon a Summertime, Give Him the Ooh-La-La* features a great collection of tunes from the high point of her recording career. The dilemma is not which recording to get, but where to start. *— Stephen Cook*

Once Upon a Summertime / Sep. 12, 1958-Sep. 13, 1958 / Verve ✦✦✦✦

Marlene Dietrich

b. Dec. 27, 1901, Schöneberg, Germany, **d.** May 6, 1992, Paris, France
Vocals / Traditional Pop, Cabaret, Torch Songs, Nostalgia
The most exotic actress of the '30s and '40s, Marlene Dietrich performed her cabaret act around the world and recorded for Decca, Columbia and Capitol in the post-war period, after her film career had slowed. A thick German accent and her odd sung-spoken vocal style proved no barrier to international popular success and adoration. She worked in the German theater and film world during the '20s, gradually assuming star status until her international breakout at the end of the decade, when she appeared in *The Blue Angel*. The film's success led directly to Hollywood, where she became one of the major female stars of the 1930s, in such films as *Song of Songs, The Scarlet Empress, Knight Without Armour,* and *Destry Rides Again*. She had recorded music in Germany as early as the late '20s, but Dietrich returned again to the vocal industry in the '50s, first with Decca and then a long-standing contract with Columbia. The label released many live albums, preserving her wild cabaret act from various European capitals (several of them recorded with a young Burt Bacharach serving as musical director). *— John Bush*

The Cosmopolitan Marlene Dietrich / 1993 / Columbia/Legacy ✦✦✦✦✦
Cosmopolitan Marlene Dietrich is a terrific 18-track collection that showcases the seductive, sophisticated pop songs Dietrich recorded for Columbia Records. Among the tracks included on the disc are "Lili Marlene," "Mean to Me," "Time on My Hands," "Taking a Chance on Love," "I Never Slept a Wink Last Night," "No Love, No Nothin" and "Miss Otis Regrets." *— Stephen Thomas Erlewine*

- **Falling in Love Again** / Sep. 22, 1998 / MCA ✦✦✦✦✦
La Femme Dietrich's career lasted several decades, and when she inked a deal with Decca Records in 1939, her first recording assignment was to produce an album of her "greatest hits," so already pervasive was her fame. This 16-track collection rounds up selections recorded over a 25-year period between her signing to Decca and her later recordings for Dot and Kapp, all of which parent company MCA-Universal now owns. Besides the definitive, elegant orchestral reading of the title track, Marlene also puts her pipes and personality to other hits like "The Boys in the Backroom" and "You've Got That Look (That Makes Me Weak)" from the movie *Destry Rides Again*, as well as a batch of classy readings of "You Do Something to Me," "You Go to My Head," and uncharacteristic, almost surreal 1957 rock & roll stabs at "Near You," and "Kisses Sweeter Than Wine" and the campy spins of her final single in 1965, "If He Swing By the String" and "Such Trying Times." All in all, a great little career overview to add to the pop vocal side of the collection. *—Cub Koda*

Jimmy Durante

b. Feb. 10, 1893, New York, NY, **d.** Jan. 29, 1980, Santa Monica, California
Vocals, Piano / Vaudeville, Traditional Pop, Nostalgia
If any performer can truly be said to have carved out his own comedic turf, made a huge success out of it lasting over several decades, while completely owning that piece of turf lock, stock and barrel, then that performer would have to be Jimmy Durante. There never has been a stylistic school of Durante; the man and his character are of one piece and ingrained in the national consciousness to the extreme. On the surface, Durante's mega-success defied all commonly understood show-business laws. He didn't sing good, he didn't look good while having the audacity to keep bringing it up, he dressed like a bum and couldn't say a complete sentence without screwing up some (or all) of the words. Not much of a show-business resume on the surface of it, but Durante's uncloneable charm gathered its main strength from being just that, an average guy. There was not one subtle thing about Jimmy Durante; whether it was wrecking a piano and throwing the resultant debris at the audience, singing a song like "I Know Darn Well I Can Do Without Broadway (But Can Broadway Do Without Me—)," or doing a complete about face and providing a brief glimpse of the wistful side of his character, he tapped the deepest of emotions every single time and did it at full bore. *—Cub Koda*

- **As Time Goes By: The Best of Jimmy Durante** / Oct. 5, 1993 / Warner Brothers ✦✦✦✦✦
As Time Goes By: The Best of Jimmy Durante compiles all of the highlights from Jimmy Durante's stint with Warner Brothers, which is where he had his biggest hits. All of his hits, including "September Song," are included on the disc, making it the definitive compilation. *—Stephen Thomas Erlewine*

Michael Feinstein

b. 1956
Vocals, Piano / Traditional Pop, Show Tunes, Nostalgia
Michael Feinstein was born in Columbus, OH, and developed an interest in the piano and in show music at an early age. After moving with his family to Los Angeles in 1976, he met Oscar Levant's widow, who in turn introduced him to Ira Gershwin. He was hired by Gershwin in 1977 to help organize The Gershwin archives, and continued to work with the lyricist until Gershwin's death in 1983.

In 1984, Feinstein launched a career as a pianist and singer devoted to the music of the '30s and '40s, playing at private parties in the Los Angeles area. He had a seven-month residence at the Mondrian Hotel, during which Liza Minnelli threw a party in his honor (February 1985) that got his name around. In January 1986, he opened at the Algonquin Hotel in New York, where a six-week engagement stretched to 16 weeks.

Feinstein's debut album, *Live at the Algonquin*, mixed the songs of Irving Berlin and Oscar Levant with more current material by Stephen Sondheim and Gretchen Cryer. By 1988 he had been signed to Elektra Records, for whom he has recorded a series of albums spotlighting the work of specific composers, among them 1998's *Michael & George: Feinstein Sings Gershwin*, as well as a children's album. *—William Ruhlmann*

Live at the Algonquin / 1986 / Asylum ✦✦✦

- **Pure Gershwin** / 1987 / Asylum ✦✦✦✦✦
Pure delight. Feinstein's reading of other composers is very, very good, but his feeling for Gershwin (as might be expected from a man who worked with Ira Gershwin for years) is near perfect. Feinstein's piano playing is excellent here, and he relishes every syllable of the words. 'S wonderful. *—William Ruhlmann*

Remember: Michael Feinstein Sings Irving Berlin / 1987 / Asylum ✦✦✦

Michael Feinstein Sings the Burton Lane Songbook, Vol. 1 / Nov. 1990 / Elektra/Nonesuch ✦✦✦
Though Michael Feinstein had previously devoted an entire album to one songwriter, this album marked the formal beginning of his Songbook series, and he worked closely with Broadway and Hollywood composer Burton Lane, who accompanied him on piano and duetted on the leadoff track, "Applause, Applause." In addition to performing such familiar Lane works as "How Are Things In Glocca Morra?" (as part of a *Finian's Rainbow* medley), "How About You?" (as part of a *Babes on Broadway* medley), and "How Could You Believe Me When I Said I Love You When You Know I've Been a Liar All My Life," Feinstein also premiered two new Lane compositions, "I Can Hardly Wait" (lyrics by Alan and Marilyn Bergman) and "And Suddenly It's Christmas" (lyrics by Ervin Drake). Since Lane never attracted the kind of anthologies devoted to the work of his peers, this album is especially valuable. Note, however, that Lane's best-known song, "On a Clear Day You Can See Forever," is missing. *—William Ruhlmann*

Michael Feinstein Sings the Burton Lane Songbook, Vol. 2 / 1992 / Elektra ✦✦✦✦
Burton Lane's extensive song catalogue more than justifies a second volume of his collaboration with Michael Feinstein, who sings to the composer's piano accompaniment. There are hits like "Everything I Have Is Yours" and "The Lady's in Love With You," and interesting obscurities, such as "It's Time for a Love Song," from the flop musical, *Carmelina*, and "Your Head on My Shoulder," from *Kid Millions*, one of the dozens of films to which Lane contributed music. And the album concludes with a lengthy medley of songs from *On a Clear Day You Can See Forever*, including the title song, Lane's most famous composition (which answers the question of why it was missing from the first volume). Since Lane is unaccountably less renowned than he should be, this collection and its predecessor perform an especially valuable function. *—William Ruhlmann*

Such Sweet Sorrow / 1995 / Atlantic ✦✦✦

Nice Work If You Can Get It: Songs by the Gershwins / Feb. 13, 1996 / Atlantic ✦✦✦✦✦
Nice Work If You Can Get It: Songs by the Gershwins is Michael Feinstein's second all-Gershwin album. His first, *Pure Gershwin*, was his best record, probably because, as a former secretary to Ira Gershwin, he knew his way around the material. This time, Feinstein puts his extensive knowledge of the Gershwin catalogue to good use, unearthing lost songs—"Anything for You" and "Will You Remember Me?" are given their first-ever recordings—resurrecting original arrangements, and singing rarely used lyrics to favorites like "Someone to Watch over Me." The album's tour de force is the seven-and-a-half-minute "Fascinating Rhythm (Medley)," which travels through time to trace the development of the song and its subsequent versions in successive musical styles. The effect is to demonstrate both the timelessness and the endless versatility of George Gershwin's music. All of this is far more elaborate than the piano accompaniment on *Pure Gershwin*, and Feinstein has developed enough as a singer to keep up. The man has the heart of a research assistant, but few history lessons are this much fun. *—William Ruhlmann*

Big City Rhythms / Oct. 12, 1999 / Concord Jazz ✦✦✦✦

Romance on Film/Romance on Broadway / Oct. 10, 2000 / Concord Jazz ✦✦✦✦✦

José Feliciano

b. Sep. 8, 1945, Lares, Puerto Rico
Vocals, Guitar / Folk-Rock, Soft Rock, Pop
One of the most prominent Latin-born performers of the pop era, singer/guitarist Jose Feliciano was born blind and spent much of his childhood in New York's Spanish Harlem area. Though his first few LPs reflected his early folk direction, Feliciano returned to his roots in the mid-'60s and scored on the Latin pop charts. With 1968's *Feliciano!*, he scored a breakthrough hit with a soulful reading of the Doors' "Light My Fire" that launched him into the mainstream pop stratosphere. His idiosyncratic Latin-jazz performance of the national anthem during the 1968 World Series proved highly controversial, though a later recording became a hit and secured his status as an emerging counterculture hero. He never again equalled the success of "Light My Fire," but remained an active performer in the '70s, touring annually and issuing a number of LPs in both English and Spanish. In 1980 Feliciano was the first performer signed to the new Latin division of Motown, making his label debut with an eponymous effort the following year; his recorded output tapered off during the course of the decade, although he occasionally resurfaced. *—Jason Ankeny*

- **All-Time Greatest Hits** / 1989 / RCA ✦✦✦✦✦
Included are his versions of "Light My Fire, " "California Dreamin', " "Suzy Q, " and "Walk Right In." *—AMG*

Absolutely the Best / Jun. 6, 2000 / Varese ✦✦✦✦

Eddie Fisher

b. Aug. 10, 1928, Philadelphia, PA
Vocals / Traditional Pop, Vocal Pop
One of the most popular male vocalists of the early '50s despite a throwback style that recalled Al Jolson and Tin Pan Alley, Eddie Fisher scored four number one hits between 1952 and 1954 but is probably known best for his celebrity circles—his wives included Debbie Reynolds, Elizabeth Taylor and Connie Stevens. Born in Philadelphia, Fisher began singing at an early age and made his first radio appearance while still in high school, singing with Buddy Morrow and Charlie Ventura. While working the borscht belt in upstate New York, he met Eddie Cantor and appeared on his highly rated radio show during 1949. The exposure naturally led to a recording contract, and his first few singles for RCA, including "Thinking of You" and "Turn Back the Hands of Time," spent time near the top of the chart.

Two consecutive million-sellers, 1952's "Any Time" and "Tell Me Why," really made Eddie Fisher's reputation as a major attraction. After one more big hit ("Wish You Were Here") that year, he scored with the biggest year of his career in 1953; both "I'm Walking Behind You" and "Oh! My Pa-Pa" spent many weeks at the top of the charts. Fisher then gained his own top-rated television programs, *Coke Time* and *The Chesterfield Supper Club*. His success continued apace in 1954 with "I Need You Now," and he starred in his first movie, *Bundle of Joy*, in 1956—co-billed with his first wife, Debbie Reynolds. His second film, 1960's *Butterfield 8*, teamed him with Elizabeth Taylor, whom he married soon after. The blitz of media publicity over the woman who lured him away from his wife boosted the public exposure of all three stars. Still, he never entered the Top 40 after 1956.

His live album, 1963's *Eddie Fisher at the Winter Garden*, was recorded for his own Ramrod label. A return to RCA in the mid-'60s yielded a moderate hit with the LP *Games That Lovers Play*. After one more RCA album, Fisher rarely recorded during the rest of his career, though he continued to perform around America. *—John Bush*

- **All-Time Greatest Hits #1** / 1991 / RCA ✦✦✦✦✦
All-Time Greatest Hits, Vol. #1 is a terrific overview of Eddie Fisher's hit-making years at RCA Victor, featuring most of his biggest pop hits, including "I Need You Now," "Count Your Blessing," "Heart," "Dungaree Doll," "Everbody's Got a Home But Me" and "Cindy, Oh Cindy." *—Stephen Thomas Erlewine*

Ella Fitzgerald

b. Apr. 25, 1917, Newport News, VA, **d.** Jun. 15, 1996, Beverly Hills, CA
Vocals / Vocal Jazz, Traditional Pop, Standards, Swing, Bop, Classic Female Blues
"The First Lady of Song," Ella Fitzgerald was arguably the finest female jazz singer of all time (although some may vote for Sarah Vaughan or Billie Holiday). Blessed with a beautiful voice

and a wide range, Ella could outswing anyone, was a brilliant scat singer and had near-perfect elocution; one could always understand the words she sang. The one fault was that, since she always sounded so happy to be singing, Ella did not always dig below the surface of the lyrics she interpreted and she even made a downbeat song such as "Love for Sale" sound joyous. However, when one evaluates her career on a whole, there is simply no one else in her class. Starting in 1935, Ella began recording with Chick Webb's Orchestra and by 1937 over half of the band's selections featured her voice. "A-Tisket, A-Tasket" became a huge hit in 1938 and "Undecided" soon followed. She already had a beautiful voice but did not improvise or scat much; that would develop later. On June 16, 1939 Chick Webb died. It was decided that Ella would front the orchestra even though she had little to do with the repertoire or hiring or firing the musicians. She retained her popularity and when she broke up the band in 1941 and went solo, it was not long before her Decca recordings contained more than their share of hits. On tour with Dizzy Gillespie's big band, she adopted bop as part of her style and started including exciting scat-filled romps in her set. Her recordings of "Lady Be Good," "How High the Moon" and "Flying Home" during 1945-47 became popular and her stature as a major jazz singer rose as a result. At the peak of her powers around 1960, Ella's hilarious live version of "Mack the Knife" (in which she forgot the words and made up her own) from *Ella in Berlin* is a classic and virtually all of her Verve recordings are worth getting. *—Scott Yanow*

☆ **75th Birthday Celebration** / May 2, 1938-Aug. 5, 1955 / GRP ♦♦♦♦♦
This attractive two-CD set, released to celebrate Fitzgerald's 75th birthday, is a perfect greatest-hits collection spanning the first half of her very productive career. All 39 songs are winners, highlighted by "A-Tisket, A-Tasket," "Undecided," "Flying Home," "Lady Be Good," "How High the Moon," "Smooth Sailing," "Airmail Special," "Lullaby of Birdland" and "Hard Hearted Hannah." During the period covered by this package, she developed from a fine big-band pop vocalist into the definitive jazz singer, one who could scat and swing with the best musicians. This set is a perfect introduction to her magic. *—Scott Yanow*

Ella: The Legendary Decca Recordings / May 2, 1938-Aug. 5, 1955 / GRP ♦♦♦♦
The four-CD retrospective *The Legendary Decca Recordings* represented both an attempt to present the essence of Ella Fitzgerald's two-decade tenure at Decca Records and to defend that period against the conventional wisdom that not until she moved to Verve Records in the mid-'50s was her talent given full rein. Divided into four sections, the collection begins with "The Very Best Of Ella," not exactly a greatest-hits set, though it began with her first big hit, "A-Tisket, A-Tasket," and included such chart successes as "Undecided," "Cow-Cow Boogie," and "Stone Cold Dead in the Market." Also included were such classics of scat singing as "Oh, Lady Be Good" and "How High the Moon" and the signature song "You'll Have to Swing It (Mr. Paganinni)." Thus, with only one disc Keepnews and Dorn had accomplished their goals of including Fitzgerald's most memorable work for Decca and demonstrating that that work was as good as any she ever did. The second disc, "Ella & Friends," featured duets with Louis Armstrong, the Ink Spots, Louis Jordan, and the Mills Brothers, among others. With the third disc, "Ella Sings Gershwin & Others," the producers went on to show how her Decca recordings anticipated the ones on Verve. Of course, the popular Verve songbooks featured not only song standards but also name arrangers, and the fourth disc, "Ella & The Arrangers," demonstrated that, again, Decca had gotten there first, pairing her with many gifted arrangers. Ella Fitzgerald recorded a great deal of material for Decca over the years, and some of it certainly justifies the criticisms made of the catalog in general. But *The Legendary Decca Recordings* presented it in the best possible light and included the most impressive sides from the period. *—William Ruhlmann*

The First Lady of Song / Sep. 18, 1949-Jul. 29, 1966 / Verve ♦♦♦♦
This attractive three-CD set gives listeners an overview of Ella Fitzgerald's Verve recordings, although the inclusion of seven previously unissued cuts (in addition to 44 that are mostly available in more complete form elsewhere) will frustrate some completists. However the careful selection of representative performances along with the informative and lengthy text make this highly enjoyable reissue (which captures her in prime form) recommended even to collectors who have most of the singer's albums. *—Scott Yanow*

☆ **The Complete Ella Fitzgerald Song Books** / Feb. 7, 1956-Oct. 21, 1964 / Verve ♦♦♦♦♦
With her signing to Verve in 1956, Ella Fitzgerald (under producer Norman Granz's guidance) began a series of *Songbook* projects in which the singer (backed by orchestras) performed the works of various major composers. Her *Cole Porter Song Book* was so well-received that it was followed by ones featuring the music of Rodgers And Hart, Duke Ellington (half of which featured his band), Irving Berlin, a massive salute to George and Ira Gershwin, Harold Arlen, Jerome Kern and Johnny Mercer. This 16-CD box set is not for everyone (due to its cost) and is not the most jazz-oriented of Ella Fitzgerald's recordings (she does not scat much and some of the string arrangements weigh the music down a little) but her voice is in peak form and this was a very classy (and extensive) project. The reissue (which uses miniature reproductions of the original LPs along with a definitive book, all placed in a red box) is a gem, perfectly done. *—Scott Yanow*

Sings the Cole Porter Song Book / Feb. 7, 1956-Mar. 27, 1956 / Verve ♦♦♦♦♦

The Complete Ella Fitzgerald & Louis Armstrong on Verve / Aug. 16, 1956-Oct. 14, 1957 / Verve ♦♦♦♦♦
Almost all of these summit meetings have been in print virtually since CDs first appeared in our lives, but never in one package. Here, you get all of *Ella and Louis,* the double album sets *Ella and Louis Again* and *Porgy and Bess,* and two live tracks recorded at the Hollywood Bowl in 1956—all in an unusual 3-CD album that partially unfolds into an accordion-file (what will Verve's inventive packaging wizards think of next—). There are two booklets, one of which contains a rare recent interview with producer Norman Granz, and the other the notes from the original albums. Of the two wonderfully relaxed *Ella and Louis* albums, with their Oscar Peterson-driven rhythm quartets, the sequel strikes me as a more diverse, more involving collection, although Satch doesn't play as much trumpet on *Again* as he does on the first album. Also, the two go it alone on several tracks, but one is not at all inconvenienced by the inclusion of solo gems like Armstrong's sly catalog of intercouplings on "Let's Do It."
The *Porgy* session is an entirely different creature, a big, formal presentation with Russ Garcia's lush yet atmospheric and even powerful orchestrations, reverberant sound (normally a Granz no-no), grandly moving vocal performances by the two, and a handful of tremendous trumpet solos from Pops. Alas, no unissued tracks turn up here, and of course, MCA still controls all of the earlier Decca duets (hence the disclaimer "Complete On Verve")—so veteran Ella/Louis collectors may opt to hang on to earlier issues. But for those who don't have everything, this is irresistible. *—Richard S. Ginell*

☆ **Sings the Rodgers & Hart Song Book, Vols. 1-2** / Aug. 21, 1956-Aug. 31, 1956 / Verve ♦♦♦♦♦
The second of Ella Fitzgerald's famed *Songbook* series features her singing 34 of the best songs co-written by Richard Rodgers & Lorenz Hart. The arrangements by Buddy Bregman for the string orchestra and big band only border on jazz but she manages to swing the medium-tempo numbers and give sensitivity to the ballads. With such songs as "You Took Advantage of Me," "The Lady Is a Tramp," "It Never Entered My Mind," "Where or When" "My Funny Valentine" and "Blue Moon," it is not too surprising that these recordings (originally released on a two-LP set) were so popular. After being released on CD as part of the massive box set *The Complete Ella Fitzgerald Song Books,* it was also released as a separate two-disc package in 1997. *—Scott Yanow*

Sings the Duke Ellington Song Book / Sep. 4, 1956-Oct. 17, 1957 / Verve ♦♦♦♦♦

Like Someone in Love / 1957 / Verve ♦♦♦

Get Happy / Jul. 24, 1957-Jul. 11, 1959 / Verve ♦♦♦

At the Opera House / Sep. 29, 1957–Oct. 7, 1957 / Verve ♦♦♦

Ella in Rome: The Birthday Concert / Apr. 25, 1958 / Verve ♦♦♦♦♦

Ella Swings Brightly with Nelson / Jan. 5, 1959-Dec. 27, 1961 / Verve ♦♦♦

Sings the George & Ira Gershwin Song Book / Jan. 5, 1959-Jul. 18, 1959 / Verve ♦♦♦♦♦

☆ **The Complete Ella in Berlin: Mack the Knife** / Feb. 13, 1960 / Verve ♦♦♦♦♦
Ella Fitzgerald was at the peak of her form during her 1960 tour of Europe. Her Berlin concert is most remembered for her hilariously inventive version of "Mack the Knife" during which she forgot the words and substituted ones of her own that somehow fit, amazing herself in the process. In addition to the original LP program, this CD has two previously unissued titles and a pair of others only briefly released on a very rare LP. With fine support from her quartet (pianist Paul Smith, guitarist Jim Hall, bassist Wilfred Middlebrooks and drummer Gus Johnson), Fitzgerald is brilliant throughout the well-rounded set with highlights including "Misty" (a version very different from Sarah Vaughan's), "The Lady Is a Tramp," "Too Darn Hot" and a scat-filled "How High the Moon." This is essential music. *—Scott Yanow*

The Intimate Ella / Apr. 14, 1960-Apr. 19, 1060 / Verve ♦♦♦♦
This is a most unusual Ella Fitzgerald recording, reissued on CD by Verve. Recorded around the time when she performed some of these songs for the film *Let No Man Write My Epitaph,* the masterful singer is heard in duets with pianist Paul Smith interpreting 13 songs (even "I Cried for You," "I Can't Give You Anything but Love" and "Who's Sorry Now") at slow expressive tempoes. Listeners who feel that Ella Fitzgerald was mostly a scat singer who had trouble giving the proper emotional intensity to lyrics will be surprised by this sensitive and often-haunting set. *—Scott Yanow*

Ella Returns to Berlin / Feb. 11, 1961 / Verve ♦♦♦♦

Ella Swings Gently with Nelson / Nov. 13, 1961-Dec. 27, 1961 / Verve ♦♦♦

Rhythm Is My Business / Jan. 30, 1962-Jan. 31, 1962 / Verve ♦♦♦

☆ **Sings the Jerome Kern Song Book** / Jan. 5, 1963-Jan. 7, 1963 / Verve ♦♦♦♦♦
By 1963, Ella Fitzgerald's *Songbook* series had almost run its course and was becoming much less ambitious in scope. Her Jerome Kern set features her interpretations of 14 songs while backed by an orchestra arranged by Nelson Riddle. Treatments of such classics as "A Fine Romance," "All the Things You Are" and "Yesterdays" are pretty straightforward and would have pleased the composer. All of her songbooks are now included in the massive 16-CD box set *The Complete Ella Fitzgerald Song Books.* *—Scott Yanow*

Ella and Basie / Jul. 16, 1963–Jul. 17, 1963 / Verve ♦♦♦♦♦

These Are the Blues / Oct. 28, 1963 / Verve ♦♦♦

Sings the Johnny Mercer Song Book / Oct. 19, 1964-Oct. 21, 1964 / Verve ♦♦♦♦♦

Dream Dancing / Jun. 12, 1972–Feb. 13, 1978 / Pablo ♦♦♦♦

Ella in London / Apr. 11, 1974 / Pablo/OJC ♦♦♦♦♦
This is one of Fitzgerald's most enjoyable recordings from her later years. With pianist Tommy Flanagan, guitarist Joe Pass, bassist Keter Betts and drummer Bobby Durham serving as a backup group (not a bad band), she swings everything from "Sweet Georgia Brown," and "It Don't Mean a Thing" to "Lemon Drop" and even Carole King's "You've Got a Friend." Her ballad interpretations are only topped by her scatting talents. This set serves as a perfect introduction to the mature Ella Fitzgerald. *—Scott Yanow*

Lady Time / Jun. 19, 1978-Jun. 20, 1978 / Pablo/OJC ♦♦♦

Pure Ella: The Very Best of Ella Fitzgerald / Mar. 31, 1998 / Verve ♦♦♦♦

● **Something to Live For** / Nov. 2, 1999 / Verve ♦♦♦♦♦
Ella Fitzgerald recorded so much, and so much of what she recorded was so good, that the notion of one album summing her up is all but ludicrous. That said, this two-disc set, a companion to a television documentary by the same title, comes the closest of any album so far. It is the first album to span the two most important eras of her recordings, the Decca years, 1935-1955, and the Verve years, 1956-1966. The eight Decca performances include Fitzgerald's first big hit, "A-Tisket, A-Tasket"; the 1947 scat masterpiece "How High the Moon"; and a selection from the voice-and-piano album *Ella Sings Gershwin,* "But Not for Me," which foreshadowed the singer's songbook albums of the late '50s and '60s. The Verve recordings get their official start with the appropriate inclusion of "Ridin' High" from 1956's *Ella Fitzgerald*

Sings the Cole Porter Song Book, one of five selections from the celebrated songbook albums. The rest of the choices are gems from Fitzgerald's career, including some stunning scat features, notably a version of "Airmail Special" from the 1957 *Newport Jazz Festival*. The memorable 1960 Berlin performance of "Mack the Knife," with its improvised lyrics, is included, as is a live 1962 recording of "Bill Bailey" which finds this uncanny mimic doing impressions of Della Reese and Pearl Bailey. The uptempo material is offset with some wonderful ballads, among them a version of "Angel Eyes" with only Barney Kessel providing a guitar accompaniment. Fitzgerald fans could cite dozens (if not hundreds) of other stellar performances, many of them from after the 1966 cut-off point of this album, but this is the first time such a long period of Fitzgerald's career has been captured on a single album. Many of the recordings that nearly all fans would agree rank among her best are here. *—William Ruhlmann*

George Formby (George Hoy Booth)

Vocals, Banjo / Music Hall, Show Tunes, Nostalgia

In a career tragically cut short in mid-stride by a brain tumor, George Gershwin (1898-1937) proved himself to be not only one of the great songwriters of his extremely rich era, but also a gifted "serious" composer who might bridge the worlds of classical and popular music. The latter is all the more striking, given that, of his contemporaries, Gershwin was the most influenced by such styles as jazz and blues.

Gershwin's first major hit, interpolated into the show *Sinbad* in 1919, was "Swanee," sung by Al Jolson. Gershwin wrote both complete scores and songs for such variety shoes as George White's *Scandals* (whose annual editions thus were able to introduce such songs as "I'll Build a Stairway to Paradise" and "Somebody Loves Me").

After 1924, Gershwin worked primarily with his brother Ira as his lyricist. the two scored a series of Broadway hits in the '20s and early '30s, starting with *Lady Be Good* (1924), which included the song "Fascinatin' Rhythm." 1924 was also the year Gershwin composed his first classical piece, "Rhapsody in Blue," and he would continue to work in the classical field until his death.

By the '30s, the Gershwins had turned to political topics and satire in response to the onset of the Depression, and their *Of Thee I Sing* became the first musical to win a Pulitzer Prize. In the mid '30s, Gershwin ambitiously worked to meld his show music and classical leanings in the creation of the folk opera *Porgy and Bess*, with lyrics by Ira and by Dubose Heyward. The Gershwins had moved to Hollywood and were engaged in several movie projects at the time of George Gershwin's death. *—William Ruhlmann*

● **Ultimate Collection** / Apr. 11, 2000 / Castle ✦✦✦✦✦

The Four Aces

f. 1949, Chester, PA, **db.** 1959

Group / Vocal Pop

One of the most successful pre-rock vocal groups, the Four Aces did well during the early '50s with a narrow range of pop material but burned out before decade's end. Founded by Navy shipmates Al Alberts and Dave Mahoney, the act added Lou Silvestri and Sol Vaccaro before making a name for themselves around their native Philadelphia. After failing to find a distributor for their debut single "(It's No) Sin," Alberts founded his own Victoria label to release the single. It became a big hit in late 1951 and sold a million copies. Signed to Decca before the end of the year, their debut single for the label, "Tell Me Why," just barely missed the top of the charts and sold a million copies as well. A few Top Ten hits followed during the early '50s before the theme to *Three Coins in the Fountain* hit number one in 1954. Another movie theme, "Love Is a Many-Splendored Thing," spent over a month at the top during 1955.

For several singles during 1955, the group had been billed as the Four Aces Featuring Al Alberts; one year later, he departed for a solo career (but never even reached the charts). Along with the rise of rock & roll, the Four Aces appeared to be doomed. They scraped the charts with a novelty song ("Bahama Mama") and a rock take-off ("Rock and Roll Rhapsody"), but failed to come through with any hits after 1959. Al Alberts continued to perform into the '90s, leading a newer edition of the act. *—John Bush*

● **The Four Aces' Greatest Hits** / 1993 / MCA ✦✦✦✦✦

The Four Freshmen

f. 1948, Indianapolis, IN, **db.** 1960

Vocals / Vocal Pop

A vocal group from the 1950s taking inspiration from barbershop quartets and Mel Tormé's Mel-Tones, the Four Freshmen's close-harmony vocals went on to become a major influence on pop groups like the Beach Boys as well as the jazz-oriented Manhattan Transfer. Originally formed as the barbershop group Hal's Harmonizers by brothers Ross and Don Barbour, the duo became a small jazz band named the Toppers, but later that year, they added lead vocalist Bob Flanagan (their cousin) and Hal Kratzsch to become the Four Freshmen. Soon after coming together, the quartet gained the notice of both Woody Herman and Stan Kenton, the latter of whom connected the group with Capitol Records. Early in the 1950s, the Four Freshmen gained their first hit with "It's a Blue World;" several moderate hits followed during the years 1953-56, including "It Happened Once Before," "Mood Indigo," "Day by Day" and "Graduation Day." The group entered the LP era in the late '50s with several album hits, including their instrument series (*Four Freshmen and 5 Trombones*, *4 Freshmen and 5 Trumpets*, etc.). Though Don Barbour left in 1960, the group kept on going with replacements, with Bob Flanagan becoming the only original member still left after Ross Barbour's departure in 1977. In one form or another, the Four Freshmen continued to tour into the 1990s. *—John Bush*

Four Freshmen and 5 Trombones / 1956 / Capitol ✦✦✦

A trombone quintet backs the Freshmen on this otherwise typical cleanly arranged and sung selection of standards by the likes of Gershwin, Kern, Weill, Mercer, and Hammerstein. *—Richie Unterberger*

4 Freshmen and 5 Trumpets / Mar. 6, 1957 / Capitol ✦✦✦

The previous year, the Freshmen had sung with a trombone quintet on *4 Freshmen and 5 Trombones*. Here's a mild spin on that vocals-with-brass concept, substituting trumpets for trombones on a collection of light romantic fare. *—Richie Unterberger*

● **Capitol Collectors Series** / Jan. 21, 1991 / Capitol ✦✦✦✦✦

This is an excellent and well-annotated collection of the best of this '60s harmony group. *—Charles S. Wolfe*

Spotlight on Four Freshmen / Jan. 23, 1996 / Capitol ✦✦✦

The *Capitol Collectors Series* CD has their most popular material; this concentrates on their LP tracks, offering 18 cuts that they recorded between 1954 and 1961. As is par for the course on Capitol's *Spotlight* series, the emphasis is on orchestrated standards. *—Richie Unterberger*

Judy Garland

b. Jun. 10, 1922, Grand Rapids, MN, **d.** Jun. 22, 1969

Vocals / Traditional Pop, Standards, Show Tunes

Like so many of Hollywood's most enduring icons, Judy Garland was also among the industry's most tragic figures. An entertainer from virtually infancy onward, she lived and died in the intense glare of the spotlight, leaving behind a legacy encompassing not only classic movies and musical performances but also a catalogue of personal setbacks and career disasters truly horrifying in their sheer number and scope. The subject of an adoring cult following, Garland remains a star on the strength of timeless motion pictures like *The Wizard of Oz* and *Meet Me in St. Louis* along with albums like *Judy at Carnegie Hall;* an engaging actress and a powerful singer, she also remains the subject of considerable public scrutiny and rumor, and as time wears on it becomes increasingly difficult to separate the woman from the myth. 1939's *The Wizard of Oz* was Garland's definitive on-screen moment, and she was forever associated with its perennial number "Over the Rainbow." However, at the peak of her success also began her tragic downward trajectory: to keep her fluctuating weight in check, Garland was administered any number of drugs, with amphetamines and barbiturates also prescribed to guide her through torturous shooting schedules. Soon she was a drug addict. In 1942 she won her first "adult" role in Busby Berkeley's *For Me and My Gal*, which scored a smash radio hit with its title track, and in 1944 she starred in Vincente Minnelli's classic *Meet Me in St. Louis*, earning another hit with "The Trolley Song." Garland and Minnelli later married, and had daughter Liza in 1946. Personal turmoil dogged her throughout her life, however, and on June 22, 1969 Garland was found dead of an apparently accidental overdose of barbiturates. *—Jason Ankeny*

Judy at Carnegie Hall / 1961 / Capitol ✦✦✦✦✦

This 40th anniversary edition of Garland's seminal *Judy at Carnegie Hall* recording is a completely fresh experience even for those intimately familiar with previous versions. By accessing tapes which have not been used on any other release—including the pricey DCC gold disc—many sonic foibles which plagued the original have now been repaired. The overwhelming success of this album, which initially spent 95 weeks on the charts and garnered five Grammy Awards, makes it a prime candidate for a sonic overhaul. By reclaiming tapes that were once considered MIA, the sound is now notably more balanced. In addition, much of the fake applause has been thoughtfully removed, unveiling previously masked dramatic pacing and audience interplay between songs. But the highlight of the entire package is the return of "Alone Together" from the actual *Carnegie Hall* performance. The song had been replaced by a studio version on the 1989 CD reissue due to missing master tapes. Since then, those tapes have been put back into commission and provide the jaw-dropping sound on this delightful set.

There is a good reason that Garland historian Scott Schechter titled his specially-penned liner notes essay "Two Hours of POW!" With relentless verve, Garland takes on her entire musical catalogue with astonishing aplomb. There is little sign of the decades of self-abuse which had left her frail by the early '60s. But what we are fortunate enough to have is the magic and youth of her voice. Especially poignant are "You Go to My Head," "Just You, Just Me," and her quintessential reading of "Somewhere Over the Rainbow." *Judy at Carnegie Hall* is far and away the finest live performance to be issued during her lifetime. The numerous improvements made on this 40th anniversary edition will no doubt serve her legacy well. *—Lindsay Planer*

All-Time Greatest Hits / 1990 / Curb ✦✦✦

This 12-track album consists of five recordings Judy Garland made for Decca Records during her tenure there in the 1930s and '40s and seven made during her stint at Capitol in the '50s and '60s. They include favorites like "Over the Rainbow" (for Capitol), "You Made Me Love You," "The Trolley Song," "Chicago," and "Swanee." There are two distinctly different Garlands here, first the exuberant, pure-voiced teenage movie star of the Decca tracks, then the more hard-edged, but still fascinating cabaret performer of the Capitol tracks. This is by no means a comprehensive collection of Garland's best-known material, but it is notable for combining two catalogs that are usually presented separately, and it will give the novice a good sense of the singer's repertoire. *—William Ruhlmann*

Spotlight on Judy Garland / Jan. 23, 1996 / Capitol ✦✦✦✦✦

Eighteen tracks from her 1955-1960 Capitol recordings, often with orchestral conduction from Nelson Riddle. As expected, standards are the order of the day, the most famous being "That's Entertainment!," "Zing! Went the Strings of My Heart," "Me and My Shadow," and a 1955 version of "Over the Rainbow." *—Richie Unterberger*

● **The Best of Judy Garland in Hollywood** / Oct. 27, 1998 / Rhino ✦✦✦✦✦

Judy Garland may have reached more ears via her movie roles than with any other medium, and this 23-track anthology assembles some of her most noteworthy performances from 1936 to 1963. All of these are the original soundtrack versions, not re-recordings, which means that while the fidelity on some cuts isn't as good as what you might be used to from renditions you've heard elsewhere, these are the real deal, not re-creations. A bunch of familiar standards are here: "Over the Rainbow," "The Trolley Song" (from *Meet Me in St. Louis*), "Dear Mr. Gable," "The Texas Tornado," "I'm Nobody's Baby," "I Could Go on Singing," and two cuts from *A Star Is Born*, "Gotta Have Me Go With You" and "The Man That Got Away." As a retrospective of her musical career, this serves almost as well as a standard greatest-hits collection, with scrupulously detailed liner notes and photos in the enclosed booklet. *—Richie Unterberger*

George Gershwin (Jacob Gershvin)

b. Sep. 26, 1898, New York, NY, **d.** Jul. 11, 1937, Beverly Hills, CA
Piano, Composer / Tin Pan Alley Pop, Traditional Pop, Standards, 20th Century Classical/Modern Composition, Show Tunes

In a career tragically cut short in mid-stride by a brain tumor, George Gershwin (1898-1937) proved himself to be not only one of the great songwriters of his extremely rich era, but also a gifted "serious" composer who might bridge the worlds of classical and popular music. The latter is all the more striking, given that, of his contemporaries, Gershwin was the most influenced by such styles as jazz and blues.

Gershwin's first major hit, interpolated into the show *Sinbad* in 1919, was "Swanee," sung by Al Jolson. Gershwin wrote both complete scores and songs for such variety shoes as George White's *Scandals* (whose annual editions thus were able to introduce such songs as "I'll Build a Stairway to Paradise" and "Somebody Loves Me").

After 1924, Gershwin worked primarily with his brother Ira as his lyricist. the two scored a series of Broadway hits in the '20s and early '30s, starting with *Lady Be Good* (1924), which included the song "Fascinatin' Rhythm." 1924 was also the year Gershwin composed his first classical piece, "Rhapsody in Blue," and he would continue to work in the classical field until his death.

By the '30s, the Gershwins had turned to political topics and satire in response to the onset of the Depression, and their *Of Thee I Sing* became the first musical to win a Pulitzer Prize. In the mid '30s, Gershwin ambitiously worked to meld his show music and classical leanings in the creation of the folk opera *Porgy and Bess*, with lyrics by Ira and by Dubose Heyward. The Gershwins had moved to Hollywood and were engaged in several movie projects at the time of George Gershwin's death. *—William Ruhlmann*

Gershwin Plays Gershwin: The Piano Rolls / 1993 / Takoma ✦✦✦✦✦
George Gershwin made 130 piano rolls between 1916-27; 28 were recorded and released in 1998 on two Nonesuch CDs. This particular release has quite a few obscure Gershwin songs, including his very first tune, "When You Want 'Em, You Can't Get 'Em, When You've Got 'Em, You Don't Want 'Em." Certainly such tunes as "Novelette In Fourths," "So Am I," and "Idle Dreams" are long forgotten but worth reviving. Among the other highlights of the fascinating and highly enjoyable recital are "Sweet and Lowdown," "Swanee" and a 14-minute rendition of "Rhapsody In Blue." The 1933 item is a bit unusual, for it is a two-piano rendition of "An American In Paris" that lasts over 16 minutes and was arranged by Frank Milne. Well worth exploring. *—Scott Yanow*

● **George and Ira Gershwin in Hollywood** / May 27, 1997 / Rhino ✦✦✦✦✦
Although George and Ira Gershwin were already well established as Broadway's hottest and finest writing team, they had to wait until the movies started talking to come westward to work their magic in films. This two-disc, 40-track deluxe anthology is largely produced through the auspices of Turner Classic Movies, which now owns the enormous MGM library. Along with pre-recorded soundtrack acetates—free from dialogue and sound effects—from RKO (the first pre-recording playback discs from *A Damsel In Distress* and *Shall We Dance*), this collection brings for the first time to compact disc items like "Delishious, "Summertime" and "135th Street Blues (Blue Monday)," Oscar Levant's "Third Prelude" and Ray Heindorf's original "Overture" from Gershwin's biopic *Rhapsody In Blue*. With the original film appearances of "Swanee," "Love Is Here to Stay," "Fascinating Rhythm," The Man I Love," "Embraceable You," 'They All Laughed," "A Foggy Day," "But Not for Me," "Let's Call the Thing Off," "Nice Work If You Can Get It," "Strike Up the Band," "Oh Lady, Be Good" and "I Got Rhythm" aboard, this compilation stands as textbook American popular songwriting of the highest order. Produced by Michael Feinstein, George Feltenstein and Bradley Flanagan, this was a labor of love, and the work put into finding the rare one-of-a-kind playback discs was the extra mile gone in making this such a thorough overview within the confines of a two-disc anthology. And no, they really *don't* write them like that anymore. *—Cub Koda*

The Ultimate Collection / May 12, 1998 / London ✦✦✦✦
George Gershwin: The Ultimate Collection is a nice double-disc set that collects definitive performances of Gershwin standards from *Rhapsody in Blue* to *Funny Face*. It's a wildly eclectic collection, containing cuts from Billie Holiday, Louis Armstrong, Audrey Hepburn, Sarah Vaughan, Bing Crosby, Ella Fitzgerald, Nina Simone, and the Boston Pops Orchestra, thereby offering a good portrait of the depth of Gershwin's material and the way it lends itself to so many different styles. It's not necessarily a definitive collection—he wrote so much great music, it's nearly impossible to condense it all into one set—but it's one terrific sampler. *—Stephen Thomas Erlewine*

Astrud Gilberto

b. Mar. 30, 1940, Salvador, Bahia, Brazil
Vocals / Mood Music, Brazilian Jazz, Vocal Pop, Bossa Nova

The honey-toned chanteuse on the surprise Brazilian crossover hit "The Girl from Ipanema," Astrud Gilberto parlayed her previously unscheduled appearance (and professional singing debut) on the song into a lengthy career that resulted in nearly a dozen albums for Verve and a successful performing career that lasted into the '90s. Though her appearance at the studio to record "Girl from Ipanema" was due only to her husband Joao, one of the most famed Brazilian artists of the century, Gilberto's singular, quavery tone and undisguised naiveté propelled the song into the charts and influenced a variety of sources in worldwide pop music.

Born in Bahia, Gilberto moved to Rio de Janeiro at an early age. She'd had no professional musical experience of any kind until 1963, the year of her visit to New York with her husband, João Gilberto, in a recording session headed by Stan Getz. Getz had already recorded several albums influenced by Brazilian rhythms, and Verve teamed him with the cream of Brazilian music, Antonio Carlos Jobim and João Gilberto, for his next album. Producer Creed Taylor wanted a few English vocals for maximum crossover potential, and as it turned out, Astrud was the only Brazilian present with any grasp of the language. After her husband laid down his Portuguese vocals for the first verse of his and Jobim's composition, "The Girl from Ipanema," Astrud provided a hesitant, heavily accented second verse in English.

Not even credited on the resulting LP, *Getz/Gilberto*, Astrud finally gained fame over a year later, when "The Girl from Ipanema" became a number five hit in mid-1964. The album became the best-selling jazz album up to that point, and made Gilberto a star across America. Before the end of the year, Verve capitalized on the smash with the release of *Getz Au Go Go*, featuring a Getz live date with Gilberto's vocals added later. Her first actual solo album, *The Astrud Gilberto Album*, was released in May 1965. Though it barely missed the Top 40, the LP's blend of Brazilian classics and ballad standards proving quite infectious with easy-listening audiences.

Though she never returned to the pop charts in America, Verve proved to be quite understanding for Astrud Gilberto's career, pairing her with ace arranger Gil Evans for 1966's *Look to the Rainbow* and Brazilian organist/arranger Walter Wanderley for the dreamy *A Certain Smile, A Certain Sadness*, released later that year. She remained a huge pop star in Brazil for the rest of the 1960s and '70s, but gradually disappeared in America after her final album for Verve in 1969. In 1971, she released a lone album for CTI (with Stanley Turrentine) but was mostly forgotten in the US until 1984, when "Girl from Ipanema" re-charted in Britain on the tails of a neo-bossa craze. Gilberto gained worldwide distribution for 1987's *Astrud Gilberto Plus the James Last Orchestra*. *—John Bush*

The Shadow of Your Smile / Oct. 21, 1964-May 27, 1965 / Verve ✦✦

The Astrud Gilberto Album / Jan. 27, 1965–Jan. 28, 1965 / Verve ✦✦✦
Demure Brazilian vocalist Astrud Gilberton became a hit artist in 1963 with the song "The Girl from Ipanema." She recorded it with her husband Joao Gilberto, plus tenor saxophonist Stan Getz and Antonio Carlos Jobim. The resulting furor eventually got her a solo album, this 1965 work. It's got some charming moments, and she was ideal for the light bossa nova sound. But the jazz content was and still is minimal. *—Ron Wynn*

Look to the Rainbow / Nov. 22, 1965-Feb. 4, 1966 / Verve ✦✦✦✦✦
For this CD reissue the music on singer Astrud Gilberto's album *Look to the Rainbow* is combined with half of the songs from her following album *A Certain Smile*. The former session was one of the bossa nova singer's best (11 perfectly suitable songs on which her soft voice is accompanied by an orchestra arranged by Gil Evans and Al Cohn) while on the latter she interacts successfully with a trio led by organist Walter Wanderley. *—Scott Yanow*

A Certain Smile, A Certain Sadness / Sep. 20, 1966-Sep. 23, 1966 / Verve ✦✦✦✦

Beach Samba / May 25, 1967-Jun. 30, 1967 / Verve ✦✦✦

The Silver Collection: The Astrud Gilberto Album / Feb. 6, 1991 / Verve ✦✦✦✦✦
Harder to find than *Compact Jazz*, this also repeats about half of the tracks from that collection and makes the major boo-boo of not including "The Girl From Ipanema." But if you want more Gilberto, this is recommended. It has 25 songs, most of which do not duplicate *Compact Jazz*, all but three dating from 1965, and leans heavily on material by Antonio Carlos Jobim and Luiz Bonfa. *—Richie Unterberger*

● **Compact Jazz: Astrud Gilberto** / Verve ✦✦✦✦✦
The best compilation of her peak years. Gilberto's brand of breathy bossa nova-jazz has a romantic (if slightly cheesy) charm of its own, and these 16 tracks, including "The Girl From Ipanema," show her to her best advantage, with support from Stan Getz, Antonio Carlos Jobim, Joao Gilberto, and Gil Evans, among others. *—Richie Unterberger*

Robert Goulet (Stanley Applebaum)

b. Nov. 26, 1933, Lawrence, MA
Vocals / Traditional Pop, Vocal Pop, Show Tunes

His face is more famous than his voice, but Robert Goulet recorded a string of popular albums for Columbia during the 1960s, striking the pop charts with several hits and earning a 1962 Grammy award. He appeared on Canadian television in the early '50s, but moved to New York and by the end of the decade was fit into a prime Broadway role: Sir Lancelot, in Lerner & Loewe's *Camelot* (with Julie Andrews and Richard Burton). He began singing in the early '60s as well, and after an appearance on *The Ed Sullivan Show*, Goulet signed to Columbia in 1962. His single "What Kind of Fool Am I?" became a modest hit later that year, and early in 1963, he won a Grammy for Best New Artist. Like many vocal artists of the day, however, Goulet became a bankable LP seller rather than a chart success, and though he made a surprise Top 20 showing of "My Love, Forgive Me (Amore, Scusami)" in 1964, it was his last hit. The album *My Love Forgive Me* reached number five and became a gold seller, and Goulet continued recording until 1970, when he moved into concert and television work. *—John Bush*

● **Greatest Hits** / 1969 / Columbia ✦✦✦✦✦
Includes "If Ever I Should Leave You" and all the rest. *—Bil Carpenter*

16 Most Requested Songs / 1989 / Columbia/Legacy ✦✦✦
16 Most Requested Songs is a midline-priced collection that spotlights many of Robert Goulet's best-known and most popular performances for Columbia Records, including "If Ever I Would Leave You," "What Now My Love," "Real Live Girl," "If I Ruled the World," "Take Me In Your Arms," "Sunrise Sunset," "For Once In My Life," "Somewhere My Love," "Who Can I Turn To?" and "The Impossible Dream." Although it's far from a perfect retrospective of his career, it's still a nice sampler of familiar items, and it may satisfy the needs of some casual fans who only want the hits. *—Stephen Thomas Erlewine*

Richard Harris

b. Oct. 1, 1930, Limerick, Ireland
Vocals, Actor / Pop, Show Tunes

The notion of Richard Harris—macho, heavy drinking, two-fisted man's man—as a popular singer would have seemed an absurdity to anyone who knew his work in 1967, ten years into his career. In less than a year from that time, however, Harris would be the most popular actor-singer in the history of popular music, with a gold record to his credit and radio play that rivalled the Beatles. His stage debut took place in 1956, and he made his first film appearance in 1958 in *Alive and Kicking,* later appearing in key supporting roles in big-budget movies like *The Guns of Navarone* and *Mutiny on the Bounty.* His performance in *This Sporting Life* (1963) propelled him to a major international career, and for most of the mid-'60s, Harris was among the most visible of British (or, more properly, Irish) actors in international cinema. It was his performance as King Arthur in Warner Bros.' 1967 screen version of Lerner and Loewe's musical *Camelot* that made people begin to think of Harris as a singer. The soundtrack album on Warner Bros. remained in print for decades, and was more profitable than the movie itself. A year later, he was approached by his friend, songwriter Jimmy Webb, with a proposed epic-length pop project, and Harris agreed to record it. "MacArthur Park," clocking in at seven-and-a-half minutes, rose to number two on the American charts and shattered AM radio's established prohibition against playing singles of greater than three-and-a-half minutes' length. The accompanying album *A Tramp Shining* was one of the great pop LPs of the '60s, a sophisticated and extraordinarily well-produced concept album (which owed a considerable debt to *Sgt. Pepper's*) to rival any of Sinatra's efforts in that direction. *—Bruce Eder*

A Tramp Shining / 1968 / MCA ✦✦✦✦
Harris' first collaboration with composer-producer Jimmy Webb, now reissued as a mid-priced CD, is a powerful record, made up of lushly arranged orchestrations and Harris' strained, pleading voice, generally singing of bittersweet romance and romantic recollections. Women understandably swooned over it, while their husbands and boyfriends felt safe listening to a man's man like Harris singing of such matters, and the result was a massive hit, although the next album was superior in many ways, recorded as it was with Harris in mind (Webb had already recorded the orchestral tracks for "MacArthur Park" before Harris agreed to do the single or the album, and the awkward fit of his almost-cracking voice straining to meld with the orchestrations made the song and album work better emotionally). *—Bruce Eder*

The Yard Went on Forever . . . / 1969 / Dunhill ✦✦✦✦✦

● **The Webb Sessions 1968-1969** / 1996 / Raven ✦✦✦✦✦
Richard Harris' biggest hit, "MacArthur Park," was pulled from *A Tramp Shining,* an album recorded, and largely written, by Jimmy Webb. After its success, the pair teamed up for the followup, *The Yard Went On Forever,* which wasn't quite as successful commercially. *The Webb Sessions* combines both albums onto a single disc. *—Stephen Thomas Erlewine*

Johnny Hartman

b. Jul. 3, 1923, Chicago, IL, **d.** Sep. 15, 1983, New York, NY
Vocals / Vocal Jazz, Traditional Pop, Standards, Ballads
Though he was never the most distinctive vocalist, Johnny Hartman rose above others to become the most commanding, smooth balladeer of the 1950s and '60s, a black crooner closely following Billy Eckstine and building on the form with his notable jazz collaborations, including the 1963 masterpiece *John Coltrane and Johnny Hartman.* Born in Chicago, he began singing early on and performed while in Special Services in the Army. Hartman studied music while at college and made his professional debut in the mid-'40s, performing with Earl Hines and recording his first sides for Regent/Savoy. After Hines' band broke up later in 1947, Hartman moved to the Dizzy Gillespie Big Band and stayed for two years, recording a few additional sides for Mercury as well.

Johnny Hartman's first proper LP came in 1956 with *Songs from the Heart,* recorded for Bethlehem and featuring a quartet led by trumpeter Howard McGhee. He recorded a second (*All of Me*) later that year, but then was virtually off-record until 1963, when his duet album *John Coltrane and Johnny Hartman* appeared on Impulse. A beautiful set of ballad standards including top-flight renditions of "Lush Life" and "My One and Only Love," the album sparked a flurry of activity for Hartman, including two more albums for Impulse: 1963's *I Just Dropped by to Say Hello* and the following year's *The Voice That Is.* During the late '60s and early '70s, he recorded a range of jazz and pop standards albums for ABC, Perception and Blue Note. Hartman recorded sparingly during the 1970s, but returned with two albums recorded in 1980, one of which (*Once in Every Life*) earned a Grammy nomination just two years before his death in 1983. *—John Bush*

Songs from the Heart / Oct. 1956 / Bethlehem Archives/Avenue Jazz ✦✦✦✦✦
Johnny Hartman's album debut is a set of tender ballads, each word of which is treasured by Hartman's expansive, evocative voice. The ballads appear not only especially chosen, but practically written with Hartman in mind. He shines on highlights like "I Fall in Love Too Easily," "We'll Be Together Again," "Moonlight in Vermont," and "I See Your Face Before Me," often transforming midtempo songs into completely downtempo ballads and shifting the emphasis on different beats with his phrasing. The backing—from drummer Ralph Sharon, trumpeter Howard McGhee, bassist Jay Cave, and drummer Christy Febbo—is soft, spare, and completely supportive. A CD reissue by Bethlehem Archives adds six bonus tracks, alternate takes of tracks from the original LP. *—John Bush*

All of Me / Nov. 1956 / Bethlehem Archives/Avenue Jazz ✦✦✦

★ **John Coltrane and Johnny Hartman** / Mar. 7, 1963 / Impulse! ✦✦✦✦✦
John Coltrane's matchup with singer Johnny Hartman, although quite unexpected, works extremely well. Hartman, who had not recorded since 1956, was in prime form on the six ballads, and his versions of "Lush Life" and "My One and Only Love" have never been topped. Coltrane's playing throughout the session is beautiful, sympathetic and still exploratory; he sticks exclusively to tenor on the date. At only half an hour, one wishes there were twice as much music, but what is here is classic, essential for all jazz collections. *—Scott Yanow*

I Just Dropped by to Say Hello / Oct. 9, 1963–Oct. 17, 1963 / Impulse! ✦✦✦✦✦
This 1995 GRP CD reissue brings back ballad singer Johnny Hartman's second Impulse session, following his classic collaboration with John Coltrane. Hartman is heard in peak form throughout these 11 pieces which include "In The Wee Small Hours Of The Morning," "Sleepin' Bee," "Stairway To The Stars" and even "Charade." Tenor-saxophonist Illinois Jacquet is on five of the songs, guitarists Kenny Burrell and Jim Hall help out on a few tunes and Hartman is consistently accompanied by pianist Hank Jones, bassist Milt Hinton and drummer Elvin Jones. This is one of his finest recordings. *—Scott Yanow*

The Voice That Is! / Sep. 22, 1964-Sep. 24, 1964 / Impulse! ✦✦✦✦

For Trane / Nov. 29, 1972–Dec. 1, 1972 / Blue Note ✦✦✦

Unforgettable / 1995 / Impulse! ✦✦✦✦

Today/I've Been There / Nov. 4, 1997 / Collectables ✦✦

Collection 1947-1972 / Sep. 22, 1998 / Hip-O ✦✦✦
Just where Johnny Hartman's name ends up in the pantheon of great jazzy pop singers is still left open to debate. But his talents and mastery of a lyric come to the fore on this marvelous two-CD set of tunes cherry-picked from his long, if not particularly prolific, career, leaving no doubt about his prodigious talents. Hartman went through label affiliations like some folks go through underwear, and this 38-track overview samples his best for RCA Victor, Regent, Bethlehem, Mercury, Jubilee, ABC-Paramount, Roost, Impulse! and the Japanese branch of Capitol, beginning in 1947 and winding up in 1972. Marvelous one-off singles proliferate throughout this collection providing sparkling performances with the Dizzy Gillespie Orchestra ("I Should Care"), Perez Prado Orchestra ("Wild") and versions of "The World Was Mine" and "I See Your Face Before Me" (featuring Howard McGhee) well worth the price of admission. Other highlights include his work with jazz giants like John Coltrane ("My One and Only Love," "Lush Life"), Hank Jones, Kenny Burrell ("In the Wee Small Hours of the Morning") and Illinois Jacquet ("Don't You Know I Care") and two 1996 string-section dates that produce stellar readings of "The Very Thought of You," "Unforgettable," "If I Had You," "As You Desire Me," "When I Get the Time" and "I Cover the Waterfront." An artist of immeasurable talent certainly deserving of a wider audience. *—Cub Koda*

Dick Haymes (Richard Benjamin Haymes)

b. Sep. 13, 1916, Buenos Aires, Argentina, **d.** Mar. 28, 1980, Los Angeles, CA
Vocals, Composer / Traditional Pop, Standards, Ballads
Dick Haymes was one of the most splendid ballad singers of his era, the near-equal of Crosby and Sinatra on classics of the form like "It Can't Be Wrong," "Till the End of Time" and "It Might as Well Be Spring." Though he was unable to cash in during the '50s golden era of adult-pop (due to alcoholism and a few tempestuous relationships), Haymes continued performing and recording until his death in 1980.

Born of British parents, Haymes spent his childhood in Paris and later the United States, where his mother performed as a singer. He left school to move to Hollywood, and worked as an extra on several films before he was hired by Harry James to replace his male singer, Frank Sinatra. During 1941-42, Haymes recorded several hits with James, though their biggest collaborative success—"I'll Get By (As Long as I Have You"—actually hit number one in 1944, three years after its recording date. Two of his first solo singles, 1943's "It Can't Be Wrong" and "You'll Never Know," also reached the top of the charts (the latter spent almost two months there). Haymes finally succeeded in Hollywood with 1945's *State Fair,* and he won an Oscar for his rendition of "It Might as Well Be Spring." He spent much of the mid-'40s near the top of the charts, though his professional and personal life began to decline after a bitter divorce, mishandled finances, and heavy drinking. (A whirlwind romance and two-year marriage to Rita Hayworth hardly settled things down.) He began a professional comeback in 1955 with two LPs for Capitol and finally kicked his habit drinking habit ten years later. Haymes performed numerous club dates and last recorded in 1978 before losing a long bout with cancer two years later. *—John Bush*

● **The Very Best of Dick Haymes** / Sep. 30, 1997 / Taragon ✦✦✦✦✦
"Faultless" would be a good word to describe this 20-song compilation, which contains every one of Dick Haymes' Top 20 hits from the start of his solo career in 1943 to the fall of 1945, a period when he was one of the most successful recording artists in the U.S. His biggest hit of the period was the gold-selling chart-topper "You'll Never Know," but he also waxed the most popular versions of the Top Ten hits "It Can't Be Wrong," "In My Arms," "Put Your Arms Around Me, Honey (I Never Knew Any Girl Like You)," "I Wish I Knew" and "The More I See You" (the last two from the film Billy Rose's *Diamond Horseshoe,* in which he starred), and a clutch of duets with Helen Forrest including "Long Ago (And Far Away)," "Together," "I'll Buy That Dream" and "Some Sunday Morning." All are included here in their original Decca recordings. Due to the musicians union recording ban, the first eight tracks were recorded a cappella with a vocal chorus, but with any backing Haymes' smooth voice delivers the songs' romantic sentiments beautifully. There are excellent liner notes by Joseph F. Laredo. *Volume 2* is also recommended. *—William Ruhlmann*

The Very Best of Dick Haymes, Vol. 2 / Sep. 30, 1997 / Taragon ✦✦✦✦✦
This flawless 20-song compilation picks up right where *Volume 1* left off: in the fall of 1945 with the Top Ten hit "It Might as Well Be Spring" from the film *State Fair* (in which Dick Haymes appeared). From there, it presents the rest of his major hits through 1950, when his popularity tailed off. In fact, Haymes was just past his peak as this compilation begins. Though 13 of the tracks made the Top Ten, none hit number one—only "Little White Lies," went gold, and only that song and "Maybe It's Because" were the most successful versions of these songs. More often, as on "It's Magic" (a signature song for Doris Day) or "Room Full of Roses" (for *Swing and Sway with Sammy Kaye*), Haymes' version was a cover. Nevertheless, he turned in excellent versions of these songs, offering stiff competition to the originators. He was helped by the arrangements and conducting of Gordon Jenkins and others (among them Artie Shaw, who was co-billed on his last major hit, "Count Every Star") and was joined by such guests as Judy Garland (on the Gershwins' "For You, For Me, For Evermore" from the film *The Shocking Miss Pilgrim,* in which he starred) and the Andrews Sisters (on "Teresa"). Also included are his last three hit duets with Helen Forrest ("I'm Always Chasing Rainbows," "Oh! What It Seemed to Be" and "In Love in Vain." Haymes' decline after the

recordings made here is one of the mysteries of popular music (he had well-documented personal problems, but they still don't fully explain it), and the mystery is deepened by listening to this album and its predecessor, which clearly reveal one of the most accomplished and popular singers of the 1940s. *— William Ruhlmann*

The Complete Columbia Recordings / Oct. 20, 1998 / Collectors' Choice Music ♦♦♦♦♦

Al Hibbler (Albert George Hibbler)

b. Aug. 16, 1915, Tyro, MS, **d.** Apr. 24, 2001

Vocals / Vocal Jazz, New York Blues, Traditional Pop, Vocal Pop

Not just a distinctive singer but a true vocal wonder, Al Hibbler featured with Duke Ellington's Orchestra throughout the 1940s and recorded a few hits ("Unchained Melody," "After the Lights Go Down Low," "He") on his own for Decca and Atlantic during the 1950s and '60s. His frequent use of a Cockney accent and non-subtle growling techniques kept listeners on their toes, though far from a novelty act, Hibbler's voice was strong, emotive and masculine, with a steady vibrato that carried every record he made.

Born blind in Mississippi, he sang soprano in the choir of a school for the blind. Inspired by lush ballad singers like Bing Crosby and Russ Columbo, Hibbler's voice soon deepened and he began singing the blues at area roadhouses. He joined Jay McShann in 1942 and debuted with Duke Ellington's Orchestra just one year later. One of the most important singers Ellington ever showcased, Hibbler appeared on a range of Ellington standards including "Do Nothin' 'Til You Hear from Me," "Ain't Got Nothin' But the Blues," and "Don't Be So Mean to My Baby." He left after eight years with Ellington's band, releasing three records at Verve before moving to Decca. There, he hit the pop charts with two million-selling singles, "Unchained Melody" and "He." In 1956, Hibbler hit the Top Ten again with "After the Lights Go Down Low, " but it proved to be his last hit.

Hibbler began taking an interest in the civil-rights movement, and his active involvement in protests eventually led to two arrests. Though the major labels backed away from the potential controversy of owning his contract, Hibbler recorded *Monday Every Day* in 1961 for Frank Sinatra's Reprise Records. He also collaborated with Rahsaan Roland Kirk for a 1972 LP, but resurfaced only occasionally afterward. *— John Bush*

● **Best of Al Hibbler** / May 19, 1998 / Varese ♦♦♦♦♦
This popular vocalist, long a fixture with the Duke Ellington band, had a long and distinguished run on the pop charts in the dark days of 1950s pre-rock & roll. Much was made of his blindness (Hibbler knocked down many a door for vision-impaired performers, paving the way for Ray Charles in particular), but the real glory was his voice, an instrument that could soar with the best of them. His two million-selling singles, "Unchained Melody" and "He" (later fodder for the Righteous Brothers), are both aboard, along with "After the Lights Go Down Low," "11th Hour Melody," "Honeysuckle Rose," "All or Nothing at All," "Don't Get Around Much Anymore" and "The Very Thought of You." For all his popularity and long-range influence on everyone from Ray Charles to Albert King, it seems almost inconceivable that a best-of package would have taken this long to come together, but fans of righteously sung pop music can rejoice that it has finally come to pass. *— Cub Koda*

Billie Holiday (Eleanora Harris)

b. Apr. 7, 1915, Philadelphia, PA, **d.** Jul. 17, 1959, New York, NY

Vocals / Vocal Jazz, Traditional Pop, Swing, Ballads, Classic Female Blues

Decades after her death, Billie Holiday remains the most famous of all jazz singers. "Lady Day" (as she was named by Lester Young) had a small voice and did not scat but her innovative behind-the-beat phrasing made her quite influential. The emotional intensity that she put into the words she sang (particularly in later years) was very memorable and sometimes almost scary; she often really did live the words she sang. During 1935-42 she would make some of the finest recordings of her career, jazz-oriented performances in which she was joined by the who's who of swing. Holiday sought to combine together Louis Armstrong's swing and Bessie Smith's sound; the result was her own fresh approach. In 1937 Lester Young and Buck Clayton began recording with Holiday and the interplay between the three of them was timeless. Holiday made history in 1939 by recording the horribly picturesque "Strange Fruit," a strong anti-racism statement that became a permanent part of her repertoire. Her records of 1940-42 found her sidemen playing a much more supportive role than in the past, rarely sharing solo space with her. Although the settings were less jazz-oriented than before (with occasional strings and even a background vocal group on a few numbers) Billie Holiday's voice was actually at its strongest during her period with Decca (1944-49). Billie Holiday's story from 1950 on is a gradual downhill slide— unhappy relationships distracted her, the heroin use and excessive drinking continued and by 1956 she was way past her prime. *— Scott Yanow*

Billie Holiday: The Legacy Box 1933-1958 / Nov. 27, 1933-Feb. 19, 1958 / Columbia ♦♦♦
The logic behind this sampler is puzzling. Rather than reissue the very best of Billie Holiday's Columbia recordings on a three-CD box set or a package of her rare alternate takes, CBS tries it both ways by including 60 common selections already available in the *Quintessential* series along with 10 rarities that were either unissued or alternates. This otherwise attractive box (which includes a colorful booklet) will drive completists and veteran collectors crazy. The music (mostly from 1933-42 with three weaker performances from 1957-58) is often classic but duplicates more coherent reissues. *— Scott Yanow*

☆ **The Quintessential Billie Holiday, Vol. 1 (1933-1935)** / Nov. 27, 1933-Dec. 3, 1935 / Columbia ♦♦♦♦♦
After years of reissuing her recordings in piecemeal fashion, Columbia finally got it right with this nine-CD *Quintessential* series. All of Lady Day's 1933-42 studio recordings (although without the alternate takes) receive the treatment they deserve in this program. *Vol. 1* has Holiday's first two tentative performances from 1933 and along with her initial recordings with Teddy Wilson's all-star bands. Highpoints include "I Wished On the Moon," "What a Little Moonlight Can Do," "Miss Brown to You," and "Twenty-Four Hours a Day." *— Scott Yanow*

☆ **The Quintessential Billie Holiday, Vol. 2 (1936)** / Jan. 30, 1936-Oct. 21, 1936 / Columbia ♦♦♦♦♦
The second of nine volumes in this essential series (all are highly recommended) continues the complete reissue of Billie Holiday's early recordings (although the alternate takes are bypassed). This set is highlighted by "I Cried for You" (which has a classic alto solo from Johnny Hodges), "Billie's Blues" (from Holiday's first session as a leader), "A Fine Romance" and "Easy to Love." Holiday's backup crew includes such greats as pianist Teddy Wilson, baritonist Harry Carney, trumpeters Jonah Jones and Bunny Berigan and clarinetist Artie Shaw. There's lots of great small-group swing. *— Scott Yanow*

☆ **The Quintessential Billie Holiday, Vol. 3 (1936-1937)** / Oct. 28, 1936-Feb. 18, 1937 / Columbia ♦♦♦♦♦
The third of nine CDs that document all of Billie Holiday's studio recordings of 1933-42 for Columbia has classic versions of "Pennies from Heaven," "I Can't Give You Anything but Love" (on which she shows the influence of Louis Armstrong) and "My Last Affair," along with Lady Day's first meeting on record with tenor-saxophonist Lester Young. Their initial encounter resulted in four songs including "This Year's Kisses" and "I Must Have That Man." All nine volumes in this admirable series (if only the alternate takes had been included!) are highly recommended. *— Scott Yanow*

☆ **The Quintessential Billie Holiday, Vol. 4 (1937)** / Mar. 31, 1937-Jun. 15, 1937 / Columbia ♦♦♦♦♦
The fourth of nine CDs in this essential series of Billie Holiday's studio recordings of 1933-42 features the great tenor Lester Young on eight of the 16 performances. Prez and Lady Day make a perfect match on "I'll Get By" (although altoist Johnny Hodges steals the honors on that song), "Mean to Me," "Easy Living," "Me Myself and I" and "A Sailboat in the Moonlight." Other strong selections without Young include "Moanin' Low," "Let's Call the Whole Thing Off" and "Where Is the Sun." It's highly recommended along with all of the other CDs in this perfectly done Billie Holiday reissue program. *— Scott Yanow*

★ **The Quintessential Billie Holiday, Vol. 5 (1937-1938)** / Jun. 15, 1937-Jan. 27, 1938 / Columbia ♦♦♦♦♦
The fifth of nine CDs in the complete reissue of Billie Holiday's early recordings (sans alternate takes), this great set has 18 selections, all but four featuring tenor-saxophonist Lester Young and trumpeter Buck Clayton. Among the classics are "Getting Some Fun out of Life," "Trav'lin' All Alone," "He's Funny That Way," "My Man," "When You're Smiling" (on which Prez takes a perfect solo), "If Dreams Come True" and "Now They Call It Swing." All nine volumes in this series are highly recommended, but if one can only acquire a single entry, this is the one. *— Scott Yanow*

☆ **The Quintessential Billie Holiday, Vol. 6 (1938)** / May 11, 1938-Nov. 9, 1938 / Columbia ♦♦♦♦♦

The Quintessential Billie Holiday, Vol. 7 (1938-1939) / Nov. 28, 1938-Jul. 5, 1939 / Columbia/Legacy ♦♦♦♦♦

★ **Commodore Master Takes** / Apr. 20, 1939-Apr. 8, 1944 / GRP ♦♦♦♦♦
If you're a completist who insists on having everything that Billie Holiday recorded, *The Complete Commodore Recordings* is required listening. But for the more casual listener, it's best to pass on that two-CD set and stick with *The Commodore Master Takes.* While *The Complete Commodore Recordings* contains all of the alternate takes that Holiday recorded for Commodore in 1939 and 1944, this collection only concerns itself with the master takes (which total 16). Holiday never singed an exclusive contract with Commodore— she only freelanced for the label, and the ultra-influential jazz singer spent a lot more time recording for Columbia in the 1930s and early 1940s, and for Decca from 1944-1950. But her Commodore output was first-rate, and Lady Day excels whether she's joined by trumpeter Frankie Newton's octet at a 1939 session or by pianist Eddie Heywood's orchestra at three sessions in 1944. The CD gets off to an impressive start with the controversial "Strange Fruit," a bone-chilling account of lynching in the Deep South that ended up being released on Commodore because Columbia was afraid to touch it. Holiday is also quite expressive on performances that range from "Fine and Mellow," "I Got a Right to Sing the Blues" and "Yesterdays" in 1939 to "My Old Flame," "Billie's Blues," "I'll Be Seeing You," and "He's Funny That Way" in 1944. For those with even a casual interest in Holiday's legacy, this superb CD is essential listening. *— Alex Henderson*

The Complete Commodore Recordings / Apr. 20, 1939-Apr. 8, 1944 / GRP ♦♦♦

☆ **The Quintessential Billie Holiday, Vol. 8 (1939-1940)** / Jul. 5, 1939-Sep. 12, 1940 / Columbia/Legacy ♦♦♦♦♦

The Quintessential Billie Holiday, Vol. 9 (1940-1942) / Oct. 15, 1940-Feb. 10, 1942 / Columbia/Legacy ♦♦♦♦♦

Billie's Blues / Jan. 12, 1942-Jan. 5, 1954 / Blue Note ♦♦♦♦♦
Most of this excellent CD features one of Billie Holiday's finest concert recordings of the 1950s. Recorded in Europe before an admiring audience, this enjoyable set finds Lady Day performing seven of her standards with her trio and joining in for jam session versions of "Billie's Blues" and "Lover Come Back to Me" with an all-star group starring clarinetist Buddy DeFranco, vibraphonist Red Norvo and guitarist Jimmy Raney. These performances (which find Holiday in stronger voice than on her studio recordings of the period) have also been included in Verve's massive CD box set. This program concludes with Holiday's four rare sides for Aladdin in 1951 (between her Decca and Verve periods) which are highlighted by two blues and "Detour Ahead," and her 1942 studio recording of "Trav'lin' Light" with Paul Whiteman's Orchestra. *— Scott Yanow*

★ **The Complete Decca Recordings** / Oct. 4, 1944-Mar. 8, 1950 / GRP ♦♦♦♦♦
Billie Holiday is heard at her absolute best on this attractive two-CD set. During her period on Decca, Lady Day was accompanied by strings (for the first time), large studio orchestras and even background vocalists, so jazz solos from her sidemen are few. But her voice was at its strongest during the 1940s (even with her personal problems) and to hear all 50 of her Decca performances (including alternate takes and even some studio chatter) is a real joy. Among the highpoints of this essential set are her original versions of "Lover Man" (Holiday's biggest selling record), "Don't Explain," "Good Morning Heartache," "Tain't Nobody's Busi-

ness if I Do," "Now or Never," "Crazy He Calls Me" and remakes of "Them There Eyes" and "God Bless the Child." *—Scott Yanow*

☆ **The Complete Billie Holiday on Verve 1945-1959** / Feb. 12, 1945-Mar. 1, 1959 / Polygram ✦✦✦✦✦
This is a rather incredible collection: ten CDs enclosed in a tight black box that includes every one of the recordings Verve owns of Billie Holiday, not only the many studio recordings of 1952-57 (which feature Lady Day joined by such jazz all-stars as trumpeters Charlie Shavers and Harry "Sweets" Edison, altoist Benny Carter, and the tenors of Flip Phillips, Paul Quinichette and Ben Webster). Also included are prime performances at *Jazz at the Philharmonic* concerts in 1945-1947, an enjoyable European gig from 1954, her "comeback" Carnegie Hall concert of 1956, Holiday's rather sad final studio album from 1959, and even lengthy tapes from two informal rehearsals. It's a perfect purchase for the true Billie Holiday fanatic. *—Scott Yanow*

Lady in Autumn: The Best of the Verve Years / Apr. 1946-Mar. 1959 / Verve ✦✦✦✦✦

Lady Sings the Blues / 1954-1956 / Verve ✦✦✦

Songs for Distingué Lovers / Jun. 6, 1956-Jun. 7, 1956 / Verve ✦✦✦

Lady in Satin / Feb. 19, 1958-Feb. 21, 1958 / Columbia ✦✦✦✦✦
This is the most controversial of all Billie Holiday records. Lady Day herself said that this session (which finds her accompanied by Ray Ellis's string orchestra) was her personal favorite, and many listeners have found her emotional versions of such songs as "I'm a Fool to Want You," "You Don't Know What Love Is," "Glad to Be Unhappy" and particularly "You've Changed" to be quite touching. But Holiday's voice was essentially gone by 1958, and although not yet 43, she could have passed for 73. Ellis's arrangements do not help, veering close to Muzak; most of this record is very difficult to listen to. Late in life, Billie Holiday expressed the pain of life so effectively that her croaking voice had become almost unbearable to hear. The 1997 CD reissue adds two alternate takes of "I'm a Fool to Want You," part of which were used for the original released rendition, plus the stereo version of "The End of a Love Affair" (only previously released in mono) and examples of Lady Day rehearsing the latter song, including a long unaccompanied stretch. There is certainly a wide range of opinion as to the value of this set. *—Scott Yanow*

Greatest Hits / Nov. 17, 1998 / Columbia/Legacy ✦✦✦

Ken Burns Jazz / Nov. 7, 2000 / Verve ✦✦✦✦

Shirley Horn

b. May 1, 1934, Washington, D.C.
Vocals, Piano / Vocal Jazz, Traditional Pop, Standards, Mainstream Jazz, Ballads
A superior ballad singer and a talented pianist, Shirley Horn put off potential success until finally becoming a major attraction while in her 50s. She studied piano from the age of four. After attending Howard University, Horn put together her first trio in 1954 and was encouraged in the early '60s by Miles Davis and Quincy Jones. She recorded three albums during 1963-65 for Mercury and ABC-Paramount but chose to stick around Washington D.C. and raise a family instead of pursuing her career. In the early '80s she began recording for SteepleChase but Shirley Horn really had her breakthrough in 1987 when she started making records for Verve, an association that continues to the present day on records like 1998's *I Remember Miles. You're My Thrill* followed in early 2001. *—Scott Yanow*

Travelin' Light / 1965 / ABC/Paramount ✦✦✦
This CD reissue brings back a historic session, vocalist-pianist Shirley Horn's last before she drifted into semi-retirement so she could raise her daughter. Among her sidemen on this date include trumpeter Joe Newman, the flutes of Frank Wess and Jerome Richardson and guitarist Kenny Burrell but the main star throughout is Horn. Not all of the material is equally strong and none of the very concise dozen performances clock in even at three minutes so this is not an essential session. But Shirley Horn fans and completists will want the generally enjoyable vocal date. *—Scott Yanow*

I Thought About You / May 12, 1987–May 13, 1987 / Verve ✦✦✦✦✦
This live set (recorded at Hollywood's Vine St. Bar and Grill) was Shirley Horn's "comeback" album after many years in which she purposely maintained a low profile as she raised her daughter. Typical of Horn's music ever since, she sings intimate ballads with her trio (which includes bassist Charles Ables and drummer Steve Williams*) and plays very effective piano behind her vocals, taking "Isn't It Romantic" as an instrumental.* —Scott Yanow

● **Close Enough for Love** / Nov. 14, 1988-Nov. 16, 1988 / Verve ✦✦✦✦✦
Shirley Horn's second Verve recording consolidated the success that she had had with her previous release, *I Thought About You*, and resulted in her gaining a large audience for her ballad vocals and solid jazz piano playing. Performing with her usual trio (which includes bassist Charles Ables and drummer Steve Williams) and guest tenor Buck Hill on five of the 13 tracks, Horn is heard in definitive form throughout these studio sessions. Highlights include "Beautiful Friendship," "Baby, Baby All the Time," "This Can't Be Love," "I Wanna Be Loved," "But Beautiful," "Get out of Town" and "It Could Happen to You." *—Scott Yanow*

You Won't Forget Me / Jun. 12, 1990-Aug. 1990 / Verve ✦✦✦✦

Loads of Love/Shirley Horn with Horns / 1963 / Verve ✦✦✦

Here's to Life / 1991-1992 / Verve ✦✦✦

I Love You, Paris / Mar. 7, 1992 / Verve ✦✦✦✦
The highlights of a 2Ω-hour concert recorded in Paris, this CD has even more ballads than a typical Shirley Horn set because, due to the monitor malfunctioning during the second half of the performance, Horn chose to stick exclusively to ballads during that portion of the show. Accompanied by bassist Charles Ables and drummer Steve Williams, Horn is in peak form throughout this program, often sounding exquisite and using silence and pauses quite expertly. Among the highlights are "Wouldn't It Be Loverly," "Do It Again," a medley of "I Loves You Porgy" and "Here Comes De Honey Man," and a lengthy version of "A Song for You" that eventually becomes "Goodbye." Highly recommended. *—Scott Yanow*

Light out of Darkness (A Tribute to Ray Charles) / Apr. 30, 1993-May 3, 1993 / Verve ✦✦✦✦

The Main Ingredient / May 15, 1995-May 18, 1995 / Verve ✦✦✦✦
This Shirley Horn CD is a little unusual, as it was recorded at her home. The four sessions utilized some of her favorite musicians, including bassists Steve Novosel and Charles Ables, drummers Steve Williams, Elvin Jones and Billy Hart, trumpeter Roy Hargrove (on "The Meaning of the Blues") and Joe Henderson and Buck Hill on tenors. As usual, virtually all of the songs are taken at slow tempos, with "All or Nothing at All" given a definitive treatment. Other highlights include "The Look of Love," "Fever" and Henderson's playing on "You Go to My Head." *—Scott Yanow*

I Remember Miles / Dec. 2, 1997-Dec. 5, 1997 / Verve ✦✦✦

Lena Horne

b. Jun. 30, 1917, Brooklyn, NY
Vocals / Vocal Jazz, Traditional Pop, Swing, Show Tunes
An ageless beauty and a very appealing personality, Lena Horne was never really a jazz singer as much as a superior pop vocalist since she does not improvise. Horne started performing when she was six, sang and danced at the Cotton Club as early as 1934, was with Noble Sissle's Orchestra (1935-36), recorded with Teddy Wilson in the late '30s and sang with Charlie Barnet's big band during 1940-41. She also recorded with Artie Shaw (1941) and made major impressions in the films *Boogie Woogie Dream* (actually a jazz short), *Cabin in the Sky* and especially *Stormy Weather.* Married to arranger/pianist Lennie Hayton, Horne has been a popular attraction since the 1940s but her connection with jazz (even when she sings veteran swing standards) is peripheral. A collection of songs made during World War II was released in early 2001 and included live recordings from the late 1950's. *—Scott Yanow*

● **Stormy Weather: The Legendary Lena (1941-1958)** / Jan. 7, 1941-Jun. 9, 1958 / Bluebird/RCA ✦✦✦✦✦
Although the very attractive Lena Horne has never really been a jazz singer, her vocals are generally of interest to jazz listeners and she has occasionally recorded in jazz settings. This Bluebird CD is pretty definitive of the first half of her career. Horne sings a pair of ballads with Charlie Barnet's 1941 Orchestra and two songs (including "Don't Take Your Love From Me") with a unique Artie Shaw-led all-star band that includes Benny Carter, Red Allen and a string section. The remainder of the disc features Lena backed by studio orchestras and the results are superior (if sometimes overly dramatic) renditions of standards as rendered by a topnotch cabaret singer. Highlights include "Stormy Weather," "Ill Wind," "Moanin' Low," "As Long As I Live" and "It's All Right With Me." *—Scott Yanow*

Lena Horne at M-G-M: Ain't It the Truth / 1942-1956 / Rhino ✦✦✦✦
Lena Horne appeared in many MGM musicals during the '40s but almost always in cameos, singing one or two songs and then disappearing. This Rhino CD collects together 23 songs (six of which were actually outtakes) from Horne's films. Although generally not jazz, these swinging middle-of-the-road pop performances are quite enjoyable and give one a well-rounded musical portrait of Lena Horne. Highlights include "Honeysuckle Rose," "Somebody Loves Me," a medley from *Showboat* and "The Lady Is a Tramp. " *—Scott Yanow*

Lena in Hollywood / 1966 / United Artists ✦✦✦
After a lengthy recording association with RCA Victor Records ended in 1963, Lena Horne cut a couple of albums for Charter Records and one for 20th Century-Fox Records before landing on United Artists Records in 1965. There she made four albums, of which this was the second. It found her in familiar territory, singing songs associated with motion pictures. Some, such as "In Love in Vain," the Jerome Kern-Oscar Hammerstein II song from *Centennial Summer,* and Kern and Dorothy Fields' "A Fine Romance" from *Swing Time,* were standards of decades' standing, while others were recent. Horne treated them all with the same enthusiasm, shining especially on uptempo numbers like Henry Mancini and Johnny Mercer's "It Had Better Be Tonight" from *The Pink Panther.* Ray Ellis' charts were sometimes surprising, notably the unusual arrangement of "Singin' in the Rain" that kicked the album off. The result was a typically classy effort for Horne, but one that had little to do with the pop marketplace of late 1965. *— William Ruhlmann*

Lena & Gabor / Oct. 11, 1969 / Gryphon ✦✦✦

Live on Broadway (Lena Horne: The Lady & Her Music) / 1981 / Qwest ✦✦✦✦

An Evening with Lena Horne / Sep. 19, 1994 / Blue Note ✦✦✦✦✦

Being Myself / 1998 / Blue Note ✦✦✦✦

The Best of the RCA Years / Oct. 20, 1998 / Koch ✦✦✦✦
Primarily thought of as a nightclub singer, Lena Horne gained her greatest visibility as a recording artist during several stints with RCA Victor Records, 1941-45, 1955-62, 1975-76, and 1983. This 16-track, 57-and-a-half-minute compilation draws its material from the 1955-62 period, during which she recorded six singles, eight solo albums, a duo album of *Porgy And Bess* with Harry Belafonte, and the original Broadway cast album of *Jamaica,* activities that resulted in several chart entries and Grammy nominations. This album contains "Love Me or Leave Me," her sole chart single for RCA, from 1955, and it relies heavily on her live recordings, including selections from the albums *Lena Horne at the Waldorf Astoria* and *Lena Horne at the Sands,* and the EP *Lena Horne at the Coconut Grove.* It also emphasizes the singer's affinity for such classic pop writers as Cole Porter, the Gershwins, and Harold Arlen. There are some surprising omissions, among them a version of her signature song, "Stormy Weather" (the title of one of her RCA albums of the period), and such *Jamaica* songs as "Push De Button." Maybe that's just to say that Horne deserved a more ambitious compilation of this title, a full-length two-CD set encompassing her entire time at the label. As it is, this is an adequate sampler of the recordings she made during a seven-year period in her late thirties and early forties. Even for the RCA catalog, it's only a part of the story. *— William Ruhlmann*

Engelbert Humperdinck (Arnold George Dorsey)

b. May 3, 1936, Madras, India
Vocals / Traditional Pop, Standards, Vocal Pop, Ballads
The smooth-voiced ballad singer Engelbert Humperdinck was born in India and raised in Leicester, England. In the middle '50s, he launched a career as a dance-band singer under the name Gerry Dorsey, but only recorded one single and later contracted tuberculosis. Then in 1966, Dorsey contacted his former roommate, songwriter and manager Gordon Mills. Mills decided to re-invent Dorsey, gave him the name of the 19th-century classical German opera composer (*Hansel and Gretel*), and introduced him to the world as the enigmatic balladeer Engelbert Humperdinck. To maintain his mysterious image, he always disappeared after every show—never meeting his fans. This often involved climbing out of bathroom windows and the like. Armed with his new name, a vivid stage presence, rugged good looks, smooth style, and three-and-a-half octave singing range, Humperdinck broke into full stardom in 1967 with his version of the country song "Release Me." He remained in the charts until the early '70s and was often the biggest selling artist in the U.K. He had another huge hit, "After the Lovin'," in 1976 but, for the most part, he has toured the cabaret circuit for the last 27 years. *—Michael Erlewine*

★ **Ultimate Collection** / Jan. 25, 2000 / Hip-O ♦♦♦♦♦
It took the powers-that-be at Universal Music a long time to get around to compiling an Engelbert Humperdinck collection more extensive than the ten-track *His Greatest Hits* that came out on Parrot Records in December 1974 as the singer was leaving the label. Thankfully, 25 years later, we finally have the appropriately named *Ultimate Collection*, which includes Humperdinck's 17 most successful U.S. pop singles chart entries, including not only favorites like "Release Me (And Let Me Love Again)," "Winter World of Love," "Am I That Easy To Forget," and "A Man Without Love," but also two major hits of the late 1970s that came while he was contracted to Epic Records, "After the Lovin'" and "This Moment in Time." Humperdinck may not have gotten into the charts since the end of the '70s, but these songs have allowed him to please audience for another two decades, and they hold up well, both because of their consistency as engaging, European-flavored love songs and because the singer's smooth voice puts them across convincingly. *—William Ruhlmann*

Julio Iglesias

b. Sep. 23, 1943, Madrid, Spain
Vocals / Adult Contemporary, Latin Pop
Julio Iglesias was the most popular Latin singer of the '70s and '80s; a smooth, romantic crooner, his appeal translated to many different countries in many different languages. A onetime goalkeeper for the Real Madrid football team, his career as an athlete was ended after an automobile accident in the mid-'60s. While he was recovering, Iglesias started playing guitar and writing songs. During the '70s, he toured Europe and Latin America, gaining a large fan base with hits like 1975's "Manuela." At the turn of the decade, Iglesias began to pursue the American and British markets by concentrating on his English recordings. His major crossover success was 1984's *1100 Bel Air Place*, a collection of duets. Featuring the Top 10 hit duet with Willie Nelson "To All the Girls I've Loved Before," the album sold over three million copies in America and peaked at number five on the pop charts; it also spawned "All of You," a hit duet with Diana Ross. Iglesias' popularity continued to grow throughout the '80s, although he only had one more pop crossover hit, 1988's "My Love," a duet with Stevie Wonder. By the '90s, he had stopped courting the English pop market and concentrated on recording mainly in Spanish, as well as a handful of other languages. His popularity did not diminish at all in his third decade of recordings—he was still capable of selling millions of records and selling out concerts around the world. *—Stephen Thomas Erlewine*

● **My Life: Greatest Hits** / Oct. 6, 1998 / Columbia ♦♦♦♦♦
It's a little surprising to consider that Julio Iglesias didn't have a comprehensive hits collection until *My Life: The Greatest Hits* was released in the fall of 1998, but the result was so strong that it made the wait worthwhile. Featuring no less than 37 songs over the course of two CDs, *My Life* has all of his biggest hits, most popular duets and fan favorites, including "To All the Girls I've Loved Before," "All of You," "My Love," and "Summer Wind," a duet with Frank Sinatra. With only a couple of exceptions, the first disc is devoted to English-language hits, the second entirely to Latin hits. For some listeners, it may be too much material to digest, especially in one sitting, but there's little question that this is the definitive Julio Iglesias compilation. *—Stephen Thomas Erlewine*

The Ink Spots

f. 1938
Group / Vocal Pop, Pop, R&B
The Ink Spots played a large role in pioneering the Black vocal group-harmony genre, helping to pave the way for the doo-wop explosion of the '50s. The quavering high tenor of Bill Kenny presaged hundreds of street-corner leads to come, and the sweet harmonies of Charlie Fuqua, Deek Watson, and bass Hoppy Jones (who died in 1944) backed him flawlessly.

Kenny's impeccable diction and Jones's deep drawl were both prominent on the Ink Spots' first smash on Decca in 1939, the sentimental "If I Didn't Care." From then through 1951, the group was seldom absent from the pop charts, topping the lists with "We Three (My Echo, My Shadow, and Me)" (1940), "I'm Making Believe" and "Into Each Life Some Rain Must Fall" (both in 1944), and "The Gypsy" and "To Each His Own" (both in 1946).

Watson eventually split to form his own group, the Brown Dots, and appeared in numerous low-budget film musicals, while Kenny attempted a solo career, notching a solo hit in 1951 with the uplifting "It Is No Secret." Countless groups masquerading as the Ink Spots have thrived across the nation since the '50s. *—Bill Dahl*

★ **The Anthology** / Jun. 16, 1998 / MCA ♦♦♦♦♦
The Ink Spots are far more influential than people realize. The genetic-spliced brotherhood of their voices were the virtual blueprint for not only most of the doo wop groups, but groups like the Brothers Four, the Hi-Lo's, the Four Lads, and many others. This leads, ultimately, to even the Beach Boys. The Ink Spots had amazing harmony, really, really funny songs, and an incredible approach. This anthology, a double, is really the one thing that you need of theirs if you're interested in the group. Most of the songs sound the same, and are actually in the same key. But guess what? It doesn't matter. All of the tracks are extremely enjoyable, and aside from the historical significance, this is just a great listening experience. Listing tip: Listen to this on a warm, lazy afternoon with the libation of your choice. You can't miss. *—Matthew Greenwald*

20th Century Masters—*The Millennium Collection: The Best of The Ink Spots* / *Oct. 5, 1999 / MCA* ♦♦♦♦
MCA's *20th Century Masters: The Millennium Collection* is a good, basic collection of the Ink Spots' biggest hits—including "If I Didn't Care," "My Prayer," "Java Jive," "Don't Get Around Much Anymore," "I'm Making Believe," "The Gypsy," "I'm Beginning to See the Light," "Prisoner of Love,"and "To Each His Own"—available at a budget price. Although there are a couple of hits and good songs missing, this has enough of the best-known tunes to make it worthwhile for casual listeners on a budget. *—Stephen Thomas Erlewine*

Al Jarreau

b. Apr. 12, 1940, Milwaukee, WI
Vocals / Contemporary Jazz, Soft Rock, Pop
The only vocalist in history to net Grammy awards in three different categories (jazz, pop and R&B, respectively), Al Jarreau was born in Milwaukee, Wisconsin on April 12, 1940; the son of a vicar, he earned his first performing experience singing in the church choir. After receiving his Masters degree in psychology, Jarreau pursued a career as a social worker, but eventually he decided to relocate to Los Angeles and try his hand in show business, playing small clubs throughout the West Coast. In the mid-1960s, he recorded an LP but largely remained an unknown, not re-entering the studio for another decade. Upon signing to Reprise, Jarreau resurfaced in 1975 with *We Got By*, earning acclaim for his sophisticated brand of vocalese and winning positive comparison to the likes of Billy Eckstine and Johnny Mathis. After 1976's *Glow*, Jarreau issued the following year's *Look to the Rainbow*, a two-disc live set which reached the Top 50 on the U.S. album charts. With 1981's *Breakin' Away*, he entered the Top Ten, scoring a pair of hits with "We're in This Love Together" and the title track. After recording 1986's *L Is for Lover* with producer Nile Rodgers, Jarreau scored a hit with the theme to the popular television program *Moonlighting*, but his mainstream pop success was on the wane, and subsequent efforts like 1992's *Heaven and Earth* and 1994's *Tenderness* found greater success with adult contemporary audiences. *—Jason Ankeny*

Look to the Rainbow / Jan. 1977-Feb. 1977 / Warner Brothers ♦♦♦♦♦
Singer Al Jarreau's double album is easily the most jazz-oriented of all of his Warner Bros. recordings. Cut shortly before Jarreau permanently switched to a more mundane version of R&B, these performances feature him as a brilliant scat singer (able to emulate practically any instrument) and a superior ballad interpreter. Joined by vibraphonist Lynn Blessing, keyboardist Tom Canning, bassist Abe Laboriel and drummer Joe Correro, Jarreau is in top form on such numbers as "Better Than Anything," "Look to the Rainbow" and "Take Five." Unfortunately, Al Jarreau essentially started on top, artistically speaking, and has since been intent on emphasizing potential commercial appeal over any possible innovations or chancetaking. *—Scott Yanow*

● **The Best of Al Jarreau** / 1996 / Warner Brothers ♦♦♦♦♦
This is one intelligently programmed greatest-hits album, for after leading with two fine, new 1996 tracks, "Compared to What" and "Goodhands Tonight," the CD actually becomes a cogent chronological account of Jarreau's twenty years with the label—and a most revealing one at that. Early Latin-flavored tracks from the mid-'70s like "Agua De Beber," "Take Five" and "Spain" reveal a unique jazz voice, with extraordinary rhythmic flexibility and an angular, scattershot, unpredictable approach to a tune that must have been as startling to audiences as Lambert, Hendricks and Ross were when they broke through. With "Never Givin' Up" and "Roof Garden," the transition away from jazz begins; by the time we reach the feel-good hit "Mornin'," the productions have become more intricate, polished and comfortable, suitable either for dancing or making out, with little room for the old vocal spontaneity. And things go downhill from there. Curiously, one of Jarreau's best crossover albums, *L Is for Lover*, is ignored, but guest appearances on Bob James/David Sanborn's *Double Vision* ("Since I Fell For You") and *Symphonic Bossa* (a surprisingly lethargic "Like a Lover"), plus the saccharine theme from *Moonlighting*, are included. Jazz listeners who feel that Jarreau's talents had been gradually eroded by avarice in the record industry can present this program as Exhibit A, but at the same time, it serves as a good introduction for the newcomer and a fine refresher course for the faithful. *—Richard S. Ginell*

Al Jolson (Asa Yoelson)

b. May 26, 1885, Seredzius, Lithuania, **d.** Oct. 23, 1950, San Francisco, CA
Vocals, Actor, Dancer / Minstrel, Traditional Pop, Nostalgia
An entertainment dynamo who quickly established himself as Broadway's leading star by the dawn of the 20th century, Jolson was America's first superstar, years before the phrase was ever coined. A truly competitive and high-energy performer, Jolson left most of the competition in the dust with his impassioned singing, dancing, and jokes (borrowing much from Black ragtime music and early jazz and performing in the then-popular minstrel blackface style). His place in popular history was assured when he starred in the first successful talking picture, *The Jazz Singer*, in 1927. His tireless efforts performing for American troops during World War II (he almost single-handedly started The USO) won him a whole new audience who had never seen him perform in his halcyon days. When the film biography of his life became a major hit twenty years later, Jolson's popularity leapt to legendary status, making no one doubt his title of "The World's Greatest Entertainer." *—Cub Koda*

You Ain't Heard Nothin' Yet: Jolie's Finest Columbia Recordings / 1994 / Columbia ♦♦♦♦♦
After starting off his recording career for Victor in 1911, Jolson switched to Columbia two

years later, and that's where these recordings begin, a 24-track single-disc set that truly lives up to its title. Here's the young and irreverent Jolson of the Winter Garden, doing novelties like "Sister Susie's Sewing Shirts for Soldiers" and "Where Did Robinson Crusoe Go With Friday On Saturday Night," and finding and recording signature songs like "Swanee," "Avalon," "Toot Toot Tootsie (Goodbye)," and "Rock-A-Bye Your Baby With a Dixie Melody." If Jolie truly was the Moses of modern popular culture, then this set goes a very long way toward capturing the essence of why that's so. *—Cub Koda*

● **Let Me Sing & I'm Happy: At Warner Bros. 1926-1936** / Nov. 19, 1996 / Rhino ✦✦✦✦✦
Many of Al Jolson's greatest performances were on the soundtracks to the seven movies he made as a star for Warner Brothers pictures in the late 1920s and early 1930s. His performances in these early talkies were live and, as a result, this is the closest link we have to the electric performances Al brought to Broadway during his peak years of performing. The 23 selections included here give the best possible overview of Jolson's movie career in its early stages.

Al Jolson in A Plantation Act, a one reel short Jolson made before *The Jazz Singer,* is heard for the first time on this compilation and his performances on "April Showers" and "Rock-A-Bye Your Baby with a Dixie Melody" are stunning. The true believer moment would probably be "Toot, Toot, Tootsie!" from *The Jazz Singer.* Bursting at the seams with energy, it reveals Jolson's myriad talents, all set to a driving performance. Even Jolson's directions to his bandleader on this track ('give it to 'em hard and heavy') presages rock terminology by a good 40 years—Al Jolson was America's first high energy entertainer and this proves it. Jolie's way with a ballad are well served by his galvanic reading of "It All Depends On You." Comparing these tracks with the latter-day recordings is a minor revelation as the energy on these tracks is palpable, revealing Al as a performer with plenty of gas left in the tank. Hard to imagine that this performing dynamo was already 40 when the first of these tracks were cut and all of 50 by his final appearance in his last Warner Bros. starring role. This is an unbelievably fine collection, making it an essential purchase for Jolson fans the world over. *—Cub Koda*

Etta Jones

b. Nov. 25, 1928, Aiken, SC
Vocals / Vocal Jazz, Standards
An excellent singer who is always worth hearing, Etta Jones grew up in New York and at 16 toured with Buddy Johnson. She debuted on record with Barney Bigard's pickup band (1944) for Black & White, singing four Leonard Feather songs, three of which (including "Evil Gal Blues") were hits for Dinah Washington. She recorded other songs during 1946-47 for RCA and worked with Earl Hines (1949-52). Jones's version of "Don't Go to Strangers" (1960) was a hit and she made many albums for Prestige during 1960-65. Jones toured Japan with Art Blakey (1970) but was largely off record during 1966-75. However starting in 1976 Etta Jones (an appealing interpreter of standards, ballads and blues) began recording regularly for Muse, often with her husband, the fine tenor-saxophonist Houston Person. Some of her finest work has been form the last two decades. *—Scott Yanow*

● **Don't Go to Strangers** / Jun. 21, 1960 / Prestige/OJC ✦✦✦✦✦
Etta Jones had been on the jazz scene for over a decade when she recorded this Prestige set (which has been reissued on CD in the OJC series) but it was this album that gave her a breakthrough, specifically the memorable song "Don't Go to Strangers." Actually Jones is in superb form throughout the other nine songs too, mixing together the dramatic ability of Abbey Lincoln and some of the expressive qualities of Billie Holiday in the 1950s. With perfectly suitable accompaniment from Frank Wess (doubling on flute and tenor), pianist Richard Wyands, guitarist Skeeter Best, bassist George Duvivier and drummer Roy Haynes, Etta Jones is heard at her early peak on "Yes Sir, That's My Baby" (a warhorse that she greatly uplifts), "Fine and Mellow," "If I Had You" and "Bye Bye Blackbird." *—Scott Yanow*

Something Nice / Sep. 16, 1961-Mar. 30, 1961 / Prestige/OJC ✦✦✦✦
This CD reissue features singer Etta Jones during two recording sessions in 1960-61. Jones is joined by two separate rhythm sections, and there is a guest appearance for tenor saxophonist Oliver Nelson (on "Easy Living"), two by vibraphonist Lem Winchester, and three from guitarist Wally Richardson. Influenced by Billie Holiday during this era, Jones is at her best during straightforward and sincere renditions of such songs as "My Heart Tells Me," "Till There Was You," "Almost Like Being In Love" and "Canadian Sunset." *—Scott Yanow*

My Buddy: Songs of Buddy Johnson / May 19, 1998 / High Note ✦✦✦✦✦

Jack Jones (John Allen Jones)

b. Jan. 14, 1938, Los Angeles, CA
Vocals / Traditional Pop, Standards, Vocal Pop, Ballads, Show Tunes
A two-time Grammy winner in the early '60s, Jack Jones has made a fine living since, blending vocal standards from traditional pop with swinging renditions of contemporary pop and rock hits. Jones was the son of the romantic lead actor and recording artist Allan Jones (who had a hit with "The Donkey Serenade") and actress Irene Hervey. He began studying the vocal arts in high school, and after graduation joined his father's successful act on the nightclub circuit. Jack left less than a year later, determined to make it on his own, and began playing small clubs around the country. Several years after forging his independence, Jones was spotted in San Francisco and signed to Kapp Records in 1961. Though he was called into the army soon after, he managed to record the single "Lollipops and Roses," a moderate 1962 hit which earned him a Grammy for Best Performance by a Male Singer. He earned another Grammy for his best-known hit, the Burt Bacharach-Hal David chestnut "Wives and Lovers." Jones became a successful LP seller, touring artist (especially in Great Britain), and occasional television performer. He also mounted a successful act in Las Vegas during the 1980s and '90s. *—John Bush*

● **Greatest Hits** / Sep. 12, 1995 / MCA ✦✦✦✦✦
Featuring 18 songs, including "The Impossible Dream," "Call Me Irresponsible," and "Lollipops and Roses," *Greatest Hits* is the definitive Jack Jones collection. *—Stephen Thomas Erlewine*

Sheila Jordan

b. Nov. 18, 1928, Detroit, MI
Vocals / Vocal Jazz, Post-Bop, Bop
One of the most consistently creative of all jazz singers, Sheila Jordan has a relatively small voice but has done the maximum with her instrument. She is one of the few vocalists who can improvise logical lyrics (which often rhyme!), she is a superb scat singer and is also an emotional interpreter of ballads. Yet despite her talents, Jordan spent much of the 1960s and '70s working at a conventional day job! She studied piano when she was 11 and early on sang vocalese in a vocal group. Jordan moved to New York in the 1950s, was married to Duke Jordan (1952-62), studied with Lennie Tristano and worked in New York clubs. George Russell used her on an unusual recording of "You Are My Sunshine" and she became one of the few singers to lead her own Blue Note album (1962). However it would be a decade before she appeared on records again, working with Carla Bley, Roswell Rudd and co-leading a group with Steve Kuhn in the late '70s. Jordan recorded a memorable duet album with bassist Arild Andersen for SteepleChase in 1977 and has since teamed up with bassist Harvie Swartz on many occasions. By the 1980s Sheila Jordan was finally performing jazz on a fulltime basis and gaining the recognition she deserved 20 years earlier. She recorded as a leader (in addition to the Blue Note session) for East Wind, Grapevine, SteepleChase, Palo Alto, Blackhawk and Muse, resurfacing in 1999 with *Jazz Child. From the Heart* and *Very Thought of Two* followed a year later. *—Scott Yanow*

★ **Portrait of Sheila Jordan** / Sep. 19, 1962–Oct. 12, 1962 / Blue Note ✦✦✦✦✦
Sheila Jordan's debut recording was one of the very few vocal records made for Blue Note during Alfred Lion's reign. Accompanied by the subtle guitarist Barry Galbraith, bassist Steve Swallow and drummer Denzil Best, Jordan sounds quite distinctive, cool-toned and adventurous during her classic date. Her interpretations of Oscar Brown Jr.'s "Hum Drum Blues" and 11 standards (including "Falling In Love With Love," "Dat Dere," "Baltimore Oriole" and "I'm a Fool to Want You") are both swinging and haunting. Possibly because of her originality, Sheila Jordan would not record again for over a dozen years, making this highly recommended set quite historic. *—Scott Yanow*

Sheila / Aug. 27, 1977-Aug. 28, 1977 / Steeple Chase ✦✦✦✦✦

Old Time Feeling / Oct. 15, 1982 / Muse ✦✦✦✦
In 1977, Sheila Jordan had recorded an album with only the accompaniment of bassist Arild Andersen. In 1982, she began an occasional duet partnership with bassist Harvie Swartz, and this LP (unfortunately out of print) was their first recorded collaboration as a duo. Jordan's solid sense of swing, subtle creativity, wit and willingness to take chances are very much in evidence as she walks a tightrope on such numbers as "Sleeping Bee," "Tribute (Quasimodo)," "It Don't Mean a Thing," "Lazy Afternoon" and "Some Other Time." This is a classic set that deserves to be reissued on CD. *—Scott Yanow*

The Crossing / Oct. 1, 1984-Oct. 2, 1984 / Black Hawk ✦✦✦✦✦

One for Junior / Sep. 1991 / Muse ✦✦✦✦✦
This CD is a real gem. Singers Sheila Jordan and Mark Murphy both possess unusual and immediately recognizable voices and are among the top jazz improvisers around. On a typically intelligent and chancetaking program there are many highlights including a humorous conversation between hipsters on "Where or When," a couple of ballad medleys and Jordan's witty lyrics on "The Bird." Assisted by pianist Kenny Barron, bassist Harvie Swartz, drummer Ben Riley and Bill Mays on occasional synthesizer, the two vocalists sound mutually inspired. *—Scott Yanow*

Jazz Child / May 11, 1999 / High Note ✦✦✦✦

From the Heart / Aug. 1, 2000 / 32 Jazz ✦✦✦

Danny Kaye (David Daniel Kominsky)

b. 1913, **d.** Mar. 3, 1987
Vocals / Traditional Pop, Nostalgia
A gifted mimic and peerless physical comedian, Danny Kaye ranked among America's most popular entertainers in the years during and following World War II. Rubber-faced and manic, he rose to stardom in film and in television, on record and on Broadway, easily adapting from outrageous novelty songs to tender ballads. Born in Brooklyn, Kaye dropped out of high school at the age of 14 and began working in various vaudeville acts. He later met pianist and songwriter Sylvia Fine, who became not only his performing partner but also his wife. Fine wrote many of Kaye's best known songs, including "Stanislavsky," "Pavlova" and "Anatole of Paris"; much of the material he then performed on Broadway in *The Straw Hat Revue,* which opened in 1939. Kaye subsequently appeared in Moss Hart's *The Lady in the Dark,* in what became a star-making performance.

In 1945, Danny Kaye began hosting his own CBS radio program, launching a number of hit songs including "Dinah," "Minnie the Moocher," and "Ballin' the Jack"; "I've Got a Lovely Bunch of Coconuts," his lone U.S. chart hit, was released in 1950. Amidst a flurry of performance activity during the late '40s and early '50s, Kaye continued his film career and found success with *Hans Christian Andersen;* two of its Frank Loesser-penned songs, "The Ugly Duckling" and "Wonderful Copenhagen," reached the Top Five on the U.K. pop charts. From 1963 to 1967, he hosted his own television variety program, *The Danny Kaye Show.* In the '70s and '80s Kaye regularly conducted classical orchestras; he also appeared frequently on television. From the early '50s on, however, much of Kaye's time was spent in support of UNICEF, and he served as the charitable organization's ambassador-at-large for 34 years. After suffering a heart attack, Danny Kaye died in 1987. *—Jason Ankeny*

● **The Best of Danny Kaye** / Aug. 31, 1999 / Prism ✦✦✦✦✦
The multi-talented Kaye had a career that spanned the stage, screen, and television. He also made a surprising number of records along the way as well and this collection brings together 23 of them in a nice overview of his career. While the majority of them are novelties like "The Babbitt and the Bromide," specialty numbers like "Tchaikovsky (And Other Russians)," or children's fare like "Tubby the Tuba," occasionally Kaye would do a number rea-

sonably straight like "Dinah," "Jenny," or "Molly Malone." A collection that's off the beaten path, difficult to categorize, and totally delightful, just like the man himself. *—Cub Koda*

Sammy Kaye

b. Mar. 31, 1910, Rocky River, OH, **d.** Jun. 2, 1987
Reeds (Multiple), Bandleader / Traditional Pop, Swing, Big Band
Reeds, bandleader. Kaye's band was a textbook example of "sweet" dance bands: large groups whose arrangements seldom swung in the true sense, but were very popular among those who enjoyed overly sentimental light pop and novelty tunes. Kaye began building his reputation in college, then became a hit on radio in Cincinnati. He moved to Pittsburgh and eventually became a national staple. His radio show *Sunday Serenade* was a huge hit in the '40s and '50s. Kaye had many pop hits, some of them adapted for Broadway shows. His gimmick of having fans volunteer to lead his band was highly popular and was transferred to television in the '50s. Perry Como and Nat King Cole had hits with Kay material. This was far from being a jazz band in the real sense, but made enjoyable material of its kind and is a big favorite to this day. *—Ron Wynn*

● **Swing and Sway with Sammy Kaye: 21 of His Greatest Hits** / Sep. 15, 1998 / Collectors' Choice Music ✦✦✦✦✦
History has not been kind to the sweet bands of the swing era, enormously popular in their time, but never given any critical notice, and therefore neglected by record company reissue people ever since, even though there is still a public nostagically clamoring to hear them. A good example is the band with the unlikely moniker of Swing and Sway with Sammy Kaye. It ranked behind only Glenn Miller and Tommy Dorsey as the most successful big band of the '40s. Nevertheless, Kaye's recordings are hard to come by. This compilation, done by a mail-order company and licensing RCA Victor (and one Columbia) recordings, partly redresses the wrong, presenting less than a third of the chart records he scored between 1939 and 1950. There were also hits in the '30s on Vocalion, and more hits in the '50s on Columbia, but the most popular songs—among them the chart-toppers "Daddy," "Chickery Chick," "I'm a Big Girl Now," "The Old Lamp-Lighter," and "Harbor Lights"—from the band's most popular period are here. There are even some modest annotations, and the sound has been spiffed up. For anyone else of Kaye's popularity, this would be the bare minimum; in his case, it's reason to rejoice. *—William Ruhlmann*

Gene Kelly (Eugene Curran Kelly)

b. 1912, Pittsburgh, PA
Vocals / Traditional Pop, Show Tunes
Gene Kelly was already a successful dance teacher in his hometown when he began his ascent in the original Broadway production of Rodgers and Hart's *Pal Joey*. This led to a film contract with David O. Selznick, which was sold to MGM before Kelly even reported to Hollywood. The allegiance with MGM proved a godsend for both the studio and Kelly, who (with the help of producer Arthur Freed) came to energize the film company's musical output for the next 15 years. Kelly quickly revealed himself to be a quintuple threat: dancer, actor, singer, choreographer, and director. Kelly was never a popular singer, despite the fact that he acquitted himself onscreen alongside even the likes of Frank Sinatra in several films, but his on-screen geniality and overall popularity—as a younger, more masculine, and more conventionally handsome rival to Fred Astaire (who was at MGM at exactly the same time)—allowed him to effectively repopularize many songs by George Gershwin, Arthur Freed, Nacio Herb Brown, and others through his performances of them in films such as *An American in Paris* and *Singin' in the Rain*. His most popular and influential work as a singer can be found on the soundtracks for those films, plus *Brigadoon, It's Always Fair Weather, Summer Stock*, and the compilation soundtrack *That's Entertainment Part 2*. *—Bruce Eder*

★ **'s Wonderful** / Jun. 1996 / Rhino ✦✦✦✦✦
And indeed it is wonderful, a fitting memorial to the late Gene Kelly, starting out with the ever-wonderful rendition of "Singin' in the Rain," a recording that never becomes tiresome or boring. The selection of songs is just fine, hitting solo high points along with duet and ensemble numbers that still delight—"Good Morning," with Donald O'Connor and Debbie Reynolds, "The Babbitt and the Bromide" with Fred Astaire, and a delightfully funny version of "I Got Rhythm." Many of these numbers are best enjoyed, of course, in their original context, with Kelly's dance work carrying them, but fans will doubtless be grateful for this compilation. Wonderful mastering and extensive annotation complete a superb package. *—Steven McDonald*

Eartha Kitt

b. Jan. 17, 1927, North, SC
Vocals / Traditional Pop, Vocal Pop
This alluring vocalist enjoyed a series of pop hits in 1953 and 1954, including the seductive Yuletide perennial "Santa Baby." Kitt's exotic style was first showcased in the Broadway production of *New Faces of 1952* (a film version was made in 1954), and she waxed the enticing "C'est Si Bon" in 1953 for RCA Victor. "Santa Baby" arrived in time for the 1953 holidays, and her 1954 output included "Somebody Bad Stole De Wedding Bell (Who's Got De Ding Dong)." Kitt has remained active as an actress and singer; she was a convincing Catwoman on the campy mid-'60s TV series "Batman," and she costarred in the recent movies *Pink Chiquitas* and *Erik the Viking*. *—Bill Dahl*

The Best of Eartha Kitt / 1975 / MCA ✦✦✦✦✦
Decent overview that concentrates on her pop-oriented material. *—Ron Wynn*

● **Miss Kitt to You** / Jul. 1992 / RCA ✦✦✦✦✦
On this smoky 16-track compilation of classics, legendary temptress Eartha Kitt tells it like it is on "Je Cherche Un Homme (I Want a Man)," and W.C. Handy's "St. Louis Blues," Cole Porter's "My Heart Belongs to Daddy" and "Let's Do It," and a dozen others. *—Roundup Newsletter*

Diana Krall

b. Nanaimo, Canada
Vocals, Piano / Vocal Jazz, Traditional Pop, Contemporary Jazz, Neo-Bop, Swing, Torch Songs
Singer/pianist Diana Krall got her musical education when she was growing up in Nanaimo, British Columbia, from the classical piano lesson she began at age four and in her high-school jazz band, but mostly from her father, a stride piano player with an extensive record collection. "I think Dad has every recording Fats Waller ever made," she said, "and I tried to learn them all." Krall attended the Berklee College of Music on a music scholarship in the early '80s, then moved to Los Angeles, where she lived for three years before moving to Toronto. by 1990, she was based in New York, performing with a trio, and singing. After releasing her first album on Justin Time Records, Krall was signed to GRP for her second, *Only Trust Your Heart* and transferred to its Impulse! division for her third, a Nat King Cole Trio tribute album called *All for You. Love Scenes* followed in 1997, and in late 1998 she issued the seasonal *Have Yourself a Merry Little Christmas. When I Look in Your Eyes* followed in 1999. *—William Ruhlmann*

Steppin' Out / 1993 / Justin Time ✦✦✦
Krall's first recording remains an eye and ear opener. Without the overt schmaltz, Krall proves a sincere singer and, more so, a fine pianist whose talent in this area would later become sublimated. If you want to hear not only the roots of Krall's jazzier and romantic side, not to mention the fun, you'll get it all on this remastered CD, with a bulletproof rhythm section of the peerless bassist John Clayton and always on-the-money/in-the-pocket drummer Jeff Hamilton. The program contains several songs that have become Krall's signature tunes. "Straighten Up & Fly Right" is typically cute as she nicely modifies the lyric. "Frim Fram Sauce" is easily swung and wittily rendered. Several standards such as the easy swinging, bluesy "I'm Just a Lucky So & So" with its impressive bridge piano or the straight read of "Do Nothin' 'Til You Hear From Me" seem like child's play. She uses delayed, staggered phrasings with energetic pianistics during "As Long As I Live," jumps in more pronounced and driving tones for "This Can't Be Love," and cleverly deviates from the melody in now typical Krall-ian fashion for the previously unreleased "On the Sunny Side of the Street." She's most convincing on the unaccompanied take of the classic "Body & Soul" and goes into semi-classical mode with Clayton's bowed bass during her lone original "Jimmie." There are two instrumentals: "42nd Street" swings very well with flourishes inserted here and there on a slight re-arrange, while Klaus Suonsaari's (not Charlie Parker's) "Big Foot" sports heavy modal introductory chords, impressive stop starts on a blues strut, and the most interaction during this set. Krall's fans should consider this an essential recording in her growing discography, and perhaps in many ways her best. *—Michael G. Nastos*

Only Trust Your Heart / Sep. 13, 1994-Sep. 16, 1994 / GRP ✦✦✦✦✦

● **All for You** / Oct. 3, 1995-Oct. 8, 1995 / Impulse! ✦✦✦✦✦
Pianist/vocalist Diana Krall pays tribute to the Nat King Cole Trio on her Impulse set. In general the medium and up-tempo tunes work best, particularly such hot ditties as "I'm an Errand Girl for Rhythm," "Frim Fram Sauce" and "Hit That Jive Jack." Krall does not attempt to directly copy Cole much (either pianistically or vocally) although his influence is obviously felt on some of the songs. The slow ballads are actually as reminiscent of Shirley Horn as Cole, particularly the somber "I'm Through with Love" and "If I Had You." Guitarist Russell Malone gets some solo space on many of the songs and joins in on the group vocal of "Hit That Jive Jack" although it is surprising that he had no other opportunities to interact vocally with Krall; a duet could have been delightful. Bassist Paul Keller is fine in support, pianist Benny Green backs Krall's vocal on "If I Had You" and percussionist Steve Kroon is added on one song. Overall this is a tasteful effort that succeeds. *—Scott Yanow*

Love Scenes / 1997 / Impulse! ✦✦✦✦
Vocalist/pianist Diana Krall was a very hot property by the time this Impulse CD was released. Teamed in a trio with her regular guitarist Russell Malone and bassist Christian McBride, Krall here mostly emphasizes ballads having something to do with love. She is at her best on "I Don't Know Enough About You," "I Don't Stand a Ghost of a Chance With You" and "How Deep Is the Ocean." However, Krall's earlier Nat King Cole tribute had more variety in tempos and moods and is recommended first. A decent but not essential release. *—Scott Yanow*

When I Look In Your Eyes / 1998 / GRP ✦✦✦✦
With this CD, the young Canadian singer/pianist/arranger joins forces with producer Tommy LiPuma who places his orchestral stamp on eight of the 13 tracks. It is the latest attempt to push Krall to an even wider pop/smooth jazz audience than she already enjoys. After all, Nat Cole, Wes Montgomery, and George Benson, among others, went this route. Wonder if she'd agree the cuts sans strings were more fun and challenging? Krall does get to it with central help from bassists John Clayton and Ben Wolfe, drummers Jeff Hamilton and Lewis Nash, and guitarist Russell Malone, all stellar players. Krall's voice is sweet and sexy. She's also flexible within her range and at times a bit kitschy, mostly the hopeless romantic. On this CD of love songs, it's clear she's cool but very much in love with this music. Bob Dorough's "Devil May Care" and the insistent "Best Thing for You" really click. Favorites are a decent Shearing-esque "Let's Fall in Love" with vibist Larry Bunker; a suave slow bossa on the opening number, "Let's Face the Music"; the lusher-than-lush title track; and especially an incredible horn-fired fanfare intro/outro on the hip "Pick Yourself Up." Some might call this fluff or mush, but it depends solely on your personal taste. This will certainly appeal to Krall's fans, lovers, and lovers at heart. *—Michael G. Nastos*

Cleo Laine (Clementina Dinah Campbell)

b. Oct. 28, 1927, Southall, Middlesex, England
Vocals / Traditional Pop, Jazz-Pop, Ballads, Cool, Bop
With a multi-octave voice similar to Betty Carter's, incredible scatting ability, and ease of transition from a throaty whisper to high-pitched trills, Cleo Laine was 25 when she first sang professionally, after a successful audition with the big band led by Johnny Dankworth. Both

Laine and the band recorded for Esquire, MGM and Pye during the late '50s, and by 1958, she was married to Dankworth. With him by her side, Laine began her solo career in earnest with a 1964 album of Shakespeare lyrics set to Dankworth's arrangements, *Shakespeare: And All That Jazz*. Laine also gained renown for the first of three concert albums recorded at New York's Carnegie Hall, 1973's *Cleo Laine Live! At Carnegie Hall*. She has proved a rugged stage actress as well, winning a Theater World award for her role in the Broadway musical *The Mystery of Edwin Drood*. In 1976 she recorded a jazz version of *Porgy and Bess* with Ray Charles, and also recorded duets with James Galway and guitarist John Williams. Laine and Dankworth continued to tour into the '90s, and she received perhaps her greatest honor when she became the first jazz artist to receive the highest title available in the performing arts: Dame Commander. *—John Bush*

- **The Very Best of Cleo Laine: 34 Classic Hits** / May 20, 1997 / RCA ✦✦✦✦✦
- **Ridin' High: The British Sessions 1960-1971** / Jan. 20, 1998 / Koch ✦✦✦✦✦

Well-chosen anthology of LP and 45 tracks issued by Laine in Britain, before she was widely known outside of the country. It's solid evidence of her versatility, which found her able to handle smoky jazz, show tunes, pop, and movie themes, all in her well-paced, multi-octave delivery (most effective when she reached for deep notes). The vaudeville-like charge through "I'm Just Wild About Harry" may be dispensable, but otherwise most of this is pretty stately, including a couple nice entries into mainstream pop: "You'll Answer to Me" (a Top Five hit in the U.K. in 1961) has lyrics by Hal David, and 1965's "If We Lived on the Top of a Mountain" could easily pass for a Bacharach-David tune, although it was actually penned by Les Reed (author of Tom Jones' "It's Not Unusual"). Another high spot is "All Gone," the lugubrious theme to the classic 1963 film *The Servant*. *—Richie Unterberger*

Frankie Laine (Frank Paul Lo Vecchio)

b. Mar. 30, 1913, Chicago, IL
Vocals / Traditional Pop

Though his influence proved less durable than his record sales, Frankie Laine was one of the most popular vocalists of the 1950s, swinging jazz standards as well as half a dozen Western movie themes of the time with his manly baritone. Laine's somewhat artificial Western nature proved more successful in far-off England, where he set a chart record in 1953 when his version of "I Believe" stayed at number one for an incredible 18 weeks. A nightclub singer while still of high-school age, Laine replaced Perry Como as the vocalist in a regional big band and signed to Mercury in the mid-'40s. By the end of the decade, he had placed three singles at the top of the charts—"That Lucky Old Sun," "Mule Train" and "The Cry of the Wild Goose." After moving to Columbia soon after, Laine moved toward husky country-pop with arrangements by '50s pop impresario Mitch Miller. Though his debut Columbia single, "Jezebel"/"Rose, Rose, I Love You" was a double-sided Top Five hit, he never again reached number one in America. Laine proved to be far more popular in Europe than America during this time, and after his last American Top Ten hit ("Love Is a Golden Ring" in 1957), he turned to lavish cabaret tours that criss-crossed the world. He retired to his home in California during the mid-'80s. *—John Bush*

- **Frankie Laine's Greatest Hits** / 1958 / Columbia ✦✦✦✦✦

Frankie Laine made a commercial comeback with the gold-selling "Moonlight Gambler" during the winter of 1956-57, his first Top Ten hit since 1953. With the further impetus being the success of the recent Johnny Mathis compilation, *Johnny's Greatest Hits* (the first ever "greatest hits" album), Columbia Records assembled *Frankie Laine's Greatest Hits*, a 12-track album leading off with "Moonlight Gambler" and also featuring Laine's biggest hits of the early '50s on Columbia, "Jezebel," "Rose, Rose, I Love You," "Jealousy (Jalousie)," "High Noon (Do Not Forsake Me)," and "I Believe." The label eschewed Laine's duet hits with Jo Stafford, Doris Day and Jimmy Boyd, and also ignored some Top Ten hits, in favor of rerecordings of two of the singer's biggest hits during his Mercury Records period, "That's My Desire" and "That Lucky Old Sun," a couple of lesser hits and a couple of non-hits. The result was not as good as it could have been, and though the album has remained in the Columbia Records catalogue for over 40 years, it is long-since due for an overhaul in the CD era. *—William Ruhlmann*

16 Most Requested Songs / 1989 / Columbia/Legacy ✦✦✦✦✦

16 Most Requested Songs is a midline-priced collection that spotlights many of Frankie Laine's best-known and most popular performances for Columbia Records, including ""Jezebel," "Moonlight Gambler," "The Rock of Gibraltar," "High Noon," "I Believe," "That Lucky Old Sun," "Hey! Joe" and "Cool Water." Although it's far from a perfect retrospective of his career, it's still a nice sampler of familiar items, and it may satisfy the needs of some casual fans who only want the hits. *—Stephen Thomas Erlewine*

The Frankie Laine Collection: The Mercury Years / 1991 / Mercury ✦✦✦✦✦

This starts with studio chatter and runs through 22 tracks, dated 1946-1950. It's far more bluesy/jazzy than his later Columbia material. *—Hank Davis*

The Very Best of Frankie Laine (ABC Years) / Jul. 16, 1996 / Taragon ✦✦✦✦

Frankie Laine did most of his best and most popular recording for Mercury Records (in the 1940s and early '50s) and for Columbia Records (in the '50s and early '60s). But in 1966, he signed to ABC Records and made a surprising comeback, placing nine songs in the pop charts through 1969, including three Top 40 hits, "I'll Take Care Of Your Cares," "Making Memories," and his biggest late-period record, "You Gave Me a Mountain," which was written for him by Marty Robbins, though it has since become better known in renditions by Elvis Presley and Willie Nelson. Laine did even better in the easy listening charts, placing 12 songs, six of them in the Top Ten, including the above-mentioned tunes plus "You Wanted Someone to Play With (I Wanted Someone to Love)," "You, No One But You," and "To Each His Own." Though in his fifties, Laine was still in good voice and the material suited his bravura style. Taragon's compilation (the first CD release of this material) contains all of the chart material in chronological order, plus a final non-chart single, "Allegra"/"If I Didn't Believe In You." The ABC years may not have been the very best of Frankie Laine, but they were very good, and *The Very Best Of (ABC Years)* (although, at 41-and-a-half minutes, it could be longer) contains everything it should to live up to its name. *—William Ruhlmann*

Mario Lanza

b. Jan. 31, 1921, Philadelphia, PA, **d.** Oct. 7, 1959, Rome, Italy
Vocals / Traditional Pop, Standards, Ballads

Dubbed by Arturo Toscannini "the greatest voice of the 20th century," Mario Lanza was one of America's most successful singers and movie stars in the years immediately following World War II. From the age of 15, he studied to be a professional vocalist, later signing to Columbia Artistes Management as a concert singer. He gained fame while performing for fellow infantrymen while in the US Army, and relocated to New York after being discharged. One of his audition tapes gained him a contract via MGM studio chief Louis B. Mayer, who signed the singer to a seven-year contract. Lanza made his MGM debut in 1949's *The Midnight Kiss*, scoring a hit with the soundtrack's "Celeste Aida." *The Toast of New Orleans* followed, launching his first million-selling hit, "Be My Love." In 1951 Lanza starred as his idol in the biopic *The Great Caruso*, scoring another million seller with "The Loveliest Night of the Year." The title song of 1952's *Because You're Mine* earned an Academy Award nomination, and became Lanza's third and final million-selling effort. After living as a recluse for several years, he briefly resumed his film career during 1956 but then moved to Italy. In 1958, Lanza toured the UK and made one final film, *For the First Time*. He died in 1959 of a heart attack. *—Jason Ankeny*

The Mario Lanza Collection / 1991 / RCA ✦✦✦✦

RCA's *The Mario Lanza Collection* is a terrific, three-disc set that contains 61 highlights from his time at the label. Many of his best-known songs are here, all in their familiar hit versions. While casual listeners may find the sheer bulk of this set somewhat intimidating, its comprehensiveness makes it ideal for the serious fan. *—Stephen Thomas Erlewine*

- **Be My Love: Mario Lanza's Greatest Performances at MGM** / Mar. 17, 1998 / Rhino ✦✦✦✦✦

Be My Love: Mario Lanza's Greatest Performances at MGM contains 20 tracks culled from five Joe Pasternak films Lanza performed in between 1949 and 1954: *That Midnight Kiss, The Toast of New Orleans, The Great Caruso, Because You're Mine*, and *The Student*. All of these selections are taken from the original motion picture soundtracks, which means nineteen of these songs have never been officially released. That doesn't necessarily mean that this record is for collectors only, because these are the versions that many casual listeners will be familiar with, since they were in the films. Lanza was at his peak during these five years, and this collection provides proof that Lanza was one of the greatest tenors of all time. *—Stephen Thomas Erlewine*

Steve Lawrence (Sidney Leibowitz)

b. Jul. 8, 1935, Brooklyn, NY
Vocals / Traditional Pop, Vocal Pop

Both as a solo performer and in tandem with wife Eydie Gorme, traditional pop stylist Steve Lawrence enjoyed success on record, on Broadway and on the club circuit. Lawrence made his debut at the age of 16 with the King Records single "Mine and Mine Alone," later garnering wide exposure through his appearances on Steve Allen's *Tonight Show;* there he first met and performed with singer Gorme, whom he subsequently married in 1957, the year he scored his first major hit with "The Banana Boat Song." Also in 1957, Lawrence's cover of Buddy Knox's "Party Girl" reached the Top Five; a string of hits followed, including "Pum-Pa-Lum," "Can't Wait for Summer," "Fabulous" and "Fraulein." He and Gorme scored their biggest joint hits with 1963's "I Want to Stay Here" and "I Can't Stop Talking About You." In 1959 the couple also hosted their own television variety program. Lawrence also maintained a successful solo career, scoring 21 Top 100 hits between 1957 and 1964; among his most popular releases were "Pretty Blue Eyes," "Footsteps" and the chart-topping "Go Away Little Girl." Throughout the 1980s and 1990s he and Gorme regularly toured clubs and often appeared in Las Vegas, many times in support of Frank Sinatra. *—Jason Ankeny*

- **The Best of Steve Lawrence & Eydie Gorme: 1954-1960** / May 26, 1998 / Music Club ✦✦✦✦

Peggy Lee (Norma Deloris Egstrom)

b. May 26, 1920, Jamestown, ND
Vocals / Vocal Jazz, Traditional Pop, Vocal Pop, Pop, Swing, Show Tunes

Peggy Lee's alluring tone, distinctive delivery, breadth of material, and ability to write many of her own songs made her one of the most captivating artists of the vocal era. From her breakthrough on the Benny Goodman hit "Why Don't You Do Right" to her many solo successes, Lee displayed a bewitching vocal power, balanced equally between sultry swing and impeccable musicianship. Born in North Dakota, she spent a difficult childhood, but made her radio debut at the age of just 14. After working in several different bands, Lee finally got her big break in 1941, when Benny Goodman heard her at a club in Chicago. She began recording with Goodman just a few days later and the collaboration resulted in two 1941 hits, "I Got It Bad (And That Ain't Good)" and "Winter Weather." Two years later, "Why Don't You Do Right" became her first major hit, but she left the Goodman band (and the music industry altogether) later that year after marrying Goodman's guitarist, Dave Barbour.

Peggy Lee returned to music just one year later however, signing to Capitol and hitting the charts with her first shot, "Waitin' for the Train to Come In." She continued to score during the late '40s, with over two dozen chart entries before the end of the decade, including "It's a Good Day," the massive hit "Mañana (Is Soon Enough for Me)," and "I Don't Know Enough About You." She recorded one major hit ("Lover") while at Decca between 1952 and 1957, but later moved back to Capitol and recorded a wide variety of material, including the blues, Latin, and cabaret as well as pop.

By the mid-'60s, Lee was an open advocate of rock. Given her depth and open mind for great songs no matter the source, it wasn't much of a surprise that she sounded quite comfortable covering the more song-oriented end of the rock spectrum. She even hit the Top Ten in 1969 with Leiber-Stoller's "Is That All There Is?" After leaving Capitol in the early '70s, Lee recorded sparingly for scattered labels before effectively retiring in the early '80s. Though she recorded two albums in 1988 and one more in 1992, her voice was effectively silenced after a 1998 stroke. *—John Bush*

The Best of the Decca Years / Apr. 28, 1952-Jan. 16, 1956 / MCA ✦✦✦✦✦
16-track survey of Lee's recordings for Decca in the early and mid-'50s, much of it from film and stage musicals like *The Jazz Singer, Lady and the Tramp,* and *Johnny Guitar.* Includes the hits "Lover," "Just One of Those Things," and "Be Anything (But Be Mine)," as well as duets with Bing Crosby and the Mills Brothers. One of the songs, "The Possibility's There," was previously unreleased in the U.S. "Lover," with its stormy, jittery arrangement, is a highlight, as is the dramatic theme to "Johnny Guitar"; "The Siamese Cat Song," on the other hand, is a ridiculous novelty. *—Richie Unterberger*

Beauty and the Beat / Apr. 28, 1959 / Capitol ✦✦✦✦✦

Latin ala Lee! / Mar. 1960 / DCC ✦✦✦

Basin Street East / Feb. 9, 1961–Mar. 8, 1961 / Blue Note ✦✦

Bewitching-Lee: Greatest Hits / 1962 / DCC ✦✦✦✦✦
DCC's reissue of Peggy Lee's 1962 album *Bewitching-Lee: Greatest Hits* preserves the first, and still one of the best, of Lee's greatest hits albums. Her most famous early hits, from "Fever" and "Hallelujah I Love Him So" to "My Man" and "Alright Okay, You Win," are here, and while there have been more extensive compilations assembled on this same material, few have been as punchy and continually entertaining as this one. The DCC reissue boasts fine remastered sound, plus all the original artwork. *—Stephen Thomas Erlewine*

Mink Jazz / 1963 / Blue Note ✦✦✦

★ **Capitol Collectors Series, Vol. 1: The Early Years** / May 21, 1990 / Capitol ✦✦✦✦✦
Like Frank Sinatra and Ella Fitzgerald, Peggy Lee started out as a big band vocalist but was destined to enjoy her greatest success as a solo artist. The band leader who gave Lee her first major break and featured her prominently in the early 1940s was Benny Goodman, much as Tommy Dorsey did with Sinatra and Chick Webb did with Fitzgerald. Commercially, the big bands were on the decline after World War II, and Lee was among the former band vocalists who was a huge solo act in the post-War years. This generally excellent collection, released in 1990, focuses on Lee's early solo output and boasts 25 recordings that she made from 1945 to1950. Most of the singer's essential solo hits of the 1940s are provided, including such Top Ten smashes as "I Don't Know Enough About You," "Golden Earrings," the cowboy ballad "Ghost Riders in the Sky," and "Waiting for the Train to Come In" (one of the many 1940s gems that was about waiting for your serviceman sweetheart to come home from the War). This CD also contains Lee's swinging 1947 remake of "Why Don't You Do Right" (which had been one of her big hits with Goodman), the number 22 hit "Don't Smoke in Bed," and "Mañana," a cute novelty item that went to number one even though it wasn't among Lee's more essential recordings. The vocalist, to her credit, didn't inundate listeners with novelty songs—Capitol, unlike Columbia and other major labels, wasn't interested in flooding the market with them. Capitol also deserves credit for its impressive digital remastering of these 78-era recordings. If you're exploring Lee's music for the first time, this collection is highly recommended and should be among your first purchases. *—Alex Henderson*

Miss Peggy Lee / Apr. 21, 1998 / Capitol ✦✦✦✦✦
Except for four hit-making years for Decca in the middle of the '50s, Peggy Lee spent the balance of her career with Capitol. And though her many LPs were among the best recorded at the label, most still lay unreleased by the late '90s. Capitol rectified the situation somewhat with the release of its four-disc treatment, *Miss Peggy Lee.* Including well over one hundred songs spanning the early '40s through the early '70s and a heavy booklet (with an extended interview/reminiscence written by Gene Lees plus extensive track notations by Jim Pierson), the box set frames Lee as one of the most distinctive vocalists of the era, able to transform herself from coquettish to impassioned to utterly destitute with no lack of conviction. Though her voice was less strident and not as wide-ranging as other female vocalists of the time, Lee frequently proved herself equal to Billie Holiday for her ability to use her vocal limitations to even better effect on her songs. *Miss Peggy Lee* may be a tad confusing for neophytes—it skips around through her career with little chronological order—but the selections and flow are impeccable. *—John Bush*

● **The Complete Recordings 1941-1947** / Jun. 15, 1999 / Columbia/Legacy ✦✦✦✦✦
Although the whole collection ranges across six years, 32 of the 35 cuts on this two-CD set were recorded within a year of Peggy Lee's joining Benny Goodman's band, and the vast majority within a six month period through the winter of 1942. It is possible during that span to hear Lee evolve from a competent but scarcely confident vocalist ("Elmer's Tune") into a bold interpreter, equally adept at blues ("Blues in the Night"), ballads ("When the Roses Bloom Again"), rhythm numbers ("My Little Cousin," "I Threw a Kiss in the Ocean"), and everything in between. Aside from an improvement in sound over 1993's *Best of the Big Bands: Benny Goodman Featuring Peggy Lee,* the real beauty here is in the material that wasn't on that earlier disc, most notably the small-group sides "Where or When" (perhaps the most beautiful rendition of that song ever cut), "On the Sunny Side of the Street," and "Blues in the Night," the latter one of Lee's earliest blues numbers. Equally important, the band is captured in a nice, close rich sound, which goes double for the solos by Goodman, Mel Powell et al. Speaking of Powell, the timing of recording of the songs on this set makes it one of the best showcases of Powell's piano playing and arranging. Lee's 32 sides with Goodman on Columbia and OKeh have been augmented by three additional numbers, cut by the two as part of Goodman's postwar Capitol Records contract—they're brighter and fuller, but not outrageously superior to his early Columbia sides; but they show off the work of a fully mature artist with five years' more confidence and skill. *—Bruce Eder*

The Lettermen

f. 1960, Los Angeles, CA
Group / Traditional Pop, Vocal Pop, Pop
The Lettermen's close-harmony pop songs with light and easy arrangements made them quite a successful group with adult audiences during the 1960s, when changing styles and tastes made many older listeners feel just a bit left behind in the music world. Formed in 1960 by two students at Brigham Young University, Jim Pike and Bob Engemann, with a lounge singer named Tony Butala, the Lettermen recorded without success for about a year until they signed to Capitol Records. The group's first single for Capitol, "The Way You Look Tonight," did very well on the pop charts, and its follow-up, "When I Fall in Love," reached the Top Ten in late 1961. Though the group only reached that plateau one more time, with the 1968 medley "Goin' Out of My Head/Can't Take My Eyes Off You" (the same year Jim's brother Gary Pike stepped in for Engemann), successful album sales to adult listeners and popular concert tours kept the group going long after many of their similar contemporaries had died off. Another Pike brother, Donny, replaced Jim in 1974, and the Lettermen formed their own Alfa Omega Records in 1979, sporadically releasing albums of new material even into the 1990s. Jim Pike and Bob Engemann later formed Reunion (with Ric de Azevedo), a group which released several albums for Collectables. *—John Bush*

● **Capitol Collectors Series** / 1992 / Capitol ✦✦✦✦✦
All six of The Lettermen's Top 40 hits are here, along with a generous selection of lesser-known singles and album tracks. Informative liner notes and excellent sound help make this the definitive Lettermen collection. *—Stephen Thomas Erlewine*

Julie London

b. Sep. 26, 1926, Santa Rosa, CA, **d.** Oct. 18, 2000, Los Angeles, CA
Vocals / Vocal Jazz, Traditional Pop, Standards, Vocal Pop, Pop, Cool, Show Tunes
A sultry, smoky-voiced master of understatement, Julie London enjoyed considerable popularity during the "Cool Era" of the 1950s. London never had the range of Ella Fitzgerald or Sarah Vaughan, but often used restraint, softness and subtlety to maximum advantage. An actress as well as a singer, London played with heavyweights like Gregory Peck and Rock Hudson in various films, and was married to Jack Webb of *Dragnet* fame for seven years before marrying songwriter Bobby Troup (*Route 66*). London performed her biggest hit, "Cry Me a River," in the Jayne Mansfield film *The Girl Can't Help It.* After recording her last album, *Easy Does It,* in 1967, she continued to act—playing a nurse on the NBC medical drama *Emergency* from 1974-78. Despite her "sex symbol" image—London was known for her sexy LP covers, which make them collector's items—she was surprisingly shy, and left show biz altogether in the late '70s. In the mid-'90s London suffered a stroke, which led to a half-decade of poor health and ultimately contributed to her death on October 18, 2000. *—Alex Henderson*

Julie Is Her Name, Vol. 1 / 1955 / Liberty ✦✦✦✦
For a time, Julie London was as famous for her sexy album covers as for her singing. Her debut is her best, a set of fairly basic interpretations of standards in which she is accompanied tastefully by guitarist Barney Kessel and bassist Ray Leatherwood. "Cry Me a River" from this album, was her biggest hit, and her breathy versions of such numbers as "I Should Care," "Say It Isn't So," "Easy Street," and "Gone With the Wind" are quite haunting. London's LPs have yet to be comprehensively reissued on CD, but can sometimes be found in specialty shops. They certainly stick in one's mind. *—Scott Yanow*

● **Time for Love: The Best of Julie London** / 1955-1965 / Rhino ✦✦✦✦✦
A collection of dusky, atmospheric mood music released as a CD in 1990, *Time for Love* serves as a superb overview of the jazz-pop songstress in her prime. Seductive and personal interpretations of "No Moon at All," "You'd Be So Nice to Come Home To," "Cry Me a River" (a major hit for her) and other classics beautifully demonstrate that, like June Christy and Helen Merrill, London realizes just how effective subtlety can be. While the big-band accompaniment on some sides (including a soul-bearing version of Thelonious Monk's "Round Midnight") is nothing to complain about, London is best served by intimate, minimalist small groups—some boasting only Barney Kessel's guitar and Ray Leatherwood's bass. *—Alex Henderson*

Make Love to Me / 1957 / Liberty ✦✦✦✦
Julie London's concise and melodic versions of standards were quite popular during the latter half of the 1950s. Her subtle sensuality and lightly swinging style made for a potent combination. This album (which has not yet reappeared on CD) matches London's voice with an orchestra arranged by Russ Garcia on standards and a couple of newer tunes, including Bobby Troup's "It's Good to Want You Bad." Among the more memorable selections are "If I Could Be With You," "Alone Together," "I Wanna Be Loved" and "You're My Thrill." *—Scott Yanow*

The Good Life / 1964 / Liberty ✦✦✦

Calendar Girl/Your Number Please / 1997 / EMI ✦✦✦✦

Sophisticated Lady/For the Night People / Nov. 3, 1998 / EMI ✦✦✦

Wild Cool and Swingin' / Jun. 29, 1999 / Capitol ✦✦✦✦

Vera Lynn (Vera Welch)

b. Mar. 20, 1919, London, England
Vocals / Traditional Pop, Vocal Pop, Nostalgia
England's sweetheart during the trying times of World War II, Vera Lynn appeared on radio broadcasts with the Joe Loss Orchestra as early as 1935, and sang with Charlie Kunz and Ambrose. After first performing solo in 1940, she became the host of the BBC radio program *Sincerely Yours;* the show became incredibly popular with overseas servicemen who missed their girlfriends, and her regular songs included such hopeful/heartsick ballads as "White Cliffs of Dover," "We'll Meet Again," "Wishing" and "Yours." She returned to the spotlight in 1947, touring the variety circuit and gaining another BBC radio program. Her recording la-

bel, Decca, seized a golden opportunity in 1948 by releasing Vera Lynn material in America during a musicians strike that had crippled the stateside music industry, and Lynn gained a Top Ten hit that year with "You Can't Be True, Dear." In 1952, she became the first British artist to hit number one on the American charts when "Auf Wiederseh'n Sweetheart" spent nine weeks at the top spot. Her first (and only) British number one came two years later, with "My Son My Son," and she gradually moved from radio/variety work to television spots during the '50s in order to round out her schedule, recording increasingly contemporary material during the 1960s and '70s. *—John Bush*

● **We'll Meet Again** / 1994 / ASV/Living Era ✦✦✦✦✦

Vera Lynn Collection / May 9, 2000 / EMI ✦✦✦✦
Vera Lynn was the Sweetheart of World War II over in England, her patriotic and tearful songs great fodder for the fighting lads. This 20-track collection rounds up her best, including "I'll Be Seeing You," "As Time Goes By," "The White Cliffs of Dover," "This Is the Army, Mr. Jones," "We'll Meet Again," "Wish Me Luck (As You Wave Me Goodbye)," and "There'll Always Be an England." This two-disc set features her older, more well-known sides while the second disc features her tackling later material like "By the Time I Get to Phoenix," "Everybody Loves Somebody," "It's Impossible," and "The Look of love," still sounding wonderful on the new stuff as well. A great little introductory set to this marvelous lady of song. *—Cub Koda*

Manhattan Transfer

f. 1969, New York, NY
Vocals / Vocal Jazz, Mainstream Jazz, Vocalese, Contemporary Jazz, Adult Contemporary
Riding a wave of nostalgia in the '70s, the Manhattan Transfer resurrected jazz trends from boogie-woogie to bop to vocalese in a slick, slightly commercial setting that sometimes failed to gel with the group's close harmonies. Originally formed in 1969, the quartet recorded several albums of jazz standards as well as much material closer to R&B/pop. Still, they were easily the most popular jazz vocal group of their era, and the most talented of any since the heyday of Lambert, Hendricks & Ross during the early '60s.

Though they were a hippie cornball act for their first album, member Tim Hauser reformed the group in 1972 with Laurel Masse, Janis Siegel, Alan Paul. The group recorded their own eponymous debut with help from Zoot Sims, Randy Brecker, Jon Faddis and Mel Davis. The album rejuvenated the field of vocalese (dormant since the mid-'60s) and made the quartet stars in the jazz community across Europe as well as America. The Manhattan Transfer's next two albums, *Coming Out* and *Pastiche*, minimized the jazz content in favor of covers from around the music community, though the ballad "Chanson d'Amour," hit number one in Britain. Cheryl Bentyne replaced Masse in 1979 and that same year, *Extensions* introduced their best-known song "Birdland," the ode to bop written by Weather Report several years earlier.

Throughout the 1980s, the group balanced retreads from all aspects of American song. The 1981 LP *Mecca for Moderns* gained Manhattan Transfer their first American Top Ten hit with a cover of the girl-group classic "The Boy from New York City." The group's 1985 tribute to vocal pioneer Jon Hendricks, titled *Vocalese*, marked a shift in Manhattan Transfer's focus, in that subsequent works managed to keep the concepts down to one per album, and the results greatly improved. *—John Bush*

The Manhattan Transfer / 1975 / Atlantic ✦✦✦

Pastiche / Dec. 1976 Sep. 1977 / Rhino ✦✦✦

Extensions / 1979 / Atlantic ✦✦✦

Mecca for Moderns / 1981 / Atlantic ✦✦✦✦✦
After the deserved artistic, critical and popular success of *Extensions*, the Manhattan Transfer went back to ace producer Jay Graydon for this one, which almost matches its predecessor in its contemporary energy while drawing selectively from the past. Outstanding is the handclapping treatment of the 1965 rock tune "The Boy from New York City" (a No. 7 hit single) and the happily swinging vocalese of the Basie band's "Until I Met You (Corner Pocket)," although their version of Charlie Parker's difficult "Confirmation" isn't nearly as assured. There is also an ample dose of the inventive weirdness that invaded *Extensions:* the African/Caribbean "(Wanted) Dead Or Alive," with its checklist of dictators, that segues right into a tongue-in-cheek secret agent spoof, "Spies In the Night"; or the ambitious, wordless composition "Kafka." No longer a mere nostalgia act, the Manhattan Transfer had not only caught up with the times, they were now slightly ahead of them as well. *—Richard S. Ginell*

Bodies and Souls / 1983 / Atlantic ✦✦✦

Bop Doo-Wopp / 1983-1984 / Atlantic ✦✦✦✦

Vocalese / 1985 / Atlantic ✦✦✦✦✦
Many of the Manhattan Transfer recordings up to this point showed off their diversity and covered a wide variety of music, including jazz. This set was quite a bit different, for it is dedicated to the vocalese of the great Jon Hendricks. The Manhattan Transfer (singers Cheryl Bentyne, Tim Hauser, Alan Paul and Janis Siegel) perform a dozen songs using Hendricks' lyrics, including "That's Killer Joe," "Rambo," "Ray's Rockhouse" and "Sing Joy Spring." Utilizing their regular band of the period (which includes guitarist Wayne Johnson), the Count Basie Orchestra (directed at the time by Thad Jones), the Four Freshmen (on "To You"), tenorman James Moody, Bobby McFerrin (guesting on "Night In Tunisia"), McCoy Tyner, Dizzy Gillespie (on "Sing Joy Spring"), altoist Richie Cole, and Hendricks himself, among many others, the Transfer gives these boppish tunes definitive vocal treatments. This is one of their finest jazz recordings and a classic of its kind. *—Scott Yanow*

The Anthology: Down in Birdland / 1975-1987 / Rhino ✦✦✦✦✦

● **The Very Best of the Manhatan Transfer** / 1994 / Rhino ✦✦✦✦
This eclectic collection of songs encompasses jazz, bebop, swing, doo wop, rock & roll and gospel; all are trimmed in an attractive pop texture. These sixteen compositions are taken from the vocal quartet's albums, which span twelve years (1975-1987). Each selection is inviting as all four song stylists display their individual vocal skills and admirable harmonies. Laurel Masse appears on recordings up until 1979, when Cheryl Bentyne replaced her. Other members include Tim Hauser, Janis Siegel and Alan Paul. *—Craig Lytle*

Swing / 1997 / Atlantic ✦✦✦✦✦

Dean Martin (Dino Paul Crocetti)

b. Jun. 7, 1917, Steubenville, OH, **d.** Dec. 25, 1995
Vocals / Traditional Pop, Vocal Pop, Pop
Enjoying great success in music, film, television and the stage, Dean Martin was less an entertainer than an icon, the eternal essence of cool. A member of the legendary Rat Pack, he lived and died the high life of booze, broads and bright lights, always projecting a sense of utter detachment and serenity; along with Frank Sinatra, Sammy Davis Jr. and the other chosen few who breathed the same rarefied air, Martin—highball and cigarette always firmly in hand—embodied the glorious excess of a world long gone, a world without rules or consequences. He originally rose to superstardom in a comedy duo alongside Jerry Lewis; after they parted ways in mid-1956, most onlookers predicted continued success for Lewis, while the general consensus was that Martin would falter as a solo act—after all, outside of the 1953 smash "That's Amore," his solo singing career had never quite hit its stride, and in light of the continued ascendancy of rock & roll, his future looked dim. Martin's first move was to appear in the 1958 drama *The Young Lions*, starring alongside Montgomery Clift and Marlon Brando; that same year he also hosted *The Dean Martin Show*, the first of his color specials for NBC television. Both projects were successful, as were his live appearances at the Sands Hotel in Las Vegas; in particular, *The Young Lions* proved him a highly capable dramatic actor. Combined with another hit single, "Volare," Martin was everywhere that year, and with the continued success of his many TV specials, he effectively conquered movies, music, television and the stage all at the same time—a claim no other entertainer, not even Sinatra, could make. In 1964, at the peak of Beatlemania, he knocked the Fab Four out of the top spot on the charts with his single "Everybody Loves Somebody," and that same year starred in Billy Wilder's acrid *Kiss Me, Stupid*, a film which crystallized his persona as the lecherous but lovable lush. In 1965, after years of overtures from NBC, Martin finally agreed to host his own weekly variety series; *The Dean Martin Show* was an enormous hit, running for nine seasons before later spawning a number of hit *Celebrity Roast* specials during the 1970s. *—Jason Ankeny*

★ **Capitol Collectors Series** / Oct. 25, 1989 / Capitol ✦✦✦✦✦
This was one instance where the Capitol Collector's series got it right on target. Released in 1989, this 20-song collection is the best and most reasonably priced collection of Dean Martin's hits that one can buy, covering his chart career from his 1948 single "That Certain Party," co-authored by and featuring Jerry Lewis, to 1960 and his work in connection with the movie *Oceans Eleven*. In that time, Martin moved from being the singing straight man in an up-and-coming comedy act into the orbit of Frank Sinatra at the heart of the entertainment world and racked up over a dozen major chart hits. He had successful singles after that, principally in association with Reprise Records, but was mostly known as a television personality from the mid-'60s onward. The dozen years here represent Martin at his most musically ambitious and focused, and also a time when he was breaking new ground in music—"Memories Are Made of This," for example, which he cut with Terry Gilkyson and the Easy Riders (who wrote the song), was a refreshing folk-inspired pop hit in 1955/1956. This disc has all of the essentials, superb sound, and, as a bonus, the first stereo appearance of his 1960 single "Ain't That a Kick in the Head," as well as thoroughly detailed notes. *—Bruce Eder*

☆ **Capitol Years** / 1996 / Capitol ✦✦✦✦✦
Spanning two discs and 40 songs, *The Capitol Years* is the most thorough retrospective of Dean Martin's Capitol recordings. From "Memories Are Made of This" to "Return to Me" and "Volare," all of his major hits for the label are included, as are several album tracks, lesser-known singles, and a handful of rarities. The collection may have a few too many songs for some casual fans, but it's the only album that presents all the important Capitol tracks with care, thought, and first-class sound. *—Stephen Thomas Erlewine*

Memories Are Made of This / Dec. 24, 1997 / Bear Family ✦✦✦✦✦
This eight-CD box set, containing 225 tracks and running almost nine-and-a-half hours, traces Dean Martin's singing career from July 1946, when he cut his first singles for Diamond Records, to November 18, 1955, the last song being "Innamorata," which became a Top 40 hit. (Actually, the studio recordings take up only six of the eight discs, with the remaining two given over to soundtrack recordings.) This was a period when the single was the dominant record format, and many of these tracks are being reissued for the first time since they turned up on 78- and 45-r.p.m. discs. A few are previously unreleased. The only sessions recorded for LPs were for *Dean Martin Sings* (his first ten-inch) and *Swingin' Down Yonder* (his first 12-inch). Though Martin was a major star during this period, his renown derived primarily from his comic partnership with Jerry Lewis in nightclubs and on radio, television and film. In fact, relatively few of the tunes heard here became hits—only "Powder Your Face with Sunshine (Smile! Smile! Smile!)," "That's Amore" and "Memories Are Made of This" reached the Top Ten—and few deserved to do any better. Martin treated his singing career cavalierly for much of this period, recording whatever was put in front of him—an inconsistent mix of ballads, novelties, ethnic tunes and revivals of standards—without much apparent preparation. While his performances were competent and characteristically relaxed, the results ranged from entertaining to embarrassing. Little of it was essential, and this massive album, while a boon to collectors and completists, contains little that is necessary to a collection of the best of the artist. John Chintala's liner notes are meticulously researched, and there is a thorough discography, both contained in a beautifully illustrated hardcover book. *—William Ruhlmann*

☆ **The Long-Lost Reprise Hits of Dean Martin** / 1998 / Collectors' Choice Music ✦✦✦✦✦
Dean Martin's Reprise Records recordings, the masters of which were owned by the artist, remained out of print during the last years of his life. After his death, his estate made an agreement with Capitol Records, which controls his catalog from the late '40s to the early

'60s, to reissue the material. Capitol, in turn, has licensed this set to mail-order firm Collectors' Choice Music. All of which means that, for the first time domestically on CD, his Reprise hits are available here. The compilers have taken a straightforward approach, simply including, in order, the 20 Martin recordings that made the pop charts from 1964 to 1969, starting with the number one gold hit "Everybody Loves Somebody." (It's worth noting that Martin scored hits on other charts that are not included.) It's an appropriate selection, since "Everybody Loves Somebody" set a pattern—very different from Martin's Capitol recordings—that he followed thereafter for his singles. Indeed, the sequencing of the album emphasizes just how similar they were. But it was in this period that Martin finally (and surprisingly) found a commercial groove after a long but inconsistent recording career. After five sound-alike follow-ups to "Everybody Loves Somebody" (same quickstep snare drum pattern, same style of female backup vocals, similar string charts), Martin and Bowen finally varied the formula with the Bill Justis arrangement of Lee Hazlewood's "Houston," a Roger Miller-like country-pop tune. Then they went right back to the old sound for "I Will" (and back into the Top Ten), but later they tried other styles, such as the bluesy party track "(Open Up the Door) Let the Good Times In." When the string of chart successes ran out, Martin did very little subsequent recording—so the re-release of these hits, long overdue, is more than welcome. *— William Ruhlmann*

Return to Me / May 20, 1998 / Bear Family ♦♦♦
Bear Family's *Return to Me* is the follow-up to its *Memories Are Made of This*, a second eight-CD, over-nine-hours box set finishing reissue of the complete Capitol recordings of Dean Martin—in this case, from 1956 to 1961. (These take up the first six discs; the seventh contains soundtrack material from films released between 1956 and 1961, and the eighth contains airchecks dating from 1944 to 1953.) As on its predecessor, the material on *Return to Me* is a sprawling collection of 221 tracks (some of them not reissued since they appeared as singles, a few never released before) by a singer for whom studio recording came well behind live performing and film acting on his list of priorities. Inadvertently, Martin did record a few hit singles during this period, notably the title song and a cover of "Volare," but it was only on the relatively rare occasions that he undertook an album session with some strong figure at the helm—Frank Sinatra, who conducted 1959's *Sleep Warm*, Nelson Riddle on *This Time I'm Swingin'!* (1960)—that the results really displayed what the singer was capable of at his best. There are also occasional moments that approach those efforts, such as the Italian-flavored material he takes on here and there, and his songs for the 1960 movie based on the musical *Bells Are Ringing*. But there is also a lot of pedestrian stuff here that will be of interest only to collectors and fans. John Chintala's annotations lay out Martin's activities in detail and with understanding, but Billy Vera's essay, essentially cribbed from Nick Tosches' exaggerated biography of Martin, could have been done without. Both are contained, along with a discography and many photographs and movie posters, in a hardcover book included in the box. *— William Ruhlmann*

Greatest Hits: King of Cool / Jun. 2, 1998 / Capitol ♦♦♦♦♦
This album is the first product of the agreement between Capitol Records (which controls Dean Martin's 1948-61 recordings) and Martin's estate (which controls the recordings he made from 1962 on). It contains eight tracks from Capitol and eight originally released on Reprise Records, including (for the first time on one album) all of Martin's biggest hits, seven Top Ten tracks, among them the gold singles "That's Amore," "Memories Are Made of This" and "Everybody Loves Somebody." Beyond the major hits, the selection mostly consists of other chart records, though not necessarily the most successful ones, and the non-chronological sequencing makes for a curious listen, since the style of Martin's '50s and '60s hits is so different. Though it runs less than 42 minutes and leaves a lot to be desired, as of the date of its release, it is the only place to get Martin's most popular recordings on a single disc. *— William Ruhlmann*

Hurtin' Country Songs / Sep. 14, 1999 / Capitol ♦♦♦♦

Late at Night with Dean Martin / Sep. 14, 1999 / Capitol ♦♦♦♦

Al Martino (Alfred Cini)

b. Oct. 7, 1927, Philadelphia, PA
Vocals / Traditional Pop, Vocal Pop
Italian singer Al Martino had four hits from 1952 to 1953 and then vanished until the end of the decade—the result of being too young to handle his success and having various disreputable elements vying for control of his career. Martino tried to continue recording in England, to no avail, and returned to America in 1958. After re-signing to Capitol Records the following year, he launched a string of 34 Hot 100 singles that would last until 1977. During the '60s Martino blended country elements with pop songs, blurring the lines between the two genres. In 1972 he appeared in Francis Ford Coppola's masterpiece, *The Godfather*, as singer Johnny Fontaine, a role that strongly resembled Frank Sinatra's life. In 2000, after a 20-year hiatus from recording, Martino released *Style*, a new collection of pop standards. *— Stephen Thomas Erlewine*

● **I Love You Because** / Apr. 13, 1999 / Razor & Tie ♦♦♦♦♦
I Love You Because paints a definitive portrait of Al Martino's career, assembling 20 of the singer's biggest hits from between 1952 and 1977; the many highlights include the Top 20 smashes "Spanish Eyes," "I Love You More and More Every Day," "Tears and Roses," "To the Door of the Sun" and "Painted, Tainted Rose." *— Raymond McKinney*

Johnny Mathis (John Royce Mathis)

b. Sep. 30, 1935, Gilmer, TX
Vocals, Guitar / Traditional Pop, Vocal Pop, Pop, Ballads
One of the last and most popular in a long line of traditional male vocalists who emerged before the rock-dominated 1960s, Johnny Mathis concentrated on romantic readings of jazz and pop standards for the ever-shrinking adult-contemporary audience of the '60s and '70s. Though he debuted with a flurry of singles-chart activity, Mathis later made it big in the album market, where a dozen of his LPs hit gold or platinum and over sixty made the charts. Unsurprisingly, given his emphasis on long sustained notes and heavy vibrato, he studied with an opera coach prior to his teenage years. His other inspirations were the smoother crossover jazz vocalists of the 1940s—Nat King Cole, Billy Eckstine and Lena Horne. After he signed to Columbia, Mathis' self-titled 1957 debut, a standards album, was mostly ignored. He switched to period-pop balladry and gained major hits with "It's Not for Me to Say" and "Chances Are" (the latter his first number one). Hit singles were surprisingly rare for Mathis during the late '50s and '60s, so he focused instead on the burgeoning LP market. He moved into soft rock during the '70s, and found his second number one single, "Too Much Too Little Too Late," in 1978. Mathis continued to record throughout the '90s, and remained a popular concert attraction. *— John Bush*

★ **Johnny's Greatest Hits** / 1962 / Columbia ♦♦♦♦♦
The original greatest-hits package, which stayed on the charts for ten years; includes "Chances Are," "It's Not for Me to Say," "Wonderful! Wonderful!" and "The Twelfth of Never." It seldom gets more romantic than this. *— Cub Koda*

● **Johnny Mathis' All-Time Greatest Hits** / 1972 / Columbia ♦♦♦♦♦
Johnny Mathis' *All-Time Greatest Hits*, a 20-track double-LP set released in 1972, was the most comprehensive compilation of the singer's best-known material up to its time. With the 11-track 1958 album *Johnny's Greatest Hits* the "greatest hits" concept was invented, and Columbia Records followed with *More Johnny's Greatest Hits* in 1959 and *Johnny's Newest Hits* in 1963. Mathis hadn't made much of an impression on the singles charts since, but in 1969 he returned with "Love Theme from 'Romeo and Juliet,'" which grazed the pop charts and hit the Top Ten on easy-listening charts. That song is the concluding track here; otherwise, most of his initial hits from the late 1950s—such as "It's Not for Me to Say," "Chances Are," and "The Twelfth of Never"—are included, along with early-'60s hits like "Gina" and "What Will Mary Say?" and late-'60s easy-listening chart entries like "Venus" and "Misty Roses." Toward the end of the set, there are some non-hits from the early '70s. *Johnny Mathis' All-Time Greatest Hits* is not a perfect compilation of the singer's most successful singles, but it is more complete than any of its popular predecessors, and it became his first million-selling album since 1959. *— William Ruhlmann*

The Best of Johnny Mathis (1975-1980) / 1980 / Columbia ♦♦♦
Johnny Mathis didn't have many hits in the latter half of the '70s—actually, he only had two, which were both duets with Deniece Williams. The low number of hits would make *Best of Johnny Mathis (1975-1980)* unfamiliar territory for anyone but diehard fans, and matters are made worse by the fact that only the number one single "Too Much, Too Little, Too Late" is featured on the record; its successor—the number 47 "You're All I Need to Get By"—is nowhere to be seen. Nevertheless, there are many good performances on this ten-track collection, including "The Best Days of My Life," "The Last Time I Felt Like This" and "What I Did for Love," which makes it worthwhile for the fan who wants to dig a little deeper. *— Stephen Thomas Erlewine*

The Ultimate Hits Collection / Apr. 21, 1998 / Columbia ♦♦♦♦♦
The title may be a little presumptuous, but *The Ultimate Hits Collection* lives up to its billing. Spanning over 20 years, from Johnny Mathis' first entry on the charts ("Wonderful! Wonderful!") in 1957 to his last chart-topper ("Too Much, Too Little, Too Late") in 1978, the collection offers no less than 18 hits. Yes, there are some hits missing, such as the Top Ten singles "Gina" and "What Will Mary Say," but the majority of the heavy-hitters are here: "It's Not for Me to Say," "Chances Are," "The Twelfth of Never," "Wild Is the Wind," "A Certain Smile," "Misty" and "Maria." The original 1962 collection *Johnny's Greatest Hits* remains the definitive Mathis collection, but this is a good substitute, especially for listeners that want to hear songs released after 1962. *— Stephen Thomas Erlewine*

Bobby McFerrin

b. Mar. 11, 1950, New York, NY
Vocals / Vocal Jazz, Neo-Bop
Vocal virtuoso Bobby McFerrin ranks among the most distinctive and original singers in contemporary music—equally adept in jazz, pop and classical settings, his octave-jumping trademark style, with its rhythmic inhalations and stop-on-a-dime shifts from falsetto to deep bass notes, often sounds like the work of at least two or three singers at once, while at the same time sounding quite unlike anyone else. The son of husband-and-wife classical singers, McFerrin was born in New York City on March 11, 1950, later studying piano at California State College at Sacramento and Cerritos College. After touring behind the Ice Follies, he performed with a series of cover bands, cabaret acts and dance troupes before making his vocal debut in 1977. While living in New Orleans, he sang with the group Astral Projection before relocating to San Francisco. There he met legendary comedian Bill Cosby, who arranged for McFerrin to appear at *the 1980 Playboy Jazz Festival*.

A performance at *the 1981 Kool Jazz Festival* led to a contract with Elektra, and the following year McFerrin issued his self-titled debut LP. With 1984's *The Voice*, he made jazz history, recording the first-ever solo vocal album (sans accompaniment or overdubbing) to be released on a major label. His Blue Note debut *Spontaneous Inventions* followed in 1985 and featured contributions from Herbie Hancock, the Manhattan Transfer (on the Grammy-winning "Another Night in Tunisia") and comic Robin Williams; McFerrin also earned mainstream exposure through his unique performance of the theme song to the television hit *The Cosby Show* as well as a number of commercial spots. With 1988's *Simple Pleasures*, he scored a chart-topping pop smash with "Don't Worry, Be Happy"; around that time, he also formed the ten-member a cappella group Voicestra, featured on 1990's *Medicine Music*.

With 1992's *Hush*, McFerrin shifted gears to team with acclaimed cellist Yo-Yo Ma; the record remained on the *Billboard* Classical Crossover charts for over two years. The jazz release *Play*, a collaboration with pianist Chick Corea, appeared in 1992 as well. McFerrin returned to classical territory in 1995 with *Paper Music*, a collection of interpretations of works by Mozart, Bach and Tchaikovsky recorded with the Saint Paul Chamber Orchestra, (which he joined as Creative Chair a year prior). For 1996's *Bang! Zoom* he teamed with members of the Yellowjackets; a second collaboration with Corea, *The Mozart Sessions*, appeared later that same year. With 1997's *Circlesongs*, McFerrin returned to his roots, recording an entire album of improvised vocal performances. *—Jason Ankeny*

Bobby McFerrin / 1982 / Elektra ✦✦✦✦

The Voice / Mar. 17, 1984-Mar. 26, 1984 / Elektra ✦✦✦✦✦
The Voice was a milestone in jazz history; it was the first time a jazz singer had recorded an entire album solo, without accompaniment or overdubbing, for a major label. Bobby McFerrin's amazing ability to switch back and forth between bass notes and falsetto, along with his talent for jumping octaves made this record quite a virtuoso showcase. For those interested in the potential of the human voices and in an important jazz talent, *The Voice* is recommended without reservations. *—Scott Yanow*

● **The Best of Bobby McFerrin** / 1985-1990 / Blue Note ✦✦✦✦✦
The highlights of vocal acrobat Bobby McFerrin's eclectic career are featured on this collection, which includes samples of his work with the St. Paul Chamber Orchestra, Chick Corea, the Yellowjackets, Manhattan Transfer and Jon Hendricks; among the selections are "Spain," "Blue Bossa" and the cloying hit "Don't Worry, Be Happy." *—Jason Ankeny*

Spontaneous Inventions / 1985 / Blue Note ✦✦✦✦✦

Simple Pleasures / 1988 / EMI ✦✦✦✦
This CD will always be remembered for including Bobby McFerrin's surprise hit "Don't Worry, Be Happy." Actually, overall, this album is not quite up to the level of his previous two, for instead of taking unaccompanied vocals, the remarkable singer overdubbed his voice many times, which reduces the miraculous nature of his talents. However, McFerrin's renditions of "Drive My Car," "Drive," and "Sunshine of Your Love" (the program is quite diverse), plus the catchy "Don't Worry," are generally unique and worth hearing. *—Scott Yanow*

Hush / Aug. 1991 / Columbia ✦✦✦✦

Circlesongs / 1997 / Columbia ✦✦✦✦

The McGuire Sisters

f. 1949, Middletown, OH, **db.** 1968
Group / Traditional Pop, Vocal Pop
The McGuire Sisters offered sanitized covers of doo-wop and rhythm & blues songs to notch several of the first pop/rock crossover hits in the mid-'50s. Including Christine, Dorothy and Phyllis, the McGuires got their big break in 1952 when they tried out for *Arthur Godfrey's Talent Scouts* and became semi-regulars. After also appearing on Kate Smith's radio show, the vocal group signed a contract with Coral Records and first hit the charts in 1954. Their first of two Top Ten entries that year, "Goodnight, Sweetheart, Goodnight," was a rather timid version of the Spaniels' R&B hit. The following year, a cover of the Moonglows' "Sincerely" spent ten weeks at the top of the pop charts, followed closely by the Top Ten hits "Something's Gotta Give" and "He." The group's last big hit ("Sugartime") came in 1957, however, and after touring the cabaret circuit during the 1960s, they disintegrated (though Phyllis remained popular as a solo act in Las Vegas). Surprisingly, the McGuire Sisters re-formed in 1985 and began touring again, adding only several contemporary showtunes to their set-list of old favorites. *—John Bush*

★ **Greatest Hits** / 1989 / MCA ✦✦✦✦✦
There are more complete compilations of the McGuire Sisters' music, but this 12-song, 32-minute compilation, which covers six years in their history from 1954 through 1960, is as simple and charming a body of work as you can find for the price. Perhaps it's the purity of their voices and the arrangements behind them that make this one of the few MCA CDs of the 1980s, apart from a couple of blues titles, with sound quality that still holds up at the dawn of the 21st century. It's also a good representation of the pop side of 1950s music, which isn't spoken of very often. While one would like to dismiss the McGuire Sisters as creators of pop product, they were actually extraordinary musicians, as proven here. True, "Sugartime," "Something's Gotta Give," and "He" were far from rock 'n roll. And while their version of "Sincerely" (an R&B hit by the Moonglows authored by Moonglows leader/founder Harvey Fuqua) was a world away from R&B, no one can complain about its craftsmanship or the radiance of the trio's singing. (This rendition of "Sincerely," and not the Moonglows' version, was the one that your parents or grandparents likely knew.) The McGuire Sisters' soaring vocals, like a fuller and more lyrical edition of the Andrews Sisters, are seductive to anyone able to hear them without prejudice against the genre. The programming here doesn't follow any release order except in the most general way, while offering some interesting reminders of what was going on away from the worlds of rock & roll and R&B at the time (including some restrained but prominent use of electric guitars in some of the arrangements). The liner notes feature comments from McGuire Sisters admirers like Neal Hefti. *—Bruce Eder*

The Anthology / Jun. 15, 1999 / MCA ✦✦✦✦✦
The first significant reissue of the McGuire Sisters' classic recordings features 50 songs, covering the years 1952-1965 (the latter from their final ABC-Paramount album), remastered in the late 1990s and, at times, very impressive. Their music can be an acquired taste, evocative as it is of a pre-rock & roll environment and, indeed, competing at the time with R&B acts on the same songs, such as "Goodnight My Love" and "Sincerely." On the other hand, their singing is so radiant, that it's hard to find fault with too much of it. Producer Bob Thiele, who was responsible for guiding most of the recordings contained here, was the founder of the Signature Jazz label, among other top-flight independent jazz imprints, and he didn't slouch on getting the McGuires the best players . So even on numbers like "Heart," which is pure pop, the playing has an edge that, coupled with their harmonies, makes the work compelling. Additionally, the quality of the masters brings out the Andrews Sisters-based edge in their singing: the McGuires come off like three trumpets, exactly like the Andrews Sisters only "played" with a bit more restraint. The overall sound is '50s pop, but with lingering traces in spots of the bounce and swing of '40s big-band. There is absolutely pure pop here, to be sure, such as "He," but the surrounding numbers add bite to the contents where none is expected. The notes are very thorough, and the illustrations, recreating publicity photos and magazine appearances, are also impressive. Disc one is all mono, and disc two, covering the later part of their career, is largely stereo. *—Bruce Eder*

Carmen McRae

b. Apr. 8, 1920, New York, NY, **d.** Nov. 10, 1994, Beverly Hills, CA
Vocals / Vocal Jazz, Traditional Pop, Standards, Bop
Carmen McRae always had a nice voice (if not on the impossible level of an Ella Fitzgerald or Sarah Vaughan) but it was her behind-the-beat phrasing and ironic interpretations of lyrics that made her most memorable. She had her first important job singing with Benny Carter's big band (1944) but it would be another decade before her career really had much momentum. In 1954 she began to record as a leader and by then she had absorbed the influences of Billie Holiday and bebop into her own style. McRae would record pretty steadily up to 1989 and, although her voice was higher in the 1950s and her phrasing would be even more laidback in later years, her general style and approach did not change much through the decades. Championed in the 1950s by Ralph Gleason, Carmen McRae was fairly popular throughout her career. *—Scott Yanow*

Here to Stay / Jun. 14, 1955-Nov. 12, 1959 / GRP ✦✦✦✦✦
One of several CDs that reissue singer Carmen McRae's early Decca recordings, this release draws its material from the 1955 small group album *By Special Request* and a 1959 record with the Ernie Wilkins Orchestra (*Something to Swing About*). McRae excels in both settings. While tenor saxophonist Zoot Sims, trumpeter Richard Williams and pianist Dick Katz get some solo space on the latter album, the former one showcases McRae either with Dick Katz's quartet, accordion player Mat Mathews' quintet (with flutist Herbie Mann) or (on "Something to Live For") with its composer Billy Strayhorn on piano. During an emotional rendition of "Supper Time," McRae herself plays piano. Throughout the 20 selections, the singer is heard in her early prime, hitting high notes that she would not even think of attempting in her later years. Recommended. *—Scott Yanow*

Carmen McRae Sings Great American Songwriters / Jun. 16, 1955-Mar. 4, 1959 / GRP/Decca ✦✦✦✦

Blue Moon / Mar. 28, 1956-Mar. 30, 1956 / Verve ✦✦✦

Sings Lover Man and Other Billie Holiday Classics / Jun. 29, 1961–Jul. 26, 1961 / Columbia/Legacy ✦✦✦✦✦
This CD reissues one of Carmen McRae's best recordings of the 1960s. McRae always considered Billie Holiday to be her primary influence, so a tribute album was a natural project for her. Joined by her regular trio (pianist Norman Simmons, bassist Bob Cranshaw and drummer Walter Perkins) and three guests (cornetist Nat Adderley, tenorman Eddie "Lockjaw" Davis and guitarist Mundell Lowe), the singer interprets a dozen songs associated with Lady Day. Although Holiday's influence can be felt, McRae already had her own distinctive voice and phrasing, resulting in fresh versions of such songs as "Them There Eyes," "Miss Brown to You," "I Cried for You" and even "God Bless the Child." A coolly emotional version of "Strange Fruit" (in which she is accompanied just by Lowe's guitar) is a highlight. In addition, two songs not originally included on the LP ("If the Moon Turns Green" and the slightly out-of-place but still satisfying "The Christmas Song") were added to the reissue. Recommended. *—Scott Yanow*

Alive / 1965 / Columbia/Legacy ✦✦✦

★ **The Great American Songbook** / Oct. 1972 / Atlantic ✦✦✦✦✦
On this popular two-LP set, singer Carmen McRae interprets songs by Duke Ellington, Cole Porter, Michel Legrand, Warren & Dubin, Henry Mancini and Jimmy Van Heusen, among others, but it is her rendition of a humorous Jimmy Rowles novelty ("The Ballad of Thelonious Monk") that is best remembered. Joined by pianist Rowles, guitarist Joe Pass, bassist Chuck Domanico and drummer Chuck Flores, McRae had what was at the time a rare opportunity to record a live, spontaneous, jazz-oriented set. She sounds quite enthusiastic about both her accompaniment and the strong repertoire, which includes "At Long Last Love," "I Only Have Eyes for You," "Sunday," "I Cried for You" and "I Thought About You." *—Scott Yanow*

Two for the Road / Jun. 1980 / Concord Jazz ✦✦✦✦✦

For Lady Day / Dec. 31, 1983 / Novus ✦✦✦✦✦
Carmen McRae always considered Billie Holiday to be the most important influence not only on her singing but on her life. Six years before she recorded her monumental tributes to Thelonious Monk and Sarah Vaughan, McRae performed a Billie Holiday set at New York's *Blue Note Club* that was broadcast over the radio; on the first of two volumes, McRae, who talks movingly about Lady Day at the beginning of the set and accompanies herself on piano on "I'm Pulling Through," is heard in prime form, combining the power and range of her earlier years with the emotional depth and behind-the-beat phrasing of her last period. Accompanied by her rhythm section of the time (pianist Marshall Otwell, bassist John Leftwich, and drummer Donald Bailey) and occasionally the tenor of Zoot Sims, McRae really digs into the material, interpreting the songs in her own style but with a knowing nod toward Holiday. This wonderful set is far superior to most of the Billie Holiday tribute albums and reminds one how much Carmen McRae is missed. *—Scott Yanow*

Any Old Time / Jun. 23, 1986 / Denon ✦✦✦✦✦

Fine and Mellow: Live at Birdland West / Dec. 1987 / Concord Jazz ✦✦✦✦

☆ **Carmen Sings Monk** / Jan. 30, 1988-Feb. 1, 1988 / Jive/Novus ✦✦✦✦✦
Carmen McRae, a good friend of Thelonious Monk, sang 13 of his songs (two of which are also heard in different live versions) on this memorable project. Half of the lyrics are by Jon Hendricks while the remainder were written by Abbey Lincoln ("Blue Monk"), Bernie Hanighen, or more Sally Swisher and Mike Ferro. On all but the two concert performances, Carmen is assisted by tenor saxophonist Clifford Jordan, pianist Eric Gunnison, bassist George Mraz, and drummer Al Foster; Mraz's solos are particularly impressive although everyone is in sensitive form. The live recordings give listeners two more chances to ac-

knowledge the uniqueness of tenor saxophonist Charlie Rouse's tone. As for McRae, her phrasing has rarely sounded better than on this classic set and it is a particular pleasure to hear her interpret the intelligent lyrics and unusual melodies. "Dear Ruby (Ruby, My Dear)" and "Listen to Monk (Rhythm-A-Ning)" are among the highpoints of the essential and very delightful CD. An inspired idea and one of the best recordings of Carmen McRae's career. *—Scott Yanow*

Dream of Life / Sep. 29, 1998 / Warner Brothers ✦✦✦✦
This 1998 CD features singer Carmen McRae late in her career, after recording her notable Thelonious Monk tribute but before cutting her final album, a set of Sarah Vaughan-associated songs. Joined by the WDR Big Band and performing arrangements by John Clayton, McRae is in fine form on a wide-ranging program. Among the better selections are "In Walked Bud," "For All We Know," "I Didn't Know What Time It Was" and "You're a Weaver of Dreams"; on the latter, McRae accompanies herself on piano. Pianist Eric Gunnisson is a major asset in the ensembles and on "Miss Brown to You" both Jon Eardley and a 20-year-old Roy Hargrove have trumpet solos. A rare opportunity to hear McRae accompanied by such a large orchestra. *—Scott Yanow*

Johnny Mercer

b. Nov. 18, 1909, Savannah, GA, **d.** Jun. 25, 1976, Los Angeles, CA
Vocals, Lyricist, Composer / Tin Pan Alley Pop, Traditional Pop, Standards
Johnny Mercer's main claim to immortality is his incredible songwriting output, penning the lyrics or music and lyrics to roughly 1,500 songs. Marked by a sophisticated, occasionally whimsical mastery of language and rhymes, many of Mercer's songs have become standards regularly covered by jazz artists. Yet Mercer was also a successful singer, with a relaxed, Southern-accented, jazzy, rhythmically agile delivery that resulted in several major hits in the 1940s. His first charted songwriting hit was Ted Lewis' 1933 recording of "Lazybones." By 1938 he was recording duets with Bing Crosby for Decca and the following year, he was on Benny Goodman's Camel Cavalcade radio program as a featured singer. In 1942, he co-founded Capitol Records, which would eventually become an industry behemoth, and Mercer reeled off a string of hits for his label, including "Atchison, Topeka and Santa Fe," "Ac-Cent-Tchu-Ate The Positive," "Candy" and "Personality." While running Capitol, Mercer the talent scout attracted the likes of Nat Cole, Stan Kenton, Jo Stafford, Peggy Lee and Margaret Whiting to the label, where they had their greatest successes. Among Mercer's most durable lyrics—a highly abbreviated list—are those for "One For My Baby," "Blues in The Night," "Come Rain Or Come Shine," "My Shining Hour," and "Early Autumn," and his many collaborators have included Harold Arlen, Hoagy Carmichael, Duke Ellington, Jerome Kern, Gordon Jenkins, and Harry Warren. *—Richard S. Ginell*

● **Capitol Collectors Series** / Apr. 6, 1942-Mar. 18, 1949 / Capitol ✦✦✦✦✦
Today we know Johnny Mercer mainly as the genius songwriter from Savannah, GA, and perhaps tend to forget that he was also one of the most prolific hitmaking singers of the 1940s. This excellent compendium of his hit singles, plus a pair of his most famous songs ("Blues in the Night" and "One for My Baby") from 78 rpm albums, will definitely give you the idea. Though not the owner of an overpowering, world-beating voice—to his everlasting and needless regret—Mercer had his own Southern hipster charm, with slippery grace-notes and swinging turns of phrase that any jazzer would envy. An irony for today's audience is that many of Mercer's biggest hits here—"Candy," "Personality," "Baby, It's Cold Outside"—were not written by him, for he truly was a recording star in his own right and not merely a songwriter out to plug his own material. Paul Weston dresses up most of the charts in period big-band garb, decorated with tasty streaks of strings; the Pied Pipers chirp away most of the time, and Benny Goodman's Orchestra and the King Cole Trio chip in on a track apiece. These records are completely saturated in World War II, GI jivey, moon-June, sentimental atmosphere that place them precisely in their time—and as such, they generate gobs of nostalgia. Informative liner notes, a thorough discography of these 20 sides, and reproductions of some of the original 78s and sheet music round out this appealing package. *—Richard S. Ginell*

V-Disc Recordings: For Our Armed Forces Overseas / Jan. 19, 1999 / Collectors' Choice Music ✦✦✦

Ethel Merman (Ethel Agnes Zimmermann)

b. Jan. 16, 1909, New York, NY [Astoria, Queens], **d.** Feb. 15, 1984
Vocals / Vaudeville, Traditional Pop, Swing, Nostalgia
Possessing one of the richest, most powerful voices in the history of theater, the Queen of Broadway strutted her way across the stage during five decades of show-business success, beginning with her breakout in 1929's *Girl Crazy* and continuing on to memorable parts in *Annie Get Your Gun* and *Gypsy,* meanwhile recording several hits for Brunswick and Decca during the 1930s and '40s. Her breakout came in 1929's *Girl Crazy,* where she stopped the show by belting a brassy anthem of self-confidence, "I Got Rhythm." Also, her recording career began with several hits on Brunswick, including "Eadie Was a Lady," "An Earful of Music" and "You're the Top"/"I Get a Kick Out of You." Merman played several other career-making parts on Broadway during the 1930s, including spots in *Scandals* by George White plus *Red Hot and Blue!* and *Anything Goes* by Cole Porter. She found the greatest success of her career in 1946 with the mounting of Irving Berlin's *Annie Get Your Gun,* which ran for over one thousand performances and gave her an undisputed theme song, "There's No Business Like Show Business." Merman's last major stage role was another important one: the antic stage mother Gypsy Rose Lee in 1959's *Gypsy.* She died in 1984, just one year after her appearance at a Carnegie Hall benefit. *—John Bush*

● **There's No Business Like Show Business: The Collection** / Dec. 2, 1940-May 24, 1959 / Razor & Tie ✦✦✦✦✦
Ethel Merman was about halfway through her 30-year career of creating roles on Broadway when the record companies finally started recording original cast albums on a regular basis in the mid-1940s. Nevertheless, Merman had preserved contemporary performances of some of her best-known songs from her shows of the 1930s for such labels as RCA Victor, Brunswick (now controlled by Sony), and Decca. Decca recorded Merman's 1946 hit musical *Annie Get Your Gun,* and in 1947 she re-recorded her early hits for the Decca album *Songs She Has Made Famous.* She also made a non-cast album of songs from her 1950 show *Call Me Madam* for Decca and cut some non-show recordings for the label as well. Along with three tracks licensed from Sony's cast album for the 1959 musical *Gypsy,* it is the Decca material that makes up the present collection. Short of more extensive licensing, it may be the most comprehensive Merman compilation we can hope for. The obvious weak spot is the seven re-recordings of songs like "I Got Rhythm," "You're the Top," and "I Get a Kick Out of You," but Merman had lost none of her 1930s vocal power by the 1940s, so the performances are strong. Most of the classic songs associated with Merman are included, and the sound quality is excellent. *—William Ruhlmann*

Bette Midler

b. Dec. 1, 1945, Honolulu, Hawaii
Vocals / Soft Rock, Pop, Adult Contemporary, Show Tunes, Nostalgia
Bette Midler counts singing as only one of her talents; at times, since 1972, when she first came to national recognition, it has seemed to be the least of her talents. Still, she has managed to score a number of major hits in a roller-coaster career as a recording artist. Midler first emerged with a nightclub act that included comedy and singing of a variety of kinds of material, including show tunes, pop hits, and even a takeoff on The Andrews Sisters, and appeared with increasing frequency in New York with her accompanist, Barry Manilow. She was signed to Atlantic Records and released *The Divine Miss M* (1972), which went gold and included a Top Ten single cover of The Andrews Sisters' "Boogie Woogie Bugle Boy." Midler's album sales fell off during the rest of the '70s, though her records always reached the Top 100 in the album chart. But in 1979 she starred in the film *The Rose,* a fictional account of the life of Janis Joplin, and the title track became a Top Ten hit. Midler made a cinematic comeback with *Down and Out in Beverly Hills* (1986), but it wasn't until 1989 that she had another pop hit, when her version of "Wind Beneath My Wings" from her film *Beaches* became a number one hit. This rejuvenated her singing career, and 1990's *Some People's Lives* became a Top Ten, million-selling album, with the song "From a Distance" hitting number two. *—William Ruhlmann*

● **The Divine Miss M** / 1972 / Atlantic ✦✦✦✦✦
Bette Midler's debut album displays how raw her talent was at the beginning of her career, a coarseness that has been lost as she's honed her persona into something brassier. Not that brassy's bad; she's just matured as a performer. But listen to this, then throw in 1990's fine *Some People's Lives* to see how she shines with both voices. On *The Divine Miss M,* the atmosphere is so intimate it's like she and the band are right in front of you, so when she turns "Superstar" into a quiet portrait of stunned heartbreak it's almost uncomfortable to bear witness to her breakdown. And when she and her backup singers turn in superior versions of "Chapel of Love" and "Boogie Woogie Bugle Boy," it's like having a front row seat to a girl-group concert. By turns bawdy and melancholy (and in an anguished "Delta Dawn," she pulls off both in the same song), this is a superstar at her finest. Every cut's a gem. Few contemporary vocalists can pull off the bleakness of "Hello in There" or the forlornness of "Am I Blue?" with such genuine shades of feeling. Perhaps because she is an accomplished actress as well, Midler's emotions always ring true. Though her talent hasn't wavered in the years since this debut, few of the collections that followed have been as consistent, revealing, or of such high quality. *—Bryan Buss*

Broken Blossom / 1977 / Atlantic ✦✦✦✦

Some People's Lives / 1990 / Atlantic ✦✦✦✦

For the Boys / Nov. 12, 1991 / Atlantic ✦✦✦

● **Divine Collection** / Jun. 22, 1993 / Atlantic ✦✦✦✦✦
Bette Midler's first compilation features most of her hits, including "Wind Beneath My Wings," "The Rose," "Boogie Woogie Bugle Boy," "From a Distance," and her version of "One More for My Baby (And One More for the Road)," recorded on one of the final episodes of *The Tonight Show* starring Johnny Carson. *Divine Collection* is the greatest-hits collection that Midler has needed for quite some time. *—AMG*

Bathhouse Betty / Sep. 15, 1998 / Warner Brothers ✦✦

Bette / Oct. 17, 2000 / Warner Bros. ✦✦✦✦

Mitch Miller

b. Jul. 11, 1911, Rochester, NY
Oboe, Producer, Conductor, Arranger / Classical Pop, Traditional Pop
For almost 15 years, beginning in 1950, Mitch Miller was a major force in the recording industry. Not only was he one of the most most powerful men in that industry, as the head of AR at Columbia Records, but he was one of the most popular recording artists at Columbia Records, responsible for dozens of chart singles and also hosting his own top-rated network television show. Miller showed an interest in music very early in life, and attended the prestigious Eastman School of Music. He earned his first success in the late '40s while at the fledgling Mercury label, where he moved from the classical division to become head of pop AR and produced a series of huge hits for Frankie Laine and Patti Page. In 1950, Miller became head of AR for Columbia Records' pop music division. He proved a marketing and strategic genius, finding massive hits for singers including Guy Mitchell, Doris Day, Jerry Vale, Rosemary Clooney, Tony Bennett, and Johnny Ray.

It was in 1950 that Miller's own recording career as a pop artist and conductor began, big-scale choral recordings credited to "Mitch Miller and His Gang." The group chalked up a six-week run at the number one spot with "The Yellow Rose of Texas." In 1958, Miller began a series of albums referred to as "Sing Along With Mitch," in which he led an all-male chorus in rousing, spirited versions of mostly older tunes. These generated 19 Top 40 hits between 1958 and 1962. Unfortunately, rock & roll never figured large in Columbia's game plan under Miller, and the company's market share was slowly undercut by changes in public taste during the '60s. Miller occasionally re-emerged as a conductor of light classical recordings, but otherwise disappeared from the music scene. —*Bruce Eder*

16 Most Requested Songs / 1988 / Columbia ✦✦✦
16 Most Requested Songs is a midline-priced collection that spotlights many of Mitch Miller's best-known and most popular performances for Columbia Records, including "Yellow Rose of Texas," "Do-Re-Mi," "Shine On Harvest Moon/For Me and My Gal," "You Are My Sunshine" and "Side By Side." Although it's far from a perfect retrospective of his career, it's still a nice sampler of familiar items, and it may satisfy the needs of some casual fans who only want the hits. —*Stephen Thomas Erlewine*

● **Greatest Hits** / Feb. 23, 1999 / Columbia/Legacy ✦✦✦✦✦
Okay, this is the kind of dorky music that your parents listened to when you weren't playing Elvis, Buddy Holly, or Dave Brubeck on the phonograph; and it was the kind of MOR pop of the '50s and early '60s that rock & roll battled tooth-and-nail for supremacy—but this is also some of the most infectiously tuneful dorky music there is, and some of the most captivating of its '50s nerd-appeal idiom. The 15 tracks, all beautifully remastered for maximum impact, range from straight sing-along numbers like "You Are My Sunshine" by Mitch Miller and the Gang to instrumentals such as "Song for a Summer Night" by Mitch Miller with His Orchestra. Marches like "Bonnie Blue Gal" and "Colonel Bogey" from *Bridge on the River Kwai* work best but ballads ("Autumn Leaves"), movie songs ("The Longest Day"), novelty songs ("Tzena Tzena Tzena"), and show tunes ("Do-Re-Me") were also at the center of Miller's repertory, and represented here. For all of the care lavished on it, this disc may still work best as a gag gift, although it's also sure to evoke strong memories in anyone over 40 of camp sing-alongs and watching Miller on television with the family. —*Bruce Eder*

The Mills Brothers

f. Piqua, OH
Group / Traditional Pop, Classic Jazz, Vocal Pop, Swing, Show Tunes
An astonishing vocal group that grew into one of the longest-lasting oldies acts in American popular music, the Mills Brothers quickly moved from novelty wonders to pop successes and continued amazing audiences for decades. Originally billed as "Four Boys and a Guitar," the group was so proficient at recreating trumpets, trombones, and saxophones with only their voices that early singles like "Tiger Rag" and "St. Louis Blues" sounded closer to a hot Dixieland combo than a vocal group. And even after the novelty wore off, the group's intricate harmonies continued charming audiences for decades.

The Mills Brothers—all born in Piqua, Ohio during the 1910's—began as a harmony quartet and vaudeville novelty group. After moving to New York, the group became a sensation during 1931 and early 1932 with the singles "Tiger Rag" and "Dinah." Dumb-founded listeners hardly believed the notice accompanying the records: "No musical instruments or mechanical devices used on this recording other than one guitar." The exposure continued during 1932, with appearances in the film *The Big Broadcast* and more hits including "St. Louis Blues" and "Bugle Call Rag." John, Jr.'s sudden death in 1936 was a huge blow to the group, but father John, Sr. took over as bass singer. Though the novelty appeared to wear off by the late '30s, all that changed in 1943 however, with the release of "Paper Doll," a sweet, intimate ballad that became one of the biggest hits of the decade.The group hit number one again in 1944 with "You'll Always Hurt the One You Love." The influence of middle-of-the-road pop slowly crept into their material during the 1940s, and in 1952, "The Glow Worm" became their last number one hit. The group soldiered on, and three remaining siblings continued performing on the oldies circuit until 1982. The last surviving brother, Donald, continued performing with his son until his own death in 1999. —*John Bush*

Chronological, Vol. 1 / Oct. 12, 1931-Apr. 14, 1932 / Storyville ✦✦✦✦✦
The English JSP label, on six CD's, has reissued in chronological order all of the Mills Brothers recordings from the 1931-39 period. Although they became a best-selling middle-of-the-road pop vocal group in the 1940's, the Mills Brothers were most notable during their first decade for their uncanny ability to imitate instruments, particularly trumpet, trombone, and bass. Using only a rhythm guitar, the Mills Brothers were able to sound like an instrumental quintet. This first volume has plenty of hot numbers (including "Nobody's Sweetheart," three versions of "Tiger Rag," and a remarkable rendition of "Sweet Sue"); a couple of medleys with the Boswell Sisters, Bing Crosby, and the not-so-hot singer Frank Munn; an appearance on a radio commercial; and versions of "Shine" and "Dinah" with Bing Crosby. All of these CDs are highly recommended, particularly to listeners not familiar with the Mills Brothers' earliest (and best) period. —*Scott Yanow*

★ **The Mills Brothers: The Anthology (1931-1968)** / 1931-1968 / MCA ✦✦✦✦✦
The Mills Brothers: The Anthology is a comprehensive 48-song overview of the vocal group's career, spanning their entire career and featuring 32 of their biggest hits. Most of their most famous songs—including "Paper Doll, " "Glow-Worm, " "Lazy River, " and "Rockin' Chair"—are included on this double disc set and the sound is the best it has ever been. In short, it is the definitive retrospective of this ground-breaking vocal quartet. —*Stephen Thomas Erlewine*

Chronological, Vol. 2 / May 1932-Feb. 24, 1934 / Storyville ✦✦✦✦✦
The second of six CDs from the British JSP label to trace all of the Mills Brothers' recordings from their first eight years on record has 23 performances covering a 21 month period. In addition to their solo records in which the four vocalists are accompanied only by an acoustic guitar, there are collaborations with Duke Ellington ("Diga, Diga, Do"), Cab Calloway and the Don Redman Orchestra ("Doin' the New Low Down"), Alice Faye ("Dinah"), and Bing Crosby (two versions of "My Honey's Lovin' Arms"); the last selection also includes short spots for future bandleaders Benny Goodman, Tommy Dorsey, and Bunny Berigan. The studio recordings are augmented by two numbers from a soundtrack of a film. Some of the other highpoints of this quite fascinating release include "The Old Man of the Mountain," "Bugle Call Rag," a haunting version of "Smoke Rings," and "I've Found a New Baby." The Mills Brothers at their best. —*Scott Yanow*

20th Century Masters—*The Millennium Collection: The Best of the Mills Brothers* / Mar. 7, 2000 / MCA ✦✦✦✦
The Mills Brothers' *20th Century Masters* features some of the vocal group's biggest hits, such as "Lazy River," "The Glow Worm," "Paper Doll," and "Someday You'll Want Me to Want You." A pleasant, nostalgic collection from some of the biggest hitmakers of the '40s and '50s. —*Heather Phares*

Liza Minnelli

b. Mar. 12, 1946, Hollywood, CA
Vocals / Traditional Pop, Pop, Show Tunes
Liza Minnelli has been one of the leading entertainers in the world for over twenty-five years, as well as a best-selling recording artist, Tony Award-winning actress, and celebrity. In the public eye for most of her life due to her famed pedigree (she is the daughter of Hollywood great Judy Garland and director Vincente Minnelli), she learned a great deal about the entertainment industry from her parents, sitting on the set while her father directed pictures and watching her mother perform from the wings of theaters and nightclubs. Living in New York after both parents told her she would have to make it on her own, Minnelli traveled with several productions and gained a recording contract with Capitol for 1964's *Liza! Liza!*.

After her mother's death and the collapse of her marriage to Australian songwriter Peter Allen, Liza Minnelli bounced back in the 1970s with the production that would make her career: *Cabaret*. The 1972 film version of Kander & Ebb's Broadway smash won nine Academy Awards, including Best Picture and Best Actress for Minnelli. That same year, her television special *Liza with a "Z"* won an Emmy and became her biggest album hit, peaking in the Top 20. A subsequent worldwide solo tour confirmed her status as one of the top entertainers in the world, and a series of solo shows performed at New York's legendary Winter Garden in 1974 broke several Broadway records. Though virtually retired during the early '80s (except for a highly visible appearance in 1981's *Arthur* opposite Dudley Moore), Minnelli returned with a vengeance durinh 1985, touring the world with several shows. In 1991, her concert series at Radio City Music Hall based around the British comedy *Stepping Out* broke the venue's box-office records, spawning performances at London's Royal Albert Hall as well. —*John Bush*

● **Liza with a "Z"** / 1972 / Columbia ✦✦✦✦✦

Liza Minnelli at Carnegie Hall [The Complete Concert] / Oct. 1987 / Telarc ✦✦✦
Having set a record by selling out 11 concerts at *Carnegie Hall* in 1979, Liza Minnelli bettered her own mark when she spent three weeks at the prestigious venue in 1987, and Telarc issued a two-disc version of "the complete concert" later in the year. (A one-disc highlights version followed in 1989.) Though Minnelli was successful on Broadway and in the movies (and even recorded the occasional album), the core of her career was always her stage act, written for her by Fred Ebb and continually updated. By 1987, the 41-year-old singer had committed several versions of her one-woman show to record already, but *Liza Minnelli at Carnegie Hall* turned out to be nearly definitive. Performing before a full orchestra, she mixed vintage standards with theater songs of her own era including, of course, the songwriting team that penned so many of her signature songs, John Kander and Ebb. And she even found places for such contemporary pop tunes as "You Better Sit Down Kids," "I Can See Clearly Now," and "Somewhere out There." The best part of the show was the extended medley of Kander and Ebb songs that came at the end and ran nearly 29 minutes, including the *Cabaret* songs "Money, Money," "Mein Herr," "Maybe This Time," and the title song, and concluding inevitably with the theme from the film *New York, New York*. The result was a concert—and a recording—that summed up Minnelli's career brilliantly. Appropriately, it was her first album to reach the charts in 13 years. —*William Ruhlmann*

Gently / 1996 / Angel ✦✦✦✦✦
If anyone is entitled to cash in on the renewed renaissance of classic pop (not to mention space-age bachelor pad) music, it's Liza Minnelli, who not only has a pedigree to match the likes of Natalie Cole but also has been at it longer. At 50, Minnelli no longer has to choose between her heritage and her generation, and the assurance with which she tackles material like George and Ira Gershwin's "Embraceable You" and Irving Berlin's "I Got Lost in His Arms" is striking. But she is equally at home with such rock era work as "Chances Are" (on which she's accompanied by Johnny Mathis, who made it a hit) and Leiber & Stoller's "Some Cats Know" (which was bringing down the house on Broadway in *Smokey Joe's Cafe* at the time of the album's release). If this album does not live up to its title or to Minnelli's liner notes description ("sentimental, romantic and sometimes foolish" songs sung "hopefully, tenderly, and most of all... gently"), that's only to say that among the many favorable things you could say about the material and Minnelli's performance of it, "gentle" is not one of them. The singer's intensity is always tempered with warmth, her power checked by careful attention to details of lyric meaning and the nuances of feeling available through her phrasing. But Liza Minnelli just isn't a gentle singer. Maybe she should have stuck with the title scrawled on the back of the CD booklet: "The Makeout Album." —*William Ruhlmann*

Minnelli On Minnelli / Feb. 29, 2000 / Angel ✦✦✦

Guy Mitchell

b. Feb. 27, 1927, Detroit, MI, **d.** Jul. 1, 1999
Vocals / Traditional Pop, Vocal Pop
To some listeners, the name Guy Mitchell evokes contempt—as the singer whose pop-styled covers of "Singin' The Blues" and "Knee Deep In The Blues" cut the legs out from under Marty Robbins' country-styled original renditions. To others, Mitchell evokes the last period of America's innocence, the mid-'50's, when he periodically ascended the pop charts in the company of singers like Frankie Laine. Mitchell was all of those things and more, in some ways a trail-blazer—he was the first major recording artist whose career was crafted in the studio, by a record company, and sold to the public by way of records and the radio, not concerts. He was the precursor to the late '50's teen idols crafted by the industry as an alternative to the burgeoning success of rock 'n roll. In contrast to some of the younger male singing

idols of that era, however, Mitchell had a genuinely good voice as his starting point in music. *—Bruce Eder*

Heartaches by the Number / 1970 / Bear Family ✦✦✦✦✦
But for the absence of his duet "You're Just In Love" with Rosemary Clooney, this 25-song disc would be the perfect, definitive Guy Mitchell compilation, containing his first two Columbia hits and its follow-ups, his other recordings in the folk-ish/novelty vein that was big then, as well as his late-'50s smashes "Singin' the Blues" and "Knee Deep In the Blues," going right to the end of Mitchell's career with the label. It is all mastered exceptionally well, and heavily annotated. *—Bruce Eder*

16 Most Requested Songs / 1991 / Columbia/Legacy ✦✦✦
16 Most Requested Songs is a midline-priced collection that spotlights many of Guy Mitchell's best-known and most popular performances for Columbia Records, including "My Heart Cries for You," "The Roving Kind," "Knee Deep In the Blues," "There's Always Room At the Top," "Chicka-Boom," "My Truly, Truly Fair," "Crazy With Love" and "Singing the Blues." Although it's far from a perfect retrospective of his career, it's still a nice sampler of familiar items, and it may satisfy the needs of some casual fans who only want the hits. *—Stephen Thomas Erlewine*

● **The Definitive Guy Mitchell** / Jun. 13, 2000 / Collectors' Choice Music ✦✦✦✦✦

Matt Monro (Terrence Parsons)

b. Dec. 1, 1932, London, England, **d.** Feb. 7, 1985
Vocals / Traditional Pop, Vocal Pop
Though Matt Monro is known best to worldwide audiences as the voice of one of the best James Bond themes, "From Russia with Love," the British vocalist produced a lifetime of great work. Often criticized as a second-rate Sinatra imitation because of his light, expressive style of swing, Monro hit the British Top Ten frequently during the 1960s but managed only two moderate hits in America.

Born Terrence Parsons in London, he began his career singing for television commercials and performed with a few British bands (including Cyril Stapleton's Orchestra) during the early '50s. After a few sides recorded for various labels, he signed to Decca for an album of standards, 1957's *Blue and Sentimental.* His career really took off one year later when producer George Martin asked him to lend his deep voice to a Peter Sellers album of Sinatra satires, *Songs for Swingin' Sellers.* Monro's straight-faced contribution, "You Keep Me Swingin'," gained him a contract from Parlophone, and he hit number three in the British charts with 1960's "Portrait of My Love."

Both "My Kind of Girl" and "Softly, As I Leave You" also hit the Top Ten during the subsequent two years; the former became his first transatlantic hit, reaching number 18 in America. Monro also proved quite proficient in the growing realm of the full-length; his 1962 LP for Parlophone, *Matt Monro Sings Hoagy Carmichael,* was a very accomplished songbook collection for a pop singer. Though his theme to the second *James Bond* vehicle, *From Russia with Love,* only hit the Top 20 in Britain, it increased his exposure around the world. His next single, "Walk Away," hit number four in Britain and just missed the Top 20 in America.

Monro gained his last British Top Ten in 1965, after his association with George Martin and Parlophone gave him the distinction of being the first artist of thousands to cover the Beatles' "Yesterday." After moving to America that year, his British chart fortunes declined (except for the moderate 1973 hit "And You Smiled"). He continued performing his nightclub routine, and recorded sparingly during the '70s. The 1980 collection *Heartbreakers* rejuvenated his career somewhat, though his health suffered during the time. He finally died of cancer in 1985. *—John Bush*

● **Spotlight on Matt Monro** / Aug. 1, 1995 / Capitol ✦✦✦✦✦
Spotlight on Matt Monro is an excellent 18-track overview of his recordings for Capitol Records. Although it doesn't contain all of his biggest hits, it does have a represenative sampling of hits and lesser-known gems, making it a good introduction to the vocalist's work. Among the highlights are "My Kind of Girl, " "I'm Glad There Is You, " "I'll Take Romance, " "Laura, " "Autumn Leaves, " "Ebb Tide, " "From Russia with Love, " "When Joanna Loved Me, " "The Good Life" and "September Song." *—Stephen Thomas Erlewine*

Vaughn Monroe

b. Oct. 7, 1911, Akron, OH, **d.** May 21, 1973
Vocals, Trombone / Traditional Pop, Swing
Despite an early talent for the trumpet, Vaughn Monroe's desire to become an opera singer eventually landed him almost ten number one hits during the 1940s as well as a host of nicknames for his rich baritone, including the Voice with Hairs on Its Chest and Old Leather Tonsils. Born in Akron, Ohio, Monroe moved to Wisconsin while still a child and focused on his trumpet talent for most of his boyhood. Another early ambition, to be an opera singer, resulted in his signing on as a vocalist with territory bands led by Austin Wylie, Larry Funk (for whom he made his recording debut) and Jack Marshand. While based in Boston with Marshand, Monroe formed his first orchestra and began recording for Victor's low-priced Bluebird label. One of his first singles, "There I Go," spent three weeks at the top of the Hit Parade in 1940. Though his orchestra was rather tame (even for the time), it was voted top college band that year. His long-time theme song "Racing with the Moon" debuted in 1941, and the following year and a half brought no less than three number one hits: "My Devotion," "When the Lights Go on Again (All Over the World)" and "Let's Get Lost."

Monroe's first few years of recording had been quite successful, but all his biggest hits were to come. During 1945, "There! I've Said It Again" and "Let It Snow! Let It Snow! Let It Snow!" both spent more than a month at the top of the charts. And his two biggest hits, "Ballerina" and "Riders in the Sky," came in 1947 and 1949, respectively. The latter, an old Western chestnut, presaged Monroe's attempt at moving into Hollywood's singing-cowboy genre with a couple of early-'50s B-movies including *The Singing Guns* and *The Toughest Man in Arizona.* He also disbanded his orchestra, and continued to work television and radio (he hosted *Camel Caravan* for many years). Except for a few mid-'50s novelties (including "They Were Doin' the Mambo" and "Black Denim Trousers and Motorcycle Boots"), Monroe never again hit the charts. He worked as a spokesman for RCA Victor, and continued to perform into the early '70s. *—John Bush*

● **The Best of Vaughn Monroe** / 1987 / MCA ✦✦✦✦✦
These big band leader's original hits are here, including "Ghost Riders in the Sky, " "Racing with the Moon, " and "Ballerina." Until RCA reissues its collection, these versions will suffice. *—Hank Davis*

Ella Mae Morse

b. Sep. 12, 1924, Mansfield, TX, **d.** Oct. 16, 1999
Vocals / Traditional Pop, Jump Blues, Big Band
One of the most talented and overlooked vocalists of the '40s, Ella Mae Morse blended jazz, country, pop, and R&B; at times she came remarkably close to what would be known as rock & roll. When she wasn't yet 14, Morse had her first taste of the big time, when Jimmy Dorsey's band came to Dallas for a stay at the Adolphus Hotel and she called for an audition. Unbeknownst to her, the band needed a new female vocalist. Believing that Morse was indeed 19, as she and her mother claimed, Dorsey hired her. When he received a letter from the school board declaring that he was responsible for The Morse's care, Dorsey fired her. Morse joined former Dorsey pianist Freddie Slack's band in 1942; she was only 17 when they cut "Cow Cow Boogie," which became Capitol Records' first gold single. The following year, Morse began recording solo. Although her recordings were consistently solid and sold fairly well (frequently charting better on the Black charts than on the pop charts), Morse never obtained a huge following. She retired from recording in 1957, and died of respiratory failure on October 16, 1999. *—Stephen Thomas Erlewine*

★ **Capitol Collectors Series** / 1992 / Capitol ✦✦✦✦✦
After being out of print for many years, a well-chosen sampling of Morse's groundbreaking recordings are now available on this splendid compilation. Her ten charting solo singles are here, along with sides recorded with Freddie Slack and some obscure tracks. Morse blazes through every song, particularly "House of Blue Lights," "Milkman, Keep Those Bottles Quiet," "Pig Foot Pete," "The Blacksmith Blues," and her first recording, "Cow Cow Boogie." The album has terrific liners and superlative sound. *—Stephen Thomas Erlewine*

Barrelhouse, Boogie & Blues / Aug. 19, 1997 / Bear Family ✦✦✦✦✦

Nana Mouskouri

b. Oct. 13, 1934, Athens, Greece
Vocals / Vocal Pop, Pop
Nana Mouskouri grew up on American jazz and black gospel. She attended a classical music conservatory, but was thrown out when it was learned that she was playing jazz on the side. She later worked with Harry Belafonte and Quincy Jones. She's an articulate, resonant soprano. The best selling female artist of all time worldwide, she is to Europe what Streisand is to America, her career spanning across four decades; among her many releases were 1964's *Favorite German Christmas Songs,* 1971's *Turn On the Sun,* 1986's *Tu M'Oubiles,* 1997's *Return to Love* and 2000's *Meisterstucke.* *—Bil Carpenter*

● **Only Love: The Best of Nana** / 1991 / Philips ✦✦✦✦✦
Includes Nana's English covers of '80s hits like Cyndi Lauper's "Time After Time." *—Bil Carpenter*

Jim Nabors

b. Jun. 12, 1932, Sylacauga, AL
Vocals / Traditional Pop, Standards, Vocal Pop, Ballads
While better known as an actor thanks to his immortal role as television's bumbling Gomer Pyle, Jim Nabors also enjoyed a successful career as an easy-listening balladeer. Born June 12, 1932 in Sylacauga, Alabama, he graduated from the University of Alabama with a degree in business administration, but later found himself working in TV as an apprentice editor; at much the same time, he also pursued a career as a cabaret singer. In 1963 Nabors was hired to guest star on an episode of the popular *Andy Griffith Show;* although his role as the hayseed Gomer was originally intended as a one-shot, the character proved such a hit with audiences that he went on to become a featured player for the next two seasons. In 1965 Nabors even received his own spin-off series, *Gomer Pyle U.S.M.C.,* in which Gomer appeared as a hapless Marine Corps private. During a 1964 guest appearance on *The Danny Kaye Show,* Nabors first displayed his vocal prowess; his baritone subsequently graced dozens of albums, including a number of gospel and country efforts. From 1969 to 1972, he hosted his own variety program, *The Jim Nabors Show,* and also regularly performed in concert; while touring in a production of *Man of La Mancha,* Nabors popularized the song "The Impossible Dream." *—Jason Ankeny*

● **16 Most Requested Songs** / Jun. 6, 1989 / Columbia/Legacy ✦✦✦✦✦
16 Most Requested Songs is a midline-priced collection that spotlights many of Jim Nabors' best-known and most popular performances for Columbia Records, including "The Impossible Dream," "Try to Remember," "Love Is Blue," "Somewhere My Love," "My Cup Runneth Over," "Just a Closer Walk with Thee," "You'll Never Walk Alone," "Jean" and "Sunrise Sunset." Although it's far from a perfect retrospective of his career, it's still a nice sampler of familiar items, and it may satisfy the needs of some casual fans who only want the hits. *—Stephen Thomas Erlewine*

Country Side of Jim Nabors / 1994 / Sony Special Products ✦✦✦✦
Sony Music Special Products' *The Country Side of Jim Nabors* is a generous collection of 16 country-pop songs he cut for Columbia Records over the years. Nabors never actually had a single on the country charts, but he could nevertheless deliver a country tune as convincingly as he could a pop or gospel tune, as this collection proves. Any fan of his wishing to hear the highlights of his country work should turn here. It may be a budget-line collection, but it's one of the rare budget-line discs that provides a thorough, successful overview of a specific portion of an artist's work. *—Stephen Thomas Erlewine*

Anthony Newley

b. Sep. 24, 1931, London, England, **d.** Apr. 14, 1999
Vocals / Traditional Pop, Film Music, Music Hall, Vocal Pop
Anthony Newley was one of entertainment's genuine triple threats—an actor, singer, and composer with an international following, equally adept and prodigious in all three fields. Moreover, he enjoyed success as a performer in such seemingly mutually exclusive fields as rock & roll and the legitimate stage. And even more improbably, he did it with a working class, Cockney persona that should never have found much currency outside of England. Born in Hackney, a working-class section of London, Newley was cast in the best of his boyhood film parts as the Artful Dodger in 1948's *Oliver Twist.* The 1959 film *Idle on Parade* yielded Newley's first chart-topping hit, "I've Waited So Long", and from 1959 to 1961 he charted seven more Top 10 British hits in a pop-rock vein, including the number one singles, "Why" and "Do You Mind."

Invited to devise his own stage production in 1961, Newley teamed up with Leslie Bricusse to create *Stop the World—I Want to Get Off,* a mix of songs, dance, pantomime, and dialogue that became a huge hit and yielded three hit songs: "What Kind of Fool Am I," "Once in a Lifetime," and "Gonna Build a Mountain." By that time, Newley and Bricusse were one of the hottest songwriting teams in music, and among their subsequent hits was the title song to *Goldfinger.* They returned to the stage in 1965 with *The Roar of the Greasepaint—The Smell of the Crowd,* and scored with the 1971 musical *Willy Wonka and the Chocolate Factory,* a box-office success and the source of the pop standard, "The Candy Man". Newley's career stalled from the mid-'70s on though, and his last new collection of material was the 1978 album *The Singer and His Songs. —Bruce Eder*

● **Once in a Lifetime: The Collection** / Jul. 15, 1997 / Razor & Tie ✦✦✦✦✦
Anthony Newley was always a distinctly British phenomenon, since he specialized in the British form of vaudeville and burlesque known as music hall. However, his music became the touchstone for all the pop-rock acts who tried to incorporate music hall into their sound. In particular, David Bowie borrowed from Newley on his pre-fame recordings for Derham. So, in a weird way, he became a minor cult figure outside of England, which may explain Razor & Tie's release of *Collection,* the first CD collection of Newley's material to be released in America. Although it isn't as good as some British collections, which contain more charting hits, it's a fine introduction, relying on Leslie Bricusse compositions like "Gonna Build a Mountain," "On a Wonderful Day Like Today," "Once in a Lifetime," "People Tree," "I Do Not Love You," "Good Old, Bad Old Days," "Candy Man" and "Talk to the Animals." These over-the-top tunes allow Newley to be as theatrical and campy as he wants, which means that *Collection* serves as a good introduction to the essence of his music, even if it doesn't have too many hits. *—Stephen Thomas Erlewine*

Wayne Newton

b. Apr. 3, 1942, Roanoke, VA
Vocals, Guitar / Traditional Pop, Vocal Pop, Show Tunes
At several times close to joining George Hamilton in the select group of persons more famous for their celebrity status than for any active artistic creation, Wayne Newton recorded for the 1960s album market and scored several hits during that time, but has become most renowned for his connections to Las Vegas, where he commanded up to $1 million per month at his peak and invested heavily into the city's real estate. Newton's early singles charted well, led by 1963's Top 20 hit "Danke Schoen" (a staple of his act for the rest of his life), but the rest of the '60s saw only one upper-reaches chart entry, "Red Roses for a Blue Lady" (the corresponding album was his only Top 20 entry). The beginning of the '70s saw Newton cut the biggest hit of his life, the number four "Daddy Don't You Walk So Fast," He began focusing more and more on his Las Vegas show after his voice began to lower. Remaking his image into a slick Mr. Entertainment instead of the wide-eyed innocent of his "Danke Schoen" days, Newton became the king of Las Vegas by the 1980s; he won the Entertainer of the Year award more than any other performer, set a record as the highest-paid nightclub performer in history, and bought the Aladdin casino. Despite the acres of fame and riches, Newton was forced to file bankruptcy after he lost a libel lawsuit against a 1991 NBC documentary which questioned if mob money had helped buy the Aladdin. Several multi-million dollar performances around the world cured his financial blues, and in no time he was back on top. *—John Bush*

The Best of Wayne Newton Now / 1985 / Curb ✦✦✦
Best of Wayne Newton Now is a ten-track budget-priced collection that features re-recordings of some of his biggest hits, including "U.S. Male, " "Danke Schoen, " "Daddy Don't You Walk So Fast, " "She's My Saturday Night Special" and "Red Roses for a Blue Lady." Although this isn't a bad budget-priced disc, there are better collections available, offering more songs and better sound, as well as the actual hit versions, for not much more money. *—Stephen Thomas Erlewine*

★ **Capitol Collectors Series** / 1989 / Capitol ✦✦✦✦✦
Thorough overview of his best sides for that label, with great fidelity and comprehensive notes. *—Cub Koda*

The Nylons

f. 1979, Canada
Group / Acappella, Adult Contemporary
The Nylons signed with Attic Records in 1981, just two years after forming in Toronto. Though the original members were Denis Simpson, Paul Cooper, Marc Connors and Claude Morrison, Simpson soon left. Ralph Cole replaced him for a year, but Arnold Robinson replaced Cole in 1980. The a cappella group's self-titled debut appeared in 1982, as did *One Size Fits All.* After 1984's *Seamless,* the Nylons hit the Top 30 with a remake of Steam's "Na Na Hey Hey Kiss Him Goodbye." The album it appeared on, *Happy Together,* also did well. Paul Cooper left the quartet after 1989's *Rockapella* and was replaced by Micah Barnes. *Four on the Floor* was released in 1991, but Mark Connors died the same year. New addition Billy Newton-Davis had been a successful solo artist (*Love Is a Contact Sport, Spellbound*) prior to joining the Nylons for 1992's *Live to Love. Run For Cover* was released in 1996 and *Wish For You* followed four years later. *—John Bush*

Happy Together / 1987 / Windham Hill ✦✦✦✦✦

● **The Best of the Nylons** / 1993 / Windham Hill ✦✦✦✦✦

Hits of the 60's: A Cappella Style / May 27, 1997 / Scotti Bros. ✦✦✦
The Nylons had their biggest hit with a cover of Steam's "Na Na Na Na (Kiss Him Good Bye)," so it isn't a big surprise that they eventually decided to record an album like *Hits of the '60s: A Cappella Style,* where they arrange a selection of familiar oldies in their signature style. The songs might not be particularly challenging ("Time of the Season," "My Cherie Amour," "The Shoop Shoop Song (It's in His Kiss)," "Lady Madonna," "One Fine Day"), but the Nylons make the album into a pleasant nostalgia trip for baby boomers. *—Rodney Batdorf*

Anita O'Day (Anita Belle Colton)

b. Oct. 18, 1919, Chicago, IL
Vocals / Vocal Jazz, Traditional Pop, Swing, Bop
One of the finest singers to emerge from the swing era, Anita O'Day at her prime was a masterful scat singer and a true improviser whose interpretations of standards uplifted and altered even the most familiar songs. Her big break was hooking up with the Gene Krupa Orchestra—during her two years with the drummer's big band (1941-43), O'Day had hits in "Let Me Off Uptown," "Thanks for the Boogie Ride," and "Bolero at the Savoy." She was with Stan Kenton for a year (1944-45), scoring with "And Her Tears Flowed like Wine." After a period back with Krupa (during which she recorded popular versions of "Opus No. 1" and "Boogie Blues"), O'Day went out on her own. She recorded for Signature in 1947 and London in 1950 but did not appear on records on a regular basis until she began her association with Verve in 1952. The singer's finest recordings were for Verve during 1952-63, both with big bands and small groups. Very open to the innovations of bebop, O'Day was one of the top singers of the decade. *—Scott Yanow*

Verve Jazz Masters 49 / 1952-1963 / Verve ✦✦✦✦✦
This is an excellent one-disc roundup of Anita O'Day's output for Clef, Norgan and Verve—arguably her most important, most experimental period—and it is especially valuable because Anita and her manager Alan Eichler made the selections themselves. It was during this decade of activity that O'Day made the transition from a spent former big-band thrush to an acclaimed jazz diva, despite the turmoil in her personal life and her feeling that she was playing second-fiddle to Ella in Norman Granz' recording stable. The selection is remarkably wide-ranging, sampling from twelve of O'Day's sixteen albums for Granz and his successor at Verve, Creed Taylor, with lots of loosely swinging mid- and uptempo numbers and ballads that can be alternately world-wise and innocent. Among the many highlights that illustrate the diversity of O'Day's Verve period are "No Soap, No Hope Blues," from O'Day's first rare ten-inch album for Granz; her saucy remake of "Boogie Blues" with the innovative Gary McFarland orchestra; and the sexy, swaggering title track of *Waiter, Make Mine Blues.* Anyone seeking an entryway into the tough yet vulnerable song world of Anita O'Day will get a lot of helpful direction from this album. *—Richard S. Ginell*

Pick Yourself Up with Anita O'Day / Dec. 15, 1956–Dec. 17, 1956 / Verve ✦✦✦✦✦
For this well-rounded CD reissue that adds nine cuts to the original program, Anita O'Day, in her prime period, is mostly heard accompanied by Buddy Bregman's Orchestra, but there are also a few tracks on which she is joined by a jazz combo featuring trumpeter Harry "Sweets" Edison. Highlights include "Don't Be That Way," "Stompin' at the Savoy," "Pick Yourself Up," "Sweet Georgia Brown" and "I Won't Dance." Virtually all of Anita O'Day's 1950s recordings are recommended, for her drug use had not yet affected her voice and her creativity was generally at its height. *—Scott Yanow*

★ **Anita Sings the Most** / Jan. 31, 1957 / Verve ✦✦✦✦✦
Anita O'Day recorded many rewarding albums in the 1950s when her voice was at its strongest, and this collaboration with the Oscar Peterson Quartet (comprised of pianist Peterson, guitarist Herb Ellis, bassist Ray Brown and drummer John Poole) may very well be her best. Not only is the backup swinging, giving a *Jazz at the Philharmonic* feel to some of the songs, but O'Day proves that she could keep up with Peterson. "Them There Eyes" is taken successfully at a ridiculously fast tempo, yet the singer displays a great deal of warmth on such ballads as "We'll Be Together Again" and "Bewitched, Bothered and Bewildered." While Peterson and Ellis have some solos, O'Day is never overshadowed (which is saying a lot) and is clearly inspired by their presence. The very brief playing time (just 33 minutes) is unfortunate on this straight CD reissue of the original LP, but the high quality definitely makes up for the lack of quantity. A gem. *—Scott Yanow*

Anita O'Day Sings the Winners / Apr. 2, 1958-Apr. 3, 1958 / Verve ✦✦✦✦✦
For this CD, which is greatly expanded from the original LP, Anita O'Day sings standards associated with other musicians, including "Four" (Miles Davis), "Early Autumn" (Stan Getz), "Four Brothers" (Woody Herman), "Sing, Sing, Sing" (Benny Goodman and Gene Krupa) and "Peanut Vendor" (Stan Kenton). Some of the material is unusual for a singer to interpret, but O'Day, one of the top jazz vocalists of the decade, improvises when the lyrics are not that strong (or barely exist). The backup by the Russ Garcia Orchestra is not all that memorable, but the focus is entirely on the vocalist, and O'Day really comes through. *—Scott Yanow*

Anita O'Day Swings Cole Porter with Billy May / Apr. 2, 1959-Apr. 9, 1959 / Verve ✦✦✦✦

Cool Heat / Jul. 1959 / Verve ✦✦✦✦✦
This LP, reissued in limited edition on CD in Japan, finds Anita O'Day's swinging singing backed by cool-toned arrangements from Jimmy Giuffre. Although the orchestra is surprisingly anonymous, the ensembles fit O'Day's voice well on tunes such as "Mack the Knife," "Gone with the Wind," "Come Rain or Come Shine," "The Way You Look Tonight" and even "Hooray for Hollywood." All of O'Day's recordings for Verve in the 1950s are recommended, and this set is no exception. *—Scott Yanow*

Trav'lin' Light / Jan. 18, 1961-Jan. 19, 1961 / Verve ✦✦✦✦

All the Sad Young Men / Oct. 16, 1961 / Verve ✦✦✦✦✦
When Creed Taylor took over the production reins from Norman Granz when the latter sold Verve to MGM, he continued to place Anita O'Day in imaginative settings that challenged her creativity. On this LP, she was served with a collection of brilliant, difficult big-band charts, courtesy of a 27-year-old emerging master named Gary McFarland who mixed instrumental voices and tempo changes in querulous, turbulent combinations. Even a truly odd pick like "You Came a Long Way From St. Louis" is enlivened with sprouting shafts of outlaw muted brass and reeds. Another highlight is the contemporary update of O'Day's old flag-waver with the Krupa band, "Boogie Blues," complete with one of her patented flip upturned glissandos at the end. This album must have been a traumatic experience for O'Day, for as she tells the story, the tapes of McFarland's arrangements arrived by mail from New York and she had to overdub her vocals in an empty studio in Los Angeles. Yet it is a tribute to O'Day's abilities that she makes it all sound easy, exhibiting a freedom in phrasing and improvising that is extraordinary even for her. *—Richard S. Ginell*

Time for Two / Feb. 26, 1962-Feb. 28, 1962 / Verve ✦✦✦✦
In another experiment, producer Creed Taylor teams O'Day with the alternately Latin and bop-grounded quartet of vibraphonist Cal Tjader—and he gets some amazing performances from this team. O'Day sounds as if she is delighted with Tjader's polished Afro-Cuban grooves, gliding easily over the rhythms, toying with the tunes, transforming even a tune so locked into its trite time as "Mr. Sandman" into a stimulating excursion. Indeed, O'Day's freewheeling phrasing becomes downright sexy on "That's Your Red Wagon" and Dave Frishberg's delicious parody of a spoiled honeybunch, "Peel Me a Grape." Also, thanks to Taylor's obsession with good engineering and tasteful applications of reverb, O'Day's voice sounds much fuller and more attractive in his productions than on her Norman Granz-produced albums. *—Richard S. Ginell*

I Get a Kick Out of You / Apr. 25, 1975 / Evidence ✦✦✦✦

Let Me Off Uptown: The Best of Anita O'Day / Jun. 15, 1999 / Columbia/Legacy ✦✦✦✦✦
If Gene Krupa's band needed a signature tune during Anita O'Day's tenure with the group, it was "Kick It!," track 11 of this collection, which includes her exhortation to "keep the rhythm moving." The 18 songs on this CD come primarily from O'Day's first stint with the band, when she was frequently paired with singer-trumpeter Roy Eldridge in one of the great ensembles of the last great years of the big band era. This collection starts with the name-dropping "Opus One" from her second stint with Krupa in 1945, which showed no slackening of her ability to twist a song with the best players. The earlier numbers, pairing her with Eldridge, are even better. In particular, "Thanks for the Boogie Ride" was the basis for a hot little soundie (which Columbia ought to find a way to re-release) featuring the two of them. "Barrelhouse Bessie From Basin Street" also features a duet between the two as well as Krupa in a featured spot that isn't played fast for a change. O'Day could also sound just plain sultry, as on her rendition of "Georgia on My Mind" from her earliest session with Krupa. This CD slots in perfectly as the complement to Columbia's earlier *Drum Boogie* CD, which covers the Krupa band's work during 1940 and early 1941. *Let Me Off Uptown* picks up where *Drum Boogie* leaves off, basically distilling the best cuts from Columbia's earlier Krupa double LP, processing them with a good amount of care to provide a level of fidelity that is a genuine pleasure to hear. *—Bruce Eder*

Patti Page (Clara Ann Fowler)

b. Nov. 8, 1927, Muskogee, OK
Vocals / Traditional Pop, Nashville Sound/Countrypolitan, Vocal Pop, Country-Pop
The best-selling female singer during the 1950s, Patti Page in many ways defined the decade of earnest, novelty-ridden adult pop with throwaway hits like "The Doggie in the Window" and "I Went to Your Wedding." By singing a wide range of popular material and her own share of novelty fluff, she proved easily susceptible to the fall of classic adult pop, but remained a chart force into the mid-'60s. After singing professionally on radio and touring with a band, Page ended up in Chicago by 1947, where she sang in a small-group outing by Benny Goodman and gained a recording contract with Mercury. After a few hits, Page gained her first million-seller in 1950 for "With My Eyes Wide Open I'm Dreaming." Also in 1950, "All My Love" became her first number one hit and spent several weeks at the top. Already having an incredible year, Page hit with one more song, "The Tennessee Waltz." Notched at number one for months, it eventually became one of the best-selling singles of all time and prompted no less than six Top 40 covers during the following year.

During 1952-53, Patti Page scored two more huge hits, "I Went to Your Wedding" and "The Doggie in the Window," both of which spent more than two months at number one.

Page also proved more resilient than her contemporaries to the rise of rock & roll, hitting big during 1956-57 with "Allegheny Moon" and "Old Cape Cod." Indeed, she kept reaching the charts (if only in moderate placings) throughout the '60s, paced by the Top Ten theme to the film *Hush, Hush, Sweet Charlotte* in 1965. Though she stopped recording for the most part in 1968, she continued performing into the '90s. *—John Bush*

In the Land of Hi Fi / 1956 / EmArcy ✦✦✦
A better title for this album might have been "Patti Page tries to pull a Sinatra," as she delves into swinging jazz, seemingly far removed from "Doggie In the Window" and much of her other pop material from this period. The original notes on *In the Land of Hi-Fi* tell us that Patti Page "has never been too far removed from jazz." That's not in dispute, since she came of age in a time—the big-band era—when the influence of jazz was at its peak. But she is fundamentally a pop singer, regardless of her influences or the rhythmic qualities of her phrasing. Page's persona as a singer is more dramatic than anything else, and even in those moments where she lightens up (as on some verses of "A Foggy Day"), she's still giving more of an emotional, almost acting performance than a musical performance. Some of the rest, including "Mountain Greenery," "My Kind of Love," and "I Didn't Know About You." work better, all more comfortable fits between singer, band, and song, but there's still not enough to make this record more than an offbeat curio in Page's career. For this album, she was joined by Pete Rugolo and His Orchestra, who sometimes seem rather ham-fisted, trying to punch home jazz and swing elements—Buddy Childers' trumpet on "Mountain Greenery" and the alto sax heard on "I've Got My Eyes on You" are enjoyable enough, and the band is sometimes more diverting than Page. On other occasions, as on "Love for Sale," the band is so busy behind Page's surprisingly tender and edgy singing, that it's almost a distraction. *—Bruce Eder*

16 Most Requested Songs / 1991 / Columbia/Legacy ✦✦✦✦
16 Most Requested Songs is a midline-priced collection that spotlights many of Patti Page's best-known and most popular performances for Columbia Records, including "Tennessee Waltz," "Green, Green Grass of Home," "Scarlet Ribbons (For Her Hair)," "I'll Never Fall in Love Again," "Little Green Apples," "Call Me Irresponsible," "The Days of Wine and Roses," "How Much is That Doggie in the Window" and "Raindrops Keep Falling on My Head." Although it's far from a perfect retrospective of her career, it's still a nice sampler of familiar items, and it may satisfy the needs of some casual fans who only want the hits. *—Stephen Thomas Erlewine*

★ **The Patti Page Collection: The Mercury Years, Vol. 1** / Jan. 1991 / Mercury ✦✦✦✦✦
When Mercury Records finally got around to compiling a Patti Page's hits for the CD era (the ten-track LP *Golden Hits* had been in print since 1960), the label opted to create two separate volumes, one containing the singer's early hits, the other her later ones. While fans might have preferred a single-disc greatest hits album containing all of her biggest singles, the two-volume approach allowed Mercury to bring back into print many of Page's lesser hits of the 1950s. The first volume, a 20-track collection, includes most of the 26 chart entries she achieved between 1948 and 1952. All 13 Top Ten hits from the period are included, among them the chart-toppers "All My Love," "The Tennessee Waltz," "Mockin' Bird Hill," and "I Went to Your Wedding." Below the Top Ten, however, compiler Ron Furmanek has made judgment calls so that, for example, "So In Love," which made the Top 20, is not here, while "Evertrue Evermore" is, which only made the Top 30. This is a solid collection which contains some excellent material that, despite its popularity, rarely gets onto compilations, such as Page's recording of "I Don't Care If the Sun Don't Shine," later cut by Elvis Presley. But fans wanting any of her hits from after 1952, starting with "The Doggie in the Window," will have to invest in the second volume as well. *—William Ruhlmann*

The Patti Page Collection: The Mercury Years, Vol. 2 / Feb. 1991 / Mercury ✦✦✦✦✦
20 hits from 1952-1962 include "Old Cape Cod" and "Allegheny Moon" include informative packaging. *—Hank Davis*

Mandy Patinkin (Mandel Bruce Patinkin)

b. Nov. 30, 1952, Chicago, IL
Vocals / Traditional Pop, Soundtracks, Musicals, Cast Recordings, Show Tunes
Actor/singer Mandy Patinkin carved out a varied career onstage, in films, in the recording studio, and on television. Though he was possessed of a flexible tenor voice with a wide range and was known for his bravura performing style, few of his movie appearances made use of his musical ability, and he was more widely known as a dramatic actor on television than for anything else. Nevertheless, he was one of the major American musical theater performers of his generation. Patinkin studied at the Juilliard School of Drama, and got his big break in 1979 when cast as Che in the Broadway production of *Evita,* a role that won him the Tony Award. In the early '80s, Patinkin appeared in a series of films, but made a triumphant return to the Broadway stage in 1984, starring in the musical *Sunday in the Park with George.* His performance established him as an important interpreter of the music of Stephen Sondheim, Broadway's most respected songwriter, and he consolidated that status with his appearance in a 1985 concert version of Sondheim's 1971 musical *Follies.* Signed to CBS, he released his debut album *Mandy Patinkin,* in 1989.

Patinkin returned to Broadway in a big way in 1991 with the successful musical *The Secret Garden.* While fans adored his energetic, committed style (which reminded some of the days of Al Jolson and Ethel Merman), detractors often criticized him for the same tendencies, which they found exaggerated. Patinkin earned an Emmy for his work on the television drama *Chicago Hope,* but left the program soon after largely due to family considerations. His fourth album, *Oscar & Steve,* was a tribute to Oscar Hammerstein II and Stephen Sondheim. In 1998, he released his fifth album, *Mamaloshen,* which found him singing traditional and other material in Yiddish. *—William Ruhlmann*

● **Mandy Patinkin** / 1989 / Columbia ✦✦✦✦✦
Patinkin has reserves of emotion that seem boundless on this tour de force collection mainly given over to show songs. Employing a vocal range that begins in a clear high tenor and plunges to a gruff baritone, Patinkin is able to act and sing duets with himself or sing beautifully alone. But feeling—sometimes overflowing feeling—is the core of his sense of interpretation. As a result, some very old songs sound newly written in his hands. *—William Ruhlmann*

Dress Casual / 1990 / Columbia ✦✦✦✦✦
An enormously ambitious collection of show and film music dominated by suites and medleys taken from Stephen Sondheim's obscure *Evening Primrose* (with guest Bernadette Peters) and *Pal Joey.* *—William Ruhlmann*

Experiment / May 17, 1994 / Nonesuch ✦✦✦

Oscar & Steve / Oct. 24, 1995 / Nonesuch ✦✦✦
The relationship between Oscar Hammerstein II and Stephen Sondheim is among the most confounding in the American musical theater. On the one hand, Hammerstein was Sondheim's spiritual father, the guiding force that led him to become a writer of theater songs. On the other, the optimistic, wholesome attitude expressed in Hammerstein's lyrics and librettos could not be more different from the skeptical, subversive wit of Sondheim. Mandy Patinkin confronted this dichotomy head-on in his fourth album, alternating songs by the two, following Hammerstein's "If I Loved You" with Sondheim's "I Wish I Could Forget You," Hammerstein's "Honey Bun" with Sondheim's "Not A Day Goes By." Those juxtapositions emphasized the differences, but Patinkin also found similarities in some pairings. The odd

thing was that, though Patinkin is identified with Sondheim, here he was more comfortable with Hammerstein. He is able to appreciate the ambivalent anguish of "I Wish I Could Forget You" and the savage wit of "Remember," but he's too nice to plumb the cruelty of either song. On the other hand, Hammerstein's embrace of sentiment is similar to Patinkin's, and in songs like "If I Loved You," "Bali Ha'i," and "Honey Bun," he was able to indulge his energy and back-wall-of-the-theater bellow. Sondheim can thank Patinkin for making his songs seem more conventional and acceptable than they really are. Here, Patinkin even found surprising warmth in two of the austere songs from *Passion*. But, despite Patinkin's obvious affection for Sondheim, that doesn't make him the ideal interpreter. On the other hand, listening to this record makes you wonder what he could do with Hammerstein standards like "Ol' Man River" or "Oklahoma!" *—William Ruhlmann*

Mamaloshen / Feb. 17, 1998 / Nonesuch ✦✦✦✦

Les Paul (Lester William Poifus)

b. Jun. 9, 1915, Waukesha, WI
Guitar (Electric), Guitar / Traditional Pop, Vocal Pop, Swing
Les Paul has had such a staggeringly huge influence over the way American popular music sounds today that many tend to overlook his significant impact upon the jazz world. Before his attention was diverted toward recording multi-layered hits for the pop market, he made his name as a brilliant jazz guitarist whose exposure on coast-to-coast radio programs guaranteed a wide audience of susceptible young musicians. Heavily influenced by Django Reinhardt at first, Paul eventually developed an astonishingly fluid, hard-swinging style of his own, one that featured extremely rapid runs, fluttered and repeated single notes, and chunking rhythm support, mixing in country & western licks and humorous crowd-pleasing effects. No doubt his brassy style gave critics a bad time, but the gregarious, garrulous Paul didn't much care; he was bent on showing his audiences a good time. Though he couldn't read music, Paul had a magnificent ear and innate sense of structure, conceiving complete arrangements entirely in his head before he set them down track by track on disc or tape. Even on his many pop hits for Capitol in the late '40s and early '50s, one can always hear a jazz sensibility at work in the rapid lead solo lines and bluesy bent notes—and no one could close a record as suavely as Les. And of course, his early use of the electric guitar and pioneering experiments with multitrack recording, guitar design and electronic effects devices have filtered down to countless jazz musicians. Among the jazzers who acknowledge his influence are George Benson, Al DiMeola, Stanley Jordan (whose neck-tapping sound is very reminiscent of Paul's records), Pat Martino and Bucky Pizzarelli. *—Richard S. Ginell*

The Complete Decca Trios—*Plus (1936-1947)* */ May 11, 1936-Jul. 25, 1947 / MCA* ✦✦✦✦✦
The Complete Decca Trios—Plus is a double-disc, 50-track collection containing all of the recordings Les Paul made for Decca between 1936 and 1947, including all of his released and unreleased masters, plus several tracks he cut with fellow Decca recording artists. These are the recordings that earned Paul's reputation as an excellent guitarist and they show his extraordinary range. He could play jazz and Hawaiian music, swing with big bands or subtly support singers like Bing Crosby, Helen Forrest and the Andrews Sisters. All of that is featured here, on a collection that is essential for anyone with an interest in Paul or the history of the electric guitar. *—Stephen Thomas Erlewine*

☆ **The Legend and the Legacy** / Feb. 1948-Dec. 23, 1957 / Capitol ✦✦✦✦✦
If you're going for the big gulp, you could do no better than this excellent four-disc box set, which covers all the highlights of Les Paul and Mary Ford's tenure with the label. Sparkling sound abounds throughout (even on the old acetate masters like "Lover"), with the first three discs covering not only the best issued Capitol masters, but three of Paul and Ford's radio shows for NBC and assorted catchy radio commercials for Robert Hall clothiers and Rheingold beer. The fourth disc in the set features no less than 34 previously unreleased tracks (most worked up for the *Les Paul & Mary Ford at Home* television show) with absolutely no letdown in the quality, musical or otherwise. Combined with all this great music is a booklet that is exemplary in its scope, chock-full of great photos, the best liners you could ask for on the duo by Stephen K. Peeples, and, best of all, a track-by-track running commentary from Les himself, right down to what guitar he used. Exhaustive and illuminating, both legend and legacy are served well here. *—Cub Koda*

16 Most Requested Songs / Jul. 13, 1958-Oct. 5, 1961 / Columbia/Legacy ✦✦✦
Paul and Ford were coming to the end of both their personal and professional partnership when these sides were recorded for Columbia between 1958 and 1961. Their reign on the charts was finishing, too; only a couple of these ("Put a Ring on My Finger" and "Jura") made the lower reaches of the Top 40. Their Columbia output hasn't played too well with critics, and while you should certainly head for the Capitol material first, this disc is hardly disgraceful. Paul's guitar chops and double-tracking wizardry are still much in evidence, all imbued with that hollow reverb that sounds like no one else. Some of this has a pop-rockabilly feel, as if the team was trying to be a bit trendy, out of commercial desperation; nonetheless, those tunes, as well as Les' instrumental showcases, have worn better than the pop ballads that fill out the rest of the compilation. Includes one previously unissued cut, "I Am My Love's." *—Richie Unterberger*

★ **The Best of the Capitol Masters: Selections from "The Legend and the Legacy" Box Set** / Jul. 20, 1992 / Capitol ✦✦✦✦✦
A good single-disc distillation of the highlights of Les Paul's epic four-disc box set, *The Legend and the Legacy, Best of the Capitol Years* is all most casual fans will need to own. *—Stephen Thomas Erlewine*

Edith Piaf (Edith Giovanna Gassion)

b. Dec. 15, 1915, Paris, France, **d.** Oct. 11, 1963, Paris, France
Vocals / French Pop, Cabaret, Vocal Pop, Torch Songs, Nostalgia
Probably the most popular French singer ever due to her *chansons* performed with passion and force, Edith Piaf's inimitable voice conquered millions of listeners during several decades. Some of the songs she wrote herself ("La vie en rose," "L'hymne a l'amour"), the others were the results of her long-time collaboration with such composers as R. Asso ("Mon Legionnaire"), Georges Moustaki ("Milord") and Charles Dumont ("Non, je ne regrette rien"). She was often affectionately called 'Sparrow of Paris' ('Piaf' means 'sparrow' in French). *—Yuri German*

★ **The Very Best of Edith Piaf: Voice of the Sparrow** / Jul. 22, 1991 / Capitol ✦✦✦✦✦

Mon Legionnaire / Nov. 11, 1997 / Arkadia Chansons ✦✦✦✦✦
The most revered and celebrated French singer of the 20th Century, Edith Piaf was only 20 when she first recorded for Polydor's French division in 1936. But even on her early recordings, Piaf sang with the wisdom, maturity and depth of a seasoned veteran artist—a fact that's hard to miss on *Mon Legionnaire*. Spanning 1937-1940, this superb CD focuses on Piaf's early work and boasts many of the gems that put her on the map in France, including "Je N'en Connais Pas La Fin," "J'entends La Sirene," "Le Chacal" and the title song. Though Piaf was never a jazz singer, some of the orchestral arrangements are influenced by the American big-band swing of the 1930s, as well as American sweet bands (whose focus was pop with jazz overtones). The sound quality isn't ideal—one wishes that Arkadia's digital remastering had filtered out more of the noise and that classics like "C'est Lui Que Mon Couer A Choisi" and "Le Voyage Du Pauvre Negre" could be heard without so many pops, crackles and clicks. Even so, the richness of the music comes through loud and clear. *Mon Legionnaire* is a CD to savor. *—Alex Henderson*

The Pied Pipers

Group / Traditional Pop, Vocal Pop
Originally consisting of eight members, the Pied Pipers had their greatest success after nearly half of the members left the group. The remaining Pipers (Billy Wilson, Chuck Lowry, Jo Stafford, and her then-husband John Huddleston) joined the Tommy Dorsey Band in 1939, backing Sinatra on many classic recordings. In 1942 the Pied Pipers broke away from Dorsey, and Huddleston joined the army, to be replaced by Hal Hopper, one of the original eight members. The group backed Johnny Mercer on several tracks during the early 40s, including "Candy" and "Blues in the Night." Their first single ("Deacon Jones"/"Pistol Packin' Mama") was released in 1943. Stafford had become quite busy with her solo career and left the group in 1944, to be replaced by June Hutton. Throughout the rest of the decade the Pied Pipers charted frequently, yet their popularity waned in the '50s. A group bearing the Pied Pipers' name still tours today. *—Stephen Thomas Erlewine*

★ **Capitol Collectors Series** / 1992 / Capitol ✦✦✦✦✦
A terrific 20-track overview of this early vocal group featuring all of their best-known songs, including "The Trolley Song, " "Dream, " "Open the Door, Richard, " "Mam'selle, " and "My Happiness." The remastering is top-notch, and the liner notes contain many anecdotes and a great deal of information. *—Stephen Thomas Erlewine*

The Best of the Pied Pipers Featuring Jo Stafford / 1997 / Collectors' Choice Music ✦✦✦✦✦
This 25-track compilation presents the ten tracks the Pied Pipers recorded for Capitol Records in 1943 and 1944 while Jo Stafford was still a member of the group, plus three tracks on which the Pipers, with Stafford's replacement, June Hutton, backed up their former lead singer, and 12 tracks by the Hutton-era group recorded through 1948. Capitol Records' own 1992 compilation, the 20-track *Capitol Collectors' Series*, focused more on the Hutton period, including only four Stafford tracks and featuring more of the Hutton-era hits. This set is more varied, including the Pipers' biggest hits, "The Trolley Song," "Dream," "Mam'selle" and "My Happiness," but also featuring such guest performers as Johnny Mercer and Andy Russell. And, of course, it will find favor with Jo Stafford fans. *—William Ruhlmann*

Whatcha Know Joe: The Best of the Dorsey Years / Apr. 13, 1999 / Razor & Tie ✦✦✦✦
The Pied Pipers' tenure with Tommy Dorsey's swing band is fondly recalled on *Whatcha Know Joe*, an excellent 21-track compilation capturing the group's biggest war-era hits. Although Jo Stafford is spotlighted on songs including "Embraceable You" and "The Night We Called It a Day," even more noteworthy are four tracks featuring Frank Sinatra ("Dolores," "I'll Take Tallulah," "You Might Have Belonged to Another" and "Let's Get Away from It All," the latter two duets with Connie Haines). *—Raymond McKinney*

Cole Porter

b. Jun. 9, 1891, Peru, IN, **d.** Oct. 15, 1964, Santa Monica, CA
Piano, Composer / Tin Pan Alley Pop, Standards
Many arguements could be generated over whether Cole Porter or Irving Berlin should be considered America's greatest tunesmith. Both wrote music and lyrics; it's clearly a pick 'em situation. The list of Porter shows and films is immense; his lyrics were literate, sophisticated, yet could be charming, suggestive, even naughty. His first show was *Paris* in 1928; it included "Let's Do It." That was followed by *Frenchmen* in 1929 containing "You Do Something to Me." *Wake Up and Dream, The New Yorkers, The Gay Divorcee, Jubilee, Leave It to Me* and *Kiss Me Kate* are only a few of his marvelous shows. The song list is just as impressive; "What Is This Thing Called Love," "Love for Sale," "Anything Goes," "You're the Top," "Begin the Beguine," and "Count Your Blessings" for starters. There were also such films as as *Silk Stockings, Born To Dance, Broadway Melody of 1940, High Society* and *Night and Day*. Porter's legs were crushed by a horse in 1937, and he endured numerous operations the rest of his life, as well as being a semi-invalid. He finally lost his right leg in 1958, only four years after his wife died. *—Ron Wynn*

● **The Cole Porter Collection** / 1926-1941 / Jass ✦✦✦✦
This is a delightful 25-song anthology of vintage (1928-1941) recordings of obscure but equally arch Porter songs. Performers include Ethel Waters, the Dorsey Brothers, the Paul Whiteman Orchestra, and others. *—Mark A. Humphrey*

Cole Porter: A Centennial Celebration / Nov. 22, 1932-Dec. 7, 1987 / RCA ✦✦

Louis Prima

b. Dec. 7, 1911, New Orleans, LA, **d.** Aug. 24, 1978, New Orleans, LA
Vocals, Trumpet / Traditional Pop, Jump Blues, Swing, Dixieland, R&B
Louis Prima became very famous in the 1950s with an infectious Las Vegas act co-starring his wife (singer Keely Smith) that mixed together R&B (particularly the honking tenor of Sam Butera), early rock & roll, comedy and Dixieland. Always a colorful personality, Prima was leading a band in New Orleans when he was just 11. In 1934 he began recording as a leader with a Dixieland-oriented unit and soon he was a major attraction on 52nd Street. His early records often featured George Brunies and Eddie Miller, and Pee Wee Russell was a regular member of his groups during 1935-36. Prima, who composed "Sing, Sing, Sing" (which for a period was his theme song), recorded steadily through the swing era, had a big band in the 1940s and achieved hits in "Angelina" and "Robin Hood." In 1954 he began having great success in his latter-day group (their recordings on Capitol were big sellers and still sound joyous today), emphasizing vocals and Butera's tenor, but he still took spirited trumpet solos. Although he eventually broke up with Keely Smith, Louis Prima (who voiced a character in Walt Disney's animated film *The Jungle Book* in 1966) remained a popular attraction into the 1970s. *—Scott Yanow*

★ **Capitol Collectors Series** / Apr. 19, 1956-Feb. 23, 1962 / Capitol ✦✦✦✦✦
What Louis Prima accomplished musically in the company of Sam Butera and the Witnesses and vocalist Keely Smith is in hard evidence on this excellent 26-track compilation. All the classics are aboard with excellent liner notes from Scott Shea and crisp transfers of the original masters ("Angelina-Zooma Zooma," "That Old Black Magic," "I've Got You Under My Skin," "Buona Sera"—which includes a great snippet of studio chatter kicking it off—"Oh Marie," and the obligatory "Just a Gigolo-I Ain't Got Nobody"). Although this duplicates several tracks with Rhino's *Zooma! Zooma!* compilation (now long out of print), with the addition of several singles and unissued tracks, this stands as the best single-disc collection available of Prima's tenure with Capitol Records. The perfect place to start your Louis Prima collection. *—Cub Koda*

☆ **The Wildest!** / Jan. 1957 / DCC ✦✦✦✦✦
A veritable greatest-hits album, *The Wildest!* is the gem of Louis Prima's catalogue. None of his other efforts transcend its raunchy mix of demented gibberish, blaring sax, and explosive swing, which rocked as hard as anything released at the time. Almost all of Prima's signature songs are found here: "Just a Gigolo/I Ain't Got Nobody," "Oh Marie," "Jump, Jive, an' Wail," and "Buona Sera," to name a few. A plethora of greatest-hits packages (especially Capitol's *Collectors Series*) may offer wider song selection and greater value, but the reissue of Prima's masterpiece is a welcome event that's been a long time coming. *—Jim Smith*

1935-1936 / Jan. 11, 2000 / Melodie Jazz Classics ✦✦✦

Flora Purim

b. Mar. 6, 1942, Rio de Janeiro, Brazil
Vocals / Vocal Jazz, Brazilian Jazz, Latin Jazz, Fusion
Influenced by both traditional Brazilian singers and the improvisations of American jazz divas like Ella Fitzgerald and Sarah Vaughan, Flora Purim was one of the most adventurous singers of the 1970s. After meeting and marrying her husband, percussionist Airto Moreira, in their native Brazil, Purim moved with him to the U.S. in the late 1960s. Though she worked with Stan Getz and pianist Duke Pearson before the decade ended, it wasn't until joining Chick Corea, Joe Farrell, Stanley Clarke and Moreira in the original Return to Forever in 1972 that she became well known in the States. Purim showed considerable promise on Forever classics like "500 Miles High" and "Light as a Feather" and lived up to it when she went solo with 1973's *Butterfly Dreams.* Ranging from superb to passably decent, Purim's Milestone dates of the mid- to late '70s kept her quite visible in the jazz world. Purim's work grew erratic and uneven in the 1980s, and she wasn't recording as often (though she did provide one album for Virgin and three with Moreira for Concord's Crossover label). Purim didn't record very often in the early to mid-'90s either, but she continued to be highly regarded in Brazilian jazz circles. *—Alex Henderson*

● **Butterfly Dreams** / Dec. 1973 / Milestone/OJC ✦✦✦✦✦
This is the album that launched Flora Purim's solo career with great promise following her magnificent stint with Chick Corea's first incarnation of Return to Forever. Most of the tracks on this album sound like they would have fit very nicely onto one of RTF's first two LPs, with bandmate Stanley Clarke not only lending support on electric and acoustic bass, but also contributing original compositions and arrangements to the mix. The rest of the supporting cast is not too shabby either, including sax and flute man Joe Henderson, keyboard whiz kid George Duke, guitarist David Amaro, and Flora's other half, percussion legend Airto Moreira. Clarke's funky "Dr. Jive" and lyrical "Butterfly Dreams" are standout tracks here, as is the upbeat Egberto Gismonti composition "Moon Dreams." Duke shows his light Brazilian side on "Love Reborn," featuring Henderson's tenor sax solo and Amaro's lovely acoustic guitar. Purim delivers a gorgeous take on Jobim's well-known ballad "Dindi," and reshapes the standard "Summer Night" into a wordless vocal in her unmistakable style. The disc closes with a fine reworking of Clarke's now-classic "Light as a Feather," which strays not too far from the original RTF version. Neatly capturing Flora Purim's many vocal strengths, *Butterfly Dreams* delivered on the great expectations generated by her work with Corea and turned out to be a high point in her recording career. *—Jim Newsom*

Stories to Tell / May 1974-Jul. 1974 / Milestone/OJC ✦✦✦✦
Though her recordings for Chick Corea's *Return to Forever* provide a better introduction to her vocal talents, *Stories to Tell* is an excellent outing by Flora Purim and friends. Assisted by a cast of jazz/fusion all-stars led by husband Airto Moreira, Purim shows off the wide range of her abilities: from wordless vocal soaring to songs with lyrics in English and Portuguese, from uptempo percussion-driven workouts to beautiful ballads. In addition to Airto, the assembled cast includes bassists Miroslav Vitous and Ron Carter, keyboard wunderkind George Duke, guitarists Earl Klugh and Oscar Castro Neves, and trombonist Raul de Souza. Also, Carlos Santana turns in one of his patented sizzling guitar solos on "Silver Sword." With material from Antonio Carlos Jobim, Vitous, Milton Nascimento, McCoy Tyner, and Purim herself, this is an album worth savoring. *—Jim Newsom*

500 Miles High / Jul. 6, 1974 / Milestone/OJC ✦✦✦✦✦

Open Your Eyes You Can Fly / 1976 / Milestone/OJC ✦✦✦

Encounter / Apr. 1976 / Milestone/OJC ✦✦✦✦✦
This was one of Flora Purim's finest all-around jazz recordings, and it is luckily available on CD. Purim is featured in a variety of challenging and stimulating settings: on two numbers ("Above the Rainbow" and "Tomara") with pianist McCoy Tyner, teamed up with tenor saxophonist Joe Henderson on Chick Corea's "Windows" and "Black Narcissus," and utilizing such players as bass trombonist Raul de Souza, keyboardists Hemeto Pascoal and George Duke, and singer Urszula Dudziak (who is heard on "Encounter") plus Flora's husband, percussionist Airto. The music is primarily group originals and finds Flora Purim in peak form. Highly recommended. *—Scott Yanow*

The Ravens

f. 1946, New York, NY, **db.** 1956
Group / Doo Wop, R&B
The Ravens were among the pioneering post-World War II R&B groups, and also among the earliest R&B groups named for birds. In both their musicality and their nomenclature, they influenced two generations of performers that followed, as well as selling lots of records in the process. Formed by a quartet based in Harlem, the Ravens were booked into a club and proved themselves sufficiently talented to rate a national tour. The group's sound was unusual for its time, featuring bass singer Jimmy Ricks as the lead voice—this would become their trademark and one of their most often emulated attributes over the next decade.

The Ravens enjoyed their first hit in 1947 with a version of "Old Man River," perhaps the best of a succession of eight Top Ten R&B hits over the next decade. By 1948, the Ravens were already an influence on dozens, perhaps hundreds of R&B vocal groups coalescing around the variety of sound that they were bringing to the charts. Though they only enjoyed one major chart hit ("Rock Me All Night Long"), the group was commanding a fee of $2000 a night for their performances during the early '50s. The end came for the group when Jimmy Ricks left for a solo career in 1956. As an indication of the flexibility of Jimmy Ricks' singing voice and the respect he commanded even after more than 25 years as an R&B vocalist, he joined the Count Basie band as its vocalist in the early '70s, a capacity in which he was serving at the time of his death in 1974. The Ravens never recorded as much as their main rival group, the Orioles, and have never received the kind of comprehensive retrospective accorded the latter group. *—Bruce Eder*

● **The Greatest Group of Them All** / 1978 / Savoy ✦✦✦✦✦

Johnnie Ray

b. Jan. 10, 1927, Dallas, OR, **d.** Feb. 25, 1990, Los Angeles, CA
Vocals / Traditional Pop, Vocal Pop
Although practically deaf, Johnnie Ray's tear-inflected delivery tabbed him as an early-'50s sensation. Leaving Oregon for Detroit, Ray found a gig at the Flame Club, an R&B and jazz institution. In 1951, Ray signed with Columbia's R&B subsidiary Okeh Records, although "Cry," his histrionic million-seller that year, was a pop entry all the way, with background vocals by the Four Lads. Produced by Mitch Miller, "Cry" remained perched atop the pop charts for nearly three months. Ray encored with "The Little White Cloud That Cried" before moving to the parent Columbia logo and enjoying a steady stream of pop hits, including "Walkin' My Baby Back Home" in 1952 and a cover of The Prisonaires' "Just Walking in the Rain" in 1956. Ray's frenzied antics set off riots among female admirers during his heyday, but the advent of rock soon dulled his hitmaking powers. By 1959, the hits were through. *—Bill Dahl*

★ **16 Most Requested Songs** / 1991 / Columbia/Legacy ✦✦✦✦✦
Johnny Ray's cultural significance—which was only slightly less substantial than that of Elvis Presley—can be summed up with this 45-minute compilation of his hits from 1951 through 1956. The singles are an amazing array of jazz and blues-inflected performances by a white singer, not unheard of at the time, but seldom spoken of as a desirable trait in the pop field in those days. Among those tracks, "All of Me," "Whiskey and Gin," "Walkin' My Baby Back Home," "Don't Blame Me," and "As Time Go By" are worth the price of the CD. There's also a good deal of pop music here, including the duet "Let's Walk That-A-Way" with Doris Day, which, unfortunately, fits easily into her '50s pop music output, and the pop choruses backing him on "Just Walkin' in the Rain" break the spell created by his most interesting vocal performances, but this CD is still a vivid portrait of a singer who broke lots of barriers—and annoyed a lot of critics while doing it—while Elvis Presley was still in high school. The sound is excellent, incidentally, and the notes by Will Friedwald are thorough, though one wishes there were recording and release dates attached to each song. *—Bruce Eder*

High Drama: The Real Johnnie Ray / Oct. 21, 1997 / Columbia/Legacy ✦✦✦✦
Except for the inevitable inclusion of "Cry," the 17 track, 44-and-a-half minute *High Drama: The Real Johnnie Ray* is a rarities compilation. Two tracks, an early version of "She Didn't Say Nothin' at All" and "Paths of Paradise," also recorded in 1951, are previously unreleased; "Ooh! Aah! Oh!," recorded with the Les Elgart Orchestra, "The Lonely Ones," backed by Duke Ellington and His Orchestra, and a live take of "Such a Night" from *the London Palladium* are given their first U.S. issue; and "I Want to Be Loved" and "I'll Make You Mine" are presented in stereo for the first time. Ray alternated between the pre-rock R&B style for which he's best remembered and a more conventional classic pop approach. As its title suggests, this collection's thesis is that the former represents the highly dramatic sound of the "real" Johnnie Ray, and compilation producer Al Quaglieri supports that contention by using bluesy and rockish material, such as "Flip, Flop and Fly" and "Such a Night," songs later covered by Elvis Presley. Five tracks are drawn from Ray's 1957 album *The Big Beat,* which found him confronting the rock & roll trend, albeit with backing by orchestras led by Ray Ellis and Ray Conniff. The result doesn't quite enlist Ray in the rock & roll revolution, but it more than justifies the notion that he was a major precursor to it. *—William Ruhlmann*

Helen Reddy

b. Oct. 25, 1942, Melbourne, Australia
Vocals / Soft Rock, Pop
Helen Reddy began performing at the age of four in her native Australia; by the early 60s she had her own television series. Between 1971 and 1978, Reddy hit the Top 40 fourteen times with her smooth, airy light-pop singles, including #1s "Delta Dawn," "Angie Baby," and "I Am Woman." As her hits petered out toward the end of the '70s, her acting work increased, including roles in *Pete's Dragon, Sgt. Pepper's Lonely Hearts Club Band,* and *Airport 1975.* *— Stephen Thomas Erlewine*

● **I Am Woman: The Essential Helen Reddy Collection** / Sep. 15, 1998 / Razor & Tie ✦✦✦✦✦
This compilation lives up to its name—everything anyone could possibly need to know about Reddy's heyday is included, and more. Dwelling largely on her years at Capitol, and concentrating almost exclusively on single releases, *I Am Woman* is a more comprehensive round-up than 1975's *Greatest Hits.* Among the highlights are "I Am Woman," "Delta Dawn" and "Angie Baby," her hat-trick of US number ones. Album favorite "The West Wind Circus" is here, too, along with a couple of moments from her short and unfruitful 1980s MCA period, and some soundtrack work. Fortunately, the weaker Capitol albums are ignored. Reddy's best work is impressive listening, particularly when shorn of the poor quality album fodder. *— Charles Donovan*

Dianne Reeves

b. 1956, Detroit, MI
Vocals / Vocal Jazz, Traditional Pop, Standards, Vocal Pop, Urban
Dianne Reeves has thus far had a rather confusing career. Blessed with a very attractive voice and the ability to be the premiere jazz singer of this era, Reeves seems reluctant to stick to jazz. Her recordings are often rather schizophrenic affairs, rarely reaching the heights of her exciting live performances. Reeves sang (and recorded) with her high school band and was encouraged by Clark Terry, performing with him while a college student at the Univesity of Colorado. She did session work in Los Angeles starting in 1976, toured with Sergio Mendes (1981) and Harry Belafonte (1984) and first started recording as a solo artist in 1982, soon becoming a familiar name on the festival circuit. Finally in 1994 after shifting back and forth between jazz, pop and African music, Reeves started to commit herself more to jazz, recording the first of several strong jazz sets for Blue Note. It is not yet too late for the singer to fulfill her enormous potential. *— Scott Yanow*

★ **I Remember** / Apr. 27, 1988-Sep. 11, 1990 / Blue Note ✦✦✦✦✦
When she wants to sing jazz, Dianne Reeves has always had the ability to reach the top of her field, but she has long seemed unable to make up her mind between jazz, R&B, world music and pop. This Blue Note disc fortunately finds her mostly sticking to jazz and in consistently superb form. Reeves' treatments of such numbers as "Afro Blue" (which is particularly memorable), "Love for Sale," "Softly as in a Morning Sunrise," "How High the Moon" and McCoy Tyner's "You Taught My Heart to Sing" all border on the classic. Joined by such illustrious sidemen as pianists Billy Childs, Mulgrew Miller and Donald Brown, bassists Charnett Moffett and Chris Severin and drummers Billy Kilson and Marvin "Smitty" Smith plus guest appearances by vibraphonist Bobby Hutcherson, altoist Greg Osby and guitarist Kevin Eubanks, Reeves sounds inspired by the company. If only she would stick to this direction! Highly recommended. *— Scott Yanow*

Quiet After the Storm / 1994 / Blue Note ✦✦✦✦✦
Dianne Reeves, who has always had a beautiful voice and the potential for greatness in jazz, has conducted a rather directionless career, performing many concerts filled with spontaneity while at the same time recording erratic albums that usually feature both veteran jazz ballads and newer material that is closer to pop and folk music. There are some strong jazz moments on this CD. "Comes Love" has an inventive arrangement that uses a riff from the Miles Davis version of "'Round Midnight" and a familiar rhythmic phrase from "Star Eyes" in surprising ways. "Detour Ahead" is fine and "The Benediction" ("Country Preacher" with Reeves's lyrics) is a sincere tribute to Cannonball Adderley (who makes a brief appearance on soprano via sampling) but on some of the other pieces Reeves wanders far away from jazz. She sings a couple of folk songs with guitarist Dori Caymmi, introduces the heartwarming if poppish original "Nine" and performs a very straight version of Joni Mitchell's "When Morning Comes" that makes the song sound like a Broadway show tune. Perhaps Dianne Reeves's eventual niche will be as a jazz-influenced folk-pop singer; someday she should probably make up her mind. *— Scott Yanow*

The Grand Encounter / Apr. 4, 1996-Apr. 9, 1996 / Blue Note ✦✦✦✦✦

That Day . . . / Nov. 4, 1997 / Blue Note ✦✦✦✦
After two solid jazz recordings, this effort by Dianne Reeves finds her returning a bit to her eclectic ways. She sounds joyous and swinging on "Exactly Like You," and making one wonder why she still spends so much time singing R&B and pop. Other highlights include the sexy and saucy "That Day," a spacy version of "Blue Prelude," and the folkish "The Twelfth of Never," but there are also several less interesting numbers that are only worthwhile due to Reeves' attractive voice. The singer is assisted by a small group that includes pianist Mulgrew Miller and drummer Terri Lyne Carrington. *— Scott Yanow*

In the Moment: Live in Concert / Jul. 18, 2000 / Blue Note ✦✦✦

Paul Robeson

b. Apr. 9, 1898, Princeton, NJ, **d.** Jan. 23, 1976, Philadelphia, PA
Vocals / Traditional Gospel, Traditional Pop
Paul Robeson's commanding voice was capable of many wonders—he powerfully sang spirituals and acted in Shakespearean plays and numerous movies (including *Emperor Jones* in 1933 and *King Solomon's Mines* in 1937). Robeson recorded for Victor in 1925, the same year he began collaborating with pianist Lawrence Brown, and his immortal "Ol' Man River" was immensely popular in 1928. As the decades passed, Robeson proved an eloquent spokesman for equality and freedom. *— Bill Dahl*

Paul Robeson Sings "Ol' Man River" & Other Favorites / 1972 / Angel ✦✦✦✦✦
Unlike many Paul Robeson collections of recordings that have been licensed or otherwise obtained and reissued by small labels, this one comes from EMI and purports to be "a collection of his greatest hits." That isn't strictly true, if only because Robeson had few "hits" in the accepted sense, but the 20-track, hour-long album is a good sampler of Robeson's studio recordings made between 1928 and 1939, starting with his signature song, "Ol' Man River." After an earlier association with Victor Records in the U.S., Robeson lived in England and recorded for EMI during this period, and the label gave him supportive symphonic arrangements of traditional material and songs crafted to resemble the spirituals the singer favored. This album is sparsely annotated, and the sound is full of hiss and crackles that later sound technology could remove. But as an accessible, well-chosen compilation of Robeson's best, it earns high marks. *— William Ruhlmann*

● **The Essential Paul Robeson** / 1987 / Vanguard ✦✦✦✦✦
The Essential Paul Robeson is an excellent 30-track collection that contains many of his best performances for Vanguard Records. Everything from folk and gospel songs to Shakespearean readings are featured on the disc, making this a great collection of the extraordinarily talented and diverse vocalist. *— Leo Stanley*

★ **Songs of Free Men: Recital** / Dec. 9, 1997 / Sony Classical ✦✦✦✦✦
Culled from six concerts given in the 1940s, with most of its tracks previously released on 78 rpm albums in that decade, this disc, as annotator Paul Robeson, Jr., notes, presents Paul Robeson at the peak of his singing career (from age 44 to 49) and recreates a typical recital. Robeson sings spirituals, folk songs from various countries in various languages, classical pieces and theater music, including works by Felix Mendelssohn, Marc Blitzstein (a brilliant "The Purest Kind of Guy" from *No for an Answer*), Earl Robinson, George Gershwin, and, of course, Jerome Kern and Oscar Hammerstein II ("I Still Suits Me" and "Ol' Man River" from *Show Boat*). Robeson is accompanied by his usual pianist, Lawrence Brown, on the first 17 tracks and by the Columbia Concert Orchestra on the remaining eight. The sound quality is remarkably clear, showing little evidence of the 50-year-old (and older) sources. As a result, Robeson's amazing bass-baritone is revealed in all its power, as is a sense of enunciation and presentation that perfectly suits a wide range of material. Released shortly before Robeson's centenary, this album is a fitting tribute to him. *— William Ruhlmann*

Patrice Rushen

b. Sep. 30, 1954, Los Angeles, CA
Vocals, Keyboards, Piano, Synthesizer / Quiet Storm, Crossover Jazz, Urban
Keyboardist/singer/songwriter/arranger/musical director Patrice Rushen has had an outstanding career with several Top Ten R&B hits, including "Haven't You Heard," "Forget Me Nots," "Feels So Real," and "Watch Out." "Forget Me Nots" was the basis of Will Smith's "Men in Black" from the blockbuster movie of the same name on *Big Willie Style.* R. Kelly's "Remind Me" was sampled from her "You Remind Me," a popular radio-aired LP track from *Straight From the Heart.* Others who have sampled Rushen's music are Def Jeff (Rushen's "Hang It Up") and Zhane ("Groove Thang").

Born September 30,1954, in Los Angeles, CA, Rushen's parents enrolled her in music classes at U.S.C. when she was three. In her teens, she won a solo competition at the 1972 *Monterey Jazz Festival.* The attention garnered from this earned her a contract with Prestige Records. After recording three albums and becoming an in-demand session player, Rushen signed with Elektra Records in 1978. Forging an engaging jazz/R&B/funk fusion, she regularly hit the R&B charts. Her five albums for the label were *Patrice, Pizzazz, Posh, Straight From the Heart,* and *Now.* Some of these sides can be found on *Haven't You Heard:The Best of Patrice Rushen.*

In 1993, Rushen signed with Disney's Hollywood Records. Her first and only release was the excellent *Anything but Ordinary,* which yielded the inspiring single "My Heart, Your Heart." Hollywood wasn't satisfied with the album and shelved it. Sindrome Records bought the rights to the album and reissued it with the single, and some LP tracks received airplay on R&B and smooth jazz radio stations. Rushen became a member of the jazz collective the Meeting, appearing on several releases. Her busy schedule includes session dates and being the musical director for several different tours and TV specials. 1997's *Signature* found Rushen returning to her jazz roots for this solid album of instrumentals.

In fall 2000, Patrice Rushen appeared as a part of Sisters Being Positively Real, an act on Brown Baby Entertainment Group. *— Ed Hogan*

Shout It Out / 1976 / Prestige ✦✦✦

Straight from the Heart / 1982 / Rhino ✦✦✦

Anything But Ordinary / Nov. 1, 1994 / Sindrome ✦✦✦

Prelusion/Before the Dawn / Nov. 10, 1998 / Prestige ✦✦✦✦
This 1998 CD reissues keyboardist Patrice Rushen's first two recordings as a leader except for one selection ("Puttered Bopcorn") from the first date that was left out due to lack of space. Twenty at the time of the earlier set, Rushen showed a great deal of potential for the future, potential that (at least in the jazz world) was unfortunately never realized. Rushen is heard on the *Prelusion* album heading a septet that includes tenor-saxophonist Joe Henderson (the most memorable soloist), trumpeter Oscar Brashear, trombonist George Bohanon and Hadley Caliman on reeds; the music is essentially advanced hard bop with touches of fusion. The later date has a similar group (without Henderson) and with guest spots for flutist Hubert Laws and guitarist Lee Ritenour. The R&Bish vocal by Josie James on "What's the Story" hints at where Rushen would be going in the future: straight to the pop market. So overall this CD, which should have served as a bright beginning for the young keyboardist, is practically the artistic highpoint of Patrice Rushen's erratic career. *— Scott Yanow*

● **Haven't You Heard: The Best of Patrice Rushen** / Elektra/Rhino ✦✦✦✦✦
Nearly every one of Patrice Rushen's R&B hits—including the Top 10 singles "Haven't You

Heard," "Forget Me Nots," "Feels So Real (Won't Let Go)," and "Watch Out"—are featured on the single-disc anthology *Haven't You Heard: The Best of Patrice Rushen.* With the exception of "Watch Out," her only Top 40 hit for Arista Records, the material is entirely drawn from Rushen's heyday at Elektra Records, when she was fusing jazz with R&B and pop. The songs on *Haven't You Heard* represent the highwater mark of her fusions, which makes the compilation both an excellent introduction and a comprehensive career retrospective. *—Stephen Thomas Erlewine*

Diane Schuur

b. 1953, Seattle, WA

Vocals, Piano / Vocal Jazz, Standards, Contemporary Jazz

Diane Schuur, who has often been on the periphery of jazz, has the potential to be an important jazz singer although she still includes a large dose of pop tunes in her repertoire. Early in her career she had the tendency to screech in her upper register but with maturity that flaw has largely disappeared and she has become a very impressive singer. Blinded at birth due to a hospital accident, Schuur (who would later be nicknamed "Deedles") imitated singers as a child. She had her first gig at a Holiday Inn when just ten and originally sang country music. The turning point in her career occurred when she sang "Amazing Grace" at the 1979 Monterey Jazz Festival, greatly impressing Stan Getz. After Getz featured her singing at a televised concert from the White House in 1982, Schuur was signed to GRP and began recording regularly. Although her 1987 collaboration with the Count Basie Orchestra was a highpoint, Diane Schuur's recordings tend to be a mixed success from the jazz standpoint; hopefully her best work is still in the future. *—Scott Yanow*

Collection / 1986-1989 / GRP ✦✦✦✦

1989's *Collection* sums up Diane Schuur's first five GRP albums, a period when she achieved a level of acclaim that tailed off somewhat in the '90s. What has been gathered together here is often very impressive, her rich, full voice keening over carefully-wrought, beautifully recorded lush backdrops (with real or electronic strings), swinging over some fine big bands, or coming to terms with '80s jazz funksters. Strangely, there is only one selection from her live-in-the-studio collaboration with the posthumous Count Basie Orchestra which is the best overall album from this period (it features guitarist Freddie Green's last recorded performance)—while the other albums (*Deedles, Schuur Thing, Timeless, Talkin' 'Bout You*)get multiple representation. It's quite possible that Schuur has never topped the leadoff track, Ivan Lins' beguiling "Love Dance"—with her sponsor Stan Getz weaving a magic spell a great example of the right material meeting the right singer and the right backing. Dave Grusin, Johnny Mandel, Billy May, Pat Williams and Jeremy Lubbock are the arrangers whose tracks were chosen—and everything has the brilliant sonic sheen that turned on the audiophile crowd early in the CD era. *—Richard S. Ginell*

Diane Schuur & the Count Basie Orchestra / 1987 / GRP ✦✦✦✦✦

This CD features a logical combination: singer Diane Schuur with the Count Basie big band. In what would be longtime rhythm guitarist Freddie Green's final performance, Schuur and the Basie ghost band (under the direction of Frank Foster) perform material that includes her standards (such as "Deedles' Blues" and "Climbing Higher Mountains"), Dave Brubeck's "Travlin' Blues" and the Joe Williams-associated "Everyday I Have The Blues." Unfortunately, the Basie band is mostly used in accompaniment without any significant solos, but Schuur sounds quite comfortable in this format and her voice is in prime form. *—Scott Yanow*

Love Songs / 1993 / GRP ✦✦✦✦✦

The jazz content on this CD from singer Diane Schuur is rather slight but this is actually one of her finest recordings. Schuur (who has a lovely voice) sings straightforward versions of ten veteran ballads while accompanied by one of two string orchestras. Tom Scott on reeds and trumpeter Jack Sheldon have short spots but this is very much Schuur's show. She really excels in the restrained setting, making this a superior middle-of-the-road pop recording. *—Scott Yanow*

Love Walked In / 1995 / GRP ✦✦✦✦

Blues for Schuur / 1997 / GRP ✦✦✦✦

Diane Schuur is in prime voice throughout this swinging date. Backed by an 11-piece group arranged by Greg Adams, Schuur emphasizes the blues feeling on a variety of mostly older but fresh material, including "Stormy Monday," "Save Your Love For Me," "When Did You Leave Heaven" and four Charles Brown songs. There are occasional solos from the backup crew (most notably guitarist David T. Walker and an uncredited altoist on "Save Your Love for Me" that might be Gary Herbig), but the emphasis is on Schuur's voice. An infectious outing from the talented singer. *—Scott Yanow*

● **The Very Best of Dianne Schuur** / Oct. 21, 1997 / GRP ✦✦✦✦✦

The Very Best of Diane Schuur is a fine collection of 13 of the vocalist's most popular recordings for GRP, featuring such tracks as "All Right, OK, You Win (I'm In Love With You), " "Try a Little Tenderness, " "Sunday Kind of Love, " "Deed I Do, " "Time for Love, " "'Round Midnight, " "Stormy Monday Blues, " "Deedles' Blues" and "New York State of Mind." For collectors and serious fans, this has no purpose, but for casual fans and neophytes, this is an ideal purchase. *—Stephen Thomas Erlewine*

Friends for Schuur / Sep. 26, 2000 / Concord Jazz ✦✦✦✦✦

Little Jimmy Scott

b. Jul. 17, 1925, Cleveland, Ohio

Vocals / Vocal Jazz, Traditional Pop, Standards, R&B

Through historical circumstances and the various labels he's recorded for, jazz balladeer Jimmy Scott (formerly known as "Little Jimmy Scott") has been lumped into the rhythm & blues category since the 1950s. In the '50s, he would perform with blues singers like Ruth Brown and Big Maybelle. But Scott has always insisted he's a jazz balladeer. He should know. Despite his misinformed dealings with unscrupulous record-company executives over the years and the misclassification of his artistry, he's emerged from a lot of difficult circumstances relatively unscathed. His last three albums for Warner Bros. prove it. Now in his early 70s, Scott still retains his unique, behind the beat phrasing. Offstage, his eternally optimist spirit has touched the hearts and minds of many fans, friends, admirers and associates. What Scott does so well is put his own stamp on the standards, and while his voice is not what it once was, it's still one of the most captivating voices in the world of jazz. *—Richard Skelly*

The Fabulous Little Jimmy Scott F / 1959 / Savoy ✦✦✦✦✦

Regal Records Live in New Orleans / Oct. 29, 1992 / Specialty ✦✦✦

Certainly, this rough live recording of a 1951 club gig is primarily a historical document, and not one of the first discs you'd turn to if you want to hear some vintage Jimmy Scott. On its own terms, though, it's pretty enjoyable. The band cooks in an R&B/jazz crossover style, yielding a sound that's rawer than what you'll find on most of Scott's studio sides. Scott himself sings well in his inimitable half-man/half-woman style, sounding like a higher-pitched version of the pre-Atlantic Records-era Ray Charles. Only five of the nine songs, by the way, actually feature Scott's vocals; the rest are instrumentals by the backing band, including a smoking, honking sax battle between Ray Abrams and guest Sam Butera on "Dueling Tenors." *—Richie Unterberger*

Lost and Found / 1993 / Rhino ✦✦✦✦

In the late 1960s and early 1970s, Scott recorded some sessions for Atlantic that were either withdrawn from the market for legal reasons, or unissued entirely. *Lost and Found* couples five unreleased songs from a 1972 session with five tracks that were originally included on the 1969 LP *The Source* (which was available only briefly). Top talents like Richard Davis, Billy Cobham, Eric Gale, Junior Mance, and Ron Carter back Scott on these ballad standards, which are augmented by string sections. Scott's higher-pitched Ray Charles style (which sounds to most like a woman rather than a man) is in good form here, though the relentlessly slow tempos can enervate, and the routine choice of material is on the staid side. *—Richie Unterberger*

Heaven / Sep. 24, 1996 / Warner Brothers ✦✦

Holding Back the Years / Oct. 6, 1998 / Artists Only ✦✦✦✦

Everybody's Somebody's Fool / Mar. 9, 1999 / GRP ✦✦✦✦

● **The Savoy Years and More** / Sep. 21, 1999 / Savoy Jazz ✦✦✦✦✦

The three-CD box set includes 66 songs, arranged in chronological order, opening with six tracks cut in 1952 and concluding with nine tunes recorded in Chicago in 1972. Charles Mingus and sax player Budd Johnson can be heard on Disc One, tracks 10-13, which include Scott's inspired version of "When Did You Leave Heaven." When it comes to interpreting a ballad, Scott takes hold of a lyric and fills it with light and space. Even when performing obscure material, he always seems to find his way to the center of the song. As a stylist, he's positively elegant, but he complements this with a certain edgy quality that comes from his singular interpretive gift. He's not a predictable singer; he'll surprise the listener with the choices he makes in terms of inflection and timing. Some of the best material featured on this box set includes "Someone to Watch Over Me," "I'm Through With Love," "Close Your Eyes," "After I'm Gone," "Never Peace of Mind," "When It Comes to Love" and "I'll Be Around." *—Philip Van Vleck*

Mood Indigo / May 16, 2000 / Milestone ✦✦✦✦

Dinah Shore (Frances Rose Shore)

b. Mar. 1, 1917, Winchester, TN, **d.** Feb. 24, 1994, Beverly Hills, CA

Vocals / Traditional Pop, Vocal Pop, Show Tunes

One of America's most popular entertainers long after her mid-'40s commercial peak, Dinah Shore was the first major vocalist to break away from the big-band format and begin a solo-billed career. During the '40s, she recorded several of the decade's biggest singles—"Buttons and Bows," "The Gypsy," and "I'll Walk Alone"—all of which spent more than a month at number one on the Hit Parade. After launching a television variety series in 1951, Shore appeared on one program or another, with few gaps, into the 1980s.

Born in rural Tennessee, Dinah Shore was performing on Nashville radio while still a teenager. Her professional career later took her to New York, where she sang with Xavier Cugat. After failing auditions with Benny Goodman and Tommy Dorsey however, she decided to simply become a solo singer. Shore signed to Bluebird, and recorded several hits during 1940-41, including "Yes, My Darling Daughter," "I Hear a Rhapsody" and "Jim." Her first million-seller came in 1942 with the prototypical blues crossover nugget, "Blues in the Night." Later that year, she moved to Victor and hit big with "You'd Be So Nice to Come Home To" and her first number one hit, 1944's "I'll Walk Alone." Shore also began appearing in films, including 1944's *Up in Arms* and 1946's *Till the Clouds Roll By.*

The late '40s proved to be her most popular era for recording. Between 1946 and 1949, she hit big with several songs, including "The Gypsy," "I Love You for Sentimental Reasons," "Anniversary Song," "I Wish I Didn't Love You So," "Buttons and Bows" and "Dear Hearts and Gentle People." Though her records didn't chart as high during the '50s, Dinah Shore enjoyed even more exposure with her top-rated variety show, *The Dinah Shore Chevy Show.* For many, Shore's opening and closing every show with "See the USA in your Chevrolet, America's the greatest land of all" practically defined the '50s. Her Chevrolet sponsorship lasted until 1963, but she returned in the '70s with a new format, the daytime talk-show. During the 1980s, she began performing once again, but returned to television once more with a series that ran for two years. She died of cancer in 1994. *—John Bush*

Dinah Sings, Andre Previn Plays/Somebody Loves Me / May 1998 / EMI ✦✦✦✦✦

Dinah Shore was an established TV star but rather forgotten as a recording artist when she cut the two albums reissued on this CD in 1960, which may help explain why they were not big sellers. It certainly had nothing to do with the quality of the music. Both sessions feature collaborations with André Previn: on the first ten songs (actually cut after the last ten), Previn is the pianist leading a rhythm section, the tempos are slow and the mood is romantic. On the second half, Previn leads the orchestra in lush arrangements at equally slow speed. The songs are mostly standards, and Shore performs them with an assurance that makes you wonder why she isn't ranked with some of her contemporaries as an accomplished pop-jazz vocalist. Maybe the TV-star tag again. Here's a chance to rediscover her. —*William Ruhlmann*

The Dinah Shore Collection: Columbia and RCA Recordings 1942-1948 / Nov. 16, 1999 / Dutton Vocalion ♦♦♦♦

● **16 Most Requested Songs** / Columbia/Legacy ♦♦♦♦♦

Nina Simone

b. Feb. 21, 1933, Tryon, NC

Vocals, Piano / Vocal Jazz, Standards

Of all the major singers of the late 20th century, Nina Simone is one of the hardest to classify. She's recorded extensively in the soul, jazz, and pop idioms, often over the course of the same album; she's also comfortable with blues, gospel, and Broadway. It's perhaps most accurate to label her as a "soul" singer in terms of emotion, rather than form. Like, say, Aretha Franklin, or Dusty Springfield, Simone is an eclectic, who brings soulful qualities to whatever material she interprets. These qualities are among her strongest virtues; paradoxically, they also may have kept her from attaining a truly mass audience. The same could be said of her stage persona; admired for her forthright honesty and individualism, she's also known for feisty feuding with audiences and promoters alike. In the late '50s, Simone began recording for the small Bethlehem label (a subsidiary of the vastly important early R&B/rock & roll King label). In 1959, her version of George Gershwin's "I Loves You Porgy" gave her a Top 20 hit—which would, amazingly, prove to be the only Top 40 entry of her career. Nina wouldn't need hit singles for survival, however, establishing herself not with the rock & roll/R&B crowd, but with the adult/nightclub/album market. A performer of nearly unsurpassed eclecticism, her records encompassed everything from Ellingtonian jazz and Israeli folk songs to spirituals and movie themes. Simone's best recorded work was issued on Philips during the mid-'60s. Her moody-yet-elegant vocals are like no one else's, presenting a fiercely independent soul who harbors enormous (if somewhat hard-bitten) tenderness. —*Richie Unterberger*

☆ **Nina at Town Hall** / Sep. 12, 1959 / Colpix ♦♦♦♦♦

One of Nina Simone's finest recordings, this Colpix LP features the unique singer/pianist performing classic versions of "Black Is the Color of My True Love's Hair," "The Other Woman," and "Wild Is the Wind." With supportive work from bassist Jimmy Bond and drummer Al "Tootie" Heath, she also sounds fine on a few instrumentals. "Summertime" is performed twice, once as a vocal. From the start of her career, Nina Simone carved out her own unique niche, meshing together her classical piano technique with folk singing, civil rights protest lyrics and jazz. All of those elements are in evidence on this highly recommended set. —*Scott Yanow*

Anthology: The Colpix Years / 1959-1964 / Rhino ♦♦♦♦♦

Simone recorded prolifically during her affiliation with Colpix in the late '50s and early '60s. This 40-song, two-CD set presents choice extracts from approximately ten albums worth of material. It isn't quite as impressive as what she recorded for Philips in the mid-'60s, sticking to a more pop- and light jazz-based approach, and not mining blues and soul nearly as heavily. She was also writing hardly any of her own tunes, and had yet to fully expound upon issues of black pride and social justice. These are ultimately minor quibbles; it's a fine set, in which Simone already demonstrates commanding vocals and a wide-ranging stylistic base that incorporates material by Duke Ellington, Rodgers & Hart, Billie Holiday, Nat Adderley, "House of the Rising Sun," and even a Hebrew tune. It also has three non-LP cuts, including the self-penned, African-tinged "Blackbird," and "Come on Back, Jack," an answer record to Ray Charles' "Hit the Road, Jack." By the way, this doesn't make the single-disc *Colpix Years* CD on Roulette totally redundant, as that release has half a dozen tracks which don't appear on this anthology. —*Richie Unterberger*

★ **The Best of the Colpix Years** / 1959-1963 / Roulette ♦♦♦♦♦

Nineteen tracks from her Colpix label recordings. Dating from 1959 to 1963, this mix of studio and live material is considerably more weighted toward jazz and standards by the likes of Ellington, Cole Porter, Rodgers & Hammerstein, and Irving Berlin than the more eclectic albums she would later cut in the '60s and '70s for Philips and RCA. The highlights are when she steps out of the soulful supper club style into more earthier settings, as on "House of the Rising Sun," "Forbidden Fruit," "Gin House Blues," "Work Song," and her own "Children Go Where I Send You" (all of which she would considerably rework over the years). Includes three previously unreleased tracks in a traditional jazz style with minimal arrangements. Note: The version of "(I Loves You) Porgy," her sole Top 20 entry, is not her 1959 hit single, but a live 1960 version. —*Richie Unterberger*

Nina Simone at the Village Gate / 1961 / Roulette ♦♦♦♦♦

Nina Simone has the rare ablity of really being able to dig into material and bring out unexpected meaning in familiar lyrics. On "Just In Time" from this CD reissue, she gives one the impression that if she had not been found "Just In Time," she would have committed suicide. During "He Was Too Good To Me," Simone sounds absolutely stunned about the end of a love affair. "Brown Baby" is both hopeful and defiant in its call for freedom while "Zungo" is an African work song. Also from her 1961 trio performance at the Village Gate, Simone performs the overly serious "If He Changed My Name," the goodtime gospel piece "Children Go Where I Send You," a regretful rendition of "House Of The Rising Sun" and an unpredictable instrumental version of "Bye Bye Blackbird." Nina Simone, who was always in a category by herself, is heard throughout in her early prime. —*Scott Yanow*

The Ultimate Nina Simone / Mar. 21, 1964-Aug. 1966 / Verve ♦♦♦♦

On this celebrity's choice tour through the Verve archives, singer Dianne Reeves comes up with a most interesting, idiosyncratic selection of the Philips recordings of Nina Simone, intuitively sequencing the tracks herself. Reeves zeroes in on the experimental side of Simone, celebrating her differences from Tin Pan Alley-oriented singers, even equivocating a bit on the term "jazz singer" in describing her style. Reeves mostly avoids standards like the plague, opting for unusual songs like the stark a cappella "Images," the chain-gang-styled "Be My Husband," the hypnotic, percussion-backed "Come Ye," or an example of Nina on piano only ("Blue On Purpose"). Besides being her congenitally feisty self, Simone is also caught displaying poignant moodiness on "The Other Woman," a live remake of her hit "I Loves You, Porgy," and "Don't Explain"—all sequenced together. Any adventurous listener coming to Nina Simone for the first time through this collection will definitely be tempted to explore some more of her output. —*Richard S. Ginell*

Pastel Blues / May 19, 1965-May 20, 1965 / Mercury ♦♦♦

If this is blues, it's blues in the Billie Holiday sense, not the Muddy Waters one. This is one of Nina Simone's more subdued mid-'60s LPs, putting the emphasis on her piano rather than band arrangements. It's rather slanted toward torch-blues ballads like "Strange Fruit," "Trouble In Mind," Billie Holiday's own composition "Tell Me More and More and Then Some," and "Nobody Knows You When You're Down and Out." Simone's then-husband, Andy Stroud, wrote "Be My Husband," an effective adaptation of a traditional blues chant. By far the most impressive track is her frantic ten-minute rendition of the traditional "Sinnerman," an explosive *tour de force* that dwarfs everything else on the album. *Pastel Blues* has been combined with the 1966 LP *Let It Out* onto a single-disc CD reissue. —*Richie Unterberger*

The Blues / Dec. 19, 1966-Jun. 24, 1971 / Jive/Novus ♦♦♦♦♦

Live at Ronnie Scott's / Nov. 17, 1984 / DRG ♦♦♦♦

A Single Woman / 1993 / Elektra/Asylum ♦♦♦

Tomato Collection / 1994 / Tomato ♦♦♦

A ragtag double-CD anthology that ranges all over the place: solo jazz piano, show tunes, soul, and live versions of many of her best-known songs, seemingly taken from the '50s, '60s, and '70s. Annoyingly—and, sadly, typically for the Tomato label—there is absolutely no information about when and where the tracks were recorded. Despite the drawbacks, in a way this is about the most wide-ranging Simone collection available, and much of the live material is good and quite different from the studio versions, although the fidelity on these is sometimes hissy. —*Richie Unterberger*

The Very Best of Nina Simone / Jul. 28, 1998 / RCA ♦♦♦♦

Nina Simone recorded for RCA Records between 1967 and 1972. While she was in fine form during those years, she didn't make her best records there and she particularly sounded a little ill at ease whenever she did pop-rock covers, which was more often than she should. However, these songs are selling points for a certain audience, namely the audience RCA is targeting with their generous 40-track collection, *The Very Best of Nina Simone*. True, her recordings during these five years were a little inconsistent, as she covered the classics, performed new songs and tackled contemporary material, so perhaps it's fitting that this compilation is also a little schizophrenic. Nevertheless, that doesn't make the compilation much more than an interesting summation of a conflicted, occasionally rewarding, era of Simone's career that will be useful for already dedicated fans that want to explore a little deeper than her classic recordings. —*Stephen Thomas Erlewine*

The Amazing Nina Simone/Nina Simone at Town Hall / Jun. 22, 1999 / Collectables ♦♦♦♦♦

A good and sensible single-disc reissue of two early Simone albums, both recorded in the late 1950s and both among her more jazz-oriented outings. *The Amazing Nina Simone*, a 1959 studio LP, is rather on the pop and standards side of things, with cuts like "It Might as Well Be Spring," "Willow Weep for Me," and "Stompin' at the Savoy," but that's not to its detriment. The mood is varied, with some sad orchestral arrangements that would have made these suitable for theater or movie productions; upbeat gospel on "Children Go Where I Send You" and "Chilly Winds Don't Blow"; and quite respectable upbeat jazz on "You've Been Gone Too Long." The live *At Town Hall*, recorded in September 1959, is un-orchestrated and more spontaneous, and puts the accent more on Simone's fine, even, stirring piano playing. Here again, Simone evidences her determination to have the most eclectic repertoire of anyone around with standards like "Exactly Like You," traditional folk tunes such as "Black is the Color of My True Love," and Billie Holiday's "Fine and Mellow." Most interesting, perhaps, are the several forceful instrumentals in which Simone really gets down, hammering the notes or trilling delicately as the mood takes her, quite audibly grunt-humming along as she gets absorbed in the music. The production on both of these LPs is rather uneven and undernourished from a technical standpoint, with odd echoes and balances throughout. If anything, though, that dated feel embellishes the unusual moods which Simone excelled at creating. —*Richie Unterberger*

Frank Sinatra (Francis Albert Sinatra)

b. Dec. 12, 1915, Hoboken, NJ, **d.** May 14, 1998, Los Angeles, CA

Vocals / Vocal Jazz, Traditional Pop, Standards, Vocal Pop, Soft Rock, Pop, Swing, Ballads, Show Tunes, Big Band

Though Frank Sinatra's reputation as celebrity, icon, bad boy, and possibly the greatest singer of American popular songs of the century are paramount to the general public, he has always been valued highly in the jazz community, especially among musicians. Though not a jazz singer per se, he was a child of the big-band era, incubated with an ability to swing in a relaxed, ingratiating way in all kinds of material. Whenever he had the chance, Sinatra would credit Billie Holiday as a primary influence on his vocal style—even recording a tribute song called "Lady Day" in 1970—and he learned circular breathing at the feet of trombonist Tommy Dorsey. Particularly from the mid-1950s into the mid-1960s, Sinatra would use expert jazzmen prominently in his recording orchestras, as well as arrangers who cut their teeth in the big-band era. He was at his freest and loosest when paired with a great big band like that of Count Basie, where he would bend to the rhythm, embroider the melody, and stray from the tune to the point where non-jazz-oriented aficionados of singing would become disoriented. Indeed, the theory has been advanced that during the '60s, flinging himself head-on against the rock & roll tide of the time, Sinatra was actually able to revive the big-band era in terms of mass popularity, record sales, concert receipts, and media exposure—although this time, the orientation was in favor of the singer rather than the band. Had he chosen to explore it more, Sinatra could have also been the most important bossa nova singer of his time; even so, the two albums he did make with Antonio Carlos Jobim display an uncanny emotional affinity for the idiom. Other than Brazilian music, though, Sinatra stayed away from developments in jazz beyond swing (unless one counts a quirk like his notorious "do-be-do-be-do" scatting at the close of "Strangers In the Night"). *—Richard S. Ginell*

☆ **The Song Is You** / Feb. 1, 1940-Jul. 2, 1942 / RCA ✦✦✦✦✦
This very attractive five-CD boxed set has every studio recording that Frank Sinatra recorded with Tommy Dorsey's Orchestra plus a full disc of mostly unreleased radio broadcasts. Since Sinatra has never really been a jazz singer and most of the selections are ballads, jazz listeners may not consider this box essential but Frank Sinatra fans will not need to be told of its existence twice. Sinatra's first session as a leader (from early 1942) is also included (along with a large and colorful booklet), giving listeners a very definitive look into his early days. *—Scott Yanow*

☆ **The Best of the Columbia Years: 1943-1952** / 1943-1952 / Columbia ✦✦✦✦✦
A four-disc distillation of the mammoth 12-disc box *The Columbia Years (1943-1952): The Complete Recordings, The Best of the Columbia Years 1944-52* provides everything most listeners need to know about Frank Sinatra's early career. Nearly all of his classic performances of the era are included in these 100 tracks, which are sequenced chronologically. Completists will need the 12-disc set, but *The Best of the Columbia Years* will satisfy the needs of most fans. *—Stephen Thomas Erlewine*

The Columbia Years (1943-1952): The Complete Recordings / 1943-1952 / Columbia/Legacy ✦✦✦✦✦

★ **Portrait of Sinatra: Columbia Classics** / 1943-1952 / Columbia ✦✦✦✦✦
Portrait of Sinatra: Columbia Classics is a double-disc, 36-track collection that features Sinatra's biggest hits from his Columbia years, including "Someone to Watch Over Me," "The House I Live In," "All or Nothing at All" and "Stormy Weather." Although the compilation contains eight unreleased cuts that will appeal only to collectors, it remains the best and most affordable overview of Sinatra's early years. *—Stephen Thomas Erlewine*

The V-Discs: Columbia Years: 1943-45 / 1943-1945 / Columbia/Legacy ✦✦✦

Swing and Dance with Frank Sinatra / Dec. 1, 1944-Jul. 19, 1951 / Columbia ✦✦✦✦✦
When Columbia decided to reissue Frank Sinatra's early '50s albums on CD, they did it right, choosing to expand each of the original albums with bonus tracks and release them at a budget price. Such is the case with *Sing and Dance with Frank Sinatra,* a record originally released in 1950. Although Sinatra's star wasn't shining as brightly in 1950 as it was in the '40s, he still was capable of turning out a charming recording, which is exactly what *Sing and Dance* is. Although it will never be remembered as one of his masterpieces, it's quite engaging on its own terms—George Siravo's arrangements may not be as lush as Axel Stordahl's, but they're quite good and very enjoyable. This expanded CD collection contains all of Sinatra's 18 recordings with Siravo for these sessions, including six alternate takes. This disc is primarily for the devoted, but it's useful in illustrating that even when Sinatra wasn't at the peak of his stardom, he could record some extraordinary music. *—Stephen Thomas Erlewine*

Complete Capitol Singles Collection / Apr. 2, 1953-Sep. 12, 1961 / Capitol ✦✦✦✦✦

The Capitol Years: The Best of Frank Sinatra / 1953-1961 / Capitol ✦✦✦✦✦

☆ **In the Wee Small Hours** / Mar. 1, 1954-Mar. 4, 1955 / Capitol ✦✦✦✦✦
Expanding on the concept of *Songs for Young Lovers, In the Wee Small Hours* was a collection of ballads arranged by Nelson Riddle. The first 12-inch album recorded by Sinatra, *Wee Small Hours* was more focused and concentrated than his two earlier concept records. It's a blue, melancholy album, built around a spare rhythm section featuring a rhythm guitar, celesta, and Bill Miller's piano, with gently aching strings added every once and a while. Within that melancholy mood, is one of Sinatra's most jazz-oriented performances—he restructures the melody and Miller's playing is bold throughout the record. Where *Songs for Young Lovers* emphasized the romantic aspects of the songs, Sinatra sounds like a lonely, broken man on *In the Wee Small Hours.* Beginning with the newly-written title song, the singer goes through a series of standards that are lonely and desolate. In many ways, the album is a personal reflection of the heartbreak of his doomed love affair with actress Ava Gardner, and the standards that he sings form their own story when collected together. Sinatra's voice had deepened and worn to the point were his delivery seems ravished and heartfelt, as if he were living the songs. *—Stephen Thomas Erlewine*

☆ **Songs for Young Lovers/Swing Easy** / 1955 / Capitol ✦✦✦✦✦
Combining Frank Sinatra's first two 10-inch albums for Capitol, the compact disc *Songs for Young Lovers/ Swing Easy* not only contains some of the best music Sinatra recorded, it captures a turning point in popular music. *Songs for Young Lovers* was the first album Frank Sinatra recorded for Capitol, as well as his first collaboration with Nelson Riddle. It was also one of the first—arguably the very first—concept album. Sinatra, Riddle, and producer Voyle Gilmore decided that the new album format should be a special event, featuring a number of songs arranged around a specific theme; in addition, the new format was capable of producing a more detailed sound, which gave Riddle more freedom in his arrangements and orchestrations. *Songs for Young Lovers* is a perfect example of this. Supported by a small orchestra, Sinatra and Riddle create an intimate, romantic atmosphere on the record, breathing new life to standards like "My Funny Valentine," "They Can't Take That Away from Me," "I Get a Kick Out of You," and "A Foggy Day." There is a breezy confidence to Sinatra's singing, and Riddle's arrangements are more complex than they initially appear. Sinatra and Riddle expanded this approach on his second Capitol album, *Swing Easy!* As the title implies, the record concentrates on up-tempo swingers. Again, the songs were all standards—"Just One of Those Things," "Wrap Your Troubles In Dreams," "All of Me"—that benefitted from the new thematic setting, the new arrangements, and, of course, Sinatra's increasingly playful and textured vocals. Sinatra plays around with the melodies without leaving them behind, delivering each line with precision. It ranks as one of his most jazzy performances, as well as one of his most fun and carefree records. *—Stephen Thomas Erlewine*

★ **Songs for Swingin' Lovers!** / Oct. 17, 1955-Jan. 16, 1956 / Capitol ✦✦✦✦✦
After the ballad-heavy *In The Wee Small Hours,* Frank Sinatra and Nelson Riddle returned to uptempo, swing material with *Songs for Swingin' Lovers,* arguably the vocalist's greatest swing set. Like Sinatra's previous Capitol albums, *Songs for Swingin' Lovers* consists of reinterpreted pop standards, ranging from the ten-year old "You Make Me Feel So Young" to the 20-year old "Pennies From Heaven" and "I've Got You Under My Skin." Sinatra is supremely confident throughout the album, singing with authority and joy. That joy is replicated in Riddle's arrangements, which manage to rethink these standards in fresh yet reverent ways. Working with a core rhythm section and a full string orchestra, Riddle writes scores that are surprisingly subtle. "I've Got You Under My Skin," with its breathtaking middle section, is a perfect example of how Sinatra works with the band. Both swing hard, stretching out the rhythms and melodies but never losing sight of the original song. *Songs For Swingin' Lovers* never loses momentum. The great songs keep coming and the performances are all stellar, resulting in one of Sinatra's true classics. *—Stephen Thomas Erlewine*

Close to You / 1957 / Capitol ✦✦✦✦

☆ **A Swingin' Affair!** / 1957 / Capitol ✦✦✦✦✦
In some ways, *A Swingin' Affair* is *Songs for Swingin' Lovers!, Pt. 2,* following the same formula of Sinatra's hit album of the previous year. Beneath the surface, there are enough variations on *A Swingin' Affair* to make it a distinctive, and equally enjoyable listen. The most noticible difference between the two records is their basic approach. Where *Songs for Swingin' Lovers!* swung hard but managed to stay rather light, *A Swingin' Affair* is a forceful, brassy album—it exudes a self-assured, confident aura. It is a hard, jazzy album However, the attack is more brash, *—Stephen Thomas Erlewine*

☆ **Where Are You?** / 1957 / Capitol ✦✦✦✦✦
Following the hard-driving *A Swingin' Affair,* Frank Sinatra released another all-ballads record, *Where Are You?* The album was the first he recorded at Capitol without Nelson Riddle, as well as the first he recorded in stereo. Where Riddle's down beat albums are stately and sullen, Jenkins favors lush, melancholy arrangements played by large, string-dominated orchestras. Jenkins' arrangements suggested classical textures, although the tempos alluded to Billie Holiday's ballad style. *Where Are You?* primarily consists of torch songs, including "The Night We Called It a Day," "I Cover the Waterfront," and "Lonely Town." Throughout the record, Sinatra blends with Jenkins' sumptuous strings, making his voice sound rich, relaxed and regretful. It doesn't have the stark despair of *In the Wee Small Hours,* but its luxurious sadness makes *Where Are You?* a majestic experience of its own. *—Stephen Thomas Erlewine*

☆ **Come Fly with Me** / Oct. 1, 1957-Oct. 8, 1957 / Capitol ✦✦✦✦✦
Constructed around a light-hearted travel theme, *Come Fly With Me,* Frank Sinatra's first project with arranger Billy May was a breezy change of pace from the somber *Where Are You.* From the first swinging notes of Sammy Cahn and Jimmy Van Heusen's "Come Fly With Me"—which is written at Sinatra's request—it's clear that the music on the collection is intended to be fun. Over the course of the album, Sinatra and May travel around the world in song, performing standards like "Moonlight In Vermont" and "April In Paris," as well as humorous tunes like "Isle of Capri" and "On the Road to Mandalay." May's signature bold, brassy arrangements give these songs a playful, carefree, nearly sarcastic feel, but never is the approach less than affectionate. In fact, *Come Fly With Me* is filled with varying moods and textures, as it moves from boisterous swing numbers to romantic ballads, and hitting any number of emotions in between. There may be greater albums in Sinatra's catalog, but few are quite as fun as *Come Fly With Me.* *—Stephen Thomas Erlewine*

☆ **Only the Lonely** / 1958 / Capitol ✦✦✦✦✦
Originally, Frank Sinatra had planned to record *Only the Lonely* with Gordon Jenkins, who had arranged his previous all-ballads album, *Where Are You?* Jenkins was unavailable at the time of the sessions, which led Sinatra back to his original arranger at Capitol, Nelson Riddle. The result is arguably his greatest ballads album. *Only the Lonely* follows the same formula as his previous down albums, but the tone is considerably bleaker and more desperate. Riddle used a larger orchestra for the album than he had in the past, which leant the album a stately, nearly classical atmosphere. At its core, however, the album is a set of brooding saloon songs, highlighted by two of Sinatra's tour de forces—"Angel Eyes" and "One for My Baby." Sinatra never forces emotion out of the lyric, he lets everything flow naturally, with grace. It's a heartbreaking record, the ideal late-night album. *—Stephen Thomas Erlewine*

☆ **Come Dance with Me!** / Dec. 9, 1958-Dec. 23, 1958 / Capitol ✦✦✦✦✦
Working with Billy May again, Frank Sinatra recorded his hardest swing album ever with *Come Dance With Me!* Driven by an intensely swinging horn section, the album has a fair share of slower numbers, but the songs that make the biggest impression are the uptempo cuts. With May's charts wildly careening all over the place, Sinatra relies on his macho swagger; as a result, *Come Dance With Me!* is an intoxicating rush of invigorating dance songs. *—Stephen Thomas Erlewine*

No One Cares / 1959 / Capitol ✦✦✦✦✦

With Red Norvo Quintet: Live in Australia 1959 / Mar. 31, 1959–Apr. 1, 1959 / Blue Note ✦✦✦✦✦

☆ **Nice 'N' Easy** / 1960 / Capitol ✦✦✦✦✦
Breaking slightly from his pattern of a swing album following the release of ballads set, Frank Sinatra followed *No One Cares* with *Nice 'N' Easy,* a breezy collection of mid-tempo numbers arranged by Nelson Riddle. Not only is it the lightest set that he recorded for Capitol, it is the one with the loosest theme. Sinatra selected a collection of songs he had sang early in his career, having Riddle rearrange the tunes with warm, cheery textures. Unlike his previous ballads albums, *Nice 'N' Easy* doesn't have a touch of brooding sorrow—it rolls along steadily, charming everyone in its path. *—Stephen Thomas Erlewine*

The Complete Reprise Studio Recordings / Dec. 19, 1960-Dec. 18, 1979 / Warner Brothers ✦✦✦✦✦

Ring a Ding Ding / Dec. 19, 1960-Dec. 21, 1960 / Reprise ✦✦✦
Ring A Ding Ding, Frank Sinatra's first album for his own record label, broke somewhat from the strict concepts of his Capitol Records; in the process, it set a kind of template for the rest of his '60s Reprise albums. Instead of following a theme, the record captures the atmosphere of Sinatra in 1961—a time when he was running the Rat Pack, so it's no coincidence that the album is named after one of his favorite phrases of the era. The title track was written especially for Sinatra by Sammy Cahn and Jimmy Van Heusen. And that song reflects the brassy, swaggering feeling of the record—even the ballads are arrogant and self-confident. —*Stephen Thomas Erlewine*

Sinatra's Swingin' Session!!! And More / 1961 / Capitol ✦✦✦✦✦
Sinatra's Swingin' Session is a fast, driving album, the speediest and hardest swing collection Frank Sinatra ever recorded. The majority of the album is a re-recording of six of the eight songs from his first LP, *Sing and Dance With Frank Sinatra,* as rearranged by Nelson Riddle. Sinatra performed the songs twice as fast as was expected; consequently, it's one of his jazziest swing sets, with the musicians spitting out energetic, forceful solos and providing tough, gutsy support. Not only do the uptempo numbers speed by, the ballads are sprightly. It doesn't have the brassy verve of *A Swingin' Affair,* but *Sinatra's Swingin' Session* does have a confident, swaggering flavor of its own that makes it nearly as enjoyable. —*Stephen Thomas Erlewine*

Come Swing with Me / Mar. 20, 1961-Mar. 22, 1961 / Capitol ✦✦✦

I Remember Tommy / May 1, 1961-May 3, 1963 / Reprise ✦✦✦
As the title suggests, *I Remember Tommy* is an affectionate tribute to Tommy Dorsey, the legendary bandleader who helped elevate Frank Sinatra to stardom. Arranged by Sy Oliver, who also gained attention through Dorsey, the album contains a number of songs that were part of the Sinatra/Dorsey repertoire, given slightly new readings. Though the intentions were good, the new versions pale in comparision to the originals. Nevertheless, there are a handful of gems included on the record, making it worthwhile for dedicated Sinatra aficionados. —*Stephen Thomas Erlewine*

Swing Along with Me / May 18, 1961-May 23, 1961 / Reprise ✦✦✦

Point of No Return / Nov. 11, 1961-Nov. 12, 1961 / Capitol ✦✦✦

Frank Sinatra's Greatest Hits! / 1961-1968 / Reprise ✦✦✦✦✦

The Reprise Collection / 1961-1975 / Reprise ✦✦✦✦✦

★ **Sinatra Reprise: The Very Good Years** / 1961-1975 / Warner Brothers ✦✦✦✦✦
Sinatra Reprise: The Very Good Years is an excellent single-disc retrospective of Sinatra's career at Reprise, including most of his signature songs from the '60s, '70s, and '80s. Hits like "My Way," "That's Life," "Summer Wind," "Strangers in the Night," "It Was A Very Good Year" and "New York, New York" are present, as are songs that were never singles but were extremely popular, like "Luck Be A Lady," "Fly Me to the Moon," "Love and Marriage," and "The Way You Look Tonight." For many casual fans, this disc captures the essence of Sinatra as an icon and provides a perfect introduction to the singer. —*Stephen Thomas Erlewine*

Sinatra & Sextet: Live in Paris / 1962 / Reprise ✦✦✦✦✦
If you've cringed at the quality of recent Sinatra projects, this 1962 session will remind you of his glorious past. The 26 cuts include many Sinatra signature pieces ("I've Got You Under My Skin," "The Second Time Around," "Night And Day," "Moonlight In Vermont") with backing from an intimate small band that provides lush, supportive frameworks around which Sinatra can build and create his inimitable charm. The session also shows Sinatra at his most loutish, with some crude (even for the time) commentary during the beginning of "One For My Baby," and borderline racist cracks at the end of "Ol' Man River" and start of "The Lady Is A Tramp." But Sinatra's vocal excellence often overcame his idiocy and bad manners, and it does on this fine set. —*Ron Wynn*

Sinatra and Swingin' Brass / 1962 / Reprise ✦✦✦

Sinatra Sings Great Songs from Great Britain / 1962 / Warner Brothers ✦✦

Sinatra and Strings / Jan. 1962 / Reprise ✦✦✦
Sinatra and Strings, Frank Sinatra's first album with arranger Don Costa, is an exquisite, romantic collection of ballads and is one of his most sensual records. Costa has given the songs—which consist entirely of standards [the CD version added two newer songs]—exceedingly lush, heavily orchestrated arrangements that sound like updated, contemporary versions of Axel Stordahl's ornate charts. Sinatra responds with smooth, nuanced, yet powerful vocals that make these traditional songs sound fresh. The pair take some chances with their arrangements—"Stardust" never reaches the chorus, for instance—but *Sinatra and Strings* remains a definitive ballads album, complete with impassioned readings and endlessly rich, detailed arrangements. —*Stephen Thomas Erlewine*

All Alone / Jan. 15, 1962-Jan. 17, 1962 / Reprise ✦✦✦
Originally, *All Alone* was going to called *Come Waltz With Me.* Although the title and the accompanying specially written title song were dropped before the album's release, the record remained a stately collection of waltzes, arranged and conducted by Gordon Jenkins. Out of all the arrangers Sinatra regularly worked with, Jenkins had the most overt classical influences in his writing, making him the perfect choice for the project. Nevertheless, *All Alone* is an uneven album, even as it is one of the most intriguing records Sinatra recorded. Divided between standards and relatively recent tunes, the most distinctive element of the album are the rich, neoclassical arrangements by Jenkins. Sinatra doesn't strictly follow Jenkins' intentions. Instead of playing close to the vest, he wrenches the emotions out of the songs. Most of the time, the results are quite moving, especially on the opening and closing Irving Berlin ballads, "All Alone" and "The Song Is Ended." When the results aren't quite as successful, they are still interesting, and the elegant, rumanative music makes *All Alone* a necessary listen for dedicated Sinatra fans. —*Stephen Thomas Erlewine*

Sinatra-Basie / Oct. 2, 1962-Oct. 3, 1962 / Reprise ✦✦✦✦

The Concert Sinatra / Feb. 18, 1963-Feb. 21, 1963 / Reprise ✦✦✦

Sinatra's Sinatra / Apr. 29, 1963-Apr. 30, 1963 / Reprise ✦✦✦

Softly, As I Leave You / Jul. 31, 1963-Oct. 4, 1964 / Reprise ✦✦✦

America, I Hear You Singing / 1964 / Reprise ✦✦✦

Sings Days of Wine and Roses, Moon River & Other Academy Award Winners / Jan. 27, 1964-Jan. 28, 1964 / Reprise ✦✦✦

It Might as Well Be Swing / Jun. 9, 1964-Jun. 12, 1964 / Reprise ✦✦✦

My Kind of Broadway / 1965 / Reprise ✦✦✦

Sinatra '65 / 1965 / Reprise ✦✦

☆ **September of My Years** / Apr. 13, 1965-May 27, 1965 / Reprise ✦✦✦✦✦
September of My Years is one of Frank Sinatra's triumphs of the '60s, an album that consolidated his strengths while moving him into new territory, primarily in terms of tone. More than the double disc set *A Man and His Music*—which was released a year after this album—*September of My Years* captures how Sinatra was at the time of his 50th birthday. Gordon Jenkins rich, stately and melancholy arrangements give the album an appropriate reflective atmosphere. Most of the songs are new or relatively recent numbers; every cut fits into a loose theme of aging, reflection and regret. Sinatra, however, doesn't seem stuck in his ways—though the songs are rooted in traditional pop, they touch on folk and contemporary pop. As such, the album offered a perfect summary, as well as suggesting future routes for the singer. —*Stephen Thomas Erlewine*

Moonlight Sinatra / Nov. 29, 1965-Nov. 30, 1965 / Reprise ✦✦✦

Greatest Hits, Vol. 2 / 1965-1972 / Reprise ✦✦✦

Strangers in the Night / Apr. 11, 1966-Apr. 16, 1966 / Reprise ✦✦✦
Strangers in the Night marked Frank Sinatra's return to the top of the pop charts in the mid-'60s, and it consolidated the comeback he started in 1965. Although he later claimed he disliked the title track, the album was an inventive, rich effort from Sinatra, one that established him as a still-viable star to a wide, mainstream audience without losing the core of his sound. Combining pop hits ("Downtown," "On a Clear Day (You Can See Forever)," "Call Me") with show tunes and standards, the album creates a delicate but comfortable balance between big band and pop instrumentation. Using strings, horns, and an organ, Riddle constructed an easy, deceptively swinging sound that appealed to both Sinatra's dedicated fans and pop radio. And Sinatra's singing is relaxed, confident, and surprisingly jazzy, as he plays with the melody of "The Most Beautiful Girl in the World" and delivers a knockout punch with the assured, breathtaking "Summer Wind." Although he would not record another album with Riddle again, Sinatra would expand the approach of *Strangers in the Night* for the rest of the decade. —*Stephen Thomas Erlewine*

Sinatra at the Sands / Oct. 18, 1966-Nov. 18, 1966 / Reprise ✦✦✦✦
In many ways, *Sinatra at the Sands* is the definitive portrait of Frank Sinatra in the '60s. Recorded in April of 1966, *At the Sands* is the first commercially released live Frank Sinatra album, recorded at a relaxed Las Vegas club show. For these dates at the Sands, Sinatra worked with Count Basie and his Orchestra, which was conducted by Quincy Jones. Like any of his concerts, the material was fairly predictable, with his standard show numbers punctuated by some nice surprises. Throughout the show, Sinatra is in fine voice, turning in a particularly affecting version of "Angel Eyes." He is also in fine humor, constantly joking with the audience and the band, as well as delivering an entertaining, if rambling, monologue halfway through the album. Some of the humor has dated poorly, appearing insensitive, but that sentiment cannot be applied to the music. Basie and the orchestra are swinging and dynamic, inspiring a textured, dramatic and thoroughly enjoyable performance from Sinatra. —*Stephen Thomas Erlewine*

That's Life / Oct. 18, 1966-Nov. 18, 1966 / Reprise ✦✦✦

Frank Sinatra and the World We Knew / 1967 / Reprise ✦✦

Francis Albert Sinatra and Antonio Carlos Jobim / Jan. 30, 1967-Feb. 1, 1967 / Reprise ✦✦✦✦✦
By 1967, bossa nova had become quite popular within jazz and traditional pop audiences, yet Frank Sinatra hadn't attempted any Brazil-influenced material. Sinatra decided to record a full-fledged bossa nova album with the genre's leading composer, Antonio Carlos Jobim. Arranged by Claus Ogerman and featuring Jobim on guitar and backing vocals, *Francis Albert Sinatra and Antonio Carlos Jobim* concentrated on Jobim's originals, adding three American classics—"Baubles, Bangles and Beads," "Change Partners," and "I Concentrate on You"—that were rearranged to suit bossa nova conventions. The result was a subdued, quiet album that used the Latin rhythms as a foundation, not as a focal point. Supported by a relaxed, sympathetic arrangement of muted brass, simmering percussion, soft strings, and Jobim's lilting guitar, Sinatra turns in an especially noteworthy performance; he has never sounded so subtle, underplaying every line he delivers and showcasing vocal techniques that he never had displayed before. *Francis Albert Sinatra and Antonio Carlos Jobim* doesn't reveal its pleasures immediately; the album is too textured and understated to be fully appreciated within one listen. After a few plays, the album begins to slowly work its way underneath a listener's skin, and it emerges as one of his most rewarding albums of the '60s. —*Stephen Thomas Erlewine*

Francis A. Sinatra & Edward K. Ellington / Dec. 12, 1967 / Reprise ✦✦✦

Cycles / 1968 / Reprise ✦✦
Cycles was Frank Sinatra's first full-fledged pop/rock-oriented album, concentrating on a more orchestrated variation on the popular folk-rock of the late '60s. The foundation of the arrangements on *Cycles* are guitars, bass, and drum kits, all played gently and unobtrusively; the strings are layered on top of the pop rhythm section. Appropriately, Sinatra sang a variety of material associated with folk-rock, particularly Joni Mitchell's "Both Sides Now" and Glen Campbell's "Gentle on My Mind" and "By the Time I Get to Phoenix." Sinatra responds to the softer material by phasing out most of the edginess in his phrasing. He doesn't sing with the nuanced textures of his Jobim albums—he is simply restrained. That doesn't result

in an embarrassing album, yet *Cycles* isn't the successful rock and traditional pop fusion that it might have been. Some of the material isn't well-suited for Sinatra—neither "Little Green Apples" or "Pretty Colors" sound convincing—but the main problem is with Don Costa's arrangements and production. There simply isn't enough variety to sustain interest throughout the course of the short, ten-song album. Certain sections work well, particularly the Glen Campbell numbers, but there isn't anything distinctive about the record, which makes it one of the weakest albums Sinatra ever released. *—Stephen Thomas Erlewine*

The Sinatra Family Wish You A Merry Christmas / 1968 / Reprise ✦✦✦

My Way / Feb. 13, 1969-Feb. 24, 1969 / Reprise ✦✦✦
Although it follows the same patterns and approach as *Cycles, My Way* is a stronger album, with a better, more varied selection of material and a more focused, gutsy performance from Sinatra. Built around the hit single "My Way," the album again alternates between rock covers ("Yesterday," "Hallelujah, I Love Her So," "For Once In My LIfe," "Didn't We," "Mrs. Robinson"), a couple of adapted French songs, and a handful of standards. This time out, Don Costa has written more engaging charts than the previous *Cycles*. The Beatles' "Yesterday" is given an affecting, melancholy treatment that brings out the best in Sinatra, as does the new arrangment of "All My Tomorrows," which is lush and aching. If Sinatra doesn't quite pull off the R&B of "Hallelujah, I Love Her So," the does sing the light Latin stylings of "A Day in the Life of a Fool" beautifully, and he has fun with Paul Simon's "Mrs. Robinson," changing the lyrics dramtically so they become a tongue-in-cheek, swinging hipster tribute. For that matter, most of the record is successful in creating a middle ground between the traditional pop Sinatra loves and the contemporary pop/rock that dominated the charts in the late '60s. *My Way* doesn't have the macho swagger of his prime Rat Pack records, but its reflective, knowing arrangements show that Sinatra could come to terms with rock & roll at some level. *—Stephen Thomas Erlewine*

A Man Alone & Other Songs of Rod McKuen / Mar. 19, 1969-Mar. 21, 1969 / Reprise ✦✦

Watertown / Jul. 14, 1969-Jul. 17, 1969 / Reprise ✦✦✦✦✦
Watertown is Frank Sinatra's most ambitious concept album, as well as his most difficult record. Not only does it tell a full-fledged story, it is his most explicit attempt at rock-oriented pop. Since the main composer of *Watertown* is Bob Gaudio, the author of the Four Seasons' hits "Can't Take My Eyes Off of You," "Walk Like a Man," and "Big Girls Don't Cry," that doesn't come as a surprise. With Jake Holmes, Gaudio created a song cycle concerning a middle-aged, small-town man whose wife had left him with the kids. Constructed as a series of brief lyrical snapshots that read like letters or soliloquies, the culminating effect of the songs is an atmosphere of loneliness, but it is a loneliness without much hope or romance—it is the sound of a broken man. Producer Charles Calello arranged musical backdrops that conveyed the despair of the lyrics. Weaving together prominent electric guitars, keyboards, drum kits, and light strings, Calello uses pop/rock instrumentations and production techniques, but that doesn't prevent Sinatra from warming to the material. In fact, he turns in a wonderful performance, drawing out every emotion from the lyrics, giving the album's character depth. *—Stephen Thomas Erlewine*

Sinatra & Company / 1969-1971 / Warner Brothers ✦✦✦
In 1969, Frank Sinatra recorded a second album with Antonio Carlos Jobim. For unknown reasons, Reprise decided not to release *Sinatra-Jobim*, but seven of the ten songs intended for the record did appear on the first side of 1971's *Sinatra & Company*. The selections from *Sinatra-Jobim* have a decidedly different flavor than the material on *Francis Albert Sinatra and Antonio Carlos Jobim*, largely due to the charts of arranger Eumir Deodato. Where Claus Ogerman's arrangements were quite subdued and understated, Deodato's charts are looser and more relaxed; consequently, the music is lighter, more immediate, and arguably more fun. Sinatra responds to the arrangements with more forceful singing than on the previous Jobim collaboration, but his phrasing is still more nuanced than even his soft pop/rock-oriented material. Nevertheless, that subtle phrasing carries over into the second side of *Sinatra & Company*, a collection of pop-oriented tracks. Although the music on the second half of the album is neither as adventerous or as compelling as that on the first, it is still highly entertaining. The seven songs were arranged by Don Costas, who keeps the material shiny and commercially oriented. In the case of "Close to You," "Leaving on a Jet Plane," "I Will Drink the Wine," "Bein' Green," and "Sunrise in the Morning," that isn't bad—this is material that demands to be delivered in slick, polished arrangements. Under Costas' direction, these songs are given arrangements that feature both strings and gentle folk-rock underpinnings, particularly strummed acoustic guitars. Taken on its own terms, the second half of *Sinatra & Company* ranks as some of his best soft rock-influenced material of the late '60s, even if it doesn't sit comfortably with the excellent bossa nova that comprises the first side of the record. *—Stephen Thomas Erlewine*

Ol' Blue Eyes Is Back / Jun. 4, 1973-Aug. 20, 1973 / Reprise ✦✦

Some Nice Things I've Missed / Dec. 10, 1973-May 21, 1974 / Reprise ✦✦

The Main Event—*Live* */ Oct. 1974 / Reprise* ✦✦

Trilogy / Sep. 17, 1979-Dec. 18, 1979 / Reprise ✦✦
By the time the triple-record set *Trilogy* was released, Frank Sinatra had become somewhat of a recluse from the recording studio. An audacious, ambitious way to stage a comeback, each of the album's three records was conceived as an individual work, and each was arranged by one of Sinatra's major collaborators—Billy May ("The Past"), Don Costa ("The Present"), and Gordon Jenkins ("The Future"). As a concept, *Trilogy* certainly has its flaws, as does some of the music on the lengthy set. However, the best moments are triumphant, proving that the Voice was still vital in his fourth decade of recording. "The Past" is easily the best record on the album. For the first time since the early '60s, Sinatra made a record of standards ("The Song Is You," "It Had to Be You," "All of You"), which is the material best suited for his talents. "The Present" isn't quite as accomplished, concentrating on pop hits like "Love Me Tender," "Something," "Song Sung Blue," "MacArthur Park," and "Just the Way You Are." Some of the material is mediocre, but Don Costa's arrangements are lovely, as is Sinatra's singing. Together, they make mid-level songs like "Theme from New York, New York" into anthems. However good the first two records are, "The Future" is an unqualified mess. Written by Jenkins, the songs are ambitious, experimental, and self-referential—in fact, it's more of a free-form suite than a set of songs. Most of the record is devoid of melody, and Sinatra sounds lost singing clichéd, trite lyrics about peace, space travel, and his past. It might be an anticlimatic way to end an otherwise enjoyable set, but "The Future" doesn't ruin the pleasures of *Trilogy*, it just puts them into greater perspective. *—Stephen Thomas Erlewine*

She Shot Me Down / 1981 / Reprise ✦✦✦
She Shot Me Down is Frank Sinatra's last great album, a dark, brooding record of saloon songs delivered with an understated authority by Sinatra. Arranged and conducted by Gordon Jenkins and produced by Don Costa, the record largely consists of contemporary material, including five that were basically tailored for Sinatra. It's a dense, moody record that works spectacularly—Sinatra's vocals are more alive and rich in detail than on *Trilogy*, and the concept is more concise and well-executed. *She Shot Me Down* might not consist of the classic saloon songs, but it has that feeling more than any of his other albums. *—Stephen Thomas Erlewine*

L.A. Is My Lady / May 17, 1984 / Qwest ✦✦

Duets / 1993 / Capitol ✦

Duets II / 1994 / Capitol ✦

Everything Happens to Me / Feb. 6, 1996 / Reprise ✦✦✦✦

Kate Smith

b. May 1, 1907, Greenville, AL, **d.** Jun. 17, 1986
Vocals / Traditional Pop, Show Tunes
The "Songbird of the South," vocalist Kate Smith was one of the most popular stars of the pre-World War II era; she remains best remembered for her definitive version of the patriotic anthem "God Bless America," which became a hit on no less than three separate occasions. The owner of a thunderous soprano, Smith signed to Columbia in 1927, debuting with "One Sweet Letter From You," backed by Red Nichols' Charleston Chasers. In 1931 she began hosting her own radio show; its theme song, "When the Moon Comes Over the Mountain," subsequently became her first major hit, selling some 19 million copies. In 1932, Smith scored her second smash with "River, Stay 'Way From My Door," recorded with Guy Lombardo and His Royal Canadians; they later backed her on "Too Late," another Top Ten success issued that same year—in all, she recorded two dozen hits for Columbia between 1927 and 1946. While American listeners looked to Smith for assurance throughout the Depression era, she became an icon in 1938, when she recorded Irving Berlin's "God Bless America" for Victor; within a year its success established it as a kind of unofficial national anthem. *—Jason Ankeny*

The Best of Kate Smith / 1970 / Curb ✦✦✦✦✦
The Best of Kate Smith is a 13-track budget-priced collection that features some of her biggest hits, including "God Bless America, " "Ridin' High, ' "Love Walked In, " "The Very Thought of You, " "Love Is Here to Stay, " "If I Had You, " "But Not for Me, " "'S Wonderful, " "They Can't Take That Away from Me" and "It Could Happen to You." Although this isn't a bad budget-priced disc, there are far better collections available, offering more songs and better sound for not much more money. *—Stephen Thomas Erlewine*

★ **16 Most Requested Songs** / 1991 / Columbia/Legacy ✦✦✦✦✦
16 Most Requested Songs is a midline-priced collection that spotlights many of Kate Smith's best-known and most popular performances for Columbia Records, including "When You Wish Upon a Star," "I've Got a Gal in Kalamazoo," "Be Careful, It's My Heart," "Tumbling Tumbleweeds," "My Melancholy Baby," "Memories of You," "The Last Time I Saw Paris," "My Buddy," "Embraceable You" and "We'll Meet Again." Although it's far from a perfect retrospective of her career, it's still a nice sampler of familiar items, and it may satisfy the needs of some casual fans who only want the hits. *—Stephen Thomas Erlewine*

The Voice of America / Dec. 14, 1999 / Vintage Jazz Band ✦✦

Stephen Sondheim

b. 1930
Composer / Musicals, Show Tunes
According to most cirtics and theater historians, Stephen Sondheim stands among Broadway show composers and lyricists not only as the greatest of his generation but as the *only* great one of his generation. There may be many reasons why Broadway failed to produce consistently great writers to follow the Rodgers and Hammersteins of the '40s and '50s, but the fact remains that, though he operates without serious competition, Sondheim clearly ranks with such masters, as well as with the Jerome Kerns and Irving Berlins of an even earlier generation. He got his first big break when he was hired to write lyrics to Leonard Bernstein's score for *West Side Story* (1957), which turned out to be one of the biggest hits and most memorable works of its time. He also worked with Jule Styne on *Gypsy* (1959), then scored his first success as both a composer and lyricist with 1962's *A Funny Thing Happened on the Way to the Forum*. It was his last hit until *Company* (1970), a show about contemporary life and mores that did much to revolutionize the Broadway musical. Since that time, Sondheim's shows of the '70s and '80s—such as *A Little Night Music, Sweeney Todd* and *Sunday in the Park with George*—have been amazingly daring in terms of subject matter, with unusual musical ideas and stunningly original lyrics. In recent years, he has turned more to the films (he wrote a score for Stravinsky in the '70s), writing songs for Madonna in *Dick Tracy* in 1990 and reportedly currently working on an original movie musical. *—William Ruhlmann*

★ **Sondheim: A Musical Tribute** / 1973 / RCA ✦✦✦✦✦
A two-disc recording of a special benefit show held Mar 11, 1973, featuring many of the original performers from Stephen Sondheim musicals, reprising their performances of his songs. Thus, the album is a kind of "Sondheim's Greatest Hits," with the added excitement of being a one-time event. Originally isssued as a two-LP set by Warner in 1973, it was reissued by RCA on CD/cassette with previously unreleased tracks. *—William Ruhlmann*

☆ **Side by Side by Sondheim** / May 1976 / RCA ♦♦♦♦♦
A two-disc London cast recording of a revue culled from songs written by Stephen Sondheim for such musicals as *A Funny Thing Happened on the Way to the Forum, Company, A Little Night Music, Follies, Anyone Can Whistle, Pacific Overtures, Do I Hear a Waltz?, West Side Story,* and *Gypsy,* and more obscure works such as "Evening Primrose" (a TV show), *The 7% Solution,* and *The Mad Show.* In anthology and presented starkly, the songs are (if possible) even more impressive than when heard in the shows for which they were written. If there was any doubt that Stephen Sondheim is the greatest talent writing contemporary musicals, this show erased it. *— William Ruhlmann*

Jo Stafford

b. Nov. 12, 1920, Coalinga, CA
Vocals / Vocal Jazz, Traditional Pop
One of the most technically gifted and popular vocalists of the immediate post-war period, Jo Stafford effortlessly walked the line between breezy pop and the more serious art of post-big-band jazz singing. With the help of her husband, top-flight arranger and Capitol A&R director Paul Weston, Stafford recorded throughout the '40s and '50s for Capitol and Columbia. She also contributed (with Weston) to one of the best pop novelty acts of the period, a hilariously inept and off-key satire that saw the couple billed as Jonathan and Darlene Edwards.

After singing from an early age, Stafford became the first female voice in a seven-man vocal act known as the Pied Pipers. Soon after the group joined Tommy Dorsey's Orchestra in 1939 however, it was pruned to a quartet. The group appeared on several of the Dorsey band's hits of the early '40s. Stafford finally left the Pied Pipers for a solo contract in 1944, though the group provided back-up for many of her initial solo hits. Not only signed to Capitol but able to preview hit songs as the co-host of label-founder Johnny Mercer's radio program, Stafford hit the charts with the mid-'40s songs "Long Ago (And Far Away)," "I Love You" and "Candy." The latter, a duet with Mercer and the Pied Pipers, became her first number one. She later moved to Columbia and recorded the two biggest hits of her career, 1952's "You Belong to Me" and 1954's "Make Love to Me." Though she slipped from the charts in the late '50s and retired from performance, Stafford continued to record and issued the LP *Getting Sentimental over Tommy Dorsey* on Reprise in 1963. She also founded Corinthian Records, with Weston, to reissue the couples' various recordings. *—John Bush*

Jo + Jazz / Jul. 15, 1960-Aug. 10, 1960 / Corinthian ♦♦♦♦♦
The closest Stafford ever came to being a jazz singer. This early '60s release had instrumental touches and a jazz tone, and Stafford sang with more energy and less gimmickry. *— Ron Wynn*

Big Band Sound / 1960-1970 / Corinthian ♦♦♦♦♦

Portrait Edition / Aug. 30, 1994 / Columbia/Legacy ♦♦♦♦♦
For over 30 years, Jo Stafford was one of America's top middle-of-the-road pop singers, admired for her ability to always sing in tune and to uplift every lyric she interpreted while actually singing very straight. This three-CD retrospective, which was released in 1994, has 76 selections covering a 40-year period, with most of the numbers dating from the 1940s and '50s. On the minus side, the music is not programmed in chronological order, and the complete personnel is not given, but since Stafford's style was unchanged through the years and she tended to be the main star of her records (except when sharing vocals with the likes of Frankie Laine, Vic Damone, Gordon McRae, Nelson Eddy, Gene Autry and even Liberace), these are minor faults. It is unfortunate that Stafford's odd hillbilly hit "Tim-tay-shun" was not included, but all of her other big sellers are here. As an extra "bonus" at the end of each CD are one or two selections from the Jo Stafford/Paul Weston alter-egos Darlene and Jonathan Edwards, which features satirical cocktail piano from Weston and remarkable singing by Stafford that is consistently just a little bit out of tune—pretty painful stuff! Recommended. *— Scott Yanow*

Spotlight on Jo Stafford / Jan. 23, 1996 / Capitol ♦♦♦♦♦
Spotlight on Jo Stafford is an excellent 18-track overview of her recordings for Capitol Records. Although it doesn't her biggest hits, it does have a good selection of lesser-known gems from later in her career, featuring such highlights as "(It Was) Just One of Those Things," "Too Marvelous for Words," "In the Still of the Night," "Fools Rush In," "I Remember You," "Over the Rainbow" and "(I'll Be With You In) Apple Blossom Time." *— Stephen Thomas Erlewine*

★ **Coming Back Like a Song: 25 Hits 1941-47** / May 19, 1998 / ASV/Living Era ♦♦♦♦♦
The selection on this compilation of Jo Stafford's early recordings is flawless. A legend on the sleeve reads "25 hits 1941-1947", and that is nearly accurate, as the 74Ω-minute disc contains every Top Ten hit—all 18 of them—on which Stafford sang a lead vocal in the almost seven years under consideration. Stafford began that period as one of four members of the Pied Pipers, the vocal group that was part of Tommy Dorsey's orchestra, but Dorsey gradually let her sing without the group, notably on the hits "Yes, Indeed!" (a duet with its composer and arranger, Sy Oliver) and "Manhattan Serenade." Leaving Dorsey, the Pipers signed to Capitol Records, and Stafford also signed as a solo artist, though she continued to record with the group at first, scoring with their reading of "The Trolley Song" even as she was having solo hits that started with "It Could Happen to You." By 1945, she had left the Pipers, though she rejoined them and Capitol label head Johnny Mercer on the chart-topping "Candy." Ironically, her only other number one hit during this period came with her comic country rendition of "Temptation," credited to Red Ingle & the Natural Seven, under the pseudonym Cinderella G. Stump. In addition to including all the major hits in chronological order by recording date, compiler Peter Dempsey has thrown in a few obscurities, notably two jazzy recordings, "Baby, Won't You Please Come Home—" and "I'll Be with You in Apple Blossom Time," on which Stafford is backed by the King Cole Trio and two horns. Mastered from 78s, the tracks are not in the best sound quality, but they are adequate, and the selection makes this the essential early Jo Stafford collection. *— William Ruhlmann*

V Disc: A Musical Contribution by America's Best for Our Armed Forces Overseas / Aug. 18, 1998 / Collectors' Choice Music ♦♦♦♦
Emerging as a solo performer in 1944 and then ranking second only to Dinah Shore as the most popular female singer of the decade, Jo Stafford was a particular favorite of American troops. So, it is appropriate that she contributed 20 tracks to the V-Disc program. Typically, she often sings of the romantic separations and reunions that were so much a part of the experience of World War II—"Gee, It's Good to Hold You," "Baby Won't You Please Come Home," "I Remember You," "Yesterdays," "I'll Be Seeing You." The song selection is curious: many are tunes associated with other singers of the day, such as Peggy Lee's "I Didn't Know About You" and the Bing Crosby/Andrews Sisters hit "Tallahassee," and there are also standards like "Blue Moon" and "Carry Me Back to Old Virginia." But Stafford sings her hit "That's For Me," as well as a couple of songs from her days with Tommy Dorsey—"Manhattan Serenade" and "Yes, Indeed!" It would be interesting to know who the backing musicians are, since some of them solo effectively. It sounds like some of these tracks, notably the two Dorsey-associated numbers among others, are actually big band tracks on which Stafford or her former group, the Pied Pipers, were featured, rather than Stafford solo tracks per se. Nevertheless, this is one of the better single-disc releases in Collectors' Choice Music's V-Disc series, especially because there is relatively little Stafford in print on CD. (1-800-923-1122) — *William Ruhlmann*

Kay Starr

b. Jul. 21, 1922, Dougherty, OK
Vocals / Traditional Pop, Standards, Swing, Classic Female Blues
A solid jazz singer whose early recordings tended to be forgotten after her ascendancy into the commercial sphere during the mid-'50s, Kay Starr was among the first pop singer to capitalize on the "rock fad" with her 1955 novelty "Rock and Roll Waltz." Her biggest hit came with the era-defining "Wheel of Fortune," a prime slice of '50s adult pop with a suitably brassy reading. Born in Oklahoma, she moved to Dallas at a young age and made her debut on radio while still in school. A brief stay with Glenn Miller & His Orchestra precipitated her working with groups led by Bob Crosby, Joe Venuti and finally Charlie Barnet. She recorded a few numbers with Barnet that earned her a solo contract with Capitol.

By 1948, Starr made her Hit Parade breakthrough with "You Were Only Foolin' (While I Was Falling in Love)." Subsequent hits like "Hoop-Dee-Doo," "Oh, Babe!" and "I'll Never Be Free" (the latter with Tennessee Ernie Ford) framed her in an emerging vein of the popular market that also looked back to traditional country and folk. In 1952, "Wheel of Fortune" became her biggest hit and one of the signature songs of the '50s pop sound. She struggled to reach a similar chart peak for several years afterwards, though "Comes A-Long A-Love" topped the British charts. With her move to RCA in 1955, though the comical "Rock and Roll Waltz" spent several weeks at number one. It was her last major hit, followed by just one additional Top Ten entry, 1957's "My Heart Reminds Me." By the 1960s, she had begun to concentrate more on performing (especially in Las Vegas) than recording, despite moving back to Capitol in 1961. In the '90s, she played several oldies packages, including the 3 Girls 3 tour with Helen O'Connell and Margaret Whiting. *—John Bush*

● **Capitol Collectors Series** / 1948-1962 / Capitol ♦♦♦♦♦
A good collection of Starr's '50s pop material includes "Hoop Dee Doo," "If You Love Me (Really Love Me)," "Changing Partners," and "Wheel of Fortune." *— Richard Lieberson*

Barbra Streisand

b. Apr. 24, 1942, Brooklyn, NY
Vocals / Traditional Pop, Standards, Musicals, Cast Recordings, Soft Rock, Pop, Adult Contemporary, Show Tunes
Barbra Streisand's status as one of the most successful singers of her generation is all the more remarkable not only because her popularity has been achieved in the face of a dominant musical trend—rock & roll—which she did not follow, but also because, despite an amazing singing voice that has enthralled practically anyone who has heard it, she has always used singing as a mere stepping stone to other careers, as a stage and film actress and as a film director. Parts in two Broadway shows during the early '60s gained her a contract through Columbia, and her first album became a Top Ten hit in 1963. Streisand turned her back on potentially lucrative concert bookings in favor of a long-running starring role in the Broadway show *Funny Girl.* "People" from that show became her first Top Ten single, and the *People* album her first chart-topping LP. Though subsequent film roles were flops, she returned to hit-making during the '70s and successfully married her musical and film acting interests, gaining film roles and #1 hits with *The Way We Were* (the title theme) and *A Star Is Born* ("Evergreen"). In 1983, Streisand's first directorial effort, *Yentl,* became a successful film with a Top Ten soundtrack album, and 1985's *The Broadway Album* brought her to the top of the charts once again. She returned to the concert stage in 1994, resulting in the Top Ten, million-selling album *The Concert.* *— William Ruhlmann*

☆ **The Barbra Streisand Album** / Feb. 25, 1963 / Columbia ♦♦♦♦♦
Of course, the first thing that strikes you listening to the first Barbra Streisand album, recorded and released before the singer's 21st birthday, is *that great voice.* And it isn't just the sheer quality of the voice, its purity and its strength throughout its register, it's also the mastery of vocal effects that produce dramatic readings of the lyrics—each song is like a one-act musical. Streisand opens with Julie London's signature torch song, "Cry Me A River," and she doesn't only surpass London, she sets off a thermonuclear explosion. From there, versatility and novelty are emphasized—a breakneck version of "Who's Afraid Of The Big Bad Wolf—," a slow, emotion-drenched performance of "Happy Days Are Here Again." But Streisand's debut, inventively arranged and conducted by Peter Matz, is notable as much for the surprising omissions as the surprising selections. Arriving in 1963, ten years into the revival of sophisticated interwar theater songs led by Frank Sinatra and followed by all other adult pop singers, Streisand virtually ignores the modern masters like Gershwin and Berlin. When she does do Rodgers and Hart or Cole Porter, she picks obscure songs; her idea of a good 1930s number is Fats Waller and Andy Razaf's "Keepin' Out Of Mischief Now." She is much more comfortable with recent theater material, choosing two songs from *The Fantasticks* (1960) and the title song from the stage play *A Taste Of Honey* (1962). *The Barbra Streisand Album* is an essential recording in the field of pop vocals because it redefines that

genre in contemporary terms. (*The Barbra Streisand Album* won Grammy Awards for Album of the Year, Best Female Vocal Performance, and Best Album Cover.) *— William Ruhlmann*

The Second Barbra Streisand Album / Oct. 1963 / Columbia ✦✦✦

The Third Album / Feb. 1964 / Columbia ✦✦✦

People / Sep. 1964 / Columbia ✦✦✦✦✦
After two less successful albums, Barbra Streisand returned to form on her fourth album with a selection of songs that showed some of the imagination of her debut album. Much of the material was new: The album opened and closed with songs by Jule Styne and Bob Merrill, first "Absent Minded Me," and then the Top Ten title song that was the hit from Streisand's triumphant Broadway show, *Funny Girl*. Streisand introduced Cy Coleman and Carolyn Leigh's "When In Rome (I Do As The Romans Do)," a lively song that allowed her to display some of the spirit and humor that had been missing on her last two outings. And when picking from older songs, she again found obscure or atypical tunes from prominent composers or lost gems she could make her owm. In the former category were Irving Berlin's "Supper Time," a blues song unlike any the composer had ever done, and "My Lord And Master," from Rodgers and Hammerstein's *The King And I*. In the latter was the delightful "Fine And Dandy," from the 1930 show of the same name, with a lyric by Kay Swift. Add in some obvious choices like James Van Heusen and Sammy Cahn's "Love Is A Bore" (a companion to the previously recorded "Down With Love") and "Don't Like Goodbyes," another selection from Harold Arlen and Truman Capote's *House Of Flowers*, from which Streisand had earlier picked "A Sleepin' Bee," and you have an album fashioned to play to the singer's strengths and musical tastes instead of trying to fit her into existing ones. That wasn't quite enough to match the quality of the debut album, but it was a definite improvement over the second and third albums. (*People* won Grammy Awards for Best Vocal Performance and Best Album Cover.) *— William Ruhlmann*

My Name Is Barbra / 1965 / Columbia ✦✦✦✦✦
An album containing many of the songs used in Barbra Streisand's TV special of the same name, *My Name Is Barbra* followed the general outline of two of the three sections of the show. The first side was a concept set of songs about childhood and growing up that allowed Streisand, in the songs "I'm Five" and "Sweet Zoo," to take a comic approach for the first time in several albums. The second side was a set of adult songs performed in Streisand's big, dramatic style. "I Can See It," her third borrowing from *The Fantasticks*, was the best yet, and Streisand's first attempt at a Gershwin tune, "Someone To Watch Over Me," was at least a qualified success. "I've Got No Strings," from the movie *Pinocchio*, was no "Who's Afraid Of The Big Bad Wolf" (one of the highlights of her debut album), but it wasn't bad. And best of all was Streisand's reading of "My Man," Fanny Brice's signature song, though it had not been used in *Funny Girl*, the Broadway show about her life, in which Streisand had starred. After this demonstration, however, it would be interpolated into the movie version. (*My Name Is Barbra* won a Grammy Award for Best Female Vocal Performance.) *— William Ruhlmann*

My Name Is Barbra 2 / Oct. 1965 / Columbia ✦✦✦

Color Me Barbra / 1966 / Columbia ✦✦✦

Je M'appelle Barbra / Nov. 1966 / Columbia ✦✦✦

Simply Streisand / Oct. 1967 / Columbia ✦✦✦
After three albums related to television specials and one of French songs, *Simply Streisand* was Barbra Streisand's first "regular" new album since *People* three years earlier and her first new release of any kind in a year. (Before, her albums came regularly every six months.) By now, the singer was spending her time in Hollywood shooting movies, and the music scene had moved heavily into rock, developments that made this a perfunctory set and one released into an indifferent climate; unlike her previous eight albums, *Simply Streisand* missed the Top Ten. But it isn't *that* bad. Streisand is not an accomplished performer of classic pop standards like "My Funny Valentine" and "More Than You Know," largely because she seems too intimidated by the material to put an individual stamp on it, but she is a great singer, and if arranger Ray Ellis's charts lack the invention of Peter Matz, they are conventionally competent. If this were the only Streisand album you ever heard, you'd still think she was good. It's only in comparison to what went before that it seems mediocre. *— William Ruhlmann*

A Happening in Central Park / 1968 / Columbia ✦✦✦

What About Today— / 1969 / Columbia ✦✦

● **Greatest Hits** / 1970 / Columbia ✦✦✦✦✦
At a time when Barbra Streisand's career was in decline, what turned out to be only her first greatest hits album seemed to serve as both a summing up and a kiss-off of her 1960s recordings. Streisand was not primarily a singles artist; between 1964 and 1969, she enjoyed nine chart singles, of which only one, "People," made the Top Ten, with only one other, "Second Hand Rose," reaching the Top 40. But in that time, she scored seven gold-selling, Top Ten albums. This hits collection contained seven of her chart singles, plus her non-charting early single, "My Coloring Book," "Happy Days Are Here Again," which was one of the highlights of her debut album (heard here in the live version from *A Happening In Central Park*), and "Don't Rain On My Parade" from the *Funny Girl* soundtrack. For casual fans, that made for a good sampling of Streisand's most prominent '60s work, and if at the time it seemed likely that this was all the hits there would be, instead the '60s proved to be only the first chapter in Streisand's career. *— William Ruhlmann*

On a Clear Day You Can See Forever / Jul. 1970 / Columbia ✦✦✦
The film version of the Broadway musical *On A Clear Day You Can See Forever* was something of a disaster, but the soundtrack album is better because the focus is on the Burton Lane/Alan Jay Lerner songs and on the primary singer, Barbra Streisand, who has six vocals out of ten selections. Far less impressive is co-star Yves Montand, whose singing voice is as suspect as his English, such that the album is a mixed success. *— William Ruhlmann*

Stoney End / Feb. 1971 / Columbia ✦✦✦✦✦
Barbra Streisand scored her second Top Ten hit in early 1971 by treating Laura Nyro's recording of her song "Stoney End" as a demo and copying it practically note for note. "Mama, let me start all over," she sang, and her wish was granted. The followup album of the same title was in its way as surprising as Streisand's debut album eight years earlier. Where that record had redefined the role of the traditional pop singer in contemporary terms for the early '60s, *Stoney End* redefined Streisand as an effective pop-rock singer, which her last outing, *What About Today?*, had failed to do. Maybe she listened as closely to Nyro and Joni Mitchell as she had to Ethel Merman and Judy Garland a decade earlier, but somehow she reoriented her approach to music, adapting herself to vocal demands that were very different in terms of dynamics, expressiveness, and especially rhythm from the traditional pop and theater music she had sung previously. Producer Richard Perry may have eased the transition by using session men like Randy Newman, who played piano on two of his own compositions, and who bridged the worlds of show music and rock. But Streisand herself found something to identify with in songs like Gordon Lightfoot's "If You Could Read My Mind" (maybe that passage about the movie queen) and Mitchell's "I Don't Know Where I Stand." *Stoney End* was not a perfect album—the reliance on minor Brill Building material and two more Nyro copies kept it from classic status—but it was so far removed from what Streisand's fans and her detractors thought her capable of that it stands as one of her major triumphs. It was also her biggest seller in four years and launched the comeback that saw her through the '70s. *— William Ruhlmann*

Barbra Joan Streisand / Aug. 1971 / Columbia ✦✦✦✦✦
On her followup to the comeback album *Stoney End*, Barbra Streisand tried to do for (or to) Carole King what she had done the last time around with Laura Nyro, i.e., redo her material in a similar manner and essentially hijack it (while providing a big jump in songwriter royalties, of course). This was not so easy to do in the case of "Beautiful," "Where You Lead," and "You've Got A Friend," however, since, unlike the Nyro songs, by the time Streisand got to these tunes, they were already on King's own chart-topping album, *Tapestry*. Nevertheless, Steisand, who after all is a much more powerful singer than King, did them well and even eked out a Top 40 single on "Where You Lead." And the album contained other gems, such as a delicate reading of John Lennon's "Love" (a take on his "Mother" was far less successful) and the only recording of "I Mean To Shine," written by Donald Fagen and Walter Becker, soon to launch Steely Dan. Streisand was not able to make the final transition into the pop-rock realm for the simple reason that she wasn't a writer, but she had spent a career making other people's songs her own, and she was as effective doing that here as she had been on very different material in the '60s. *— William Ruhlmann*

Live Concert at the Forum / Oct. 1972 / Columbia ✦✦✦

The Way We Were / Jan. 1974 / Columbia ✦✦✦

ButterFly / Oct. 1974 / Columbia ✦✦✦
Barbra Streisand's first album of newly recorded, non-soundtrack studio material in three years, *ButterFly* was ridiculed at the time of its release because its credited producer was her boyfriend, Jon Peters, whose musical credentials were non-existent. In retrospect, the real power on the album was arranger Tom Scott, a reed player who had perfected a light jazz-pop style in his work on Joni Mitchell's *Court And Spark* earlier in the year. *ButterFly* backed off from the pop-rock style of its predecessors, *Stoney End* and *Barbra Joan Streisand*, but it still found Streisand essaying contemporary material by such writers as Bob Marley, Graham Nash, and David Bowie. Unlike Richard Perry, who had produced those albums, Scott adapted the songs to Streisand's powerful and individual vocal style rather than having her ape existing versions of the songs. The result was more of a compromise with contemporary pop that, while it sold only to Streisand's existing fan base, nevertheless had its charms. *— William Ruhlmann*

Funny Lady / 1975 / Arista ✦✦

Lazy Afternoon / 1975 / Columbia ✦✦✦

Classical Barbra / Feb. 1976 / Columbia ✦✦✦

A Star Is Born / Nov. 1976 / Monument ✦✦

Streisand Superman / 1977 / Columbia ✦✦✦
Appearing only seven months after *A Star Is Born*, *Streisand Superman* seemed to continue much of its rock-oriented feel, even including several songs that had been intended for the film. It was unusual in featuring all recently written songs, many first recorded here. Streisand co-wrote the rockish "Don't Believe What You Read," an attack on her negative press coverage, while Alan Gordon contributed both the discoish "I Found You Love" and the album's Top Ten single ballad "My Heart Belongs To Me." *Streisand Superman* seemed to be an unusually personal album for the singer, reflecting her feelings and viewpoints. That did not make it one of her best, however. *— William Ruhlmann*

★ **Barbra Streisand's Greatest Hits, Vol. 2** / 1978 / Columbia ✦✦✦✦✦
Between the release of Barbra Streisand's first hits collection in 1970 and her second in 1978, she essentially became a different kind of recording artist. In the 1960s, she made a series of consistent albums devoted largely to show music material, but she scored precious few singles hits, with only one, "People," and reaching the Top Ten. But in the 1970s, she shifted to contemporary soft-rock and released a series of highly successful ballad singles, while her albums became largely inconsistent. For that reason, the hit quotient of her second hits album was much higher—"The Way We Were," "Love Theme From 'A Star Is Born' (Evergreen)," and the duet version of "You Don't Bring Me Flowers," sung with songwriter Neil Diamond and released on album here for the first time, all were #1 hits, while "Stoney End" and "My Heart Belongs To Me" were Top Tens and "Sweet Inspiration/Where You Lead," "Songbird," and "Love Theme From 'Laura Mars' (Prisoner)" reached the Top 40. That was enough material to make *Volume 2* Streisand's definitive hits collection, so much so that later compilations like *Memories* and *A Collection/ Greatest Hits... And More* would be forced to cannibalize it. It was also a genre-defining album in terms of the emergence of a post-'60s contemporary pop music that drew upon the rock revolution to redefine classic pop for a new generation. *— William Ruhlmann*

Songbird / 1978 / Columbia ✦✦✦
Songbird was a competent, professional effort from Barbra Streisand, typical of the soft-rock

style of her '70s work, but unexceptional. Gary Klein, who had produced *Streisand Superman*, guided a middle course between bombast and balladry, resulting in, for example, perhaps the least objectionable version possible of the frankly awful "Tomorrow" from the Broadway musical *Annie* and a good reading of Neil Diamond's "You Don't Bring Me Flowers" that would help inspire the hit duet version a year later. But though Streisand now seemed to have access to the efforts of a raft of good songwriters, most of the material here was not memorable. The intended hit, obviously, was the title song, which was patterned after Streisand's recent string of hit ballads. But it was not as effective as its predecessors and didn't perform as well as they had in the charts, only breaking into the Top 40. *— William Ruhlmann*

Wet / 1979 / Columbia ♦♦♦
A concept album of sorts in the sense that each of the songs has something to do with water, *Wet* was the third of a trilogy of albums produced by Gary Klein in a soft-rock vein increasingly set in the synth-pop style of the late '70s and early '80s. The concept allowed for a range of material, from old favorite Harold Arlen's "Come Rain Or Come Shine" to an updated version of the old Bobby Darin hit "Splish Splash." The album's *1 hit was "No More Tears (Enough Is Enough)," a disco duet with Donna Summer.* But most of the songs were newly written ballads attempting to recreate the "Evergreen"/"The Way We Were" style of Streisand's recent hits. "Kiss Me In The Rain" grazed the Top 40, but most of that material was substandard. Yet there was enough variety on the album to make it an average Streisand outing. *— William Ruhlmann*

The Main Event / Jun. 1979 / Columbia ♦♦

Guilty / 1980 / Columbia ♦♦♦♦♦
The biggest selling album of Barbra Streisand's career is also one of her least characteristic. The album was written and produced by Barry Gibb in association with his brothers and the producers of the Bee Gees, and in essence it sounds like a post-*Saturday Night Fever* Bee Gees album with vocals by Streisand. Gibb adapted his usual style somewhat, especially in slowing the tempos and leaving more room for the vocal, but his melodic style and the backup vocals, even when they are not sung by the Bee Gees, are typical of them. Still, the record was more hybrid than compromise, and the chart-topping single "Woman In Love" has a sinuous feel that is both right for Streisand and new for her. Other hits were the title song and "What Kind of Fool," both duets with Gibb. (The song "Guilty" won a Grammy Award for Best Pop Vocal by Duo or Group.) *— William Ruhlmann*

Memories / Nov. 1981 / Columbia ♦♦♦

Yentl / 1983 / Columbia ♦♦♦

Emotion / Oct. 1984 / Columbia ♦♦♦
Barbra Streisand's first album of contemporary material in four years was a typical '80s "Adult Contemporary" superstar release, each track written and produced as a potential "power ballad" single by an extensive team of other performers, in this case including Richard Perry, Kim Carnes, Maurice White of Earth, Wind and Fire, Jim Steinman, Albhy Galuten (the Bee Gees' producer), Richard Baskin, Diane Warren, John Mellencamp, and Streisand herself. Streisand proved capable of handling everything from White's space-age R&B to Steinman's melodramatic overproduction. (He was the man who brought you Meat Loaf.) But as usually happens with such big budget efforts, the album lacked consistency, and as Columbia tried to pull several singles off it without notable success it sold only to Streisand's million-member base audience. *— William Ruhlmann*

☆ **The Broadway Album** / 1985 / Columbia ♦♦♦♦♦
Barbra Streisand's abandonment of Broadway was the worst thing that happened to the theater in the '60s. Her retreat from theater music on record was less of a loss, if only because she had tended to focus on second-rank composers and obscure songs by first-rate ones, while practically ignoring, for example, Stephen Sondheim. When she returned to show songs in 1985, she reversed these failings. Now, the singer who had never done much with Rodgers and Hammerstein, Frank Loesser, George Gershwin, or Jerome Kern finally felt confident enough to take on "If I Loved You" from *Carousel*, "Adelaide's Lament" from *Guys and Dolls*, "Can't Help Lovin' That Man" from *Showboat*, and a medley from *Porgy and Bess*, and she did them well. Even better, on seven tracks with Sondheim's name on them, she proved the perfect intepreter of the most contemporary and intellectual of Broadway's writers, whether singing his lyrics over the music of Leonard Bernstein (another composer she'd largely neglected) from *West Side Story* or making the most of material drawn from shows like *Company, A Little Night Music, Sweeney Todd,* and *Sunday in the Park With George.* Sondheim collaborated with Streisand, penning special lyrics for songs like "Putting It Together" and even his standard, "Send in the Clowns." The result was an album that repositioned some of Broadway's best in a pop context and showed that Streisand was still at her best when presenting the dramatically satisfying story songs of the theater. Apparently, many long-time fans agreed: At sales over three million, *The Broadway Album* was Streisand's most commercially successful album in five years. *— William Ruhlmann*

One Voice / Apr. 1987 / Columbia ♦♦♦

Till I Loved You / Oct. 1988 / Columbia ♦♦♦

Greatest Hits . . . and More / Sep. 1989 / Columbia ♦♦♦

Just for the Record . . . / Sep. 24, 1991 / Columbia ♦♦♦♦♦
As they evolved in the 1980s, boxed set retrospectives tended to contain a full complement of an artist's essential recordings, plus enough rarities to suggest the artist's inspirations and ambitions. Not all boxed sets conformed to this outline, however. Barbra Streisand was unusual, in that she had a large base of devoted fans interested in the minutiae of her career, and in that her entire recorded catalog remained in print. She had also worked with the same record company for her entire career and maintained her status as a frontline artist, so she had complete creative control over this retrospective. The result was a four-disc box devoted almost entirely to rare, previously unreleased material. Here and there, Streisand tossed in one of her most familiar recordings, such as the hit version of "People." But the overwhelming bulk of *Just for the Record...* was given over to homemade demonstration tapes, live recordings, television appearances, and outtakes from unfinished album projects, not to mention other special material.To Streisand's army of fans, that made it a delight, but practically by definition, that did not make it a great Barbra Streisand album unto itself. Unlike most boxed sets, this was not a one-stop shopping item that gave you the best and the rest of Barbra Streisand. That is not to say that there weren't some fascinating and terrific performances included. Especially notable was a set of eight songs recorded at a nightclub in 1962 and originally intended for Streisand's debut album. A duet with Judy Garland from her TV show and a rendering of "In the Wee Small Hours of the Morning" from a Las Vegas show were equally impressive. Nevertheless, *Just for the Record...* was an album to buy in addition to her hits collections and landmark albums, not in place of them. *— William Ruhlmann*

Prince of Tides / Nov. 12, 1991 / Columbia ♦♦♦

Back to Broadway / Jun. 29, 1993 / Columbia ♦♦♦

Barbra: the Concert / Sep. 1994 / Columbia ♦♦♦♦♦
Barbra Streisand's fourth live album was the only one to be drawn from a concert tour and not a one-time occasion, but it is no less special for that. For her first tour in 28 years, Streisand didn't just come out and sing her greatest hits for an hour and a half. Instead, she wove a selection of her best-known songs together with what she considered career highlights and added new and special material, starting with the customized lyrics of "As If We Never Said Goodbye" and "I'm Still Here" and including "Ordinary Miracles," by her conductor, Harvin Hamlisch and her house lyricists, Alan and Marilyn Bergman. The show was a musical autobiography crafted (as her 1991 boxed set *Just For The Record...* had been) for fans who would catch the references and agree with the artist on her viewpoints about her life, her career, the entertainment business, and politics. (And it was an abridged resume—rockers like "Stoney End" and disco hits like "Enough Is Enough" were omitted.) There was no denying that the 52-year-old singer, backed by a large orchestra and singing the songs that had kept her at the forefront of popular music for 30 years, was an impressive concert performer. But Streisand insisted that her listeners also encounter everything from her film directing ambitions to her psychoanalyst which made this an idiosyncratic performance from an artist determined to make public art out of her private story. As a result, *The Concert* may not be the place for neophytes to be introduced to her, though for fans it was the culmination of decades of wishing. *— William Ruhlmann*

Mirror Has Two Faces / Nov. 12, 1996 / Columbia ♦♦

Higher Ground / Nov. 4, 1997 / Columbia ♦♦♦

A Love Like Ours / Sep. 21, 1999 / Columbia ♦♦♦

Timeless: Live in Concert / Feb. 8, 2000 / Columbia ♦♦♦

Maxine Sullivan (Marietta Williams)

b. May 13, 1911, Homestead, PA, **d.** Apr. 7, 1987, New York, NY
Vocals / Vocal Jazz, Standards, Swing
A subtle and lightly swinging jazz singer, Maxine Sullivan's delivery was very likable, and she did justice to all of the lyrics she sang during her long career. After moving to New York, Sullivan sang during intermissions at the Onyx Club and was discovered by pianist Claude Thornhill. Thornhill recorded her with a sympathetic septet singing a couple of standards and two Scottish folk songs performed in swinging fashion—"Annie Laurie" and "Loch Lomond." The latter became a big hit and Sullivan's signature song for the rest of her career. Future sessions found her singing vintage folk tunes such as "Darling Nellie Gray," "I Dream of Jeanie," "Drink to Me Only With Thine Eyes" and "If I Had a Ribbon Bow." Even if lightning did not strike twice, she was now a popular attraction. From 1940-42, Sullivan often sang with her husband, bassist John Kirby's Sextet, a perfect outlet for her cool sound, and then in the mid-1950s became a trained nurse. In 1968, the singer began making a comeback; now married to pianist Cliff Jackson, Sullivan (whose style and appealing voice were unchanged from earlier years) sometimes appeared with the World's Greatest Jazz Band, and she recorded frequently. *— Scott Yanow*

1937-1938 / Jun. 14, 1937-Jun. 29, 1938 / Classics ♦♦♦♦♦
The basic and pleasing vocals of Maxine Sullivan are quite enjoyable. This CD has her first 23 recordings, including three songs originally released under pianist Claude Thornhill's name; Thornhill (who helped discover the singer) is on all of the selections. The original version of "Loch Lomond" is among the highlights and became a huge hit, leading to Sullivan's lightly swinging renditions of other folk songs such as "Darling Nellie Gray" and "Dark Eyes." Joined by such fine musicians as trumpeters Manny Klein, Frank Newton, Charlie Shavers and Bobby Hackett (all of whom are heard from briefly), along with the future members of the John Kirby Sextet, Maxine Sullivan is heard throughout in her early prime (she was 26-27 years old during this period). Recommended. *— Scott Yanow*

The Biggest Little Band in the Land / Oct. 10, 1940-Jan. 20, 1941 / Circle ♦♦♦♦

Loch Lomond / 1940-1941 / Circle ♦♦♦♦

Close as Pages in a Book / Jun. 11, 1969–Jun. 13, 1969 / Audiophile ♦♦♦♦♦

We Just Couldn't Say Goodbye / Feb. 6, 1978-1983 / Audiophile ♦♦♦♦

It Was Great Fun / 1983 / Audiophile ♦♦♦♦♦

Uptown / Jan. 1985 / Concord Jazz ♦♦♦♦

Swingin' Sweet / Sep. 1986 / Concord Jazz ♦♦♦♦♦

● **Ruban Bleu Years: Complete Recordings 1944-1949** / 1944 / Baldwin Street Music ♦♦♦♦♦
All of Maxine Sullivan's recordings from 1944-49 are on this single CD; she would only record two songs during the 1950-54 period before making some full-length records in 1955. This reissue is more complete than the previous Tono recording that covered the same period, for it adds nine additional cuts. The previous 18 numbers find Sullivan in the studios

with a couple of groups that utilize string sections and Larry Johnson's Orchestra, and best of all, six swinging numbers with pianist Ellis Larkins' trio. The "new" cuts feature Sullivan with the Teddy Wilson Sextet, Benny Carter's big band, and on the radio with backing by Jimmie Lunceford's Orchestra. Although these recordings overall did not sell that well, the appealing singer (who interprets lyrics fairly straight but with a solid sense of swing) was very much in her prime, as can be heard on such numbers as "Every Time We Say Goodbye," "Mad About the Boy," "Skylark," "Taking My Time," "Legalize My Name" and remakes of "Loch Lomond" and "If I Had a Ribbon Bow." Recommended. *—Scott Yanow*

1938-1941 / Dec. 10, 1938-Apr. 1, 1941 / Classics ♦♦♦♦

1941-1946 / Jun. 17, 1941-1946 / Classics ♦♦♦♦

Mel Tormé (Melvin Howard Tormé)

b. Sep. 13, 1925, Chicago, IL, **d.** Jun. 5, 1999, Los Angeles, CA
Vocals, Drums / Vocal Jazz, Traditional Pop, Swing, Ballads, Bop, Show Tunes
Mel Tormé was a genuine Renaissance man—one of the top jazz singers of the last third of the century but also a superb writer, a good arranger, a more-than-competent drummer, a songwriter with a number of standards to his credit, a versatile actor, and a most engaging raconteur. Known in his youth as the "Velvet Fog" for his high, murky, sustained vocals, Tormé gradually developed into a first-class jazz baritone with great scatting ability, superb control and a sophisticated way with ballads. Indeed, his voice actually grew stronger and more flexible in his later years, shedding old mannerisms and developing an ever-more-powerful sense of swing. Though Tormé notes that it took him an agonizingly long time to write them, his arrangements for orchestra and big band are sonorous and intelligently conceived. Furthermore, Tormé was probably as fine a writer as he was a singer; his autobiography *It Wasn't All Velvet*, his memoir of Judy Garland *The Other Side of the Rainbow* and his biography of his friend Buddy Rich *Traps, The Drum Wonder*, are compulsively readable, chatty, and full of insight. At 19, he also assured himself of immortality by co-writing "The Christmas Song," which in the wake of Nat King Cole's 1946 hit record has become an imperishable holiday standard. Amidst several parallel careers in show business and literature, Torme still continued to refine his vocal abilities through the decades.. *—Richard S. Ginell*

☆ **The Mel Tormé Collection** / 1944-Sep. 18, 1985 / Rhino ♦♦♦♦♦
Up until he suffered a stroke at age 70 in 1996, singer Mel Tormé continued to improve with age and seemed to have inexhaustible energy. This four-CD set from Rhino does a fine job of covering Tormé's pre-Concord output although the omission of his Concord work of 1986-95 is unfortunate for that catalog contains many of Tormé's most exciting recordings. In general the earlier selections (some of which were with his vocal group the Mel-Tones) feature Tormé on hip (for the period) swing tunes and ballads. By the time he cut the sessions included on this set from 1954, the singer was quite mature and sounding very much like himself. The small group dates of the 1950s are generally much more rewarding than some of the slower numbers in which Tormé is accompanied by string orchestras and the 1956-60 collaborations with the Marty Paich Dek-tette are classic. But once the '60s hit, Tormé's career (at least on records) started to quickly decline. Although disc four (which covers 1962-85) does its best to focus on Tormé's better recordings of the period, a few of the tracks (such as "Strangers in the Night," "A Day in the Life of Bonnie and Clyde" and "Yesterday When I Was Young") are pretty sappy. Things greatly improve once the singer reaches the year 1975 and there are enough highpoints throughout the set to justify its purchase by Tormé's many fans. Three previously unreleased selections (best is "Walkin' Shoes" with Shorty Rogers in 1962) are a plus and the colorful 84-page booklet is quite definitive. *—Scott Yanow*

Spotlight on Mel Tormé / Jan. 17, 1949-Oct. 4, 1951 / Capitol ♦♦♦♦
This very interesting CD gives listeners a cross section of Mel Tormé's Capitol recordings. Caught fairly early in his career, Tormé's voice was already quite recognizable and appealing. Ballads alternate with occasional romps including several arranged by Frank DeVol in 1949 that are surprisingly boppish; Pete Rugolo, Nelson Riddle, and Sonny Burke take care of the other charts. Highlights of the 18 cuts (four of which were previously unreleased) include a wild "Oh, You Beautiful Doll," "Stompin' at the Savoy," "Blue Moon," a spirited "Sonny Boy," and "You're a Heavenly Thing" (which finds Mel Tormé playing piano in a quartet with guitarist Mary Osborne). *—Scott Yanow*

In Hollywood / Dec. 15, 1954 / GRP/Decca ♦♦♦

It's a Blue World / Aug. 28, 1955-Aug. 30, 1955 / Bethlehem ♦♦♦♦♦
Mel Tormé had spent the first decade of his solo career being treated by record companies as a pop singer when Bethlehem offered to treat him as a jazz artist in 1955. The label requested that his first album be a collection of ballads, probably noting the recent success of Frank Sinatra's *In the Wee Small Hours*. But Tormé picked the songs, ranging from Jerome Kern and P.G. Wodehouse's "Till the Clouds Roll By" from 1917 to Duke Ellington and Paul Webster's "I've Got It Bad and That Ain't Good" from 1941. The 15-piece orchestra assembled by his accompanist Al Pellegrini backed the singer, and Pellegrini, Sandy Courage, Andre Previn, Marty Paich, and Russ Garcia wrote the arrangements Tormé sang with delicate precision, caressing the lyrics. Despite the album title, his interpretations had none of the darkness of Sinatra. Rather, Tormé invested the songs with warmth and confidence. Recorded and released around the time he turned 30, *It's a Blue World* marked a turning point in Mel Tormé's recording career. *—William Ruhlmann*

★ **Lulu's Back in Town** / Jan. 1956 / Rhino ♦♦♦♦♦
The up-tempo, swinging album that naturally followed *It's a Blue World* (Tormé's languorous debut for Bethlehem), *Lulu's Back in Town* is a vocal masterpiece, an extremely satisfying record achieved only by a fusion of an excellent voice, an excellent band and excellent material. Tormé had been inspired musically by the swinging West Coast cool group of Gerry Mulligan; accordingly, he made sure that his new musical arranger, Marty Paich, was of a similar mind. The two came up with the "Dek-tette," a group including no more than ten pieces and heavy on the stinging brass (including Pete Candoli and Don Fagerquist on trumpet, Bob Enevoldsen on trombone and two French horns). The band is incredibly sympathetic and appears to hang on Tormé's every word. The material, as well, is pure gold: Tormé is as buoyant and exuberant as he's ever been, resulting in fantastic, definitive versions of inimitable standards like "Lullaby of Birdland," "Fascinating Rhythm" and "The Lady Is a Tramp." There are a few down-tempo numbers ("The Blues," "Keeping Myself for You") but even on these Tormé sounds like he can't wait to get to the next song and really stretch out. After its first release in 1956 as *Mel Tormé with the Marty Paich Dek-tette*, the album was reissued many times under various titles (*Lulu's Back in Town, The Tormé Touch*), but surprisingly never on CD. Rhino finally rectified the situation with the album's first CD release (as *Lulu's Back in Town*) in 1999. *—John Bush*

☆ **Sings Fred Astaire** / Nov. 1956 / Bethlehem Archives/Avenue Jazz ♦♦♦♦♦
Though it's sometimes relegated to second or third place among Tormé's best albums of the '50s (behind *Lulu's Back in Town* and *It's a Blue World*), it's difficult to hear how *Mel Tormé Sings Fred Astaire* can't be the best album of his entire career. Featuring an artist at the peak of his ability and talent, a collection of top-drawer songs from the best pop composers ever, and a swinging ten-piece that forms the perfect accompaniment, *Sings Fred Astaire* is one of the best up-tempo vocal albums ever recorded. Coming hot on the heels of *Lulu's Back in Town* in 1956, this tribute to Hollywood's most stylish dancer finds Tormé obliging with his nimblest and most elegant singing. Even while Marty Paich's band takes "The Way You Look Tonight" and "Cheek to Cheek" at a breakneck pace that Astaire himself would've had trouble with, Tormé floats over the top with death-defying vocal acrobatics. He's breezy and sophisticated on "They Can't Take That Away from Me," ecstatic and effervescent on "Top Hat, White Tie and Tails" (matching an exuberant solo by trumpeter Pete Candoli), and even breaks out an affectionate croon for "A Foggy Day." A collection of perfect hard-swinging pop with a few ballads thrown in for good measure makes *Sings Fred Astaire* a masterpiece of the vocal era. *—John Bush*

Mel Tormé's California Suite [II] / Mar. 1957 / Bethlehem Archives/Avenue Jazz ♦♦♦♦

Tormé / Jun. 26, 1958-Jun. 27, 1958 / Sound Products ♦♦♦♦
Most of Mel Tormé's albums for Verve and Bethlehem during the 1950s concentrated on material either carefree (usually uptempo) or reflective (mostly downtempo), but 1958's *Tormé* blended the two. For every bouncy single like "That Old Feeling" or "I'm Gonna Laugh You Out of My Life," Tormé sinks into the depths with "Gloomy Sunday," "The House Is Haunted by the Echo of Your Last Goodbye" or his dramatic eight-minute reading of "Blues in the Night." All this makes for a bit of emotional confusion while listening to *Tormé*, but the LP pulls together for the most part. *—John Bush*

Mel Tormé Swings Shubert Alley / Jan. 21, 1960-Feb. 11, 1960 / Verve ♦♦♦♦♦
Though the nominal concept for *Swings Shubert Alley* is Broadway standards, this last moment of Mel Tormé brilliance swings much too fast and hard for the concept to be anything but pure swing. Of course it starts out with a bang, the punchy "Too Close for Comfort." Tormé sounds like he's racing the band to the finish of the song on this one and many others ("Too Darn Hot," "Surrey with the Fringe on Top"), repeating the title over and over again in a purely exuberant voice. As with his other classic swing albums, Tormé does insert a few slower songs; here, "Once in Love with Amy," "A Sleepin' Bee" and "Old Devil Moon" are down-tempo—with a smile. The overall mood is unrestrained enthusiasm, and it makes for an excellent record. *—John Bush*

Swingin' on the Moon / Aug. 3, 1960-Aug. 5, 1960 / Verve ♦♦♦

The Duke Ellington and Count Basie Songbooks / Dec. 12, 1960–Feb. 2, 1961 / Verve ♦♦♦♦♦

My Kind of Music / Jul. 18, 1961-Jul. 21, 1961 / Verve ♦♦♦

That's All / 1965 / Sony Special Products ♦♦♦
This 1997 CD reissues Mel Tormé's 1965 album *That's All*, ten songs only previously out as singles, and two unreleased titles. Tormé sings beautifully throughout the set, but there are a few problems. The arrangements (mostly by Robert Mersey and also including a few charts from Dick Hazard, Mort Garson and Pat Williams) are essentially unimaginative middle-of-the-road pop with an orchestra and occasional strings and background singers greatly weighing down the proceedings. The 24 selections (all ballads) are mostly taken at slow tempos and were clearly geared for radio airplay, clocking in around the three-minute mark, which means that Tormé's improvising is held to a minimum. So if the melody is not strong, the singer was not given a chance to improve it, and if the tune was excellent, Mel's straightforward version added nothing to the song's legacy. At best, this CD makes for a pleasant listen, but get Mel Tormé's Concord releases instead. *—Scott Yanow*

London Sessions / 1977 / Sandstone ♦♦♦

Encore at Marty's, New York / Mar. 27, 1982 / DCC ♦♦♦♦
This CD reissues a full set of music from Mel Tormé with his 1982 trio: pianist Mike Renzi, bassist Jay Leonhart and drummer Donny Osborne. No editing took place except for the excision of some chatter yet the music is consistently rewarding. Tormé, who was already 56, was amazingly just entering his musical prime. His well-paced set mixes together older songs (highlighted by a Fred Astaire medley) with some newer but worthy pieces (including the debut of Tormé's own "I'm Gonna Miss You"), alternating scat-filled romps with lyrical ballad interpretations. Throughout it all Tormé succeeds at everything he tries with a humorous rendition of "I Like to Recognize the Tune" and some heated scatting on "Day In, Day Out" begin among the memorable moments. This CD reissue of an album originally put out on the Flair label is recommended. *—Scott Yanow*

An Evening with George Shearing / Apr. 15, 1982 / Concord Jazz ♦♦♦♦

An Evening at Charlie's / Oct. 1983 / Concord Jazz ♦♦♦♦♦
Mel Tormé and pianist George Shearing had recorded together twice for Concord prior to this live set; both dates (*An Evening with George Shearing and Mel Tormé* and *Top Drawer*) gave Shearing top billing. For their third outing, the dynamic duo are up to their usual high

level, with assistance from bassist Don Thompson and drummer Donny Osborne. Among the high points are "Nice's Dream," "Love Is Just Around the Corner" and a medley of "Just One of Those Things" and "On Green Dolphin Street." *—Scott Yanow*

☆ **Mel Tormé, Rob McConnell and the Boss Brass** / May 1986 / Concord Jazz ✦✦✦✦✦
This was a very logical matchup that came out as well on record as it looked on paper. Valve trombonist/arranger Rob McConnell has long led one of the top mainstream jazz big bands, while Mel Torme blossomed into one of the truly great jazz singers in the 1980s. McConnell's charts suited Torme perfectly, and the result is this consistently enjoyable and swinging album. The singer is quite enthusiastic and in top form on "Just Friends," a touching "September Song," "Don'cha Go 'Way Mad," "A House Is Not a Home," "The Song Is You," a whimsical "Cow Cow Boogie," a "Stars" medley and an exciting six-song Duke Ellington medley. Highly recommended. *—Scott Yanow*

A Vintage Year / Aug. 1987 / Concord Jazz ✦✦✦✦✦

Night at the Concord Pavilion / Aug. 1990 / Concord Jazz ✦✦✦✦✦

Mel and George Do WWII / Sep. 2, 1990-Sep. 3, 1990 / Concord Jazz ✦✦✦✦✦

The Great American Songbook: Live at Michael's Pub / Oct. 1992 / Telarc ✦✦✦✦

Sing Sing Sing / Nov. 1992 / Concord Jazz ✦✦✦✦

Velvet & Brass / Jul. 5, 1995-Jul. 6, 1995 / Concord Jazz ✦✦✦✦

At the Movies / Jun. 15, 1999 / Rhino ✦✦✦
Though Mel Tormé's film work was better than most, he's always been known as a jazz singer, best suited to formats like a live concert or a concept LP. During the '40s and '50s, the Hollywood movie machine spit out a lot of subpar pop material, luring singers to croon dozens of conservative songs with "champagne music" backing. Though it spans his entire career, from the mid-'40s into the '90s, *At the Movies* includes much material from the '40s, in the singer's much-maligned *Velvet Fog* period. Fortunately, the collection includes not only songs Tormé sang expressly for films but also his own versions of songs made famous in the movies, like "Blue Moon," "Sunday in New York," and "Puttin' on the Ritz." It's a solid compilation for collectors (six unreleased tracks), but isn't an incredibly good start for anyone unfamiliar with Tormé's best work. *—John Bush*

☆ **The Best of the Concord Years** / Sep. 28, 1999 / Concord Jazz ✦✦✦✦✦
For nearly 20 years, critics have been praising Mel Tormé's recordings for Concord, the label he spent the last 13 years of his career recording for, in a variety of settings. Fans of his '50s and '60s heyday, however, have often had difficulty approaching the work of Tormé's last 13 years. *The Best of the Concord Years* presents two hours of his best on the label, including a mix of live and studio sessions recorded with groups both small and large, originally issued on solo albums as well as his excellent collaborations with George Shearing, Rob McConnell, Marty Paich, and the Frank Wess/Harry Edison Orchestra. No, Tormé wasn't at his performing peak on "Hi-Fly, " recorded in 1983, but his emphatic delivery and scatting finale will surprise listeners unaware that he was nearing the age of 60. The selections are roughly chronological and include many gems from Tormé's later career: "Lullaby of Birdland" with George Shearing taking one careful run-through before Tormé himself storms through the song; his perennial "Too Close for Comfort," delivered with just as much emotion and exuberance as it had been 40 years earlier; and a languid, touching "These Foolish Things" recorded at the *Fujitsu-Concord Jazz Festival* in 1992. Yes, the polish was wearing off what had once been the most able voice to ever grace an American popular song, but these songs reveal a depth of experience and consistency unmatched during the 1950s. *—John Bush*

The Velvet Fog / Feb. 22, 2000 / ASV/Living Era ✦✦✦✦✦
Covering the first five years of Mel Tormé's solo career (from 1944 to 1949), *The Velvet Fog* features 25 tracks of the vocalist at his dreamiest and most reminiscent of dreaded nicknames like the one found in the title and "The Singer with Gauze in His Jaws." The collection begins with his biggest hit of the era (1949's "Careless Hands"), then cycles through the best of his Capitol recordings in what is roughly chronological order. The seven tracks in which Tormé leads his superb vocal group, the Mel-Tones (usually with Artie Shaw & His Orchestra), are among the best here, from the aching ballad "A Stranger in Town" to the wonderful, uptempo harmony numbers "I Got the Sun in the Morning" and "What Is This Thing Called Love—." As for the solo tracks, there's a focus on ballads that may disappoint fans of Tormé's '50s work. Still, whereas many ballad singers of the '40s doing period material sound insufferable today, Tormé's voice is sweet and irresistible on "Until the Real Thing Comes Along," "Gone With the Wind," and "A Foggy Day." Also, a few of the more swinging numbers ("Night and Day," "Little White Lies," the Peggy Lee duet "The Old Master Painter") show him reflecting the bop influence at an early age, scatting for more than 32 bars at a time and setting tracks on fire with an energy that few (if any) vocal artists were capable of before him. For listeners who've been turned off by the many confusing reissues of Tormé's '40s material (often from budget labels with inferior mastering), *The Velvet Fog* is a perfect collection. However, those who own his Rhino box set, *The Mel Tormé Collection,* may find some overlap on the first disc. *—John Bush*

Jerry Vale (Genaro Louis Vitaliano)

b. Jul. 8, 1932, New York, NY [The Bronx]
Vocals / Traditional Pop, Vocal Pop, Ballads
Jerry Vale's beautiful high-tenor voice graced many of the most enchanting pop songs of the '50s and '60s, including a parade of Italian-American favorites like "Innamorata (Sweetheart)," "Volare," "Amore, Scusami," and his signature song, "Al Di La." Vale, born Genaro Louis Vitaliano in 1932, learned the Italian repertoire from an early age; his mother often sang around the house and trotted out the old songs at extended-family gatherings. While shining shoes at a local barber shop at the age of 11, young Vitaliano began singing popular songs for customers while he worked. He was soon sent to a vocal coach, where he learned piano as well as voice. Over the course of just four years, he'd progressed from school productions to paying gigs to residencies at supper clubs around New York City.

After Guy Mitchell caught his set at one club, Jerry Vale began recording demonstration discs for Columbia. When A*R supremo Mitch Miller* heard his excellent voice, however, he signed Vale to his own contract. Vale first hit the charts in 1953 with "You Can Never Give Me Back My Heart" (arranged by Percy Faith), and continued during the mid-'50s with "Two Purple Shadows," "I Live Each Day," and his biggest hit, "You Don't Know Me." Though his first explicitly Italian recording, "Innamorata (Sweetheart)," finally appeared in 1956, it wasn't until 1962 that Vale convinced the notoriously conservative Miller to record a full album of Italian songs. *I Have But One Heart* proved a big seller and was followed one year later by *Arrivederci, Roma* and a continental LP, *The Language of Love,* both of which placed even higher than the first on the album charts.

Though the mid-'60s were a trying time for traditional pop singers, Vale continued to be successful, with singles like "Have You Looked Into Your Heart" and "For Mama," and Top 40 LPs like *There Goes My Heart* and *It's Magic.* And even after his albums began failing to make the charts in the early '70s, Vale remained a popular name in clubs and on television throughout the '70s and '80s. *—John Bush*

I Remember Buddy / 1958 / Columbia/Legacy ✦✦✦

I Remember Russ / 1958 / Columbia/Legacy ✦✦✦

Till / Jan. 18, 1969 / Columbia/Legacy ✦✦✦

Jerry Vale Sings the Great Hits of Nat King Cole / Jan. 5, 1972 / Columbia/Legacy ✦✦✦

● **Greatest Hits** / Sep. 1, 1998 / Columbia/Legacy ✦✦✦✦✦
Until Columbia/Legacy released *Greatest Hits* in the fall of 1998, there weren't any definitive collections of Jerry Vale's biggest hits available on CD. Legacy's disc makes the wait worthwhile, since it's hard to imagine assembling a better single-disc collection of his most popular songs than *Greatest Hits.* The album focuses on Vale's heyday of the '50s and early '60s, containing nearly all of his charting hits between 1954 and 1965—"Two Purple Shadows," "Innamorata (Sweetheart)," "You Don't Know Me," "Pretend You Don't See Her," "Go Chase a Moonbeam," "Have You Looked Into Your Heart," "For Mama"—plus several tunes produced by Mitch Miller and other well-known tunes, like his first record "And No One Knows" and "Somewhere," from the film *Marco the Magnificent.* Certainly, Vale recorded plenty of worthwhile material that didn't make this collection—the concurrently released collection *Sings the Great Italian Hits* offers ample proof of that—but this *Greatest Hits* is ideal either as a one-stop collection of hits or as an introduction to the incomparable baritone. *—Stephen Thomas Erlewine*

Jerry Vale Sings the Great Italian Hits [Compilation] / Sep. 1, 1998 / Columbia/Legacy ✦✦✦✦✦
Released as a companion piece to Columbia/Legacy's *Greatest Hits* collection, *Jerry Vale Sings the Great Italian Hits* features 18 Italian songs Vale recorded for Columbia Records during the '50s, '60s and 1970. Like any Italian-American crooner, he learned these songs from his family and continually returned to them over the years. He didn't record a full album of Italian songs until 1962, when he cut two that year. Ten tracks from those two albums are featured here—the remaining cuts date from 1955, 1966, 1967 and 1970. The remarkable thing about *Sings the Great Italian Hits* is that it all sounds as if it comes from the same recording session. That's how consistent Vale's performances are—even though this disc contains sessions helmed by four different producers, it all holds together. Also, these 18 songs—including "Innamorata (Sweetheart)," "Volare," "Ciao, Ciao, Bambina," "O Sole Mio," "Arrivederci, Roma," "Summertime in Venice," "You Don't Have to Say You Love Me" and "More"—are among his best vocal performances, illustrating what a fine vocalist he could be. For some tastes, the collection may be a little ballad-heavy, but this remains one of the very best Vale compilations released in the CD era. *—Stephen Thomas Erlewine*

Rudy Vallée (Herbert Pryor Vallée)

b. Jul. 28, 1901, Island Pond, VT, **d.** Jul. 3, 1986, Hollywood, CA
Vocals / Traditional Pop, Vocal Pop, Nostalgia
One of the most popular entertainers of the 1930s, Rudy Vallée was one of the few vocalists to begin crooning before the advent of Bing Crosby. Famed for singing through a megaphone and introducing his performances with a salutary "Heigh-Ho, Everybody," Vallée recorded into the mid-'40s and enjoyed a renaissance during the '60s after high-profile appearances on Broadway. After studying at Yale and the University of Maine, he was leading his first band (the Connecticut Yankees) by 1928. During the following year, he gained a large audience through radio, vaudeville appearances, and a feature film, *The Vagabond Lover.* He'd begun recording that year, and burst out of the gate with the immensely popular singles "Marie," "Honey" and "Weary River."

In 1930, he paid tribute to his alma mater and gained the biggest hit of his career. "Stein Song (The University of Maine)" spent more than two months as the most popular song in America, and later became the official theme song for the school. He continued to appear in films during the 1930s, though Vallée later moved from romantic lead to eccentric character actor. He led a Coast Guard orchestra during World War II, and found his last big hit—thanks to the film *Casablanca*—with 1946's "As Time Goes By," a reissue recorded more than fifteen years earlier.

After the war, Vallée returned to Hollywood for work in film, radio, performance and later television. The biggest acting part of his career came in 1961, when he portrayed a bombastic company president in the Broadway hit *How to Succeed in Business Without Really Trying* (he reprised his role for the 1967 film as well). Vallée continued to appear in films until the mid-'70s, and performed around the country up to his death ten years later. *—John Bush*

● **Heigh-Ho Everybody, This Is Rudy Vallee** / 1981 / ASV/Living Era ✦✦✦✦✦
This collection of Vallee favorites includes "Life Is Just a Bowl of Cherries," "Let's Do It," "I Love the Moon," "Life Is a Song" and others. *—Jason Ankeny*

As Time Goes By / May 19, 1998 / Varese ✦✦✦✦✦
Originally issued in 1956 on RKO's Unique label under the title *The Kid from Maine,* this captures Vallee on one of his more successful late-career missions in recutting his old hits for a new audience. Unlike most of his contemporaries who had trouble bridging their mu-

sic from old 78s to the LP high-fidelity format, Vallee shows himself to be in good voice throughout. The title track, "Rain," "Life Is Just a Bowl of Cherries," "Sweet Music," "Honey," his "Vieni, Vieni" and "Deep Night" show him firmly in command of the material with none of the platinum missing off the old pipes. This 1998 CD reissue also adds three bonus tracks: "The Whiffenpoof Song," "Maine Stein Song" and a raunchy (for Rudy) version of "There's a Tavern in the Town." Succinct liner notes from Ian Whitcomb are an added bonus. *—Cub Koda*

Sarah Vaughan

b. Mar. 27, 1924, Newark, NJ, **d.** Apr. 3, 1990, Los Angeles, CA

Vocals / Vocal Jazz, Traditional Pop, Standards, Ballads, Cool, Bop

Possessor of one of the most wondrous voices of the 20th century, Sarah Vaughan ranked with Ella Fitzgerald and Billie Holiday in the very top echelon of female jazz singers. She often gave the impression that with her wide range, perfectly controlled vibrato, and wide expressive abilities, she could do anything she wanted with her voice. After winning an amateur contest at the Apollo Theatre, she sang with big bands led by Earl Hines and Billy Eckstine during the early-to-mid-'40s; influenced by a couple of both leaders' sidemen, Charlie Parker and Dizzy Gillespie, Vaughan became one of the first singers to fully incorporate bop phrasing (and have the vocal chops to pull it off). Her 1946-48 solo selections for Musicraft found her rapidly gaining maturity and adding bop-oriented phrasing to popular songs. Signed to Columbia from 1949 to 1953, Vaughan continued to build on her popularity with sessions that were quite commercial. During the 1950s, she recorded middle-of-the-road pop material with orchestras for Mercury, and jazz dates for the label's subsidiary, EmArcy. During the '60s, she was signed to Roulette and Mercury once again; after a surprising four years off records, she also recorded for Mainstream during the early '70s. Vaughan was with Norman Granz's Pablo label from 1977-82, and only during her last few years did her recording career falter a bit. She continued touring the world for several years, as her miraculous voice stayed in prime form. *—Scott Yanow*

One Night Stand: The Town Hall Concert 1947 / Nov. 8, 1947 / Capitol ♦♦♦♦

This 1997 CD has music from a previously unreleased *Town Hall* concert. The program is split between the Lester Young sextet and Sarah Vaughan with the two principals only coming together on the final song, "I Cried for You." The recording quality is listenable, if not flawless, and it features the two giants at interesting points in their careers. Tenor great Lester Young sounds excellent on his seven features, but his backup group is sometimes a bit shaky, particularly during uncertain moments on "Just You, Just Me" and "Sunday"; bassist Rodney Richardson does not mesh well with the eccentric pianist Sadik Hakim. The young Roy Haynes is fine, although some of his "bombs" are overrecorded, while trumpeter Shorty McConnell comes across as a second-rate Howard McGhee, sincere but streaky. But the reason to acquire this CD is Sarah Vaughan, who at age 23 was already a marvel; what a voice! Very influenced by Dizzy Gillespie and Charlie Parker, Vaughan mostly lays way behind the beat during her ballad-oriented performances, swirling between notes like a first altoist and often settling on very unlikely (and boppish) notes. She gives the impression that she could do anything with her voice, and some of her flights (particularly on "Don't Blame Me," "I Cover the Waterfront" and "Mean to Me") border on the miraculous. *—Scott Yanow*

Sarah Vaughan in Hi-Fi / Dec. 21, 1949-Jan. 5, 1953 / Columbia/Legacy ♦♦♦♦

Most of Sarah Vaughan's Columbia recordings were on the commercial side, but not the memorable selections on this wonderful CD reissue. She recorded eight selections in 1950 with an octet that included trumpeter Miles Davis, trombonist Benny Green, the remarkably cool clarinetist Tony Scott and tenorman Budd Johnson. This CD adds alternate takes to seven of the numbers, increasing the discography of both Sassy and Miles. This version of "Ain't Misbehavin'" is a true classic (with memorable eight-bar solos by each of the four horns); "Mean to Me" and "Nice Work If You Can Get It" are gems, and the other performances are not far behind. In addition, Vaughan sings two versions of "The Nearness of You" in 1949; there is also a previously unknown recording of "It's All In the Mind," and three orchestra numbers from 1951 and 1953 wrap up the outstanding reissue. Sassy has rarely sounded better. Highly recommended. *—Scott Yanow*

16 Most Requested Songs / 1949-1953 / Columbia/Legacy ♦♦♦

☆ **Complete Sarah Vaughan on Mercury, Vol. 1** / Feb. 10, 1954-Jun. 21, 1956 / Mercury ♦♦♦♦♦

Sarah Vaughan's years on Mercury (and its subsidiary EmArcy) feature inspired jazz performances, commercial recordings with string orchestras and big-band sides that fall in between jazz and middle-of-the-road pop music. All of her recordings for Mercury are on four impressive box sets that add up to 23 CDs. The first set (six CDs) is the best overall of the four for it has a full set with her trio, the famous session with trumpeter Clifford Brown, a date with the Ernie Wilkins Orchestra (featuring altoist Cannonball Adderley) and a variety of orchestral sides. As with all of these sets, there are many previously unissued performances included too. More selective fans may want to get some of Sassy's individual packages instead (particularly the Clifford Brown date) but completists and true Sarah Vaughan fanatics will consider these four perfectly done sets to be essential. *—Scott Yanow*

★ **Sarah Vaughan with Clifford Brown** / Dec. 16, 1954-Dec. 18, 1954 / Verve ♦♦♦♦♦

This 1954 studio date, a self-titled album recorded for Emarcy, was later reissued as *Sarah Vaughan with Clifford Brown* to denote the involvement of one of the top trumpeters of the day. Vaughan sings nine intimate standards with a band including Brown on trumpet, Herbie Mann on flute, and Paul Quinichette on tenor, each of which have plenty of space for solos (most of the songs are close to the five-minute mark). Vaughan is arguably in the best voice of her career here, pausing and lingering over notes on the standards "April in Paris," "Jim," and "Lullaby of Birdland." As touching as Vaughan is, however, Brown almost equals her with his solos on "Lullaby of Birdland," "Jim," and "September Song," displaying his incredible bop virtuosity in a restrained setting without sacrificing either the simple feeling of his notes or the extraordinary flair of his choices. Quinichette's solos are magnificent as well, his feathery tone nearly a perfect match for Vaughan's voice. Ironically though, neither Brown nor Quinichette or Mann appear on the album's highlight, "Embraceable You," which Vaughan performs with close accompaniment from the rhythm section: Jimmy Jones on piano, Joe Benjamin on bass, and Roy Haynes on drums. Vaughan rounds the notes with a smile and even when she's steeping to reach a few low notes, she never loses the tremendous feeling conveyed by her voice. In whichever incarnation it's reissued, *Sarah Vaughan With Clifford Brown* is one of the most important jazz-meets-vocal sessions ever recorded. *—John Bush*

The Gershwin Songbook / 1954-1957 / Mercury ♦♦♦♦♦

In the Land of Hi-Fi / Oct. 26, 1955-Oct. 27, 1955 / EmArcy ♦♦♦♦♦

This single CD (whose contents are also included in the box set *The Complete Sarah Vaughan on Mercury Vol. 1*) has one of the great singer's best jazz dates for EmArcy. Accompanied by an all-star orchestra arranged by Ernie Wilkins and featuring altoist Cannonball Adderley (who was near the beginning of his career), Vaughan is in superior form during these concise (around three minutes apiece) performances, particularly on "Soon," "Cherokee," "I'll Never Smile Again" and "An Occasional Man." A strong session. *—Scott Yanow*

Complete Sarah Vaughan on Mercury, Vol. 2: Sings Great American Songs (1956-1957) / Oct. 29, 1956-Jul. 12, 1957 / Mercury ♦♦♦♦♦

This five-CD box set, the second of four volumes that reissue all of Sarah Vaughan's recordings for Mercury and EmArcy (plus many previously unissued performances) contains her exploration of Gershwin songs, 13 vocal duets with her close friend Billy Eckstine and just five jazz numbers with her trio; all of the other selections feature Vaughan backed by large studio orchestras, usually led by Hal Mooney. Most of the material is a bit commercial (certainly the arrangements tend to be) but Sarah Vaughan generally uplifts the songs and overcomes her surroundings. Still, listeners strictly interested in her jazz performances are advised to get some of her single CD collections instead. *—Scott Yanow*

At Mister Kelly's / Aug. 6, 1957-Aug. 8, 1957 / EmArcy ♦♦♦♦♦

The Complete Sarah Vaughan on Mercury, Vol. 3: Great Show on Stage (1954-1956) / Aug. 6, 1957-1959 / Mercury ♦♦♦♦♦

The third of four Sarah Vaughan Mercury box sets (this one has six CDs) traces her career during the last two and a half years of the 1950s. There are several very interesting sessions (expanded greatly by the inclusion of many previously unissued performances) on this box including 21 numbers from a gig at *Mister Kelly's* in Chicago with her trio (led by pianist Jimmy Jones), a meeting with the Count Basie Orchestra that resulted in the album *No Count Sarah*, and a live set with a septet (which includes cornetist Thad Jones and the tenor of Frank Wess) at the London House in Chicago. In addition, there are quite a few commercial sides with large orchestras (including some sessions arranged by Quincy Jones), so overall this box lets one hear the many sides of Sarah Vaughan; a special highlight is her first recorded version of "Misty." The reissue (and the other three volumes) is a must for Sarah Vaughan's greatest fans although more general listeners may want to acquire one of the less expensive) single CDs instead. *—Scott Yanow*

The Roulette Years / 1960-1964 / Roulette ♦♦♦

This CD contains 24 selections so one cannot complain about its brevity, but it would have been preferable to have Sarah Vaughan's Roulette albums reissued in full (a few have been) rather than putting out this sampler. For the beginner there are many fine performances on the jazz-oriented set with Sassy's accompaniment ranging from guitar-bass duets and the Count Basie Big Band to string orchestras. Exact recording dates are not given (which is rather inexcusable) but the music is consistently enjoyable with some of the highpoints being "Just in Time," "Have You Met Miss Jones," "Perdido," "'Round Midnight," "I'll Be Seeing You" and "Spring Can Really Hang You up the Most." *—Scott Yanow*

You're Mine You / 1962 / Roulette ♦♦♦

Sarah Sings Soulfully / Jun. 6, 1963–1963 / Roulette ♦♦♦♦♦

Sarah Vaughan's final Roulette session before going back to Mercury was one of her best. Some of the tunes (such as "A Taste of Honey," "What Kind of Fool Am I" and "The Good Life") do not look all that promising but Sassy was near the peak of her powers during this era. Plus her renditions of "I Guess I'll Hang My Tears out to Dry," "Sermonette," "Gravy Waltz," "Moanin'," "'Round Midnight" and "Midnight Sun" are classics. Assisted by a sextet arranged by Gerald Wilson and including organist Ernie Freeman, trumpeter Carmell Jones and the tenor of Teddy Edwards, Vaughan is brilliant throughout this highly enjoyable CD reissue. *—Scott Yanow*

Sassy Swings the Tivoli / Jul. 18, 1963-Jul. 21, 1963 / Mercury ♦♦♦♦♦

Complete Sarah Vaughan on Mercury, Vol. 4, Pts. 1 and 2: (1963-1967) / Jul. 19, 1963-Jan. 1967 / Mercury ♦♦♦♦♦

The fourth of four box sets reissuing every recording Sarah Vaughan made for the Mercury and EmArcy labels (including many previously unreleased performances) starts off (after four orchestra tracks) with its strongest selections, no less than 32 songs recorded during a live four-day engagement in Copenhagen during which the singer is accompanied by the Kirk Stuart Trio. Everything else on this six-CD set is somewhat anticlimactic in comparison, for Vaughan is otherwise hindered a bit by string orchestras, a big band and/or a choir. Better to get the live sessions (released as *Sassy Swings the Tivoli* in addition to a Japanese set by the same name that has extra material) instead although lovers of Vaughan's voice will want to pick up this large reissue anyway. *—Scott Yanow*

Jazz Fest Masters / Jul. 1969 / Scotti Bros. ♦♦♦♦

How Long Has This Been Going On— / Apr. 25, 1978 / Pablo ♦♦♦♦♦

The Duke Ellington Songbook, Vol. 1 / Aug. 15, 1979-Sep. 13, 1979 / Pablo ♦♦♦♦♦

The Duke Ellington Songbook, Vol. 2 / Aug. 15, 1979-Sep. 13, 1979 / Pablo ♦♦♦♦♦

Send in the Clowns / Feb. 16, 1981-Mar. 16, 1981 / Pablo ♦♦♦

Crazy and Mixed Up / Mar. 1, 1982–Mar. 2, 1982 / Pablo ♦♦♦♦♦

In the City of Lights / Nov. 2, 1985 / Justin Time ♦♦♦♦

Bobby Vinton (Stanley Robert Vinton)

b. Apr. 16, 1935, Canonsburg, PA
Vocals, Clarinet / Traditional Pop, Vocal Pop, Pop
Every era needs its crooner, and in the early '60s, it was Bobby Vinton. Vinton's sentimental balladeering and orchestral, middle-of-the-road arrangements were a throwback to a decade earlier, before rock & roll had found its mass market. If Vinton is sometimes identified with a rock & roll audience, it's only because his music was bought by young listeners for a time, and because he still catches some airplay on oldies stations. What he sang was vocal pop, landing some of the biggest hits of the early '60s with "Roses Are Red (My Love)," "Blue on Blue," "There! I've Said It Again," "Mr. Lonely," and "Blue Velvet," the last of which has become his signature song in the wake of its notorious prominence in David Lynch's *Blue Velvet*. *—Richie Unterberger*

● **16 Most Requested Songs** / 1991 / Columbia/Legacy ✦✦✦✦✦
16 Most Requested Songs is a midline-priced collection that spotlights many of Bobby Vinton's best-known and most popular performances for Columbia Records, including "Blue Velvet," "Tell Me Why," "Take Good Care of My Baby," "Halfway to Paradise," "Blue on Blue," "L-O-N-E-L-Y," "Just as Much as Ever," "Mr. Lonely" and "Roses are Red (My Love)." Although it's far from a perfect retrospective of his career, it's still a nice sampler of familiar items, and it may satisfy the needs of some casual fans who only want the hits. *—Stephen Thomas Erlewine*

Dinah Washington (Ruth Lee Jones)

b. Aug. 29, 1924, Tuscaloosa, AL, **d.** Dec. 14, 1963, Detroit, MI
Vocals / Vocal Jazz, Traditional Pop, Standards, Jump Blues, Ballads
Dinah Washington was at once one of the most beloved and controversial singers of the mid-20th century—beloved to her fans, devotees and fellow singers; controversial to critics who still accuse her of selling out her art to commerce and bad taste. Her principal sin, apparently, was to cultivate a distinctive vocal style that was at home in all kinds of music, be it R&B, blues, jazz, middle-of-the-road pop—and she probably would have made a fine gospel or country singer had she the time. Hers was a gritty, salty, high-pitched voice, marked by absolute clarity of diction and clipped, bluesy phrasing. Dinah's personal life was turbulent, with seven marriages behind her, and her interpretations showed it, for she displayed a tough, totally unsentimental, yet still gripping hold on the universal subject of lost love. She has had a huge influence on R&B and jazz singers who have followed in her wake, notably Nancy Wilson, Esther Phillips and Diane Schuur, and her music is abundantly available nowadays via the huge seven-volume series *The Complete Dinah Washington on Mercury*. *—Richard S. Ginell*

The Best in Blues / Dec. 29, 1943-Jun. 10, 1953 / Mercury ✦✦✦

Mellow Mama / Dec. 10, 1945-Dec. 13, 1945 / Delmark ✦✦✦✦✦
Dinah Washington's first solo recordings (with the exception of a session supervised by Lionel Hampton in 1943) are included on this Delmark repackaging of her Apollo sides. Recorded in Los Angeles during a three-day period, the 12 selections feature the singer with a swinging jazz combo that has tenor-saxophonist Lucky Thompson, trumpeter Karl George, vibraphonist Milt Jackson and bassist Charles Mingus among its eight members. The 21-year-old Washington was already quite distinctive at this early stage and easily handles the blues and jive material with color and humor. Recommended despite the brevity (34 minutes) of the CD. *—Scott Yanow*

★ **The Complete Dinah Washington on Mercury, Vol. 1 (1946-1949)** / Jan. 14, 1946-Sep. 27, 1949 / Mercury ✦✦✦✦✦
All of Dinah Washington's studio recordings from 1946-61 have been reissued in definitive fashion by Polygram on seven three CD sets. *Volume 1* finds the youthful singer (who was 21 on the earliest sessions) evolving from a little-known but already talented singer to a best-selling R&B artist. Ranging from jazz and spirited blues to middle-of-the-road ballads, this set (as with the others in the *Complete* series) includes both gems and duds but fortunately the great majority fall into the former category. The backup groups include orchestras led by Gerald Wilson, Tab Smith, Cootie Williams, Chubby Jackson and Teddy Stewart and there are a dozen strong numbers with just a rhythm section. The first five volumes in this series are highly recommended. *—Scott Yanow*

☆ **The Complete Dinah Washington on Mercury, Vol. 2 (1950-1952)** / Feb. 7, 1950-May 6, 1952 / Mercury ✦✦✦✦✦
Dinah Washington was a best-selling artist on the R&B charts during this period but she was also a very versatile singer who could easily handle swinging jazz, schmaltzy ballads, blues and novelties with equal skill. The second of these seven three-CD sets in Mercury's *Complete* program mostly finds Washington being accompanied by studio orchestras although the Ravens join her on two numbers and drummer Jimmy Cobb heads a couple of jazz groups (including one with both Ben Webster and Wardell Gray on tenors). Not every selection is a classic but the quality level is quite high and the packaging is impeccable. Recommended. *—Scott Yanow*

☆ **The Complete Dinah Washington on Mercury, Vol. 3 (1952-1954)** / 1952-Aug. 14, 1954 / Mercury ✦✦✦✦✦
Of the seven three-CD sets in Mercury's *Complete* series of Dinah Washington recordings, this is the most jazz-oriented one. The versatile singer participates in a very memorable jam session with an all-star group (featuring Clifford Brown, Maynard Ferguson and Clark Terry on trumpets!), meets up with Terry and tenor-saxophonist Eddie Lockjaw Davis on another spontaneous date (highlighted by uptempo rops on "Bye Bye Blues" and "Blue Skies") and has several classic collaborations with the warm Lester Youngish tenor of Paul Quinichette. There are a few commercial sides with studio orchestras that are included (since they took place during the same period) but those are in the great minority on this essential volume. *—Scott Yanow*

Dinah Jams / Aug. 15, 1954 / PSM ✦✦✦✦✦

☆ **The Complete Dinah Washington on Mercury, Vol. 4 (1954-1956)** / Nov. 2, 1954-Apr. 25, 1956 / Mercury ✦✦✦✦✦
The fourth of seven three-CD sets in Mercury's *Complete* series alternates between strong swinging jazz with the likes of trumpeter Clark Terry, tenor-saxophonist Paul Quinichette, pianist Wynton Kelly and altoist Cannonball Adderley, and middle-of-the-road pop performances with studio orchestras. The third volume is the strongest in this series but the first five sets all contain more than enough jazz to justify their purchase. *Vol. 4* really attests to Dinah Washington's versatility. *—Scott Yanow*

☆ **The Complete Dinah Washington on Mercury, Vol. 5 (1956-1958)** / Jun. 25, 1956-Jul. 6, 1958 / Mercury ✦✦✦✦✦
Mercury has given the great singer Dinah Washington the complete treatment with seven three-CD sets that contain all of her recordings during the 1946-61 period, practically her entire career. *Vol. 5* is the final volume to be highly recommended, since it has her final jazz recordings. On many of these performances she is backed by orchestras led by Quincy Jones, Ernie Wilkins (including a tribute to Fats Waller) or Eddie Chamblee in arrangements that often leave room for short statements from some of the sidemen; one of the albums with Chamblee has a full set of songs associated with Bessie Smith. *Vol. 5* (which contains only a few commercial sides) concludes with her strong performance at the 1958 *Newport Jazz Festival*. *—Scott Yanow*

Dinah! / 1956 / EmArcy ✦✦✦✦✦

The Fats Waller Songbook / Oct. 1957 / EmArcy ✦✦✦✦✦

The Bessie Smith Songbook / Dec. 30, 1957-Jan. 20, 1958 / EmArcy ✦✦✦

Dinah Washington Sings Bessie Smith / Dec. 30, 1957-Jan. 20, 1958 / EmArcy ✦✦✦✦✦
Gifted with a strong, beautiful voice and very precise phrasing, Dinah Washington translated Bessie Smith's irrepressible spirit and flair even better than Billie Holiday, Smith's most famous devotee. For her tribute album, Washington avoided Smith's best-known songs ("Tain't Nobody's Bizness If I Do," "Nobody Knows You When You're Down and Out," "Baby Won't You Please Come Home"). Instead, she wisely concentrated on the more defiant standards from "The Empress of the Blues," including "Send Me to the 'Lectric Chair," "Jailhouse Blues," and "You've Been a Good Ole Wagon." Washington sounds simply glorious, focused on alternating Smith's phrasing to emphasize her own gospel roots. The accompaniment, by Eddie Chamblee and His Orchestra, emphasizes the vaudeville and Dixieland sound of early-century blues, heavy on the slide trombone, growling trumpet, and skeletal, rickety percussion. Reissued several times (occasionally under the title *The Bessie Smith Songbook*), *Dinah Washington Sings Bessie Smith* charts a perfect balance between tribute and genuine artistic statement. A Verve master edition reissue added alternate takes of "Trombone Butter" and "Careless Love," plus three songs taken from a Newport performance later in 1958. *—John Bush*

The Ultimate Dinah Washington / 1957-1961 / Verve ✦✦✦

What a Diff'rence a Day Makes! / Feb. 19, 1959-Aug. 1959 / Mercury ✦✦✦✦✦
One of the more notorious albums in the history of vocal music, *What a Diff'rence a Day Makes!* is the lush session that bumped up Dinah Washington from the "Queen of the Blues" to a middle-of-the-road vocal wondress—and subsequently disenfranchised quite a few jazz purists. Washington had been praised in the same breath as Holiday and Fitzgerald for more than a decade, but Mercury nevertheless decided to back her with mainstream arrangements (by Belford Hendricks), heavy strings, and wordless vocal choruses similar to the radio hits of the day. Apparently, the mainstream backings didn't faze Washington at all; she proves herself with a voice as individual and evocative as ever. To be honest, the arrangements are quite solid for what they're worth; though it's a bit jarring to hear Washington's voice wrapped in sweet strings, the effect works well more frequently than not. Most of the songs here are familiar standards ("I Remember You," "I Thought About You," "Cry Me a River," "Manhattan," "Time After Time"), but they've been transformed by Washington as though they'd never been sung before. The Top Ten title track is by no means the best song on the album, but its title proved prophetic for Washington's career. Though her vocal style hadn't changed at all, one day she was a respected blues singer; the next, according to most of the jazz cognoscenti, she had become a lowbrow pop singer. Thankfully, the evidence against Washington's "transformation" is provided right here. *—John Bush*

Andy Williams (Howard Andrew Williams)

b. Dec. 3, 1928, Wall Lake, IA
Vocals / Traditional Pop, Film Music, Standards, Vocal Pop, Soft Rock, Pop, Show Tunes
Easily the most solid and long-lasting vocalist of his era, Andy Williams' laidback delivery and expansive voice charmed audiences for decades, from his first appearance with a brother quartet into his seventh decade of performance as the head of his own dinner theater in Branson, Missouri. Williams began singing in his church choir and later formed the Williams Brothers Quartet with his three brothers. (The group can be heard on Bing Crosby's 1944 hit "Swinging on a Star.") He finally began his solo career in 1952, and recorded his first Top Ten hit while at Cadence with 1956's "Canadian Sunset." One year later, his soft-toned cover of the Charlie Gracie rockabilly nugget "Butterfly" spent three weeks at number one (it's still his biggest hit). Additional Top Ten entries "Are You Sincere," "Lonely Street" and "The Village of St. Bernadette" followed before Williams moved to Columbia in 1961.

Despite another big hit in 1963, "Can't Get Used to Losing You," Williams failed to generate much action on the singles charts during the 1960s. Instead, his high-rated variety program on NBC-TV spurred interest in the ever-growing LP market for adult and middle-of-the-road audiences. The popular 1962 album *Moon River and Other Great Movie Themes* launched the song he's most identified with, and the following year's *Days of Wine and Roses* spent 16 weeks at the top of the album charts. Nine more LPs hit the Top Ten for Andy Williams during the '60s, many organized around loose themes—Broadway, ballads, and one album that featured members of his family. Though his television show was cancelled in 1971, Andy Williams remained very popular during the '70s, especially for British audiences.

He released relatively few LPs during the '80s, but returned to the pop world in the early '90s when he founded his own theatre/resort in the home-grown entertainment capital of Branson, Missouri. Williams continued to headline shows there during the rest of the decade. *—John Bush*

Lonely Street / 1959 / Varese ✦✦✦✦✦
A reissue of Williams' 1960 best-selling Cadence album with bonus tracks added from *Andy Williams' Best* and *Two Times Winners*. This is Williams making—for him—a very bluesy and jazzy album, full of melancholy and longing on tracks like "You Don't Know What Love Is," "In the Wee Small Hours of the Morning," "When Your Lover Has Gone," "Twilight Time," and two versions of the title track, the single version reconstructed from mono and stereo sources. Not enough o's in smooth to describe this one, Williams is nothing but spot on in this collection. *—Cub Koda*

Greatest Hits, Vol. 2 / 1981 / Columbia ✦✦✦

16 Most Requested Songs / 1990 / Columbia/Legacy ✦✦✦✦✦
16 Most Requested Songs is a midline-priced collection that spotlights many of Andy Williams' best-known and most popular performances for Columbia Records, including "Butterfly," "Are You Sincere," "Lonely Street," "Charade," "On the Street Where You Live," "Music to Watch Girls By," "Where Do I Begin," "Happy Heart" and "Speak Softly Love." Although it's far from a perfect retrospective of his career, it's still a nice sampler of familiar items, and it may satisfy the needs of some casual fans who only want the hits. *—Stephen Thomas Erlewine*

★ **I Like Your Kind of Love: The Best of the Cadence Years** / Mar. 26, 1996 / Varèse Vintage ✦✦✦✦✦
All of Andy Williams' biggest late '50s hits—including "Butterfly," "Are You Sincere," "Lonely Street," and "The Village of St. Bernadette"—are included on *I Like Your Kind of Love: Best of Andy Williams*, making it the definitive retrospective of his early career. *—Stephen Thomas Erlewine*

Under Paris Skies / Aug. 12, 1997 / Varese ✦✦✦

Cadence Collection / Apr. 7, 1998 / Recall ✦✦✦✦✦
This two-CD, 40-track British compilation was, at the time of its release in 1998, the most comprehensive collection of Andy Williams's early recordings in print. Williams recorded for Cadence Records from 1955 to 1961, a period that coincided with the birth of rock & roll, and though he, six years Elvis Presley's senior and in the business since childhood, was uncomfortable with the new style, Cadence pushed him to try it as a means of breaking through. And break through he did, topping the singles charts in 1957 with the rockish "Butterfly." After a few more experiments with rock, however, he settled into the ballad style he pursued for the rest of his career. This set, which contained "Butterfly" along with Williams's 15 other chart singles for Cadence (both A- and B-sides, in chronological order), also selected from Wiliams LPs of the era such as *Andy Williams Sings Rodgers & Hammerstein, Two Time Winners* (in which he covered other people's hits), and *Under Paris Skies* (French songs) for a thorough, coherent anthology that summed up the first part of the singer's solo career effectively. *—William Ruhlmann*

Days of Wine & Roses/Moon River & Other Great Movie Themes / Columbia ✦✦✦

Joe Williams (Joseph Goreed)

b. Dec. 12, 1918, Cordele, GA, **d.** Mar. 29, 1999
Vocals / Vocal Jazz, Traditional Pop, Standards, Swing
Joe Williams was the last great big-band singer, a smooth baritone who graced the rejuvenated Count Basie Orchestra during the 1950s and captivated audiences well into the '90s. After forming his own gospel vocal quartet as a teenager, Williams appeared with orchestras led by Jimmie Noone, Coleman Hawkins, Lionel Hampton and Andy Kirk during the late '30s and early '40s. Still, a lingering bout of tuberculosis from childhood kept him sidelined from active touring, and he worked menial jobs before his first minor hit for Checker, 1952's "Every Day I Have the Blues."

Williams finally got his big break in 1954, when he was hired as the male vocalist for Count Basie's Orchestra. He soon helped audiences forget the absence of Basie's long-time vocalist, Jimmy Rushing with his first (and best) LP, 1955's *Count Basie Swings/Joe Williams Sings*. A definitive version of "Every Day I Have the Blues" (already his signature song) hit number two on the R&B charts, and the success sparked another LP, 1957's *The Greatest! Count Basie Swings/Joe Williams Sings Standards*. He also made his solo-billed debut LP in 1956, and followed it with a trio of albums for Roulette. Despite an inevitable parting from Basie in 1961, Williams recorded with a host of great jazzmen for many of his mid-'60s LPs, including 1963's *Jump for Joy* and 1966's *Presenting Joe Williams and the Thad Jones-Mel Lewis Orchestra*.

Though Williams toured consistently during the 1970s, his recordings fell off until a pair of mid-'80s LPs, *Nothin' But the Blues* and *I Just Wanna Sing*. He then landed a recurring role on the popular television series *The Cosby Show* and signed a contract for Verve. Live appearances at Vine St. resulted in material for his first two Verve albums, *Every Night: Live at Vine St.* and *Ballad and Blues Master*. Still in extraordinarily fine voice, Williams recorded two more albums for Verve, toured constantly, and remained one of the most talented jazz vocalists in the world right up until his death in 1999. *—John Bush*

The Best of Joe Williams: The Roulette, Solid State & Blue Note Years / 1951-1968 / Blue Note ✦✦✦✦✦
The Best of Joe Williams: The Roulette, Solid State & Blue Note Years is an excellent sampler of Williams' work for Roulette and Solid State, providing a terrific overview of Williams' early records. Most of these 18 tracks feature Williams with the Count Basie Orchestra; there are also several cuts with Jimmy Jones, Harry "Sweets" Edison, Horace Ott, Jimmy Mundy, the Thad Jones-Mel Lewis Orchestra and Lambert, Hendricks and Ross. For anyone wondering why Williams is considered one of the great blues and big band vocalists, this offers a reason why. *—Stephen Thomas Erlewine*

A Night at Count Basie's / Oct. 22, 1955 / Vanguard ✦✦✦

A Man Ain't Supposed to Cry / 1958 / Roulette ✦✦✦✦

A Swingin' Night at Birdland / 1962 / Blue Note ✦✦✦✦
In 1961, after six years as one of the main attractions of Count Basie's orchestra, Williams (with Basie's blessing) went out on his own. One of his first sessions was this live recording, cut at Birdland with a strong quintet that featured trumpeter Harry "Sweets" Edison and Jimmy Forrest on tenor. Williams mostly sings standards and ballads, but also tosses in a few of his popular blues (including "Well Alright, OK, You Win" and "Goin' to Chicago") during a well-rounded and thoroughly enjoyable set. *—Scott Yanow*

Me and the Blues / Jan. 2, 1963-Dec. 5, 1963 / RCA ✦✦✦✦✦
This recording features singer Joe Williams backed by a studio orchestra headed and arranged by Jimmy Jones. Williams mostly sticks to blues-oriented material but there is a surprising amount of mood variation on the dozen selections along with short solos by trumpeters Thad Jones and Clark Terry, altoist Phil Woods and Seldon Powell on tenor; Ben Webster has a guest spot on "Rocks in My Bed." Williams, heard at the peak of his powers, is at his best on "Me and the Blues," "Rocks in My Bed," "Work Song," and "Kansas City." *—Scott Yanow*

The Overwhelmin' / Feb. 6, 1963-Jun. 18, 1965 / Bluebird/RCA ✦✦✦✦✦
A CD sampler taken from five former LPs, this fine CD features Joe Williams doing three songs from Duke Ellington's play *Jump for Joy*, five numbers at the 1963 *Newport Jazz Festival* (during which he is joined by trumpeters Clark Terry and Howard McGhee, and tenor greats Coleman Hawkins, Zoot Sims, and Ben Webster), four blues numbers backed by an all-star jazz group, and five ballads in front of an orchestra. Although it would be preferable to have each of the five original albums intact, this superb collection features Joe Williams on a wide variety of material, and he is heard close to his peak throughout. *—Scott Yanow*

Then and Now / Apr. 29, 1965-Nov. 23, 1983 / Sea Breeze ✦✦✦✦✦

☆ **Presenting Joe Williams and the Thad Jones-Mel Lewis Jazz Orchestra** / Sep. 30, 1966 / Blue Note ✦✦✦✦✦
This CD reissues one of Joe Williams's finest recordings. Accompanied by the Thad Jones/Mel Lewis Orchestra, the singer is heard at the peak of his powers. The big band primarily functions as an ensemble (Snooky Young gets off some good blasts on "Nobody Knows the Way I Feel This Morning") but the inventive Thad Jones arrangements insure that his illustrious sidemen have plenty to play. Many of the selections (half of which have been in the singer's repertoire ever since) are given definitive treatment on this set (particularly a humorous "Evil Man Blues," "Gee Baby Ain't I Good to You—" and "Smack Dab in the Middle") and Williams scats at his best on "It Don't Mean a Thing." Get this one. *—Scott Yanow*

Joe Williams Live / Aug. 7, 1973 / Fantasy/OJC ✦✦✦✦

Dave Pell's Prez Conference / 1979 / GNP Crescendo ✦✦✦✦✦
Dave Pell's Prez Conference was to Lester Young what Supersax is to Charlie Parker. Pell's short-lived group featured harmonized Lester Young solos recreated by three tenors and a baritone; their matchup with singer Joe Williams is quite enjoyable. Since Young was in Count Basie's orchestra when Jimmy Rushing was the vocalist, Joe Williams has a rare opportunity to give his own interpretation to Rushing and Bilie Holiday classics like "I May Be Wrong," "You Can Depend on Me," "If Dreams Come True" and "Easy Living." A delightful and swinging date. *—Scott Yanow*

Nothin' But the Blues / Nov. 16, 1983-Nov. 17, 1983 / Delos ✦✦✦✦

I Just Wanna Sing / Jun. 29, 1985-Jun. 30, 1985 / Delos ✦✦✦✦

Every Night: Live at Vine St. / May 7, 1987-May 8, 1987 / Verve ✦✦✦✦✦

In Good Company / Jan. 19, 1989-Jan. 21, 1989 / Verve ✦✦✦✦

Live at Orchestra Hall, Detroit / Nov. 20, 1992 / Telarc ✦✦✦✦

● **Every Day: The Best of the Verve Years** / Nov. 16, 1993 / Verve ✦✦✦✦✦
In effect, this double-disc set, released in anticipation of Joe Williams' 75th birthday, is two compilation albums in one. The first CD, containing material recorded between 1955 and 1957, presents the artist singing with Count Basie and His Orchestra at the start of Williams' national career, when he and Basie scored a major R&B hit with the title song and made albums like *Count Basie Swings/Joe Williams Sings, One O'Clock Jump*, and *The Greatest! Count Basie Swings/Joe Williams Sings Standards*. Along with *The Count Basie Band and the Dizzy Gillespie Band at Newport*, these provide most of the selections included, among them memorable Williams performances such as "Teach Me Tonight," "I'm Beginning to See the Light," and "The Comeback." The second CD chronicles Williams' return to Verve Records in the years 1987 to 1990, for such albums as *Every Night* and *Ballad and Blues Master*, both of which were recorded live May 7-8, 1987, at *the Vine St. Bar and Grill* in Hollywood. So, we have the (relatively) young Williams and a much older Williams towards the end of his career. In both cases, however, he displays considerable dexterity in his blues-tinged jazz singing, and he gets tremendous support from his instrumentalists. The 30-year gap from one disc to another prevents this from being a definitive look at his career, but for the periods covered the anthology is well-chosen. *—William Ruhlmann*

Feel the Spirit / Sep. 20, 1994-Sep. 23, 1994 / Telarc ✦✦✦

Ultimate Joe Williams / Sep. 28, 1999 / Verve ✦✦✦✦

Cassandra Wilson

b. Dec. 4, 1955, Jackson, MS
Vocals / Vocal Jazz, Standards, Free Funk, Contemporary Jazz, M-Base, World Fusion
Although her recording career has been somewhat erratic, Cassandra Wilson is one of the top jazz singers of the 1990s, a vocalist blessed with a distinctive and flexible voice who is not afraid to take chances. She began playing piano and guitar when she was nine and was working as a vocalist by the mid-'70s, singing a wide variety of material. Following a year in New Orleans, Wilson moved to New York in 1982 and began working with Dave Holland

and Abbey Lincoln. After meeting Steve Coleman, she became the main vocalist with the M-Base collective. Although there was really no room for a singer in the overcrowded free funk ensembles, Wilson did as good a job of fitting in as was possible. She worked with New Air and recorded her first album as a leader in 1985. By her third record, a standards date, she was sounding quite a bit like Betty Carter. After a few more albums in which she mostly performed original and rather inferior material, Cassandra Wilson changed directions and performed an acoustic blues-oriented program for Blue Note called *Blue Light 'Til Dawn*. By going back in time, she had found herself and Wilson has continued interpreting in fresh and creative ways vintage country blues and folk music up until the present day. During 1997 she toured as part of Wynton Marsalis' *Blood on the Fields* production; *Traveling Miles*, her tribute to Miles Davis, followed two years later. *—Scott Yanow*

Songbook / Mar. 1985-Aug. 1991 / JMT ✦✦✦✦

Point of View / Dec. 14, 1985-Dec. 15, 1985 / JMT ✦✦✦✦
Cassandra Wilson's debut as a leader features the chancetaking singer in a funky M-Base setting. The overcrowded ensembles (played by altoist Steve Coleman, trombonist Grachan Moncur III, guitarist Jean-Paul Bourelly, bassist Lonnie Plaxico and drummer Mark Johnson) did not leave much space for a singer, but the flexible Wilson did her best to find a role for her voice, and she sounds enthusiastic. In addition to group originals, the sextet performs "Blue in Green" (which has Wilson's lyrics) and "I Wished on the Moon." *—Scott Yanow*

Blue Skies / Feb. 1988 / JMT ✦✦✦✦

★ **Blue Light Til Dawn** / 1993 / Blue Note ✦✦✦✦✦
Cassandra Wilson has steadfastly refused to be pigeonholed or confined to any stylistic formula. Her highly anticipated Blue Note debut may stir renewed controversy, as she is once again all over the place. She begins the set with her intriguing version of "You Don't Know What Love Is." Then she moves from two Robert Johnson covers ("Come On In My Kitchen" and "Hellhound On My Trail") to rock compositions from Van Morrison and Joni Mitchell, then to her own title track and blues cut "Redbone" and a piercing version of "I Can't Stand The Rain" that can hold up to comparisons with Ann Peebles' classic. She doesn't have Johnson's menacing quality (who does—), but does invoke an equally compelling air. Wilson has great timing, pacing and delivery and certainly has blues sensibility in her sound. *—Ron Wynn*

New Moon Daughter / 1995 / Blue Note ✦✦✦✦✦
Singer Cassandra Wilson, who has had a rather diverse career that has ranged from the free funk of M-Base to standards a la Betty Carter, has in recent times adopted a folk-oriented style a little reminiscent of Nina Simone. On this CD her repertoire ranges from U2 to Son House, from Hoagy Carmichael to Hank Williams ("I'm So Lonesome I Could Cry"); it is certainly the only album ever that contains both the Monkees' "Last Train to Clarksville" and "Strange Fruit" This CD is a surprise best-seller, for Wilson's voice actually sounds quite bored and emotionally detached. She deserves great credit for stretching herself but one has to dig deep to find any warmth in her overly cool approach. *—Scott Yanow*

Traveling Miles / Mar. 23, 1999 / Blue Note ✦✦✦

Nancy Wilson

b. Feb. 20, 1937, Chillicothe, OH
Vocals / Vocal Jazz, Traditional Pop, Standards
Diva Nancy Wilson was among contemporary music's most stylish and sultry vocalists; while often crossing over into the pop and R&B markets—and even hosting her own television variety program—she remained best known as a jazz performer, renowned for her work alongside figures including Cannonball Adderley and George Shearing. Wilson first attracted notice performing the club circuit in Columbus, OH; she quickly earned a growing reputation among jazz players and fans, and was recording regularly by the late 1950s. Her dates with Shearing, including 1960's *The Swingin's Mutual*, solidified her standing as a talent on the rise, and her subsequent work with Adderley—arguably her finest recordings—further cemented her growing fame and reputation. In the years to follow, however, Wilson often moved away from jazz, much to the chagrin of purists; she made numerous albums, many of them properly categorized as pop and R&B outings, and toured extensively. She even hosted her own Emmy-winning variety series for NBC, *The Nancy Wilson Show;* hits of the period included "Tell Me the Truth," "How Glad I Am," "Peace of Mind," and "Now, I'm a Woman." Regardless of how far afield she traveled, Wilson always maintained her connections to the jazz world, and in the 1980s, she returned to the music with a vengeance. *—Jason Ankeny*

● **Swingin's Mutual** / Jun. 29, 1960-Jan. 7, 1961 / Capitol ✦✦✦✦✦
Singer Nancy Wilson has only made a few recordings throughout her career that are of any interest to jazz listeners. This CD reissue brings back her third album, an excellent collaboration with the George Shearing Quintet. Originally Wilson participated on six of the 12 selections but since five new tracks (with only one vocal) have been added, she is now on seven out of 17. Very much under the influence of Dinah Washington at this point, Nancy Wilson is in generally good form particularly on "The Nearness of You," "All Night Long," and "The Things We Did Last Summer." As far as the instrumentals by pianist Shearing's Quintet go, "I Remember Clifford," "Evansville," "Blue Lou," and "Lullaby of Birdland" are most memorable with short solos heard from vibraphonist Warren Chiasson and guitarist Dick Garcia. *—Scott Yanow*

Hello Young Lovers / 1962 / Capitol ✦✦✦

Nancy Wilson & Cannonball Adderley / Sep. 1, 1962 / Capitol ✦✦✦✦✦
This is a reissue of an excellent collaboration of the Nancy Wilson voice with the Cannonball Adderley alto sax from the early '60s. While this 1961 recording was the first time Wilson was with Adderley in the studio, it was not the first time they had worked together. After singing with Rusty Bryant's band, Wilson worked with Adderley in Columbus, OH. It was there that Adderley encouraged her to go to N.Y.C. to do some recording, eventually leading to this session.

Not entirely a vocal album, five of the 12 cuts are instrumentals. The additional cut added to the reissue, "Little Unhappy Boy," tips the scales in favor of Wilson's vocalizing. A highlight of the album is the gentle cornet playing of Nat Adderley behind Wilson, especially on "Save Your Love for Me" and on "The Old Country." Cannonball Adderley's swinging, boppish sax is heard to excellent effect throughout. Joe Zawinul's work behind Wilson on "The Masquerade Is Over" demonstrates that he is a talented, sensitive accompanist. On the instrumental side, "Teaneck" and "One Man's Dream" are especially good group blowing sessions. On the other end of the spectrum, Adderley's alto offers a lovely slow-tempo treatment of the Vernon Duke-Ira Gershwin masterpiece, "I Can't Get Started." To keep the listeners on their musical toes, the first couple of bars of "Save Your Love for Me" are quotes from "So What" from the Miles Davis Sextet seminal *Kind of Blue* session.

Given the play list and the outstanding artists performing it, why any serious jazz collection would be without this classic album is difficult to comprehend. *—Dave Nathan*

Yesterday's Love Songs/Today's Blues / 1963 / Blue Note ✦✦✦

Today, Tomorrow, Forever / 1964 / Capitol ✦✦✦

A Touch of Today / 1966 / Capitol ✦✦✦

Welcome to My Love / 1968 / Blue Note ✦✦✦✦

But Beautiful / 1969 / Blue Note ✦✦✦✦
Nancy Wilson has been on the fringes of jazz throughout her career, mostly performing middle-of-the-road pop and R&B. Most of her albums were major productions, but this CD reissue is quite different. On a relaxed and tasteful program of ballads (including three previously unreleased numbers), Wilson sounds properly expressive and a bit influenced by Dinah Washington while backed by a flawless rhythm section comprised of pianist Hank Jones, guitarist Gene Bertoncini, bassist Ron Carter and drummer Grady Tate. Her performances are straightforwrd, a little soulful and very mindful of the melody and the lyrics. There is little of jazz interest, but this is superior ballad singing and one of Nancy Wilson's finest recordings to date. *—Scott Yanow*

Forbidden Lover / Jan. 19, 198787 02 / Columbia ✦✦✦✦✦

With My Lover Beside / 1991 / Columbia ✦✦✦✦✦
A superbly arranged, produced, and mastered session from a wonderful vocalist. Wilson's singing, delivery, and tone are enticing and sensual throughout, even when the songs threaten to get overly sentimental or just sappy. Although the album was aimed at the adult contemporary audience, Wilson never coasted through any number, and this was about as polished and effective as this kind of session could get. *—Ron Wynn*

● **Anthology** / Jun. 6, 2000 / Capitol ✦✦✦✦
Wilson is a vexing artist to summarize with a best-of compilation, due both to her versatility and her prolific discography. This two-set CD concentrates on her pop- and R&B-influenced recordings for Capitol in the 1960s and '70s. While that means that her jazziest and most standard-inclined sides are relatively lightly represented (although not ignored), it does mean that this is the material most likely to be familiar to the general audience. In truth the soul influence is quite light; this is really pop material, not R&B, soul, or rock, even as it might show some traces of those genres (as well as jazz and cabaret). As a whole, this easy-listening soul music was light fare, but Wilson was probably better at it (and certainly more successful at it) than anyone else. The first disc, covering 1962-1970, is the better of the pair, with the big 1964 hit "(You Don't Know) How Glad I Am" and a couple of nice non-LP singles in 1963's bluesy "Tell the Truth" and 1965's "Where Does That Leave Me." Her reading of Stevie Wonder's "Uptight" is actually respectable, and some of her better mid-'60s singles show the influence of New York uptown soul production. The second disc charts the decline of pop-soul as a whole, even if it does lead off with a couple of 1970 Gamble-Huff-affiliated tracks. Much of the rest marks Wilson as one of the mothers of adult contemporary music, which is not the highest badge of honor one can bear. Is this *the* anthology you should have if you only get one Wilson collection— If your tastes run to pop rather than jazz, it probably is, though it should be cautioned that it's uneven and does not reflect the full scope of her repertoire. *—Richie Unterberger*

Various Artists

20 Centuries of Hits / Jan. 19, 1999 / Rhino ✦✦✦
As the title suggests, Rhino's *20 Centuries of Hits* collects some of the most memorable sacred, traditional, and contemporary songs—from "The First Delphic Hymn to Apollo" to the Kingsmen's "Louie Louie." Atrium Musicae de Madrid performs "Epitaph of Seiklos," "Hymn to the Muse," and other sacred pieces from ancient Greece, and the Monks of Ampleford Abbey sing "Ave Maris Stella," "Hymn to the Virgin Mary," and "Te Deum Laudamus." Alfred Deller & the Deller Consort contribute "Gloria From 'Notre Dame Mass'" and "Greensleeves," while Bing Crosby's "Star Dust" and Paul Robeson's version of "The Old Folks at Home (Swannee River)" bring the listener into more modern times. *20 Centuries of Hits* does an admirable job of highlighting two millennia of music history, and is worthwhile for anyone looking for an overview of popular music's evolution. *—Heather Phares*

50's Remembered: Pop Vocalists Era—*Male* */ Feb. 11, 1997 / Varese* ✦✦✦✦
A multi-volume retrospective of the pop-vocalists era (although neither volume is individually designated from the other; a curious twist or perhaps a mere oversight), the first entry into the series features a 16-track collection of sides from male singers who recorded with success primarily for Decca and Coral Records. Make no mistake about it, there is nothing remotely rock & roll about any of these sides; this is lush, romantic pop music of the highest order, the pre-Elvis side of the '50s equation. The compilation starts right on the cusp of the decade with big-band singer Dick Haymes contributing five tracks to the fray, including the pop hit version of "Room Full of Roses" and duets with Eileen Wilson and Ethel Merman. Next up is Alan Dale, still a year or so away from playing fake rocker Arnie Haynes in the Alan Freed/Bill Haley movie *Don't Knock the Rock doing business with &"Cherry Pink and*

Apple Blossom White" and a trio effort with Buddy Greco and Johnny Desmond on the jaunty and venerable "East Side, West Side." Which sets the stage perfectly for big-voiced Johnny Desmond with his big hit, "The High and the Mighty." Closing things out are four tracks from pop smoothie Don Cherry, culling three of his early-'50s Decca singles and one stray Columbia side, his 1955 pop hit, "Band of Gold." A nice collection of sides seldom heard anywhere today. *—Cub Koda*

Billboard Pop Memories: 1940-1944 / 1994 / Rhino ✦✦✦✦
Billboard Pop Memories: 1940-1944 is a fine retrospective of the era in question—although it contains only ten tracks, each is a gem, and for baby-boomers onward it's a solid introduction to the music of the war years. Highlights include such perennials as Glenn Miller's "In the Mood," Bing Crosby's "Swinging on a Star," Artie Shaw's "Stardust" and the Mills Brothers' "Paper Doll." *—Raymond McKinney*

Billboard Pop Memories: 1945-1949 / 1994 / Rhino ✦✦✦✦
As the 1940s wore on, the end of the big band/swing era resulted in changes on the pop music horizon. This fourth disc in Rhino's latest pre-rock series shows how sophisticated, jazzy fare declined, and forgettable, novelty/humorous numbers reigned. Peggy Lee's "Manana," with its phony Afro-Latin vocal and exaggerated rhythms, Dinah Shore's "Buttons and Bows" and Frankie Carle's "Rumors Are Flying" were symptomatic of the lightweight lyrical fare that dominated the era's popular music. The CD also features breezy, pleasant but ultimately trivial material from Ted Weems, Les Brown, Russ Morgan and Vaughn Monroe. *—Ron Wynn*

Billboard Pop Memories: 1950-1954 / 1994 / Rhino ✦✦✦✦
Rock and roll seemed the farthest thing from anyone's mind during the early '50s. Elaborate, highly arranged songs such as Tony Bennett's "Rags To Riches," Rosemary Clooney's "Come On-A My House" and Kay Starr's "Wheel Of Fortune" were the norm, plus the overwrought and frenzied vocals of Eddie Fisher and Johnny Ray with the Four Lads. There were also sentimental tunes by Patti Page, Jo Stafford and folk from Gordon Jenkins and his Orchestra with The Weavers. Only "How High The Moon" by Les Paul and Mary Ford provide any inkling of what's on the horizon—songs with a more pronounced rhythm and emotional vocal style. *—Ron Wynn*

Billboard Pop Memories: 1955-1959 / 1994 / Rhino ✦✦✦
The final disc in Rhino's pre-rock pop series moves through the middle and end of the 1950s, with mainstream pop still mostly avoiding the emerging rock revolution. The lush sound of Dean Martin and the Four Aces remained prominent, although Tommy Edwards did break the embargo somewhat with "It's All In The Game." Perez Prado capitalized on the mambo craze with "Cherry Pink and Apple Blossom White," while orchestral background music reaped dividends. A couple of songs outlined the industry's basic strategy to deal with early rock; Pat Boone's "Love Letters In The Sand" was a teen pop attempt at presenting an alternative to such feared artists as Little Richard, and the McGuire Sisters' saccharine remake of "Sincerely" was one of many R&B hits reworked by white groups because they were deemed too harsh (i.e., black) for the mainstream market. *—Ron Wynn*

Billboard Pop Memories: The 1920s / 1994 / Rhino ✦✦✦✦
Another in Rhino's continuing line of pre-rock popular music anthologies featuring ten hits from the 1920s. This six-disc slate accents tunes that were hits as determined by *Billboard.* The first disc contains seminal country from Vernon Dalhart alongside light fluff from Guy Lombardo and Selvin's Novelty Orchestra. The dominant acts are Paul Whiteman & His Orchestra, Al Jolson and Gene Austin, who have six of the 10 selections, including "Valencia," "Sonny Boy" and "My Blue Heaven." The mastering is superb. *—Ron Wynn*

Billboard Pop Memories: The 1930s / 1994 / Rhino/RCA ✦✦✦✦✦
The second Rhino pre-rock hits CD covers the 1930s, showcasing the rise of big bands and the phasing out of novelty/comic types such as Rudy Vallee. Bing Crosby's majestic sound, as well as the orchestras of Artie Shaw, Duke Ellington, Benny Goodman and Glenn Miller are featured. Two of the least musically interesting tracks were huge hits, Vallee's "Stein Song" and "Deep Purple" by Larry Clinton and His Orchestra. They're more than balanced by Crosby's wondrous "Pennies From Heaven" with George Stoll and His Orchestra, and "Night And Day," with Fred Astaire's stately lead vocal and Leo Reisman And His Orchestra. *—Ron Wynn*

Blues in the Night: the Johnny Mercer Songbook / Mar. 25, 1997 / Verve ✦✦✦
Contrary to Verve's blurb on the sticker of this CD, this is not the first songbook album devoted to the lyrics of Johnny Mercer; indeed, none other than Verve was responsible for an Ella Fitzgerald/Mercer songbook back in 1964. Needless to say, Ella is here, as is an all-star gallery of Verve, Mercury. MGM and Mars artists in an anthology spanning some 40 years of recording history and about 16 years of Mercer's work (1936-52). There are some enterprising choices like Buddy Rich *singing* "Goody Goody" quite competently in front of a big band, the first recording of the lyrics to "Early Autumn" via a rare Woody Herman recording on his own Mars label, and Helen Merrill drifting over the dissonantly loose Gil Evans Orchestra in "Any Place I Hang My Hat Is Home." Of the most famous songs identified with Mercer, Louis Armstrong's marvelous meeting with the Oscar Peterson Quartet on "Blues in The Night," Anita O'Day's buoyant "Come Rain Or Come Shine" with Jimmy Giuffre's off-center ensemble, and Billie Holiday's hard-boiled treatment of "One For My Baby" (with sweet and sultry obligatos by Harry "Sweets" Edison and Ben Webster) stand out. Other artists heard here include Bing Crosby, Sarah Vaughan, Dinah Washington, Billy Eckstine, Margaret Whiting, Mel Tormé, Joe Williams, and Dee Dee Bridgewater. Throughout, when not distracted by the musical quick-changes, the listener is seduced by Mercer's facility with lingering images and interior rhymeplay. And even though a single disc isn't quite enough to sum up Mercer's achievement—after all, it isn't easy to choose 16 songs out of some 1, 500—this is only Volume One. *—Richard S. Ginell*

Capitol from the Vaults, Vol. 1: The Birth of a Label 1942-1943 / Jun. 6, 2000 / Capitol ✦✦✦✦
From the Vaults is a multi-disc series commemorating the 60th anniversary of Capitol Records. Volume one, *Birth of a Label,* compiles 25 of the earliest sides issued by the label's collective brain trust: songwriters Buddy DeSylva, Johnny Mercer, and record shop proprietor Glenn Wallichs. Although many of these tunes quickly became pop standards, several have never been issued on CD before—and of those that have previously entered the digital domain, most were transferred from sonically challenged vinyl. Tremendous care has been taken on the *From the Vaults* series to track down the best possible source materials. The extra effort pays off immeasurably. Capitol's incipient recordings were, as one might imagine, an ideal vehicle for Mercer's dynamic compositions. "Strip Polka," "Trav'lin' Light," and "G.I. Jive" are among his earliest pieces for the label and are included on this volume. However, the label quickly became recognized for the variety of sounds released under their moniker. Some of Capitol's earliest hits were taken from motion picture soundtracks. "My Ideal," "You'd Be So Nice to Come Home To," "Moonlight Becomes You," and the seasonal favorite "White Christmas" are among the baker's dozen of movie songs featured on this release. Other genres to be represented by Capitol ranged from jazz ("Trav'lin' Light") to boogie-woogie ("Cow Cow Boogie"), and even early R&B ("Riffette"). A 10-page liner notes booklet contains memorabilia, vintage photos, and other previously unpublished eye candy, as well as an essay by musician and music historian Billy Vera. Initial pressings—limited to 10,000—are cleverly packaged in a digi-pack designed to replicate the 78 rpm records and sleeves of the era. With such attention to sonic as well as visual detail, *Vol. One: Birth of a Label* is a promising start to the series. *—Lindsay Planer*

Capitol from the Vaults, Vol. 2: Vine Street Divas / Jun. 6, 2000 / Capitol ✦✦✦✦
This volume of From the Vaults highlights early Capitol Records hits by the ladies of the tower, so to speak. Individual talents such as Jo Stafford, Anita O'Day, and Peggy Lee began to emerge from many top orchestras and soon became Vine Street divas in their own right. The timing for this incipient wave of girl power couldn't have been better, since WW II was preoccupying many of the country's top male vocalists. The extensive selection of musical genres on the label didn't hurt either. Among the most popular of these were \show tunes. Jo Stafford led her fellow female artists scoring Top Ten hits with songs from both stage and screen. *Vine Street Divas* includes two Stafford classics: "Long Ago (And Far Away)" from the film *Cover Girl,* as well as "Some Enchanted Evening" from the stage adaptation of South Pacific. Among the other soundtrack or cast recordings featured on this compilation are Ella Mae Morse's "*Shoo-Shoo Baby*" from the motion picture Three Cheers for the Boys," and Betty Hutton's classic "Doctor, Lawyer, Indian Chief" as featured in The Stork Club. This volume has cleverly gathered rare and hard to find early recordings by ladies who quickly gained international acclaim, such as Anita O'Day ("*And Her Tears Flowed Like Wine*"), June Christy ("*It's Been a Long, Long Time*"), and Margaret Whiting (who is featured with no less than three different orchestras on this collection). *Vine Street Divas* is accompanied by a ten-page liner notes booklet containing vintage memorabilia, photos, and other previously unpublished eye candy. Plus, to fill in the details is an essay by musician and music historian Billy Vera. Initial pressings—limited to 10,000—are cleverly packaged in a digipack designed to replicate the 78-rpm records and sleeves of the era. *—Lindsay Planer*

Capitol From the Vaults, Vol. 3: Capitol Jumps / Jun. 6, 2000 / Capitol ✦✦✦
The \swing era and pre-\bop \jazz age of the '40s was a zenith for Capitol Records, which was jumpin' not only on radios and jukeboxes nationwide, but at cash registers as well. This third volume in the venerable label's From the Vaults series is an indispensable guide to Capitol's ever-increasing talent roster, highlighting this unique period in American popular music. Aptly subtitled *Capitol Jumps,* the album does considerably more, ranging from the erudite cool of the Nat "King" Cole Trio on "Sweet Loraine" to decidedly more "alternative" \bop classics such as Dizzy Gillespie's "You Stole My Wife You Horse Thief." On the lighter side are remnants of \big-band orchestras led by Benny Goodman ("On a Slow Boat to China") and Johnny Mercer ("One More for My Baby (And One More for the Road)"). The passing of the \pop music baton from \big band to \jazz is reflected in this volume most notably by the Four Freshmen's brilliant interpretation of "Tuxedo Junction" and the intoxicating one-two punch of Ella Mae Morse's "Buzz Me" and "Juice Head Baby by Cootie Williams & His Orchestra, featuring vocalist Eddie "Cleanhead" Vinson. One trend continuing for Capitol was that of hitmaker. Among the seven Top 40 hits on *Capitol From the Vaults, Vol. 3* are Alvino Rey's ultra-danceable "Cement Mixer (Put-Ti, Put-Ti)", Benny Carter & His Orchestra with "Poinciana," and the Johnny Mercer conducted orchestra on "My Sugar Is So Refined." This all-star recording also features labelmates the Pied Pipers, accompanied by Paul Weston & His Orchestra. As with other volumes in this collection, the sonic transfer is superior, making it an essential component to any comprehensive overview of American popular music. The 12-page liner notes booklet contains lots of memorabilia wrapped around another installment of Billy Vera's informative essays. *—Lindsay Planer*

Capitol Sings, Vol. 13: Over the Rainbow Harold Arlen / 1995 / Capitol ✦✦✦
The 13th volume of the *Capitol Sings series of compilations concerns itself with Harold Arlen,* who collaborated with label co-founder Johnny Mercer on eight of the 20 songs heard here, among them the opener, "Ac-cent-tchu-ate the Positive," which is Mercer's own hit recording from 1944. (The set closes appropriately with Arlen's performance of the same song.) That turns out to be the only original hit on the disc, though Judy Garland recordings of two of her signature songs, "Over the Rainbow" and "The Man That Got Away," turn up in later renditions, as does a version of "Blues in the Night" by Dinah Shore, whose 1942 record on Bluebird was a hit. Indeed, the compilers seem to have avoided familiar Capitol recordings of Arlen tunes, passing over, for example, Louis Prima and Keely Smith's version of "That Old Black Magic" in favor of Margaret Whiting's, then skipping Whiting's hit version of "Come Rain or Come Shine" to include one by Peggy Lee. Of course, the recordings that are really missed here are those of Frank Sinatra. Capitol must not have the right to anthologize Sinatra's work with the label; otherwise, it's hard to imagine we'd have Louis Prima's comic but slight reading of "I've Got the World on a String" or Lou Rawls' "One for My Baby (And One More for the Road)." That said, Capitol's formidable roster of classic pop singers proves an excellent group of interpreters of the bluesiest classic pop songwriters. Like

the other volumes in the series, *Over the Rainbow* is an effective survey of Capitol's vaults of the '40s, '50s, and '60s. — *William Ruhlmann*

Capitol Sings Jimmy Mchugh, Vol. 17: I Feel a Song Comin' On / 1995 / Capitol ✦✦✦
Jimmy McHugh is one of the lesser-known songwriters to be included in the *Capitol Sings* series of compilations, but several of his songs, including "I Can't Give You Anything But Love," "On the Sunny Side of the Street," and "I'm in the Mood for Love," are standards, and many more, written during a 40-year career mostly devoted to Broadway and Hollywood, are familiar. McHugh's most successful work was written with lyricist Dorothy Fields in the late '20s and early '30s, and much of his catalog predates the founding of Capitol Records in 1942. So, necessarily, most of the selections here are 1950s recreations of songs written in previous decades. (One exception: Nat "King" Cole's popular recording of "Too Young to Go Steady," drawn from McHugh's unsuccessful attempt to return to Broadway with Strip for Action in 1956.) That means lots of vibrant studio orchestra music conducted by Nelson Riddle and Billy May, among others, and lots of bravura singing by people like Judy Garland, Peggy Lee, Dinah Washington, and Sarah Vaughan. But there are also some performances that provide a change of pace, such as Julie London's smoky "I'm in the Mood for Love," accompanied only by bass and guitar, and Chet Baker's jazzy reading of "Let's Get Lost." The result is more a grab bag than a definitive McHugh compilation, but there are some excellent individual interpretations. — *William Ruhlmann*

• **Celebrate Broadway, Vol. 1: Sing Happy** / 1994 / RCA Victor ✦✦✦✦✦
The first in a series of compilations of songs from Broadway shows recorded by RCA Victor, this album puts together an hour's worth of what used to be called "eleven o'clock numbers." These were the show-stoppers that woke you up shortly before the end of the show and got you ready to hit the street with a smile on your face. (Although, to tell the truth, some of these are first act finales meant to send you into the lobby anticipating the rest of the evening.) "Blow, Gabriel, Blow," from Anything Goes, "I've Gotta Crow," from *Peter Pan*, "Oklahoma!" from Oklahoma; these are the big, bright Broadway songs audiences have hummed to themselves for generations. The RCA catalog is mixed—not all of these performances are taken from the original casts, and the notes don't make that clear—but this is a good sampler for the casual fan who likes Broadway's stirring songs. — *William Ruhlmann*

Celebrate Broadway, Vol. 2: You Gotta Have a Gimmick / 1994 / RCA Victor ✦✦✦
For this collection, RCA has scoured its vaults for Broadway novelty songs, comic numbers frequently performed by the supporting players in shows that provide a change of pace and some laughs. Songs like "I Cain't Say No," from *Oklahoma!*, and "Arthur In The Afternoon," from *The Act*, show that being risque is not a problem, but just as often these songs are just odd: what else to say about the celebratory "Lizzie Borden," from *New Faces Of 1952*? That song, from a revue, had no real context in a show, and some of these songs are actually ringers, such as Fats Waller's "Your Feet's Too Big" from *Ain't Misbehavin'* and the "Caribbean Plaid" medley from *Forever Plaid*, material not actually written for Broadway. This is an episodic album, to be sure, but you won't get through it without laughing a few times. — *William Ruhlmann*

Celebrate Broadway, Vol. 3: Lullaby of Broadway / 1994 / RCA Victor ✦✦✦✦✦
Broadway has always had a great ability to celebrate itself, actually, and that ability is showcased on the third volume of RCA's anthology series in songs about show business, starting with the title track (actually written for the movie musical Forty-Second Street, which then became a Broadway musical) and ending, inevitably, with & "There's No Business Like Show Business." In between are songs by Sondheim, Coleman, Styne, Herman, Kern, Yeston, and Kander, all exploring aspects of the biz. As with the other volumes in this series, the caveat is that these songs come from various sources including but not limited to original Broadway cast albums—concert versions, revivals, revues, etc.—but there isn't a performance here that isn't good, and the selection makes a powerful case for Broadway. — *William Ruhlmann*

Celebrate Broadway, Vol. 4: Overtures! / 1994 / RCA Victor ✦✦✦
Overtures introduce Broadway audiences to the music they're going to hear during the course of the evening. Played one after another, they can take on the quality of Muzak, not unpleasant but not compelling. This collection of 12 overtures taken from shows that played on Broadway between the '40s and '80s displays the consistency of style in Broadway music. Much of it is appealing, but then, that's the problem: it's like trying to make a dinner out of appetizers. — *William Ruhlmann*

Cheek to Cheek: The Irving Berlin Songbook / Dec. 1952-Nov. 16, 1988 / Verve ✦✦✦

The Complete Gershwin Songbooks / Oct. 24, 1995 / Verve ✦✦✦✦✦
The Complete Gershwin Songbooks collects three discs also released separately: *'S Wonderful*, *'S Marvelous* and *'S Paradise*. The first two discs include the greatest vocalists Verve had to offer, including Ella Fitzgerald, Billie Holiday, Louis Armstrong, Anita O'Day, Shirley Horn, Sarah Vaughan, Dinah Washington, Bing Crosby, Joe Williams, Fred Astaire and even Antonio Carlos Jobim. Obviously, the songs are all classics and the versions presented are quite legendary themselves. The third disc in the set includes instrumental versions of Gershwin standards (by Bill Evans, Coleman Hawkins, Stan Getz, Clifford Brown, Art Tatum, Oscar Peterson) which focus on the composer's stunning gift of melody and harmonic interplay—just as the vocalists' versions highlight his lyrical prowess. Not all the versions are definitive, but *The Complete Gershwin Songbooks* includes many treats for fans of classic traditional pop. —*John Bush*

Eh Paisano! 100% Italian-American Classics / Jan. 14, 1997 / Rhino ✦✦✦✦
The concept behind *Eh Paisano: Italian-American Classics* namely, 18 tracks of pop standards and Italian songs from the '50s and '60s, sung by crooners like Dean Martin, Louis Prima and Lou Monte—may be a little cutesy, but it works surprisingly well. Even with tracks by pop acts like Jay & the Americans and Connie Francis, the album is a focused, if occasionally campy, collection of classics like "Volare," "That's Amore," and "Eh Cumpari." It may be designed to appeal to the kitsch-addled hipsters of the '90s cocktail nation, but the music on *Eh Paisano* is so strong, such quibbles doesn't matter—it's one of the most enjoyable collections of mainstream pop assembled in the mid-'90s. — *Stephen Thomas Erlewine*

The Fabulous Forties: That Golden Age of Song / Apr. 2000 / Perennial Music ✦✦✦
A two-disc set of big hits from the wartime era. With a generous 24 tracks per disc, the selections include classics from Frank Sinatra, Bing Crosby, Ella Fitzgerald, Billie Holiday, Doris Day with Les Brown, the Andrews Sisters, the Ink Spots, Peggy Lee, Helen Forrest with Harry James, Nat "King" Cole, and Judy Garland. Also aboard are pop and big-band singers like Tex Beneke, Vera Lynn, Dinah Shore, Dick Haymes, Anne Shelton, Ethel Smith, Ray Eberle, Deanna Durbin, Al Jolson, Russ Morgan, Bob Eberle and Kitty Kallen, Marjorie Hughes, and even a stray track from Spike Jones. A pretty great collection of old favorites, cleanly remastered with informative notes to recommend it. — *Cub Koda*

The Forties / Jun. 27, 2000 / Pearl ✦✦✦
Flapper's *The 'Forties* is a British compilation of 25 recordings popular in that decade, and it will help a lot in the appreciation of the disc if the listener is British, too. While there was considerable overlap between U.S. and U.K. popular music in the '40s, more in terms of songs than artists, there was also far more separation than there would be in later decades. The compilation does contain some recordings that were successful stateside, notably such American chart-toppers as Russ Morgan's "Cruising Down the River" and Glenn Miller's "I've Got a Gal in Kalamazoo"; major U.S. stars like Bing Crosby and Frank Sinatra are included, and such popular songs as "Seems Like Old Times" and "G.I. Jive" are featured. But some of the songs and many of the artists will be unfamiliar to Americans. Joe Loss, Vera Lynn, and Edmundo Ros had some impact on the west side of the Atlantic, but names like Carroll Gibbons, Billy Cotton, the Squadronaires, Nat Gonella, Harry Roy, Archie Lewis, Flanagan and Allen, Steve Conway, and Geraldo remained British-only favorites. Yet they turn out to be engaging performers, and if U.S. listeners may be hearing such war-themed songs as the ally-friendly "Yankee Doodle Came to London Town" or the democratic "The Smiths and the Jones" for the first time, they may become welcome additions to a list of '40s favorites. — *William Ruhlmann*

Great Songs of George Gershwin / Nov. 17, 1998 / Columbia/Legacy ✦✦✦
George Gershwin wrote so many standards during his shortened life that his music has been recorded by a vast variety of singers. This 1998 reissue CD has 18 different vocalists interpreting Gershwin tunes, recorded during a 30-year period and programmed loosely in chronological order. The swing era is represented by the first seven records, which feature Fred Astaire, Billie Holiday ("Summertime"), Helen Forrest (with Benny Goodman), Helen Ward (with Teddy Wilson), Mildred Bailey, Woody Herman ("Somebody Loves Me" in 1947 with his Four Chips) and Lee Wiley ("I've Got a Crush On You"). The other Gershwin tunes are performed by a variety of mostly middle-of-the-road pop singers with a few departures: Dorothy Kirsten, Mary Martin (a bombastic "I Got Rhythm"), Jo Stafford, Doris Day, Johnny Mathis, Aretha Franklin, George Benson ("A Foggy Day"), Mel Torme, Andy Williams, Judy Garland (an over-the-top version of "Swanee") and Tony Bennett. Overall, this hodge-podge CD is more highly recommended to listeners who want to hear straightforward readings of George Gershwin tunes than to completists or jazz fans. — *Scott Yanow*

Jackpot! the Las Vegas Story / Nov. 19, 1996 / Rhino ✦✦✦✦✦
Designed to cash-in on the lounge music fad of the mid-'90s, *Jackpot: The Las Vegas Story* is a swinging collection of 18 tracks from the city's glory days of the '50s and '60s. Many of the biggest names that ever played in Las Vegas are included on the album, including Dean Martin, Sammy Davis, Jr., Wayne Newton, Robert Goulet, Engelbert Humperdinck, Mel Torme, Liberace, Jerry Vale, Louis Prima & Keely Smith, Jack Jones, Paul Anka and Tom Jones. With their big, brassy arrangements and off-hand humor (which is occasionally unintentional), this music was almost always bordered on kitsch, which actually makes the album more entertaining, because kitsch and camp is the essence of Las Vegas. And with classics like "The Lady Is a Tramp," "Danke Schoen," "That Old Black Magic," "Delilah," "Release Me (And Let Me Love Again)," and "My Way," *Jackpot* truly does capture the sound and feeling of Las Vegas. — *Stephen Thomas Erlewine*

Let's Be Frank: A Tribute to Sinatra / Jun. 30, 1998 / Hip-O ✦✦✦
So when is a tribute album not *really* a tribute album— When it's made up of tracks recorded over a period of years that were never originally intended to be part of a tribute album in the first place. None of the folks here—everyone from Mel Torme ("The Second Time Around"), Ella Fitzgerald ("The Tender Trap"), and Billie Holiday ("All the Way") to ring-a-ding-ding pretenders to the throne like Buddy Greco ("The Lady Is a Tramp"), Jack Jones ("Strangers in the Night") and Paul Anka ("My Way")—ever did an actual Sinatra tribute album during his lifetime and all the tracks here were album filler, buried on a side two where they wouldn't get much comparison to the definitive reading by the Chairman of the Board. So with all that said and with this released less than a month after Sinatra's death in 1998 (although to be fair, it was compiled and annotated before his death), the odd thing is how well this collection actually *does* hang together. Nobody tries to cut Sinatra on his own turf here and you walk away realizing what an enormous influence the man had on 20th century song interpretation and the majority of its practitioners. On that level, it's a true success. — *Cub Koda*

Lullaby of Broadway: The Music of Harry Warren / 1992 / Pearl Flapper ✦✦✦
Perhaps the most prolific Hollywood song composer of the 1930s and '40s, Harry Warren is represented here in a sampling of some of his biggest hits, primarily from the '30s, including "You're Getting to Be a Habit With Me," "You Must Have Been a Beautiful Baby," "Jeepers Creepers," and "I Only Have Eyes for You," in recordings made between 1924 and 1948. For the most part, the compilers have not presented any of the actual hit recordings of these songs, perhaps because they didn't have access to them. (The three exceptions are all by Bing Crosby.) Instead, they have tended to favor records made by the stars who sang the songs in the films, especially Carmen Miranda, who is on two tracks, Dick Powell, who is on three, and Al Jolson, who is on four, the first an obscure B-side, "Home In Pasadena" (here titled "Pasadena") and the others "private" recordings dated 1948, much later than the rest of the tracks. There is also a recording taken directly from a film soundtrack of Winifred Shaw singing "Lullaby of Broadway," and an Andrews Sisters recording of a non-hit, "Love Is Where You Find It." The remaining nine tracks on this British compilation are by British acts,

most of whom will be unfamiliar to Americans (the exception is Al Bowlly) and present pale imitations of American originals. The result is a mixed bag of vintage recordings, some of which show off Harry Warren's abilities as a songwriter to their best advantage. *— William Ruhlmann*

Moonlight Becomes You: Songs of Jimmy Van Heusen / May 23, 2000 / ASV/Living Era ♦♦♦♦
This collection includes over 20 performances of songs penned by legendary pop composer Jimmy Van Heusen. Most of the included songs were co-written with Van Heusen's songwriting partner, lyricist Johnny Burke, as well as with previous partner Eddie De Lange. *Moonlight Becomes You: Songs of Jimmy Van Heusen* compiles the original (mono) recordings of Van Heusen's biggest hits as performed by some of the biggest names of the time, including "It's the Dreamer in Me" by Helen Humes with Harry James and his orchestra; the million-seller "Swinging on a Star," sung by Bing Crosby in the Academy Award-winning movie *Going My Way;*"Like Someone in Love," also performed by Bing Crosby; and "Yah-Ta-Ta, Yah-Ta-Ta (Talk, Talk, Talk)," which finds Crosby in a duet with Judy Garland. Frank Sinatra appears several times, while Dinah Shore also performs a couple of numbers, including "Personality." Other included performers are such legendary, influential artists as Fats Waller, Ella Fitzgerald, Artie Shaw, Benny Goodman, and more. Finally, Van Heusen admirer Frank Sinatra closes the collection with his performance of "But Beautiful." *—Joslyn Layne*

New York Songs / Jul. 6, 1999 / Rhino ♦♦♦

Nipper's Greatest Hits: 1901-1920 / 1991 / RCA ♦♦♦♦♦
Most record companies of any tenure have vaults of issued and unissued material. But with the exception of Columbia (now Sony), no American company has a longer history than RCA Victor (now BMG). This multi-volume set cherry picks and highlights the best-selling records from all the decades in its long history. Starting at the turn of the century, the earliest entries are John Philip Sousa's Band's "In the Good Old Summertime" from 1905 and George M. Cohan's "Grand Old Rag" by Billy Murray from 1906. The standards "Shine On, Harvest Moon" (sung here by Miss Walton & Mister MacDonough) and Len Spencer's "The Arkansas Traveler" are from 1908, while the following year saw the release of Ada Jones' "Yama Yama Man" and Billy Murray returning with "In My Merry Oldsmobile" and also dueting with Miss Jones on "Come Josephine in My Flying Machine." Al Jolson also started his recording career with Victor, and his "That Haunting Melody" from 1911 was his first hit. Nora Bayes is represented here by two of her biggest numbers, "Has Anybody Here Seen Kelly?" and a duet with "Mister Moon Man, Turn Off the Light." By 1918, America was in the throes of the First World War, and even Enrico Caruso joined the fray with George M. Cohan's "Over There." But the jazz age was starting to rear its head, and selections from the decade's end, like John Steel's "A Pretty Girl Is Like a Melody," Ben Selvin's "I'm Forever Blowing Bubbles," and the Original Dixieland Jazz Band's "Tiger Rag" all pointed to the decade to come. Given that some of these tracks are 90-plus years old, the CEDAR restoration used on these battered old '78s is amazing, preserving a time in our history long since gone, but not forgotten. *— Cub Koda*

Nipper's Greatest Hits: The 20's / Aug. 21, 1990 / RCA ♦♦♦
The 1920s evoke an era of gangsters, flappers, bootleg gin, and a nation gone jazz crazy right down to the raccoon coats. This second entry in RCA's *Nipper's Greatest Hits* series evokes that era in a big way on this 20-track compilation. While there were jazz recordings by the carload from the '20s, it's the pop tunes that drove the decade, and kicking off with the triple punch of Irving Aaronson & His Commanders' "Let's Misbehave," Gene Austin's "My Blue Heaven," and Fred Waring & His Pennsylvanians' "Collegiate" sets both the mood and ambience for this set. Other highlights in this excellent collection include Maurice Chevalier's "Louise," Eddie Cantor's "Makin' Whoopee," Paul Whiteman's "Whispering" and "Charleston," Fanny Brice's "My Man," George Gershwin's "Rhapsody in Blue," and Duke Ellington's "Black and Tan Fantasy." But ultimately it's the one-off novelties, like the Coon-Sanders Nighthawks' "Little Orphan Annie," Nat Shilkret's "Lucky Lindy," and George Olsen's "The Varsity Drag" that make this compilation such a wonderful listening experience. While the transfers are moderately clean (given that few real masters of any kind exist), everything on here is 70 years old or older, so don't expect modern recording miracles—just a nice ride back in time. *— Cub Koda*

Nipper's Greatest Hits: The 30's, Vol. 1 / 1990 / RCA ♦♦♦♦♦
The 1930s were a tumultuous decade, and the record business almost went under after the stock market crash of 1929 and the Depression that gripped the nation. But in adverse times, America still wanted to be entertained, and Victor provided much of the soundscape for that decade. This first of two volumes features escapist fare like Bing Crosby's "Wrap Your Troubles In Dreams," Leo Reisman's optimistic "Happy Days Are Here Again," Fred Astaire's "We're In the Money," Cole Porter's "You're the Top," Tommy Dorsey's "The Music Goes 'Round and 'Round" and Kate Smith's patriotic flag waver "God Bless America." But it was also the beginning of jazz taking the nation by storm, with tracks like Fats Waller's "Honeysuckle Rose," Benny Goodman's "Life Goes to a Party," Meade "Lux" Lewis' "Honky Tonk Train Blues," Glenn Miller's "Moonlight Serenade" and Bunny Berigan's "I Can't Get Started With You" counted in the mix. And great torch songs like Hoagy Carmichael's "Stardust" and Mae West's (with Duke Ellington) "My Old Flame" and infectious novelties like Wayne King's "Josephine" and Maurice Chevalier's "Mimi" help to give the big picture of this decade in this marvelous collection. Transfers are still a bit grainy, as we're still a good decade and a half away from the invention of magnetic tape, but nothing sounds like a battered 78 on here either. *— Cub Koda*

Nipper's Greatest Hits: The 30's, Vol. 2 / Apr. 19, 1991 / RCA ♦♦♦♦♦
The second volume of hit songs from Victor's vaults follows the format of its predecessor, using an all-over-the-road approach that mixes pop tunes with big-band swing classics. Starting with Rudy Vallee and his Connecticut Yankees' "Maine Stein Song" from 1930, we now enter the age of the vocalist in front of the big band with Bing Crosby fronting Duke Ellington's on "Three Little Words," Mildred Bailey with Paul Whiteman on "Rockin' Chair," Skinnay Ennis with Hal Kemp on "Got a Date With an Angel," and Russ Columbo (Crosby's predecessor) on "Paradise." Pop and torch songs were still big, and Leo Reisman's "Brother Can You Spare a Dime—" Helen Morgan's "Frankie and Johnny," and Jeanette MacDonald and Nelson Eddy's "Ah! Sweet Mystery of Life" were all indicative of the era. But the big news was jazz making the pop charts, and Glenn Miller's "In the Mood," Louis Armstrong's "St. Louis Blues," Coleman Hawkins' classic "Body and Soul" and Benny Goodman's "Sing Sing Sing" were as much signposts of an era as anything else. Transfers using the CEDAR noise reduction system make these old tracks shine brightly, especially given that most of them are 60 years old or older. *— Cub Koda*

Nipper's Greatest Hits: The 40's, Vol. 1 / 1940-1949 / RCA ♦♦♦♦♦
We now officially enter the age of the big band with this first volume of pop hits from Victor's vaults. This 20-track collection features numerous highlights from the big-band era, including "Frenesi" and "Stardust" by Artie Shaw, "Don't Get Around Much Anymore" and "I'm Beginning to See the Light" by Duke Ellington, "Pompton Turnpike" and "I Hear a Rhapsody" by Charlie Barnet, "Chattanooga Choo Choo," "Moonlight Cocktail" and "Pistol Packin' Mama" from Glenn Miller, and "There Are Such Things" and "Boogie Woogie" by Tommy Dorsey. The big-band singers and solo vocalists of the day are also represented with the inclusion of Frank Sinatra's "Night and Day," Lena Horne's "Stormy Weather," Vaughn Monroe's "There! I've Said It Again," and Dinah Shore's "Blues In the Night." But as always, America couldn't resist a great novelty song, and Spike Jones' "Cocktails for Two" and the King Sisters' "The Hut-Hut Song" were as good as the decade had to give. Transfers are well done, and given the wartime restrictions on shellac (the compound used to make records back then), the sound is astonishingly clear. *— Cub Koda*

Nipper's Greatest Hits: The 50's, Vol. 1 / RCA ♦♦♦
The 1950s are generally seen as the first blooming of rock & roll, but there was still an awful lot of pop music on the charts, and this set spotlights a large chunk of it. In between a breakthrough record like "Heartbreak Hotel" there was sprightly fare on either side of it, like Pee Wee King's "Slow Poke," Eddie Fisher's "Dungaree Doll," Perry Como's "Catch a Falling Star," and Lou Monte's "Lazy Mary." Although Jesse Belvin ("Guess Who") and Neil Sedaka ("Oh! Carol") make appearances here, this is by and large a pop collection with only a smattering of the rock & roll style that would soon dominate the charts. Tracks by Dinah Shore, Mario Lanza, the Browns, Jim Reeves, Harry Belafonte, Don Gibson, the Ames Brothers, Kay Starr, Eddy Arnold, Perez Prado, and Eartha Kitt complete the package. *— Cub Koda*

Number 1 Greatest Hits / Mar. 10, 1998 / RCA Victor ♦♦♦♦
No. 1 Hits: Greatest Hits contains 18 big hits culled from RCA Victor's traditional pop and jazz vaults. Everything on the collection was recorded in the first half of the 20th century, and there are a number of truly classic songs and performances on the disc. Although a handful of songs sound dated, few samplers of this kind are quite as consistently entertaining as this. Among the featured artists on the disc are Duke Ellington ("Cocktails for Two"), Glenn Miller ("Elmer's Tune," "Over the Rainbow"), Fats Waller ("It's a Sin to Tell a Lie"), Sammy Kaye ("Daddy"), Artie Shaw ("They Say," "Frensi"), Larry Clinton ("Deep Purple"), Fats Waller ("Two Sleepy People"), Sammy Kaye ("The Old Lamplighter") and Frank Sinatra & Tommy Dorsey ("In the Blue of the Evening"). *— Stephen Thomas Erlewine*

Radio Classics of the 50s / 1989 / Columbia ♦♦♦
This 14-track collection brings home the fact that it wasn't all rock & roll on the charts back in the 1950s. Pure pop from beginning to end, this features Top Ten favorites like Tony Bennett's "Rags to Riches," Doris Day's "Que Sera, Sera," Johnny Mathis' "Chances Are," Johnnie Ray's "Cry," Marty Robbins' "El Paso," Guy Mitchell's "Singin' the Blues," and Rosemary Clooney's "Hey There." Selections from the Four Lads, the Brothers Four, Johnny Horton, Joan Weber, Terry Gilkyson and the Easy Riders, and Louis Armstrong (a nice cover of "Mack the Knife") complete the package. *— Cub Koda*

☆ **Rodgers and Hart Revisited, Vol. 1** / 1990 / Painted Smiles ♦♦♦♦♦
This was Ben Bagley's first compilation of the little-known songs of Broadway composers, recorded in 1960. Bagley, who had a background assembling and producing stage revues, conceived a kind of revue album, using four performers, Dorothy Loudon, Danny Meehan, Charlotte Rae, and Cy Young, to sing songs that had been cut from shows written by Richard Rodgers and Lorenz Hart in the 1920s and 1930s or, if used, long since forgotten. He began with the first song from the team's first successful show, *The Garrick Gaieties* in 1925, and demonstrated that Hart's wit and Rodgers' melodic gifts were just as apparent in songs like "At the Roxy Music Hall" and "I Blush" as they were in their more famous compositions. The spirited performances gave life to songs that, often through no fault of their own, happened to have been written for shows that failed or scenes that were replaced. Theater buffs were delighted, and Bagley went on to record dozens of follow-ups, including four more volumes of Rodgers and Hart. The 1990 CD reissue added eight newly recorded songs, all from the unsuccessful 1940 musical *Higher and Higher*, performed by Ann Hampton Callaway, Arthur Siegel, and Sandy Stewart, among them "It Never Entered My Mind," which had gone on to become a standard. *— William Ruhlmann*

☆ **Sentimental Journey, Vol. 1** / Jun. 15, 1993 / Rhino ♦♦♦♦♦
The first volume of Rhino's pop vocal collection, *Sentimental Journey* covers the years 1942-1946 and includes such vocalists as Bing Crosby, Doris Day, Judy Garland, Jo Stafford, Vaughn Monroe and Frank Sinatra (with "Swinging on a Star," "Sentimental Journey," "The Trolly Song," "Candy," "There! I've Said It Again," and "Night and Day," respectively). Not only does the music sound great, but the liner notes are extensive, with complete musician credits. *—AMG*

☆ **Sentimental Journey, Vol. 2** / Jun. 15, 1993 / Rhino ♦♦♦♦♦
Sentimental Journey: Pop Vocal Classics, Vol. 2 (1947-1950) includes Dinah Shore's "Buttons and Bows," Patti Page's "The Tennessee Waltz," "Again" by Mel Torme, Eileen Barton's "If I Knew You Were Comin' I'd've Baked a Cake," and (on CD) "Goodnight Irene" by The Weavers and "Music! Music! Music!" by Teresa Brewer among its 18 tracks. *—AMG*

☆ **Sentimental Journey, Vol. 3** / Jun. 15, 1993 / Rhino ♦♦♦♦♦
Sentimental Journey: Pop Vocal Classics, Vol. 3 (1950-1954) includes Johnny Ray's "Cry," Tony Bennett's "Because of You," "Come On-A My House" by Rosemary Clooney, Jo Stafford's

"You Belong to Me," Kay Starr's "Wheel of Fortune," Dean Martin's "That's Amore" and "How High the Moon" by Les Paul & Mary Ford. It's another good installment in the Rhino pop vocal series. *—AMG*

☆ **Sentimental Journey, Vol. 4** / Jun. 15, 1993 / Rhino ✦✦✦✦✦
Arguably the best, most consistent entry in Rhino's pop vocal series, *Sentimental Journey: Vol. 4 (1954-1959)* includes "Mack the Knife" by Bobby Darin, Peggy Lee's "Fever," Dinah Washington's "What A Diff'rence a Day Makes," Guy Mitchell's "Singing the Blues," Doris Day's "Whatever Will Be, Will Be (Que Sera, Sera)," Dean Martin's "Memories Are Made of This," and "Chances Are" by Johnny Mathis. *—AMG*

September Songs: The Music of Kurt Weill / Aug. 19, 1997 / Sony ✦✦✦✦
German-born composer Kurt Weill's music has aged quite well through the years and has been rediscovered and reinterpreted by such diverse artists as Louis Armstrong, Bobby Darin, Willie Nelson, the Doors and Teresa Stratas. Just prior to the 70th anniversary of the classic *Three Penny Opera,* which made its debut in 1928, producer Hal Wilner, who supervised the brilliant 1985 Weill tribute *Lost in the Stars,* in association with filmmaker *Larry Weinstein,* gave fans old and new *September Songs,* a collection of interpretations from the film project of the same name.

Weinstein, inspired by hearing the *Lost in the Stars project,* developed his film as a visual follow-up to the record, hiring Wilner to reprise his role as music supervisor. Wilner once again chose a wide array of artists for the project, ranging from pop musicians such as Polly Harvey and Elvis Costello to jazz vocalist Betty Carter, opera soprano Teresa Stratas, beat author William S. Burroughs and the gospel stylings of the Persuasions. Among the true joys of *September Songs,* aside from the wonderful new renditions, is the inclusion of recordings by Weill's wife Lotte Lenya from 1955 on "Pirate Jenny," lyricist Bertolt Brecht performing "Mack the Knife" in 1930 in its original German, and Weill himself, joined via modern recording technology by bassist Charlie Haden, singing the beautiful "Speak Low."

Without a weak performance on the entire album, Wilner once again has done an excellent job of capturing the beauty and scope of one of the 20th century's greatest composers. *—Brett Hartenbach*

The Thirties / Jun. 27, 2000 / Pearl ✦✦✦✦
British reissue label Flapper's compilation *The Thirties* is a generous selection of 25 songs from that decade. It is essentially a miscellaneous collection, consisting of many well-known songs, only a few of which are presented in their most popular recordings, with several curiosities and, as a nod to the country of origin, a distinct bias toward tracks by British artists. The only one of the most popular songs of the decade found here in its most successful recording is "A-Tisket, A-Tasket" by Chick Webb and His Orchestra with vocals by Ella Fitzgerald. "Goodnight Sweetheart" and "Isle of Capri" were also among the biggest songs of the '30s, and while there are recordings of them featured here, they are not the most successful ones but covers by British performers. Other major hits from the decade include "This Year's Kisses" (in a rendition by Alice Faye, who sang it in the movie *On the Avenue);* "Marie" (in the hit version by Tommy Dorsey); "Nice Work If You Can Get It" (as performed by the Andrews Sisters); and "Please Be Kind" (by the British Joe Loss Orchestra). There are also standards recorded by the artists long associated with them, such as "Over the Rainbow" by Judy Garland and "Let's Face the Music and Dance" by Fred Astaire, and major artists such as Louis Armstrong ("Flat Foot Floogie") and Bing Crosby ("The Folks Who Live on the Hill," "Basin Street Blues," "Can I Forget About You—") are also represented. But the set gives evidence of being constructed from a limited number of records, making for more of a sampler than any sort of comprehensive survey of the '30s. *—William Ruhlmann*

What Did They Do Before Rock'n'Roll? / Sep. 29, 1998 / Westside ✦✦✦
A companion volume to *Rockin' Is Not Our Business!,* Westside's look at RCA's whiter-than-white pop attempts at coming to grips with the rise of rhythm & blues, this 20-tracker is heavy on the pop crooners and especially tunes that would later find their way into the recorded repertoire of one Elvis Presley, like Tony Martin's "I Don't Care If the Sun Don't Shine," and Don Cornell's "Are You Lonesome Tonight," and Jimmie Rodgers Snow's "Love Me." Vaughn Monroe turns in the most surreal attempts here on "They Were Doing the Mambo" and an even nuttier "Black Denim Trousers and Motorcycle Boots" that must be heard to be believed. An oddball collection for sure, here's some early-'50s pop sides that meets rock & roll at the crossroads. Full of pop legends like Eartha Kitt, Billy Eckstine, Perry Como and Gogi Grant, it's also a good place to start investigating the best of the highly underrated Ziggy Talent. *—Cub Koda*

Easy Listening

The first genre of music created with the specific purpose of assisting relaxation and providing background instead of active attention, easy listening usually focuses on nothing more than a solid performance of a great song by talented musicians or, occasionally, singers. Until a critical and commercial resurrection in the '90s (the latter partly a result of its kitsch quality), easy listening was also the most scorned of music genres. It was often thought of as an artistic ghetto, populated by tame big-band-era arrangers, Hollywood film music sellouts, and those who refused to acknowledge the passing of either time or new musical forms. With the benefit of hindsight, though, it's easier to see the genre for what it was: a form tailor-made for the millions of listeners increasingly alienated by the radio and popular charts during the '50s and '60s. For a generation of Americans who'd lasted the Depression and fought a world war, the great songs of earlier decades were more than just musical entertainment—they were pieces of nostalgia and the perfect background music for living. Impulses like these didn't always make for the most artistic music, but the easy listening genre kept alive hundreds of classic American popular songs, as well as the notion of simple, lasting, good music performed by musicians with techniques perfected over decades.

Easy listening emerged in the '50s, though sweet or champagne music pre-existed the term. Orchestras led by Guy Lombardo and Glenn Miller had played sentimental jazz music during the '30s and '40s, and the torch was carried into the '50s by Lawrence Welk, Ray Conniff, Paul Weston, Percy Faith, and others. Many of these artists had worked in the big bands, either as musicians or as arrangers, and aside from conducting and writing arrangements for the new brand of star vocalists (Frank Sinatra, Ella Fitzgerald, Peggy Lee), they led their own orchestras on the side. As rock & roll gradually took over the charts during the '50s and '60s (and as jazz itself splintered into more challenging forms), a generation of popular figures began arranging simple charts, with little improvisation, for their bands to play before the vast majority of Americans. It was perfect background music for everything from dinner parties to movie titles, and it was soon reviled by fans of jazz and rock for its lack of innovation and challenge to listeners.

Even the field of easy listening had its pioneers, though, and several bandleaders soon began experimenting within the format. Esquivel, a bespectacled Mexican futurist, wrote radical charts and incorporated an array of oddball instruments and percussion, including newer electrical innovations like the theremin and ondes martenot. This space-age pop surely wasn't background music—it was nearly impossible to ignore, and appealed not only to average record-buyers but also genuine music fans and audiophiles (many of his LPs flaunted contemporary innovations in stereo sound). Les Baxter and Martin Denny stretched the form as well, evoking the music of the world with instruments, album concepts, and covers devoted to Polynesia, Asia, the Caribbean, and all sorts of exotic locales. It was perfect for the millions of suburban stay-at-homes, and the style (termed exotica) was one of the most popular in easy listening during the '50s.

As rock began to take hold in the '60s, easy listening figures (and traditional pop singers) came to grips with the shifting winds by covering many of rock's most popular songs (or, to put a finer point on it, those most capable of crossover to their own audiences). Many easy listening artists found it easier to relate to '60s popsters like Burt Bacharach or Brian Wilson, but a new generation of easy figures—Sergio Mendes & Brasil '66, Herb Alpert & the Tijuana Brass, the Sandpipers, the 5th Dimension—proved quite capable of crossover during an era when audiences appeared to disagree on almost everything.

As jazz-based music became increasingly ignored by the mainstream during the '70s, the easy listening genre branched out even farther, embracing folk and new age, as well as an approach based more on individual instrumentation with artists like Zamfir, James Galway, and Richard Clayderman. The reissue culture of the '90s eventually rescued easy listening from critical oblivion, and a lounge revival soon appeared, led by indie rockers like Combustible Edison, the Coctails, and Love Jones. *—John Bush*

Artist Reviews

Eden Ahbez

b. Brooklyn, NY, **d.** 1995

Vocals / Obscuro, Beat Poetry, Exotica

One of the genuinely strange characters of pre-rock American popular music, Eden Ahbez's main claim to fame was as the composer of "Nature Boy." The melodically and lyrically beguiling song was a huge pop hit for Nat King Cole; it would be covered by many other reputable performers, including Frank Sinatra, John Coltrane, Sarah Vaughan, and the Great Society (Grace Slick's pre-Jefferson Airplane band). A hippie a good 20 years before his time, he cultivated a Christ-like appearance with his shoulder-length hair and beard. He claimed to live on three dollars a week, sleeping outdoors with his family, eating vegetables, fruits, and nuts. His most comprehensive statement as a recording artist was the 1960 LP *The Music of an Enchanted Isle*, which wedded Martin Denny-style exotica to Ahbez's near-stereotypical beatnik poetry. It rates as one of the goofiest efforts in the goofy exotica genre—and brother, that's saying something, given the stiff competition.*—Richie Unterberger*

● **Eden's Island** / 1960 / Del-Fi ✦✦✦✦

Musically, Ahbez' 1960 outing was squarely in line with the exotica fad, utilizing then-unusual combinations of instruments (flutes, bongos, vibes) and sound effects like creaking boats to conjure up the aural equivalent of a tropical breeze. Unlike Martin Denny or Arthur Lyman, Ahbez often added his own spoken poetry, speaking of coves, paradise, and other idyllic subjects. Occasionally he even sang in a thin voice (he's no Nat King Cole). Even those who share Ahbez' yearning for heaven on earth must concede that his recorded effort to invoke these states is, to put it bluntly, sophomoric. Yes, it's good for some snickers from the exotica revival crowd, but that's almost definitely not what he had in mind when he was making this. *—Richie Unterberger*

Steve Allen (Stephen Valentine Patrick William Allen)

b. Dec. 21, 1921, New York, NY, **d.** Oct. 30, 2000, Encino, CA

Piano / Lounge, Bop, Instrumental Pop

For someone of Steve Allen's versatility and staggering capacity for work, jazz occupies a small yet significant portion of his biography. Yet despite his crowded agenda, Allen can still spin out facile, competent, bop-and-cocktail-flavored piano in fast jazz company—nothing particularly original but always pleasurable to hear. Best-known as a comedian and the first host of the American TV institution *The Tonight Show* (1954-57), Allen frequently played piano and sang on his shows and used them as a forum to present guests from the jazz world. He also played the lead role in the film *The Benny Goodman Story* in 1955, produced the TV series *Jazz Scene USA* in 1962, and narrated a history of jazz on records *The Jazz Story* (Coral). Allen recorded frequently during the peak of his TV fame and as late as 1992, taped an enjoyable mainstream set for Concord Jazz, *Plays Jazz Tonight*. Allen claims to have written (as of 1994) more than 4, 700 songs, of which only a bare handful—"This Could Be The Start Of Something (Big)," "Gravy Waltz," "Impossible"—have staked claims in the repertoire. Ultimately Allen's most valuable contribution to jazz has been as a cheerleader in the mass media. *—Richard S. Ginell*

● **Plays Hi-Fi Music for Influentials** / 1957-1966 / Varese ✦✦✦✦✦

Sixteen tracks selected from various albums released between 1957 and 1966. Allen distributes the material fairly evenly between his own compositions and interpretations of standards by the likes of Cole Porter, Johnny Mercer, and Irving Berlin. As cocktail jazz goes, it's very straightahead (though some cuts take a bossa nova approach), and perhaps not eccentric enough to appeal to the lounge revival crowd. *—Richie Unterberger*

Herb Alpert

b. Mar. 31, 1935, Los Angeles, CA

Trumpet, Producer, Arranger / Jazz-Pop, Soft Rock, Pop, Adult Contemporary, Instrumental Pop

One of the most successful instrumental performers in pop history, trumpeter Herb Alpert was also one of the entertainment industry's shrewdest businessmen: A&M, the label he co-founded with partner Jerry Moss, ranks among the most prosperous artist-owned companies ever established. Alpert had already written songs for Sam Cooke and worked on production for the surf duo Jan & Dean before founding A&M in 1962 and scoring a Top Ten hit with the single "The Lonely Bull." Even after A&M grew to become the world's biggest independent label, Alpert and his backing unit the Tijuana Brass remained the label's flagship act. His 1965 LP *Whipped Cream and Other Delights* topped the charts and popularized his Latin-influenced style (dubbed "Ameriachi"). Four follow-ups also hit number one and in 1968, Alpert scored his first chart-topping single, a rare vocal turn for Burt Bacharach's "This Guy's in Love with You." As his commercial fates fell in the early '70s and A&M continued to thrive, he moved his primary focus from music to industry. In 1979, Alpert staged a major artistic comeback with a Top Ten LP (*Rise*) and a number one single (the title track). In 1987 Alpert enjoyed another renaissance with the Top Five single "Diamonds." He continued recording throughout the 1990s, and with Moss founded a new label (Almo Sounds) after selling A&M to PolyGram. Alpert also tackled other forms of media, exhibiting his abstract expressionist paintings and co-producing a number of Broadway successes including *Angels in America* and *Jelly's Last Jam*. *—Jason Ankeny*

The Lonely Bull / Dec. 1962 / A&M ✦✦✦

The colossus that is A&M Records starts right here with the first album by the '60s instrumental juggernaut known as the Tijuana Brass. True, there was no "Tijuana Brass" per se at this time; just Herb Alpert and a coterie of Los Angeles sessionmen, with Alpert overdubbing himself on trumpet to get that bullring effect. Also, Alpert was just getting the TJB concept underway; the textures are leaner, the productions less polished, and the accent is more consciously on a Mexican mariachi ambience—the relatively square rhythms, the mandolins, the mournful, wistful siesta feeling—than the records down the road. The hit title track (originally a tune called "Twinkle Star"!) is a cleverly structured, exciting and haunting piece of record-making—and its composer, Sol Lake, becomes the charter member of Alpert's team of TJB tunesmiths with several more ethnic-flavored numbers. In accordance with the newly emerging bossa nova movement, Alpert does a nice, straightforward, authentic cover of "Desafinado," even departing a bit from the tune with some spare jazz-inspired licks, and "Crawfish" pleasingly adapts the mariachi horn sound to a bossa beat. Still a charming record, still in print on CD. *—Richard S. Ginell*

Whipped Cream & Other Delights / Apr. 1965 / A&M ✦✦✦✦✦
We'll never know exactly what made this album Herb Alpert's big commercial breakthrough—the music or the LP jacket's luscious nude model covered almost entirely with simulated whipped cream. Probably both. In any case, Alpert's most famous album is built around a coherent concept; every song has a title with food in it. Within this concept, Alpert's musical tastes are still refreshingly eclectic; he uses Brazilian rhythms on "Green Peppers" and "Bittersweet Samba," reaches back to the big-band era for the haunting "Tangerine," uses Dixieland jazz on "Butterball," and goes to New Orleans for the Allen Toussaint-penned title track (familiar to viewers of TV's *The Dating Game*). He also has developed a unique sense of timing as a producer, using pauses for humorous effect, managing to score his second Top Ten hit with a complex, tempo shifting version of "A Taste of Honey." No wonder Alpert drew such a large, diverse audience at his peak; his choices of tunes spanned eras and generations, his arrangements were energetic enough for the young and melodic enough for older listeners. This album, number one in the nation for eight weeks, is available on CD, though the cover obviously doesn't make as alluring an impression as it did on LP. *—Richard S. Ginell*

Going Places / Sep. 1965 / A&M ✦✦✦

Greatest Hits / Mar. 1970 / A&M ✦✦✦
Released in 1970, a bit too late to capitalize on the Tijuana Brass at the peak of their appeal, this early hits collection compounded the error of its tardy timing by only including selections from the TJB's first five albums. Still, since the CDs of three of the five albums are currently out of print, this can serve as a decent, if brief, overview of the development of Herb Alpert's vehicle from its clever ethnic novelty beginnings into a cosmopolitan septet that could actually bridge the yawning generation gap of the 1960s. But for a more sweeping look at the TJB, there are better, more economical packages around. *—Richard S. Ginell*

Four Sider / Nov. 1973 / A&M ✦✦✦

Rise / Sep. 1979 / A&M ✦✦✦✦✦
Fresh from his Masekela experience and hoping to dabble in the then-raging disco movement, Herb Alpert recorded a soaring dance-beat tune composed by his nephew Randy Badazz and friend Andy Armer, slowed the tempo way down, and put it out as a 12-inch disco single. Hardly anyone except Alpert and Badazz thought it would sell, but almost as if on command, "Rise" inexorably rose up the charts, landing at number one to provide Alpert with the biggest hit of his life. Faced with following up a sudden huge hit, Alpert quickly put together an album brimming with renewed confidence and an instinct for the contemporary jugular, assimilating then-current dance beats and electronic backing instruments. He even goes beyond the contemporary with the avant-garde, electronic loop stunt piece "Rotation," which still sounds fascinating today. And Alpert's trumpet playing has newfound authority and power; a number one hit can do wonders for your adrenaline level. *Rise* brought Alpert back to the upper reaches (No. 6) of the album charts, and discophobes will always be grateful to "Rise"'s laidback beat for having the ironic effect of letting the hot air out of the disco craze, which soon faded from sight. *—Richard S. Ginell*

● **Classics, Vol. 1** / Jan. 1987 / A&M ✦✦✦✦✦
All the high points from the ten-year dominance of Alpert and the Tijuana Brass; includes "A Taste of Honey," "Spanish Flea," and others. *—Cub Koda*

● **Classics, Vol. 20** / Feb. 1987 / A&M ✦✦✦✦✦
This set features Alpert's solo hits from "This Guy's in Love with You" to "Rise." *—Cub Koda*

Keep Your Eye on Me / Feb. 1987 / A&M ✦✦✦

North on South St. / 1991 / A&M ✦✦✦

Midnight Sun / Jun. 9, 1992 / A&M ✦✦✦

Second Wind / Apr. 1996 / Almo Sounds ✦✦

Passion Dance / Apr. 29, 1997 / Almo Sounds ✦✦✦✦

Colors / Jun. 15, 1999 / Almo Sounds ✦✦✦✦

Leroy Anderson

b. Jun. 29, 1908, Cambridge, MA, **d.** May 18, 1975
Composer / Classical Pop, Orchestral Pop
Leroy Anderson was a light-classical pop composer, most popular in the '40s and '50s. Anderson was a student at both the New England Conservatory of Music and Harvard University. At Harvard, he was the orchestral director, choirmaster and organist for six years, between 1929-1935.

Anderson began his professional musical career in 1935, writing and arranging for the Boston Pops Orchestra and Arthur Fiedler. In 1942, he entered the US Army; four years later, he returned to writing music.

The sound effects Anderson incorporated into many of his compositions became his musical signature. Among his most popular songs are the Christmas classic "Sleigh Ride," "The Syncopated Clock" (the old *Late Show* theme), "Blue Tango," and "Forgotten Dreams." Anderson's witty, melodic compositions gained wide acceptance in both pop and classical circles. *—Kenneth M. Cassidy*

★ **The Best of Leroy Anderson: Sleigh Ride** / Nov. 18, 1997 / Decca/MCA ✦✦✦✦✦
This collects 20 of Leroy Anderson's best-known recordings. Anderson produced little "orchestral miniatures": original compositions that utilized much of the trappings of classical music put in the confines of a pop single. Decca Records signed him in 1950 to conduct his music for a gigantic, 55-piece orchestra (one that Anderson often said could never be put together in a live situation), producing pieces that were quirky ("The Syncopated Clock"), offbeat ("The Typewriter"), and just plain whimsical and fun ("Fiddle Faddle" and "Plink, Plank, Plunk!"). Best known of all is the title track, composed during a July heat wave in 1948. Though his music is seldom revived today, it was enormously catchy and popular in the pre-rock & roll days of pop music and sounds wonderful collected here. *—Cub Koda*

Les Baxter

b. Mar. 14, 1922, Detroit, MI, **d.** 1996
Saxophone, Piano, Conductor, Composer, Arranger / Lounge, Exotica
Les Baxter is a pianist who composed and arranged for the top swing bands of the '40s and '50s, but he is better-known as the founder of an exotica, a variation of easy listening that glorified the sounds and styles of Polynesia, Africa, and South America, even as they retained the traditional string-and-horn arrangements of instrumental pop. Exotica became a massively popular trend in the '50s, with thousands of record buyers listening to Baxter, Martin Denny, and their imitators. Baxter also pioneered the use of the electronic instrument the theremin, which has a haunting, howling sound. In 1948, he released a triple-78 album called, *Music Out of the Moon* which ushered in space age pop with its use of the theremin. Four years later, he began recording exotica albums with *Le Sacre Du Sauvage*. On his early '50s singles Baxter was relatively straightforward, performing versions of standards like the number one hits "Unchained Melody" and "The Poor People of Paris," but on his albums he experimented with all sorts of world musics, adapting them for his orchestra. Although he continued to compose and record in the '70s, his output was sporadic. Nevertheless, a cult following formed around his exotica recordings that persisted into the '90s. *—Stephen Thomas Erlewine*

Space Escapade / 1958 / Capitol ✦✦✦✦✦
A real period piece, *Space Escapade* is a definitive slice of lounge/bachelor pad music. The music, of course, is a bit dated, although it certainly shows off Baxter's chops as a big-band leader. One reason to get the record, however, is the cover—two astronauts holding goblets of exotic (and potentially lethal) cocktails, surrounded by three *very* attractive Martian women, and in the background, a silhouette of a rocket. All cloaked in dry ice. This record has sold for decades on the cover artwork alone, and you'll see why if (and when) you pick it up. *—Matthew Greenwald*

The Lost Episode / 1995 / Dionysus ✦✦✦

● **Baxter's Best** / Jun. 25, 1996 / Capitol ✦✦✦✦✦
This may not be his "best" if you favor his more adventurous and weirder outings; these are the kind of Baxter productions that became building blocks of the easy listening genre. However, these 16 tracks from 1951-1961 are among his most popular successes, including the hits "The Poor People of Paris," "Blue Tango," "Wake the Town and Tell the People," and "Unchained Melody." *—Richie Unterberger*

Exotic Moods of Les Baxter / Jul. 1996 / Capitol ✦✦✦✦✦
Over the course of two compact discs, *The Exotic Moods of Les Baxter* collects most of Baxter's biggest hits, plus a selection of rare and previously unreleased material. For casual fans, the collection is fine, if a little long—two discs is a lot of Baxter for listeners with a passing interest in exotica. For the more dedicated easy listening/exotica collector, this compilation is useful, if a little frustrating, since much of this material is available on other collections. Still, this gives a good overview of the scope and variety of his music and it emphasizes his wilder, unpredictable side more effectively than *Baxter's Best*. *—Stephen Thomas Erlewine*

Tamboo!/Skins! / Oct. 17, 2000 / Collectables ✦✦✦

Ray Charles (Charles Raymond Offenberg)

b. Sep. 13, 1918, Chicago, IL
Arranger, Producer / Easy Pop, Vocal Pop
Reaching number three on the pop charts in 1964 with one of the most successful easy listening singles of the '60s, "Love Me with All Your Heart (Cuando Caliente el Sol), " the Ray Charles Singers made numerous genteel albums of choral mood music throughout the '50s and '60s. Although they were led by a man named Ray Charles, this group had no connection whatsoever to Ray Charles the famous soul singer, and certainly no connection whatsoever to soul music. The coincidence of two such different artists sharing the same name led the Ray Charles of the Ray Charles Singers, in fact, to bill himself as "The Other Ray Charles" when he was given a TV credit.

This Ray Charles was born Charles Raymond Offenberg on September 13, 1918 in Chicago. Working in radio, Broadway, and local bands, he got his major break when he landed a job as an arranger for Perry Como's radio backing group in the late 1940s, remaining in that position when Como got a TV program. By the mid-1950s, the group called the Ray Charles Singers replaced the Fontaine Sisters as Como's TV backing ensemble. The Ray Charles Singers recorded on their own for Essex, MGM and Decca before hitting their commercial stride on Enoch Light's Command label in the 1960s, with arrangements emphasizing lush instrumentation and soft, breathy singing.

There is little music from the era more whitebread than records by the Ray Charles Singers, with vocals and instrumentation smooth and saccharine enough to fit onto elevator Muzak programs, and almost too wholesome sounding for TV milk commercials. For material, the group favored interpretations of popular standards, also including some Mexican and South American pop and bossa nova songs. "Love Me with All Your Heart, " in fact, was a translation of a Mexican song, "Cuando Caliente el Sol, " which Charles first heard aboard a cruise ship. Originally the B-side of a cover of "Hello Dolly!," it became an unexpected hit in 1964. The group had several more Top 40 singles that year—"Al-Di-La" and "One More

Time"—and hit number 11 with the album *Something Special for Young Lovers.* After the Ray Charles Singers (who rarely appeared live in concert) passed their prime as a recording act, Charles continued to work in musical direction on TV programs like *Sha Na Na* and *The Muppet Show.* —*Richie Unterberger*

● **Love Me with All Your Heart** / 1995 / Varese ✦✦✦✦✦
Compilation of 1964-68 tracks for the Command label, concentrating most heavily on his popular 1964 material. Includes the hits "Love Me With All Your Heart," "Al-Di-La," and "One More Time," the last of which sounds like a Bacharach-David tune. Other points of interest include some songs from the 1965 *Songs for Latin Lovers* album. —*Richie Unterberger*

Richard Clayderman

b. 1954, Paris, France
Piano / Contemporary Instrumental, Instrumental Pop, Neo-Classical
With his lush, sophisticated, instrumental, approach to pop music, Richard Clayderman (born: Phillipe Pages) is, according to *The Guinness Book Of World Records,* "the most successful pianist in the world." Clayderman's albums routinely sell millions of copies and his concerts are quickly sold out. In a review of his 1985 Carnegie Hall concert, *Variety* wrote, "(Clayderman's) main appeal lies in his youth and boyish good looks.... .coupled with his gentlemanly charm and his thick French accent, they promise to rope in the romantically inclined middle aged Yank ladies who cotton to this ilk of soothing entertainment." Nancy Reagan referred to Clayderman as "the prince of romance." Instructed in classical piano by his father, Clayderman enrolled in the Paris Conservatory of Music at the age of twelve. Four years later, he placed first in a piano competition at the school. Despite his classical background, Clayderman opted for popular music when he launched his professional career. A tour as opening act for French rock musician Johnny Hollyday introduced him to an international following. Clayderman's debut album, *Ballade Pour Adeline,* recorded at the urging of producers and composers Oliver Toussaint and Paul De Senneville in 1977, sold more than twenty million copies and was distributed in thirty-eight countries. Clayderman, who took his stage name from his Swedish grandmother, has continued to tour throughout the world to enthusiastic audiences. A live concert, broadcast on Chinese television in 1987 attracted more than 800 million viewers. —*Craig Harris*

● **Romance of Richard Clayderman** / Dec. 1, 1995 / Sony Special Products ✦✦✦✦✦

Ray Conniff

b. Nov. 6, 1916, Attleboro, MA
Trombone, Arranger, Strings / Easy Pop, Traditional Pop, Vocal Pop, Orchestral Pop
The man who popularized wordless vocal choruses and light orchestral accompaniment on a mix of popular standards and contemporary hits of the 1960s, Ray Conniff was a trombone player for Bunny Berigan's Orchestra and Bob Crosby's Bobcats before being hired as an arranger by Mitch Miller for Columbia Records in 1954. After he wrote the charts for several sizeable Columbia hits during the mid-'50s, Conniff became a solo artist as well, applying his arranging techniques to instrumental easy-listening for the booming adult album market. The result, twelve Top Ten LPs and well over 50 million total albums sold, cemented his status as one of the top LP sellers of all time, but his increasingly watered-down and commercially focused arrangements gained few young fans by the end of the 1960s. Though he continued recording and touring the world into the 1990s, Conniff's albums slipped off the charts in the early '70s. —*John Bush*

'S Wonderful / Mar. 1957 / Columbia ✦✦✦✦✦
Ray Conniff had a solid career of big band arranging and conducting the orchestras backing Columbia Records' stable of 1950s pop singers before he managed to get his name on a record himself. But that didn't prepare anybody for the success of this album, named after the Gershwin song he first arranged when he was working for Artie Shaw. Conniff updated the big band sound to the 1950s, retaining its danceable tempos and building upon the unison section innovations of Glenn Miller, his own added idea being a vocal chorus that hummed and sang syllables as an extra part of the ensemble. Employing standards with familiar melodies, the imaginativeness of his work became all the more noticeable, and *'S Wonderful!* became a substantial hit that kicked off a run of successful albums in the same style. —*William Ruhlmann*

'S Marvelous / Dec. 1957 / Columbia ✦✦✦✦✦
After the less-successful *Dance the Bop,* on his third album Ray Conniff returned to the formula with which he had found success on his first album, *'S Wonderful!,* once again turning out a set of lively arrangements of standards featuring a wordless chorus, with the deliberately similar title *'S Marvelous,* again evoking the Gershwin song. Along with Gershwin, the featured composers included Cole Porter, Richard Rodgers and Jerome Kern, and the album was even more popular than its predecessor, lodging in the Top Ten and going gold. With that, Conniff was off to the races, cloning this style on dozens of subsequent releases. —*William Ruhlmann*

'S Awful Nice / Jun. 1958 / Columbia ✦✦✦
The third entry in Ray Conniff's series of neo-swing easy listening albums, *'S Awful Nice* followed *'S Wonderful!* and *'S Marvelous* into hit status, reaching the Top Ten and spending a year in the charts. As ever, Conniff's writing was danceable, with his wordless choir carrying the melodies, doubled by the horn and reed sections. The song selection remained blue chip, especially in the Jerome Kern standards "Smoke Gets in Your Eyes," "All The Things You Are" (dominated by Bernie Glow's trumpet) and "Lovely to Look At." —*William Ruhlmann*

Somewhere My Love / Jul. 1966 / Columbia ✦✦✦

★ **16 Most Requested Songs** / 1986 / Columbia/Legacy ✦✦✦✦✦
Featuring most of his biggest hits, including "Somewhere, My Love" and "Love Is A Many Splendored Thing," *16 Most Requested Songs* offers a good overview of Ray Conniff's career. Though it isn't as comprehensive as some other discs, it is easy to find and has a representative track selection, making it a good introduction to Conniff. —*Stephen Thomas Erlewine*

Songs from the Big & Small Screen / 1993 / Columbia ✦✦✦
This compilation of 1970s (and a couple of late '60s) movie and TV themes will be entertaining to those who think back fondly on the decade. The Conniff touch (in which everything is filtered through a 1940s swing sensibility) works best on music already close to his buoyant style, such as "Love Is All Around," the theme from *The Mary Tyler Moore Show.* Even the slower tunes work well, as long as they already have a nostalgic glow, notably "The Way We Were." Elsewhere, however, Conniff is forced to adapt himself to the rock-oriented sounds of "Stayin' Alive" and "Theme From S.W.A.T.," and he can't really do much more than ape the arrangements from the original recordings, which makes the musicians and singers sound uncomfortable. But if you were already an adult in the 1970s, this may be the right approach for you. —*William Ruhlmann*

The Essence of Ray Conniff / Jun. 1, 1993 / Columbia ✦✦✦✦✦

Xavier Cugat

b. Jan. 1, 1900, Gerona, Spain, **d.** Oct. 27, 1990, Barcelona, Spain
Violin, Bandleader, Arranger / Cha Cha, Lounge, Afro-Cuban Jazz, Rhumba, Mambo, Latin Jazz, Pop, Instrumental Pop, Big Band
Remembered for his highly-commercial approach to pop music, Xavier Cugat (born: Francisco De Asis Javier Cugat Mingall De Cru Y Deulofeo) made an even greater mark as one of the pioneers of Latin-American dance music. During his eight decade long career, Cugat helped to popularize the tango, the cha-cha, the mambo and the rhumba. His hits included "El Manicero" in the 1930s, "Perfida" in 1940 and the original recording of "Babalu" in 1944. Members of Cugat's band included Desi Arnaz, Miguelito Valdes, Tito Rodriguez, Luis Del Campo, Yma Sumac and his third (of four) wives, Abbe Lane. Cugat used the success of his musical career as a springboard for appearances in many films throughout the '30s, '40s and '50s, which, in turn helped fuel sales of his albums.

Born in Spain, he was raised in Havana. Trained as a classical violinist, he played with the Orchestra of the Teatro Nacional in Havana at the age of twelve. Emigrating to the United States, sometime between 1915 and 1918, he quickly found work accompanying an opera singer. At the height of the tango craze, in 1918, Cugat joined a popular dance band, The Gigolos. He left music briefly, taking a job as a cartoonist for *The Los Angeles Times.* Cugat returned to music in 1920, forming his own group, The Latin American Band. The group had its greatest success after moving to New York and became the house band for the Waldorf Astoria Hotel. That job helped him develop the listener-friendly amalgamation of Latin styles that made him a recording sensation. Upon his retirement in 1970, Cugat returned to Spain. He died in Barcelona on October 27, 1990. His band, which was led by Tito Puente following his retirement, continues to perform under the direction of dancer, musician and vocalist Ada Cavallo. —*Craig Harris*

16 Most Requested Songs / Apr. 26, 1993 / Columbia/Legacy ✦✦✦
16 Most Requested Songs is a midline-priced collection that spotlights many of Xavier Cugat's best-known and most popular performances for Columbia Records, including "Chica Chica Boom Chic," "Brazil," "Amor," "Tico-Tico," "My Shawl," "You, So It's You," "Walter Winchell Rhumba," "Miami Beach Rhumba" and "South America, Take It Away." Although it's far from a perfect retrospective of his career, it's still a nice sampler of familiar items, and it may satisfy the needs of some casual fans who only want the hits. —*Stephen Thomas Erlewine*

Cugie A-Go-Go / May 13, 1997 / Varese ✦✦✦
This collection compiles 16 tracks from several of Xavier Cugat's albums recorded for Decca Records in the mid-1960s. This marks a time in Cugat's career when he was largely chasing after trends (Herb Alpert's Tijuana Brass and Brasil '66) and recasting current pop tunes in an effort to regain entry into the pop mainstream. The track highlights include Sonny and Cher's "Bang Bang," "Theme From Zorba the Greek," "Moon Over Naples," "Charade" and "La Playa (Aruba-La Plage)" from the album *Bang Bang;* "Judith," "Thunderball," "Zip-A-Dee-Doo-Dah," and "Adios" from *Dance Party;* "Jungle Rhumba," "Compadre Pedro Juan," "The Jewish Wedding Song," and "Music to Watch Girls By" from *Today;* and "Chim, Chim, Cheree" and "Goldfinger" from *Feeling Good.* Most of the tracks are making their CD debut with the release of this collection. These four albums were dismal sellers upon release, but in light of the current interest in Latin music, they now almost seem like guides to the changing face of the genre. No matter how seemingly incongruous the material at hand, all feature that distinctive Cugat touch: the touch of a true master. —*Cub Koda*

● **The Greatest RCA Sides** / Oct. 3, 2000 / Collectors' Choice Music ✦✦✦✦✦
As the title promises, Xavier Cugat's *Greatest RCA Sides* delivers the best of his classic RCA material, including hits such as "Frenesi," "Perfidia," "Cumparsita," and 17 other highlights from his easy-on-the-ears interpretations of Latin rhythms. "Cielto Lindo," "Quierme Mucho," and "Whatever Happened to You" capture Cugat at the peak of his powers. —*Heather Phares*

Martin Denny

b. 1911, New York, NY
Piano, Composer, Arranger / Space Age Pop, Exotica
In 1957 pianist Denny popularized the "exotica" style of ethnic pop music with the release of *Exotica.* This record—with beautiful artwork and the hit single "Quiet Village"—briefly influenced a generation and has found new favor since the mid-1980s. Supposedly reminiscent of tropical jungles and beaches, the soothing, natural sounds evoke the tranquility and mystery of Southeast Asian and Pacific islands. Strong melodies are highlighted by such exotic instruments as Japanese samisen and koto, boobams, gong, temple bells, and the trademark bird calls of first vibes player Arthur Lyman (who left after the first record to lead his own group) and then percussionist August Colon (two solo records). The first and most intriguing records rely heavily on the compositions of Les Baxter, essentially stripping Baxter's seminal exotic "tone poem" *Ritual of the Savage* of strings but adding exotic percussion. Following the deep exotica period, Denny turned to light jazz (including bossa nova), cocktail-lounge piano, and covers of standard pop hits, showtunes, and film themes. Highlights of Denny's

later career include *Exotic Moog*, a highly desired, unique electronic record; *A Taste of India*, with its sitar cover of "Incense and Peppermints"; and *Latin Village*. Otherwise the steam runs out during the mid-1960s. *—Tony Wilds*

★ **Exotica: The Best of Martin Denny** / 1990 / Rhino ♦♦♦♦♦
Drawing from eight of his late-'50s albums, this 20-track compilation includes everything that all but the truly hard-bitten will need to hear by the "King of Exotica," complete with informative liner notes. Includes "Quiet Village," of course, as well as Denny's only other Top 40 hit, "The Enchanted Sea." *—Richie Unterberger*

Afro-Desia: The Exotic Sounds of Martin Denny / 1995 / Scamp ♦♦♦♦♦
Nominally, this represents Denny's attempt to evoke the ambience of the African continent, after having done the same for the South Pacific via a series of early albums. Denny does use marimba, vibes, bongos, congas, and timbales—not to mention sound effects of a buzzing tsetse fly and the rainforest. But the result is even less genuinely African (to the nth degree) than, say, Paul Simon's *Graceland*. Not to mention that The Randy Van Horne Singers, who contribute backing vocals (as they did for the Flintstones and Jetsons cartoons), were probably about as authentically African as a Disneyland voodoo doll. Denny never pretended to offer a genuinely ethnic experience, though. This is, despite any impressions generated by the title, more exotica music, pure and simple. There isn't much Denny on CD, but almost everyone will be content to pick up the Rhino best-of (which admittedly only duplicates a few cuts from *Afro-Desia*) and leave it at that. *—Richie Unterberger*

The Exotica 1/Exotica 2: Exciting Sounds of Martin Denny / 1996 / Scamp ♦♦♦♦♦
The two Denny albums that gave the genre its name and popularized its sound, originally released circa 1957, are here combined onto one compact disc. If you want more Martin Denny after you're finished with Rhino's best-of, this should be the next stop. Only seven of the 24 tracks here duplicate the Rhino set, Martin Denny wrote the extensive liner notes, and the sound is better than what you'll find on the beat-up original vinyl. The earlier album (featuring "Quiet Village") is jazzier and more boistrous than you might expect; *Exotica 2* is considerably mellower, and heavier on the cocktail lounge vibe. *—Richie Unterberger*

Forbidden Island/Primitiva / 1996 / Scamp ♦♦♦
Denny's third and fourth LPs, combined into one single-disc CD reissue, with new liner notes by Martin himself augmenting the original artwork. If you're interested enough in this exotica bandleader to want more than a greatest hits collection, it's a good investment. The fidelity's much better than what you're likely to find if you manage to locate battered copies of the original vinyl, and only three of the 24 tracks appear on Rhino's best-of. *—Richie Unterberger*

Quiet Village/The Enchanted Sea / Jul. 29, 1997 / Scamp ♦♦♦♦♦
Martin Denny is rightfully known as the king of exotica/lounge music. The music is defined by breezy, middle of the road, early-60's pop arrangements buttressed by sound effects of ocean, wildlife, birds, and other natural phenomenon. Scamp Records out of New York has done an excellent job of reissuing his original albums, and this CD, which contains two albums on one disc, is one of the best of the lot. The first album, *Quiet Village*, has a distinct Hawaiian air, with songs like "Hawaiian War Chant," "Pagan Love Song," "Paradise Found," and others. It's a gorgeous mood album, wonderfully recorded and produced (by Simon Waronker). The second set, *The Enchanted Sea*, is equally exotic, using the ocean as a motif. The packaging is excellent, with extensive liner notes by Denny himself. With lounge music enjoying a resurgence in the past years, this disc is quite obviously the place to start. *—Matthew Greenwald*

Robert Drasnin

Sax (Alto), Flute, Clarinet / Television Music, Lounge, Exotica
Drasnin has a host of television compositions under his belt, including work for *Lost in Space, Playhouse 90, The Man from U.N.C.L.E., Mission Impossible*, and *The Twilight Zone*. From 1977 until the early '90s, he was the Director of Music for CBS Entertainment. Before all of that, he played alto, clarinet, and flute in the jazz bands of such leaders as Tommy Dorsey and Red Norvo. His current status as an *artiste*, however, rests upon an album that he might have considered as a trifle at the time. *Voodoo*, issued around the late '50s on the tiny Tops label, closely approximated the exotica sound of Martin Denny—under, apparently, instructions from the Tops A&R chief himself. Drasnin devised a satisfying approximation of Denny's tropical-Latin-lounge jazz hybrid, in somewhat of a more low-key fashion than Denny himself. Indeed, Drasnin later arranged Denny's *Latin Village* album. The rare *Voodoo* LP was reissued on CD in 1996. *—Richie Unterberger*

Voodoo / Feb. 13, 1996 / Dionysus ♦♦♦
Exotica fans will treat the reissue of this super-rare album as a Holy Grail of sorts, akin to, say, the re-release of a highly-rated, locally pressed '60s rock LP by garage band collectors. The rest of you are probably better off sticking with the Martin Denny best-of, if you get that far. In other words, if you swoon over Martin Denny, you're not going to be disappointed with this somewhat more sedate and dignified effort; otherwise, you'll find it competent but superfluous. *—Richie Unterberger*

Esquivel

b. Jan. 20, 1918, Tampico, Mexico
Piano / Tropical, Lounge, Space Age Pop, Exotica
In the mid-'90s, Juan Garcia Esquivel enjoyed one of the most unexpected resurgences of popularity—and hipness—in the annals of 20th-century pop. The composer and arranger skirted the lines between lounge music, eccentric experimentalism, and stereo sound pioneer in the late '50s and early '60s on a series of albums aimed at the easy-listening market. Both cheesy and goofily unpredictable, these records were forgotten by all but thrift-store habitues for decades. With the space age pop/exotica revival of the mid-'90s, however, Esquivel was not just being rediscovered, but was being championed as a cutting-edge innovator by certain segments of the hipper-than-thou alternative crowd. In an era in which stereo albums were first starting to be marketed, Esquivel—along with several other of "space age pop"'s leading lights—took advantage of this development to use his albums as laboratories of sorts to explore the spectrum of recorded sound, as reflected in LP titles like *Other Worlds, Other Sounds*, and *Four Corners of the World*. He employed then-exotic instruments such as the theremin, the ondioline, early Fender-Rhodes keyboards, Chinese bells, bass accordion, and boo-bams (a 24-bongo kit tuned to F) to get what he wanted. What kept Esquivel from serious critical appreciation at the time are, perhaps, the same factors that exert a strange fascination upon listeners of the 1990s. In its form and content, Esquivel's material was lightweight martini mixing fare, more geared toward suburban easy listening than challenging innovation. He threw in just enough sly, oddball quirks, however, to make one wonder whether he was in fact deftly satirizing the form, or at least using it as a forum to slip in some unbridled zaniness. *—Richie Unterberger*

To Love Again / 1957 / RCA Victor ♦♦♦♦
Esquivel records are typically considered the ultimate way to show off the magic of stereo sound. It hardly seems possible that the full effect could come from a monaural recording. But his debut LP, *To Love Again*, is easily his finest work. By 1957, greatness already had been conferred on Esquivel in Mexico (where the album was recorded) and among music professionals in the United States. It was only a matter of introducing the man to the American public, and *To Love Again* clearly indicates a great concentration of effort, the culmination of years of preparation, professionalism, and perfectionism. The material generally is of the exotic, Latin variety associated with Lecuona. Xavier Cugat's "Nightingale," "Nocturnal," "Besame Mucho," and "Siboney" all are first-rate and compare with any of Esquivel's best later work. The remainder of the album really is about as good, making it consistently excellent from start to finish. The trademark chorus is present throughout. Note that Esquivel's arrangement of "Jungle Drums" makes its first LP appearance here; it is updated on his second greatest album, the historic stereo masterpiece *Latin-Esque*. And "Besame Mucho" is reworked on 1967's *The Genius of Esquivel*. *—Tony Wilds*

Four Corners of the World / 1958 / RCA Victor ♦♦

Other Worlds Other Sounds / 1958 / RCA Victor ♦♦♦♦
Other Worlds Other Sounds may be the best known Esquivel album because of its sensational jacket art portraying a red-caped woman prancing across a green planetary landscape. Its real significance is as the moment where Esquivel takes control of his production and develops his signature sound. The chorus (the Randy Van Horne Singers) begins the "zu zu zu" nonsense beloved by Esquivel fans, and the playfulness with stereophonic separation begins here. But the material is not his best. "Ballerina" and "Night and Day" are cheesy, while most of the album seem like slow song outtakes from *To Love Again*. It is a different mood, one that never really hits its stride until the closing track: the astounding arrangement of "It Had to Be You." This is the promise of the future. *—Tony Wilds*

Latin-Esque / 1962 / RCA Victor Stereo Action ♦♦♦♦
This album has several musical and historical significant aspects, making it Esquivel's most desirable. First, it is one of only three or so truly great RCA Stereo Action ("The Sound Your Eyes Can Follow") albums. The music is deliberately scored for channel separation, but there is more to the stereo gimmickry than the arrangements. Not counting layered-track (multi-dubbing) efforts, *Latin-Esque* was the first album recorded with total stereo separation—two separate orchestras in two separate studios performed, connected by headphones. The results are fairly fantastic. *Latin-Esque* also is Esquivel's first stereo album in the Latin-esque style of his great first album, *To Love Again*. ("Jungle Drums" from that LP is updated here.) The artist's jaw-dropping masterpiece of zany pop, "Mucho Muchacha," is a highlight. "Carioca," "La Paloma," and several other standards also were well-chosen for this project. This album was essential to the renaissance of Esquivel's popularity in the 1990s. *—Tony Wilds*

More of Other Worlds, Other Sounds / 1962 / Reprise Archives ♦♦♦♦
Traditionally the most sought after and highest valued Esquivel record, *More of Other Sounds Other Worlds* should be considered in context. First, it is not a sequel to the RCA record of three years earlier. The title only reflects Stanley Wilson's desire to record Esquivel since having heard the earlier LP. Second, the label switch is significant. Reprise, a division of Warner Bros., started out giving old masters a fresh shot (hence the name). While the dual 35mm film recording process is played up, it is more important that new people are involved after hi-fi and stereo have become old hat. (Another great, similar "Reprise" from this period is Les Baxter's return to exotica in *The Primitive and the Passionate*.) The album begins with "The Breeze and I (Andalucia)," a brassy bullfighting number. "Street Scene" and "One for My Baby (And One More for the Road)" belong to the bluesy urban crime jazz idiom. The rest of the album is typical of the style of Esquivel's later U.S. RCA work. While not his quirkiest or most sensational, it is among his best and most interesting. *—Tony Wilds*

★ **Space Age Bachelor Pad Music** / 1994 / Bar/None ♦♦♦♦♦
Esquivel was one of the most interesting easy-listening composers of the 1950s and '60s, creating open, futuristic sonic landscapes. Part of his music's appeal is its pure campiness; "Mucha Muchacha," with its bad puns and exaggerated Latin rhythms and vocals, is hilarious. *Esquivel*, a collection of his "greatest hits," makes it apparent that the humor is at least partially intentional. Using dissonance and aural humor, along with intricately structured arrangements, Esquivel created records that were indeed "space-age bachelor pad music"—they sounded out of this world and they swung. The music may sound dated, but it also sounds peculiarly fresh; no one made music like this then, and no one makes music like this now. *—Stephen Thomas Erlewine*

Music from a Sparkling Planet / 1995 / Bar/None ♦♦♦♦♦
Bar/None's second collection of Esquivel tracks from the '60s, *Music From A Sparkling Planet* isn't quite as infectiously listenable as *Space Age Bachelor Pad Music*, containing nothing quite as mind-bending as the best moments of the first compilation. Nevertheless, there is plenty of wonderful music to found on the album, even though most of it sounds like pleasant soundtrack or elevator music, devoid of much of the quirkiness that fueled *Space Age*. *—Stephen Thomas Erlewine*

Cabaret Manana / Nov. 1995 / RCA ♦♦♦♦♦
Esquivel's output is pretty diverse, yet it's hard to rate one compilation against another.

They're of such a similar qualitative standard that none can be singled out as definitive, or even recommended above the others. *Cabaret Manana* is as good as any a place to start (and no worse or better than the compilations on Bar/None). The 20 tracks are drawn from RCA releases spanning 1958 to 1967, including both original compositions and oddball versions of standards like "Harlem Nocturne," "Night and Day," "Malaguena," and "Take the 'A' Train." Whether this rings your chimes or not, it's certainly different, unpredictable, and full of idiosyncratic touches like whistlers, berserk organ solos, choruses of "zu-zu" vocals, Bugs Bunny cartoon slide guitar, and sassy horn sections that blow with an energy more savage than anything else you'll hear on "easy" listening recordings. *—Richie Unterberger*

Exploring New Sounds in Stereo/Strings Aflame / Sep. 16, 1997 / Bar/None ♦♦♦♦
Exploring New Sounds in Stereo is the first of the "typical" Esquivel albums from which the CD compilations draw heavily, and there is a lot to recommend it. "Whatchamacallit" is probably his second best-loved tune (released also as a single backed with the non-LP track, "I Feel Merely Marvelous"). The track features the ondioline, an electronic-organ-like instrument often associated with the theremin. And on *Exploring New Sounds in Stereo,* there is indeed theremin in Esquivel's spacy treatment of "Spellbound" (from the movie of the same name). Other highlights include the exotic "Bella Mora," the cheesy "My Number One Love," and "The 3rd Man Theme." *Strings Aflame,* the second album reissued on this two-fer, is one of the easier Esquivel records to find, no doubt because many people were turned off by the material. As with *Four Corners of the World,* Esquivel seems to be proving his chops (this time with arrangements of popular string pieces), rather than doing what he does best or what his fans want most. Nevertheless, it is a fine album, well worth having in stereo. "Turkish March," "Parade of the Wooden Soldiers," "Gypsy Lament," "Guadalajara," and "Misirlou" all receive semi-exotic, unusual treatments. About four or so tunes feature the chorus's patented "zu zu zu" wordless vocal. *—Tony Wilds*

Percy Faith

b. 1908, Toronto, Ontario, Canada, **d.** 1976, Los Angeles, CA
Piano, Conductor, Composer, Arranger / Easy Pop, Traditional Pop, Orchestral Pop
Percy Faith was one of the most popular film composers and easy listening recording artists of the '50s and '60s. Not only did he have a number of hit albums and singles under his own name, but Faith was responsible for arranging hits by Tony Bennett, Doris Day, Johnny Mathis and Burl Ives, among others as the musical director for Columbia Records in the '50s. A child piano prodigy whose career was cut short when he injured his hands in a fire, Faith then moved into arranging and worked for CBC radio. After moving to America in 1940, he recorded for both Decca and RCA Victor, then joined Columbia in 1950 as musical director and a recording artist. While he arranged traditional pop songs, as well as show tunes, folk songs, and traditional pop songs for the label's vocalists, Faith became a pioneer of easy listening "mood music" with his own albums. He had his first number one single, "Song from the Moulin Rouge (Where Is Your Heart)," in 1953. In the mid-'50s, he began composing film scores; his work for the 1960 film *A Summer Place* earned another number one hit with "Theme to A Summer Place." After rock & roll took over popular music in the early '60s, Faith slowly withdrew from a professional career and released his last album in 1970. *—Stephen Thomas Erlewine & Cub Koda*

★ **16 Most Requested Songs** / 1978 / Columbia ♦♦♦♦♦
Conductor-arranger Percy Faith made his greatest direct impact on popular music during the 1950's, and fully half of this 16 song collection represents the highlights of his output from that decade, from the spritely "Swedish Rhapsody" and "Moulin Rouge" through his instrumental of "A Summer Place". Highlights of this very nicely mastered compilation include "Delicado", which features Stan Freeman's rippling harpsichord, and the ethereal "Baubles, Bangles and Beads" . Faith and other makers of pop instrumental music were put on the defensive by rock 'n roll, to the point of fighting a rear guard action in the 1960's, but it had its virtues—the articulation of the individual instrumental voices is rather bracing for the listener who can appreciate those attributes, and Faith does manage to capture the essence of the original material, no more so than in "A Summer Place". One of Max Steiner's final triumphs as a composer, the instrumental came to richer, more vibrant life in Faith's hands, so much so that the composer relinquished the baton to Faith at a recorded live performance in 1963. The 60's material here is more uneven—"I Will Follow You", adapted from the Petula Clark/Peggy March hit, fares very nicely in the hands of Faith's string section, reeds, and winds. "The Girl From Ipanema" is nothing to write home about, however, and it's clear by the mid-1960's the conductor-arranger was selling tracks like "MacArthur Park" by emphasizing sides of the song that were markedly different from their chart hit renditions. The sound is superb and the annotation is excellent, although one wishes that more information about specific songs were included. *—Bruce Eder*

Percy Faith's Greatest Hits / 1978 / Columbia ♦♦♦♦

Tara's Theme from Gone with the Wind/Jealousy / Jul. 1, 1997 / Collectables ♦♦♦

Camelot/My Fair Lady / Jan. 5, 1998 / Collectables ♦♦♦♦

Bim! Bam!! Boom!!!/Theme from the "In" Crowd / Aug. 15, 2000 / Collectables ♦♦♦

Ferrante & Teicher

Group / Classical Pop, Lounge, Orchestral Pop
A piano duo, Arthur Ferrante and Louis Teicher met while both were studying at Juilliard in the late '40s. After years of being guests in front of large orchestras and cutting several cleverly arranged duo albums, they hit their stride in the early '60s with a string of lush orchestrated hit singles and albums based around their interlocking piano style. *—Cub Koda*

Blast Off! / 1958 / Varese ♦♦♦♦♦
The reissue of Ferrante and Teicher's pricey 1958 album *Blast Off!* with four additional tracks is a welcome one. The piano duo was not originally budgeted for a full orchestra for the recording of its third album for ABC-Paramount. Undaunted, the pair experimented and created the necessary sounds through modifications to their concert grands. Strategically placed pieces of rubber, wood, metal, and wads of paper achieved the desired instrumental effects. Unlike John Cage, who was performing similar modifications for art's sake, Ferrante and Teicher were doing it for the masses.

Though much of the repertoire on *Blast Off!* are standards other lounge artists were covering at the time ("S'Wonderful," "Ain't Misbehavin'," "I Got Rhythm"), Ferrante and Teicher's approach is novel enough to sustain interest. Even today, it's amazing the sounds they were able to coax out of concert grand pianos—at times they sound as otherworldly as synthesizers, or as down to earth as harps, zithers, and celestes. The best quality about the album is that it doesn't sound like a novelty or a gimmick, just two guys using their imagination to surmount the obstacle of not having the necessary instrumentation to create the sounds they desired. *—Jim Powers*

★ **Greatest Hits** / 1965 / Curb ♦♦♦♦♦
Curb's *Greatest Hits* is a budget-line collection that contains Ferrante & Teicher's greatest hits, including "Theme From the Apartment," "Exodus," "Tonight," "Lisa," and "Midnight Cowboy," as well as five other tracks. It's a brief collection, but it gives a good sense of what the easly listening group was all about. *—Stephen Thomas Erlewine*

James Galway

b. Dec. 8, 1939, Belfast, Northern Ireland
Flute / Celtic Pop, Instrumental Pop
James Galway gained fame as one of Ireland's most popular flautists in the late '70s. Over the next two decades, Galway's smooth, lightly Celtic instrumental stylings were internationally popular, selling numerous records. Galway began playing music with penny whistles and mouth-organs as a child, soon moving to flute. At the age of ten, he was the winner of all three classes of the Irish Flute Championships, which earned him a BBC radio session, as well as a spot in the Belfast Youth Orchestra. Galway earned scholarships first at London's Guildhall School of Music, then the Paris Conservatoire; he would occasionally busk on the subways to earn extra money. After spending some time at Sadlers Wells, Galway became the Berlin Philharmonic's principal flautist in 1969. His time with the orchestra was popular, which led his manager, Michael Emerson, to persuade the flautist to go solo in 1975. Galway was instantly successful as a solo artist, both as a live performer and a recording artist. He was soon playing 120 concerts a year, as well as recording both both classical and popular albums. In 1978, his version of John Denver's "Annie's Song" became an international hit. While his pop recordings were commercially successful, his classical albums were warmly recepted by critics and peers alike, as his records of Mozart and Vivaldi compositions won awards. Though he wasn't able to replicate the success of "Annie's Song" in the '80s, he continued to sell out concerts around the world well into the '90s and his infrequent records have proven nearly as successful. *—Stephen Thomas Erlewine*

● **Greatest Hits** / 1988 / RCA ♦♦♦♦
Although there are a couple of tracks missing, *Greatest Hits* has the majority of James Galway's best-loved numbers and offers a good introduction to the popular flautist. *—Sara Sytsma*

Jackie Gleason (Herbert John Gleason)

b. Feb. 26, 1916, Brooklyn, NY, **d.** Jun. 24, 1987
Vocals / Mood Music, Orchestral Pop
Not only was he one of the finest comedians America has ever produced, Jackie Gleason applied his prodigious talents to music as well. With a strong jazz roots background (leaning to mesmerized idolatry when dealing with good trumpet players), Gleason developed a chart-topping series of mood music albums in the '50s, citing his reason for their existence: "Every time I ever watched Clark Gable do a love scene in the movies, I'd hear this really pretty music, real romantic, come up behind him and help set the mood. So I'm figuring that if Clark Gable needs that kinda help, then a guy in Canarsie has gotta be dyin' for somethin' like this!" Gleason rose to stardom in the early '50s, thanks to the television series *The Life of Riley* and *Cavalcade of Stars.* His television stardom led to a contract with Capitol Records, who released his first album, *Music for Lovers Only,* in 1953. As a musician, Gleason favored lush, dramatically orchestrated instrumentals; he wasn't a trained musician, but he was responsible for the musical direction of his records. Gleason continued to release albums into the '60s, but his popularity dipped dramatically after 1957. His records have continued to be popular cult items and they have come to be regarded as definitive mood music albums. *—Cub Koda & Stephen Thomas Erlewine*

Lonesome Echo / Jun. 1955 / Collectors' Choice Music ♦♦♦
Gleason's 1955 chart-topper *Lonesome Echo* features more lush interpretations of standards such as "I'm Always Chasing Rainbows," "The Thrill Is Gone," "Deep Purple," and "How Deep Is the Ocean." The album also features striking cover artwork by surrealist master Salvador Dali; Collector's Choice's 2000 reissue also includes three bonus tracks, "After My Laughter Came Tears," "Can This Be Love," and "Down Among the Sheltering Palms." *—Heather Phares*

Merry Christmas / Dec. 1956 / Razor & Tie ♦♦♦♦♦
With its soft-blanket strings and romantic bent, Gleason's orchestra was perfectly suited for \Christmas music. His haunting arrangements make for some wonderful interpretations, especially the wistful baritone chorus of "White Christmas" and a dreamy reworking of "Santa Claus Is Comin' to Town." One of the warmest \holiday albums of all time. *—Jim Smith*

The Best of Jackie Gleason / 1993 / Capitol/Curb ♦♦♦♦♦
Although the track selection is skimpy and there are no liner notes to speak of, *The Best of Jackie Gleason* is an effective, inexpensive introduction to his lush, romantic music, featuring a good cross-section of his Capitol hits.. *—Stephen Thomas Erlewine*

And Awaaay We Go! / 1996 / Scamp ♦♦♦
Divided about equally between easy-listening orchestral works and comedy routines, with the latter decidedly outshining the former. On the musical side, "Melancholy Serenade" is here, as well as some familiar themes from *The Honeymooners,* one of which is built around

Gleason's famous "One of These Days—Pow!" schticks. Highlights of the comedy routines include Gleason's recitation of "Casey at the Bat" and his "Reggie Van Gleason III" character. The music means virtually nothing to anyone except *Honeymooners* fanatics, and as for the comedy, it's a lot funnier to see Gleason's characters than only hear the dialog. —Richie Unterberger

• **How Sweet It Is! The Jackie Gleason Velvet Brass Collection** / 1996 / Razor & Tie ✦✦✦✦✦
How Sweet It Is! The Jackie Gleason Velvet Brass Collection is a nice 20-track compilation of Gleason's easy-listening brass records, containing lush, appealing versions of such standards as "You're Driving Me Crazy," "But Not for Me," "The Man I Love," "Me and My Shadow," "Take the 'A' Train," "Am I Blue," "What's New—," "Girl of My Dreams," "September Song" and "My Buddy." There's also a handful of fine original compositions, such as "Melancholy Serenade" and "To a Sleeping Beauty," that may not be as strong as the standards, but they're lovely songs nonetheless, and they add value to what already is the strongest compilation of Gleason's lush brass recordings yet assembled. *—Stephen Thomas Erlewine*

Marty Gold

b. Dec. 26, 1915, New York, NY
Piano / Lounge, Space Age Pop
Space-age pop arranger and composer Marty Gold was born December 26, 1915 in New York City; after spending the early decades of his career as a big-band pianist, during the early 1950s he became a studio arranger at Decca Records, and also authored the Four Aces' 1951 smash "Tell Me Why." Gold later jumped to RCA, where he collaborated on a series of LPs by the Three Suns; he also arranged and conducted numerous sessions for Peter Nero. For RCA and its affiliates Vik and X, Gold and his orchestra recorded a series of LPs—among them *Organized for Hi-Fi, Stereo Action Goes Hollywood, Soundpower! Music to the Limits of Audibility* and *Soundaroundus*—much prized by today's collectors of space-age lounge-pop. *—Jason Ankeny*

Stereo Action Goes Hollywood / 1961 / RCA Victor ✦✦✦

Tony Hatch

Arranger, Producer / Television Music, Pop, Orchestral Pop
Although Tony Hatch had success in various segments of the entertainment industry from the '60s onwards, he'll be best remembered for his work as a producer and songwriter for several British pop and rock stars in the '60s. As a staff producer at Pye Records, Hatch worked with the Searchers, Petula Clark, his wife, Jackie Trent and on several early singles by David Bowie. Hatch's productions boasted a clean and well-arranged sound that, particularly on his collaborations with Petula Clark, displayed some traces of mainstream pop and Broadway. His most significant role in straight British rock music was as producer during the Searchers' 1963-66 commercial prime, a span which saw them ring up all of their big hits. He left his biggest imprint, however, by producing and often writing the big international hits by Petula Clark in the mid-'60s, including "Downtown, " "My Love, " "I Know a Place, " "Don't Sleep in the Subway, " and "A Sign of the Times, ". These had enough mod swing to sell to a rock audience, but also enough showbizzy horns and theatrical-type piano to bring in older listeners.

Hatch also had a fair amount of success with Jackie Trent, a singer-songwriter who somewhat recalled *Petula Clark* and hit number one with "Where Are You Now (My Love)." Moody balladeer Scott Walker also had a British hit with Hatch-Trent's "Joanna." Hatch recorded a few duets with Trent and made some instrumental recordings under his own name, which gathered some belated hipness when they were included on some CD compilations geared toward the lounge revival crowd. During the '70s, he and Trent wrote a couple of musicals and some television music, including the theme song to "Neighbors." *—Richie Unterberger*

• **The Best of Tony Hatch & His Orchestra** / Feb. 11, 1997 / Sequel ✦✦✦
The third volume in Sequel's *The Easy Project* series includes no less than 30 themes by Tony Hatch & His Orchestra, originally recorded for Pye between 1961 and 1975. Hatch's brand of easy listening was well-constructed orchestral pop, though it was often even blander than the average easy-listening fare. He only charted one single (1962's "Out of This World," obviously included here). Still, there are great versions of "Music to Watch Girls By," "Downtown," and "The Surrey with the Fringe on Top," as well as Hatch's own themes to numerous TV series: "Emmerdale," "Naked City," "Sportsnight," "The Champions," "Mr. and Mrs.," and "Best in Football," among others. It's wonderful to see such a solid collection for this important figure in British pop, but since most of his best work was in service of star vocalists, this compilation of original material is best for only devoted listeners of easy listening. *—John Bush*

Hatchback / Jan. 27, 1998 / Sequel ✦✦

Bert Kaempfert

b. Oct. 16, 1923, Hamburg, Germany, **d.** Jun. 21, 1980, Switzerland
Arranger, Conductor, Prodcuer, Composer / Orchestral Pop
Though best known for the dozens of lush orchestral pop albums he recorded for Decca during the '60s, conductor, arranger and producer Bert Kaempfert was also a hugely successful composer, responsible for perennials including "Spanish Eyes," "Danke Schoen" and "Strangers in the Night"; ironically enough for a figure most closely associated with the rise of easy listening, he also made the very first studio recordings of the Beatles. Kaempfert was born October 16, 1923 in Hamburg, Germany, learning piano as a child and later attending the Hamburg Conservatory of Music. During World War II he performed with the Hans Bussch Orchestra and also worked in radio; after the war, he signed on with the A&R department at Polydor Records, going on to produce Ivo Robic's international hit "Morgen." In 1959, Kaempfert and his studio orchestra released the LP *April in Portugal*, a year later topping the U.S. pop charts with the single "Wonderland"; in all, he scored four Top 40 hits, including 1961's "Tenderly" and a pair of 1965 entries, "Red Roses for a Blue Lady" and "Three O'Clock in the Morning."

Kaempfert's popularity as a recording artist soon brought an end to his A&R duties, although not before he produced a 1961 Hamburg session for singer Tony Sheridan which featured the then-unknown Beatles in support. After completing work on two Sheridan tracks, "My Bonnie" and "When the Saints Go Marching In," Kaempfert also recorded a pair of Beatles cuts, "Ain't She Sweet" and "Cry for a Shadow"—in all, the four songs comprise the Fab Four's earliest official output. In the meantime, Kaempfert continued producing his own material for Decca, generating over 30 LPs for the label between 1959 and 1973; concurrently he composed a series of hits including Al Martino's "Spanish Eyes," Wayne Newton's "Danke Schoen," Nat King Cole's "L-O-V-E," Billy Vaughn's "Swingin' Safari," and Joe Dowell's "Wooden Heart" (the latter originally sung by Elvis Presley in the film *G.I. Blues*). Perhaps his best-known song is "Strangers in the Night," a number one hit for Frank Sinatra in 1966. After leaving Decca, Kaempfert recorded for MCA and Polydor; he died while on vacation in Majorca, Spain on June 21, 1980. *—Jason Ankeny*

Bye Bye Blues / Feb. 14, 1966 / Taragon ✦✦✦

• **The Very Best of Bert Kaempfert** / 1995 / Taragon ✦✦✦✦✦
The Very Best of Bert Kaempfert collects 16 of the easy listening composer's biggest hits, including "Red Roses for a Blue Lady," "Spanish Eyes (Moon Over Naples)," and "Three O'Clock in the Morning." Not all of his hits are inlcuded, but it is the best American CD collection available of Kaempfert's singles. *—Stephen Thomas Erlewine*

That Latin Feeling/Blue Midnight / Dec. 9, 1997 / Taragon ✦✦✦✦

Andre Kostelanetz

b. Dec. 22, 1901, St. Petersburg, Russia, **d.** Jan. 13, 1980, Port-au-Prince, Haiti
Composer / Classical Pop, Orchestral Pop
Andre Kostelanetz arranged classical pieces as easy listening numbers, bringing the music to a broad, middle-brow audience that wouldn't normally have listened to the music. In the process, he inadvertently invented easy listening music. Kostelanetz grasped the power of radio and he adapted his arrangements to fit the conventions of mass communications. In 1924, he made his radio debut, conducting an orchestra. In the '30s, he assembled a 65-piece orchestra, which happened to be the largest orchestra broadcast on radio, for the national show *Andre Kostelanetz Presents*. By the mid-'30s, he was one of the most popular radio stars in the U.S., as evidenced by the sheer amount of awards he won and polls he topped. Not only was he popular, he was quite innovative as well. Kostelanetz understood the potential of recording as a way to expose mass audiences to music. Consequently, he also grasped the technological necessities of recording, and helped promote the value of recording engineers. But his most noteworthy technological advance was his invention of a mechanical tuning instrument, which told musicians whether they were in pitch or not. The device was adapted by the military and used as a way to track submarines. Kostelanetz never lost his popularity, even as musical styles shifted dramatically over the next four decades. Over the course of his career, he sold over 52 million records. *—Stephen Thomas Erlewine*

• **16 Most Requested Songs** / 1972 / Columbia ✦✦✦✦✦
16 Most Requested Songs is a midline-priced collection that spotlights many of Andre Kostelanetz's best-known and most popular performances for Columbia Records, including "My Favourite Things," "Theme From Love Story," "Theme From Romeo and Juliet," "The Way We Were," "All the Things You Are," "Bolero," "Tenderly," "The Godfather Love Theme," "The Impossible Dream," "Till There Was You" and "I Get a Kick Out of You." Although it's far from a perfect retrospective of his career, it's still a nice sampler of familiar items, and it may satisfy the needs of some casual fans who only want the hits. *—Stephen Thomas Erlewine*

Erich Kunzel

Conductor / Instrumental Pop, Orchestral Pop
The most successful Classical/Crossover recording artist in chart history, Erich Kunzel rose to fame during his lengthy reign as the conductor of the Cincinnati Pops Orchestra. He studied under French conductor Pierre Montreux, later serving as his personal assistant; in 1965, Kunzel was invited by music director Max Rudolph to join the Cincinnati Symphony Orchestra, soon taking over their Eight O'Clock Pops series. His affinity for the pops repertoire was immediate, and in 1970 Arthur Fiedler invited him to conduct the Boston Pops; in the years to follow, he returned to Boston annually to assume guest conductor duties, and by the time the Cincinnati Pops Orchestra was officially established in 1977, Kunzel was the obvious choice for conductor. Many of his recordings with the Cincinnati Pops—among them *The Sound of Music, Victory at Sea* and *Chiller*—topped *Billboard*'s chart of best-selling classical crossover records; in total, over three dozen of his works made chart appearances, a number unpredecedented for pops recordings. *—Jason Ankeny*

• **Big Band Hit Parade** / 1988 / Telarc ✦✦✦✦✦

Magical Musical / Sep. 28, 1999 / Telarc ✦✦✦

James Last

b. Apr. 17, 1929, Bremen, Germany
Bass, Conductor, Composer / Cabaret, Big Band
James Last is a German big band leader with a large fan base in Europe, although he has never had a comparable following in the United States. Last's trademark is arranging pop hits in a big band style; his series of "party albums" is equally well-known. Over the course of his career, he has sold well over 50 million albums. Last released his first album, *Non-Stop Dancing*, in 1965. The record of brief renditions of popular songs, all tied together by an insistent dance beat and joyous crowd noises. It was a hit and helped make him a major European star. Over the next two decades, Last released over 50 records, including several more volumes of *Non-Stop Dancing*. On these records, he varied his formula by adding different songs from different countries and genres, as well as guest performers like Richard Clayderman and Astrud Gilberto. Though his concerts and albums were consistently successful—especially in England, where he had 52 hit albums between 1967-86, which made him second to Elvis Presley in terms of number of charting records—he only had one hit single with "The Seduction," the theme from *American Gigolo* (1980). *—Stephen Thomas Erlewine*

● **The Very Best of James Last** / Jan. 1996 / Polydor ✦✦✦✦✦

Liberace (Wladziu Valentino Liberace)

b. 1919, Milwaukee, WI, **d.** Feb. 4, 1987
Piano / Classical Pop, Orchestral Pop
Liberace (born Wladziu Valention Liberace) was the most flamboyant, popular easy listening pianist of the '60s and '70s by a wide margin. His campy, theatrical appearance and performances often disguised his prodigious talent. When he was 11, he debuted as a concert soloist. When he was in his teens, he was performing with symphony orchestras. Instead of following the accepted path of classical recitals and university courses, Liberace chose to be a showman. At encores at his concerts, he began playing novelty songs like "Mairzy Doats." In the late '40s, he signed with Columbia Records and, under the direction of producer Mitch Miller, recorded an over-the-top rendition of "September Song." Along with a live concert album, the single helped bring Liberace to a national audience. Liberace became a star in the '50s, both through his records and assorted television and film appearances. His appearance and repertoire was becoming increasingly campy, as he dressed himself in rhinestone, gold lame, furs, and sequins while playing everything from Gershwin and show tunes to lounge jazz and light classical pieces, with a candelabra placed on his piano. Liberace's star rose rapidly in the early '50s, as he had his own television show, appropriately titled *The Liberace Show.* His celebrity reached a peak in the mid-'50s. Liberace remained a celebrity and a popular performer until his death in 1987. *—Stephen Thomas Erlewine*

● **The Best of Liberace** / 1972 / MCA ✦✦✦✦✦
This is an excellent sampler that showcases the flamboyant, semi-classical style of the pianist, including "Shubert's Serenade." *—David Szatmary*

16 Most Requested Songs / 1990 / Columbia/Legacy ✦✦✦
16 Most Requested Songs is a midline-priced collection that spotlights many of Liberace's best-known and most popular performances for Columbia Records, including "Begin the Beguine," "Stella by Starlight," "Stardust," "Indian Love Call," "I'll Be Seeing You" and "Chopsticks." Although it's far from a perfect retrospective of his career, it's still a nice sampler of familiar items, and it may satisfy the needs of some casual fans who only want the hits. *—Stephen Thomas Erlewine*

The Golden Age of Television, Vol. 1 / 1991 / Curb ✦✦✦

Loungin' with Lee / Jul. 14, 1998 / Hip-O ✦✦✦
Loungin' with Lee is a compilation targeted at the lounge revivalists of "Generation X." Unfortunately (for Hip-O at least), when the disc appeared in 1998, the cocktail nation was beginning to gather moss, thereby shrinking the audience for the disc, leaving Liberace fans with a 15-track collection of some of the pianist's kitschiest, silliest tracks. As a camp exercise, there's little arguing that this is pretty entertaining—it's hard to believe Liberace attempted "Overture from Tommy," but here it is, along with Neil Diamond and Burt Bacharach medleys, Beatles covers, "Send in the Clowns," "You Don't Send Me Flowers," "Strangers in the Night," "El Bimbo" and "Na Na Hey Hey Kiss Him Goodbye." Liberace fans, in all likelihood, probably won't get the arch humor that the compilers intended and simply enjoy this as one of the few Liberace compilations assembled with any care or thought. Those Gen-X kids, however, will know when to laugh and they'll probably have a good time chuckling along. *—Stephen Thomas Erlewine*

Super Hits / May 4, 1999 / Columbia/Legacy ✦✦✦✦
Liberace recorded for a number of different labels during his career, and in the years following his death, a number of budget-line compilations surfaced on a variety of cut-rate labels, so it's easy to forget where he recorded the records that made his career. It was at Columbia, and the 1999 *Super Hits* compilation features ten of those celebrated waxings with Mitch Miller. Since it's only ten songs, it's hardly definitive, but those ten songs are all winners, containing such staples as "Begin the Beguine," "September Song," "Kitten on the Keys," "Warsaw Concerto," "Fantasie Impromptu Op. 66," "Beer Barrel Polka" and "Chopsticks." There are a few other compilations of his Columbia material on the market, but this actually contains more hits than the others, even if it has fewer tracks—and that's why it's a better buy. *—Stephen Thomas Erlewine*

Enoch Light

b. 1935, Canton, OH, **d.** Jul. 31, 1978, New York, NY
Producer / Exotica
Enoch Light was a popular bandleader of the '40s and '50s, best known for his *Persuasive Percussion* and *Provocative Percussion* albums of the mid-'50s, which were some of the first albums to exploit the capabilities of stereo recording and 35mm film as a recording devise. During the '30s, he headed the Enoch Light and the Light Brigade big band, which managed a hit in 1937 with "Summer Night." After the Light Brigade disbanded, Light became a session musician; during the '40s, he recorded versions of popular hits for budget-labels, for sale in discount stores. Light's career bounced back in the late '60s, when the Charleston City All-Stars, under his direction, had a series of hit albums entitled *Roaring Twenties.* He then founded the Command label, which gave him an outlet for his sonically adventurous records. Light happened to begin the label around the time stereo became widely available, and he exploited the new technology to its fullest, creating albums that used the full sonic spectrum of stereo. *—Stephen Thomas Erlewine*

I Want to Be Happy Cha Cha's / 1958 / Grand Award ✦✦✦✦✦
A famous album and a smash success, *I Want to Be Happy Cha Chas* probably can be blamed as much as any Grand Award LP for all the Command records to follow. Actually, *I Want to Be Happy Cha Chas* is less offensive. The percussion and channel separation is not yet pushed to extremes, and the organ duplicates that of the Prado outfit. ("Patricia" and "Guaglione" are covered.) Latin fans may despise North American tunes that were adapted to the cha cha cha and cheesily arranged, but it is certainly a classic album of its kind. *—Tony Wilds*

☆ **Persuasive Percussion, Vol. 1** / 195 / Command ✦✦✦✦✦
Persuasive Percussion, Vol. 1 collects a number of tracks featuring layers of exotic percussion. Primarily, this record—like its companion, *Provocative Percusssion*—was designed to showcase hi-fi equipment, but it's weird, inventive polyrhythms made it a cult favorite. *—Stephen Thomas Erlewine*

Brass Menagerie, 1973 / 1973 / Project 3 ✦✦✦

★ **Persuasive Percussion** / 1995 / Varese ✦✦✦✦✦
Between 1959 and 1961, Enoch Light released three LPs called *Persuasive Percussion* and two called *Provocative Percussion,* and it was all pretty much the same sort of stuff, i.e., instrumental treatments of pop standards in bouncy, exotic arrangements that emphasized the rhythm section and such unusual instruments as bongos and car horns. Each of the albums hit the Top Ten. Confusingly enough, this 40-track reissue, which adopts the name *Persuasvie Percussion,* is actually a compilation of those five albums—11 tracks from the original *Persuasive Percussion,* eight from *Persuasive Percussion, Volume 2,* two from *Persuasive Percussion, Volume 3,* 12 from *Provocative Percussion* (the whole record, though not in exact sequence), and seven from *Provocative Percussion, Volume 2.* But since it is pretty much the same sort of stuff, the re-sequencing works as well as the original did, and you don't have to get up off the couch so often to turn over the record. *—Tony Wilds*

Guy Lombardo

b. Jun. 19, 1902, London, Ontario, Canada, **d.** Nov. 5, 1977
Vocals, Violin, Conductor / Sweet Bands, Traditional Pop, Dance Bands, Show Tunes, Orchestral Pop, Big Band
"The Sweetest Music This Side of Heaven" was the logo of Guy Lombardo & His Royal Canadians, who by 1930 had established themselves as America's top dance band. Unfairly lumped in with unswinging "mickey mouse" bands of the era, the music of Lombardo's outfit was actually top-notch, and they were constantly cited by Louis Armstrong as his favorite band for their purity of intonation. A cache of early sides for Gennett reveals that the band was capable of playing "hot" any time they wanted to, but sweet music is what the public wanted, and Lombardo never failed to disappoint. He became a national institution hosting televised New Year's Eve broadcasts from New York, making his rendition of "Auld Lang Syne" part of our national memory chest and his lasting legacy. Lombardo formed his first band in 1924, with brothers Lebert, Carmen, and Victor. After moving from Canada to Cleveland, they inevitably ended up in New York and began a long string of hits in 1927 that ran all the way to 1954. Between those years, Lombardo and his Royal Canadians sold well over 100 milllion records on a variety of labels, including Columbia, Brunswick, Decca, and RCA/Victor. Lombardo continued to lead musical productions at New York's Marine Theatre until his death in 1977. *—Cub Koda & Stephen Thomas Erlewine*

16 Most Requested Songs / 1989 / Columbia/Legacy ✦✦✦

★ **Enjoy Yourself: The Hits of Guy Lombardo** / Oct. 22, 1996 / MCA ✦✦✦✦✦
Enjoy Yourself: The Hits of Guy Lombardo is the finest collection ever assembled of Lombardo's biggest hits, including "Penny Serenade," "Nicaragua," "The Band Played On," "Enjoy Yourself (It's Later than You Think)," and "Auld Lang Syne." It's the most comprehensive compilation of Lombardo recordings ever assembled, touching on all aspects of his career and featuring the original versions of his best-known material. *—Stephen Thomas Erlewine*

The V-Disc Recordings / Nov. 17, 1998 / Collectors' Choice Music ✦✦✦✦

Norman Luboff

b. May 14, 1917, Chicago, IL, **d.** Sep. 22, 1987
Vocals, Arranger, Choir / Chanukah, Film Music, Vocal Pop, Choral, Christmas
The Norman Luboff Choir was among the most popular choral ensembles of their day, releasing a series of hit easy-listening LPs during the late 1950s and 1960s. Luboff was born May 14, 1917 in Chicago, where he began his career as a vocalist and arranger for area radio programs; in 1948 he relocated to Hollywood, signing on to compose movie music for Warner Bros. The first incarnation of the Norman Luboff Choir was formed during the mid-1950s, and in the years to follow they released a series of albums on Columbia that drew on music from a variety of genres and geographic locales, with titles including *Calypso Holiday, Broadway!, Songs of the Cowboy* and *Songs of the Caribbean.* The choir also backed a number of vocalists including Harry Belafonte and Doris Day, and although their recording career came to a halt during the late 1960s, they continued touring until Luboff's cancer-related death on September 22, 1987. *—Jason Ankeny*

Ticket to the Movies / Oct. 12, 1999 / Taragon ✦✦✦✦
Positioned somewhere between the grand chorales of Europe and the populism of Mitch Miller stood Norman Luboff, who could move his choir between the twin poles of classical and popular music. On this set, he puts the choir members through their paces on a number of movie song favorites with typical results. Highlights include "All the Things You Are," "High Noon," "Stella by Starlight," "Laura," "Unchained Melody," "Ruby," "An Affair to Remember," and "It's Magic." *—Cub Koda*

● **Songs of the South/Songs of the Sea** / Nov. 23, 1999 / Collectables ✦✦✦✦

Arthur Lyman

b. 1934, Kauai, HI
Vibraphone, Conga, Bongos, Piano, Guitar, Arranger / Lounge, Exotica
As the vibraphonist for Martin Denny's group, Lyman was instrumental in crafting the sound of exotica. Lyman didn't stay with Denny for long, however, leaving the ensemble in 1957 to start a solo career that was nearly as successful as Denny's. To no one's surprise, Lyman's albums sounded very much like Denny's, with even more of a somnambulent feel. Much of the public wanted to relax, though, and they sent his debut, *Taboo,* to #6 in the album charts in 1958. In addition to playing vibes on his group's recordings, Lyman also played some guitar, piano, and drums, as well as paying careful attention to using stereophonic sound.

Lyman also had a few hit singles, with "Taboo" and "Love For Sale" reaching the middle of the charts, and "Yellow Bird" (the only big exotica hit besides Denny's "Quiet Village") making *4 in 1961. Like Denny* (though to a lesser extent), Lyman experienced a resurgence in popularity in the 1990s, when the space age pop revival made it acceptable to drag out his old LPs and sit in tiki bars again. *—Richie Unterberger*

The Legend of Pele: Sounds of Arthur Lyman / 1957 / Rykodisc ✦✦✦
Arthur Lyman's enchanted vibraphone conjures exotic magic on this Rykodisc reissue. *The Legend of Pele* is a series of material loosely based on the elusive and transforming Hawaiian volcano goddess, creating soundscapes of land and fauna in awe of a powerful and unpredictable force. Lyman's vibe-powered lounge music is subtle as a tropical mist on "Cumana." Lyman's use of four-mallet vibes (a pair in each hand) and added instrumentation of guitar, ukulele, flute, and glockenspiel result in a mix that is unhindered by much mid- and low-range instrumentation. Thus soaring, Lyman provides aerial views of mysterious and beautiful oceanic utopias and dresses up such varied standards as "76 Trombones" and Rimsky-Korsakov's "Scherezade." *—Tom Schulte*

Taboo / 1958 / Rykodisc ✦✦✦
Lyman's debut album, recorded shortly after he left Martin Denny's group, was almost as popular as the concurrent releases by his former mentor, reaching the Top Ten. Purists may hang me for this, but I honestly don't detect much difference between Lyman's late '50s releases and Denny's. Meaning, if you like one, you'll most likely want the other, and if you're not all that excited about exotica to begin with, one Denny compilation should be all you need. If there are any subtle differences between the pair, Lyman may have a slightly sedate, jazzier sound, though he too uses a wide variety of ethnic instruments, percussions, and bird calls. The CD reissue adds four tracks from the *Bwana A* album. *—Richie Unterberger*

Leis of Jazz: Jazz Sounds of Arthur Lyman / Feb. 19, 1959 / Rykodisc ✦✦

The Best of the Arthur Lyman Group / 1996 / DCC ✦✦✦
For those that are hooked on Martin Denny and want something similar—or, for those who find Martin Denny just a tad too upbeat and extroverted. This has 18 of Lyman's vintage tracks, including the modest hits "Taboo" and "Love For Sale." Oddly, his Top Ten single "Yellow Bird" is missing, although it's on DCC's *More Of The Arthur Lyman Group*. *—Richie Unterberger*

● **More of the Best of the Arthur Lyman Group** / 1996 / DCC ✦✦✦✦✦
When you choose between vintage Arthur Lyman compilations, there's really no specific criteria to use. You're about as well off with this one as DCC's *The Best of*—if you like Lyman a lot, you'll want both, and if you're lukewarm about his brand of exotica, you shouldn't get either. The only reason this gets a slight edge is for the inclusion of "Yellow Bird," ahis 1961 Top Ten hit. It also has Lyman's version of "Quiet Village," a Top Ten hit for his former employer, Martin Denny. *—Richie Unterberger*

Yellow Bird / 1998 / Rykodisc ✦✦✦

Taboo, Vol. 2: New Exotic Sounds of Arthur Lyman / Mar. 17, 1998 / Rykodisc ✦✦✦
This stands up to any Martin Denny album as an example of exotica in full flight, decorated with lots of bird noises and soft vibraphone. The songs do tend to melt into each other without much in the way of striking differences, and it's not likely it would be played often except by those who can't get enough Lyman in the house. "Jungle Fantasy," though, is notable as an example of exotica at its most frenetic, with exuberant bird-calls from the band and a fast tempo that has more in common with rumbas than Hawaiian music. The CD reissue restores the original sleeve, whose distorted tikified heads were considered "too gruesome" upon its initial release. *—Richie Unterberger*

Henry Mancini

b. 1924, Cleveland, OH, **d.** Jun. 14, 1994
Piano, Conductor, Composer, Arranger, Strings / Spy Music, Movie Themes, Television Music, Original Score, Lounge, Mood Music, Television Soundtracks, Instrumental Pop, Orchestral Pop, Christmas

If the recognition of one's peers is the true measure of success, then few men are as successful as composer, arranger, and conductor Henry Mancini. In a career that spanned 40 years, Mancini won more Grammy awards than any other pop artist (five for 1961's *Breakfast at Tiffany's* alone). Though a stint in the military during World War II curtailed his musical study, Mancini worked for the post-war Glenn Miller Orchestra as a pianist and arranger, then began writing scores for film studios—his first was the Abbot and Costello film *Lost in Alaska*. Soon, he was working on a large number of films and television programs, including Orson Welles' *Touch of Evil* and the TV show *Peter Gunn*. Mancini's scores frequently straddled the line between jazz and Hollywood dramatics, making his music both distinctive and influential.

Mancini's heyday was the early '60s, when his score for *Breakfast at Tiffany's* (1961) yielded the Oscar-winning hit single "Moon River," arguably one of the finest pop songs of the last 50 years. Just one year later, he won another Oscar for the title song to *Days of Wine and Roses*. Throughout the next three decades, he continued to be one of the most successful film composers in the world (as well as a popular concert conductor), his work constantly fresh due to his ability to write in almost any style imaginable and his successful experimentations with unusual sounds and instruments. *—Kenneth M. Cassidy & Stephen Thomas Erlewine*

☆ **The Music from Peter Gunn** / 1959 / Buddha ✦✦✦✦✦
This is not only a great CD but a key piece of jazz and pop music history. Back in 1958, *Peter Gunn* was one of the unexpected hits of the new television season, capturing the imagination of millions of viewers by mixing private eye action with a jazz setting. Composer Henry Mancini was more than fluent in jazz, and his music nailed down the popularity of the series. With the main title theme, a driving, ominous, exciting piece of music to lead off the album, *The Music from Peter Gunn* became a huge hit, charting extraordinarily high for a television soundtrack and doing so well that RCA Victor came back the next year asking for a second helping (*More Music From Peter Gunn*) from Mancini. The music holds up: "Session at Pete's Pad" is a superb workout for the trumpets of Pete Candoli, Uan Rasey, Conrad Gozzo, and Frank Beach, while Barney Kessel's electric guitar gets the spotlight during "Dreamsville"; and "Sorta Blue" and "Fallout" are full-ensemble pieces that constitute quintessential "cool" West Coast jazz of the period. In other words, it's all virtuoso orchestral jazz, presented in its optimum form.

In 1999 the reactivated Buddha Records label gave *The Music from Peter Gunn* a new and sharper digital transfer and added the four best tracks on *More Music from Peter Gunn*. The improved sound and the extra tracks definitely justify the upgrade for those who own the old CD, and make this a doubly valuable addition to any jazz or soundtrack collection of the era. *—Bruce Eder*

Charade / 1963 / RCA ✦✦✦✦✦
Reflecting the European setting of Stanley Donen's 1963 comedy thriller *Charade*, Henry Mancini's soundtrack provides an easy listening tour of continental musical history: Parisian café songs on "Bistro," Eastern European gypsy music on "Bateau Mouche," Schubert quartets on "Bye Charlie," and some beer barrel polka on "Punch and Judy." Thrown in for variety's sake are dashes of Bond soundtracks, Cossack songs, and Strauss waltzes. With Mancini's typically cohesive approach, though, *Charade* doesn't become a messy pastiche (even with his mix of Latin rhythms and classical music on some tracks). And in the spirit of inclusiveness, Mancini also shows his south of the border touch on "Mambo Parisienne" (picture Perez Prado sporting an accordion), "Latin Snowfall" (transcendentally gorgeous bolero, one of his best), and "Mégève" (bossa nova for the Biarritz set). Also don't overlook one of his biggest hits and finest melodies, "Charade" (done here in instrumental, vocal, and carousel— versions). A great Mancini recording made during the same fruitful, early-'60s period that produced two other fine soundtracks of his, *Breakfast at Tiffany's* and *The Pink Panther*. *—Stephen Cook*

☆ **Days of Wine and Roses** / Oct. 10, 1995 / RCA ✦✦✦✦✦
Days of Wine and Roses is a comprehensive three-disc box set featuring all of Henry Mancini's most popular and best-known works in their original versions. For some, the sheer extensiveness of the set may be a bit intimidating—after all, three discs is a lot for casual fans—but for serious fans of the composer, it's an essential purchase. *—Stephen Thomas Erlewine*

★ **Greatest Hits** / Sep. 26, 2000 / RCA ✦✦✦✦✦
Greatest Hits is a terrific compilation of 22 digitally remastered Henry Mancini favorites, including his soundtrack themes "Peter Gunn," "The Pink Panther Theme," "Love Theme From Romeo and Juliet," "Mr. Lucky," and "Breakfast at Tiffany's," among many others. The collection also includes well-known Mancini tunes like "Moon River," "The Days of Wine and Roses," "Baby Elephant Walk," and "Dear Heart" to name a few. The sound is crystal clear and the track selection demonstrates over and over again Mancini's gifts for melody and mood. Overall, it's probably the best single-disc introduction to Mancini's work yet assembled. *—Steve Huey*

Breakfast at Tiffany's / 1961 / RCA ✦✦✦✦✦
This soundtrack to the movie adaptation of Truman Capote's novel *Breakfast at Tiffany's* is one of Henry Mancini's best. The pleasing blend of pop (the perennial "Moonriver") and swing stays fresh over the album's 12 tracks and shows off Mancini's considerable writing and arranging skills. The cuts range from the layered, big-band mambo "Something for Cat" to the transcendently smooth lounge number "Sally's Tomato" with some vaudeville moments coming via "Mr. Yunioshi" (check out that banjo eating up the faux Japanese scales) and "Hub Caps and Tail Lights" (sounds like the "Adams Family Theme"). Mancini keeps the lounge/easy listening mood from collapsing in on itself with many fine jazz solos, a driving rhythm section, and his expert (yet pleasantly cheesy) handling of the liquid-toned chorus parts. He also strikes a nice balance here between his crime-jazz backdrops for the *Peter Gunn* TV show and *Touch of Evil* and the later, more streamlined soundtracks for *The Pink Panther* and *Charade*. Through *Breakfast at Tiffany's* solid program, Macnini makes it clear that he isn't just a peddler of muzak but a fine composer. *—Stephen Cook*

Mantovani (Annunzio Paolo Mantovani)

b. Nov. 15, 1905, Venice, Italy, **d.** Mar. 30, 1980, England
Violin, Conductor, Composer, Arranger, Strings / Mood Music, Instrumental Pop, Orchestral Pop

Violinist, composer, and conductor Annunzio Paolo Mantovani was born in Venice, Italy. He started working in London at 16 and was conducting The Hotel Metropal Orchestra by 1925. Mantovani was a major pioneer in the heavy use of strings and one of the first to be almost exclusively interested in recorded rather than live music. He also was one of the first popular artists to concentrate on producing albums rather than singles. He had seven million-selling albums, including *Immortal Classics* (1954) and *Exodus and Other Great Themes* (1960). In 1935-1936 Mantovani had hits in the US with "Red Sails in the Sunset" and "Serenade to the Night." He was soon recognised as the undisputed king of easy listening, or mood music, as it was called then. He had 51 hit albums in the U.S. alone. *—Michael Erlewine*

● **Mantovani's Golden Hits** / Mar. 1967 / London ✦✦✦✦✦

Paul Mauriat

b. 1925, France
Arranger / Easy Pop, Instrumental Pop

French composer/conductor Paul Mauriat is a classically trained musician who decided to pursue a career in popular music. Throughout the '40s and the '50s, he worked primarily as an arranger for other musicians. Mauriat began a solo career in the early '60s, recording a series of instrumental albums that were distinguished by their sweeping, melodic strings and gently insistent contemporary rhythms. Using the pseudonym Del Roma, he co-wrote "Chariot" which became a hit for Petula Clark in 1962. The following year, the song was given a new, English lyric by Arthur Altman and Norman Gimbel and recorded by Little Peggy March as "I Will Follow Him"; it became a number one hit in the U.S. Throughout the '60s, Mauriat continued to record his pop instrumental albums, which became more popular as the decade progressed. His popularity peaked in 1968, when his version of "L'Amour Est Bleu" ("Love Is Blue"), which was Luxembourg's submission to the 1963 Eurovision Song contest, became an international hit, reaching number one on a number of charts, including America. *—Stephen Thomas Erlewine & Kenneth M. Cassidy*

● **Love Is Blue** / 1967 / Mercury ♦♦♦♦

Meco (Meco Monardo)

b. Nov. 29, 1939, Johnsonburg, PA
Producer / Disco

Producer and studio musician Meco marked a confluence of the two dominant pop-culture preoccupations of the late '70s, shooting to fame on the heels of a chart-topping disco rendition of the theme to *Star Wars.* Born Meco Monardo in Johnsonburg, Pennsylvania in 1939, he took up the trombone at the age of nine, and later earned a scholarship to the Eastman School of Music in Rochester, New York. There Meco formed a jazz trio with fellow students Chuck Mangione and Ron Carter, later enlisting with the West Point Army Band. From 1965 to 1974, Meco worked as a studio player, and also landed a number of arranging gigs, most notably on Tommy James' "Crystal Blue Persuasion." He additionally arranged and performed the music on a series of television commercials.

Meco's breakthrough arrived in 1974 when he co-produced the Gloria Gaynor smash "Never Can Say Goodbye," followed by the Carol Douglas masterpiece "Doctor's Orders." In 1977, Meco saw the George Lucas film *Star Wars* on the day of its release and quickly became obsessed, seeing the picture numerous times; while admiring producer John Williams' score, he felt the music lacked commercial possibilites, and soon contacted Casablanca Records chief Neil Bogart about the possibility of a disco version. Working with veteran Broadway arranger Harold Wheeler, Meco recorded *Star Wars and Other Galactic Funk;* soon the first single, "Star Wars Theme/Cantina Band," rose to number one. Although he recorded similar music inspired by films including *The Wizard of Oz* and *Close Encounters of the Third Kind,* Meco remained most closely associated with *Star Wars,* even recording a highly successful Christmas album based on the movie; he retired from music in 1985, later working as a commodities broker in Florida. *—Jason Ankeny*

● **The Best of Meco** / Feb. 4, 1997 / Mercury ♦♦♦♦
The Best of Meco is an exhaustive and carefully assembled collection of the producer/keyboardist's disco-fied renditions of popular movie themes; opening with his biggest hit, "Star Wars Theme/Cantina Band," the disc also includes singular performances of "Theme From Close Encounters," "Themes From the Wizard of Oz," and "Love Theme From Superman (Can You Read My Mind—)," plus most of his breakout recording *Star Wars & Other Galactic Funk.* While certainly a one-of-a-kind document of the cultural forces at work during the late '70s, at over 74 minutes in length, it's nevertheless guaranteed to tax the endurance of all but the most devoted fans. *—Jason Ankeny*

Sergio Mendes

b. Feb. 11, 1941, Niteroi, Brazil
Piano, Producer, Composer, Arranger / Lounge, Soft Rock, Bossa Nova, Samba, Pop, Latin Pop

For most of the second half of the 1960s, Sergio Mendes was the top selling Brazilian artist in the United States, charting huge hit singles and LPs that regularly made the top five. His records with his group Brasil '66 regularly straddled the domestic pop and international markets in America, getting played heavily on AM radio stations, both rock and easy listening, and he gave his label, A&M, something to offer light jazz listeners beyond the work of the company's co-founder, Herb Alpert. During this period, he also became an international music star and one of the most popular musicians in South America.

His early music, represented on albums like *Bossa Nova York* and *Girl from Ipanema,* was heavily influenced by Antonio Carlos Jobim. After recording for Capitol without attracting too much notice, Mendes and his group Brasil '66 was successful upon the release of their first album for A&M, with its mix of light jazz, a bossa nova beat, and contemporary soft pop melodies. The group's third album, *Look Around,* rose to No. 5 behind a cover of the Beatles' "Fool on the Hill". Depending upon one's sensibilities, cover versions like "Fool on the Hill", "Scarborough Fair", and Otis Redding's "(Sittin' On) The Dock of the Bay" were either legitimate internationalized pop versions of the originals, or they were "elevator music."

Mendes seemed to lose his commercial edge with the turn of the decade, though, and his next two A&M albums, *Stillness* and *Primal Roots,* failed to make any impression on the charts whatsoever. The group moved to the much smaller Bell Records label in 1973, and then Mendes jumped to Elektra for his first official solo album, the self-titled *Sergio Mendes.* He re-launched his recording career two years later with *Sergio Mendes & Brasil '77,* to little avail, though his 1983 comeback album, *Sergio Mendes,* was his most popular album in over a decade and was accompanied by his biggest chart single ever, "Never Gonna Let You Go". Since then, Mendes has had limited chart success, though he has remained a popular figure internationally. *—Bruce Eder*

Quiet Nights / 1963 / Philips ♦♦♦

In the Brazilian Bag / 1965 / Tower ST ♦♦♦♦♦

The Great Arrival / 1966 / Atlantic ♦♦♦

Sergio Mendes & Brasil 66 / 1966 / A&M ♦♦♦♦♦
After bouncing around Philips, Atlantic, and Capitol playing Brazilian jazz or searching for an ideal blend of Brazilian and American pop, Sergio Mendes struck gold on his first try at A&M (then not much more than the home of Herb Alpert & the Tijuana Brass and the Baja Marimba Band). He came up with a marvelously sleek, sexy formula: dual American female voices singing in English and Portuguese over a nifty three-man bossa nova rhythm/vocal section and Mendes' distinctly jazz-oriented piano, performing tight, infectious arrangements of carefully chosen tunes from Brazil, the U.S., and the U.K. The hit was Jorge Ben's "Mais Que Nada," given a catchy, tight bossa nova arrangement with the voice of Lani Hall soaring above the swinging rhythm section. But other tracks leap out as well; the obvious rouser is the Brazilian go-go treatment of the Beatles' "Day Tripper," but the sultry treatment of Henry Mancini's "Slow Hot Wind" and the rapid-fire "Tim Dom Dom" also deserve mention. Miraculously, Mendes' original Brasil '66 still sounds fresh today; Mendes' piano especially appears not to have dated at all. *—Richard S. Ginell*

Equinox / 1967 / A&M ♦♦♦♦♦
Equinox continues the scrumptiously winning sound that Sergio Mendes cooked up in the mid-'60s, this time a bit more fleshed out with John Pisano's guitar, a slightly thicker texture, and even an imitation sitar (this was, after all, 1967). Again, the mix of American pop tunes old and new and Brazilian standards and sleepers is impeccable (although it didn't yield any substantial hits), and the treatments are smooth, swinging, and very much to the point. While Mendes reaps a predictable harvest from Antonio Carlos Jobim—he was one of the first to discover and record "Triste" and "Wave"—he also likes to explore the work of other outstanding Brazilian writers like Jorge Ben, Joao Gilberto, and especially Edu Lobo (whose "For Me," with its bright flashes of combo organ, is one of the album's highlights). Lani Hall's star was just rising at this time, and it is her cool, clear voice that haunts the memory most often. Like its predecessor, *Equinox* is exceedingly brief in duration, yet not a motion is wasted. *—Richard S. Ginell*

Fool on the Hill / 1968 / A&M ♦♦♦♦♦
Having hit upon another smash formula—cover versions of pop/rock hits backed by lavish strings, a simplified bossa nova rhythm, and the leader's piano comping—Sergio Mendes & Brasil '66 produced two more chart-busting singles, again turning to the Beatles for sustenance with the title track (number six) and Simon & Garfunkel for "Scarborough Fair" (number 16). But again, the bulk of the album was dominated by Brazilians, and by one in particular: the hugely gifted Edu Lobo, whose dramatic "Casa Forte" and infectious "Upa, Neguinho" were the best of his four songs. The tracks were longer now, the string-laden ballads (arranged by Dave Grusin) more lavish and moody, and Lani Hall emerged as the vocal star of the band, eclipsing her new partner, Karen Philipp (although Hall is upstaged on "Lapinha" by future Brasil '77 member Gracinha Leporace). Even though he had become thoroughly embedded in the consciousness of mainstream America, Mendes still managed to have it three ways, exposing first-class tunes from little-known Brazilian talent, garnering commercial hits, and also making some fine records. Cultural note: the striking foldout cover art, depicting Brasil '66 at sunset seated on top of a nude woman, somehow made it past the uptight censors of the day and no doubt boosted sales; it was Mendes' highest-charting album at number three. *—Richard S. Ginell*

Look Around / 1968 / A&M ♦♦♦♦♦
Sergio Mendes took a deep breath, expanded his sound to include strings lavishly arranged by the young Dave Grusin and Dick Hazard, went further into Brazil, and out came a gorgeous record of Brasil '66 at the peak of its form. Here Mendes released himself from any reliance upon Antonio Carlos Jobim and rounded up a wealth of truly great material from Brazilian fellow travelers: Gilberto Gil's jet-propelled "Roda" and Joao Donato's clever "The Frog," Dori Caymmi's stunningly beautiful "Like a Lover," Harold Lobo's carnival-esque "Tristeza," and Mendes himself (the haunting "So Many Stars" and the title track). Mendes was also hip enough to include "With a Little Help From My Friends" from the Beatles' *Sgt. Pepper* LP. As things evolved, though, the one track that this album would be remembered for is the only other non-Brazilian tune, Burt Bacharach's "The Look of Love," in an inventive, grandiose arrangement with a simplified bossa beat. The tune just laid there on the album until Mendes and company performed it on the Academy Awards telecast in 1968. The performance was a sonic disaster, but no matter; the public response was huge, a single was released, and it become a monster, number four on the pop charts. So much for the reported demise of bossa nova; in Sergio Mendes' assimilating, reshaping hands, allied with Herb Alpert's flawless production, it was still a gold mine. *—Richard S. Ginell*

Crystal Illusions / 1969 / A&M ♦♦♦♦

Ye-Me-Le / 1969 / A&M ♦♦♦

★ **Greatest Hits of Brasil '66** / 1970 / A&M ♦♦♦♦♦
A 1970 release, along with a slew of other A&M greatest-hits collections, *Greatest Hits* takes us through a dozen Sergio Mendes and Brasil '66 tunes from the albums *Herb Alpert Presents* through *Crystal Illusions.* Not all of these were hits—indeed, not all of them were singles—and they are not representative of the wide range of Brazilian material that Mendes cut during this period. But you do get a good idea of how Mendes' winningly sexy blend of American female voices, simplified bossa nova rhythms, and lavish Dave Grusin orchestrations captivated mainstream America in the late 1960s. *Look Around* receives by far the most attention, with five tracks—which is only fitting, since in retrospect, that appears to be Mendes' most irresistibly memorable album. For a more comprehensive overview of Sergio Mendes on CD, though, *Classics Volume 18* is a better bet. *—Richard S. Ginell*

Pais Tropical / 1971 / A&M ♦♦♦

In Concert / 1972 / A&M ♦♦♦♦

Four Sider / May 27, 1988 / A&M ♦♦♦♦♦
Covering the extent of Brasil '66's output from 1966-1972, *Four Sider* is the best available retrospective for those new to Mendes' successful Brazilian pop outfit (the 45-song *Very Best of Sergio Mendes & Brasil '66* offers a more comprehensive, yet potentially daunting overview). Typical of the band's original albums, *Four Sider* includes a mix of Brazilian material and '60s pop hits. Also on display is Mendes' winning blend of bossa nova rhythms and lounge-a-go-go elements (churning organ riffs and rock bass lines), complimented by a variety of percussion, airy vocal harmonies, and his own jazz-informed keyboard contributions and horn charts. Highlights include renditions of the Beatles' "Nowhere Man" and Joni Mitchell's "Chelsea Morning," in addition to several Brazilian hits, like Jorge Ben's "Mais Que Nada" and Antonio Carlos Jobim's "Wave." Other Brazilian luminaries are represented as well, in-

cluding Edu Lobo, Dori Caymmi, and Oscar Neves, not to mention Mendes himself ("Look Around"). Wrapping up the set are a few Brasil '77 cuts, which spotlight the post-bossa nova sounds of tropicalismo (Ben's "Pais Tropical" and Mendes' "Promise of a Fisherman"). This is a fine collection; one that shows Mendes wasn't simply another space-age bachelor, but an innovative musician and arranger as well. *—Stephen Cook*

The Very Best of Sergio Mendes & Brasil 66 / 1997 / A&M ✦✦✦✦✦
Although it's not assembled chronologically, the 48-track, double-disc *The Very Best of Sergio Mendes & Brasil 66* is a near-definitive collection, featuring all of the group's hits plus a good selection of their album tracks and lesser-known singles. For fans who want a little more than a single-disc collection, this is an ideal purchase, even if it might be a little bit too much for some listeners. *—Stephen Thomas Erlewine*

Hugo Montenegro

b. 1925, New York, NY, **d.** Feb. 6, 1981
Conductor, Arranger / Spy Music, Movie Themes, Film Music, Instrumental Pop, Orchestral Pop
Hugo Montenegro was a composer, arranger, and conductor, who is primarily known for his movie work in the '60s, as well as his adaptations of film scores like *The Good, the Bad, and the Ugly*. Initially, Montenegro was the staff manager to Andre Kostelanetz at Columbia Records in New York, which eventually led to a job as a conductor/arranger for several of the label's artists, most notably Harry Belafonte. By the mid-'50s, Montenegro was making his own albums of easy listening orchestral music. Montenegro moved to California in the mid-'60s and began to write film scores, starting with Otto Preminger's *Hurry Sundown* in 1967. That same year, he recorded a version of the theme to *The Good, the Bad and the Ugly*, which was written by Ennio Morricone. Featuring an arrangement that relied on a chorus, electric instruments, and special effects, the single was a major hit, reaching number one in the U.K. and number two in the U.S.; internationally, it sold over a million copies. Montenegro began to branch out after the *Hang 'Em High* album, recording a diverse array of albums, ranging from show tunes to electronic experiments. *—Stephen Thomas Erlewine*

☆ **The Good, the Bad & the Ugly** / 1992 / RCA ✦✦✦✦✦
Certainly purists will prefer the versions of these classic Ennio Morricone spaghetti Western soundtracks conducted by Morricone himself to the ones on this compilation, which were arranged and conducted by Hugo Montenegro. Still, anyone who likes prime Morricone from that era will probably enjoy this CD quite a bit. Containing pieces from three of the most famous Morricone-scored films, all of the material was released in 1967, and it must be said that Montenegro didn't miss a trick, employing the low twangy guitars, weeping horns, and ghostly whistles that are usually identified as Morricone trademarks. Perhaps these are a tad more bombastic, orchestrated, and pop-slanted than Morricone's own versions but, if anything, Montenegro's touches enhance the grandiose sadness of the melodies. Contains the massive hit version of the theme from *The Good, the Bad and the Ugly*, which went to number two in 1968. *—Richie Unterberger*

All-Time Greatest Movie Themes & Schemes / Aug. 24, 1999 / RCA ✦✦✦✦
All-Time Greatest Movie Themes & Schemes presents only the tautest of strings and brassiest of arrangements; that is, Hugo Montenegro's versions of the most famous spy and Western themes of the '60s, including "Secret Agent Man," "The Man From U.N.C.L.E.," "Get Smart," "Goldfinger," "The Godfather," and "The Good, the Bad & the Ugly." Though most of these aren't going to be the versions most listeners recognize, Montenegro's wonderful arrangements and impeccable sense of sound make every song fun to listen to. Definitely a notch above the average novelty collection. *—John Bush*

Peter Nero

b. May 22, 1934, Brooklyn, NY
Piano / Classical Pop, Mainstream Jazz, Swing, Instrumental Pop
Peter Nero (born Bernard Nierow, 1934, Brooklyn) is a pianist and New York native who started with Paul Whiteman, then moved up to symphony until the early '60s, when RCA Victor signed him and successfully promoted him into a pop music interpreter. His lush orchestrated albums continued through the early '70s, when he returned to a harder jazz format, recording with a trio. For several years, he played New York's club circuit before he came to the attention of Stan Greeson, an executive at RCA Records. Convinced that Nierow had star potential, Greeson signed the pianist and had him change his name to Peter Nero; he also persuaded Nero to add pop songs like "Over the Rainbow" to his repertoire. *Piano Forte*, Peter Nero's first album, was released in 1961 and he began touring the country. Nero's popularity continued to rise throughout the early '60s; his jazzy hybrid of pop, classical, swing, and bop became one of the most popular mainstream sounds of the era. *—Cub Koda*

Hail the Conquering Nero / 1963 / RCA ✦✦✦✦✦

Nero Goes "Pops" / 1965 / RCA ✦✦✦
An interesting, largely successful album with Arthur Fiedler and the Boston Pops Orchestra. *—Cub Koda*

● **Peter Nero's Greatest Hits** / 1974 / Columbia ✦✦✦✦✦

Nelson Riddle

b. Jun. 1, 1921, Oradell, NJ, **d.** Oct. 6, 1985, Los Angeles, CA
Trombone, Conductor, Arranger / Television Music, Traditional Pop, Film Music, Orchestral Pop
While Nelson Riddle had experience as a trombonist and arranger for Charlie Spivak, Jerry Wald, and Tommy Dorsey in the '40s and was a staff arranger for NBC radio later in that era, he achieved his greatest success and notoriety during the '50s. Riddle was the arranger and conductor for Judy Garland, Jimmy Wakely, Betty Hutton, Ella Mae Morse, and many others in the early '50s, including Nat King Cole, but became the top arranger in Hollywood through his collaborations with Frank Sinatra during 1953. Riddle's orchestrations and careful, intelligent use of first-class jazz musicians accented Sinatra's voice perfectly, without obscuring, challenging, or threatening. No one was better at knowing when to increase the brass section's volume, how to support a singer, and what soloist to spotlight and for how long.. *—Ron Wynn*

Joy of Living/Love Is a Game of Poker / 1997 / EMI ✦✦✦✦
British EMI repackages two Nelson Riddle albums on one CD, revealing the arranger, conductor, and (sometime) composer's evolution from his bouncy 1950s style to a more melodramatic approach in the early '60s. During the period covered by *The Joy of Living* (1959), Riddle was writing charts for Frank Sinatra, Nat "King" Cole, and others, and his work on the album had some of the smooth style of later Capitol Sinatra concept albums like *Nice 'n' Easy*. By the time of *Love Is a Game of Poker* (1962), Riddle, following on from Henry Mancini's *Peter Gunn* breakthrough, was writing music and arrangements for TV shows like *The Untouchables* and *Route 66*, and his work on the album was harder-edged and jazzier. Juxtaposed on the same CD, therefore, the music seems to perk up halfway through, though Riddle never loses his tasteful emphasis on melody. *—William Ruhlmann*

Hey . . . Let Yourself Go!/C'mon . . . Get Happy! / Sep. 12, 2000 / Collectors' Choice Music ✦✦✦✦
Hey . . . Let Yourself Go!/C'mon . . . Get Happy! puts Nelson Riddle's 1957 and 1958 albums, both of which reached the Top 20, onto one CD. Smooth, artfully arranged versions of "September in the Rain," "Let's Face the Music and Dance," "Younger Than Springtime," and "Am I Blue—" are some of the highlights of this collection of sophisticated instrumental pop. *—Heather Phares*

★ **The Best of Nelson Riddle** / Capitol ✦✦✦✦✦
The Best of Nelson Riddle doesn't offer a comprehensive overview of the composer/arranger's career, but it does have enough highlights to make it an effective introduction. *—Stephen Thomas Erlewine*

David Rose

b. Jun. 15, 1910, London, England, **d.** Aug. 23, 1990, Burbank, CA
Vocals, Keyboards, Piano, Conductor, Composer, Arranger / Traditional Pop
David Rose was one of the most popular and distinctive mainstream instrumental pop composers of the '40s,'50s and '60s, writing a number of pieces that became part of the nation's collective memory. From "Holiday for Strings" to "The Stripper," his music was usually distinguished by a loose, humorous approach. In addition to his signature songs, Rose composed scores for many films and television programs, including *Bonanza* and *Little House on the Prairie*. For most of the '30s, Rose was a conductor, pianist and arranger for NBC. He left New York in 1938 for Hollywood, assembling the David Rose Orchestra for the Mutual Broadcast System. In 1941, MGM Studios hired Rose as a musical director. One of his trademark tunes, "Holiday for Strings," became a major hit in 1943 while Rose served in World War II; the following year, "So in Love"—a song he wrote with lyricist Leo Robin—was nominated for an Oscar after appearing in the Danny Kaye film *Wonder Man*.

After the war, Rose moved to TV, where he wrote music for over 20 series in the '50s,'60s, and '70s, including *Bonanza*, which earned him several Emmy awards, and *Little House on the Prairie*. He also released albums of show tunes, film themes and mood music, but his biggest pop chart success was with 1962's number one hit "The Stripper," taken from the television program *Burlesque*. The accompanying album, *The Stripper and Other Fun Songs for the Family*, peaked at number three. During the '70s and '80s Rose conducted a number of symphony concerts and recorded the occasional album. David Rose died in 1990. *—Stephen Thomas Erlewine*

● **The Very Best of David Rose** / 1996 / MGM ✦✦✦✦✦
The Very Best of David Rose offers a good cross-section of his light easy listening pop instrumentals of the '50s and functions as an excellent introduction to his career. *—Stephen Thomas Erlewine*

The Sandpipers

Group / Folk Revival, Vocal Pop, Pop, Folk-Pop
The Sandpipers were a male vocal trio that recorded a handful of easy listening pop hits in the mid-'60s. The group was distinguished by their light, breezy harmonies, which floated over delicate, breezy string arrangements, as well as the occasional appearance of a wordless female backing vocalist who drifted in and out of the music. None of the singles the Sandpipers released on A&M were successful until their producer, Tommy LiPuma, recommended that they record a South American folk song called "Guantanamera." Once "Guantanamera" was released in 1966, it became a major hit, reaching the Top Ten in both the United States and Britain. The Sandpipers managed to follow "Guantanamera" with several minor hits, including versions of "Louie Louie" and "Kumbaya." Though they continued to record into the '70s, their audience diminished with each successive year. After spending five years without any chart success, the group disbanded in the mid-'70s. *—Stephen Thomas Erlewine*

Greatest Hits / 1970 / A&M ✦✦✦✦
Though *Greatest Hits* doesn't quite live up to its title—only one of the Sandpipers' four Top 100 singles appear on the collection—it offers a good sampling of the band's sound and does include their big hit, "Guantanamera." *—Stephen Thomas Erlewine*

● **Guantanamera/The Sandpipers** / Oct. 3, 2000 / Collectors' Choice Music ✦✦✦✦✦
Guantanamera/The Sandpipers collects two albums' worth of the group's gentle, folk-tinged pop. These are the group's first—and highest-charting—releases, which include mellow, charming renditions of "Michelle," "Strangers in the Night," "Cast Your Fate to the Wind," and "I'll Remember You," as well as other contemporary and classic pop standards and the number one hit "Guantanamera." Though it's not as representative a collection as their *Greatest Hits*, *Guantanamera/The Sandpipers* offers nearly as many highlights. *—Heather Phares*

John Schroeder

Arranger / Space Age Pop, Orchestral Pop
Arranger/conductor/producer Schroeder does have a few pop/rock credentials: he wrote a number one U.K. hit for British singer Helen Shapiro ("Walkin' Back to Happiness") in the

early '60s, made the first licensing deal for Motown product on British shores, and formed Sounds Orchestral, which had a Top Ten hit on both sides of the Atlantic in 1965 with "Cast Your Fate to the Wind." To the current space-age pop crowd, however, he's known as one of the chief exponents of what the British call "easy"—recordings, mostly instrumental, which welded easy-listening pop arrangements to soul, rock, and psychedelic source material. At the time, naturally, it was critically ignored, as his work was really aimed at creating background music for those who found the original versions way too intense to handle. In the mid-'90s, of course, it's all the rage in London clubs, where his blaring horn charts and pumping Hammond organs provide—um—suitable background music for those looking for the cutting edge in retro sounds. Placed in the home CD unit rather than the dancefloor, it tends to sound rather trivial, if occasionally possessed of an inspired oddball charm. The demand is there, though (maybe for the first time), which paved the way for the reissue of some of his recordings decades after they made a beeline for the cutout bin. *—Richie Unterberger*

Working in the Soul Mine / 1966 / Pye ✦✦✦
All but two of these 14 tracks were covers of mid-'60s American soul favorites like "You've Lost That Lovin' Feelin'," "Sunny," and "Rescue Me," in which Schroeder bled most of the funk (and vocals) from the originals to craft instrumentals that were at once more tolerable to elderly ears than the originals, but still mildly rhythmic and danceable. It sounds silly now—it sounded silly *then*. But that hasn't prevented the album from being reissued in its entirety on Sequel's *Space Age Soul*, which adds seven other (rather more interesting) tracks that Schroeder recorded in the '60s. *—Richie Unterberger*

● **Space Age Soul** / Sep. 17, 1996 / Sequel ✦✦✦✦
This 21-track compilation includes the entirety of his 1966 *Working in the Soul Mine* LP (which consisted mostly of covers of American soul hits), as well as some other tracks from the '60s, some credited to Sounds Orchestral and a couple previously unreleased (!). As much hip appeal as this may have in certain quarters, it's hard to fathom why you'd want to hear an easy listening-cum-go-go instrumental arrangement of "Papa's Got a Brand New Bag" or "You Can't Hurry Love," except for a laugh (once). Occasionally, soulful female vocals wander in for a phrase or two, as if they've accidentally stumbled on the session without realizing that it's supposed to be instrumental. The relatively few originals (mostly found on the non-*Working in the Soul Mine* cuts) have the advantage of more, well, originality, as the arranger's working in a vein more akin to his experience. "Soul Coaxing," for instance, has some gorgeous strings and spectral moaning female vocals worthy of Ennio Morricone, and "Lovin' You Girl" weds some jelly-thick Hammond organ grooves to suitably mournful brass. *—Richie Unterberger*

Jimmy Sturr

Sax (Alto), Clarinet / Polka
An orchestra leader with over 100 albums to his credit since the 1960s, clarinetist Jimmy Sturr won six straight Grammy awards for Best Polka Album. His band mixes pop, country and Cajun influences with polka; his latter-day albums include *Polka Your Troubles Away, I Love to Polka*, Polkapalooza and *Touched By A Polka*. *—John Bush*

When It's Polka Time at Your House / 1991 / Vanguard ✦✦✦

Polka! All Night Long / 1996 / Rounder ✦✦✦✦

● **Dance with Me** / Aug. 18, 1998 / Rounder ✦✦✦✦✦
On his 100th album, Jimmy Sturr, the polka man on a mission, succeeds in honoring the basic traditions of polka music while broadening its appeal. The songs and influences vary, but the underlying spirit and strength of the music remains. This time out, guests include the Oak Ridge Boys, (polished and professional as usual) Flaco Jimenez, the Jordannaires, and the Rocco Sisters. The recording starts out strong with two big band sounding polka tunes, "Make Mine Polka" and "My Dot Polka." Four of the remaining cuts are instrumentals, and all are played with an effervescent spirit and solid musicianship. Of particular note is "E String Polka," which begins with fast-paced country fiddle before transitioning into more traditional polka instrumentation. Another cut which combines two styles is "Borracho *1*," bridging the gap between the Jimmy Sturr style and the Tex-Mex style of polka (featuring an excellent accordion solo by Flaco Jimenez). The only two cuts which seem subpar are "May All Your Dreams Come True" and the good time staple "Wasn't That a Party." The former is a waltz that goes a little too far into schmaltz territory (though sentimentalists may love it) and the latter suffers from too generic an arrangement. But, overall, this is a very good recording and should be enjoyed by those who enjoy first-rate dance music and can leap beyond the stereotype of polka music being only for the gray-haired generation. *—Michael Ofjord*

Polkapalooza / Aug. 10, 1999 / Rounder ✦✦✦✦

Yma Sumac

b. 1928
Vocals / Exotica
A singer with an amazing four-octave range, Yma Sumac was said to have been a descendant of Inca kings. Her offbeat stylings became a phenomenon of early '50s pop music. While her album covers took advantage of her strange costumes and voluptuous figure, rumors abounded that she was, in actuality, a housewife named Amy Camus. It mattered little, since there has been no one like her before or since in the annals of popular music. She began performing with a group named the Inca Taqui Trio, which moved from Peru to New York and played radio and television variety programs. In 1950, her first album for Capitol, the 10-inch *Voice of Xtabay*, became a hit. She continued to release hit records and sell out concerts during the '50s, though she retired in the early '60s. Though Sumac did not perform frequently in the '90s, she experienced a popular revival, as a cult of alternative music fans discovered the exotica records of the '50s. The on-going interest in exotica and Sumac led to the CD release of her catalog in 1996. *—Stephen Thomas Erlewine & Cub Koda*

● **Voice of the Xtabay** / 1950 / The Right Stuff ✦✦✦✦✦
Sumac's first and most popular release, and also one of her least hokey or pop-oriented. That's not to say it's without its mass-appeal elements, especially in the arrangements, conducted by Les Baxter. Originally issued as a 10-inch LP, the latest CD reissue combines the eight tracks with the eight others contained on another of her early albums, *Inca Taqui*. *—Richie Unterberger*

Legend of the Sun Virgin / 1954 / The Right Stuff ✦✦✦
One of Sumac's most operatic and melodramatic outings, incantationally performed to approximate an Incan ritual. The cinematic string arrangements, though, are pure Hollywood. *—Richie Unterberger*

Mambo / 1954 / The Right Stuff ✦✦✦✦✦
Capitol got on top of two '50s fads at once by issuing an album of Sumac tackling mambo. Yma (characteristically) held nothing back, and the result was one of her more enjoyable LPs, with respectably swinging mambo grooves crafted by Billy May. "Five Bottles Mambo" is one of her most astonishing vocal workouts, dropping into guttural growls that are downright bestial, and making one wonder how exactly they got away with that in the conservative milieu of the 1950s. *—Richie Unterberger*

Fuego del Ande / 1959 / The Right Stuff ✦✦✦
Even those who find Sumac unbearable would have to admit that she was nothing if not adaptable. *Fuego Del Ande* has her interpreting South American folk songs with characteristic panache, although it's not one of her better '50s albums. *—Richie Unterberger*

● **The Ultimate Yma Sumac Collection** / Jan. 11, 2000 / Capitol ✦✦✦✦
The Ultimate Yma Sumac Collection may very well live up to its title; at the very least, it's likely the most comprehensive overview of her recordings yet assembled. Therefore, the question is, is it better to go with a collection (which contains three previously unreleased cuts and four rare stereo mixes) or an official album, namely her *Voice of the Xtabay*, which Richie Unterberger calls her "first and most popular release." Since that first album isn't quite as pop-oriented as some of the material on *The Ultimate*, it may seem that the collection is preferable, yet that's not really the case. Sumac is a bit of a cultural artifact, so she makes the most sense in the context; hence, the album makes a bit more sense than the compilation. However, there is very, very little overlap between *Voice of the Xtabay* and *The Ultimate*, so the collection not only functions as a nice supplement to the record, but neophytes who decide they want to sample an overview instead of diving into the proper albums will not be disappointed by repeated tracks when they go to the *Voice*. Any way you look at it, *The Ultimate Yma Sumac Collection* is a good compilation of a difficult artist to anthologize. *—Stephen Thomas Erlewine*

The Three Suns

Group / Traditional Pop, Lounge, Exotica, Vocal Pop, Pop
The postwar-era pop trio the Three Suns comprised vocalist/organist Artie Dunn, guitarist Al Nevins and accordionist Marty Nevins. Although formed in 1939, the group did not achieve widespread success until their 1944 Top 20 rendition of "*Twilight Time*," co-written by the trio with Buck Ram, sold over a million copies. In 1947 the Three Suns topped the charts with "*Peg o' My Heart*," but by the 1950s line-up shuffles plagued the group—first Al Nevins was replaced by Johnny Buck, who later gave way to Joe Negri. After disbanding, Dunn briefly reformed the trio in 1957 with guitarist Johnny Romano and accordionist Tony Lovello; a largely-forgotten curio for several decades, by the 1990s the Three Suns had accrued hipster cache thanks to the lounge-music revival, and their original recordings resurfaced on any number of exotica and "*space-age bachelor pad*" reissues. Al Nevins also etched his name in pop history as the co-founder, with Don Kirshner, of Aldon Music, the songwriting house which served as the epicenter of the Brill Building music factory. *—Jason Ankeny*

Love in the Afternoon / 1957 / RCA Victor ✦✦✦✦✦

Swingin' on a Star / 1959 / RCA Victor ✦✦✦✦✦

Twilight Memories / 1960 / RCA Victor ✦✦✦

● **The Very Best of the Three Suns** / Oct. 12, 1999 / Taragon ✦✦✦✦✦
A nice 20-track roundup of this little remembered group, drawing on their biggest hits as both EP and album tracks. Highlights include "Peg of My Heart," "Don't Take Your Love From Me," "Moonlight and Roses," and nice takes of "Perdido," *Just One More Chance*," "Ain't Misbehavin'," and "Let's Call the Whole Thing Off." The Three Suns were the epitome of smooth, with their blend of guitar, accordion, Hammond organ, and smooth vocals, but the group also had a unique—almost quirky—quality to them that made these tracks stand out then, as they do now. *—Cub Koda*

Billy Vaughn

b. Apr. 12, 1919, Glasgow, KY, **d.** Sep. 14, 1991, Palomar, CA
Vocals / Traditional Pop, Orchestral Pop
Billy Vaughn was one of the most popular orchestra leaders and pop music arrangers of the '50s and early '60s. In fact, he had more pop hits than any other orchestra leader during the rock & roll era. Vaughn was also the musical director for many of the hitmakers on Dot Records, including Pat Boone, the Fontane Sisters, and Gale Storm. As a pop music arranger, his most distinctive feature was his clean, non-offensive mainstream adaptations of rock & roll and R&B hits. Vaughn was also a recording artist, and he cut a number of albums of easy listening, instrumental music that were very popular throughout the '60s. Beginning with 1954's "Melody of Love," Vaughn had a string of easy listening U.S. hit singles that ran for over a decade. He also recorded numerous hit albums, with 36 of his records entering the U.S. album charts between 1958 and 1970. Though he was the most successful orchestra leader of the rock & roll era, he wasn't able to sustain an audience in the late '60s. *—Stephen Thomas Erlewine*

★ **Melody of Love: Best of Billy Vaughn** / Oct. 25, 1994 / Varese ✦✦✦✦✦
Melody of Love: The Best of Billy Vaughn is a definitive 18-track collection that contains the great majority of Billy Vaughn's biggest hits, including "Melody of Love," "The Shifting Whis-

pering Sands (Parts 1 & 2)," "Sail Along Silvery Moon," and "Blue Hawaii." *—Stephen Thomas Erlewine*

Lawrence Welk

b. Mar. 11, 1903, Strasburg, ND, **d.** May 17, 1992, Santa Monica, CA
Accordion, Bandleader / Polka, Instrumental Pop
Long a butt of comedians and music fans, Lawrence Welk survived into the '90s as America's most successful bandleader. From dirt-poor beginnings in rural North Dakota, the relatively uneducated and heavily accented Welk seemed an unlikely candidate to carve out a successful, 60-plus-year career in the music business, but through sheer dogged persistence and belief in himself, that's exactly what transpired. His "Champagne music" style (lighter and less rhythmic than Guy Lombardo's) remained remarkably unchanged over the years. Changes in music have been constant—the end of the big band era, rock & roll, country & western, the Beatles, disco—with Welk seemingly impervious to it all, and a built-in audience that felt the same way. While jazz legends like Coleman Hawkins were lucky to land a Timex jazz special once a year, Welk was on ABC-TV twice a week! After being dropped by that network, he was one of the first to successfully move into television syndication, ending up more visible than he had been on ABC at his peak. Expanding his musical family to include tap dancers, jazz musicians (notably Pete Fountain), and multitudes of singers (The Lennon Sisters, etc.), Welk made no pretense of being remotely hip, merely delivering simple, well-played music and solid, family-oriented entertainment year after year. *—Cub Koda*

22 All Time Big Band Favorites / 1987 / Ranwood ✦✦✦✦✦
Lawrence Welk, the man who entertained America for 29 consecutive years on television, was as famous for his accent as much as his music. But beyond being the brunt of many jokes, the man knew what America wanted. On this collection of big-band favorites, Welk and company come up with a thoroughly entertaining collection. Whether performing their renditions of Count Basie's "One O'Clock Jump," Duke Ellington's "Take the 'A' Train," or other classics of the era, the playing is impressive. Especially effective are the brass and piano solos (though unfortunately there are no liner notes to say who played what). Rhythmically the playing might be toned down a bit, and the vocals might be stylized. Still, there is a spirit beyond mere professionalism that can't be denied. For those who enjoyed Lawrence Welk over the years, or are fans of the big-band era, this is an easy collection to enjoy. *—Michael Ofjord*

★ **16 Most Requested Songs** / 1989 / Columbia/Legacy ✦✦✦✦✦
Though it's far from a comprehensive collection, Lawrence Welk's *16 Most Requested Songs* contains most of the bandleader's best-known songs, presented in top-notch versions. It's a good way to get acquainted with his laid-back style. *—Stephen Thomas Erlewine*

Paul Weston

b. Mar. 12, 1912, Springfield, MA, **d.** Sep. 20, 1996, Santa Monica, CA
Arranger, Conductor / Traditional Pop, Mood Music, Swing, Instrumental Pop
Paul Weston was one of the most diverse and talented arrangers and conductors of the '40s and '50s, moving from mainstream swing and jazz to instrumental easy listening pop in the course of his career. Though he began his career playing hard swing, Weston is the father of mood music—lush, relaxing instrumental orchestral pop designed to provide a soundtrack to everyday events like romance and dining. His early work arranging for Rudy Vallee and Tommy Dorsey made his reputation. While with Dorsey, he wrote jumping, swinging charts for the band and vocalists like Dinah Shore and Jo Stafford, who he would marry in the mid-'40s. Adjusting his music to suit the gentler public tastes, Weston released his first album of mood music, *Music for Dreaming,* in 1945. The album was a major success, and he recorded many albums of smooth, string-laden music for the next five years (prompting the press to coin the term mood music). He moved to Columbia in 1950, continuing to record albums and write arrangements for artists like Sarah Vaughan, Ella Fitzgerald, Dinah Shore and Doris Day. Weston returned to Capitol by the end of the '50s and stayed throughout the '60s. In the early '70s, Weston and Stafford both retired, later forming a reissue label, Corinthian Records. *—Stephen Thomas Erlewine*

★ **Music for Memories/Music For Dreaming** / Jan. 20, 1992 / Capitol ✦✦✦✦✦
Music for Memories / Music For Dreaming combines Paul Weston's two groundbreaking 10-inch albums of lush, romantic mood music. It offers a perfect introduction to Weston, as well as the entire genre of mood music. *—Stephen Thomas Erlewine*

Columbia Album of Jerome Kern / Columbia ✦✦✦✦✦
Yeah, this is the stuff your parents probably listened to on the record player when you weren't playing Elvis or Chuck Berry, but it's still great music, and Weston was one of the top interpreters of pop standards of the 1950s. His recordings of Jerome Kern's hits (two LPs on a 70-minute-plus CD) are among the best work he ever did. The sound is moody and lush, without being overwhelmingly sweet—the achingly beautiful melodic nuances of a piece like "You Are Love" still come through amid the harps and strings, even if it's better to hear it sung. Amazingly, some of Kern's best known pieces, including "Ol' Man River" and "Till the Clouds Roll By," are not here, but that's good, because it gives Weston room to work with slightly lesser-known songs, including "Can I Forget You." The sound is mono, but very clean and pretty sharp. *—Bruce Eder*

Mason Williams

b. Aug. 24, 1938, Abilene, TX
Vocals, Recorder, Guitar, Banjo / Classical Pop, Instrumental Pop
Mason Williams reached his peak in the late '60s. A humorous scriptwriter and virtuosic acoustic guitar player and composer, Williams reached the top of the hit parade in 1968 with his classical folk guitar instrumental, "Classical Gas." Although it took six months for the single to become a chart-topping smash, it went on to win Grammy awards as Best Instrumental (Theme) Composition and Best Instrumental (Theme) Performance, as well as a Best Instrumental Orchestral Arrangement award for arranger Mike Post. An album featuring a re-recorded version of the tune with Mannheim Steamroller and Fresh Aire, *Classical Gas,* sold more than a million copies in 1987. Williams has recorded several other memorable albums and compositions. An acoustic Christmas/holiday season album, *A Gift of Song,* was released in 1992, while his composition "Symphony Bluegrass" has been performed by more than 40 symphony orchestras. Although Williams attracted attention with his melodic 12-string guitar and banjo playing in the early 1960s, he initially attracted attention as a writer for *The Smothers Brothers Comedy Hour.* *—Craig Harris*

● **Music 1968-1971** / 1969 / Vanguard ✦✦✦✦✦

Roger Williams (Louis Weertz)

b. 1925, Omaha, NE
Vocals, Piano / Instrumental Pop, Orchestral Pop
Pianist Roger Williams' sweeping, sparkling arpeggios, showy technique, and gentle, easy listening arrangements made him one of the most popular pop instrumentalists of the late '50s and '60s. Like many other easy listening musicians, he blurred the boundaries between pop, jazz, and classical, creating a smooth, relaxing hybrid. Between 1955 and 1972, he had 38 hit albums and 22 hit singles, including the number one hit, "Falling Leaves." He studied at Juilliard, and got his big break after a Juilliard vocalist he was to accompany on *Arthur Godfrey's Talent Scouts* failed to show up, leaving the pianist to play a solo spot. Kapp signed him, and after a few singles, Roger Williams had his first hit with the arpeggio-laden "Autumn Leaves" in 1955. The single reached number one on the US charts and began a streak of 22 hit singles, including the Top Ten hits "Near You" and "Born Free." Williams was equally successful on the album charts, hitting the Top Ten with *Songs of the Fabulous Fifties* (1957), *Till* (1958), *Maria* (1962), and *Born Free* (1966). Though his audience faded in the early '70s, he continued to record into the '80s and remains one of the most popular pianists of the postwar era. *—Stephen Thomas Erlewine*

Roger Williams' Greatest Hits / 1971 / MCA ✦✦✦✦✦
Roger Williams' Greatest Hits is a good single-disc sampling of the pianist's biggest hits and should satisfy most of his casual fans. Listeners that want to dig deeper should pick up the double-disc set, *The Artist's Choice.* *—Stephen Thomas Erlewine*

☆ **The Greatest Popular Pianist/The Artist's Choice** / 1992 / MCA ✦✦✦✦✦
The Artist's Choice is a splendid, double-disc set featuring all of Roger Williams' biggest hits, as well as a select amount of the pianist's favorite tracks. Devoted Williams fans will find this compilation a treasure, but those that want just a taste of his easy listening should stick with MCA's single-disc *Greatest Hits* collection. *—Stephen Thomas Erlewine*

★ **Collection** / Apr. 21, 1998 / Varese ✦✦✦✦✦

Softly As I Leave You: A Tribute to Frank Sinatra / Nov. 3, 1998 / Varese ✦✦✦

Pop Goes the Ivories / Jan. 25, 2000 / Gold Label ✦✦✦✦✦

Frankie Yankovic

b. Jul. 28, 1915, Davis, WV, **d.** Oct. 14, 1998
Accordion / Polka
Frankie Yankovic was one of the most popular polka band leaders of the '40s and '50s. Yankovic taught himself how to play the accordion when he was a child. At the age of 15, he began playing professionally. Soon, he was leading one of the most popular polka bands in the country. He was at the peak of his popularity at the end of the '40s, when his version of the Czechoslovakian song "Blue Skirt Waltz" was a hit single. Although they never sold many records, Yankovic and his band continued to perform into the '70s, selling out concerts across the United States. He died October 14, 1998. *—Stephen Thomas Erlewine*

● **Greatest Hits** / Columbia ✦✦✦✦✦
Featuring all of his best-known numbers, *Greatest Hits* offers a solid introduction to the master of the accordion, Frankie Yankovic. *—Stephen Thomas Erlewine*

Greatest Polka Hits / Mar. 21, 2000 / RCA ✦✦✦
Frank Yankovic's *Greatest Polka Hits* collects 23 of the polka king's most popular numbers, including *Just Because, Pretty Polly Polka, Blue Skirt Waltz,* and *Ten Swedes. Town Tap Polka, Pretty Music,* and *Jo Ann Waltz* are some of the other highlights of this entertaining compilation, which is a fine overview of Yankovic's late-'60s work for RCA. It's not only for newcomers, it's an enjoyable piece of nostalgia for longtime fans. *—Heather Phares*

Zamfir

Pan Flute, Nai, Flute / Instrumental Pop
Romanian panpipe player Gheorghe Zamfir first reached #4 on the U.K. charts in 1976 with an ethereal hit called "Doina De Jale"—a traditional Eastern funeral piece. He has gone on to make dozens of albums and entrance millions of buyers with the other-worldly sound of the pan pipes. His repertoire includes Romanian folk music and classical melodies, but most of all popular film themes; among his releases were 1973's *Solitude,* 1984's *Lonely Shepherd,* and 1997's *Songs of Romance, Volume 1.* *—Michael Erlewine*

Romance of the Panflute / 1982 / Philips ✦✦✦
Romance of the Pan Flute offers a good introduction to the ethereal yet lovely sound of Zamfir, showcasing his mastery of tone and his light, romantic phrasing. Nearly all of Zamfir's albums are of equal quality—if you enjoy this, you should enjoy his other records. *—David Jehnzen*

● **The Best of Zamfir** / Philips ✦✦✦✦✦
The Best of Zamfir offers a good cross-section of the pan flautist's best material, making it an effective introduction. Then again, all of Zamfir's albums are remarkably similar, so any of them are a good starting point. *—David Jehnzen*

Various Artists

Cigar Classics, Vol. 1: The Standards / Mar. 25, 1997 / Hip-O ♦♦♦
Now obviously, there's absolutely no such animal as "cigar smoking music," but never let it be said that a major record company (in this case, MCA, through their Hip-O imprint) would let a yuppie-derived social fad—in this case, the rise of cigar smoking in the politically correct '90s—go by without cobbling together a four-volume series to profit from it. The initial entry in this tenuous series is called *The Standards* and this volume is obviously targeted at the parents (and grandparents) of baby boomers, loaded up as it is with 14 tracks aimed at the AARP set and inveterate cigar smoker Milton Berle doing the liner notes. Actually, as an entry in the "pop vocal" section, this compilation holds up remarkably well, with Dooley Wilson's "As Time Goes By," The Four Aces' original "Mister Sandman," "Near You" by Francis Craig, "Takes Two To Tango" by Pearl Bailey, "Don't Fence Me In" by Bing Crosby and the Andrews Sisters, "Embraceable You" by Judy Garland, and "I Don't Want To Set The World On Fire" by the Ink Spots holding sway next to sweet big band sides like "Smoke Rings" by Glen Gray's Casa Loma Orchestra. Left-field additions also include Peggy Lee's sultry "Black Coffee," Louis Jordan's "Let The Good Times Roll," and the out-of-time-frame "Smoke Gets In Your Eyes" by the Platters. *—Cub Koda*

Cocktail Mix, Vol. 1: Bachelor's Guide to the Galaxy / Jan. 23, 1996 / Rhino ♦♦♦
This 18-track compilation is largely devoted to lounge/cocktail/easy listening outings of the late '50s and early '60s that were aimed at exploiting the new dimensions of stereo sound. The actual musical content was often trifling; what was more interesting were the somewhat unusual arrangements and utilization of sonic textures. Shimmering percussion, often with a Latin rhythm, was a big element, as were blaring horns and unexpected swoops on the keyboards, along with some embellishments of sound effects and weird (by the era's standards) instruments. It was daring, in a very limited sense, for the time, and charmingly dated several years later. But the slight nature of the material is often tiring, as is its tendency to wander into novelty territory. *—Richie Unterberger*

Cocktail Mix, Vol. 2 / Jan. 23, 1996 / Rhino ♦♦♦♦♦
Certainly the best of Rhino's *Cocktail Mix* series, focusing on the most dance-oriented aspects of "space age pop." This 18-song compilation could be said to stretch the boundaries of that newly coined genre a bit. After all, Mose Allison, Cal Tjader, Brother Jack McDuff, and Pucho & the Latin Soul Brothers were not so much cocktail musicians as respected jazzmen who drew liberally from Latin music, blues, and pop. Mel Torme (represented by the classic "Comin' Home Baby") and Nancy Wilson were respected "straight" pop vocalists; Quincy Jones and Connie Francis wandered into the playing field with their bossa nova novelties. Ann-Margaret, Sergio Mendes, and Walter Wanderley are more the kind of chintzy good-bad acts you'd expect, but it's silly to get bogged down in classification. The bottom line is that this is infectious suave vintage dance music. It may be suitable for cocktail lounges, but only raucous ones—which is a compliment. *—Richie Unterberger*

Cocktail Mix, Vol. 3 / Jan. 23, 1996 / Rhino ♦♦♦♦♦
A look at the roster of cuts assembled for this 18-cut compilation may have you anticipating a staid set of pre-rock pop, with the likes of Rosemary Clooney, Sammy Davis, Jr., Tony Bennett, Dean Martin, Mel Torme, Bobby Darin, and Peggy Lee. Actually, this is lounge music at its most hepped-up, even getting a bit raucous in spots, and often deploying Latin rhythms to raise the energy level. As for the Rat Packers and Vegas habitues, this is about as hard as they ever swang; from the other direction, we get some of the more dance-conscious sides from performers with higher critical credentials, like Della Reese, Sarah Vaughan, Ella Fitzgerald, and Stan Kenton. Robert Mitchum (singing calypso), Henry Mancini (with one of his best instrumentals, "Something for Cat"), and Latin bandleader Xavier Cugat add variety and novelty to a set that may appeal even to those who disdain adult pop, lounge or otherwise. *—Richie Unterberger*

Cocktail Mix, Vol. 4: Soundtracks with a Twist / Nov. 19, 1996 / Rhino ♦♦♦♦♦
Because it sticks to a specific theme, *Cocktail Mix, Vol. 4: Soundtracks with a Twist!* is the best installment in the *Cocktail Mix*. Concentrating entirely on film scores, *Soundtracks with a Twist!* features a cross section of movie music from the '60s, including songs written by Burt Bacharach, Henry Mancini, Nelson Riddle, Herbie Hancock, Ennio Morricone, Quincy Jones, John Barry, Alex North and George Duning. Nearly all of the music on the collection features light strings, swinging brass, psuedo-rock & roll beats and incessently catchy melodies. The album largely draws from British films like Lolita, What's Up Pussy Cat, Grand Slam, Blow-Up, and The Knack ... And How to Get It, with a few American and French films thrown in for good measure. But the whole sound of the album is the sound of swinging London, complete with "la-la-la" backing vocals, muted horns and bright, punchy hooks. And it's not just kitsch or nostalgia, either—this is good music, pure and simple. *—Stephen Thomas Erlewine*

● **The History of Space Age Pop, Vol. 1: Melodies and Mischief** / 1995 / RCA ♦♦♦♦♦
"Space age pop" wasn't called by that name during its heyday; it's a label that was dreamed up in the '90s, when this sort of experimental easy listening music, which was in vogue in the '50s and early '60s, had a mini-revival among collectors and pop culture historians. These 16 tracks, all taken from the vaults of RCA, date from the early days of the LP format, when many easy listening albums were aimed at the market of adults who had recently bought their first hi-fi equipment. Accordingly, the records often featured innovative (for the time) stereophonic effects, organ timbres, elaborate orchestration, and ersatz big-band/cool jazz/lounge music designed both to soothe and to utilize the full range of recorded sound. The hybrids that resulted were not just imaginative in the kitschiest fashion, but sometimes downright bizarre, as cornball melodies and vocals collided head-on with idiot savant-like quirkiness. There are actually a few big artists here (Henry Mancini, Perez Prado, Esquivel), but the bulk of these names are long forgotten. Is it fun? Certainly. Is it important? Not really. Does it stand up to repeated listenings? Not unless you're a nut for this stuff, in which case it's one of the top (and few) compilations available. Highlight: Sir Julian's zany, bouncing arrangement of "Caravan" for organ, featuring some of densest, most explosive clusters of tones that could be squeezed from the instrument. *—Richie Unterberger*

● **The History of Space Age Pop, Vol. 2: Mallets in Wonderland** / 1995 / RCA ♦♦♦♦♦
The focus of this volume of *Space Age Pop*, as the title implies, is on percussion instruments. Within the space age pop rubric, this didn't just mean drums, but all sorts of exotic (by the standards of the '50s and early '60s) touches on vibes, xylophones, bongos, steel drums, and even some instruments more associated with ethnomusicology studies, such as the Burmese gong. The music itself, though, isn't much different from what's found on other *Space Age Pop* volumes: imaginative easy listening, sometimes goofy, sometimes bizarre. In fact, some of the same artists on other volumes reappear here (the Three Suns, Henry Mancini, Esquivel, Perez Prado). Fun, if hardly profound, stuff with some cheesy quasi-ethnic flourishes of Latin and South Pacific rhythms. Martin Denny fans will enjoy the exotica-like outings of the wonderfully named Markko Polo Adventurers, particularly on "Rain in Rangoon." *—Richie Unterberger*

● **The History of Space Age Pop, Vol. 3: Stereo Action Dimension** / 1995 / RCA ♦♦♦♦♦
RCA's *Stereo Action* series of the early '60s was designed to showcase the possibilities of the then-new medium, particularly the separation of instruments and the "panning" effects that could be created with more than one speaker. This collection concentrates on the kinds of arrangements that highlighted these characteristics: rapid up-and-down scales and glissandos, chimes of bells and glockenspiels for decorative flavor, vibrant organs that run the gamut of high and low timbres, nifty sound effects, and pieces that seem to have been recorded specifically to simultaneously highlight different ends of the sonic spectrum. It still, however, doesn't sound all that much different than the other *Space Age Pop* volumes. That's not a criticism; what you, the modern-day jaded listener, want from this stuff is good clean kitschy fun, not a demonstration of stereo technology, which you've been familiar with for decades. And on that count, this delivers, with cuts from RCA space age pop faves Esquivel, the Three Suns, and Henry Rene, and similar easy-listening-with-a-strange-twist from several other names that are more obscure. *—Richie Unterberger*

★ **Instrumental Gems of the '60s** / 1995 / Collectors' Choice Music ♦♦♦♦♦
A good concept for a collection, one that will appeal to many rock listeners, although this is mostly not rock. Two CDs and 40 tracks, covering most of the biggest non-rock instrumental hits of the '60s, songs that were played on the AM dial right next to the Beatles and Motown. Think of the biggest songs of the type from the era, and they're likely to be here: "Love Is Blue" (Paul Mauriat), "Theme From a Summer Place" (Percy Faith), "Calcutta" (Lawrence Welk), "Classical Gas" (Mason Williams), "Washington Square" (the Village Stompers), "Bonanza" (Al Caiola), and so on, including some more obscure numbers and some nearly forgotten one-shot hits by the likes of Arthur Lyman and Bill Purcell (whose "Our Winter Love" has some of the most overmodulated electric bass ever captured on record). A few rock instrumentals do pop up by the String-A-Longs, the T-Bones, and Bill Black, but by and large this doesn't have much to do with rock, encompassing movie themes, pseudo-classical, bossa nova jazz, cocktail jazz, novelties, and more. Sure, some of this is sappy, but many of the tunes are enduring, and sometimes imaginative (or even innovative) in a way found in few easy listening/popular instrumental recordings from subsequent decades. *—Richie Unterberger*

Let's Dance: The Best of Ballroom Foxtrots & Waltzes / Nov. 11, 1997 / Rhino ♦♦♦
Let's Dance: The Best of Ballroom Foxtrots & Waltzes was designed to cash-in on the swing and lounge revival of the '90s by offering a selection of foxtrots and waltzes, along with a choreography and beats-per-minute-guide, designed for hip young swingers. Despite a few selections that are a little too slick or schmaltzy, the music on the collection is generally first-rate, offering eight foxtrots and seven waltzes. The featured artists—including Andy Williams, Harry James, the Manhattan Transfer, Mel Torme, Percy Faith, 101 Strings, Melissa Manchester, Engelbert Humperdinck and Henry Mancini—are uniformly strong, but what really matters is the rhythm, sway and music, and on that level, *Let's Dance: The Best of Ballroom Foxtrots & Waltzes* fulfills its purpose quite well. *—Stephen Thomas Erlewine*

Let's Dance: The Best of Ballroom Swing, Lindy, Jitterbug & Jive / Nov. 11, 1997 / Rhino ♦♦♦
Let's Dance: The Best of Ballroom Swing, Lindy, Jitterbug & Jivewas designed to cash-in on the swing and lounge revival of the '90s by offering a selection of uptempo swing and jump blues songs, along with a choreography and beats-per-minute-guide, designed for hip young swingers that want to dance the Lindy, jitterbug and jive. Despite a few selections that indicate the compilers didn't really understand the idea behind the swing revivalJoe Jackson's "Jump, Jack, You're Dead" and the Manhattan Transfer are good examples of the revival, while tracks by the Commitments, Aretha Franklin, Buddy Guy & Junior Wells and James Cotton, Junior Wells, Carey Bell & Billy Branch's are simply not suited for this kind of ballroom dancing—the music is generally first-rate, offering a selection of eight "swing" songs, three Lindy numbers and five jive blues. Ultimately, the rhythm of the music is what matters on *Let's Dance*, and while this disc takes a few wrong steps here and there, it ultimately serves the modern-day ballroom dancer quite well. *—Stephen Thomas Erlewine*

Lounging at the Nick at Nite Club / May 13, 1997 / Columbia ♦♦♦

Music for a Bachelor's Den / 1995 / DCC ♦♦♦
As space age bachelor pad music goes, these were among the most widely heard examples of the genre. Over half of these 15 cuts, in fact, were hit singles, including such smashes as "Quiet Village" (Martin Denny), "So Rare" (Jimmy Dorsey), "Moritat" (Dick Hyman, and later to be changed into "Mack the Knife" by Bobby Darin), "Yellow Bird" (Arthur Lyman), "Theme from Route 66" (Nelson Riddle), and "Moonglow and Love Theme from Picnic" (Morris Stoloff). This means that experts might sniff and deride this collection as too "mainstream." Popular lounge music, however, was no less interesting than collectible lounge music, and perhaps more so. Which means that this is a good sampler of the style that was a subordinate but notable part of American popular music in the late '50s and early '60s, especially if you weren't around when these hits were played on AM radio. *—Richie Unterberger*

Music for a Bachelor's Den, Vol. 2: Exotica / 1995 / DCC ✦✦✦✦✦
This 14-track survey isn't the most extensive exotica compilation, and lacks the single-minded depth of those Martin Denny and Arthur Lyman anthologies. What it lacks in depth, however, it more than compensates for in breadth, especially as it's not limited to the back catalog of a single specific label. Cuts by some of the standard-bearers of the genre are here (Arthur Lyman, Les Baxter, Yma Sumac, the South Sea Serenaders), as well as more unexpected contributions from Duke Ellington and Percy Faith. The absence of Martin Denny excludes this from the top of the field, but it's one of the better introductions to the strange world of exotica, with the expected more or less equal doses of kitsch and off-the-wall goofiness. *—Richie Unterberger*

Music for the Jet Set / Nov. 5, 1996 / Hi Fi/Tradition ✦✦✦
Fourteen vintage cocktail/lounge/exotica outings from the archives of the Tradition label, offering a kind of soundtrack to a slide show of the world as it might have been presented at a 1965 travel agency. Exotica by Arthur Lyman; jungle percussion from Soubri Moulin; silly "China Nights Mambo" from Jack "Bongo" Burger; nightclub soul from Gloria Lynne (whose "Bali Ha'i" is one of the set's highlights); faceless white vocal muzak from the Ray Ventura Singers. Flamenco guitarist Bernabe de Moron and Woody Herman/Charlie Byrd (who combine jazz and latin music on "Prelude a La Cha Cha Cha"), might be insulted at finding themselves in this company. As far as '90s lounge reissues go, it's okay but a bit of an also-ran; more focused compilations will probably have greater appeal for most listeners. *—Richie Unterberger*

The Sound Gallery, Vol. 1 / Mar. 26, 1996 / Scamp ✦✦✦✦
The mainstream always lags way behind the cutting edge, so it wasn't until the end of the '60s that easy listening began reflecting such pop innovations as psychedelia and funk. *The Sound Gallery* is a collection of 24 tracks cut between 1968 and 1976 for British "mood music" LPs. This is "easy listening" at its peppiest, with considerably more bite (if that's the right word) than its American lounge/cocktail cousin. Go-go horn charts, wah-wah guitars, and vaguely rockish drums make these sound like nothing so much as soundtrack pieces to late '60s/early '70s movies that were trying desperately to be mod and trendy. Occasionally something packs some real oomph—Neil Richardson's "The Riviera Affair," for instance, is brisk and uplifting '60s soundtrack music at its finest, and other tracks have touches akin to the more mainstream work of great film composers like Morricone. But it's really stretching credibility to try and pretend that this stuff is any less lightweight in the '90s, when the whole easy listening genre is undergoing rehabilitation at the hands of collectors desperate to find something new to excavate. *—Richie Unterberger*

Take It Off!: Strip Tease Classics / Apr. 1, 1997 / Rhino ✦✦✦

Ultra Lounge, Vol. 1: Mondo Exotica / Feb. 1996 / Capitol ✦✦✦
An 18-song exhumation of the Capitol exotica back catalog, placing old standbys like Martin Denny, Les Baxter, and Yma Sumac alongside lesser-knowns like Webley Edwards, Bas Sheva, and the wonderfully-named 80 Drums Around the World. This favors easy listening-friendly exotica, rather than the style at its most outrageous. It may be too naroticizing for some, but connoisseurs will appreciate the inclusion of the rarer material; a couple of the cuts were even previously unreleased. *—Richie Unterberger*

Ultra Lounge, Vol. 2: Mambo Fever / Feb. 1996 / Capitol ✦✦✦
When Latin bandleaders popularized mambo in the early 1950s, this set many pop and big band acts scrambling to get in on the action. *Mambo Fever,* part two of Capitol's *Ultra-Lounge series, takes 18 such examples from the vaults, spanning the mid-'50s to the early '60s. Yma Sumac* (an exotica singer, not a bandleader) and Billy May are the only readily recognizable names on this compilation, which is akin to hearing competent, somewhat Whited-out derivations of Perez Prado. There are odd touches like Sumac's high-frequency warbles, John Buzon's roller-rink organ runs, and the sheer silliness of Chuy Reyes' "Oink, Oink Mambo." But the results are oddly similar, on one level, to hearing some White bands try to play the blues—in comparison to the most genuine article, it's somewhat sanitized for broader consumption. That's not to deny its considerable fun (if lightweight) qualities; this usually works up respectable heat, in addition to evoking the slightly kitschy '50s mentality that is a necessary ingredient of the space age pop revival. *—Richie Unterberger*

Ultra Lounge, Vol. 3: Space Capades / Feb. 1996 / Capitol ✦✦✦
In the late 1950s and early 1960s, this was the easy listening music that tried to anticipate the space age. Utilizing theremin or spooky organ figures helped, as did then-novel tricks like stereo separation and then-exotic instruments and hi-fi effects. It wasn't just novelty artists that got in on the act; bandleaders Les Baxter and David Rose, who perform some of the 18 tracks assembled here, also tried their hands. This compilation still falls closer to novelty than either innovation or period kitsch (although there's plenty of the latter). Some will complain that I'm not getting into the spirit of the thing, but there's more banality than entertainment here. As amusing as some of these gimmicky records sound upon first or second hearing, it lends itself even less to repeated plays than most of the space age bachelor pad reissues. *—Richie Unterberger*

Ultra Lounge, Vol. 4: Bachelor Pad Royale / Feb. 20, 1996 / Capitol ✦✦✦
As the title implies, the songs on this 18-song compilation were intended for bachelors who wanted to create a suitably suave atmosphere between the mid-1950s and mid-1960s. So although the music draws from jazz (both big band and cool), lounge pop, and film/TV soundtracks, it's primarily designed to set a mood or background. That means that when it's pushed to the foreground, it really doesn't sound all that entertaining, even as it evokes archetypical (and oft-silly) vibes of a certain era. Martin Denny, Julie London, Nelson Riddle, and a host of no-names from the Capitol vaults bring you that sound here. When an occasional element of excitement, even danger, creeps in (Riddle's "Theme From Route 66," Elliott Fisher's "Theme From Our Man Flint," Jimmie Haskell's "A Shot in the Dark"), the interest level rises, as it does for any slice of good soundtrack music. Otherwise, these days it makes the ambience stuffier, not cooler. *—Richie Unterberger*

Ultra Lounge, Vol. 5: Wild Cool & Swingin / Feb. 20, 1996 / Capitol ✦✦✦
This 18-song compilation is the showbiz-encased, Vegasized school of late '50s and early '60s pop vocals. The emphasis is certainly more on the "cool" than the wild and swinging; if it ever breaks out a sweat, there will be a martini-dipped silk handkerchief on hand to wipe it away. You get selections from Rat Packers (Dean Martin, Sammy Davis, Jr.), African-American mainstream pop (Nat King Cole, Lou Rawls), adult pop stars (Bobby Darin, Peggy Lee, Julie London), adult pop with a dash of vaudevillian slapstick (Louis Prima & Keely Smith), and those for whom Vegas was always the prize (a teenaged Wayne Newton). Targeted toward the nuevo cocktail crowd (it's volume five of Capitol's *Ultra Lounge* series), it's not the most satisfying survey of the form. Serious fans of pop vocals will find it too scattershot, and its packaging too flippant; space age poppers will find it too old-school cornball for their tastes, even if they're told it's part of some sort of cutting edge. *—Richie Unterberger*

Ultra Lounge, Vol. 6: Rhapsodesia / Feb. 20, 1996 / Capitol ✦✦✦
The sixth volume of Capitol's *Ultra Lounge* series, this focuses on the most sedate face of space age bachelor pad music: the sounds designed for dimming the lights, unwinding with martinis, and (stated implicitly; this was the '50s, remember) seduction. It might not have worked for those purposes then, and it certainly won't now, since prospective partners will be giggling too much at the cheesiness of it all to get it on. As far as sheer listening value, this, even more than other reissues of this sort, needs to be taken lightly or not at all. Julie London, Les Baxter, April Stevens, and a host of nonentities from the Capitol vaults may produce relaxing sounds, but not very involving ones. Those creepy organ lines that form the undercurrent of some of the selections provide the most fascination. At its worst, though, it's barely any better than the music you'll hear after you're put on hold by the airlines or the phone company. *—Richie Unterberger*

Ultra Lounge, Vol. 7: Crime Scene / Jul. 1996 / Capitol ✦✦✦
One of the kitschier installments in the *Ultra Lounge* series, *Vol. 7, Crime Scene* features a cross-section of easy-listening and movie music culled primarily from Capitol Records' vaults. All of the songs are allegedly "about" or inspired by detective and crime novels and films, so you have movie and television themes (Nelson Riddle's "The Untouchables," "Peter Gunn Suite" as performed by Ray Anthony), as well as songs whose titles imply a crime connection of some sort. It's an enjoyable collection, but it's too incoherent and campy to really be consistently entertaining. *—Stephen Thomas Erlewine*

Ultra Lounge, Vol. 8: Cocktail Capers / 1996 / Capitol ✦✦✦✦✦
If you've been following the *Ultra-Lounge series this far, you know what to expect: a mixture of stars (Les Baxter,* Nelson Riddle) and no-names from the Capitol vaults, playing space age pop/cocktail music of all hues in the 1950s and 1960s. Yet this has an edge over most of the previous titles in the series: there's more of a sense of swing, groove, even (dare we say) *danger* on much of this, albeit danger of a very safe sort. Hints of rock'n'roll and spy music even creep in from time to time, with James Bond-type reverb guitar decorating cuts like Al Caiola's "Underwater Chase," and top rock & roll session drummer Earl Palmer getting into the bongo/lounge vibe on "Binga Banga Bongo/Percolator." Another highlight is the highly sought-after theme song to Stanley Kubrick's 1962 film *Lolita, performed as a tongue-in-cheek rock & roll satire by Nelson Riddle* (with surfish twangy guitar, orchestration, and a chipper chorus of young girls adding wordless "ya-ya" vocals throughout). *—Richie Unterberger*

Ultra Lounge: On the Rocks, Pt. 1 / Apr. 8, 1997 / Capitol ✦✦✦
Extending their kitschy Ultra-Lounge series to its logical conclusion, Capitol Records prepared its own variation of Rhino's Golden Throats discs with the two volumes of *On the Rocks.* The idea is to gather a number of '60s rock & roll staples—"Light My Fire," "Mellow Yellow," "A Hard Day's Night," etc.—as they were covered by mainstream pop and easy listening acts, from Mel Torme, Martin Denny, and Julie London to the Lettermen, Buddy Morrow, and Zacharias. In short, it's supposed to be a laugh riot, since these artists are so, you know, square. However, the concept reads better than it plays—ten tracks of this stuff is entertaining, 22 winds up being an endurance test. A handful of cuts are quite funny—after all, it's hard not to be amused at London's "Mighty Quinn (Quinn the Eskimo)," Wayne Newton's "Love Grows (Where My Rosemary Goes)," and the Lettermen's unbelievable Doors medley, "Hello, I Love You/Touch Me"—and the song selection on whole is more entertaining than *Pt. 2,* yet *On the Rocks* remains a disc that can only be enjoyed in moderation. *—Stephen Thomas Erlewine*

AVANT GARDE

Categories are at best relative, and this is especially true in avant garde music. In this section, you'll find music made with stones and symphony orchestras, home-built computers and the unadorned human voice. The subjects are diverse—from personal political concerns to meditations on natural phenomena. Of course there are innovations in all genres of music. What these pieces have in common are composers who pursued unique visions intertwined with their lives—composers whose works have a deep conceptual component. This may be born in the quiet of the night, in sudden insights, in desires to go beyond prescribed behavior and the usual outcomes of circumscribed fate, in surprising social interactions, in contact with ancient cultural and religious traditions, and in many other life experiences. The works that result go beyond any recognized categories, and help enhance our sensitivity to both physical and imaginary worlds (both of which are "real" because, after all, we do the imagining).

The wide range of musical intervention includes:

(1) pattern music, that gradually evolves over a steady pulse into complex and changing forms incidentally mimicking natural processes such as the "divine proportion" patterns of the chambered nautilus, or the splitting of an amoeba (for example, the pieces of Terry Riley, Steve Reich, Tom Johnson, John Adams, Philip Glass, Jon Gibson);

(2) music which takes single sounds and other elements from pop music's song forms and formally expands on them to make music of universal vision (Glenn Branca, the Residents, Rhys Chatham);

(3) music employing chance procedures (something called "aleatory" which is actually a limited special case of chance operations) that produce the unexpected at every moment for performer, listener and even composer—compositions are often described as indeterminate of their "realization" (a one-time performance like sand painting erased after a particular ceremony, with the basic tradition or score remaining until the next realization); this music gives the performer both greater responsibility and freedom, and encourages us to fully experience the myriad events of every moment outside and inside ourselves, a sort of "ecology of the mind" (John Cage, Earle Brown, Christian Wolff, Morton Feldman, Marcel Duchamp); in a very real sense, this music is not "about" something, but is that "thing" itself;

(4) music is based on psychoacoustic illusions and natural phenomena—brainwaves, sonic blasts from sand dunes, chaotic vibrations, a plant's apparent response to emotional even telepathic stimuli (the Backster Effect used in Tom Zahuranec's unrecorded *Plant Music* of 1972), a bat's echolocation sense, whistling "sferics" from outer space, analogues of brain sytems, shadowing and intense amplification of environmental sound, and much more (Alvin Lucier, Maryanne Amacher, Paul DeMarinis, David Tudor, Maggi Payne, Annea Lockwood, "Blue" Gene Tyranny Hildegard Westerdamp);

(5) compostions for home-built and composer-built instruments (Harry Partch, David Behrmann, Fast Forward, Ellen Fullmann);

(6) sound-installations and other pieces designed to happen in places other than the usual concert halls (Ron Kuivila, Bill Fontana, Gordon Monahan);

(7) music in alternate tunings that creates new sensations of hearing (Ben Johnston, Ivan Wychnegradsky, LaMonte Young) and music that explores new ways of playing traditional instruments (Malcom Goldstein, Guy Klucevsek, Joseph Celli, Jin Hi Kim);

(8) unique approaches to melody, harmony and rhythm, and to traditional music (Alan Hovhaness, Virgil Thomson, Peter Garland, Toshio Hosokawa, Toru Takemitsu, Moondog), including what could be called "the downtown sound" where pop/world/techno/folk/concert sounds have all become part of the general vocabulary, not "collaged" in some artificial way but a result of the musicians having grown up hearing and playing these musics (Lenny Pickett, Peter Gordon, John Zorn);

(9) New Narrative opera with its political, humanitarian, and spiritual concerns, text-sound pieces, and other unusual uses of language and the voice (Robert Ashley, Kenneth Atchley, Beth Anderson, Ben Neill, Mikel Rouse, Lars Gunnar-Bodin, Joan LaBarbara, Christopher Butterfield, Gregory Whitehead, Carlos Santana);

(10) deeply meditative music of an altered and expanded time sense (Lois Vierk, Phill Niblock, Eliane Radique, Pauline Oliveros, Jerry Hunt);

(11) unique "crossover" pieces from jazz, rock, etc. (Ornette Coleman's "Skies of America," Lou Reed's "The Amino Ring),

(12) super-formalist pieces, even by academics who are even seen by their fellows as somewhat out of the fold (Stefan Wolpe, Jean Barraqui, Milton Babbitt, Elliot Carter, Iannis Xenakis);

(13) the whole array of electronic and tape music—generated by digital computers (John Chowning, Joel Chadabe, James Tenney, Larry Polansky, Joel Ryan, David Rosenboom) by analog synthesizers (Sun Ra, Walter Carlos, Morton Subotnick), "musique concrite" made with manipulation of tape speed and editing (also sound accumulation by covering the erase head, delay by multiple tape loops, etc., pioneers like Pierre Henry, Vladmir Ussachevsky), "live electronic" performance and interactive performance with acoustic instruments and voices (the Bifurcators, John Cage, David Tutor, Max Neuhaus, Gordon Mumma, Karlheinz Stockhausen, Richard Teitelbaum), sampling of acoustic and electronic sounds and modulating them with waveshaping synthesis etc.—including the outrageous "plunderphonics" cultural commentaries of John Oswald and others—computer-controlled installation and acoustic instruments, electronically amplified instruments and environmental sounds, like computer music (Jim Horton, John Bischoff, the Hub) and much more;

(14) collective improvisation and group "process"/"procedural" work (the Deep Listening Band, Machine for Making Sense, Cornelius Cardew and the Scratch Orchestra, Yankees, Jacques Bekaert); and, of course,

(15) composers/performers and their pieces that can be described as employing several of the techniques, aesthetics and influences mentioned above. *—"Blue" Gene Tyranny*

Artist Reviews

John Adams

b. Feb. 15, 1947, Worcester, MA

Composer / Classical Crossover, Minimalism

Former professor San Francisco Conservatory of Music, founder of the New Music Ensemble. Conductor of many new music premieres. Best known for opera Nixon in China. Adapted pattern music minimalism to rich melodic and harmonic studies in such works as Harmonielehrer. *–"Blue" Gene Tyranny*

Grand Pianola Music/Eight Lines / Aug. 1985 / Angel ✦✦✦

By the early '80s, John Adams' reputation as a second-generation minimalist had been established through works such as "Shaker Loops" for string septet and "Phrygian Gates" for solo piano. That tag seemed a bit uncomfortable, however, as Adams never appeared to fully subscribe to such rigorous systems as those employed by Steve Reich or Philip Glass. With "Grand Pianola Music," Adams took a confident stride toward a more all-embracing type of American music; one might even say toward Americana. The work, scored for a small wind orchestra, two pianos, and four sopranos, uses delicate minimalist patterns as an underlying basis for much of its duration, but there are hints of other concerns: the odd brass fanfare here, a thumping bass drum there, as if a neighborhood marching band is practicing in the distance. By the third movement, that band explodes onto the scene with a strutting, rousing melody that might sound more at home in a work by Blitzstein or Copland than one by a supposed minimalist. Much of the success of the composition is due to Adams' straightforward, unapologetic use of such "old-fashioned" material. As on the cover painting, Charles Demuth's "My Egypt," a non-ironic appreciation of certain uniquely American sources of beauty provides this work with unusual strength. *—Brian Olewnick*

● **Shaker Loops/Phrygian Gates** / 1990 / Arch ✦✦✦

An exceptionally good performance … rushing, trembling sounds represent the practices of the utopian religious sect the Shakers and also the musical "shake"… the two lovely inner movements "Hymning Slews" and "Loops and Verses" are Adams' best harmonic writing … a lot of activity for a so-called "minimal" music. *–"Blue" Gene Tyranny*

Harmonielehre / 1993 / EMI Classics ✦✦✦

The City of Birmingham Symphony Orchestra, conducted by S. Rattle, give a bright, spirited performance of this intriguing work by Adams; a thrilling study in new harmonies and orchestral textures. One of Adam's finest scores. *–"Blue" Gene Tyranny*

☆ **Earbox: A 10-CD Retrospective** / Oct. 12, 1999 / Elektra ✦✦✦✦✦

Maryanne Amacher

b. Feb. 25, 1943

Composer / Multimedia, Sound Sculpture, 20th Century Classical/Modern Composition, Avant-Garde

Modern American composer Maryanne Amacher has almost exclusively created huge multimedia installations from the '70s through (at least) the close of the '90s. Amacher's installments combine sculpture and layers of loud sound and low, resonating tones. She has developed her craft mainly in Europe, by experimenting with the acoustics of varying architectural spaces. In 1993, Amacher became the first Rosekrans Artist in Residence at Mills College. She has toured with Merce Cunningham collaborator David Behrman, teamed with Mark Trayle on the *Capp Street Project* in San Francisco (1985), and worked with composer Alvin Curran. In 1999, the Tzadik label released a recording of pieces that Amacher chose for CD, entitled *Sound Characters (making the third ear)*. *—Joslyn Layne*

● **Stain: The Music Rooms/In "Imaginary Landscapes"** / 1989 / Elektra/Nonesuch ✦✦✦✦✦

Amacher has created some of the finest pieces and sound-installations based on psychoacoustic illusions. Until the advent of CDs, most of her work was unrecordable partly because of the extreme ranges of pitch and dynamics, the duration of the piece necessary to create some illusions, and the stability of the medium. The "music rooms" are literally that—installed on floors of a house or in adjacent rooms that the audience walks through and creates their own mix from enormously amplified environmental and electronic sounds. —*"Blue" Gene Tyranny*

Sound Characters (Making the Third Ear) / Feb. 16, 1999 / Tzadik ✦✦✦
The "Making the Third Ear" part of the title refers to the phenomenon which listeners experience when listening to Maryanne Amacher's compositions—played at the right volume, sounds seem to emit from within the listener's head! Even though these works were written for installations in specific spaces, and not for recording, the "third ear" still happens (but not with headphones). The included pieces range from a rather comforting wash of tones ("Synaptic Island," *3) to boggling, bleeping loops (&"Dense Boogie 1",* and are, necessarily, often excerpts of longer works. —*Joslyn Layne*

Ambiances Magnétiques

f. 1982
Improvisation / Avant-Garde Jazz, Experimental Rock, 20th Century Classical/Modern Composition, Avant-Garde
Although the name Ambiances Magnétiques is mostly known for (and perceived as) the Montreal experimental music record label, there is also a specific artists' collective which preceded it. This nucleus of musicians has built what is now known as the Montreal experimental music scene.

It all started in 1982 when guitarist René Lussier and saxophonist/flutist Jean Derome presented a few duo concerts in Montreal under the name Ambiances Magnétiques (which translates to "Magnetic Atmospheres"). They teamed up with guitarist André Duchesne and clarinetist Robert Marcel Lepage and launched the label Ambiances Magnétiques in 1983, an entity managed by the members of the collective that would release records of the members, with occasional guests that would always have some sort of connection to the nucleus—up until the late 1990s, when the label started to broaden its horizons. In 1986 the group was extended to include Joane Hétu, Diane Labrosse and Danielle P. Roger, three hard-working musicians performing together in various avant-pop girl groups (Wondeur Brass, Justine). Hétu would soon be left in charge of the label itself. Radio DJ and drummer Michel F. Côté was enlisted in 1988 and finally turntablist/record manipulator Martin Tétreault (discovered accidentally as he was overheard by his unsuspecting neighbor André Duchesne in the late 1980s) officially joined in the mid-1990s.

The collective only performed a couple of times as a group, an event documented on the 1992 CD *Une Théorie des Ensembles.* They work more as a pool of musicians and a cooperative and they succeeded in creating their own underground network to support an experimental scene. This includes the record label, but also Distributions Ambiances Magnétiques Etc. (DAME), a distribution outlet, and production companies such as Productions Super-Mémé which orchestrates concert series and events in Montreal. By late 2000, the label had 90 titles under its belt and all Ambiances Magnétiques members had become keystones in the development of demanding music in Canada. —*François Couture*

- **Une Theorie Des Ensembles: Ambiances Magnétiques en Concert** / Jul. 19, 19929Aug. 2 02 / Ambiances Magnetiques ✦✦✦✦
This CD was an event: the first live album from the Ambiances Magnétiques label in almost ten years, and the only album ever to be credited to the Ambiances Magnétiques artists' collective. Recorded in February 1992 at the *Maison de la Culture Frontenac* in Montreal, the CD presents performances from all eight members of the collective at the time: founders René Lussier, Jean Derome, André Duchesne, and Robert Marcel Lepage; 1986 inductees Diane Labrosse, Danielle Palardy Roger, and Joane Hétu; and 1988 last addition Michel F. Côté. The album opens and closes on two ensemble pieces. "Ambulances en Plastique" is a Derome-penned rock fanfare, while "Montréal, 7 A.M." bears the typical rock guitar-driven Duchesne stamp. This fantastic guitarist/composer worked so rarely in the 1990s that every bit of material is a delight to hear. Between these two pieces, five Ambiances Magnétiques groups show their chops. Duchesne's Locomotive plays renditions of three tracks from its CD. Côté's Bruire delivers two very nice improvs in the same direction as its second album *Les Fleurs de Léo.* Two tracks from the all-girl group Justine are mostly improvised, although the first one is recognizable as "Vidanges Domestiques" from the *Langages Fantastiques* CD. The album's highlight is Les Granules' 13-minute suite "Le Bizarre ...chevelé," a never-recorded piece and the last thing Lussier and Derome's duo put on disc. It's a pity that the two tracks from La Flore Laurentienne are the only crumbs remaining from this Lepage project; the music is a very good blend of extended clarinet techniques and a more rock/techno approach. *Une Théorie Des Ensembles* is a very enjoyable CD that adds valuable material to these artists' discographies. —*François Couture*

Amm

f. 1965
Group / Improvisation, Avant-Garde Jazz, Experimental Rock, Free Jazz, Avant-Garde
Usually a trio of drummer Eddie Prévost, saxophonist Lou Gare and guitarist Keith Rowe, AMM has explored the minimalist fringe of avant-garde chance operations and improvisational jazz since its inception in 1965. The group debuted with *AMMMusic* in 1967, and released two additional albums during the late '60s. Much more quiet during the following decade, AMM became jazz-oriented for a brief period when only Prévost and Gare remained. The addition of composer Cornelius Cardew, and frequent classical musicians (cellist Rohan de Saram, pianist John Tilbury), tilted the balance back towards classical minimalism.

AMM's recording activity resumed again in the mid-'80s, with a parade of live releases and re-releases on Prevost's own Matchless Records, but very few original pieces; one exception is the Tom Phillips opera *Irma,* with contributions from Lol Coxhill, among others. Prévost also contributed to a new generation of experimentalists by recording with Jim O'Rourke, as well as Sonic Boom's EAR project. —*John Bush*

The Crypt: 12th June 1968, The Complete Session / 1968 / Matchless ✦✦✦✦

- **AMM III: It Had Been an Ordinary Enough Day in Pueblo, Colorado** / 1980 / Japo ✦✦✦✦
Including Eddie Prévost on drums and Keith Rowe on guitar, prepared guitar and transistor radio, AMM work through five selections of improvisatory music. —*John Bush*

- **Combine + Laminates + Treatise '84** / 1984 / Matchless ✦✦✦✦✦
In his liner notes to this recording, percussionist Eddie Prevost writes that there is "the tacit acknowledgement of potential failure at every music making moment. we can only ever be, at best, in the twilight world of the controlled accident." Since the group's inception in 1965, the various members of AMM have proven themselves masters of the "controlled accident," practicing the unforgiving art of non-idiomatic free improvisation with generally stellar results. This recording is one of their finest. "Combine + Laminates" tends to seesaw between aggressive, noisy sections dominated by Prevost and softer drone-like territories with Tilbury's muffled piano tones in the foreground. Both areas are given immense structural support by Keith Rowe's tabletop guitar arsenal: earthshakingly deep tremors in the louder portions, quietly keening harmonics in the more serene ones. Tilbury's unique genius in integrating the piano's more "traditional" sound into the alien environment created by the unorthodox use of percussion and guitar-electronics is very clear here.

Originally issued on vinyl by the Pogus label, the CD reissue includes another piece from the same date, a 32-minute interpretation of a section of Cornelius Cardew's masterwork, "Treatise." Cardew, a founding member of AMM, wrote this lengthy piece entirely in graphic notation. The performance sounds to the listener not substantially different than a "typical" one by this group. It tends toward the subdued with perhaps an emphasis on drier sounding textures, all seeming to be carefully considered even as they are improvised. This is one of AMM's great accomplishments: proving that free improvisation can be as thoughtful, demanding, and precise as composed music. Perhaps more so, judging from this beautiful document. —*Brian Olewnick*

The Inexhaustible Document / 1987 / Matchless ✦✦✦✦✦
By the early '80s, AMM's core group had come to consist of founding members Keith Rowe, Eddie Prevost, and its latest contributor, pianist John Tilbury. Periodically, musicians who shared their appetite for uninhibited and expansive improvisatory landscapes would join them. In this 1987 recording, the guest artist is Rohan de Saram, cellist with the Arditti String Quartet. *The Inexhaustible Document* is a fine example of AMM's mature style where the pieces, though necessarily lengthy, have an entirely unforced character; the music unfurls in a manner as natural as breathing. Most of this session is quiet and serene, de Saram's cello at first emitting soft sighs over Tilbury's surprisingly stately piano chords. Rowe and Prevost provide subtle underpinnings, complex washes of sound bearing little resemblance to the standard sonic qualities associated with guitar and drums. The storm clouds break on only a couple of occasions during the second piece, the rumbles surfacing into eruptions. Toward the end of the composition, de Saram improvises some moving romantic chords while Tilbury pounds ferociously at the keyboard and Prevost unleashes a barrage of old-fashioned drum kit work. This is electro-acoustic improvisation at a very high level, with sounds both unexpected and inevitable and with music no less stirring for being so abstract. —*Brian Olewnick*

Newfoundland / 1992 / Matchless ✦✦✦✦✦
Since its inception in 1966, the cooperative group AMM has been uncompromising in its commitment to freely improvised music. Often, especially early in its existence, this resulted in a harsh, aggressive sound field, one that even the most inquisitive newcomer might have difficulty approaching. By the mid-'80s, perhaps due to the mellowing that comes with age or the addition of pianist John Tilbury, AMM's music took a turn toward the quieter, more contemplative music evidenced on this release. In fact, *Newfoundland,* in addition to being one of their finest albums, is also one of the easiest entries not only into AMM, but into electro-acoustic improvisation in general. For this live recording, AMM consists of its founding members, Keith Rowe (guitar and electronics) and Eddie Prevost (percussion), in addition to Tilbury. The disc is a single, 77-minute piece in which the group constructs a breathing, evolving sonic space, ranging from the quietest whispers of softly brushed cymbals to raging electronic maelstroms, all sounding unforced and flowing. Tilbury, well known as one of the world's finest interpreters of Morton Feldman, inserts surprisingly melodic fragments into the proceedings, leavening the more severe sounds emanating from Rowe's guitar (which *never* sounds like a guitar) and Prevost's percussion arsenal. When, late in the piece, Rowe tunes in a radio program, it somehow sounds perfectly appropriate; it is the exact accent needed at that point. While this recording is a must for fans of AMM or freely improvised music in general, it is also one of the best possible introductions to the genre. —*Brian Olewnick*

Live in Allentown USA / 1994 / Matchless ✦✦✦✦✦

Before Driving to the Chapel We Took Coffee with Rick and Jennifer Reed / 1996 / Matchless ✦✦✦✦✦

Beth Anderson

b. Jan. 3, 1950, Lexington, KY
Vocals, Composer / 20th Century Classical/Modern Composition, Electronic
In 1981 Beth Anderson wrote, "The idea that beauty is revolutionary is a revelation to me... I've discovered the part of my brain that can't decode anything, can't add, can't work from verbalized concepts, but that does make melodies with pitch and rhythm... beauty is enough." That same year she wrote a piece demonstrating these ideas called *Revelation,* and in 1984 Barney Childs and the University of Redlands commissioned a shortened version that was called *Revel.* It is made up of five themes: (1) a six-note scale that turns around on itself until it becomes a b-minor melody, (2) a "dueling trumpets" sequence, (3) a Tune in F sharp related to the first theme, (4) a spanish gypsy-*Ben Hur* Brassy theme, and (5) a brass chorale that summarizes all the themes.

Beth Anderson was born in Kentucky and studied there, in California and in New York and John Cage, Terry Riley, Robert Ashley and Larry Austin. She has written an opera (*Queen*

Christian), an oratorio (*Joan*), numerous works for soloists and tape, and two off-broadway shows. She has received commissions from the Cabrillo Music Festival, the Staten Island Symphony, the San Francisco Conservatory; her awards have come from BMI, the NEA, National Public Radio, and others. Ms. Anderson says, "My own mystic bent leads me to believe that musical variations, collage, reiteration and process, or evolution, are beautiful. Life is worth living and beauty is worth making." *Revel* has been recorded by the Richmond Symphony conducted by Jacques Houtmann. It is still available on vinyl disc from Opus One (#100) *—Philip Krumm*

● **Torero Piece (1973) in "10 + 2 " 12 American Text Sound Pieces"** / 1974 / 1750 Arch ✦✦✦✦✦
This unfortunately not-yet-reissued disc contains this duet for the composer and her mother in which the mother describes her relationship to her daughter while the daughter makes unrelated phonemic sounds decoded from a paint-by-number picture she found in a junk antique store. An imaginative and drolly humorous piece by this very original composer who is also known for her opera about Queen Christina. *— "Blue" Gene Tyranny*

Revel (1981/1984) / 1984 / Opus One ✦✦✦
Performed by The Richmond Symphony conducted by Jacques Houtmann. Romantic music that combines rock harmony and an interest in world music. *— "Blue" Gene Tyranny*

Laurie Anderson (Laura Phillips Anderson)

b. Jun. 5, 1947, Chicago, IL
Vocals, Violin / Multimedia, Experimental Rock, Experimental
After briefly entering the mainstream pop radar in 1981 with her lone hit "O Superman," Laurie Anderson enjoyed a public visibility greater than virtually any other avant-garde figure of her era. Her infrequent forays into rock aside, Anderson remained firmly grounded in performance art, her ambitious multimedia projects encompassing music, film, mime, visual projections, dance, and—most importantly—spoken and written language, the cornerstone of her work.

In her teens, she studied violin, and at 20 moved to NYC, earned an art history degree from Barnard College in 1969, and an M.F.A. in sculpture from Columbia University in 1972. She taught, then staged her first public performances in 1973. By 1976, Anderson was performing throughout North America and Europe. Based on the power of words and language, her work also emphasized visual imagery and cutting-edge technology. Anderson recorded "O, Superman," for the tiny NY label 110 Records; at eleven-minutes, built around electronic drones, with opaque half-spoken, half-sung lyrics, "O, Superman" was a most unlikely hit. Nevertheless, it was a smash in Britain, reaching #2 on the pop charts in late 1981. Now signed to Warner Bros., Anderson issued *Big Science* (1982), a work drawn from the seven-hour multi-media performance *United States*. 1984's *Mister Heartbreak* was her most overtly pop-oriented work, included artists Peter Gabriel and Adrian Belew, and reached the American Top 100. That same year she also issued the complete *United States Live*, spread across a five-LP set. Her next project was concert film *Home of the Brave*, followed by the score for *Swimming to Cambodia*. The studio album, *Strange Angels*, came out in 1989. Anderson and boyfriend Lou Reed teamed with producer Brian Eno on *Bright Red* (1994), but she focused more on performing, including "The Nerve Bible" (1995) and "Songs and Stories from Moby Dick" (1999) tours. *—Jason Ankeny*

● **Big Science** / 1982 / Warner Brothers ✦✦✦✦✦
Big Science is essentially a chunk of the more elaborate and difficult four-part multi-media performance piece *United States*. But, that said, *Big Science* never sounds like a portion, it is in fact a meal in itself. The music is moody and minimalistic, and Anderson's wry observations are perspicacious, smartalecky and, at times, laugh-out-loud funny. There have been numerous artists attempting work like this since *Big Science;* few, however, equal Anderson's panache. Not your average pop record. Oh yeah, "O Superman" is here in all its glory. *—John Dougan*

Mister Heartbreak / 1984 / Warner Brothers ✦✦✦✦
A more pop-oriented record (there are songs here and musicians like Adrian Belew and Peter Gabriel), Anderson displays a functional singing voice that graces such wonderful songs as "Sharkey's Day" and "Excellent Birds" (a duet with Gabriel). More accessible than *Big Science*, but in some ways a record indicating that while she may not be a musician herself, Anderson certainly knows how to pick them, work with them, and challenge them. A thoroughly wonderful record. *—John Dougan*

Strange Angels / Oct. 1989 / Warner Brothers ✦✦✦✦✦
Purists may disagree, but I think *Strange Angels* is Anderson's most stunning work. It may be due to its nearly giddy selection of pop songs (including the supremely ecstatic "Babydoll"), but here Anderson sounds supremely confident—as a pop singer/songwriter. Rather than weighing down her songs with avant-gardisms, *Strange Angels* positively luxuriates in this conflation of the avant-garde and the popular. Hence, there is a relentless joyfulness that imbues this record, but never sacrifices intelligence one iota. A brilliantly conceived record, *Strange Angels* offers the best of both worlds to the benighted and aficionados. *—John Dougan*

Bright Red / Oct. 25, 1994 / Warner Brothers ✦✦✦

The Ugly One with the Jewels and Other Stories / Mar. 14, 1995 / Warner Brothers ✦✦✦✦✦
On her later albums, Laurie Anderson had moved from her earlier spoken word-plus-effects style to a more overtly musical approach, with less effective results. *The Ugly One With the Jewels*, a recording of a live performance of readings from her book *Stories From the Nerve Bible*, returned her to speaking instead of singing, and it was her best album since *Big Science*. The 18 stories reflected Anderson's extensive travels, including forays into the Third World and to convents, although she made Los Angeles and Houston sound just as exotic. In fact, telling her stories over sounds from birds, guitars, and electronic beeps, she seemed an anthropologist from another world, always finding the natives friendly but strange. And she didn't fail to recognize that she could appear just as odd to them: "The Ugly One With the Jewels" was a name used by one of her subjects to describe her. *— William Ruhlmann*

Jorge Antunes

b. Apr. 23, 1942, Rio de Janeiro, Brazil
Composer / Electro-Acoustic, Electronic
Avant-garde composer Jorge Antunes is known as the man who pioneered electronic music in Brazil. During the '50s and '60s, he studied the violin, conducting, composition, and physics, and as a result of the latter wrote his "Cromoplastofonias" series. Starting in the late '60s, he worked in electronic studios in Buenos Aires (with Alberto Ginastera and Umberto Eco, among others) and Paris, with Groupe de Recherches Musicales (with Pierre Schaeffer). He served as a professor, studio director, and orchestra conductor at the University of Brasilia. Over the years, he founded the Chromo-Music Research Studio and the new music ensemble Group of Musical Experimentation. In his compositions, Antunes has explored the relationship between sound and colors, flavors and odors (in "Ambiente I"), and 'commented' on work by Claude Levi-Strauss with a percussive performance art piece. He has won several awards including the International Tribune of Composer's UNESCO prize twice in the '90s. *—Joslyn Layne*

Musica Electronica / Joias Musicais ✦✦✦
This is the first of electronic music made in Brazil. Antunes is a wonderful composer who constructed the Center for Chomo-Musical Research in Rio de Janeiro and thereby became the first composer of electronic music in his country. "Valso Sideral" (1962) and "Contrapunctus Contra Contrapunctus" (1965) are early uses of patterning in "rhythmic cells" where the rhythms are gradually distorted. In "Cintra Cita" (1969) the composer has a "bande rendezvous" (tape meeting) with himself over materials and chance rhythms and thoughts used throughout his work. The fascinating "Auto-Retrato Sonre Paisaje Porteno" (1969) used a scratch in an old 78 rpm record played on a wind-up phonograph as the basic rhythmic element for the construction of an electronically modified samba where the words are inflected by the composer's voice and lose all actual meaning. "Historia de un Pueblo" (1970) is a dramatic work alternating between sweet persuasion and aggression, a not explicitly narrative story that can nevertheless be understood by anyone. *— "Blue" Gene Tyranny*

Robert Ashley

b. Mar. 28, 1930, Ann Arbor, MI
Composer / Experimental, Minimalism, Electro-Acoustic, Opera
Studied with Ross Lee Finney, Roberto Gerhard, Leslie Bassett. Music degrees from Univ. of Michigan and Manhattan School of Music, worked in Speech Research Lab (psychoacoustics and cultural speech patterns) and was a Research Assistant in acoustics at the Architectural Research Lab. Co-founder legendary ONCE Group in the 1960s, co-director Center for Contemporary Music at Mills College in 1970s. Created new kind of opera (sometimes called the New Narrative opera) in works like *That Morning Thing* (1967), *Combination Wedding and Funeral* (1964), *Perfect Lives* an opera-for-TV (1980), *e/L Aficionado* (1991). Social behavior and and language illusion studies like *The 4th of July* for tape (1960), *The Wolfman* (1964), *in memoriam… Crazy Horse (symphony)* (1963), *The Trial of Anne Opie Wehrer and Unknown Accomplices for Crimes Against Humanity* (1968). *— "Blue" Gene Tyranny*

She Was a Visitor in "Extended Voices" / 1968 / Odyssey ✦✦✦
The Brandeis University Chamber Chorus, cond. by Alvin Lucier. Describes musically how "rumor" is spread among people, with leaders of a group selecting phonemes of the chanted line "she was a visitor" and the group sustaining each individual sound. The amassed sound, a "surface" of normalized little disturbances, in which an audience could also participate, begins to resemble airplanes, cars, trains… or perhaps the subatomic world. *— "Blue" Gene Tyranny*

Music with Roots in the Aether / 1980 / Lovely Music ✦✦✦
The legendary 14-hour videotape series (seven two-hour programs) with interviews and performances by post-serial, post-Cage composers David Behrman, Philip Glass, Alvin Lucier, Gordon Mumma, Pauline Oliveros, Terry Riley and Robert Ashley. Not mere MTV or PBS, the series is actually a "music-theater piece in color video" that finds new ways to show music being performed in highly unusual, visually exciting and continuous-shot (un-cut) approaches. *— "Blue" Gene Tyranny*

Music Word Fire and I Would Do It Again: the Lessons / 1981 / Lovely Music ✦✦✦

Atalanta (Acts of God) / 1985 / Lovely Music ✦✦✦

● **In Sara Mencken Christ and Beethoven There Were Men and Women** / 1991 / Cramps ✦✦✦✦✦
This uniquely original work for voice and electronics dates from 1972. A 128-stanza poem by the legendary John Barton Walgamot traces a hidden story of social progress and influence within the gradual repetition of a single grand phrase. For example, "In its very truly great manners of Ludwig Van Beethoven, very heroically the very cruelly ancestral death of Sara Powell Haardt had very ironically come amongst his very really grand men and women to Rafael Sabatini, George Ade, Margaret Storm Jameson, Ford Madox Hueffer, Jean-Jacques Bernard, Louis Bronfield, Friedrich Wilhelm Nietzsche and Helen Brown Norden very titanically." In the other verses names are added and subtracted, and there occurs a subtlety organized variation of syntactical parts leading to further mysterious integration of meanings. The voice part is read with as few inflections and breaths as possible—in the first realization prepared on tape, all pauses were removed, so that the voice has this eternal quality. (Gertrude Stein once mentioned that she aimed for this same quality while in the 1934-35 recording of her works, but had to settle for reading in long breaths). The voice activates electronic sounds that respond with inflected sounds; in the initial realization for records, electronic sounds designed by composer Paul DeMarinis were variously beautiful and humorous. The musical effect is that of an internal voice stimulating involuntary ideas and feelings. This piece, together with Ashley's "Automatic Writing" (1979), "The Wolfman" (1964), "Fancy Free, or It's There" (1970), "Purposeful Lady Slow Afternoon" (1968, from *The Wolfman Motorcity Revue*) and "She Was a Visitor" (1967, from the opera *That Morning Thing*) offer a profound musical exploration of the relation between the physical nature of the voice and social/language behaviors. *— "Blue" Gene Tyranny*

★ **Perfect Lives** / 1991 / Lovely Music ♦♦♦♦♦
Available on CD and videotape, *Perfect Lives* is part of a trilogy of operas for TV, including *Atalanta (Acts of God)* and *Now Eleanor's Idea*. A total of 39 half-hour episodes, *Perfect Lives* was realized for Channel Four of British television. In this epic work set in the American Midwest, the rhythms of the music, the geometry of the scenes, and the relations of the characters all seem to be from the same cloth, as if being described by the martyred first natural scientist Giordano Bruno, who is a background character never appearing in this work. For the characters who do appear, this is the basic plot: "Raoul de Noget (No-zhay), a singer, and his friend, Buddy, 'The World's Greatest Piano Player,' have come to a small town in the Midwest to entertain at the Perfect Lives Lounge. For some unexplained reason, they have fallen in with two people from the town, Isolde ('nearing 30 and not yet spoken for') and her brother 'D,' just out of high school and known as 'The Captain of the Football Team' (his parents call him Donnie), to commit the perfect crime, a metaphor for something philosophical: in this case, to remove a sizable amount of money from The Bank for one day (one day only) and 'let the whole world know it was missing.'" The seven episodes are "*The Park (Privacy Rules)*," "*The Supermarket* (Famous People)," "*The Bank (Victimless Crime)*," "*The Bar (Differences)*," "*The Living Room (The Solutions)*," "*The Church* (After the Fact)," and "*The Backyard (T'Be Continued)*." "*Perfect Lives* is nothing less than the first American opera" (Allan Evans, *Fanfare*). The opera, taken as a whole, is a giant metaphor for the rebirth of the soul. *— "Blue" Gene Tyranny*

☆ **Improvement (Don Leaves Linda)** / 1992 / Elektra/Nonesuch ♦♦♦♦♦
In the past 15 years, Ashley, both as composer and writer, has invented a new kind of opera of far-ranging narrative discourse and vocal inflection that replaces the older romantic opera where the characters exist only to move along the plot. This new form arrived in a series of operas-for-TV that speak with remarkable feeling and intelligence of contemporary society, history and mind—*Perfect Lives* (seven episodes), *Atalanta (Acts of God)* (three episodes), and *Now Eleanor's Idea* (four episodes).

"Improvement" from *Now Eleanor's Idea* is for voices and electronic orchestra, and has an uniquely original sound. The basic premise of the opera is presented in the prelude called "The Argument": "To continue I must explain an idea I am inadequate to communicate… Now Eleanor's Idea conceived as if in a flash of light, the offering of images is a radical form of Judaism which has come to us unacknowledged in the same form as Protestantism, Modernism, Science and Theater as we know it… Her idea explains… how all of these things have come together… For the sake of argument Don is Spain in 1492, and Linda is the Jews." We are taken through genuinely humorous, surreal and poignant modern situations which serve as metaphors: "The Airline Ticket Counter" (where Don explains why his wife or her luggage are not with him), "Back Home Some Days She Pretends She's Someone Else," "The Contents of Her Purse," "He Tries to Teach Junior Jr. to Play Golf Left Handed," "North (Berlin/A Tango)," "The Doctor (All Things Rolled Into One)," "The Big City (But Only As If in a Dream)," etc. Through these touching incidents and characters, and a music that is equally intimate and dramatically universal, we are presented with a sense of the "eternal present." A masterpiece. *— "Blue" Gene Tyranny*

Superior Seven: Concerto for Flute and Orchestra/Tract for Orchestra and Voice / 1995 / New World ♦♦♦

Automatic Writing and Other Works / 1996 / Lovely Music ♦♦♦
Re-release of three new music landmarks: *Automatic Writing* (1979), in which the composer explores spontaneous speech unfiltered (as much as is possible) by his normal language behavior ("My mind is censoring my own mind"); *Purposeful Lady Slow Afternoon* (1968) from the *Wolfman Motor City Review*, a sensual and captivating study of random vocal reactions (sung by the vocal trio of Mary Ashley, Mary Lucier, and Barbara Lloyd) with a personal story (by Cynthia Liddell) about the sense of touch, which with smell is repressed in Western society; and *She Was a Visitor* (1967) from the opera *That Morning Thing*, performed by the Brandeis University Chamber Chorus, conducted by Alvin Lucier—this wonderful piece describes musically how rumor is spread, with leaders of a chorus group selecting phonemes of the chanted line "she was a visitor" and the group sustaining each individual sound. The amassed sound, a surface of normalized little disturbances, in which an audience could also participate, begins to resemble airplanes, cars, trains—or perhaps the subatomic world. *— "Blue" Gene Tyranny*

Kenneth Atchley

b. Nov. 7, 1954
Composer / 20th Century Classical/Modern Composition, Electronic
Studied at Mills College with Robert Ashley and David Behrman. Describes himself as "listening to news & noise" and as "a dilletante Buddhist." Many performances. A comprehensive article on his work is published in *An Introduction to the Operatic Works of K. Atchley Including an In-Depth Discussion of an Original Opera Titled 'Don Giovanni'*, pub. in Leonardo Music Journal (Jan. 1991). His writings and scores also appear in *The Guests Go In To Supper* (Burning Books). Other works: *Light of Hand (Lumiére de Main)* (1982) for voices and computer, *Cabinet (Enclosed Spaces)* from the opera *Edison's Last Projection* (1985), *Wasserglocken mit Electronics* (1985), *Marconi—The Last Seven Words* (1986). *— "Blue" Gene Tyranny*

Don Giovanni, Act I, Scenes 1—4/ in "Anthology of Music for the 21st Century" / 1991 / Leonardo Music Journal, Vol. 1 #1 ♦♦♦♦♦
A musical conversation with the characters of Da Ponte's libretto for Mozart's opera about the cultural myth of Don Juan and the history of our attitudes about sexuality (and "going to hell" for sharing sensual feeling). A subtle, surreal evocation for voices and electronics with a highly poetic and intelligent text by the composer. *— "Blue" Gene Tyranny*

Larry Austin

b. Sep. 12, 1930, Duncan, OK
Composer / Improvisation, Electro-Acoustic, Electronic
Austin received his education at North Texas State University and taught at University of California-Davis, and later at University of South Florida and at the Center of the Creative and Performing Arts of SUNY in Buffalo, NY. He was a principal founder and editor of *Source*, a journal of avant-garde music. He achieved his first success with his composition *Improvisations for Orchestra and Jazz Soloists* in 1961, performed by the New York Philharmonic and commercially recorded. He experimented with an open style in which sections of the composition are designated for free improvisation by the performers and the work's overall form is controlled by analogue notation. He also uses electronic and theatrical devices in his composition. *— Lynn Vought*

Hybrid Music: Four Compositions: Quadrants/Event/Complex No. 1/Second Fantasy on Ives / 1980 / Irida ♦♦♦
The early music of prolific acoustic and electronic music composer Larry Austin combined elements of jazz improvisation and advanced compositional techniques, as in his "Cantana for Soprano and Jazz" at the University of California, Davis (1963) and composed works in his "open style" such as "Catharsis: Open Style for Two Improvisational Ensembles, Tape and Conductor" (1967) and the theater piece "The Maze" (1966) for percussionists, dancer, tape, and films. He later developed combinatorial pieces (the "event/complexes" of the '70s), wrote fantasies for voice and the legendary *Source* magazine anthology of new music, and composed many other electro-acoustic works. His recent work with computers documented on CD continues to combine electronics and acoustic instruments/voices by transforming—with a sense of humor—recognized historical material into "mini opera-buffas." *— "Blue" Gene Tyranny*

Milton Babbitt

b. May 10, 1916, Philadelphia, PA
Composer / Musique Concrète, Atonal, Electronic, Classical
Studied with Marion Bauer, Roger Sessions. Teacher at Juilliard and Princeton. Co-director Columbia-Princeton Electronic Music Center, consultant in creation of Mark II RCA Synthesizer. Early use of serialist techniques in America. *Generatrix* for orchestra (1935), *Composition for Four Instruments* (1948), *Vision and Prayer* for soprano and synthesized tape (1961), *String Quartet No. 4* (1970). *— "Blue" Gene Tyranny*

All Set, for Jazz Ensemble (1957) / 1990 / Elektra/Nonesuch ♦♦♦
Formal writing for a jazz group… like experiments for other "progressive jazz" ensembles of the late '40s and '50s—the Sauter-Finegan Orchestra, the Stan Kenton Orchestra etc.—this is a piece of its decade, but still interesting. Other works on this CD are by other well-known formalist composers George Rochberg (1918-), Lalo Schifrin (1932-), Richard Wernick (1934-), and Stefan Wolpe. *— "Blue" Gene Tyranny*

● **Correspondences for String Orchestra and Synthesizer Tape (1967) in "Cage/ Carter/ Bab** / 1994 / Deutsche Grammaphon ♦♦♦♦
A fascinating classic of electro-acoustic illusions within a formalist style. *— "Blue" Gene Tyranny*

Ensembles for Synthesizer / Columbia ♦♦♦
One of the first composers in America to employ Arnold Schöenberg's method of composition with 12 tones, Babbitt also extended this method—before the young European school of Boulez/Stockhausen/Nono/Berio—into the even more highly organized system of serial composition in the mid-'40s, with his pieces "Three Compositions for Piano" (1947) and "Composition for Four Instruments" (1948). This electronic composition from 1964 was realized at the Columbia-Princeton Electronic Music Center, and demonstrates Babbitt's methods applied to this medium. His primary musical material employs the 12 tones of the even tempered scale, and a vast array of pitch, rhythmic, registral, textural, and timbral degrees, which are contained within interrelating collections or ensembles. Babbitt uses the synthesizer primarily for this ability to move very quickly and accurately among these delineated parameters. The result is a kaleidoscope of electronic timbres. *— "Blue" Gene Tyranny*

Tadeusz Baird

b. Jul. 26, 1928, Grodzisk Mazowiecki, Poland, **d.** Sep. 2, 1981, Warsaw, Poland
Composer / 20th Century Classical/Modern Composition, Atonal
Polish composer Tadeusz Baird was interested in expressionism (although his definition of this changed during his career), and wrote many works for voice. Baird studied under Piotr Rytel and Tadeusz Witulski, among others, in Warsaw. He co-founded Group 49 in 1949 with the goal of writing music that expressed the state's ideology. In 1956, he and Group 49 cohort Kazimierz Serocki organized a festival of international contemporary music. Around this time, Baird's style underwent a change, with subsequent works such as "12-Tone String Quartet" (1957) and "Four Essays for Orchestra" (1958) demonstrating a more emotional aspect. He scored films by Andrzej Wajda in the late '50s and early '60s. His works for voice include a song cycle of Halina Poswiatowska's poems. Baird received numerous awards and honors, including the Polish Composers' Union Award, the Honegger Prize, the Koussevitzky prize, the Award of the Andrzej Jurzykowski Foundation (NY), and the UNESCO International Composer's Rostrum three times during the '50s and '60s. He taught composition at the Academy of Music in Warsaw beginning in the late '70s. *— Joslyn Layne*

Psychodrama for Orchestra / Concert for Oboe and Orchestra / Scenes for Cello, Harp And / 1993 / Koch ♦♦♦
Works with an interesting blend of dramatic Schöenbergian romanticism, serial pointillism and original orchestral colors written by a composer who went from a rather bland style of what was then imagined to be "people's music" to a radical change in the '60s. *— "Blue" Gene Tyranny*

Llorenç Barber

b. 1948, Aielo de Malferit, Spain
Composer / Experimental, 20th Century Classical/Modern Composition, Avant-Garde
Modern composer Llorenç Barber is best known as the author of large-scale pieces played on all of the church bells within a town. Throughout the '90s, he was commissioned by a number of European cities and music festivals to create these unique pieces. The Catalan

composer has also collaborated on works with Javier Maderuelo, choreographer Antonio Aparisi (for "Gargoyles," basend on Valencia's Lonja building), and singer/performance artist Fatima Miranda, with whom Barber co-founded the group Taller de M'sica Mundana. Barber was also a founding member of l'Ensemble Actum, in the early '70s. Several CDs of his work, including *Linguopharincampanology,* have been released in Europe. *—Joslyn Layne*

Concierto de Campanas Sacra Lucus [The "Sacra Lucus" Concerto for Church Bells] / 1992 / Unio Musics ✦✦✦

Written for more than 100 musicians located in 14 bell towers in Lugo, this astonishing piece, similar to many that Barber has presented in Spanish cities, was presented on June 8, 1991. All traffic ceased during performance, and suddenly Lugo was transported back in time, as the persistent rhythm of "Hymn of the Ancient Kingdom of Galicia," with the "Alabado Sea el Santisimo" played simultaneously on a cathedral carrillon, began to ring from the outermost bell towers toward the center of the city, the queen tower of the cathedral. The sound is stunning, floating over the area like a sonorous "decibel net" or mystical blanket, or the humming of UFOs. The performers were given chronometers and a precise time score for their various parts, which required exercising prior to and strenuous playing during the 40-minute performance. Barber has recently received cooperation from the Spanish navy for a piece that uses modern battle cruisers, ancient frigates, cannon, and cathedrals on shore—and again the involvement of an entire city—for a performance. *—"Blue" Gene Tyranny*

Jean Barraqué

b. Jan. 17, 1928, Puteaux, France, **d.** Aug. 17, 1973, Paris, France

Composer / 20th Century Classical/Modern Composition, Atonal, Chamber Music

French composer of chamber music; a contemporary of Messiaen; one of the first serialists. His unique style combined a rich impressionism with extremely formal pointillism. The use of jazz instrumentalists in classical ensembles playing his serial music led to social stigmatization in the late '50s. The pieces *… au delà du hasard* and *Chant après Chant* (1966) for six percussionists, voice, and piano were inspired by *The Death of Virgil,* by Hermann Broch. These pieces do not merely set the text but reflect upon it, as shown in "Unable to evolve or regress," "Before the quotation," and "On a thought without night." *—"Blue" Gene Tyranny*

… Au Dela Du Hasard (… Beyond Mere Luck) (1959) for Four Instrumental Formations And / 1981 / Astree ✦✦✦

Barraque was one of the first serialists with a unique style that combined a rich impressionism and extremely formal pointillism. His beautiful "Sonate Pour Piano" (1950-1952) (recorded by Claude Helffer on Astre AS 36, out of print disc) was praised by jazz critic Andre Hodeir in an early book; this praise and Barraque's use of jazz instrumentalists (playing his serial music) sitting together with classic ensembles led to Barraque being stigmatized socially—this was the late '50s after all. "… Au Dela du Hasard," like "Chant Apres Chant" (1966) for six percussionists, voice, and piano, was inspired by Hermann Broch's poem *The Death of Virgil,* not merely setting the text, but reflecting upon it. The titles of the movements give some idea of this impulse: "The Night Without Rays," "Unable to Evolve or Regress," "Which Ephemeral Signs—," "Abusive Exaggerations," "In the Wandering Multitude," "For the Unknown Edge of Chance," "Before the Quotation," "Blinded by the Dream (Quotation)," "Beyond the Direct Line of Sight," and "On a Thought Without Night." *—"Blue" Gene Tyranny*

● **Le Temps Restitu (1968) Excerpt from "La Mort De Virgile" (The Death of Virgil) by Herm** / 1987 / Harmonia Mundi ✦✦✦✦✦

A work similar in many aspects to "… au dela du Hasard" although more in the pointillistic serial style. Beautiful performance by mezzo-soprano Anne Bartelloni. On the same CD is the virtuosic "Concerto" (1962–1968) for alternating trios of instruments (eg. violin-bassoon-trumpet, violoncello-flute-tenor saxophone etc.). *—"Blue" Gene Tyranny*

Louis and Bebe Barron

Group / Film Music, Electro-Acoustic, Electronic

Wrote electronic music for film. The Barrons also assisted John Cage in making "Williams Mix." *—"Blue" Gene Tyranny*

Forbidden Planet (1954) / 1988 / Planet ✦✦✦

The first Hollywood filmscore to use electronic music (the first all-electronic soundtrack was for Anais Nin's "The Bells of Atlantis" in 1952). Music from cybernetic (controlled feedback) circuitry especially designed by the Barrons… music of the Krells, monsters from the Id. The Barrons also assisted John Cage in the making of "Williams Mix." *—"Blue" Gene Tyranny*

Martin Bartlett

b. 1939, Great Britain, **d.** 1993

Composer / Computer Music, 20th Century Classical/Modern Composition, Avant-Garde, Electronic

Martin Bartlett (1939-1993) was a West Coast-based composer who worked with, among others, the composers/performers Pauline Oliveros and David Tudor, but his work, unfortunately, largely eluded wider recognition. As represented on the album *Burning Water,* he was very involved with interactive electronics, programming both computers and synthesizers to interact in real time with live performers. *—Brian Olewnick*

Pythagoras' Ghost / 1993 / Front ✦✦✦

The title piece on this CD is for four electronic wind instruments and contains sections that are lighthearted, even goofy in their sense of humor ("Akousmata—ear whisperings," "Xenomelophilia—love of strange melodies") one movement of elegant transparency ("Chromopneuma—breath colours"), and a tiny pedantic march ("Gymnosophia—naked philosophies or nude philosophers"). My favorite work is "The Arrival Of Sir John Franklin In Paradise" (1988) for a wonderful variety of synthesized sounds surrounding and supporting Bartlett's chanting and sometimes electronically-modified voice on texts from Dante. A composer with a definitely original manner. *—"Blue" Gene Tyranny*

● **Burning Water** / Jan. 1, 1998 / Periplum ✦✦✦✦

Martin Bartlett's "Hexachords," which opens the album, provides a lovely example of his work with interactive electronics. Patterns played on soprano recorder are "listened to" by a computer, which reacts with its own elaborations on those patterns and signals a synthesizer to play them, creating a constant back and forth between performer and program. The result is a beautiful, many-layered tapestry of sound, smooth yet unpredictable, the general character perhaps a bit reminiscent of Terry Riley's late '60s organ improvisations (both Bartlett and Riley studied with Indian vocalist Pandit Pran Nath). Two versions of "Etats," one each with George Lewis (trombone) and Frances-Marie Uitti (cello) are different affairs, much less mellifluous and somewhat more turbulent in nature. Uitti is especially impressive, using dark, melancholy lines to summon equally brooding gurgles and tremblings from the computer. The title piece, which finds Bartlett interacting with his own program, begins much as the first, with subtle inferences of Carnatic singing, but segues into a small flurry of rising tones like a cluster of tornadoes and finally subsides into several minutes of gentle sighs, pings, and whirrs. Overall, this is a fine and rewarding series of compositions from a composer who should be far better known. *—Brian Olewnick*

David Behrman

b. Aug. 16, 1937, Salzburg, LA

Composer / Sound Sculpture, Improvisation, Computer Music, Avant-Garde, Electronic

Holds degrees from Harvard and Columbia. Produced *Music of Our Time* series for Columbia Records in 1960s. Co-founder Sonic Arts Union. Tours with Merce Cunningham Dance Company in 1970s and 1990s. Co-director Center for Contemporary Music, Mills College (1975-80). Also taught at Ohio State Univ. and CAL Arts, designed children's computer games at Children's Television Workshop. Toured under friendship grants from the Japan-United States Friendship Commission and the DAAD (Berlin). Many sound installations, that can be played by non-professionals at Whitney Museum, Museum of Contemporary Art in Chicago, Für Augen und Ohren (For Eye and Ear) in Berlin, DeCordova Museum in Lincoln, MA, La Villette in Paris, etc. *—"Blue" Gene Tyranny*

On the Other Ocean/Figure in a Clearing / 1978 / Lovely Music ✦✦✦✦✦

Leapday Night / 1990 / Lovely Music ✦✦✦

★ **Unforeseen Events** / 1992 / Experimental Intermedia ✦✦✦✦✦

Two 1991 suites—"Unforeseen Events" (in four parts) and "Refractive Light" (in three parts)—make up this beautiful CD of interactive music. In "Unforeseen Events," instrumentalists trigger computer programs that in turn control sound-making electronic modules, which the acoustic instrumentalist freely responds to. The first version of "Unforeseen Events" was created with composer/performer Ben Neill in mind, playing his invention the mutantrumpet—a brass instrument with three separate bells. In the first section, "View Finder," the computer responds to the trumpet with immediate and slightly delayed chords that are also slightly shifted in pitch and timbre over time. Part Two is "Fishing for Complements," a trio in which the interchange is noted by a "listener" at a keyboard who enters changes into the computer. In Part Three, "Witch Grass," when the soloist pauses, the sustained chords begin to gradually slip away from their tonal centers until the performer begins to play again. In the last part, entitled "Canyon," single notes trigger a shimmering chord that fades away in pitch-shifted trails into a seemingly borderless canyon depth. "Unforeseen Events II" (1998) is the latest version of the software program that was made for the artistry of Jon Gibson on flutes and soprano saxophone and *"Blue" Gene Tyranny* on MIDI-keyboard. In the three sections of "Refractive Light," aharmonic changes occur as "deflections" off of dying sustained tones. "Harbinger" is a kind of introduction that begins with delicate bell patterns and sliding chords. "Crisscrossed Eights" is similar in tonal structure and also has bell-like sounds mixed with sliding chords, koto-like arpeggios and strumming, and high string-like swells, all in very elastic, "breathing" quasi-random rhythms. The third section, "Ein Glaesele Warems" (A Little Glass of Warmth), features sounds "… made with intervals and timbres meant to create a feeling of remoteness from the modern world." *—"Blue" Gene Tyranny*

Cathy Berberian

b. Jul. 4, 1928, Attleboro, MA, **d.** Mar. 6, 1983, Rome, Italy

Vocals / International Folk, 20th Century Classical/Modern Composition, Opera

Berberian's education included the study of mime, writing and opera at Columbia and New York Universities, Hindu and Spanish dancing, a position as soloist for the Armenian Dance Group and vocal study with Vigo. She debuted in Naples in 1957 and in the USA in 1960 at Tanglewood. Many composers have written works for her, including Stravinsky and Henze. Her repertoire covers a wide range of material, from 17th century opera to folksongs. She is also a composer, and *Stripsody* (1966) for solo voice and *Morsicat(h)y* (1971) for piano are examples of her work. *—Lynn Vought*

Cathy Berberian, Voice / Mainstream ✦✦✦

Astonishing performances by one of new music's first vocal sound experimenters, Berberian (1925–1983) had many pieces written especially for her. Includes Luciano Berio "Circles" (text by e.e. cummings), Bussotti "Frammento", and an especially noteworthy presentation of the John Cage "Aria with Fontana Mix". You may also wish to hear her "Stripsody for solo voice" (1966) on Wergo WER 60054-50. *—"Blue" Gene Tyranny*

Luciano Berio

b. Oct. 24, 1925, Oneglia, Italy

Composer / Musique Concrète, Experimental, 20th Century Classical/Modern Composition, Atonal, Electronic

A major force in the development of postwar-era experimental music, avant-garde composer and theorist Luciano Berio brought a sense of lyricism and personal expression to even the most complex techniques of electronic and aleatoric music, his modernist approach lending itself to a variety of idioms while incorporating resources including folk traditions, choreography, mime, and acrobatics. Born in 1925, Berio studied composition and conducting in Milan before travelling to the U.S. to study and compose his first major work, *Chamber Music for Mezzo-Soprano, Clarinet, Cello, & Harp (After James Joyce).* He returned to Italy in 1954, and co-founded the Studio di Fonologia Musicale, among the top electronic music centers in Europe.

While heading the studio, Berio began pursuing a means of reconciling electronic music with musique concrète. In 1958, Berio completed his breakthrough electro-acoustic piece *Thema/Omaggio a Joyce*, which manipulated a sound source of a reading from *Ulysses*. In 1960, he relocated to America, where over the next dozen years he taught at several schools and became increasingly fascinated by rock and folk music. Indeed, Berio's major works of the era—*Visage, Passagio, Folk Songs, Laborintus II* and the *Sequenza* series among them—seem to draw upon virtually every major Western musical tradition, with an increasing emphasis on electronic media and tape.

Berio's other primary focus was the voice, primarily that of his longtime wife and muse Cathy Berberian, the mezzo-soprano who gave the debut performances of '70s-era works including a revised *Folk Songs*. The head of the electro-acoustic department of ICRAM in Paris until 1980, in 1987 Berio founded the Tempo Reale research institute in Milan. The occasion of Berio's 70th birthday in 1995 brought with it not only a number of musical celebrations, but also new recordings of many of his greatest pieces. —*Jason Ankeny*

Coro for 40 Voices and 40 Instruments (1976) / 1991 / Deutsche Grammaphon ✦✦✦
Performed by the Cologne Symphony Orchestra and Chorus conducted by the composer, *Coro* is Berio's masterpiece in his romantic-pointillism style. —*"Blue" Gene Tyranny*

Johanna Magdelena Beyer

b. Jul. 11, 1888, Leipzig, Germany, **d.** Jan. 9, 1944, New York, NY
Composer / Minimalism, Atonal, Electronic
Born in Leipzig, Johanna Beyer came to New York City in 1924. A mysterious "enigma" who led a solitary life with few friends, she nonetheless left over 50 compositions—pieces that anticipated techniques and sounds half a century before their re-discovery by other composers—many of which are still unperformed. She was also very active within the new music community, and studied composition with such notable moderns as Dane Rudhyar, Ruth Crawford, Charles Seeger, and Henry Cowell. Her death in 1944 of ALS ("Lou Gehrig's Disease") makes it likely that her reputation as an alcoholic resulted from the unfair assumptions of casual observers who mistook her symptoms for drunkeness. —*"Blue" Gene Tyranny*

IV for Percussion (1935) / 1991 / Aerial ✦✦✦
Performed by the group Essential Music. This remarkable score is written for nine percussion instruments, which are left unspecified and open to the tastes of the performers—a purely modernist gesture that was to re-appear only in the 1950s New York School (John Cage, Morton Feldman et al). A gradually accelerating and decelerating shuffling rhythm alternately energizes and puts the brakes on non-periodic and short, single percussive stabs and rolls. At the end of this brief composition, the runner has reached the goal line and grabs a few deep breaths as the beat stops in its final emphatic beats. This is music for (or of) an unknown culture, completely unique but at the same time appealing to a fundamental feeling. —*"Blue" Gene Tyranny*

John Bischoff

b. Dec. 7, 1949, San Francisco, CA
Computers/Sound Tracks, Composer / Computer Music, Electronic
Studied at CA Institute of the Arts, Mills College. Comp. with Robert Moran, James Tenney, Robert Ashley. Founding member of League of Automatic Music Composers, the first computer network band, and the Hub, a computer performance collective. Published writings on computer music. Currently on faculty and staff of Center for Contemporary Music, Mills College. *Outdoor Memory* constructed in 1970 is a computer-implemented listening system that responds to tuning in environmental sounds. —*"Blue" Gene Tyranny*

● **Artificial Horizon** / 1989 / Artifact ✦✦✦✦✦
Originally composed for a dance entitled "Crosses and Veils" by Evangel King, this piece uses two sound sources that respectively represent the "crosses" and "veils" and that are mixed and filtered in live performance: the sound of a steel foundry in Oakland, California recorded by the composer, and the sound of an digital oscillator that creates just-tuned harmonies. Bischoff's title "refers to an imaginary line that I envisioned as a setting upon which the motions of the dance could be traced." A mysterious low white-noise wind with occasional beeps opens the work. Slow resonate filterings and an airplane motor-like sound are gradually added to the texture. Pure wave, evocative melodic patterns emerge in double counterpoint toward the center of the sound image. A single bang of a metal sheet. Everything disappears but the sustained tones which slowly fade away. —*"Blue" Gene Tyranny*

Audio Wave / 1989 / Artifact ✦✦✦✦

Happy Trails / 1989 / Artifact ✦✦✦✦
This wonderfully humorous piece is made from musical phrases written by Bischoff played on a computer-controlled instrument, and "exclamations" created on the Mouse Guitar played by Perkis. A rhythmic plucky bass underscores the piece, over which glide wheezy chromatic organ figures. Around this instrumental fly very smile-inducing boings, bings, bangs and squiggly cartoony blasts, and gurgling white noise and long-distance transmission-like ring modulations, and quickly amplitude-modulated metallic sounds. (Where are the words to describe such a rich variety?) —*"Blue" Gene Tyranny*

Perry Mason in East Germany / 1989 / Artifact ✦✦✦✦✦
This work was originally created for the microcomputer network band called the Hub. Its overall design was created by Bischoff, with each of the six players running a program of his own design. Each program sends three variables to the Hub configuration to be used by the other three performers. Each program "also must use three variables it reads from three different performers in making its own musical decisions... the persistent diversity of the parts is complemented by moments of change that appear to propagate from one part to the next" which gives the work a unique kind of musical coherence—a global change "giving the music structure beyond any individual's planning." This web is also like the interactions in any society, including a network of spies. This may be how the composer derived his title. In any case, the sounds—rhythmically pulsed chords varied in many ways, rattlings, clickings, humorous little beeps and pops, tiny car horns, "pregnant" silences, events like tiny violins, industrial noises (tiny), etc.—while not specifically programmatic, do have a sophisticated sense of humor to them. And the listener can actually hear the web or global activity without necessarily resorting to program notes. —*"Blue" Gene Tyranny*

The Glass Hand / 1994 / Centaur ✦✦✦

Jaap Blonk

b. 1953, Woerden, Netherlands
Voices, Vocals / Improvisation, Avant-Garde
Hearing Jaap Blonk for the first time can be an ear-opening experience. Blonk is a self-taught, self-described sound poet, who twists and bends language (English and others) in engagingly disturbing ways. Working solo, and with different sized groups, Blonk has performed extensively, particularly in Europe, where he has collaborated with John Tchicai, Tristan Honsinger, and Matts Gustafsson, among others. Blonk founded and leads Splinks, a small orchestra that plays his compositions, and BRAAXTAAL, an avant-rock trio with synthesizer and drums. A concert by Blonk falls under the rubric of Performance Art, as he shows remarkable stage presence. Using original poetry as well as the words of others, Blonk clicks, blurts, and snaps his voice, creating unusual sounds and noises, mimicking nature and often injecting offbeat humor. While his performances sometimes offend, and they are not easily categorized, they nonetheless reflect considerable creativity and often contain large amounts of improvisation. —*Steve Loewy*

Braxtaal / Jun. 1991 / Kontrans ✦✦✦✦

Splinks / Feb. 1992-Mar. 1992 / Kontrans ✦✦✦✦✦
Perhaps Blonk's most accessible album to date, the vocalist leads his jazz septet through all sorts of gyrations for eleven very different numbers. Using fairly traditional instrumentation of trumpet, trombone, alto saxophone, plus guitar, bass, and drums (with Blonk on vocals, as well as doubling on alto and tenor saxophones), the band shows strong jazz roots, with plenty of solid mainstream improvisation, as well as Blonk's signature left-of-center humor and abstract forays. Trumpeter Angelo Verploegen, bassist Jacko Schoonderwoerd, and guitarist Lorand Sarna display strong chops, and longtime collaborator alto saxophonist Bart van der Putten is sensational. But, as always, what makes this recording so special is the way Blonk arranges the tunes, each a unique collage of sounds, with the vocalist's elastic vocal cords at the fore. Blonk's slapstick rendition of the Dutch reaction to bebop and his humorous take on Soviet Soul are among the highlights. —*Steve Loewy*

Improvisors / Feb. 4, 1996 / Kontrans ✦✦✦✦✦
Documenting a complete, unedited session recorded in Stockholm, there is a visceral excitement as each of the eleven cuts of this recording explores the extremes of the avant-garde. Blonk is found here in a startlingly original and totally improvised trio with free music stylists Matts Gustafsson and Michael Zerang. A departure from Blonk's other recordings, this is the first of two stunning interactions with some of the finest free-style musicians on the scene. For this CD, Swedish woodwind whiz Gustafsson brings his full arsenal of soprano, tenor, and baritone saxophones, flute, fluteophone, and french flageolet, while Chicagoan Zerang powerfully and gracefully fills the percussion slot. Blonk's voice is both horn and percussionist, and the three performers seem to enjoy the interactive flow of pings, pops, and scratches. Stimulating and ever-changing, this recording demands close listening, but the rewards are clearly there for the adventuresome. Not to be missed, this version of *Improvisors* is laced with humor, along with buckets of extraordinary noises/sounds. Certain to drive your spouse (or significant other) out the door. —*Steve Loewy*

● **Speechlos** / Jan. 1997-Mar. 1997 / Kontrans ✦✦✦✦✦
Working with his BRAXTAAL group, Blonk combines wit with sputters, twists, and loose social commentary to demonstrate his extraordinary ability to mold the human voice into often unrecognizable forms. Vocalizing in English (and other tongues, some nonsensical), this recording is not easy listening. In fact, it may disrupt and even annoy with its unique vocabulary of noise/sound. Nonetheless, there is much here to savor, and Blonk's utterly unique style and marvelous technique are quite astonishing. Performances by Blonk are not for the squeamish (he has been known to simulate the sounds of bodily functions), and this one is no exception. But for those open to something entirely different that is challenging as well as entertaining, though sometimes upsetting, a fling with Jaap Blonk might do the trick. Especially gripping are his renditions of the entertaining "Speechlos," and the prescient "Rational," and the provocative "As I Was Saying." —*Steve Loewy*

Vocalor / Aug. 4, 1998 / Staalplaat ✦✦✦

Lars-Gunnar Bodin

b. Jul. 15, 1935, Stockholm, Sweden
Liner Notes, Composer / Electro-Acoustic, Electronic
Swedish composer and visual artist Lars-Gunnar Bodin was a pioneer of electro-acoustic music and text-sound compositions, who also educated through teaching and through radio presentations, was an integral part of electronic music's presence in the Fylkingen society, and was director of the Electronic Music Studio (EMS). Bodin's early works and his involvement—which includes three years as Chairman—in Fylkingen (a society for the promotion of new art forms since the '30s) were crucial to the development of electronic music in Sweden. The Stockholm-born composer studied with Lennart Wenström during the last half of the '50s and first became involved at the Fylkingen society in the early '60s. Bodin was already using computer processing in his visual art when he met up with Göran Sundqvist; the process improved as the two collaborated during the '60s and their work was part of the L¥Artiste et L¥Ordinateur exhibition. With fellow Swedish composer Bengt-Emil Johnson, Bodin began staging concerts and festivals of text-sound composition—works of music in which language and voice are used for their sound, not their meaning. He and Johnson were among the first to write in this mode, along with Sten Hanson and others. One compilation

documenting their work is *The Pioneers: Five Text-Sound Artists* (Phono Sueco, 1992). Bodin wrote electro-acoustic music, instrumental theater music, multimedia works, compositions utilizing tape in live performance, and the text that he used in many of his pieces. Two notable works are "Commenting on Traces I" (1970), and "In Clouds" (1972-1976). Lars-Gunnar Bodin was composer-in-residence at California's Mills College in 1972, and became the Director of Stockholm's EMS in the late '70s. *—Joslyn Layne*

For Jon (Fragments of a Time to Come)(1977) / 1978 / Folkways ✦✦✦
An out-of-print disc well worth searching for. A "surrealistic science fiction," even cyberpunk (the term wasn't in wide usage at the time) cantata for narrator, chamber choir and electronics with the text processed through and triggering the electronics… reflects Bodin's continuing concern with concepts connected with modern science and technology, and the role of art in a post-revolutionary (Marcuse-ian sense) society. *— "Blue" Gene Tyranny*

• **Anima (1984)/ in "Computer Music Currents 7"** / 1990 / Wergo ✦✦✦✦✦
A brief work perfectly depicting a profound psychic process… the unification of consciousness with the higher self… the human voice (soprano) hears its counterpart in the computer voice, and gradually the two merge throughout the course of the piece. Beautiful. *— "Blue" Gene Tyranny*

David Borden

b. Dec. 25, 1938, Boston, MA
Keyboards, Composer / Minimalism, Electronic
An innovator in electronic and minimalist music since the 1970s, David Borden made his mark as the leader of Mother Mallard, the world's first all-synthesizer ensemble. In the period 1973-1976, Mother Mallard released two albums, *Mother Mallard's Portable Masterpiece Company* and *Like a Duck to Water.*

After Mother Mallard disbanded in the late 1970s, Borden developed his compositional skills, releasing *Music for Amplified Keyboard Instruments* in 1981. Mother Mallard regrouped and recorded *Anatidae* for Cuneiform in 1986. *Migration* (1988) added jazz improvisation to the mix.

Between 1976 and 1987 Borden composed *The Continuing Story of Counterpoint,* a 12-part work released on three CDs. Combining electronics, classical concepts, strict counterpoint and musical density, this groundbreaking work is entertaining and pleasing to the ear.

Borden released *Cayuga Night Music,* a more introspective work, on the Linden Music label. *Places, Times & People* (Cuneiform) consists mostly of solo keyboard works. *—Jim Dorsch*

The Continuing Story of Counterpoint, Parts 1-4 + 8 (Complete) / 1990 / Cuneiform ✦✦✦✦✦

The Continuing Story of Counterpoint Pts. 5-8 / 1990 / Cuneiform ✦✦✦✦✦

• **The Continuing Story of Counterpoint, Pts. 9-12** / 1990 / Cuneiform ✦✦✦✦✦
Borden composed *Parts 9-12* of his *Counterpoint* series mainly between 1986 and 1987, about a decade after the series' earliest pieces. At this point, he seems somewhat more adventurous, pushing against the boundaries of his own rules. Consequently, there is a noticeable development in the contrapuntal language, with somewhat softer timbres and perhaps a bit more melodic invention. "Part 11" features a continually shifting tonal center and many related (but varying) melodic themes. Compared to the tightly controlled structures of the earlier *Counterpoint* recordings, this is extravagant and occasionally almost giddy, and almost certainly the most colorful part in the entire series. "Part 9" and "Part 10" feature the wordless soprano of Mother Mallard regular Ellen Hargis and sometimes sound like Brian Eno's prototypical *Music for Airports* ambience combined with the rhythmic pulse of early Steve Reich. According to Borden, "Part 10" is further distinguished as the only part in the series that includes improvisation, supposedly on alto flute, although solos by tenor and soprano saxes are written in a loose, improvisational style. (Many listeners will probably find the alto solos sounding the most improvised.) "Part 12A" starts with a lovely interlocking mallet pattern, very reminiscent of Reich, from which Borden builds a musical structure, with some vocalese from Hargis and two related patterns of long notes contrasting with the busy mallet progression. In "Part 12B," tuned electronic percussion is prominent for the first time in the series, and the relentless repetition and shrill timbres acquire an urgency that begins to suggest a touch of Gothic prog rock in the manner of Univers Zero. Borden's monumental *Counterpoint* series is brought to a close with "12C," a limpid, strangely muted piece that Borden indicates is meant to sound "dreamlike" and "inconclusive." *—Bill Tilland*

Double Portrait (1987) / In Double Edge "U.S. Choice" / 1992 / ✦✦✦
Influenced by other pattern music composers (Glass, Reich, Riley), Borden's music nevertheless has its own character made from rich layers of freewheeling solos over the patterns with some very lovely textures. The structure of the music is built on composer and performers' names and birthdates in an elevated soap opera structure. Performed by Mother Mallard's Portable Masterpiece Co., a well-known East Coast synthesizer group in the early 1970s (original members: David Borden, Linda Fisher, Steve Drews) which used many modern techniques in their pieces from chance procedures to pattern music and various forms of improvisation. *— "Blue" Gene Tyranny*

Places, Times & People / Mar. 29, 1995 / Cuneiform ✦✦✦

Linda Bouchard

b. May 21, 1957, Val-d'Or, Québec, Canada
Conductor, Composer / 20th Century Classical/Modern Composition, Chamber Music, Opera
Quebec composer Linda Bouchard has written a variety of works, from orchestral pieces to dance scores. After living and working in N.Y.C. for 11 years, Bouchard organized festivals and workshops and conducted a number of ensembles and orchestras (New York Children's Free Opera, San Francisco Contemporary Music Players), was music director at Banff, and resident composer of the National Arts Centre Orchestra, which she also directed. In the 1990s, Bouchard has won the Canada Council for the Arts' Joseph S. Stauffer Prize, first prize in competitions such as the Princeton Composition Contest, four PROCAN Awards, and was named Composer of the Year by the Conseil Quebecois de la Culture's Prix Opus. Her works have been recorded for the Analekta, CRI, Marquis Classics, and ECM labels. *—Joslyn Layne*

Black Burned Wood / in Dora Ohrenstein's "Urban Diva" / 1993 / CRI ✦✦✦
An accomplished composer of more than 50 works in various genres from opera to chamber works, Bouchard has created an intense song concerning a mysterious girl Sara running through woods, obsessed, who may have murdered her parents. See also Bouchard's "Lung Ta" for string quartet in "Bang On A Can, Vol. 3." *— "Blue" Gene Tyranny*

Andre Boucourechliev

b. Jul. 28, 1925, Sofia, Bulgaria, **d.** Nov. 13, 1997, Paris, France
Piano, Composer / Tape Music, 20th Century Classical/Modern Composition
Boucourechliev started his musical career as a pianist, studying at the Sofia Conservatory and the Ecole Normale de Musique in Paris. In 1951 he earned his "licence de concert" and pursued a career as a concert pianist and a teacher. He began to compose in 1954 and has since then been active in that area as well as music criticism and musicology. Boucourechliev has composed with tape and indeterminate elements. The series *Archipels* (1967-72) gained him a respected reputation as a composer. The score for this work resembles a large navigational chart that contains an "archipelago" of musical structures which are designed as possibilities for the performer to employ. Although the structure is determined by the course of the performance, the players must listen and communicate in order for the work to be successful. *—Lynn Vought*

Ombres (Shades) (Hommage a Beethoven) / EMI ✦✦✦
Performed by the National Chamber Orchestra of Toulouse—Louis Auriacombe, director. Recordings of Boucourechliev's music are difficult to find but well worth the effort. This is an homage to the Father of Modern Music—Beethoven's *Third Symphony* "Eroica" and sometimes other works are often credited with being the first modernist compositions partly because they were built from small kernels of ideas rather than as variations on full melodies, and also because the music did not need outside references to justify it. Instead of falling for the rather obvious idea of collaging Beethoven's works, Boucourechliev creates an impression of the interior nature of Beethoven's democratic and universal pieces. This is difficult to put in words, but is something like the feeling you have left after the music has ended. This is a transcendental and sustained piece, unique in character. *— "Blue" Gene Tyranny*

Pierre Boulez

b. Mar. 26, 1925, Montbrison, France
Conductor, Composer / Musique Concrète, 20th Century Classical/Modern Composition, Electro-Acoustic, Atonal, Electronic, Classical
After initially studying mathematics, Boulez entered the Paris Conservatoire as a student in theory and harmony (he failed the pianists' entrance examination). His principal teacher was Messiaen, and he also studied counterpoint privately with Andrée Vaurabourg. According to Boulez, composition is a form of aesthetic research and should be pursued logically. He viewed personal stylistic development as having no importance and deemed atonality as necessary. He adopted 12-tone serialism after being exposed to it by Liebowitz, a student of Schoenberg. In *Structures* for two pianos (1952), Boulez utilized a serial control of rhythm, dynamics and tone. These works brought him initial public recognition, but it was his *Le Marteau sans Maître* (1954) that was to become a landmark of 20th century music. Scored for small ensemble, it is rhythmically monotonous with sudden tempo changes and large sections of improvisatory melodies. The success of these pieces led to an invitation to teach at Darmstadt, as a professor of composition. It was here that he gave a series of lectures that was to become the book *Musikdenken Heute,* an outline of his ideas concerning total serialization. At this time Boulez was expanding his serial techniques to include open form, or "organized delirium." He also developed techniques that allowed performer and conductor to make many more creative choices in form and tonal duration. Boulez is also an active conductor, his performances marked by analytical clarity. He has served as head conductor for the BBC Symphony in London and the New York Philharmonic. *—Lynn Vought*

Improvisations Sur Mallarmé I & II / 1957 / Hungaroton ✦✦✦✦✦
This composition, together with "Le Marteau Sans Maitre" (The Hammer Without a Master), established the particular sound of Boulez's approach to serialist composition, a poetic pointillism with a Debussy-ian sense of timbres, which has characterized most of his works, and is more interesting than most of the later rather arid pieces that followed it. This CD also contains two lovely classics of 12-tone music (upon which serialism is based) by Arnold Schöenberg ("Pierrot Lunaire, Op. 21") (1912) and Anton Webern ("5 Canons on Latin Texts") for soprano and instrumental ensemble, op. 16 (1923-24) and two of his songs. *— "Blue" Gene Tyranny*

Paul Bowles

b. Dec. 30, 1910, New York, **d.** Nov. 18, 1999, Tangier, Morocco
Composer / 20th Century Classical/Modern Composition, World Fusion, Opera
Bowles studied with Copland, Thomson and Boulanger during the '20s and early '30s, while living in Europe and North Africa. For the next three decades he wrote music for the New York theatre. In 1941 he received a Guggenheim Fellowship to compose the opera *The Wind Remains.* He returned to Tangier in 1948 to write his second opera, *Yerma,* for blues singer Libby Holman. He conducted ethno-musicological research in Tangier under a Rockefeller grant during the 1960s. Most of his compositions were written before 1949. In that year his novel about travellers, *The Sheltering Sky,* was published. As a composer, Bowles wrote in short forms. Even his operas are constructions of suites of songs. They draw heavily upon American jazz, Moroccan rhythm and Mexican dance for inspiration. His fiction is generally dark in character and centers around insights of psychological perception. *—Lynn Vought*

Black Star at the Point of Darkness / 1992 / Sub Rosa ♦♦♦
A wonderful sound and soul journey featuring the voice of Paul Bowles reading narrations and poems, his recordings of ritual Moroccan music and the six Preludes for piano. *—"Blue" Gene Tyranny*

● **Baptism of Solitude** / Sep. 12, 1995 / Meta ♦♦♦
Bowles is the famous author of *The Sheltering Sky* and several other novels, not to mention numerous short stories, essays and poems. His permanent, self-imposed North African exile helped to put that region on the map of EuroAmerican letters; the influence of Moroccan culture and of the sun-blasted expanses of its desert milieu pervades his writing. *Baptism of Solitude* is a collection of excerpts read by Bowles himself, accompanied by Bill Laswell's suitably bleak, spacious sound sculptures. There's little music to speak of on this album; instead, as Bowles intones his prose in a laconic, slightly stentorian voice, Laswell lends sonic context to his words with echoey washes and distant, windy howls. The texts are sometimes intensely evocative (as on the title track) and sometimes almost Zen-like in their obscurity, as on "You Are Not I." Others are downright disturbing—one describes matter-of-factly the sexual mutilation of a young boy by a Bedouin raider. The stark power of Bowles' writing is such that it's hard not to feel parochial in objecting to such stuff on the grounds of taste, but the faint of stomach should take warning. In any case, this is a remarkable debut release from what promises to be an exciting new label. *—Rick Anderson*

The Voices of Paul Bowles / Tellus ♦♦♦♦♦
Audio portrait on cassette of the author/composer with stories, selected works, early compositions ("Music for a Farce," "Interlude and Prelude *2*," long unavailable) and environmental recordings made near his Moroccan home. In a library you may still find his wonderful pieces "A Picnic Cantata" (1955) for four women's voices, two pianos, and percussion (including a milk bottle and cigar box) (Columbia LP with pianists Gold and Fizdale), "The Wind Remains" (1943) (an opera which is based on an abstraction of the third act of Garcia Lorca's "Asi Que Pasen Cinco Anos") (MGM Records disc E3549, contains also composer Peggy Glanville-Hick's "Letters From Morocco," which are settings of texts by Bowles). *—"Blue" Gene Tyranny*

Glenn Branca

b. Oct. 6, 1948, Harrisburg, PA
Guitar, Composer / Microtonal, No Wave, Experimental, Instrumental Rock
Formed late-'70s bands Theoretical Girls and the Static. Influenced by Dane Rudyhar's harmonic theories, dense rock guitar music, minimalist-style cyclic organization, tone cluster music. *—"Blue" Gene Tyranny*

Symphony No. 6 (Devil Choirs at the Gates of Heaven) / 1989 / Atavistic ♦♦♦
Studies in gradually denser sonorities ("resultant masses") with a rock-steady pulse, this music digs deep into the mind/feeling to elicit bardo-like sensations often approached by the profoundest Buddhist chant. (Cage and Branca once had a disagreement about Branca's music being "fascist." Cage argued that densities creating a "sustained climax" restrict the mind from opening up. I doubt that fascists would like these symphonies.) *—"Blue" Gene Tyranny*

Symphony No. 2 (The Peak of the Sacred) / 1992 / Atavistic ♦♦♦♦♦
The legendary live performance at St. Mary's Church on May 14, 1982. Scored for eight mallet guitars, taped harmonic guitars, bass drums, metal percussion and drums. The first movement, "Slow Mass," has magnificently dense, giant clusters and scale patterns describing the image of a slowly moving soundmass. The second movement, entitled "Radioactive Poltergeist Kitchen 1955," features Z'ev on metal percussion with gradually more massive electronically amplified crashing and random forms, punctuated at times by blasts from the drums and guitars. The third movement, "Melodrama and Nuclear Physics in the Global Theater," features sustained soft and sharp, densely layered harmonic textures that float in and around the space. The fourth movement, "Sacred Field," brings in a mass of drum rhythms, rattling metal sheets, and gradually building harmonic masses. "In the Late 20th Century the Impossible Becomes Possible (short excerpt)" is the concluding movement, and begins with mallet guitar strokes that sound like church bells. *—"Blue" Gene Tyranny*

Symphony Nos. 8 & 10 (The Mysteries) / 1994 / Atavistic ♦♦♦
Subtitled "The Mystery" and "The Mystery Pt. 2," these two symphonies concern themselves with the two big questions: Life and Death. They are both scored for eight guitars, two basses, keyboard, drums, vocal and two conductors. *Symphony No. 8* has two movements: "The Passion" and "Spiritual Anarchy" that both build upon sustained tones that create a counterpoint by means of delays in scale and other patterns and microtunings. The effect is tremendously intense and beautiful. There are also two movements in *Symphony No. 10:* "The Final Problem" and "The Horror." These are built in a similar manner to the techiques in *No. 8* but the tuning and scales employed are different, creating another sensation yet still as intense and continuous in rhythm as *No. 8*. Especially successful is the final movement, "The Horror," which employs masses of moving clusters that are very close in tuning and thoroughly convincing in the image they portray. It is a gigantic chant of worlds never before imagined. Incidentally, the CD comes with a nifty holographic cover that visually simulates Branca's dense textures. *—"Blue" Gene Tyranny*

● **Symphony No. 9 "L'Eve Future"** / 1995 / Point ♦♦♦♦♦
Performed by the Polish Radio National Symphony Orchestra, Katowice, with vocals by the Camerata Silesia Singers Ensemble, conducted by Christian van Borries. The beginning expands melodic patterns, many of them scalar and in close intervals, played by instruments and doubled by voices. These are surrounded by an aura of sustained, chromatically shifting harmonies—the effect is one of great longing and possibly of desolation (this writer is reminded of the textures of Richard Yardumian's little-known orchestra work "Desolate City"). Around 11 minutes into the work, the patterns become approximately two times faster and more telegraphic and chantlike. This develops into an almost waltz figure (12/8). Then a warm, low strings melody is added against the triplet accompaniment. Descending scales interrupt this, and with the doubling voices it sounds like derisive laughter. This idea is developed. Then the telegraphic patterns are combined with the longer string melodies, descending scales and patterns from the start of the work. All of these elements are varied and recombined to produce a continuously unfolding movement of approximately 47 minutes. The additional movement is a "Freeform" in which duple and triple time are integrated by varying them within a theme, or in contrasting orchestral sections. Again Branca uses scales, telegraphing figures, rhythmic variation and chromatic modulation in direct ways, that, by combination, create dense activity, a kind of Beethovenesque minimalism. This last movement, of approximately 11Ω minutes duration, is very bright and seemingly hopeful in its effect. This is a very unique work and highly recommended. *—"Blue" Gene Tyranny*

● **Selections from the Symphonies (Works for Electric Guitar)** / Oct. 1, 1996 / Atavistic ♦♦♦♦
This compilation album offers excerpts from Glenn Branca's second, third, fifth, sixth, eighth, and tenth symphonies. The tracks have been selected among Branca's loudest and noisiest works, representing his best writing for walls of electric guitars. The hardcore fan will not find anything new (all the material is already available), but the newcomer is offered a chance to enter Branca's world and then work his way through the complete symphonies. Heavy fabrics of distorted sound unfold through anguishing moods ranging from the almost relaxed atmosphere of "Symphony *2 2nd Movement"* to a terrible degree of oppression and suffocation in "Symphony *3 2nd movement"* and the apocalyptic "Symphony *10 2nd movement."* Drums are heavy, almost tribal and sometimes reminiscent of Magma. For someone who would like to enter the post-apocalyptic world of an avant-rock composer who's been a major influence on bands like Sonic Youth, this disc is the perfect compendium. *—François Couture*

Henry Brant

b. Sep. 15, 1913, Montreal, Quebec, Canada
Composer / 20th Century Classical/Modern Composition, World Fusion, Atonal, Classical
Studied with George Antheil, Aaron Copland, Wallingford Riegger, Rubin Goldmark. Scoring and arranging radio brodcasts and films. Taught at Columbia, Juilliard, Bennington. *Variations for Any Four Instruments* composed using original concept of "oblique harmony," the *Music for a 5c and 10c Store* (1932) for violin, piano, kitchen utensils and alarm clocks, *Angels and Devils* (1931, 1956, 1979) for three piccolos, five flutes and two alto flutes, *Encephalograms II* (1955), *Spatial Concerto (Questions from Genesis)* (1976), Ives/Brant *The Concord Symphony* (30 years of composition, premiered in 1996). *—"Blue" Gene Tyranny*

☆ **Angels and Devils for Flute and Flute Orchestra (1932, Rev. 1947)** / 1991 / Centaur ♦♦♦♦♦
Played by the Eastman Wind Ensemble. Brant is the composer who re-introduced spatial distribution as a parameter of musical expression, such as it was in Gabrieli's time. This is Brant's classic work of "spatial music" for 14 flutes with performers standing on ladders or on different levels. *—"Blue" Gene Tyranny*

● **Henry Brant** / 1999 / CRI ♦♦♦♦
For most of his long career as a composer, Henry Brant has been toying with space. Whether inside a theater or in the great outdoors, Brant searched for a way to include a spatial dimension in his music. As a result, he wrote for enormous musical ensembles. The score for "Western Spring" calls for two symphony orchestras, two choirs, and two jazz combos with four conductors following different tempi. "Orbits" is written for church organ, soprano voice, and 80 trombones, an orchestration that, needless to say, gives the piece a lot of power. This CRI CD was released in 1999 in the *American Masters* series. It reissues material previously released on LP by CRI in 1971, 1980, and 1985. On one disc, the listener can experience Brant's musical vision, something of gigantic proportions. *—François Couture*

Chris Brown

b. Sep. 9, 1953
Piano / Sound Sculpture, Avant-Garde Jazz, 20th Century Classical/Modern Composition
Chris Brown began his music career as a classical pianist, but became increasingly influenced by American experimental and improvised music. These influences, combined with studies of Indonesian, Indian & Cuban musics, led Brown further into free jazz. Since the late '70s, Brown has been building personal electronic instruments, using analog circuits to modify acoustic devices' sounds, and mixing these with concrete & synthetic sounds. He created an installation of networked rhythm machines, called Talking Drum, that made stops in San Francisco, Montreal and Holland. Brown has received commissions from Abel-Steinberg-Winant Trio, Rova Saxophone Quartet and the Berkeley Symphony Orchestra. He was a member of The Hub from 1986 to 1998, and of Glenn Spearman's Double Trio. Brown has performed piano music by James Tenney, Henry Cowell, Luc Ferrari, and more, and recorded and performed in the free-jazz tradition at venues including the San Francisco, Monterey, Du-Maurier and Victoriaville Festivals. The end of the '90s found Brown working on a new series of concert pieces called "Inventions; " they are based around the results of a polyrhythm generating software. In addition to this, he has been developing "The Eternal Network Music Site, " playing in Room, a new music trio with Larry Ochs of Rova and William Winant. *—Joslyn Layne*

● **Snakecharmer** / 1989 / Artifact ♦♦♦♦♦
Five pieces for solo performer and live electronics: in each piece a different acoustic instrument is played through an electronic system that responds automatically to the sounds and actions of the performer. Performed by the composer on piano, keyboards, voice and electronics with William Winant, percussion. *—"Blue" Gene Tyranny*

Chain Reaction for Electronics, Airdrums, Sax and Piano (1991) / 1994 / Centaur ♦♦♦♦♦
In the collection "CDCM Computer Music Series, Vol. 17," performed by the group ROOM. Similar to the setup of the composer's computer-network piece "Rol'Em" (1988), Brown continues to experiment "with music in which the musicians cross the boundaries of each other's instrumental territory, where their instruments interact and influence each other directly, and where every player is responsible for a different parameter of the same sound." In this approximately 13-minute piece, the Airdrums (a MIDI-based instrument controller with two

tubes, each of which has six accelerometer-based triggers that respond to motion on three axes) controls several parameters such as transposition, delay and reverberation of bass-like and percussion-like sounds, and triggers electronic sound in the last section of the piece; similarly, the saxophone controls transposition through a pitch-follower. The first section of the piece begins the slow unfolding of richly harmonic and melodically angular new jazz lines for piano and sax in a dense and intense texture. This develops into a nervous telegraphic rhythmic pulsing with additional Airdrums and other electronics, at times engagingly humorous in its gestures. Cymbal-like sounds evoke dense and propulsive accumulative delays of notes and sax breath and lipping noises. The piece concludes with a gradual dissolution of sounds. *— "Blue" Gene Tyranny*

Lava / 1995 / Tzadik ✦✦✦✦
Composed in 1992, this dramatic and gritty electro-acoustical work is scored for brass quartet, four percussionists and live electronics. "Aspects of the physical structure of a volcano are applied to control musical elements... the change from a solid (earth) to a liquid (lava) is modeled by the transformation of the acoustic sounds into electronic sounds... a primordial state of flux" (C. Brown). The electronics create fascinating "3D imaging" illusions. *— "Blue" Gene Tyranny*

Earle Brown

b. Dec. 26, 1926, Lunenburg, MA
Composer / 20th Century Classical/Modern Composition, Minimalism
Studied with Roslyn Brogue Henning and Schillinger Method. Pianist. Innovative graphic notational methods influenced by Schillinger and Calder. Collaborated with John Cage on the *Project for Music for Magnetic Tape* (1952-55). Other compositions include: *Music for "Tender Buttons"* for speaker, flute, horn, and harp (1953), *Indices* for chamber orchestra (1954), *Calder Piece* for four perc. and mobile (1967), *Modules I-II* for orchestra (1966), *Event: Synergy II* for 11 woodwinds and eight strings (1968), *Time Spans* for orch. (1972), *Tracer* for ensemble and tape (1984), *Tracking Pierrot* for ensemble (1992). *— "Blue" Gene Tyranny*

Available Forms II / in New Music / 1968 / RCA Victrola ✦✦✦
Ethereally beautiful performance conducted by Bruno Maderna. The score is constructed in blocks of music ("available forms") that the conductor cues and guides with various signals, like an engineer with tracks of recorded material to mix... a combination of spontaneous music making and pre-composed intentions that works well. Enthusiasts may also want to check out his "Four Systems For Four Amplified Cymbals" (1964) in "Electronics and Percussion," Max Neuhaus, percussion, Columbia MS 7139 disc, currently out-of-print. *— "Blue" Gene Tyranny*

Folio (1952/53) / Music for Cello and Piano (1954)/ in "The New York School" / 1993 / hatHUT ✦✦✦
Two classic works by Brown, including four realizations of the famous multi-dimensional graph score "Folio." *— "Blue" Gene Tyranny*

Music for Piano(s), 1951-1995 / 1996 / New Albion ✦✦✦

• **Times Five (1963) / Octet 1 (1953) / December (1952) / Novara (1962)** / CRI ✦✦✦✦✦
Elegant kaleidoscopic mobiles for various instrumental combinations and electronics realized from graphic scores. In contrast to his "open form" compositions, the fascinating *Octet 1 (for 8 loudspeakers)* for magnetic tape, composed in 1953 at the Project for Music for Magnetic Tape, employs random sampling tables employed in statistical research. The choice of sounds again points to the composer's fascination with "inarticulate, uncharacteristic" timbres—only brief fragments of the Project's city/country and electronic/instrumental sounds were used to create complex densities and sequences, so that the sounds themselves were not recognizable.

Composed in 1963, the timbrely rich and fascinating *Times Five* is for a group of five instrumentalists who are seated in the center of a square described by four loudspeakers placed evenly about them which broadcast an eceltronic tape made from the processed sounds of an 11-piece acoustic ensemble. There are five sections to the work: the first contains microtonal frequencies around F sharp with speeded-up harp and bass figurations on the tape; the second is "variations of density and harmonic fields throughout the available instrumental range as washes of texture and color"; the third section is made from "noisy sounds" or those kind of not fully articulated "uncharacteristic" sounds which occur on the instrument body, in underblown winds, soft bowings, etc. By contrast, the fourth section is articulate, containing "musical" sounds with notated phrasing; while the fifth and final section is percussively energetic on the tape with material from the third and fourth sections juxtaposed as a "commentary to the tape." —"Blue" Gene Tyranny

Four Systems, 1954 / Oct. 19, 1995 / hatART ✦✦✦✦✦

Gavin Bryars

b. Jan. 16, 1943, Goole, England
Cello, Percussion, Composer / Experimental, Minimalism
Bryars studied philosophy at Sheffield University as well as music on a private basis. He played in jazz groups during the 1960s and has lectured at Leicester Polytechnic since 1970. Bryars is an experimental composer, influenced by Satie and Cage and also modern literature. He often writes for unusual forces and locations. These works are published by Experimental Music Catalogue. *— Lynn Vought*

First Viennese Dance (M.H.) (1985-86) in "Three Viennese Dancers" / 1986 / ✦✦✦
Scored for French Horn and percussion, this ethereal, slowly unfolding music is different from Bryars' other "sound" of jauntingly repeating, minimally changing chords that he shares with Michael Nyman. M.H. equals Mata Hari, the famous World War One spy and one of three famed dancers in Vienna in late 1906. *— "Blue" Gene Tyranny*

• **Jesus' Blood Never Failed Me Yet** / 1993 / Point ✦✦✦✦
Six realizations for orchestra and the gravelly old man's voice of Tom Waits (who sounds very much like the original tape recorded voice of a street singer used in the earlier Obscure Records recording of this piece). Each realization shows Bryars' gift for invention and variation and simple, appealing emotionality. A very touching and beautiful recording of nearly 75 minutes duration, highly recommended. *— "Blue" Gene Tyranny*

Buckethead (Brian Carroll)

Guitar (Electric) / Progressive Metal, Guitar Virtuoso, Funk Metal, Experimental, Heavy Metal, Prog-Rock/Art Rock, Fusion
Buckethead is one of the most bizarre and enigmatic figures in American underground and experimental music since Parliament-Funkadelic birthed their bevy of cosmic characters in the mid-'70s. An accomplished multi-instrumentalist best known for his virtuosic command of the electric guitar, Buckethead is one of the instrument's most recognizable contemporary innovators, his rapid-fire riffing, near-robotic fretwork, and idiosyncratic lead lines combining elements of Yngwie Malmsteen, Adrian Belew, Slayer's Kerry King, P-Funk's Eddie Hazel, and avant-improv artist John Zorn's Scud-attack sax abuse. His first group, the San Francisco-based metal-funk combine the Deli Creeps, was a regional success, but disbanded before they could release anything. Buckethead's solo career has been more productive, thanks mostly to the motivation of Zorn and Bill Laswell, the latter of whom Buckethead has also recorded and toured with in Praxis. Laswell has also produced a number of Buckethead's solo albums (including *Dreamatorium* and *Day of the Robot*) and included him on more than a dozen one-off recordings with the likes of Hakim Bey, Bootsy Collins, Anton Fier, Jonas Hellborg, and Bernie Worrell. In addition to releases including 1998's *Colma*, Buckethead has also contributed soundtrack material to such films as *Last Action Hero* and *Street Fighter*. Buckethead returned in 1999 with *Monsters and Robots*, after which he joined Guns n' Roses. *— Sean Cooper*

• **Day of the Robot** / Apr. 30, 1996 / Subharmonic ✦✦✦✦
The most consistent and coherent-sounding of Buckethead's releases to date (two qualities usually absent from his earlier works). Most often referred to as his "jungle album" (it features rhythm tracks by U.K. beat scientist DJ Ninj), the hyperspeed breaks are actually the least interesting aspect of the album, which is instead notable for its steady and inspired, chaos-by-design integration of diverse elements (treated guitars, keyboards and pianos, loping bass, etc.). Much of the credit for this goes to Laswell's excellent production. *— Sean Cooper*

Colma / Mar. 24, 1998 / CyberOctave ✦✦✦
For a guy who takes his sartorial cues from teenage horror flicks (he plays onstage with a weird sort of hockey mask on his face), Buckethead sure does make pretty music. It was not always thus—his work with Praxis, for example, has often been pretty challenging. But on this solo project, on which he plays both guitar and bass and is helped out on all tracks by drummer Brain, the material is surprisingly pleasant, bordering at times on the banal. Titles like "Hills of Eternity" and "Wishing Well" are something of a giveaway—though Brain's beats are fairly funky (and DJ Disc throws in a bit of far-off turntable scratching on a few tracks), these compositions are mostly pretty contemplative, occupying a space just one step away from the new age section. That's not necessarily a bad thing, but there are a couple of problems: the first is that Buckethead is a lousy bass player. Like many guitarists, he seems to think that playing bass is simply a matter of hitting the root of the chord on the downbeat of the measure. A real bassist could have contributed enormously to the proceedings (as Bill Laswell does in his guest turn on "Machete"). Another problem is the unimaginative production, which is overly soft and sweet. That said, "Big Sur Moon" is a cool solo guitar piece, and "Machete" really does cook. The rest is merely very pleasant. *— Rick Anderson*

Harold Budd

b. May 24, 1936, Los Angeles, CA
Piano, Synthesizer, Producer, Composer / Experimental, Avant-Garde, Ambient, Electronic, Neo-Classical
The American ambient/neo-classical composer who has most closely allied himself with the increasingly sympathetic independent-rock underground—through his collaborations with the Cocteau Twins' Robin Guthrie—Harold Budd is also one of the very few who can very rightly be called an ambient composer. His music, a sparse and tonal wash of keyboard treatments, was inspired by a boyhood spent listening to the buzz of telephone wires near his home in the Mojave Desert town of Victorville, CA. He became a respected name in the circle of minimalist and avant-garde composers based in Southern California during the late '60s, premiering his works *The Candy-Apple Revision* and *Unspecified D-Flat Major Chord and Lirio* around the area. In 1976, Budd gained a recording contract with the Brian Eno-affiliated EG Records, and released his debut album *The Pavilion of Dreams* in 1978. Two years later, he collaborated with Eno on one of the landmark albums of the ambient style, *Ambient 2: The Plateaux of Mirrors*. A contract with Eno's Opal Records resulted in one of Budd's most glorious albums, *The White Arcades*, recorded in Edinburgh with the Cocteau Twins' Guthrie. *— John Bush*

• **The Pearl** / 1984 / EG ✦✦✦✦✦
Hearing Budd's piano slowly fade in with the start of "Late October" is just one of those perfect moments—it's something very distinctly him, made even more so with Eno's touches and slight echo, and it signals the start of a fine album indeed. Acting in some respects as the understandable counterpart to *Ambient 2*, with the same sense of hushed, ethereal beauty the partnership brought forth on that album, *Pearl* is so ridiculously good it instantly shows up much of the mainstream new age as the gloopy schlock that it often is. Eno himself is sensed as a performer on the album, if not by his absence then by his very understated presence. The merest hints of synth and whisper play around Budd's performances, ensuring the latter takes center stage. Eno and Daniel Lanois handle the production side of things, their teamwork once again overseeing a winner. When they bring themselves a little more to the fore, it still always is in the subtlest of ways, as with the artificially higher-pitched notes from Budd on "Lost in the Humming Air." Part of the distinct charm of the album is how the song titles perfectly capture what the music sounds like—"A Stream With Bright Fish" is almost

self-defining. Another key point is how Budd truly captures what ambience in general can and does mean. "Against the Sky" is a strong example—it can be totally concentrated upon or left to play as atmospherics and is also at once both truly beautiful and not a little haunting in a disturbing sense. Other highlight tracks include the deceptively simple title track, as serene a piece of music as was ever recorded, and the closing "Still Return," bringing *Pearl* to a last peak of beauty. *—Ned Raggett*

The Room / Aug. 15, 2000 / Atlantic ✦✦✦✦
With *The Room*, Harold Budd makes his major-label debut. Expanding on a track from *The White Arcades*, he crafts 13 pieces with a simple, childlike innocence that also contain rich textures beneath, inducing a calm, meditative state—perfect for relaxation therapy or cloud watching. As he has been a longtime master of ambient atmospherics, Budd is able to create a benign, peaceful aural gallery as each piece slowly, quietly unfolds into a different "room," heard in the shimmering bells of "The Room Alight," the chanted voices of "The Candied Room," and the somber "Room of Forgotten Children" (note the wonderfully evocative titles). Though some of the synthesizer textures verge on a little too much new age sweetness, his piano is always a thing of tranquil beauty, veiled in layers of eerie echo, evoking a half-remembered dream. After many interesting collaborative records, this is an impressive return to form to Budd's early to mid-'80s heyday. *—Jason Gross*

Sylvano Bussotti

b. Oct. 1, 1931, Florence, Italy
Composer / 20th Century Classical/Modern Composition, Opera
Bussotti was a gifted child musician and entered the Florence Conservatory in 1940. He left four years later to pursue independent study in composition and was influenced by Deutsch, Metzger, Boulez and Cage, among others. His music participates in and also criticizes the decadence of modernism. He uses graphic notation in a flamboyant style that is often difficult to perform, in works that are erotic and artificial and often refer to his personal life, which is seemingly colorful. *La passion selon Sade* (1969) and *Lorenzaccio* (1972) are his main works for theatre. In addition to music he has worked in the fields of painting, graphic art and journalism. *—Lynn Vought*

Rara Requiem / Bergkristall / Lorenzaccio Symphony, The / 1992 / Deutsche Grammaphon ✦✦✦
A talented graphic artist, Bussotti has made some of the most amazing looking graph scores, like the famous "Five Pieces for David Tudor," a 1959 score made from a 1949 drawing. There are lines running in every direction, wild squiggles and vortices, small icons of imaginary characters, laconic word phrases, and formless dark areas. Likewise, the score for "Coeur Pour Batteur" on Max Neuhaus' out of print Columbia disc *Electronics and Percussion* is as defined as it is open to subjective readings by the performer. Neuhaus divides the score into spatial directions for sound-producing body movements; the piece also allows for the effects of inadvertent body movements and instruments set up to vibrate sympathetically out of the performer's control. In Bussotti's later works heard in this two-CD reissue of recordings from 1976 and 1978, the composer's approach is more traditional but the sounds are not. "Bergkristall" is a ballet based on Adalbert Stifter's tale of a young boy and girl who become lost in a Christmas Day snowstorm while returning home from the valley where their grandparents live. Following the spirit of a baker's boy who had once become lost, they wander off toward the "regions of eternal ice." Nature takes on supernatural forms—snow spirits, comets—that dance with the children to keep them awake (together with their mouthfuls of coffee), and in the morning the children are rescued. The music is often presented in brief illustrations, as dense (in a good sense) as the multicolored drawings in a children's book. If Charles Ives had decided to write with serialistic gestures and sounds, the result would probably be close to this unusual and exciting score. *—"Blue" Gene Tyranny*

Christopher Butterfield

b. Nov. 17, 1952, Vancouver, Canada
Composer / Experimental Rock, 20th Century Classical/Modern Composition, Chamber Music
Sang in King's College Choir as a child, comp. at University of Victoria and State University of New York at Stony Brook. Co-founded rock group Klo. Collaborated with writer John Bentley Mays on music drama *Project for an Opera of the Twentieth Century G.S.: something that happened once and it is very interesting.* Has composed for many of Canada's principal ensembles. Teacher of composition at University of Victoria. *—"Blue" Gene Tyranny*

Music for Klein and Beuys (1987) / Pillar of Snails (1984-87) / 1993 / Artifact ✦✦✦
Highly original chamber music ("Music for Klein and Beuys") by this Canadian composer with snatches of delightful tune-like passages that are somewhat more like melodic gestures, brief responses, bon mots, to the accompaniment of percussion that often sounds like amplified crumpled bags. But it's not "joke music." It's something else. "Pillar of Snails" is a piano piece that begins with single unharmonized melodic line statements separated by an appropriate silence, and gradually glorious chords are added but only briefly as a shading. The title refers to a tower or pillar, a massive black basalt cube that once sat on a pedestal but has now fallen and is half-submerged in a marsh in a mausoleum on a hill (The Spindles) in the once ancient Phoenician port of Amrit in what is now Syria. This CD is literally not for sale but came included in a package from the Canadian *Musicworks* magazine, who may still have some. Butterfield also excellently performs Kurt Schwitter's "Ursonate" (Sonate in Urlauten) on this CD. *—"Blue" Gene Tyranny*

Michael Byron

b. Sep. 7, 1953
Composer / 20th Century Classical/Modern Composition
Influential as a writer and commentator on new music, and an editor of new music anthologies while living in NYC. *—"Blue" Gene Tyranny*

● **Marimbas in the Dorian Mode in "Cold Blue Anthology"** / 1990 / Cold Blue ✦✦✦✦✦
Unusual fluttering sounds from four marimbas played sustained and very quietly… absolutely peaceful. Also grab a copy of the lovely orchestral pieces on "Tidal" on the defunct Neutral Records if you run across one. *—"Blue" Gene Tyranny*

Music of Nights without Moon or Pearl / Nov. 10, 2000 / Cold Blue ✦✦✦
Music of Nights Without Moon or Pearl presents three works by New York composer Michael Byron. The first two, the title piece and "Invisible 'Seeds' for James Tenney," were both written in 1998 for the same instrumentation (string quintet, two pianos, one synthesizer) and are related as each other's negative reflection. Recorded in 2000, they are performed by the CalArts New Century Players, conducted by David Rosenboom. Two principal elements constitute "Music of Nights Without Moon or Pearl": staccato playing from the strings and rolled piano chords acting like washes of sound. Synthesizer soundscapes add to the pianos' effect. The delicate, textural, and organized keyboard playing contrasts heavily with the seemingly random harsh string plucks. The piece begins with soundscapes and sparse staccato notes, then builds up to a climax where strings become more and more busy, adding the pianos along the way and finally reverting to its first state. On "Invisible 'Seeds' for James Tenney" the colors are inverted: the strings play arco throughout and the pianists drop bombshell-staccato chords. The first piece is softer, more textural, while the second is more troubled and has greater impact on the listener. "Entrances" completes the program. Recorded in 1982, this is an impressive piece for four pianos. All parts are performed by David Rosenboom. It starts as a disjointed contemporary piece—nice, but still an exercise—but builds up into rhapsodic frenzy, taking the listener into its maelstrom, putting a surprising exclamation point at the end of this album. *—François Couture*

George Cacioppo

b. Sep. 24, 1927, **d.** Apr. 4, 1984
Composer / 20th Century Classical/Modern Composition, Avant-Garde
Composer and educator George Cacioppo was a co-founder of the ONCE Group, a 1960s Ann Arbor composing collective that included Robert Ashley, Gordon Mumma, Donald Scavarda, Roger Reynolds, and Robert Sheff (*"Blue" Gene Tyranny*). While some of Cacioppo's experimental works are important in themselves, including "Time on Time in Miracles," "Holy Ghost Vacuum," and "Cassiopeia," Cacioppo's biggest impact was through his decades of teaching. His former student Gérard Pape composed "In Memoriam: George Cacioppo" for eight trombones, tape, and percussion, upon hearing of Cacioppo's death in April, 1984. Other composer friends and collaborators were similarly inspired, resulting in "Four Fold Heart Sutra" by Robert Morris, Mumma's "Epifont," and "Sonata for Alto Saxophone and Piano" by William Albright. *—Joslyn Layne*

☆ **Time on Time in Miracles** / 1966 / Advance ✦✦✦✦✦
Composed in 1964, for soprano voice and chamber ensemble, this piece is a study of sounds that gradually evolve from the "distinct crystallizations" of single tones, through a midpoint of tone clusters, to "noise" at the other end of the spectrum. This procedure "make(s) possible diverse transformations with respect to time, including, for example, the exploration of timbre as a function of intensity" (Cacioppo). There are also many complexities produced by the sum-and-difference interferences of sung (by the instrumentalists) and played pitches, and the "artificial" partials (harmonics) of the extreme upper registers of instruments. Breath and whistling sounds through brasses, single note to crunching sounds produced by extreme pressure on the cello, minor second intervals in the brass like Tibetan horns, harsh and very gentle articulations and many other timbres unique and original for that time constitute this piece which is equally a fascinating sonic study and a mysterious contemporary tone poem. Cacioppo produced other remarkable scores for ensembles—the graph score based directly on the form of the constellation Cassiopeia, "Two Worlds" (1962) which contrasts the worlds of instrumental and vocal sounds, "Advance of the Fungii" based on ideas in the book by E.C. Large which describes various plagues that overwhelm plants and animals from time to time, and "Bestiary 1 Eingang." Several of these works had their pitches and overall forms generated from Markov chains. *—"Blue" Gene Tyranny*

John Cage

b. Sep. 5, 1912, Los Angeles, CA, **d.** Aug. 12, 1992, New York, NY
Composer / Process-Generated, 20th Century Classical/Modern Composition, Minimalism, Electronic
The most influential and controversial American experimental composer of the 20th century, John Cage was the father of indeterminism, a Zen-inspired aesthetic which expelled all notions of choice from the creative process. Rejecting the most deeply-held compositional principles of the past—logical consequence, vertical sensitivity and tonality among them—Cage created a groundbreaking alternative to the serialist method, deconstructing traditions established hundreds and even thousands of years earlier; the end result was a radical new artistic approach which impacted all of the music composed in its wake, forever altering not only the ways in which sounds are created but also how they're absorbed by audiences. Indeed, it's often been suggested that he did to music what Karl Marx did to government—he leveled it.

Born in Los Angeles, Cage traveled across Europe during the early '30s, but returned to America to study with Henry Cowell and Arnold Schoenburg. Around this time he published his earliest compositions, a series of Varèse-inspired works. During the late '30s, Cage began experimenting with both musique concrète (the landmark *Imaginary Landscape No. 1*), and the "prepared piano," in which he placed a variety of household objects between the strings of a grand piano to create sounds suggesting a one-man percussion orchestra. His work of the 1940s took a variety of shapes, including scores for percussion, sound montage, and heavily-muted prepared piano.

Though Cage's innovations were widely recognized by the end of the decade, his most visionary work was still to come: in 1951, he completed Imaginary Landscape No. 4, which limited its sound sources to only a dozen radios, with the end result dependent entirely on the broadcast material at the time of performance. One year later, pianist and longtime associate David Tudor premiered Cage's *4'33"*, known colloquially as "Silence"; the composer's most notorious work, it asks the performer to sit at his instrument but play nothing, the environmental sounds instead produced by a typically uncomfortable audience. Cage began to immerse himself in electronics during the '50s, most famously in works like 1960's Cartridge Music. He also turned to writing, teaching and lecturing across the globe. *—Jason Ankeny*

Four Walls / 1989 / Tomato ✦✦✦✦✦
This beautiful piece for piano solo (Richard Bunger), with a scene for the unaccompanied solo voice of Jay Clayton in the middle, is of approximately one hour's duration. It was written originally as music for a theater piece, a "dance play" psychodrama about a family conceived by the dancer Merce Cunningham, which had only one performance in Steamboat Springs, CO on August 22, 1944. The music is played entirely on the white keys of the piano, which gives the work natural modal qualities, and the music is not complex, as it was designed to be easily played by a pianist unknown to either Cage or Cunningham, and there was no travel money for Cage to attend the rehearsals with the pianist. All of these circumstances resulted in a work of direct, evocative, mesmerizing musical gestures, some set off by silences of varying length, some of insistent rhythm with simple variation. There are 14 Scenes, plus two sections for dance alone, each with a different dynamic—the text they were to accompany, now lost, can only be imagined by the listener. The text for the solo singer in Scene VII reads "Sweet love, my throat is gurgling, the mystic mouth, leads me so defted, and the black nightingale, turned willowly by love's tossed treatment, berefted." Written at a time when Cage was considering the serious move of ceasing to write music in order to devote time to being psychoanalyzed, the title (as in the expression "staring at four walls" for intense, cabin-fever boredom) must have taken on poignant personal significance for the composer. He resolved to keep on with music, which lead to the radical and highly influential solutions of his post-1950 work. *—"Blue" Gene Tyranny*

Cheap Imitation / 1991 / Cramps ✦✦✦
With the composer at the piano. A lovely performance of melodies which are fragments and transformations of melodies for Erik Satie's opera "Socrate" on the death of Socrates. Cage had to produce "cheap imitations" of these melodies for a performance when the rights for the Satie score could not be obtained. *—"Blue" Gene Tyranny*

☆ **Empty Words (Part III, Live Teatro Lyrico Di Milano 2 Dec. 1977)** / 1991 / Cramps ✦✦✦✦✦
Cage reading a gradually fragmenting text based on Thoreau's "Walden Pond"... this heartwarming piece shows how Cage's chance procedures serve to enhance, rather than distance, human feeling and attention. The entire "Empty Words" (Parts I-IV) was slated for reissue on 8 CDs in the '90s by Lovely Music. *—"Blue" Gene Tyranny*

Music for Marcel Duchamp (1947) / Music for Amplified Toy Pianos (1960) / R / 1991 / Cramps ✦✦✦✦✦
Wonderful performances of these modern classics by composer/performers Juan Hidalgo, Marchetti, Simonetti, and Stratos. *4'33",* with its alternative realization *0'00" (Solo to Be Performed in Any Way by Anyone, 4'33" No. 2),* is perhaps the most elegantly simple and controversial in all of Cage's works. The score consists of the notations I. Tacet, II. Tacet, III. Tacet. The seeming intent is to create an action that will give a sense of three moments in time, and will also make the presence of an undisturbed, eternal silence felt; not a negative act, but an affirmation of that element necessary for any meaningful sound gesture, an awareness of silence. David Tudor first realized this piece, quietly opening and closing the keyboard lid of a piano to create a performance of 4 minutes and 33 seconds duration, and thus giving the piece the title by which it is best known. It can, of course, be performed for any duration, and has been. The version written for Yoko Ono and Toshi Ichiyanagi elucidates this experience further through a kind of non-clock time, or eternal presence, and indicating that the piece can also have the other extreme of infinite compression or loudness. There are probably as many reactions, meanings, and interpretations in linear time (e.g., a "blank wall" on which the mind involuntarily projects itself) of *4'33"* as there are possible realizations. And that will always be the undisturbed, elusive, quite timeless beauty of this piece. Aside from all these considerations, it is charmingly warm and disarming to simply share this peaceful moment (unselfconsciously) with the rest of the audience. *—"Blue" Gene Tyranny*

★ **Singing Through/ Vocal Compositions by John Cage** / 1991 / New Albion ✦✦✦✦✦
Beautifully performed pieces from 1942 to 1985 by vocalist Joan LaBarbara with piano and percussion. Contains: *A Flower* (1950), *Mirakus* (1984), *Eight Whiskus* (1984), *The Wonderful Widow of 18 Springs* (1942) for voice and closed piano, *Nowth upon Nacht* (1984), *Sonnekus* (1985), *Forever and Sunsmell* (1942), *Solos for Voice (from the Songbooks) #'s 49, 52, 67* (1970), *Music for Two (by One)* (1984). *—"Blue" Gene Tyranny*

Concert for Piano and Orchestra / Atlas Eclipticalis / 1993 / Wergo ✦✦✦✦✦
This has got to be one of the finest recordings of Cage's music ever. The careful consideration given to musical and sonic details by the Orchestra of the S.E.M. Ensemble with conductor Petr Kotik, and the wonderful performance of piano soloist Joseph Kubera finally makes understandable in sound Cage's philosophical and poetical insights. In the performance of "Atlas Eclipticalis," for example, we finally hear the ongoing universe of stars, planets, solar winds and asteroids (etc.) much as Cage may have imagined a performance of his work. These musicians play the music with respect, accuracy and a more than ordinary sense of what is beautiful. *—"Blue" Gene Tyranny*

Music of Changes, Books I-IV / 1996 / Lovely Music ✦✦✦✦✦
An exquisitely played and beautiful recording of Cage's masterpiece, one of the most technically difficult pieces in all of piano repertoire. After studying the details of the work with David Tudor, who premiered it, and refining his interpretation in live performance over several years, pianist Joseph Kubera has applied his amazing range of touch and inflection to this accurate and highly musical recording. Because of advanced recording techniques we are able to hear the fine harmonic and resonant combinations that were scored by Cage, and that forms a sort of interior life of the piece. One unique and surprising sound follows the next over wide dynamic (pppp to ffff applied to each individual event), durational (blazingly fast grace note figures to events or silence held for a page), and pitch ranges (the entire tessitura of the piano is employed). This is one of the first compositions to use organized parameters and chance-operations (using the Chinese *Book of Changes* or -I-Ching) in its composition. It provides a continually fascinating listening experience. *—"Blue" Gene Tyranny*

Litany for the Whale / 1998 / Harmonia Mundi ✦✦✦✦
Named after the longest work on the CD, this is an excellent and beautifully performed collection of familiar and rarely given vocal works by John Cage. It is performed by the Theatre of Voices, directed by Paul Hillier, with guest performer/composer Terry Riley. These include: "Litany for the Whale" (for two voices), "Aria No. 2" (for voice and electronics... rolling thunderclouds and other weather and sounds, with vowels and consonants from five languages), "Five" (for five voices... sustained, pure tones... Cage indicates that the notes "should be brushed into being"), "The Wonderful Widow of Eighteen Springs" (the classic song for voice and closed piano, 1942), "Solo for Voice 22 from the Songbooks" (for two voices and electronics... the multiple "meanings" of breath inflections), "Experiences No. 2" (for solo voice, 1948), "36 Mesostics and not re Marcel Duchamp" (two voices and electronics, 1970), "Aria" (for two voices and electronics... a fascinating new realization for two voices... interesting to compare with the classic solo Cathy Berberian realization, 1958), and "The Year Begins to Be Ripe" (from *Songbooks–Solo for Voice 49, Song With Electronics–Relevant: The Year Begins To Be Ripe,* using a text from Henry David Thoreau's journal... for voice and closed piano, 1970). *—"Blue" Gene Tyranny*

Cornelius Cardew

b. May 7, 1936, Winchcombe, England, **d.** Dec. 13, 1981, London, England
Cello, Piano, Composer / Improvisation, 20th Century Classical/Modern Composition
Cardew was a chorister at Canterbury Cathedral for eight years, and he later studied at the RAM. He received a scholarship from the RAM in 1957 to study electronic music in Köln. He served as an assistant to Stockhausen from 1958-60 and collaborated with him on the composition *Carré.* After a period as a graphic designer, Cardew became professor of composition at the RAM in 1967. Influenced by Cage and Tudor, Cardew was interested in the idea of performer participation in the creation of a work. He composed music that could be realized in several ways with notation that is a suggestion of the possible interpretations of the score. His most important work with this method is his graphic score *Treatise* (1963-7). In it, the performers must interpret the work as a sound version of how they see the score. This score can also be read as an abstract visual artwork. Cardew was also a frequent performer of the work of Stockhausen, Cage, Feldman and Wolff. Together with pianist John Tilbury, Cardew became known as a leading interpreter of experimental and indeterminate music in England. *—Lynn Vought*

☆ **Memorial Concert 16th May 1982: First Movement for String Quartet / Octet '71 / Trea** / Gelbe Musik ✦✦✦✦✦
A retrospective of this musically and morally influential British composer's work played by his composer-friends Bryars, Nyman, Dave Smith, John White, John Tilbury, Rzewski, Tom Philips, Christopher Hobbs, Balanescu, Janos Negyesy, and members of the "Scratch Orchestra," a collective performing group for musicians and non-musicians which Cardew cofounded in 1969. In their constitution draft they stated that "the word music... is here not understood to refer exclusively to sound... (but) is flexible and depends entirely on the members... " (see- "Scratch Music," aed. by C.C., M.I.T. Press, MIT 239, paperback issued 1974). *—"Blue" Gene Tyranny*

Elliott Carter

b. Dec. 11, 1908, New York, NY
Composer / 20th Century Classical/Modern Composition, Atonal, Classical
Studied with Walter Piston, Gustav Holst at Harvard, Nadia Boulanger in Paris. Teacher at Juilliard School of Music. Early works in neo-classical idiom, eg. *Holiday Overture* (1944), *Pocahantas* ballet for orchestra (1939). Later pieces in atonal chromatic style with "metric modulation" and great rhythmic complexity, eg. *Variations for Orchestra* (1955), *Double Concerto for Harpsichord and Piano with Two Chamber Orchestras* (1961). *—"Blue" Gene Tyranny*

● **String Quartet No. 3 (1971)/ Elegy (1943) in "The Music for String Quartet, Vol. Ii"** / 1988 / Etcetera ✦✦✦✦✦
Amazing performances by the renowned Arditti String Quartet. Pieces that illustrate the best of his early and later styles... the dense "abstract expressionist" complexity of the 3rd Quartet... instrumental conversations... and the unpredictable but warm, advanced-Coplandesque harmonies of the "Elegy." *—"Blue" Gene Tyranny*

Holiday Overture (1944, Revised 1961) / Suite from Pocahontas / Syringa / 1991 / CRI ✦✦✦
Reissues of Carter in his early style. Sweeping energetic performance of the "Holiday Overture." *—"Blue" Gene Tyranny*

Variations for Orchestra (1954-55) in "Cage/ Carter/ Babbitt/ Schuller" / 1994 / Deutsche Grammaphon ✦✦✦
The shocking classic that was a signal of Carter's change into a radically new American serialist style. *—"Blue" Gene Tyranny*

Joseph Celli

b. Mar. 19, 1944
Oboe, Horn (English), Composer / Multimedia, 20th Century Classical/Modern Composition, World Fusion
Developed new performing techniques for oboe and English horn, and plays many double reed instruments including Korean p'iri, tae'ponso, Indian Mukha Veena, Japanese hickiricki, and employs electronics in his performances. Created first American satellite performance piece with Jerry Hunt entitled *PHALBA.* Has produced over 1500 contemporary concerts and art activities, and commissioned works from many composers, including Ornette Coleman, Pauline Oliveros, Roberta Friedman, etc. Has premiered over 35 inter-media works by various artists. *—"Blue" Gene Tyranny*

Organic Oboe / 1968 / O.O. Discs ♦♦♦♦
Wonderful performances by Joseph Celli in this historic recording re-released on CD. Contains the only American release of Stockhausen's "Spiral" (1968) for soloists on short-wave radio and other instruments, Celli's "Sky:S for J" (1976), Elliott Schwartz' "Extended Oboe" (1973-74) for oboe and electronic tape, and Malcolm Goldstein's "A Summoning of Focus" (1977) for wind instruments. *—"Blue" Gene Tyranny*

No World (Trio) Improvisations / 1992 / O.O. Discs ♦♦♦
Imaginative group improvs by Joseph Celli, double reeds, and Jin Hi Kim, komungo and electric komungo, in trio format with different guest soloists, including Alvin Curran, electronics, Shelley Hirsch, voice, and Malcolm Goldstein, violin. *—"Blue" Gene Tyranny*

No World Improvisations / 1992 / ♦♦♦♦
Virtuoso solo and duo improvisations with Jin Hi Kim (b.1956) on Korean komungo, changgo, and electric komungo and Celli on Indian Mukha Veena, english horn without reeds and Yamaha WX-7 MIDI-breath controller. Wonderful.—No World (trio) *—"Blue" Gene Tyranny*

Sky: S for J (1976) for Five English Horns Without Reeds / in "Organic Oboe" / 1992 / O.O. Discs ♦♦♦
New and startling techniques for the english horn. *—"Blue" Gene Tyranny*

● **Video Ears Music Eyes** / 1995 / O.O. Discs ♦♦♦♦♦
A collection of five works of music written to accompany multi-channel video presentations. *36 Strings* (1992) is for the Korean komungo, played here with much expression and feeling by Jin Hi Kim, and five channels of video. It is dedicated to the reconciliation of North and South Korean families. "8 Mallets Four Brian" (1986) is for marimba, vibraphone, xylophone and orchestra bells and three channels of video. It is an evocative work with dense, sustained textures. "Andes" (1990) was realized by seven Peruvian musicians, and is set amongst a "Mountain of Televisions." It is played here by the Grupo de Musica Folklorica del Peru on cajon, mama cuena, cuena, zampoona, cahita, and charango, and was recorded at *Peruvian National Television* in Lima with submachine-gunned guards standing around while the musicians obliged with simultaneous rhythms of African 4/4 and Spanish 3/4. "Video Sax" (1993) is for various saxes and five channels of video. It begins with slow, dissonantly meshing scale patterns, and then begins to accelerate and get stuck in repeating rhythmic nodes; the slow process is started again and winds its way to a free-for-all wailing jam for a coda. "Violin & Video" (1988), for multi-tracked solo violin and three channels of video, is a triple counterpoint of stereo pulsing chops, a descending sustained tone track and a wild central improvised solo track. This entire CD is a richly rewarding listening experience. *—"Blue" Gene Tyranny*

Eugene Chadbourne

b. Jan. 4, 1954, Mount Vernon, NY
Guitar / Avant-Garde Jazz, Experimental, Prog-Rock/Art Rock, Alternative Pop/Rock, Fusion, Avant-Garde
A seemingly endless—and endlessly eclectic—series of releases made the innovative guitarist Eugene Chadbourne one of the underground community's most well-known and well-regarded eccentrics. Chadbourne was raised in Boulder by his mother, a refugee of the Nazi death camps. Inspired by the Beatles to learn guitar at age 11, Chadbourne began experimenting with distortion pedals and fuzzboxes after hearing Jimi Hendrix. Ultimately, however, he became dissatisfied with rock and pop conventions, traded in his electric guitar for an acoustic one, and began playing bottleneck blues.

When Chadbourne discovered jazz, he initially drawn to John Coltrane and Roland Kirk, and later became an acolyte of the avant excursions of Derek Bailey and Anthony Braxton. He studied to become a journalist, and during Vietnam, the vociferously left-wing Chadbourne fled to Canada rather than fight, and wasn't allowed back in the country until 1976 when President Jimmy Carter's declared amnesty for conscientious objectors. Chadbourne moved to NYC and plunged headlong into the downtown music scene, released his 1976 debut, *Solo Acoustic Guitar,* and began collaborating on purely improvisational music with visionary saxophonist John Zorn and acclaimed guitarist Henry Kaiser.

Chadbourne carved out a singular style, comprised of equal parts protest music, free improvisation and avant-garde jazz, topped off with his absurd, squeaky vocals. His subsequent collaborations and genre workouts form a lengthy list, indeed, including recordings with artists ranging from Fred Frith and Elliott Sharp to Evan Johns and Mothers of Invention drummer Jimmy Carl Black. His better-known projects include fronting the demented rockabilly-revisionist outfit Shockabilly, with well-known producer Kramer, in the early '80s, and collaborating with the members of Camper Van Beethoven for a one-off covers project in 1987. That same year Chadbourne released an album of his own idiosyncratic brand of country and folk, accurately dubbed *LSD C&W.* For decades now, Chadbourne has explored unique styles inspired by music from all over the globe, with numerous releases on labels including his own, Parachute, and Leo. He also wrote the hilarious and helpful book *I Hate the Man Who Runs This Bar! The Survival Guide for Real Musicians. —Jason Ankeny*

● **LSD C&W: The History of the Chadbournes in America** / 1987 / Fundamental ♦♦♦♦♦
The ultimate Chadbourne, featuring medleys of The Beatles, Roger Miller, and Burl Ives, plus much more insanity filtered through post-avant-garde brilliance. *—Jeff Tamarkin*

Worms With Strings / 1993-1998 / Leo ♦♦♦♦
Ignore the puerile musings by the good professor, and instead enjoy his slightly demented music, which includes a collection of tracks from four different conglomerations, recorded over the course of five years. Concentrating on various combinations of strings, Chadbourne leads with his acoustic banjo and guitar. Most of the pieces are multitracked performances with Chadbourne overdubbing on guitars, banjos, and assorted homemade instruments, while one features mandolin soloist Barry Mitterhof with a trio. Others add accordion, bassoon, and oboe, and the results, if not electrifying, should please admirers of Chadbourne. While some might find the extensive doodling tiresome, there is no question that the humor, creativity, and incomprehensible melange add up to a good time. *—Steve Loewy*

The Hellingtunes / Mar. 23, 1997-Mar. 24, 1997 / Intakt ♦♦♦♦
This unusual tribute to Duke Ellington uses the cut-up techniques of author William Burroughs to sketch scores for pieces only peripherally sounding like the big band master. Nonetheless, this largely successful recording is a creative and imaginative pastiche of styles, featuring strong improvising, particularly from piano basher Pat Thomas and clarinetist and alto saxophonist Alex Ward. The group's leader, Eugene Chadbourne, displays remarkable arranging skills while subordinating his fine banjo and guitar to the total sound. While blips of old Ellington recordings are occasionally inserted, don't expect to hear too much from the Duke's repertoire. These are freestyle transformations, with dissonance, blues, swing, and outside styling all blending in a stew that jumps and bubbles. Rounding out the sextet are Paul Lovens on drums and cymbals, Carrie Shull on oboe, and Leslie Ross on bassoon and shawm. One of Chadbourne's finer efforts. *—Steve Loewy*

Beauty and the Bloodsucker / Sep. 1997-Feb. 1999 / Leo ♦♦♦♦
Another in Chadbourne's infamous "insect" series, this may be the jazziest yet of the fine Doctor's work. This recording is actually a compilation of tracks during the span of slightly more than a year. While Chadbourne is the unifying factor, there are an additional 15 musicians (including tenor saxophonist Ellery Eskelin, percussionists Garth Powell and Gino Robair, and saxophonist Dan Plonsey) who pop up from time to time. Chadbourne plays acoustic and electric guitars, Dobro, and five-string banjo, and his jazz roots are clearly evident. Still, as with all his recordings, the results are off-kilter, with overdubs, superimposed excerpts, and turntables adding to the mix. Chadbourne fans should be pleased with the variety, goofiness, genre-bashing, and off-the-wall humor. Others should find this never less than fascinating. *—Steve Loewy*

● **Young at Heart/Forgiven** / Jun. 27, 2000 / Leo ♦♦♦

Rhys Chatham

b. Sep. 19, 1952, New York, NY
Composer / No Wave, 20th Century Classical/Modern Composition, Avant-Garde, Electronic
Post-minimalist composer and New York downtown music figure Rhys Chatham was involved in music at an early age. He studied classical flute, and was already playing works by contemporary composers such as Luciano Berio and Pierre Boulez by the time he began studying composition (including serialism) in his early teens. Chatham started writing electronic works after meeting Morton Subotnick in college, and came into contact with Eliane Radigue, Maryanne Amacher, and Ingram Marshall, among others, at NYU's Studio for Electronic Music. Starting in the '70s, Chatham began composing in just intonation, and made a living tuning instruments, sometimes in trade for lessons, as he did with LaMonte Young. He played in Young's Dream House band and in a group with Tony Conrad during this time. Later in the '70s, Chatham began incorporating rock elements into his music and explored non-notated forms. The rock part of his work mainly focused on electric guitars which he was inspired to love after seeing the Ramones play at *CBGB*'s. Chatham's guitar works—the first of which, "Guitar Trio," was premiered by a trio including Glenn Branca—were played at high volumes, revealing the overtones, which can sound like voices, but also resulted in tinnitus for him by the early '80s. Chatham's better-known guitar works include "Drastic Classicism" (1982) for four guitars with alternate tunings, and the symphony "An Angel Moves Too Fast to See" (1989) for 100 electric guitars (with bass and drums). Performances of his large-scale works utilized guitarists including Bill Brovold (who went on to form Larval) and Robert Poss (Band of Susans). Chatham began composing for brass (such as "Factor X") in addition to guitar, and resumed notating his works. After years of living in NYC, he relocated to Paris. Chatham also began incorporating his trumpeting (often electrified, with effects) after about a decade of studying the instrument. You can hear his trumpet on *Hard Edge* (1999, Wire Editions) and *Neon* (1996, NTone), an album by Chatham and Martin Wheeler. In the late '90s, Chatham co-founded the group Septile with a Bronx DJ and ex-Swans drummer Jonathan Kane. *—Joslyn Layne*

Die Donnergotter / 1987 / Homestead ♦♦♦
Rhys merges both pattern rock-influenced riffs (like Peter Gordon) and dense sonorities (like Glenn Branca) to produce music of an extended time sense... with imagery of thundergods, Waterloo complete with the requisite drums and massed trumpets, and the '60s rock trio. *—"Blue" Gene Tyranny*

● **An Angel Moves Too Fast to See** / 1994 / New Tone ♦♦♦♦♦
Like the composer's works *Warehouse of Saints, Songs for Spies* and *Symphony No. 3,* this innovative and dynamic piece is scored for the unusual ensemble of 100 specially tuned electric guitars, drums and electric bass.

Patterns of bell-like resonances are interchanged in wide spatial distribution among the various massed groups above a continuous rock beat. These first patterns are then alternated with fast tremolos of accumulating tone clusters and later ascending scales. The effect is indeed vast and, if this is your idea of heaven, angelic. *—"Blue" Gene Tyranny*

John Chowning

b. Aug. 22, 1934, Salem, NJ
Composer / Spectral Music, Computer Music, Electronic
The father of the digital synthesizer, inventor and composer John Chowning forever altered the face of modern music. Born in 1934, he was first exposed to electronic music while studying in Paris, and visited computer-music pioneer Max Mathews after returning to America. With only a box stuffed with computer punch cards, he discovered the technology to play them in the university's artificial intelligence department. Chowning's breakthrough followed in 1967: while experimenting with high-speed vibratos, he also began toying with a pair of oscillators. What he discovered was a recognizable, richly harmonic tone color which he was able to manipulate to approximate the sound of clarinets, bassoons and the like. Having hit upon frequency modulation (FM) synthesis, Chowning spent several years exploring his findings before sending out feelers to organ manufacturers. Only the Japanese corporation Yamaha understood the possibilites Chowning's dis-

covery offered. Yamaha licensed the FM synthesis patent and in 1973 built the MAD, the first known all-digital synth.

Though Chowning was dismissed from his position at Stanford, when Yamaha came back to license a ten-year deal for the FM rights, the situation proved highly embarrassing for university officials. They quickly rehired him as Director of the University's Center for Computer Research and Musical Acoustics, with a professorship to follow in 1979. The GS-1 digital synth—the first fruits of Chowning's research and Yamaha's development—rolled out of Yamaha's Japanese factories in 1981. Two years later, Yamaha released the DX-7 and overnight, the industry was seemingly turned upside down. The DX-7's success and influence aside, Chowning also left his mark as a composer of computer music; his most notable works included 1971's *Sabelithe*, 1972's *Turenas*, 1977's *Stria* and 1981's *Phone*. *—Jason Ankeny*

★ **Phone (1980-1981) / Turenas (1972) / Stria (1977)/ Sabelithe (1971)** / 1988 / Wergo ✦✦✦✦✦

Lyrical and sophisticated FM synthesis computer music with mysterious and surprising psychoacoustic illusions, like in *Turenas*, the first piece to create the impression of sound sources moving in a 360-degree space. *— "Blue" Gene Tyranny*

Jay Cloidt

b. Oct. 5, 1949

Engineer, Composer / 20th Century Classical/Modern Composition, Electronic

Has collaborated and performed with Paul Dresher Enseble, Margaret Jenkins Dance Company, ODC San Francisco and Kronos String Quartet. *Exploded View* is a live performance work with digital sampling electronics. Works with Paul Dresher's *Looking West to the East* as composer, sound engineer and performer. Other works: *Light Fall* (1989) for Margaret Jenkins Dance Co., *Meteorology* (1988) and *Love It to Death* (1989) for G. Palmer Dance Co. *— "Blue" Gene Tyranny*

Light Fall / 1995 / Inial ✦✦✦

In the collection *Views from the Perfect City*. Exquisite and mysterious electronic sound from many sources: modified bell-tones, city environments, a sampled housefly, "singing" frequencies of a chainsaw at varying speeds, disembodied and indistinct public-information voices, etc. And somehow the composer has made them all combine beautifully. *— "Blue" Gene Tyranny*

● **Kole Kat Krush** / 1999 / Starkland ✦✦✦✦

Composer Jay Cloidt has been called "the Spike Jones of the Bay Area's new music scene," and while there's certainly something to that comparison, it's not entirely fair. There's no missing the sense of humor that pervades many of these pieces; titles like "Jimi's Fridge" and "DixieLurch Music" are dead giveaways, and it takes not only a deeply talented but also a slightly twisted composer to fashion compelling music out of samples of cats meowing and babies cooing. But the humor is only part of this music's charm. The excellent title piece, presented in two very different realizations, one by the Kronos Quartet and one by the Paul Dresher Ensemble, includes quotes from "Sunshine of Your Love" and Stravinsky's "Rite of Spring," as well as some very original and attractive thematic development. The title of "Karoshi," for bass instrument and sampled percussion, has reference to a medical syndrome first observed in Japan in which businessmen drop dead without warning due to job-related stress. The meowing cats and gurgling babies are excerpts from a larger composition entitled "Exploded View" and are actually samples controlled by members of the Kronos Quartet playing Zeta MIDI instruments. Need I say more— This is a wonderful, accessible, and yet challenging album from one of new music's brightest lights. *—Rick Anderson*

Nicolas Collins

b. Mar. 26, 1954, New York, NY

Electronics, Composer / Experimental, Electronic

Before Oval brought the artful use of CD-skipping to the attention of a larger audience, Nicolas Collins was using CD (and CD player) manipulation, as well as a variety of electronics, in his compositions. After studying with Alvin Lucier, the New York native went on to work with John Cage, Christian Marclay, David Tudor, Peter Cusack, and Guy Klucevsek, among others. He was among the first to use computers in performance, and is responsible for installations and shows all over the West and in Japan. Collins has lived and worked in Amsterdam (as an art director for STEIM), Berlin (on a DAAD residency), and Chicago. He has recordings available on Trace Elements and New Tone. *—Joslyn Layne*

● **100 of the World's Most Beautiful Melodies** / 1989 / Trace Elements ✦✦✦

This album is played by an all-star downtown group: Nicolas Collins, Pippin Barnett, Anthony Coleman, Tom Cora, Peter Cusack, Shelley Hirsch, George Lewis, Christian Marclay, Ben Neill, Zeena Parkins, Robert Poss, Ned Rothenberg, Elliott Sharp, Davey Williams, John Zorn, and Peter Zummo. A tongue-in-cheek title, perhaps, depending on your idea of "beautiful melody," as the sounds range from electronically and physically modified instruments with a definite edge to the barely perceptible, awakening the ear. Collins is also part of the Impossible Music group (with David Weinstein, David Shea, Ted Greenwald, and Tim Spelios) who, performing live, manipulate CD players in the spirit of Plunderphonics and rap-scratch style, creating a new style of electronic ensemble with works like the spatial and surreal "Simulcatastrophy," a performance of Collin's "In CD" (a title pun on Riley's "In C," of course) often humorously re-thinking Beethoven and Mozart cadences and form (he has made some recent work with Ben Neill along this same line), and the dense work "Salvador Dali's Digital Cinema." *— "Blue" Gene Tyranny*

It Was a Dark and Stormy Night / 1992 / Trace Elements ✦✦✦

More ensemble work with a sound like "100 Melodies" but with a more through-composed style. *— "Blue" Gene Tyranny*

Devil's Music / 1994 / New Tone ✦✦✦✦✦

Like many composers of electronic music (in particular, John Cage, Karlheinz Stockhausen, Ned Sublette, Phil Harmonic and others), Collins employs the richness and surprise of live radio broadcasts for his initial sound sources to make this piece. Here, radio transmissions are "digitally sampled, looped, retriggered, reversed, and de-tuned" through a "cheap sampling system (consisting of two Electro Harmonix Super Replays and one 16 second Delay) to develop the quirky rhythmic interplay that characteristizes the piece" (Collins). The result is a contemporary rhythm collage that could also be at home in techno, house, hip-hop and other dance music situations. This work has been performed in concert versions and was also issued as a regular dance LP, an "encyclopedia of break" (Collins), which the composer later discovered was selling like hotcakes several years after its initially commercially unsuccessful release—perhaps, the price of being ahead of your time. Collins shares sensibilities with many contemporary composers who are familiar with and often perform both advanced and pop styles of music. *— "Blue" Gene Tyranny*

Loren Mazzacane Connors

b. 1949, New Haven, CT

Vocals, Guitar / Improvisation, Experimental Rock, Indie Rock, Experimental, Avant-Garde

The eclectic music of improvisational avant-garde guitarist Loren Mazzacane Connors is difficult to describe; experimental, jazz, and blues all fit, and even hints of Irish music are evident. Often creating albums out of extensively edited recordings, Connors is incredibly prolific; he released over 30 albums on countless labels from 1978 on, many in extremely limited quantities. Connors' obscure albums met with indifference until the early 1990s, when supporters such as Sonic Youth's Thurston Moore and Lee Ranaldo, Gastr Del Sol's Jim O'Rourke, and Alan Licht began to sing his praises. Connors studied art in college during the early 1970s, but decided his music was more original than his painting. Between 1978 and 1980, he released eight albums of solo acoustic guitar improvisations on his own Connecticut-based Daggett label; just 75 to 100 copies of each were pressed (these albums were re-released in 1999 as a four-CD set). Between 1984 and 1989, Connors was largely inactive musically; he married vocalist Suzanne Langille and dabbled in writing, winning a haiku award in Japan. He moved to New York City in 1990 and a year later began releasing albums on labels other than his own. Connors was diagnosed with Parkinson's disease in 1992, and it changed the direction of his music; instead of short acoustic pieces, he began experimenting with longer electric guitar works, complete with feedback and distortion. Much of Connors' late-'90s output was released on Road Cone Records, a small label based in Portland, OR. *—Bret Adams*

● **Come Night** / 1991 / What Next ✦✦✦✦✦

This highly original CD is one of those cross-category musical experiences, a netherworld of avant-garde song-form jazz (like some 1960s ESP groups) and laid-back non-tonal improvisation, that it is truly something different and should be mentioned here. With Suzanne Langille (vocals), Loren Mazzacane (guitar), Brian Johnson (percussion), and the remarkable playing of George Cartwright (tenor sax), the selections—many of which are solely instrumental—proceed through the bardos of conscious and pre-conscious worlds with contained emotion. Some of the selections are "Take Me Up," "The Dream Comes," "Never the Blues," "Almost You," "Tell Me Where," "Still Bound," "Too Late," "Cross Town" and "No Words." *— "Blue" Gene Tyranny*

Moonyean / Jan. 1, 1996 / Road Cone ✦✦✦✦

Loren Mazzacane Connors is truly a master of minimal guitar compositions; the incredibly sparse and bare touches of guitar that make up *Moonyean* drift along gorgeously, tending far more toward prettiness than they do desolation. This is the sound that originally defined Connors' work, and with good reason—even as he moved into fuller, fuzzier, and more ambient textures, it was this minimal guitar style that formed the basis and the true interest of his compositions. *—Nitsuh Abebe*

Calloden Harvest / Road Cone ✦✦

Mercury / Road Cone ✦✦✦

Another gorgeous collaboration between Licht and Connors—as usual, the two present two-guitar duets with a subliminal, atmospheric beauty, but the presence of drones, ambient swells, and generally more atmosphere makes *Mercury* fall slightly closer to Licht's general aesthetic than Connors' (as opposed to *Two Nights*, on which the opposite seems to be true.) *—Nitsuh Abebe*

Tony Conrad

b. 1940, Baltimore, MD

Violin / Experimental Rock, Kraut Rock, Avant-Garde

A pioneering force behind the evolution of minimalism, violinist and composer Tony Conrad introduced the idea of "Eternal Music," a droning, mesmerizing performance idiom which employed long durations, amplification and precise pitch to explore new worlds of sound; through both his solo work and through collaborations with artists including LaMonte Young, John Cale and Faust, he forged new creative directions which proved enormously influential on successive generations of artists ranging in background from pop to the avant-garde. Born in 1940, Conrad studied music at Harvard and, by the early '60s, became immersed in New York's burgeoning underground music scene; there he first joined forces with composer/saxophonist LaMonte Young and the young Welsh musician John Cale, with whom he formed an ensemble variously dubbed the Dream Syndicate and the Theater of Eternal Music. Sustaining notes for hours at a time, their improvised dissections of specific harmonic intervals rejected the compositional process, instead elaborating shared performance concepts.

The Dream Syndicate disbanded in 1965, with Conrad, Young and Cale all later staking claim to authoring of the "Eternal Music" aesthetic. Still, Conrad continued collaborating with Cale, though he also channeled his energies into filmmaking. He directed several features (*The Flicker, Film Feedback*), and also composed their scores. By the early '70s, Conrad began recording with members of the nascent Kraut-rock scene, resulting in the 1973 Faust collaboration *Outside the Dream Syndicate*, his first-ever proper recording. However, he largely abandoned performing to teach at the University at Buffalo. Finally, in 1993, he performed with Faust at a music festival recorded *Slapping Pythagoras* two years later. In 1996, he issued *Four Violins*, a piece dating back to 1964. A year later, Conrad released *Early Minimalism*, a four-disc collection including not only the aforementioned *Four Violins* but also newly-recorded recreations of vintage Dream Syndicate performances. *—Jason Ankeny*

Outside the Dream Syndicate [With Faust] / 1972 / Table of the Elements ✦✦✦✦
Recorded over a span of three days in 1973, *Outside the Dream Syndicate* was Tony Conrad's first official release; though also credited to the celebrated Krautrock band Faust, it's primarily a showcase for Conrad's minimalist drone explorations, an aesthetic fascinatingly at odds with the noisy, fragmented sound of his collaborators. Consisting of three epic tracks, each topping out in excess of 20 minutes, the album is hypnotically contemplative; the music shifts in subtle—almost subliminal—fashion, and the deeper one listens, the more rewarding it becomes. *—Jason Ankeny*

● **Early Minimalism, Vol. 1** / Nov. 18, 1997 / Table of the Elements ✦✦✦✦✦
The four-disc *Early Minimalism, Vol. 1* is probably the closest modern listeners will come to experiencing the visionary brilliance of the Theatre of Eternal Music at their peak—with an official release of the ensemble's original mid-'60s recordings still nowhere in sight, Tony Conrad has instead assembled a number of latter-day experimentalists (including the always-intriguing Jim O'Rourke) in an attempt to recreate the group's groundbreaking explorations of sound. It's impossible to know to just what extent these new recordings (dating from between 1994 and 1996) have succeeded in recapturing the past, of course, but taken on its own terms this is compelling stuff—minus LaMonte Young's blistering saxophone and Marian Zazeela's vocals, the emphasis is instead on Conrad's violin, which wails with starkly hypnotic power as it weaves through these difficult but rewarding live performances. *—Jason Ankeny*

Henry Cowell

b. Mar. 11, 1897, **d.** Dec. 10, 1965
Composer / 20th Century Classical/Modern Composition, World Fusion, Atonal
Of all the early-20th-century American musical revolutionaries, it is composer Henry Cowell whose influence was most vivid and far-reaching. Born in 1897, Cowell studied the violin briefly at age five, and began to write his own music by his eleventh birthday. Until he began musical studies with Charles Seeger at the University of California at Berkeley in 1914 Cowell remained a basically self-taught musician (as well as a young man who had never spent so much as a day in school during his life). Free of the often confining attitudes which govern formal musical education, Cowell had come to view any sound as musical substance with which he could work, and his early music owes more to the influence of birdsong, machine noises and folk music than it does to any knowledge of earlier masterworks.

However, Seeger felt that without structure and guidelines Cowell would remain an unskilled, if impressively inventive, musician, and he encouraged the young composer to make a rigorous study of traditional harmony and counterpoint. Concert appearances throughout North America and Europe during the 1920s earned Cowell countless friends and enemies throughout the musical establishment. Although he had earned the respect of such luminaries as Bartok and Schoenberg, his concerts frequently caused audience riots and invoked the wrath of critics who wondered if Cowell's headstrong independence disguised a lack of true musical craftsmanship. Later music, such as the "Amerind Suite for piano" (1939) and the "26 Simultaneous Mosaics" (1964) incorporate generous helpings of indeterminacy, though from the 1930s on Cowell's compositional language grew increasingly tonal and rhythmically simple. He died in 1965 after several years of serious illness. *—Blair Johnston*

Quartet Euphometric (1916-19) / 1977 / New World ✦✦✦✦✦
Like "Quartet Romantic" (1915-17) and "Concerto for Rhythmicon and Orchestra," this brief two-minute work, played here by the Emerson String Quartet, is built on yet another of Cowell's groundbreaking resources: converting pitch intervals into rhythms (all tones vibrate in rhythmic cycles but you can only hear the separate beats on very low notes). Although these works were too difficult for players of that decade, they are quite playable now. Cowell was the prime mover of the ultramodernist (the term used then) music scene in the early part of the century, who established the vitally important new music editions publishing some modern classics and who produced many concerts of new music (see Rita Mead's "Henry Cowell's New Music 1925-1936—The Society, the New Music Editions and the Recordings" UMI [University Microfilms International, Ann Arbor, MI] Research Press 1981). He invented many technical musical devices (see his 1930 book New Music Resources), such as playing inside the piano (in his famous work "Banshee"), producing artificial harmonics on the piano, and, like Charles Ives, was writing atonally before the similar technique reached America from Europe (Schonberg, Berg, Webern, Hauer). His interest in the musical techniques of other cultures led to attempts at synthesizing a world music, and greatly influenced his later more conservative works (his writing seemed to change after the sad episode of his undeserved imprisonment—see Michael Hicks' article "The Imprisonment of Henry Cowell" in the Journal of the American Musicological Society. Nevertheless, he made the best of the situation, organizing and inspiring prison bands and continuing his editing and correspondence with the help of friends). A recording of his piano works is essential to any new music collection, but there are (amazingly) none available. *—"Blue" Gene Tyranny*

Persian Set / 1993 / Koch ✦✦✦
This is a collection of Cowell's more conservative but still original later works that reflect a fascination with "world music" and re-defining traditional harmony and counterpoint. Performed beautifully by The Manhattan Chamber Orchestra, conducted by Richard Aulden Clark, this CD contains: "Persian Set", "Old American Country Set", "American Melting Pot", "Hymn and Fuguing Tune", "Air" and "Adagio" from "Ensemble". *—"Blue" Gene Tyranny*

● **Piano Music** / Jun. 1, 1993 / Smithsonian/Folkways ✦✦✦
At last, a re-issue of the 1963 recording of Cowell playing several of his piano works in his casual style, so that the listener regards the unusual sounds and techniques as completely natural within the context of each piece's imagery. A recording of the complete piano works is definitely needed, but this CD, with Cowell's spoken commentary at the end, is a precious thing to have at the moment. *—"Blue" Gene Tyranny*

Ruth Crawford Seeger

b. Jul. 3, 1901, East Liverpool, OH, **d.** Nov. 18, 1953, Chevy Chase, MD
Transcription, Composer / 20th Century Classical/Modern Composition, Atonal, Traditional Folk
Ruth Porter Crawford Seeger was a remarkable composer, admired greatly among the few who knew her music, and one of the most stylistically advanced composers of her time. She was also a leading ethnomusicologist and an excellent teacher and academic. Born in 1901, she worked as a piano teacher and later attended the American Conservatory in Chicago. On graduation she began teaching at the Conservatory and at nearby Elmhurst College of Music. Her music began to appear in the "New Music Editions," and she also studied under Charles Seeger in New York. Meanwhile, her music was becoming more chromatic and dissonant until she approached the forefront of the American avant garde of the day.

After she returned to the United States she married Seeger, becoming the step-mother of Pete Seeger and soon the mother of Michael and Peggy Seeger, all of whom later became noted folk-singers. Her husband introduced her to the music and theoretical writing of Arnold Schoenberg, as a result of which she became one of the first Americans to write a twelve-tone piece, her 1931 String Quartet. During the mid-'30s, Ruth joined John and Alan Lomax in working for the Library of Congress on its collection of American folksong. Together they published the great volume *Our Singing Country*.

After abandoning composition in the 1930s, she returned in the early '50s, though any further development was prevented by her early death in 1953. By the end of the 20th century her music was only in the early stages of being "discovered." The music is imaginative, personal, and often strongly dissonant, with the impression of a bold spirit on the part of its author. *—Joseph Stevenson*

Sonata for Violin and Piano/Study in Mixed Accents for Piano (1930) / 9 Preludes For / 1993 / CRI ✦✦✦
A CD re-issue of mostly earlier pieces by Crawford showing her innovations and originality. *—"Blue" Gene Tyranny*

● **Nine Preludes for Piano (1924-1928)** / CRI ✦✦✦✦✦
Performed by J. Bloch, these wonderful *Preludes* are clearly articulated, brief studies for the piano. Each is written in a basic ABA form with striking textural and timbral contrasts between the A and B sections. In the *1st Prelude*, winding chromatic lines contrast with jazz-like smeared notes. The *2nd Prelude* opens with short repeated chords followed by flashing ascending arpeggios. A harp-like texture soon emerges, quickly leading back into the initial gestures. The *3rd Prelude* begins with a lovely, lyrical chromatic melody, then a jazzy, loping rhythm provides a lively contrast before a return to the first texture. For the *4th Prelude*, a lovely, winding chromatic melody is contrasted with quick reiterated tones. The music climbs dramatically toward the higher registers before returning to the opening idea. In the *5th Prelude*, a slowly pulsing and evolving left-hand chord underscores flighty, mellismatic figures; bits of a more serious melody emerge in the foreground occasionally. The *6th Prelude* opens with light, starry dissonances in even pulse that are surrounded and eventually engulfed by massive arpeggios; a brief coda of extremely low and high tones ends this piece. The energetic *7th Prelude* features ascending arpeggios in the constant rhythm of a long tone followed by five speedy ones; this idea is contrasted against single melody notes. In the *8th Prelude*, energetic, jumpy fifths are interspersed with slides, and the hint of a tango emerges. For the concluding *9th Prelude*, the composer obsesses on mysterious low gong-like pulses with slowly unwinding intervals above; a full, sonorous chordal development in the middle provides the contrast, and a slow repeat of the chromatically wandering intervals finishes the piece. *—"Blue" Gene Tyranny*

Quartet 1931 / in "Arditti String Quartet" / Gramavision ✦✦✦✦✦
A highly expressive piece and an innovative breakthrough in its use of harmonics and extended tones; she invented structural techniques that have had great influence on avant-garde music. *—"Blue" Gene Tyranny*

Study in Mixed Accents (1929) / CRI ✦✦✦✦

Alvin Curran

b. Dec. 13, 1938, Providence, RI
Piano, Composer / 20th Century Classical/Modern Composition, Avant-Garde, Electronic
American composer Alvin Curran co-founded the group Musica Elettronica Viva and has been active with solo performances, international radio concerts and large-scale sound installations since the 1960s. Born in Providence, Rhode Island, Curran studied composition under Ron Nelson at Brown University, and afterward with Elliott Carter at Yale. After completing his studies—which also included piano and trombone—in 1963, Curran went with Carter to Berlin, where he remained for a year before moving to Rome. In 1966, Curran cofounded the free music collective Musica Elettronica Viva with Richard Teitelbaum and Frederic Rzewski. In the '70s, Curran focused on solo performances that utilized keyboards, taped sounds, voice and more; over the years, he has also performed on sampler and electronics. The '80s found Curran creating large-scale environmental works in quarries, ports, caverns, and on lakes, etc. During this time, he also staged radio concerts of three and six ensembles performing simultaneously from various parts of Europe. From 1990 on, Curran has occasionally collaborated on sound installations with artist Melissa Gould. He has also workted with dance companies and composed for avant-garde theater in Rome. Curran's instrumental works have been commissioned by Kronos Quartet, Aki Takahashi, Rova, the St. Paul Chamber Orchestra and more. Some of his awards include those from Ars Acoustica International, NPR and the NEA. He taught briefly at the Academia Nazionale d'Arts, and later starting in the mid-90s was a guest professor at California's Mills College. Recordings of Curran's works appear on several labels, including CRI, New Albion and Tzadik. *—Joslyn Layne*

Electric Rags II / 1990 / New Albion ✦✦✦✦✦
Rova Saxophone Quartet with Curran, electronics, Scot Gresham-Lancaster, Oberheim expander. Lots of tuneful and rhythmic material ("Z Train", "Corny Island", "Scusami, I walk alone", "Continental shelf-dance" etc.) The computer spontaneously structures the concert

while the sax players control synthesizers and all is constantly transformed in real time. —*"Blue" Gene Tyranny*

Songs and Views of the Magnetic Ocean / 1994 / Catalyst ♦♦♦
Sounding a bit like Terry Riley plus sound effects, this CD is a lovely, almost New Age mix of environmental, vocal and synthesized sounds. Sections include "At Harmony Ranch" and "Crystal Aires". —*"Blue" Gene Tyranny*

• **Animal Behavior** / 1995 / Tzadik ♦♦♦♦♦
Two very different compositions are featured on this album. "Animal Behavior" is a wholly sampled collection of blips and moans, musical bits, and animal sounds interspersed with the spoken word fragments of President George Bush. The samples are run through loops, slowed down, speeded up, and otherwise altered to produce a cacophonous sound that is jarring to the ear and mind. Like his fellow *Mills College* colleagues, Alvin Curran has, on this piece and the one that follows, made use of technology to bend and chip music into a form that he likes. The second piece on the album, "Why Is This Night Different Than All Other Nights—," takes a perhaps more conventional approach with its mostly acoustic sound, but produces a result that is equally experimental—prepared piano and "unleavened percussion" combine with accordion, violin, and tuba to make a piece that was originally composed for the Trisha Brown dance company and intended to be danceable without any melody or rhythmic direction—not surprisingly, she rejected it for being "too powerful." Indeed, it is powerful, if extremely minimal, and acts as an interesting counterpoint to the chaos of *Animal Behavior.* This album is not always easy to listen to, but there is some thought behind it, and it gives some promise of future good things to come from Alvin Curran. —*Stacia Proefrock*

Holger Czukay

b. Mar. 24, 1938, Danzig, Germany
Vocals, Bass / Experimental Rock, Prog-Rock/Art Rock, Avant-Garde, Electronic
A founding member of the enormously influential Krautrock group Can, Holger Czukay was one of the pivotal underground figures of his era; he successfully bridged the gap between pop and the avant-garde, pioneering the use of samples and exploring the significance of world music on Western culture. Czukay spent his formative years studying to be a composer and conductor, but his ideas were frequently too radical for mainstream tastes. Under the tutelage of avant-garde composer Karlheinz Stockhausen, Czukay continued to refine his ideas, and also gained his first exposure to rock & roll. After picking up the bass, Czukay formed Can in early 1968, and a series of visionary albums established the band as one of the truly seminal artists of the period. In 1969, Czukay teamed with Rolf Dammers to release an LP titled *Canaxis 5;* sculpted from thousands of recordings dubbed from short-wave radio broadcasts, the album instituted primitive sampling techniques (achieved with tape splices) and positioned Czukay as an early proponent of world music appropriation. After Can disbanded, Czukay issued his acclaimed 1980 solo debut *Movies,* a marked refinement of his short-wave sonic collage techniques; he subsequently began work on a number of outside projects. Czukay's next official solo release was 1982's *On the Way to the Peak of Normal,* a collaboration with bassist Jah Wobble. 1984's *Der Osten Ist Rot* and 1987's *Rome Remains Rome* (featuring the controversial "Blessed Easter," which contained a sample of Pope John Paul II) followed amidst a variety of production work, plus collaborations with David Sylvian. In 1989, Czukay re-formed Can to record a new studio LP, *Rite Time.* Apart from the 1991 solo effort *Radio Wave Surfer* and 1993's *Moving Pictures,* Czukay spent much of the 1990s focusing on production work, before releasing *Good Morning Story* in 1999. —*Jason Ankeny*

• **Rome Remains Rome** / 1987 / Virgin ♦♦♦♦♦

Good Morning Story / 1999 / Tone Casualties ♦♦♦♦
If you know his name at all, it's as one of the founding members of the legendary experimental German rock group Can. But he's been mighty busy on his own over the last few decades, collaborating with the likes of David Sylvian, Brian Eno, and Jah Wobble; he's been remixed by the Orb and U.N.K.L.E.; and he's probably the first musician ever to have applied Edgard Varese's principles of musique concrete to rock & roll (though he's certainly not the last). So with such an impressive resume, what does his first solo album in six years sound like— Well, lots of things. The first four tracks are spoken-word compositions with funky, multi-layered backing; the words that are spoken can sometimes get embarrassing in an English-as-a-second-language sort of way ("The invisible man is all around me!"), but the music is mostly very compelling. "Dancing in Wild Circles" is especially cool, with its busy percussion, "forged ethno samples" and David Byrne-esque guitar. "Atlantis" betrays a clear drum'n'bass influence, but is much more sonically and rhythmically complex. Fully half of the program is contained in "Mirage," a 22-minute long composition that sounds like equal parts Jon Hassell and African Head Charge—that is, until it bogs down into drones about halfway through and stays bogged down for the remaining ten minutes. Still, you'll have lots of fun before getting to that soggy place. Recommended. —*Rick Anderson*

Deep Listening Band

f. 1988
Group / 20th Century Classical/Modern Composition, Avant-Garde
The Deep Listening Band was formed in late 1988 by Pauline Oliveros (accordion and electronics), Stuart Dempster (trombone and didjeridu), and David Gamper (keyboards and electronics). The group has chosen acoustically interesting recording spaces, including caves and a two million gallon cistern at Fort Warden, WA. The Deep Listening Band has recorded seven albums for a number of labels in addition to the members' many other projects. —*Joslyn Layne*

• **Troglodyte's Delight (1989)** / 1990 / What Next? ♦♦♦♦
Exploring the sound properties of The Tarpaper Cave in Rosendale, New York, this group of renown improvisors (Stuart Dempster on trombone and didjeridu, Pauline Oliveros on accordion with voice and whistles, the vocals of Panaiotis and Julie Lyon Balliett, and the percussion of Fritz Hauser). Satisfying natural and meditative beauty with even two cuts featuring just the cave water ("Cave Water"). My favorite cut "After Dinner With The Trogs". —*"Blue" Gene Tyranny*

The Ready Made Boomerang / 1991 / New Albion ♦♦♦
This time our intrepid new music crew are found enchantingly mucking around underground in the Cistern Chapel, Fort Worden Cistern, Olympic Peninsula, Washington… exploding a balloon ("Balloon Payment") to demonstrate the natural reverberation time of the space, making suspended vocal ("CCCC" / Cistern Chapel Chance Chants) and unusual instrumental sounds, and dropping percussive stuff. Lovely and mysterious. —*"Blue" Gene Tyranny*

Aurelio de la Vega

b. Nov. 28, 1925, Havana, Cuba
Composer / 20th Century Classical/Modern Composition, Avant-Garde
Studied with Fritz Kramer in Havana (1943-46) and with Ernst Toch in Los Angeles (1947-48). Dean, School of Music, University of Oriente; Executive Advisor, National Institute of Culture (Cuba); Vice-President, Havana Philharmonic Orchestra; President, Cuban Section of the ISCM. Received Outstanding Professor Award, California University system. Many awards and grants. Lecturer and essayist on contemporary music. Early works, eg. *The Infinite Foundation,* are post-impressionist, *Elegy for String Orchestra* (1954) is freely chromatic, *String Quartet* is serialist. Graph scores of '70s include *Olep ed Arudamot, The Infinite Square, Astralis, The Magic Labyrinth.* Other works: *Undici Colori* (1981) for solo bassoon and projections of abstract drawings, *Inflorescencia* (1976) for soprano, bass clarinet and tape, *Magias e Invenciones* (1986) a song cycle for soprano and piano. —*"Blue" Gene Tyranny*

Tropimapal / Opus One ♦♦♦
In the collection *Latin American Composers in the U.S.* Scored (1983) for flute, clarinet, bassoon, trombone, percussion (one player), violi, viola, cello and double bass. It is written in a free, post-serialist style, with indeterminate sections and textures that wander between a dreamy mysteriousness, and intense, explosive, and multi-rhythmic sound events. Although not programmatic, these are sounds of a wild, untamed landscape. —*"Blue" Gene Tyranny*

Robert Dick

b. Jan. 4, 1950, New York, NY
Flute, Composer / Avant-Garde Jazz, 20th Century Classical/Modern Composition, Post-Bop
A brilliant and very adventurous flutist pushing the limits of his instrument, Robert Dick's New World CD *Third Stone From the Sun* (in which he interprets tunes by Jimi Hendrix) is a classic of its kind; imagine a flute imitating an electric guitar. Dick, who graduated from the Yale School of Music, has played with a who's who of "new music," including Steve Lacy, Evan Parker, George Lewis, John Zorn, Marty Ehrlich, New Winds and Tambastics. Robert Dick's recordings as a leader have been on the Attacca Babel, O.O. Discs, GM and New World labels, and he has the potential to be one of the more important flute players in improvised music. —*Scott Yanow*

Venturi Shadows / 1992 / O.O. Discs ♦♦♦
It would be easy to argue that Robert Dick is the most important living 20th century flutist. He might bridle at being called avant garde (and then again, he might not), but his explorations of extended flute technique have helped do for his instrument what Bertram Turetsky did for the string bass and John Cage for the piano—opened up a new realm of tonal possibilities that had either never occurred to those before him, or which had never been extended quite as far as they could have been. Harmonic vocalization and the percussive smacking of keys, for example, are not new techniques, but they sound brand new in Dick's work. That said, *Venturi Shadows* is not for the faint of heart—don't go looking for humalong melodies here. "A Black Lake With a Blue Boat on It" features nifty backwards sampling courtesy of computer whiz Neil Rolnick, while "Further Down" showcases Dick's astounding tonal palette; his use of vocalisms and his ability to coax an enormous range of timbres from his flute will make you reassess the limitations of acoustic instruments. "Bassbamboo" is a charming piece in which Dick plays a percussion part on his bass flute while Steve Gorn (his frequent collaborator) traces an oriental melody around it on the bamboo bansuri. Much of the music on this disc is rather severe, but it's all rewarding. —*Rick Anderson*

• **Third Stone from the Sun** / Feb. 14, 1993-Feb. 15, 1993 / New World ♦♦♦♦♦
This is a most unusual CD with flutist Robert Dick paying tribute to rock guitar-great Jimi Hendrix. Dick creates a wide variety of sounds throughout this release that seem electronically altered but are actually totally acoustic. He plays chords, sings through his flute and uses circular breathing and overdubbing to cast new light on four of Jimi Hendrix's compositions (along with three of his own). The "power trio" also features bassist Jerome Harris and drummer Jim Black while The Soldier String Quartet makes a memorable appearance on "Tycho." Robert Dick not only manages to recapture the spirit of Jimi Hendrix in ingenuous ways but also creates some startling new music; this version of "It's Still Like It Wouldn't Be Yesterday" with its six flutes and piccolos is absolutely spooky. —*Scott Yanow*

Steel & Bamboo / 1993 / O.O. Discs ♦♦♦♦

Die Toedliche Doris (Deadly Doris)

f. 1980, **db.** 1987
Group / Multimedia, Avant-Garde
Die Tödliche Doris ("Deadly Doris") was a German performance art/music group that were together from 1981-1987, long enough to record a few albums, singles and enough video tape to warrant a couple of releases. The three band members—Käthe Kruse, Wolfgang Müller, and Nikolaus Utermöhlen—formed in reaction against the suddenly popular Neue Wilde painting in Berlin. Die Tödliche Doris combined rather dadaist theatrics with their music. Even the new wave sound of the band's second album, *Unser Debüt,* wasn't as straightforward as it seemed; with their next album, Sechs, the band revealed that the two albums were meant to be listened to simultaneously, creating a third, 'invisible' album. —*Joslyn Layne*

Naturkatastrophen (Natural Catastrophes) (1985) / 1984 / Gelbe Musik ✦✦✦
7" disc with booklet in German and English. Instructions on how to produce do-it-yourself disasters—a way of dealing with "the dread generated by State, society and nature" like kids do by means of fairy tales, and others do by forms of resistance. Tödliche Doris, Deadly Doris, is three visual artists, centered in Berlin, who manifest a good sense of humor, a very raw and raucous approach to music, a lot of well-placed angst, and who refer to their group as "she." This record is one of their milder productions, but be warned: Playing this album will definitely not endear you to the neighbors. *—"Blue" Gene Tyranny*

Lucia Dlugoszewski

b. Jun. 16, 1931, Detroit, MI, **d.** Apr. 11, 2000, New York, NY
Choreographer, Composer / Experimental, 20th Century Classical/Modern Composition, Atonal
Studied with Edgard Varése, Grete Sultan, devised "timbre piano," scores for Living Theater, Erick Hawkins dances, devised over 100 percussion instruments, teacher NYU, New School for Social Research, Foundation for Modern Dance, many awards and orchestral commissions. *—"Blue" Gene Tyranny*

• **Angels of the Inmost Heaven** / 1975 / Folkways ✦✦✦✦✦
Performed by a brass ensemble conducted by Gerard Schwarz. Music for a dance by Erick Hawkins, these "Angels" are described by transformations called Nova (bursts of energy), Corona (transparent densities), and Clear Core (tiny distinctions in static walls, a nervous surface of extremely quick pulses)... extraordinary variations of glissandos, fast lip and finger trills, constant shifting of mutes are the ingredient techniques of a very unique style that flows with high energy and also the eloquence of a Debussy orchestral brass section. *—"Blue" Gene Tyranny*

Fire Fragile Flight / 1979 / Candide ✦✦✦
This gorgeous piece, performed by The Orchestra Of Our Time, is totally unique in sound and conception: A chamber orchestra with an unusual percussion section (4 players on slide whistles, hanging bells, playing inside the piano, etc.) re-create the physical phenomena of falling leaves in early March in the Great Lakes country... the music has 65 freely chosen, musically dangerous "leap-points" which trigger whirling "startle-juxtapositions" of varying speed, like the reflected light on turning and falling leaves will sometimes appear to set them on fire. *—"Blue" Gene Tyranny*

Tender Theatre Flight Nageire (1971 / 1978) / CRI ✦✦✦
A "series of musical rituals involved... with the poetic roots of erotic experience... Nageire is an oriental aesthetic principle of non-development, of non-linear..leap... it uses constant and extreme surprise... leaping into unknown material... for the flexibility of the mind... one drop of water can unhinge my throat into miracles of swallowing... the sudden shiver of a delicate paper rattle or an unusually sensitive tonguing on a brass instrument becomes transparency utterly alive." (from notes by the composer) For brass ensemble with the composer playing on many of her 100 percussion instruments..lovely silence... surprising sounds. *—"Blue" Gene Tyranny*

Charles Dodge

b. Jun. 5, 1942, Ames, IA
Composer / Computer Music, Electro-Acoustic, Electronic
Studied with Richard Hervig, Gunther Schuller, Jack Beeson, Chou Wen-chung, Otto Luening, electronic music with Ussachevsky, computer music with Godfrey Winham. Research at IBM Thomas J. Watson Research Center, Bell Telephone Labs, University of CA at San Diego. Taught at Columbia, Princeton, Brooklyn College. *Rota* for orchestra (1966), *Changes* for computer-synthesized sound (1970), *Earth's Magnetic Field* for computer-synthesized sound (1970), *Any Resemblance Is Purely Coincidental* (1980) for piano and synthesized voice on tape. *—"Blue" Gene Tyranny*

Earth's Magnetic Field (1970) / 1971 / Nonesuch ✦✦✦
Realized at the Columbia University Computer Center, this piece is built from directly translating a record of the magnetic changes (Kp indices) for planet Earth in 1961— 8 values a day are read from graphic charts that look so much like music they are popularly known as Julius Bartel's "musical diagrams". An interesting experiment. *—"Blue" Gene Tyranny*

In Celebration / Speech Songs / the Story of Our Lives / 1990 / CRI ✦✦✦
Re-issue of a 1978 disc in which readings of poetry, etc. are digitized and restructured in the computer to modify vocal sounds, etc. *—"Blue" Gene Tyranny*

• **Any Resemblance Is Purely Coincidental** / 1992 / New Albion ✦✦✦
A collection of Dodge's compositional modifications of pre-existing material. Includes: "Any Resemblance is Purely Coincidental" for voice (Enrico Caruso) and pianist (Alan Feinberg), "Speech Songs" (see below), "The Waves" and "Viola Elegy." *—"Blue" Gene Tyranny*

Paul Dolden

Composer / Tape Music, Electro-Acoustic
Solo concerts with violin, guitar, and cello with tape, and improvisation. Works with up to 400 tracks or parts occuring simultaneously (70-80 parts are traditional Western instruments and the rest are gamelan, hand percussion, drum kits, electric guitar, and voice). Winner of 18 Canadian and international awards for composition, including Canada's Jean A. Chalmers Award for "L'Ivresse de la Vitesse." *—"Blue" Gene Tyranny*

The Threshold of Deafening Silence / 1992 / Tronia ✦✦✦
Wonderfully uninhibited and compact densities of amassed acoustic sounds, like the 400 tracks of "Below The Walls of Jericho", or the modulated galactic racket of "In The Natural Doorway I Crouch" for alternately-tuned balalaikas. Highly recommended. *—"Blue" Gene Tyranny*

Paul Dresher

b. Jan. 8, 1951, Los Angeles, CA
Guitar, Composer / World Fusion, Electronic, Opera
Studied with Robert Erickson, Roger Reynolds, Pauline Oliveros, Bernard Rands. Ghanaian drumming with C.K. and Kobla Ladzekpo, Hindustani classical music with Nikhil Banerjee, and Balinese and Javanese music. Guitarist with live delay systems. Organizer Electro-Acoustic Band, artistic director Paul Dresher Ensemble. Collaborations about American culture *Slow Fire* (1985-88), *Power Failure* (1988-89), and *Pioneer* (1990). *The Gates* (1993) for dancer Margaret Jenkins. Many awards and orchestral, opera commissions. *—"Blue" Gene Tyranny*

Other Fire (1984) in "Another Coast" / 1988 / Music & Arts ✦✦✦
A rich mix of naturally occuring rhythmic and cycling environmental sounds (birds, temple bells, etc.) from tape recordings made during Asian and Southeast Asian travels that nonetheless gives the illusion of electronic synthesis. *—"Blue" Gene Tyranny*

• **This Same Temple** / 1996 / Lovely Music ✦✦✦
A re-release of two lovely pattern music works *This Same Temple* and *Liquid and Stellar Music* with two additional new works *Water Dreams* and *Destiny.* Beautiful guitar work through sound processing (delay) systems; brilliant performances by the internationally-renowned Double Edge piano duo (Nurit Tilles and Edmund Niemann). *—"Blue" Gene Tyranny*

Mark Dresser

b. 1952
Bass (Upright) / Avant-Garde Jazz, 20th Century Classical/Modern Composition, Fusion, Modern Creative
Bassist and composer Mark Dresser has developed a recognizable sound and masterful technique through the years—from the L.A. avant garde jazz scene of the early '70s, to '80s European tours in Anthony Braxton's Quartet, to the late '90s' NYC downtown scene of musicians who frequently are booked at such venues as *the Knitting Factory* and *Tonic.* In addition to his acclaimed work as a composer, Mark Dresser has emerged as a master of the contrabass and has played in all manner of improvisatory and composed settings with just about every major experimental, creative and/or improviser around—including Misha Mengelberg, Evan Parker, Henry Threadgill, Tim Berne, John Zorn, and even Diamanda Galas! He has worked as a professional musician since he was 20 years old. In the early '70s, he played in Stanley Crouch's Black Music Infinity, a group that included Bobby Bradford, Arthur Blythe, James Newton and David Murray. Also during this time, Dresser was playing in the San Diego Symphony. He earned his M.A. at UCSD (where he also studied as an undergraduate), went to Italy on a Fulbright Fellowship, then moved to New York in 1986, when he was invited to join the Anthony Braxton Quartet. Dresser toured Europe and recorded with the Quartet, which included pianist Marilyn Crispell and drummer Gerry Hemingway through the early '90s. In NY, Dresser also focused on composing for the Arcado String Trio, and Tambastics, two groups he performed in which toured extensively, won awards, and combined recorded six CDs. Dresser has received several commissions including from Germany's WDR Radio of Cologne, and the McKim fund. Dresser has led his many recordings, including those of his own quintet, *Force Green,* and recordings of his original scores for two classic silent films, including *The Cabinet of Dr. Caligari.* In 1995, the Knitting Factory label released a CD of some of his solo contrabass recordings, *Invocation,* and two years later, Tzadik issued two of his chamber works, *Banquet.* Dresser has guest lectured at Juilliard, UCSD and the National Superior Conservatory of Paris. By the late '90s, he had performed on over 70 CDs, was still based out of New York, and continued wowing audiences in a variety of musical settings. *—Joslyn Layne*

Invocation / 1980-1995 / Knitting Factory ✦✦✦
Invocation is something every die-hard fan of the upright bass should hear. The excellent techniques and talents of leading avant-garde jazz bassist Mark Dresser are here heard solo, although not necessarily live—some tracks are overdubbed, and "Trains" includes recordings of (you guessed it) trains. These compositions are all very active, as opposed to minimal, and highlight cuts include Dresser's delivery of the Gerry Hemingway work, "Threnody for Charles Mingus," the title track, and "Polystop for Multiple Solo Bass," both written by Mark Dresser. And while this album may be less accessible than some of the grooves found on Michael Formanek's solo bass release, *Am I Bothering You?*, *Invocation* is certainly more varied than Dave Holland's *Emerald Tears,* and Dresser's performance will not fail to intrigue, astonish, and thoroughly impress those who listen. *—Joslyn Layne*

Banquet / Nov. 18, 1997 / Tzadik ✦✦✦

• **Sonomondo** / Mar. 14, 2000 / Cryptogramophone ✦✦✦✦
Contrabassist Mark Dresser and cellist Frances-Marie Uitti are both respected members of the avant-garde and improvisational music establishment. Dresser, who is based in Brooklyn, was a member of Anthony Braxton's quartet for nine years and has also worked with Robert Dick, Bob Ostertag, John Zorn, and others, while Uitti has collaborated with John Cage, Luigi Nono, Brian Ferneyhough, and Iannis Xenakis. Both players make great use of extended string techniques. Dresser's approach is a grab bag of battuto and col legno techniques, as well as "double glissandi" and creative amplification; Uitti, even more interestingly, uses two bows at once on her cello, permitting her to play four-voice chords and contrasting simultaneous dynamics. The seven improvisations that make up this program are consistently fascinating and frequently lovely. The title track occasionally sounds like two people trying to tune to each other, but passes repeatedly into passages of subdued beauty, and on "Montebell," Uitti's artificial harmonics swoop over Dresser's 5/8 digressions to stunning effect. Though perhaps not for the faint of heart, this is "instant composition" of very high quality. *—Rick Anderson*

James Drew

b. Feb. 9, 1929

Piano, Composer / Musical Theater, 20th Century Classical/Modern Composition, Avant-Garde

This very original composer studied with Wallingford Riegger and Edgard Varése. He has taught at Northwestern University, Yale University, UCLA, Cal State, and other institutions, and also teaches privately. He has performed with and co-founded several musical groups: the Crossfire Mission Orchestra in the late '60s in New Haven (radical performances often behind barbed wire), the Mysterious Traveling Cabaret, the American Music Theater in CA, the Blast Opera Theater and has undertaken concerts and arts education work with the Grey Wolf Project. His works include: *Survivors in Pale Light* a theater piece recently taped for PBS-TV with the Blast Opera players both singing and acting (he refers to the form as an opera "ostrannie" (Russian word meaning laid bare, or everything exposed, for example, the actors are acting and at the same time not "acting")); *Hypothetical Structures, Books I and II, Cantalobosolo* (1995) a monodrama for contrabassist/singer/actor, *Dances of the Tunnel Saints* (1995) for two pianos and percussion, and *Powder Songs of the Lady Magicians* (1996) staged in a ritualistic circle for singer-actor, percussion, and droning strings. *— "Blue" Gene Tyranny*

The Celestial Cabaret, a Concerto for Pianist and Chamber Orchestra Symphony No. 3 / 1991 / Artistry Production ♦♦♦

Called by Nicolas Slonimsky "an authentic American original," Drew has received many awards for composition, taught at Yale University and U.C.L.A. in the 70's, but he is also a illusive figure, a legendary underground jazz pianist who has played with Elvin Jones, Clark Terry, Donald Byrd, and Earl Turbinton. He has created a style entirely his own, each piece beautifully conceived—"Symphony No. 3" is in one movement of long slow melodies that create a mysterious yet hopeful feeling with very brief percussion punctuations and chordal brass writing, none of these elements suggesting anything you've heard before yet somehow you understand the meaning. The remarkable "Celestial Cabaret" is built featuring the unaccompanied piano soloist in a lyrical, flowing style that is not romantic but like a commentary, free-flowing thought suddenly surrounded by brief strange versions of cabaret music of a very refined type, not satirical and not immediately recognizable. You must hear his music to really get the idea. *— "Blue" Gene Tyranny*

William E. Duckworth

b. Jan. 13, 1943, Morgantown, NC

Composer / 20th Century Classical/Modern Composition, Minimalism

Composer William Duckworth, who had composed over 100 works by the late 1990s, is often regarded as the founder of postminimalism because of works like his *Southern Harmony* and *Time Curve Preludes*. For his education, Duckworth attended the University of Illinois, where he studied with Ben Johnston, and went on to teach at Bucknell. In 1997, Duckworth put an interactive piece on the web *Cathedral* scheduled to culminate, years later, in a live, on-line 48 hour concert. *—Joslyn Layne*

Thirty-One Days (1987) for Alto Saxophone / 1990 / Lovely Music ♦♦♦♦♦

Singing and wailing sax… solo and multi-tracked in ensemble, great playing by Michael Swartz who uses movement in the stereo space to change presence and "throw" sounds. *— "Blue" Gene Tyranny*

Time Curve Preludes (1982) : Books 1 and 2, Preludes 1-24, The / 1990 / Lovely Music ♦♦♦

Described quite accurately by a reviewer as a "new age Well-Tempered Clavier"… played elegantly by pianist Neely Bruce. *— "Blue" Gene Tyranny*

★ **Southern Harmony** / 1994 / Lovely Music ♦♦♦♦♦

The Gregg Smith Singers, assisted by The Rooke Chapel Choir of Bucknell Uiversity, conducted by Gregg Smith create the first complete recording of this exceptionally fascinating and moving choral work… by concentrating and sampling only certain aspects—rhythm, a single gesture, etc.—of shaped-note ("sacred harp") singing, a style of the rural South, the interior nature of these hymns is brought to the surface… a very different idea than merely "setting" the hymns with new harmonies. *— "Blue" Gene Tyranny*

David Dunn

b. May 22, 1953

Composer / Process-Generated, Sound Sculpture, Computer Music, 20th Century Classical/Modern Composition

Studied with David Ernst, Norman Lowrey, Pauline Oliveros, and Kenneth Gaburo. From 1970-74 he was assistant to Harry Partch and performed in the Harry Partch ensemble for over a decade. Co-founded the Independent Media Labs in Santa Fe, NM. International tours and presentations. Featured artist at international sound festival SoundCulture in Tokyo, Japan. Author of *Music, Language, and Environment* and *Skydrift* a large environmental sound project. Many theoretical writings incl. *Harry Partch: An Anthology of Critical Perspectives*. *— "Blue" Gene Tyranny*

● **Angels and Insects** / 1992 / What Next? ♦♦♦

"Tabula Angelorum Onorum 49" is based on alchemist John Dee's psychic communications (see also Jerry Hunt's work along these lines). Computer-fractal voices, disembodied informants. Includes an extended remix of "Chaos and the Emergent Mind of the Pond," an assembly of micro bio-acoustical underwater events recorded very (macro-) closely—insect dronings, buzzings, clickings—that lets listeners listen to a burgeoning level of liege not normally heard. Dunn has also edited a splendid book, *Pioneers of Electronic Art*, available from Nonsequitor. See also his "… With Zitterings of Flight Released (in Memoriam Kenneth Gaburo)" in the collection *Views From the Perfect City*. *— "Blue" Gene Tyranny*

Music, Language and Environment / 1996 / Innova ♦♦♦♦♦

This double-CD set collects a wide variety of Dunn's fascinating and innovative environmental sound works/interactions from 1973-1985. *Nexus 1* (1973) features a series of trumpet gestures, played by a trio of performers, sounded into the interior of the Grand Canyon. *Entrainments 1* (1984) accumulates square-wave oscillations played in a California state park glen, simulating the resonant characteristics of the environment. *Entrainments II* (1985) is a complex interaction for three speaking vocalists giving their spontaneous impressions of an outdoor environment, which are amplified through self-carried small loudspeakers. The sound and movement of small oscillators they carry are picked up by a microphone and input to a computer, which triggers sound blocks also played back into the environment. All persons and instruments (except the computer and its operator) are constantly moving in circles. The beautiful *Skydrift* (1977) features ten voices, 16 instrumentalists, and four channels of electronic sound generated from materials gathered at the performance site. The instrumentalists move outward from a central circle while their playing responds to environmental sounds; the circle becomes enlarged up to half a mile from its original formation. Inspired by the extraordinary mimicking ability of the mockingbird, *Mimus Polyglottos* (1976) is an unintentionally humorous (i.e., delightful) study for electronically generated birdlike sounds and an actual mockingbird in a park. (Some kind of dialogue happened, linguistic, and/or musical.) *(espial)* (1979) was recorded by a solo violinist performing gestures composed by Dunn over three-and-a-half hours in a harsh California desert environment. The results were then played back in a layering of seven half-hour segments on cassette machines and re-recorded. The barebones essence of the arid landscape is overwhelmingly present. *— "Blue" Gene Tyranny*

Robert Erickson

b. Mar. 17, 1917, Marquette, MI, **d.** Apr. 24, 1997, San Diego, CA

Composer / Tape Music, 20th Century Classical/Modern Composition, Atonal

American maverick and Modernist Robert Erickson was among the first U.S. composers to write in the 12-tone system and to experiment with tape manipulation. As a teacher at a number of universities and co-founder of the UCSD Music Dept. in the mid-'60s, he influenced countless musicians and composers including Morton Subotnick, Pauline Oliveros, Terry Riley, and Paul Dresher. He also wrote two books: *The Structure of Music: A Listener's Guide* (he claimed that writing this 1950s book helped him overcome a "contrapuntal obsession") and *Sound Structures in Music* (1975).

Born in Marquette, MI, Erickson played music from a young age and later studied under Ernst Krenek. After receiving his master's degree, he began his long and successful teaching career at a number of institutions. He went on to co-found the UCSD Music Dept. and help start the San Francisco Tape Music Center. As a composer, Erickson wrote for a variety of lineups including string quartet, orchestra, chorus, and voice, tape, and solo instruments. He was commissioned by a number of cities, by the NEA (1976), by Kronos Quartet, SONOR, and other ensembles. During his career, Erickson was the recipient of many honors and awards including Yaddo Fellowships in the '50s and '60s, the Guggenheim Fellowship (1966), and the 1985 Friedham Award for Chamber Music for his string quartet "Solstice."

In addition to sometimes working with tape, Erickson also wrote pieces that incorporated another unusual element: resonating metal rods, which can be heard in "Taffy Time" (1983) and a few other works. His final work was "Music for Trumpet, Strings, and Tympani" (1990). Sadly, Erickson spent his last 15 years bedridden with polymyositis. He is the subject of two biographies and a retrospective disc by CRI. *—Joslyn Layne*

Robert Erickson / 1991 / CRI ♦♦♦

The "Ricercar 3" (1967) is a bass solo with an improvised quality played sensitively by Bertram Turetzky. "Sierra" (1984), with text by Erickson and sung here by Philip Larson with The SONOR Ensemble, is a very peculiar recitative with instrumental colors about the California environs interspersed with greetings to friends. Erickson's writing is built from "academic" elements but is always personal, unique and lively. *— "Blue" Gene Tyranny*

Fast Forward

b. Mar. 24, 1954

Composer / Avant-Garde, World Fusion

Studied with Stuart Marshall in Newcastle, and Robert Ashley, David Behrman at Center for Contemporary Music, Mills College (1976-78). Owned and operated Pink Noise Studios, a research center for experimental audio and video techniques. Lives in NYC and Amsterdam, Netherlands. Worldwide tours. *The Accident* (1993) nine evenings of performance music with the Wooster Group. Numerous grants and commissions. *— "Blue" Gene Tyranny*

Panhandling / 1990 / Lovely Music ♦♦♦♦♦

Not your usual percussion music. Sometimes studies of a single sound… a bullroarer (Africa, Australia) in "Bullroarer" and a metal ball rolled about a waterfilled tuned oil drum producing beautiful harmonics in "Waterball"… and assemblies of metals from life… a bathtub, metal snake and two temple bells in "Precious Metals"… to the bright emotion of steel pan solos in "Red Dance", "The Big Wind" and "Stix" exploring closely placed tones moving on a steady rhythm figure, like some guitar picking, Bach Prelude or African marimba music. *— "Blue" Gene Tyranny*

Fast Forward / 1995 / Experimental Intermedia

● **Same Same** / Experimental Intermedia ♦♦♦

Three wonderful ensemble compositions from the uplifting, lighthearted, and generous mind of Forward. *Simultaneous Music* is for six players who prepare their parts independently, never rehearse together, and are asked not to listen to each other for cues, etc. In this recording, the combination of melodic strings with percussion, voice, electronics, pedal steel, television sound, telephone books, dishes, turntables, stamping, etc., provides some rare moments. *The Yin-Yang Merger* is intended as "a meeting ground for acoustic and electronic music" and is scored for a battery of percussionists, voice, electronics, and Ben Neill's "mutatrumpet." *Feeding Frenzy* is a project about the "fabrication, composition, and consumption of food"—food and cooking hardware are used as instruments, and the score for the work is a set menu listing each of the courses. A delight for the unhurried. [Fans may also want to pick up Fast's *The Caffeine Effect* on Ear Rational Records and *Rotorblade* on Obsolete Music]. — *"Blue" Gene Tyranny*

Morton Feldman

b. Jan. 12, 1926, New York, **d.** Sep. 3, 1987, Buffalo, NY

Composer / 20th Century Classical/Modern Composition, Minimalism

Studied piano with Madame Maurina-Press, comp. with Wallingford Riegger, Stefan Wolpe. Was Edgard Varése Professor at State University of New York at Buffalo. Began graphic works, with open pitch and rhythm, and music "free from a compositional rhetoric" in early '50s, eg. *Structures* for string quartet (1951). Music with pitches given but with freedom of rhythm, eg. *The Swallows of Salagan* (1960). Later, fully notated works, mostly quiet (in order to perceive timbre and overtone material) with non-dramatic gestures, eg. *Piano and Orchestra* (1975). Last works of long durations up to six-hour *String Quartet No. 2* (1983). — *"Blue" Gene Tyranny*

★ **Rothko Chapel (1971) for Chorus, Viola and Percussion/Why Patterns — (1978)** / 1991 / New Albion ✦✦✦✦✦

After inventing graph notation in the early 50's ("Projection I" for solo cello in 1950), Feldman began to write works that used long tones, wordless singing, and were played very quietly (allowing sounds that could not be otherwise heard) creating a changing but unbroken "surface". In the 70's, he began to work with gently pulsing mobile-like rhythmic figures of which "Why Patterns —" is a good example.. — *"Blue" Gene Tyranny*

Viola in My Life (1970) / False Relationships and the Extended Ending (1968) / Why Patt / 1992 / CRI ✦✦✦✦✦

Re-issues of some wonderful pieces. "False Relationships and the Extended Ending" alternates between exact proportions and "free time" in the vertical style (slowly changing chords, common-tone suspensions etc. in works such as "Atlantis" (1958) and *"The Swallows of Salangan"*) which came after the counterpoint style of the early 50's graph pieces. "The Viola in My Life" was the next development adding melody-like gestures. Ethereal, heartfelt. — *"Blue" Gene Tyranny*

For Bunita Marcus / 1994 / hatHUT ✦✦✦✦✦

This piano work, composed near the end of Feldman's life, is perhaps his signature composition for the instrument, and reveals his truly original method of opening up time and space by restricting the movement of sound within them. As Feldman grew older and his compositions became longer (for example, the 4 CD-long "For Philip Guston"), his obsession with the space between sounds (how long it took to hear one before another was introduced) became a driving force in his work. It moved him to constrain the palette he wrote from, in this case to contain only two pitches (C sharp and D), and within these two pitches, an equally restrictive and systematic sequence of meters (alternating 3/8, 5/16). Add to this his direction to the pianist to push the keys just enough to make the slightest sound (*ppp*), and directions to the listener to playback at very low volume, and you have a very small world to peer into.

The paradox is what emerges from this tiny space, played out over an hour. Time and space drop away. Inside the intervals where notes are played, and chords are built in miniature, is the role that silence itself plays, where it becomes the biggest presence in the work. Pianist Hildegard Kleeb understands these methods instinctually; there isn't so much as an extra nuance here. Her ability to exercise the tension and restraint in performing such a lengthy work creates for the listener an endless expanse. *For Bunita Marcus* reveals Feldman thinking not only of musical forms, but also of memory forms, in which memory is formed as a relationship, not of the fragment to the whole, but rather, from fragment remembered as fragment to the next, unto the entire work. While Feldman would make time "disappear" into his works, his intent here is not so much putting weight on time itself, but on time as a visual analogy of structure and duration. With *For Bunita Marcus,* he has created a memory system in which lapses are freely accepted, because resolution doesn't happen within a structured piece of music, but in the memory of silence itself. — *Thom Jurek*

String Quartet (1979) / 1994 / Koch ✦✦✦

Astonishingly well played by the Group for Contemporary Music, this piece is a masterwork. Continually new inventions of harmonic colors, mobile-like patterns, and crystalline to shockingly rich timbres occur in an unpredictable but ultimately aesthetically satisfying time placement, and the whole performance of 78 minutes and 27 seconds takes the listener through a wide range of transcendental mental spaces. — *"Blue" Gene Tyranny*

For Franz Kline (1962) / The O'Hara Songs (1962) / De Kooning (1963) / 1996 / Wergo ✦✦✦✦✦

Feldman often referred to the inspirations and ideas of painters and poets, perhaps more than to those of fellow composers, as influencing his own aesthetics. These ensemble works, played by the Ensemble Avantgarde (except for the "O'Hara Songs" with wordless solo voices used as instruments) are perfectly and sensitively played on this CD—many of Feldman's works of this time are to be performed quietly so that delicate harmonic combinations and a certain "purity" of sound, not possible at louder dynamics, are perceivable, and as with most of Feldman's work, the presence of a universal stillness makes itself manifest. The rarely performed "The O'Hara Songs" are a major revelation and innovation—chants on central resonances and vowels of isolated individual words adds a new kind of meaning, a deeply interior feeling to the text. — *"Blue" Gene Tyranny*

Durations I-V (1960-61) / Coptic Light (1986) for Orchestra / 1997 / Cpo ✦✦✦✦✦

Performed by the Ensemble Avantgarde, and the Deutsches Symphonie-Orchester Berlin conducted by Michael Morgan, this is a very sensitive and fine performance of the new music classic "Durations I-V". In these five innovative pieces, the composer gave over control of the duration parameter entirely to the performers (there are only notes without stems, therefore no divided rhythm)—the pulse (ictus) is slow, all is quiet, the tones have a minimum of attack. Thus, each performance is unique, and creates its own timbre combinations and exquisite beauty of a transparent sound texture. By contrast, "Coptic Light" for orchestra is of an extremely dense, polyrhythmic texture that shifts slowly by rhythmic staggering (phase shifting) within orchestral groups, creating the unique effect of a shimmering of sound analogous to the shimmering of light on water. The specific visual analog in Feldman's mind was the fine interweaving of ancient Coptic textiles he had seen in a museum. He was also attempting to create the effect of a piano's sustaining pedal for the orchestra, which allows tones to continue resonating and to blend together and overlap. — *"Blue" Gene Tyranny*

● **Madame Press Died Last Week at Ninety** / Elektra/Nonesuch ✦✦✦✦✦

In the collection *American Elegies,* performed by the Orchestra of St. Luke's, and conducted by composer John Adams, this piece was written in 1970 as an elegy to Feldman's adored Russian piano teacher (who reportedly tutored the Czar's children) with whom he had studied since age 12, and whom he always credited as a great influence on his sense of music: "The way she would put her finger down, in a Russian way of just the finger. The liveliness of just the finger. And produce a B-flat, and you wanted to faint." (Feldman). This composition is one of Feldman's first pieces in which he used continuous rhythm and some repetition. A repeated major-third figure in the flute, and a few times in the trumpet, suggests a cuckoo clock and is played throughout the piece—a cuckoo clock that has gone cuckoo. Each time it is stated it is re-harmonized by the small orchestra. A chime further suggests a clock. This charming, attractively sentimental (without being syrupy) piece is atypical of Feldman's music, though it shares the quiet attitude, the peacefulness and the ensemble sound of many of his works. It is an easy introduction for the listener new to his music. — *"Blue" Gene Tyranny*

Luc Ferrari

b. Feb. 5, 1929, Paris, France

Composer / Musique Concrète, 20th Century Classical/Modern Composition, Electronic

20th century French composer Luc Ferrari has been a major contributor to musique concrète since the late '50s, when he began collaborating with the "Groupe de Musique Concrete" (a relationship which lasted until 1966) and helped Pierre Schaeffer found the "Groupe de Recherches Musicales," a group and studio dedicated to the electronic medium where Iannis Xenakis and Karlheinz Stockhausen also worked.

Ferrari studied composition with Arthur Honegger, piano with Alfred Cortot, and musical theory with Olivier Messiaen. After hearing a live radio broadcast of Varese's *Déserts for tape and orchestra,* Ferrari went to NY to meet Varese. In the '60s, Ferrari created the ambient musical tale *Hétérozygote,* and produced films about the rehearsal processes of Messiaen, Varése, Stockhausen and others. By 1970, he finished *Presque Rien No. 1,* a 'musical photography' piece, which contained no readily apparent music, making quite an impact upon it's release on Deutsche Grammophon. Using the ambient sounds of a Yugoslavian village, zooming in and out on particular sound sources, it demonstrated that music was, as John Cage had said, all around us.

Ferrari founded the studio, Billig (early '70s), and La Muse en Circuit (1982). His musical theatre piece, *Journal intime,* was successfully staged in Paris in 1989. Throughout his career, he taught in cities such as Cologne, Stockholm, and Paris. Ferrari has received various awards, including the 1987 Prix Italia for the symphonic tale "Et si toute entiere maintenant", the Karl Sczuca prize for the radio play "Je me suis perdu ou labyrinthe-portrait", and the International Kossevitzky Prize for his symphony "Histoire du plaisir et de la désolation" (found on *Luc Ferrari Matin et Soir*). His body of work was awarded the Grand Prix National from the French Ministry of Culture in 1988. Recordings of Ferrari's work are found on various independent labels including BVHaast and Tzadik. — *Joslyn Layne*

Brise-Glace (Et Si Toute Entiere Maintenant . . .) (Icebreaker . . . Supposing Now I Were To.) / 1991 / Adda ✦✦✦✦✦

For this composition, which was the winner of the Prix Italia 1987, the composer combined electronically-transformed recordings made over a two-weeks sail aboard the icebreaker Frej with rich orchestral music and a text by Colette Fellous, delivering intimate, sensual, imaginary impressions as if in an interior monologue as a passenger on shipboard near the Arctic Circle—from sequence 5, "The Cabin": "The pilot comes very close to one's face to speak… that's what drew me to him immediately… I can still recognize the smell of him and the taste of his mouth, even though he is far away." A beautiful and original blend of superb orchestral writing, electronic and natural sound, premiered on Radio-France. — *"Blue" Gene Tyranny*

Cellule 75 / Apr. 21, 1998 / Tzadik ✦✦✦

Cellule 75 presents two of music concrète composer Luc Ferrari's 1970s creations: the title track from 1975 followed by "Place des Abbesses," created in 1977 at his own Studio Billig. "Cellule 75" tampers with the percussive function of the instruments, and plays with instrumental role-switching and layering. It opens with simple, repeating melodies provided by pianist Chris Brown and percussionist William Winant, backed by a humming machinery ambience. Layers and notes get added onto successive loops, until the phrases become relatively lengthy and complex. After establishing this theme and structure, the variations begin, as the piano switches to soloing, referencing parts of the theme out of different layers, and usurping the phrasing of the other electronic sounds present. The piece is a continuous build-up of musical layers, imperceptibly segued into the beginning's stripped-down simplicity, from which the process starts again, but never turns out the same. After continually playing with the expectations of the close listener, it appropriately closes with several false stops. The second piece begins with slowly turning loops overlaying small electronic swells that pan between channels. This turns into an electronic atmosphere that's a seeming precursor to the "space" of '90s space rock bands, followed by a repeating of the opening form, this time with vocal samples. The panning continues, echoing from side to side, while newly added electronic sounds rise out of the center. About halfway through the piece, Ferrari switches briefly to saxophone and water sounds, providing organic contrast to all of the electronic construction. — *Joslyn Layne*

● **Acousmatrix 3: Luc Ferrari: Petite symphonie intuitive pour un paysag** / BVHaast ✦✦✦✦✦

Simon Fisher-Turner

b. Nov. 21, 1954, Dover, England
Composer / Film Music, Experimental, Avant-Garde
U.K. composer and sound designer Simon Fisher-Turner is perhaps best known for his film scores of independent films, including a number of Derek Jarman's and his Oscar-nominated score for Anna Campion's *Loaded.* In his youth, he was a child television actor who recorded a pop LP and some 45s (self-described as "appalling") for UK Records and Ariola in the '70s. Later, he and Colin Lloyd Tucker were involved in the early days of the The, but soon went off as a duo (1982), recording two albums as Deux Filles (two French girls), then one as Jeremy's Secret. After Fisher-Turner went solo, his film score work for Derek Jarman began, starting with the film *Caravaggio* and including his later score for *Blue.* He also recorded two albums (for El) and toured under the name the King of Luxembourg in the late '80s. The late '90s found him collaborating with Robin Rimbaud (Scanner) on live improvisations and the album on *Travelcard;* Fisher-Turner also collaborated with choreographer Rosemary Butcher for several years and, more recently, played in the Hangovers, a band led by Gina Birch of the Raincoats. He has recorded for Creation, Mute, and other labels under a variety of aliases (not including those previously mentioned): Simon Turner, SFT, Loveletter, Live Blue Roma, and in collaborations as Kendall Turner Overdrive and Bad Dream Fancy Dress. *—Joslyn Layne*

Blue (Music for the Film by Derek Jarman) / 1994 / Mute ♦♦♦
To write music to underscore a political message, to protest war, to promote human rights, or, in this case, to respond to the current AIDS plague are difficult enough assignments. To also be sensitive to a brilliant and moving text, that contains an artist's deepest feelings in the forms of ironic personal stories ("With yellow infection bubbling at the corner I said this looks like a planet The doctor says 'Oh, I think it looks like a pizza' ") and transcendent poetic expression, is an even more challenging task. On the screen, and on the CD booklet and disc label, we see only the color blue, no images. And in the soundtrack, with some additional music—Brian Eno, Szymanowski ("Scheherazade" from "The Masques") "Disco Hospital," Satie etc.—and several excellent surreal environment ambience seques, Turner succeeds in inventing a dramatic score of great variety. It works best when the total sound avoids directly illustrating one-for-one the images in the text; otherwise, at times the effect is like Orson Welles delivering a mythological radio play, which overwhelms the humanity and directness of the text. "From the bottom of your heart, pray to be released from image," Jarman exhorts us, "Blue is the universal love in which man bathes—it is the terrestial paradise." *—"Blue" Gene Tyranny*

Bill Fontana

b. Apr. 25, 1947, Cleveland, OH
Composer / Sound Sculpture, Electronic
Preeminent sound installation artist Bill Fontana has created a variety of sound projects from the late '60s into the next century, including radio projects, compositions for modern dance, installations for spaces such as museums, and dozens of sound sculptures that were commissioned for spots all over the U.S. and Europe, including San Francisco, N.Y.C., North Carolina's State Revenue Building, London, Venice, Paris, Cologne, and Berlin. Born in 1947 in Cleveland, OH, Fontana has lived in Paris and San Francisco and has received fellowships from the NEA, the Guggenheim Foundation, the Japan-U.S. Friendship Commission, and the Berliner Künstlerprogramm des DAAD (twice in the '80s). *—Joslyn Layne*

• **Landscape Sculpture with Fog Horns (Installation Version, 1981; Live Radio Version, 198** / 1982 / KQED-FM ♦♦♦♦♦
This installation, created for *the San Francisco New Music America '81 Festival,* involved eight loudspeakers each playing a broadcast of ambient sound from distant locations in the Bay Area, as listeners walked along the 600 foot pier (East Wall of Pier 2, Fort Mason Center) on a trajectory toward Angel Island three miles away. A changing and drifting configuration of echo and delay patterns was created by the uncoordinated pulses of the horns and the wide spatial placement of the microphones at Point Blunt, West Garrison, Treasure Island, Yacht Harbor, Fort Point, China Beach, the Legion of Honor, and the Cliff House. Four locations were used for the live radio version. The sound of a fog horn can travel about five miles. Under certain atmospheric conditions, the fog will mask certain pitches (on the radio version, the horns form a mysteriously beckoning major chord with a flat second added, plus seagulls and some brief unintelligible conversation by passersby). Certain horns are louder at a distance than at close proximity. These variations make for a beautiful listening experience. *—"Blue" Gene Tyranny*

Australian Sound Sculptures / Edition Block ♦♦♦
Fascinating sounds by one of the pioneers of sound installation pieces. This work was made while he was a producer for the Australian Broadcasting Commission from 1975-1978, and is based on eight-channel field recordings he made for a tape archive of Australian environmental sounds, which were presented as an exhibition called "Sound Sculpture" at the National Gallery of Victoria in Melbourne. *—"Blue" Gene Tyranny*

Fred Frith

b. Feb. 17, 1949, Heathfield, England
Multi Instruments, Keyboards, Violin, Guitar, Bass / Experimental, Prog-Rock/Art Rock, Avant-Garde
Brilliant British avant-garde electric guitarist and multi-instrumentalist specializing in improvisation incorporating trace-elements of free jazz and progressive rock with lots of noise and "treated" guitars á la John Cage's "treated" pianos. Solo, duo, and group (see Henry Cow) recordings range from flat-out noise (*Guitar Solos, With Enemies Like These, Who Needs Friends*), to lovely, airy, almost lullaby-like compositions (parts of *Gravity*), to industrial dance music (side two of *Speechless*). Even the prettiest tunes have an edge, and the others (the majority) may make you re-evaluate what you consider music. Challenging and complex. It is hard to be halfway about Frith's music; you either love it or hate it. Definitely not for the weak-hearted, weak-minded, or weak-spirited. *—Niles J. Frantz*

Guitar Solos / 1974 / East Side Digital ♦♦♦
Made in four days, improvised, some to a roughly preconceived idea. "Glass c/w Steel"..."four layers of sound in an eerie haze out of which bounds a rubbery, animal-like line" (Cole Gagne in the book *Sonic Transports*)... "Ghosts" distorted chords appearing and disappearing, "Out of Their Heads (On Locoweed)"..."like being harangued by an automobile accident" (Gagne)... "Hello Music" a cheery welcome... "No Birds" is a tour through imaginary landscapes... a remarkable album that pre-dated so much radical guitar playing of the next decades, and still has a lot of originality to offer. *—"Blue" Gene Tyranny*

With Enemies Like These, Who Needs Friends— / Jul. 8, 1979-Jul. 17, 1979 / SST ♦♦♦

Speechless / 1981 / East Side Digital ♦♦♦♦
This one of the most important guitar-based, experimental guitar titles from the avant-guitarist and founding Henry Cow member Fred Frith. Frith's second solo album, *Speechless,* includes appearances by Estron Fou Leloublan, Massacre, and Bill Laswell. This is a studio Frankenstein of live clips and found sounds. While Frith states attests to the occurrence of many "happy accidents," the album comes across confidently and more often more coherent than merely challenging. Six bonus tracks appear on this CD version. This is often cited as Frith's best solo record and its inspired manipulations hold up under repeated scrutiny. There is a bit of European folk influence here, too, but not as obvious as on *Gravity. —Thomas Schulte*

Technology of Tears (And Other Music for Dance) / Jul. 1988 / SST ♦♦♦♦♦

• **Step Across the Border** / 1990 / East Side Digital ♦♦♦♦
Although this is technically the soundtrack to a film of the same name by Nicolas Humbert and Werner Penzel, *Step Across the Border* actually serves as an excellent overview of Fred Frith's groundbreaking work as a soloist, bandleader, and collaborator. There's an example of his "guitars on the table" approach ("Romanisches Cafe"), and a couple of excellent duos with tape manipulation whiz Bob Ostertag ("Voice of America Part 3," from the lost and lamented *Voice of America* album they made for the defunct Metalanguage label). There are also scraps of material from his work with Skeleton Crew as well as numerous other well-chosen miniatures that vary from tuneful and charming to stark and forbidding. Perhaps the best thing this album accomplishes is that it puts some of the material from the astounding (but, sadly, long out-of-print) album of avant-garde power trio compositions and improvisations Frith recorded with Bill Laswell and Fred Maher under the name Massacre back into circulation: the very fine "Legs" is included here, as is a previously unreleased live track from 1983. Very highly recommended. *—Rick Anderson*

Previous Evening / Dec. 23, 1997 / ReR ♦♦♦♦
The Previous Evening is a composition in three parts, each of them a tribute to a major contemporary classical composer. The first is a homage to John Cage, and, accordingly, it consists of music and texts (taken from Cage's book *Silence*) organized according to chance processes. It's in this piece that Frith's personal instrumental voice is most clearly identifiable, with snippets of prepared guitar advancing and retreating through the mix. The second part is a tribute to Morton Feldman on which Frith plays piano accompanied by a percussionist and clarinetist. As befits a tribute to Feldman, the piece unfolds with almost painful slowness, making only limited use of the clarinet and almost subliminal use of percussion, the piano playing only one or two notes every few seconds and rarely any chords. Part three, in honor of Earle Brown, is the more challenging of the three, incorporating as it does a jagged piano part, scraps of prerecorded found sounds, and even an Australian-dawn chorus. Long-standing fans of Fred Frith may not recognize his voice easily in this music, but all of it is worth listening to. *—Rick Anderson*

Pacifica / Jun. 16, 1998 / Tzadik ♦♦♦♦

Friends & Enemies / May 15, 1999 / Cuneiform ♦♦♦♦
In 1979, guitarists Fred Frith and Henry Kaiser made an album titled *With Friends Like These...* on the Metalanguage label. It was one of the defining documents of the downtown avant-garde scene, a collection of improvised duets on which both players essentially redefined the sound of the guitar, Frith with his physically altered (and sometimes beaten) instruments, and Kaiser with his virtuosic and harmonically adventurous technique. Four years later they reunited to make *Who Needs Enemies?,* again on Metalanguage, and on this second album they expanded their arsenal to include the Linn drum and sequencer. Metalanguage went belly up not too long after, and until now the only in-print remnant from those two albums was a condensed single-disc package on SST. The Cuneiform reissue improves on the SST item enormously, first of all by including the entirety of both albums, secondly by adding another full album's worth of previously unreleased live material, and thirdly by adding on top of that another half hour of new studio performances. In short, this set offers everything Frith and Kaiser have recorded together, and at mid-price. Absolutely a must for noise fans, skronk hounds, and adventurous guitarheads. *—Rick Anderson*

• **Traffic Continues** / Mar. 14, 2000 / Winter & Winter ♦♦♦♦♦
For the past quarter century the varied recordings of musical renegade Fred Frith have provided a far-flung tour of the worldwide avant-garde fringe. On *Traffic Continues,* he composes for and plays guitar with Ensemble Modern, the venerable 21-piece German new music assemblage. This handsomely packaged CD is one of the strongest statements of Frith's career, a finely balanced work that contains concert hall and street sensibilities in equal measure. There are two lengthy pieces, the 29-minute "Traffic Continues" and the 35-minute "Traffic Continues II: Gusto (for Tom Cora)," an homage to the phenomenal cellist who with Frith was a member of the avant rock band Skeleton Crew. Scored for 15 musicians, the first composition nearly summarizes all the diverse strains of Frith's music, with varied instrumental groupings vertically layered in polyrhythmic counterpoint; wild improvisations scattered between, over, and through the scored sections; and rubato passages punctuated by crisp pointillistic gestures. "Gusto" moves through a series of vignettes performed by Frith, harpist Zeena Parkins, Ikue Mori on drum machines, and Ensemble Modern members. The piece mixes the ragged energy of downtown New York improv with the Ensemble's massed instruments, while going straight for the heart with samples of Cora at his most lyrical and

evocative. At the closing, the music hovers in stasis with Cora's cello a ghostly presence; the full Ensemble then gradually reenters in a stunningly beautiful passage. Tom Cora's untimely death was a tremendous loss, and anyone listening to "Gusto" will realize that Cora was not only a wonderful collaborator to Frith, but also a fellow life traveler and friend. The closing elegiac minutes of this CD prove that even the most cutting-edge new music is most meaningful when there is emotional resonance at its core. *—Dave Lynch*

Ellen Fullman

b. 1957, Memphis, TN
Composer / Sound Sculpture, 20th Century Classical/Modern Composition
Ellen Fullman is an artist, musician, and sculptor of sound. Combining her longtime loves of sound and form into new artistic directions is something Fullman pursues by design and by chance. After graduating with a BFA in sculpture from the Kansas City Art Institute, one of her first performances was 1980's "Streetwalker," in which she wore her "Metal Skirt Sound Sculpture" for New Music America in Minneapolis.

Not long after, Fullman noticed the the haunting, seemingly endless tones made by long, vibrating wires. This accidental discovery sparked one of her longest-running projects, the Long String Instrument. The instrument consists of 100 wires, with 90-foot long bass string and 30 to 60-foot long treble strings, all tuned with just intonation. It is played by three performers rubbing the strings gently, bringing out its eerie sound. Not surprisingly for such an ambitious project, it took a while to develop and record this instrument; Fullman's first recording with it was 1985's *Long String Instrument,* released by the Dutch label Apollo Records. *Change of Direction,* was released in 1999.

While the Long String Instrument has been one of main projects of Fullman's career, she has pursued many other works during that time. In 1986, she received a New York Foundation for the Arts Fellowship; some of her other awards and grants include NEA Visual Artists Fellowship in New Genres in 1989 and 1990, and a New Forms Regional Initiative project grant for her collaboration with vocalist Tina Marsh in 1992. Fullman's other collaborations include a 1986-1989 Composer/Choreographer Project with choreographer Deborah Hay, "The Man Who Grew In Common Wisdom," in Austin, Texas, and an appearance on Poi Dog Pondering's 1992 album *Volo Volo.*

She continues to collaborate with the Deep Listening band, and her albums *Body Music* and *Staggered Stasis* appear on their Deep Listening label. Fullman currently teaches composition classes and leads sound meditations at her Candy Factory studio in Austin. *—Heather Phares*

Body Music / 1993 / Experimental Intermedia ✦✦✦

● **Change of Direction** / Apr. 20, 1999 / New Albion ✦✦✦✦
Ellen Fullman's third album, *Change of Direction,* culminates her Long String Instrument project, which began in 1981 when she discovered the haunting tones created by long wires stretched over great distances. The Long String Instrument consists of 100 wires strung over a 90-foot span, and is rubbed by three performers for a flowing, resonant sound. *Change of Direction's* 11 tracks capitalize on this quality, resulting in songs that sound like ghostly blues. Pieces like "Nocnoca/Aconcon Flip" and "Aconcon Progression" are variations on a theme, set to a walking cadence that is both comforting and eerie. *—Heather Phares*

Diamanda Galás

b. Aug. 29, 1955, San Diego, CA
Vocals / No Wave, Experimental, Alternative Pop/Rock
A fiercely confrontational avant-garde performer noted for her wailing, four-octave vocal range, Diamanda Galas was born and raised in San Diego, California. The daughter of Greek Orthodox parents, her singing was roundly discouraged, although her prowess as a classical pianist was nurtured; ultimately, her strict upbringing resulted in a reckless, drug-fueled youth prior to her entrance into the University of California's music and visual arts program.

Galas made her performing debut in 1979 at France's Festival d'Avignon, which led to an invitation to assume the lead role in composer Vinko Globokar's politically-charged opera *Un Jour Comme un Autre.* In subsequent solo performance-art pieces like *Wild Women With Steak Knives* and *Tragouthia apo to Aima Exon Fonos,* Galas further honed her unique, shattering vocal style, inspired by the Schrei ("shriek") opera of German expressionism (a form employing a system of four microphones and a series of echoes and delays).

Galas made her recorded debut in 1982 with *The Litanies of Satan,* a provocative work comprised of a vocal adaptation of a poem by Charles Baudelaire. After the prison-themed performance piece *Panoptikon* (documented on a self-titled 1984 release), she began developing a trilogy of albums known collectively as *The Masque of the Red Death;* released independently between 1986 and 1988 as *The Divine Punishment, Saint of the Pit* and *You Must Be Certain of the Devil,* the three records catalogued Galas' litany against the AIDS epidemic, which claimed her brother, playwright Philip-Dimitri Galas, in 1986.

With 1990's *The Singer,* she made her first subtle advances into the realm of pop music; reprising some of the same gospel material which snaked through *The Masque of the Red Death,* the record also featured her covers of Willie Dixon's "Insane Asylum" and Screamin' Jay Hawkins' "I Put a Spell on You." 1993's *Vena Cava,* an a cappella effort, preceded 1994's *The Sporting Life,* a collaboration with former Led Zeppelin bassist John Paul Jones. A record of Galas' 1994 radio work *Schrei X* followed in 1996, in tandem with her first book collection, *The Shit of God.* She returned two years later with *Malediction and Prayer. —Jason Ankeny*

● **Divine Punishment** / 1986 / Mute ✦✦✦✦✦

Masque of the Red Death Trilogy (You Must Be Certain of the Devil) / 1989 / Mute ✦✦✦
Contains: "The Divine Punishment", "Saint of the Pit", and "You Must Be Certain of the Devil (A Plague Mass in 3 Parts)". A 2-CD set with pieces similar in intensity to the "Plague Mass". *—"Blue" Gene Tyranny*

☆ **Plague Mass (1984 End of the Epidemic)** / 1991 / Mute ✦✦✦✦✦
Galas, who has been known for both her own work and as a singer of extremely demanding modern scores, has created this heart-wrenching cry about the physical suffering caused by the AIDS plague being compounded by the shameful arrogance of self-appointed moralists. Maintaining an incredible intensity and depth for over an hour's solo vocal (recorded live at The Cathedral of St. John The Divine, NYC, with suitably minimal band and electronics backup), Galas proceeds through Mahalia Jackson-influenced spiritual singing, saxophone-like wails, to dramatic dialogues in many dialects and languages ("there are no more tickets to the funeral") to engrossing Portugese "fado" singing to taking on the attributes of Satan (in "Sono L'Antichristo", *I Am The Anti-Christ*) in order to challenge the concept of a vengeful, instead of compassionate deity (and society), much as Nina Simone did in her controversial song "God is a Killer" in the 60's... the Mass ends with the heart-felt lyrics "I go to sleep each evening now dreaming of the grave and see the friends I used to know calling out my name. O Lord Jesus, do you think I've served my time —". At times, the singing is "self-indulgent", but, well... *—"Blue" Gene Tyranny*

Malediction & Prayer / Apr. 21, 1998 / Asphodel ✦✦✦✦
Diamanda Galas' CD of live covers (of B.B. King, the Supremes, Johnny Cash and Billie Holiday songs, among others) is one of her most accessible works to date. Her screaming, demonic, cacophonous vocal style has been tamed, and throughout Greek anti-ballads to blues, spirituals, and flamenco-classical hybrids, Galas' voice is shown to be a stunningly flexible instrument. Galas croons, intones, grooves and laments with enormous agility and beauty, and accents her singing with minimalism, classical, blues and improvised piano. "Si La Muerte," the highlight of this recording, is an old-style Spanish ballad with hints of flamenco vocal rhythm, enhanced by both classical and minimalist piano. *Live: Malediction and Prayer* is a dynamic, phenomenal recording. *—Lisa Schwartzman*

Ge Gan-Ru

b. 1954
Composer / Film Music, 20th Century Classical/Modern Composition, Avant-Garde, World Fusion, Atonal
China's first avant-garde composer. After receiving degrees in violin and composition from the Shanghai Conservatory of Music, he was forbidden to play anything but scales during the Cultural Revolution and later incarcerated and tortured. In 1983, he was awarded a fellowship to Columbia University where he studied with Chou Wen-chung and Mario Davidovsky and received his Doctor of Musical Arts degree. He has composed concert music, as well as music for dance, theatre, and several film scores: "Tang Dynasty," "Who Killed Vincent Chin" (1988 Oscar nominee for Best Documentary Film), and "A Great Wall," the first Chinese-American feature film collaboration. His dramatic and effective music combines "contemporary Western compositional techniques with my Chinese feeling and experience along with Chinese musical characteristics inherited from thousands of years ago, so as to set up a universal music world expressing natural and primitive beauty." Watch for a future recording of his composition "Wu" (*Rising to Height*) (1986) for piano and chamber orchestra. *—"Blue" Gene Tyranny*

Gu Yue In "Sonic Encounters" / 1990 / Mode ✦✦✦
China's first avant-garde composer. After receiving degrees in violin and composition from the Shanghai Conservatory of Music, he was forbidden to play anything but scales during the Cultural Revolution and later incarcerated and tortured. In 1983, he was awarded a fellowship to Columbia University where he studied with Chou Wen-chung and Mario Davidovsky and received his Doctor of Musical Arts degree. He has composed concert music, as well as music for dance, theatre, and several film scores: *Tang Dynasty, Who Killed Vincent Chin* (1988 Oscar nominee for Best Documentary Film), and *A Great Wall,* the first Chinese-American feature film collaboration. His dramatic and effective music combines "contemporary Western compositional techniques with my Chinese feeling and experience along with Chinese musical characteristics inherited from thousands of years ago, so as to set up a universal music world expressing natural and primitive beauty." Watch for a future recording of his composition "Wu" ("Rising to Height") (1986) for piano and chamber orchestra. *—"Blue" Gene Tyranny*

Orlando Jacinto Garcia

b. 1954, Havana, Cuba
Composer / 20th Century Classical/Modern Composition
Emigrated to Miami, Florida, 1961; then to Maryland. Doctorate in composition from University of Miami where he studied with Dennis Kam. Studied privately with David Del Tredici, John Corigliano and Morton Feldman. President and Founder of the South Florida Composers Alliance. Director of the New Music Ensemble and the Electronic Music Studio at the State University of Florida. *—"Blue" Gene Tyranny*

● **La Belleza del Silencio (The Beauty of Silence)** / 1992 / O.O. Discs ✦✦✦✦✦
Beautiful groups of sounds, soft sharp sustained dissonances in constantly varying permutations characterize the music by this Cuban-born, Miami-based composer, who studied with Morton Feldman. Perfect performances by Joan LaBarbara, voice, The Gregg Smith Singers, Jan Williams, percussion and other musicians. *—"Blue" Gene Tyranny*

Celestial Voices / Oct. 27, 1998 / O.O. Discs ✦✦✦✦
Five compositions as rich in atmosphere as they are intelligent in structure. "Music for Berlin" (1990) for one performer on flute, piccolo, C flute, alto flute, and bass flute, and one pianist, slowly develops a haunting low flute melody. The pianist plays briefly on the strings of the piano, then plays ascending arpeggios in broken, jagged rhythms, a pattern that a higher flute then imitates. After the wind player changes to another instrument, the rhythm patterns occur in arpeggiated chromatic clusters in the piano part, while the flute continues with slow tones. Then the work simply stops, as if this strange new land has been charted and there is no more to be said. "Canciones Fragmentadas" (1996) is for solo contrabass, and employs strong pizzicati contrasted with fleeting, barely audible harmonics, multiple and simultaneous sliding tones, little popping sounds, and many other techniques. "Retratos I" (1989), for piano and electronics on tape, employs slowly developing and rhythmically lay-

ered patterns of a moody, sultry personality. The composition "2 from Three Pieces" (1990), for double bass and tape, contrasts sighing/sliding patterns in the high registers of the bass with slowly swelling/intermodulating, deeply pitched chords and slides in the electronics. The brilliant concluding selection "Voces Celestiales" (1993) is for two contrabasses and orchestra. Opening with a roar of instruments and intermittent percussion, the two basses begin harmonic slides like lone birds in the sky. Deep, sonorous sustained chords are each presented singly, and examined for their unique timbres. Dense textures like the increasing acceleration of a string rhythm–are often interrupted by simple percussion events. Garcia's harmonic sense is remarkable and surprising in its invention, his original "sound" infused with a dramatic foreboding yet realized with a thorough-going modern formality. *— "Blue" Gene Tyranny*

Peter Garland

b. Jan. 27, 1952, Portland, ME

Composer / 20th Century Classical/Modern Composition

American composer Peter Garland was born in Portland, Maine, in 1952. He began composing before the age of 20 while studying under Harold Budd and James Tenney at Cal Arts in the early 1970s. During this time, Garland also studied performance art and video with Wolfgang Stoerchle, and American literature with poet Clayton Eshleman. Garland has had at least four recordings of his compositions released by labels including Tzadik, New Albion and Avant. In addition to composing, Garland is also a musicologist and essayist. As a musicologist, he specializes in traditional U.S. and Mexican musics and 20th century American composers. He researched while living in Mexican villages for some years during the 1970s and 1990s. Garland spent the '80s in Santa Fe, where he had his own performing ensemble and could also study Southwestern Indian and Hispanic musical traditions. In 1991, he ceased publishing Soundings Press, a unique source of new music information and new composers' scores. He then traveled the world for four years, visiting twelve countries over five continents. These travels yielded Garland's third book of published essays, *Gone Walkabout*. Garland also authored a six volume work, *Collected Studies of Nancarrow & Paul Bowles*. In 1997, Garland returned to Mexico to compose, work on his fourth book of essays and study Jarocho music and culture. The Tzadik label released an album of solo piano works in early 2000 called *the Days Run Away*. *— Joslyn Layne*

Walk in Beauty / 1992 / New Albion ♦♦♦

Two piano pieces and an ensemble work with Aki Takahashi, piano, and the Abel-Steinberg-Winant trio. The title piece "Walk in Beauty", named after the Beauty Way chant of Navajo curing and peyote ceremonies, is a bit stiff and uninflected in performance and composition, but the final piano work "Jornada del Muerto (in memoriam Lew Welch)" (*Journey of the Dead One* - name of a place in southern New Mexico in which travelers have perished in its desert and where the first atomic bomb was exploded) has much interesting and beautiful patterning especially in the final section "The View From Vulture Peak;" the 8-section ensemble piece "Sones de Flor" (Flower Songs), based structurally on the Japanese poetic form renga, a chain of linked couplets, played on violin, piano, vibraphone and tom-tom, is beautiful, clear and a full realization of Garland's folk music-minimalist-formal aesthetic and also makes for good listening. Listeners may also enjoy checking out Garland's "Nana + Victorio" (1993) on the Avant label. *— "Blue" Gene Tyranny*

● **The Days Run Away** / Jan. 25, 2000 / Tzadik ♦♦♦♦♦

Days Run Away presents some of Peter Garland's piano compositions that will stun you with their beauty and spacious simplicity. All are compositions from the '70s except the opener, "Bright Angel-Hermetic Bird," which Garland wrote in 1996. Through the intuitive performance by Aki Takahashi, the music quietly develops into a stillness of beauty and calm honesty. Simple notes of light and gratitude become more powerful the more gently they are played in graceful repetitions. *— Joslyn Layne*

Janice Giteck

b. Jun. 27, 1946, New York

Composer / Contemporary Folk, 20th Century Classical/Modern Composition, Contemporary Instrumental, World Fusion

Seattle-based composer and teacher Janice Giteck studied with Darius Milhaud in the '60s, with Oliver Messiaen in Paris, and, later, percussion and gamelan music with Obo Addy and Daniel Schmidt, respectively. World and ritual music have strongly influenced Giteck's own compositions, including the award-winning works "Breathing Songs From a Turning Sky" (which won the NEA's Composer's Award in the '80s) and "Thunder, Like a White Bear Dancing" (1977 Norman Fromm Composers Award). Giteck has received commissions and grants from Meet the Composer and the San Francisco Symphony, and has written music for two films by Pat Ferrero. In the mid-'80s, she also earned a degree in psychology, and worked several years for a Seattle mental health organization. *— Joslyn Layne*

Home (Revisited) / 1992 / New Albion ♦♦♦

An album of pieces dedicated to people living with AIDS, this is music of hope and humanity rather than overt raging. Giteck's music is influenced by the gamelan and cyclic music traditions, especially in the lovely "Om Shanti". "Home (revisited)" is a heart-filling piece for choir (mostly singing the word "home") and instruments, sung here by the Philandros of The Seattle Men's Choir. There is also the touching "Tapasya" for viola and percussion. See also Giteck's "Breathing Songs From A Turning Sky (excerpt)" in the collection "Music From Mills". *— "Blue" Gene Tyranny*

Philip Glass

b. Jan. 31, 1937, Baltimore, MD

Keyboards, Conductor, Composer / Original Score, 20th Century Classical/Modern Composition, Avant-Garde, Minimalism, Ethnic Fusion

Philip Glass was unquestionably among the most innovative and influential composers of the 20th century; postmodern music's most celebrated and high-profile proponent, his myriad orchestral works, operas, film scores and dance pieces proved essential to the development of ambient and new age sounds, and his fusions of Western and world music were among the earliest and most successful global experiments of their kind. Born in 1937, Glass was accepted to the University of Chicago at the age of 15. After graduation he spent time at Julliard and also in Paris, under the tutelage of the legendary Nadia Boulanger. Glass' admitted artistic breakthrough came while working with Ravi Shankar on transcribing Indian music; the experience inspired him to begin structuring music by rhythmic phrases instead of by notation.

During the late '60s, he began to develop his distinctively minimalist compositional style, consisting of hypnotically repetitious circular rhythms. After forming his own imprint, Glass self-released his first recording, 1971's *Music with Changing Parts*. Subsequent efforts like 1973's *Music in Similar Motion/Music in Fifths* earned significant notoriety overseas, and in 1974 he signed to Virgin U.K. Glass rose to international fame with his 1976 "portrait opera" *Einstein on the Beach*, an early masterpiece that toured Europe and was performed at the Metropolitan Opera House. In the years to follow, Glass focused primarily on theatrical projects, including 1980's *Satyagraha*, an operatic portrayal of the life of Gandhi. Similar in theme and scope was 1984's *Akhnaten*, which examined the myth of the Egyptian pharoah.

While remaining best known for his theatrical productions, Glass also enjoyed a successful career as a recording artist. In 1981, he signed to CBS Masterworks and issued the highly successful *Glassworks*. 1986's *Songs of Liquid Days*, meanwhile, featured lyrics from luminaries including Paul Simon and Laurie Anderson, and became Glass' best-selling effort to date. By this time he was far and away the avant-garde's best-known composer, and in 1992, Glass was even commissioned to write "The Voyage" for the Met in honor of the 500th anniversary of Christopher Columbus' arrival in the Americas. *— Jason Ankeny*

Einstein on the Beach / 1979 / Elektra/Asylum ♦♦♦♦♦

This opera, composed in 1975 and premiered in 1976, is scored for four principal actors, 12 singers doubling as dancers and actors, a solo violinist, and an amplified ensemble of keyboards, winds and voices. It is imbued with the postmodern spirit both in its non-linear, poetic, mystic narrative and the floating, eternal world created by the shifting, mathematically precise patterns of Glass' modal music. There are three primary visual sets linked to three musical themes that recur within the work: trains (recalling the metaphors Einstein used to illustrate the theory of relativity, and with which he played as a child), a trial setting (modern life and modern science examined), and a spaceship (a metaphor for transcendence, and/or an escape from nuclear disaster). Also Einstein himself appears midway between the orchestra and the stage as a violinist (his hobby) and observer/witness. There are also additional spoken texts written by Christopher Knowles, Samuel M. Johnson and Lucinda Childs, which appear in various arrangements for single and multiple voices. This work locates itself as a midpoint between the composer's early-'70s work linking rhythmic and harmonic structures and his later series of operas and vocal works and filmscores employing expanded narrative and/or timbral experiments. *— "Blue" Gene Tyranny*

☆ **Koyaanisqatsi** / 1982 / Wea International ♦♦♦♦♦

Parodied more than once, derided, blessed, hailed as a wonder and decried as a travesty, this (abbreviated) soundtrack is capable of generating fascination and annoyance, often simultaneously. The truth is that this isn't merely minimalism—it's expressive minimalism, with some impressive nuances. Given the space to breathe, the music here is breathtaking, and becomes even more so when properly linked, in its full form, with the film's visuals. The later *Powasqaatsi* did not live up to the first film in either a visual or musical respect. *— Steven McDonald*

Songs from Liquid Days / 1986 / CBS ♦♦♦♦♦

Songs From Liquid Days became Philip Glass' most popular and successful recording. The title holds the clue to the music's accessibility: These are songs, providing a more familiar and comfortable format for appreciating the world of minimalism than Glass' operas or instrumental pieces. Working with such lyrical collaborators as David Byrne and Suzanne Vega, he created art music which sounds radio friendly. There is also great variety displayed on this album. While the musical backing is unmistakably Philip Glass, the arrangements and vocal treatments range from the coolly subdued chamber music of "Freezing," featuring the Kronos Quartet and Linda Ronstadt, to the appropriately electrifying and almost new wave-ish "Lightning." The album's highlight, however, is the opener, a ten-minute opus called "Changing Opinion." With unusually oblique lyrics courtesy of Paul Simon, it condenses the odd excitement and drama of a minimalist opera into a single, creative burst of melody, rhythm, and momentum. The minimalist composers originally wanted to reconnect Western art music with a broad, popular audience. On that basis, *Songs From Liquid Days* may be their single greatest achievement. *— Freddy Stidean*

★ **Music in 12 Parts** / 1990 / Venture ♦♦♦♦♦

Philip Glass is renowned for his style of pattern music, presented in its most developed form in this early work, still one of his best. Glass developed a method of writing that simultaneously retained the sense of the timeless "present" while bringing new thoughts about melody and harmony in a non-virtuosic sense. On *Music in 12 Parts* (as well as his opera *Akhnaten*), these ideas are very elegant and profound, while at times Glass verges on the direct appeal of a movie-music sensibility as in *1000 Airplanes on the Roof*. For having this range, he remains a very controversial composer. *— "Blue" Gene Tyranny*

Glassworks / 1993 / Columbia ♦♦♦

With a richer sound and variation of timbres than in the usual Glass keyboard renditions, Donald Joyce plays, with great attention and feeling, various solo works by Glass on a large church organ. Appealing. *— "Blue" Gene Tyranny*

Music with Changing Parts / 1994 / Elektra/Nonesuch ♦♦♦

A re-issue of the 1971 recording. Glass at his most fundamental and best. *— "Blue" Gene Tyranny*

Kundun / Nov. 25, 1997 / Elektra ♦♦♦♦♦

Philip Glass' soundtrack to Martin Scorsese's Dalai Lama epic *Kundun* captures the grace, beauty, joy and melancholy within the film. Glass uses familiar minimalist structures, but works with traditional Tibetan instrumentation and monks, giving the music an alluringly otherworldly feel. It's an entirely original, evocative score, and one of Glass' high-water marks in the field. *—Stephen Thomas Erlewine*

Vinko Globokar

b. Jul. 7, 1934, Anderny, France

Trombone, Composer / 20th Century Classical/Modern Composition, Avant-Garde

Avant-garde trombonist and composer Vinko Globokar has written over 80 works, from solo to chamber to opera, many of which explore the voice and speech and leave room for improvisation. He has premiered works by composers such as Mauricio Kagel, Toru Takemitsu, and Louis Andriessen. His technique on his instrument is such that many compositions have been written for him by composers, including Karlheinz Stockhausen, Henri Pousseur, and Luciano Berio, with whom Globokar studied. He also studied under Rene Leibowitz and Andre Hodeir in Paris.

Although born in France in 1934, Globokar spent his teens in Slovenia. Starting out as a jazz musician there, his studies in Paris included not only trombone, but also conducting (incidentally, he went on to conduct the Warsaw Philharmonic and Jerusalem Symphony Orchestra, among others). In 1967, he began an almost ten-year tenure as a music professor in Cologne, where he also co-founded the improvising group, New Phonic Art. He spent much of the '70s as a department head of IRCAM and, beginning in the mid-'80s, was head of 20th century music at the Scuola di Musica de Fiesole/Firenze. He has performed with world-renowned improvisers Derek Bailey, Evan Parker, and many more. *—Joslyn Layne*

Les Emigrés (The Emigrants) (1982-1986) / 1991 / Harmonia Mundi ✦✦✦

Performed by the Ensemble Musique Vivante. A music-theatre work by this composer/jazz trombonist, who lives in Paris and whose works are nearly impossible to classify—"any model of organisation existing in nature or in culture can become music." Five narrators singing, shouting, and speaking in many languages "give the impression of sitting in a court that is in the process of judging the public," the listener also placed in a similar situation. You are dealing with people who left their countries in order to survive or improve their way of life—the first part "Miserere" is an historical allegory, letters from Italians who had emigrated to Brazil and also from Turkish emigrants, interviews with women who follow their husbands, and so on. The second part "Réalitiés/Augenblicke (Realities/Flashes)" contrasts hope accompanied by dance music against projected images of potential misery. The third part "Sternbild der Grenze (Border Constellation)" with a text by Peter Handke is a series of nine tableaux performed by giant puppets contriving to cross "a hermetically sealed border" in a clandestine way. At various points, the singers cross the border of the stage and go into the audience. There are also parts for an orchestra, a small choir, two vocal soloists, and a jazz trio. *—"Blue" Gene Tyranny*

Malcolm Goldstein

b. Mar. 27, 1936, Brooklyn, NY

Violin / Improvisation, Avant-Garde

American avant-garde violinist, improviser, and composer Malcolm Goldstein has been exploring the sounds possible with the violin since the early '60s, when he, Philip Corner, and James Tenney founded the Tone Roads Ensemble. In addition to receiving commissions for his own work from a number of arts councils and vocalists, other composers (including John Cage, Christian Wolff, and Ornette Coleman) have written works specifically for Goldstein. He has performed all over Europe and North America, in groups, solo, and with dance troupes. Recordings of Goldstein's music (including his 1997 solo performance at the Fire in the Valley festival) finally started becoming more readily available during the '90s. *—Joslyn Layne*

Daniel Goode

b. Jan. 24, 1936, New York, NY

Clarinet, Composer / Gamelan, 20th Century Classical/Modern Composition, Electronic

New York born modern composer and clarinetist Daniel Goode has composed innovative works for clarinet in addition to ensemble and multimedia works. Goode first studied philosophy, then music under such modern composers as Henry Cowell and Pauline Oliveros. He was Rutgers University's Director of the Electronic Music Studio from 1971 to 1998. In 1976, Goode joined Gamelan Son of Lion, as composer and performer, and in 1983, co-founded NY's DownTown Ensemble, which he co-directed from then on. His composed works have been performed throughout North America, Eastern and Western Europe, Japan and Australia at festivals including the 1991, '92 and '96 Bang On a Can Festivals, and the 1994 Pfeifen im Walde festival in Berlin. In July, 1996, Goode toured Java with Gamelan Son of Lion, in July 1996. The toured included the performance of his *Eine Kleine Gamelan Music* at the Second Yogyakarta International Gamelan Festival—recordings of Goode's gamelan works, *Gamelan in the New World vol.1 & 2*, can be found on the Folkways label. Other compositions of note include his pieces for solo clarinet, *Circular Thoughts* (1974) and *Clarinet Songs* (1979-91) which was released in 1993 on the Experimental Intermedia (XI) label, a work for solo bass recorder, *Thrush From Upper Dunakyn*, recorded for Opus One records, and a piece for 15 instruments *Tunnel-Funnel*, which was performed in 1989 at the New Music America festival, and was recorded for the Tzadik label for 1996 release. Goode also has book of writings, *From Notebooks*, and of music, *One PagePieces*, that were published by New Hampshire's Frog Peak Music. *—Joslyn Layne*

Clarinet Songs / 1993 / Experimental Intermedia ✦✦✦

A fascinating collection of short pieces for solo clarinet skillfully played by the composer. Each piece features a different playing technique. My personal favorites are "Clarinet Drum", the odd tunings of "Six New Fractal Fingers", the almost-Tibetan "Clarinet Trumpet", and the lovely double stop harmonies of "Long Distance". Daniel Goode is one of the founders of the well-known Downtown Ensemble in New York City and has created many other larger works such as the nixed media piece "Managua-Matagalpa-Music" about the Nicaraguan revolution and "Three Talking Sculptures for Election Day" (1992) about guns, pornography and sexual expression. *—"Blue" Gene Tyranny*

● **Tunnel-Funnel** / Jan. 20, 1998 / Tzadik ✦✦✦✦✦

Tunnel-Funnel presents two works by New York composer Daniel Goode. Performed by the Crosstown Ensemble, the title track is something of a modern pastoral, and very pleasant. With its friendly dissonance, it's less crisp than what "20th century composition" normally refers to. The second composition, "Fiddle Studies," was inspired by Goode's work with traditional Scotch-Canadian fiddlers in Nova Scotia, and is light, lovely, and hypnotic. It's too bad there aren't more compositions on this release, as it is a really enjoyable listen. *—Joslyn Layne*

Michael Gordon

b. Jul. 20, 1956, Miami, Florida

Keyboards, Composer / 20th Century Classical/Modern Composition

Composer Michael Gordon is the co-founder and co-director of New York's *Bang on a Can* new music festival. Although he was born in Florida, Gordon grew up in an Eastern European community in Nicaragua. He eventually returned to the U.S. and studied composition with Martin Bresnick at Yale, and played in various rock bands in N.Y.C. His works have been performed by the Icebreaker ensemble of London ("Trance" and "Yo Shakespeare"), Ensemble Modern ("Love Bead"), and the Michael Gordon Philharmonic. Icebreaker has recorded a couple of Gordon's works for releases on Argo, and performed his score for the Jeyasingh Dance Company piece "Intimacies of a Third Order." Formed in 1983, the Michael Gordon Philharmonic adds string instruments to a rock group's instrumentation. In the years since its founding, the Philharmonic has toured North America and Europe. Gordon began working in the music theater in the early '90s, collaborating with video artist Elliot Caplan on +Van Gough Video Opera (1991). He has since worked on other operas, including *Chaos*, and comic-book opera *The Carbon Copy Building* (1999). *—Joslyn Layne*

Big Noise from Nicaragua / 1992 / Composers ✦✦✦

Complex works from the 80's by this dynamic composer—"Thou shalt not! Thou shalt not!" (1983) with passages of triple meter rhythms in strings and winds counter to quarter notes in the percussion, "The Low Quartet" (1985/86) for four bass clarinets, "Four Kings Fight Give" (1988) for chamber strings and winds which has a passage in seven tempi at once, performed by the Michael Gordon Philharmonic conducted by Linda Bouchard, and "Acid Rain" (1986) played by The Spectrum ensemble conducted by Guy Proteroe. *—"Blue" Gene Tyranny*

Peter Laurence Gordon

b. Jun. 20, 1951

Saxophone, Composer / Experimental, Prog-Rock/Art Rock, Avant-Garde

Studied at Center for Contemporary Music, Mills College. Plays saxes and other winds, keyboards. Organized "Trust in Rock" concerts of art-rock in 1976 at University of California at Berkeley. Producer of many records included early Laurie Anderson, Arthur Russell, David Van Tieghem, etc. Many film scores including incidental music for Spielberg's *Joe Vs. the Volcano*. Founder the Love of Life Orchestra. Many international tours. Opera *The Strange Live of Ivan Osokin* (1994), settings of Kathy Acker songs and collaborative theater work at BAM, *Otello*. After 1995's *Peter Gordon and the Love of Life Orchestra Quartet*, he issued 1996's *Yellow Box*. *—"Blue" Gene Tyranny*

● **Leningrad-Xpress** / 1990 / New Tone ✦✦✦✦✦

Music from dance and theatre productions in a musical language equally informed by world music, tough New York City rock, pattern music, Albert Ayler jazz, and electronic music... Gordon makes it all work in these highly original tone poems from the almost Weill-ian "Leningrad Express" and "Warsaw", to the disco-Italian folk music of "Toscana", to the electronic and dissonant "In The Fields", "Trinity Site" and "Inside The Nuclear Power Plant" (text-Kathy Acker), the sublime "atonal" chamber music of"Inside Marie", the Chopinesque-Tibetan "Woyzeck's Dream", the 1920's Berlin-style "Der Kindertotentanz", and the unabashedly pretty "Pastis" acoustic guitar solo. *—"Blue" Gene Tyranny*

Geneva & Extended Niceties / 1992 / New Tone ✦✦✦

Imaginative polytonal rock songs and instrumentals re-issued from post-art-rock times of the early 80's. Bold and beautiful genuine lyricism and humor with various combinations of The Love Of Life Orchestra. *—"Blue" Gene Tyranny*

Still Life and the Deadman / 1994 / New Tone ✦✦✦

From the lush string orchestra of the first piece "Awareness" to the excellent performances of the Balanescu and Parsley Club string quartets (respectively in "De Dode (The Dead Man)" music for a Bataille drama and in "Rembrandt Suite"), this melodic, evocative album fulfills the promise of the thorny rose on its cover—romantic harmonies with strange melodic turns, the sweet with the dissonant, the humorous with the plaintive, and the traditional with the "downtown" This CD, with additional winds and percussion, presents a turning point and a maturing of style in Gordon's work. *—"Blue" Gene Tyranny*

Peter Gordon & The Love of Life Orchestra Quartet / 1995 / New Tone ✦✦✦

A terrific overview of this cross-genre composer's music that lies somewhere between new music tone poems and pop styles. Contains: "Nannies and Chauffeurs," a three-part political suite "Nightmare in Tobaccoland," two pieces influenced by Gordon's study of Korean music ("Chejudo" and "Sorak San), a rock commentary "Gnarly Youth," a lovely ballad "My Bed" from Gordon's recent opera *The Strange Life of Ivan Osokin*, "The Khazars," "Ivan's Rag," and a live performance recording of "Raw Chihuahua" featuring the quartet playing at breakneck speed for a wildly enthusiastic audience. With P. Gordon on saxes and Farfisa organ, Jeffrey Berman on percussion, Paul Nowinski on bass, and *"Blue" Gene Tyranny* on piano. *—"Blue" Gene Tyranny*

The Yellow Box / 1996 / Resurgent ✦✦✦

Henryk Mikolajj Górecki

b. Dec. 6, 1933, Czernica, Poland
Composer / 20th Century Classical/Modern Composition, Sacred Choral, Classical
Studied at Katowice Conservatory. First premiere at 1958 Warsaw Autumn Festival. International success with his *Third Symphony.* Changed styles from highly experimental early compositions to tonal, melodic recent work. *— "Blue" Gene Tyranny*

The Essential Gorecki / Olympia ✦✦✦
A collection of the earlier more radical and interesting works by this Polish composer whose current tonal style is a kind of syrupy sentimentalism that has a certain popularity. Included are excellent performances of "Epitafium" (Epitaph) for mixed choir and instrumental group (1958), "Zderzenia-Scontri" (Collisions) (1960), "Genesis II: Canti strumentali per 15 esecutori" (Genesis II: Instrumental songs for 15 performers) (1962), "Refren" (Refrain) (1965), and "Muzyka staropolska" (Old Polish Music) (1969). Performances by the Polish national Orchestra And The National Philharmonic Choir. *— "Blue" Gene Tyranny*

Gerard Grisey

b. Jun. 17, 1946, Belfort, France, **d.** Nov. 11, 1998, Paris, France
Composer / Spectral Music, 20th Century Classical/Modern Composition, Atonal
Gerard Grisey taught at University of California, Berkeley from 1982-1986. One of the founders of "spectralism" composition, which involves sustained and modulated, hypnotic harmonic colors. Recent work includes *L'icone paradoxale* (title refers to a painting of the Virgin Mary by Piero della Francesca) for orchestra distributed low instruments on left, high on right, trumpets and flutes in front, 17 gongs around the hall, instruments tuned in quarter-tones, two voices on phonemics. *— "Blue" Gene Tyranny*

• **Gerard Grisey** / 1995 / Accord ✦✦✦
Beautiful chamber works in the "spectralism" style. Includes *Talea for ensemble* (1986), *Prologue* for alto and resonators (1976), *Anubis* for sax (1983), *Nout* for sax (1983), *Jour Contre Jour* for ensemble (1979). *— "Blue" Gene Tyranny*

Partiels for 16 or 18 Musicians/ Derives for 2 Orchestral Groups / Erato ✦✦✦
Ensemble Ars Nova, dir. Boris de Vinogradov; Orchestre National de France, dir. Jacques Mercier. Extremely quiet washes of harmonic colors over the orchestral surface with other unusual timbres. *— "Blue" Gene Tyranny*

Bernhard Günter (Bernd Günter)

b. 1957, Neuwied, Germany
Composer / Computer Music, 20th Century Classical/Modern Composition, Avant-Garde, Electro-Acoustic, Electronic
Bernhard Günter is a leading example of post-Cagian composers. His first album, *Un Peu de Neige Salie*, was cited by *Wire Magazine* as one of the 'top 100 records that shook the world,' and was at the forefront of the minimal, post-techno music known as microwave or lowercase. His music evolved from the very quiet 'microwave' clicks and pops to a more expansive, but equally quiet and tranquil, music which owes more to Morton Feldman than any pop figure. His interest in Japanese esthetics and haiku is reflected in the economy of, and the use of silence in, his work. While his earliest compositions used computer-generated sound, he had better results with the more complex overtone structures of sampled sound. But unlike other sample-based composers, such as John Oswald or David Shea, his approach is non-referential and contemplative, and doesn't call attention to the original sample source.

Günter started out playing drums and guitar in rock and jazz bands before moving to Paris in 1980 and studying at IRCAM. He returned to Germany in 1986 and began work on computer compositions. After his first two albums (originally released on the Selektion label, and now reissued on Table of the Elements), he focused on remixes and collaborations with sound artists, including John Duncan, Asmus Tietchens, and Merzbow. In 1995 Günter founded the electroacoustic Trente Oiseaux label. Since 1998, Günter measured the duration of his work in three-second units, a concept he calls DIM ("Duree, Ici, Maintenant"—Duration, Here, Now), based on the neurological finding that our perception of the present lasts only about three seconds; everything else is memory or anticipation. The decade's close saw a resurgence in solo compositions, with new works reflecting his growing interest in harmony, and the influence of Feldman and Luigi Nono. *—Caleb Deupree*

• **Un Peu de Neige Salie** / 1993 / Table of the Elements ✦✦✦✦
Günter's first album brings together works from 1992 and 1993. The title of the album comes from one of his haiku: "elle fonderait/dans ma main... /un peu de neige salie" (roughly "it would melt in my hand—a bit of soiled snow"). The first piece uses computer generated sounds, but all of the others display his use of samples, which is still his preferred type of sounds. All of the pieces collected here are subtle and reward careful listening, but as they are all extremely quiet, they can get lost in a noisy listening environment. Each piece uses silence very effectively, as well as unpitched drones and clicks. The clicks can be fast and rhythmic, as in "Untitled I/92," or varied and sounding like fireworks, as in "Untitled III/92." "Untitled II/92" and "Untitled IV/92" deal strictly with sustained tones, white noise, and delicate swirls of sound, and foreshadow Günter's more recent, Feldman-influenced pieces. "Untitled I/93" combines slow rhythmic clicks over white noise, a low drone, and quiet booms. When this album was first released in 1993, it was greeted with bewilderment, since at the time the direction of avant-garde music was anything but quiet. Even the original label executive and CD manufacturer called the artist to tell him the master tape was defective, nothing remaining but clicks and pops. But with the growing recognition of Morton Feldman's importance and the increasing awareness of John Cage's late works, known as the Number pieces (which are very quiet and serene), over the course of the 1990s, this album isn't the shocker it once was. Nevertheless, the pieces remain as interesting and challenging as they were in 1993. *— Caleb Deupree*

• **Time, Dreaming Itself** / 1999 / Trente Oiseaux ✦✦✦✦✦
Time, Dreaming Itself is the most Feldman-like release in Günter's growing discography. Gone are the trademark clicks and pops; instead you are treated to long pitched gestures, many of which sound like they could have been played by acoustic instruments (and are, in fact, treated samples). The sounds have a richness that shows Günter's continued mastery of his instrument and his materials. There is still excellent use of silence and tranquillity, almost meditational or devotional in nature. Günter's entire oeuvre has been about treating his listeners to small sounds, cleansing the system of the environmental noise pollution, and *Time, Dreaming Itself* is an excellent continuation of his exploration. *— Caleb Deupree*

Brown, Blue, Brown on Blue (For Mark Rothko) / 1999 / Trente Oiseaux ✦✦✦✦

Univers Temporel Espoir / Nov. 23, 1999 / Trente Oiseaux ✦✦✦✦✦

Hafler Trio

f. 1980, Sheffield, England
Group / Experimental Rock, Ambient
Prolific and enigmatic, the Hafler Trio masterminded some of the most challenging and innovative sonic experiments of their time—defining music as simply organized sound, their unique synthesis of electronics, samples and tape loops probed the psychoacoustic power of noise, exploring not only its sensory effects but its physical ramifications as well. Formed in Sheffield, England in 1980 by Cabaret Voltaire alum Chris Watson and Andrew McKenzie, the Hafler Trio was never a three-piece in any actual sense—in fact, the third member originally credited to the line-up, one Dr. Edward Moolenbeek, was (according to an interview with McKenzie in the March/April 1991 issue of *Option* magazine) reportedly an expert in psychoacoustic research who edited the journal *Science Review* during the 1930s.

Much of the Hafler Trio's mystique stems from the deliberate misinformation the group consistently set forth—although their records regularly came packaged with deluxe graphs, diagrams and essays detailing the purported effects of sound on the listener, the scientific authenticity of their "findings" is debatable; for example, their 1984 debut, *Bang! An Open Letter,* claims to be based on the studies of an acoustic researcher named Robert Spridgeon, complete with bibliography. Spridgeon later proved to be a complete fabrication, however, and over the course of subsequent efforts including 1985's *Alternation, Perception and Resistance: A Comprehension Exercise* EP, 1986's *Three Ways of Saying Two–The Netherlands Lectures* and *Dislocation,* the Hafler Trio continued baffling audiences with a deluge of propaganda, clouding perceptions to increase the visceral impact of their music.

By 1987's double-LP *A Thirsty Fish* Watson had exited H30, leaving McKenzie the sole constant member; its follow-up, *intoutof,* heralded a new approach, rejecting the cut-and-paste noise and abrasive drones of earlier releases in favor of a more hypnotically ethereal sound. 1991's *Kill the King* announced the beginning of a trilogy which continued on with *Mastery of Money* and *How to Reform Mankind;* acclaimed in many quarters as the Hafler Trio's finest work, these three records diametrically oppose the soothing, placating effects of most ambient musics—*Mastery of Money,* with its extensive use of low-frequency tones, is a particularly unnerving and discomforting experience. Subsequent releases include 1992's *Fuck* and 1994's *One Dozen Economical Stories,* a collaboration with filmmaker Peter Greenaway. In 1996, the Hafler Trio also mounted *Who Sees Goes On,* a series of thematically-linked limited-edition releases. *—Jason Ankeny*

• **Kill the King** / 1991 / Silent ✦✦✦✦✦

Mastery of Money / 1992 / Touch ✦✦✦
Mastery of Money is the second part of a trilogy the Hafler Trio released in the early 1990s. Each release in the series (the others are *Kill the King* and *How to Reform Mankind*) has similar oversize packaging, including a booklet with texts and photos for each piece on the CD. Musically the trilogy explores similar territory as well, with less emphasis on recognizable voices and more on field recordings, layered loops, and drones. "Empty Rooms and Their Occupants," for example, is a long drone piece with active inner sounds, fading in and out, subtly changing pitch while maintaining a steady state. "Callibre" and "Eloise C" are both based on field recordings. The former contains sirens, church bells, car horns, sounds of walking, announcement voices, all surrounded by a gentle outdoor-like ambience. The latter is more abstract, with wind sounds combined with radio static and frequency manipulation. The group still plays with perceptions, but additionally they have now moved their attention to the CD itself. Although there are titles and credits for seven pieces, the album contains 34 tracks which bear no relation to the pieces at all, but instead comprise two very long tracks (46:34 and 27:50) which sandwich 34 tracks so short that they are under the standard for track length, all one to three seconds in duration. All of the short tracks are contained within *Splitting the Stick.* The album's closing moments are the laugh box, a toy from the late 1960s with a built-in belly laugh, an echoing and reverberating commentary from this mysterious group. *— Caleb Deupree*

Bang! An Open Letter/Walk Gently Through the Gates of Joy / 1995 / Grey Area/Mute ✦✦✦✦✦
As the Hafler Trio's experimental sound is far from everyone's cup of tea, the two-fer release *Bang! An Open Letter/Walk Gently Through the Gates of Joy* is a smart way for budget-minded consumers to pick up a large chunk of the group's music without a great deal of risk. The first, Hafler Trio's debut album, is stil one of their best efforts, and the second includes several previously unreleased tracks as well as the 1985 EP *Alternation, Perception and Resistance.* It's easily the best document of Hafler Trio's abrasive post-punk period still available. *—Jason Ankeny*

Keiji Haino

b. 1952
Guitar (Electric) / Noise, Experimental Rock, Noise-Rock, Avant-Garde
When attempting to describe what Keiji Haino does to a guitar, the verb "play" seems terribly insufficient. Mauling might be a more appropriate choice, maybe even destroying. Whatever, whether it is as a solo performer or leading his tremendous trio Fushitsusha, Haino has been leading the loud, free form, noise-loaded, jazz/rock guitar movement in Japan for nearly three decades, starting with seminal noise-jazz/rockers Lost Aaraaff in 1971. He remains a virtual unknown, even among the music connoisseurs in his own country (I once

asked a group of Japanese students, all of whom admitted to being eclectic music fans, about him, not one had heard of him) but his music as beautiful as it is coruscating is jarring, unpredictable and well worth hearing, especially by those enamored of those on the fringes of music performance.

Affecting a rock star pose (long black hair, ever-present sunglasses) Haino is an accomplished player who enjoys experimenting with undulating sheets of metallic sound. His solo recordings are frequently done live with no overdubbing, and Haino adds to the frenetic improvisatory mood by emitting shrieks and yelps as he strangles the neck of his Gibson SG. If you need a familiar example think of the more extreme moments of the late, great Sonny Sharrock, or Pete Cosey's envelope-pushing soloing with Miles Davis in the mid-70s. With Fushitsusha, however, Haino's playing is more nuanced and restrained, kind of like Bill Frisell or an introspective Fred Frith. That doesn't mean however that Haino and Fushitsusha are afraid of cutting loose and tearing it up, they are well-known (hell, revered) for turning up the volume and kicking out the jams, and the aural chaos is frequently stunning.

Not for the faint of heart or for those who compare every guitar player to Edward Van Halen, Keiji Haino is a tremendously exciting player. Granted his entire output is not essential (some of his solo recordings are repetitive), but when it comes to pushing the boundaries of music, noise, and where the guitar fits in this discourse, he has few peers. *—John Dougan*

Affection / 1991 / Poor Strong Factory ♦♦♦♦
An excellent Haino solo recording, dark and disturbing, yet reaching the manic noisy moments that grace virtually all of his work. Recorded live, this is another example of Haino's take-no-prisoners approach to improvised music. Caveat: this disc is hard to find and expensive once you have. *—John Dougan*

Double Live / 1993 / Poor Strong Factory ♦♦♦♦♦
Perhaps the best recording of Haino with Fushitsusha. Live and unrestrained, this double-CD with over two hours of music might be like jumping into the deep end of the pool when it comes to music this intense, but what the hell, you only live once. This is careening, no-holds-barred improvisatory jazz-rock, part Sonny Sharrock, part heavy metal thunder, part '60s garage-rock rant. Haino's playing is jaw-droppingly great, making this a free music masterpiece. Made loud to be played loud. Crank it up and invite the neighbors. *—John Dougan*

Tenshi No Gijinka / 1995 / Tzadik ♦♦♦♦♦
Tenshi no Gijinka finds Keiji Haino solo and without guitar. Focusing entirely on percussion and vocals, Haino builds a unique, meditative space out of drones, cymbal smacks, rings, and reverberations. Bizarre yet also beautiful, Haino creates a personalized and esoteric ritual that alternately serves as repeated tension release and representation of the inner sounds of existence. The result is a captivating immersion in sustains and overtones. *—Joslyn Layne*

● **Execration That Accept to Acknowledge** / Jun. 21, 1996 / Forced Exposure ♦♦♦♦
A very strong representation of Haino cutting loose in a solo context. Recorded live in Japan, this 40-minute chunk of skronk is built upon some predictable structural dynamics (loud to very loud to soft to sudden silence), but there's enough density and variance in the piece to make this relentless ferocity accessible. Uncompromising and berserk, this is a thrilling, unclassifiable hybrid. It's as if AC/DC's Angus Young discovered Pete Cosey's soloing on Miles' *Agharta* and created a whole new trick bag. Not for those who are made woozy by extreme noise damage. *—John Dougan*

Lou Harrison

b. May 14, 1917, Portland, OR
Composer / Microtonal, World Fusion
Studied with Henry Cowell, Arnold Schoenberg, Virgil Thomson, and Korean, Chinese, and other Asian musics. Built gamelans, taught at many colleges, holds Honorary Doctorate, many awards and commissions. Dance and film scores for dancer Erick Hawkins and filmmaker James Broughton among many others. *—"Blue" Gene Tyranny*

● **La Koro Sutro** / 1988 / New Albion ♦♦♦♦♦

● **Double Music (1941), Collaboration with John Cage, for 4 Percussionists/ in the New Mus** / 1990 / New World ♦♦♦
A wild and wacky by-now-classic percussion piece, using a small range of pitches, that begins as a modest melody and winds up like a heated and joyous village celebration for many unusual instruments. Excellent example of a successful collaboration in composition. This CD is especially recommended as a good collection of percussion music. *—"Blue" Gene Tyranny*

☆ **Music for Guitar and Percussion** / 1990 / Etcetera ♦♦♦♦♦
Thanks to John Schneider's well-tempered guitar and the Cal Arts Percussion Ensemble conducted by John Bergamo, listeners are presented with a good overview of Harrison's sometimes pastoral and sometimes crashingly celebratory "Canticle No. 3" (1941) for ocarina, guitar, and percussion. The ocarina suggests Native American and Japanese folk melodies; the guitar is used as a percussion instrument along with gamelan-like suspended brake drums and shaker (more melodic, but still unusual in Pythagorean and just tuning and Babylonian/Arabic and artificial scales). Excellent performances. *—"Blue" Gene Tyranny*

Gamelan Music / 1992 / Music Masters ♦♦♦
Beautiful and meditative pieces that reflect Harrison's abiding affection for the gamelan that has dominated his musical thought in the last few decades. *—"Blue" Gene Tyranny*

Henry Cow

f. 1968, **db.** 1978
Group / Canterbury Scene, Experimental Rock, Jazz-Rock, Prog-Rock/Art Rock
The progressive-rock genre spawned many groups who became top-grossing arena acts—Pink Floyd and Genesis are two—as well as many who progressed right into obscurity. Henry Cow was one of the best-known and most widely traveled English bands of the progressive era (though only a cult-favorite in the U.S.), and their music has aged amazingly well over the last 20 years due to diverse influences (Oliver Messiaen, Kurt Weill, Frank Zappa, and Soft Machine were a few) and uncompromising creativity. The group functioned more or less as a collective, with a true group identity that changed from album to album as members came and went. This turnover was one factor in the consistent vitality of Henry Cow; another was the dedicated core of the band, a serious, politicized trio whose interest in improvisation served to leaven the complexity they supplied as primary writers.

Tim Hodgkinson played keyboards and reeds; Chris Cutler (later of Pere Ubu) played drums, Fred Frith provided a variety of instruments, specializing in strings (the guitar in particular); all of them sang. The three appear on all of the Henry Cow albums recorded between 1973 and 1978. Other longtime members included multi-reedist Lindsay Cooper, bassist John Greaves, and German singer Dagmar Krause, who worked with Frith and Cutler in the spin-off Art Bears band and later recorded bilingual renditions of songs by Brecht & Weill. Together, their sound was so mercurial and daring that they had few imitators, even though they inspired many on both sides of the Atlantic with a blend of spontaneity, intricate structures, philosophy, and humor that has endured and transcended the "progressive" tag.

Since the demise of Henry Cow, its members have continued in creative directions, mostly working in Europe with rock-based or improvising ensembles. Over the years they have reunited in various units, with resultant recordings being distributed worldwide through the Recommended Records network spearheaded by active improviser Chris Cutler. *—Myles Boisen*

● **Leg End** / 1973 / East Side Digital ♦♦♦♦♦
The first album from this Cambridge University-spawned group explores its initial influences: serial music, free jazz, and the early prog-rock that had come about in the Cambridge scene a few years before. Imagine a humorless Soft Machine making a jazz noise and you may be close to the sound of Leg End (there is humor, however, in the bad pun of the album title). Of interest now is how the debuts of members Chris Cutler and Fred Frith are already informed with the sound that would carry through their careers: Frith especially employing the Eastern European scales and tuning, Cutler's freewheeling drumming and percussion. There is a certain unbalance in the album: the very energetic rockish jams of "Teenbeat Reprise" and others throw into light the rather paltry and painful free jazz moments (future Hatfield and the North member Geoff Leigh's sax takes some getting used to). On the whole, however, a mature effort. *—Ted Mills*

Unrest / 1974 / East Side Digital ♦♦♦♦
By this point Henry Cow consisted of guitarist Fred Frith, drummer Chris Cutler, bassist John Greaves, keyboardist Tim Hodgkinson, and, of particular importance to the band's sound at this point, bassoonist Lindsay Cooper. As is so often the case with avant-garde rock & roll, it's the composed pieces that work best, and the fact that Frith is responsible for the majority of them is significant. "Bittern Storm Over Ulm" is an absolutely brilliant demolition of the Yardbirds' "Got to Hurry," while the brief but lovely "Solemn Music" unfolds in a stately manner with atonal but pretty counterpoint between Frith and Cooper. The improvised material succeeds in a more spotty way. "Upon Entering the Hotel Adlon" demonstrates how fine the line can be between bracing free atonality and mindless cacophony. The unsettling but eventually gorgeous "Deluge," on the other hand, shows how well Henry Cow could walk that line when they tried; in this piece, random guitar skitterings, scattershot drum clatter, and pointillistic reed grunts are eventually snuck up on and overtaken by softly massed chords and Cooper's gently hooting bassoon. The effect is startlingly moving. Overall, this is one of Henry Cow's better efforts. *—Rick Anderson*

In Praise of Learning / 1975 / East Side Digital ♦♦♦
A team-up with Slapp Happy may seem an obvious meeting of minds in 2000, but not at the time (1975) when all they really shared was a Marxist outlook and a record label (Virgin). The two bands had already recorded *Desperate Straights*, which focused more on songs and Dagmar Krause's vocals. Here, Krause gets one good song, the terrific Kurt Weill-esque "War" (subsequently covered by the Fall many years later), which leads off the album. "Living in the Heart of the Beast" takes up the rest of side one, and in long form Kraus seems lost. There's some free noise on side two, and it's a bit of a waste seeing Mongezi Feza among others play on the album. The best thing to take away from this meeting is that it went on to produce Art Bears, News From Babel, and several other groups made up from this spectacular personnel. *—Ted Mills*

Pierre Henry

b. Dec. 9, 1927, Paris, France
Synthesizer, Composer / Musique Concrète, Electronic
The celebrated French composer Pierre Henry was among the pivotal forces behind the development of musique concrète, becoming the first formally educated musician to devote his energies to the electronic medium. Born in 1927, he began training at the Paris Conservatoire at the age of ten. Still, Henry had little regard for traditional musical instruments, preferring instead to privately experiment with non-musical sound sources; over time, he grew fascinated with the notion of incorporating noise into the compositional process, and perhaps unsurprisingly first attracted notice in performing circles for his prowess as a percussionist.

In 1949, Henry joined the staff of the RTF electronic studio, founded by Pierre Schaeffer five years earlier; he soon immersed himself completely in electronic music, heading the Groupe de Research de Musique Concrète throughout the greater part of the 1950s. In 1952, Henry produced the first musique concrète ever commissioned for a commercial film, and frequently collaborated with choreographer Maurice Béjart, a pairing which yielded 1962's *Le Voyage* and 1967's *Messe pour le temps présent*, among others. By the 1960s, Henry began incorporating the electronic aesthetics pioneered in other areas of the world at his own private workshop (the Apsone-Cabasse Studio), with the 1960 piece *La noire a soixante* fusing musique concrète with pure electronics. Throughout the decade to follow his music adopted increasingly spiritual and meditative qualities. In 1969, he premiered *Ceremony*, which included music by the pop band Spooky Tooth. By the 1970s, his primary interest was large-scale works complete with elaborate lighting effects, among them *Mise en musique de corticolart* and *Kylderstück*. Henry continued to work reguarly throughout the years that followed in a vast range of musical contexts—even collaborating with the American alternative rock trio Violent Femmes. —*Jason Ankeny*

- **Messe Pour Le Temps Présent** / 1967 / Philips ✦✦✦✦

Though it's perhaps Henry's best-known work, *Messe Pour le Temps Présent* isn't the best display of the powers of *musique concrète*. Similar to the glut of crossover Moog rock albums around the same time, Henry's occasional bursts of searing computer static are accompanied by a faux '60s go-go beat. It's an intriguing release, but works better for novelty fans and beginners who would rather have a gradual immersion into *musique concrète*. It earns its stars, however, for its reissue on a French CD that also includes several of Henry's other compositions, including "Variations Pour une Porte et un Soupir." —*John Bush*

Futuriste / 1980 / ✦✦✦

All hauntingly beautiful albums from this composer's over forty years of work in electronic and "musique concrète" and collaborations with Pierre Schaeffer. Watch for a future re-issue of a collection of these currently out-of-print discs. —*"Blue" Gene Tyranny*

Lejaren Hiller

b. Feb. 23, 1924, New York, NY, **d.** Jan. 26, 1994, Buffalo, NY
Composer / Tape Music, Computer Music, Atonal, Electronic
Studied with Harvey Officer, oboe with Joseph Marx, Ph.D. in Chemistry from Princeton, composition with Milton Babbitt, Roger Sessions. Founded Experimental Music Studio at Univ. of Illinois in late '50s. Slee Professor of Composition at State University of NY at Buffalo. Collaborated on first significant computer music composition *Illiac Suite* (1957) with Leonard Issacson. Later employed techniques of indeterminancy, serialism, tonality. Collaborated with John Cage on *HPSCHD* for one to seven Harpsichords and 51 tapes (1968). Also *Computer Cantata* for soprano, tape and chamber ensemble (1963), *Midnight Carnival* (1976) for principal tape and indeterminate number of subsidiary tapes and other events. —*"Blue" Gene Tyranny*

Illiac Suite (Excerpt)/ in "The Voice of the IBM 7090 Computer" / 1960 / Bell Telephone Labs ✦✦✦

The "Illiac Suite" composed with engineer L.M. Issacson was the first computer music piece. It demonstrated possibilities for complex rhythms, transpositions of melody, and suggested a spectrum of controlled to quasi-random systems for composition... the IBM 7090 computer occupied two rooms with the computing ability now possessed by a modest personal computer... included on this disc are brief experiments by Drs. J.R. Pierce, M.V. Mathews, Newman Guttman, David Slepian, David Lewin, M.E. Shannon. —*"Blue" Gene Tyranny*

- **Algorithms, Versions 1 and 4 (1968)** / 1969 / Deutsche Grammaphon ✦✦✦

An interesting ensemble piece for acoustic instruments and magnetic tape, composed using the IBM 7094 computer. Titles of the three sections reflect some of the mathematical constructs represented—"The Decay of Information", *"Icosahedron"*, and "The Incorporation of Constrants". —*"Blue" Gene Tyranny*

Metaphors/ in the Buffalo Guitar Quartet's "New Music for Guitars" / 1990 / New World ✦✦✦

Jim Horton

b. Sep. 6, 1944, Minnesota, **d.** Jun. 8, 1998, Berkeley, CA
Composer, Computer / Computer Music
Studied with Robert Ashley at Center for Contemporary Music, Mills College. Co-founder League of Automatic Music Composers, member of RotaLeague, founding member of Just Intonation Network and the Cactus Needle Project. Currently compiling texts toward a history of experimental music in northern California. Since 1976 has created interactive real-time computer music. —*"Blue" Gene Tyranny*

Simulated Winds and Cries / 1996 / Art ✦✦✦

Finally, an album of real-time, performer-manipulated computer works in various alternative tunings by one of the Bay Area's most delightfully creative composer/philosopher/visionaries. Selections include: "I Heard a Thousand Blended Notes" (title from a 1794 poem by William Wordsworth), "Simulated Winds and Cries" (1992) made from justly intoned sliding intervals selected by 1/f fractal patterns, "Some Pointillism" (1990), "Rebirth" (1990) in which "the computer, empty of suffering (running the language Formula), simulates high-speed attainment of Nirvana by playing (a) medieval Tibetan Buddhist game," and "Rave Patterns" (1992) created for a rave dance party that the police shut down before it got going ("... Thus was the underground confirmed in its oppositions.") The composer has this to says about the various pieces: "I like to imagine that they are precursors to uplifting, slightly alien musical A.I.s of the 21st century. Oh, how I hope and wish that contemporary cyber-culture will lead to a beautiful utopian compassionate world of Good!" —*"Blue" Gene Tyranny*

Toshio Hosokawa

b. Oct. 23, 1955, Hiroshima, Japan
Piano, Composer / 20th Century Classical/Modern Composition, World Fusion, Classical
The classical tradition has been combined with highly innovative imagination by Japan-born pianist and composer Toshio Hosokawa. The first place winner in a composition celebrating the one hundredth anniversary of the Berlin Philharmonic Orchestra in 1982, Hosokawa has continued to pave his own path. In an early-1990s interview, he explained that his music is "calligraphy with notes in space and time, notes that come from the world of silence and also return to it."

A native of Hiroshima, Hosokawa studied piano and composition in Tokyo as a teenager. He continued to study while living in West Berlin between 1976 and 1986. The artistic director of *the Akiyoshidai International Contemporary Music Seminar and Festival* since 1989, Hosokawa returned to live in his birthplace in 1994.

Hosokawa's masterpiece is his composition, "In Die Tiefe Der Zeit (Into The Depths Of Time)," written for cello and accordion. Initially featured on an album shares with avant garde composer John Cage, the piece was later featured on an album recorded by viola player Nobuko Imai and accordionist Mie Miki. According to Hosokawa, the viola "symbolizes the male principal, the accordion a sympathetic response to that voice, a fertile womb embracing it." —*Craig Harris*

Seeds of Contemplation (Mandara) for Shomyo and Gagaku Ensemble (1986) / Fragmente I Fo / 1990 / Fontec ✦✦✦

Two exquisitely spare compositions combining ancient court music gestures with matrix-combinatory European compositional techniques. Beautifully paced performances in the "breath" tempo of traditional Gagaku ensembles. Hosokawa studied with Isang Yun and Witold Szaloneck in (West) Berlin and has received commissions and prizes in Japan, Europe and the United States. His "pure" use of The Gagaku ensemble is different from Takemitsu's somewhat more romantic approach. For comparison with the tradition, listen to the still excellent *Gagaku: The Imperial Court Music Of Japan* by The Kyoto Imperial Court Music Orchestra, re-issued on CD on Lyrichord. —*"Blue" Gene Tyranny*

François Houle

Clarinet / Improvisation, Avant-Garde Jazz, Avant-Garde
François Houle is a creative and extremely active clarinetist, composer and improviser of avant-garde jazz and modern classical music. A Vancouver native, Houle has been an active developer of contemporary Canadian music during the '90s through his participation in Standing Wave and the Vancouver New Music Ensemble, among others. He has developed a personalized improvisational language, getting all manner of sounds from his instrument and its individual parts. Houle has performed with many extraordinary musicians, from Wayne Horvitz to Evan Parker, collaborated with composers including Paul Dolden, and released several albums on Canada's Songlines and Red Toucan labels. He is also involved in a trio, including guitarist Scott Fields and bassist Jason Roebke, which recorded *Hornet's Collage* (1999) for the Nuscope label. *Cryptology* followed in early 2001. In addition to his lively music career, Houle created graphic score settings of Catriona Strang's poems that were published by ECW Press & various North American poetry magazines. —*Joslyn Layne*

- **Hacienda** / Mar. 28, 1992 / Songlines ✦✦✦✦✦

In retrospect, this early recording led by avant-garde clarinetist François Houle surprises not only for its melodic content but also for its range of styles. Houle has developed a reputation as a refreshingly freestyle clarinetist and has produced a series of very fine albums. Here, he leads an all-Vancouver (Canada) septet called François Houle Et Cetera, with a talented four-horn front line backed by a piano-less trio. Each of the horns doubles or triples on other instruments, the result being tightly arranged pieces with the sound of a much larger group. Houle proves himself a formidable soprano saxophonist, in addition to a clarinetist, and the inclusion of alto sax, bass trombone, euphonium and tuba, among others, is revelatory. This is the sort of in-and-out performance that attractively incorporates multiple influences without sacrificing its soul. —*Steve Loewy*

- **In the Vernacular: The Music of John Carter** / Jul. 7, 1998 / Songlines ✦✦✦✦✦

One has the feeling that if Francois Houle played saxophone he might be a household name. Alas, it is his destiny to play the disfavored clarinet, but Houle performs with such consistent creativity that his improvisations have to be numbered among the supreme joys of modern jazz. Here, he leads an all-star quintet through the compositions of John Carter with splendid results. Carter was a clarinetist and writer of enormous depth, a true iconoclast; an original who followed his own path, merging sophisticated folk and jazz harmonies. Houle is joined by eclectic trumpeter Dave Douglas, new music cellist Peggy Lee, bassist Mark Dresser, and drummer Dylan van der Schyff in reinterpreting Carter's works. With that kind of talent, and with the extraordinary arranging skills of the leader, it should not be surprising that this one is as good as it is. —*Steven Loewy*

Au Coeur Du Litige / 2000 / Spool ✦✦✦✦

Very rarely does clarinetist François Houle produce a recording that is less than excellent, and this is no exception. Beautifully packaged, with extensive liner notes in French and English, this concept album is based on "The Great Ice Storm of '98" that afflicted Quebec. Using bilingual clips, electronics, tapes, prepared piano, along with some conventional instrumentation (including the leader's clarinets and flutes), Houle gently pulls the listener through collages of sound, pastels of layered figments, and coats of many colors. Distorted clarinet mixed with heavy synthesizers blend to give way to jumbled, confused voices. There is a majestic symphonic feeling at times, with its sheer beauty, but there are also moments of bleak, spare iciness, a reflection of the immediate emotions. Houle is superb on clarinet, as always, although his palette is broadened here with his attention to a panoply of diversionary offerings. It holds together well, even if it takes intense concentration to appreciate its secrets. —*Steven Loewy*

Alan Hovhaness (Alan Vaness Chakmakjian)

b. Mar. 8, 1911, Somerville, MA, **d.** Jun. 21, 2000, Seattle, WA
Liner Notes, Composer / 20th Century Classical/Modern Composition, World Fusion
A world view was incorporated into the symphonic compositions of Somerville, Massachusetts-born Alan Hovhaness (born: Alan Chakmakjian). While much of his music reflects his Armenian heritage, Hovhaness utilized elements of Indian ragas, Japanese gugaku music and natural sounds. Hovhaness' 1970 composition, "And God Created Great Whales," was composed for a full orchestra and the recorded song of a humpback whale.

Hovhaness began stirring controversy with his music during the 1930s. While many established musicians criticized his compositions, others praised him for his global approach. Although his "Symphony No. 1" was denounced by Leonard Bernstein as "filthy ghetto music", Hovhaness was embraced by such musicians as Leopold Stokowski who conducted the American premiere of his 1936 composition, "The Exile," inspired by the persecution and exile of Armenians in Turkey, and Andre Kostalanetz recorded his 1975 composition, "Rubiyat Of Omar Khayyam."

The son of Armenian and Scottish immigrants, Hovhaness composed his first pieces at the age of four. By the time he reached his teens, he was composing operatic works. As pianist and organist for a local Armenian church, he became known for his skill at improvising on ancient modes. He sharpened his compositional talents through study with Frederick Converse at the New England Conservatory of Music in Boston and Bohuslav Martinu at Tanglewood.

Hovhaness, who was given his professional name by his high school librettist, was extremely prolific. Although he destroyed many of his early compositions in 1940, the works that survived number in the hundreds. Among Hovhaness' best known compositions are "Lousadzak (The Coming Of Light)," written for piano and strings in 1945, "The Prayer Of Saint Gregory," written for trumpet and symphony orchestra in 1952, and, "Seventeen Prayers," written for oud, lute or guitar and string quartet or string orchestra in 1975. Hovhaness' composition, "Symphony No. 3" has been described as "a tribute to the Mozartian classical sonata form." He died June 21, 2000 at the age of 89. *—Craig Harris*

And God Created Great Whales (1970) for Orchestra and Whale Songs / Concerto No. 8 For / 1989 / Crystal ✦✦✦

A magnificently beautiful recording of an orchestra in an old abbey, *Alleluia and Fugue for String Orchestra* is one of Hovhaness' best-known works, a two-part composition from 1942. The "Alleluia" varies between parallel chords in rhythm, somewhat like a Russian Orthodox chant, with an Eastern European-influenced melismatic melody in imitative canon style. The effect is plaintive, praising with a restrained passion. The "Fugue" melody, first stated by the cellos, is likewise a melismatic, flowing creation. The voices develop in a classic fugue form, but there are few key modulations. At times, two or three voices are heard in high, angelic registers, and during the middle and end sections the entire string orchestra fills the air with a heartfelt richness of sound. This is classic 20th century music. *And God Created Great Whales* (1970) is for orchestra and the taped songs of whales, including humpback, bowhead, and killer whales. The piece begins with rushing sounds in the strings and a simple melody that emerges in the brass and high bells. The music becomes quieter, and a lovely and light pentatonic melody like a sea chantey occurs in the high winds and strings, with lovely harmonies beneath. Low tremulous strings appear and recede quietly while the sounds of whales are heard. The initial melody is played again above lower rushing string sounds, and then sliding trombones imitate the whales. The whale sounds return among a rolling, swelling timpani, random bells and harp glissandi, and staccato winds (suggesting "tiny sea creatures"). When the whales are next heard, the accompaniment includes high strings and rolling tympani, the simple sea chantey, and dissonant horns layered on top. Three gigantic waves of random sounds, the last with whale sounds, build and ebb, concluding the work. *—"Blue" Gene Tyranny*

★ **Lousadek (Dawn of Light), Op. 48 (1945) for Piano and Orchestra /Symphony No. 2, Op.132** / 1990 / Music Masters ✦✦✦✦✦

Performed by the American Composers Orchestra, Dennis Russell Davies conducting, with Keith Jarrett as piano soloist. Informed by the highly melliferous, floating melodic sense of Armenian song together with simple, refined orchestration, "Lousadek" is a lovely work that nearly caused a riot at its New York premiere as it innocently stepped on the mental toes of the academic chromaticists and the American nationalists in the audience. The symphony "Mysterious Mountain" combines many of the elements of Hovhaness' later style: parallel chordal passages of universal religious feeling (similar to Eastern Orthodox Church chanting), the treatment of canon and fugue in an entirely original manner (more of a variation form), quasi-random pizzicati and strange transparent bells on odd harmonics which suggest landscapes at long distances from civilization. Hovhaness is a prolific composer of nearly 500 compositions to date, but these two pieces will give the listener a good idea of his general instrumental approach. *—"Blue" Gene Tyranny*

Armenian Rhapsodies Nos. 1, 2, 3 / Symphony No. 38, Op. 314 (3rd and 4th mo / Koch ✦✦✦✦✦

The Hub

Group / Computer Music, Experimental, Avant-Garde

Electronic musicians John Bischoff, Chris Brown, Scot Gresham-Lancaster, Tim Perkis, and Phil Stone are the Hub—a band via their computer network of the same name which grew out of an earlier project of Bischoff's. The first computer network band, the League of Automatic Music Composers, was founded in the late '70s by Bischoff, Jim Horton, and Rich Gold. Their system didn't work as well when more musicians were connected, and changes to remedy this eventually led to the Hub. The group has been performing and recording since the mid-'80s and have several albums on the Artifact label; they have collaborated with Rova Saxophone Quartet and Alvin Curran, as heard on two cuts on *Wreckin' Ball*. *—Joslyn Layne*

The H.U.B. / 1989 / Artifact ✦✦✦✦✦

A totally new idea in live electronic music, the six composers of the Hub play computer music live by interacting with musically sensitive responses to each other's programs, the computers often physically connected through complex networks that make many aspects of their performances spontaneous—contains: John Bischoff's terrific "Perry Mason in East Germany," and Tim Perkis "Farabi," Chris Brown "Rol'Em", Phil Stone "Borrowing and Stealing," Scot Gresham-Lancaster "Whackers," Perkis Brown Stone "Hot Pig," Bischoff Perkis Trayle "Dovetail," Perkis "The Minister of Pitch," and Mark Trayle "Simple Degradation." *—"Blue" Gene Tyranny*

Jerry Hunt

b. Nov. 30, 1943, Waco, TX, **d.** Nov. 27, 1993, Canton, TX

Composer / Multimedia, 20th Century Classical/Modern Composition, Avant-Garde, Electronic

One of the most original composers of our time, Hunt, often creating scores of complex physical moves in space, made a concert into an occasion that re-creates music's role in divination of all countries and ages... for example, his "Sur John Dee" (1966) in John Cage's thought-provoking compilation "Notations"(1969, Something Else Press). Hunt was also an innovative computer systems designer and created mysterious alliances of computers and primal energy in his installation pieces (one a voodoo hut with computerized proximity detectors triggering electronic sounds for the New Music America festival in Houston). *—"Blue" Gene Tyranny*

★ **Fluud for Dual Synclaviers** / 1988 / Centaur ✦✦✦✦✦

Contained in the CDCM Computer Music series, *Vol. 1*, and composed in 1988, this otherworldly procedural score provides ceremonial moves for an audio-visual performance, and is based on Robert Fluud's "monochordum mundi syphiphoniacum" (1622). Templates of patterns are generated from the text, which give rise to sound-making gestures modulated by other isolated features of the text. This results in sound events like the mysterious ringing of small bells, sliding melodies, rhythmic shakings, and other unusual percussion patterns. One of the most original composers of our time, Hunt often created scores of complex physical moves in space, making a concert into an occasion that re-creates music's role in divination. Hunt was also an innovative computer systems designer and created mysterious alliances of computers and primal energy in his installation pieces (one a voodoo hut with computerized proximity detectors triggering electronic sounds for the New Music America festival in Houston). *—"Blue" Gene Tyranny*

Haramand Plane: Three Translation Links / 1994 / What Next? ✦✦✦

Lattice (1979) / Transform (Stream) (1977) / Cantegral Segment 18, 17 / Transphalba (19 / 1997 / CRI ✦✦✦

Jerry Hunt was a brilliant pianist and electronics designer, and, as a composer, created a unique musical terminology and sound vocabulary that enabled him to realize subtle musical and spiritual goals. This is the welcome CD re-release of highly innovative and engaging music that formerly appeared on two vinyl discs on Hunt's Irida label. "Lattice" is one of the root scores used to realize many of Hunt's performances, to form a "stream" as he would have termed it. Much of Hunt's music is built from the gradual transformation of repeated sounds, a kind of real-time signal analysis that in concert took on the appearance of mysterious ceremonies of evocation and conjuring. The piano realizations of the score produce a background resonance of non-harmonics. The "Cantegral Segments" (repeatable materials) are realized from a 1972 compositional procedure called "Haramand Plane: parallel/regenerative," which used signal analysis techniques. "Transform (stream)" is a transformation of "Cantegral Segment 16"—built on slow variations on the building-blocks of human speech—and "Cantegral Segment 7." In a concert performance, several voices independently respond to a soloist using many kinds of small percussive instruments. Combined with the breath sounds and human speech fragments, the result is one of great mystery and incantation. "Cantegral Segment 18" electronically emulates a collection of speech fragments, and "Cantegral Segment 17" produces changes in these electronic emulations. The sonic result is a fascinating journey among mysterious planes of electronically modified speech sound. "Cantegral Segment 19" consists of material for lip-vibrated aerophone in two versions, one for solo mechanical instrument and one for that instrument "in an electronically extended environment." "Cantegral Segment 16" uses the language structures of remote cultures, and formulates a context for the individual performer's vocal mechanism. In "Cantegral Segment 7," strange melismatic incantations punctuated by small percussive rattles and shakers hypnotize the listener. *—"Blue" Gene Tyranny*

● **Song Drapes** / Jun. 22, 1999 / Tzadik ✦✦✦✦✦

This intriguing release presents some of innovator Jerry Hunt's SongDrapes and Strings. "Strings" refers to Hunt's linear bits of transitional music that are open-ended and include an onomatopoeic influence. "SongDrapes" are the settings for vocal performance he created for his collaboration with performance artist Karen Finley, *the Finley-Hunt Report*, which was staged at New York City's *Kitchen* in 1992. This Tzadik release alternates instrumentals with readings, in all presenting seven SongDrapes—three without their accompanying vocals—and 12 Strings, some with vocals. Finley's performances are most powerful and transfixing, and are not for easily offended sensibilities. Also appearing are vocalists Shelley Hirsch, and on "Song Drape 7," Mike Patton. Jerry Hunt's soundscapes are unique, well-executed, and versatile. This posthumous release of a series of his works provides an important volume, be it introduction or addition, in the lineage of true originals. *—Joslyn Layne*

David Hykes

b. Mar. 2, 1953, Taos, NM

Vocals, Composer / Ambient, World Fusion, Choral

The work of David Hykes focuses on a few throat singing traditions, including Mongolian and Tuvan. In 1975, he combined this singing form and the harmonic series, and five years later founded his Harmonic Awareness practice in meditation. While Hykes was born in New Mexico in 1953, he grew up in the Northwest and lived in N.Y.C. from the mid-'70s through the late '80s. Beginning in the arts in performance and as a filmmaker, Hykes eventually moved toward composition and teaching meditation. He has recorded almost ten CDs with his Harmonic Choir. *—Joslyn Layne*

Hearing Solar Winds / 1983 / Ocora ✦✦✦

An extended choral work made from Hoomi singing of western Mongolia and the overtone chanting of Tantric Buddhism. Spectacular shimmering surfaces (overtones from clusters of fundamentals beating against each other) and other effects. Some titles are "Multiplying Voices at the Heart of the Body of Sound, " "Gravity Waves" and "Rainbow Voice." *—"Blue" Gene Tyranny*

Harmonic Meetings / 1986 / Celestial Harmonies ✦✦✦

1990 A re-issue of the two-disc set on CD. Lovely as always. *—"Blue" Gene Tyranny*

Current Circulation / 1992 / Celestial Harmonies ✦✦✦

A re-issue of the well-known 1984 album. More like single studies of the singing techniques. Includes "Free Ascents, " "Subject to Change, " "Ascending Mount Summation." *—"Blue" Gene Tyranny*

● **Earth to the Unknown Power** / 1996 / Catalyst/BMG ✦✦✦

With the Harmonic Choir. Four lovely, spiritual, meditative vocal compositions. *Flight of Prayer, Brotherhood Returning, Le Souffle du Seigneur,* and *Earth to the Unknown Power*. *—"Blue" Gene Tyranny*

Toshi Ichiyanagi

b. Feb. 4, 1933, Kobe, Japan

Composer / 20th Century Classical/Modern Composition, Avant-Garde, World Fusion, Classical

Toshi Ichiyanagi is one of Japan's most imaginative composers. Inspired by the avant garde works of John Cage, Ichiyanagi has consistently found new ways to express his musical vision. His 1960 composition, "Kaiki," combined Japanese instruments, sho and koto, and western instruments, harmonica and saxophone. His 1967 piece, "Extended Voices" was written for a chorus accompanied by Moog and Buchla synthesizers. "Orchestral Space," recorded in 1978 by the Yomiuri Nippon Symphony Orchestra conducted by Seiji Ozawa, was composed for electronic modulators, magnetic tape and orchestra. Ichiyanagi's most eccentric piece might be "Music For Piano *5: Fluxvariation,"* featuring darts thrown into the back of a piano. Ichiyanagi, who studied in New York at the Julliard School of Music and the New School for Social Research, was the recipient of the Serge Koussevitzky prize at the Berkshire Music Camp. *—Craig Harris*

Solo Compositions / 1991 / Camerata ✦✦✦

Includes "Cloud Figures for Solo Oboe"; "Hoshi-No-Wa" for sho; "Scenes III for Solo Violin"; "Time Sequence for Piano". Lovely pieces by the composer who introduced much of new music to Japan by organizing concerts and exhibitions of graph music, and whose early pieces such as "Kaiki" (1960) for sho, organ, koto, harmonica and saxophone, and early theatre music works, such as "Sapporo" (1963) are classics. See also his work "Extended Voices" in the collection *Extended Voices. —"Blue" Gene Tyranny*

Violin Concerto "Junkansuru Fukei" (Circulating Scenery) / 1994 / Camerata ✦✦✦

Performed at *the Min-On Contemporary Music Festival* with Paul Zukofsky, violin, and the Tokyo Philharmonic Orchestra conducted by Tadaaki Otaka, this dramatic concerto in three movements was composed in 1983, and is described by Ichiyanagi as a "violin solo with an orchestra attached." The title *Circulating Scenery* is applicable to the concerto's evocative, mysteriously rotating patterns of "memory... linked with a scene." Sometimes impressionistically cloudy, sometimes rhythmically propulsive patterns continuously segue into new and unexpected territories. The complex and virtuosic solo violin writing provides lyrical and at times impassioned commentaries on evoked memories. The orchestration is a rich palette with the depth of an Alban Berg score and the transparencies of the best contemporary composers, such as Takemitsu. But Ichiyanagi's voice is unique and convincing. This concerto and the five pieces for violin and piano from the years 1976 through 1982 form a new departure into narrative music for a composer previously involved with more Cage-ian influences. However, his earlier works always possessed the internal dramatics externalized by this 1983 concerto. Ichiyanagi was also responsible for bringing much European and American new music to Japan in the 1960s by organizing concerts and exhibitions of graph music. His late-'80s solo works and larger pieces also provide engaging listening. *—"Blue" Gene Tyranny*

● **Cosmos of Toshi Ichiyanagi** / 1995 / Camerata ✦✦✦

A wonderful overview of the composer's chamber instrumental work ranging from his lyrical to conceptual compositions. Includes: "Paganini Personal" for marimba and piano, "Flowers Blooming in Summer" for harp and piano, "Two Existences" for 2 pianos, "Scenes II" for violin and piano, and the splendid "Cloud Atlas" for piano. In the series "New Aspect of Japanese Music—3." *—"Blue" Gene Tyranny*

Charles Ives

b. Oct. 20, 1874, Danbury, CT, **d.** May 19, 1954, New York, NY

Composer / 20th Century Classical/Modern Composition, Classical

Highly original American composer of orchestral, chamber, and solo vocal and piano music who used and anticipated polytonality, atonality, and polymeter/polytone clusters. A unique quality of his music is the combination of well-known hymns and popular tunes with a complex dissonant accompaniment. Notable works include *Three Places in New England* (1914) and the *Sonata for Piano no. 2, "Concord, Mass"* (1920). *—Mary K. Scanlan*

The Orchestral Music of Charles Ives / 1990 / Koch ✦✦✦

With The Orchestra New England conducted by J. Sinclair. Includes: *Calcium Night Light,* "Country Band" March, *Largo Cantabile, Postlude in F, Set for Theatre Orchestra, Set of Four Ragtime Dances, Three Places in New England,* and *the Yale-Princeton Football Game...* great performances... collection does not include other orchestra works like the "Orchestral Set No. 2" (probably the best performance of this was Stokowski conducting The London Symphony Orchestra on the out-of-print disc London Records SPC 21060), or the visionary "Tone Roads"... twelve-tone music written many years before that technique found its way from Europe to the States. *—"Blue" Gene Tyranny*

● **Symphony #4 (1910-16) / Robert Browning Overture (1908-12), Songs: an Election; Lincol** / 1991 / Sony Classical Masterworks ✦✦✦✦✦

With Leopold Stokowski conducting The American Symphony Orchestra, and The Gregg Smith Singers. A magnificent transcendental vision of life... performed with full spirit by Stokowski's orchestra with attention to the polyrhythms, transparent "memory" textures, harmonic layerings, etc. of Ives completely innovative writing. The songs, especially "Lincoln, the Great Commoner" with its amazing tone-cluster glissandos for voices and strings, are a perfect complement to the Symphony. *—"Blue" Gene Tyranny*

The Complete Piano Music of Charles Ives / Voxbox ✦✦✦

A welome re-issue on CDs of the marvellous performances by pianist Alan Mandel. Includes the two Sonatas, masterpieces of 20th-century music, and the shorter works *The Three-Page Sonata, Song Without (Good) Words, Baseball Take-off, The Seen and Unseen,* and many of the *Studies,* and other works. *—"Blue" Gene Tyranny*

Ives Plays Ives / Record # 4 in "Charles Ives, the 100th Anniversary" / Columbia ✦✦✦

This out-of-print 5 disc set is a treasure of music and memoribilia. Ives playing spontaneously (improvising) on published and unpublished material/ideas... reveals the creative process in its searching mode (apart from the necessary structural work), with Ives enthusiastically letting his hands discover what cannot be pre-conceived. Especially remarkable are the so-called "X, Y, Z Improvisations". *—"Blue" Gene Tyranny*

☆ **Unanswered Question (1908) / Central Park in the Dark (1898-1907) / "Holidays" Symphony** / CBS ✦✦✦✦✦

This recording by The Chicago Symphony is particularly interesting because both the original and revised versions of "The Unanswered Question" are performed... the dissonant flute-clusters and trumpet theme are played completely free of the consonant, serene chords of the strings in the original version... another of Ives' innovations. *—"Blue" Gene Tyranny*

Terry Jennings

b. Jul. 19, 1940, Eagle Rock, CA, **d.** Dec. 11, 1981, San Pablo, CA

Composer / 20th Century Classical/Modern Composition, Avant-Garde

Modern avant-garde composer Terry Jennings is one of the founders of minimalist keyboard music, whose best known works include "Winter Trees." He was deeply involved in the style and ideas of his main influence, so that when his name and work comes up, discussion of his teacher La Monte Young is not far away.

Born in 1940 in Eagle Rock, CA, Jennings showed a predilection for music at a young age, and began studying piano before he enrolled in elementary school. He studied the compositions of John Cage before reaching his teens, and arranged music for his junior high school's band. Jennings went on to study music with La Monte Young, as well as Robert Erickson, and saxophone with William Green, and was composing by the late '50s. Following in the footsteps of Young's earlier work, Jennings explored what became known as minimalism: prolonged tones and spaces with repetitive patterns (to simplify in lieu of a more thorough definition here). La Monte Young also gave him what could be called his first big break, opening an avant-garde concert series in New York with works by Jennings. His work—which is not all for piano—has gone on to be performed (by musicians including Young, Jon Gibson, Cornelius Cardew, and Peter Garland) all over the U.S. and Europe in the decades since.

In early '60s NY, Jennings became part of Young's Dream Syndicate/Theater of Eternal Music, performing and recording with Young, Tony Conrad, Marian Zazeela, John Cale, and Angus MacLise (the latter two went on to the Velvet Underground from here), but eventually relocated back to the West Coast, where he taught Harold Budd, among others. He continued to compose through the '70s, and died in San Pablo, CA in December, 1981. *—Joslyn Layne*

☆ **Terry's G Dorian 12-Bar Blues (9 X 5) + 3 (1962)/ in "Jon Gibson"** / 1992 / Point ✦✦✦✦✦

Gibson on sax with two synthesizers and percussion. Terry Jennings was one of the first players on any wind instrument to play multi-phonic chords, which are produced by a combination of unusual fingering and overblowing. Classics of extended time-sense music, his ethereally beautiful piano music and especially the remarkable "String Quartet" (September 1960) (see score in La Monte Young's *An Anthology*) have yet to be recorded. *—"Blue" Gene Tyranny*

Scott Johnson

b. May 12, 1952, Madison, WI

Guitar, Composer / 20th Century Classical/Modern Composition, Minimalism

American composer and guitarist Scott Johnson incorporates modern instrumentation such as the electric guitar into his works. The New York-based composer started out in Wisconsin, where he was raised, and studied visual arts at the University. In addition to his major, Johnson played in local rock bands and took music theory courses during this time. After relocating to N.Y.C. in 1975, he focused solely on visual arts for a few years before his music interest was re-ignited by working on a sound sculpture. Johnson has gone on to compose works for ensembles including Kronos Quartet ("How It Happens"), and the Scott Johnson Ensemble. He has toured Europe and North America both with his ensemble and on solo tours. "John Somebody" is the most acclaimed of his compositions, which have been recorded for the Point Music and Nonesuch labels. *—Joslyn Layne*

John Somebody / 1986 / Elektra/Nonesuch ✦✦✦✦✦

"Remember that guy... John Somebody— ... He was a... sort of a b'..." asks the repeating master tape loop of a woman's voice, as other smaller loops join in, and then pop jazz instrumental figures imitate the rhythm and add funky melodies and cross-rhythms (built on the smaller samples of the loop) in accumulating levels which suddenly break and start again with interpretations of the loops. We find ourselves tapping our feet and wanting to dance. An original and appealing album where Johnson clearly demonstrates for his listeners the relation between ordinary speech and musical rhythms. Speech in this case also includes the laughter of "Involuntary Songs". "No Memory" is also built on this speech sampling idea but is more complex in its modulation of both the loop sounds and the layering of the more chromatic instrumental phrases. *—"Blue" Gene Tyranny*

● **Confetti of Flesh in Dora Ohrenstein "Urban Diva"** / 1993 / CRI ✦✦✦

A sensual rhapsody about New York City living with text by Jayne Cortez (" i am new york city of blood police and fried pies"), this chamber piece shows Johnson in a more melodious and somewhat more "uptown" mode than in his previous compositions, the whole texture grown from a three-note motive, but still with an underlying hip beat. Beautifully performed. *—"Blue" Gene Tyranny*

Tom Johnson

b. Nov. 18, 1939, Greeley, CO

Piano, Composer / 20th Century Classical/Modern Composition, Minimalism

Village Voice music critic and modern composer Tom Johnson has published two books, and created over 70 musical works, including for piano (1971's "An Hour for Piano"), with text (1987's "Eggs and Baskets"), for radio ("J'Entends un Choeur," 1993), and, most notably, opera. After obtaining his undergraduate and master's degrees from Yale, Johnson studied some with composer Morton Feldman, and has since composed for a variety of settings. His most highly regarded opera, "The Four Note Opera," has gone on to be performed dozens of times, and in a number of languages, since its 1972 premiere. Another oft-performed work is "Failing: A Difficult Piece for Solo String Bass," which requires the performer to speak throughout the already-challenging composition. While living in New York, Tom Johnson wrote about modern composition for *The Village Voice* from 1972-1982, before moving to Paris, which has been his home since 1983. His articles for the New York paper can be found in the book *The Voice of New Music* (Apollohuis, 1991). Johnson also wrote a book on his music theories, -Self-Similar Melodies (Editions 75, 1996). *—Joslyn Layne*

An Hour for Piano / 1985 / Lovely Music ♦♦♦
A terrific and intense performance by composer-performer Frederic Rzewski on piano of this trance music piece made up of repeating 4/4 cells in which an absolutely steady eight-note motion predominates, resulting in large-scale shifts in density and tonality over the time span. *— "Blue" Gene Tyranny*

● **Music for 88** / 1993 / Experimental Intermedia ♦♦♦
Just the disc to give to those people who remark inquisitively about the relationship of music and mathematics. Johnson actually explains out front before and at times during each piece about the math being used, and at times how musicians and mathematicians differ in their views. Many charming and lovely minimalist pieces for voice and very well recorded piano with sometimes unintentionally droll humor. A very original piece (as in "why didn't I think of that—"). (See also his piece "Failing: A Very Difficult Piece for Solo Bass" in *Bang on a Can Live, Vol. 1* in collections.) *— "Blue" Gene Tyranny*

Rational Melodies (1982) / 1993 / hatART ♦♦♦
Lovely conceptual pieces performed by Eberhard Blum on piccolo, flute, alto flute, bass flute. *— "Blue" Gene Tyranny*

Ben Johnston

b. Mar. 15, 1926, Macon, GA
Composer / Microtonal, 20th Century Classical/Modern Composition
Studied with Darius Milhaud, Harry Partch, Burrill Phillips, Robert Palmer, John Cage. Professor of theory and composition at University of Illinois. Selected works: *Somewhere i have never traveled* (1949) for tenor and piano, *Knocking Piece Collage* (1969) for tape, *In Memory, Harry Partch, 1975* (1975) for soprano, computer tape, tape, string quartet, eight percussionists, and slide show, *Suite for Microtonal Piano* (1978), *Twelve Partials* (1980) for flute and microtonal piano. *— "Blue" Gene Tyranny*

★ **Amazing Grace (String Quartet No. 4) 1973** / 1991 / Elektra/Nonesuch ♦♦♦♦♦
Heart-rendingly beautiful microtonal setting with variations on this traditional melody played by The Kronos Quartet. It is also called the "String Quartet No. 4" on out-of-print vinyl Gasparo GS-205, where it is played in more accurate tuning by The Fine Arts Quartet. *— "Blue" Gene Tyranny*

Calamity Jane to Her Daughter / in Dora Ohrenstein "Urban Diva" / 1993 / CRI ♦♦♦
With a text based on a section from a disputed diary (which includes a receipe for a "20 year cake") that may or may not be the authentic account of the historical Calamity Jane's secret marriage to James Butler (Wild Bill) Hickok, Johnston spins a wonderfully melodious vocal line in just intonation with beautiful consonances and dissonances amongst the accompanying instruments. *— "Blue" Gene Tyranny*

Ponder Nothing: Chamber Music of Ben Johnston / 1993 / New World ♦♦♦
Compelling works in just intonation played by Music Amici: "Septet," "Three Chinese Lyrics," "Gambit," "Five Fragments," "Trio," and "Ponder Nothing" for clarinet solo. *— "Blue" Gene Tyranny*

Mauricio Kagel

b. Dec. 24, 1931, Buenos Aires, Argentina
Composer / 20th Century Classical/Modern Composition, Classical
Born in Buenos Aires, Argentina, Kagel proved to be one of the most versatile, creative and witty composers to come of age in the second half of the 20th century. He studied piano, theory, violoncello, organ, singing, and conducting, and was self-taught as a composer. Kagel also studied philosophy and literature extensively during his college years, and his career eventually included film and drama.

His early career found Kagel filling positions that drew upon all of these interests. He took a position in Colón as conductor of the Chamber Opera and Theater, also conducting new-music concerts in the late '50s. The 1960s found Kagel in the United States, where he undertook a lecture tour and taught briefly at the University of Buffalo. He then returned to Europe, where he filled Stockhausen's shoes as the director of the Institute of New Music at the Rheinsiche Musikschule. He was also a presence at the West German Radio electronic music studio, and produced several of his own films and plays.

One can find in Kagel's output elements ranging from serialism to expressionism to musique concrete to Dada to aleatoria. Many of his works also employ musical collage techniques, such as his "Music for Renaissance Instruments" and the music for the film *Ludwig Van.* The influence of Satie and Cage can be seen in "Der Schall" and "Unter Strom," two chamber pieces which call for a variety of archaic, invented, or "nonmusical" instruments. Again, however, these sounds are not thrown together with reckless abandon; as Kagel himself stated, "An essential aspect of my work is strict composition with elements which are not themselves pure." *—J. Neal*

Quodlibet / 1991 / Col Legno ♦♦♦
Composed between 1986 and 1988, this work is scored for female voices and orchestra. Introduced toward the middle of the 16th century, the "quodlibet" vocal music form was a collage or compression of melodies currently in fashion. Kagel recalls one example 58 measures long that contained fragments of 39 songs, "a kind of Reader's Digest for the listeners of the time" (Kagel). This was also related to the practices of "disputations of quodlibet," an exercise of rhetoric on subjects chosen at random at the Sorbonne during the Renaissance. By employing French song texts of the 15th century, Kagel is able to present a social overview and analysis of that time with all its contradictions, not so different from ours—chastity is valued but matters of the heart and "virtuous sensuality" are equally praised, chivalry is highlighted but that is also used to excuse political wrangling and weapon making (arms development). Love and dream texts are interwoven with martial texts. The complex, dissonant yet melodic and highly entertaining Weill-like music exaggerates the sentimentality and the martiality into grotesque and humorous portraits. *— "Blue" Gene Tyranny*

★ **String Quartet I (1965-67) / Pan (1985) for Piccolo and String Quartet / String Quarte** / 1991 / Disques Montaigne ♦♦♦♦♦
Played with great sensitivity by the Arditti String Quartet. The marvelous first and second quartets take some late Bartok string techniques (snap string, tremolos of bow wood (col legno) rebounding off strings, non-vibrato glassy textures, etc.) to the max (maximum bow "crunch," random pizzicato, playing on the wood of the instrument, etc.) and beyond, treating the quartet compositionally like electronic music—at turns mysterious, dramatic, and lyrical. With scale-like fragments and operatic "bird" figures, "Pan" seems to reset "The Magic Flute." The third quartet, like "Pan," contains elements of past musical gestures treated for their sound value (not as quotes or satire), combined with techniques from the first quartets—all this makes for a very original music. *— "Blue" Gene Tyranny*

Der Tribun (The Tribune) / . . . Nach Einer Lektüre Von Orwell (. . . After a Lecture by Orw / 1996 / Wergo ♦♦♦
Two brilliant and insightful satiric political works. *The Tribune* (1979) is scored "für einer politischen Redner, Marschklänge und Lautsprecher" (for a political orator, march sounds and loudspeaker). *. . . After a lecture by Orwell* was composed later in 1984. *— "Blue" Gene Tyranny*

Staats Theater (1967-70) / Deutsche Grammaphon ♦♦♦
Kagel takes apart the apparatus of the State Theater of operas, plays, and other spectacles and examines in detail the images and sounds you are presented with apart from plot, libretto, and subject matter. Not a satire but a surreal concentration. Many of Kagel's original instruments and sound-making devices (listen to "Akustica" (1968-1970), a two-disc set on Deutsche Grammaphon, if you can find a copy) are used, both for the sound they make and because of their symbolic value: a steel strip partially strapped to the player's feet (he is part of the circuit) is in the form of a Mobius loop which is associated with getting from one side, the "real," to the other side, "the figurative," without going over the edge, likewise, tape music, choral and operatic ensembles, stage sets (Wagner-ian to pop art large soda bottles) and stock characters (The Barber, The Imaginary Invalid, Amor, and the troubadour Knight) and stock themes (Concern, Virginity, Iron Curtain, Investigation, Nighttime), movement (Contradance), the players in the pit, performers calisthenics for keeping in shape, and even the resultant waste paper of programs and notices are all presented in their physical and imaginary contexts. *— "Blue" Gene Tyranny*

Udo Kasemets

b. Nov. 16, 1919, Tallinn, Estonia
Composer / Process-Generated, 20th Century Classical/Modern Composition, Electro-Acoustic
Music reviewer for *Toronto Daily Star* (63), organizer multi-media and new music performances at Issacs Gallery (1965-67), director "Sightsoundsystems" festival (1968) a branch of Experiments in Art and Technology (E.A.T., New York). Taught sound studies at Ontario College of Art (1970-87). Influenced by ideas of John Cage, Marshall McLuhan and Buckminster Fuller. *— "Blue" Gene Tyranny*

Timetrip to Big Bang, Big Bang and Back / 1993 / Artifact Music ♦♦♦
Subtitled "A sonic celestial voyage from here and now to the end of the universe and from the beginning of time a sonic cosmological journey to here and now," this music attempts, quite literally, to describe in electro-acoustic sound the ultimate trip (at least as far as science can conceive). "Part One: Astronomics" "is based on the premise that when we look at the night sky, we see TIME . . . in Part One we travel from EARTH and NOW . . . at ever-accelerating speed until we arrive at the limit of the universe where there is NOTHING ON THE OTHER SIDE: NO SPACE, NO TIME." (Kasemets, his emphasis). In "Part Two: Big Band or Turning the TimeGlove Inside Out," in order to return "we take our imaginary glove of time—the five fingers . . . pointed . . . to the five phases of our trip (via the moon, the planets, the comets, the stars and the galaxies)—and turn it inside out . . . (to) follow time's forward motion through five phases of cosmological evolution." The concluding "Part Three: Chaosmosis" ". . . charts the course of the emergence of cosmic life from the beginnings of nuclear evolution through the pivotal fusions of the chemical evolution to the structuring of the DNA double-helix and the formation of the protein chain. Quite a program (!) but it is achieved through a thorough-going structural minaturization of the stages of the journey, and by use of deceptively simple musical means." This is a piece to study in detail. *— "Blue" Gene Tyranny*

Jin Hi Kim

b. 1957, Inchon, Korea
Electric Komungo, Komungo / Computer Music, 20th Century Classical/Modern Composition, World Fusion
Studied komungo, a zither of six silk strings most often used for meditation of male Confucian scholars, at an early age, breaking tradition where most girls study kayagum, a brighter, more popular zither. Studied at Seoul National University, electronic music and composition at Mills College. Has worked with Derek Bailey, Bill Frisell, Oliver Lake, Elliott Sharp, Eugene Chadbourne. Co-founder No World Improvisations quartet. Designed electric version of komungo, and MIDI-version of changgo, a Korean percussion instrument in collaboration with Danny Ferrington. Collaborated on computer music works. Several awards and commissions. *— "Blue" Gene Tyranny*

Living Tones / 1995 / O.O. Discs ♦♦♦
Four elegantly composed and expressively played compositions influenced by Korean music

and conceptual music. *Nong Rock* (1992) for komungo and string quartet employs many shaken, sliding, multiple vibratos to move the tones, giving the sense of each sound being a living being. Midway through, the music employs a more steady, rock & roll-influenced texture, almost as an interlude. Then the tonalities become cosmic. A thoroughly engaging, deeply felt work. *Tchong* (1995) for daegum and flutes is built from a haunting series of calls. *Yoeum* (1995) for kagok singer and baritone is a moving duet with incidental harmonies, subtle overtones, and contrasting vocal styles. The ancient and eternal are expressed in the nobility of the music. *Piri Quartet* (1993) for three piri (reed flutes) and oboe/English horn is simply intense and wonderful, with the combined piri suggesting the Japanese sho of courtly Gagaku music, and the Western reeds providing an almost electronic artificial harmonic texture. At times, the winds flit like birds among the trees and sometimes they wail (with joy—with hurt—) definitely from the heart. A great CD. *—"Blue" Gene Tyranny*

Guy Klucevsek

b. Feb. 26, 1948

Accordion / Avant-Garde Jazz, Klezmer, Minimalism, World Fusion, Modern Creative

Accomplished accordionist and composer Guy Klucevsek has stunned audiences around the world with his mastery of the unwieldy instrument in jazz- and world-influenced avant-garde concerts. Included on compilations from Tzadik's Burt Bacharach tribute, to the more mainstream Ellipsis Arts release *Planet Squeezebox*, Klucevsek has also led nearly ten of his own recordings for labels including Ewa and CRI. He has composed extensively for modern dance, and was awarded a BESSIE in 1995 for the score for "Hey" by choreographer David Dormanis. Since at least the mid-'80s, Klucevsek has performed and recorded with a variety of creative musicians such as John Zorn, Bill Frisell, Anthony Braxton, and Kronos Quartet. In 1996, he co-founded Accordion Tribe with master accordionists from around the world including Maria Kalaniemi (Finland) and Bratko Bibic (Slovenia). In 1998, *Accordion Tribe* came out on Intuition, and Winter & Winter released an album by another new group with Klucevsek, Dave Douglas' new project *Charms of the Night Sky*, with Klucevsek, bassist Greg Cohen, and violinist Mark Feldman. While Accordion Tribe could only get together for the rare festival appearance, the *Charms of the Night Sky* group toured North America and Europe for parts of the next three years, and recorded *A Thousand Evenings* for RCA. Klucevsek has also performed solo at festivals all over the world, and can be heard providing music accompaniment on the audio book version of *Accordion Crimes*, a novel by E. Annie Proulx. *—Joslyn Layne*

• **Manhattan Cascade** / Apr. 1991 / Composers ✦✦✦✦✦

A marvellous, uplifting concert of twisted tunes and new uses for the "free bass accordion" containing Mary Ellen Childs' charming Pygmymusic-like "Oa Poa Polka", Anthony Coleman's plaintive "Below 14th Street, Above 125th Street", Rolf Groesbeck's tone cluster and conjuring "Polka 1", Aaron Kernis's cinematic joke "Phantom Polka" (Kernis is also a composer of some brilliant orchestral music, watch for future recordings), John King's hymn-based "All Together Now", Guy Klucevsek's "Samba D Hiccup" and the lovely "An Air of Gathering Pipers", Christian Marclay's "Ping Pong Polka" with wildly modulated record collage, Lois Vierk's "Manhattan Cascade" (see review under composers), and John Zorn's humorous "Road Runner". *—"Blue" Gene Tyranny*

• **Stolen Memories** / Aug. 20, 1996 / Tzadik ✦✦✦✦

World-renowned master accordionist Guy Klucevsek joins with the string trio Bantam Orchestra on his original compositions, some of which were commissioned for dance companies. The album opens with a breathing, dirge-like piece, followed by one with more of a gypsy feel. "Wave Hill" is peaceful, with an overlapping, repeating melody—a seeming precursor to a tune Klucevsek would later play on Dave Douglas' *Charms of the Night Sky*, "Sea Change." The next piece, "Tesknota," written in memory of John Cage, is beautiful and meditative, with erhu-like string work and introspective slides and drones. The mood and pace lift considerably for the title track, and the closing piece features a string whistle call-and-response across a lake of accordion. Filled with beautiful instrumentals—except for the unnecessary, goofball song "Donut Ask, Donut Tell"—Klucevsek's *Stolen Memories* is a strong offering from a premier music maker. *—Joslyn Layne*

Gottfried Michael Koenig

b. Oct. 5, 1926, Magdeburg, Germany

Composer / Musique Concrète, Computer Music, Atonal, Electronic

Composing and generating sound via computer technology as early as the mid-'60s, Gottfried Michael Koenig was a pivotal force in cementing the emerging relationship between music and electronics. Born in Magdeburg, Germany in 1926, Koenig studied composition at the Detmold School of Music before relocating to Bonn, where he pursued his interest in computer engineering. Between 1954 and 1964, he worked alongside Karlheinz Stockhausen at the electronic music studios of the Westdeutscher Rundfunk (WDR) in Cologne, collaborating with other aspiring composers including György Ligeti and Mauricio Kagel; in 1956, Koenig completed his first major electronic piece, *Klangfiguren II*, followed a year later by *Essay*.

During the early '60s, Koenig began writing a program—named simply Project 1, or PR1—designed to compose and generate music via the computer; when in 1964 he accepted the position of creative director with the Institute for Sonology in Utrecht, Holland, he took the software with him, putting on the finishing touches three years later. While at Utrecht, Koenig also began experimenting with the Variable Function Generator, a machine developed by physics student Stan Templaars able to generate sound using roughly the same technology as an analog sequencer. Hitting upon the idea of treating the VFG as an oscillator, between 1967 and 1969 Koenig used the machine to compose a series of groundbreaking pieces known collectively as the *Funktionen*.

In 1968, Koenig also began work on a second program, PR2; its complicated design made it difficult to use, however, and so PR1 remained his primary outlet for computerized composition. He continued tinkering with PR1 for years to follow, in 1978 introducing VOSIM oscillators to the project to create an extended program christened PRIX; a series of subsequent additions resulted in another upgrade, PRIXM, and the completion of 1979's *Output*. When the Institute of Sonology was relocated to the Hague in 1986, Koenig retired from his post to focus full-time on computerized composition as well as developing new musical programs; in 1991, he also published the first in a series of theoretical writings titled *Aesthetic Practice*. *—Jason Ankeny*

• **Langfiguren II (Soundfigures 2) (1955-56)/ Essay (1957-58)/ Terminus 1 (1962) / Termin** / 1990 / BVHaast ✦✦✦✦✦

This collection of material by electronic pioneer Gottfried Michael Koenig includes three classic pieces, *Langfiguren II, Essay* and *Terminus*. It's classic pointillistic electronic music. *—"Blue" Gene Tyranny*

Jill Kroesen

b. 1949

Composer, Multi-Media, Vocals / Multimedia, Musical Theater, Avant-Garde

Performer and writer Jill Kroesen has not only participated in a number of rock bands and avant-garde productions, but has also produced original music theater works and written for independent publications. In the mid-'70s, after earning her M.F.A. at Mills College (where she studied with Terry Riley and Robert Ashley), Kroesen moved to N.Y.C. There, she worked briefly in Rhys Chatham's group before focusing on her own musical theater works and performance art works. Other performing credits include a role in Robert Ashley's early-'80s opera-for-TV project +Perfect Lives, and her own recording for Lovely Music, *Stop Vicious Cycles*. Kroesen's work in graphic and visual arts led to her receiving a video fellowship from the New York Foundation for the Arts in 1985, after which she continued her work as a video engineer. *—Joslyn Layne*

Stop Vicious Cycles / 1982 / Lovely Music ✦✦✦

Like the albums of Ned Sublette and Laurie Anderson, this disc presents only the songs that make up part of the material for her extended and inventive performance pieces. Jill Kroesen, a performer as intense as Diamanda Galas and Lydia Lunch but more flexible, has made stage works, including a ballet *The Lou and Walter Story*, that reduce historical and social icons, like Alexander the Great and even *The History of the World* as an icon in itself, to the personal and emotional, thereby stripping away much of the pomposity and abstraction that often accompanies the cant of the historical imperative—one European fan said to her "You try to make everything so simple whereas we try to make everything complex." These songs with a beat also make use of electronic and acoustic noise, free-style brass playing, bizarre percussion and mixing, and a totally new approach to the idea of pitched/non-pitched singing. Some of the pieces are "I'm Sorry I'm Such a Weenie," "I Am Not Seeing That You Are Here," "I'm Just a Human Being" ("I'm just a human being who can hardly keep her own house clean. And I lie in bed and think how the president is just a human being and it scares me to think about the life he leads"), "Alexander the Great" ("... I want to travel all around and get lost conquering everybody's ground. And send plunder to my mother and kill my threatening brother, I'm Alexander and I'm pretty and I ain't in no hurry to get home"), and the legendary "Fay Shism Blues." *—"Blue" Gene Tyranny*

Philip Krumm

b. Apr. 7, 1941

Composer / 20th Century Classical/Modern Composition, Avant-Garde, Electronic

Studied with Raymond Moses, and Frank Sturchio at St. Mary's University, Rackham Graduate School at University of Michigan with Ross Lee Finney. Comp. with Karlheinz Stockhausen at UC Davis, CA. Presented new music festivals at McNay Art Institute with *"Blue" Gene Tyranny* in late '50s, early '60s. Traveled with ONCE Group, appeared with Yoko Ono, George Brecht, Terry Jennings at Carnegie Hall. Tours with Jerry Hunt, including Roger Shattuck's Pataphysics Festival in Austin, TX. Host for ten years of radio show *Musica Nova* on Texas Public Radio. Owner of Clipper Ship Book Store in San Antonio, TX since 1982. *—"Blue" Gene Tyranny*

• **Sound Machine (1966) in "Texas Music"** / 1979 / Irida ✦✦✦✦✦

An electronic but somehow also a living being with a gently insistent pulse (or is it a purr—) that sometimes emits quasi-random tiny beeps and sighs. A lovely short piece from the composer of much innovative music: "Music for Clocks" (for multiple clock/metronomes and orchestra composed several years before Ligeti's "Poeme Symphonique" (1965) for 100 metronomes and before Ichiyanagi's "Music for Electronic Metronome" (1961) was published), the "Piano Variations" (all on one C chord, the "variations" are in fingering changes which affect the pressure and consequently the timbre of the chord), the outer space "Formations" (score of heavenly lattices), and much more. *—"Blue" Gene Tyranny*

Concerto for Bass Clarinet / Opus One ✦✦✦

In the collection *The Orchestra According to the Seven*. Performed by soloist Scott Vance, with the University of Redlands Chamber Ensemble, conducted by Barney Childs. Composed in 1964, this unique conceptual work has received many performances since that time. Each of the instrumental parts, written in innovative notation, are in large formats, about four feet by six feet, and are placed on the floor, so that all the players except for the soloist and the pianist move about while playing the piece. Surreal artificial harmonics and many other unusual playing techniques are employed. The resulting textures, although not intentionally programmatic, can evoke an untamed landscape, a protean world of delicate and primal sounds and unfettered expression. *—"Blue" Gene Tyranny*

Ron Kuivila

b. Dec. 19, 1955, Boston, MA

Composer / Sound Sculpture

Sound installation artist and composer Ron Kuivila often uses electronic instruments of his own design, but is also noteworthy as an early user of ultrasounds and live sound sampling. Throughout the '80s and '90s, Kuivila has received commissions and honors from a number of sources, including the NYSCA, NEA, Jerome Foundation, and Austria's Ars Electronica. He has performed and exhibited all over North America and Europe, collaborating with composers and choreographers such as Nicolas Collins, Anthony Braxton, and Merce Cunningham. His pieces incorporate a range of sound sources, from his unique electronic devices to stun guns. Recordings of some of Kuivila's works have been released on labels including Lovely Music, Tellus, and Nonesuch. *—Joslyn Layne*

Blurred Genres / Slowscan #6 ♦♦♦♦♦
Electronic music by a composer renown for his evocative and beautiful sound-installation pieces based on subtle concepts and realized with self-designed and built electronics, his latest work being a high-voltage arcing sound sculpture entitled "Dolci Mura" (Sweet Walls). *—"Blue" Gene Tyranny*

Joan La Barbara

b. Jun. 8, 1947, Philadelphia, PA
Vocals, Organ, Composer / 20th Century Classical/Modern Composition, Avant-Garde
Virtuoso vocalist Joan La Barbara has explored the possibilities of voice and extended techniques such as multiphonics and glottal clicks since the '70s. She has performed with orchestras all over the world, from the New York Philharmonic to the Orchestra of the Hague, and has premiered operas including Robert Ashley's "Now Eleanor's Idea," and "Jacob's Room," by Morton Subotnick, with whom La Barbara cowrote "The Misfortune of the Immortals." This piece (also co-written by Mark Coniglio) is an example of her work melding electronics and technology into performance. Morton Feldman, Philip Glass, and James Tenney are among the American composers who have written works specifically for her. As a composer, she has also written chamber pieces, works for radio, television, and a number of filmscores including the score for *Anima* (1991). She has worked with choreographers and artists, such as Merce Cunningham, Kenneth Goldsmith and Lita Albuquerque. Her own recordings can be found on the Lovely Music, Music & Arts, and New World labels; she has produced a number of modern classical recordings, as well. She is the recipient of fellowship awards and commissions from the NEA, Meet The Composer, Akustische International Competition Award, the San Francisco Contemporary Music Players, and more. In addition to performing and recording, Joan La Barbara has spent much of her time educating vocalists during the '80s and '90s. *—Joslyn Layne*

Sound Paintings / 1990 / Lovely Music ♦♦♦♦♦
Extended vocal techniques (circular breathing, multiphonics like that in Buddhist chant, imitation of environmental sounds, speech just on the edge of comprehensibility, etc.) multi-tracked into some beautiful pieces… esp. liked "Erin"… on a photograph of an Irish child with his father's coffin… and "Klee Alee"..inspired by the imagery of Paul Klee's paintings and the squiggles and brushstrokes when viewed close-up. *—"Blue" Gene Tyranny*

● **ShamanSong** / Dec. 1, 1998 / New World ♦♦♦♦♦
A beautiful CD of three elegant, subtle, and evocative compositions. *ShamanSong* (1991, 1998) is a mysterious 25-minute "concert suite" of excerpts from the soundtrack for a film entitled *Anima*, which concerns a woman who journeys to the desert to leave her former life behind and enter "the world where magic happens" by performing certain rituals and labors. We hear La Barbara's recorded voice (sighs, whispers, lamentations, ululations, calls, echoing cries, lullabies, and "vocal winds") and percussion sounds (Balinese gamelan, tar and dumbek hand drums, shakuhachi, music box tines, rainstick, and African rattles) on location high in the rocky cliffs of Diablo Canyon, NM. Several sounds are also modified by computer. *ROTHKO* (1986) is an approximately 24-minute work designed for the Rothko Chapel. La Barbara wished to emulate painter Mark Rothko's layering techniques in sound. The mood is somber, meditative, and intense, as sounds from several tapes of multiphonic and microtonal voice choirs and bowed pianos move through the space, with a pervasive, constantly moving drone filling and reconfiguring itself as a living presence. The listener's attention is drawn both to this resonance but also to the small, fine sounds that ring throughout. The score of *Calligraphy II/Shadows* (1995) for voice and Chinese wind, string, and percussion instruments attempts "to reflect the gestural qualities and physicality of calligraphy," with the "shadows" of the title referring "to the musical score as a shadow or reflection of the movements and gestures of both calligraphy and dance." La Barbara succeeds beautifully with an engaging piece built from gentle evocative gestures and mysterious vocalisms that seem to tell a private story. *—"Blue" Gene Tyranny*

Bun-Ching Lam

b. 1954, Macao, China
Producer, Composer / 20th Century Classical/Modern Composition, World Fusion
Composer Bun-Ching Lam was born in 1954 in Macao. First trained as a pianist, she earned a bachelor's degree in performance from the Chinese University in Hong Kong. Upon receiving a scholarship from the University of California, San Diego, in 1976, Lam moved to the U.S. and began composing under the tutelage of Robert Erickson, Pauline Oliveros, and Roger Reynolds. She received a Ph.D. in composition in 1981. From then until 1986, taught at the Cornish College of the Arts in Seattle. Lam now lives in New York, where she works with such Chinese musicians as pipa virtuoso and composer Wu Man, tenor Chen Shi-Zheng, and is also active in Chinese Shadow Theater. In fact, her second release, *The Child of God*, is of three compositions based on Chinese texts, including shadow opera (with English narration). Lam has received numerous grants—including the Rome Prize for Composition—as well as fellowships from the NEA, Meet the Composer, and the New York Foundation for the Arts. She has been commissioned by the Hong Kong Chinese Orchestra, the American Composers Orchestra, and Swiss percussionist Fritz Hauser, to name a few. Lam's works have been featured at prestigious venues and festivals worldwide, from *Carnegie Hall* to *Aspekte*. Mixing Eastern and Western traditions, Bun-Ching Lam's music can be heard on two releases on the Tzadik label. *—Joslyn Layne*

● **… Like Water** / Mar. 18, 1997 / Tzadik ♦♦♦♦♦
Like Water is a fitting title for a composition that is, overall, very soft and quiet without being inorganically sparse. Bun-Ching Lam kept three Chinese sayings in mind while composing: "Years flow by like water," "Relations between gentlemen are plain like water," and "Love tender like water." Through the exquisite musicianship of the Abel-Steinberg-Winant Trio, Lam slowly unwraps her water emotive vignettes. An overall balance is realized as percussive melodic bursts and dramatic runs provide intermittent release after sections of patience and musical tension, and refocus attention after the more delicate stretches. With this release, Tzadik presents a strong, understated modern composition of mature beauty. *—Joslyn Layne*

Bill Laswell

b. Feb. 12, 1955, Salem, IL
Bass, Producer, Arranger / Electronica, Dark Ambient, Club/Dance, Experimental, Dub, M-Base, Prog-Rock/Art Rock, Fusion, Ambient, Modern Creative
A longtime linchpin of the New York City underground music scene, Bill Laswell was among the most prolific artists in contemporary music; as a performer, producer and label chief, his imprint is on literally hundreds of albums, the majority of them characterized by a signature sound fusing the energy of punk with the bone-rattling rhythms of funk. In 1978 Laswell formed Material, an outlet for his experimental approach towards sounds ranging from jazz to hip-hop to worldbeat. He concurrently scored his first major production credit with the self-titled debut from Public Image Limited; Laswell also mounted a solo career, issuing *Baselines* in 1982 on Celluloid, a label he partly owned and operated. Appearances on key recordings from the likes of David Byrne, John Zorn, Fred Frith and the Golden Palominos established Laswell as a virtual nexus of the downtown NYC community, and in 1983 he broke into the mainstream with his production work on Herbie Hancock's smash "Rockit." Throughout the mid-1980s Laswell was everywhere, playing bass on LPs from artists including Mick Jagger, Peter Gabriel, Yoko Ono and Laurie Anderson; he also joined the avant group Curlew, and produced a number of African acts. In 1986, Laswell joined the group Last Exit; another project, the hip-hop-flavored Praxis, was resumed after close to a decade of inactivity with 1992's *Transmutation (Mutatis Mutandis)*. In 1990, Laswell formed another label, Axiom, to explore his interest in the new sounds of ambient and techno. *—Jason Ankeny*

Destruction: Celluloid Recordings / 1993 / Restless ♦♦♦♦
A more than adequate overview of Laswell's work at Celluloid, where he successfully blurred the division lines between hip-hop, rap, reggae, African music, jazz, and avant-garde, this two-CD anthology includes his work as a producer as well as solo and band recordings. Laswell displays both his strengths and weaknesses (brilliant bass playing, over-reliance on some technotoys, an ear for combinations, a tendency to lock down in one place). One of his strongest pieces, "World Destruction" (Timezone, featuring Afrikaa Bambaataa and John Lydon) kicks the album off, and after that it's a true roller-coaster ride that sails through various line-ups of Material via Manu Dibango, Massacre, Fela Anukulapo Kuti, The Last Poets, and Ginger Baker, amongst others. Some listeners will explore further, which they will most likely find beneficial. *—Steven McDonald*

Web / 1995 / Subharmonic ♦♦♦
Some of the most abrasive, industrial leaning ambient of either of these composers' careers. Chains rattle, voices whisper menacingly, and dark, dissonant textures and deep bass drones collide on a trio of extended tracks united by the questionably thematic topic of digital communications technology. Difficult but rewarding. *—Sean Cooper*

Equations of Eternity / 1996 / WordSound ♦♦♦

Sacred System, Chapter 2 / 1997 / ROIR ♦♦♦♦
On *Sacred System: Chapter Two,* bassist and producer extraordinaire Bill Laswell makes good on the partly unfulfilled promise of 1996's *Sacred System Chapter One: Book of Entrance.* The difference, in this case, is a small ensemble of guest musicians who include Material guitarist Nicky Skopelitis, a tabla virtuoso named Bill Buchen, and jazz cornettist Graham Haynes (son of legendary bop drummer Roy Haynes). Whereas *Chapter One* was a rather arid solo project, *Chapter Two* comes completely to life with the various contributions of its ensemble players: Skopelitis mostly lays back and contributes lovely textures, while Haynes defines cavernous aural spaces with his echoey, jazzy horn lines and Buchen delivers almost impossibly intricate percussion figures. Laswell himself seems more energized, as well, and his bass lines sound deeper, heavier, happier. This is a deeply satisfying compilation of groove music from one of groove's greatest living exponents. *—Rick Anderson*

● **Invisible Design** / Mar. 23, 1999 / Tzadik ♦♦♦♦♦
Though Bill Laswell is no stranger to his inner creative genius, there is something about the complete free reign that the Tzadik label routinely gives its artists that seems to bring out their best work. So it is not surprising that *Invisible Design,* his first Tzadik album, hums with energy and the poetic grace of a well-executed thought. The overwhelming element throughout is a kind of meditative flow—with synth elements and lingering bass notes floating in and out like breath. The percussive element of some of his other albums is not to be found here—this is a work of pure contemplation. Deeply spiritual, the album also creates a landscape of chill and emptiness. It is nearly never dark, but sometimes gives the impression of light viewed from a place of shadow. A few pieces show contrast—"Black Aether" alternates the atmospheric elements with swaths of grind and buzz, and "Oceans of Borrowed Money" trades the slow, lingering bass of many of the other tracks for something more uptempo and funky. The result is active, but never frenetic or tense. *Invisible Design* may echo elements of Laswell's other ambient projects, but this is a unique project and nowhere yet has he produced a record that is so consistently good from start to finish. *—Stacia Proefrock*

Imaginary Cuba / Sep. 14, 1999 / RCA ♦♦♦♦

Dub Chamber 3 / Apr. 25, 2000 / ROIR ♦♦♦♦

Mary Jane Leach

b. 1949, Vermont
Composer / 20th Century Classical/Modern Composition
Composer Mary Jane Leach grew out of a strong grounding in the arts, singing at church as a child, playing bass clarinet in high school, writing theater pieces in college, and finally get-

ting into New York City's performance art scene in the late '70s while studying music at Columbia. Leach decided in the early '80s that she wanted to make her name as a composer and began to experiment with slow-paced pieces and layered tapes, as well as compositions for voices. She has worked with the New York Treble Singers and the Western Wind, and has released several albums, including *Celestial Fires*. *—Steve Huey*

Celestial Fires / 1993 / Experimental Intermedia ✦✦✦
Beginning from simple means—close harmonies with phasing rhythms —, each of the 6 compositions on this CD gradually blossom in the intricacy of their exquisite movement and sound. Each uses an ensemble of instruments or voices of a similar family, which emphasizes the textural binding—"Bruchstuck," "Green Mountain Madrigal," "Mountain Echoes" and "Ariel's Song" for 8 treble voices, "Feu de Joie" for solo bassoon and 6 taped bassoons, and the illusionary "Trio for Duo" for live and taped alto flute and voice. Truly beautiful. *—"Blue" Gene Tyranny*

● **Adriadne's Lament** / 1998 / New World ✦✦✦✦✦
A CD of remarkably beautiful and innovative new vocal works with instruments, reminiscent of both modern European choral sounds like those of Ligeti, Renaissance composers like Thomas Tallis, and containing a distinct New York "downtown" energy. Performances are by the New York Treble Singers, the Rooke Chapel Choir, and the Cassatt String Quartet, with splendid vocal and instrumental soloists. The six pieces are: "O Magna Vasti Creta" (1997), "Call of the Dance" (1997), "Windjammer" (1995), "Tricky Pan" (1995), "Ariadne's Lament" (1993), and the "Song of Sorrows" (1995). *—"Blue" Gene Tyranny*

Joëlle Léandre

b. Sep. 12, 1951, Aix-en-Provence, France
Bass (Upright), Composer / Improvisation, Avant-Garde Jazz, Experimental, Free Jazz, 20th Century Classical/Modern Composition, Avant-Garde
Contrebassist and improviser Joëlle Léandre counts John Cage among her close mentors and has remained under-acknowledged for the amount—and quality—of her work since she began recording in 1981. Léandre has performed and recorded with many of the best, and most interesting, musicians in improvised music, including German bassist Peter Kowald, American reedsman and composer Anthony Braxton, Swiss pianist Irène Schweizer, Australian violinist Jon Rose, vocalist Lauren Newton, and British guitarist Fred Frith, among others.

Born in Aix-en-Provence, France, Léandre played recorder and piano before deciding upon the double bass. She won honors and scholarships during her studies for her outstanding musicianship and first met composers such as John Cage, Giacinto Scelsi, and Morton Feldman while in Buffalo, NY, on a scholarship. Léandre recorded works by Cage and Scelsi and performed in a number of new music ensembles including 2E2M and l'Ensemble Intercontemporain. She got to know Cage personally and he had a strong influence upon her music and perception of sound. Within jazz, Léandre was attracted to free playing and found another influence in Derek Bailey; the two later recorded together. Léandre has also recorded in duos with bassist William Parker and trombonist Sebi Tramontana and as a member of the European Women's Improvising Group, the Marilyn Crispell Quartet, the Canvas Trio with violinist Carlos Zingaro and clarinetist Rüdiger Carl, and a trio with pianist Georg Graewe and clarinetist François Houle. Joëlle Léandre has held residencies in Berlin and in Metz, France, during the '90s, and continues to write and paint in addition to making music and teaching. She has recorded for FMP, Intakt, Leo, Hat, and (most of all) Chris Cutler's Recommended Records (or ReR). *—Joslyn Layne*

E'Vero / Nov. 16, 1999 / Leo ✦✦✦✦
Canadian string bassist Leandre and Italian trombonist Sebi Tramontana engage in nine improvised conversations that bring out the best in each performer. Equal partners, the two bounce off one another, along the way engaging in some extremely passionate, if low-key interaction. Tramontana continues to develop as one of the most exciting of the young free-style trombonists. Emphasizing mutes and a unique style that owes as much to American George Lewis as to Italian Giancarlo Schiaffini, Tramontana listens carefully, never becoming too self-absorbed. Leandre gurgles vocally and coaxes remarkable sounds from the bass, her exquisite technique subsumed by her remarkable vision. Together, this is an example of how a duo can transcend its inherent limitations and produce something tasteful, unique, and compelling. *—Steve Loewy*

Tricotage / 2000 / Ambiances Magnétiques ✦✦✦
In May 1999, French bassist Joëlle Léandre was in Montreal for a concert and a recording session with drummer Danielle P. Roger (ex-Justine, Les Poules, Wondeur Brass). The result of this encounter was released in early 2000 by Ambiances Magnétiques under the tittle *Tricotage* (Knits), a feminine title for an album soaked in feminine sensibility. The two improvisers make one with their instruments, Léandre letting sighs and moans escape along the way (like on the beautiful "Knit One, Purl Three"). The pretentiousness found on Ambiances Magnétiques' releases from the same period is absent on this CD; the music goes down to the roots of improvising, taps into the unconscious: a bass that can sound like a drum playing with a delicate drum set that could almost sound melodious. *Tricotage* is a very organic record, quite sensual at times, and makes an enjoyable listen. *—François Couture*

● **Joelle Leandre Project** / Apr. 11, 2000 / Leo ✦✦✦✦✦
Highly regarded improvising bassist Joelle Leandre aligns herself with a multinational, all-star entourage of forward thinking and like-minded improvisers on this 2000 release simply titled *Joelle Leandre Project*. Essentially this outing represents a series of works that interweave in somewhat of a seamless manner as the overall tone and flow might suggest a multi-part suite. Some of the highlights of this project are rooted within Leandre's angular, craftily executed and often-emotive arco-bass lines during episodes of fervent interplay with violinist Carlos Zingaro, pianist Marilyn Crispell, and keyboards/electronics expert Richard Teitelbaum. Throughout these expressive and at times free-flowing improvisations, the listener will hear fluttering dialogue amid drummer Paul Lovens' undulating rhythmic structures and multihued backwashes of crashing cymbals and gongs. And while Richard Teitelbaum provides supple statements via his acute utilization of analog synths, Crispell occasionally employs a cavalcade of huge block chords intertwined with pensive harmonies and swirling clusters of sound.

The band often pursues vertical movement in concert with curiously interesting dialogue as they create grooves and motifs that announce a distinct sense of urgency atop temperate crosscurrents. Despite a few lulls in the momentum where the dialogue seems to flounder, *The Joelle Leandre Project* is a relatively strong outing, teeming with impassioned interplay and abstract thematic invention, brought to listeners by an assemblage of celebrated stylists. *—Glenn Astarita*

Anne Lebaron

b. May 30, 1953, Baton Rouge, LA
Harp, Composer / Improvisation, 20th Century Classical/Modern Composition, Avant-Garde
Studied with Frederick Goosen, Bulent Arel, Daria Semegen, Mauricio Kagel, György Ligeti, Chour Wen-Chung, Jack Beeson, Mario Davidowsky. Harpist, improvisor with many groups, including LeBaron/Smith/Dixon trio and LeBaron Quintet. Taught at Stony Brook, University of Alabama, Columbia University. *Concerto for Active Frogs* (1975), *Strange Attractors* for large orchestra (1987), many awards and commissions. *—"Blue" Gene Tyranny*

Dish / in Dora Ohrenstein's "Urban Diva" / 1993 / CRI ✦✦✦
A sensual and humorous chamber work based on the texts "Seeing You Again Makes Me Wanna Wash the Dishes," "On Being Irresponsible About Lovers and Those Who Swoop on You," and "The Swooper and the Swoopee." LeBaron is an accomplished composer with chamber music recorded on the Mode label, and the German Ear-Rational label features her jazz group the Anne LeBaron Quintet With the Phantom Orchestra. The voice in "Dish," especially at the beginning of the piece, is amplified and echoed to create tactile effects. See also LeBaron's "Blue Harp Study 1" and "Blue Harp Study 2" in the collection *Jewel Box*. Listeners may also enjoy checking out her new album with several ensemble works on MODE records (1993). *—"Blue" Gene Tyranny*

Richard Lerman

b. Dec. 5, 1944, San Francisco, CA
Composer, Multi-Media / Sound Sculpture
The work of sound artist Richard Lerman centers around his custom-made contact microphones of unusually small size. Numerous well-placed mics are essential to his work recording environmental sounds not easily heard (or noticed) by humans, as in his project of sonically mapping the Sonoran Desert. While growing up in Milwaukee, Lerman played trombone, listened to jazz, and upon hearing Darius Milhaud's "Le Creation du Monde" was inspired to begin studying modern composition on his own while still in high school. Lerman then studied film, as well as composition, at Brandeis College. There, he worked in the electronic music studio, first started working with piezoelectric transducers, and studied with Alvin Lucier, Gordon Mumma, and mentor David Tudor. His sound installations often depend on natural stimuli, such as the wind moving on strings or tuning forks. Yet much of his work centers on capturing the sounds we miss altogether. In "Travelon Gamelon" (1977), Lerman amplified the sounds and reverberations of a moving bicycle; a recording of this was released on Smithsonian Folkways in 1982. For the collaborative work "Threading History," Lerman recorded the barbed wire of a prison camp. "A Seasonal Mapping of the Sonoran Desert" includes the sound of cactus needles plucked like strings by rainfall. Since he first began performing in the late '60s, Lerman has traveled to Europe and across the U.S. with his creations, including a film show at MOMA. In addition to working on his own creations, Lerman has taught arts in Boston and Arizona. *—Joslyn Layne*

Within Earreach / 1994 / Artifact ✦✦✦✦
Sounds from the composer's site-specific sound installations using self-made microphones and transducers, and also composed "soundscapes." The recordings are from all around the world—Australia, Newfoundland, Hong Kong, Bali, Argentina, Jerusalem—with the devices attached to trees, metal objects, strings, leaves etc. Fascinating and mind-expanding. *—"Blue" Gene Tyranny*

George Lewis

b. Jul. 14, 1952, Chicago, IL
Trombone, Composer / Avant-Garde Jazz, 20th Century Classical/Modern Composition
Trombonist and composer George Lewis studied his crafts with Dean Hey and Muhal Richard Abrams. Lewis' compositions and improvisations are found on over 80 recordings, and he has performed with such important musicians, composers and improvisers as Steve Lacy, Anthony Braxton, Count Basie, Derek Bailey and John Zorn. A Yale University, Philosophy graduate, Lewis has been a member of the Association for the Advancement of Creative Musicians (AACM) since the 1970s. His residencies include IRCAM (Paris), STEIM (Amsterdam), and Alberta's Banff Centre for the Arts. Lewis has been an NEA Fellow, was hosted as Visiting Artist by the Art Institute of Chicago, and curated the music program of NY's The Kitchen Center. Lewis also programmed interactive music systems for computers, has lectured at computed art workshops, and has worked as a computer installation artist, with interactive installations shows at Paris' Musee de la Villette, in Boston and Chicago. *—Joslyn Layne*

★ **Homage to Charles Parker** / 1979 / Black Saint ✦✦✦✦✦
This tribute to bop icon Charlie Parker is not a program of his famous tunes but a representation of his spirit that still exists. Through means of improvised music with a variety of significant signposts, George Lewis offers two 18-minute texture pieces that display a haunting quality by combining natural elements and electronically generated waves of sound, passion, and a little fury. Moog synthesizer programmer Richard Teitelbaum provides the landscape, pianist Anthony Davis the skyscapes, and Douglas Ewart on alto sax and bass clarinet provides the Bird-like characteristics. Lewis, on trombone and electronics, directs the ensemble from within this quiet storm's eye. "Blues" starts with tonal fragmented phrases in no time

with trombone, bass clarinet, and piano circling Teitelbaum's occasional synthesized insertions. The inquisitive nature of the counterpointed horns is strikingly bold and pervasive, as if Parker was cueing various icons of blues legends like Leadbelly, Howlin' Wolf, and T-Bone Walker to speak up for themselves. Long-held tones in the midsection lead to Teitelbaum's spacey, blue, Sun Ra-like touches. The title cut starts with reverent, spiritual, hovering washes from cymbals and soft synths, and a languid alto solo from Ewart signifies the ghost of Bird has arrived. Davis plays some absolutely gorgeous piano, like delicate beacons of light cutting through fog, while an organ-sounding synth urges a more sweeping piano solo. Lewis, on a poignant trombone, waxes lyrical and poetic, aware of the transfiguration of bop while addressing its contemporary, contemplative needs. Pretty stunning music. As heavy and stylistically different as this music is, the point is clear and well-taken. Lewis and his group make a statement unique in creative jazz and unto itself. This is an important recording in many ways, and a *magnum opus* for the leader. *—Michael G. Nastos*

☆ **Chicago Slow Dance (1977)** / 1981 / Lovely Music ✦✦✦✦✦
Chicago Slow Dance for acoustic instruments and electronics is an elegantly slow, evolving introspective portrait of Chicago life. It contains gentle surreal dream sounds and melodies evoking many images: the sound of shakers like the clacking of overhead subway rails, perhaps a bird lost in the city, kids playing in vacant lots, night sounds on the edge of town, a passing police car, boats on the lake, your neighbors' noises through the walls of an apartment house... This is an exquisite work. *—"Blue" Gene Tyranny*

Changing with the Times / Mar. 15, 1993-Mar. 17, 1993 / New World ✦✦✦✦✦
Innovative pieces, each with a speaker, poet, or singer reflecting on modern living. Titles include "Chicago Dadagram, " "So You Say, " *"The View From Skates In Berkeley, "* "Airplane, " *"Epilogue." —"Blue" Gene Tyranny*

The Usual Turmoil and Other Duets / Jul. 21, 1998 / Music & Arts ✦✦✦✦✦
George Lewis records so infrequently as a leader that any new release featuring him on trombone is itself an event. Here, he is featured on trombone in a series of duets with kotoist Miya Masaoka. (Masaoka's koto is a sort of modified Japanese zither.) The results, as expected, are superb, as Lewis and Masaoka negotiate twelve improvised pieces, swerving, interacting, bouncing, and complementing each other in spectacular ways. Lewis is up to his usual bag of tricks, totally dominating his horn with rapid displays of notes bursting forth like shooting stars, extremely precise phrasing, and extended range. Masaoka is a fine dueling partner, stroking her koto in different avenues, jabbing here and there with atonal forays. While the sound quality suffers a bit on the two lengthy live numbers, Lewis fans will nonetheless savor the extended 'bone solos, not to mention the outstanding koto work of Masaoka. *—Steve Loewy*

György Ligeti

b. May 28, 1923, Tirnaveni, Transylvania
Composer / 20th Century Classical/Modern Composition, Atonal, Electronic, Classical
Influential modern composer György Ligeti broke much ground for late 20th century composition, moving through phases of unique techniques and styles exploring the use of micropolyphony, counterpoint, microintervals, and polyrhythms, among other things. He strongly influenced avant-garde composition, including the development of cluster composition in the '60s.

Born and raised in Romania, Ligeti studied composition under Ferenc Farkas and others, both before being sent to a Jewish labor camp in 1943 and after his release. Even after WWII and the Nazi occupation ended, Ligeti's growth was stifled by the restrictive political climate (his works from this time were safely based in folk traditions). After graduating from Budapest's Liszt Academy in 1949, he taught there until fleeing Hungary in 1956. But before this, he had already come up with sketches for Apparitions and Atmospheres during the slight reprieve following Stalin's death in 1953.

After leaving Hungary for Vienna in 1956, Ligeti met avant-garde composers such as Karlheinz Stockhausen and Herbert Eimert and joined the Electronic Music Studio in Cologne the following year. 1958 saw the completion of his electronic work Artikulation and the birth of Apparitions, an orchestral work which premiered at the city's 1960 ISCM festival. This work brought Ligeti international acclaim that was only reinforced by his next piece, Atmosphères (1961). With these, Ligeti used micropolyphonies—dense textures that hid distinct pitches of rhythms and melodies—instead of serialism or tonal language. Over the decades that followed, Ligeti composed a number of innovative works, including Aventures and Nouvelles Aventures (1962-1965) (which imitated the sounds of language; the elaborate contrapuntal techniques of the mid-'60s work Requiem, winner of the 1967 Bonn Beethoven prize), Lux Aeterna (1966) (heard in *2001: A Space Odyssey*), his reactions (including 0'00") against John Cage's work, and the polyrhythmic complexity of the Piano Concerto (1985-1988).

Besides living in Cologne and Austria, Ligeti taught at the music academies of Stockholm, Hamburg, and Stanford. His many awards and honors include Hamburg's 1975 Bach Prize and the 1996 Music Prize of the International Music Council. *—Joslyn Layne*

★ **Atmospheres (1961) for Large Orchestra/ Lontano (1967) for Large Orchestra/ in "Wien Mo** / 1990 / Deutsche Grammaphon ✦✦✦✦✦
Performed by the Vienna Philharmonic and conducted by Claudio Abbado, transparent washes of neo-impressionistic colors paint inter-dimensional landscapes in this evocative piece. Composed in 1961, *Atmosphéres for Large Orchestra* is in the radical tradition (not a contradiction) of sustained-surface compositions (perhaps beginning with Schönberg's "Summer Morning by a Lake" from the *Five Pieces for Orchestra,* or the opening of Ravel's *Daphnis et Chloe*). The beginning of the piece involves a quiet but huge chromatic cluster covering over five octaves of the orchestra; from this cluster sections eventually fall out leaving masses of natural notes (scale clusters) only or sharp/flat notes (pentatonics) only. Among the sounds are: shimmering rapid vibrato, multiple high glissandi, waves of string harmonics in different meters, notes moving along the same path but at varying speeds from each other (like a celestial highway), and the sound of breathing only through brass instruments (without producing tones). Like Ligeti's *Lux aeterna,* parts of this composition were also used in Stanley Kubrick's famous movie *2001.* Composed in 1967, *Lontano for Large Orchestra* depicts the opening and closing of "a window on long submerged dream worlds of childhood" (Ligeti). *—"Blue" Gene Tyranny*

Lux Aeterna, for 16-Voice Mixed Chorus (1966) / Deutsche Grammaphon ✦✦✦✦✦
Performed by the North German Radio Chorus conducted by H. Franz. The famed "sound of the monolith" in Stanley Kubrick's film *"2001"* was lifted from "Lux Aeterna" here in a lovely performance... a surface of sustained and overlapping clusters of multi-timbral quality that suggest universality without "bigness." *—"Blue" Gene Tyranny*

Alvin Lucier

b. May 14, 1931, Nashua, NH
Liner Notes, Composer / 20th Century Classical/Modern Composition, Minimalism, Electronic
A trailblazing force in psycho-acoustic music, avant-garde composer and performer Alvin Lucier was born in Nashua, New Hampshire in 1931; educated at Yale and Brandeis, he also spent two years in Rome on a Fulbright Scholarship before returning to Brandeis in 1962 to teach and conduct the university's chamber chorus. His breakthrough composition, *Music for Solo Performer (1964-65) for Enormously Amplified Brain Waves and Percussion,* was the first work to feature sounds generated by brain waves in live performance; biological stimuli played an increasing role in Lucier's subsequent work as well, most notably through his notation of performers' physical movements. Acoustical phenomena, meanwhile, was the subject of 1970's landmark *I Am Sitting in a Room,* in which several sentences of recorded speech were simultaneously played back into a room and re-recorded there dozens of times over, the space gradually filtering the speech into pure sound. 1980's *Music on a Long Thin Wire* was a further extension of Lucier's fascination with the physics of sound—a conceptual piece featuring a taut 50-foot wire passed through the poles of a large magnet and driven by an oscillator, the amplified vibrations yielded beautifully ethereal results. A professor at Wesleyan University from 1970 onward, Lucier's later works additionally included a number of sound installations as well as works for solo instruments, chamber ensembles, and orchestra. *—Jason Ankeny*

Music on a Long Thin Wire / 1980 / Lovely Music ✦✦✦
Recording of an installation made on May 10, 1979 in the Rotunda of the US Customs House, Bowling Green, New York City. The wire was extended 80 feet through the oval of the Rotunda and was driven by one pure wave oscillator. The wire played itself: all changes in volume, timbre, harmonic structure, rhythmic and cyclic patterning, and other sonic phenomena. *—"Blue" Gene Tyranny*

Music for Solo Performer (1964-65) for Enormously Amplified Brain Waves and Percussion / 1982 / Lovely Music ✦✦✦✦✦
The first musical work to use brain waves to generate sound. World instruments, as well as a cardboard box and a trash can are vibrated by loudspeakers placed near and under them, as bursts and trains of the amplified alpha waves disturb the cones of the speakers. *—"Blue" Gene Tyranny*

★ **I Am Sitting in a Room** / 1990 / Lovely Music ✦✦✦✦✦
A new music classic. 32 repetitions of a simple line of text over 40 minutes, constantly broadcast and re-recorded in a room until the nodal tones of the room and the voices undergo a magical transformation of a sense of person and place into a sense of universal presence. Lucier is the dean of psychoacoustic music. *—"Blue" Gene Tyranny*

Crossings / Lovely Music ✦✦✦✦✦
Pure, profound and classic. Complex ideas realized simply. This CD includes the pieces "In Memoriam Jon Higgins" (1984) / "Septet for Three Winds, Four Strings and Pure Wave Oscillator" (1985) / "Crossings" (1982) for small orchestra with slow-sweep pure wave oscillator. *—"Blue" Gene Tyranny*

Witold Lutoslawski

b. Jan. 25, 1913, Warsaw, Poland, **d.** Feb. 9, 1994, Warsaw, Poland
Piano, Composer / 20th Century Classical/Modern Composition, Atonal, Classical
Born in Warsaw, Poland, Lutoslawski's musical talents surfaced early, with his first compositions dating from 1922. He studied piano, violin and composition (with Witold Maliszewski, a pupil of Rimsky-Korsakov), graduating from the Warsaw Conservatory in 1937. His first substantial orchestral work, *the Symphonic Variations,* was premiered in 1939. Lutoslawski survived the difficult war years and Stalinist period by writing for radio, film and theatre, and doing folk-song arrangements and music for children. Considered too formalist, his concert music was rarely performed. He continued, however, to develop his musical language on his own, culminating in the folk-influenced *Concerto for Orchestra* (1954). With the cultural thaw of 1955, his reputation began to grow, at home and abroad, as did his compositional style, with twelve-tone harmonies appearing in *Funeral Music* (1958), and aleatoric rhythmic textures (passages where the musicans are unsynchronized) in *Jeux Venitiens* (1960). Having achieved his mature style by this point, Lutoslawski went on to compose nearly twenty major orchestral works, including *Symphony No. 3* (1982), for which he was awarded the prestigious Grawemayer Award, and his last, *Symphony No. 4* (1992), for the Los Angeles Philharmonic. He also composed works for distinguished soloists such as Dietrich Fischer-Dieskau, Heinz Holliger, Anne-Sophie Mutter, Peter Pears, Mstislav Rostropovich and Krystian Zimerman. His extensive experience conducting his own works helped him to refine his musical language, later works becoming more lyrical and harmonically transparent. *—James Harley*

Preludes and Fugue (1972) for 13 Solo Strings/ Mi-Parti (1976) for Orchestra / Novelett / 1989 / Polskie Nagrania ✦✦✦
Performed by The National Chamber Orchestra in Warsaw and The Polish Radio National Symphony Orchestra with the composer and Holliger as conductors. Totally re-defines "preludes" as mysterious sound-pieces, and re-makes the "fugue" with aleatoric, sliding, perpen-

dicular lines. Both "Mi-Parti" (French for a whole with two parts not the same) and the "Novelette" both imply non-specified narratives. *—"Blue" Gene Tyranny*

- **Les Espaces Du Sommeil (The Spaces of Sleep)** / 1990 / Philips ✦✦✦

Performed by the Berlin Philharmonic, conducted by the composer, with the superb singing of Dietrich Fischer-Dieskau, *Les Espaces du Sommeil* contains some lovely timbral effects beautifully set to the poem by Robert Desnos. The text concerns the discovery of one's soul and of the presence of others ("There is you undoubtedly whom I do not know…") during the internal wanderings of sleep.

Symphony No. 3, completed and premiered in 1983, is built from a love of sounds. The large form of the two movements is described by the composer in normal terms of episodes, refrains and themes, but the substance is built from recurrent simple trumpet-call figures on one pitch (later played in unison by a single chime and a French horn, or the amassed brass section), between which occur swirling sounds in the winds and sometimes in the strings, little fragments of the beginnings of melodies that just as suddenly trail off in the distance, quick rushes in the strings that come to rest in sustained chords, sliding sounds and spinning sounds combined—in short, events that continually approach, stop, then approach further with even more mass, until the suppressed tension explodes as the whole orchestra has joins in. The entire 30-minute work played without pause retains a suspense built on illusions that keeps you on the edge of your seat. *—"Blue" Gene Tyranny*

Postlude I for Orchestra (1958) / Paroles Tissees (Weaving Songs) (1965) for Tenor, Str / 1990 / Polskie Nagrania ✦✦✦

Although his pre-1960 works are almost 19th-century-style in their gestures and development, the pieces on this CD are strikingly different in their tone-colors and organization. Premiered in 1968, the *Livre pour Orchestre* (Book for Orchestra) is made up of four movements called "chapters" separated by three short intermediate pieces of relatively static nature. The changing and inventive textures emerge in a constant flow: sighing and sliding tones, a field of flowing colors, mystery movie-like basses, flurries of brass sounds, densely beautiful undulating textures for full orchestra, cycles of swirling tones and rhythmic pulsations, glassy textures, and melodic wind solos.

Premiered in 1965, the *Paroles Tissées* (Weaving Songs) is a setting for tenor solo, strings, harp, piano and percussion of a mysterious and elaborate four-part poem by Jean-François Chabrun entitled "Quatre tapisseries pour le Chatelaine de Vergi" (Four Tapestries for the Chatelaine [lady of the manor] of Vergi), the subject of which is the tragic romance in the Middle Ages of that lady and the Duke of Burgundy. The spinning motion is suggested by steady harp arpeggios, often with random string pizzicati above. Suddenly the music takes a more dramatic turn with the ringing of tubular bells and multiple pizzicati at different rhythmic rates, as well as attacked notes followed by glissando slides, all of which also suggest a "weaving" motion but of a frantic nature. The piece ends in a mysterious bewilderment that describes the death of the two lovers.

Written during the years 1968-1970 and premiered by the famous cellist Mstislav Rostopovich, the *Cello Concerto* is in four movements—intense dialogues at turns dramatic, mocking, and forgiving between soloist and orchestra are played without pause. *—"Blue" Gene Tyranny*

The Machine for Making Sense

Group / Avant-Garde

Australian avant-garde cooperative Machine for Making Sense was founded in the late '80s to blend speech and improvisation and has since performed in Europe and North America, as well as Australia.

The group consists of hurdy-gurdy player and violinist Stevie Wishart, poets/vocalists Amanda Stewart and Chris Mann, Jim Denley on winds, and Rik Rue on samples and tape, all of whom are involved in a variety of other projects. They have been described as similar in spirit to AMM and Jon Rose and have recorded for O.O. Discs. *—Joslyn Layne*

On Second Thoughts / 1994 / O.O. Discs ✦✦✦

A, well, bizarre concept music group of Sydney, Australian-based composer-performers. The tracks (26, A-Z) take the kind of (mostly vocal) inflections associated with "making sense" in all its forms, and explore these in a musical manner that is at turns humorous, mysterious, lyrical, rambunctious, the music of an unsuspected culture, the birth noises of a new species. Wonderfully, barely readable and appropriately dense notes accompany the disc. Performers are Jim Denley (flutes, sax, and voice), Chris Mann (voice and text), Rik Rue (digital and analogue samples and tape manipulation), Amanda Stewart (voice and text), Stevie Wishart (violin, live electronics, hurdy-gurdy, and voice). (See also their great short piece in the collection *Aerial #5*). *—"Blue" Gene Tyranny*

Angus Maclise

b. Mar. 14, 1938, Bridgeport, CT, **d.** Jun. 21, 1979, Katmandu, Nepal

Percussion / Proto-Punk, Experimental, Avant-Garde, Minimalism, Rock & Roll

Angus MacLise is best known as the original drummer of the Velvet Underground, although he left the band before their first recording session. MacLise was also extremely active in the experimental and film music world. As a percussionist, MacLise merged avant-garde and world (particularly Asian) music, and collaborated with avant-garde musician La Monte Young, among others. His contributions have been difficult to assess due to the scarce availability of recordings including him—a situation that changed with the release of some compilations decades after his death.

By the early '60s, MacLise was a poet and beatnik who co-founded Dead Language Press with poet/filmmaker Piero Heliczer. From the early to mid-'60s, he played bongos in La Monte Young's the Theatre Of Eternal Music, and through bandmate violist John Cale, met Lou Reed and Sterling Morrison and became the first drummer of the Velvet Underground. MacLise's role in the early Velvets is uncertain as there are almost no recordings with him, but it could be that his strongest contribution was his connection to New York's multimedia underground. MacLise quit the band in late 1965, returning for a brief stint in 1966 to fill in for a hepatitis-stricken Lou Reed. Live versions of "Heroin" and "Venus in Furs" from this time appear in Ronald Nameth's film, *Exploding Plastic Inevitable.* MacLise collaborated extensively with musicians including Terry Riley, Tony Conrad, Terry Jennings, and Yoko Ono. His extensive film work includes soundtracks for Ron Rice's *Chumlum* (1964), and Gerard Malanga's *The Children* (1969); the score for Heliczer's *The Autumn Feast;* and collaborations with Jerry Jofen (on *Voyage*), and Jonas Mekas.

In the late 1960s, MacLise married illustrator Hetty McGee, a bandmate in the psychedelic trance band the Universal Mutant Repertory Company. The collection *The Invasion of Thunderbolt Pagoda* (1999) includes a 1970 performance by this group, Another compilation of 1968-72 material, *Brain Damage in Oklahoma City,* came out in 2000, but was considerably more dissonant and difficult, and less interesting. During the '70s, MacLise lived in India and Nepal, making music, but also focusing on poetry, calligraphy and his literary magazine, *Ting-Pa.* He died of hypoglycemia in Nepal in 1979. *—Richie Unterberger*

- **Invasion of Thunderbolt Pagoda** / Dec. 21, 1999 / Siltbreeze ✦✦✦✦

The best available recorded documentation of MacLise's work has imperfect fidelity and sketchy details about the five tracks, recorded between 1968 and 1972. It does, however, reveal multiple facets of the percussionist's adventurous music, and firmly establishes him as a significant force in experimental sound in projects not at all related to the Velvet Underground. The most powerful and ambitious of the five cuts is the 39-minute title song, an improvised soundtrack to Ira Cohen's avant-garde film of the same name. MacLise's polyrhythmic hand drum anchors a spooky, hypnotic piece in which organ, tanpura (both played by his wife Hetty MacLise), flute, guitar, dulcimer, and disturbing vocal chants ebb and subside like a Halloween dream soundscape. Although it's not detailed in the liner notes, ghostly reverb seems to be employed on both the flute and vocals, adding to a otherworldly ambience in which psychedelia, shamanistic rhythm, avant-garde drone, and Indian music weave shifting prisms around each other. The other four selections are a real mixed bag, in the best sense of that expression. "Shortwave-India" is a one-minute blast of radio static and white noise; "Heavenly Blue Pt. 4 & 5," credited to the Universal Mutant Repertory Company, is another combination of drum and drone that puts a greater accent on Indian and Asian music influences; and "Blastitude" is a more rhythmic construction that might remind some listeners of Moroccan trance music, with periodic unascribed orgiastic yelps and sighs. The concluding "Humming in the Night Skull," featuring MacLise on song bells, Hetty MacLise on harmonium, and others on flute and guitar, is a soothing combination of tones (punctuated by a couple of baby cries), demonstrating that Angus was not entirely devoted to angst. *—Richie Unterberger*

Brain Damage in Oklahoma City / Sep. 5, 2000 / Siltbreeze ✦✦

Jackson Mac Low

b. Sep. 12, 1922, Chicago, IL

Poetry, Composer / Multimedia, Avant-Garde

Mac Low began writing music and poetry when he was 15, and later he developed his "simultaneities" after 1953 for speakers, vocalists, instrumentalists, and/or projectionists. His poetry, published to date in 25 volumes, is written following the many indeterminate / non-intentional procedures which he has invented. *—"Blue" Gene Tyranny*

Open Secrets / 1994 / Experimental Intermedia ✦✦✦

This CD provides a good overview of Mac Low's creativity: the "1st Milarepa Gatha" (1976), "Thanks" (1960), the "38th and 39th Merzgedichte in Memoriam Kurt Schwitters" (1989), "Phoneme Dance in Memoriam John Cage" (by Mac Low and Anne Tardos) (1993), "Free Gatha 1" (1978), and "Free Gatha 2" (1981) are works for massed, multi-tracked voices speaking/singing at the same time with complex compositional procedures described in the notes; the "Milarepa Quartet for Four Like Instruments" (1982) employs a letter-to-pitch-class code that translates text into music in the manner of procedures used by Messiaen, Ashley, Cage, et al. "Winds/Instruments" (1980) is for voices and instrumentalists who sometimes speak, and "Lucas 1 to 29: For One or More Instrumentalists (In Memoriam Morton Feldman and for the Musicians of Germany)" (1990) is based on the Lucas sequence. *—"Blue" Gene Tyranny*

David Mahler

b. Aug. 13, 1944, Plainfield, NJ

Composer / Tape Music, Computer Music, 20th Century Classical/Modern Composition, Electro-Acoustic

Seattle-based composer David Mahler works with tape to create unique, sometimes humorous works, from teaching the theme song to *The Mickey Mouse Club* backwards ("Speech With Interpreter"), to parodying text-sound composition and its Swedish roots in "(Singing in the Style Of) The Voice of the Poet," his most acclaimed composition. Mahler has been active in Seattle's experimental music scene since the '70s. In 1989, he created "Washington State Centennial Bell Garden," a permanent installation for downtown Seattle consisting of 28 bells controlled by computer that not only announce the time but also play new compositions. His creations are published by the composers' collective Frog Peak Music, and have been recorded for the Artifact and Tzadik labels. *—Joslyn Layne*

- **The Voice of the Poet** / 1997 / Artifact ✦✦✦✦✦

This important CD contains six beautifully innovative compositions using the richness of acoustic sound and voices processed through or mixed with electronics. In *Cup of Coffee* (1980), a woman's voice delivers the phrase "I could really use a cup of coffee" in wide-ranging and fantastical pitch and rhythmic modulations via electronics. In other works, David Mahler has used similar techniques to deconstruct human speech and reveal its hidden aspects. *The King of Angels* (1977-1978) uses the voice of Elvis Presley singing the intro to his classic "Heartbreak Hotel." Initially, the voice is cut and widely modulated in pitch, using a process similar to that employed in *Cup of Coffee,* but then a low, growling amplitude modulation is employed, Mahler says, "in an attempt to coax the King to speak his own first name." Amazingly, that slowly begins to happen within a loop that emerges from deepening feedback, although the accent is strangely displaced on the second syllable (el-VIS). In an analog system, this is true techno magic. *Rising Ground* (1979-1980) is "a study of the crescendo/decrescendo and pitch characteristics of spinning objects" like coins, metal washers, an aluminum hoop, and a Chinese yo-yo. *The Voice of the Poet* (1982) is based on a Seattle radio interview between composer Ingram Marshall and announcer Jim Wilke; the syntax is deconstructed into a gigantically reverberated and disembodied illogical dialogue of vocal sounds and phrases. *For Thom Miller* (1986) effectively combines a 1973 audio letter from composer Miller, singing voices from a 1975 workshop, and tracks of bells and organ produced in 1984. *Wind Peace* (1972), dedicated to Harold Budd, is a lovely work that uses the sounds of crystal glassware and aluminum pie pans. *— "Blue" Gene Tyranny*

The King of Angels / Frog Peak Music ✦✦✦
Two tributes to Elvis Presley: the song "Every Song You Sang," and the tape piece "The King of Angels." Also the word piece "Cup of Coffee." Surprising works by this important Seattle-based composer. *— "Blue" Gene Tyranny*

Christian Marclay

b. 1955, San Rafael, CA
Noise, Turntables, Producer / Improvisation, Turntablism, Experimental, Avant-Garde
Christian Marclay was the first non-rap DJ to make an artform out of the turntable, treating the instrument as a means to rip songs apart, not bridge them together. A longtime associate of Downtown improv figures John Zorn, Elliott Sharp and Butch Morris as well as Kronos Quartet. After a period studying at the Massachusetts College of Art, Marclay was inspired artistically by Joseph Beuys and musically by Cage and the Fluxus group. He noted the experimental applications made possible by using the turntable in ways hardly recommended by owners manuals, and began performing as early as 1979. Marclay's methods included standard scratching, playback on damaged turntables, the actual destruction (and reassembly) of vinyl to record the results, and creating musical juxtapositions by mixing together a variety of radically different artists. His 1985 installation *Footsteps* included a gallery floor lined with thousands of records for people to walk over (the results were packaged and sold). His 1988 LP *More Encores* featured tributes to a variety of musical figures, including "John Cage" (recorded by gluing together pieces of several records to create one) and "Louis Armstrong" (using a hand-cranked gramophone to alter the pitch). Though he recorded much more sparingly in the 1990s, Marclay continued to appear on Zorn projects including several editions of his *Filmworks* series. The Atavistic label has released the retrospective *Records 1981-1989. Moving Parts* was released in mid-2000. *— John Bush*

● **Records 1981-1989** / Jun. 10, 1997 / Atavistic ✦✦✦✦✦
Records 1981-1989 is a fascinating collection of Marclay's work during the 1980s, the results of hours of home recordings—using up to eight turntables and various other instruments of his own making—plus many live performances (one track comes from a nationally televised appearance on the David Sanborn/Hal Willner program *Night Music*). Marclay did much more than just scratching and sampling for these tracks—"One Thousand Cycles" uses an increasing variety of repeated samples and clicks to create a complex rhythm of its own, while "Pandora's Box" varies the speed on its array of plunderphonics. (Though the latter sounds like an easy contemporary of late-'90s major-label turntablist LPs, it was originally released on a 1984 avant-indie compilation from Sweden that also featured Sonic Youth and Live Skull.) *— John Bush*

High Noon / 2000 / Intakt ✦✦✦✦✦
This duo of tone manipulator and distorter Christian Marclay and electric guitarist and synthesizer whiz Elliott Sharp pushes the limits with twisted sounds galore. Like a painting by Dali, there is a surreal feel to it all, a dreamlike trance interrupted repeatedly by never-ending nightmares. Pops, clicks, warbles, bangs, and dizzy bubblegum-like twists are interspersed with clanking metal to produce collages of some of the weirdest stuff on disk. Marclay is so seldom heard from that each of his recordings is a treasure, and this one is no exception. He takes Sharp's already disfigured lines and manages to mangle them further so that they are barely recognizable in their sliced and diced, transformed evolutionary state. It is hard to identify all of Sharp's instruments, but there is touch of what sounds like bass clarinet, shriveled by Marclay's deconstruction. The results are highly disturbing, but gloriously so. Unadulterated noise/music, there is a clear "take no prisoners" approach, one which is sure to delight or incite. *— Steven Loewy*

Ingram Marshall

b. May 10, 1942, Mount Vernon, NY
Liner Notes, Composer / 20th Century Classical/Modern Composition, Minimalism, Electronic
While composer Ingram Marshall's earliest compositions were electronic works, he has increasingly written for live musicians, including the Kronos Quartet. In the mid-'60s, he studied under Vladimir Ussachevsky, among others, while in another program at Columbia. Marshall then learned from Morton Subotnick, first (briefly) in Greenwich Village, then at Cal Arts as his assistant during the early '70s. It was while earning his masters at Cal Arts that Marshall was first exposed to Indonesian music, which he then added to his studies. While he blended his current musical interests in his own work (writing pieces for electronics and Balinese flute, for instance), Marshall continued to explore other styles of composition as well, as when he traveled to Sweden in the mid-'70s on a Fulbright Fellowship to study text-sound composition. "Fog Tropes" (1982) is the best known of his works that incorporate live (real time) electronic manipulation. From the mid-'80s on, Marshall has written ensemble music, not necessarily with electronics. His work for the Kronos Quartet includes "Voces Resonae" (1984) and, more recently, "Fog Tropes II." He also composed the orchestral, one-movement piece "Sinfonia 'Dolce far Niente.'" *— Joslyn Layne*

Fog Tropes/Gradual Requiem / 1990 / New Albion ✦✦✦✦✦
Composed for brass sextet, fog horns and ambient textures, Marshall's "Fog Tropes" stands in sharp contrast to his "Gradual Requiem," a piece typified by the use of tremelando effects on its mandolins and keyboards. It also employs the gambuh, an end-blown flute descended from Bali. *— Jason Ankeny*

● **Alcatraz** / 1991 / New Albion ✦✦✦✦✦

Three Penitential Visions/Hidden Voices / 1993 / Elektra/Nonesuch ✦✦✦
Atmospheric, subtle with almost "new age" transparency but more ideas, Marshall creates here two of his best albums… the "Fog Tropes" creating the beautiful landscape suggested by the title with gently phasing orchestral brass and taped ocean sounds. *— "Blue" Gene Tyranny*

Richard Maxfield

b. Feb. 27, 1927, Seattle, WA, **d.** Jun. 27, 1969, Los Angeles, CA
Composer / 20th Century Classical/Modern Composition, Atonal, Electronic
Groundbreaking electronic composer Richard Maxfield was born in Seattle in 1927. As a child he studied piano and played clarinet, even writing a symphony while still in high school. During the late '40s, he studied under composer Roger Sessions and, after graduation, befriended the likes of Pierre Boulez and Karlheinz Stockhausen while travelling in Europe. After spending 1958 in New York studying under John Cage, he assumed Cage's teaching duties and tapped LaMonte Young as his assistant; instructing his students in the art of creating music from exclusively electronic sources, he is widely believed to be the first true teacher of electronic music in America.

Also in 1959, Maxfield completed his first major electronic piece, "Sine Music (A Swarm of Butterflies Encountered Over the Ocean)." Over the next five years he created many new works, primarily via a cut-and-paste method assembled from randomly-chosen pieces of tape spliced together with blank passages of assorted duration, often creating what he dubbed inter-masters—i.e., multiple tape reels played simultaneously to generate a new master recording. Maxfield was likely the first American to generate electronic music by means of building his own equipment, and may also have been the first outside of European circles to compose pure electronic music removed from the principles of musique concrète.

Maxfield's visibility in the New York art underground was raised considerably by his standing as a member of the Fluxus movement, with performances at the famous concert series mounted by LaMonte Young at Yoko Ono's loft during 1960-61. During the mid-'60s, Maxfield taught at San Francisco State College for two years. While there, he released his best-known work, a 1967 recording titled simply *Electronic Music* that featured both tape constructions and ensemble performance pieces. In 1968, Maxfield relocated to Los Angeles, though he tragically committed suicide the following year. *— Jason Ankeny*

Richard Maxfield: Electronic Music / 1992 / Mela Foundation ✦✦✦✦✦
A cassette reissue of the original out of print Advance Recordngs disc (1969), this collection contains some of the most beautiful and imaginative electronic and "live electronic" music ever made using only pre-synthesizer Army-surplus store electronics: "Pastoral Symphony" (1960) for three channels, one behind the audience, a lovely work like the "Night Music" on Odyssey records and his "A Swarm of Butterflies Encountered on the Ocean." "Bacchanale" (1963) is made from a noise-improv-collage ensemble: poetry by Edward Fields, folk music recordings (many from Henry Cowell), jazz hangouts, scraping violin noises, underwater clarinet, drum and typewriter, as well as parts of Maxfield's "African Symphony" and the poetic "Wind" made of events separated from each other by beautifully timed silence; the sounds are composed of wind and the sounds of things that wind moves, like squeaking rusty gates; Maxfield makes it all into an intriguing piece, "Piano Concert for David Tudor (1961) for piano and tapes made from the performer's improvisations. & "Amazing Grace" (1960) a mass of tape loops, cut to a score (like Maxfield's "Cough Music" (1959-61) and "Italian Folk Music"), which are humorous samples from a religious revival; part of the sketches for Maxfield's opera "Stacked Deck". A very interesting essay "Composers, Performance and Publication" can be read in La Monte Young's *An Anthology*. *— "Blue" Gene Tyranny*

● **Night Music in "New Sounds in Electronic Music"** / Odyssey ✦✦✦✦✦
Exquisite pre-synthesizer electronic music made—like his pieces "Sine Music" (1959) and "Trinity Piece" (1960)—with only the supersonic bias signal of a tape recorder and a supersonic sawtooth waveform from an oscilloscope producing audio range difference tone "ghosts". Identical in feeling to a response to the sound of birds and insects on a summer night in a city park. *— "Blue" Gene Tyranny*

Toshiro Mayuzumi

b. Feb. 20, 1929, Yokohama, Japan, **d.** Apr. 10, 1997, Kawasaki, Japan
Composer / Musique Concrète, World Fusion, Atonal, Electronic
Toshiro Mayuzumi was the first Japanese composer to create works of musique concrète and electronic music. In 1951, he graduated from a Tokyo university and enjoyed a successful premiere of his composition, "Sphenogrammes," at the ISCM festival. While spending the next year studying in Paris, Mayuzumi discovered the musique concrète scene. He returned to Tokyo and formed the composer group Sannin no kai ("Group of Three") and write the first musique concrète work ["X, Y, Z" (1955)] and first electronic piece ["Shusaku I" (1955)] in Japan. His experimentations also include the use of prepared piano and unusual instrumentations. From the late '50s on, Mayuzumi's music was increasingly influenced by traditional Japanese music and Buddhism, and was awarded the Otaka Prize twice (in 1958 and 1967) for work in this vein. He also composed for theater (including his collaborations with Mishima) and for film, including his award-winning electronic score for *Tokyo Olympic* in the mid-'60s. Later in his career, Mayuzumi also hosted a television show and served as the President of the Japan Federation of Composers. *— Joslyn Layne*

Mandala Symphony (1960) / Odyssey ✦✦✦
Performed by the NHK Symphony Orchestra conducted by Hiroyuki Iwaka. Although bordering on a large contemporary romantic work, this symphony attempts to express a Japanese "Buddhist view of the omnipotent universe," and uses only collections of sounds to achieve this aim. The two parts of the mandala are expressed in the two parts of the symphony: "Kongokai-Mandala symbolizes spiritual awakening through contemplation and

oneness with eternity; "Taizokai-Mandala" represents the world of Sokushin Jyobutsu, which is made up of the phases of life, such as Gakido (a place of hunger and thirst where sinners go in the afterlife) or Shurado (passage of pandemonium, the world of the immature until they attain spiritual awakening)". *— "Blue" Gene Tyranny*

- **Prelude for String Quartet (1964)** / Deutsche Grammaphon ♦♦♦♦♦
Performed by the LaSalle Quartet and composed in 1964, this piece introduces its basic musical material right at the beginning: mysterious and gently shifting single long tones are played non-vibrato, the middle strings play tremolos and high harmonics, and occasional koto-like pizzicati develop into fuller, almost humorous gestures that are echoed among the players. After several minutes the various materials are moved closer and closer together, are given shorter durations, and the tempo becomes very active. All the strings join in several mutual fast glissandi upwards, followed by a gradually de-tuned and very rhythmic strummed guitar effect. The *Prelude for String Quartet* ends as it began with several high sustained tones. *— "Blue" Gene Tyranny*

Merzbow (Masami Akita)

b. 1956, Tokyo, Japan
Guitar, Effects, Producer / Noise, Dark Ambient, Experimental
Merzbow is the alias of Masami Akita, one of the world's most prolific practitioners of eardrum-assaulting Japanese noise. Starting in 1981, Merzbow issued literally dozens of releases on a monthly basis; however, his first official U.S. collection, *Venereology,* did not come out until 1994. His second stateside release, the psychedelia-tinged *Pulse Demon,* appeared in 1996; like its predecessor, the record was mastered at abnormally high audio levels to further amplify the extreme nature of Merzbow's work. *—Jason Ankeny*

Pulse Demon / May 28, 1996 / Release ♦♦♦

- **Scumtron: A Tribute to Merzbow** / Aug. 19, 1997 / Mute ♦♦♦♦
Standing next to two deafening Merzbow originals ("Eat Beat Eat 1," "Eat Beat 2"), remixers Autechre, Jim O'Rourke, Panasonic and Russell Haswell can't help but come off a bit muted. The best contribution is Bernhard Günter's atmospheric mix, which comes off as a photographic negative of the usual Merzbow material. *—John Bush*

- **1930** / May 19, 1998 / Tzadik ♦♦♦♦♦
There's a wider variety of unexpected sounds than those normally heard in a Merzbow listening session in this sonic inundation. Unguessed-at dimensions are accessed through *1930* via sensory overload of oscillations, infinitely layered static, frequencies from pitch to buzz—an explosion could get lost in this, and many do. It is the sounds of tuning in the radio, only to catch the low-end frequencies of an earthquake. Music has long explored—and exploited—its ties to emotions; the genre of noise, it seems, has moved on to exploring sound's physical effects. Merzbow, the leader of Japanese noise, has learned how to use sound to operate on your brain; he utilizes indiscernible frequencies to poke pinholes in your eardrums and bleed out your preconceived notions of sound, music, and how they can affect you. This listening experience is not simply a result of sheer volume (Merzbow is generally listened to *very* loudly): Even while turned down low, the sounds all combine into an irresistible force that messes with your physical being. It will scramble your brain, until consciousness barely registers anything but sound. [Note: This is, however, a somewhat temporary effect.] *—Joslyn Layne*

Olivier Messiaen

b. Dec. 10, 1908, Avignon, France, **d.** Apr. 28, 1992, Paris, France
Organ, Composer / Musique Concrète, 20th Century Classical/Modern Composition, World Fusion, Atonal, Electronic, Classical
The classical music tradition was expanded to include the sounds of nature and world music by French composer Oliver Messiaen. His composition *Turangalila Symphonie,* premiered by the Boston Symphony Orchestra in 1949, fused rhythms of classical Indian music and western pop influences. From 1930 until his death in 1992, Messiaen served as organist and composer at Eglise De La Trinite in Paris.

Messiaen inherited his creative skills from his parents. His mother was poet Cecile Sauvage, while his father helped to translate Shakespeare into French. Composing music by the age of eight, Messiaen advanced quickly. After learning to read music, he successfully tackled the operatic scores of Mozart, Gluck, Berlioz, and Wagner. He was only 11 years old when he began studying at the Paris Conservatory.

Accepting a position as organist at La Trinite in 1930, Messiaen was inducted into Ecole Normale de Musique in Paris six years later. Messiaen's musical career was interrupted when he enlisted as a medical orderly in the French army in 1939. Captured by German forces the following year, he was taken to a prisoner of war camp in Silesia. While imprisoned, he continued to work on his music. Despite the lack of a piano, he composed, *The Quartet for the End of Time,* premiering the piece for an audience comprised of more than five-thousand prisoners.

In 1941, after securing his freedom and being discharged from the army, Messiaen taught harmony at the Paris Conservatory. Between 1943 and 1947, he conducted seminars on musical analysis and composition to a small, private group that included Pierre Boulez and Karlheinz Stockhausen.

Messiaen continued to balance his work at Eglise de la Trinite with commissioned compositions. The French government commissioned him to compose a piece, *Et Expecto Resurrectionem Mortuorum,* in memory of those who died in the World Wars. The following year, he taught composition at the Paris Conservatory. *— Craig Harris*

★ **Des Canyons Aux Etoiles (From the Canyons to the Stars) (1971-1974) / Oiseaux Exotiques** / 1991 / CBS ♦♦♦♦♦
Performed by the London Sinfonietta and directed by Esa-Pekka Salonen, this is a terrific collection of Messiaen's later style, with pointillistic tone paintings and good performances. However, I still prefer the earlier vinyl recording of "Des Canyons aux Étoiles" on Erato with Marius Constant conducting. Five passages from the Book of Revelations were the stimulus for "Couleurs de la cité céleste," including the lines "And the light of the Holy City was like a jasper stone, clear as crystal, and the foundations of the wall of the City were garnished with all manner of precious stones, jaspar, sapphire, chalcedony." Greek and Hindu rhythms, plainsong, birdsongs (including the shattering cry of the Brazilian araponga), and a sustained rainbow of symbol soundcolors are all used in the composition of the work for the unusual combination of piano solo, three clarinets, three xylophones, brass and metallic percussion. An ancient, raw and almost primitive religious feeling prevades this dynamic piece from 1963. *— "Blue" Gene Tyranny*

O Sacrum Convivium in of Eternal Light / 1993 / Catalyst ♦♦♦
A warm, hopeful religious work in Messiaen's early style in a beautifully subtle performance by Musica Sacra, conducted by Richard Westenburg. This CD also contains the enchanting and energetic "Return to Earth" by Meredith Monk, and works by Moran and Ligeti. *— "Blue" Gene Tyranny*

Eclairs Sur L'au-Dela . . . (1992) / 1994 / Jade ♦♦♦
The generally agreed upon translation for this title, "Illuminations From the Beyond . . . ," and is a little tame compared to the equally appropriate and somewhat more apt "Lightning-Flashes From the Beyond . . ."—the full brass unisons with whipcracks and deep rolls from bass drum and gong in the section "Seven Angels With Seven Trumpets" elicits the most chilling majestic feelings from a pre-modern sense of the eternal mystery, "The Way to the Invisible" likewise opens gates of the subconscious with beautifully bizarre harmonic sweeps in the strings, full chordal annunciations in the brass, and "total chromatic" backdrops for the song of the Pied Butcherbird to wander through. As in several other Messiaen works, the birds are seen as intermediaries between the heavenly and the earthly—there is a gorgeous menagerie of 25 bird songs played freely and simultaneously in the section "Several Birds From the Trees of Life," and birds appear throughout the piece. Lovely, unique melodic strains appear in several sections: "God Will Wipe Every Tear From Their Eyes . . . ," the very moving (yet not sensual in the usual manner) "Dwelling in Love," and the final "Christ, Light of Paradise." This piece is a testament to faith in the natural revelation of the Great Mystery expressed in clear, beautiful musical imagery, neither over-emotional nor over-austere. Recorded in live performance, Antoni Wit conducting the National Polish Radio Orchestra of Katowice. *— "Blue" Gene Tyranny*

L' Ascension (Four Symphonic Meditations for Orchestra) (1933) / Koch Schwann ♦♦♦
Performed by The Bavarian Radio Orchestra, dir. Karl Anton Rickenbacher. Compassionate, sacramental, similar to "Les Offrandes oubliees"(1930) . . . unlike the severe religious works of his later style. CD includes "Chronochromie" (1959/60). *— "Blue" Gene Tyranny*

Trois Petites Liturgies (Three Brief Liturgies) (1943-44) for Women's Chorus, Chamber O / Erato ♦♦♦
A very curious, Bzyantine work with a poetic and controversial text by the composer, the poetry of gems and colors mixed with reflections on the presence of the Creator, in us, in others, in things. *— "Blue" Gene Tyranny*

Phil Minton

b. Nov. 2, 1940, Torquay, England
Vocals, Trumpet / Improvisation, Avant-Garde Jazz, Avant-Garde
Avant-garde vocalist Phil Minton has a large vocabulary of voices and extended vocal techniques and an extensive discography cataloguing his numerous projects from 1969 on. Born near the Southern coast of England in 1940, he started out on the trumpet, and began playing in jazz bands in the late '50s. After moving to London in the mid-'60s, Minton began doubling as trumpeter/vocalist for the Mike Westbrook Orchestra, then lived in the Canary Islands for a year, and in Sweden for five before returning to London (and Westbrook's band) in the early '70s. The mid-'70s found him working in a variety of settings, from improvised duos to theatre groups, and in his vocal trio Voice with Julie Tippetts and Maggie Nicols. As an improviser, Minton has toured throughout the world, working with a great many creative musicians, including Peter Brötzmann, Fred Frith, John Butcher, Derek Bailey's Company, and an ongoing collaboration with Veryan Weston. In addition to Voice, he was in another trio during the '90s called Axon (with Marcio Mattos & Martin Blume, which recorded for another collaborator Georg Graewe's label Random Acoustics), led the Phil Minton Quartet, and was a member of the quartet Roof. *—Joslyn Layne*

A Doughnut in Both Hands (1975-1982) / Aug. 15, 1975-1982 / Emanem ♦♦♦♦
Not to be confused with the more recent FMP recording, *A Doughnut in One Hand,* this Emanem release includes the reissue of vocalist Phil Minton's first record (*Rift 3*), plus six previously unissued tracks. Remarkable chiefly for showing the unusual places the human voice can travel, this CD is a poignant lesson in extended vocalese. While its musical value is debatable, and it can be difficult listening at one sitting for its full fifty minutes, Minton nonetheless astonishes with his incredible range. He can be gruff or silly, majestic or morose, or even filled with whimsy, all in the same tune. He sputters, growls, simulates spitting and vomiting, gurgles, yodels, yells, clicks, and clacks. At times he is a meditative monk, and at others a wild animal. How he does it is anybody's guess, but unaccompanied Minton is a romp through an amusement park where every ride is a roller coaster in a haunted house. *— Steve Loewy*

Gordon Monahan

b. Jun. 1, 1956, Kingston, Canada
Piano, Composer / Sound Sculpture, Avant-Garde
Musician and multimedia artist Gordon Monahan has created works ranging from piano compositions to loudspeaker installations since the late '70s. He played in rock bands for several years, starting in the late '60s. From the mid-'70s throughout the '80s, Canadian-born Monahan studied physics, then piano and composition in Ottawa and New Brunswick, spending two years during this time as the pianist in John Cage's Etudes Australes, and studying with Cage. Monahan began mounting multimedia installations and constructing sound sculptures in the late '70s. He often used natural forces in his work; the wind-activated string

installation *Long Aeolian Piano* is an example of these kinetic sculptures. The '80s also brought compositions for piano, including "Piano Mechanics." From the mid- to late '90s, Monahan worked on "Multiple Machine Matrix" (MMM), a network of unique instruments made from recycled materials that are controlled via a MIDI computer. By then, Monahan was based in Berlin, where he collaborated with Laura Kikauka not only on art projects but also on running an underground bar for a few years. Berlin also houses a permanent display by Monahan, his interactive work "Silicon Lagoon" (2000). Monahan has been commissioned by CBC Radio, *the DAAD Festival*, and more. One work, commissioned by an organization in Miami, was banned from the city's 1988 *New Music America* festival. "When It Rains" (2000) was commissioned by Canada Musique; "Earworks" (1983) and "Music From Nowhere" (1992) are among his other important works. Monahan plays organ in a pop group called Fuzzy Love, and is the artistic director of irreverent multimedia group KB Zed. He has had several residencies in North America and has written for various music publications. A few of his recordings, initially self-released, were reissued by Swerve Editions and Musicworks. *—Joslyn Layne*

● **The Long Aeolian Piano** / 1990 / Musicworks ✦✦✦✦✦
A lovely "aeolian harp", sculpted with Thaddeus Holownia, made from strings attached to an upright piano, stretched down a hill, and set in resonance by the wind. (Incidentally, another lovely "aeolian harp" with metal resonators bult by Doug Hollis lives as a permanent installation atop the Exploratorium in San Francisco.) See also Canadian composer Monahan's piece "Speaker Swinging" (excerpt) in the collections *Imaginary Landscapes* and *Soundviews*. *—"Blue" Gene Tyranny*

This Piano Thing / 1992 / Swerve Editions ✦✦✦
Studies in producing unusual sounds from both an unaltered acoustic piano in "Piano Mechanics" and a prepared piano in "This Piano Thing." Monahan has invented several original playing techniques ("Fingers and Arms Becoming Four Hands," "High Trills Becoming Difference Tones," "Voices Emerging Along High Tension Wires") that also require an ear sensitive to the momentary buildups of rushing waveforms and overtone changes. Fascinating and original work. *—"Blue" Gene Tyranny*

Meredith Monk

b. Nov. 20, 1942, New York, NY
Vocals, Keyboards, Piano, Composer / 20th Century Classical/Modern Composition, Avant-Garde
The career of composer, vocalist and filmmaker Meredith Monk has been understandably diverse, resulting in a dozen albums—most for ECM New Series—plus several documentaries and numerous awards for both careers. Born in 1942, she attended Sarah Lawrence College and began composing while there. In 1968, Monk formed the House, a record company-of-sorts for interdisciplinary works relating both to music, dance and film. She signed to the ECM label in the late '70s and has recorded consistently since, avant-garde works encompassing jazz, classical and theater music. *—John Bush*

● **Key** / 1977 / Lovely Music ✦✦✦
Re-release on CD of the 1973 classic. Monk's modern folk music from her beautiful and noble performance-ceremonies that recall former times and a lineage of human understanding beyond the present state of things. Songs include "Porch," "Under Street," "What Does it Mean—," "Vision," "Fat Stream," "Do you be—" "Vision" (reprise), "Change," and "Dungeon" with Meredith Monk, voice, organ, jew's harp; Daniel Ira Sverdlik, Dick Higgins, Colin Walcott, Lanny Harrison, and Mark Monstermaker, voices. See also her beautiful "Phantom Waltz" in the collection *U.S. Choices* by the piano duet Double Edge. *—"Blue" Gene Tyranny*

Dolmen Music / Mar. 1980 / ECM ✦✦

Moondog (Louis Hardin)

b. May 26, 1916, Marysville, KS, **d.** Sep. 8, 1999, Germany
Vocals, Keyboards, Percussion, Harmonica, Composer / 20th Century Classical/Modern Composition, Avant-Garde, Minimalism
A mostly self-taught composer, Louis Hardin was born in 1916 and grew up in Wyoming. After his father brought him to an Arapho Sun Dance, he began playing drums and tomtoms. The constant "tomtom" beat became incorporated in many of his later pieces, such as the complex canon for marimbas "Wind River Powwow: arapa-host, arapa-home, arapa-hope." He played drums in high school in 1929, but lost his sight in his early teens when a dynamite cap exploded. Hardin finished high school at the Iowa School for the Blind, and in 1933 studied braille at the Missouri School for the Blind in St. Louis. He lived in Arkansas until 1942 when he got a scholarship to study in Memphis. However, he mostly taught himself ear training and other musical skills and theory from books in braille. In 1943, he came to New York and met Artur Rodzinski, Leonard Bernstein, and then Toscanini. Hardin began using the name Moondog as a pen name in 1947. His music, built mostly from pure modal themes expanded by sophisticated counterpuntal techniques, would now receive the avant-garde label of "minimal" or pattern music but this sound has characterized his music since the late '40s, and is thus a precursor of this postmodern compositional style.

In New York, Moondog began to meet legendary jazz performer-composers, such as Charlie Parker and Benny Goodman, and to incorporate jazz inflections as well as humorous philosophical couplets and environmental sounds into his recorded compositions. Moondog also sold his printed music and records as well as performed on the streets of Manhattan. His music truly expressed a universal vision with the best of American musical sensibilities. Moondog passed away in Germany at the age of 83. *—"Blue" Gene Tyranny*

More Moondog/The Story of Moondog / 1956-1957 / Prestige/OJC ✦✦✦✦✦
CD re-issues of two lp's on the Prestige label from 1956 and 1957. Moondog on the street and everywhere else. The sources in everyday life with music and life blending as a whole. A soundtrack to spur the imagination. Contains: *Softshoe and Hardshoe (7/4)*, a duet with *The Queen Elizabeth Whistle And Bamboo Pipe, Ostrich Feathers Played on Drums, All Is Loneliness, 5/8 in Two Shades, Violetta's Barefoot Dance, A Portrait of Ninon-A Cocker Spaniel*, etc. *—"Blue" Gene Tyranny*

● **Moondog [CBS]** / 1969 / Columbia ✦✦✦✦✦

● **Moondog [Compilation]** / 1969 / Columbia ✦✦✦✦✦
Although this is not Moondog's most characteristic release—he barely appears on it himself, for one thing—this collection of orchestral treatments of his compositions may be his most appealing work. Dozens of string and wind instruments were enlisted to expound upon the composer's circular themes (which are sometimes canons). The results were tracks that were both dramatic and melodic, building in impact and tension instead of driving listeners up the wall with repetition, often propelled by lightly insistent, rattling percussion. Jazz stars Ron Carter and Hubert Laws are among the musicians, yet Moondog only contributes some bass, and brief snippets of enigmatic spoken phrases, to the recording. It's fine contemporary classical music, however, produced by—of all people—James Guercio, who also produced Chicago. The CD reissue is excellent value, adding the entirety of his 1971 album Moondog 2, fitting both LPs onto a single disc. *—Richie Unterberger*

☆ **The Music of Moondog** / 1990 / Columbia ✦✦✦✦✦
A re-issue of two LPs recorded in 1969 and 1972. Rounds, canons, and other pieces that are the precursor of much pattern music. Incidentally, John Fahey has made a wonderful arrangement of Moondog's "Theme and Variations" (1952) for guitars, percussion and synthesizer on *John Fahey: Rain Forests, Oceans and Other Themes* Varrick CD 019. *—"Blue" Gene Tyranny*

Sax Pax for a Sax / Nov. 11, 1997 / Atlantic ✦✦✦✦✦
As the name implies, this album consists of pieces composed with the saxophone in mind. Nine saxophonists in all (from the London Saxophonic) pitch in on the disc, which also features some piano, folk-rock vet Danny Thompson on contra bass, several percussionists, piano, and occasional ensemble vocals; Moondog himself contributes bass drum, bongos, and (as a member of the ensemble) vocals throughout. In its swaying (at times even sing-along) melodicism, intricate arrangements, and light bounce, it's strongly reminiscent of his excellent 1969 *Moondog* album; in fact, "Bird's Lament" makes an appearance on both records. This is more enjoyable, toe-tapping, and life-affirming than most any other jazz or avant-garde music around in the 1990s, demonstrating that Moondog's talents remain undimmed in his eighties; it's impossible to hear the ebullient choral vocals on "Paris" without smiling. *—Richie Unterberger*

Robert Moran

b. Jan. 8, 1937, Denver, CO
Composer / Multimedia, Sound Sculpture, 20th Century Classical/Modern Composition, Minimalism
Studied with Apostel, Berio, Milhaud. Co-founder San Francisco New Music Ensemble at the San Francisco Conservatory of Music in '60s. Composed large-scale event "Pachelbel Promenade" for city of Graz, Austria in '70s. Composer-in-residence Northwestern University. Operas *From the Towers of the Moon* (1992) for Minnesota Opera, *The Dracula Diary, Night Passage* (1995) for 180 male voices of Seattle Men's Chorus about Oscar Wilde trial and sentence. *—"Blue" Gene Tyranny*

Arias, Interludes and Inventions from "Desert of Roses" / Ten Miles High over Albania F / 1993 / Argo ✦✦✦
A very original composer whose orchestral sound has touches of exotic color, phase music, tuneful invention. Moran collaborated with Philip Glass on the opera "The Juniper Tree." Highly recommended. *—"Blue" Gene Tyranny*

Rocky Road to Kansas/Requiem: Chant Du Cygne (Requiem: Swan Song) / 32 Cryptograms Fo / 1995 / Argo ✦✦✦
The title of the title work comes from the name given to a Pennsylvania quilt pattern, circa 1865, that reminded the composer of the multi-tracked quartet design (thick layers, repeated patterns, etc.) for this charming percussion piece, featuring a variety of African, Isreali and Moroccan drums. Premiered in 1990, the *Requiem: Swan Song* is an inspired piece for four choruses and four chamber orchestras dispersed throughout a cathedral. The text is based on the last words of Mozart as recorded by his wfe and sister ("I compose this Requiem for my self... I can smell death... And now I must leave my art behind"). The rhythmic units of the words closely match those of the instrumental parts—for example, short words occur with pizzicato string notes, choral swells with complementary brass and string sustains. Moran views the work as a "gigantic sound-tapestry... the sounds of some unearthly musical ping-pong game," no doubt an image that would have delighted Mozart who loved dice and billiards and created compositional methods using them. *32 Cryptograms for Derek Jarman* is a delightful, highly rhythmic work from 1995, painted in bright timbres for chamber orchestra. Borrowing the bass line of a well-known aria from Henry Purcell's *Dido and Aeneas*, Moran builds cryptograms from pitch aggregates pitches, consulting the *I-Ching* (John Cage's well-known procedure) to determine the "sound-thickness." Dynamics and repetitions may be altered by performers and conductor. Derek Jarman was the brilliant British filmmaker who was once chosen by Moran to direct his opera *Desert of Roses*. *—"Blue" Gene Tyranny*

● **Desert of Roses/Ten Miles High** / Polygram ✦✦✦✦

Ikue Mori

b. 1953, Tokyo, Japan
Drum Machine, Drums, Composer / Film Music, No Wave, Experimental, Avant-Garde
Ikue Mori has been a key member of the downtown music scene since moving to New York from Tokyo in 1977. She began her career playing drums for the seminal "no wave" group DNA, which she formed with guitarist Arto Lindsay and keyboardist Tim Wright. After the short-lived but highly influential group broke up in 1982, Mori began improvising live and recording with experimental musicians like Fred Frith, Tom Cora and, most notably, John Zorn. By 1985, Mori had completely abandoned the standard drum set in favor of her own unique drum machine/sampler set-up. Her signature instrument evolved into a highly cus-

tomized arrangement of three self-programmed drum machines which she could trigger simultaneously to perform live, as well as for use recording.

In 1990, Mori received an NEA grant to work with filmmaker Abigail Child, which marked the beginning of several soundtrack projects for the musician. Throughout the 90s, Mori played and recorded with countless musicians, including projects/albums *Death Praxis* with vocalist Tenko, *Painted Desert* with guitarists Marc Ribot and Robert Quine and *Death Ambient* with guitarist Frith and bassist Kato Hideki. Mori's career-defining compositions on *Hex Kitchen* (1995) incorporate impressive performances by several of Mori's most frequent collaborators, including electric harp player Zeena Parkins, vocalist Catherine Jauniaux and trombonist Jim Staley. In 1996, Mori released her first solo drum machines album, *Garden,* followed by *B/Side* (1998), a collection of tracks originally recorded for Child's films. Mori continued to work with a myriad of performers in the avant-garde and electronic scenes in the late 1990s, including collaborations with gifted trumpeter Dave Douglas, Mr. Bungle vocalist Mike Patton, Sonic Youth's Kim Gordon, free jazz bassist William Parker and extensive work with composer/saxophonist John Zorn. Mori had several performance highlights in 1999, including an appearance on stage with Sonic Youth, a debut performance of new compositions with DJ Olive in New York City and an improvised duo with Chicago electronic musician Jim O'Rourke. Ikue Mori is one of the most respected musicians in the downtown scene, renowned for her abilities as an accomplished composer and improviser and as one of the foremost electronic music innovators. *—Matthew Carlin*

● **Hex Kitchen** / 1995 / Tzadik ✦✦✦✦✦
Hex Kitchen showcases downtown New York musician Ikue Mori at the height of her compositional abilities. While her unique manipulation of samples and drum machines always yields interesting sounds, some of her improvisatory and recorded work leaves something to be desired in terms of musical structure. This release, however, offers the fascinating percussive and machine sounds Mori is known for, along with some highly inventive, yet listenable songs. Most of the tracks even clock in at the three- to four-minute range, making for the closest approximation of a conventional album that will ever come from this purely experimental electronic musician. Boasting an appearance by John Zorn on clarinet, *Hex Kitchen* is an all-star avant-garde ensemble piece with some inspired playing by Zeena Parkins on electric harp and accordion, trombonist Jim Staley, and violinist Hahn Rowe. The real highlights of the album come with the first three tracks, though. Album opener "Slush" showcases Mori's unique approach to rhythm with driving, syncopated solo drum machines and sampler. "Woke Up Aghast" is rather catchy with a rolling bass line courtesy of Hideki Kato and surprising use of bagpipes by David Watson. Here, Mori also introduces her haunting use of vocals, which have a sort of lullaby-ish quality that portrays a frightening innocence when coupled with Mori's abrasive samples. Zorn's clarinet work, coupled with Parkins' accordion and the odd vocalizations of Catherine Jauniaux on "Angler Fish" make for the album's best moments. *Hex Kitchen* remains consistently solid, however, with Mori laying a solid foundation for the other musicians to work on top of, using drum machines and samplers to create alternately strong rhythmic bases and brief blasts of utter chaos. The sum total is an engaging experimental work that would be a good starting point for the uninitiated. *—Matthew Carlin*

B-Side / Jan. 20, 1998 / Tzadik ✦✦✦✦
B-Side presents soundscapes and music that Ikue Mori composed for the films of Abigail Child, spanning 1992 through 1996. The piece for *Geek Love* is a sad cello narrative lightly screened by clunky action in the foreground. Most of this recording, created for the 1996 film *B-Side,* is an atmospheric collage of well-built samples seeded with surprises and electronics that intertwine nicely with the live instrumentation. This release has enough examples of Ikue Mori's tasteful and clever drum machine and sampling work to make it a worthwhile listen both for fans and for the simply curious. *—Joslyn Layne*

● **One Hundred Aspects of the Moon** / Feb. 22, 2000 / Tzadik ✦✦✦✦✦
Ikue Mori's *One Hundred Aspects of the Moon* (Tzadik, 2000) is a wonderful and multifaceted modern chamber suite similar in nature to her film music, as opposed to, say, her work in Death Ambient. The work is named for Mori's inspiration in composing this music, a woodblock print series by Yoshitoshi, the last master of Japanese Ukiyoe. The pieces ranges from a section reminiscent of John Zorn's cartoon music, called "Monkey Music Moon," to the interim piece heard during "Like a Reflection in the Moon" to the disturbed and repetitive "Cloth-Beating Moon." Mori performs on her drum machines, joined by pianist and organist Anthony Coleman, violinist Eyvind Kang, cellist Erik Friedlander, bassist Kato Hideki, and the vocals (acrobatics, speaking, and singing) of Theo Bleckmann. *—Joslyn Layne*

David Moss

b. Jan. 21, 1949, New York
Vocals, Percussion / Improvisation, Experimental, Avant-Garde
Innovative percussionist and vocalist David Moss has been based out of Berlin since 1991. Improviser and provocateur, Moss' music ranges from extreme to experimental to 20th century, and includes compositions, sound collages, and tough jazz rock hybrids—as in his Dense Band. Commissioned by New American Radio for the second time in the mid-80s, he created an 'operadio,' *Language Linkage,* based on and around the texts of Italo Calvino. He has performed solo worldwide—including NYC, Koln and Tokyo—in prestigious places that like the Whitney Museum. Moss has also led the group Direct Sound, and served as Musical Director for the Leipzig Opera (for "Survival Songs"). Among his honors: a 1991 Guggenheim Fellowship and a DAAD Kunstlerprogram stipend for a one-year residency in Berlin; the Preis der Deutschen Schallplatten Kritik in 1992 and 1994; the Horspeil des Monats from the Deutsche Akademie des Darstellenden Kunste in 1995 for "Moss Tales." There's a clear record of experimental achievement and an openness to variety found in Moss' past that includes his solo performances; his work with music makers Heiner Goebbels, Fred Frith, and Jon Rose; and his collaborations with dancers Steve Paxton, Kei Takei, and Kenneth King. *—Joslyn Layne*

Language Linkage (1988) / 1990 / Aerial ✦✦✦
Energetic setting of Italo Calvino text for many processed voices, electronic sounds, percussion. Like a parallel universe. A very different sound. *—"Blue" Gene Tyranny*

Raphael Mostel

Composer / 20th Century Classical/Modern Composition, World Fusion
New York composer Raphael Mostel is known for his use of Tibetan singing bowls in his ritualistic works. In 1983, he founded the Tibetan Singing Bowl Ensemble, which has recorded his compositions for a variety of labels including Angel and Digital Fossils. Mostel composed music commemorating the bombings of Hiroshima and Nagasaki, which was performed at ceremonies in 1987 and can be heard on *Blood on the Moon.* He has received fellowships, commissions, and grants from a number of organizations, and has worked as a lecturer, freelance writer, and conductor. In the latter half of the '90s, two multimedia retrospectives of Mostel's work were put on in N.Y.C. In 2000, his score for the children's story "Travels of Babar" premiered, incorporating slides and narrators. *—Joslyn Layne*

● **Nightsongs** / 1991 / Digital Fossils ✦✦✦
Not a new age group, this ensemble is described on their first CD cover as creating "new music for old instruments," and that's what they do. Raphael Mostel resonates Tibetan brass meditation bowls, gradually introducing sharp and startling sounds that will awake the chakras. "Jacob's Ladder" combines didgeridoos, water, and breaking sounds with wailing thighbone trumpets. John Charles Thomas produces a solo on the ancient lyzarden with jazzline inflections in "Nightsong," and the brilliant singer and instrumentalist Mieczyslaw Litwinski is also featured throughout. *—"Blue" Gene Tyranny*

Blood on the Moon / 1992 / Digital Fossils ✦✦✦

Ceremonial for the Equinox (1985) / 1995 / Digital Fossils ✦✦✦✦
This impressive, dreamy and dramatic large-scale spatial piece was commissioned by the Cathedral of St. John the Divine in New York City, and this CD is a recording of the 1985 premiere. The orchestra, consisting of instruments from the whole world, spread throughout the cathedral or moving with the performers, is made up of a bodhran (Celtic frame drum), four bass drums at the altar and five bass drums at the entrance played by friction on the membranes (which sounds like horns or electronics), one 12-foot bass drum hit with baseball bat, Mayan rainsticks, Japanese shakuhachi, Tibetan singing bowls played by 23 performers, seven shofar (Jewish ram's horns) players, saxophone, oboe, bassoon, clarinet, English horn, Brazilian wood bird whistles, three large Wu Han tam-tams, tube trumpets. The sound is further transformed by the Cathedral's resonant enormity and variety of architectural shapes, the sound of burning torches, and sounds from the audience which is set in rows facing each other, so that all seats were equally in the best location. The Ceremonial proceeds through four sections: Fire (torches in darkness, a "Processional" with solo bodhran, an "Invocation of Furies" with tube trumpets and drums, and "The Duel" of opposing percussion ensembles, which approaches thunderstorm intensity), Water (the "Grace of Rain" with rainsticks and birdwhistles), Earth (the hauntingly beautiful "Holy Songs of Thanksgiving" in the mode of the Book of Job, six solo "Songs" and seven "Ecstatic Dances" played by solo woodwinds with drums, and ensemble winds) and Air ("Oracle of the Sun" for the large tamtams with droning winds, "Starry Night" for Tibetan singing bowls, and "Ram's Horns Tocsin" for shofar septet with drums). The initial Celtic frame drum is heard briefly concluding the piece. *—"Blue" Gene Tyranny*

Gordon Mumma

b. Mar. 30, 1935, Framingham, MA
Composer / Minimalism, Electronic
Gordon Mumma is a cofounder, with Robert Ashley, of the Cooperative Studio for Electronic Music in Ann Arbor, MI, which has been in existence since the early 60s. *—AMG*

Hornpipe (1967)/ in "The Sonic Arts Union" / 1970 / Mainstream ✦✦✦
Piece for French horn played with unusual reed mouthpieces etc. and cybersonic feedback circuitsry. We hear the sound of the processing circuits balancing and unbalancing themselves, as the horn player's chosen responses gradually build an "orchestra" of accumulated decisions. A mysterious live performance. *—"Blue" Gene Tyranny*

Dresden Interleaf 13 February 1945/ Music from the Venezia Space Theatre/ Megaton for W / Lovely Music ✦✦✦✦✦
Live electronic music created for multi-media theatres performances by The ONCE Group on tour. Fascinating and mysterious. *—"Blue" Gene Tyranny*

★ **Mesa/Pontpoint/Fwyyn** / Lovely Music ✦✦✦✦✦
The composer with Pauline Oliveros, David Tudor on bandoneons. "Fwyyn" is a lament to bring back to life a dancing princess who had been enchanted. Beautiful, slowly evolving textures. "Mesa" describes expansive, eroded mesa landscapes, and "Pontpoint" interprets a bridge in a rural French village through an analogous bridging movement in the acoustical space. Pure electronic music, by a co-founder with Robert Ashley of the Cooperative Studio for Electronic Music in Ann Arbor, Michigan from 1960—1970. *—"Blue" Gene Tyranny*

Conlon Nancarrow

b. Oct. 27, 1912, Texarkana, AK, **d.** Aug. 10, 1997, Mexico City, Mexico
Composer / 20th Century Classical/Modern Composition, Fusion, Atonal
Nancarrow composed some of the most rhythmically intricate music ever written, almost all of it for the player piano. Indeed, his music is so dense—with multiple lines of counterpoint, contrasting tempi, and time signatures—it's virtually inconceivable that it could be played by a single human pianist. Nancarrow did his work in isolation, away from the musical establishment, and was unrecognized for his achievements until very late in his long life. As a teenager, Nancarrow played trumpet in early jazz bands. He studied at the Cincinnati College Conservatory of Music from 1929-1932; while there, he heard a performance of Stravinsky's the Rite of Spring, which cemented his desire to become a composer. He moved to Boston in 1934, where he studied privately with Nicolas Slonimsky, Walter Piston, and Roger Sessions (according to his first wife, Helen Rigby, he also met Schoenberg after the latter had fled to this country following the Nazi takeover).

In 1936, he worked his way to Europe as a ship's musician and visited London, Paris, and

Germany. The next year, he joined the Abraham Lincoln Brigade and fought against Franco's fascists in the Spanish Civil War. While in Spain, Slonimsky published Nancarrow's first works: the Toccata for Violin and Piano and the Prelude and Blues for Piano (1938). After the defeat of the Spanish republicans, Nancarrow smuggled himself back to the U.S. in the hold of a freighter. He returned to Texarkana for a time, then moved to New York, where he made the acquaintance of many of the era's finest composer's, including Elliott Carter, Aaron Copland, Wallingford Riegger, and Minna Lederman. He wrote for the journal Modern Music and read composer Henry Cowell's treatise on contemporary music, New Musical Resources. Cowell's theories involving multiple time signature and tempi intrigued Nancarrow, as did his idea that such inhumanly elaborate rhythms could be realized on the player piano. In order to avoid harassment from the U.S. government over his leftist politics, he moved to Mexico City in 1940. In 1947 he traveled to New York to buy a player piano; he also had a machine made that would punch holes in piano rolls. While in New York, he also heard John Cage's Sonatas and Interludes (a piece for prepared piano) performed. He returned to Mexico in 1948, where he married painter Annette Margolis, who was an assistant to the painter Diego Rivera. The couple built a house on the outskirts of Mexico City, where the composer would live for the rest of his life.

Nancarrow began writing his Studies for Player Piano. In 1951, Elliott Carter had Nancarrow's Rhythm Study No. 1 for Player Piano published in New Music. In 1955, Nancarrow became a Mexican citizen. For most of the next two-plus decades, his profile remained very low. Merce Cunningham choreographed several of his piano studies in 1960; in 1962, Nancarrow gave a public performance of his music. In 1969, Columbia issued an LP of Nancarrow's Player Piano Studies (the record was deleted in 1973).

During the '70s, Nancarrow had a few random publications and recordings, but it wasn't until the '80s that his stardom began to rise. In 1981, he secured the services of an agent, who convinced him to tour. He visited San Francisco for New Music America '81, his first visit to his homeland since 1948. The next year he received a MacArthur Grant in the amount of 300,000 dollars. He was named composer-in-residence at the Cabrillo Festival, also in 1982. Public performances of his work increased during the '80s; in 1986, his non-player-piano music was played at Lincoln Center by the group Continuum and in 1987, he traveled to the Holland Festival for performances of his work. In 1988, the noted critic and composer Kyle Gann undertook to write Nancarrow's biography, visiting the composer in Mexico City.

The University of Mexico presented a two-day festival of Nancarrow's music in 1991. The composer suffered a stroke that year, beginning a physical decline. After years in the writing, Gann's book was published in 1995. It's appearance helped to further elevate Nancarrow's reputation. At the time of his death in 1997, Nancarrow had never been held in higher esteem. His uniqueness lay in part on his choice of medium, combined with the depth of his imagination. Because Nancarrow did not have to consider the physical limitations of a human performer, he was able to indulge his every idea, no matter how complex or arcane. *—Chris Kelsey*

★ **Studies for Player Piano, Vols. 1-5** / 1990 / Wergo ✦✦✦✦✦
Secluded in a quiet suburban district of Mexico City, Conlon Nancarrow has spent decades composing these incomparable pieces, punching the player piano rolls himself; these studies, of unparalleled rhythmic complexity and fascinating energy, were begun in 1949. A jazz trumpeter in the 1930s, the composer also studied world music in great detail, giving special attention to the musics of Africa and India. The consideration given to all those musical structures shows up in the studies, not in stylistic imitation but in re-thinking shared musical "problems" (in the good sense) and coming up with his own solution.

A brief discussion of selected studies will give some idea of their breadth. One of the best-known is the delightful five-movement "Boogie Woogie Suite," (study 3a-3e.) Number 3a is based on traditional boogie and jazz (like studies 1-10) but is maniacally sped-up and eventually attains eight superimposed layers of activity. Study number 20 is a more "pure music" piece (like numbers 21-27), a three-voice canon on aperiodic rhythmic patterns. Each pattern is given a certain restricted set of pitches, which are first introduced in a staggered, gentle manner, then later played in octaves over the full range of the piano resulting in a dramatic, impassioned angularity. All of Nancarrow's innovations and experiments make for wonderful listening. *— "Blue" Gene Tyranny*

Studies / 1991 / RCA Victor Red Seal ✦✦✦
Composed in 1986, "Piece No. 2 for Small Orchestra" begins with an enthusiastic and bright but stumbling march tempo, with piano offbeat accents and staggered fast-tonguing horn, trumpet and wind figures in rhythms that begin to get gradually slower and slower. Then the music begins to build toward its former energy, sort of half succeeds, then stops. A version of the music returns with the same rhythms slowed down, but orchestrated with a jazzy pizzicato bass, with wheezy winds above. When the winds stop, the bass continues, and muted chords in two pianos in multiple rhythms replace the winds. This music also ceases, and coquettish oboe solos, and a bassoon and trombone have a very tenuous duet over very subdued fragments of the bass, muted piano chords, and pizzicato strings. The effect is very droll and charming. Gradually other instruments are added into the pointillistic, hocketing texture, and the beginning music gradually tries to reassemble itself by drawing together fragments in multiple tempi. It doesn't succeed in doing that, but does recreate a new body that seems satisfied enough to proceed with a strong ending cadence. A delightful piece and an interesting extension of Nancarrow's rhythmic compositional procedures for player piano. *— "Blue" Gene Tyranny*

Study No.15 (1950s), Transcribed for Piano Four-Hands by Yvar Mikhashoff in "Continuum / 1992 / Music Masters ✦✦✦
The same surprising rhythmic complexities and drive as the piano rolls played here by live performers. *— "Blue" Gene Tyranny*

Ben Neill

b. Nov. 14, 1957, North Carolina
Keyboards, Trumpet, Producer / Multimedia, Electronica, Jungle/Drum 'N Bass, Ambient
Trumpeter Ben Neill successfully bridged the gap between ambient music and the avant-garde, further blurring aesthetic boundaries with the development of his mutantrumpet, a revolutionary electro-acoustic hybrid of conventional trumpet and synthesized sound. A native of North Carolina and a product of classical training, Neill relocated to New York City during the mid-'80s, immersing himself in the downtown experimental music scene; increasingly fascinated with minimalism, he studied under the legendary La Monte Young, and with the aid of the synthesizer pioneer Robert Moog designed the first mutantrumpet, an instrument fit with three bells, six valves, a trombone slide and an analog processing system whch allowed him to create any number of open, muted and electronic sounds.

In 1984, Neill completed *Orbs*, his first major composition for mutantrumpet, percussion and audio/visual projections; pieces including 1985's *Mainspring*, 1987's *Money Talk* and 1988's *Abblasen House* followed prior to his breakthrough work *ITSOFOMO (In the Shadow of Forward Motion)*, a 1989 collaboration with visual artist David Wojnarowicz. A year later Neill travelled to Amsterdam's Steim Studios to develop a new, MIDI-capable mutantrumpet; the upgrade resulted in the addition of a number of switches, knobs and pressure-sensitive pads allowing the player to trigger and modify a variety of sounds and sequences, as well as lights and projections, all in real time. *After Haydn*, a collaboration with electronic composer Nicolas Collins, followed in 1991.

Neill then began a six-year stint as curator of the downtown NYC performance space The Kitchen, a position which served as his gateway into the burgeoning electronic music scene. Presenting performances by everyone from John Cage to Jim O'Rourke to Future Sound of London, he began increasingly absorbing electronic influences into his work and was particularly fascinated by the local "illbient" movement; originally created as an installation/performance piece, Neill's 1995 album *Green Machine* instead evolved into a full-blown dance music project, complete with 12-inch remixes from the likes of Single Cell Orchestra and DJ Spooky. The latter resurfaced on 1996's *Triptycal*, and Neill also spent the better part of 1997 appearing with Spooky and video sampling innovator's Gardner Post "Sci-Fi Lounge" tour. *Goldbug* followed a year later. *—Jason Ankeny*

Mainspring / 1992 / Ear-Rational ✦✦✦✦✦
Pieces featuring Neill's invention the "mutatrumpet," a combination of three trumpets plus slide, which makes rapid change between a variety of sonorities possible; an electronic processing system by Robert Moog and a computer program by David Behrman have both been designed to work with the mutatrumpet. This CD exemplifies the idea of "unified multi-sidedness" in the sounds and the compositional style. For example, in "Mainspring" (1985), which is really delightful and peculiar. "Dis-solution 2" (1986) is for mutatrumpet, percussion, and pitch-sensing electronics (David Behrman) providing a lovely treble shadow, and "No More People" (1988) with text by Stevie Smith for soprano and band is a classic aria over constantly intense telegraphic figures. Wow. *— "Blue" Gene Tyranny*

ITSOFOMO (In the Shadow of Forward Motion) (Complete Works) / 1993 / Robi Droli/New Tone ✦✦✦
The raw truth of a personal experience of anti-gay violence... the energetically telegraphing style of the music is excellently imagined and perfectly complements the impassioned text and delivery by the late Wojnarowicz. Extraordinarily moving. *— "Blue" Gene Tyranny*

678 Streams / 1994 / New Tone ✦✦✦✦

● **Goldbug** / Jun. 16, 1998 / Antilles/I.L.S. ✦✦✦✦✦
For a trumpet player, Neill proves himself a masterful drum'n'bass merchant and an excellent keyboardist to boot on his 1998 album *Goldbug*. From the opening track "Tunnel Vision," Neill's blend of breakbeats and occasional mutantrumpet solos sounds better than many producers in the drum'n'bass community. There are some notable guests (including DJ Spooky and Page Hamilton), but they appear on few tracks and never take the focus away from Neill's excellent album. *—Keith Farley*

Phill Niblock

b. Oct. 2, 1933, Anderson, IN
Photography, Composer / Multimedia, Minimalism, World Fusion, Electronic
American minimalist composer Phill Niblock has been active in his multimedia endeavors since the mid-'60s. His shows usually incorporate film footage (generally are long takes of non-Western people working), or other visual elements such as slides, video and photography, often presenting more than one of these simultaneously with his music. His music itself is characterized by multiple tones sounding simultaneously for long stretches, creating a very dense, seemingly static sound. Niblock has relatively few recordings, but some argue that his music is so inseparable from whatever physical space it's performed in, that recordings don't do justice anyway. Nevertheless, he began curating the CD series of the Experimental Intermedia Foundation, along with David Behrman and Lois V. Vierk, to remedy this situation for himself and other modern composers. He has been involved in EIF since the late '60s, became producer of their presentations in the early '70s, and director of the organization in 1985.

after becoming the organization's director in the '80s. His shows have visited a number of art museums and spaces in North America and Europe, including MoMA, London's Institute of Contemporary Art, and Palais des Beaux Arts in Brussels. He has received numerous grants from organizations including the NEA and the Guggenheim Foundation, and has taught at the City University of New York since 1971. *—Joslyn Layne*

Four Full Flutes / 1991 / Experimental Intermedia ✦✦✦✦✦

● **Music by Phill Niblock** / 1993 / Experimental Intermedia ✦✦✦
This CD contains two compositions "Five More String Quartets" and "Early Winter", both of which are long, sustained sound universes which slowly change in pitch and timbre, redefining the form of the sonic space they simultaneously create and occupy. For example, in "Early Winter" for string quartet, multi-tracked bass flute, sampled and synthesizer voices and flute, harmonics slowly appear and vanish like the slow onset of winter weather. "Five More String Quartets" creates ghostly difference tones by the detuning/retuning of pitches from multi-tracked strings. *— "Blue" Gene Tyranny*

Luigi Nono

b. Jan. 29, 1924, Venice, Italy, **d.** May 8, 1990, Venice, Italy

Composer / 20th Century Classical/Modern Composition, Atonal, Electronic, Classical

Italian composer in the 12-tone or atonal style, whose work encompasses many forms, including opera and electronic music. Many fundamental works by Nono are out of print—"y su sangre ya viene cantando (And Even Your Blood Comes Singing)," for flute, strings, and percussion, from *Epitaffio per Garcia Lorca* ("Epitaph for Garcia Lorca," RCA Victrola VICS 1313, 1968); the choral settings of texts by Cesare Pavese; and the operas *Intolleranze* ("Intolerance," 1960, which attacks segregation, the bomb, and Nazism); *Al Gran Sole Carico d'Amore* ("To the Great Sun Charged with Love," 1975, about the Paris Commune of 1871). *—"Blue" Gene Tyranny*

● **Floresta E Jovem E Cheja De Vida (1965-66) for Soprano, Voices, Clarinet, Copper Plate** / 1979 / Deutsche Grammaphon ✦✦✦

This is a good example of Nono's pieces (like "Non Consumiamo Marx" and "La Fabricca Illuminata," both for voices and tape) that call for attention to immediate situations: in this case, the escalation of the Vietnam War by American forces. Tapes mix multiphonics played on the clarinet with various electronic sounds produced at the studios of national radio RAI. Texts—from pro- and antiwar groups and individuals, a Vietnamese partisan, American workers, and students—are vocalized by the legendary New York-based group the Living Theatre. In live performance with this tape, a soprano and other live voices sing a lament and deliver other texts, accompanied by five suspended copper metal plates of various thicknesses (ancient sounds of the call to war). *—"Blue" Gene Tyranny*

Liebeslied (Love Song) for mixed choir and instruments (1954) / 1990 / Deutsche Grammaphon ✦✦✦✦✦

La fabbrica illuminata (The Illuminated Factory) (1964) for voice and tape / H / 1992 / Wergo ✦✦✦✦✦

"La Fabbrica Illuminata" (The Illuminated Factory) is for woman's voice and four-channel magnetic tape that uses noises and speech sounds recorded in a factory. These were combined with choral and electronic sounds and taken through multiple transformations. The woman sings a commentary on the situation represented by the fixed sound events on the tape: the trial of the work process in the factory and the social injustice and unfairness that are tied to the social forms of capitalism. Massive vocal tone clusters followed by declarative, fragmented political chants begin the work.

Steel-on-steel electronics accompany the voices. The live soprano's text is likewise punctuated and fragmentary ("... electronic... machinery... and..."). Imagery is created by deep rolling sounds, wind-like roars of empty landscapes, voices of muscle-exhausted workers and the sounds of their expended effort, cars rushing past, and the actual and electronically described sounds of turning gears.

Nono has created an empathetic, mysteriously toned and moving work, which is also compelling, convincing and original with "Ricorda cosa ti hanno fatto in Auschwitz" (Remember what they did to you in Auschwitz) (1965). Strangely modified children's voices in a nightmarish landscape are heard followed by a distorted national anthem (unrecognizable). Trumpets like sirens of war, sounds like bullets striking metal, and horrific bellowing creatures fill the soundscape. Odd echoes of a damp, dreary jail, moaning voices, screeching machinery, and deep unison gasps of a multitude of people complete the horrible picture. One of the most moving and effective depictions of this instance of inhumanity. *—"Blue" Gene Tyranny*

Fragmente—*Stille, an Diotima (1980) (Fragments*—Stillness, to Diotima) / 1992 / Disques Montaigne ✦✦✦

Diotima was Socrates' teacher, and is associated with the concept of time. Performed by the Arditti String Quartet, this music is guided by lines from Holderlin's famous poem, which are present only as an unspoken meditation and guidepost written into the score in 52 places. Nono poses the fundamental questions "Where am I, and who am I—" by examining old music and memories from the distant past as producers of both pain and hope. The composer seeks to "externalize as fully as possible that which has been internalized.... " He concludes, "That is what matters today." In writing this music for the *Beethoven Festival* in Bonn, Nono used Beethoven's piano sonata instruction "mit innigster empfindung" (roughly, "with innermost searching of the heart") to imply a readiness to break out of the habitual and "into the open air." This quartet produces a positive sensation that has been also used as an instruction in several of John Cage's works: "Play until you feel the presence of silence." There is also a lovely performance by the LaSalle Quartet on Deutsche Grammaphon 415 513-2 (issued in 1986), which you may also want to check out. *—"Blue" Gene Tyranny*

La Lontananza Nostalgica Utopica Futura (Nostalgia for a Far Away Future Utopia) for Vi / 1992 / Disques Montaigne ✦✦✦✦✦

Intolleranza 1960 (Intolerance 1960) / 1995 / Teldec ✦✦✦✦✦

This magnificent and controversial opera is performed here by vocal soloists David Rampy and Urszula Koszut as refugees, among others, with Chor der Staatsoper Stuttgart and Staatsorchester Stuttgart conducted by Bernhard Kontarsky. Premiered as *Intolleranza 1960* and later revised as *Intolleranza 1970*, this is Nono's first opera. Its premiere was an internationally reported scandal (even *Time* magazine gave the event a full page) similar to that of other groundbreaking works, with people attempting to shout down the musicians and political leaflets raining from the upper balconies. Some of the protest related to Nono's membership in the Italian Communist party, and had little to do with the opera itself. In fact, the text attacks segregation, the atomic bomb, and Nazism, concluding with a plea to prevent civilization from destruction. Like D.W. Griffith's famous movie epic of the same name with its widely ranging historical periods, Nono's opera journeys through a vast contemporary scene, drawing from European history but applicable worldwide. The cast includes the two refugees as well as demonstrators, police, Algerians, farmers, miners, torturers, and fanatics. Additionally, a scene focusing on "some absurdities of contemporary life" includes projections, voices, magnetic tape, and mimes. The colorful and pointillistic orchestral music is brilliant and dramatic, giving full rein to Nono's techniques of dividing and overlapping the text syllables to create new dimensions of meaning. Nono has written that the opera concerns "the wakening of human awareness in a man who has rebelled against the demands of necessityÖand searches for a reason and a 'human' basis for life." Although experiencing intolerance and domination before being "swept away in a flood with other people," he remains certain of "a time when man will be a help to man." "Symbol— Reportage— Fantasy—" Nono asks. "All three, in a story of our time." *—"Blue" Gene Tyranny*

Prometeo: Tragedia Dell'ascolto (Prometheus: a Tragedy About Listening) / 1995 / EMI Classics (Ricordi) ✦✦✦

Pauline Oliveros

b. May 20, 1932, Houston, TX

Electronics, Accordion, Composer / Free Jazz, 20th Century Classical/Modern Composition, Minimalism, Electronic

Avant-garde composer Pauline Oliveros pioneered the concept of Deep Listening, an aesthetic based upon principles of improvisation, electronic music, ritual, teaching and meditation designed to inspire both trained and untrained performers to practice the art of listening and responding to environmental conditions in solo and ensemble situations. Born in Houston, Texas on May 20, 1932, Oliveros received her first musical instruction from her mother and grandmother—equally inspired by the sounds of nature, she committed to pursuing a career in music early in life, studying composition at San Francisco State College during the early '50s and playing french horn in an improvisational group which also included pianist Terry Riley. Later recognized primarily for her prowess on the accordion, during the mid-'60s she served as the first director of the Tape Music Center at Mills College, followed by a 14-year teaching stint at the University of California at San Diego which concluded upon her relocation to Kingston, New York in 1981. In the intervening years Oliveros established herself among the most original thinkers in contemporary music, known initially for the "Sonic Meditations," her earliest attempts at absorbing environmental sounds into the musical process. The same concept was at the heart of the Deep Listening series, a collection of 30 pieces composed between 1971 and 1990. During the mid-'80s, she also established the Pauline Oliveros Foundation, which spread the Deep Listening gospel through recordings, lectures and retreats. *—Jason Ankeny*

I of IV (1966)/ in "New Sounds in Electronic Music" / 1968 / Odyssey ✦✦✦✦✦

This is a good example of Oliveros' earlier electronic music using a configuration of tape recorders patched into each other with magnetic tape spliced in loops so that a form of "automatic generation" system was created by feedback. Similar to Richard Maxfield, Oliveros used bias frequencies of tape recorders and difference, or lower "ghost tones" produced by the interference of very high frequencies. *—"Blue" Gene Tyranny*

★ **The Roots of the Moment** / 1988 / hatART ✦✦✦✦✦

Oliveros with accordion in just intonation within an interactive electronic environment created by Peter Ward. An amazing hour-long live creation (improvisation)... images of valleys, other universes, whatever comes to mind... an exercise in true "deep listening"as she refers to the concerts her foundation presents in upstate New York. *—"Blue" Gene Tyranny*

Duo for Accordion and Bandoneon with Possible Mynah Bird Obbligato (See-saw / 1998 / Musicworks ✦✦✦✦✦

In the collection *Musicworks #70* with Pauline Oliveros on accordion, David Tudor on bandoneon, and Ahmed the Mynah bird, this piece is an absolute delight with punctuated accordion, bandoneon sounds, hissings and a kind of bird barking and squeaking. Another wonderful experiment in interspecies communication. *—"Blue" Gene Tyranny*

Bob Ostertag

b. Apr. 19, 1957, Albuquerque, NM

Synthesizer, Composer / Tape Music, Electronic

An electronic musician and avant-garde composer since the late '70s, Bob Ostertag pioneered techniques later simplified by the sampler by using reel-to-reel machines to create sound loops which could be re-used and manipulated. Basing varied compositions on everything from the plight of an El Salvadoran boy whose father has been murdered by his country's National Guard to a piece centering on AIDS, Ostertag recorded for Elektra/Nonesuch as well as Avant and Recrec. He's also worked with the Kronos Quartet and Bill Frisell, among others. *—John Bush*

Sooner or Later (Tarde O Temprano) / 1991 / Seeland ✦✦✦✦✦

Known for his technique of live performance sampling before there were samplers (by recording performance, cutting the tape, and making a loop, then playing it back on a tape recorder with the tape guards held up by balloons), Ostertag has created a stark and moving work based on the recorded voice of a young Salvadoran boy burying his father who had been killed by El Salvador's National Guard. "There is the sound of the boy's voice, a fly buzzing nearby, and the shovel digging the grave. In part two, there are additional sounds from a 20-second sample of the guitar playing of Fred Frith." Ostertag spent the last ten years working in or around El Salvador. "I saw a lot of death... In that culture, which is both Catholic and highly politicized, death gets surrounded with all kinds of trappings that are intended to make it heroic and purposeful... God's will, or else as irrevalent, since the victims 'live on in the struggle.' It's all glorious and heroic... but some 70,000 people have died there, most because they were in the wrong place at the wrong time... they didn't want to... there was no plan... there was no glory... even for the heroes there is a starker, more immediate side to their death... sooner or later... no angels sang and no one was better... if there is a beauty, we must find it in what is really there... the boy, the shovel, the fly... if we look closely, despite the unbearable sadness, we will discover it." *—"Blue" Gene Tyranny*

● **Say No More** / 1993 / RecRec Music ✦✦✦✦✦

With *Say No More*, Bob Ostertag elevated the sampler to the rank of musical instrument and gained recognition as a true visionary and an avant-garde artist that could not be ignored anymore. This CD is the start of a project in four phases which ended in 1999 with the release of *Verbatim, Flesh and Blood.* Ostertag asked drummers Joey Baron and Gerry Hemingway, vocalist Phil Minton, and bassist Mark Dresser to record some solo improvisations in studio, without giving them any specifications. He took the tapes, loaded them in a computer, fragmented them, and recombined the fragments into two pieces. His aim was to use the musicians' personal vocabulary but apply his own syntax. In Ostertag's previous albums, his hand could always be seen: he manipulated and transformed. This time, 80 percent of the music feels like it is played by an actual band. Some samples are almost a minute long, others a tenth of a second, and the musicians' playing are put together as if they improvised the same piece. The result is simply incredible. Ostertag did leave some traces of his intervention—there is a Phil Minton "solo" in the middle of "Tongue-Tied" where the reconstruction is obvious, some percussion parts are humanly impossible, etc. The border between free improvisation and musique concrete will never be the same. Any serious fan of avant-garde music needs to hear this, one of the rare avant-garde albums where the relevance of the artistic argument equals the relevance of the result. A classic. *—François Couture*

Verbatim, Flesh and Blood / Feb. 15, 2000 / Seeland ✦✦✦✦

John Oswald

b. May 30, 1953, Toronto, Canada

Sax (Alto), Sample Arrangements / Sound Collage, Experimental, Avant-Garde

Canadian composer, saxophonist, and sound collage artist John Oswald is best known for his plunderphonics, which involves using samples of existing recordings to create a new work. A year before Negativland got sued for their *U2* EP, Oswald was taken to court for his 1989 *Plunderphonics* CD by one of the many sample sources, Michael Jackson. *Plunderphonics* was deemed a copyright infringement and all unsold copies were destroyed. He has since recorded *Rubiyat Plunderphonics* and the demonstrative *Nine Examples of Plunderphonic Techniques,* as well as written papers and given lectures on related topics. Oswald is also well-known for his *Grayfolded* releases, a plunderphonics-like treatment of recordings of the Grateful Dead's "Dark Star." In the mid-'70s, he co-founded Pitch with Marvin Green; the project consisted of playing music in the dark. His improvisational work includes leading an (improvising) orchestra weekly for most of the 1980s and performing as an alto saxophonist in a variety of lineups as well as solo. He has composed numerous scores for dance, and has conducted an improvised dance workshop for over a decade. Oswald is the research director for Toronto's Mystery Laboratory experimental studio, and NorthAmerican Experience's music director. He has produced a number of recordings, and has his own releases on the Swell and Musicworks labels, among others. *—Joslyn Layne*

Discosphere / 1991 / Cuneiform ✦✦✦

This is a wonderful compilation of short, effective, single themed pieces written for dance, or that had dances made to them or with them. From very delicate studies like "Skindling Shades" made from incendiary sounds, the wild rhythmic rock of "Angle" to the thousand-fold overdubbing of a tiny bell sound in "Amina" and the hilarious fractured mystery-tale "The Case of Death." Oswald points out the bones and flesh of our illusions with a funny kind of love. *— "Blue" Gene Tyranny*

● **Nine Examples of Plunderphonic Techniques** / 1992 / Musicworks ✦✦✦✦✦

These are the techniques used to make the legendary, not for sale, but nevertheless illegal to possess "Plunderphonics" (1989). Copies were destroyed by the Canadian Recording Industry Association even though the quoted recordings were so distorted by creative sampling that no one would mistake them for the real thing. Canadian composer Oswald comments hilariously and surrealistically on sound material that has become the archtypical if not the downright kitsch-geck detritus of civilization. A procedure and attitude reminiscent of pre-samplers James Tenney ("Collage *1 : Blue Suede"* 1961), Richard Maxfield ("Amazing Grace" and "Cough Music" from the early '60s), and Gordon Mumma ("Epoxy"). *— "Blue" Gene Tyranny*

Plexure / 1993 / Avant ✦✦✦

Grayfolded : Transitive Axis / 1995 / Swell/Artifact ✦✦✦

In 1994, Oswald was invited to "plunderphonicize" the music of the legendary rock band the Grateful Dead, and he went through over a hundred performances from 1969 upward (onward) to accumulate over 40 hours of tape. The music he chose was the unnamed song, sometimes simply referred to as "It," a open, simple modal improvisation that suggests a kind of celestial yearning or universal understanding. He has a soloist "harmonizing with himself over the years," interrelates and studies details of isolated gestures, and creates multiple overlays of the band that add a depth and texture perhaps more in the mind of the group than was actually realized, or realizable, in live performance. After analyzing and organizing the original material over several years, two separate CDs were made (the last shortly before Jerry Garcia's death) from this compositional process: *Grayfolded: Transitive Axis* (utilizing 51 of the original performances) and *Grayfolded: Mirror Ashes.* These are now available as a two-CD set. [See also his *Bell Speeds* in the collection *...lectro Clips.*] *— "Blue" Gene Tyranny*

Grayfolded : Mirror Ashes / 1996 / Swell/Artifact ✦✦✦

Oval

f. 1993

Group / IDM, Glitch, Minimal Techno, Experimental Techno, Electronica, Ambient Techno, Post-Rock/Experimental, Electronic

Although Oval are perhaps more well-known for how they make their music than for the music they actually make, the German experimental electronic trio have provided an intriguing update of some elements of avant-garde composition in combination with techniques of digital sound design, resulting in some of the most original, if somewhat challenging electronic music of the contemporary scene. Originally composed of Markus Popp, Sebastian Oschatz, and Frank Metzger, Oval gradually became the work of just Popp, with Metzger providing most of the visual and design work. The bulk of Popp's work, released through the Force Inc.-related Mille Plateaux label, incorporates elements of what could be described as "prepared compact disc"—manually marred and scarified CDs played and sampled for the resultant, somewhat randomly patterned rhythmic clicking. Layered together with subtle, sparse melodies and quirky electronics, the results are often as oddly musical as they are just plain odd. Popp brought this approach to bare on the first full-length Oval releases— *Wohnton, Systemische* and *94 Diskont*–as well as a number of compilation tracks. Although a rung below marginal in their home country and even more obscure in the States, Oval's remixes of Chicago post-rock group Tortoise brought them in contact with American audiences; both *Systemische* and *94 Diskont,* as well as Markus Popp's work as Microstoria (with Mouse on Mars' Jan St. Werner) were reissued domestically by Thrill Jockey in 1996. One year later, the *Dok* LP featured Oval's collaboration with Christophe Charles. After 1999's *Szenario* EP, Popp and co. returned in 2000 with *Ovalprocess. — Sean Cooper*

Wohnton / 1993 / Thrill Jockey ✦✦✦

Even on their debut album back in 1993, Oval was heavy into CD-skip experimentation, though the big surprise on this skeleton-in-the-closet is the surprising number of vocal tracks. The resulting collision between experimental techno and pop actually works quite well, and several songs here (notably "Allesin Gedanken" and "Hallodrauflen") work better with vocals than they would've as simple tracks. The production is years ahead of its time as well, pointing the way toward futurist techno at the same time many electronic groups were attempting to sound like the Orb. *—John Bush*

● **94 Diskont** / 1995 / Thrill Jockey ✦✦✦✦✦

Oval's second proper collection of digitally damaged electronica adds a far wider range of sound and texture to the blender than the previous *Systemische.* The vinyl Mille Plateaux version included a bonus 12-inch of remixes by Scanner, Mouse on Mars, and Jim O'Rourke. *— Sean Cooper*

Ovalprocess / Jun. 20, 2000 / Thrill Jockey ✦✦✦✦✦

By the time of *Ovalprocess,* Oval's fifth full album, the clicks-and-cuts style of experimental ambience Markus Popp and company helped develop nearly a decade before was being championed all over the world, from Tokyo (Nobukazu Takemura) to Berlin (Pole) to Sheffield (SND) to San Francisco (Kit Clayton). All of which makes it a bit of a surprise that *Process* remains a distinctive work. The scratchy bass hum and high-pitched, atonal effects heard on most every track are very nearly Oval trademarks, and despite the focus on experimentation, *Ovalprocess* retains yet another hallmark of the group's productions: it's a remarkably beautiful album. Granted, this won't quite signify to listeners unfamiliar with the genre, but when the album climaxes (on the ninth untitled track) with a droning organ melody heard faintly above a cacophony of glitch static, electronics fans might just find themselves wiping their eyes from the wonder of it all. Even among considerable competition, Oval remains the very best at making beautiful music out of civilization's sonic detritus. *— John Bush*

Harry Partch

b. Jun. 24, 1901, Oakland, CA, **d.** Sep. 3, 1974, San Diego, CA

Composer / Microtonal, Experimental, 20th Century Classical/Modern Composition, Avant-Garde, World Fusion

Grew up in Tombstone, AZ, taught by family to play clarinet, harmonica, reed organ, guitar. Self-taught composer. Rode the rails during the early Depression years. Original theorist on tuning systems, wrote the extraordinary book *Genesis of a Music* (1949), instrument designer and builder from 1938 onward. His operas, in micro-tonal tunings played on his self-made instruments, were often designed for performers who would take multiple roles, eg. singer-instrumentalist-dancer. His songs were often open as to vocal pitch, pre-cursors of the New Narrative Opera. Several innovative filmscores. A number of collections came out in the late '90s: four volumes on CRI label, and 3-CD set *Enclosure Five* on Innova. *— "Blue" Gene Tyranny*

And on the Seventh Day, Petals Fell on Petaluma/The Bewitched: Final Scene And / 1964 / CRI ✦✦✦

Revelation In The Courthouse Park / Oct. 12, 1987 / Tomato ✦✦✦✦

During Harry Partch's lifetime, only one production of his play +Revelation in the Courthouse Park took place. That was at the University of Illinois in 1960. Not until 1987—11 years after Partch's death—was another production held. Recorded in *the Great Hall* at Philadelphia's University of the Arts on October 12, 1987, that posthumous production was recorded for broadcast on public radio and can be heard on this double CD. The Philadelphia production was a creative triumph, and it's amazing that all of the pieces fell into place so well. Partch's outlook on music and theater was very abstract and left of center—depending on who you talk to, Partch was either a genius or was too eccentric for his own good. Partch (born Oakland, CA, Jun. 24, 1901, died La Jolla, CA, 1976) created his own instruments, and the musicians who took part in this production had to learn to play them. To say that this production of *Revelation* (which could be described as an unorthodox and quirky American adaptation of ancient Greek theater) took a lot of hard work and preparation on the part of the Philadelphia actors and musicians would be a major understatement. It must have been *insanely* challenging! But it was a challenge that the participants were obviously capable of meeting head on, and this fine recording bears that out. *—Alex Henderson*

Enclosure Two: Harry Partch / 1995 / Innova ✦✦✦

A four-CD set of historic speech music recordings from the Partch archives. A captivating assemblage of Partch's vocal works (outside of the operas) played on his original instruments and tunings, recorded near the times of their composition. Includes several pithy, humorous, and pointed commentaries by Partch, such as *A Wagnerian Wrestling Match, The Use of English in Serious Music, Life Is Too Precious to Spend It With Important People, You Are Charged With Being Guilty. Are You Drunk or Not Drunk*– recorded mostly in his later years, and the pieces By the Waters of Babylon, the lovely Ten Li Po Lyrics, Barstow Eight Hitchhiker's Inscriptions From a Highway Railing at Barstow, California, San Francisco Newsboy Cries, U.S. Highball A Musical Account of Slim's Transcontinental Hobo Trip, While My Heart Keeps Beating Time, Two Settings From Joyce's Finnegan's Wake, Dark Brother, A Quarter-

Saw Section of Motivations and Intonations, 36 Extracts from Bitter Music, a hobo journal, Y.D. Fantasy–On the Words of an Early American Tune, O Frabjous Day!, Ring Around the Moon, and Bless This Home. — *"Blue" Gene Tyranny*

- **Enclosure Five** / Nov. 17, 1998 / Innova ✦✦✦✦✦
This three-CD set of works from American composer and instrument creator Harry Partch consists of two major works, "King Oedipus" and "The Bewitched," along with a half dozen smaller works or portions of works. A spoken introduction to "Oedipus," by Partch, explains his aims in seeking an historically rooted purity of theater unifying the importance of dialogue, story and music. The lyrics to "King Oedipus" is none other than the verse of the great wordsmith, W. B. Yeats. Through most of the work, Partch's music is played on such exotic creations as diamond marimbas, chromelodeons and adapted microtonal stringed instruments which take a backseat to the exchange of dialogue. One is reminded that Partch spent part of his life as a Depression-era hobo when one hears the potent language exchanged, as if by rootless cynics over a bowl of Mulligan stew. I would image a production of Steinbeck's *Tortilla Flat* would bear the same curious juxtaposition. "The Bewitched," subtitled "A Ballet Satire," is a purer exhibition of Partch's musical vision. Constantly underpinned by marimba, the angular melodies of flutes and strings, along with vocalizations, gives an edgy, Oriental feel to interpretive pieces like "Background for the Demonic Descent of the Cognoscenti while Shouting over Cocktails" and "Background for the Visions of a Defeated Basketball Team in the Shower Room." Greek themes are treated in "Ulysses Departs from the Edge of the World" and "Revelation in the Courthouse Park based on Euripides." Originally written for an interested Chet Baker, "Ulysses" is perhaps the most accessible piece, thanks to the constant presence of a trumpet melody. Partch is a large intelligence, full of creative vision. *Enclosure* goes very far toward giving proper treatment to his under appreciated body of work. — *Thomas Schulte*

Maggi Payne

b. Dec. 23, 1945, Temple, TX
Flute, Composer / Tape Music, Multimedia, Avant-Garde, Electronic
Studied at Northwestern University, University of Illinois, Mills College. Several grants and awards. Music for two of dancer Carolyn Brown's works *Synergy II* and *House Party*. Recording engineer and instructor-in-music, and co-Director at Center for Contemporary Music, Mills College. Her multi-media performances often involve the use of video, film, abstract slides, and/or dance. — *"Blue" Gene Tyranny*

Airwaves (Realities) (1987)/ in "Another Coast" / 1988 / Centaur ✦✦✦
A comparison of consensual reality in desert and urban cultures by slow sound-imaging. One step beyond the idea of the tone poem into a kind of reality-based illusionism. — *"Blue" Gene Tyranny*

- **Crystal** / 1991 / Lovely Music ✦✦✦
These seven beautiful and well-crafted electronic music compositions suggest vast internal and universal dimensions. Events within the interior of a humble flute become a gigantic sonic landscape in the stunning *Scirocco* (1983) for flute and tape. Taped flute sounds—whistles, tones, multiphonics, humming, and so on—are processed through a digital delay and layered in up to 32 tracks to create dense and massive structures. A low motoring sound is suddenly swept into an angelic siren. Electronic vocals, like an ululating chorus, are underscored with a low wind resonance. A slow crescendo of low winds sweeps from side to side as high sustained sounds sail above, seeming to morph into a gigantic buzzing string, and then high crystalline clusters. More than once, everything is swept aside into silence. Extremely soft winds gradually build into an overwhelming air storm and the piece concludes. *Crystal* (1982), an elegantly beautiful and sensitive study in electronic timbres created on a Moog synthesizer with multi-track recording, opens on a thin, icy surface of emerging tones with gentle wind and chant-like sounds resonating in the background. Winds begin to build and sweep in a massive crescendo of overlapping waves. A slow organ-like sustained texture—a positive light appearing after the ice and wind—soon spreads across the surface, concluding the work. After this music was completed, Payne created a video to accompany the tape, with prismatic, colorful crystals seen forming in real time as if magnified by a microscope. Other compositions on this CD are *Subterranean Network, White Night*, and *Solar Wind* (based on shockwave interactions of Saturn and Venus with the solar wind). — *"Blue" Gene Tyranny*

Krzysztof Penderecki

b. Nov. 23, 1933, Debica, Poland
Conductor, Composer / 20th Century Classical/Modern Composition, Atonal, Classical
An internationally known composer and conductor, Krzysztof Penderecki is best known for his 1965 composition "St. Luke's Passion." His style reflects the changes in music from the '60s to the present day. He has played with and conducted several orchestras and has won numerous awards for his composition and conducting. Born in Poland in 1933, Penderecki studied at a music school and quickly became an accomplished composer in Poland. His early works, such as "Emanations," "Strophes" and "Threnody for the Victims of Hiroshima," reflect his early avant-garde style, in which he combined sound with social issues of the time. With inspiration from the Orthodox liturgy, Penderecki composed several religious choral works including 1965's "St. Luke's Passion," 1971's "Utrenia" and 1974's "Magnificat." While teaching at Yale from 1973 to 1978, Penderecki began to restructure his music, changing his style to reflect contemporary neo-Romanticism.

Aside from being a noted composer, Krzysztof Penderecki also established himself as a musical dramatist during the late '60s and '70s.His first opera was *The Devils of Loudon*, followed by 1978's *Paradise Lost*. *The Black Mask*, his third opera, received rousing acclaim at the Salzburg Festival in 1986. During the '80s, his compositions ("Cello Concerto No. 2," "Viola Concerto") began to reflect both sounds of his first period and romantic gestures of the second. Two of his works, "Violin Concerto No. 2" and "Symphony No. 3," premiered at Carnegie Hall in 1996. Penderecki has conducted the Berlin Philharmonic Orchestra and orchestras in France, England, Italy, Austria, Sweden and Switzerland. He also holds two permanent positions: the guest conductor of the NDR Orchestra in Hamburg and the music director of the Casals Festival in Puerto Rico. Several universities have honored him with honorary doctorates. — *Kim Summers*

"K. Penderecki, Vol. 1": Threnody for the Victims of Hiroshima for 52 Strings (1959) / / 1989 / Vienna Modern Master ✦✦✦

Jutrznia I (Utrenya I: The Entombment of Christ) (1969-70)/Jutrznia II (Utrenya II: Th / 1989 / Polskie Nagrania ✦✦✦

Volume 4: Cello Concerto No. 2 (1982)/ The Awakening of Jacob (1974)/ Adag / 1989 / Polskie Nagrania ✦✦✦✦✦
Another wonderful assembly in the extensive 1989 Polskie Nagrania series of Penderecki releases, this CD contains powerful works performed by the Polish Radio National Symphony Orchestra conducted by Antoni Wit. Composed in 1974 for the celebration of Prince Rainier III of Monaco's 25th year of accession to the throne, *The Awakening of Jacob* is a brief work, sometimes translated as *The Dream of Jacob*. Premiered by soloist Mscislav Rostropovich and the Berlin Philharmonic, *Cello Concerto No. 2* (1982) is a dramatic, energetic work that opens with a pulsating, gradually descending line and a brooding, romantic melody built on two tone repetitions. Great variety is achieved through unique orchestrations; the melody is fragmented into statement-like passages, the non-pitched percussion instruments imitate the melodic material, etc. The orchestra complements and supports the musical developments of the soloist, rather than acting as a contrasting adversary. As in all of Penderecki's work, the music is well-defined and the gestures easily distinguished; punctuations as gestures begin and end and percussive doubling of instruments with "softer" timbres are Penderecki characteristics. *Concerto for Viola and Orchestra* (1983) is a dynamic example of Penderecki's more melodic style. The work is built on its opening motif, a line of short sighing phrases. There are gradual buildups in energy and several returns to the sighing line throughout the piece. In the last few minutes, the sighing quality is restored until, in an elegant conclusion, the soloist reaches a single high note and continues to hold it as the full orchestra joins in imitation. — *"Blue" Gene Tyranny*

- **Matrix 5: Krzysztof Penderecki Anaklasis (1959)/Threnody for the Victims of Hiroshima** / 1994 / EMI Classics ✦✦✦
Excellent and moving performances of Penderecki's orchestral music performed by the Polish Radio National Symphony Orchestra. A unique and original work in the musical literature for voices and instruments, *Canticum Canticorum Salomonis* (1970-1973) is a setting for choir and small orchestra of an erotic text drawn from the *Song of Solomon*. Crashing, clattering percussion, showers of high bell sounds, bowed gongs and harmonium dissonances, sensual string glissandos, and other unique orchestral timbres underline dense vocal clusters and dreamily erotic choral patterns. Composed in 1966, *De Natura Sonoris No. 1* (Concerning the Nature of Sound) is an orchestral study of sonorities and harmonic tension that marked a new creative direction for the composer. He fused several earlier compositional elements with electronic music ideas (applied to acoustic instruments), creating a triptych with the first and third sections open to free playing on notated ideas (including some "walking bass" jazz-influenced passages). In contrast, the middle section uses densely structured serial logic. The result is highly dramatic music with highlighted sound combinations and a forward momentum usually found in more fully notated styles. *De Natura Sonoris No. 2* (1971) is a second sound study using a smaller instrumental group than the preceding piece. Texturally creating a sustained and mysterious landscape, it features a large and unusual percussion section including a sliding bird whistle, musical saw, and piece of railway track. Midway into the piece the orchestra breaks loose with a highly dramatic, dense, and compelling sound aggregation featuring huge scrapings on the strings, trombone glissandos, and a brass section that sounds like many oncoming trains. The mysterious texture returns after a few string stabs reminiscent of *De Natura Sonoris No. 1*, and the piece concludes. — *"Blue" Gene Tyranny*

Matrix 17: Penderecki : Emanationen (Emanations) for two string orchestras / 1995 / EMI Classics ✦✦✦✦✦
Performed by the Polish Radio Symphony Orchestra and the London Symphony Orchestra, conducted by the composer, and written in 1958, "Emanationen (Emanations)" (for two string orchestras tuned a semi-tone apart) presents many of the sounds and sound-painting compositional style that would constitute his later works of the '60s and early '70s. It is an essay on unstable but energetic sounds.

The "Partita" is a dynamic composition set for harpsichord and an orchestra of nine woodwinds, 22 strings, celesta and various percussion instruments. At the onset, long tones a semitone apart begin pulsing, followed by clusters, tremolo tones, fast cycles and whirls of sound in similar pulsations. The harpsichords play fast cycles in different rhythms, backed up by splattering horns, and a wildly avant-garde jazz combo of amplified instruments. The harpsichordist begins to sound like Cecil Taylor on speed. The orchestra mutates the texture into a heavenly shimmer.

The symphony's form was inspired by a painting of two angels in an arch which the composer saw during a visit to Ravenna. This arch suggested the structural form of the work. The pulsing sound of a solo slapstick or whipcrack makes for a surprising beginning to the work. The slapped gourd rattle and other percussion soon join in accompanied by a host of pizzicato strings all in different rhythms, the whole effect like some gigantic clockworks factory. Sighing dissonant brass take over, their attacks inverted like taped sounds heard in reverse. Then there is stillness, the bass strings briefly pulse, and then descending "whistling" glissandos appear en masse in the strings ending in a quietly pulsing tone cluster wall that gradually thins out to a solo string with a slight "cry" like a lonely animal. The massed strings begin to develop on this, into a cascading of multi-dimensional glissandos and sustained brass. — *"Blue" Gene Tyranny*

Philip Perkins

b. Aug. 24, 1951, Coatesville, PA
Piano, Composer / Electro-Acoustic, Electronic
Electronic music composer Philip Perkins has worked in film and collaborated with a variety of West Coast avant-garde musicians, including the Residents and the Hub. The Penn-

sylvanian first started working with tape during high school, while playing in pop rock bands. He directed experimental films throughout the '70s, including *Crownfire* (1973), *Patchwork* (1977), and *Gila* (1979), and co-founded the Eugene Filmmaker's Cinemateque in Oregon with Scott Fraser, among others. After graduating with a liberal arts degree from the University of the Pacific in 1973, Perkins studied filmmaking with David Foster for a couple of years, then moved to San Francisco, where he served on the board of the Canyon Cinema Cooperative from 1978-81. During this time, Perkins changed his focus to making electronic music. With Fraser, *"Blue" Gene Tyranny*, and others, Perkins ran the Fun Music label, formed in 1979. His collaborations with the Residents also began that year. For the next five years, Perkins made videos for Ralph Records artists, and recorded and toured with the Residents. He went on to collaborate with conductor and vocalist Frederick Goff and computer group the Hub (*Computer Network Music*). Perkins has also received commissions for his radio works, resulting in "South Florida Remote" (1988), "Berkeley Remote" (1989), and "San Francisco Remote," which feature live musicians interacting with custom electronics. — *Joslyn Layne*

● **Neighborhood with a Sky** / 1982 / Fun Music ♦♦♦
A beautiful album of compositions where the electronic and "natural sounds" are barely distinguishable; significantly, Perkins does not try to simulate the natural sounds but lets their dynamic form and movement influence his electronic sounds (somewhat in the way that Cage, using chance methods, tries to imitate nature not in its appearance but in its manner of working)—the neighborhood for Perkins is that of the disc itself, where the natural and the artificial co-exist successfully. Contains: "Bird Variations," "The Black and White Cat," "Este's Request," "The Fountain," "Equinox Weather," "Rico in the Birdhouse" for trombone solo in an environment, and "Retreat." — *"Blue" Gene Tyranny*

The Flame of Ambition / 1986 / Fun Music ♦♦♦
A collection of pieces about people "burning literally with ambition… the root of both mankind's greatest triumphs and worst self-made calamities" with scenes from a corporate skyscraper, the company fort: "Taking the Stairs", "Worrisome Fanfare / Weekend with the Kids", "At The Bar", "Talk/Exit (for Corazon Aquino)". A good blend of Perkins' electronic, natural sound, and tuneful mixes. — *"Blue" Gene Tyranny*

☆ **The Remotes (I) (1990)** / 1990 / Fun Music ♦♦♦♦♦
A mix on cassette tape of nine live radio broadcasts of "The Remotes", a live performance work for interactive electronic system and various guest musicians, where spontaneous playing and processing allows for all sorts of interesting, communal, and intuitive music making. — *"Blue" Gene Tyranny*

Larry Polansky

b. Oct. 16, 1954, New York, NY
Composer / Process-Generated, Experimental, 20th Century Classical/Modern Composition
Composer, performer, guitarist, and educator Larry Polansky has written and arranged over 40 works for a variety of instrumentations. He is a core member of the Frog Peak Music composer's collective, and a widely published music theorist who co-wrote HSML, or Hierarchical Music Specification Language, with Phil Burk and David Rosenboom, as well as other computer software. He taught at Mills College for ten years, then went to Dartmouth, where he teaches electro-acoustic music, is department Chair, and co-director of its electronic music studio. Recordings of some of his compositions appear on the Artifact and Tellus labels; *The Theory of Impossible Melody* features the use of HMSL. —*Joslyn Layne*

● **The Theory of Impossible Melody** / 1989 / Artifact ♦♦♦♦♦
Fascinating formal (transformational) logic programs generating electronic and acoustic pieces, using the HMSL (Hierarchical Music Specification Language, designed by Phil Burk, Polansky and David Rosenboom). A feeling of the Cabalistic mysteries. Contains: *B'rey'sheet* (In the beginning…)… computer-aided melodic transformations of traditional Hebrew tropes and melodies used for singing the Torah / Cantillation Study No. 1 for Jody Diamond, for voice and electronics / Four Voice Canons Nos. 3-6(#3 for computer, #4 for marimbas, #5 for percussion, #6 for computer) / Simple Actions—Rules Of Compossibility for voice and live computer /Psaltery for Lou Harrison. — *"Blue" Gene Tyranny*

Simple Harmonic Motion / 1994 / Artifact ♦♦♦
A collection of four works for instruments in experimental intonation from the '70s to the late '80s, with a recent work entitled *Horn* for French Horn and live interactive electronics. The other three compositions are *Another You* 17 variations for harp in just intonation, *Movement for Andrea Smith* for string quartet in just intonation, and *Movement for Lou Harrison* for bass quartet in just intonation. — *"Blue" Gene Tyranny*

Movement for Andrea Smith (My Funny Valentine for Just String Quartet) in "Just Intonat" / Tellus ♦♦♦
An extremely slowed-down angular-ized ballad. How can I possibly describe the pleading feeling? — *"Blue" Gene Tyranny*

Henri Pousseur

b. Jun. 23, 1929, Malmédy, Belgium
Composer / 20th Century Classical/Modern Composition, Atonal, Electronic
Belgian modern composer Henri Pousseur has written well over 100 works in a variety of styles, and has served as a music educator for several decades. By the time he was finished with his music studies in the early '50s, Pousseur was already active in avant-garde music, influenced by and creating music not unlike that of Stockhausen and Berio. Pousseur's works included serial music, experimental operas like "Electre" (1961), and electronic music such as "Scambi" (1957). He began his longstanding collaboration with Michel Butor in the early '60s; the duo have gone on to write over 20 works, including "La Rose Des Voix" (1982). Pousseur founded the Centre de recherches et de formation musicales de Wallonie in Liège, the magazine *Marsyas*, and taught in several countries (but mostly at the University and Conservatory of Liège) until his retirement in 1994. —*Joslyn Layne*

● **Scambi (Exchanges) (1954)/Trois Visages De Liege (Three Faces of Liege) (1961)/ Parab** / 1990 / BVHaast ♦♦♦♦♦
The pure evolving electronic masses of "Scambi", a portrait of the city of the composer's youth comissioned by the city of Liege, and a semi-improvised live electro-acoustic mixture changed every evening of the performance (containing a "love duet," "Viva Cuba", "Hymn to the ornithological Zeus", "aerial view of Haiphong, Massachusetts"…) by this wonderfully poetic composer. — *"Blue" Gene Tyranny*

Traverser La Foret (1987) / 1993 / Adda ♦♦♦
Although it can be a bit coy at times, this odd mythological Cantata for narrator, two solo voices, choir and 12 instruments has its charms and probably a hidden meaning that I'm not getting. The vocal writing and harmonies are exquisite and transparent in texture. — *"Blue" Gene Tyranny*

Dichterliebesreigentraum (Dream of the Round of the Poet's Loves) (1993) fo / 1995 / Cyprés ♦♦♦♦♦
Performed here by the Choeur de Chambre de Namur (dir. Pierre Cao) and the Orchestra Philharmonique de Liege (dir. Pierre Bartholomée), this fascinating work is based upon compositional procedures derived from Schumann's famous *Dichterliebe* song cycle—Pousseur's work culminated in the essay "Schumann, le poéte (vingt-cinq moments d'une lecture de Dichterliebe)" [Paris, Mérdiens-Klincksieck, 1993]. The 16 love poems chosen by Schumann were modified by him to form a deeper level, a philosophical and autobiographical journey, and the music contains many symbolic interplays. Similarly, the design approach to Pousseur's work is equally deconstructionist and high symbolism: notes are organized in elaborate matrices (rounds, distorting prisms) and "amorous" elements in the Heinrich Heine text are equally philosophical (therapeutic/alchemical) and autobiographical. Pousseur combines the poems to interrelate their meanings thereby creating new ones, and also incorporates personal correspondence between Robert and Clara Schumann before their marriage (Pousseur dedicated his work to his own wife), the first three lines of Heine's *Mnémosyne* (which concerns a lost language and the "forgotten word" spoken by a beloved one), and Pousseur's own reflections and mental reactions to the text. The music has the lyricism and gracefulness of Romantic tonality but with the elements seemingly freely interpolated—there is frequent richly timbred polytonality, serialist gestures restricted to normal scale modes, folksong-like phrases, rhythmic accents that may go from Bartók to jazz to Carl Orff within one line. But none of this comes off as mere collage—Pousseur somehow makes the elements create an impressive and enjoyably original style. — *"Blue" Gene Tyranny*

Eliane Radigue

b. 1932, Paris, France
Composer / Tape Music, Minimalism, World Fusion, Electronic
Electronic composer Eliane Radigue has created lovely, meditative works based on Tibetan Buddhism using tape and an Arp synthesizer. After studying electro-acoustic music under Pierre Henry and Pierre Schaeffer in the late '50s, the Parisian learned to play the piano and harp and delved into classical music. She spent one year (1967-68) as Pierre Henry's assistant, one (1970-71) at New York University, then spent some time in residency at universities including California Institute of the Arts in the early '70s. By this time, Radigue was making her music with tape and an Arp synthesizer. After converting to Tibetan Buddhism in 1975, she took a four-year hiatus from music. The French composer's works have since included compositions for ballet and commissioned works on the life of Milarepa, an influential Tibetan poet and saint. —*Joslyn Layne*

● **Kyema, Intermediate States** / 1992 / Experimental Intermedia ♦♦♦♦♦
Profound and serenely meditative electronic music inspired by *the Bardo Thodol* (Tibetan Book of the Dead). Six states: *Kyene (Birth), Milam (Dream), Samten (Contemplation), Chikai (Death), Chonye (Clear Light), Sippai (Becoming).* This is the real thing. — *"Blue" Gene Tyranny*

Mila's Journey Inspired by a Dream / 1992 / Lovely Music ♦♦♦
With Tibetan singing by Lama Kunga Rinpoche, and English singing by Robert Ashley. Wonderful images and stories from the "100, 000 Songs of Milarepa," the musical setting of which is Radigue's lifelong project. — *"Blue" Gene Tyranny*

Songs of Milarepa / 1998 / Lovely Music ♦♦♦
This two-CD set combines two vinyls previously issued by Lovely Music. Disc I contains four of the *Songs of Milarepa:* "Mila's Song in the Rain," "Song of the Path Guides," "Elimination of Desires," and "Symbols for Yogic Experience." Deeply meditative, compassionate and inspiring, these settings for voices and electronics from the Buddhist classic *The 100, 000 Songs of Milarepa* were realized in 1981-83 in Paris. Disc 2 contains the complete 63-minute "Mila's Journey Inspired by a Dream," both discs with Tibetan singing by Lama Kunga Rinpoche and English singing by Robert Ashley. Radigue's electronic music is rich in harmonics and slowly changing harmonies with a real sense of the eternal that moves the depths of the soul. — *"Blue" Gene Tyranny*

Trilogie de la Mort (Trilogy on Death) / 1998 / XI (Experimental Intermedia) ♦♦♦♦♦
This profound work of electronic music on three CDs is based on the composer's complete immersion in Tibetan Buddhist teaching, and takes its title from Thomas Merton's *Trilogy on Death:* "Going beyond death in this life, beyond the dichotomy of life and death, and so to become a witness to life itself." The first "chapter" is *Kyema*, composed during the years 1985-1988. It was inspired by texts of the Bardo-Thödol (a book of the dead) and "evokes the six intermediate states which constitute the 'existential continuity' of being: Kyene (birth), Milam (dream), Samtem (contemplation and meditation), Chikai (death), Chönye (clear light) and Sippai (crossing and return)." The slowly changing timbres create quite physical resonances and density modulations, suggesting encounters with traveling personalities, some comforting, some evoking deep and strange spirits. *Kyema* is dedicated to the composer's son Yves Arman, who passed away in a car accident shortly before its completion. The second chapter, *Kailasha* (1988-1991), is "an imaginary journey around the most sacred of the Himalayan mountains, Mount Kailash," but since the mountain is considered a "natural man-

dala," the work also attempts to recreate the illusion found in works of visual artists Albers and Escher, where one perspective overlaps and flips over into another, involuntarily. The composer considers *Kailasha* to be "the most chaotic part of the trilogy" and deeply unnerving. *Koumé*, the third chapter, emphasizes the transcendence of death. The title of *Koumé*'s fourth subsection quotes the Bible in Corinthians XV ("O Death, where is thy victory?"): "Ashes of illusion becoming light. Descent to the deepest, where the spark of life is. There, Death is born. Death becomes birth. Actively re-beginning. Eternity—a perpetual becoming." *—"Blue" Gene Tyranny*

Steve Reich

b. Oct. 3, 1936, New York, NY

Composer / Tape Music, 20th Century Classical/Modern Composition, Avant-Garde, Minimalism

Following in the footsteps of La Monte Young and Terry Riley, composer Steve Reich is widely considered the third major pioneer of minimalism; credited as the innovator behind phasing—a process whereby two tape loops lined up in unison gradually move out of phase with each other, ultimately coming back into sync—his early experiments in tape manipulation also anticipated the emergence of hip-hop sampling by well over a decade. Born in 1936, Reich studied philosophy at Cornell before turning to composition at the Juilliard School of Music. He finally landed at Mills College in Oakland, California under the tutelage of avant-garde composers Luciano Berio and Darius Milhaud.

In the early '60s, Reich completed his first major compositions, *Pitch Charts* and the experimental film score *Plastic Haircut*. 1964's *Music for Three or More Pianos* was his first work to make use of tape loops, followed a year later by the landmark phased piece *It's Gonna Rain*. Reich again applied his phasing manipulations to the recorded voice on 1966's *Come Out*, but with 1967's *Piano Phase* and *Violin Phase* he began employing the process on acoustic instruments. Subsequent works continued expanding the parameters of the phasing concept—1971's extended *Drumming* was scored for four pairs of bongos, three marimbas, three glockenspiels, and voice.

Reich's subsequent work veered from quintessential minimalism (1972's self-explanatory *Clapping Music*) to orchestral compositions (1976's *Music for Eighteen Musicians*), with the latter aesthetic becoming his primary focus in later years. Rarely recorded throughout his first decades as an artist, during the 1980s Reich's major works finally began appearing on album, among them 1988's brilliant *Different Trains*. Reich's Jewish heritage continued playing a central role in his later work as well—1994's multi-media piece *The Cave* retold the story of the prophet Abraham. As Reich's trailblazing work came into fashion with the wave of late-'90s electronica, the remix album *Reich Remixed* appeared in 1999. *—Jason Ankeny*

The Desert Music / 1985 / Elektra/Nonesuch ♦♦♦♦

★ **Early Works** / 1987 / Elektra/Nonesuch ♦♦♦♦♦

These historical recordings were difficult to find (usually on out-of-print compilations) for a long time so it's gratifying to have them readily available in one place. The two important tape pieces here from the mid-sixties, "Come Out" and "It's Gonna Rain", have their sound sources originating in police brutality and apocalyptic evangelism. Reich takes his sources and turns them into two short tape loops repeated rapidly as they gradually go out of synch with each other- what's revealed are the intricacies of the human voice. "Come Out" takes the voice fragment and turns it into a hall-of-mirror set of voices over shuffling beat and wah-wah that are actually a by-product of subtleties of the voice and almost unrecognizable as the original vocal sample. It becomes a scary psychedelic funk piece that Funkadelic or Can would have been proud of. "It's Gonna Rain" is similarly looped and phased as the preacher's admonition is transformed, moving in and out of synch as the piece progresses with the second part of the piece especially full of fierce, terrifying swirls of noise. After taking musique concrete to another level, Reich decided to try to make similar strides with instrumental music. The two other pieces here, "Piano Phase" and "Clapping Music", represent this new direction in his work. Re-recorded here in 1986 and 1987, their intricate, layered patterns should be familiar to fans of another one of Reich's masterpieces, "Music for 18 Musicians". *Early Works* is a must-have introduction for anyone interested in the roots of minimalist music. *—Jason Gross*

Different Trains/Electric Counterpoint / 1989 / Elektra/Nonesuch ♦♦♦♦♦

In an acoustic equivalent to interactive electronics, Reich creates a rhythmic tape of train whistles of the 1930s and '40s and of speakers recalling train rides of the past in the U.S.A. and in Nazi-occupied lands . The natural pitch inflections of the voices are then transferred to pitches for the instruments. A rich emotional experience akin to his earlier pieces "It's Gonna Rain" (1965) and the shocking "Come Out" (1966) (both on Elektra / Nonesuch 79169-2)... a more interesting use of the rather mechanistic edge of his pattern music. *—"Blue" Gene Tyranny*

☆ **Another View of Counterpoint** / 1993 / Amiata ♦♦♦♦♦

Reich compositions from 1973, 1967, 1985, and 1979 are brought into new focus by the Amadinda Percussion Group, pianists Kinga Szekely and Bela Farago, and their ensemble Group 180. They bring new brightness, meaning, and substance to the composer's already iridescent, thematically gradual process music. The utterly beautiful "Music for Mallet Instruments, Voices & Organ," played by Amadinda, creates wintertime holiday images, phasing in and out of time and harmonic focus with dual glockenspiels and marimba, organ, female siren songs, mixed vocals, and metallic percussion. The piece is liquid, luminescent, exacting, almost surreal. In "Piano Phase," the two pianists bounce off one another, using a Reich signature technique, with phrases moving in and out of rhythmic convergence. At times the effect is polyphonic to the delightfully maddening saturation point. Over 26 minutes long, "Sextet" (by Amadinda without voices and organ) is one of Reich's most demanding, complex, and multi-faceted works. It's in an ABCBA form: the head and tail are intense, the B sections somewhat patient in their inquisitive construct or stark drama, the midpoint heavy and deliberate or somewhat spatial. Group 180 performs "Octet," with 11 instruments—including strings, oboe, bassoon, and trombone—playing no more than eight lines at one time. A 5/4 rhythm rules throughout these incredible 17-and-a-half minutes of music. String accents and lovely flute inserts set the group off into a frenzy of bronzed, polished contrapuntal and individualistic dissertations. Reich has viewed this as a fresh and playful interpretation, filled with good humor and precise teamwork. The result is a wonderful alchemy of chamber music, improvised jazz, African percussive phraseology, and galactic vistas. Of the many fine recordings documenting Reich's music, this is one that every follower must have. The master of musical juxtaposition has perhaps been represented as well on previous CDs, but no better than on this masterpiece. *—Michael G. Nastos*

☆ **Works: 1965-1995** / 1997 / Elektra/Nonesuch ♦♦♦♦♦

Of the composers generally referred to as "minimalist" (a label almost universally rejected by those to whom it is applied), three have had a substantial and direct impact on modern music both popular and classical since the 1960s: Philip Glass, Steve Reich and, to a somewhat lesser degree, John Adams. Glass has had the greater commercial success and Adams has worked in larger forms with more prestigious orchestras, but Reich has made the most consistently interesting music in both harmonic and rhythmic terms, successfully setting repetitious, slow-changing patterns into interesting and musically compelling structures. As he has repeatedly and adamantly stated, his is not "trance" music; he expects the listener to pay close attention, and his music amply rewards those who do. This monumental ten-CD retrospective collects the original recordings of Reich's published music, except for the new recordings of "New York Counterpoint," "Eight Lines," "Four Organs," and "Music for 18 Musicians." It documents his progression from early tape pieces (deceptively simple, foreshadowing later work with phase shifting and canonic structures), to more recent choral/orchestral works that demonstrate conclusively that Reich's music is far from "minimal." His most famous works are included, notably "Music for 18 Musicians," "The Desert Music," and "Different Trains," widely regarded as his masterpiece. There are, however, some curious exclusions: His groundbreaking "Violin Phase" is missing, not to mention the charming "Music for Pieces of Wood" ("Clapping Music," from the same period, is included), and his gorgeous composition for flutist Ransom Wilson, "Vermont Counterpoint." Nevertheless, this box set is an essential purchase for anyone with a serious interest in modern art music. The packaging is beautiful, and the accompanying booklet includes full track and personnel listings, a chronology of Reich's career, appreciative notes from fellow musicians, and an excellent new interview by Jonathan Cott. *—Rick Anderson*

● **Music for 18 Musicians** / Mar. 31, 1998 / ECM ♦♦♦♦♦

After Reich's initial experiments with phase music, he moved on to exploring pulse—music that had no relation to melody, but would repeat phrases of either one or several notes, increasing then decreasing in volume as long as the musician had the stamina. When repeated with several musicians playing around one key and starting them off at different times, the result was a piece that continuously evolved, sounding like a night drive through a neon city with bright sounds appearing on the horizon, coming closer, then disappearing behind. The original recording in 1978 on ECM records was a major step forward for Reich and legitimized his music beyond the experimentation of such works as "Violin Phase." Where the phase work felt insular and looped, *Music for 18 Musicians* stretches as far as the eye can see. The piece was rerecorded in the late '90s, but this original recording is worth checking out, even more now for the historical value. *—Ted Mills*

The Residents

f. 1966, Shreveport, LA

Group / Multimedia, No Wave, Post-Punk, Experimental, Avant-Garde

Over the course of a recording career spanning several decades, the Residents remained a riddle of Sphinx-like proportions; cloaking their lives and music in a haze of willful obscurity, the band's members never idenitified themselves by name, always appearing in public in disguise—usually tuxedos, top hats and giant eyeball masks—and refusing to grant media interviews. Drawing inspiration from the likes of fellow innovators including Harry Partch, Sun Ra and Captain Beefheart, the Residents channelled the breadth of American music into their idiosyncratic, satiric vision, their mercurial blend of electronics, distortion, avant-jazz, classical symphonies and gratingly nasal vocals reinterpreting everyone from John Philip Sousa to James Brown while simultaneously expanding the boundaries of theatrical performance and multimedia interaction.

Finding no takers for their oddball sounds, the Residents issued their first records on their own Ralph Records. The 1973 full-length *Meet the Residents* prompted a lawsuit from Capitol Records over its cover, a twisted, dadaesque Beatles parody. 1976's *Third Reich 'N' Roll* was a collection of pop oldies covers, followed one year later by an abrasive cover of the Rolling Stones' "Satisfaction," which became an underground hit on both sides of the Atlantic at the peak of the punk movement.

During the early '80s, the Residents embarked upon a trilogy of prog-rock albums and also mounted another ambitious project, the "American Composer" series, although only two of the projected titles ever appeared. Instead, in the wake of financial and corporate difficulties which resulted in the creation of a New Ralph label, the Residents issued the one-off *God in Three Persons* and 1989's *The King and Eye*. The 1990 album *Freak Show* was reissued as a CD-ROM four years later, marking the group's first leap into the new digital interactive technology. In 1997, the band celebrated their silver anniversary with the release of the career-spanning overview *Our Tired, Our Poor, Our Huddled Masses*. *—Jason Ankeny*

Eskimo / 1979 / East Side Digital ♦♦♦♦♦

The most rewarding, the most difficult, and the most accomplished of all the Residents' albums, this was their departure into the field of imaginary ethno-musicography that they had begun on "Six Things to a Cycle" on *Fingerprince*. Ostensibly a musical documentary on the Eskimo, this is an album of icy atmospheres, poetic electronics, and imaginary landscapes, concocted around a loose narrative told in the liner notes. There's also a subtheme of indigenous populations overrun by western commercialism (is that native chant actually "Coca Cola is Life"—). Ex-Henry Cow member Chris Cutler plays a lot of the percussion on the album, especially on the finale, "Festival of Death," the only real piece of rhythmic music here, which shines out as anything but dark or sinister. In any other group's hands this would have been a pretentious disaster, but the Residents pull it off through spirit, humor, and sheer bravado. *— Ted Mills*

The Commercial Album / Nov. 1980 / East Side Digital ✦✦✦✦
Here's the concept: The structure of most pop songs consists of only two parts, the verse and the chorus. Since the verse and chorus usually repeat three times in a three-minute song, a pop tune really only consists of one minute of music. Cut out the repetition and you can, therefore, fit 40 pop songs onto a 40-minute record. And that's exactly what the Residents have done on *The Commercial Album*, the title of which comes from the band's deduction that since pop songs only consist of one minute of music and most advertisements are about a minute long also, ad jingles are "therefore the music of America." Got it— Whatever the concept behind it, this album is not only weird in that special way that only Residents albums are, but it's also surprisingly musically satisfying. A few of its 40 tracks ("Secrets" and "The Simple Song," for example) feel like throwaways, but most of them are surprisingly well organized and complete. The instrumental "Japanese Watercolor" is particularly impressive, as are the songs "Picnic Boy" and "Troubled Man." This album would make a great introduction to the Residents for anyone who hasn't yet been exposed to the band's unique brand of whimsy. *— Rick Anderson*

13th Anniversary Show—*Live in Japan* / *1986 / East Side Digital* ✦✦✦✦✦
The 13th Anniversary Tour marked the last live appearance of Snakefinger with the Residents and was the only time the group took to the stage with an armload of career spanning material, not centered around one concept album. Expanded from the original Torso release by eight tracks, the song list ranges from the early "Eloise" (from *Vileness Fats*) to their angst-ridden cover of James Brown's "Man's World." The band, relying heavily on the Emulator synth and the fiery angular distortion of Snakefinger's guitar, bring life to even the slightest of their material, rendering "Monkey and Bunny" from their snoozy team-up with Renaldo and the Loaf into something approaching a frightening beauty. The lead Resident's vocals burst forth with bile and confusion, letting out a cathartic wail on the show closing "Cry for the Fire." The remaster adds some applause into an original mix that was once all the more devastating when it seemed like they were playing for an enthusiastic crowd of three in an echoing hall. That quibble aside, this is one of the finest live documents of this mysterious group. *— Ted Mills*

★ **God in Three Persons** / 1988 / Rykodisc ✦✦✦✦✦
Employing the same stress-scheme as Poe's "The Raven" throughout its 62 minutes, "God In Three Persons" is an extended work in "talking-blues" style for narrator, electronic instruments, and a chorus providing comments not to be found in the libretto—they sing production credits at the beginning, and lines like "something's coming, but not real soon", and "this is a sad part, oh, such a sad part". This surreal and yet directly delivered work is as lovingly human as it is comic with profound experience simply expressed... in short, an original masterpiece of American music, directly in the tradition of the Thomson-Stein and Robert Ashley operas. As in all Residents pieces, the voices are modified electronically and the musical elements are deceptively minimal—most of its 14 episodes have only two chords which, however, still manage to instantly produce the correct atmosphere (Phil Glass-like Wagnerian thirds for mythic import, tonic-dominant in triplets for 50's teenage love story, etc.). There are only passing riffs, more like comments, and the only melody in the whole piece is a wheezy organ quote of the standard doxology hymn "Holy, Holy, Holy (God in Three Persons)".The subject matter is, in part, the derivation of religious and other symbolic images from the naturally erotic... but that's only part of it. Please give this one a listen. *— "Blue" Gene Tyranny*

Roger Reynolds

b. Jul. 18, 1934, Detroit, MI
Composer / Electro-Acoustic, Atonal, Electronic
Studied with Ross Lee Finney, Roberto Gerhard. Undergraduate degree in engineering physics. Founding member ONCE Group. Teacher at University of California at San Diego, founded Center for Music Experiment and Related Research (1979). Composer-in-residence, IRCAM, Paris, France. *The Emperor of Ice Cream* (1962), *Blind Men* (1966) for 24 voices and chamber ensemble, *I/O: A Ritual for 23 Performers* (1970), *Fiery Wind* for orchestra (1978). *— "Blue" Gene Tyranny*

Distant Images / 1985 / Lovely Music ✦✦✦
A delicate and mysterious vinyl LP release of two works for chamber ensemble in which Reymolds addresses the dualistic nature of aural perception, approaching the elusive territory between the polarized pair and the unified whole. *— "Blue" Gene Tyranny*

Voicespace: Still (1975)/A Merciful Coincidence (1976) / Eclipse (1979) / the Palace (1 / 1992 / Lovely Music ✦✦✦✦✦
A reissue of the two-record set, featuring four pieces for computer electronics and voices that amplify to an extreme degree the components and expressive qualities of the voice. "Still," with a text from Samuel Coleridge's *The Wanderings of Cain* (1798), moves extremely slowly in a "vocal fry" across the aspirate clicks and wind of the performer; "A Merciful Coincidence," on a text from Samuel Beckett's *Watt* (1953), uses the aggressive-passive inflections of the frog performers croaking, which seems to have intent, if not syntactical "meaning"; "Eclipse," with a combined text from Jorge Luis Borges, Gabriel Marquez, Issa, James Joyce, Melville, and Wallace Stevens, eclipses strains of modulated texts into each other; and "The Palace," on a translated text by Borges (1976), is a dramatic monodrama about how The Self imagines its confines within the space of The Mind, with the prerecorded modified voice added to the singer onstage, yielding an enormous, suprahuman quality. *— "Blue" Gene Tyranny*

• **Electroacoustic Music** / 1993 / New World ✦✦✦
Dramatic new works for instruments and electronics: *Versions / Stages* (1988–1991) and *The Ivanov Suite* (1991) created for Tadashi Suzuki's version of Chekhov's play. *— "Blue" Gene Tyranny*

Terry Riley

b. Jun. 24, 1935, Colfax, CA
Keyboards, Piano, Composer / Tape Music, 20th Century Classical/Modern Composition, Minimalism, Ambient, World Fusion, Atonal
Minimalist pioneer Terry Riley was among the most revolutionary composers of the postwar era; famed for his introduction of repetition into Western music motifs, he also masterminded early experiments in tape loops and delay systems which left an indelible mark on the experimental music produced in his wake. Riley began performing professionally as a solo pianist during the 1950s, and studied composition in San Francisco and Berkeley. Influenced by John Coltrane and John Cage, he began exploring open improvisation and avant-garde music, and in 1960 composed the musique concrète piece *Mescalin Mix.*

By the early '60s, Riley was regularly holding all-night solo harmonium performances. His next major work, 1963's *Music for the Gift*, was among the first pieces ever generated by a tape delay/feedback system, it employed two tape recorders. The loop effect sparked Riley's interest in repetition as a means of musical expression, and in 1964 he completed his most famous work, the minimalist breakthrough *In C.*

In time, Riley also learned to play saxophone, introducing the instrument into his so-called all-night flights; these epic improvisational performances became the basis for his most successful recordings, 1968's *Poppy Nogood and the Phantom Band* and the following year's *A Rainbow in Curved Air.* During the early '70s, Riley made the first of many trips to India to study and collaborated with John Cale for *Church of Anthrax*, arguably Riley's most widely-known recording outside of experimental music circles. Throughout the 1970s, he also taught composition and North Indian Raga at Mills College in Oakland, California.

A pair of early 1970s live performances—one in L.A., the other in Paris—resulted in the 1972 album *Persian Surgery Dervishes*, a work of meditative machine music clearly prescient of the trance sound to follow. He also recorded a total of nine string quartets with the help of violinist David Harrington of the Kronos Quartet. Another Riley/Kronos collaboration, 1989's *Salome Dances for Peace*, was even nominated for a Grammy. *—Jason Ankeny*

★ **Rainbow in Curved Air/Poppy Nogood and the Phantom Band** / 1990 / Columbia ✦✦✦✦✦
A CD reissue of the classic 1969 recording. After several graph compositions and early pattern pieces with jazz ensembles in the late '50s and early '60s (see "Concert for Two Pianists and Tape Recorders" and "Ear Piece" in La Monte Young's book *An Anthology*), Riley invented a whole new music which has since gone under many names (minimal music—a category often applied to sustained pieces as well—pattern music, phase music, etc.) which is set forth in its purest form in the famous "In C" (1964) (for saxophone and ensemble, CBS MK 7178). "Rainbow in Curved Air" demonstrates the straightforward pattern technique but also has Riley improvising with the patterns, making gorgeous timbre changes on the synthesizers and organs, and presenting contrasting sections that has become the basic structuring of his works ("Candenza on the Night Plain" and other pieces). Scored for large orchestra with extra percussion and electronics, some of this work's seven movements are: "Star Night," "Blue Lotus," "The Earth Below," and "Island of the Rhumba King." *— "Blue" Gene Tyranny*

Persian Surgery Dervishes / 1993 / New Tone ✦✦✦
A welcome re-issue on two CDs of Riley's 1970s masterpiece. Exquisite playing and a phenomenal experience of constantly evolving creation. *— "Blue" Gene Tyranny*

Terry Riley: Zeitgeist-Intuitive Leaps / 1994 / Work Music London ✦✦✦
This CD by the group Zeitgeist contains two works by Riley which he personally supervised and created in close cooperation with the group. These performances are perhaps the best ones recorded of Riley's music played by others. "The Room of Remembrance" (1987) is built around five melodic phrases, each of which serves as a door. When the musicians go out they are in the realm of improvisation and must construct ways to re-enter the room. The internal story of the piece is built around the image of a medicine man, having expired in the wintry north of future America, being carried slowly up an icy incline as "snow clams" chant the Om Mane Padme Hum. A beautiful hymn in steady jazz-voiced chords opens the first section, and is interrupted at times by jolly phrases that recall gamelan music; snowflake patterns and windy tremolos are added, making the aural landscape wintry. Rushing patterns follow. The piece concludes with a subdued but fuller textured repeat of the initial hymn in steady chords. "Salome's Excellent Extension" (1989) is in four sections for quartet (piano, marimba, sax, vibraphone/steel drum) and part of a series of works with a similar title: the string quartets called "Salome Dances for Peace." This work offers a unique combination of the rich harmonic and gestural field of American West Coast jazz with Riley's pattern and Indian music sensibilities, with occasionally themes of a 1920s French "Les Six" turn. *— "Blue" Gene Tyranny*

Reed Streams / Apr. 20, 1999 / Cortical Foundation ✦✦✦✦
Terry Riley's debut work, 1966's *Reed Streams*, has been unavailable for over 30 years. 1999's reissue on the Cortical Foundation label features Riley's groundbreaking keyboard trance pieces, remastered from the original tapes, in all their droning, psychedelic glory. Along with "Untitled Organ (1964-66)" and "Dorian Reeds (1966)," the reissue includes a psychedelic big-band version of "In C—*Mantra," the classic minimalist favorite.* —Heather Phares

Jean-Claude Risset

b. Mar. 13, 1938, Le Puy, France
Composer / Spectral Music, Computer Music, Atonal, Electronic
Composer Jean-Claude Risset was a pioneer in the field of computer music and recipient of a great many honors for this music and research (especially in the area of sound synthesis). After studying the sciences, in addition to composition and piano with teachers like André Jolivet (Le Jeune France co-founder), Risset went on to work at Bell Labs, with Max Matthews, for a few years in the late '60s, working on applications that would imitate instruments and others sounds. He brought sound synthesis to Orsay in the early '70s, and Marseille and Paris—to the Institute for Acoustic Music Research and Creation, with Pierre Boulez—in the

mid-'70s. He became IRCAM's computer music director from 1975-1979, after which he served as Director of Research at facilities including CNRS; Risset received the CNRS Bronze Medal in 1971, the Silver Medal in 1987, and the Gold Medal in 1999, for his work and related writings, such as his computerized sound synthesis catalogue of 1969. His other awards include the Dartmouth Prize (1970), first place in the Bourges Digital Music competition (1980), Ars Electronica Austria (1987), Grand Prix National de la Musique (1990), Musica Nova Prague (1995), and an Honorary Doctorate of Music by the University of Edinburgh in the mid-'90s. His best work spans decades and includes "Sud" (1985), "Aventure de lignes, Profiles" (1981), "Mirages" (1978), "Inharmonique" (1977), "Musique pour Little Boy" (1968), and "Fantasie pour Orchestre" (1963). *—Joslyn Layne*

Songes (Dreams) (1979) /Passages (1982) for Flute and Tape / Computer Suite from Little / 1988 / Wergo ✦✦✦
One of the early developers of computer music with Max Matthews at Bell Laboratories and at IRCAM in Paris. Exquisite textures in an aural space that constantly changes it dimensions… soft velvet to digital glacier edges to the ringing of huge bells after they are struck."Sud" is filled with electronic tropical sounds and washes like extended raindrops and wind chimes… a delight to the ear. *— "Blue" Gene Tyranny*

Neil B Rolnick

b. Oct. 22, 1947, Dallas, TX
Composer / Multimedia, Computer Music, 20th Century Classical/Modern Composition
Composer and performer Neil B. Rolnick has been working in the field of computer music since the late '70s. He has written works for theater and for multi-media presentation, and has worked as an educator for many years. The Fulbright grant recipient was composer-in-residence at a number of institutions, and later became the director of the iEAR Studio ("integrated Electronic Arts at Rensselaer") and a teacher at Rensselaer Polytechnic Institute. He has performed all over North America and Europe, and collaborated with ensembles including Gamelan Son of Lion (on the 1992 album *Macedonian Air Drumming*), Relache (on 1987's *A La Mode & Real Time*), and the California E.A.R. Unit. While recordings generally feature Rolnick on keyboards and synthesizers, he operates a MIDI performance system for some works, including "Balkanization" (1988). His mid-'90s multi-media tour, "Requiem: Songs for the Victims of Nationalism," was also performed before the U.S. House of Representatives. *—Joslyn Layne*

ElectriCity / 1992 / O.O. Discs ✦✦✦
Great performances of Rolnick's music by George Lewis, trombone, The New York Contemporary Music Ensemble, and Robert Dick, flute. *— "Blue" Gene Tyranny*

● **Macedonian Air Drumming** / 1992 / Bridge ✦✦✦
Contains: "Sanctus" a computer-generated tape, the complete "Balkanization" (see also *Imaginary Landscapes* under collections), "ReRebong" for the gamelon Son of Lion, and "Macedonian Air Drumming" for MIDI-controlled instruments. *— "Blue" Gene Tyranny*

Requiem Songs: for the Victims of Nationalism (1993) / Screen Scenes (1995) / 1996 / Albany ✦✦✦
Moving and poignant *Requiem Songs* with lyrics by Ed Sanders, Rolnick and from traditional songs, scored for vocals, violin, percussion and sampling electronics. Selections include: "Bosnia's Mountains," "Ethnic Cleansing" and "Home Is a Ghost." The second composition *Screen Scenes* is divided into Playlists 1-4 and is scored for flute and tenor sax, violin, bass, percussion, synthesizer and prepared piano. *— "Blue" Gene Tyranny*

David Rosenboom

b. Sep. 9, 1947, Fairfield, IA
Viola, Piano, Composer / Sound Sculpture, Electronic
Pianist, violinist. Studied at University of Illinois with Salvatore Martirano. Early work in brainwaves and nervous system, cross-cultural collaborations, compositional algorithms. Dean of the School of Music and Co-Director of the Center for Experiments in Art, Information and Technology at CAL Arts since 1990. Taught at Mills College 1979-1990, Professor of Music, Head of the Music Department, Director of the Center for Contemporary Music, and held the Darius Milhaud Chair from 1987 to 1990. Worked and taught at Center for Creative and Performing Arts at SUNY Buffalo, the Electric Circus, York University in Toronto—*Professor of Music and Interdisciplinary Studies, University of Illinois, NYU, Banff Center for the Arts, Simon Fraser University, Aesthetic Research Centre of Canada, San Francisco Art Institute, California College of Arts and Crafts. — "Blue" Gene Tyranny*

Systems of Judgment (1987) / 1990 / Centaur ✦✦✦
A many-timbred computer music composition, sweeping in scope… dynamic sonic illusions of natural sound… mythical and philosophical worlds meeting. *— "Blue" Gene Tyranny*

● **Precipice in Time (1966)/in CDCM Computer Music Series, Vol. 10, A** / 1991 / ✦✦✦✦✦
A unique blend of "free jazz," live "phantom doubles" (computer re-synthesis of acoustic instruments), and graphed structure. From high energy to quiet anticipations with interior tension. Terrific playing. *— "Blue" Gene Tyranny*

Mikel Rouse

b. Jan. 26, 1957, St. Louis, MO
Producer, Composer / Multimedia, 20th Century Classical/Modern Composition, Electronic, Opera
Studied at Kansas City Art Institute, Conservatory of Music at Univ. of Missouri. African and World Musics, Schillinger Method of Composition. Formed Mikel Rouse Broken Consort which recorded many pop music CDs. Electronic works: *Colorado Suite* (1984), *Quorum* (1984). Music for Alvin Ailey Dance Co. *Autorequiem* (1994) for strings, percussion and voices, *Book One* for string quartet, *Two Paradoxes Resolved*, a piano suite. *— "Blue" Gene Tyranny*

● **Living Inside Design** / 1994 / Robi Droli/New Tone ✦✦✦
In "Soul Menu" there is some excellent, positive spirited pattern music combined with rock and soul music instrumentation and rhythmic support, material developed for one of Rouse's groups Broken Consort, which plays his more concert-oriented music. (Tirez Tirez is his pop group.) Simultaneous gamelan-like phrases of seven and eight beats occur in "Hope Chest," a tongue in cheek jazz riff in the lively "Ranger," group rhythm studies in "Copperhead" and "Leading the Machine." The CD *Living Inside Design* continues many of these sounds and techniques but applies them to an excellently produced sequence of songs that goes from the almost-pop "Forever Tonight" to the heartfelt "Kiss Him Goodbye" ("Mouth congress: a kiss, a second parade/An orgy of logic, a romance replayed/And up to the minute, a best out of three"), in which multiple voices occur in an overlay and deconstruction technique Rouse calls "counterpoetry," backed up with vocal and instrumental drones over a beat. Like Arthur Russell, Rouse at times creates that peculiar cosmically "airy" sound associated in pop music with Julee Cruise, the Cocteau Twins, early Fleetwood Mac, and even the Tuff Records version of "Sally, Go 'Round the Roses." After this, Rouse worked on an opera based on Truman Capote's *In Cold Blood. — "Blue" Gene Tyranny*

Failing Kansas / 1995 / Robi Droli/New Tone ✦✦✦

Dennis Cleveland / 1996 / New World ✦✦✦✦✦
The second part of the new narrative opera trilogy (between *Failing Kansas* and *The End of Cinematics,*) about the nature of corporate entertainment, *Dennis Cleveland* is a spectacular piece, a multimedia opera in the form of a television talk show. Its host, Dennis Cleveland, is the central "catalyst and provocateur" surrounded by soloists (audience members) and a chorus (the on-stage guests). Stories of lost love, obsession, crime and regrets, describe both personal events in the participants lives and also by implication unfold the story of the show's host. Live video of the audience, the singers in the audience, studio lighting, and so on are employed to obscure the difference between the opera stage and attending audience. The content of the text is a critique of modern society that depends only on reason, the ability to "deliver, " to the exclusion of intuition, feeling, creativity and even common sense. Many contemporary rhythmic styles are suggested and the text is a subtle and highly involving "counterpoetry." *— "Blue" Gene Tyranny*

Dane Rudhyar (Daniel Chenneviere) (Daniel Chennevière)

b. Mar. 23, 1895, Paris, France, **d.** Sep. 13, 1985, San Francisco, CA
Composer / 20th Century Classical/Modern Composition, Avant-Garde
American composer Dane Rhudyar was known not only for his music, but for pioneering a humanist approach to astrology, and writing about both topics. Born Daniel Chennevière in Paris, before the turn of the century, he heard Stravinsky's "Rite of Spring" when it premiered. He emigrated to the U.S. during the teens (but his early 20s), and continued composing. One of his works, "Paens," was included in a program with works by Ruggles and Copland, organized by Henry Cowell, and in Cowell's first *New Music Editions* in the late '20s. While he may be best known for the piano piece, "Stars," it was his orchestral work "Soul Fire" which earned him a prize by the LAPO. Despite this, and the influence that his writings on music—specifically, Dissonant Harmony (1928) and The New Sense of Sound (1930)—had on many composers, Rudhyar was little known for his music until late in life when composers James Tenney and Peter Garland helped bring him to the attention of the music world. Garland wrote that Rudhyar's "best works occurred in the 1920s and … 1970s!" For at this time, he began composing again, experiencing a revival at the age of 80, mostly writing piano and chamber music. Regardless of his musical ups and downs, Rudhyar remained creatively active throughout his life, taking up painting in New Mexico in the late '30s, writing about music, exploring religion, philosophy, and theosophy (which led to his name change based on a Sanskrit term). He eventually came to form a different conception of astrology that was more spiritual, and wrote many books on this topic, as well as his own biography. *—Joslyn Layne*

● **Five Stanzas for String Orchestra (1927), Epic Poem for Piano (1979)** / 1983 / CP2 ✦✦✦
Performed by the Sinfóníuhljómsveit Aeskunnar and conducted by Paul Zukofsky, this piece was written in 1927, and scored in early 1928. The composer wrote of the "poem" *Five Stanzas for string ensemble* that he had "no story or personal drama in mind when I composed it." The music is nevertheless a completely subjective music of dramatic emotions: "it is meant to speak directly to the inner nature… it is never 'made' as an object according to… patterns." Theoretically, the piece is an excellent exposition of his idea of "dissonant harmony," and of "music of speech," and— which is built from the accumulation of gestures as distinguished from music based on dance rhythms. For example, the fifth and concluding stanza, a Moderato and the longest of the movements, opens with wild telegraphic figures in fifths above tortuous development in the lower strings. Then the lower strings tremolo and move in deep rumbling counterpoint while the upper strings play widely octave-ranging, speech-like and wildly declamatory passages. Out of this comes a brief coda of a gigantic chord in fifths that covers the entire tessiturae of the strings, that is reiterated gradually slower, stretching the telegraphic rhythm of the opening. A truly breath-taking movement. *— "Blue" Gene Tyranny*

Syntony / Pentagram III for Piano / Orion ✦✦✦
Rudhyar's sense of large, cyclic phases of life and civilization and individuation led him to write the brilliant classic *The Astrology of Personality* in 1936, but his compositional style remained non-cyclic, linear, asymmetrical, and highly emotional. "Five Stanzas" is almost unremittingly tense in sweeping writing reminiscent of Carl Ruggles, but contains an otherworldly andante espressivo mid-movement. Piano works "Epic Poem" (played by Robert Black), "Syntony," "Penentagram III" (played by Michael Sellers), and "Transformation" (played brilliantly by Marcia Mikulak) alternate dissonant counterpoint melodies with massive chords (reminding one of Ives' *First Sonata*). The two string quartets "Advent" and "Crisis and Overcoming" move through constant statement-like passages to describe psychic processes—in "Advent" with its movements Visitation, Tumult in the Soul, Tragic Vision, Summons and Response, and Acceptance (referring to Christ's mother Mary), and in "Crisis and Overcoming" from a troubled minor key to a calm major key "realization" at the end. A unique voice. *— "Blue" Gene Tyranny*

Carl Spaque Ruggles

b. Mar. 11, 1876, East Marion, MA, **d.** Oct. 24, 1971, Bennington, VT

Composer / 20th Century Classical/Modern Composition, Atonal

Ruggles' eclectic education included private lessons in theory and composition from professors at Harvard. While supporting himself as an engraver, Ruggles honed his compositional craft and gave lectures on modern music. The year 1907 marked the beginning of an active musical period during which Ruggles taught at the Mar d'Mar School of Music in Minnesota, founded The Winona SO and began work on the opera *The Sunken Bell*. A move to New York in 1917 brought Ruggles private patronage and acquaintances with Varese and Ives, relationships that opened many professional doors for Ruggles. Ruggles' largest work, *Sun Treader* for orchestra, was performed in Paris and Berlin in 1932. In addition to a position at University of Miami as director of composition from 1938-43, Ruggles continued composing and revising his scores. Though he received many honors for his musical work, in later years he began to shift his creative emphasis to painting. Although not a serial composer, Ruggles wrote melodies so that no note was repeated until a set number had been played. His music is atonal with an emphasis on the chromatic. His love for American and English literature is evident in his use of the work of Whitman and Browning for settings for his work. *—Lynn Vought*

★ **Sun-Treader (1926-31)** / 1990 / Deutsche Grammaphon ✦✦✦✦✦
Dramatic and soaring peformance by The Boston Symphony Orchestra, conducted by Michael Tilson Thomas. Ruggles like Ives shared the same Emersonian transcendentalist vision of society and the soul's possibilities, and this work is his most eloquent expression of that insight. Ruggles would work by placing enormous scores on the floor and craft every note and passage in detail. An earlier recording of the orchestral "Lilacs" and "Portals", played by The Juillard String Orchestra, Frederick Prausnitz, conducting, is also recommended. *—"Blue" Gene Tyranny*

Evocations (4 Chants) for Piano (1935—43, revised 1954) / Music & Arts ✦✦✦✦✦
Performed by J. Jensen, the four pieces assembled under the title *Evocations* were composed respectively during 1937, 1941, 1943 and 1940 for piano solo. These movements were also orchestrated by the composer from 1942 to the next few years, and continually revised through 1956. The opening "Largo" starts with a motif that gradually re-starts several times, each time extending its melodic range until it achieves large and passionate arches. The music quickly descends again to the lower ranges with a still and quiet concluding chord covering a wide range. The second piece, marked "Andante sempre poco rubato" in the orchestral version and "Andante con fantasia" in the piano solo version, opens with a steady, wandering melody, which is made into a more angular version, and then varied in slow tempo, and in tense double counterpoint that has two dramatic arching points and then subsides. The initial wandering idea returns for a brief statement and the music peacefully concludes. The third movement is a "Moderato appassionato" and is built of many short flowing melodic arches and highly dramatic chordal statements. The final "Adagio sostenuto" is built on accumulations of arching gestures in irregular rhythms, often rushing forward, balanced mid-way by a tense bridge of ascending double counterpoint. The music then becomes exceedingly quiet but still maintains its dissonant, tense character, before it evaporates into silence. *—"Blue" Gene Tyranny*

Organum for Large Orchestra (1944-47) / CRI ✦✦✦✦✦

Vox Clamans in Deserto (A Voice Crying in the Wilderness) (1923) / in "The Complete Wor / CBS Masterworks ✦✦✦✦✦
A magnificent work with texts by Robert Browning, Walt Whitman and C.H. Meltzer, years ahead of its time. Sweeping performance. Performed by Beverly Morgan, mezzo-soprano, with The Speculum Musicae conducted by M. Tilson Thomas. *—"Blue" Gene Tyranny*

Ruins

f. 1985

Group / Noise-Rock, Prog-Rock/Art Rock, Alternative Pop/Rock, Avant-Garde

Ruins, who are Tatsuya Yoshida (drums/vocals) and Hisashi Sasaki (bass/vocals), play a unique form of manic and twisted progressive rock for these millennial times. This duo's compositions are complex and can be disorientating to the listener who is accustomed to less innovative, dynamic and demanding musics. Tatsuya Yoshida, the founding member of Ruins, formed the band in 1985. Since that time there have been a number of different bass players, including Ryuichi Masuda, Hisashi Sasaki, and Kimoto Kazuyoshib. Bandleader/drummer/singer Yoshida credits such diverse influences as progressive-rock stalwarts Magma, classical composers such as Chopin, and traditional throat singing from Tuva. Though hints of these and other influences (e.g. Bill Bruford, Rush, Pink Floyd, Gong, King Krimson, Magma, Yes, and Genesis) often come through in the Ruins sound, there is no mistaking them for anyone else. Many of their compositions employ odd time signatures, sudden tempo changes, and passages of heavily processed noise. The bass, which unlike most has six strings, is often threaded through various effects. Both members of the band sing vocables that complement one another. These vocables are meant to be nonsensical and that's how they sound. They are usually improvised, as are portions of their songs. Their overall sound is chaotic yet precise, noisy yet harmonious, catchy yet repelling, frenetic yet disciplined. As if the demands of Ruins were not enough, both Yoshida and Masuda keep themselves busy with various musical side projects (e.g. Vasilisk, YBO*2*, Men of the Continent Versus the Mountain Women). From time to time Ruins will collaborate with others. These people have included saxophonist/producer John Zorn, keyboardist Kenichi Oguchi, vocalists Eleonola Emi and Aki Kubota, the acrobatic punkers Schlong, Kazutoki Umezu, producer Steve Albini and guitarists Derek Bailey and Jason Willet. Ruins have many releases in the form of singles, collaborations, and full length CDs. Among these full-length albums are *Stonehenge* (1990), *Burning Stone* (1992), *Refusal Fossil* (1997), and *Symphonica* (1998). The latest release from Ruins, *Pallaschtom* (2000), is comprised of three tracks: a classical music medley, a hard rock medley, and a progressive rock medley. *—John Vallier*

Burning Stone / 1992 / Shimmy Disc ✦✦✦✦✦

● **Hyderomastgroningem** / 1995 / Tzadik ✦✦✦✦✦
Hyderomastgroningem is a wild release of frenzy á la Ruins; it is tough, metal-punk Japanese rock that is the soundtrack of an attack and fight in a lion's den played at 78 rpm. Percussionist Yoshida Tatsuya and bassist Masuda Ryuichi also provide sporadic vocals that work well with the music. This album is a sonic fireworks display of powerful bass and percussion. *—Joslyn Layne*

Refusal Fossil / Jan. 19, 1998 / Skin Graft ✦✦✦
The first Ruins release to feature new bassist Sasaki Hishashi, a longtime vet of the Japanese grindcore scene, *Refusal Fossil* doesn't deviate at all from the pattern of previous releases—this is music of extreme intensity, unforgiving bass-and-drum noise typified by stop-on-a-dime tempos and time signatures and lyrics sung in a language plainly not of this earth. *—Jason Ankeny*

Stonehenge / Shimmy Disc ✦✦✦✦✦
Stonehenge is the first CD made by the Japanese post-punk prog rock duo Ruins. Ruins, who is drummer/bandleader Tatsuya Yoshida and bassist/vocalist Kimoto Kazuyoshi on this album, released *Stonehenge* in 1990. In what has become a characteristically Ruins sound, this CD contains a series of angular, aggressive, adroit, and sometimes catchy songs. The shortest song, "Plexus," lasts for only one minute. It consists of tortured vocals and a repeated distorted bass and syncopated drum set ostinato in odd time. The longest song on the CD, "B.U.G.," rampages for over six minutes. It is characterized by an extended section of spine-crushing quarter notes and then a slippery groove in five. The liner notes, which are written in something close to two-point font, list the CD as having 14 songs. In actuality, *Stonehenge* has 21 serpentine songs that may leave you panting for more. *—John Vallier*

Arthur Russell

b. 1951, Oskaloosa, IA, **d.** Apr. 4, 1992, New York

Cello, Producer, Composer / Minimalism, Classical, Disco, Hip-Hop

Arthur Russell was a formally trained cellist and composer with a background in Indian classical music, a resume highlighted by collaborations with Allen Ginsberg and Philip Glass, and involvement in Manhattan's downtown performance scene of the '70s. The same Arthur Russell was also a quirky songwriter, a producer of one-shot disco singles, a founding partner of seminal hip-hop/dance label Sleeping Bag, and a principle designer of the dubby, underground club sound that bridges the gap between the disco era and the first stirrings of house and garage music. Yet, despite a career that seemed contradictory on the surface, he produced a body of work notable for its focus, integrity, and singularity.

Russell moved to San Francisco in the early '70s and studied at a school founded by Hindustani (North Indian) music master Ali Akbar Khan. He provided musical accompaniment for many of Allen Ginsberg's performances. Russell moved to New York later in the '70s and made his reputation as a dance music producer with tracks like "Kiss Me Again" and Loose Joint's "Is It All Over My Face" for West End. In 1982, under the name Dinosaur L, Russell released *24-24 Music* on his own Sleeping Bag label. A Francois Kevorkian remix of the album's "Go Bang" single epitomized the loose, jazzy, somewhat minimalist underground sound that would inform Chicago house.

In 1983, Russell released a portion of a larger instrumental composition as the *Tower of Meaning* LP. His 1986 *World of Echo* was a one-man show of quietist original songs in a solo cello and vocal format that seemed designed to be overheard. Though it received a favorable critical reception in the British music press, Russell remained relatively obscure throughout his life, which was ended by AIDS in 1992. In 1994, a retrospective of previously unissued material was released as *Another Thought*. *—Richard Pierson*

● **Tower of Meaning** / 1983 / Chatham Square ✦✦✦✦✦
Julius Eastman conducting an almost medievally pure music in which tone combinations of two or three notes tuned to modal/raga scales are played by various instrumental groups. There is a love of listening to the pure combinations per se, as they are delivered at a regular, moderate pace . . . then, unpredictibly, rich or dissonant chords will be held that open your mind's ear, and take your breath away. . . . the sudden ceasing of the music at certain points also has a similar effect. *—"Blue" Gene Tyranny*

World of Echo / 1986 / Upside ✦✦✦
An incredible assemblage of solo versions of this influential and unique downtown musician. Contains the songs and instrumentals written from 1980-1986: "Soon-To-Be Innocent Fun/Let's See," "Tower of Meaning / Rabbit's Ear/Home Away from Home," "Tone Bone Kone," "Answers Me," "Being It," "Place I Know/ Kid Like You," "She's the Star/ITake This Time," "Treehouse," "See-Through," "Hiding Your Present from You," "Wax the Van," "All-Boy All-Girl," "Lucky Cloud," and "Let's Go Swimming." Subtle, transcendental with gentle rock beats and new music influences in patternings and textures. *—"Blue" Gene Tyranny*

Joel Ryan

b. Jan. 1, 1945

Composer, Electronics / Electronic

Studied with Jose Barroso (Mexican film composer and guitarist), Ravi and Lakshmi Shankar, Robert Ashley, David Behrman, and influenced by live concerts of John Coltrane. Collaborated with composers and artists including George E. Lewis, Malcolm Goldstein, Evan Parker, Steina and Woody Vasulka, and "Blue" Gene Tyranny. Has been creating digital sound processing instruments for live electronic music since 1979. Currently Director of Research at STEIM in Amsterdam, and Docent at the Institute of Sonology of the Royal Conservatory in The Hague. International performances. *—"Blue" Gene Tyranny*

☆ **The Number Readers** / OR Ltd (London) ✦✦✦✦✦
One of our most original writers on the aesthetics of new music, Ryan also has been associated as an original software designer with the STEIM studios in Amsterdam. This elegant work for live computer-driven electronics, video, and spoken text is based on evening shortwave radio transmissions of women's voices reading numbers with great precision in German, and sometimes Spanish and Czech, sometimes preceded by electronic chime patterns.

"No nation or agency has claimed authorship of these broadcasts." Joel observed a middle-aged woman who sat with pad and pencil in semi-darkness by an old-style model radio at the front window of a well-kept old house in Amsterdam; he soon began to realize that there was a "synchrony of the number readers broadcasts with the woman's vigils." Ryan weaves a variety of musical imagery using this central "coding" idea as a stepping stone: "Codes to Protect Property," "Julius Caesar's Code to Confuse the Gauls Equals C + 3Mod24," "Code as Reason Contradicting Itself," "The Language of Flowers," "Codes You Can Eat," and many others. Fascinating, innovative work. *— "Blue" Gene Tyranny*

Frederic Rzewski

b. Apr. 13, 1938, Westerfield, MA

Piano, Conductor, Composer / 20th Century Classical/Modern Composition, World Fusion, Atonal

Avant-garde composer and pianist Frederic Rzewski studied with many of the best-known names in 20th century music: Randall Thompson, Walter Piston, Roger Sessions, Milton Babbitt, Luigi Dallapiccola, and Elliott Carter. Rzewski studied at Harvard and Princeton and taught at schools including the Royal Conservatory of Music at Liege and Yale. He was awarded a Fulbright Fellowship in 1960 and co-founded Musica Elettronica Viva in Rome in 1966.

A virtuoso pianist, much of Rzewski's music is written for piano, including what is arguably his best-known work, the politically driven "The People United Will Never Be Defeated! (36 variations on "El pueblo unido jamas sera vencido")" (1975), which pushes the extreme of both instrument and pianist.

Rzewski has written works that explore timbres in not only the piano, but also in electronics and incorporating spoken word. An example of this type of experimental voicing is "Coming Together", written for speaking voice and instrumental octet, commemorating the uprising at New York's Attica State Prison. The text comes from a prisoner involved in the riot who later died and the combination of emotional text with instrumental work employing extended techniques, silence, and unique instrumental sounds allow for a unique type of emotional response to the music itself.

Although Rzewski's exploration of a multitude of techniques, sounds, and styles is impressive, but doesn't allow for very much work in any one area. However, his music will continue to serve as an example of exploration in these different styles. *— Michael Blostein*

☆ **Winnsboro Cotton Mill Blues (1980) in Double Edge "Us Choice"** / 1992 / CRI ✦✦✦✦✦

The whirring and clanging of the factory mixed with the rhythmic blues of the workers. Thrilling music played with a lot of heart by this astonishingly talented duo. *— "Blue" Gene Tyranny*

De Profundis / 1994 / hatART ✦✦✦

Two moving examples of how political concerns can be expressed with rich human emotions. *— "Blue" Gene Tyranny*

A Decade: Zeitgeist Plays Rzewski / 1994 / O.O. Discs ✦✦✦

Four chamber works— *Wails* (1984), *Spots* (1986), *The Lost Melody* (1989), and *Crusoe* (1993)—beautifully and energetically played by the Zeitgeist chamber ensemble. Highly tuneful, often playful, riff-like melodies over colorful harmonies equally reminiscent of the '20's "Les Six" composers and the voicings of Duke Ellington. *— "Blue" Gene Tyranny*

● **People United Will Never Be Defeated, The** / 1994 / New Albion ✦✦✦✦

The thrilling, virtuoso, political classic for piano... 36 variations on "El Pueblo Unido Jamas Sera Vencido!" played brilliantly by Stephen Drury, with excerpts from a live performance in Buenos Aires of the tune by Quillapayun. *— "Blue" Gene Tyranny*

Erik Satie

b. May 17, 1866, Honfleur, France, **d.** Jul. 1, 1925, Paris, France

Piano, Composer / 20th Century Classical/Modern Composition, Fusion, Minimalism, Atonal, Classical

Satie's music, in sound and aesthetics, was fundamentally different from the prevailing 19th-century German school that prized ideals of continuity and development. It is music as sound per se (*Musique d'ameublement*, i.e., "Furniture Music" or "Music for Furnishing", 1920). In *Musiques intimes et secretes* ("Intimate and Secret Music") and the famous "Vexations" (from *Pages mystiques*, 1892-1895), Satie describes the conceptual nature of human mental activity and then requires the performers to experience and scrutinize, simultaneously, the exact moments of shifting psychological states. "Vexations" is a short musical passage of neutral feeling (augmented and diminished chords) repeated 840 times very slowly. Satie emphasizes natural and spontaneous mentation apart from "ideas" in *The Dreaming Fish, Heures séculaires et instantanées* ("Ordinary and Snapshot Times"), and *Véritables préludes flasquers–pour un chien* ("Authentic Flabby Preludes—for a Dog"). Ironic titles and commentaries poke fun at pomposity, as in *Le duc de Connaught et le President aux manoeuvers* ("The Duke of Connaught and the President on Manouvers") and *Enfantines* ("Infantile Pieces," 1913 which go by such titles as "The Bean-King's War Chant"; "Importune Peccadillos, I"; "Being Jealous of His Comrade with the Big Head, II"; "Him Eat His Cookie, III"; and "Taking Advantage of His Corns to Steal His Hoop"). Satie's religious feeling was of a mystical, pre-clerical kind, expressed in works such as *Première pensée Rose + Croix* ("First Rosey Thought + Cross," 1891, French word play on "Rosicrucians"); the beautiful and compassionate *Messe des Pauvres* ("Mass for the Poor," 1893-1895); and the moving *Socrate* (1918) on the death of Socrates and based on texts by Plato. Satie invented many musical techniques—the use of whole-tone scales, chords built in fourths, pattern melodies, unresolved "dissonances" used for their value as sounds, "open" large forms without contrasting or developing sections, and others. Perhaps more important, he was the first conceptual composer. *— "Blue" Gene Tyranny*

● **Piano Works, Vol. 1 "First and Last Works" / Piano Works, Vol. 2 "Mystical Works" / Pia** / 1989 / Angel ✦✦✦

Pianist Aldo Ciccolini produced the first complete recordings of all of Satie's piano works, and his playing of them is still the best. He treats them with clarity, lightness, and the appropriate humor but never with the rubato sweetness that some performers slip into. In these piano works, Satie can probably be most clearly seen creating a music that, in both its sound and aesthetics, is fundamentally different from that produced under the ideals of continuity and development prized by the 19th century Germanic school (which until about the 1950s still held the most influence in the United States). With originality from the root of the soul and some amazing titles, Satie focuses on music as "sound" per se. With Buddhist-like attention and perhaps the first true attempt to describe the "conceptual" nature of human mental activity, he requires the performer(s) to simultaneously experience and examine in detail the exact moments of shifting psychological states. He used ironic titles and written commentaries in his scores to poke fun at pomposity and officialism, as with titles like "Importune Peccadillos," "I. Being Jealous of His Comrade With the Big Head," "II. Him Eat His Cookie," etc. Satie's religious feeling was of a mystical pre-cleric kind expressed in works like "Premiere Pensee Rose + Croix" (1891) ("First Rose + Cross Thought"). Satie invented many musical techniques—use of whole tone scales, chords built in fourths, pattern melodies, unresolved "dissonances" used for their value as sounds, "open" large forms without contrasting or developing sections, etc.—but perhaps more importantly, he was the first conceptual composer. *— "Blue" Gene Tyranny*

The Complete Ballets / 1990 / Vanguard Classics ✦✦✦

With wonderful performances by Maurice Abravanel conducting the Utah Symphony Orchestra, this recording includes "Parade" (1917, realist ballet after Jean Cocteau), "Mercure" ("Mercury," 1924, plastic poses in 13 scenes, designed by Pablo Picasso), "Relache" ("Respite," 1924, instantaneous ballet in two acts, a cinematic intermission, and a dog's tail, designed by Francis Picabia, film by Rene Clair), "Jack in the Box" (1899, pantomime, orchestrated by Milhaud, 1923), "Gymnopedies 1 and 3" (1888, orchestrated by Debussy, music for ancient Greek gymnastic exercises written in old modal scales), "Trois Morceaux en Forme de Poire" (1903, "Three Pieces in the Form of a Pear," orchestrated by Desormiere), "Cinq Grimaces Pour 'Le Songe d'une Nuit d'Ete'" ("Five Grimaces for a Planned Cocteau Production of "A Midsummer Night's Dream"," 1914), and "The Grand Ritournelle" from "La Belle Excentrique" ("The Beautiful Eccentric Lady," 1920). *— "Blue" Gene Tyranny*

Giacinto Scelsi

b. Jan. 8, 1905, La Spezia, Italy, **d.** Aug. 8, 1988, Rome, Italy

Composer / 20th Century Classical/Modern Composition, Minimalism, Atonal, Classical

Giacinto Scelsi's music was largely unknown throughout most of his life, as he refused interviews, rarely sought out performances, and would not even have his photograph taken, preferring instead to be represented by the symbol of a horizontal line placed under a circle. The attitudes behind his musical creations can be tied in with this reclusiveness, as from the 1940s he saw music as a type of spiritual revelation, with the composer as creator of circumstances through which the secrets in sounds could be revealed—a result of the Eastern philosophies encountered during his earlier travels, which he had time to reflect upon following a breakdown around the time of WWII. Before this, he had composed 12-tone and atonal music (usually for piano, which he played), revealing his own influences—instructors Walter Klein, a pupil of Schoenberg's, and Scriabin enthusiast Egon Koehler. After his revelation, Scelsi began composing works which involved very static harmony with surface fluctuations of timbre and microtonal inflection. This type of harmonic minimalism was developed independently of other minimalists and was received with fascination by the music world when Scelsi's music finally received performances and recordings in the 1980s.

He wrote over one hundred works, including pieces for orchestra, chamber ensemble, string quartets, and solo and duo performers. His fascination with microtones made itself felt in his work, beginning in the '50s, as in String Quartet No. 4 (1964), Khoom (1962) (which also displayed his interest in the human voice during this period, developed through his collaborations with singer Michiko Hirayama), and was at its most pronounced in the Quattro Pezzi Su Una Nota Sola (Four pieces each on a single note) (1959), for chamber orchestra. From the 1970s, Scelsi's pieces became generally shorter and more succinct. Many of his pieces were worked out in improvisation and subsequently written down, but dating his compositions has been difficult as he re-dated manuscripts deliberately to confuse musicologists. *— Rachel Campbell*

● **Pfhat (1974) for Chorus and Orchestra** / 1988 / Accord ✦✦✦

Unlike the heaviness with which Scelsi at times depicts mythologies of Buddhist, Egyptian, Latin and other ancient cultures (in a ponderous style sometimes called "the new religiosity"), "Pfhat" employs a concentrated pallette of sounds and compositional ideas... breathing sounds from the chorus, imitation of a single giant ringing bell, and a lovely finale for two flutes holding a dissonance surrounded by (about) a hundred small, tinkling bells. For comparison, this CDC also contains "Aion" (1961) and "Konx-om-pax" (1969). *— "Blue" Gene Tyranny*

Botba / 1992 / hatART ✦✦✦

Marianne Schroeder, piano. Somewhat more conservative but more concentrated early works, beautifully played. Includes "Un Adieu," the "*Sonata No. 2*" and the interesting "Suite No. 8" (1952) which is an evocation of Tibet with its monastaries, rituals, prayers and dances. *— "Blue" Gene Tyranny*

Pierre Schaeffer

b. Aug. 14, 1910, Nancy, France, **d.** Aug. 19, 1995, Les Milles, France

Composer / Tape Music, Musique Concrète, 20th Century Classical/Modern Composition, Atonal, Electronic

The father of musique concrète, French composer Pierre Schaeffer was among the most visionary artists of the postwar era; through the creation of abstract sound mosaics divorced from conventional musical theory, he pioneered a sonic revolution which continues to resonate across the contemporary cultural landscape, most deeply in the grooves of hip-hop and electronica. Not a trained musician or composer, Schaeffer was working as a radio engineer when he founded the RTF electronic studio in 1944 to begin his first experiments in what would ultimately be dubbed "musique concrète." Working with found fragments of sound—both musical and environmental in origin—he assembled his first tape-machine pieces, collages of noise manipulated through changes in pitch, duration and amplitude; the end result heralded a radical new interpretation of musical form and perception.

Though the 1948 radio broadcast of his first public piece provoked a range of response from comic disbelief to genuine outrage, many composers and performers were intrigued, among them Pierre Henry, who in 1949 joined the RTF staff. Working with the classically-trained Henry on subsequent pieces including *Variations Sur une Flute Mexicaine* and *Orphee 51* clearly informed Schaeffer's later projects, as he soon adopted a more accessible musical approach. Together, the two men also co-founded the Groupe de Recherches Musicales, a studio that became the launching pad behind some of the most crucial electronic music compositions of the era. By the end of the '50s, though, Schaeffer announced his retirement from music.

Leaving the GRM in the hands of Francois Bayle, Schaeffer worked as the director of the research center at the Office of French Television Broadcasting and also explored areas of psycho-acoustic research which he dubbed Traite de Objets Musicaux (TOM). He also hit the lecture circuit and agreed to produce radio presentations. —*Jason Ankeny*

● **Erotica "Symphonie Pour Un Homme Seul" (Collaboration with Pierre Henry) in "Concert Im** / 1984 / INA.GRM - INA ♦♦♦♦

A short and sweetly humorous feuilleton (or bob-bon as the case may be) by the composer who led early French work on composing with environmental, extra-musical sounds or "musique concrete"... resulting in his "Concert de Bruits" (*Concert of Noises*) broadcast in 1948 and the establishment in 1951 of The Groupe de Recherches de Musique Concrete, and in 1958 The Group for Musical Research of the Office of French Radio-Television (O.R.T.F.). "Musique concrete" now also includes electronic and world music. —*"Blue" Gene Tyranny*

Klaus Schulze

b. Aug. 4, 1947, Berlin, Germany

Electronics, Keyboards, Guitar, Synthesizer, Composer / Space Rock, Kraut Rock, Electronic

As both a solo artist and as a member of groups including Tangerine Dream and Ash Ra Tempel, Klaus Schulze emerged among the founding fathers of contemporary electronic music, his epic, meditative soundscapes a key influence on the subsequent rise of the new age aesthetic. While Schulze's previous recorded work had been in a typically noisy Krautrock vein, as a solo artist he quickly became more reflective; although he acquired his first synthesizer in 1972, it did not enter into his solo debut *Irrlicht*, its long, droning peices instead assembled from electronic organ, oscillators and orchestral recordings. *Blackdance* was his first recording to feature synths; *Timewind*, regarded by many as Schulze's masterpiece, appeared in 1975. *Dig It* was his first fully digital recording. By the 1990s, Schulze had immersed himself in contemporary dance music, occasionally working in conjunction with Pete Namlook (as Dark Side of the Moog). —*Jason Ankeny*

☆ **Irrlicht** / 1972 / Thunderbolt ♦♦♦♦♦

Schulze's solo debut is a masterful album featuring some of the most majestic instances of space music ever recorded, all the more remarkable for being recorded without synthesizers. "Satz Gewitter," the first of two tracks and the highlight here, slowly progresses from oscillator static to a series of glowing organ lines, all informed by Schulze's excellent feel for phase effects. —*John Bush*

Cyborg / 1973 / Gramavision ♦♦♦♦♦

From the early days of electronic experimentation in the pop field, Klaus Schulze's second solo album still today it stands as one of the most powerful examples of ambient pulse music ever conceived. The dense layers of rhythm and synthetic tone colors melt into a seamless, flowing soundscape of melody, motion and spatial effects. It's a monumental double album of "cosmic music." —*Archie Patterson*

Timewind / 1975 / Blue Plate ♦♦♦♦

X / 1978 / Thunderbolt ♦♦♦♦

Each track on *X* or "Ten" (since it's Schulze's tenth release) is titled after famous German personalities, but it's the provocative electronic music within the names that makes this one of his best albums. On this two-CD set, Schulze's sequencer is joined by electric guitar and drums, that pleasingly brings an earthy, simplistic feel into his pastiches. Still captivating and alluring with his multi- keyboard entourage, the tracks each exhibit a personality all their own. "Friedrich Nietzsche" is the most vibrant of all six, harboring a complex but attractive aura. The 24 minutes of this synthesized voyage involve imaginative sculpturing using both the Moog and Mellotron. Extreme washes of sturdy tones and pulses make up this wonderfully crafted track, one of Schulze's best. In the same manner, the rest of the album is pure electronic bombardment. With 12 different types of sequencers and synthesizers molded, merged, and fused together, the musical landscape created is overwhelming. On both the 29-minute "Ludwig II Von Bayern" and the equally lengthy "Heinrich Von Kleist," a foreign atmosphere is bred through the multitude of variable electronics, both of the guitar and keyboard type. As each track begins to take shape, the music is dissected and laid out, but not before it forms lasting images and intricately conveys mood. A true pioneer at his craft, Schulze's *X* is one of the more definitive albums of his career, since it's length and instrumental combinations make for a multifaceted electronic piece. —*Mike DeGagne*

● **Essential (1972-1993)** / Feb. 11, 1994 / Plan 9/Caroline ♦♦♦♦

The Essential 72-93 is a makeshift best-of, piecing together some of Klaus Schulze's most alluring and interesting electronic offerings. With 14 tracks from over ten albums, this compilation is a generous retrospection into this former Tangerine Dream member's material. Many of his masterpieces are included on this double CD, like the swirling electronic breeze of "Wahnfried 1883" from 1975's *Timewind*, or the out-of-body atmospheric waves of "Floating" from *Moondawn*. Also breathtaking is the ten minute synthesized soup of "Ludwig II Von Bayern" off of the monumental *X* album, and the chilling glaze of "Freeze", a superb example of keyboard artistry as Schulze precipitates an icy climate from basic tonal applications. A good cross section of his work can be regarded all at once throughout this compilation, making for an insightful trip across this musician's many different periods. While his single albums convey one precise mood or atmosphere from beginning to end, this set investigates a variance of his electronic compositions, and is pleasing on that aspect alone. As an historical journey, this album serves it's purpose, but Schulze's albums should still be heard in completion to fully admire this genius' ability to produce phenomenal electronic music. —*Mike DeGagne*

Ramon Sender (Ramon Sender Barayon)

b. Oct. 29, 1934, Madrid, Spain

Composer / Avant-Garde, Electronic

Electronic and experimental composer Ramon Sender co-founded the San Francisco Tape Music Center with Morton Subotnick in 1961. He studied under George Copeland, Elliott Carter, and Robert Erickson in California colleges including Mills College (M.A., 1965). In the S.F. Tape Music Center's early days, Sender, Subotnick, Pauline Oliveros, Tony Martin, and Terry Riley were the core composers. In the late '60s, Sender also became a part of Lou Gottlieb's Morning Star/Wheeler (Ahimsa) Ranch communes, and in the '90s, became involved in the Peregrine Foundation, which helps people "living in or exiting from experimental social groups." His works include "Desert Ambulance" (1964) for accordion, tape, slides, and film, and "Audition for Three Small Harps in Mode 28" (1981). Sender is a performer in some of his compositions, playing, among other instruments, the dilruba harp. —*Joslyn Layne*

Audition (Excerpt) / 1986 / Music from Mills ♦♦♦

One of my favorite composers ever since I heard, at a *ONCE Festival* in the mid 60's, both his electronic tape "Kore" (1962) and "Information", the score, a huge roll of transparent material, for performer(s) giving improvised "information"... a few receiving instructions on headphones while performing on accordion with his wonderful electronic tape "Desert Ambulance". —*"Blue" Gene Tyranny*

Elliott Sharp

b. Mar. 1, 1951, Cleveland, OH

Electronic Sounds, Sax (Tenor), Clarinet (Bass), Guitar, Composer / Microtonal, Experimental Rock, Soundtracks, Experimental, Free Jazz, Avant-Garde

Perhaps next to John Zorn the most eclectic and outrageous member of the '90s "downtown" group, Elliott Sharp does free, ethnic, rock and a wild mixture of everything else in the musical spectrum. The composer/performer plays electric and steel guitar, electric bass, soprano sax, bass clarinet and many other things and with his band Carbon brings to his dates a spirit of adventure, bizarre antics and rampaging musical experimentation that makes it difficult to assess much of his material. It may be improvisational, but it's also deliberately chaotic, sometimes horrendous, other times quite insightful. He's recorded for the Enemy label, and has been featured on Knitting Factory sessions. Sharp's one musician who's truly not for all tastes. —*Ron Wynn*

Blackburst Psycho-Acoustic / Nov. 11, 1996 / Victo ♦♦♦♦

Psycho-Acoustic is guitarist Elliott Sharp and harpist Zeena Parkins, and *Blackburst* is their first album together under that name (their first album was titled *Psycho-Acoustic* and simply credited to Sharp and Parkins). As with their first project, this one finds them exploring the sonic frontiers of their various instruments, which include double-neck guitar/bass, bass clarinet, synthesizers and rhythm machines, and a mysterious instrument called the "Buchla Thunder." *Blackburst* is somewhat more accessible than *Psycho-Acoustic*, but it's still thoroughly weird. "Specific Gravity" features a percolating beat that hops along under a one-chord vamp, allowing Sharp and Parkins to lay down layers of moaning, shrieking instrumental lines on top. "Peregrine" is episodic in nature and epic in length, but ultimately proves to be more interesting than enjoyable. The best track of the album is "Massive Apatite" (sic), which weaves together subtle vocal samples, a staggering beat and a recurring synth pattern that sounds like R2D2 in ecstasy. Cool. —*Rick Anderson*

● **In the Land of the Yahoos** / 1987 / SST ♦♦♦♦♦

Elliott's "pop" album, made as sort of a joke, features lots of sampled vocals on top of dance-club beats. It's certainly his most accessible: his other recordings have more of his trademark guitar turbulence and mathematically oriented compositional style. —*Myles Boisen*

● **Hammer, Anvil, Stirrup** / 1989 / SST ♦♦♦♦♦

An excellent rendering by the Soldier String Quartet of some of Sharp's best music: visceral patterns with searing harmonic content and new string techniques. The unique title piece, present in two takes interesting to contrast, seems to be partly a gritty and humorous take-off on hoe-down/cowboy horseback-riding music (as depicted in movies) and then wanders into some strange slithery tuning zones traversed by squiggly melodies. Using the Fibonaccis series to generate tunings, rhythms, and forms, the next selection, "Tessalation Row," delivers an electrifyingly gorgeous image as geometric and scintillating as the Zapotec design from Oaxaca, Mexico, on the CD's cover. "Digital" is a toe-tapping rhythmic study that uses a strip of spring steel woven into the strings near the bridge as a preparation, the instruments then all played with a two-handed hammering technique. "Diurnal" and "Ringtoss" study massed and unison melodic gestures using looping and deconstruction techniques. "Re/Iterations" is for string orchestra (made here by overdubbing the Quartet) with contact microphones attached to the instruments to pick up the subtle difference or "ghost" tones produced by the combinations of high harmonics, dense masses of swirling frequency/rhythm patterns lovely in their rawness. —*"Blue" Gene Tyranny*

Amusia / 1993 / Atavistic ♦♦

Terraplane / Aug. 5, 1994 / Homestead ♦♦

Figure Ground / Mar. 18, 1997 / Tzadik ♦♦♦♦♦

Though composed for four very different films (among them two documentaries—one on the life of gay erotic artist Tom of Finland and the other on transvestites who live in the salt warehouses of New York City), the music on *Figure Ground* hangs together as a cohesive collection. Somewhat confusing liner notes make it a bit difficult to assign all of the songs to specific films, but a general idea of their distribution is given. The songs seethe and hum with an often erotic energy, with long, vibrating synth tones stretched over layers of shuffling rhythm. A kind of dark minimalism pervades, especially on the first track, "Incandescent," which lumbers on like a somnambulent slave. A strong dance influence can be felt in places, with somewhat tribal drums setting the pace for rhythmic scratching. Indeed, the influence of many kinds of music can be felt on these works, with Sharp pulling musical tricks out of his hat to suit the mood he is trying to create, from bluesy to icy to hyperactive. The nearly frenetic "Letha" is one of the most interesting tracks on the album, combining hypnotizing rhythms and guitar gurgles. Two tracks later, "Nightmare" seems like a score for the yawning gates of hell. This is one of Sharp's most complex and varied albums—nevertheless, it rarely manages to miss the mark. *—Stacia Proefrock*

Laetitia Sonami

b. 1957, France

Engineer / Sound Collage

Laetitia Sonami incorporates music and spoken word with technology and improvisation, also utilizing an instrument made out of an elbow-length formal glove fitted with sensors that allow her to manipulate electronic sounds. Although born in France in 1957, Sonami has lived in the U.S. since 1975. The late '90s brought increased recognition for Sonami and her electronic pursuits, as she performed around the world at a number of major avant-garde festivals as well as in the American Embassy's Interlink Festival. She has collaborated with Lou Mazzolli, Donald Swearingen, and Visual Brains, among others. *—Joslyn Layne*

Pie Jesu: Sounds from Empty Spaces No. 3/ in "Another Coast" / 1988 / Music and Art ✦✦✦✦✦

We hear Moslem song, sweet synthesizer tones, CB radio, the beginnings of an anxious explanation, a dog bark and other environmental sounds that depict an imaginary world built from the drama of "unforeseen change." See also her compositions "What Happened" in the collection *Imaginary Landscapes* (1989), and "Story Road" in the collection *Jewel Box* (1992). *—"Blue" Gene Tyranny*

Bernadette Speach

b. Jan. 1, 1948, Syracuse, NY

Piano / Improvisation, 20th Century Classical/Modern Composition

Studied at College of Saint Rose in Albany, Columbia University, courses in Siena, Italy, State University of NY at Buffalo. Composition with Nicolas Roussakis, Jacques-Louis Monod, Morton Feldman, Lejaren Hiller. President of Buffalo New Musi Ensemble, Board of Directors of the Musicians of Brooklyn Initiative (MOBI), Executive Director of Composers' Forum, Inc. in NYC. *—"Blue" Gene Tyranny*

Dualities / 1991 / Mode ✦✦✦

Featuring the duo of Jeffrey Schanzer on electric and classical guitars and Bernadette Speach on piano, this CD presents sensitive pieces that successfully combine advanced harmonies and compositional techniques with some gestures suggesting folk music and jazz/pop genres. "Two in the Morning" begins with a nocturnal mysterious ballad feel and a hint of Spanish guitar, works its way through more aggressive fast pointillism, and returns to a moody, introspective time-to-close-up-the-bar coda. "3 1/2" is a fascinating pattern piece that gradually shifts phase and accents in this complex time signature, becoming splendidly aggressive with guitar string snaps and massive piano clusters. "It's Your Turn" has a lovely, pensive baladic feel; "Tracings" for solo guitar is likewise a lyrical piece with an introspective and at times even eerie nature. A lyric piece in an improvisatory style for solo piano, "A Page Upon Which..." has a romantic yet clear texture in which patterns are reexamined and constantly varied along a fascinatingly rich path of their gradual unfolding, sensitively and beautifully performed by the composer. "Blue" for guitar and piano is a joyous, pointillistic, pattern blues with complex rhythms and harmonies. "Ajiaco" by composer/conductor Tania León is the last piece and, like the Speach/Schanzer duo's pieces, also combines advanced writing with a variety of American rhythmic styles. *—"Blue" Gene Tyranny*

● **Without Borders** / Mode ✦✦✦✦✦

A collection of some of the composer's finest work, beautifully performed. The pieces are each gems of instrumental color, original combinations of pop and folk musics with advanced compositional techniques. "Moto" (1982), performed by the Bowery Ensemble, is a study of momentum with lovely patterns and figures somewhere between pointillism and American minimalism. "Pensées" ("Thoughts") (1983), for solo guitar, is a portrait of the composer's husband, each movement representing aspects of his personality; it again achieves that wonderful blending of folk music emotion with an advanced compositional technique. "Trajet" (1983), for percussion and trombone, is a charmingly humorous and, at times, rhythmically dancelike and tongue-in-cheek journey through interactive "colors, patterns and designs... inspired by the motions and movements of our tropical fish." "Sonata" (1986), for piano, is a 12-minute "sonata" in the older sense of the term signifying "soundpiece"; it moves among serialist statements, gently rocking loops that create a suspended-in-the-air sensation, and extended, suspenseful melody. "Shattered Glass" (1987), for percussionist, presents distinct motives of multi-rhythmic character and gesture—playful, aggressive, and extremely gentle—which are fragmented and "enhanced, recalled, accelerated, slowed down and sometimes almost entirely eliminated until they resolve into a singular sound." "Telepathy: Poetry/Music Suite" (1987), for reciter and bass, trombone, alto sax, piano, and guitar, is a collaboration with poet Thulani Davis and is in three parts: the first (Contessas and Cardsharks) is a portrait of Malcolm X's early life, the second (Telepathy) is a kind of love poem about people separated by a great distance (with motifs suggesting Coltrane's "Naima" and the descending chords of his "Giant Steps"), and the third (Boppin' Is Safer Than Grindin') recalls dancin' and romancin' and is a mix of blues, rocksteady bass, and advanced harmonic comping. *—"Blue" Gene Tyranny*

Laurie Spiegel

b. Sep. 20, 1945

Composer / Computer Music

Studied at Oxford University, comp. with J.W. Duarte, Vincent Persichetti, Hall Overton, Jacob Druckman, Emmanuel Ghent. Plays guitar and lute. Worked at Bell Labs from 1973-74 and in computer graphics. Created computer music program Music Mouse which eliminates reliance on keyboards, sampled or acoustic sounds. Numerous soundtracks, video projects with Nam June Paik and others, her realization of Kepler's Music of the Spheres was sent into space by NASA. Many grants and awards, director of computer music at Aspen Music Festival, Bucks Count Community College, Cooper Union, NYU. Freelance computer consultant. *—"Blue" Gene Tyranny*

● **Unseen Worlds** / 1991 / Scarlet ✦✦✦✦✦

This album gives a good overview of her approaches to digital synthesis, from folk music-like steady sequences of single sounds to the stately, galactic "Sound Zones," a beautiful and original piece using sweeps of clusters, sounds-within-sounds, images-within-images, tunings never before experienced. A truly moving experience. A similar mix can be heard in her currently out-of-print CD *The Expanding Universe* on Philo PH 9003. *—"Blue" Gene Tyranny*

Cavis Muris (1986) / in Cdcm Computer Music Series, Vol. 13 / 1993 / Centaur ✦✦✦

A charming piece in five parts, computer-generated using Spiegel's self-designed computer program "Music Mouse—An Intelligent Instrument." The title meaning "mouse hole" or "the mouse's cave," was a result of her imaging what it would be like for mice to experience our ordinary human spaces—"such a vast and foreign world from their tiny perspectives." *—"Blue" Gene Tyranny*

Jim Staley

b. 1950

Trombone / Avant-Garde Jazz, 20th Century Classical/Modern Composition, Fusion

Jim Staley occupies a unique position among trombonists, crossing genres freely between post-modern classical music and avant-garde jazz. He boasts spectacular technique, including the ability to spit forth clusters of notes at rapid speed. Usually concentrating in the mid-to-lower registers of the trombone, his big, gruff tone hearkens to an earlier era, though his wondrous abilities and style plant him firmly in the free music world. Raised in Illinois, Staley served in the armed forces as a member of a U.S. Army Band in Berlin, before receiving Bachelor and Masters degrees in music from the University of Illinois in the late 1970s. Since 1978, Staley has lived in lower Manhattan, where he has actively performed and recorded with many cutting edge innovators, including composer/alto saxophonist John Zorn, guitarist Elliott Sharp, and vocalist Shelley Hirsch. In addition to recordings under his leadership, he appears on several of Zorn's CDs. He also performs and records with a classical ensemble, the Tone Road Ramblers. *—Steve Loewy*

● **Don Giovanni** / 1992 / Einstein ✦✦✦✦

The allusion to Mozart may be a bit stretched, but this is another superb effort by Staley, who again shows his ability to create a connected set of improvisatory gems. The groups range from trio to quintet, with wildly outrageous helpings of contorted notes the norm. Tenko's vocals add a Fluxus effect, while Zeena Parkins chimes in with pointillistic harps. Staley takes the lead throughout, and his trombone playing has never been better. Unlike some others on the instrument, he sticks to the middle and lower registers of his horn, where his magnetically rough blotches of sound steal the show. The changing timbres, instruments, and colors help all 19 tracks to hit the mark, and the recording demands to be listened to over and over to mine its many rewards. Davey Williams' electric guitar and Ikue Mori's electrifying (and electric) drums are an added bonus. *—Steve Loewy*

Mumbo Jumbo / 1994 / Einstein ✦✦✦✦

Jim Staley is one of the best trombonists you've never heard. His playing combines the technique of George Lewis with the playfulness of Jack Teagarden to produce wonders on his instrument. This recording is a series of four trio groupings with elite members of New York's downtown crowd in the mid-'80s, and fairly represents some of the state-of-the-art performances at the time. Among Staley's partners are John Zorn (alto saxophone), Bill Frisell (guitar), Shelley Hirsch (vocals), and Elliott Sharp (double-neck guitar/bass and soprano saxophone). While the novelty of these unions has paled somewhat over time, the playing is first-rate, and the self-effacing, under-recorded Staley is featured throughout. Most of the pieces sound like snippets, without melody or linear development. Still, they are fascinating structures, both for the quality of improvisation and for capturing a slice of an important freestyle genre. *—Steve Loewy*

Northern Dancer / 1996 / Einstein ✦✦✦✦

Recorded nearly a decade after the epochal *Mumbo Jumbo,* and using some of the same musicians, Jim Staley continues to effectively utilize the trio format, although he adds an effective duo piece with John Zorn (again on alto sax) and a deliberative solo statement on trombone. Every one of the nine tracks has its moments, but the emphasis on longer pieces and greater atmosphere mitigates the edge that made the earlier release so compelling. Still, admirers of Staley's gorgeously subversive trombone will not be disappointed, as he continues to impress with knotty runs, fat, globular splats, and riveting, muted jabs. The two tracks with electric harpist Zeena Parkins take awhile to get moving, but the attractive work of Ikue Mori on drum machines and Davey Williams on guitar adds nicely to the mix. *—Steve Loewy*

Karlheinz Stockhausen

b. Aug. 22, 1928, Mödrath, Germany

Composer / Musique Concrète, 20th Century Classical/Modern Composition, Electronic

The most innovative and influential German composer of the postwar era, Karlheinz Stockhausen laid much of the foundation of modern experimental music; through his pioneering work in electronics, he left an indelible imprint not only in contemporary classic circles but throughout the creative spectrum, where echoes of his genius still reverberate everywhere from the avant-garde to rock to dance music. Born in 1928, Stockhausen studied music in

Cologne and began exploring long-range serial composition with 1951's *Kreuzspiel* and the following year's *KontraPunkte*. He first delved into electronic music while studying under Olivier Messiaen in Paris, and continued his pursuits during the mid-'50s with his first breakthrough, 1956's *Gesang der Jünglinge*–among the first tape-loop pieces ever assembled. Stockhausen made his first trip to the US in 1958, a journey which triggered a new relaxation in his music attributed largely to the influence of John Cage. One key work completed as the decade drew to its close was *Zyklus*, conceived as a physical and musical circle with the soloist surrounded by a large array of instruments on all sides.

In 1960, Stockhausen premiered the landmark *Kontakte*, heralded as a watershed in the evolution of modern experimental music; composed for electronic tape, either alone or in tandem with live piano and percussion, it was among the first pieces of its kind to fuse prerecorded material with live instrumentation. By the mid-'60s, Stockhausen's immersion in electronics was almost total, and in 1964 he assembled a touring ensemble for his latest composition, *Mikrophonie I*. He also created a pair of major tape works, 1966's *Telemusik* and 1967's *Hymnen*, constructed from recordings assembled from across the globe.

Stockhausen's next period found him less in the role of creator than "process planner," and 1968's *Kurzwellen* was little more than a series of procedural instructions for performers to imitate short-wave radio broadcasts. With 1970's *Mantra*, Stockhausen returned to more conventional compositional techniques, resulting in a fully-notated piece for piano and electronics built around transformations of its melodic theme. His major works in the years that followed—1971's *Trans*, 1974's *Inori* and 1977's *Sirius*–were similarly thematic, albeit more dramatic than his earlier material. Remaining active as the century drew to its end, he was celebrated as a trailbrazing force behind the rise of contemporary electronic music. —*Jason Ankeny*

★ **Kontakte** / 1959 / Ecstatic Peace ✦✦✦✦✦
Kontakte is the epitome of Stockhausen's pioneering "moment form," characterized by long periods of inactivity broken by sudden changes. The prepared tape used in the work consists of a variety of metallic effects, some sped up to create radically different sounds and timbres. Probably Stockhausen's most famous work, *Kontakte* has been performed in two versions, one with four-channel tape and another with four-channel tape with added piano and percussion. The only widely available version, released on Ecstatic Peace, was recorded in Toronto in 1978 with tape plus pianist James Tenney and percussionist William Winant. —*John Bush*

Klavierstucke (Piano Pieces) / David Tudor, Piano / 1994 / hatHUT ✦✦✦
A reissue of the incredible performances of the "Piano Pieces" in their first recording made on September 19, 1958, and September 27, 1959, at WDR Radio in Cologne, Germany. At that time, Tudor was the renowned pianist of avant-garde music (having played Boulez' monumentally complex "First Piano Sonata" from memory, for instance) and the exponent of the new "indeterminate" music of Cage. At some point after these performances, Tudor swore that he would never play a piece of Stockhausen's again, probably for political reasons. Anyhow, these are astonishing concerts of the "Klavierstucke I-VIII," and four versions of "Klavierstuck XI." Highly recommended. —*"Blue" Gene Tyranny*

Inori / Anbetungen Für Einen Der Zwei Soloisten Und Orchester (Inori / Adorations for O / Deutsche Grammaphon ✦✦✦
In the mid-'60s, Stockhausen began to be influenced by non-European meditative practices and musics in his composition—for example "Stimmung" with overtone singing on a low Bb tone like Tibetan Buddhist chant and the use of "magic names" to give mouth positions, etc., the 15 conceptual pieces known as "Aus dem Sieben Tagen" (From the Seven Days), performances of "Kurzwellen" (Shortwaves) in the dark, etc. "Inori" is based around rhythmic variations on a single note center, like a chant. Surrounding this are reiterated and rhythmically varied tones which change their basic pitches, timbres and overtone structures over various time cycles. Gradually these pitches take on the character of quasi-melodic gestures which include sliding tones. There is a brilliant variety of orchestral colors and combinations and uses of profound silences—the overall effect is that of a grand meditative ceremony that leads into deep psychological states. —*"Blue" Gene Tyranny*

Konkrete Und Elektronische Musik: Etude/ Studie I U. Ii/ Gesang Der Jÿnglinge (Song O / Stockhausen Gesamtausgabe CD #3 ✦✦✦✦✦
A great collection of Stockhausen's classic and well-crafted electronic music. An electronic composition realized on tape during the years 1955-1956, "Gesang der Jünglinge" is perhaps the best-known of Stockhausen's compositions. It was originally scored for five loudspeaker groups, but has been most widely heard in the mono and stereophonic versions prepared for vinyl records by the composer. The basic sound and emotional image described by the title is that of the well-known story of the youths who miraculously survive being thrown into the fiery furnace, from the *Bible*, Book of Daniel, chapter three. Stockhausen successfully combines the sound of the natural sung voice with beautiful electronic sound, in what today would be termed audio-morphing, as the voice and electronic tones subtly interchange and blend. "Wherever the music's audible signals momentarily become human speech, it is always in the praise of God" (Stockhausen). —*"Blue" Gene Tyranny*

Carl Stone

b. Feb. 10, 1953, Los Angeles, CA
Producer, Composer / Computer Music, Ambient Techno, Experimental, Electro-Acoustic, Electronic
American electro-acoustic and computer musician Carl Stone works primarily in sampler-based composition, emphasizing the slow evolution of sound through thematic variation and recurrence. A Los Angeles native, Stone currently lives in San Francisco, a base of sorts for his ongoing involvement in the international avant-garde scene. A student of computer music innovators Morton Subotnick and James Tenney, Stone studied composition formally at the California Institute of the Arts. Focusing strictly on electro-acoustic composition since the early '70s, Stone's commissioned works have been performed in the U.S. (under such auspices as the National Endowment for the Arts and the LA Museum of Modern Art), as well as in Canada, Europe, South America, Australia, and, most often, Japan, where he's collaborated with dance companies and composed for film, video, radio broadcast, and multimedia installation. More recent works have included 1992's "Kamiya Bar," an evening-length composition for Tokyo-FM based on the city's urban soundscape, as well as the 1993 piece "Ruen Pair," commissioned by the Paul Dresher Ensemble. Although his recorded output represents only a small percentage of his total compositional work, Stone has released a number of albums through similarly eclectic means—from self-distributed cassettes and independent labels such as New Albion and Em:t, to larger, more recognizable names like Sony and EMI. Stone's passion for food usually works its way into his music in titular fashion—"Nayala," "Mom's," "Sukothai," and "Kamiya Bar" are all named for favorite restaurants. —*Sean Cooper*

● **Woo Lae Oak** / 1983 / Wizard ✦✦✦✦✦
Lovely, sustained and slowly changing music made by classic "musique concrete" means... a rubbed string, blowing in a bottle, etc. are made into tape loops and changed by means of precise tape speed change, layering, etc. —*"Blue" Gene Tyranny*

Mom's / 1992 / New Albion ✦✦✦
Captivating by their simplicity, Stone has an underlying feeling for modality and rhythm from American folk music without ever imitating it. "Banteay Srey" for example has a simple two-note pulse to which is gradually added a walking bass line and harmonies, transparent in their textures in a West Coast way, creating an engaging romantic and also otherworldly feeling. "Mom's" has a guitar riff that goes on simply for a while when suddenly a whole slew of salsa-sampling musicians step in, a sheer delight. Other selections are beautiful character studies. An original and widely listenable composer. —*"Blue" Gene Tyranny*

Carl Stone 1196 / Jul. 1, 1996 /

Ned Sublette

b. 1951, Lubbock, TX
Guitar / Salsa, Avant-Garde, World Fusion
Ned Sublette was one of the most unclassifiable talents in the late-twentieth-century New York music scene—quite a statement, considering that New York new music specializes in unclassifiable talents. His forte is the unlikely combination of Cuban and country styles. Born in Texas and a resident of New York since 1976, he went through a lot of phases before discovering salsa, with a background including conservatory study of classical guitar and composition, musicology field work in New Mexico, and work with John Cage, LaMonte Young, Glenn Branca, and Peter Gordon. His Ned Sublette Band, in the early 1980s, was a cowpunk group of sorts, though more sophisticated than the usual such outfit.

Sublette got into salsa music in the 1980s, and Cuban music in particular after his first trip to Cuba in 1990. His Qbadisc label is devoted to releasing Cuban music in the United States, and he has executive-produced releases by Latin musicians such as Ritmo Oriental and Isaac Delgado. He's also worked as senior co-producer of *Public Radio International*'s "Afropop Worldwide" show, and as of 1999 was working on a book about Cuban music. His 1999 release *Cowboy Rumba* combined the Texan country of his roots with Latin music, as he collaborated with musicians from Cuba, Puerto Rica, the Dominican Republic, and the New York salsa community. —*Richie Unterberger*

Western Classics with the Southwesterners / 1980 / Lovely Music ✦✦✦

● **Ships at Sea, Sailors and Shoes** / 1993 / Excellent ✦✦✦
To unbelievably great texts by Lawrence Weiner, Ned Sublette sings, in his decidedly cowboy accent, with the Persuasions—yes, those Persuasions (!), really stretching *out*–on this entertaining CD of fractured doo wop art songs/pieces. There is an underlying philosophical earnestness ("There Is No Light at the End of the Tunnel," "Ever Widening Circles of Remorse"), and topics include ecological concerns ("Big Bang/New Flora," with its lyric "Row row row your boat as the shit flows gently down the stream/What we don't flush away we'll blow away another day") and transcendent situations ("Postcards From Heaven," like the title of Cage's piece for harps, with a collage of Spanish dialogue, seashore, and a choir from somewhere). Poetry is also read, and the pieces never "develop" in any ordinary song fashion. Deserves to be placed in both pop and avant-garde bins in the record outlets. Highly recommended. —*"Blue" Gene Tyranny*

Cowboy Rumba / Apr. 6, 1999 / Palm ✦✦✦
Although Sublette had been playing and recording for about two decades before this release, this is the first disc to feature his own music and lyrics. As the title indicates, it's a fusion of country music and Latin sounds. It's not the most organic of combinations, and while there's no doubt that Sublette is sincere in his ambitions—you don't get rich by devoting yourself to such a goal—the results are not wholly enticing. Sublette has a laconic, dry voice and delivery that doesn't quite match the habitual energy of the salsa, Cuban, Dominican Republican and Puerto Rican musicians (including Yomo Toro) that provide much of the backing; Texas country producer and session ace Lloyd Maines adds touches of pedal steel and dobro. The cover of "Not Fade Away," with its Afro-Cuban-type percussive arrangement, sounds more like it's trying to prove a musicological point than it does anything else. All credit to Sublette and crew for trying something new, but this brew doesn't quite sound comfortable yet. —*Richie Unterberger*

Morton Subotnick

b. Apr. 14, 1933, Los Angeles, CA
Composer / 20th Century Classical/Modern Composition, Atonal, Electronic
Long at the vanguard of American electronic music, composer Morton Subotnick also pioneered the rise of multi-media performance through his extensive work in connection with interactive computer systems. Born in 1933, he studied under Darius Milhaud at Oakland's Mills College. (From 1959 to 1966, Subotnick himself taught at Mills as well.) His earliest major work was 1959's *Sound Blocks*, the first of his compositions to focus on the relationship between musical, visual and verbal components.

In 1967, Subotnick released the landmark *Silver Apples of the Moon*, the first electronic work commissioned by a recording company (Nonesuch). Realized via the Buchla modular synthesizer which he in turn helped design and develop, the album sold remarkably well, its success widely perceived as recognition of the home-stereo system as a legitimate medium for present-day chamber music. Subotnick returned a year later with *The Wild Bull*, shortly followed by the two-part *Reality*. Much of his late-'60s work shared sophisticated timbres, contrapuntal textures and pulsing undercurrents—in fact, many were so rhythmic they were adapted for modern dance performances. Subnotnick's next major plunge into multi-media was 1973's *Four Butterflies*, a piece for four-track tape and three films. Concurrent was his work on the "ghost box," a modification device designed to control real-time sound processing. Since none of the equipment contained any actual sounds, Subotnick dubbed the end result a "ghost score," introducing the concept in 1977's *Two Life Histories*.

Computer technology assumed greater and greater importance in Subnotnick's later work, with pieces like *The Key to Songs, Return* and *all my hummingbirds have alibis* taking full advantage of MIDI technology. Latter-day compositions—among them *Jacob's Room*, a multimedia opera premiered in 1993—also regularly made full use of computerized sound generation, specially designed software and "intelligent" interactive computer controls. *—Jason Ankeny*

• **Silver Apples of the Moon for Electronic Music Synthesizer** / 1968 / Nonesuch ♦♦♦♦♦
Over the course of thirty minutes, *Silver Apples of the Moon* presented a change for serious electronic music. Unlike many other early synthesizer records, the music here is continuous, powerful, almost overwhelming. The work is also reliant on a breathtaking variety of sounds: clicks, chirps, buzzes, gongs, hums, sirens. Some of these are *de rigeur* for an academic synthesizer record, but many continued to sound fresh decades after its recording. *Silver Apples of the Moon* deserves credit not just because it's one of the earliest albums produced by a modular synthesizer, but because it's a great piece of music. A 1994 reissue by Wergo added Subotnick's 1968 work "The Wild Bull" to the CD program. *—John Bush*

Key to Songs (1985) / Return (1985—86), The / 1986 / New Albion ♦♦♦♦♦
Subotnick's music from the electronic music classics *Silver Apples of the Moon* and *The Wild Bull* has always been descriptive of poetic, lyrical imagery… similarly, *The Key to Songs* is based on Max Ernst's collage novel "Une Semaine de Bonte" (*A Week of Kindness or the Seven Deadly Elements*) and *Return: A Triumph of Reason* refers to the change from dread and foreboding to reason that was accomplished by Edmond Halley upon explaining the circuit of his well-known comet… a good example of modern "tone poem" electronic music. *—"Blue" Gene Tyranny*

Yuji Takahashi

b. Sep. 21, 1938, Tokyo, Japan
Piano, Composer / 20th Century Classical/Modern Composition, Avant-Garde
A pianist with over 100 Japanese releases to his his credit, Yuji Takahashi first attracted notice as an avant-garde composer in the early '60s while a member of the New Directions group along with Toshi Ichiyanagi and Kenji Kobayashi. After premiering Iannis Xenakis' *Herma*, a piano composition dedicated to him, Takahashi studied stochastic music under Xenakis between 1963 and 1966.

After leaving Xenakis' tutelage, Takahashi focused his energies largely on composing, working with a variety of forms including orchestral, operatic, improvisational and even pop music. In 1978, he returned to performing, organizing the Suigyu Band to play Asian protest songs. He also recorded his own work in addition to compositions by John Cage, Earle Brown, Roger Reynolds and Toru Takemitsu. For the Denon label, he released a number of recordings by Bach and Satie.

Throughout his long career, Takahashi worked with a number of collaborators, including John Zorn, Ryuichi Sakamoto, Musica Elettronica Viva, Ned Rothenberg and Carl Stone. Despite the breadth of his huge back catalog, none of his own music was released on an American label until the appearance of *Finger Light* in 1995. *—Jason Ankeny*

Iki to Ishi (Breath and Stone)(1990) for voice and computer performance sythesizer / 1992 / Classic Masters ♦♦♦♦♦
In the collection "Music From Japan, Vol. 1"; changing and relatively unchanging aspects of matter are contrasted in this work, and generate their own kinds of time (as pulse). A voice heard over loudspeakers at the outset explains: " Breath is vibrating, invisible time. Stone is the fixed point in space. Breathing changes slightly with each repetition; stone remains unchanged in a state of flux. Breath is blown sound; stone is the sound of striking." We hear a dense rhythmic texture of computer-manipulated and modified digital samples of gongs, bamboo buzzers, wooden bells for water buffalo—sounds of Asian life layered and spread across a stereo landscape. The sounds are first hard-edged, banging, twanging and collapsing; every once in a while a human call appears in the distance. Then all is still, everything disappears. *—"Blue" Gene Tyranny*

Tree (1991) for MIDI piano, trombone & computer performance system, CPS / 1992 / Classic Masters ♦♦♦♦♦
In the collection "Music From Japan, Vol. 1"; the composer's central image for this seven-movement composition for MIDI piano, trombone, and CPS (computer performance system) is the tree-shaped puppet seen at the opening of Javanese shadow plays—it's various names are the Tree of Heaven, the Tree of Mystery, the Tree of Life, the Tree of Wisdom, the Tree of Time, the Tree of Hope. The music has a simple, almost gamelan quality about it—a simple five-note scale pattern is reiterated in slightly changed rhythmic cycles, with only one other voice in occasional duets. Each movement is constructed from certain "melodic formulas, simultaneous melodic variations, ornamentations, random events, and other algorithms for improvisation… layered and mixed in different timbres (using) a different five-tone scale." *—"Blue" Gene Tyranny*

• **Finger Light** / Feb. 1996 / Tzadik ♦♦♦
Finger Light is the first record of Takahashi's music released on an American label. The record features compositions for shamisen, double shamisen and sho (the Japanese mouth organ), in addition to piano. *—Jason Ankeny*

New Music for Piano / Mainstream ♦♦♦
Excellent performances of Xenakis "Herma", Reynolds "Fantasy for Pianist", Takahashi "Metatheses", and especially Earle Brown's "Corroboree". *—"Blue" Gene Tyranny*

Toru Takemitsu

b. Oct. 8, 1930, Tokyo, Japan, **d.** Feb. 20, 1996, Tokyo, Japan
Composer / 20th Century Classical/Modern Composition, World Fusion, Atonal
Largely self-taught, worked with the Experimental Workshop in Tokyo in early '50s. Guitarist, pianist. Received Italia Prize in 1958. Influenced by John Cage, jazz, serialism, Debussy, ancient Japanese music, and many world cultures. Unique polyrhythmic and open scoring methods combined with traditional Western notation. First combinations of Western orchestra with traditional Japanese instruments and Gagaku ensembles. Filmscores include *Woman in the Dunes* (1964), *Dode'skaden* (1970), *Ran* (1985), *Kwaidan* (1964), *Under the Cherry Blossoms* (1975), *Empire of Passion* (1978). *—"Blue" Gene Tyranny*

★ **Music of Toru Takemitsu IV: Music of Tree (1961) / Coral Island (1962) / Kaidan (1966)** / 1988 / JVC ♦♦♦♦♦
A great collection of Takemitsu's innovative electronic tape music and two beautiful early orchestral pieces. *Coral Island (An Atoll)* is an early and exquisite work for soprano and orchestra from 1962 that already shows many of the compositional procedures and aesthetics that would concern Takemitsu throughout his life: the kaleidoscope of sound timbres, the smooth and lush orchestra of Debussy combined with the more earthly percussion of the moderns, and the expressive inflections of traditional Japanese music. The underlying image or "program" of this piece is a dichotomy—in this case, between the abstract and the concrete. The composition is in five sections. Through wind and percussion that accumulate around string sonorities, "Introduction and Accumulation I" depicts "the play of the surf ringing an atoll… the horizon appears, then disappears gradually into tranquility." In "Poem I" (words by Makoto Ohka) the voice flows on a horizontal line and the instruments in verticalities; when they intersect "a magic sound-space of colors" occurs. "Intermezzo and Accumulation II" expands upon the sound material of the previous sections. "Poem II," with a musical approach similar to that of "Poem I," speaks of many earthly concerns and sighs, "Ah, but I remain an island when the sun penetrates into my wood of shells, I become a transparent coral island, a foaming crest of love." In "Finale and Accumulation III," "voices from a far place" are heard. "An endless horizon. An atoll is not an island; neither is it an ocean… the coral island may be one's desire, physical love or memory—or might it be man's prayer—" The tape piece *Vocalism A-I* uses a human voice on the word "AI" (meaning "love" in Japanese) modulated through tape and electronic methods; it was used as the soundtrack for a charming animated film in which a man is pursued by his overenthusiastic beloved. *—"Blue" Gene Tyranny*

Dreamtime/Nostalghia/Vers, L'arc-En-Ciel, Palma (Verse, Rainbow, Palma)/Far Calls / 1993 / ABC Classics ♦♦♦
One of the finest CDs of Takemitsu's music, performed by the Melbourne Symphony Orchestra conducted by Hiroyuki Iwaki. "Far Calls, Coming, Far !" is scored for solo violin and orchestra. The title, a quote from James Joyce's *Finnegan's Wake* is what Anna Livia sings out upon sighting the River Liffy meeting the sea. The music, likewise, attempts to depict a flowing river, taking winding routes, rushing or barely in motion, until it finally reaches a great C-major tonal sea. "Vers, L'Arc-En-Ciel, Palma (Verse, Rainbow, Palma)" for guitar and oboe d'amore soloists with orchestra is an homage to the painter Joan Miró whom Takemitsu met in 1970. The lovely, nostalgic music rises with orchestral imitations of rising guitar arpeggios, constantly adding more rich harmonies to the texture. *—"Blue" Gene Tyranny*

Mi-Yo-Ta / 1997 / Denon ♦♦♦♦♦
Five hip and beautiful pop/jazz songs sung by the well-known Seri Ishikawa followed by five instrumental versions of the same tunes. In English translation the songs are: "Mi-yo-ta" (a person's name), "Burning Autumn," "Wings," "What is the thing that the dead man left—" and "Little Sky." This CD is an excellent example of Takemitsu's ability to work in pop styles, as well as his own filmscore and avant-garde concert styles. *—"Blue" Gene Tyranny*

Tsubasa (Wings): A String Around Autumn (1989) for viola and orchestra / An / 1997 / Philips ♦♦♦♦♦

From me flows what you call Time / Twill by Twilight (In Memory of Morton F / 1998 / Sony Classical ♦♦♦♦♦
Performed by the percussion group Nexus, and the Pacific Symphony Orchestra conducted by Carl St. Clair. "From me flows what you call Time" is a concerto for percussion ensemble of five players and orchestra was written in 1990 for the centennial of Carnegie Hall. The title is from Makoto Ooka's poem "Clear Blue Water," and was intended by the composer to refer to the music that flowed from Carnegie Hall during its lifetime. Takemitsu was also inspired by two meditative elements from Tibetan Buddhism in the creation of this work: the number five and its association with the five colors of the Wind Horse—blue for water, red for fire, yellow for earth, green for wind, and white for sky. There is a wide variety of percussion timbres employed in this work: gentle surface textures of small bells, vibraphone solos, virtuosic chromatic passages for steel drums, exotic rolling patterns on marimbas, the eerie nighttime calling of slow glissandi on a bowed saw combined with bells, the sound of a rainstick (or, alternatively, a suspended cymbal) combined with a rich chorale for strings to make an intriquing and innovative combination, galloping patterns on log drums in which you can image the Wind Horse flashing the power of the dharmic colors as it tears across a landscape only partially earthly, a thrilling stereo duet for high and low congas in complex rhythms. As the piece slowly closes, we hear, in the distance, bells located in the top balcony of the concert space gently rung by five long colored streamers (blue, red, yellow, green, white) attached to them and pulled by the performers on the stage. *—"Blue" Gene Tyranny*

Seasons (1970) for percussion / Munari by Munari (1967) for percussion / To / Deutsche Grammaphon ♦♦♦♦♦
A welcome re-release on CD of the original 1972 and 1975 vinyl recordings of these three very innovative and mysterious works for percussion ensembles. Most of the percussion in-

struments are non-traditional (snapping metal rods, rubbed metal bowls, vibraslaps, glass plates and chimes, large temple bells etc. etc.) or played in unusual ways. The percussion timbre effects are often indistinguishable from electronic music. Speech fragments are also often mixed with the percussion. *— "Blue" Gene Tyranny*

Richard Teitelbaum

b. May 19, 1939, New York, NY

Synthesizer, Composer / Multimedia, Early Creative, Electronic

Composer and electronic musician Richard Teitelbaum was born in NYC in 1939. After graduating from Haverford College, he went on to get a Master of Music degree from Yale in 1964. Teitelbaum studied with composers Luigi Nono and Goffredo Petrassi in Italy on a Fullbright scholarship, after which he brought the first Moog synthesizer to Europe. Teitelbaum performed hundreds of concerts with it, and co-founded the pioneering live electronic music group Musica Elettronica Viva with Frederic Rzewski and Alvin Curran in Rome, 1966. An opera of his, *Golem*, was performed at the *Ars Electronica Festival in Linz*, Austria (1991), and Teitelbaum himself has performed throughout the U.S., Japan and Europe. His music is heard on Cantaur, Hat Hut, Tzadik, and other labels. Besides making music and working with interactive computer systems, Teitelbaum has taught electronic music and composition at New York's Vassar College, and Bard College where he has also been Director of the Electronic Music Studio. *—Joslyn Layne*

● **Blends (1977)** / 1985 / Lumina ✦✦✦✦✦

As the title promises, one of the most perfect blends of world music with Katsuya Yokoyama on shakuhachi, Trilok Gurtu on tabla and other percussion, and Teitelbaum on synthesizer.The score is written in different notations based on Japanese, Indian and American practices. *— "Blue" Gene Tyranny*

James Tenney

b. Aug. 10, 1934, Silver City, NM

Keyboards, Piano, Composer / Spectral Music, Experimental, 20th Century Classical/Modern Composition, Atonal, Electronic

Studied piano with Eduard Steuermann. Composition with Chou Wen-chung, Lionel Nowak, Paul Boepple, Henry Brant, Carl Ruggles, Kenneth Gaburo, Lejaren Hiller, Edgard Varése. Associate Member of the Technical Staff at Bell Telephone Labs from 1961-64. Developed computer systems at Yale and Polytechnic Institute of Brooklyn. Co-founder Tone Roads Chamber Ensemble (1963-70), and performer with many ensembles including those of Steve Reich, Philip Glass, Harry Partch, John Cage, Fluxus. Lecturer at New School for Social Research. Also teacher at University of South Florida, University of California at Santa Barbara, Stanford University etc. Respected theorist he has written *META + HODOS* (1961), *John Cage and the Theory of Harmony* (1984), *A History of Consonance and Dissonance* (1988). *— "Blue" Gene Tyranny*

Collage No. 2, Viet Flakes (1967) / 1992 / Musicworks ✦✦✦

A tape collage with silences utilizing snatches of pop music urging love and sensibility ("think about it") contrasted with ominous classical phrases and folk music. Very subtle way to make political/ humanist music. *— "Blue" Gene Tyranny*

Selected Works: 1961-1969 / 1992 / Artifact ✦✦✦

Some of the earliest and most imaginative electronic and computer-generated music. Tenney was one of the first composers to use Max Mathew's computer music synthesis system at Bell Labs, and this CD includes some works created there: "Ergodos II (For John Cage)" and "Analog *1: Noise Study.*" Also included are his humorous study of Elvis Presley's voice in "Collage *1 (Blue Suede)*"; the terrifying "Fabric for Che"; and the illusionary "For Ann (Rising)," an audio version of the persistence-of-motion visual illusion (e.g., when a stopped train still seems to be moving to a passenger), in which tones rise but get nowhere—until the final ascension. Also included is a Nancarrow-like player piano piece but with stochastically generated notes. *— "Blue" Gene Tyranny*

Bridge & Flocking / 1996 / hatHUT ✦✦✦✦✦

"Bridge" (1984) and "Flocking" (1993) are scored for four and two pianos respectively and in alternate tunings. It takes a while to re-orient one's listening habits to hear beyond the intial impression of "out-of-tuneness." Then the rich interplay of tuning and timbre and harmonic combinations/relations comes into play. Shared octaves become shocking, bell-like timbres (cathedrals, gamelans) come to mind, normal consonances are kind of touching. The vocabulary of "Bridge" is the pointillistic, gestural world of 1950s and '60s serial music, but gradually evolves into more sustained overlaps as the piece progresses. Part One is performed mostly with hard attacks that emphasize the cross-piano effects of the tuning. Part Two shares the vocabulary of Part One but begins with muted dynamics until mightily resonant low tones arise for dramatic crossplay. "Flocking" is a graph score for two pianos tuned a quarter-tone apart. A delightful variation of timbre occurs as the pianists hand mute the strings, occasionally allowing normally struck tones to emerge, occasionally plucking or striking the strings with the fingers. The massed effect is indeed like the flocking of birds or animals with its rapid, quasi-random flow and accumulation and de-accumulation. *— "Blue" Gene Tyranny*

The Solo Works for Percussion / 1998 / hatART ✦✦✦✦

★ **Music of James Tenney: Selected Works 1963-1984** / Musicworks ✦✦✦✦✦

This recording includes "Three Indigenous Songs No. 3 (Hey When I Sing These Songs Hey Look What Happens)" (1979), with words based on Iroquois chants coded into instrumental music; "Phases" (1963), a computer-generated tape composition; "Quiet Fan for Erik Satie" (1970-1971), for an ensemble of 13 instruments (lyrical, hypnotically phase-modulated, Satie-like pastoral melodies); "For Ann (Rising)" (1969), a tape composition; "Spectral CANON for CONLON Nancarrow" (1974), for harmonic player piano; "Bridge" (1982-1984, excerpt), for two pianos, eight-hands; and "Voice(s)" (1982-1984), for instrumental ensemble, voice(s), tape, and tape delay (like a field of supernatural rainbows). See also his "Septet for Electric Guitars" in Tellus number 14 (collections), "Koan" in Malcolm Goldstein's *Sounding the New Violin*, and "Critical Band" played by the Relache Ensemble on MODE. *— "Blue" Gene Tyranny*

Virgil Thomson

b. Nov. 25, 1896, Kansas City, MO, **d.** Sep. 30, 1989, New York, NY

Composer / 20th Century Classical/Modern Composition

Thomson is one of the few true modernists in America. Thomson's music is almost disconcertingly spare and direct. In the consciously American pieces especially, there is a kind of aural equivalent to Cubist collage, as ragtime, waltzes, tangos, two-steps, fiddle tunes, and hymns get pasted onto the texture. Unlike Ives, there's an unsentimental distance and clarity to it all, like someone without illusions able to state exactly what's on his mind. Thomson gets this effect in his prose, too.

Although overshadowed by Copland (who, by the way, always ackowledged his debts to Thomson), Thomson achieved far more in the realm of opera and vocal music, in which almost everyone acknowledges him a master. Try the powerful (and, to my ear, deeply American) *5 Songs from William Blake*, the incredibly beautiful *Feast of Love* for baritone and chamber ensemble (a real lesson in how to vary orchestral texture and how to continue a musical line), *4 Southern Hymns* (a choral classic), the sinewy cello concerto, the *Symphony on a Hymn Tune*, *Acadian Songs and Dances* (which deserve the recognition given to the sister suite "Louisiana Story"), *Praises and Prayers*, the delicate *4 Songs to Poems of Thomas Campion* for voice and chamber group, and the heartbreaking *Stabat Mater* for mezzo and string quartet. *— Steven Schwartz*

The Mother of Us All (1947) / 1990 / New World ✦✦✦✦✦

The text for this opera, performed by the Santa Fe Opera, is again by Gertrude Stein, but the organization is somewhat more narrative with even semblances of a plot. The theme is the life and struggles of suffragette Susan B. Anthony: the weariness of leading a totally public life and the seemingly endless fight for rights—deep reflections about the meaning of "family" and humanity versus laws. The musical writing is beautifully atmospheric. Much of Thomson's other writing is very lyrical and always with a sound of his own, but conventional in structure; however, if you love this opera try "Sonata da Chiesa" ("Church Sonata") (1926), the award-winning film scores for *The River* (1937), "The Plow That Broke the Plains" (1936), "Louisiana Story" (1948), and *A Portrait Album* (Elektra/Nonesuch D4-79024), which contains selections from Thomson's 147 musical portraits of friends—a task similar to Stein's many portraits in writing. *— "Blue" Gene Tyranny*

★ **Four Saints in Three Acts (1934)** / Elektra/Nonesuch ✦✦✦✦✦

A setting of the magnificent text by Gertrude Stein (1874-1946). For this opera, Thomson employed her writing technique of having characters and images just appear on the landscape of the stage; there is no linear plot line, only a real/historical/imaginary connection to a specified subject. This frees the creative process to attempt great character and language combinations that hopefully will provide insights, making for a completely modern opera where melodies, moods, etc., follow in surprising sequences, but always presenting a sense of the whole (or what Stein called "the eternal present"). There are humorous choruses about "pigeons on the grass, alas" and "Lucy Lily," as well as subtle lines about perception ("the garden inside and outside of the wall"), St. Ignatius predicting the Last Judgment, and St. Teresa painting flowers on very large eggs. An all African-American cast gave the first productions of this opera, because Thomson wanted clear American speech. Thomson had set three songs to Stein's texts before attempting this opera. *— "Blue" Gene Tyranny*

Asmus Tietchens

b. 1947

Synthesizer, Producer / Musique Concrète, Experimental, Avant-Garde

Synthesizer experimentalist and musique concrète producer Asmus Tietchens began recording in the mid-'60s and continued to record three decades after that. Born in 1947 and based in Hamburg, Tietchens listened to German radio as a child and heard pioneering electric transmissions by the likes of Stockhausen and Gottfried Michael Koenig. He began recording his own home experiments in 1965 with crude reverb devices and picked up a MiniMoog several years later. Also influenced by atonal Kraut-rockers like Cluster and Faust, Tietchens met Okko Bekker and began a partnership that lasted for decades (Bekker has produced most of Tietchens' work). After Tangerine Dream's Peter Baumann heard a tape of his work, he produced Tietchens' debut album *Nachtstücke*, released in 1980 on Sky Records. His four albums for Sky during the early '80s focused on surprisingly accessible electronic pop, though 1984's *Formen Letzter Hausmusik* (recorded for Nurse with Wound's United Dairies label) began a period of more abstract, concrète recordings that often use tape experiments as well as synthesizers. During the '90s, Tietchens recorded for experimental labels Barooni, Staalplaat and Syrenia, the latter a 1996 collaboration with Vidna Obmana. Since 1990, he has also taught sound at a Hamburg university. *—John Bush*

Das Fest Ist Zu Ende. Aus. / 1995 / Barooni ✦✦✦

Tietchens constructed this album from his ten-year audio diary, beginning at age 15 (1962), altering the vocals and adding occasional accompaniment. *—John Bush*

● **Asmus Tietchens & Vidna Obmana** / 1996 / Syrenia ✦✦✦✦

The German Syrenia label's second release combines old and new-school ambient talent, with electro-acoustician Tietschens combining his more surly, difficult style with Obmana's warm, flowing ambience. Three cuts in collaboration and a solo cut a piece fill out the hour of this disc, with mostly formless, textured program music the focus. Subtlety beautiful, with treated samples and found sounds accenting cycling synth passages and alternately stern and gentle melodies. *— Sean Cooper*

Yasunao Tone

b. 1935, Tokyo, Japan

Producer, Composer / Process-Generated, Computer Music, Experimental, Avant-Garde

Japanese composer Yasunao Tone became involved in the Fluxus movement in the early '60s and has since been active as an organizer of events, an improviser, a performer in a number of groups, and, more recently, he creates pieces with manipulated CDs. His work as a composer ranges from environmental art to computer-oriented, also including pieces for theatre, radio, film, and dance, including Merce Cunningham scores.

Although he graduated with a degree in Japanese literature in 1957, three years later he encountered Group Ongaku, who improvised and put on "event music" and began participating himself in 1962, starting with a solo concert. He has also participated in the groups Hi-Red Center and Team Random, purportedly the first Japanese computer art group. In 1966, Team Random hosted a process music festival, which included Tone's "Theater Piece for Computer."

After relocating to the U.S. in the early '70s, Tone continued to perform (at New York's Roulette and the Kitchen, among others), participate in Fluxus concerts, and compose for the Merce Cunningham Dance Company. One of his works for a Cunningham dance, "Geography and Music," was also played at several new music festivals, including the John Cage Festival in San Juan. He has received numerous grants and commissions for his work. Some of his compositions have been recorded for independent labels such as Lovely Music and Tzadik. *—Joslyn Layne*

● **Musica Iconologos** / 1994 / Lovely Music ✦✦✦
Tone continues his refined, elegant work in the transformation of one sense sphere into another (for example, flute tones into computer haiku in "Lyrictron" on Barbara Held's CD in collections), in this beautiful CD: here, the sound is an encoded description, via a video-to-sound transformation array (which brings to mind David Behrman's 70's installation piece "Clouds") which scans Chinese character "poems" describing photographic images into an optical music recognition computer program, a very direct process bypassing the electronicness of the devices. Intriguing. *—"Blue" Gene Tyranny*

Solo for Wounded CD / 1997 / Tzadik ✦✦✦
A pioneer of the Fluxus movement since the early '60s, Yasunao Tone has committed many sound experiments to vinyl and CD. This work is the second of his experiments on CDs themselves. Like the first of its kind, *Music for 2 CD Players* (premiered at *the Experimental Intermedia Foundation* on March 16, 1986), this album is a recording of the sound that results when a CD is altered so that instead of producing the recording it contains, it skips, squeaks, stutters, and otherwise produces error-generated sounds. Yet unlike *Music for 2 CD Players*, which used a number of original CDs and allowed fragments of the original music to come through, *Solo for Wounded CD* uses only one prepared CD, a copy of Tone's *Musica Iconologos*—a work that he claims is excellent for his purposes because its high tone and discordant sound help produce a variety of fascinating sounds. The result is interesting, to a point. The most fascinating things about Tone's work are the ideas behind it: his surrender of control in the musicmaking process and his lack of desire to communicate specific musical idioms. However, because of these characteristics the pieces on *Solo for Wounded CD* lack distinctness and one begins to wonder if their value would be changed if they were half or twice as long as the versions on the album. This is an interesting, one-time experiment, but Tone cannot revisit this project again without significant changes to his method. Otherwise, the results will certainly seem tired and stale. *—Stacia Proefrock*

Mark Trayle

b. 1955, California
Synthesizer, Composer / Sound Sculpture, Computer Music
Studied at University of Oregon and at Mills College with Robert Ashley, David Behrman and David Rosenboom. Artist-in-residence at STEIM (Amsterdam) and at the Lab. Collaborated with Maryanne Amacher at the Capp Street Project in SF (1985). Created soundtrack for *Menagerie*, a virtual-reality installation shown at Centre Pompidou in Paris. Article "Nature, Networks, Chamber Music" published in the *Leonardo Music Journal*. *—"Blue" Gene Tyranny*

● **Etudes and Bagatelles** / 1994 / ART ✦✦✦
Found sounds, found processes, and homebrew gear, "the flotsam and jetsam of popular culture." Trayle using a data-glove to manipulate sounds stored in the "virtual shelves" before him in live performance. Terrific. *—"Blue" Gene Tyranny*

Megabitichin' / 1994 / Inial ✦✦✦
In the collection *Views from the Perfect City.* Composed in (1989-92), this live electronic piece uses surf-guitar and cymbal samples, with modifying electronics triggered by a performer wearing a "dataglove." The result is a surreally beautiful homage to '60s surf music and Gordon Mumma's *Megaton for William Burroughs'* (a live electronics classic from the early '60s). *—"Blue" Gene Tyranny*

David Tudor

b. Jan. 20, 1926, Philadelphia, PA, **d.** Aug. 13, 1996, Tomkins Cove, NY
Piano, Producer, Composer / Experimental, Avant-Garde
American experimental music's foremost performer, pianist David Tudor remains as inextricably linked to many of the most groundbreaking pieces in the modern canon as their respective composers; long John Cage's most intimate associate, he also delivered virtuoso early performances of landmark works by Boulez, Feldman, Stockhausen and Young, many of them written expressly with Tudor in mind. After playing organ in Philadelphia churches and later studying theory and composition, Tudor delivered the American premiere of Boulez's *Deuxième Sonate pour Piano* in 1950, which immediately launched him to the vanguard of the experimental community.

Tudor's extended collaboration with Cage began during the early '50s, and in 1952 he premiered the composer's notorious *4'33"*. Widely praised for his imaginative solutions to the often deliberate challenges of notation and performance presented by the pieces he tackled, Tudor's genius in time began to directly influence the composers whose work he interpreted, becoming an essential component of their creative processes. During the late '50s he began experimenting with electronic modification of sound sources.

As the next decade approached, Tudor began initiating the move away from taped sources towards live electronic music. Manufacturing and designing his own equipment, he mounted works that were closely tied to visual media. While collaborating on design at Expo '70 in Japan, Tudor composed and performed several new works, among them an early version of the seminal *Microphone*. As his work in electronic music continued, he increasingly experimented with new components, circuitry and interconnections, with the end results determining both compositional and performing strategies. Much of Tudor's major work of the period was commissioned by the Merce Cunningham Dance Company, with whom he'd been affilitated since their 1953 inception. After Cage's 1992 death, Tudor succeeded him as the Cunningham troupe's musical director, until he himself died in 1996. *—Jason Ankeny*

★ **Microphone (1975)** / 1991 / Cramps ✦✦✦✦✦
A re-issue on CD of this classic. One of the great and wild "live electronic" pieces with sounds that Tudor once described as sounding to him like dinosaur howls echoing in pre-historic caves to timid, sweet calls of unidentifiable creatures.The original circuitry was designed by Tudor and Gordon Mumma. *—"Blue" Gene Tyranny*

Neural Synthesis, Nos. 6-9 / 1995 / Lovely Music ✦✦✦✦✦
Derived from the score "Neural Synthesis Plus," used to accompany Merce Cunningham's dance +Enter. The primary electronic instrument employed in the piece is a synthesizer with 64 non-linear amplifiers (metaphorical neurons) with 10,240 programmable interconnections, emulating neuron cells in the human brain and capable of processing many analog signals in parallel. Sound oscillators are created by connecting 16 of the 64 "neurons" in feedback circuits, with tank circuits to control their frequencies. During a performance, Tudor chooses up to 14 channels of output, further modifying them with other electronic devices, while he also listens, learns patterns (heuristically), and responds and modifies his actions. In this recording, Tudor uses a new binaural technique for translating sound into out-of-head localizations, seeming to surround the listener. For all this technology, the results still reflect Tudor's love of simple sounds that are full of character and often drolly humorous, even if not identifable in any ordinary context. *—"Blue" Gene Tyranny*

Three Works for Live Electronics: Pulsers/Untitled /Phonemes / 1996 / Lovely Music ✦✦✦

Rainforest / Apr. 21, 1998 / Mode ✦✦✦✦
Rainforest (Version I, Music for Dance) is a wonderful live electronic work that has become a new music classic since its creation in 1968 for the Merce Cunningham Dance Company. Performed throughout the world, the 21-minute dance was also notable for its stage set that included helium-filled reflective silver mylar pillows designed by Andy Warhol. *Version I* was performed by Takehisa Kosugi and David Tudor in eight channels for a sound system that surrounded the audience. Long sustained tones produce a mysterious sustained atmosphere, semi-melodic phrases seem like small bagpipes, a pulse of short string-plucking sounds is produced, and a variety of raw and pure waveforms create a dense forest of electronic birds, frogs, and other unnamed creatures. *Sliding Pitches in the Rainforest in the Field: Rainforest (Version IV, Electro-Acoustical Environment)* was first created in 1968 at Chocorua, NH. Inside a large barn, many unique, vibrating resonant objects (bells, beams held between the teeth, dual metal transducers, parabolic reflectors attached to circular hat-like cages, etc.) were suspended from the ceiling, and the audience moved throughout the space interacting with the ear-level objects and appreciating the gentle sounds emitted by them. This piece was developed by Tudor with many other composers and artists (Phil Edelstein, Bill Viola, Andres Zravic, John Driscoll, Michael Quigly, Nick Collins, Ralph Jones, Martin Kalve, Linda Fisher, Prent Rodgers) from 1968 to 1982. The electronics heard as sources in *Version I?*—the calls of electronic birds and other creatures—now cause the objects' vibration over a seemingly vast and dense landscape. *—"Blue" Gene Tyranny*

"Blue" Gene Tyranny

b. 1945, San Antonio, TX
Keyboards, Piano, Composer / Fusion, Minimalism, Electronic
Avant-garde pianist and composer "Blue" Gene Tyranny has created over 50 electronic and acoustic for instruments, voice, and dance. After studying in the '50s with pianist Meta Hertwig, and composer Frank Hughes, among others, Tyranny promoted new music in Texas with composer Philip Krumm, premiering works by Cage, Maxfield, and others. After relocating to Ann Arbor, MI, Tyranny performed in the ONCE concerts and other events. During the 60's and 70's, he toured with jazz and rock groups Carla Bley Band, Iggy Pop, and more. 1971-1982, he worked as a music educator at Mills College and elsewhere. He moved to NY in 1983, and worked as an audio consultant, and composer/performer. He produced, recorded and performed on recordings such as Laurie Anderson's *Strange Angels*, and John Cage's *Cheap Imitation* and has created over 40 soundtracks for film and video, collaborating on projects with video artists Kenn Beckman and Kit Fitzgerald. His theater collaborations include work with the Talking Band, performance artist Pat Oleszko, *Prisoner of Gravity* (1996), and live electronic music for Stefa Zawerucha's *The Black Box* (1993), and the Otrabanda Company's *Brain Café* (1987). He's composed dance music for Timothy Buckley's *Barn Fever* (1983), and Trisha Brown and Steve Paxton's *Long and Dream* (1996). Tyranny received the 1961BMI Student Composers Award, a 1988 Composer Award at the Bessies, and various grants, fellowships and residencies in the '80s and '90s, and has written extensively about contemporary music. Tyranny has performed extensively in hundreds of concerts throughout the US, Canada and Europe, and also in Mexico, Brazil and Japan. Recordings of his music include *Country Boy Country Dog / How To Discover Music In The Sounds Of Your Daily Life*, (a 25-year project for electronics, orchestra and environmental sounds), and *Free Delivery*'s live keyboard concerts, both on Lovely Music. *—AMG*

Real Life and the Movies / 1981 / Fun Music ✦✦✦
A cassette retrospective of electro-acoustic pieces from 1958-1980. Includes: some hi-and-low-fi soundtracks for independent movies, "Closed Transmission" (1966) realized on a IBM 7090 computer, "The White Night Riot" (1979) based on recordings made while running from police during the riot that followed Dan White's light sentencing for the murders of mayor George Moscone and gay civil-rights leader Harvey Milk, and the parapsychological experiment/illusion "Pals/Action at a Distance." *—AMG*

The Intermediary / 1982 / Lovely Music ✦✦✦✦✦

Free Delivery / 1990 / Lovely Music ✦✦✦✦✦
These live keyboard performances from1983-1989 include "Five Takes on the Nocturne With and Without Memory" (1989) for solo piano, "The Country Boy Country Dog Intro" (1984) for piano and tape, "The Intermediary Following Traces of the Song" (1988) for acoustic piano and live sampling keyboard, "The Intermediary With a Rendition of Stardust" (1983) for solo piano and electronics, and "Sunrise or Sunset in Texas" (1983) from a film soundtrack. Kyle Gann of *The Village Voice* describes "Blue" Gene Tyranny as possessing "Cecil Taylor's keyboard energy, Morton Feldman's ear," and states, "The most original aspect of (his) works is the way they create continuity: they're tonal, yet rigorously asymmetrical. They satisfy the ear without letting it take anything for granted. They evolve... with the labyrinthine irreversibility of deep psychic forces." *—AMG*

• **Country Boy Country Dog / How to Discover Music in the Sounds of Your Daily Life** / 1994 / Lovely Music ✦✦✦
In a small Midwestern town, a natural mystery that's always been there is revealed. Using the procedural score "How To Discover Music In The Sounds of Your Daily Life" (1967), a rich variety of orchestral, electronic and natural sounds describe the interaction between mental events and the daily environment: the "inside"—intuitive decision, spontaneous mental activity, feeling—and the "outside" that make up reality. The score sets up an ecological chain in which natural sounds and voices are recorded and analyzed electronically (for hidden rhythmic codes, continuous melodic streams, harmonic attractions), and then electro-acoustical pieces are made from these analyses and played back into the environment. The five parts form an "audio-storyboard" (a movie soundtrack independent of a film): "A Dream Without Images" (before dawn, inside), "The CBCD Intro" (sunrise, outside), "Country Boy Country Dog" (midday, inside and out), "X Marks The Spot (Daydream)" (afternoon, inside), and "The CBCD Variations for Soloist and Orchestra" (twilight, outside). "Like any true artist, however, Tyranny reaches for the heart, not only the mind, through the tender and solemn hymn of 'The CBCD Intro' with its grand recurring motif, and the delightful 'CBCD Variation' for soloist and orchestra, one of the crowning achievements of his career... the schizophrenic babble of our lives becomes order and beauty... to these ears the electro-acoustic pieces rank among the more developed and seductive music that Tyranny has composed." (Piero Scaruffi, i/e No. 7) *—AMG*

Nocturne with and Without Memory/In Lois Svard's "With and Without Memory" / 1994 / Lovely Music ✦✦✦
A lovely and mysterious work beautifully played by pianist Lois Svard in her premier CD. "With and without memory" refers to sections that resonate (like memories from the day into the evening) contrasted with light, dry, non-resonant sections; and also refers to the second and third movements that sometimes do and sometimes don't recall passages from the first movement. *—AMG*

Just for the Record / Lovely Music ✦✦✦✦✦
"Blue" Gene Tyranny plays multi-keyboard works by Robert Ashley "Sonata" with "Trio: Christopher Columbus Crosses to the New World in the Nina, the Pinta and the Santa Maria Using Only Dead Reckoning and a Crude Astrolabe", John Bischoff "Rendezvous", Phil Harmonic "Timing", and Paul DeMarinis "Great Masters of Melody". *—AMG*

Vladimir Ussachevsky

b. Nov. 3, 1911, Hailar, Manchuria, **d.** Jan. 4, 1990, New York, NY
Composer / Musique Concrète, 20th Century Classical/Modern Composition, Atonal, Electronic
A leading catalyst behind the rise of American electronic music, composer Vladimir Ussachevsky was born November 3, 1911 in Hailar, Manchuria; he emigrated to the U.S. in 1930, and after graduating from Pomona College went on to study at the Eastman School of Music. There he composed his first major works, among them 1935's *Theme and Variations* and 1938's *Jubilee Cantata*, as well as various other pieces for piano, vocal, choral and orchestral performance. Upon earning his Ph.D. in 1939, Ussachevsky joined the faculty at Columbia University in 1947; around this time he began making his first forays into electronic music, culminating a few years later with his acquisition of an Ampex tape recorder. In 1952, he and colleague Otto Luening presented the first tape music performance ever given in the U.S., where among the pieces premiered was Ussachevsky's musique concrète landmark *Sonic Contours;* key works including 1954's *Poem of Cycles and Bells* and 1956's *Piece for Tape Recorder* followed, and in 1958 Ussachevsky and Luening received a Rockefeller Foundation grant to open the Columbia-Princeton Electronic Music Center, the first such electro-acoustic facility in America. Complete with four analog tape studios for electronic composition as well as the room-sized RCA Mark II Synthesizer, the CPEMC was the launching pad for countless experimental works, not the least of which were those written by Ussachevsky himself. He died January 4, 1990. *—Jason Ankeny*

• **Electronic Film Music** / 1990 / New World ✦✦✦✦✦
Electronic Film Music includes two lyric, eerie and innovative filmscores, for the film of J.P. Sartre's play *No Exit* and Lloyd William's avant-garde film *Line of Apogee* by the master of the Columbia-Princeton electronic music sound. Also employs vocal, animal and environmental sounds. *— "Blue" Gene Tyranny*

Galina Ustvolskaya

b. Jun. 17, 1919, Petrograd, Russia
Composer / 20th Century Classical/Modern Composition
Studied with Dimitri Shoshtakovitch until 1947 and Conservatory of Petrograd from 1937-1939. Often criticized for her modernism, she was defended by Shoshtakovitch. Also an instrument builder of unique instruments for her pieces. *— "Blue" Gene Tyranny*

Composition I/Composition II/Composition III / 1995 / Philips ✦✦✦
A Shostakovich pupil, Ustvolskaya for many years remained in isolation from Western musical styles, while refusing to kowtow to those in official Russian musical circles who attacked her for modernism. Her music is thus imbued with a freshness in its aesthetic and sound, and an almost prehistoric love of directness. This cycle of works, here performed by the Schönberg Ensemble conducted by Reinbert De Leeuw, is intended to be played in a church, forming a kind of instrumental version of the mass. "Composition I—Dona Nobis Pacem" (1970-1971), a plea for world peace, is scored for the odd combination of piccolo, tuba, and piano. The shiftings and rhythmic variations are subtly complex; the listener is always aware of the raw, bracingly direct expression. "Composition II—Dies Irae" (1972-1973) is evocative like ancient Coptic Christian music. Scored for eight double basses, a cubical drum, and piano, it features some orchestral combinations that are almost brutal with prehistoric vigor. "Part X" moves through very peaceful quiet notes, an insistent chant pattern, and loud drum knocks; the effect is deeply shocking. The third section of this religious triptych, "Composition III—Benedictus Qui Venit" (1974-1975), is scored for another unusual ensemble combination: four flutes, four bassoons, and piano. Perhaps the purest of the pure, it utilizes only two primary elements: a steady beat chant harmonized in clusters distributed amongst the ensemble, and more sustained cluster groups from which a single note steadily emerges like a plea. The effect is that of people first discovering music, directly connecting their instruments to their range of feeling—though (to borrow Buckminster Fuller's expression), not barbarically, but with little distance between emotion and the expressive medium. *—"Blue" Gene Tyranny*

Peter Van Riper

d. Nov. ??, 1998
Saxophone, Composer / Sound Sculpture, Electro-Acoustic
Peter Van Riper was an artist and musician who worked with light and was among the first to work in holography. In the late '60s, Van Riper and artist Gerry Pethick teamed with laser physicist Lloyd Cross (a former classmate at Cranbrook) to form the first company dealing with holographic art. From the '60s on, Van Riper composed music for his sound and light environments, music which increasingly drew from nature and world music traditions following his graduate studies in Tokyo and the Japanese exhibitions and performances that followed. He has since performed in Spain, Holland, Canada, N.Y.C., and around California. The late '70s found him collaborating with dancer Simone Forti; he later composed music for numerous installations by Eugenia Balcells, edited a 1994 video by performer Regina Frank, produced music for the NASA video *Seven Days in Space*, and collaborated with performance artist Sha Sha Higby. He died unexpectedly in November, 1998. *—Joslyn Layne*

Heart (From Acoustic Metal Music) / 1992 / Aerial #4 ✦✦✦
Playing on a twirling metal strip about eight feet long which a sculptor-friend used to make interlocking heart constructions, Van Riper makes a transparently beautiful and almost electronic effect. *— "Blue" Gene Tyranny*

Sound to Movement / VRBLU ✦✦✦
Beautiful sax music sometimes played while spinning, sometimes mixed with natural sounds. Similar work can be heard in *Room Space* (VRBLU 13) and *Indian Circle* (VRBLU 16). *—AMG*

• **Windows to the Sky** / Van Riper Editions ✦✦✦
Windows to the Sky features a vocal duo, with high sliding tones and low drones, performing subtly mixed and modified pieces based on mysterious environmental and pre-verbal human sounds. "Synchronies" features wood, glass, and mechanical sounds in some mysterious place; in "Nook and Cranny," suspended bells and tuned bowls underscore delicate vocal intoning; "Sustainable Music: Acoustic Cups" is a mix of strange breathing sounds (like blowing up a balloon) with light chimes and rain and the sounds of moving, unidentifiable objects; "Susmusic I" is a set of variations on bells with water sounds (and in the background a family pet is being called by name); "Susmusic II (In Memory of John Cage)" is made from environmental sounds, children voices with sustained bell resonances, bird squawks, various drier percussion rattles, and a "coda" of light bell sounds; for "Limits," a highly reverberated rainstick is the primary sound with mysterious low rolling and clicking sounds gradually added into the mix; the pertinently titled "What's Going On" is composed of rain, bird, walking around, and sustained bell sounds; the final "d'Accord" contrasts electronic pulsing and reverberated clicking that is interrupted at times by duet drone singing. *— "Blue" Gene Tyranny*

Edgard Varèse

b. Dec. 22, 1883, Paris, France, **d.** Nov. 6, 1965, New York, NY
Composer / Musique Concrète, 20th Century Classical/Modern Composition, Atonal, Electronic
Criminally unknown during his lifetime, composer Edgard Varèse was among the century's true creative visionaries. Imagining music as bodies of sound in space—its impact most profound as a physical experience—he sought to strip away convention and tradition; his work's massive, cacophonic power anticipated much of the experimental music to follow in its wake.

The Parisian studied under Roussel, among others, was encouraged by Debussy and Romain Rolland, and befriended Richard Strauss and Erik Satie after moving to Berlin in 1907. Varèse theorized that music should imitate scientific principles, and became increasingly fascinated by the possibilities of electronic instrumentation. After his earliest compositions were destroyed by fire, Varèse conducted, then settled in the U.S. (1915), formed the New Symphony Orchestra and proposed new electronic instruments to little interest. In 1921, Varèse completed *Amériques*, and founded the International Composers' Guild. The ICG premiered key works by Berg, Ives, Cowell, Webern, and Varèse, including his *Offrandes* (1922), and *Intégrales* (1925). In 1930, Varèse composed his most renowned non-electronic work, the percussion piece *Ionisation*.

After being denied several funding and grant requests, Varèse suffered from severe depression. Aside from *Ecuatorial* (1934), and *Density 21.5* (1936), he was largely silent until an anonymous donor bought him an Ampex tape recorder in 1951. The gift allowed Varèse to finally start realizing the music he'd been striving towards for decades; he compiled sound fragments for *Déserts*, begun in acoustic form nearly 30 years prior. Varèse traveled to Paris to work alongside musique concrète trailblazer Pierre Schaeffer and, in 1955, *Déserts* became the first piece transmitted in stereo sound over French airwaves. Varèse returned to NY, then was invited to compose for the 1958 World's Fair in Brussels, resulting in his most admired and famous work.

Produced in collaboration with architect Le Corbusier, *Poeme Electronique* was a completely electronic work designed for broadcast over 400 speakers scattered throughout the pavilion. Its impact won Varèse long-overdue recognition; his work began to be recorded, and he received prestigious awards and honors. Apart from 1961's *Nocturnal*, Varèse focused on revising earlier work—many of his earliest ideas now possible with recent technological advances. His final project, *Nuit*, was unfinished at the time of his death. *—Jason Ankeny*

Offrandes (1921)/Integrales(1925) /Octandre (1923)/Ecuatorial (1934) / 1990 / Elektra/Nonesuch ✦✦✦✦
The Contemporary Chamber Ensemble, Arthur Weisberg, conductor. Simply the very best performances available of Varese's acoustic and vocal works. Ancient forests, Queen of the Polar Dawns, the sacred Mayan texts, musical and verbal imagery par excellence. *— "Blue" Gene Tyranny*

Poeme Electronique (1958) in "Electroacoustic Music : Classics" / 1990 / Neuma ✦✦✦✦
A visionary piece..."opacities and rarefactions," the jungle, outer space, The Golden Section, strange ceremonies... CD booklet includes a spectrogram score of the music. *— "Blue" Gene Tyranny*

★ **Music of Edgard Varèse** / Apr. 1996 / One Way ✦✦✦✦✦
The pioneering composer's best-known works are included on this reissue by One Way. On the first five tracks, Robert Craft conducts an ensemble of woodwinds, brass and percussion in the performance of such famous Varèse works as "Ionisation" and "Density 21.5." The sixth and final selection is a 1958 recording of "Poème »lectronique" created by the composer onto magnetic tape for the 1958 World's Fair in Brussels. *—John Bush*

Edgard Varèse : The Complete Works / 1998 / London ✦✦✦✦
Wonderfully performed by the Royal Concertgebouw Orchestra, the Asko Ensemble, dir. Riccardo Chailly. At long last, the complete work of this brilliant composer, including the original version of "Amériques," as well as several previously unpublished works. The entire project was assembled with the assistance of composer Chou Wen-Chung, who had worked directly with Varèse. This massive undertaking includes the following works: "Tuning Up," "Amériques," "Arcana," "Poème ...lectronique," "Nocturnal," "Un Grand Sommeil Noir" (in both the original and orchestral versions),"Offrandes," "Hyperprism," "Octandre," "Intégrales," "Ecuatorial," "Ionisation," "Density 21.5," "Déserts," and "Dance for Burgess." *— "Blue" Gene Tyranny*

Lois V. Vierk

b. Aug. 4, 1951, Lansing, IL
Composer / 20th Century Classical/Modern Composition, Minimalism, World Fusion
American modern composer Lois V. Vierk has been based mostly out of NYC, where she has collaborated with artists including choreographer Anita Feldman. Born outside of Chicago in 1951, Vierk went to California for college, studying under Morton Subotnick and Leonard Stein, among others. Her music studies then turned to gagaku (Japanese court music) for a dozen years, first in L.A. then in Tokyo where she studied with Sukeyasu Shiba, a lead flutist of the Imperial Court Orchestra. The gradual build in Vierk's compositions are one manifestation of gagaku's influence upon her own music. She also composed the gagaku work "Silversword" (1996), which was commissioned for performance by an ensemble led by former teacher Shiba; the premiere occurred at New York's *Lincoln Center*. Vierk's work first became prominent in the '80s, and since then she has received commissions from musicians including pianists Aki Takahashi and Frederic Rzewski, and accordionist Guy Klucevsek. Her compositions have been performed by a number of esteemed ensembles such as Kronos Quartet, Ensemble Modern, and Relâche, and at music festivals in Europe and North America. Vierk's music has been recorded for CRI, O.O. Discs, Tzadik, XI, and Sony. *—Joslyn Layne*

Simoom / 1992 / Experimental Intermedia ✦✦✦✦✦
Cuts incl. "Go Guitars" for 5 electric gts., "Cirrus" for 6 trumpets, "Simoom" for 8 cellos. Sighing, sliding tones, rhythmic pulse, strange harmonics. Reaches an indescribable state like music from an unknown culture. Japanese Buddhist chant influenced, seriously meditative. *— "Blue" Gene Tyranny*

Go Guitars / 1994 / New Tone ✦✦✦✦✦
The word "go" can be translated from the Japanese as the number "five," and thus this composition is for five guitars playing repeated rhythms in slowly changing, sliding microintervals. Vierk uses her compositional technique based on "exponential structures" (for modulating time, pitch movement and rates of change) to create gradually building and gripping emotional tension. A fascinating and unique work in a soundworld of its own. *— "Blue" Gene Tyranny*

● **River Beneath the River** / Apr. 25, 2000 / Tzadik ✦✦✦✦✦
River Beneath the River features four compositions, covering a ten-year span in the life and work of the composer. It is meant to be a kind of introduction to Lois V. Vierk's work, a primer for the uninitiated, or a "greatest hits" for the aficionado, and is one of the prestigious Tzadik catalog's most welcome additions. The title track, a string quartet from 1993 commissioned by Kronos—but played here by violinists Eva Gruesser and Patricia Davis, cellist Bruce Wang, and violist Lois Martin—features several Vierk trademarks. First there is the sense of stillness that slowly evolves into glissando movement. It begins as a downward slide into the point of stillness, but before reaching it, the second trademark comes into play, as systematic activity and movement travel ever upward to a polyphonic epiphany. Energy accumulates until the violins become almost free within the score, placing you on the edge of your seat. Next is a string quartet commissioned by a dance troupe, the flowing "Into the Brightening Air," first written in 1994 and reworked in 1999. The third piece, "Jagged Mesa," is perhaps the most serene and beautiful piece on the album. So gradual is its unfolding, so long are the intervals between the predominate fourths and fifths, that it feels as if the piece is one long unraveling ball of yarn. Perhaps the best-known work here is "Red Shift" (1989), for electric guitar, synthesizer (played by Vierk herself), cello, and percussion (courtesy of Jim Pugliese). It is as close as possible to rock in the post-classical age. Glissando is the strategy here, as the work slides from its somber, spare beginnings into a near-operatic frenzy. "Red Shift" has yet to be equaled as a single piece that brings the visceral dynamics of rock together with the sophistication and emotional control of classical music. *—Thom Jurek*

Gregory Whitehead

Composer, Multi-Media / Sound Collage, Experimental
Gregory Whitehead has done a variety of work in the arts. He is best known for his 50 plus "radiophonic" works, radio features which mix the human voice, text, sounds, and music. These radio pieces were preceded by performing in experimental theater and improvised music. Whitehead's accomplishments also include his recorded experiments with voice, essays on language, directing the Nantucket production studio Sea-Crow Media, and co-editing the book of essays -Wireless Imagination: Sound, Radio and the Avant-Garde (MIT Press, 1994). Several of his radio works were commissioned by American Radio, including "Display Wounds" (1986), "Lovely Ways to Burn" (1990), "Shake, Rattle and Roll" (1992), and "The Thing About Bugs" (1994), the last a collaboration with Christof Migone. Another work of note is his "Pressures of the Unspeakable" (1991), which resulted from setting up a "national scream line," with answering machine, to collect screams to create this piece for the Australian Broadcasting Corporation. This work won the 1992 Prix Italia; Whitehead has also received the 1993 Prix Futura and the BBC Award. *—Joslyn Layne*

William S. Burroughs Tape Worm Mutation (1991), The / 1992 / Musicworks ✦✦✦
A hilarious piece for speaker and audience response in which the degenerative re-recording of a voice leads one through human ageing and the gradual complete breakdown of spoken language. The phase chosen to be treated to 327 degenerations is aptly "I am a degenerate." See his radio piece "Pressure of the Unspeakable" in the collection *Radius #2*. *— "Blue" Gene Tyranny*

Christian Wolff

b. Mar. 8, 1934, Nice, France
Piano, Guitar, Composer / Experimental, 20th Century Classical/Modern Composition
Studied a few weeks with John Cage, but otherwise self-taught. Pianist, guitarist. Ph.D. in Comparative Literature from Harvard. Pioneered scores in open instrumentation, in open cueing systems, scores for non-musicians, and, along with others, scores in verbal instructions only. Teacher, Classics Department at Harvard (1962-70), lecturer Darmstadt 1972 and 74, Classics/Comp. Lit. & Music at Dartmouth. *Changing the System* (1973), *Peace Marches 1, 2 & 3* (1984), *Black Song Organ Preludes* (1987), *Play* (1968), *For Five or Ten Players* (1962). *— "Blue" Gene Tyranny*

For 1,2, or 3 People (1964)/In "A Second Wind for Organ" / 1968 / Odyssey ✦✦✦
A sensitive, imaginative realization by David Tudor using the baroque organ like a synthesizer... sounds never to be expected from a baroque organ... great recording in wide stereo adds to the effect... Tudor has a refined sense of timing. *— "Blue" Gene Tyranny*

★ **Mayday Materials (In CDCM Computer Music Series, Vol. 6)** / 1990 / Centaur ✦✦✦✦✦
A "mix of abstraction, lightheartedness and perhaps political suggestiveness," an interesting combination of Wolff's earlier new music sensibilities and his later use of folk songs as guiding lines (rather than directly quoted). 9 out of 20 pieces made for a dance by Lucinda Childs. *— "Blue" Gene Tyranny*

For Prepared Piano (1951)/For 1,2, or 3 People (1964)/In "The New York School" / 1993 / hatHUT ✦✦✦
Two classic turning points in contemporary music. Concerning "For Prepared Piano," Wolff was once asked to close the window while he was playing (I believe it was) this piece. But he declined saying that all the sounds happening at that moment constituted the music. Excellent performances and realizations of the score. *— "Blue" Gene Tyranny*

I Like to Think of Harriet Tubman / Oct. 20, 1998 / Mode ✦✦✦✦✦
A wonderful overview of the variety of Wolff's work from 1950 thru 1987. One of the legendary members of the now-called New York School (John Cage, Morton Feldman, Earle Brown and Wolff), this album clearly ted with avant-garde music at Mills College, both in the Tape Music Center and the Center for Contemporary Music (much of this rich interchange is covered in the generous liner notes). The CD begins with Cage's famous "silent piece" "4:33" in which we hear the ambient surroundings of the concert hall which can be opened onto an ampitheater in the back, and onto gardens on the side. Julie Steinberg is seated silently at the piano performing some unseen (to the CD listener) action that delineates the 3 movements of the silence "I. tacet, II. tacet, III. tacet". A performance of Cage's "Variations II" by the live computer-music band The Hub and David Gamper's EIS (The Expanded Instrument System environment) contains legendary composer Ramon Sender Barayon as Zero the Clown playing Mairzy Doats on an accordion which is processed electronically. Which seques seamlessly into "Traffic Prayers and Amnesia" written and narrated by Wendy Jeanne Burch, accompanied by Joe Catalano on the electric rebab with the ensemble. Another version of Cage's silent (or maybe "nothing special happening") piece is recorded with the audience enjoying a reception in the entrance hall, their sounds reflected and echoed from side hallways. The instruments begin again with David Gamper's "Deep Hockets", a lovely Terry Riley-like phase piece with the Deep Listening Band, which seques into a fabulous 45-minute improvisation with everyone called "The Last Chances". This CD delivers the meditative spirit inherent in American new music, the richness that comes from trusting fellow musicians to spontaneously produce from the deepness of their understanding. *— "Blue" Gene Tyranny*

Stefan Wolpe

b. Aug. 25, 1902, Berlin, Germany, **d.** Apr. 4, 1972, New York, NY
Composer / 20th Century Classical/Modern Composition, Atonal
Stefan Wolpe was a composer of atonal works notable for providing one alternative mode of atonal writing to that developed by Schoenberg. Despite excursions into popular, folk and jazz idioms at different periods, Wolpe continued to compose in atonal styles throughout times when he wrote other types of pieces. His works are often characterized by cross cutting and discontinuity between different musical gestures and textures, an influence of the artistic movement Dadaism. Wolpe was an influential teacher in the United States, where his pupils included Morton Feldman, George Shapey and Charles Wuorinen.

Wolpe spent the early part of his life in Berlin, associated with the Bauhaus group. He supported himself as a jazz pianist in cabaret and cinemas. His early compositions use the twelve-note serialist techniques of Schoenberg and right from the outset he seems to have used irregular rhythms and contrapuntal textures. He was also influenced by jazz and popular dance music, in such pieces as Tango (1927), and his socialist convictions led him to reflect on the function of music in society. When the Nazis rose to power, Wolpe fled Germany, studying in Vienna with Webern during 1933-34 and continuing on to Palestine. There he became more interested in his Jewish musical heritage, and used it in such works as 1938's "Songs from the Hebrew."

In 1938 Wolpe moved on to New York, where his mature style crystallized. He retained atonal writing, but developed a technique of intense variation. The forms of the pieces did not operate on the principle of contrasts between different sections, but rather evolved cumulatively. Important works from this period are "Enactments" (1950-1953) for three pianos, "Battle Piece" (1947) for solo piano, and the notorious "Symphony" (1956) which had to be renotated because the score was so difficult. From 1952-1956, he taught at Black Mountain College whilst John Cage, David Tudor and Lou Harrison were also on the faculty. *—Rachel Campbell*

● **String Quartet (1968-1969)** / 1991 / CRI ✦✦✦✦✦
Performed by The Juilliard String Quartet. Although writing in a strict atonal style, Wolpe wrote clear, angular music that weaved gestures directly appealing to the body senses, sometimes with a sense of humor; a non-abstract academic composer (not always recognized as one by contemporary academics). This Quartet is one of his finest works, and stands out among the other two works on this CD by Roger Sessions and Milton Babbitt. Also recommended are "Enactments for 3 pianos" (1950-53) on Elektra/Nonesuch 78024-4 (cassette tape), and the "Passacaglia" from Four Studies of Basic Rows (1936) on New World NW-344-2. *— "Blue" Gene Tyranny*

Quartet (Piece) for Oboe, Cello, Piano and Percussion (1954-55) / Cantata f / 1997 / Cpo ✦✦✦✦✦
Performed by the Gruppe Neue Musik "Hanns Eisler" Leipzig (the Hanns Eisler New Music Group of Leipzig), the Robert Schumann Kammerorchester (Chamber Orchestra), and the Silesian String Quartet. Wolpe's "Quartet (Piece)" is a nearly 25-minute work of quickly flashing colors, and flighty speech-like melodic lines in solo and dialogues. The percussionist employs a wide variety of instruments, vibraphone, kitchen utensils, biscuit tins, little bells, steel brushes, aluminum and glass containers. The percussive accents, especially in rhythmic unison with other instruments, heighten the pointillistic textures, and the continuous counterpoint of the whole ensemble makes for fascinating and imagination-stimulating listening. The Quartet opens with some "early morning music" which fades "as if it hasn't ended yet." Lovely passages of plaintive melodies follow, interspersed with popping restrained energy, and little comical sections. Truly enjoyable yet tonally complex music. Texts from Hölderlin, Herodotus, and Robert Creeley are set for the "Cantata," which draw marked contrasts between modern American life and the ancient world, between buying "a god-damned big car" to keep away "the darkness that surrounds us" or becoming intoxicated by the smell of a burning fruit "as the Hellenes are with wine." The wonderfully crafted vocal music ranges from intensely dramatic to warmly thoughtful. The "String Quartet" of 1969 features Wolpe's trademark outbursts of energy separated by silences, and interludes of rich countrapuntal melodies. There is much imitative crosstalk between the strings, and interweaving of lines often in tense close harmonic clusters. *— "Blue" Gene Tyranny*

Quartet for Trumpet, Tenor Saxophone, Percussion and Piano / Nonesuch ✦✦✦
Written in 1950 and revised in 1954, this piece marked the beginning of a new phase of Wolpe's complex work in the mid-'50s. However, it is highly accessible music with gestures and melodic arcs clearly defined, original and emotionally appealing. Wolpe was always influenced by the socially-conscious Gebrauchmusik (music for everyday use) movement in the '20s and '30s in Europe. In the first movement of the piece performed here by the Contemporary Chamber Ensemble conducted by Arthur Weisberg, a central rising and falling somewhat wistful melodic gesture is shared and reinterpreted by each player. In the second movement, the influence of American jazz can be clearly felt in the almost Dixieland complexity of counterpoint; it is still a European idea of jazz, however, recalling textures of Darius Milhaud's *La Création du Monde* of 1923. New methods of nonlinear continuity (partial canonic imitation, for example) are explored by Wolpe in this work as in others appearing at this time, so the music has fluidity and a captivating modern tunefulness throughout. *— "Blue" Gene Tyranny*

Ivan Wyschnegradsky

b. May ??, 1893, St. Petersburg, Russia, **d.** Sep. 29, 1979, Paris, France
Composer / 20th Century Classical/Modern Composition, Atonal
Microtonal composer Ivan Wyschnegradsky was a pioneer in quarter-tone music. He studied music under Nicolas Sokolov and stopped studying law around the same time he began composing. Although his first compositions were written in the normal chromatic system, within three years he adopted the quarter-tone system and was notating 1/12-tones in 1919. The following year, he and his family emigrated from St. Petersburg to France. During the early '20s, he travelled from France to Germany a number of times, meeting Alois Hába, among others. He and Hába commissioned the building of a quarter-tone piano which was built by the decades' end. In addition to his compositions, Wyschnegradsky published a book, *Manuel d'harmonie à quarts de ton*, in 1932. He met up with Olivier Messiaen a few years later and continued to compose in the quarter-tone and 1/6-tone systems for decades to come. Ivan Wyschnegradsky died at the age of 86 in 1979. *—Joslyn Layne*

Compositions for String Quartet and String Trio / 1990 / Edition Block ✦✦✦
Performed by the Arditti String Quartet. Includes the three microintervallic string quartets, a Composition (op.43), and a Trio (op.53). A pioneer (with Willy Moellendorf, Joerg Mager, Alois Haba and Fredrich Trautwein) in quarter-tone and "ultrachromatic" music... the "Trio" with its tone leaps that collapse into each other, and, the first Quartet are probably the most unique discoveries. *— "Blue" Gene Tyranny*

Iannis Xenakis

b. May 22, 1922, Braïla, Romania, **d.** Feb. 4, 2001, Paris, France
Composer / Musique Concrète, 20th Century Classical/Modern Composition, Atonal, Electronic, Classical
In applying mathematical and physical laws to the composition of music, Iannis Xenakis exposed the implicit connections between science and art—rooted in theories of statistical probability, his stochastic method revolutionized not only the composition of music but also its performance, exploring the boundaries of sound and space. Born of Greek parentage in Braïla, Romania on May 22, 1922, Xenakis returned to Greece at age ten, later studying engineering at Athens Polytechnic University. He relocated to Paris in 1947, honing his skills as a composer under the tutelage of Honegger, Milhaud and Messiaen, and in 1954 completed his first major work, *Metastasis for Orchestra.* For over a decade Xenakis also worked with the renowned French architect Le Corbusier, most notably contributing to the design of the Philips Pavilion for the 1958 Brussels International Fair.

Xenakis' engineering studies and architectural work directly impacted his musical ideas (and vice versa)—on the belief that composition develops outside of music, he built upon mathematical and philosophical principles to develop his stochastic theory (adapting the name from "stochos," the Greek word for "goal"). Xenakis explored the inner structural organization of composing, applying theories of statistical probability to discover the interrelationships between organized sound and music; with the advent of computer technology, he translated his findings into programs which created new compositional families. Xenakis broke further ground in his studies of spatial dynamics—positioning musicians throughout an auditorium according to kinetic principles, he pursued a perfect sonic balance based upon the distribution of sound from a multitude of directions.

Works including 1956's *Pithoprakta* and 1957's *Diamorphoses* launched Xenakis to the forefront of the avant-garde, and he continued pushing the envelope with subsequent pieces including 1958's *Duel* (a composition based on the principles of game theory) and 1962's *Bohor* (his first major electronic project). As the complex rhythms of ensemble compositions like 1963's *Eonta* gave way to full-blown orchestral scores including 1969's *Oresteia*, in the interim Xenakis directed much of his energies towards guiding the Centre d' ...tudes de Mathématique et Automatique Musicales (CEMAMu), which he founded at the Sorbonne in 1966. Although his oeuvre includes works for ballet and theatre, tape constructions and even vocal music, from the mid-'70s onward the majority of Xenakis' compositions grew from orchestral and instrumental origins. After suffering poor health for some years, Iannis Xenakis died at his home in Paris on February 4, 2001. *—Jason Ankeny*

Medea for Male Choir, Hand-Held Stones and Orchestra / 1969 / Erato ✦✦✦✦✦
Perfomed by the Orchestra and Choir of the French Radio-Television directed by Marius Constant. A good combination of Xenakis' more spare abstract music combined with ancient Greek chant... more involving than the often violent-themes or forced humor of his music based on stochastic procedures, transformation groups, Poisson's law of probabilities, etc, where structure is the only content... but some people like that sort of thing... This record also includes "Syrmos" for 18 strings, and "Polytope for 4 orchestras disseminated in the audience." *— "Blue" Gene Tyranny*

Mycenae-Alpha (1978)/ in "Electroacoustic Music: Classics" / 1990 / Neuma ✦✦✦
Composed in 1978 on the !UPIC graphic computer system at the *Centre d'Etudes de Mathematique et Automatique Musicales* (Center for the Study of Mathematics and Automatic Music) in Paris, this electronic work is for mono tape manipulated between two or among four speakers. The work has become a classic of computer-generated music. By taking the shapes and movements of natural phenomena, such as molecules in a gas, Xenakis developed a method of digitally mapping those images into the computer and using them to trigger sound events of similar aural shapes. The result is a nine-minute 38-second composition of dense and intense textures, of phase-shifting waveforms rich in harmonics that cascade, flutter, crash, and scream like sirens in a vast cosmological territory. *— "Blue" Gene Tyranny*

La Legende d'Eer / 1995 / Montaigne ✦✦✦✦
Xenakis' 46-minute electro-acoustic masterpiece for eight-track tape, "La Légende d'Eer" is based loosely on the Myth of Er the Pamphylian, which closes Plato's *Republic.* Like the comparatively more succinct "Concret PH" (composed for the 1958 World's Fair and played within the sweeping eaves of the Philips Pavilion), "La Légende" was conceived as an architectural sound event. It was originally planned for the opening of the Centre George Pompidou in 1978 and, as at the Philips Pavilion, was to have been played within a structure of Xenakis' design. "La Légende d'Eer" also incorporates some of Xenakis' first experiments with the !UPIC, a compositional device he designed to translate hand-drawn sketches into audible sound. *—Sean Cooper*

● **Kraanerg (1968)** / Jul. 7, 1997 / Asphodel ✦✦✦✦
Xenakis' 1968 work for tape and orchestra, "Kraanerg" was performed several times after its composition, though synchronizing tape effects with the orchestra often proved difficult. Charles Zacharie Bornstein, conductor of the ST-X Ensemble, conceived the brilliant idea of hiring turntablist philosopher Paul D. Miller (aka DJ Spooky) to take over the tape effects (prerecorded by Xenakis in 1968) for a new 1996 recording, supervised and attended by the

composer himself. The result is an excellent recording that dovetails nicely with Xenakis' late-'60s compositional aims—reflecting the world's exploding population base (and the fact that much of it will be youth). The recording itself and sound quality are excellent, with much care devoted to the wide frequencies of the ST-X Ensemble (which includes many strings plus trumpets, trombones, contrabassoon, and contrabass clarinet). Miller's contributions are not large, but the concrète atmospheres of Xenakis' tape exerts a certain dominance over the proceedings. Though it might be a difficult album for listeners not used to the work of early electronic composers, *Kraanerg* is a rewarding recording. *—John Bush*

Otomo Yoshihide

b. Aug. 1, 1959, Yokohama, Japan

Guitar (Electronic), Sampling, Turntables, Scratching, Composer / Japanese Rock, Noise, Electronica, Experimental, Avant-Garde, Ambient

Improvisational guitarist, turntablist and composer Otomo Yoshihide was born August 1, 1959 in Yokohama, Japan; the son of an engineer, as a child he built his own radio and electronic oscillator, and as a teen began creating sound collages by means of open-reel tape recorders. During high school, Yoshihide performed in a local rock band before moving on to free jazz, influenced primarily by saxophonist Kaoru Abe and guitarist Masayuki Takayanagi; while a university student, he also became fascinated with ethnic music, and in 1981 travelled to Hainan, China to research the area's musical culture. Upon returning to Tokyo, Yoshihide began regularly performing free improvisational sets at the local Goodman club, although he maintained a relatively low profile until 1987, when he appeared in a duo with saxophonist Junji Hirose in addition to concurrent stints in the bands No Problem and ORT. In 1990, Yoshihide joined bassist Hideki Kato's group Player Piano and also formed his own noise rock group, Ground Zero. From 1992 to 1994, he also led the Double Unit Orchestra. Other Yoshihide-helmed groups of the period included Mosquito Paper and Sampling Virus Project; following the 1998 dissolution of Ground Zero, his work moved increasingly towards minimalism in projects including I.S.O. and Filament. *—Jason Ankeny*

Cathode / Oct. 19, 1999 / Tzadik ♦♦♦♦

With 1999's *Cathode*, Otomo Yoshihide presents a mix of his experimental material. On the opening and closing tracks, "Modulation *2*" and "Modulation *1*" respectively, he makes full use of sine waves alongside the sounds of the sho, a traditional Japanese instrument. It should be noted that while some listeners find sine waves refreshing and mind-expanding, as they penetrate areas of your mind that sound does not normally hit so directly, other listeners—specifically, those with tinnitus or other sensitivity to high-pitched sounds—will find these frequencies unbearable. In contrast, "Cathode *1*" presents an improvising ensemble of samplers and electronics, and traditional instruments, from cello to shamisen. The following cut, "Cathode *2*" finds Yoshihide working solo, sampling on a hard disk recorder. Yoshihide continues to explore sound experimentation with this release, never looking back to past projects such as Ground Zero. *—Joslyn Layne*

• **Bits, Bots and Signs** / Nov. 15, 2000 / Erstwhile ♦♦♦♦

It's hard to believe one had to wait until 2000 for Otomo Yoshihide and the Swiss duo Voice Crack (Norbert Möslang and Andy Guhl), two influential artists in the field of free electronic improvisation, to first meet on stage. It happened on March 27, 2000, in St. Gallen (Switzerland), and Erstwhile released the document under the title *Bits, Bots and Signs*. Since Ground Zero's conclusion, Yoshihide has continued to develop his very personal musical language made of low-fi electronics and sampler treatments. The duo Voice Crack has been cracking everyday household machines in order to extract unusual noises out of them since the early '80s. Their music was compatible from the start and the result is a mind-boggling soundscape, a rough terrain with burbling low frequencies, ethereal sustained tones, piercing high-pitched electronic screams, and haunting noises. These five improvisations stay clear of monotony: gradually but quickly changing form, always on the verge of redefining themselves. Both entertaining and ear opening, *Bits, Bots and Signs* is more convincing than Yoshihide's CDs with *I.S.O.* and *Filament* and somehow less aggressive than Voice Crack's *Poire'z* project with Erik M and Günter Müller. Fans of free electronic improv have no reason to pass on this one. Strongly recommended. *—François Couture*

Gayle Young

b. 1950

Composer / Sound Sculpture, 20th Century Classical/Modern Composition

Canadian modern composer and performer Gayle Young is known not only for her compositions, but also for her musical invention (the amaranth), for her use of unusual tunings, and as the editor of Musicworks magazine. She has created sound sculptures and music since the late '70s and, in 1980, built the amaranth, a 24-stringed instrument with a moveable bridge (she had previously designed another microtonal instrument called the Columbine). In addition to this, she has composed for installations by sculptor Reinhard Eaitzenstein, performed in the Test Tubes, and authored a biography of Canadian composer and scientist Hugh LeCaine. *—Joslyn Layne*

Amaranth / Musicworks ♦♦♦

A fascinating work bu this important Canadian composer, instrument builder, author and editor of the Musicworks magazine. *—"Blue" Gene Tyranny*

La Monte Young

b. Oct. 14, 1935, Bern, ID

Piano, Composer / Multimedia, 20th Century Classical/Modern Composition

One of the principal architects of the minimalist aesthetic, La Monte Young was among the true innovators of 20th century music, his rejection of traditional melody and structure in favor of hypnotic drone epics influencing not only the avant-garde music created in his wake but also proving seminal in the development of punk, Krautrock and ambient. In 1959, Young composed *Trio for Strings*, regularly cited as the earliest work in the minimalist canon. Three years later, he first began to conceive of the Dream House, a continual sound and light environment related to his composition *The Four Dreams of China;* the project remained in limbo for some years to follow, but was a clear forerunner of the principle to guide his subsequent career—music with no beginning and no end. By the beginning of the 1970s, Young's approach to eternal music required tours of six to eight players, slide projectionists, a technician and over two tons of electronic equipment; needing a week for set-up time alone, these multi-media Dream House installations then remained intact for another week, with sine-wave generators and shifting light patterns creating continuous sounds and images throughout the residency. Rarely recorded throughout much of his career, Young signed to Gramavision in 1987, with a flurry of releases—*The Well-Tuned Piano, The Second Dream of the High-Tension Line Stepdown Transformer from the Four Dreams of China* and *Just Stompin',* a raga-blues effort recorded with his Forever Blues Band, among them—soon appearing. Still, throughout his career Young remained a largely shadowy figure, often discussed but seldom heard; his influence on the rise of ambient music and drone-rock is undeniable, yet almost subliminal. *—Jason Ankeny*

The Well Tuned Piano / 1973 / Gramavision ♦♦♦

The legendary just intonation work in a set of five CDs. The booklet goes on a bit much justifying Young's place in history, so just listen to the music which is non-virtuosic in the usual sense, and pleasant. *— "Blue" Gene Tyranny*

• **90 XII 9C. 9:35-10:52 PM NYC, The Melodic Version (1984) of the Second Dream of the Hig** / 1991 / Gramavision ♦♦♦♦♦

Composed in 1984, this piece presents a form of group improvisation based on timelessness—each performance is "woven out of an eternal fabric of silence and sound (which) evanesces back into silence until a group of musicians picks up the same set of pitches again" (Young). Each listing of this title in a program or recording will also contain the specific date, time, and city of the performance. Like Harry Partch, Ben Johnston, and others, Young is known for basing his compositions on alternative tunings, especially "The Well-Tuned Piano" of 1964-1981. For one recorded realization, eight trumpets with Harmon mutes provide an amazing recreation of the title's sonic experience as they play four pitches in frequency ratios of the complete quadrad 18/17/16/12 which "can be isolated in the harmonic structures of the sounds of power plants and telephone poles." There are also macro-structure outlines which guide the larger sections of the work. Young recalls two such listening experiences in his life: one next to a telephone pole in Bern, ID, and the other near 20 transformers outside of Montpelier where his grandfather ran a gas station. *— "Blue" Gene Tyranny*

Just Stompin': Live at the Kitchen / 1993 / Gramavision ♦♦♦♦

"I consider much of my music... to be blues-based," claims La Monte Young, the acknowledged father of minimalism. This might not seem so bizarre considering his early collaborations with jazz musicians and the undoubted minimal qualities of blues pioneers like Howlin' Wolf and Muddy Waters. Like many of his works, Young has been developing the piece here, "Young's Dorian Blues in G," since its inception in 1960, including his work with his Theatre of Eternal Music ensemble with John Cale and Tony Conrad. Here the piece is presented as a two-hour live performance which he did at *the Kitchen* in New York in 1993 with a guitar/bass/drums line-up headed by Young's synthesizer in his "just intonation" tuning. Beginning with an elegiac opening, the piece soon evolves into a rollicking, driving, gradually-evolving epic featuring Jon Catler's searing guitar runs and Young's keyboard mimicking a barrelhouse piano—because the two of them trade solo spots so effectively, this never gets tedious or drawn-out. With its extensive liner notes, *Just Stompin'* serves an excellent introduction to the work of one of the most important composers of the 20th century, especially for anyone interested in Young's work but frightened off by the scope of the 5-LP *The Well-Tuned Piano. —Jason Gross*

89 VI 8C. 1:42-1:52 AM Paris Encore from "Poem for Chairs, Tables, Benches, Etc." (1960 / Tellus ♦♦♦

A piece with a verbal instruction score (what we used to call "music without notes," "procedural music," "events," etc... see the FluxTellus collection) which uses the floor sounds of precisely moved furniture in a resonate space. Young's "early style." *— "Blue" Gene Tyranny*

John Zorn

b. Sep. 2, 1953, New York, NY

Sax (Alto), Composer / Improvisation, Jewish Music, Avant-Garde Jazz, Film Music, Soundtracks, Free Jazz, 20th Century Classical/Modern Composition, Post-Bop, Avant-Garde

It is possible to call John Zorn a "jazz" musician, but that would be much too limiting a description. While jazz feeling is present in a good deal of his work, and the idea of improvisation is vitally important to him, Zorn doesn't operate within any idiom's framework, drawing from just about any musical, cultural or noise source that a fellow who grew up in the TV and LP eras could experience. This eclecticism gone haywire can result in such wildly jump-cutting works as *Spillane*, whose plethora of diverse and incompatible styles makes for a listening experience akin to constantly punching the station buttons on a car radio. Zorn believes that the age of the composer as an "autonomous musical mind" had come to an end in the late 20th century; hence the collaborative nature of much of his work, both with active musicians and music and styles of the past. Like Mel Brooks, the zany film director, many of Zorn's works are tributes to certain musical touchstones of his—such as Ennio Morricone, Sonny Clark and Ornette Coleman—all filtered through his unpredictable hall of mirrors. While it would be foolhardy to single out a handful of dominant influences, Zorn's music seems very close in spirit to that of Warner Bros. cartoon composer Carl Stalling, both in its transformation of found material and manic, antic moods.*—Richard S. Ginell*

Yankees / 1984 / Charly ♦♦♦♦

• **The Big Gundown: John Zorn Plays the Music of Ennio Morricone** / Sep. 1984-Sep. 1985 / Tzadik ♦♦♦♦♦

On this intriguing concept album, altoist John Zorn (who also "sings" and plays harpsichord, game calls, piano, and musical saw) utilizes an odd assortment of open-minded avant-garde players (with a couple of ringers) on nine themes originally written for Italian films by Ennio Morricone, plus his own "Tre Nel 5000." These often-radical interpretations (which Morricone endorsed) keep the melodies in mind while getting very adventurous. Among the musicians heard on the colorful and very eccentric set (which utilizes different personnel and instrumentation on each track) are guitarists Bill Frisell and Vernon Reid, percussionist Bobby Previte, keyboardist Anthony Coleman, altoist Tim Berne, pianist Wayne Horvitz, organist Big John Patton, and even Toots Thielemans on harmonica and whistling among many others. There are certainly no dull moments on this often-riotous program. *—Scott Yanow*

Voodoo: The Music of Sonny Clark / Nov. 25, 1985-Nov. 26, 1985 / Black Saint ♦♦♦♦♦
This unusual album is an unlikely success. Altoist John Zorn, who is best-known for his avant-garde flights and rather eccentric concept albums, here plays it fairly straight. He interprets seven compositions (all fairly obscure) by the somewhat forgotten hard bop pianist Sonny Clark including "Cool Struttin'," "Voodoo" and "Sonny's Crib." With alert support from pianist Wayne Horvitz, bassist Ray Drummond and drummer Bobby Previte, Zorn creates fairly boppish solos with occasional hints at more advanced improvising techniques. Worth checking out. *—Scott Yanow*

Classic Guide to Strategy / 1985 / Tzadik ♦♦♦
The Classic Guide to Strategy, Volumes One & Two presents two Zorn albums from the mid-'80s which have long been out of print. Featuring a variety of manipulated saxophones, clarinets, and duck calls, the album plays at the edges of sounds traditionally associated with reed instruments. The album is not entirely accessible, especially *Volume One*—if it were produced by a college student sowing his experimental oats after a giddy term at *BAM*, it would probably be labeled a failure for its eccentricity, abruptness, and lack of a coherent theme. However, when a line is drawn through Zorn's previous work, it ends up here—the playfulness of sound, the variety of textures, the use of silence and space as part of the composition—if the listener approaches this album expecting to find musical genius, he or she will not have to look too far. Zorn manufactures the sounds of animals, voices, squeaks, scraps of melodic lines, drowning (or at least dampened) beasts, and cartoon worlds with his reeds, paying homage to the work of Carl Stalling, as well as the sounds of Anthony Braxton and Evan Parker. The first two tracks on this collection represent the original volume one; the last five belonged to the original volume two. Stylistically, they are similar, with the second volume containing less spacial breaks between the musical bursts and each song paying tribute to avant-garde Japanese artists like Mori Ikue, Enoken, Kondo Toshinori, Katsumi Shigeru, Aoyama Michi, and Togawa Jun. *—Stacia Proefrock*

☆ **News for Lulu** / Aug. 30, 1987 / hatHUT ♦♦♦♦♦
Avant-garde altoist John Zorn teams up with trombonist George Lewis and guitarist Bill Frisell to form a unique trio. Without the benefit of piano, bass, or drums, they interpret the hard bop compositions of Kenny Dorham, Hank Mobley, Sonny Clark, and Freddie Redd, generally not even the better-known ones. The performances are quite concise (Dorham's "Windmill" is covered in 40 seconds), respectful to the melodies, and unpredictable. There are hints of the avant-garde here and there, but also plenty of swinging, bop-oriented solos and coherent ensembles. Very intriguing music that is highly recommended to a wide audience of jazz and general listeners. *—Scott Yanow*

More News for Lulu / Jan. 18, 1989-Jan. 19, 1989 / hatART ♦♦♦♦♦

● **Torture Garden** / 1989-1990 / Shimmy Disc ♦♦♦♦
From the violent cover art to the Japanese text inside the album, at first glance one might mistake *Torture Garden* for a fetishist soundtrack. But jazz madman John Zorn and Boredoms frontman Yamatsuka Eye assembled another group of open-minded musicians to carry on their vision of grindcore and jazz uniting. Distinguished musicians Wayne Horovitz and Bill Frisell help Zorn and Eye take this from a curious side project to a fantastic metal band. Songs blur together but never get boring, no lyrics are actually sung, and few songs last longer than a minute. It also never takes itself seriously, a nice relief from Zorn's heavy-handed ambient collaborations. This would make a great introduction to the noise/jazz efforts that this group of musicians pioneered in the early '90s. *—Bradley Torreano*

Black Box: Torture Garden/Leng Tch'e / 1992 / Tzadik ♦♦♦♦

Kristallnacht / 1993 / Tzadik ♦♦♦♦♦
This release documents an intense musical representation of *Kristallnacht*, or the Night of Broken Glass, a coordinated attack on Jews throughout the German Reich that occurred on November 9, 1938, during which Nazis, SS members, and Hitler youth broke into Jewish homes and businesses, assaulting the people and their property. The official German report tallied 7,500 businesses destroyed, 267 synagogues burned (with 177 totally destroyed), and 91 Jews killed. John Zorn has created a musical work that powerfully represents the different stages of this historical event. "Shtetl (Ghetto Life)" is beautiful yet apprehensive klezmer, interspersed with sound bites of German rallies and speeches that become more frequent, increasingly crowding the life from the music. This segues into "Never Again," which, Zorn warns in the liner notes, "contains high frequency extremes at the limits of human hearing and beyond, which may cause nausea, headaches and ringing in the ears." While nearly unbearable, it is a fitting sound representation of *Kristallnacht*, as thousands of layers of shattering glass assault the ears. "Never Again" is both effective and affecting, if you can listen. This onslaught is followed by the loud silence and emptiness of "Gahelet (Embers)", a walk through the immediate aftermath of wind, darkness, and destruction. Alley echoes are heard as sound is overwhelmed by a dread and horror beyond expressing, and no words can contain what might begin to form in the midst of shock. This is a heavy silence. Strings have gone haggard on the next composition, and from this point the album becomes less literal and explicit, moving away from poignancy and focus into more chaos. Zorn's forceful undertaking is realized through the expert and passionate musicianship of violinist Mark Feldman, guitarist Marc Ribot, keyboardist Anthony Coleman, bassist Mark Dresser, and percussionist William Winant, as well as guest trumpeter Frank London and clarinetist David Krakauer. *—Joslyn Layne*

● **Execution Ground** / Nov. 15, 1994 / Subharmonic [Ltd. Edition] ♦♦♦♦♦
A trio consisting of alto saxophonist John Zorn, bassist Bill Laswell,and drummer Mick Harris, Painkiller was a novel blend of free improv, jazz, dub, and death metal. Although the lineup occasionally expanded to include the uniquely gifted Japanese vocalist Yamantaka Eye and other guests, *Execution Ground* is an investigation of the power and range of the core trio. The first disc of this inventive and unsettling two-disc set features three long improvisations that show off the band's dub influence. The second disc, subtitled "Ambient Dub," is a rethinking/remix of the third and first improvs on the first disc. Overall less thrashy than some Painkiller excursions, the improvisations here are striking for their greater sonic space without sacrificing any of the heaviness. At times, the band rests, making way for ominous breathing and distant sustained screams, which recur throughout. The transitions from silence to groove to noise and back are relentless and dramatic. Harris proves to be an astonishingly inventive drummer, consistently varying the foundation in surprising ways. Laswell's tone varies from the brightness of flanged round-wound strings scraping the frets to a clean, menacing low-frequency pulse, and sticks mostly to elemental, non-flashy lines that keep the mood deep and dark. Zorn's playing is excellent here, varying between extremely overblown piercing tones (perhaps the best way of being heard over such a rhythm section) and nearly conventional jazzy lines that confidently ride atop the din. An occasional microtonal chorus effect warps his playing, and the effect is so disturbing that it's surprising he soon abandoned this technique. *—Maurice Rickard*

Masada, Vol. 3: Gimel / Mar. 28, 1995 / DIW ♦♦♦♦♦

Elegy / Oct. 1995 / Tzadik ♦♦♦♦♦
A mysterious, elegant, exotic tone poem built around Jean Genet's image relating flowers and prisoners. There are four parts entitled *Blue, Yellow, Pink* and *Black*. A constantly changing soundscape of images—sweet, tortured, folk ceremony, hellishly cosmic, dungeon sounds of chains and locks, breathing and much more—highlighted by silences. Brilliantly evocative. With Barbara Chaffe, alto and bass flutes, David Abel, viola, Scummy, guitar, David Shea, turntables, David Slusser, sound effects, William Winant, percussion, and Mike Patton, voice. *—"Blue" Gene Tyranny*

Masada, Vol. 5: Hei / Nov. 21, 1995 / DIW ♦♦♦♦

Bar Kokhba / Aug. 20, 1996 / Tzadik ♦♦♦♦♦
Bar Kokhba encompasses the wealth of material John Zorn has composed with his eminent quartet Masada. The album is a collection of Masada songs that have been rearranged for chamber ensembles. For this effort, Zorn enlists some of New York's finest musicians: John Medeski, Marc Ribot, Anthony Coleman, and Erik Freedlander, among others. The compositions range from groups of four to solo performances by Ribot, Medeski, and Coleman. While some compositions retain their original structure and sound, some are expanded and probed by Zorn's arrangements, and resemble avant-garde classical music more than jazz. But this is the beauty of the album; the ensembles provide a forum for Zorn to expand his compositions. The album consistently impresses, and the highlights include "Gevurah," "Paran," and "Mochin." Zorn's genius as both songwriter and arranger are evidenced, and the recording sits well among the traditional Masada material. *—Marc Gilman*

Film Works, Vol. 5: Tears of Ecstasy / Nov. 19, 1996 / Tzadik ♦♦♦

● **Film Works, Vol. 3** / Mar. 18, 1997 / Tzadik ♦♦♦♦
The third volume cataloguing John Zorn's film scores is a quality release that offers the scores from two films, a rare piece of music cues that would lead to *Cynical Hysterie Hour*, and music spots for commercials. First comes the 1993 score for *Thieves Quartet*, which is warm, solid, smoky jazz written with Miles Davis' *Escalator to the Scaffold* soundtrack in mind. This score also marks the first recording of the quartet that would later be known as Masada. Combining musicians of the highest caliber and compatibility, this strong first outing gives full indication of the rapport between bassist Greg Cohen, trumpeter Dave Douglas, drummer Joey Baron and Zorn. Guitarist Robert Quine also guests on the closer, "End Titles." The track of music sketches for Japanese cartoonist Kiriko Kubo, "Music for Tsunta (nine cues)," separates the two film scores. Following this track is the score from 1994, for L.A. filmmaker Mei-Juin Chen's *Hollywood Hotel*. This recording joins a long, impressive list of Zorn's sax collaborations with electric guitarists that includes Eugene Chadbourne, Henry Kaiser, Derek Bailey, and Keiji Haino. Here is his saxophone duo with exemplary guitarist Marc Ribot; Ribot most often provides fabric and rhythm for Zorn's solos, in addition to his crucial role in a few atmospheric and a few splurtey pieces. The remaining 31 tracks on the album are shorts composed for a commercial advertising firm with which Zorn had an excellent and open working relationship. The musicianship and stylistic range found here is commendable. The reed and brass-less instrumentation varies between tracks, as guitarists Arto Lindsay, Quine, and Ribot provide a strong front, seamlessly relaxed in southwestern and surf. *—Joslyn Layne*

Film Works, Vol. 7: Cynical Hysterie Hour / Aug. 19, 1997 / Tzadik ♦♦♦
Cynical Hysterie Hour is John Zorn's music for four animated shorts by Japanese cartoonist Kiriko Kubo. Bursts of TV rock, synth whistles & barks, banjo licks, and sound effects intensify the caffeinated jumping through genre hoops of this slick and cinematically silly music. Clocking in at 25 minutes, this CD's value lies in that (1) it is Zorn's first venture into cartoon music, which he has long revered, and (2) it was in print on Sony for merely months in 1990, before being yanked out of print, making it the most sought-after rarity of Zorn's recordings. In late 1996, Zorn finally attained the rights for his music, and remastered and rereleased the album on his own label, Tzadik. *—Joslyn Layne*

Film Works, Vol. 4: S&M / 1997 / Tzadik ♦♦♦

Film Works, Vol. 8 / Feb. 17, 1998 / Tzadik ♦♦♦♦♦
Film Works 8 contains the scores for two films. First is music for *The Port of Last Resort*, a documentary about the Jewish refugees who fled to Shanghai from 1930s Nazi Germany. The music is a continuation of the Masada Chamber project, elegant klezmer jazz of as high a worth as *Bar Kokhba* or *Circle Maker* (the other two releases drawing from the Masada songbook that are not performed by the quartet). The Masada String Trio—violinist Mark Feldman, cellist Erik Friedlander, and bassist Greg Cohen—is joined by guitarist Marc Ribot, pianist Anthony Coleman, and pipa virtuoso Min Xiao Fen. The second half of this release is film music for *Latin Boys Go to Hell*, whose final edit, incidentally, barely used the music

heard here. The low-key music of this score, with wind chime trances and pieces with a subtle tribal low-end, is performed entirely by the excellent percussionists Cyro Baptista and Kenny Wolleson. The sophisticated music of *Film Works 8* stands apart for its cosmopolitan assuredness, high level of musicianship, and beauty. *—Joslyn Layne*

★ **Circle Maker** / Mar. 17, 1998 / Tzadik ♦♦♦♦♦
This two-disc release captures beautiful and refined music that makes full use of the ensembles' extraordinary musicianship. Drawing from John Zorn's *Masada* songbook are the Masada String Trio and the Bar Khokba Sextet. Each ensemble fills one CD with beautiful chamber jazz woven around a heart of Jewish melodies. Superb and elegant music, Zorn skeptics will find the music on *Circlemaker* surprisingly stable and accessible. This is a fitting successor to the other *Masada* works that Zorn doesn't actually perform on—the first *Masada* chamber project, *Bar Khokba*, and *Film Works, Vol. 8*, whose recording session wrapped up weeks before this weekend date of December 1997. Issachar is the name of the disc on which bassist Greg Cohen, cellist Erik Friedlander, and violinist Mark Feldman perform. Zevulun is the *Bar Khokba* sextet: the Masada String Trio plus drummer Joey Baron, percussionist Cyro Baptista, and guitarist Marc Ribot. All of these musicians are accomplished in jazz and improvised music, and have performed extensively in world and/or classical settings, as well. *Circlemaker* is a very necessary recording for all appreciaters of chamber jazz, new Jewish music, or any of these stellar musicians. *—Joslyn Layne*

Bribe / Sep. 15, 1998 / Tzadik ♦♦♦♦♦
John Zorn's *Bribe* is a continuation and extension of his album *Spillane*. Like its predecessor, this album features almost the same line-up of extraordinary NYC improvisers including pianist Anthony Coleman, drummer Bobby Previte, organist Wayne Horvitz, turntablist Christian Marclay, and harpists Zeena Parkins and Carol Emanuel. Unlike the fast-spliced pace of *Spillane*, which functioned as its own narrative, the music on *Bribe* is allowed to stretch and develop because it was composed as a background for the dialogue in three 30-minute radio plays by Terry O'Reilly (it was later adapted to a stage production). O'Reilly described his creation as "low art; " along the lines of little respected categories such as pulp fiction and B-movies. Zorn then constructed appropriate music, continually switching styles and filling it with pop references. The overall mood of *Bribe* is also different from *Spillane* and much of Zorn's work (excluding *Film Works, Vol. 7*), in that it maintains a light-hearted approach, weaving music box chimes and carnival sounds into the music. A nicer mood pervades this release, yet given its kaleidoscopic and slightly demented tone, it certainly can't be described as relaxed. Then again, maybe "relaxed" isn't too far off, after all—perhaps by playing a supporting role to the production's cast instead of driving the concept, the musicians were able to enjoy themselves a little more. *—Joslyn Layne*

Masada: Live in Jerusalem / Apr. 20, 1999 / Tzadik ♦♦♦♦♦

★ **Godard/Spillane** / Jul. 20, 1999 / Tzadik ♦♦♦♦♦
"Godard" and "Spillane" were the two first (and purest) examples of the "file card" composition technique developed by John Zorn and inspired by theater director Richard Foreman. The compositions were constructed from independent scraps of music inscribed on file cards; the two principal works here called for assembly of the cards ("Spillane" used 60 cards within roughly 25 minutes) to create compositions within the conceptual frame of work by *Mickey Spillane* and Jean-Luc Godard. The goal was to translate imagery from Godard's films and *Spillane's* crime novels (and probably the films based on those novels) into unified compositions. Bits of text weave through musical fragments including gentle lounge piano, spacy electronic music, violent sonic crashes, and dive-bar jazz. Ironically, "Godard" and "Spillane" both work as unified compositions because they are made of fragments. The ideas of the filmmaker and the writer would have been too complex to be tackled by an overblown, operatic score; such a work could only scratch the surface of a few of their ideas without seeming disjointed. But Zorn's file card snippets bounce around like thoughts, overlapping and intruding on each other, reversing direction like a changed mind. Careful selection and arrangement make all the snippets seem essential and irreplaceable, despite their remarkable diversity. This album's execution is aided by a truly impressive cast of supporting musicians, whose close relationships with Zorn made it possible for the musical nuances to be communicated through interpersonal interaction. As a result, every piece sounds like a pure fragment of its genre instead of mere imitation. Perhaps most impressive were the contributions of Anthony Coleman and Bill Frisell, both of whom wrenched an amazing variety of sounds from their instruments. This collection, issued by Tzadik in 1999, also contains a delightful Christmas song, "Blues Noël," which applies the file card method in a much shorter, but charming, piece. *—Stacia Proefrock*

The String Quartets / Jul. 20, 1999 / Tzadik ♦♦♦♦
This fine CD from Tzadik includes all four of John Zorn's works for string quartet. The first piece was composed and recorded in 1988, while the rest were recorded for the first time in 1999, specifically for this release. Zorn describes *Cat O'Nine Tails* as being "about the visual." Full of humor and musical games, this fun composition is subtitled "Tex Avery Meets the Marquis de Sade," and includes beauty, dynamism, strain, and melodrama. *The Dead Man* (1990) is the "sensual" piece that Zorn considers—as he does *Torture Garden*—a soundtrack to S&M scenes. Appropriately, the strings portray the pulling of taut wires and painful screeching throughout the piece's13 sections, each less than two minutes long. *Memento Mori*, from two years later, is the CD's "emotional" work, dedicated to Ikue Mori. Listening to the strings' wavering, plummeting, dipping, and plucking is a journey toward inner depths. With its 29-minute length and unique approach, *Memento Mori* requires special attention; Zorn refers to it as a "complexly hermetic work." The final string quartet is the "spiritual" piece, *Kol Nidre* (1996), related in name (and spirit) to the song of the same name that opens Yom Kippur services. The holy day is a time for forgiveness and reflection; according to the Torah, it is a time to afflict your soul. The composition is a weeper with a slow sway of bowed drones beneath unfurling meditative melodies. Maybe Zorn's genius isn't that he creates entirely unique music, but he certainly has an ear for great musical ideas, gleaned from his years of deep listening. And so, while these compositions may not be landmarks among string quartet works, they are exceedingly well done. *—Joslyn Layne*

● **Masada: Live in Sevilla 2000** / Jul. 25, 2000 / Tzadik ♦♦♦♦♦
Live in Sevilla, recorded and released in the year 2000, is arguably the finest document in this extremely prolific jazz quartet's catalog. If there's anyone who still believes that John Zorn is nothing more than an avant-garde screamer, look no further. The interplay between Zorn's alto and the trumpet of Dave Douglas is nothing short of amazing, and each one's soloing is focused and intense. Joey Baron and Greg Cohen are a fantastic rhythm section; Cohen acts as anchor while Baron playfully dances around the beat, simultaneously supplying a driving pulse. Even when Zorn and Douglas enter the realm of extended techniques (as on the end of "Ne'eman"), Cohen and Baron keep things firmly grounded. Of course, the real stars of the show are Zorn and Douglas; their solos are never less than dazzling, and each has an utterly unique style. Zorn's trademark alto wails are delightful and Dave Douglas has a warm and buttery tone all his own. This might also be the best recorded of the live Masada releases, making it a real jewel in an already glittering discography. *Live in Sevilla* proves that Masada is one of the most exciting jazz ensembles in the world, bar none. *—Sean Westergaard*

Parachute Years, 1977-1980 / Tzadik ♦♦♦♦
The Parachute Years is a seven-CD box of John Zorn's first self-produced recordings, including his systems for structured improvisation based on games (namely "Lacrosse," "Hockey," "Pool," and "Archery"), as well as over two hours of previously unreleased outtakes, rehearsals, etc. Zorn first began developing his game-based ideas in 1974, inspired by the works of such modern composers as Braxton, Kagel, Stockhausen, and Wolff. Two discs worth of "Lacrosse" are here: the first (from June 1978) offers six takes ranging from six to 20 minutes in length performed by Zorn, Mark Abbott, Polly Bradfield, Eugene Chadbourne, and LaDonna Smith; the second presents the original "Lacrosse" recording (from one year earlier) featuring Zorn, Chadbourne, Henry Kaiser, and Bruce Ackley. Next comes a single disc of "Hockey." Two lineups offer their interpretations: first, there are four electric takes (1978) by Chadbourne, Wayne Horvitz, and Bob Ostertag; these are followed by 13 acoustic interpretations by Bradfield, Zorn, and Mark E. Miller. "Pool" was written in March 1979, and the recording included here took place one year later with musicians Zorn, Bradfield, Ostertag, Miller, and Charles K. Noyes, with prompter Lesli Dalaba. The three CDs of "Archery" (one of which is all rehearsals) document a 12-piece ensemble organized in 1981 and consisting of Robert Dick, George Lewis, Anthony Coleman, Kramer, Bill Laswell, Tom Cora, David Moss, Wayne and Bill Horvitz, Chadbourne, Bradfield, and Zorn. This box set is for dedicated fans already intrigued by the early annals of Zorn and his musical game theories. However, Zorn skeptics and listeners with less patience for theory (or history) should definitely avoid *The Parachute Years*. This set will not win anyone over; nor will the theories become more clear upon listening. The recordings in *The Parachute Years* helped the participants—inspired and creative musicians, all—to grow, but they also have more historical value than listening interest. *—Joslyn Layne*

Peter Zummo

b. 1948
Trombone / Improvisation, Avant-Garde, Electronic
Instrument training, trombone and other winds with the legendary Carmine Caruso. Also studied with Roswell Rudd, Jim Fulkerson, didgeridoo with Stuart Dempster, electronic music with Alvin Lucier, and was in the World Music program at Wesleyan University. Zummo's many compositions for ensemble (incl. Zummo Labs, the Environmental Combo, etc.) build on original melody and melodic fragments, generating interactive situations for musicians. *Radical Filtering* premiered at the BAM Next Wave Festival, *Semiotic Handgun* premiered at Lincoln Center Out-Of-Doors, *Fast Dream* at Boston Opera House. Many commisions and grants. Music for dancer Trisha Brown's *Newark* and *Lateral Pass*, and several other dance and theater works. *— "Blue" Gene Tyranny*

Zummo with an X: Contains: Instruments (1980)/Song IV from the Suite Six Songs / 1985 / Loris Bend Foundation ♦♦♦♦♦
"Instruments" is a pure, spare study of musical intervals with a gently humorous quality, using phase (mobile) techniques to produce variations… the "Six Songs" are all played over the same peacefully persuasive tabla pulse from Bill Ruyle… Arthur Russell's singing and cello playing (harmonics, counter-rhythms) together creating one warm voice… and Peter Zummo's open and muted trombone statements (simple riffs, sweet pleas and, sometimes, snores)… all combine to make an irresistible mental dance. Highly recommended. *— "Blue" Gene Tyranny*

● **Experimenting with Household Chemicals** / 1995 / Experimental Intermedia ♦♦♦

Slybersonic Tromosome / 2000 / Penumbra ♦♦♦♦
Acoustic versus synthesized, breathing versus bleeping, live versus studio: *Slybersonic Tromosome* is all about contrasts and opposites meeting. Peter Zummo is a virtuoso on the trombone. His extended technique covers a lot of aural ground, an impression emphasized by his use of unusual instruments like didgeridoo and irrigation hose. Tom Hamilton plays electronics and synthesizers. They have been working together since 1993 but *Slybersonic Tromosome* is their first recording as a duet. Both instrumentalists been recorded separately and then integrated through digital mixing. Although there was live interaction at the session, there was also subsequent studio tampering. This work method allows better mixing of the electronics (stereo panning, depth in the mix), resulting in a more lively and—paradoxically enough—interactive performance on CD. It sounds like Zummo and Hamilton relate to each other on a subconscious level as they anticipate the other's move. The electronics take at times an almost electroacoustical quality, dressing up the music in an almost "thoroughly composed" fashion. The music contains a healthy dose of humor tha translates into track titles like "Neural Sturgeon" and "Trance for the Bopanon Set." A very enjoyable CD requiring a lot of the listener's attention, *Slybersonic Tromosome* was released in a numbered limited edition of 600. *—François Couture*

Various Artists

20 Ans De Musique Contemporaine i Metz (20 Years of Contemporary Music at Metz) / 1991 / Col Legno ✦✦✦
A five-CD set with booklet containing premieres of important contemporary works, mostly orchestral. The set contains works by Rolf Gehlhaar ("Phase," 1972), Yoshihisa Taïra ("Radiance," 1973), Morton Feldman ("Piano and Orchestra," 1975), Pierre Boulez ("Rituel in Memoriam Bruno Maderna," 1976), Kazimierz Serocki ("Pianophonie," 1978), Iannis Xenakis ("Jonchaies," 1981), Michaël Levinas ("Les Rires du Gilles" ["The Laughter of Gilles"], 1981), Bernd Alois Zimmermann ("Musique Pour les Soupers du Ubu Roi" ["Music for the Suppers of King Ubu"], 1982), György Ligeti ("Magyar Etüdök" ["Hungarian Etudes for 16-Voice A Cappella Choir"], 1983), Paul Méfano ("La Scéne III," 1984), Klaus Huber ("2. Streichquartett Erster Satz" ["Second String Quartet, First Movement"], 1985), Younghi Pagh-Paan ("Nim," 1987), John Cage ("ASLSP Organ 2," 1987), Luigi Nono ("A Carlo Scarpa Architetto Ai Suoi Infiniti Possibili" ["To Carlo Scarpa, Architect, To His Infinite Possibilities"], 1987), Mauricio Kagel ("Quodlibet," 1988), Carlos Roqué Alsina ("Suite Indirecte," 1989), Bruno Maderna ("Giardino Religioso" ["The Religious Garden"], 1989), and Hans Zender ("Furin No Kyo" [literal translation: "Wind Bell Stillness Mute"], based on a Zen text sung in four languages, 1989). *—"Blue" Gene Tyranny*

The Aerial # 2: A Journal in Sound / 1990 / Aerial ✦✦✦✦✦

The Aerial # 3: A Journal in Sound / 1991 / Aerial ✦✦✦✦✦
Another wonderful compilation covering a variety of styles. Contains: Ellen Fullman Staggered Stasis, Mark Barreca Messier Crosses the Blue Line, Nicolas Collins Tobabo Fonio, Peter Cusack Dandelion Clock, Tom Guralnick Over Time, Johanna Beyer/Essential Music IV for Percussion, Zae Munn Interface, Myra Melord/Marion Brandis Duo Three Interludes, William Hooker The Dream:Red, and Lesli Dalaba *Core Sample* (Sylvan). *—"Blue" Gene Tyranny*

The Aerial # 5: A Journal in Sound / 1992 / Aerial ✦✦✦✦✦
A compilation of great spoken and radiophonic works. Contains: Willem De Ridder & Hafler Trio *Report,* Helen Thorington In the Dark, Gustavo Matamoros Portrait: Bob Gregory, Sarah Peebles Excerpts from Kai, Sydney Davis Star Axis Philip Corner Gong/Ear Richard Klein & Mark Hosler Wildman The Machine for Making Sense Changing the Subject and Derek Bailey *In My Studio.* *—"Blue" Gene Tyranny*

The Alternative Schubertiade / 1999 / CRI Emergency Music ✦✦✦
1997 marked the 100th anniversary of Franz Schubert's death. All around the world, schubertiades took place in various forms. The contemporary classical label CRI contributed to the commemoration by inviting a handful of more experimental composers (mainly taken from their Emergency Music roaster) to revisit and reinterpret Schubert. A concert was organized by Phil Kline on September 12, 1997, and the best results are featured on *The Alternative Schubertiade.*

For a theme album, this one holds the road very well. Schubert's music is used as inspiration, sound source, or simply as a starting point. Nick Didkovsky tampers with the "Impromptu in Eb Major" by adding computer-analyzed performance statistics. Phil Kline sees a journey into the underworld behind a trill of the "Bb Major Piano Sonata." Roger Kleier creates a soundscape with a fragment of a melody taken from the "Ninth Symphony." But the most surprising results are David First's treatment of nine measures from "Gretchen Am Spinnrade" and the very moving "URWhatU8," an interpretation of the "Unfinished Symphony" on electric guitars by John Myers. Of the meeting between old and new comes a fascinating collection of works. *—François Couture*

Ambiances Magnétiques, Vol. 1: La Bastringue Migratoire / 1996 / Ambiances Magnétiques ✦✦✦

Ambiances Magnétiques, Vol. 3: Inedits / 1998 / Ambiances Magnetiques ✦✦✦
For the third installment in its compilation series, the label Ambiances Magnétiques decided to give the fans something new: The first two volumes comprised only previously available material and were targeted toward the neophyte, but *Inédits* (Unreleased) was a fan pleaser. This CD contains tracks from all nine members of the Ambiances Magnétiques collective: René Lussier, André Duchesne, Jean Derome, Robert Marcel Lepage, Joane Hétu, Diane Labrosse, Danielle Palardy Roger, Michel F. Côté, and Martin Tétreault. Most pieces were recorded at Studio 270 with engineer Robert Langlois (*Ambiances Magnétiques* members' usual hangout, therefore, sound quality is often excellent) and represent transitional experiments. Some others were recorded by Radio-Canada (Canada's national radio) and document live projects that never made it on record. It is interesting to note that some performances already hinted at the direction these musicians would take in the late '90s (especially Côté's trio Klaxon Gueule, Lussier, and Hétu). *Inédits* contains valuable contributions from Lussier and a noisier than usual suite from Derome (very nice) but the album is most noticeable for the contributions of more discreet musicians. Since his 1992 CD *Locomotive,* André Duchesne has been very quiet and even though his "Les Barrages" (The Dams) is an unremarkable excerpt from a symphonic work, "Les Toasts Brûlées" (Burned Toasts) is the only existing document from his short-lived band Diesel. Danielle Palardy Roger is another discreet artist; her two performances exemplify her work outside Ambiances Magnétiques' "girl groups" (Wondeur Brass, Les Poules, Justine). Finally, the excerpt from Martin Tétreault's "Chronique Du Disque" (an unreleased radio piece) is one of his best performances. Fans of Ambiances Magnétiques will find a lot to explore and be surprised about on *Inédits.* *—François Couture*

☆ **Another Coast (New Works from the West)** / Music & Arts ✦✦✦✦✦

Anthology of Music for the 21st Century Leonardo Music Journal Vol.1 No.1 / ✦✦✦
This recording contains music by Marc Battier, Sarah Hopkins, Larry Austin, Ed Osborn, Daniel Goode, I.Wayan Sadra (gamelan), Craig Harris, Amnon Wolman, Graeme Gerrard, and Steven Paxton with Paula Claire, David Rothenberg, Simon Running, and Erling Wood. Last, but not least, the compilation includes Kenneth Atchley's take on *Don Giovanni* (Act 1, Scenes 1-4); it's a musical conversation with the characters of Da Ponte's libretto for Mozart's opera about the cultural myth of Don Juan and the history of our attitudes about sexuality (and "going to hell" for sharing sensual feeling). A subtle, surreal evocation for voices and electronics with a highly poetic and intelligent text by the composer. *—"Blue" Gene Tyranny*

Bang on a Can Live, Vol. 1 / 1991 / CRI ✦✦✦✦✦
A collection of live performances from the annual new music festival in Manhattan—includes: Alison Cameron "Two Bits", Bill Doerfeld "Evening Chant", Michael Gordon "Strange Quiet", Tom Johnson "Failing", Scott Lindroth "Relations to Rigor", Julia Wolfe "The Vermeer Room" and Evan Ziporyn "Luv Time". *—"Blue" Gene Tyranny*

Cassette Mythos Audio Alchemy CD/K7 / 1991 / What Next? ✦✦✦
A great deal of the newest music is found only on cassettes or computer discs that are freely exchanged through the mail or available through word-of-mouth contacts and small publications soliciting contributions. (One might be reminded of Frankie Mann's remark that some of the best music in the country is made by "12 year olds in their attics with cassettes.") This is a collection with some of the most inspired, sometimes gawd-awful, but always unique samplings of the cassette culture—maybe more in the air than underground. There are 21 selections: Heather Perkins' "What You Think Will Happen Will," Ric E. Braden's "Columbus Ave. 10 PM," Jim Steele's "Splatter Experience of the Green Gods," Daniel Johnston's "Grievances," John Wiggins' "Timbre Melody," Yximalloo's "China-Pong," Qubais Ghazala's "The Delphian Oracle," Frederick Lonberg-Holm's "The Second Minuet," Costes' "Oh Fortuna," the Kitchen Table Ensemble's "Exploded Views," Solomonoff & Von Hoffmanstahl's "Banzai Noir," Vosch's "Tunnel at Dawn," Philip Perkins' "Remoting (Excerpt From Berkeley Remote)," Minyy's "Sspress," Triptic of a Pastel Fern's "Shiny Things," Gregory Whitehead's "It Makes Me Blush . . . ," Mystery Laboratory's "Excerpt From V.T.," Bat Lenny's "Delphi ((tm) +)," Collapse/Relapse's "Webs," Hope Organ's "Sneaky," and a piece for which no composer is given entitled "Tentatively, a Convenience Drying Clothes Made Entirely From Zippers (Partial Cycle)." *—"Blue" Gene Tyranny*

CDCM Computer Music Series Vol. 10: The Virtuoso in the Computer Age—*I, The* / Centaur ✦✦✦✦✦
This recording features music by Paul Lansky ("As If" for string trio and computer-synthesized sound), Larry Austin ("Montage: Themes and Variations for Violin and Computer Music on Tape" [1985]), and John Melby ("Concerto No. 1 for Flute and Computer-Synthesized Tape" [1984]). Also included are David Rosenboom's "A Precipice in Time" (1966), a unique blend of "free jazz," live "phantom doubles" (computer resynthesis of acoustic instruments), and graphed structure, and an excellent performance of Anthony Braxton's 1982 "Composition No. 107 (Excerpt)", a "dry and glass-like sound universe" punctuated with high-energy improvisation. Braxton has taken the "graph score" to a new level for his compositions involving a combination of spontaneous and charted playing, and has extended his imagination into the future—like Charles Ives in his "Universe Symphony" to be played from mountaintops—to pieces to be played from planet to planet. *—"Blue" Gene Tyranny*

CDCM Computer Music Series Vol. 17: Music from the Center for Contemporary Music (Ccm) / 1994 / Centaur ✦✦✦
A great collection of unique compositional interests that somehow adds up to a West Coast sound. The recording includes works by John Bischoff ("The Glass Hand," 1992), Chris Brown ("Chain Reaction," 1991 [performed by ROOM with Chris Brown, piano and MIDI-piano, William Winant, Airdrums MIDI-controller, Larry Ochs, tenor sax, and Scot Gresham-Lancaster, computer and electronics]), and Tom Erbe ("After a Day," 1991). Also included are Maggi Payne's "Resonant Places" (1992), Alvin Curran's "Animal Behavior" (1992), and the collaborative composition "CCM Flotsam" (1993), which consists of short segments that can be ordered any way the listener desires on a programmable CD player. Highly recommended. *—"Blue" Gene Tyranny*

CDCM Computer Music Series Vol. 25: The International Computer Music Assoc / 1997 / Centaur ✦✦✦✦✦
A collection of five notable recent computer music compositions: Stephen Montague's "Silence: John, Yvar and Tim" (1994) is a set of three elegies for composers John Cage (employing Cage's ideas of the prepared piano and strings), Yvar Mikhashoff (employing material from a tango written for Mikhashoff's tango collection project), Tim Souste (which borrows material from Souster's "Hambledon Hill" string quartet); Canadian composer Jonty Harrison's "Unsound Objects" (1995, rev. 1996) is a well-crafted piece in the tradition of classic early electronic music; Canadian composer Michael Matthews' "In Emptiness, Over Emptiness" (1994) is an eerie and dynamic work for soprano and computer music on tape, existing both as an independent concert piece and also as part of a music theater work entitled "Madrugada" ("I wish plants in the fields could talk, They must have tears! They must have songs! To hatch a crow, a black rainbow bent in emptiness over emptiness but flying . . ."); the Buenos Aires-based composer Ricardo Dal Farra's "Tierra y Sol" (Earth and Sun) (1996) was built from ancient woodwind instruments of the Andes, more contemporary cross-cultural instruments and the relatively recent guitar introduced during the Spanish colonization . . . it is an attempt to express "the people's vital cycle living high on the mountains of Ecuador, Peru, Bolivia, northern Chile and Argentina" (Dal Farra); the concluding composition is Frances White's poetic "Birdwing" (1996) for shakuhachi and computer music on tape. *—"Blue" Gene Tyranny*

CDCM Computer Music Series Vol. 7: Ear Studios at Rensselaer Polytechnic Institute, Tro / Centaur ✦✦✦
Music by Neil B. Rolnick "Vocal Chords" (1988) for voice and digital processors, and "A Robert Johnson Sampler" (1987), Pauline Oliveros "Lion's Tale" (1989) for digital sampler, Julie Kabat "Child and the Moon-Tree" (1989) for vocalist and electronics, Barton McLean "Visions of a Summer Night" (1989) (nocturnal tone poems, beautifully formed computer sounds expressing different night sensations, for MIDI-based computer system), and Joel Chadabe "Modalities" (1989) for interactive computer music system. *—"Blue" Gene Tyranny*

Century XXI—*UK, A—M* / 1996 / New Tone ♦♦♦
Fascinating new works from composers residing in the British Isles: Steve Martland "Re-Mix," and Graham Fitkin "Flak," Orlando Gough "Drowning" (Parts 1—3), John Godfrey "Euthanasia . . . ," David Cunningham "Canta," and Laurence Crane "The Swim." *—"Blue" Gene Tyranny*

Century XXI—*UK, N—Z* / 1996 / New Tone ♦♦♦
More fascinating new works from composers residing in the British Isles: Michael Nyman "Waltz," and Jocelyn Pook "Oppenheimer," Howard Skempton "Lullaby," Andrew Poppy "Poems and Toccatas No. 10," Jeremy Peyton Jones "Deadwood," Nicholas Wilson "Darwin," Glyn Perrin "Cri/Me," and John Stanley "Spire." *—"Blue" Gene Tyranny*

Century XXI—*USA I*—Electronics / 1995 / New Tone ♦♦♦
Five electronic compositions from some of the most productive imaginations in the States: Carl Stone "Kamiya Bar (excerpts)," Ben Neill "678 Streams," Mikel Rouse "Autorequiem," Kyle Gann "Ghost Town," Nicholas Collins "Devil's Music (remixed version)." *—"Blue" Gene Tyranny*

Century XXI—*USA II*—Electroacoustics / 1995 / New Tone ♦♦♦
Newly issued and rare tracks by Rhys Chatham "An Angel Moves Too Fast To See (5th Movement)", Evan Ziporyn "Be In", Dave Soldier "Utah Dances (Jig, Fugue in One Voice, Cortijo, Allemande, Forty-nine and double)", Michael Gordon, "Strange Quiet", Glenn Branca "Les Honneurs du Pied (parts I and II)", and Lois Vierk "Go Guitars". *—"Blue" Gene Tyranny*

Cold Blue Anthology / Cold Blue ♦♦♦♦♦

Concert Imaginaire, GRM (Imaginary Concert) / Adda ♦♦♦
A good collection of "musique concrete" pieces by The GRM (Groupe de Recherches Musicales, Group for Musical Research) : J. Schwarz "And Around", Bernard Parmegiani "La Roue Ferris", Pierre Schaeffer-Pierre Henry "Erotica —symphonie pour un homme seul", Michel Chion "La Ronde". Jacques Lejeune "L'invitation au depart", Ivo Malec "Reflets", Jean Schwarz "Suite N", Christian Zanesi "D'un jardin a l'autre", Denis Dufour "Bocalises", Philippe Mion "Puzzlasept", Francois Bayle "Erosphere". *—"Blue" Gene Tyranny*

A Confederacy of Dances, Vol. 1: Live Recordings From The Roulette Series / Einstein ♦♦♦♦♦

A Confederacy of Dances, Vol. 2 / 1994 / Einstein ♦♦♦
Smashing genres, this collection of live recordings from a music series at Roulette in New York City is an interesting look at some of the leading postmodernists of the '80s and early '90s. Irène Schweitzer has never sounded better than on her solo piece, "Unexpected Demand," where she seems to encompass the whole history of the instrument. The same cutting-edge quality is found on the duo number featuring LaDonna Smith on viola and voice and Davey Williams on electric guitar. The other tracks are a mixed bag, with Robert Ashley's fine premiere of "Love Is a Good Example" a good introduction to his work, and Jerome Cooper's eerie multi-instrumentalist musical recitation on "They Told Me This—But They Did That" curiously appealing. Well-packaged with extensive liner notes, this avant-garde smorgasbord should turn a few heads. *—Steve Loewy*

Cultures Electroniques / 6 : Les Magisteres Du 19e Concours International De Musique El / Harmonia Mundi ♦♦♦
An excellent compilation of elegant, subtle and poetic electronic works including Bernard Parmegiani (1927-) "Exercisme 3" (Exercise/ Exorcism 3) (1986), Barry Truax (1947-) "Riverrun" (1986), Wilhelm Zobl (1950-) "Andere die Welt, Sie brauchtes" (Change the World, It Needs Changing) (1973), and James Dashow (1944-) "Whispers Out of Time" (1976). *—"Blue" Gene Tyranny*

Cultures Electroniques / 6 : Prix Quadrivium / Bourges 1991" / Harmonia Mundi ♦♦♦
Another interesting collection of prize-winning electro-acoustic pieces, although sometimes their "tastefulness" makes them seem somewhat similar. Especially unique are Andrew Lewis' (from Great Britain, born 1963) "Time and Fire," Mike Vaughan's (from Great Britain, born 1954) "Ensphered" for soprano sax and tape, Ake Parmerud's (from Sweden, born 1953) "Alias," Justice Olsson's (from France, born in Johannesburg in 1949) "Up!," and Alicyn Warren (United States, 1955) "Longing for the Light." Other compositions are Cort Lippe's (United States, 1953) "Music for Harp and Tape," David Arzouman's (United States, 1955) "Precipitation," Jon Appleton's (United States, 1939) "Stereopticon," Roderik De Man's (Pays Bas, born in Indonesia, 1941) "Chordis Canam," and Georg Katzer's (West Germany, 1935) "Rondo." *—"Blue" Gene Tyranny*

Electro Clips (25 Instantanés Électroacoustiques / 25 Électroacoustic Snaps / 1990 / Empreintes Digitales ♦♦♦

☆ **Electroacoustic Music: Classics** / Neuma ♦♦♦♦♦

Electronic Music / Folkways ♦♦♦

Emre (Dark Matter) / Nov. 1, 2000 / SouRce Research Recordings ♦♦♦♦♦
A project directed by SouRce Research Recordings' Ian Mackinnon, *Emre (Dark Matter)* has at its basis a proposition to work on darkness and light. The resulting gloomy album of avant-garde electronics shows that selected artists decided to concentrate on the former. Each track was created for the purpose of this album and one of its strengths is its cohesion. SouRce Research opens and closes the album with two short pieces of bleeping electronics. Cyclobe contributes a demented track, haunted by cat-like supplicating meows and claustrophobic atmospheres: delightfully deranged, although very restrained decibel-wise. Andrew Poppy's "Blind Fold" brings anticlimactic contrast with its stripped-down electric piano piece. The sparse notes and erratic playing recalls pianist Ernesto Diaz-Infante (but deprived from his usual serenity). This piece is much more convincing than Poppy's CD *Time at Rest Devouring Its Secret.* COH gets very close to *musique concrète* while Leif Elggren's association with SouRce Research gave birth to a disquieting piece of soft hiss, burbling electronics, and treated voice (reminiscent of Elggren's "Mother!?" on the Ash International compilation album *Hiss*). Coil blends noise with electronics, samples, and a male voice reciting "As I fell into the water, I slipped and broke my aura": the album's highlight. Ovum provides a slice of noise before the soft closing electronics. *Emre (Dark Matter)* is a compelling journey into the darkest regions of the psyche, demented cutting-edge electronic experimentation, and one of the strongest compilation albums in this field. Very strongly recommended. *—François Couture*

Essential Music: Ten Years of Essential Music / 1997 / Monroe Street ♦♦♦♦♦
An excellent assembly of truly innovative and engaging music from 8 very different composers: Johanna M. Beyer "Music of the Spheres" (1938), an eerie and mysterious work for cello, lion's roar, other strings and small percussion; Robert Ashley "in memoriam . . . Kit Carson (opera)" (excerpt) (1963), an early graph work that forms a dense soundscape for multiple instrumental groups; Peter Garland "A Green Pine" (1990), a lovely and moving simple melody for soprano and accordion; John Kennedy "Chant" (1988) for low-pitched intoning percussion; Christian Wolff "Merce" (excerpt) (1993) for percussion, sounding a bit like deconstructed Chinese opera; Malcolm Goldstein "The Seasons:Vermont Winter" (excerpt) (1980-82) for chamber orchestra including Ben Neill on his instrument the mutantrumpet, an evocative tone poem of isolated sounds and gestures that is truly in love with its subject; Kyle Gann "Snake Dance No. 2" (1995) for percussion and keyboard, a spirited and spirit-evoking polyrhythmic study; and Charles Wood "Land's Shadow, Visible World" (1988), a mysterious study of massive surfaces and sound-edges (reminding this writer of white noise ganzfelds that evoke pre-conscious feeling/thought, eg. voices in the wind) for percussion. *—"Blue" Gene Tyranny*

Experimental Theater / Tellus ♦♦♦
Sound from "performance art" presentations: Spalding Gray "Sex and Death to the Age 14 (excerpt)"/ Vulcan Death Grip with Ann Magnuson "Get It Up Or Get Out" (1986) vocals with band/ Mike Kelley with Sonic Youth "Plato's Cave, Rothko's Chapel, Lincoln's Profile" (1986) / Jerri Allyn "Queer Revolution" (1984)/ Ann Magnuson "Arachnae X. Pudenda" (1987) / Lydia Lunch "The Cancer Has Finally Become Contagious" (1987). *—"Blue" Gene Tyranny*

☆ **Extended Voices; the Brandeis University Chamber Chorus, Alvin Lucier, Director** / Odyssey ♦♦♦♦♦

Flies in the Face of Logic: Piano Music by Didkovsky, MacLean and Vrtacek / 1994 / Pogus ♦♦♦♦♦
Twenty-three tracks for, or rather, about the piano by three composers, none of whom play the piano. *—"Blue" Gene Tyranny*

Futura 1-5 (Soundtext Poetry) / Cramps ♦♦♦
A great series of poetry utilizing vocal sounds as well as words, called "soundtext" in the States. It isn't necessary to know the base language in which the poem-performances are given. Futura 1—"La declamazione futurista (The futurist declamation)", and "Lo Zaum', linguaggio trasmentale (Zaum', the transmental language)"; Futura 2—"Simultaneismo francese (French simultaneism)", and "Precursori e dadaisti in Germania (Forerunners and dadists in Germany)"; Futura 3—"L'urlo: Antonin Artaud (The howl: ultralettristes)" and "La poesia sonora oggi (Sound poetry today)"; Futura 4 and 5— "La poesia sonora oggi (Sound poetry today)". *—"Blue" Gene Tyranny*

Gay American Composers / 1996 / CRI ♦♦♦
An incredible overview of contemporary music from academic to eclectic styles, wonderfully performed by various groups including the Kronos Quartet. The CD was assembled to present the question "Is there a gay sensibility to American classical music—" Contains: Robert Helps Homage á Rachmaninoff, Lee Hoiby I Was There, Lou Harrison from String Quartet Set: Variations; Estampe, Chester Biscardi Invitation to Desire: Tango, Ned Rorem from The Nantucket Songs, David Del Tredici Fantasy Pieces, Robert Maggio Desire Movement, Conrad Cummings In the Department of Love, William Hibbard Bass Trombone, Bass Clarinet, Harp, Jerry Hunt Lattice, Lou Harrison Serenade for Betty Freeman & Franco Assetto, Chris DeBlasio Walt Whitman in 1989, and Robert Helps Homage á Fauré. *—"Blue" Gene Tyranny*

Haikus Urbains / 1997 / Cave 12 ♦♦♦♦
The Cave 12 Disques label of Geneva has produced a diverse compilation of music experimentalists and improvisers from around the world. *Haikus Urbains* ("urban haikus") is a concept album similar to the Resurgent compilation *Miniatures,* in which artists are asked to contribute a piece of approximately one minute in length. On *Haikus Urbains,* each artist also remixes their piece for an out-of-order appearance for the last half of the disc. The album features a lineup of world-renowned new music artists such as turntablist and sine wave experimenter Otomo Yoshihide; violinists Iva Bittova, Jon Rose, and Carlos Zingaro; guitarist Fred Frith; multi-instrumentalist Frank Pahl; Hoahio's Haco, Luc, Andy Ex, late NY cellist Tom Cora, and many more. The result is a variety of instrumental styles and sounds, with interest for any experimental ears. *—Joslyn Layne*

☆ **Hallelujah, Anyway—*Remembering Tom Cora*** */ May 18, 1999 / Tzadik* ♦♦♦♦♦
Hallelujah Anyway is an important retrospective of underrecognized and versatile cellist Tom Cora. A worthy eulogy, released one year after his death, this double-disc set includes songs written in his memory, songs that he composed for others, and a great cross-section of the myriad projects and musical contexts that Cora embraced. And that means a cross-section of all the creative experimenters and improvisers in avant garde rock, jazz, etc. spanning the late '70s through the late '90s. This collection includes some of Cora's solo recordings, as well as projects with John Zorn, Carlos Zingaro, Richard Teitelbaum, the Ex, Barre Philips, and the bands Curlew, Roof, Third Person (with Samm Bennett), the Chadbournes, and Skeleton Crew (with Fred Frith). Upbeat, eclectic, eccentric, beautiful—it's all here. This release is not only emotional, for the intense, loving commitment it shows to Cora's music, but also important, in that it illuminates the undervalued brilliance of a significant improviser and extraordinary cellist. Highly recommended for all with open ears. *—Joslyn Layne*

☆ **Imaginary Landscapes: New Electronic Music** / Elektra/Nonesuch ♦♦♦♦♦

Island of Sanity: New Music from New York City / 1987 / Review ♦♦♦♦♦

Jewel Box / Tellus 26 / 1992 / Tellus ♦♦♦
An excellent collection of works by women composers in avant-garde styles. Contains: Anne

LeBaron *Blue Harp Study 1, Laetitia Sonami Story Road, Sussan Deiham Navai, Bun Ching Lam EO-9066, Catherine Jauniaux* & Ikue Mori *Smell, Sapphire Boys Love Baseball, Mary Ellen Childs Ruler Etude: A Work in Progress, Michelle Kinney Coordinated Universal Time and Anne LeBaron* &Blue Harp Study 2. *— "Blue" Gene Tyranny*

Jon Gibson / Point Music ✦✦✦
The essential collection for understanding the variety of expressions possible in pattern or phase music (sometimes rather misleadingly called "minimal" music), with amazingly gorgeous saxophone playing by Jon Gibson. The recording includes Terry Riley's "Tread the Trail" (1964-65); Steve Reich's "Reed Phase" (1967); Philip Glass' "Bed From Einstein on the Beach (Act IV/2)" (1976); John Adams' "Pat's Aria From Nixon in China (Act II/I)" (1987); Philip Glass' "Gradus for Jon Gibson" (1968); Jon Gibson's "Waltz" (1981), "Song Three" (1976), and "Extensions II" (1981/1982) for sound environment and saxophone; Terry Jennings' "Terry's G Dorian 12-Bar Blues (9 X 5) + 3" (ca. June 1962); and LaMonte Young's "Any Integer (To Henry Flynt)" (April 1960). *— "Blue" Gene Tyranny*

Lesbian American Composers / 1998 / CRI ✦✦✦✦✦
Ten interesting works in diverse styles by as many composers: Pauline Oliveros' "Poem of Change" (1992) a powerful and thoughtful piece for evocative sound effects and voice and accordion, Nurit Tilles' alternatively sultry and light-hearted virtuosic piano work "Raw Silk (A Rag)" (1994), Linda Montano's mysterious "Portrait of Sappho" (1997) for voice, low drum and piano, Lori Freedman and Marilyn Lerner's "Barbie's Other Shoe" (1997) a lively jazzy work, Paula Kimper's lyrical and operatic "I Want To Live" from "Patience & Sarah" (1997), Eve Beglarian's "Wolf Chaser" (1995) a truly innovative work full of rich and intriguing timbres for violin, wolf chaser, percussion and electronics, Jennifer Higdon's wildly energetic ensemble work "running the edgE" (1996), Annea Lockwood's moving solo for soprano "I Give You Back" (1993), Madelyn Byrne's computer music composition "Winter" (1997) rich in imagery and mystery, and Ruth Anderson's sound collage "SUM (State of the Union Message)" (1973 /revised 1997). In the liner notes, the various composers discuss their thoughts about participating in this collection, as well as the musical ideas of the compositions. I've heard some people ask why "Lesbian American" should be used as a designation, but after centuries of musical dictionaires like "Men in Music" and the "Great Composers" (i.e. male, European) some alternative emphasis certainly seems long overdue; but more than that, we now live in a multi-cultural, and multi-everything else world, and, to quote from the album's liner notes "As beautiful, strong and diverse as the voices of women in America today, the music of these ten lesbian American composers speaks to the heart, soul and conscience of our times." So in answer to the question why? Why not? *— "Blue" Gene Tyranny*

Life is a Killer / Giorno Poetry Systems ✦✦✦✦✦
A Dial-A-Poem Poets life-centering collection of different ensembles of speakers with and without instrumental music. Works by Amiri Baraka, William S. Burroughs, Jim Carroll, Jayne Cortez, The Four Horsemen (B.P. Nichol, Steve McCaffery, Paul Dutton, Rafael Barreto Rivera), John Giorno, Brion Gysin, Rose Lesniak, Ned Sublette. *— "Blue" Gene Tyranny*

Music from Mills / Mills College ✦✦✦
A centennial anthology produced and compiled at the *Center for Contemporary Music at Mills College, this recording contains Lou Harrison*'s "Sonata No. 2" for cembalo, Terry Riley's "The Ethereal Time Shadow (Excerpt)," Luciano Berio's "Chamber Music," Dave Brubeck's "Summer Song," David Rosenboom's "In the Beginning: Etude 1 (Trombones)," Robert Ashley's "Flying Saucer Dialogue From the Opera Atalanta (Acts of God)," Anthony Braxton's "Composition No. 62 (+ 30 + 96)," David Behrman's "Interspecies Smalltalk, Part 2 (Excerpt)," Elinor Armer's "Thaw," Steve Reich's "Melodica," Maggi Payne's "Subterranean Network (Excerpt)," Darius Milhaud's "Segoviana," Pauline Oliveros' "Alien Bog (Excerpt)," Anthony Gnazzo's "Asparagas," Katrina Krimsky's "Apparitions," Larry Polansky's "Four Voice Cannon 3," Pandit Pran Nath's "Dira Dira Ta Na in Raga Bhairavi (Excerpt)," Janice Giteck's "Breathing Songs From a Turning Sky (Excerpt)," *"Blue" Gene Tyranny*'s "Remembering," Ramon Sender's "Audition (Excerpt)," and Morton Subotnick's "The Key to Songs (Excerpt)." *— "Blue" Gene Tyranny*

Music from the Once Festival / Advance ✦✦✦✦✦
The only recording of compositions from this legendary festival that presented the newest in avant-garde music, film and dance from 1961-1968. Contains: Gordon Mumma "Music from the Venezia Space Theatre", Robert Ashley "Crazy Horse Symphony", George Cacioppo "Time on Time In Miracles", Donald Scarvarda "Landscape Journey". *— "Blue" Gene Tyranny*

Music with Memory / Tellus ✦✦✦✦✦
A collection of works by composers who use microcomputers as their instruments. Includes Nicolas Collins "Devil's Music" (1985), John Driscoll "Stall" (excerpt) with Phil Edelstein and Peter Labiak's rotating robotic loudspeaker system (1981), Brenda Hutchison "Interlude from Voices of Reason" (1984), Ron Kuivila "Parodicals" and "Cannon Y for C.N." (1985), Paul DeMarinis "Eenie Meenie Chillie Beenie" (1983) and "Yellow Yankee" (1983). *— "Blue" Gene Tyranny*

Musicworks #55: Sound Ecology / 1993 / Musicworks ✦✦✦✦✦
With many interesting music selections/installations/ideas/talks prepared for the ~7e Printemps ...lectroacoustique (7th Electroacoustic Spring) held in Montreal in 1992, this CD contains 32 works concerned with the audio environment, appreciating it, preserving it, performing with it, changing it. Fascinating views and inventions, like Jacques Dudon's "Synthése Photosonique" (1992), a photo-sonic synthesizer which uses semi-transparent discs that reproduce imaginary soundwaves when light is shown through them. *— "Blue" Gene Tyranny*

Musicworks #60 : Plunderphonia & Vox / 1994 / Musicworks ✦✦✦✦✦
Several wonderful and wacky works built from sampled sounds of contemporary culture, recontextualized and de-constructed with the "plunderphonics" technique, and also several beautiful vocal works: John Oswald's "Power" (1975), "7th" (1988), "More from the Case of Death," by Agatha Smith (1991), "Urge/Manifold" from "Plexure" (1992-93); The Residents "Beyond the Valley of a Day in the Life" (from "The Residents Play the Beatles" (1977); Tibor Szemzö 's "The Sex Appeal of Death (in memoriam T.H.)" (1981) and "Airy Wedding" (1991); Gary Barwin's "Down to the Middle and Back Again" (1992); Christian Marclay's "Maria Callas" (1988); Paul Rapoport's "De spiritu sancto" (1993); Philip Strong's "plunderPHILe" (1992, 94); and Louis Andriessen's "Dubblespoor" (Double Track) for chamber ensemble. *— "Blue" Gene Tyranny*

Musicworks #68 : Tearing Down Borders / 1997 / Musicworks ✦✦✦✦✦
A wide variety of recent vocal and acoustic works including: a solo vocal improvisation (1996) by Sainkho Namtchylak; Ned Rothenberg (shakuhachi) and Sainkho Namtchylak (vocal) in "Ancient Garden" (1995); excerpts from "De puro amor" (On pure love) (1991) and "En amor duro" (In untiring love) (1991) by Maria de Alvear, performed by Eve Egoyan on piano; John Beckwith's "After images, after Webern" (1995) for guitar and cello; "Cage d'oiseau" (a pun on "birdcage" and "Cage for the birds" and John Cage's book For the birds) (1962) by Serge Garant for soprano and piano; David Demnitz's & "Graffiti Removal" (1983) and "Second Hand" (1985) both performed by the renowned group Gamelan Son of Lion. *— "Blue" Gene Tyranny*

Musique Expèrimentale Groupe De Recherches Musicales De La R.T.F. (Musical Research Gro / Disques ✦✦✦✦✦
This is an exquisite collection of musique concrète pieces. "Volumes" (1960) by Francois-Bernard Mache for 12-track tape and a chamber orchestra (consisting of seven trombones, two pianos, and two percussionists) creates cosmic sounds of great import on the distant horizon that slowly approach and suddenly disappear; there are small rattlings and great ones like crickets and breaking, impacting percussion. "Crucifixion (Excerpts)" by Romuald Vandelle is based on a poem by Poe spoken by a fragmented voice, gloomy and terrifying; the surreal, elegant "Ambiance II (Toast Funabre)" by Michel Philippot for woman's spoken voice and tape is based on a Mallarme text. One of the best musique concrète compositions and a soundtrack to stimulate the imagination, "Tautologos II" by Luc Ferrari features masses of speech-inflected, tape-manipulated sounds like conversations amongst alien beings, bizarre glasslike drones (rotating metal resonators on piano strings), and humorous mobiles of sounds that combine and recombine. "Texte II" (1953) by Andre Boucourechliev, described as "a form in movement" employing "controlled chance," was recorded on two tapes that are played simultaneously on two tape recorders so that coincidences of the mono tracks are always variable from performance to performance; for such an early piece, "Texte II" creates an astonishingly rich palette of sounds. *— "Blue" Gene Tyranny*

New Music China / Tellus ✦✦✦
Contains both new popular and folk music as well as new music: Fred Houn "I Wor Kuen (The Boxers)" from *Bamboo That Snaps Back*/Chen Yi "Xie Zi"/ Ge Gan-Ru "Yi Feng (Ancient Wind)" for solo cello/ Zhou Long "Kong Gu Liu Shui (Valley Stream)" for traditional ensemble/ Wu Wen Guang "Liu Shui (Flowing Water)" for guqin (ancient 7-string zither) / Tan Dun "Plucking Instruments Suite" (excerpt) / R.I.P. Hayman "Nightsongs" score from film about immigrant life in Chinatown/ Jing Jing Luo "Monologue Part 1"..she also writes for large orchestra and traditional Chinese ensembles. *— "Blue" Gene Tyranny*

New Music for Electronic and Recorded Media / 1750 Arch ✦✦✦
A great collection of music by contemporary women composers writing from 1938—1977. Contains a realization of Johanna Beyer's "Music of the Spheres" (1938), Annea Lockwood "World Rhythms", Pauline Oliveros "Bye Bye Butterfly" (1965), Laurie Spiegel "Appalachian Grove I", Megan Roberts "I Could Sit Here All Day", Ruth Anderson "Points", Laurie Anderson "New York Social Life", "Time to Go" and "For Diego". *— "Blue" Gene Tyranny*

New Music for Orchestra / Opus One ✦✦✦✦✦

☆ **OHM: The Early Gurus of Electronic Music** / Apr. 25, 2000 / Ellipsis Arts ✦✦✦✦✦
This three-CD, 42-track compilation, spanning 1937-1982 (though largely comprised of performances from the '60s and '70s), includes pieces by many of the big names in experimental electronic music: John Cage, Pauline Oliveros, Steve Reich, Terry Riley, Karlheinz Stockhausen, Milton Babbitt, Laurie Spiegel, Robert Ashley, LaMonte Young, Morton Subotnick, and Iannis Xenakis. That alone would make this anthology impressive, but there are also contributions from composers who have made some impact with rock and pop recordings (Brian Eno, Klaus Schulze, Holger Czukay of Can, Jon Hassell), along with some names that are not commonly discussed in highbrow serious music circles (Raymond Scott), some composers not always associated with electronic music (Olivier Messiaen, Edgard Varese), and a host of names that aren't too well known beyond the avant-garde community. What is most impressive about this set, however, is that is not only serves as a reasonable overview of pre-1980 electronic music, but also is much more accessible in content to non-experts than many such compilations would have been. Contrary to the stereotype of serious electronic music as being difficult to listen to, many of the pieces are quite engaging for novices and electronic specialists alike. That's not to say there aren't plenty of more jarring or abstract pieces with minimal ambience or cut-up assemblages, or even occasional tracks that most listeners might find downright annoying (such as MEV's cacophonous "Spacecraft," mercifully placed at the very end of the first disc). On the whole, however, the set achieves the effect of both educating and entertaining, and is likely to expand the audience for a music that is too often unwilling to offer inviting introductions that might incite listeners to explore further. The 98-page booklet includes detailed track descriptions and comments, usually by the composers/performers themselves. *— Richie Unterberger*

Panorama Alectronique / Mercury Limelight ✦✦✦✦✦
Classic pure electronic and musique concrete compositions from studios in Paris and Cologne. Includes: Pierre Henry "Entite", Gyorgy Ligeti "Artikulation", Herbert Eimert "Selection I", Mauricio Kagel "Transition I", Andre Boucourechliev "Texte I", and Henri Pousseur "Scambi". *— "Blue" Gene Tyranny*

Pioneers of Electronic Music / CRI ✦✦✦✦
The Columbia-Princeton sound from 1952 to 1971—compositions by Ussachevsky, Otto Luening (b. 1900), Pril Smiley, Bulent Arel, Mario Davidovsky, Alice Shields... recommended

cuts: "Incantation" by Luening and Ussachevsky, "Stereo Electronic Music" by Arel. — *"Blue" Gene Tyranny*

Pulse, the New Music Consort / New World ♦♦♦
A great collection with some classic percussion music. Contains: John Cage and Lou Harrison "Double Music" (1941), John Cage's rhythmically sophisticated "Second Construction" (1940) and jazzy "Third Construction" (1941), Henry Cowell "Pulse" (1939) for 6 percussionists, Harvey Sollberger "The Two and The One" (1972), and Lukas Foss "Percussion Quartet" (1983). — *"Blue" Gene Tyranny*

Radius #1: Transmissions from Broadcast Artists / 1993 / What Next? ♦♦♦
Imaginative, entertaining and definitely different sound creations for radio on strange subjects performed by even stranger subjects. Contains: Sheila Davies *What is the Matter in Amy Glennon?, Helen Thorington Partial Perceptions, and Terry Allen* &Bleeder. — *"Blue" Gene Tyranny*

Radius #2: Transmissions from Broadcast Artists / 1993 / What Next? ♦♦♦

Site-Less Sounds / Tellus ♦♦♦♦♦
Powerful personal and political visions by Shelley Hirsch *"39"/ Gregory Whitehead* "How To Pronounce 'Prothesis'", "M is for the Million Things", and "This Is Not A Test"/ David Moss "Conjure"/ Jacki Apple, Keith Antar Mason, Linda Albertano, Akilah Nayo Oliver "Redefining Democracy in America:Episodes in Black and White"/David Wojnarowicz and Ben Neill "The Collapse of the Illusory One-Tribe Nation from ITSOFOMO (In The Shadow of Forward Motion)" / Constance DeJong with Brenda Hutchinson "Vanishing Act". Highly recommended. — *"Blue" Gene Tyranny*

Sound Forms for Piano / 1995 / New World ♦♦♦
A welcome re-release on CD of great performances of works by four composers. Contains: Henry Cowell *The Banshee, &Aeolian Harp, and &Piano Piece (Paris 1924), John Cage* from *Sonatas and Interludes, Ben Johnston Sonata for Microtonal Piano, and Conlon Nancarrow* &Studies for Player Piano: # 1, # 27, # 36. — *"Blue" Gene Tyranny*

Tango / Apr. 8, 1997 / Tellus ♦♦♦♦♦
Re-takes on the idea and spirit of the tango. Includes works by Carlos Gardel, David Garland with Cinnie Cole and Zeena Parkins, Chris DeBlasio, Keith Keeler, B. Hutchinson with Gerry Lindahl, A. Tomlinson, Elodie Lauten, Jo Basile and Orchestra, *"Blue" Gene Tyranny*, Molly Elder, Mathew Nash, Christopher Berg, Fast Forward and Mader. — *"Blue" Gene Tyranny*

Timebomb: Live at the Clocktower Gallery / 1997 / Clock Tower ♦♦♦♦♦
A collection from "Timebomb," a series of four powerful and innovative performance events during the Fall of 1966 at the *Clocktower Gallery, New York City. The Selections include a wildly racuous and energized improv entitled "Zeitsite" (Timesite) with Elliott Sharp* (guitar) and John Zorn (sax); Bob Holman's poem "Comet" for voice with belltower and environmental sounds; Tracey Morris's rhythmically accumulative recitation "Chaingang"; Todd Colby's hilarious loud-mouthed neighborhood poem with variation on normal speech inflections "Ken and Kathy Had Twins!"; Emily XYZ's wonderfully rhythmic "They Don't Get It" for multiple voices; Edwin Torres enthusiastically de-constructed and interwoven Spanish and English poem "Edwin Tourist"; Rebecca Moore's noise blues "Niagara" for singer, two electric guitars, electric cello, and bass guitar; Zeena Parkins mysterious and fascinating "At Land (excerpt)" for electric harp and sampler; Judith Ren-Lay fast as a bat out of hell poem "Raging Bats (excerpt)"; Bradley Eros eerie soundtrack "illusion travels by" (film performance) excerpt from "Ocula" with electronically processed visual and sound loops from "Dracula"; Prema Murthy "Descending Staircase" for guitar and processed tape loops from a gallery tour (—); Mike Tyler's poetic ambiguity "You're Soaking In It"; Maggie Estep's love's almost over and almost out the door poem "You Suck"; and Lin Culbertson and Katie O'Looney's "Six on Four," a rhythmic extravaganza for keyboards and percussion. — *"Blue" Gene Tyranny*

Utopia Americana: Compilation Of American Music / New Tone ♦♦♦♦♦

Views from the Perfect City / 1995 / Inial ♦♦♦

Voice of the Computer / Decca ♦♦♦
Bell Labs computer music from the 1960's. Contains James Tenney "Stochastic Quartet", Max Mathews "Masquerades", "Slider" and "Swan Song", J.R. Pierce "Eight-Tone Canon" and J.C. Risset "Computer Suite From Little Boy." Risset is one of the early developers of computer music with Max Matthews at Bell Laboratories and at IRCAM in Paris; he creates exquisite textures in an aural space that constantly changes it dimensions. — *"Blue" Gene Tyranny*

Wergo Collection: Music of Our Century / Wergo ♦♦♦♦♦
An excellent sampler of 15 works giving a quick "taste" of many composers: Herbert Henck, Cage, Ligeti, Penderecki, Henze, Stockhausen, etc. — *"Blue" Gene Tyranny*

JAZZ

For all of its attributes and for all of its faults, Ken Burns' Jazz series did accomplish one remarkable thing—it got people interested in jazz again. Not just jazzbos or record hounds that are always interested in music, always interested in new acquisitions, but listeners that just love music. The kind of listener that always found jazz to be a little scholarly, or a little distant, something that just wasn't for them. The miniseries proved that wasn't the case, but it really just hit the tip of the iceberg. This jazz section digs deeper, delving deep into the catalogs of such titans as Duke, Louis, and Miles, while covering artists like Monk and Mingus that the series barely touched—and then digging further, revealing how jazz is still a vital, breathing life form today.

That's not to say that this is complete or definitive—for more detailed information and artists that aren't covered here, please turn to our edition devoted to jazz or search our website, allmusic.com. Yet this section is dense with information, enough to make a neophyte drunk with knowledge, and enough to make it interesting for those that know *Kind of Blue* and *Giant Steps* by heart, or hum "Big Butter and Egg Man" in their sleep.

The section plays to both audiences because there's so much there. In a sense, jazz music really does reflect the history of the 20th century, the history of what's commonly referred to as the American century. Jazz was the first popular music to be recorded, and it has remained a fixture of American culture ever since it exploded in the 1910s. It may not always have been at the forefront of American culture—once rock & roll captured the minds and wallets of American teenagers, it retreated to the background—but it was always there. There were always sects looking to keep the music pure, relying on classic music (thankfully preserved on classic recordings) as a template for their own music. These groups—whether it was the Dixieland revivalists of the '50s and '60s or the neo-bop classicists led by Wynton Marsalis in the '80s—did keep the music alive in a sense, since they kept the focus on the great musicians and innovators of jazz. Then, there've always been the restless explorers, intent on redefining what music (not just jazz) can do and what it means. These are the musicians whose music breaks boundaries, just like that of the accepted greats did in their era, but the modern innovators—anybody who's followed through with the innovations of John Coltrane and Ornette Coleman—make music that's not easily assimilated, so they can be marginalized at present, only to have their music discovered as breathtakingly fresh years later.

This section intends not to satiate both camps, but to perhaps draw a bridge between them, to possibly illustrate that while they have their differences, they do originate from the same source. True, some of these connections may arise from careful reading on the readers' part, but they are there, and neither camp is presented disparagingly. Neither are smooth jazz, fusion, revivalists, or any other contingent that is frequently dismissed by hardcore jazzbos. This gives everybody, no matter what their taste or jazz persuasion, something they like—and it might just help them discover another style or musician while they're at it. And what is jazz about, if it's not about discovery? *—Stephen Thomas Erlewine*

Jazz Styles

Because jazz in its 100 years has consistently inspired musicians to develop their own individual approaches to self-expression, there are almost as many different styles as there are innovators. The 19 categories listed in this section are a simplification that makes it possible to give readers a hint as to what particular musicians sound like. It should be assumed that the most original players do not fit neatly into any one style and that the boundaries between these terms are not absolute or uncrossable.

RAGTIME—Although not really jazz (ragtime does not have improvisation or the feeling of the blues), this style, at its prime during 1899-1915, was a strong influence on the earlier forms of jazz. Best-known as a piano music, ragtime (which is totally written-out) was also performed by orchestras. Its syncopations and structure, blending together aspects of classical music and marches, hint strongly at jazz and some of its melodies were played in later years by dixieland musicians.

NEW ORLEANS JAZZ—The first style of jazz, the music played in New Orleans from the time that Buddy Bolden formed his first band in 1895 until Storyville was closed in 1917 went totally unrecorded. However with the success of the Original Dixieland Jazz Band in 1917 and the many performances documented in the '20s, that situation changed. Ensemble oriented with fairly strict roles for each instrument, New Orleans jazz generally features a trumpet or cornet providing a melodic lead, harmonies from the trombone, countermelodies by the clarinet and a steady rhythm stated by the rhythm section (which usually consists of piano, banjo or guitar, tuba or bass and drums). This music is a direct descendant of marching brass bands and, although overlapping with dixieland, tends to de-emphasize solos in favor of ensembles. Due to its fairly basic harmonies and the pure joy of the ensembles, it is consistently the happiest and most accessible style of jazz.

CLASSIC JAZZ—The '20s were a rich decade with jazz-influenced dance bands and a gradual emphasis on solo (as opposed to collective) improvisations. Whether it be the stride pianists, the increasingly adventurous horn soloists or arranged music that predates swing, much of the jazz from this decade can be given the umbrella title of "Classic Jazz." Some of the modern-day revivalists who look beyond the dixieland repertoire to the music of Fletcher Henderson, Clarence Williams and Bix Beiderbecke (to name three examples) can be said to be playing in this open-ended style.

DIXIELAND—A style that overlaps with New Orleans jazz and classic jazz, dixieland has also been called "Chicago jazz" because it developed to an extent in Chicago in the '20s. Most typically the framework involves collective improvisation during the first chorus, individual solos with some riffing by the other horns, and a closing ensemble or two with a four bar tag by the drummer being answered by the full group. Although nearly any song can be turned into dixieland, there is a consistent repertoire of forty or so songs that have proven to be consistently reliable. This music has had a fairly large audience since its revival in the '40s.

SWING—Due to the utilization of more than three or four horns in big bands, it became necessary for ensembles to be written out. Swing caught on in the mid-'30s as dance music of the era and the saxophone grew in importance as did the role of the arranger. Swing differs from New Orleans jazz and dixieland in that the ensembles (even for small groups) are simpler and generally filled with repetitious riffs while in contrast the solos are more sophisticated. Individual improvisations still pay close attention to the melody but, due to the advance in musicianship, the solo flights are more adventurous while staying accessible.

BEBOP—Also known as bop, bebop was a radical new music that developed gradually in the early '40s and seemed to explode in 1945 with the emergence of Charlie Parker and Dizzy Gillespie. The main difference between bop and swing is that in the former the soloists engage in chordal (rather than melodic) improvisation, often discarding the melody altogether after the first chorus and using the chords as the basis for the solo. The virtuosic pacesetters of the style divorced themselves from the pop music world yet their once-futuristic style became a conservative alternative by the '60s to the avant-garde.

COOL (OR WEST COAST) JAZZ—Cool jazz is a mixture of bop with certain aspects of swing that had been overlooked or temporarily discarded. Dissonances were smoothed out, tones were softened, arrangements became important again and the rhythm section's accents were less jarring. Many of the style's leaders were based near the studios of Los Angeles, some of the recordings were experimental in nature (hinting at classical music) and for a period in the '50s this was a very popular style.

MAINSTREAM—The term "mainstream" was coined by critic Stanley Dance to describe the style that veterans of the swing era) were playing in the '50s, music between dixieland and bop. Although this idiom was overshadowed for quite awhile, with the rise of tenor saxophonist Scott Hamilton and trumpeter Warren Vache in the '70s and the beginning of the Concord label (which emphasized the music), mainstream (which is essentially small group swing) has become a potent force.

THIRD STREAM—"Third stream" (a term invented by composer Gunther Schuller in 1957) means a mixture of jazz and classical music. During the mid-to-late '50s, serious experiments took place although most attempts at fusing the two very different idioms have been at best mixed successes with non-improvising string sections tending to weigh down jazz soloists. Overshadowed by the avant-garde in the '60s, the idea of the third stream lives on and more recent projects have sometimes shown great promise.

LATIN (OR AFRO-CUBAN) JAZZ—Of the post-swing styles, Latin jazz has been the most consistently popular and it is easy to see why. The emphasis on percussion and Cuban rhythms make the style (essentially a mixture of loop-oriented jazz with Latin percussion) quite danceable and accessible. Among the pioneers in mixing together the two styles in the '40s were the big bands of Dizzy Gillespie and Machito and the music (which has never gone out of style) has remained a viable force through the '90s.

Artist Reviews

John Abercrombie (John L. Abercrombie)

b. Dec. 16, 1944, Port Chester, NY

Guitar / Post-Bop, Chamber Jazz

John Abercrombie's tying together of jazz's many threads made him one of the most influential acoustic and electric guitarists of the 1970s and early '80s; his recordings for ECM have helped define that label's progressive chamber-jazz reputation. More recently his star has faded somewhat, due largely to the general conservatism that's come to dominate jazz, though he has remained a vital creative personality. Abercrombie's style draws upon all manner of contemporary improvised music; his style is essentially jazz-based, but he also displays a more-than-passing familiarity with forms that range from folk and rock to Eastern and Western art musics.

Abercrombie attended Boston's Berklee College of Music from 1962 to 1966. While at Berklee, the guitarist toured with bluesman Johnny Hammond. After relocating to New York in 1969, Abercrombie spent time in groups led by drummers Chico Hamilton and Billy Cobham. It was with the latter's Spectrum group that Abercrombie first received widespread attention. Abercrombie's first album as leader was *Timeless*, a trio album with drummer Jack DeJohnette and keyboardist Jan Hammer. That was followed by *Gateway*, another trio with DeJohnette and bassist Dave Holland replacing Hammer. Abercrombie's subtle and lyrical style is heard to best effect in small, intimate settings—with the recurring *Gateway* trio, or as captured in duos with fellow guitarist Ralph Towner. *—Chris Kelsey*

• **Timeless** / Jun. 21, 1974-Jun. 22, 1974 / ECM ✦✦✦✦✦
Guitarist John Abercrombie's first in a long line of recordings for ECM was also his debut as a leader. Teamed up with Jan Hammer (who here plays organ, synthesizer and piano) and drummer Jack DeJohnette, Abercrombie plays four of his originals plus two by Hammer. These performances differ from many of the guitarist's later ECM dates in that Hammer injects a strong dose of fusion into the music and there is plenty of spirited interplay between those two with fine support by DeJohnette. Thought-provoking and occasionally exciting music that generally defies categorization. *—Scott Yanow*

Gateway / Mar. 1975 / ECM ✦✦✦✦✦
Guitarist John Abercrombie was one of the stars of ECM in its early days. His playing on this trio set with bassist Dave Holland and drummer Jack DeJohnette is really beyond any simple categorization. Abercrombie's improvisations are sophisticated, yet, because his sound is rockish and sometimes quite intense (particularly on the nearly 11-minute "Sorcery 1"), there is really no stylistic name for the music. Holland contributed four of the six originals while DeJohnette brought in the other two (one of which was co-written with Abercrombie). The interplay between the three musicians is quite impressive although listeners might find some of the music to be quite unsettling. It takes several listens for one to digest all that is going on, but it is worth the struggle. *—Scott Yanow*

Sargasso Sea / May 1976 / ECM ✦✦✦

Gateway 2 / Jul. 1977 / ECM ✦✦✦✦
Unlike the first Gateway album, this CD reissue puts more of an emphasis on the rockish side of guitarist John Abercrombie's style. Abercrombie (who also plays some electric mandolin) still indulges in close interplay with bassist Dave Holland and drummer Jack DeJohnette (who doubles a bit on piano) but the playing on the five group originals is generally more fiery than introspective. None of the individual selections are all that memorable but the group improvising does have plenty of surprising moments. *—Scott Yanow*

Characters / Nov. 1977 / ECM ✦✦✦✦
Always unique and uncompromising, John Abercrombie gained a good deal of his popularity from his solo playing. Not the virtuoso of his primary influences—Django Reinhardt, Tal Farlow and Jim Hall—Abercrombie is much more the introvert. He often bypasses traditional techniques to pursue experimental sounds and rhythms. Along with Ralph Towner, whom he has recorded with before (see *Sargasso Sea*), Abercrombie makes excellent use of space within both his compositions and solos. Upon the first listen there may not appear to be very much here; however, this music needs to be absorbed over several listens to appreciate Abercrombie's brilliance. *—Robert Taylor*

Witchcraft / Jun. 24, 1986-Jun. 25, 1986 / Justin Time ✦✦✦✦

Animato / Oct. 1989 / ECM ✦✦

While We're Young / Jun. 1992 / ECM ✦✦✦✦

Speak of the Devil / Jul. 1993 / ECM ✦✦✦

Gateway: Homecoming / Dec. 1994 / ECM ✦✦✦✦✦
The trio heard on this CD (guitarist John Abercrombie, bassist Dave Holland, and drummer Jack DeJohnette) recorded *Gateway* and *Gateway 2* for ECM back in 1975 and 1977. Although each of the musicians have grown musically since that time and has piled up plenty of accomplishments, the style of music that they perform when they come together as Gateway has remained largely unchanged. One could call it "creative fusion" or "post bop;" whatever the name, the music's success depends on a great deal of intuitive interplay between the talented players. John Abercrombie's often-distorted tone and use of color show hints of Bill Frisell (who must have learned from the example of the older guitarist). Dave Holland's bass is never predictable nor subservient to Abercrombie, and, even if the other musicians were allowed to coast, Jack DeJohnette's constantly rumbling drumming would keep the performances from ever getting too comfortable. Although the original music (which concludes with a quiet piece for DeJohnette's piano) is not for all jazz fans (Abercrombie's rockish sound may scare some off), the high improvisational level makes this a set deserving of close listens. *—Scott Yanow*

Open Land / Sep. 1998 / ECM ✦✦✦✦
Here, Abercrombie grafts three soloists—trumpeter Kenny Wheeler, tenor saxman Joe Lovano, and violinist Mark Feldman—onto his organ trio and comes out with an absorbing set of elegantly textured, poly-styled music laced with his drifting, occasionally jagged yet never overbearing guitar. On the title track and, not unexpectedly, on "Free Piece Suit(e)," the sextet veers onto the outside, but they always do so in a relaxed ECM manner, without jangling any nerves. "Little Booker," a reversal of the names of the short-lived trumpeter, is the nicest track, outfitted with a memorable tune, and "That's for Sure" has an off-kilter, loose-jamming country feeling. Both Lovano and Wheeler play sparely and tastefully, and Feldman occasionally emits a gust of shock fiddling but mostly stays within lyrical bounds. Adam Nussbaum's drumming is loose, unpredictable, and adaptable; Dan Wall's organ discreetly lays in the background or steps forth in the usual Jimmy Smith-derived idiom. *—Richard S. Ginell*

The Hudson Project / Oct. 17, 1998 / Stretch ✦✦✦

Muhal Richard Abrams

b. Sep. 19, 1930, Chicago, IL
Piano, Composer / Avant-Garde Jazz, Free Jazz, M-Base
Although somewhat underrated through the years due to his behind-the-scenes work, Muhal Richard Abrams was one of the most important figures to emerge from the Association for the Advancement of Creative Musicians (AACM), an organization whose successes would have been much fewer without his participation. Influential as an avant-garde pianist who bridged the gap between hard bop, free jazz and (to a certain extent) contemporary classical music, Abrams's additional significance as a composer, arranger and bandleader has long put him near the top of the avant-garde field. Abrams gained some early attention for his playing on the MJT+3's album *Branching Out*, and through the years gigged and/or recorded with such musicians as Max Roach, Sonny Stitt, Dexter Gordon, Eddie Harris, Ruth Brown and Woody Shaw. On May 8, 1965, he was a major force in the founding of the AACM, a still-active Chicago-based organization that emphasizes self-reliance by performing original compositions, organizing one's own concerts and educating the community (including younger musicians) about the new music. The innovators who emerged from the AACM (including the Art Ensemble of Chicago, Anthony Braxton and Henry Threadgill) invigorated the avant-garde, taking the music out of the potential dead-end of consistently intense improvisations into an appreciation of the value of space and silence and a logical mix of compositions with individual expression. *—Scott Yanow*

Levels and Degrees of Light / Jun. 7, 1967–Dec. 21, 1967 / Delmark ✦✦✦✦

Young at Heart/Wise in Time / Jul. 2, 1969–Aug. 20, 1969 / Delmark ✦✦✦
Muhal Richard Abrams, as the founder of the AACM in Chicago, has been one of the unsung leaders of the avant-garde ever since the mid-'60s. A versatile pianist, Abrams is heard in two different settings on this, his second session as a leader. "Young at Heart" finds him stretching out on a solo piano performance that hints at earlier styles while exploring the potential sounds and silence of free jazz. *Wise in Time* has Abrams functioning as part of an explorative quintet with trumpeter Leo Smith and altoist Henry Threadgill, both of whom were unknown youngsters at the time. Fascinating music, it is recommended strictly for the open-eared listener who does not demand that all jazz swing conventionally. *—Scott Yanow*

Things to Come from Those Now Gone / Oct. 10, 1972 / Delmark ✦✦✦
A masterpiece and one of the finest works in the contemporary (post-'50s free) jazz vernacular. Muhal Richard Abrams' compositions and piano solos illuminate multiple traditions, from stride and ragtime to the percussive style of the '50s and '60s. *—Ron Wynn*

Afrisong / Sep. 9, 1975 / India Navigation ✦✦✦

Sightsong / Oct. 13, 1975-Oct. 14, 1975 / Black Saint ✦✦✦✦✦
The reputation of members of the AACM (Association for the Advancement of Creative Musicians), of which Abrams is a founding member, has long been one of adventurous, dangerous, and difficult music. But in fact, much of the music created out of this organization shows enormous appreciation of the blues and earlier jazz forms. *Sightsong* is a splendid case in point. The album opens with four duets (two dedicated to Chicago legends Wilbur Ware and Johnny Griffin) which have a swing, a groove, and a delicacy that no fan of "straight-ahead" jazz could ignore. Favors, always one of the great underrated bassists in the music, provides a thick, soulful pulse and solos with huge imagination while Abrams always stays within the song's parameters which provide ample room for his creativity. As fine as these more "traditional" numbers are, the standout piece is perhaps Favors's solo feature, the wonderfully titled "Way Way Way Down Yonder." Opening with what sounds like the riffled pages of a book, Favors then states the deep, bluesy theme with strutting authority and proceeds through one of the richest investigations of the string bass the listener is ever likely to hear. *Sightsong* is one of Abrams's finest recordings and is also perhaps the best showcase for Malachi Favors's talents outside of his seminal work with the Art Ensemble of Chicago. *—Brian Olewnick*

1-OQA+19 / Nov. 1977-Dec. 1977 / Black Saint ✦✦✦

Lifea Blinec / Feb. 1978 / Novus ✦✦✦

• **Rejoicing with the Light** / Jan. 8, 1983-Jan. 25, 1983 / Black Saint ✦✦✦✦✦
Muhal Richard Abrams blended vintage and progressive sensibilities on this outstanding 1984 session. It was a large band outing, and Abrams assembled many of the finest active improvisers. His orchestra did not include just saxophones and trumpets but also French horns, bass clarinets, cello, guitar, vibes and timpani. This assured Abrams a varied, rich sound with multiple options. He led the orchestra through pieces that were sometimes introspective and other times jubilant and swinging, but never simple or predictable. This session was a challenging, instructive and entertaining lesson in modern big-band writing, arranging and performing. *—Ron Wynn*

The Hearinga Suite / Jan. 17, 1989-Jan. 18, 1989 / Black Saint ✦✦✦✦✦
Pianist Muhal Richard Abrams leads an 18-piece orchestra on his seven originals that make up the *Hearinga Suite*. Much of the music is quite adventurous although "Oldfotalk" is fairly conventional. Although the personnel includes such fine players as trumpeters Jack Walrath and Cecil Bridgewater and saxophonists John Purcell and Marty Ehrlich, the emphasis is on group interplay and the colorful arrangements. Throughout this very interesting set, Abrams shows how a big band can logically be utilized in freer forms of jazz. *—Scott Yanow*

Blu Blu Blu / Nov. 9, 1990-Nov. 10, 1990 / Black Saint ✦✦✦✦

Think All, Focus One / Jul. 1994 / Black Saint ✦✦✦✦
The seven compositions by Muhal Richard Abrams on this release can be considered part of a suite. Although there are no memorable melodies, the music flows from one piece to another and stays consistently stimulating; the only exception is the closing "Think All, Focus One" which has Abrams on synthesizer and seems quite directionless. Otherwise many moods are covered, from a dirge-like "The Harmonic Veil" and the complex but often exu-

berant "Crossbeams" to the swinging (in its own fashion) "Scaledance" and a funky jam on "Encore." The highly expressive trumpeter Eddie Allen (who is masterful with a wa-wa mute) is often the lead voice although guitarist David Gilmore also makes a strong impression and the leader's piano (which often drops out) keeps the musicians on track; tenorman Eugene Ghee, trombonist Alfred Patterson, bassist Brad Jones and drummer Reggie Nicholson complete the unit. Due to the frequently dense ensembles of the septet and the complexity of the music, this set will take several listens to fully absorb, but it is well worth the effort. *—Scott Yanow*

One Line, Two Views / Jun. 23, 1995-Jun. 24, 1995 / New World ♦♦♦♦♦

George Adams

b. Apr. 29, 1940, Covington, GA, **d.** Nov. 14, 1992, New York, NY
Sax (Tenor), Flute / Avant-Garde Jazz, Post-Bop
A passionate tenor and flute player who was not shy to break up chordal improvising with an unexpected scream or roar, George Adams was an original voice who (like his friend Don Pullen) crossed over several stylistic boundaries. He started on piano but by the time he was in high school he was playing tenor in funk bands. In 1961 he toured with Sam Cooke and in 1963 Adams moved to Ohio where he played with organ groups from the next few years. In 1968 he relocated to New York where he played with Roy Haynes, Gil Evans and Art Blakey among others. However it was his association with Charles Mingus (1973-76) that gave him his initial fame. After playing a bit with McCoy Tyner, Adams co-led a stimulating quartet with Don Pullen that made many records. Late in life Adams (who enjoyed taking an occasional raspy blues vocal) teamed up with James "Blood" Ulmer in the group Phalanx and occasionally played with Mingus Dynasty. *—Scott Yanow*

Don't Lose Control / Nov. 2, 1979-Nov. 3, 1979 / Soul Note ♦♦♦

Paradise Space Shuttle / Dec. 21, 1979 / Timeless ♦♦♦

Life Line / Apr. 5, 1981-Apr. 6, 1981 / Timeless ♦♦♦♦
George Adams and Don Pullen led a quartet featuring some of the best players in post-bop jazz, but with often less than sensational results. This recording is no exception to the rule, as the leaders are joined again by bassist Cameron Brown and drummer Dannie Richmond. There is some sensational music throughout, but the listener is left with a sense that this is not all that it could have been. There is much in the nature of the jam, and Adams's vocals, while perhaps commercially attractive, exude less than perfect intonation. When playing tenor saxophone, Adams is never short of brilliant; he always seems to place his notes perfectly. Don Pullen strokes the keyboard characteristically, with a fine feel for the blues. Dannie Richmond is given plenty of solo space, and he fills it to great advantage. While not the best effort by the quartet, it is one with plenty of rewarding moments. *—Steven Loewy*

Melodic Excursions / Jun. 6, 1982–Jun. 9, 1982 / Timeless ♦♦♦

City Gates / Mar. 27, 1983-Mar. 28, 1983 / Timeless ♦♦♦♦♦
By 1983, the quartet was at a musical peak, and this may be their best recording. Everything gels: The choice of tunes, the solos, and the arrangements all come together to produce one of the leading post-bop albums of the 1980s. Adams and Pullen perform magnificently and soulfully on "Nobody Knows the Trouble I've Seen," while the other three originals by pianist Don Pullen and two by Adams include a lengthy tribute to Charles Mingus and a shorter one for Thelonious Monk. Thankfully, there are no vocals by Adams. When these fellows get it right, as they do here, there is a synergy and energy that just can't be beat. Adams soars on tenor, building to a frenzied crescendo without losing control, while Pullen is right at his side. Drummer Dannie Richmond and bassist Cameron Brown seem inspired by the date. *—Steven Loewy*

Live at the Village Vanguard, Vol. 1 / Aug. 19, 1983 / Soul Note ♦♦♦♦♦
The George Adams-Don Pullen Quartet was one of the top jazz groups of the 1980s, although it tended to be overlooked in the U.S. Tenor saxophonist Adams and pianist Pullen (who were assisted by bassist Cameron Brown and drummer Dannie Richmond) were both flexible players easily capable of playing both inside and outside music, sometimes simultaneously. This first of two volumes from a night at the Village Vanguard has four lengthy performances: a tune apiece by Adams, Pullen, Charles Mingus and Duke Ellington ("Solitude"). Passionate music. *—Scott Yanow*

Live at the Village Vanguard, Vol. 2 / Aug. 19, 1983 / Soul Note ♦♦♦♦♦
The second album taken from a strong performance by the George Adams-Don Pullen Quartet, this set features three compositions by pianist Pullen (including his catchy "Big Alice") and tenorman Adams's "City Gates." The music swings in its own way while being quite unpredictable, intense, and sometimes avant-garde. There is nothing sleepy or routine about the chance-taking (and frequently exciting) music. *—Scott Yanow*

Nightingale / Aug. 1988 / Blue Note ♦♦

● **America** / May 24, 1989-Jul. 18, 1989 / Blue Note ♦♦♦♦♦
This is one of tenor saxophonist George Adams's funnest records. He takes eight songs, all of which now qualify as American folk songs (along with two originals), and gives them melodic but inventive treatments. "America the Beautiful" starts out with a Sousa march before Adams takes a chorus fairly straight, leading to interesting tonal variations. "Georgia" is treated as a tasteful ballad, "You Are My Sunshine" is given a funky background, and, best of all, "Take Me out to the Ballgame" becomes an unaccompanied tenor solo—at one point Adams makes clicking sounds that are very similar to a ball hitting a mitt. He sings three numbers, the rhythm section (comprised of pianist Hugh Lawson, bassist Cecil McBee, and drummer Mark Johnson) is fine in support, and Adams (who plays both his humming flute and tenor on "Old Folks at Home") is heard in top form. This CD is accessible, patriotic, and a highly recommended and continually surprising set. *—Scott Yanow*

Old Feeling / Mar. 11, 1991-Mar. 12, 1991 / Blue Note ♦♦♦♦
Old Feeling ranks as one of George Adams's most exciting and eccentric sessions. Unlike some other avant-gardists who seem to lose their personality and purpose when they play standard material, Adams turns even overplayed songs into his own inventive devices; three standards get the Adams treatment on this CD. *—Scott Yanow*

Pepper Adams (Pepper Park Adams III)

b. Oct. 8, 1930, Highland Park, MI, **d.** Sep. 10, 1986, New York, NY
Sax (Baritone) / Hard Bop
Pepper Adams was one of the all-time great baritonists, ranking at the top with Harry Carney, Serge Chaloff and Gerry Mulligan. But Mulligan overshadowed Adams throughout virtually his entire career, which is a little strange because Pepper had a much different sound (heavier and more intense) than the light-toned and playful Mulligan.

Adams grew up in Rochester, NY, and when he was 16 he moved to Detroit where he became an important part of the very fertile local jazz scene. Other than a period in the military (1951-53), Adams was a major fixture in Detroit, playing with such up-and-coming musicians as Donald Byrd, Kenny Burrell, Tommy Flanagan, Barry Harris and Elvin Jones. Adams had opportunities to tour with Stan Kenton, Maynard Ferguson and Chet Baker and he moved to New York in 1958. In addition to recording both as a leader and a sideman, Adams played with Benny Goodman (1958-59) and Charles Mingus (off and on between 1959-63) and co-led a quintet with Donald Byrd (1958-62). He was a longtime member of the Thad Jones/Mel Lewis Orchestra (1965-78) and a major stylist up until his death. *—Scott Yanow*

Pepper Adams Quintet / Jul. 10, 1957 / VSOP ♦♦♦

Pure Pepper / Nov. 19, 1957 / Savoy ♦♦♦
Originally titled The Cool Sound Of Pepper Adams, this 1984 reissue LP features the great baritonist on an early session as a leader with the euphonium of Bernard McKinney, pianist Hank Jones, bassist George Duvivier and drummer Elvin Jones. The unusual frontline blends together better than expected and the often-explosive baritonist (who brought a new sound to his instrument) is heard in his early prime on the straightahead material. *—Scott Yanow*

● **10 to 4 at the 5-Spot** / Apr. 15, 1958 / Riverside/OJC ♦♦♦♦♦
Most of the recordings by the Donald Byrd-Pepper Adams Quintet were released under the trumpeter's name but this near-classic (reissued on CD) is an exception. With pianist Bobby Timmons, bassist Doug Watkins and drummer Elvin Jones completing (and inspiring) the group, Adams and Byrd make for a potent team on "You're My Thrill" and some originals; hard bop at its best. *—Scott Yanow*

Encounter! / Dec. 11, 1968-Dec. 12, 1968 / Prestige/OJC ♦♦♦♦
Baritonist Pepper Adams and tenor saxophonist Zoot Sims (who rarely performed together) make a surprisingly compatible team on this CD reissue of a 1968 Prestige session. With pianist Tommy Flanagan, bassist Ron Carter and drummer Elvin Jones forming a fairly adventurous rhythm section, Pepper and Sims sound inspired on material that includes obscurities by Flanagan, Thad Jones and Adams in addition to the Ellington-Strayhorn ballad "Star-Crossed Lovers" and a pair of Joe Henderson songs. The setting is more advanced than usual for Sims, who rises to the challenge. *—Scott Yanow*

Julian / Aug. 13, 1975 / Enja ♦♦♦♦
Recorded five days before Julian "Cannonball" Adderley's death, the title cut of this album was retitled and dedicated to the late altoist. The powerful baritonist Pepper Adams is well showcased with a quartet comprised of pianist Walter Norris, bassist George Mraz and drummer Makaya Ntshoko on three of his originals, one by Norris and two ("Three And One" and "'Tis") by Thad Jones. Adams is in typically excellent form, playing intense solos that push but stay within the boundaries of hard bop. *—Scott Yanow*

Pepper / Aug. 13, 1975–Feb. 25, 1986 / Enja ♦♦♦♦

Live / Sep. 18, 1977 / Just Jazz ♦♦♦♦
Baritonist Pepper Adams had a rare chance to really stretch out on this live set from Half Moon Bay, CA. The music, released for the first time on this 1995 CD, really showcases Adams since pianist John Marabuto, bassist Bob Maize and drummer Ron Marabuto are subtle and quite supportive. Adams performs three standards (including versions of "Dewey Square" and "How Long Has This Been Going On" that are over 13 minutes apiece) plus a couple of original blues. A good showcase. *—Scott Yanow*

Conjuration: Fat Tuesday's Session / Aug. 19, 1983-Aug. 20, 1983 / Reservoir ♦♦♦♦♦
The great baritonist Pepper Adams is teamed up with the adventurous trumpeter Kenny Wheeler and veteran pianist Hank Jones for this live quintet date. Wheeler, although often associated with the avant-garde, has never had any difficulty playing changes and his strong style clearly inspired Adams. Together they perform three of the baritonist's originals, Thad Jones's "Tis," Wheeler's "Old Ballad," and the standard "Alone Together." *—Scott Yanow*

Cannonball Adderley (Julian Edwin Adderley)

b. Sep. 15, 1928, Tampa, FL, **d.** Aug. 8, 1975, Gary, IN
Sax (Alto) / Hard Bop, Soul-Jazz
One of the great alto saxophonists, Cannonball Adderley had an exuberant and happy sound (as opposed to many of the more serious stylists of his generation) that communicated immediately to listeners. His intelligent presentation of his music (often explaining what he and his musicians were going to play) helped make him one of the most popular of all jazzmen. With his younger brother, cornetist Nat, Cannonball formed a quintet that struggled until its breakup in 1957. Adderley then joined Miles Davis, forming part of his super sextet with John Coltrane and participating on such classic recordings as *Milestones* and *Kind of Blue*. Adderley's second attempt to form a quintet with his brother was much more successful for in 1959 with pianist Bobby Timmons he had a hit recording of "This Here." From then on, he always was able to work steadily with his band. During its Riverside years (1959-63), the Adderley Quintet primarily played soulful renditions of hard bop and Cannonball really excelled in the straightahead settings. The collapse of Riverside resulted in Adderley signing with Capitol and his recordings became gradually more commercial. He later started doubling on soprano and the Quintet's later recordings emphasized long melody statements, funky rhythms and electronics. *—Scott Yanow*

Presenting Cannonball Adderley / Jul. 26, 1955 / Savoy ♦♦♦

With Strings/Jump for Joy / Oct. 27, 1955-Aug. 21, 1958 / Mercury ♦♦♦♦
This CD reissues two complete LPs from near the beginning of altoist Cannonball Adderley's career. The first session is quite unusual for Adderley (who was completely unknown just a few months earlier) was given a very early opportunity to record with strings. He sounds fine on 11 standards and Terry Gibbs's "Lonely Dreams" but mostly sticks near the melody while Richard Hayman's Orchestra sounds rather anonymous. The 1958 sessions finds him performing ten songs from the early-'40s Duke Ellington show *Jump for Joy* (including "Just Squeeze Me," "I Got It Bad" and "Jump for Joy") while accompanied by a string quartet, a rhythm section and trumpeter Emmett Berry; Bill Russo provided the generally stimulating arrangements. The formerly rare music on this CD is enjoyable but not as essential as Adderley's slightly later Riverside albums. *—Scott Yanow*

Sophisticated Swing: The EmArcy Small Group Sessions / Jul. 12, 1956-Mar. 6, 1958 / EmArcy ♦♦♦♦♦
Reissued in this two-CD set are all of the recordings from the first Cannonball Adderley Quintet, a group that despite its talents failed commercially. With Cannonball on alto, cornetist Nat Adderley, pianist Junior Mance, bassist Sam Jones, and drummer Jimmy Cobb, it is surprising that the group did not make it, but the Adderleys were fairly unknown at the time. The music is quite bop-oriented, bluesy but not as soulful as it would be when Cannonball put together a new group in 1959. This set reissues all of the music originally included on Nat Adderley's *To the Ivy League From Nat*, and Cannonball's *Sophisticated Swing*, *Cannonball Enroute*, and *Sharpshooters* (except for one trio feature without the horns) plus a few cuts not released until the CD era. The generous reissue not only gives one a fine sampling of the first Cannonball Adderley Quintet but everything they recorded. Highly recommended to bop fans. *—Scott Yanow*

★ **Somethin' Else** / Mar. 9, 1958 / Blue Note ♦♦♦♦♦
It isn't too difficult to understand why MFSL considered this album to be a worthy candidate for an Ultradisc reissue—aside from Adderley, you have a lineup that includes Miles Davis, Hank Jones, Sam Jones and Art Blakey. This is a group that could take on a Barry Manilow number and turn it into a jazz masterpiece.

MFSL have done the purchaser a favor, too, by including an additional track that was left off the original album. This sixth track, "Alison's Uncle," closes out the album on a high note, changing the flow of energy in an interesting way (purists can still finish up on a quieter note, as with the original, by programming "Dancing In the Dark" as the final track). In many ways it's a surprise that this track was left off originally—it's an excellent piece, with Adderley and Davis trading licks and solos while Jones and Blakey keep pace. Blakey also takes some terrific solos.

The remastering job is the usual superb MFSL effort, producing clear sound with almost no background noise. Due to the original recording (made in 1958), Davis's trumpet sometimes seems a little shrill and metallic, but it's not an overwhelming problem—certainly not when you consider Davis's style. Altogether, an excellent addition to any jazz collection. *—Steven McDonald*

Portrait of Cannonball / Jul. 1, 1958 / Riverside/OJC ♦♦♦♦
Altoist Cannonball Adderley's debut for Riverside (which has been reissued in the Original Jazz Classics CD series along with additional alternate takes of "Minority" and "Nardis") was recorded while he was a member of the legendary Miles Davis Sextet. He utilized pianist Bill Evans and drummer Philly Joe Jones from Davis's group along with trumpeter Blue Mitchell and bassist Sam Jones for a set of soulful bop. Highlights include "Minority," "Straight Life" and "A Little Taste." *—Scott Yanow*

☆ **Things Are Getting Better** / Oct. 28, 1958 / Riverside/OJC ♦♦♦♦♦
Cannonball Adderley teams up with vibraphonist Milt Jackson, pianist Wynton Kelly, bassist Percy Heath and drummer Art Blakey for a jubilant and often-explosive session on this CD reissue. On tunes such as "Things Are Getting Better," "Just One Of Those Things" and a memorable "Sidewalks Of New York," the altoist-leader is quite joyful in his solos, really ripping into the material. This set is a very good example of early Cannonball Adderley, recorded a year before his quintet caught on. *—Scott Yanow*

Cannonball Adderley Quintet in Chicago / Feb. 3, 1959 / Mercury ♦♦♦♦♦

Cannonball and Coltrane / Feb. 3, 1959 / EmArcy ♦♦♦♦♦
This LP (whose contents have been reissued many times) features the Miles Davis Sextet of 1959 without the leader. Altoist Cannonball Adderley and tenor-saxophonist John Coltrane really push each other on these six selections with this version of "Limehouse Blues" really burning. Coltrane's very serious sound is a striking contrast to the jubilant Adderley alto; the latter is showcased on "Stars Fell on Alabama." With pianist Wynton Kelly, bassist Paul Chambers and drummer Jimmy Cobb playing up to their usual level, this gem is highly recommended. *—Scott Yanow*

Cannonball Adderley Quintet in San Francisco / Oct. 18, 1959–Oct. 20, 1959 / Riverside/OJC ♦♦♦♦♦
Cannonball Adderley had struggled unsuccessfully with a quintet during 1955-57, giving up for a time to play with Miles Davis' group. In 1959 his new quintet suddenly caught on with the release of this very exciting live album, which has been reissued on CD in the Original Jazz Classics series. With cornetist Nat Adderley, pianist Bobby Timmons, bassist Sam Jones and drummer Louis Hayes, Cannonball had the top new jazz group of 1959. Their version of Timmons' "This Here" was a major hit and the other numbers on this famous date (which include "Spontaneous Combustion," "Hi-Fly," "You Got It," "Bohemia After Dark" and "Straight No Chaser") are also quite enjoyable, showing why Cannonball Adderley's group was a pacesetter in funky soul jazz and proving that they could outswing most of their competition. This gem is essential for all jazz collections. *—Scott Yanow*

Coast to Coast / Oct. 18, 1959-Jan. 14, 1962 / Milestone ♦♦♦♦
This two-LP set combines together two of Cannonball Adderley's finest recordings. The earlier session, recorded live at The Jazz Workshop in San Francisco, made his new quintet (which also featured cornetist Nat Adderley, pianist Bobby Timmons, bassist Sam Jones, and drummer Louis Hayes) into a very popular attraction. In addition to a previously unissued version of "Straight No Chaser," a classic rendition of "High Fly," and two originals by the altoist, this is the set that featured the debut recording of Bobby Timmons's hit "This Here," which by itself defined the term "soul-jazz" or "funk." The second half of this two-fer is not exactly lightweight material either, a live album by Adderley's 1962 sextet with the great tenor Yusef Lateef and pianist Joe Zawinul. Their version of "Dizzy's Business" is quite memorable. These two sessions (which are also available on CD) contain plenty of essential music. *—Scott Yanow*

Them Dirty Blues / Feb. 1, 1960 - 19 / Capitol ♦♦♦
Recorded in early 1960, *Them Dirty Blues* contains two classic jazz compositions: Nat Adderley's "Work Song" and Bobby Timmons' "Dat Dere," the sequel to "This Here." This was alto saxophonist Cannonball Adderley's second quintet with brother Nat Adderley (cornet), and features Bobby Timmons on piano (who plays on four tracks and was replaced by Barry Harris on the remaining five), Sam Jones on bass, and Louis Hayes on drums. *Them Dirty Blues* was originally released on Riverside until Adderley made the switch to Capitol where he brought several master tapes with him, including these sessions. The CD reissue contains an alternate version each of "Work Song" and "Dat Dere." *—Al Campbell*

What Is This Thing Called Soul? / Nov. 22, 1960-Nov. 23, 1960 / Pablo/OJC ♦♦♦♦
Cannonball Adderley's 1960 Quintet (with cornetist Nat Adderley and pianist Victor Feldman) was in top form during their tour of Europe. Norman Granz did not release the music heard on this CD until almost 25 years after the fact but the strong solos and enthusiastic ensembles had not dated nor faded with time. These versions of "The Chant," "What Is This Thing Called Love?" and "Big 'P'" make for interesting comparisons with the better-known renditions. Adderley fans will want this set. *—Scott Yanow*

African Waltz / Feb. 8, 1961-May 15, 1961 / Riverside/OJC ♦♦♦

Nancy Wilson/Cannonball Adderley / Jun. 27, 1961-Aug. 24, 1961 / Capitol ♦♦♦♦
Adderley's abilities as a talent scout have long been overlooked. He helped discover Nancy Wilson early in her career, and by 1961, she was already on her way to becoming a popular middle-of-the-road singer. Instead of alternating instrumental performances by his quintet with Wilson's vocals, as on the LP, this CD (which adds a previously unissued "Little Unhappy Boy" to the original LP) sounds like two separate sets, due to the placement of the seven vocals at the beginning of the program. Never really a jazz singer, Nancy Wilson sounds more influenced by jazz on these numbers (particularly on "Never Will I Marry," "The Masquerade Is Over," and "A Sleepin' Bee") than she would later on. The instrumentals include fine versions of "I Can't Get Started" and "Unit 7." *—Scott Yanow*

Cannonball's Bossa Nova / Dec. 7, 1962 / Riverside ♦♦

In New York / Jan. 12, 1962–Jan. 14, 1962 / Riverside/OJC ♦♦♦♦
This album (reissued on CD) was the recording debut of altoist Cannonball Adderley's strongest group, his sextet with brother Nat on cornet, Yusef Lateef on tenor, oboe and flute, pianist Joe Zawinul, bassist Sam Jones and drummer Louis Hayes. All of Lateef's 1962-63 recordings with Adderley are well worth acquiring. This live set (recorded at the Village Vanguard) has plenty of variety and is highlighted by "Gemini," the boppish "Dizzy's Business" and "Scotch And Water." *—Scott Yanow*

Dizzy's Business / Sep. 21, 1962-Jul. 19, 1963 / Milestone ♦♦♦♦
Although the nine songs on this new Cannonball Adderley reissue were originally done live at concerts in Japan and San Francisco in 1963, they nevertheless make a nice tribute to departed jazz giant Dizzy Gillespie. The assembled group was among the finest Adderley ever led, with Yusef Lateef providing a dynamic, unpredictable third solo voice on flute, tenor sax, and oboe, contrasting with Cannonball's pungent alto sax and Nat Adderley's pithy cornet solos. Bassist Sam Jones and drummer Louis Hayes were a top-flight tandem, while Joe Zawinul was then playing bluesy, funky piano in his pre-synthesizer, Miles Davis/Weather Report phase. Everything is illustrative of a prime band enjoying some great nights. *—Ron Wynn*

Nippon Soul / Jul. 14, 1963–Jul. 15, 1963 / Riverside/OJC ♦♦♦

☆ **Mercy, Mercy, Mercy! Live at 'The Club'** / Oct. 20, 1966 / Blue Note ♦♦♦♦♦
This set (reissued on CD) is one of Cannonball Adderley's finest albums of his last decade. "Mercy, Mercy, Mercy," a soulful Joe Zawinul melody that is repeated several times without any real improvisation, became a surprise hit but the other selections on this live date ("Fun," "Games," "Sticks," "Hippodelphia" and "Sack O'Woe") all have plenty of fiery solos from the quintet (which is comprised of the leader on alto, cornetist Nat Adderley, pianist Joe Zawinul, bassist Victor Gaskin, and drummer Roy McCurdy). Cannonball sounds quite inspired (his expressive powers had expanded due to the unacknowledged influence of the avant-garde) and Nat shows just how exciting a player he was back in his prime. "Sack O'Woe" is particularly memorable. This CD, which is far superior to most of Cannonball's later Capitol recordings, is highly recommended. *—Scott Yanow*

Phenix / Feb. 1975-Apr. 1975 / Fantasy ♦♦♦♦

Nat Adderley

b. Nov. 25, 1931, Tampa, FL, **d.** Jan. 2, 2000
Cornet / Hard Bop, Soul-Jazz
Nat Adderley's cornet was always a complementary voice to his brother Cannonball in their popular quintet. His career ran parallel to his older brother for quite some time. After a period with Lionel Hampton (1954-55), Nat made his recording debut in 1955, joined Cannonball's unsuccessful quintet of 1956-57 and then spent periods with the groups of J.J. Johnson and Woody Herman before hooking up with Cannonball again in Oct. 1959. This time the group became a major success and Nat remained in the quintet until Cannonball's death in 1975, contributing such originals as "Work Song," "Jive Samba" and "The Old Country" along with many exciting hard bop solos. Nat Adderley, who was at the peak of his powers in the early to mid-'60s and became adept at playing solos that dipped into the subtone register of

his horn, has led his own quintets since Cannonball's death; his most notable sidemen were altoists Sonny Fortune and Vincent Herring. Although his own playing has declined somewhat (Adderley's chops no longer have the endurance of his earlier days), Nat has continued recording worthwhile sessions. *—Scott Yanow*

That's Nat Adderley / Jul. 26, 1955 / Savoy ✦✦✦
Early material from Nat Adderley. His pithy, pungent trumpet and cornet work is effective in a hard bop context, although his own work outside his brother's group has never seemed quite as effective. His backing group included Kenny Clarke in a non-Modern Jazz Quartet role, plus pianist Hank Jones, bassist Wendell Marshall, and Jerome Richardson on tenor sax and flute, playing with more punch than on either his Quincy Jones or Oliver Nelson large group dates. *—Ron Wynn*

Branching Out / Sep. 1958 / Riverside/OJC ✦✦✦✦
Cornetist Nat Adderley's debut for Riverside (reissued on CD in the OJC series) was recorded about a year before he permanently rejoined his brother Cannonball Adderley's Quintet. Teamed with tenor-saxophonist Johnny Griffin and the Three Sounds (the popular soul jazz rhythm section comprised of pianist Gene Harris, bassist Andy Simpkins and drummer Bill Dowdy), Nat is in excellent form on such tunes as "Well You Needn't," "Don't Get Around Much Anymore" and "I Never Knew" in addition to two of his lesser-known originals. Adderley and Griffin made for an exciting frontline. *—Scott Yanow*

● **Work Song** / Jan. 25, 1960-Jan. 27, 1960 / Riverside/OJC ✦✦✦✦✦
This CD reissue brings back a near-classic by cornetist Nat Adderley. Utilizing a cornet-cello-guitar frontline (with Sam Jones and Wes Montgomery) along with a top-notch rhythm section (pianist Bobby Timmons, Percy Heath or Keter Betts on bass and drummer Louis Hayes), Adderley performs a fine early version of his greatest hit ("Work Song") and helps introduce Cannonball Adderley's "Sack O' Woe." Four songs use a smaller group with Timmons absent on "My Heart Stood Still" (which finds Keter Betts on cello and Jones on bass), "Mean to Me" featuring Nat backed by Montgomery, Betts and Hayes and two ballads ("I've Got a Crush on You" and "Violets for Your Furs") interpreted by the Adderley-Montgomery-Jones trio. No matter the setting, Nat Adderley is heard throughout in peak form, playing quite lyrically. Highly recommended. *—Scott Yanow*

Work Songs / Jan. 25, 1960-Sep. 15, 1960 / Riverside ✦✦✦✦✦
This out-of-print two-LP set combines together two of cornetist Nat Adderley's finest albums: *Work Song* and *That's Right*. Both dates have since been reissued separately on CD. The former set features Nat with guitarist Wes Montgomery, cellist Sam Jones and a strong rhythm section (some selections are played by a smaller group from this band); highlights include "Work Song," "Sack O' Woe," and "Violets for Your Furs." The latter session is quite a bit different for Nat is joined by five saxophonists (including brother Cannonball on alto and Yusef Lateef on tenor, flute and oboe) and a four-piece rhythm section. Jimmy Heath (one of three tenors on the date) did most of the arrangements and gets to solo along with Lateef and Charlie Rouse. Most memorable is Nat's "The Old Country" and the ballad "The Folks Who Live on the Hill." Superb music worth acquiring in one form or another. *—Scott Yanow*

That's Right!: Nat Adderley & The Big Sax Section / Aug. 9, 1960-Sep. 15, 1960 / Riverside/OJC ✦✦✦✦✦
Nat Adderley has seldom played with more fire, verve and distinction than he did on *That's Right!* It placed him in the company of an expanded sax section that included his brother Cannonball on alto, Yusef Lateef on tenor, flute and oboe, Jimmy Heath and Charlie Rouse on tenor and baritone saxophonist Tate Houston. Solos crackled, the backing was tasty and stimulating, and the eight songs ranged from brisk standards to delightful originals. This CD reissue, despite lacking any new or alternate material, is most welcome due to the full, striking sound that the big reed section provided. *—Ron Wynn*

In the Bag / May 9, 1962 / Jazzland/OJC ✦✦

Sayin' Somethin' / Feb. 16, 1966 / Atlantic ✦✦✦

Air

f. 1971, **db.** Aug. 6, 1974
Group / Avant-Garde Jazz, Free Jazz, Modern Creative
Comprised originally of Henry Threadgill on reeds, bassist Fred Hopkins and drummer Steve McCall, Air emphasized equality of roles by the instruments (without any clear-cut leader) and a smooth mixture of advanced arrangements and free improvisations. In 1971 Threadgill was asked to arrange some of Scott Joplin's songs for a production at Columbia College in Chicago. He teamed up with Hopkins and McCall as the trio Reflection. A few years later in 1975 the musicians came together again as Air, touring Europe, Japan and America and recording 11 records for such labels as Nessa, India Navigation, Black Saint, Novus and Antilles. By far their most popular release was 1979's *Air Lore* which found the group performing abstract versions of tunes by Joplin and Jelly Roll Morton. In 1982 when McCall returned to Chicago and was replaced by Pheeroan AkLaff, the group changed its name to New Air. A year before their breakup in 1986 Andrew Cyrille took over the drum slot. Since then all of the musicians (other than McCall who passed away in 1989) have had very productive careers. *—Scott Yanow*

Air Song / Sep. 10, 1975 / India Navigation ✦✦✦✦
Air Song was the first recording by Air, a trio comprised of altoist Henry Threadgill (who also plays tenor, baritone and flute on this date), bassist Fred Hopkins and drummer Steve McCall. The idea behind this unit was always to have all three members on an equal footing and, although Threadgill consistently comes across as the lead voice, their advanced interplay and consistently strong solos on these four lengthy performances make this a rather successful outing. *—Scott Yanow*

Live Air / Jul. 1, 1976-Oct. 28, 1977 / Black Saint ✦✦✦

Air Raid / Jul. 15, 1976 / India Navigation ✦✦✦✦
Air's third recording (following two others recorded during the previous ten months) once again features Henry Threadgill (who contributed all four compositions) as the main lead voice, switching between alto, tenor, Chinese musette, flute and hubkaphone (a percussive instrument that he put together made of hubcaps). Threadgill's close interaction with bassist Fred Hopkins and drummer Steve McCall should make this obscure album of strong interest to avant-garde collectors. *—Scott Yanow*

Air Time / Nov. 17, 1977-Nov. 18, 1977 / Nessa ✦✦✦✦
The trio Air aimed to have close interplay between three musical equals. This Nessa release (their first recording for an American label) has plenty of explorative solos and is highlighted by Threadgill's three extended compositions; check out his hubkaphone feature on "G.V.E." *—Scott Yanow*

● **Air Lore** / May 11, 1979-May 12, 1979 / Bluebird/RCA ✦✦✦✦✦
This was the most unusual and accessible recording ever made by Air. Instead of performing their complex originals as usual, this group (in addition to Threadgill's brief "Paille Street") stretches out on two songs apiece by Jelly Roll Morton and Scott Joplin. Most memorable is their investigation of Joplin's "The Ragtime Dance." Threadgill's solos in particular really fit the mood of these classic pieces. *—Scott Yanow*

Air Mail / Dec. 28, 1980 / Black Saint ✦✦✦✦
The Chicago trio Air was at a high point on this 1980 date, thanks in part to remarkable percussive foundations provided by the late Steve McCall and his interaction with bassist Fred Hopkins, plus the amazing solos and versatility of nominal leader Henry Threadgill. Besides alto and tenor sax, flute, and bass flute, Threadgill plays his own unique instrument called the hubkaphone and makes it just as memorable a weapon as the other horns. *—Ron Wynn*

Air Show No. 1 / Jun. 2, 1986-Jun. 3, 1986 / Black Saint ✦✦✦✦
The second and final Air recording after drummer/percussionist Pheeroan AkLaff took Steve McCall's place is a bit unusual, for vocalist Cassandra Wilson is heard on three of the six selections. She does an expert job of fitting into this complex music, giving a strong blues feeling to some of altoist Henry Threadgill's originals; bassist Fred Hopkins is also in top form on these unpredictable and dynamic performances. *—Scott Yanow*

Gerald Albright

b. 1957, Los Angeles, CA
Sax (Tenor), Sax (Alto) / Smooth Jazz, Crossover Jazz, Contemporary Jazz, Jazz-Pop, Urban
Gerald Albright has occasionally shown the ability to play jazz (most notably on his Atlantic set *Live at Birdland West*) but has chosen to make his career as an R&B saxophonist. Originally he studied piano before switching to tenor, and in college he began doubling on electric bass. Through the years Albright has performed in a variety of R&Bish settings (with Patrice Rushen, Anita Baker, Quincy Jones, the Temptations, etc.), content to play simplistic music and, disappointingly, little jazz. *—Scott Yanow*

● **Live at Birdland West** / 1991 / Atlantic ✦✦✦✦
Virtually all of saxophonist Gerald Albright's previous recordings were in the pop/R&B field, making this mostly straightahead session a major surprise. Albright, alternating between alto and tenor, plays quite well throughout this set which is highlighted by versions of "Impressions," "Georgia on My Mind" and "Limehouse Blues." Tenorman Kirk Whalum helps out on three tracks and Eddie Harris makes a guest appearance on "Bubblehead McDaddy." This is easily Gerald Albright's most rewarding session to date. *—Scott Yanow*

Smooth / Feb. 22, 1994 / Atlantic ✦✦✦
After a feisty live album recorded at *Birdland* gave this soulful saxman a chance to stretch his straight-ahead chops, the super cool side of Albright came back on this one. *Smooth* is indeed the operative word here, as this is a tasty if somewhat typical journey through the land of quiet storm and light funk. Albright's sharp, distinctive tone (bearing both melody and unexpected improvisations) heats up a too long series of pleasant but unremarkable melodies and grooves—the one instrumental exception being the blazing dual energy provided on "glee" by the breezy guitar of Lee Ritenour. As background for those seductive night moves, the silky vocals by the likes of Howard Hewett and Will Downing are can't miss. Though Albright himself dazzles, more sax and less commercial slickness would make this a triumph rather than just another fine but generic rhythm and jazz effort. After you've heard his real jazz chops, the lack of a true traditional piece is a notable omission as well. *—Jonathan Widran*

Live to Love / 1997 / Atlantic ✦✦✦
Live to Love finds Gerald Albright returning to urban R&B, turning in an album of laidback, polished soul and smooth jazz. Several vocalists, including Albright's daughter Selina, his longtime partner Will Downing, and the Whispers' Walter and Wallace Scott, contribute their skills to these well-crafted tracks. The vocal cuts form the core of *Live to Love*, making it more of interest to an urban audience than to fusion jazz fans, although there are a few instrumental interludes as well. However, the key thing distinguishing *Live to Love* is focus—Albright hasn't had such a consistently engaging set of songs in years, and that's what makes the album such a pleasure for fans of his work. *—Leo Stanley*

Monty Alexander (Montgomery Bernard)

b. Jun. 6, 1944, Kingston, Jamaica
Piano / Hard Bop, Bop
Monty Alexander long ago combined together the influence of Oscar Peterson with the soul of Gene Harris and Nat King Cole to form his own appealing and personable style. Long a bit underrated (due to the shadow of Peterson), Alexander has recorded more than a score of excellent albums. Monty Alexander began piano lessons when he was six and he played professionally in Jamaica clubs while still a teenager; his band, Monty and the Cyclones, was quite popular locally during 1958-60. He first played in the U.S. when he appeared in Las Vegas with Art Mooney's Orchestra. Soon he was accompanying a variety of top singers, formed a friendship with vibraphonist Milt Jackson and began gigging with bassist Ray Brown. With the recording of a pair of Pacific Jazz albums in 1965, an RCA date in 1967 and a Verve session in 1969, Alexander began to gain a strong reputation. His series of exciting albums for

MPS during 1971-77 found him in prime form and later recordings (most notably on Pablo and Concord) found him building on his original style. Alexander, who often pays tribute to his Jamaican heritage, performs regularly with his own trio and swings hard in his own voice. *—Scott Yanow*

Live! Montreux Alexander / Jun. 10, 1976 / MPS ♦♦♦
Pianist Monty Alexander did some of his finest recordings for the MPS label. This live trio set with bassist John Clayton and drummer Jeff Hamilton (reissued on CD) features Alexander playing his usual repertoire of the period with blues, standards ("Satin Doll," "Work Song" and "Battle Hymn of the Republic") and a version of "Feelings" that uplifts the song a bit (although not enough). His soulful approach to the generally familiar melodies makes them sound fresh and swinging. *—Scott Yanow*

Jamento: The Monty Alexander 7 / Jun. 15, 1978-Jun. 16, 1978 / Pablo/OJC ♦♦♦♦
Monty Alexander's Jamaican heritage is combined with his bop-oriented piano on this date to create some enjoyable music. This was his first recording to make use of a steel drummer (Vince Charles), and Alexander also uses an oversized rhythm section with Jamaican guitarist Ernest Ranglin, bassist Andy Simpkins, both Duffy Jackson and Roger Bethelmy on drums and percussionist Larry McDonald. The repertoire (which includes four Alexander originals and George Benson's poppish "Weekend In L.A.") is mostly obscure, but the interpretations are lively and full of spirit. *—Scott Yanow*

Ivory & Steel / Mar. 1980 / Concord Jazz ♦♦♦♦
This well-rounded set features Monty Alexander exploring his West Indian heritage by utilizing the steel drum of Othello Molineaux and performing both straightahead jazz and calypsos. The music is often quite joyous and even the more familiar material (such as "Work Song," "Stella By Starlight" and a medley of "Impressions" and "So What") sounds fresh. Whether it be the Milt Jackson blues "S.K.J." or the Crusaders' hit "Street Life," this is a very successful outing that is quite enjoyable. *—Scott Yanow*

● **Triple Treat, Vol. 1** / Mar. 1983 / Concord Jazz ♦♦♦♦♦
One can excuse pianist Monty Alexander if his playing on this Concord set recalls Oscar Peterson, for his sidemen in the trio are O.P.-alumni guitarist Herb Ellis and bassist Ray Brown. The combination lives up to its potential with the group romping on such songs as "The Flintstones," Blue Mitchell's "Fungi Mama" and an uptempo "Small Fry." *—Scott Yanow*

Triple Treat, Vol. 2 / Jun. 1987 / Concord Jazz ♦♦♦♦♦
Five years after the original *Triple Treat*, pianist Monty Alexander has a reunion with guitarist Herb Ellis and bassist Ray Brown in a program that is in the tradition of both Oscar Peterson and Nat King Cole. A special bonus is violinist John Frigo who sits in on four of the eight songs. Highpoints include Ray Brown's "Lined with a Groove," "Straighten up and Fly Right," "Seven Come Eleven" and "Lester Leaps In." *—Scott Yanow*

Echoes of Jilly's / Dec. 20, 1996-Dec. 21, 1996 / Concord Jazz ♦♦♦♦
From 1963-67, pianist Monty Alexander played regularly at Jilly's in New York City, a popular hangout where Frank Sinatra would occasionally drop in and, on very rare occasions, sing a song or two. This trio set with bassist John Patitucci and drummer Troy Davis gives Alexander an opportunity to pay tribute to both Jilly's and Sinatra. Performing 13 of the many hundreds of songs associated with the singer, Alexander plays melodic and swinging versions of such tunes as "I've Got You Under My Skin," "Just One of Those Things," "Fly Me to the Moon," "Come Fly With Me" and "Here's That Rainy Day," among others. The songs are mostly pretty familiar, and Alexander does not stretch himself all that much (the only real departure is his haunting unaccompanied melodica solo on "Strangers In the Night"), but his renditions are quite enjoyable and accessible. *—Scott Yanow*

Stir It Up: The Music of Bob Marley / Oct. 10, 1998-Oct. 12, 1998 / Telarc ♦♦♦

Island Grooves: Jamboree & Ivory and Steel / Mar. 1980-Mar. 1988 / Concord Jazz ♦♦♦♦♦

Rashied Ali (Robert Patterson)

b. Jul. 1, 1935, Philadelphia, PA
Drums / Avant-Garde Jazz, Free Jazz
It must have been daunting for Rashied Ali to follow Elvin Jones as John Coltrane's drummer, but when Coltrane was transcending limitations, it seems proper that he would complement Jones' polymetric intractability with the addition of Rashied Ali's skittish, asymmetrical flexibility. The two drummers shared the bandstand briefly, then Jones left the band, marking Coltrane's last and most extreme step away from the jazz tradition. In contrast to Jones, Ali almost completely abandoned a steady pulse, adopting instead a rhythmically irregular, textural, hyperactive approach that propelled the music in a manner at odds with Jones' more literal style. The removal of a steady beat, and the multitude of implied meters set by Ali and bassist Jimmy Garrison freed Coltrane to an unprecedented extent, truly beginning his free period.

Ali started out playing with local jazz and R&B bands around Philadelphia. In 1963, he toured Japan with Sonny Rollins, then moved to New York, and into the city's free jazz scene. Associations with Pharoah Sanders, Albert Ayler, Bill Dixon, and Sunny Murray preceded his 1965 to 1967 tenure with Coltrane. Ali continued playing with pianist Alice Coltrane, before becoming a bandleader and musical organizer. In 1972, he helped coordinate the New York Musicians Festival, formed his label, Survival, in 1973, and opened the NYC performance loft, Ali's Alley, which presented free jazz until the summer of 1979. In the '80s and '90s, his presence on the scene was sporadic; occasionally performing with saxophonist Makanda Ken McIntyre, and recording with multi-instrumentalist Zusaan Kali Fasteau, and tenor saxophonist David Murray. In 1987 he recorded as a member of Phalanx (with guitarist James "Blood" Ulmer). Ali made the critically acclaimed *Touchin' on Trane* (1991) with bassist William Parker and tenor saxophonist Charles Gayle, then helmed Prima Materia (initially co-led with Parker), an ensemble dedicated to interpreting the late works of Coltrane and Albert Ayler. *—Chris Kelsey*

Duo Exchange / 1972 / Survival ♦♦♦♦
Thankfully, Knitting Factory Records has reissued much of Rashied Ali's long-defunct and much-sought-after Survival Records catalog. *Duo Exchange* is the original first release from that label, and the recording lends much credibility to Ali's choice to start his own label. The interaction between Ali and Frank Lowe is exciting and of a consistently high level, making this recording a worthy and historical addition to the collections of all fans of avant-garde duos. *—Wilson McCloy*

● **New Directions in Modern Music** / 1971 / Survival ♦♦♦♦♦
Recorded live at *the East: A Cultural and Educational Center for People of African Descent, New Directions in Modern Music* is yet another rewarding recording from the Survival archives. "As-Salaam-Alikum" begins with the quick statement of a memorable theme, which fades into a fiery Carlos Ward improvisation ranking amongst the finest moments in spiritual avant-garde playing. In fact, the album calls to mind Alice Coltrane's *P'tah the El'Daoud* and Franklin Kiermyer's *Solomon's Daughter*, with Fred Simmons' punchy, sparse chords and Tyner-inspired runs complementing the group well. All of the early Survival albums include long Ali solo sections, so be forewarned; but be aware that these musicians will be pushing the limits of jazz expression. The music is the reward. *—Wilson McCloy*

The Rings of Saturn / Aug. 9, 1997–Aug. 1997 / Knitting Factory ♦♦♦
Rashied Ali was 62 when, in August 1997, he recorded *Rings of Saturn*, a collection of duets with tenor saxophonist Louie Belogenis. But the drummer was showing no signs of mellowing with age—he was still committed to avant-garde jazz and outside improvisation, and he still had an uncompromising take-it-or-leave-it mindset. Because of its tenor/drums format, *Rings of Saturn* is bound to be compared to *Interstellar Space*, Ali's 1967 duet with John Coltrane. Belogenis, in fact, has been greatly influenced by late-period Trane as well as the innovations of Albert Ayler. But he's also his own man, and the saxman makes that clear on original material as well as fiery, intensely emotional performances of the Trane pieces "Saturn" (which was heard on *Interstellar Space*) and "Seraphic Light." *Rings of Saturn* falls short of essential, but it's a heartfelt, satisfying date that admirers of free jazz will enjoy. *—Alex Henderson*

Moon Flight / Aug. 26, 1975 / Knitting Factory ♦♦♦♦
The Survival label was started by Rashied Ali on a shoestring budget in the mid-70s. These discs were rare when they were first issued, so it is to the credit of Knit Classics for reissuing them and allowing a second chance to hear them. On *Moon Flight* drummer Rashied Ali assembles a group of musicians who didn't have to struggle to keep up with the polyrhythms he inflicted. Joined by James Vass on alto sax, Marvin Blackman on tenor, Charles Eubanks on piano, and Benny Wilson on bass, this ensemble rages through Ali's "Blood on the Cross," Blackman's "Moon Flight," Vass's "A Light," and fellow drummer Zahir Batin's "Face of Forgotten Thought," while veering into a free jazz landscape while oddly juggling jagged hard bop roots. Acting as a balance to this intensity are tributes to John Coltrane in the form of two beautiful compositions—Mal Waldron's "Soul Eyes" and Coltrane's "Naima," which Ali had played live with Coltrane, as documented on the *Village Vanguard Again* sessions on Impulse. *—Al Campbell*

Geri Allen

b. Jun. 12, 1957, Pontiac, MI
Piano / Improvisation, M-Base, Post-Bop
Geri Allen is the quintessence of what a late-'90s mainstream jazz musician should be. Well versed in a variety of modern jazz styles, from bop to free, Allen steers a middle course in her own music, speaking in a cultivated and moderately distinctive voice, respectful of, but not overly impressed with the doctrine of conservatism that rules the scene at the end of jazz's first century. There is little conceptually that separates her from her most obvious models—Keith Jarrett, Herbie Hancock and Bill Evans primary among them—yet Allen plays with a spontaneity and melodic gift that greatly transcends rote imitation. Her improvisational style is at various times both spacious and dense, rubato and swinging, blithe and percussive. After forming an association with the Brooklyn "MBase" crowd in the mid-'80s, Allen played on several of scene-leader Steve Coleman's albums, including his first, 1985's *Motherland Pulse*. Allen's own first album, *The Printmakers*, from a year earlier, showcased the pianist's more avant-garde tendencies. In 1988 came perhaps her first mature group statement, Etude, a cooperative trio effort with Charlie Haden and Paul Motian. In the '90s, Allen signed first with Blue Note, then Verve. Her subsequent records placed her in ever more conventional contexts, supported by the cream of the mainstream "young lion" crop. *—Chris Kelsey*

Segments / Apr. 6, 1989-Apr. 8, 1989 / DIW ♦♦♦♦
Reissued from the original 1989 recording, *Segments* features three of the finest modern jazz musicians: pianist Geri Allen, bassist Charlie Haden and drummer Paul Motian. At the time, the trio performed and recorded frequently, and the collaborative energy they shared is palpable on this album. Along with original pieces, they perform smart, unique versions of Ornette Coleman's "Law Years," Charlie Parker's "Marmaduke" and "Segment," along with the standards "I'm All Smiles" and "You'll Never Know." *—Heather Phares*

Twenty One / Mar. 23, 1994-Mar. 24, 1994 / Blue Note ♦♦♦♦
Pianist Geri Allen has thus far been a very consistent performer, and all of her recordings are easily recommended. This particular set finds her in a trio with bassist Ron Carter and drummer Tony Williams performing six of her originals along with six jazz standards. Allen's style is fairly original, with hints of Herbie Nichols, and her chancetaking but logical solos are generally quite stimulating. *—Scott Yanow*

● **Some Aspects of Water** / Mar. 15, 1996–Mar. 17, 1996 / Storyville ♦♦♦♦♦
In 1996, pianist/composer Geri Allen was awarded the prestigious Jazzpar Prize. She flew to Denmark to pick up the award and performed at a few concerts that were recorded. This CD showcases her at her best. Allen performs two originals (including "Feed the Fire" which eventually becomes Miles Davis' "Dig") in a trio with bassist Palle Danielsson and drummer Lenny White. Veteran trumpeter Johnny Coles (a year before his death) contributes a faltering but heartfelt statement to "Old Folks" and is part of an international nonet (along with Danielsson, White and five other horns) on the two remaining pieces; the highpoint is Allen's

complex and nearly 19-minute "Some Aspects of Water." Throughout the date, Geri Allen shows why she is one of postbop's top stars. Highly recommended. *—Scott Yanow*

Gathering / Feb. 19, 1998-Feb. 25, 1998 / Verve ♦♦♦♦
Geri Allen, a brilliant jazz pianist since the '80s, wrote all 11 pieces on this moody and atmospheric CD. Although not a major composer, her arrangements, and her use of colors overall, make the music quite haunting. The personnel varies from track-to-track and includes Allen, trumpeter Wallace Roney, trombonist Robin Eubanks, Dwight Andrews on bass clarinet, flutes and piccolo, guitarist Vernon Reid, Ralphe Armstrong and Buster Williams on basses, drummer Lenny White and percussionist Mino Cinelu. Allen, whose playing on this date sometimes is reminiscent of Herbie Hancock, always records music that grows in interest with each listen. *—Scott Yanow*

Henry "Red" Allen

b. Jan. 7, 1908, New Orleans, LA, **d.** Apr. 17, 1967, New York, NY
Vocals, Trumpet / New Orleans Jazz, Swing, Dixieland
One of the last great New Orleans trumpeters to emerge during the post-Louis Armstrong era, Henry "Red" Allen has long been overshadowed by Satch and his successors but actually had a fresh new approach of his own to offer. Allen sounded modern no matter what the setting and the rhythmic freedom he achieved made his solos consistently unpredictable and exciting. He recorded with King Oliver and Clarence Williams, and then Allen joined Luis Russell's superb orchestra and began his own solo recording career. Signed by Victor as an alternative to Okeh's Louis Armstrong, Allen's solos were original and brilliant from the start (particularly "It Should Be You"); throughout the 1930s his trumpet and gruff vocals would be heard on dozens of recordings and, even when the material was indifferent, he was usually able to uplift the music. *—Scott Yanow*

1929-1933 / Jul. 16, 1929-Nov. 9, 1933 / Classics ♦♦♦♦♦
The first of a five-volume CD series released by the European Classics label that reissues all of the recordings led by trumpeter Red Allen during 1929-41 is one of the best. The great trumpeter is first heard fronting the Luis Russell Orchestra for such classics as "It Should Be You" and "Biff'ly Blues," he interacts with blues singer Victoria Spivey, and on the selections from 1933 (two of which were previously unreleased) he co-leads a group with tenor-saxophonist Coleman Hawkins. Not all of the performances are gems but there are many memorable selections including "How Do They Do It That Way," "Pleasin' Paul," "Sugar Hill Function," and "Patrol Wagon Blues." Other soloists include trombonists J.C. Higginbottham and Dicky Wells, clarinetist Albert Nicholas and altoist Charlie Holmes. *—Scott Yanow*

The Rhythmakers / Apr. 16, 1932-Oct. 8, 1932 / IAJRC ♦♦♦
This LP from the collector's label may look like a bootleg album, but the music is quite exciting. Trumpeter Red Allen teams up with Pee Wee Russell (heard on both clarinet and tenor) and either Joe Sullivan or Fats Waller on piano for eight selections originally released under singer Billy Banks's name, seven from the Rhythmakers and one number ("Who Stole the Lock on the Hen House Door") from a date headed by guitarist Jack Bland. The heated interaction between Allen and Russell (particularly on the later version of "Oh Peter") is quite inspired, and, even with the many Billy Banks vocals, this music should greatly satisfy Dixieland and New Orleans jazz fans. *—Scott Yanow*

Ride, Red, Ride in Hi-Fi / Mar. 21, 1957-Apr. 10, 1957 / RCA ♦♦♦♦♦
This 1957 LP (which has since been reissued as *World on a String* on CD) was one of trumpeter Henry "Red" Allen's finest hours. He leads a potentially unruly group of all-stars (which includes Coleman Hawkins on tenor, clarinetist Buster Bailey and trombonist J.C. Higginbotham) through a variety of heated standards. The highpoints are Red's abstract solo on "I Cover the Waterfront," the catchy "Algiers Bounce" and the hot ensembles of the Dixielandish "Love Is Just Around the Corner." *—Scott Yanow*

★ **World on a String** / Mar. 21, 1957-Apr. 10, 1957 / Bluebird/RCA ♦♦♦♦♦
This CD is a true classic. Trumpeter Red Allen is heard at the peak of his creative powers with a remarkable octet also featuring trombonist J.C. Higginbotham, clarinetist Buster Bailey and the great tenor Coleman Hawkins. "I Cover the Waterfront" has a wonderfully abstract statement from Allen, "Love Is Just Around the Corner" is joyous Dixieland, "Let Me Miss You, Baby" is a particularly strong blues (featuring Allen's vocal) and the simple blues line that serves as a melody on "Algiers Bounce" is quite catchy. The other seven selections from the classic veterans are also quite enjoyable. Although the music has its basis in Dixieland and swing, the solos of Allen and Hawkins in particular look ahead toward the future. There is nothing dated about these essential performances; highly recommended. *—Scott Yanow*

Henry Red Allen Meets Kid Ory / 1960 / Verve ♦♦♦♦♦

Mose Allison

b. Nov. 11, 1927, Tippo, MS
Vocals, Piano, Lyricist / Vocal Jazz, Jazz Blues, Hard Bop
Not unlike his namesake, Luther Allison, pianist Mose Allison has suffered from "categorization problem," given his equally brilliant career. Although his boogie woogie and bebop-laden piano style is innovative and fresh sounding when it comes to blues and jazz, it is as a songwriter that Allison really shines. Allison's songs have been recorded by the Who ("Young Man Blues"), Leon Russell ("I'm Smashed"), and Bonnie Raitt ("Everybody's Cryin' Mercy"). Other admirers include Tom Waits, John Mayall, Georgie Fame, the Rolling Stones and Van Morrison. But because he's always played both blues and jazz, and not one to the exclusion of the other, his career has suffered. As he himself admits, he has a "category" problem that lingers to this day. "There's a lot of places I don't work because they're confused about what I do," he explained in a 1990 interview in *Goldmine* magazine. Despite the lingering confusion, Allison remains one of the finest songwriters in 20th century blues. *—Richard Skelly*

Back Country Suite / Mar. 7, 1957 / Prestige/OJC ♦♦♦♦
Mose Allison's very first recording finds the 29-year old pianist taking just two vocals (on his "Young Man Blues" and "One Room Country Shack") but those are actually the most memorable selections. The centerpiece of this trio outing with bassist Taylor LaFargue and drummer Frank Isola (which has been reissued on CD) is Allison's ten-part "Back Country Suite," a series of short concise folk melodies that puts the focus on his somewhat unique piano style which, although boppish, also looked back toward the country blues tradition. Very interesting music. *—Scott Yanow*

● **Greatest Hits** / Mar. 7, 1957-Feb. 13, 1959 / Prestige/OJC ♦♦♦♦♦
Basic, no-frills anthology of 13 of his better late-'50s Prestige sides, all of which feature his vocals. It has most of his most famous songs, particularly to listeners from a rock background, including his versions of "The Seventh Son," "Eyesight to the Blind" (covered by The Who on *Tommy,* though Sonny Boy Williamson did it before Allison), "Parchman Farm" (done by John Mayall), and "Young Man's Blues" (also covered by The Who). Were it not for the significant omission of "I'm Not Talking" (retooled by The Yardbirds), this would qualify as the basic collection for most listeners, although more thorough retrospectives are available (particularly Rhino's *Anthology*). *Greatest Hits* does include liner notes by Pete Townshend, originally penned for a 1972 collection. *—Richie Unterberger*

Local Color / Nov. 8, 1957 / Prestige/OJC ♦♦♦
This CD reissue brings back Mose Allison's second of six Prestige recordings. Allison performs eight instrumentals in a trio with bassist Addison Farmer and drummer Nick Stabulas, displaying his unusual mixture of country blues and bebop and even taking an effective trumpet solo on "Trouble In Mind." However it is his vocals on "Lost Mind" and particularly the classic "Parchman Farm" that are most memorable. *—Scott Yanow*

★ **Allison Wonderland: Anthology** / 1957-1989 / Rhino ♦♦♦♦♦
Only Dave Frishberg and possibly Mark Murphy can rival Mose Allison when it comes to creative use of irony in lyric writing and neither compares as an instrumentalist. He's a fine bop pianist able to play challenging instrumentals and eclectic enough to integrate country blues and gospel elements into his style. Allison's unique mix of down-home and uptown styles has made him a standout since the '50s. He's one of the few jazz musicians on Atlantic's roster ideally suited for Rhino's two-disc anthology format. Allison recorded so many different kinds of songs and was always as much, if not more, a singles than an album artist. In addition, Rhino thankfully sequenced the selected songs—which span over 40 years, from 1957 to 1989, and include all of his best-known songs—chronologically. Allison does reflective duo and trio pieces, moves into uptempo combo numbers with a jump beat, then returns to the intimate small group sound. His ability to highlight key lyrics, delivery, timing and packing is superb. The set includes such classics as "Back Country Blues," "Parchman Farm," "Western Man," and "Ever Since the World Ended," plus definitive covers of of Willie Dixon's "The Seventh Son" and Sonny Boy Williamson II's "Eyesight to the Blind." It's an essential introduction to Allison's catalog. *—Ron Wynn*

Creek Bank / Jan. 24, 1958–Aug. 15, 1958 / Prestige ♦♦♦♦
When Mose Allison recorded his six early albums for Prestige, he was best-known as a bop-based pianist who occasionally sang. This single CD (which reissues in full *Young Man Mose* and *Creek Bank*) has 15 instrumentals including a rare appearance by Allison on trumpet ("Stroll") but it is his five typically ironic vocals that are most memorable, particularly Allison's classic "The Seventh Son" and "If You Live." His piano playing, even with the Bud Powell influence, was beginning to become original and he successfully performs both revived swing songs and moody originals. *—Scott Yanow*

Autumn Song / Feb. 13, 1959 / Prestige/OJC ♦♦♦♦

Transfiguration of Hiram Brown / Dec. 21, 1959-Jan. 11, 1960 / Columbia/Legacy ♦♦♦♦
Mostly instrumental, this ingratiating release features outstanding playing by this exceptionally talented yet largely unknown songwriter/singer/pianist. The album begins with the eight-part "Hiram Brown" suite, in which a naïve country boy loses his illusions and optimism in the big city. Five standards complete the album in fine style. "Baby Please Don't Go" and "'Deed I Do" offer Mose's unique, smoky singing at its most touching. This album was released with two others in a delightful 1994 collection called *High Jinks*. *—Mark Allan*

I Love the Life I Live / Jun. 28, 1960-Sep. 9, 1960 / Columbia/Legacy ♦♦♦♦♦
When this album was recorded in 1960, this laconic Mississippian wasn't the brilliant lyricist he would later become. But he had great taste. The title track, written by Willie Dixon, sure sounds like a Mose song; "Fool's Paradise" is another gem. Mose's four tunes are instrumentals. The production by Teo Macero makes it feel like you're perched on one end of the piano bench. This album was released with two others in a delightful 1994 collection called *High Jinks*. *—Mark Allan*

V-8 Ford Blues / Apr. 1961 / Epic/Legacy ♦♦♦♦
Besides cool playing and his uniquely smoky singing, Mose has great taste in material. "Hey Good Lookin'" fits right in with revisited versions of "I Love the Life I Live," "I Ain't Got Nobody," and "Baby Please Don't Go," complete with what the singer himself calls his distinctive "involuntary groan" during the piano solo. Teo Macero's intimate production makes it feel like you're right there in the studio. This album was released with two others in a delightful 1994 collection called *High Jinks*. *—Mark Allan*

I Don't Worry About a Thing / Mar. 15, 1962 / Rhino ♦♦♦♦♦
Mose Allison was already 34 and had recorded nine records as a leader before cutting his debut for Atlantic (which has been reissued on CD by Rhino) but this was his breakthrough date. One of jazz's greatest lyricists, at the time, Allison was making the transition from being a pianist who occasionally sang to becoming a vocalist who also played his own unusual brand of piano. In addition to the original versions of "Your Mind Is on Vacation," "I Don't Worry About a Thing (Because I Know Nothing Will Turn out Right)," and "It Didn't Turn out That Way," he sings bluish versions of two standards ("Meet Me at No Special Place" and "The Song Is Ended") and plays five instrumentals with his trio. There are only 33 1/2 minutes of music on this straight reissue of the orignal LP, but the set is one of Mose Allison's most significant recordings. *—Scott Yanow*

The Best of Mose Allison / 1962-1970 / Atlantic ♦♦♦♦♦
The Mose Allison installment in Atlantic's Jazz Anthology series of 1970 is superior to most in that line simply on the grounds of time. Since Mose's songs were usually brief, Atlantic was able to fit 12 of them onto a single LP and thus provide a wider selection of his output, unlike others in that series which included only five or six tracks, making it serve as a pretty good capsule introduction to one of American music's most idiosyncratic individualists. Many of his most famous songs are here—"ßYour Mind Is on Vacation," "New Parchman," "I'm the Wild Man," "I Don't Worry About a Thing," "Your Molecular Structure," etc., along with covers like "Rollin' Stone" and a rushed live remake of his biggest "hit," Willie Dixon's "Seventh Son." For a more comprehensive—and well-packaged—overview of most of his career, turn to the double-CD box *Allison Wonderland* on Rhino/Atlantic. *—Richard S. Ginell*

The Word from Mose / Mar. 10, 1964 / Atlantic ♦♦♦
Despite his continuing popularity, many of Mose Allison's Atlantic records remain out of print, including this 1964 Lp. The program, which has the vocalist-pianist being accompanied by bassist Ben Tucker and drummer Ron Lundberg, is most notable for the inclusion of such originals as "One of These Days," "New Parchman" and "I'm Not Talking" plus memorable cover versions of Muddy Waters' "Rollin' Stone" and "Your Red Wagon." *—Scott Yanow*

Mose Alive! / Oct. 22, 1965-Oct. 31, 1965 / Atlantic ♦♦♦

I've Been Doin' Some Thinkin' / Jul. 9, 1968-Jul. 10, 1968 / Atlantic ♦♦♦♦
Unaffected so far by the rock and electronic revolutions, the Mose kept on doing his inimitable thing through the late '60s, developing his chromatic acoustic piano idiom, wryly observing life, covering an occasional standard. This album yielded at least three Allison classics—the clever chemical love song "Your Molecular Structure," and his trenchant rebuke to platitude criers of all stripes "Everybody Cryin' Mercy," and the urban warning that probably didn't go over too well with the drug crowd at the time, "If You're Goin' to the City." The standard under consideration this time is Gov. Jimmie Davis' "You Are My Sunshine." Red Mitchell (bass) and Bill Goodwin (drums) provide the backing, and that's all Mose needed for another entertaining, thought-provoking set. *—Richard S. Ginell*

Western Man / Feb. 2, 1971-Mar. 4, 1971 / Atlantic ♦♦♦

Mose in Your Ear / Apr. 25, 1972-Apr. 26, 1972 / Atlantic ♦♦♦♦

Your Mind Is on Vacation / Apr. 5, 1976-Apr. 9, 1976 / Koch International ♦♦♦♦♦
It seems strange to realize that this was Mose Allison's only recording during the 1973-1981 period. In addition to his trio with bassist Jack Hannah and drummer Jerry Granelli, such guests as altoist David Sanborn, Al Cohn, and Joe Farrell on tenors and trumpeter Al Porcino pop up on a few selections. However, Mose Allison is easily the main star, performing ten of his originals (including a remake of the famous title cut, "What Do You Do After You Ruin Your Life," and "Swingin' Machine") plus renditions of the standards "Foolin' Myself" and "I Can't See for Lookin'." *—Scott Yanow*

Pure Mose / 1978 / 32 Jazz ♦♦♦

Ever Since the World Ended / May 11, 1987-Jun. 2, 1987 / Blue Note ♦♦♦

My Backyard / Dec. 5, 1989-Dec. 7, 1989 / Blue Note ♦♦♦

The Earth Wants You / Sep. 8, 1993-Sep. 9, 1993 / Blue Note ♦♦♦♦
Mose Allison, one of the top lyricists of the '90s, shows throughout this entertaining CD that his powers as a pianist and singer are also very much intact. The album introduces a few new classics in "Certified Senior Citizen," "This Ain't Me" and "Who's in, Who's Out." His voice is still in prime form and his piano playing remains quite unique. It is true that the guests on the set (guitarist John Scofield, altoist Joe Lovano, Bob Malach on tenor and trumpeter Randy Brecker) are not all that necessary but Allison's performance makes this an excellent showcase for his music. *—Scott Yanow*

Gimcracks and Gewgaws / May 17, 1997-May 18, 1997 / Blue Note ♦♦♦♦♦
The older Mose Allison gets, the sharper his mind becomes, the more idiosyncratic his music sounds, and the more pleasure the aficionado gets for spending the better part of an hour with his latest stuff. By this time, the 70-year old philosopher from Tippo, Miss. had sharpened his wit and insight on life to an even keener edge, musing wryly on materialism, technology, aging, death, even his own name ("MJA, Jr."). The tunes seem to have disappeared almost entirely but it doesn't matter; the lyrics are so damned clever and as hilarious as ever, even when they are obviously sequels to previous masterworks like "Your Mind Is On Vacation" ("What's With You") or "Young Man's Blues" ("Old Man Blues"). Mose's piano style by now has been pared down to its unique essentials, a ceaseless, swinging linear flow drawing from the three Bs—Bach, Bartok and bop—and his voice has barely aged since his Prestige days. Mark Shim muses ably on tenor sax now and then, and guitarist Russell Malone ranges all over the stylistic lot between R&B and jazz. At this rate, waiting four years or so between albums in the '90s, Allison has kept his creative batteries fresh every time out. *—Richard S. Ginell*

Albert Ammons

b. Sep. 23, 1907, Chicago, IL, **d.** Dec. 2, 1949, Chicago, IL
Piano / Swing, Boogie-Woogie, Piano Blues
Albert Ammons was one of the big three of late-'30s boogie-woogie along with Pete Johnson and Meade Lux Lewis. Arguably the most powerful of the three, Ammons was also flexible enough to play swing music. Ammons played in Chicago clubs from the 1920s on although he also worked as a cab driver for a time. Starting in 1934 he led his own band in Chicago and he made his first records in 1936. In 1938 Ammons appeared at Carnegie Hall with Pete Johnson and Meade Lux Lewis, an event that really helped launch the boogie-woogie craze. Ammons recorded with the other pianists in duets and trios, fit right in with the Port of Harlem Jazzmen on their Blue Note session, appeared regularly at Cafe Society, recorded as a sideman with Sippie Wallace in the 1940s and he even cut a session with his son, the great tenorman Gene Ammons. Albert Ammons worked steadily throughout the 1940s, playing at President Harry Truman's inauguration in 1949; he died later that year. Many of his recordings are currently available on CD. *—Scott Yanow*

☆ **Complete Blue Note Recordings of Albert Ammons and Meade Lux Lewis** / Nov. 21, 1935-Apr. 22, 1944 / Mosaic ♦♦♦♦♦
This magnificent three-LP box set was issued as part of the first release by the Mosaic label. The out of print collection has all of the music recorded during Blue Note's first session (nine piano solos by Albert Ammons, eight including a five-part "The Blues" by Meade Lux Lewis, and a pair of Ammons-Lewis duets) plus Lewis' 1935 version of "Honky Tonk Train Blues" and his complete sessions of October 4, 1940, April 9, 1941 (four songs on harpsichord), and August 22, 1944. The music emphasizes boogie-woogie and both Ammons (quite memorable on "Boogie Woogie Stomp") and Lewis are heard in prime form. Incidentally, one of their duets (which is mistakenly titled "The Sheik of Araby") is actually "Nagasaki." This box is well worth bidding on at an auction. *—Scott Yanow*

Boogie Woogie Stomp / 1938-Oct. 31, 1939 / Delmark ♦♦♦
The classic boogie-woogie performances of Albert Ammons, Meade Lux Lewis and Pete Johnson have never been put out completely and in chronological order, although some sessions have been reissued many times. This 1998 Delmark CD confuses the matter a bit because some of the live recordings that it includes formerly came out on Euphonic LPs, and some are unknown. The selections alternate between solo tracks by Ammons (nine), Lewis (six) and Johnson (two); there is also a lone piano duet ("Saturday Night") by Ammons and Lewis. Because the performances (recorded at *the Hotel Sherman* in 1939 and in an obscure studio session in 1938 that adds bassist Herbert Marshall) are not issued in chronological order, and since the music switches between the pianists, it can be a bit confusing trying to figure out who is playing when. Musically, the three pianists are quite consistent and since the music is taken from their prime period, it is easily recommended to boogie-woogie collectors despite one's reservations about the order of the performances. *—Scott Yanow*

● **The First Day** / Jan. 6, 1939 / Blue Note ♦♦♦♦♦
Producer Alfred Lion, who had attended John Hammond's Spiritual to Swing concert of Dec. 23, 1938 which had introduced boogie-woogie pianists Albert Ammons and Meade Lux Lewis to New York audiences, was very impressed. Two weeks later he started the Blue Note label by recording nine Ammons solos, eight by Lewis and a pair of heated duets during a single day. All of the music (except an untitled original by Meade Lux Lewis slated to be issued by Blue Note in the future) is on this single CD. Ammons, the more forceful (relatively speaking) of the two pianists, generally takes honors but there are plenty of rewarding performances including Lewis' five-part "The Blues," Ammons' "Boogie Woogie Stomp" and their duet on "Nagasaki." Highly recommended to collectors who do not already own Mosaic's more extensive three-LP limited-edition Ammons/Lewis set. *—Scott Yanow*

1939-1946 / Apr. 8, 1939-Apr. 2, 1946 / Classics ♦♦♦♦♦
This CD offers three distinct periods in the development of boogie-woogie pianist Albert Ammons. Kicking off with solo tracks recorded in 1939 and 1944 for the Solo-Art and Commodore labels, the next batch follows him into a small-band format with Hop Lips Page practically stealing the show in his demonstrative style. The final ten selections emanate from Chicago sessions for Mercury—again with a small group—featuring vocals from Sippie Wallace and Mildred Anderson. Ammons was a giant in his chosen field of endeavor, and these sides make a marvelous addition to his too-short discography. *—Cub Koda*

Gene Ammons

b. Apr. 14, 1925, Chicago, IL, **d.** Aug. 6, 1974, Chicago, IL
Sax (Tenor) / Hard Bop, Soul-Jazz, Bop
Gene Ammons, who had a huge and immediately recognizable tone on tenor, was a very flexible player who could play bebop with the best (always battling his friend Sonny Stitt to a tie) yet was an influence on the R&B world. Some of his ballad renditions became hits and, despite two unfortunate interruptions in his career, Ammons remained a popular attraction for 25 years. Son of the great boogie-woogie pianist Albert Ammons, he left Chicago at age 18 to work with King Kolax's band. He originally came to fame as a key soloist with Billy Eckstine's orchestra during 1944-47, trading off with Dexter Gordon on the famous Eckstine record *Blowing the Blues Away*. Other than a notable stint with Woody Herman's Third Herd in 1949 and an attempt at co-leading a two tenor group in the early '50s with Sonny Stitt, Ammons worked as a single throughout his career, recording frequently in settings ranging from quartets and organ combos to all-star jam sessions. Drug problems often landed him in prison, and when Ammons returned to the scene in 1969 he opened up his style a bit, including some of the emotional cries of the avant-garde while utilizing funky rhythm sections. *—Scott Yanow*

All-Star Sessions / Mar. 5, 1950-Jun. 16, 1955 / Prestige/OJC ♦♦♦♦♦
This is an excellent recording that pieces together three separate sessions. The first, with Art Farmer and Lou Donaldson marked Ammons' return to jazz after exploring R&B for a period of time. The second and third sessions find "Jug" teaming up with his musical soulmate Sonny Stitt for two separate dates. Their interplay over the years produced some of jazz's most stimulating moments and they don't disappoint here. The songs are short, but the addition of numerous outtakes make for a long, satisfying listen. Essential. *—Robert Taylor*

The Gene Ammons Story: The 78 Era / Mar. 5, 1950-Nov. 4, 1955 / Prestige ♦♦♦♦
This CD contains 26 of the 30 selections included on the two-LP set of the same name (and catalog number). Although mostly cut during an era when Ammons co-led a two-tenor group with Sonny Stitt, the focus is almost entirely on Ammons. All but the final five titles are from the 1950-51 period and these concise performances were originally on 78s. Even at this early stage Ammons's tone was quite distinctive and he was able to combine the innovations of bop with the simplicity of R&B in his forceful and direct solos; also, few could play ballads with the passion he possessed. This CD is recommended to listeners who do not already own the two-fer. *—Scott Yanow*

Greatest Hits: The 50's / Mar. 5, 1950-May 2, 1958 / Prestige/OJC ♦♦♦♦
Ten long years after the release of *Vol. 1* of Gene Ammons' *Greatest Hits: The 60s*, the de facto *Vol. 2* finally emerged in 1998, summing up the 1950s on a single disc of short-play singles and long, glorious blowing sessions. The three singles, all succinct little summaries

of progressive bop, cover the years 1950 and 1955 and then the real meat and potatoes kick in, five extended tracks (including the definitive jam of this period, "The Happy Blues") with plenty of ecstatic blowing room for Jackie McLean's alto, Art Farmer's and Donald Byrd's trumpets, and Mal Waldron's piano. Throughout, Ammons' massive, booming tone hovers over the disc like a majestic yet benign presence, always funky, always in charge. Unlike the first volume, *Vol. 2* is sequenced in chronological order, which makes more programmatic sense, and almost all of Ammons' Prestige LPs from the '50s are touched upon. With this and *Vol. 1,* you can acquire a decent overview of the soulful Ammons mystique, with only the final period (1969-1974) missing. *—Richard S. Ginell*

☆ **The Happy Blues** / Aug. 23, 1956 / Prestige/OJC ♦♦♦♦♦
This is one of the great studio jam sessions. Tenor saxophonist Gene Ammons is teamed up with trumpeter Art Farmer, altoist Jackie McLean, pianst Duke Jordan, bassist Addison Farmer, drummer Art Taylor, and the congas of Candido for four lengthy selections. Best is "The Happy Blues," which has memorable solos and spontaneous but perfectly fitting riffing by the horns behind each others' solos. The other numbers ("The Great Lie," "Can't We Be Friends," and "Madhouse") are also quite enjoyable, making this a highly recommended set. *—Scott Yanow*

Jammin' with Gene / Jul. 13, 1956 / Prestige/OJC ♦♦♦♦
This tenor-saxophonist led a series of excellent all-star jam sessions for the Prestige label during the mid-'50s that took advantage of the extra time available on LPs (as opposed to the three-minute 78). This album features versions of "Jammin' with Gene" (a blues), "We'll Be Together Again" (which evolves from being an Ammons ballad feature into a group jam and then back again) and "Not Really the Blues" that clocks in between ten and over 16 minutes. With such sidemen as trumpeters Art Farmer and Donald Byrd, altoist Jackie McLean, pianist Mal Waldron, bassist Doug Watkins, and drummer Art Taylor, this is an excellent (and rather spontaneous) straightahead session. *—Scott Yanow*

Jammin' in Hi Fi with Gene Ammons / Apr. 12, 1957 / Prestige/OJC ♦♦♦♦

Groove Blues / Jan. 3, 1958 / Prestige/OJC ♦♦♦♦
On Jan. 3, 1958, Gene Ammons led one of his last all-star jam sessions for Prestige. The most notable aspect to this date (which resulted in two albums of material) is that it featured among its soloists John Coltrane, on alto. This CD, a straight reissue of one of the original LPs, includes baritonist Pepper Adams, the tenor of Paul Quinichette and Coltrane on two of the four selections and Jerome Richardson's flute during three of the songs in addition to a fine rhythm section (pianist Mal Waldron, bassist George Joyner and drummer Art Taylor). This set consists of three of Waldron's originals in addition to the standard ballad "It Might as Well Be Spring" and it (along with the CD *The Big Sound*) fully documents the productive day. *—Scott Yanow*

Boss Tenor / Jun. 16, 1960 / Prestige/OJC ♦♦♦♦♦
There are many Gene Ammons recordings currently available on CD in Fantasy's Original Jazz Classics since the versatile tenorman was a longtime Prestige recording artist. Unlike his earlier jam sessions, this particular outing finds Ammons as the only horn, fronting a talented rhythm section (pianist Tommy Flanagan, bassist Doug Watkins, drummer Art Taylor, and Ray Barretto on congas). Jug explores standards (including a near-classic version of "Canadian Sunset"), blues and ballads in his usual warm, soulful and swinging fashion. This is a fine outing by one of the true "bosses" of the tenor. [A 20-bit remaster of *Boss Tenor* was released in October 1999.] *—Scott Yanow*

The Gene Ammons Story: Organ Combos / Jun. 17, 1960–Nov. 28, 1961 / Prestige ♦♦♦♦

Soul Summit / Jun. 13, 1961-Apr. 13, 1962 / Prestige ♦♦♦♦
This single CD reissues all of the music from two LPs titled *Soul Summit* and *Soul Summit, Vol. 2.* The latter session is one of the lesser known of the many collaborations of tenors Gene Ammons and Sonny Stitt, who are joined by organist Jack McDuff and drummer Charlie Persip. Their six performances are primarily riff tunes with "When You Wish upon a Star" taken at a medium pace and "Out in the Cold Again" the lone ballad. The second half of this CD features Ammons on two songs ("Love I've Found You" and a swinging "Too Marvelous for Words") with a big band arranged by Oliver Nelson, jamming "Ballad for Baby" with a quintet, sitting out of "Scram" (which stars McDuff and the tenor of Harold Vick) and backing singer Etta Jones on three numbers, of which, "Cool, Cool Daddy" is the most memorable. Overall, this is an interesting and consistently swinging set that adds to the large quantity of recordings that the great Ammons did during the early '60s. *—Scott Yanow*

We'll Be Together Again / Aug. 26, 1961 / Prestige/OJC ♦♦♦♦
The title of this exciting meeting between the tenors of Gene Ammons and Sonny Stitt was rather poignant, because this recording was released in the late '60s, when Ammons was serving a long jail sentence for possession of heroin, and it appeared that he and Stitt might never meet up again. Backed by pianist John Houston, bassist Buster Williams and drummer George Brown, Ammons, and Stitt (who had co-led a regular group a decade before) proved once again to be a perfect team, jamming on a variety of standards, blues and ballads while also revisiting "New Blues Up and Down." The two tenors always brought out the best in each other, and luckily, they would get back together in the early '70s. This is high-quality bebop. *—Scott Yanow*

★ **Boss Tenors: Straight Ahead from Chicago 1961** / Aug. 27, 1961 / Verve ♦♦♦♦♦
There are perhaps no better tenors, no better jazz. This is definitive. With Sonny Stitt. *—Michael G. Nastos*

Up Tight / Oct. 17, 1961-Oct. 18, 1961 / Prestige ♦♦♦♦

Preachin' / May 3, 1962 / Prestige/OJC ♦♦♦♦
This is a most unusual session. The great tenor performs 11 religious hymns with accompaniment by organist Clarence "Sleepy" Anderson (along with bassist Sylvester Hickman and drummer Dorral Anderson) that is straight from the church. Ammons mostly sticks very closely to the themes but gives such melodies as "Abide with Me," "You'll Never Walk Alone," "What a Friend," and "Holy Holy" passion, soul and honest feelings. This little-known album (now available on CD) is a rather touching and emotional outing and quite unique. *—Scott Yanow*

The Boss Is Back / Nov. 10, 1969-Nov. 11, 1969 / Prestige ♦♦♦♦
The executives at Prestige must have been felt ecstatic when they heard Gene Ammons first play after his release from a very severe seven-year jail sentence. The great tenor proved to still be in his prime, his huge sound was unchanged and he was hungry to make new music. This CD, which completely reissues the first two LPs Ammons cut after his return (*The Boss Is Back!* and *Brother Jug!*) rewards repeated listenings. The first date (in an acoustic quintet with pianist Junior Mance) hints at his earlier bop-based music while the numbers from the following day (with organist Sonny Phillips) find Ammons playing over a couple of boogaloo vamps very much of the period. Actually it is his ballad statements (particularly "Here's That Rainy Day," "Feeling Good" and even "Didn't We") that really make this CD memorable, although on "He's a Real Gone Guy" Ammons shows that he had not forgotten how to jam the blues either. *—Scott Yanow*

Ernestine Anderson

b. Nov. 11, 1928, Houston, TX
Vocals / Vocal Jazz, Standards
Positioned squarely in the mainstream camp, at home in the worlds of jazz and pop standards as well as the blues, comfortable with small groups and big bands, Ernestine Anderson regularly receives a lot of airplay on traditional jazz radio stations these days. She fits those demographics well with her tasteful, slightly gritty, moderately swinging contralto, someone who doesn't probe too deeply into emotional quagmires (and thus doesn't disturb the dispositions of those who use the radio as background) but always gives you an honest, musical account. After making her first recording with Shifty Henry's Orchestra in 1947 for the Black-And-White label, she converted over to the jazz side, working with Lionel Hampton in 1952-53 and recording with a band featuring Illinois Jacquet, Milt Jackson, and Quincy Jones in 1953 and with Gigi Gryce in 1955. During a three-month Scandinavian tour Anderson made a recording called *Hot Cargo* that ironically established her reputation in America. Once back in the U.S., she signed with Mercury and made a number of albums for that label until the early 1960s, when her career went into a decline. An appearance at the 1976 Concord Jazz Festival led to a Concord contract which immediately bore fruit with the albums *Live From Concord to London* and *Hello Like Before.* These and other comeback albums made her a top-flight jazz attraction in the U.S. again—this time for the long haul. *—Richard S. Ginell*

Live from Concord to London / Aug. 1, 1976–Oct. 11, 1977 / Concord Jazz ♦♦♦♦♦
The first half of this CD is quite historic—17 minutes from Ernestine Anderson's comeback concert at the 1976 Concord Jazz Festival. One can feel excitement throughout the performance as the audience rediscovers the talented singer, who had not recorded in a decade. Four songs ("Don't Get Around Much Anymore," "Days of Wine and Roses," "Stormy Monday," and a soulful "Am I Blue") have swinging and stimulating accompaniment by pianist Hank Jones, bassist Ray Brown and drummer Jake Hanna, while a brief "Take the 'A' Train" has Anderson joined by Bill Berry's Big Band. The "London" half of the disc is from a year later and is more laidback and routine, although enjoyable. Backed by an English rhythm section, the singer interprets "My Romance," a four-song Duke Ellington medley, and "Love for Sale" in winning fashion. Overall, this is one of the best in Ernestine Anderson's string of Concord recordings. *—Scott Yanow*

● **Never Make Your Move Too Soon** / Aug. 1980 / Concord Jazz ♦♦♦♦♦
The title cut of this near-classic album became a sort of theme song for Ernestine Anderson, but it is not the only high point. The singer sounds in top form on such fine material as "As Long As I Live," a touching "Old Folks," "My Shining Hour" and "Poor Butterfly." With fine assistance from pianist Monty Alexander, bassist Ray Brown and drummer Frank Gant, Ernestine Anderson is heard throughout in prime form, sounding quite enthusiastic and powerful. Highly recommended. *—Scott Yanow*

Be Mine Tonight / Dec. 1986 / Concord Jazz ♦♦♦♦
Backed by a fine rhythm section (pianist Marshall Otwell deserves a date of his own) and assisted by Benny Carter's alto on several selections, Anderson sounded as if she really enjoyed this session. Best were a rare vocal version of "In a Mellotone" and a Dinah Washington-inspired treatment of "Christopher Columbus," the two most jazz-oriented tracks on this well-rounded album. *—Scott Yanow*

Ballad Essentials / Feb. 22, 2000 / Concord Jazz ♦♦♦
Though Ernestine Anderson is best known for her sassy and upbeat interpretations, *Ballad Essentials* gathers some of her finest renditions of ballads like "Body and Soul," "Spring Is Here," "Summertime," and "T'Ain't Nobody's Bizness If I Do." A welcome look at some of her more underrated performances. *—Heather Phares*

Fred Anderson

b. Mar. 22, 1929, Monroe, LA
Sax (Tenor) / Avant-Garde Jazz, Free Jazz, Modern Creative
Despite being an "old school" musician in terms of grounding and early influences, Fred Anderson was a founding member of the Association for the Advancement of Creative Musicians (AACM) and headed several AACM groups in the '60s. Anderson had formally studied music theory and was strongly influenced by Lester Young, Coleman Hawkins and Gene Ammons. He reflected that training throughout his career, always having a full, huge tone and being a capable blues and ballad stylist. But he also absorbed the new ideas pioneeed by Ornette Coleman and other free theorists; it was this ability to merge old and new that made Anderson a seminal figure among Chicago musicians in the '60s. Anderson later toured Europe with a quintet that included Douglas Ewart, and later toured Germany with another new band that had both Ewart and George Lewis. *Another Place* on Moers (1978) is a fine early recording of Anderson as a leader, and he has many excellent recordings from the 1990s on Chicago's Okkadisk label. *—Ron Wynn*

Birdhouse / Apr. 7, 1994-Feb. 20, 1995 / Okka Disk ♦♦♦
Named for his Chicago jazz club which closed in the late '70s, *Birdhouse* finds tenor sax great Fred Anderson leading his quartet through four originals that cover a spectrum of moods. It opens with the casual (and tasteful) burner "Birdhouse," an 18-minute number that places drummer Hamid Drake and bassist Harrison Bankhead in the role of often-swinging rhythm section while pianist Jim Baker backs up Anderson's playing with occasional, parallel solos and, 10 minutes in, takes a nice solo that leaves plenty of room in which to stretch out. A few minutes later, Baker also steps back, letting Bankhead step in with an interesting solo of his own. Finally, he too drops out of the mix, leaving Drake the responsibility of keeping both time and melodies going during his hot drum solo. The whole group then jumps in again and neatly ties up the entire piece in the remaining minute. Next comes "Bernice," a drawn-out, slow wailer, beautifully played. Next, the group lets loose with rocketing intensity on "Like Sonny," dedicated to bop saxophonist Sonny Stitt. The closing number is a hot Anderson-Drake improvisation, "Waiting for MC," which was recorded while the two awaited the arrival of pianist Marilyn Crispell for a rehearsal of what would become Okkadisk's 1995 release, *Destiny*. *—Joslyn Layne*

● **Fred Anderson & DKV Trio** / Dec. 3, 1996 / Okka Disk ♦♦♦♦♦
Fred Anderson & DKV Trio is an excellent jazz album that captures the high level of musicianship possessed by these top Chicago players. Heard here are saxophonist Fred Anderson (founding member of the AACM), percussionist Hamid Drake, bassist Kent Kessler, and reeds man Ken Vandermark. With this group, there *is* no "warming up"; they're hot from the opening notes. "Planet E" is the first cut, and within no time the fire is stoked and the musicians move, wail, plummet, and shine. The breadth of playing hard and now—of playing to live—comes through quite clear; each tune reveals a different side of what exquisite players can do, from the walking-bass, standards feel of "Lady's in Love" to the rollicking urgency of "Aaron's Tune." Moments that, alone, are enough to justify this album's place in your jazz collection include "Black Woman," a heartbreaking, harmonizing saxophone duet that occasionally recalls "Gloomy Sunday," and a particularly brooding rendition of "Dark Day," an Anderson piece that appears on some of his other recordings, including *Fred Anderson Quartet, Vol. 1* on Asian Improv. This take of "Dark Day" finds Vandermark on clarinet and Kessler bowing the bass in a manner that's alternately reflective and emotional. Hamid Drake's playing is faultless throughout. *Fred Anderson & DKV Trio* cannot disappoint any free-jazz fan; with its lyrical beauty, passion, and warmth, it will convert many a jazz enthusiast who thinks "free" means "squalling." *—Joslyn Layne*

Fred Anderson Quartet, Vol. 1 / 1998 / Asian Improv ♦♦♦
Recorded live at Fred Anderson's Chicago jazz club, *the Velvet Lounge*, this release captures a jazz show of the converting caliber—a show so full of ability and style that audience members are inspired to love and stand behind the musicians from that point on. This great concert opens with extended saxophone fluttering from Anderson. His horn has a time-carved warmth that somewhat recalls the warm sound of Hank Mobley and early Ben Webster, but remains entirely Anderson's own sound; when he blows, you can hear all the years of playing behind that sound. Bass-bending moves through the background of "The Moon Song," as Brimfield's trumpet comes in for a nice solo that is striking at first, but rather snuffs itself out. Each musician takes a solo and as soon as the song is brought back to a solid group groove, they stop the song cold—and crack up. The rendition of "Dark Day" found on this release is the old-time spiritual, done justice instrumentally. Rising with a slow cry, the saxophone lets out wails and moans while the rhythm section stays sparse and in the background. (There's another great version of this tune on Okkadisk's *Fred Anderson/DKV Trio*). "Get It Right" changes the mood from heavy to dance bop, starting with a percussive slap-bass solo. The drums join in, and finally the horn steps into the circle, touching all over it in a thorough six-minute solo. The last piece meets this album's high standards and includes some really interesting warps coming from Aoki's bass. This album is essential for any fans of the new scene, the Chicago jazz scene, the freer jazz scene, or any of the musicians found here. *—Joslyn Layne*

Fred Anderson Quartet, Vol. 2 / 1999 / Asian Improv ♦♦♦♦
A sequel to *Fred Anderson Quartet, Vol. 1*, this two-CD set also documents the tenor saxman's performances at his Velvet Lounge on Chicago's South Side. But there are some important differences. *Vol. 2* was recorded in 1999, not 1998. And while *Vol. 1* found Anderson being joined by bassist Tatsu Aoki, trumpeter Bill Brimfield, and drummer Chad Taylor, *Vol. 2* has different personnel and a different combination of instruments. Aoki is still on acoustic bass, but there is no trumpeter this time—instead, Anderson features guitarist Jeff Parker. Meanwhile, Hamid Drake is on drums instead of Taylor. But there are some definite parallels between *Vol. 1* and *Vol. 2*. Both favor an inside/outside approach, and both of them offer avant-garde jazz that is challenging but, for the most part, relatively accessible. "Relatively" is the key word; probing pieces like the 34-minute "Jeff's Turnaround," the 15-minute "December 4th," and the 37-minute "Road Trip" are hardly the work of someone who's trying to sound like Stan Getz in 1948. But they are more accessible than the very angular opener "Look Out!," and they are less extreme than things Anderson had done in the past. Of course, how accessible one finds a particular Anderson piece can depend on one's likes and dislikes—the more you can accept Anderson on his own terms, the more rewarding you'll find *Vol. 2* to be. The Chicagoan was 70 when these excellent performances were recorded, and he continues to play with the authority of someone who is very much in his prime. *—Alex Henderson*

Live at the Velvet Lounge / Jun. 1, 1998 / Okka Disk ♦♦♦♦♦
Anderson opens it up with a strong, lyrical solo, and soon bassist Peter Kowald comes in low, followed by the rolling and cymbal-shading addition of drummer Hamid Drake. "Straight, But Not Straight" tells it like it is, both musically and by its very name: it's free jazz that doesn't abstract into "formlessness"—and even has sections of very straight-ahead, or inside, playing—yet the detailed development of the piece (over 30 minutes) will be enough to take most straight jazz listeners further outside of their listening territory than is comfortable. The next piece is "To Those Who Know," a suspenseful, restrained ballad in which the trio plays the blues by playing under, over, and around it. The piece is very low-key, with both loveliness and pain, until about eight minutes in, when Anderson's saxophone lets go a heavy stream of notes and Drake drops out, while Kowald switches to a circular-saw bowing. Drake only comes back in on this song for a few, sporadic cymbal accents and hi-hat punctuations. "Multidimensional Reality"—another long one, clocking in at almost 30 minutes—starts with a feathery hand-drumming solo by Drake. After a couple of minutes, Anderson and Kowald join in, each translating Drake's finger rolls and hand slaps through the sounds of his own instrument. Then Kowald twists things around by picking up his bow and imitating the sounds of Anderson's imitation and building from there. Before you know it, the trio is in the midst of a lively musical display that melds Anderson's all-out blowing, Kowald's extended techniques, and Drake's skill in hand percussion. *—Joslyn Layne*

Louis Armstrong

b. Aug. 4, 1901, New Orleans, LA, **d.** Jul. 6, 1971, New York, NY
Vocals, Trumpet / Vocal Jazz, Traditional Pop, New Orleans Jazz, Classic Jazz, Swing, Dixieland

Louis Armstrong was the most important and influential musician in jazz history. Although he is often thought of by the general public as a lovable, clowning personality, a gravel-voiced singer who played simple but dramatic trumpet in a New Orleans-styled Dixieland setting, Armstrong was much much more.

One of the first soloists on record (although he was preceded by Sidney Bechet), Louis was more responsible than anyone else for jazz changing from an ensemble-oriented folk music into an art form that emphasized inventive solo improvisations. His relaxed phrasing was a major change from the staccato style of the early '20s (helping set the stage for the swing era) and Armstrong demonstrated that it was possible to have both impressive technique and a strong feeling for the blues. One of jazz's first true virtuosos, his influence over his contemporaries was so powerful that nearly every trumpeter to record between 1927 and 1940 sounded to an extent like one of his followers. Armstrong's unique singing voice was imitated by a countless number of listeners through the years, he popularized scat singing (using nonsense syllables rhythmically rather than words) and his phrasing (carried over from his horn playing) affected virtually every singer to emerge after 1930, including Bing Crosby, Billie Holiday and Frank Sinatra. In addition, Armstrong's accessible humor and sunny stage personality were major assets in popularizing jazz with larger audiences. Many youngsters were inspired to take up the trumpet after hearing or seeing him and millions more were introduced to jazz through Armstrong; in later years, his worldwide tours resulted in him being widely known as "America's goodwill ambassador." *—Scott Yanow*

Louis Armstrong and King Oliver / Apr. 6, 1923-Dec. 22, 1924 / Milestone ♦♦♦♦♦
King Oliver's Creole Jazz Band was the most important jazz group to record in 1923 and did wonders to popularize the new music beyond Chicago. With Louis Armstrong on second cornet, clarinetist Johnny Dodds and trombonist Honore Dutrey, cornetist King Oliver was able to feature jazz that was state of the art for 1923, emphasizing melodic group improvisations during that pre-solo age. This Milestone CD is a duplicate of the original two-LP set except that the two King Oliver-Jelly Roll Morton duets have been moved to a Morton reissue. The 18 performances by Oliver's band (with "Chimes Blues," "Dippermouth Blues," "Snake Rag" and "Mabel's Dream" among the classics) are joined by the 1924 recordings by The Red Onion Jazz Babies, a small group with Armstrong, soprano great Sidney Bechet and singer Alberta Hunter. *—Scott Yanow*

Portrait of the Artist as a Young Man / Apr. 6, 1923-Oct. 1934 / Columbia/Legacy ♦♦♦♦
This very attractive four-CD box set has definitive liner notes from Dan Morgenstern and draws its 81 selections from Louis Armstrong's prime period. Why then does it not receive the highest rating— Armstrong's immortal *Hot Five* and *Hot Seven* recordings, along with his early big-band sides, had already been reissued complete and in chronological order on seven Columbia CDs and his less interesting performances as an accompanist to various blues singers (some of which are on this set) have also been reissued in similar fashion. Therefore this box is of no real interest to veteran collectors and, although a good introduction to beginners just starting to explore Satch's classic music, they too will eventually be moved to duplicate many of these recordings by getting the more complete series. As for the music, this set has literally dozens of influential classics and 19 performances that actually predate The Hot Fives but, since everything is available elsewhere, this box is recommended only for the informative booklet. *—Scott Yanow*

☆ **Hot Fives, Vol. 1** / Nov. 12, 1925-Jun. 23, 1926 / Columbia ♦♦♦♦♦
To say that the performances on this CD (plus the ones on Vols. 2-4) are classic would be an extreme understatement. With these first 16 recordings by Louis Armstrong's Hot Five, the trumpeter revolutionized jazz, changing it from an ensemble-oriented music into an art form dominated by virtuoso soloists. The most powerful jazz improviser of the 1920's, Louis Armstrong's beautiful tone, his sense of swing (which set the stage for the big band era) and his chancetaking yet melodic improvisations amazed his contemporaries and permanently altered the future of jazz. Among the many gems on this first volume are "Come Back, Sweet Papa," "Heebies Jeebies" (which is highlighted by Armstrong's highly influential scat vocal), the brilliant "Cornet Chop Suey," the debut of Kid Ory's "Muskrat Ramble" and the joyous "Don't Forget To Mess Around." With clarinetist Johnny Dodds (the pacesetter on his instrument), trombonist Kid Ory, pianist Lil Armstrong and banjoist Johnny St. Cyr all making strong contributions, the music is consistently memorable and innovative. *—Scott Yanow*

Hot Fives & Hot Sevens, Vol. 2 / Jun. 28, 1926-May 13, 1927 / Columbia ♦♦♦♦♦
More excellent Hot Fives and Hot Sevens transfers from the JSP label. Beyond being bowled over by the presence and clarity of these perennial Armstrong performances, listeners get a chance to really hear the fine solos and group interplay by Hot Fives regulars Johnny Dodds, Kid Ory, Lil Armstrong, and Johnny St. Cyr. In addition to turning in inspired work on standout cuts like "Struttin' With Some Barbecue," the group holds its own on numbers featuring Armstrong and famed Chicago blues guitarist Lonnie Johnson, including the classic "Hotter Than That." Adding tuba player Peter Briggs, drummer Baby Dodds, and trombonist John Thomas (who replaces Kid Ory), the Hot Fives become the Hot Sevens and reel off immortal

tracks like "Potato Head Blues" and "S.O.L. Blues." And as a taste of the superb work Armstrong did with pianist Earl Hines, "Chicago Breakdown"—the only Sunset Stompers recording made—is included as well. (Hines and Armstrong would go on to record several more famous sides in 1928 as part of Carroll Dickerson's Savoyagers and various Armstrong-led groups, including classics like "Weather Bird" and "West End Blues.") As is the case with the other Hot Fives/Hot Sevens discs on JSP, this collection of 1927 sides is highly recommended. *—Stephen Cook*

☆ **The Louis Armstrong Collection, Vol. 4: Louis Armstrong and Earl Hines** / May 9, 1927-Dec. 12, 1928 / Columbia ♦♦♦♦♦
It can easily be argued that Louis Armstrong was at his most advanced during the 1928 recordings that featured him with the Savoy Ballroom Five. Constantly challenged by the equally adventurous pianist Earl Hines, Armstrong is consistently remarkable throughout the 18 selections that are on this CD. First there are three tracks with big bands during 1927-28 ("Chicago Breakdown," "Symphonic Raps" and "Savoyagers' Stomp") that also include Hines; then the chronology picks up where Vol. III left off. The startling "West End Blues" (with its classic trumpet cadenza) was always Armstrong's personal favorite recording, "Weather Bird" is a hair-raising duet with Hines and other highlights include "Sugar Foot Strut," "Beau Koo Jack" and the earliest recorded versions of "Basin Street Blues" and "St. James Infirmary." Although the other musicians in the Savoy Ballroom Five (trombonist Fred Robinson, Jimmy Strong on clarinet and tenor, banjoist Mancy Cara and for some selections Don Redman on clarinet and alto) is excellent, it is the interplay between Hines, drummer Zutty Singleton and Satch that really make the music classic. The first four volumes in this series are essential for all serious jazz collections. *—Scott Yanow*

★ **Hot Fives & Sevens, Vol. 3** / May 13, 1927-Jun. 28, 1928 / Columbia ♦♦♦♦♦
Louis Armstrong's 1925-28 recordings with his Hot Fives and Hot Sevens belong in every serious jazz collection, even those owned by listeners who otherwise do not listen to music before bebop. Armstrong's remarkable trumpet solos of the 1920's were so advanced that they indirectly led the way not only toward swing but bop of 20 years later. On the third of seven CD volumes that have all of Louis' earliest records, Armstrong is featured with three separate groups. His Hot Seven (with the brilliant clarinetist Johnny Dodds, trombonist John Thomas, pianist Lil Armstrong, banjoist Johnny St. Cyr, Pete Briggs on tuba and drummer Baby Dodds) plays three numbers (including the humorous "That's When I'll Come Back To You"). There are nine of the greatest Hot Five performances (with Dodds, trombonist Kid Ory, Lil on piano and St. Cyr), including a perfectly constructed Louis Armstrong solo on the original version of "Struttin' With Some Barbeque," "Once In A While," and exciting guest appearances by guitarist Lonnie Johnson on three numbers (most notably "Hotter Than That"). This set concludes in 1928 with Louis Armstrong's new recording group The Savoy Ballroom Five (a sextet with pianist Earl Hines, drummer Zutty Singleton, trombonist Fred Robinson, Jimmy Strong on clarinet and tenor and banjoist Mancy Cara); their four songs include the initial version of Hines' "A Monday Date" and the tricky "Fireworks." Essential music. *—Scott Yanow*

Louis Armstrong Collection, Vol. 5: Louis in New York / Mar. 5, 1929-Nov. 26, 1929 / Columbia ♦♦♦♦♦
By 1929, Louis Armstrong had switched from New Orleans jazz to fronting a variety of larger orchestras, widening his repertoire to include pop tunes but always leaving room for closing trumpet solos. This set includes all known versions (including a few new alternates) of his recordings of this era, including appearances by backing singers Seger Ellis and Victoria Spivey. Highpoints include "Mahogany Hall Stomp" and "Ain't Misbehavin'." *—Scott Yanow*

Louis Armstrong Collection, Vol. 6: St. Louis Blues / Dec. 10, 1929-Oct. 9, 1930 / Columbia ♦♦♦♦
Using different big bands purely as a backdrop by 1930, Louis Armstrong was free to stretch out with flashy virtuosic trumpet solos and often scat-filled vocal choruses. "St. Louis Blues," "Body and Soul" and "Tiger Rag" are classics but his rendition of "I'm a Ding Dong Daddy" (which has a solo that gradually builds to a tremendous finish) is a true gem. *—Scott Yanow*

Louis Armstrong Collection, Vol. 7: You're Driving Me Crazy / Oct. 16, 1930-Nov. 3, 1931 / Columbia ♦♦♦♦♦
It took domestic Columbia until the late 1980's before the label finally started a program reissuing complete and in chronological order all of Louis Armstrong's earliest recordings as a leader; only 60 years after the classic music was originally recorded. The series reached its seventh CD by 1992 but thusfar an eighth and final album has not been compiled to complete the essential task of making Louis' greatest recordings available. Vol. 7 has 17 big band selections from 1930-31 (plus an alternate take of "You're Drivin' Me Crazy") and, even if the first six volumes are a bit more essential, this one contains plenty of gems. Lionel Hampton made his first recorded appearance on vibes during "Memories Of You" and "Shine" and the other memorable selections include "Sweethearts On Parade," Armstrong's theme song "When It's Sleepy Time Down South," "I'll Be Glad When You're Dead, You Rascal You," "Lazy River" and "Chinatown, My Chinatown." Recommended. *—Scott Yanow*

Rhythm Saved the World / Oct. 3, 1935-Feb. 4, 1936 / GRP ♦♦♦

Pops / Apr. 27, 1946-Aug. 1, 1956 / Bluebird/RCA ♦♦♦♦♦

Pops: 1940's Small Band Sides / Sep. 6, 1946-Oct. 16, 1947 / Bluebird/RCA ♦♦♦♦

The Complete Town Hall Concert / May 17, 1947 / RCA ♦♦♦♦

The Complete Decca Studio Louis Armstrong All Stars / Apr. 26, 1950-Oct. 8, 1958 / Mosaic ♦♦♦♦

☆ **Louis Armstrong Plays W.C. Handy** / Jul. 12, 1954-Jul. 14, 1954 / Columbia/Legacy ♦♦♦♦♦
This recording was not only Louis Armstrong's finest record of the 1950's but one of the truly classic jazz sets. Out of print for years, it was reissued quite shoddily in 1986 on a Columbia CD with alternates in place of many of the original versions and no real explanation. It was a complete and inexcusable mess and should be avoided by all but completists. Ten years later, Columbia finally got around to bringing back the original gem, and the music is at last available on CD. Armstrong and his All-Stars (trombonist Trummy Young, clarinetist Barney Bigard, pianist Billy Kyle, bassist Arvell Shaw, drummer Barrett Deems and singer Velma Middleton), were clearly inspired by the fresh repertoire, 11 songs written by W.C. Handy. Their nearly nine-minute version of "St. Louis Blues" (with witty vocals, roaring Young trombone and a couple of long majestic trumpet solos) is arguably the greatest version of the oft-recorded song. Other highlights include "Loveless Love," "Beale Street Blues" and a romping version of "Ole Miss Blues." This CD also includes rehearsal versions of three songs, Louis Armstrong telling a joke and a brief George Avakian interview with W.C. Handy. Essential music for all serious jazz collections. *—Scott Yanow*

Satch Plays Fats: The Music of Fats Waller / Apr. 26, 1955-May 3, 1955 / Columbia/Legacy ♦♦♦♦♦
Armstrong and Waller only worked together twice, briefly in 1925 in Erskine Tate's band and four years later in the New York revue, *Connie's Hot Chocolates*. But Waller made an indelible enough impression for Satchmo to record this tribute album in 1955 when such ideas were new. The original nine-track lineup forms the centerpiece of the reissue, with Armstrong ably supported by his All-Stars on such classics as "Honeysuckle Rose," "Squeeze Me," and "Ain't Misbehavin'." But this reissue delivers over twice the tracks of the original LP issue, with four edited alternate takes from the same session, plus seven more tracks of Waller material recorded by Armstrong in the 1920s and '30s. The mid-'50s was a fertile time for Armstrong and coupled with the '20s and '30s bonus tracks, this makes for a stellar overall package. *—Cub Koda*

Ella and Louis / 1956 / Verve ♦♦♦♦♦

Great Chicago Concert 1956 / Jun. 1, 1956 / Columbia ♦♦♦♦
Originally out on a double LP, this is a definitive set of the Louis Armstrong All-Stars of 1956. The music and many of the solos will be familiar to longtime Armstrong fans, but whether it be "Struttin' with Some Barbecue, " "Basin Street" or his new hit, "Mack the Knife, " the spirit and enthusiasm of this music is irresistible. This is his best live set in the '50s. The CD reissue, a two-CD set, is slightly more complete than the two-fer LP in that it adds a version of Armstrong's theme song, "When It's Sleepy Time Down South, " a closing "Saints" that allows Satch to introduce his band and a straightforward rendition of "The Star Spangled Banner." *—Scott Yanow*

I've Got The World On A String/Louis Under The Stars / Aug. 14, 1957 / Verve ♦♦♦♦♦
Recorded in one marathon session in Hollywood's Capitol Records Tower, these two albums were joined together in a double-CD set in 1999, with new notes, repros of the original LP covers, and a liberal sprinkling of outtakes tacked onto each disc. That these once-overlooked albums have been given so exhaustive a treatment—at full price—is a sign that they are finally being appreciated as prime samplings from the autumn of Louis's recording career. Even in the pressure-cooker of a marathon session, even when confronted with standards not often associated with him, Armstrong finds the essence of each tune, bending and projecting them with his patented joie de vivre and gravel-voiced warmth every time. There are also lots of examples of his trumpet—pithy, soulful, belonging to no one else—although the index markings indicate that some solos are composite takes. While annotator Richard M. Sudhalter doesn't think much of arranger Russ Garcia's contribution, in fact, Garcia pulls off several charts for big band and/or strings that are among the most atmospheric ever accorded to Armstrong. "When Your Lover Is Gone" in particular is sublime, with its signature riff of blasé, sighing horns and responding, rising string tremelos—and Garcia frames "Body And Soul" with a lovely string chart whose penultimate stroke is a perfectly-placed blue note. The strings of incomplete takes are particularly interesting, for they reveal the working relationship between Armstrong and Norman Granz, with Armstrong basically subservient to his producer. At their best, these albums create a seductive nighttime ambience that'll draw you in every time. *—Richard Ginell*

Louis Under the Stars / Aug. 14, 1957 / Verve ♦♦♦

Porgy and Bess / Aug. 18, 1957 / Verve ♦♦♦

Hello, Dolly / Dec. 3, 1963-Apr. 18, 1964 / MCA ♦♦♦♦

What a Wonderful World / 1968 / GRP ♦♦♦

★ **The Complete Hot Five and Hot Seven Recordings** / 1925-1929 / Columbia/Legacy ♦♦♦♦♦
This four-CD set brings together all the recordings made during the period of the Hot Five and Hot Sevens along with all the attendant recordings that Armstrong was involved in during this breakthrough period. Although this material has been around the block several times before—and continues to be available in packages greatly varying in transfer quality—this is truly the way to go, and certainly the most deluxe packaging this material has ever received with the greatest sound retrieval yet employed. In addition to sounding better than the competition, it also sensibly lays out all the recordings Satchmo made during this period, grouping all the original Hot Five recordings from 1925 to 1927 (and all attendant material) together on the first two discs, all of the Hot Sevens on disc three, with the final disc devoted to the second coming of the Hot Five in 1928 along with the attendant material from the following year. There are also several categories of "bonus tracks" aboard this deluxe set, including the "Lil's Hot Shots" 1926 Hot Five Vocalion recordings, a 1927 Johnny Dodds session that became the prototype for the Hot Seven recordings that soon followed, and the only known alternate take of "I Can't Give You Anything but Love." You can't have a Louis Armstrong collection without this historic set. Come to think of it, you can't have any kind of respectable *jazz* collection without it, either. Beyond indispensable. *—Cub Koda*

The Great Summit: The Master Takes / Jan. 9, 2001 / Blue Note ♦♦♦♦♦

The Art Ensemble of Chicago

f. 1966

Group / Avant-Garde Jazz, Free Jazz, Avant-Garde

Originally comprised of saxophonists Roscoe Mitchell and Joseph Jarman, trumpeter Lester Bowie, bassist Malachi Favors, and later, drummer Famoudou Don Moye, the Art Ensemble of Chicago was a unique collective of composers and improvisers that enjoyed a critical reputation as one of the finest and most influential avant-garde jazz ensemble of the 1970s and '80s. While that reputation is debatable, the Art Ensemble was unquestionably a groundbreaking band. In the late '60s and early-'70s, they blended jazz with European art music and indigenous African musics, combining a modernist spirit of experimentation with elements of jazz history and pre-history (from gospel to minstrel music) and theatrics.

Established jazzman Favors and college students/veterans Mitchell and Jarman were in pianist Muhal Richard Abrams' early-'60s Experimental Band, and all were early members of the Association for the Advancement of Creative Musicians (AACM). Bowie met Mitchell after arriving from St. Louis in 1966, and the Roscoe Mitchell Sextet (with Bowie and Favors) recorded the first AACM album, *Sound.* The four musicians who would become the Art Ensemble first recorded together in 1967 on Bowie's *Numbers 1 & 2* Delmark). The drummerless band performed as the Roscoe Mitchell Art Ensemble for two years before moving to Paris in 1969. There, they met and hired American "Sun Percussionist" Don Moye. Renamed the Art Ensemble of Chicago, the group was successful in Europe, recording several classic albums including *People in Sorrow.* They returned to Chicago in 1971; *Live At Mandel Hall* captures their 1972 homecoming concert. The band's renown grew in the '70s, and they formed the label AECO in 1978.

The group recorded a series of critically-acclaimed albums for ECM through the early '80s, topping critic's polls. But as the '80s progressed, critical enthusiasm for—and interest in—the avant-garde declined, and members focused more on other projects. Still, the group continued performing and recording through the '90s, becoming a quartet in 1993, when Jarman left to focus on spiritual matters. When Bowie was stricken with liver cancer, he was replaced by saxophonist Ari Brown for a June 1999 festival appearance. Bowie died five months later. In January, 2000, for its first concert following Bowie's death, the Art Ensemble performed as a trio, but its future seemed in doubt. —*Chris Kelsey*

Art Ensemble: 1967/68 / May 18, 1967-Mar. 11, 1968 / Nessa ✦✦✦✦✦
This limited-edition five-CD set available directly from Nessa not only reissues the important free jazz albums *Old/Quartet, Numbers 1 & 2,* and *Congliptious* but contains quite a bit of music taken from rehearsals by the members of the group that would by 1969 become known as the Art Ensemble of Chicago. With such advanced improvisers as trumpeter Lester Bowie, Roscoe Mitchell and Joseph Jarman on reeds, bassist Malachi Favors, drummer Phillip Wilson, and appearances from bassist Charles Clark, drummers Robert Crowder and Thurman Barker, the music is usually very emotional and sometimes quite scary. There are meandering sections and individual performances that do not work all that well, but in general the music is quite colorful, adventurous, and innovative: in many ways the beginning of the modern avant-garde. Open-eared listeners are advised to search for this important historical set. —*Scott Yanow*

People in Sorrow / Jul. 7, 1969 / Nessa ✦✦✦
In 1969, the Art Ensemble of Chicago (which had recorded just one official record, *Congliptious,* as a group at that point in time), moved to Paris for two years and recorded eight albums during their first year overseas alone. This particular LP has the innovative band (which was then a quartet consisting of trumpeter Lester Bowie, bassist Malachi Favors, and both Roscoe Mitchell and Joseph Jarman on multiple reeds) performing the 40-minute group original "People in Sorrow." The still-startling music, which uses space, dynamics, and a wide range of emotions expertly, is not for everyone's taste (the high-energy tenors of the mid-'60s are actually easier to get into), but worth the struggle. —*Scott Yanow*

Les Stances A Sophie / Jul. 22, 1970 / Nessa ✦✦✦✦✦
In 1970, the members of the Art Ensemble of Chicago were living as expatriates in Paris. The group had only recently expanded to its permanent quintet status with the addition of drummer/percussionist Don Moye when they were asked by New Wave director Moshe Misrahi to provide the soundtrack for his movie, *Les Stances a Sophie.* The music was never used in the film but, luckily, it was recorded. The result was one of the landmark records of the burgeoning avant-garde of the time and, simply put, one of the greatest jazz albums ever.

On two of the tracks, the Art Ensemble is joined by vocalist Fontella Bass, at the time the wife of trumpeter Lester Bowie and riding the success of her pop-soul hit *Rescue Me.* She's featured most prominently on the opening number, *Theme De Yoyo,* an astounding piece that has achieved legendary status as the finest fusion of funk and avant-garde jazz ever recorded. The mix is indeed seamless, with Moye and Favors laying down a throbbing, infectious groove, Bass singing the surreally erotic lyrics with enormous soul and the horn players soloing with ecstatic abandon.

The remaining pieces cover a wide range stylistically with no less beauty and imagination, including two variations on a theme by Monteverdi, intense free improvising and soft, deeply probing sonic investigations.Their extensive knowledge of prior jazz styles, love of unusual sound sources (the so-called "little instruments") and fearless exploration of the furthest reaches of both instrumental and compositional possibilities came into full flower on this record. —*Brian Olewnick*

● **Live at Mandel Hall** / Jan. 15, 1972 / Delmark ✦✦✦✦✦
The Art Ensemble of Chicago had just returned to Chicago after several years in Europe when they recorded this continuous 76-minute concert. Drummer Don Moye (who had recently joined the classic avant-garde group) was proving to be a major asset, holding his own with trumpeter Lester Bowie, the reeds of Joseph Jarman and Roscoe Mitchell and bassist Malachi Favors. Although there are some meandering moments during their lengthy set, the music almost always holds on to one's interest (a humorous drunken march is a highpoint) and gives listeners a very good idea of how the Art Ensemble sounded in its early days when it was not at all shy about exploring music's outer limits. —*Scott Yanow*

Bap-Tizum / 1972 / Koch Jazz ✦✦✦✦✦
This was the Art Ensemble's breakthrough—however short-lived—onto a major U.S. label (Atlantic), as well as a document of the freewheeling band's first appearance at an American festival (the Ann Arbor Blues and Jazz Festival). With activist John Sinclair delivering the introduction, politics is in the air; the crowd is young and predisposed to radical ideas and the Art Ensemble holds back nothing in a chaotic, meandering, exasperating, outrageous—and thus, always fascinating—performance. The band seems to be clearing its collective throat in the first half of the concert, opening with a battering all-percussion prelude. Roscoe Mitchell and Malachi Favors go at it at length in a staggered, honking tenor sax/bass duet on "Unanka," and Mitchell ratchets up the gears into screeching overdrive on "Oouffnoon." Finally, after a mocking intro by Lester Bowie, the 15-minute "Ohnedaruth" puts the Art Ensemble on full, ultra-colorful, wailing, freeform display (complete with a few vocal obscenities) before signing off with the "relatively" straight-ahead "Odwalla." It is interesting that Atlantic would lease these way-out recordings to Koch at a time (1998) when it was simultaneously putting out new, safer-sounding releases by the current Art Ensemble and its members. —*Richard S. Ginell*

Fanfare for the Warriors / 1974 / Koch International ✦✦✦✦
The Art Ensemble of Chicago's first (and arguably most significant) period concluded with this high-quality studio session. The quintet (trumpeter Lester Bowie, Roscoe Mitchell and Joseph Jarman on reeds, bassist Malachi Favors and drummer Don Moye) provides concise but adventurous performances. Highpoints include Mitchell's "Nonnaah," Bowie's humorous "Barnyard Scuffel Shuffle" and "Tnoona," but all of the selections have their own musical personality. It's a fine showcase for this important avant-garde unit. —*Scott Yanow*

Nice Guys / May 1978 / ECM ✦✦✦✦
Nice Guys was the first Art Ensemble of Chicago album released after a five-year recording hiatus and the group's first for the ECM label. During those five years, the Art Ensemble toured Europe and continued to expand its compositional, improvisational, and theatrical jazz fundamentals, captured abundantly on *Nice Guys.* Broken up into six pieces, two each from Roscoe Mitchell and Joseph Jarman and one each from Lester Bowie and Don Moye, the album reveals how the AEC managed to turn individual compositions into a fully realized, surprisingly accessible, avant garde group collective. *Nice Guys* maintains its edge while incorporating reggae, New Orleans marches, and a wide use of space complemented by "little instruments" (car horn, whistles, etc.). The strongest portion of the disc is the finale "Dreaming of the Master," dedicated to Miles Davis and sounding not unlike Davis' mid-'60s quintet—while maintaining the AEC edge. —*Al Campbell*

Urban Bushmen / May 1980 / ECM ✦✦✦✦✦
Recorded at a 1980 concert in Munich, *Urban Bushmen* not only provides an excellent summation of the Art Ensemble of Chicago's work since 1966, but also substantiates the group's reputation for putting on intense and inspired shows. The album centers around three extended pieces: reed player Joseph Jarmen's "Theme for SCO," the group's "Urban Magic," and reed player Roscoe Mitchell's "Uncle." Over the course of these multi-part "suites," the group effectively blurs the lines between jazz and free jazz, deftly working through New Orleans' marches, turbulent hard bop, highlife/reggae rhythms, and minimalist sound sculptures; while Jarmen, Mitchell, and trumpeter Lester Bowie come up with consistently varied and surprising solo/tandem contributions, drummer Don Moye and bassist Malachi Favors expand the sound with an array of percussion effects and humorous interjections (sirens, car horns, megaphone rants). Moye and Favors are also featured on the percussion vehicles "Promenade: Cote Bamako I & II," "Bush Magic," and "Sun Preconditions II." The set is balanced out by melancholic and sweet ballads by Bowie and Mitchell ("New York Is Full of Lonely People" and "Peter and Judith," respectively). This is one of the Art Ensemble's best recordings, but due to its intense breadth it might not be an ideal first purchase for newcomers. The best entry point into the group's catalog would be a studio record like *Nice Guys* (1978) or *Third Decade* (1984). —*Stephen Cook*

Ancient in the Future, Vol. 1 / Mar. 17, 1987-Mar. 19, 1987 / DIW ✦✦✦✦

Coming Home Jamaica / Dec. 27, 1995-Jan. 16, 1996 / Atlantic ✦✦✦

The Association for the Advancement of Creative Musicians
(AACM)

Group / Avant-Garde Jazz, Free Jazz
Since its founding by a group of forward-thinking jazz musicians that included pianist/composer Muhal Richard Abrams, pianist Jodie Christian, drummer Steve McCall, and composer Phil Cohran, the AACM has been a force for innovation within the jazz community. The Chicago-based organization is a registered non-profit organization dedicated, according to the AACM's statement, "to nurturing, performing, and recording serious, original music." In the '60s and especially the '70s, the AACM was widely acknowledged as being in the forefront of experimental jazz. Early AACM members such as Abrams, Henry Threadgill, Anthony Braxton, Jack DeJohnette, and the members of the Art Ensemble of Chicago-Lester Bowie, Roscoe Mitchell, Joseph Jarman, Famadou Don Moye, and Malachi Favors-created music that would have creative implications that reached far beyond the city of Chicago. It's motto is "Great Black Music, Ancient to the Future." Although there is no one "typical" AACM artist, it can be said that the membership in general has attempted to transcend common practice by absorbing into their work various influences lying outside the jazz domain (African indigenous musics, and European classical forms, for example).

The AACM grew out of a rehearsal band led by Muhal Richard Abrams in 1962. The group-known informally as the Experimental Band-never performed, but existed to read down scores written by Abrams, Cohran, DeJohnette, Jarman, Mitchell, Troy Robinson, and Maurice McIntyre, among others. Many of the band's writers employed compositional techniques taken from contemporary classical music—serialism, polytonality, chromaticism. The group's first rehearsals were held in a South Side tavern, but the band eventually moved to Abraham Lincoln Center, one of the city's oldest settlement houses. Obviously inspired by the high level of creativity and frustrated by a lack of performance opportunities, Abrams, Christian, Cohran, and McCall instigated the formation of a cooperative that would produce concerts, and opened membership to their cohorts in the Experimental Band. In May of 1965 the AACM was chartered by the state of Illinois as a non-profit organization. Six groups comprised the original AACM: Christian's hard bop quintet, Cohran's Artistic Heritage Ensemble, the Experimental Band, and the groups of Robinson, Jarman, and Mitchell. The next year,

Delmark recorded Mitchell's band. The resulting album-*Sound*-was the first of many to come out of the AACM.

In addition to its function as a concert producer, the AACM runs a free training program for inner city youth. The AACM School of Music offers instruction on all instruments and vocals, as well as classes in music theory. The faculty is made up entirely of AACM members, many of whom are, themselves, graduates of the program. Although the cooperative's influence in the jazz world waned a bit in the '80s and '90s, affiliated artists continued to produce bold and compelling music. Newer members like saxophonist/composer Edward Wilkerson, percussionist Kahil El-Zabar, and saxophonist Ari Brown continued the AACM's tradition of high creative achievement into the new millennium. *—Chris Kelsey*

Roy Ayers

b. Sep. 10, 1940, Los Angeles, CA
Vibraphone / Jazz-Pop, Fusion, Soul-Jazz, Jazz-Funk
Once one of the most visible and winning jazz vibraphonists of the 1960s, then an R&B bandleader in the 1970s and '80s, Roy Ayers' reputation in the 1990s is now that of one of the prophets of acid-jazz, a man decades ahead of his time. A tune like 1972's "Move to Groove" has a crackling backbeat that serves as the prototype for the shuffling hip-hop groove that became, shall we say, ubiquitous on acid-jazz records. Yet Ayers' own playing has always been rooted in hard bop—crisp, lyrical, rhythmically resilient. Ayers became involved in the West Coast jazz scene in the early '60s, and played with Herbie Mann for four years. The experience gave Ayers tremendous exposure and opened his ears to styles of music other than the bebop that he had grown up with. After recording three solo albums for Atlantic under Mann's supervision, Ayers left the group in 1970 to form the Roy Ayers Ubiquity. An R&B-jazz-rock band at first, the Ubiquity gradually shed its jazz component in favor of commercially successful R&B/funk and disco. As the merger of hip-hop and jazz took hold in the early '90s, Ayers made a guest appearance on Guru's seminal *Jazzmatazz* album in 1993 and played at New York clubs with Guru and Donald Byrd. *—Richard S. Ginell*

Virgo Vibes / Jan. 18, 1967-Mar. 6, 1967 / Atlantic ✦✦✦
Long before he switched to playing disco and pop music, Roy Ayers was considered a promising young jazz vibraphonist. This LP, his second as a leader, was one of his finest. On four of the five selections (obscurities and pieces by group members), Ayers teams up with trumpeter Charles Tolliver, tenor saxophonist Joe Henderson, bassist Reggie Workman, drummer Bruno Carr, and the mysterious pianist Ronnie Clark (Herbie Hancock under a disguised name). On "Glow Flower," Ayers and Tolliver are joined by Harold Land on tenor, pianist Jack Wilson, bassist Buster Williams, and drummer Donald Bailey. The music is primarily advanced hard bop with some freer moments on Tolliver's "The Ringer." This underrated music is long overdue to be reissued on CD and displays Roy Ayers' lost potential. *—Scott Yanow*

Daddy Bug & Friends / Mar. 6, 1967-Dec. 11, 1969 / Atlantic ✦✦✦✦
During 1967-69, vibraphonist Roy Ayers (a few years before he turned to disco music) recorded three excellent albums for Atlantic. This 1976 LP has selections from two of the records, plus a pair of selections ("In the Limelight" and "Virgo Vibes") that were previously unreleased. On the fine sampler, Ayers' sidemen include Herbie Hancock, Joe Henderson, Charles Tolliver and Ron Carter. "Slow Motion," the latest selection (from Dec. 1969), hints at the commercial direction that Ayers would be emphasizing from 1970 on. *—Scott Yanow*

Stoned Soul Picnic / Jun. 20, 1968 / 32 Jazz ✦✦✦
Stoned Soul Picnic dates from the earlier part of Roy Ayers' career as a leader, before he delved heavily into R&B and funk fusions and instead concentrated more on soul-jazz grooves. Ayers leads a septet including such big names as pianist Herbie Hancock, altoist Gary Bartz, bassist Ron Carter, and flutist Hubert Laws. The Laura Nyro-penned title track foreshadows Ayers' later forays beyond the boundaries of pure jazz, and the group keeps the groove percolating nicely throughout, making *Stoned Soul Picnic* one of Ayers' better jazz-oriented outings. *—Steve Huey*

● **Evolution: The Polydor Anthology** / 1970-1981 / Polydor Chronicles ✦✦✦✦✦
Evolution charts Roy Ayers' 12 years and 20 LPs with Polydor, a rich time where his gliding, loose-groove jazz-funk gained many fans—though perhaps fewer than it did 20 years later in the midst of the rare groove/acid jazz revival. During the 1970s, Ayers and his band Ubiquity progressed from political- and social-commentary funk to blaxploitation to disco to some surprisingly touching R&B ballads, and this two-disc set covers it all with grace and a smooth flow. Fans of hip-hop, groove music, funk, and jazz will all be able to find something to enjoy on the collection. Highlights include "We Live in Brooklyn Baby," "Evolution," "Running Away" and "Get on Up, Get on Down," among others. *—John Bush*

Mystic Voyage / 1975 / Polydor ✦✦✦✦✦
Nice outing, although there's minimal jazz content. Ayers, once a Downbeat New Star winner, decided at end of the '60s to forego the rigors of straight jazz life and investigate the world of funk and R&B. He would (and still does) dabble back into light soul-jazz, but has become far more known for his funk and R&B releases like this one. *—Ron Wynn*

Everybody Loves the Sunshine / 1976 / Polydor ✦✦

The Best of Roy Ayers: Love Fantasy / 1979 / Polydor ✦✦✦✦
Vibist Roy Ayers' proto-acid-jazz is collected on this best-of compilation, which features performances of "Running Away," "Don't Stop the Feeling," "What You Won't Do for Love" and "Mystic Voyage." *—Jason Ankeny*

Albert Ayler

b. Jul. 13, 1936, Cleveland, OH, **d.** Nov. 5, 1970, New York, NY
Sax (Tenor), Sax (Alto) / Avant-Garde Jazz, Free Jazz, Avant-Garde
One of the giants of free jazz, Albert Ayler was also one of the most controversial. His huge tone and wide vibrato were difficult to ignore and his 1966 group sounded like a runaway New Orleans brass band from 1910—it could be said of Ayler's music that he was so far advanced that he came in at jazz's beginning. Unable to find work in the U.S. due to his uncompromising style, he spent time in Sweden and Denmark during 1962-63, making his first recordings (which reveal a tone with roots in Sonny Rollins) and working a bit with Cecil Taylor. Ayler's prime period was during 1964-67. In 1964 he toured Europe with a quartet that included Don Cherry and was generally quite free and emotional. Folk melodies (which had been utilized a bit with Cherry) had a more dominant role as did collective improvisation and yet, despite the use of spaced-out marches, Irish jigs and brass-band fanfares, tonally Ayler remained quite free. His ESP recordings from this era and his first couple of Impulses find Ayler at his peak and were influential; John Coltrane's post-1964 playing was definitely affected by Ayler's innovations. However during his last couple of years Albert Ayler's career seemed to become a bit aimless and his final Impulse sessions, although experimental (with the use of vocals, rock guitar and R&Bish tunes), were at best mixed successes. In November 1970 Ayler was found drowned in New York's East River under mysterious circumstances. *—Scott Yanow*

Swing Low Sweet Spiritual / Feb. 24, 1964 / Osmosis ✦✦✦
This LP contains one of Albert Ayler's most unusual projects. The free jazz tenor innovator (who doubles here on his less assured soprano) performs six traditional melodies including "Going Home," two versions of "Old Man River," "Nobody Knows the Trouble I've Seen" and even "When the Saints Go Marching In." Ayler works well with his backup group (pianist Call Cobbs, bassist Henry Grimes and drummer Sunny Murray) and creates very emotional music (really hangning on to the themes), all of which has been reissued (with additional tracks) on CD by Black Lion. *—Scott Yanow*

Witches and Devils / Feb. 24, 1964 / 1201 Music ✦✦✦✦
This album was recorded the same day as a lyrical spiritual album, and on this session, tenor saxophonist Albert Ayler really lets his emotions loose. Teamed with primitive trumpeter Norman Howard, Henry Grimes and/or Earle Henderson on bass and drummer Sunny Murray, Ayler plays quite freely on his four originals, "Witches and Devils" (a dirge), "Spirits," the melodic "Holy Holy" and "Saints." The often-intense music (which has been reissued on CD) is not for everyone, and this is one of Ayler's more forbidding releases, but open-eared listeners will find these radical explorations quite colorful. *—Scott Yanow*

Prophecy / Jun. 14, 1964 / ESP ✦✦✦
The first of Albert Ayler's ESP recordings (but one of the last to be released) is this live session with bassist Gary Peacock and drummer Sunny Murray. The tenor is heard on the earliest versions of his most famous theme, "Ghosts" (two renditions are included), along with such melodies as "Spirits," "Wizard," and "Prophecy." Ayler alternated the simple march-like themes with wild and very free improvisations which owe little if anything to the bop tradition or even his contemporaries in the avant-garde. Ayler always had his own individual message, and his ESP sessions find him in consistently explorative form. *—Scott Yanow*

Spiritual Unity / Jul. 10, 1964 / ESP ✦✦✦✦
Tenor saxophonist Albert Ayler seemed to burst on the scene in 1964, playing heated free-form solos that put an emphasis on emotion over melodic development. Ironically, many of his themes (particularly "Ghosts," which is heard twice on this brief set) were quite catchy, reminiscent of pre-1910 folk music, but his improvisations need an open mind for one to fully appreciate them. On this ESP date (reissued on CD but under a half-hour long), Ayler also performs "The Wizard" and "Spirits" with bassist Gary Peacock and drummer Sunny Murray. The intense music has not lost any of its fire through the decades. *—Scott Yanow*

Vibrations / Sep. 14, 1964 / Freedom ✦✦✦✦
1964 was a busy year for Albert Ayler, who recorded at least seven albums worth of material. This particular session, a quartet date with trumpeter Don Cherry, bassist Gary Peacock and drummer Sunny Murray, was probably his most significant of the period. Switching between tenor and alto, Ayler is often ferocious on the six performances, jumping from simple melodies (of which "Ghosts" is the most memorable) to intense sound explorations overflowing with emotion; he even makes Cherry seem conservative. It helps greatly to have open ears to appreciate this music, although Ayler's jams would become a bit more accessible the following year. Recommended. *—Scott Yanow*

Bells / May 1, 1965 / ESP ✦✦✦
Albert Ayler teamed up with his brother, trumpeter Donald Ayler, on this record for the first time, with the exception of one slightly earlier track issued on an Impulse sampler. The concert performance with both Aylers, Charles Tyler on alto, bassist Lewis Worrell, and drummer Sunny Murray is their entire 20-minute set from a *Town Hall* concert and originally came out as a one-sided LP (with the flipside being blank). What is here is quite interesting, with some ferocious ensembles, military-like themes (most of the music is taken up by "Holy Ghost"), and a couple of tenor solos from Albert. This music should have been combined with some other dates so the release would not be so ridiculously brief, but it's worth getting (if found at a budget price) anyway. *—Scott Yanow*

Spirits Rejoice / Sep. 23, 1965 / ESP ✦✦✦✦
Tenor saxophonist Albert Ayler's 1965 group (with trumpeter Donald Ayler, altoist Charles Tyler, both Henry Grimes and Gary Peacock on basses, drummer Sunny Murray and an appearance by Call Cobbs on harpsichord) is a fairly strong and sometimes riotous effort. As is often true of the ESP releases, the playing time is brief (32 minutes), but the quality of the free-form improvisations is high and the music is somewhat groundbreaking while always being stimulating. *—Scott Yanow*

At Slug's Saloon, Vol. 1 / May 1, 1966 / Get Back ✦✦✦✦
One of two CDs that originated from the Albert Ayler Quintet's May Day 1966 appearance at *Slug's* in New York, this is the better of the pair although Ayler fans will want both. The leader's tenor is both melodic and ferocious in spots, and his group (with trumpeter Donald Ayler, violinist Michel Sampson, bassist Lewis Worrell, and drummer Ronald Shannon Jackson) was one of his finest. The adventurous performances of lengthy versions of "Truth Is Marching In," "Our Prayer," and "Bells" often sound a bit like a runaway turn-of-the-century

marching band, and although the droning violin sometimes gets in the way, the spirit of this rambunctious and often-wild set is memorable. *—Scott Yanow*

At Slug's Saloon, Vol. 2 / May 1, 1966 / ESP ♦♦♦
The second of two CDs from the Albert Ayler Quintet's engagement at Slug's on May 1, 1966 has long versions of "Ghosts" (over 23 minutes) and "Initiation" performed by the tenor/leader, trumpeter Donald Ayler, violinist Michel Sampson, bassist Lewis Worrell and drummer Ronald Shannon Jackson. The music is both futuristic (with extroverted emotions expressed in free improvisations) and ancient (New Orleans marching band rhythms, group riffing and folkish melodies). Although *Vol. 1* gets the edge, most avant-garde collectors will want both releases. *—Scott Yanow*

Live at Lorrach: Paris, 1966 / Nov. 7, 1966–Nov. 13, 1966 / hatART ♦♦♦♦♦
Originally released as a double LP (with the second half being a 45), this single CD finds tenor saxophonist Albert Ayler in top form in 1966. At the time, his music could be considered to have been so advanced that it came in at the beginning of jazz. The folk melodies and some of the ensembles sound very much like an out-of-control New Orleans brass band circa 1900, yet the individual improvisations are as explorative as any heard in free jazz. Ayler heads a quintet with his brother Donald on trumpet, violinist Michel Sampson (whose sawing often sets a drone effect), bassist William Folwell and drummer Beaver Harris. Together they perform two versions of "Ghosts" and such group originals as "Bells," "Jesus," "Our Prayer," "Spirits," "Holy Ghost" and "Holy Family." Due to the accessible nature of some of the melodies, this is the perfect place for open-eared listeners unfamiliar with Albert Ayler's unique music to start. *—Scott Yanow*

Love Cry / Aug. 31, 1967–Feb. 13, 1968 / Impulse! ♦♦♦
From the time he was signed to Impulse in 1966, it was assumed that Albert Ayler's releases on that label would be motivated by an attempt at commercialism. While the music was toned down from his earlier ESP recordings, by no means did Ayler ever make commercial records. Much in the same way John Coltrane's later-period Impulse releases weren't commercial, Ayler simply took advantage of a larger record company's distribution, trying to expose the music to more people. Ayler's uncompromising musical freedom mixed with his catchy combination of nursery rhythms and brass band marches remained prominent on *Love Cry*. The interplay between the Ayler brothers also remained fiery as younger sibling Donald is heard playing trumpet for the last time on a recording with his brother. Donald was fired from the band (at the suggestion of Impulse) and, unfortunately, was committed to a mental institution for a short stay after these sessions were made. The rhythm section of Alan Silva on bass and Milford Graves on drums continually instigates and propels this music into furious militaristic march territory. Unhappily, the four tracks in which Call Cobbs is featured on harpsichord tend to drag the music down; it's unfortunate his gospel-inspired piano or organ playing couldn't have been utilized instead. The CD reissue contains alternate takes of "Zion Hill" and "Universal Indians." *—Al Campbell*

New Grass / Sep. 5, 1968–Sep. 6, 1968 / Impulse! ♦♦♦
Possibly the most notorious Albert Ayler release and universally misunderstood (i.e., hated) by fans and critics alike. When *New Grass* was released in 1968 it received a hostile outcry of sellout. Listening to *New Grass* in hindsight it must be taken into account that even though commercial elements are apparent—a soul horn section, backup singers, boogaloo drumming from Bernard Purdie, and electric rock bass—Ayler's vocals and tenor playing could hardly gain commercial radio exposure at any time. It's likely Impulse prodded Ayler to move into a more pronounced blues-oriented sound and he went willingly. Ayler wasn't a stranger to R&B or gutbucket blues; he had started his career playing saxophone with Chicago bluesman Little Walter in the '50s. Ayler's screeching tone remains intact on New Grass but it's mixed with definite R&B riffs like the obvious honkin' nod to "Slippin and Sliddin" on "New Generation." Ayler's attempt to explain himself on the opening track "Message From Albert Ayler" reveals his impending dread over controversy concerning the material. It is a problem many artists face at some point in their careers when trying to move in a different direction, no matter what the reason; they may end up losing a majority of their audience by taking a foreign approach. The fact that this material remains out of print in the United States speaks volumes for the lasting commercial contempt still attributed to this album, not only by fans and critics but the record company. Proving that New Grass wasn't commercial when it was first released and remains less so 30 years later. *—Al Campbell*

• **Live in Greenwich Village: The Complete Impulse Sessions** / Mar. 28, 1965-Feb. 26, 1967 / GRP ♦♦♦♦♦
This double-CD from 1998 combines all of the music on tenor-saxophonist Albert Ayler's *In Greenwich Village* recording with a two album set from the same sessions, titled *The Village Concerts* (these latter are taken from two concerts in 1966-67). In addition, there is the one number from 1965, originally included on the sampler, *The New Wave in Jazz*, and a previously unissued (and incomplete) "Universal Thoughts," from the 1967 date, one of the very few examples of Ayler using a trombonist (the forgotten George Steele). Taken as a whole, these are among the most rewarding recordings that the controversial Ayler ever made. They will not convince detractors of the radical saxophonist's music but they are more accessible than much of his music. Teamed up with brother Donald Ayler on trumpet, violinist Michel Sampson, sometimes cellist Joel Freedman, two bassists (Bill Fowell and either Henry Grimes or Alan Silva) and drummer Beaver Harris, Ayler uses simple marchlike melodies, that could have come from 1905, as the basis for his improvisations, which often become quite violent. Among the pieces are "Truth Is Marching On," "Spirits Rejoice," "Angels" (an Albert Ayler duet with pianist Call Cobbs), "For John Coltrane" and "Change Has Come." Donald Ayler's bugle-like fanfares and the droning violin certainly make the ensembles sound quite unique! *—Scott Yanow*

Derek Bailey

b. Jan. 29, 1932, Sheffield, Yorkshire, England
Guitar / Improvisation, Avant-Garde Jazz, Experimental Rock, Free Funk, Free Jazz, Avant-Garde

At first glance, Derek Bailey possesses almost none of the qualities one expects from a jazz musician—his music does not swing in any appreciable way, it lacks a discernible sense of blues feeling—yet there's a strong connection between his amelodic, arhythmic, atonal, uncategorizable free-improvisatory style, and much free jazz of the post-Coltrane era. His music draws upon a vast array of resources, including indeterminacy, rock & roll, and various world musics. Indeed, this catholic acceptance of any and all musical influences is arguably what sets Bailey's art outside the strict bounds of "jazz." The essential element of his work, however, is the type of spontaneous musical interrelation that evolved from the '60s jazz avant-garde. Sound, not ideology, is Bailey's medium. He differs in approach to almost any other guitarist who preceded him. Bailey uses the guitar as a sound-making, rather than a "music"-making, device. Meaning, he rarely plays melodies or harmonies in a conventional sense, but instead pulls out of his instrument every conceivable type of sound using every imaginable technique. His timbral range is quite broad. On electric guitar, Bailey is capable of the most gratingly harsh, distortion-laden heavy-metalisms; unamplified, he's as likely to mimic a set of windchimes. His guitar is much like John Cage's prepared piano; both innovations enhanced the respective instrument's percussive possibilities. *—Chris Kelsey*

Domestic & Public Pieces (1975-77) / May 22, 1975-Mar. 1977 / Emanem ♦♦♦♦♦
The first eight tracks of this album were recorded at home, with Bailey performing on six-string acoustic guitar. Clearly comfortable in his environment, the master improviser voices a range of emotion and sound, from shimmering beauty to fast and furious intensity to scraping and cutting. The next cuts are from a concert performance in which Bailey adds two volume pedals on six tracks and a practice amplifier on the other two. The breathtaking results reflect his spare and effective use of electronics. However, it is the last piece, "Happy Birthday to You," that takes the cake. The guitarist accompanies himself as he reads, with his disarmingly British accent, from Simone de Beauvoir's acutely accurate and detailed description of the aging process. Bailey's astonishing ability to deliver consistently marks him as a true original, a national (and even international) treasure. *—Steve Loewy*

★ **Outcome** / Jun. 25, 1983 / Potlatch ♦♦♦♦♦
This is only the second recorded collaboration between guitarist Derek Bailey and soprano saxophonist Steve Lacy, and while the rarity of the event adds to the thrill, there is little question of the outstanding results produced on this particular occasion. As critic Jon Morgan points out in the liner notes, Lacy and Bailey embrace different concepts of improvisation, yet neither sacrifices any of his individuality to meet the other on common ground. There is little of the conversational quality so often found when musical giants play in tandem. Instead, the five pieces reflect two performers in peak form, each of whom displays his abilities to the fullest. Lacy has rarely sounded better, taking full advantage of the freedom of Bailey's electric guitar. While you are not likely to hear an ounce of familiarity in Bailey's contribution (he always seems *sui generis*), the guitarist continues to amaze with his independence and originality. Anyone even modestly interested in either Lacy or Bailey will wish to hear this one. *—Steven Loewy*

Saisoro / 1995 / Tzadik ♦♦♦♦
Okay, so it's a strange teamup: Derek Bailey, the grizzled veteran of free-improv guitar, and the Ruins, a Japanese bass-drums duo who usually play rock & roll and had never improvised in the studio before this meeting. It may have been lunacy, but it was lunacy of the inspired kind; Yoshida Tatsuya's frenetic-but-solid drumming and creepy, otherworldly vocals give Bailey a lot to react to, and bassist Masuda Ryuishi runs along next to him with infectious glee, frequently playing in the upper registers and sounding like a twin guitar. The disc opens with the rocking "Yagimbo" and then moves into a more impressionistic, almost pointillistic mode, with Tatsuya muttering, yammering and crooning while Bailey makes his guitar sound like a robot being drawn and quartered. Excellent. Then it gets better. "Odangdoh" is fractured and jerky in a surprisingly cool way, while "Manugan Melpp" (were the titles improvised, too?) is beautiful in a surprisingly fractured and jerky way. In fact, the key adjectives for the album as a whole may be "surprising," "beautiful," "fractured" and "jerky." Highly recommended, as long as you don't have a headache or a cat. *—Rick Anderson*

Music & Dance / Jul. 4, 1980-Jul. 6, 1980 / Revenant ♦♦♦♦
Min Tanaka is a dancer, and although one can hear the sporadic shuffling or stomping of feet or the slapping of hands against a wall, one gets the impression that Derek Bailey is being more directly influenced by the dance movements themselves and adjusting his improvisations accordingly. A photo inside the disc package shows Bailey walking and playing around Tanaka who, in this instance, is huddled nude, pressing himself into a wall.

The ambience of the recording site, a glass-ceilinged, abandoned forge in Paris, plays the other significant role here. Several minutes into the first track, a heavy rainstorm erupts, creating a low roar that briefly threatens to overwhelm the music. Bailey, with his classic English ability to take things in stride, simply uses the sound as material to work with and accompanies the downpour with aplomb. When the leaking roof causes a small fusillade of water drops, these too are incorporated into the fabric of the piece, and quite beautifully. In fact, on occasion Bailey sits out entirely, allowing the rain splatters, the dancer's movements and the passing car engine to fully inhabit the sound space.

As is the case with many of his releases, Bailey consistently amazes the listener both with his extraordinary ability to coax sounds from his guitar that may have never before been heard or imagined and, more importantly, his unerring sense of exactly when to utilize those sounds. While Bailey remains maligned in so-called traditional circles, it's clear that he's admired by one of the musicians most deeply involved with the entire tradition of the guitar. *—Brian Olewnick*

Mirakle / Nov. 29, 1999 / Tzadik ♦♦♦♦♦
In one of the most unlikely groupings in music history, avant-skronk guitar godfather Derek Bailey teams up with the harmolodic, free funk rhythm section of Jamaaladeen Tacuma and Calvin Weston. Weston and Tacuma have been the anchor for Ornette Coleman, James Blood Ulmer, and James Carter's first electric album; Weston has been a member of the Lounge Lizards, so these guys can clearly cut a groove. You'd be hard pressed to say that Derek Bailey has ever grooved in his recorded career. That's what makes this recording so much fun. No one compromises their individual sound or strengths, but each is a good enough listener and improviser to make things happen as a group. Weston and Tacuma lay it down super

funky, while Derek Bailey does his thing over the top, and it works! Who says the avant garde can't be a rocking good time? *—Sean Westergaard*

No Waiting / May 1997 / Potlatch ✦✦✦✦✦
Derek Bailey has recorded many LPs and CDs, yet his style never fails to invigorate. This one is no exception. These five totally improvised duos between Bailey and string bassist Joëlle Leandre, live in concert at *Les Instants Chavirés* in Montreuil, France, are some of the most interesting examples of the free music genre. Bailey's electric guitar reverberates ever so spasmodically next to Leandre's scratchy, then hyper-technical bass. Leandre can play with such virtuosity and intensity, but Bailey can counter with space and atmospherics before concentrating on little sounds. Call it a symphony of tiny, sometimes busy, sounds, and you get the idea. The entire album is a lesson in interaction: Leandre and Bailey duel, but only peripherally; they blend not as one, but as a two-headed dragon. In all, a cause for celebration. *—Steve Loewy*

Chet Baker (Chesney Henry Baker)

b. Dec. 23, 1929, Yale, OK, **d.** May 13, 1988, Amsterdam, The Netherlands
Vocals, Trumpet / Vocal Jazz, West Coast Jazz, Cool
A popular cool-toned trumpeter and a fragile singer whose charisma made up for his limited voice, with his good looks Chet Baker probably could have been a movie star. Instead he became a drug addict in the mid-'50s and had an extremely erratic lifestyle with horrific episodes alternating with some wonderful musical moments. Baker certainly started out on top. After getting out of the Army, he gigged with Charlie Parker on the West Coast in 1952 and then joined the Gerry Mulligan Quartet, a pianoless unit that soon became among the most popular in jazz. He began to win polls on both trumpet and vocals, toured Europe in 1955 and seemed on his way to a lucrative career. But by 1960 Baker was in an Italian jail and, although he made a few worthy recordings in the '60s, by the end of the decade his teeth had been knocked out after a botched drug deal and he was out of music. Against all odds Chet Baker made a gradual comeback in the 1970s. Although Baker recorded far too much during his final 15 years, his nomadic lifestyle (never kicking drugs and essentially wandering all over Europe) was unstable and his occasional vocals (always an acquired taste) were generally poor, his trumpet playing actually improved as the decade progressed. In fact despite everything, Chet Baker was still in his musical prime when he fell out of a second story window (pushed or slipped—) to his death in 1988. He remains one of the great cult figures of jazz. *—Scott Yanow*

The Pacific Jazz Years / Oct. 15, 1952-Dec. 9, 1957 / Pacific Jazz ✦✦✦
This attractive four-CD box set gives one a good overview of trumpeter Chet Baker's 1952-57 recordings, a period when he became unexpectedly popular. Baker is heard on four numbers with Gerry Mulligan, with his own quartet (which featured pianist Russ Freeman), in quintets with either altoist Art Pepper or tenor-saxophonist Phil Urso and with larger groups that also include altoist Herb Geller, valve trombonist Bob Brookmeyer, and altoist Bud Shank among others. Perfect as an introduction for those just beginning to appreciate Chet Baker, this set will also interest veteran collectors for, in addition to its attractive booklet, it contains four previously unissued selections with Stan Getz (including a 17-minute version of "All the Things You Are") and four selections from what was thought to be a long-lost session in which the trumpeter is backed on some Bob Zieff arrangements by French horn, bass clarinet, bassoon, cello and bass. *—Scott Yanow*

West Coast Live / Jun. 12, 1953-Aug. 17, 1954 / Blue Note ✦✦✦✦✦
This two-CD set, released in 1997, has 20 formerly rare selections (seven previously unreleased and the remainder mostly put out in Europe) that feature trumpeter Chet Baker and/or tenor saxophonist Stan Getz. The Baker-Getz relationship was never too friendly, but they teamed up on at least four occasions, two of which are represented here. The bulk of the set is taken from June 12, 1953 and features the Gerry Mulligan Quartet with Getz in place of the jailed baritonist. With bassist Carson Smith and drummer Larry Bunker offering quiet support, the tenor tries his best to fit into the ensembles but is much more comfortable when taking solos, with Baker sometimes playing background harmonies. Actually, the trumpeter steals the show and has rarely sounded better, coming up with consistently inventive improvisations on such tunes as "Strike Up the Band," "Winter Wonderland," "Move," "Bernie's Tune" and "Whispering." The second date is from a year later and has Getz sitting in with Chet's regular quartet (which also includes pianist Russ Freeman, bassist Carson Smith and drummer Shelly Manne). A 17 1/2-minute version of "All the Things You Are" holds one's interest, while Baker is absent on the two other Getz features. It is a pity that Baker and Getz disliked each other, for their cool-toned sounds and bop/swing styles were potentially very complementary. In any case, this two-fer is essential for all serious bop collectors. *—Scott Yanow*

Chet Baker Quartet Featuring Ross Freeman / Jul. 24, 1953-Oct. 1953 / Blue Note ✦✦✦✦

The Best of Chet Baker Plays / Jul. 29, 1953-Oct. 31, 1956 / Pacific Jazz ✦✦✦

Grey December / Dec. 22, 1953-Feb. 28, 1955 / Pacific Jazz ✦✦✦✦
This excellent CD reissues two Chet Baker sessions. The trumpeter is heard in a septet from 1953 with tenor-saxophonist Jack Montrose (who contributed the arrangements), altoist Herb Geller, baritonist Bob Gordon and p.anist Russ Freeman, and backed by strings on four vocal numbers from 1955, The latter cuts are passable but the former session (which is augmented by five alternate takes, two being issued for the first time) is frequently superb, West Coast jazz at its best. *—Scott Yanow*

Chet Baker with Strings / Dec. 30, 1953-Feb. 20, 1954 / Columbia/Legacy ✦✦✦
Trumpeter Chet Baker was an up-and-coming star when he recorded these three sessions during 1953-54 with a full string section. Reissued on CD in 1998 with two additional alternate takes (this music last came out in 1991) and updated liner notes, the music is strictly instrumental; Baker had not begun to sing very extensively yet. The emphasis is on his mellow horn; the string arrangements (by Johnny Mandel, Shorty Rogers, Marty Paich and Jack Montrose) are not too harmful, and there are short spots for tenor saxophonist Zoot Sims, altoist Bud Shank and pianist Russ Freeman (who contributed "The Wind" for this date). Not essential, but the melodic music (which includes such numbers as "You Don't Know What Love Is," "Love Walked In," "I Married an Angel" and Rogers' "Trickleydidlier") is quite pleasant and lightly swinging. *—Scott Yanow*

● **The Best of Chet Baker Sings: Let's Get Lost** / Oct. 27, 1953-Jul. 30, 1956 / Capitol/Pacific Jazz ✦✦✦
To much of the pop (as opposed to the jazz) audience, Chet Baker was known not as an able cool jazz trumpeter, but as a romantic balladeer. The two classifications were not mutually exclusive; Baker's vocal numbers would also feature his trumpet playing, as well as fine instrumental support from west coast cool jazzers. For those who prefer the vocal side of the Baker canon, this is an excellent compilation of his best vintage material in that mode. The 20 tracks draw from sessions covering the era when he was generally conceded to be at his vocal peak (1953-56), and are dominated by standards from the likes of Rodgers & Hart, Carmichael, Gershwin, and Kern. Baker's singing was white and naive in the best senses, with a quavering, uncertain earnestness that embodied a certain (safe) strain of mid-'50s bohemianism. That's the Chet we hear on this collection, which contains some his most famous interpretations, including "My Funny Valentine," "Time After Time," "There Will Never Be Another You," and "Let's Get Lost." *—Richie Unterberger*

Young Chet / Feb. 15, 1954-Jul. 31, 1956 / Blue Note ✦✦✦
This CD brings together some leftover tracks from trumpeter Chet Baker's Pacific Jazz sessions. The first five songs originally featured Baker's overdubbed vocals but Richard Bock had a change of heart and also had "alternate" versions made with either tenor-saxophonist Bill Perkins or (on one song) clarinetist Jimmy Giuffre overdubbed where Baker's vocals had been. It is those renditions that form the first half of this CD. The remainder is from a 1956 session by Baker with his quintet when it included tenor-saxophonist Phil Urso and pianist Bobby Timmons. Baker plays well on five songs from this set but is actually not present on "It's Only a Paper Moon" (an Urso feature) and "Autumn in New York" (which is played by the trio). Although there is some good music on the CD, this release is mostly for Baker completists since there are many more essential Chet Baker albums currently available. *—Scott Yanow*

Complete Pacific Jazz Live Recordings / May 9, 1954-Oct. 1954 / Mosaic ✦✦✦✦✦
Chet Baker and his popular Quartet (pianist Russ Freeman, bassist Carson Smith, and drummer Bob Neel) recorded live for Pacific Jazz on three different occasions in 1954. While their appearance in Ann Arbor was released, less than half of the music recorded in Los Angeles and none of the five selections cut in Santa Cruz, CA, were issued until this limited-edition four-LP box set was put out by Mosaic. Throughout this instrumental set Baker and Freeman are in their early peak form, showing that their variations of bop was not as cool as the stereotype of West Coast jazz might lead one to expect. Get this gem while you can. *—Scott Yanow*

Chet Baker Big Band / Sep. 9, 1954-Oct. 26, 1954 / Pacific Jazz ✦✦✦✦
Despite the title, only four of the 16 titles that comprise this CD are actually performed by a big band. Trumpeter Chet Baker is featured with an 11-piece group for those selections, plays in a nonet for six others and with a sextet for the remainder. The arrangements of Jimmy Heath, Jack Montrose, Johnny Mandel, Bill Holman, Christian Chevallier, Pierre Michelot and Phil Urso really bring out the best in Baker, making this a highly enjoyable and varied set. *—Scott Yanow*

Chet Baker & Crew / Jul. 24, 1956-Jul. 31, 1956 / Pacific Jazz ✦✦✦✦
This CD brings back one of his lesser-known bands, the quintet with tenor-saxophonist Phil Urso and pianist Bobby Timmons. Urso's cool tenor blended in perfectly with Baker's relaxed trumpet while Timmons's funky piano (which in three years would make him famous with Art Blakey and Cannonball Adderley) inspired the soloists. The fresh repertoire heard on this consistently enjoyable set contains many songs begging to be revived. *—Scott Yanow*

The Route / Jul. 26, 1956 / Pacific Jazz ✦✦✦✦
One of two CDs that team Baker and altoist Art Pepper, this one also features tenor-saxophonist and pianist Pete Jolly; all four players get their own showcases. The often-heated results make it obvious that there was no strict borderline between artists associated with West Coast jazz and hard bop for some of these performances burn. It's strange that both Baker and Pepper could play such consistent music while conducting chaotic lifestyles. *— Scott Yanow*

Playboys / Oct. 31, 1956 / Pacific Jazz ✦✦✦✦
This is the second CD (following *The Route*) to team trumpeter Chet Baker and altoist Art Pepper, two masterful players who had similar (and rather strange) life stories, with so many ups and downs as to be almost unbelievable. None of the chaos of their lives appears in the fine music they created. This sextet session (which has five Jimmy Heath compositions in addition to two originals from Pepper) also contains spots for excellent solos by tenor-saxophonist Phil Urso and pianist Carl Perkins. *—Scott Yanow*

The Art of the Ballad / Aug. 1958-Aug. 25, 1965 / Prestige ✦✦✦
All but two of these 13 tracks date from the late 1950s (the other two were done in 1965), and while Baker's talents were undimmed at this point, this wasn't his best era recording-wise, in terms of either material or bands. For his best you should turn to the earlier Pacific Jazz discs, but this is still a good set of slow and sentimental Baker for those who have heard the peak stuff in this vein and want yet more. "Autumn in New York," recorded in Italy with a string orchestra, is one extreme of his sentimental predilections, yet there's also stuff in a far more straight-ahead vein with the likes of Bill Evans and Kenny Burrell among the backup musicians. "Almost Like Being in Love" is a standout, Baker's trumpet taking on an oddly echoing tone, though with its sharp bebop rhythm it's not really a ballad. Not many vocals on this set, but it does close out with a couple of good Baker-sung standards, "I'm Old Fashioned" and "My Heart Stood Still." *—Richie Unterberger*

Chet Baker Sings It Could Happen to You / Aug. 1958 / Riverside/OJC ✦✦✦

Chet Baker in New York / Sep. 1958 / Riverside/OJC ✦✦✦✦

Chet Baker in Milan / Sep. 25, 1959-Oct. 6, 1959 / Jazzland/OJC ♦♦♦

The Italian Sessions / Mar. 1962 / Bluebird/RCA ♦♦♦♦♦
Throughout the 1950s Chet Baker gained fame as a quiet low-register trumpeter with a cool tone and a relaxed style. This CD therefore should be a major surprise to listeners who believe he was incapable of playing heated material or of utilizing the upper register of his horn. Assisted by a fine European sextet (including Bobby Jaspar on tenor and flute and guitarist Rene Thomas), Baker is heard in peak form throughout this memorable and frequently exciting bop date. *—Scott Yanow*

Baker's Holiday: Plays & Sings Billie Holiday / May 1965 / EmArcy ♦♦♦

● **Lonely Star** / Aug. 23, 1965-Aug. 25, 1965 / Prestige ♦♦♦♦♦
In 1964, trumpeter Chet Baker returned to the United States after five sometimes-traumatic years spent overseas (which included a long stay in an Italian jail for drug abuse). Baker recorded prolifically during his first 14 months back in the States, including a set for Colpix, two records for Limelight and, in a busy three-day period, five albums for Prestige titled *Groovin', Comin' On, Cool Burnin', Smokin'* and *Boppin' With the Chet Baker Quintet.* The Prestige sets have been long overlooked and only partially reissued in the past, but in 1997 they reappeared as three CDs. Teamed up with tenorman George Coleman (fresh from his notable period with Miles Davis), the young pianist Kirk Lightsey (who sometimes takes solo honors) and the supportive bass-drums team of Herman Wright and Roy Brooks, Chet Baker (sticking exclusively to flugelhorn) is heard throughout in top form. Although his cool style was very much intact (sometimes hinting strongly at both Miles Davis and Shorty Rogers), Baker also plays with surprising fire in spots. Of the trio of CDs, this particular one has a slight edge due to a well-rounded repertoire (two standards, Tadd Dameron's appealing blues "So Easy" and seven often-catchy Richard Carpenter originals), but all three sets (which also include *On a Misty Night* and *Stairway to the Stars*) are easily recommended to straight-ahead jazz fans. *—Scott Yanow*

On a Misty Night / Aug. 23, 1965-Aug. 25, 1965 / Prestige ♦♦♦♦

Stairway to the Stars / Aug. 23, 1965-Aug. 25, 1965 / Prestige ♦♦♦♦
During a three-day period in 1965, trumpeter Chet Baker (who during the era was exclusively playing flugelhorn) recorded five albums for Prestige that were soon forgotten, despite their quality. In 1997, the entire program was reissued on three CDs (which also include *Lonely Star* and *On a Misty Night*), showing that Baker was in excellent form at the time. Chet is teamed with tenor saxophonist George Coleman, pianist Kirk Lightsey (in top form), bassist Herman Wright and drummer Roy Brooks; the one-time gathering group on the whole sometimes recalls the Miles Davis Quintet of 1956. There are some occasional missteps (Baker gets a bit lost during the rapid rendition of "Cherokee" that opens this CD), but overall, the music (some light swingers and a few more heated tracks) is quite rewarding. Producer Richard Carpenter (Baker's manager at the time and best known for writing "Walkin'") contributed three songs to this set (and 13 others to the other two CDs), which also includes three jazz standards, a few obscurities, and three Tadd Dameron originals. Enjoyable straight-ahead music. *—Scott Yanow*

You Can't Go Home Again / Feb. 16, 1977-May 13, 1977 / A&M ♦♦♦

Blues for a Reason / Sep. 30, 1984 / Criss Cross ♦♦♦♦♦
This combination works quite well. For what might have been the only time in their careers, trumpeter Chet Baker and tenor-saxophonist Warne Marsh were teamed together in a quintet (which also includes pianist Hod O'Brien, bassist Cecil McBee and drummer Eddie Gladden) for this Criss Cross session. The CD reissue adds two alternate takes to the original six songs which consist of "If You Could See Me Now," "Imagination," Marsh's "Well Spoken" and three Baker originals. Recommended. *—Scott Yanow*

Chet Baker in Tokyo / Jun. 14, 1987 / Evidence ♦♦♦♦

The Legacy, Vol. 1 / Nov. 14, 1987 / Enja ♦♦♦♦

My Favourite Songs, Vols. 1-2: The Last Great Concert / Apr. 28, 1988 / Enja ♦♦♦♦♦

Billy Bang (William Vincent Walker)

b. Sep. 20, 1947, Mobile, AL
Violin / Avant-Garde Jazz, Free Jazz
Although he plays an instrument that's more closely identified with uptown concert halls than downtown jazz clubs, there's no mistaking the primary source of Billy Bang's musical inspiration. While his violin technique is extensive and his familiarity with contemporary classical forms apparent, Bang's rough-edged, sometimes almost guttural tone, his old-fashioned sense of swing, and his lexicon of vocalic expressive devices define him as a jazz musician. Whether in the abstract (as a solo violinist, elaborating on skeletal melodic material) or as part of a greater whole (with Sun Ra's Arkestra, for example), a Bang performance is always awash with surprise.

Prompted by a fascination with Afro-Cuban rhythms, Billy Bang switched from violin to percussion while in high school. After being drafted into the service and sent to Vietnam, he became radicalized upon returning to the US and worked in the anti-war movement. Inspired by the free jazz of the mid-'60s, Bang began playing music again in the late '60s and studied violin with Leroy Jenkins. He formed his own group—the Survival Ensemble—in the early '70s, and co-founded (with bassist John Lindberg and guitarist James Emery) the String Trio of New York in 1977. He also played with bassist Bill Laswell's Material and drummer Ronald Shannon Jackson's Decoding Society, and led his own groups.

In the '90s Bang fronted his own ensembles and occasionally led ad hoc groups on record dates. A 1992 session with Sun Ra produced *Tribute to Stuff Smith.* Bang recorded *Spirits Gathering* for the CIMP label in 1996. The next year he made his most straight-ahead jazz album, *Bang On!,* for Justin Time. That same year he recorded *Commandment (for the sculpture of Alain Kirili)* an album of solo violin, for Alan Schneider's NoMore label. *—Chris Kelsey*

Rainbow Gladiator / Jun. 10, 1981-Jun. 11, 1981 / Soul Note ♦♦♦♦
Ever since his emergence in the late '70s, Billy Bang has been one of the top violinists in the jazz avant-garde (along with his predecessor Leroy Jenkins), a musician not shy to play either melodies or sound explorations. This set, his first as a leader, finds Bang holding his own with a strong cast of players including Charles Tyler on alto and baritone and pianist Michele Rosewoman. All six compositions are Bang's, making this a good introduction to his music for those who have an open mind toward adventurous jazz. *—Scott Yanow*

● **Live at Carlos 1** / Nov. 23, 1986 / Soul Note ♦♦♦♦♦
Violinist Billy Bang uses the same instrumentation on this set as on his previous *The Fire from Within* although his sextet had two new members: trumpeter Roy Campbell and drummer Zen Matsuura. A more rhythmic album, this melodic avant-garde set rewards repeated listenings and has an impressive amount of variety. *—Scott Yanow*

Tribute to Stuff Smith / Sep. 1992 / Soul Note ♦♦♦
The connection to the past is worth pointing out here: Sun Ra and violinist Stuff Smith once played together, back in 1953 or 1954. Bassist John Ore has also been a staple in Ra's bands, and Andrew Cyrille is no stranger to any of this crew. That said, those who like their violin "inside" will want to start their Bang collections with this recording: It is the last avant-garde of his oeuvre. For Sun Ra lovers, this recording will be important for being probably the very last thing he did before passing on to the interplanetary spaceways. The entire date is relaxed and highly structured. Like Smith, Bang plays here well within established boundaries, but still manages to place his notes somewhere just out of reach, in a place that's difficult to put a finger on, and all the more rewarding because of this enigma. *—Scot Hacker*

Bang On! / Apr. 21, 1997-Apr. 23, 1997 / Justin Time ♦♦♦♦♦
Bang is well-regarded as one of the premier progressive jazz violinists, and this recording, not surprisingly, shows him balancing music both inside and out. Pianist D.D. Jackson follows these modern traditionalist lines, while unheralded bassist Akira Ando holds up things nicely, and drummer Ronnie Burrage constructs and deconstructs rhythms in rapid-fire fashion. Of the standards, played within the tradition, all are easily identifiable and enjoyable. "Sweet Georgia Brown" is a most vibrant rendition of the other side of Stephane Grappelli—straight, swinging, and yes, incorporating some low-atmosphere blasts and scrapings. "Yesterdays" has Jackson setting off sparklers with his now characteristic Don Pullen-like, hand-turned rumblings. "Willow Weep for Me" is a neat changeup on the well-known ballad; instead, it's a down-home blues, flowing from wistful crying to a river of tears. Bang writes engaging material for this quartet, and likes to mix messages. The R&B bass ostinato against bubbling Latin rhythm sets Burrage ablaze during "Don's Dream," while more funky blues and a simple melody works with a complex, acid-tinged Bang solo on "Three Faces of Eve." The hippest of modern compositions, "Spirits Entering" is rambunctious, loaded with changes—many on the spot—and framed by modal piano. Jackson constantly challenges rhythmic parameters and melodic barriers, while Bang follows suit. Both are at the top of their game on this one. "'Bama Swing" might turn out to be a standard; certainly it's a signature piece for the violinist, a very tuneful, straight swinger wiith both plucked and bowed melody lines which any listener should appreciate. This is Billy Bang's finest recorded hour—a hallmark for modern jazz violin in the 1990s, and a strong candidate for best jazz CD of 1997. *—Michael G. Nastos*

Big Bang Theory / -08 / Justin Time ♦♦♦
Billy Bang long ago earned his reputation as an engaging leader and violin soloist in avant-garde circles. Luckily that has not stifled his abilities and ambition to play in more straight-ahead settings as he does on *Big Bang Theory.* Bang's assembled drummer Codaryl Moffett, pianist Alexis Pope, and bassist Curtis Lundy—musicians easily capable of improvisation while maintaining a cohesive balance. Bang scored five originals including "At Play in the Fields of the Lord" providing Pope and Lundy ample solo space to shine and "One For Jazz", a tribute to drummer Dennis Charles that starts with voice and drum and hauntingly falls into full quartet momentum. The inclusion of Freddie Hubbard's exuberant composition "Little Sunflower and a joyous funky version of the traditional "Swing Low, Sweet Chariot" sum up the projects overt statement of spirituality that borders on experimentation while maintaining conventional structures. *—Al Campbell*

Patricia Barber

b. Chicago, IL
Vocals, Piano / Vocal Jazz, Cabaret, Contemporary Jazz
Patricia Barber is a difficult performer to easily categorize. A singer with an unusual voice and a talented jazz pianist, Barber has sought to expand the repertoire that singers have today by not only taking obscurities from the pop world but writing her own material. A fixture at Chicago's Gold Star Sardine Bar since 1984 (switching in more recent years to the Green Mill), Barber is the daughter of a saxophonist who played with Glenn Miller (Floyd Barber). She studied classical piano, played saxophone in her high-school band and mostly stuck to classical while at the University of Iowa before switching permanently to jazz. She worked locally in Iowa, moved back to Chicago and formed a regular trio. Beginning in 1989 Barber started appearing regularly at the North Sea Jazz Festival. Thus far she has recorded for her own Floyd label (1989's *Split*), Antilles (1992's *A Distortion Of Love*) and more recently for Premonition, including 1994's much-acclaimed *Cafe Blue* and 1998's *Modern Cool.* Two years later *Night Club* was released. *—Scott Yanow*

A Distortion of Love / Nov. 25, 1991-Nov. 29, 1991 / Antilles ♦♦♦♦
Pianist and singer Patricia Barber's second album (and major-label debut) is a consistently interesting, but not always completely rewarding, array of original instrumentals, vocal standards, and surprise cover versions. The arrangement of "Summertime" that opens the program is eerie almost to the point of creepiness, and all the more effective for it: after a long instrumental prelude, Barber sings the lyrics over the most minimal bass-and-piano unison pedal point, her voice goosed with reverb and wailing softly like a ghost. "Subway Station 5," the original composition that follows, is nervous, jumpy, barely tonal, and moves niftily from a contrapuntal and polyrhythmic introduction into a straight swing section. The problem is that it lasts almost ten minutes, and by the seventh or eighth minute, its ideas seem pretty well played out. "Or Not to Be" and "Yet Another in a Long Series of Yellow Cars" suf-

fer from similar treatment. But her singing on "You Stepped Out of a Dream" and, especially, her sweet and touching rendition of the soul classic "My Girl" are quietly spectacular. There's every reason to expect great things of her in the future. *—Rick Anderson*

• **Café Blue** / Jun. 28, 1994-Jul. 1, 1994 / Blue Note ♦♦♦♦
Patricia Barber, who is both a fine keyboardist and an atmospheric singer, contributes roughly half of the material to her Premonition debut. Her dark voice and the generally esoteric program takes awhile to get used to (listeners will have to be patient) but after two or three listens this thought-provoking and rather moody set becomes more accessible. The music ranges stylewise from sophisticated pop sensitivities to the avant-garde and even touches of minimalism while not fitting securely into any category. Barber gives a new slant to "The Thrill Is Gone," "Ode to Billy Joe" and even "A Taste of Honey" and her vocals are all quite haunting and contemporary. An added plus to this unusual music is the adventurous guitarist John McLean. *—Scott Yanow*

Companion / Jul. 17, 1999-Jul. 19, 1999 / Blue Note ♦♦♦♦
Companion was recorded in a special three-night series of shows in July, 1999 at Chicago's famed *Green Mill* jazz club—an unusually short amount of time to produce a live album. To mine as much material as possible from those nights the performances were run more like recording sessions than live shows, with the crowd reverently hushed. Patricia Barber is in her element and the only thing that seems to have suffered for the recording circumstances is the album's length—at seven songs and 40 minutes, it walks the line between standard EP and full-length size. One surmises that it might have been longer had there been more album-quality material from the performances. Recalling the energy that was present on her critically worshipped *Café Blue* album, there is an ease and creativity on *Companion* which makes her fans' devotion understandable. Barber has been criticized for being a jazz singer in the loosest sense—her style borrows heavily from R&B and she often covers pop songs (Sonny Bono's "The Beat Goes On" is a sheer stylish delight), and her song "If This Isn't Jazz" answers that criticism with a thumb to the nose. What many critics fail to notice, however, is the strength of her musicianship. Sexism within the industry keeps many from seeing female jazz performers playing roles other than those of vocalists—Barber's warm, breathy voice and creative phrasing are wonderful, for sure, but what really shines are her arrangements. With a talented band behind her, on *Companion* Barber has made magic with her compositions, her piano playing, and yes, her voice. Intended to be a companion to *Modern Cool*, this album of mostly previously unrecorded material serves as an excellent introduction to all of her work. *—Stacia Proefrock*

Night Club / May 15, 2000-May 9, 200 / Blue Note ♦♦♦

Gato Barbieri (Leandro J. Barbieri)

b. Nov. 28, 1934, Rosario, Argentina
Sax (Tenor) / Jazz-Pop, Latin Jazz
Gato Barbieri is the second Argentinian musician to make a significant impact upon jazz—the first being Lalo Schifrin, in whose band Barbieri played as a teenager. His story has been that of an elongated zigzag odyssey between his homeland and North America. He started out playing to traditional Latin rhythms in his early years, turning his back on his heritage to explore the jazz avant-garde in the '60s, reverting to South American influences in the early '70s, playing pop and fusion in the late '70s, only to go back and forth again in the '80s. North American audiences first heard Barbieri when he was a wild bull, sporting a coarse, wailing, John Coltrane/Pharoah Sanders-influenced tone. Yet by the mid-'70s, his approach and tone began to mellow somewhat in accordance with ballads like "What a Diff'rence a Day Makes" (which he always knew as the vintage bolero "Cuando Vuelva a tu Lado") and Carlos Santana's "Europa." Still, regardless of the idiom in which he works, the warm-blooded Barbieri has always been one of the most overtly emotional tenor sax soloists on records, occasionally driving the voltage ever higher with impulsive vocal cheerleading. *—Richard S. Ginell*

Gato Barbieri and Don Cherry / 1965 / Inner City ♦♦♦
This LP features tenor-saxophonist Gato Barbieri (at the beginning of his career) and trumpeter Don Cherry teaming up with a French rhythm section for the trumpeter's five-part "Togetherness." While Cherry plays pretty free, he sounds conservative next to the often-violent wails of Barbieri. This interesting set (long out-of-print) is for the open-minded only. *—Scott Yanow*

In Search of the Mystery / Mar. 15, 1967 / ESP ♦♦♦
Gato Barbieri's ESP album finds the Argentine tenor playing some ferocious solos on four of his originals. Joined by cellist Calo Scott, bassist Sirone and drummer Bobby Kapp, Barbieri is virtually the whole show so this set is mainly interesting for listeners who enjoy the intense tone he had in his early days. *—Scott Yanow*

The Third World / Nov. 24, 1969–Nov. 25, 1969 / Flying Dutchman ♦♦♦

• **Fenix** / Apr. 27, 1971-Apr. 28, 1971 / Flying Dutchman ♦♦♦♦♦
The manic album that won him fame on college campuses in early 70s. *—Ron Wynn*

Last Tango in Paris / Nov. 20, 1972-Nov. 25, 1972 / United Artists ♦♦♦♦♦
Although some of the smoky sax solos get a little uncomfortably close to 1970s fusion cliche, Gato Barbieri's score to Bertolucci's 1972 classic is an overall triumph. Suspenseful jazz, melancholy orchestration, and actual tangos fit the film's air of erotic longing, melancholy despair, and doomed fate. "Last Tango in Paris" is a particular standout, its orgiastic, wordless vocal yelps reflecting, whether by design or not, the actual content of the movie. The 1998 CD reissue is by no means just a substitute for the old vinyl; it more than doubles the length of the original release with a "Last Tango in Paris Suite," put together by Barbieri himself from 29 cues from the original score as used in the film. *—Richie Unterberger*

Chapter 1: Latin America / 1973 / Impulse! ♦♦♦♦
The four "Chapters" in this series found Gato Barbieri rediscovering his South American roots and displaying his intense tone in melodic settings where his energy would be better focused than it had been on his earlier avant-garde albums. Joined by a large group of Argentinian musicians, Barbieri is in top form throughout this heated set, particularly on "Encunetros" and "India." Each of the "Chapters" is recommended although *Chapter Three* is the only one currently available on CD. *—Scott Yanow*

Latino America / Apr. 18, 1973-Oct. 17, 1973 / Impulse! ♦♦♦♦♦

Chapter 3: Viva Emiliano Zapata / Jun. 25, 1974–Jun. 26, 1974 / Impulse! ♦♦♦♦♦
On the third of four "Chapters," the intense tenor-saxophonist Gato Barbieri is accompanied by a big band playing Chico O'Farrill arrangements. The charts really showcase Barbieri at his peak, performing four of his melodic originals, "Milonga Triste" and "What a Difference a Day Makes." This CD (a straight reissue of the original LP) is highly recommended. *—Scott Yanow*

Che Corazon / Apr. 27, 1999 / Columbia ♦♦♦♦
An improvement on tenor saxophonist Gato Barbieri's previous Columbia debut, this outing mostly features his romantic and passionate horn in the spotlight. One song is primarily a vocal feature for Gato. His backup band (which usually includes bassist Mark Egan and guitarist Chuck Loeb) is generally quite spirited, but it is the tenor who stars throughout. Even when sticking to the melody (Gato and Loeb wrote most of the material), there is so much feeling in Barbieri's playing that he largely possesses each song, even an oddly memorable rendition of "Auld Lang Syne." And, although the performances are a bit commercial in spots, Barbieri's sincere emotionalism consistently uplifts this recording. *—Scott Yanow*

The Best of the Early Years / 1970-1973 / RCA ♦♦♦

Last Tango in Paris / Nov. 20, 1972-Nov. 25, 1972 / United Artists ♦♦♦♦♦
Although some of the smoky sax solos get a little uncomfortably close to 1970s fusion cliche, Gato Barbieri's score to Bertolucci's 1972 classic is an overall triumph. Suspenseful jazz, melancholy orchestration, and actual tangos fit the film's air of erotic longing, melancholy despair, and doomed fate. "Last Tango in Paris" is a particular standout, its orgiastic, wordless vocal yelps reflecting, whether by design or not, the actual content of the movie. The 1998 CD reissue is by no means just a substitute for the old vinyl; it more than doubles the length of the original release with a "Last Tango in Paris Suite," put together by Barbieri himself from 29 cues from the original score as used in the film. *—Richie Unterberger*

Kenny Barron

b. Jun. 9, 1943, Philadelphia, PA
Piano / Hard Bop, Post-Bop
In recent years Kenny Barron has been recognized one of the giants of modern mainstream piano. The younger brother of the late saxophonist Bill Barron (who was 16 years older), he started on piano when he was 12 and played with Mel Melvin's R&B band in 1957. Barron moved to New York in 1961 where he worked briefly with James Moody, Lee Morgan, Roy Haynes and Lou Donaldson. Most significant were his four years (1962-66) playing and recording with Dizzy Gillespie. Barron followed that important association with periods in the groups of Freddie Hubbard (1966-70), Yusef Lateef (1970-75) and Ron Carter's two-bass quartet (1976-80). Barron was a co-leader of the group Sphere in the 1980s and since then has generally been the leader of his own trios. The pianist was on Stan Getz's final session (a series of brilliant duets) and has recorded many dates as a leader. In the 1990s Barron received long overdue recognition for his talents. *—Scott Yanow*

Peruvian Blue / Mar. 14, 1974 / 32 Jazz ♦♦♦♦
Reissued in 1998, this set (which was originally put out by Muse) has more than its share of variety. Kenny Barron is heard on piano, electric piano and clavinet on various tracks, and is joined some of the time by guitarist Ted Dunbar, bassist David Williams, drummer Albert "Tootie" Heath and percussionists Richard Landrum and Sonny Morgan. Dunbar in particular is in top form, dueting with Barron on an explorative version of "Blue Monk" and being an important part of the ensemble on some of the more electric jams (the four Barron originals), all of which are fairly colorful. The leader takes a lengthy unaccompanied piano solo on "Here's That Rainy Day," another of the date's highlights. This is a CD that rewards repeated listenings. *—Scott Yanow*

At the Piano / Feb. 13, 1981 / Prevue ♦♦♦♦
Up until the original release of *At the Piano* in 1982, Kenny Barron had yet to record an entire album of solo piano pieces. Although this would not to be his last in this context, it would be his most honest and representative. The set is a fine mix of standards and originals, with the highlights being a beautiful interpretation of "The Star Crossed Lovers", and a memorable original, "Enchanted Flower." Along with the duets he recorded with Stan Getz, this stands as the high-water mark in his stellar recording career. *—Robert Taylor*

Green Chimneys / Jul. 9, 1983–Dec. 31, 1987 / Criss Cross ♦♦♦♦
In the 1980s, Kenny Barron was recognized as one of jazz's top pianists, a modern mainstream master who two decades later is still in prime form. His 1983 trio date with bassist Buster Williams and drummer Ben Riley, *Green Chimneys*, originally consisted of six songs highlighted by "Softly As in a Morning Sunrise," "Straight No Chaser," and a lengthy version of "There Is No Greater Love." The CD reissue adds a second alternate take of "Time Was," plus three numbers ("Skylark," "When Lights Are Low," and Barron's "Morning Blues") recorded with the same musicians in 1987. The additions are of equally high quality as the earlier set, making this swinging program (which has almost 68 minutes of music) a bargain. *—Scott Yanow*

Scratch / Mar. 11, 1985 / Enja ♦♦♦♦
Kenny Barron, one of those talented pianists who always seems to be underrated, breaks away from playing standards and conventional bebop on this frequently exciting trio date. Matched up with bassist Dave Holland and drummer Daniel Humair, Barron explores five of his originals and Carmen Lundy's "Quiet Times." The fresh material and close interplay between the musicians make this set one of Barron's best trio recordings to date. *—Scott Yanow*

• **Live at Maybeck Recital Hall, Vol. 10** / Dec. 3, 1990 / Concord Jazz ♦♦♦♦
Producing a darker tone from the Maybeck Yamaha piano than do some other participants

in the series, Kenny Barron gets a chance to flaunt a wider range of his influences than he usually does in a group format. Barron opens with a stride-ish "I'm Getting Sentimental Over You," which sports a few minor fluffs (this is live, folks), and then explores a number of diverse styles under the bop umbrella. Barron's "Bud-Like" has reminiscences of "Un Poco Loco," built on an ostinato bass pattern most of the way, with a witty "Bemsha Swing." As usual with Maybeck, the sound of the hall's bright, brittle Yamaha piano is brilliantly captured. *—Richard S. Ginell*

Invitation / Dec. 20, 1990 / Criss Cross ✦✦✦✦✦
Kenny Barron has been a respected jazz pianist since the early '60s, but it wasn't until the mid-'70s that he began coming into his own as a composer; deftly working complex time signatures and mercurial melodies into seamlessly swinging numbers, agile sambas, and lovely ballads. Fifteen years on, *Invitation* finds Barron in full maturity as a writer and in the sympathetic company of tenor saxophonist Ralph Moore, bassist David Williams, and drummer Lewis Nash. Barron's democratic pen runs the gamut here as he distills Monk's angular jubilance on "And Then Again," produces one of his most beautiful ballads in "Dewdrop," and works a fine bossa nova groove on "Joanne Julia." The covers are no less impressive. Barron and the group swing solid and fleet on Bronislaw Kaper's caustically subdued "Invitation" and place John Lewis' "Parisian Afternoon" in a gently swinging light. "You Don't Know What Love Is" is read solo by Barron with mysterious aplomb, and "Blue Monk" gets a strong blues reading. Throughout, Ralph Moore's choice tenor lines glide over the notes, Lewis Nash's tasteful drumming impressively anchors the group, and Barron's inventive solos ride atop the band in full stride. With great material, solid playing, and the full *Criss Cross* sound, *Invitation* ends up as one of Kenny Barron's finest outings of the 1990s. *—Stephen Cook*

Wanton Spirit / Feb. 22, 1994-Feb. 23, 1994 / Verve ✦✦✦✦✦

Things Unseen / Mar. 17, 1995–Mar. 18, 1995 / Verve ✦✦✦✦

Soft Spoken Here / Apr. 2, 1973-Apr. 18, 1980 / 32 Jazz ✦✦✦✦✦
Two of pianist Kenny Barron's earlier LPs (*Sunset to Dawn* and *Golden Lotus*) are reissued in full on this double CD from 1997. The 1973 date has its moments of interest, with Barron doubling on electric piano as part of a five-piece rhythm section, performing five of his originals and a song by drummer Freddie Waits. Those post-bop sides hint a bit at fusion and funk while still remaining reasonably creative. However, it is the later set (a quintet outing with John Stubblefield on tenor and soprano, vibraphonist Steve Nelson, bassist Buster Williams and drummer Ben Riley) that is of greatest interest; the group performs four Barron tunes, including "Golden Lotus," plus "Darn That Dream." Nelson's playing at that early stage showed great potential that he has since largely realized. An excellent two-fer. *—Scott Yanow*

Count Basie (William Basie)

b. Aug. 21, 1904, Red Bank, NJ, **d.** Apr. 26, 1984, Hollywood, FL
Piano / Swing, Piano Blues, Big Band
Throughout his career the name of Count Basie was synonymous with swing. Basie, whose influence remains huge over a decade after his death, not only led two of the finest jazz orchestras ever but he redefined the role of the piano in the rhythm section. Originally a stride pianist in the vein of his idol Fats Waller, Basie had such a strong rhythm section in the mid-'30s that he pared down his style drastically, eliminating the oom-pah timekeeping function of his left hand. With bassist Walter Page, rhythm guitarist Freddie Green and drummer Jo Jones filling in the spaces, Count stuck to simple phrases that were strategically placed to add momentum to the ensembles and he unwittingly acted as a transitional figure towards the bop of Bud Powell. After a period of struggle in which the orchestra had some rough moments, by late 1937 the Count Basie band had caught on. With such important soloists as the cool-toned tenor Lester Young, trumpeters Buck Clayton and Harry "Sweets" Edison, trombonist Dicky Wells, vocalist Jimmy Rushing (and for a period Billie Holiday), Basie's orchestra could hold its own against any other swing band. Its theme "One O'Clock Jump" soon became widely recorded (almost serving as an anthem for the era) and "Jumpin' at the Woodside" became a standard. In the 1940s the band's arrangements (many of which were originally thought up by sidemen while on the bandstand) became more formalized. Bad money management and the change in the public's musical taste led Basie to reluctantly break up his orchestra at the end of 1949 and use a small group; in 1952, during a period when very few jazz orchestras were being formed, he put together what became known as his "New Testament" (as opposed to the earlier "Old Testament") band. Against all odds, Basie's orchestra caught on, especially after recording "April in Paris" in 1954 and after singer Joe Williams signed on the following year. Although there was a lot of turnover in the 1960s, the Basie sound never changed and the orchestra did not decline nor stop travelling. *—Scott Yanow*

☆ **The Complete Decca Recordings (1937-1939)** / 1937-Feb. 4, 1939 / GRP ✦✦✦✦✦
This magnificent three-disc set has the first 63 recordings by Count Basie's Orchestra, all of his Deccas. The consistency is remarkable (with not more than two or three turkeys) and the music is the epitome of swing. With such soloists as Lester Young and Herschel Evans on tenors, trumpeters Buck Clayton and Harry "Sweets" Edison, the great blues singer Jimmy Rushing and that brilliant rhythm section of Basie, guitarist Freddie Green, bassist Walter Page and drummer Jo Jones, the music is timeless. It's all here: "One O'Clock Jump," "Sent for You Yesterday," "Blue and Sentimental," "Jumpin' at the Woodside," "Jive at Five" and many others. This is the first Count Basie collection to acquire and should be in every jazz collection. *—Scott Yanow*

Count Basie Featuring Anita O'Day & the Tadd Dameron Trio (1945-1948) / May 14, 1945-Sep. 25, 1948 / EPM Musique ✦✦✦✦✦
It's discs like this that give the European pirates a good name—the opener alone, "High Tide," cut at *Radio City* in May of 1945, justifies the price, a scatting, bouncy jam built on a number by Freddie Green and Rudy Rutherford (who takes a great clarinet solo). "The Peacock" and "Swedish Pastry" come from the band's Royal Roost engagments in September of 1948, but hardly any of it overlaps with Drive Archive's Royal Roost release on Basie. O'Day actually sings with the Basie band on only five of the 13 numbers on which they appear, and on the last two (also from the Royal Roost) appears with the Tadd Dameron Trio. The band is fine throughout, O'Day dazzles with her singing and scatting, and the repertory is a mix of Basie ("High Tide") and O'Day ("Hi-Ho Trailus Boot Whip"), with the sultry R&B-flavored "That's That" a major highlight for band and singer alike. The recording, as is the tendency of transciptions, tends to be a bit bass-heavy at some expense to the upper range, but isn't distractingly poor. *—Bruce Eder*

★ **Count Basie Swings, Joe Williams Sings** / Jul. 17, 1955-Jul. 26, 1955 / Verve ✦✦✦✦✦
Joe Williams' debut as the featured vocalist in Count Basie's band was one of those landmark moments that even savvy observers don't fully appreciate when it occurs, then realize years later how momentous an event they witnessed. Williams brought a different presence to the great Basie orchestra than the one Jimmy Rushing provided; he couldn't shout like Rushing, but he was more effective on romantic and sentimental material, while he was almost as spectacular on surging blues, up-tempo wailers, and stomping standards. Basie's band maintained an incredible groove behind Williams, who moved from authoritative statements on "Every Day I Have the Blues" and "Please Send Me Someone to Love" to brisk workouts on "Roll 'Em Pete" and his definitive hit, "All Right, OK, You Win." *—Ron Wynn*

☆ **April in Paris** / Jul. 26, 1955-Jan. 5, 1956 / Verve ✦✦✦✦✦
A true classic, this studio album includes Count Basie's hit versions of "April in Paris," ""Shiny Stockings" and "Corner Pocket"; these three tunes have remained in the Basie band's repertoire ever since. Actually all ten selections are very enjoyable, and this exciting and of course swinging record is definitive of '50s Count Basie. With such soloists as trumpeters Joe Newman and Thad Jones, the tenors of Frank Foster and Frank Wess (who doubles on flute) and the leader-pianst, the Basie Orchestra was well on its way to exceeding the success of its earlier ccounterpart. This CD reissue adds seven alternate takes to the original program, showing that Thad Jones' famous "Pop Goes the Whistle" quote on "April in Paris" was planned in advance! *—Scott Yanow*

Count Basie in London / Sep. 7, 1956 / Verve ✦✦✦

★ **Count Basie at Newport** / Jul. 7, 1957 / Verve ✦✦✦✦✦
At the 1957 Newport Jazz Festival the music was consistently inspired and often historic. Count Basie welcomed back tenor-great Lester Young and singer Jimmy Rushing for part of a very memorable set highlighted by "Boogie Woogie" and "Evenin'"; Young plays beautifully throughout and Rushing is in prime form. An exciting full-length version of "One O'-Clock Jump" features Young, Illinois Jacquet and trumpeter Roy Eldridge; the Basie band stretches out on "Swingin' at Newport"; and five previously unreleased selections (put out for the first time on this CD) include four Joe Williams vocals. It's a great set of music. *—Scott Yanow*

The Complete Roulette Studio Count Basie / Oct. 21, 1957-Jul. 26, 1962 / Mosaic ✦✦✦✦✦
Some of Count Basie's finest recordings were cut for the Roulette label during 1957-1962, and all of his studio performances are included on this massive Mosaic ten-CD boxed set. Among the classic former LPs that are reissued here are *The Atomic Mr. Basie, Basie Plays Hefti, Chairman of the Board, Everyday I Have the Blues,* and *Kansas City Suite.* With such soloists as trumpeters Thad Jones and Joe Newman, the tenors of Frank Foster and Eddie Lockjaw Davis, Frank Wess on alto and flute, vocals by Joe Williams, and the timeless arrangements of Neal Hefti, Thad Jones, Frank Foster, Ernie Wilkins, and Frank Wess among others, this essential (but unfortunately limited-edition) set features the second Count Basie Orchestra at its very best. *—Scott Yanow*

The Complete Roulette Live Recordings of Count Basie and His Orchestra (1958-1962) / 1958-1962 / Mosaic ✦✦✦✦
Count Basie is one jazz musician who was amply recorded throughout his career and has been the subject of numerous domestic and foreign reissue lines; yet, Mosaic has managed to release Count Basie material in a valuable fashion. This eight-disc set contains Basie recordings for the Roulette label from 1959 to 1962, the first of a two-part series covering his full Roulette output. These are live recordings; the studio sessions are coming on their own set. There are plenty of blues, relaxed swingers, and superb vocals. There is nothing revolutionary about this music, but its consistency and celebratory fiber remain impressive through every disc. While eight discs is a lot of time for one band, no matter how great (and they do frequently repeat some songs), the set provides a chance to replicate the experience of life on the road for a touring band. *—Ron Wynn*

First Time! The Count Meets the Duke / Jul. 6, 1961 / Columbia ✦✦✦✦

Count Basie and the Kansas City 7 / Mar. 21, 1962 / MCA ✦✦✦✦

Basie's Beatle Bag / May 3, 1966-May 5, 1966 / Verve ✦✦✦✦✦
The Count and his orchestra tackle the music of the Fab Four, without any hint of condescension or lassitude. Indeed, the 11 songs by John Lennon and Paul McCartney and one ("Kansas City") by Leiber & Stoller are treated with the same kind of dignity and enthusiasm that the band would give to the likes of Johnny Mercer or Harold Arlen. "Kansas City" is the bluesiest number here, and the one with which the band is obviously the most comfortable—it's the only number here that could have appeared, as is, on any Basie album of the previous decade. But "Michelle" is the best track here, a gently swinging rendition in which Basie's piano is featured in some pleasing flourishes and the band slips into a satisfying groove. The rest also comes off well—the ballads fare the best, showing off the quieter side of the band, stretching out and luxuriating on pieces like "Do You Want to Know a Secret." But they also rise to the occasion on rockers like "I Wanna Be Your Man" and "Can't Buy Me Love," taking big bites out of the beat and the principal melodies with some hot ensemble playing and solos. In the end, the songs and the band are both well served by Chico O'Farrill's arrangements, which manage to maintain the familiar and emphasize some surprises. Even "Yesterday," the most overrecorded of the Beatles' songs, gets a moving jazz vocal treatment from Bill Henderson, supported by Basie's engaging organ fills and a quietly soaring trombone and sax section, comes off fresh. The band romps, and the soloists, in addition to Basie, include Eddie "Lockjaw" Davis and Al Grey. *—Bruce Eder*

Basie and Zoot / Apr. 9, 1975 / Pablo/OJC ✦✦✦✦✦
This is a classic encounter that has been reissued on CD in the Original Jazz Classics series. Pianist Count Basie (in his best-small group outing of the 1970's) and tenor-saxophonist Zoot Sims were mutually inspired by each other's presence and, with the tasteful assistance of bassist John Heard and drummer Louie Bellson, they can be heard playing at the peak of their creative powers. Every listener interested in swinging jazz should pick up this disc, if only to hear these hard-charging versions of "I Never Knew," "It's Only A Paper Moon" and "Honeysuckle Rose." A gem, essential music. *—Scott Yanow*

I Told You So / Jan. 12, 1976-Jan. 14, 1976 / Pablo/OJC ✦✦✦✦

Prime Time / Jan. 18, 1977-Jan. 20, 1977 / Pablo ✦✦✦✦

Basie Jam: Montreux '77 / Jul. 15, 1977 / Pablo/OJC ✦✦✦✦
From Norman Granz's marathon series of performances recorded at the 1977 Montreux Jazz Festival, this set finds Count Basie fronting a jam session featuring trumpeter Roy Eldridge, altoist Benny Carter, Zoot Sims on tenor and the trombones of Vic Dickenson and Al Grey. Despite the possibility of being overcrowded, a bit of planning by Basie made this into a very coherent set with a blues, a long ballad medley and the closing "Jumpin' at the Woodside." Lots of nice moments. *—Scott Yanow*

On the Road / Jul. 12, 1979 / Pablo/OJC ✦✦✦✦
This release gives one a definitive look at the Count Basie Orchestra during its final years. Trumpeter Pete Minger, trombonist Booty Wood and Eric Dixon on tenor and flute are the main soloists, but it is the classic Basie ensemble sound (which never seems to get dated or lose its charm and power) that carries the day. Whether it is "Wind Machine," "Splanky" or "In a Mellow Tone," this is a highly enjoyable set. *—Scott Yanow*

☆ **The Complete Atomic Basie** / 1994 / Roulette ✦✦✦✦✦
One of the reasons that some major labels love to license big chunks of their catalogs to smaller independent outfits for box set reissues is that they never know that those licensees will turn up in putting those sets together, and it all becomes fair game for the parent company. Thus, in 1994, a year after Mosaic unearthed five previously unissued tracks from the October 1957 sessions that yielded *The Atomic Mr. Basie* on Roulette, Capitol Records (which had acquired the Roulette library) issued this expanded version of the original album. The original 11 songs are here, remastered into proper mono (there was an impossible to listen to duophonic stereo master made at the time of release that was in circulation on LP for a time), along with five outtakes consisting of material written and arranged by Jimmy Mundy: the instrumentals "Silks and Satins," "Sleepwalker's Serenade" (two different takes), and "The Late Late Show" and a vocal version of the latter featuring Joe Williams. These were apparently part of a proposed Jimmy Mundy album that never got completed, and were forgotten; they fit in surprisingly well with the Neal Hefti arrangements comprised the original recording, and Joe Williams turns in some of the best work of his career on the vocal version of "The Late Late Show," a sultry, richly intoned performance that positively seduces the listener, with the band blowing beautifully behind him. *—Bruce Eder*

Count Basie, Lester Young and the Stars of Birdland On Tour: Recorded Live in Topeka, K / Feb. 1955 / Jazz Classics ✦✦✦✦
Double CD release of a February 1955 show from Topeka, Kansas, with Count Basie and his Orchestra on three numbers, backing Basie alumnus Lester Young on three more, and Joe Williams (who had just joined the group) on three songs (including a jazzy version of "Shake, Rattle & Roll"), Stan Getz on four numbers (including an exciting version of "Little Pony"), and Sarah Vaughan on eight songs. Additionally, the George Shearing Quintet featuring Toots Thielemans does seven numbers (including a medley of Shearing hits), and the Errol Garner Trio has a set, and two more Basie numbers with Joe Williams close the show. That's two hours of music, and while the initial burst of sound is ominously distorted, the audio quality settles down comfortably to a nice level with excellent fidelity. Young's sax, in particular, is up close and personal on "I'm Confessin'." Collectors will prize this artifact from the boom years for Birdland. *—Scott Yanow & Bruce Eder*

At Birdland 1956 / Nov. 18, 1997 / Storyville ✦✦✦✦

Count Basie Encounters Oscar Peterson / Feb. 11, 1998 / Pablo/OJC ✦✦✦✦

Atomic Swing / Oct. 21, 1957-Jul. 3, 1962 / Blue Note ✦✦✦✦✦
Released in 1999 to cash in on the resurgence of interest in swing music among post-baby boomers, *Atomic Swing* manages to transcend its immediate commercial purpose. It is the first 20-bit remastering of the Roulette library, and the sound quality alone makes it worth picking up. The 13 tracks present were cut by Basie over a six-year period with Morris Levy's Roulette Records, and they're a strong mix despite only three of the numbers coming off of the legendary *Atomic Mr. Basie* album. Most of the rest is from afterwards—amazingly, only two of the numbers here—"The Late, Late Show" and "Taps Miller"—overlap with Capitol's existing *Best of the Roulette Years*, so duplication is a minimum, and the sound is amazingly good. The brass on "Moten Swing" and the broader numbers has equally impressive measures of richness and presence, while softer, moodier pieces like "The Midnight Sun Never Sets" display surprising warmth (but Eddie Jones' bass and Freddie Green's guitar also seem very close). There are no notes, but that's not a problem—the session listing says most of what needs saying. *—Bruce Eder*

Sidney Bechet

b. May 14, 1897, New Orleans, LA, **d.** May 14, 1959, Paris, France
Sax (Soprano), Clarinet / New Orleans Jazz, Classic Jazz, Dixieland
Sidney Bechet was the first important jazz soloist on records in history (beating Louis Armstrong by a few months). A brilliant soprano saxophonist and clarinetist with a wide vibrato that listeners either loved or hated, Bechet's style did not evolve much through the years but he never lost his enthusiasm or creativity. A master at both individual and collective improvisation within the genre of New Orleans jazz, Bechet was such a dominant player that trumpeters found it very difficult to play with him. After spending time in New Orleans, Chicago and even Europe (courtesy of a 1919 tour by Will Marion Cook), Bechet made his recording debut in 1923 with Clarence Williams. He was with Duke Ellington's early orchestra for a period, but spent the last four years of the '20s overseas. Most of the 1930s were comparatively lean times for Bechet, though in 1938 he had a hit recording of "Summertime." Soon he was signed to Bluebird where he recorded quite a few classics during the next three years. After moving overseas permanently, Bechet became a major celebrity and national hero in France even though the general public in the U.S. never did know who he was. Bechet's last decade was filled with exciting concerts, many recordings and infrequent visits back to the US before his death from cancer. *—Scott Yanow*

The 1923-1936 / Oct. 1923-Mar. 1936 / Classics ✦✦✦✦
The first in a series of Classics CDs focusing on the recordings of Sidney Bechet, this disc features the clarinetist/soprano-saxophonist on two early titles with blues singer Rosetta Crawford, his torrid 1932 session with The New Orleans Feetwarmers (which also features trumpeter Tommy Ladnier and is highlighted by "Shag" and "Maple Leaf Rag") and sides from Noble Sissle's somewhat commercial orchestra. Fortunately Sissle was wise enough to give Bechet plenty of solo space on some of his selections, most notably "Polka Dot Rag." Even with a few indifferent vocals, this CD is recommended to those not already owning this music. *—Scott Yanow*

The Complete, Vols. 1-2 / Sep. 15, 1932-Jan. 8, 1941 / RCA ✦✦✦✦✦
Of all the overlapping Bechet reissue series, this series of two-LP sets released by French RCA is easily the best, with all of the Victor sides by the great soprano-saxophonist and clarinetist (including the valuable alternate takes) being issued complete and in chronological order. The first two-fer is highlighted by the blazing session by The New Orleans Feetwarmers from 1932, four selections from the "Really the Blues" date with trumpeter Tommy Ladnier and clarinetist Mezz Mezzrow, and such Bechet classics as "Indian Summer," "Old Man Blues" and "Nobody Knows The Way I Feel 'Dis Mornin'." *—Scott Yanow*

★ **Master Takes: Victor Sessions (1932-1943)** / Sep. 15, 1932-Dec. 8, 1943 / Bluebird/RCA ✦✦✦✦✦
This three-CD set has most of the finest recordings ever made by soprano-saxophonist and clarinet master Sidney Bechet. Although the alternate takes have unfortunately been left out (making the three sadly out of print French RCA double-LPs the absolute best way to acquire this timeless music), there are a remarkable amount of exciting performances in this box. Bechet jams with trumpeter Tommy Ladnier and the New Orleans Feetwarmers on a 1932 session (including torrid versions of "I've Found a New Baby," "Maple Leaf Rag," and "Shag") and then is heard mostly during 1940-1941 on his other Victor recordings. Among the highlights are "Indian Summer," "One O'Clock Jump," Duke Ellington's "Old Man Blues," an emotional and definitive "Nobody Knows the Way I Feel 'Dis Mornin," "Blues in Thirds," "Stompy Jones," "Egyptian Fantasy," Bechet's one-man band version of "The Sheik of Araby," "Swing Parade," "The Mooche," and "What Is This Thing Called Love." Although the supporting cast (17 different combinations of musicians are utilized) is quite impressive, it is Sidney Bechet who makes these performances quite classic. This music is essential (in one form or another) for every serious jazz collection. *—Scott Yanow*

☆ **Complete Blue Note Recordings** / Jul. 8, 1939-Aug. 25, 1953 / Mosaic ✦✦✦✦✦
Mosaic, a mail-order company, has compiled a series of remarkable box sets that feature the complete recordings of various immortal musicians at the peak of their careers. This limited-edition six-LP set (get it while you can) has all of Sidney Bechet's recordings for Blue Note including three songs with the Port of Harlem Seven (climaxed by his hit version of "Summertime"), two blues with guitarist Josh White, and Bechet's sessions from 1940, 1944, 1945, 1946, 1949, 1950, 1951, and 1953 in which he shares the frontline with such trumpeters as Sidney DeParis, Max Kaminsky, Bunk Johnson, Wild Bill Davison, and Jonah Jones. The music ranges from hot swing to exuberant Dixieland, and Bechet somehow always sounds inspired. *—Scott Yanow*

Port at Harlem Jazzmen / Apr. 7, 1939-Feb. 12, 1946 / Blue Note ✦✦✦✦✦

Live in New York, 1950-51 / Apr. 1, 1950-Oct. 19, 1951 / Storyville ✦✦✦✦
Neglected in his homeland, the great soprano-saxophonist Sidney Bechet first moved to France (where he quickly became known as a national hero) in 1949 but made a couple of trips back to the United States during the next few years. His Storyville CD features Bechet in the U.S. during two occasions, leading a quartet/quintet with only a trombone joining him in the frontline; at least he was not compelled to battle for the lead with a trumpeter. There are eight selections with trombonist Vic Dickenson, pianist Ken Kersey, bassist Herb Ward and drummer Cliff Leeman that include individual features for Dickenson and Kersey along with spirited renditions of "Muskrat Ramble," "High Society" and "Royal Garden Blues"; in addition Bechet caresses the melody of "Laura" and romps through "Just One of Those Things." However it is the other 11 numbers (which were only previously released on LP by Pumpkin) that are most notable for these are probably the finest recordings of the underrated trombonist Big Chief Russell Moore. With pianist Red Richards and drummer Art Trappier functioning quite well as the entire rhythm section (without a bassist), the trombonist stays out of Bechet's way and adds some robust and humorous solos of his own. During memorable versions of "I Found a New Baby," "Bugle Call Rag," "Panama" and even "Casey Jones," Bechet never runs out of infectious riffs and is in consistently exciting form. *—Scott Yanow*

Sidney Bechet's Blue Note Jazzmen / Jan. 21, 1949-Apr. 19, 1950 / Blue Note ✦✦✦✦✦

The Best of Sidney Bechet / May 3, 1994 / Blue Note ✦✦✦✦

Runnin' Wild / Jan. 21, 1949-Apr. 19, 1950 / Blue Note ✦✦✦✦
After Blue Note switched to bop in 1947, it was the end of trad jazz on the label, with the exception of a few sessions led by Sidney Bechet and George Lewis. The masterful soprano saxophonist Bechet led no less than nine dates for Blue Note, as well as appearing as a sideman on four others, all of which were included in Mosaic's now out-of-print comprehensive Bechet box set. Three of Bechet's outings for Blue Note co-featured cornetist Wild Bill Davison, and all of that music is on this single 1998 CD. Since Bechet was generally quite dominant in ensembles, he did not usually get along well with trumpeters, and since Davison could be quite

fiery, it is surprising that this matchup works so well. Bechet actually enjoyed Wild Bill's playing because the cornetist played fairly simply and left plenty of space. Davison had great respect for Bechet and is slightly more restrained than usual throughout these numbers, although he does let loose with some heated blasts here and there. This excellent Dixieland collection features one quintet and two sextet sessions with Bob Diehl or Jimmy Archey on trombone, Art Hodes or Joe Sullivan on piano, Pops Foster or Walter Page on bass and Freddie Moore or Slick Jones on drums; there are lots of hot moments on the warhorse material from the two principals. A surprise success. *— Scott Yanow*

Greatest Hits / Oct. 14, 1949-Jul. 4, 1958 / RCA ♦♦♦♦

Sidney Bechet, Vol. 12: 1942-1943 / Aug. 1942-Nov. 1943 / Masters of Jazz ♦♦♦♦♦
This 12-song collection zeroes in on Bechet's recording activities between 1942 and early 1943 and showcases him in three different settings. The centerpiece is a private recording from August 1942 with Bechet and his New Orleans Feetwarmers running through such classics as "Honeysuckle Rose," "Bugle Call Rag," "Royal Garden Blues," and "That's A-Plenty." This is followed by more private wartime recordings, three of which showcase Sidney playing piano (one of which is his original composition, "Negro Rapsodie No. 1"), the closing three being a three-part rendition of Hadyn's "Toy Symphony" recorded at a private party. Some very interesting Bechet that didn't make it onto commercial recordings, this accounts for some important music that deserves to be reissued. Expertly annotated and plenty of exhaustive notes and session information, this volume is just as potent as the others in the set. *— Cub Koda*

Bix Beiderbecke (Leon Bix Beiderbecke)

b. Mar. 10, 1903, Davenport, IA, **d.** Aug. 6, 1931, New York, NY
Cornet / Classic Jazz
Bix Beiderbecke was one of the greatest jazz musicians of the 1920s. His colorful life, quick rise and fall and eventual status as a martyr made him a legend even before he died and he has long stood as proof that not all the innovators in jazz history were black. Possessor of a beautiful distinctive tone and a strikingly original improvising style, Bix's only competitor among cornetists in the '20s was Louis Armstrong. Influenced by the original Dixieland Jazz Band, Beiderbecke became a full-time musician after dropping out of college and became the star cornetist of the Wolverines by 1923. He spent time during the mid-'20s in Chicago and St. Louis (the latter with Frankie Trumbauer's Orchestra), and really broke out in 1927; he recorded his piano masterpiece "In a Mist," cut many classic sides with a small group headed by Trumbauer, and then signed up with Paul Whiteman's huge and prosperous orchestra. With Whiteman, Bix's solos tended to be short moments of magic, sometimes in odd settings; his brilliant chorus on "Sweet Sue" is a perfect example. He was productive throughout 1928 but by the following year his drinking really began to catch up with him. After brief comebacks in 1929 and 1930, he died that year at the age of 28. *— Scott Yanow*

And the Chicago Cornets / Feb. 18, 1924-Jan. 26, 1925 / Milestone ♦♦♦♦
Not only does this superior double-LP set contain all of cornetist Bix Beiderbecke's recordings with The Wolverines in 1924 (much of which is classic), but it features him with The Sioux City Six and his Rhythm Jugglers (highlighted by the original version of "Davenport Blues"), the two titles cut by The Wolverines after Beiderbecke departed (with Jimmy McPartland in his spot) and seven performances by The Bucktown Five in 1924 (the recording debut of cornetist Muggsy Spanier). Collectors of '20s jazz should be familiar with most of this music, especially The Wolverines sides. Bix Beiderbecke, although only 21 years old at the time, already demonstrated the lyricism, inventiveness and beautiful tone that one associates with him. *— Scott Yanow*

The Indispensable / Nov. 24, 1924-Sep. 15, 1930 / RCA ♦♦♦♦
This double-CD from French RCA in their Jazz Tribune series (a reissue of an earlier double-LP) gives one a good overview of cornetist Bix Beiderbecke's Victor recordings. More serious collectors will want to acquire this music as part of a more complete series (since all of his solos are significant) while beginning collectors are advised to pick up his Columbia reissue CDs (which feature Beiderbecke in smaller groups) first. The 36 performances on this two-fer mostly focus on his sideman appearances with the large dance orchestras of Jean Goldkette and Paul Whiteman during 1926-28 although there is one 1924 track ("I Didn't Know") with Goldkette and a few later sessions from 1930. Highlights include "Clementine," "San," "There Ain't No Sweet Man," "From Monday On" and "You Took Advantage of Me." *— Scott Yanow*

★ **Bix Beiderbecke, Vol. 1: Singin' the Blues** / Feb. 4, 1927-Sep. 30, 1927 / Columbia ♦♦♦♦♦
Cornetist Bix Beiderbecke's greatest recordings were mostly made in 1927. This definitive CD (reissued in 1990) has most of Bix's best-loved work, including "Singin' the Blues," "I'm Coming Virginia," "Ostrich Walk," "Way Down Yonder In New Orleans," and his solo piano classic "In a Mist." Most of the recordings were cut with Frankie Trumbauer's Orchestra, although there are also two titles from the Broadway Bellhops, a similar group. The beauty of Bix's horn outshone virtually every other brassman in the 1920s other than Louis Armstrong, and he never sounded better than on these records. Beiderbecke is joined by such notables as C-melody saxophonist Trumbauer, guitarist Eddie Lang, clarinetist Jimmy Dorsey, trombonist Bill Rank and clarinetist Don Murray, among others. In addition to the titles mentioned, the renditions of "Clarinet Marmalade," Hoagy Carmichael's "Riverboat Shuffle" and "Wringin' and Twistin'" are among the other highlights. Essential music that in one form or another belongs in every serious jazz collection. *— Scott Yanow*

Bix Beiderbecke, Vol. 2: At the Jazz Band Ball / Oct. 1, 1927-Apr. 3, 1928 / Columbia ♦♦♦♦♦
This second installment into Bix's recorded career focuses on the sides he made while working as a member of Paul Whiteman's band. Cutting dates with old friends and bandmates like Frank Trumbauer, Adrian Rollini, Pee Wee Russell, Bill Rank, Eddie Lang, and drummer Chauncey Morehouse, these sides chronicle Bix's activities in the studios away from the "king of jazz" between 1927 and 1928. But don't consider all these sides as some sort of hot jazz oasis away from the more stilted arrangements of the Whiteman band; there's more than enough corn aboard on sides like "Mississippi Mud," two takes of "Clorinda," "Our Bungalow of Dreams," and "There'll Come a Time," several of these tracks clumsily adorned with annoying glee-club vocals. But sides like the two takes of "Three Blind Mice," "Sorry," "Jazz Me Blues," "Royal Garden Blues," and "Since My Best Gal Turned Me Down" show Bix still was full of creative ideas galore and a tone to die for. While conventional wisdom has this period as the start of Bix's musical decline, these sides show that there was much great music left in him. *— Cub Koda*

Han Bennink

b. Apr. 17, 1942, Zaandam, Netherlands
Percussion / Avant-Garde Jazz, Free Jazz
In the niche-oriented world of major-league jazz, it's almost unfashionable to be so multi-faceted a player as Han Bennink. Bennink is one of the unfortunately rare musicians whose abilities and interests span the music's entire spectrum, from Dixieland to free. His straight-ahead playing is absolutely convincing—his time is solid, his sense of swing strong, and his technique flawless. He also possesses the requisite qualities of a free jazz virtuoso; Bennink's ability to interact quickly and creatively with horn players and pianists is great, as is his ear for timbral contrasts. What ultimately makes Bennink special is his manifest love for the music—a love that inclines him to tear down the cardboard walls that too often separate different schools of jazz. At his best, with colleagues who share his all-encompassing stylistic embrace, Bennink plays the continuum of jazz as an instrument unto itself.

Bennink began playing drums while in his teens, under the influence of his father, a classical percussionist. He played with hometown musicians in the early '60s. Between 1962 and 1969, Bennink backed local American jazz greats like Dexter Gordon, Sonny Rollins, and Eric Dolphy on their visits to Holland (he was the drummer on Dolphy's *Last Date* album, from 1964). In 1963, he formed a quartet that included the pianist Misha Mengelberg, which played the Newport Jazz Festival in 1966. In the mid-'60s, Bennink began to play free jazz with the likes of Mengelberg and Willem Breuker. In 1967, those three founded the Instant Composer's Pool, a not-for-profit organization designed to promote the Dutch jazz avant-garde. Around that same period, Bennink began continuing associations with the saxophonist Peter Brotzmann, guitarist Derek Bailey, trombonist Alex Schlippenbach, trumpeter Don Cherry, and the Globe Unity Orchestra. In the '70s and '80s, Bennink led and played as sideman on a number of sessions on the FMP, Incus, and Soul Note labels; he made a notable contribution to Steve Lacy's Herbie Nichols tribute album, *Regeneration,* with Mengelberg, bassist Kent Carter, and trombonist Roswell Rudd. In the late '80s Bennink started, with the cellist Ernst Reijseger and saxophonist Michael Moore, the Clusone Trio, which has since become perhaps the percussionist's most ideal performance vehicle. Both Reijseger and Moore share Bennink's extraordinarily wide range of musical interests, to say nothing of his absurdist sense of humor. It is, in fact, Bennink's rather whimsical theatricality that mitigates—for some, at least—the seriousness and depth of his art. *— Chris Kelsey*

● **Jazz Bunker** / Feb. 0, 1980 / Golden Years of New Jazz ♦♦♦♦
Featuring a trio of Dutch drummer Han Bennink, American electric guitarist Eugene Chadbourne, and Japanese trumpeter Toshinori Kondo, this double CD promises a bit more than it delivers. Nonetheless, it is an absolutely fascinating exposition of free jazz. Recorded live in Holland (in less than high fidelity), the three musicians fly high, with more than a dozen different instruments represented. Just the chance to hear Han Bennink play piano, tenor and soprano saxophones, clarinet, trombone, and harmonica is alone worth the price of the CDs. His skills should surprise more than a few of his admirers. Fans of Chadbourne can expect his usual silliness, along with some tasty string work. Kondo adds a couple of euphoniums to his usual virtuoso trumpet work, and the whole conglomeration is outrageously wild. While sometimes it all seems somewhat anarchic, there are nonetheless plenty of rewarding moments. *— Steven Loewy*

Serpentine / Jan. 30, 1996 / Songlines ♦♦♦
Serpentine is a hearty, exploratory meeting between percussionist Han Bennink and trumpeter Dave Douglas. The seemingly over-caffeinated nervous energy of "Neck Four" and "Delft," and the extended technique showcases such as "Stekelbaarsje," are somewhat offset by "Alap"'s meditative development and the straighter cuts "Too Close for Comfort" and "Serpentine." These last two feature more lyrical trumpet playing from Douglas and the softened accompaniment of Bennink's brushes. Each musician also gets a brief solo piece: the percussive "Rein" and Douglas' "Greenleaf." While not as wowing as some of Bennink's other duo work—namely, *Dissonant Characters* with tenor saxophonist Ellery Eskelin—this 1996 studio recording captures the good interaction of two excellent creative musicians. *— Joslyn Layne*

Nerve Beats: 1973 / Sep. 27, 1973 / Atavistic ♦♦♦♦

David Benoit

b. 1953, Bakersfield, CA
Keyboards, Piano, Producer, Arranger / Crossover Jazz, Contemporary Jazz
One of the more popular performers in the idiom somewhat inaccurately called "contemporary jazz," David Benoit has mostly performed light melodic background music, what critic Alex Henderson has dubbed "New Age with a beat." Benoit has done a few fine jazz projects (including a tribute to Bill Evans and a collaboration with Emily Remler) but most of his output for GRP has been aimed clearly at the charts. He studied composition and piano at El Camino College and in 1975 played on the soundtrack of the film *Nashville.* After recording with Alphonse Mouzon and accompanying singer Gloria Lynne, he was signed to the AVI label when he was 24, recording sets that paved the way towards his later output. Benoit has been been a solo artist for GRP since 1986. Albums like 1989's *Waiting For Spring* and 1999's *Professional Dreamer* showcase his smooth, lyrical style, while projects like his 2000 tribute to Vince Guaraldi's Peanuts scores, *Here's to You, Charlie Brown: 50 Great Years,* demonstrate where his own tastes lie. *— Scott Yanow*

Freedom at Midnight / 1987 / GRP ♦♦♦

The Best of David Benoit 1987-1995 / 1987-1995 / GRP ✦✦

● **Waiting for Spring** / Feb. 5, 1989–May 25, 1989 / GRP ✦✦✦✦
After making so many forgettable albums with commercial radio in mind, David Benoit took a break from the type of "smooth jazz" fluff he usually records and delivered a respectable straightahead CD with *Waiting for Spring*. Instead of shamelessly wasting his improvisatory skills, he actually lets loose on the acoustic piano and makes some meaningful statements. Bill Evans is obviously a great influence on Benoit, whose vulnerability makes his love of the late piano legend obvious on originals as well as lyrical interpretations of standards like "My Romance" and "Secret Love." Benoit has a fine soloist in the late guitarist Emily Remler, who is consistently warm, melodic and inviting. Though the album isn't breathtaking, it's satisfying and heartfelt. *—Alex Henderson*

Benoit/Freeman Project / 1994 / GRP ✦✦✦✦✦
The Benoit/Freeman project is a reunion of sorts, as both smooth jazz icons worked on 1986's landmark Rippingtons debut *Moonlighting* and together wrote Benoit's hit "Every Step of the Way." Since then, Freeman's career with that band and Benoit's as a solo artist spearheaded the smooth jazz movement while expanding the rules on just what modern jazz is. The new project combines the radio-friendly pleasures inherent in their separate endeavors with an exciting expansion and interplay of fresh and innovative ideas. Though the focus is clearly on the interplay between guitar and piano, the two are surrounded by all-star backing talent like Nathan East, Abe Laboriel, John Robinson, and former Rippingtons members Steve Reid and Tony Morales. Much attention was directed to Kenny Loggins' wonderful vocal performance of "When She Believed in Me," but the Phil Perry sung version of "After the Love Is Gone" is superfluous; it's beautiful but adds nothing to the original Earth, Wind & Fire arrangement. Instrumental highlights include "Mediterranean Nights" (a seven-minute meditation featuring symphonic elements and Freeman's rich electric guitar work), the percussive "Swept Away," moody "The End of Our Season," and a remake of "Mirage," one of *Moonlighting*'s most beautiful tunes. The two seem to have been too busy for a follow-up, but smooth jazz could definitely benefit from another tandem brainstorm like this. *—Jonathan Widran*

Shaken Not Stirred / 1994 / GRP ✦✦✦✦
Unlike most genre superstars, David Benoit never seems content to stick strictly with any pop formula for very long. While his hummable ivory spirit always shines through, his many attempts to shake and stir the typical expectations make him perhaps the most artistic pop jazz artist around. *Shaken Not Stirred* is thus an appropriate moniker for this wildly eclectic collection, which makes overwhelmingly effective use of orchestral grandeur (the enrapturing "Carmel"), and comes across more as a smashing musician's playground than a lightweight, radio friendly stab. he treads just enough familiar territory to keep old fans pleased but enjoys experimenting with percussive explosions, wild jamming, and traditional smoky club blues. The genuine simple warmth of the acoustic tribute "Jacqueline" (Jackie Kennedy Onassis died the year this was released) reminds us, however, that behind the crazy, genre-busting navigations is a gentle man full of grace. Hopefully the mixed bag of vocals—a solid effort by David Pack undercut by a meandering schmaltzer by Kenny Rankin—won't detract from the wide-ranging and powerful instrumental tracks. The only voice Benoit needs is in his fingers. *—Jonathan Widran*

Professional Dreamer / Jun. 1, 1999 / GRP ✦✦✦✦
The pairing of smooth jazz's premier veteran pianist and trumpeter/producer Rick Braun is remarkable. The six tracks produced by the latter offer a unique contrast between thick, hip-hoppy bass grooves and Benoit's peppy, angst-free ivory musings. On the in-your-face "Rejoyce," Benoit's swirling, high-register melody combines with Pat Kelley's Wes Montgomery-like electric licks (and Benoit's own Hammond B-3 harmony coloring) for a floating ride above a jumpy retro-soul rhythm. The underpinnings are even chunkier on "Jump Start," which finds Benoit's piano and Andy Suzuki's playful alto making light, bluesy conversation over a throbbing hip-hop pattern. Braun also gives Benoit space here for some lower-toned piano improvisations. Braun indeed lets Benoit be Benoit on the graceful ballad "Something You Said," whose melody—enhanced by Marc Antoine's tender acoustic guitar harmony—glides over a sparse, easy shuffling percussion scheme. Braun mostly plays keyboards, but picks up his muted trumpet to go strutting with Benoit's joyous exclamations over a laid-back but still pulsating groove as if they were joining "Miles After Dark." Longtime Benoit fans who fear change can rest assured; the four remaining tunes produced by the pianist and longtime engineer Clark Germain are vintage. "Golden Gate" and "Dad's Room" (a sweeping film score like tribute to Benoit's ailing father) are simple and sweet, orchestrally enhanced piano reflections, while "Gothic Jazz Dance" combines Benoit's equal loves for pop, chamber music (the hypnotic piano flurries in the intro), and Brazilian rhythms. *—Jonathan Widran*

Here's to You, Charlie Brown: 50 Great Years! / Sep. 13, 1999 - 20 / GRP ✦✦✦

George Benson

b. Mar. 22, 1943, Pittsburgh, PA
Vocals, Guitar / Smooth Jazz, Quiet Storm, Crossover Jazz, Contemporary Jazz, Jazz-Pop, Hard Bop
George Benson is simply one of the greatest guitarists in jazz history, but he is also an amazingly versatile musician—and that frustrates critics to no end who would paint him into a narrow bop box. He can play in just about any style—from swing to bop to R&B to pop—with supreme taste, a beautiful rounded tone, terrific speed, a marvelous sense of logic in building solos, and always, an unquenchable urge to swing. His inspirations may have been Charlie Christian and Wes Montgomery—and he can do dead-on impressions of both—but his style is completely his own. Not only can he play lead brilliantly, he is also one of the best rhythm guitarists around, supportive to soloists and a dangerous swinger, particularly in a soul-jazz format. Yet Benson can also sing in a lush soulful tenor with mannerisms similar to those of Stevie Wonder and Donny Hathaway—and it is his voice that has proved to be more marketable to the public than his guitar. Benson is the guitar-playing equivalent of Nat Cole—a fantastic pianist whose smooth way with a pop vocal eventually eclipsed his instrumental prowess in the marketplace—but unlike Cole, Benson has been granted enough time after his fling with the pop charts to reaffirm his jazz guitar credentials, which he still does at his concerts. *—Richard S. Ginell*

George Benson/Jack McDuff / May 1, 1964–Oct. 19, 1965 / Prestige ✦✦✦✦✦
Guitarist George Benson spent an important period early in his career as a sideman with organist Jack McDuff. This two-LP set brings back two albums that they recorded together; one was originally under Benson's name while the other was led by McDuff. With tenor saxophonist Red Holloway adding his distinctive solo voice, this quartet/quintet (depending on whether they use a bassist) was an exciting blues-oriented unit that was rightfully popular in the mid-'60s. The two-fer gives one a valuable look at George Benson in his early years. *—Scott Yanow*

The New Boss Guitar / May 1, 1964-May 14, 1964 / Prestige/OJC ✦✦✦✦
George Benson was only 21 when, on May 1, 1964, he recorded his first album as a leader, *The New Boss Guitar of George Benson*. At that point, the guitarist had yet to become a huge name in jazz, although many of those who knew Benson for his work with Jack McDuff's group (which he joined in 1962) agreed that he showed great potential. Benson still had some growing to do in 1964, but even so, this is an impressive debut. The guitarist had developed a distinctive, recognizable sound on his instrument, and he plays with both feeling and technique on five Benson originals (including the sly "Shadow Dancers," the exuberant "Rock-A-Bye," and the earthy blues "I Don't Know") as well as interpretations of "Easy Living" and "Will You Still Be Mine." Benson, of course, had an insightful teacher in McDuff, who plays both organ and piano on this hard bop/soul-jazz date. Tenor saxophonist Red Holloway, another member of McDuff's early '60s group, is also on board, as are bassist Ronnie Boykins and drummer Montego Joe. Originally released on LP by Prestige, *The New Boss Guitar of George Benson* was reissued on CD for Fantasy's *Original Jazz Classics* series in 1990 (where Fantasy added "My Three Sons," a driving bonus track that finds Benson, McDuff and Holloway appearing on drummer Joe Dukes' *The Soulful Drums* session of May 14, 1964). In 1964, Benson's best work was yet to come—nonetheless, this album is historically important as well as rewarding. *—Alex Henderson*

The George Benson Cookbook / Aug. 1, 1966-Oct. 19, 1966 / Columbia/Legacy ✦✦✦
The second of Benson's John Hammond-produced albums is far and away the superior of the pair, mixing down-to-basics, straight-ahead jazz with soul-drenched grooving. Suddenly Benson's backup group—same as that of *Uptown*, with Benny Green added on trombone now and then—has found its bearings and apropos to the title, they can cook, even sizzle. The effect upon Benson's own playing is striking; with something to react against, his sheer ability to swing advances into the realm of awesome. The rapid-fire work on "The Cooker" and "Ready And Able" will make you gasp. Only one vocal here, an exuberant "All Of Me." *—Richard S. Ginell*

Giblet Gravy / Feb. 1968 / Verve ✦✦✦✦
No, you're not in Creed Taylor country yet, but you might as well be, for many of the ingredients that would garnish Benson's albums with Taylor are already present in this often enjoyable prototype. The immediate goal was to groom Benson as the next Wes Montgomery (who was about to leave Verve)—and so he covers hit tunes of the day ("Sunny," "Along Comes Mary," "Groovin'"), playing either with a big band plus voices or a neat quintet anchored by Herbie Hancock, and the sound is contoured to give his guitar a warm mellow ambience. But the eclectic Benson is his own man, as his infectious repeated-interval rhythm trademark tells us on his self-composed title track, and despite Tom McIntosh's mostly lame arrangements, George's work is always tasty and irresistibly melodic. *—Richard S. Ginell*

Blue Benson / 1967-1968 / Polydor ✦✦✦✦✦
Another sampler spotlighting his bluesy, funky material, this time taken from his brief period on Verve, when he recorded with The Sweet Inspirations and also played in a quintet with Herbie Hancock and Ron Carter. It's fine material, but not as strong as the Columbia or Prestige fare that preceded it. *—Ron Wynn*

☆ **Shape of Things to Come** / Aug. 27, 1968-Oct. 22, 1968 / A&M ✦✦✦✦✦
Upon Wes Montgomery's sudden death June 15, 1968, Creed Taylor signed Benson up and immediately thrust him onto the master's pedestal—or so the line has it. While this smashing debut for A&M has some of the Wes trappings—Don Sebesky's charts, Herbie Hancock and Ron Carter in the rhythm team—Benson triumphantly stamps his own image on the sessions with his infectious riffing, R&B slant, and solid jazz licks, propelled by Wes Covington's soulful organ and Leo Morris' driving drums. Just once, Benson tries a Varitone hookup with multi-speed overdubbings a la Les Paul on the title track; he would never use it again on discs but it is a great, futuristic electronic guitar trip, driven hard by a sizzling rhythm section and decorated sparingly by Sebesky. This superbly-produced record made Benson a formidable pop/jazz guitar star, not a mere Montgomery clone. *—Richard S. Ginell*

Tell It Like It Is / Apr. 29, 1969-May 20, 1969 / A&M ✦✦✦

The Other Side of Abbey Road / Oct. 22, 1969-Nov. 9, 1969 / A&M ✦✦✦✦✦
Just three weeks after the U.S. release of the Beatles' swan song *Abbey Road*, Creed Taylor ushered Benson into the studio to begin a remarkably successful pop/jazz translation of the record (complete with a parody of the famous cover, showing George with guitar crossing an Eastern urban street). It is a lyrical album, with a hint of the mystery and a lot of the cohesive concept of the Beatles' original despite the scrambled order of the tunes. Benson is given some room to stretch out on guitar, sometimes in a bluesy groove, and there are more samples of his honeyed vocals than ever before (oddly, his voice would not be heard again by record-buyers until he signed with Warner Bros.). Don Sebesky's arrangements roam freely from baroque strings to a full-throated big band, and Freddie Hubbard, Sonny Fortune and Hubert Laws get some worthy solo space. Yet for all its diversity, the record fits together as a whole more tightly than any other George Benson project, thanks to his versatile talents and the miraculous overarching unity of the Beatles' songs. One wonders if the Fab Four liked it, too. *—Richard S. Ginell*

★ **Beyond the Blue Horizon** / Feb. 2, 1971-Feb. 3, 1971 / Columbia/Legacy ✦✦✦✦✦
Having taken Benson along with him when he founded CTI, Creed Taylor merely leaves the

guitarist alone with a small group on his first release. The payoff is a superb jazz session where Benson rises to the challenge of the turbulent rhythm section of Jack DeJohnette and Ron Carter, with Clarence Palmer ably manning the organ. Benson is clearly as much at home with DeJohnette's advanced playing as he was in soul/jazz (after all, he did play on some Miles Davis sessions a few years before), and his tone is edgier, with more bite, than it had been for awhile. The lyrical Benson is also on eloquent display in "Ode To A Kudu" (heard twice on the CD, as is "All Clear"), and there is even a somewhat experimental tilt toward Afro-Cuban-Indian rhythms in "Somewhere To The East." A must-hear for all aficionados of Benson's guitar. *—Richard S. Ginell*

White Rabbit / Nov. 23, 1971-Nov. 30, 1971 / Columbia ✦✦✦✦
For Benson's second CTI project, producer Creed Taylor and arranger Don Sebesky successfully place the guitarist in a Spanish-flavored setting full of flamenco flourishes, brass fanfares, moody woodwinds and such. The idea works best on "California Dreamin'" (whose chords are based on Andalusian harmonies), where, driven by Jay Berliner's exciting Spanish rhythm guitar, Benson comes through with some terrifically inspired playing. On "El Mar," Berliner is replaced by Benson's protege Earl Klugh (then only 17) in an inauspicious—though at the time, widely-heralded—recorded debut. The title track is another winner, marred only by the out-of-tune brasses at the close, and in a good example of the CTI classical/jazz formula at work, Heitor Villa-Lobos's "Little Train of the Caipira" is given an attractive early-'70s facelift. Herbie Hancock gets plenty of nimble solo space on Rhodes electric piano, Airto Moreira contributes percussion and atmospheric wordless vocals, and Ron Carter and Billy Cobham complete the high-energy rhythm section. In this prime sample of the CTI idiom, everyone wins. *—Richard S. Ginell*

Body Talk / Jul. 17, 1973-Jul. 18, 1973 / Columbia ✦✦✦✦
With an eye and ear on what was happening on the soul charts—James Brown in particular—Benson made a decided swerve toward R&B on this release. Indeed the JB's Pee Wee Ellis turns up as a big band arranger on three tracks, and he no doubt had a direct influence on the distinct JB groove of one of the non-big-band tunes, "Dance." It should come as no surprise by now that this formidable guitarist has no problem handling any kind of groove, although the mixed rhythm section of Jack DeJohnette, Ron Carter, electric pianist Harold Mabern, and percussionist Mobutu sometimes sends mixed messages. Earl Klugh has a few tasty moments on his own, and there are some reconnaissance flights back to the jazz side of George, which he handles with his usual confident aplomb. *—Richard S. Ginell*

In Concert-Carnegie Hall / Jan. 11, 1975 / Columbia ✦✦✦

Good King Bad / Jul. 1, 1975-Dec. 5, 1975 / Columbia ✦✦✦✦✦

Breezin' / Jan. 6, 1976-Jan. 9, 1976 / Rhino ✦✦✦
All of a sudden, George Benson became a pop superstar with this album, thanks to its least representative track. Most of *Breezin'* is a softer-focused variation of Benson's R&B/jazz-flavored CTI work, his guitar as assured and fluid as ever with Claus Ogerman providing the suave orchestral backdrops and his crack then-working band (including Ronnie Foster on keyboards and sparkplug Phil Upchurch on rhythm guitar) pumping up the funk element. Yet it is the sole vocal track (his first in many years), Leon Russell's "This Masquerade"—where George unveiled his new trademark, scatting along with a single-string guitar solo—that reached No. 10 on the pop singles charts and drove the album all the way to No. 1 on the pop (!) LP charts. The attractive title track also became a minor hit single, although Gabor Szabo's 1971 recording with composer Bobby Womack is even more fetching. In the greater scheme of Benson's career, this is really not so much a breakthrough as it is a transition album; the guitar is still the core of his identity. *—Richard S. Ginell*

In Flight / Aug. 1976-Nov. 1976 / Warner Brothers ✦✦✦
In the wake of "This Masquerade," and the balance of power now shifts for the first time toward Benson's suddenly marketable voice; four of the six tracks are vocals. By this time, Benson was tailoring his tenor toward soulful pitch-bending a la Stevie Wonder on tunes as diverse as "Nature Boy" and "The World Is A Ghetto," and the unison scatting with the guitar that caught fire with the public on "Masquerade" is now pulled out whenever possible. Benson's backing band from *Breezin',* still set in its funk mode, is intact, and Claus Ogerman again contributes gentle orchestral cushions. The two instrumentals, particularly Donny Hathaway's "Valdez In The Country," prove that Benson remained a brilliantly inventive melodist on guitar, in full possession of his powers. Yet there is every indication here that Benson was set upon becoming primarily a pop star. *—Richard S. Ginell*

The Best of George Benson: The Instrumentals / 1976-1979 / Warner Brothers ✦✦✦✦
Anyone who despaired about the total lack of instrumentals on Warner's unrepresentative *The Best of George Benson* will be overjoyed by this sequel, which contains nothing but instrumentals (that may have been the game plan all along). Admittedly, the instrumental pickings in the Warner catalog are slimmer than, say, those for Benson's pre-"This Masquerade" recordings on CBS/CTI and A&M/Verve, and the style is often slanted toward the kind of easy jazz heard on *The Wave* radio format. But Benson could still create funky fireworks with his guitar on tunes like "Dinorah, Dinorah," "Affirmation," and "Weekend In L.A.," and Benson's off-the-cuff fluency is shown off to stunning effect all alone on "Tenderly." The range of albums is more inclusive than that of the earlier set, spanning Benson's long Warner period and even reaching out to the funky-butt title track from his first GRP album, *That's Right.* If you combine this album and the vocal *Best Of* collection, you'll get an excellent summary of George Benson over a span of 20 years. *—Richard S. Ginell*

Livin' Inside Your Love / Feb. 1, 1977 / Warner Brothers ✦✦✦

Weekend in L A / Sep. 30, 1977-Oct. 2, 1977 / Warner Brothers ✦✦✦✦

In Your Eyes / 1978 / Warner Brothers ✦✦

Give Me the Night / 1980 / Warner Brothers ✦✦✦✦✦
This is the peak of Benson's courtship of the mass market—a superbly crafted and performed pop album with a large supporting cast—and wouldn't you know that Quincy Jones, the master catalyst, is the producer. Q's regular team, including the prolific songwriter Rod Temperton and the brilliant engineer Bruce Swedien, is in control, and Benson's voice, caught beautifully in the rich, floating sound, had never before been put to such versatile use. On "Moody's Mood," Benson really exercises his vocalese chops and proves that he is technically as fluid as just about any jazz vocalist, and he become a credible rival to Al Jarreau on the joyous title track. Benson's guitar now plays a subsidiary role—only two of the ten tracks are instrumentals—but Q has him play terrific fills behind the vocals and in the gaps, and the engineering gives his tone a variety of striking, new, full-sounding timbres. The instrumentals themselves are marvelous: "Off Broadway" is a kick driving, danceable and Ivan Lins' "Dinorah, Dinorah" grows increasively seductive with each play. Benson should have worked with Quincy Jones from this point on, but this would be their only album together. *—Richard S. Ginell*

Tenderly / 1989 / Warner Brothers ✦✦✦✦✦

Big Boss Band / 1990 / Warner Brothers ✦✦✦✦

● **The George Benson Anthology** / May 1, 1964-Jun. 7, 1982 / Rhino ✦✦✦✦✦
George Benson's two-disc *Anthology* from Rhino ultimately manages to encapsulate Benson's career. These 32 tracks not only highlight the obligatory vocal pop hits "Turn Your Love Around," "Give Me the Night," and "On Broadway," but dish out a heavy dose of his early jazz recordings that followed in the footsteps of Wes Montgomery, and his many appearances throughout the years with Brother Jack Mcduff, Lonnie Smith, Hubert Laws, Aretha Franklin, Jimmy Smith, Earl Klugh, and the Count Basie Orchestra. If you're only accustomed to Benson's pop/jazz crossover work, check out this definitive overview. *—Al Campbell*

Bunny Berigan (Rowland Bernart Berrigan)

b. Nov. 2, 1908, Hilbert, WI, **d.** Jun. 2, 1942, New York, NY
Vocals, Trumpet / Swing
During the late '30s, Bunny Berigan was arguably the top trumpeter in jazz (with his main competition being Louis Armstrong and Roy Eldridge). Blessed with a beautiful tone and a wide range, Berigan brought excitement to every session he appeared on. He was not afraid to take chances during his solos and could be a bit reckless but his successes and occasional failures were always colorful to hear, at least until he drank it all away. Berigan began playing in Midwestern college groups, and joined Fred Rich's CBS studio band in 1931. In 1935 he spent a few months with Benny Goodman's Orchestra and had classic solos on Goodman's first two hit records ("King Porter Stomp" and "Sometimes I'm Happy"). In 1937 he joined Tommy Dorsey's band and was once again largely responsible for two hits: "Marie" and "Song of India." After leaving Dorsey, Bunny Berigan finally put together his own orchestra and scored early on with his biggest hit "I Can't Get Started." Unfortunately, alcoholism pushed him into bankruptcy by 1940, and he was forced to break up his band. Though he rejoined Tommy Dorsey for a few months, he never stopped drinking and was not happy being a sideman again. His health began declining and in 1942, he died. *—Scott Yanow*

Portrait of Bunny Berigan / Sep. 27, 1932-Aug. 7, 1937 / ASV/Living Era ✦✦✦
'92 reissue covering some mid-'30s Bunny Berigan sessions with The Dorsey Brothers, Artie Shaw, and Connie Boswell, among others. This set is weighted toward his most popular tunes, not necessarily the most jazz-oriented, although everything presented rates as prime Berigan. *—Ron Wynn*

● **The Pied Piper** / Jul. 1, 1935-Aug. 3, 1940 / Bluebird/RCA ✦✦✦✦✦
This is the best single-CD compilation of Bunny Berigan recordings issued to date. Although all of the trumpeter's big-band sides for Bluebird have come out on three double LPs, this set gives more general collectors a better overview of his talents. One of the top trumpeters active during the 1935-39 period (only Louis Armstrong and the up and coming Roy Eldridge were on his level), Berigan was largely responsible for the success of important hit records for Benny Goodman ("King Porter Stomp" and "Sometimes I'm Happy") and Tommy Dorsey ("Marie" and "Song of India"), in addition to having a best-seller of his own ("I Can't Get Started"). Unfortunately, Berigan's alcoholism eventually did him in, but this CD has all of the hits, plus appearances with Gene Gifford's Orchestra (a majestic solo on "Nothin' But the Blues"), Frankie Trumbauer, jamming with Fats Waller, and with the Metronome All-Stars, plus more titles as a leader, with BG, and with Dorsey (including a radio broadcast version of "I've Found a New Baby" from 1940). This is a well-conceived reissue of important and often exciting swing by one of the greats. *—Scott Yanow*

Devil's Holiday, Vol. 2: 1938 / Jun. 27, 1938-Aug. 9, 1938 / Jass ✦✦✦✦

Tim Berne

b. 1954, Syracuse, NY
Sax (Alto) / Improvisation, Avant-Garde Jazz, Free Jazz, Modern Creative
Alto and baritone saxophonist, composer and bandleader Tim Berne is an important member of the NYC's creative music community whose contributions invite comparison to those of fellow New Yorker John Zorn. Like Zorn, Berne asserts a strong musical personality throughout his diverse works, has influenced many later improvisers, and knows his way around the music business. The last attribute has led to Berne founding independent record labels, when necessary, to get his music recorded and released.

While attending college in Oregon, Berne was more interested in R&B and Motown until he heard jazz saxophonist Julius Hemphill's album *Dogon A.D.* Taken with Hemphill's soulful creative jazz, Berne went to NYC to find him in 1974. Hemphill became Berne's biggest influence, as mentor and friend, until his death in 1995.

Five years after first meeting Hemphill, Berne founded the Empire label and released four albums featuring such up-and-coming musicians as Paul Motian, and the Cline brothers. He began recording for Soul Note in the mid-'80s, then landed a major label deal with Columbia, which lasted for two albums: *Fulton Street Maul* (1987), and *Sanctified Dreams* (1988). Over the next six years, Berne recorded for Stefan Winter's JMT label, recording with his groups Miniature and Tim Berne's Caos Totale.

In the early '90s, Berne formed a quartet with bassist Michael Formanek and drummer

Jim Black, and clarinetist/saxophonist Chris Speed. Bloodcount played escalating, fiery pieces that could stretched up to 50 minutes. After the releases of their first three live albums, with guitarist Marc Ducret, JMT was purchased by Polygram and shut down. As a result, Berne formed the Screwgun label and continued to release albums by Bloodcount, Paraphrase (his trio with bassist Drew Gress and drummer Tom Rainey), and more. He also recorded for other labels including Winter & Winter. In 2000, Berne premiered his new ensembles, Quicksand and Composure. *—Dave Lynch*

Ancestors / Feb. 19, 1983 / Soul Note ♦♦♦

Mutant Variations / Mar. 5, 1983-Mar. 6, 1983 / Soul Note ♦♦♦♦
Definitely not part of the new traditional scene, alto saxophonist Tim Berne keeps moving forward. This '83 quartet set of all originals is reminiscent at times of mid-'50s Ornette Coleman, notably due to Herb Robertson's pocket trumpet solos and the dynamics generated by Berne and Robertson's interaction with bassist Ed Schuller and percussionist Paul Motian. *—Ron Wynn*

Fulton Street Maul / 1986 / Koch Jazz ♦♦♦♦
How did avant-gardist Tim Berne get signed to Columbia? During his relatively brief alliance with that media giant, the passionate altoist was somehow able to continue recording his uncompromising music with apparently no real interference. On this set, he teams up with the amazing guitarist Bill Frisell, cellist Hank Roberts and percussionist Alex Cline for five explorative pieces that one can safely bet did not receive much airplay. *—Scott Yanow*

Diminutive Mysteries / Sep. 1992 / JMT ♦♦♦♦
This is certainly the most unusual David Sanborn recording to date. Avant-gardist Tim Berne (heard here on alto and baritone) and the popular R&B star Sanborn (mostly leaving his trademark alto behind to play sopranino) share a great respect for altoist Julius Hemphill and the St. Louis free jazz movement. Along with guitarist Marc Ducret, cellist Hank Roberts and drummer Joey Baron, they perform seven often-emotional Hemphill pieces plus Berne's "The Maze." Sanborn is to be congratulated for successfully stretching himself although this is very much Berne's date. *—Scott Yanow*

● **Discretion** / 1997 / Screwgun ♦♦♦♦♦
Some musicians become increasingly concise over the years, aiming to use fewer notes, more succinct tunes. Tim Berne, however, has merely grown out of any inclination to curb—much less apologize for—his standard of long compositions (15 minutes is an average length, but 40 minutes isn't unheard of). What's great about these notorious burners, though, is that they don't grow tiresome. The musicians are brilliantly creative and experienced enough not to get lost in all the room provided by these large time frames. Each player has boundless creative energy, matched only by technical ability—they never seem to tire, only to get more worked up and inspired. In the always-live recordings, Bloodcount constantly morph and shape-shift musical ideas, and keep the compositions breathing through exploitation of the whole range of dynamics: There are sections of whispery brushes and soft-touch saxophone flits (when the sounds of fingers moving on keys are as audible as the tones created); there are apexes of shooting fireballs and bellowing frenzy. As a unit, they can be intuitively tight and inseparable. Conversely, they can be like electrons zipping around the nucleus of a shared mental conception of a composition. As a result, the same compositions turn out differently each time they're played—notice how songs like "Byram's World" and "The Opener" show up on several albums—so even if some of the songs on *Discretion* are familiar, it's guaranteed to be a new listening experience. *—Joslyn Layne*

● **Big Satan** / Feb. 8, 1996-Feb. 10, 1996 / Winter & Winter ♦♦♦♦♦

Ornery People / 1998 / little brother ♦♦♦♦

Chu Berry (Leon Brown Berry)

b. Sep. 13, 1910, Wheeling, WV, **d.** Oct. 30, 1941, Conneaut, OH
Sax (Tenor) / Swing
Chu Berry was considered one of the top tenor-saxophonists of the 1930s, just below Coleman Hawkins (his main influence), Lester Young and Ben Webster. Particuarly strong on uptempo numbers (although his ballad statements could be overly sentimental), Berry might have become an influential force if he had not died prematurely. After playing alto in college, he switched to tenor in 1929 when he joined Sammy Stewart's band. In 1930 he moved to New York, playing with Benny Carter's band and Charlie Johnson's Orchestra. He was prominently featured in Spike Hughes 1933 recording sessions, was a star with the bands of Teddy Hill (1933-35) and Fletcher Henderson (1936) (to whom he contributed his song "Christopher Columbus") and then found a permanent home with Cab Calloway in 1937. Berry was used on many sessions including with his friend Roy Eldridge, Lionel Hampton (a classic version of "Sweethearts on Parade"), Teddy Wilson and Calloway (his version of "Ghost of a Chance" became well-known); in addition he led a couple of his own fine dates. Chu Berry died from the effects of a car crash when he was just 31. *—Scott Yanow*

Chu / May 14, 1936-Jul. 3, 1941 / Columbia ♦♦♦♦♦
One of the finest tenor saxophonists of the 1930s (he died in a car crash in late 1941), Leon "Chu" Berry made a lot of exciting music during his 31 years. He only led five sessions in his career (including two for Commodore and a rare date with Charlie Ventura). The first two four-song dates lead off this well-conceived LP. Berry is heard jamming with trumpeter Hot Lips Page (who sings "Too Marvelous for Words") and clarinetist Buster Bailey on the first date, and with trumpeter Irving Randolph and trombonist Keg Johnson on the later session; highlights include "Indiana," "Limehouse Blues," and "Chuberry Jam." Rounding off the album of hot swing is 1936's "Warmin' Up" (from a Teddy Wilson date on which Berry teams up with trumpeter Roy Eldridge) and seven of his feature numbers with Cab Calloway's Orchestra, including Chu's most famous ballad recording, "Ghost of a Chance." A definitive set. *—Scott Yanow*

● **The Indispensable** / 1936-1939 / RCA ♦♦♦♦♦
A wide variety of sessions (1936-39) from an immortal stylist are included. With Gene Krupa (d), Lionel Hampton (vib), Cab Calloway (v), Fletcher Henderson (leader), and Wingy Manone's bands. *—Michael G. Nastos*

A Giant of Tenor Sax / Nov. 1938-Aug. 1941 / Commodore ♦♦♦♦
Struggling for notoriety amidst well-known peers like Coleman Hawkins, Ben Webster, and Lester Young, tenor saxophonist Chu Berry gained the respect of his fellow jazz musicians while obtaining some fame over in Europe. His quest for wider exposure in U.S., though, was put to rest when he passed after a car wreck in 1941. Luckily the alumnus of bands led by Fletcher Henderson, Benny Carter, and Cab Calloway was recorded on a good number of solo date sides between 1938-1941. Berry's entry in Commodore Records *Giants of the Tenor Sax* series includes some of the highlights. Aided by the bands of Roy Eldridge and Hot Lips Page, Berry reels of a very engaging program of ballad standards like "Body and Soul" and "Stardust" and jam session cuts like "Sittin' In." Like Webster and Hawkins, Berry displays incredible suppleness on slower numbers, while handling fast tempos with power and intelligence (next to Young, he probably was the smoothest of the big tenor players). Also featured on this collection, equally unsung and talented tenor man Lucky Thompson. Even though he eventually found wide exposure via dates with Miles Davis, Dizzy Gillespie, and Stan Kenton, Thompson, like Berry, never really made it into the upper echelon of jazz soloists in the public's eye; but similar to Berry in another aspect, Thompson won the respect of his fellow musicians and the devotion of expansive jazz fans around the world. Backed by trumpeter Hot Lips Page's group on four numbers from 1944, Thompson comes off more modern sounding than Berry, sacrificing some of his peer's tonal sophistication for more advanced harmonic ideas. Page compliments the solo fireworks with a few of his indomitable vocal performances and some fine soloing of his own. A great showcase of two of the underground giants of jazz. *—Stephen Cook*

Andy Bey

b. 1939, Newark, NJ
Vocals, Piano / Vocal Jazz, Standards, Hard Bop, Soul-Jazz
One of the great unsung heroes of jazz singing, Andy Bey is a commanding interpreter of lyrics who has a wide vocal range and a big, rich, full voice. Bey enjoys a small following that swears by him; nonethless, he isn't nearly as well known as he should be. Born and raised in Newark, NJ not far from from New York, Bey was exposed to jazz as a child and starting singing in front of local audiences as early as eight. At some gigs, an eight-year-old Bey was accompanied by tenor sax great Hank Mobley. Bey was 13 when, in 1952, he recorded his first solo album, *Mama's Little Boy's Got The Blues*, and he was 17 when he formed Andy & The Bey Sisters with his siblings Salome and Geraldine in 1956. The group did a 16-month tour of Europe and recorded three albums (one for RCA Victor in 1961, two for Prestige in 1964 and 1965) before breaking up in 1967. In the 1960s and 1970s, Bey's vocals were featured by Max Roach, Duke Pearson and Gary Bartz (for whom he delivered very socio-political lyrics, including some searing condemnations of U.S. involvement in the Vietnam War). The 1970s also found Bey recording *Experience And Judgement* for Atlantic and beginning a long association with pianist Horace Silver, who featured him prominently on many of the religious-themed albums he put out own his own Silveto label in the 1970s and 1980s. The LPs contained what Silver termed "metaphysical self-help music" and preached a sort of religious self-help philosophy that wasn't unlike Reverend Ike's message—unfortunately for Silver and Bey, this appproach meant limited distribution and little commercial appeal. Bey continued to work with Silver into the 1990s, when he was featured on Silver's 1993 Columbia date *It's Got To Be Funky* (which marked a return to hard bop's mainstream and did much better commercially than his "self-help music"). Labels Bey recorded for as a leader in the 1980s and 1990s included Jazzette, Zagreb and Evidence, which in 1996, released the superb *Ballads, Blues And Bey*. *—Alex Henderson*

● **Now Hear** / Aug. 17, 1964–Aug. 20, 1964 / Prestige ♦♦♦♦♦
Expressive vocalists hook up with Jerome Richardson (sax and fl), Kenny Burrell (g) for expansive treatments of jazz. *—Michael G. Nastos*

Ballads, Blues & Bey / May 19, 1995-May 20, 1995 / Evidence ♦♦♦♦
Andy Bey was 56 when he recorded *Ballads, Blues and Bey* in 1995, and despite the fact that his voice had more rough edges than it did in the 1960s and '70s, he still had an impressive range and was among jazz's most expressive male singers. For this project, the Newark, NJ native didn't employ a band—his only accompaniment is his own acoustic piano, and this spare, intimate approach really makes Bey's heartfelt vocals stand out on such chestnuts as "Someone to Watch Over Me," "Embraceable You" and "You'd Be So Nice to Come Home To." This time, the Duke Ellington songbook is a high priority for Bey, who demonstrates how marvelous an interpreter of lyrics he is on "In a Sentimental Mood," "Day Dream" and other Ellington gems. Unfortunately, Bey still wasn't nearly as well known in jazz circles as he deserved to be, and he continued to be one of the great unsung heroes of jazz singing. *—Alex Henderson*

Shades of Bey / Dec. 16, 1997-Feb. 21, 1998 / Evidence ♦♦♦♦
Andy Bey's bass-baritone voice has aged over the last thirty-odd years, but it's aged well; he now sings in a husky drawl that sounds all the more warm and intimate for being a bit ragged around the edges. When he goes into falsetto, as on "Midnight Blue," athe sound is so dark that you don't recognize it as falsetto at first. This album peaks early on with "Like a Lover," a wistful love song with only the gentlest, sparest guitar accompaniment. But there are many other beautiful moments, the best of which always come on the slow numbers: the Billy Strayhorn classic "Pretty Girl," on which Bey sounds like Billy Eckstine with a weathered patina to his voice, and the surprising Nick Drake cover, the moody and intense "Dark Shadows." His vocal version of Thelonious Monk's "Straight, No Chaser" is fun, but it tends to expose the limitations of his range; however, he makes the uptempo "Believin' It" work beautifully—Geri Allen's edgy, modernist piano contrasts nicely with Bey's effusive, bop-inflected delivery. *—Rick Anderson*

Eubie Blake (James Hubert Blake)

b. Feb. 7, 1883, Baltimore, MD, **d.** Feb. 12, 1983, New York, NY
Piano, Composer / Ragtime
Eubie Blake had a rather unique career. Although his main importance was as a songwriter

for Broadway shows in the 1920s, late in life he became known as the last living link to ragtime. Blake always had a colorful life. He wrote his first rag "The Charleston Rag" in 1899, spent years playing with medicine shows and in sporting houses and by 1915 was teaming up with singer Noble Sissle in vaudeville. Sissle and Blake wrote for the 1921 hit show *Shuffle Along* (the first all-Black musical) and it was followed by *Revue Negre, Plantation Review, Rhapsody in Black* and *Bamville Review*. Among Blake's hit songs of the 1920's were "I'm Just Crazy About Harry," "You're Lucky to Me" and "Memories of You." Although he made some recordings in 1931, Eubie Blake generally had a lower profile for the next three decades. He was largely forgotten until 1969, when he recorded an LP, *The Eighty-Six Years of Eubie Blake*, that amazed listeners who had never heard of him. During his remaining 14 years, Eubie Blake was a very popular perfomer, playing and singing ragtime-era pieces, charming audiences, making new records, appearing on Broadway in the 1978 show *Eubie* (he was 95 at the time) and running his own label Eubie Blake Music. He continued performing until he was 98 and made it to his 100th birthday with five days to spare. *— Scott Yanow*

Memories of You / Sep. 1915-May 1973 / Biograph ♦♦♦

• **Blues and Rags (1917-1921)** / 1917-1921 / Biograph ♦♦♦♦♦
This record was the first volume of two which reproduced some of Eubie Blake's earliest piano rolls on a vintage 1910 Steinway player piano with Blake-approved tempos. As typical for piano rolls, some of them were doctored (i.e., had extra notes added) by the issuing company in order to give them a "fuller" sound—as if you needed that with a pianist the caliber of Eubie Blake. Highlights include the earliest known performance of Blake's first composition, "Charleston Rag," plus a rare piano duet with Milton Suskind on "Goodnight Angeline." The remaining tracks are predominantly covers of tunes by Perry Bradford and Broadway composers like Creamer & Layton and Irving Berlin. While Eubie clearly had strong chops as a young ragtime player, he was as good or better in his nineties. This historical release is worth seeking. *— Ken Dryden*

Blues & Spirituals (1921) / Mar. 1921-Dec. 1921 / Biograph ♦♦♦♦♦

The 86 Years of Eubie Blake / Dec. 25, 1968-Mar. 12, 1969 / Columbia ♦♦♦♦♦

Live Concert / May 22, 1973 / Eubie Blake Music ♦♦♦

Ran Blake

b. Apr. 20, 1935, Springfield, MA
Piano / Avant-Garde Jazz, Third Stream, Post-Bop
Third Stream pianist and music educator Ran Blake has recorded a number of unique, often solo, jazz albums since the early '60s that showcase his dramatic contrasts of silence and "outbursts" and fresh reinventions of older standards. He has also made his mark on music by influencing music students for many decades at Boston's New England Conservatory of Music.

He was born in Springfield, MA on April 20, 1935, and eventually got his degree from Bard College, in addition to studying at Columbia University and at the School of Jazz in his homestate. In 1957, Blake began collaborating with vocalist Jeanne Lee, and the duo went on a European tour in 1963. His debut album, *The Newest Sound Around* was awarded the RCA Album First Prize in Germany in 1963. The follow-up to his debut, *Ran Blake Plays Solo Piano*, was released on ESP in 1965. Two years later, Blake began teaching jazz at Boston's New England Conservatory of Music. 30 years later, Blake was still educating students at NEC, and also served as chairman of the school's Contemporary Improvisation department.

Blake is the recipient of fellowships from the Massachusetts Artists Foundation, the Guggenheim Foundation, Mac Arthur Foundation and the NEA. His recording has been sporadic and, most often, solo. His discography includes *Blue Potato* (Milestone, 1969); *Third Stream Today* (Golden Crest, 1977); *Film Noir* (Novus, 1980); *Duke Dreams* (Soul Note, 1981); a double disc journey through jazz standards and international folk music alike called *Painted Rhythms: The Compleat Ran Blake* (GMRecordings, 1985); one of his duos with Anthony Braxton, *A Memory of Vienna* (Hatology, 1988); his duo with Clifford Jordan, *Masters From Different Worlds* (Mapleshade, 1989).

He recorded even less during the 1990s, but did create, among others: a tribute to Sarah Vaughan, *Unmarked Van* (Soul Note, 1995), and a revisiting of film noir material and other tunes in a duo with flugelhorn player and trumpeter Enrico Rava, entitled *Duo en Noir* (2000), recorded for composer Franz Koglmann's new label, Between the Lines. Other labels that have released Blake albums over the decades include the Owl, Horo, Crest, RCA and Arista labels. In addition to his previously mentioned collaborators, Blake has also worked with Oscar Peterson, Jaki Byard, Mary Lou Williams, Mal Waldron, Houston Person, William Russo, Gunther Schuller, Kate Wolf and Ricky Ford. *—Joslyn Layne*

The Newest Sound Around / Nov. 15, 1961-Dec. 7, 1961 / Bluebird/RCA ♦♦♦♦♦

• **Duke Dreams** / May 29, 1981-Jun. 2, 1981 / Soul Note ♦♦♦♦♦
Although Ran Blake plays nine Duke Ellington and Billy Strayhorn songs on this set (plus his own "Duke Dreams," and Dave Brubeck's "The Duke," and the ancient and rather delightful "Animal Crackers," which Ellington recorded in 1926), he does not try to emulate the masters; instead, Blake interprets their music on his own terms, making each note count and each performance into a dramatic solo recital. While hinting at Duke's piano style, Ran Blake often reharmonizes and greatly reinvents his music, including such pieces as "Drop Me Off in Harlem," "It Don't Mean a Thing" and "Take the 'A' Train." Highly recommended. *— Scott Yanow*

Painted Rhythms: The Compleat Ran Blake, Vol. 1 / Dec. 1985 / GM ♦♦♦♦
The first of two Ran Blake solo albums cut for the GM label, this CD may not offer the "compleat" Blake, but it does feature the dramatic pianist (who constantly improvises while making every note count) in particularly inventive form and is a strong introduction to his unique playing. With one exception ("Impresario of Death"), the pianist sticks to standards, but he makes them sound unlike any previous rendition. He interprets three very different versions of "Maple Leaf Rag" (a fourth is on the second volume), three Duke Ellington songs (including "Drop Me Off in Harlem"), and numbers by Mary Lou Williams, George Russell, Pete Rugolo, Stan Kenton and Jerome Kern, plus the standard "Moonlight on the Ganges." Highly recommended, as are most of Ran Blake's unique recordings. *— Scott Yanow*

Short Life of Barbara Monk / Aug. 26, 1986 / Soul Note ♦♦♦
Ran Blake has recorded fairly often during his career, but this was his first full set with a standard quartet. Tenor saxophonist Ricky Ford works surprisingly well with Blake, whose phrasing and use of space are unusual, while his interpretations are sometimes based on the feeling he gets from song titles rather than the chord changes. Bassist Ed Felson and drummer Jon Hazilla (former students) were very familiar with Blake's music. The repertoire is as unusual as usual for a Ran Blake date, including "I've Got You Under My Skin," "Artistry in Rhythm," obscurities, and originals including the emotional "Short Life of Barbara Monk." Another intriguing Ran Blake set. *— Scott Yanow*

Masters from Different Worlds / Dec. 26, 1989-Dec. 30, 1989 / Mapleshade ♦♦♦

Epistrophy / Apr. 19, 1991–Apr. 20, 1991 / Soul Note ♦♦♦

Round About / Dec. 19, 1992–Sep. 29, 1993 / Music & Arts ♦♦♦♦
Ran Blake has long been a very emotional pianist whose use of space and sometimes-thunderous outbursts are always stimulating if unpredictable. For this set he performs solos and duets with the straightforward but very effective vocalist Christine Correa, alternating stirring versions of standards with five of his songs. Among the more memorable selections are "Angel Eyes," "Drop Me off in Harlem," "The Short Life of Barbara Monk," "Long as You're Living" and "I Get a Kick Out of You." Thought-provoking music. *— Scott Yanow*

Art Blakey (Abdullah Ibn Buhaina)

b. Oct. 11, 1919, Pittsburgh, **d.** Oct. 16, 1990, New York, NY
Drums / Hard Bop
In the '60s, when John Coltrane and Ornette Coleman were defining the concept of a jazz avant-garde, few knowledgeable observers would have guessed that in another thirty years, the music's mainstream would virtually bypass their innovations, in favor of the hard bop style that free jazz had apparently supplanted. As it turned out, many listeners who had come to love jazz as a sophisticated manifestation of popular music were unable to accept the extreme esotericism of the avant-garde; their tastes were rooted in the core elements of "swing" and "blues," characteristics found in abundance in the music of the Jazz Messengers, the quintessential hard bop ensemble led by drummer Art Blakey. In the '60s,'70s, and '80s, when artists on the cutting edge were attempting to transform the music, Blakey continued to play in more or less the same bag he had since the '40s. By the '80s, the evolving mainstream consensus had reached a point of overwhelming approval in regard to hard bop: this is what jazz is, and Blakey—as its longest-lived and most eloquent exponent—was its master. The Jazz Messengers had always been an incubator for young talent. A list of the band's alumni is a who's-who of straight-ahead jazz from the '50s on—Lee Morgan, Wayne Shorter, Freddie Hubbard, Johnny Griffin, Jackie McLean, Donald Byrd, Bobby Timmons, Cedar Walton, Benny Golson,Branford Marsalis, Freddie Hubbard, Keith Jarrett and Chuck Mangione, to name several of the most well-known. In the '80s, precocious graduates of Blakey's School for Swing would continue to number among jazz's movers and shakers, foremost among them being trumpeter Wynton Marsalis. Marsalis became the most visible symbol of the '80s jazz mainstream; through him, Blakey's conservative ideals came to dominate the public's perception of the music. At the time of his death in 1990, the Messenger aesthetic dominated jazz, and Blakey himself had arguably become the most influential jazz musician of the past twenty years. *— Chris Kelsey*

New Sounds / Dec. 22, 1947-1948 / Blue Note ♦♦♦♦
This historically significant CD collects together two sessions led by tenor saxophonist James Moody in 1948 (when he was a member of Dizzy Gillespie's big band) along with drummer Art Blakey's first recording date as a leader. Moody's music features boppish arrangements by Gil Fuller and solos by trumpeter Dave Burns, altoist Ernie Henry and baritonist Cecil Payne while the Blakey set (originally released under the title of *Art Blakey's Messengers*) features an octet that includes trumpeter Kenny Dorham, altoist Sahib Shihab and pianist Walter Bishop. Classic and formerly rare music. *— Scott Yanow*

A Night at Birdland, Vols. 1-3 / Feb. 21, 1954 / Blue Note ♦♦♦♦♦
Art Blakey Quintet. 1987 CD reissue of early editions of the group. How can you overlook the sets with Horace Silver (p) and others— Many feel they are his best live dates. I agree. — *Michael G. Nastos*

At the Cafe Bohemia, Vol. 1 / Nov. 23, 1955 / Blue Note ♦♦♦♦
This first of two volumes features the original version of The Jazz Messengers, the quintet co-led by drummer Art Blakey and pianist Horace Silver that also featured trumpeter Kenny Dorham, Hank Mobley on tenor and bassist Doug Watkins. Caught live, the band stretches out on such numbers as "Soft Winds," "Minor's Holiday," "Alone Together" and Dorham's "Prince Albert." Highly enjoyable and still timeless music. *— Scott Yanow*

At the Cafe Bohemia, Vol. 2 / Nov. 23, 1955 / Blue Note ♦♦♦

The Jazz Messengers / Apr. 15, 1956–May 4, 1956 / Columbia/Legacy ♦♦♦
This CD reissue brings back the music on the earlier LP titled *Art Blakey with the Original Jazz Messengers*, plus five other selections (just one of which is an alternate) from the same two sessions that were formerly out on imported sets; "Deciphering the Message" was previously unreleased altogether. These were the last recordings by the Art Blakey-Horace Silver Jazz Messengers before pianist Silver went out on his own and the first edition disbanded. Trumpeter Donald Byrd, tenor saxophonist Hank Mobley and bassist Doug Watkins (along with Silver and Blakey) are in excellent form. Silver's "Nica's Dream" is heard here in the original version, and the band is typically hard-swinging throughout the 76-minute-plus program. *— Scott Yanow*

Second Edition 1957 / Mar. 13, 1957-Apr. 8, 1957 / Bluebird/RCA ♦♦♦♦
This is an interesting CD reissue of formerly rare material from the second version of Art Blakey's Jazz Messengers. The first six selections are the full contents of a long-out-of-print

Vik LP which find the Messengers (with tenor-saxophonist Johnny Griffin, trumpeter Bill Hardman, pianist Sam Dockery, bassist Spanky DeBrest and the drummer/leader) playing six songs by Lerner and Loewe including "Almost Like Being in Love," "On the Street Where You Live" and "I Could Have Danced All Night." In addition, the same group is heard on two previously unreleased alternate takes with altoist Jackie McLean (who was actually Griffin's predecessor) making the band a sextet, and there are three numbers (including two "new" takes) from an expanded unit (called "The Jazz Messengers Plus Two") which features such players as a very young Lee Morgan (making his debut with Blakey a year before he joined the group), Hardman, trombonist Melba Liston, Griffin and pianist Wynton Kelly. But rarity aside, the performances should please straightahead jazz fans. *—Scott Yanow*

Orgy in Rhythm, Vol. 1-2 / Mar. 7, 1957 / Blue Note ♦♦♦♦
This CD reissues one of the first percussion-oriented jazz records, although it was preceded two weeks earlier by Art Blakey's obscure Columbia set *Drum Suite*. For the Blue Note date, which was originally released as two LPs and is now available as a single CD, Blakey enlisted quite a lineup—the leader, Art Taylor, Jo Jones, and Specs Wright on drums (with the latter two doubling on tympani), five percussionists, flutist Herbie Mann, pianist Ray Bryant and bassist Wendell Marshall. Mann plays a variety of African wood flutes, except on the final number, a conventional blues featuring his regular flute. With percussionist Sabu leading the chanting and taking three vocals (Blakey himself sings a little on "Toffi"), the music is quite African-oriented and generally holds one's interest, preceding Max Roach's *M'Boom* by over 20 years. Mostly for specialized tastes, this is a set that drummers should consider essential. *—Scott Yanow*

Mirage / Mar. 8, 1957-Mar. 9, 1957 / Savoy ♦♦♦

Theory of Art / Apr. 2, 1957-Apr. 8, 1957 / Bluebird/RCA ♦♦♦

Art Blakey's Jazz Messengers with Thelonious Monk / May 14, 1957–May 15, 1957 / Rhino ♦♦♦♦
This was an ideal matchup, one that should have been repeated in future years. Art Blakey was always one of the perfect drummers for Thelonious Monk's music, matching the innovative pianist's percussive excitement while leaving him plenty of space. Blakey's tenorman Johnny Griffin also proved to have a perfect understanding of Monk's music, joining Monk's quartet the following year. With trumpeter Bill Hardman and bassist Spanky DeBrest completing the quintet, five of Monk's finest compositions plus Griffin's "Purple Shades" are explored on this LP. *—Scott Yanow*

★ **Moanin'** / Oct. 30, 1958 / Blue Note ♦♦♦♦♦
The third version of Art Blakey's Jazz Messengers debuted with this stunning album. Tenor saxophonist Benny Golson helped give the quintet its own personality with his compositions and arrangements (contributing "Blues March," "Along Came Betty," "Are You Real" and "The Drum Thunder Suite" to this set), 20-year old trumpeter Lee Morgan quickly emerged as a powerful soloist and the funky pianist Bobby Timmons's "Moanin'" became The Messengers' first real hit. This classic album, a major influence on hard bop, is highly recommended. *—Scott Yanow*

Paris 1958 / Dec. 18, 1958-Dec. 19, 1958 / Bluebird/RCA ♦♦♦♦
Originally part of an 11-song three-LP set, this six-song CD (not counting the 28-second "Theme") features the Lee Morgan-Benny Golson-Bobby Timmons version of The Jazz Messengers stretching out on their "hits" (including "Blues March," "Moanin'" and "Whisper Not"), giving one alternate versions of their studio recordings. This was one of the finest bands of the period, and this CD serves as a perfect introduction to the exciting music of The Jazz Messengers. *—Scott Yanow*

Art Blakey & The Jazz Messengers / Nov. 2, 1958-Mar. 29, 1959 / Blue Note ♦♦♦♦
Drum legend Art Blakey was heading a streamlined edition of The Messengers when they came to Birdland on April 15, 1959. It was a two-horn, piano, bass, and drum configuration, with trumpeter Lee Morgan, tenor saxophonist Hank Mobley, bassist Jymie Merritt and pianist Bobby Timmons in the lineup alongside Blakey. This two-CD set combines the original two volumes issued as *At The Jazz Corner Of The World*, and it was galvanizing hard bop at its best. No recent Blue Note series has been more on target than the Doubletime line; this one is no exception. *—Ron Wynn*

At the Jazz Corner of the World, Vol. 1-2 / Apr. 15, 1959 / Blue Note ♦♦♦♦♦
This two-CD set is a logical reissue, combining both volumes (formerly Lp's) of a live performance by Art Blakey and his 1959 Jazz Messengers. Recorded shortly after tenor-saxophonist Benny Golson had left the group, this particular version of Blakey's classic band featured trumpeter Lee Morgan, Hank Mobley on tenor (his only recordings with the band), pianist Bobby Timmons, bassist Jymie Merritt and the drummer-leader. Surprisingly Morgan, Timmons and the departed Golson did not contribute any compositions to the set although there are three Hank Mobley songs. In addition, the band performs songs by Thelonious Monk ("Justice"), Ray Bryant, Randy Weston ("Hi-Fly") and Gildo Mahones plus the standard "Close Your Eyes" and two versions of "The Theme." The music falls short of being essential but hard bop collectors will find much to savor on the twofer. *—Scott Yanow*

Africaine / Nov. 10, 1959 / Blue Note ♦♦♦♦
Not released until over 20 years after it was recorded, this set (reissued on CD in 1998) features tenor saxophonist Wayne Shorter in his first recording with the Jazz Messengers. The quintet at the time also featured the great trumpeter Lee Morgan, pianist Walter Davis, Jr., bassist Jymie Merritt, and the drummer/leader Art Blakey. The highpoint is easily Shorter's memorable composition "Lester Left Town" (written after Lester Young's passing). Overall, this forgotten session contains plenty of excellent hard bop. *—Scott Yanow*

The Big Beat / Mar. 6, 1960 / Blue Note ♦♦♦♦
In 1960, Art Blakey led one of the greatest versions of his Jazz Messengers. The particular edition heard on this CD features three distinctive soloists (trumpeter Lee Morgan, tenor saxophonist Wayne Shorter and pianist Bobby Timmons). Highlights of *The Big Beat* include Timmons's "Dat Dere" and Shorter's "Lester Left Town" in addition to a colorful arrangement of "It's Only a Paper Moon," heard in two versions. A gem. *—Scott Yanow*

Like Someone in Love / Aug. 7, 1960-Aug. 14, 1960 / Blue Note ♦♦♦

A Night in Tunisia / Aug. 7, 1960–Aug. 14, 1960 / Blue Note ♦♦♦♦
The lengthy title track on this CD easily overshadows the rest of the program for it is one of the most exciting versions ever recorded of Dizzy Gillespie's "A Night in Tunisia." Trumpeter Lee Morgan (then only in his early 20s), tenor saxophonist Wayne Shorter, pianist Bobby Timmons and bassist Jymie Merritt formed one of the strongest of the many versions of Art Blakey's Jazz Messengers and are actually in fine form during the remainder of the satisfying (if anticlimatic) set. [The CD augments the LP by adding a version of "When Your Lover Has Gone" and an alternate take of "Sincerely Diana" to the original program.] *—Scott Yanow*

Roots & Herbs / Feb. 18, 1961 / Blue Note ♦♦♦

The Witch Doctor / Mar. 14, 1961 / Blue Note ♦♦♦
The 1960-61 Jazz Messengers featured three distinctive soloists (trumpeter Lee Morgan, Wayne Shorter on tenor and pianist Bobby Timmons), perfectly suitable accompaniment by bassist Jymie Merritt and typically powerful drumming from its leader, Art Blakey. *Witch Doctor* has two compositions apiece from Morgan and Shorter in addition to Timmons's "A Little Busy" and Clifford Jordan's "Lost and Found." None of these songs became standards, but the fine solos and strong group sound make this album worth picking up. *—Scott Yanow*

The Freedom Rider / Feb. 12, 1961-May 27, 1961 / Blue Note ♦♦♦♦♦
The final recording by this edition of The Jazz Messengers (featuring trumpeter Lee Morgan, tenor saxophonist Wayne Shorter, pianist Bobby Timmons, bassist Jymie Merritt and drummer/leader Art Blakey) finds the group consolidating their year-and-a-half of experience into yet another exciting document. Blakey's unaccompanied drum feature on "The Freedom Rider" is full of drama while the rest of the program (two compositions apiece by Morgan and Shorter) makes this last chapter for this particular band quite memorable. *—Scott Yanow*

Art Blakey Jazz Messengers / Jun. 13, 1961-Jun. 14, 1961 / Impulse! ♦♦♦

Mosaic / Oct. 2, 1961 / Blue Note ♦♦♦♦
The first studio recording by Art Blakey's all-star Messengers of 1961-64 features five group originals (including "Mosaic," "Arabia" and "Crisis") and exciting solos from the great frontline (trumpeter Freddie Hubbard, trombonist Curtis Fuller and tenor saxophonist Wayne Shorter). All of the recordings by this classic hard bop group are well worth acquiring. *—Scott Yanow*

Buhaina's Delight / Nov. 28, 1961–Dec. 18, 1961 / Blue Note ♦♦♦♦
Arguably the finest lineup of the Jazz Messengers (with the possible exception of the Lee Morgan edition), this incarnation of the band—Blakey, saxophonist Wayne Shorter (here playing tenor), young trumpeter Freddie Hubbard, trombonist Curtis Fuller, pianist Cedar Walton, and bassist Jymie Merritt—set the tone for the hard bop movement of the '60s. This release features six classic modern-jazz icons and four alternate takes. Starting with Shorter's "Backstage Sally," the band jump into a happy, staccato horn chart and the groove-style shuffle that was their signature sound. Shorter's tenor-led ballad "Contemplation" finds the brassmen solidly behind him as he unleashes a breathtaking solo, while the Fuller-penned "Bu's Delight" is a supersonic hard bopper featuring Blakey's cage-rattling drum breaks and a formidable Walton solo. Written and led by Shorter, "Reincarnation Blues" is another good swinger, with counterpoint and unison lines sprinkled in together. The stunner of the set is Walton's "Shaky Jake," a low, moaning melody with deep-blue harmony soaring over a groove shuffle. On "Moon River," a frisky bopper featuring substantial solos from Hubbard and Fuller and a joyous arrangement modified from the original blue waltz, the song's staggered phrases are introduced and interrupted by drum breaks. The second takes of "Moon River" and "Backstage Sally" are fairly close to the first takes, while the alternate versions of "Reincarnation Blues" and "Bu's Delight" run one to two minutes shorter than the originals. Overall, you won't find a better representation of what modern mainstream jazz sounds like. Blakey and his band are on it from start to finish. *—Michael G. Nastos*

The African Beat / Jan. 24, 1962 / Blue Note ♦♦♦

Three Blind Mice, Vol. 1 / Mar. 9, 1962–Mar. 18, 1962 / Blue Note ♦♦♦

Three Blind Mice, Vol. 2 / Mar. 9, 1962-Mar. 18, 1962 / Blue Note ♦♦♦

Caravan / Oct. 23, 1962-Oct. 24, 1962 / Riverside/OJC ♦♦♦♦
Art Blakey led many strong versions of his Jazz Messengers over a 30 year period. This particular unit featured five young greats: trumpeter Freddie Hubbard, tenor-saxophonist Wayne Shorter, trombonist Curtis Fuller, pianist Cedar Walton and bassist Reggie Workman. On the CD reissue (which adds a pair of alternate takes to the original Lp program), the group is heard in prime form with the highlights including "Caravan," "Thermo" (two versions are included) and "Skylark." *—Scott Yanow*

Ugetsu / Jun. 16, 1963 / Riverside/OJC ♦♦♦♦
Art Blakey's 1963 Jazz Messengers (which included trumpeter Freddie Hubbard, tenor-saxophonist Wayne Shorter, trombonist Curtis Fuller, pianist Cedar Walton and bassist Reggie Workman in addition to the drummer-leader) was one of his finest. The CD reissue (which adds two songs to the seven on the original LP) has plenty of strong moments, particularly on "Ping-Pong," Shorter's feature ("I Didn't Know What Time It Was") and the memorable "One By One." This high-quality hard bop session is recommended. *—Scott Yanow*

A Jazz Message / Jul. 16, 1963 / Impulse! ♦♦♦

Free for All / Feb. 10, 1964 / Blue Note ♦♦♦♦
During most of 1961-64 Art Blakey's Jazz Messengers (except for bassist Reggie Workman replacing Spanky DeBrest) managed to keep the same personnel, a remarkable feat when one considers the strong talent (which included trumpeter Freddie Hubbard, trombonist Cur-

tis Fuller, Wayne Shorter on tenor and pianist Cedar Walton). *Free for All* was this particular group's last recording before Freddie Hubbard went out on his own, and it includes lengthy versions of two Shorter tunes, Hubbard's "The Core" and the standard "Pensativa." Fine music. *—Scott Yanow*

Kyoto / Feb. 20, 1964 / Riverside/OJC ♦♦♦
Reissued on Fantasy's OJC series, this album finds Art Blakey's Jazz Messengers paying tribute to Japan (where they had toured to great acclaim) on two selections, featuring Art Blakey's cousin as a vocalist on "Wellington's Blues" (a real rarity in The Jazz Messengers' discography) and debuting Curtis Fuller's "The High Priest." With trumpeter Freddie Hubbard, tenorman Wayne Shorter and trombonist Fuller in fine form, this is one of literally dozens of recommended Jazz Messengers recordings. *—Scott Yanow*

Indestructible / Apr. 24, 1964–May 15, 1964 / Blue Note ♦♦♦♦
In 1964, trumpeter Lee Morgan rejoined The Jazz Messengers, replacing his original replacement, Freddie Hubbard. The hard-swinging style of this influential unit remained unchanged with drummer/leader Art Blakey still insisting on distinctive solos and constant new material. Typically, the music on this fine LP consists of five then-recent compositions by bandmembers, one apiece from Morgan, pianist Cedar Walton ("When Love Is New") and tenor saxophonist Wayne Shorter and two from trombonist Curtis Fuller. Enjoyable music. *—Scott Yanow*

Keystone 3 / Jan. 1982 / Concord Jazz ♦♦♦♦♦

Coast to Coast / May 1984-Apr. 1985 / Concord Jazz ♦♦♦♦♦

☆ **The Complete Blue Note Recordings of Art Blakey's 1960 Messengers** / Mosaic ♦♦♦♦♦
Drummer Art Blakey led many great editions of The Jazz Messengers from the inaugural mid-'50s sessions until his death in the '90s. While arguments rage regarding which was his best, there is no doubt that the 1960-61 unit figures in the debate. This wonderful six-disc set, notated with care and painstaking detail by Bob Blumenthal, covers studio and live sessions from March 6, 1960 to May 27, 1961 with the same personnel on all but two songs. Producer Michael Cuscuna used only first issue dates, and while he included some alternate takes, he did not litter the discs with second-rate vault material. They smoothly detail the band's evolution, cohesion and maturation. This set, as with all Mosaic boxes, goes beyond essential. Get it post haste. *—Ron Wynn*

Terence Blanchard

b. Mar. 13, 1962, New Orleans, LA
Trumpet / Hard Bop, Post-Bop
Although he originally rose to prominence in the shadow of Wynton Marsalis, Terence Blanchard was one of the first Young Lions to develop his own sound, mixing in elements of Freddie Hubbard and Marsalis. He studied piano from the age of five and took up trumpet in 1976. Blanchard was with Lionel Hampton during 1980-82 and then replaced Marsalis with Art Blakey's Jazz Messengers. He found fame while with Blakey during 1982-86 and then co-led a group with Donald Harrison. After taking time off to work on his embouchure (and returning with a greatly increased range), Blanchard became active writing film scores for Spike Lee. He played in the films *Do the Right Thing* and *Mo' Better Blues* and then wrote for *Jungle Fever* and *Malcolm X*, launching a potentially lucrative second career. Fortunately Blanchard has not neglected his own playing and he has recorded several superior sets of advanced hard bop music. *—Scott Yanow*

Nascence / Jan. 28, 1986-Jan. 31, 1986 / Columbia ♦♦♦
This Columbia album was recorded shortly after trumpeter Terence Blanchard and altoist Donald Harrison left Art Blakey's Jazz Messengers to form their own group although it was their third recording project together co-leading a quintet. Pianist Mulgrew Miller, bassist Phil Bowler and drummer Ralph Peterson Jr. give the horns solid and stimulating support on two Blanchard pieces, three Harrison originals, "Alabama" and "She's Out Of My Life." Harrison has rarely sounded as advanced and as distinctive as he did in this group while Blanchard shows a great deal of potential that he later realized. *—Scott Yanow*

Eric Dolphy & Booker Little Remembered Live at Sweet Basil, Vol. 1 / Oct. 3, 1986-Oct. 4, 1986 / Evidence ♦♦♦♦
In memory of the great tandem of alto saxophonist/flutist/bass clarinetist Dolphy and trumpeter Little, Blanchard and Harrison team with the same rhythm section—Mal Waldron on piano, Richard Davis on bass, Ed Blackwell on drums—who backed those modern jazz pioneers, who played 25 years hence at *the Five Spot* (*The Great Concert of Eric Dolphy* on Prestige.) These sessions at *Sweet Basil*/NYC do great justice to that historic juncture while creating a little history of their own in the process. There are three lengthy selections. "The Prophet" is almost 22 minutes of the sheer joy and bluesy madness that so typified the Dolphy sound. The band captures a sourdough, bluesy swagger. Harrison's solo is less edgy but just as frantic as Dolphy's, while Blanchard is Blanchard, capturing the melodicism but not the bite of Little. Blackwell spontaneously doubles the time during the trumpeter's solo, settles it back, and then lets Waldron and Davis rest in a solid groove. "Aggression" is the highlight: a lightning fast, ribald-toned hard-bop line played perfectly. This is where Waldron's signature vamping comes to the forefront; his deep, blue-grey chords express his completely individual sound during the trio-only section. "Booker's Waltz" has Harrison switching to bass clarinet, with not quite the same childlike depth as Dolphy, and mixed a little thin. This is a beautiful, 3/4-paced song that ebbs and flows naturally, all members listening and responding in less dramatic ways. Despite eventual stylistic comparisons, which are truthfully minor, the intentions of this recording and its execution produce more than delightful results. It's a major coup for Blanchard and Harrison. Further proof is found on the companion disc *Fire Dance*. Recommended. *—Michael G. Nastos*

Crystal Stair / Apr. 1, 1987-Apr. 3, 1987 / Columbia ♦♦♦♦

Black Pearl / Jan. 22, 1988-Jan. 30, 1988 / Columbia ♦♦♦♦
The fifth and final recording by the Terence Blanchard-Donald Harrison Quintet uses the same notable rhythm section that was on their previous Crystal Stair release: pianist Cyrus Chestnut, bassist Reginald Veal, and drummer Carl Allen. In addition, two songs add vibraphonist Monte Croft and percussionist Steve Thornton while guitarist Mark Whitfield sits in on "Infinite Heart." With the exception of Leonard Bernstein's "Somewhere," the repertoire is split between compositions by the co-leaders. Harrison (who contributed tributes to two notable trumpeters, "Selim Sivad" and "Dizzy Gillespie's Hands") was heard at his best during his period with this group. All five of the Quintet's releases (two for the George Wein Collection on Concord and three for Columbia) are worth picking up for this was one of the most stimulating acoustic jazz groups of the mid- to late '80s. *—Scott Yanow*

The Malcolm X Jazz Suite / Dec. 10, 1992-Dec. 14, 1992 / Columbia ♦♦♦♦♦
Trumpeter Terence Blanchard continues to grow and develop with each year. He wrote the score for *Malcolm X* and this set finds him exploring 11 of his themes from the movie with his quintet (which also includes Sam Newsome on tenor, pianist Bruce Bath, bassist Tarus Matten and drummer Troy Davis). Many moods are explored and the fresh material really invigorates the quintet. Newsome's Trane-isms blend well with Blanchard (whose range has become quite impressive) and the performances (which easily stand apart from the film) are quite memorable. It's one of Terence Blachard's finest recordings. *—Scott Yanow*

The Heart Speaks / Aug. 28, 1995-Aug. 31, 1995 / Columbia ♦♦♦♦

Jazz in Film / Mar. 17, 1998-Apr. 7, 1998 / Columbia ♦♦♦♦

● **Wandering Moon** / 1999 / Columbia ♦♦♦♦♦
Trumpeter Blanchard has released some fine recordings in the '90s, but this one may be the best of them all, as he asserts himself as a composer of truly original modern jazz. He wrote seven selections, utilizing one or two of three saxophonists per cut—Branford Marsalis and Brice Winston (tenor) or Aaron Fletcher (alto). It's the rhythm section that boils this pot over; bassist David Holland and especially pianist Edward Simon are *en fuego*, while young drummer Eric Harland continues to show steady progress en route to becoming a first-rate trappist.

The first piece, "Luna Viajera," harkens back to the composition "Black Pearl." It's a dark, tick-tock, well-after-hours siren's song, with Fletcher and Winston crying uncle for romantic mercy. A patented, masterful bass solo from Holland intros "My Only Thought of You," an easy waltz with moaning, clarion horns by the leader and Marsalis, with a tick-tock beat going back to 3/4 informing the tenorman's solo. Three later numbers feature Winston: the very slow ballad "Sweet's Dream" has a lonely trumpet line from Blanchard; "Sidney" metamorphoses "End of a Love Affair" snippets into a completely new tune; while Simon's lone composition "The Process" is a deep midnight-blue waltz. The 11-minute "Joe & O" has steadily swung, introspective fragments of hip melody strewn throughout from Blanchard and Marsalis, while the resolute token standard finale "I Thought About You" is a languid blues-drizzled ballad for only the leader and his astute trio.

Sparks fly, and unrequited moods coalesce during this prismatic epic of emotions, swing, and truly new mainstream jazz from Blanchard and his cohorts. It comes highly recommended, and is a strong candidate for Jazz CD of Y2K. *—Michael G. Nastos*

Carla Bley (Carla Borg)

b. May 11, 1938, Oakland, CA
Piano, Organ, Composer / Avant-Garde Jazz, Post-Bop, Progressive Big Band
Post-bop jazz has produced only a few first-rate composers of larger forms; Carla Bley ranks high amongst them. Bley possesses an unusually wide compositional range; she combines an acquaintance with and love for jazz in all its forms with great talent and originality. Her music is a peculiarly individual type of hyper-modern jazz. Bley is capable of writing music of great drama and profound humor, often within the confines of the same piece. As an instrumentalist, Bley makes a fine composer; she plays piano and/or organ with most of her bands, and while her playing is always quite musical, it's clear that her strengths lie elsewhere. Bley's asymmetrical compositional structures subvert jazz formula to wonderful effect, and her unpredictable melodies are often as catchy as they are obscure. In the tradition of jazz's very finest composers and improvisers, Bley has developed a style of her very own, and the music as a whole is the better for it. *—Chris Kelsey*

Escalator over the Hill / Nov. 1968-Jun. 1971 / ECM ♦♦♦

● **Tropic Appetites** / Sep. 1973-Feb. 1974 / ECM ♦♦♦♦♦
Following their superb "chronotransduction," *Escalator Over the Hill*, composer Carla Bley and poet Paul Haines once again teamed up for *Tropic Appetites*, a somewhat different, but equally compelling effort. The instrumentation is scaled down to an octet and the lyrics revolve around trips to Southeast Asia, particularly Bali, made by Haines over the preceding years. Bley makes an inspired choice for lead vocalist by enlisting the extraordinary Julie Tippetts who had attained rock stardom in the late '60s (as Julie Driscoll) in Brian Auger's Trinity.

After a powerful introductory "overture" led by the still incendiary Gato Barbieri who, for contractual reasons, is referred to in the credits as "Unidentified Cat," the hothouse atmosphere of the recording is established by the next song, "In India," with its humid, surreal lyrics. Bley consistently provides rich, imaginative, and varied underpinnings for Tippett's crystalline vocal work. From the ferocious and angry "Enormous Tots" to the yearning "Caucasian Bird Riffles" to the delightful singsong "Funnybird Song" featuring priceless vocals from Howard Johnson and Bley's very young daughter Karen Mantler (who would go on to a career of her own), the music is strong and memorable throughout.

All of the musicians are in top form, but special mention should be made of the dream rhythm team of David Holland and Paul Motian. Their tonal colors and supple interplay is a major factor of the success of this album. *Tropic Appetites* is one of Carla Bley's greatest successes; one could only wish that she had continued in this vein rather than opting for the jazz-funk bands she led from 1980 forward. *—Brian Olewnick*

Dinner Music / Jul. 1976-Sep. 1976 / ECM ♦♦♦♦♦
First excursion on a funky trail, executed immaculately. Near essential. *—Michael G. Nastos*

European Tour (1977) / Sep. 1977 / Watt ♦♦♦♦♦

One of Carla Bley's most rewarding recordings, this set features her tentet playing such numbers as "Wrong Key Donkey," "Drinking Music" and the 19-minute "Spangled Banner Minor and Other Patriotic Songs." Bley's wry humor is often felt and she utilizes such colorful players as trumpeter Michael Mantler, Gary Windo on tenor, trombonist Roswell Rudd and Bob Stewart on tuba in this unusual, somewhat innovative and always fun music. *—Scott Yanow*

Musique Mecanique / Aug. 1978-Nov. 1978 / Watt ♦♦♦♦

Social Studies / Sep. 1980-Dec. 1980 / ECM ♦♦♦♦♦

Fleur Carnivore / Nov. 14, 1988-Nov. 16, 1988 / ECM ♦♦♦♦♦
On *Fleur Carnivore,* pianist Carla Bley deftly integrates her beautiful melodies into five complex, yet effortless sounding pieces. Taken from 1988 live dates at Copenhagen's *Montmartre* club, *Carnivore* spotlights Bley's very accomplished big band, which includes, amongst several others, trumpeter Lew Soloff, alto saxophonist Wolfgang Pusching, trombonist Gary Valente, tenor saxophonist Andy Sheppard, and organist/harmonica player Karen Mantler (Bley's daughter). The title track is a romantically bittersweet ballad swinger, which includes impassioned solos from Pusching and Soloff, while, in nice contrast, there's the buoyant, Latin-tinged "Song of the Eternal Waiting of Canute," featuring rousing solos by Valente and tenor saxophonist Christof Lauer. In addition to these extended pieces, there is the suite composition, "The Girl Who Cried Champagne (Parts 1/2/3)." This breezily swinging bossa nova features meaty tenor work from Sheppard and a minimalist harmonic solo by Mantler. Rounding out the set are the whimsical "Ups and Downs" and the gospel R&B tune "Healing Power." Combining surprising arrangements and pop song melodies, Bley creates a unique jazz language, setting herself apart from both traditionalist bandleaders (Wynton Marsalis, Thad Jones) and more avant-garde stylists (Muhal Richard Abrams, George Russell). *Fleur Carnivore* is one of Bley's best titles and good place to start for newcomers. *—Stephen Cook*

Carla Bley Big Band Goes to Church / Jul. 19, 1996-Jul. 21, 1996 / ECM ♦♦♦♦♦
This unusual set (recorded live in Italy) features Carla Bley's 17-piece big band playing a set of her originals that hint at times at church hymns without getting particularly somber. Most memorable is the complex "Beads," but all of the music is full of colorful surprises and often rambunctious solos; the nearly 24-minute "Setting Calvin's Waltz" is episodic and frequently fascinating. The key soloists include tenor saxophonist Andy Sheppard, trumpeter Lew Soloff, altoist Wolfgang Puschnig and the extroverted trombonist Gary Valente, while the ensembles are both loose and tight. One of Carla Bley's finest recordings of the 1990s. *—Scott Yanow*

Fancy Chamber Music / Dec. 5, 1997-Dec. 6, 1997 / ECM ♦♦♦♦

Are We There Yet— / Oct. 1998 / ECM ♦♦♦♦
Carla Bley and Steve Swallow's third outing as a duo captures them live on their 1998 European tour sounding fabulous. Three of the seven tunes are by Bley: "Major," an infectious triadic shell game; "King Korn," a whimsical run through rhythm changes in the keys of E flat and C; and "Musique Mecanique," an ambitious three-part suite adapted from Bley's 1978 album of the same name. Three other compositions are by Swallow: "A Dog's Life," a Ray Charles-style tune in a slow 6/8; "Satie for Two," an affecting tribute to the minimalist composer; and "Playing With Water," a bossa nova previously performed by Swallow's 1991 sextet. The only non-original of the set is Kurt Weill's ballad "Lost in the Stars," which Bley and Swallow play beautifully.

Bley's piano is remarkably versatile and passionate, and Swallow's signature electric bass sound tickles the senses, especially during the Weill song where one moment he makes the room vibrate with low notes, and the next reaches the stratosphere of his range with singing melodies. *—David R. Adler*

Paul Bley

b. Nov. 10, 1932, Montreal, Quebec, Canada
Keyboards, Piano / Avant-Garde Jazz, Free Jazz, Avant-Garde
Paul Bley has long offered avant-garde pianists an alternative approach to improvising than that of Cecil Taylor. Bley has been able to use melody and space in inventive ways while performing fairly free improvisations. After recording for Charles Mingus' Debut label in 1953, he moved to New York. Following a stint with Jackie McLean's quintet, he relocated to Los Angeles. Bley played with Chet Baker and then in 1958 played at the Hillcrest with musicians who would soon form the Ornette Coleman Quartet: Coleman, Don Cherry, Charlie Haden and Billy Higgins. Married to the talented up-and-coming pianist/composer Carla Bley, Paul Bley spent much of 1963 with Sonny Rollins' group. He participated in the famous October Revolution in Jazz in 1964 and was a founding member of the Jazz Composers Guild. He recorded frequently with his trios, for a few years experimented with electronics with his second wife Annette Peacock, and then in 1974 founded his Improvising Artists label. A key link between Bill Evans and Keith Jarrett, Bley's adventurous yet thoughtful playing sounds like no one else. *—Scott Yanow*

Improvisations: Introducing Paul Bley / Nov. 30, 1953 / Debut/OJC ♦♦♦
Pianist Paul Bley's debut as a leader features the 21-year old in a trio with bassist Charles Mingus and drummer Art Blakey for Mingus' Debut label. The CD reissue, which adds four performances to the original program, finds Bley developing his voice within the bebop tradition. Mixing together stimulating originals such as "Opus 1" and "Spontaneous Combustion" with a few standards, Horace Silver's "Split Kick" and a surprisingly effective version of "Santa Claus Is Coming To Town," Paul Bley may not have been distinctive this early on but he clearly had a potentially strong future. *—Scott Yanow*

Live at the Hillcrest Club (1958) / Oct. 1958 / Inner City ♦♦♦♦
This out of print LP is quite valuable, for it features altoist Ornette Coleman live in concert shortly after making his first studio sessions. Musicians from what would be the Coleman Quartet (with trumpeter Don Cherry, bassist Charlie Haden, and drummer Billy Higgins) are heard at a live gig in Los Angeles under the leadership of pianist Paul Bley. Bley's piano is mostly pretty sparse, and Coleman is the dominant force, particularly on his melodic "The Blessing" and the well-titled "Free." It is particularly interesting to hear Coleman and Cherry improvising freely on Charlie Parker's "Klactoveesedstene" and Roy Eldridge's "I Remember Harlem." The recording quality is decent for the period, and avant-garde collectors will want to search for this pioneering effort. *—Scott Yanow*

Barrage / Oct. 20, 1964 / ESP ♦♦♦♦
Pianist Paul Bley's early ESP free jazz session combines the influence of the Jazz Composer's Guild with Ornette Coleman. On *Barrage,* Bley is joined by alto saxophonist Marshall Allen (in one of his few appearances outside of Sun Ra's Arkestra), trumpeter Dewey Johnson (who would go on to play on Coltrane's *Ascension* the following year), Eddie Gomez on bass, and Milford Graves taking care of percussion. All compositions are by Bley's former wife, Carla Bley, with a definite nod to Coleman's hyperactive stop-start punctuation (Paul Bley had fronted one of the earliest incarnations of the original Coleman quartet). Graves and Allen are especially irrepressible here, making *Barrage* a lost free jazz classic. *—Al Campbell*

● **Open, to Love** / Sep. 11, 1972 / ECM ♦♦♦♦♦
This set is one of Paul Bley's finest solo outings which, considering how often he has recorded during the past 30 years, is really saying something. His rendition of "Ida Lupino" is classic and his other interpretations (of originals by Carla Bley and Annette Peacock in addition to his own "Harlem") are close to definitive. Loose yet logical, these piano solos (which make expert use of space) always hold one's interest. *—Scott Yanow*

Paul Bley Quartet / Nov. 1987 / ECM ♦♦♦♦♦
Paul Bley Quartet. One of his stronger groups. John Surman (sax) and Bill Frisell (g) especially sharp. *—Ron Wynn*

Plays Carla Bley / Dec. 1991 / Steeplechase ♦♦♦♦
Most of Carla Bley's earliest compositions were first recorded by her then-husband, pianist Paul Bley, during the first half of the 1960s. For this 1991 trio date with bassist Marc Johnson and drummer Jeff Williams, Bley revisits ten of his former wife's songs, most of which date from the early era. While "Ida Lupino" has been explored in more definitive fashion by Bley elsewhere, his versions of such songs as "Vashkar," "Seven," "Turns" and "Ictus" work quite well. The music falls somewhere between advanced bop and the avant-garde, often swinging but with surprising turns and twists and often-unusual chord sequences. An intriguing set. *—Scott Yanow*

Chaos / Mar. 28, 1994-Mar. 29, 1994 / Soul Note ♦♦♦♦♦
This is a fascinating set. Although the instrumentation (pianist Paul Bley, bassist Furio Di-Castri and Tony Oxley on drums and percussion) may lead one to expect a conventional piano trio, in reality the 13 selections consist of four drum solos, one unaccompanied bass piece, two piano solos, a piano-drums duet and just five trio numbers. Bley's use of space and dynamics gave free jazz pianists in the 1960s an alternative approach to Cecil Taylor; here he sounds quite creative and his opening "Chaos" is a near-classic. DiCastri, who is very inventive on his unaccompanied "Touching Bass," is intuitive and displays a huge tone. However, it is Oxley who often steals one's attention. His wide array of equipment makes one think that he raided a junkyard, and his four solos are full of color rather than technique, surprises rather than swing. While many drum/percussion solos lose a great deal when the visual element is not present, Tony Oxley's transfer very well to disc. This set of concise free improvisations is highly recommended to open-minded listeners. *—Scott Yanow*

Not Two, Not One / Jan. 1998 / ECM ♦♦♦♦
Like a good wine, Paul Bley seems only to improve with age. Re-united with bassist Gary Peacock and percussionist Paul Motian (their last recording together for ECM was made more than two decades earlier), the trio revisits the quirky "Fig Foot," and explores colors, moods, and even a touch of blues on a set of all original compositions. Bley is especially effective exploring the lower sonorities, while Peacock's full-sounding bass throbs with joy. Motian is characteristically exquisite, his soft, layered, sensitive strokes prodding his colleagues. None of the pieces drift, as these three masters contribute a mature perspective that comes from varied experience. Remarkable interplay, chamber-free harmonies, and loose improvisations add up to some special sounds. *—Steven Loewy*

Hamiet Bluiett

b. Sep. 16, 1940, Lovejoy, IL
Sax (Baritone) / Avant-Garde Jazz
The most prominent baritone saxophonist of his generation, Hamiet Bluiett combines a blunt, modestly inflected attack with a fleet, aggressive technique, and (maybe most importantly) a uniform hugeness of sound that extends from his horn's lowest reaches to far beyond what is usually its highest register. Probably no other baritonist has played so high, with so much control. His technical mastery aside, Bluiett's solo voice is unlikely to be confused with any other. Enamored with the blues, brusque and awkwardly swinging—in his high-energy playing, Bluiett makes a virtue out of tactlessness; on ballads, he assumes a considerably more lush, romantic guise. Like his longtime collaborator, tenor saxophonist David Murray, Bluiett incorporates a great deal of conventional bebop into his free playing. In truth, Bluiett's music is not free jazz at all, but rather a plain-spoken extension of the mainstream tradition. After playing sideman roles with Lester Bowie, Sam Rivers and Charles Mingus, in 1976 he recorded the material that would comprise his first two albums as a leader, *Endangered Species* and *Birthright.* Later that year, he began performing with Murray, Oliver Lake, and Julius Hemphill as the World Saxophone Quartet, which in the '80s became arguably the most popular free jazz band ever. Bluiett continued lead his own ensembles and recorded a number of strong albums for Black Saint/Soul Note. By the mid-'90s, Bluiett was recording for Mapleshade. *—Chris Kelsey*

Ebu / Feb. 1, 1984-Feb. 13, 1984 / Soul Note ♦♦♦
As a founding member of the World Saxophone Quartet, baritone saxophonist Hamiet Bluiett acquired a well-deserved reputation as an avant-gardist. However, as this album proved in 1984 (and others have proven countless times since), his talents also run to the more conventional. Though Ebu has a taste of the arcane, it is mostly a collection of relatively straigh-

tahead Bluiett-penned blowing vehicles done with fire and invention. Bluiett has the biggest sound in town; his phrasing and articulation is a little heavy, as one would expect, but he plays with a strength and conviction that's rarely equalled by other baritonists. And, of course, he has an immediately identifiable style. His band—John Hicks, piano; Fred Hopkins, bass; Marvin "Smitty" Smith, drums—is well-attentive to the music's needs, and ambitious enough to take it to places not commonly explored. An interesting album, given the perspective of the years that have passed since it was made. It's very straightahead; however, it's wildly different from the mannered product that's usually presented as mainstream jazz in the late '90s. This music has a manifest unruliness, a spirit of adventure; it leaps outrageously into the unknown and usually lands square on its feet—unlike it's contemporary equivalent, which can rarely be bothered to scuff it's polished Gucci loafers. If jazz remains content to continually re-examine its past, this would be a great place to revisit. *—Chris Kelsey*

Live at Carlos I / 1986 / Just a Memory ♦♦♦

• **Young Warrior, Old Warrior** / Mar. 1, 1995-Mar. 3, 1995 / Mapleshade ♦♦♦♦

Live at the Knitting Factory / Jun. 1997 / Knitting Factory ♦♦♦♦♦

Same Space / Jul. 20, 1997-Jul. 21, 1997 / Justin Time ♦♦♦♦♦

Baritone saxophonist and World Saxophone Quartet cofounder Hamiet Bluiett teamed up with Canadian-born, Brooklyn-based pianist D.D. Jackson and Senegalese percussion master Mor Thiam to create *Same Space*, their first release for the Canadian label Justin Time. This is an exciting but surprisingly accessible trek through a fusion of jazz/world originals. Accessibility is not normally associated with the music of Bluiett or Jackson, which typically leans toward the avant-garde. However, pigeonholing these musicians is a mistake, as apparent on Thiam's opening infectious African groove "Aseeko" followed by Jackson's gospelized ballad "Closing Melody." Bluiett's contributions are powerful but not dominating—he is more prone to step back and let his cohorts exceed while the organized unrest of his baritone, bass clarinet, and wood flute weave in and out of the proceedings. The centerpiece to these sessions is the diversity and strength of material split between Jackson and Thiam. *Same Space* also serves as a tribute to the late pianist Don Pullen. Thiam was a member of Don Pullen & the African-Brazilian Connection; in fact, all three musicians played with Pullen, and Jackson was his protégé. The influence of Pullen and the combination of these artists' diverse backgrounds fuse to create a uniquely versatile music style. *—Al Campbell*

Arthur Blythe (Arthur Murray Blythe)

b. Jul. 5, 1940, Los Angeles, CA

Sax (Alto) / Avant-Garde Jazz, Post-Bop

For a time in the late '70s and early '80s, it seemed as if jazz's avant-garde was on the verge of a popular breakthrough in the person and music of Arthur Blythe. Blythe was signed by Columbia Records; the label's hype-heavy promotion of the saxophonist almost made him a star. It didn't work; Blythe was too "out" for the masses. Columbia realized that it had made a mistake by expecting too much of the public, and threw its promotional weight behind a more malleable, less threatening young prince by the name of Wynton Marsalis. He was no young lion—Blythe was 37 years old when his first records, *The Grip* and *Metamorphosis*, were released. By then, he was a fully developed, mature artist, a free-influenced player who was also capable of playing older styles in an utterly personal and borderline iconoclastic way. When Blythe played a standard, he imbued it with all that had happened in jazz since it was written, up to and including the free techniques that were integral to his concept; one can hear traces of his predecessors, but as an affectionate remembrance, not an affectation. Blythe's style varied mostly in the form of his contexts. He possesses one of the most easily recognizable alto sax sounds in jazz—big and round, with a fast, wide vibrato and an aggressive, precise manner of phrasing. His lines are frequently quite baroque and always well-defined; Blythe's playing has been criticized (unfairly, some would say) as being overly ornamental, but he is certainly capable of improvising melodies of great character and originality. *—Chris Kelsey*

Bush Baby / Dec. 1977 / Adelphi ♦♦♦

During this outstanding and challenging recital, altoist Arthur Blythe (who at the time went by the title of "Black Arthur") stretches out on four originals in a sparse trio with Bob Stewart on tuba and Ahkmed Abdullah on conga. Blythe had an original sound from the start and his soulful yet adventurous and intense style is heard in its early prime on what was his second recording session as a leader, cut just before he was surprisingly signed to Columbia. *—Scott Yanow*

Lenox Avenue Breakdown / 1978 / Koch Jazz ♦♦♦♦

The signing of Arthur Blythe to Columbia in 1978 received a great deal of attention. Fortunately, the adventurous altoist was able to record for that giant label for a few years without being pressured to water down his sound or his music. This set matchs Blythe with such talents as flutist James Newton, guitarist James "Blood" Ulmer, bassist Cecil McBee, drummer Jack DeJohnette, tuba player Bob Stewart and percussionist Guillermo Franco; no weak spots to this group. The band performs four of Blythe's diverse originals with creativity and a strong bluesy feeling. *—Scott Yanow*

In the Tradition / Oct. 1978 / Columbia ♦♦♦♦♦

Sometimes the easiest way to get "in" to someone's music is to see how they handle standards. Altoist Arthur Blythe, who—although he has been associated somewhat with the avant-garde—does not fit easily into any category, is heard on this 1978 studio session exploring four veteran songs plus two of his originals. The instrumentation of his quartet is conventional but the musicianship is exceptionally high (pianist Stanley Cowell, bassist Fred Hopkins, and drummer Steve McCall), and it is quite interesting to hear how they stretch such songs as "In a Sentimental Mood," "Jitterbug Waltz," and "Caravan," making them sound fresh and original. *—Scott Yanow*

Illusions / Apr. 1980-May 1980 / Koch Jazz ♦♦♦♦

It is surprising how artistically productive altoist Arthur Blythe was during his period on Columbia. Despite the hype and Columbia's reputation for pressuring artists to play mass-appeal music, Blythe's recordings for that label are inventive and creative. For this, his third Columbia release, Blythe uses two different groups: an "in the tradition" quartet with pianist John Hicks, bassist Fred Hopkins, and drummer Steve McCall, and a more eccentric unit with guitarist James Blood Ulmer, cellist Abdul Wadud, tuba player Bob Stewart, and drummer Bobby Battle. No matter the setting, the distinctive alto of Blythe is heard in top form on six of his unusual originals. It's recommended. *—Scott Yanow*

Light Blue: Arthur Blythe Plays Thelonious Monk / Jan. 27, 1983 / Columbia ♦♦♦

Altoist Arthur Blythe and his unique quintet (comprised of guitarist Kelvyn Bell, cellist Abdul Wadud, Bob Stewart on tuba and drummer Bobby Battle) perform six underplayed Thelonious Monk songs ("We See," "Light Blue," "Off Minor," "Epistrophy," "Coming On The Hudson" and "Nutty") and these creative players (and the unusual instrumentation) put a fresh slant on Monk's music. Blythe's passionate sound throughout this inspired set is consistently memorable. *—Scott Yanow*

• **Retroflection** / Jun. 25, 1993-Jun. 26, 1993 / Enja ♦♦♦♦♦

Arthur Blythe, whose alto tone has been quite original ever since the start of his career, is joined by pianist John Hicks, bassist Cecil McBee and drummer Bobby Battle on this superior quartet date from Enja. Blythe really stretches out at this "Live at the Village Vanguard" set, with six of the seven songs being over nine minutes long. "Jana's Delight" (which is based on a five-note pattern), "JB Blues," a remake of Blythe's "Lenox Avenue Breakdown" and one of the best versions ever of Thelonious Monk's "Light Blue" are the highpoints of the explorative program. Arthur Blythe fans are strongly advised to pick up this particularly strong effort. *—Scott Yanow*

Spirits in the Field / Jun. 24, 1999 / Savant ♦♦♦

Claude Bolling

b. Apr. 10, 1930, Cannes, France

Piano / Swing, Big Band

Claude Bolling has found his greatest fame in the U.S. for his jazzy classical collaborations with Jean-Pierre Rampal, Maurice Andre, Elena Duran and Yo Yo Ma while in Europe he is best-known as the leader of various swing big bands. Bolling formed his first group when he was 14 in 1944. In 1948 he recorded with Rex Stewart and accompanied blues singer Chippie Hill at a jazz festival. Bolling also recorded with Roy Eldridge (1951) and Lionel Hampton (1953 and 1956), led big bands since the 1950s and recorded ragtime, tributes to Duke Ellington and his own original music. Although not an innovator, Claude Bolling has been an important fixture in the French jazz scene since the 1950s. *—Scott Yanow*

• **Suite for Flute and Jazz Piano Trio** / 1975 / Milan ♦♦♦♦

This was a very popular album of jazz/classical fusion. *—Myles Boisen*

Concerto for Classical Guitar & Jazz Piano / 1975-1982 / Milan ♦♦♦♦♦

With the success of his *Suite for Flute and Jazz Piano Trio*, Claude Bolling had stumbled upon a cottage industry: round up a willing classical soloist regardless of instrument, let him be himself, insert a piano part that plays ambassador between the classical and jazz camps, and voila! a neat little crossover record. *The Guitar Concerto* is one of the best manifestations of Bolling's personal solution to the perennial Third Stream puzzle, incorporating Spanish ideas into the guitar part, moving his piano in and out of the jazz rhythms with an easy Continental elegance, coming up with attractive pastiche tunes in the baroque and classical idioms. The 5/4 theme and guitar/piano juxtapositions of "Hispanic Dance" remind one of Dave Brubeck's famous experiments in odd meters, and "Serenade" makes delicious use of a bossa nova groove. The Greek/Italian classical guitarist Alexander Lagoya is the sharp-edged soloist; Bolling is equally at home in both stylistic camps (though the piano is sometimes a wee bit out of tune), and Michel Gaudry (bass) and Marcel Sabiani (drums) make up the rhythm section. Note: the first version of this performance, released on RCA in 1976, contains the six-movement edition of the *Concerto;* Bolling later added a seventh movement that was tacked onto this recording when CBS reissued it in 1982. Also, the Finale features a different rhythm section (Marc Michel, bass; André Arpino, drums). *—Richard S. Ginell*

Suite for Violin and Jazz Piano / 1977 / Milan ♦♦♦♦

Now besieged with requests for classical/jazz "suites" for himself and big-time classical performers, Bolling took up violinist Pinchas Zukerman's commission, and out came another attractive confection that allows a classical cat to play quasi-jazzman for a day. This time, Bolling chooses mostly classical dance forms for his eight movements, still inserting mostly mainstream jazz segments (and a few vintage ones) around and under his soloist without getting him involved. Although he isn't asked to play jazz, Zukerman's warm, Romantic-era-grounded virtuosity doesn't betray even a hint of feeling for it; that makes Bolling's close-knit merger even more remarkable. On "Tango," the compulsively restless Zukerman switches to viola; elsewhere he sticks to the violin. Max Hediguer (bass) and Marcel Sabiani (drums) provide the propulsive rhythm in chosen spots, and Bolling still manages to swing hard even when playing underneath the square, heavy Zukerman tone. *—Richard S. Ginell*

Jazz Brunch / Oct. 1984-Apr. 1985 / CBS ♦♦♦♦

In the 1984-85 Parisian concert season, the big band of Claude Bolling held court in the expansive lounge of L'Hotel Méridien in a series of "jazz brunches"; from the evidence of this live recording, they must have been splendidly high-spirited affairs. Though colored by the Ellington and New Testament Basie manners of swinging and voicing, Bolling's band still has a perceivable, clearly etched Continental flavor that gives this music its own signature. Bolling's ten fingers are in an unquenchably swinging mode on his "Canonette" and Ernie Wilkins' "Sixteen Men Swingin'"; Annette Lowman provides sassy vocals (in English, fortunately) on five of the eleven tracks, scatting up a storm on "Cotton Tail." The centerpiece of the disc is a remarkably coherent, 20-minute, three-part suite for Basie, "From CB to CB With Love," that seamlessly merges various Basie arrangers' trademarks within the lighter Bolling sound. Though technically this is music out of its time and place, more often than not, this band could achieve liftoff. *—Richard S. Ginell*

Bolling's Greatest Hits / 1975- 198 / Columbia ✦✦✦✦
CBS attempts to summarize Claude Bolling's voluminous output of classical/jazz suites with this single disc of excerpts from eight of them. All of the CBS issues up to 1987 except *Suite For Chamber Orchestra and Jazz Piano Trio* are represented; the list of classical collaborators is impressive—Jean-Pierre Rampal, Maurice André, Alexandre Lagoya, Yo-Yo Ma, Pinchas Zukerman. Along with Bolling's changing French rhythm sections, we also hear from American jazzmen like Hubert Laws, Bud Shank, Chuck Domanico and Shelly Manne. While CBS' mad programmer manages to choose the best cut on the *Cello Suite* ("Baroque In Rhythm"), the most famous numbers on the *First Suite* ("Baroque and Blue," "Sentimentale") and the most astonishing piece in the *Second Suite* ("Jazzy"), the *Toot Suite* is poorly represented by "Mystique" and "Rag-Polka." Yet this disc will give you the basic idea about Bolling's likable mergers of idioms, and casual browsers may not need anything else. —*Richard S. Ginell*

A Tribute to Duke Ellington / Jan. 19893-198 / Milan ✦✦✦
After meeting Duke Ellington in 1950 and working with him for the first time in 1962 on a production of *A Drum is a Woman*, bandleader Claude Bolling has consistently paid homage to Ellington. His allegiance continues with *Tribute to Duke Ellington*, a double CD set that includes Bolling's live recordings of "Black, Brown & Beige" and "A Drum Is A Woman" among other tracks, spanning Ellington's career. Bolling's reputation as a stylish, thoughtful bandleader is reinforced with this classy, heartfelt tribute. —*Heather Phares*

Earl Bostic

b. Apr. 25, 1913, Tulsa, OK, **d.** Oct. 28, 1965, Rochester, NY
Sax (Alto) / Soul-Jazz, R&B
Earl Bostic's roots and foundation were steeped in jazz and swing, but he later became one of the most prolific R&B bandleaders. His searing, sometimes bluesy, sometimes soft and moving, alto-sax style influenced many players, including John Coltrane. His many King releases, which featured limited soloing and basic melodic and rhythmic movements, might have fooled novices into thinking Bostic possessed minimal skills; but Art Blakey once said, "Nobody knew more about the saxophone than Bostic, I mean technically, and that includes Bird." A soloist in the bands of Don Redman, Edgar Hayes, and Lionel Hampton, Bostic also led his own combos, whose members included Jimmy Cobb, Al Casey, Blue Mitchell, Stanley Turrentine, Benny Golson and Coltrane. Bostic toured extensively through the '50s, while cutting numerous sessions for King. His recording of "Flamingo" in 1951 was a huge hit, as were the songs "Sleep," "You Go to My Head," "Cherokee," and "Temptation." Bostic recorded for Allegro, Gotham and King from the late '40s to the mid-'60s. He made more than 400 selections for King; his mid-'60s albums were more soul-jazz than R&B. —*Ron Wynn and Michael Erlewine*

☆ **That's Earl, Brother** / 1943-Dec. 1945 / Spotlite ✦✦✦✦✦
Earl Bostic was one of the most technically gifted of all saxophonists, having complete control of his alto including a huge range. Because he became famous for his R&B hits of the 1950s, Bostic has tended to be underrated in jazz circles, but this set from the British Spotlite label shows how powerfully he could play in swing settings. Bostic is featured on four rare numbers apiece with Lionel Hampton's big band (broadcasts from 1943-1944), a studio set with an octet headed by cornetist Rex Stewart in 1945, and with his own ensemble in concert in late 1945; the latter numbers are the earliest documented examples of Bostic leading a band. This set is highly recommended to swing and bop collectors and even to fans of R&B; Bostic's brilliant playing crossed many musical boundaries. —*Scott Yanow*

● **All His Hits** / Jul. ??, 1946-Jul. 17, 1964 / King ✦✦✦✦
This definitive recording is not entirely made of altoist Earl Bostic's "hits"; in fact, "Arrivederci Roma" was never previously released. However, virtually all of Bostic's best-selling numbers are here, including the two-part "That's the Groovy Thing," "Flamingo," "Sleep," and "845 Stomp," plus later tunes taken from albums. 1964's "Walk on the Wild Side" is from Bostic's final King record, cut a year before his death. Listeners wanting to be introduced to Earl Bostic's popular R&B-ish music cannot do better than picking up this album. —*Scott Yanow*

The Best of Earl Bostic / 1951-1956 / King ✦✦✦✦
A nice cross-section of this fiery alto-saxist's '50s output, it includes his hits "Sleep" and "Flamingo." —*Bill Dahl*

Dance Time / 1957 / King ✦✦✦✦✦
These are mostly uptempo instrumental R&B, pop, and dance/novelty tunes delivered with style and flair by the great Earl Bostic. He was among the finest honking saxophonists, and King kept pumping out collections of his singles throughout the '50s. —*Ron Wynn*

Let's Dance with Earl Bostic / 1957 / King ✦✦✦

Lester Bowie

b. Oct. 11, 1941, Frederick, MD, **d.** Nov. 8, 1999
Multi Instruments, Flugelhorn, Trumpet / Avant-Garde Jazz, Free Jazz
From the 1970s on, Lester Bowie has been the preeminent trumpeter of the jazz avant-garde—one of the few trumpet players of his generation to successfully and completely adopt the techniques of free jazz. Indeed, Bowie has been the most successful in translating the expressive demands of the music—so well-suited to the tonally pliant saxophone—to the more difficult-to-manipulate brass instrument. Like a saxophonist such as David Murray or Eric Dolphy, Bowie invests his sound with a variety of timbral effects; his work has a more vocal quality, compared with that of most contemporary trumpeters. In a sense, he's a throwback to the pre-modern jazz of Cootie Williams or Bubber Miley, though Bowie is by no means a revivalist. Though he's certainly not afraid to appropriate the growls, whinnies, slurs, and slides of the early jazzers, it's always in the service of a thoroughly modern sensibility. And Bowie has chops; his style is quirky, to be sure, but grounded in fundamental jazz concepts of melody, harmony, and rhythm. —*Chris Kelsey*

Numbers 1 & 2 / Aug. 11, 1967–Aug. 25, 1967 / Nessa ✦✦✦
The music on this LP has been reissued in Nessa's limited edition multi-CD box set which traces the beginnings of the Art Ensemble of Chicago. Trumpeter Bowie meets up with bassist Malachi Favors and Roscoe Mitchell, who is heard on alto, soprano, flute, clarinet and miscellaneous instruments; Joseph Jarman joins the trio on the second selection, playing alto, soprano, clarinet, bassoon and bells. The pretty spontaneous music often wanders and rambles a bit, reaching some surprising conclusions and showing expert use of space; very advanced for 1967. —*Scott Yanow*

The 5th Power / Apr. 12, 1978–Apr. 17, 1978 / Black Saint ✦✦✦✦
1978 quintet with Arthur Blythe (as), Amina Myers (p). Creative jazz and a progressive gospel segment. Bowie at his eclectic best. Essential. —*Michael G. Nastos*

★ **The Great Pretender** / Jun. 1981 / ECM ✦✦✦✦✦
This is one of trumpeter Lester Bowie's most accessible albums; certainly his brief versions of "It's Howdy Doody Time" and "When the Moon Comes over the Mountain" are not difficult to understand. But actually the bulk of this album is taken up with the 16-minute title cut and a variety of Bowie's colorful originals. The highly expressive trumpeter is mostly heard with a quartet (although "The Great Pretender" also adds two vocalists and baritonist Hamiet Bluiett) and this set offers many fine examples of his original approach to making music, technically avant-garde but also borrowing aspects of earlier styles in unusual combinations. —*Scott Yanow*

All the Magic! / Jun. 1982 / ECM ✦✦✦
Two very different sessions are combined on this two-LP set. Trumpeter Lester Bowie and a quintet also including Ari Brown on tenor and soprano, pianist Art Matthews, bassist Fred Williams, and drummer Phillip Wilson, are often used to accompany the soulful and gospel-oriented vocals of Fontella Bass and David Peaston (in addition to taking colorful solos). The 12-minute "For Louie" and a suite that is dominated by an emotional version of "Everything Must Change" are highlights; also memorable is a brief version of Albert Ayler's "Ghosts." The second album is quite a bit different, a set of unaccompanied trumpet solos by Bowie that are often quite humorous. On "Miles Davis Meets Donald Duck," the meeting does seem to take place; "Thirsty—" is a funny joke, and some of the other pieces (including "Organic Echo," "Dunce Dance" and "Fraudulent Fanfare") are brief but effective wisecracks. All in all, this two-fer shows off both Lester Bowie's playing abilities and his sense of humor. —*Scott Yanow*

The Organizer / Jan. 14, 1991-Jan. 16, 1991 / DIW ✦✦✦
Trumpeter Lester Bowie grew up in St. Louis with a musical backdrop provided by the popular organ combos of the era. In 1991, while on hiatus from the Art Ensemble of Chicago and Lester Bowie's Brass Fantasy, the trumpeter revisited his organ roots. He wisely matched the soulful, gospel influences of organist Amina Claudine Myers and the exhilarating tenor powerhouse James Carter with trombonist Steve Turre and drummers (fellow AEC members past and present) Famoudou Don Moye and Phillip Wilson, making for invigorating yet reverent sessions. The six cuts on *The Organizer* include three by Bowie, one apiece from Turre and Myers, and a nod to Gene Ammons with the inclusion of "Angel Eyes." Carter and Myers receive the majority of solo space throughout the disc; however, by the session's concluding "Brooklyn Works Suite," Bowie unabashedly takes the solo spotlight. Bowie released a companion disc the same year with the same personal (also on DIW) called *Funky T Cool T.* —*Al Campbell*

Odyssey of Funk & Popular Music, Vol. 1 / Sep. 27, 1997-Oct. 4, 1997 / Atlantic ✦✦✦
Songbook albums were considered cool and trendy in the late '90s, and that seemed to fit into Lester Bowie's pop-tune agenda with the Brass Fantasy. But he wouldn't be bound to the usual worshipful homages on bended knee to a single composer, directing his Brass Fantasy (brass ensemble plus drums/percussion) toward a mind-boggling assortment of sources that are often thoroughly contemporary. Hence a record that pits Cole Porter back-to-back with Marilyn Manson, Andrew Lloyd Webber with the Spice Girls, or how about Notorious B.I.G. with Giacomo Puccini! Bowie's Brass Fantasy is at the ensemble's best when they swagger irreverently through "The Birth of the Blues" or a doo wop "In the Still of the Night"—and the Manson track, "Beautiful People," is savage, even raucous fun. Other songs are taken quite seriously; the Spice Girls' "Two Become One" becomes a sophisticated ballad chart. However, the Bowie band cannot relieve the tedium of Lloyd Webber's quasi-tango "Don't Cry for Me Argentina" by doing it relatively straight, and they seem a bit intimidated by Puccini's "Nessun Dorma"—which is probably beyond the reach of a jazz treatment anyway. At the very least, the brasses sound fresh and interested in what they're doing, so there is pleasure to be had here. —*Richard S. Ginell*

American Gumbo / Sep. 1974-Jun. 17, 1975 / 32 Jazz ✦✦✦✦✦
32 Jazz's double-disc set *American Gumbo* reissues two of Lester Bowie's best albums, *Fast Last!* and *Rope-A-Dope*, with each album occupying a single disc on the compilation. These two albums were recorded in the mid-'70s and played a large part in establishing Bowie as one of the leaders of the contemporary avant-garde jazz movement. He may have recorded more accessible albums, but these two provided the cornerstone of his reputation, and are essential for any listener with interest in Bowie or cutting-edge jazz in the '70s. —*Stephen Thomas Erlewine*

Bobby Bradford

b. Jul. 19, 1934, Cleveland, MS
Cornet, Trumpet / Avant-Garde Jazz, Post-Bop
One of the best trumpeters to emerge from the avant-garde, Bobby Bradford largely fulfiled the potential of Don Cherry (whose chops declined through the years due to the amount of time allocated to performing on flute and other instruments). Bradford grew up in Dallas, playing trumpet locally with such local players as Cedar Walton and David Newman. In 1953 he moved to Los Angeles where he met and played with Ornette Coleman and Eric Dolphy. Bradford spent time in the military and in school before becoming Don Cherry's replacement with the Ornette Coleman Quartet in 1961-63, a period when the group unfortunately rarely worked. After moving to Los Angeles, Bradford became a school teacher and also began a

longtime association with clarinetist John Carter; his mellow trumpet blended in well with Carter's dissonant flights. He recorded with Ornette Coleman in 1971 but otherwise is best-known for his playing and recordings with Carter. Since the clarinetist's death, Bradford has frequently led a quintet (the Mo'tet) featuring Vinny Golia and occasionally Marty Ehrlich. He has also performed since the early '90s with John Stevens's Freebop, the David Murray Octet and Charlie Haden's Liberation Music Orchestra. *— Scott Yanow*

● **In Time Was** / Jul. 1986 / Circulasione Totale ♦♦♦♦♦
There aren't too many quartets whose members were more far-flung than these; cornetist Bobby Bradford hails from Los Angeles, tenor saxophonist Frode Gjerstad from Norway, bassist Johnny Mbizo Dyani from South Africa, and drummer John Stevens from London. Together they formed a free-jazz group called Detail, which with this lineup made one tour of England, a double studio album titled *Ness for Impetus*, and this startling live recording in Cambridge for a Norwegian label. The entire disc consists of one freely conceived piece in three sections, "In Time Was," yet the progression of events is virtually seamless; your attention will not waver as you follow Detail's fantastic, telepathic interplay out on the fringe. Bradford plays brilliantly throughout, with on-the-button attacks of every note in every free flurry, while Gjerstad is a bit fuzzy in tone and somewhat further out there in conception. Stevens' drumming is a crisp and unpredictably volatile, which coupled with Dyani's asymmetrical, staggered, extraordinarily charged-up bass makes for quite a stimulating rhythm engine. Alas, the amazing Dyani died just days after the alleged date of this recording, which is dedicated to his memory. *— Richard S. Ginell*

Comin' On / May 29, 1988 / hatART ♦♦♦♦
Clarinetist John Carter and cornetist Bobby Bradford teamed up many times during a 25-year period. Nearly all of their joint recordings were issued under Carter's name, but this CD is an exception. Carter's often intense flights on clarinet served as a contrast to Bradford's mellower sound. What is unusual about this set, which also includes bassist Richard Davis and drummer Andrew Cyrille, is the participation of pianist Don Preston, who often doubles on synthesizer. His synth adds some otherworldly sounds on several of the selections (such as "Encounter") and takes some getting used to. Bradford contributed two of the pieces, while Carter brought in three, including "Sunday Afternoon Jazz Society Blues." The music is advanced, but not as forbidding as it sometimes was from Carter and Bradford, making this one of their more accessible releases. *— Scott Yanow*

No Saints Walkin' / Jan. 9, 2001 / Appaloosa ♦♦♦♦

One Night Stand / Nov. 11, 1986 / Soul Note ♦♦♦♦♦
A melodic player with a healthy sense of humor who has become more expressive through the years, Bobby Bradford really got a chance to stretch out on this fine session. Although pianist Frank Sullivan is essentially a bop player, he did a good job of keeping up during the more adventurous performances. Bassist Scott Walton (who has learned from the innovations of Charlie Haden) and drummer Billy Bowker were excellent in support. "Ashes" (a calypso version of "I Got Rhythm") and the mysterious "Woman" were the highpoints of this highly recommended disc. *— Scott Yanow*

Ruby Braff (Reuben Braff)

b. Mar. 16, 1927, Boston, MA
Cornet, Trumpet / Dixieland Revival, Mainstream Jazz, New Orleans Jazz, Swing
One of the great swing/Dixieland cornetists, Ruby Braff went through long periods of his career unable to find work because his music was considered out-of-fashion but his fortunes improved by the 1970s. A very expressive player who in later years liked to build his solos up to a low note, Braff's playing is instantly recognizable within seconds.

Braff mostly worked around Boston in the late '40s. He teamed up with Pee Wee Russell when the clarinetist was making a comeback (they recorded live for Savoy) and after moving to New York in 1953 he fit easily into a variety of Dixieland and mainstream settings. Braff recorded for Vanguard as a leader and with Vic Dickenson, Buck Clayton and Urbie Green. He was one of the stars of Buck Clayton's Columbia jam sessions and in the mid-'50s worked with Benny Goodman. But despite good reviews and occasional recordings, work was hard for Braff to come by at times. In the 1960s he was able to get jobs by being with George Wein's Newport All-Stars and at jazz festivals, but it was not until the cornetist formed a quartet with guitarist George Barnes in 1973 that he became more secure. Since that time Braff has been heard in many small-group settings including duets with Dick Hyman and Ellis Larkins (he had first met up with the latter in the 1950s), quintets with Scott Hamilton and matching wits with Howard Alden. He remains one of the greats of mainstream jazz. *— Scott Yanow*

The Best of Ruby Braff / Mar. 17, 1955-Mar. 18, 1955 / Bethlehem Archives/Avenue Jazz ♦♦♦♦♦
Rhino's *The Best of Braff* is a reissue of a Bethlehem collection that featured highlights from two ten-inch albums, *A Ruby Braff Omnibus* and *Holiday in Braff*, which is also released as *Adoration of the Melody*. Braff was at the beginning of his career as a leader here, yet he was already playing with ease, as these 12 songs illustrate. He may have gained greater popularity in the years following these recordings, but these remain among his finest waxings—and this is a nice way to acquire them. *— Stephen Thomas Erlewine*

★ **Two by Two: Ruby and Ellis Play Rodgers and Hart** / Oct. 14, 1955 / Vanguard ♦♦♦♦♦
In 1955 trumpeter Ruby Braff recorded two duet album with the sensitive pianist Ellis Larkins and both projects were very well-received. This CD reissue brings back the second session in which they perform a dozen songs written by Rodgers and Hart. The passionate Braff and Larkins (a masterful accompanist) work quite well together. Although the emphasis is on ballads, there are a few hotter pieces that find Braff pushing Larkins a bit. Highlights include "Mountain Greenery," "Blue Moon," "My Romance" and "You Took Advantage of Me." *— Scott Yanow*

☆ **Ruby Braff with Buddy Tate & the Newport All Stars** / Oct. 28, 1967 / Black Lion ♦♦♦♦♦
Cornetist Ruby Braff and tenor-saxophonist Buddy Tate make for a very complementary team on this fine CD reissue which also includes pianist George Wein, bassist Jack Lesberg and drummer Don Lamond. Several alternate takes and a previously unreleased "Lullaby of the Leaves" expand this fine session which has among its highlights enjoyable versions of "Mean to Me," "My Monday Date," "Take the 'A' Train" and "The Sheik of Araby" among others. This is high-quality small-group swing by some of the best which was recorded at a time when the idiom was considered very much out-of-style by the modernists. *— Scott Yanow*

The Grand Reunion / Oct. 14, 1972 / Chiaroscuro ♦♦♦♦
In 1955 cornetist Ruby Braff and pianist Ellis Larkins recorded a well-received set of duets. In 1972 they had a reunion which has not yet been reissued on CD. Since Larkins is a superior ballad player and accompanist, the emphasis on this date is on slower numbers although Braff does provide some fiery moments. The ten duets include "Fine and Dandy," "Skylark," "If Dreams Come True," "Liza" and "Love Walked In." Twenty years later Braff and Larkins would get together again with equally successful results. *— Scott Yanow*

The Concord Jazz Heritage Series / Jul. 1974-Sep. 1995 / Concord Jazz ♦♦♦♦
Cornetist Ruby Braff recorded so many rewarding albums for Concord that it must have been quite difficult to put this single-disc 1998 sampler together. Braff is heard in his popular quartet with guitarist George Barnes, in duets with pianists Dick Hyman and Roger Kellaway and interacting with such players as tenor saxophonist Scott Hamilton, guitarist Howard Alden, clarinetist Ken Peplowski, and pianist Dave McKenna, among others. Most of the dozen selections are hot swing standards (including "A Sailboat In the Moonlight," "Shoe Shine Boy" and "Dinah"), along with a few slightly later show tunes and Braff's original "Here's Carl." An excellent buy for mainstream jazz fans with a limited budget, although all of Ruby Braff's numerous Concord sets are well worth acquiring. *— Scott Yanow*

Plays Rodgers & Hart / Oct. 1974 / Concord Jazz ♦♦♦♦
For the fourth of five recordings made by the classic Ruby Braff-George Barnes Quartet, ten songs by Rodgers and Hart are given melodic, swinging, creative treatment. Cornetist Braff and guitarist Barnes fed off of each other and worked very well together, while rhythm guitarist Wayne Wright and bassist Michael Moore always gave them impeccable support. Highlights of this enjoyable set include "Isn't It Romantic," "Blue Room," "You Took Advantage of Me" and "The Lady Is a Tramp." *— Scott Yanow*

A First / Feb. 1985 / Concord Jazz ♦♦♦♦♦

A Sailboat in the Moonlight / Feb. 1985 / Concord Jazz ♦♦♦♦♦
Taken from the same sessions as *A First*, this collaboration between veteran cornetist Ruby Braff and the relatively young tenor great Scott Hamilton lives up to its potential. With strong assistance from pianist John Bunch, guitarist Chris Flory, bassist Phil Flanigan and drummer Chuck Riggs, Braff and Hamilton are a perfect team on such joyful swing tunes as "A Sailboat in the Moonlight," "'Deed I Do," "Jeepers Creepers" and "Sweethearts on Parade." All eight selections (even the obscure "Milkman's Matinee") are well wotth hearing, making this a highly recommended set. *— Scott Yanow*

☆ **Music from My Fair Lady** / Jul. 1989 / Concord Jazz ♦♦♦♦♦
The many Lerner and Loewe songs written for the play *My Fair Lady* have long been rightfully acclaimed. Even with several decades of fine recordings, this duet set by cornetist Ruby Braff and pianist Dick Hyman is one of the finest interpretations of the famous music. Braff and Hyman come up with new ideas during melodic versions of such songs as "Wouldn't It Be Loverly," "I Could Have Danced All Night," "On the Street Where You Live" and "Get Me to the Church on Time" among others. Every Braff-Hyman collaboration is well worth getting and this set is no exception. *— Scott Yanow*

Music from South Pacific / Jun. 12, 1990-Jun. 13, 1990 / Concord Jazz ♦♦♦♦♦
This CD is much better than it looks. Cornetist Ruby Braff and pianist Dick Hyman can always be relied upon to create exciting music but the songs from *South Pacific* (best-known are "Some Enchanted Evening" and "Younger than Springtime") would not seem to have much potential. However, through witty frameworks and creativity, Braff and Hyman greatly uplift the music, particularly their two versions of "Bali Ha'i." This consistently surprising CD is well worth checking out. *— Scott Yanow*

Ruby Braff & His New England Songhounds, Vol. 1 / Apr. 29, 1991 / Concord Jazz ♦♦♦♦♦
Cornetist Ruby Braff and tenor-saxophonist Scott Hamilton have teamed up on several memorable occasions. On the first of two CD volumes Braff and Hamilton are joined by a fine quartet ("The New England Songhounds") which is comprised of guitarist Howard Alden, pianist Dave McKenna, bassist Frank Tate and drummer Alan Dawson. Alternating stomps with warm ballads, the horns sound at their best on such numbers as "I'm Crazy 'Bout My Baby," "This Can't Be Love," "My Shining Hour," "Down in Honky Tonk Town" and "More than You Know." Highly recommended to mainstream and straightahead jazz fans. *— Scott Yanow*

Live at the Regattabar / Nov. 22, 1993 / Arbors ♦♦♦♦♦

Play Nice Tunes / Jul. 2, 1994 / Arbors ♦♦♦♦

Duets, Vol. 2 / Feb. 22, 2000 / Vanguard ♦♦♦♦

Anthony Braxton

b. Jun. 4, 1945, Chicago, IL
Sax (Alto), Reeds, Piano, Flute, Clarinet / Avant-Garde Jazz, Free Jazz, Avant-Garde
Of all the current leaders of the avant-garde, Anthony Braxton's music has possibly the least chance of ever being accepted by the bebop establishment. His complex lines, staccato attack and enormous quantity of compositions have a logic all their own. Some detractors (like Wynton Marsalis) may deny that Braxton's music is even jazz but, because it does contain a large amount of improvisation and the feeling of the blues, it is unquestionably jazz. And for what it is worth, this writer regards him as an obvious genius although the huge quantity of his work can be rather daunting. In 1968, Braxton made his recording debut, and his second recording as a leader was an unprecedented double-LP of unaccompanied alto explorations. In 1970, he teamed up with Chick Corea, Dave Holland and Barry Altschul in the mostly

freeform unit Circle. After Corea left, Braxton kept Holland and Altschul and added trumpeter Kenny Wheeler to his quartet. Braxton has cut duet albums with Joseph Jarman, Muhal Richard Abrams, Evan Parker, Derek Bailey and Max Roach, utilized a big band (the Creative Music Orchestra), performed standards with a trio headed by Tete Montoliu, paid tribute (in an abstract way) to the music of Charlie Parker, Thelonious Monk and Warne Marsh, and recorded more unaccompanied alto solos. In addition, Braxton has been a teacher at Mills College and Wesleyan University. *—Scott Yanow*

Three Compositions of New Jazz / Mar. 27, 1968–Apr. 10, 1968 / Delmark ♦♦♦♦♦
Anthony Braxton's first record as a leader (which has been reissued on this CD) features the innovative saxophonist coming up with an alternative to the dense high-energy freedom music of the era. Utilizing space, dynamics, "little instruments" and ideas gained from associations with the AACM, Braxton teams up with violinist Leroy Jenkins, trumpeter Leo Smith and (on one selection) pianist Muhal Richard Abrams for three lengthy originals. The music frequently takes a while to get going but rewards repeated listenings and eventually builds up to some furious interplay. *—Scott Yanow*

For Alto Saxophone / Oct. 1968 / Delmark ♦♦♦♦
Anthony Braxton's second recording as a leader is a stunning and somewhat unpredecented two-Lp set, eight unaccompanied alto solos. Braxton's sound and innovative style were already quite distinctive and his very advanced playing, which combines together emotional intensity with logic and a dramatic use of space, is memorable if sometimes startling. This twofer was not as influential as some of his later recordings but it does show that Braxton was a somewhat forbidding master musician from virtually the start of his very productive career. *—Scott Yanow*

☆ **News from the '70s** / May 22, 1972-Nov. 1976 / New Tone ♦♦♦♦♦
This rare collection of recordings from the 1970s features Braxton at the height of his power and makes an indispensable contribution to his discography. Personally selected by esteemed Italian musicologist Franceso Martinelli from long forgotten cassettes stored in the saxophonist's home, these six tracks were not released commercially until 1999. While the sound quality is mixed, the music is some of Braxton's best. There are two solo performances ("Composition 8g" and "Composition 8c"); three classic quartets ("Four Winds" with trombonist George Lewis, bassist Dave Holland, drummer Barry Altschul, and Braxton on sopranino, clarinet, and piccolo; "Composition 23E" and "Composition *2*" with Kenny Wheeler on flugelhorn; and an impressive duo between Braxton on clarinet and Dave Holland on cello). Sparks fly throughout, as this collection enthralls with some of the best jazz of the era. *—Steve Loewy*

Five Pieces (1975) / Jul. 1, 1975-Jul. 2, 1975 / Arista ♦♦♦♦♦

★ **Anthony Braxton Live** / Jul. 20, 1975–Nov. 4, 1976 / Bluebird ♦♦♦♦♦
With the exception of a 23-minute classical piece that was left out, this single CD has all of the music from Anthony Braxton's two-LP set *The Montreux/Berlin Concerts.* There are three Braxton originals apiece taken from two concerts and featuring either trumpeter Kenny Wheeler or trombonist George Lewis, bassist Dave Holland, and drummer Barry Atschul; the leader switches between alto, soprano, contrabass sax, flute, and clarinet. The six compositions (all of which have diagrams for titles) are among Braxton's strongest, and the improvisations (particularly the interplay between Braxton and Lewis) are continually fascinating. Those listeners who claim that Anthony Braxton does not have a strong sense of humor and is incapable of swinging are particularly recommended to acquire this colorful disc. A gem. *—Scott Yanow*

★ **The Montreux/Berlin Concerts** / Jul. 20, 1975 / Arista ♦♦♦♦♦
Anthony Braxton has recorded so extensively during the '80s and '90s that it is potentially foolhardy to call any of his recordings "definitive," but this two-LP set comes close. Braxton (mostly on alto and clarinet but also playing contrabass clarinet, flute, and sopranino) is heard with two of his best quartets on these live performances. Featured are either trumpeter Kenny Wheeler or trombonist George Lewis along with bassist Dave Holland and drummer Barry Altschul in exciting group improvisations based on six of Braxton's difficult compositions. There is a surprising amount of humor on one of these selections, and the interplay between these masterful musicians (making expert use of space and dynamics) sometimes borders on miraculous. The fourth side of this two-fer contains a lengthy performance of Braxton and Lewis playing with the Berlin New Music Group that is of slightly lesser interest; the CD reissue leaves out that selection. In either form, this music is highly recommended and by itself demonstrates the greatness and uniqueness of Anthony Braxton's music. This important set (other than side four) has been reissued on CD. *—Scott Yanow*

Donaueschingen (Duo) 1976 / Oct. 23, 1976 / hatART ♦♦♦♦♦
A live set featuring duets by trombonist George Lewis and the reeds of Anthony Braxton might seem as if it would be a bit tedious, but the instant communication between the two keep the music continually fascinating. Braxton (who is heard on alto, sopranino, clarinet, contrabass clarinet, flutes, and contrabass saxophone) and Lewis engage in some colorful sound explorations on their compositions on a continuous basis for 41-and-a-half minutes, showing off not only their technique but their very sharp imagination. As an encore they surprised everyone by playing an effective three-and-a-half-minute version of Charlie Parker's "Donna Lee." Listeners with open ears will enjoy this colorful set. *—Scott Yanow*

★ **Dortmund (Quartet-1976)** / Oct. 31, 1976 / hatART ♦♦♦♦♦
This is the perfect Anthony Braxton recording for listeners to start with. The innovative multireedist (heard here on alto, clarinet, soprano, flute and the remarkable contrabass sax) led a particularly strong group during part of 1976, a quartet with trombonist George Lewis, bassist Dave Holland and drummer Barry Altschul. This CD releases for the first time the often-stunning music they performed at their final concert. Braxton's complex but exciting compositions are among his most accessible (one of them is based on a circus march and another is a hard-swinging original dedicated to Lou Donaldson), both Braxton and Lewis take consistently emotional solos, Holland really drives the group, Altschul contributes his colorful percussion and the ensembles are very spirited. Give this recording to a bebopper who claims that what Anthony Braxton plays is not jazz. *—Scott Yanow*

Creative Orchestra (Koln) 1978 / May 12, 1978 / hatART ♦♦♦♦♦
Although Anthony Braxton does not play on this double CD (whose contents were released for the first time in 1995), his presence is certainly felt. He conducts the band through a fairly free improvisation and five of his compositions. Braxton showed a great deal of insight in originally picking the personnel for nearly every one of the 21 musicians has had an important career in advanced jazz, particularly Marty Ehrlich, Vinny Golia, Michael Mossman, Leo Smith, Kenny Wheeler, Ray Anderson, George Lewis, Marilyn Crispell, and John Lindberg. The music is often dense and atonal but never dull, and the closing composition is a superb piece that displays Braxton's love of marching band music! Although one wishes that Anthony Braxton himself had played, this is a set easily recommended to his fans. *—Scott Yanow*

Composition No. 96 / May 30, 1981 / Leo ♦♦♦
Composition No. 96 has loomed large in Braxton's oeuvre. He not only refers to it often as a key work, crucial to his own development, but it is also one of the most common "sound territories" to appear in recordings by various of his groups.The present recording is by a 37-piece student orchestra with only two ringers: clarinetist Bill Smith and trombonist Julius Priester.

Composition No. 96, composed in 1979-1980, is structured in alternating blocks, one dense and turbulent, the other soft and serene. The style in the former is that of somewhat academic serial technique, which is to say there is no "straight" thematic material (certainly nothing remotely "jazz" oriented) and no set meter. The listener is jostled about as if in an instrumental sea. Sometimes the writing is a bit reminiscent of Ornette Coleman's symphonic work, *The Skies of America,* which Braxton is known to admire, but more often it sounds like a slightly freer version of much contemporary serialist composing since the '50s. The quieter sections are more consonant though still complex, forming a rich stasis, a raft to which the listener lost at sea may easily grasp. Braxton biographer Graham Lock offers highly detailed liner notes both on the structure of the piece as well as its philosophical foundations.

For confirmed Braxaholics, *Composition 96* is a must-have, if only for its historical significance in his career. Listeners familiar with his jazz work, however, may be put off by its relatively severe classical orientation, lack of improvisation, and absence of overt themes. Also, note that Braxton does not play on this recording, but only conducts. *—Brian Olewnick*

Six Compositions: Quartet / Oct. 21, 1981-Oct. 22, 1981 / Antilles ♦♦♦♦
Anthony Braxton (who on this album switches between alto, tenor, clarinets and contrabass clarinet) heads an all-star avant-garde quartet for a set also including pianist Anthony Davis, bassist Mark Helias and veteran drummer Ed Blackwell. There is plenty of diversity in Braxton's six originals and it is quite interesting to hear him perform with this unique one-time group. *—Scott Yanow*

Four Compositions (Quartet) 1984 / Oct. 10, 1984-Oct. 11, 1984 / Black Saint ♦♦♦♦

Five Compositions (Quartet), 1986 / Jul. 2, 1986-Jul. 3, 1986 / Black Saint ♦♦♦♦♦
Anthony Braxton has spent his career plying a mostly inspired blend of complex compositions and free group improvisation, reserving choice spots in his works for the parade of talented jazz musicians he's employed. In the '70s, lean years for the avant-garde jazz set, his forbidding form of music forced him to make the occasional buck hustling chess games in New York's Washington Square Park. Fortunately, those days were short lived. Now Braxton is utilizing his considerable talents in the Wesleyan University music department as a professor. By the time of this mid-'80s quartet date, Braxton was just starting to get better compensated for his music and was also formalizing his heady compositional formula; this advance was helped along considerably by his stellar quartet, including pianist Marilyn Crispell, percussionist Gerry Hemingway, and bassist Mark Dresser. *Five Compositions* features this group minus Crispell (ably replaced by David Rosenboom). Things kick off with the relatively straightforward, Braxtonized bebop number "Composition No. 131," featuring a complex head statement followed by some swinging passages, albeit with plenty of gritty horn work by the leader. Some deliberate and mercurial chamber jazz follows on "Composition No. 88" and the livelier "Compostion No. 122," spotlighting Hemingway's incredibly intuitive and sophisticated drum work. Braxton loosens up a bit on the more free-form "Composition No. 124" and "Composition N. 101"; these last two feature Braxton's engaging soprano work and a distortion-riddled, bowed bass solo by Dresser. Knotty music to be sure, but some of Braxton's most rewarding. *—Stephen Cook*

Six Monk's Compositions (1987) / Jun. 30, 1987–Jul. 1, 1987 / Black Saint ♦♦♦♦
Altoist Anthony Braxton and drummer Bill Osborne are joined on this quartet outing by two musicians with a strong affinity for the music of Thelonious Monk: pianist Mal Waldron and bassist Buell Neidlinger. Together they perform hard-driving renditions of four of Monk's more difficult compositions ("Brilliant Corners," "Played Twice," "Four In One" and "Skippy") plus two of Thelonious' more enduring ballads: "Reflections" and the wistful "Ask Me Now." Braxton's improvisations are sometimes quite fiery and abstract but he clearly studied this music and keeps the melodies of Monk's tunes in mind. Worth checking out. *—Scott Yanow*

Victoriaville 1988 / Oct. 8, 1988 / Victo ♦♦♦♦♦
Recorded live at the *Festival Musique de Actuel* in Quebec, Anthony Braxton's *Victoriaville 1988* features a star-studded, avant-garde jazz ensemble, including tenor saxophonist Evan Parker, trombonist George Lewis, trumpeter Paul Smoker, drummer Gerry Hemingway, vibraphonist Bobby Naughton, and bassist Joëlle Léandre. Braxton's lengthy "Composition No. 141 (–20–96–120D)" opens the set in Schoenbergian fashion, sporting knotty, expressionistic arrangements and plenty of inspired unison and solo improvisation for balance; in spite of its sprawling structure, the solid and empathetic rhythm section keeps the piece running smoothly. The other ensemble members make quality contributions as well, with Smoker's humorous, muted trumpet work and Lewis' fervid trombone solos standing out in particular. The shorter "Composition No. 142" closes the performance with an intriguing mix of frenetic and languid group improvisation. A top-notch Braxton release. *—Stephen Cook*

Eugene (1989) / Jan. 31, 1989 / Black Saint ♦♦♦

☆ **Eight (-3) Tristano Compositions, 1989: For Warne Marsh** / Dec. 10, 1989-Dec. 11, 1989 / hatART ✦✦✦✦✦
Critics can bitch all they want about Anthony Braxton's "cerebral" approach to composition and improvisation, because their words—like these—are only words. None of them could handle the jazz canon like Braxton in his taste and execution as a soloist or as a bandleader, and such criticisms are therefore easy to make. This set was recorded as an homage to late saxophone great Warne Marsh (who was alive at the time of this recording) as well as to Lennie Tristano and his band of the late '40s and early '50s, which also included alto saxophonist Lee Konitz and guitarist Billy Bauer. Braxton's own band mirrors Tristano's, with Jon Raskin on baritone saxophone, Dred Scott on piano, Cecil McBee on bass, and Andrew Cyrille on drums. The first four tracks are all Tristano's. His songbook—which incorporated Charlie Parker's sense of harmony and his own sense of lyrical melody and counterpoint—is executed flawlessly by this band, with a different sense of clarity and emotional intensity that only history can bring to bear. Interestingly, it's on "Lennie's Pennies" that Braxton and Raskin really dig in to the melodic invention that is so subtle in the original from 1952. They look from the downside up in the way they play through the front line and then take out the harmony and turn it inside out. On Irving Berlin's "How Deep Is the Ocean," a favorite of Marsh's, they turn a lilting lyrical line into a force for beauty and complexity. On Marsh's own "Sax of a Kind," Braxton's most emotional playing ever comes to the fore. He doesn't sweat the technique, he's already got that. He's interested in Marsh's feeling that came across when he heard the tune and the feeling Marsh got out of his horn, and, of course, he's grateful for that influence. Braxton sails with no edges, slowly allowing the tune to build from his soprano and inverting the tune's mode just as the line slips into improvisation. It's a ballad without a backbone, just a feeling, spreading over the entire body of the track until all that's left are the mode changes in the solos—truly beautiful. Braxton has done numerous recordings of standards, and even a double CD on this same label of his readings of Charlie Parker. But as fine as most of those recordings are, none of them matches the lyrical brilliance and subtle grace of this tribute. *—Thom Jurek*

☆ **Willisau (Quartet) 1991** / Jun. 2, 1991-Jun. 5, 1991 / hatART ✦✦✦✦✦
This mammoth document of the final year of the famous Braxton Quartet shows exactly why that group finally split: They had reached a creative apex as a group that—arguably—could not be furthered. The music on this collection features two live CDs and two studio CDs, and gives a completely different picture of the same band who recorded for Black Saint on the *Six Compositions for Quartet* (1984) record.

The concert reveals the quartet able to execute any notion from Braxton's theoretical yet soulful music almost instinctually. As the compositions get stacked up, such as "No. 67–147–96"), some element of each of those compositions enters into the playing of this piece, whether it be in Marilyn Crispell's piano solo or line, Mark Dresser's bass line or changes, or a particular shift in rhythm from drummer Gerry Hemingway. The empathy of the players saturates Braxton's music, and he appears, giant that he is, not so much as a soloist on his many saxophones and clarinets, but as another player in a band that spoke with multi-lingual possibilities, but with one voice.

This group is all lightning and fire; there is no hesitation, nor is there any room for any. They challenge each other and their leader to the breaking point and somehow ride the wave into yet another new territory, where the process begins again. The studio discs in this collection show another side of the band. Here, dynamic and harmonic possibility are the concern of Braxton—each note is played, at least in the opening lines, and is carefully nuanced as if it were finding its own place in space. There is a freedom for the composer to seek out color and dexterity, texture and surface, as the band is all about making it anyway.

Braxton's quartet was easily the most creative band he played with, and his longest running. Since that time, in duet and solo performance, he has found the fire he needs to continue exploring the musical ground his mind conjures up on composition paper. But he has been lost in band settings. Since 1994 he has not found a group that has, member for member, this much musical talent or empathetic dexterity. With this band, he never had to assert himself as a leader because they could instinctively follow his cues. Since that time, he has had to assert himself more and more. And while the music he's writing has every bit of the wonder, awe, and irritation of his earlier work, it has never been played with this virtuosity. This set is a worthy companion to the Leo Records "Coventry Concerts" series. What a swan song. *—Thom Jurek*

4 (Ensemble) Compositions: 1992 / Dec. 5, 1992 / Black Saint ✦✦✦✦
Two of the compositions on this recording were written around 1980, two in 1992, but all are representative of the more "classical" side of Braxton's work. Unlike several previously recorded examples of this facet of his oeuvre, however, an ensemble made up largely of jazz musicians is utilized and, partially as a result, this is one of his most successful orchestral albums. The instrumental palette also contributes to the luscious and rich sound with a group consisting of winds, accordions, an organ, and a percussion section of vibes, marimbas, and steel drums.

"Composition 96," for example, had been recorded by a student orchestra in 1981 (*Composition 96*, Leo Records) where it retained a slightly academic tinge. Here, in a shortened version, it opens up and breathes with the fine organ work of Amina Claudine Myers featured prominently. Elsewhere, the twin accordions of Guy Klucevsek and Ted Reichman are in the fore, providing colors not usually associated with Braxton. In the reed section, he shows a predilection for clarinets that also serves to amplify the creamy, liquid sound world achieved here. Additionally, it seems clear that Braxton allowed room for improvisation (though it's difficult to ascertain exactly when this is the case), which, of course, adds life and passion to the proceedings. It should be noted that Braxton conducts the ensemble but does not perform on this album.

Listeners who might be cautious about the more arcane aspects of his work will find a relatively accessible introduction to Braxton's "classical" leanings herein as will others interested in the state of contemporary, creative orchestral writing. A rewarding, challenging effort. *—Brian Olewnick*

(Victoriaville) 1992 / Oct. 10, 1992 / Victo ✦✦✦

Charlie Parker Project 1993 / Oct. 21, 1993-Oct. 23, 1993 / hatART ✦✦✦✦

Knitting Factory (Piano/Quartet) 1994, Vol. 1 / 1994 / Leo ✦✦✦✦
Braxton debuted as a small-group pianist during a week-long engagement at *the Knitting Factory* in late 1994. This gargantuan two-disc set documents that semi-auspicious occasion. The band is made up of solid downtown N.Y.C. professionals—Marty Ehrlich on saxes and clarinet, Joe Fonda on bass, and Pheeroan Aklaff on drums; the repertoire comprised of several not-too-familiar standards by Charles Mingus, Lennie Tristano, and Thelonious Monk, among others. Braxton's pianistic style is much like his alto style. His rhythms are not even subdivisions of the beat. Braxton treats the pulse as a fence on which to hang the rhythms when he feels the urge, though he's just as likely to run alongside it, or ignore its existence altogether; he treats the harmonies with a similar bashful regard. His technique is that of an ingenious autodidact; he can definitely play, in his own way, but the way he treats the music is almost too personal. There's not much here that relates to tradition, and this vein of jazz is inextricably bound to tradition. This album is interesting in its way, but better to hear Braxton perform his own compositions in his native tongue than someone else's tunes in a borrowed language, even if he speaks that language in such a colorful and discerning dialect. *—Chris Kelsey*

11 Compositions / Mar. 24, 1995 / Leo ✦✦✦✦
Here is another example of the remarkable versatility of Anthony Braxton. For this series of nearly eighty minutes of carefully arranged duets, Braxton performs on flute; contra-alto, contrabass, Bb, and soprano clarinets; and sopranino, alto, and F saxophones. Brett Larner joins him on traditional 13-string koto and 17-string bass koto. The combinations of sounds are utterly fascinating; the duo allures with deceptive simplicity. While some of the compositions lean toward familiar abstraction, others are surprisingly melodic. Larner is a fine foil for Braxton's explorations, which demonstrate a slightly off-kilter bop sensibility. Braxton is particularly strong on the contrabass clarinet, where he mines the lower strata. Larner's koto can be sweet or acerbic, and even mellow. While not an essential part of the ever-growing Braxton discography, *11 Compositions* is nonetheless a highly rewarding session. *—Steve Loewy*

14 Compositions (Traditional) 1996 / 1996 / Leo ✦✦✦✦✦
It seemed that Anthony Braxton has done it all, but this recording of fourteen tunes from the first half of the century is a major addition to Braxton's remarkable discography. Here, he takes old standards, songs like "Ja Da," "Star Dust," and "Rosetta," and gives them new twists. The variety is astonishing, as Braxton and Gillmor try every variation imaginable. Thus, "Star Dust" has Braxton on alto sax with Gillmor in unison on French horn, while "Rosetta" finds Braxton romping through an energized variation with Gillmor playing it straight on piano. With Braxton alternating among soprano, alto, tenor, and bass saxophones, plus flute, clarinet, and contrabass clarinet, and Gillmor chiming in on piano, trumpet, and French horn, the combinations are endless. Often the melodies and solos are true to the era, though there are enough surprises to make this an entirely entertaining and fascinating collection. *—Steve Loewy*

Composition No. 173 / 1996 / Black Saint ✦✦✦✦

Composition No. 94: For Three Instrumentalists / Golden Years of New Jazz ✦✦✦✦✦
A major find, this recording captures the only trio appearance of Braxton, trombonist Ray Anderson, and guitarist James Emery during a performance in Bologna, Italy. Everything gelled that evening as the group played two versions of Braxton's monumental "Composition No. 94," the second one an incredible reading of the piece backwards! All the musicians were in perfect synch, as Braxton utterly impresses with lengthy forays on sopranino, soprano, alto and tenor saxophones, and contrabass clarinet, while Anderson is stunning on both alto and tenor trombones, cornet, and slide trumpet. Add Emery's extraordinary manipulations on electronics and major efforts on both acoustic and electric guitars, and the results should please even the most discerning critic of free jazz. Surprises abound, as this is one of the finest examples of extraordinary free music from the 1980s. The poor sound quality diminishes the thrill somewhat, but this CD remains an important document and a major contribution to Braxton's discography. *—Steve Loewy*

Michael Brecker

b. Mar. 29, 1949, Philadelphia, PA
Sax (Tenor) / Crossover Jazz, Contemporary Jazz, Fusion
A remarkable technician and a highly influential tenor-saxophonist (the biggest influence on other tenors since Wayne Shorter), Michael Brecker took a long time before getting around to recording his first solo album. He has spent much of his career as a top-notch studio player who often appeared backing pop singers, leading some jazz listeners to overlook his very strong improvising skills.

Michael Brecker originally started on clarinet and alto before switching to tenor in high school. Early on he played with rock and R&B-oriented bands. In 1969 he moved to New York and soon joined Dreams, an early fusion group. Brecker was with Horace Silver during 1973-74, gigged with Billy Cobham and then co-led the Brecker Brothers (a commercially successful funk group) with his brother-trumpeter Randy Brecker for most of the 1970s. He was with Steps (later Steps Ahead) in the early '80s, doubled on an EWI (electronic wind instrument) and made a countless number of studio sessions during the 1970s and '80s, popping up practically everywhere (including with James Taylor, Yoko Ono and Paul Simon). With the release of his first album as a leader in 1987 (when he was already 38), Brecker started appearing more often in challenging jazz settings. He recorded additional sets as a leader (in 1988 and 1990), teamed up with McCoy Tyner on one of 1995's most rewarding jazz recordings and toured with a reunited Brecker Brothers band. *Two Blocks from the Edge* followed in 1998, and a year later, Brecker returned with *Time Is of the Essence*. *—Scott Yanow*

★ **Michael Brecker** / Dec. 1986-1987 / Impulse! ✦✦✦✦✦
Although he had been a major tenor saxophonist in the studios for nearly 20 years and was

quite popular for his work with the Brecker Brothers, this MCA/Impulse set was Michael Brecker's first as a leader. Playing in a quintet with guitarist Pat Metheny, keyboardist Kenny Kirkland, bassist Charlie Haden and drummer Jack DeJohnette, Brecker performs three of his originals, two by producer Don Grolnick and Mike Stern's "Choices." The music in general is straightahead but far from predictable; the tricky material really challenges the musicians and Michael Brecker is in consistently brilliant form, constantly stretching himself. Highly recommended. *—Scott Yanow*

Don't Try This at Home / 1988 / Impulse! ✦✦✦✦✦
Michael Brecker's second album as a leader is almost the equal of his first. Surprisingly, only one song ("Suspone") uses his working quintet of the period (which consists of guitarist Mike Stern, pianist Joey Calderazzo, bassist Jeff Andrews and drummer Adam Nussbaum) although those musicians also pop up on other selections with the likes of pianists Don Grolnick and Herbie Hancock, bassist Charlie Haden, drummer Jack DeJohnette and violinist Mark O'Connor. Brecker (on tenor and the EWI) is in superb form, really ripping into the eight pieces (mostly group originals). Recommended. *—Scott Yanow*

Tales from the Hudson / 1996 / Impulse! ✦✦✦✦
Michael Brecker, a major influence on today's young saxophonists, shows off his own influences a bit throughout this fine modern straightahead set. Brecker sounds surprisingly like Stanley Turrentine on parts of "Midnight Voyage" and otherwise displays his roots in Ernie Watts and John Coltrane. With the exception of Don Grolnick's "Willie T," the music on the CD is comprised of group originals (five by the leader) and falls into the 1990's mainstream of jazz. While the tenor-saxophonist has plenty of blowing space (really letting loose on the exciting closer "Cabin Fever"), Pat Metheny is mostly pretty restrained (in a Jim Hall bag) except for his wild solo on guitar synth during "Song For Bilbao." Pianist Joey Calderazzo starts out sounding a bit like McCoy Tyner on "Slings And Arrows" before his own musical personality is revealed. When Tyner himself plays on "Song For Bilbao" (one of two guest appearances), one can certainly tell the difference between master and pupil. All of Michael Brecker's recordings as a leader (as opposed to his cameos as a sideman on pop records) are easily recommended and show why he is considered a giant by many listeners. *—Scott Yanow*

Two Blocks from the Edge / 1997 / Impulse! ✦✦✦✦✦
Although Michael Brecker made his initial reputation as a greatly in-demand studio player able to play quite credibly in commercial settings, his recordings for Impulse have all been strictly straight-ahead. Displaying his roots in John Coltrane and Ernie Watts, Brecker has developed his own approach to sheets-of-sound playing while not being shy of playing quite lyrically. From the opening medium-tempo blues "Madame Toulouse" and the catchy "Bye George" (which could almost have been written by Horace Silver) to the funky and slyly humorous closer "Delta City Blues," this is a particularly strong outing. With pianist Joey Calderazzo often emulating to at least a small degree McCoy Tyner, and the alert and intuitive rhythm section (bassist James Genus, drummer Jeff "Tain" Watts and percussionist Don Alias), Brecker often creates fiery solos that linger to their optimum length before the mood changes. Recommended. *—Scott Yanow*

Randy Brecker

b. Nov. 29, 1945, Philadelphia, PA
Flugelhorn, Trumpet / Crossover Jazz, Contemporary Jazz, Hard Bop, Fusion
Randy Brecker is essentially a fine hard bop trumpet soloist but one versatile enough to fit into nearly any setting including in the pop world, funk bands and electronic fusion. He studied classical trumpet and attended Indiana University. Brecker was with Blood, Sweat & Tears in 1967 and spent 1968-69 playing with Horace Silver's Quintet. He also appeared with the big bands of Clark Terry, Duke Pearson, Frank Foster and the Thad Jones/Mel Lewis Orchestra. After playing with the early fusion group Dreams in 1969, he worked with Larry Coryell's Eleventh House and Billy Cobham in addition to keeping very busy with studiowork. He teamed up with Michael Brecker in the popular funk-oriented Brecker Brothers (1974-79), in the 1980s often collaborated with his wife, pianist/vocalist Eliane Elias, and in the '90s toured with the reunited Brecker Brothers. But Randy Brecker still sounds best when in a freewheeling bebop combo and fortunately he occasionally records in that type of spontaneous setting. *—Scott Yanow*

Score / Jan. 24, 1969–Feb. 3, 1969 / Blue Note ✦✦✦✦
Considering the emphasis on group originals on this set and his work around the period with Dreams (not to mention the Brecker Brothers), trumpeter Randy Brecker's debut as a leader is often surprisingly straight-ahead and has some worthwhile solos along with period trappings. This CD reissue of a Solid State album features Brecker with two overlapping groups, utilizing his brother Michael on tenor, guitarist Larry Coryell, keyboardist Hal Galper, either Eddie Gomez or Chuck Rainey on bass, Mickey Roker or Bernard Purdie on drums, and alto flutist Jerry Dodgion. Overall this is an effective (if somewhat obscure) set. *—Scott Yanow*

● **Live at Sweet Basil** / Nov. 18, 1988–Nov. 20, 1988 / GNP Crescendo ✦✦✦✦
Trumpeter Brecker is at the top of his game in a live club setting. This one, done at *Sweet Basil* in NYC with a quintet sans brother Michael but with Bob Berg on tenor sax, showcases not only Brecker's fleet, sweet, bright tonal style, but also his mettle as a composer, penning all seven pieces here. Pianist David Kikoski, bassist Dieter Ilg, and drummer Joey Baron comprise a rhythm section playing together with the Brecker-Berg tandem for the first time. Brecker specializes in elongated, complicated core melodies. Two of his very best are included, including the absolutely gorgeous "Moontide," done originally on his *In the Idiom* recording. Kikoski tosses in some synth washes, but as on all of this, they are very much in the background, undermixed. "Thrifty Man" for Horace Silver is uncharacteristic of the soul jazz godfather—a dauntingly stretched melody on top of an easy rhythmic bed, and pristine sonic union from Brecker's piquant trumpet and Berg's brash tenor. The most popping numbers—"Ting Chang" for Tony Williams and Elvin Jones, or "Mojoe" for Joe Henderson—are real-time jams, hard-driving, forward-thinking hard bop. Baron is particularly animated, excited, and on the mark with every measure. "The Sleaze Factor" is the most intriguing number, one that purposefully slows as the piece wears on in its slippery leech, lugubrious, funky samba fashion.

Kikoski is consistently excellent on piano and Baron's really on it, while Brecker with Berg instrumentally sing melodies of hope, freedom, and joy. As much fun as this is to listen to, it was obviously a blast for the musicians to create as well. A fine addition to Randy Brecker's too-small discography as a leader. *—Michael G. Nastos*

Into the Sun / Dec. 1995 / Concord Jazz ✦✦✦

Willem Breuker

b. Nov. 4, 1944, Amsterdam, The Netherlands
Sax (Tenor), Sax (Soprano), Reeds, Clarinet / Film Music, Progressive Big Band, Avant-Garde
Dutch saxophonist, clarinetist, composer and bandleader Willem Breuker is probably the best known and most prolific figure in 20th century Dutch music. His accomplishments span from his '60s free jazz playing, to his role decades later as leader of the successful Willem Breuker Kollektief. Breuker also instigated the reform of government funding for improvisers, co-founded two important independent Dutch labels, and unabashedly mixed genres and incorporated humor and theater into his compositions.

Breuker's early musical influences ran the gamut from Ives and Schoenberg to Count Basie and altoist Piet Noordijk. He studied voice and bass clarinet, and was gigging and composing by the early '60s. He also won a few jazz competitions, and through those performances, was invited to join pianist Misha Mengelberg's quartet, which also included Noordijk. The group changed direction and went through line-up changes, resulting in a trio of Mengelberg, Breuker, and Bennink. Out of these three arose the ICP (Instant Composers Pool) label and a variety of groups and projects, but a split occurred in the '70s, eventually resulting in the Willem Breuker Kollektief and Mengelberg's ICP Orchestra. When Breuker's focus was still on free music, he collaborated with musicians including drummer Pierre Courbois, Peter Brötzmann (including his 1968 landmark recording *Machine Gun*), and bandleader Gunter Hampel.

Breuker tired of free jazz and focused more on composing, including film scores, music theater, and more experimental works. He lobbied for what became BIMHuis and grants for improvisers, and co-founded the BVHaast label with then-songwriting partner, pianist Leo Cuypers. The Kollektief began in the mid-'70s and their theatrical, humorous shows went over well with audiences all over the world for several decades, recording over 30 albums, mostly for BVHaast. Breuker was awarded the 1970 Dutch National Jazz Prize, among other honors, and continued to receive many commissions through the years. *—Joslyn Layne*

Live in Berlin / Nov. 1975 / FMP ✦✦✦
Recorded about a month after their BASF release *The European Scene, Live in Berlin* is almost as fine an example of their earliest roots. The basic elements are all here, from the shameless purloining of themes from all conceivable genres (especially those not normally associated with the avant-garde) and their conflation with free jazz soloing to the revitalization of schmaltzy pop standards. There's still a certain roughness to the arrangements and performance, but Breuker's determination to set himself apart from the European free jazz scene as represented by the work of musicians with whom he collaborated early on, like Peter Brötzmann and Evan Parker, is very clear. As they and others moved more and more into abstract and non-idiomatic improvisation, Breuker attempted to balance those ideas with a structure that relied on song forms (especially those of composers like Kurt Weill) and the more classically influenced compositions of musicians like Carla Bley. He also insisted on the injection of large doses of humor, an anathema to most of his contemporaries. The Kollektief's spirited rendition of "Our Day Will Come" shows how successful this approach can be, and the album as a whole makes a good case for Breuker's stance. There is a somewhat muted recording quality here and, of the two earliest examples of this band, one would have to give the nod to the BASF release for musical and audio quality, but both are essential to a full understanding of Breuker's music. *—Brian Olewnick*

● **In Holland** / Apr. 21, 1981-May 6, 1981 / BVHaast ✦✦✦✦✦
Simply put, this is the finest album ever released by the Willem Breuker Kollektief as a jazz tentet (as opposed to the repertory ensemble they later became). *In Holland* contains the most creative orchestrations, and the most thrilling solo work by the Kollektief, and ranks among the best jazz albums of the '80s. Two of the songs here ("Tango Superior/Interruptie" and "To Be With Louis P.") were released on the compilation disk *The Parrot*, but the remainder were only available on vinyl as of 2001.

The first record of this two-LP set is essentially designed as a suite, beginning with a powerful overture, and continuing on through an uproarious tango featuring a comically frustrated Breuker on alto, a drunkenly careening showcase for the brilliant trumpeter Boy Raaymakers, a loving homage to Prokofiev, and a fleeting reference to Wagner. Altoist Bob Driessen soloing never sounded better, and the driving bass work of the invaluable Arjen Gorter causes one's jaw to drop. Next comes "To Be With Louis P.," a surging R&B number with Breuker in the hilarious role of sleazy lounge singer who nonetheless matches Maarten van Norden's wondrous tenor sax shouting note for note.

The second LP consists of four compositions, including a concertino by an obscure 17th century Swiss composer, and a ferocious reel called "Hopsa, Hopsa" that builds up, morphs, and goes bananas. It's an album highlight, featuring a breathtaking performance by WBK, and composed by the newcomer (who'd stick around) pianist Henk de Jonge. Also included is one of Breuker's most beautiful and moving compositions, "Marche Funèbre" (from his musical production –De Vuyle Wasch, or 'Dirty Laundry'), whose themes are at once rich, somber, romantic, and inspired. Though the group lost quite a bit of freshness after the mid-'80s, *In Holland* qualifies as an extraordinary record by one of the most creative and enjoyable jazz ensembles to have emerged from Europe. *—Brian Olewnick*

Willem Breuker Kollektief / Oct. 31, 1983 / About Time ✦✦✦✦
The only occasion that the Kollektief recorded for an American label, this 1983 session is one of the ensemble's best, documenting the band near the end of the ten-year period when it was one of the most exciting musical groups in jazz. Though the individual instrumentalists

in the ensemble have always been undersung, they were some of the finest in the music and several are given particularly bright spots to shine herein. Belgian altoist Andre Goudbeek, German trumpeter Andy Altenfelder, and Breuker mainstay Maarten van Norden all demonstrate what creative and fiery players they could be. Additionally, the record features two of Breuker's most accomplished compositions: "Amsterdam Rhapsody Overture" and the intriguingly titled "Women's Voting Rights." The latter uses a deliciously lopsided rhythmic pattern to support several rich and juicy melodies and some sublime soloing by the aforementioned Altenfelder. "Preparations and Farewell," a fun conflation of a few national anthems, among other things, was recorded earlier for the *Driebergen-Zeist* album (under the title "Wolkbreuk III"), as was the Kurt Weill song "Benares." Tenorist van Norden's "Kontrafunkt" is a loose, lively number giving the band some room to rock out, and the record closes with yet another Weill piece, the sprightly and delicious "Road to Mandalay." Long a collector's item as a vinyl release, *Willem Breuker Kollektief* was finally issued to disc by About Time in 2000. Highly recommended. *—Brian Olewnick*

Pakkepapèn / Sep. 23, 1997-Sep. 24, 1997 / BVHaast ♦♦♦♦
William Breuker is back to form with this full-spirited 11-tet performance of ten original compositions by the leader. While Breuker only solos on one piece, there are some nice improvisations from trumpeter Andy Altenfelder, tenor saxophonist Alex Coke (who also narrates one track), and trombonist Bernard Hunnekink. The loud and dense harmonies are a matter of taste, but those who enjoy the composer's jazz side should not be disappointed. While there is no new ground broken, there is a joyous ambience and a forward motion that pull the listener into the orbit of the band. Naturally, it would not be properly Breukerian without some humor, and that is here, too, on occasion. Not likely to win new converts, this should satisfy the leader's longtime admirers. The utterly original plastic design (with the notes imprinted in the casing) is an attractive bonus. *—Steve Loewy*

Psalm 122 / Feb. 1988 / BVHaast ♦♦♦♦
Of the many diverse projects the Breuker Kollektief have involved themselves in, this might be their most ambitious. They are joined by member violinist Lorre Lynn Trytten's eight-piece string ensemble, vocalist/narrator Peter Halpern, Huub Kerstens conducting the New Music Ensemble and 40-member choir, and barrel organist Andre DeBoer. The theme of Psalm 122 (from Deuteronomy 16:1-17 of *the Bible*) is the story of a pilgrimage to a city later know as Jerusalem, and the settlers who established that city. The piece defies description, except that it is a continuous live performance at *the Poothoorn Church* in Amsterdam, combining Breuker's signature written music with Dutch libretto recited by American-born Halpern. The 76-plus minute production opens with fanfare and insect-buzzing strings to Andy Altenfelder's mournful trumpet, moves into a segment where the Kollektief briefly quote "Groove Merchant," ham up calliope sounds with DeBoer, then go into the actual Psalm, the arrival. Trytten's string octet evoke a hang-gliding feel under flutist Alex Coke's skittering solo for the instrumental highlight "Psalm 122, Pt. II." Halpern switches to English for the second fanfare "I Was Glad When They Said to Me." The final three segments are introduced by an organ short, the uplifting choir in unison with instruments leading into some pure dissonance for "Peace Be Within Thy Walls." As dramatic as Breuker's music is already, the accompanying entourage adds even more. It must be heard or witnessed as a whole, either on this disc or in performance. Likely this was a one shot, but what a blast it was. [This recording documents the performance of longtime Breuker alto saxophonist Peter Barkema, who died shortly after this concert.] *—Michael G. Nastos*

Celebrating 25 Years on the Road / Nov. 5, 1975 / BVHaast ♦♦♦♦♦
The Willem Breuker Kollektief occupies a unique place in the history of jazz. By the end of the 20th century, the Dutch orchestra was possibly the longest regularly performing one in the world, with no signs of abating. This beautifully packaged double CD collects almost three dozen representative tracks from the Kollektief's output over a quarter of century. Not all of the pieces were previously released, and even among the ones that were, several never made it to CD, being relegated to out of print LPs at the time of this release in 1999. In addition to the music, which covers the gamut from swing, show tunes, and avant-garde orchestrations, the packaging includes a valuable 128-page full-size book filled with hundreds of black and white photographs of the band through the years (with generous portions of the band's characteristic zaniness), and color reproductions of album covers and historical flyers. The results are a veritable feast for Breuker fans and others interested in any way in his unusual conglomeration of sounds. *—Steven Loewy*

Heibel / BVHaast ♦♦♦♦♦
This is the famous "cheese box" issue, where the CD is actually packaged in a small round wooden container just large enough to fit the disk and (circular) leaflet. While the novel packaging will likely attract attention, the orchestra's efforts are among the better releases of many that Willem Breuker has issued through the years. Although there remains a heaviness that has permeated many Breuker's large group performances, there is also some very exciting soloing and arranging. The second half of the album features a mini-opera by the leader, replete with vocals by Greetje Bijma and Breuker himself. Classical influences lie just beneath the surface, with Lorre Lynn Trytten's violin and Bijma's voice singing half-mockingly. As good a place as any for an introduction to Breuker's work, this CD should satisfy Breuker's devotees and attract new fans. *—Steven A. Loewy*

Dee Dee Bridgewater (Dee Dee Garrett)

b. May 27, 1950, Memphis, TN
Vocals / Vocal Jazz, Standards, Contemporary Jazz
One of the best jazz singers of her generation, Dee Dee Bridgewater (who was married to trumpeter Cecil Bridgewater in the early '70s) had to move to France to find herself. She performed in Michigan during the 1960s and toured the Soviet Union in 1969 with the University of Illinois big band. She sang with the Thad Jones/Mel Lewis Orchestra (1972-74) and appeared in the Broadway musical *The Wiz* (1974-76). Due to erratic records and a lack of direction, Dee Dee Bridgewater was largely overlooked in the jazz world by the time she moved to France in the 1980s. She appeared in the show *Lady Day* and at European jazz festivals, and eventually formed her own backup group. By the late '80s Bridgewater's Verve recordings were starting to alert American listeners as to her singing talents. Her 1995 Horace Silver tribute disc (*Love and Peace*) is a gem and resulted in the singer extensively touring the U.S, reintroducing her to American audiences. She would find even more success with her tribute album, *Dear Ella*, which won a Grammy in 1997. *—Scott Yanow*

In Montreux / Jul. 18, 1990 / Verve ♦♦♦♦
Dee Dee Bridgewater's move to France awhile back has resulted in her having a relatively low profile in jazz. This excellent live set should help restore her reputation. Whether it be a three-song Horace Silver medley, the warhorse "All of Me," Jobim's "How Insensitive," "Night in Tunisia" or the rarely performed "Strange Fruit," Bridgewater (who is backed by a French rhythm section) is in top form, singing with swing and sensitivity. *—Scott Yanow*

● **Love and Peace: A Tribute to Horace Silver** / Dec. 1994 / Verve ♦♦♦♦♦
Dee Dee Bridgewater performs 13 of Horace Silver's songs on her very well-conceived release. On most selections she is accompanied by her French quintet but there are also two guest appearances apiece for organist Jimmy Smith and pianist Silver ("Nice's Dream" and "Song for My Father"). Bridgewater uplifts Silver's lyrics, proves to be in prime form and swings up a storm. Other highpoints include "Filthy McNasty," "Doodlin"' and "Blowin' the Blues Away." A gem. *—Scott Yanow*

Dear Ella / Jan. 29, 1997-Feb. 19, 1997 / Verve ♦♦♦♦
Bridgewater's heartfelt tribute to Ella Fitzgerald is a resounding testament not only to the legendary jazz vocal icon, but also to Bridgewater's own faithful singing style, rich in Ella's tonal quality particularly on the high end. Her inflections are also quite natural, rather than self-effacing or forced. Some of the tracks vary in group size, as duo (with Kenny Burrell), trio (with Lou Levy leading on piano), or combo (with Milt Jackson, Antonio Hart, Grady Tate, Slide Hampton, and brother Cecil Bridgewater). Nine of the total 13 cuts have big-band backing, or orchestral settings arranged and conducted by John Clayton. "Midnight Sun" is perhaps the best of all ballads, and here Dee Dee sings with ravishingly lush, near-frightening efficiency. She cops Ella best on "Stairway to the Stars," with the piano trio leading and strings following along. She picks up on Ella's cutesiness for "A-Tisket, A-Tasket," while starting balladic, then swinging well during "Mr Paganini." Brother/trumpeter/arranger Cecil writes a neat call-and-response with horns and the singer on "Undecided," and they wail together in convincing, authentic fashion on "Lady Be Good." Andre Cecceralli, with the trio on "Mack the Knife," adds a dash of contemporary flavor. Bridgewater's finale "Dear Ella" is the end-all tribute with guitarist Burrell only as accompanist and author. They thank the legend for her enormous contributions which need no additional comment. This is certainly Dee Dee Bridgewater's most ambitious, and finest recorded production. You have to appreciate the reality of Fitzgerald's influence on thousands of musicians, but on this CD, it all comes home to roost. Highly recommended, for the singer's attitude and the brilliant backup musicians who nod in total agreement. *—Michael G. Nastos*

Live at Yoshi's / Apr. 23, 1998-Apr. 25, 1998 / Verve ♦♦♦♦

Bob Brookmeyer

b. Dec. 19, 1929, Kansas City, MO
Trombone (Valve), Piano, Arranger / West Coast Jazz, Post-Bop, Cool
Bob Brookmeyer has long been the top valve trombonist in jazz and a very advanced arranger whose writing is influenced by modern classical music. He started out as a pianist in dance bands but was on valve trombone with Stan Getz (1953). He gained fame as a member of the Gerry Mulligan quartet (1954-57), was part of the unusual Jimmy Giuffre Three of 1957-58 (which consisted of Giuffre's reeds, Brookmeyer's valve trombone and Jim Hall's guitar) and then rejoined Mulligan as arranger and occasional player with his Concert Jazz Band. Brookmeyer, who was a strong enough pianist to hold his own on a two-piano date with Bill Evans, occasionally switched to piano with Mulligan. He co-led a part-time quintet with Clark Terry (1961-66), was an original member of the Thad Jones/Mel Lewis Orchestra (1965-67) and became a busy studio musician. Brookmeyer was fairly inactive during much of the 1970s but made a comeback in the late '70s with some very advanced arrangements for the Mel Lewis band (of which he became musical director for a time). Brookmeyer has since moved to Europe where he continually writes and occasionally records on his distinctive valve trombone, issuing *Old Friends* in 1998. *New Works Celebration* appeared a year later, and in 2000 Brookmeyer issued *Together*. *—Scott Yanow*

The Dual Role of Bob Brookmeyer / Jan. 6, 1954–Jun. 30, 1955 / Prestige/OJC ♦♦♦
This CD reissue has four selections apiece from two different bands, both of which feature subtle interplay and cool tones. Bob Brookmeyer plays valve trombone and piano on two songs apiece with his 1955 quartet, a group also including guitarist Jimmy Raney, bassist Teddy Kotick and drummer Mel Lewis. The other half of this disc is actually led by vibraphonist Teddy Charles who features Brookmeyer on both of his instruments along with bassist Teddy Kotick and drummer Ed Shaughnessy; Nancy Overton takes a vocal on "Nobody's Heart." Although the overall set is not all that essential, the music is pleasing and reasonably creative. *—Scott Yanow*

Bob Brookmeyer with Phil Urso / Apr. 30, 1954 / Savoy ♦♦♦♦♦

The Ivory Hunters-Double Barrelled Piano / Mar. 12, 1959 / United Artists ♦♦♦♦
This is a rather surprising session, since Bob Brookmeyer, normally a valve trombonist, switched to piano and is heard playing in a quartet with pianist Bill Evans, bassist Percy Heath and drummer Connie Kay. The two-piano experiment was supposed to be for just a couple of songs, but the interplay between Brookmeyer and Evans was so delightful that they decided to make a full album out of it. Brookmeyer brought out the playful side of Evans on the six standards, making this straight CD reissue of the original LP a swinging success. *—Scott Yanow*

Live at Sandy's Jazz Revival / Jul. 28, 1978-Jul. 29, 1978 / DCC ♦♦♦
This double-LP (which will hopefully be reissued on CD someday) is an excellent showcase

for Bob Brookmeyer's valve trombone playing. Joined by the complementary guitarist Jack Wilkins, bassist Michael Moore and drummer Joe LaBarbera, Brookmeyer stretches out on ten standards, two songs by Andy Laverne, the obscure "Passages" plus a pair of his own songs. The two-fer is one of the best examples of Brookmeyer's playing since his permanent return from semi-retirement earlier in 1978. *—Scott Yanow*

Paris Suite / Oct. 15, 1993-Jan. 5, 1994 / Challenge ♦♦♦♦
Veteran valve-trombonist/composer Bob Brookmeyer has not recorded many small group dates during the 1980s and '90s, making this Challenge CD with a young European rhythm section (pianist Kris Goessens, bassist Riccardo Del Fra and drummer Dre Pallemaerts) a bit special. Brookmeyer plays eight obscurities (four by him and three by his pianist) that are complex, harmonically advanced and yet still able to be swung. Well worth searching for. *—Scott Yanow*

● **New Works Celebration** / Jul. 28, 1997-Jul. 30, 1997 / Challenge ♦♦♦♦♦
This stunning release features the recording debut of Bob Brookmeyer's New Art Orchestra, made up mostly of young Europeans recruited by the valve trombonist while touring the Continent. The four-part suite "Celebration" was originally written as a feature for the late baritone sax great Gerry Mulligan for a special concert in 1994, two years before his death. Scott Robinson fills Mulligan's role admirably on this initial recording of this extended work, and Brookmeyer's incredible voicings within the haunting ballad movement "Remembering" are also worth noting. The tracks following the suite are a diverse lot, but all of them merit strong praise. The leader's solo on the closer, "Boom Boom," demonstrates that his playing is as exciting as ever. Highly recommended! *—Ken Dryden*

Together / Oct. 9-1998 , 1998 / Challenge ♦♦♦♦
This duet CD shows the supportive bassist Vinding using his solid tones to underline the bright, clean, literate, tonally improvised lines of valve trombonist Brookmeyer. The result is a very pleasant experience that presents both musicians at their empathetic best. Brookmeyer also plays piano on three of the nine cuts, two of which he composed himself. Liner note writer Michael Stephans suggests the peaceful, relaxed "New Song" evokes the airiness of Satie and the warmth of Bill Evans. "Pretty Song" is a pure wedding anthem, while a take on the standard "Everything Happens to Me" moves effortlessly from pensive to slightly agitated and back. Brookmeyer loves to re-harmonize established melodies and circle them like a hawk without nailing the exact line. This is best demonstrated during the totally off-the-cuff "How Deep Is The Ocean" and "I Can't Get Started." Happy, wholesome, full bodied, fat, and crisp lines are perfectly stated by the two during the entire body of "Anything Goes." The pretty waltzing "Someday My Prince Will Come" and lightly swinging "Time on My Hands" with a hefty bass solo by Vinding, shows their romantic leanings. "Nobody Knows" is most bluesy and interactive using some unison, some counterpoint, and some trading of fours. Usually heard more frequently in much larger bands as an arranger, Brookmeyer proves quite a player, and the underrated Vinding should get just due as a premier European jazz bassist that America needs to pay more attention to. Recommended. *—Michael G. Nastos*

Peter Brötzmann

b. Mar. 6, 1941, Remscheid, Germany
Tarogato, Sax (Tenor), Sax (Bass), Sax (Alto), Saxophone, Clarinet / Improvisation, Avant-Garde Jazz, Free Jazz, Avant-Garde
Peter Brötzmann is a longtime champion of Europe's avant-garde, and a self-taught saxophonist famous for animated, swirling solos and lengthy, twisting dialogues. Brötzmann played initially in local dixieland bands in Germany, then was an early member of the Fluxus movement and began playing free jazz by 1964. A year later, Brötzmann, Peter Kowald and Sven-Ake Johannsson formed a group. Brötzmann toured Europe in 1966 with a quintet that included Mike Mantler and Carla Bley. He also began working with the Globe Unity Orchestra, and continued with them until 1981. Brötzmann was a founder of the co-operative FMP in 1969, an organization that sponsors and issues free jazz releases. He also founded a trio with Han Bennink and Fred Van Hove that became extremely influential through its blend of European theater and folk music and African rhythms. Van Hove left the group in 1976, but continued playing with Bennink until 1979. During the '80s his associations included Harry Miller, Louis Moholo, Willie Kellers, Andrew Cyrille, the Alarm Orchestra, Cecil Taylor and Last Exit. Among the most ferocious of the free jazz players, Peter Brötzmann has also recorded on baritone, bass sax, clarinet, alto, soprano and bass clarinet. *—Ron Wynn*

★ **Machine Gun** / May 1968 / FMP ♦♦♦♦♦
This historic free jazz album is a heavy-impact sonic assault so aggressive it still knocks listeners back on their heels decades later. Recorded in May 1968, *Machine Gun* captures some top European improvisers at the beginning of their influential careers, and is regarded by some as the first European—not just German or British—jazz recording. Originally self-released by Peter Brötzmann, the album eventually came out on the FMP label, and set a new high-water mark for free jazz and "energy music" that few have approached since. Brötzmann is joined on sax by British stalwart Evan Parker and Dutch reedsman Willem Breuker (before Breuker moved away from free music, his lungs were as powerful as Brötzmann's). The rest of the group consists of drummers Han Bennink (Dutch) and Svenske Johansson (Swedish), Belgian pianist Fred van Hove, and German bassists Peter Kowald and Buschi Niebergall. Brötzmann leads this octet in a notoriously concentrated dose of the relentless hard blowing so often characteristic of his music. While Brötzmann has played this powerfully on albums since, never again is it with a group of this size playing just as hard with him. The players declare and exercise their right to bellow and wail all they want; they both send up the stereotype of free playing as simply screaming, and unapologetically revel in it. The sound of *Machine Gun* is just as aggressive and battering as its namesake, blowing apart all that's timid, immovable, or proper with an unrepentant and furious finality. The years have not managed to temper this fiery furnace blast from hell; it's just as relentless and shocking an assault now as it was then. Even stout-hearted listeners will nearly be sent into hiding—much like standing outside during a violent storm, withstanding this kind of fierce energy is a primal thrill. *—Joslyn Layne*

Nipples / Apr. 18, 1969-Apr. 24, 1969 / Atavistic ♦♦♦
Due to its previous rarity, *Nipples* has been something of a free jazz cult item, even championed by Sonic Youth's Thurston Moore. Now with a more easily found CD available, listeners can hear that it's not quite a lost classic but still comes by its reputation honestly. To be fair, the slightly muffled sound quality doesn't help music this detail-oriented, but perhaps listeners should be glad it was even recorded. The 18-minute title track (the original LP's first side) is a performance by improvisers who would become well-known names but were still making their marks in 1969. Brotzmann, of course, is on tenor sax with Evan Parker also playing tenor (instead of his usual alto), guitarist Derek Bailey, pianist Fred Van Hove, drummer Han Bennink, and the now mostly forgotten Buschi Niebergal on bass. They create a swirl of sound with saxes locking into repeated riffs that generally change slowly but sometimes take abrupt leaps while the drum, bass, and guitar roll in waves and the piano jumps in with hyperactive runs. The music's dense, everything-at-once nature sometimes makes it seem like a hot-headed competition, but in the end it's the musician's construction of intricately detailed patterns that really matter. The 15-minute "Tell a Green Man" finished the album. A performance by just Brotzmann, Van Hove, Niebergall, and Bennink, the piece offers a contrast by a closer focus on each instrument instead of group improvisation. The piece opens with Bennink alone on drums at a mid-tempo before Niebergall enters with bowed bass. Brotzmann and Van Hove eventually jump in, pushing the others. *Nipples* is certainly not the best introduction to these musicians but nevertheless offers a fascinating look at their early careers. *—Lang Thompson*

3 Points And A Mountain . . . Plus / Feb. 25, 1979-Feb. 26, 1979 / FMP ♦♦♦♦♦
Three Points and a Mountain is a surprisingly balanced meeting between hard-blowing reedsman Peter Brotzmann, pianist Misha Mengelberg, and percussionist Han Bennink, who also plays some clarinet and tenor here. Recorded over the course of two days in February, 1979 in Berlin, the results are all that you might hope for from these three, and even more light-hearted than you might expect. Brotzmann travels the range of dynamics (as opposed to his all-out, power-blowing sessions), and there are several duet sections, as well as solo moments for all. The three musicians take turns riling each other as the trio whips up engaging, lively music, and have a grand time doing it—Mengelberg even lets out an occasional howl in the background. There are also odd moments of the trio swerving into early American piano jazz forms, but by the time this sinks in, Brotzmann, Mengelberg, and Bennink have taken it back out, wiping away the previous moment's impressions. Overall, this is a great and enjoyable session from three of the most creative and unique musicians in European avant-garde music. *—Joslyn Layne*

Die Like A Dog: Fragments Of Music, Life & Death Of Albert Ayler / Aug. 19, 1993 / FMP ♦♦♦♦
This first recording of the *Die Like a Dog Quartet* is fittingly subtitled *Fragments of Music, Life and Death of Albert Ayler.* In the liner notes (in both German and English), Peter Brötzmann writes of his passionate empathy for a musician whom he considers a kindred spirit; Brötzmann feels a link with Ayler since each were doing a similar thing "at the same point in time" although neither musician had heard the other. And so, lightly scattered throughout this first meeting of the Die Like a Dog Quartet are fragments of quotes from Ayler's *Bells,* "Ghosts," "Prophet," and more. In August 1993 Brötzmann was joined for a live concert in Berlin by legendary free jazz trumpeter Toshinori Kondo (who also occasionally utilizes electronics effects) and the wondrous rhythm section (although they are no straight timekeepers) of bassist William Parker and percussionist Hamid Drake. And so here, on one recording, you get four musicians who, whenever they're playing, play with every ounce of their attention, passion, and ability. Add to this each musician's great ability on his respective instrument and you get music that is alternately moving, invigorating, and astonishing. The dynamics range from rattles, long, low breaths, and short staccato blurts to the kind of exploding intensity and energy that is usually associated with Brötzmann. There are also two takes (one, just over a minute long) on Don Redman's "Saint James Infirmary" that come at the beginning and end of the three-part "No. 2." *—Joslyn Layne*

The WELS Concert / Nov. 8, 1996 / Okka Disk ♦♦♦♦♦
This live recording from a 1996 Austrian music festival is a powerful interaction of three musicians from different countries, each of whom have extraordinary improvisational abilities and deep, grounded technique. A somewhat unusual instrumentation is heard from this free jazz trio: German saxophonist Peter Brotzmann also performs on e-flat clarinet and tarogato (a Hungarian single-reed woodwind), American percussionist Hamid Drake plays a drum kit, a frame drum, and tablas, and Moroccan master musician ("maleem") Mahmoud Gania plays the guembri, a three-chord lute drum with a low register. The concert is broken up into three parts, totaling over an hour's worth of a set that is "meditative" in the ecstatic-trance sense of the word, meaning that the music's energy level has a natural ebb and flow. This current results in an outside-of-time atmosphere that's meditative even while remaining very musically active. The album opens with Gania's guembri playing, and Brotzmann and Drake soon come in, picking up a conversation midway (there are no buffering introductions with Brotzmann). The guembri is used in rituals by Gnaoua people to call in supernatural beings to possess believers, and European-oriented ears may find Brotzmann's thickly passionate horn to be the very sound of possession. Regardless, this recording captures a performance that really cooks! As a warning, it should be noted that the sound quality will leave audiophiles unhappy: There are moments when Brotzmann apparently moves away from the mic, and when Gania's vocal chants have a shifting sound quality. The music, however, outweighs those concerns. These three musicians come together in a successful melding of musical backgrounds. The result is a unified, energetic, affecting, free performance. *—Joslyn Layne*

● **Little Birds Have Fast Hearts, No. 1** / Nov. 7, 1997-Nov. 8, 1997 / FMP ♦♦♦♦♦
The Die Like a Dog Quartet came together four years after recording their first album for the *30th Total Music Meeting* festival in Berlin that took place in November 1997. The sets that the quartet performed over the course of the three day festival were subsequently released by the FMP label in two volumes entitled *Little Birds Have Fast Hearts.* Peter Brötzmann plays tenor, of course, as well as some tarogato and clarinet, and he is joined by bassist Wil-

iam Parker, drummer Hamid Drake, and trumpeter Toshinori Kondo who occasionally utilizes electronic effects. On this first volume, the quartet is in it for the long run; there are just two parts, totaling over an hours' worth of music. They go long, but not without pause, for there are definite let-ups over the course of "Part 1" (which remains engaging and varied throughout its 45 minutes), and "Part 2" is a relatively low-key piece. But "calm" and "low-key" for this group are still strongly out; there is no "casual" mode, there is no collapsing into old forms, this is a work-out, and all four musicians give 100 percent as they are known to do. This is not music for people wanting to hear some nice jazz, some hum-along-able standards; this is music for listeners who want to take a journey and are willing to let this quartet steer. The Die Like a Dog Quartet is not improvising for an audience, they are improvising because. Because that is how you find music. *Little Birds Have Fast Hearts, No. 1* is a great example of why that is important. *—Joslyn Layne*

Chicago Octet/Tentet / Jan. 29, 1997-Sep. 17, 1997 / Okka Disk ♦♦♦♦♦
This three-CD box documents a landmark 1990s avant-garde jazz band. Between the recorded lineup and the live concert lineup (replacing Mars Williams and Joe McPhee with William Parker and Toshinori Kondo for a three-date North American tour in May, 1999), Peter Brotzmann's *Chicago Octet/Tentet* brings together some of the greatest innovators in free jazz—first generation and new blood alike—who gel beautifully *and* energetically.

The first disc opens cacophonously with Brotzmann's "Burning Spirit." Midway through comes a Brotzmann solo, during which the other musicians interject dotted echoes and blurted mimicry. Their interference grows until all players simultaneously deliver their own take of Brotzmann's solo (which he's still playing)! The rest of this box covers a variety of compositional styles, from Michael Zerang and Hamid Drake's groove-oriented "Makapoor" to Ken Vandermark's slow build of a blues squall, "Other Brothers" to Mats Gustafsson's sound painting, "Old Bottles, No Wine" (included twice, since each outcome is different). With several pieces clocking in at over 20 minutes each, there is plenty of time for the band to work the listener up—and over. Even those with long attention spans may lose any sense of the path or direction that the group is taking—until they bring it back around, that is. There is structure; there is fire; there is passion; and there is supreme musicianship. There's also such a thing as "unique voice," and it's heard all over this box set. With excellent interplay and soloing from all of the musicians—both live and in the studio (the studio half starts with "Immediate Music")—Brotzmann's Tentet shoots sparks when they're low-key, and explodes into grande finale fireworks once they warm up. *—Joslyn Layne*

Clifford Brown

b. Oct. 30, 1930, Wilmington, DE, **d.** Jun. 26, 1956, Pennsylvania
Trumpet / Hard Bop, Bop
Clifford Brown's death in a car accident at the age of 25 was one of the great tragedies in jazz history. Already ranking with Dizzy Gillespie and Miles Davis as one of the top trumpeters in jazz, Brownie was still improving in 1956, but accomplished a great deal in the short time he had. He started on trumpet when he was 15 and by 1948 was playing regularly in Philadelphia. In 1952 Brown made his recording debut with Chris Powell's Blue Flames (an R&B group). The following year he spent some time with Tadd Dameron and from August to December was with Lionel Hampton's band, touring Europe and leading some recording sessions. In early 1954 he recorded some brilliant solos at Birdland with Art Blakey's quintet and by mid-year had formed a quintet with Max Roach. Considered one of the premiere hard bop bands, the group lasted until Brown's death, featuring Harold Land (and later Sonny Rollins) on tenor and recording several superb sets for Emarcy. Just hours before his death, Brownie appeared at a Philadelphia jam session that was miraculously recorded and played some of the finest music of his short life. Clifford Brown had a fat warm tone, a boppish style quite reminiscent of the equally ill-fated Fats Navarro and a mature improvising approach; he was as inventive on melodic ballads as he was on rapid jams. *—Scott Yanow*

★ **The Beginning and the End** / Mar. 21, 1952–Jun. 25, 1956 / Columbia/Legacy ♦♦♦♦♦
This CD, a straight reissue of the original LP, has some incredible music. Trumpeter Clifford Brown is heard at the beginning of his tragically brief career, taking solos on a pair of R&B sides by Chris Powell's Blue Flames. The remainder of the package features Brown on the last night of his life, just a few hours before his death in a car accident. Performing in his hometown of Philadelphia before a loving crowd, the 25-year-old is heard playing at his absolute peak. He performs "Walkin" with a local sextet that includes Billy Root on tenor and pianist Sam Dockery (a future member of Art Blakey's Jazz Messengers), "A Night in Tunisia" with a quintet and concludes both his night and his career with a quartet rendition of "Donna Lee" that is simply brilliant. Brownie's death was one of the great tragedies of jazz history and his "goodbyes" to the audience are ironic and in retrospect quite sad; don't listen to it twice. But Clifford Brown's playing on this date is so memorable that the CD is essential for all jazz collections. *—Scott Yanow*

Clifford Brown Quartet in Paris / 1953 / Prestige/OJC ♦♦♦♦♦
This straight CD reissue of a Clifford Brown LP features the great trumpeter with a quiet rhythm section consisting of pianist Henri Renaud, bassist Pierre Michelot and drummer Benny Bennett. There are six songs and six alternate takes (including three versions apiece of "I Can Dream, Can't I" and "You're a Lucky Guy") but each of Brownie's solos are different and his tone is so warm that every performance is well worth hearing. Ironically the finest solo, a classic version of "It Might as Well Be Spring," was improvised in one take. Highly recommended. *—Scott Yanow*

Complete Blue Note-Pacific Jazz / Jun. 9, 1953-Aug. 13, 1954 / Pacific Jazz ♦♦♦♦♦
This four-CD set has the exact same music as an earlier Mosaic five-LP box, but is highly recommended to those listeners not already possessing the limited-edition set. Trumpeter Clifford Brown is heard on the most significant recordings from the first half of his tragically brief career. Whether co-leading a date with altoist Lou Donaldson, playing as a sideman with trombonist J.J. Johnson, interacting with an all-star group of West Coast players, or jamming with the first (although unofficial) edition of Art Blakey's Jazz Messengers (a two-disc live performance with a quintet that also includes the drummer/leader, Donaldson and pianist Horace Silver), Brown is the main star. Highlights are many, including versions of "Brownie Speaks," Elmo Hope's "De-Dah," "Cherokee," "Get Happy," "Daahoud" and "Joy Spring." The attractive packaging, with its 40 pages of text and many rare pictures, is an added bonus. *—Scott Yanow*

Memorial [OJC] / Jun. 11, 1953-Sep. 15, 1953 / Prestige/OJC ♦♦♦
Trumpeter Clifford Brown is heard here in two unusual and unrelated sessions. On four selections, Brown is featured with arranger/pianist Tadd Dameron's Orchestra; other soloists include Benny Golson on tenor and altoist Gigi Gryce. The other date was recorded in Sweden while Brown was touring with Lionel Hampton's Orchestra. Clifford Brown and fellow trumpeter Art Farmer play four Quincy Jones arrangements with a Swedish group that includes altoist Arne Domnerus, baritonist Lars Gullin and pianist Bengt Hallberg. "Lover Come Back to Me" really cooks and Brownie and Farmer get to trade off in exciting fashion during "'Scuse These Blues." *—Scott Yanow*

Memorial [Blue Note] / Aug. 28, 1953–Jun. 9, 1953 / Blue Note ♦♦♦
This was a grab-bag of sessions Clifford Brown cut for Blue Note in the '50s with many great players, among them Lou Donaldson, Art Blakey, Gigi Gryce, Charlie Rouse, and Elmo Hope. This has been reissued on a double CD, although there was some material from this date also released on the vinyl album *Alternate Takes* that has not yet been reissued on disc. *—Ron Wynn*

Clifford Brown & Max Roach / Aug. 1954 May 2, - 19 / EmArcy ♦♦♦♦♦
According to the original 1955 liner notes to *Clifford Brown and Max Roach*, the announcement that Clifford Brown and Max Roach had begun recording and playing together sent shock waves throughout the jazz community and predictions ran rampant about how the two might shape bop to come. The last duo to really shape the music had begun over ten years earlier, with the relationship between Bird and Diz. This recording was early fruit from a tree that would only live as long as Clifford Brown was around to water it (1956, the year of his tragic auto accident). The result is by far some of the warmest and most sincere bebop performed and committed to tape. Brown's tone is undeniably and characteristically warm, and he keeps the heat on alongside Roach's lilting vamps and pummeling solos. What really keeps this record on the orange side of things (other than the decidedly orange cover) is the solo work of saxophonist Harold Land, who plays part Bird and part Benny Goodman. His tone is as delightful as it gets on the sultry "Deliah" and as bop-expressive as it gets on "The Blues Walk" and "Parisian Thoroughfare," where he and Brownie go head to head blowing expressive runs of sheer New York-style jazz. This collection of songs runs a nice gamut between boplicity and pleasant balladry. It represents bop at its best and is recommended for collectors and casual fans alike. [The 2000 Verve reissue includes alternate takes of "The Blues Walk," "Daahoud," and "Joy Spring."] *—Jack LV Isles*

Brown and Roach, Inc. / Aug. 2, 1954-Aug. 6, 1954 / Trip ♦♦♦♦
The first of the EmArcy recordings of the Clifford Brown/Max Roach Quintet, this album features trumpeter Brown, drummer Max Roach, tenor-saxophonist Harold Land, pianist Richie Powell and bassist George Morrow in fine form. Highpoints include "Stompin' at the Savoy," "I Get a Kick Out of You" and Brownie's ballad feature on "Ghost of a Chance." Near-classic music from a legendary group. *—Scott Yanow*

☆ **Brownie: The Complete Emarcy Recordings of Clifford Brown** / Aug. 3, 1954-Feb. 25, 1956 / EmArcy ♦♦♦♦♦
Although undoubtedly an expensive acquisition, this ten-CD set is perfectly done and contains dozens of gems. The remarkable but short-lived trumpeter Clifford Brown has the second half of his career fully documented (other than his final performance) and he is showcased in a wide variety of settings. The bulk of the numbers are of Brownie's Quintet with co-leader and drummer Max Roach, either Harold Land or Sonny Rollins on tenor, pianist Richie Powell and bassist George Morrow (including some previously unheard alternate takes) but there is also much more. Brown stars at several jam sessions (including a meeting with fellow trumpeters Clark Terry and Maynard Ferguson), accompanies such singers as Dinah Washington, Helen Merrill and Sarah Vaughan and is backed by strings on one date. Everything is here including classic versions of "Parisian Thoroughfare," "Joy Spring," "Daahoud," "Coronado," a ridiculously fast "Move," "Portrait of Jenny," "Cherokee," "Sandu," "I'll Remember April" and "What Is This Thing Called Love." Get this set while it stays in print. *—Scott Yanow*

Clifford Brown with Strings / Jan. 18, 1955-Jan. 20, 1955 / EmArcy ♦♦♦
There are two schools of thought regarding this Clifford Brown with strings session (which has been reissued on CD). Brownie plays quite beautifully and shows off his warm tone on such numbers as "Portrait of Jenny," "Memories of You," "Embraceable You" and "Stardust." But on the other hand the string arrangements by Neal Hefti border on muzak and Brown never really departs from the melody. So the trumpeter's tone is the only reason to acquire this disc which to this listener is a slight disappointment, not living up to its potential. *—Scott Yanow*

A Study in Brown / Feb. 23, 1955-Feb. 25, 1955 / EmArcy ♦♦♦♦
This CD reissue features the 1955 version of the Clifford Brown/Max Roach Quintet, a group also including tenor-saxophonist Harold Land, pianist Richie Powell and bassist George Morrow. One of the premiere early hard bop units, this band had unlimited potential. Highlights of this set are "Cherokee" (during which trumpeter Brownie is brilliant), "Swingin"' and "Sandu." All of the group's recordings (which have been included in the Clifford Brown ten-CD box set) are well worth acquiring. *—Scott Yanow*

At Basin Street / Jan. 4, 1956-Feb. 17, 1956 / PSM ♦♦♦♦♦
The last official album by the Clifford Brown/Max Roach Quintet is the only one that featured the great Sonny Rollins on tenor. With pianist Richie Powell and bassist George Morrow completing the group, this CD reissue is a hard bop classic. Brownie and Rollins fit together perfectly on memorable versions of "What Is This Thing Called Love," "I'll Remember

April" and a witty arrangement of "Love Is a Many Splendored Thing." Highly recommended. *—Scott Yanow*

The Immortal Clifford Brown / May 1965 / Pacific Jazz ♦♦♦
Although he was working here in a less intense, relaxed "West Coast" sphere, Brown still made some striking music on this 1954 date. It showed he could turn to mellow material, but retain his fire and grit. Tenor saxophonist Zoot Sims and pianist Russ Freeman were among the distinguished guests. *—Ron Wynn*

Alone Together: The Best of the Mercury Years / Aug. 3, 1954-Oct. 1960 / Verve ♦♦♦♦

Complete Paris Sessions, Vol. 1 / Sep. 28, 1953–Sep. 29, 1953 / Vogue ♦♦♦♦
The music on this 1997 CD made available by RCA features the great trumpeter Clifford Brown on two sessions originally led by altoist Gigi Gryce. When the Lionel Hampton Orchestra was touring France, the leader for unknown reasons forbade his sidemen from making records; fortunately most of them disobeyed. Brown is heard with a big band filled with both Americans and Frenchmen performing arrangements of three Gryce originals and two alternate takes. In addition to Brown and Gryce, trombonist Jimmy Cleveland and tenor saxophonist Clifford Solomon get worthwhile solo space. the second half of the disc matches Brown and Gryce in a two-horn sextet with guitarist Jimmy Gourley and pianist Henri Renaud, playing two versions of "Conception," Brownie's obscure "Goofin' With Me" and a pair of standards ("I Cover the Waterfront" and two renditions of "All the Things You Are"). Although falling just short of classic, these two dates are excellent examples of mainstream bop from the period and are recommended to listeners who do not already own the material. *—Scott Yanow*

Marion Brown

b. Sep. 8, 1935, Atlanta, GA
Sax (Alto), Flute / Avant-Garde Jazz, Free Jazz
One of the brightest and most lyrical voices of the 1960s avant-garde, Marion Brown participated in many stimulating recordings during the '60s and '70s while never really becoming an influential force. He played alto in high school and in Army bands and attended Clark College. In 1965 Brown moved to New York and recorded the monumental *Ascension* with John Coltrane and *Fire Music* with Archie Shepp. Soon Brown was leading his own dates for ESP and Impulse. He worked with Sun Ra, lived in Europe during 1968-70 and in the early '70s in the U.S. played with Leo Smith. Since recording with Gunter Hampel in 1983 and making an unaccompanied solo date in 1985, ill health has limited Marion Brown's musical activities. *—Scott Yanow*

Marion Brown Quartet / Nov. 1965 / ESP ♦♦♦♦♦
Altoist Marion Brown's debut as a leader is a typical ESP free form blowout. He performs three numbers (two are quite lengthy) with either trumpeter Alan Shorter or tenor-saxophonist Bennie Maupin (who was at the beginning of his career), both Ronnie Boykins and Reggie Johnson on basses and drummer Rashied Ali. The fiery performances feature the musicians stretching themselves and playing with great intensity; at this early point Marion Brown was already recognizable. *—Scott Yanow*

Why Not? / Oct. 23, 1966 / ESP ♦♦♦
Marion Brown's second of two ESP discs is an excellent showcase for his advanced alto in a quartet with pianist Stanley Cowell, bassist Norris Jones and drummer Rashied Ali. None of the four Brown compositions caught on elsewhere but they serve as fine vehicles for his adventurous flights. *—Scott Yanow*

● **Three for Shepp** / Dec. 1, 1966 / Impulse! ♦♦♦♦♦
As a sort-of answer to Archie Shepp's album *Four For Trane*, altoist Marion Brown recorded *Three For Shepp*, a set split evenly between Brown and Shepp compositions. This album features Brown interacting with either Dave Burrell or Stanley Cowell on piano, bassist Norris Jones and Bobby Capp or Beaver Harris on drums. Although none of the selections (including the Shepp songs) ever became well-known, Marion Brown is heard in prime form throughout the colorful performances. It seems strange that he would not get a chance to record for Impulse again until 1973. *—Scott Yanow*

Porto Nova / Dec. 14, 1967-Dec. 1970 / Black Lion ♦♦♦
This was one of altoist Marion Brown's best recordings. Although a very adventurous improviser, Brown usually brought lyricism and a thoughtful (if unpredictable) approach to his music. Accompanied by bassist Maarten van Regteben Altena and drummer Han Bennink for this stimulating session (recorded in Holland), Brown stretches out on five of his compositions and is heard at the peak of his creative powers. *—Scott Yanow*

Live in Japan / Nov. 8, 1979 / DIW ♦♦♦♦

Oscar Brown, Jr.

b. Oct. 10, 1926, Chicago, IL
Vocals, Lyricist / Vocal Jazz, Standards
The multi-talented Oscar Brown, Jr. has written several classic pieces including the lyrics to "Dat Dere," "Work Song," "Watermelon Man" and "The Entertainer" (the latter a bittersweet biography of Scott Joplin) and the compositions "Signifyin' Monkey" and "But I Was Cool." An important social commentator and playwright, Oscar Brown, Jr. acted on a regular network radio soap opera while in high school. After a wide variety of careers (including public relations, real estate, ad copy and running unsuccessfully for political office), he became a professional songwriter, starting with "Brown Baby" (which was recorded by Mahalia Jackson) and collaborating with Max Roach on the "Freedom Now Suite." A dramatic singer, Brown was signed to Columbia in 1960 where he recorded several classic albums. In 1962 he was the MC on the legendary *Jazz Scene USA* television series (some episodes of which have been made available on video). Brown has performed and written many shows through the years and served as artist-in-residence at several colleges. After recording steadily, he was off records altogether during 1975-94 until returning with *Then & Now* for the Weasel Disc label in 1995, a disc full of both fresh remakes and new material. *—Scott Yanow*

● **Sin & Soul & Then Some** / Jun. 20, 1960-Oct. 23, 1960 / Columbia/Legacy ♦♦♦♦♦
Oscar Brown Jr.'s debut recording, which was finally reissued on CD in 1996, is a true classic. A brilliant lyricist, a dramatic singer, and a highly individual genius in his own way, Brown performed a dozen memorable selections for this album. His lyrics to "Work Song," "Watermelon Man," "Afro-Blue" and particularly "Dat Dere" are famous, "But I Was Cool" and "Signifyin' Money" are humorous, "Bid 'Em In" is a chilling depiction of a slave auction, and "Rags and Old Iron" is quite touching. In addition to the original program, five previously unreleased selections from the same sessions (most of which were later remade) were added to this reissue, including four from the Brown musical *Kicks and Company.* Decades later, Oscar Brown, Jr. still performs many of these pieces. Essential music from an underrated great. *—Scott Yanow*

Mr. Oscar Brown Goes to Washington / 1964 / Verve ♦♦♦♦
Although this date sounds political due to its title, most of the lyrics by the talented Oscar Brown Jr. deal with more universal and timeless topics. Recorded live at the Cellar Door in Washington D.C., Brown is accompanied by pianist Floyd Morris, guitarist Phil Upchurch, bassist Herbert Brown and drummer Curtis Boyd on a set of a dozen originals. Most memorable are "Maggie" (a tribute to his young daughter), "Living Double In a World of Trouble" (about having two girlfriends at once), "Forty Acres and a Mule" and "Brother Where Are You." For this 1998 limited-edition CD reissue (the recording was originally cut for Fontana), an unedited second version of the latter tune is added to the original program. Although not quite up to the level of his classic *Sin & Soul,* this CD is a worthy acquisition. *—Scott Yanow*

Movin' On / May 30, 1972 / 32 Jazz ♦♦♦
Oscar Brown Jr.'s vocal and lyrical talents shine on this reissue of his 1972 album *Movin' On.* Brown's witty, politically conscious scats meld art and humor into innovation. *Movin' On*'s nine songs, including highlights like "A Dime Away From a Hot Dog," "Ladiesman" and "No Place To Be Somebody, " enhance Brown's reputation as an inventive jazzman. *—Heather Phares*

Ray Brown

b. Oct. 13, 1926, Pittsburgh, PA
Bass / Bop
The huge and comfortable sound of Ray Brown's bass has been a welcome feature on bop-oriented sessions for a half-century. Although not a soloist on the level of an Oscar Pettiford, Brown's quick reflexes and ability to accompany soloists in a swinging fashion put him near the top of his field. After playing with Jazz at the Philharmonic, he married Ella Fitzgerald (their marriage only lasted during 1948-52) and for a time led his own trio to back the singer. Brown recorded with an early version of the Modern Jazz Quartet (under Milt Jackson's leadership) and then became a permanent member of the Oscar Peterson Trio (1951-66). With Peterson the bassist travelled the world, guested with other top jazz artists, was featured on JATP tours, became famous and recorded constantly. *—Scott Yanow*

Bass Hit! / Nov. 21, 1956–Nov. 23, 1956 / Verve ♦♦♦♦
Ray Brown's earliest date as a leader features him prominently in the solo spotlight with arrangements by Marty Paich. They collaborated on a swinging original blues, "Blues for Sylvia," and the snappy "Blues for Lorraine." The rest of the release concentrates on familiar standards, with the addition to the reissue of several complete and incomplete takes of "After You've Gone," which didn't appear on the original release. The supporting cast includes the cream of the crop of musicians living on the West Coast at the time: Jimmy Rowles, Harry "Sweets" Edison, and Jimmy Giuffre among them. Out of print for a long time, this record was reissued in 1999, though as a limited-edition title in the Verve Elite series, so it will not remain available for long. *—Ken Dryden*

Ray Brown with Milt Jackson / Jan. 4, 1965-Jan. 5, 1965 / Verve ♦♦♦♦♦

Live at the Concord Jazz Festival / Aug. 1979 / Concord Jazz ♦♦♦♦

Soular Energy / Aug. 1984 / Concord Jazz ♦♦♦♦
This album is important as an early milestone in pianist Gene Harris' second career. Harris, who had led the popular Three Sounds in the 1960's, had been living in obscurity in Boise, Idaho for several years before he was urged by bassist Ray Brown to come to the West Coast for some recording sessions. Harris became a permanent member of Brown's regular trio for quite a few years before launching his own quartet. He had lost none of his technique, soul or swing in the interim as he shows throughout this fine release. Seven of the eight numbers (highlighted by "Exactly Like You," "Teach Me Tonight" and "Sweet Georgia Brown") feature Brown, Harris and drummer Gerryck King playing soulful bop while "Mistreated But Undefeated Blues" adds guitarist Emily Remler and the tenor of Red Holloway. An excellent effort. *—Scott Yanow*

Summer Wind: Live at the Loa / Jul. 1988 / Concord Jazz ♦♦♦♦
Brown's trio with Gene Harris (k) and Jeff Hamilton (d). Perhaps Brown's very best. *—Michael G. Nastos*

Black Orpheus / May 23, 1989-Feb. 7, 1991 / Evidence ♦♦♦♦
Whether accompanying or leading a band, bassist Ray Brown has long been among jazz's greatest players. These cuts, mostly from 1989 except for two numbers done in 1991, feature Brown backing soulful pianist Gene Harris and steady drummer Jeff Hamilton on a program combining Afro-Latin material with standards from Johnny Mercer, Fats Waller and others, as well as an excellent rendition of Percy Mayfield's blues/R&B standard "Please Send Me Someone to Love." The songs are long enough to display each musician's skills, but not so lengthy that they become repetitious. It's a well-played, delightful example of the kind of high-powered material that's been Ray Brown's stock-in-trade. *—Ron Wynn*

● **Don't Get Sassy** / Apr. 21, 1994-Apr. 22, 1994 / Telarc ♦♦♦♦
Bassist Ray Brown, pianist Benny Green and drummer Jeff Hamilton make for a perfect team on their Telarc CD. The tight yet swinging arrangements are full of subtle surprises and serve as a perfect format for the players, particularly Green. Highlights include Thad Jones' "Don't

Get Sassy," Oscar Peterson's "Kelly's Blues," "Tanga," "Brown's New Blues" and a three-song Duke Ellington medley. Recommended. *—Scott Yanow*

Seven Steps to Heaven / May 22, 1995-May 23, 1995 / Telarc ✦✦✦✦✦
The Ray Brown Trio in 1995 featured pianist Benny Green and drummer Gregory Hutchinson along with the leader/bassist. In the tradition of the mid-'50s Oscar Peterson Trio, the group featured tight arrangements with concise but consistently brilliant solos. For this Telarc session, guitairst Ulf Wakenius (a little reminiscent of Herb Ellis) fits in perfectly. Highlights include "Seven Steps to Heaven" and "Cotton Tail." *—Scott Yanow*

Some of My Best Friends Are . . . The Sax Players / Nov. 20, 1995-Feb. 13, 1996 / Telarc ✦✦✦✦
As a follow-up to bassist Ray Brown's previous record in which he collaborated with several of his favorite pianists, for this set he features six major saxophonists (tenors Joe Lovano, Ralph Moore, Joshua Redman and Stanley Turrentine plus altoists Benny Carter and Jesse Davis) on two songs apiece with his regular trio. Although more than 60 years separate the ageless Carter from Redman, each of the saxes originally developed their own voice in the straightahead jazz tradition. Highlights of the colorful set include Benny Carter's playful rendition of "Love Walked In," Moore's cooking solo on "Crazeology" (a Benny Harris bop classic which the record mistakenly lists as written by Bud Freeman), Davis ripping through "Moose the Mooche" and Turrentine's romp on the blues "Port of Rico." Pianist Benny Green and drummer Gregory Hutchinson provide suitable accompaniment (Green's solos are consistently excellent) and all dozen of the songs are successful and swinging. As an extra bonus, on the latter part of the CD each of the saxophonists has a brief chat (between 26 seconds and a minute apiece) with Brown about their early influences. There is so much good feeling and obvious mutual respect shown that one wishes these talks were at least twice as long; the Benny Carter segment is most memorable. This well-conceived project is easily recommended. *—Scott Yanow*

Some of My Best Friends Are . . . Singers / Dec. 15, 1997- 199 / Telarc ✦✦✦✦✦
What does a bass player do when he's recording an album as a leader— Surely not an hour's worth of bass solos! Ray Brown solved the bass player's dilemma with a series of recordings under the *Some of My Best Friends Are* . . . heading. This 1998 release is the third in the series, following the earlier *. . . Piano Players* and *. . . Saxophonists* albums, and it's a gem. Featuring a sextet of fine vocalists, ranging from the well-established to the unknown, this CD is a class act from beginning to end. The rising jazz vocal superstar of the late '90s, Diana Krall, is showcased to great effect on "I Thought About You" and "Little Boy." Well-established female vocal veterans Etta Jones, Dee Dee Bridgewater, and Marlena Shaw deliver superb performances, soulfully giving master lessons in the art of singing. The lone male singer spotlighted here, Kevin Mahogany, wraps his smooth baritone around the ballad, "Skylark," and swings gently on "The Party's Over."

The one unknown in this collection is Oregonian Nancy King. This veteran of the San Francisco and Pacific Northwest scenes shows she has a fine way with a ballad on "But Beautiful," and scats her way across the upbeat Brown original, "The Perfect Blues," that closes this set. Both of these songs also feature Antonio Hart's alto saxophone. In addition to Brown's trio mates Geoff Keezer and Gregory Hutchinson, musical support includes guitarist Russell Malone on two tracks and tenor saxman Ralph Moore cooking alongside Ms. Bridgewater on "Cherokee." *—Jim Newsom*

Dave Brubeck

b. Dec. 6, 1920, Concord, CA
Piano, Composer / West Coast Jazz, Cool
Dave Brubeck has long served as proof that creative jazz and popular success can go together. Although critics who had championed him when he was unknown seemed to scorn him when the Dave Brubeck Quartet became a surprise success, in reality Brubeck never watered down or altered his music in order to gain a wide audience. Creative booking (being one of the first groups to play regularly on college campuses) and a bit of luck resulted in great popularity and Dave Brubeck today remains as one of the few household names in jazz. From nearly the start Brubeck enjoyed utilizing polyrhythms and polytonality (playing in two keys at once). During 1946-49 Brubeck led a group mostly consisting of fellow Mills College classmates and they recorded as the Dave Brubeck Octet; their music (released on Fantasy in 1951) still sounds advanced today with complex time signatures and some polytonality. The octet was too radical to get much work so Brubeck formed a trio with drummer Cal Tjader (who doubled on vibes) and bassist Ron Crotty. In 1951, Brubeck was persuaded by altoist Paul Desmond to make the group a quartet. Within two years the band had become surprisingly popular. Desmond's cool-toned alto and quick wit fit in well with Brubeck's often heavy chording and experimental playing; both Brubeck and Desmond had original sounds and styles that owed little to their predecessors. The huge success of Paul Desmond's "Take Five" (1960) was followed by many songs played in "odd" time signatures such as 7/4 and 9/8; the high-quality soloing of the musicians kept these experiments from sounding like gimmicks. *—Scott Yanow*

The Dave Brubeck Octet / 1946-Jul. 1950 / Fantasy/OJC ✦✦✦✦
On infrequent occasions during 1946-50, pianist Dave Brubeck led an octet that was dominated by students of the composer Darius Milhaud. This pioneering West Coast outfit combined bop with modern classical music to form an interesting new blend of styles but, since they only recorded one LP's worth of material (which has remained obscure through the decades), the octet's life and general influence were limited. With such players as trumpeter Dick Collins, altoist Paul Desmond, Bill Smith on clarinet and baritone, tenor-saxophonist Dave Van Kreidt and a rhythm section comprised of Brubeck, bassist Ron Crotty and Cal Tjader on drums, this fascinating group performs highly original music throughout this CD reissue. *—Scott Yanow*

Time Signatures: A Career Retrospective / 1946-May 7, 1991 / Columbia/Legacy ✦✦✦✦
This four-CD boxed set does a near-perfect job of summing up Dave Brubeck's extensive recorded legacy. Drawing its recordings from not only Columbia but Fantasy, Atlantic and Music Masters, the attractive package also includes an extensive booklet written by Doug Ramsey that can serve as a mini-biography. The focus is naturally on Brubeck's quartet with altoist Paul Desmond but there is also music from before and after their association, even including one otherwise unissued performance, a remarkable polytonal polyrhythmic version of "Tritonis." Although completists will prefer to acquire Dave Brubeck's individual releases, this set is perfect for those just beginning to explore the magic of his music. *—Scott Yanow*

The Dave Brubeck Trio with Gerry Mulligan & the Cincinnati Symphony Orchestra / Sep. 1949-Nov. 1950 / MCA ✦✦✦✦
This collaboration with Eric Kunzel and the Cincinnati Symphony Orchestra was Dave Brubeck's third, but the addition of guest Gerry Mulligan and the purely instrumental nature of this release make it very different from the two albums of sacred music that preceded it. "Happy Anniversary" is a big and brassy opener that features brief, effective solos by both Mulligan and Brubeck, while Frank Proto's arrangement of "The Duke" adds a mysterious introduction that includes tidbits of several of Ellington's landmark songs. "Blessed Are the Poor" is impressive even without it's lyric, while "Forty Days" (probably Brubeck's best known composition among his sacred songs) is highlighted by Brubeck's aggressive solo and Mulligan's soulful tone. The extended work "Elementals" is superior to the original version recorded for Columbia and marks a finale to a rather brief but essential CD. *—Ken Dryden*

Dave Brubeck/Paul Desmond / Sep. 1952-Mar. 30, 1954 / Fantasy ✦✦✦✦
This CD reissues two earlier Fantasy LPs titled *Jazz at the Black Hawk* and *Jazz at Storyville.* Pianist Dave Brubeck and altoist Paul Desmond are the two main constants while bassists Ron Crotty and Wyatt Ruther and drummers Lloyd Davis, Herb Barman and Joe Dodge are heard on some tracks. There are many high points to this interesting set including Brubeck-Desmond duets on "Over the Rainbow" and "You Go to My Head," an unaccompanied piano solo on "My Heart Stood Still" and quartet versions of "Jeepers Creepers," "Trolley Song" and "Crazy Chris." *—Scott Yanow*

Jazz at Oberlin / Mar. 2, 1953 / Fantasy/OJC ✦✦✦✦
Although a touch underrated, this is one of the early Dave Brubeck classic recordings. The interplay between the pianist-leader and altoist Paul Desmond on "Perdido" borders on the miraculous and their renditions of "The Way You Look Tonight," "How High The Moon" and "Stardust" are quite memorable. Brubeck's piano playing on "These Foolish Things" in one spot is so percussive and atonal as to sound like Cecil Taylor, who would not emerge for another two years. With bassist Ron Crotty and drummer Lloyd Davis giving the Quartet quiet and steady support, Brubeck and Desmond were free to play at their most adventurous. Highly recommended. *—Scott Yanow*

Jazz at the College of the Pacific / Dec. 14, 1953 / Fantasy/OJC ✦✦✦✦✦
This CD brings back a near-classic (one of many from this period) by the Dave Brubeck Quartet. Drummer Joe Dodge had just joined the group and he joins with bassist Ron Crotty in laying down a solid and subtle foundation. However the real action takes place up front with pianist Dave Brubeck and altoist Paul Desmond. Their individual solos are full of creative ideas on six standards (most memorable are "All The Things You Are," "Laura" and "I'll Never Smile Again") and their interaction and tradeoffs are timeless. Recommended. *—Scott Yanow*

☆ **Jazz Goes to College** / Mar. 1954 / Columbia ✦✦✦✦✦
A true classic, this CD reissues the original LP. Altoist Paul Desmond's lengthy solo on the blues "Balcony Rock" was one of the greatest of his career with one fresh idea leading (through repetition and gradual development) logically into another; pianist Brubeck's improvisation on this piece almost reaches the heights of Desmond's. Bassist Bob Bates and drummer Joe Dodge give a solid and quiet accompaniment to Desmond and the unpredictable pianist/leader with other highlights including "Out of Nowhere," "The Song Is You" and "Don't Worry 'Bout Me." This is the Brubeck Quartet at its best. *—Scott Yanow*

Interchanges '54: Featuring Paul Desmond / Oct. 1954-Nov. 1954 / Columbia ✦✦✦✦
This excellent CD reissues the LP *Brubeck Time* plus half of *Red Hot and Cool.* One of the few early studio (as opposed to club) recordings by the early Dave Brubeck Quartet (this version has bassist Bob Bates and drummer Joe Dodge in addition to pianist Brubeck and altoist Paul Desmond), the fine unit performs nine standards plus three new compositions: "Stompin' for Mili," "Audrey" (dedicated to Audrey Hepburn) and Brubeck's classic, "The Duke." *—Scott Yanow*

Brubeck Plays Brubeck / Apr. 18, 1956–Apr. 19, 1956 / Columbia ✦✦✦
Dave Brubeck has had a strikingly original style ever since he appeared on records, avoiding the usual Bud Powell runs and instead expressing his training in classical music and his interest in polyrhythms and polytonality while never forgetting to swing. On his first solo piano record, Brubeck not only plays quite well but introduces such new compositions as "In Your Own Sweet Way" and "One Moment Worth Years" in addition to performing a remake of "The Duke." *—Scott Yanow*

Dave Digs Disney / Jun. 29, 1957-Aug. 3, 1957 / Columbia/Legacy ✦✦✦✦
This CD contains the original LP of the same name plus two previously unissued songs ("Very Good Advice" and "So This Is Love"). Inspired by a trip with his family to Disneyland, Dave Brubeck recorded eight songs taken from four Disney movies (*Alice in Wonderland, Pinocchio, Snow White* and *Cinderella*), including such melodies as "Give a Little Whistle," "Heigh Ho," "When You Wish Upon a Star" and "Someday My Prince Will Come." The funny part is that all of these songs were already in the Brubeck Quartet's repertoire. The results are pleasing although, due to a misprint, the CD booklet only contains half of the original liner notes. *—Scott Yanow*

Jazz Impressions of Eurasia / Jul. 28, 1958-Aug. 23, 1958 / Columbia/Legacy ✦✦✦✦
In 1958 Dave Brubeck's Quartet, one of the most popular jazz groups in the world, played 80 concerts in 14 countries during a three-month period. To salute the marathon road trip, the pianist/leader composed six songs for a new recording (which is now out on this CD). "Nomad" and "Brandenburg Gate" are the best-known originals but all of the other selections are equally enjoyable, featuring fine solos from Brubeck and altoist Paul Desmond. *—Scott Yanow*

★ **Time Out** / Jun. 25, 1959-Aug. 18, 1959 / Columbia/Legacy ✦✦✦✦✦
This is one of the most popular jazz recordings of all time. Altoist Paul Desmond's memorable "Take Five" became a huge hit, showing that it is possible for creative jazz to sell. In addition to "Take Five" (which is still a standard), other highpoints of this classic album include "Blue Rondo A La Turk" and "Three to Get Ready." Bassist Eugene Wright and drummer Joe Morello (whose talents made it possible for Brubeck's Quartet to play in different time signatures) are superb in support of the two lead voices. This classic set (which has been reissued many times including on a 1997 CD) is essential for all jazz collections. *—Scott Yanow*

Brubeck & Rushing / Jan. 29, 1960-Aug. 4, 1960 / Columbia/Legacy ✦✦✦
Although associated with the more modern styles of jazz, Brubeck always had a great respect (if not reverence) for the masters of the past. On ten standards Brubeck, altoist Paul Desmond and the Quartet fit in perfectly behind the great swing/blues singer Jimmy Rushing who sounds rejuvenated by the fresh setting. This LP, a surprising success, is well worth searching for. *—Scott Yanow*

Time Further Out / May 3, 1961-1963 / Columbia/Legacy ✦✦✦✦✦
Unlike most sequels, *Time Further Out* is a worthy successor to *Time Out*. Among the numbers introduced on this impressive set are "It's a Raggy Waltz" and "Unsquare Dance" (the latter an ancestor of Don Ellis's "Pussy Wiggle Stomp"). The selections, which range in time signatures from 5/4 to 9/8, are handled with apparent ease (or at least not too much difficulty) by pianist Brubeck, altoist Paul Desmond, bassist Eugene Wright and drummer Joe Morello on this near-classic. The 1996 CD reissue adds a previously inissued "Slow and Easy" and a version of "It's a Raggy Waltz" from the Quartet's 1963 Carnegie Hall concert to the original program. *—Scott Yanow*

Real Ambassadors / Sep. 12, 1961-Sep. 19, 1961 / Columbia/Legacy ✦✦✦✦
In 1961 Dave Brubeck put together a remarkable musical show. Using the talents of Louis Armstrong and his All-Stars, Carmen McRae, the innovative bop vocal group Lambert, Hendricks And Ross and his own rhythm section, Brubeck and his wife, lyricist Iola, wrote a largely upbeat play full of anti-racism songs and tunes that celebrated human understanding. Although it had only one live performance (at the 1962 Monterey Jazz Festival), *The Real Ambassadors* was recorded for posterity and now, with its reissue on CD, the original 15 selections have been augmented by five more. It is important to listen to this music without prior expectations because Paul Desmond is nowhere to be found, Louis Armstrong does not play that much trumpet here and Lambert, Hendricks And Ross essentially function as background singers. However Satch and Carmen McRae make for a very potent team and there are many touching and surprising moments. *—Scott Yanow*

Bravo! Brubeck! / May 12, 1967-May 14, 1967 / Columbia/Legacy ✦✦✦✦
One of the better Dave Brubeck LPs from the later period of the Quartet with altoist Paul Desmond, this set is unusual in that it only contains one Brubeck original. On such tunes as "Cielito Lindo," the beautiful "La Paloma," "Besame Mucho" and "Estrellita," the Quartet is augmented by guitarist Chamin Correa and percussionist Rabito Agueros. The results are melodic but swinging treatments of a variety of famous themes. *—Scott Yanow*

Live at the Berlin Philharmonic / Nov. 7, 1970 / Columbia/Legacy ✦✦✦✦✦
Out of the 13 selections included on this double CD, six were originally released just in Europe, two ("Out of Nowhere" and "Mexican Jumping Bean") were never out before and only five songs were on the American LP. Considering how inspired the Dave Brubeck Quartet sounds, it is surprising that the music has been so obscure for so long. Baritonist Gerry Mulligan is particularly heated on the opening two numbers (the unreleased tracks), pianist Dave Brubeck really stretches himself (check him out on "Things Ain't What They Used to Be" where he progresses from stride to free), and bassist Jack Six and drummer Alan Dawson, in addition to their solo space, are quite alert and constantly pushing the lead voices. Not only are the musicians in top form but the audience is very enthusiastic, demanding three encores. The extensive liner notes by Geoffrey Smith are also a major plus. Highly recommended. *—Scott Yanow*

All the Things We Are / Jul. 17, 1973-Oct. 3, 1974 / Atlantic ✦✦✦✦
This album is a bit unusual in the Dave Brubeck discography. The pianist is heard in a quartet with altoist Lee Konitz on "Like Someone in Love" and a brief "Don't Get Around much Anymore," avant-garde giant Anthony Braxton (also on alto) is featured on "In Your Own Sweet Way" and both Konitz and Braxton team up for "All the Things You Are." In addition, the Brubeck Trio (with bassist Jack Six and drummer Alan Dawson) plays an exquisite and frequently exciting 21-minute five-song "Jimmy Van Heusen Medley." A total success, this "experimental" Brubeck set is highly recommended. *—Scott Yanow*

25th Anniversary Reunion / Mar. 10, 1976-Mar. 12, 1976 / A&M ✦✦✦✦
This classic recording was the last time that pianist Dave Brubeck recorded with the late altoist Paul Desmond. The reunion of the most famous version of Brubeck's Quartet (which also included bassist Eugene Wright and drummer Joe Morello) found all of the players enthusiastic and still in their prime (although Morello's eyesight was failing). "St. Louis Blues," the tender "Don't Worry 'Bout Me," "Three to Get Ready" and yet another version of "Take Five" are among the highpoints of this historic final session. *—Scott Yanow*

Paper Moon / Sep. 1981 / Concord Jazz ✦✦✦✦✦
The third of three Concord albums by this version of the Quartet (with Jerry Bergonzi on tenor, Chris Brubeck on bass and bass trombone and drummer Randy Jones) is the most rewarding of the trio although each one is recommended. Brubeck and the Coltrane-influenced tenor Bergonzi take consistently exciting solos on seven standards which are highlighted by "Music, Maestro, Please," "I Hear a Rhapsody" and "It's Only a Paper Moon"; Brubeck's solo version of "St. Louis Blues" is also noteworthy. *—Scott Yanow*

Blue Rondo / Nov. 1986 / Concord Jazz ✦✦✦✦
The 1987 edition of the Brubeck Quartet featured pianist Brubeck, his son Chris on electric bass and bass trombone, clarinetist Bill Smith and drummer Randy Jones. In addition to remakes of "Blue Rondo à la Turk," "Strange Meadowlark" and "Swing Bells," the leader contributed six new originals including "I See, Satie" and a tribute to Dizzy Gillespie and Stan Getz called "Dizzy's Dream." Bill Smith, who uses electronics with taste on his clarinet during a few songs, has long been a major asset to the later Brubeck Quartets. This is one of their better Concord CDs. *—Scott Yanow*

Moscow Nights / Mar. 1987 / Concord Jazz ✦✦✦✦
In 1987 Brubeck, after decades of trying, finally had an opportunity to perform with his Quartet in the Soviet Union. The enthusiastic crowd (many of whom had grown up on Brubeck's music) clearly inspired the musicians which included clarinetist Bill Smith, electric bassist Chris Brubeck and drummer Randy Jones. Together they perform exciting versions of a variety of the leader's tunes plus Howard Brubeck's "Theme for June," "St. Louis Blues" and of course "Take Five." *—Scott Yanow*

Nightshift / Oct. 5, 1993-Oct. 10, 1993 / Telarc ✦✦✦✦
This is a particularly well-balanced set with pianist Dave Brubeck (then 73) in typically creative form. Although Brubeck (who is accompanied throughout by bassist Jack Six and drummer Randy Jones) is actually the real star of every selection (coming up with continually inventive ideas whether in ensembles, behind soloists or during his own solos), he is joined by three of his favorite horn players on some of the numbers. Bobby Militello shows a great deal of versatility with some blazing alto on "Yesterdays," melodic playing in a Paul Desmond vein on "I Can't Give You Anything but Love," soulful tenor on "Travelin' Blues" and plenty of intensity on "Knives." Clarinetist Bill Smith is well featured on "You Go to My Head" and the boisterous bass trombone of Chris Burbeck makes several welcome appearances. This recommended set has more than its share of variety and surprising moments. *—Scott Yanow*

Late Night Brubeck / Oct. 5, 1993-Oct. 7, 1993 / Telarc ✦✦✦✦
Dave Brubeck teams up with Bobby Militello (heard here on alto, tenor and flute), bassist Jack Six and drummer Randy Jones for a set that emphasizes ballads and slower tempos. Militello brings back the spirit of Paul Desmond while Brubeck's own playing continues to be full of surprises. On "Theme for June" he breaks out into stride, a Duke Ellington medley seems to develop quite spontaneously and "Mean to Me" really works well. With bassist Jack Six and drummer Randy Jones fine in support, this CD is a strong effort from Dave Brubeck, who has nearly 100 worthwhile recordings currently in print. *—Scott Yanow*

40th Anniversary Tour of the U.K. / Nov. 10, 1998-Nov. 12, 1998 / Telarc ✦✦✦✦
Forty years after his classic quartet's first triumphant tour of the U.K. in 1958, Dave Brubeck took his current group back for an anniversary visit, playing a mixed bag of old and new for audiences both old and new. This time out Brubeck's working quartet included two British natives, drummer Randy Jones and bassist Alec Dankworth (the son of British jazz superstars Cleo Laine and John Dankworth). Brubeck himself was the obvious draw for the crowds, but it's saxman Bobby Militello who is truly the musical star of the show. The highly regarded Militello shows he can roam across the entire spectrum of alto saxophone tonality, employing a light, delicate tone a la Paul Desmond one minute, then bearing down for some gritty, deep-throated improvisations the next. Brubeck's unmistakable pianism remains as identifiable as ever, comping and soloing with the same energy he undoubtedly had 40 years earlier. "Goodbye Old Friend," his solo farewell to friend Gerry Mulligan, is beautiful. The new material is more interesting than the older stuff, with Brubeck's tango "The Time of Our Madness" and blues-inflected "Oh You Can Run (But You Can't Hide)" particular standouts. However, Militello enlivens even the old warhorse "I Got Rhythm," and Brubeck himself digs fresh ideas out of "Deep Purple." *—Jim Newsom*

One Alone / Sep. 3, 1997-Feb. 24, 2000 / Telarc ✦✦✦✦
Dave Brubeck rarely recorded as a solo pianist, but beginning in the late '90s, he started performing occasional solo pieces in concert and recorded two first-rate solo dates for Telarc. His third solo CD for the label is full of rich harmonies that any Brubeck fan can identify as his in seconds, including a mix of memorable but overlooked songs from the 1920s through the 1940s, plus a few choice standards and a pair of his timeless originals. Brubeck clearly loves old ballads like "That Old Feeling" and "I'll Never Smile Again," and there are several classics that are perfect vehicles for Brubeck. "Someone to Watch Over Me" is yet another lush ballad, while his unusual chord substitutions to the very familiar "Over the Rainbow" are dazzling. He ventures into Duke Ellington's repertoire, obviously having fun with the jaunty "Just Squeeze Me" but at a slower tempo than one would expect; his percussive swinging take of "Things Ain't What They Used to Be" is just as fun but wilder. Brubeck only features two of his own works, but they are among his best. "Weep No More" is the obscure song, appearing first as a part of his 1956 solo piano LP for Columbia, *Brubeck Plays Brubeck;* this poignant melody deserves to be better known than it is. "Summer Song," written as a vocal feature for Louis Armstrong in Dave & Iola Brubeck's short-lived production *The Real Ambassadors*, has gradually become a jazz standard. This highly recommended CD is yet another of his finest hours. *—Ken Dryden*

Rusty Bryant

b. Nov. 25, 1929, Huntington, WV, **d.** Mar. 25, 1991, Columbus, OH
Sax (Tenor) / Hard Bop, Post-Bop, Soul-Jazz
Among the finest funky and soul-jazz tenors of the '70s, Bryant is noted for his thick tone, robust sound, and jam-session-style albums. Rusty Bryant is one of the original bar-walking sax players.

Royal G. "Rusty " Bryant was born on November 25, 1929 in Huntington, West Virginia, but was raised in Columbus, Ohio. He credits Gene Ammons and Sonny Stitt as his main influences. He played with and learned from Tiny Grimes and Stomp Gordon, and was leading his own groups by 1951. Bryant toured with Hammond organist Mike Marr during the 1960s. He settled in Columbus, Ohio. *—Michael Erlewine & Ron Wynn*

Rusty Bryant Returns / Feb. 17, 1969 / Prestige/OJC ✦✦✦✦
Rusty Bryant, a veteran R&B tenor player, was somewhat forgotten at the time of his debut Prestige album, but due to the commercial success of this recording, Bryant would record seven more sessions for Prestige during the next five years. Actually, this date is a bit sur-

prising, with Bryant sticking exclusively to alto and sometimes using an electrified model similar to what Lou Donaldson was playing at the time. The music (mostly blues-oriented originals) is enjoyable, with plenty of boogaloos and soulful vamps. In addition to Bryant, the main soloists are guitarist Grant Green, in excellent form, and organist Sonny Phillips. *—Scott Yanow*

● **Legends of Acid Jazz** / Oct. 6, 1969–Jun. 15, 1970 / Prestige ✦✦✦✦✦
Presenting both the 1969 album *Night Train Now!* and the 1970 follow-up *Soul Liberation* in their entirety, this 73-minute disc is the best document of Bryant at his soul-jazz peak. *—Richie Unterberger*

Legends of Acid Jazz, Vol. 2 / Feb. 22, 1971–Oct. 1971 / Prestige ✦✦✦
A single-CD reissue that combines two 1971 albums, *Fire-Eater* and *Wildfire*. *Fire-Eater* is just four long cuts, all between seven and ten minutes in length, on a session that has Bryant stretching out his meaty tone and improvisations a bit further than usual. This is respectable soul-jazz with a lot of funk, but no fusion, employing the tenor sax-organ-guitar-drums lineup. All of the material was written by Bryant or members of the quartet, and favors a laid-back groove that's on the slow side, except for "Mister S.," on which guitarist Wilbert Longmire has a particularly engaging solo. *Wildfire* is dependable, if rather predictable, early-'70s soul-jazz from Bryant, on one of the several sessions from the era that benefited from the forceful groove of drummer Idris Muhammad. It's the kind of music that network television used to employ at the time as background on film clips summarizing the week's pro basketball highlights—not a mocking criticism, just an observation. There are a couple of originals penned by Bryant and organist Bill Mason, but most of the album is given over to rock, soul, and pop covers, including an unlikely jaunty reading of the Doors' *"Riders on the Storm."* On Stevie Wonder's "If You Really Love Me," Bryant takes off into some pretty impressive improv flights. *—Richie Unterberger*

Jane Bunnett

b. Oct. 22, 1956, Toronto, Ontario, Canada
Sax (Soprano), Flute / Afro-Cuban Jazz, Post-Bop, Latin Jazz, Worldbeat
One of the finest soprano-saxophonists in jazz of the 1990s, Jane Bunnett originally studied classical piano but tendonitis cut short that career. After seeing the Charles Mingus group in San Francisco, Bunnett was inspired to play advanced jazz. On soprano she recalls Steve Lacy a bit (who she has studied with) while her flute playing is quite distinctive. Bunnett has always had major players on her records; in addition to her husband trumpeter Larry Cramer, the late pianist Don Pullen had been a fixture on her records, her 1988 debut for Dark Light also featured Dewey Redman and she has utilized Sheila Jordan and Jeanne Lee.

Bunnett has recorded for Dark Light, Music & Arts (a series of duets with Pullen) and Denon. Her most adventurous work thus far is 1991's *Spirits of Havana* which matches her playing with many of Cuba's top jazz musicians in Cuba. In recent years Jane Bunnett has been living in Paris. *—Scott Yanow*

● **Spirits of Havana** / Sep. 27, 1991-Oct. 4, 1991 / Messidor ✦✦✦✦✦
On this remarkable CD, Jane Bunnett (doubling on flute and soprano) performs Cuban music on its own terms quite successfully. Bunnett and a pair of fellow Canadians (trumpeter Larry Cramer and bassist Kieran Overs) recorded in Havana with some of the top Cuban musicians including Guillermo Barreto (who supervised the sessions, played some timbales and was an inspiration to Bunnett), singer Merceditas Valdes, pianists Hilario Duran, Gonzalo Rubalcaba and Frank Emilio, several top percussionists and others. The very original music (including a fresh rendition of Thelonious Monk's "Epistrophy") is well worth several listens and is a classic of its kind. *—Scott Yanow*

Water is Wide / Aug. 18, 1993-Aug. 19, 1993 / Evidence ✦✦✦✦
This intriguing set has more than its share of variety. Jane Bunnett pays tribute to Rahsaan Roland Kirk with some speechlike flute on "Serenade to a Cuckoo," recalls Steve Lacy a bit with her soprano on two Thelonious Monk pieces ("Pannonica" and "Brake's Sake") and her originals (along with those of trumpeter Larry Cramer) range from advanced bop to fairly free improvising. Vocalists Sheila Jordan (wonderful on "You Must Believe in Spring") and Jeanne Lee have individual features and are both major parts of the ancient hymn "The Water Is Wide" while the rhythm section (pianist Don Pullen, bassist Kieran Overs and drummer Billy Hart) consistently displays flexibility and creative reactions to the directions of the lead voices. *—Scott Yanow*

Rendez-Vous Brazil/Cuba / May 20, 1995-May 21, 1995 / Justin Time ✦✦✦✦
Jane Bunnett has done a great deal to document the modern Cuban jazz scene. On this CD, she mixes aspects of Cuban music with Brazilian jazz, a combination not often utilized. The music overall is a bit softer and mellower than some of her previous sets, but Bunnett is in superb form on both soprano and flute and has her fiery moments. Guitarist Filo Machado (who along with his brother, percussionist Celso Machado, is largely responsible for the Brazilian flavor) contributed five of the ten selections, while Bunnett brought in two originals. Other soloists include trumpeter Larry Cramer and pianist Hilario Duran. A continually intriguing date that grows in interest with each listen. *—Scott Yanow*

Ritmo & Soul / 1992 / Blue Note ✦✦✦✦

Kenny Burrell (Kenneth Earl Burrell)

b. Jul. 31, 1931, Detroit, MI
Guitar (Electric), Guitar / Hard Bop, Cool, Bop
Kenny Burrell has been a very consistent guitarist throughout his career. Cool-toned and playing in an unchanging style based in bop, Burrell has always been the epitome of good taste and solid swing. Duke Ellington's favorite guitarist (though he never actually recorded with him), Burrell started playing guitar when he was 12 and he debuted on records with Dizzy Gillespie in 1951. Part of the fertile Detroit jazz scene of the early '50s, Burrell moved to New York in 1956. Highly in-demand from the start, Burrell has appeared on a countless number of records during the past 40 years as a leader and as a sideman. Among his more notable associations have been dates with Stan Getz, Billie Holiday, Milt Jackson, John Coltrane, Gil Evans, Sonny Rollins, Quincy Jones, Stanley Turrentine and Jimmy Smith. Starting in the early '70s Burrell began leading seminars and teaching, often focusing on Duke Ellington's music. He toured with the Phillip Morris Superband during 1985-86 and has led three-guitar quintets but generally Kenny Burrell plays at the head of a trio/quartet. *—Scott Yanow*

Introducing Kenny Burrell / May 29, 1956 / Blue Note ✦✦✦✦
Despite its title, this LP was actually guitarist Kenny Burrell's second Blue Note album, although the first to be released. Teamed with pianist Tommy Flanagan, bassist Paul Chambers, drummer Kenny Clarke and the conga of Candido, Burrell displays what was already an immediately recognizable tone. At 24, Burrell had quickly emerged to become one of the top bop guitarists of the era, and he is in particularly excellent form on "This Time the Dreams on Me," "Weaver of Dreams" and "Delilah." A bonus of this set is a percussion duo by Clarke and Candido on "Rhythmorama." Enjoyable music. *—Scott Yanow*

All Day Long/All Night Long / Dec. 28, 1956–Jan. 4, 1957 / Prestige/OJC ✦✦✦✦
Two of guitarist Kenny Burrell's finest sessions from the 1950s are combined on this appealing double-LP; the music is also available now on two separate CDs. The high point of the earlier date is the nearly 17-minute "All Night Long," a jam featuring guitarist Burrell, trumpeter Donald Byrd, Hank Mobley on tenor, Jerome Richardson doubling on flute and tenor, pianist Mal Waldron, bassist Doug Watkins and drummer Art Taylor. The group of young all-stars also performs three shorter originals. That particular session was so successful that the same group (with Tommy Flanagan in Waldron's place and Frank Foster replacing both Mobley and Richardson) came back into the studio a week later and recorded the 18-minute "All Day Long" and three other originals. Both of these swinging dates were somewhat inspired and are recommended either as this two-fer or as CDs. *—Scott Yanow*

Blue Moods / Feb. 1, 1957 / Prestige ✦✦✦✦✦
Smooth, cool, yet musically impressive late '50s date that has both blowing session fervor and soulful undergirding. Burrell's fluid guitar voicings and Cecil Payne's robust baritone make nice partners, while Tommy Flanagan adds his usual sparkling piano riffs and solos, and bassist Doug Watkins teams with Elvin Jones, who shows he can drive a date without dominating things on drums. *—Ron Wynn*

Two Guitars / Mar. 5, 1957 / Prestige/OJC ✦✦✦
For this 1957 studio session (which has been reissued on CD in the OJC series), the two distinctive but complementary guitarists Kenny Burrell and Jimmy Raney are teamed together in a septet with trumpeter Donald Byrd, altoist Jackie McLean, pianist Mal Waldron, bassist Doug Watkins and drummer Art Taylor. The full group gets to stretch out on originals by Watkins, McLean ("Little Melonae"), and three from Waldron, while the two standards ("Close Your Eyes" and "Out of Nowhere") are individual features for Burrell and Raney. This is a well-rounded set that may not contain any real surprises but will be enjoyed by collectors of hard bop. *—Scott Yanow*

Kenny Burrell & John Coltrane / Mar. 7, 1958 / Prestige/OJC ✦✦✦✦
John Coltrane recorded many interesting jam session-type dates in the 1950s. This matchup with guitarist Kenny Burrell (in a quintet with pianist Tommy Flanagan, bassist Paul Chambers and drummer Jimmy Cobb) finds the group stretching out on two Flanagan compositions, Burrell's "Lyresto," and the standard "I Never Knew." In addition, Coltrane and Burrell play a short duet on "Why Was I Born." Overall, the music is excellent for the time period, with Coltrane displaying some of his sheets of sound and Burrell sounding inspired by 'Trane's presence. It was formerly available as the first half of a two-LP set, *Kenny Burrell/John Coltrane*. *—Scott Yanow*

☆ **Blue Lights, Vols. 1-2** / May 14, 1958 / Blue Note ✦✦✦✦✦
The music on this 1997 two-CD set was originally on two LPs and already previously reissued as a pair of CDs. Guitarist Kenny Burrell leads a very coherent jam session in the studio with a particularly strong cast that also includes trumpeter Louis Smith, both Junior Cook and Tina Brooks on tenors, either Duke Jordan or Bobby Timmons on piano, bassist Sam Jones and drummer Art Blakey. The material consists of basic originals and standards and has excellent playing all around; six of the nine tunes are over nine minutes long. At that point in time, Cook and Brooks had similar sounds, but fortunately, the soloists are identified in the liner notes for each song. The solo star is often trumpeter Louis Smith, who fell into obscurity after a few notable appearances on Blue Note during the period (including his own brilliant date, *Here Comes Louis Smith*). He was one of the finest of the Clifford Brown-influenced players of the period and deserves much greater recognition. This is a recommended reissue for hard bop collectors who do not already have the two individual CDs. *—Scott Yanow*

On View at the Five Spot Cafe / Aug. 25, 1959-Aug. 26, 1959 / Blue Note ✦✦✦✦
This likable live set from guitarist Kenny Burrell has a strong supporting cast (Tina Brooks on tenor, either Bobby Timmons or Roland Hanna on piano, bassist Ben Tucker and drummer Art Blakey) and the original five-song program has been expanded on this CD to eight tunes. The swinging music, highlighted by "Lady Be Good," "Birks Works," the blues "36-23-36" and Burrell's feature on "Lover Man," is quite mainstream for the period and predictably excellent. *—Scott Yanow*

★ **Midnight Blue** / Jan. 7, 1963 / Blue Note ✦✦✦✦✦
This album is one of guitarist Kenny Burrell's best-known sessions for the Blue Note label. Burrell is matched with tenor saxophonist Stanley Turrentine, bassist Major Holley, drummer Bill English and Ray Barretto on conga for a blues-oriented date highlighted by "Chitlins Con Carne," "Midnight Blue," "Saturday Night Blues" and the lone standard "Gee Baby Ain't I Good to You." *—Scott Yanow*

Freedom / Mar. 27, 1963-Oct. 22, 1964 / Blue Note ✦✦✦✦

Blue Bash / Jul. 16, 1963-Jul. 26, 1963 / Verve ✦✦✦

Soul Call / Apr. 7, 1964 / Prestige/OJC ✦✦✦
Guitarist Kenny Burrell alternates blues and ballads on this swinging quintet set with pianist Will Davis, bassist Martin Rivera, drummer Bill English and Ray Barretto on congas. The mu-

sic is melodic and boppish, although no real surprises occur. By this time, Burrell was a very respectful player, upholding the tradition rather than offering any real innovations. This CD reissue will still be enjoyed by his fans. *—Scott Yanow*

Guitar Forms / Dec. 4, 1964-Apr. 12, 1965 / Verve ✦✦✦✦
Though this ranks as one of arranger Gil Evans' minor achievements in the grand scheme of things, for Kenny Burrell it was a career-defining moment, one of his most individual, most multi-faceted, most emotionally affecting recordings. Whether playing straight-ahead and countrified blues on electric guitar, dipping into the bossa nova and brooding post-*Sketches of Spain* backgrounds on acoustic guitar, or interpreting classical music, Burrell quietly lets the world know that he can be as versatile as he is tasteful. Evans collectors should know that Evans' charts only appear on five of the selections. On three others, Burrell is featured with a swinging conga-accented combo that includes pianist Roger Kellaway, and Burrell goes solo on a transcribed excerpt from George Gershwin's "Prelude No. 2" for piano. What is special about this release is not so much the improved sound as the inclusion of a truckload of outtakes from the small-group sessions, which have the effect of doubling the length of the original album. All of them—four takes each of the bluesy "Downstairs" and "Breadwinner" and three of "Terrace Theme"—are worth hearing, for Burrell's invention rarely flags, and what fluffs there are do not upset the group's swinging rapport. The outtakes, though, are grouped by title at the end of the CD in a way that might induce fatigue; you could shuffle the order with your programming controls and get a more listenable lineup that way. *—Richard S. Ginell*

☆ **Ellington Is Forever, Vol. 1** / Feb. 4, 1975-Feb. 5, 1975 / Fantasy ✦✦✦✦✦
This two-CD set is a splendid and well-conceived tribute to Duke Ellington by guitarist Kenny Burrell. In a variety of settings, he utilizes such special players as trumpeters Thad Jones, Snooky Young and Jon Faddis, tenors Joe Henderson and Jerome Richardson, organist Jimmy Smith and a fine rhythm section headed by pianist Jimmy Jones. Ernie Andrews has two vocals, all of the horn players get their chances to solo and 15 Ellington and Strayhorn songs receive tasteful yet inventive treatments. It's recommended along with the second volume. *—Scott Yanow*

Ellington Is Forever, Vol. 2 / Dec. 1975 / Fantasy ✦✦✦✦
The second two-CD set to result from guitarist Kenny Burrell's marathon tribute to Duke Ellington is even wider ranging than the first. In addition to such stars as guitarist Burrell, trumpeters Snooky Young and Thad Jones, tenors Joe Henderson and Jerome Richardson, organist Jimmy Smith, pianist Jimmy Jones, and singer Ernie Andrews, this release has solo space for cornetist Nat Adderley, trombonist Quentin Jackson, altoist Gary Bartz and pianist Roland Hanna. By varying the personnel and instrumentation from track-to-track, Kenny Burrell pays homage in a memorable fashion to 15 classic songs by Ellington and Strayhorn. It comes recommended, as does the first volume. *—Scott Yanow*

Sunup to Sundown / Jun. 10, 1991-Jun. 12, 1991 / Contemporary ✦✦✦✦
Guitarist Kenny Burrell has a strong all-around showcase on this release from Contemporary. Assisted by pianist Cedar Walton, bassist Rufus Reid, drummer Lewis Nash and percussionist Ray Mantilla, Burrell swings harder than he usually does when paying tribute to the past, coming up with fresh statements on the varied material. Although there are a few standards in the program (such as "I'm Old Fashioned," "Autumn Leaves" and "Speak Low"), there are also such obscurities as "Out There" (a medium-uptempo blues), "Sunup to Sundown" and "Love Dance." This set serves as an excellent introduction to Kenny Burrell's enjoyable brand of straightahead playing. *—Scott Yanow*

12-15-78 / Dec. 15, 1978 / 32 Jazz ✦✦✦✦
32 Records' *12-15-78* is a double-disc set that reissues the entirety of his concert at *the Village Vanguard.* Originally, the show was released as two separate albums—*Live at the Village Vanguard* and *In New York*—but this excellent collection features all of the music from both records, which happened to be among the finest Burrell recorded in the '70s. *—Stephen Thomas Erlewine*

Gary Burton

b. Jan. 23, 1943, Anderson, IN
Vibraphone / Post-Bop
One of the two great vibraphonists to emerge in the 1960s (along with Bobby Hutcherson), Gary Burton's remarkable four-mallet technique (best displayed on an unaccompanied version of "No More Blues" from 1971) can make him sound like two or three players at once. He has recorded in a wide variety of settings and always sounds distinctive. Self-taught on vibes, Burton made his recording debut with country guitarist Hank Garland when he was 17, started recording regularly for RCA in 1961 and toured with George Shearing's Quintet in 1963. He gained some fame while with Stan Getz's pianoless quartet during 1964-66 and then put together his own groups. In 1967 with guitarist Larry Coryell, he led one of the early "fusion" bands. Burton recorded duet sets with Chick Corea, Ralph Towner, Steve Swallow and Paul Bley, and collaborated on an album apiece with Stephane Grappelli and Keith Jarrett. Among his sidemen in the late '70s/'80s were Makoto Ozone, Tiger Okoshi and Tommy Smith. *—Scott Yanow*

3 in Jazz / Feb. 14, 1963-Mar. 11, 1963 / RCA ✦✦✦✦
This CD, a straight reissue of an RCA LP, has three unrelated but consistently interesting sessions that were recorded in 1963. Three selections with tenor-saxophonist Sonny Rollins (the only performances currently available elsewhere) are rather free (and fascinating) versions of standards and also feature cornetist Don Cherry, bassist Henry Grimes and drummer Billy Higgins. Vibraphonist Gary Burton's quartet (with trumpeter Jack Sheldon, bassist Monty Budwig and drummer Vernell Fournier) is fine if not overly memorable on their four numbers but flugelhornist Clark Terry (with pianist Hank Jones, bassist Milt Hinton, drummer Osie Johnson and Willie Rodriguez on Latin percussion) is in superior form, playing with great exuberance on "When My Dream Boat Comes Home" and "Cielito Lindo." Well worth picking up. *—Scott Yanow*

Artist's Choice / Aug. 15, 1963-Aug. 16, 1967 / Bluebird/RCA ✦✦✦✦✦
This session traces vibist Gary Burton's musical evolution during 1963-1968 with selections taken from eight of Burton's 13 RCA LPs. Burton was among the very first to incorporate elements of rock, pop and freer forms of jazz into his own music without trivializing any of the styles. *Artist's Choice* is a fine retrospective of the early Gary Burton, although one wishes these sessions were available in full rather than piecemeal. *—Scott Yanow*

Duster / Apr. 18, 1967-Apr. 20, 1967 / Koch ✦✦✦✦✦
This CD reissue is quite important and in some ways can be considered one of the first fusion records. Vibraphonist Gary Burton had just added the young rock/blues guitarist Larry Coryell to his quartet (which also included bassist Steve Swallow and drummer Roy Haynes), and Coryell's influence can be felt throughout the performances. Highlights include Michael Gibbs' "Sweet Rain," Swallow's "General Mojo's Well Laid Plan," Coryell's exploratory and speedy "One, Two, 1-2-3-4" and Carla Bley's "Sing Me Softly of the Blues." Although Burton's basic sound had not changed during from the previous year, his openness toward other styles made his Quartet one of the most significant jazz groups of the period. This was the first of the four Burton-Coryell recordings. This important set was reissued on a 1997 Koch CD. *—Scott Yanow*

A Genuine Tong Funeral / Nov. 20, 1967 / One Way ✦✦✦✦✦
One of vibraphonist Gary Burton's most intriguing recordings, *A Genuine Tong Funeral* (Carla Bley's suite which musically depicts attitudes toward death) was called by its composer a "Dark Opera Without Words." Burton's classic Quartet (which also includes guitarist Larry Coryell, bassist Steve Swallow and drummer Bob Moses) is augmented by six notable all-stars: soprano saxophonist Steve Lacy, trumpeter Mike Mantler, Gato Barbieri on tenor, trombonist Jimmy Knepper, Howard Johnson on tuba and baritone and Bley herself on piano and organ. The music is dramatic, occasionally a little humorous, and a superb showcase for Gary Burton's vibes. *—Scott Yanow*

★ **Gary Burton & Keith Jarrett/Throb** / Jun. 2, 1969-Jul. 23, 1970 / Rhino ✦✦✦✦✦
Two of vibraphonist Gary Burton's albums from 1969-70 and reissued in full on this single CD. Burton teams up with pianist Keith Jarrett for five numbers (including four of Jarrett's originals) in 1970, using a quintet that also features guitarist Sam Brown, bassist Steve Swallow and drummer Bill Goodwin. The other session has more of an avant-country flavor with Burton, Swallow and Goodwin joined by guitarist Jerry Hahn and violinist Richard Greene; Michael Gibbs and Steve Swallow contributed most of the obscurities. Burton was at his most explorative during this period which is why he can be considered one of the pioneers of fusion (although his music never really fit into a tight category). This is excellent music that mostly still sounds fresh. *—Scott Yanow*

Paris Encounter / Nov. 4, 1969 / Atlantic ✦✦✦✦✦
Atlantic has thus far been very slow to reissue its six valuable Gary Burton records. This particular set is the most accessible of the group, for it matches the advanced vibraphonist with the classic violinist Stephane Grappelli in a quartet also including electric bassist Steve Swallow and drummer Bill Goodwin. The music alternates between standards and originals (including Swallow's famous "Eiderdown"), and both Grappelli and Burton prove to be flexible enough to have much common ground despite a 35-year difference in age. A frequently delightful set. *—Scott Yanow*

Gary Burton & Keith Jarrett / Jan. 12, 1971 / Atlantic ✦✦✦✦✦
This combination works. Vibraphonist Gary Burton and pianist Keith Jarrett (along with guitarist Sam Brown, bassist Steve Swallow and drummer Bill Goodwin) play five Jarrett originals plus Steve Swallow's "Como en Vietnam." Elements of pop music, rock, country and the jazz avant-garde are used in the mixture of styles and the results are quite logical. Burton and Jarrett should have a reunion and see how their styles have grown since this early effort. *—Scott Yanow*

Crystal Silence / Nov. 6, 1972 / ECM ✦✦✦✦✦
Debut on ECM with Corea (k). The first of many successful pairings of the two. *—Ron Wynn*

Reunion [With Pat Metheny] / May 6, 1989-May 10, 1989 / GRP ✦✦✦✦✦

Face to Face / Oct. 31, 1994-Nov. 1, 1994 / GRP ✦✦✦✦✦
This set of duets between vibraphonist Gary Burton and pianist Makoto Ozone is a bit of a surprise, not the quiet and introverted date one might expect but a consistently exciting outing. The duo (who first started working together back in 1982) clearly inspires each other and a lot of sparks fly. The music ranges from three of Ozone's diverse originals and Astor Piazzola's "Laura's Romance" to a pair of Thelonious Monk tunes, a few standards and a romping version of the Benny Goodman-associated "Opus Half"; on the latter Ozone plays some creditable stride piano. More than half of the selections are taken at medium-to-fast tempos and, whether it be "Blue Monk," a memorable version of Jobim's "O Grande Amor" or a heated rendition of Steve Swallow's "Eiderdown," this is a highly enjoyable outing, one of Burton's finest of the past decade. *—Scott Yanow*

Astor Piazzolla Reunion: A Tango Excursion / Dec. 2, 1996-Dec. 5, 1996 / Concord Jazz ✦✦✦✦
Gary Burton has had many stellar moments over the years, and in the 1990s, one of his finest achievements was *Astor Piazzolla Reunion,* a heartfelt tribute to the late Argentinean tango innovator and bandoneon master. Having toured and recorded with Piazzolla in the 1980s, Burton clearly had a strong appreciation of his legacy, and that appreciation comes through in a major way on arrangements of "Tanguedia," "Romance Del Diablo," and other gems by Piazzolla (whose risk-taking approach to tango generated as much controversy in tango circles as Charlie Parker, Ornette Coleman, and John Coltrane did in jazz). But as passionately as Burton expresses his love of Piazzolla's distinctive music, the vibist's own identity doesn't become buried or obscured. The CD's only major flaw is "Mi Refugio"; Burton has taken Piazzolla's 1970 solo performance of that Juan Carlos Cobian classic and overdubbed his vibes to make it sound like they're performing a duet. Even if Burton had the best of intentions, the end result is deception and cheap, crude exploitation. But otherwise, this album is outstanding. *—Alex Henderson*

Like Minds / Dec. 15, 1997-Dec. 17, 1997 / Concord Jazz ✦✦✦✦✦
Talk about all-star groups—this quintet date matches together vibraphonist Gary Burton with pianist Chick Corea, guitarist Pat Metheny, bassist Dave Holland and drummer Roy Haynes. Burton and Corea have recorded frequently through the years, while Metheny gained some early fame working with Burton; Holland was with Corea in Miles Davis' late-1960s group, and Haynes was formerly with both Burton and Corea. However, not all of these musicians had played together before—Corea had never worked with Metheny previously, nor Burton with Holland. No matter; the masterful players fit together quite well. The vibraphonist is the lead voice in the ensembles, where Metheny at times sounds close to Jim Hall and seems a bit restrained, but everyone gets a chance to contribute to the success of the CD. Metheny contributed five songs (including "Question and Answer" and "Elucidation," which deserves to be a standard), while Burton brought in two; Corea's three contributions include his classic "Windows." The lone standard is George Gershwin's "Soon." The music is modern straight-ahead jazz; the solos are concise and the rhythm section is quite tight. In fact, this sounds like a regularly working band. Highly recommended. *—Scott Yanow*

Libertango: The Music of Astor Piazzolla / Jan. 20, 1999-Jan. 24, 1999 / Concord Jazz ✦✦✦✦
Gary Burton's *Libertango: The Music of Astor Piazzolla* continues the vibraphonist's homage to Piazzolla's nuevo tango, which began with 1996's *Astor Piazzolla Reuninon: a Tango Excursion*. Here, as on that album, Burton collaborates with former Piazzolla players such as pianist Pablo Ziegler, violinist Fernando Suarez-Paz, and guitarist Horacio Malvicino on stylized updates of the composer's best-known tangos. Burton's vibes weave in and out of interpretations of "Escualo," "Fuga Y Misterio," and "Adios Nonino," which dance along on brisk, jazzy rhythms that nevertheless capture the tango's elegant passion. *Libertango* is another fresh and worthwhile exploration of Piazzolla's music from an artist *—Heather Phares*

Jaki Byard (John A. Byard, Jr.)

b. Jun. 15, 1922, Worcester, MA, **d.** Feb. 11, 1999, Queens, NY
Piano / Mainstream Jazz, Free Jazz, Stride, Post-Bop
Possessor of a very eclectic style, Jaki Byard was long able to play stride, swing, bop, completely free and funky in addition to being able to imitate closely both Erroll Garner and Dave Brubeck. His playing fit perfectly with Charles Mingus' band in 1964 during their famous European tour with Eric Dolphy but otherwise he was never given the recognition he deserved. As a youth he played piano and trumpet, switched to trombone while in the army and then (back on piano) gigged with Earl Bostic (1949-50). Byard (also a fine tenor-saxophonist) played with the big bands of Herb Pomeroy and Maynard Ferguson (1959-61) and then gigged and recorded with Dolphy, Don Ellis, Booker Ervin, Charlie Mariano and Mingus (1962-65 and 1970); he also recorded as a leader frequently in the 1960s and collaborated with Rahsaan Roland Kirk. Although he recorded fairly often through the years (including duet albums with Earl Hines and Ran Blake) and headed a big band (the Apollo Stompers), Byard was mostly active as an educator from the late '60s onward. He was found murdered in his Queens, New York home on February 11, 1999 at the age of 76. *—Scott Yanow*

Blues for Smoke / Dec. 16, 1960 / Candid ✦✦✦✦✦
Pianist Jaki Byard's first recording as a leader was not released domestically until this 1988 CD. That fact seems strange for Byard is absolutely brilliant on the solo piano set. Many of his selections (all nine tunes are his originals) look both backwards to pre-bop styles and ahead to the avant-garde including such numbers as "Pete and Thomas (Tribute to the Ticklers)," "Spanish Tinge No. 1," and "One, Two, Five." The most remarkable selection is "Jaki's Blues Next" which has Byard alternating between James P. Johnson-type stride and free form à la Cecil Taylor; at its conclusion he plays both styles at the same time. A highly recommended outing from a very underrated pianist. *—Scott Yanow*

Here's Jaki / Mar. 14, 1961 / New Jazz/OJC ✦✦✦

Out Front! / Mar. 14, 1961-May 28, 1964 / Prestige/OJC ✦✦✦

Hi-Fly / Jan. 30, 1962 / New Jazz/OJC ✦✦✦✦
Following the success of *Here's Jaki*, the eclectic pianist continued his explorations in a trio format, with Pete La Roca replacing Roy Haynes on the drums. The set mixes standards with some forgotten gems, plus three originals. The "Excerpts from Yamecraw" is an updated version of the nearly forgotten James P. Johnson orchestral suite, which is complimented here by the Byard original "There Are Many Worlds," which was also written for an orchestra. "Tillie Butterball" is a fun blues romp based on a puppy and a bowling alley. Byard's distinctive approach is evident on Randy Weston's title track "Hi-Fly" and George Shearing's "Lullaby of Birdland," while his debt to Thelonious Monk, sprinkled throughout this session, is obvious on "'Round Midnight." What makes this session special, however, is his original "Here to Hear." His multi-influenced compositional style matched by his versatile technique is explored at length. There are certain pieces that can never be interpreted by anyone else but the composer, and that is the case here, for it would be virtually impossible, and futile, to try and duplicate the individual genius of Jaki Byard. This stands as one of his best. *—Robert Taylor*

Live! / Apr. 15, 1965 / Prestige ✦✦✦✦✦
Except for a ballad medley, this CD reissues all of the music from two earlier LPs featuring pianist Jaki Byard, Joe Farrell (who plays tenor, soprano, flute, and even some drums), bassist George Tucker, and drummer Alan Dawson (doubling on vibes). The set, recorded live at *Lennie's-on-the-Turnpike* in Massachusetts, is a superior outing for all of the players. Farrell shows just how strong a player he was while Byard's versatility (and full knowledge of all jazz piano styles) keeps the proceedings continually unpredictable. Recommended. *—Scott Yanow*

Freedom Together! / Jan. 11, 1966 / Prestige/OJC ✦✦✦✦
Pianist Jaki Byard's best recordings were done for Prestige in the 1960s, and fortunately, they have been gradually seeing reissue on CD in the Original Jazz Classics series. This is a particularly unusual and colorful set, for Byard not only plays piano, but makes appearances on celeste, electric piano, vibes, drums and tenor sax. His tenor playing (best heard on "Just You, Just Me") is particularly excellent, while his piano solos show his usual diversity, hinting at 50 years of jazz styles. With the assistance of bassist Richard Davis (who doubles on cello) and drummer Alan Dawson (who also contributes some tympani on "Ode to Prez," plus some vibes), Byard is in excellent form. Only the two rather ponderous vocals of Junior Parker are a minus, but this should not discourage listeners from acquiring this largely successful set. *—Scott Yanow*

★ **The Jaki Byard Experience** / Sep. 17, 1968 / Prestige/OJC ✦✦✦✦✦
Pianist Jaki Byard and the wondrous Roland Kirk (here switching between tenor, clarinet, and manzello) were two of the few jazz musicians who could play in literally every jazz style, from New Orleans to bop and free form. If only they had recorded a history-of-jazz album. Fortunately, they did meet up on a few occasions, including this brilliant quartet session with bassist Richard Davis and drummer Alan Dawson. They romp on Bud Powell's "Parisian Thoroughfare," Thelonious Monk's "Evidence," "Shine on Me," and "Teach Me Tonight." Byard duets with Davis on his own "Hazy Eve," but best of all is the pianist's duet with Kirk on "Memories of You." This set was also reissued as half of the Roland Kirk two-LP set *Pre-Rahsaan*. *—Scott Yanow*

Live at Maybeck Recital Hall, Vol. 17 / Sep. 8, 1991 / Concord Jazz ✦✦✦✦
Jaki Byard has to be considered one of the most underrated jazz pianists of all time. Very few other keyboardists have mastered as many styles as he has and yet Byard generally sounds like himself. This solo piano CD finds Byard revisiting his lengthy "Family Suite," doing a three-song Thelonious Monk medley, showing respect for the early stride pianists on "Tribute to the Ticklers" and uplifting a pair of standards. an excellent outing, one of Jaki Byard's few recordings in the 1990s. *—Scott Yanow*

Solo/Strings / Sep. 12, 2000 / Prestige ✦✦✦✦✦
Few jazz pianists could honestly claim to be more eclectic than the late Jaki Byard. Depending on the mood he was in, the Bostonian could acknowledge anyone from Dave Brubeck to James P. Johnson to Cecil Taylor. Byard wasn't afraid to take chances, and his open-mindedness served him well. The pianist's eclectic nature is impossible to miss on *Solo/Strings*, which is the 2000 reissue of his Prestige dates *Jaki Byard with Strings* (1968) and *Solo Piano* (1969) on a single 78-minute CD (minus, unfortunately, "Hello, Young Lovers" from *Solo Piano*). While *Solo Piano* is exactly that—an album of unaccompanied solo piano—*Jaki Byard With Strings* is somewhat misleading. That title implies that Byard is accompanied by a large string orchestra, but in fact, he leads a sextet that includes four string instruments (George Benson's guitar, Ray Nance's violin, Ron Carter's cello, and Richard Davis' bass) along with Byard's piano and Alan Dawson's drums. Byard is unpredictable in both settings, although *Solo Piano* is even more of a rollercoaster ride. Unaccompanied, Byard shows his appreciation of different eras of jazz piano and has fun with everything from stride and boogie woogie to modal post-bop, free jazz, and the avant-garde. "The Hollis Stomp" manages to combine stride piano à la James P. Johnson or Fats Waller with elements of Cecil Taylor, while "New Orleans Stomp" is a playful blues that offers an unlikely combination of Taylor, McCoy Tyner, and Professor Longhair. "Spanish Tinge 2," meanwhile, isn't as Jelly Roll Morton-influenced as its title implies (Morton described the Latin influences in his music as "the Spanish tinge"). Rather, the tune brings to mind Miles Davis' work with Gil Evans on the innovative *Sketches of Spain*. Full of surprises, this superb CD is recommended to anyone who appreciates a wide variety of jazz. *—Alex Henderson*

Don Byas (Carlos Wesley Byas)

b. Oct. 21, 1912, Muskogee, OK, **d.** Aug. 24, 1972, Amsterdam, The Netherlands
Sax (Tenor) / Swing, Bop
One of the greatest of all tenor players, Don Byas' decision to move permanently to Europe in 1946 has resulted in him being vastly underrated in jazz history books. His knowledge of chords rivalled Coleman Hawkins and, due to their similarity in tones, Byas can be considered an extension of the elder tenor. He played with many top swing bands including those of Lionel Hampton (1935), Buck Clayton (1936), Don Redman, Lucky Millinder, Andy Kirk (1939-40) and most importantly Count Basie (1941-43). An advanced swing stylist, Byas' playing looked towards bop. He jammed at Minton's Playhouse in the early 1940s, appeared on 52nd Street with Dizzy Gillespie and performed a pair of stunning duets with bassist Slam Stewart at a 1944 Town Hall concert. After recording extensively during 1945-46 (often as a leader), Byas went to Europe with Don Redman's band and (with the exception of a 1970 appearance at the Newport Jazz Festival) never came back to the U.S. He lived in France, the Netherlands and Denmark, often appeared at festivals and worked steadily. Whenever American players were touring, they would ask for Byas who had opportunities to perform with Duke Ellington, Bud Powell, Kenny Clarke, Dizzy Gillespie, Jazz at the Philharmonic (including a recorded tenor battle with Hawkins and Stan Getz), Art Blakey and (on a 1968 recording) Ben Webster. Byas also recorded often in the 1950s but was largely forgotten in the U.S. by the time of his death. *—Scott Yanow*

Midnight at Minton's / 1941 / High Note ✦✦✦✦✦
Tenor saxophone legend Don Byas is heard with great clarity on this, a relative jam session, as is vocalist Helen Humes (the first two cuts) and ostensible leader/trumpeter Joe Guy, whose high energy solos are very good in spots. Less audible in the mix are pianist Thelonious Monk and drummer Kenny Clarke, working in this band while bebop was fermenting. These two would lead the bop charge later in the '40s at *Minton's Playhouse, the* bebop concubine/jazz club in N.Y.C. The music is pretty much swing material, with Humes tossing in a ballad ("Stardust") and a bluesy number ("Exactly Like You") while the instrumental "Indiana" is all fired up, and they typically chill down "Body & Soul." Present on the dates is an unidentified tenor saxophonist and trumpeter tossing in his/her less than two-cents worth solos. Even annotator Dan Morgenstern, with his detailed and informative liner notes, can't ID the pair. The star is clearly Byas. His well-rounded tenor inflections and characteristic

quarter-to-eight note slurve is on throughout the performance. He can be at once warm, witty, smooth, precise, and consistently wonderful. He's one of the first original jazz voices on his horn and emphatic to boot on these tunes. These are true club date "field recordings," from the then Columbia University student Jerry Newman's portable unit, replete with crowd noise in the background (one can hear Humes rebuffing a heckler/admirer) annoying kicking of the stage area, and a brief drop out or distortion. Total time is barely 39 minutes. But the overall sound quality is quite acceptable, at most times remarkable. The music itself is priceless, the document of a transitional period from swing to bop, and some of the people that made it happen, especially the underappreciated genius Byas. *—Michael G. Nastos*

● **1944-1945** / Jul. 28, 1944-Mar. 1945 / Classics ✦✦✦✦✦
Don Byas was one of the great tenor-saxophonists of the 1940's, a Coleman Hawkins-influenced improviser who developed a complex style of his own. His permanent move to Europe in 1946 cut short any chance he had of fame but Byas recorded many worthy performances during the two years before his departure. On Classics' first Don Byas CD (which contains his first 21 numbers as a leader), Byas matches wits and power with trumpeter Charlie Shavers on two heated sessions with pianist Clyde Hart and bassist Slam Stewart, plays swing with trumpeter Joe Thomas and pianist Johnny Guarnieri in a 1945 quintet and leads a quartet that on four of its eight numbers welcomes the great blues guitarist-singer Big Bill Broonzy. Highlights include "Riffin' And Jivin'," "Don's Idea," the two-part "Savoy Jam Party," "1944 Stomp" (which has been adopted by 1990's saxophonist James Carter), "Pennies From Heaven," "Jamboree Jump" and "Just A Dream." This music was originally put out by Savoy, Jamboree and Hub. Highly recommended. *—Scott Yanow*

Savoy Jam Party: The Savoy Sessions / Jul. 28, 1944-Aug. 21, 1946 / Savoy ✦✦✦✦
What a lazy way to reissue music: a former two-LP set with 32 tracks becomes a single CD consisting of the first 25 numbers. The packaging was shrunk to the point where the liner notes (which refer to all 32 songs) is so microscopic as to be completely unreadable. But at least it is "an exact reproduction." Although this reissue from the Japanese Denon label is utterly ridiculous, the music is excellent. Don Byas, one of the great tenors of the 1940s, is featured with groups ranging from a quartet to a sextet; the sideman include trumpeters Charlie Shavers, Emmett Berry and Benny Harris, altoist Rudy Williams, pianists Clyde Hart, Dave Rivera, Jimmy Jones, Teddy Brannon and Sanford Gold, bassists Slam Stewart and Milt Hinton and drummers J.C. Heard and Max Roach. Byas is in superior form on these late-period swing performances but the packaging is so dumb that I advise collectors who have the original two-LP set (put out by Arista in the 1970s) to keep it. *—Scott Yanow*

A Tribute to Cannonball / Dec. 15, 1961 / Columbia/Legacy ✦✦✦✦
The title of this album is misleading for, although Cannonball Adderley produced the session, no "tribute" takes place. Adderley could always recognize talent and he was wise to get the veteran tenor Don Byas (who had not recorded since 1955) back on record. Teamed in Paris with trumpeter Idrees Sulieman, pianist Bud Powell, bassist Pierre Michelot and drummer Kenny Clarke, Byas proved to be in prime form on a variety of jazz standards including "Just One of Those Things," "Cherokee" and "Jeannine." This set has also been reissued on CD under Bud Powell's name. *—Scott Yanow*

A Night in Tunisia / Jan. 13, 1963-Jan. 14, 1963 / Black Lion ✦✦✦✦
The first of two CDs documenting two nights at the Montmartre in Copenhagen, this release features the great tenor Don Byas in a quartet with pianist Bent Axen, bassist Niels Pederson (still a teenager) and drummer William Schiopffe. Alternating romps with ballads, Byas tears into such songs as "I'll Remember april," "Anthropology" and "A Night in Tunisia." He shows that, despite being overseas since 1946, he had lost nothing of his power and inventiveness. This release (along with *Walkin'*) is easily recommended, among the best recordings from Byas' European years. *—Scott Yanow*

Charlie Byrd

b. Sep. 16, 1925, Chuckatuck, VA, **d.** Dec. 2, 1999
Guitar / Brazilian Jazz, Latin Jazz, Bossa Nova, Bop
Charlie Byrd has two notable accomplishments to his credit—applying acoustic classical guitar techniques to jazz and popular music and helping to introduce Brazilian music to mass North American audiences. Tasteful, low-key, and ingratiatingly melodic, Byrd is always a pleasure to listen to in concert. Byrd experienced his first brush with greatness while a teenager in France during World War II, playing with his idol Django Reinhardt. He started recording for Savoy as a leader in 1957, and also recorded with the Woody Herman band in 1958-59. A tour of South America under the aegis of the U.S. State Department in 1961 proved to be a revelation, for it was in Brazil that Byrd discovered the emerging bossa nova movement. Once back in D.C., he played some bossa nova tapes to Stan Getz, who then convinced Verve's Creed Taylor to record an album of Brazilian music with himself and Byrd. That album *Jazz Samba* became a pop hit in 1962 on the strength of the single "Desafinado" and launched the bossa nova wave in North America. *—Richard S. Ginell*

Classical Byrd / 1958-1960 / Milestone ✦✦✦✦✦
Single-disc, 77-minute compilation of two long-unavailable classical LPs that Byrd recorded in 1958-60 for the Washington label, *An Anthology of Music for the Guitar–The Sixteenth Century* and *Lodovico Roncalli Suites.* (Unfortunately, one of the tracks from *An Anthology of Music for the Guitar–The Sixteenth Century,* "Tres Fantasies (Three Fantasies)," was deleted for space reasons). Byrd interprets courtly dances and folk songs of Spanish composers of the 16th century on *Anthology*, and presents four longer (average track length: ten minutes) suites from the 17th century by the little-known Italian composer Lodovico Roncalli on *Lodovico Roncalli Suites.* It's a fine compendium of Byrd's talents as a virtuoso classical interpreter, and one would guess that works such as this were an influence on guitarist Sandy Bull in the 1960s. *—Richie Unterberger*

Mr. Guitar / 1959-1960 / Riverside ✦✦✦✦✦
A delightful trio outing with an adroit and light feel, also featuring Keter Betts on bass and Bertell Knox on drums. Byrd's playing combines jazz swing with influences from both Spanish guitar and classical music on a session comprised of both Byrd originals and covers, usually of Gershwin and Ellington tunes. Betts and Knox are both nimble players who flesh out Byrd's arrangements without encumbering them, Knox exhibiting a deft touch on the snares in particular. Byrd swings pretty hard on numbers like "Gypsy in My Soul," and gets more into the Spanish sound on the original "Funky Flamenco"; there is one chance for the musicians to stretch out into more space, on the six-minute "Lay the Lily Low." It sounds like this album was a substantial influence upon the noted eclectic British folk guitarist Davy Graham, whose debut LP from the early '60s, *Guitar Player,* has arrangements that are similar to much of what's on *Mr. Guitar.* *—Richie Unterberger*

The Guitar Artistry of Charlie Byrd / 1960 / Riverside ✦✦✦✦✦
Before he toured South America and discovered bossa nova, guitarist Charlie Byrd already had his recognizable sound formed. A master on the acoustic guitar who was well trained in classical music, Byrd performed regularly in Washington D.C. from 1958-60, recording for the tiny Offbeat label. This CD reissue of a set originally on Offbeat and then put out by Riverside features Byrd and his regular trio (with bassist Keter Betts and drummer Buddy Deppenschmidt) performing concise versions of eight jazz standards, including two songs under two minutes, and longer versions of three obscurities, plus "The House of the Rising Sun." The melodic music is pleasing (if not too substantial), predictable and reasonably enjoyable, with the highlights including "Moonlight In Vermont," "Nuages," "Django" and the lengthy "Taboo." *—Scott Yanow*

Charlie Byrd at the Village Vanguard / Jan. 15, 1961 / Riverside/OJC ✦✦✦
Shortly before departing on his epochal 1961 State Department tour of South America, the one that ignited his love affair with bossa nova—and subsequently, ours—Charlie Byrd played this trio gig at New York City's Village Vanguard. At first, "Just Squeeze Me" goes at an easygoing stroll as Byrd adheres swingingly to the beat, and "Why Was I Born" isn't terribly eventful. But then, there are definitely hints of things to come in the fluid samba-like rhythm that the trio kicks up on "You Stepped Out of a Dream." The 20-minute fantasia on the old union rouser "Which Side Are You On—" also has a Brazilian-tinged groove, and the combination of that and Byrd's low-key classical savvy keeps you as mesmerized as the quiet audience must have been. It is also significant that both of Byrd's cohorts on the date, bassist Keter Betts and drummer Buddy Deppenschmidt, would play on Byrd's historic *Jazz Samba* album with Stan Getz a year later. The direction is clear; Byrd was about to open the door to bossa nova, and you can hear him inching up to the starting gate here. *—Richard S. Ginell*

● **Latin Byrd** / 1961-1963 / Milestone ✦✦✦✦✦
This single CD reissues two complete Charlie Byrd Lp's (*Latin Impressions* and *Charlie Byrd's Bossa Nova*), some of which had been available previously on a 1970's twofer. Byrd, the master of the acoustic guitar whose gentle and lyrical style perfectly fit bossa-nova, is heard in prime form on 23 rather pretty numbers. There are six unaccompanied solos and many workouts with his quartet which is sometimes augmented by four cellos, a French horn, trumpeter Hal Posey, vibrahonist Tommy Gwaltney and/or extra percussionists. Surprisingly there are only two Antonio Carlos Jobim songs among the ones performed but the other selections (which include five Byrd originals) are very much in the idiom. This CD shows that pretty music does not have to be muzak or New Age. Highly recommended. *—Scott Yanow*

Byrd at the Gate / May 9, 1963-May 10, 1963 / Riverside/OJC ✦✦✦✦✦
This CD reissue has a rare straightahead set by guitarist Charlie Byrd, whose trio with bassist Keter Betts and drummer Bill Reichenbach welcomes trumpeter Clark Terry and tenor saxophonist Selden Powell to a few numbers. the emphasis is on swing and a repertoire mostly filled with standards (including "Shiny Stockings," "Butter and Egg Man," "I Left My Heart in San Francisco" and "Broadway"). the CD adds two unissued selections to the original program: "Let's Do It" and "Jive at Five." Recommended. *—Scott Yanow*

Brazilian Byrd / Dec. 21, 1964-Feb. 8, 1965 / Columbia ✦✦✦✦
The arrangements by Tommy Newsome for strings, brass and woodwinds may be a bit sweet and the 13 performances (which on the CD reissue includes a previously unreleased take of "Engano") may be overly concise (often under three minutes), but the resulting music is strangely pleasing. Acoustic guitarist Charlie Byrd always had a strong affinity for Brazilian jazz and he sticks exclusively to Antonio Carlos Jobim songs (including "So Danco Samba," "Corcovado," "Dindi" and "The Girl From Ipanema") during this tasteful and melodic effort. Truly beautiful music. *—Scott Yanow*

Great Guitars / Jun. 28, 1974 / Concord Jazz ✦✦✦✦
Charlie Byrd was teamed up with Barney Kessel and Herb Ellis (along with bassist Joe Byrd and drummer John Rae) for this rather exciting concert. While Ellis and Kessel have three unaccompanied duets, the inclusion of Byrd (thought of as a Brazilian specialist rather than a bopper) is the wild card that makes this set a major success. While Byrd is excellent on his features "Charlie's Blues" and "O Barquinho," it is the three stomps featuring all the guitarists ("Undecided," "Topsy" and "Benny's Bugle") that are most memorable. *—Scott Yanow*

Blue Byrd / Aug. 1978 / Concord Jazz ✦✦✦✦✦
This delightful album (reissued on CD) is one of Charlie Byrd's finest for Concord. Teamed up with bassist Joe Byrd and drummer Wayne Phillips, the acoustic guitarist had a real chance to show off his versatility on a wide-ranging repertoire. Highlights include "It Don't Mean a Thing" (which really cooks), "Jitterbug Waltz," the memorable "Carinhoso" and "Isn't It a Lovely Day." Joe Byrd made his vocal debut on spirited versions of "I Ain't Got Nothin' but the Blues" and an uptempo "Saturday Night Fish Fry," sounding like a cross between Bob Dorough and Mose Allison. This set is particularly recommended to listeners who think that Charlie Byrd could only play Brazilian music. *—Scott Yanow*

My Inspiration: Music of Brazil / May 12, 1998-May 14, 1998 / Concord Jazz ✦✦✦✦
When he recorded *My Inspiration: Music of Brazil* in May 1998, a 72-year-old Charlie Byrd was considered an elder statesman of Brazilian jazz as well as bebop. The guitarist had been involved with Brazilian jazz for 37 years, and his name was always among the first that came up in a discussion of the bossa nova. One of the many Brazilian-oriented projects he has recorded, *My Inspiration* finds the guitarist joined by the Brazilian group Trio Da Paz (which

consists of guitarist Romero Lubambo, bassist Nilson Matta and drummer Duduka Da Fonseca) as well as vocalist Maucha Adnet, Chuck Redd (who is heard on vibes instead of drums) and tenor saxman Scott Hamilton. Byrd embraces a few well known Jobim standards on this CD, including "Agua de Beber" and "So Danco Samba," but thankfully, he doesn't limit himself to obvious choices—he also turns his attention to material that ranges from Chopin's "Freddie's Tune" to the traditional Brazilian song "Violao Quebrada" and the 1930s show tune "My Inspiration." Hamilton, who is heard on half of the songs, enjoys an undeniably strong rapport with Byrd, which isn't surprising because they're both very lyrical and melodic. *My Inspiration* was a welcome addition to Byrd's sizable catalog. *—Alex Henderson*

Best of the Concord Years / Sep. 26, 2000 / Concord Jazz ✦✦✦✦✦

Donald Byrd (Donaldson Toussaint L'Ouverture II)

b. Dec. 9, 1932, Detroit, MI

Trumpet / Smooth Soul, Crossover Jazz, Hard Bop, Fusion, Jazz-Funk, Funk

In the late '50s and early '60s, Donald Byrd carved out a niche for himself as one of the most adept hard boppers of his generation. Never a wildly original player, Byrd nevertheless captured the tenor of his times as a solid, clean-toned, lyrical improviser in the manner of contemporaries like Clifford Brown and Freddie Hubbard. In the mid-'50s, he recorded for the Prestige, Riverside, Blue Note and Savoy labels (among others), both as a leader and as a sideman. Following stints with the likes of Max Roach, Art Blakey, and Sonny Rollins, Byrd co-led a band with the baritone saxophonist Pepper Adams from 1958-61. After releasing a number of fine straight-ahead Blue Note albums throughout the '60s, in the '70s his music took a decidedly commercial turn. Byrd recorded a number of heavily produced, pop-oriented albums on which his horn was subjugated by disco-fied vocals and string sections. In the '80s and '90s Byrd returned to his jazz roots, recording with peers such as Joe Henderson and Bobby Hutcherson, and with younger musicians like Kenny Garrett and Mulgrew Miller. *—Chris Kelsey*

First Flight: Yusef Lateef with Donald Byrd / Aug. 23, 1955 / Delmark ✦✦✦

Byrd in Hand / May 31, 1959 / Blue Note ✦✦✦✦✦

For this excellent album, trumpeter Donald Byrd teams up with tenor saxophonist Charlie Rouse, baritonist Pepper Adams, pianist Walter Davis, Jr., bassist Sam Jones and drummer Art Taylor. Together the sextet performs three Byrd originals, two Davis songs and the standard "Witchcraft." Although none of the new tunes caught on, the group (which includes two distinctive saxophonists and the rapidly maturing trumpet of Donald Byrd) plays consistently creative and spirited solos in the hard bop idiom. *—Scott Yanow*

Fuego / Oct. 4, 1959 / Blue Note ✦✦✦✦

This CD reissue brings back a typically excellent Donald Byrd Blue Note session; virtually all of the trumpeter's most rewarding dates were for that label. Teamed with altoist Jackie McLean, pianist Duke Pearson, bassist Doug Watkins and drummer Lex Humphries, Byrd plays six of his originals with the most memorable ones being "Fuego," "Funky Mama" and "Amen." An above-average hard bop set that still sounds fresh nearly 40 years later. *—Scott Yanow*

Byrd in Flight / Jan. 17, 1960-Jul. 10, 1960 / Blue Note ✦✦✦✦✦

Two separate dates are combined on this Blue Note album. Trumpeter Donald Byrd, pianist Duke Pearson and drummer Lex Humphries are heard in both quintets with either tenorman Hank Mobley or altoist Jackie McLean and Doug Watkins or Reggie Workman on bass. The consistently strong originals by Pearson and Byrd ("Little Boy Blue" is the lone standard) give this set its own personality and purpose. An excellent example of early '60s hard bop. *—Scott Yanow*

Donald Byrd at the Half Note Cafe, Vol. 1-2 / Nov. 11, 1960 / Blue Note ✦✦✦✦✦

This 1997 two-CD set was last available as a pair of single CDs. Trumpeter Donald Byrd and huge-toned baritonist Pepper Adams always made for a potent combination, and fortunately, they recorded together quite a bit from 1960-61. The live set has four originals apiece by Byrd and pianist Duke Pearson, plus four standards. The material is consistently rewarding (including the definitive jazz version of Henry Mancini's "Mr. Lucky"); the quintet (which also includes pianist Duke Pearson, bassist Laymon Jackson and drummer Lex Humphries) sounds quite inspired, and the often joyful music is quite inventive within the hard bop genre. Highlights include "My Girl Shirl," "Chant," "A Portrait of Jennie" and "Jeannine." Highly recommended to straight-ahead fans not already owning the previous CDs. *—Scott Yanow*

Chant / Apr. 17, 1961 / Blue Note ✦✦✦✦✦

Not released until 1979, this excellent quintet session features the always formidable team of trumpeter Donald Byrd and baritonist Pepper Adams. The accompanying rhythm section includes pianist Herbie Hancock shortly before he joined Miles Davis. The repertoire consists of six likable tunes including an uptempo "I'm an Old Cowhand," "That's All," "Sophisticated Lady," two Byrd originals and Duke Pearson's "Chant." This is superior hard bop from the early '60s. *—Scott Yanow*

The Cat Walk / May 2, 1961 / Blue Note ✦✦✦

Royal Flush / Sep. 21, 1961 / Blue Note ✦✦✦

Donald Byrd was at his peak as a straight-ahead hard bop band leader in the early '60s, turning a series of remarkably solid, enjoyable sessions for Blue Note. *Royal Flush* is no exception to the rule. Recorded in the fall of 1961, *Royal Flush* finds Byrd once again working with baritionist Pepper Adams, but adding bassist Butch Warren, drummer Billy Higgins, and, most importantly, a young pianist named Herbie Hancock. For the most part, the quintet plays a set of vital hard bop, swinging hard on the bluesy groove "Hush" and laying back on the pop standard "I'm a Fool to Want You." But what's really interesting is when they begin pushing the boundaries of bop. All three of Byrd's original pieces—"Jorgie's," "Shangri-La," "6M's"—are harmonically complex and have subtly shifting rhythms; all three are successful, but "Shangri-La" is particularly noteworthy. Similarly, Hancock's graceful "Requiem" calls attention to its fluid melodic lines and rhythm. Throughout the date, Byrd and Adams are typically impressive, alternating between punchy, hard-hitting, and graceful solos, but Hancock is just as good, signaling early on in his career his deep, unique talent. *—Stephen Thomas Erlewine*

Free Form / Dec. 11, 1961 / Blue Note ✦✦✦

Trumpeter Donald Byrd was in his prime during the 1960s and this CD reissue (which adds "Three Wishes" to the original five-song program) finds him stretching the limits of hard bop. With the assistance of four other young forward-thinking musicians (tenor saxophonist Wayne Shorter, pianist Herbie Hancock, bassist Butch Warren and drummer Billy Higgins), Byrd plays some of his more adventurous originals. Highpoints include "Pentecostal Feeling," Hancock's ballad "Night Flower" and the unpredictable "Free Form." Highly recommended. *—Scott Yanow*

● **A New Perspective** / Nov. 12, 1963 / Blue Note ✦✦✦✦✦

This unusual set (reissued on CD by Blue Note) was one of the most successful uses of a gospel choir in a jazz context. Trumpeter Donald Byrd and a septet that also includes tenor saxophonist Hank Mobley, guitarist Kenny Burrell and pianist Herbie Hancock are joined by an eight-voice choir directed by Coleridge Perkinson. The arrangements by Duke Pearson are masterful and one song, "Cristo Redentor," became a bit of a hit. This is a memorable effort that is innovative in its own way, a milestone in Donald Byrd's career. *—Scott Yanow*

Mustang! / Jun. 4, 1966 / Blue Note ✦✦✦

Donald Byrd, a talented hard bop trumpeter during his prime (although rarely reaching the technical heights of Lee Morgan and Freddie Hubbard), performs a varied repertoire on this CD reissue. "Dixie Lee" has dated rhythms, and "Mustang" was an attempt to achieve a hit on the level of Morgan's "The Sidewinder." However, Byrd sounds fine on those numbers; he digs into the complex chord changes of "Fly Little Bird Fly," is sensitive on "I Got It Bad," swings on his "I'm So Excited By You" and performs his memorable countermelody to "On the Trail," which had been recorded earlier by several other musicians. Teamed with a typically impressive Blue Note crew (altoist Sonny Red, tenor saxophonist Hank Mobley, pianist McCoy Tyner, bassist Walter Booker and drummer Freddie Waits), Byrd performs high-quality straight-ahead jazz that fits the modern mainstream of the era. Also on this CD are a pair of selections ("Gingerbread Boy" and "I'm So Excited By You") from an earlier quintet date (with tenorman Jimmy Heath, Tyner, bassist Walter Booker, and drummer Joe Chambers) that, despite being excellent, went unissued until this 1997 CD. *—Scott Yanow*

Blackjack / May 27, 1963–Jan. 1967 / Blue Note ✦✦✦

One of three Donald Byrd albums from 1967 (the end of his hard bop period), this recording features the trumpeter/leader with altoist Sonny Red, tenor saxophonist Hank Mobley, pianist Cedar Walton, bassist Walter Booker and drummer Billy Higgins. The six tunes (five of which are originals by Byrd or Red) are all quite obscure and to one extent or another quite explorative. One can sense that Byrd wanted to break through the boundaries and rules of hard bop but had not yet decided on his future directions. The music does swing and highlights include "West of the Pecos" and "Beale Street"; Byrd and Red in particular are in excellent form throughout the date. *—Scott Yanow*

Slow Drag / May 12, 1967 / Blue Note ✦✦✦

The Creeper / Oct. 5, 1967 / Blue Note ✦✦✦

Fancy Free / May 9, 1969-Jun. 6, 1969 / Blue Note ✦✦✦

This CD reissue brings back trumpeter Donald Byrd's final jazz recording before going completely commercial with his R&B group The Blackbyrds; he would not return to jazz until the 1980s and by then the many years of not playing his horn would clearly show. *Fancy Free* was Byrd's first to use electric keyboards and on it the trumpeter found a highly satisfying balance between jazz improvisation and funky rhythms, the acoustic and the electric; pity that he did not continue in that direction. The melody of "Fancy Free" is memorable, a few of the songs are danceable without being simplistic and Byrd and tenor-saxophonist Frank Foster have lyrical solos on the ballad "I Love the Girl." *—Scott Yanow*

Kofi / Dec. 16, 1969-Dec. 4, 1970 / Blue Note ✦✦✦

This previously unreleased material (taken from two sessions in 1969-70) contains some of trumpeter Donald Byrd's final jazz recordings before he shifted completely to R&B-funk. On "Kofi" Lew Tabackin's flute solo easily takes honors while "Fufu" (which is also from the earlier date) has some fine Byrd trumpet in a Miles Davis vein. The other three performances from a year later feature Byrd and Foster in excellent form on moody material which merges together hard bop with early fusion; it is remarkable how much Byrd sounds like Miles Davis of the period on some of these numbers. Unfortunately he would not be pursuing this path in the future, making this transitional CD a historic and somewhat unique venture that is well worth investigating. *—Scott Yanow*

Electric Byrd / May 15, 1970 / Blue Note ✦✦✦

This CD brings back trumpeter Donald Byrd's last worthwhile jazz recording before his descent into commercial success (and artistic oblivion) in the R&B/funk world. Byrd contributed three of the four originals (the fourth is from percussionist Airto) and he explores music that combines together the vestiges of hard bop, Miles Davis-style fusion, modern Brazilian music and touches of R&B. There are some worthwhile solos by the leader along with such saxophonists as Frank Foster and Lew Tabackin on tenors and his old friend baritonist Pepper Adams. The funky rhythm section (which includes the electric piano of producer Duke Pearson, guitarist Wally Richardson, bassist Ron Carter and drummer Mickey Roker in addition to Airto) keeps the proceedings interesting and this set is far superior to Byrd's work throughout the rest of the 1970s. *—Scott Yanow*

Black Byrd / Apr. 3, 1972-Apr. 4, 1972 / Blue Note ✦✦✦

Starting in 1969 with some transition projects, trumpeter Donald Byrd gradually moved away from hard bop into funk and R&B. This particular set (which has been reissued on CD) is completely outside of jazz and was a major seller when it was released in 1972. The only problem is that the very dated R&B/pop music (which earned Byrd the reputation of being a sellout) sounds even worse now than it did at the time. Under the direction of producer Larry Mizell, who contributed all of the arrangements and compositions, the music is even weak and derivative from the R&B standpoint, unless one thinks of Donald Byrd as being a great vocalist. It would take the label's death and subsequent rebirth before Blue Note recovered its earlier credibility. *—Scott Yanow*

Street Lady / Jun. 13, 1973-Jun. 15, 1973 / Blue Note ✦✦✦

Places and Spaces / Aug. 1975-Sep. 1975 / Blue Note ✦✦

Complete Blue Note Donald Byrd/Pepper Adams Studio Session / 2000 / Mosaic ✦✦✦✦✦

Don Byron

b. Nov. 8, 1958, New York, NY

Clarinet (Bass), Clarinet / Avant-Garde Jazz, Klezmer, M-Base, Post-Bop

An inspired eclectic, Byron has performed an array of musical styles with great success. Byron first attained a measure of notoriety for playing Klezmer, specifically the music of the late Mickey Katz. While the novelty of a black man playing Jewish music was enough to grab the attention of critics, it was Byron's jazz-related work that ultimately made him a major figure. Byron is an exceptional clarinetist from a technical perspective; he also possesses a profound imagination that best manifests itself in his multifarious compositions. Byron's at heart a conceptualist. Each succeeding album seems based on a different stylistic approach, from the free jazz/classical leanings of his first album, *Tuskegee Experiments* (Nonesuch, 1992), to the hip-hop/funk of *Nu Blaxpoitation* (Blue Note, 1998). Byron's composition ìThere Goes the Neighborhoodî was commissioned by the Kronos Quartet and premiered in London in 1994. He's also composed for silent film, served as the director of jazz for the Brooklyn Academy of Music, and scored for television. Byron was born and raised in New York City, the son of a mailman who also occasionally played bass in calypso bands, and a mother who dabbled on piano. As a child, Byron developed asthma; his doctor suggested he take up a wind instrument as therapy. Byron chose clarinet. His South Bronx neighborhood had a sizeable Jewish population, which partly explains his fascination with Klezmer. Byron was encouraged by his parents to learn about all different kinds of music, from Leonard Bernstein to (Dizzy Gillespie. Byron's models on clarinet included Tony Scott, Artie Shaw, and especially Jimmy Hamilton. As an improviser, Joe Henderson was a prominent influence. As a teenager Byron studied clarinet with Joe Allard. Byron attended the New England Conservatory of Music, where he studied with George Russell. While at NEC, Byron was recruited to play in Hankus Netsky's Klezmer Conservatory Band. Byron moved from Boston back to New York in the mid-80s, where he began playing with several of the city's more prominent jazz avant-gardists, including David Murray, Craig Harris, and Hamiet Bluiett. A year after recording *Tuskegee Experiments*, Byron made *Plays the Music of Mickey Katz*(Nonesuch), which put something of an end to his Klezmer career (at least in terms of recording). Byron's career built steadily over the course of the '90s. By the end of the decade he had signed with Blue Note records. While hardly a radical, Byron is an original voice within the bounds of whatever style he happens to embrace. *—Chris Kelsey*

● **Tuskegee Experiments** / Nov. 1990-Jul. 1991 / Elektra/Nonesuch ✦✦✦✦

Clarinetist Don Byron immediately became famous in the jazz world after the release of his debut CD as a leader. The strong themes (all but a melody apiece from Robert Schumann and Duke Ellington are originals), the advanced yet logical improvising, and the often-dramatic music make this a particularly memorable set. Byron, doubling on clarinet and bass clarinet, is heard in settings ranging from an unaccompanied solo and duets with bassist Reggie Workman and pianist Joe Berkovitz to medium-size groups with such sidemen as guitarist Bill Frisell, bassist Lonnie Plaxico, drummer Ralph Peterson, Jr., pianist Edsel Gomez and others. Although several songs involve justifiable social protest (including the title cut which has a poem by Sadiq), the music also stands alone outside of the issues. Highly recommended. *—Scott Yanow*

Bug Music / May 1996 / Nonesuch ✦✦✦✦✦

This CD is a tribute to the music of Raymond Scott's Quintette, John Kirby's Sextet and Duke Ellington headed by the remarkably versatile clarinetist Don Byron. Raymond Scott's legendary compositions feature eccentric song titles (including on this set "Siberian Sleighride," "Tobacco Auctioneer" and "War Dance For Wooden Indians"), complex and thoroughly-composed arrangements (all of which were originally memorized rather than being written out) and unique melodies. Kirby's brand of swing, which is quite complementary to Scott's novelties, often utilized themes from classical music and had solos, but were also tightly arranged (even "St. Louis Blues" and "Royal Garden Blues"). The CD begins and ends with four Ellington/Strayhorn pieces that fit well into the idiom (particularly "The Dicty Glide" and "Cotton Club Stomp"). In addition to Byron, the key players on the project include altoist Steve Wilson (one of the best of the younger swing stylists), trombonist Craig Harris and pianist Uri Caine, in addition to four other horns and several rhythm sections. Other than a silly rendition of Ellington's "Blue Bubbles" and an adventurous interpretation of "Snibor," the selections are played with respect and great understanding of the somewhat forgotten style. None of the modern musicians sound as if swing were only their second language, making the continually surprising set a major success. *—Scott Yanow*

Nu Blaxploitation / Dec. 27, 1997-Jan. 5, 1998 / Blue Note ✦✦✦✦✦

Jazz clarinetist Don Byron likes to focus on specific musical styles. He's released albums filled with Latin jazz (*Six Musicians*), the klezmer music of Mickey Katz (*Don Byron Plays the Music of Mickey Katz*), and the repertory works of Duke Ellington, John Kirby, and Raymond Scott (*Bug Music*). Now for his sixth solo release, *Nu Blaxploitation*, Byron offers up a musical evocation of '70s funk, including a nod to hip-hop by way of a Biz Markie guest spot. The poet Sadiq is prominently featured, recalling his fine performance on Byron's debut, *Tuskeegee Experiments*, with ruminations on Princess Diana's vilified boyfriend Dodi Al Fayed ("Dodi") and Haitian immigrant Abner Louima's brutal interrogation by N.Y.C. police ("Blinky"), among other topics. Byron mirrors Sadiq's wide-ranging commentary via some somber, chamber jazz arrangements and a bevy of funky, swinging charts, bolstering the overall mix with fine renditions of songs by '70s Latin-funk group Mandrill ("Mango Meat," "Fencewalk," "Hagalo"). Other highlights include the humorous and intelligent discussions of black life heard on "Domino Theories, Parts 1 & 2" and an inventive cover of Hendrix's "If 6 Was 9." The disc is topped off with stellar performances by both Byron and Existential Dred band members pianist/organist Uri Caine, drummer Ben Wittman, and bassist Reggie Washington. Highly recommended. *—Stephen Cook*

Romance with the Unseen / Jan. 1999/Mar. 1999 / Blue Note ✦✦✦✦

With *Romance With the Unseen*, Don Byron decides to not focus on a particular musical style, as he has done for most of his albums. Instead, he chooses to craft an album of songs that live up to the record's title; these are songs that feel romantic, but aren't love songs. Like most of Byron's albums, there's an abundance of technique and emotion, yet each track feels distinctly different from the others, while managing to form a cohesive whole. The most impressive thing about *Romance With the Unseen* is that, while it takes chances (how could it not, with Bill Frisell, Jack deJohnette, and Drew Gress forming Byron's backing band—), it never sounds inaccessible. It's a shining example of mainstream jazz at its best—stimulating, provocative, and entertaining, all at once. *—Stephen Thomas Erlewine*

A Fine Line: Arias and Lieder / Nov. 7, 2000 / Blue Note ✦✦✦✦

Arias and lieder are forms strongly associated with classical music, yet clarinetist Don Byron defines them in a newly expansive way for this remarkable project. To Byron, arias and lieder belong not only to classical figures, but also to writers as diverse as Ornette Coleman, Roy Orbison, Stevie Wonder, Henry Mancini, and Stephen Sondheim.

Byron's right-hand man in this endeavor is pianist Uri Caine. The two play a series of duets throughout the program: "Zwielecht (Twilight)" by Robert Schumann, "Basquiat" by Byron himself, "Nessun Dorma" by Puccini, and "Reach Out (I'll Be There)," the 1966 Holland/Dozier/Holland hit sung by the Four Tops. Byron concludes the album with a solo clarinet rendition of the "Larghetto" from Chopin's second piano concerto.

These duo and solo vignettes frame the full ensemble pieces, on which Byron and Caine are joined by Jerome Harris, Paulo Braga, and a number of very effective guest vocalists. Former Pat Metheny Group vocalist Mark Ledford is wispy and ethereal on Ornette Coleman's "Check Up," deep-toned and far more dramatic on Roy Orbison's "It's Over." Patricia O'-Callaghan takes a turn on Leonard Bernstein's "Glitter and Be Gay," an epic piece which Byron infuses with a strong dose of calypso. Both vocalists are joined by Dean Bowman and Harris to form a four-voice choir on Henry Mancini's "Soldier in the Rain." And finally, the great Cassandra Wilson turns in a spellbinding performance on Stephen Sondheim's "The Ladies Who Lunch."

The juxtapositions are unusual, and almost certain to be rejected by purists of any stripe. But at a time when more and more creative artists are bringing together classical, jazz, and pop influences, Byron's attempt surely ranks as one of the most personal and least calculating. *—David R. Adler*

Larry Carlton

b. Mar. 2, 1948, Torrance, CA

Guitar / Smooth Jazz, Crossover Jazz, Contemporary Jazz, Fusion

Like so many other Los Angeles studio musicians, guitarist and composer Larry Carlton was faced with a choice: whether to go solo under his own name, or to continue the less risky, more lucrative existence as a session guitarist. Fortunately, he chose the former, and has recorded for major labels Warner Bros., MCA and GRP since 1978. In addition to his dozens of eclectic studio credits, Carlton's theme music for TV and films include *Against All Odds, Who's the Boss*, and the theme for *Hill Street Blues*. Carlton began taking guitar lessons when he was six. After hearing Joe Pass on the radio, he was inspired to play jazz and blues; Wes Montgomery and Barney Kessel became important influences soon after. Carlton toured with the Fifth Dimension in 1968 (the year he recorded his first album under his own name) and began doing studio sessions in 1970. In 1971, he was asked to join the Crusaders, and he remained with the group until 1976, developing the highly rhythmic, often bluesy style he has now. Carlton delivered his self-titled debut for Warner Bros. in 1978; he released four more albums before being dropped from the label. He continued studio session work and touring in between, emerging again in 1986 on MCA with an all-acoustic album, *Discovery;* its instrumental remake of Michael McDonald's "Minute by Minute" won a Grammy Award for Best Pop Instrumental Performance. While working on 1989's *On Solid Ground*, Carlton was shot in the throat outside his private studio near Burbank, California; the bullet shattered his vocal cord and caused significant nerve trauma, but through intensive therapy, Carlton completed the album. Carlton's output has remained steady through the '90s; he seems to have slowed down his touring schedule a bit, but certainly not his recordings. *—Richard Skelly*

Playing/Singing / 1973 / Edsel ✦✦✦✦

This is Larry Carlton's second independent recording, which has finally been reissued on CD. The trademark 'Carlton' guitar sound is evident throughout, as is his toneless singing. The tracks here have a more earthy feel, as opposed to the over-produced stylings he would later employ; however, the overall results are disappointing. The guitar playing is certainly impressive (especially the distortion-filled "Free Way"), but there is simply not enough of it. Regardless, this is an interesting part of Carlton's beginnings and there are enough moments here that foreshadow his evolvement into one of the most distinctive voices in the history of electric guitar. *—Robert Taylor*

● **Larry Carlton** / 1978 / Warner Brothers ✦✦✦✦✦

Sleepwalk / 1981 / MCA ✦✦✦

Slightly better than *Strikes Twice* thanks in part to the absence of Carlton's toneless singing. "Last Nite" and "10:00 P.M." have become staples in Carlton's live set. The legendary Carlton feel is evident throughout this session, but "Blues Bird" stands as the high-water mark. "Sleepwalk" is played beautifully, almost preventing the listener from noticing the sap-heavy strings in the background. Carlton's faceless rhythm section does little to enhance the music (as is usually the case with his solo efforts), but his playing more than makes up for this. Despite sounding a bit dated, this is still worth exploring, especially for guitarists. *—Robert Taylor*

Friends / 1983 / MCA ♦♦♦
By the time Larry Carlton recorded *Friends*, his status as a guitar legend had already been established. In addition to being admired by musicians, he was also loved by Muzak programmers. His blend of happy pop-jazz was the perfect background music for dentist offices. For those who care to listen closer, there is some excellent guitar work being performed. A good example of this would be his creative improvisation on the introduction to "South Town." His duet with B.B. King on "Blues for TJ" is wonderful. It is refreshing to hear two players that are more interested in sharing ideas than showing off. The scat version of "Tequila," courtesy of Al Jarreau, was also interesting. As with most Carlton recordings, there is something here for just about everyone—just not enough of it. *—Robert Taylor*

Discovery / 1986 / MCA ♦♦♦
Following up his surprise hit debut on acoustic guitar, *Alone/But Never Alone*, Carlton offers a collection of easygoing, laid-back, Wave-oriented smooth jazz that slowly reveals hints of the full range of his capabilities. At first, it sounds as if the guitarist would be merely killing time here, but starting with the funky "Knock on Wood," things get progressively more interesting as Carlton seems to find his funky bearings. "Discovery" is actually quite nice with its cushiony vamp; "My Home Away From Home" finds Carlton flashing his acoustic chops quite effectively; the shuffling "Minute By Minute" garnered a lot of airplay. Kirk Whalum can be relied upon for stock, crowd-pleasing R&B tenor solos on several tracks, while Terry Trotter plays digital synths, John Pena handles the bass, and Rick Marotta is on drums. Nice stuff, not too demanding, but it wears well. *—Richard S. Ginell*

Last Nite / Feb. 17, 1986 / MCA ♦♦♦♦
This live set is one of Larry Carlton's best recordings because the guitarist stretches himself. Joined by keyboardist Terry Trotter, bassist Abraham Laboriel, drummer John Robinson and percussionist Alex Acuna (and an occasional three-piece horn section), Carlton plays five- to eight-minute versions of four originals (including "The B.P. Blues"), plus Miles Davis's "So What" and "All Blues." Recorded at the Baked Potato in North Hollywood in California, Carlton is heard throughout at his very best, making one wonder why he has recorded so few albums of a similar spontaneous nature in his career. *—Scott Yanow*

The Larry Carlton Collection, Vol. 2 / 1987-1992 / GRP ♦♦♦♦♦
Creatively, Larry Carlton has had his ups and downs over the years. The guitarist has recorded his share of throwaways, but when he really digs in and plays, Carlton can be thrilling. Spanning 1986-1996 and drawing on five of his albums, this compilation illustrates Carlton's ability to bore one minute and captivate the next. Carlton is at his worst on "Heart to Heart," "Those Eyes" and "Pure Delight," all of which are embarrassing examples of the sort of lightweight, passionless background Muzak he has stooped to recording at times. But on much meatier fusion offerings like "Honey Samba" and the insistent "Remembering J.P.," Carlton's sizable chops are put to good use. Very much a mixed bag, *The Larry Carlton Collection, Vol. 2* would hardly be an ideal introduction to his work. Newcomers would do well to skip this CD in favor of 1986's *Last Night* or 1989's *On Solid Ground*. *—Alex Henderson*

On Solid Ground / 1989 / MCA ♦♦♦
This is a fairly typical Larry Carlton date, with a mixture of music (funky jazz, R&B, some rock influences and a bit of pop) and some distinctive if unadventurous guitar playing. Carlton, who is joined by an electric rhythm section (including keyboardists Terry Trotter and Alan Pasqua) and occasionally saxophonist Kirk Whalum, sounds fine, but the music appears to have been geared toward potential radio airplay. The biggest surprise is a version of Eric Clapton's "Layla." *—Scott Yanow*

Kid Gloves / 1992 / GRP ♦♦♦
From the opening melody of "Kid Gloves," it is obvious that Carlton's commercial direction wasn't about to change here. It is too easy to dismiss most of this session's output as insipid fluff; however, a closer listen to the "The Preacher" finds an intense Carlton playing a very George Benson-like melody. There is also a bit of an edge to his playing in "Where Be Mosada—." There are of course the standard "lite" songs geared for radio airplay, such as "Oui Oui" and "Terry T." The session's best performance is Carlton's solo rendition of "If I Could I Would," a beautiful chordal solo. Another solid recording which can be appreciated by commercial jazz fans and guitarists. *—Robert Taylor*

Fingerprints / Feb. 2000 / Warner Brothers ♦♦♦
After a period of recording with Fourplay in the late '90s, Larry Carlton comes back under his own name with a collection that is typically both tantalizing and frustrating. It's tantalizing in that you get flashes and streaks of what this extremely gifted and eloquent guitarist can do when the material is good enough to inspire him. It's frustrating, however, because there isn't enough of it; Carlton can only do so much with the weak-to-middling tunes that take up the majority of the disc. Nevertheless, the title cut is a fine example of the smooth jazz genre at its most ingratiating, with a nice groove and tasty guitar work. "Slave Song" is even better, spangled with intriguing instrumental touches (including the multi-tracked saxes of Kirk Whalum); some great, funky octave work right in the pocket; and most unusually in the smooth jazz arena, a passionate instrumental chorus on the way to the fade. "Gracias," a Latin-flavored acoustic-guitar duet between Carlton and country music's Vince Gill, may be the album's masterpiece; together, the two create the disc's most beautiful tunes and licks, evoking memories of Chet Atkins' best celebrity duo sessions. Too often, though, the disc settles for the mediocre and the innocuous, the most obvious example being "Til I Hurt You," an undistinguished tune carefully tooled for airplay, featuring the indecipherably mumbled vocals of Michael McDonald. Yet *Fingerprints'* best stuff, in addition to Carlton's sterling efforts to make the rest come alive, redeems the package. *—Richard S. Ginell*

Benny Carter (Bennett Lester Carter)

b. Aug. 8, 1907, New York, NY
Sax (Alto), Trumpet, Composer, Arranger / East Coast Blues, Jump Blues, Swing
To say that Benny Carter has had a remarkable and productive career would be an extreme understatement. As an altoist, arranger, composer, bandleader and occasional trumpeter, Carter has been at the top of his field since at least 1928, and in 1996 Carter was as strong an altoist at the age of 88 as he was in 1936. His gradually evolving style has not changed much through the decades but neither has it become at all stale or predictable except in its excellence. Benny Carter has been a major figure in every decade since the 1920s and his consistency and longevity are unpredecented. Essentially self-taught, he formed his first big band in 1928 and began contributing arrangements to Fletcher Henderson and even Duke Ellington. By the mid-'30s, Carter was considered one of the two top altoists in jazz (along with Johnny Hodges) as well as a skilled arranger and composer. He relocated to Los Angeles in 1943, wrote for the film studios and made a few tours with Jazz at the Philharmonic. After hardly playing alto at all during the '60s, he made a full "comeback" by the mid-'70s. Even after the rise of such stylists as Charlie Parker, Cannonball Adderley, Eric Dolphy, Ornette Coleman and David Sanborn (in addition to their many followers), Benny Carter still ranks near the top of active altoists. *—Scott Yanow*

The 1929-1933 / Sep. 18, 1929-May 19, 1933 / Classics ♦♦♦♦
The European Classics series has been reissuing on CD the complete output of many top jazz artists of the '20s and '30s. Benny Carter's music at last receives the treatment it deserves in this program. His first volume features the great altoist with a pickup group (the Chocolate Dandies) from 1929-30 that showcases sidemen from Fletcher Henderson's Orchestra, with his own orchestra in 1932-33 (three of the five numbers have rare vocals from Carter) and on 11 sides with Spikes Hughes's all-star band, an orchestra that also features trumpeter Red Allen, trombonist Dicky Wells, Wayman Carver on flute and the tenors of Coleman Hawkins and Chu Berry. This is wonderful and, in many cases, formerly rare music. *—Scott Yanow*

The 1933-1936 / May 19, 1933-Apr. 1936 / Classics ♦♦♦♦
The second volume of the complete early Benny Carter from the European Classics label features Carter on alto, trumpet, clarinet and as arranger (in addition to contributing a bit of piano and even a vocal) on three numbers with Spike Hughes's all-star orchestra, as part of the 1933 edition of The Chocolate Dandies (an interracial outfit put together by Mezz Mezzrow) and with his own big band in 1933-34 and in England two years later. Highlights include "Symphony in Riffs," "Blue Lou" and "Everybody Shuffle." *—Scott Yanow*

The Chocolate Dandies / 1933-1935 / DRG ♦♦♦
Classic early swing and combo material written and arranged by the great Benny Carter. Carter's alto playing was joyous, concise, and bluesy, while his arrangements emphasized both ensemble cohesion and individual freedom, giving his soloists just enough space to express themselves, yet never letting the pace waver or the ensemble stop swinging. *—Ron Wynn*

The 1937-1939 / Jan. 11, 1937-Jun. 29, 1939 / Classics ♦♦♦♦
The fourth CD in Classics' complete chronological reissue of Benny Carter's early recordings as a leader finds Carter (on alto, trumpet, clarinet, tenor and even one vocal) leading orchestras in London, Laren, the Hague, Paris and (for the final three selections) New York. Highpoints include "Nagasaki," "I'm in the Mood for Swing," "Blues in My Heart," "I'm Coming Virginia" (from a three-song session that also features Django Reinhardt) and "Melancholy Lullaby." In addition, the great tenor Coleman Hawkins plays a prominent role on four of the performances. Carter is in top form throughout these often formerly rare but very vital swing recordings. His fans should quickly acquire all of these invaluable Classics releases. *—Scott Yanow*

The 1940-1941 / May 25, 1940-Oct. 16, 1941 / Classics ♦♦♦♦
Most of the selections on the sixth and final Classics' CD to reissue all of Benny Carter's prewar recordings as a leader feature the altoist's commercially unsuccessful big band. With such major soloists as the leader, trumpeter Jonah Jones and Sidney DeParis, trombonists Benny Morton and Jimmy Archey and pianist Sonny White, it is surprising that this orchestra did not make it. The October 23, 1940 recording session (which has three vocals by Roy Felton including one in which he is joined by the Mills Brothers) is quite rare while the opening set from eight days earlier is a small group date with Bill Coleman and Benny Morton that features a pair of W.C. Handy blues sung by Big Joe Turner. Excellent swing music overall. *—Scott Yanow*

Cosmopolite: The Oscar Peterson Verve Sessions / Sep. 18, 1952-Nov. 12, 1954 / Verve ♦♦♦♦
These timeless Benny Carter performances match the great altoist with pianist Oscar Peterson, bassist Ray Brown, either Barney Kessel or Herb Ellis on guitar, Buddy Rich, J.C. Heard or Bobby White on drums, and, on four numbers, trombonist Bill Harris. The 17 standards (four of which are also heard in alternate versions) are treated with respect, taste and swing. Carter always sounds flawless and is in excellent form throughout this enjoyable set. *—Scott Yanow*

The Urbane Sessions / Sep. 18, 1952-1955 / Verve ♦♦♦♦♦
This excellent double CD wraps up the complete reissuance of altoist Benny Carter's Verve recordings of the 1950s. The first CD features his horn backed by strings, and although not all of the arrangements are inspiring, Carter consistently uplifts the music. Although ballad-oriented, there are swinging versions of "With a Song in My Heart" and "Symphony" (the latter a classic rendition); the 16 selections are joined by ten alternate takes. The second disc features Carter in small group sessions. There are nine performances (including a ballad medley and one alternate take) in a quintet with the fiery trumpeter Roy Eldridge, pianist Bruce McDonald, bassist John Simmons, and drummer Alvin Stoller. In addition there are four selections that feature the unusual (but quite coherent) duo of Eldridge (who overdubbed on piano for one track) and Stoller; apparently Art Tatum did not show up for that hoped-for trio session. There are two jam session-style numbers that match Carter with trumpeter Dizzy Gillespie and trombonist Bill Harris, and the two-fer is rounded off by an alter-

nate version of "Street Scene" featuring Carter with the Oscar Peterson Quartet. This important release is both a historical gap-filler and overflowing with great music. *—Scott Yanow*

3, 4, 5: The Verve Small Group Sessions / Mar. 1955 / Verve ♦♦♦♦
Has there ever been a more consistent performer in jazz history over a longer period of time than Benny Carter— The classic altoist, who had fully formed his sound by the early '30s (he first recorded in 1927), has not altered his style much in the past 65 (and counting) years. The music on this Verve reissue CD features Carter in three settings: in a trio with pianist Teddy Wilson and drummer Jo Jones (those performances were only previously out in Japan), heading a quartet with pianist Don Abney, bassist George Duvivier and drummer Louis Bellson and showcased on three previously unissued tracks with the Oscar Peterson trio plus drummer Bobby White. Carter knew most of these standards extremely well and he glides effortlessly over the chord changes, infusing the music with swing and subtle creativity. *—Scott Yanow*

Jazz Giant / Jul. 22, 1957-Apr. 21, 1958 / Contemporary/OJC ♦♦♦♦
Benny Carter had already been a major jazz musician for nearly 30 years when he recorded this particularly strong septet session for Contemporary. With notable contributions from tenor saxophonist Ben Webster, trombonist Frank Rosolino and guitarist Barney Kessel, Carter (who plays a bit of trumpet on "How Can You Lose") is in superb form on a set of five standards and two of his originals. This timeless music is beyond the simple categories of "swing" or "bop" and should just be called "classic." *—Scott Yanow*

★ **Further Definitions** / Nov. 13, 1961-Nov. 15, 1961 / GRP/Impulse! ♦♦♦♦♦
This essential single-CD combines altoist/arranger Benny Carter's classic *Further Definitions* with the related *Additions to Further Definitions*. The former set was a revisit, instrumentation-wise, to the famous 1937 session that Carter and tenor saxophonist Coleman Hawkins made in France with two top European saxophonists (Andre Ekyan and Alix Combelle) and guitarist Django Reinhardt. The all-star group (which also includes Hawkins, altoist Phil Woods, Charlie Rouse on second tenor, pianist Dick Kats, guitarist John Collins, bassist Jimmy Garrison and drummer Jo Jones) performs a particularly inspired repertoire. Carter's charts, which allow Hawkins to stretch out on "Body and Soul," give everyone a chance to shine. "Honeysuckle Rose" and "Crazy Rhythm" hold their own with the 1937 versions, and "Blue Star" and "Doozy" prove to be two of Benny's finest originals. The second date does not quite reach the same heights, but is enjoyable in its own right. This time, Carter contributed six of the eight selections (including a remake of "Doozy"), and the band was gathered from jazzmen then working in the L.A. studios, including Carter and Bud Shank on altos, and tenors Teddy Edwards and either Buddy Collette or Bill Perkins. Although Benny Carter was not actively playing much at the time (this was his only small-group recording during 1963-75), he is heard in typically prime form. Very highly recommended. *—Scott Yanow*

B.B.B. & Co. / Apr. 10, 1962 / Swingville/OJC ♦♦♦
One of Benny Carter's last jazz recordings before he became totally immersed in writing for the studios, this set matches his alto and trumpet with tenor great Ben Webster, clarinetist Barney Bigard and trumpeter Shorty Sherock on a pair of lengthy blues and Carter's "Lula" and "When Lights Are Low." All of the swing all-stars are in fine form, making one wish that they were not being so neglected by critics and fans alike during this era; Webster soon left the U.S. permanently for Europe. Although not essential, this set is fun. *—Scott Yanow*

Carter, Gillespie, Inc. / Apr. 27, 1976 / Pablo/OJC ♦♦♦

Live and Well in Japan / Apr. 29, 1977 / Pablo/OJC ♦♦♦♦

Meets Oscar Peterson / Nov. 14, 1986 / Pablo/OJC ♦♦♦
Altoist Benny Carter had recorded with pianist Oscar Peterson back in the early '50s for Norman Granz's Verve label. More than 30 years, later he teamed up with Peterson again, this time for Granz's Pablo company. There was no sign of decline or disillusionment in either of the co-leaders' playing; in fact, if anything, they had improved with age. Joined by guitarist Joe Pass, bassist Dave Young and drummer Martin Drew, Carter and Peterson are both in a joyous mood and in typically swinging form on six standards and a blues. *—Scott Yanow*

Songbook / Jun. 26, 1995-Aug. 26, 1995 / Music Masters ♦♦♦♦♦

James Carter

b. Jan. 3, 1969, Detroit, MI
Baritone, Sax (Tenor), Sax (Soprano), Sax (Baritone), Sax (Alto), Clarinet (Bass) / Avant-Garde Jazz, Contemporary Jazz, Hard Bop, Post-Bop, Soul-Jazz
James Carter caused a sensation in the mid-'90s with his DIW and Atlantic recordings. Similar in some ways to Rahsaan Roland Kirk (although he only plays one instrument at a time!), Carter has the ability to play in any jazz style from the slap-tongue staccato of early '20s tenors and Dixieland to swing, bop, 1950's R&B, free form and funk while still sounding like himself. A high-powered player skilled on most reeds (with tenor being his main instrument), Carter often switches quickly and unexpectedly between styles and the effect can be exhilarating or numbing. Carter started played sax when he was 11, performed in the Blue Lake Monster Ensemble with Marcus Belgrave and before he graduated high school in 1986 he gigged with Wynton Marsalis. In 1988 Carter played with Lester Bowie in New York and he soon appeared on two Bowie DIW recordings with the New York Organ Ensemble. He has since worked with the Charles Mingus Big Band, the Lincoln Center Jazz Orchestra, Julius Hemphill, recorded with the Tough Young Tenors and led his own highly versatile group. James Carter has unlimited potential and he seems destined to be one of the giants of jazz. *—Scott Yanow*

JC on the Set / Apr. 14, 1993-Apr. 15, 1993 / DIW/Columbia ♦♦♦♦♦
Twenty-five at the time of this CD, James Carter had already absorbed much of the tradition. His debut as a leader includes compositions by the classic tenors Don Byas and John Hardee, Duke Ellington's "Sophisticated Lady" and even a Sun Ra ballad. He also shows that he has the courage to play completely outside whenever it seems logical to him; in fact on the title cut Carter moves from Gene Ammons and Illinois Jacquet to outbursts a la David Murray in the stratosphere. But most importantly, at this early stage James Carter already had his own sound. He switches between the tenor (his main ax) to alto and baritone, shows self-restraint on the ballads and fills his improvisations with continual surprises. Joined by the supportive pianist Craig Taborn, bassist Jaribu Shahid and drummer Tani Tabbal, James Carter puts on quite a tour-de-force throughout this very impressive set. *—Scott Yanow*

Jurassic Classics / Apr. 16, 1994-Apr. 17, 1994 / DIW/Columbia ♦♦♦♦♦
The young but already great saxophonist James Carter explores seven jazz standards with pianist Craig Taborn (himself a young master capable of playing in several styles), bassist Jaribu Shahid and drummer Tani Tabbal. Among the most versatile and knowledgeable of today's saxophonists, Carter draws on many top stylists during these lengthy solos yet always sounds quite individual. His violent depiction of a train whistle on "Take the 'A' Train" perfectly launches that romp and he also really stretches out on "Epistrophy," plays the blues on John Coltrane's "Equinox" and shows quite a bit of fire on "Oleo." A very stimulating session. *—Scott Yanow*

Real Quiet Storm / Oct. 6, 1994-Nov. 20, 1994 / Atlantic ♦♦♦
Despite this CD's title and a slight emphasis on ballads, this is not an easy-listening record. James Carter, one of the great new discoveries of the 1990s (and whose versatility, brilliance on a variety of reed instruments and seeming encyclopedic knowledge of jazz styles makes him a possible successor to Rahsaan Roland Kirk) is heard playing tenor, alto, soprano, baritone, bass clarinet and bass flute on the nine selections with the impressive pianist Craig Taborn, either Dave Holland or Jaribu Shahid on bass and Leon Parker or Tani Tabbal on drums. Although some of the ballad statements (such as his statements on baritone on "'Round Midnight" and "Eventide") are fairly straightforward, Carter also has some explosive moments. His rendition (on soprano) of Don Byas's "1944 Stomp" is memorable as is his interpretations of "Born to Be Blue" and two originals. The results are a bit restrained compared to his live performances, but this is an enjoyable and unpredictable outing, music that will not be played on the "Quiet Storm." *—Scott Yanow*

Conversin' with the Elders / Oct. 2, 1995-Feb. 5, 1996 / Atlantic ♦♦♦
The brilliant saxophonist James Carter and his quartet (which also includes pianist Craig Taborn, bassist Jaribu Shahid and drummer Tani Tabbal) welcome some of Carter's musical heroes as guests throughout this CD. Carter matches wits with the eccentric trumpeter Lester Bowie on "Freereggaehibop" and the often-hilarious "Atitled Valse"; he also features the legendary (but rarely recorded) Detroit altoist Larry Smith on "Parker's Mood," showcases Count Basie veterans Harry "Sweets" Edison and Buddy Tate on two swing standards apiece (Tate's work on clarinet during "Blue Creek" is memorable), and interacts with baritonist Hamiet Bluiett on "Naima" and an Anthony Braxton march. Switching between tenor, alto, baritone and bass clarinet, Carter makes each of his guests feel at home while pushing them to stretch themselves. A consistently colorful and generally swing-oriented set. *—Scott Yanow*

In Carterian Fashion / May 19, 1998 / Atlantic ♦♦♦♦
James Carter is the Arturo Sandoval of the reeds, a remarkable virtuoso who can seemingly do anything he wants on his horns. It is just a matter of time passing and the accomplishments accumulating before Carter is thought of as one of the all-time greats. This particular CD differs from his earlier ones in that Carter (who switches between tenor, soprano, baritone sax and bass clarinet) is joined by one of three organists (Henry Butler, Cyrus Chestnut and his regular pianist Craig Taborn) instead of piano, which of course changes the sound of the ensembles. However, only a few of the songs come across as Jimmy Smith-style soul-jazz. Carter stretches from bluesy tunes to Don Byas' swinging mid-'40s romp "Don's Idea," and some avant-garde explorations, and a few strong hints at Rahsaan Roland Kirk (particularly on the soprano feature "Trouble in the World") and Eddie "Lockjaw" Davis. Trumpeter Dwight Adams sounds fine during his four appearances, particularly when trading off with Carter on "Don's Idea," and altoist Cassius Richmond (who is on three of the trumpet pieces) is also excellent. However, the dominant voice throughout is James Carter, who in general is a little more restrained, which makes his fiery explosions and colorful tonal distortions really stand out. Recommended. *—Scott Yanow*

● **Chasin' the Gypsy** / Jun. 6, 2000 / Atlantic ♦♦♦♦♦
James Carter celebrated 2000 by putting out two vastly different albums at the same time, an amazing concession from a major label for a jazz artist who doesn't sell in Kenny G-like proportions. *Chasin' the Gypsy,* as you might guess, is an homage to Django Reinhardt, whose music Carter used to dig on Detroit radio when he was a teenager, but Carter doesn't take the predictable reverent path in paying his respects. He rummages through his closet and pulls out a rarely used bass saxophone on three cuts—the bumpy sounds are often comic yet a comfortable fit for his antic style—and even tries out an F mezzo sax on the exotically relaxed "Oriental Shuffle." Back on tenor, Carter's slippery playing often doesn't hesitate to approach the outside; he keeps his sense of humor and his individual quirks intact. Most of the tunes are Django's yet the one that comes closest to evoking the frantic *Hot Club Quintette* drive is Carter's own title track, a madcap chase indeed with Carter on wild soprano sax this time. A nostalgic accordion underpins the tango-like "Nuages" á la Piazzolla; violinist Regina Carter provides the Stephane Grappelli-like foil on a few tracks (she does all right but could be a bit looser); and Jay Berliner and Romero Lubambo occasionally summon the ghost of Django with their respectively steel and nylon-stringed solo and rhythm guitar work. Mostly, this is a delightful departure for Carter, though probably destined to be a one-off excursion. *—Richard S. Ginell*

Layin' in the Cut / Jun. 6, 2000 / Atlantic ♦♦♦
The second of James Carter's pair of 2000 releases shifts wildly, and perhaps trendily, toward electric funk, as the title cut proclaims within seconds. It's really a loose, collective electric jam session with all of the risks, occasional hot streaks, and passages of torpor that the term implies. Oddly enough, the tracks that really make it are those that are credited to only one composer: guitarist Jef Lee Johnson's stimulating Prime Time-like melee, "Terminal 8," that gathers momentum like a freight train; Carter's cooking "There's a Puddle" that explodes into a freeform burst on cue at the end; and Carter's "GP." The collectively credited pieces are the

ones that tend to go nowhere, often desperately in need of editing or clear direction. At all times, though, Carter is a freewheeling dynamo on soprano and tenor saxes, not afraid to reach wildly to the outside even when the funk backgrounds are merely mild mannered. Carter draws from the New York City avant-garde scene for help: Marc Ribot is the other electric guitarist, Jamaaladeen Tacuma plays bass, and the volatile drummer G. Calvin Weston tries with partial success to mix things up. Carter says that he intends to pursue this direction in the future—with hopefully less diffuse results. *—Richard S. Ginell*

John Carter (John Wallace Carter)

b. Sep. 24, 1929, Fort Worth, TX, **d.** Mar. 31, 1991, Inglewood, CA
Clarinet / Avant-Garde Jazz, Free Jazz
John Carter was one of the very few free jazz players to concentrate exclusively on clarinet, and one of not very many to place an emphasis on the music's composed elements. Carter studied alto saxophone and clarinet early in his career. He played with fellow Fort Worth-native Ornette Coleman in the late '40s. In 1949, he received his Bachelors degree from Lincoln University in Jefferson City, Missouri. In 1956, he earned a Masters degree from the University of Colorado. He taught in the Fort Worth Public schools from 1949-61 and in the Los Angeles school system from 1961-82. In 1964, while living in Los Angeles, Carter formed the New Art Jazz Ensemble with trumpeter BobbyBradford (who would also work with Coleman). The next year he conducted a program of Coleman's music at UCLA. In the late-'60s he played and recorded with pianist Horace Tapscott and saxophonist Arthur Blythe, among others. Carter switched to clarinet full-time in 1974. He recorded as a leader for the Flying Dutchman, Moers Music, and Revelation labels in the late-'60s and early-'70s. In the 1970s, Carter became an elder statesman to a group of young Los Angeles free jazz that included the multi-instrumentalist Vinny Golia. In 1983, Carter formed a school for improvisation called the Wind College, with flutist James Newton, bassist/tubaist Red Callender, and saxophonist Charles Owens. Carter's activities in the '80s included participation in Clarinet Summit, a multi-generational, multi-stylistic quartet with David Murray, Alvin Baptiste, and Jimmy Hamilton; the group recorded for India Navigation and Black Saint. Carter's major focus in his last decade was, however, a five-part set of multi-movement compositions entitled "Roots and Folklore: Episodes in the Development of American Folk Music." The first suite was recorded for Black Saint, the final four for Gramavision. As a player, Carter comes very much out of the free melodic tradition of Coleman, Bradford, and Dewey Redman. He navigated the notoriously difficult B-flat clarinet with extraordinary fluidity and a rare certainty of execution. Carter had a comprehensive technique and a prodigious imagination; in his compositions, Carterharnessed the looseness of collective improvisation without compromising spontaneity. *—Chris Kelsey*

West Coast Hot / 1969 / Jive/Novus ✦✦✦✦✦
This very valuable release documents two important but underrated avant-garde units that were based in Los Angeles. Clarinetist John Carter (here also heard on tenor and alto) and trumpeter Bobby Bradford co-led bands for many years in virtual obscurity. With bassist Tom Williamson and drummer Buzz Freeman, they are both abstract and logical on four originals with Carter's passionate sounds contrasting, as usual, with Bradford's lyricism. The second half of this disc features L.A.'s great undiscovered legend, pianist Horace Tapscott. He is heard in superlative form on four tracks (including the 17-minute "The Giant Is Awakened") in a two-bass quintet also co-starring the young altoist Arthur Blythe. *—Scott Yanow*

Self-Determination Music / 1969-1970 / Flying Dutchman ✦✦✦

● **Dauwhe** / Feb. 25, 1982-Mar. 8, 1982 / Black Saint ✦✦✦✦✦
The first of clarinetist John Carter's five-part series in which he musically depicts the history of Black Americans is one of the strongest. For the only set on Black Saint (the following chapters were released by Gramavision), Carter utilizes a notable octet which also includes cornetist Bobby Bradford, flutist James Newton, Charles Owens on soprano, oboe and clarinet, bassist Roberto Miranda, the veteran Red Callender on tuba, drummer William Jeffrey and Luis Peralta on percussion. The five originals pay tribute to life in Africa a few centuries ago, mixing together folk melodies with very advanced improvising; Newton and Callender in particular really excel in this setting. Highly recommended for open-eared listeners. *—Scott Yanow*

Castles of Ghana / Feb. 1985 / Gramavision ✦✦✦✦
The second of clarinetist John Carter's five-part depiction of the history of African Americans deals with the capture of many Africans for shipment as slaves to the New World. Carter's octet on this date features such fine players as bass clarinetist Marty Ehrlich, cornetist Bobby Bradford, trombonist Benny Powell and trumpeter Baikida Carroll, and the music is as dramatic as the episodes it portrays. *—Scott Yanow*

Regina Carter

Violin / Post-Bop
A talented player with a beautiful tone, Regina Carter has the potential to become the most significant new violinist in jazz since Jean-Luc Ponty in the late 1960s. Carter began playing violin when she was four and, after graduating from Cass Technical High School, the New England Conservatory and Michigan's Oakland University, she became a member of Straight Ahead. In 1994, she left the band (which had recorded for Atlantic) to move to New York. Carter has since worked with the Uptown String Quartet, the String Trio of New York, Oliver Lake and Max Roach. Her debut set as a leader for Atlantic was a bit R&B- and pop-oriented, but her appearance near the end of Wynton Marsalis' Pulitzer Prize-winning *Blood On the Fields* during 1996-97 nearly always stole the show. Carter's second solo effort, *Something for Grace*, also appeared in 1997; her debut for the Verve label, *Rhythms of the Heart*, followed two years later. In 2000 she returned with a tribute to her home town, *Motor City Moments*. *—Scott Yanow*

Regina Carter / 1995 / Atlantic ✦✦

Something for Grace / Apr. 1, 1997 / Atlantic ✦✦✦
Regina Carter (who has a beautiful tone and a swinging style) is one of the top new jazz violinists of the 1990s, and the more memorable selections on this CD are so strong that they almost allow one to overlook the three throwaway pop/R&B songs. Unfortunately, the opening "Downtown Underground" is one of the losers, and the Nicki Richards vocal piece "Late Night Mood" (which recording executive talked Carter into recording that turkey—) is so lightweight that it should have been released on another album. In contrast are near-classic renditions of Eddie Harris' "Listen Here" and Mal Waldron's "Soul Eyes"; Carter's haunting ballad "Reflections" deserves to become a standard. A mixed bag, but overall this CD is recommended, with reservations. *—Scott Yanow*

Rhythms of the Heart / Nov. 24, 1998-Dec. 8, 1998 / Verve ✦✦✦
Regina Carter definitely has a lot of room to run in the jazz world with the violin, an instrument that has been selected by relatively few for compelling reasons; a)., the sheer difficulty of mastering the contraption, and b)., the rigorous, non-swinging, non-improvising classical training that usually produces that mastery. Some of the conservatory still lingers in Carter's formal stage stance and in traces of the music, but there is no doubt that she can swing mightily, if not yet with the consistently eloquent ease of the old masters. Kenny Barron contributes his unshakeably solid piano to four cuts and Werner Geirig handles four more; Rodney Jones serves up jazz and wah-wah guitars; Peter Washington (bass) and Lewis Nash (drums) back most of the tracks. A good deal of the CD places Carter in a straight-ahead setting, where she shows her Stuff Smith stuff particularly winningly on "Lady Be Good." Luckily, she hasn't been roped into the mainstream to the exclusion of all else: hence, the brave, if slightly inhibited, reggae/funk version of the Temptations' "Papa Was A Rollin' Stone" with an idiosyncratic moaning vocal by guest Cassandra Wilson. Carter also tries out a mild salsa groove on "Mojito, " and a nice, revolving African beat on "Mandingo Street" in the manner of early-'90s Jean-Luc Ponty. In all, a decent, all-purpose major-label debut, designed to present a table of contents for her emerging career. *—Richard S. Ginell*

● **Motor City Moments** / Sep. 26, 2000 / Verve ✦✦✦✦
Two years after her stunning debut on Verve, violinist Regina Carter offers listeners her exceptional string virtuosity on ten great songs inspired by her hometown of Detroit, Michigan. *Motor City Moments* features a stellar collection of songs written by some of the best musicians from Detroit including Marvin Gaye, Stevie Wonder, Thad Jones, and Milt Jackson. Regina Carter applies her pure skill, pizzicato, and arco passages to "Don't Mess With Mr. T" and "Higher Ground" with impeccable tuning and multiple approaches. Her string virtuosity on Milt Jackson's "For Someone I Love," is a masterful performance backed adeptly by Mayra Casales on percussion and spotlights a brilliant piano solo by Werner "Vana" Gierig. Two originals, "Forever February" and "Up South," which was co-written with guitarist Russell Malone, provide an interesting contrast of the artist's use of reflective temperament and folk-ornamented cadences. Each song also emphasizes Carter's adept techniques with melodic phrasing and song forms. Accompanied by her touring band of Daryl Hall on bass, Alvester Garnett on drums, percussionist Mayra Casales, Marcus Belgrave on trumpet and flugelhorn, James Carter on bass clarinet and tenor sax, Barry Harris on piano, Lewis Nash, as well as several special guests, Regina Carter has rapidly become one of the most exciting and original violinists to arrive on the jazz scene. *—Paula Edelstein*

Ron Carter

b. May 4, 1937, Ferndale, MI
Piccolo Bass, Cello, Bass / Hard Bop, Post-Bop
The epitome of class and elegance, though not stuffy, Ron Carter has been a world class bassist and cellist since the '60s. He's among the greatest accompanists of all time, but has also done many albums exhibiting his prodigious technique. He's a brillant rhythmic and melodic player, who uses everything in the bass and cello arsenal; walking lines, thick, full, prominent notes and tones, drones and strumming effects and melody snippets. Carter's nearly as accomplished in classical music as jazz, and has performed with symphony orchestras all over the world. He began playing cello at age ten, but had switched to bass by the time he moved to New York and began playing in Chico Hamilton's quintet with Eric Dolphy. In 1963, he was tapped to become a member of Miles Davis' band, and remained until 1968, appearing on every crucial mid-'60s recording and teaming with Herbie Hancock and Tony Williams to craft a new, freer rhythm section sound. The high-profile job led to the reputation that's seen Carter become possibly the most recorded bassist in jazz history (some sources have claimed as many as 1000 credits). He's led his own bands at various intervals since 1972, using a second bassist to keep time and establish harmony so he's free to provide solos. He eventually landed at Blue Note for LPs including 1997's *The Bass and I* as well as the next year's *So What?* *—Ron Wynn*

● **Where?** / Jun. 20, 1961 / New Jazz/OJC ✦✦✦✦
Essential session with Carter on both bass and cello. Awesome solos by Eric Dolphy (sax)—stunning pieces. W/ Mal Waldron. *—Ron Wynn*

Piccolo / Mar. 25, 1977-Mar. 26, 1977 / Milestone ✦✦✦✦✦
This double album is mostly recommended to lovers of bass solos. With Ron Carter functioning as the main soloist on piccolo bass, only the solos of pianist Kenny Barron offer a bit of contrast. Bassist Buster Williams and drummer Ben Riley, who complete the quartet, are mostly featured in support. These performances, which are well-played, are almost all quite long, so listeners who prefer more variety in their music are advised to look elsewhere. *—Scott Yanow*

Parade / Mar. 1979 / Milestone/OJC ✦✦✦✦
Bassist Carter heads a sterling mid-sized band with three trumpeters and saxophonists and two trombones, but no bass or drums. He handles the job of being both the primary and secondary rhythm support, while guests Joe Henderson, Jon Faddis, and Frank Wess, among others, provide some standout solos. The ensemble interaction clicks as well. *—Ron Wynn*

Patrao / May 19, 1980-May 20, 1980 / Milestone/OJC ✦✦✦✦

☆ **Telephone** / Aug. 1984 / Concord Jazz ✦✦✦✦✦

A live performance—a concert. Lots of space, and a slow pace. Music to listen to, perhaps a tad too intellectual. Still... lovely. —*Michael Erlewine*

Panamanhattan / Jul. 23, 1990 / Evidence ♦♦♦

Mr. Bow Tie / 1995 / Blue Note ♦♦♦♦

Bassist Ron Carter varies the personnel often enough to keep one's interest throughout this CD. Carter, who contributed six of the ten compositions (which alternate with four familiar standards) takes his share of bass solos but also showcases pianist Gonzalo Rubalcaba (who is pretty restrained throughout) on the opening "Mr. Bow-Tie" and allocates a generous amount of solo space on some selections to trumpeter Edwin Russell (inspired by Miles Davis but possessing his own fire) and Javon Jackson, who often sounds like a close relative of Joe Henderson. Rubalcaba sits out on four of Carter's originals, making the group occasionally a pianoless quartet/quintet (depending on whether percussionist Steve Kroon is present). All of the music is straightahead and the playing is consistently colorful. This is an impressive effort that is easily recommended. —*Scott Yanow*

Bass and I / Sep. 23, 1997 / Blue Note ♦♦♦♦

Orfeu / Nov. 2, 1999 / Blue Note ♦♦♦

Joe Chambers

b. Jun. 25, 1942, Stoneacre, VA

Drums, Piano / Avant-Garde Jazz, Post-Bop

Joe Chambers is an extremely versatile, tasteful, master of all post-bop idioms. Chambers drives an ensemble with a light hand; his time is excellent, and his grasp of dynamics superb. He's not a flashy drummer by any means, but he's a generous collaborator who makes any group of which he's a part as good as it can possibly be. Chambers worked around Washington, D.C. in his late teens. After moving to New York in 1963, he played with Eric Dolphy, Freddie Hubbard, Jimmy Giuffre, and Andrew Hill. In the mid-'60s, Chambers played with a number of the more progressively inclined musicians associated with the Blue Note Label, such as vibist Bobby Hutcherson and saxophonists Joe Henderson, Wayne Shorter, and Sam Rivers. In 1970, Chambers joined Max Roach's percussion ensemble, M'Boom, as an original member. During the '70s, Chambers played with a great many of jazz's most prominent elder statesmen, including Sonny Rollins, Tommy Flanagan, Charles Mingus, and Art Farmer. With Flanagan and bassist Reggie Workman, Chambers formed the Super Jazz Trio. In the late '70s, he co-led a band with organist Larry Young. Chambers recorded with bands led by trumpeter Chet Baker and percussionist Ray Mantilla in the early '80s. He's maintained his association with Roach into the '90s. Chambers has recorded infrequently as a leader; his output as a sideman, however, continues to be sizable. —*Chris Kelsey*

• **Phantom of the City** / Mar. 8, 1991-Mar. 9, 1991 / Candid ♦♦♦♦

Drummer Joe Chambers works with an intriguing lineup on this '91 quintet set. Young lion trumpeter Phillip Harper teams with journeyman Bob Berg, who holds his own with the lyrical, energetic Harper. Chambers never hurries or crowds the soloists, and he interacts easily and fully with pianist George Cables and bassist Santi Debriano. —*Ron Wynn*

Mirrors / 1998 / Blue Note ♦♦♦♦

This long-anticipated date by drummer Chambers, his first domestic production since the mid-'70s, is the personification of what modern jazz in the '90s can be. Immaculately played and programmed, collectively inspired by brilliant musicianship, and triggered by the creative juices of its fearless leader, the date commands interest throughout, and upon repeated listenings. That's the mark of a truly great recording. Chambers explores many veins of contemporary jazz, from the New Orleans-derived, modern modal "Tu-Way-Pock-E-Way," the Jazz Messenger-ish title track, the darker, modal "Caravanserai," the tearjerker "Ruth," and the more hopeful, upbeat trio finale "Ruthless" to the delicate take on Janet Jackson's "Come Back to Me." The middle section hints at Chambers' polyphonic notions, on the fast samba modification of Andrew Hill's "Catta" (previously recorded on Chambers' '70s Muse/32 Jazz date *The Almoravid*) retitled "Mariposa," plus a more multi-instrumental focus; there are overdubs of vibes and drums with the trio of astounding pianist Mulgrew Miller and bassist Ira Coleman on Rod Temperton's "Lady in My Life," and more as Chambers duets with himself on drums and vibes for "Circles." Saxophonist Vincent Herring and trumpeter Eddie Henderson are lockstep in harmonic interplay, forming a frontline that is as attractive as any. The rhythm section can do no wrong, and Chambers is right on with every step. In case you hadn't heard, Chambers is one of the all-time greats, as he proves on every track of this exceptional modern jazz date. Footnote: Chambers is also a fine pianist, yet another side that hopefully will come to the forefront on a follow-up that we should not have to wait twenty years for. —*Michael G. Nastos*

Paul Chambers

b. Apr. 22, 1935, Pittsburgh, PA, **d.** Jan. 4, 1969, New York, NY

Bass / Hard Bop

One of the top bassists of 1955-65, Paul Chambers was among the first in jazz to take creative bowed solos (other than Slam Stewart who hummed along with his bowing). He grew up in Detroit where he was part of the fertile local jazz scene. After touring with Paul Quinichette, Chambers went to New York where he played with the J.J. Johnson-Kai Winding quintet and George Wallington. He spent the bulk of his prime years (1955-63) as a member of the Miles Davis Quintet, participating in virtually all of Davis' classic recordings of the era. When he left "Mr. P.C." (as John Coltrane called him in one of his originals) worked with the Wynton Kelly Trio (1963-66) and freelanced until his death. Chambers, a consistently inspired accompanist who was an excellent soloist, made many recordings during his brief period including some with Sonny Rollins, Coltrane, Cannonball Adderley, Donald Byrd, Bud Powell and Freddie Hubbard in addition to a few as a leader —*Scott Yanow*

Whims of Chambers / Sep. 21, 1956 / Blue Note ♦♦♦♦

Of the seven songs on this Blue Note CD reissue, four are more common than the other three because they contain solos by tenor saxophonist John Coltrane and have therefore been reissued more often. Actually there are quite a few solos in the all-star sextet (which includes the bassist-leader, Coltrane, trumpeter Donald Byrd, guitarist Kenny Burrell, pianist Horace Silver and drummer Philly Joe Jones) and all of the players get their chances to shine on this fairly spontaneous hard bop set. Coltrane's two obscure compositions ("Nita" and "Just for the Love") are among the more memorable tunes and are worth reviving. "Tale of the Fingers" features the quintet without Coltrane, the rhythm section stretches out on "Whims of Chambers" and "Tale of the Fingers" is a showcase for Chambers bowed bass. This is a fine effort and would be worth picking up by straightahead jazz fans even if John Coltrane had not participated. —*Scott Yanow*

• **Bass on Top** / Jul. 14, 1957 / Blue Note ♦♦♦♦♦

Bass on Top is another thoroughly engaging set of straight-ahead, mainstream jazz from Paul Chambers. The bassist leads a quartet comprised of guitarist Kenny Burrell, pianist Hank Jones and drummer Art Taylor through a selection of standards, including "Yesterdays," "You'd Be So Nice to Come Home To" and "Dear Old Stockholm," as well as a handful of contemporary jazz numbers and originals. There's a relaxed, friendly atmosphere to the music, both in its tone and in the fact that Chambers lets Jones and Burrell have some time in the spotlight. The result is a warm, entertaining collection of mainstream jazz that nevertheless rewards close listening. —*Stephen Thomas Erlewine*

Go / Feb. 2, 1959-Feb. 3, 1959 / Vee-Jay ♦♦♦♦

This interesting but out of print Vee Jay LP is headed by bassist Paul Chambers and features four all-stars as sidemen: altoist Cannonball Adderley, pianist Wynton Kelly, drummer Jimmy Cobb, and (on four of the six numbers) the young trumpeter Freddie Hubbard who was at the beginning of his career. Other than Hubbard, all of the musicians were currently members of the Miles Davis Sextet, but the fiery and sometimes funky music sounds much more extroverted than much of Davis' output at the time. Cannonball and Kelly are the solo stars on three standards and a trio of Chambers originals while Hubbard sounds promising. Hopefully Vee-Jay will reissue this set (along with its follow-up *1st Bassman*) on CD eventually; the unavailable Japanese reissue has added quite a few alternate takes. —*Scott Yanow*

Just Friends / Feb. 2, 1959-Feb. 3, 1959 / Vee-Jay ♦♦♦

Rare 1959 and 1960 sessions Chambers led for Vee Jay label. These were once available as poorly remastered bootleg; they are tough to locate. —*Ron Wynn*

1st Bassman / May 12, 1960 / Vee-Jay ♦♦♦♦

Paul Chambers was one of the top bassists of the 1955-65 period, so it is somewhat surprising to realize that this out-of-print Vee Jay LP was his final one as a leader. Actually tenor saxophonist Yusef Lateef, who contributed all five selections, is the most prominent musician on the album although trumpeter Tommy Turrentine, trombonist Curtis Fuller, pianist Wynton Kelly, drummer Lex Humprhies and Chambers are all strong assets. The music is straightahead without being overly predictable, falling into the hard bop idiom and containing many fine moments. —*Scott Yanow*

Teddy Charles (Theodore Charles Cohen)

b. Apr. 13, 1928, Chicopee Falls, MA

Vibraphone / Cool

Teddy Charles is a true rarity: a jazz musician who largely retired from the business. A skillful if not overly distinctive vibraphonist and (early in his career) quite capable on piano and drums, Charles was as important for his open-minded approach in the 1950s towards more advanced sounds as he was for his playing. He moved to New York to study percussion at Juilliard in 1946, but instead became involved in the jazz world. He had short stints with the big bands of Randy Brooks, Benny Goodman, Artie Shaw, Buddy DeFranco and Chubby Jackson from 1948-51 and then played with combos headed by Anita O'Day, Oscar Pettiford, Roy Eldridge and Slim Gaillard. He also became a member of the Jazz Composers' Workshop (1953-55) along with Charles Mingus and Teo Macero, opening his style up to the influences of classical music and freer improvising. Charles began leading his own stimulating record dates in 1951, and by 1953 he was also working as a record producer, a field that took much more of his time from 1956 on. —*Scott Yanow*

Collaboration: West / Dec. 23, 1952-Aug. 31, 1953 / Prestige/OJC ♦♦♦

Vibraphonist Teddy Charles heads three West Coast-style sessions on this CD reissue that look a bit toward Third Stream and the avant-garde experiments of the early '60s. Although there are some swinging sections, much of the music is quite complex with difficult arrangements and some polytonality. One session has Charles (who doubles on piano) in a quartet with guitarist Jimmy Raney (those four numbers were not on the original LP) while the other originals feature trumpeter Shorty Rogers, bassist Curtis Counce, drummer Shelly Manne and sometimes Jimmy Giuffre on tenor and baritone. The music is thought-provoking if a bit cold and clinical, easier to respect than to love. —*Scott Yanow*

Evolution / Aug. 31, 1953–Jan. 6, 1955 / Prestige/OJC ♦♦♦♦

Although somewhat overlooked in the jazz history books, vibraphonist Teddy Charles was for a period an important participant in the early Third Stream movement, using aspects of classical music to revitalize West Coast-style jazz. This CD reissue features trumpeter Shorty Rogers, tenor saxophonist Jimmy Giuffre, bassist Curtis Counce and drummer Shelly Manne on a couple of advanced originals (one apiece by Giuffre and Rogers) from 1953. After moving to New York, Charles teamed up for a short time with bassist Charles Mingus, performing six other numbers in a quartet with tenor saxophonist J.R. Monterose and drummer Gerry Segal. This session alternates cookers with sensitive ballads and is one of the better recorded showcases for Charles' vibes. Recommended. —*Scott Yanow*

• **Tentet** / Jan. 6, 1956-Nov. 12, 1956 / Atlantic ♦♦♦♦♦

Most of this CD features vibraphonist Teddy Charles heading an advanced tentet in 1956, a unit including the likes of trumpeter Art Farmer, altoist Gigi Gryce, tenor saxophonist J.R. Monterose, pianist Mal Waldron, and guitarist Jimmy Raney. The arrangements of George Russell ("Lydian M-1"), Gil Evans (a year before *Miles Ahead*), Jimmy Giuffre, Mal Waldron, and Charles are quite advanced but often leave room for some swinging spots. The final three selections on the CD are actually taken from a slightly later album. Of these, "Blue Greens" is a change of pace, a quartet outing for Charles, pianist Hall Overton, bassist Charles Mingus, and drummer Ed Shaughnessy. All in all, this CD is pretty definitive of Teddy Charles' more adventurous music of the 1950s and it grows in interest with each listening. *—Scott Yanow*

A Word From Bird / Oct. 12, 1956–Oct. 16, 1956 / Koch International ✦✦✦
This Koch reissue brings to light a forgotten 1957 Atlantic session from vibraphonist Teddy Charles. Although much of this material falls under the category of cool jazz, the leadoff and title track "Word From Bird" features a full ensemble and caused some controversy for its third stream approach. Commissioned for *the Stuttgart Light-Music Festival* in 1956, the festival directors ended up rejecting it, insisting it was too musically advanced and serious for a "light music" festival. The swinging uptempo Bob Brookmeyer composition "Show Time" features admirable soloing from Charles, Hal Stein on alto, Robert Newman on tenor, trumpeter Art Farmer, and Jimmy Rainey on guitar. The four remaining tracks feature the rhythm section only with Hall Overton on piano, Charles Mingus on bass, and Ed Shaughnessy on drums. Cole Porter's "Just One of Those Things", a haunting version of "Laura," "When Your Lover Has Gone," and the midtempo "Blue Greens" lazily gallops along with Mingus receiving ample solo space. *Word From Bird* is an enjoyable reissue. *—Al Campbell*

Coolin' / Apr. 14, 1957 / New Jazz/OJC ✦✦✦✦
Although this sextet session was officially a co-op, vibraphonist Teddy Charles and pianist Mal Waldron were really the main organizers. The group plays five originals by bandmembers that often have complex melodies but familiar chord changes. Trumpeter Idrees Sulieman excels on the one standard ("Everything Happens to Me"), altoist John Jenkins (making his recording debut) has some worthy solos and both bassist Addison Farmer and drummer Jerry Segal are fine in support. This obscure session (reissued on CD in the OJC series) is an excellent outing. *—Scott Yanow*

New Directions / Nov. 16, 1999 / Prestige/OJC ✦✦✦✦
Vibraphonist Teddy Charles was turning people's heads when he recorded these tracks in the early 1950s. Originally released on one LP (entitled *Teddy Charles and His Trio*) and two EPs (both titled *New Directions*, one credited to the Teddy Charles Quartet and one to Teddy Charles, Hall Overton, and Ed Shaughnessy), these performances find him taking standards like "Ol' Man River" and "Basin Street Blues" down strange paths and creating unusually challenging "modern" music in collaboration with pianist and pedagogue Hall Overton. The trio that performs the first eight tracks consisted of Charles, guitarist Don Roberts, and bassist Kenny O'Brien; without a drummer, their sound is somewhat fragile, which doesn't benefit Charles's boppish arrangement of "Ol' Man River" but nicely serves his almost ethereal conception of "I'll Remember April." The last four tracks on this collection are the most interesting and challenging: titled "Mobiles," "Antiphony," "Metalizing," and "Decibels," they are compositions based on organizational concepts rather than melodic ideas and sound something like a cross between John Cage and Charles Mingus. Not everyone will love this stuff, but anyone with an interest in jazz theory and history will want to hear it at least once. *—Rick Anderson*

Doc Cheatham (Adolphus Anthony Cheatham)

b. Jun. 13, 1905, Nashville, TN, **d.** Jun. 2, 1997, Washington, D.C.
Vocals, Trumpet / Swing, Dixieland
Doc Cheatham was without question the greatest 90-year old trumpeter of all time; in fact no brass player over the age of 80 had ever played with his power, range, confidence and melodic creativity. Most trumpeters fade while in their 60s due to the physical difficulty of their instrument, but Cheatham did not truly find himself as a soloist until he was nearly 70. Doc Cheatham's career reaches back to the early '20s when he played in vaudeville theatres backing such travelling singers as Bessie Smith and Clara Smith. He moved to Chicago, recorded with Ma Rainey, subbed for Louis Armstrong (his main idol) and had his own group in 1926. Due to his wide range and pretty tone, Cheatham worked as a nonsoloing first trumpeter with McKinney's Cotton Pickers and Cab Calloway throughout the 1930s He spent time with Teddy Wilson's big band and was with the commercially successful Eddie Heywood Sextet. In the 1950s Cheatham alternated between Dixieland (Wilbur DeParis, guest spots with Eddie Condon) and Latin (Perez Prado, Herbie Mann) bands. He was with Benny Goodman during 1966-67 but it was not until the mid-'70s that Cheatham felt truly comfortable as a soloist. Duet sets with pianist Sammy Price launched his new career and until his death in 1997 he recorded fairly prolifically. Cheatham was also a charming singer whose half-spoken, half-sung vocals took nothing away from his chance-taking trumpet flights. *—Scott Yanow*

● **The Fabulous** / Nov. 16, 1983-Nov. 17, 1983 / Parkwood ✦✦✦✦✦
The ageless trumpeter Doc Cheatham (who was 78 years old at the time of this studio session) is remarkable. Most trumpeters fade when they hit their 60s, but he continues to gain in strength, hitting reasonably high notes with confidence and power; his melodic invention also continues to develop. This quartet session with the late pianist Dick Wellstood is one of his finest recordings. Cheatham is in particularly top form on "Deed I Do," "Swing That Music" and "I Double Dare You" but all nine selections (which also feature his charming whispered vocals) are quite enjoyable. *—Scott Yanow*

Echoes of New Orleans / Apr. 18, 1992 / Big Easy ✦✦✦✦
The remarkable Doc Cheatham, two months shy of 87 at the time, leads a fine sextet through a variety of Dixieland and swing numbers on this live set. Clarinetist Sammy Rimington has some good solos; trombonist Jerry Zigmont, pianist Jon Marks and drummer John Russell are competent without leaving much of an impression; and bassist Arvell Shaw is in top form, taking a couple of spirited vocals. However, it is Cheatham who dominates the upbeat performances, which range from "Clarinet Marmalade" and "Pennies From Heaven" to "Ain't Misbehavin'" and "Struttin' With Some Barbecue." *—Scott Yanow*

The Eighty-Seven Years of Doc Cheatham / Sep. 17, 1992–Sep. 18, 1992 / Columbia ✦✦✦✦✦
There has never been a trumpeter in recorded history over the age of 80 on Doc Cheatham's level. Age 87 at the time of this CD, he plays with power, creativity and confidence on this quartet set of swing standards. He dominates the music with his trumpet solos and quiet but charming vocals and, even with the participation of a strong rhythm section led by pianist Chuck Folds, Cheatham is the obvious star. This historic set is a real gem on several levels and is highly recommended. *—Scott Yanow*

Doc Cheatham & Nicholas Payton / Oct. 9, 1994 / Verve ✦✦✦✦
This matchup between trumpeters Doc Cheatham (91 at the time) and Nicholas Payton (just 23) is quite logical and delightful. Cheatham, one of the few survivors of the 1920s, was still in remarkably fine form, while Payton (a flexible New Orleans player capable of ranging from Dixieland to Freddie Hubbard) is both respectful and inspiring. With Doc contributing occasional vocals and the settings ranging from a quartet to an octet with clarinetist Jack Maheu and pianist Butch Thompson, the brassmen explore a variety of 1920s and '30s standards, including a couple of obscurities ("Do You Believe in Love at Sight—" and "Maybe"). The interplay between the co-leaders, the many subtle tributes to Louis Armstrong, and the consistent enthusiasm of this swinging set make this a historic success and a very enjoyable outing. *—Scott Yanow*

Swinging Down in New Orleans / 1995 / Jazzology ✦✦✦✦✦
Although it has not gotten the publicity that his Columbia and Verve CDs received, this is one of the finest of all Doc Cheatham albums. Age 88 at the time, Cheatham had not lost a thing and plays miraculously well. He is teamed up with clarinetist Brian O'Connell, pianist Butch Thompson, Les Muscutt (doubling on guitar and banjo), Bill Huntington (on bass and guitar), bassist Peter Badie and drummer Ernest Elly. Cheatham plays melodic, swinging and frequently exciting solos, taking personable and whispery vocals on such likeable numbers as "When I Grow Too Old to Dream," "You're Lucky to Me," "Never Swat a Fly," "I Would Do Anything for You" and "I've Got the World on a String." This somewhat overlooked CD is highly recommended. *—Scott Yanow*

Don Cherry

b. Nov. 18, 1936, Oklahoma City, OK, **d.** Oct. 19, 1995, Malaga, Spain
Cornet, Flute / Avant-Garde Jazz, Free Jazz, Avant-Garde, World Fusion
The second track from *Tomorrow is the Question?*Ornette Coleman's 1959 wake-up call to the hard bop movement—is a medium tempo blues, "Tears Inside." After the statement of the tune's two-beat, countrified-bebop theme, trumpeter Don Cherry plays a solo that—for all its frail beauty and general adherence to modern jazz's harmonic conventions—sounds as if it might have been played by Miles Davis or Chet Baker. Coleman and Cherry were vanguardists, to be sure, and they were received as such by critics, musicians, and audiences alike. Even so, today, in listening to these early free jazz sides, one wonders what all the fuss was about, for it's clear that both musicians—especially Cherry—played in a style derived from the mainstream of jazz's development. Naturally, the passing of four decades provides us a perspective denied listeners at the time; changes that seem slight to us today were magnified then. Coleman and Cherry's elastic relationship to pitch and swing-time were certainly a liberation from the tyranny of equal temperament and literal pulse. Despite the music's revolutionary characteristics, however, no one would now deny that the work of these men is an extension or interpretation of the jazz tradition. This is particularly obvious in Cherry's case; abstracted from his contexts, Don Cherry's style was in a real sense grounded in bebop. Evaluating Cherry in classic terms is a mistake, for like Miles Davis—and Coleman, for that matter—concepts of Western musical objectivity were nearly irrelevant to his work. Cherry was not gifted with extraordinary chops, but those are classicist concerns, and his was a wholly romantic art. Cherry's greatest strength was less easily quantified, less tangible: an ability to convey emotional depth via a subtle manipulation of musical elements. Like Coleman, Cherry's sound came as close to the expressive qualities of the human voice as was instrumentally possible. And his playing was utterly spontaneous; Cherry was among the most unpredictable of improvisers. *—Chris Kelsey*

The Avant-Garde / Nov. 29, 1961 / Atlantic ✦✦✦✦✦
Misleading title, but substantial session that was really Cherry's, though John Coltrane (ts) plays with fire. *—Ron Wynn*

The Complete Blue Note Recordings of Don Cherry / Dec. 24, 1965-Nov. 11, 1966 / Mosaic ✦✦✦✦
This limited-edition two-CD set reissues trumpeter Don Cherry's three Blue Note albums: *Complete Communion, Symphony for Improvisers* and *Where Is Brooklyn*. The avant-garde cornetist is teamed with the tenors of Gato Barbieri and Pharoah Sanders on one album apiece and with both of them on the explosive *Symphony*. All of the music (much of which is performed as continuous medleys) is quite fiery and free and displays Cherry's musical direction during his post-Ornette Coleman and pre-world music phase. These sessions are not essential but they make for stimulating listening. *—Scott Yanow*

Complete Communion / Dec. 24, 1965 / Blue Note ✦✦✦
Trumpeter Don Cherry, best known for his association with altoist Ornette Coleman, matched his innovative—but relatively mellow—horn with ferocious tenors on his three Blue Note albums (all of which have since been reissued in a Mosaic box set). This LP, which finds Cherry, bassist Henry Grimes, and drummer Ed Blackwell joined by the passionate tenor of the young Gato Barbieri, consists of two four-song suites that were all composed by Cherry. The unexpected twists and turns of the music and Gato's high-register screams will excite some listeners and turn off others. This is chance-taking and intense music. *—Scott Yanow*

● **Symphony for Improvisers** / Sep. 19, 1966 / Blue Note ✦✦✦✦✦
Don Cherry's second of three Blue Note albums (all have been included in a Mosaic box set) is quite a heated affair. That fact is not too surprising when one considers that the lyrical cornetist is joined by the tenors of the young Gato Barbieri and Pharoah Sanders in addition to a four-piece rhythm section that includes two bassists. This stirring music (eight of Cherry's

originals) is performed continuously and has plenty of heated moments full of classic avant-garde fire. *—Scott Yanow*

Where is Brooklyn / Nov. 11, 1966 / Blue Note ♦♦♦
Don Cherry's third Blue Note album (each has been reissued in full on a Mosaic box set) features the cornetist in a quartet with bassist Henry Grimes, drummer Ed Blackwell and the fiery tenor of Pharoah Sanders. Although the instrumentation is not that much different than it had been with the Ornette Coleman Quartet, the presence of Sanders keeps the music quite passionate and stirring. This group plays the lengthy "Unite" and four shorter pieces, all composed by Cherry and full of the passion of the mid-'60s avant-garde fire. *—Scott Yanow*

Don Cherry / Apr. 22, 1971 / BYG ♦♦♦♦♦
Cherry is accessible and full of surprises. Percussive, slightly electric, and always potent. Easy to recommend. *—Michael G. Nastos*

Brown Rice / 1975 / A&M ♦♦♦
This CD (a reissue of Horizon 717) has always been a bit of a disappointment. Don Cherry's trumpet playing is only heard sparingly (he only plays piano on the title cut) and little memorable occurs. "Brown Rice" is closer to R&B than jazz and Cherry's verbal recitation on "Degi-Degi" is not something one needs to hear twice. He also "vocalizes" a bit on "Chenrezig," and, although bassist Charlie Haden is a strong asset and the leader's trumpet is fine on "Malakauns," this release can be safely passed by. *—Scott Yanow*

El Corazón / Feb. 1982 / ECM ♦♦♦♦
Trumpet and drum duets are not exactly commonplace, making this collaboration between Don Cherry and Ed Blackwell something special. The music is often quite sparse (Cherry also plays a little bit of piano, melodica and organ) and the colorful Blackwell often steals the show (although the trumpeter's unaccompanied "Voice of the Silence" is a highpoint). The use of space is consistently impressive and those listeners with open ears will find this thoughtful date quite interesting. *—Scott Yanow*

Art Deco / Aug. 27, 1988-Aug. 30, 1988 / A&M ♦♦♦♦
Although it is not mentioned anywhere on the outside of this CD, this session is very much a reunion. Trumpeter Don Cherry is reunited with bassist Charlie Haden and drummer Billy Higgins from the early Ornette Coleman Quartet and, most importantly, tenor saxophonist James Clay. Clay, who after playing with Cherry in Los Angeles in the 1950s and doing a few recordings moved back to Texas, had been in obscurity for decades. Fortunately, his playing is quite strong on what turns out to be a surprising bop-oriented session. Comprised of superior standards, a few group originals and three Ornette Coleman tunes (including the classic "The Blessing"), this set is quite accessible and finds all of the musicians in top form. *—Scott Yanow*

M.U. [Complete Session] / Sep. 17, 1996 / Affinity ♦♦♦

Charlie Christian

b. Jul. 29, 1916, Dallas, TX, **d.** Mar. 2, 1942, New York, NY
Guitar (Electric), Guitar / Swing, Bop
It can be said without exaggeration that virtually every jazz guitarist that emerged during 1940-65 sounded like a relative of Charlie Christian. The first important electric guitarist, Christian played his instrument with the fluidity, confidence and swing of a saxophonist. Although technically a swing stylist, his musical vocabulary was studied and emulated by the bop players and when one listens to players ranging from Tiny Grimes, Barney Kessel and Herb Ellis to Wes Montgomery and George Benson, the dominant influence of Christian is obvious. Christian's time in the spotlight was terribly brieff. He began to utilize an amplified guitar in 1937, after becoming a student of Eddie Durham, a jazz guitarist who invented the amplified guitar. Beginning in 1939 he was featured with Benny Goodman's Sextet, where had the opportunity to jam at Minton's Playhouse with such up-and-coming players as Thelonious Monk, Kenny Clarke and Dizzy Gillespie. Tragically he contracted tuberculosis in 1941 and died at the age of 25 on March 2, 1942. It would be 25 years before jazz guitarists finally moved beyond Charlie Christian. *—Scott Yanow*

Solo Flight (1939-1941) / Aug. 19, 1939-Jun. 1941 / Vintage Jazz Classics ♦♦♦♦♦
Charlie Christian, who died in 1942 at the age of 25, was the first important electric guitarist, and his solos would be the basis of jazz guitar for the next 25 years. This CD is filled with live performances (mostly from radio shows) of the Benny Goodman Sextet featuring Christian solos on every track. With such sidemen as vibraphonist Lionel Hampton and later tenor saxophonist Georgie Auld and trumpeter Cootie Williams, this unit was a perfect outlet for both Christian and Benny Goodman. And, in addition to a big band performance of "Solo Flight" (virtually a tour-de-force for the guitarist), there are five selections from a remarkable all-star group comprised of Goodman, Christian, trumpeter Buck Clayton, Lester Young on tenor, and Count Basie along with his rhythm section. This CD is highly recommended as an example of some of the very best in small-group swing and as a tribute to Charlie Christian's highly influential style. *—Scott Yanow*

★ **The Genius of the Electric Guitar** / Oct. 2, 1939-Mar. 13, 1941 / Columbia ♦♦♦♦♦
This set contains some of guitarist Charlie Christian's greatest recordings (although he did not live long enough to record any bad ones). Christian is heard with the Benny Goodman Sextet on famous versions of "Seven Come Eleven," "Benny's Bugle" and "Air Mail Special"; is showcased with Goodman's orchestra on "Solo Flight"; and jams with the members of the Sextet (minus their leader) on "Blues in B" and a fascinating ad-lib, "Waitin' for Benny." This important release belongs in every jazz collection and contains a great deal of essential music. *—Scott Yanow*

The Immortal Charlie Christian / 1939-1941 / Legacy ♦♦♦♦♦

Circle

f. 1970, **db.** 1971
Group / Free Jazz
During their short time together (1970-71), Circle was a virtual super-group of '70s free jazz, with the talents of Chick Corea on piano, Anthony Braxton on reeds and flute, Dave Holland on bass and cello, and Barry Altschul on drums. Circle came out of Corea and Holland's desire to do something less commercial than where they were heading with Miles Davis in the late '60s. Altschul had some previous avant-garde jazz experience from playing with Paul Bley, among others, and the three formed a trio which Anthony Braxton soon joined. Braxton had lately been making ends meet by playing chess in New York, and probably was drawn into the project not only by the quartet's rapport, but perhaps also by the possibility of relatively more commercial success on the kind of labels that would want Corea's new effort. And so the avant-garde jazz quartet Circle was born, resulting in six releases—some on ECM and Blue Note. Even though some of these recordings were taken from concert performances (including the best of the bunch, *Paris-Concert*), this is still quite an output for Circle's one year. They were an exciting, intense group whose sets included compositions by each of them, as well as some very fine group improvisations, long solo pieces, and the combinations in between. By '71, Corea had decided that he was more interested in the kind of thing that Miles was doing after all, and went on to form his own, more accessible, fusion group Return to Forever. The other three continued in the free vein, sometimes together, as on Holland's stellar *Conference of the Birds* with Sam Rivers, recorded a year after Circle called it quits, and in the Braxton Quartet for the next several years. *—Joslyn Layne*

Paris Concert / Feb. 21, 1971 / ECM ♦♦♦♦♦
Of all of the recordings from the short-lived avant-garde quartet Circle, this double-LP is the most rewarding. Cut live in Paris, this set features pianist Chick Corea, the reeds of Anthony Braxton, bassist Dave Holland, and drummer Barry Altschul playing a wide variety of fairly free explorations. Highlights include their reinterpretation of the standard "There Is No Greater Love," the playful "Toy Room—Q & A," Braxton's "73 Degrees Kelvin," and "Nefertiti." The music is often quite abstract but generally colorful and innovative; Chick Corea would soon break up the band for other musical adventures, but this set remains one of the high points of his productive career. *—Scott Yanow*

Sonny Clark (Conrad Yeatis Clark)

b. Jul. 21, 1931, Herminie, PA, **d.** Jan. 13, 1963, New York, NY
Piano / Hard Bop, Bop
Before drugs drastically shortened his life, Sonny Clark was one of the top Bud Powell-inspired bop pianists. He worked in San Francisco with Vido Musso and Oscar Pettiford in the early '50s, settled in Los Angeles, made his first recordings with Teddy Charles and then worked with Buddy DeFranco's quartet (1953-56); all of his records with DeFranco have been reissued by Mosaic on a deluxe limited-edition box set. During the same period he worked with Sonny Criss, Frank Rosolino and the Lighthouse All-Stars. Moving to New York in 1957, Clark became a fixture on Blue Note, recording several classics as a leader (*Dial S for Sonny, Cool Struttin'* and *Sonny's Crib* to name three from 1957 alone) and appearing as a sideman with Sonny Rollins, Hank Mobley and Curtis Fuller among many others. Sonny Clark's premature death (at age 31) was a major loss to jazz. *—Scott Yanow*

Dial "S" for Sonny / Nov. 10, 1957 / Blue Note ♦♦♦
Dial "S" for Sonny, Sonny Clark's first session for Blue Note Records and his first session as a leader, is a terrific set of laidback bop, highlighted by Clark's liquid, swinging solos. Clark leads a first-rate group—Art Farmer (trumpet), Curtis Fuller (trombone), Hank Mobley (tenor sax), Wilbur Ware (bass), Louis Hayes (drums)—through four originals and two standards, balancing the selections between swinging bop and reflective ballads. There are traces of Bud Powell in Clark's style, but he's beginning to come into his own, developing a style that's alternately edgy and charmingly relaxed. Mobley, Farmer and Fuller have their moments, but Clark steals the show in this set of fine, straight-ahead bop. *—Stephen Thomas Erlewine*

● **Sonny's Crib** / Oct. 9, 1957 / Blue Note ♦♦♦♦♦
One of the great Sonny Clark albums, this is the one that is best-known for featuring John Coltrane. Actually 'Trane's tenor is only one of six distinctive voices in a sextet also including trumpeter Donald Byrd, trombonist Curtis Fuller, the pianist-leader, bassist Paul Chambers and drummer Art Taylor. The CD reissue adds alternate takes to three of the five performances ("With a Song in My Heart," "Speak Low" and "Sonny's Crib"); every song but "Come Rain or Come Shine" and "News for Lulu." The now-legendary musicians are a joy to hear on this classic Blue Note set. *—Scott Yanow*

Sonny Clark Trio / Sep. 13, 1957 / Blue Note ♦♦♦♦
Pianist Sonny Clark sounds very much at home on this trio set with bassist Paul Chambers and drummer Philly Joe Jones. Sticking to bop standards, Sonny Clark essentially plays his version of Bud Powell, carving out his own approach to the influential style. The CD reissue adds three alternates to the six selections and includes such gems as "Two Bass Hit," "Be-Bop" and "Tadd's Delight." *—Scott Yanow*

Cool Struttin' / Jan. 5, 1958 / Blue Note ♦♦♦
Pianist Sonny Clark leads a quintet comprised of young hard bop all-stars on this 1958 session which has been reissued on CD. Trumpeter Art Farmer, altoist Jackie McLean, bassist Paul Chambers, drummer Philly Joe Jones and the leader stretch out on seven numbers (originals and standards) including three performances that were previously only out in Japan. Clark's title cut is a highpoint. *—Scott Yanow*

Leapin' and Lopin' / Nov. 13, 1961 / Blue Note ♦♦♦♦♦
Sonny Clark's final recording as a leader gives no hint as to his increasingly erratic lifestyle (he passed away in January 1963). Heading a quintet with trumpeter Tommy Turrentine, tenor saxophonist Charlie Rouse, bassist Butch Warren and drummer Billy Higgins, Clark introduces such originals as the modestly-titled "Somethin' Special," "Melody for C" and "Voodoo"; "Deep in a Dream" was the date's only standard. The CD reissue adds Clark's formerly unknown "Zellmar's Delight" and the alternate of "Melody for C" to the original six-song program. The music is high-quality hard bop and keeps Sonny Clark's record perfect. During his shortened life, every one of the albums that Clark led were excellent. *—Scott Yanow*

Kenny Clarke

b. Jan. 9, 1914, Pittsburgh, PA, **d.** Jan. 26, 1985, Paris, France
Drums / Bop
Kenny Clarke was a highly influential if subtle drummer who helped to define bebop drumming. He was the first to shift the time-keeping rhythm from the bass drum to the ride cymbal, an innovation that has been copied and utilized by a countless number of drummers since the early '40s. After stints with Roy Eldridge (1935) and the Jeter-Pillars band, Clarke joined Edgar Hayes' Big Band (1937-38). He made his recording debut with Hayes and showed that he was one of the most swinging drummers of the era. Stints with the orchestras of Claude Hopkins (1939) and Teddy Hill (1940-41) followed and then Clarke led the house band at Minton's Playhouse (which also included Thelonious Monk). The legendary after-hours sessions led to the formation of bop and it was during this time that Clarke modernized his style. A flexible drummer, he was still able to uplift the more traditional orchestras of Louis Armstrong and Ella Fitzgerald (1941) and the combos of Benny Carter (1941-42), Red Allen and Coleman Hawkins; he also recorded with Sidney Bechet. However after spending time in the military, Clarke stayed in the bop field, working with Dizzy Gillespie's big band and leading his own modern sessions; an original member of the Modern Jazz Quartet (1951-55), from 1956 onward Clarke worked in France and was a major figure on the European jazz scene. *—Scott Yanow*

Bohemia After Dark / Jun. 26, 1955-Jul. 26, 1955 / Savoy ♦♦♦♦
The June 26, 1955 session is most notable for being the recorded debut of the recently discovered altoist Cannonball Adderley and his brother, cornetist Nat (who is also featured on the lone number from July 26, a quartet version of "We'll Be Together Again"). Although drummer Kenny Clarke is the nominal leader and the other sidemen include trumpeter Donald Byrd, Jerome Richardson on tenor and flute, pianist Horace Silver and bassist Paul Chambers, the impressive performance by the young Adderleys makes this a historic session that has often been reissued under Cannonball's name. *—Scott Yanow*

Kenny Clarke Meets the Detroit Jazzmen / Apr. 30, 1956–May 9, 1956 / Savoy ♦♦♦
Drummer Kenny Clarke, who was the first to record with Cannonball Adderley, was an underrated talent scout. On this album, Clarke utilizes bassist Paul Chambers and three relative unknowns who had recently arrived in New York from Detroit: baritonist Pepper Adams, pianist Tommy Flanagan and guitarist Kenny Burrell. During what would be the drummer's last date as a leader before permanently moving to Europe, the quintet performs one original apiece by each of the Detroiters plus four jazz standards. This high-quality hard bop set in 1956 showed that the latest NY imports were already major leaguers. *—Scott Yanow*

Clarke-Boland Big Band: Handle With Care / 1962 / Koch International ♦♦♦♦
Kenny Clarke's 11-year collaboration with Francy Boland produced many fine records, but most of them have not reappeared as CDs. Happily, this 1962 session is once again available, showcasing the Clark-Boland Big Band's mix of top-notch European and expatriated American musicians. Boland wrote all of the arrangements and four of the six songs, with his "Long Note Blues (Here Is Cecco Peppe)" opening the album with a flourish. Cole Porter's "Get out of Town" has a Thelonious Monk-like introduction and recurring motif, alternating with the muted brass. Clarke's "Sonor" is another burning blues, featuring tenor saxophonist Ronnie Scott and Billy Mitchell along with trumpeters Benny Bailey and Idrees Suileman. Although pretty brief by CD standards at just 34 minutes 26 seconds, there's absolutely no filler in this highly recommended CD. *—Ken Dryden*

• **Clarke-Boland Big Band** / Oct. 29, 1969 / RTE ♦♦♦♦♦
One of the great jazz orchestras of the 1960s and '70s and one rarely heard (either live or on record) in the United States was the Kenny Clarke-Francy Boland Big Band. This overseas group (which was equally filled with Americans and Europeans) was a hard-swinging modern mainstream ensemble, analogous in ways to Rob McConnell's Boss Brass of the 1980s and '90s. Its double CD (which was put out in 1992 but not made available in the U.S. until 1995) has a particularly exciting live concert performance by the big band. Overflowing with soloists (including trumpeters Benny Bailey, Art Farmer, and Idrees Sulieman, trombonist Ake Persson, and a sax section comprised of Derek Humble, Johnny Griffin, Sahib Shihab, Tony Coe, and Ronnie Scott), the band is quite powerful throughout the set with Griffin generally taking solo honors. Easily recommended. *—Scott Yanow*

Pieces of Time / Sep. 16, 1983-Sep. 17, 1983 / Soul Note ♦♦♦
Standout session late in his career, with fellow drummers Andrew Cyrille, Milford Graves, and Don Moye. *—Ron Wynn*

Stanley Clarke

b. Jun. 30, 1951, Philadelphia, PA
Bass / Contemporary Jazz, Post-Bop, Fusion, Jazz-Funk
A brilliant player on both acoustic and electric basses, Stanley Clarke has spent much of his career outside of jazz although he has the ability to play jazz with the very best. He played accordion as a youth, switching to violin and cello before settling on bass. He worked with R&B and rock bands in high school but after moving to New York he worked with Pharoah Sanders in the early '70s. Other early gigs were with Gil Evans, Mel Lewis, Horace Silver, Stan Getz, Dexter Gordon and Art Blakey; everyone was impressed by his talents. However Clarke really hit the big time when he started teaming up with Chick Corea in Return to Forever. When the group became a rock-oriented fusion quartet, Clarke mostly emphasized electric bass and became an influential force, preceding Jaco Pastorius. But starting with his *School Days* album (1976) and continuing through his funk group with George Duke (the Clarke/Duke Project) up to his current projects writing movie scores, Stanley Clarke has largely moved beyond the jazz world into commercial music; his 1988 Portrait album *If This Bass Could Only Talk* and his 1995 collaboration with Jean Luc Ponty and Al DiMeola on the acoustic *The Rite of Strings* are two of his few jazz recordings of the past decade. *—Scott Yanow*

Stanley Clarke / 1974 / Epic ♦♦♦♦
Definitive early-period funk/fusion. Clarke's finger-pop bass is up front. *—Michael G. Nastos*

Journey to Love / 1975 / Epic ♦♦♦
Prolific bassist Stanley Clarke's second jazz-rock album in the early '70s marked the beginning of what proved to be an extremely profitable collaboration with keyboardist George Duke. The album includes guest appearances from Chick Corea, John McLaughlin, Lenny White, and rocker Jeff Beck. *—Ron Wynn*

Live (1976-1977) / Jun. 1976-Sep. 1977 / Epic ♦♦♦♦
After giving Clarke's fans a taste of some live tapes of the School Days band on *I Wanna Play for You*, Epic waited until 1991 to put another batch of them out, well after it would have been commercially feasible to do so. But no matter, for this CD captures one of Clarke's best electric bands—maybe his best band, period—in a number of gigs in the U.S. and U.K., mixing up the jazz, funk and rock into a high-energy, musically literate brew. A lot of this album recycles then-existing material, but the live conditions add flashes of spontaneity and sometimes considerable interest to jazz fans. Along with the core of Raymond Gomez (guitar), Peter Robinson or David Sancious (keyboards) and Gerry Brown (drums), Clarke used a four-piece horn section to which he gives sophisticated voicings, several solos, and on "The Magician," quasi-baroque turns. There is a thinly stretched (at times) acoustic cat-and-mouse dialogue between Clarke and Sancious on "Bass Folk Song No. 3," plus, in a departure from the format, an Indian-flavored studio outtake of "Desert Song" (with John McLaughlin) from the *School Days* sessions. *—Richard S. Ginell*

• **School Days** / Jun. 1976 / Epic ♦♦♦♦♦
Every pro electric bass player and his mother wore out the grooves of this record when it first came out, trying to cop Clarke's speedy, thundering, slapped-thumb bass licks. Yet ultimately, it was Clarke's rapidly developing compositional skills that made this album so listenable and so much fun for the rest of us, then and now. The title track not only contributed a killer riff to the bass vocabulary, it is a cunningly organized piece of music with a well-defined structure. Moreover, Clarke follows his calling card with two tunes that are even more memorable—the sauntering ballad "Quiet Afternoon" and an ebullient, Brazilian percussion-laced number with a good string arrangement and a terrific groove, "The Dancer." Clarke also brings out the standup bass for a soulful acoustic dialogue with John McLaughlin on "Desert Song." Evidently enthused by their leader's material, David Sancious (keyboards) and Raymond Gomez (guitars) deliver some of their best solos on records—and with George Duke on hand on one cut, we hear some preliminary flickerings of Clarke's ventures into the commercial sphere. But at this point in time, Clarke was triumphantly proving that it was possible to be both good and commercial at the same time. *—Richard S. Ginell*

I Wanna Play for You / Sep. 1977-1979 / Epic ♦♦♦♦
Clarke stretches his muscles and comes up with a mostly impressive, polystylistic, star-studded double album (now on one CD) that gravitates ever closer to the R&B mainstream. Clarke's writing remains strong and his tastes remain unpredictable, veering into rock, electronic music, acoustic jazz, even reggae in tandem with British rocker Jeff Beck. Clarke's excursion into disco, "Just a Feeling," ais surprisingly and infectiously successful, thanks to a good bridge and George Duke's galvanizingly funky work on the Yamaha electric grand piano (his finest moment with Clarke by far). The brief "Blues for Mingus," a wry salute from one master bassist to another (Mingus died about six months before this album's release), is a cool acoustic breather for piano trio, and the eloquent Stan Getz can be detected, though nearly buried under the garish vocals and rock-style mix, on "The Streets of Philadelphia." Yet even the talented Clarke in full creative flower couldn't quite fill a double set with new material, so he has a tendency to reprise some of his old memorable riffs a lot, and there are several energetic snapshots of his live band in action. In its zeal to get this two-LP set onto one disc, Epic deleted three of the original 15 tracks—including at least one gem, the sizzling hard rocker "All About"—and scrambled the order of the remaining tunes. Which is dumb, because the missing tracks only take up a bit less than 12 minutes of playing time, not enough to overload a 65-minute disc. Hunt for the double-LP version if you can still play vinyl. *—Richard S. Ginell*

If This Bass Could Only Talk / 1988 / Portrait ♦♦♦♦
This was bassist Stanley Clarke's twelfth solo set, and one of his very few that would be recommended to jazz (as opposed to funk and R&B) listeners. On the instrumental set, Clarke's bass is featured in a wide variety of settings, including duets with tap dancer Gregory Hines and drummer John Robinson, a quartet with Wayne Shorter ("Goodbye Pork Pie Hat"), in a power trio with guitarist Allan Holdsworth and drummer Stewart Copeland, a piece with George Duke (on acoustic piano for a change) and soprano saxophonist George Howard, a quartet with the synthesizers of Steve Hunt, and "Funny How Time Flies," which has a colorful Freddie Hubbard trumpet solo. Throughout, Clarke's bass has plenty of solo space, and he shows how strong a player he can be when given decent material. *—Scott Yanow*

Live at the Greek / 1993 / Epic ♦♦♦♦♦

Rite of Strings / Apr. 1995 / Gai Saber ♦♦♦♦

Buck Clayton (Wilbur Dorsey Clayton)

b. Nov. 12, 1911, Parsons, KS, **d.** Dec. 8, 1991, New York, NY
Trumpet, Arranger / Mainstream Jazz, Swing
An excellent bandleader and accompanist for many vocalists including Billie Holiday, Buck Clayton was a valued soloist with the Count Basie orchestra during the '30s and '40s, and later was a celebrated studio and jam session player, writer and arranger. His tart, striking tone and melodic dexterity were his trademark, and Clayton provided several charts for Basie's orchestra and many other groups. During a 1936 visit to Kansas City, he was invited to join Basie's orchestra and remained in the band until 1943, also featuring on sessions with Lester Young, Teddy Wilson and Holiday. Clayton also did arrangements for Benny Goodman and Harry James before forming a small combo in the late '40s that lasted in some form throughout the '50s. He also organized a series of outstanding recordings for Columbia in the mid-'50s under the title *Jam Session*. Clayton joined Eddie Condon's band in 1959, toured

Japan and Australia with the group, and continued to revisit Europe throughout the '60s. After health problems virtually ended his playing career in the late '60s, Clayton returned as a nonplaying arranger, providing arrangements and compositions for a 1974 Lyttleton and Buddy Tate album. He led a group of Basie sidemen on a European tour in 1983, then headed his own big band in 1987 that played almost exclusively his compositions and arrangements. *—Ron Wynn*

The Classic Swing of Buck Clayton / Jun. 26, 1946-Jul. 24, 1946 / Riverside/OJC ✦✦✦
This limited-edition CD features small-group swing originally issued on the H.R.S. label from three different sessions in 1946. On one date, the great trumpeter Buck Clayton heads an octet with both Trummy Young and Dicky Wells on trombones; on another occasion he leads an unusual pianoless quartet that also includes clarinetist Scoville Brown, guitarist Tiny Grimes and bassist Sid Weiss. In addition, Clayton is heard as a sideman with Trummy Young's septet, which also features clarinetist Buster Bailey. Swing was going very much out of style at the time, and these somewhat obscure dates can be considered among the final small-group swing sessions of the classic era. More importantly, all of the principals sound creative and full of spirit. *—Scott Yanow*

Dr. Jazz Series, Vol. 3 / Dec. 13, 1951-Jan. 24, 1952 / Storyville ✦✦✦✦
Storyville has released a series of CDs taken from the legendary *Dr. Jazz* radio series of 1951-52, a program which each week featured some of the top Dixieland bands then currently playing in New York clubs. Trumpeter Buck Clayton was a swing rather than a Dixieland player but during this era he decided to increase his versatility (and potential for getting jobs) by learning the basic Dixieland repertoire. He fares pretty well in a sextet that also has plenty of solo space for trombonist Herb Flemming, clarinetist Buster Bailey and pianist Kenny Kersey. Highlights of these fairly well-recorded jams include "There'll Be Some Changes Made," "Struttin' with Some Barbecue," "'Deed I Do" and "Crazy Rhythm." *—Scott Yanow*

☆ **Complete CBS Buck Clayton Jam Sessions** / Dec. 14, 1953-Mar. 5, 1956 / Mosaic ✦✦✦✦✦
Trumpeter Buck Clayton led a series of exciting studio jam sessions during the mid-'50s. All of the performances are on this superlative three-CD box set including a few "new" alternate takes and several that have been restored to their full length. Among the many soloists (most of them swing-oriented stylists) are Clayton, Joe Newman, $Joe Thomas, Billy Butterfield, and Ruby Braff on trumpets; trombonists Urbie Green, Benny Powell, Henderson Chambers, Trummy Young, Bennie Green, Dicky Harris, J.C. Higginbotham, and Tyree Glenn; altoist Lem Davis; tenors Coleman Hawkins, Al Cohn, and Buddy Tate; Julian Dash doubling on tenor and alto; baritonist Charlie Fowlkes; several rhythm sections with pianists Sir Charles Thompson, Jimmy Jones, Billy Kyle, Ken Kersey, and the forgotten Al Waslohn; and a guest appearance by Woody Herman on clarinet. These generally lengthy performances contain plenty of spontaneous riffing behind soloists and lots of special moments; "How Ili the Fi" is quite memorable. *—Scott Yanow*

Buck Clayton Jam Session / Mar. 25, 1974 / Chiaroscuro ✦✦✦

Goin' to Kansas City / Oct. 5, 1960-Oct. 6, 1960 / Riverside/OJC ✦✦✦✦
Although trumpeter Buck Clayton gets top billing, this CD reissue actually features Tommy Gwaltney's *Kansas City Nine*, an unusual group sporting arrangements by Gwaltney and tenor-saxophonist Tommy Newsom (who decades later became famous for his work on *The Tonight Show*). The group has an unusual combination of major names (Clayton, trombonist Dickie Wells, guitarist Charlie Byrd, pianist John Bunch, bassist Whitey Mitchell and drummer Buddy Schutz) along with Gwaltney (who doubles on reeds and vibes), Newsom and Bobby Zottola (playing second trumpet and peck horn). Although the nonet performs a variety of songs associated with Kansas City Jazz of the swing era, the arrangements are modern and unpredictable. *—Scott Yanow*

Buck and Buddy / Dec. 20, 1960 / Swingville/OJC ✦✦✦
Count Basie veterans Buck Clayton and tenorman Buddy Tate teamed up during 1960-61 for a pair of Swingville recordings. This CD reissues the first one, a quintet outing with pianist Sir Charles Thompson, bassist Gene Ramey and drummer Mousie Alexander. The repertoire is split between three standards (including "When a Woman Loves a Man") and three Clayton originals. The melodic music consistently swings and practically defines "mainstream" jazz. Worth picking up. *—Scott Yanow*

Buck Clayton All-Stars, 1961 / Apr. 1961 / Storyville ✦✦✦

Swiss Radio Days Jazz Series, Vol. 7: Basel 1961 / May 2, 1961 / TCB ✦✦✦✦
In 1961, trumpeter Buck Clayton toured Europe with an octet filled with swing-era veterans, many formerly with the Count Basie Orchestra: trumpeter Emmett Berry, trombonist Dickie Wells, altoist Earle Warren, tenor saxophonist Buddy Tate, pianist Sir Charles Thompson, bassist Gene Ramey and drummer Oliver Jackson. This 1997 CD features the all-star band at a typical concert that was broadcast over the radio in Switzerland. Although mainstream swing was way out of style by 1961 (a period when the John Coltrane Quartet was becoming very influential, not to mention hard bop and soul-jazz), many of the swing-era stars were still in their musical prime; Clayton was still only 49. On the well-recorded set, the group jams through such numbers as Buck's catchy "Swinging at the Coppers' Rail," "Robbins' Nest," "Swingin' the Blues" and "St. Louis Blues" with spirit and consistently inventive ideas. Although Wells was a little past his peak, his statements are full of color and wit, and it is a pleasure to hear the contrasting trumpets of Clayton and Berry soloing on the same songs. *—Scott Yanow*

★ **Buck Clayton All-Stars** / Shanachie ✦✦✦✦✦
Two half-hour Swiss television shows from 1961 feature trumpeter Buck Clayton with such swing all-stars as fellow trumpeter Emmett Berry, altoist Earle Warren, tenorman Buddy Tate, trombonist Dickie Wells, pianist Sir Charles Thompson, bassist Gene Ramey, drummer Oliver Jackson and singer Jimmy Witherspoon. There are 11 complete songs in all, and each of the musicians has plenty of space to stretch out during the series of informal but hard-swinging performances. *—Scott Yanow*

Arnett Cobb

b. Aug. 10, 1918, Houston, TX, **d.** Mar. 24, 1989, Houston, TX
Sax (Tenor) / New York Blues, Jump Blues, Soul-Jazz, Swing
A stomping Texas tenor player in the tradition of Illinois Jacquet, Arnett Cobb's accessible playing was between swing and early rhythm & blues. After playing in Texas with Chester Boone (1934-36) and Milt Larkin (1936-42), Cobb emerged in the big leagues by succeeding Illinois Jacquet with Lionel Hampton's Orchestra (1942-47). His version of "Flying Home No. 2" became a hit and he was a very popular soloist with Hampton. After leaving the band, Cobb formed his own group but his initial success was interrupted in 1948 when he had to undergo an operation on his spine. After recovering he resumed touring. But a major car accident in 1956 crushed Cobb's legs and he was reduced to using crutches for the rest of his life. However by 1959 he returned to active playing and recording. Cobb spent most of the 1960s leading bands back in Texas but starting in 1973 he toured and recorded more extensively including a tenor summit with Jimmy Heath and Joe Henderson in Europe as late as 1988. Arnett Cobb made many fine records through the years for such labels as Apollo, Columbia/Okeh, Prestige (many of the latter are available on the OJC series), Black & Blue, Progressive, Muse and Bee Hive. *—Scott Yanow*

● **Blows for 1300** / May 1947-Aug. 1947 / Delmark ✦✦✦✦✦
This Delmark CD reissues all 15 of Arnett Cobb's recordings for Apollo. The spirited tenor (who straddled the boundaries between swing and early R&B) is in prime early form with his sextet on a variety of basic material, much of it blues-oriented. Milt Larkin takes vocals on three of the tracks and there are short solos by either Booty Wood or Al King on trombone, but otherwise the main focus is on Cobb's tough tenor. This very accessible music is both danceable and full of exciting performances that were formerly rare. *—Scott Yanow*

Blow, Arnett, Blow / Jan. 9, 1959 / Prestige/OJC ✦✦✦✦
Arnett Cobb's debut for Prestige and his first recording as a leader in three years (due to a serious car accident in 1956) is an explosive affair. Cobb is matched up with fellow tough tenor Eddie "Lockjaw" Davis and there are plenty of sparks set off by their encounter. With organist Wild Bill Davis, bassist George Duvivier and drummer Arthur Edgehill keeping the proceedings heated, Cobb and Davis tangle on a variety of basic material, alternating uptempo romps such as "Go Power" and "Go Red Go" with slightly more sober pieces highlighted by "When I Grow Too Old Tto Dream." This is a great matchup (reissued on CD in the OJC series) that lives up to its potential. *—Scott Yanow*

Smooth Sailing / Feb. 27, 1959 / Prestige/OJC ✦✦✦
This CD reissue brings back a typically swinging date by tenor saxophonist Arnett Cobb. The colorful trombonist Buster Cooper (who was not featured in enough small group sessions through the years) seems to inspire Cobb; the rhythm section (organist Austin Mitchell, bassist George Duvivier and drummer Osie Johnson) is also a strong asset for this music. Four standards (three from the swing era plus Cobb's "Smooth Sailing") alternate with a blues and a couple of uptempo riff numbers. Arnett Cobb's solos are typically emotional and generally exciting during the fine set. *—Scott Yanow*

Party Time / May 14, 1959 / Prestige/OJC ✦✦✦✦
Tenor saxophonist Arnett Cobb, who was inactive between 1957 and 1958 due to a serious auto accident, recorded three strong albums for Prestige during the first half of 1959. This CD reissue is the only one of the trio that features Cobb as the only horn and backed by a pianist (Ray Bryant) instead of an organ player. With bassist Wendell Marshall, drummer Art Taylor and Ray Barretto on conga completing the group, most of the focus is on Cobb's tough yet flexible tenor. Such songs as "When My Dreamboat Comes Home," "Blues in the Closet" and a remake of "Flying Home" make this the definitive Arnett Cobb album from the era. Highly recommended. *—Scott Yanow*

More Party Time / Feb. 16, 1960–Feb. 17, 1960 / Prestige/OJC ✦✦✦✦✦
During 1959-60, the tough-toned but sentimental tenor saxophonist Arnett Cobb recorded six albums for Prestige; his next recording as a leader would not be until 1971. On this particular CD reissue, Cobb performs quintet selections with pianist Tommy Flanagan, bassist Sam Jones, drummer Art Taylor and Danny Barrajanos on conga; on "Down by the Riverside" (from Feb. 17) pianist Bobby Timmons and Buck Clarke on congas join Jones, Taylor and Cobb. The tenor's treatments of "Blue Me" and five veteran songs ("Lover Come Back to Me," "Blue Lou," "Swanee River," "Down by the Riverside" and "Sometimes I'm Happy") are melodic, soulful and swinging. An excellent if (at 36 minutes) brief effort. *—Scott Yanow*

Tenor Tribute, Vol. 1 / Apr. 30, 1988 / Soul Note ✦✦✦✦
This blowing session (comprised of Charlie Parker's "Steeple Chase," Arnett Cobb's "Smooth Sailing," "Lester Leaps In," a four-song ballad medley and "I Got Rhythm") is of greatest interest for featuring the contrasting styles of tenors Arnett Cobb, Joe Henderson and Jimmy Heath; the latter also plays a bit of soprano and flute. This being one of Cobb's final recordings (he died less than a year later), he holds his own against the younger tenors during this German concert, taking "Smooth Sailing" as his feature. One should have little trouble telling the three tenor masters apart. *—Scott Yanow*

Billy Cobham (William C. Cobham)

b. May 16, 1946, Panama
Drums / Post-Bop, Fusion
Considered the definitive fusion drummer in the 1970s, Billy Cobham's fame has subsided a bit since then but he remains a very capable player who is more flexible than one might think. His family moved to New York from Panama when he was three. After spending time performing with a military band in the Army, Cobham spent eight months with Horace Silver (1968). He then became a busy session musician, played with the jazz-rock band Dreams (1969-70), appeared on some very important Miles Davis records (*Bitches Brew, Live-Evil* and *Jack Johnson*) and joined John McLaughlin in the Mahavishnu Orchestra (1971-73) where he became an influential force. Cobham led his own band (Spectrum) from 1973 on, making a strong initial impact but by the late '70s he was mostly freelancing. Since that time

he has led electric bands on an occasional basis, been involved in teaching and remains a busy studio player. *—Scott Yanow*

● **Spectrum** / May 14, 1973-May 16, 1973 / Atlantic ✦✦✦✦
Drummer Billy Cobham was fresh from his success with the Mahavishnu Orchestra when he recorded his debut album, which is still his best. Most of the selections showcase Cobham in a quartet with keyboardist Jan Hammer, guitarist Tommy Bolin and electric bassist Lee Sklar. Two other numbers include Joe Farrell on flute and soprano and trumpeter Jimmy Owens with guitarist John Tropea, Hammer, bassist Ron Carter and Ray Barretto on congas. The generally high-quality compositions (which include "Red Baron") make this fusion set a standout, a strong mixture of rockish rhythms and jazz improvising. *—Scott Yanow*

Crosswinds / 1974 / Wounded Bird ✦✦✦
Billy Cobham's second date as a leader was one of his better sessions, although, as with most of his Atlantic recordings, it has gone out of print. Four songs (all originals by the leader/drummer) comprise "Spanish Moss—A Sound Portrait," and, in addition, Cobham contributed three other pieces. The selections team him with guitarist John Abercrombie, both of the Brecker Brothers, trombonist Garnett Brown, keyboardist George Duke, bassist John Williams, and Latin percussionist Lee Pastora. In general, the melodies and the vamps are reasonably memorable. Cobham also takes an unaccompanied drum solo on "Storm." Worth searching for by fusion collectors. *—Scott Yanow*

Inner Conflicts / 1977 / Wounded Bird ✦✦✦✦
A solid effort that has been dismissed based upon its associations with two Cobham lemons, *Simplicity of Expression/Depth of Thought* and *B.C.*, all recorded around the same time. This recording finds Cobham continuing to explore the funk genre; however, the overall mood here is quite darker and more introspective, similar to *Crosswinds*. "Inner Conflicts" is a haunting song that includes Cobham's experimentation with electronic percussion and synthesizer. "Nickles and Dimes" is a page out of Cobham's early work, while "El Barrio" is heavily influenced by African rhythms. Of note, Prince's former sidekick Sheila E performs here with her father Pete. The closer, "Arroyo," is another of Cobham's memorable compositions that he continues to perform. *—Robert Taylor*

Billy Cobham Live: Flight Time / Jun. 1980 / Peter Pan ✦✦✦✦✦
A lesser known Cobham recording that has only been available in the U.S. as an import. Cobham also seems to push guitarists to new heights (i.e. Tommy Bolin, John Abercrombie, John Scofield) and does so here with Barry Finnerty. Their interaction on the tune "Flight Time" is reminiscent of Cobham/Bolin on *Spectrum*. Yet, despite the intensity and chops of Finnerty and Cobham, this session is remarkably restrained thanks in large part to the thoughtful playing of keyboarist Don Grolnick. There is a definite sense of a band here, rather than just a collection of all-stars playing Billy Cobham songs; in fact, the only Cobham retread is "Antares" (from *Magic*). Whether it is Don Grolnick's piano solo on "6 Persimmons" or his opening duet with Barry Finnerty on "Princess," Cobham should get just as much credit for what he did not play. It is a shame that this unit did not become Cobham's regular band as this is one of his most cohesive efforts. *—Robert Taylor*

The Best of Billy Cobham / 1988 / Atlantic ✦✦✦✦
Drummer Billy Cobham became a star during his tenure with the Mahavishnu Orchestra. His output during the 70's was inconsistent, but he did record two fusion classics, *Spectrum* and *Crosswinds*, which are both well represented here. There are also good selections from *Total Eclipse, A Funky Thide Of Sings* and *Live' On Tour In Europe*. Recommended for the casual listener, but fans seeking a deeper understanding of this drumming genius are encouraged to explore Cobham's expansive discography. *—Robert Taylor*

The Traveler / Nov. 1993 / Cleopatra ✦✦✦✦
The overall feel of this recording is very similar to *Incoming*. Peter Wolpl remains on guitar, as does Nippy Noya on percussion. The pianist has been changed to Joe Chindamo; however, his style is similar to Rita Marcotulli's on *Incoming*. The music is very dense and cannot be listened to casually or infrequently if one wants to absorb the full impact of the recording. The underrated Wolpl provides an excellent acoustic guitar solo on "Alfa Waves." There are three vocal tracks here, which means a meager attempt at pop on a majority of contemporary jazz recordings. Fortunately, this is not the case here. Carole Rowley does a fine job of "jazz" singing and seems to be a cohesive part of the band, rather than a novelty. Cobham's mastery of rhythm (not technique) is evident on "Balancing Act." This is an aspect of his playing that is often overlooked due to his overwhelming power behind the traps. For fans just interested in that aspect of his playing, "On the Inside Track" features a mini-drum battle with drummer extraordinaire Gary Husband. As a whole, *The Traveler* is a very good recording and clearly shows Cobham's constant striving to grow as both a composer and musician. *—Robert Taylor*

Billy Cobham/George Duke Live / Oct. 25, 1998 / Atlantic ✦✦✦
Following two studio recordings, this impressive band hit the road and cut this session with keyboardist George Duke. Their encounter provided for an uneven, but infectious, recording. "Hip Pockets," composed by Cobham, and "Ivory Tatoo," composed by Scofield, begin the session with some intense playing. Things get a bit goofy with "Space Lady" (a song which probably worked better live), and a bit melodramatic with "Almustafa the Beloved." "Do What Cha Wanna" features Duke on vocals and, ironically, made it onto Cobham's *Best of Billy Cobham*. The closer, "Frankentein Goes to the Disco," is primarily a vehicle for Cobham, while "Sweet Wine" and "Juicy" are good jam sessions. Despite some corny moments, this is a fun session that continues to be one of Cobham's most sought after recordings, leading to its release on CD. *—Robert Taylor*

Holly Cole

b. 1963, Halifax, Nova Scotia, Canada
Vocals / Traditional Pop, Standards, Cabaret
Holly Cole's music is difficult to classify. She takes familiar standards and casts them in a new ironic light that is sometimes sinister and occasionally humorous. She also performs sets of diverse music that have more variety than one would think could possibly be successful; somehow it works. Both of her parents are classical musicians and she studied classical piano for a time. But after discovering Sarah Vaughan when she was 15, she switched to jazz. Cole sang with a big band in Toronto and in 1985 she formed a permanent trio with pianist Aaron Davis and bassist David Piltch. Their first album *Girl Talk* (released only in Canada) was a success and led to three records (thus far) for Manhattan: *Blame It on My Youth, Don't Smoke in Bed* and a nonjazz set of Tom Waits' music. *—Scott Yanow*

● **Don't Smoke in Bed** / Feb. 1993-Mar. 1993 / Manhattan ✦✦✦✦
Holly Cole explores a number of styles on her second album, *Don't Smoke in Bed*, without overreaching her grasp. Adding pop, blues, country, and a French ballad to her standard, low-key jazz, Cole demonstrates that not only does she have impeccable taste, but she has the talent to make all of the material sound convincing. *—Stephen Thomas Erlewine*

Girl Talk / 1994 / Alert Canada ✦✦✦✦✦
Girl Talk was recorded live to two-track using a single microphone. The liner notes state that Holly Cole's intention in doing so was to preserve the "quintessence of her live performances," and the result is dazzlingly successful. The air of intimacy between artist and listener is so great that, if anything, the feeling of being present in the moment is greater here than on the 1996 live album *It Happened One Night*. On an album recorded "live in concert," the ambient noises that occur when a large number of people are gathered in one place can seem discordant or inappropriate when you're listening to the CD in your car or your living room; the atmosphere can exclude rather than include you. Put on this disk, however, and you can imagine that Holly Cole is singing for you alone. It's easy to focus on Cole's emotionally compelling delivery, and at first you can be so mesmerized that you forget that the vocalist is one part of a trio. Listen more carefully, and it becomes apparent that the piano and bass accompaniments are deceptively simple—that they are, in fact, providing a counterpoint to the sung lyrics that is almost conversational. Suddenly, these simple arrangements feel quite complex. The most entertaining song on the album may well be Cole's interpretation of the traditionally sunny and euphoric "Downtown." In her expert hands it moves from near cynicism to a guarded openness that makes this standard seem to have a range of meaning you may never have considered. *—Maya Geryk*

It Happened One Night / Jun. 28, 1995 / Metro Blue ✦✦✦✦
It Happened One Night is a nice overview of Holly Cole and her band doing their night club act live. Containing such Cole standards as "Cry (If You Want To)" and "Que Sera Sera," this disc has all the charm of a late night club date without the smoky atmosphere or the drunks to detract you from the pleasures of listening. Recorded on a one-night stand in Montreal, Cole and her band work their charms well indeed. *—James Chrispell*

The Best of Holly Cole / Jun. 1991-1997 / Blue Note ✦✦✦
As leader of the Holly Cole Trio, the smoky-voiced jazz chanteuse has created an impressive catalog over the last decade with her longtime cohorts Aaron Davis (piano) and David Piltch (string bass), seamlessly mixing blues, pop, and jazz. This collection gathers tunes which allow the sultry singer to stand out above sparse yet often playful arrangements. The first three tracks epitomize the diversity of her approach. On "Trust in Me," she plays it subtle and sly, asking her lover to "trust in me," sometimes singing a few bars a capella. She shows her wares as a torch singer on "Calling You," while a spry arrangement of Lyle Lovett's "God Will" offers a glimpse of her blues persona. Part of Cole's charm comes from the way she interacts with her mates; the first verse of "I Can See Clearly Now" is sung richly over Piltch's plucky solo bass before Davis' piano and a gentle string section glide in. Many people were puzzled that a singer who excels at jazz standards would tackle the Tom Waits catalog, but some of the best tracks from the Waits tribute *Temptation* show up here as well. "Jersey Girl" is particularly impressive, with Cole's low voice rising above a chorus of "sha-la"s and Davis and Piltch's simple percussive magic. *—Jonathan Widran*

Nat King Cole (Nathaniel Adams Cole)

b. Mar. 17, 1917, Montgomery, AL, **d.** Feb. 15, 1965, Santa Monica, CA
Vocals, Piano / Vocal Jazz, Traditional Pop, Jump Blues, Swing
Nat King Cole had two overlapping careers. He was one of the truly great swing pianists, inspired by Earl Hines and a big influence on Oscar Peterson. And he was a superb pop ballad singer whose great commercial success in that field unfortunately resulted in him greatly de-emphasizing his piano after 1949. He left his native Chicago in 1936 to lead the band for the revival of the revue *Shuffle Along*, and settled in Los Angeles when the show ended. After putting together a trio with guitarist Oscar Moore and bassist Wesley Prince, the group eventually settled in for a long residency in Hollywood. The group first recorded for Decca in 1940, and Nat King Cole soon gained confidence in his own singing. Nat Cole recorded a great deal of exciting jazz during the 1940s including dates featuring Lester Young and Illinois Jacquet plus the first Jazz at the Philharmonic concert (1944). After "Mona Lisa" became a number one hit in 1950, suddenly Nat King Cole became famous to the nonjazz public as a singer, and he mostly recorded pop ballads during the 1950s and '60s. The popularity of his records and public appearances remained at a remarkable level until his death from lung cancer in 1965. *—Scott Yanow*

★ **Hit That Jive Jack: The Earliest Recordings** / Dec. 6, 1940-Oct. 22, 1941 / Decca ✦✦✦✦✦
Nat King Cole's 16 trio recordings for Decca have been reissued many times (including on this CD) and rightfully so. Cole was already one of the top swing pianists by 1940, his vocal style (best displayed on his first hit "Sweet Lorraine") was quite recognizable and his trio with guitarist Oscar Moore and bassist Wesley Prince had a memorable sound. Cole's Decca records (his first for a major label) were a breakthrough for Nat although his Capitol recordings (which started in 1943) really paved the way toward major success. In addition to "Sweet Lorraine," highlights of this fine CD include "Honeysuckle Rose," "I Like to Riff" and "Hit That Jive, Jack" (which has the Trio's most famous group vocal). *—Scott Yanow*

☆ **The Complete Capitol Trio Recordings** / Oct. 11, 1942-Mar. 2, 1961 / Mosaic ✦✦✦✦✦
This 18-CD box set lives up to its title, containing not only all of the Nat King Cole Trio's recordings for Capitol during 1943-1949 but a remarkable amount of previously unavailable

radio transcriptions owned by Capitol. Also, all of Cole's post-1949 recordings that at least have the presence of the trio are here, including the entire *After Midnight* sessions of 1956 and various odds and ends that feature Cole's piano—349 selections in all with a countless number of formerly unissued tracks. This is a limited-edition set. *—Scott Yanow*

Jumpin' at Capitol / Nov. 30, 1943-Jan. 5, 1950 / Rhino ✦✦✦✦✦
For those who cannot afford or get a hold of the magnificent Mosaic 18-CD box set, this single CD offers a fine sampling of Nat King Cole's talents as a pianist and jazz singer with his popular trio in the 1940s. These 16 selections (highlighted by "Straighten up and Fly Right," "Sweet Lorraine" and "Route 66") are still quite enjoyable a half-century later. *—Scott Yanow*

☆ **Nat King Cole** / Nov. 30, 1943-Jun. 3, 1964 / Capitol ✦✦✦✦✦
For an overview of Nat King Cole's years as a remarkably popular singer, this four-CD box would be difficult to top. Containing 100 songs spanning a 20-year period, this box has virtually all of Cole's hits, some of his best jazz sides and more than its share of variety including a humorous previously unreleased version of "Mr. Cole Won't Rock & Roll." Recommended to beginners and veteran collectors alike, its attractive booklet is also a major asset. *—Scott Yanow*

★ **The Greatest Hits** / 1944-1963 / Capitol ✦✦✦✦✦
For all the resurgence in interest in Nat King Cole since 1991, when his daughter Natalie recorded a duet patching her new vocal with his from 40 years earlier and scored a gold-selling hit, Capitol Records lacked a single-disc hits collection that covered Cole's most successful singles for the label. This 22-track, 62-plus-minute CD/cassette collection does the trick. Cole scored 21 Top Ten hits between 1944 and 1963, and 19 of them are here, from "Straighten Up And Fly Right" to "Those Lazy-Hazy-Crazy Days Of Summer." The only ones missing are seasonal hits, "The Christmas Song" and "Frosty The Snow Man." In their places, you get the original and later versions of "Unforgettable" (neither of which, as it happens, quite made the Top 10). You also get Cole's four number one songs, "Mona Lisa," "Nature Boy," "(I Love You) For Sentimental Reasons," and "Too Young," along with such memorable tunes as "Walkin' My Baby Back Home," "Smile," and "(Get Your Kicks On) Route 66." The non-chronological sequencing emphasizes the stylistic and qualitative consistency of $Cole's work; it doesn't much matter if you juxtapose a song recorded in the '40s ("Nature Boy") against one recorded in the '60s ("Ramblin' Rose"), you still get the same warmth and assurance in Cole's singing, the same tastefulness in the arrangements. One might have hoped for more in the way of packaging (there are no liner notes), but this is the single album to buy to hear Nat King Cole's best-known vocal performances. *—William Ruhlmann*

★ **Jazz Encounters** / Mar. 30, 1945-Jan. 5, 1950 / Capitol ✦✦✦✦✦
This CD has many of Cole's most interesting Capitol dates away from his trio. The great jazz pianist is heard with the 1947 Metronome All-Stars, jamming with the all-star Capitol International Jazzmen, backing the straight vocals of Jo Stafford and collaborating with Nellie Lutcher, Woody Herman (on a remarkable version of "Mule Train") and Johnny Mercer (highlighted by the joyful "Save the Bones for Henry Jones"). This colorful set is highly recommended. *—Scott Yanow*

Lush Life / Mar. 29, 1949-Jan. 11, 1952 / Capitol ✦✦✦✦✦
This is a very interesting transitional collection featuring Nat King Cole when he was gradually emphasizing his vocals over his jazz piano playing and phasing out his Trio. All 25 of the selections on this generous set feature the arrangements of Pete Rugolo; highlights include "Lush Life," "Time Out for Tears," "That's My Girl," "Red Sails in the Sunset," "It's Crazy" and "You Stepped out of a Dream." There is enough jazz content and popular appeal on this CD to satisfy both of Cole's audiences. *—Scott Yanow*

Big Band Cole / Aug. 16, 1950-Sep. 6, 1961 / Capitol ✦✦✦✦✦
Cole's collaborations with the Count Basie and Stan Kenton Orchestras (all of which are included on this CD) found him mostly sticking to singing but enjoying the jazz-oriented backgrounds. He first met up with Kenton in 1950, recording the memorable "Orange Colored Sky" and starring on piano during the instrumental "Jam-Bo." They had a reunion in 1960-61, cutting a remake of "Orange Colored Sky" and two more poppish songs. The matchup with Basie showcased Cole purely as a singer in 1958; Gerald Wiggins took Basie's place at the keyboards. One of Cole's better vocal sessions, he is in top form on a variety of standards (particularly on "The Late Late Show" and "Welcome to the Club"); pity he did not sit in with the band on piano. This CD is recommended for its rare examples of Nat King Cole as a big-band singer. *—Scott Yanow*

Penthouse Senenade / Jan. 2, 1952-Jul. 14, 1955 / Capitol ✦✦✦✦✦
The year after he had formally disbanded his trio to turn his attention to vocal pop music, Nat "King" Cole reversed himself and went into the studio with guitarist John Collins, bassist Charlie Harris, and drummer Bunny Shawker and recorded the eight-song 10" LP *Penthouse Serenade*, a quiet, reflective set of standards like "Somebody Loves Me" and "Laura" that he performed instrumentally at the piano. The album confirmed that, whatever success he might be having as a singer, he hadn't lost his touch. In 1955, with the 12" LP gaining dominance, Cole went back into the studio with Collins, Harris, and drummer Lee Young and cut four more songs to create a 12-track reissue of *Penthouse Serenade* that was his first full-length LP release. In 1998, Capitol Jazz again expanded the album, putting out a 19-track CD version by appending an alternate take of "I Surrender Dear" from the 1955 session and six tracks recorded with Collins and Harris (and, on most of them, percussionist Jack Costanzo) from January 1952, four of which were previously unreleased. The justification for these inclusions was that they featured the same personnel, and they are interesting in that they include alternate, non-orchestrated versions of Cole hits like "Too Young," "Walkin' My Baby Back Home," and "Unforgettable." But they are not in keeping with the rest of the album in that they are vocal tracks. Nevertheless, it's hard to argue with an album that, over the years, has grown from 23 to 51 minutes in length. *—William Ruhlmann*

The Complete After Midnight Sessions / Aug. 15, 1956-Sep. 2, 1956 / Capitol ✦✦✦✦
After several years of hearing criticism from the jazz press about his decision to break up his trio and become a pop singer, Nat "King" Cole was persuaded to record this jazz set. Joined by a strong rhythm section (including guitarist John Collins), Cole welcomed four guests for several selections apiece: altoist Willie Smith, trumpeter Harry "Sweets" Edison, violinist Stuff Smith, and valve trombonist Juan Tizol. The performances on this CD (which include five selections released for the first time) are quite enjoyable, highlighted by "Just You, Just Me," "Sweet Lorraine," "It's Only a Paper Moon," and "Route 66." Cole did hedge his bet a bit by not recording any instrumentals or having any performances feature his trio without a guest. Despite that, this is a great set, and the last time that Nat King Cole would perform an album's worth of jazz material. *—Scott Yanow*

Nat King Cole Sings/George Shearing Plays / Dec. 19, 1961-Dec. 22, 1961 / Capitol ✦✦✦✦
Although it would have been interesting to hear Nat Cole play some piano and perhaps accompany a vocal by George Shearing instead of exclusively the other way around, this session was a big success. Cole is in prime form on such songs as "September Song," "Pick Yourself Up," and "Serenata." Shearing's accompaniment is tasteful and lightly swinging, and the string arrangements help to accentuate the romantic moods. This CD adds three "new" selections from the same sessions to the original program. *—Scott Yanow*

☆ **The Christmas Song** / Sep. 1963 / Capitol ✦✦✦✦✦
Cole recorded the definitive version of "The Christmas Song" in 1946, and while this 1960 rerecording is sublime, seek out the original. Although there is a heavy-handed use of orchestras and choruses on this record, Cole rises above the dreck with stellar versions of "Adeste Fidelis," "O Holy Night" and more. Originally released in September 1963, *The Christmas Song* [Capitol 1967) was reissued on CD in 1990 [Capitol 46318]. *—Dennis MacDonald*

Live at the Circle Room / Sep. 21, 1999 / Capitol ✦✦✦✦✦
A number of live broadcasts by the Nat King Cole Trio have turned up on European independent labels, but this is the first to appear on Capitol. In spite of the usual background noise from a night club, including a cash register, rattling glasses, and the inevitable audience conversations, the sound of these newly discovered performances is far superior to the unauthorized releases of other live dates on labels like Musidisc, Duke, and Swing House. Most of the songs covered were recorded by the trio for Capitol, but there are exceptions: "C Jam Blues," two takes of "My Sugar Is So Refined"—which deserved a better fate—and, surprisingly, "I Found a New Baby." Cole's warm vocals are flawless, and the trio's playing is more than up to par. Needless to say, this is an essential release for anyone who enjoys Nat "King" Cole. *—Ken Dryden*

Ornette Coleman

b. Mar. 9, 1930, Fort Worth, TX
Sax (Alto), Violin, Trumpet, Composer / Multimedia, Avant-Garde Jazz, Free Funk, Free Jazz
One of the most important (and controversial) innovators of the jazz avant-garde, Ornette Coleman gained both loyal followers and lifelong detractors when he seemed to burst on the scene in 1959 fully formed. Although he and Don Cherry in his original quartet played opening and closing melodies together, their solos dispensed altogether with chordal improvisation and harmony, instead playing quite freely off of the mood of the theme. Coleman's tone (which purposely wavered in pitch) rattled some listeners and his solos were emotional and followed their own logic. In time his approach would be quite influential and the Quartet's early records still sound advanced over 35 years later. During 1959-61 Coleman recorded a series of classic and somewhat startling quartet albums for Atlantic. With Don Cherry, Charlie Haden, Scott LaFaro or Jimmy Garrison on bass and Billy Higgins or Ed Blackwell on drums, Coleman created music that would greatly affect most of the other advanced improvisers of the 1960s including John Coltrane, Eric Dolphy and the free jazz players of the mid-60s. One set, a nearly 40-minute jam called *Free Jazz* (which other than a few brief themes was basically a pulse-driven group free improvisation) had Coleman, Cherry, Haden, LaFaro, Higgins, Blackwell, Dolphy and Freddie Hubbard forming a double quartet. In the early '70s Coleman entered the second half of his career. He formed a "double quartet" comprised of two guitars, two electric bassists, two drummers and his own alto. The group, called "Prime Time," featured dense, noisy and often-witty ensembles in which all of the musicians are supposed to have an equal role but the leader's alto always ended up standing out. He now calls his music "Harmolodics" (symbolizing the equal importance of harmony, melody and rhythm) although "free funk" (combining together loose funk rhythms and free improvising) probably fits better. *—Scott Yanow*

Tomorrow Is the Question! / Jan. 16, 1959-Mar. 10, 1959 / Contemporary/OJC ✦✦✦
Ornette Coleman's second of two studio albums for Contemporary, which has been reissued on CD in the OJC series, finds him dropping the piano and interacting closely with trumpeter Don Cherry. The rhythm section (Percy Heath or Red Mitchell on bass and drummer Shelly Manne) is still not loose enough for the music (nine Coleman originals, of which "Turnaround" and "Tears Inside" are the best-known), but the freedom heard in the playing of the two horns is quite notable, particularly for 1959. A very interesting session. *—Scott Yanow*

The Art of the Improvisers / May 22, 1959-Mar. 27, 1961 / Atlantic ✦✦✦✦
The seven selections on this recording are performances by various versions of the Ornette Coleman Quartet that were not released until this 1988 album came out; all of the contents were then also reissued in Rhino's large Coleman CD box set. The very original altoist is in excellent form and joined by cornetist Don Cherry, either Charlie Haden, Scott LaFaro or Jimmy Garrison on bass and Billy Higgins or Ed Blackwell on drums. The lyrical ballad "Just for You" is one of the highlights, and some of the song titles ("The Legend of Bebop" and "The Fifth of Beethoven") allude both to Coleman's often overlooked wit and his roots. The music is quite advanced, unpredictable and stimulating. *—Scott Yanow*

☆ **Beauty Is a Rare Thing: The Complete Atlantic Recordings** / May 22, 1959-Mar. 27, 1961 / Rhino/Atlantic ✦✦✦✦✦
This six-CD box set (which includes a very informative and, colorful 70-page booklet) has all of altoist Ornette Coleman's recordings for the Atlantic label. These performances, considered quite revolutionary at the time since Coleman did not use any chord changes, still sound futuristic today. Not only is all the music included from the albums *The Shape of Jazz to*

Come, This Is Our Music, Free Jazz, Ornette and *Ornette on Tenor* along with the two later sets of unissued material (*The Art of the Improvisers* and *Twins*) but a record only previously out in Japan (*To Whom Who Keeps a Record*), two songs that feature Coleman on a Gunther Schuller album and six cuts never out before. Although more general listeners may be content with one or two of Ornette Coleman's albums, serious collectors will want to get this very valuable set while it is still around for it contains some of the most important jazz recordings of the early '60s. *—Scott Yanow*

★ **The Shape of Jazz to Come** / May 22, 1959 / Atlantic ✦✦✦✦✦
Altoist Ornette Coleman's first Atlantic recording was his first with his somewhat revolutionary quartet, which included cornetist Don Cherry, bassist Charlie Haden and drummer Billy Higgins. Because the solos did not follow any set chord pattern, this music became known as "free jazz." This CD reissue, which has also been included in Rhino's six-CD Ornette Coleman box set, is highlighted by the original version of Coleman's most famous composition, "Lonely Woman," plus "Peace" and "Congeniality." This music would greatly influence jazz of the mid-'60s and still sounds quite advanced. *—Scott Yanow*

Change of the Century / Oct. 8, 1959-Oct. 9, 1959 / Atlantic ✦✦✦✦✦
Altoist Ornette Coleman originally recorded six albums for Atlantic (not counting later releases of temporarily discarded tracks), and this particular one was his second. With Don Cherry (on pocket trumpet), bassist Charlie Haden and drummer Billy Higgins, Coleman introduces such interesting and unpredictable "free" pieces as the rhythmic "Una Muy Bonita," "Ramblin'" and "Bird Food." This is important (and still advanced) music that deserves to be heard either in this set or as part of the comprehensive Rhino six-CD box of Coleman's Atlantic recordings. *—Scott Yanow*

This Is Our Music / Jul. 19, 1960-Aug. 2, 1960 / Atlantic ✦✦✦✦✦
The third of altoist Ornette Coleman's six Atlantic albums (not counting later compilations of unreleased material) is most notable for his lyrical and childlike interpretation of the only non-original recorded during this era, "Embraceable You," and for the memorable "Blues Connotation." The other five numbers are lesser known, but "Beauty Is a Rare Thing" and "Humpty Dumpty" also stick in one's mind. Ornette, trumpeter Don Cherry, bassist Charlie Haden, and drummer Ed Blackwell, the latter making his recording debut with the group, formed a classic unit in which each musician was somehow able to quickly figure out in what direction the others were heading. Their brand of "free jazz" or "avant-garde jazz" caused quite a stir during this era and indirectly influenced many groups later in the 1960s. *—Scott Yanow*

☆ **Free Jazz (A Collective Improvisation)** / Dec. 21, 1960 / Atlantic ✦✦✦✦✦
This was one of the most controversial jazz recordings of the period, although when compared to John Coltrane's *Ascension* of five years later, *Free Jazz* sounds quite melodic and even slightly conservative. Altoist Ornette Coleman gathered together a "double quartet" comprised of bass clarinetist Eric Dolphy, Don Cherry and Freddie Hubbard on trumpets, Scott LaFaro and Charlie Haden on basses and both Billy Higgins and Ed Blackwell on drums. Although there is an opening melody, a steady pulse and loose but organized parts between the solos, otherwise this music (which is continuous for around 36 1/2 minutes) is completely free. While one player improvises, the other musicians are free to "comment" behind the solo. The ten-minute stretch when Ornette Coleman is the lead voice and the other three horns come up with free "riffs" is the high point of this very interesting recording (which has also been reissued in Rhino's six-CD Coleman box set). *—Scott Yanow*

Ornette on Tenor / Mar. 22, 1961–Mar. 27, 1961 / Atlantic ✦✦✦
Altoist Ornette Coleman's final album in a series of classic and highly influential Atlantic recordings (which have been reissued in Rhino's *Complete Ornette* six-CD box set) is most unusual because Coleman sticks exclusively to tenor. His gutbucket sound makes his music even more passionate and inaccessible than usual, although listeners who study this record closely will be able to grasp its logic. The "free jazz" improvising by Coleman, trumpeter Don Cherry, bassist Jimmy Garrison (shortly before he joined the John Coltrane Quartet) and drummer Ed Blackwell is quite original and impressive; the often-startling "Cross Breeding" is a high point. *—Scott Yanow*

Town Hall Concert 1962 / Dec. 21, 1962 / Get Back ✦✦✦

At the "Golden Circle" in Stockholm, Vol. 2 / Dec. 3, 1965-Dec. 4, 1965 / Blue Note ✦✦✦✦✦
The second of two volumes (reissued on CD) documenting a series of concerts in Stockholm, Sweden by the 1965 Ornette Coleman Trio is almost the equal of the first. Coleman plays his primitive violin and trumpet on "Snowflakes and Sunshine" but sticks to alto (at its prime during this period) during his other three originals ("Morning Song," "The Riddle" and "Antiques"). The interplay between brilliant bassist David Izenson and drummer Charles Moffett is also quite impressive on this recommended set of free jazz. *—Scott Yanow*

At the "Golden Circle" in Stockholm, Vol. 1 / Dec. 3, 1965-Dec. 4, 1965 / Blue Note ✦✦✦✦✦
Ornette Coleman was at the peak of his powers by 1965. His alto playing had become quite a bit stronger than in his early days, and Coleman's trio with bassist David Izenson and drummer Charles Moffett was as exciting as his earlier quartet. On this CD reissue of a Blue Note LP, he stretches out on four of his originals ("Faces and Places," "European Echoes," "Dee Dee" and "Dawn") and plays consistently innovative and surprising solos that probably confused the majority of his audience while delighting others. This set is recommended, as is the second volume. *—Scott Yanow*

Empty Foxhole / Sep. 9, 1966 / Blue Note ✦✦✦

Love Call / Apr. 29, 1968–May 7, 1968 / Blue Note ✦✦✦✦✦
Ornette Coleman's 1968 Quartet featured the explorative tenor of Dewey Redman (who blended in very well with Coleman's alto), bassist Jimmy Garrison and drummer Elvin Jones. For this CD reissue, which was recorded at the same sessions that resulted in *New York Is Now,* the original four songs are augmented by two "new" alternate takes and "Just for You," which was previously available only in Japan. The interplay between Coleman and Redman on these free jazz jams and the similarity of their approaches, even though they had different sounds, make this unit a particularly strong group. This CD is about as accessible as Ornette Coleman ever became. *—Scott Yanow*

New York Is Now / Apr. 29, 1968–May 7, 1968 / Blue Note ✦✦✦✦✦
Altoist Ornette Coleman had a particularly strong group at the time of his 1968 Blue Note recordings, which resulted in the music heard on this CD and its companion, *Love Call.* Dewey Redman was the equivalent of Coleman on tenor, while bassist Jimmy Garrison and drummer Elvin Jones were alumni of John Coltrane's Quartet. For the CD reissue, a "new" alternate take of "Broad Way Blues" was added to the original program and, although none of the melodies caught on, the complementary playing by Coleman and Redman in particular is quite impressive, making this free jazz set highly recommended. *—Scott Yanow*

Friends and Neighbors / Feb. 14, 1970 / Flying Dutchman ✦✦✦

Science Fiction / Sep. 9, 1971-Sep. 13, 1971 / Columbia ✦✦✦
This LP has quite a bit of variety and finds altoist Ornette Coleman joined by most of his alumni. Three pieces feature a reunion of his original quartet with trumpeter Don Cherry, bassist Charlie Haden and drummer Billy Higgins; three others match Coleman with trumpeter Bobby Bradford, Dewey Redman on tenor, Haden and drummer Ed Blackwell; and the remaining three pieces utilize either Indian vocalist Asha Puthli or poet David Henderson. The generally dissonant and still radical music will take several listens to absorb, but it is worth the effort. *—Scott Yanow*

Skies of America / Apr. 17, 1972-Apr. 20, 1972 / Columbia/Legacy ✦✦✦
At the time it was unveiled, *Skies of America* was a watershed for Ornette Coleman, for not only was it his first important orchestral work, it was here that he introduced the word "harmolodics" as a concept. Alas, the so-far sole recording of the piece is a travesty that does not represent Coleman's intentions. At the recording sessions in London, he was prohibited from using his quartet by arcane British union rules; the piece was heavily cut by over a third in order to fit a single LP, the London Symphony Orchestra (led by David Measham) is clearly lost at sea, and the results are poorly recorded. From what one can make out here, Coleman's writing for a symphony orchestra is uncompromisingly dissonant, pitched deliberately in the high register, often in unrelieved homophonic unison. Occasionally, a rhythm section breaks through the acid texture, and Coleman's harshly pitched alto flies in the face of angry strings and thundering tympani. Some familiar strands of material turn up in later Coleman pieces, such as a repeated riff that later became "Theme From a Symphony." In light of a revelatory live performance by Coleman and the New York Philharmonic that opened the *1997 Lincoln Center Festival,* one cannot gain any idea of the work's structure from this album, although repeated hearings soften the initial shock and reveal the uneasy serenity of the Charles Ives-like conclusion. As a piece of music, *Skies of America* is a problem child and probably always will be, but this fascinating clash between American and European elements does make sense when heard in its entirety, and this album does the piece a disservice. *—Richard S. Ginell*

Dancing in Your Head / Jan. 1973-Dec. 28, 1975 / A&M ✦✦✦✦
Following the symphonic explorations of 1972's *Skies of America,* Ornette Coleman became fascinated with the music of Morocco. *Dancing in Your Head* is the chaotic result of that experimental period with the formation of Prime Time. "Theme From a Symphony" (Variation One and Two) is a 27-minute dervish whirlwind mixed with funk. This was the first opportunity listeners had to hear the two-guitar assault of Charles Ellerbee and Bern Nix. With its infectious danceable melody, Coleman fused these musics together in a unique unpredictable way that had not previously been attempted. "Midnight Sunrise" is a field recording with Ornette playing in Morocco alongside the Master Musicians of Jajouka during a religious ceremony. Music critic Robert Palmer, the first to expose Ornette to the music and culture of Morocco, plays clarinet. Unfortunately this fascinating piece clocks in at only 4:36, with an alternative take not on the original album, at 3:50 featuring Coleman and Palmer playing in an absolute frenzy. *Dancing In Your Head* sustained Ornette Coleman's role of controversial innovator. *—Al Campbell*

Body Meta / Dec. 19, 1976 / Verve ✦✦✦✦
The short-lived but classy Artists House label debuted with this early Prime Time album by Ornette Coleman. At that point Coleman was utilizing guitarists Bern Nix and Charlie Ellerbee, bassist Jamaaladeen Tacuma and drummer Roland Shannon Jackson. The music (five Coleman originals) features dense ensembles with free funk rhythms. Although the musicians were supposed to be given an equal status, Ornette Coleman's alto always stands out above the complex and overlapping rhythms. *—Scott Yanow*

Soapsuds, Soapsuds / Jan. 30, 1977 / Artists House ✦✦✦✦

Of Human Feelings / Apr. 25, 1979 / Antilles ✦✦✦✦
When one thinks of Ornette Coleman's innovative Prime Time Band, it is of crowded ensembles played by the altoist/leader, two guitars, two electric bassists, and two drummers. Actually, Jamaaladeen Tacuma, who plays enough for two musicians, is the only bassist on this date, but guitarists Charlie Ellerbee and Bern Nix, along with drummers Denardo Coleman and Calvin Weston, keep the ensembles quite exciting. None of the eight Coleman originals (which includes a tune titled "What Is the Name of That Song—") would catch on, but in this context they serve as a fine platform for Coleman's distinctive horn and often witty and free (but oddly melodic) style. *—Scott Yanow*

In All Languages / Feb. 1987 / Caravan of Dreams ✦✦✦✦
This is an unusual and very stimulating double CD. On the first CD, Ornette Coleman, on alto and tenor, has a reunion with his original quartet, which is comprised of trumpeter Don Cherry, bassist Charlie Haden and drummer Billy Higgins. The second CD features Coleman's then-current edition of his "double quartet" Prime Time with guitarists Charlie Ellerbe and Bern Nix, electric bassists Jamaaladeen Tacuma and Al MacDowell, and drummers Denardo Coleman and Calvin Weston. Five of the ten songs the quartet plays are also heard in versions by Prime Time, and the latter electric group almost makes the acoustic unit sound conservative in comparison. While the quartet displays subtle use of space and inter-

play between the musicians, Prime Time comes across as overcrowded and loud, but no less stimulating. Highly recommended to fans of Ornette Coleman. *—Scott Yanow*

Tone Dialing / Oct. 1995 / Harmolodic/Verve ✦✦✦✦
Ornette Coleman's first album in several years and first recording for a major label in quite some time features his 1995 version of Prime Time with two guitars, two bassists, son Denardo Coleman on drums and Badal Roy on tables and percussion. In addition the band includes Dave Bryant, Coleman's first keyboardist in decades (although his part is actually fairly minor). The ensembles are funky and quite dense, Coleman really wails on alto (also playing a bit of violin and trumpet) and, despite the inclusion of one obnoxious rap, this free funk set is well worth picking up by open-minded listeners. *—Scott Yanow*

Hidden Man / 1996 / Verve ✦✦✦

Three Women / 1996 / Harmolodic/Verve ✦✦✦

Colors: Live from Leipzig / Aug. 31, 1996 / Verve ✦✦✦✦
Ornette Coleman is certainly full of surprises in his 60s, recording a duo album with—believe it or not—a pianist. For this project, he chose the German pianist Joachim Kühn, who gratefully claims that it was Ornette's example that originally led him down the road to free jazz, and they recorded eight Coleman compositions live in the opera house of Kühn's hometown, Leipzig. Yet their collaboration is not really a radical departure from Ornette's sound worlds in his acoustic groups or in the electric Prime Time. The two seem to exist on parallel planes, not interacting or reacting rhythmically or harmonically, but carving out their occasionally entwined melodic lines separately. Nor does Ornette change his own alto sax manner; at times, he performs in the same rhetorical fashion as he does with Prime Time, while venturing on the outside far more often and scraping away on the violin or burbling on his trumpet when the odd impulse strikes. The music ranges from the relatively funky "Faxing"—no doubt a spinoff from *Tone Dialing*?to the atonal complexity of "Three Ways to One," and the technically formidable Kühn gets an ovation for his extremely intricate solo passage in the latter. Here is an example of the artist having it both ways, reintroducing an instrument that he became famous for banishing, yet without compromising the artistic conception that led to its banishment in the first place. Thus, *Colors* is a fascinating addition to the Ornette Coleman catalogue. *—Richard S. Ginell*

Complete Science Fiction Sessions / Sep. 7, 1971-Sep. 13, 1971 / Columbia/Legacy ✦✦✦✦

Steve Coleman

b. Sep. 20, 1956, Chicago, IL
Sax (Alto) / Free Funk, M-Base, Post-Bop
The leader of what he termed "M-Base" (short for macro-basic array of structured extemporization), Steve Coleman has a strikingly original alto style (very different from bebop) and his groups through the years have utilized funk rhythms and some nonjazz elements in an unpredictable and creative fashion. Coleman started on alto when he was 15 and played R&B in his early days. After moving to New York in 1978, Coleman played with the Thad Jones-Mel Lewis Orchestra, Cecil Taylor and Sam Rivers. After the mid-'80s he has usually been heard either with his group Five Elements or with such M-Base players as Greg Osby, Gary Thomas, Graham Haynes, Robin Eubanks, Geri Allen and Cassandra Wilson. Coleman has recorded sessions as a leader for JMT and Novus and been a sideman with David Murray, Dave Holland and Branford Marsalis. He is one of the most potentially significant saxophonists of the 1990s. *—Scott Yanow*

On the Edge of Tomorrow / Jan. 1986–Feb. 1986 / JMT ✦✦✦✦
Steve Coleman's second recording as a leader introduces his M-Base music in its prime. Essentially creative and avant-garde funk, the performances feature dense but coherent ensembles and crowded grooves. The altoist is teamed up with trumpeter Graham Haynes, Geri Allen (on synthesizer), guitarist Kelvyn Bell, electric bassist Kevin Bruce Harris, both Marvin "Smitty" Smith and Mark Johnson on drums and percussion, and the up and coming singer Cassandra Wilson. Not for everyone's taste, this frequently exciting set hints at a future that has not yet come. *—Scott Yanow*

● **Black Science** / 1991 / Jive/Novus ✦✦✦✦
The mixture of complex funk rhythms and inside/outside soloing performed by the "M-Base" stylists, although similar to Ornette Coleman's "free funk," is quite different from any other earlier idiom. Altoist Steve Coleman's CD is recommended as a good example of his music. The improvisations are dynamic, unpredictable and quite original and the ensemble (which includes pianist James Weidman, guitarist David Gilmore and three guest vocals by Cassandra Wilson) is tight. Coleman, who wrote all but one of the originals, is the dominant force behind this often-disturbing but generally stimulating music. *—Scott Yanow*

Phase Space / Jan. 1991 / DIW ✦✦✦✦

Curves of Life / Mar. 29, 1995 / RCA ✦✦✦✦
The innovative altoist Steve Coleman and his Five Elements constantly prove that it is possible to play creative funk. When one thinks of modern funk (as opposed to the Horace Silver variety), it is of repetitious basslines and drum machines but Coleman's music is actually quite spontaneous. The bass and drum parts are danceable but unpredictable and Coleman's improvising is fresh and distinctive. On this live session, Coleman and his quartet jam through a mostly continuous set with one song flowing into another. David Murray (on tenor) sits in on two pieces and for a change of pace Coleman duets with pianist Andy Milne on a rhapsodic and respectful version of "The Gypsy." The one flaw to the set is the final selection, a 13-minute "I'm Burnin' Up" which is dominated by three annoying rappers. *—Scott Yanow*

The Sonic Language of Myth: Believing, Learning, Knowing / May 18, 1999 / RCA Victor ✦✦✦✦✦
Alto saxophonist Coleman conceives his music as "a symbolic language used to express the nature of the Universe," and it goes much deeper as his extensive liner notes attest. It probes dissonant recesses of space with spiritual and ancient thematic parallels, his rambling, tart saxophone lines placed squarely in the middle of either chaos or orderly settings, both being quite prevalent. The varying instrumentation and connectedness of the seven compositions lends to a suite-like concept. Haunting violins and violas act nearly as synthesizers. Hard blues funk is more prevalent rhythmically, but there are many instances of no time spaciness. Vocals as on "Maat" and "Seth" are shaman sounding and hymnal. Help on select tracks from saxophonist Craig Handy for "Precessional," vibist Stephon Harris soloing on a processional "The Twelve Powers," and tenor saxophonist Ravi Coltrane with trombonist Tim Albright and Coleman only for the minimalist ebony framed trio workout "The Gate" show Coleman a benevolent leader, time sharing ideas and concepts. Jason Moran's dramatic piano on three cuts shows his ever-growing prowess. "Seth" and "Ausar" are odes to a dead Pharaoh reincarnated, then resurrected. Polyphonic harmonies and stealth tones dominate the recording from start to finish. There's also some impressive unison playing among front liners. This is yet another bold statement for Coleman. It holds a strangely exotic, alluring beauty that challenged listeners should appreciate and fans will recognize as another step ahead. *—Michael G. Nastos*

Buddy Collette (William Marcell Collette)

b. Aug. 6, 1921, Los Angeles, CA
Sax (Tenor), Sax (Alto), Flute, Clarinet / West Coast Jazz, Cool, West Coast Blues
An important force in the Los Angeles jazz community, Buddy Collette was an early pioneer at playing jazz on the flute. Collette started on piano as a child and then gradually learned all of the woodwinds. He played with Les Hite in 1942, led a dance band while in the Navy during World War II and then freelanced in the L.A. area with such bands as the Stars of Swing (1946), Edgar Hayes, Louis Jordan, Benny Carter and Gerald Wilson (1949-50). An early teacher of Charles Mingus, Collette became the first Black musician to get a permanent spot in a West Coast studio band (1951-55). He gained his greatest recognition as an important member of the Chico Hamilton Quintet (1955-56) and he recorded several albums as a leader in the mid-to-late '50s for Contemporary. Otherwise he mostly stuck to the L.A. area, freelancing, working in the studios, playing in clubs, teaching and inspiring younger musicians. Although a fine tenor player and a good clarinetist, Collette's most distinctive voice is on flute; he recorded an album with one of his former students, the great James Newton (1989). In addition Collette participated in a reunion of the Chico Hamilton Quintet and recorded a two-disc "talking record" for the Issues label in 1994 in which he discussed some of what he had seen and experienced through the years. *—Scott Yanow*

● **Man of Many Parts** / Feb. 13, 1956-Apr. 17, 1956 / Contemporary/OJC ✦✦✦✦✦
This CD reissue of a Contemporary session shows off the many parts of multireedist Buddy Collette. Collette is showcased on tenor, alto, clarinet and his strongest ax, flute; he also contributed nine of the dozen selections. The cool jazz set (which sometimes uses advanced harmonies) also features among the sidemen trumpeter Gerald Wilson, guitarist Barney Kessel and pianist Gerald Wiggins, ranking with Buddy Collette's best work of the 1950s. *—Scott Yanow*

Nice Day with Buddy Collette / Nov. 6, 1956-Feb. 18, 1957 / Contemporary/OJC ✦✦✦✦
A Nice Day is a nice recording for multireedist Buddy Collette who plays alto, clarinet, flute and tenor during the three sessions heard on the CD reissue. Five of the ten selection's are Collette's originals and, although the title cut and "Fall Winds" (which was renamed "Desert Sands") are both better-known for the versions he recorded with the Chico Hamilton Quintet than for these renditions, the original runthroughs are also excellent. Collette is the main voice throughout this set of lightly swinging music although he gets support from the fine rhythm sections (which include either Don Friedman, Dick Shreve or Calvin Jackson on piano). Overall this set serves as a good all-around showcase for Buddy Collette's playing and writing talents. *—Scott Yanow*

Warm Winds / 1964 / World Pacific ✦✦✦

Flute Talk / Jul. 4, 1988–Jul. 5, 1988 / Soul Note ✦✦✦✦✦
Other than a couple of releases for tiny labels in 1973, this Soul Note CD was Buddy Collette's first session as a leader since 1964. Collette and his former pupil, the great flutist James Newton, team up with pianist Geri Allen, bassist Jaribu Shahid, and drummer Gianpiero Prina for six of Collette's melodic originals (including "Blues in Torrance"), one of Newton's, and a free improvisation created by the two flutists. Collette, who also plays some alto and clarinet on the date, sounds quite happy to be reunited with Newton and to finally be recording again. Although the music is primarily straight-ahead, there are some adventurous moments. *—Scott Yanow*

Live from the Nation's Capital / Jun. 6, 1996 / Bridge ✦✦✦✦
Multi-instrumentalist Collette came to front a 20-piece group for this in-concert date at *the Lincoln Theatre* in Washington, D.C., as part of a *Library Of Congress Jazzfest*. For this hour program, Collette presents his original compositions, many modern charts adapted to larger accompaniment. Besides the world-class flute, sax, and clarinet of the leader, you get exceptional solo and ensemble work from clarinetist/saxophonist Jack Kelson; supplemental saxophonists Ann Patterson, John Stephens, and Louie Taylor; trombonists George Bohanon, Garnett Brown, Maurice Spears, and Britt Woodman; trumpeters Al Aarons and Ron Barrows; pianist Gerald Wiggins; guitarist Al Viola; and other notables. The band starts with the bright flute-driven bopper "Magali" with a drum break from Ndugu Leon Chanceler and a handsome sub melody from the other horns, then all join together on this memorable line. Call and response splendor is extant during "Andre," the bridge having an Afro-Cuban rhythm and a good swing section for Collette's tenor sax. Kelson's clarinet lead intro and free improv with Viola's guitar prompts the band into insistent swing on "Mr. & Mrs. Goodbye" from an easier wrought, older-type tradition. Brown's piquant trombone takes the initial foray for "Blues *4,*" the group supporting his extended wailing. Special guests Chico Hamilton and Ernie Fields Jr. make cameo appearances on the finale "Buddy Boo," as the drummer's signature roiling samba-tango swing leads to a happy swing that elevates the alto sax solo of Fields to a high level as Viola's tiny plucked notes tiptoe around the orchestral monster. This is a wonderful recording that gives further proof to the notion that Buddy Collette continues to be one of the greatest jazz musicians of them all, and also an unsung hero of

big-band legerdemain. The band being absolutely loaded can't hurt. Highly recommended. *—Michael G. Nastos*

Alice Coltrane

b. Aug. 27, 1937, Detroit, MI
Harp, Piano, Organ / Avant-Garde Jazz, Free Jazz
Music obviously ran in Alice Coltrane's family; her older brother was bassist Ernie Farrow, who in the '50s and '60s played in the bands of Barry Harris, Stan Getz, Terry Gibbs and especially, Yusef Lateef. As a young woman she played the bands of such musicians as Lateef and Kenny Burrell before traveling to Paris in 1959 to study with Bud Powell. She met John Coltrane while touring and recording with Gibbs around 1962-63; she married the saxophonist in 1965, and joined his band—replacing McCoy Tyner—a year later. Alice stayed with John's band until his death in 1967. Subsequently, she formed her own bands with players such as Pharoah Sanders, Joe Henderson, Frank Lowe, Carlos Ward, Rashied Ali and Jimmy Garrison. She became increasingly concerned with spiritual matters, founding a center for the study of Eastern religions in 1975. Since the mid-'70s, Coltrane has performed with decreasing frequency. By most accounts, Alice Coltrane was a fine bebop pianist in her early years. With John Coltrane, on albums like *Live at the Village Vanguard Again* or *Concert in Japan*, her playing is characterized by rhythmically ambiguous arpeggios and a pulsing thickness of texture. *—Chris Kelsey*

A Monastic Trio / Mar. 7, 1967-Jun. 6, 1968 / Impulse! ✦✦✦✦
This 1998 CD reissue has Alice Coltrane's first recordings since her husband John Coltrane's death. The original six-song program has been augmented by two selections recorded the same day and originally released as part of John Coltrane's *Cosmic Music* (the material bypassed from that album actually did feature 'Trane and is from 1966). In addition, there is a previously unreleased piano solo by Alice Coltrane that was recorded during one of the sessions that resulted in her husband's last album, *Expression*. Other than for the latter piece, pianist Coltrane is joined by bassist Jimmy Garrison and either Ben Riley or Rashied Ali on drums. The first three numbers (including the two from *Cosmic Music*) have appearances by Pharoah Sanders, who on one song apiece is heard on tenor, very much in the background on flute, and bass clarinet, respectively. In addition, the final three trio pieces find Coltrane switching to harp. Overall, the music is spiritual, well played and sets a mood before staying in the same place. Unfortunately, Alice Coltrane (whose harp playing is atmospheric but little more) would never evolve much from this point on, but overall, this is one of her better recordings. *—Scott Yanow*

● **Ptah the El Daoud** / Jan. 26, 1970 / Impulse! ✦✦✦✦✦
After John Coltrane's death in 1967, his widow Alice Coltrane recorded a few albums and then dropped out of the jazz scene to raise a family and become much more involved in her religious life. This album was arguably her finest post-1967 recording. Playing piano and harp in a quintet with the tenors of Pharoah Sanders and Joe Henderson, bassist Ron Carter and drummer Ben Riley, Coltrane stretches out on four of her compositions, sounding both soulful and spiritual. She had grown as a pianist during the past three years and it is a pity that she did not continue after this session on a full-time basis. *—Scott Yanow*

Journey in Satchidananda / Jul. 4, 1970–Nov. 8, 1970 / Impulse! ✦✦✦
Harp and strings with jazz and Indian influences. Extraordinarily beautiful. *—Michael G. Nastos*

World Galaxy / Nov. 15, 1971-Nov. 16, 1971 / Impulse! ✦✦✦✦✦
Inspired by Indian mystic Swami Satchidananda, the wife of the late tenor sax titan John Coltrane shoots for the stars—and at times, she reaches them. The titles of her three compositions here include the word galaxy, indicating the sweep of her objective. Sixteen strings help to create a feeling of God's power and majesty, especially on "Galaxy Around Olodumare" and "Galaxy in Turiya." Like many astral travellers, she veers off into the ozone, but the magnificent high points linger in your head. *—Mark Allan*

John Coltrane

b. Sep. 23, 1926, Hamlet, NC, **d.** Jul. 17, 1967, New York, NY
Sax (Tenor), Sax (Soprano), Composer / Avant-Garde Jazz, Modal Music, Free Jazz, Hard Bop, Post-Bop, Avant-Garde
Despite a relatively brief career (he first came to notice as a sideman at age 29 in 1955, formally launched a solo career at 33 in 1960, and was dead at 40 in 1967), saxophonist John Coltrane was among the most important, and most controversial, figures in jazz. It seems amazing that his period of greatest activity was so short, not only because he recorded prolifically, but also because, taking advantage of his fame, the record companies that recorded him as a sideman in the 1950s frequently reissued those recordings under his name and there has been a wealth of posthumously released material as well. Since Coltrane was a protean player who changed his style radically over the course of his career, this has made for much confusion in his discography and in appreciations of his playing. There remains a critical divide between the adherents of his earlier, more conventional (if still highly imaginative) work and his later, more experimental work. No one, however, questions Coltrane's almost religious commitment to jazz or doubts his significance in the history of the music. *—William Ruhlmann*

The Last Giant: Anthology / 1946-1967 / Rhino ✦✦
This deluxe two-CD set is a major disappointment. It contains a few revelations (a brief 1946 recording of "Hot House" featuring a 20-year-old Coltrane, an aircheck with Dizzy Gillespie and a rare side by Gay Crosse's Good Humor Six in 1952) but mostly repackages familiar material and includes nothing from Coltrane's very important years with Impulse. Why weren't all four of the 1946 sides included and why are only the first 90 seconds heard from Coltrane's final performance before it fades out— The accompanying booklet is quite attractive but this set (which will greatly frustrate completists) only gives an incomplete picture of the great saxophonist. *—Scott Yanow*

☆ **John Coltrane: The Prestige Recordings** / May 7, 1956-Dec. 26, 1958 / Prestige ✦✦✦✦✦
During 1956-58 Coltrane participated in 27 recording sessions for the Prestige label (not counting his three dates with the Miles Davis Quintet), both as a leader and as a sideman. Although these recordings are not as significant on a whole as Coltrane's later Impulse albums, there are many gems among the jam sessions and all of the music (except The Davis sessions) have been released in their entirety on this somewhat remarkable 16-CD set. Coltrane and a constantly changing all-star cast perform such classics as "Tenor Madness" (his one-time meeting on records with Sonny Rollins), "On a Misty Night," "While My Lady Sleeps," "Like Someone in Love," "Black Pearls" and "Stardust" among many others. This expensive box may not be for all jazz collections, but any true fan of John Coltrane will have to acquire it. *—Scott Yanow*

Dakar / Mar. 22, 1957-Apr. 20, 1957 / Prestige/OJC ✦✦✦

Bahia / May 17, 1957-Dec. 26, 1958 / Prestige/OJC ✦✦✦

Cattin' with Coltrane and Quinichette / May 17, 1957 / Prestige/OJC ✦✦✦✦✦
Although John Coltrane gets top billing, this CD reissue from DCC Jazz is really an excellent set by tenor Paul Quinichette who was always most notable for the similarity of his sound and style to Lester Young in the 1950s. There are the five selections from the original album which, in addition to Quinichette (who has "Exactly like You" as his feature) and Coltrane, includes pianist Mal Waldron, bassist Julian Euell and drummer Ed Thigpen, plus an unreleased version of "Tea for Two" without Coltrane and three previously unknown numbers from a 1952 Quinichette session with a four-piece rhythm section. The sound quality on this CD is superb and the swing/bop music has plenty of strong moments. There were not that many recordings made by Paul Quinichette and most are out-of-print, making this rare release fairly significant. *—Scott Yanow*

Lush Life / May 31, 1957-Jan. 10, 1958 / Prestige ✦✦✦✦
The music on this CD reissue is taken from three separate sessions led by John Coltrane. Most rewarding are memorable versions of "Like Someone in Love," "I Love You" and "'Trane's Slo Blues" that feature the masterful tenor accompanied by just bassist Earl May and drummer Art Taylor; "Like Someone in Love" in particular is given definitive treatment. Of the two other songs, "I Hear a Rhapsody" finds Coltrane accompanied by pianist Red Garland, bassist Paul Chambers and drummer Al "Tootie" Heath while "Lush Life" is played with a quintet also featuring trumpeter Donald Byrd, Garland, Chambers and drummer Louis Hayes. *—Scott Yanow*

The Last Trane / Aug. 16, 1957-Mar. 26, 1958 / Prestige/OJC ✦✦✦

Traning In / Aug. 23, 1957 / Prestige/OJC ✦✦✦
This CD brings back a good session but one that does not quite live up to its great potential. Tenor saxophonist John Coltrane, halfway through his one-year hiatus from Miles Davis' group, performs five songs with the assistance of pianist Red Garland, bassist Paul Chambers and drummer Art Taylor. Although "Traneing In" and "You Leave Me Breathless" have their moments, in general this set is less memorable than one might expect; inspiration was lacking that day. *—Scott Yanow*

★ **Blue Train** / Sep. 15, 1957 / Blue Note ✦✦✦✦✦
This CD is a true classic, one of the highpoints of John Coltrane's early career. A few steps above most of his Prestige recordings, his only Blue Note session is a very special and consistently inspired outing with trumpeter Lee Morgan, trombonist Curtis Fuller, pianist Kenny Drew, bassist Paul Chambers, and drummer Philly Joe Jones. "Blue Train," with its brilliant solos by Coltrane and Morgan, really amazed listeners at the time, while "Moment's Notice" was one of Coltrane's finest compositions. The other numbers ("I'm Old Fashioned," "Lazy Bird," and "Locomotion") are close behind, making this an essential acquisition for all serious jazz collections. In addition to the Blue Note reissue, Mobile Fidelity has come out with an audiophile version of the timeless recording. *—Scott Yanow*

The Bethlehem Years / Oct. 1957-Dec. 1957 / Bethlehem Archives ✦✦✦✦
The title of this double CD is rather humorous for John Coltrane only recorded two albums for Bethlehem and both as a sideman within a two-month period. Coltrane was part of *The Winner's Circle* (an all-star octet) and also recorded with drummer Art Blakey in a big band and a quintet. Among the other key sidemen were trumpeter Donald Byrd, tenorman Al Cohn, trombonist Jimmy Cleveland, and pianist Walter Bishop, Jr. The double CD greatly expands upon the original sessions, adding 15 alternate takes to the 12 songs. Obviously this two-fer is not for general collectors, but John Coltrane completists will have to get it. *—Scott Yanow*

Black Pearls / Jan. 10, 1958-May 23, 1958 / Original Jazz Classics ✦✦✦✦
Four of the six performances on this two-LP set are over ten minutes long, giving tenor-saxophonist John Coltrane (heard at the peak of his "sheets of sound" period), trumpeter Donald Byrd, pianist Red Garland, bassist Paul Chambers and drummer Art Taylor plenty of space in which to stretch out. 'Trane takes some miraculous solos (by 1958 he was the leading tenor-saxophonist in jazz and already long on his way to becoming a giant), sounding ten years ahead of his sidemen. The young trumpeter Freddie Hubbard makes an appearance on "Do I Love You Because You're Beautiful—" and this two-fer also finds Coltrane for the first time playing a McCoy Tyner composition ("The Believer"), two years before Tyner joined his Quartet. *—Scott Yanow*

Soultrane / Feb. 7, 1958 / Prestige ✦✦✦✦
Tenor saxophonist John Coltrane, who had recently rejoined Miles Davis' group, teams up with pianist Red Garland, bassist Paul Chambers and drummer Art Taylor for a fine set which has been reissued on CD. Coltrane performs his earliest rendition of "I Want to Talk About You" (although without a closing cadenza), "Good Bait," "You Say You Care," "Theme for Ernie" and "Russian Lullaby." This is excellent music that falls short of being classic but Coltrane and Garland always made for a complementary team. [A 20-bit remaster of *Soultrane* was released in October 1999.] *—Scott Yanow*

Settin' the Pace / Mar. 26, 1958 / Prestige/OJC ✦✦✦✦
Tenor saxophonist John Coltrane recorded quite a few records with the rhythm section of pi-

anist Red Garland, bassist Paul Chambers and drummer Art Taylor during 1957-58. On this particular CD reissue, Coltrane performs "Rise and Shine," "I See Your Face Before Me," "If There Is Someone Lovelier than You" and "Little Melonae." But more significant than the material are Coltrane's searching and passionate improvisations which were pointing the way toward the future. This music (along with Trane's other Prestige recordings) is also available as part of his huge *Complete on Prestige* box set. *—Scott Yanow*

Coltrane Time / Oct. 13, 1958 / Blue Note ♦♦♦♦
This is a most unusual CD due to the inclusion of Cecil Taylor on piano. Although Taylor and John Coltrane got along well, trumpeter Kenny Dorham (who is also on this quintet date) hated the avant-garde pianist's playing and was clearly bothered by Taylor's dissonant comping behind his solos. With bassist Chuck Israels and drummer Louis Hayes doing their best to ignore the discord, the group manages to perform two blues and two standards with Dorham playing strictly bop, Taylor coming up with fairly free abstractions and Coltrane sounding somewhere in between. The results are unintentionally fascinating. *—Scott Yanow*

☆ **Heavyweight Champion: The Complete Atlantic Recordings** / Jan. 15, 1959-May 25, 1961 / Rhino/Atlantic ♦♦♦♦♦
The Heavyweight Champion is a box set that lives up to its title. Collecting all of John Coltrane's Atlantic recordings, including a fair number of unreleased takes as well as an entire disc of alternate tracks and studio chatter, the seven-disc box set documents a pivotal moment in Coltrane's career, as he was moving from hard-bop and sweet standards to a more daring, experimental style of playing influenced by the avant-garde. Much of the music is hard-bop (*Giant Steps*) or lushly melodic (*My Favorite Things*), but the latter discs show the saxophonist developing coming to terms with the more experimental movements in jazz, as he performs with musicians like Ornette Coleman. The scope of this music is, quite simply, breathtaking—not only was Coltrane developing at a rapid speed, the resulting music encompasses nearly every element that made him a brilliant musician and it is beautiful. *—Stephen Thomas Erlewine*

★ **Giant Steps** / Apr. 1, 1959-Dec. 2, 1959 / Atlantic ♦♦♦♦♦
This is one of John Coltrane's classic sets; in fact this CD reissue (which adds alternate takes to five of the seven original recordings) almost doubles one's pleasure. In "Giant Steps" Coltrane built a tongue-twister of chord changes (stretching bop to its logical breaking point) which he would soon abandon in favor of long drones on simpler patterns. Not only does this CD give one the two earliest versions of "Giant Steps" but also "Naima," "Cousin Mary," "Spiral," "Syeeda's Song Flute," the underrated but remarkable "Countdown" and "Mr. P.C." Recorded while Coltrane was still with Miles Davis's group, this CD (which mostly features pianist Tommy Flanagan, bassist Paul Chambers and drummer Art Taylor) made it obvious that Coltrane had something very important of his own to say and that he would need his own band in the future to fully express himself. *—Scott Yanow*

Coltrane Jazz / Nov. 24, 1959-Oct. 21, 1956 / Atlantic ♦♦♦♦♦
The first album to hit the shelves after *Giant Steps, Coltrane Jazz* was largely recorded in late 1959, although one of the eight songs ("Village Blues") was done in late 1960. On everything save the aforementioned "Village Blues," Coltrane used the Miles Davis rhythm section of pianist Wynton Kelly, bassist Paul Chambers, and drummer Jimmy Cobb. While not the groundbreaker that *Giant Steps* was, *Coltrane Jazz* was a good consolidation of his gains as he prepared to launch into his peak years of the 1960s. There are three standards aboard, but the group reaches their peak on Coltrane's original material, particularly "Harmonique" with its melodic leaps and upper-register saxophone strains and the winding, slightly Eastern-flavored principal riffs of "Like Sonny," dedicated to Sonny Rollins. The moody "Village Blues" features the lineup of McCoy Tyner on piano, Elvin Jones on drums, and Steve Davis on bass; with the substitution of Jimmy Garrison on bass, that personnel would play on Coltrane's most influential and beloved 1960s albums. The 2000 CD reissue on Atlantic/Rhino adds four bonus tracks: alternate takes of "Like Sonny" and "I'll Wait and Pray" that were first issued on *Alternate Takes* and alternate takes of "Like Sonny" and "Village Blues" that came out on the *Heavyweight Champion: The Complete Atlantic Recordings* box. *—Richie Unterberger*

The Avant-Garde / Jun. 20, 1960-Jul. 8, 1960 / Atlantic ♦♦♦♦
This CD is a straight reissue of the original LP. Despite the title, it is actually a fairly relaxed and somewhat conservative session for these players. Tenor-saxophonist John Coltrane (who on "The Blessing" makes his debut on soprano) works well with the sidemen of the Ornette Coleman Quartet (trumpeter Don Cherry, bassist Charlie Haden or Percy Heath and drummer Ed Blackwell) on three Coleman compositions (this version of "The Blessing" is a classic), Don Cherry's "Cherryco" and Thelonious Monk's "Bemsha Swing." It's an enjoyable set of early freebop. *—Scott Yanow*

Coltrane Plays the Blues / Oct. 24, 1960 / Atlantic ♦♦♦♦♦
Coltrane's sessions for Atlantic in late October 1960 were prolific, yielding the material for *My Favorite Things, Coltrane Plays the Blues*, and *Coltrane's Sound. My Favorite Things* was destined to be the most remembered and influential of these, and while *Coltrane Plays the Blues* is not as renowned or daring in material, it is still a powerful session. As for the phrase "plays the blues" in the title, that's not so much an indicator that the tunes are conventional blues (which they aren't). It's more indicative of a bluesy sensibility, whether he is playing muscular saxophone or, on "Blues to Bechet" and "Mr. Syms," the more unusual-sounding (at the time) soprano sax. Elvin Jones, who hadn't been in Coltrane's band long, really busts out on the quicker numbers, such as "Blues to You" and "Mr. Day." The 2000 reissue on Rhino adds five bonus tracks: two alternates apiece of "Blues to Elvin" and "Blues to You" (which were originally released on the 1995 *Heavyweight Champion: The Complete Atlantic Recordings* box), and "Untitled Original (Exotica)." This last track first appeared on the 1970 compilation *The Coltrane Legacy* and, like every other one on this CD, was recorded on October 24, 1960. *—Richie Unterberger*

Coltrane's Sound / Oct. 24, 1960–Oct. 26, 1960 / Atlantic ♦♦♦♦
Although one may not think of *Coltrane's Sound* as being one of John Coltrane's most famous recordings, when one looks at its contents it quickly becomes obvious that this set ranks near the top. This CD reissue contains such classic material as "Central Park West," "Equinox," a reharmonized (and influential) version of "Body and Soul," the underrated "Satellite," "Liberia" and an intense rendition of "The Night Has a Thousand Eyes." Also included on this reissue is an alternate version of "Body and Soul" and the lesser-known "262." Co-starring pianist McCoy Tyner, bassist Steve Davis and drummer Elvin Jones, this set is highly recommended. *—Scott Yanow*

★ **My Favorite Things** / Oct. 24, 1960-Oct. 26, 1960 / Atlantic ♦♦♦♦♦
This album was very influential when it came out and remains a classic. The first full album by the classic John Coltrane Quartet (with pianist McCoy Tyner, drummer Elvin Jones and their bassist of the time Steve Davis) consists of a fiery "Summertime," the lyrical "But Not for Me," a nice ballad for 'Trane's soprano on "Everytime We Say Goodbye" and most importantly, the lengthy "My Favorite Things." On the latter Coltrane, who had used a seemingly endless number of chords on the prior year's "Giant Steps," reduces the chords to a minimum and plays passionately over a repetitious vamp, creating startlingly new music. *—Scott Yanow*

Complete Africa/Brass Sessions / May 23, 1961–Jun. 4, 1961 / Impulse! ♦♦♦♦♦
John Coltrane's first recordings for Impulse are different than any of his later ones for they feature the saxophonist accompanied by large brass-heavy 14-17 piece groups. This two-CD set has all of the music which was originally released on *Africa/Brass*, the later *Africa/Brass Sessions, Vol. 2* and *Trane's Modes*. In general the arrangements are essentially an expansion of the style and sound of the John Coltrane Quartet with much of the improvising ("Blues Minor" excepted) taking place over two-chord vamps. Eric Dolphy wrote all but a pair of the charts (there are one apiece from McCoy Tyner and Calvin Massey) and he based his orchestrations on the piano voicings of Tyner. The only soloists are Coltrane (on both tenor and soprano) and his regular quartet members; it is disappointing that Dolphy, Freddie Hubbard and Booker Little are not really heard from. While Massey's "The Damned Don't Cry" falters and sounds under rehearsed, the three renditions of "Africa" are quite colorful. But since over half of the performance time is taken up by "Africa," this two-CD set is not for everyone. *—Scott Yanow*

Olé Coltrane / May 25, 1961 / Atlantic ♦♦♦♦
One of John Coltrane's most interesting sessions for Atlantic was also his last before exclusively switching to Impulse. This CD, which contains the original three selections from the LP ("Ole," "Dahomey Dance" and "Aisha") in addition to one item from the same date that was not released until decades later ("To Her Ladyship"), features the great saxophonist leading an all-star group (Eric Dolphy on alto and flute, trumpeter Freddie Hubbard, pianist McCoy Tyner, bassists Reggie Workman and Art Davis and drummer Elvin Jones) on a variety of very interesting material. "Ole" is quite haunting and "Dahomey Dance" became a minor standard. The solos are more concise than is usual on a Coltrane session and this set is quite accessible even to listeners who prefer his earlier "sheets of sound" recordings. *—Scott Yanow*

Complete 1961 Village Vanguard Recordings / Nov. 1, 1961-Nov. 5, 1961 / GRP ♦♦♦♦♦
All of the music that survives from John Coltrane's famous 1961 five-day engagement at the Village Vanguard has been released on this 1997 four-CD box set. The original *Live at the Village Vanguard* album just had three selections; 16 others came out on various releases through the years, and this attractive box has all 19 of those cuts, plus three previously unreleased performances. During the period, the great tenor and soprano saxophonist was joined by pianist McCoy Tyner, both Reggie Workman and Jimmy Garrison on bass, drummer Elvin Jones, and usually Eric Dolphy on alto and bass clarinet; "India" usually adds Ahmed Abdul-Malik on oud and Garvin Bushell on oboe and contrabassoon, while Bushell also appears on "Spiritual," and Roy Haynes sits in for Jones on "Chasin' Another Trane." Although the band was considered controversial and branded as "anti-jazz" by critic John Tynan, the music is not as "far out" as was once thought with the benefit of decades of hindsight. Coltrane and Dolphy do take plenty of extended and adventurous solos, often over one or two-chord vamps, but the improvising seems quite logical and properly emotional. There are multiple versions of most of the songs, with all of the treatments holding one's interest. Included are "Brasilia," "Chasin' Another Trane," "Softly As In a Morning Sunrise," two versions of "Chasin' the Trane," "Greensleeves," a thinly disguised "Naima" and "Miles' Mode," three of "Impressions," and four of "India" and "Spiritual." All true John Coltrane fans have to own this set. *—Scott Yanow*

Newport '63 / Nov. 2, 1961-Jul. 7, 1963 / Impulse! ♦♦♦♦♦
Three of the four lengthy performances on this CD are taken from one of the John Coltrane Quartet's greatest performances: the 1963 Newport Jazz Festival. With pianist McCoy Tyner, bassist Jimmy Garrison and drummer Roy Haynes (filling in for an absent Elvin Jones), Coltrane performs what is arguably his greatest version of "My Favorite Things" along with memorable renditions of "Impressions" and "I Want to Talk About You." Two of those selections originally appeared on the LP *Selflessness* while "Impression" was included in a later collection. This set is rounded out by "Chasin' Another Trane," the only recording from 'Trane's famous Nov. 1961 engagement at the Village Vanguard that had Roy Haynes sitting in for Elvin Jones; altoist Eric Dolphy is also heard from on that heated selection. *—Scott Yanow*

Impressions / Nov. 3, 1961-Apr. 29, 1963 / Impulse! ♦♦♦♦
This LP is a hodgepodge of memorable John Coltrane performances from the 1961-63 period. "India" and "Impressions" are taken from 'Trane's famous Nov. 1961 engagement at the Village Vanguard; bass clarinetist Eric Dolphy is heard on the former while the latter features a marathon solo from Coltrane on tenor. Also included on this set are 1962's "Up 'Gainst the Wall" and the classic of the album, 1963's "After the Rain." *—Scott Yanow*

Ballads / Dec. 21, 1961-Nov. 13, 1962 / Impulse! ♦♦♦♦
Stung by criticism from conservative jazz critics, Coltrane decided to show his detractors that he had not forgotten how to embrace a melody; the problem is that on this brief set (reissued on CD by GRP in an attractive fold-out package) he never really gets away from the themes.

While Trane (who sticks to tenor) plays quite pretty, pianist McCoy Tyner actually has the more interesting solos. Coltrane shows the tunes an excess of respect, making this outing with his classic quartet enjoyable as background music but lacking much passion. *—Scott Yanow*

The Gentle Side of John Coltrane / 1961-1964 / GRP ♦♦♦♦
"Gentle" is a relative term, for while this collection of material is mostly pitched at a slower set of tempos and more lyrical frame of mind, Coltrane was no less passionate in a ballad as he was in a roaring frenzy. Originally issued on two LPs and now excellent value on a single CD, *The Gentle Side* draws nine tracks from the legacy of the classic Coltrane quartet (with McCoy Tyner, Jimmy Garrison and Elvin Jones), adding a pair of tracks each from his collaborations with Duke Ellington and Johnny Hartman. You can say all you want about how a collection like this disregards the musical flow of the original albums—which is true—and still be caught up helplessly in the staggering emotional power of this man's playing. Even when heard in this context, performances like "After the Rain" and "Welcome" remain breathtaking in their spiritual beauty, and the combination of Coltrane's eloquence and the warm, masculine baritone of Hartman can still break your heart with their most-likely-untopped interpretation of "My One and Only Love." Above all, if you know anyone who has resisted Coltrane because of the fearsome reputation of his more agitated music, lay this CD on them. *—Richard S. Ginell*

Coltrane / Apr. 11, 1962-Jun. 29, 1962 / Impulse! ♦♦♦♦
John Coltrane and his classic Quartet (pianist McCoy Tyner, bassist Jimmy Garrison and drummer Elvin Jones) are in fine form for this 1962 studio LP. High points include a passionate "Out of This World" (what did Johnny Mercer think of this version—) and a classic version of Mal Waldron's "Soul Eyes." The remainder of the program includes "The Inch Worm" and the two Coltrane compositions "Tunji" and "Miles' Mode." Not as intense as many of 'Trane's other albums, this is still a recommended, enjoyable set. *—Scott Yanow*

☆ **John Coltrane and Johnny Hartman** / Mar. 7, 1963 / Impulse! ♦♦♦♦♦
John Coltrane's match-up with singer Johnny Hartman, although quite unexpected, works extremely well. Hartman, who had not recorded since 1956, was in prime form on the six ballads and his versions of "Lush Life" and "My One and Only Love" have never been topped. Coltrane's playing throughout the session is beautiful, sympathetic, and still explorative; he sticks exclusively to tenor on the date. At only a half-hour one wishes there were twice as much music, but what is here is classic, essential for all jazz collections. *—Scott Yanow*

Dear Old Stockholm / Apr. 29, 1963-May 26, 1965 / Impulse! ♦♦♦♦
This CD contains five excellent performances by the John Coltrane Quartet from two occasions when drummer Roy Haynes filled in for Elvin Jones. A definitive "Dear Old Stockholm" and Coltrane's mournful ballad "After the Rain" are from Apr. 29, 1963 while the beautiful "Dear Lord" and two long and raging performances ("One Down, One Up" and "After the Crescent") date from May 26, 1965. Although Haynes had a different approach on the drums than Jones, he fit in perfectly with the group, stimulating Coltrane to play brilliantly throughout these two sessions. *—Scott Yanow*

☆ **Live at Birdland** / Mar. 6, 1963-Nov. 18, 1963 / Impulse! ♦♦♦♦♦
Arguably John Coltrane's finest all-around album, this recording has brilliant versions of "AfroBlue" and "I Want to Talk About You"; the second half of the latter features Coltrane on unaccompanied tenor tearing into the piece but never losing sight of the fact that it is a beautiful ballad. The remainder of this album ("Alabama," "The Promise" and "Your Lady") is almost at the same high level. *—Scott Yanow*

Crescent / Apr. 27, 1964–Jun. 1, 1964 / Impulse! ♦♦♦
One of only two studio albums cut by the John Coltrane Quartet during 1964, *Crescent* is most notable for including five Coltrane compositions including the title cut, "Lonnie's Lament" and the swinging "Bessie's Blues." The music is excellent although not as fiery as the Quartet's live performances of the period. *—Scott Yanow*

★ **A Love Supreme** / Dec. 9, 1964 / Impulse! ♦♦♦♦♦
John Coltrane recorded more exciting albums than this one (which has been reissued on CD but GRP) but the highly influential *A Love Supreme* is the project that meant the most to him, his gift to God. In addition to the famous chanting of the title, Coltrane performs a couple of particularly memorable themes (it is surprising that "Resolution" did not become a standard) and the soloing is on a consistently high level. This recording (which also features pianist McCoy Tyner, bassist Jimmy Garrison and drummer Elvin Jones) closed the book on what could be considered 'Trane's most significant period for he would begin to more fully explore atonality with the coming of 1965. *—Scott Yanow*

The John Coltrane Quartet Plays / Feb. 17, 1965-May 17, 1965 / Impulse! ♦♦♦♦

Transition / May 26, 1965-Jun. 10, 1965 / Impulse! ♦♦♦♦
The title of this CD (a straight reissue of the LP) fits perfectly for Coltrane was certainly at an important transitional point in his career at the time. Although he was still utilizing the same Quartet that he had had for over three years (pianist McCoy Tyner, bassist Jimmy Garrison and drummer Elvin Jones) and his music had always been explorative, now he was taking his solos one step beyond into passionate atonality, usually over simple but explosive vamps. Other than the tender ballad "Welcome," most of this set is uncompromisingly intense; in fact the closing 9-minute "Vigil" is a fiery tenor-drums duet. The 21-minute "Suite," even with sections titled "Prayer And Meditiation: Day" and "Affirmation," is not overly peaceful. It must have seemed clear, even at this early point, that McCoy Tyner and perhaps Elvin Jones would not be with the band much longer. *—Scott Yanow*

Kulu Se Mama / Jun. 16, 1965-Oct. 14, 1965 / Impulse! ♦♦♦

☆ **Ascension** / Jun. 28, 1965 / 151549 ♦♦♦♦♦
This historic outing can be looked at as John Coltrane's answer to Ornette Coleman's *Free Jazz* of four years earlier. Coltrane, who progressed steadily throughout 1965 until he was largely specializing in atonality, is heard leading a large ensemble through a 40-minute piece that, except for some brief passages, is freely improvised. While the rhythm section (pianist McCoy Tyner, both Jimmy Garrison and Art Davis on basses, and drummer Elvin Jones) kept the music moving, seven adventurous horn players performed emotional and sometimes violent solos and fiery ensembles. With Coltrane, Archie Shepp and Pharoah Sanders on tenors, John Tchicai and Marion Brown on altos, and trumpeters Freddie Hubbard and Dewey Johnson, the results are pretty ferocious and a bit scary. This performance (plus a rarer alternate take and some other long pieces) has been reissued on the two-CD set *The Major Works of John Coltrane*. *—Scott Yanow*

☆ **The Major Works of John Coltrane** / Jun. 28, 1965-Oct. 14, 1965 / Impulse! ♦♦♦♦♦
Some of John Coltrane's more adventurous and eccentric works from 1965 have been reissued on this important two-CD set. The two versions of the 38-40 minute "Ascension" (one of which was formerly quite rare) dominate the program. The innovative tenor saxophonist, other than on a few short transitions, allowed his expanded group to play very freely on the rather violent work Such musicians as tenors Pharoah Sanders and Archie Shepp, altoists John Tchicai and Marion Brown, trumpeters Freddie Hubbard and Dewey Johnson, pianist McCoy Tyner, bassists Jimmy Garrison and Art Davis and drummer Elvin Jones were turned loose for solos and furious ensembles. Also on the stimulating twofer are "Om," "Kulu Se Mama" and "Selflessness." Among the musicians added to Coltrane's classic quartet for these pieces are tenor saxophonist Pharoah Sanders, Donald Garrett on bass clarinet and second bass, flutist Joe Brazil (on "Om") and the oddly memorable vocalizing and percussion of Juno Lewis (on "Kulu Se Mama"). Far from Coltrane's most accessible recordings, the groundbreaking and influential explorations are all worthy of several listens by openminded listeners. *—Scott Yanow*

New Thing at Newport / Jul. 2, 1965 / 151549 ♦♦♦♦
The classic John Coltrane Quartet made one of its final appearances at the *Newport Jazz Festival* in 1965. The tension among band members is evident on the advanced versions of "One Down, One Up" and "My Favorite Things." Coltrane's performance is moving... yet weary. It's apparent the saxophonist wasn't getting the sound he wanted and by the end of the year he would take a different direction, hiring Pharoah Sanders and wife Alice Coltrane for the band. Tenor saxophonist Archie Shepp's earlier afternoon *New Thing* performance includes engaging versions of "Call Me By My Rightful Name" and "Gingerbread, Gingerbread Boy" (included as a bonus track on this package) with Bobby Hutcherson on vibes. *—Al Campbell*

Sun Ship / Aug. 26, 1965 / Impulse! ♦♦♦♦
Other than *First Meditations*, which was not released at the time, *Sun Ship* (reissued on CD by Impulse) was the final studio album by John Coltrane's classic quartet (with pianist McCoy Tyner, bassist Jimmy Garrison and drummer Elvin Jones) before Pharoah Sanders joined the band on second tenor. At this point in time, Coltrane was using very short repetitive themes as jumping off points for explosive improvisations, often centered around one chord and a very specific spiritual mood. Tyner sounds a bit conservative in comparison, but Jones keeps up with 'Trane's fire (especially on "Amen"). Even in the most intense sections (and much of this music is atonal), there is a logic and thoughtfulness about Coltrane's playing. *—Scott Yanow*

First Meditations / Sep. 2, 1965-Sep. 22, 1965 / Impulse! ♦♦♦♦

Live in Seattle / Sep. 30, 1965 / Impulse! ♦♦♦♦
This double CD features John Coltrane at a concert in Sept. 1965 with his expanded sextet (which included pianist McCoy Tyner, bassist Jimmy Garrison, drummer Elvin Jones, Pharoah Sanders on tenor and Donald Garrett doubling on bass clarinet and bass). Coltrane experts know that 1965 was the year that his music became quite atonal and, with the addition of Sanders, often very violent. This music, therefore, is not for fans of Coltrane's earlier sheets of sound period or for those who prefer jazz as melodic background music. The program from the original double LP (the nearly free "Cosmos," an intense workout on "Out of This World," a bass feature and the truly wild "Evolution") is augmented by previously unissued versions of "Body and Soul" and a 34-minute "Afro Blue" that is incomplete because the tape ran out. Throughout much of this set Coltrane plays some miraculous solos, Sanders consistently turns on the heat, Garrett makes the passionate ensembles a bit overcrowded, Tyner is barely audible, Garrison drones in the background and Jones struggles to make sense of it all. This is innovative and difficult music that makes today's young lions (not to mention the pop saxophonists) sound very old-fashioned in comparison. *—Scott Yanow*

Om / Oct. 1, 1965 / Impulse! ♦♦♦

Meditations / Nov. 23, 1965 / Impulse! ♦♦♦♦♦
This CD reissues what was arguably the finest of the John Coltrane-Pharoah Sanders collaborations. On five diverse but almost consistently intense movements ("The Father and the Son and the Holy Ghost," "Compassion," "Love," "Consequences" and "Serenity"), the two tenor saxophonists, pianist McCoy Tyner, bassist Jimmy Garrison and both Elvin Jones and Rashied Ali on drums create some powerful, dense and emotional music. Unlike some of the live jams of 1966, the passionate performances never ramble on too long and the screams and screeches fit logically into the spiritual themes. This would be the last recording of Coltrane with Tyner and Jones. *—Scott Yanow*

Live in Japan / Jul. 11, 1966–Jul. 22, 1966 / Impulse! ♦♦♦
This very interesting four-CD set contains two sets of music by the 1966 John Coltrane Quintet, recorded in Tokyo, Japan. Most of the music had not been released in the United States until 1991. Coltrane (heard on tenor, soprano and alto) engages in some ferocious interplay with Pharoah Sanders (on tenor, alto and bass clarinet), pianist Alice Coltrane, bassist Jimmy Garrison and drummer Rashied Ali; fans of Trane's earlier records may not like these atonal flights. However listeners who enjoy avant-garde jazz will find many stirring moments among the very lengthy performances. The shortest piece is the 25-minute version of "Peace on Earth" and "My Favorite Things" goes on for over 57 minutes. *—Scott Yanow*

Expression / Feb. 15, 1967-Mar. 7, 1967 / Impulse! ♦♦♦♦
This music came from John Coltrane's final recording sessions, although no one at that time knew it. It was emblematic of his work in that era—unpredictable, experimental, restless, sometimes remarkable, sometimes more noteworthy for what was being attempted than presented. GRP's recently reissued CD includes a great bonus cut, the nearly 12-minute "Number One" with surging, raw Coltrane tenor contrasted by Pharoah Sanders' piccolo and

flute. But while the new material was valuable, the compelling cut here remains "To Be," the 16-minute-plus Coltrane/Sanders dialogue on flutes and piccolo. It was the only time on record that Coltrane played flute (at least for any lengthy period), and his singing lines, blend of raspy and lyrical phrases and overall approach were as identifiable on that instrument as any of his saxes. *—Ron Wynn*

Stellar Regions / Feb. 15, 1967 / Impulse! ✦✦✦✦✦
This is a major set, "new" music from John Coltrane that was recorded February 15, 1967, (five months before his death) but not released for the first time until 1995. One of several "lost" sessions that were stored by Alice Coltrane for decades, only one selection ("Offering" which was on *Expression*) among the eight numbers and three alternates was ever out before. The music, although well worth releasing, offers no real hints as to what Coltrane might have been playing had he lived into the 1970s. The performances by the quartet (with pianist Alice Coltrane, bassist Jimmy Garrison and drummer Rashied Ali) are briefer (2:48-8:54) than Coltrane's recordings of the previous year but that might have been due to the fact that this music was played in the studio (as opposed to the marathon live blowouts with Pharoah Sanders) or to Coltrane's worsening health. Actually 'Trane (who sticks here exclusively to tenor) is as powerful as usual, showing no compromise in his intense flights and indulging in sound explorations that are as free (but with purpose) as any he had ever done. Coltrane's true fans will want to go out of their way to acquire this intriguing CD. *—Scott Yanow*

Interstellar Space / Feb. 22, 1967 / Impulse! ✦✦✦✦
Not released for the first time until 1974 but now available in expanded form as a CD, this set of duets by tenor saxophonist John Coltrane and drummer Rashied Ali are full of fire, emotion and constant abstract invention. The original four pieces ("Mars," "Venus," "Jupiter" and "Saturn") are joined by "Leo" and "Jupiter Variation." Coltrane alternates quiet moments with sections of great intensity, showing off his phenomenal technique and ability to improvise without the need for chordal instruments. Rousing if somewhat inaccessible music. *—Scott Yanow*

☆ **The Classic Quartet: Complete Impulse! Studio Recordings** / Dec. 21, 1961-Sep. 22, 1965 / Impulse!/GRP ✦✦✦✦✦
In 1998, Impulse released this logical eight-CD set, which contains every studio recording by the quartet of John Coltrane (on tenor and soprano), pianist McCoy Tyner, bassist Jimmy Garrison and drummer Elvin Jones. In addition to those musicians, Roy Haynes is heard subbing for Jones on a few occasions, and Art Davis plays second bass on one session. Reissued in full are the albums *Coltrane, Ballads, Crescent, A Love Supreme, The John Coltrane Quartet Plays, Transition, Sun Ship, First Meditations* and *Infinity*. In addition, there are three numbers that were included in *The Definitive Jazz Scene*, plus the studio quartet performances that formed part of *Impressions, Live at Birdland* and *Kulu Se Mama*. The final disc consists of previously unreleased performances (all alternate takes) including "Crescent," "Bessie's Blues" and the "Resolution" section of *A Love Supreme*. What is missing are 'Trane's collaborations with Johnny Hartman and Duke Ellington, plus any selections that add other players (including Pharoah Sanders in 1965). The music is in strict chronological order, rather than being programmed as it was released; it is surprising how conservative many of the selections sound (particularly from the *Ballads* set), at least until 1965 arrives. However, when it came to "One Down, One Up," "Sun Ship" and the tenor/drums duet on "Vigil" in 1965, the music was blazing new paths and still sounds fairly radical. On a whole, this box (which includes such highlights as "Soul Eyes," "Out of This World," "Bessie's Blues," the complete "A Love Supreme," "Nature Boy," "Dear Lord," "One Down, One Up," "Welcome," "Sun Ship" and "Meditations") contains a great deal of wondrous music. Essential recordings, a must in every serious jazz collection in one form or another. *—Scott Yanow*

Eddie Condon (Albert Edwin Condon)

b. Nov. 16, 1905, Goodland, IN, **d.** Aug. 4, 1973, New York, NY
Guitar / Swing, Dixieland, Big Band
A major propagandist for freewheeling Chicago jazz, an underrated rhythm guitarist and a talented wisecracker, Eddie Condon's main importance to jazz was not so much through his own playing as in his ability to gather together large groups of all-stars and produce exciting, spontaneous and very coherent music. In 1927 he co-led (with Red McKenzie) the McKenzie-Condon Chicagoans on a record date that helped define Chicago jazz; although Condon had to an extent laid low since the beginning of the Depression, in 1938 with the opportunity to lead some sessions for the new Commodore label, he became a major name, utilizing top musicians in racially mixed groups. He started a long series of exciting recordings (which really continued on several labels up until his death) and his Town Hall concerts of 1944-45 (which were broadcast weekly on the radio) were consistently brilliant and gave him an opportunity to show his verbal acid wit. Condon opened his own club in 1945, recorded for Columbia in the 1950s and wrote three colorful books including his 1948 memoirs *We Called It Music*. *—Scott Yanow*

● **Dixieland All Stars** / Aug. 11, 1939-Mar. 27, 1946 / GRP/Decca ✦✦✦✦✦
Some but not all of Eddie Condon's studio recordings for Decca are included on this single CD. Since five of the 20 selections are actually previously unissued alternate takes and several songs are bypassed altogether, this release will probably drive some collectors mad, but the music is consistently enjoyable. The rhythm guitarist heads an impresssive outfit (with trumpeter Max Kaminsky, valve trombonist Brad Gowans, clarinetist Pee Wee Russell, Bud Freeman on tenor and pianist Joe Sullivan) on four titles from 1939 along with a variety of groups from 1944-46 that feature other top stylists including trumpeters Billy Butterfield, Bobby Hackett, Yank Lawson, Max Kaminsky and Wild Bill Davison, trombonists Jack Teagarden and Lou McGarity, baritonist Ernie Caceres, clarinetist Edmond Hall, Tony Parenti and Joe Dixon; the latter bands perform a variety of standards including eight George Gershwin songs. Dixieland and small-group swing fans will enjoy this set which serves as a strong example of Eddie Condon's music, at least until a more complete reissue of the valuable recordings takes place. *—Scott Yanow*

Town Hall Concerts, Vol. 1 / May 20, 1944-Jun. 10, 1944 / Jazzology ✦✦✦✦✦
Eddie Condon's *Town Hall Concerts* were historic in several ways. These weekly half-hour radio shows were very uncommercial (in fact they could not attract a sponsor), featured interracial bands and gave Condon an opportunity to put together well-paced programs. He would gather together a core band of Condonites who would have ensemble jams and individual features, and there were always a couple of numbers set aside for guest artists who would also join in on the show's concluding jam (titled "Impromptu Ensemble") with the regulars. Plus Condon, despite making a few too many jokes at the expense of Pee Wee Russell, proved to be a perfect host. After decades of only being available as incomplete excerpts, these programs have finally been issued complete and in chronological order on a series of two-CD sets by George Buck of Jazzology. The first volume, which has four complete shows, features such classic players as trumpeters Billy Butterfield, Bobby Hackett, Max Kaminsky, Hot Lips Page and Rex Stewart, clarinetists Pee Wee Russell and Edmond Hall, trombonists Bill Harris, Miff Mole and Benny Morton, the greatly underrated baritonist Ernie Caceres, and pianists James P. Johnson and Gene Schroeder. Although the recording quality of the very first show is subpar (the only one in the series that is less than flawless technically), all of the volumes in this wonderful series (which find the participants at the peak of their powers) are highly recommended. *—Scott Yanow*

Town Hall Concerts, Vol. 2 / Jun. 17, 1944-Jul. 8, 1944 / Jazzology ✦✦✦✦✦
This two-CD set has four complete radio shows featuring Eddie Condon's all-star groups during their legendary series of Town Hall concerts. Despite having large ensembles of classic players, Condon was able to feature virtually everyone on every show, still leaving room for ensemble pieces and interplay between the unique musicians. In addition, the verbal commentary of Condon and announcer Fred Robbins is informative and witty (even if they picked on Pee Wee Russell a bit too much). Among the musicians heard on the well-recorded set (which like the other volumes in this extensive series is highly recommended to fans of Chicago jazz) include trumpeters Bobby Hackett, Hot Lips Page, Max Kaminsky, Jonah Jones and Billy Butterfield, trombonists Bill Harris and Benny Morton, clarinetists Pee Wee Russell, Joe Marsala and Edmond Hall, baritonist Ernie Caceres and pianists James P. Johnson, Willie "The Lion" Smith and Gene Schroeder. *—Scott Yanow*

Town Hall Concerts, Vol. 3 / Jul. 15, 1944-Aug. 5, 1944 / Jazzology ✦✦✦✦✦
The third volume in this very valuable series of two-CD sets contains four half-hour weekly radio shows featuring Eddie Condon's all-star ensembles at Town Hall concerts. Condon (who supplies verbal commentary along with annnouncer Fred Robbins) programmed each show quite skillfully, featuring the large groups of all-stars in logical fashion. This set (which is highly recommended along with the other volumes in the series to followers of traditional jazz) features quite a roster: trumpeters Bobby Hackett, Jonah Jones, Max Kaminsky and Sterling Bose, trombonist Benny Morton, baritonist Ernie Caceres (who is really in peak form throughout the Condon programs), clarinetists Edmond Hall and Pee Wee Russell, guitarists Carl Kress and Tony Mottola, pianist Harry "The Hipster" Gibson (taking a couple of rare solos), Willie "The Lion" Smith, Jess Stacy and Gene Schroeder, bassist Bob Haggart, drummers Gene Krupa, Joe Grauso and George Wettling and singer Lee Wiley. *—Scott Yanow*

The Complete CBS Eddie Condon All Stars / Nov. 24, 1953-Sep. 4, 1962 / Mosaic ✦✦✦✦✦
Chicago jazz and Dixieland fans should go out of their way to pick up this limited-edition five-CD boxed set. The first four discs date from 1953-1957 and feature freewheeling performances (originally out on seven LPs) with such classic soloists as cornetists Wild Bill Davison and Bobby Hackett, trumpeter Billy Butterfield, trombonists Cutty Cutshall, Lou McGarity, and Vic Dickenson, clarinetists Edmond Hall, Peanuts Hucko, Bob Wilber, and Pee Wee Russell and tenorman Bud Freeman among others. Eddie Condon's comments during his band's waterlogged performance at the 1957 *Newport Jazz Festival* alone are worth the price. The final disc of material (all from 1962) is somewhat commercial but still has its moments of interest. *—Scott Yanow*

Ballin' the Jack / Commodore ✦✦✦✦✦
Eddie Condon & Band. Set-piece Condon, as old and conservative as ever. *—Michael G. Nastos*

Norman Connors

b. Mar. 1, 1947, Philadelphia, PA
Drums / Smooth Jazz, Quiet Storm, Crossover Jazz, Post-Bop, Fusion, Jazz-Funk, Urban
Like Roy Ayers, George Benson and Patrice Rushen, Norman Connors is best known for his major R&B hits but started out as a jazz improviser. The drummer/composer was born and raised in Philadelphia, where he lived in the same neighborhood as Bill Cosby and became interested in jazz when he was only a child. As a kid in elementary school, Connors was exposed to jazz extensively thanks to such schoolmates as drummer Lex Humphries and the younger brother of bassist and Jazz-Messenger-to-be Spanky De Brest. Connors was in junior high when he began sneaking into jazz clubs and sat in for Elvin Jones at a John Coltrane gig. At 13, he first got to meet his idol, Miles Davis, and started expressing his admiration for the famous trumpeter by dressing like him. Connors went on to study music at Philly's Temple University and the Juilliard School of Music in New York. Gigs with Jackie McLean, Jack McDuff and Sam Rivers followed, and he was first recorded as a sideman when Archie Shepp employed him on his 1967 Impulse! session *Magic of JuJu*. After touring with Pharoah Sanders and playing on several of his albums, Connors signed with Buddah's Cobblestone label in 1972 and recorded his first album as a leader, *Dance of Magic*. A few more jazz-oriented Cobblestone and Buddah dates followed, and it was in 1975 that Connors made R&B his main priority with *Saturday Night Special* (which included the *10 soul hit "Valentine Love"). The rest of the 1970s found $Connors* featuring R&B singers prominently (including Michael Henderson, Jean Carn and the late Phyllis Hyman) and scoring such R&B hits as "We Both Need Each Other," "Once I've Been There" and the lovely "You Are My Starship." Connors, who signed with Arista in 1977, wasn't as popular or as visible in the 1980s, although in the 1990s, he would make a comeback by signing with Motown's MoJazz label and focusing on both urban contemporary and crossover. *—Alex Henderson*

Norman Connors / Nov. 18, 1997 / BMG Special Products ♦♦♦
BMG Special Products' *Norman Connors: The Encore Collection* is a fine budget-priced collection that contains many of his most popular hits and best-known tunes. All of his pop hits and biggest R&B singles are here—"Valentine Love, " "We Both Need Each Other, " "You Are My Starship, " "Betcha By Golly Wow, " "Once I've Been There" and "This Is Your Life." It may not be a definitive collection, but any budget-minded casual fan looking for a basic colleciton of his mid-'70s fusion crossover hits will not be disappointed with this disc. *—Stephen Thomas Erlewine*

● **The Best of Norman Connors: Melancholy Fire** / Apr. 27, 1999 / Razor & Tie ♦♦♦♦
This excellent 1999 set is an overview of drummer and producer Connors' 1975-88 work. During the mid-'70s to the '80s he was leader of the fusion of jazz and R&B during its most influential and successful era. Unlike other compilations on similar artists, *The Best of Norman Connors: Melancholy Fire* centers on what made Connors such a popular and enduring artist and zeroes in on his skill as a bandleader and a hitmaker. After the relative failure of his early '70s efforts, Connors finally attained the jazz/R&B mix that suited him best. Tracks like "You Are My Starship," "Valentine Love," and "Betcha by Golly Wow" with its poignant reading from Phyllis Hyman, created the blueprint for Connors' sophisticated and emotional productions. Although most are familiar with Jean Carn, Phyllis Hyman, the collection also highlights many other of Connors' vocalists. Eleanor Mills' soulful and precise vocals can be heard on the flawless cover of Jimmy Webb's "This Is Your Life" and the funky and refined "Wouldn't You Like to See." By the late '70s, and perhaps due to lessened jazz content, Connors' hitmaking acumen began to wane. Tracks like "Invitation" and "Handle Me Gently" lack the necessary jazz quotient and challenging melodic sense of his earlier work. The masterful 1980 title track, featuring Glenn Jones, is more in line with Connors' production gifts. This album is one of a handful of compilations that doesn't attempt to rewrite history with unreleased tracks and failed experiments. This set is a necessity for Connors fans and lovers of intelligent jazz and R&B. *—Jason Elias*

Bob Cooper

b. Dec. 6, 1925, Pittsburgh, PA, **d.** Aug. 5, 1993, Hollywood, CA
Sax (Tenor), Oboe / West Coast Jazz, Hard Bop, Cool
One of the great West Coast tenors, Bob Cooper made even the most complex solos sound swinging and accessible. Coop joined Stan Kenton's big band in 1945 and he was a fixture with several of the editions (including the Innovations Orchestra) through 1951; in 1947 he married Kenton's singer, June Christy. After leaving Kenton, Cooper settled in Los Angeles where he was a busy studio musician for the next four decades. He was a regular member of the Lighthouse All-Stars from 1952-62, sometimes playing oboe and English horn (being the first strong jazz soloist on both of those instruments). The cool-toned tenor (whose sound fit into the "Four Brothers" style) was on many records in the 1950s (including those of Shorty Rogers, Pete Rugolo and June Christy) and continued working steadily in Los Angeles-area clubs up until his death. He appears on records with the big bands of Frank Capp/Nat Pierce, Bob Florence and the 1980s version of the Lighthouse All-Stars and participated in the 1991 Stan Kenton 50th-anniversary celebration. As a leader Coop recorded for Capitol in the 1950s, Contemporary, Trend, Discovery and Fresh Sound. *—Scott Yanow*

Shifting Winds / Apr. 26, 1955-Jun. 14, 1955 / Capitol ♦♦♦♦
Always a bit underrated, Bob Cooper (best-known for his fine tenor saxophone playing) was the first significant jazz improviser on oboe and English horn. This out-of-print LP features Coop in 1955 playing all three of his axes with a couple of overlapping all-star West Coast jazz groups. The octets consist of either Stu Williamson (on trumpet and valve trombone) or John Graas on French horn, Bob Enevoldsen tripling on valve trombone, tenor and bass clarinet, Bud Shank on flute, alto and tenor, Jimmy Giuffre on clarinet, tenor and baritone, pianist Claude Williamson, either Joe Mondragon, Max Bennett or Ralph Pena on bass, and Stan Levey or Shelly Manne on drums. The music is all arranged by Cooper and ranges from inventive reworkings of standards to jazz chamber music; despite the cool tones, the results are consistently exciting. These high-quality performances will hopefully be reissued on CD, for they feature Bob Cooper in prime form. A little-known gem, with this version of "'Round Midnight" (one of the highlights) showcasing Cooper's English horn. *—Scott Yanow*

● **Coop! The Music of Bob Cooper** / Aug. 26, 1958-Aug. 27, 1958 / Contemporary/OJC ♦♦♦♦♦
Tenor saxophonist Bob Cooper's only Contemporary album (reissued on CD in the Original Jazz Classics series) is a near-classic and one of his finest recordings. Coop, along with trombonist Frank Rosolino, vibrahonist Victor Feldman, pianist Lou Levy, bassist Max Bennett and drummer Mel Lewis, performs colorful versions of five standards (best are "Confirmation," "Easy Living" and "Somebody Loves Me") that show off his attractive tone and ability to swing at any tempo. Half of the release consists of his "Jazz Theme and Four Variations," a very interesting work that holds together quite well throughout 23Ω-minutes and five movements; three trumpeters (including Conte Candoli) and one trombone are added to make the ensembles richer. This set is an underrated gem. *—Scott Yanow*

Bob Cooper/Conde Candoli Quintet / Jun. 25, 1993 / VSOP ♦♦♦♦
It is difficult to believe, listening to this enthusiastic bop date, that tenor saxophonist Bob Cooper would pass away only 41 days after the recorded concert. Cooper never declined, and he certainly seems right in his prime, jamming eight standards with trumpeter Conte Candoli (long an underrated great), pianist Ross Tompkins, bassist John Leitham and drummer Paul Kreibich. Whether it be a romping "Confirmation," "Airegin," "Hackensack" or a medium-tempo "Come Sunday," this is a highly enjoyable straight-ahead set with everyone in excellent form. Bob Cooper certainly went out on top. *—Scott Yanow*

Chick Corea (Armando Anthony Corea)

b. Jun. 12, 1941, Chelsea, MA
Piano (Electric), Keyboards, Piano, Composer / Free Jazz, Post-Bop, Fusion
Chick Corea has been one of the most significant jazzmen of the past 30 years. Not content at any time to rest on his laurels, Corea has been involved in quite a few important musical projects and his musical curiosity has never dimmed. A masterful pianist who along with Herbie Hancock and Keith Jarrett was one of the top stylists to emerge after Bill Evans and McCoy Tyner, Corea is also one of the few electric keyboardists to be quite individual and recognizable on synthesizers. Initially, Corea picked up experience during the mid-'60s playing with several leaders including Mongo Santamaria, Herbie Mann and Stan Getz. He made his debut as a leader with 1966's *Tones for Joan's Bones* and two years later, joined Miles Davis as Herbie Hancock's gradual replacement. About a year after he left Davis, Corea formed Return to Forever, which started out as a melodic Brazilian group but soon embraced a pacesetting and high-powered brand of fusion. While the music was rock-oriented, it still retained the improvisations of jazz and Corea remained quite recognizable, even under the barrage of electronics. When RTF broke up in the late '70s, Corea generally emphasized his acoustic playing and appeared in a wide variety of contexts. During the mid-'80s, he formed a new fusion group, the Elektric Band, plus, to balance out his music, an Akoustic Trio. He remains an important force in modern jazz and every phase of his development has been well-documented on records. *—Scott Yanow*

Music Forever and Beyond: The Selected Works of Chick Corea / 1949-1996 / GRP ♦♦♦♦♦
This very attractive five-CD set does an excellent job of summing up the rather productive career of pianist-keyboardist Chick Corea. The first two discs have highlights from the 1964-82 period including a few sideman appearances, a previously unissued version of "Windows" played with Stan Getz, the original version of "Spain," four pieces from the Return to Forever days and numbers from his freelance projects of the late '70s (highlighted by the exciting "Central Park"). The third disc concentrates on Corea's GRP projects (1986-94), particularly his Elektric and Akoustic Bands (two selections were previously unissued) while the fourth CD is quite a grab-bag that includes collaborations with Herbie Hancock (a version of "Liza" that progresses from stride to free), Gayle Moran, John McLaughlin, Paco DeLucia, Gary Burton, Bobby McFerrin and Miles Davis (a new duet version of "I Fall in Love So Easily" from 1969). In addition Corea is heard as an eight-year old in 1949 on a privately recorded 78 playing a short piano solo and on a version of "'Round Midnight" with strings that was recorded for this 1996 box. In fact the fifth disc consists exclusively of new recordings of standards (plus one original) by Corea in an acoustic quartet with tenor saxophonist Bob Berg (who has rarely sounded more exciting). This well-conceived set is highly recommended even to Chick Corea fans who might have some of his earlier records. A gem. *—Scott Yanow*

Inner Space / Nov. 30, 1966-Jan. 196 / Atlantic ♦♦♦♦
This double album reissues Chick Corea's first album as a leader, *Tones for Joan's Bones,* adding two previously unissued tracks from the same session plus a pair of performances from a Hubert Laws date of the period that feature Corea's piano and writing. With such players as Joe Farrell on tenor and flute, trumpeter Woody Shaw, bassist Steve Swallow and drummer Joe Chambers on this Corea date, the pianist performs five of his originals plus "This Is New" while The Laws cuts include Corea's "Windows." Throughout, this advanced hard bop music, which keeps an open attitude toward the avant-garde innovations of the period, is consistently stimulating. Even at this early stage, Chick Corea's playing is quite recognizable. *—Scott Yanow*

Tones for Joan's Bones / Nov. 30, 1966-Dec. 1, 1966 / Atlantic ♦♦♦♦♦
Youthful Corea makes quick splash. This is an extremely rare album. *—Ron Wynn*

Now He Sings, Now He Sobs / Mar. 14, 1968-Mar. 27, 1968 / Blue Note ♦♦♦♦♦
The original LP (using the same title) only had five selections, but this CD contains 13, with the added eight (from the same sessions) having first been released on the double-LP *Circling In.* Age 26 at the time, and on the brink of gaining major recognition in the jazz world, pianist Chick Corea is featured with a very strong trio that also includes bassist Miroslav Vitous and drummer Roy Haynes. The music includes 11 of Corea's originals including "Matrix," "Windows" and "Samba Yantra," Thelonious Monk's "Pannonica" and the standard "My One and Only Love" and is essentially advanced hard bop with an open-minded attitude toward free jazz. Listen to how part of "Steps-What Was" has hints of Corea's future composition "Spain." *—Scott Yanow*

Song of Singing / Apr. 7, 1970-Apr. 8, 1970 / Blue Note ♦♦♦♦
This LP features the rhythm section of Circle (pianist Chick Corea, bassist Dave Holland and drummer Barry Altschul) playing rather advanced improvisations on group originals (highlighted by Holland's "Toy Room") and "Nefertiti." Influenced by the early Art Ensemble of Chicago, this music is rather free and avant-garde but rewards close listenings. *—Scott Yanow*

Early Circle / Apr. 8, 1970-Oct. 18, 1970 / Blue Note ♦♦♦♦
Chick Corea's most esoteric music of his career was performed when he was a member of Circle, an avant-garde quartet that during 1970-1971 featured pianist Corea, the reeds of Anthony Braxton, bassist Dave Holland, and drummer Barry Altschul. This CD contains some of their briefer performances including bass/piano and clarinet/piano duets, two versions of "Chimes," "Percussion Piece," a free ballad, and Braxton's "73 Degrees—A Kelvin." These free explorations are worth listening to closely, but one has to put away any preconceptions that they have about Corea. The title of this CD is a bit silly though, for Circle broke up only a few months after these recordings. —Scott Yanow

Circulus / Apr. 8, 1970-Aug. 21, 1970 / Blue Note ♦♦♦♦♦
Chick Corea has had a very diverse career and has consistently been among the most popular of all jazzmen, but his avant-garde music of 1970-1971 certainly will not appeal to fans of his fusion band, Return to Forever. His group, Circle, is well-showcased on this two-LP set which finds Corea, reed master Anthony Braxton, bassist Dave Holland, and drummer Barry Altschul performing three lengthy group improvisations. In addition, Altschul is showcased on "Percussion Piece," and Braxton sits out on the trio selection "Drone." The music is generally quite difficult with sound explorations emphasized over melodic development, and is much closer to the direction that Braxton would explore than what Corea would be playing

two years later. But open-eared listeners who enjoy avant-garde jazz will find much to savor during these fascinating performances from one of the new music's top (if short-lived) regular groups. *—Scott Yanow*

A.R.C. / Jan. 11, 1971–Jan. 13, 1971 / ECM ♦♦♦♦
This LP features pianist Chick Corea, bassist Dave Holland and drummer Barry Altschul during the brief period that, along with Anthony Braxton, they were members of the fine avant-garde quartet Circle. The music heard on this set is not quite as free as Circle's but often very explorative. Four of the six songs are Corea originals which, in addition to Holland's "Vedana" and Wayne Shorter's "Nefertiti," form a very viable set of adventurous jazz, recorded just a few months before Corea changed direction. *—Scott Yanow*

Paris Concert / Feb. 21, 1971 / ECM ♦♦♦♦♦
Of all of the recordings from the short-lived avant-garde quartet Circle, this double-LP is the most rewarding. Cut live in Paris, this set features pianist Chick Corea, the reeds of Anthony Braxton, bassist Dave Holland, and drummer Barry Altschul playing a wide variety of fairly free explorations. Highlights include their reinterpretation of the standard "There Is No Greater Love," the playful "Toy Room—Q & A," Braxton's "73 Degrees Kelvin," and "Nefertiti." The music is often quite abstract but generally colorful and innovative; Chick Corea would soon break up the band for other musical adventures, but this set remains one of the high points of his productive career. *—Scott Yanow*

☆ **Return to Forever** / Feb. 2, 1972-Feb. 3, 1975 / ECM ♦♦♦♦♦
Chick Corea's original version of Return to Forever (featuring Joe Farrell on flute and soprano, bassist Stanley Clarke, Airto on drums and percussion and singer Flora Purim along with the pianist/leader) only was in existence long enough to record two albums. This self-titled set is highlighted by a sidelong medley of "Sometime Ago" and "La Fiesta" and demonstrates that it is possible to create music that is both strong jazz and popular. *—Scott Yanow*

★ **Light As a Feather** / Oct. 1972 / Polydor ♦♦♦♦♦
The 1998 re-release of Return To Forever's *Light as a Feather*?the second, final, and most popular album of the band's first edition—as a two-CD set had the effect of nearly doubling the band's released output. The first disc contains the original album as sequenced, while the second contains over an hour of outtakes, including some new titles and tracks that were reconstructed from a number of takes. The actual album as originally released was a splendidly light, fluid, fleeting exercise in electric jazz with a strong whiff of Brazil, featuring Corea's lyrical, probing work on Rhodes electric piano and containing a number of Corea tunes—especially the Rodrigo-based "Spain"—that became standards. Airto Moreira was a whirlwind on trap drums and overdubbed percussion, Flora Purim's vocals gave the band some commercial appeal; Stanley Clarke made his first astounding impact on electric and standup basses; Joe Farrell contributed superb wind solos. The outtakes are of uniformly high quality, all but one unmarked by post-production, with excellent solos all around. The major surprise is four takes of an unreleased tune, "What Games Shall We Play Today?," a great little Chick Corea boogaloo with a delicate wah-wah pedal applied to the Rhodes. It was heartening to see the jazz industry finally starting to document its electric music heritage with the same thoroughness once reserved only for acoustic jazz landmarks. *—Richard S. Ginell*

Crystal Silence / Nov. 6, 1972 / ECM ♦♦♦

Romantic Warrior / Feb. 1976 / Columbia/Legacy ♦♦♦

★ **My Spanish Heart** / Oct. 1976 / Polydor ♦♦♦♦♦
Chick Corea has long been one of the most distinctive of all electric keyboardists, being able to transfer his mastery of the acoustic piano successfully to synthesizers. This double-LP, a classic of its genre, is full of delightful new melodies (particularly the last section of "El Bozo") and masterful keyboard playing along with a few guest appearances by a string quartet, a small brass section, singer Gayle Moran, bassist Stanley Clarke and drummer Steve Gadd. *—Scott Yanow*

Friends / 1978 / Polydor ♦♦♦♦
Although this set contains eight lesser-known Chick Corea compositions, it is in reality a fine blowing date. Corea, on both acoustic and electric pianos, is joined by his old friend Joe Farrell on reeds, bassist Eddie Gomez and drummer Steve Gadd for some fine straightahead jazz. *—Scott Yanow*

Live in Montreux / 1981 / Stretch ♦♦♦♦♦
This important live recording from 1981 features the great pianist with a stunning group: Joe Henderson on tenor sax, Gary Peacock on bass, and Roy Haynes on drums. Haynes worked with Corea on many prior occasions, and Henderson was about to collaborate with him on the Griffith Park albums of the early '80s, but this is the first time the three appear together. Peacock's presence is an additional delight. The probing bassist contributes the multi-layered, magnificent "Up, Up and.... "

Three of Corea's compositions here—"Hairy Canary," "Folk Song," and "Slippery When Wet"—would later wind up as bonus tracks on Stretch's 1994 reissue of the 1981 CD *Three Quartets*. In addition, there are valuable renditions of two dense and challenging Corea tunes, "Psalm" and "Quintet 2," along with two standards: Thelonius Monk's "Trinkle, Tinkle" and Cole Porter's "So in Love." The latter culminates in a four-minute Haynes drum solo.

Overall, the record is essential for fans of any and all of the four musicians involved. *—David R. Adler*

Trio Music / Nov. 1981 / ECM ♦♦♦♦
Pianist Chick Corea had a reunion with bassist Miroslav Vitous and drummer Roy Haynes for this double LP, 13 years after they had recorded *Now He Sings, Now He Sobs*. The first half of this two-fer consists of duet and trio-free improvisations and is sometimes a touch lightweight even with moments of interest; playing free was not as natural to Corea by this time as it had been in the 1960s. However, the second album, seven Thelonious Monk compositions, comes across quite well as Corea does justice to the spirit of Monk without losing his own strong musical personality. *—Scott Yanow*

Trio Music: Live in Europe / Sep. 1984 / ECM ♦♦♦♦
Pianist Chick Corea had a reunion with bassist Miroslav Vitous and drummer Roy Haynes for this well-rounded set of trio performances. In addition to three standards (including "I Hear a Rhapsody" and "Night and Day"), the group performs a touch of classical music and four originals. *—Scott Yanow*

Light Years / 1987 / GRP ♦♦♦♦
The second recording by Chick Corea's Elektric Band was the first to feature altoist Eric Marienthal and guitarist Frank Gambale in addition to bassist John Patitucci, drummer Dave Weckl and the leader/keyboardist. Unlike most other fusion groups, these musicians displayed original musical personalitites and Corea's compositions tended to be memorable. This is one of The Elektric Band's better releases. *—Scott Yanow*

Eye of the Beholder / 1988 / GRP ♦♦♦♦♦
During an era when the word "fusion" was applied to any mixture of jazz with pop or funk, Chick Corea's Elektric Band reinforced the word's original meaning: a combination of jazz improvisations with the power, rhythms and sound of rock. *Eye of the Beholder,* which found guitarist Frank Gambale, saxophonist Eric Marienthal and bassist John Patitucci displaying increasingly original solo voices, is one of this group's finest recordings and ranks with the best fusion of the latter half of the 1980s. *—Scott Yanow*

Akoustic Band / Jan. 2, 1989–Jan. 3, 1989 / GRP ♦♦♦♦
As a contrast to his Elektric Band, Chick Corea formed The Akoustic Band with bassist John Patitucci and drummer Dave Weckl. This trio gave him a chance to stretch out acoustically in a straightahead setting on a variety of standards and originals. Their debut release is highlighted by "Bessie's Blues," "My One and Only Love," "Someday My Prince Will come" and Corea's "Spain." *—Scott Yanow*

Inside Out / 1990 / GRP ♦♦♦♦

Expressions / 1993 / GRP ♦♦♦♦
Although Chick Corea has recorded quite a few releases throughout his career, solo albums are rare, particularly ones in which he explores standards. This acoustic set (which he dedicated to Art Tatum) finds Corea performing such songs as "Lush Life," "My Ship," Bud Powell's "Oblivion" and even the veteran warhorse "I Want to Be Happy" with individuality, respect and creativity. *—Scott Yanow*

Paint the World / 1993 / GRP ♦♦♦♦

Remembering Bud Powell / 1997 / Stretch ♦♦♦♦♦
Pianist Chick Corea in 1996 gathered together some notable young all-stars (tenor-saxophonist Joshua Redman, trumpeter Wallace Roney, altoist Kenny Garrett, bassist Christian McBride, plus veteran drummer Roy Haynes) for explorations of tunes by the innovative pianist Bud Powell. Although "Bouncin' With Bud," "Tempus Fugit" and "Celia" have been occasionally recorded by others, most of the complex songs (including "Mediocre," "Dusk In Sandi," "Oblivion" and "Glass Enclosure") have rarely been played in recent decades. Rather than play revivalist bebop, Corea and his associates (after authentically stating the melody) perform modern post bop improvisations in their own styles, so much of the music is way beyond bop. In addition to nine Powell songs, Corea contributed a song rightfully titled "Bud Powell." All of the talented musicians have a fair amount of solo space and sound consistently inspired, making this a very successful and easily recommended project. *—Scott Yanow*

Change / Jun. 8, 1999 / Rykodisc ♦♦♦♦
Following the massive live outpouring of music that marked the debut of Corea's band Origin, this studio album begins to fulfill some of the sextet's possibilities; hence, the completely appropriate title. The front line is unchanged from the live albums (Steve Wilson and Bob Sheppard on reeds and flutes, Steve Davis on trombone), Avishai Cohen remains on bass, and Jeff Ballard replaces Adam Cruz on drums. Again, though everyone solos and interacts intelligently and energetically, Corea is still Origin's most distinctive presence, and he reinforces his dominance by being the album's sole composer, save for Cohen's "Lylah." Corea makes his debut on marimba on the leadoff track, "Wigwam," which he plays in an Afro-Cuban-spiced manner (his Spanish tinge on marimba is even more pronounced in live performance). "Armando's Tango" sends the Latin explorations further South, while "Little Flamenco" is a busy, highly syncopated, high-energy outing driven by a simulation of flamenco hand-clapping by Ballard with nice flute work by Wilson. But when "Early Afternoon Blues" harkens back to bedrock hard bop in every respect, straight out of Blue Note, the CD settles pretty much back into the mainstream with a few quirky compositional motifs to pique your interest. The best tune on the CD is the closer, "Awakening," which echoes all the way back to Corea's triumphant RTF album *Where Have I Known You Before*. *—Richard S. Ginell*

Piano Originals / Nov. 14, 1999-Nov. 30, 1999 / Concord Jazz ♦♦♦♦
Perhaps hearkening back to 1971's two-volume *Piano Improvisations*, pianist Chick Corea issues this majestic, two-part solo recording, the first disc of which features his original compositions. The music spans Corea's career thus far: opening with "Brasilia" and then "Yellow Nimbus"—the latter written for flamenco guitarist Paco De Lucia—he goes on to play "Armando's Rhumba," three selections from the 1983 solo piano album *Children's Songs*, and then a short, to-the-point "Spain," probably his most famous piece. (The finale, "Children's Song *12*," runs over thirteen minutes.) Curiously, he also includes two preludes by classical composer Alexander Scriabin—one of which he also played solo on 1986's *Trio Music: Live in Europe*. In an engaging twist, Corea plays four consecutive free improvisations, each inspired by an image or idea solicited from members of the concert audience: "April Snow," "The Chase," "The Falcon," and "Swedish Landscape" (The last title came from Corea himself). Each is a marvel of improvisational ingenuity and technical poise. To give credit where it is due, the idea of a two-part series featuring originals and standards was executed earlier by a much younger pianist, Ethan Iverson on *Construction Zone* and *Deconstruction Zone*. But regardless, Corea's two-disc opus serves as a sort of state-of-the-union address for his mu-

sicianship and piano mastery. While his chameleonic ways over the years have yielded some mixed results, this is Corea "unplugged," if you will, and at his very best. *—David R. Adler*

Piano Standards / Nov. 15, 1999-Nov. 30, 1999 / Stretch ♦♦♦♦
Part two of Corea's solo piano series features standard tunes. There is a preponderance of Thelonious Monk music: "Monk's Dream," "Blue Monk," "Ask Me Now," and "'Round Midnight." Bud Powell, another piano legend whose music Corea has recorded and studied closely over the years, is represented by "Dusk in Sandi" and "Oblivion." The more universally familiar selections are "But Beautiful," "Thinking of You," "Yesterdays," "It Could Happen to You," "So in Love," "How Deep Is the Ocean," and "Brazil." Corea knows this music intimately and is uniquely able to mine each selection for fresh insights and possibilities. There are few pianists alive who equal Corea in stature and influence, and this beautiful concert recording reminds us of his continuing importance as an interpreter of jazz tradition. *—David R. Adler*

Larry Coryell

b. Apr. 2, 1943, Galveston, TX
Guitar / Post-Bop, Fusion
As one of the pioneers of jazz-rock—perhaps *the* pioneer in the ears of some—Larry Coryell deserves a special place in the history books. He brought what amounted to a nearly alien sensibility to jazz electric guitar playing in the 1960s, a hard-edged, cutting tone, phrasing and note-bending that owed as much to blues, rock and even country as it did to earlier, smoother bop influences. Yet as a true eclectic, he is comfortable in almost every style, from the most decibel-heavy, distortion-laden electric work to the most delicate, soothing, intricate lines on acoustic guitar. After moving to New York in 1965, he made a startling recorded debut on Chico Hamilton's *The Dealer*, played with the proto-jazz-rock band the Free Spirits and spread his name even further during 1967-68 with Gary Burton's combo and on Herbie Mann's popular *Memphis Underground*. He also formed a group called Foreplay (later 11th House) in 1969, and issued a string of well-received solo records for Vanguard (including 1970's *Spaces*). By 1975 however, Coryell had pulled the plug and begun concentrating on acoustic guitar. He recorded Brazilian music with Dori Caymmi, mainstream jazz for Muse, solo guitar for Shanachie and Acoustic Music, and an album of classical transcriptions. Coryell will probably remain as eclectic as ever throughout his career, which will no doubt make life difficult for musicologists with a yen for pigeonholing. *—Richard S. Ginell*

The Essential Larry Coryell / 1968-1975 / Vanguard ♦♦♦♦♦
When Larry Coryell recorded the sides gathered on this 70-minute CD, fusion was still a new and radical idea—and the guitarist was one of the adventurers who did more than his part to get the ball rolling. Coryell's diehard followers will be familiar with most of this material, but for novices, *The Essential Larry Coryell* can serve as a splendid introduction to his Vanguard output. This diverse compilation ranges from 1968's landmark "Stiffneck" (a duet with drummer Elvin Jones that is among the earliest examples of fusion) to the abrasive, Jimi Hendrix-influenced "The Jam with Albert" to the haunting "Spaces (Infinite)," which unites Coryell with another very influential fusion guitarist: John McLaughlin. It's hard to miss Miles Davis' influence on "Yin," a gem underscoring the initial excellence of Coryell's *Eleventh House*. But even so, there's no mistaking the fact that Coryell was very much a visionary in his own right. *—Alex Henderson*

Barefoot Boy / 1971 / One Way ♦♦♦♦♦
Produced by Bob Thiele and recorded at *Electric Lady* studios with engineer Eddie Kramer, *Barefoot Boy* is one of Larry Coryell's finest recordings as a leader. "Gypsy Queen" was recorded prior to bassist Mervin Bronson's arrival at the studio, and features the percussion section locking into a groove over which Coryell lays down a riff and Steve Marcus cuts loose with a fiery soprano sax solo. When it's his turn to solo on this opening number, Coryell turns up the heat, sounding like a cross between Jimi Hendrix and Sonny Sharrock. (Coryell played with Sharrock on Herbie Mann's *Memphis Underground*.) "The Great Escape" finds Coryell cooking over a bass and percussion groove, with Marcus on tenor sax. "Call to the Higher Consciousness" is a side-long 20-minute jam in which all the players take a ride, with Marcus once again cooking on the soprano sax. Roy Haynes is superb throughout, working in tandem with the percussionists to keep the music moving. This recording is a noteworthy example of the possibilities inherent in the early days of fusion, blending the electrifying energy of rock with the improvisational excitement of jazz. *—Jim Newsom*

● **Introducing Larry Coryell & The 11th House** / 1972 / Vanguard ♦♦♦♦♦
The Eleventh House during 1972-1975 was one of the stronger working groups in fusion, led by one of the unsung heroes of the idiom, guitarist Larry Coryell. This CD reissue brings back the Eleventh House's first recording and, in addition to Coryell's guitar, most heavily featured are trumpeter Randy Brecker (who would later be replaced by Mike Lawrence) and keyboardist Mike Mandel; bassist Danny Trifan and drummer Alphonse Mouzon are strong in backup roles. The influence of Miles Davis, Weather Report, and Herbie Hancock is apparent, but the Eleventh House also offered a sound of their own. Brecker's solos are often both fiery and lyrical (although his use of an occasional electric wah-wah device is less interesting). Coryell and Mandel blend together quite well, and the original grooves on this set often have distinctive personalities. Pity that the reissue does not have any liner notes, otherwise it is easily recommended to fans of early fusion. *—Scott Yanow*

Bolero / Apr. 18, 1981-Nov. 1983 / Evidence ♦♦♦♦
Among the most flexible of jazz guitarists, Larry Coryell performs ten unaccompanied and largely acoustic solos and plays four duets with fellow guitarist Brian Keane (who has "A Piece for Larry" to himself). The intimate selections often come across as improvised classical music (although all but a couple of Ravel themes were composed by one of the two guitarists), with Coryell emphasizing the beauty of his tone and the melodic side of his style. This CD reissue was originally issued by the German String label. *—Scott Yanow*

Just Like Being Born / 1984 / Flying Fish ♦♦♦♦
With Brian Keane (g), it features soothing acoustic guitar duets by two excellent players. *—Paul Kohler*

Together / Aug. 1985 / Concord Jazz ♦♦♦♦♦
This interesting and one-time matchup features Larry Coryell and Emily Remler on a set of guitar duets. It is easy to tell the two players apart, yet their styles were quite complementary. Highlights of the date (which has four standards, Pat Martino's "Gerri's Blues," and two Coryell originals) include "Joy Spring," "How My Heart Sings" and "How Insensitive." *—Scott Yanow*

Spaces Revisited / Feb. 25, 1997-Feb. 26, 1997 / Shanachie ♦♦♦♦
What started as a project to reunite Coryell with Billy Cobham on drums in order to take a second look at the sound and style of the Coryell's *Spaces* ended up creating a whole new chapter instead. With Richard Bona on bass and Bireli Lagrene on guitar, these nine songs capture the spirit of that 30-year-old session with new, adventuresome playing and vigor. Coryell takes great pride in the spontaneity of this project—one day rehearsal, two days recording—and well he should, since it contains musicians interacting with each other in a loose yet totally on-top-of-their-game manner. Bireli shines on the 9/8 section "Variations on Goodbye Pork Pie Hat," while Bona solos beautifully on "Blues for Django and Stephane." Yet it's ultimately Coryell's and Cobham's show, and their playing throughout is sublime with the on-the-spot recording of "Hong Kong Breeze"—an off the cuff head arrangement done in one take—showcasing their two players/one mind interplay. Maybe you can't go home again, but this album clearly proves you can always take your luggage with you and build a whole new house. *—Cub Koda*

Monk, 'Trane, Miles & Me / May 28, 1998 / High Note ♦♦♦♦
This recording properly acknowledges Coryell's main influences, swings nicely, delves into his underappreciated mellow side, and reaffirms his status as an enduring jazz guitarist who still has plenty to say. Gone are the flash and the kamikaze riffs in favor of lean chords and structured, sensible, slightly gritty linear improvisations.

Tributes to his heroes fall along standard company lines. Still, there's a lingering trace of the steely, hair-trigger old days of fusion in his interpretation of Thelonious Monk's spastic "Trinkle Tinkle" with tenor saxophonist Willie Williams. For contrast is the warm, spiritual blanket of John Coltrane's "Naima" and the forthright reading of the twelve-bar blues "Up 'Gainst the Wall" featuring Williams. The elongated lines of Miles Davis's "All Blues" almost lull you into a false sense of security, so beautifully subtle, understated and cool are they. Coryell always chooses extraordinary sidemen, and when you pick pianist John Hicks (on four cuts, including the gorgeous "Naima") bassist Santi Debriano and drummer Yoron Israel, you've got a winning team. It's also great that Coryell introduces new material, like the soulful, swinging "Fairfield County Blues," Hicks and Coryell in complete accord, with a tip of the chordal-and-single-line-combo hat to Wes Montgomery. "Almost a Waltz," also written by the leader, is molasses slow, in 4/4, and a calm ending to this fulfilling disc. Coryell's virtuosity is evident; harnessed, and sounding better than ever, utilizing a prototype Cort LCS-1 model he designed. Several recent efforts can also be easily recommended, but this finely crafted recording ranks with any of his many better-to-best dates. *—Michael G. Nastos*

Coryells / Jan. 25, 2000 / Chesky ♦♦♦♦
Like father, like sons, acoustic guitarist Larry Coryell and sons Julian and Murali get together for their first recorded project, and it sounds fine. Larry tends to dominate improv space, but doesn't get in the way of his kids, who are adept in their own bluesy ways. Bassist Brain Torff and percussionist Alphonse Mouzon (no drum kit, only hand drums and tambourine) join on several selections. Murali sings in his down-home, slightly affectated manner for three cuts, quite soulfully on the Rahsaan Roland Kirk lyric re: Lester Young on "Goodbye Porkpie Hat," on the original pop blues "Somebody's Got to Win-Lose," and on Al Green's simple, funk-blues "Love & Happiness." Julian has two features by himself, with Torff only on the easy two-beat "Something Pretty" and the nice waltz "Song for Emily." The hippest workout between the three occurs during the bulk of Julian's "Sink or Swim," while up and down, cascading and tumbling, waterfall crystalline-clear guitars shine on Larry's "Transparance." Two tracks are unearthed from Larry's days with the Eleventh House: the stunning "Low-Lee-Tah" is dark, moody, and ominous, with Larry playing the intricate melody first all the way through and his sons joining in with heavy embellishments and startling improvisation; "Funky Waltz" is not so much funky as the loud original, but shaded with Native American punctuations from Mouzon. Though some speedy lines crop up here and there, this is a more musical than pyrotechnical display that proves quite enjoyable throughout. A very good first step for the Coryell family's musical bonding recorded for public display, this is definitely recommended. *—Michael G. Nastos*

Curtis Counce

b. Jan. 23, 1926, Kansas City, MO, **d.** Jul. 31, 1963, Los Angeles, CA
Bass / West Coast Jazz, Hard Bop
Curtis Counce was an in-demand session bassist and one of the first African-Americans to get heavily involved in the West Coast jazz movement in the 1940s. He studied violin and tuba in addition to bass before leaving his native city for employment with the Nat Towles Band in Omaha at the age of 16. He moved to L.A. in 1945, taking a job with Johnny Otis at the Club Alabam and made his recording debut with Lester Young the following year. He recorded prolifically as a sideman (Shelly Manne, Lyle Murphy, Teddy Charles, Clifford Brown) before starting his famous quintet in 1956. His premature death from a heart attack was a tragic loss to jazz. All of Counce's Contemporary dates as a leader have been reissued, as has the once rare *Exploring the Future*. An added bonus was the appearance of previously unreleased Contemporary masters on the 1989 CD *Sonority*. *—Ken Dryden*

● **Landslide** / Oct. 8, 1956-Oct. 15, 1956 / Contemporary/OJC ♦♦♦♦♦
During 1956-57 bassist Curtis Counce led an excellent Los Angeles-based hard bop quintet comprised of trumpeter Jack Sheldon, tenor saxophonist Harold Land, pianist Carl Perkins, bassist Curtis Counce and drummer Frank Butler. They recorded four albums worth of material for Contemporary, all of which have been reissued on CD (three as part of the Original Jazz Classics series). For their debut album, the group performs selections by Land ("Landslide"), Perkins, Sheldon and two by Gerald Wiggins (including "Sonar") plus the lone

standard "Time After Time." All of Counce's recordings (which include a slightly later album for Dootone) are well worth getting by collectors interested in 1950s straightahead jazz; this disc is an excellent place to start. *—Scott Yanow*

You Get More Bounce with Curtis Counce / Oct. 8, 1956-Sep. 3, 1957 / Contemporary/OJC ♦♦♦♦
Although the title and even the cover photo have been changed, this CD reissue has the same music as was earlier issued as *Counceltation;* the "bonus cut" "Woody'n You" has also been reissued on *Sonority.* In any case, the program features the underrated but talented Curtis Counce Quintet of 1956-57, a group consisting of the bassist-leader, trumpeter Jack Sheldon, tenor saxophonist Harold Land, pianist Carl Perkins and drummer Frank Butler. Counce contributed two originals but otherwise the band sticks to jazz standards with some of the best moments being on "Too Close for Comfort," "Mean to Me" and Charlie Parker's "Big Foot." *—Scott Yanow*

Carl's Blues / Aug. 29, 1957-Jan. 6, 1958 / Contemporary/OJC ♦♦♦♦
Although the Curtis Counce Quintet was not a commercial success, their four Contemporary albums (which have been reissued on CD) were all timeless in their own way, undated examples of high-quality hard bop from the late '50s. This set features the bassist-leader, either Jack Sheldon or Gerald Wilson on trumpet, tenor saxophonist Harold Land, pianist Carl Perkins and drummer Frank Butler interpreting both jazz standards (including "Love Walked In" and Clifford Brown's "Larue") and originals (such as the drummer's "The Butler Did It"). Excellent music that still sounds fresh four decades later. *—Scott Yanow*

Hank Crawford (Bennie Ross Crawford, Jr.)

b. Dec. 21, 1934, Memphis, TN
Sax (Alto) / Hard Bop, Soul-Jazz, R&B
Hank Crawford's greatest contribution to music has been his soulful sound, one that is immediately idenitifiable and flexible enough to fit into several types of settings. Early on he played with B.B. King, Bobby Bland and Ike Turner in Memphis before moving to Nashville to study at Tennessee State College. He gained fame with Ray Charles (1958-63), at first playing baritone before switching to alto and becoming the music director. During 1959-69 Crawford recorded a popular series of soul jazz albums for Atlantic that made his reputation. His 1970s sets for Kudu were more commercial and streakier but in 1982 Crawford started recording regularly for Milestone, often matched up with organist Jimmy McGriff or pianist Dr. John. An influence on David Sanborn, Crawford's very appealing sound can still be heard in prime form in the mid-'90s. *—Scott Yanow*

Heart and Soul: The Hank Crawford Anthology / Jul. 5, 1958-Sep. 9, 1992 / Rhino/Atlantic ♦♦♦
This is one of the better of Rhino's two-CD samplers of Atlantic jazz artists. Altoist Hank Crawford, one of the most soulful stylists to emerge during the 1960s, is heard on 31 of his best recordings, 27 as a leader plus sideman appearances with Ray Charles, David "Fathead" Newman, B.B. King and Etta James. Crawford's sound and style were virtually the same in the 1990s as they were in the '60s although the settings changed a bit. Highlights of this well-conceived introduction include "Please Send Me Someone to Love," "Two Years of Torture," "Don't Get Around Much Anymore," "The Very Thought of You," "Trouble in Mind" and "Hank's Groove." Recommended to listeners not familiar with the beauty of Hank Crawford's playing. *—Scott Yanow*

After Hours / Oct. 19, 1965-Jan. 19, 1966 / Atlantic ♦♦♦
The most unusual aspect to this straight CD reissue of a Hank Crawford Atlantic Lp is that the altoist plays some very effective piano on two numbers including a lengthy feature on "After Hours." Fortunately his alto playing is not neglected and he really shows off his appealing tone on "Who Can I Turn To," "Makin' Whoopee" and "When Did You Leave Heaven." A fine soulful crossover set that is quite accessible and melodic. *—Scott Yanow*

Indigo Blue / Aug. 22, 1983-Aug. 23, 1983 / Milestone ♦♦♦♦
All of altoist Hank Crawford's many Milestone recordings of the 1980s and '90s are fine examples of his soulful approach to playing straightahead jazz. This CD, which ranges in repertoire from "The Very Thought of You" and "Things Ain't What They Used to Be" to Willie Nelson's "Funny," showcases Crawford's immediately distinctive alto in a quintet with pianist-organist Dr. John and guitarist Melvin Sparks that is augmented by a four-piece horn section arranged by the leader. Accessible and reasonably creative music. *—Scott Yanow*

Soul Survivors / Jan. 29, 1986-Jan. 30, 1986 / Milestone ♦♦♦♦
Hank Crawford's fifth in his long string of Milestone recordings was the first of several to team the soulful altoist with organist Jimmy McGriff. Guitarists George Benson and the lesser-known Jim Pittsburgh are on three songs apice while Bernard Purdie is on drums except on "Frim Fram Sauce" where Mel Lewis takes his spot. The superior material and the infectious swing supplied by McGriff and his rhythm mates inspire Hank Crawford to some of his best playing of the era. Recommended. *—Scott Yanow*

Steppin' Up / Jun. 15, 1987-Jun. 16, 1987 / Milestone ♦♦♦♦
Altoist Hank Crawford and organist Jimmy McGriff met up for a second time on this 1987 CD, and the results are predictably soulful and pleasing. With guitarist Jimmy Ponder and drummer Vance James completing the quartet and pianist Billy Preston (rarely heard in this type of setting) sitting in successfully on three of the seven numbers, this is a highly enjoyable outing, easily recommended for soul-jazz fans. Among the highlights are "River's Invitation," "Tippin' In" and McGriff's "Steppin' Up." *—Scott Yanow*

● **On the Blue Side** / Apr. 4, 1989–Aug. 9, 1989 / Milestone ♦♦♦♦♦
With Jimmy McGriff on Hammond organ and Jimmy Ponder on guitar. Funky, mellow, and gritty. *—Ron Wynn*

Road Tested / Jun. 30, 1997-Jul. 1, 1997 / Milestone ♦♦♦♦
Jimmy McGriff continued on a high roll on his second tour with Milestone, taping another dual-billed soul-jazz album with the redoubtable Hank Crawford. You know what to expect by now—hardass, down-home, blues-drenched organ trio-plus-sax grooving—but this is a really potent gusher of that genre, rising to the level of McGriff's idiom-defining *The Dream Team* from 1996. Throughout, Crawford produces some sterling roadhouse tenor work and guitarist Wayne Boyd stays resolutely in the pocket. Drummer Bernard Purdie stokes the engines from the opening crack of the funky "Peanuts," and contributes to a refreshingly kicking transformation of "I Only Have Eyes for You," and lays on a devastating backbeat whenever asked. John Coltrane's minor blues "Mr. P.C." also responds well to the soul-jazz treatment. Recorded the old-fashioned Prestige way—in two sessions, with Bob Porter producing in Rudy Van Gelder's studio—it's amazing and gratifying that bluesicians are still allowed to make records this way. *—Richard S. Ginell*

World of Hank Crawford / Feb. 8, 2000 / Milestone ♦♦♦♦
Rather than stick completely with the down-home soul-jazz rituals that have served him well in his previous several releases, Crawford mixes up his pitches in this more-inclusively titled outing—or he seems to. For once the semi-samba stylings and straight-ahead jazz solos of "Grab the World" and funky gospel flavor of the Crusaders tune "Way Back Home" are disposed of, and Crawford returns to the Mother Church, as it were, for the core of the disc. To cite two examples, Duke Ellington's "Come Sunday" is exactly what you might expect from this soulmeister: slow and soulful, with organ swimming underneath the bluesy alto sax wailings and overdubbed gospel piano. "Sonnymoon for Two" gets right down to the bedrock soul-jazz groove on the blues. Then, two cuts from the end, Tadd Dameron's "Good Bait" and "Star Eyes," take us back to Crawford's bop side. Melvin Sparks gets a lot of solo space with his soulful urban guitar, Danny Mixon takes care of business on both piano and organ, spelling out the bass on the pedals when bassist Stanley Banks sits out, and Kenny Washington is on drums. Marcus Belgrave (trumpet) and Ronnie Cuber (baritone saxophone) form a new front line on the stylistically varied outer tracks. Nice change of pace, though not that big of a change for this soulful veteran. *—Richard Ginell*

Low Flame, High Heat / Oct. 7, 1960-Mar. 21, 1966 / Label M. ♦♦♦

Marilyn Crispell

b. Mar. 30, 1947, Philadelphia, PA
Piano / Avant-Garde Jazz, Avant-Garde
One of the finest modern jazz pianists, Marilyn Crispell first emerged as an exciting, adventurous soloist and composer on the free scene in the early '80s. She was a member of the Anthony Braxton Quartet during the '80s and '90s, and also led a number of her own dates (mostly for Leo and Music & Arts) during this period. Although not as widely acclaimed as she deserves, Crispell is nevertheless gaining increased respect, and fewer write-offs as simply a pianist in the Cecil Taylor vein.

Crispell is a rarity in that she's not interested in hard bop nor jazz/hip-hop or fusion. Her style, with its slashing phrases, percussive mode, clusters and speed, pays homage to Cecil Taylor (whom she reveres), but isn't merely an imitation. She's not as dance-oriented, and her use of space, African rhythms and chording also recall Thelonious Monk and Paul Bley, two others she cites as influences, along with Leo Smith.

Crispell started piano lessons at seven at the Peabody Music School in Baltimore. She later studied piano and composition at the New England Conservatory in Boston. Crispell abandoned music for marriage and medical work in 1969. But she returned to the music world six years later, moving to Cape Cod after a divorce and being introduced to the sound of transitional John Coltrane (*A Love Supreme*) by pianist George Kahn. Crispell attended Karl Berger's Creative Music Studio and studied jazz harmony with Charlie Banacos in Boston. She met Anthony Braxton at the studio, and toured Europe with his Creative Music Orchestra in 1978, recording on his *Composition 98* album in 1981. Crispell began playing solo and leading groups in the '80s, teaming with Billy Bang and John Betsch in one band. She made several albums on the Music & Arts and Leo labels, among others, working with Reggie Workman, Doug James, Andrew Cyrille, Anthony Davis, Tim Berne, Marcio Mattos, Eddie Prevost and several others.

Crispell continued recording throughout the '90s, yielding a number of incredible albums and interesting line-ups that included her Braxton Quartet bandmates Mark Dresser and Gerry Hemingway, as well as sessions with Paul Motian, Irene Schweizer, Workman, Georg Graewe, Braxton, Gary Peacock, Fred Anderson and many others, not to mention a few solo recordings including *Live at Mills College 1995.* Marilyn Crispell has performed at a large number of jazz and avant-garde festivals, occasionally as a solo artist, as with her set at FIMAV (aka Victoriaville) 2000, which preceded a solo set by Cecil Taylor. *—Ron Wynn*

● **Spirit Music** / May 15, 1981–Jan. 13, 1982 / Cadence ♦♦♦♦♦
Marilyn Crispell is one of the most significant piano voices of the avant-garde. A powerful player influenced by Cecil Taylor but who has her own way of using space, Crispell has been closely associated with Anthony Braxton's group during the past decade. This Cadence release, however, finds her leading her own trio, an unusual group which also includes violinist Billy Bang and drummer John Betsch. On one of the four lengthy improvisations heard on this set, guitarist Wes Brown makes the band a quartet. These stirring performances serve as a fine introduction to the passionate music of Marilyn Crispell. *—Scott Yanow*

For Coltrane / Jul. 10, 1987 / Leo ♦♦♦♦

Labyrinths / Oct. 2, 1987 / Victo ♦♦♦♦♦
Taken from a 1987 solo date at Quebec's venerable *Festival Musique Actuelle, Labyrinths* finds avant garde jazz pianist Marilynn Crispell balancing Cecil Taylor's cataclysmic and staunchly free piano style with her own melodic and spacious take on free improvisation. The connection to Taylor is made clear on the dedication piece "Au Chanteur Qui Danse (For Cecil Taylor)" and on "Encore," both of which feature the kind of rhythmically muscular piano runs Taylor favored. Other Taylor touches include the frantic, high-note excursions found on "Labyrinths" and the emphatic, slammed-down piano chords employed throughout the set. Crispell, though, finds her own ground with a seamless mix of introspectively romantic phrasing and charged improvisation; "Still Womb of Light (For Ann Sheldon)" exemplifies this best, with its melancholic buildup and subsequent rhythmic "roughhousing" of the once

delicate themes. Her keen way with cover material is also on display, as evidenced by the expert blending of major and minor chords on "You Don't Know What Love Is" and Coltrane's "After the Rain"; Crispell's abiding love of Coltrane is further expressed by excellent readings of the tenor saxophonist's "Lasy Bird" and "Over the Rainbow." One of the few solo releases from this highly original composer and improviser, *Labyrinths* provides a great introduction to Marilyn Crispell's catalogue. *—Stephen Cook*

Live in Zurich / Apr. 12, 1989 / Leo ✦✦✦✦
Crispell keeps cranking out furious, aggressive free dates for the European market. They're devoid of any devices now in vogue on the jazz circuit: no standards, no electronics, no hard bop, Adult Contemporary, strings, or fusion. If you enjoy hearing spirited dialogues between Crispell, bassist Reggie Workman, and drummer Paul Motian, this one's for you. *—Ron Wynn*

Live in San Francisco / Oct. 20, 1989 / Music & Arts ✦✦✦✦
This is the Marilyn Crispell CD to start out with. The avant-garde pianist, most influenced by Cecil Taylor but increasingly original through the years, explores eight selections during a dynamic live set. In addition to five originals, Crispell plays very fresh (and unpredictable) versions of "When I Fall in Love," Thelonious Monk's "Ruby, My Dear," and John Coltrane's spiritual "Dear Lord." In addition, the 55 minutes of solo piano are joined by two numbers featuring Crispell that were also released on other Music & Arts releases: a duet with Anthony Braxton and "Wha's Nine" from a very adventurous Reggie Workman set with vocalist Jeanne Lee and clarinetist Don Byron. Invigorating music. *—Scott Yanow*

Circles / Oct. 7, 1990 / Victor ✦✦✦✦

Images / Aug. 1991 / Music & Arts ✦✦✦✦✦
The current piano favorite among the new generation of outside players, Crispell doesn't tone down the intensity until she concludes the session. Her approach, attack, tone, and phrasing have often been compared to her mentor Cecil Taylor, but she's not quite as percussive (no one is). However, this is as close as any living being can get to duplicating his energy and power. *—Ron Wynn*

Crispell & Hemingway Duo / 1992 / Knitting Factory ✦✦✦✦

Nothing Ever Was, Anyway: The Music of Annette Peacock / 1997 / ECM ✦✦✦✦
Marilyn Crispell's double-disc *Nothing Ever Was Anyway: The Music of Annette Peacock* is an enchanting, ambitious tribute to Peacock. Crispell is backed by Gary Peacock (double bass) and Paul Motian (drums), two musicians who have worked with and interpreted Annette Peacock's music since the '60s, and the trio created a wonderful, complex salute to her music that emphasizes the strength of the compositions, as well as Crispell's complex, intricate playing. Peacock herself sings on "Dreams (I Time Weren't)." *—Leo Stanley*

Sonny Criss (William Criss)

b. Oct. 23, 1927, Memphis, TN, **d.** Nov. 19, 1977, Los Angeles, CA
Sax (Alto) / Hard Bop
A talented bop altoist, Sonny Criss was influenced by Charlie Parker but had his own heavier sound. He spent most of his life in the Los Angeles area starting in 1942. In 1946 he worked in Howard McGhee's band with Charlie Parker and Teddy Edwards and can be heard on several jam sessions on Savoy in 1947. Criss spent periods playing with Johnny Otis, Gerald Wilson, and Billy Eckstine (1950-51) and was with Stan Kenton in 1955. He also worked with Howard Rumsey's Lighthouse All-Stars and Buddy Rich's quartet (1958) in addition to leading his own groups, recording three albums for Imperial in 1956. Criss lived in Europe during 1962-65, recorded some excellent sets for Prestige during 1966-69 and in the 1970s headed sessions for Fresh Sound, Xanadu, Muse and a couple of commercial efforts for Impulse. After European tours in 1973 and 1974, Sonny Criss' career seemed on an upswing. But due to the pain of cancer, he chose to commit suicide in 1977. *—Scott Yanow*

This Is Criss! / Oct. 21, 1966 / Prestige/OJC ✦✦✦✦
The first of seven Prestige albums that altoist Sonny Criss made during 1966-69 (all are excellent in their own way) was Criss' first record for an American label since 1959. Joined by pianist Walter Davis, bassist Paul Chambers and drummer Alan Dawson, Criss is in fine form on eight selections; the CD reissue adds a previously unissued "Love Ffor Sale." He displays his usual distinctive tone and shows that the years of critical neglect had not lessened his creativity within the bop idiom. *—Scott Yanow*

Portrait of Sonny Criss / Mar. 12, 1967 / Prestige/OJC ✦✦✦✦
Sonny Criss' second of seven Prestige albums (which has been reissued on CD in the OJC series) finds the passionate altoist using the same rhythm section as on the earlier date: pianist Walter Davis, bassist Paul Chambers and drummer Alan Dawson. Criss is in fine form on five jazz standards (including a heated "Wee" and an emotional version of "Smile") plus Davis' gospellish "A Million or More Times." An excellent outing. *—Scott Yanow*

Sonny's Dream (Birth of the New Cool) / May 8, 1968 / Prestige/OJC ✦✦✦✦
For Sonny Criss this was an unusual date. The altoist is backed for the set by a nonet arranged by the great Los Angeles-legend Horace Tapscott. The arrangements are challenging but complementary to Criss's style and he is top form on the six Tapscott originals. The CD reissue includes two additional alternate takes and is highly recommended for both Criss's playing and Tapscott's writing. *—Scott Yanow*

I'll Catch the Sun / Jan. 20, 1969 / Prestige/OJC ✦✦✦✦
Altoist Sonny Criss made some of his finest recordings for Prestige during the mid-to-late '60s; *I'll Catch the Sun* was the seventh and final. Since this CD reissue is only 35 minutes long, it is overly brief but the straightahead music (featuring Criss with pianist Hampton Hawes, bassist Monty Budwig and drummer Shelly Manne) is often excellent as the altoist performs two blues, two standards (including a passionate "Cry Me a River") and two forgotten pop tunes from the era. *—Scott Yanow*

★ **Crisscraft** / Feb. 24, 1975–Oct. 20, 1975 / 32 Jazz ✦✦✦✦✦
This is one of the very best Sonny Criss albums. The distinctive altoist, who is here joined by guitarist Ray Crawford, pianist Dolo Coker, bassist Larry Gales and drummer Jimmy Smith, is in prime form on a lengthy "The Isle of Celia," Benny Carter's "Blues in My Heart," the boppish blues "Crisscraft" and two shorter pieces. Criss, who had not recorded as a leader in six years, was really ready for this session, making this his definitive set to get. The CD reissue adds an alternate version of "Blues in My Heart" plus a slightly later version of "Out of Nowhere" to the original (and memorable) program. *—Scott Yanow*

The Complete Imperial Sessions / Jan. 26, 1956-Oct. 3, 1956 / Blue Note ✦✦✦
This double disc reissue on Blue Note contains the three releases that alto saxophonist Sonny Criss did for Imperial: *Jazz U.S.A., Go Man!,* and *Plays Cole Porter.* These sessions were all recorded in 1956 at a time when Criss had honed his amazing bebop alto precision. These 34 performances contain only five of his originals and are surrounded by mainly standards. The bands consisted of solid lineups with Sonny Clark or Kenny Drew on piano; Barney Kessel on guitar; Leroy Vinnegar, Buddy Clark or Bill Woodson on bass; Larry Bunker on vibes; and Lawrence Marable or Chuck Thompson taking care of drumming duties. While Criss had a career that erratically spanned the '70s, these Imperial sessions (reissued in glorious mono) contained highly regarded performances of passionate blues, moving ballads, and energetic up-tempo pieces. *—Al Campbell*

The Crusaders

f. 1960, Houston, TX, **db.** 1988
Group / Crossover Jazz, Hard Bop, Fusion, Soul-Jazz
Back in 1954 Houston pianist Joe Sample teamed up with high-school friends tenor saxophonist Wilton Felder and drummer Stix Hooper to form the Swingsters. Within a short time they were joined by trombonist Wayne Henderson, flutist Hubert Laws and bassist Henry Wilson and the group became the Modern Jazz Sextet. With the move of Sample, Felder, Hooper and Henderson to Los Angeles in 1960, the band (a quintet with the bass spot constantly changing) took on the name of the Jazz Crusaders. The following year they made their first recordings for Pacific Jazz and throughout the 1960s the group was a popular attraction, mixing together R&B and Memphis soul elements with hard bop; its trombone/tenor frontline became a trademark. By 1971 when all of the musicians were also busy with their own projects, it was decided to call the group simply the Crusaders so it would not be restricted to only playing jazz. After a few excellent albums during the early part of the decade (with guitarist Larry Carlton a strong asset), the group began to decline in quality. In 1975 the band's sound radically changed when Henderson departed to become a full-time producer. 1979's "Street Life" was a hit but also a last hurrah. With Hooper's decision to leave in 1983, the group no longer sounded like the Crusaders and gradually disbanded. In the mid-'90s Henderson and Felder had a reunion as the Crusaders but in reality only Joe Sample has had a strong solo career. *—Scott Yanow*

Freedom Sounds / May 1961 / Pacific Jazz ✦✦✦✦
The first album by the Jazz Crusaders (which started an extensive series for Pacific Jazz) introduced the colorful quintet. With trombonist Wayne Henderson and tenor saxophonist Wilton Felder giving the ensembles a unique sound, the group (also featuring regular members pianist Joe Sample and drummer Stix Hooper along with guests Jimmy Bond on bass and guitarist Roy Gaines) managed to strike a balance between creative hard bop and accessible soul-jazz. In addition to their version of "Theme From Exodus" (hoping to jump on the bandwagon created by Eddie Harris' hit rendition), the Jazz Crusaders perform originals by Felder, Henderson, and Sample ("Freedom Sound"). *—Scott Yanow*

Live at the Lighthouse '66 / Jan. 14, 1966-Jan. 16, 1966 / Pacific Jazz ✦✦✦✦✦
Because the Jazz Crusaders in the early '70s dropped the "Jazz" from their name and later in the decade veered much closer to R&B and pop music than they had earlier, it is easy to forget just how strong a jazz group they were in the 1960s. This CD reissues one of their rarer sessions, augmenting the original seven-song LP program (highlighted by "Blues Up Tight," "Doin' That Thing," and "Milestones") with previously unissued versions of "'Round Midnight" and John Coltrane's "Some Other Blues." The Jazz Crusaders (comprised of tenor saxophonist Wilton Felder, trombonist Wayne Henderson, pianist Joe Sample, drummer Stix Hooper, and, during this period, bassist Leroy Vinnegar) are heard in prime form. Felder shows the strong influence of Coltrane, Henderson recalls J.J. Johnson, Sample displays the most originality and the quintet on a whole (with its tenor-trombone frontline) sounds quite distinctive. An excellent set of primarily straight-ahead (but soulful) jazz. *—Scott Yanow*

Uh Huh / May 15, 1967 / Pacific Jazz ✦✦✦✦✦
One of the best of the Jazz Crusader LPs, this outing features fairly lengthy investigations of six group originals including "Uh Huh" and "Watts Happening." Tenor saxophonist Wilton Felder, trombonist Wayne Henderson, pianist Joe Sample, drummer Stix Hooper, and guest bassist Buster Williams all sound as if they are pushing each other. Their brand of soulful hard bop (utilizing their distinctive tenor-trombone frontline) is heard throughout at its prime. *—Scott Yanow*

● **1** / 1971 / MCA ✦✦✦✦✦
The Jazz Crusaders dropped the "jazz" from their name in 1971 but fortunately jazz remained a significant part of their music throughout the remainder of their existence. This double LP stands as one of the highpoints of the (Jazz) Crusaders' productive career. In addition to the founding members (Wilton Felder on tenor and electric bass, trombonist Wayne Henderson, keyboardist Joe Sample, and drummer Stix Hooper), the band is joined by three guitarists (most notably Larry Carlton) and electric bassist Chuck Rainey. "Put It Where You Want It" was a minor hit at the time, and the other compositions are excellent, but best is a colorfully reworked (and nearly 12-minute) exploration of Carole King's "So Far Away," the only non-original among the dozen songs. *—Scott Yanow*

Chain Reaction / 1975 / MCA ✦✦✦✦✦
One of the tastiest concoctions of the mid-seventies jazz-fusion era, *Chain Reaction* finds the Crusaders at the top of their form. The compositions are both accessible and memorable, and the playing is uniformly excellent. Guitarist Larry Carlton delivers some of his finest licks

and funkified rhythm work. Wayne Henderson shows there is a place in fusion for the trombone. Wilton Felder does double duty, delivering smoking saxophone lines and funky bass riffs. Joe Sample's Fender Rhodes piano provides a solid chordal foundation and great solos. And the stickman, Stix Hooper, keeps the groove solid. The band employs a variety of rhythms and tempos, and gives the members plenty of room to strut their individual and collective stuff. In fact, "collective" may be the key word here, for this is the sound of a band, not just a group of guys thrown together for a recording session. *Chain Reaction* was one of the albums that helped lure young, rock and soul-oriented listeners over to check out the jazz side, and should not be missed by those interested in the more accessible, funky side of fusion. *—Jim Newsom*

☆ **Free as the Wind** / Dec. 1976 / MCA ✦✦✦✦✦
There's a terrific reason why the triple-CD Crusaders retrospective *The Golden Years* included six of *Free as the Wind*'s eight tracks—the material. Indeed, Side One of the LP version may be the strongest single side of original tunes that the band ever put together. It opens with Joe Sample's driving, tense title cut, and flows flawlessly through Stix Hooper's subtly funky "I Felt the Love," Pops Popswell's infectiously finger-popping "The Way We Was" (a high point in the Crusaders' groove collection) and Larry Carlton's steamy vehicle for Wilton Felder, "Nite Crawler." Even the two tracks that the box set left out—the galvanic "Feel It," driven by Sample's clavinet and Hooper's tom-toms, and "River Rat"—are as funky as you can stand it. And from out of the blue, Sample concludes the album with a lovely, wistful tune that may have become a standard, "It Happens Everyday." When the material is this good, everything falls into place from there; the grooves are deeper, the soloing by all five Crusaders is more melodic and probing, and while Sample provides a few brass and string arrangements, this is just harmless decoration, neither a necessity nor a hindrance. This would be the Crusaders' high-water mark in the post-Wayne Henderson years, and it can stand tall with anything they've done. *—Richard S. Ginell*

Street Life / 1979 / MCA ✦✦✦✦
Although the Crusaders could not have known it at the time, their recording of "Street Life" (which features a memorable vocal by Randy Crawford) was a last hurrah for the 20-year old group. Their recordings of the next few years would decline in interest until the band gradually faded away in the 1980s. However this particular set is well worth picking up for the 11-minute title cut and there is good playing by the three original members (Wilton Felder on tenor, soprano and electric bass, keyboardist Joe Sample and drummer Stix Hooper) along with guitarist Barry Finnerty; horn and string sections plus additional guitarists are utilized on Sample's commercial but listenable arrangements *—Scott Yanow*

Live in Japan / Jan. 18, 1981 / GRP ✦✦✦✦
This CD contains selections from a triumphant Japanese tour which saw three-fourths of the original lineup augmented by such guest stars as guitarists Barry Finerty and Roland Bautista, percussionist Rafael Cruz and bassist Alphonso Johnson. But the interaction and contributions of Sample, Felder and Hooper make this memorable, plus the fact that this is the first time the complete concert has ever been available on a domestic release. It's really a "greatest hits live" CD, with such familiar numbers as "Spiral," "Rainbow Seeker," "So Far Away" and "Put It Where You Want It" part of the menu. While not in the class of such classic releases as *Crusaders I, Scratch* or *Second Crusade*, this is still a welcome addition to the legacy of a sorely underrated group. *—Ron Wynn*

Andrew Cyrille

b. Nov. 10, 1939, New York, NY
Drums / Avant-Garde Jazz, Free Jazz, Post-Bop
Andrew Cyrille is perhaps the preeminent free-jazz percussionist of the 1980s and '90s. Few free-jazz drummers play with a tenth of Cyrille's grace and authority. His energy is unflagging, his power absolute, tempered only by an ever-present sense of propriety. Cyrille is at his best in an utterly free context, as on his encounters with the ambidextrous pianist Borah Bergman, where his serrated rhythms and variable textures are given maximum latitude. In the late '50s and early '60s, he worked with such mainstream jazzers as Mary Lou Williams, Roland Hanna, Roland Kirk, Coleman Hawkins, and Junior Mance. He recorded with Hawkins, as well as tenor saxophonist Bill Barron, for the Savoy label. Cyrille succeeded Sunny Murray as Cecil Taylor's drummer in 1964. He stayed with the pianist until 1975, during which time he played on many of Taylor's classic albums. Cyrille, Rashied Ali, and Milford Graves collaborated on a series of mid-'70s concerts entitled "Dialogue of the Drums." Beginning in 1975 and lasting into the '80s, Cyrille led his own group, called Maono, which included the tenor saxophonist David S. Ware, trumpeter Ted Daniel, pianist Sonelius Smith, and at various times bassists Lisle Atkinson and Nick DiGeronimo. *—Chris Kelsey*

● **Metamusicians' Stomp** / Sep. 1978 / Black Saint ✦✦✦✦✦

Nuba / Jun. 1979 / Black Saint ✦✦✦✦
Drummer Andrew Cyrille and alto saxophonist Jimmy Lyons developed an impressive chemistry during their years with Cecil Taylor. Cyrille's array of percussion instruments and mastery of multiple styles, from hard bop to Afro-Latin, enabled him to play rippling rhythms or light, tinkling lines, attack or lay back. Lyons' alto solos were alternately driving and soft, sometimes searing in their intensity, sometimes more laidback and introspective. Those seeking a standard trio or straight jazz date are advised to look elsewhere; there was nothing conventional or predictable about this one. *—Ron Wynn*

My Friend Louis / Nov. 18, 1991-Nov. 19, 1991 / DIW/Columbia ✦✦✦✦
Fiery, rampaging session with drummer Andrew Cyrille anchoring a stirring set featuring the dynamic tenor saxophonist David S. Ware. This is uncompromising, exciting material, far from sedate standards or derivative hard bop recitations. *—Ron Wynn*

Ode to the Living Tree / Dec. 18, 1994–Dec. 19, 1994 / Evidence ✦✦✦

Good to Go: A Tribute To Bu / Oct. 17, 1995-Oct. 18, 1995 / Soul Note ✦✦✦✦
This is an intriguing set, featuring the combination of drummer Andrew Cyrille, flutist James Newton and bassist Lisle Atkinson, a different kind of power trio. The music ranges from fairly free flights to "Inch Worm" (arranged by Sheila Jordan) and two versions of "A Tribute to Bu" (for Art Blakey). Due to the variety of the material (mostly originals) and the consistent brilliance of Newton, this CD is recommended to fans of advanced jazz. *—Scott Yanow*

Tadd Dameron (Tadley Ewing Peake Dameron)

b. Feb. 21, 1917, Cleveland, OH, **d.** Mar. 8, 1965, New York, NY
Piano, Composer, Arranger / Bop
The definitive arranger/composer of the bop era, Tadd Dameron wrote such standards as "Good Bait," "Our Delight," "Hot House," "Lady Bird." and "If You Could See Me Now." Not only did he write melody lines but full arrangements and he was an influential force from the mid-'40s on even though he never financially prospered. Dameron started out in the swing era touring with the Zack Whyte and Blanche Calloway bands, he wrote for Vido Musso in New York and most importantly contributed arrangements for Harlan Leonard's Kansas City Orchestra, some of which were recorded. Soon Dameron was writing charts for such bands as Jimmie Lunceford, Count Basie, Billy Eckstine and Dizzy Gillespie in addition to Sarah Vaughan. However drug problems started to get in the way of his music. After recording a couple of albums (including 1958's *Mating Call* with John Coltrane) he spent much of 1959-61 in jail. After he was released, Dameron wrote for Sonny Stitt, Blue Mitchell, Milt Jackson, Benny Goodman but was less active in the years before his death from cancer. *—Scott Yanow*

1947-1949 / Aug. 1947-Apr. 1949 / Classics ✦✦✦✦✦
Although Tadd Dameron was a talented pianist, he never considered piano playing his strong point—the bebopper was best known for his writing and arranging, and when he recorded as a leader (which wasn't all that often), Dameron was quite happy to let his sidemen take most of the solos. Dameron can hardly be accused of hogging the solo space on *1947-1949*, a collection of small-group and big-band sides he recorded as a leader for Blue Note and Savoy, among others, from August 1947-April 1949. The material, most of it superb, falls into two main categories: hard-swinging bop instrumentals and romantic ballads featuring vocalists. On the instrumentals (which include "Our Delight," "Dameronia," "The Squirrel," "Lady Bird," and other Dameron originals), he features some of early bop's heavy-hitting soloists, including trumpeter Fats Navarro (a major influence on Clifford Brown), tenor saxman Wardell Gray, and alto saxman Ernie Henry (who, like Sonny Stitt, was a Charlie Parker disciple but not a clone). And Dameron's romantic side takes over when he features Kay Penton (a delightful though underexposed vocalist) on several ballads (including "What's New" and "Gone With the Wind") and employs the Billy Eckstine-influenced Kenny Hagood on "I Think I'll Go Away." Meanwhile, singer Rae Pearl (who later went by Rae Harrison) provides a wordless vocal on Dameron's dreamy "Casbah." Boasting some of Dameron's most essential work, this French release is recommended without hesitation to lovers of early bop. *—Alex Henderson*

Fontainebleau / Mar. 9, 1956 / Prestige/OJC ✦✦✦✦✦
Pianist-composer-arranger Tadd Dameron led relatively few sessions in his career, making the half-hour of music on this CD reissue quite valuable. Dameron performs five of his originals (best-known are the complex "Fontainebleau" and "The Scene Is Clean") with an octet comprised of trumpeter Kenny Dorham, trombonist Henry Coker, altoist Sahib Shihab, tenor saxophonist Joe Alexander, baritonist Cecil Payne, bassist John Simmons, drummer Shadow Wilson and the leader's sparse piano. As is usual with most Dameron dates, the emphasis is on his inventive arrangements although there is space (most notably on the 11-minute blues "Bula-Beige") for individual solos. Recommended. *—Scott Yanow*

Mating Call / Nov. 30, 1956 / Prestige/OJC ✦✦✦✦✦
Sometimes issued under John Coltrane's name, this excellent quartet session features pianist Tadd Dameron (who contributed all six compositions) with the great tenor, bassist John Simmons and drummer Philly Joe Jones. Dameron (who was a fairly basic pianist) has a rare opportunity to stretch out and his originals (best-known are "Soultrane" and "On a Misty Night") clearly inspire Coltrane. Available on CD, this set is a gem. *—Scott Yanow*

● **The Magic Touch of Tadd Dameron** / Feb. 27, 1962 / Riverside/OJC ✦✦✦✦✦
Tadd Dameron's final session as a leader (he died in 1965) is a definitive set that sums up much of his career. Some of Dameron's best-known originals are here (including "On a Misty Night," "Fontainebleau," "If You Could See Me Now" and "Our Delight"), and this CD reissue has three previously unreleased alternate takes. For once, Dameron had a large group of all-stars at his exposure (up to 14 pieces) and could concentrate on providing the arrangements, while Bill Evans took care of the piano playing. Among the featured sidemen are tenor saxophonist Johnny Griffin, trumpeters Charlie Shavers, Joe Wilder and Clark Terry, trombonist Jimmy Cleveland, Julius Watkins on French horn and drummer Philly Joe Jones; Barbara Winfield takes two fine vocals. Highly recommended to all bop collectors. *—Scott Yanow*

Eddie Daniels

b. Oct. 19, 1941, New York, NY
Sax (Tenor), Clarinet / Hard Bop
One of the truly great jazz clarinetists (ranking at the top with Benny Goodman, Artie Shaw and Buddy DeFranco), Daniels makes the impossible look effortless. On his first GRP release *Breakthrough* in 1984, Daniels switched back and forth on a second's notice between jazz and classical and he has since explored Charlie Parker, Roger Kellaway tunes, crossover and even swing with consistent brilliance. He is also a dazzling (if underrated) tenor player. Daniels appeared at the 1957 Newport Jazz Festival in Marshall Brown's Youth band (playing alto) and after graduating from Juilliard in 1966 he played tenor with the Thad Jones/Mel Lewis Orchestra for six years. Daniels recorded *First Prize* as a leader (1966) and made albums with Freddie Hubbard (1969), Richard Davis, Don Patterson and duets with Bucky Pizzarelli (1973). Although he recorded as a leader for Muse and Columbia during 1977-78, Eddie Daniels did not make it big until he started specializing on clarinet and recording reg-

ularly for GRP in 1984. In 1992 he started doubling on tenor again now that his reputation on clarinet was secure. *—Scott Yanow*

First Prize / Sep. 8, 1966–Sep. 12, 1966 / Prestige/OJC ✦✦✦✦✦
When one hears this early Eddie Daniels CD (a straight reissue of the original LP), it is surprising to realize that he would remain in relative obscurity for almost another 20 years. As shown on the three of the eight selections on which he plays clarinet, Daniels (even at this early stage) ranked near the top while his tenor playing on the remaining numbers was already personal and virtuosic. With the assistance of the Thad Jones/Mel Lewis rhythm section of the time (pianist Roland Hanna, bassist Richard Davis and drummer Mel Lewis), Daniels is in top form on three standards, four originals and the pop tune "Spanish Flea." *—Scott Yanow*

★ **Breakthrough** / 1986 / GRP ✦✦✦✦✦
This classic recording is a breakthrough in several ways. One of the most successful of all "third stream" efforts, the arrangements by Jorge Calandrelli, Torrie Zito, and Nan Schwartz for the London Philharmonia Orchestra are a superior blend of aspects of jazz and classical music. This album (reissued on CD) was also a major breakthrough for clarinetist Eddie Daniels who finally became a major name. Daniels proved that (with the possible exception of Buddy DeFranco) he was on a higher level than any other clarinetist of the post-swing era. He effortlessly switches back and forth between rapid classical music passages and inventive jazz on "Solfeggietto/ Metamorphosis" and easily holds one's interest througout Calandrelli's 22-minute three-part "Concerto for Jazz Clarinet and Orchestra." To call Eddie Daniels' playing "brilliant" on this release would be an understatement. Essential music. *—Scott Yanow*

To Bird with Love / 1987 / GRP ✦✦✦✦✦
Following his remarkable classical/jazz recording *Breakthrough*, clarinetist Eddie Daniels performed a set of Charlie Parker tunes with pianist Fred Hersch, bassist John Patitucci and drummer Al Foster; "This Is the Time" (an abstract rendition of "Now's the Time" has pianist Roger Kellaway sitting in. Daniels' playing is often quite remarkable throughout the program and the highlights include "East of the Sun" (which finds Hersch utilizing a synthesizer to simulate strings), "Just Friends," "Passport" and a Bird medley of three of his blues lines. Recommended. *—Scott Yanow*

Under the Influence / 1993 / GRP ✦✦✦✦✦
After a decade of exclusively playing clarinet (and establishing himself as one of the greats), Eddie Daniels began doubling on tenor again on this recording. Switching between his two axes, Daniels sounds in top form on some diverse but consistently rewarding originals and a few standards ("I Hear a Rhapsody," "Weaver of Dreams," "I Fall in Love Too Easily" and an exciting version of Bill Evans's "Five"). Joined by pianist Alan Pasqua, bassist Mike Formanek and drummer Peter Erskine, Eddie Daniels really digs into these tunes and both his virtuosity and his inventive improvisations are quite impressive. *—Scott Yanow*

Eddie "Lockjaw" Davis

b. Mar. 2, 1922, New York, NY, **d.** Nov. 3, 1986, Culver City, CA
Sax (Tenor) / Hard Bop, Latin Jazz, Soul-Jazz, Swing, Bop
Possessor of a cutting and immediately identifiable tough tenor tone, Eddie "Lockjaw" Davis could hold his own in a saxophone battle with anyone. Early on he picked up experience playing with the bands of Cootie Williams (1942-44), Lucky Millinder, Andy Kirk (1945-46) and Louis Armstrong. He began heading his own groups from 1946 and Davis' earliest recordings as a leader tended to be explosive R&B affairs with plenty of screaming from his horn; he matched wits successfully with Fats Navarro on one session. Davis was with Count Basie's Orchestra on several occasional (including 1952-53, 1957 and 1964-73) and teamed up with Shirley Scott's trio during 1955-60. During 1960-62 he collaborated in some exciting performances and recordings with Johnny Griffin, a fellow tenor who was just as combative as Davis. After temporarily retiring to become a booking agent (1963-64), Davis rejoined Basie. In his later years Lockjaw often recorded with Harry "Sweets" Edison and he remained a busy soloist up until his death. Through the decades he recorded as a leader for many labels including Savoy, Apollo, Roost, King, Roulette, Prestige/Jazzland/Moodsville, RCA, Storyville, MPS, Black & Blue, Spotlite, SteepleChase, Pablo, Muse and Enja. *—Scott Yanow*

The Eddie Lockjaw Davis Cookbook, Vols. 1-3 / Jun. 20, 1958-Dec. 15, 1958 / Prestige ✦✦✦✦✦

Jaws / Sep. 12, 1958 / Prestige/OJC ✦✦✦
Tenorman Eddie "Lockjaw" Davis and organist Shirley Scott co-led a popular combo during 1956-60, recording many albums and helping to popularize the idiom. This particular CD finds the quartet (with bassist George Duvivier and drummer Arthur Edgehill) interpreting eight swing standards, alternating ballads with romps. It's a fine all-around showcase for the accessible group. *—Scott Yanow*

Smokin' / Sep. 12, 1958–Dec. 5, 1958 / Prestige/OJC ✦✦✦✦
Tenor-saxophonist Eddie "Lockjaw" Davis cut enough material during these two sessions to fill up four records. The seven selections included on this brief 36-minute CD which was recorded during the same period as Davis's better-known *Cookbook* albums) also include Jerome Richardson (switching between flute, tenor and baritone) on three of the numbers, bassist George Duvivier and drummer Arthur Edgehill. Together the group swings hard on basic originals, blues and an occasional ballad, showing why this type of accessible band was so popular during the era. *—Scott Yanow*

Trane Whistle / Sep. 20, 1961 / Prestige/OJC ✦✦✦✦✦
This CD reissue brings back an Eddie "Lockjaw" Davis session in which the distinctive tenor saxophonist is joined by a 13-piece big band arranged by Oliver Nelson. Most significant is the inclusion of the original version of "Stolen Moments" (here called "The Stolen Moment" and predating the more famous Oliver Nelson recording by several months). Eric Dolphy is in the backup group but is not heard from in a solo capacity. There are some spots for trumpeters Richard Williams, Clark Terry and Bobby Bryant along with Nelson on alto but this is primarily Davis' showcase. On a set comprised of four Oliver Nelson originals, the ballad "You Are Too Beautiful" and the leader's "Jaws," Lockjaw as usual shows plenty of emotion during his driving solos. *—Scott Yanow*

★ **Live at Minton's—*First Set* / *Jan. 6, 1961*** / Prestige ✦✦✦✦✦
This duo (tenor saxophonists Eddie "Lockjaw" Davis and Johnny Griffin) made about a dozen LPs together, most for Jazzland and Prestige, and they are all worth investigating. They had a special affinity for pianist Thelonious Monk's music, and while there were other sets which emphasize that better, the Monk pieces ("Straight No Chaser"/"In Walked Bud") included in the program on this live set were among the highlights. *—Bob Rusch, Cadence*

Lookin' at Monk / Feb. 7, 1961 / Jazzland ✦✦✦✦✦

Afro Jaws / May 4, 1961–May 12, 1961 / Riverside/OJC ✦✦✦✦
This set was a change of pace for tenor saxophonist Eddie "Lockjaw" Davis. Backed by three trumpeters (Clark Terry gets some solos), a rhythm section (pianist Lloyd Mayers, bassist Larry Gales and drummer Ben Riley) and a percussion section led by Ray Barretto, Lockjaw performs four compositions by Gil Lopez (who arranged all of the selections) plus "Tin Tin Deo," "Star Eyes" and his own "Afro-Jaws." The Afro-Cuban setting is perfect for the tough-toned tenor, who romps through the infectious tunes. *—Scott Yanow*

Blues Up and Down / Jun. 5, 1961 / Milestone ✦✦✦✦

Jawbreakers / Apr. 18, 1962 / Riverside/OJC ✦✦✦

Streetlights / Nov. 15, 1962 / Prestige ✦✦✦✦✦
This CD combines together the music from two complete LPs (*I Only Have Eyes for You* and *Trackin'*) that were recorded the same day with the identical personnel. Eddie "Lockjaw" Davis's tough tenor is well featured with his regular group of the time, a combo consisting of the powerful organist Don Patterson (who dominates many of the ensembles), guitarist Paul Weeden (talented but quite obscure), drummer Billy James and guest bassist George Duvivier. The emphasis is on standards and intense blowing (even on the ballads) with the set being a good example of a strong tenor organ band. *—Scott Yanow*

All of Me / Aug. 23, 1983 / Steeple Chase ✦✦✦✦✦
Tenorman Eddie "Lockjaw" Davis had already been a potent force in jazz for 35 years when he recorded this set but as it turned out his SteepleChase date (his next-to-last session) was one of the strongest of his career. Accompanied by a trio led by pianist Kenny Drew, Lockjaw really tears into these standards which are highlighted by "I Only Have Eyes for You," two versions of "There Is No Greater Love" (the alternate version was released for the first time on this CD reissue), "Four" and the title cut. Davis was at the peak of his powers during this recording, making his lone SteepleChase outing one of his very best. *—Scott Yanow*

Straight Blues / Sep. 12, 1958-May 5, 1976 / Prestige ✦✦✦✦
As earthy and true-blue as the disc's title, the huge, abrasive yet joyous tenor sax of Jaws is showcased in a variety of settings in this compilation from Prestige's heyday in the '50s and '60s. Since the CD is constantly expanding and contracting in personnel, from the Red Garland Trio to a big band with several stops in between, there is no listener fatigue even though the menu is mostly blues. Shirley Scott's grunting organ can be heard pumping up the truckin' Lockjaw rhythm section on "Heat 'N' Serve," "Pots and Pans" and "The Rev"; these tracks helped launch her in the soul-jazz world. We also hear the fine, wailing, little-known first version of "Stolen Moments" with a big band led by the composer Oliver Nelson (with Nelson and Eric Dolphy in the ranks); indeed, Lockjaw can be said to have launched Nelson the arranger, too. The stray Pablo track from 1976 is a combo date with Count Basie and "Sweets" Edison on open horn, "Edison's Lights." Everything here has been reissued on CD previously, so the Lockjaw completist fringe needn't apply. *—Richard S. Ginell*

Miles Davis (Miles Dewey Davis III)

b. May 26, 1926, Alton, IL, **d.** Sep. 28, 1991, Santa Monica, CA
Trumpet, Organ, Composer / Jazz-Rock, Modal Music, Hard Bop, Post-Bop, Fusion, Cool, Bop, Jazz-Funk
Miles Davis had quite a career, one with so many innovations that his name is one of the few that can be spoken in the same sentence with Duke Ellington. As a trumpeter, Davis was never a virtuoso on the level of his idol Dizzy Gillespie but by 1947 he possessed a distinctive cool-toned sound of his own. His ballad renditions (utilizing a Harmon mute) were exquisite yet never predictable, he mastered and then stripped down the bebop vocabulary to its essentials and he generally made every note count; as with Thelonious Monk, less was more in Miles' music. But Davis was much more than just a trumpeter. As a bandleader he was a brilliant talent scout, able to recognize potential in its formative stage and bring out the best in his sidemen. Among the musicians who greatly benefitted from their association with Davis were Gerry Mulligan (virtually unknown when he played with Miles' Birth of the Cool Nonet), Gil Evans, John Coltrane, Red Garland, Paul Chambers, Philly Joe Jones, Cannonball Adderley, Bill Evans, Jimmy Cobb, Wynton Kelly, George Coleman, Wayne Shorter, Herbie Hancock, Ron Carter, Tony Williams, Chick Corea, Jack DeJohnette, Dave Holland, John McLaughlin, Joe Zawinul, Keith Jarrett, Steve Grossman, Gary Bartz, Dave Liebman, Al Foster, Sonny Fortune, Bill Evans (the saxophonist), Kenny Garrett, Marcus Miller, Mike Stern and John Scofield. This partial list forms a who's who of modern jazz. In addition to his playing and nurturing of young talent, Miles Davis was quite remarkable in his rare ability to continually evolve. Most jazz musicians (with the exceptions of John Coltrane and Duke Ellington) generally form their style early on and spend the rest of their careers refining their sound. In contrast Miles Davis every five years or so would forge ahead, and due to his restless nature he not only played bop but helped found cool jazz, hard bop, modal music, his own unusual brand of the avant-garde and fusion. Jazz history would be much different if Davis had not existed. *—Scott Yanow*

★ **Birth of the Cool** / Jan. 21, 1949-Mar. 9, 1950 / Blue Note ✦✦✦✦✦
So dubbed because these three sessions—two from early 1949, one from March 1950—are where the sound known as cool jazz essentially formed, *The Birth of the Cool* remains one

of the defining, pivotal moments in jazz. This is where the elasticity of bop was married with skillful, big-band arrangements and a relaxed, subdued mood that made it all seem easy, even at its most intricate. After all, there's a reason why this music was called cool; it has a hip, detached elegance, never getting too hot, even as the rhythms skip and jump. Indeed, the most remarkable thing about these sessions—arranged by Gil Evans and featuring such heavy-hitters as Kai Winding, Gerry Mulligan, Lee Konitz, and Max Roach—is that they sound intimate, as the nonet never pushes too hard, never sounds like the work of nine musicians. Furthermore, the group keeps things short and concise (probably the result of the running time of singles, but the results are the same), which keeps the focus on the tones and tunes. The virtuosity led to relaxing, stylish mood music as the end result—the very thing that came to define West Coast or "cool" jazz—but this music is so inventive, it remains alluring even after its influence has been thoroughly absorbed into the mainstream —*Stephen Thomas Erlewine*

And Horns / Jan. 17, 1951–Feb. 19, 1953 / Prestige/OJC ✦✦✦

☆ **Chronicle: The Complete Prestige Recordings (1951-1956)** / Jan. 17, 1951-Oct. 26, 1956 / Prestige ✦✦✦✦✦
This eight-CD set does indeed have all 17 of trumpeter Miles Davis' Prestige sessions. The music is also available in separate CDs in the *Original Jazz Classics* series. Most significant are the many performances by Davis' classic quintet of 1955-1956 with tenor saxophonist John Coltrane, pianist Red Garland, bassist Paul Chambers, and drummer Philly Joe Jones but there are also dates featuring Sonny Rollins, Charlie Parker (on tenor), Thelonious Monk, Milt Jackson, Jackie McLean, Lee Konitz, Lucky Thompson, and J.J. Johnson among others. Much of this music is classic and dates from the period when Miles Davis was really beginning to emerge as an innovator. —*Scott Yanow*

Collector's Items / Oct. 5, 1951-Mar. 16, 1956 / Prestige/OJC ✦✦✦✦✦

Dig / Oct. 5, 1951 / Prestige/OJC ✦✦✦
Although his lifestyle was erratic during this period, trumpeter Miles Davis is in fine form for a sextet outing with two of the top young saxophonists of the early '50s: Sonny Rollins and Jackie McLean. Pianist Walter Bishop, bassist Tommy Potter (Charles Mingus takes his place on "Conception") and drummer Art Blakey complete the impressive group that is heard on the OJC CD reissue. In addition to two standards ("My Old Flame" and "It's Only a Paper Moon"), there are four obscure originals and McLean's "Dig" (based on "Sweet Georgia Brown"). Excellent early hard bop. —*Scott Yanow*

Miles Davis, Vol. 1 / May 9, 1952-Mar. 6, 1954 / Blue Note ✦✦✦✦
Miles Davis's recordings of 1951-54 tend to be overlooked because of his erratic lifestyle of the period and because they predated his first classic quintet. Although he rarely recorded during this era, what he did document was often quite classic. The two sessions included on this CD (which includes three alternate takes) are among the earliest hard bop recordings and would indirectly influence the modern mainstream music of the 1960s. The first session features Davis in a sextet with trombonist J.J. Johnson, altoist Jackie McLean, pianist Gil Coggins, bassist Oscar Pettiford and drummer Kenny Clarke; highlights include "Dear Old Stockholm," "Woody'n You" and interpretations of "Yesterdays" and "How Deep Is the Ocean." The remaining six numbers showcase Davis in a quartet with pianist Horace Silver, bassist Percy Heath and drummer Art Blakey, really stretching out on such numbers as "Take Off" and "Well You Needn't." However on "It Never Entered My Mind," Davis's muted statement (his only one on this set) looks toward his treatments of ballads later in the decade. —*Scott Yanow*

Miles Davis, Vol. 2 / Apr. 20, 1953 / Blue Note ✦✦✦✦
This CD contains all of the music recorded by a particularly strong sextet in 1953, six selections and five alternate takes. With trumpeter Miles Davis, trombonist J.J. Johnson, tenor-saxophonist Jimmy Heath, pianist Gil Coggins, bassist Percy Heath and drummer Art Blakey all in fine form, "Tempus Fugit" and "C.T.A." receive definitive treatment along with two Johnson compositions. —*Scott Yanow*

Blue Haze / May 19, 1953-Apr. 3, 1954 / Prestige/OJC ✦✦✦

Walkin' / Apr. 3, 1954 / Prestige/OJC ✦✦✦✦✦
In 1954 Miles Davis was on the verge of making a comeback. Somewhat obscure during 1951-53 due to his erratic lifestyle and low-profile gigs, Davis at 28 was entering his creative prime. On April 3 of that year he recorded three fine numbers (including his "Solar") in a quintet with the forgotten altoist Dave Schildkraut and pianist Horace Silver, but the real reasons to acquire this set are for the exciting versions of "Walkin'" and "Blue 'N' Boogie" performed by Davis, Silver, trombonist J.J. Johnson and tenor-saxophonist Lucky Thompson. [A 20-bit remaster of *Walkin'* was released in October 1999.] —*Scott Yanow*

☆ **Bags Groove** / Jun. 29, 1954–Dec. 24, 1954 / Prestige/OJC ✦✦✦✦✦
The title track of *Bags Groove* comes from December 24, 1954, the classic date that matched together trumpeter Miles Davis, vibraphonist Milt Jackson, pianist Thelonious Monk, bassist Percy Heath and drummer Kenny Clarke. Davis and Monk actually did not get along all that well and the trumpeter did not want Monk playing behind his solos, but a great deal of brilliant music occured on the day of their encounter. There are two very different versions apiece of "Bags' Groove", and Monk's solo on the first take was one of his best. The rest of the album is taken from a session the previous June which included Sonny Rollins and Horace Silver doing Rollins' own "Airegin" as well as "Oleo" and "But Not for Me." Timeless music that defies easy classification, this set belongs in every jazz collection. —*Scott Yanow*

☆ **Miles Davis & the Modern Jazz Giants** / Dec. 24, 1954–Oct. 26, 1956 / Prestige ✦✦✦✦✦
Including sessions recorded the same day as those on *Bags Groove*, this album includes more classic performances from the date that matched together trumpeter Miles Davis, vibraphonist Milt Jackson, pianist Thelonious Monk, bassist Percy Heath, and drummer Kenny Clarke. Davis and Monk actually did not get along all that well, and the trumpeter did not want Monk playing behind his solos. Still, a great deal of brilliant music occurred on the day of their encounter, including "The Man I Love," "Bemsha Swing," and "Swing Spring." [A 20-bit remaster of *Miles Davis and the Modern Jazz Giants* was released in October 1999.] —*Scott Yanow*

Circle in the Round / Oct. 27, 1955-Jan. 27, 1970 / Columbia/Legacy ✦✦✦✦
This two-CD set is highly recommended to collectors for it contains many interesting performances, all but one of which were previously unissued at the time of this two-fer's release. Spanning 15 years, this program includes a 1955 version of "Two Bass Hit" from Davis's first classic quintet, an extended version of "Love for Sale" by his 1958 sextet, a reunion between Miles and drummer Philly Joe Jones in 1961, the side long "Circle in the Round" from Davis's 1967 quintet (with guest guitarist Joe Beck), a few unfinished works from his transitional 1968 band and a lengthy workout by Davis's fusion group in early 1970. There are lots of unusual performances on this worthy collection. —*Scott Yanow*

★ **Round About Midnight** / Oct. 27, 1955-Sep. 10, 1956 / Columbia/Legacy ✦✦✦✦✦
Recorded while Miles Davis was still signed to Prestige—and still owed the label several albums—*Round About Midnight* finds Miles' first classic quintet hitting its stride, cutting an album that set the standard for hard bop. This is classic music not just because it's so exceptionally performed, capturing a terrific group at its peak, but because it perfectly summarizes all the attributes of hard bop. This, for the casual jazz fan, is what a jazz band should sound like, as Miles' cool trumpet pushes and pulls against the hot saxophone of John Coltrane, with pianist Red Garland, bassist Paul Chambers, and drummer Philly Joe Jones providing supple, sympathetic support. Needless to say, the more sophisticated listener will find much to treasure within the interplay of this group, since it not only captures a phenomenal group at its absolute peak, it demonstrates what hard bop should be—searching, surprising, accessible, but never predictable. This is what makes it worthwhile to jazzbos, but the great thing about this record is that it isn't for snobs. This is vital music that remains lively decades after its original release. While the trio of *Workin', Relaxin',* and *Steamin'* impresses because of the three albums' sheer drive and sustained energy, this is more concentrated, eloquent, and elegant, perhaps the best way to hear Miles and Coltrane in a pure hard bop setting. [Columbia/Legacy's 2001 reissue contains four bonus tracks from the sessions—"Two Bass Hit," "Little Melonae," "Budo," and "Sweet Sue, Just You"—which may not provide revelations, but certainly nicely enhance an already classic album.] —*Stephen Thomas Erlewine*

☆ **Cookin'** / Nov. 16, 1955-Oct. 26, 1956 / Prestige/OJC ✦✦✦✦✦
Trumpeter Miles Davis (along with tenor-saxophonist John Coltrane, pianist Red Garland, bassist Paul Chambers and drummer Philly Joe Jones) are heard on this CD reissue performing such tunes as "My Funnny Valentine" (Davis's earliest version of this standard), "Blues by Five," "Airegin" and a medley of "Tune Up" and "When Lights Are Low." Both the quintet and the music qualify as classic; all four of their Prestige albums are easily recommended. [A 20-bit remaster of *Cookin'* was released in October 1999.] —*Scott Yanow*

☆ **Relaxin'** / May 11, 1956-Oct. 26, 1956 / Prestige/OJC ✦✦✦✦✦
One of the strongest of Miles Davis' recordings with his first classic quintet (a group also including the young tenor saxophonist John Coltrane, pianist Red Garland, bassist Paul Chambers and drummer Philly Joe Jones), this CD reissue is highlighted by "If I Were a Bell," "I Could Write a Book" and Sonny Rollins' "Oleo." Actually all six selections are quite rewarding and helped set the standard for bands of the era. —*Scott Yanow*

☆ **Steamin'** / May 11, 1956-Oct. 26, 1956 / Prestige/OJC ✦✦✦✦✦
This classic Prestige session (one of four cut for the label by Davis' first permanent group) has been reissued many times. Davis is heard with his classic quintet of 1956 (which featured tenor-saxophonist John Coltrane, pianist Red Garland, bassist Paul Chambers and drummer Philly Joe Jones) performing six numbers, all of which are somewhat memorable. Highpoints are "Surrey with the Fringe on Top," "Diane" and "When I Fall in Love;" Davis's muted tone rarely sounded more beautiful. —*Scott Yanow*

☆ **Workin'** / May 11, 1956-Oct. 26, 1956 / Prestige/OJC ✦✦✦✦✦
Miles Davis's 1956 Quintet was one of his classic groups, featuring tenor-saxophonist John Coltrane, pianist Red Garland, bassist Paul Chambers and drummer Philly Joe Jones. They recorded four albums for Prestige in two marathon sessions. Among the highlights are "It Never Entered My Mind," "Four," "In Your Own Sweet Way" and two versions of "The Theme." The music is essential in one form or another. —*Scott Yanow*

Miles Davis: The Columbia Years 1955-1985 / Jun. 5, 1956-Feb. 27, 1985 / Columbia ✦✦✦

★ **Miles Ahead** / May 6, 1957-May 27, 1957 / Columbia/Legacy ✦✦✦✦✦
Miles Davis' first collaboration with arranger Gil Evans since *The Birth of the Cool* recordings of 1949-50 resulted in this classic album. Reissued three times on CD (the first one, which substituted alternate takes in places, was a disaster), the third version (which came out in 1997) augments the original ten selections with four excellent and complete alternates. An advantage that this CD reissue has over the LP is that, since the music was recorded as a continuous suite, there is no break between the fifth and sixth songs. Davis' trumpet (backed by Evans' 19-piece orchestra) is heard at its best on such classics as "The Duke," "My Ship," "Miles Ahead," "Blues for Pablo" and "I Don't Wanna Be Kissed." Highly recommended for all collections. —*Scott Yanow*

☆ **Miles Davis & Gil Evans: The Complete Columbia Studio Recordings** / May 6, 1957-Feb. 16, 1968 / Columbia/Legacy ✦✦✦✦✦
Over the course of six compact discs, *Miles Davis & Gil Evans: The Complete Columbia Studio Recordings* collects every bit of music the legendary duo recorded together between the years 1957 and 1968. Each of the original albums—*Miles Ahead, Porgy and Bess, Sketches of Spain,* and *Quiet Nights*—are presented in their original running order on separate discs; each individual disc is augmented with revealing alternate takes and rarities, like the duo's long-unavailable music for "The Time of the Barracudas" at the end of the *Quiet Nights* disc. The remaining two discs are filled with alternate takes, rehearsals, overdubbed solos, studio chatter, and outtakes. All of the music sounds splendid and often revelatory—for instance, in addition to being released in stereo for the first time ever, *Miles Ahead* is presented in its original version for the first time on compact disc. Each disc is enclosed in a sleeve that replicates

the original album release (both covers of *Miles Ahead* are included within the set) and housed in an immense, detailed, gold-bound 197-page book. In fact, if there is any fault with the set it is this—since the notes, sleeves, track listings and discs are bound together within one thick book, the set feels like a library piece instead of a functional, listenable retrospective. This is vital music that will be accessed often by anyone willing to invest in the set, so the box set should have been designed with that in mind. Nevertheless, *Miles Davis & Gil Evans: The Complete Columbia Studio Recordings* is filled with so much visionary and beautiful music, it makes the slight flaws in packaging forgivable. *—Stephen Thomas Erlewine*

☆ **Milestones** / Apr. 2, 1958-Apr. 3, 1958 / Columbia/Legacy ♦♦♦♦♦
Kind of Blue might have received most of the acclaim but *Milestones*, the recorded debut of the Miles Davis Sextet, is in the same league. This remarkable super group (featuring Davis's trumpet, tenor-saxophonist John Coltrane, altoist Cannonball Adderley, pianist Red Garland, bassist Paul Chambers and drummer Philly Joe Jones) was arguably the greatest one Miles Davis ever led. "Two Bass Hit" features the two saxes trading off with fire and "Billy Boy" showcases the Red Garland trio (showing what they learned from Ahmad Jamal), but "Straight No Chaser" really demonstrates what a powerhouse band this was. *—Scott Yanow*

58 Sessions Feat. Stella by Starlight / May 26, 1958-Jul. 28, 1958 / Columbia ♦♦♦♦

☆ **Porgy and Bess** / Jul. 22, 1958-Aug. 18, 1958 / Columbia/Legacy ♦♦♦♦♦
The second of the three great Miles Davis-Gil Evans collaborations features the trumpeter backed by Evans's 18-piece orchestra on 13 selections from George Gershwin's *Porgy and Bess*. This version of "Summertime" (with Evans's countermelody) is definitive and the entire suite should be savored in one sitting. Other highlights include "Bess, You Is My Woman Now," "My Man's Gone Now" and "I Loves You Porgy." In 1997 this classic was reissued on CD and augmented by alternate versions of "I Loves You, Porgy" and "Gone." A more expanded documentation is currently available on Columbia's complete Miles Davis/Gil Evans box. *—Scott Yanow*

★ **Kind of Blue** / Mar. 2, 1959-Apr. 22, 1959 / Columbia/Legacy ♦♦♦♦♦
Kind of Blue isn't merely an artistic highlight for Miles Davis, it's an album that towers above its peers, a record generally considered as *the* definitive jazz album, a universally acknowledged standard of excellence. Why does *Kind of Blue* posses such a mystique? Perhaps because this music never flaunts its genius. It lures listeners in with the slow, luxurious bass line and gentle piano chords of "So What." From that moment on, the record never really changes pace—each tune has a similar relaxed feel, as the music flows easily. Yet *Kind of Blue* is more than easy listening. It's the pinnacle of modal jazz—tonality and solos build from chords, not the overall key, giving the music a subtly shifting quality. All of this doesn't quite explain why seasoned jazz fans return to this record even after they've memorized every nuance. They return because this is an exceptional band—Miles, Coltrane, Bill Evans, Cannonball Adderly, Paul Chambers, Jimmy Cobb—one of the greatest in history, playing at the peak of its power. As Evans said in the original liner notes for the record, the band did not play through any of these pieces prior to recording. Davis laid out the themes and chords before the tape rolled, and then the band improvised. The end results were wondrous and still crackle with vitality. *Kind of Blue* works on many different levels. It can be played as background music, yet it amply rewards close listening. It is advanced music that is extraordinarily enjoyable. It may be a stretch to say that if you don't like *Kind of Blue*, you don't like jazz—but it's hard to imagine it as anything other than a cornerstone of *any* jazz collection. *—Stephen Thomas Erlewine*

☆ **Sketches of Spain** / Nov. 15, 1959-Mar. 10, 1960 / Columbia/Legacy ♦♦♦♦♦
The third and final of the great Miles Davis-Gil Evans collaborations of 1957-59 was also their most ambitious. This set finds Davis in the forefront improvising on two numbers associated with Spanish music and three Evans compositions in that idiom. Much of the music is quite dramatic and emotional (notably "Saeta") and Davis plays at his best throughout, really stretching the boundaries of jazz. The 1997 CD reissue adds the brief "Song of Our Country" plus an alternate take of "Concierto De Aranjuez" to the original program. *—Scott Yanow*

Directions / Mar. 11, 1960-Feb. 27, 1970 / Columbia ♦♦♦

Someday My Prince Will Come / Mar. 7, 1961-Mar. 21, 1961 / Columbia/Legacy ♦♦♦♦
Miles Davis's 1961 Quintet was more relaxed and less adventurous than his earlier groups with John Coltrane. The trumpeter was at the peak of his powers in the early '60s and comfortable with his own playing. This CD, a straight reissue of the earlier LP, features Davis, tenor-saxophonist Hank Mobley, pianist Wynton Kelly, bassist Paul Chambers, either Jimmy Cobb or Philly Joe Jones on drums and, as a special bonus, guest appearances by John Coltrane (the last time he would record with Miles) on "Teo" and the title cut. *—Scott Yanow*

In Person: Friday Night at the Blackhawk / Apr. 21, 1961 / Columbia ♦♦♦♦

At Carnegie Hall / May 19, 1961 / Columbia/Legacy ♦♦♦♦
On May 19, 1961, Miles Davis was showcased at a Carnegie Hall concert, performing with his quintet of the time (tenor saxophonist Hank Mobley, pianist Wynton Kelly, bassist Paul Chambers and drummer Jimmy Cobb) and, for the first time in public, the Gil Evans Orchestra. Although thought of by some later on as being in an off period since he was between innovations, Miles' trumpet chops were actually in prime form during 1961-63, as he shows throughout the date. All of the music on this 1998 two-CD set has been out before, either on the original LP of the same name or on the later album *More Music From the Legendary Carnegie Hall Concert*, but this is the first time that the two sets have been reproduced in their original order. While the first half of the show includes good versions of "So What" (which has the only interaction of the orchestra with Davis' small group) and "Walkin'," the second set (highlighted by "Oleo" and "No Blues") clearly found the trumpeter in better form. He concluded the performance with a lengthy rendition of "Adagio" from "Concierto De Aranjuez" with Evans' ensemble. While not quite essential (there are many other classic Miles Davis recordings currently available), this twofer will be wanted by the trumpeter's many fans. *—Scott Yanow*

Quiet Nights / Jul. 27, 1962-Nov. 6, 1962 / Columbia/Legacy ♦♦♦

Sorcerer / Aug. 23, 1962-May 24, 1967 / Columbia/Legacy ♦♦♦♦♦
Sorcerer, the third album by the second Miles Davis Quintet, is in a sense a transitional album, a quiet, subdued affair that rarely blows hot, choosing to explore cerebral tonal colorings. Even when the tempo picks up, as it does on the title track, there's little of the dense, manic energy on *Miles Smiles*—this is about subtle shadings, even when the compositions are as memorable as Tony Williams' "Pee Wee" or Herbie Hancock's "Sorcerer." As such, it's a little elusive, since it represents the deepening of the band's music as they choose to explore different territory. The emphasis is as much on complex, interweaving chords and a coolly relaxed sound as it is on sheer improvisation, though each member tears off thoroughly compelling solos. Still, the individual flights aren't placed at the forefront the way they were on the two predecessors—it all merges together, pointing toward the dense soundscapes of Miles' later '60s work. It's such a layered, intriguing work that the final cut, recorded in 1962 with Bob Dorough on vocals, is an utterly jarring, inappropriate way to end the record, even if it's intended as a tribute to Miles' then-wife, Cicely Tyson (whose image graces the cover). *—Stephen Thomas Erlewine*

Seven Steps to Heaven / Apr. 16, 1963-May 14, 1963 / Columbia ♦♦♦♦♦
In 1963 Miles Davis was at a transitional point in his career, without a regular group and wondering what his future musical direction would be. At the time he recorded the music heard on this CD he was in the process of forming a new band, as can be seen from the personnel: Tenor-saxophonist George Coleman, Victor Feldman (who turned down the job) and Herbie Hancock on pianos, bassist Ron Carter, and Frank Butler and Tony Williams on drums. Recorded at two seperate sessions, this set is highlighted by the classic "Seven Steps to Heaven," "Joshua" and slow passionate versions of "Basin Street Blues" and "Baby Won't You Please Come Home." *—Scott Yanow*

The Complete Concert: 1964 (My Funny Valentine & "Four More" / Feb. 12, 1964 / Columbia ♦♦♦♦♦
This two-CD set, which completely reissues the two lengthy LPs *My Funny Valentine* (a set of lyrical ballads) and *Four & More* (which is filled with very rapid versions of Davis's standard repertoire), features the 1963-64 Quintet at its best. This particular unit consisted of the greatly underrated tenor-saxophonist George Coleman and the young rhythm section of pianist Herbie Hancock, bassist Ron Carter and drummer Tony Williams. Since Davis's future studio albums with this group (after Wayne Shorter replaced Coleman) would be sticking exclusively to group originals, this exciting set gives one the opportunity to hear this band really stretching out on older tunes, showing off the influence of the avant-garde along with the players' own individual styles. It's highly recommended transitional music. *—Scott Yanow*

Miles in Tokyo / Jul. 14, 1964 / Columbia ♦♦♦♦
After George Coleman left the Miles Davis Quintet, tenor-saxophonist Sam Rivers took his place for a short period including a tour of Japan. Davis did not care for Rivers's avant-garde style (they failed to develop any chemistry) and soon replaced him, but this live LP (originally only issued in Japan) survived to document this brief association. The music (five lengthy versions of standards) is actually of high quality with both Davis and Rivers in fine form and the young rhythm section (pianist Herbie Hancock, bassist Ron Carter, and drummer Tony Williams) pushing the trumpeter/leader to open up his style. *—Scott Yanow*

☆ **E.S.P.** / Jan. 20, 1965-Jan. 22, 1965 / Columbia/Legacy ♦♦♦♦♦
ESP marks the beginning of a revitalization for Miles Davis, as his second classic quintet—saxophonist Wayne Shorter, pianist Herbie Hancock, bassist Ron Carter, and drummer Tony Williams—gels, establishing what would become their signature adventurous hard bop. Miles had been moving toward this direction in the two years preceding the release of *ESP* and he had recorded with everyone outside of Shorter prior to this record, but his addition galvanizes the group, pushing them toward music that was recognizably bop but as adventurous as jazz's avant-garde. Outwardly, this music doesn't take as many risks as Coltrane or Ornette Coleman's recordings of the mid-'60s, but by borrowing some of the same theories—a de-emphasis of composition in favor of sheer improvisation, elastic definitions of tonality—they created a unique sound that came to define the very sound of modern jazz. Certainly, many musicians have returned to this group for inspiration, but their recordings remain fresh, because they exist at this fine dividing line between standard bop and avant. On *ESP*, they tilt a bit toward conventional hard bop (something that's apparent toward the end of the record), largely because this is their first effort, but the fact is, this difference between this album and hard bop from the early '60s is remarkable. This is exploratory music, whether it's rushing by in a flurry of notes or elegantly reclining in Hancock's calm yet complex chords. The compositions are brilliantly structured as well, encouraging such free-form exploration with their elliptical yet memorable themes. This quintet may have cut more adventurous records, but *ESP* remains one of their very best albums. *—Stephen Thomas Erlewine*

☆ **The Miles Davis Quintet, 1965-68: The Complete Columbia Studio** / Jan. 20, 1965-Jun. 21, 1968 / Columbia/Legacy ♦♦♦♦♦
There's little argument that the quintet Miles Davis led between 1965 and 1968 was one of the classic combos in the history of jazz. By teaming with the adventurous young musicians Wayne Shorter (tenor sax), Herbie Hancock (piano), Ron Carter (bass) and Tony Williams (drums), Davis pushed mainstream jazz toward the avant-garde, expanding on the modal jazz he inaugurated with *Kind of Blue* and laid the groundwork for fusion. Four of their five studio albums—*ESP, Miles Smiles, Sorcerer, Nefertiti*—were essential, and even when they were slightly off the mark, as on *Miles in the Sky*, they were still filled with provocative sounds and ideas. That's the reason why *The Miles Davis Quintet 1965-'68: The Complete Columbia Studio Recordings* is an essential release. It contains all the music from each of the five studio records, plus half of the material released on *Filles De Kilimanjaro* and *Water Babies*, as well as several alternate takes and 13 previously unreleased selections. There's no question that this material is necessary for any jazz collection, but this may not necessarily be the best way to acquire it. The strict chronological sequencing is according to session order, which means the sequencing of the original albums—which was quite effective

in conveying the combo's ideas—is thrown out of line, and the long stretches where alternates and master takes are back to back may be tedious to some listeners. Also, packaging all the discs within cardboard mock-record sleeves in a bound booklet may look attractive, but it's impractical and not designed for heavy listening. In other words, this music is essential, and this set will appea to most serious jazz fans and historians, but less dedicated listeners are better served by the original albums. *—Stephen Thomas Erlewine*

☆ **The Complete Live at the Plugged Nickel** / Dec. 22, 1965-Dec. 23, 1965 / Columbia/Legacy ♦♦♦♦♦
All of the music that trumpeter Miles Davis and his second classic quintet (with tenor saxophonist Wayne Shorter, pianist Herbie Hancock, bassist Ron Carter and drummer Tony Williams) played at the Plugged Nickel in Chicago on two nights in 1965 have been released on this eight-CD box. The packaging is a bit confusing because Davis's group actually performed seven full sets, but, since their second one on the 22nd ran over, it has been issued on two CDs but placed inside the same package. In any case, the music during these two nights, primarily explorative versions of standards (as opposed to Miles's all-original studio albums of the period), is continually fascinating. A few titles are repeated, but the interpretations differ greatly from each other. The trumpeter's chops are actually not quite in peak form (although his creativity is) but Wayne Shorter (who often takes solo honors) is consistently brilliant and the rhythm section (propelled by Tony Williams) was one of the best of the period. Although some of this music had been issued earlier on three LPs, most of it had been out previously only in Japan. This was a very significant group (even if it were somewhat overshadowed by John Coltrane's Quartet at the time) and their advanced versions of such Miles Davis standards as "Walkin, "" "My Funny Valentine," "I Fall in Love Too Easily," "If I Were a Bell," "Stella by Starlight" and "So What" are among the many highlights. One of the top releases of 1995. *—Scott Yanow*

★ **Miles Smiles** / Oct. 24, 1966-Oct. 25, 1966 / Columbia/Legacy ♦♦♦♦♦
With their second album, *Miles Smiles*, the second Miles Davis Quintet really began to hit their stride, delving deeper into the more adventurous, exploratory side of their signature sound. This is clear as soon as "Orbits" comes crashing out the gate, but it's not just the fast, manic material that has an edge—slower, quieter numbers are mercurial, not just in how they shift melodies and chords, but how the voicing and phrasing never settles into a comfortable groove. This is music that demands attention, never taking predictable paths or easy choices. Its greatest triumph is that it masks this adventurousness within music that is warm and accessible—it just never acts that way. No matter how accessible this is, what's so utterly brilliant about it is that the group never brings it forth to the audience. They're playing for each other, pushing and prodding each other in an effort to discover new territory. As such, this crackles with vitality, sounding fresh decades after its release. And, like its predecessor, *ESP*, this freshness informs the writing as well, as the originals are memorable, yet open-ended and nervy, setting (and creating) standards for modern bop that were emulated well into the new century. Arguably, this quintet was never better than they are here, when all their strengths are in full bloom. *—Stephen Thomas Erlewine*

☆ **Nefertiti** / Jun. 7, 1967-Jul. 19, 1967 / Columbia/Legacy ♦♦♦♦♦
Nefertiti, the fourth album by Miles Davis' second classic quintet, continues the forward motion of *Sorcerer*, as the group settles into a low-key, exploratory groove, offering music with recognizable themes—but themes that were deliberately dissonant, slightly unsettling even as they burrowed their way into the consciousness. In a sense, this is mood music, since, like on much of *Sorcerer*, the individual parts mesh in unpredictable ways, creating evocative, floating soundscapes. This music anticipates the free-fall, impressionistic work of *In a Silent Way*, yet it remains rooted in hard bop, particularly when the tempo is a bit sprightly, as on "Hand Jive." Yet even when the instrumentalists and soloists are placed in the foreground—such as Miles' extended opening solo on "Madness" or Hancock's long solo toward the end of the piece—this never feels like showcases for virtuosity, the way some showboating hard bop can, though each player shines. What's impressive, like on all of this quintet's sessions, is the interplay, how the musicians follow an unpredictable path as a unit, turning in music that is always searching, always provocative, and never boring. Perhaps *Nefertiti*'s charms are a little more subtle than those of its predecessors, but that makes it intriguing. Besides, this album so clearly points the way to fusion, while remaining acoustic, that it may force listeners on either side of the fence into another direction. *—Stephen Thomas Erlewine*

Water Babies / Jun. 1967-Jul. 1969 / Columbia ♦♦♦

Miles in the Sky / Jan. 16, 1968-May 17, 1968 / Columbia/Legacy ♦♦♦♦
With the 1968 album *Miles in the Sky*, Miles Davis explicitly pushed his second great quintet away from conventional jazz, pushing them toward the jazz-rock hybrid that would later become known as fusion. Here, the music is still in its formative stages, and it's a little more earth-bound than you might expect, especially following on the heels of the shape-shifting, elusive *Nefertiti*. On *Miles in the Sky*, much of the rhythms are straightforward, picking up on the direct 4/4 beats of rock, and these are illuminated by Herbie Hancock's electric piano—one of the very first sounds on the record, as a matter of fact—and the guest appearance of guitarist George Benson on "Paraphernalia." All of these additions are tangible and identifiable, and they do result in intriguing music, but the form of the music itself is surprisingly direct, playing as extended grooves. This meanders considerable more than *Nefertiti*, even if it is significantly less elliptical in its form, because it's primarily four long jams. Intriguing, successful jams in many respects, but even with the notable additions of electric instruments, and with the deliberately noisy "Country Son," this is less visionary than its predecessor and feels like a transitional album—and, like many transitional albums, it's intriguing and frustrating in equal measures. *—Stephen Thomas Erlewine*

Filles de Kilimanjaro / Jun. 19, 1968-Sep. 24, 1968 / Columbia ♦♦♦♦♦
Since it's billed as "Directions in Music By Miles Davis," it should come as little surprise that *Filles de Kilimanjaro* is the beginning of a new phase for Miles, the place that he begins to dive headfirst into jazz-rock fusion. It also happens to be the swan song for his second classic quintet, arguably the finest collective of musicians he ever worked with, and what makes this album so fascinating is that it's possible to hear the breaking point—though his quintet all followed him into fusion (three of his supporting players were on *In a Silent Way*), it's possible to hear them all break with the conventional notions of what constituted even adventurous jazz, turning into something new. According to Miles, the change in "direction" was as much inspired by a desire to return to something earthy and bluesy as it was to find new musical territory, and *Filles de Kilimanjaro* bears him out. Though the album sports inexplicable, rather ridiculous French song titles, this is music that is unpretentiously adventurous, grounded in driving, mildly funky rhythms and bluesy growls from Miles, graced with weird, colorful flourishes from the band. Where *Miles in the Sky* meandered a bit, this is considerably more focused, even on the three songs that run over ten minutes, yet it still feels transitional. Not tentative (which *In the Sky* was), but certainly the music that would spring full bloom on *In a Silent Way* was still in the gestation phase, and despite the rock-blues-n-funk touches here, the music doesn't fly and search the way that *Nefertiti* did. But that's not a bad thing—this middle ground between the adventurous bop of the mid-'60s and the fusion of the late '60s is rewarding in its own right, since it's possible to hear great musicians find the foundation of a new form. For that alone, *Filles de Kilimanjaro* is necessary listening. *—Stephen Thomas Erlewine*

☆ **In a Silent Way** / Feb. 18, 1969 / Columbia ♦♦♦♦♦
The beginning of fusion (although other groups such as Gary Burton's Quartet with Larry Coryell had hinted strongly at it), this set found Miles Davis for the first time really combining jazz improvising with the rhythms and power of rock. On this LP, Davis jams with an octet (which includes the magical names of tenor-saxophonist Wayne Shorter, keyboardists Herbie Hancock, Chick Corea, and Joe Zawinul, guitarist John McLaughlin, bassist Dave Holland, and drummer Tony Williams; all future bandleaders) on two lengthy side-long medleys. Those jazz purists with their minds closed toward electronics of any kind are advised to check out this fairly accessible date before tackling *Bitches Brew*. The strong solos on this early fusion classic might very well win them over. *—Scott Yanow*

★ **Bitches Brew** / Aug. 19, 1969-Aug. 21, 1969 / Columbia/Legacy ♦♦♦♦♦
No jazz collection is complete without *Bitches Brew*, an influential set that was one of the first successful attempts to form a new music (soon termed fusion) by combining jazz solos with rock rhythms. "Miles Runs the Voodoo Down" is the most memorable of the six lengthy selections, featuring a fascinating ensemble with Davis's trumpet, Wayne Shorter's soprano, Bennie Maupin's bass clarinet, guitarist John McLaughlin, the keyboards of Chick Corea and Larry Young (Joe Zawinul is on some of the other selections), Dave Holland and Harvey Brooks on basses, drummers Jack DeJohnette, Charles Alias, and Lenny White, and percussionist Jim Riley. Not for the close-minded, this music brought many rock listeners into jazz and gave jazz musicians new possibilities to explore. *—Scott Yanow*

The Complete Bitches Brew Sessions (August 1969-February 1970) / Aug. 19, 1969-Feb. 6, 1970 / Columbia/Legacy ♦♦♦♦♦
Columbia's continuing summation of the career of Miles Davis through lavish box-set reissues resumed in 1998 with *The Complete Bitches Brew Sessions*, a four-disc set including all the music from the original 1970 double album *Bitches Brew* plus over two additional hours of music from the six-month period during which the album was recorded. (Some of those tracks were previously released on compilations like *Big Fun* and *Circle in the Round*, but almost one-third of the material lay unissued until this release.) The music is simply fabulous—the simultaneous birth and peak of jazz-rock/fusion, with a host of major players (John McLaughlin, Chick Corea, Joe Zawinul, Wayne Shorter, Jack DeJohnette) and many innovations. There is a bit more evidence of tape hiss than in Columbia's last American remastering of the album, but the revelations of depth and timbre more than make up for it. Though the unreleased selections are distinctly inferior to those released on *Bitches Brew*, "Yaphet," "Corrado," and "Trevere" are intriguing jam sessions that reveal much about the creative process between Davis and producer Teo Macero during recording. Unlike Columbia's previous sets in the series (one treating Miles' period of collaboration with Gil Evans and one featuring the music of his second classic quintet), the *Bitches Brew* sessions lend themselves well to a box set of this type—presenting the music in chronological order does no harm to original LP configurations as it did on previous sets, and the music here is another glowing testament to Miles Davis' importance to the development of jazz in 1969, as in 1949. *—John Bush*

Big Fun / Nov. 19, 1969-Jun. 12, 1972 / Columbia/Legacy ♦♦

Live-Evil / Feb. 6, 1970-Dec. 19, 1970 / Columbia/Legacy ♦♦♦♦♦
The first in a continuing series of double-LP extravaganzas released only in Japan in the early '70s, *Live-Evil* mixes four studio tracks from 1970 with four live ones taken from a Washington, D.C. performance in December of that year. Amidst heavy competition, the live tracks—including "What I Say," "Sivad" and "Funky Tonk"—are the highlights, featuring some of Miles' best playing of the decade, plus aggressive work on extended solo spots by John McLaughlin on guitar, Keith Jarrett on keyboards, and Jack DeJohnette on drums. Alternating chaotic deep-groove passages with a few more atmospheric, *Live-Evil* held up for two decades as one of the great import-only Miles Davis albums, until it was reissued in America by Columbia/Legacy in 1997. *—John Bush*

A Tribute to Jack Johnson / Apr. 7, 1970 / Columbia ♦♦♦♦♦
Davis's odd soundtrack for a documentary on the boxer Jack Johnson did not really fit the movie (it was far too modern) but stands alone very well as a strong piece of music. On this straight reissue of the original LP, the two lengthy jams (25-minute-plus versions of "Right Off" and "Yesternow") feature fine playing by a sextet comprised of Davis's trumpet, Steve Grossman's soprano sax, keyboardist Herbie Hancock, guitarist John McLaughlin, electric bassist Michael Henderson and drummer Billy Cobham. Even listeners who write off the fusion years will find moments of interest on this set. *—Scott Yanow*

Black Beauty: Miles Davis at Fillmore West / Apr. 10, 1970 / Columbia/Legacy ♦♦♦
Prior to 1997, when the music was finally released domestically on a double CD, this particular Miles Davis concert was only available in Japan. The trumpeter used what was essen-

tially a stripped-down *Bitches Brew* sextet (with Steve Grossman on soprano, Chick Corea on Fender Rhodes, electric bassist Dave Holland, drummer Jack DeJohnette, and percussionist Airto) to play a continuous 80-minute set. Grossman's soprano playing gets a bit limited at times, and Corea's banging of the electric piano is sometimes a little monotonous, but Davis is heard in superior form, and the rhythm section (with Airto adding many colorful sounds) is excellent. The jam (which includes "Directions," a very brief "I Fall in Love Too Easily," Wayne Shorter's "Sanctuary," and "Bitches Brew," among others) is quite intriguing, high-quality fusion with plenty of surprising turns. *—Scott Yanow*

Miles Davis at Fillmore: Live at the Fillmore East / Jun. 17, 1970-Jun. 20, 1970 / Columbia/Legacy ✦✦✦

On the Corner / Jun. 1, 1972-Jun. 6, 1972 / Columbia/Legacy ✦✦✦
On the Corner is Miles Davis's most controversial album. Jazz purists detest the album, dismissing it out of hand for the very reason that its fans celebrate it—there are no fully formed songs on the record, just funky rhythmic vamps. Davis assembled a large group of musicians, who aren't credited on the record, and had them play one groove, which demonstrated a heavy debt to Sly Stone. Miles rarely plays trumpet on the record, and when he does, it is distorted and processed. Instead, he plays organ, blending into the dense, electric funk. None of the players take extended solos and all of the songs are brief, but improvisation isn't the point of the record. *On the Corner* is about funk and rhythm, not about jazz. With this record, Davis laid the foundation of the genre-blurring hip-hop and acid jazz revolutions in popular music in the '80s and '90s. *—Stephen Thomas Erlewine*

Get Up with It / Sep. 6, 1972-Oct. 7, 1974 / Columbia/Legacy ✦✦✦
This double LP, featuring a variety of Miles Davis' electric ensembles of 1974, has plenty of variety, ranging from a sidelong dirge for Duke Ellington ("He Loved Him Madly") and a dumb but interesting "Red China Blues" to heated jams on "Honky Tonk," "Calypso Frelimo," and "Mtume." Although Davis plays organ rather than trumpet half the time, the dense ensembles and passionate improvisations are creative rather than predictable. *—Scott Yanow*

In Concert: Live at Philharmonic Hall / Sep. 29, 1972 / Columbia/Legacy ✦✦

Dark Magus / Mar. 3, 1974 / Sony ✦✦✦
The music on this double CD, released domestically for the first time in 1997, was only previously out in Japan and was formerly among the rarest of Miles Davis recordings. Featured is one of the trumpeter's most controversial bands, a noisy ensemble with three guitarists (Reggie Lucas, Pete Cosey, and Dominique Gaumont), electric bassist Michael Henderson, drummer Al Foster, percussionist Mtume, Dave Liebman on tenor, soprano, and flute, and guest tenorman Azar Lawrence. The spontaneous music has plenty of repetitive funk sounds from the guitars and bits of aimless rambling, along with some strong moments from Davis and Liebman. If drastically edited, the double CD would have made a killer single disc, for there are some very interesting stretches when magic occurs, but these are often succeeded by overlong vamps. Worth checking out, but not essential. *—Scott Yanow*

Agharta / Feb. 1, 1975 / Columbia ✦✦✦

Pangaea / Feb. 1, 1975 / Columbia ✦✦✦✦
Although Davis's health was shaky at the time of this two-CD set (recorded the same day as the weaker *Agharta*), he has a few strong trumpet solos on these two very lengthy pieces ("Zimbabwe" and "Gondwana"); Davis would drift into retirement for six years shortly after this concert. The music is actually quite rewarding (at least it will be for listeners with open ears) with the dense ensembles and heated solos (Sonny Fortune on soprano, alto, and flute and the guitars of Pete Cosey and Reggie Lucas) being quite dangerous, as opposed to the safe fusion of the 1990s. *Pangaea* is the finest recording from the least-understood period of Davis's career (1971-1975). *—Scott Yanow*

The Man with the Horn / 1981 / Columbia ✦✦✦

We Want Miles / Jun. 27, 1981-Oct. 4, 1981 / Columbia ✦✦✦✦

Star People / Sep. 1, 1982-Jan. 5, 1983 / Columbia ✦✦✦✦

Decoy / Jun. 30, 1983-Sep. 11, 1983 / Columbia ✦✦

You're Under Arrest / 1985 / Columbia ✦✦

Aura / Jan. 31, 1985-Feb. 4, 1985 / Columbia ✦✦✦

Tutu / Jan. 6, 1986-Mar. 25, 1986 / Warner Brothers ✦✦✦

Music from Siesta / Jan. 19, 1987-Mar. 1987 / Warner Brothers ✦✦✦

Amandla / 1989 / Warner Brothers ✦✦✦✦

Miles & Quincy Live at Montreux / Jul. 8, 1991 / Warner Brothers ✦✦✦

☆ **The Complete Birth of the Cool** / May 19, 1998 / Blue Note ✦✦✦✦✦
Capitol's *The Complete Birth of the Cool* is a double-disc set that's separated into two halves. The first contains all 12 tracks Davis cut in the studio in January 1949 with Gil Evans. The second contains three radio broadcasts that the Bright of the Cool nonet performed in September 1948 at the Royal Roost in New York City. All the recordings have been completely remastered, resulting in the best ever sound for these recordings. The set also features brand new liner notes from Phil Schapp, plus the original liners. All the added features help make *The Complete Birth of the Cool* the definitive chronicle of one of the most important eras in jazz history. *—Stephen Thomas Erlewine*

The Complete Columbia Recordings 1955-1961 / Oct. 26, 1955-Mar. 21, 1961 / Columbia/Legacy ✦✦✦✦✦
As the fourth (fifth, if you count the *Complete Plugged Nickel*) entry in Columbia's celebrated series of Miles Davis box sets, *The Complete Columbia Recordings: Miles Davis & John Coltrane* was perhaps the most anticipated set, and it's easy to see why. The push and pull between Miles and Coltrane resulted in dynamic recordings that set the standard for modern jazz—and this was for their Prestige recordings, before they even moved to Columbia. Once Miles relocated to Columbia, he began to push the boundaries of his music. The progression from the sublime, after-hours *Round About Midnight* to the modal *Milestones* is remarkable—all the more so when *Kind of Blue*, the culmination of Davis's modal direction, is taken into the equation. Over the course of six discs, *The Complete Columbia Recordings* traces this progression, including the entirety of *'Round About Midnight, Milestones*, and *Kind of Blue*, plus selections from *Someday My Prince Will Come*, the live album *Miles & Coltrane 57*, and 18 unreleased tracks, all alternate takes. Even if you're familiar with this music—and any jazz fan will be—the chronological, session-order sequencing keeps it fresh, and it's possible to marvel at how quickly their talents deepened. For neophytes, this isn't really an ideal way to dive into these remarkable recordings, since there's not only too much, but it's arranged in a way that doesn't ease the listener into the music. It's designed to be a library piece for collectors, fans, and historians that have already absorbed the music fully. After all, the original album covers are not reproduced anywhere in the notes, and the discs themselves are cryptically identified with dots that parallel the numbers on a clock. For anyone that knows and loves this music though, this is an essential addition to a comprehensive jazz library. *—Stephen Thomas Erlewine*

Walter Davis, Jr.

b. Sep. 2, 1932, Richmond, VA, **d.** Jun. 2, 1990, New York, NY
Piano / Hard Bop, Bop
In 1959 Walter Davis, Jr. led one of the great Blue Note sessions, a quintet set with Donald Byrd and Jackie McLean called *Davis Cup*. It seems strange that not only did he not have an opportunity for an encore but his next session as a leader was for Denon, in 1977! An excellent bop-based pianist, Walter Davis picked up early experience in the late '40s working with Babs Gonzales' Three Bips and a Bop before playing and recording with Charlie Parker in 1952. Following were associations with Max Roach (1952-53), Dizzy Gillespie's big band (1956), Donald Byrd (1959) and Art Blakey's Jazz Messengers (1959). After a long period outside of music Davis came back to play with Sonny Rollins (1973-74), the Jazz Messengers (1975-77) and then as leader of his own group. He was on the soundtrack of the film *Bird* and recorded extensively as a leader during 1977-79 (for Denon, Bee Hive, Red and Owl) and in 1987-89 (for Jazz Heritage, Jazz City, Mapleshade and SteepleChase). *—Scott Yanow*

● **Davis Cup** / Aug. 2, 1959 / Blue Note ✦✦✦✦✦
Walter Davis Jr.'s debut record as a leader for Blue Note is a terrific hard bop session, a driving collection of six original tunes that emphasize the strengths not only of the pianist himself, but also his supporting band: trumpeter Donald Byrd, alto saxophonist Jackie McLean, bassist Sam Jones, and drummer Art Taylor. Apart from the lovely ballad "Sweetness," *Davis Cup* moves along at a brisk pace, with the rhythm section urging the soloists to new heights. Byrd has rarely sounded better, and on this date, McLean provides ample evidence that he was moving beyond the conventions of hard bop and developing his own unique style. Davis, of course, does more than acquit himself—he contributes an engaging, energetic performance that keeps the music grounded. His compositions are just as captivating, whether it's the swinging "Rhumba Nhumba" or the darkly invigorating "Minor Mind." It all adds up to a wonderful straight-ahead hard bop date, one that's so good it's a wonder that Davis didn't receive another chance to lead a session until 1979. *—Stephen Thomas Erlewine*

In Walked Thelonious / Apr. 1987- 198 / Mapleshade ✦✦✦✦✦
Pianist Walter Davis, Jr. led relatively few recording sessions throughout his career despite his obvious talent. In fact this CD was his first opportunity to head a date for an American label since his lone Blue Note set back in 1959! Davis performs 14 Thelonious Monk songs (including two versions of "'Round Midnight") unaccompanied. To his credit he does not avoid the more difficult and obscure works (including "Gallop's Gallop," "Trinkle Twinkle," and "Criss Cross"), and he consistently plays with creativity and a dose of the famous Monk wit. Walter Davis, Jr. knew Thelonious Monk both personally and musically, and his familiarity really shows on this easily recommended release. *—Scott Yanow*

Wild Bill Davison (William Stethen Davis)

b. Jan. 5, 1906, Defiance, OH, **d.** Nov. 14, 1989, Santa Barbara, CA
Cornet / Dixieland Revival, Dixieland
One of the great Dixieland trumpeters, Wild Bill Davison had a colorful and emotional style that ranged from sarcasm to sentimentality with plenty of growls and shakes. His unexpected placement of high notes was a highlight of his solos and his strong personality put him far ahead of the competition. In the 1920s he played with the Ohio Lucky Seven, the Chubb-Steinberg Orchestra (with whom he made his recording debut), the Seattle Harmony Kings and Benny Meroff. After he was involved in a fatal car accident that ended the life of Frankie Teschemacher in 1932 (his auto was blindsided by a taxi), Davison spent the remainder of the 1930s in exile in Milwaukee. By 1941 he was in New York and in 1943 made some brilliant recordings for Commodore (including a classic version of "That's a Plenty") that solidified his reputation. After a period in the Army, Davison became a fixture with Eddie Condon's bands starting in 1945, playing nightly at Condon's. In the 1950s he was quite effective on a pair of albums with string orchestras but most of his career was spent fronting Dixieland bands either as a leader or with Condon. Wild Bill toured Europe often from the 1960s, recorded constantly, had a colorful life filled with remarkable episodes and was active up until his death. A very detailed 1996 biography (*The Wildest One* by Hal Willard) has many hilarious anecdotes and shows just how unique a life Wild Bill Davison had. *—Scott Yanow*

★ **The Commodore Master Takes** / Nov. 27, 1943-Jan. 4, 1946 / GRP ✦✦✦✦✦
This 1997 CD contains some of the most rewarding Dixieland ever recorded. On November 27, 1943 cornetist Wild Bill Davison, trombonist George Brunies (in peak form), clarinetist Pee Wee Russell, pianist Gene Schroeder, rhythm guitarist Eddie Condon, bassist Bob Casey and drummer George Wettling cut a classic version of "That's a Plenty," along with three other songs that show just how exciting the style can be. Also on this CD are Davison's other Commodore sessions as a leader, 24 titles in all that include such outstanding players as clarinetists Edmond Hall, Joe Marsala and Albert Nicholas, trombonist Lou McGarity, pianists Dick Cary and Joe Sullivan, and drummers Danny Alvin and Dave Tough. With definitive

versions of such tunes as "Muskrat Ramble," "At the Jazz Band Ball," "Jazz Me Blues," "Sensation" and "I'm Coming Virginia," this is an essential acquisition for anyone even remotely interested in freewheeling Chicago Dixieland jazz. *—Scott Yanow*

And His Jazz Band, 1943 / Dec. 3, 1944–Oct. 13, 1955 / Jazzology ✦✦✦✦
This CD contains the complete Wild Bill Davison session of December 3, 1944 (which was originally made as radio transciptions) and part of a date led by the cornetist in 1955. The former set has five songs, plus five alternate takes, from a particularly mighty outfit also including trombonist George Brunis, clarinetist Pee Wee Russell, pianist Gene Schroeder, Eddie Condon on rhythm guitar, bassist Bob Casey and drummer George Wettling. Highlights include "That's a Plenty," the many different versions of "Royal Garden Blues" and "Muskrat Ramble." Only three songs are included from the later session, which matches Davison with trombonist Lou McGarity, clarinetist Tony Parenti, pianist Hank Duncan, bassist Pops Foster and drummer Zutty Singleton, but there are also 12 false starts and 11 alternate takes, eight of which are incomplete. Obviously this CD is mostly for true Dixieland completists and fanatics, but fans of Wild Bill Davison will find his many consistently colorful variations worth hearing. *—Scott Yanow*

☆ **Showcase** / Dec. 27, 1947-Oct. 19, 1976 / Jazzology ✦✦✦✦✦
Two unrelated but rewarding sessions by the great Dixieland cornetist Wild Bill Davison are combined on this delightful CD. The first session, a six-song ballad-oriented date that also includes trombonist Jimmy Archey, Garvin Bushell on clarinet and (on "Yesterdays") bassoon, pianist Ralph Sutton, bassist Sid Weiss and drummer Morey Feld, has some particularly ferocious playing from Davison (who takes his first recorded vocal on "Ghost of a Chance"). The remaining dozen tunes come from a very successful matchup in 1976 between Davison and the Classic Jazz Collegium Orchestra, a talented ten-member Czechoslovakian group. Some of the numbers (most notably a classic rendition of "Sunday") have inventive arrangements that make the band sound like a unit from the 1920s. Wild Bill is quite inspired throughout, making this one of his most rewarding sets of the 1970s. Highly recommended. *—Scott Yanow*

Sweet and Lovely / Aug. 6, 1976-Aug. 8, 1976 / Storyville ✦✦✦✦
The arrangements for the 12-piece string section on this Storyville set may not be all that inspiring (functioning primarily as background music) but cornetist Wild Bill Davison's solos are thoughtful, very expressive and consistently inspired. Wild Bill performs a dozen of his favorite ballads and, although violinist Finn Ziegler has a few solos and there are guest spots for clarinetist Jesper Thilo and trombonist Ole "Fessor" Lindgreen, Davison is largely the entire show. His warm playing on such numbers as "Sugar," "Serenade in Blue," "She's Funny That Way" and "If I Had You" is sometimes both haunting and memorable. *—Scott Yanow*

Together Again / May 23, 1977-May 24, 1977 / Storyville ✦✦✦✦
Cornetist Wild Bill Davison and the masterful stride pianist Ralph Sutton team up on this Copenhagen session with five fine Danish musicians, including Jesper Thilo (who switches between tenor, clarinet, and soprano) and trombonist Ole "Fessor" Lindgreen. The program emphasizes swing standards and finds Davison (71 at the time) still in exciting form. Among the memorable selections on the exuberant set are "Everybody Loves My Baby," "Shine," "Running Wild," and Davison's vocal on "After I Say I'm Sorry." The superior playing of Wild Bill and Sutton make this one of the better Storyville trad sets of the past few decades. *—Scott Yanow*

With Fessor's Big City Band / Mar. 3, 1998 / Storyville ✦✦✦✦
Cornetist Wild Bill Davison spent a good amount of time in Scandinavia during the 1970s where he enjoyed playing with both Papa Bue's Vikings and Fessor's Big City Jazz Band. The latter group, led by trombonist Ole "Fessor" Lindgreen, is heard on this 1997 CD performing with the exciting cornetist in 1973, 1974, 1977 and 1978. The repertoire is primarily Dixieland and swing standards with a few departures (Johnny Hodges' "Open Ears," Neal Hefti's "Duet" and an original, "My Friend Bill") working out quite well. Some selections have Finn Otto Hansen or Verner Work Nielsen on trumpets, Steen Vig helps out on tenor and soprano and, on "Sweet Lorraine," the great pianist Ralph Sutton sits in. A typically spirited Dixieland-oriented set from Wild Bill. *—Scott Yanow*

Pretty Wild/With Strings Attached / Feb. 22, 1956-Jan. 11, 1957 / Arbors ✦✦✦✦✦
The commercial success of Charlie Parker's *Bird With Strings* sessions of 1949-1950 inspired countless jazz musicians to follow his lead and record albums with string orchestras in the 1950s and 1960s. One of them was Wild Bill Davison, who was joined by lush string orchestras on two Columbia dates: 1956's *Pretty Wild* (which employs Percy Faith's band) and 1957's *With Strings Attached*. In 2000, Arbors reissued those two albums back to back on this CD, which was long overdue because they were out of print for many years. These recordings are, for the most part, a departure from the type of hard-swinging Dixieland that Davison is best known for. Some jazz purists cried foul when *Pretty Wild* and *With Strings Attached* first came out in the late 1950s-as they saw it, jazzmen who recorded with strings were pandering to the pop market. But purists be damned; Davison's playing is simply gorgeous on lyrical versions of "Prelude to a Kiss," "Our Love Is Here to Stay," and other standards. He was a superb ballad player, and there is nothing wrong with the cornetist allowing his romantic side to prevail. This superb CD is recommended to anyone who is looking for a collection of five-star mood music. *—Alex Henderson*

Joey de Francesco

b. Apr. 10, 1971, Philadelphia, PA
Organ (Hammond), Trumpet, Organ / Hard Bop, Soul-Jazz
The comeback of the organ in jazz during the late '80s was partly due to the rise of Joey DeFrancesco, a brilliant and energetic player whose style is heavily influenced by Jimmy Smith.

Joey DeFrancisco was born April 10, 1971 in Springfield, PA and was raised in the Philadelphia area. The son of Papa John DeFrancisco, a fierce Hammond organ player himself, Joey got an early start on piano when he was five and within a year had switched to his father's instrument, the organ.

He won all kinds of major awards in high school including the Philadelphia Jazz Society's McCoy Tyner Scholarship. In the first Thelonious Monk International Jazz Piano Competition in 1987 he was a finalist at the age of 16. More. He is a decent player too.

He had a record contract with Columbia, was playing with Miles Davis (1988) by the time he left high school and has led his own groups ever since. DeFrancesco is the most important new organist to emerge during the past decade. He recorded for Columbia, Muse and Big Mo before signing to High Note for 1998's *All in the Family; The Champ: Dedicated to Jimmy Smith* followed a year later, and in 2000 DeFrancesco returned with *Incredible*. *—Scott Yanow & Michael Erlewine*

All of Me / 1989 / Columbia ✦✦✦✦✦
Organist Joey DeFrancesco's debut as a leader would be impressive even if he had not been 17 at the time! DeFrancesco, whose sound has always been strongly influenced by Jimmy Smith (sounding like an exact duplicate on "All of Me"), is backed by an eight-piece horn section on two songs and a 16-piece string section on three others but more important to the music is the playing of guitarist Lou Volpe, drummer Buddy Williams and the electric bass of Alex Blake. Houston Person's tenor is also a strong asset on two of the eight numbers in a program that ranges from swing to more modern funk. A strong start to a colorful career. *—Scott Yanow*

● **Where Were You—** / Jun. 1990 / Columbia ✦✦✦✦✦
On his second recording, organist Joey DeFrancesco is heard in settings ranging from a quartet to a large orchestra. Although he is generally the main star, DeFrancesco welcomes such guests as tenors Illinois Jacquet and Kirk Whalum (heard on two songs apiece including both jamming on "Red Top") and guitarist John Scofield. DeFrancesco holds his own and is in top form on such selections as "Teach Me Tonight," "Where Were You," "But Not for Me" and "Love Attack." *—Scott Yanow*

Live at the 5 Spot / 1993 / Columbia ✦✦✦
Organist Joey DeFrancesco clearly had a good time during this jam session. His fine quintet (which has strong soloists in altoist Robert Landham, trumpeter Jim Henry and especially guitarist Paul Bollenback) starts things off with a runthrough of "rhythm changes" during "The Eternal One" and the hornless trio cuts loose on a swinging "I'll Remember April," but otherwise all of the other selections feature guests. Tenors Illinois Jacquet, Grover Washington, Jr., Houston Person and Kirk Whalum all fare well on separate numbers (Jacquet steals the show on "All of Me") and on the closing blues DeFrancesco interacts with fellow organist Captain Jack McDuff. Few surprises occur overall (the tenors should have all played together) but the music is quite pleasing and easily recommended to DeFrancesco's fans. *—Scott Yanow*

The Champ / May 27, 1998 / High Note ✦✦✦✦
In a way, Joey DeFrancesco's entire career has been devoted to Jimmy Smith. Ever since he arrived in the late '80s, DeFrancesco was known for his dexterous assimilation of Smith's tasteful soul-jazz, and he expanded on that basic sound as the '90s progressed. It was likely just a matter of time before he sat down and recorded a full-fledged tribute to the Master of the Jazz Organ—which is exactly what he did with *Champ: Dedicated to Jimmy Smith*. Working with bassist Randy Johnston and drummer Billy Hart, DeFrancesco keeps the spirit of Smith's classic Blue Note sessions alive, and *Champ* is indeed an expert emulation of that clean yet funky sound—so much so that certain listeners may wonder what the point is and why not just listen to Smith's own albums. That's a valid complaint, since DeFrancesco rarely finds a voice of his own on this record, but the album itself is a good listen for that very reason. *—Stephen Thomas Erlewine*

Joey DeFrancesco's Goodfellas / Mar. 17-18, 1998 / Concord Jazz ✦✦✦
Try to imagine the best Italian-American wedding you've every been to—the people, the food, the style, the love—then set it to some great jazz music, Joey DeFrancesco's Goodfellas. Add this killer band to your next wedding party and be prepared to have the time of your life. Plain and simple, this album is 55 minutes of unabated fun. Joey DeFrancesco (Hammond B-3 organ), Frank Vignola (guitar), and Joe Ascione (drums), three outstanding musicians who grew up in typical Italian-American families, play some of the music on which they were raised. Highlights abound on this brilliant concept piece: the kicked-up, jazzy "Volare," the groovy, tasty "Fly Me to the Moon," the energetic, rollicking "Malafemmena," and the beautiful slow dance "Young at Heart." Even Monk's "Evidence," taken at a blistering pace, is right at home in this setting. The Goodfellas wrote a couple of tunes for the occasion as well, none better than the bluesy, gutbucket title track. This band has big-time chops, and this music swings like mad. *—Brian Bartolini*

Incredible! / Oct. 28, 1999 / Concord Jazz ✦✦✦✦

Buddy DeFranco (Boniface Ferdinand Leonardo DeFranco)

b. Feb. 17, 1923, Camden, NJ
Clarinet / Post-Bop, Bop
Buddy DeFranco is one of the great clarinetists of all time and, until the rise of Eddie Daniels, he was indisputably the top clarinetist to emerge since 1940. It was DeFranco's misfortune to be the best on an instrument that after the swing era dropped drastically in popularity and, unlike Benny Goodman and Artie Shaw, he has never been a household name for the general public. After working with the big bands of Gene Krupa (1941-42) and Charlie Barnet (1943-44), he was with Tommy Dorsey on and off during 1944-48. DeFranco, other than spending part of 1950 with Count Basie's septet, was mostly a bandleader from then on. Among the few clarinetists to transfer the language of Charlie Parker onto his instrument, DeFranco recorded frequently in the 1950s (among his sidmeen were Art Blakey, Kenny Drew and Sonny Clark), and participated in some of Norman Granz's Verve jam sessions. However work was difficult to find in the 1960s, leading DeFranco to accept the assignment of leading the Glenn Miller ghost band (1966-74). He has found more artistic success coleading a quintet with Terry Gibbs off and on since the early '80s and has recorded through the decades for many labels. *—Scott Yanow*

★ **Complete Verve Recordings of Buddy De Franco with Sonny Clark** / Apr. 7, 1954-Aug. 26, 1955 / Mosaic ♦♦♦♦♦
Clarinetist Buddy DeFranco recorded extensively for Norgran and Verve during 1953-1958. For a little over a year, Sonny Clark was his regular pianist and all of their small-group recordings have been reissued on this limited-edition five-LP set. With bassist Eugene Wright (a couple years before he joined the Dave Brubeck Quartet) and drummer Bobby White completing the quartet, and guitarist Tal Farlow making the group a quintet on its final 11 numbers, DeFranco had one of his strongest bands. The majority of the 39 selections on the typically attractive Mosaic box are standards or based on a familiar tune's chord changes. Buddy DeFranco had no real competitors (other than Benny Goodman) during the era, while Sonny Clark was one of the most talented of the Bud Powell-influenced pianists; they made for a mutually inspiring team. *—Scott Yanow*

☆ **Like Someone in Love** / Mar. 11, 1989 / Progressive ♦♦♦♦♦
An all-star quintet comprised of clarinetist Buddy DeFranco, guitarist Tal Farlow, pianist Derek Smith, bassist George Duvivier and drummer Ronnie Bedford performs two obscure DeFranco originals, Jim Gillis' "Coasting at the Palisades," a couple of Gershwin classics and the title cut. DeFranco and Farlow made for an appealing team in the mid-'50s when they briefly played together regularly and the old magic (fueled by Derek Smith's fine swing solos) was still present for this excellent 1977 session. *—Scott Yanow*

Hark / Apr. 30, 1985 / Pablo/OJC ♦♦♦♦♦
This CD reissue of a Pablo date by clarinetist Buddy DeFranco teams him with pianist Oscar Peterson, guitarist Joe Pass, bassist Niels Pedersen and drummer Martin Drew. They perform a few obscure originals plus Duke Ellington's "All Too Soon," "By Myself" and Clifford Brown's "Joy Spring." DeFranco has been very consistent throughout his long recording career but the presence of Peterson and Pass clearly inspired him to play even better than usual. Recommended. *—Scott Yanow*

Holiday for Swing / Aug. 22, 1988-Aug. 23, 1988 / Contemporary ♦♦♦♦♦
The two virtuosoes clarinetist Buddy DeFranco and vibraphonist Terry Gibbs always inspire each other. Gibbs is such a hyper player and DeFranco can play very fast with no difficulty, so they make for a perfectly compatible team. Most of their joint projects have been released under Gibbs' name but on this occasion, DeFranco received first billing. With pianist John Campbell, bassist Todd Coolman and drummer Gerry Gibbs forming a powerhouse rhythm section, DeFranco and Gibbs romp on such material as "Holiday for Strings," "Seven Come Eleven," "Carioca," Bud Powell's "Parisian Thoroughfare" and Gibbs' "Fickle Fingers." Joyous music. *—Scott Yanow*

Mr. Lucky / Jan. 5, 1981–Jan. 6, 1981 / Pablo/OJC ♦♦♦
Considering that he recorded extensively for Norman Granz's Norgran and Verve labels in the 1950s, it is surprising that it took until 1984 before clarinetist Buddy DeFranco finally led a session for Granz's Pablo Records. On the first of his two Pablo dates, DeFranco is joined by the cool-toned guitarist Joe Cohn, pianist Albert Dailey, bassist George Duvivier and drummer Ronnie Bedford for some standards along with obscurities by Victor Feldman ("Your Smile"), Al Cohn, Bernie Senensky and Eddie Higgins; he also greatly uplifts Henry Mancini's "Mr. Lucky." To his credit, DeFranco (who at that point had ranked near the top for 40 years) had not given up his search for fresh material in which to test himself. *—Scott Yanow*

Jack DeJohnette

b. Aug. 9, 1942, Chicago, IL
Keyboards, Drums / Avant-Garde Jazz, Post-Bop, Fusion
At his best, Jack DeJohnette is one of the most consistently inventive jazz percussionists extant. His style is wide-ranging, yet, while capable of playing convincingly in any modern idiom, he always maintains a well-defined voice. DeJohnette has a remarkably fluid relationship to pulse. His time is excellent; even as he pushes, pulls and generally obscures the beat beyond recognition, a powerful sense of swing is ever-present. His tonal palette is huge as well; no drummer pays closer attention to the sounds that come out of his kit than DeJohnette. He possesses a comprehensive musicality rare among jazz drummers. DeJohnette's professional career began in the mid-'60s, when he became involved with the Chicago-based AACM. His big break came from 1966 to 1968, when he was a member of the very popular Charles Lloyd Quartet. The drummer's first record as a leader, 1968's *The DeJohnette Complex,* came soon after. One year later, DeJohnette replaced Tony Williams in Miles Davis' band; later in 1969, he played on the seminal *Bitches Brew.* He left Davis in 1972, and became something like a house drummer for ECM, recording both as leader and sideman with such label mainstays as Jan Garbarek, Kenny Wheeler, and Pat Metheny. *—Chris Kelsey*

The DeJohnette Complex / Dec. 26, 1968-Dec. 27, 1968 / Milestone/OJC ♦♦♦♦
Drummer Jack DeJohnette's debut as a leader (which has been reissued on CD) has quite a bit of variety. The music ranges from advanced swinging to brief free improvisations and some avant-funk. DeJohnette (who doubles on melodica) is joined by Bennie Maupin (on tenor and flute), keyboardist Stanley Cowell, bassists Miroslav Vitous and Eddie Gomez, and drummer Roy Haynes. He uses six different combinations of musicians on the eight songs (five of his originals, John Coltrane's "Miles' Mode," Cowell's "Equipoise" and Vitous' "Mirror Image"). Intriguing and generally successful music. *—Scott Yanow*

★ **Special Edition** / Mar. 1979 / ECM ♦♦♦♦♦
The debut recording by Jack DeJohnette's Special Edition is a classic. The drummer (who also plays some piano and melodica) is joined for three of his stimulating originals (including "Zoot Suite") and a pair of John Coltrane songs ("Central Park West" and "India") by tenor saxophonist David Murray (doubling on bass clarinet), altoist Arthur Blythe and bassist Peter Warren (who also plays some cello). The challenging frameworks are full of color, variety and highly expressive moods that push the musicians (both collectively and individually) to play at their very best and most explorative. This was one of the great groups of the late '70s and the finest version of DeJohnette's Special Edition; highly recommended. *—Scott Yanow*

Inflation Blues / Sep. 1982 / ECM ♦♦♦♦♦
The only recording by Jack DeJohnette's Special Edition to use a trumpeter (guest Baikida Carroll), this is a particularly strong outing by the 1982 edition of the group. With Chico Freeman (on tenor, bass clarinet and soprano), John Purcell (alto, flutes and baritone), bassist Rufus Reid and the leader-drummer (who also contributes some piano), it is not surprising that the music is adventurous yet quite coherent, with the solo and group statements being both spontaneous and logical. Recommended. *—Scott Yanow*

Album, Album / Jun. 1984 / ECM ♦♦♦♦♦
Most of Special Edition's recordings are quite rewarding and this set is no exception. Drummer/keyboardist Jack DeJohnette contributed five of the six compositions (all but "Monk's Mood") and they cover a wide range of styles and moods, from "New Orleans Suite" and "Festival" to the ambitious "Third World Anthem" and a revisit to his "Zoot Suite." This was one of the most stimulating jazz groups of the 1980s and this particular lineup (with John Purcell on alto and soprano, tenor saxophonist David Murray, Howard Johnson doubling on tuba and baritone, and bassist Rufus Reid) was one of DeJohnette's strongest. *—Scott Yanow*

Irresistible Force / Jan. 1987 / MCA ♦♦♦♦
Jack DeJohnette's first Special Edition recording in five years finds him using completely different personnel than earlier. Greg Osby (on alto and soprano) and Gary Thomas (doubling on tenor and flute) bring M-Base influences to the band (their improvisations have a fresh new logic) while guitarist Mick Goodrick, bassist Lonnie Plaxico, percussionist Nana Vasconcelos and the leader-drummer (who doubles on keyboards) all make strong contributions. Other than Osby's "Osthetics," the repertoire is comprised of DeJohnette's originals and the somewhat unique music gives all of the musicians opportunities to express themselves and inspire each other. *—Scott Yanow*

Dancing with Nature Spirits / May 1995 / ECM ♦♦♦♦
For Jack DeJohnette's 1995 ECM release, the drummer teams up in an unusual trio with pianist Michael Cain (who has his own sound) and the atmospheric reeds of Steve Gorn (who is heard on soprano, clarinet and bansuri flute). The five group originals (two of which are over 20 minutes long) build gradually to a high level of intensity. Although there is no bass, the music swings in its own way and DeJohnnette's drums and percussion are consistently stimulating. This thoughtful but often-fiery music is worth a close listen. *—Scott Yanow*

Oneness / Jan. 1997 / ECM ♦♦♦♦

Paul Desmond (Paul Emil Breitenfeld)

b. Nov. 25, 1924, San Francisco, CA, **d.** May 30, 1977, New York, NY
Sax (Alto) / Cool
The definitive "cool" alto saxophonist, Paul Desmond (who had a beautiful floating tone that owed little to Charlie Parker) took his time in his solos (rarely double-timing) but his melody ideas were full of surprising twists and turns. He played his first and his last gigs with Dave Brubeck and spent his prime years (1951-67) with Brubeck's popular quartet. Early on he studied clarinet in school and then during 1948-50 recorded and gigged on alto with the Dave Brubeck octet. During the years with the quartet, Desmond was a key part of the sound, indulging in counterpoint with the pianist-leader, writing "Take Five" (in his will he left the huge royalties of this hit to the Red Cross) and taking witty and logical solos that inspired Brubeck. Away from the group, Desmond occasionally recorded as a leader (usually in pianoless settings) including a couple of encounters with Gerry Mulligan and a series of records with Jim Hall. After the quartet broke up, Desmond was mostly semi-retired although a concert with the Modern Jazz Quartet (1971) was recorded and he teamed up with guitarist Ed Bickert on a few live albums. The altoist also had reunions with Brubeck during 1972-75 before his death from cancer. His Jim Hall sets have been reissued in a Mosaic box set, most of the Brubeck albums are currently in print and Desmond also recorded as a leader for Fantasy, A&M, Finesse, CTI, Telarc and Artists House. *—Scott Yanow*

Gerry Mulligan Quartet/Paul Desmond Quintet / Sep. 2, 1952 / Fantasy ♦♦♦♦♦

The Complete RCA Victor Recordings / Jun. 19, 1961-Jun. 1, 1965 / RCA ♦♦♦♦♦
This set is similar to but not exactly the same as a limited-edition Mosaic six-LP box from the early 1990s. The latter included a Warner Bros. LP that is replaced here by a Paul Desmond date with strings, plus one song formerly bypassed. Desmond recorded fairly regularly from 1961-65 for RCA while on brief hiatuses from Dave Brubeck's constantly traveling quartet. Included on this five-CD set are the complete contents of *Desmond Blue* (the string session with suitable arrangements by Bob Prince), *Take Ten, Glad to Be Happy, Bossa Antigua* and *Easy Living;* there are no previously unreleased selections. Most of the songs feature the cool-toned altoist in a pianoless quartet with the very complementary guitarist Jim Hall. The interplay between the two stylists is so subtle and logical that it takes several listens to fully appreciate their magic. Frequently exquisite music, mixing together standards with some melodic originals. *—Scott Yanow*

● **Two of a Mind** / Jun. 26, 1962-Aug. 13, 1962 / Bluebird/RCA ♦♦♦♦♦
Altoist Paul Desmond and baritonist Gerry Mulligan always made for a perfect team during their infrequent collaborations. Both of the saxophonists had immediately distinctive light tones, strong wits and the ability to improvise melodically. For this RCA CD (a series that reissued some of the earlier Bluebirds under the RCA banner), the two masterful reed players are featured in pianoless quartets that also include Wendell Marshall, Joe Benjamin or John Beal on bass and Connie Kay or Mel Lewis on drums. The songs all utilize common chord changes including the two "originals" ("Two Of A Kind" and "Blight Of The Fumble Bee") and the interplay between Desmond and Mulligan is consistently delightful. Highly recommended. *—Scott Yanow*

Take Ten / Jun. 5, 1963-Jun. 25, 1963 / Bluebird/RCA ✦✦✦✦✦
Now listeners enter the heart of the Paul Desmond/Jim Hall sessions, a great quartet date with Gene Cherico manning the bass (Gene Wright deputizes on the title track) and MJQ drummer Connie Kay displaying other sides of his personality. Everyone wanted Desmond to come up with a sequel to the monster hit "Take Five"; and so he did, reworking the tune and playfully designating the meter as 10/8. Hence "Take Ten," a worthy sequel with a solo that has a Middle-Eastern feeling akin to Desmond's famous extemporaneous excursion with Brubeck in "Le Souk" back in 1954. It was here that Desmond also unveiled a spin-off of the then-red-hot bossa nova groove that he called "bossa antigua" (a sardonic play-on-words meaning "old thing"), which laid the ground for Desmond's next album and a few more later in the decade. Two of the best examples are his own tunes, the samba-like "El Prince" (named after arranger Bob Prince), an infectious number with on-the-wing solo flights that you can't get out of your head, and the haunting "Embarcadero." Hall now gets plenty of room to stretch out, supported by Kay's gently dropped bombs, and he is the perfect understated swinging foil for the wistful altoist. There is not a single track here that isn't loaded with ingeniously worked out, always melodic ideas. *—Richard S. Ginell*

Paul Desmond & Modern Jazz Quartet / Dec. 25, 1971 / Columbia/Legacy ✦✦✦✦
The MJQ made their annual Christmas gig at New York's *Town Hall* one year, and who should show up after intermission but Paul Desmond, who would hardly bring himself to play with anyone in those days, save a Creed Taylor record date or two. The cool classical modernists and the dry-martini altoist are not unexpectedly a close fit—after all, Percy Heath and especially Connie Kay had been fixtures on Desmond's solo sessions—and they do some relaxed swinging turns on some congenial standards, adaptations of P.D. tunes ("La Paloma," "Greensleeves"), one current hit ("Jesus Christ Superstar" in a cute John Lewis arrangement), and the inevitable "Bags' Groove" (here entitled "Bags' New Groove"). Again, Desmond softly intones perhaps his favorite standard in the repertoire (he recorded it countless times), "You Go to My Head," tumbling contrapuntally around Milt Jackson in the tune, while "East of the Sun" has a fine chase sequence between the two down the stretch. Though they had been friends since the 1950s, this was apparently the only time the MJQ and Desmond ever performed in public, making this one-off album (issued well after Desmond's death through Lewis's efforts) a thing to savor for fans of all five musicians. *—Richard S. Ginell*

Like Someone in Love / Mar. 29, 1975 / Telarc ✦✦✦✦
In 1992, Telarc unveiled a series of performances from the vault on a short-lived label punningly entitled "Telarchive," beginning with this long-delayed encore to the original releases from Paul Desmond's "Canadian" quartet. Recorded live in Toronto's *Bourbon Street Jazz Club* several months before the live dates released on Horizon and Artists House, it finds Desmond growing comfortable with his new Toronto friends but not quite settled into their laid-back ways quite yet. There are passages in this session where Desmond sounds a bit uncharacteristically scattered and unfocused, where guitarist Ed Bickert becomes the more fluid and stable solo partner, and bassist (and engineer) Don Thompson takes a lengthy solo on every track. Desmond seems to produce his best work in the material that he seems most familiar with. The title track is the one that catches fire most brightly (with a wry assist from "We're in the Money") and "Things Ain't What They Used to Be" finds him working in some clever asides from, yes, Ravel's "Daphnis et Chloe." The wistful European melancholy of Django Reinhardt's "Nuages" suits him perfectly and Jobim's "Meditation" makes its first appearance on a Desmond recording. The boxy, confined live sound doesn't suit the late saxophonist—nor, obviously, the perfectionist standards at Telarc—but every precious unreleased note from Desmond is definitely worth sampling at whatever sonic level. *—Richard Ginell*

The Paul Desmond Quartet Live / Oct. 25, 1975-Nov. 1, 1975 / A&M ✦✦✦✦
During his post-Brubeck years, altoist Paul Desmond was semiretired, only playing in public on an occasional basis. When he did perform, it was often with the tasteful Canadian guitarist Ed Bickert in a quiet pianoless quartet. This double LP, put out by John Snyder's Horizon subsidiary for A&M, is melodic, subtle and consistently swinging. Desmond and Bickert (along with bassist Don Thompson and drummer Jerry Fuller) clearly enjoyed themselves matching wits and wisdom on the altoist's "Wendy" and the seven superior standards (which include Desmond's "Take Five"). *—Scott Yanow*

Lemme Tell Ya 'Bout Desmond: The Music of Paul Desmond / Sep. 9, 1961-Sep. 26, 1974 / Label M. ✦✦✦

Vic Dickenson

b. Aug. 6, 1906, Xenia, OH, **d.** Nov. 16, 1984, New York, NY
Trombone / Swing, Dixieland
A distinctive trombonist with a sly wit and the ability to sound as if he were playing underwater, Vic Dickenson was an asset to any session in which he appeared. He stated out in the 1920s and '30s playing in the Midwest. Associations with Blanche Calloway (1933-36), Claude Hopkins (1936-39), Benny Carter (1939), Count Basie (1940), Carter again (1941) and Frankie Newton (1941-43) preceded a high-profile gig with Eddie Heywood's popular sextet (1943-46); Dickenson also played and recorded with Sidney Bechet. From then on he was a freelancing soloist who spent time on the West Coast, Boston and New York, appearing on many recordings (including some notable dates for Vanguard) and on the legendary *Sound of Jazz* telecast (1957). In the 1960s Dickenson co-led the Saints and Sinners, toured with George Wein's Newport All-Stars and worked regularly with Wild Bill Davison and Eddie Condon. During 1968-70 he was in a quintet with Bobby Hackett, in the 1970s he sometimes played with the World's Greatest Jazz Band and Vic Dickenson was active up until his death. *—Scott Yanow*

★ **The Essential Vic Dickenson** / Dec. 29, 1953-Nov. 29, 1954 / Vanguard ✦✦✦✦✦
This single CD reissues ten of the dozen songs originally on a double LP of the same name. Trombonist Vic Dickenson did not get to lead that many sessions, and he is generous in allocating solo space on these mainstream sessions. Trumpeters Ruby Braff and/or Shad Collins, along with the distinctive clarinetist Edmond Hall and pianist Sir Charles Thompson (who often sounds here like Count Basie), are well featured, and the music is enjoyable; highlights include "Russian Lullaby," a 12-minute rendition of "Jeepers Creepers," "Old Fashioned Love" and "Everybody Loves My Baby." *—Scott Yanow*

Mainstream / Oct. 28, 1958 / Koch Jazz ✦✦✦✦

Gentleman of the Trombone / Jul. 25, 1975 / Storyville ✦✦✦✦

Plays Bessie Smith: "Trombone Cholly" / Mar. 31, 1976 / Gazell ✦✦✦✦✦

Walt Dickerson

b. 1931, Philadelphia, PA
Vibraphone / Post-Bop
Walt Dickerson made an impact when he first emerged in the early '60s—he won the *Down Beat* Critic's Poll as "New Star" in 1962—but as the years have passed, he's become much less visible. Dickerson graduated from Morgan State College in 1953. After serving in the Army from 1953-1955, he settled in California, where he led a band that included Andrew Cyrille and Andrew Hill. In his early-'60s heyday, Dickerson played the clubs on the New York scene. He worked with Sun Ra, recording *Impressions of a Patch of Blue* in 1965. Shortly thereafter, Dickerson retired from performing for nearly a decade and returning in 1975. In the years 1977-78, he made the bulk of his for the Steeplechase label, which included duos with Sun Ra, guitarist Pierre Dorge, and bassist Richard Davis. Also in '78, Dickerson recorded in a quartet with pianist Albert Dailey. Dickerson has been one of the few vibists to exhibit an awareness of free-jazz techniques, though he's manifestly conversant in the language of post-bop. Dickerson reportedly still performs around his native Philadelphia, though his recording career is—for now, at least—at a standstill. *—Chris Kelsey*

This Is Walt Dickerson! / Mar. 7, 1961 / Prestige/OJC ✦✦✦✦
This CD reissue of vibraphonist Walt Dickerson's debut as a leader finds Dickerson (in a quartet with pianist Austin Crowe, bassist Bob Lewis and drummer Andrew Cyrille) performing six of his moody and generally advanced originals. One can hear the influence of Ornette Coleman in the soloing which does not stick exclusively to standard bebop chordal improvisation. The purposely monotonous backup on "Death and Taxes" and such songs as "The Cry" and "Infinite You" show that Dickerson was trying to get beyond the dominant Milt Jackson influence that affected most of the other vibists at the time. It's an interesting outing. *—Scott Yanow*

● **A Sense of Direction** / May 5, 1961 / New Jazz/OJC ✦✦✦✦✦
Vibraphonist Walt Dickerson's second recording as a leader (reissued on CD in the OJC series) utilizes talented if obscure sidemen (pianist Austin Crowe, bassist Edgar Bateman and drummer Eustis Guillemet, Jr.) on a variety of challenging originals and three standards ("What's New," "You Go to My Head" and "If I Should Lose You"). Although Dickerson would not become an influential force himself, he was one of the first vibraphonists of the era to develop his voice away from Milt Jackson's influence, predating Bobby Hutcherson by a few years. *—Scott Yanow*

Relativity / Jan. 16, 1962 / New Jazz/OJC ✦✦✦✦
Vibraphonist Walt Dickerson always had a fairly unique sound, predating Bobby Hutcherson with his ability to straddle the boundaries between hard bop and the emerging avant-garde. On this quartet date with pianist Austin Crowe, bassist Ahmed Abdul-Malik and drummer Andrew Cyrille, Dickerson plays a fairly accessible program (three standards and four diverse originals) that serve as a strong introduction to his talents for the uninitiated. *—Scott Yanow*

Impressions of a Patch of Blue / 1965 / MGM ✦✦✦✦
Vibraphonist Walt Dickerson has had an erratic recording career but this session interpreting music from the film *A Patch of Blue* is one of the highlights of his discography. Dickerson's approach to vibes is very different from better known players like Lionel Hampton, Milt Jackson, Gary Burton, and Red Norvo because he plays with very little vibrato. The inspired choice of Sun Ra to play piano and harpsichord adds to the interesting rhythms and dissonance of the arrangements. Long out of print and a sought after collectable LP, this 1999 reissue CD won't be around long either, as it is part of the Verve Elite limited-edition series which have a tendency to sell out in a hurry. *—Ken Dryden*

Al DiMeola

b. Jul. 22, 1954, Jersey City, NJ
Guitar (Electric), Guitar / Guitar Virtuoso, Jazz-Rock, Fusion, World Fusion
Al DiMeola has had a dual career as a blazing fusion electric guitarist and as an acoustic player eager to explore music from other cultures. DiMeola burst upon the scene by replacing Bill Connors with Return to Forever in 1974 before he turned 20. He had been attending Berklee but essentially started out on top, immediately becoming an influential fusion guitarist. Criticized for playing an excess of notes and not showing enough feeling in his playing (faults he has since overcome), DiMeola has matured through the years. After Return to Forever broke up, he went on several tours with John McLaughlin and Paco DeLucia in an acoustic guitar trio. (1980-83). Since that time DiMeola has led his own groups, alternating between electric and acoustic guitars and changing musical direction a few times. DiMeola, who toured with the Rite of Strings in 1995 (a trio with Jean Luc Ponty and Stanley Clarke), has recorded sets as a leader since 1976 including dates for Columbia, Manhattan and Tomato. *—Scott Yanow*

Land of the Midnight Sun / 1976 / Columbia ✦✦✦✦✦
One of the guitar heroes of fusion, Al DiMeola was just 22 years old at the time of his debut as a leader but already a veteran of Chick Corea's *Return to Forever.* The complex pieces (which include the three-part "Suite-Golden Dawn," an acoustic duet with Corea on "Short Tales of the Black Forest" and a brief Bach violin sonata) show DiMeola's range even at this early stage. With assistance from such top players as bassists Jaco Pastorius and Stanley Clarke, keyboardist Barry Miles and drummers Lenny White and Steve Gadd, this was a very impressive beginning to DiMeola's solo career. *—Scott Yanow*

☆ **Elegant Gypsy** / 1976 / Columbia ✦✦✦✦✦
Guitarist Al DiMeola's second record as a leader is generally an explosive affair, although it

does have a fair amount of variety. With Jan Hammer or Barry Miles on keyboards, electric bassist Anthony Jackson, drummer Lenny White (Steve Gadd takes his place on the "Elegant Gypsy Suite"), and percussionist Mingo Lewis on most of the selections, DiMeola shows off his speedy and rockish fusion style. He was still a member of Return to Forever at the time and was a stronger guitarist than composer, but DiMeola did put a lot of thought into this music. The brief "Lady of Rome, Sister of Brazil" (an acoustic guitar solo) and "Mediterranean Sundance" (an acoustic duet with fellow guitarist Paco DeLucia) hints at DiMeola's future directions. A near-classic in the fusion vein. *—Scott Yanow*

☆ **Casino** / 1977 / Columbia/Legacy ♦♦♦♦♦
Guitarist Al DiMeola's third album as a leader (which has been reissued on CD) is still one of his finest recordings. The compositions (which include "Fantasia Suite for Two Guitars" and Chick Corea's "Senor Mouse") are strong and diverse, DiMeola is joined by a sympathetic backup group (which includes keyboardist Barry Miles, bassist Anthony Jackson and drummer Steve Gadd) and his own playing shows impressive growth since his period with Return to Forever (which had ended two years before.). Some of the music is no-nonsense fusion/rock but the set also displays DiMeola's growing love for flamenco and the hot "Fantasia Suite" is purely acoustic. Recommended. *—Scott Yanow*

★ **Splendido Hotel** / 1979 / Columbia ♦♦♦♦♦
Talk about ambitious, this two-LP set finds guitarist Al DiMeola performing with his quintet of the time (featuring keyboardist Philippe Saisse), with studio musicians, solo, in a reunion with pianist Chick Corea, singing a love song and welcoming veteran Les Paul for a version of "Spanish Eyes." Most of the music works quite well and it shows that DiMeola (best-known for his speedy rock-oriented solos) is a surprisingly well-rounded and versatile musician. *—Scott Yanow*

Kiss My Axe / Sep. 24, 1988-May 1991 / Tomato ♦♦♦♦♦
Despite the aggression its title implies, *Kiss My Axe* is the work of a softer, more reflective Al DiMeola, who had become greatly influenced by Pat Metheny's subtle lyricism, but still had a very recognizable and distinctive sound. DiMeola's new approach was perfectly summarized when, in 1991, he told *JazzTimes* he wanted to be "enchanted" by the music instead of dazzling listeners with his considerable chops. DiMeola still has fine technique, but avoids overwhelming us with it, and shows more restraint than before. One thing that remains is the guitarist's strong interest in world music—this imaginative session liberally incorporates Latin influences (Brazilian, Spanish, Peruvian and Afro-Cuban) as well as Middle Eastern and African elements. In that *JazzTimes* interview, DiMeola explained that this CD's title resulted in part from his frustration over the fact that many labels and commercial radio stations were choosing bloodless "elevator muzak" over more adventurous fusion. Consistently rewarding, *Axe* makes it clear that DiMeola did the right thing by refusing to compromise. *—Alex Henderson*

DiMeola Plays Piazzolla / Oct. 1990-Sep. 1990 / Atlantic ♦♦♦♦
Latin music has been a strong influence on Al DiMeola since his early years, and in the '90s, he paid especially close attention to the music of Argentina. A welcome addition to his already impressive catalogue, *DiMeola Plays Piazzola* pays homage to the late Argentinean tango master Astor Piazzolla (whose distinctive and very poetic brand of romanticism was considered quite daring and radical in Argentina). It would have been easy for an artist to allow his own personality to become obscured when saluting Piazzolla's legacy, but the charismatic DiMeola is too great an improvisor to let that happen. Though his reverence for Piazzola comes through loud and clear on these haunting classics, there's no mistaking the fact that this is very much an Al DiMeola project. *—Alex Henderson*

World Sinfonia / Oct. 1990 / Tomato ♦♦♦♦♦
Comparing early Al DiMeola dates like *Land of the Midnight Sun* and *Casino* to his albums of the 1990s, it's clear how much his playing has softened. The exceptional *World Sinfonia*, an entirely acoustic CD, makes it clear that what hasn't changed is his unpredictable, spontaneous nature. DiMeola's right-hand man throughout this highly introspective date is the soulful bandonean player Dino Saluzzi, with whom he enjoys an undeniably strong rapport. A long-time lover of world music, DiMeola incorporates South American, Spanish and Middle Eastern elements, and makes Argentinean tango a very high priority. The improvisor's reverence for Argentina's musical heritage is especially evident on Astor Piazzola's haunting "Tango Suite" and DiMeola's soulbearing ode to the tango legend "Last Tango for Astor." But *World Sinfonia*'s standout track and most pleasant surprise of all is a 12-minute interpretation of Chick Corea's 1975 Return to Forever classic "No Mystery," which works quite well in an acoustic setting. *—Alex Henderson*

The Dirty Dozen Brass Band

f. 1975, New Orleans, LA
Group / New Orleans Brass Bands, New Orleans Jazz
The Dirty Dozen Brass Band in its prime successfully mixed together R&B with the instrumentation of a New Orleans brass band. Featuring Kirk Joseph on sousaphone playing with the agility of an electric bassist, the group revitalized the brass band tradition, opening up the repertoire and inspiring some younger groups to imitate their boldness. Generally featuring five horns (two trumpets, one trombone and two saxes) along with the sousaphone, a snare drummer and a bass drummer, the DDBB was innovative in its own way, making fine recordings for Rounder, Columbia and the George Wein Collection (the latter released through Concord); guest artists have included Dr. John, Dizzy Gillespie and Danny Barker. Unfortunately in recent years the group has become much more conventional, still using R&B riffs but now with a standard (and less distinctive) rhythm section. *—Scott Yanow*

★ **My Feet Can't Fail Me Now** / 1984 / Concord Jazz ♦♦♦♦♦
The Dirty Dozen Brass Band's *My Feet Can't Fail Me Now* is a rollicking, infectious set that captures the spirit of classic New Orleans R&B and jazz because it isn't enslavened to those traditions. The group is willing to play around and have fun, adding different rock, pop and R&B influences to their sound. The result is a wonderful, unpredictable album that is as wild and rich as New Orleans itself. *—Leo Stanley*

Live: Mardi Gras in Montreux / Jul. 1985 / Rounder ♦♦♦

Voodoo / Aug. 1987-Sep. 1987 / Columbia ♦♦♦♦
The Dirty Dozen Brass Band certainly knew how to have a good time while playing their music. Their spirited blending of New Orleans jazz parade rhythms with R&Bish horn riffs made them flexible enough to welcome guests Dr. John (who sings and play piano on "It's All Over Now"), Dizzy Gillespie ("Oop Pop A Dah") and Branford Marsalis ("Moose the Mooche") to their Columbia debut without altering their music at all. With Gregory Davis and Efrem Towns playing strong trumpet in the ensembles and occasional solos, and with sousaphonist Kirk Joseph not letting up for a moment, this is a typically spirited set by the unique DDBB. *—Scott Yanow*

New Orleans Album / Aug. 1989-Dec. 1989 / Columbia ♦♦♦♦
A bit of a hodge-podge, this CD features the Dirty Dozen Brass Band (comprised of two trumpets, two saxes, sometimes one trombone, the sousaphone of Kirk Joseph, snare drum and bass drum) welcoming such guests as singer Eddie Bo, guitarist-vocalist Danny Barker (showcased on "Don't You Feel My Leg"), trumpeter Dave Bartholomew (heard on "The Monkey") and rock singer Elvis Costello. However it is the R&Bish parade band that is the main star, romping through group originals plus Cannonball Adderley's "Inside Straight" and "Kidd Jordan's Second Line." *—Scott Yanow*

Open Up: Whatcha Gonna Do for the Rest of Your Life— / Jan. 1991-Apr. 1991 / Columbia ♦♦♦♦
The Dirty Dozen Brass Band sticks to originals (except for Johnny Dyani's "Eyomzi") on this fairly adventurous set. The octet (which consists of two trumpets, two saxes, one trombone, sousaphone, snare drum and bass drum) still had a unique sound in 1991 but three songs on the date only used part of the unit and the DDBB seemed to be trying to escape the sound of the brass band tradition (they had long had a more modern repertoire). Not all of the pieces work although the music in general is pretty colorful and somewhat unpredictable, even if it falls short of essential. *—Scott Yanow*

Jelly / Aug. 1992-Jan. 1993 / Columbia ♦♦♦

Buck Jump / May 25, 1999 / Mammoth ♦♦♦♦

DKV Trio

f. 1994
Group / Avant-Garde Jazz, Free Jazz
By the close of the 1990s, DKV Trio was one of the leading free jazz trios based out of Chicago. The highly skilled and passionate members—Hamid Drake (percussion), Kent Kessler (bass) and Ken Vandermark (reeds)—initially came together in 1994, for Vandermark's *Standards* release on Quinnah records. The trio worked so well together that they continued to perform, eventually recording several strong albums, including their debut, *Baraka*, and the two-disc *Live in Wels & Chicago, 1998*, both on Okkadisk. DKV Trio has also recorded with legendary Chicago tenor saxophonist Fred Anderson, and guitarist Joe Morris. All three also perform and record in several other acclaimed groups, such as the Brotzmann Tentet, Fred Anderson Trio and Vandermark 5. DKV Trio has performed at Austria's *Music Unlimited '98 Festival, the 1999 Chicago Jazz Festival*, and regularly at Chicago jazz clubs including *the Empty Bottle* and *the Velvet Lounge*. *—Joslyn Layne*

● **Live in Wels & Chicago, 1998** / Nov. 8, 1998-Jan. 2, 1998 / Okka Disk ♦♦♦♦♦
Live in Wels & Chicago, 1998 is an incredible two-disc release from premiere Chicago musiciansHamid Drake, Kent Kessler, Ken Vandermark. These live recordings document some of the exciting—and engaging—live improvisations that make the DKV Trio one of the top groups in free jazz of the late 1990s and beyond. The only pre-composed theme used by the group is heard on the "Wels CD," disc one. It is the theme from Don Cherry's "Complete Communion," around which DKV base their six-part "Complete Communion Suite," performed at *the Music Unlimited '98 Festival* in Wels, Austria. By "Part 2" of the suite, the rhythm section is kicking a funky counter-emphasis leading into a drum solo before the wind down at the track's end. A bass solo opens "Part 3," which is also the section where DKV bring the suite to a full boil. A late November, 1998 concert at Fred Anderson's *Velvet Lounge* is heard on disc two, or the "Chicago CD." It opens with a bowed bass of circular overtones which is soon joined by hand drums and bass, along with a beautiful melody of patiently held saxophone notes. The band cooks, steams, and finally, screams with an all-out intensity and an urgency that lifts "Open Door." Next comes "Blues for Tomorrow," a soft and tasteful breather from which a clarinet blues eventually emerges. "Burning Sky" is a transcendent piece that opens with saxophone pulses, muted drum rolls, and bass bows for a slow and suspenseful, esoteric mood. The music continues to grow until, almost halfway through, it escalates into a storm of melodic grit chaos that's something like the climaxes of the Dirty Three. A must-have for those who believe music taps into—and creates—something greater. *—Joslyn Layne*

Johnny Dodds

b. Apr. 12, 1892, New Orleans, LA, **d.** Aug. 8, 1940, Chicago, IL
Clarinet / New Orleans Jazz, Classic Jazz
One of the all-time great clarinetists and arguably the most significant of the 1920s, Johnny Dodds (whose younger brother Baby Dodds was among the first important drummers) had a memorable tone in both the lower and upper registers, was a superb blues player and held his own with Louis Armstrong (no mean feat) on his classic Hot Five and Hot Seven recordings. He did not start on clarinet until he was 17 but caught on fast, being mostly self-taught. Dodds was with Kid Ory's band during most of 1912-19, played on riverboats with Fate Marable in 1917, and joined King Oliver in Chicago in 1921. During the next decade he recorded with Oliver's Creole Jazz Band, Jelly Roll Morton, Louis Armstrong and on his own heated sessions, often utilizing trumpeter Natty Dominique. He worked regularly at Kelly's Stables during 1924-30. Although Dodds continued playing in Chicago during the 1930s, part of the time was spent running a cab company. The clarinetist led recording sessions in 1938 and 1940 but died just before the New Orleans revival movement began. *—Scott Yanow*

Wild Man Blues: 24 Clarinet Classics / Apr. 6, 1923-Jun. 5, 1940 / ASV/Living Era ✦✦✦✦✦
This ASV/Living Era disc charts Johnny Dodds through his many recordings with jazz greats, from a 1923 recording with King Oliver and Louis Armstrong to trio sessions with Jelly Roll Morton. Also included are six tracks recorded by Dodds' New Orleans Wanderers (or Bootblacks) and the Black Bottom Stompers. *—John Bush*

☆ **The 1926** / May 1926-Dec. 1926 / Classics ✦✦✦✦✦
Dodds was one of the very finest New Orleans clarinetists, and the only non-creole among them. The peak experiences here, and some of the finest small-group recordings ever made, are The New Orleans Wanderers sessions—Armstrong's Hot Five with George Mitchell instead of Armstrong. Also present are Freddie Keppard's only two recordings and a bunch of marginally lesser cuts that Dodds transmutes into gold. *—John Storm Roberts, Original Music*

● **Blue Clarinet Stomp** / Dec. 11, 1926-Feb. 7, 1929 / Bluebird/RCA ✦✦✦✦✦
A French RCA double-LP from the late '70s had the complete Johnny Dodds on Victor, 30 selections in all. This single CD just has 21 of the performances, leaving out most alternates and a few other numbers. A good introductory set to the recordings of the great New Orleans clarinetist (but sure to frustrate veteran collectors and completists), this set features the masterful Dodds with a couple of trios, heading his own sextets and as a sideman with Jelly Roll Morton ("Wolverine Blues" and "Mr. Jelly Lord") and the Dixieland Jug Blowers. Classic New Orleans jazz by arguably the finest jazz clarinetist of the 1920s, this CD is recommended until something better comes along. *—Scott Yanow*

☆ **1927** / Jan. 1927-Aug. 10, 1927 / Classics ✦✦✦✦✦

☆ **The 1927-1928** / Oct. 5, 1927-1228 / Classics ✦✦✦✦✦

Eric Dolphy

b. Jun. 20, 1928, Los Angeles, CA, **d.** Jun. 29, 1964, Berlin, Germany
Sax (Alto), Clarinet (Bass), Flute / Avant-Garde Jazz, Free Jazz, Post-Bop
Eric Dolphy was a true original with his own distinctive styles on alto, flute and bass clarinet. His music fell into the "avant-garde" category yet he did not discard chordal improvisation altogether (although the relationship of his notes to the chords were often pretty abstract). While most of the other "free jazz" players sounded very serious in their playing, Dolphy's solos often came across as ecstatic and exuberant. His improvisations utilized very wide intervals, a variety of nonmusical speechlike sounds and its own logic. Although alto was his main ax, Dolphy was the first flutist to move beyond bop (influencing James Newton) and he largely introduced the bass clarinet to jazz as a solo instrument. He was also one of the first (after Coleman Hawkins) to record unaccompanied horn solos, preceding Anthony Braxton by five years. *—Scott Yanow*

☆ **The Complete Prestige Recordings** / Apr. 1, 1960-Sep. 8, 1961 / Prestige ✦✦✦✦✦
During his 19 months with Prestige, Eric Dolphy recorded 13 sessions as a leader and sideman. All are included in this massive nine-CD set and, even when absorbed in two or three sittings, there is enough variety to hold on to any true jazz fan's attention. Dolphy, whether on alto, bass clarinet, flute and even on a couple of occasions clarinet, was a true original with distinctive sounds of his own and very unique (but ultimately logical) styles. Included in this box (which has no previously unissued material) are the complete contents of the albums *Outward Bound, Here & There, Dash One,* Oliver Nelson's *Screamin' the Blues,* Ken McIntyre's *Looking Ahead, Out There, Caribe* (with the Latin Jazz Quintet), Eddie Lockjaw Davis's *Trane Whistle* (during which Dolphy is an anonymous section player), *Far Cry,* Oliver Nelson's *Straight Ahead,* Ron Carter's *Where,* Mal Waldron's *The Quest, At the Five Spot* and *Eric Dolphy in Europe.* Even with the many impressive sidemen (which include trumpeters Freddie Hubbard, Richard Williams, and Booker Little, saxophonists Oliver Nelson, Ken McIntyre, Booker Ervin and Eddie Lockjaw Davis, pianists Jaki Byard, Richard Wyands, Walter Bishop, Jr. and Mal Waldron, bassists George Tucker, George Duvivier, Sam Jones, Ron Carter (who doubles on cello), Joe Benjamin and Richard Davis and drummers Roy Haynes, Art Taylor, Charlie Persip and Ed Blackwell), Eric Dolphy consistently emerges as the solo star. This often-remarkable music stands apart from the other styles prevalent during the era. *—Scott Yanow*

Here and There / Apr. 1, 1960-Sep. 6, 1961 / Prestige/OJC ✦✦✦✦
This CD reissue has rarities from three different Eric Dolphy sessions. "April Fool" and the alternate take of "G.W." are drawn from Dolphy's initial date as a leader, a quintet outing with trumpeter Freddie Hubbard and pianist Jaki Byard. "Don't Blame Me" is taken from a Copenhagen concert but it is the two remaining numbers ("Status Seeking" and an unaccompanied rendition on bass clarinet of "God Bless the Child") that are of greatest interest. The latter cuts are taken from Dolphy's legendary gig at the Five Spot Cafe with trumpeter Booker Little, pianist Mal Waldron, bassist Richard Davis and drummer Ed Blackwell, not duplicating the seven more famous performances that are often thought of as the group's entire output. Although it is easy to think of this set on a whole as containing "leftovers," Dolphy's strong playing on alto, flute and bass clarinet makes the music of strong interest to his fans. *—Scott Yanow*

Outward Bound / Apr. 1, 1960 / New Jazz/OJC ✦✦✦✦✦
This very likable set, Eric Dolphy's first as a leader, has been reissued as a single CD and (along with some alternate takes) on Dolphy's huge Prestige box set. Teamed up with the young trumpeter Freddie Hubbard, pianist Jaki Byard, bassist George Tucker and drummer Roy Haynes, Dolphy introduces his tribute to Gerald Wilson, "G.W.," and rips into "On Green Dolphin Street," stretches out on flute on "Glad to Be Unhappy," and takes a memorable bass clarinet solo on the delightful "Miss Toni." Hubbard and Byard are also both in good form. A perfect introduction to Eric Dolphy's versatile talents, this boppish set is more accessible than many of Dolphy's more innovative recordings. Recommended. *—Scott Yanow*

Other Aspects / Jul. 8, 1960-1962 / Blue Note ✦✦✦✦
Other Aspects is unlike any other title in Eric Dolphy's catalog. The startling 15-minute composition "Jim Crow," recorded in 1962 with an unidentified rhythm section and operatic singer, shows his embracing of 20th century classical composition. Strong Indian influence is heard on 1960's "Improvisations and Tukras," featuring Dolphy's flute mixed with tabla and tamboura. The final three pieces were also recorded in 1960: "Inner Flight 1 and 2" are solo flute pieces, while "Dolphy'n" is a collaboration with bassist Ron Carter featuring Dolphy on alto. This music remained in the private collection of Dolphy's friend Hale Smith until the recordings were handed over to Blue Note in 1985. While *Other Aspects* is fascinating, and in its own way essential, it should be one of the final discs obtained for your Dolphy library. *—Al Campbell*

☆ **Out There** / Aug. 15, 1960 / New Jazz/OJC ✦✦✦✦✦
Eric Dolphy's second session as a leader is one of his most intriguing. On this CD reissue, Dolphy is heard performing two songs apiece on alto, bass clarinet and flute along with a rare appearance ("Eclipse") on clarinet. Joined by Ron Carter on cello, bassist George Duvivier and drummer Roy Haynes, Dolphy's playing is quite explorative and the hypnotic and somewhat spooky "Out There" finds both Dolphy's bass clarinet and Carter's cello sounding as if they are talking. *—Scott Yanow*

Far Cry / Dec. 21, 1960 / New Jazz/OJC ✦✦✦✦✦
Charlie Parker's influence permeates this 1960 session. Beyond the obvious acknowledgment on song titles ("Mrs. Parker of K.C. ['Bird's Mother']" and "Ode to Charlie Parker"), his restless spirit is utilized as a guiding light for breaking bebop molds. *Far Cry* finds multi-reedist Eric Dolphy in a transitional phase, relinquishing Parker's governing universal impact and diving into the next controversial phase that critics began calling "anti-jazz." On this date Booker Little's lyrical trumpet and Jackie Byard's confident grasp of multiple piano styles (though both steeped in hard bop) were sympathetic to the burgeoning "avant-garde" approach that Dolphy displays, albeit sparingly, on this session. *Far Cry* contains the initial performance of Dolphy's future jazz classic "Miss Ann," along with his first recorded solo alto sax performance on "Tenderly," in which Dolphy bridges the gap between the solo saxophone performances of Coleman Hawkins and Anthony Braxton. *—Al Campbell*

The Great Concert of Eric Dolphy / Jul. 16, 1961 / Prestige ✦✦✦✦✦
For two weeks, the multi-instrumentalist (alto, flute, and bass clarinet) Eric Dolphy appeared at *the Five Spot* in New York with a quintet comprised of trumpeter Booker Little (who would pass away before the year ended), pianist Mal Waldron, bassist Richard Davis, and drummer Ed Blackwell. One night, July 16, 1961, was fully recorded and the results released on three LPs. This three-LP box set contains all of the music, and despite an out-of-tune piano, the results are consistently brilliant. The seven selections (all over 12 minutes long with "The Prophet" going on for over 21) give the principles plenty of space in which to stretch out, and the long improvisations consistently hold one's interest. All of the material (except the standard "Like Someone in Love") was composed by Dolphy, Little, or Waldron. Classic and adventurous music. *—Scott Yanow*

Live! at the Five Spot, Vol. 1 / Jul. 16, 1961 / New Jazz/OJC ✦✦✦✦
On July 16, 1961, multi-instrumentalist Eric Dolphy and trumpeter Booker Little were extensively documented during the finish of a two-week engagement at the Five Spot in New York. Pianist Mal Waldron (overcoming an out-of-tune piano), bassist Richard Davis and drummer Ed Blackwell completed the quintet which on the first of three CD reissues from this gig performs Waldron's "Fire Waltz," Dolphy's "The Prophet" (which lasts 21 minutes) and two versions of Little's "Bee Vamp." Dolphy and Little during their short musical partnership always inspired each other and their playing on the challenging tunes is quite stimulating. *—Scott Yanow*

Live! at the Five Spot, Vol. 2 / Jul. 16, 1961 / Prestige/OJC ✦✦✦✦
The second of three CDs that document the Eric Dolphy/Booker Little Quintet's playing at the Five Spot (the third volume is titled *Memorial Album*) features the group (with pianist Mal Waldron, bassist Richard Davis and drummer Ed Blackwell) really stretching out during long versions of Little's "Aggression" and the standard "Like Someone in Love." Dolphy's playing (whether on alto, bass clarinet or flute) always defied categorization while Little (who passed away less than three months later) was the first new voice on the trumpet to emerge after Clifford Brown's death in 1956. An excellent set although, at just 36 minutes, one wishes that it had been combined with one of the other two volumes. *—Scott Yanow*

The Illinois Concert / Mar. 10, 1963 / Blue Note ✦✦✦✦✦
The 1999 discovery of a previously unknown 1963 concert by Eric Dolphy makes it one of the finds of the decade. Taped for broadcast at the University of Illinois at Champaign, it was mentioned in an Eric Dolphy Internet chat room and eventually relayed to producer Michael Cuscuna. The sound is very good, except for overly prominent drums throughout the concert and an under-miked flute on "South Street Exit." Dolphy's playing is consistently rewarding, including a lengthy workout of "Softly, As in a Morning Sunrise," a miniature of "Something Sweet, Something Tender," and his always superb solo feature of "God Bless the Child." He switches to alto sax for an adventurous new work, "Iron Man" (which he would record a few months later for Douglas International), also inserting a hilarious quote of "Comin' Through the Rye." A 23-year-old Herbie Hancock on piano, Eddie Locke on bass, and drummer J. C. Moses make up the solid rhythm section. The last two tracks, "Red Planet" and Dolphy's "G.W.," add the support of the University of Illinois Brass Ensemble, which included a young Cecil Bridgewater on trumpet. Highly recommended!- *—Ken Dryden*

☆ **Conversations** / May 1963-Jun. 1963 / Restless ✦✦✦✦✦
For those who want all the Dolphy out there. Often brilliant material, but haphazardly compiled. *—Ron Wynn*

Iron Man / May 1963-Jun. 1963 / Restless ✦✦✦✦
Recorded between Dolphy's initial and adventurous hard bop releases for Prestige and the wholly unique and fully realized chamber jazz collection *Out to Lunch, Iron Man* appropriately includes both sprawling, yet mostly straight-ahead, bop as well as some somberly abstract and searching pieces. Mistakenly tagged with the free jazz label, Dolphy did bring new compositional textures to the music and at times played with unmatched sonic and rhythmic intensity, but his approach generally fit into the confines of traditional jazz playing. In

many ways, by plying a very individual style, Dolphy was able to transcend the somewhat fractured landscape of jazz during the first half of the '60s. His unique vision certainly is given a fine reading here with the help of top players like vibraphonist Bobby Hutcherson, trumpeter Woody Shaw Jr., flutist Prince Lasha, bassist Richard Davis, and saxophonist Clifford Jordan. With Davis and drummer J.C. Moses supplying provocative and rock-solid support, Dolphy, Shaw, and Hutcherson particularly shine on extended originals like the title track and "Burning Spear." Dolphy scales things back with a couple of starkly beautiful ballad duets with Davis, playing bass clarinet and flute respectively on renditions of Ellington's "Come Sunday" and Jaki Byard's "Ode to C.P." A great disc for jazz fans whose tastes fall somewhere between hard bop and free jazz. *—Stephen Cook*

★ **Out to Lunch** / Feb. 25, 1964 / Blue Note ✦✦✦✦✦
Eric Dolphy's debut as a leader on Blue Note was also his last American recording before his unexpected death four months later. On this brilliant set, Dolphy performs five of his colorful originals with quite an all-star group (even though at the time none of these young players were all that well-known): trumpeter Freddie Hubbard, vibraphonist Bobby Hutcherson, bassist Richard Davis and drummer Tony Williams. Whether playing alto, flute or bass clarinet, Dolphy had a highly original style, and this set remains one of his finest statements. *—Scott Yanow*

☆ **Last Date** / Jun. 2, 1964 / Verve ✦✦✦✦✦
Although one slighty later session has since been discovered, *Last Date* remains a near-classic with the great Eric Dolphy (heard on alto, flute and bass clarinet) backed by a top European rhythm section—pianist Misha Mengelberg, bassist Jacques Schols and drummer Han Bennink—performing exciting versions of "Epistrophy," "You Don't Know What Love Is" and four of his originals. The innovative music points out what a giant loss Dolphy's premature death was; he passed away just 27 days after this memorable performance. *—Scott Yanow*

Lou Donaldson

b. Nov. 1, 1926, Badin, NC
Sax (Alto) / Hard Bop, Soul-Jazz, Bop
Lou Donaldson has long been an excellent bop altoist influenced by Charlie Parker, but with a more blues-based style of his own. His distinctive tone has been heard in a variety of small-group settings, and he has recorded dozens of worthy and spirited (if somewhat predictable) sets through the years. Donaldson first gained attention when he moved to New York and in 1952 started recording for Blue Note as a leader. At the age of 25, his style was fully formed, and although it would continue growing in depth through the years, Donaldson had already found his sound. In 1954, he participated in a notable gig with Art Blakey, Clifford Brown, Horace Silver and Tommy Potter that was extensively documented by Blue Note and that directly predated the Jazz Messengers. However, Donaldson was never a member of the Messengers, and although he recorded as a sideman in the 1950s and occasionally afterwards with Thelonious Monk, Milt Jackson and Jimmy Smith, among others, he has been a bandleader from the mid-1950s up until the present. Donaldson's early Blue Note recordings were pure bop. In 1958, he began often utilizing a conga player, and starting in 1961 his bands often had an organist rather than a pianist. Donaldson's bluesy style was easily transferable to soul-jazz, and he sounded most original in that context. *—Scott Yanow*

The Lou Donaldson Quartet/Quintet/Sextet / Jun. 10, 1952-Aug. 22, 1954 / Blue Note ✦✦✦✦✦
Since *Quartet/Quintet/Sextet* is Lou Donaldson's first full-length album, it's not surprising that it captures the alto saxophonist at the height of his Charlie Parker influence. Throughout the album—on CD, the collection features all the music on the 12" LP, music from its 10" incarnation, and three alternate takes—Donaldson plays in a straight bop vein, whether on up-tempo swingers or ballads. Most of the songs on the collection are standards, with a couple of fine originals from Donaldson and pianist Horace Silver spicing the mix; in particular, Silver's rollicking, Latin-tinged "Roccus" is a standout. While Donaldson's tone isn't quite as full as it would be within just five years, he impresses with his bold, speedy technique and fine phrasing. He doesn't play anything out of the ordinary, but he plays it very, very well, and his playing is enhanced by the three stellar bands that support him on these sessions. Among his fellow musicians on *Quartet/Quintet/Sextet* are Silver, bassist Gene Ramey, drummer Art Taylor, trumpeter Blue Mitchell, pianist Elmo Hope, and trumpeter Kenny Dorham. Everyone plays in a straight bop and hard bop tradition, contributing fine performances to a strong debut effort by Donaldson. *—Stephen Thomas Erlewine*

Lou Takes Off / Dec. 15, 1957 / Blue Note ✦✦✦✦✦
The influence of Charlie Parker can be heard in virtually every modern jazz musician, particularly players of the alto saxophone. Although considered to be one of "Bird's children," Lou Donaldson absorbed and synthesized other pre-Parker influences, such as Johnny Hodges and Benny Carter. This recording marks a period in his development prior to a stylistic shift away from bop and toward a stronger rhythm and blues emphasis. Three up-tempo tunes are pure bebop; the remaining number is a medium blues in B flat, quite characteristic of the hard bop period. The front line on this set includes Donald Byrd and Curtis Fuller; the rhythm section is Sonny Clark, George Joyner, and Art Taylor. Overall, *Lou Takes Off* breaks no new musical ground, but it is a solid, swinging session of high-caliber playing. *—Lee Bloom*

★ **Blues Walk** / Jul. 28, 1958 / Blue Note ✦✦✦✦✦
This early session from Lou Donaldson is pure bebop with the altoist romping on such pieces as "Blues Walk," "Move," "Play Ray" and "Callin' All Cats." The rhythm section (pianist Herman Foster, bassist Peck Morrison, drummer Dave Bailey) is supportive if not particularly distinctive, although the congas of Ray Barretto add some color to the accompaniment. No matter; Lou Donaldson is the main star of this swinging and enjoyable set. *—Scott Yanow*

Light Foot / Dec. 14, 1958 / Blue Note ✦✦✦
In many ways, *Blues Walk* marked the culmination of Lou Donaldson's prime period as a hard-driving, straight-ahead bop saxophonist. Until that point, he had been turning out intense, furious bop workouts—afterward, as its successor *Light Foot* shows, he began to slow down a bit. With *Light Foot,* Donaldson still was pretty firmly grounded in bop, but the tempos began to slow down, and his blues influence came to the forefront; furthermore, the bop tracks are hard bop, not straight bop, which tended to dominate his previous recordings. That diversity makes *Light Foot* an interesting listen, but the record suffers from slightly uneven material and performances. His quintet—featuring pianist Herman Foster, bassist Peck Morrison, drummer Jimmy Wormsworth, and conga player Ray Barretto—is usually up to the task at hand, but they tend to play conventionally. And, ultimately, that's what *Light Foot* is—an entertaining but conventional release from an alto saxophonist capable of greatness. *—Stephen Thomas Erlewine*

LD + 3: Lou Donaldson with the Three Sounds / Feb. 18, 1959 / Blue Note ✦✦✦✦✦
Lou Donaldson and the Three Sounds both had a tendency to slip into low-key grooves, which is what makes the hard-driving bop of the opener "Three Little Words" a little startling. Donaldson is at a fiery peak, spinning out Bird-influenced licks that nevertheless illustrate that he's developed a more rounded, individual style of his own. The Three Sounds are equally as impressive, working bop rhythms with a dexterity that their first albums only hinted at. That high standard is maintained throughout the album, one of the finest in either of their catalogs. Albums like this and *Blues Walk* established Donaldson's reputation as a first-rate alto saxophonist, since he flaunts a full, robust tone, a fondness for melody, and nimble solos over the course of the record. *LD + 3* is pretty much straight bop and hard bop, with little of the soul-jazz the two artists would later explore, but this collection of swinging standards, bop staples, and a pair of Donaldson originals ranks as one of Lou's finest straight bop sessions. *—Stephen Thomas Erlewine*

Sunny Side Up / Feb. 5, 1960+Feb. 29, 1960 / Blue Note ✦✦✦
Sunny Side Up is closer to hard bop than the straight-ahead bop that characterized Lou Donaldson's '50s Blue Note records. There's a bit more soul to the songs here, which pianist Horace Parlan helps emphasize with his lightly swinging grooves. The pair help lead the group—which also features trumpeter Bill Hardman, drummer Al Harewood and bassist Sam Jones (Laymon Jackson plays bass on two of the eight songs)—through a mellow set of standards and bluesy originals from Donaldson and Parlan. Even the uptempo numbers sound relaxed, never fiery. Despite the general smoothness of the session, Donaldson stumbles a little—the quotation of "Flight of the Bumblebee" on "Blues for J.P." is awkward, as is the snippet of "Pop Goes the Weasel" on "Politely," and "Way Down Upon the Swanee River" sounds lazy—but there's enough solid material to make *Sunny Side Up* a worthwhile listen for fans of Donaldson and early-'60s hard bop. *—Stephen Thomas Erlewine*

Here 'Tis / Jan. 23, 1961 / Blue Note ✦✦✦✦✦

Gravy Train / Apr. 27, 1961 / Blue Note ✦✦✦

The Natural Soul / May 9, 1962 / Blue Note ✦✦✦✦

Good Gracious / Jan. 24, 1963 / Blue Note ✦✦✦✦
Good Gracious may be Lou Donaldson's record, but guitarist Grant Green and organist John Patton steal the show. Working with a tight, soulful groove laid down by drummer Ben Dixon, the guitarist and organist trade hot lines that often steal the thunder from Donaldson, who nevertheless turns in a robust, tuneful performance. Donaldson's tone is richer and fuller than it is on many of his early '60s records, and he really connects with the laid-back R&B grooves and soul-jazz vamps on *Good Gracious,* turning in melodic, memorable solos. However, Grant and Patton take the songs even further with their intense solos and fills; Patton, in particular, sounds on fire even when the tempo is mellow. *Good Gracious* still falls prey to some of the lazy tempos that pop up on most Lou Donaldson records, but it remains one of his finest soul-jazz sessions. *—Stephen Thomas Erlewine*

Lush Life / Jan. 20, 1967 / Blue Note ✦✦✦✦✦
After brief sojourns at Argo and Cadet, Lou Donaldson marked his 1967 return by recording *Lush Life,* the grandest project he ever attempted. With its plush arrangements and unabashedly pretty melodies, *Lush Life* stands in stark contrast to everything else he cut in the '60s. There are no blues, no stabs at soul-jazz grooves, no hard bop—only sweet, sensitive renditions of romantic standards. Donaldson shone on ballads before, but it's nevertheless surprising how successful he is on this set of slow love songs. His tone is full and elegant—it's easy to get lost in his rich readings of these familiar melodies, as well as his slyly seductive improvisations. Of course, it helps that his instrumental backdrops are as lovely as those his nine-piece backing band provide. Nonets are unwieldy, to be certain, but Duke Pearson's arrangements are clean, sparkling, and attractive, and the superstar band—Wayne Shorter (tenor sax), Jerry Dodgion (alto sax, flute), Pepper Adams (bari sax), Freddie Hubbard (trumpet), Garnett Brown (trombone), McCoy Tyner (piano), Ron Carter (bass), Al Harewood (drums)—knows enough to provide sympathetic support and not steal the show. When they do take solos, it enhances Donaldson's original statements, and helps make *Lush Life* the singularly enchanting record it is. *—Stephen Thomas Erlewine*

Alligator Bogaloo / Apr. 17, 1967 / Blue Note ✦✦✦✦
Altoist Lou Donaldson had a big hit at the time with the catchy title cut. This CD reissue (a straight reproduction of the original LP) features Donaldson in a quintet with cornetist Melvin Lastie, Sr., guitarist George Benson, organist Lonnie Smith and drummer Leo Morris. The material (originals by Donaldson, Smith and Freddie McCoy along with the standard "I Want a Little Girl") is pretty basic (generally bluesy and funky) but there are fine solos on this session from Donaldson, Benson and Smith. *—Scott Yanow*

The Midnight Creeper / Mar. 15, 1968 / Blue Note ✦✦✦✦
As he delved deeper into commercial soul-jazz and jazz-funk, Lou Donaldson became better at it. While lacking the bite of his hard bop improvisations or the hard-swinging funk of *Alligator Bogaloo, Midnight Creeper* succeeds where its predecessor, *Mr. Shing-A-Ling* failed: it offers a thoroughly enjoyable set of grooving, funky soul-jazz. The five songs—including two originals by Donaldson and one each by Lonnie Smith (who also plays organ on the record), Teddy Vann, and Harold Ousley—aren't particularly distinguished, but the vibe is important, not the material. And the band—Donaldson, Smith, trumpeter Blue Mitchell, gui-

tarist George Benson, and drummer Leo Morris—strikes the right note, turning in a fluid, friendly collection of bluesy funk vamps. Donaldson could frequently sound stilted on his commercial soul-jazz dates, but that's not the case with *Midnight Creeper.* He rarely was quite as loose on his late-'60s/early-'70s records as he is here, and that's what makes *Midnight Creeper* a keeper. *—Stephen Thomas Erlewine*

Hot Dog / Apr. 25, 1969 / Blue Note ✦✦

Everything I Play Is Funky / Aug. 22, 1969+Jan. 9, 1970 / Blue Note ✦✦

Birdseed / Apr. 28, 1992-Apr. 29, 1992 / Milestone ✦✦✦✦

Man with a Horn / Sep. 25, 1961+Jun. 7, 1963 / Blue Note ✦✦✦
These sessions were recorded for Blue Note in 1961 and 1963. The first date features five cuts with Jack Mcduff on organ, Grant Green on guitar, and Joe Dukes on drums. The four remaining cuts were recorded two years later with John Patton on organ, Ben Dixon on drums, and the addition of Irvin Stokes on trumpet. This is a mainly mellow affair with six of the nine tracks exchanging the hard bop and soul-jazz of the times for ballads and slow blues. However, the occasional up-tempo funky surprise does pop up on "My Melancholy Baby" and the Donaldson originals "Hipty Hop" and "Soul Meetin'." *—Al Campbell*

Kenny Dorham

b. Aug. 30, 1924, Fairfield, TX, **d.** Dec. 5, 1972, New York, NY
Trumpet / Hard Bop
Throughout his career Kenny Dorham was almost famous for being underrated since he was consistently overshadowed by Dizzy Gillespie, Fats Navarro, Miles Davis, Clifford Brown and Lee Morgan. Dorham was never an influential force himself but a talented bop-oriented trumpeter and an excellent composer who played in some very significant bands. In 1945 he was in the orchestras of Dizzy Gillespie and Billy Eckstine, he recorded with the Be Bop Boys in 1946 and spent short periods with Lionel Hampton and Mercer Ellington. During 1948-49 Dorham was the trumpeter in the Charlie Parker Quintet. After some freelancing in New York in 1954 he became a member of the first version of Art Blakey's Jazz Messengers and for a short time led a group called the Jazz Prophets which recorded on Blue Note. After Clifford Brown's death, Dorham became his replacement in the Max Roach Quintet (1956-58) and then he led several groups of his own. He recorded several fine dates for Riverside (including a vocal album in 1958), New Jazz and Time but it is his Blue Note sessions of 1961-64 that are among his finest. Dorham was an early booster of Joe Henderson (who played with his group in 1963-64). After the mid-'60s Kenny Dorham (who wrote some interesting reviews for *Downbeat*) began to fade and he died in 1972 of kidney disease. Among his many originals is one that became a standard, "Blue Bossa." *—Scott Yanow*

Kenny Dorham Quintet / Dec. 15, 1953 / Debut/OJC ✦✦✦✦
Kenny Dorham's debut as a leader found the 29-year-old trumpeter more than ready to take control; unfortunately he spent virtually his entire career in the shadows of other trumpeters (such as Dizzy Gillespie, Miles Davis, Clifford Brown and Lee Morgan). This set was originally released by the Debut label as a six-song ten-inch LP and then reissued with two alternate takes as a regular album. Now available on CD with two additional blues and another alternate, the fine playing by the quintet (with Jimmy Heath on tenor and baritone, pianist Walter Bishop, bassist Percy Heath and drummer Kenny Clarke) is not watered down by the extra material. A special bonus is the fine arranging of Dorham for the ensemble, a much overlooked talent of a continually underrated musician. *—Scott Yanow*

★ **Afro-Cuban** / Jan. 30, 1955+Mar. 29, 1955 / Blue Note ✦✦✦✦✦
This is a particularly strong set from trumpeter Kenny Dorham, for it has the debut versions of "Lotus Flower," "Minor Holiday" and "La Villa," three of his most rewarding compositions. The first half of the set is Afro-Cuban in nature due to the inclusion of Carlos "Potato" Valdes's conga; also on the four songs (plus a previously unreleased alternate take of "Minor's Holiday") are trombonist J.J. Johnson, Hank Mobley on tenor, baritonist Cecil Payne, pianist Horace Silver, bassist Oscar Pettiford and drummer Art Blakey. The final four numbers (including a "new" song added to the CD reissue, "K.D.'s Cab Ride") are more straightahead in nature and drop out Valdes and Johnson while substituting Percy Heath for Pettiford. In both cases, Dorham has an all-star group of young hard boppers eager to play his challenging and memorable originals. *—Scott Yanow*

'Round About Midnight at the Cafe Bohemia, Vol. 1 / May 31, 1956 / Blue Note ✦✦✦✦
This CD plus its second volume has been recently reissued as a two-CD set. The first volume has the original six songs from the LP of the same name (featuring trumpeter Kenny Dorham's short-lived hard bop group The Jazz Prophets) plus three previously unreleased performances. Dorham and his sextet (with tenor-saxophonist J.R. Monterose, guitarist Kenny Burrell, pianist Bobby Timmons, bassist Sam Jones and drummer Arthur Edgehill) are in fine form, performing high-quality hard bop with some of the best performances including "Monaco," "'Round Midnight," "Night in Tunisia" and "K.D's Blues." *—Scott Yanow*

Jazz Contrasts / May 21, 1957+May 27, 1957 / Riverside/OJC ✦✦✦✦✦
Some of trumpeter Kenny Dorham's finest recordings were his sessions as a leader for Riverside in the 1950s and fortunately all of that music has been reissued on CD. This album is a bit brief in time (41 minutes) but contains many memorable selections. Three of the songs ("Falling in Love with Love" a 12-minute version of "I'll Remember April" and the trumpeter's "La Villa") match Dorham in an all-star quintet with the great tenor Sonny Rollins, pianist Hank Jones, bassist Oscar Pettiford and drummer Max Roach. The other three numbers (of which only "My Old Flame" includes Rollins) adds a fine harp player (Betty Glamman) and focuses on Dorham's lyricism. *—Scott Yanow*

2 Horns, 2 Rhythms / Nov. 13, 1957+Dec. 1957 / Riverside/OJC ✦✦✦✦
Trumpeter Kenny Dorham was one of the most underrated talents of the bop and hard bop eras. Although he did not hit high note or influence a lot of players, Dorham's appealing sound and consistently creative ideas should have made him a star in the jazz world instead of just a journeyman. On this CD reissue (which adds an alternate take of "'Sposin'" to the original eight-song LP program), Dorham and altoist Ernie Henry (on his final session) are heard in a pianoless quartet (with either Eddie Mathias or Wilbur Ware on bass and drummer G.T. Hogan) playing three of the trumpeter's originals (including "Lotus Blossom") and four standards. Highlights include "I'll Be Seeing You" and a rare revival of "Is It True What They Say About Dixie—" The sparse setting (unusual for a Dorham session) works quite well. *—Scott Yanow*

Blue Spring / Jan. 20, 1959+Feb. 18, 1959 / Riverside/OJC ✦✦✦✦
This is one of trumpeter Kenny Dorham's most intriguing sessions. His arrangements of five songs that have "Spring" in their title plus the tune "Poetic" are colorful, making use of altoist Cannonball Adderley, baritonist Cecil Payne, the french horn of Dave Amram and a fine rhythm section. Plus, Dorham's melodic solos (he was never just a bop stylist) are often memorable. *—Scott Yanow*

Quiet Kenny / Nov. 13, 1959 / New Jazz/OJC ✦✦✦

Whistle Stop / Jan. 15, 1961 / Blue Note ✦✦✦✦✦
Kenny Dorham was always underrated throughout his career, not only as a trumpeter but as a composer. This CD reissue features seven of his compositions, none of which have been picked up by any of the "Young Lions" of the 1990s despite their high quality and the many fresh melodies. Dorham teams up with tenor-saxophonist Hank Mobley (who he had recorded with previously with Art Blakey and Max Roach), pianist Kenny Drew, bassist Paul Chambers and drummer Philly Joe Jones for a set of lively, fresh and consistently swinging music. This is a generally overlooked near-classic set. *—Scott Yanow*

Matador/Inta Somethin' / Nov. 1961-Apr. 15, 1962 / Blue Note ✦✦✦✦
Two full LPs are combined on this single CD. Both dates feature trumpeter Kenny Dorham and altoist Jackie McLean (two very compatible players) although the rhythm sections (pianist Bobby Timmons or Walter Bishop, bassist Teddy Smith or Leroy Vinnegar and drummer J.C. Moses or Art Taylor) differ between the two sessions. McLean was beginning to look forward and be influenced by the avant-garde; the passion he puts into his tone on such tunes as "Smile," "Beautiful Love," "It Could Happen to You" and "Lover Man" is memorable. Dorham was able to keep up with the times during this era and his three compositions (particularly "El Matador" and "Una Mas") add a lot to the music. This generous CD is worth picking up as an example of veteran players stretching the boundaries of hard bop. *—Scott Yanow*

☆ **Una Mas** / Apr. 1, 1963 / Blue Note ✦✦✦✦✦
When one thinks of great talent scouts in jazz, the name of Kenny Dorham is often overlooked. However, many top young players benefited from playing in his groups, and for proof one need look no further than the lineup on this 1963 CD reissue: tenor-saxophonist Joe Henderson, bassist Butch Warren, and (before either player joined Miles Davis) pianist Herbie Hancock and drummer Tony Williams. Together the quintet performs three of the trumpeter's originals ("Una Mas" is the most famous) along with the standard ballad "If Ever I Would Leave You." Even if the playing time (under 37 minutes) is a bit brief, the explorative yet swinging music lives up to its potential. *—Scott Yanow*

Trompeta Toccata / Sep. 4, 1964 / Blue Note ✦✦✦✦
It seems strange and somewhat tragic that this was trumpeter Kenny Dorham's last full album as a leader for he was only 40 at the time and still in his prime. Dorham contributed three of the four selections to the session (Joe Henderson's catchy "Mamacita" also receives its debut), and his very underrated abilities as a writer, trumpeter, and talent scout are very much in evidence. This modern hard bop quintet set with Henderson on tenor, pianist Tommy Flanagan, bassist Richard Davis, and drummer Albert "Tootie" Heath served as a strong (if premature) ending to Dorham's impressive career as a solo artist. *—Scott Yanow*

Bob Dorough

b. Dec. 12, 1923, Cherry Hill, AR
Vocals, Piano, Composer / Vocal Jazz, Vocalese, Cool, Bop
Although neglected and underexposed most of his life, Bob Dorough is an adventurous, risk-taking master of vocalese (the process of writing and singing lyrics to instrumental jazz solos) and scat singing who has directly or indirectly influenced Mark Murphy, Michael Franks, Mose Allison and most recently, Kurt Elling. The Arkansas native started out on piano in the 1940s, then took up singing in the early 1950s (when he played for boxer Sugar Ray Robinson, an entertainer at the time). From 1954-55, Dorough lived in Paris, where he recorded with singer Blossom Dearie. The improviser launched his own recording career when he signed with Bethlehem in 1955 and recorded the excellent *Devil May Care,* which introduced the defiant title song and lyrics to Charlie Parker's "Yardbird Suite." But sadly, he recorded only sporadically after that. In 1962, Dorough co-wrote "Comin' Home Baby" (a hit for Mel Torme) with Ben Tucker, and in 1966, he recorded his second album, *Just About Everything,* for Focus. In the early 1970s, he began writing and directing the series of educational children's TV programs, *Schoolhouse Rock.* Though instructional material became his bread and butter, Dorough recorded obscure jazz dates for 52 Rue East, Orange Blue, Pinnacle, Boomdido, Laissez-Faire and other tiny labels in the 1970s and 1980s. In 1997, a 73-year-old Dorough received some long-overdue attention from a major label when the Capitol-distributed Blue Note released *Right on My Way Home. Too Much Coffee Man* followed in the spring of 2000. *—Alex Henderson*

Devil May Care / Oct. 1956 / Bethlehem Archives/Avenue Jazz ✦✦✦✦✦
Vocalist-pianist-lyricist Bob Dorough's first record as a leader is a pretty definitive set that has been reissued on CD through Evidence. Assisted by his longtime bassist Bill Takas, drummer Jerry Segal and sometimes trumpeter Warren Fitzgerald and vibraphonist Jack Hitchcock, Dorough performs near-classic renditions of such songs as "Old Devil Moon," "Yardbird Suite," "Baltimore Oriole," "Devil May Care" and "Johnny One Note." Recommended. *—Scott Yanow*

● **Just About Everything** / Mar. 17, 1966+Mar. 21, 1966 / Evidence ✦✦✦✦✦
This CD reissue brings back Bob Dorough's definitive album. The vocalist-pianist, who is joined by guitarist Al Schackman, bassist Ben Tucker and drummer Percy Brice, was in top creative form for the set. His renditions of "Baltimore Oriole" and "Lazy Afternoon" are

haunting while his versions of "I've Got Just About Everything," "Better Than Anything" and "Tis Autumn" are quite memorable. Dorough even manages to do a credible job on Bob Dylan's "Don't Think Twice" and in 1966 must have been one of the few jazzmen to cover a current rock tune. Dorough's unusual voice and swinging piano are heard at their best throughout the highly recommended release. *—Scott Yanow*

Right on My Way Home / Apr. 30, 1997-May 6, 1997 / Blue Note ♦♦♦♦
As one of the key voices of *Schoolhouse Rock*, Bob Dorough acquired many fans, but no one ever knew his name. Even after the series ended, he was reluctant to pursue a full-fledged recording career, which made 1997's *Right on My Way Home*?an album he recorded when he was 73—something of an event. It was one of the rare occasions that Dorough was able to demonstrate the depth and range of his talent. Like Mose Allison, he has a friendly, idiosyncratic variation on bluesy scat and bop that sounds equally at home on standards ("Moon River," "Spring Can Really Hang You Up the Most") or originals ("I Get the Neck of the Chicken," "Something for Sidney," "Up Jumped a Bird"). Some tastes might Dorough find a bit too cutesy, yet there's no denying that he can make a song his own, and *Right On My Way Home* is one of the best proofs of that statement. *—Stephen Thomas Erlewine*

Too Much Coffee Man / Apr. 18, 1998-Dec. 14, 1998 / Blue Note ♦♦♦♦
There's no decaf on *Too Much Coffee Man*, Bob Dorough's second album for Blue Note. But there is plenty of bouquet, flavor, and remarkable stylistic diversity. Dorough is 76, idiosyncratic, goofy, and creative. He worked with Miles Davis decades ago; he's also worked with Blossom Dearie, Art Farmer, and John Zorn. Dorough's voice is nasal, penetrating, and conversational; the way he stretches a tune to maximize its impact and his obvious camaraderie with technically dizzying players such as Phil Woods, Ray Drummond, Billy Hart and Jamey Haddad is exceptional in its naturalness. A natural all the way, Dorough is as authoritative on love ballads such as "There's Never Been a Day" as on novelty songs, like Dave Frishberg's "Oklahoma Toad." But it's not his style alone that's so striking, it's his sensibility. Dorough has been many emotional places and is eager to tell their stories. At times, his attitude evokes Randy Newman, and his eclecticism suggests a more worldly, slightly more commercial Van Dyke Parks. Dorough is energetic. Check the way he effortlessly integrates samba into the cutting "Marilyn" (a relative of Dylan's "Leopardskin Pillbox Hat"). Despite his debonair delivery, he also can transmit deep emotion. Perhaps the best example is "Where Is the Song—," one of the meditations on transience that mark the latter half of this notable album. Here, Dorough negotiates a tricky rhythm, stepping between the stones of a marvelous Woods obbligato as the rhythm section underlines his storyline of missed, yearned-for connections. The album ends with "Late in the Century," Dorough's nosegay to the late, lamented 19th century. It's a plea for patience and tolerance, replete with Hammond B3, a sweet chorus, and Dorough's rubato piano. The tune looks backward and forward, like Dorough himself. *—Carlo Wolff*

Jimmy Dorsey

b. Feb. 29, 1904, Shenandoah, PA, **d.** Jun. 12, 1957, New York, NY
Sax (Alto), Clarinet / Swing, Big Band
The older of the two Dorsey Brothers, Jimmy was the superior jazz player. An excellent clarinetist and one of the finest altoists to emerge during the 1920s, JD's jazz playing was overshadowed during the swing era by the commercial hits of his orchestra. He started out playing with his brother Tommy in Dorsey's Novelty Six, the Scranton Sirens and the California Ramblers and his solos with Red Nichols' Five Pennies made a strong impression. Dorsey recorded with Frankie Trumbauer, Jean Goldkette and Paul Whiteman and became a busy studio musician during the Depression. In addition, starting in 1928 he co-led the Dorsey Brothers Orchestra with Tommy. Jimmy took over the nucleus of the band and, after a period of struggle, the orchestra hit it big in the early '40s with a series of vocal records featuring Bob Eberle and Helen O'Connell. By late in the decade Dorsey was alternating between some boppish big band performances (Maynard Ferguson was among his sidemen) and Dixieland jams with his Dorseyland Band. In 1953 he broke up the band to join Tommy in a new Dorsey Brothers Orchestra that emphasized dance music. After Tommy's sudden death in late 1956, Jimmy took over the orchestra and had a surprise hit in "So Rare" before passing away from cancer. *—Scott Yanow*

★ **Contrasts** / Jul. 7, 1936-Oct. 7, 1943 / Decca/GRP ♦♦♦♦♦
This CD, virtually the only example of Jimmy Dorsey's orchestra currently available on CD, puts the emphasis on his jazz sides rather than the vocal best-sellers. Popular singer Helen O'Connell does make three appearances (including the hit, "Tangerine") but most of these selections are instrumentals with Dorsey's alto and clarinet in outstanding form (it was easy to forget how talented an instrumentalist he was during these commercial years). Most of the other fine soloists are lesser names although they include future-bandleaders Ray McKinley (on drums) and pianist Freddie Slack. Highlights are "Parade of the Milk Bottle Caps," "I Got Rhythm," "John Silver," "Ducks in Upper Sandusky," Dorsey's theme "Contrasts," and "King Porter Stomp" although there isn't a weak track on this release. Recommended, this is Dorsey's definitive set. *—Scott Yanow*

America's Premier Dixieland Jazz Band Live 1950 / Aug. 25, 1998 / Jazz Crusade ♦♦♦♦
In 1949 Jimmy Dorsey formed his Original Dorseyland Jazz Band, a Dixieland combo taken out of the personnel of his big band. While Dorsey had been emphasizing his alto playing since the late 1930s and became famous for his pop hits, the Dorseyland band featured nononsense and often hyperactive trad jazz. The music on this 1998 CD, some of which had been put out earlier on an obscure Jazz House British LP, is taken from two full-length radio broadcasts. Dorsey (on clarinet except for some alto on "Sweet Lorraine") is matched with the underrated but hot trumpet of Charlie Teagarden, either Bud Hackman or Cutty Cutshall on trombone, Frank Mayne or Buddy Bardach on tenor, Al Waslohn or Bob Carter on piano, bassist Bill Lallotte and either Ray Bauduc or Karl Kiffe on drums. In addition, Pat O'Connor has a couple vocals, including "Charley My Boy," in which she is assisted by Teagarden. The repertoire is chiefly comprised of warhorses, but JD and his men play with such spirit and drive that this is very easy music to enjoy. It is as if Dorsey was finally liberated from his roles as a big bandleader and could at last devote his energy completely to jamming among near-equals. Easily recommended to Dixieland fans. *—Scott Yanow*

Live at the Edgewater / Jul. 12, 1950+Aug. 4, 1952 / Jerden ♦♦♦♦♦
A fine live performance by the Jimmy Dorsey band near the tail-end of its history, captured live at the *Edgewater Starlite Roof*, on the shores of Lake Mendota in Madison, Wisconsin. The big-band era was coming to a close, but you'd scarcely know it from the elegant playing here, before a crowd of 2500 eager listeners and dancers. The emphasis tends toward "sweet" (i.e., pop) rather than swing (jazz), but the band still takes flight on "Wimoweh" (a then-current single as well as a recent hit for the Weavers) and "That's a Plenty," a piece better known for Jackie Gleason's appropriation of it as "a little traveling music" on his TV show. "Perfida" makes a supremely elegant and lyrical opening, and vocalist Eleanor Russell turns in a sultry performance on "Don't You Worry 'Bout Me." The source for this show are radio transcription discs from the original 25-minute live broadcast, and these have been cleaned up nicely—there are still some pops and clicks, but the noise only becomes obstrusive in the quiet parts. They were also very well recorded, with excellent balances; every section of the band, from the drums to the brass, is sharply delineated throughout, and Dorsey's extended clarinet solo on "Delicado" justifies the price of the disc. Paired with a 30-minute Woody Herman show from the same venue. *—Bruce Eder*

Tommy Dorsey

b. Nov. 19, 1905, Shenandoah, PA, **d.** Nov. 26, 1956, Greenwich, CT
Trombone / Sweet Bands, Swing, Big Band
Tommy Dorsey was the definitive ballad player of the swing era, possessing a beautiful tone and very impressive breath control. A better jazz player than he thought, Dorsey enjoyed playing Dixieland now and then but preferred later in life to stick to ballads. In his early days he played with older brother Jimmy in Dorsey's Novelty Six before moving to New York and appearing on records with Jean Goldkette, Paul Whiteman and Red Nichols. He was a busy studio player during the Depression until agreeing to co-lead the Dorsey Brothers Orchestra in 1934. Late in 1935 a blowup on stage led to Tommy leaving and forming his own big band, taking over the Joe Haymes Orchestra. After a short struggle, major hits in 1937 ("Marie" and "Song of India," made the Tommy Dorsey Orchestra into a major attraction. In the early '40s with the hiring of Sy Oliver as chief arranger, drummer Buddy Rich and a vocal group featuring Frank Sinatra and Jo Stafford, the orchestra evolved and continued to have hits including "I'll Never Smile Again" and "Opus One." In 1942 Dorsey was able to hire the string section of the Artie Shaw Orchestra, greatly expanding his band. By the end of World War II and the collapse of the swing era, TD had to drop the strings and cut back a bit, even breaking up his band for a period after 1946. *—Scott Yanow*

The Complete Tommy Dorsey, Vol. 1 (1935) / Sep. 26, 1935-Dec. 21, 1935 / Bluebird ♦♦♦♦
The most complete series of Tommy Dorsey reissues was a two-fer LP program that succeeded in issuing in chronological order all of his recordings from the beginnings of his big band in September 1935 up to March 1939 (eight volumes in all), before corporate indifference brought the program to a halt at its halfway mark. Since Dorsey led a dance band that performed novelties and commercial vocal features in addition to jazz, not all of their recordings were classics. General collectors might be more satisfied with samplers rather than getting everything. *Volume I* in this series has as its highpoints: "Weary Blues," Dorsey's theme "I'm Getting Sentimental Over You," and the first sides by his Clambake Seven, including "The Music Goes Round and Round." *—Scott Yanow*

Music Goes Round and Round / Dec. 9, 1935-Feb. 25, 1947 / Bluebird/RCA ♦♦♦♦♦
In 1935, Tommy Dorsey first jammed with musicians from his big band in a Dixieland format, calling the little band the Clambake Seven. He recorded frequently with the unit up until 1939 and then on a rare basis up until 1950. This particular CD has 21 of the Clambake's better performances, and although it would have been preferable to reissue all of the group's recordings, this serves as a strong introduction to their music. With such soloists as trumpeters Yank Lawson, Max Kaminsky, and Pee Wee Erwin, clarinetists Johnny Mince and Joe Dixon, tenorman Bud Freeman, and TD himself, this music was quite joyous and spirited. Edythe Wright ably sings on many of the songs which are highlighted by the title cut, "At the Codfish Ball," two versions of "The Sheik of Araby," and "When the Midnight Choo-Choo Leaves for Alabama." These are Dixieland recordings that predated the New Orleans revival of 1940. *—Scott Yanow*

★ **Yes, Indeed!** / Jun. 15, 1939-Sep. 20, 1945 / Bluebird/RCA ♦♦♦♦♦
This CD includes many of Tommy Dorsey's very best recordings from 1939-1942 along with four selections dating from 1944-1945. During this period the sound of his orchestra had changed from the earlier days, thanks in large part to Sy Oliver's arrangements and the hard-driving drums of Buddy Rich. With such soloists as trumpeter Ziggy Elman, tenor-saxophonist Don Lodice, and clarinetist Johnny Mince (in addition to Dorsey's trombone), this orchestra could play jazz with the best of their contemporaries, although many of their other recordings (not included here) actually showcased vocals and dance music. Highlights of this recommended disc include "Well, All Right," "Stomp It Off," "Quiet Please," "Swing High," "Swanee River," "Deep River," and "Well, Git It!," while the later tracks include "Opus I," the Charlie Shavers feature "At the Fat Man's," and a guest appearance by Duke Ellington on "The Minor Goes Muggin'." *—Scott Yanow*

All-Time Greatest Dorsey/Sinatra Hits, Vol. 1-4 / 1940-1942 / RCA ♦♦♦♦
When RCA decided to issue its early 40s Tommy Dorsey recordings containing Frank Sinatra vocals on compact disc, it abandoned the chronological sequencing found on the Grammy-winning album series *The Dorsey/Sinatra Sessions* and instead jumped back and forth through the catalog. This first volume of four contains some of the biggest hits, notably "I'll Never Smile Again" and "I'll Be Seeing You," and thus is the best selection for beginners. But be sure to move on to Vol. 2 and Vol. 3 and, especially, Vol. 4, which contains Sinatra's first solo session. *—William Ruhlmann*

All-Time Greatest Dorsey/Sinatra Hits, Vol. 2 / 1940-1942 / RCA ♦♦♦
W/ Frank Sinatra. Fine companion volume to first Dorsey/Sinatra overview set. *—Ron Wynn*

All-Time Greatest Dorsey/Sinatra Hits, Vol. 3 / 1940-1942 / RCA ✦✦✦

Stardust / Feb. 26, 1940-Jul. 1, 1942 / Bluebird/RCA ✦✦✦

Stop, Look & Listen / Sep. 26, 1935-Jul. 1, 1942 / ASV/Living Era ✦✦✦✦
Having remastered everything that Tommy Dorsey and His Orchestra ever cut with Frank Sinatra, BMG now turns its attention to Dorsey's pre-Sinatra catalog, more or less doing with Dorsey's late-'30s catalog what the two-CD *Essential Glenn Miller* did with Miller's output of hits. The 21 tracks here have been remastered very carefully using the CEDAR system, which run circles around any previous collections of Dorsey's work. The range of sounds among these 64 minutes of music is impressive, from hot swing like Lew Pollack's "That's a Plenty" and jazzed classics like "Mendelssohn's Spring Song" and "Song of India" (from Rimsky-Korsakov) to smooth pop like "After You've Gone," with lots of room in between for hot dance numbers ("Keepin' Out of Mischief Now") and future pop standards (including Irving Berlin's "Marie," sung by Jack Leonard). Regardless of the music, whether pop or jazz, the playing is impeccable—the singing by Edythe Wright on "The Goona Goo," is forgettable, but there are only three vocal numbers here. It's still not easy to pick out the sound of the rhythm guitar, but boy does the bass bounce here, and the reeds, trumpets (Bunny Berigan excels throughout), and trombones are radiant in their clarity. Berigan's solos of "Song of India" and "Marie" are worth the price of this disc. The notes are a bit of a puzzle, presented as a quotes from opposed legal-style briefs, alternately attacking and defending Dorsey's jazz credentials. —*Bruce Eder*

Swingin' in Hollywood / 1998 / Rhino ✦✦✦
Although credited to Tommy and Jimmy Dorsey jointly, this is not a collection of collaborations or duets, just an anthology of tracks that one or the other of the brothers filmed and recorded for MGM soundtracks in 1942-45. It's actually much more weighted toward Tommy (who has 13 of the 21 sides) than Jimmy; it's mostly instrumental, but vocalists like Bob Eberly, Helen O'Connell, and Nancy Walker are featured on some of the selections. The sound is good, and as a dozen of the items were previously unreleased (with 13 appearing for the first time in stereo), Dorsey collectors will consider this indispensable. For the more general fan, it's not the first place to get acquainted with their work, but it's quite respectable early-'40s swing. In general, it's more effective the harder and faster it swings—as on Jimmy's extended version of "One O'Clock Jump," and Tommy's "Battle of the Balcony Jive" and "Opus One"—and the less it resembles movie musicals. —*Richie Unterberger*

Homefront: 1941-1945 / May 19, 1998 / RCA ✦✦✦✦
Released to coincide with the arrival of Memorial Day, *The Homefront 1941-1945* is a worthwhile compilation of many of Tommy Dorsey's most popular and enduring wartime favorites. Among the selections: "I'm Getting Sentimental Over You," "Just as Though You Were Here," "Kiss the Boys Goodbye," "All the Things You Are" and "Yes Indeed!" —*Jason Ankeny*

Dave Douglas

Trumpet / Avant-Garde Jazz, Post-Bop, Modern Creative
Dave Douglas has arguably become the most original trumpeter/composer of his generation. Douglas's stylistic range is broad, yet unaffected; his music is not a pastiche, but, rather, a personal aesthetic that reflects an wide variety of interests—he explicitly cites such diverse influences as Igor Stravinsky, Stevie Wonder, and John Coltrane. As a composer, Douglas adapts and synthesizes unusual forms and creates his own out of disparate elements. As a trumpeter, Douglas possesses a comprehensive jazz technique; certainly, one hears the ghost of Lester Bowie in Douglas's expressive manipulations of timbre and pitch, but more pronounced is the integration of distinctive compositional and improvisational conceptions that ultimately defines his work.

Douglas grew up in the New York City area. He started playing piano at the age of five, then trombone at seven before discovering the trumpet at nine. He learned jazz harmony in high school, and began playing improvised music as an exchange student in Barcelona, Spain. From 1981-83, he studied in Boston, first at Berklee School of Music, then the New England Conservatory. He moved to New York City in 1984, where he attended New York University and studied with Carmine Caruso. In 1987, he toured Europe with Horace Silver. The early '90s saw Douglas begin to record in earnest; he led or co-led dates for the Hat Art, Soul Note, New World, and Arabesque labels. His various bands include the Tiny Bell Trio, a self-described "jazz-Balkan-improv" group with drummer Jim Black and guitarist Brad Schoeppach; his String Group, which includes violinist Mark Feldman, cellist Erik Friedlander, and bassist Mark Dresser; and his Quartet and Sextet, which includes notably drummer Joey Baron. Douglas has also recorded as a sideman with Myra Melford, John Zorn, and Anthony Braxton, among others. —*Chris Kelsey*

In Our Lifetime / Dec. 7, 1994-Dec. 8, 1994 / New World ✦✦✦✦✦
Trumpeter Dave Douglas's New World CD is consistently intriguing, the type of music that gains in interest with each listening. Douglas is quick to acknowledge the influence of Booker Little (the early-'60s trumpeter who was among the first to emerge from Clifford Brown's shadow) and on this set he performs three of Little's tunes plus his own "Four Miniatures After Booker Little." However it is the two lengthier pieces, "In Our Lifetime" and "Bridges" (the latter over 17 minutes long), that are of greatest interest. Douglas's originals, which are episodic and avant-garde (but not afraid to swing) while expertly mixing together improvisation with composition, are consistently colorful. His flexible band (Chris Speed on tenor and clarinet, trombonist Josh Roseman, pianist Uri Caine, bassist James Genus, drummer Joey Baron and guest bass clarinetist Marty Ehrlich on the title cut) is able to switch grooves quickly and interpret the frequently dramatic music with sensitivity and wit. —*Scott Yanow*

• **Constellations** / Feb. 27, 1995+Feb. 28, 1995 / hatHUT ✦✦✦✦✦
Constellations was the second album that Dave Douglas recorded with his Tiny Bell Trio, which excluded piano and bass and united the experimental trumpeter with electric guitarist Brad Schoeppach (subsequently changed to Shepik) and drummer Jim Black. Douglas described the trio as a "jazz-Balkan improv" group, and to be sure, East European music is a strong influence on abstract inside/outside originals like "Unhooking the Safety Net," "Hope Ring True," and the probing "Scriabin." Some of Douglas' writing is inspired by sociopolitical situations. "Taking Sides" is an emotional piece that was influenced by the bloody fighting that, in the 1990s, took place in the former Yugoslavia, while "Maquiladora" takes its name from a Spanish word for American-operated factories along the U.S./Mexican border—the infamous *maquiladoras* are known for their low pay and dangerous working conditions, and the song's somber mood paints a depressing picture of such an environment. Another high point of the CD is Douglas' interpretation of Herbie Nichols' "The Gig"; the late Nichols is among the unsung heroes of jazz pianism, and Douglas deserves credit for embracing his work. *Constellations* isn't easy to absorb on the first listen; like a lot of avant-garde jazz, this is music that reveals more and more of its power with each listen. —*Alex Henderson*

Five / Jul. 31, 1995-Aug. 1, 1995 / Soul Note ✦✦✦✦
Trumpeter Dave Douglas' unusual string group (which also includes violinist Mark Feldman, cellist Erik Friedlander, bassist Drew Gross and drummer Michael Sarin) is reminiscent in some ways of Ornette Coleman's free-jazz quartet despite not playing any of Ornette's originals and having a very different instrumentation. All of the musicians function as equals, the interaction is often intuitive, and the improvising on eight Douglas originals (including tunes dedicated to Steve Lacy, Wayne Shorter, Mark Dresser, Woody Shaw, John Cage and John Zorn), Thelonious Monk's "Who Knows," and Rahsaan Roland Kirk's "The Inflated Tear" is on a high level. Well worth exploring. —*Scott Yanow*

Charms of the Night Sky / Sep. 18, 1997+Sep. 19, 1997 / Winter & Winter ✦✦✦✦✦
Trumpeter Dave Douglas has participated in so many styles of music that listing them all would be mesmerizing. Some of his best work has been performed in free style and hard bop jazz groups. Here, he charts a different path, albeit one that he has pursued successfully before, in a mellow, lovely vein. Douglas is the only horn, backed by Guy Klucevsek's eclectic accordion, Mark Feldman's gloriously sweet violin, and Greg Cohen's acoustic string bass. With some exceptions, the dynamics are generally low, the tempos slow, and the mood serene. There is almost a post-minimalism to it all, capped by the exquisite sound of Douglas' trumpet. Often, the tunes (mostly written by Douglas) have an Eastern European flair, at times hinting at Klezmer or Jewish wedding music. The group's exacting technical skills eclipse limitations and transcend the immediate moment with gorgeous sound and forward-looking harmonies. —*Steve Loewy*

Songs for Wandering Souls / 1999 / Winter & Winter ✦✦✦✦✦
The irrepressible Dave Douglas delivers another installment in the life of the Tiny Bell Trio, which features his own inimitable trumpet style, but the rhythmic invention of Jim Black on drums, and Brad Shepik's emotionally vulnerable yet volatile guitar playing. Where previous Tiny Bell outings have focused on the possibilities for texture, dynamic, and atmospheric possibilities within a given compositional structure, *Songs for Wandering Souls* places its eye firmly on group execution this set of compositions—all but two of which are by Douglas, the others arranged by him especially for this of his many groups. The disc opens with "Sam Hill," a beautiful "song," where the lead "call" voice is carried by Douglas, but its "response" is in the lyrical flow of Shepik's string interplay. Theme and melody are stated repeatedly throughout the piece, and soloing is kept to merely three or four measures, but it's enough. The tenderness and empathy that these musicians, especially Jim Black's approach to "song," is nothing less than emotionally moving. Elsewhere, on "Loopy"—with Black leading a kind of rhythmic chant for Shepik to play the melody from, which starts from the inside out, seemingly, and Douglas chiming in on the last note—the band plays for seven minutes on the off-kilter side of the three different harmonic structures present in the composition. It swings, easily, lightly, and with enough grace to make the listener forget its odd stylistic attributes. The deep listening this band plays with is truly remarkable. Each tune swings, dances, and shimmies with the skill and enthusiasm this band shows toward lyrical improvising, and turn-on-a-pin attention to compositional detail, dynamic, and the value of a fragment to solo in. The cover of Rahsaan Roland Kirk's "Breath-A-Thon" is noteworthy because it was originally a solo piece, here reconstructed for the entire trio. The modal invention here, and the melodic sentiment in Kirk's original, come shining through here, as well as his warm sense of humor. *Songs for Wandering Souls* is a truly wonderful installment in this revelatory band's journey. May it be long and prosperous. —*Thom Jurek*

Convergence / Jan. 22, 1998-Jan. 23, 1998 / Soul Note ✦✦✦✦✦
To hear many hard bop hard-liners tell it, all avant-garde jazz is nothing more than atonal screaming. The problem with such sweeping generalizations is that some avant-garde jazz is, in fact, quite musical. A perfect example is Dave Douglas' *Convergence*, an experimental, adventurous outing that incorporates everything from classical and chamber music to Jewish, Middle Eastern, and East European music. Joined by violinist Mark Feldman, cellist Erik Friedlander, bassist Drew Gress, and drummer Michael Sarin, the New York-based trumpeter doesn't shy away from the eccentric and the unorthodox, but he also provides his share of discernible, substantial melodies. The inside/outside approach works impressively well on pieces ranging from Douglas' "Goodbye Tony" (a passionate ode to the late drummer Tony Williams), his Miles Davis-influenced "Tzotzil Maya," and his probing "Meeting at Infinity" to the traditional Burmese song "Chit Kyoo Thwe Tog Nyin Hmar Lar" (to which he brings a strong Jewish element). You can hear a variety of influences in Douglas' playing—everyone from Lester Bowie and Don Cherry to Miles Davis and Booker Little—but *Convergence* leaves no doubt that he is very much an original himself. —*Alex Henderson*

• **Soul on Soul** / Sep. 14, 1999-Sep. 15, 1999 / RCA Victor ✦✦✦✦✦
Trumpeter Dave Douglas continues on his remarkable journey to document some of his primary musical influences. This one, a celebration of Mary Lou Williams, comes on the heels of similar tributes to Booker Little and Wayne Shorter. While only four of the 13 compositions were penned by Williams (the rest are by Douglas), her uniquely upbeat, sophisticated style is well captured. For those who know Douglas only for his forays into the avant-garde, this recording should open some eyes; the trumpeter has a strong handle on the tradition. Actually, this is nothing new, as he has been remarkably at home with a broad collection of styles for years. Douglas leads one of his most versatile and exciting groups here: pianist Uri Caine (who improvises all over the map), bassist James Genus, drummer Joey Baron, trom-

bonist Joshua Roseman, and tenor saxophonist/clarinetist Chris Speed. Greg Tardy sits in on clarinet, bass clarinet, and tenor saxophone on a few numbers. *— Steven Loewy*

A Thousand Evenings / Oct. 10, 2000 / RCA ✦✦✦✦
By 2000 trumpeter Dave Douglas had etched himself as one of the most versatile, intriguing, and important players and composers on the scene. By leading several groups that successfully focus on particular styles, Douglas had been able to be not only one of the best but also one of the most recorded. *A Thousand Evenings* was his second album for BMG and his third release of that year. *A Thousand Evenings* features his so-called *Charms of the Night Sky* group (also the name of the quartet's 1998 Winter & Winter label debut) with Mark Feldman on violin, Greg Cohen on bass, and the marvelous Guy Klucevsek playing accordion. As with the initial *Charms of the Night Sky* release, the set list is comprised of flowing chamber jazz pieces that lend themselves to a strange mix of tango, Eastern European folk, and klezmer, all in the framework of the New York downtown jazz scene. The title song is a beautiful engaging opening number that floats along with Douglas blowing right on top. One of the most important factors of this group is Klucevsek's accordion: he adds a great deal to the density and also to the rhythm of this music. Highlighting his role, "Variety" is an interesting solo accordion piece. There's also an entertaining reworking of the James Bond theme "Goldfinger." *A Thousand Evenings* is an example of great musicians keeping their ideals straight in the oft-murky landscape of major-label contemporary jazz and is highly recommended. *— Jack L. V. Isles*

Kenny Drew

b. Aug. 28, 1928, New York, NY, **d.** Aug. 4, 1993, Copenhagen, Denmark
Piano / Hard Bop
A talented bop-based pianist (whose son has been one of the brightest pianists of the 1990s), Kenny Drew was somewhat underrated due to his decision to move permanently to Copenhagen in 1964. He made his recording debut in 1949 with Howard McGhee and in the 1950s was featured on sessions with the who's who of jazz including Charlie Parker, Coleman Hawkins, Lester Young, Milt Jackson, Buddy DeFranco's quartet, Dinah Washington and Buddy Rich (1958). Drew led sessions for Blue Note, Norgran, Pacific Jazz, Riverside and the obscure Judson label during 1953-60; most of the sessions are currently available on CD. He moved to Paris in 1961 and relocated to Copenhagen in 1964 where he was co-owner of the Matrix label. He formed a duo with Niels-Henning Orsted Pederson and worked regularly at the Montmartre. Drew recorded many dates for SteepleChase in the 1970s and remained active up until his death. *— Scott Yanow*

The Kenny Drew Trio / Sep. 20, 1956+Sep. 26, 1956 / Riverside/OJC ✦✦✦✦
Kenny Drew, with the assistance of bassist Paul Chambers (whose bowed solos are always welcome) and drummer Philly Joe Jones, explores six standards and two of his originals. Although Drew would have to move to Europe in the early '60s in order to get the recognition he deserved, it is obvious (in hindsight) from this enjoyable date that he was already a major improviser. *— Scott Yanow*

Plays the Music of Harry Warren and Harold Arlen / Feb. 1957 / Milestone ✦✦✦✦
This CD reissue combines together the complete contents of two similar sessions by pianist Kenny Drew. With the assistance of bassist Wilbur Ware, Drew performs a dozen songs apiece from the Harry Warren and Harold Arlen songbooks. The interpretations, originally released on the Judson label, are quite melodic, tasteful and lightly swinging. Drew does come out with any new revelations while playing songs such as "Lullaby of Broadway," "I Only Have Eyes for You," "That Old Black Magic" and "It's Only a Paper Moon" but neither do these versions sound overly nostalgic or tired. This is a nice set if not all that essential. *— Scott Yanow*

★ **Pal Joey: Stage and Screen Classic** / Oct. 15, 1957 / Riverside/OJC ✦✦✦✦✦
It seems strange that (with the exception of a 1960 session for Blue Note) this would be pianist Kenny Drew's last session as a leader until 1973. With bassist Wilbur Ware and drummer Philly Joe Jones, Drew interprets eight Rodgers and Hart tunes, five written for the play *Pal Joey* and three of their earlier hits that were included in the film version. Drew contributes swing and subtle bop-based improvising to these superior melodies (which are highlighted by "Bewitched, Bothered and Bewildered," "I Could Write a Book," and "The Lady Is a Tramp"), and the results are quite memorable. *— Scott Yanow*

Undercurrent / Dec. 11, 1960 / Blue Note ✦✦✦✦✦
Kenny Drew recorded fairly frequently in the 1950s but after his Blue Note album (reissued on this CD), he moved to Europe and did not appear as a leader on records until 1973. Still just 32 in 1960, Drew was teamed with the young trumpeter Freddie Hubbard (who already showed great potential), tenor saxophonist Hank Mobley, bassist Sam Jones and drummer Louis Hayes on six of his originals (including "Undercurrent," "The Pot's On" and "Groovin' the Blues"). A fine hard bop set. *— Scott Yanow*

Paquito d'Rivera

b. Jun. 4, 1948, Havana, Cuba
Sax (Soprano), Sax (Alto), Clarinet / Afro-Cuban Jazz, Post-Bop, Latin Jazz
Cuba-born and New York-based saxophonist and clarinet player Paquito D'Rivera has balanced a career in Latin jazz with commissions as a classical composer and appearances with symphony orchestras. D'Rivera inherited his understanding of music from his father, Tito, a classical saxophonist and conductor. By the age of ten, he performed with the National Theater Orchestra of Havana. D'Rivera also played with the Cuban National Symphony Orchestra, the Cuban Army Band, and the Orchestra Cubana de Musica Moderna, then joined with eight members of the latter band to form Irakere in 1973. The group, which fused jazz, rock, classical and traditional Cuban music, became the first post-Castro Cuban group to sign with an American record label.

D'Rivera defected from Cuba in 1981, and his debut solo album, *Paquito Blowin',* appeared later that year. In 1988, D'Rivera was invited to become a charter member of Dizzy Gillespie's fifteen-piece all-star United Nations Orchestra. In addition to performing with his own big band, quintet, chamber music group (TrianguIo), and calypso/salsa band, he began to accept commissions to compose for chamber groups and orchestras. In 1997, D'Rivera's album, *Portraits Of Cuba,* received a Grammy award. D'Rivera is artist-in-residence for the New Jersey Performing Arts Commission and artistic director in charge of jazz programming for the New Jersey Chamber Music Society. The album *Live at the Blue Note* appeared in the spring of 2000. *— Craig Harris*

Blowin' / 1981 / Columbia ✦✦✦✦
Altoist Paquito D'Rivera's first American recording after defecting from Cuba is an often-jubilant affair. D'Rivera, who also plays some soprano and flute on this album, is heard in groups ranging from a duet with pianist Jorge Dalto to a septet. The impressive lineup also includes pianist Hilton Ruiz, bassist Eddie Gomez and drummer Ignacio Berroa, among others. The music is high-quality modern bebop with a strong dose of Latin rhythms—a fine example of D'Rivera's talents. *— Scott Yanow*

● **Taste of Paquito** / 1981-1987 / Columbia ✦✦✦✦✦
Not a "greatest hits" album (like he was shooting for "hits"), nor a thoroughgoing anthology of Paquito D'Rivera's Columbia period (only the first five of his seven albums are covered), the word "taste" is an intriguing choice, though at 74 minutes, the CD is a bit more than just a taste. But then, since Sony has done a real number on his catalog by not reissuing those first five albums, *A Taste* is all that CD buyers can sample from Paquito's first American recordings. Up to a point, we receive a pretty good idea as to what the commotion was initially about, starting from the time two years after D'Rivera's defection from Cuba, when he was primarily a joyous, shouting Latin bopper with a hot hand on the alto sax. The CD concentrates upon smaller group sessions, leaving off at the point where Paquito was starting to incorporate larger groups and more eclectic wanderings into his music. Two of the more memorable tracks are the poignant "Song To My Son" (recorded when Paquito's wife and son were still left behind in Cuba) and the robust Dizzy-inspired humor of "Just Kidding." Watch out for some booboos in the track credits, such as the listing of Hilton Ruiz on acoustic bass instead of piano on "Miami" and omitting mention of Toots Thielemans on "Brussels in the Rain," which was merely written for the Belgian harmonica virtuoso in the first place. *— Richard S. Ginell*

Mariel / 1982 / Columbia ✦✦✦✦✦
Paquito D'Rivera's string of Columbia albums (his first in the United States after defecting from Cuba) are consistently enjoyable. This LP features D'Rivera (mostly on alto but also playing a bit of soprano) performing four originals, two obscurities and John Coltrane's "Moment's Notice." The Afro-Cuban jazz set (which has some more commercial sections) features among Paquito's sidemen trumpeter Randy Brecker, keyboardist Hilton Ruiz, drummer Ignacio Berroa and percussionist Daniel Ponce among others; Brenda Feliciano has a guest vocal on "New York Is You." *— Scott Yanow*

Return to Ipanema / Mar. 1, 1989-Mar. 2, 1989 / Town Crier ✦✦✦✦
Return to Ipanema has a strong dose of Brazilian music (along with strong hints of the leader's roots in Cuba), featuring Paquito D'Rivera co-starring with trumpeter Claudio Roditi. The octet (which includes tenor saxophonist Ralph Moore, trombonist Jay Ashby, and pianist Danilo Perez) performs two songs apiece from Lobo, Antonio Carlos Jobim (including "No More Blues"), and Roditi, plus D'Rivera's "To Brenda," an obscurity, and a fresh rendition of "Summertime." D'Rivera and Roditi always make for an appealing team, and it is more fun to hear them in a larger group than usual. *— Scott Yanow*

Tico! Tico! / Jun. 28, 1989-Aug. 16, 1989 / Chesky ✦✦✦✦
Paquito D'Rivera's alto and clarinet skills were ably displayed on this session, which featured him working in Afro-Latin, salsa, funk, swing and hard bop. Compositions ranged from intense, jam-flavored numbers with torrid solos, like "Recife's Blue" and the title tune, to introspective ballads, group pieces with rhythmically explosive sections and numbers displaying classical influences. The unifying force was D'Rivera, who also played tenor, but was most prominent on clarinet, doing both swing-oriented and looser, freer solos. While not as strict a jazz vehicle as his Columbia dates, this session presented a more eclectic, versatile Paquito D'Rivera. *— Ron Wynn*

Havana Cafe / Aug. 28, 1991-Aug. 29, 1991 / Chesky ✦✦✦✦
This excellent all-round session features Paquito D'Rivera on alto, clarinet and soprano with his sextet which is comprised of either Fareed Haque or Ed Cherry on guitar, the great pianist Danilo Perez, bassist David Finck, drummer Jorge Rossy and percussionist Sammy Figueroa. The program has some strong group originals (such as "Havana Cafe," "Jean Pauline," "Who's Smoking" and "Bossa Do Brooklyn") and the result is an often-fiery set of modern Afro-Cuban jazz. *— Scott Yanow*

A Night in Englewood / Jul. 1993 / Messidor ✦✦✦✦✦
After Dizzy Gillespie's death in 1991, his colorful Afro-Cuban United Nation Orchestra (which was formed in 1988) was headed by altoist-clarinetist Paquito D'Rivera. With the better-known sidemen on this 1993 CD including first trumpeter Byron Stripling, trombonist Conrad Herwig and tenor saxophonist Mario Rivera, additional solo space allocated to some of the other talented players and guest spots for trumpeter Claudio Roditi, trombonist Slide Hampton and vibraphonist Dave Samuels, this is an easily recommended set. The music is very Latin-oriented and shows that the orchestra had moved away from Gillespie's usual repertoire to exclusively featuring originals by bandmembers (including D'Rivera's "I Remember Diz"). Definitely worth investigating. *— Scott Yanow*

Portraits of Cuba / Feb. 6, 1996-Feb. 7, 1996 / Chesky ✦✦✦✦✦
Because Paquito D'Rivera is such a compelling improviser, one greets a heavily arranged and orchestrated session like *Portraits of Cuba* with some apprehension. But as it turns out, such apprehension is unwarranted, for the Cuban saxman/clarinetist still has enough room to solo and say what needs to be said. With this 1996 session, which was arranged and conducted by Carlos Franzetti and finds D'Rivera backed by combinations of up to 14 musicians, D'Rivera envisioned an Afro-Cuban equivalent of Miles Davis' *Sketches of Spain*—and, to be sure, there are some parallels. Franzetti's classical-influenced arrangements recall Gil Evans'

work with Davis, and D'Rivera paints an orchestral jazz picture of Cuba much as Davis painted an orchestral jazz picture of Spain. The key phrase here is "jazz picture"—D'Rivera approaches famous Cuban songs like Ignacio Pineiro's "Echale Salsita" and Ernesto Lecuona's "Como Arrullo de Palmas" from an instrumental jazz perspective; this is jazz with both Afro-Cuban and classical elements, but it's jazz first and foremost. Recorded in New York around the time of the infamous Blizzard of 1996—which dumped up to three feet of snow on parts of the Northeastern U.S.—*Portraits of Cuba* is among D'Rivera's most essential recordings. —*Alex Henderson*

Charles Earland

b. May 24, 1941, Philadelphia, PA, **d.** Dec. 11, 1999, Kansas City, MO
Organ (Hammond), Synthesizer, Organ / Hard Bop, Soul-Jazz, Jazz-Funk
Charles Earland came into his own at the tail end of the great 1960s wave of soul-jazz organists, gaining a large following and much airplay with a series of albums for the the Prestige label. While heavily indebted to Jimmy Smith and Jimmy McGriff, Earland comes armed with his own swinging, technically agile, light-textured sound on the keyboard and one of the best walking-bass pedal techniques in the business. Though not an innovative player in his field, Earland can burn with the best of them when he is on. He made his first recordings for Choice in 1966, then joined Lou Donaldson for two years (1968-69) and two albums before being signed as a solo artist to Prestige. Earland's first album for Prestige, *Black Talk!*, became a best-selling classic of the soul-jazz genre; a surprisingly effective cover of the Spiral Starecase's pop/rock hit "More Today Than Yesterday" from that LP received saturation airplay on jazz radio in 1969. —*Richard S. Ginell*

★ **Black Talk!** / Dec. 15, 1969 / Prestige/OJC ✦✦✦✦✦
This CD reissue of a Prestige date is one of the few successful examples of jazz musicians from the late '60s taking a few rock and pop songs and turning them into creative jazz. Organist Charles Earland and his sextet, which includes trumpeter Virgil Jones, Houston Person on tenor and guitarist Melvin Sparks, perform a variation of "Eleanor Rigby" titled "Black Talk," two originals, a surprisingly effective rendition of "Aquarius" and a classic rendition of "More Today than Yesterday." Fans of organ combos are advised to pick up this interesting set. —*Scott Yanow*

☆ **Living Black!** / Sep. 17, 1970 / Prestige ✦✦✦✦✦
One of the best Charles Earland albums ever released, *Living Black!* is noteworthy not only for his inspired organ playing, but also for the dynamic tenor sax of Grover Washington, Jr. When *Living Black!* was recorded live at the Key Club in Newark, N.J. in 1970, Washington was only 26, and he wouldn't record for the first time as a leader until *Inner City Blues* the following year. But Earland, who knew Washington from his native Philadelphia, realized that the saxman showed enormous promise, and it's evident that Earland's faith in him was completely justified when they dig into Miles Davis' "Milestones" and Benny Golson's "Killer Joe," as well as the funky "Westbound #9." After being out of print for many years, *Living Black!* was finally reissued on CD in 1997 with two previously unreleased bonus tracks: "More Today Than Yesterday" (which was first a hit for the soul-flavored pop group the Spiral Staircase in 1969, but soon became Earland's theme song) and a passionate version of the Motown tune "Message From a Black Man." Rounding out the lineup are guitarist Maynard Parker, trumpeter Gary Chandler, drummer Jesse Kilpatrick and percussionist Buddy Caldwell—all of them competent and hard-swinging, though little known. *Living Black!*'s debut on CD was long overdue. —*Alex Henderson*

Intensity / Feb. 16, 1972+Feb. 17, 1972 / Prestige/OJC ✦✦✦✦
Even if the performances on *Intensity* weren't excellent, this Charles Earland session would be required listening for jazz historians because it marked the last recorded documentation of Lee Morgan. Only two days after *Intensity* was recorded at Rudy Van Gelder's famous New Jersey studio on February 17, 1972, the influential trumpeter was shot and killed by a girlfriend at the age of 33. Refusing to confine himself to hard bop, Morgan was exploring soul-jazz and fusion during the last years of his life—and his enthusiasm for soul-jazz is hard to miss on Earland's funky "'Cause I Love Her" as well as inventive interpretations of Chicago's "Happy 'Cause I'm Goin' Home" and the Shirelles' "Will You Still Love Me Tomorrow." Originally released on LP by Prestige, *Intensity* was out of print for many years but was reissued on CD in 1999 for Fantasy's *Original Jazz Classics* (OJC) series. For the CD, Fantasy added two bonus tracks: a passionate remake of Morgan's "Speedball" and a driving version of Chicago's "Lowdown," which shouldn't be confused with Boz Scaggs' 1976 hit. The importance of this reissue cannot be denied. —*Alex Henderson*

Blowing the Blues Away / 1997 / High Note ✦✦✦✦

Jazz Organ Summit / May 24, 1997 / Cannonball ✦✦✦✦
When four masters of the Hammond B-3 are on the same bill, it's a major event for lovers of soul-jazz and hard bop organ. Charles Earland is listed the leader, but the Philadelphia native is only one of four organists who take the spotlight on this superb live date, which was recorded at the DuSable Museum of African-American History in Earland's adopted home of Chicago. The other B-3 icons are Jimmy McGriff, Dr. Lonnie Smith and the late Johnny "Hammond" Smith, all of whom are equally indebted to the seminal Jimmy Smith—and all of whom are, like Earland, among the all-time greats of the instrument. Sadly, this special concert turned out to be the last live appearance of "Hammond" Smith, who was in the advanced stages of cancer and had less than two weeks to live. Nonetheless, he finds the strength to play convincingly on "The Masquerade Is Over" and an unaccompanied "Summertime." The latter is incredibly tough to listen to—its stark, haunting, naked quality sounds like the work of a man who knew he didn't have long to live and was telling his supporters good-bye. Earland is in fine form on his signature tune "More Today Than Yesterday," and McGriff demonstrates his mastery of the 12-bar form on "Gospel Slow Blues" and "Groovin' Blues." Especially surprising is Smith's version of "Cherokee," which he plays as a ballad instead of at the breakneck speed that has so often characterized hard bop and soul-jazz performances of this standard. The disc ends on a high note when all four organists are united for the catchy blues "Summit Time." Documenting a truly historic concert, *Organ Summit* is a CD that no B-3 enthusiast should be without. —*Alex Henderson*

Organomically Correct / 1977-1978 / 32 Jazz ✦✦✦

Cookin' with the Mighty Burner / May 7, 1997 / High Note ✦✦✦✦
Organist Earland is known far and wide as one of the more inventive, awe-inspiring, soul-sending practitioners of the B-3. On this set, he still sounds like the man to beat, but in many instances he instead allows his bandmates to shine. Those mates include younger firebrands (trumpeter Jim Rotundi and saxophonist Eric Alexander), as well as longtime sidemen (guitarist Melvin Sparks and drummer Bobby Durham), helped by percussionist Gary Fritz. Of course, when Earland wants to burn, he can, and does on many occasions. He recapitulates a piece from *Front Burner* which was titled "Mom & Dad," but is re-named "Seven of Nine." It's a modal cooker in 10/8 that is even more relentless than the original with a reworked head for the horns. Earland leads the way on Carole King's half-speed "Will You Love Me Tomorrow," but the trumpet and tenor, separately or together, inspire the change on other cuts; Rotundi quite naturally on "Seven Steps to Heaven," "Milestones," and "Stella By Starlight." Alexander is really hitting his stride, getting fluttery and animated on "Seven Steps" and "Seven of Nine." And Sparks, who is woefully underdocumented these days, proves why he is still one of the all-time greats. His shimmering chords on "Milestones" and fleet single lines in the middle of "Seven Steps" provide plenty of evidence for this contention. At first you think this is a head-solo-tail fest, with the first four cuts running true to predictable form. But then Earland steps forward, turns up the heat, and things cook along nicely until the end. This is one of Earland's better efforts in the last ten years of his life, consistent from start to finish. The burner is in the house, and mightier than ever. —*Michael G. Nastos*

The Almighty Burner / 1976 Jan. - 19 / 32 Jazz ✦✦✦
Organist Charles Earland, who many referred to as "The Mighty Burner," passed away in 1999. On this 2000 release titled *The Almighty Burner*, 32 Jazz eternalizes the memory of a musician who was among the finest practitioners of jazz/groove organ-led ensembles. Earland, ever the protagonist, performed with fiery intensity amid soul-drenched lines, which is most evident on this set of originals and sprightly jazzed-up renditions of pop hits such as Gordon/Bourne's "Unforgettable" and P. N. Upton's "More Today Than Yesterday." Consisting of 11 tracks spanning 1976 through 1991, the listener should benefit from this comprehensive overview of Earland's stylistic melding of funk, pop, and mainstream jazz into a vernacular that proclaimed his shrewd rhythmic sensibilities and predilection for reconstructing themes and melodies. The organist also performs a bouncy, finger-snapping version of Miles Davis' "Milestones," as this set reaches its finale with a radiant post-bop translation of saxophonist Joe Henderson's composition "The Kicker." Artists such as saxophonists Houston Person, Eric Alexander, and trombonist Clifford Adams represent some of the more notable jazz performers who supported Earland on these often-vivacious pieces. Hence, *The Almighty Burner* offers a worthy snapshot of this time-honored yet sorely missed artist. —*Glenn Astarita*

Billy Eckstine

b. Jul. 8, 1914, Pittsburgh, PA, **d.** Mar. 8, 1993, Pittsburgh, PA
Vocals / Vocal Jazz, Traditional Pop, Standards, Bop
An influential ballad singer with a very appealing baritone voice, Billy Eckstine made a very important contribution to jazz early on, leading one of the first bebop big bands and keeping it together (while turning down lucrative offers to work as a single) as long as possible. He worked in Chicago starting in 1937 and was with the Earl Hines Orchestra during 1939-43, having a few hit records including the blues "Jelly, Jelly." Near the end of his stay with Hines, the big band had become bop-oriented with such sidemen as Dizzy Gillespie, Charlie Parker and the young Sarah Vaughan. After leaving Hines, Eckstine hired those three as part of his very modern orchestra and other members of his band during parts of 1944-47 included Gene Ammons, Dexter Gordon, Frank Wess, Miles Davis, Kenny Dorham, Fats Navarro, Sonny Stitt, Leo Parker and Art Blakey; virtually all of the musicians were fairly unknown at the time. Eckstine was forced financially to give up the band, switching to middle-of-the-road pop ballads; Mr. B. became a very popular attraction (in a later era he would have been a romantic movie star), recording many string-filled arrangements for MGM that were best-sellers. But he never lost his feeling for jazz and a 1959 collaboration with Count Basie finds Eckstine swinging with the best. —*Scott Yanow*

☆ **Mister B and the Band** / May 2, 1945-Oct. 6, 1946 / Savoy ✦✦✦✦✦
Unlike other big-band singers who regarded the other musicians in the orchestra as little more than backup to their generally sugarcoated stylings, Billy Eckstine was a man with wide-ranging tastes and a musicality he brought to everything he lent his honeyed baritone voice to. When it was time for him to start his own band to capitalize on his growing fame, he didn't settle for hiring some hacks to read charts framed around his vocals. Instead, he put together what is now, in hindsight, the first big band to feature almost exclusively young, emerging bop players. Both Bird and Diz did time in the band and, at one time or another, Eckstine featured Sonny Stitt, Dexter Gordon, Wardell Gray, Lucky Thompson, Fats Navarro, Miles Davis and Kenny Dorham on his bandstand. The band was far, far ahead of its time, appealing more to musicians than White America, but making extraordinary music nonetheless. This single-disc collection brings together a delightful batch of tunes that band recorded for the tiny National label between 1945 and the following year. With Art Blakey, Tommy Potter and Leo Parker also in the lineup, this is no nostalgic "remember the big bands" anthology by any stretch of the imagination, and B's vocals on "A Cottage for Sale," "Prisoner of Love" and "I'm In the Mood of Love" are every bit as fine as the band's two takes of Gillespie's "Oo Bop Sh'Bam." Originally a 32-track, two-disc vinyl album set, the compact disc configuration lops off the last five tunes from that original collection due to time restrictions. —*Cub Koda*

★ **Everything I Have Is Yours: The Best of the M-G-M Years** / May 20, 1947-Apr. 26, 1957 / Verve ✦✦✦✦✦
This two-CD set improves upon the original two-LP package by adding 14 more songs. The

pop side of Billy Eckstine was emphasized during his period with MGM and many of these selections (including hit versions of "Everything I Have Is Yours," "Blue Moon," "Caravan," "My Foolish Heart" and "I Apologize") feature his warm baritone backed by string sections. There are some exceptions including "Mr. B's Blues" (which gives Eckstine a chance to solo on valve trombone), dates with Woody Herman and George Shearing, eight numbers on which the singer is accompanied by the Bobby Tucker Quartet and a pair of wonderful performances with the Metronome All-Stars in 1953 (a group that includes trumpeter Roy Eldridge, both Lester Young and Warne Marsh on tenors and vibraphonist Terry Gibbs). Although not as essential from the jazz standpoint as Billy Eckstine's earlier big-band dates, this two-fer features the singer at the peak of his powers; five ballad duets with Sarah Vaughan are a highlight. *—Scott Yanow*

No Cover, No Minimum / Aug. 30, 1960 / Roulette ♦♦♦♦
This CD has an unusual cover picture showing Billy Eckstine singing while holding a trumpet. He does indeed take a few short trumpet solos on the well-rounded program, 24 songs (13 previously unissued) performed during one night in Las Vegas. Eckstine, who is backed by an orchestra arranged by his pianist Bobby Tucker, is heard in prime form on a variety of standards. His baritone voice (which was quite influential) straddles the boundary between middle-of-the-road pop and jazz on such numbers as "I've Grown Accustomed to Her Face," "Without a Song," "Prisoner of Love," "I Apologize", "Alright, Okay, You Win" and "'Deed I Do." A good example of his talents. *—Scott Yanow*

Mr. B / 1962 / Ember ♦♦♦♦
This Ember collection includes Billy Eckstine and His Orchestra's 1944 recordings for Deluxe Records. Eckstine's band featured some of the best sidemen of the big band era—Dizzie Gillespie, Dexter Gordon, Sarah Vaughan, Art Blakey, Gene Ammons, Maxine Sullivan, Benny Carter, Oscar Pettiford—and they swung harder than anyone else on numbers like "Good Jelly Blues," "Blowing the Blues Away," and "I Got a Date with Rhythm." Unfortunately, the sound quality hasn't been remastered at all since this same sequence was first reissued (in 1962), and all of this material is also available on the superb 1944-1945 collection. *—John Bush*

1944-1945 / Apr. 13, 1944-Oct. 1945 / Classics ♦♦♦♦♦

Harry "Sweets" Edison

b. Oct. 10, 1915, Columbus, OH, **d.** Jul. 27, 1999
Trumpet / Mainstream Jazz, Swing
Harry "Sweets" Edison got the most mileage out of a single note, like his former boss Count Basie. Edison, immediately recognizable within a note or two, long used repetition and simplicity to his advantage while always swinging. He played in local bands in Columbus and then in 1933 joined the Jeter-Pillars Orchestra. After a couple years in St. Louis, Edison moved to New York where he joined Lucky Millinder and then in June 1938 Count Basie, remaining with that classic orchestra until it broke up in 1950. During that period he was featured on many records, appeared in the 1944 short *Jammin' the Blues* and gained his nickname "Sweets" (due to his tone) from Lester Young. In the 1950's Edison toured with Jazz at the Philharmonic, settled in Los Angeles and was well-featured both as a studio musician (most noticeably on Frank Sinatra records) and on jazz dates. He had several reunions with Count Basie in the 1960s and by the '70s was often teamed with Eddie "Lockjaw" Davis; Edison also recorded an excellent duet album for Pablo with Oscar Peterson. One of the few swing trumpeters to be influenced by Dizzy Gillespie, Sweets led sessions through the years for Pacific Jazz, Verve, Roulette, Riverside, Vee-Jay, Liberty, Sue, Black & Blue, Pablo, Storyville and Candid among others. Although his playing faded during the 1980s and '90s, Edison could still say more with one note than nearly anyone; he died July 27, 1999 at age 83. *—Scott Yanow*

Harry "Sweets" Edison—*Eddie "Lockjaw" Davis & Richard Boone* */ Feb. 27, 1976-Dec. 19, 1976 / Storyville* ♦♦♦
Although trumpeter Harry "Sweets" Edison gets top billing on this Storyville LP, he is only on half of the selections and none of the ones that feature tenor saxophonist Eddie "Lockjaw" Davis and vocalist Richard Boone (who mostly sings his three features straight). Leonardo Pedersen's Jazzkapel (a Danish 11-piece group) is a small big band that sometimes bows in the direction of Count Basie and backs the three guests. Actually nothing all that essential occurs but Edison and Davis completists and fans of mainstream jazz may want to get this set. *—Scott Yanow*

★ **Edison's Lights** / May 5, 1976 / Pablo/OJC ♦♦♦♦♦
Although trumpeter Harry "Sweets" Edison and tenor saxophonist Eddie "Lockjaw" Davis recorded several albums together in the 1970s, this CD reissue was their only Pablo date as a team. Edison is the nominal leader and he contributed four of the eight selections (which alternate with four veteran standards) but the competitive Lockjaw gets in his fiery licks too. While bassist John Heard and drummer Jimmie Smith are part of the quintet and pianist Dolo Coker is on half of the program, Count Basie himself drops by for four songs to cheer on his former sidemen. All of the musicians sound quite inspired and are heard throughout playing at their best and most colorful. *—Scott Yanow*

Simply Sweets / Sep. 22, 1977 / Pablo/OJC ♦♦♦
Trumpeter Harry "Sweets" Edison and tenor saxophonist Eddie "Lockjaw" Davis always made a potent pair. They both possessed immediately identifiable sounds, were veterans of Count Basie's Orchestra and never had any difficulty swinging. The repertoire of this Edison album is not too creative with five blues among its eight songs and one of the others, "Feelings," being quite forgettable. However, the playing of the principals (along with pianist Dolo Coker who also makes a couple of surprising appearances on electric keyboard) holds one's interest throughout. *—Scott Yanow*

Swinger/Mr. Swing / Jul. 27, 1999 / Verve ♦♦♦♦
The late Harry "Sweets" Edison was one of the acknowledged masters of swing trumpet; this reissue combines the original LPs *The Swinger* and *Mr. Swing* into a two-CD set with the addition of the previously unreleased "How Am I to Know—" and an Edison original "Blues in the Closet" (no relation to the Oscar Pettiford piece with the same name). Edison and tenor saxophonist Jimmy Forrest work well together, inspiring one another with lyrical lines on the ballads like "The Very Thought of You" and Edison's easygoing blues "Pussy Willow," but also heat up the session with their playing on an up-tempo Basie-like blues like "Nasty." Edison switches to open horn during most of the second CD. Forrest's vibrato-filled solo on "Ill Wind" and Edison's memorable rendition of "Baby, Won't You Please Come Home?," including both open and muted trumpet solos, are second-half highlights. Pianist Jimmy Jones, bassist Joe Benjamin, drummer Charlie Persip, and rhythm guitarist Freddie Greene make up the capable rhythm section. Because this reissue is a part of the Verve Elite limited-edition series with only 6,500 copies pressed, collectors should not delay in picking up this highly recommended session. *—Ken Dryden*

Teddy Edwards

b. Apr. 26, 1924, Jackson, MS
Sax (Tenor) / West Coast Jazz, Hard Bop, Bop
Teddy Edwards was, with Dexter Gordon and Wardell Gray, the top young tenor of the late '40s. Unlike the other two, he chose to remain in Los Angeles and has been underrated through the years but, even in his early 70s, Edwards remains in prime form. Early on he toured with Ernie Fields' Orchestra, moving to L.A. in 1945 to work with Roy Milton as an altoist. Edwards switched to tenor when he joined Howard McGhee's band and was featured in many jam sessions during the era, recording "The Duel" with Dexter Gordon in 1947. A natural-born leader, Edwards did work briefly with Max Roach and Clifford Brown (1954), Benny Carter (1955) and Benny Goodman (1964) and he recorded in the 1960s with Milt Jackson and Jimmy Smith. But it is his own records for Onyx (1947-48), Pacific Jazz, Contemporary (1960-62), Prestige, Xanadu, Muse, SteepleChase, Timeless and Antilles that best show off his playing and writing; "Sunset Eyes" is Edwards' best-known original. *—Scott Yanow*

★ **Teddy's Ready** / Aug. 17, 1960 / Contemporary/OJC ♦♦♦♦♦
Tenor saxophonist Teddy Edwards' debut for Contemporary (which has been reissued on CD in the OJC series) gives listeners a strong sampling of the underrated tenor's talents. Edwards, a contemporary of Dexter Gordon and Wardell Gray but sometimes overlooked due to his decision to spend most of his life living in Los Angeles, is showcased on a quartet set with the obscure but talented pianist Joe Castro, bassist Leroy Vinnegar and drummer Billy Higgins. Performing three standards, three originals (of which "Higgins' Hideaway" is most memorable) and Hampton Hawes' "The Sermon," Edwards has a chance to stretch out and he makes the most of the opportunity, creating some excellent straightahead music. *—Scott Yanow*

Back to Avalon / Dec. 7, 1960-Dec. 13, 1960 / Contemporary ♦♦♦
Although rejected at the time it was recorded, this octet session by tenor-saxophonist Teddy Edwards sounded pretty good when it was finally released in 1995. There are some minor slip-ups in some of the ensembles and Edwards is the only significant soloist (although altoist Jimmy Woods and baritonist Modesto Brisenio were talented players) but the leader is in fine form and his arrangements manage to be both complicated and swinging Five of the nine songs (all but "You Don't Know What Love Is," "Sweet Georgia Brown" and two versions of "Avalon") are Edwards', highlighted by "Our Last Goodbye" and "Good Gravy." A worthwhile if not essential release. *—Scott Yanow*

Good Gravy! / Aug. 23, 1961-Aug. 25, 1961 / Contemporary/OJC ♦♦♦♦
Teddy Edwards has long been one of the most underrated of the bop tenors, due in large part to his decision to settle in Los Angeles. Edwards is in typically swinging form on this quartet date with either Phineas Newborn, Jr., or Danny Horton on piano, bassist Leroy Vinnegar and drummer Milt Turner. The tenor contributed four originals and also performs the obscure "A Little Later" and four standards with warmth and creativity within the hard bop genre. *—Scott Yanow*

Horn to Horn / Dec. 27, 1994 / 32 Jazz ♦♦♦♦♦
This is a logical and very successful collaboration featuring the East Coast tenor Houston Person and L.A.'s legendary Teddy Edwards. Although one can generally tell the two veterans apart (Person has a heavier sound than the comparatively light-toned Edwards), the coleaders are quite complementary and work together well in the tradition of Sonny Stitt and Gene Ammons. With fine backup from pianist Richard Wyands, bassist Peter Washington, and drummer Kenny Washington, Edwards and Person pay tribute to eight great tenors of the past (John Coltrane, Ben Webster, Lester Young, Stan Getz, Coleman Hawkins, Gene Ammons, Dexter Gordon, and Eddie "Lockjaw" Davis) through their renditions of eight standards. Highlights include a romp on "Lester Leaps In," a surprisingly successful version of "The Girl From Ipanema" and a spirited "Red Top." Recommended. *—Scott Yanow*

Midnight Creeper / Mar. 7, 1997 / High Note ♦♦♦♦♦
This CD is really two recordings in one. It starts off with three fine originals by tenor saxophonist Teddy Edwards, who is featured with a quintet also consisting of the underrated trumpeter Virgil Jones, pianist Richard Wyands, bassist Buster Williams and drummer Chip White. However the music really becomes memorable when Edwards performs a slower than usual, 10Ω-minute version of "Lady Be Good." He also has melodic and swinging renditions of "Don't Blame Me," "Tenderly" and "Almost Like Being in Love" as warm quartet features and jams "Sunday" with Jones. 52 years after his recording debut, Teddy Edwards proved to still be in his musical prime. *—Scott Yanow*

Close Encounters / Nov. 6, 1996 / High Note ♦♦♦♦

Roy Eldridge (David Roy Eldridge)

b. Jan. 30, 1911, Pittsburgh, PA, **d.** Feb. 26, 1989, Valley Stream, NY
Trumpet / Mainstream Jazz, Swing
One of the most exciting trumpeters to emerge during the swing era, Roy Eldridge's combative approach, chancetaking style and strong musicianship were an inspiration (and an in-

fluence) to the next musical generation, most notably Dizzy Gillespie. After arriving in New York in 1931, he worked with Elmer Snowden, McKinney's Cotton Pickers, Teddy Hill, Billie Holiday and Fletcher Henderson. With the decline of Bunny Berigan and the increasing predictability of Louis Armstrong, Eldridge was arguably the top trumpeter in jazz during the late '30s. During 1941-42 Eldridge sparked Gene Krupa's Orchestra with classic versions of "Rockin' Chair," "After You've Gone" and "Let Me Off Uptown." Eldridge had a short-lived big band of his own, toured with Jazz at the Philharmonic and spent several years during the early '50s in France. He recorded steadily for Norman Granz in the 1950s, and by 1956 was often teamed with Coleman Hawkins in a quintet. The 1960s were tougher as recording opportunities and work became rarer, but he was leading his own group by the end of the decade. He recorded for Pablo during the '70s, though a serious stroke halted his horn in 1980. *—Scott Yanow*

★ **Little Jazz** / Feb. 26, 1935-Apr. 2, 1940 / Columbia ✦✦✦✦✦
This CD contains the best recordings from the early years of the fiery trumpeter Roy Eldridge. Eldridge, one of the great swing trumpeters and a powerful player into the 1970s, is heard with Teddy Hill's Orchestra, backing singer Putney Dandridge, on four titles with Fletcher Henderson (including the hit "Christopher Columbus"), starring on a four-song session with Teddy Wilson, joining Billie Holiday on "Falling in Love Again," soloing on two numbers with Mildred Bailey (his "I'm Nobody's Baby" solo is years ahead of its time) and, best of all, leading a small group through six songs (plus an alternate) from his own explosive sessions of January 1937. This brilliant music is essential for all serious jazz collections. *—Scott Yanow*

After You've Gone / Feb. 5, 1936-Sep. 24, 1946 / GRP ✦✦✦✦
This excellent CD features the great swing trumpeter Roy Eldridge shortly after the breakup of the Gene Krupa Orchestra. Eldridge is heard leading his own recording groups (mostly big bands) and, although his own orchestra never really caught on, the trumpet solos are always quite exciting. This CD skips over five of Eldridge's Decca sides (it should have been a "complete" set) but does include three previously unissued performances plus a recently discovered jam on "Christopher Columbus" from 1936. *—Scott Yanow*

Uptown / May 8, 1941-May 9, 1949 / Columbia ✦✦✦✦✦
The Krupa band of 1941 to 1943 had two great forces in it with the addition of trumpeter Roy Eldridge and vocalist Anita O'Day replacing Irene Day. Eldridge almost singlehandedly transformed the orchestra from a pop-based dance band to a more jazz-inspired one, and O'-Day was simply the most swinging singer Krupa ever had in the fold. Highlights include a wild "After You've Gone," "Stop! The Red Light's On," "Let Me Off Uptown," "Thanks for the Boogie Ride," "Knock Me a Kiss," "Bop Boogie," and the previously unissued "Barrelhouse Bessie From Basin Street." Those interested in Krupa's career as a bandleader should start with this one. *—Cub Koda*

Roy and Diz / Oct. 29, 1954 / Verve ✦✦✦

Just You Just Me, Live in 1959 / 1959 / Stash ✦✦✦✦✦
In the late '50s trumpeter Roy Eldridge and tenor-saxophonist Coleman Hawkins teamed up on a fairly regular basis. Since they always brought out the best in each other (their solos could be quite competitive and fiery), all of their joint recordings are recommended. Two LPs from their gig at Washington D.C.'s Bayou Club in 1959 were previously released on the Honeysuckle Rose label. Five of those selections plus four previously unissued cuts are included on this Stash CD. Most of the tunes are medium-tempo jams such as "Just You, Just Me," "Rifftide," and "How High the Moon," but there is also an excellent ballad medley. Backed by a local rhythm section, Eldridge and Hawk are both in superior form, making this a highly recommended disc even for those listeners who already have the earlier LPs. *—Scott Yanow*

Mexican Bandit Meets Pittsburg Pirate / Aug. 24, 1973 / Fantasy ✦✦✦✦✦
Interesting title for this wonderful collaboration between Eldridge and Paul Gonsalves (ts); a delightful date. *—Ron Wynn*

☆ **Montreux 1977** / Jul. 13, 1977 / Pablo Live/OJC ✦✦✦✦✦
Eldridge's final recording as a leader is a real gem. Although his chops were no longer in prime form, he was still pushing himself to the limit. With a brilliant rhythm section egging him on (pianist Oscar Peterson, bassist Niels Pedersen and drummer Bobby Durham), Eldridge still went for the high notes (and generally hit them) during this exciting set from the 1977 Montreux Jazz Festival. Although the musicians did not know it at the time, the last two songs ("Perdido" and "Bye Bye Blackbird") were a perfect ending to a brilliant career. This dramatic CD reissue is highly recommended. *—Scott Yanow*

Roy Eldridge & Vic Dickenson / May 20, 1978 / Storyville ✦✦✦✦
Roy Eldridge is in better-than-expected form for what would be his final recording before a heart attack forced him to give up the trumpet. Teamed up with trombonist Vic Dickenson, tenorman Budd Johnson, pianist Tommy Flanagan, bassist Major Holley and drummer Eddie Locke (who was actually the organizer of the date), Eldridge and his friends play a lengthy ad-lib blues and eight familiar standards. This Storyville CD is well worth picking up by straightahead, swing and mainstream jazz fans. *—Scott Yanow*

☆ **Essential Keynote Collection, Vol. 4: Roy Eldridge & the Swing Trumpets** / Jul. 1, 1991 / Mercury ✦✦✦✦✦
A very good collection of 40s Eldridge done for Keynote. The Coleman Hawkins quintet sides are particularly tasty. *—Ron Wynn*

Eliane Elias

b. Mar. 19, 1960, Sao Paulo, Brazil
Vocals, Piano / Brazilian Jazz, Brazilian Pop, Post-Bop, Latin Jazz
The classical tradition meets the spontaneity of jazz through the virtuosic playing of Brazilborn and New York-based pianist Eliane Elias. A former member of jazz ensemble, Steps Ahead, Elias has continued to explore two distinct musical streams through her solo recordings and her performances for the past decade. In 1993, she became own of the few artists to simultaneously release jazz and classicalalbums. In a review of a concert in her homeland, "Brazzil" magazine praised Elias for "her dazzling right hand runs, executed often at frightening speeds. Her command of the keyboard was total. Her harmonic sensibility caused a sense of wondermint". Elias inherited her musical talents from her mother, Lucy, a classical pianist who often played jazz records in the family home. After studying for six years at the *Free Center of Music Apprenticeship* in Sao Paulo, she continued to study classical technique with Amilton Godoy and Amaral Vieria. By her teens, Elias was composing her own pieces and performing in jazz clubs. While touring in Europe in 1981, she met jazz bassist Eddie Gomez and was encouraged to travel to New York. Arriving in the Big Apple, the following year, she studied privately with Olegna Fuschi at the Julliard School of Music. Elias' professional career received a boost when she was invited to join Steps Ahead, a jazz "supergroup" featuring Michael Brecker, Peter Erskine, Mike Manieri and Eddie Gomez. She recorded one album with the group—"*Steps Ahead*"—in 1983. Shortly after leaving Steps Ahead, Elias began collaborating with trumpet player Randy Brecker, whom she subsequently married. Their sole duo album, released in 1985, was named after their daughter, Amanda. The following year, Elias launched her career as a bandleader. Since then, she's alternated tours with two different trios, one featuring Jack DeJohnette and Eddie Gomez and the other featuring Peter Erskine and Marc Johnson. Elias has also performed with a third trio, featuring Marc Johnson on bass and Satoshi Takaeshi on drums. Her 1995 album, "*Solos And Duets*", featured a billiantly-executed duet with Herbie Hancock. While most of her recordings have been instrumental, Elias introduced her soft, but coarse, vocals on her 1989 album, "*Eliane Elias Plays Jobim*". In addition to working periodically with Toots Thielman's Brasil Project, Elias has served as musical director for Gilberto Gil's group. *—Craig Harris*

Eliane Elias Plays Jobim / Dec. 1989 / Blue Note ✦✦✦✦

Fantasia / Mar. 1992 / Blue Note ✦✦✦✦✦
Eliane Elias continues exploring Brazilian music on this latest release, doing both classics such as "The Girl From Ipanema" and a Milton Nasciemento medley, plus several Ivan Lins tunes. She uses alternating bassists and drummers, with Eddie Gomez, Marc Johnson, Jack DeJohnette, and Peter Erskine dividing time, plus Nana Vasconcelos on percussion, with Lins helping out on vocals. *—Ron Wynn*

● **Solos & Duets** / Nov. 18, 1994+Dec. 1994 / Blue Note ✦✦✦✦✦
This release is a change of pace for Eliane Elias. Instead of interpreting Brazilian songs, fusion or modern bop, Elias shows off her classical technique on a set of acoustic solos plus six duets with Herbie Hancock. She really digs into the standards (sometimes sounding a little like Keith Jarrett) and creates some fairly free and unexpected ideas while putting the accent on lyricism. Some of the music is introspective and there are wandering sections but the net results are logical and enjoyable. As for the duets, Elias and Hancock mostly stay out of each other's way, which is an accomplishment when one considers that the four-part "Messages" is a series of free improvisations. There are playful spots (particularly on the adventurous tenminute rendition of "The Way You Look Tonight") and, since Elias knows Hancock's style well (and was clearly thrilled to have him on the date), their collaborations work quite well. A successful outing. *—Scott Yanow*

Three Americas / 1996 / Blue Note ✦✦✦
Two sides of Eliane Elias are on display on this CD. She is heard as an effective soft-toned singer of bossa nova and (particularly on the last few numbers) as a strong post-bop jazz pianist. The bossas (which often feature guitarist Oscar Castro-Neves and flutist Dave Valentin) are enjoyable, if a bit lightweight, and "Chorango (which has Gil Goldstein on accordion and violinist Mark Feldman) is a modern tango. But it is as a pianist that Elias is most significant, and fortunately, there are enough instrumentals on this release to make it worth picking up by jazz listeners. *—Scott Yanow*

Sings Jobim / Jul. 28, 1998 / Blue Note ✦✦✦
Elias has considerable chops as an acoustic pianist, although as a singer, she is definitely limited and doesn't have a great range by any means. No one's going to mistake Elias' singing for that of Flora Purim, Astrud Gilberto, Gal Costa or Tania Maria. But while her voice is paper-thin, Elias sings with enough feeling and sincerity to make *Eliane Elias Sings Jobim* a decent, if conventional, Brazilian jazz offering. Her second tribute to Antonio Carlos Jobim (the first was 1989's all-instrumental *Eliane Elias Plays Jobim*), this CD finds her staying away from instrumentals and embracing familiar, oft-recorded bossa nova standards like "The Girl From Ipanema," "So Danco Samba," "One Note Samba" and "Desafinado." Elias' singing (most of it in Portuguese) is the focal point, although she gets in a few nice piano solos. Unfortunately, Elias plays it safe and doesn't offer a lot of surprises. As many great but lesser-known songs as Jobim wrote, one wishes she had been less conservative and more adventurous in her choice of material. Although pleasant enough, this isn't one of Elias' essential releases. *—Alex Henderson*

Kurt Elling

b. Nov. 2, 1967, Chicago, IL
Vocals / Vocal Jazz, Post-Bop
During an era when the number of significant male jazz singers under the age of 60 can be counted on one hand, Kurt Elling's arrival is very welcome. Influenced by Mark Murphy, Elling combines poetry with jazz and is a chancetaking improviser who often makes up lyrics as he goes along. He discovered jazz while attending college and, although he had planned to become a professor in the philosophy of religion, he eventually became a professional singer instead. After a period of struggle Elling recorded a demo tape that was accepted by Blue Note, resulting in the impressive 1995 release *Close Your Eyes. Messenger* followed in 1997, and a year later he issued *This Time It's Love*. *—Scott Yanow*

The Messenger / Jul. 1994-Dec. 1996 / Capitol ✦✦✦✦✦
This is one of the most interesting jazz vocal sets to be released in 1997. Kurt Elling covers a wide range of music, continually taking chances and coming up with fresh approaches. He is assisted by his longtime pianist Laurence Hopgood, different bassists and drummers, and on various tracks trumpeter Orbert Davis and the tenors of Edward Petersen and Eddie Johnson. Among the more memorable selections are Elling's vocalese version of Dexter Gordon's

solo on the lengthy "Tanya Jean," and his spontaneous storytelling on "It's Just a Thing" (a classic of its kind), some wild scatting on "Gingerbread Boy," the fairly free improvising of "Endless," and his mostly straightforward renditions of "Nature Boy," "April In Paris" and "Prelude to a Kiss." Cassandra Wilson drops by for "Time of the Season," but does not make much of an impression. This rewarding and continually intriguing set is particularly recommended to listeners who feel that jazz singing has not progressed much beyond bop. *—Scott Yanow*

● **This Time It's Love** / Dec. 1997-Jan. 1998 / Blue Note ✦✦✦✦✦

Live In Chicago / Jul. 14, 1999+Jul. 15, 1999 / Blue Note ✦✦✦✦
Fans of Kurt Elling have long known that his recordings, as clever and well-orchestrated as they might be, don't quite match up to the power and charm of his live performances. Years of holding court at *the Green Mill* and other Chicago clubs are what really have brought Elling his most devoted followers, so it is exciting to see that Blue Note's new Elling album is a document of three special nights spent recording at the legendary *Uptown* jazz club. And indeed, with a few small exceptions, the album shows off Elling at his best—loose, uninhibited, creative, and solid. His standard backing trio has never been tighter and more balanced, and the performance of pianist (and Elling collaborator) Lawrence Hobgood really shines. Three saxophonists—Von Freeman, Ed Petersen and Eddie Johnson—manage to blend together in perfectly balanced harmonies, as well as command attention in solos of their own. Chicago's own Khalil El'Zabar makes a fine appearance, and a rare contribution by legendary jazz vocalist Jon Hendricks shows that he can still steal a show. The enthusiasm of the highly appreciative audience is captured, as well as more than a little evidence of the noise in the surrounding bar. The three nights of recording produced some fine versions of new and classic songs, including "Esperanto," Elling's pairing of the poetry of Pablo Neruda with the music of Vince Mendoza's jazz classic, "Esperança"; and "The Rent Party," which recalls Elling's jazz-poet days at the beginning of his career. *—Stacia Proefrock*

Duke Ellington (Edward Kennedy Ellington)

b. Apr. 29, 1899, Washington, D.C., **d.** May 24, 1974, New York, NY
Piano, Composer, Arranger / Orchestral Jazz, Film Music, Standards, Swing, Progressive Big Band, Big Band
Duke Ellington's contributions to jazz and American music were simply enormous. As a bandleader, his orchestra during 1926-74 was always among the top five, whether it be 1929 or 1969. As a composer, Ellington ranked with George Gershwin, Cole Porter, Irving Berlin and their contemporaries. He wrote literally thousands of songs (the exact number is not known) of which hundreds became standards. As an arranger Ellington was particularly innovative, writing for his very individual players rather than for an anonymous horn section and, not being content to play his songs the same way every time, he constantly rearranged them; "Mood Indigo" sounded different in 1933 than it did in 1953 or 1973. As a pianist Duke Ellington was originally an excellent stride player who gained the respect of such giants as James P. Johnson, Fats Waller and his main influence Willie "The Lion" Smith. Unlike virtually all of his contemporaries (other than Mary Lou Williams), Duke was able to modernize his style through the years, keeping the percussive approach of the stride players but leaving more space and using more complex chords; his playing was an influence on Thelonious Monk and (in a more abstract fashion) Cecil Taylor.Duke Ellington always considered his orchestra to be his main instrument and with it he recorded constantly from 1926 on. In the early days he recorded for many labels, sometimes under pseudonyms, and by the 1950s he often seemed to live in the studios when not performing before audiences, trying out new material and fresh versions of older songs. The result is that there are currently a countless number of Ellington albums available (way over 200) with "new" (previously unissued) ones coming out nearly every month as if he were still alive. What is more remarkable than the quantity is the consistently high quality; there are few if any throwaways in Ellington's entire discography. *—Scott Yanow*

☆ **Early Ellington: The Complete Brunswick Recordings (1926-1931)** / Nov. 29, 1926-Jan. 20, 1931 / Decca/GRP ✦✦✦✦✦
This three-CD set, which has all of Duke Ellington's recordings for the Brunswick and Vocalion labels, dwarfs all of the earlier reissues that Decca and MCA have put out of this important material. Starting with the first session in which the Ellington Orchestra sounds distinctive ("East St. Louis Toodle-oo" and "Birmingham Breakdown" from November 29, 1926) and progressing through *the Cotton Club* years, this essential release (which contains 67 performances) adds a few "new" alternate takes and rare items ("Soliloquy" and a few titles by the "Six Jolly Jesters") to make this collection truly complete, at least for MCA's holdings (since Ellington also recorded for Columbia- and Victor-owned labels during the same period). With such major soloists as trumpeters Bubber Miley (and his replacement Cootie Williams), Freddy Jenkins, and Arthur Whetsol, trombonist Tricky Sam Nanton, clarinetist Barney Bigard, altoist Johnny Hodges, baritonist Harry Carney, and the pianist/leader, along with the classic arrangements/compositions, this set is essential for all serious jazz collections. *—Scott Yanow*

Okeh Ellington / Mar. 22, 1927-Nov. 8, 1930 / Columbia ✦✦✦✦
Although generally not as celebrated as his Victor recordings of the same period, Duke Ellington's performances for OKeh (late acquired by Columbia) are among the best of the period, featuring distinctive solos by the likes of trumpeter Bubber Miley (and later his replacement Cootie Williams), trombonist Tricky Sam Nanton (who, like Miley, was an expert with wa-wa mutes), clarinetist Barney Bigard and altoist Johnny Hodges among others These 50 performances (which bypass Ellington's alternate takes) contain many classics including his original theme "East St. Louis Toodle-oo," "Black and Tan Fantasy," "The Mooche," "Mood Indigo" and his two earliest solo piano sides. This is one of the best sets of early Ellington currently available. *—Scott Yanow*

★ **Duke's Men: The Small Groups, Vol. 1** / Dec. 12, 1934-Jan. 19, 1938 / Columbia ✦✦✦✦✦
In the '30s Ellington started recording prolifically with small groups taken from his big band. It gave him an opportunity to both debut new works and to let his sidemen stretch out and act as leaders once in awhile (under his direction). This two-disc set contains 45 recordings, almost all of them brilliant, including sessions ostensibly under the leadership of cornetist Rex Stewart (including two selections cut before he joined Ellington), clarinetist Barney Bigard, trumpeter Cootie Williams and altoist Johnny Hodges. In addition to early versions of such future standards as "Caravan," "Stompy Jones" and "Echoes of Harlem," there are many hot stomps performed that feature strong solos from these very distinctive stylists. Brilliant music, highly recommended. *—Scott Yanow*

Duke's Men: The Small Groups, Vol. 2 / Mar. 28, 1938-Mar. 20, 1939 / Columbia ✦✦✦✦✦
This second two-disc set, like the first, includes all of the master takes (no alternates) from the small-group sessions led by Duke Ellington's sidemen. During the year covered on this volume, Johnny Hodges, Cootie Williams and Rex Stewart all had opportunities to head sessions and the results included early versions of "Jeep's Blues," "Pyramid," "Prelude to a Kiss," "The Jeep's Jumping" and "Hodge Podge" along with many hot obscurities. There are few duds and many memorable performances during these 43 recordings. *—Scott Yanow*

☆ **The Blanton-Webster Band** / 1939-1942 / Bluebird/RCA ✦✦✦✦✦
This attractive three-CD set contains the master takes of all 66 selections recorded by Duke Ellington's Orchestra during what many historians consider its peak period. Left out are the many alternate takes, last released by European labels, and the Duke Ellington-Jimmy Blanton duets, which are available on a different CD. Included are dozens of classics, including "Ko-Ko," "Concerto for Cootie," "Cottontail," "Harlem Air Shaft," "All Too Soon," "In a Mellotone," "Warm Valley," "Take the 'A' Train," "Jumpin' Punkins," "I Got It Bad," "Jump for Joy," "Rocks in My Bed," "Chelsea Bridge," "Perdido," "The C Jam Blues" and "Johnny Come Lately," among many others. The arrangements and originals of Ellington and Billy Strayhorn are full of surprises, and even the lesser-known pieces are generally gems. With such soloists as trumpeter Cootie Williams, cornetists Rex Stewart and Ray Nance, trombonists Tricky Sam Nanton and Lawrence Brown, clarinetist Barney Bigard, altoist Johnny Hodges, tenor saxophonist Ben Webster, baritonist Harry Carney, bassist Jimmy Blanton and the leader/pianist (plus singers Ivie Anderson and Herb Jeffries), Ellington led quite a remarkable unit. This music is essential for all jazz collections. *—Scott Yanow*

★ **The Carnegie Hall Concerts (January 1943)** / Jan. 23, 1943-Jan. 28, 1943 / Prestige ✦✦✦✦✦
This two-CD set captures one of the milestones in Duke Ellington's long and extremely productive career, highlighted by his monumental suite "Black, Brown and Beige" in the only full-length version ever recorded by his orchestra; soon it was only performed as excerpts. In addition, Ellington's all-star orchestra (including such stylists as trumpeters Rex Stewart, Ray Nance and Shorty Baker, trombonists Tricky Sam Nanton and Lawrence Brown and a saxophone section boasting Johnny Hodges, Ben Webster and Harry Carney) excels on the shorter pieces, a mixture of older and recent compositions. Every serious jazz library should contain this set. *—Scott Yanow*

The Carnegie Hall Concerts (December 1944) / Dec. 19, 1944 / Prestige ✦✦✦✦
The Ellington orchestra was undergoing some personnel (and personality) changes during this era, none of it unexciting. This Carnegie Hall concert (available on two CDs) introduced Ellington's "Perfume Suite," and includes a half-hour series of selections from "Black, Brown and Beige," but also in the shorter pieces shows the impact of tenorman Al Sears and high-note wizard Cat Anderson on the band's sound, making it a more potentially boisterous and extroverted ensemble. Lots of great moments from this brilliant orchestra occured during this concert. *—Scott Yanow*

The Carnegie Hall Concerts (December 1947) / Dec. 27, 1947 / Prestige ✦✦✦✦✦

Great Times! Piano Duets with Billy Strayhorn / Sep. 13, 1950-Oct. 3, 1960 / Riverside/OJC ✦✦✦✦
This CD reissues three unusual combo dates by Duke Ellington. Two of the sessions feature Ellington and his longtime musical partner Billy Strayhorn both playing piano (while assisted by either Wendell Marshall or Joe Shulman on bass and sometimes an unidentified drummer). The futuristic "Tonk" is the best-known performance but all eight numbers (which include "Cotton Tail" and "Johnny Come Lately") are quite fascinating. The remaining date has four songs that primarily serve as features for the cello of Oscar Pettiford who is accompanied by Ellington, bassist Lloyd Trotman, drummer Jo Jones and (on two tunes) the celeste of Strayhorn; "Perdido" and "Take the 'A' Train" are most memorable. Intriguing music. *—Scott Yanow*

☆ **Uptown** / Dec. 7, 1951-Dec. 8, 1952 / Columbia ✦✦✦✦✦
Although some historians have characterized the early '50s as Duke Ellington's "off period" (due to the defection of alto-star Johnny Hodges), in reality his 1951-52 orchestra could hold its own against his best. This set has many classic moments, including Betty Roche's famous bebop vocal on "Take the 'A' Train," a version of "The Mooche" that contrasts the different clarinet styles of Russell Procope and Jimmv Hamilton, a hot "Perdido" that is highlighted by some great Clark Terry trumpet, Louie Bellson's drum solo on "Skin Deep," a definitive version of "The Harlem Suite" and the two-part "Controversial Suite" which contrasts New Orleans jazz with futuristic music worthy of Stan Kenton. One of the great Duke Ellington sets. *—Scott Yanow*

1952 Seattle Concert / Mar. 28, 1952 / Bluebird/RCA ✦✦✦

The Complete Capitol Recordings of Duke Ellington / Apr. 6, 1953-May 19, 1955 / Mosaic ✦✦✦✦✦
This five-CD box set from Mosaic documents Duke Ellington's least-known period, his two years on Capitol. Although thought of by some as his off years because of the absence of Johnny Hodges, the set serves as evidence that a great deal of viable music was created. The problem was basically one of the times themselves, coupled with weaknesses at Capitol and its approach to marketing jazz. Ellington's move to Capitol followed four frustrating years at Columbia Records, where he was kept out of the studio for 20 months by a combination of the Musicians' Union strike and the label's laziness, and then allowed to record two startlingly ambitious LPs, only to see his sales (in an era dominated by singers and novelty tunes) plummet. He felt the new label would be able to sell his records better than Colum-

bia, but it wasn't to be—Capitol, although an aggressive, upstart company, wasn't well focused on jazz.

In fact, however, during this period, Ellington's orchestra had 11 distinctive soloists including four very different trumpeters (Clark Terry, Cat Anderson, Willie Cook and Ray Nance), and they were playing and even writing good music. In addition, there's a well-known trio set (sounding better here than on Capitol's own reissue) that showcases Ellington's underrated piano playing. Toss in the original version of "Satin Doll" plus the unusual *Ellington '55* album, and one has a highly enjoyable reissue that Duke Ellington fans should pick up immediately. Two other virtues of this set that fans should consider are the extraordinary sound quality and the thoroughness of the historical annotation. To properly appreciate all of Ellington's best work during the period covered by the Mosaic set, one should also grab hold of the Discovery Records reissue of those Reprise recordings, Symphonic Ellington. *—Scott Yanow & Bruce Eder*

Piano Reflections / Apr. 13, 1953-Dec. 3, 1953 / Capitol ♦♦♦♦♦
At the time of its release this was a true rarity, a full album of Duke Ellington featured with a trio sans his orchestra. Although his talents at the piano sometimes have been overshadowed by his many accomplishments as a composer, arranger, and bandleader, Ellington was actually one of the very few stride pianists (along with Mary Lou Williams) to effectively make the transition into more modern styles of jazz without losing his own musical personality; in fact Duke was an early influence on both Thelonious Monk and Cecil Taylor. Throughout this CD (which contains one previously unissued track), Ellington sounds modern (especially rhythmically and in his chord voicings) and shows that he could have made a viable career out of just being a pianist. *—Scott Yanow*

☆ **Ellington at Newport** / Jul. 7, 1956 / Columbia ♦♦♦♦♦
Duke Ellington's appearance at the 1956 *Newport Jazz Festival* has long been famous, and justifiably so. Paul Gonsalves' 27-chorus tenor solo on "Diminuendo in Blue and Crescendo in Blue" practically started a riot at *Newport* and made headlines around the world. The momentum generated by this concert led to Ellington's "comeback" and never let up during his 18 remaining years. A double CD put out in 1999 presents the entire concert performance, previously unheard material, and a few revelations. After a brief truncated set that was cut short because four of Ellington's musicians could not be found, the Ellington Orchestra returned to the stage three hours later. They played "Take the 'A' Train," "Newport Jazz Festival Suite," a showcase for Harry Carney on "Sophisticated Lady" and a so-so Jimmy Grissom vocal outing on "Day In, Day Out." Then came "Diminuendo in Blue and Crescendo in Blue." The saxophone "interlude" caused crazed dancing, and soon the crowd was as loud as the band. When the crowd would not quiet down, Ellington saved the day by closing with a long version of "Skin Deep". But unknown to most people is that on July 9, the orchestra went to the studios to reproduce the program. The earlier version of the "Newport Jazz Festival Suite" had been a bit sloppy and Gonsalves' famous tenor solo on "Diminuendo" had actually been played into the wrong microphone. Ellington's band therefore performed the entire "Newport Jazz Festival Suite" again and it was issued (with phony applause, introductions and crowd noises) on the original LP. Happily, a second version of the *Newport* concert had since been discovered so Gonsalves' solo is a bit louder here than on the LP. And by combining the two tapes, one can hear the Duke Ellington Orchestra in stereo in 1956. Highly recommended. *—Scott Yanow*

Such Sweet Thunder / Apr. 1957-May 1957 / Columbia/Legacy ♦♦♦♦♦
The 1999 reissue of this album marks a total reconstruction and rethinking of the original LP, and such a complete break from the original album that its story could fill a book. *Such Sweet Thunder* was originally announced as a stereo and mono release, but only showed up in mono, thanks to the technical problems, inherent in early stereo, in creating a concert-like ambience in which the performance seemed continuous. The reissue presents the original album as it was intended, using alternate takes from the original sessions, plus the stereo masters of the takes used on the original album, all rounded out with a mono outtake or two. The music itself counts among Ellington's most well-realized "concept projects," all inspired by Shakespeare's work and filled with memorable melodies and ample opportunities for solos by Cat Anderson, Johnny Hodges, Paul Gonsalves and Quentin Jackson. The Ellington-Strayhorn compositions treat their soloists like actors doing scenes and, in effect, playing parts, even quoting lines after a fashion—Clark Terry "plays" Puck in "Up and Down, Up and Down (I Will Lead Them Up and Down),"and Johnny Hodges turns in one of the most sensuous performances of his career for "Half the Fun," from *Antony and Cleopatra*. These moments more than justify the cost of the CD, and the bonus tracks, many of which are different takes and others are simply material that came from the same sessions, more than double the length of the original LP. The extended notes by Phil Schaap deserve some kind of award for detail and clarity. *—Bruce Eder*

☆ **Black, Brown & Beige** / Feb. 4, 1958-Feb. 12, 1958 / Columbia/Legacy ♦♦♦♦♦
Duke Ellington originally wrote the 50-minute "Black, Brown and Beige" in 1943 for a *Carnegie Hall* concert, where critics dismissed it as overreaching for a jazz composer. Over the next 15 years, he periodically resurrected it for performances of excerpts or, as in the case of his 1958 Columbia album, transmuting it into what was essentially a new work. Long out-of-print on vinyl, and only available as an import on CD until 1999, the original Columbia *Black, Brown and Beige* album was one of the most extraordinary products of Ellington's second stay with the label, growing out of his 1956 *Newport* triumph, and it was received somewhat more readily than the original 1943 "Black, Brown and Beige." The main problem for those who knew the piece and its history lay in the absence of Johnny Hodges, who was hardly ever with the Ellington band during 1958, and on whose talents "Come Sunday," the centerpiece of the original work and even more the core of the revamped *Black, Brown and Beige,* was built. Instead, Mahalia Jackson sings a version of "Come Sunday" that is, if anything, equally affecting, backed by the orchestra led by Ray Nance's violin. The result on the original album was a piece that started off in big-band-style blues and led to one of Ellington's most moving, wrenching pieces of work, and music that, had it been better known, might also have done more to raise people's consciousnesses about civil rights than a hundred folk songs of the period. An expanded 1999 reissue has ten bonus tracks, including eight flawed but fascinating alternate takes of the complete work. There's not a note of music that isn't worth hearing anywhere on the CD, and the album is a welcome restoration to the catalog. *—Bruce Eder*

Anatomy of a Murder / May 29, 1959-Jun. 2, 1959 / Rykodisc ♦♦♦
By the time of Ellington's engagement to write and record the music for Otto Preminger's *Anatomy of a Murder,* he was an elder statesman of jazz. He'd performed in, and contributed music to, various movies before, but those were almost all short subjects or B-musicals, or confined to a handful of numbers (*Belle of the Nineties*)—*Anatomy of a Murder,* by contrast, was a four-star feature film with a first-class cast (led by James Stewart, Lee Remick and Ben Gazzara) and director. He rose to the occasion, creating a virtuoso jazz score—moody, witty, sexy and, in its own quiet way, playful. Ellington naturally subordinated his music to the action in the film, but "Midnight Indigo," "Flirtibird," "Happy Anatomy" and "Sunswept Sunday" (the latter highlighted by Jimmy Hamilton's clarinet theme) would have slotted in nicely in other contexts, on any of his standard albums. The 1999 reissue (Columbia-Legacy 65569) includes several unedited studio performances by the band, and some variant performances and arrangements, an open-ended Ellington interview intended to publicize the film and the album, and rehearsal excerpts. The main difference from the original LP or the earlier foreign CD reissue is that, in going to the original session tapes, this reissue misses the heavy layer of echo added to the original LP, bringing the detail and presence of the original band performances much closer. *—Bruce Eder*

Three Suites / Mar. 3, 1960-Oct. 10, 1960 / Columbia ♦♦♦♦♦

First Time! The Count Meets the Duke / Jul. 6, 1961-Jul. 7, 1961 / Columbia/Legacy ♦♦♦♦♦
The 1999 remastering (Columbia-Legacy 65571) supercedes all previous editions, CD or vinyl, of the 1961 album, *First Time! The Count Meets the Duke,* and not just because of the superior sound and the presence of five bonus tracks that add 27 minutes to the running time, although that's a big part of it. The sound is improved, making the original CD release seem like a copy of the LP, from the opening bars of the rollicking "Battle Royal," with that bass right up front. The Sonny Cohn and Ray Nance trumpet dialogue, and the Jimmy Hamilton clarinet and Budd Johnson tenor sax duet on "Take the A-Train" are more thickly textured and more "there" than on any previous incarnation, and Willie Cook's trumpet and Paul Gonsalves' tenor sax solo on "Corner Pocket" are gorgeously vivid. As important as anything else here, the closer sound captures the really hard, swinging nature of the performance on numbers like the bluesy "Segue in C" and "Jumpin' at the Woodside,". The new notes, by bassist Aaron Bell and reissue co-producer Phil Schaap, also provide extraordinary insights into the making of this record—with the album recorded more as a genial get-together than an old-style battle-of-the-bands, and packaging only awaiting the approval of Basie, the Count balked at the *"Battle Royal"* title and jacket design, and his manager, Teddy Reig, supposedly flushed the only copy of the latter down the men's room toilet, thus forcing a reconsideration of the whole concept. The result was a hastily designed cover for an obscurely titled album that Columbia was never fully behind in marketing—that it's lingered this long is, thus, even more of a testament to the power of the music and the good feelings from the sessions. *—Bruce Eder*

Money Jungle / Sep. 17, 1962 / Blue Note ♦♦♦♦♦
George Wein, in his liner notes for this classic session, says that "to hear this album is to believe fully in the validity and lasting qualities of jazz." How right he is. Ellington was between recording contracts at the time, and producer Alan Douglas, hustling to get some product out on United Artists, brought him together with two modern musicians who practically idolized him. The results, which sound much better on CD than they did on LP, reveal the continuity of jazz, grounded in the blues. Mingus was reportedly quite nervous at the session, and perhaps it's this tension that contributes to his energized conversational style. Roach is an equal partner in the group, with his precise and flowing rhythms. It's one of the great piano trio records. *—Stuart Kremsky*

☆ **Duke Ellington and John Coltrane** / Sep. 26, 1962 / Impulse! ♦♦♦♦♦
For this classic encounter, Duke Ellington "sat in" with the John Coltrane Quartet for a set dominated by Ellington's songs; some performances have his usual sidemen (bassist Aaron Bell and drummer Sam Woodyard) replacing Jimmy Garrison and Elvin Jones in the group. Although it would have been preferable to hear Coltrane play in the Duke Ellington Orchestra instead of the other way around, the results are quite rewarding. Their version of "In a Sentimental Mood" is a high point, and such numbers as "Take the Coltrane," "Big Nick" and "My Little Brown Book" are quite memorable. Ellington always recognized talent, and Coltrane seemed quite happy to be recording with a fellow genius. *—Scott Yanow*

☆ **The Reprise Studio Recordings** / Nov. 29, 1962-Apr. 14, 1965 / Mosaic ♦♦♦♦♦
Not much has been said about Duke Ellington's Reprise Records period, and even less that's enthusiastic, mostly owing to the fact that his output there ran between two extremes: dazzlingly inventive conceptual pieces juxtaposed with re-recordings of classic big-band material, and pop-jazz efforts built around covers of current popular songs. Amid that wildly divergent body of work, it's no surprise that the live material from *The Great Paris Concert* and *Ellington's Greatest Hits* eclipsed much of his Reprise studio work. Thus, this five-CD box is the first opportunity that most listeners will have had to assess the music properly. As with all Mosaic issues, it's in recording session order, and Disc One opens with Ellington's 1962 covers of classic big-band material. Disc Two is where things not only get interesting but downright spellbinding, containing the entirety of the *Afro-Bossa Album*?this is some of the most beautiful, engaging, and forward-looking music of Ellington's 1960s output, and the varied rhythms and textures are coupled with some truly luscious playing. Disc Three is largely given over to the material off of *Symphonic Ellington,* mixed band and orchestra pieces dating from the period in which Ellington began writing concert music for orchestra. Disc Four is devoted to the *Ellington '65* and *Ellington '66* albums, renditions of current pop and rock & roll hits. Few of Ellington's serious fans have ever professed much love for his *Mary Poppins* album, the contents of which open Disc Five, but the material holds up quite

well, mostly because the soloists are enjoying themselves. As usual with Mosaic, the annotation and sessionography material are thoroughly detailed. *—Bruce Eder*

The Great Paris Concert / Feb. 1, 1963-Feb. 23, 1963 / Atlantic ♦♦♦♦♦
This set came about, in part, as a result of Ellington's signing to Frank Sinatra's Reprise label in November 1962, with the ending of his exclusive contract to Columbia. Six numbers from the three Paris dates were initially edited and released by Reprise as part of the ten-song *Duke Ellington's Greatest Hits*, but the bulk of the performances from those shows didn't surface until many years later as *The Great Paris Concert* on two LP's; for the CD reissue, the two separate releases were merged with the ten *Greatest Hits* songs appended to the double-LP's contents. The stuff from *The Great Paris Concert* is raw and largely unedited, and depicts the full Ellington band in extraordinary form, oozing excitement—from the saxophone showcase on the opener, "Rockin' in Rhythm," the various sections of the band take flight at different points throughout this set, which includes such contemporary numbers as Ellington's theme music for an all-but-forgotten television series, *The Asphalt Jungle*, and excerpts from *Such Sweet Thunder*. Johnny Hodges is showcased in several solos, most notably on "Suite Thursday," a work whose original studio incarnation he missed appearing on; Cootie Williams ("Tutti for Cootie"), Paul Gonsalves ("Cop Out"), Ray Nance ("Bula") and Cat Anderson ("Jam with Sam") get their own moments in the spotlight. The editing and equalization on the Reprise tracks is considerably smoother and more obtrusive, in terms of closing fades, from that on the Atlantic release, where the sound is rougher and more realistic, and one wishes that original tapes could have been found and the complete 26 numbers from the Paris shows reassembled together in an integrated fashion. *—Bruce Eder*

☆ **And His Mother Called Him Bill** / Aug. 28, 1967-Sep. 1, 1967 / Bluebird/RCA ♦♦♦♦♦
Shortly after Billy Strayhorn's early death in 1967, the Duke Ellington Orchestra recorded a dozen of his compositions during a series of emotional and passionate sessions. The results are consistently inspired with such selections as "Blood Count" (Strayhorn's final composition), "Rain Check," "Lotus Blossom" and "The Intimacy of the Blues" receiving definitive versions. In addition, this CD reissue also contains an alternate take of "Lotus Blossom" and remakes of three more Strayhorn classics that were previously unissued. This was one of Duke Ellington's finest sessions and, considering his huge recorded legacy, that is saying a lot. *—Scott Yanow*

70th Birthday Concert / Nov. 25, 1969-Nov. 26, 1969 / Blue Note ♦♦♦♦♦

● **The Best of the Duke Ellington Centennial Edition** / Oct. 26, 1927-Aug. 30, 1967 / RCA ♦♦♦♦♦
This latest compilation of some of Ellington's most popular, enduring, and important RCA Victor sides from a period of 40 years (October 26, 1927, to August 30, 1967) consists of 18 tracks, drawn from the remastered tracks on BMG's 24-CD *Ellington Centennial* box. That's hardly enough to address the range of changes in Ellington's style, but it does give the casual listener a glimpse of that range—"Mood Indigo" sounds light years beyond "Black and Tan Fantasy" or "East St. Louis Toodle-o," and it's only four tracks in, and the development of Ellington's musical language only got more sophisticated, so this is a rushed history lesson, a handy "Monarch notes"-type look at the man's work. The producers have very shrewdly included the "Mood Indigo-Hot and Bothered-Creole Love Call" experimental long-play (for 1932) medley, clocking in at more than seven minutes, and presented here in stereo, one of the unique elements of the box, to wet the appetite of the budgetary-challenged. Otherwise, all of the expected bases are touched ("Take the 'A' Train," etc.), up through the soaring, lyrical "Come Sunday" from the First Concert of Sacred Music and the upbeat, energetic "Raincheck," from Ellington's 1967 memorial to Billy Stayhorn. As with the box, the sound is largely impeccable, with stunning delineating of the soloists' work and a rich, full texture to the ensemble sections. There's a little sloppiness in the annotation, which could've been cleaner, but this is a otherwise a handy mid-priced compilation and a worthy teaser for a monumental career survey. *—Bruce Eder*

V-Disc Recordings / Apr. 20, 1999 / Collectors' Choice Music ♦♦♦♦
This triple-CD set fills in some important holes around Duke Ellington's '40s RCA-Victor output. The World War II-era V-Disc program helped raise morale among soldiers, and it also gave an opportunity—overlapping as it did with two ill-advised Musicians' Union strikes against the record companies—for many artists to capture the sounds of certain lineups that might otherwise have been lost. The Ellington V-Discs are amazingly ambitious, including conceptual material which was not easily accessible, and certain important compositions that were never well-represented in the catalogs of his major labels. The most notable component of Disc One of this three-disc set is a live recording of two parts of "Black, Brown & Beige," done in late 1944 or early 1945, long after the piece's *Carnegie Hall* premiere. The postwar "Deep South Suite, Parts 1-4" occupies 20 minutes of the same disc, and is a far more topical and biting piece reflecting the lot of Black Americans in the South in the immediate aftermath of World War II. The concerto-like "New World A Comin' (Parts 1 and 2)" opens Disc Three with more of the man's brilliant playing, and depicts Ellington's band in full, lyrical flight; the only other extant version of this piece, incidentally, is on the MusicMaster *Great Chicago Concert* double-CD set. The other treats to be found here are the extended versions of pieces that never would have gone so long on any commercial release of the day. Apart from a few flawed sources, most of the material is in better than decent shape. The notes are virtually non-existent, which means that one must deduce a good deal of the personnel and dates. *—Bruce Eder*

★ **At Newport 1956 Complete** / Jul. 7, 1956 / Columbia/Legacy ♦♦♦♦♦
One of the greatest live jazz festival recordings ever has gotten better, and more interesting as well, with this 1999 reissue, a result of the kind of effort that most record companies normally won't even discuss. Ellington's original 1956 *Newport* album was his best-selling long-player ever, and re-established him, after a two-year drought in the wake of his unsuccessful stay at Capitol, as a vitally popular jazz artist, perceived as worth courting by the major labels. But that record was, in keeping with Columbia's standard operating proceedure of the day, a cut-and-paste job made up of studio re-recordings of the festival's repertory. The producers of the 1999 double-CD reissue, containing 20 tracks, have assembled the complete live performance in true, real stereo as well as the studio-produced tracks. The result is the first complete consideration of the actual *Newport* performance, as well as a complete account of the studio-generated portions of the original release. The highlight is an extraordinarily vivid account of Paul Gonsalves' legendary 27-chorus tenor sax solo on "Diminuendo in Blue and Crescendo in Blue." The latter ends Disc One, and Disc Two gives a vivid account of the aftermath of Gonsalves' moment of glory and finishes the live set. The concert portion is followed by the original LP's studio-generated fake-live productions, which aren't as exciting as the live renditions, but are worth hearing. *—Bruce Eder*

☆ **Centennial Edition: Complete RCA Victor Recordings: 1927-1973** / Jan. 10, 1927-Dec. 1, 1973 / RCA-BMG ♦♦♦♦♦
This 24-CD box, which dwarfs even most Bear Family sets in scope, is essentially everything Ellington cut for RCA-Victor over a 46-year period. There are gaps, especially after 1946 when he jumped to Columbia, but otherwise, this is all of it. One quickly discovers that, by virtue of its leader's taste, combined with the good sense of RCA-Victor's recording managers, this was a band that did little, if any, wrong on record. Better yet, from the opening cut on Disc One (which encompasses 1927 and part of 1928), there's scarcely a trace of tinniness, and the bass and middle are rich and natural. Disc Three takes us from 1929 into 1930, and even only two years into their recording career, the Ellington band was evolving into something more sophisticated than a dance band. Disc Five includes the 1930 session that yielded the first recording of "Mood Indigo," where the band sort of announces to the world that they're the most musically sophisticated and adept outfit in jazz. Disc Eight picks up in 1940—this is the Blanton-Webster band transferred properly to CD, and it never got any better than this, at least within the context of big-band swing. The excerpts from "Black, Brown and Beige" included on Disc 14 are among the most famous parts of this body of work, and they've never sounded better. Discs 18 through 20 encompass the complete trio of *Sacred Concerts*, and Discs 21 thru 24 cover the *Far East Suite*, Ellington's mid-'60s recuttings of his classic hits, and his tribute to Billy Strayhorn, through to his final concert release from 1973. This material is all worthwhile, and the 122-page book that comes with the set is chock full of extraordinarily informative and well-written essays, plus vital sessionography information. The set is also, alas, incredibly unwieldy, the individual CDs sliding out too easily from their separate sleeves. They're still a bargain, of course, but someone should have given more thought to the needs of real listeners. *—Bruce Eder*

Beyond Category: The Musical Genius of Duke Ellington / Jun. 29, 1999 / Buddah ♦♦♦♦♦
This 1999 two-CD set should *not* be confused with an identically titled double-disc set from RCA/BMG that dates from a decade earlier. That set, which came in a somewhat awkward longbox and was mastered in the '80s, was merely adequate for its time, but this Buddha-imprinted version has been remastered, upgraded, and reconfigured into a more convenient shape and size—and is even cheaper than the old collection. That's the upside of the Buddha version; the obvious downside is that representing Ellington's career within the scope of 37 tracks is a near-impossible task. But *Beyond Category* is a handy introduction nonetheless. Beginning with "East St. Louis Toodle-Oo," recorded in November of 1926, the set takes us up through "Lotus Blossom" (from 1967's *And His Mother Called Him Bill*). Along the way, it touches the expected standards ("Mood Indigo," "Take the 'A' Train"); many of the musically important pieces, including the second version of "Creole Rhapsody"; and such recording touchstones as "Concerto for Cootie," "I Got It Bad (And That Ain't Good)" (featuring Ivey Anderson), "Carnegie Blues," "Transbluency," "Harlem Suite," and "Come Sunday" (from the December 1965 *Concert of Sacred Music* recording). It's not ideal—a three-disc set would've worked better—but it does make the point of its title, illustrating the sheer scope of Ellington's music, even if it doesn't truly embrace its full range or depth. The 1999 Buddha version of *Beyond Category* is only the second compilation to make use of the remastered Ellington sides from RCA's *Centennial* set, and is preferable to the earlier, longbox version for sound as well as price. *—Bruce Eder*

☆ **The Duke: The Essential Recordings (1927-1962)** / Jun. 12, 1930-Jul. 6, 1961 / Columbia/Legacy ♦♦♦♦♦
Unlike some labels, who chose to celebrate Duke Ellington's centennial with lavish sets of his complete recordings for a label, Columbia/Legacy decided to keep things relatively simple. They assembled *Duke Ellington ?The Essential Collection: 1927-1962*, a three-disc set that features highlights of his sessions for Columbia over the years. Completists and purists may wish they have gone whole-hog with a complete sessions box, but it's hard to argue against this wonderful set. Since this spans several decades, it winds up being a terrific overview of Ellington's bands and the progression of his career, as it hits many of his best compositions in classic performances. Yes, there are great moments missing, not just from his RCA or Decca work, but from his Columbia waxings, but that ultimately doesn't matter, since this was designed as an overview for relative neophytes and for the dedicated that appreciate new contexts. On that level, it succeeds grandly, since it's hard to imagine anyone that hears this set not wanting to dig deeper into Ellington's rich body of work. *—Stephen Thomas Erlewine*

The Best of the Complete Duke Ellington RCA Victor Recordings, 1944-1946 / Apr. 4, 2000 / RCA ♦♦♦♦♦
Given that the 24-disc set *The Complete RCA/Victor Recordings* was so large it was only for specialized tastes, it was inevitable that the set would be released in excerpts. As it happens, *The Best of the Complete Duke Ellington RCA/Victor Recordings: The Mid Forties Recordings* is an excerpt of an excerpt, selecting the 18 finest cuts from the three-disc *The Complete Victor Mid-Forties Recordings (1944-1948)*. This isn't a bad thing, by any means, since only affluent fans could afford either of the multi-disc sets, and this single-disc does an excellent job of narrowing down the finest moments from these four years, arguably the best in Ellington's many years of leading superlative bands. Yes, there are some seminal recordings missing from these mere 18 tracks—how could there not—?but these all are terrific cuts that illustrate why Ellington and his band were peerless in the mid-'40s. For the fan on a budget, this is an essential sampler. *—Stephen Thomas Erlewine*

☆ **The Complete RCA-Victor Mid-Forties Recordings (1944-1946)** / Dec. 1, 1944-Sep. 3, 1946 / RCA ✦✦✦✦✦
Once Duke Ellington's complete RCA/Victor recordings were released on the 24-disc box set in 1999, it meant that it was only a matter of time before the cream of that crop was released in individual sets. RCA was sharp enough to realize that there were a number of different audiences for Ellington's timeless recordings—audiences that wanted an overview of the entire multi-decade stint, audiences that wanted to hear a particular period of his time at the label. So, they released a number of different highlight discs, including the three-disc *The Complete Victor Mid-Forties Recordings*, which contained everything Ellington recorded during the middle of the '40s. This is one of Ellington's classic bands, perhaps his greatest band, and there are certainly listeners that will only want this, and nothing else. The problem is, the completists would rather spend their money on the full set, while the curious will definitely be better-served by the single-disc *The Best of the Complete Duke Ellington RCA/Victor Recordings: The Mid Forties Recordings*, which contains the cream of this admittedly excellent crop. So, it's all a matter of knowing what consumer you are; if you just have an interest in a specific era, go for this (or the highlights if you're budget-conscious), but if you're a completist/scholar, acquire this music through the comprehensive 24-disc box set. *—Stephen Thomas Erlewine*

Highlights From the Duke Ellington Centennial Edition, 1927-1973 / Oct. 26, 1927-Dec. 1973 / RCA ✦✦✦✦✦

Don Ellis

b. Jul. 25, 1934, Los Angeles, CA, **d.** Dec. 17, 1978, Hollywood, CA
Trumpet / Avant-Garde Jazz, Post-Bop
A talented trumpeter with a vivid musical imagination and the willingness to try new things, Don Ellis led some of the most colorful big bands of the 1965-75 period. He led four quartet and trio sessions during 1960-62 for Candid, New Jazz and Pacific Jazz, mixing together bop, free jazz and his interest in modern classical music. However it was in 1965 when he put together his first orchestra that Ellis really started to make an impression in jazz. His big bands were distinguished by their unusual instrumentation (which in its early days had up to three bassists and three drummers including Ellis himself), the leader's desire to investigate unusual time changes (including 7/8, 9/8 and even 15/16), its occasionally wacky humor (highlighted by an excess of false endings) and an openness towards using rock rhythms and (in later years) electronics. Ellis invented the four-valve trumpet and utilized a ring modulator and all types of wild electronic devices by the late '60s. *—Scott Yanow*

New Ideas / May 11, 1961 / New Jazz/OJC ✦✦✦✦
It seems strange that three out of four of Don Ellis' obscure small group sessions from the early 1960s are currently available on CD, while all of his famous big band albums for Pacific Jazz, Columbia and Atlantic are out of print. On this 1961 quintet set for Prestige (with vibraphonist Al Francis, pianist Jaki Byard, bassist Ron Carter and drummer Charlie Persip), Ellis experiments with time, new chord structures and free improvising; a highlight is his brief unaccompanied workout on the free form "Solo." Ellis, who switches to piano during part of "Tragedy," already had a sound of his own, although he would change the direction of his music within a few years. Even over 35 years later, his thoughtful musical experiments of the early 1960s are often quite fascinating to hear. *—Scott Yanow*

Live In 3 2/3 4 Time / Oct. 10, 1966+Mar. 27, 1967 / Pacific Jazz ✦✦✦✦✦
The Don Ellis Orchestra really came into its own during the period covered by this CD (1966-67), playing perfectly coherent solos in ridiculous time signatures. At the time the band consisted of five trumpets, three trombones, five reeds, piano, three basses, two drummers and three percussionists. "Barnum's Revenge" has the ensemble playing a satirical brand of dixieland in 5/4, "Orientation" goes back and forth between 7/8 and 9/8 and "Upstart" is in 11/8 (3 2/3 beats to the measure!). Somehow everything swings with Ellis, Ira Schulman (on tenor and clarinet), pianist Dave Mackay and Tom Scott (on saxello) being the main soloists. In addition to the original six selections (recorded at the Pacific Jazz Festival in 1966 and at Shelly's Manne-Hole in 1967), there are five additional cuts including an alternate version of "Freedom Jazz Dance." Fun music. *—Scott Yanow*

Electric Bath / Sep. 17, 1967-Sep. 20, 1967 / Columbia/Legacy ✦✦✦✦✦
For his first studio recording with his colorful big band, Don Ellis utilized five trumpets, three trombones, five reeds, Mike Lang on keyboards, three bassists, drummer Steve Bohannon and three percussionists to perform some remarkable new music. The most memorable selection is "Indian Lady" (accurately described as a "hoedown in 5/4") which with its false endings is often quite humorous. The other four originals (the trumpeter-leader's feature on "Alone," "Turkish Bath," "Open Beauty" and the 17/4 "New Horizons"), while lesser-known, are also quite spirited. For the first time Ellis opened his band to the influence of rock (making liberal use of electronics) and the results lend themselves to some hilarity. The 1998 CD reissue has the original five selections plus the brief single versions of "Turkish Bath" and "Indian Lady." Well worth searching for. *—Scott Yanow*

★ **Autumn** / Aug. 1968 / Tristar ✦✦✦✦✦
Don Ellis' Orchestra is heard at the peak of its powers on this out of print Columbia LP. "Pussy Wiggle Stomp," a variation on "My dad's better than your dad" but performed in 7/4 time, became the band's theme song, and it has its riotous moments. The 19-and-a-half minute, six-part "Variations for Trumpet" is a major showcase for Ellis, "Scratt and Fluggs" is a brief bit of silliness, and the relatively straightforward "K.C. Blues" features altoist Frank Strozier, John Klemmer on tenor, and keyboardist Pete Robinson. However it is the 17-and-a-half minute "Indian Lady" (a live remake) that really finds the band going crazy. Ellis, trombonist Glen Ferris, and keyboardist Robinson play humorous solos before tenors John Klemmer and Sam Falzone engage in a long and nutty tradeoff that is often quite hilarious. The many false endings at the end of this performance add to the general atmosphere. This is a classic release. *—Scott Yanow*

Don Ellis at Fillmore / 1970 / Columbia ✦✦✦✦✦
This is a crazy and consistently riotous two-LP set that features the Don Ellis Orchestra at its height. The 20-piece orchestra (which finds trumpeter Ellis doubling on drums and also utilizes a regular drummer and two percussionists) often used electronic devices (such as ring modulators) at the time to really distort their sound. When coupled with odd time signatures and such exuberant soloists as Ellis, trombonist Glen Ferris, tenor-saxophonist John Klemmer (showcased on the remarkable "Excursion II"), guitarist Jay Graydon, altoists Fred Selden and Lonnie Shetter, and tenor Sam Falzone, the results are quite memorable. Highlights of the date include "Final Analysis" (which contains a countless number of false endings), a bizarre rendition of "Hey Jude," and an often-hilarious remake of "Pussy Wiggle Stomp." *—Scott Yanow*

Herb Ellis (Mitchel Herbert Ellis)

b. Aug. 4, 1921, Farmersville, TX
Guitar / Swing, Bop
An excellent bop-based guitarist with a slight country twang to his sound, Herb Ellis became famous playing with the Oscar Peterson Trio during 1953-58. Prior to that he had attended North Texas State Unversity and played with the Casa Loma Orchestra, Jimmy Dorsey (1945-47) and the sadly under-recorded trio Soft Winds. While with Peterson, Ellis was on some Jazz at the Philharmonic tours and had a few opportunities to lead his own dates for Verve including his personal favorite, *Nothing but the Blues* (1957). After leaving Peterson, Ellis toured a bit with Ella Fitzgerald, became a studio musician on the West Coast, made sessions with the Dukes of Dixieland, Stuff Smith and Charlie Byrd and in the 1970s became much more active in the jazz world. He is on the first three Concord releases, interacting with Joe Pass on the initial two, and toured with the Great Guitars (along with Byrd and Barney Kessel) through much of the 1970s into the '80s. After a long series of Concord albums, Herb Ellis cut a couple of excellent sessions in the 1990s for Justice, as well as 1999's *Burnin'* on Acoustic Music. *—Scott Yanow*

★ **Nothing But the Blues** / Oct. 11, 1957-May 1, 1958 / Verve ✦✦✦✦✦
Guitarist Herb Ellis considers this is his favorite personal album and it is easy to see why. With trumpeter Roy Eldridge and tenor-saxophonist Stan Getz contributing contrasting but equally rewarding solos and lots of inspired riffing while bassist Ray Brown and drummer Stan Levey join Ellis in the pianoless rhythm section, these performances have plenty of color and drive. Ellis does indeed stick to the blues during the original eight selections yet there is also a surprising amount of variety. This CD reissue has been augmented by four numbers from 1958 originally recorded for a European soundtrack. Getz, Eldridge and Coleman Hawkins all have their features but Dizzy Gillespie fares best. *—Scott Yanow*

☆ **Herb Ellis Meets Jimmy Giuffre** / Mar. 1959 / Verve ✦✦✦✦✦

Together / Jan. 8, 1963 / Koch Jazz ✦✦✦✦✦
This Koch CD reissues an interesting and very successful matchup between guitarist Herb Ellis and the great swing violinist Stuff Smith. Pianist Lou Levy and Bob Enevoldsen (doubling on his cool-toned tenor and valve trombone) contribute some solos and drummer Shelly Manne adds fine support. The reissue (which has three alternate takes in addition to the original six-song program) features plenty of cooking and strong interplay between Stuff and Ellis on some blues, the ancient standard "How Come You Do Me Like You Do" (which has one of the violinist's two personable vocals) and Smith's two originals "Hillcrest" and "Skip It." This is one of Ellis' personal favorite records and one of the best recordings from Stuff Smith's later years. *—Scott Yanow*

Two for the Road / Jan. 30, 1974-Feb. 20, 1974 / Pablo/OJC ✦✦✦✦✦
This recording was the third and final matchup between guitarists Herb Ellis and Joe Pass and, unlike the first two (which were both made for Concord), this is a duo date rather than a quartet session. Pass was just beginning to gain recognition for his remarkable unaccompanied solos but Ellis had not recorded in this sparse a setting before. They complement each other quite well on such tunes as "Love for Sale," "Seven Come Eleven," "Lady Be Good," "I've Found a New Baby" and two versions of "Cherokee." Highly recommended. *—Scott Yanow*

Soft Shoe / Aug. 1974 / Concord Jazz ✦✦✦✦✦
This early Concord recording (which is available on CD) is unusual in a couple of ways. Guitarist Herb Ellis and bassist Ray Brown (who are the co-leaders) are joined not only by trumpeter Harry "Sweets" Edison (who is in colorful form) and drummer Jake Hanna but pianist George Duke in one of his very few mainstream records. Their repertoire includes jazz versions of such unlikely tunes as "Inka-Dinka-Doo," "Easter Parade" and "The Flintstones Theme"; the latter version (which is based on the familiar "I Got Rhythm" chord changes) was the first of many to turn that cartoon melody into jazz. In addition Brown ("Soft Shoe"), Edison and Ellis contribute a song apiece plus there is a brief rendition of "Green Dolphin Street" that is taken as a Brown-Ellis duet. Recommended. *—Scott Yanow*

Gravy Waltz: Best Of Herb Ellis / Oct. 19, 1999 / Euphoria/Sundazed ✦✦✦✦
Ellis struts his stuff on this nicely compiled 16-track collection taken from his tenure at Epic and Columbia Records. In addition to two duets with guitarist Charlie Byrd, Herb trades licks with Roy Eldridge, Andre Previn, Stuff Smith, and Laurindo Almeida on various cuts. To put the icing on the cake, there's the inclusion of six previously unreleased tracks, including a nice reading of "You Came a Long Way From St. Louis." While any best-of collection is open to debate, this one gives a nice introduction to Herb's style and would make an excellent introductory purchase. *—Cub Koda*

Booker Ervin

b. Oct. 31, 1930, Denison, TX, **d.** Jul. 31, 1970, New York, NY
Sax (Tenor) / Avant-Garde Jazz, Hard Bop, Post-Bop
A very distinctive tenor with a hard passionate tone and an emotional style that was still tied to chordal improvisation, Booker Ervin was a true original. He was originally a trombonist but taught himself tenor while in the Air Force (1950-53). After studying music in Boston for two years, he made his recording debut with Ernie Fields's R&B band (1956). Ervin gained fame while playing with Charles Mingus (off and on during 1956-62), holding his own with the volatile bassist and Eric Dolphy. He also led his own quartet, worked with Randy Weston

on a few occasions in the '60s and spent much of 1964-66 in Europe before dying much too young from kidney disease. Ervin, who is on several notable Charles Mingus records, made dates of his own for Bethlehem, Savoy and Candid during 1960-61, along with later sets for Pacific Jazz and Blue Note, but it his nine Prestige sessions of 1963-66 (including *The Freedom Book, The Song Book, The Blues Book* and *The Space Book*) that are among the high-points of his career. *—Scott Yanow*

Cookin' / Nov. 26, 1960 / Savoy Jazz ✦✦✦✦✦

Back from the Gig / Feb. 15, 1963+Jun. 24, 1968 / Blue Note ✦✦✦✦✦
This two-LP set consists of a pair of classic Blue Note sets that were not originally released until 1976. The great tenor Booker Ervin (whose hard passionate sound was always immediately recognizable) is well-showcased with the Horace Parlan Sextet in 1963 (a group also featuring pianist Parlan, trumpeter Johnny Coles and guitarist Grant Green) and with his own all-star quintet from 1968 (which also stars trumpeter Woody Shaw and pianist Kenny Barron). The stimulating group originals and advanced solos (which fall somewhere between hard bop and the avant-garde) still sound fresh and frequently exciting. *—Scott Yanow*

Exultation! / Jun. 19, 1963 / Prestige/OJC ✦✦✦✦
Booker Ervin's debut for Prestige (which has been reissued on CD with two shorter alternate takes added) matches the intense tenor with altoist Frank Strozier, pianist Horace Parlan, bassist Butch Warren and drummer Walter Perkins for some bop-based music that is actually quite adventurous. Highlights include "Mour" (based on "Four"), "Black and Blue" and Ervin's "Mooche Mooche." Ervin and Strozier made a mutually inspiring team; pity that this was their only recording together. *—Scott Yanow*

Freedom Book / Dec. 3, 1963 / Prestige/OJC ✦✦✦✦✦
One of the finest groups that tenor saxophonist Booker Ervin ever led was the quartet that recorded *The Freedom Book* and ten months later *The Space Book.* The trio of pianist Jaki Byard, bassist Richard Davis and drummer Alan Dawson really could not be improved upon but unfortunately this band only existed in the recording studios on an irregular basis. For this CD reissue, Ervin performs four of his obscure but worthy originals plus Randy Weston's "Cry Me Not." Although the music is not as "free" as the title might hint, the music does take advantage of the recent innovations and is a couple steps beyond hard bop. These are stimulating performances which, as with the other entries in the *Book* series that were to come (*The Song Book, Blues Book* and *Space Book*), is heartily recommended. *—Scott Yanow*

Groovin' High / Dec. 3, 1963-Oct. 2, 1964 / Prestige/OJC ✦✦✦✦✦
This CD reissue has four selections from the same sessions (but not released on the original sets) that resulted in *The Freedom Book, The Blues Book* and *The Space Book.* "Groovin' High" features the intense tenor of Booker Ervin playing comparatively lighthearted bebop in a quintet with trumpeter Carmell Jones, pianist Gildo Mahones, bassist Richard Davis and drummer Alan Dawson. The other numbers ("The Second *2,*" "Bass-IX" and a brief "Stella By Starlight") match Ervin with the unbeatable trio of pianist Jaki Byard, Davis and Dawson. Although these performances are not quite classic, Booker Ervin fans will want this CD to round out their collection, for Ervin was at the peak of his powers during this era. *—Scott Yanow*

The Song Book / Feb. 27, 1964 / Prestige/OJC ✦✦✦✦
The second in tenor saxophonist Booker Ervin's *Book* series, this CD reissue may seem a bit more conservative than the others due to the inclusion of six standards (including "Come Sunday," "All the Things You Are" and "Just Friends"), but Ervin and his quartet (with pianist Tommy Flanagan, bassist Richard Davis and drummer Alan Dawson) come up with fresh interpretations of the warhorses. Booker Ervin never sounded like anyone else. *—Scott Yanow*

● **The Blues Book** / Jun. 30, 1964 / Prestige/OJC ✦✦✦✦✦
For this CD reissue in his series of *Books,* Ervin and his quintet (with trumpeter Carmell Jones, pianist Gildo Mahones, bassist Richard Davis and drummer Alan Dawson) perform four very different blues: the speedy "One for Mort," a lowdown "No Booze Blooze," the modal "True Blue" and the minor-toned "Eerie Dearie." The consistently passionate Ervin makes each of the fairly basic originals sound fresh and the performances are frequently exciting inside/outside music. *—Scott Yanow*

Space Book / Oct. 2, 1964 / Prestige/OJC ✦✦✦✦✦
Tenor saxophonist Booker Ervin's quartet with pianist Jaki Byard, bassist Richard Davis and drummer Alan Dawson was so strong and dynamic that it is surprising that it only existed in the recording studio, and only for two sessions. For the fourth and final of Ervin's series of *Books,* the music is indeed somewhat spacey. The group explores two standards ("I Can't Get Started" and "There Is No Greater Love") along with a pair of Ervin originals (the intense "Number Two" and "Mojo"), stretching the boundaries of hard bop without totally abandoning the chord changes. This CD is a fine example of Booker Ervin's unique style. *—Scott Yanow*

Settin' the Pace / Oct. 27, 1965 / Prestige ✦✦✦✦✦
This CD reissue has the complete contents of two former LPs, both recorded at the same session. With very stimulating playing by pianist Jaki Byard, bassist Reggie Workman and drummer Alan Dawson, tenors Booker Ervin and Dexter Gordon battle it out on marathon (19 and 22 1/2 minute) versions of "Setting the Pace" and "Dexter's Deck." Although Gordon is in good form, Ervin (who sometimes takes the music outside) wins honors. The other two selections ("The Trance" and "Speak Low") are by the same group without Dexter, and these long (19 1/2- and 15-minute) showcases also find Booker in top form, sounding quite distinctive and completely original playing inside/outside music. An exciting set. *—Scott Yanow*

The In Between / Jan. 12, 1968 / Blue Note ✦✦✦✦
Booker Ervin headed to Blue Note in 1968 for *The In Between,* a record that found him continuing in the vein of his later Prestige sessions. Supported by trumpeter Richard Williams, pianist Bobby Few, bassist Cevera Jeffries and drummer Lennie McBrowne, Ervin created an album that pushed the boundaries of hard bop. Every song on *The In Between* is an Ervin original designed to challenge the musicians. The music rarely reaches avant-garde territory—instead, it's edgy, volatile hard bop that comes from the mind as much as the soul. Appropriately, Ervin balances his full-bodied tone with a forceful, aggressive attack that even sounds restless on the slower numbers. The result is a satisfying, cerebral set of adventurous hard bop that finds Booker Ervin at a creative peak. *—Stephen Thomas Erlewine*

Gumbo / Jan. 31, 1963-Jun. 27, 1963 / Prestige ✦✦✦✦
Tenor saxophonist Booker Ervin joined alto and soprano saxophonist Pony Poindexter in 1963 on *Gumbo,* based around the sights and sounds of Poindexter's birthplace, the Crescent City. Poindexter penned the majority of these compositions, providing them with evocative titles of the city: "Creole Girl," "French Market," and "Gumbo Filet." *Gumbo* finds Ervin playing more straight-ahead than on his exploratory "Book" sessions, which he had begun recording under his name by this time. The rhythm section on the first 12 cuts include Gildo Mahones on piano, George Tucker on bass, and Jimmie Smith on drums, with trombonist Al Grey making an appearance on four tracks. The remaining four tunes tacked on the CD's conclusion were recorded in January and February 1964, featuring the trio of Ervin, Jerry Thomas on drums, and Larry Young's distinctive Hammond organ virtuosity. "You Don't Know What Love Is" (two takes), "Autumn Leaves," and "Old Folks" had remained unreleased until the appearance of this CD in 1999. *—Al Campbell*

Ellery Eskelin

b. Baltimore, MD
Sax (Tenor) / Avant-Garde Jazz, Modern Creative
Tenor saxophonist Ellery Eskelin was born in Wichita, Kansas in 1959. He was raised in a musical home in Baltimore, Maryland by his mother, 'Bobbie Lee, ' who played Hammond B-3 organ and led her own jazz groups during the '60s. Eskelin began playing the tenor saxophone when he was 10 years old and knew immediately that he wanted to be a jazz player. He began working professionally while still in high school, and in 1973, began attending annual week-long summer residences with the Stan Kenton Orchestra at Towson State University, where he later ('77 to '81) was a student. In 1983, Eskelin moved to NYC to study and play, and it was here that he first really listened to music by his father Rodd Keith, who worked in the song-poem industry during the '60s and '70s. Although Keith became a sort of cult figure due to his music, Eskelin was not as musically influenced by his father since he did not hear his music until this later date. Four years later, Eskelin appears on his first recording, *Joint Venture* with Drew Gress and Paul Smoker, released by the Enja label. Over the years, Eskelin has developed a strong individual approach, combining jazz roots with "various concepts of independence and role changing in an attempt to play freely, " while still paying attention to harmony, time and form. In 1994, he formed a trio with Andrea Parkins and Jim Black which has released structurally tight and enjoyable albums, mostly on the Hatology label. By 1999, Eskelin had released 10 albums as a leader, and appeared as a sideman on over 20 other releases. *—Joslyn Layne*

Jazz Trash / Oct. 27, 1994-Oct. 28, 1994 / Songlines ✦✦✦✦
Tenor saxophonist Ellery Eskelin's music is characterized by a uniquely zany American sensibility, and this recording is no exception. *Jazz Trash* is one of his earlier efforts with collaborators Andrea Parkins and Jim Black. Parkins is stunning on accordion and sampler, where she can simulate the sounds of an organ or simply project deliciously disjointed lines. Black is one of the most underrated performers on the scene, with his eclectic, propelling percussion holding down the fort. These three make an unbeatable trio, easily able to sustain interest for 70 minutes of recording time. The nine tracks explore different aspects of their playing, ranging from very subtle, luxurious textures to wildly frenetic offerings. Since this recording, the trio has continued to produce some striking CDs, but this early effort clearly sets the pace. *—Steve Loewy*

● **Kulak, 29 & 30** / Oct. 29, 1997+Oct. 30, 1997 / hatHUT ✦✦✦✦✦

Dissonant Characters / Dec. 11, 1998+Dec. 12, 1998 / hatHUT ✦✦✦✦✦

Bill Evans

b. Aug. 16, 1929, Plainfield, NJ, **d.** Sep. 15, 1980, New York, NY
Piano / Modal Music, Post-Bop, Cool
Bill Evans was (along with McCoy Tyner) the most influential pianist in jazz during the 1960s and '70s, and since his death in 1980 his influence has exceeded Tyner's. Evans, who was the next step beyond Bud Powell, had a sophisticated way of voicing chords that has been adopted by a countless number of pianists. Very popular even among nonjazz audiences to his sensitive interpretations of ballads, Evans could always swing as hard as anyone when he was inspired.

After attending Southewestern Louisiana University, working with Mundell Lowe and Red Mitchell and serving in the Army, Evans first emerged on the New York scene playing with Tony Scott in 1956 and that year he made his first trio album, *New Jazz Conceptions.* After working with George Russell and recording with Charles Mingus, Evans was part of the 1958 Miles Davis Sextet with John Coltrane and Cannonball Adderley. Other than a few live dates and "So What" from the 1959 classic *Kind of Blue,* Evans did not record all that much during his months with Davis but he made a strong impact and contributed one future standardm, "Blue in Green, " which ranks with "Waltz for Debby" as his most famous original. By 1959 Bill Evans was leading his own trio which soon utilized the great bassist Scott LaFaro and drummer Paul Motian. The interplay between the three musicians (with an almost equal role by each of the players) was highly influential and nearly telepathic. Tragically, shortly after they recorded extensively at the Village Vanguard in June 1961, LaFaro was killed in a car accident. Evans went into isolation for the remainder of the year. In 1962 he re-emerged with Chuck Israels as his new bassist and recorded the first of two classic albums in duet with guitarist Jim Hall. In future years Evans would continue touring and recording with his trio which included such sideman as bassists Israels (1962-65), Gary Peacock (1963), Eddie Gomez (1966-77) and Marc Johnson (1978-80) and drummers Motian (1959-62), Larry Bunker (1963-5), Philly Joe Jones (1967), Jack DeJohnette (1968), Marty Morell (1969-75), Eliot Zigmund (1975-78) and Joe LaBarbera (1979-80). Drug addiction cut short Bill Evans' life prematurely but he fortunately had recorded extensively from 1956 on, most notably for Riverside, Verve, Fantasy and Warner Bros. Several videos are also available of this major force in modern jazz whose innovations helped form the styles of Herbie Hancock and Keith Jarrett. *—Scott Yanow*

New Jazz Conceptions / Sep. 18, 1956-Sep. 27, 1956 / Riverside/OJC ♦♦♦♦
Bill Evans' debut as a leader found the 27-year old pianist already sounding much different than the usual Bud Powell-influenced keyboardists of the time. Even in 1956 (more than a year before he joined Miles Davis' Sextet), Evans had his own chord voicings and a lyrical yet swinging style. Three selections (including the original version of his classic "Waltz for Debby") on this CD reissue are taken solo while the other nine (including his future theme "Five," "Speak Low" and two versions of "No Cover, No Minimum") are performed in a trio with bassist Teddy Kotick and drummer Paul Motian. A strong start to a rather significant career. *—Scott Yanow*

☆ **The Complete Riverside Recordings (1956-63)** / 1956-1963 / Riverside ♦♦♦♦♦
This magnificent 12-CD set contains all of Bill Evans' Riverside recordings as a leader, an extremely important period in the influential pianist's development. The first session predates Evans' period with the Miles Davis Sextet and other significant sessions include his sets with bassist Scott LaFaro and drummer Paul Motian (highlighted by the marathon Village Vanguard session of June 25, 1961), Evans' return nearly a year after LaFaro's death in a car accident with a new trio (consisting of Motian and bassist Chuck Israels), a sideman set with altoist Cannonball Adderley, the *Interplay* sessions with either trumpeter Freddie Hubbard or tenor saxophonist Zoot Sims, an extensive and rather somber solo set and a 1963 appearance at Shelly's Manne Hole with bassist Israels and drummer Larry Bunker. Twenty sessions are released in full, 151 selections in all including 24 performances that had been previously unissued at the time. Fortunately for listeners with a budget, nearly all of this material has since been reissued on single CDs (mostly as part of the Original Jazz Classics series) but true Bill Evans fanatics will have to get this remarkable box. *—Scott Yanow*

Everybody Digs Bill Evans / Dec. 15, 1958 / Riverside/OJC ♦♦♦♦
Bill Evans' second album as a leader was made shortly after he left Miles Davis' group. Evans, whose style was already fully formed, performs seven songs in a trio with bassist Paul Chambers and drummer Philly Joe Jones, really digging in for most of the songs and playing with a stronger aggression than usual; highlights include "Minority," "Night and Day" and "Oleo." However it is his three piano solos, particularly the brilliant "Peace Piece," that are most memorable. *—Scott Yanow*

Undercurrent / Apr. 24, 1962-May 14, 1962 / Blue Note ♦♦♦♦
Other than four piano solos from April 4, 1962, this set was pianist Bill Evans' first recordings after a hiatus caused by bassist Scott LaFaro's tragic death in a car accident. The first of two meetings on record in a duo format with guitarist Jim Hall, the collaborations are often exquisite. Both Evans and Hall had introspective and harmonically advanced styles along with roots in hard-swinging bebop. The six selections on the original LP have been expanded to ten for this CD reissue with the inclusion of two alternate takes and previously unheard versions of "Stairway to the Stars" and "I'm Getting Sentimental over You." There is more variety than expected on the fine set with some cookers, ballads, waltzes and even some hints at classical music. Recommended. *—Scott Yanow*

Portrait in Jazz / Dec. 28, 1959 / Riverside/OJC ♦♦♦♦♦
The first of two studio albums by the Bill Evans-Scott LaFaro-Paul Motian trio (both of which preceded their famous engagement at the Village Vanguard), this CD reissue contains some wondrous interplay, particularly between pianist Evans and bassist LaFaro on the two versions of "Autumn Leaves." Other than introducing Evans' "Peri's Scope," the music is comprised of standards but the influential interpretations were far from routine or predictable at the time. LaFaro and Motian were nearly equal partners with the pianist in the ensembles and their versions of such tunes as "Come Rain or Come Shine," "When I Fall in Love" and "Someday My Prince Will Come" (which preceded Miles Davis' famous recording by a couple years) are full of subtle and surprising creativity. A gem. *—Scott Yanow*

Explorations / Feb. 2, 1961 / Riverside/OJC ♦♦♦♦♦
The second and final studio recording by pianist Bill Evans with bassist Scott LaFaro and drummer Paul Motian is nearly the equal of the earlier *Portrait in Jazz.* LaFaro was borrowing a bass for the date while his regular instrument was being repaired and, since it apparently sounded better in its lower register than its higher one, he tends to emphasize lower notes than usual. No matter, the interplay between the musicians once again is consistently magical, uplifting such tunes as Miles Davis' "Nardis," "Israel," "How Deep Is the Ocean" and two versions of "Beautiful Love." *—Scott Yanow*

★ **Sunday at the Village Vanguard** / Jun. 25, 1961 / Riverside/OJC ♦♦♦♦♦
Sunday at the Village Vanguard (and *Waltz for Derby,* its companion album) is one of the most important piano trio albums in history and a desert-island choice among many musicians. It marks the final appearance of bassist Scott LaFaro with Evans and drummer Paul Motian. LaFaro demonstrated a concept of jazz bass playing here that shattered traditional limits to how interactive and contrapuntal a bass line could be without totally abandoning its supportive function. He also soloed with unparalleled imagination and technical facility. The album also showed how Evans had refined an approach to solo improvisation in which the pulse was not as obvious as it had been in swing and bop approaches. And his extraordinarily high standards required that each improvised melodic idea be extensively developed, resulting in more continuity and pacing than was common to any previous modern style. The influence of what LaFaro and Evans laid out here was still being felt in the 1990s. *—Mark C. Gridley*

☆ **Waltz for Debby** / Jun. 25, 1961 / Riverside/OJC ♦♦♦♦♦
The companion to *Sunday at the Village Vanguard* (the two CD reissues bring back nearly the entire night's music), this set features pianist Bill Evans, bassist Scott LaFaro (only ten days before his death in a car accident) and drummer Paul Motian stretching the boundaries of piano trio playing. Each of the musicians have a nearly equal role (although Evans is generally the lead voice among equals) and they consistently inspire each other. There are seven selections on this disc plus three alternate takes and the highlights include the two versions of Evans' most famous original "Waltz for Debby," a touching interpretation of "My Foolish Heart," "Some Other Time" and "Milestones." Highly recommended. *—Scott Yanow*

How My Heart Sings! / May 17, 1962-Jun. 5, 1962 / Riverside/OJC ♦♦♦♦
When pianist Bill Evans returned to the active jazz scene in 1962 after taking time off due to bassist Scott LaFaro's death in a car accident, he was persuaded by producer Orrin Keepnews to record two projects: a ballad album and a set of more uptempo tunes. This CD reissue contains the latter. Evans has a reunion with drummer Paul Motian and, with the fine bassist Chuck Israels in LaFaro's place, performs such numbers as "How My Heart Sings," "34 Skidoo," "Show-Type Tune" and two versions of "In Your Own Sweet Way." *—Scott Yanow*

Moonbeams / May 17, 1962-Jun. 5, 1962 / Riverside/OJC ♦♦♦

Interplay Sessions / Jul. 16, 1962-Aug. 22, 1962 / Riverside/OJC ♦♦♦♦
Although pianist Bill Evans had been recording as a leader steadily since 1959 (with one date in 1956), the two albums included in this two-LP set were his first to use horns. The earlier date features Evans with trumpeter Freddie Hubbard, guitarist Jim Hall, bassist Percy Heath, and drummer Philly Joe Jones performing five veteran standards plus the pianist's blues "Interplay." While that session (highlighted by "You and the Night and the Music" and "Wrap Your Troubles in Dreams") came together pretty smoothly, the follow-up album, an outing with tenor saxophonist Zoot Sims, Hall, bassist Ron Carter, and Jones, had so many problems that it was not released at the time. Evans had the under-rehearsed group play seven of his recent originals, but the date was soon forgotten and lost in the vaults. When this 1982 two-fer was prepared, the "Loose Bloose" set was rediscovered and found to be better than expected; in fact, because four of the songs were never again recorded by Evans, its historic value is also quite strong. Both of these "Evans with horn quintets" have fortunately been reissued on CD. *—Scott Yanow*

Conversations with Myself / Jan. 1963-Feb. 1963 / Verve ♦♦♦♦♦
A classic of its kind, for this Verve project Bill Evans recorded three piano parts via overdubbing. Accurately-titled, the music on the CD reissue has a surprising amount of spontaneity with Evans constantly reacting to what he had just recorded, and the results are sometimes haunting. The highlights include "How About You," "The Love Theme from 'Spartacus'," "Blue Monk" and "Just You Just Me." *—Scott Yanow*

Bill Evans Trio at Shelly's Manne-Hole / May 30, 1963+May 31, 1963 / Riverside/OJC ♦♦♦♦
Pianist Bill Evans' final Riverside album, a live set with bassist Chuck Israels and drummer Larry Bunker, is reissued on this CD which also contains a previously unreleased version of "All the Things You Are." An earlier two-LP set (*Time Remembered*) actually has 16 tunes from the engagement (as opposed to nine on the CD) but will be hard to locate. After a year of steady work, the underrated Evans-Israels-Bunker Trio was in top form for an enjoyable, swinging and sensitive outing with highlights including "Isn't It Romantic," "The Boy Next Door," "'Round Midnight" and "Blues in F." *—Scott Yanow*

Trio '64 / Dec. 18, 1963 / Verve ♦♦♦♦
For this Bill Evans session (reissued on CD), bassist Gary Peacock was temporarily in Chuck Israels' place and drummer Paul Motian had returned, filling in for Larry Bunker. The pianist's playing is typically excellent and he sounds inspired by Peacock's presence; the bassist was normally associated around the period with Paul Bley. In addition to a cartoon theme ("Little Lulu"), the group sticks to standards although there are a couple of unusual choices: Noel Coward's "I'll See You Again" and an effective interpretation of "Santa Claus Is Coming to Town." Although not a major release overall, this fine outing is certainly not without interest and should please Bill Evans' fans. *—Scott Yanow*

Trio '65 / Feb. 3, 1965 / Verve ♦♦♦♦
Although all eight of the selections heard on this Verve release have been recorded on other occasions by pianist Bill Evans, these renditions hold their own. Teamed up with bassist Chuck Israels and drummer Larry Bunker (his regular trio of 1963-65), Evans plays definitive versions of such songs as Johnny Carisi's "Israel," "How My Heart Sings," "Who Can I Turn To" and "If You Could See Me Now." *—Scott Yanow*

Bill Evans at Town Hall / Feb. 21, 1966 / Verve ♦♦♦♦
This CD (which adds three songs including a previously unreleased version of "One for Helen" to the original LP program) is a superior effort by Bill Evans and his trio in early 1966. The last recording by longtime bassist Chuck Israels (who had joined the Trio in 1962) with Evans (the tastefully supportive drummer Arnold Wise completes the group), this live set features the group mostly performing lyrical and thoughtful standards; highlights include "I Should Care," "Who Can I Turn To" and "My Foolish Heart." However the most memorable piece is the 13-minute "Solo—In Memory of His Father," an extensive unaccompanied exploration by Evans that partly uses a theme that became "Turn Out the Stars." *—Scott Yanow*

Intermodulation / Apr. 7, 1966-May 10, 1966 / Verve ♦♦♦

Bill Evans at the Montreux Jazz Festival / Jun. 15, 1968 / Verve ♦♦♦♦
Bill Evans, with bassist Eddie Gomez and his drummer of the period Jack DeJohnette (just prior to him joining Miles Davis), is in excellent form on this well-rounded CD reissue. Evans performs two of his originals (including "One for Helen" which was dedicated to his longtime manager Helen Keane), Denny Zeitlin's "Quiet Now," Earl Zindars' "Mother of Earl" and a few of his favorite standards, tunes that are generally ballads and harmonically rich. The interplay between Evans and Gomez was growing month-by-month (the bassist had been with him for almost two years at this point) and is the main reason to acquire this disc although DeJohnette does offer some stimulating support. *—Scott Yanow*

Bill Evans Album / May 11, 1971-Jun. 9, 1971 / Columbia/Legacy ♦♦♦♦
On this CD reissue (which adds three "new" alternate takes to the original seven song-program), Bill Evans made his debut on electric piano, usually playing it in conjunction with his acoustic piano. Joined by bassist Eddie Gomez and drummer Marty Morell, Evans per-

forms seven of his stronger originals including "Funkallero," "The Two Lonely People," "Re: Person I Knew," "T.T.T." and "Waltz for Debby." Although not as distinctive on the electric keyboard as he was on the acoustic counterpart, Evans sounds inspired by its possibilities and is heard in top creative form throughout the date. *—Scott Yanow*

☆ **The Complete Fantasy Recordings** / Jan. 20, 1973-Nov. 6, 1978 / Fantasy ✦✦✦✦✦
Bill Evans' Fantasy recordings of 1973-79 have often been underrated in favor of his earlier work but, as this remarkable nine-CD set continually shows, the influential pianist continued to grow as a musician through the years while holding on to his original conception and distinctive sound. The collection has all of the 98 selections recorded at Evans' 11 Fantasy sessions including nine numbers from a previously unreleased 1976 concert with his trio. In addition, Evans' appearance on Marian McPartland's *Piano Jazz* radio program is tacked on as a bonus and it is actually among McPartland's finest shows, a fascinating hour of discussion and music with Evans. Nearly all of the performances on this box (which includes duets with bassist Eddie Gomez and singer Tony Bennett, trio outings with Gomez and either Marty Morell or Eliot Zigmund on drums, and a couple of quintet sets with the likes of tenors Harold Land and Warne Marsh, altoist Lee Konitz, guitarist Kenny Burrell, bassist Ray Brown and drummer Philly Joe Jones) is available individually on CD but Bill Evans' more passionate collectors will certainly want this definitive box. The only minus is Gene Lees' typically self-serving liner notes; he always seems to love to write about himself. *—Scott Yanow*

But Beautiful / Aug. 9, 1974+Aug. 16, 1974 / Milestone ✦✦✦✦✦
Pianist Bill Evans and tenor-saxophonist Stan Getz only recorded in the studio together on one occasion, making these previously unreleased concert performances (issued for the first time in 1996) quite valuable. Evans (due to a misunderstanding) sits out on much of "Stan's Blues," and there are two trio features without the tenor but otherwise the other seven numbers match Getz with Evans, bassist Eddie Gomez, and drummer Marty Morell. Although released under the pianist's name, this CD is very much Stan Getz's show and his beautiful tone sounds quite exquisite on "But Beautiful," "Emily," "The Peacocks," and the swinging "You and the Night and the Music." This historic and somewhat unique release has many enjoyable moments. *—Scott Yanow*

Intuition / Nov. 7, 1974-Nov. 8, 1974 / Fantasy/OJC ✦✦✦✦
After having played together on a regular basis for eight years, it is not surprising that this set of duets by pianist Bill Evans and bassist Eddie Gomez are intuitive and bordering on the telepathic. The material is quite fresh. Evans might have recorded "Invitation" and "Show-Type Tune" previously but the other six songs were getting their debut in his hands. Whether it be "Hi Lili, Hi Lo," Claus Ogerman's "A Face Without a Name," Steve Swallow's "Falling Grace" or "Blue Serge," the sensitive and generally introspective playing on this CD reissue definitely holds one's interest. *—Scott Yanow*

The Tony Bennett/Bill Evans Album / Jun. 10, 1975-Jun. 13, 1975 / Fantasy/OJC ✦✦✦✦

Cross-Currents / Feb. 28, 1977-Mar. 2, 1977 / Fantasy/OJC ✦✦✦✦✦
This superior set was a logical idea. One of pianist Bill Evans' earlier influences was Lennie Tristano so on the date Evans' trio (with bassist Eddie Gomez and drummer Eliot Zigmund) was teamed with Tristano's two top "students": altoist Lee Konitz and tenor saxophonist Warne Marsh. The quintet performs four standards (all of which fit easily into Evans' repertoire) plus "Pensativa" and Steve Swallow's "Eiderdown." Konitz and Marsh always worked very well together and their cool-toned improvising makes this outing by Bill Evans something special. The CD reissue adds three alternate takes to the original program. Recommended. *—Scott Yanow*

You Must Believe in Spring / Aug. 23, 1977-Aug. 25, 1977 / Warner Brothers ✦✦✦✦

I Will Say Goodbye / May 11, 1979-May 13, 1979 / Fantasy/OJC ✦✦✦✦

Turn Out the Stars: Final Village Vanguard Recordings / Jun. 4, 1980-Jun. 8, 1980 / Warner Brothers ✦✦✦✦
Just three months before his death, pianist BIll Evans was extensively recorded at the Village Vanguard. Originally, one or two LPs were to be released featuring his brilliant new trio (with bassist Marc Johnson and drummer Joe LaBarbera), but after the innovative pianist's death, the project was stalled for over 15 years. Finally, when Warner Bros. got around to it, a definitive six-CD box set was released (although unfortunately in limited-edition form). Evans sounded quite energized during his last year, Johnson was developing quickly as both an accompanist and a soloist, and the interplay by the trio members (with subtle support from LaBarbera) sometimes bordered on the telepathic. The playing throughout these consistently inventive performances ranks up there with the Evans-Scott LaFaro-Paul Motian trio of 20 years earlier. *—Scott Yanow*

The Complete Bill Evans on Verve / Aug. 20, 1962-May 27, 1970 / Verve ✦✦✦✦✦
While its sheer bulk negates its interest to a general audience, *The Complete Bill Evans on Verve* is an essential library piece for any serious jazz fan or historian. Spanning 18 CDs, 269 tracks and 21 hours, the box set includes all of Evans' recordings for the label between 1962 and 1969, including 19 albums, two previously unreleased albums and 98 previously unreleased tracks. During these years, the pianist made some of his greatest music, including his legendary Village Vanguard sessions, and the set charts all of his changes, as he plays with his trio and as a solo artist, as well as a rare session with a rhythm quartet and strings. While the set itself could be a little more user-friendly—it's encased in a steel box, with a 160-page booklet and an 18-disc fanpack on separate shelves—the music itself is nearly flawless and nearly essential for most serious jazz fans. *—Leo Stanley*

Piano Player / Jun. 10, 1957-May 17, 1971 / Columbia/Legacy ✦✦✦✦
Although this 1998 CD may at first glance seem to be a reissue, all but three of the 11 selections had never been released before. The highly influential pianist Bill Evans is heard in five different settings. An unissued (and slightly earlier rendition) of the third section of George Russell's "All About Rosie" (a showcase for Evans with Russell's 14-piece orchestra) starts off the release. Next are the three previously issued but somewhat obscure numbers: a live rendition of "My Funny Valentine" with Miles Davis in 1958 (played by just a quartet) and two songs from a 1962 set headed by vibraphonist Dave Pike. Producer Orrin Keepnews discovered and released here six long-lost selections from 1970, duets by Evans (who also plays a little bit of electric piano) and bassist Eddie Gomez that are strong enough to make one wonder why the projects was originally abandoned. Wrapping up the intriguing set is a trio number (with Evans, Gomez and drummer Marty Morell) that is an alternate take left over from *The Bill Evans Album*. The pianist's fans will definitely want this consistently enjoyable CD. *—Scott Yanow*

The Last Waltz / Oct. 10, 2000 / Milestone ✦✦✦✦✦
A moving finale to a remarkable career, *The Last Waltz* was recorded during a nine-night stand at San Francisco's legendary *Keystone Korner* one week prior to jazz piano icon Bill Evans' death at age 51. With the youthful rhythm team of Marc Johnson and Joe LaBarbera providing telepathic support, Evans turns in some of the most magnificent performances of his 25-year career. Aware that his days were numbered, he played with the creative drive and improvisational intensity with which he had long ago made his mark.

This eight-disc set's 65 tracks include takes on 32 different tunes of which nine are Evans originals. Revisiting, reworking, and revitalizing many of his signature pieces, he finds new dimensions to explore in each. The set lists range from standards like "My Foolish Heart," "If You Could See Me Now," "Autumn Leaves," and "Polka Dots and Moonbeams" to the pianist's own classics, "Turn Out the Stars," "Letter to Evan," and "Waltz for Debby." The lengthy solo piano introductions to six different renderings of Miles Davis' "Nardis" are breathtaking in their beauty.

This is simply gorgeous music, powerful and moving, a fitting farewell from one of the finest. *—Jim Newsom*

Gil Evans (Ian Ernest Gilmore Green)

b. May 13, 1912, Toronto, Ontario, Canada, **d.** Mar. 20, 1988, Cuernavaca, Mexico
Piano, Composer, Arranger / Modern Big Band, Post-Bop, Fusion, Cool, Progressive Big Band
One of the most significant arrangers in jazz history, Gil Evans' three album-length collaborations with Miles Davis (*Miles Ahead, Porgy and Bess* and *Sketches of Spain*) are all considered classics. Evans had a lengthy and wide-ranging career that sometimes ran parallel to the trumpeter. Like Davis, Evans became involved in utilizing electronics in the 1970s and preferred not to look back and recreate the past. He first gained recognition for his somewhat futuristic charts for Claude Thornhill's Orchestra during the '40s, and after meeting Miles Davis, contributed arrangements to Davis' "Birth of the Cool" nonet. Evans collaborated with Davis again in 1957 for *Miles Ahead*. In addition to his work with Miles (which also included a 1961 Carnegie Hall concert and the half-album *Quiet Nights*), he recorded several superb and highly original sets as a leader (including *Gil Evans and Ten, New Bottle Old Wine* and *Great Jazz Standards*) during the era. After his own sessions for Verve during 1963-64, Evans waited until 1969 to record again as a leader; *Blues in Orbit* was his first successful effort at combining acoustic and electric instruments. It was followed by dates for Artists House, Atlantic (*Svengali*) and a notable tribute to Jimi Hendrix in 1974. He began playing with a large ensemble on a weekly basis in New York clubs, and most of Evans' recordings were taken from live performances. *—Scott Yanow*

★ **Gil Evans and Ten** / Sep. 6, 1957-Oct. 10, 1957 / Prestige/OJC ✦✦✦✦✦
Although arranger Gil Evans had been active in the major leagues of jazz ever since the mid-'40s and had participated in Miles Davis's famous *Birth of the Cool* recordings, this set was his first opportunity to record as a leader. The CD reissue features a typically unusual 11-piece unit consisting of two trumpets, trombonist Jimmy Cleveland, Bert Varsalona on bass trombone, French horn player Willie Ruff, Steve Lacy on soprano, altoist Lee Konitz, Dave Kurtzer on bassoon, bassist Paul Chambers and either Nick Stabulas or Jo Jones on drums, plus the leader's sparse piano. As good an introduction to his work as any, this program includes diverse works ranging from Leadbelly to Leonard Bernstein, plus Evans's own "Jambangle." The arranger's inventive use of the voices of his rather unique sidemen make this a memorable set. *—Scott Yanow*

New Bottle, Old Wine / Apr. 9, 1958-May 26, 1958 / Blue Note ✦✦✦✦✦
Gil Evans' second album as a leader (a World Pacific set that has been reissued by Blue Note) features his reworking of eight jazz classics including "St. Louis Blues," "Lester Leaps In" and "Struttin' with Some Barbecue." Evans' charts utilize three trumpets, three trombones, a french horn, a prominent tuba, one reed player, altoist Cannonball Adderley and a four-piece rhythm section. Most memorable is a classic rendition of "King Porter Stomp" featuring the exuberant altoist Cannonball Adderley, who is the main soloist on most of the selections. Other key voices include Evans' piano, guitarist Chuck Wayne and trumpeter Johnny Coles. This is near-classic music that showed that Gil Evans did not need Miles Davis as a soloist to inspire him to greatness. *—Scott Yanow*

Great Jazz Standards / 1959 / Blue Note ✦✦✦✦✦
A follow-up to *New Bottle, Old Wine*, this Gil Evans set has colorful arrangements of five jazz standards plus "Ballad of the Sad Young Men" and Evans' "Theme." Using a band consisting of three trumpets, three trombones, a French horn, Bill Barber's tuba, soprano-saxophonist Steve Lacy (the first important post-swing player on his instrument), tenor saxophonist Budd Johnson (on half of the program), and a four-piece rhythm section (including the leader's piano), Evans contributes some very memorable written ensemble passages, most notably on "Straight No Chaser." In addition to Lacy and Johnson, the main soloists are trumpeter Johnny Coles, trombonists Curtis Fuller and Jimmy Cleveland, and guitarist Ray Crawford. Highly recommended. *—Scott Yanow*

Out of the Cool / Nov. 18, 1960-Dec. 15, 1960 / Impulse! ✦✦✦✦
Gil Evans recordings (particularly those without Miles Davis) were not a common occurrence in the pre-1970 era, making this set a special treat. Evans's 14-piece band (which includes trumpeter Johnny Coles, trombonist Jimmy Knepper, Budd Johnson on tenor and soprano and guitarist Ray Crawford among others) investigates a wide variety of complex material including the leader's "La Nevada" and "Sunken Treasure," John Benson Brooks's obscure "Where Flamingos Fly," George Russell's "Stratusphunk" and Kurt Weill's "Biobao"; some

reissues of this album also add Horace Silver's "Sister Sadie." The orchestrations are both thoughtful and colorful, the main reason to acquire this music. *—Scott Yanow*

Into the Hot / Sep. 14, 1961-Oct. 31, 1961 / Impulse! ♦♦♦

The Individualism of Gil Evans / Sep. 1963-Oct. 29, 1964 / Verve ♦♦♦♦
Although Gil Evans had gained a lot of acclaim for his three collaborations with Miles Davis in the 1950s and his own albums, this CD contains (with the exception of two tracks purposely left off), Evans's only dates as a leader during 1961-68. The personnel varies on the six sessions that comprise the CD (which adds five numbers including two previously unreleased to the original Lp) with such major soloists featured as tenorman Wayne Shorter, trombonist Jimmy Cleveland, trumpeter Johnny Coles and guitarist Kenny Burrell. Highlights include "Time of the Barracudas," "The Barbara Song," "Las Vegas Tango" and "Spoonful." Highly recommended to Gil Evans fans; it is a pity he did not record more during this era. *—Scott Yanow*

Blues in Orbit / 1969+1971 / Enja ♦♦♦♦♦
Arranger Gil Evans's first recording as a leader in five years found him leading an orchestra that could be considered a transition between his 1950s groups and his somewhat electric band of the 1970s. Several of these charts, particularly his reworking of George Russell's "Blues in Orbit," are quite memorable, and Evans utilizes his many interesting sidemen, including the distinctive voices of trombonist Jimmy Cleveland, Howard Johnson on tuba and baritone, tenor-saxophonist Billy Harper and guitarist Joe Beck, in unexpected and unpredictable ways. A near-classic release which has been made available on CD by Enja. *—Scott Yanow*

Svengali / May 30, 1973+Jun. 30, 1973 / Koch Jazz ♦♦♦♦♦
This is one of Gil Evans's finest recordings of the 1970s. He expertly blended together acoustic and electronic instruments, particularly on an exciting rendition of "Blues in Orbit" (which includes among its soloists a young altoist named David Sanborn). All six selections have their memorable moments (even a one-and-a-half minute version of "Eleven"); colorful solos are contributed by guitarist Ted Dunbar, Howard Johnson on tuba and flügelhorn, the passionate tenor of Billy Harper, and bassist Herb Bushler, among others; and Evans's arrangements are quite inventive and innovative. Rarely would he be so successful in balancing written and improvised sections in his later years. *—Scott Yanow*

Gil Evans' Orchestra Plays the Music of Jimi Hendrix / Jun. 11, 1974-Jun. 13, 1974 / Bluebird/RCA ♦♦♦♦♦
This CD reissue (which adds additional material to the original LP program) is much more successful than one might have expected. Jimi Hendrix was scheduled to record with Gil Evans's Orchestra but died before the session could take place. A few years later, Evans explored ten of Hendrix's compositions with his unique 19-piece unit, an orchestra that included two French horns, the tuba of Howard Johnson, three guitars, two basses, two percussionists and such soloists as altoist David Sanborn, trumpeter Hannibal Marvin Peterson, Billy Harper on tenor and guitarists Ryo Kawasaki and John Abercrombie. Evans's arrangements uplift many of Hendrix's more blues-oriented compositions and create a memorable set that is rock-oriented but retains the improvisation and personality of jazz. *—Scott Yanow*

There Comes a Time / Mar. 6, 1975-Jun. 12, 1975 / Bluebird/RCA ♦♦♦♦♦
This CD reissue differs greatly from the original LP of the same name. Not only are there three previously unreleased performances ("Joy Spring," "So Long" and "Buzzard Variation") but "The Meaning of the Blues" has been expanded from six minutes to 20, two numbers ("Little Wing" and "Aftermath the Fourth Movement Children of the Fire") have been dropped (the former was reissued on Evans's Jimi Hendrix tribute) and the remaining four tracks were re-edited and remixed under Evans's direction. So in reality, this 1987 CD was really a "new" record when it came out. The remake of "King Porter Stomp" (with altoist David Sanborn in Cannonball Adderley's spot) is a classic, the "new" version of "The Meaning of the Blues" is memorable and overall the music (which also has solos by Billy Harper and George Adams on tenors along with trumpeter Lew Soloff) is quite rewarding, creative big band fusion that expertly mixes together acoustic and electric instruments. This was one of Gil Evans's last truly great sets. *—Scott Yanow*

Bud & Bird / Dec. 1, 1986+Dec. 22, 1986 / Evidence ♦♦♦

Tal Farlow (Talmage Holt Farlow)

b. Jun. 7, 1921, Greensboro, NC, **d.** Jul. 24, 1998, New York, NY
Guitar / Cool, Bop
Nearly as famous for his reluctance to play as for his outstanding abilities, guitarist Tal Farlow did not take up the instrument until he was already 21 but within a year was playing professionally and in 1948 was with Marjorie Hyams's band. While with the Red Norvo Trio (which originally included Charles Mingus) from 1949-53, Farlow became famous in the jazz world. His huge hands and ability to play rapid yet light lines made him one of the top guitarists of the era. After six months with Artie Shaw's Gramercy Five in 1953, Farlow put together his own group which for a time included pianist Eddie Costa. Late in 1958 Farlow settled on the East Coast, became a sign painter and just played locally. He only made one record as a leader during 1960-75 but emerged a bit more often during 1976-84, recording for Concord fairly regularly before largely disappearing again. Profiled in the definitive documentary *Talmage Farlow,* the guitarist can be heard on his own records for Blue Note (1954), Verve, Prestige (1969) and Concord. He died of cancer July 25, 1998 at age 77.*—Scott Yanow*

Autumn in New York / Nov. 15, 1954 / Verve ♦♦♦♦
A generally relaxed date (only "Cherokee" is uptempo), Tal Farlow's pretty tone and tasteful improvising style are the main reasons to search for this rare LP. Pianist Gerry Wiggins, bassist Ray Brown and drummer Chico Hamilton offer quiet and swinging support of the great guitarist, who performs two originals ("And She Remembers Me" and "Tal's Blues"), plus six superior standards. All of Farlow's difficult to find Verve releases of the '50s are recommended. *—Scott Yanow*

• **The Swinging Guitar of Tal Farlow** / May 1956 / Verve ♦♦♦♦♦
In the mid-'50s, guitarist Tal Farlow led one of his finest groups, a drumless trio with pianist Eddie Costa and bassist Vinnie Burke. The same band would record the album *Tal* a week or two later. With Burke contributing a constant walking bass, the interplay between Farlow and Costa is always exciting, whether they are playing unisons or trading off. This 1999 CD reissue not only has the original seven selections but "Gone With the Wind" (which was left off of the original LP due to lack of space) plus three full-length alternate takes that are basically on the same level as the masters. Among the highpoints are "Taking a Chance on Love," "Yardbird Suite," "Like Someone in Love," and Farlow's lone original, "Meteor," which utilizes the chord changes of "Confirmation." Hot bebop that is easily recommended. *—Scott Yanow*

The Return of Tal Farlow: 1969 / Sep. 23, 1969 / Prestige/OJC ♦♦♦
After recording a series of rewarding albums in the '50s, guitarist Tal Farlow largely dropped out of the jazz scene, being quite content to be a sign painter in New England. This Prestige set (reissued on CD) was his first in a decade and would be followed by another seven years of silence. Fortunately, Farlow had continued playing on a low-profile basis in the interim, and he was still very much in top form. Joined by pianist John Scully, bassist Jack Six and drummer Alan Dawson, Farlow performs swinging versions of seven standards, including "Straight, No Chaser," "I'll Remember April" and "Crazy, She Calls Me." Recommended. *—Scott Yanow*

On Stage / Aug. 1976 / Concord Jazz ♦♦♦♦
Other than a Prestige date in 1969, this was guitarist Tal Farlow's first recording in nearly 17 years. He is heard at a reunion with vibraphonist Red Norvo and matching wits with pianist Hank Jones, bassist Ray Brown and drummer Jake Hanna. Recorded at the 1976 Concord Jazz Festival, this was Farlow's first of six Concord albums, and it led to a slightly higher profile for him than during the past decade. Highlights of the joyous occasion include Norvo's feature on "The One I Love Belongs to Somebody Else," a heated "Lullaby of Birdland" and a colorful rendition of "My Shining Hour." Highly recommended to straight-ahead jazz fans. *—Scott Yanow*

Cookin' on All Burners / Aug. 1982 / Concord Jazz ♦♦♦♦♦
On the fifth of six Concord albums (a surprising amount of activity considering that he only played locally in the New England area during most of 1957-75), the brilliant bop-based guitarist Tal Farlow performs concise renditions (none over six-and-a-half minutes) of nine standards with pianist James Williams, bassist Gary Mazzaroppi and drummer Vinnie Johnson. Highlights of the excellent straight-ahead date include "You'd Be So Nice to Come Home To," "I've Got the World on a String," "Love Letters" and "Just Friends." *—Scott Yanow*

Art Farmer

b. Aug. 21, 1928, Council Bluffs, IA, **d.** Oct. 4, 1999, New York, NY
Flugelhorn, Trumpet / Hard Bop, Cool, Bop
Largely overlooked during his formative years, Art Farmer's consistently inventive playing has been more greatly appreciated as he continues to develop. Along with Clark Terry, Farmer helped to popularize the flugelhorn among brass players. His lyricism gives his bop-oriented style its own personality. He worked in Los Angeles from 1945 on, performing regularly on Central Avenue and spending time in the bands of Johnny Otis, Jay McShann, Roy Porter, Benny Carter and Gerald Wilson among others; some of the groups also included his twin brother bassist Addison Farmer. After playing with Wardell Gray (1951-52) and touring Europe with Lionel Hampton's big band (1953) Farmer moved to New York and worked with Gigi Gryce (1954-56), Horace Silver's Quintet (1956-58) and the Gerry Mulligan Quartet (1958-9). Farmer co-led the Jazztet with Benny Golson (1959-62) and then had a group with Jim Hall (1962-64). He moved to Vienna in 1968 where he joined the Austrian Radio Orchestra, worked with the Kenny Clarke-Francy Boland Big Band and toured with his own units. *—Scott Yanow*

The Art Farmer Septet Plays Arrangents / Jul. 2, 1953-Jun. 7, 1954 / Prestige/OJC ♦♦♦♦
This CD reissue features the mellow-toned but hard-swinging trumpeter Art Farmer on a pair of four-song sessions from 1953 and 1954. Among Farmer's sidemen are trombonist Jimmy Cleveland, either Clifford Solomon or Charlie Rouse on tenor and Horace Silver or Quincy Jones on piano. In addition Farmer is showcased on a version of "When Your Lover Has Gone" that is taken from a 1956 album titled *Two Trumpets.* Highlights overall include "Mau Mau," "Up in Quincy's Room," "Evening in Paris" and "Elephant Walk." An excellent early hard bop set. *—Scott Yanow*

Farmer's Market / Jul. 2, 1953-Nov. 23, 1956 / New Jazz/OJC ♦♦♦♦
This double album consists of material taken from seven different dates led by trumpeter Art Farmer in the 1950s. These Prestige sessions give one a cross-section of Farmer's early years with such sidemen as tenor-saxophonist Sonny Rollins, pianist Horace Silver, trombonist Jimmy Cleveland, altoist Gigi Gryce and tenor-saxophonist Hank Mobley all having a generous amount of solo space. *—Scott Yanow*

Early Art / Jan. 20, 1954+Nov. 9, 1954 / New Jazz/OJC ♦♦♦♦
Two of trumpeter Art Farmer's earlier sessions as a leader are reissued on this CD in the OJC series. Farmer teams up with an all-star quintet (which includes tenor-saxophonist Sonny Rollins, pianist Horace Silver, bassist Percy Heath and drummer Kenny Clarke) for four songs and dominates a quartet (with pianist Wynton Kelly, bassist Addison Farmer and drummer Herbie Lovelle) on six other tunes. Farmer's sound is lyrical even on the uptempo pieces and he is heard throughout in his early prime. Highlights include "Soft Shoe," "I'll Take Romance," "Autumn Nocturne" and an uptempo "Gone with the Wind." One should note that the programming differs from what is listed, with "Soft Shoe" (which should have been the opener) actually appearing fifth and the songs listed as appearing second through fifth moving up to first through fourth. Despite that flaw, the music is quite enjoyable and a must for 1950s bop collectors. *—Scott Yanow*

When Farmer Met Gryce / May 19, 1954+May 26, 1955 / Prestige/OJC ♦♦♦♦
This CD features trumpeter Art Farmer, altoist Gigi Gryce and two rhythm sections with ei-

ther Horace Silver or Freddie Redd on piano, Percy Heath or Addison Farmer on bass and Kenny Clarke or Art Taylor on drums. The early hard bop music is highlighted by "Social Call" (one of Gryce's best-known compositions), "Capri," "A Night at Tony's" and "Blue Concept" but all eight numbers will easily be enjoyed by straightahead jazz fans. *— Scott Yanow*

The Art Farmer Quintet / Oct. 21, 1955 / Prestige/OJC ♦♦♦♦♦
During 1955 trumpeter Art Farmer had a short-lived quintet with altoist Gigi Gryce but, because neither of the co-leaders were big names at the time, the band did not last long. Fortunately they did record two records of material of which this CD reissue (originally known as *Evening in Casablanca*) was the second. In addition to Farmer and Gryce, the unit includes pianist Duke Jordan, bassist Addison Farmer and drummer Philly Joe Jones. With the exception of Duke Jordan's "Forecast," the cool-toned hard bop date consists entirely of Gigi Gryce compositions of which "Evening in Casablanca" and "Nice's Tempo" are best-known. Excellent music well-deserving a close listen. *— Scott Yanow*

Portrait of Art Farmer / Apr. 19, 1958+May 1, 1958 / Contemporary/OJC ♦♦♦♦♦
This CD reissue (which adds a version of "The Folks Who Live on the Hill" to the original LP program) is an excellent showcase for trumpeter Art Farmer in the 1950s. Farmer is showcased with a quartet that also includes pianist Hank Jones, bassist Addison Farmer and drummer Roy Haynes. The repertoire alternates veteran standards with lesser-known material including three of Farmer's originals and George Russell's "Nita" along with a particularly strong version of Benny Golson's "Stablemates." An excellent outing. *— Scott Yanow*

Modern Art / Sep. 10, 1958-Sep. 14, 1958 / Blue Note ♦♦♦♦
For this CD reissue from over a year before the Jazztet was formed, trumpeter Art Farmer teams up with his future co-leader tenor-saxophonist Benny Golson. With a strong rhythm section consisting of pianist Bill Evans, bassist Addison Farmer and drummer Dave Bailey, Farmer and Golson perform two of their originals and such songs as "Darn That Dream," "Like Someone in Love" and "Cool Breeze." The straightahead hard bop music (originally out on United Artists) is as successful as one would expect; Farmer and Golson always brought out the best in each other. *— Scott Yanow*

★ **Meet the Jazztet** / Feb. 6, 1960-Feb. 10, 1960 / MCA/Chess ♦♦♦♦♦
Although this CD has the same program as the original LP, it gets the highest rating because it is a hard bop classic. Not only does it include superior solos from trumpeter Art Farmer, trombonist Curtis Fuller, tenor-saxophonist Benny Golson and pianist McCoy Tyner (who was making his recording debut) along with fine backup from bassist Addison Farmer and drummer Lex Humphries, but it features the writing of Golson. Highlights include the original version of "Killer Joe" along with early renditions of "I Remember Clifford" and "Blues March." This was Fuller and Tyner's only recording with the original Jazztet and all ten selections (which also include "Serenata," "It Ain't Necessarily So," "It's All Right with Me" and "Easy Living") are quite memorable. *— Scott Yanow*

Blues on Down / Sep. 16, 1960-May 15, 1961 / Chess ♦♦♦♦

On the Road / Jul. 26, 1976-Aug. 16, 1976 / Contemporary/OJC ♦♦♦♦
This CD reissue of a Contemporary set from 1976 features a logical but only one-time collaboration between flugelhornist Art Farmer and altoist Art Pepper. With pianist Hampton Hawes, bassist Ray Brown and either Steve Ellington or Shelly Manne on drums completing the quintet, the five standards and Hawes's original "Downwind" were certainly in good hands. A special highlight is a duet version of "My Funny Valentine" featuring Farmer and Hawes. Everyone plays up to par on this spirited straightahead set. *— Scott Yanow*

Work of Art / Sep. 1981 / Concord Jazz ♦♦♦♦♦
Flugelhornist Art Farmer is in top form on this quartet set with pianist Fred Hersch, bassist Bob Bodley and drummer Billy Hart. Farmer had, if anything, grown through the years and although he had lived in Europe for 13 years at the time of this album, he was still getting better. Farmer is heard in peak form on such numbers as Charlie Parker's "Red Cross," "She's Funny That Way," "Change Partners" and "Love Walked In." A fine example of his artistry. *— Scott Yanow*

Warm Valley / Sep. 1982 / Concord Jazz ♦♦♦♦♦
The second of flugelhornist Art Farmer's two Concord albums is the equal of his first. For this Concord outing, the mellow-toned brassman performs four standards (including "Moose the Mooche," "Three Little Words" and the title cut) along with selections from Fred Hersch (who plays piano on this quartet outing), Tommy Flanagan and Benny Golson. With fine support from bassist Ray Drummond and drummer Akira Tana, Art Farmer is heard in prime form, playing in his appealing lyrical bop style. *— Scott Yanow*

Back to the City / Feb. 21, 1986-Feb. 22, 1986 / Contemporary/OJC ♦♦♦♦

☆ **Something to Live for: The Music of Billy Strayhorn** / Jan. 14, 1987-Jan. 15, 1987 / Contemporary ♦♦♦♦♦
This very logical set is a real gem. The lyrical flugelhornist Art Farmer and his quintet (which consists of tenor-saxophonist Clifford Jordan, pianist James Williams, bassist Rufus Reid and drummer Marvin "Smitty" Smith) interpret seven of Billy Strayhorn's compositions. Highlights include "Isfahan," "Johnny Come Lately," "Raincheck" and the title cut. Farmer brings the right combination of sensitivity, swing, respect for the melody and creativity to these renditions and the results are quite memorable. *— Scott Yanow*

Blame It on My Youth / Feb. 4, 1988-Feb. 8, 1988 / Contemporary ♦♦♦♦♦
This is one of the better Art Farmer recordings of the 1980s, which is saying a great deal, for the flugelhornist is among the most consistent of all jazz musicians. The two ballads that open and close this set ("Blame It on My Youth" and "I'll Be Around") give Farmer an opportunity to display his warm and attractive sound (with fine support from pianist James Williams, bassist Rufus Reid and drummer Victor Lewis), while the other five pieces (Benny Carter's "Summer Serenade" and more obscure material) add the great tenor saxophonist (and so-so soprano player) Clifford Jordan to the group. It's an enjoyable and very successful outing. *— Scott Yanow*

Central Avenue Reunion / May 26, 1989-May 27, 1989 / Contemporary ♦♦♦♦♦

Victor Feldman

b. Apr. 7, 1934, London, England, **d.** May 12, 1987, Los Angeles, CA
Vibraphone, Keyboards, Drums, Piano, Percussion / Crossover Jazz, Cool
Victor Feldman was a child prodigy who was a professional from the age of seven and sat in on drums with Glenn Miller's Army Air Force Band in 1944 when he was ten. He was active in his native England through the bebop years (mostly on drums), debuting as a leader in 1948. By 1952 Feldman was getting better-known for his vibes playing and he recorded extensively during the 1950s. After touring with Woody Herman (1956-57), he decided to move to the U.S. in 1957 where he worked at the Lighthouse with Howard Rumsey. Feldman recorded (on vibes and piano) for Mode, Contemporary and Riverside during 1957-61, a period in which he became a busy studio musician. Feldman was with Cannonball Adderley's Quintet (mostly as a pianist) for six months in 1960-61 and recorded with Miles Davis in 1963 (who offered him a job with his new quintet and recorded his original "Seven Steps to Heaven") but remained in L.A. and the studios. He cut jazz dates for Choice, Concord, Palo Alto and TBA and in the 1980s up until his death he led a soulful crossover group (The Generation Band) that often featured his son Trevor Feldman on drums. *— Scott Yanow*

★ **Suite Sixteen** / Aug. 19, 1955-Sep. 21, 1955 / Contemporary/OJC ♦♦♦♦♦
This interesting set (a CD reissue of the original LP) features Victor Feldman shortly before he left England for the United States. Feldman, mostly heard on vibes but also making strong appearances on piano and drums, heads several groups filled with English All-Stars including such notable musicians as trumpeters Jimmy Deuchar and Dizzy Reece, tenors Ronnie Scott and Tubby Hayes and pianist Tommy Pollard. The music is boppish with some surprises in the consistently swinging arrangements, giving one a definitive look at Victor Feldman near the beginning of his career. *— Scott Yanow*

With Mallets a Fore Thought / Sep. 1957 / VSOP ♦♦♦♦

Merry Olde Soul / Dec. 16, 1960-Jan. 11, 1961 / Riverside/OJC ♦♦♦

The Artful Dodger / Jan. 24, 1977-Jan. 26, 1977 / Concord Jazz ♦♦♦

Maynard Ferguson

b. May 4, 1928, Verdun, Quebec, Canada
Trumpet / Crossover Jazz, Jazz-Pop, Hard Bop
When he debuted with Stan Kenton's Orchestra in 1950, Maynard Ferguson could play higher than any other trumpeter up to that point in jazz history, and he was accurate. Somehow he has kept most of that range through the decades and since the 1970s has been one of the most famous musicians in jazz. Never known for his exquisite taste (some of his more commercial efforts are unlistenable), Ferguson has nevertheless led some important bands and definitely made an impact with his trumpet playing. In 1950 with the formation of Kenton's Innovations Orchestra, Ferguson became a star, playing ridiculous high notes with ease. In 1953 he left Kenton to work in the studios of Los Angeles and three years later led the all-star "Birdland Dreamband." In 1957 he put together a regular big band that lasted until 1965, recorded regularly for Roulette, and performed some of the finest music of his career. After economics forced him to give up the impressive band, Ferguson had a few years in which he was only semiactive in music, spending time in India and eventually forming a new band in England. After moving back to the U.S., Ferguson in 1974 drifted quickly into commercialism. *— Scott Yanow*

Verve Jazz Masters 52 / Dec. 21, 1951-Aug. 2, 1957 / Verve ♦♦♦
As part of Verve's extensive *Jazz Masters* reissue series, this CD has some highlights from trumpeter Maynard Ferguson's recordings for EmArcy and Mercury. There is one selection ("King's Riff") from a date with tenorman Ben Webster and altoist Benny Carter, five songs from an album with West Coast all-stars (*Dimensions*), a version of "Can't We Talk It Over" that features MF with arranger Pete Rugolo, and selections from Ferguson's early big band LPs *Around the Horn* and *Boy with Lots of Brass*. Best-known as a high-note trumpeter, Maynard Ferguson did his best on these performances to show off his other abilities including taking solos on valve trombone and playing jazz in the trumpet's lower register. The bop-based music is enjoyable, there are many other prominent soloists (including altoists Bud Shank, Herb Geller and Anthony Ortega) and Irene Kral sings an effective rendition of "Moonlight in Vermont." But more serious collectors are advised to search for the complete original records. *— Scott Yanow*

● **The Birdland Dream Band** / Sep. 7, 1956-Dec. 24, 1956 / Bluebird/RCA ♦♦♦♦♦
In 1956 Maynard Ferguson had the opportunity to put together a "dream band." Fortunately (in addition to a tour), the orchestra cut a pair of albums, most of which is included on this single CD. With arrangements from Al Cohn, Bob Brookmeyer, Jimmy Giuffre, Ernie Wilkins, Bill Holman, Marty Paich, Willie Maiden, Johnny Mandel, and Herb Geller, it is not too surprising that these charts sound both modern and quite exciting. In addition to Ferguson's high-note trumpet work, the main soloists are trombonist Jimmy Cleveland, altoist Herb Geller, and Al Cohn on tenor. Overall, this music serves a particularly strong start to Maynard Ferguson's career as a major bandleader. *— Scott Yanow*

The Complete Maynard Ferguson on Roulette / May 6, 1958-Mar. 1962 / Mosaic ♦♦♦♦♦
Trumpeter Maynard Ferguson led his greatest big band during the years that he was signed to Roulette and all of the music from his 13 Roulette LPs (plus 11 previously unissued selections) are included on this deluxe limited-edition ten-CD box set. Although three of the LPs were originally recorded as dance records (and stick close to the melodies), this box as a whole finds Maynard at his peak and with an orchestra that includes such talented soloists as trombonists Slide Hampton and Don Sebesky (both of whom contributed arrangements), altoist Lanny Morgan, the tenors of Carmen Leggio, Willie Maiden, Joe Farrell, and Don Menza, pianists Jaki Byard and Joe Zawinul, and drummer Rufus Jones in addition to the leader. The music is very jazz-oriented and contains more than its share of classic moments, particularly the sessions that resulted in *A Message From Newport* and *Newport Suite*. It's highly recommended. *— Scott Yanow*

Orchestra 1967 / 1967 / Just a Memory ♦♦♦♦

Maynard Ferguson's Horn, Vol. 1/Maynard Ferguson's Horn, Vol. 2 / Feb. 1970-Jan. 1972 / Columbia ✦✦✦
1970-1972. A combination of two of Ferguson's biggest hit albums, with minimal jazz content. *—Ron Wynn*

Live from London / 1993 / Avenue Jazz ✦✦✦✦

These Cats Can Swing / 1994 / Concord Jazz ✦✦✦✦

Brass Attitude / May 26, 1998-May 30, 1998 / Concord Jazz ✦✦✦✦
With one major exception, the tracks on *Brass Attitude* reflect the relatively traditional (dare we say restrained) big band sound of Maynard Ferguson's Big Bop Nouveau, whose most distinctive feature by far is—surprise, surprise—its leader. At 70, MF still has a lot left, able to blast away at those ultrasonic passages and dish out that throbbing, unctious tone in the middle regions. Yet he seems to be choosing his spots with more economy, resorting frequently to the flugelhorn for mellower passages. The soloing by MF's sidemen—the most prominently featured of whom are Tom Garling on trombone and Sal Giorgianni on tenor sax—is of a competent, energetic bop variety with few distinguishing qualities. Thankfully, an element of strangeness bursts forth at the album's midpoint, "Misra-Dhenuka," a nearly 16-minute reminder of MF's sabbatical in India. Grounded in a raga, it dissolves into a 6/8 meter vamp based on what sounds like a Spanish chordal pattern. A less welcome bit of weirdness is MF alumnus Denis DiBlasio's amateurish vocal cameo in "The Lip," which in this context fawns over MF's high-note proclivity as shamelessly as rappers have about Miles Davis. *—Richard S. Ginell*

Tommy Flanagan

b. Mar. 16, 1930, Detroit, MI
Piano / Hard Bop, Bop
Known for his flawless and tasteful playing, Tommy Flanagan received long overdue recognition for his talents in the 1980s. He played clarinet when he was six and switched to piano five years later. Flanagan was an important part of the fertile Detroit jazz scene (other than 1951-53 when he was in the Army) until he moved to New York in 1956. He was used for many recordings after his arrival during that era, cut sessions as a leader for New Jazz, Prestige, Savoy, and Moodsville and worked regularly with Oscar Pettiford, J.J. Johnson (1956-58), Harry "Sweets" Edison (1959-60) and Coleman Hawkins (1961). Flanagan was Ella Fitzgerald's regular accompanist during 1963-65 and 1968-78 which resulted in him being underrated as a soloist. However starting in 1975 he began leading a series of superior record sessions and since leaving Ella, Flanagan has been in demand as the head of his own trio, consistently admired for his swinging and creative bop-based style. Among the many labels that he has recorded for since 1975 have been Pablo, Enja, Denon, Galaxy, Progressive, Uptown, Timeless and several European and Japanese companies. For Blue Note, he cut *Sunset and Mockingbird* in 1998, followed a year later by *Samba for Felix*. *—Scott Yanow*

Montreux 1977 / Jul. 13, 1977 / Pablo/OJC ✦✦✦✦
This Pablo recording was cut at a time when pianist Tommy Flanagan was almost forgotten due to his long stint with Ella Fitzgerald's backup band. This fine trio outing with bassist Keter Betts and drummer Bobby Durham has been reissued on CD in the Original Jazz Classics series with one track ("Heat Wave") added to the original program. The two ballad medleys are enjoyable, but it is on "Barbados," "Woody'n You" and "Blue Bossa" that Flanagan shows how hard-swinging a pianist he can be. His solo career really started to take off a few years after this concert appearance. *—Scott Yanow*

Our Delights / Jan. 28, 1978 / Galaxy/OJC ✦✦✦✦
Piano duets have the potential danger of getting overcrowded and a bit incoherent, but neither happens on this rather delightful set. Hank Jones and Tommy Flanagan, two of the four great jazz pianists (along with Barry Harris and Roland Hanna) to emerge from Detroit in the '40s and '50s, have similar styles and their mutual respect is obvious. Their renditions of seven superior bop standards (including "Jordu," "Confirmation" and Thad Jones' "A Child Is Born") plus an alternate take of "Robbins Nest" on this CD reissue are tasteful, consistently swinging and inventive within the tradition. *—Scott Yanow*

Jazz Poet / Jan. 17, 1989-Jan. 19, 1989 / Timeless ✦✦✦✦✦
By the time of this recording, pianist Tommy Flanagan had been performing for decades—mostly as a sideman—for a who's who of jazz: players such as Miles Davis, J.J. Johnson, and Sonny Rollins, to name a few. His perfect, yet unassuming style made him the pianist of choice for dozens of musicians. While he has recorded as a leader from time to time, this album may be the best representation of his work available. He performs a set of great tunes ("Caravan," "Willow Weep for Me," "St. Louis Blues," "Lament," and others) in a topflight trio, with George Mraz on bass and Kenny Washington on drums. Flanagan is at the peak of his powers. Never flashy, never showy, this is just outstanding music performed by a true master who is one of the great bop pianists of the 20th century. *—Steven Loewy*

● **Beyond the Blue Bird** / Apr. 29, 1990+Apr. 30, 1990 / Timeless ✦✦✦✦✦
Veteran pianist Tommy Flanagan, in a quartet with guitarist Kenny Burrell, bassist George Mraz and drummer Lewis Nash, performs blues, ballads and some obscurities during one of his most rewarding recordings. Flanagan has never recorded an indifferent album, but this set seems more inspired than most, making it a perfect introduction to this tasteful, swinging and creative (within the bop mainstream) pianist. *—Scott Yanow*

Let's Play the Music of Thad Jones / Apr. 4, 1993 / Enja ✦✦✦✦✦
This relatively little-known trio set by pianist Tommy Flanagan (with bassist Jesper Lundgaard and drummer Lewis Nash) is a minor classic. Flanagan performs 11 of cornetist Thad Jones's compositions, the majority of which had never been played by a piano trio before. Easily the best-known selection is "A Child Is Born" with "Mean What You Say," "Three in One" and "Quietude" being the closest of the other songs to being standards. But, despite their relative obscurity, this body of work is quite diverse and flexible enough to be covered by other jazz musicians. Congratulations are due Tommy Flanagan for putting together a consistently swinging and tasteful salute to Thad Jones, a very talented composer. *—Scott Yanow*

Lady Be Good . . . For Ella / Jul. 30, 1993-Jul. 31, 1993 / Verve ✦✦✦✦✦
The exquisite musings of piano great Tommy Flanagan need no extraneous superlatives; they speak volumes on their own. Here though it's personal, as he pays tribute to First Lady of Jazz Song Ella Fitzgerald, whom he faithfully accompanied first in the summer of 1956, as well as 1962-64 and 1968-78. Of the eleven songs swung by Flanagan, bassist Peter Washington and drummer Lewis Nash, the majority come right out of Ella's fabled songbook, with a couple of zingers tossed in for kicks. By the way, Flanagan himself has never sounded better, illuminating these well-known melodies with some modifications of his own. This program starts and ends with the title cut, but the first time around it's a wistfully slow ballad packed with all the elegance and emotion Flanagan can muster. The finale has him knocking it out flat, rippling with extroversions and extrapolations quite reminiscent of Ella's vocal excursions. Everyone knows how untouchable the pianist is on ballads, shown by the lugubriously patient melody he builds on the absolutely pristine "Isn't It a Pity?," the spooky, foggy "Angel Eyes," or the soft bossa "Alone Too Long." At his excitable best, Flanagan bops away at the midtempo "How High the Moon," goes for it during "Cherokee," chases the Fitzgerald penned "Love You Madly"-type song "Rough Ridin'" full steam ahead, trading eights with the clever Nash. The pianist is at his best during the actual, easy-swinging "Love You Madly," digging into his chordal interpretations of the melody, almost overemphasizing and staggering the phrases into a totally submissive stranglehold. Although Flanagan has many high points in an exceptional career, this is certainly up there with the best, and a great set of Cliff Notes for doing the jazz piano trio right. Highly recommended. *—Michael G. Nastos*

Sea Changes / Mar. 11, 1996-Mar. 12, 1996 / Evidence ✦✦✦✦
It's easy to understand why Tommy Flanagan has been one of the most praised pianists over the '80s and '90s while listening to an excellent trio date such as this CD. With bassist Peter Washington and drummer Lewis Nash, he features a number of songs with oceanic themes, including a tantalizing "How Deep Is the Ocean—," "I Cover the Waterfront," and his own snappy title track. Flanagan also delivers a thunderous take of "Relaxin' at Camarillo" and the smoldering, savory blues "C.C. Rider." *—Ken Dryden*

Sunset and the Mockingbird: The Birthday Concert / Aug. 25, 1998 / Blue Note ✦✦✦✦
Recorded at the Village Vanguard on the night of his 67th birthday, Tommy Flanagan celebrated by recording this memorable set. Joined by bassist Peter Washington and drummer Lewis Nash, the brilliant pianist devours two uptempo bop classics by Thad Jones, "Birdsong" and "Let's," plus a trio of tunes by Tom MacIntosh (a composer who merits wider recognition). His lengthy sojourn through Dizzy Gillespie's "Tin Tin Deo" explores new ground, while the late trumpeter's lesser-known "I Waited for You" is quite enchanting. Flanagan's arrangement of the title track, a rarely performed song from Duke Ellington's "Queen's Suite," matches the elegance of the late composer's recording. His dramatic solo of "Good Night My Love" is dedicated to his wife Diana, who is not only present but heard answering her husband's call to her at the end of the night. *—Ken Dryden*

Overseas / Aug. 15, 1957 / Prestige/OJC ✦✦✦

Béla Fleck

b. 1958, New York, NY
Banjo / Post-Bop, Fusion, Progressive Bluegrass
Premiere banjo player Béla Fleck is considered one of the most innovative pickers in the world and has done much to demonstrate the versatility of his instrument, which he uses to play everything from traditional bluegrass to progressive jazz. After graduating high school, he joined the Tasty Licks, a group from Boston. They recorded two albums and dissolved in 1979. Afterwards, Fleck joined the Kentucky band Spectrum. That year, only five years after he took up the instrument, he made his solo recording debut with *Crossing the Tracks*, which the Readers' Poll in *Frets* magazine named Best Overall Album. In 1982, he joined New Grass Revival and stayed with them until the end of the decade. During this time, his reputation continued to grow and in 1990, *Frets* added his name to their Hall of Greats. In 1989, Fleck was asked by PBS television to play on the upcoming *Lonesome Pine Special;* in response he gathered together a veritable "dream team" of musicians to form the Flecktones. The original members included Howard Levy, who played piano, harmonica and ocarina, among other instruments; bass guitarist Victor Lemonte Wooten, and his brother Roy "Future Man" Wooten on the drumitar, an electronic drum shaped like a guitar. *—Sandra Brennan*

Crossing the Tracks / 1979 / Rounder ✦✦✦✦

Daybreak / 1988 / Rounder ✦✦✦✦✦

Bela Fleck & The Flecktones / 1990 / Warner Brothers ✦✦✦✦✦
After disbanding New Grass Revival, Bela Fleck began re-creating the role of the banjo in the same way Charlie Parker redefined the role of the saxophone. But Fleck may be the least-innovative member of this quartet: Howard Levy gets chromatics from his blues harp, Victor Wooten picks banjo rolls on his bass, and Roy "Future Man" Wooten plays a Frankenstein-monster drum-machine/guitar synthesizer. For all the flash, there's little pretense; the group's astonishing musicianship keeps an "aw-shucks" accessibility that lets everybody follow the melody while they marvel. *—Brian Mansfield*

● **Flight of the Cosmic Hippo** / Jan. 1991 / Warner Brothers ✦✦✦✦✦
The Flecktones owe more to bebop than bluegrass, and here the group finally names its style "blu-bop." That's why *Cosmic Hippo* topped the jazz, not the country, chart. The Flecktones continue to make it look easy, adding banjo power chords to "Turtle Rock" and reworking Lennon/McCartney's "Michelle." *—Brian Mansfield*

Tales from the Acoustic Planet / Jan. 1994-Mar. 1994 / Warner Brothers ✦✦✦✦

Tabula Rasa / Oct. 1994 / Waterlily Acoustics ✦✦✦✦✦

The Bluegrass Sessions: Tales From the Acoustic Planet, Vol. 2 / Jun. 22, 1999 / Warner Brothers ✦✦✦✦
As it turns out, the *Tales From the Acoustic Planet* albums are where Béla Fleck sounds the most comfortable in the '90s. As his jazz fusion records begin to sound played out, his acoustic experimentation and returns to straight-ahead bluegrass sound lively, vibrant, and

fresh. As a matter of fact, *The Bluegrass Sessions: Tales From the Acoustic Planet, Vol. 2* feels like one of his finest albums, due in no small part to the caliber of supporting musicians. The core band consists of Fleck, Sam Bush, Jerry Douglas, Stuart Duncan, Tony Rice, and Mark Schatz, while Vassar Clements, John Hartford, and Earl Scruggs all guest; it's a veritable who's-who of bluegrass. Fleck's idea was to record everything from the purest bluegrass to modern newgrass, giving his talented musicians the opportunity to explore every facet of their musical personality. Much of the album is devoted to Fleck originals, complimented by a handful of covers, none of which are predictable. The same can be said for the music: Even seasoned newgrass listeners will probably be surprised by some of the twists and turns here, while the sheer commitment and astonishing musicianship will win over traditionalists. But the true key to *The Bluegrass Sessions* is that even when it gets technical, it feels heartfelt, and the textures keep changing from song to song, enough to keep it interesting, even captivating, throughout 18 songs and 70 minutes. It had been easy to take Fleck for granted, but this record is a welcome reminder of what a talented and unique musician he is. *— Stephen Thomas Erlewine*

Greatest Hits of the 20th Century / Nov. 16, 1999 / Warner Brothers ♦♦♦♦
Whenever a group with the stature and critical reputation of Béla Fleck and the Flecktones issues a career-spanning collection, the quality of the work is not measured in the same way that an original album would be. The question isn't so much whether or not Béla Fleck and the Flecktones are talented musicians capable of producing worthwhile songs, but whether or not the editor of the collection has chosen wisely from their repertoire. On the satirically titled *Greatest Hits of the Twentieth Century,* someone has done a good job. In roughly chronological order (with the exception of the last song, "Sunset Road" from very early in the band's history) the collection presents a mixture of live and studio tracks, previously released and unreleased material, each song showing off a different facet of the band's style and abilities. There is the tight, funky quartet sounds of their first hit, "The Sinister Minister," the strong bluegrass influence on "The Yee-Haw Factor," the pleasant guest appearance by Dave Matthews on "Communication," and the sweetly minimal "Sunset Road." There isn't a dud in the bunch of this concise history of the Flecktones. An inventive blend of a world of influences, this collection offers an extremely pleasant listening experience. *— Stacia Proefrock*

Jimmy Forrest

b. Jan. 24, 1920, St. Louis, MO, **d.** Aug. 26, 1980, Grand Rapids, MI
Sax (Tenor) / Jump Blues, Swing
A fine all-round tenor player, Jimmy Forrest is best-known for recording "Night Train," a song that he "borrowed" from the last part of Duke Ellington's "Happy Go Lucky Local." While in high school in St. Louis, Forrest worked with pianist Eddie Johnson, the legendary Fate Marable and the Jeter-Pillars Orchestra. In 1938 he went on the road with Don Albert and then was with Jay McShann's Orchestra (1940-42). In New York Forrest played with Andy Kirk (1942-48) and Duke Ellington (1949) before returning to St. Louis. After recording "Night Train," Forrest became a popular attraction and recorded a series of jazz-oriented R&B singles. Among his most important later associations were with Harry "Sweets" Edison (1958-63), Count Basie's Orchestra (1972-77) and Al Grey with whom he co-led a quintet until his death. Forrest recorded for United (reissued by Delmark), Prestige/New Jazz (1960-62) and Palo Alto (1978). *— Scott Yanow*

● **Night Train** / Nov. 27, 1951-Sep. 7, 1953 / Delmark ♦♦♦♦♦
Jimmy Forrest had a tremendous hit in 1951 with "Night Train," a simple blues riff he lifted from Duke Ellington's "Happy Go Lucky Local." Although the tenorman was not able to duplicate that song's appeal with any other recording, he was a popular performer in the R&B circuit throughout the 1950s. Virtually all of his records from the era (originally made for the United label) are on this CD reissue, including five selections not previously released. The tough-toned Forrest was not really a screamer or a honker, and the 17 numbers on the set should be of interest both to early R&B and jazz collectors. Recorded in Chicago, Forrest fronts a rhythm section that includes either Charles Fox or Bunky Parker on piano, and sometimes trumpeter Chauncey Locke or trombonist Bert Dabney. The music is very enjoyable and highly recommended. *— Scott Yanow*

All the Gin Is Gone / Dec. 10, 1959-Dec. 12, 1959 / Delmark ♦♦♦♦
This was the first album that tenor saxophonist Jimmy Forrest made after his R&B phase ended. Particularly notable is that the set served as the recording debut of guitarist Grant Green; completing the band are pianist Harold Mabern, bassist Gene Ramey and drummer Elvin Jones. The top-notch group performs two ballads, "Caravan" and three basic Forrest originals, including the title cut. The music is essentially melodic and blues-based hard bop that looks toward soul-jazz. Everyone sounds in fine form. *— Scott Yanow*

Forrest Fire / Aug. 9, 1960 / New Jazz/OJC ♦♦♦♦
During 1961, Jimmy Forrest recorded four albums for Prestige and its subsidiary New Jazz, all of which have been reissued on CD in the Original Jazz Classics series. The appealing tenor is matched up with 20-year-old organist Larry Young, guitarist Thornel Schwartz and drummer Jimmie Smith. They perform two jump tunes ("Dexter's Deck" and Doug Watkins' "Help"), a pair of blues, a swinging version of Irving Berlin's "Remember," and a lone ballad ("When Your Lover Has Gone"). Excellent music that is also quite accessible. *— Scott Yanow*

Out of the Forrest / Apr. 18, 1961 / Prestige/OJC ♦♦♦♦
This CD reissue is an excellent example of tenor saxophonist Jimmy Forrest in a soulful but fairly straight-ahead setting. Accompanied by pianist Joe Zawinul, bassist Tommy Potter and drummer Clarence Johnston, Forrest revives his "Bolo Blues," and plays his basic "Crash Program," and otherwise sticks to melodic standards. His highly expressive powers and ability to say a lot with a few notes is very much in evidence on this excellent set. *— Scott Yanow*

Most Much / Oct. 19, 1961 / Prestige/OJC ♦♦♦♦♦
Jimmy Forrest was a very consistent tenor, able to infuse bop and swing standards with soul and his distinctive tone. With the assistance of pianist Hugh Lawson, bassist Tommy Potter, drummer Clarendon Johnson and Ray Barretto on congas, Forrest explores mostly veteran tunes, such as a jumping "Annie Laurie," and the calypso "Matilda," a sentimental "My Buddy," "Robbins Nest," and even "Sonny Boy." Enjoyable music from the warm tenor. *— Scott Yanow*

Pete Fountain (Peter Dewey Fountain, Jr.)

b. Jul. 3, 1930, New Orleans, LA
Clarinet / Dixieland Revival
One of the most famous of all New Orleans jazz clarinetists, Pete Fountain has the ability to play songs that he has performed a countless number of times (such as "Basin Street Blues") with so much enthusiasm that one would swear he had just discovered them! His style and most of his repertoire have remained unchanged since the late '50s yet he never sounds bored. In 1948 Fountain (who is heavily influenced by Benny Goodman and Irving Fazola) was a member of the Junior Dixieland Band and this was followed by a stint with Phil Zito and an important association with the Basin Street Six (1950-54) with whom the clarinetist made his first recordings. In 1955 Fountain was a member of the Dukes of Dixieland but his big breakthrough came when he was featured playing a featured Dixieland number or two on each episode of *The Lawrence Welk Show* during 1957-59. After he left, he moved back to New Orleans, opened his own club and has played there regularly since. Fountain's finest recordings were a lengthy string for Coral during 1959-65 (they turned commercial for a period after that) although he has made relatively few CDs considering his continuing popularity. *— Scott Yanow*

Pete Fountain's New Orleans / Feb. 1959 / MCA ♦♦♦
This album is an excellent showcase for Pete Fountain in his early days. The clarinetist (who is the only horn in a quartet with pianist Stan Wrightsman, bassist Morty Corb and drummer Jack Sperling) sounds typically enthusiastic on the Dixieland warhorses, turning "The Saints" into a march and coming up with fresh things to say on such songs as "Do You Know What It Means to Miss New Orleans," "Basin Street Blues" and "Tin Roof Blues." *— Scott Yanow*

Mr. New Orleans / 1961 / MCA ♦♦♦

Pete Fountain's French Quarter / 1961 / Coral ♦♦♦♦♦
In the early to mid-'60s Pete Fountain recorded a series of rewarding albums for Coral, none of which have yet been reissued on CD. This album, a quintet set with vibraphonist Godfrey Hirsch, pianist Stan Wrightsman, bassist Morty Corb, and drummer Jack Sperling, celebrated the opening of the clarinetist's New Orleans club, *the French Quarter Inn.* Fountain always sounds enthusiastic when he plays (as if he were discovering veteran Dixieland and swing standards for the first time), and he is heard in top form on such songs as "Dear Old Southland," "Someday Sweetheart," "Is It True What They Say About Dixie—," "That Da Da Strain," and even "The Birth of the Blues." *— Scott Yanow*

● **Standing Room Only** / 1965 / Coral ♦♦♦♦♦
This is one of the best Pete Fountain records for the clarinetist (who recorded so often with just a rhythm section or very subservient horns) is challenged by the presence of trumpeter Charlie Teagarden, trombonist Bob Havens and the great tenor Eddie Miller. With drummer Nick Fatool pushing the rhythm section, the band romps through eight standards (highlighted by "Muskrat Ramble," "Struttin' with Some Barbeque" and "You Are My Sunshine") and a memorable four-song "Ramblin' Medley." This LP, as with all of Pete Fountain's valuable output for Coral, has yet to be reissued on CD. *— Scott Yanow*

Pete Fountain At Piper's Opera House / Aug. 10, 1994 / Jazzology ♦♦♦♦
Clarinetist Pete Fountain leads a fairly strong group on this set, which was reissued on CD in 1993. Recorded live in Virginia City, Nevada, one has to put up with some raving from the announcer, but otherwise the music is enjoyable. Fountain is joined by the underrated trumpeter John Thomas, the great tenor Eddie Miller, trombonist Bob Havens, pianist Merle Koch, bassist Bunky Jones and drummer Nick Fatool for a straightforward set of Dixieland jams and swing-era ballads. In the repertoire are such songs as "Jazz Me Blues," "Shine," "Wolverine Blues" and "South Rampart Street Parade." A fun outing, and one of Pete Fountain's few (and best) recordings of the 1980s. *— Scott Yanow*

Fourplay

f. 1991
Group / Smooth Jazz, Crossover Jazz, Jazz-Pop
This all-star group (comprised of keyboardist Bob James, guitarist Lee Ritenour, bassist Nathan East and drummer Harvey Mason) was formed in 1991 after the quartet all came together on part of James' *Grand Piano Canyon* album. They have since recorded a number of CDs for Warner Bros. that have all been big-sellers, not surprising considering the popularity of James and Ritenour. The group's music borders on jazz with some strong improvisations mixed in with large doses of pop and R&B, about what one would expect from these studio musicians. *— Scott Yanow*

● **The Best of Fourplay** / 1991-1997 / Warner Brothers ♦♦♦♦
What looked at first like a premature marketing ploy—a greatest-hits collection after only three albums—?now makes some historical sense, for founding member Lee Ritenour left the quartet not long after the CD's release. So this is in essence a summary of Fourplay's first edition, a collection of mildly funky, ethereally voiced selections from *Fourplay, Between the Sheets* and *Elixir,* where Ritenour, Bob James, Nathan East and Harvey Mason integrate their personalities into a smoothly homogenized whole. To sweeten the pot for the hardcore fans, Fourplay recorded three new tracks for the album—Stevie Wonder's "Higher Ground" with vocals by Take 6, "4 Play and Pleasure" and "Any Time of Day"—all fairly uneventful. The musicianship is impeccable, the production velvety, and despite the suitable-for-lovemaking-and-commuting stamp of approval, one wishes that these fine players would just cut loose and really rip once in a while. *— Richard S. Ginell*

Elixir / 1994 / Warner Brothers ♦♦♦♦
The third outing from Fourplay (Lee Ritenour, Nathan East, Bob James and Harvey Mason clubbing together) is another lightly sautéed jazz offering, low-key and relaxed. Vocals this

time are contributed by Phil Collins, East, Patti Austin and Peabo Bryson (the latter two on an undistinguished version of "The Closer I Get to You"), but the main attraction for most is likely to be Ritenour's flexible guitar work. *—Steven McDonald*

4 / 1998 / Warner Brothers ✦✦✦

Yes, Please / Aug. 22, 2000 / Warner Brothers ✦✦✦
There are certain "givens" when purchasing a Fourplay album. Smooth, non-threatening, pop and R&B-inflected, groovy contemporary jazz. Mainly instrumentals with at least one vocal track contributed by a big-name artist and one or more other tracks with added vocal flavorings, usually in the form of rhythmic chanting. A clean, slick recording that is both polished and crisp. Bob James (piano), Nathan East (bass), Larry Carlton (guitar), and Harvey Mason (drums) have made their programmatic approach an art form, copied by countless contemporary jazz artists and envied by rival A&R types hoping to sell as many records as has this talented quartet (with either Lee Ritenour or Larry Carlton in the guitar chair). With respect to the basic Fourplay program, *Yes, Please!* does not disappoint. Yet, this album is a touch softer than previous releases and significantly more seductive, thus living up to the "fourplay/foreplay" double entendre. "Robo Bop" pulses to the repeated motif sounded in East's bass. "Blues Force" is a smoky temptress, with Carlton's guitar adding to the drama. James' keyboard fills romance "Go With Your Heart." "A Little Fourplay" is carried by guest artist Sheree's sexy vocals, Mason's drums, and some added R&B electronic kick in the mix. Those looking to set an after-hours mood with the one they love will say "yes, please" to this album. *—Brian Bartolini*

Bud Freeman (Lawrence Freeman)

b. Apr. 13, 1906, Chicago, IL, **d.** Chicago, IL
Sax (Tenor) / Swing, Dixieland
When Bud Freeman first matured, his was the only strong alternative approach on the tenor to the harder-toned style of Coleman Hawkins and he was an inspiration for Lester Young. Freeman, one of the top tenors of the 1930s, was also one of the few saxophonists (along with the slightly later Eddie Miller) to be accepted in the Dixieland world and his oddly angular but consistently swinging solos were an asset to a countless number of hot sessions. It took him time to develop his playing, which was still pretty primitive in 1927 when he made his recording debut with the McKenzie-Condon Chicagoans. He was starred on Eddie Condon's memorable 1933 recording "The Eel." After stints with Joe Haymes and Ray Noble, Freeman was a star with Tommy Dorsey's Orchestra and Clambake Seven (1936-38) before having a short unhappy stint with Benny Goodman (1938). He led his short-lived but legendary Summe Cum Laude Orchestra (1939-40), spent two years in the military and then from 1945 on alternated between being a bandleader and working with Condon's freewheeling Chicago jazz groups. He made scores of fine recordings and stuck to the same basic style that he had developed by the mid-'30s. *—Scott Yanow*

1928-1938 / Dec. 3, 1928-Nov. 30, 1938 / Classics ✦✦✦✦
Bud Freeman was virtually the only key tenor saxophonist of the 1928-35 period who did not sound heavily influenced by Coleman Hawkins. Freeman, whose style fell between Dixieland and swing and who has long had a distinctive sound, is heard on this Classics CD at the head of several classic groups. There are two titles from 1928 with an octet also including obscure trumpeter Johnny Mendel, pianist Dave North, drummer Gene Krupa and (on "Can't Help Lovin' That Man") singer Red McKenzie. While those performances have early examples of Freeman's style, the tenor's sound was very much formed by the time of the 1935 sextet date with the brilliant trumpeter Bunny Berigan; Bud and Bunny made for an exciting team. The bulk of this CD features Freeman in prime form jamming in a trio with pianist Jess Stacy and drummer George Wettling; these versions of "You Took Advantage of Me," "I Got Rhythm," "Keep Smiling at Trouble" and "My Honey's Loving Arms" are definitely classics. Also on this CD are five numbers on which Freeman leads an all-star octet also including cornetist Bobby Hackett, clarinetist Pee Wee Russell, Stacy and Eddie Condon. Although this music has been reissued in many different settings through the years, it is certainly essential (in one form or another) to all historical jazz collections. *—Scott Yanow*

1939-1940 / Jul. 19, 1939-Jul. 23, 1940 / Classics ✦✦✦✦
The second Bud Freeman Classics CD has all of the studio sessions (the master takes, but not the alternates) by Freeman's short-lived all-star Summe Cum Laude Orchestra. The Dixieland octet sounds very much like a well-organized Eddie Condon band, and the rhythm guitarist is among the personnel. Teaming up with Freeman (one of the first early tenormen to form a distinctive sound of his own) are such notable players as trumpeter Max Kaminsky, valve trombonist Brad Gowans, clarinetist Pee Wee Russell, pianist Dave Bowman and a rhythm section; the final set has the great trombonist Jack Teagarden (who takes a notable vocal on "Jack Hits the Road") in Gowans' place. The music, which includes eight titles originally recorded by Bix Beiderbecke's Wolverines, has more than its share of high points, and this CD is highly recommended to Dixieland fans. All of the musicians (many of whom would be performing a similar repertoire for the next few decades) sound fresh, enthusiastic, young and at the peak of their powers. *—Scott Yanow*

1945-1946 / Aug. 9, 1945-1946 / Classics ✦✦✦✦
The third Bud Freeman CD in Classics' reissues of all of his early sessions as a leader has some memorable performances. The classic tenor heads an all-star octet (with trumpeter Yank Lawson, trombonist Lou McGarity and clarinetist Edmond Hall) on four hot numbers; he creates a pair of hilarious verbal introductions to a couple of satirical V-Disc numbers ("The Latest Thing In Hot Jazz" and "For Musicians Only"); and on "The Atomic Era," Freeman performs an unusual duet with drummer Ray McKinley. However, this CD gets a lower rating than expected because 12 of the 21 performances showcase the Five De Marco Sisters, a pleasant but fairly mediocre swing vocal group. Although there are some good solos and ensembles on those selections, the recordings overall are only of interest to completists. *—Scott Yanow*

● **California Session** / Jan. 9, 1982 / Jazzology ✦✦✦✦✦
By the time of this previously unreleased 1982 concert (put out on CD in 1997), tenor saxophonist Bud Freeman was 75 and had been playing at a major-league level for over 55 years, but there was nothing tired about his timeless style. Freeman, who happened to be in Los Angeles, was invited to a concert put on by the Poor Angel Hot Jazz Society and agreed to appear on a few numbers. However, he was so impressed by the band that during the first song he quickly put his horn together and played throughout the entire performance. Freeman was joined by trumpeter Dick Cathcart, trombonist Betty O'Hara (doubling on double-belled euphonium), clarinetist Bob Reitmeier, the great swing pianist Ray Sherman, guitarist Howard Alden (just 23 at the time), bassist Phil Stephens, and drummer Nick Fatool. The repertoire on this CD consists of eight familiar standards, but the interpretations are full of inspiration and joy. On some tunes, Alden, already a masterful player, weaves lines around Freeman, and there are a few individual features for the tenorman (most notably a rollicking "Tea for Two" and a double-time rendition of "Body and Soul"). The group numbers are all enjoyable and full of high spirits, particularly "Struttin' With Some Barbecue" and "Just a Closer Walk With Thee." Highly recommended to Dixieland and straight-ahead fans. *—Scott Yanow*

Swingin' with the Eel / Dec. 16, 1927 May 2, - 19 / ASV/Living Era ✦✦✦✦
This 24-track collection follows the career highlights of this much-in-demand session whiz in recordings made between 1927 and 1945 under his own name and working as a featured sideman. With tracks aboard from McKenzie and Condon's Chicagoans, Wingy Manone, Joe Venuti, Eddie Condon, Tommy Dorsey, and Muggsy Spanier, as well as Freeman's trio and Summa Cum Laude Orchestra, Freeman's elegant tenor saxophone adds much sparkle to all of these varied sides. A little heralded figure in jazz history, Freeman left much remarkable work behind and here's a nice chunk of it. *—Cub Koda*

Bill Frisell

b. Mar. 18, 1951, Baltimore, MD
Guitar / Avant-Garde Jazz, Post-Bop, Fusion, Modern Creative
One of the most remarkable guitarists of the 1980s and '90s, Bill Frisell gets bizarre (and sometimes humorous) sounds out of his instrument that have not been heard before. Immediately recognizable, Frisell has the ability to sound like a Nashville country session guitarist, a heavy metal specialist, a Jim Hall devotee and an unusual avant-gardist. After growing up in Denver, he went to Berklee in the mid-'70s, toured England with Mike Gibbs's orchestra (1978) and recorded with Eberhard Weber (1979).

Frisell soon began appearing on many recordings for ECM including dates led by Jan Garbarek and Paul Motian. He had two ECM albums of his own during 1982-84 before forming a quartet with cellist Hank Roberts, bassist Kermit Driscoll and drummer Joey Baron. Frisell, who has recorded in several piano-less bass-less groups with Motian and has been a guest on many other artists' albums, is heard at his best on his own sessions. 1992's *Have a Little Faith* (which ranges from Sousa to Madonna with stops for Aaron Copland, Stephen Foster and Muddy Waters) is a good place to start! *—Scott Yanow*

Rambler / Aug. 1984 / ECM ✦✦✦✦✦
This relatively early set from Bill Frisell is a fine showcase for the utterly unique guitarist. Frisell has the ability to play nearly any extroverted style of music and his humor (check out the date's "Music I Heard") is rarely far below the surface. This particular quintet (with trumpeter Kenny Wheeler, tuba player Bob Stewart, electric bassist Jerome Harris and drummer Paul Motian) is not exactly short of original personalities and their outing (featuring seven Frisell compositions) is one of the most lively of all the ones in the ECM catalog. *—Scott Yanow*

Lookout for Hope / Mar. 1987 / ECM ✦✦✦✦✦
Guitarist Bill Frisell had one of the most stimulating and eccentric regular bands of the mid- to late 1980s. The highly versatile Frisell, whose playing ranges from Jim Hall to rock and Nashville while including sounds never previously heard on guitar, found complementary spirits in cellist Hank Roberts, bassist Kermit Driscoll and drummer Joey Baron. Together, the quartet performs nine of Frisell's diverse and colorful originals on this wide-ranging set, plus Thelonious Monk's "Hackensack." Well worth several listens by open-eared (and tolerant) jazz fans. *—Scott Yanow*

Live / Oct. 27, 1991 / Gramavision ✦✦✦✦✦
A Bill Frisell solo can invoke amber waves of grain, the south side of Chicago and various places in New England, all in the space of three bars. His tonal palette is hugely varied, yet his sound is completely personal—only Richard Thompson can boast a guitar style so individual and fully realized. Think of the music of Duke Ellington, Charlie Parker and Charles Mingus; jazz has always lived at the murky nexus between African music and European art music, and what makes Frisell unique is his ability to take those same two basic ingredients and come up with something that sounds brand new. That he's liable to quote Chuck Berry at the same time says something about his sweetness of spirit. This album finds Frisell onstage with bassist Kermit Driscoll and drummer Joey Baron, running through a few faves ("Throughout," "Strange Meeting," "When We Go") as well as some more obscure and surprising material. Driscoll is a sharply intuitive bassist with a reggae player's feel for silence; Baron punctuates more than he undergirds. As a result, this is largely music without groove. Instead, it hovers and floats overhead like a benevolent thunderstorm, sometimes letting loose rumbling, atonal chaos like "Crumb" and sometimes emitting bolts of pure electric light such as the utterly charming "Rag" and the yearning sweetness of "Throughout." "Pip, Squeak/Goodbye" steps briefly into tango territory, and Frisell takes the Sonny Rollins composition "No Moe" all the way back to the Delta with a bent blues solo. The John Hiatt cover, by the way, is the emotional centerpiece of the album: a deeply felt rendition of "Have a Little Faith in Me." This is a very special disc. *—Rick Anderson*

★ **Have a Little Faith** / Mar. 1992 / Elektra/Nonesuch ✦✦✦✦✦
Bill Frisell has long been one of the most unique guitarists around. Able to switch on a moment's notice from sounding like a Nashville studio player to heavy metal, several styles of jazz and just pure noise, Frisell can get a remarkable variety of sounds and tones out of his instrument. This set features Frisell in a quintet with Don Byron (on clarinet and bass clar-

inet), Guy Klucevsek on accordion, bassist Kermit Driscoll and drummer Joey Baron. To call the repertoire wide-ranging would be an understatement. In addition to eight melodies from Aaron Copland's *Billy the Kid*, Frisell and company explore (and often re-invent) pieces written by Charles Ives, Bob Dylan, Muddy Waters, Madonna, Sonny Rollins, Stephen Foster and John Phillip Sousa. This is one of the most inventive recordings of the 1990s and should delight most listeners from any genre. *—Scott Yanow*

Nashville / Sep. 1995-Nov. 1996 / Elektra/Nonesuch ✦✦✦✦✦
The vague country elements long dwelling on the fringes of Bill Frisell's music rise to the forefront on *Nashville*, an exquisitely atmospheric collection recorded in Music City with the aid of dobro legend Jerry Douglas, Union Station members Adam Steffey and Ron Block, and Lyle Lovett's Large Band bassist Viktor Krauss. Produced by Wayne Horvitz, the record is both genuine and alien—while played with real affection for the country form and without any *avant* posturing, its sound is original and distinct, a cinematic variation on C&W tenets. While primarily instrumental and comprised largely of Frisell originals, *Nashville* does welcome vocalist Robin Holcomb for a pair of more traditional numbers—Hazel Dickens' "Will Jesus Wash the Bloodstains From Your Hands" and the Skeeter Davis hit "The End of the World"—as well as a cover of Neil Young's "One of These Days." *—Jason Ankeny*

Bill Frisell Quartet / 1996 / Nonesuch ✦✦✦✦
Guitarist Bill Frisell has become well-known for his eccentric and highly versatile style. Able to sound like Jim Hall, a heavy metal player, or a Nashville studio guitarist at a moment's notice, Frisell has created sounds on the guitar that had never been heard before. This CD uses a rather unusual instrumentation, a quartet comprised of Frisell, trumpeter Ron Miles, trombonist Curtis Fowlkes and Eyvind Kang, who doubles on violin and tuba. Ten of the 13 Frisell originals on the release were originally written for films (including Gary Larson's *Tales From the Far Side* and the Buster Keaton movie *Convict 13*), and the resulting music is tightly arranged yet spontaneous, episodic, and sometimes a bit nutty, but also strangely logical. Whether it be the oldtimey theme to "Dead Ranch," athe blues "Convict 13," a few somber ballads, or hints at early Duke Ellington (particularly by Miles' wah-wah trumpet), this is a continually interesting, offbeat set. *—Scott Yanow*

Gone, Just Like a Train / 1997 / Nonesuch ✦✦✦✦
Drawing from all over the musical spectrum, Frisell selects drummer Jim Keltner (best known for his records with George Harrison, Eric Clapton and other rock stars) and bassist Viktor Krauss (a fixture in Lyle Lovett's country band), and comes up with an immensely likable, easy-grooving CD that defies one to put a label on it. If anything, Frisell leans toward a drawling country twang heavily indebted to Chet Atkins in his guitar work here, but there is a freewheeling jazz sensibility at work on every track. Keltner contributes the heavy rock element with his emphatic strokes, occasionally pushing Frisell in that direction on the title track and the lengthy "Lookout for Hope." Yet Keltner is also capable of surprising subtlety, and Krauss provides firm, unflashy underpinning. Above all, this is thoughtful, free-thinking, ear-friendly jamming that was recorded in bustling Burbank, CA. but sounds as if it was laid down in a relaxed cabin in the hills. *—Richard S. Ginell*

Good Dog, Happy Man / May 18, 1999 / Nonesuch ✦✦✦✦
No doubt pleased with his countrified direction on *Gone, Just Like A Train*, Frisell gives us a lot more of basically the same thing here—only with expanded numbers in the ranks. Bassist Viktor Krause and drummer Jim Keltner return, now accompanied by Wayne Horvitz's understated organ and piano; Greg Leisz on as assortment of fretted instruments, including the dobro, pedal steel guitar and mandolin; and on "Shenandoah, " Ry Cooder's atmospheric guitars. The first tracks of this album pick up right where *Gone, Just Like A Train* left off—low-key, perhaps too low-key—but tracks like "Big Shoe" and "Cadillac 1959" add a bit of swagger to the lope and "Poem For Eva" sports the best tune. Again, Frisell often captures a loose, evolutionary jamming quality in these sessions, playing the country accents off of his jazz sensibilities. Unlike its predecessor, though, you can't imagine this being recorded on a backwoods front porch, for there are some production tricks and distant-sounding electronic loops that give away its Burbank studio origins. Purists on either side of the jazz/country divide are hereby warned to back off so that the rest of us can enjoy this. *—Richard S. Ginell*

Ghost Town / Mar. 7, 2000 / Nonesuch ✦✦✦✦
While Bill Frisell has released plenty of albums under his own name, this is his first true solo album—the first on which he plays all of the instruments himself. These include electric and acoustic guitar, six-string banjo, and bass, as well as the occasional looped sample. To call the music he creates on this album "introspective" would be something of an understatement. This won't come as a complete surprise to his fans—there has always been a gentle and meditative quality to his music, and even when he's gotten wild with his trio or with downtown pals like John Zorn or Vernon Reid, those moments of abrasive abandon have always seemed like detours from his more natural, but no less inventive and interesting, sweetness and good humor. But there's a darkness around the edges this time out that is unusual, as if he's lonely playing by himself and a little bit unnerved at the thoughts and feelings he's being forced to face on his own. His rendition of the A.P. Carter classic "Wildwood Flower" starts out with an extended Delta-blues introduction, which is a pretty unusual choice. There are other cover versions, including Hank Williams' "I'm So Lonesome I Could Cry" and Gershwin's "My Man's Gone Now," both of which deeply explore the emotional wreckage described by the songs' lyrics; his own compositions, such as the vaguely surfy "Variation on a Theme" and the slightly ominous "Big Bob," seem to be cut out of similar cloth. There are moments of light relief, such as the gently lovely title track and the brief banjo interlude "Fingers Snappin' and Toes Tappin'," but the overall mood here is relatively dark, though consistently beautiful. *—Rick Anderson*

Dave Frishberg

b. Mar. 23, 1933, St. Paul, MN
Vocals, Piano, Lyricist / Vocal Jazz, Swing, Bop
Arguably the top living lyricist, Dave Frishberg has written more than his share of witty (yet insightful) classics including "I'm Hip," "Peel Me a Grape," "Dear Bix," "The Underdog," "Saratoga Hunch," "Slappin' the Cakes on Me," "Z's," "My Attorney Bernie," "Blizzard of Lies," "Another Song About Paris," "You Are There," "El Cajon," "Can't Take You Nowhere" and "Let's Eat Home." A fine swing pianist and a world-weary sounding vocalist, the multi-talented Dave Frishberg moved to New York in 1957. He worked early on as a pianist with Carmen McRae, Kai Winding, Gene Krupa (1960-63), Wild Bill Davison, Bud Freeman, Ben Webster, the Al Cohn-Zoot Sims Quintet and Bobby Hackett among others and cut an album with Jimmy Rushing. He recorded a commercial record for CTI (1968) that generated a surprise hit in "Van Lingle Mungo." However it was not until Frishberg moved to the West Coast (1971) and started recording for the Concord label (1977) as a vocalist/pianist that he began to make a big impression. Dave Frishberg has since cut albums for Omnisound, Fantasy, Bloomdido and a purely instrumental duet set with Dixieland trumpeter Jim Goodwin (1992) for Arbors. Many of his originals have been recorded by other vocalists. *—Scott Yanow*

Getting Some Fun out of Life / Jan. 25, 1977-Jan. 26, 1977 / Concord Jazz ✦✦✦✦✦
One of Dave Frishberg's finest albums (and a set that gained him a great deal of recognition), this album can be easily split into two. Frishberg performs six enjoyable unaccompanied piano solos (including "In a Mist," "King Porter Stomp" and the title cut) and sings six other numbers with a quintet also including trumpeter Bob Findley, altoist Marshall Royal, bassist Larry Gales and drummer Steve Schaeffer. Of the latter, his "Dear Bix" (taken in duet with Findley) is a classic, while "Lotus Blossom" and "Old Man Harlem" are also quite memorable. Highly recommended. *—Scott Yanow*

You're a Lucky Guy / Jul. 10, 1978 / Concord Jazz ✦✦✦✦
There is plenty of diversity on this prime Dave Frishberg set. Four songs (including vocal versions of "Truckin'" and "*The Underdog*") match Frishberg's piano with trombonist Bob Brookmeyer, tenor saxophonist Al Cohn, bassist Jim Hughart, and drummer Nick Ceroli. Frishberg takes "That Old Feeling," "You're a Lucky Guy" (which he sings), and "Cheerful Little Earful" as piano solos, and there are also three wonderful duets with Cohn. Only two of the ten songs were written by Frishberg, so the emphasis is on his talents as a pianist and singer rather than as a lyricist. Recommended. *—Scott Yanow*

Dave Frishberg Classics / Apr. 29, 1981-Dec. 1982 / Concord Jazz ✦✦✦✦✦
This is the essential Dave Frishberg CD. Comprised of all ten selections originally issued as an Omnisound LP (*The Dave Frishberg Songbook, Volume 1*) and seven of the ten songs from *Vol. 2*, the release features the composer/lyricist singing and playing piano on many of his best-known originals. Highlights include "I'm Hip," "Van Lingle Mungo," "Slappin' the Cakes on Me," "Z's," "Sweet Kentucky Ham," "My Attorney Bernie," "Blizzard of Lies" and "You Are There." Frishberg is one of the top lyricists of the past 20 years, and this release has plenty of convincing evidence. A gem. *—Scott Yanow*

● **Live at Vine Street** / Oct. 1984 / Fantasy/OJC ✦✦✦✦✦
Arguably the greatest living lyricist, Dave Frishberg sings and plays piano on this very enjoyable solo disc. His nine originals include such memorable (and humorous) tunes as "El Cajon" (a Johnny Mandel melody), "The Dear Departed Past," and "Blizzard of Lies." In addition, Frishberg plays a lengthy medley of Johnny Hodges-associated songs. This witty set is easily recommended. *—Scott Yanow*

Let's Eat Home / Aug. 1989 / Concord Jazz ✦✦✦✦
This CD is most significant for having the original versions of Dave Frishberg's "Let's Eat Home," "I Was Ready" and "Lookin' Good." The pianist, who also takes several instrumentals (Al Cohn and Billy Strayhorn medleys, plus "The Mooche"), is assisted by valve trombonist Rob McConnell, trumpeter Snooky Young, bassist Jim Hughart and drummer Jeff Hamilton on most selections. Although not quite essential, this is an enjoyable outing by the pianist/singer/lyricist and ranks in his top five recordings. *—Scott Yanow*

Double Play / Oct. 3, 1992-Oct. 4, 1992 / Arbors ✦✦✦✦
Dave Frishberg, best-known for his impressive abilities as a lyricist and vocalist, sticks exclusively to instrumentals on this enjoyable disc. Frishberg the pianist is teamed with cornetist Jim Goodwin on a duet set comprised of 17 trad and swing classics that mostly date from the 1920s and '30s. To their credit the duo constantly walk a musical tightrope, taking chances within the idiom and not being afraid to make mistakes; neither musician felt that the music should be edited afterward. The result is colorful classic jazz interpreted by two strong stylists who, while paying tribute to their predecessors, infuse the music with their own personalities. It is easily recommended to trad fans. *—Scott Yanow*

By Himself: Arbors Piano Series, Vol. 3 / Jun. 30, 1997-Aug. 4, 1997 / Arbors ✦✦✦✦✦
Dave Frishberg had not recorded a strictly instrumental solo piano record in many years when he cut this 1997 Arbors set. Actually he does vocalize on four numbers (most memorable is his classic "I Want To Be A Sideman" and a remake of "Can't Take You Nowhere"), the other ten songs put the focus purely on his underrated but swinging mainstream piano playing. Frishberg, whose inspirations are the swing era pianists rather than those of the bop era, even turns Dizzy Gillespie's "Groovin' High" into a swing song. Other highlights include "You Took Advantage Of Me," "Jump For Joy" and a six-song "Kansas City Medley." Recommended. *—Scott Yanow*

Satoko Fujii

Piano / Avant-Garde Jazz, Free Jazz, Progressive Big Band, Modern Creative
During a relatively brief period of time, pianist Satoko Fujii has made a strong impression on the American avant-garde jazz scene. Rather than running through chord changes, Fujii generally improvises quite freely, using a song's melody or mood as a point of departure. She started on piano in her native Japan when she was four and studied classical music for 16 years before finally deciding to switch to advanced jazz. Fujii first came to the United States in 1985 to attend the Berklee College Of Music (it only took her two years to graduate) and she spent 1993-1995 attending the New England Conservatory where her teachers included George Russell, Cecil McBee and Paul Bley. Fujii has since worked in the studios in both Japan and Europe and played with Joseph Jarman. Satoko Fujii, who had recorded previously (but her earliest dates are thus far only available in Japan) debuted in the U.S. by cutting a series of duets with fellow pianist Bley during which she held her own. Since then she has

cut a solo recital (both of the dates are on the Japanese Libra label), a dynamic set of duets with her husband trumpeter Natsuki Tamura and led a 15-piece orchestra on South Wind (released by Leo). *—Scott Yanow*

● **Kitsune-Bi** / May 7, 1998+Nov. 3, 1998 / Tzadik ✦✦✦✦✦
Pianist Satoko Fujii leads a beautiful date featuring solo pieces, duets with soprano saxophonist Sachi Hayasaka, and trio numbers with eminent bassist Mark Dresser and ingenious percussionist Jim Black. *Kitsune-Bi* sounds great the first time through, and becomes more wildly impressive with each listen, revealing multi-layered depths. The pieces are all originals (except Jimmy Giuffre's "Moonlight"). The album opens with "Hizumi," a trio tune that begins with the musicians feeling each other out. They gel within the first minute, and Dresser soon starts performing double duty, moving around rhythmically with Black while simultaneously interacting with Fujii. The clincher is Dresser's ability to mimic all the sounds of the piano theme; it's mind-boggling that he can create these sounds with a bass. "Sound of Stone" is a solo piano piece that Fujii opens by musically chalking out the boundaries. A dark chord signals the end of the sketching, and she proceeds to fill the piece with dramatic runs and stalls, momentous build-up and thinning-out contrasts, and clusters that move up the scale followed by single notes that tinkle back down. This excellent melodic piece showcases her ability without turning into a show of empty virtuosity. "Zauzy" is a duet between piano and soprano saxophone; Fujii and Hayasaka play foil to each other, giving the impression of notes flying from a large, spinning music wheel. About 18 minutes into the trio piece "Past of Life," the group recalls the groove and interaction of Tim Berne's Bloodcount. Altogether, *Kitsune-Bi* is a stunning album filled with amazing interplay and stellar compositions. The astonishing skill and distinctive style on display here is somewhat surprising, considering that this is only Satoko Fujii's second U.S. release. *Kitsune-Bi* is an achievement of constantly flowing brilliance and creativity. *—Joslyn Layne*

South Wind / Jun. 19, 1997 / Leo ✦✦✦✦✦

Double Take / Jul. 11, 2000 / East Works Entertainment ✦✦✦✦✦
Double Take is the musical statement establishing Satoko Fujii as one of the most exciting jazz composers of the late '90s, thus bringing the "ascension" phase of her career to an end. This two-CD set features two incarnations of the Satoko Fujii Orchestra: the "East" version, on Disc 1, the live Okegawa 10/99 recording, and the second disc's "West" lineup, recorded a month later in NY's Avatar Studios.

The album opens with a fresh reading of the title track from Fujii's *South Wind* (1998, Leo Lab), a work based on a Japanese scale that may be Fujii's most oriental-sounding composition. Then comes "Ruin," a suite in four parts. A series of tone poems, "Ruin" will remain one of Fujii's masterpieces. Born out of silence, it builds to a climax in "The Desert" just to come down and surprise the listener when ("The Megalopolis") begins on an urban-like frenzy. The East band (15 players from Japan's new jazz scene) is impressively tight, loud, and exuberant with an energy level close to Peter Brötzmann's Chicago tentet. Disc two opens with "Ruin," which serves as a point of comparison between the two bands. The West cohorts (which includes Briggan Krauss, Chris Speed, Andy Laster, Cuong Vu, and Stomu Takeishi) have a less in-your-face approach, playing with more nuance but, paradoxically, with a little less feeling.

The music of Satoko Fujii (and her husband, trumpeter Natsuki Tamura, since he contributes three pieces) is surprisingly easy to listen to and can appeal to a wide audience of jazz fans. Her writing on *Double Take* is packed with energy, contrasts, solid grooves (like on "Tobifudo"), and power-brass galore while staying more punchy and concise than the Orchestra's previous release, *Jo*. This one is a definitive must-have. *—François Couture*

Toward to West / May 7, 1998 / Enja ✦✦✦✦

Curtis Fuller

b. Dec. 15, 1934, Detroit, MI
Trombone / Hard Bop
Curtis Fuller belongs in the select circle with J.J. Johnson, Kai Winding and a few others who make the trombone sound fluid and inviting rather than awkward. His ability to make wide octave leaps and play whiplash phrases in a relaxed, casual manner is a testament to his skill. Fuller's solos and phrases are often ambitious and creative, and he's worked in several fine bands and participated in numerous great sessions. Fuller studied music in high school, then began developing his skills in an army band, where he played with Cannonball Adderley. He worked in Detroit with Kenny Burrell and Yusef Lateef, then moved to New York. Fuller made his recording debut as a leader on Transition in 1955, and recorded in the late '50s for Blue Note, Prestige, United Artists and Savoy. He was a charter member of The Jazztet with Benny Golson and Art Farmer in 1959, then played in Art Blakey's Jazz Messengers from 1961 to 1965. During the '70s, he experimented for a time playing hard bop arrangements in a band featuring electronic instruments. *—Ron Wynn*

New Trombone / May 11, 1957 / Prestige/OJC ✦✦✦
Trombonist Curtis Fuller's debut as a leader was a strong start to the 22-year-old's career. Already a strong player in the J.J. Johnson mold, Fuller blends in well with altoist Sonny Red, pianist Hank Jones, bassist Doug Watkins and drummer Louis Hayes on the fine straight-ahead date. The CD reissue adds "Alicia" to the original five-song program. While four of the six tunes are originals, their chord changes are generally easy to recognize (two are blues, and "Vonce #5" borrows from "I Got Rhythm"), and all of the musicians fare quite well. *—Scott Yanow*

Curtis Fuller with Red Garland / May 14, 1957 / New Jazz/OJC ✦✦✦✦
This CD reissue features trombonist Curtis Fuller in a quintet with altoist Sonny Red, pianist Red Garland, bassist Paul Chambers and drummer Louis Hayes performing a pair of originals, two blues and a couple of ballad features. Red is outstanding on "Moonlight Becomes You" (one of his finest recordings) while Fuller does a fine job on "Stormy Weather." Even with the new material, this set has a feel of a jam session; the blend between the trombone and the alto is particularly appealing. Despite the overly critical liner notes (written in 1962), this is an excellent hard-bop oriented date. *—Scott Yanow*

Curtis Fuller and Hampton Hawes with French Horns / May 18, 1957 / New Jazz/OJC ✦✦✦✦✦

The Complete Blue Note/UA Curtis Fuller Sessions / Jun. 16, 1957-Mar. 9, 1959 / Mosaic ✦✦✦✦✦
Trombonist Curtis Fuller, who developed his sound out of the style of J.J. Johnson, recorded prolifically as a leader from 1957-1962. After recording three dates for Prestige and New Jazz within a seven-day period in 1957, Fuller made four albums for Blue Note from 1957-1958, and after three albums for Savoy, he cut a lone session for United Artists in 1959. All of the five Blue Note and United Artists records (plus an alternate take of "Down Home") are on this excellent three-CD limited box set, released in 1996. Fuller is heard with four different quintets that include either tenor saxophonist Hank Mobley, baritonist Tate Houston, trumpeter Art Farmer, or (on a date only previously out in Japan) fellow trombonist Slide Hampton; the rhythm sections consist of either Bobby Timmons or Sonny Clark on piano, Paul Chambers or George Tucker on bass, and Art Taylor, Louis Hayes, or Charlie Persip in the drum slot. In addition, there is a sextet session with Lee Morgan, Mobley, Tommy Flanagan, Chambers, and Elvin Jones that has arrangements by Gigi Gryce and Benny Golson. Throughout, the music is high-quality hard bop with plenty of fine features for the underrated but talented Curtis Fuller. *—Scott Yanow*

● **Blues-ette** / May 21, 1956 / Savoy ✦✦✦✦✦
A legendary set that became very popular in Japan (leading to 1993's *Blues-ette Part II*), this is one of several pre-Jazztet recordings that teamed together trombonist Curtis Fuller and tenor saxophonist Benny Golson. The strong rhythm section (pianist Tommy Flanagan, bassist Jimmy Garrison and drummer Al Harewood), excellent material (including two songs apiece by Golson and Fuller) and inspired solos make this a hard bop gem. *—Scott Yanow*

Imagination / Dec. 17, 1959 / Savoy ✦✦✦✦
Prior to the official formation of the Jazztet with trumpeter Art Farmer, trombonist Curtis Fuller and tenorman Benny Golson made several albums together, usually with other trumpeters. This somewhat rare date has trumpeter Thad Jones, bassist Jimmy Garrison, drummer Dave Bailey, and, most significantly, pianist McCoy Tyner in his recording debut completing the sextet. Fuller arranged all five of the songs, four of which were his originals. Although the material (other than the lone standard "Imagination") is unfamiliar, the chord changes inspire the players to create some fine solos. Easily recommended to hard bop fans lucky enough to find this album. *—Scott Yanow*

Blues-ette, Pt. 2 / Jan. 4, 1993-Jan. 6, 1993 / Savoy ✦✦✦✦✦
The original *Blues-ette* album was a quintet session from 1959 featuring trombonist Curtis Fuller, tenor-saxophonist Benny Golson, pianist Tommy Flanagan, bassist Jimmy Garrison and drummer Al Harewood. Thirty-four years later the same musicians (with bassist Ray Drummond filling in for the deceased Garrison) had a reunion for this Savoy CD. Three of the songs from the original session are given new versions and there are also performances of several recent compositions by both Golson and Fuller in addition to four standards. Although Golson's sound on tenor has evolved since the earlier date, the appealing blend between the two horns remain unchanged as do the styles of Fuller and Flanagan, making this an excellent example of swinging hard bop. *—Scott Yanow*

Kenny G. (Kenneth Gorelick)

b. 1959, Seattle, WA
Sax (Soprano) / Smooth Jazz, Crossover Jazz, Jazz-Pop, Adult Contemporary
Kenny G has long been the musician many jazz listeners love to hate. A phenomenally successful instrumentalist whose recordings make the pop charts, G's sound has been a staple on adult contemporary and "smooth jazz" radio stations since the mid-1980s, making him a household name. Kenny G is a fine player with an attractive sound (influenced a bit by Grover Washington Jr.) who often caresses melodies, putting a lot of emotion into his solos. Because he does not improvise much (sticking mostly to predictable melody statements), his music largely falls outside of jazz. Like most pop stars, Kenny G now takes a long time between records, going out on occasional tours and filling stadiums. Whether he will ever choose to play jazz in the future is open to question (certainly there is no financial incentive), but he has made the soprano sax sound appealing to millions of fans, while simultaneously annoying many jazz purists. *—Scott Yanow*

● **Greatest Hits** / 1982-1992 / Arista ✦✦✦✦✦
Kenny G's music has always been pop-oriented, so a *Greatest Hits* collection serves him much better than it would if he was a straight jazz musician. The 17-track collection rounds up all of his pop Top 40 hits and many of his adult contemporary favorites, including "Songbird," "Don't Make Me Wait for Love," "Silhouette," "Forever in Love," "By the Time This Night Is Over," "How Could an Angel Break My Heart," and "Everytime I Close My Eyes." For collectors, there are a couple of non-LP tracks—his Sinatra duet "All the Way/One for My Baby" and "Theme From *Dying Young*"—plus the previously unreleased "Loving You," "Baby G," and the Michael Bolton duet "You Send Me." While the non-LP cuts are worthy inclusions, the new tracks are marginal and tend to weigh down the lengthy album. Nevertheless, all of Kenny G's hits are here, which makes it an ideal choice for casual fans. *—Stephen Thomas Erlewine*

G Force / 1983 / Arista ✦✦✦
Kenny G's work can be divided into three main categories: (1) his improvisatory fusion efforts as a Jeff Lorber sideman in the late 1970s, (2) his R&B-oriented albums of 1982-1985, and (3) the elevator Muzak he has specialized in since 1986. Falling into the second category, *G Force* is a fairly decent urban contemporary release that clearly benefits from the input of Kashif (who serves as executive producer). Kashif was hot at the time, and the R&B singer/producer/songwriter had been burning up the charts with hits by Evelyn "Champagne" King, George Benson, Howard Johnson and himself. Kashif's stamp is all over this sleek album; you can hear it on both the tunes with R&B vocals ("Hi, How Ya Doin'" and "Do Me Right") and groove-oriented instrumentals like "I've Been Missin' You" and "I Wanna Be Yours." *G Force*, Kenny's second album, is a long way from the adventurous fusion Kenny

had recorded with Lorber, and the sax solos he was taking in 1983 were hardly breathtaking. But thanks to Kashif's participation, *G Force* is an enjoyable, R&B-oriented date and is probably the best album he did as a leader (which isn't saying a lot, considering how boring most of his subsequent projects would be). *—Alex Henderson*

Gravity / 1985 / Arista ✦✦✦

Duotones / 1986 / Arista ✦✦✦✦✦
Kenny G's breakthrough effort featured the hit "Songbird," which is the definitive example of the saxophonist's smooth, lyrical playing; the rest of the album is nearly as good, highlighting his melodic jazzy pop. *—Stephen Thomas Erlewine*

Silhouette / 1988 / Arista ✦✦✦
Kenny G was at the top his form with *Silhouette,* the follow-up to his breakthrough *Duotones,* turning in a set of smooth, melodic sax that cemented his position as America's favorite pop instrumentalist. *—Stephen Thomas Erlewine*

Breathless / 1992 / Arista ✦✦✦✦
Throughout the 1990s, Kenny G was the whipping boy of the jazz world—the instrumentalist that hardcore jazz improvisers loved to bash when the subject of smooth jazz came up. Kenny's huge following responded that the attacks were silly and misguided because the saxman was the first to admit that he was primarily a pop instrumentalist and wasn't pretending to be anything else. True, it was silly for jazz artists to judge Kenny by hard bop standards when hard bop (or even soul-jazz or fusion) was a long way from what he was going for. And *Breathless* isn't bad because it's a pop album or because it's commercial; it's bad because of its complete lack of soul, substance or creativity. There's nothing even remotely tasteful about interchangeable tunes like "Sentimental," "Forever In Love" and "End of the Night," all of which are about as bloodless and schlocky as it gets. Always sounding like he's on automatic pilot, Kenny takes no risks whatsoever and sees to it that one song is as shamelessly contrived as the next. Even the presence of the great R&B crooner Aaron Neville on "Even If My Heart Would Break" can't save this one-dimensional release. Whether you're into pop or jazz, *Breathless* is unlistenable. *—Alex Henderson*

The Moment / 1996 / Arista ✦✦✦✦
Although *The Moment* followed four years after Kenny G's blockbuster *Breathless,* the saxophonist didn't change his approach at all during his time off. Kenny G remains a sweet, melodic instrumentalist, who works entirely in lush, slick adult contemporary pop settings. His playing has improved somewhat in those four years—he soars and dives with effortless skill, and his vibrato remains fleet and elegant—yet after *The Moment* is finished, you wish that he had tried some new musical territories. That said, it is true that *The Moment* ranks second to only *Breathless* in terms of sheer consistency in Kenny G's catalog, thanks to the sustained vision of producer Babyface. Of particular note are the two vocal collaborations (Babyface's "Everytime I Close My Eyes," Toni Braxton's "That Somebody Was You"), which are the best duets to yet appear on any of Kenny G's records. *—Thom Owens*

Classics in the Key of G / Jun. 29, 1999 / Arista ✦✦✦✦

Slim Gaillard (Slim Bulee Gaillard)

b. Jan. 1, 1916, Detroit, MI, **d.** Feb. 26, 1991, London, England
Vocals, Piano, Guitar / Vocal Jazz, Jive, Swing
A cult hero, Slim Gaillard was a frequently hilarious personality whose comedy (inventing his own jive language with a liberal use of the words "vout" and "oreenee") generally overshadowed his music. In the mid-'30s he had a solo act during which he played guitar while tap dancing! In 1936 Gaillard began teaming with bassist Slam Stewart as Slim and Slam. Their very first recording became his biggest hit, "Flat Foot Floogie." Slim and Slam were a popular attraction up to 1942 with such other songs as "Tutti Frutti" and "Laughin' in Rhythm." By 1945 Gaillard had a new bassist, Bam Brown (whose frantic vocals matched well with Slim's cool if nonsensical voice), and "Cement Mixer" and "Poppity Pop" caught on. Gaillard, who played electric guitar influenced by Charlie Christian, fairly basic boogie-woogie piano and vibes, led an unusual date with guests Charlie Parker and Dizzy Gillespie (1945) that was highlighted by "Slim's Jam." Throughout the 1940s in Los Angeles, Gaillard had a strong following, using such sidemen as Zutty Singleton and Dodo Marmarosa, but the popularity of jive singers (which included Harry "The Hipster" Gibson and Leo Watson) ran its course and after 1953 Gaillard only led two other record sessions (in 1958 and 1982). In the 1960s he was largely outside of music, running a motel in San Diego, but by the late '70s Slim Gaillard was back on a part-time basis, still singing "Flat Foot Floogie" and making one wonder why this comic whiz was neglected for nearly three decades. Many of his key recordings can be found on Tax (a box set has the complete Slim and Slam from 1938-42), Hep and Verve. *—Scott Yanow*

Groove Juice Special / Jan. 19, 1938-Apr. 4, 1942 / Columbia ✦✦✦
Singer/guitarist Slim Gaillard and bassist Slam Stewart made for a frequently hilarious and outrageous team. Gaillard's jive talk and the basic but memorable originals (best-known of which is "The Flat Foot Floogie") made Slim & Slam a popular group in the late '30s. All of their joint recordings were reissued in a perfectly done box set for Affinity a few years ago, so this single disc pales in comparison. and since eight of the 20 numbers that are included here are alternate takes (including "Floogie"), this is not quite a definitive introductory or greatest-hits set either, although beginners should be delighted by the music. The performances (which sometimes includes such guests as trumpeter Al Killian, clarinetist Garvin Bushell, drummers Kenny Clarke and Chico Hamilton and tenor great Ben Webster) are quite fun, but a bit more planning should have gone into the programming. *—Scott Yanow*

• **Slim & Slam** / Feb. 17, 1938-Apr. 4, 1942 / Affinity ✦✦✦✦✦
Starting with his initial recording "Flat Foot Floogie" (whose original name was actually "Flat Fleet Floogee"), guitarist/singer/jokester Slim Gaillard was a cult hero and a masterful (if somewhat limited) entertainer. Teamed with bassist Slam Stewart (who sang along with his bowed solos), Gaillard became quite popular during the latter part of the swing era. This very complete three-CD set contains all of Slim Gaillard's 82 performances (usually with Slam), including several taken from radio broadcasts and quite a few alternate takes. Among the other sidemen are the underrated tenorman Kenneth Hollon, trumpeter Al Killan, pianist Loumell Morgan, clarinetist Garvin Bushell, and Ben Webster on tenor. A definitive and perfectly realized reissue from the English Affinity label. *—Scott Yanow*

The Best of Slim Gaillard: Laughin' in Rhythm / Apr. 22, 1946-Jan. 1954 / Verve ✦✦✦✦
This CD has highlights from Slim Gaillard's 1946-47 and 1951-54 recordings for the Verve label. A fine Charlie Christian-inspired guitarist, an adequate pianist and a unique jive singer, Gaillard was always in his own category. Some of the selections on this CD are hilarious and highlights include the four-part "Opera in Vout," "Serenade to a Poodle" (which of course has plenty of barking), "Laughing in Rhythm," "Chicken Rhythm," "Potato Chips" and the previously unreleased (and modestly titled) "Genius" which features Gaillard overdubbing himself on trumpet, trombone, tenor, vibes, piano, organ, bass, drums and tap dancing. Although Gaillard's heyday was really the mid-'40s, this CD is quite memorable. *—Scott Yanow*

Ganelin Trio

f. 1971, **db.** 1990
Group / Avant-Garde Jazz, Free Jazz
Comprised of pianist Vyacheslav Ganelin (b. 1944), saxophonist Vladimir Chekasin (b. 1947) and drummer Vladimir Tarasov (b. 1947), the Ganelin Trio created quite a stir when they were discovered by the West. The group from the Soviet Union played very explorative avant-garde jazz, a rare example of freedom behind the Iron Curtain. They mixed in ethnic free music and earlier jazz styles in their lengthy, colorful and often-humorous improvisations. In addition to their work for the Russian Melodija company, most of their recordings were made for the enterprising Leo label. The group, which had a few opportunities to tour in the West, broke up when Ganelin emigrated to Israel. *—Scott Yanow*

Encores / Jun. 15, 1978-Nov. 15, 1981 / Leo ✦✦✦✦✦
This wonderfully accessible collection of live performances includes the entire LP *Con Fuoco,* along with several pieces from other long-out-of-print records. As usual, the trio is in peak form, with great playing, lots of fun, and wonderful interaction. The music for *Con Fuoco* was recorded in 1979, and the tape had to be literally smuggled out of the former Soviet Union to reach Western ears. This CD is distinguished by a couple of standards: "Summer Time" and "Mack the Knife," each played with the characteristic humor of the group. The other seven numbers are delightfully whimsical, with Vladimir Chekasin in especially good form on whatever he happens to playing at the moment: bassett horn, alto sax, tenor sax, clarinet, wooden flute, ocarina, pipes, percussion, or even his voice. Add Vladamir Tarasov's wacky percussion and leader Ganelin's piano (and even electric guitar), and you've got the ingredients for a zany, wild set of free-style Russian jazz. *—Steve Loewy*

• **Concerto Grosso** / 1978 / Melodiya ✦✦✦✦✦
Ganelin-Tarasov-Checkasin. Russian trio of wildly pure improvisers. A must-buy for the challengable listener. *—Michael G. Nastos*

Old Bottles / Jun. 26, 1982+Mar. 31, 1983 / Leo ✦✦✦✦
Old Bottles is a remarkable recording that presents two vintage, extended Ganelin pieces in new settings. The first, "Non Troppo, is an unissued live recording from 1983, while "New Wine" was previously available on LP (Leo, 112). Vyacheslav Ganelin (on piano and electric guitar, and more), Vladimir Tarasov (on all manner of drums and percussion), and Vladimir Chekasin (on saxophones, clarinets, bassett-horn, trombone, and voice) start "Non Troppo" quietly—not exactly the way they've played it in the past—with many surprises to follow. Taking on Bartok's "Microcosmos" as a foundation for group improvisation is a heady thing, but these three make it seem like a Road Runner cartoon! This is harmonic invention stretched to its most extreme, and then torn apart in the interest of something completely new and different that might not make sense, but makes sense somehow.

"New Wine" reveals, in a much more careful, though still intense way, how the group's architecture of improvisation worked, going from the inside out, including an intricate drum solo, a reinvention of "Too Close for Comfort," and time signatures colliding with key changes, as harmonic response and melodic convention are tossed into the dustbin. All of the freedom in the piece was earned by the restraint of the beginning, and a wealth of generated ideas. This track is one of the most stellar examples of how group improvising *happens. Old Bottles* is two sides of the Ganelin Trio that are most compelling: a willingness to throw convention to the dogs in order to find music's heart (and often that heart had a really funny face drawn on it) and the taste and sheer musicianship it takes to honor that tradition as a way of creating a new kind of jazz, one excluding nothing that is honest and interesting. *—Thom Jurek*

Con Affetto / Nov. 20, 1983 / Golden Years of New ✦✦✦✦✦
The Ganelin Trio has reached a sort of legendary status among devotees of free jazz. This largely unreleased live set from a concert in Moscow was originally smuggled out to the West, but took some time for its eventual release. The music is classic Ganelin, and although the first track is almost 60 minutes, it is filled with such a panoramic view of the history of jazz that it should delight even the most skeptical critics. Ganelin, Tarasov, and Chekasin spread out, to be sure, with lots of characteristic color. They also reach way back to swing and ragtime, with one of their most eclectic performances on disc. Ganelin immerses himself in his piano, but also adds some stunningly primitive work on basset and horn, while Chekasin lets loose with a funky blast from the past to complement his ambitious adventurousness. The three encores, including a subversive version of "Mack the Knife," round out the show. *—Steven A. Loewy*

Opuses / Dec. 24, 1989 / Leo ✦✦

Poco a Poco / Feb. 1978 / Leo ✦✦✦✦
The Ganelin Trio (Vyacheslav Ganelin, piano and electric guitar; Vladimir Tarasov, drums; Vladimir Chekasin, reeds, wooden flutes, and voice) is the proof that the Soviet Union could produce incredible musicianship and unbridled creativity. *Poco-a-Poco,* recorded live in Novosibirsk, February 1978, and released in 1988 on Leo Records (it was the label's first CD),

introduced the trio to Western listeners. The shock was real and invigorating. Avant-garde jazz aficionados discovered a trio of lunatics who were condensing 100 years of jazz, blending it with folkloric elements and stage antics. The resulting music is passionate, complex, ever-shifting, and very funny; it crackles with energy. Posing as a 60-minute suite, "Poco-a-Poco" sounds more like a collage of excerpts from a live show (cuts are noticeable between sections) but ultimately it matters very little: The fact remains that this is an exciting record from beginning to end. Vyacheslav Ganelin's writing could be compared to a Russian and jazzier avatar of John Zorn. The trio moves from free jazz to 2/4 upbeat themes, from sensual Coltrane-ian melodies to wacky recorder solos. Although *Catalogue,* the trio's second album for Leo Records, is stronger composition-wise, *Poco-a-Poco* remains a must. In September 2000, the label released a reissue of the CD with extensive liner notes by Steve Kulak in a limited edition of 500 copies. *—François Couture*

Jan Garbarek

b. Mar. 4, 1947, Mysen, Norway
Sax (Tenor), Sax (Soprano), Flute / Post-Bop
The Norwegian saxophonist Jan Garbarek's icy tone and liberal use of space and long tones has long been perfect for the ECM sound and as a result he is on many recordings for that label, both as a leader and as a sideman. He had won a competition for amateur jazz players back in 1962, leading to his first gigs. Garbarek worked steadily in Norway throughout the remainder of the 1960s, usually as a leader but also for four years with George Russell (who was in Scandinavia for a long stretch). Garbarek began recording for ECM in the early '70s and, although he had opportunities to play with Chick Corea and Don Cherry, his association with Keith Jarrett's European quartet in the mid-'70s made him famous, resulting in the classic recordings *My Song* and *Belonging.* In the 1980s Garbarek's groups included bassist Eberhard Weber and at various times guitarists Bill Frisell and David Torn. Garbarek, whose sound is virtually unchanged since the 1970s, collaborated with the Hilliard Ensemble in 1993 (a vocal quartet singing Renaissance music) and the result was a surprisingly popular recording. *Visible World* followed in 1995, and four years later he resurfaced with *Rites.* In April of 1999, Garbarek and the Hilliard Ensemble returned with *Mnemosyne.* *—Scott Yanow*

Afric Pepperbird / Sep. 22, 1970-Sep. 23, 1970 / ECM ✦✦✦✦
Jan Garbarek Group. His best, most exciting date from 1970. *—Ron Wynn*

● **Witchi-Tai-To** / Nov. 27, 1973-Nov. 28, 1973 / ECM ✦✦✦✦✦
One of the albums that defined the ECM Records sound. *—Michael G. Nastos*

Photo with Blue Sky, White Cloud, Wires, Windows and a Red Roof / Dec. 1978 / ECM ✦✦✦✦
Jan Garbarek's icy and haunting tones on tenor and soprano are in the forefront during much of this set. He performs six originals (which have simple but picturesque titles such as "Blue Sky," "Windows" and "The Red Roof") with the assistance of guitarist Bill Connors, pianist John Taylor, bassist Eberhard Weber and drummer Jon Christensen. Nothing too exciting occurs, but this is high-quality background music. *—Scott Yanow*

Star / Jan. 1991 / ECM ✦✦✦✦
Saxophonist Jan Garbarek, bassist Miroslav Vitous and drummer Peter Erskine have been making records for ECM for a long time, both as leaders and as sidemen. They know each other's styles well, they're familiar with ECM label head Manfred Eicher's echo-drenched production tendencies, and they know how to turn jazz formulas into hip, lyrical romanticism. On this leaderless trio album, as with most ECM releases, you get the feeling of music emerging from a vast and echoey space; Erskine's Morse-code drum accents, Vitous' thrumming basslines and the plaintive cry of Garbarek's soprano and alto saxophones are far removed from what some would consider "jazz," but that's not the point. The tunes may be somewhat interchangeable, but the music is virtuosic, thoughtful and thoroughly lovely, at times heart-tugging. Makes you wish these three would get together more often. *—Rick Anderson*

Officium / Sep. 1993 / ECM ✦✦✦✦
Fearlessly searching for new conceptions of sound and not caring where he found them, Garbarek joined hands with the classical early-music movement, improvising around the four male voices of the Hilliard Ensemble. Now here was a radical idea guaranteed to infuriate both hardcore jazz buffs and the even more pristine more-authentic-than-thou folk in early music circles. Yet this unlikely fusion works stunningly well—and even more hearteningly, went over the heads of the purists and became a hit album at a time (1994) when Gregorian chants were a hot item. Chants, early polyphonic music, and Renaissance motets by composers like Morales and Dufay form the basic material, bringing forth a cool yet moving spirituality in Garbarek's work. Recorded in a heavily reverberant Austrian monastery, the voices sometimes develop in overwhelming waves, and Garbarek rides their crest, his soprano sax soaring in the monastery acoustic, or he underscores the voices almost unobtrusively, echoing the voices, finding ample room to move around the modal harmonies yet applying his sound sparingly. Those with nervous metabolisms may become impatient with this undefinable music, but if you give it a chance, it will seduce you, too. *—Richard S. Ginell*

Rites / Mar. 1998 / ECM ✦✦✦
Jan Garbarek, long a fixture with the ECM label, had not recorded for the company in nearly three years when he came out with this diverse and generally intriguing double CD. The music ranges from trance music that develops at a very slow pace, to numbers that sound a bit like Weather Report, one piece utilizing a boys choir, and an oddity ("The Moon Over Mtatsminda") with singer Jansug Kakhidze and the Tbilisi Symphony Orchestra. Among the other musicians heard from are keyboardist Rainer Bruninghaus, bassist Eberhard Weber, drummer Marilyn Mazur and occasionally Bugge Wesseltoft on synthesizers and accordion. This set will not convert anyone to Garbarek's often stark music but it will reward repeated listenings for his fans. *—Scott Yanow*

Mnemosyne / Apr. 13, 1999 / ECM ✦✦✦✦
Garbarek and the Hilliard Ensemble waited nearly five years before trying to follow up their surprisingly successful *Officium* album, but finally they came through with an even more adventurous two-CD set of jazzman-meets-early-music-voices. Here, their range straddles no less than three milleniums (just missing a fourth by a couple of years), from the "Delphic Paean" of Athenaeus circa 127 B.C. to a lullaby by the contemporary Estonian composer Veljo Tormis, with intervening contributions by Hildegard von Bingen, William Billings, and Thomas Tallis, Iroquois Indians, Basque and Peruvian folksongs, and many more far-flung choices. Most daringly, the four voices themselves now start to improvise on scraps of ancient material culled from old book bindings and the like, though it's hard to determine exactly where this occurs (probably during some passages of wordless vocalise). Ultimately, despite the freer methods, the results are often pretty much the same as *Officium* on disc one—soothing, timeless sonic frescos reverberantly recorded in the same Austrian St. Gerold monastery, with Garbarek soaring over or threading through the texture ever more sparingly. Yet on disc two, Garbarek and the Hilliards start to move into other worlds, breaking into something more disturbing and even atonal in that ancient "Delphic Paean," the syncopated harmonies of Garbarek's own "Loiterando," or a strange-sounding Russian Psalm from the 16th century. This is a collaboration in transition, and one hopes it will continue to evolve. *—Richard S. Ginell*

Red Garland (William M. Garland)

b. May 13, 1923, Dallas, TX, **d.** Apr. 23, 1984, Dallas, TX
Piano / Hard Bop
Red Garland mixed together the usual influences of his generation (Nat Cole, Bud Powell and Ahmad Jamal) into his own distinctive approach; Garland's block chords themselves became influential on the players of the 1960s. He started out playing clarinet and alto, switching to piano when he was 18. During 1946-55 he worked steadily in New York and Philadelphia, backing such major players as Charlie Parker, Coleman Hawkins, Lester Young and Roy Eldridge but still remaining fairly obscure. That changed when he became a member of the classic Miles Davis Quintet (1955-58), heading a rhythm section that also included Paul Chambers and Philly Joe Jones. After leaving Miles, Garland had his own popular trio and recorded very frequently for Prestige, Jazzland and Moodsville during 1956-62 (the majority of which are currently available in the Original Jazz Classics series). The pianist eventually returned to Texas and was in semi-retirement but came back gradually in the 1970s, recording for MPS (1971) and Galaxy (1977-79) before retiring again. *—Scott Yanow*

The P.C. Blues / May 11, 1956-Aug. 9, 1957 / Prestige/OJC ✦✦✦✦
This CD reissues a trio album from 1957 that features pianist Red Garland with bassist Paul Chambers (the "P.C." in the title) and drummer Art Taylor. In addition to the four original titles (which are highlighted by a sensitive version of "Lost April" and the lengthy "Tweedle Dee Dee"), Garland's feature on a 1956 Miles Davis record, "Ahmad's Blues" (which features Red with Chambers and drummer Philly Joe Jones), adds to the value of this thoughtful but swinging release. *—Scott Yanow*

A Garland of Red / Aug. 17, 1956 / Prestige/OJC ✦✦✦✦✦
Thirty-three at the time of this, his first recording as a leader, pianist Red Garland already had his distinctive style fully formed and had been with the Miles Davis Quintet for a year. With the assistance of bassist Paul Chambers (also in Davis's group) and drummer Art Taylor, Garland is in superior form on six standards, Charlie Parker's "Constellation" (during which he shows that he could sound relaxed at the fastest tempos) and his own "Blue Red." Red Garland recorded frequently during the 1956-62 period and virtually all of his trio recordings are consistently enjoyable, this one being no exception. *—Scott Yanow*

Red Garland's Piano / Dec. 14, 1956+Mar. 22, 1957 / Prestige/OJC ✦✦✦✦
Red Garland's third session as a leader finds the distinctive pianist investigating eight standards (including "Please Send Me Someone to Love," "Stompin' at the Savoy," "If I Were a Bell" and "Almost Like Being in Love") with his distinctive chord voicings, melodic but creative ideas and solid sense of swing. Joined by bassist Paul Chambers and drummer Art Taylor, Garland plays up to his usual consistent level, making this an easily recommended disc for straightahead fans. *—Scott Yanow*

Groovy / Dec. 14, 1956-Aug. 9, 1957 / Prestige/OJC ✦✦✦✦
As the liner notes properly state, this CD (Red Garland's fourth as a leader for the Prestige label) has "jazz standards, ballad standards, blues ballads and just plain blues." The pianist's trio (with bassist Paul Chambers and drummer Art Taylor) swings such numbers as "C Jam Blues," "Will You Still Be Mine" (the latter from The Ahmad Jamal songbook) and "What Can I Say After I Say I'm Sorry" with spirit and subtle invention. All of Red Garland's Prestige recordings are worth getting. *—Scott Yanow*

Soul Junction / Nov. 15, 1957 / Prestige/OJC ✦✦✦✦
Pianist Red Garland's very relaxed, marathon blues solo on the 16-minute "Soul Junction" is the most memorable aspect of this CD reissue. With such soloists as tenor saxophonist John Coltrane and trumpeter Donald Byrd, plus steady support provided by bassist George Joyner and drummer Art Taylor, Garland gets to stretch out on the title cut and four jazz originals, including "Birk's Works" and "Hallelujah." Coltrane is in excellent form, playing several stunning sheets of sound solos. *—Scott Yanow*

Dig It! / Dec. 13, 1957-Feb. 7, 1958 / Prestige/OJC ✦✦✦
1989 reissue contains more from the mammoth Garland late-50s output, with Donald Byrd (tpt), John Coltrane (ts), Paul Chambers (b), Art Taylor (d), and the underrated George Joyner (b). *—Ron Wynn*

It's a Blue World / Feb. 7, 1958 / Prestige/OJC ✦✦✦✦
Of the miles of Red Garland sessions recorded in the late '50s, some of the tapes didn't see the light of day until many years later. This session, which except for "Crazy Rhythm," first appeared in the early '70s, is typical of Garland's trio work of the '50s, evoking a mid-century nightclub atmosphere from Rudy Van Gelder's studio with the perfectly-gauged help of bassist Paul Chambers and drummer Art Taylor. "Since I Fell for You" and "Teach Me Tonight" are taken at relaxed tempos, and after Garland's trademark block chords in the left

hand and octaves in the right hand take care of the themes, they ride easily and winningly. "Crazy Rhythm" zips along at the usual steeplechase pace, with a fluid bebop solo from Garland and some agile bowing from Chambers (Chambers also gets an unusually lengthy bowed solo on "This Can't Be Love"), and the title track closes the CD reissue on a jaunty note. Garland fans—and for that matter, fans of Vince Guaraldi, whose chord voicings very much resemble those of Garland—need not hesitate. —*Richard S. Ginell*

Blues in the Night / Apr. 11, 1958-Jul. 15, 1960 / Prestige ♦♦♦♦
The emphasis is on the blues (although not exclusively) on this CD reissue. The original eight-song program has been joined by "A Portrait of Jennie" by the same trio (pianist Red Garland, bassist Sam Jones and drummer Art Taylor) from an earlier date. Most unusual about the set is that Garland makes a rare (and effective) appearance on organ during "Halleloo-Y'All." Otherwise, this is a conventional but enjoyable set of bluesy bop, highlighted by "Revelation Blues," "Everytime I Feel the Spirit" and "Rocks In My Bed." —*Scott Yanow*

Can't See for Lookin' / Jun. 1958 / Prestige/OJC ♦♦♦
Pianist Red Garland recorded many sets in the late 1950s and early '60s, often (as in this case) with bassist Paul Chambers and drummer Art Taylor. Despite the LP length of this CD reissue (under 35 minutes), this is a particularly strong example of Garland's talents. His block chords are distinctive, as is his use of space, and the music always swings. The trio sounds in top form on "I Can't See For Looking," George Gershwin's "Soon," "Blackout" and a driving version of the classic blues "Castle Rock." Recommended. —*Scott Yanow*

Rojo / Aug. 22, 1958 / Prestige/OJC ♦♦♦♦
Pianist Red Garland recorded frequently with trios for Prestige during the second half of the 1950s. For this set (reissued on CD), Garland, bassist George Joyner and drummer Charlie Persip are joined by Ray Barretto on congas and the emphasis is on forceful swinging. Garland takes such ballads as "We Kiss in a Shadow" and "You Better Go Now" at faster-than-expected tempos. "Ralph J. Gleason Blues" and the Latin feel of "Rojo" are among the highlights of this enjoyable disc. —*Scott Yanow*

★ **Red Garland at the Prelude, Vol. 1** / Oct. 1959 / Prestige ♦♦♦♦♦
Originally released as two LPs (*Red Garland at the Prelude* and *Red Garland/Live!*), this single CD (which has around 77 minutes of music) features a particularly strong trio set by the pianist, bassist Jimmy Rowser and drummer Specs Wright. Garland mostly sticks to standards and the highlights include "Perdido," "Bye Bye Blackbird" (which is reminiscent of the famous Miles Davis version) and two versions of "One O'Clock Jump." Straightahead jazz fans should get this one. —*Scott Yanow*

Red Garland Revisited! / May 14, 1957 / Prestige/OJC ♦♦♦♦
Pianist Red Garland's fourth recording as a leader had often eluded reissue until this 1998 CD was released. Garland is teamed up with bassist Paul Chambers, drummer Art Taylor and (on "Four" and "Walkin'") guest guitarist Kenny Burrell. Garland plays throughout in his distinctive style and the highlights include "Billy Boy" (which was adapted from Ahmad Jamal's rendition), "I'm Afraid the Masquerade Is Over," "It Could Happen to You" and the two Burrell tracks. Predictably excellent music; Garland recorded more than 20 additional albums within the next five years. —*Scott Yanow*

The Moodsville, Vol. 1 / Dec. 11, 1959 / Prestige/OJC ♦♦♦
In the late 1950s, Prestige started a new subsidiary (Moodsville) that was designed to provide mood music for courting couples. The emphasis on this CD reissue, the very first Moodsville release is on ballads, matching pianist Red Garland, bassist Sam Jones and drummer Art Taylor with guest tenor Eddie "Lockjaw" Davis on three of the eight tunes. Due to the overly relaxed nature of much of this music and the lack of variety, this is not one of the more essential Red Garland sets, but it is still generally enjoyable. Highlights include "We'll Be Together Again," "When Your Lover Has Gone" and "Blue Room." —*Scott Yanow*

When There Are Grey Skies / Oct. 9, 1962 / Prestige/OJC ♦♦♦♦

Red Alert / Dec. 2, 1977 / Galaxy/OJC ♦♦♦♦

Crossings / Dec. 1977 / Galaxy/OJC ♦♦♦

Misty Red / Apr. 13, 1982-Apr. 14, 1982 / Timeless ♦♦♦♦

I Left My Heart in San Francisco / May 1978 / 32 Jazz ♦♦♦♦
Recorded during pianist Red Garland's final period, this enjoyable outing (a Muse LP that was reissued in 1999 as a 32 CD) has three trio numbers by Garland with bassist Chris Amberger and drummer Eddie Moore plus three selections that add altoist Leo Wright to make the group a quartet. Garland's style was unchanged from the '50s, as he shows on "Will You Still Be Mine" and "Bye Bye Blackbird." Wright's portion of the date finds him playing lyrically on two ballads (including a surprise version of "I Left My Heart in San Francisco") and swinging on "Bag's Groove." The set was recorded live at San Francisco's Keystone Korner and was clearly a happy occasion. —*Scott Yanow*

Erroll Garner

b. Jun. 15, 1921, Pittsburgh, PA, **d.** Jan. 2, 1977, Los Angeles, CA
Piano / Swing, Bop

One of the most distinctive of all pianists, Erroll Garner proved that it was possible to be a sophisticated player without knowing how to read music, that a creative jazz musician can be very popular without watering down his music, and that it is possible to remain an enthusiastic player without changing one's style once it is formed. A brilliant virtuoso who sounded unlike anyone else, Garner on medium-tempo pieces often stated the beat with his left hand like a rhythm guitar while his right played chords slightly behind the beat, creating a memorable effect. His playful free-form introductions (which forced his sidemen to really listen), his ability to play stunning runs without once glancing at the keyboard, his grunting and the pure joy that he displayed while performing were also part of the Garner magic. By 1946 he had his sound together and when he backed Charlie Parker on his famous "Cool Blues" session of 1947, the pianist was already an obvious giant. His unclassifiable style had an orchestral approach straight from the swing era but was open to the innovations of bop. From the early '50s Garner's accessible style became very popular and he never seemed to have an off day up until his forced retirement (due to illness) in early 1975. His composition "Misty" became a standard. —*Scott Yanow*

1945-1946 / Sep. 25, 1945-Feb. 1946 / Classics ♦♦♦♦
The fifth CD in the European Classics label's Erroll Garner reissue series showcases the great pianist on the 21 recordings that he cut in a five-month period during 1945-46. Garner's four trio numbers for Savoy (particularly his hit version of "Laura") helped make him famous. Those are included on this set along with four obscure piano solos for the Disc and Arco labels, 11 numbers for Mercury, and a couple of *V-Disc* performances. Despite the success of "Laura," Garner, at that early point in time, was better at medium-tempo numbers. He romps on such tunes as "Indiana," "Lady Be Good," "Bouncin' With Me" and "High Octane." This outing is not quite essential, but it does contain plenty of enjoyable numbers. —*Scott Yanow*

Long Ago and Far Away / Jun. 28, 1950-Jan. 11, 1951 / Columbia ♦♦♦♦♦
These sides from 1950-51 were the first Garner recorded for Columbia, and like the later *Body And Soul* reissue from the same label, this disc includes a sophisticated and highly enjoyable program of classic standards. In his inimitable keyboard style– a seamless mixture of swing's bounce, pianist Art Tatum's mammoth facility, and some of bebop's mercurial twists–Garner glides through fine ballad readings of "Spring Is Here" and "Long Ago and Far Away," as well as compact, medium to fast tempo swingers like "When You're Smiling" and "Lover." Garner's burgeoning knack for abstract song preludes are plentiful too, with his two minute (half the song's length) impressionistic reworking of the chords to "My Heart Stood Still" standing out in particular. Extending the process further, Garner plays cat and mouse with the chords over the entirety of both "It Could Happen to You" and "Laura," creating spectral—some might say overly florid—interpretations in the process. The pianist's soft, almost strumming touch endeared him to a millions of fans in the late '40s and early '50s, and made the complex improvisational embellishments almost seem like part of the original composition. A great disc for newcomers and fans alike ≠- nicely remastered, too. —*Stephen Cook*

Body and Soul / Jan. 11, 1951-Jan. 3, 1952 / Columbia ♦♦♦♦♦
As was the case with Fats Waller, Erroll Garner's natural and advanced musical talent ingratiated him to jazz aficionados and experts alike. Garner took to the piano intuitively, never needing to take lessons because of his exceptional ear for music. Further breaking the mold, he transcended many of the jazz styles he came up with, including both swing and bebop. You hear the power of swing pianist Earl Hines in his fleet and robust approach, and, yes, he once played with Charlie Parker, but as heard on this Columbia collection from 1951-1952, Garner concocts a unique blend of the big band's svelte rhythms and bebop's heady swing. On the 20 gems found on *Body and Soul,* Garner employs a rush of dynamics, yet never compromises the inherent lyricism of the set's many standards. This balancing act cuts across a varied set of brisk swingers (Waller's "Honeysuckle Rose"), fine ballads ("I Can't Get Started"), and medium-tempo strollers ("It's the Talk of the Town"). In light of Garner's thoroughly engaging and self-contained work at the piano, even the fact that bassist John Simmons and drummer Shadow Wilson are practically inaudible becomes negligible. Garner bolsters many of these "little symphonies" with clever intros: a miniature recasting of the song's chord and harmonic structure, heard to sublime effect here on "Summertime" and "Body and Soul" (Garner would expand these preambles in the future, particularly on solo piano outings). And in response to criticisms of his playing being too ornate (extra tremolo on the ballads), it should be said that part of Garner's charm is his "old-fashioned" phrasing, part of the romantic and urbane touch he employs to keep said indulgences in check most of the time. *Body and Soul* is a fine collection of early Garner sides. Highly recommended. —*Stephen Cook*

Too Marvelous for Words, Vol. 3 / Mar. 26, 1954 / EmArcy ♦♦♦♦♦
The third in the Polygram series of overviews. Plenty of majestic performances. —*Ron Wynn*

☆ **Erroll Garner Plays Misty** / Jul. 27, 1954-Mar. 14, 1955 / EmArcy ♦♦♦♦♦

The Original Misty / Jul. 27, 1954-Mar. 14, 1955 / Mercury ♦♦♦♦♦
Erroll Garner's first album for Mercury Records, *The Original "Misty" from the Piano Virtuoso,* is a lovely, swinging record that spotlights his light, sophisticated style. Supported by bassist Wyatt Ruther, drummer Eugene "Fats" Heard and conga player Candido Camero, Garner swings a number of standards—"You Are My Sunshine," "I've Got the World on a String," "Misty"—performing all of them in true style. It's a wonderful record from the pianist's prime. [The CD reissue includes the 45 take of "Exactly Like You."] —*Stephen Thomas Erlewine*

Solitaire / Mar. 14, 1955 / Mercury ♦♦♦
On March 14, 1955, Erroll Garner sat down at the piano and played one interesting solo after another, resulting in two albums of music. Seven pieces (all but "That Old Feeling" are taken as ballads) were originally released as *Solitaire;* this CD reissue adds four additional selections that are taken at faster paces. Although not essential, the rhapsodic and occasionally wandering but always intriguing set should greatly interest fans. —*Scott Yanow*

★ **Concert by the Sea** / Sep. 19, 1955 / Columbia ♦♦♦♦♦
Concert by the Sea was arguably the finest record pianist Erroll Garner ever made, and he made many—a few outstanding—many good recordings. But this live recording (9/19/55) with his trio (Eddie Calhoun, bass; Denzil Best, drums) presented a typical Garner program; it was a mixture of originals, show biz and pop standards delivered with his unique delivery and enthusiasm. The rhythms and brillant use of tension and release was perfectly captured. And while for many jazz listeners, Garner's deliberate structures were too orchestrated, there was an equal spontaneity in the propulsion of these orchestrations that swung as well as anything. —*Bob Rusch, Cadence*

Dreamstreet & One World Concert / Dec. 18, 1959+Aug. 25, 1962 / Telarc ♦♦♦♦
Two of pianist Erroll Garner's albums for his Octave label have been reissued on full on this single CD from Telarc. Backed by bassist Eddie Calhoun and drummer Kelly Martin, Garner is heard stretching out in the studios and playing in concert at the 1962 Seattle World's Fair. Among the most consistent of jazzmen, Garner typically romps through a variety of stan-

dards plus his own "Misty," "Dreamstreet," "Mambo Gotham" and a medley of songs from the play *Oklahoma*. Other highlights of the spirited set include "Just One of Those Things," "Blue Lou," "The Lady Is a Tramp," "The Way You Look Tonight" and "Mack the Knife." *—Scott Yanow*

Dancing on the Ceiling / Jun. 1, 1961-Aug. 19, 1965 / EmArcy ✦✦✦✦✦
The great pianist Erroll Garner is heard on these 11 selections, jamming on standards with bassist Eddie Calhoun and drummer Kelly Martin. One number is from 1964 and another from a year later, but the remainder was performed in 1961; all of the selections were previously unreleased. The music is marvelous and sometimes miraculous, with Garner's distinctive style heard at its best throughout. *—Scott Yanow*

Close-Up in Swing/A New Kind of Love / Jul. 1961-Feb. 1963 / Telarc ✦✦✦✦
Two former LPs were reissued in full on this single CD. The earlier date features pianist Erroll Garner in typically brilliant and witty form with his 1961 trio, which also included bassist Eddie Calhoun and drummer Kelly Martin. Whether it be a sly "My Silent Love," "All of Me," or a joyful "Back In Your Own Backyard," Garner is heard throughout in his prime. The later date is a bit more unusual, for the pianist improvises on ten themes that would be used in the Paul Newman film "A New Kind of Love." Joined by a big band and string orchestra conducted by Leith Stevens, Garner, who never learned to read or write music, contributed several original themes to the score (a few of which are quite catchy) in addition to jamming on such tunes as "You Brought a New Kind of Love to Me," "Louise" and "Mimi." On both former albums, the overall results are quite memorable, which is not a surprise, for Erroll Garner always seemed incapable of playing an uninspired or indifferent solo. *—Scott Yanow*

1944-1945 / Dec. 22, 1994-Mar. 9, 1945 / Classics ✦✦✦✦✦
The fourth in Classics' reissuance of all of the early recordings by the great pianist Erroll Garner has some unusual performances. The first eight numbers were private recordings cut during a jam session at Timme Rosenkrantz's apartment. Garner (who at that point in time only hinted at his emerging distinctive style and showed the influence of Fats Waller) and trumpeter Charlie Shavers constantly inspire each other and are assisted by trombonist Vic Dickenson, altoist Lem Davis, bassist Slam Stewart (in top form), drummer Cliff Leeman and on one song clarinetist Hank D'Amico. Those selections are quite extended (two songs exceed ten minutes) and sometimes a little loose but filled with excitement; the ad-lib ending of "Red Cross" is pretty humorous. Wrapping up this CD are Garner's first studio recordings: four selections cut with a trio for the Black & White label and four piano solos made for Signature. Although performed only a short time after the earlier jam session, Garner was already starting to play in his own familiar style. Recommended. *—Scott Yanow*

Campus Concert/Seeing Is Believing / Jul. 28, 1998 / Telarc ✦✦✦✦
This twofer from the Telarc label's Archive series brings together two fine but unrelated albums from jazz piano legend Erroll Garner. *Campus Concert* was recorded in the spring of 1964 at Purdue University, and shows the affinity Garner shared with his student audience in the days when jazz was considered cooler on campus than the then-teenage-oriented rock & roll. The set list for this live performance was mostly standards, done in Garner's unique barrelhouse-meets-piano-bar style. *Seeing is Believing* was released in 1970, and reflects the influence of the contemporary pop music of the time, with covers of "For Once in My Life," "Yesterday," "Spinning Wheel" and "The Look of Love" mixed in with five originals and "Strangers in the Night." The material on this half of the disc is more adventurous and consequently more interesting than the earlier live tracks. Here, Garner's usual trio setting is augmented by percussionist Jose Mangual, whose congas add a spicy rhythmic touch to the proceedings. "Paisley Eyes" and "You Turned Me Around" are especially intriguing originals, while "Mood Island" floats across a pleasantly relaxed Latin groove. *—Jim Newsom*

Complete Savoy Master Takes / Jan. 30, 1945-1949 / Savoy Jazz ✦✦✦✦

Charles Gayle

b. Feb. 28, 1939, Buffalo, NY
Sax (Tenor) / Avant-Garde Jazz, Free Jazz, Avant-Garde
Charles Gayle made his first significant impact on the free jazz scene with a series of critically-acclaimed New York performances at the *Knitting Factory* in the mid-to-late '80s. The tenor saxophonist's hyper-kinetic free expressionism draws on stylistic devices pioneered by '60s free jazz icon Albert Ayler. Like Ayler, Gayle employs a huge tone which, more often than not, he splits into its individual harmonic components. Timbral distortion is a key aspect of Gayle's work. His improvisations feature long, vibrating, free-gospel melodies; full of huge intervallic leaps, screaming multiphonics, and a density of line that evidences a remarkable dexterity in all registers of his horn (especially the altissimo). Gayle is also capable of great lyricism, imbued with the same bracing intensity present in his high-energy work.

As a teenager in the '50s, Gayle became intrigued by bebop and he became involved in New York City's nascent free jazz movement during the early '60s. He lived a mainly precarious existence for the next twenty years, poor and homeless most of the time until his "discovery" in the '80s earned him a modest income. In 1988, Gayle recorded a series of albums for Silkheart, and their 1990 release gave his music worldwide exposure. Subsequent recordings for Black Saint, FMP, and the *Knitting Factory* house label garnered him more of a reputation. In the '90s, Gayle took to performing on piano and bass clarinet in basically the same style that he displays on tenor, though the latter remains clearly his strongest instrument. By the turn of the millennium, Gayle's concerts had taken on aspects of performance art, complete with clown costumes and face paint, plus preaching a religious message to his audience. Indeed, Gayle's in-concert expressions of his religious and political views are a source of dismay to some critics and fans, and threaten at times to overshadow his music. *—Chris Kelsey*

Touchin' on Trane / Oct. 31, 1991-Nov. 1991 / FMP ✦✦✦✦✦
This is Charles Gayle's most accessible work. Gayle's mastery of free jazz is blended with a more traditional compositional style of jazz on this disc. *Touchin' on Trane* is composed of five original songs, and even includes ex-Coltrane drummer Rashied Ali. As the title insists, Coltrane is the influence for the music on this disc. The influence ranges from the upbeat tempo of "Giant Steps" in "Part A," while "Part D" is reminiscent of Coltrane's "Live in Japan" performances. Gayle, bassist William Parker, and Ali don't copy Coltrane, but rather expand on his accomplishments. Without covering any songs, *Touchin' on Trane* is the greatest John Coltrane tribute album. *—Brian Flota*

● **Repent** / Jan. 13, 1992-Mar. 2, 1992 / Knitting Factory ✦✦✦✦✦
There is absolutely no one currently playing tenor (or any other saxophone) coming close to making the kind of music created by Charles Gayle. While it's reminiscent of Albert Ayler's energetic, twisting 1960s free dates, Gayle's saxophone acrobatics and stamina are astonishing. This two-song CD was recorded live and features one number that runs 23 minutes; it's the short tune. "Jesus Christ and Scripture," the second piece, proceeds for over 50 minutes, much of that featuring Gayle's honks, bleats, turnarounds, moans and anguished cries on tenor. After listening closely to this disc, its lack of repetition and gimmickry is commendable. It's certainly not for all (or even most tastes), but those who listen fairly and intently to Charles Gayle will be rewarded. *—Ron Wynn*

More Live / Jan. 1, 1993-Feb. 22, 1993 / Knitting Factory ✦✦✦✦✦
Tenor saxophonist Charles Gayle plays with such fury and intensity that it seems he won't make it through the performances featured on these two discs. They spotlight his quartet during concerts. Hearing Gayle's overtones, screams, and blistering solos, backed by equally spirited playing from bassists Vattel Cherry and William Parker, and either Michael Wimberly or Marc Edwards on drums, it's easy to forget you're hearing it as they played it, with little pacing or variance in volume. It's impossible not to remember the 1960s and '70s free and loft jazz schools, but it's also appropriate to emphasize that Gayle doesn't sound like anyone else currently active and deserves significant attention beyond tiny jazz publications and sympathetic, but small, audiences. *—Ron Wynn*

Consecration / Apr. 17, 1993-Apr. 18, 1993 / Black Saint ✦✦✦✦✦
On *Consecration*, a studio album, the Charles Gayle Quartet show that they can play just as wild and unrestrained as they do on the *More Live* album. But the tension of Gayle's great live albums (*Repent, More Live*) is missing from *Consecration*. Despite an audience-free environment, Gayle manages to produce some of his best "songs." "Rise Up" starts with fury and immediacy. "Redemption" shows the stamina Gayle has, blowing the horn when it seems that another sound from him cannot be possible. The combination of bassist Vattel Cherry and bassist/cellist William Parker give the songs added power. Once again, these performances are not easy to listen to, given their time-free chaos, but the emotional impact of the playing achieved here, like Gayle's other work, is unrivaled. *—Brian Flota*

Delivered / May 20, 1997 / Thirsty Ear ✦✦✦✦
As could be inferred from the title, *Delivered* is Charles Gayle's fusion of propulsive free jazz with traditional gospel. Though the idea sounds unworkable, Gayle structures the album much more than on his free-flying live dates, and *Delivered* is much more focused than Gayle's other recordings as well. His quartet (including James Jones on piano, Gerald Benson on bass, drummer Kalil Madi) is given much room to soar on their frequent solos, but Gayle controls the whole effort with a fine effort, on tenor sax or bass clarinet. *—John Bush*

Daily Bread / Oct. 25, 1995-Oct. 28, 1995 / Black Saint ✦✦✦✦
Charles Gayle, who is deeply religious, is a very passionate musician. His emotional ideas on the tenor require a large variety of sounds which he has developed, from growls to squeals, purrs to screams. One could call him an extension of Albert Ayler except that Gayle usually does not utilize folkish melodies as Ayler did and he has a distinctive sound of his own. As with Ayler, though, Gayle pours a great deal of feeling into each solo. This quartet CD is a bit unusual in that Gayle (who is also heard on bass clarinet) plays piano on two songs, bassist William Parker mostly performs on cello (switching to piano on three other pieces) and two numbers feature Gayle on viola and drummer Michael Wumberly switching to violin; "Our Sins" actually has a violin-viola-cello-bass quartet! Bassist Wilber Morris is also in this very simulating and intuitive group. Charles Gayle takes some heartfelt solos on piano and fiddles up a storm on viola, but it is his very intense tenor solos that (as one would expect) leave the biggest impression. To use a cliché, this powerful recording is not for the fainthearted! *—Scott Yanow*

Ancient of Days / Sep. 20, 1999 / Knitting Factory ✦✦✦✦✦
Charles Gayle is not breaking any new ground with *Ancient of Days*, but it is the most consistent of his "restrained" albums since *Touchin' on Trane*. Each song on the album builds with a quiet intensity, gliding between standard jazz and late-era John Coltrane. Piano player Hank Johnson keeps things under control, while bassist Juini Booth sounds more like Jimmy Garrison than William Parker. Only on the last track, "Glorified Love," does Gayle show off the saxophone pyrotechnics displayed on such landmark releases as *Repent* and *More Live at the Knitting Factory*. *Ancient of Days* is an interesting listen in its demonstration of how Gayle's furious playing has evolved. Where it was once sandpaper, it's now a sanded piece of oak—smooth, yet covered with knots. *—Brian Flota*

Stan Getz

b. Feb. 2, 1927, Philadelphia, PA, **d.** Jun. 6, 1991, Malibu, CA
Sax (Tenor) / West Coast Jazz, Hard Bop, Post-Bop, Bossa Nova, Cool
One of the all-time great tenor saxophonists, Stan Getz was known as "The Sound" because he had one of the most beautiful tones ever heard. Getz, whose main early influence was Lester Young, grew to be a major influence himself and to his credit he never stopped evolving. Getz had the opportunity to play in a variety of major swing big bands while a teenager due to the World War II draft. He was with Jack Teagarden (1943) when he was just 16 and this was followed by stints with Stan Kenton (1944-45), Jimmy Dorsey (1945) and Benny Goodman (1945-46). Getz became famous during his period with Woody Herman's Second Herd (1947-49); after leaving Herman, he was a leader for the rest of his life. During the early '50s Getz broke away from the Lester Young style to form his own musical identity and he was soon among the most popular of all jazzmen. He discovered Horace Silver in 1950 and

used him in his quartet for several months. In Feb. 1962 Getz helped usher in the bossa nova era by recording *Jazz Samba* with Charlie Byrd; their rendition of "Desafinado" was a big hit. During the next year Getz made bossa nova flavored albums with Gary McFarland's big band, Luiz Bonfa and Laurindo Almeida, but it was *Getz/Gilberto* (a collaboration with Antonio Carlos Jobim and Joao Gilberto) that was his biggest seller, thanks in large part to "The Girl from Ipanema" (featuring the vocals of Astrud and Joao Gilberto). Getz could have spent the next decade sticking to bossa nova but instead he de-emphasized the music and chose to play more challenging jazz. *—Scott Yanow*

Early Stan / Mar. 14, 1949-Apr. 23, 1953 / Prestige/OJC ✦✦✦✦✦
This two-LP set includes seven sessions from 1949-50 and one from 1953 that feature the great tenor-saxophonist Stan Getz. Getz is heard with a Terry Gibbs septet, in quartets with either pianist Al Haig or Tony Aless, with Haig in a sextet that features vocals from Blossom Dearie, on a couple of collaborations with guitarist Jimmy Raney and in a classic if odd date with four other tenors (Al Cohn, Allen Eager, Brew Moore and Zoot Sims), all of whom sounded identical at the time. This two-fer (which contains several alternate takes) gives one a fine overview into the early days of Stan Getz. *—Scott Yanow*

The Complete Roost Recordings / May 17, 1950-Dec. 16, 1954 / Blue Note ✦✦✦✦
The Complete Roost Recordings is a three-disc, 59-track box set that contains all of the recordings Stan Getz made for the Roost Record label in the '50s. The set includes all of his officially released sessions—including the date led by guitarist Johnny Smith, the live performances with Count Basie, and a full disc of live performances with his quintet—as well as many unreleased and alternate takes. Roost was the first label Getz recorded for as a leader, and what's surprising about these sessions is how mature he sounds here. He had already arrived at his full, rich tone and was able to improvise with skill and grace. That's what makes this box set so rewarding—it's not only historically important, but it offers a wealth of excellent music. *—Leo Stanley*

☆ **The Complete Recordings of the Stan Getz Quintet with Jimmy Raney** / Aug. 15, 1951-Apr. 23, 1953 / Mosaic ✦✦✦✦✦
This limited-edition three-CD set will be hard to acquire but it is a gem. Tenor-saxophonist Stan Getz and guitarist Jimmy Raney had very complementary cool-toned but hard-swinging styles. Their gig at Storyville in Boston resulted in some classic music that, along with five studio sessions, is included in this box. The supporting cast includes pianists Al Haig, Horace Silver, Duke Jordan and Hall Overton; the music was originally recorded for Roost, Clef, Norgran and Prestige. This essential set is filled with exciting performances from Stan Getz when he was first becoming a highly influential force in jazz. *—Scott Yanow*

● **The Artistry of Stan Getz, Vol. 1** / Dec. 12, 1952-Mar. 21, 1967 / Verve ✦✦✦✦✦
Stan Getz was the most lyrical of jazz saxophonists. This two-disc set samples some of his best work of the 1950s and 1960s. His great range is shown here—uptempo bop and swing, ballads, bossa nova—he really could do it all. He and guitarist Charlie Byrd had a number one pop album the week of March 9, 1963, with their *Jazz Samba*, the album that introduced the Brazilian bossa nova craze to North Americans. The hit single that propelled that album to the top spot, Antonio Carlos Jobim's "Desafinado," and is included here in its six minute album version. Getz is heard with bebop king Dizzy Gillespie on "It Don't Mean a Thing (If It Ain't Got That Swing)" from 1953. He's captured in a unique setting with a string section creating a funky rhythmic bed on "I'm Late, I'm Late" from the *Focus* LP of 1961. There are two tracks from Getz's 1967 album with a young Chick Corea, *Sweet Rain*. The number five pop single, "The Girl from Ipanema," featuring vocalist Astrud Gilberto, is here from the 1964 Grammy Album of the Year *Getz/Gilberto*. Bill Evans is here, Max Roach, Oscar Peterson, Gary Burton, Elvin Jones... They had called Stan Getz "The Sound," and while no single collection could completely document this musical giant's career, this two-disc set is a good place to begin. *—Jim Newsom*

The Artistry of Stan Getz, Vol. 2 / Dec. 29, 1952-Mar. 17, 1971 / Verve ✦✦✦✦✦
With more great music from this remarkable saxophonist, *Artistry of Stan Getz, Volume 2* continues where the first volume left off, adding selections from different albums, and finding additional highlights from some of the LPs sampled on the earlier *Artistry, Volume 1*. Taken together, and the music justifies that they be, these two double-disc sets show what a versatile, imaginative, smooth and sexy improviser Stan Getz was. Listening to these discs can only whet the appetite for more servings of "The Sound." *—Jim Newsom*

Diz and Getz / Dec. 9, 1953 / Verve ✦✦✦✦✦
This is prime material with two giants playing bop and old-time standards with characteristic verve and wit. John Lewis (p) and the Oscar Peterson quartet join the masters. *—Michael G. Nastos*

Getz Meets Mulligan in Hi-Fi / Oct. 10, 1957+Oct. 12, 1957 / Verve ✦✦✦

Stan Getz and the Oscar Peterson Trio / Oct. 10, 1957 / Verve ✦✦✦✦
This very enjoyable CD for the first time gathers together all of the music recorded at this timeless session. Tenor-saxophonist Stan Getz is joined by pianist Oscar Peterson, guitarist Herb Ellis and bassist Ray Brown for a well-rounded set filled with appealing standards, three Getz originals (two of which are blues) and a fine ballad medley. Everyone is in top form and Getz clearly enjoyed playing with Peterson. *—Scott Yanow*

At the Opera House / Sep. 29, 1957-Oct. 7, 1957 / Verve ✦✦✦✦✦

Stan Getz with Cal Tjader / Feb. 8, 1958 / Fantasy/OJC ✦✦✦✦✦
In the vein of many a smooth, West Coast jazz outing, this 1958 disc finds original cool stylist Getz paired with vibraphonist Cal Tjader on a very enjoyable selection of jazz standards and Tjader originals. The lineup includes pianist Vince Guaraldi, guitarist Eddie Duran, bassist Scott La Faro, and drummer Billy Higgins (this was one of the earliest record dates for either La Faro or Higgins, both of whom were playing with Getz at San Francisco's *Black Hawk* in between recording sessions). Guaraldi's spry "Ginza Samba" kicks thing off with nimble and imaginative statements by all the soloists. Tjader's swinging originals "Crow's Nest" and "Big Bear" provide prime solo vehicles as well, while his lovely waltz number "Liz-Anne" adds some nice contrast to the set, eliciting one of Getz's best solos in the process. The group rounds things out with fine ballad readings of "I've Grown Accustomed to Her Face" and "For All We Know." A suitable title for both Getz and Tjader fans. Highly recommend. *—Stephen Cook*

Stan Meets Chet / Feb. 16, 1958 / Verve ✦✦✦
Tenor saxophonist Stan Getz and trumpeter Chet Baker never particularly liked each other and, even though they had musically compatible styles, they only worked together briefly in three periods. Their mutual hostility can be felt in subtle ways on this session which has been reissued on CD. Getz ignores Baker's attempt to state the melody of "I'll Remember April" and he plays it himself several bars after. The two horns do not meet at all on the ballad medley and, since Baker sits out on "Jordu," they only play together on two of the four performances. Getz battles a squeaky reed on "I'll Remember April" and Baker seems a bit subpar in general although he really digs in on "Half-Breed Apache" (a very fast "Cherokee"). So overall this CD (which also includes pianist Jodie Christian, bassist Victor Sproles and drummer Marshall Thompson), even with some good moments, does not live up to its potential. *—Scott Yanow*

☆ **Focus** / Jul. 1961-Oct. 1961 / Verve ✦✦✦✦✦
Stan Getz's personal favorite recording, this challenging session found the great tenor improvising over a big band performing seven songs composed and arranged by Eddie Sauter. Nothing was written out for Getz but he was up to the challenge, creating beautiful and logical statements, and interacting closely with the orchestra. Music worth hearing several times. *—Scott Yanow*

Jazz Samba / Feb. 14, 1962 / Verve ✦✦✦✦✦
This classic session which launched the bossa nova craze in the early '60s was originally recorded for Verve. The reissue from DCC Compact Classics improves the sound a bit and adds the shortened 45 version of "Desafinado" to the original program. The music, which matches Stan Getz's cool tenor with guitarist Charlie Byrd and his lightly swinging group, helped introduce Antonio Carlos Jobim's music to the United States through the hit recordings of "Desafinado" and "One Note Samba." It's essential music, no matter in what format one acquires it. *—Scott Yanow*

Jazz Samba Encore / Feb. 8, 1963-Feb. 27, 1963 / Verve ✦✦✦✦
Here's some more bossa nova from Stan Getz when the bloom was still on the first Brazilian boom. This time, however, on his third such album, Getz relies mostly upon native Brazilians for his backing. Thus, the soft-focused grooves are considerably more attuned to what was actually coming out of Brazil at the time. Two bona fide giants, Antonio Carlos Jobim and Luiz Bonfa (who gets co-billing), provide the guitars and all of the material, and Maria Toledo contributes an occasional throaty vocal. Getz injects more high-wailing passages into his intuitive affinity for the groove, even going for some fast bop on "Un Abraco No Getz," and Bonfa takes adept care of the guitar solos against Jobim's rock-steady rhythm. Clearly Jobim's songwriting contributions—"So Danco Samba," "How Insensitive," and "O Morro Nao Tem Vez"—would have the longest shelf life, and though the album didn't sell as well as its two predecessors, it certainly helped break these tunes into the permanent jazz repertoire. Avid bossa nova fans will certainly treasure this album for the lesser-known Bonfa tunes. *—Richard S. Ginell*

★ **Getz/Gilberto** / Mar. 18, 1963-Mar. 19, 1963 / Verve ✦✦✦✦✦
When bossa nova seemed in danger of being written off as a fad, this classic album came out and made bossa nova a permanent part of music. The combination of tenor saxophonist Stan Getz, pianist/composer Antonio Carlos Jobim and guitarist/singer Joao Gilberto had universal appeal (they all worked so beautifully together), and the last-minute addition of Astrud Gilberto, who had never sung professionally before, to "The Girl from Ipanema" made the record a huge hit. The 1997 CD reissue, which also includes such memorable numbers and future standards as "Desafinado," "Corcovado (Quiet Nights of Quiet Stars)" and "So Danco Samba," adds the shortened 45 versions of "Ipanema" and "Corcovado" to the original program. This music has been reissued many times and belongs in everyone's collection. *—Scott Yanow*

Getz Au Go Go Featuring Astrud Gilberto / Aug. 19, 1964 / Verve ✦✦✦

Getz/Gilberto #2 / Oct. 9, 1964 / Verve ✦✦✦✦
Justifiably overshadowed by the peerless *Getz/Gilberto* album (which featured "Girl From Ipanema") from a year before, *Getz/Gilberto #2* still holds its own with an appealing selection of fine jazz and bossa nova cuts. Unlike the first album's seamless collaboration by Getz, Joao Gilberto, Astrud Gilberto, and Antonio Carlos Jobim, here Getz and Joao Gilberto turn in separate sets recorded live at *Carnegie Hall* in October of 1964. Backed by a stellar quartet comprised of vibraphonist Gary Burton, bassist Gene Cherico, and drummer Joe Hunt, Getz turns in a sparkling performances on the seldom covered ballad "Tonight I'll Shall Sleep With a Smile On My Face," while stretching out nicely on his original blues swinger "Stan's Blues." With the support of bassist Keeter Betts and drummer Helcio Milito, Gilberto displays his subtle vocal and guitar talents on a set of bossa nova favorites, including his own "Bim Bom" and Jobim's "Meditation." The CD reissue also includes a couple of additional live vocal cuts featuring Astrud Gilberto, including somewhat lifeless versions of "Corcovado" and "Girl From Ipanema" from the *Carnegie Hall* concert, and inspired readings of "It Might As Well Be Spring" and "Only Trust Your Heart" from the club recording *Getz Au Go Go*. An appealing title amongst Getz's many bossa nova outings, but not an essential one. Newcomers should definitely start with the *Getz/Gilberto* album before checking this one out. *—Stephen Cook*

What the World Needs Now: Stan Getz Plays Bacharach and David / Aug. 30, 1967-1968 / Verve ✦✦✦

Captain Marvel / Mar. 2, 1972 / Koch Jazz ✦✦✦✦✦
This album was one of Stan Getz's most successful recordings of the 1970s. Teamed up with a younger rhythm section (keyboardist Chick Corea, bassist Stanley Clarke, drummer Tony Williams and percussionist Airto), Getz is in consistently brilliant form on "Lush Life" and

five Corea compositions. "Times Lie" and "Five-Hundred Miles High" are memorable but it is this version of "La Fiesta" (a song that perfectly fit Stan Getz's tone) that is truly classic. —*Scott Yanow*

The Peacocks / Jul. 1975 / Koch Jazz ♦♦♦♦
Although listed under Stan Getz's name, this CD is really a showcase for pianist Jimmie Rowles, an underrated stylist loved by singers and musicians alike. Rowles is heard in exquisite duets with Getz, solo, in a quartet with Getz, bassist Buster Williams and drummer Elvin Jones, and on "The Chess Players" during which the quartet is joined by four vocalists including three from Jon Hendricks's family. Most memorable are the haunting title cut, "Lester Left Town" and several of Rowles's touching vocals. —*Scott Yanow*

The Dolphin / May 1981 / Concord Jazz ♦♦♦

Spring Is Here / May 1981 / Concord Jazz ♦♦♦

Blue Skies / Jan. 1982 / Concord Jazz ♦♦♦♦
Because Stan Getz was so consistent during his lifetime—very rarely did he record a weak album—one greets a posthumous release like *Blue Skies* with enthusiasm. Although recorded in January 1982, *Blue Skies* remained in the can until 1995, four years after the saxman's death from cancer. Joined by pianist Jim McNeely, bassist Marc Johnson, and drummer Billy Hart, Getz is in excellent form on this generally caressing and introspective CD. The only up-tempo offering on *Blue Skies* is McNeely's cerebral "There We Go"; Getz is quite relaxed on Johnson's dreamy "Antigny" and interpretations of "Blue Skies," "Easy Living," "Spring Is Here," and "How Long Has This Been Going On." True to form, Getz makes the listener marvel at his tone throughout the album; without question, he had one of the sexiest, most gorgeous tones in the history of jazz. It's unfortunate that this excellent material went unreleased for 13 years. —*Alex Henderson*

Soul Eyes / Jun. 29, 1989-Jul. 27, 1989 / Concord Jazz ♦♦♦♦
Stan Getz was such a consistent performer and had such a beautiful tone that nearly all of his recordings are well worth getting. The two radio appearances heard on this 1997 CD are even on a higher level than normal. Joined by pianist Kenny Barron, either Ray Drummond or Yashuito Mori on bass, and drummer Ben Riley, Getz is heard at the peak of his powers on a pair of obscurities (Kenny Barron's "Feijada" and Gigi Gryce's "Stan's Blues") and six numbers (including "Voyage," "Blood Count" and "Warm Valley") that he recorded numerous times. To hear Getz adding even more beauty to Mal Waldron's already gorgeous "Soul Eyes" is a memorable experience. —*Scott Yanow*

People Time / Mar. 3, 1991-Mar. 6, 1991 / Verve ♦♦♦♦♦
Stan Getz's final recording, a two-CD live set of duets with pianist Kenny Barron that was cut just three months before his death, finds the great tenor in surprisingly creative form despite an occasional shortness of breath. Getz's tone is as beautiful as ever and he does not spare himself on this often exquisite set. His version of Charlie Haden's "First Song" is a highlight but none of the 14 performances are less than great. A brilliant farewell recording by a masterful jazzman. —*Scott Yanow*

My Foolish Heart: Live at the Left Bank / Sep. 26, 2000 / Label M. ♦♦♦
This previously unreleased Stan Getz performance took place at *the Famous Ballroom* in Baltimore on May 20, 1975. It was an exciting time to hear Getz live as he was exploring a harder tenor sound, much like Art Pepper was beginning to experiment with on alto. Getz surrounded himself with the propelling and modern rhythm section of Richie Beirach on piano, Dave Holland on bass, and Jack Dejohnette on drums. Getz fits into a comfortable combination of straight-ahead hard bop and ballads on this date. The 11 songs include "Spring Is Here" and "My Foolish Heart," alongside Chick Corea originals "Litha" and "Fiesta." Available from legendary producer Joel Dorn's mid-line Label M, dedicated to preserving unissued live performances. —*Al Campbell*

João Gilberto

b. Jun. 1931, Salvador, Bahia, Brazil
Vocals, Guitar / Brazilian Jazz, Bossa Nova, Tropicalia
Though Antonio Carlos Jobim set the standard for the creation of the bossa nova in the mid-'50s, the genre was brilliantly reimagined (and, arguably, defined) by the singer/songwriter and guitarist João Gilberto. In his native country he is called O Mito (The Legend), a deserving nickname, for since he began recording in the late '50s Gilberto, with his signature soft, near-whispering, croon, has set a standard few have equaled.

After playing in several bands during his youth, Gilberto lived a semi-nomadic life for years until joining forces with singer Luis Telles, a combination public-relations guru and sugar daddy who made sure the demanding Gilberto concentrated on his music. He began perfecting his unique vocal style, so breathy and nasally it is almost defies description. Not even established crooners such as Bing Crosby and Perry Como sang more quietly or with less vibrato. This, along with his rhythmically idiosyncratic approach to playing the guitar—an intensely syncopated plucking of the strings that flowed with his singing—made for some exhilarating music. By the time of his first record, 1959's *Chega de Saudade*, Gilberto became widely known as the man who made bossa nova what it is. After the success of his debut record and two follow-ups, Gilberto moved to America, where he lived until 1980. During this period he recorded some amazing records working with saxophonist Stan Getz and recording music by older Brazilian songwriters such as Dorival Caymmi and Ary Barroso. He returned to Brazil in the early '80s and since then has worked with virtually every big name in Brazilian pop including Gilberto Gil, Caetano Veloso, Maria Bethania, Gal Costa, and Chico Buarque. True to his image as enigmatic and eccentric, Gilberto lives a semi-reclusive lifestyle secure in the knowledge that, almost 40 years ago, he changed the course of Brazilian culture by making the bossa nova his music, as well as the music of Brazil. —*John Dougan*

★ **Amoroso/Brasil** / Nov. 17, 1976-Jan. 7, 1977 / Warner Brothers ♦♦♦♦♦
Two of the influential Joao Gilberto's LPs (*Amoroso* and *Brasil*) are combined on this single CD. The former session is pretty definitive with Gilberto interpreting four of Antonio Carlos Jobim's compositions (including "Wave" and "Triste") and four other songs (highlighted by "Besame Mucho," "Estate" and an odd 31-bar rendition of "'S Wonderful"). The strings (arranged by Claus Ogerman) are unnecessary but Gilberto proves to be in prime form. The later album also has its moments of interest (including a Brazilian version of "All of Me") and finds Gilberto backed by Johnny Mandel arrangements and assisted by singers Caetano Veloso, Gilberto Gil and Maria Bethania. Overall there is not much variety throughout this gently swinging program but these are a pair of Gilberto's better post-1970 recordings. —*Scott Yanow*

Live in Montreux / 1991 / Elektra ♦♦♦
The eminence grise of bossa nova steps halfway out of the shadows in a performance that, as always, adds new depth to the word reflective. Guitar of perfect simplicity backs vocals at once provisional-seeming and definitive. The songs themselves mix standards like "Aquarela do Brasil" and "Garota de Ipanema" with less familiar songs. —*John Storm Roberts, Original Music*

João / Dec. 22, 1992 / Verve ♦♦♦♦
Recent but classic jazz-bossa is played by one of its defining spirits. Vocally, Gilberto is in fine muttering form, communicating intensely with somebody in his breast pocket, and his guitar is as delicate as ever. This recording expresses the close links of bossa nova and jazz. *Joao* has Clare Fisher arranging and on some cuts playing keyboards, along with one of those saccharin string-sections even the most avant-garde Brazilians love. —*John Storm Roberts*

Dizzy Gillespie (John Birks Gillespie)

b. Oct. 21, 1917, Cheraw, SC, **d.** Jan. 6, 1993, Englewood, NJ
Trumpet, Composer / Vocal Jazz, Afro-Cuban Jazz, Jump Blues, Bop
Dizzy Gillespie's contributions to jazz were huge. One of the greatest jazz trumpeters of all time (some would say the best), Gillespie was such a complex player that his contemporaries ended up copying Miles Davis and Fats Navarro instead, and it was not until Jon Faddis's emergence in the 1970s that Dizzy's style was successfully recreated. Somehow Gillespie could make any "wrong" note fit and harmonically he was ahead of everyone in the 1940s, including Charlie Parker. Unlike Bird, Dizzy was an enthusiastic teacher who wrote down his musical innovations and was eager to explain them to the next generation, thereby insuring that bebop would eventually become the foundation of jazz. Gillespie was also one of the key founders of Afro-Cuban (or Latin) jazz, adding Chano Pozo's conga to his orchestra in 1947 and utilizing complex polyrhythms early on. The leader of two of the finest big bands in jazz history, Gillespie differed from many in the bop generation by being a masterful showman who could make his music seem both accessible and fun to the audience. With his puffed-out cheeks, bent trumpet (which occurred by accident in the early '50s when a dancer tripped over his horn) and quick wit, Dizzy was a colorful figure to watch. A natural comedian, Gillespie was also a superb scat singer and occasionally played Latin percussion for the fun of it, but it was his trumpet playing and leadership abilities that made him into a jazz giant. —*Scott Yanow*

☆ **The Complete RCA Victor Recordings 1937-1949** / May 17, 1937-Jul. 6, 1949 / Bluebird/RCA ♦♦♦♦♦
Although the sheer scope of this double-CD roundup of all of Dizzy's Victor sessions places it most obviously within the evolution of bebop, it is absolutely essential to Latin jazz collections as well. Here we find the discographical launching pad of Afro-Cuban jazz, Dec. 22, 1947, when Cuban conguero Chano Pozo added his galvanic congas and bongos to Gillespie's big band for the first time on records. One can feel the explosive effect that Pozo's subdivisions of the beat, rhythmic incantations and grooves have on the band's bebop charts. Though the musicians' styles aren't much affected, and Pozo does most of the adapting to bebop rather than vice-versa, the foundation has clearly shifted. Alas, aside from recorded live gigs, Pozo only made eight tracks with the band—four on Dec. 22 and four more eight days later, just before the second Musicians Union recording ban kicked in. Yet even after Pozo's murder the following year, Gillespie continued to expand his Latin experiments, using two Latin percussionists who brought more rhythmic variety to the sound of tunes like "Guarachi Guaro" (later popularized by Cal Tjader as "Soul Sauce") and even commercial ballads like "That Old Black Magic." The reprocessing of these late-78 RPM-era recordings through the CEDAR process sounds a bit harsh, though less so than most of RCA's earlier desecrations of vault material using NoNOISE. Even so, this is the best way yet in which to acquire these seminal Latin jazz tracks. —*Richard S. Ginell*

Groovin' High / Feb. 9, 1945-Nov. 12, 1946 / Savoy Jazz ♦♦♦

★ **Shaw Nuff** / Feb. 9, 1945+Nov. 12, 1946 / Musicraft ♦♦♦♦♦
This CD has Dizzy Gillespie's classic Musicraft sides (all except "A Handfulla Gimme"), some of the most famous recordings of his long career. These influential performances (which set the standard for bebop) include "Blue 'N' Boogie" (with tenor-saxophonist Dexter Gordon), seven gems with Charlie Parker (highlighted by "Groovin' High," "Hot House" and "Salt Peanuts"), a few numbers with Sonny Stitt and nine big-band recordings including "Our Delight," "Ray's Idea" and the futuristic "Things to Come." If Dizzy Gillespie's career had ended after these recordings, he would still be famous in the jazz world. —*Scott Yanow*

Dizzy Gillespie and His Big Band / Jul. 26, 1948 / GNP Crescendo ♦♦♦♦♦
The Dizzy Gillespie Big Band was the most innovative jazz orchestra of 1946-49, proof that bebop was not exclusively a small group music. All of its recordings are well worth acquiring and this particular CD gives one a well-rounded picture of the orchestra at a concert before an enthusiastic crowd. With prominence given James Moody's tenor, Cecil Payne on baritone and Chano Pozo on congas (he was killed a short time after this performance) in addition to the remarkable leader/trumpeter, the Dizzy Gillespie Orchestra is heard at its absolute prime. Versions of "Good Bait," "One Bass Hit" and "Manteca" are among the highlights of this recommended CD. —*Scott Yanow*

School Days / Apr. 16, 1951-Jul. 18, 1952 / Savoy Jazz ♦♦♦♦♦

The Champ / Apr. 16, 1951+Jul. 18, 1952 / Savoy ♦♦♦♦♦

Diz and Getz / Sep. 9, 1953+Oct. 16, 1956 / Verve ✦✦✦✦✦
Dizzy Gillespie was at the peak of his powers throughout the 1950s, still the pacesetter among trumpeters. This double CD matches Dizzy with Stan Getz, the Oscar Peterson Trio and drummer Max Roach. Getz, although identified with the "cool" school, thrived on competition and is both relaxed and combative on the uptempo explorations of "It Don't Mean a Thing" and "Impromptu." *—Scott Yanow*

★ **Dizzy Gillespie with Roy Eldridge** / Oct. 29, 1954 / Verve ✦✦✦✦✦
To call this music "classic" would be a great understatment. Producer Norman Granz loved to team together combative musicians in jam sessions, both live and in the studios. Since Roy Eldridge was one of the most competitive of trumpeters and Dizzy Gillespie considered him his original idol, they made a perfect matchup. This two-CD includes a ballad medley and a few slower pieces, but to hear Gillepsie and Eldridge battling on "I've Found a New Baby" and "Limehouse Blues" is to hear two of the very best trying to cut each other. Highly recommended for all jazz collections. *—Scott Yanow*

☆ **Birk's Works: Verve Big Band Sessions** / Jun. 6, 1956-Jul. 8, 1957 / Polygram ✦✦✦✦✦
Dizzy Gillespie's globetrotting big band of 1956-57 was one of his finest groups, a very exciting orchestra that at various times had such players as trumpeters Gillespie, Joe Gordon and Lee Morgan, trombonists Melba Liston and Al Grey, altoists Phil Woods and Ernie Henry, the tenors of Billy Mitchell, Ernie Wilkins and Benny Golson, and pianists Walter Davis, Jr. and Wynton Kelly. With arrangements contributed by Quincy Jones (who was in the trumpet section), Wilkins, Liston and Golson, this was a classic orchestra. Its three studio albums plus a few numbers only previously out on samplers and nine previously unreleased performances (mostly alternate takes) are on this wonderful two-CD set. The highpoints are many including "Dizzy's Business," "Jessica's Day," "The Champ," "Cool Breeze," "Birks Works," "Whisper Not," "Stablemates" and "I Remember Clifford." Essential music. *—Scott Yanow*

★ **At Newport** / Jul. 6, 1957 / Verve ✦✦✦✦✦
This CD features Dizzy Gillespie's second great big band at the peak of its powers. On the rapid "Dizzy's Blues" and a truly blazing "Cool Breeze," the orchestra really roars; the latter performance features extraordinary solos by Gillespie, trombonist Al Grey and tenor saxophonist Billy Mitchell. In addition to fine renditions of "Manteca" and Benny Golson's then-recent composition "I Remember Clifford," the humorous "Doodlin'" is given a definitive treatment, there is a fresh version of "A Night in Tunisia" and pianist Mary Lou Williams sits in for a lengthy medley of selections from her "Zodiac Suite." This brilliant CD captures one of the highpoints of Dizzy Gillespie's remarkable career and is highly recommended. *—Scott Yanow*

Sonny Side Up / Dec. 1957 / Verve ✦✦✦✦
Dizzy Gillespie brings together tenor saxophonists Sonny Stitt and Sonny Rollins for four extended cuts and in the process comes up with one of the most exciting "jam session" records in the jazz catalog. While the rhythm section of pianist Ray Bryant, bassist Tommy Bryant, and drummer Charlie Persip provide solid rhythmic support, Stitt and Rollins get down to business trading fours and reeling off solo fireworks. Apparently, Gillespie had stoked the competitive fires before the session with phone calls and some gossip, the fallout of which becomes palpable as the album progresses. On "The Eternal Triangle," in particular, Stitt and Rollins impress in their roles as tenor titans, with Stitt going in for sheer muscle as that most stout of bebop cutters and Rollins opting for some pacing as a more thematic player. In the midst of the rivalry (certainly some torch was being passed, since Rollins was soon to become the top tenor saxophonist in jazz) an embarrassment of solo riches comes tumbling out of both these men's horns. Gillespie adds his own split commentary on the proceedings with a casual solo on "After Hours" and a competitively blistering statement on "I Know that You Know." With an at-ease rendition of "On the Sunny Side of the Street" rounding things out, *Sonny Side Up* comes off as both a highly enjoyable jazz set and something of an approximation of the music's once revered live cutting session. *—Stephen Cook*

Gillespiana / Carnegie Hall Concert / Nov. 14, 1960-Mar. 4, 1961 / Verve ✦✦✦✦✦
This CD combines two complete and related LPs. When Lalo Schifrin joined Dizzy Gillespie's Quintet in 1960, he was encouraged by Gillespie to write an extended work for him. "Gillespiana" was the result, an impressive five-movement suite that showcased the trumpeter's talents with a large orchestra. The latter half of this CD was recorded at Carnegie Hall the same day that "Gillespiana" was debuted live, but those five pieces are more conventional, highlighted by remakes of "Manteca" and "Night in Tunisia" (the latter as the more involved "Tunisian Fantasy"). Only an overly silly version of "Ool Ya Koo" with Joe Carroll detracts from this otherwise superb release. *—Scott Yanow*

☆ **An Electrifying Evening with the Dizzy Gillespie Quintet** / Feb. 9, 1961 / Verve ✦✦✦✦✦
Dizzy Gillespie (along with altoist Leo Wright, pianist Lalo Schfrin, bassist Bob Cunningham and drummer Chuck Lampkin) were in peak form for this live performance. Their versions of "Kush," "Salt Peanuts" and "The Mooche" are all excellent, but it is "A Night in Tunisia," with its absolutely stunning trumpet break (which lasts half a chorus), that is most memorable. *—Scott Yanow*

The Cool World/Dizzy Goes Hollywood / Sep. 11, 1963-Apr. 23, 1964 / Verve ✦✦✦✦
This single CD reissues all of the music from two rare Dizzy Gillespie LPs. Dating from 1963-64, the set features the trumpeter's interpretation of the score of the obscure film *The Cool World* (although these are not the actual performances heard in the movie) plus 11 themes from other films. Gillespie, who is joined by James Moody (on tenor, alto and flute), pianist Kenny Barron, bassist Chris White and drummer Rudy Collins, was in peak form during that era and hopefully all of his other Philips recordings will also be reissued by Verve in the future. Although the liner notes deal only with *The Cool World*, the other set is actually of greater interest. Gillespie uplifts such tunes as the "Theme from Exodus," "Moon River," "Days of Wine and Roses," "Never on Sunday" and "Walk on the Wild Side," turning them into swinging jazz. *The Cool World* pieces (all composed by Mal Waldron) are also worth hearing although they are not as memorable overall. This set is a real historical curiosity and, although not essential, it is a release that should please Dizzy Gillespie fans while reminding others of how great a trumpeter he was before his long decline. *—Scott Yanow*

Jambo Caribe / Nov. 4, 1964-Nov. 6, 1964 / Verve ✦✦✦
The populist Dizzy Gillespie gets full rein in this lively, happy collection of tunes exploring rhythms and idioms from the Caribbean. Gillespie is in an ebullient mood, even offering some sly lead calypso vocals on three numbers (perhaps his lighthearted presidential "campaign" of 1964 contributed to the high spirits; the sessions began a day after Election Day). Much of the material comes from Dizzy's band on the session—which includes the formidable James Moody on tenor and flute, Kenny Barron on piano, and percussionist Kansas Fields—and there are some genuine calypsos by Joe Willoughby to round out the package. The cut with the biggest quota of fun is "Barbados Carnival," with guitarist Chris White doubling as a calypso singer, and the lengthy "Trinidad, Goodbye" offers the largest amount of straight-ahead playing. This slice of enjoyable minor Gillespie, originally on Limelight, was reissued on Verve with the original cover on its By Request series in 1998. *—Richard S. Ginell*

Swing Low, Sweet Cadillac / May 25, 1967-May 26, 1967 / GRP/Impulse! ✦✦✦
Although trumpeter Dizzy Gillespie was in his prime in the mid-1960's, this CD (which is a straight reissue of an Impulse Lp) is a disappointment. Gillespie mostly jokes around on "Swing Low, Sweet Cadillac" (a routine he did better in the early 1950's), the brief "Bye" is a waste and Dizzy makes the mistake of singing the forgettable "Something In Your Smile" (from *Dr. Doolittle*). Although the trumpeter has decent solos on the Brazilian "Mas Que Nada" and his lengthy "Kush" and Dizzy's interplay with the audience is sometimes humorous, this effort with his quintet (which includes James Moody on tenor, alto and flute and pianist Mike Longo) is definitely a lesser effort that does not deserve to be continually reissued. *—Scott Yanow*

Dizzy's Big 4 / Sep. 19, 1974 / Pablo/OJC ✦✦✦✦✦
Arguably Dizzy Gillespie's most rewarding recording of the 1970s, this quartet date (with guitarist Joe Pass, bassist Ray Brown and drummer Mickey Roker) finds the 57-year-old trumpeter near peak form on three of his compositions and four standards. These versions of "Tanga" and "Be Bop" are brilliant. *—Scott Yanow*

To a Finland Station / Sep. 9, 1982 / Fantasy/OJC ✦✦✦✦
This unique set finds Dizzy Gillespie (who was nearly age 65) sharing the frontline with the great Cuban trumpeter Arturo Sandoval. Backed by a fine Finnish rhythm section, Sandoval and the great trumpeter are both in good spirits playing five of Gillespie's originals including "Wheatleigh Hall" and "And Then She Stopped." Considering that it would be another decade before Sandoval was able to defect from Cuba (and finally play the music he wanted), this recording is of great historic value. *—Scott Yanow*

Live at Royal Festival Hall / Jun. 10, 1989 / Enja ✦✦✦✦

Complete Dial Masters: Modern Jazz Trumpets / Aug. 26, 1997 / Jazz Classics ✦✦✦✦✦

Jimmy Giuffre

b. Apr. 26, 1921, Dallas, TX
Sax (Tenor), Sax (Soprano), Sax (Baritone), Flute, Clarinet / Avant-Garde Jazz, Folk-Jazz, West Coast Jazz, Cool

Jimmy Giuffre had many accomplishments in a long career that has never been predictable. His composition "Four Brothers" became a hit for Woody Herman, an orchestra that Giuffre eventually joined in 1949. Settling on the West Coast, the cool-toned tenor started also playing clarinet and occasional baritone. In 1956 he went out on his own, forming the Jimmy Giuffre 3; he then had a minor hit with his recording of "The Train and the River." In 1958 Giuffre had a most unusual trio with valve trombonist Bob Brookmeyer and guitarist Hall (no piano, bass or drums!); after a couple years of reverting back to the reeds-guitar-bass format, in 1961 the new Jimmy Giuffre 3 featured pianist Paul Bley and bassist Steve Swallow and was involved in exploring the more introspective side of free jazz. *—Scott Yanow*

☆ **The Complete Capitol & Atlantic Recordings of Jimmy Giuffre** / Feb. 19, 1954-Dec. 3, 1958 / Mosaic ✦✦✦✦✦
Jimmy Giuffre has always followed his own singular musical path. In the mid- to late '50s, he was increasingly interested in folky melodies, quiet playing, and lyrical freedom. This limited-edition 1997 six-CD set has a great deal of formerly rare material (including six previously unreleased performances) that traces his career during a nearly five-year period. The cool-toned Giuffre (switching between clarinet, tenor, and baritone) is heard with a few medium-size groups of West Coast all-stars, heading a pianoless quartet that includes trumpeter Jack Sheldon, matching wits with clarinetist Pee Wee Russell ("Blues in E Flat") and cornetist Rex Stewart ("In a Mellotone"), collaborating with the Modern Jazz Quartet, playing songs from *The Music Man,* and leading the Jimmy Giuffre 3. The latter group started out also including guitarist Jim Hall and bassist Jim Atlas, but it is the two projects that match Giuffre with Hall and valve trombonist Bob Brookmeyer (no piano, bass, or drums) that are most intriguing. In addition, on one odd date, Giuffre overdubbed four tenors while joined by Hall and Brookmeyer (this time on piano). Although Jimmy Giuffre's influence was quite slight—his quiet experiments were soon overshadowed by the more fiery avant-garde—this music has dated pretty well and rewards repeated listenings. *—Scott Yanow*

The Jazzlore: The Jimmy Giuffre Three, Vol. 46 / Dec. 3, 1956-Dec. 24, 1956 / Atlantic ✦✦✦
The only one of Jimmy Giuffre's valuable Atlantic recordings to thus far be reissued on CD, this disc features the first version of Giuffre's *3.* With guitarist Jim Hall and either Ralph Pena or Jim Atlas on bass, Giuffre is heard on clarinet, tenor and baritone. The generally introverted music is wistful, has a fair amount of variety, and is melodic while still sounding advanced. In addition to the nine original songs (including the earliest recording of Giuffre's classic folk song "The Train and the River"), two previously unreleased tunes (including "Forty-Second Street") were added to the CD reissue. An excellent introduction to Jimmy Giuffre's unique (if not particularly influential) music. *—Scott Yanow*

Western Suite / Dec. 3, 1958 / Atlantic ✦✦✦✦

• **1961** / Mar. 3, 1961+Aug. 4, 1961 / ECM ♦♦♦♦
One of the most intriguing groups that Jimmy Giuffre led was the trio that he had during 1961-1962 with pianist Paul Bley and bassist Steve Swallow. As opposed to the free jazz and high-energy avant-garde players that were beginning to emerge, Giuffre (who stuck exclusively to clarinet) sought to free up his music but with subtlety, a use of space and at a quiet volume. This ECM double CD not only reissues two of the trio's three out of print LPs (*Fusion* and *Thesis*) but adds some previously unreleased selections too. The music was still tied (although sometimes loosely) to chordal improvisation, but there are spots on these originals by Giuffre, Paul Bley, and Carla Bley (plus a dramatic version of the standard "Goodbye") where the performances are nearly as advanced as Ornette Coleman's. The three musicians often act as equals and bassist Steve Swallow (years before he switched permanently to electric bass) is particularly advanced. Thought-provoking music. *—Scott Yanow*

Free Fall / Jul. 10, 1962-Nov. 1, 1962 / Columbia/Legacy ♦♦♦
The final classic version of the Jimmy Giuffre Three matched Giuffre (sticking to clarinet) with pianist Paul Bley and bassist Steve Swallow. Unlike the earlier Giuffre groups, this unit concentrated primarily on free improvisations which, even when a bit introspective, could be a little startling. Their 1998 reissue CD brings back the trio's elusive Columbia recording which has the ten selections that were on the original LP, one number only previously out on a sampler and five previously unreleased tracks. Surprisingly, the majority of the performances (10 of the 16 numbers) are unaccompanied clarinet solos; of the remainder, two are clarinet-bass duets, and only four feature the full trio. Giuffre's improvisations are a bit futuristic, although in general much gentler than the high-energy players of the mid-'60s. Even if it is a bit innovative and thought-provoking, this music is not all that essential (there isn't enough opportunities for communication between the musicians), and Giuffre's flights get a bit dull after awhile. A historical curiosity. *—Scott Yanow*

Momentum, Willisau 1988 / Sep. 3, 1988 / hatOLOGY ♦♦♦♦
A set of live duets and solos by two reed players would not seem to have much potential except maybe in avant-garde jazz, but this recital is actually quite melodic, makes use of space and holds one's interest throughout. Veteran Jimmy Giuffre (heard here on clarinet and soprano) and Andre Jaume (doubling on tenor and bass clarinet) perform obscure and mostly spontaneous originals. the fairly basic themes contrast sound and silence, and the thoughtful renditions contain subtle surprises and fine interplay. A sleeper that is well worth picking up. *—Scott Yanow*

Benny Golson

b. Jan. 25, 1929, Philadelphia, PA
Sax (Tenor), Composer, Arranger / Hard Bop
Benny Golson is a talented composer/arranger whose tenor playing has continued to evolve with time. He first worked in Philadelphia with Bull Moose Jackson's R&B band (1951); Golson then played with Todd Dameron for a period in 1953 and this was followed by stints with Lionel Hampton (1953-54), Johnny Hodges and Earl Bostic (1954-56). He came to prominence while with Dizzy Gillespie's globetrotting big band (1956-58), as much for his writing as for his tenor playing. Golson wrote such standards as "I Remember Clifford," "Killer Joe," "Stablemates," "Whisper Not," "Along Came Betty" and "Blues March" during 1956-60. His stay with Art Blakey's Jazz Messengers (1958-59) was significant and during 1959-62 he co-led the Jazztet with Art Farmer. From that point on Golson gradually drifted away from jazz and concentrated more on working in the studios and with orchestras. When Golson returned to active playing in 1977, his tone had hardened. *—Scott Yanow*

• **Benny Golson's New York Scene** / Oct. 14, 1957+Oct. 17, 1957 / Contemporary/OJC ♦♦♦♦♦
This was one of the first albums to establish Golson's reputation as a soloist and composer. *—Ron Wynn*

New York Scene / Oct. 14, 1957-Oct. 17, 1957 / Original Jazz Classics ♦♦♦♦♦
Benny Golson's debut as a leader was recorded at a time when he was better known as a composer than a tenor saxophonist. This CD reissue, which adds "B.G.'s Holiday" to the original LP program, features Golson in a quintet with fellow future Jazztet co-leader Art Farmer on trumpet, pianist Wynton Kelly, bassist Paul Chambers and drummer Charlie Persip on five selections, and with the same group plus four horns on three other songs. The set is most significant for including an early version of Golson's "Whisper Not" (which soon became a jazz standard) along with "Step Lightly," as well as for the leader's inventive and swinging arrangements; plus, there are some excellent solos from Golson and Farmer. Overall, this underrated gem served as a strong start to Benny Golson's influential solo career. *—Scott Yanow*

The Modern Touch / Dec. 19, 1957+Dec. 23, 1957 / Riverside/OJC ♦♦♦♦
Benny Golson's second album as a leader (reissued on CD in the OJC series) is a solid hard bop date featuring the tenorman in a quintet with trumpeter Kenny Dorham, pianist Wynton Kelly, bassist Paul Chambers and drummer Max Roach. The all-star group performs three Golson originals (none of which really caught on), a pair of Gigi Gryce tunes (best known is "Hymn to the Orient") and the standard "Namely You." Excellent playing on an above-average set that defines the modern mainstream of 1957 jazz. *—Scott Yanow*

The Other Side of Benny Golson / Nov. 12, 1958 / Riverside/OJC ♦♦♦♦
Tenor-saxophonist Benny Golson's third recording as a leader was significant in two ways. It was his first opportunity to work with trombonist Curtis Fuller (the two would be members of The Jazztet by 1960) and it was one of his first chances to really stretch out on record as a soloist; up to this point Golson was possibly better known as a composer. Three of the six originals on this CD reissue of a Riverside date are Golson's ("Are You Real" was the closest one to catching on) but the emphasis is on the solos of the leader, Fuller and pianist Barry Harris; bassist Jymie Merritt and drummer Philly Joe Jones are excellent in support. *—Scott Yanow*

Gone with Golson / Jun. 20, 1959 / New Jazz/OJC ♦♦♦♦
Shortly before the formation of The Jazztet, tenor-saxophonist Benny Golson and trombonist Curtis Fuller teamed up for this quintet set with pianist Ray Bryant, bassist Tommy Bryant and drummer Al Harewood. Although Golson contributed three of the six songs ("Blues After Dark" is the best-known one), the emphasis is on his playing; the tenor is quite heated on the uptempo blues "Jam for Bobbie." The CD reissue adds "A Bit of Heaven" (originally on a sampler but part of the same session) to the original program, a fine example of hard bop of the late '50s. *—Scott Yanow*

Groovin' with Golson / Aug. 28, 1959 / New Jazz/OJC ♦♦♦

Stockholm Sojourn / 1964 / Prestige/OJC ♦♦♦

Benny Golson Quartet / Jun. 20, 1990-Jun. 21, 1990 / Delta ♦♦♦♦♦
Since Laserlight is a budget CD label, it is easy not to take its releases overly seriously, particularly since its personnel listings and dates are often wrong. In the case of this CD, however, the music is excellent, and the listing of musicians (Benny Golson on tenor, pianist Mulgrew Miller, bassist Rufus Reid and drummer Tony Reedus) is accurate, although the dates are not given and there are several errors with the listing of composers for the songs. Golson is heard throughout in top form, stretching himself on Freddie Hubbard's "Up Jumped Spring" (listed as an original called "Up, Jump, Spring!"), Kenny Barron's "Voyage" and his own "Stable Mates." On the latter, Golson plays an effective and intense duet with drummer Reedus. 61 at the time, Benny Golson is heard here at the peak of his powers. *—Scott Yanow*

I Remember Miles / Oct. 5, 1992-Oct. 6, 1992 / Evidence ♦♦♦♦♦
There are a few remarkable recreations on tenor-saxophonist Benny Golson's tribute to Miles Davis, particularly "'Round Midnight" and parts of "So What" and "Bye Bye Blackbird." Trumpeter Eddie Henderson (especially when muted) comes very close to duplicating not only the sound but the spirit of Davis while Golson sometimes discards his own strong musical personality to do close impressions of John Coltrane. Trombonist Curtis Fuller, pianist Mulgrew Miller, bassist Ray Drummond and drummer Tony Reedus are also in fine form on a program that not only has five songs associated with 1950s Miles Davis but three Golson originals including "One Day, Forever (I Remember Miles)" which (although worthy) is not in the same league as his earlier classic "I Remember Clifford." This heartfelt tribute album has enough unique moments to make it easily recommended. *—Scott Yanow*

Remembering Clifford / Mar. 30, 1997+Mar. 31, 1997 / Milestone ♦♦♦♦
Benny Golson was moved by the death of bop trumpeter Clifford Brown to pen the classic "I Remember Clifford." Now presented with the opportunity to do an album in honor of his old friend, Golson assembles a sextet and presents an album that takes the idea of "I Remember Clifford," thoroughly updates it and extends it across an hour of great music on this disc. Re-doing his best known tune as "Brown Immortal," Benny also does a remake of "Five Spot After Dark," long a set-list staple. Golson's horn is pure honey, sounding every bit as wonderful at age 69 as many players would hope to be at half his age. Trading solos with tenor sax man Ron Blake, trumpeter John Swana and pianist Mike Ledonne, Peter Washington adds fine string bass support while Joe Farnsworth pushes the beat along, kicking in all the right places and never overplaying. Tito Puente and Carlos Valdes make guest appearances on Golson's "Tito Puente," but where Golson and company really shine are on new tracks like "Horizon Ahead" and the closer, "Ever More." These two spirited tracks show that Golson's playing is still edgy when need be and still philosophical on tracks like "Lullaby of Birdland" and the ballad "You're the First to Know." With some great music on tap, there's no level at which this album does not succeed. *—Cub Koda*

That's Funky / Feb. 22, 2000 / Arkadia Jazz ♦♦♦♦
As an originator of the initial soul-funk movement of the '60s when he was with Art Blakey's Jazz Messengers, Golson is eminently qualified to funkify jazz and R&B-flavored instrumental music. Nat Adderley plays cornet alongside Golson's tenor in this, one of his last recordings before he passed away. Always fresh and deep in the groove is pianist Monty Alexander, and acoustic bassist Ray Drummond plays fat notes with ultimate conviction. Also contributing here is genius drummer Marvin "Smitty" Smith, who lays out rhythms that Bernard Purdie would be envious of. All of the tunes are well-known, save Golson's original "Mississippi Windows," dedicated to the saxophonist's days with R&B icon Bullmoose Jackson. Golson also re-casts his classic "Blues March" in a New Orleans style, while the steady tick-tock to shuffle stride of "Moanin'" is not all that different from the original. The ultra-funky "Work Song" is much more so than the original, while "Sidewinder" is the single tune on the date that is most faithful to the original and not rhythmically altered. There are two versions of "Mack the Knife": one is a half-speed funk with ol' Mackie coming back with a twist; the second is the sole solid swinger of the session, as Golson and Adderley swap licks half-and-half on the melody line, then join together and slightly modify the line. Though they're not swinging, for the most part, in conventional 2/4 or 4/4 jazz beats, in a sense they *are* swinging in their own inimitable, danceable, street-derived, back-beat-driven way á la Silver, Stanley Turrentine, and Grant Green, among others. Those inventors of this boogaloo-influenced subgenre should be happy with Golson's results. *—Michael G. Nastos*

Paul Gonsalves

b. Jul. 12, 1920, Boston, MA, **d.** May 14, 1974, London, England
Sax (Tenor), Reeds / Swing, Bop
The greatest moment of Paul Gonsalves's musical career occurred at the 1956 Newport Jazz Festival when, to bridge the gap between "Diminuendo in Blue" and "Crescendo in Blue," Duke Ellington urged him to take a long solo, egging him on through 27 exciting choruses that almost caused a riot. That well-publicized episode resulted in Ellington having a major "comeback," and Gonsalves forever earning Duke's graditude.

Gonsalves had already earned a strong reputation during his stints with Count Basie (1946-49) and the Dizzy Gillespie Orchestra (1949-50). Joining Ellington in 1950, Gonsalves's warm breathy tone and harmonically advanced solos were a constant fixture for 24 years (except for a brief time in 1953 when he was with Tommy Dorsey) and he was well-featured up until his death, just ten days before Ellington passed on. In addition to his countless number of recorded performances with Ellington, Gonsalves led dates of his own on an occasional basis including for Argo, Jazzland, Impulse (highlighted by a combative meeting with Sonny Stitt), Storyville, Black Lion and Fantasy. *—Scott Yanow*

Cookin' / Aug. 6, 1957 / Argo ♦♦♦♦♦

Gettin' Together! / Dec. 20, 1960 / Jazzland/OJC ♦♦♦♦♦
The most easily available of tenor saxophonist Paul Gonsalves' infrequent sessions as a leader, this CD is a straight reissue of his original Jazzland LP. Three songs (including two ballads) showcase Gonsalves in a quartet with pianist Wynton Kelly, bassist Sam Jones and drummer Jimmy Cobb, while five other pieces add cornetist Nat Adderley (in his prime during the era) to the band. The music is straight-ahead and shows that Gonsalves was quite capable of playing with younger "modernists." *—Scott Yanow*

● **Salt and Pepper** / Sep. 5, 1963 / Jasmine ♦♦♦♦♦

Paul Gonsalves Meets Earl Hines / Dec. 15, 1970+Nov. 29, 1972 / Black Lion ♦♦♦♦
Most of this CD was recorded at the earlier date. Duke Ellington's longtime tenor, Paul Gonsalves, was a perfect match for the inventive pianist, Earl Hines, who (along with bassist Al Hall and drummer Jo Jones) is in top form on five standards, three by Ellington. The music swings hard and has its surprising moments. The one track from 1972 is a solo version of "Blue Sands" played by its composer Earl Hines. Although not essential, this CD should please the fans of Hines and Gonsalves, two masterful players who had only previously recorded together once, on a date shared by the pianist and Johnny Hodges. *—Scott Yanow*

Mexican Bandit Meets Pittsburgh Pirate / Aug. 24, 1973 / Fantasy/OJC ♦♦♦
This album teams tenor saxophonist Paul Gonsalves and trumpeter Roy Eldridge quite late in their careers. Gonsalves would pass away within a year and Eldridge would only be able to play for about five more. Actually, Eldridge is in generally good (and typically combative) form on tunes such as his "5400 North" and "C Jam Blues." The ailing Gonsalves is tentative and streaky in spots and just average throughout despite his best efforts. The rhythm section (pianist Cliff Smalls, bassist Sam Jones and drummer Eddie Locke) is perfectly up to the task and has "It's the Talk of the Town" as its feature. It's an interesting historical album although the leader has sounded much better elsewhere. *—Scott Yanow*

Benny Goodman

b. May 30, 1909, Chicago, IL, **d.** Jun. 13, 1986, New York, NY [Manhattan]
Clarinet, Bandleader / Swing, Big Band
By the time he formed his first big band in 1934, Goodman had been a pro for a decade. Born into a large and poor family in Chicago (of which he became the main support after his father's death in 1926), he joined drummer Ben Pollack's band at 16, came to New York with it in 1928, and soon was one of the Big Apple's most in-demand recording and radio studio musicians. His clarinet style, influenced at first by Jimmie Noone and Frank Teschemacher, was fluent and swinging and was widely imitated during the Swing Era, which he helped ring in. As a bandleader, Goodman was a demanding taskmaster. He lived for music and expected others to be as dedicated; this often caused friction, but the personnel of his bands, which he led full-time until 1948 and sporadically thereafter, nevertheless was quite stable. Dubbed "King of Swing," a title he neither invented nor invited but felt no need to refuse, Goodman helped break down racial barriers in popular music by hiring pianist Teddy Wilson, vibist Lionel Hampton, guitarist Charlie Christian, trumpeter Cootie Williams, and other Black stars-to-be, first for his small "bands-within-the-band," then for the full orchestra. His choice of arrangers, chief among them Fletcher Henderson (though Jimmy Mundy was the most productive), also bespoke his admiration for Black musical creativity. Goodman helped launch the band—leading the careers of Gene Krupa, Harry James, and Hampton, among others. He liked to perform classical music and commissioned compositions from Béla Bartók, Paul Hindemith, Aaron Copland, and Leonard Bernstein. Though he periodically went into semi-retirement, Goodman could never stay away from his beloved clarinet for long; at the very end of his life, he was once again leading a big band that specialized in Fletcher Henderson arrangements. Until the end, the number of his fans was legion. *—Dan Morgenstern*

B.G. & Big Tea in NYC / Apr. 1929-Oct. 1934 / GRP ♦♦♦♦♦
CD reissue of some early '30s material that doesn't feature clarinetist Benny Goodman in a leadership role. Instead, he's in bands under the direction of Red Nichols, Arthur Rollini, and Irving Mills. Yet, he's the star soloist, along with trombonist Jack Teagarden. *—Ron Wynn*

☆ **The Birth of Swing** / Apr. 4, 1935-Nov. 5, 1936 / Bluebird/RCA ♦♦♦♦♦
This three-CD set includes all of the Benny Goodman big band's recordings from April 1935 through November 1936, a period when the orchestra became the most popular and influential in the world, making both swing and Benny Goodman into household words. Augmented by some alternate takes, this set shows just how solid and musical a unit Goodman had from the start. Key soloists include trumpeters Bunny Berigan and Ziggy Elman, pianist Jess Stacy and the band's excellent singer Helen Ward, but BG usually emerges as the main star, with the tight, swinging ensembles being a close second. In addition to the hits ("King Porter Stomp," "Sometimes I'm Happy," "When Buddha Smiles," "Stompin' at the Savoy," and "Goody-Goody"), even the lesser-known numbers and pop tunes have their strong moments. This music is essential to any serious jazz collection. *—Scott Yanow*

● **Sing, Sing, Sing** / Apr. 4, 1935-Apr. 11, 1939 / Bluebird/RCA ♦♦♦♦♦
A fine all-around single CD, it sums up Benny Goodman's 1935-39 period on Victor. During this time BG became jazz's and popular music's number one attraction, achieving this impressive feat without watering down his music or emphasizing novelties. All Goodman did was play the music he loved and the audience magically responded and started dancing. This set has most of BG's better-known recordings from the era including "King Porter Stomp," "Goody Goody," "Roll 'Em," "Don't Be That Way," "One O'Clock Jump" and of course the memorable "Sing, Sing, Sing"; it serves as a good beginning for those listeners just beginning to explore Benny Goodman's music. *—Scott Yanow*

The Complete Small Group Recordings / Jul. 11, 1935-Apr. 6, 1939 / RCA ♦♦♦♦♦
The music of the Benny Goodman Trio and Quartets (with the clarinetist, pianist Teddy Wilson, drummer Gene Krupa and sometimes vibraphonist Lionel Hampton) has been put out many times through the years, including in other, earlier "complete" sets. This 1997 three-CD reissue not only has all of the regular recordings, but 20 alternate takes, two of which were previously unissued. Many of the performances (such as "After You've Gone," "Moonglow," "Dinah" and "Avalon") are quite famous, considered perfect examples of "chamber jazz," and veteran collectors will certainly enjoy hearing many of the alternates. Singers Helen Ward and Martha Tilton, trumpeter Ziggy Elman (on "Bei Mist Bist Du Schoen") and (after Krupa's departure) drummers Dave Tough and Buddy Schutz, bassist John Kirby and pianist Jess Stacy also make appearances. Classic music with many exciting moments from the King of Swing and his famous sidemen. *—Scott Yanow*

Original Benny Goodman Trio and Quartet Sessions, Vol. 1: After You've Gone / Jul. 11, 1935-Feb. 3, 1937 / Bluebird/RCA ♦♦♦♦
Although Benny Goodman came to fame as leader of a big swinging orchestra, from nearly the beginning he always allocated some time to playing with smaller groups. On July 13, 1935, the Benny Goodman Trio debuted (featuring drummer Gene Krupa and pianist Teddy Wilson) and 13 months later vibraphonist Lionel Hampton made the unit a quartet. The first interracial group to appear regularly in public, this outlet gave BG an opportunity to stretch out and interact with his peers. The CD *After You've Gone* contains the first ten Trio recordings and the initial twelve studio performances by the Quartet. Helen Ward contributes two fine vocals but the emphasis is on the close interplay between these brilliant players. *—Scott Yanow*

The Complete Small Combinations, Vols. 1-2 / Jul. 13, 1935-Jul. 30, 1937 / RCA ♦♦♦♦♦
This two-CD set from the French RCA Jazz Tribune series (a straight reissue of a two-LP set) has the first 30 recordings by the Benny Goodman Trio and Quartets, groups featuring the leader-clarinetist, pianist Teddy Wilson, drummer Gene Krupa and sometimes vibraphonist Lionel Hampton. A special bonus of this historic set is the inclusion of five formerly rare alternate takes (including "After You've Gone" and "Body and Soul" from the first trio session). Although used by BG as a brief departure from his big band, his trio and quartet became famous in their own right and their recordings are essential to any serious jazz collection. This twofer was followed by a second one tracing Goodman's small groups into 1939. *—Scott Yanow*

Stompin' at the Savoy / Jul. 1, 1935-Feb. 16, 1938 / Bluebird/RCA ♦♦♦♦♦

☆ **On the Air 1937-1938** / Mar. 3, 1937-Sep. 20, 1938 / Columbia/Legacy ♦♦♦♦♦
This two-CD set was originally issued as a deluxe multi-disc set in Columbia's Masterwork series and was intended as a companion piece to Goodman's best selling *Live At Carnegie Hall,* a record so successful that it was parceled out by Columbia in as many piecemeal configurations and vinyl speed formats as is imaginable. Mainly pulled from Goodman's appearances on the Camel Caravan radio show, these capture the swing band of the era in its defining moment, blowing audiences away on a night to night basis in a variety of locales. Carefully edited (radio broadcasts could often have announcer's remarks annoyingly inserted in the middle of performances), the sound is far cleaner than the majority of bootlegs from the same time frame. With plenty of brilliant soloing from Goodman, Harry James, Ziggy Elman, and a brace of trio and quartet sides featuring Teddy Wilson and Lionel Hampton, with Gene Krupa power-housing everything he touches, this is the swing era in all its glory. If you have the Carnegie Hall set and a good sampling of the Victor-era sides, this is your next stop. *—Cub Koda*

★ **Featuring Charlie Christian** / Oct. 2, 1939-Mar. 13, 1941 / Columbia ♦♦♦♦♦
Charlie Christian was not the first electric guitarist, but he was its first giant. He elevated the guitar from a member of the rhythm section (where it was often inaudible) to the frontline, taking solos that could challenge any saxophonist. His playing was so appealing to his contemporaries that it was not until the emergence of rock in the mid- to late '60s that more advanced guitarists emerged. By then it was over a quarter century since Christian's premature death from tuberculosis. He spent his only two high-profile years as a member of the Benny Goodman Sextet, and 18 of their best recordings are on this CD. Christian and Goodman are joined by Lionel Hampton on the first dozen performances, while the final six boast the explosive combination of trumpeter Cootie Williams and Georgie Auld's tenor. The riffing inspires heated yet melodic solos, resulting in classic music that is impossible to dislike. *—Scott Yanow*

Greatest Hits / 1939-1946 / Columbia/Legacy ♦♦♦

Best of the Big Bands / Mar. 1, 1940-Jun. 4, 1941 / Columbia/Legacy ♦♦♦

Best of the Big Bands, Vol. 2 / Aug. 15, 1941-Dec. 10, 1941 / Columbia/Legacy ♦♦♦

Small Groups: 1941-1945 / Oct. 28, 1941-Feb. 4, 1945 / Columbia ♦♦♦♦
When one thinks of Benny Goodman's small groups, it is generally his original Trio and Quartet (with Lionel Hampton, Teddy Wilson and Gene Krupa) or his sextet with Charlie Christian that comes immediately to mind. This superior set dates from a slightly later period and features a sextet with trombonist Lou McGarity and pianist Mel Powell (the clarinet-trombone blend works very well) and his 1944-45 quintet/sextet with vibraphonist Red Norvo. Vocalists Peggy Lee, Jane Harvey and Peggy Mann give this set some variety. The music (and the clarinet playing) is consistently brilliant. *—Scott Yanow*

The Best of Benny Goodman: Capitol Years / 1944-1964 / Blue Note ♦♦♦
The Best of Benny Goodman: The Capitol Years is an excellent 18-track overview of the clarinetist's stint at Capitol. He recorded for the label between 1944 and 1955, during which time he played in a wide variety of combinations, from his traditional big band to small trios. This disc captures the variety and vitality of this era, featuring both re-recordings of '30s hits like "Sing, Sing, Sing" and relatively new songs, as well as solo spots from Harry James, Lionel Hampton, Mel Powell and Ruby Braff. It's a good sampler of an underrated time in Goodman's career. *—Leo Stanley*

Sextet / Nov. 24, 1950-Oct. 22, 1952 / Columbia ♦♦♦♦
In 1950, Benny Goodman formed a new sextet, and although he used a big band for some

recordings, the small group was his main outlet for the next couple of years. This CD features this somewhat forgotten unit, a hot swing combo featuring vibraphonist Terry Gibbs and usually pianist Teddy Wilson. Rather than repeat his older hits, the clarinetist clearly enoyed playing other standards not generally associated with him. Excellent and enjoyable music. *—Scott Yanow*

B.G. in Hi-Fi / Nov. 8, 1954-Nov. 16, 1954 / Blue Note ♦♦♦♦♦
On this all-around excellent CD, Benny Goodman performs a dozen selections (mostly Fletcher Henderson arrangements) with a big band filled with sympathetic players in 1954 and eight other numbers with a pair of smaller units that also feature pianist Mel Powell and either Charlie Shavers or Ruby Braff on trumpets. Although the big-band era had been gone for almost a decade, Benny Goodman (then 46) plays these swing classics with enthusiasm and creativity and shows that there was never any reason for anyone to write him off as "behind the times." *—Scott Yanow*

Together Again! (1963 Reunion with Lionel Hampton, Teddy Wilson & Gene Krupa / Feb. 13, 1963-Feb. 14, 1963 / Bluebird/RCA ♦♦♦♦♦
The music on this CD has been reissued several times, including once previously on a Bluebird CD. This was the first full reunion in the studios of the Benny Goodman Quartet (featuring the clarinetist, vibraphonist Lionel Hampton, pianist Teddy Wilson, and drummer Gene Krupa), and although they would get together on an infrequent basis over the next decade, this was their last studio recording. In general, the classic swing stars avoided recreating their past triumphs and instead recorded veteran standards that they had missed the first time around. Krupa's bass drum work (which is meant to fill in for a bassist) gets a bit heavy-handed at times, but the good spirits of the reunion uplift the music. Highlights include "Seven Come Eleven," "I've Found a New Baby," "Runnin' Wild," and the blues "Four Once More." *—Scott Yanow*

Sextet Featuring Charlie Christian / Oct. 2, 1939-Mar. 13, 1941 / Columbia ♦♦♦♦
Over the course of Benny Goodman's career, the stars often lined up right and he found himself working in tandem with someone every bit as talented as he, whether it was Bunny Berigan, Fletcher Henderson, Harry James, Gene Krupa, Lionel Hampton or Teddy Wilson. For a brief period after most of the above had left his employ, Goodman hooked up with guitarist Charlie Christian and the jazz world was never the same. Christian played in the big band and his "Solo Flight" was one of the first big band staples built around the then new electric guitar, but his best work came with a handful of finely wrought gems as a member of Goodman's sextet. Sharing solo space with Goodman and Hampton, Christian gave the electric guitar a place in the music on sides like "Flying Home," "Air Mail Special," "Stardust" and "AC-DC Current," where his instrument seems to be bursting with ideas and ceaseless invention. Along with sides by Eddie Lang and Django Reinhart's "Hot Club of France," these are the recordings that made jazz guitar history. *—Cub Koda*

Benny Goodman and His Great Vocalists / 1995 / Columbia/Legacy ♦♦♦♦
One doesn't often think of the Goodman band as a repository for great singers, but over the course of the 1940s, the King of Swing framed the band around some vocalists who delivered the goods as well as any others, nicely documented in this 16-track collection. Swinging performances from the likes of Billie Holiday, Helen Ward, Martha Tilton, Mildred Bailey (all 1930s recordings), Helen Forrest, Peggy Lee, Dick Haymes, Art Lund, and others make this a side of the Goodman discography that seldom comes up for air. Transfers are clean and the booklet comes with excellent notes from *Jazz Singing* author Will Friedwald. *—Cub Koda*

The V-Disc Recordings / Nov. 17, 1998 / Collectors' Choice Music ♦♦♦♦♦
This four-CD set is a treasure trove of wartime Benny Goodman activity, containing 68 tracks recorded or released on behalf of the Navy V-Disc program. In addition to the full band, the Benny Goodman Trio (with Teddy Wilson and Specs Powell) is represented, along with the "V-Disc Quartette," and the Benny Goodman Quintet. There are no dates included or other information, but the recordings generally span from the second half of 1943 until the middle of 1945. These aren't Goodman's complete V-Disc issues, nor has there apparently been much effort to keep what is here in recording or release order. They have been assembled in a sensible order for listening pleasure, however, and there's a considerable amount of that to be had. Goodman, like most other artists, was sidelined from recording for much of the early '40s by the Musicians Union's recording ban, but he recorded dozens of V-Discs that served to capture his repertory and his band's sound during this era. The Goodman band, in particular, through a combination of serving the public in their work and the growing optimism of the later war years—and the plentiful work and money—developed a reputation for reckless abandon in their performances during this period that made them a wonder to hear, stretching out on every solo as though there were no tomorrow. The repertory is, thus, unique, and priceless—Goodman and his band (and trio and quartet) at the peak of their performance and innovation. The sound is uniformly good throughout this collection, with few exceptions of consequence, and the only flaw is the lack of any detailed notes. *—Bruce Eder*

Good to Go / Jun. 6, 1935 / Buddha ♦♦♦♦
In the days before he was the King of Swing, Benny Goodman had a struggling band that played hot jazz like a small combo; they were too wild and loud for the ballrooms that catered to the Guy Lombardo crowd. Money was tight so when a chance to record and make a pile of dough doing transcription work arose, Goodman and his band rose to the challenge and blasted out these 25 gems (along with 25 others) in a single session, all one-take wonders. For this, the members in the band were paid the musician union's stipulated fee of a dollar per side, a true chunk of change by Depression-era standards. Although pivotal driving force Gene Krupa is here in the drum chair, we're still a few years away from the presence of Harry James, Lionel Hampton, Teddy Wilson, or Jess Stacey. All the more amazing, then, are these performances with the band virtually running through what was their entire book at the time, playing with an on-the-edge-of-their-chairs exuberance that comes with one-take, fly-by-the-seat-of-your-pants recordings like this. There may be a few clams on a track here and there, but this is some of the true beginnings of the swing movement, a movement that changed the course of popular music forever. *—Cub Koda*

The Complete Capitol Trios / Nov. 7, 1947-Nov. 16, 1954 / Blue Note ♦♦♦♦♦
The Complete Captiol Trios is a long-overdue reissue of the five trio sessions Benny Goodman led for Capitol Records. The five sessions are easily broken down into two categories—recordings from 1947 and recordings from 1954. The highlights of the 1947 recordings are sessions with pianist Teddy Wilson and drummer Jimmy Crawford. This provided Goodman an opportunity to reunite with Wilson who he had toured with in the late '30s in a trio with drummer Gene Krupa. Goodman and Wilson have a real ease to their interaction and the results are positively joyful. There are three other recordings from 1947, featuring pianist Jimmy Rowles and drummer Tom Romersa; these are good, but not quite as delightful as their 1947 companions. However, the 1954 recordings—all featuring the great pianist Bud Powell, four featuring drummer Eddie Grady, and two featuring drummer Bobby Donaldson—are equally wonderful, filled with good humor, elegant flair, and magical interludes. These sessions have been out of circulation for too long, but *The Complete Capitol Trios* is so well-done—and its fidelity is so good—that the wait was certainly worthwhile. *—Stephen Thomas Erlewine*

★ **Live at Carnegie Hall: 1938 Complete** / Nov. 2, 1999 / Columbia/Legacy ♦♦♦♦♦
Benny Goodman's January 16, 1938, *Carnegie Hall* concert is considered the single most important jazz or popular music concert in history: jazz's "coming out" party to the world of "respectable" music, held right in that throne room of musical respectability, *Carnegie Hall*. The 1950-vintage three-album set from the concert only solidified its reputation, and an earlier CD release derived from the LP master was a choice entry in the Goodman catalog for more than ten years. For the 1999 release, producer Phil Schaap re-sourced the concert from original 78 rpm transcription discs; he has also rescued "Sometimes I'm Happy," the show's original second number, and "If Dreams Come True," its original first encore, along with the unedited version of "Honeysuckle Rose" (with Harry Carney in a two-chorus baritone sax solo and Buck Clayton's three-chorus trumpet solo), all previously lost. The detail is startling, with soloists who are more up close than ever and even details from the audience reactions. Gene Krupa's drums have an extraordinary richness of tone, and the whole rhythm section finally gets its due as well, even Freddie Green's rhythm guitar solo during "Honeysuckle Rose," which is gloriously enhanced. There will be casual listeners, however, who won't like this release because Schaap has chosen to leave a lot of surface noise, in the interest of preserving the original concert ambience. Some compromise should have been possible, however, where the worst source damage is concerned, and some casual listeners may prefer the original CD release, despite the enhancements featured here. *—Bruce Eder*

Dexter Gordon

b. Feb. 27, 1923, Los Angeles, CA, **d.** Apr. 25, 1990, Philadelphia, PA
Sax (Tenor) / Hard Bop, Bop
Dexter Gordon had such a colorful and eventful life (with three separate comebacks) that his story would make a great Hollywood movie. The top tenor saxophonist to emerge during the bop era and possessor of his own distinctive sound, Gordon sometimes was long-winded and quoted excessively from other songs, but he created a large body of superior work and could battle nearly anyone successfully at a jam session. His first important gigs came during the '40s with Lionel Hampton, Fletcher Henderson, Louis Armstrong's big band and Billy Eckstine's Orchestra. He also recorded as a leader for Savoy before becoming a major part of Los Angeles' Central Avenue scene. After 1952, drug problems resulted in some jail time and periods of inactivity during the 1950s (although Gordon did record two albums in 1955). By 1960 he was recovered and soon he was recording a consistently rewarding series of dates for Blue Note. After living in Europe for most of the 1960s and '70s, his return to America in 1976 was treated as a major media event; he signed to Columbia and remained a popular figure until his gradually worsening health made him semiactive by the early '80s. His third comeback occurred when he was picked to star in the motion picture *'Round Midnight* and, even if his playing by then was past its prime, Gordon's acting was quite realistic and touching. *—Scott Yanow*

Dexter Rides Again / Oct. 30, 1945-Dec. 11, 1947 / Savoy Jazz ♦♦♦♦♦
Taken from three separate sessions from 1945-'47, *Dexter Rides Again* showcases prime bebop sides Gordon cut for Savoy. His unique adaptation of Charlie Parker's alto conception to the tenor saxophone is displayed throughout, revealing a mix of fluid, hard-toned lines and a vibrato-heavy and vaporous ballad sound. And while Gordon's ballad mastery would come to the fore on his come-back albums for Blue Note in the '60s, the tenor saxophonist primarily sticks to up-tempo material here, a standard for most bebop sets. Abetted by a collective cast including the fine, yet rarely heard trumpeter Leonard Hawkins, baritone saxophonist Leo Parker, pianists Tadd Dameron and Bud Powell, and drummers Max Roach and Art Blakey, Gordon is in top form on a typical collection of self-penned, utility tunes, dispensing of involved head statements in favor of solo space. Standouts include "Dexter's Deck," the lone ballad "I Can't Escape From You," and the jam session number "Settin' The Pace" (Gordon recorded many extended cuts like this with fellow bebop tenor star Wardell Gray, and here teams up with Leo Parker for something like a baritone and tenor cutting contest). For those interested in where elements of both Sonny Rollins and John Coltrane's distinct style came from, check out these fine Gordon sides; besides the history lesson on wax, there's a consistent run of top-notch bebop sides to enjoy. For completists, these tracks, plus alternate takes and an excellent session featuring Fats Navarro, are included on Denon's Savoy reissue package, *Settin' the Pace*. *—Stephen Cook*

Long Tall Dexter / Oct. 30, 1945-Dec. 22, 1946 / Savoy ♦♦♦♦

The Chase! / Jun. 5, 1947-Dec. 4, 1947 / Prestige ♦♦♦♦♦
During the mid- to late '40s, Dexter Gordon, one of the top young tenors to emerge during the bop era, had nightly tenor "battles" in Los Angeles clubs with his two top competitors, Wardell Gray and Teddy Edwards. Fortunately, Gordon also had opportunities to meet up with his fellow tenors on record: "The Chase" (featuring Gray and Gordon) is a classic, and "The Duel" (which was recorded twice with Edwards) is close behind. Although issued as part of Stash's budget series, the vintage music on this CD (which has all of Dexter Gordon's

recordings for Dial in 1947) is often quite memorable. In addition the battles, Gordon teams up with trombonist Melba Liston in a quintet and leads a couple of his own quartets; "Blues in Teddy's Flat" features Edwards. Since all of the alternate takes are also included, this highly recommended release is quite definitive and recaptures some of the excitement of the period. *—Scott Yanow*

Daddy Plays the Horn / Sep. 1955 / Bethlehem Archives/Avenue Jazz ✦✦✦
One of only two Dexter Gordon recordings from the 1953-59 period, this Bethlehem set (reissued on CD through Evidence) is a fine jam session-flavored date featuring the tenor with pianist Kenny Drew, bassist Leroy Vinnegar and drummer Larence Marable. The programming differs from the listing on the liners; the fourth, fifth and sixth songs are actually first, second and third! Gordon is in particularly good form on these four standards and two fairly basic originals and his style was little different than the way he would sound in the 1960s. Recommended to straightahead jazz fans. *—Scott Yanow*

Dexter Blows Hot and Cool / Nov. 11, 1955-Nov. 12, 1955 / Boplicity ✦✦✦

The Resurgence of Dexter Gordon / Oct. 13, 1960 / Jazzland ✦✦✦

Doin' Alright / May 6, 1961 / Blue Note ✦✦✦✦
The title of this Blue Note set perfectly fit at the time, for tenor-saxophonist Dexter Gordon was making the first of three successful comebacks. Largely neglected during the 1950s, Gordon's Blue Note recordings (of which this was the first) led to his rediscovery. The tenor is teamed with the young trumpeter Freddie Hubbard, pianist Horace Parlan, bassist George Tucker and drummer Al Harewood for a strong set of music that is highlighted by "You've Changed" (which would become a permanent part of Dexter's repertoire), "Society Red" (a blues later used in the film *Round Midnight*) and "It's You or No One." *—Scott Yanow*

Dexter Calling. . . . / May 9, 1961 / Blue Note ✦✦✦✦
Tenor-saxophonist Dexter Gordon recorded seven Blue Note albums during 1960-64 and all are easily recommended. The power and creativity he showed during those performances led to his first successful comeback and display him in prime form. This particular CD (the reissue adds a version of "Landslide" not released at the time) showcases the distinctive tenor with a quartet that also includes pianist Kenny Drew, bassist Paul Chambers and drummer Philly Joe Jones. Gordon and Drew contributed six originals to the date but it is the leader's interpretations of the two standards ("End of a Love Affair" and particularly "Smile") that are most memorable. *—Scott Yanow*

★ **Go!** / Aug. 27, 1962 / Blue Note ✦✦✦✦✦
Dexter Gordon is in hard-swinging yet lyrical form throughout this particularly strong release. Accompanied by pianist Sonny Clark, bassist Butch Warren and drummer Billy Higgins, Gordon is heard at his best on "I Guess I'll Hang My Tears out to Dry," "Where Are You" and "Three O'Clock in the Morning"; three rarely performed standards. All of Dexter Gordon's Blue Note recordings (and in reality 90% of his releases) are recommended to lovers of bop and straightahead jazz. *—Scott Yanow*

A Swingin' Affair / Aug. 29, 1962 / Blue Note ✦✦✦✦
Recorded just two days after his popular album *Go* and using the same personnel (pianist Sonny Clark, bassisf-Butch Warren and drummer Billy Higgins), tenor-great Dexter Gordon stretches out on two of his originals, Warren's "The Backbone" and (best of all) three standards: "You Stepped out of a Dream," "Until the Real Thing Comes Along" and the highpoint "Don't Explain." This CD is well worth getting. *—Scott Yanow*

Our Man in Paris / May 23, 1963 / Blue Note ✦✦✦✦
Tenor-saxophonist Dexter Gordon, who had recently moved to Europe, is featured on this set with the all-star rhythm section sometimes called "the Three Bosses": pianist Bud Powell, bassist Pierre Michelot and drummer Kenny Clarke. The repertoire is strictly bop standards and Powell in particular is in excellent form. Gordon sounds fine too on such songs as "Scrapple from The Apple," "Stairway to the Stars" and "A Night in Tunisia." *—Scott Yanow*

One Flight Up / Jun. 2, 1964 / Blue Note ✦✦✦
Tenor-great Dexter Gordon and trumpeter Donald Byrd make for an excellent team on this 1964 hard bop quintet date with pianist Kenny Drew, bassist Niels Pedersen (then only 18) and drummer Art Taylor. The Blue Note album only contains three selections: an 18-minute rendition of Byrd's "Tanya," Drew's minor-toned "Coppin' the Haven" and a quartet version of "Darn That Dream" that finds Gordon in lyrical form. *—Scott Yanow*

Gettin' Around / May 28, 1965+2196 / Blue Note ✦✦✦✦
Dexter Gordon meets up with vibraphonist Bobby Hutcherson, pianist Barry Harris, bassist Bob Cranshaw and drummer Billy Higgins on this excellent hard bop date. Recorded during one of the great tenor's infrequent U.S. visits (he had moved to Europe in 1962), Gordon is in excellent form on six diverse selections that range from "Manha De Carnaval" and "Shiny Stockings" to "Heartaches" and Gordon's original "Le Coiffeur." Although underrated during this era due to his residence in Europe, Dexter Gordon was at the peak of his powers throughout this period; all of his Blue Note releases are easily recommended. *—Scott Yanow*

Body and Soul / Jul. 20, 1967 / 1201 Music ✦✦✦✦✦
Tenor-saxophonist Dexter Gordon recorded three CD's worth of material during a two-day period at Copenhagen's legendary Montmartre Club; *Take the 'A' Train* and *Both Sides of Midnight* have also been released by Black Lion on CD. Gordon and his impressive quartet (pianist Kenny Drew, bassist Neils Henning Orsted Pederson and drummer Albert "Tootie" Heath) play versions of "Like Someone in Love," "Come Rain or Come Shine," "There Will Never Be Another You," "Body and Soul" and "Blues Walk" that clock in between nine and 14 minutes. Ironically, Dexter, who was in peak form during his years in Europe, was somewhat forgotten in the U.S. at the time. This set is recommended along with the two other CDs from this well-documented engagement. *—Scott Yanow*

The Panther! / Jul. 7, 1970 / Prestige/OJC ✦✦✦✦
Although Dexter Gordon contributed three originals to this American session, it is his rendition of the three standards that are most memorable. The great tenor romps on the familiar line "The Blues Walk," digs into "Body and Soul" (giving this warhorse a fresh new interpretation) and makes a classic statement on "The Christmas Song." With the assistance of pianist Tommy Flanagan, bassist Larry Ridley and drummer Alan Dawson, Gordon is in typically spirited form for this upbeat set. *—Scott Yanow*

Generation / Jul. 22, 1972 / Prestige/OJC ✦✦✦✦
Veteran tenor-saxophonist Dexter Gordon welcomed trumpeter Freddie Hubbard to his recording group several times during his career and each collaboration was quite rewarding. For this Prestige studio set the two horns (who are joined by pianist Cedar Walton, bassist Buster Williams and drummer Billy Higgins) work together quite well on "Milestones" (a second version is included as a bonus track), "Scared to Be Alone," Thelonious Monk's "We See" and Gordon's "The Group." This CD should please collectors. *—Scott Yanow*

Bouncin' with Dex / Sep. 14, 1975 / Steeple Chase ✦✦✦✦
Dexter Gordon recorded nine albums for SteepleChase during 1975-76 (seven in 1975 alone) and was at the peak of his powers. This particular release finds Gordon joined by pianist Tete Montoliu, bassist Niels Pedersen and drummer Billy Higgins for two of his originals and three jazz standards. Gordon is in superlative form, jamming with enthusiasm and melodic creativity on these familiar chord changes. *—Scott Yanow*

Homecoming: Live at the Village Vanguard / Dec. 11, 1976-Dec. 12, 1976 / Columbia ✦✦✦✦✦
The acclaim that met Dexter Gordon when he returned to the United States after 14 years in Europe was completely unexpected. Not only did the jazz critics praise the great tenor but there were literally lines of young fans waiting to see his performances. This double CD, recorded during his historic first American tour, improved on the original double LP with the inclusion of previously unreleased versions of "Fried Bananas" and "Body and Soul." Gordon in a quintet with trumpeter Woody Shaw, pianist Ronnie Mathews, bassist Stafford James and drummer Louis Hayes frequently sounds exuberant on these lengthy performances; all ten songs are at least 11 minutes long. The excitement of the period can definitely be felt in this excellent music. *—Scott Yanow*

Settin' the Pace / Oct. 6, 1998 / Savoy Jazz ✦✦✦✦
This single CD has most but not all of Dexter Gordon's Savoy recordings. While there are previously unheard extra alternate takes included ("Dexter Digs In," "Dexter's Mood," "Dextrose," "Index" and "Dextivity") time limitations resulted in the already issued alternates to "Blow Mr. Dexter," "So Easy" and "Dexter's Riff" being left out. Hopefully, the latter three takes will be issued eventually on a sampler; in the meantime, completists should hold on to their earlier Arista/Savoy two-fer. Gordon's four Savoy sessions (which feature a lot of "originals" based on the chord changes of blues and standards) found him introducing his hard tone and fairly distinctive style to a wide audience, making him one of the first full-fledged bop tenors. The supporting cast (which includes on various dates trumpeter Fats Navarro, baritonist Leo Parker and pianist Bud Powell) is strong, and it is noteworthy that now the discographies of Powell and Navarro have been slightly expanded. Highly recommended. *—Scott Yanow*

Stephane Grappelli (Stephane Grappelly)

b. Jan. 26, 1908, Paris, France, **d.** Dec. 1, 1997, Paris, France
Violin / Swing
One of the all-time great jazz violinists (ranking with Joe Venuti and Stuff Smith as one of the big three of pre-bop), Stephane Grappelli's longevity and consistently enthusiastic playing did a great deal to establish the violin as a jazz instrument. Grappelli played in movie theaters and dance bands before meeting guitarist Django Reinhardt in 1933. They hit it off musically from the start, and together as the Quintet of the Hot Club of France (comprised of violin, three acoustic guitars and bass) during 1933-39 they produced a sensational series of recordings and performances. During a London engagement in 1939, World War II broke out. Reinhardt rashly decided to return to France but Grappelli stayed in England, effectively ending the group. The violinist soon teamed up with the young pianist George Shearing in a new band that worked steadily through the war. In 1946 Grappelli and Reinhardt had the first of several reunions although they never worked together again on a regular basis. Grappelli performed throughout the 1950s and '60s in clubs throughout Europe and, other than recordings with Duke Ellington (*Violin Summit*) and Joe Venuti, he remained somewhat obscure in the U.S. until he began regularly touring the world in the early '70s. *—Scott Yanow*

★ **1935-1940** / Sep. 30, 1935-Jul. 30, 1940 / Classics ✦✦✦✦✦
This Classics CD has all of the recordings made under violinist Stephane Grappelli's name during the 1935-40 period. The earlier selections (with his Hot Four) match his violin with Django Reinhardt's guitar in what was essentially the Quintet of The Hot Club of France. There are also nine duets with Reinhardt; a couple find Grappelli switching to piano. The set concludes in 1940 with Grappelli (in London) leading an octet on two numbers that also feature the young pianist George Shearing. *—Scott Yanow*

1941-1943 / Feb. 28, 1941-Dec. 8, 1943 / Classics ✦✦✦✦✦
This Classics CD reissues some very rare recordings made by violinist Stephane Grappelli: all of his performances as a leader during a difficult three-year period. The violinist had decided to stay in England during World War II (when Django Reinhardt returned to France) and soon had a new group featuring the young pianist George Shearing. This CD has seven sessions with quartets and quintets along with one featuring a larger group that includes other strings and a harp. Although there are vocals on eight of the numbers (by Beryl Davis and Dave Fullerton), the swinging performances and the rarity of the recordings easily compensate. *—Scott Yanow*

Violins No End / May 1957+1957 / Pablo/OJC ✦✦✦✦
Since Joe Venuti was in the middle of a long off-period, this CD reissue features arguably the two top jazz violinists of the 1950s: Stephane Grappelli and Stuff Smith. Joined by pianist Oscar Peterson, guitarist Herb Ellis, bassist Ray Brown and drummer Jo Jones, the two masterful violinists share four songs ("Don't Get Around Much Anymore," "Chapeau Blues," "No Points Today" and "The Lady Is a Tramp") in a fine studio session that contrasts the styles of

the fairly complementary fiddlers. In addition, although this set has been reissued under Grappelli's name, there are three songs from a Paris concert that took place the same day without Stephane. Stuff sounds in peak form on his "Desert Sands," "How High the Moon" and "Moonlight In Vermont." This fun set is easily recommended. *—Scott Yanow*

Stephane Grappelli Meets Barney Kessel / Jun. 23, 1969-Jun. 24, 1969 / 1201 Music ♦♦♦♦♦
This excellent set features a logical combination. Violinist Stephane Grappelli originally came to fame through his recordings with guitarist Django Reinhardt. Barney Kessel, although more influenced by Charlie Christian than by Django, was one of the top jazz guitarists of the 1950s and '60s and his style was quite complementary to Grappelli's. The two teamed up for several albums' worth of material in 1969. This CD reissues the former LP *I Remember Django,* adding four additional selections and serving as a perfect introduction to the brilliant playing of Stephane Grappelli. *—Scott Yanow*

Venupelli Blues / Oct. 22, 1969 / Charly ♦♦♦♦♦
Stephane Grappelli and Joe Venuti, arguably the two top violinists in jazz history, only made one recording together, this heated 1969 studio sesion. With pianist George Wein and guitarist Barney Kessel helping out as part of the supporting four-piece rhythm section, Grappelli and Venuti often romp during the title cut and the six standards that comprise this memorable session. This violin "battle" ends up as a dead heat, a joyous and historic occasion for all concerned. *—Scott Yanow*

☆ **Live in London** / Nov. 5, 1973 / Black Lion ♦♦♦♦♦
One of the best groups that violinist Stephane Grappelli collaborated with during the second half of his long career has been The Hot Club of London, a unit led by guitarist Diz Disley and usually including a second rhythm guitarist and a bassist. This Black Lion CD reissues the entire contents of a former two-LP set (*I Got Rhythm*) and even has room for a previously unreleased version of "Them There Eyes." Grappelli sounds particularly inspired playing with this group, very comfortable with the drumless setting and free to dominate the proceedings. *—Scott Yanow*

Young Django / Jan. 19, 1979-Jan. 21, 1979 / Verve ♦♦♦♦♦
This CD finds veteran violinist Stephane Grappelli joined by bassist Niels Pedersen and guitarists Philip Catherine and Larry Coryell for a memorable tribute to Django Reinhardt. Grappelli has recorded many Reinhardt memorial albums through the years but this one is particularly special for both Coryell and Catherine go out of their way to display the unexpected influence that Reinhardt has had on their styles. The guitarists contribute a song apiece and also enjoy playing seven compositions co-written by Django and Grappelli. *—Scott Yanow*

Stephane Grappelli and David Grisman Live / Sep. 7, 1979+Sep. 20, 1979 / Warner Brothers ♦♦♦♦♦
One of the most exciting of the many Stephane Grappelli recordings, this live session (a straight CD reissue of the original LP) teams the veteran violinist with mandolist David Grisman's band, an ensemble that (in addition to its leader) boasts hot solos from Mike Marshall on violin, guitarist Mark O'Connor (who switches to violin to battle Grappelli on a memorable "Tiger Rag"), and bassist Rob Wasserman. The first two songs ("Shine" and "Pent-Up House") are taken at breakneck tempos and then, after the group tries to cool off on "Misty," they really burn on "Sweet Georgia Brown" and "Tiger Rag." Essential music with more than its share of great solos. *—Scott Yanow*

One on One, With McCoy Tyner / Apr. 18, 1990 / Milestone ♦♦♦♦
Violinist Stephane Grappelli, although a veteran of the swing era, has always kept an open mind toward newer styles even while he has retained his own sound and veteran repertoire. This duet set with pianist McCoy Tyner might seem unlikely at first glance but it works quite well. The duo sticks to standards (including two that are associated with John Coltrane) and find plenty of common ground. The mutual respect they have for each other is obvious and they both sound a bit inspired. *—Scott Yanow*

Live at the Blue Note / Oct. 9, 1995-Oct. 11, 1995 / Telarc Jazz ♦♦♦♦

The Very Best of Grappelli & Menuhin / 1998 / Angel ♦♦♦♦

Milford Graves

b. Aug. 20, 1941, New York, NY
Drums / Avant-Garde Jazz, Free Jazz
Milford Graves has been among the flashiest drummers in the free mode, known for skillful inclusion of Asian and African rhythmic ingredients into his solos. He studied Indian music extensively, including learning the tabla from Wasantha Singh. He has unfortunately not recorded much in recent years, especially on American labels. Graves played congas as a child, then switched to trap drums at 17, before his tabla studies with Singh. During the '60s Graves worked with Giuseppi Logan and the New York Art Quartet. He recorded on ESP in the mid-'60s with Logan, and was an original member of the Jazz Composers' Orchestra Association. Graves also played with Hugh Masekela and Miriam Makeba in the early '60s. His appearance in the Bill Dixon-sponsored concert series "The October Revolution In Jazz" helped introduce Graves to a wider audience. He did two albums of duets with pianist Don Pullen at Yale in 1966. Graves worked regularly with Albert Ayler in 1967 and 1968, performing at the 1967 Newport Festival. He also played with Hugh Glover, and worked in a duo with Andrew Cyrille. During the '70s Graves participated in a series of mid-'70s concerts called "Dialogue of the Drums" with Cyrille and Rashied Ali, including several shows in Black neighborhoods. Graves taught at Bennington College alongside Bill Dixon in the '70s, and toured Europe and Japan. During the '80s, he played in percussion ensembles with Cyrille, Kenny Clarke and Don Moye. Philly Joe Jones later replaced Clarke. The late '90s found Graves enjoying a revival, collaborating with younger musicians including John Zorn, and recording albums for his Tzadik label. In 2000, the New York Art Quartet's first recording in decades, *35th Reunion,* was released by DIW. *—Ron Wynn*

● **Milford Graves Percussion Ensemble** / Jul. 1965 / ESP ♦♦♦♦

Grand Unification / Oct. 11, 1997 / Tzadik ♦♦♦
Milford Graves was one of the greatest free jazz percussionists of the '60s, mastering the traps, conga, and tabla to create a multiethnic firestorm of rhythm. He has essentially not recorded for years, making sporadic appearances on the albums of other jazz artists while making almost no recordings of his own. The very fact that he has a new album on the Tzadik label is, therefore, exciting. Fans of Graves from the '60s will be pleased to note that this is a collection of work that picks up right where he left off. Others may find it a little bit of a relic in its frenzied and jazz stylings. Regardless, the record is a tight, technical masterpiece played with passion. Combining a variety of African, Asian, and Western drums with rhythmic chanting, Graves provides all of the instrumentation on the album and creates something rare: unaccompanied jazz percussion that shows variety and consistent energy throughout a nearly hour-long album. *—Stacia Proefrock*

Bennie Green

b. Apr. 16, 1923, Chicago, IL, **d.** Mar. 23, 1977, San Diego, CA
Trombone / Swing, Bop
Bennie Green was one of the few trombonists of the 1950s who played in a style not influenced by J.J. Johnson (Bill Harris was another). His witty sound and full tone looked backwards to the swing era yet was open to the influence of R&B. After playing locally in Chicago, he was with the Earl Hines Orchestra during 1942-48 (except for two years in the military). Green gained some fame for his work with Charlie Ventura (1948-50) before joining Earl Hines's small group (1951-53). He then led his own group throughout the 1950s and '60s, using such sidemen as Cliff Smalls, Charlie Rouse, Eric Dixon, Paul Chambers, Louis Hayes, Sonny Clark, Gildo Mahones and Jimmy Forrest. Green recorded regularly as a leader for Prestige, Decca, Blue Note, Vee Jay, Time, Bethlehem and Jazzland during 1951-61 although only one further session (a matchup with Sonny Stitt on Cadet in 1964) took place. Bennie Green was with Duke Ellington for a few months in 1968-69 and then moved to Las Vegas where he spent his last years working in hotel bands although he did emerge to play quite well at the 1972 Newport Jazz Festival in New York jam sessions. *—Scott Yanow*

Trombone by Three / Oct. 5, 1951 / Prestige/OJC ♦♦♦♦♦
This bebop era trombone sampler provides a perfect way to hear early sides by J.J. Johnson, Kai Winding, and Bennie Green. Johnson appropriately kicks thing off, demonstrating his innovative adaptation of Charlie Parker's bop language to the trombone. Joined by tenor saxophonist Sonny Rollins, trumpeter Kenny Dorham, pianist John Lewis, and drummer Max Roach, Johnson works through four up-tempo cuts, including the self-penned "Fox Hunt" and "Opus V." Lewis and Dorham contribute a cut apiece and join the rest of the group in turning in many fine and fluid solos. Winding, who at first took cues from Johnson, avails himself admirably on four tracks here as well, keeping with the up-tempo groove on his original number "A Night on Bop Mountain" and Gerry Mulligan's "Waterworks." Along with Mulligan on baritone, Winding is supported by tenor saxophonist Brew Moore, pianist George Wallington, and drummer Roy Haynes, whose depth-charge bass drum accents particularly standout. In contrast to the bebop mold both Johnson and Winding fitted into, Green stuck mostly to a big band and R&B vein, sidestepping many of Parker and Dizzy Gillespie's innovations in favor of a more traditional, yet no less swinging sound. Sparked by the honking intensity of Eddie "Lockjaw" Davis' tenor solos and Art Blakey's busy, yet tight drumming, Green blazes through four cuts as well, mixing intense, grainy solos with more fluid and rounded statements. Both his duel with Davis on "Whirl-A-Licks" and the fine rendition of "Pennies From Heaven" deserve particular recognition. While the sound here is not top-notch, these recordings from 1949-'51 offer more than enough engaging moments to make this a great jazz title. The CD offers a handful of bonus tracks, including alternate takes and a title not found on the original LP. *—Stephen Cook*

● **Bennie Green Blows His Horn** / Jun. 10, 1955+Sep. 22, 1955 / Prestige/OJC ♦♦♦♦♦
Bennie Green, one of the few trombonists of the 1950s not to sound somewhat like a J.J. Johnson clone, always had a likable and humorous style. He blends in well with tenor-saxophonist Charlie Rouse on these standards, blues and jump tunes, two of which have group vocals. With a fine rhythm section (pianist Cliff Smalls, bassist Paul Chambers, drummer Osie Johnson and Candido on congas), Green and his band show that there is no reason that swinging jazz has to be viewed as overly intellectual and esoteric. This CD (a reissue of the original LP) is a fine example of Bennie Green's talents and winning musical personality. *—Scott Yanow*

With Art Farmer / Apr. 13, 1956 / Prestige/OJC ♦♦♦
Trombonist Bennie Green and trumpeter Art Farmer (with the assistance of pianist Cliff Smalls, bassist Addison Farmer and drummer Philly Joe Jones) challenge each other on these five selections which include an original apiece by the two horns and Smalls in addition to cheerful renditions of "My Blue Heaven" and "Gone with the Wind." The playing is not flawless on this recording but the soloists take chances and the music is often exciting. It's recommended to straightahead jazz fans. *—Scott Yanow*

Walking Down / Jun. 29, 1956 / Prestige/OJC ♦♦♦♦
The third of Bennie Green's three Prestige albums from 1955-56 features the personable trombonist in a quintet with the young tenor-saxophonist Eric Dixon (here showing a strong Paul Gonsalves influence) and an obscure but swinging rhythm section (pianist Lloyd Mayers, bassist Sonny Wellesley and drummer Bill English). The solos are colorful if occasionally stumbling and the arrangements of the four standards and Green's "East of the Little Big Horn" have their share of surprises; "Walkin'" and "The Things We Did Last Summer" are taken at two different tempos while "It's You or No One," normally a ballad, really cooks. *—Scott Yanow*

Benny Green

b. Apr. 4, 1963, New York, NY
Piano / Hard Bop
Although not yet an innovator himself, Benny Green has managed to combine the styles of Bobby Timmons, Wynton Kelly, Gene Harris and especially Oscar Peterson in his playing;

his fast octave runs are often wondrous. He grew up in Berkeley and played as a teenager with Joe Henderson and Woody Shaw. After moving to New York he spent important periods with Betty Carter (1983-87) and Art Blakey's Jazz Messengers (1987-89), becoming quite well-known during the latter association. In addition to working with Freddie Hubbard, Green popped up in many bop-oriented settings for a few years before joining Ray Brown's Trio in 1992. At the same time he has worked with his own trio which originally included Christian McBride and Carl Allen. When Oscar Peterson in 1992 was asked to name his protegé for a concert, Green was his choice. Benny Green has recorded for Criss Cross and Blue Note in addition to his work with Ray Brown on Telarc and his earlier Blakey dates. *—Scott Yanow*

Prelude / Feb. 22, 1988 / Criss Cross ✦✦✦
Pianist Benny Green's debut as a leader (the first of two Criss Cross releases) was indeed a prelude to his long string of Blue Note recordings. Already a brilliant player who had been in Betty Carter's group and with Art Blakey's Jazz Messengers for a year, Green was at 24 on the brink of jazz stardom. He holds his own with some notable sidemen (trumpeter Terence Blanchard, tenor saxophonist Javon Jackson, bassist Peter Washington and drummer Tony Reedus), performing Duke Ellington's "Take the Coltrane," a pair of obscurities and two of his originals. The music is advanced hard bop and easily recommended to straight-ahead jazz fans. *—Scott Yanow*

In This Direction / Dec. 29, 1988-Jan. 2, 1989 / Criss Cross ✦✦✦✦
For his second album as a leader, pianist Benny Green is showcased in a trio with bassist Buster Wiliams and drummer Lewis Nash. Nearing the end of his two-year stint with Art Blakey's Jazz Messengers, Green had mixed together elements of Bobby Timmons and Oscar Peterson in his own impressive style. He performs two numbers apiece by Buster Williams and Bud Powell (including "I'll Keep Lovin' You"), the standard "What Is There to Say," Thelonious Monk's complex "Trinkle Tinkle," and his own "Dealin' With a Feelin'" on a well-rounded and consistently swinging outing. *—Scott Yanow*

● **Testifyin'!: Live at the Village Vanguard** / Nov. 1991 / Blue Note ✦✦✦✦✦
A former member of Betty Carter's band, Green shows on this set that the word on him was correct; he's both an aggressive and sensitive stylist, able to rip through songs and make quick, yet correct chord changes. Yet he can also play a passionate ballad and not rush through it, instead developing and then completing his solos impressively. *—Ron Wynn*

That's Right! / Dec. 21, 1992-Dec. 23, 1992 / Blue Note ✦✦✦✦✦
At the time of this 1992 recording, Benny Green had developed into a masterful pianist who thought fast, swung hard, and played with soul, mixing together Oscar Peterson, Gene Harris, and Bobby Timmons. The only problem was that his music had become somewhat predictable, sticking closely to the boundaries of hard bop circa 1962. In his trio with bassist Christian McBride and drummer Carl Allen, Green is heard in top form for the period (his version of Bud Powell's "Celia" is particularly memorable) and performs a program that is easily recommended to lovers of bop. Benny Green plays with such enthusiasm and joy that it almost sounds as if he had invented the style. *—Scott Yanow*

These Are Soulful Days / Jan. 16, 1999-Jan. 17, 1999 / Blue Note ✦✦✦✦✦
As part of Blue Note's 60th anniversary gala, Benny Green was invited to record a selection of his favorite tunes from the label's venerable catalog. Green picked eight songs previously recorded by the likes of Horace Silver, Lee Morgan, Joe Henderson, and Dexter Gordon, then he recruited bassist Christian McBride and guitarist Russell Malone. Together, they recorded *These Are Soulful Days*, a splendid tribute to the glory days of Blue Note, when excellent hard bop musicians ruled the roster. Like the classic albums from the late '50s and early '60s, *These Are Soulful Days* clocks in at an economical 45 minutes and feels intimate. All eight songs were recorded directly to two-track, giving the music an immediate, vibrant feel. Since Green decided not to choose well-known standards, the songs are fresh, which is only appropriate, since the trio gives performances that are steeped in tradition, yet remain lively and unpredictable. At its best, *These Are Soulful Days* feels like a lost classic from the Blue Note vaults, and that's the highest praise that can be said about a project like this. *—Stephen Thomas Erlewine*

Grant Green

b. Jun. 6, 1931, St. Louis, MO, **d.** Jan. 31, 1979, New York, NY
Guitar (Electric), Guitar / Hard Bop, Soul-Jazz
Grant Green was one of the most creative exponents of Blue Note-style funk-jazz, during that music's heyday in the early '60s. Green's linear style steered clear of certain guitar conventions; he asserted that his greatest influences were horn players, and certainly his boppish manner of phrasing and limited use of chordal playing bears out that claim. Green's version of modern jazz was leavened with a heavy blues tinge, combining the relative harmonic intricacies of bebop with the straightforward expressivity of popular idioms.

Green played with Jimmy Forrest, Harry Edison, and Lou Donaldson in the '50s. His collaborations with Jack McDuff, Big John Patton, Gloria Willette, and Larry Young in the early '60s helped establish the popularity of the "organ trio" (organ, guitar, drums) as a performing unit. From 1961-64, Green recorded a series of albums for Blue Note that solidified his creative reputation. His sidemen on those dates included many of that label's biggest names, including Herbie Hancock, Bobby Hutcherson, McCoy Tyner, Joe Henderson, and Elvin Jones. Green also recorded under other Blue Note leaders, such as Stanley Turrentine, Johnny Hodges, Hank Mobley, Lee Morgan, and Ike Quebec. Green retreated from the scene due to drug problems during the mid-'60s; he resumed recording in the late '60s and early '70s. For the last several years of his life, Green was essentially a rhythm & blues player. *—Chris Kelsey*

Grant's First Stand / Jan. 28, 1961 / Blue Note ✦✦✦

Reaching Out / Mar. 15, 1961 / 1201 Music ✦✦✦
Green is in fine form as is pianist Gardner (better known as an organist), but the album is perhaps most valuable for the contributions of the obscure tenorman Frank Haynes who died in 1965; his sound will remind some a little of Stanley Turrentine. *—Scott Yanow*

Green Street / Apr. 1, 1961 / Blue Note ✦✦✦✦
Most of guitarist Grant Green's recordings of the 1960s feature him in larger groups, making this trio outing with bassist Ben Tucker and drummer Dave Bailey (a CD reissue of the original LP plus two added alternate takes) a strong showcase for his playing. Green, whose main competitor on guitar at the time was Wes Montgomery, already had his own singing sound and a highly individual hornlike approach. He stretches out on a full set of attractive originals plus "'Round Midnight" and "Alone Together," so this reissue is an excellent introduction to his appealing and hard-swinging style. *—Scott Yanow*

Sunday Mornin' / Jun. 4, 1961 / Blue Note ✦✦✦
Although it was Grant Green's fourth album as a leader, this date was his earliest one to utilize a pianist. Green, one of the first to cover "Exodus" (Eddie Harris' hit version had just been released) and "So What," swings here in a manner little different than Wes Montgomery during the same period other than his almost total reliance on single-note solos. The music is conventional for the early '60s although it contains enough variety to hold one's interest; "Tracin' Tracy" was released here for the first time. With pianist Kenny Drew functioning as a strong co-star and bassist Ben Tucker and drummer Ben Dixon fine in support, this is an above-average if not essential effort from the underrated Grant Green. *—Scott Yanow*

Grantstand / Aug. 1, 1961 / Blue Note ✦✦✦✦
This Blue Note CD reissue brings back a session by an unusual but ultimately logical quartet. The great guitarist Grant Green (in his third Blue Note album as a leader) welcomes Yusef Lateef (doubling on tenor and flute), organist Jack McDuff, and drummer Al Harewood for a set comprised of a pair of groovin' Green originals ("Grantstand" and "Blues In Maude's Flat"), a ballad feature for the guitarist ("My Funny Valentine"), and the standard "Old Folks." Green and Lateef never recorded together otherwise, but they blend quite well and seem to inspire each other on this fine hard bop date. *—Scott Yanow*

Standards / Aug. 29, 1961 / Blue Note ✦✦✦✦
In 1998, Blue Note released several CDs of previously unavailable (at least domestically) material from its prime years under the title of *Standards*. Some are not up to the level of the label's best output, but this outing is a definite exception. Guitarist Grant Green is heard in prime form in a sparse trio with bassist Wilbur Ware and drummer Al Harewood. Six of the eight performances were previously available in Japan as an LP but never before in the U.S. Because Green rarely ever played chords, sticking to single-note lines, hearing him in this setting is similar to hearing a tenor in a pianoless trio. Highlights include "Love Walked In," "I'll Remember April," "All the Things You Are," and two versions of "If I Had You." Recommended. *—Scott Yanow*

Born to Be Blue / Dec. 11, 1961+Mar. 1, 1962 / Blue Note ✦✦✦✦✦
Although Grant Green provided his share of groove-oriented soul-jazz and modal post-bop, his roots were hard bop, and it is in a bop-oriented setting that the guitarist excels on *Born to Be Blue*. Most of the material on this five-star album was recorded at Rudy Van Gelder's New Jersey studio on December 11, 1961, when Green was joined by tenor titan Ike Quebec, pianist Sonny Clark, bassist Sam Jones, and drummer Louis Hayes. Tragically, Quebec was near the end of his life—the distinctive saxman died of lung cancer at the age of 44 on January 16, 1963—but there is no evidence of Quebec's declining health on *Born to Be Blue*. He was playing as authoritatively as ever well into 1962, and the saxman is in fine form on hard-swinging interpretations of "Someday My Prince Will Come" and Al Jolson's "Back in Your Own Back Yard." It's interesting to hear Quebec playing bop, for his big, breathy tone was right out of swing and was greatly influenced by Coleman Hawkins and Ben Webster. Although Quebec and Green (who was 14 years younger) had very different musical backgrounds, they were always quite compatible musically. They clearly enjoyed a strong rapport on the uptempo selections as well as ballads like "My One and Only Love" and Mel Torme's "Born to Be Blue." Originally a vinyl LP, this album was reissued on CD in 1989, when Blue Note added an alternate take of the title song and a previously unreleased version of Charlie Parker's "Cool Blues." *—Alex Henderson*

★ **The Complete Quartets with Sonny Clark** / Dec. 23, 1961-Sep. 7, 1962 / Blue Note ✦✦✦✦✦
Mosaic released a four-disc box set titled *The Complete Blue Note with Sonny Clark* in 1991, rounding up everything that the guitarist and pianist recorded together between 1961 and 1962. Blue Note's 1997 version of the set, *The Complete Quartets with Sonny Clark*, trims Mosaic's collection by two discs, offering only the quartet sessions (the Ike Quebec sessions, *Born to Be Blue* and *Blue and Sentimental*, are available on individual discs). In some ways, this actually results in a more unified set, since it puts Green and Clark directly in the spotlight, with no saxophone to complete for solos, but it doesn't really matter if the music is presented as this double-disc set, the four-disc box or the individual albums—this is superb music, showcasing the gutiarist and pianist at their very best. All of the sessions are straightahead bop but the music has a gentle, relaxed vibe that makes it warm, intimate and accessible. Grant and Clark's mastery is subtle—the music is so enjoyable, you may not notice the deftness of their improvisation and technique—but that invests the music with the grace, style and emotion that distinguishes *The Complete Quartets*. Small group hard-bop rarely comes any better than this. *—Stephen Thomas Erlewine*

The Best of Grant Green, Vol. 1 / Jan. 28, 1961-Jun. 12, 1964 / Blue Note ✦✦✦
While the "best-of" format often leaves quite a bit to be desired in a jazz setting, this set contains good Green material from his most productive period, the early and mid-'60s. There's a nice mix between uptempo and slower numbers, standards and his own compositions, as well as soul jazz and straight mainstream and bop material. Although this isn't as far-reaching or comprehensive as Green's Mosaic set, this set will satisfy the needs of those unfamiliar with his work or listeners who just want a good cross-section of his cuts. *—Ron Wynn*

The Latin Bit / Apr. 26, 1962 / Blue Note ✦✦✦
Grant Green was one of the top jazz guitarists to emerge during the early '60s. For the original LP program reissued on this 1996 CD, Green and a particularly strong rhythm section (with pianist Johnny Acea, bassist Wendell Marshall, drummer Willie Bobo, and percussion-

ists Potato Valdez and Garvin Masseaux) play the very attractive melodies (including "Mambo Inn," "Besame Mucho," and "Tico Tico") with affection and swing. In fact, Green has rarely sounded happier. For this reissue a previously unissued straight-ahead piece from the same session ("Blues for Juanita") and two numbers from a slightly later date (featuring a similar group with tenor saxophonist Ike Quebec and pianist Sonny Clark) are also included. Overall, this is one of Grant Green's more delightful sets, an underrated gem. *—Scott Yanow*

Feelin' the Spirit / Dec. 21, 1962 / Blue Note ✦✦✦✦
This is a rather unusual session (reissued on CD) by guitarist Grant Green. In a quintet with pianist Herbie Hancock, bassist Butch Warren, drummer Billy Higgins, and (on tambourine) Garvin Masseaux, Green interprets six spirituals including a version of "Deep River" that was not on the original LP. All of the selections (which include "Just a Closer Walk With Thee," "Nobody Knows the Trouble I've Seen," and "Sometimes I Feel Like a Motherless Child") had been played by jazz musicians before, but to hear Green (who was primarily known as a swinging bluesy hard bop guitarist) perform with sincerity and honest emotion over the fairly simple chord structures is a bit of a revelation. This release is a surprise success. *—Scott Yanow*

☆ **Idle Moments** / Nov. 4, 1963-Nov. 11, 1963 / Blue Note ✦✦✦✦✦
This classic Grant Green album was actually recorded twice. With Duke Pearson on piano and the main head arranger Bobby Hutcherson on vibes, Joe Henderson on tenor sax, Bob Cranshaw on bass, and Al Harewood on drums, the original session on November 4, 1963, produced great versions of "Jean de Fleur," the Modern Jazz Quartet's "Django," and the title track, an extended workout lasting almost 15 minutes. But all were deemed too long to fit the confines of a vinyl album, so the entire band was reassembled on November 11 to recut shorter versions of the tunes to fit the time constraints of the original LP. This compact disc reissue brings that configuration back with alternate and longer takes from the earlier session of "Django" and "Jean de Fleur." As all Blue Note albums from this time period were recorded direct to two-track analog tape, this compact disc transfer literally sparkles with a spatial and defined sound. Green's tone is fat, wide, and bluesy throughout, as always showing consummate swing, skill, taste, and invention. The inclusion of the longer and alternate versions of the two bonus tracks shows the depth of Green's genius for improvisation and his fine interaction with Henderson, Pearson, and Hutcherson (who shines on both takes of "Jean de Fleur"), while Cranshaw and Harewood make a swinging—but never obtrusive—rhythm section. This is a record whose classic status is not diminished in the least by the inclusion of alternate takes, if anything benefiting from their presence. *—Cub Koda*

☆ **Matador** / May 20, 1964 / Blue Note ✦✦✦✦✦
Critics have often tried to typecast Grant Green, but the truth is that the guitarist (particularly in the 1960s) excelled in every setting. For this set (reissued on CD along with a previously unissued version of "Wives and Lovers") Green holds his own with quite a rhythm section: pianist McCoy Tyner, bassist Bob Cranshaw, and drummer Elvin Jones. In fact, Green leads the group (which includes two of John Coltrane's mightiest sidemen) successfully through 'Trane's signature song "My Favorite Things." The five lengthy cuts each clock in between nine to 12 minutes yet never lose their momentum or drive. Highly recommended. *—Scott Yanow*

Solid / Jun. 12, 1964 / Blue Note ✦✦✦✦✦
Not released until 1979, this set contains more challenging material than many of guitarist Grant Green's other Blue Note sessions. In a state-of-the-art sextet with tenor saxophonist Joe Henderson, altoist James Spaulding, pianist McCoy Tyner, bassist Bob Cranshaw and drummer Elvin Jones, Green performs tunes by Duke Pearson, George Russell ("Ezz-thetic"), Sonny Rollins, Henderson ("The Kicker") and his own "Grant's Tune." Perhaps this music was considered too uncommercial initially or maybe it was simply lost in the shuffle. In any case, this is one of Grant Green's finer recordings. *—Scott Yanow*

Talkin' About! / Sep. 11, 1964 / Blue Note ✦✦✦

Street of Dreams / Oct. 16, 1964 / Blue Note ✦✦✦

I Want to Hold Your Hand / Mar. 31, 1965 / Blue Note ✦✦✦✦✦
This 1997 CD, whose music had also been reissued as part of Mosaic's limited-edition Larry Young box set, finds guitarist Grant Green exploring both recent ("I Want to Hold Your Hand," "Corcovado," and "This Could Be the Start of Something Big") and more vintage material. The all-star quartet (Green, tenor saxophonist Hank Mobley, organist Larry Young, and drummer Elvin Jones) uplifts the songs—turning the Beatles tune into a bossa nova was an inspired idea—and plays very much in the modern mainstream of the era. Mobley had largely dropped his earlier Sonny Rollins influence to develop his own voice; Young was starting to grow beyond Jimmy Smith; Elvin Jones keeps the proceedings heated, and the always appealing Grant Green guitar is heard in fine form. Worth picking up. *—Scott Yanow*

His Majesty, King Funk/Up With Donald Byrd / Nov. 2, 1964-May 26, 1965 / Verve ✦✦✦
This single Verve CD reissues the complete contents of two unrelated LPs: Grant Green's *His Majesty King Funk* (great title) and *Up with Donald Byrd*. Unfortunately the music overall is not as rewarding as Green and Byrd's work of the period for Blue Note. Green is okay with a quintet that includes tenor-saxophonist Harold Vick and organist Larry Young but the material (mainly fairly simple funk riffs) is disappointing. Trumpeter Donald Byrd has a potentially strong group with both Jimmy Heath and Stanley Turrentine on tenors along with pianist Herbie Hancock and guitarist Kenny Burrell. However the three- or four-voice "Donald Byrd Singers" and the arrangements by Claus Ogerman weigh down the date. Each album watered down its music to an extent in hopes of gaining commercial success but neither really caught on. The results are interesting but somewhat forgettable. *—Scott Yanow*

Iron City / 1967 / 32 Jazz ✦✦✦
Recorded for Muse Records in 1967, as Grant Green was on an extended recording hiatus—it was his only record between 1965's *His Majesty, King Funk*, his only album for Verve, and 1969's *Carryin' On*, his return to Blue Note—*Iron City* actually captures the guitarist in fine form, jamming on six blues and R&B numbers with his longtime cohorts, organist Big John Patton and drummer Ben Dixon. The trio had long ago perfected their interplay, and they just cook on *Iron City*, working a hot groove on each song. Even the slow blues "Motherless Child" has a distinct swing in its backbeat, but most of the album finds the trio tearing through uptempo grooves with a vengeance. Green's playing is a bit busier than normal and he solos far more often than Patton, who lays back through most of the album, providing infectious vamps and lead lines. The two styles intermesh perfectly with Dixon's deft drumming, resulting in a fine, overlooked date that showcases some of Green's hottest, bluesiest playing. *—Stephen Thomas Erlewine*

Carryin' On / Oct. 3, 1969 / Blue Note ✦✦

Green Is Beautiful / Jan. 30, 1970 / Blue Note ✦✦✦

Alive! / Aug. 15, 1970 / Blue Note ✦✦✦
Grant Green was one of the most consistent and versatile guitarists of the 1960s but once 1970 came around his recording career became quite erratic. This CD reissue brings back a rather weak effort with Green's sextet (which at time included Claude Bartee on tenor, vibraphonist William Bivens and either Ronnie Foster or Earl Neal Creque on organ) playing R&B cliches while laying forever on one chord. There are many more rewarding Grant Green sets than this one. *—Scott Yanow*

Visions / May 21, 1971 / Blue Note ✦✦✦

Live at the Lighthouse / Apr. 21, 1972 / Blue Note ✦✦✦
There is lot of fat to the live jams heard on this Blue Note double album. With the many dated verbal introductions and overly lengthy one-chord funk vamps, this session should have been edited down to one album. Guitarist Grant Green's group (which includes Claude Bartee on tenor and soprano, vibraphonist Gary Coleman, organist Shelton Lester, electric bassist Wilton Felder, drummer Greg Williams and percussionist Bobbye Hall) is actually quite good and Bartee was an underrated saxophonist. But none of the six selections (which include "Betcha By Golly Wow" and Donald Byrd's "Fancy Free") are all that memorable even if there are lots of good feelings. The overall results in this stretched-out format are far from essential. *—Scott Yanow*

Johnny Griffin

b. Apr. 24, 1928, Chicago, IL
Sax (Tenor) / Hard Bop, Bop
Once accurately billed as "the world's fastest saxophonist," Johnny Griffin (an influence tonewise on Rahsaan Roland Kirk) has been one of the top bop-oriented tenors since the mid-'50s. He gained early experience playing with the bands of Lionel Hampton (1945-47) and Joe Morris (1947-50) and also jammed regularly with Thelonious Monk and Bud Powell. After serving in the Army (1951-53), Griffin spent a few years in Chicago (recording his first full album for Argo) and then moved to New York in 1956. He held his own against fellow tenors John Coltrane and Hank Mobley in a classic Blue Note album, was with Art Blakey's Jazz Messengers in 1957 and proved to be perfect with the Thelonious Monk Quartet in 1958 where he really ripped through the complex chord changes with ease. During 1960-62 Griffin co-led a "tough tenor" group with Eddie "Lockjaw" Davis. He emigrated to Europe in 1963 and became a fixture on the Paris jazz scene both as a bandleader and a major soloist with the Kenny Clarke-Francy Boland Big Band. In 1973 Johnny Griffin moved to the Netherlands but has remained a constant world traveller, visiting the U.S. often and recording for many labels including Blue Note, Riverside, Atlantic, SteepleChase, Black Lion, Antilles, Verve and some European companies. *—Scott Yanow*

Introducing Johnny Griffin / Apr. 17, 1956 / Blue Note ✦✦✦✦
This CD reissue does not have tenor saxophonist Johnny Griffin's first recording as a leader (he made a few sides for Okeh in 1953 and a full album for Argo a few months earlier in 1956), but it gained Griffin a great deal of attention. Soon billed as "the world's fastest saxophonist," Griffin was also a superior ballad interpreter with a fairly distinctive tone of his own. With strong support given by pianist Wynton Kelly, bassist Curly Russell, and drummer Max Roach, Griffin romps on three of his originals, barn-busting versions of "The Way You Look Tonight" and "Cherokee" (the latter two were released for the first time domestically on this CD), and a couple of ballads. Superior music. *—Scott Yanow*

★ **A Blowin' Session** / Apr. 6, 1957 / Blue Note ✦✦✦✦✦
A Blowin' Session is one of the greatest hard bop jam sessions ever recorded; it is filled with infectious passion and camaraderie. It's also the only time tenor saxophonists Johnny Griffin and John Coltrane would play together on record. Initially Coltrane wasn't scheduled to be on this date, but Griffin saw him on his way to Rudy Van Gelder's studio and asked him to join the remaining musicians, third tenor Hank Mobley, trumpeter Lee Morgan, pianist Wynton Kelly, bassist Paul Chambers, and drummer Art Blakey. These musicians were all associates within the same East Coast hard bop scene of the time; they came from the Jazz Messengers and Miles Davis' quintet, and many had played with Dizzy Gillespie's big band. Showcased on this April 8, 1958, session are two standards, "The Way You Look Tonight" and "All the Things You Are," along with two original Griffin compositions, "Ball Bearing" and "Smoke Stack." An added bonus on the 1999 Rudy Van Gelder remastered edition is an alternate take of "Smoke Stack." Of special note is "The Way You Look Tonight," featuring the three tenors trading off with complexity and speed that is still astonishing, especially in the case of Griffin (dubbed the world's fastest saxophonist) and Coltrane's ability to navigate complex chord changes over a fast tempo. *—Al Campbell*

☆ **The Congregation** / Oct. 23, 1957 / Blue Note ✦✦✦✦✦
The great tenor-saxophonist Johnny Griffin is heard in top form on this near-classic quartet set. Assisted by pianist Sonny Clark, bassist Paul Chambers and drummer Kenny Dennis, Griffin is exuberant on "The Congregation" (which is reminiscent of Horace Silver's "The Preacher"), thoughtful on the ballads and swinging throughout. It's recommended for bop collectors. *—Scott Yanow*

Way Out! / Feb. 26, 1958-Feb. 27, 1958 / Riverside/OJC ✦✦✦✦
This formerly obscure quartet set by tenor-saxophonist Johnny Griffin (reissued on CD in the OJC series) features the fiery soloist on five little-known originals written by Chicagoans plus

a burning version of "Cherokee." Virtually all of Griffin's recordings are worth getting and, with the assistance of pianist Kenny Drew, bassist Wilbur Ware and drummer Philly Joe Jones, the tenor is in superior form for this spirited date. *—Scott Yanow*

The Little Giant / Aug. 4, 1959-Aug. 5, 1959 / Riverside/OJC ✦✦✦
This CD reissue is a bit offbeat, for the set by tenor saxophonist Johnny Griffin features three originals by then-obscure pianist Norman Simmons, a reworking of the pop tune "Playmates," Babs Gonzalez's "Lonely One" and the tenor's "63rd Street Theme." Simmons' arrangements for the three horns (which include trumpeter Blue Mitchell and trombonist Julian Priester) are colorful; the rhythm section (pianist Wynton Kelly, bassist Sam Jones and drummer Albert "Tootie" Heath) is state-of-the-art for the period, and Griffin (who is featured in a trio with Jones and Heath on "The Lonely One") is in fine form. An interesting set of obscure straight-ahead jazz. *—Scott Yanow*

The Big Soul Band / May 24, 1960-Jun. 3, 1960 / Riverside/OJC ✦✦✦
Tenor-saxophonist Johnny Griffin is showcased with a ten-piece group on this CD reissue of a Riverside LP which is augmented by a previously unreleased version of "Wade in the Water." The repertoire is a bit unusual with some spirituals (including "Nobody Knows the Trouble I've Seen" and "Deep River"), a tune apiece by Bobby Timmons ("So Tired") and Junior Mance, and three originals from Norman Simmons who arranged all of the selections. Trumpeter Clark Terry and trombonists Matthew Gee and Julian Priester have some short solos but the emphasis is on the leader who is in typically spirited and passionate form. *—Scott Yanow*

Griff and Lock / Nov. 4, 1960+Nov. 10, 1960 / Jazzland/OJC ✦✦✦✦
Eddie "Lockjaw" Davis and Johnny Griffin co-led a combo during 1960-62, a perfect outlet for the two very competitive and distinctive tenors. This reissue set (which also features pianist Junior Mance, bassist Larry Gales and drummer Ben Riley) is highlighted by heated versions of James Moody's "The Last Train from Overbrook," "Second Balcony Jump," "I'll Remember April" and "Good Bait." Easily recommended to straightahead jazz fans. *—Scott Yanow*

Return of the Griffin / Oct. 17, 1978 / Galaxy/OJC ✦✦✦✦
Johnny Griffin recorded this studio album during his first visit to the United States in 15 years. Accompanied by a very supportive trio (pianist Ronnie Mathews, bassist Ray Drummond and drummer Keith Copeland), the great tenor is in frequently exuberant form on such tunes as "Autumn Leaves," his own "A Monk's Dream" and the funky "The Way It Is." Long one of the underrated masters, Johnny Griffin is heard at the peak of his powers on this modern bop session. *—Scott Yanow*

Tough Tenor Back Again! / Jul. 10, 1984 / Storyville ✦✦✦✦
During 1960-63, Johnny Griffin and Eddie "Lockjaw" Davis teamed up in a two-tenor quintet, inspiring each other to play at their most intense and swinging on a nightly basis. After the band's breakup, Griffin and Davis occasionally had reunions that found them playing as heatedly as ever. This 1998 CD, which released a particularly exciting encounter at Copenhagen's Montmartre in 1984 for the first time, has what might have been their last matchup since Lockjaw passed away two years later. With pianist Harry Pickens, bassist Curtis Lundy and drummer Kenny Washington keeping the momentum moving, the two tough tenors battle it out on a variety of basic material, including "Blues Up and Down" (which has a colorful chorus of conversational commentary by the two tenors before their solos), "Funky Fluke" and "Lester Leaps In." Throughout the heated bebop date, Griffin and Davis are heard at the peak of their powers, and the results are quite memorable. *—Scott Yanow*

Dave Grusin

b. Jun. 26, 1934, Denver, CO
Piano, Composer / Original Score, Film Music, Crossover Jazz
Dave Grusin has been a highly successful performer, producer, composer, record label executive, arranger and bandleader. His piano playing ranges from mildly challenging to competent to routine, but he's an accomplished film and television soundtrack composer. Grusin played with Terry Gibbs and Johnny Smith while studying at the University of Colorado. He was assistant music director and pianist with Andy Williams from 1959 to 1966, and started his television composing career. Grusin recorded with Benny Goodman in 1960, and recorded with a hard bop trio that included Milt Hinton and Don Lamond in the early '60s. He also played and did a session with a quintet including Thad Jones and Frank Foster. Grusin did arrangements and recorded with Sarah Vaughan, Quincy Jones and Carmen McRae in the early '70s. He played electric keyboards with Gerry Mulligan and Lee Ritenour in the mid-70s, then helped establish GRP Records out of a production company. GRP developed into one of the top contemporary jazz and fusion companies; they were later taken over by Arista, then by MCA. Grusin continued recording through the '80s and '90s, doing numerous projects from fusion and pop to working with symphony orchestras. He's also conducted the GRP big band, continued scoring such films as *The Fabulous Baker Boys*, and doing duet sessions with his brother Don, and Ritenour. Besides his numerous GRP releases, Grusin's also recorded for Columbia, Sheffield Lab and Polygram. *—Ron Wynn*

One of a Kind / 1977 / GRP ✦✦✦
A fairly typical Dave Grusin date from the early days of GRP, this set features five of the keyboardist/producer's originals. The music is often atmospheric and a bit cinematic, with Grusin assisted by the soprano of Grover Washington and flutist Dave Valentin (along with top rhythm section players) on two songs apiece; "The Heart Is a Lonely Hunter" has Grusin's keyboards joined just by Ron Carter's bass. The music is pleasing, but not too substantial. *—Scott Yanow*

Harlequin / 1985 / GRP ✦✦✦✦

Sticks and Stones / 1988 / GRP ✦✦✦✦✦
This set works very well. Dave Grusin and his younger brother Don Grusin use a variety of keyboards to create a series of colorful duets. Other than Dori Caymmi's "Southern Wind," all of the fairly spontaneous yet well-planned performances are originals by one or both of the brothers. Even listeners who are not that much into electronics will find much of interest on this melodic and funky, yet often unpredictable set. *—Scott Yanow*

The Gershwin Connection / 1991 / GRP ✦✦✦✦
Because many of Dave Grusin's albums have been rather commercial and overproduced, it is often forgotten how excellent a pianist he could be. This CD, which includes a 40-page booklet, features an enjoyable program of George and Ira Gershwin tunes played by a continually changing all-star lineup that includes the leader's piano, clarinetist Eddie Daniels, vibraphonist Gary Burton, altoist Eric Marienthal, trumpeter Sal Marquez, guitarist Lee Ritenour, bassist John Patitucci, drummer Dave Weckl and guest spots for pianist Chick Corea (who duets with Grusin on "'S Wonderful") and Don Grusin. A few of the numbers are given light funk rhythms and made to sound slightly "contemporary" (particularly "I've Got Plenty O' Nuthin'," which has an electric Ramsey Lewis-type groove), but overall, this is a very tasteful and respectful set—a classy package. *—Scott Yanow*

● **Homage to Duke** / 1993 / GRP ✦✦✦✦✦
Although Dave Grusin is best known as a soundtrack composer and for his jazz-pop recordings, he has always had a great admiration for jazz. This CD (released in a fairly deluxe package) gave Grusin an opportunity to pay tribute to Duke Ellington. He performs ten mostly familiar songs associated with Ellington and wisely features fluegelhornist Clark Terry on five of the selections. Other prominent soloists include tenor saxophonist Pete Christlieb, trombonist George Bohanon, tenor saxophonist Tom Scott (returning to his roots), clarinetist Eddie Daniels (on an orchestrated version of "Mood Indigo") and pianist Grusin himself. This is a respectful and well-conceived tribute. *—Scott Yanow*

Presents: West Side Story / 1997 / Digital Sound ✦✦✦✦✦
To celebrate the 40th anniversary of the opening of *West Side Story* on Broadway, Dave Grusin revived the score, giving its ten themes fresh arrangements that keep the original melodies in mind but add a stronger dose of jazz and Afro-Cuban rhythms to the music. For the most rewarding recording of this music since Stan Kenton's powerful renditions of the early 1960s, Grusin utilized an all-star big band with strings. Among the key soloists are trumpeter Arturo Sandoval, Bill Evans (who takes several superlative soprano solos), Michael Brecker on tenor, baritonist Ronnie Cuber and flutist Dave Valentin (who is featured on a purposely cute rendition of "I Feel Pretty") plus the pianist/leader, who clearly loves the music. In addition, one song apiece features vocalists Jonathan Butler ("Maria"), Gloria Estefan and Jon Secada. Although one wishes that the singers were more jazz-oriented (or that the entire date were instrumental), the overall result is a very respectful yet creative reworking of the famous score. Highly recommended. *—Scott Yanow*

Two Worlds / Jun. 2000-Dec. 1999 / Decca ✦✦✦✦
Forging a unique creative relationship, Lee Ritenour and Dave Grusin's mutual professional history extends back some two decades. Ritenour was a core artist on Grusin's label, GRP, throughout the 1980s and early '90s; in 1986, they first collaborated on the Grammy Award winning *Harlequin*, a critically-acclaimed, Brazilian-themed recording. Ritenour also appeared on many of the pianist/composer's film scores and solo recordings, and the two jammed together on *GRP Super Live* in 1987. *Two Worlds*, the classical-oriented labor of love that reunites the two legends, is more than simply a beautiful creative departure from their usual jazz-oriented projects. A blend of original compositions and respectful reworkings of timeless classics from Bach, Bartok, Villalobos, Mompov, and Segovia, the collection—which features stellar guest performances by opera star Renee Fleming, violinist Gil Shaham, and cellist Julian Lloyd-Webber—finds Ritenour and Grusin joyously reconnecting with their rich classical roots. Among the highlights are the lush, highly percussive Vivaldi/Bach piece "Bach Concerto, featuring a twenty-piece string section; "Bachianas Aria," a piece from Brazilian composer Villalobos, provides a showcase for opera diva Renee Fleming. As for the original compositions, there's the haunting, melodic "Elegia," which Grusin composed many years ago for his late father, a violinist, featuring Gil Shaham; "Lagrima (Lee's Prelude)," a graceful Ritenour original led by the classical guitar; "River's Song," Grusin's clever medley adaptation of the folk songs "The Water Is Wide" and "Shenandoah," featuring Fleming on vocals and "Canto," an Italian-styled "winter song" which Grusin originally wrote for a Ritenour project in the late '70s. Timeless yet contemporary, *Two Worlds* is beautiful reunion of these musical soul mates. *—Jonathan Widran*

Vince Guaraldi

b. Jul. 17, 1928, San Francisco, CA, **d.** Feb. 6, 1976, Menlo Park, CA
Piano, Composer / West Coast Jazz, Latin Jazz, Cool
Vince Guaraldi occupies an unusual place in jazz history. Although not a major pianist, his playing in the late '50s on ballads influenced the new age pacesetter George Winston two decades later, he was an Italian whose work in Latin-jazz impressed many and he became best-known for writing the scores for the *Peanuts* television cartoons. Guaraldi was with Cal Tjader's first trio in 1951, gigged with the Bill Harris/Chubby Jackson band (1953), Georgie Auld (1953) and Sonny Criss (1955), toured with Woody Herman's Orchestra (1956-57), gained fame playing with Tjader again (1957-59) and returned to Herman for part of 1959. Guaraldi, who recorded two albums for Fantasy during 1956-57, led his own groups from 1960 on and made seven further records for Fantasy during 1962-66 including a recording of his hit original "Cast Your Fate to the Wind" and his 1965 jazz mass. *—Scott Yanow*

Vince Guaraldi Trio / Apr. 1956 / Fantasy/OJC ✦✦✦
This CD reissue in the OJC series brings back the first full session led by pianist Vince Guaraldi. Teamed up with the fine guitarist Eddie Duran and bassist Dean Reilly, Guaraldi swings lightly and with subtle creativity on two group originals and eight standards including "Django," "Chelsea Bridge," "Fascinatin' Rhythm" and "The Lady's in Love with You." Tasteful music. *—Scott Yanow*

A Flower Is a Lovesome Thing / Apr. 16, 1957 / Fantasy/OJC ✦✦✦✦
This is one of pianist Vince Guaraldi's better sets. Showcased in a San Francisco-based trio with guitarist Eddie Duran and bassist Dean Reilly, Guaraldi plays seven standards plus his

own "Like a Mighty Rose" tastefully and with light swing, making this a program that is equally successful as both cool jazz and background music. *—Scott Yanow*

Jazz Impressions of Black Orpheus / Apr. 18, 1962 / Fantasy/OJC ✦✦✦✦✦
Here we have Vince Guaraldi's breakthrough album—musically, commercially, in every which way. After numerous records as a leader or sideman, for the first time a recognizable Guaraldi piano style emerges, with whimsical phrasing all his own, a madly swinging right hand and occasional boogie-influenced left hand, and a distinctive, throat-catching, melodic improvisational gift. The first half of the CD is taken up by cover versions of tunes from the Antonio Carlos Jobim/Luiz Bonfa score for the film *Black Orpheus,* recorded just as bossa nova was taking hold in America. These are genuinely jazz-oriented impressions in a mainstream boppish manner, with only a breath of samba from Monty Budwig (bass) and Colin Bailey (drums) in the opening minute of "Samba de Orpheus"; an edited version of this haunting song was issued as a 45 RPM single. But DJs soon began flipping the single over to play the B-side, a wistful, unforgettably catchy Guaraldi tune called "Cast Your Fate to the Wind" that opens the North American half of the album. The tune became a surprise hit; Fantasy redesigned the cover to call attention to it, and Vince was on his way to fame as one of Latin and mainstream jazz's most irresistible composers. The whole album evokes the ambience of San Francisco's jazz life in the 1960s as few others do—and such is this record's appeal that even non-jazz and non-Latin music people have been grooving to this music ever since it came out. *—Richard S. Ginell*

Greatest Hits / 1962-1966 / Fantasy ✦✦✦✦
First released on LP in 1980, this compilation concentrates upon bite-sized samples from Guaraldi's Fantasy catalogue. Naturally, Fantasy includes famous tunes like "Cast Your Fate To The Wind" and "Linus And Lucy") but there are also some superb sleepers ("Star Song," Jobim's "Outra Vez") that display Guaraldi's wonderful melodic gift and the sessions with Bola Sete are touched upon. As a chronicle of Guaraldi's Fantasy days, the set is somewhat incomplete, for it leaves out all material recorded prior to "Cast Your Fate" and Guaraldi isn't given much of a chance to stretch out. But this is definitely the place to start for someone who has not heard this whimsically inventive pianist. *—Richard S. Ginell*

● **A Boy Named Charlie Brown** / 1964 / Fantasy ✦✦✦✦✦
Originally entitled *Jazz Impressions of A Boy Named Charlie Brown,* this is an important album not only because it is Guaraldi's first *Peanuts* soundtrack, but also because the music heard here probably introduced millions of kids (and their parents) to jazz from the mid-1960s onward. Actually, this music is the score for a documentary on the *Peanuts* phenomenon called *A Boy Named Charlie Brown,* which ran before the first *Peanuts* specials per se appeared on the CBS network. The most remarkable thing, besides the high quality of Guaraldi's whimsically swinging tunes, is that he did not compromise his art one iota for the cartoon world; indeed, he sounds even more engaged, inventive and light-hearted in his piano work here than ever. It must have been quite a delightful shock back then to hear a straight-ahead jazz trio (Guaraldi, Monty Budwig, bass; Colin Bailey, drums) backing all those cartoon figures and genuine children's voices, a mordant running musical commentary that made its own philosophical points. The music on this album laid the groundwork for much that was to come; here is the first appearance of the well-known bossa nova-influenced "Linus And Lucy," and fans of the series will recognize such themes from future episodes as "Baseball Theme" and "Oh, Good Grief" (which is a rewrite of the Dixiebelles' hit "Down At Papa Joe's"). The original LP came with twelve bonus lithographs of Charles Schulz's celebrated *Peanuts* drawings; the only extra thing the CD issue offers is a gratuitous outtake of "Fly Me To The Moon." *—Richard S. Ginell*

The Latin Side of Vince Guaraldi / 1960 / Fantasy/OJC ✦✦✦✦
The Latin side for Vince Guaraldi means a brush with both the Brazilian and Caribbean strains of Latin jazz, garnished now and then by an outboard string quartet and graced by four of his own delightful tunes. On Brazilian numbers like "Corcovado" and Brazilian-treated tunes like "Mr. Lucky" and Guaraldi's lovely "Star Song," Vince has drummer Jerry Granelli deploy his distinctive brushes-and-rim-shots bossa nova beat. Jack Weeks supplies bittersweet string arrangements as he tries to grant Guaraldi's wish for a "Villa-Lobos sound," which he does, more or less. Other tunes, like Guaraldi's own happy-go-lucky "Treat Street," "Whirlpool" and Nat Adderley's "Work Song," are treated to gentle cha-cha rhythms. Guaraldi's piano is hauntingly melodic, impulsively swinging and unmistakable for anyone else's, and the sound is much improved over the LP issue—especially in the case of the strings, which sound less seedy on the CD. *—Richard S. Ginell*

A Charlie Brown Christmas / 1965 / Fantasy ✦✦✦✦✦
Peanuts creator Charles Schultz called on pianist extraordinaire Vince Guaraldi and his trio to compose and perform music that would reflect the humor, charm, and innocence of Charlie Brown, Snoopy, and the entire Peanuts gang for their 1965 Christmas TV special. It was a perfect match: Guaraldi strings together elegant, enticing arrangements that reflect the spirit and mood of Schultz's work and introduce contemporary jazz to youngsters with a grace, charm and creativity. "What Child Is This" touches on cool jazz's richly textured percussive nuances, while "The Christmas Song" reflects Christmas' relaxing, mellow moments. The renowned "Linus and Lucy" gives the Peanuts characters a fresh, energetic feel with its tantalizing meter changes, brilliant percussion, and dashing, humorous piano lines. "Christmastime Is Here", perhaps the album's most endearing and eloquent moment, is six minutes of soft, lullaby-like melodic and percussive flavors. This collection of soul-soothing melodies would not be complete without the romantic gem "Skating,", which blends musical references to falling snowflakes with the dashing feel of swing. Finally, the uplifting, emotionally stirring swing tune "Christmas Is Coming" really brings the listener into the joyous light of the Christmas spirit. Fred Marshall's alluring walking bass lines and drummer Jerry Granelli's hauntingly beautiful brush work give most of the album a warm foundation, while Monty Budwig and Colin Bailey shine through with eminent dexterity on bass and drums on "Greensleeves". As for Guaraldi, his penetrating improvisational phrases paint pictures of the first winter snowfall, myriads of glistening trees and powdery white landscapes. With its blend of contemporary jazz and lyrical mannerisms, *A Charlie Brown Christmas* is a joyous and festive meditation for the holiday season. *—Shawn Haney*

Vince Guaraldi at Grace Cathedral / May 21, 1965 / Fantasy ✦✦✦✦✦
In a year that also saw Duke Ellington, Dave Brubeck and Lalo Schifrin write jazz-based pieces for the church, Vince Guaraldi may have come up with the most effective sacred work of the four. Written for the completion of San Francisco's Grace Cathedral, Guaraldi's Mass fuses his mainstream and Latin strains comfortably and movingly underneath the plain vanilla Gregorian lines and Anglican plainchant of a 68-voice chorus. Sometimes all Vince does to create a beguiling effect is improvise arpeggios or have his trio engage in a hot bossa nova workout as the chorus chants on one note. Despite the immense size of the cathedral, this music produces an intimate, unpretentious and undeniably emotional response—and there is plenty of jazz content, particularly when Guaraldi's trio goes it alone for nearly a third of the work in the ruminative "Holy Communion Blues." By all means, check this beautiful, unusual album out. *—Richard S. Ginell*

Oh, Good Grief! / 1968 / Warner Brothers ✦✦✦
In his first album for Warner Bros., Guaraldi serves up another delightful, though pitifully short (27 minutes) helping of his themes for the *Peanuts* TV specials. By this time, like several other pianists, Guaraldi was actively exploring the new sonic horizons offered by electronic keyboards—and so, he superimposes layers of electric harpsichord on most of these tracks. Some of the old sardonic spontaneity goes over the side, replaced by an overloaded gee-whiz atmosphere that sometimes gets in the way of the quartet's willingness to swing. But the tunes are marvelous, and since so little of Guaraldi's vast *Peanuts* output was ever made available, every millisecond of these jazz waltzes, bossa novas and soulful ruminations on Charlie Brown's world becomes cherishable. *—Richard S. Ginell*

Charlie Haden

b. Aug. 6, 1937, Shenandoah, IA
Bass / Avant-Garde Jazz, Free Jazz, Hard Bop
What would Ornette Coleman have done in 1959 if Charlie Haden were not around— There was probably not another jazz bassist who fully understood Coleman's radical music that early. Haden's large and distinctive tone, his unhurried approach and his ability to state a pulse without handcuffing the lead voices to a repeated chord structure were unpredecented at the time. It was with Paul Bley at the Hillcrest Club that Haden first performed with Coleman and Don Cherry, and he soon became an important member of their quartet. Haden traveled with Coleman to New York in 1959 and was with him through 1961 including making some innovative records for Atlantic. Always outspoken against injustice and political repression, Haden's avant-garde orchestra was quite political. He also played often with Keith Jarrett (1967-75) including his excellent quintet that featured Dewey Redman, recorded with Alice Coltrane (1968-72), led a pair of diverse duet albums (1975-76) and was with Old and New Dreams in the mid-to-late '70s. *—Scott Yanow*

Liberation Music Orchestra / Apr. 27, 1970-Apr. 29, 1970 / Impulse! ✦✦✦✦✦
A fascinating reissue that comfortably straddles the lines of jazz, folk and world music, working up a storm by way of a jazz protest album that points toward the Spanish Civil War in particular and the Vietnam War in passing. Haden leads the charge and contributes material, but the real star here may in fact be Carla Bley, who arranged numbers, wrote several, and contributed typically brilliant piano work. Also of particular note in a particularly talented crew is guitarist Sam Brown, the standout of "El Quinto Regimiento/Los Cuatro Generales/Viva La Quince Brigade," a 21-minute marathon. Reissue producer Michael Cuscuna has done his best with the mastering here, but listeners will note a roughness to the sound—one that is in keeping with the album's tone and attitude. *—Steven McDonald*

As Long as There's Music / Jan. 25, 1976+Aug. 21, 1976 / Verve ✦✦✦✦
Although one would not immediately associate bassist Charlie Haden with pianist Hampton Hawes, they had performed together on an occasional basis since first meeting in 1957. This Artists House LP, a set of five duets, was their last opportunity to play together because Hawes would pass away the following year. The music includes a fairly free improvisation on "Hello/ Goodbye," the duo's intepretation of the title cut, a collaboration on "This Is Called Love" and two originals from the pianist. This quiet and often lyrical set contains a great deal of thoughtful and subtle music by two masters. *—Scott Yanow*

Closeness (Duets) / Jan. 26, 1976-Mar. 21, 1976 / Horizon ✦✦✦✦✦
In 1976, bassist Charlie Haden recorded eight duets with musicians whom he admired; the results were originally released on two Horizon LPs as *Closeness.* In 1988, A&M reissued all of the music on a pair of CDs, titled "Closeness" Duets. For this release, Haden is teamed with pianist Keith Jarrett, plays a memorable "O.C." with altoist Ornette Coleman, interprets a moody piece with harpist Alice Coltrane, and performs the highly political "For a Free Portugal" (which also utilizes excerpts from a record of Angolan music) with percussionist Paul Motian. Recommended, particularly due to the Ornette and Jarrett collaborations. *—Scott Yanow*

Golden Number / Jun. 7, 1976-Dec. 20, 1976 / A&M ✦✦✦✦
The second of two duet sets by bassist Charlie Haden (both have been reissued on A&M CDs) is the equal of the first. Haden teams up with Don Cherry (on trumpet and flutes), tenor saxophonist Archie Shepp (for the excellent "Shepp's Way"), pianist Hampton Hawes (jamming Ornette Coleman's blues "Turnaround"), and Ornette himself, who unfortunately plays trumpet this time around. In general, the music is quite intriguing and has its share of variety. *—Scott Yanow*

Folk Songs / Nov. 1979 / ECM ✦✦✦✦
One of the better ECM recordings, this collaboration by bassist Charlie Haden, Jan Garbarek on tenor and soprano, and Egberto Gismonti (switching between guitar and piano) is filled with moody originals, improvisations that blend together jazz and world music, and atmospheric ensembles. This date works well both as superior background music and for close listening. *—Scott Yanow*

The Ballad of the Fallen / Nov. 1982 / ECM ♦♦♦
The second recording by Charlie Haden's Liberation Music Orchestra utilizes a few alumni (the bassist/leader, trumpeters Don Cherry and Mike Mantler, tenor saxophonist Dewey Redman, drummer Paul Motian and pianist Carla Bley), along with other musicians who rose to prominence since the 1969 debut album (Jim Pepper and Steve Slagle on reeds, trombonist Gary Valante, guitarist Mick Goodrick, Sharon Freeman on French horn, and Jack Jeffers on tuba). As with the first set, the music mixes together some melodic but avant-garde explorations with revolutionary themes including songs from the Spanish Civil War, El Salvador, Portugal and Chile. "Too Late," a duet by Bley and Haden, serves as a change of pace. The music is quite credible and emotional, and has dated well. *—Scott Yanow*

★ **Quartet West** / Dec. 22, 1986-Dec. 23, 1986 / Polygram ♦♦♦♦♦
The debut recording by Charlie Haden's Quartet West (comprised of the bassist/leader, tenor saxophonist Ernie Watts, pianist Alan Broadbent and, at the time, drummer Billy Higgins) launched the popular acoustic group. Haden now had an opportunity to display his skill in playing bop-based music, along with his strong interest in the mood of film noir. For this CD, the quartet performs three standards plus pieces by Pat Metheny, Ornette Coleman ("The Blessing" and "The Good Life"), Charlie Parker ("Passport") and Haden. The band also gave exposure to the underrated Broadbent and helped push Watts toward his original love of Coltranish jazz. *—Scott Yanow*

Etudes / Sep. 14, 1987-Sep. 15, 1987 / Soul Note ♦♦♦
The very democratic trio of bassist Charlie Haden, drummer Paul Motian and pianist Geri Allen perform sensitive yet often exploratory group improvisations on several originals, Ornette Coleman's "Lonely Woman," and Herbie Nichols' "Shuffle Montgomery." The communication between these three masterful players is quite impressive. *—Scott Yanow*

In Angel City / May 30, 1988-Jun. 1, 1988 / Verve ♦♦♦♦
The second recording by Charlie Haden's Quartet West is similar to the music that the group (bassist Haden, tenor saxophonist Ernie Watts, pianist Alan Broadbent and drummer Larance Marable) would play for the next decade. Among the highlights of this well-rounded set (one of the band's most definitive releases) is "First Song" (Haden's most memorable composition), Miles Davis' "Blue In Green," and a lengthy exploration of Ornette Coleman's "Lonely Woman." An excellent showcase for Haden in a straight-ahead setting and for Watts, whose passionate sound perfectly fits the band. Highly recommended. *—Scott Yanow*

Dream Keeper / Apr. 4, 1990-Apr. 5, 1990 / Blue Note ♦♦♦♦♦

Haunted Heart / Oct. 27, 1991-Oct. 28, 1991 / Verve ♦♦♦♦♦
Charlie Haden loves film as much as music, combining both loves on the critically acclaimed *Haunted Heart*. Haden led his tremendous group Quartet West through 12 numbers, several, like Cole Porter's "Every Time We Say Goodbye," and Alan Broadbent's "Lady In The Lake," Arthur Schwartz and Howard Dietz's "Haunted Heart," and even the short introduction, with film ties and/or links. Haden transferred vocals on some numbers from Jeri Southern, Billie Holiday and Jo Stafford into the mix without disrupting or disturbing the group framework. Quartet West has emerged as a premier small combo, and Haden nicely paid tribute to the past without being held hostage to it. *—Ron Wynn*

Always Say Goodbye / Jul. 30, 1993-Aug. 1, 1993 / Verve ♦♦♦♦♦

Steal Away / Jun. 29, 1994-Jun. 30, 1994 / Verve ♦♦♦
This is an unusual record. Bassist Charlie Haden and pianist Hank Jones perform a variety of spirituals, hymns and folk songs as duets. The traditional music (which includes such tunes as "Nobody Knows the Trouble I've Seen," "Swing Low, Sweet Chariot," "Sometimes I Feel like a Motherless Child" and "We Shall Overcome") are all performed respectfully and with reverence. These melodic yet subtly swinging interpretations hold one's interest throughout and reward repeated listenings. *—Scott Yanow*

Beyond the Missouri Sky (Short Stories) / 1996 / Verve ♦♦♦♦

Montreal Tapes with Geri Allen / Jul. 1, 1989 / Verve ♦♦♦♦

Montreal Tapes with Gonzalo Rubalcaba / Jul. 3, 1989 / Verve ♦♦♦
In Volume Four of the Charlie Haden concerts at the 1989 Montreal Festival, Paul Motian returns as the drummer, but this time, the piano chair is occupied by the then-little-known Haden discovery, Cuban Gonzalo Rubalcaba, who proceeds to dazzle the audience with his mind-boggling speed. Rubalcaba's irresistible momentum drives this session whenever he solos; all the others can do is hang onto the whirlwind. The musicmaking in general, though, is more tied to the mainstream than that of the companion Montreal trio album with Geri Allen, and this group doesn't have quite the same internal compatibility as that of the Allen trio. There is one concession to Rubalcaba's Latin heritage, Haden's Spanish-tinged tune "La Pasionara," in which the Cuban goes bonkers with the tremolos. Haden's own soloing is massive and outgoing in tone; clearly, he was hugely enjoying this festival where he was given total carte blanche. *—Richard S. Ginell*

LMO Montreal Tapes / Jul. 8, 1989 / Verve ♦♦♦

Jim Hall (James Stanley Hall)

b. Dec. 4, 1930, Buffalo, NY
Guitar / Post-Bop, Cool
A harmonically advanced cool-toned and subtle guitarist, Jim Hall has been an inspiration to many current guitarists including some (such as Bill Frisell) who sound nothing like him. Hall attended the Cleveland Institute of Music and studied classical guitar in Los Angeles with Vincente Gomez. He was an original member of the Chico Hamilton Quintet (1955-56) and during 1956-59 was with the Jimmy Giuffre Three. After touring with Ella Fitzgerald (1960-61) and sometimes forming duos with Lee Konitz, Hall was with Sonny Rollins's dynamic quartet in 1961-62, recording *The Bridge*. He co-led a quartet with Art Farmer (1962-64), recorded on an occasional basis with Paul Desmond during 1959-65 (all of their quartet performances are collected on a Mosaic box set) and then became a New York studio musician. He has mostly been a leader ever since and in addition to his own projects for World Pacific/Pacific Jazz, MPS, Milestone, CTI, Horizon, Artists House, Concord, Music Masters and Telarc, Jim Hall recorded two classic duet albums with Bill Evans. A self-titled collaboration with Pat Metheny followed in 1999. *—Scott Yanow*

● **Alone Together** / Aug. 4, 1972 / Milestone/OJC ♦♦♦♦♦
Long considered a classic and a revelation to listeners who had taken guitarist Jim Hall for granted, this set of duets with bassist Ron Carter (reissued on CD) has near-telepathic communication between the two musicians and quiet music full of inner tension and fire. Hall and Carter brought in an original apiece and also collaborated on six standards, including "St. Thomas," "Softly As In a Morning Sunrise," "Autumn Leaves" and "Alone Together." Introspective and thought-provoking music. *—Scott Yanow*

Concierto / Apr. 16, 1975+Apr. 23, 1975 / Columbia/Legacy ♦♦♦♦♦
Jim Hall's *Concierto* was arguably the greatest LP in the history of CTI; now that it has been reissued (for a second time, as a CD), the improved sound and packaging plus three more new tracks eclipse the earlier CD reissue on CBS Associated. With Chet Baker, Roland Hanna and Paul Desmond, Hall is perfectly complemented. A master of melody who never wastes notes, the centerpiece for this release is Hall's interpretation of one movement from Rodrigo's "Guitar Concerto," arranged by Don Sebesky. New tracks include alternate takes of "You'd Be So Nice to Come Home To" and "Rock Skippin'," plus "Unfinished Business," an incomplete track that fades following Desmond's solo just as Hall starts to play (This song is actually "La Paloma Azul," a Mexican folk tune played by Paul Desmond while with the Dave Brubeck Quartet about a decade earlier, also known as "The Blue Dove"). *—Ken Dryden*

All Across the City / May 1989 / Concord Jazz ♦♦♦♦♦
Jim Hall's successful blend of contemporary and mainstream jazz should appeal to both camps on this well-crafted CD. Hall displays the subtle quiet lyricism that makes his guitar sound instantly identifiable. Gil Goldstein is a perfect choice on keyboards, because he uses synthesizer only to color rather than overpower a song, while avoiding schmaltz. Both "Beja-Flor" and the title track benefit from his contributions. Though his piano is frequently in the background, it matches Hall's hushed, effective guitar lines. Bassist Steve LaSpina and drummer Terry Clarke frequently lay out during the introductions and then enter to add either gentle shadings or full steam, if needed. One of Jim Hall's best CDs. *—Ken Dryden*

Dialogues / Feb. 3, 1995-Feb. 25, 1995 / Telarc ♦♦♦♦♦
Guitarist Jim Hall has long been one of the most open-minded of the important stylists to emerge during the 1950s and his harmonically advanced style remains quite modern while hinting at its foundations in bop. For this Telarc CD, Hall teams up with five major players on two numbers apiece: Guitarists Bill Frisell and Mike Stern, Joe Lovano on tenor, flugelhornist Tom Harrell and Gil Goldstein on accordion. Bassist Scott Colley and drummer Andy Watson are on the Frisell and Lovano tracks and part of the Harrell and Stern performances. All of the compositions but "Skylark" are Hall's originals and, although they are usually a bit dry, there are some exceptions; "Uncle Ed" and "Frisell Frazzle" are a little nutty. The emphasis throughout is on interplay between the lead voices and advanced improvising. Despite his strong sidemen (Stern and Harrell fare best), Jim Hall ends up as the dominant voice on virtually every selection, making this a set his fans will enjoy. *—Scott Yanow*

Jim Hall & Pat Metheny / Jul. 30, 1998-Oct. 1998 / Telarc ♦♦♦♦
These two guitarists—one an elder statesman, the other still a relatively young man in the midst of a stellar career—are such a natural fit that it's amazing no one's thought of getting them together for a duo album before. Both play with a gentle touch and sweet tone and both are capable of challenging experimentation, though both have spent most of their time in one mainstream tradition or another (Hall in straight-ahead jazz, Metheny in jazz-rock fusion). On this disc they focus on original compositions (Metheny's "Farmer's Trust" and "Into the Dream," Hall's "Cold Spring" and "Waiting to Dance"), but there are also tunes by Jerome Kern and Steve Swallow as well as the inevitable rendition of "Summertime." Their interplay is nothing short of astounding, and the five improvisational pieces scattered throughout the program sometimes sound as organized as the standards. The mood does get a little bit samey after a while, and the complete lack of high frequencies in both guitarists' tone might leave you wondering if you've got water in your ear. But overall, this really is a wonderful album. *—Rick Anderson*

Grand Slam: Live at the Regattabar, Cambridge Massachusetts / Sep. 26, 2000 / Telarc ♦♦♦♦♦

Chico Hamilton (Forestorn Hamilton)

b. Sep. 21, 1921, Los Angeles, CA
Drums / Crossover Jazz, Hard Bop, Post-Bop, Cool
Chico Hamilton, a subtle and creative drummer, will probably always be better-known for the series of Quintets that he led during 1955-65 and for his ability as a talent scout than for his fine drumming. He made his recording debut with Slim Gaillard, was house drummer at Billy Berg's, toured with Lionel Hampton and served in the military (1942-46). He toured as Lena Horne's drummer (on and off during 1948-55) and gained recognition for his work with the original Gerry Mulligan pianoless quartet (1952-53). In 1955 Hamilton put together his first Quintet; one of the last important West Coast jazz bands, the Chico Hamilton Quintet was immediately popular. In 1966 Hamilton started composing for commercials and the studios and he broke up his Quintet. However he continued leading various groups, playing music that ranged from the avant-garde to erratic fusion and advanced hard bop. *—Scott Yanow*

☆ **The Complete Pacific Jazz Recordings of the Chico Hamilton Quintet** / Nov. 12, 1954-Jan. 12, 1959 / Mosaic ♦♦♦♦♦
The original Chico Hamilton Quintet was one of the last significant West Coast jazz bands of the cool era. Consisting of Buddy Collette on reeds (flute, clarinet, alto, and tenor), guitarist Jim Hall, bassist Carson Smith, and the drummer/leader, the most distinctive element in the group's identity was cellist Fred Katz. The band could play quite softly, blending together elements of bop and classical music into their popular sound and occupying their own niche. This six-CD, limited-edition box set from 1997 starts off with a Hamilton drum solo from a

1954 performance with the Gerry Mulligan Quartet; it contains three full albums and many previously unreleased numbers) by the original Chico Hamilton band and also has quite a few titles from the second Hamilton group (which has Paul Horn and John Pisano in the places of Collette and Hall). In addition, there are three titles from the third Hamilton Quintet (with Eric Dolphy on flute and alto) and a 1959 Duke Ellington tribute date that featured both Collette and Horn. Most of these performances were formerly quite rare and never reissued coherently before. Highly recommended to jazz historians and to listeners who enjoy classic cool jazz, this box is sure to be sold out quickly. *—Scott Yanow*

Gongs East / Dec. 29, 1958-Dec. 30, 1958 / Discovery ✦✦✦✦✦
The best-known of all the 1950s Chico Hamilton Quintet sets, this is also the only early Hamilton music that has been fully reissued on CD. At the time, the drummer's group also included cellist Nate Gershman, guitarist Dennis Budimir, bassist Wyatt Ruther and the young Eric Dolphy on alto, bass clarinet and flute. Dolphy has quite a few short solos on this rewarding music, and the highlights of the date include "Beyond the Blue Horizon," "Passion Flower," Gerald Wilson's "Tuesday at Two" and the exotic "Gongs East." Recommended. *—Scott Yanow*

Man from Two Worlds / Sep. 18, 1962+Dec. 11, 1963 / GRP ✦✦✦✦✦
Although it tended to get overlooked at the time, one of drummer Chico Hamilton's finest groups was his 1962-63 quartet/quintet. With Charles Lloyd at his most fiery on tenor and flute and the colorful solos of the up-and-coming Hungarian guitarist Gabor Szabo, this band placed a stronger emphasis on melody and softer sounds than the more avant-garde groups of the time but still pushed away at musical boundaries. Trombonist George Bohanon is also on the final four numbers of this CD reissue which brings back all of the music from Hamilton's *Man from Two Worlds* LP and four of the six numbers originally on *Passin' Thru*. Highlights include the original version of Lloyd's most famous song, "Forest Flower." *—Scott Yanow*

The Dealer / Sep. 1966 / Impulse! ✦✦✦✦
Drummer Chico Hamilton introduced many top young players during his years as a bandleader, but few probably realize that Larry Coryell made his recording debut with Chico a year before joining Gary Burton's quartet. This CD reissue brings back Coryell's initial appearance on record, and at times he sounded oddly like Chuck Berry (especially on "The Dealer"). Also heard on this set are altoist Arnie Lawrence, bassist Richard Davis, organist Ernie Hayes (on two numbers), and, on his spirited boogaloo "For Mods Only," Archie Shepp making a rare appearance on piano. Most of the performances still sound surprisingly fresh, especially the explorative "A Trip," making this an underrated but worthy release. [The 1999 CD reissue contains four bonus tracks, plus 20-bit remastering.] *—Scott Yanow*

● **My Panamanian Friend** / Aug. 21, 1992-Aug. 28, 1992 / Soul Note ✦✦✦✦✦
My Panamian Friend is Hamilton's finest outing in several years. Part of the reason may be its purpose, paying tribute to the great Eric Dolphy. Another plus is that eight of the nine songs are Dolphy compositions, among them "Springtime," "South Street Exit," and "Something Sweet, Something Tender." But the prime reason for this disc's success is alto saxophonist/flutist Eric Person. He plays with sensitivity and a tender, yet strong, dynamic approach that proves more intriguing than his performances on his recent session as a leader. Although he's no Dolphy, Eric Person not only pays ample respects, but matures greatly as a player on this session. *—Ron Wynn*

The Original Ellington Suite / Aug. 22, 1958 / Blue Note ✦✦✦✦
This release will have fans of Eric Dolphy salivating as it includes some long-lost work that jazz scholars didn't know existed at all. When the premiere reissue producer Michael Cuscuna researched all known Pacific Jazz tapes attributed to Chico Hamilton, all he came across were three edited numbers from this session, two of which had appeared on a compilation and another only on a DJ sampler. But this release is due to the luck of a Canadian resident who was digging through a used record bin in his hometown of Brighton, England, where he found a copy of *The Ellington Suite* with the personnel listed from a later session and a near mint blank test pressing of what turned out to be the long lost Chico Hamilton original version with Dolphy. While producer Richard Bock may have thought Dolphy's playing was at times too radical, history proves him wrong. His mellow alto sax is a key ingredient of "In a Sentimental Mood," while his unique phrasing is central to the swinging "Just A-Sittin'and A-Rockin'." Dolphy's flute is not as aggressive as it would be in the next few years, but his playing on "Everything but You" provides a preview of what was to come later in his career. Dolphy's clarinet weaves underneath Nate Gershman's arco cello solo in the lovely "Day Dream." Of course, the work of guitarist John Pisano, bassist Hal Gaylor, and the leader should not be ignored, as their musicianship is of the highest order, too. Chico Hamilton's pianoless chamber jazz recordings for Pacific Jazz between 1955 and 1959 are important landmarks, but the discovery of this long-lost date adds to his many achievements. Highly recommended. *—Ken Dryden*

Lionel Hampton

b. Apr. 12, 1909, Louisville, KY
Vibraphone, Drums, Piano / New York Blues, Swing, Big Band
Lionel Hampton was the first jazz vibraphonist and has been one of the jazz giants since the mid-'30s. He has achieved the difficult feat of being musically open-minded (even recording "Giant Steps") without changing his basic swing style. Originally a drummer, Hampton became the first jazz improviser to record on vibes after being asked by Louis Armstrong to play on a 1930 recording session. He gained his big break in 1936 after joining Benny Goodman's band, and became one of the stars of the Goodman organization. In 1937 he started recording regularly as a leader for Victor and formed his first big band in 1940. Two years later, he had a huge hit with "Flying Home" and during the rest of the decade, Hampton's extroverted orchestra was a big favorite, leaning towards R&B, showing the influence of bebop after 1944 and sometimes getting pretty exhibitionistic. His popularity allowed him to continue leading big bands off and on into the mid-'90s. Despite strokes and the ravages of age, Lionel Hampton as of this writing is still a vital force. *—Scott Yanow*

1937-1938 / Feb. 8, 1937-Jan. 18, 1938 / Classics ✦✦✦✦✦

1938-1939 / Jan. 18, 1938-Jun. 13, 1939 / Classics ✦✦✦✦✦

1939-1940 / Jun. 13, 1939-May 10, 1940 / Classics ✦✦✦✦✦

● **Midnight Sun** / Jan. 29, 1946-Nov. 10, 1947 / GRP/Decca ✦✦✦✦✦
Although firmly identified with Benny Goodman and the swing era, vibraphonist Lionel Hampton led one of the most bop-oriented and forward-looking big bands of the mid-to-late '40s; for proof of that check out "Mingus Fingers" (by Charles Mingus) on this CD. This set reissues some of Hampton's most boppish sides from 1946-47 along with the original version of "Midnight Sun" and is full of extroverted solos and exciting ensembles. Although tenorman Arnett Cobb (heard in the earlier selections) and pianist Milt Buckner are the best-known sidemen, such musicians as the screaming trumpeters Jimmy Nottingham and Leo "the Whistler" Sheppard and tenors Morris Lane, John Sparrow and the young Johnny Griffin provide their own strong moments. Until Decca gets around to reissuing all of Hamp's big band sides in chronological order, this is one of the sets to get. *—Scott Yanow*

☆ **Hamp and Getz** / Aug. 1, 1955 / Verve ✦✦✦✦✦
If one were to believe the cliches and stereotypes common in some jazz history books, this matchup should not have worked. By 1955 Lionel Hampton was a veteran swing vibraphonist while Stan Getz was the leader of the "cool school" of young tenors. But what these two masters had in common (in addition to a healthy respect for each other's talents) was the ability to swing as hard as possible. Joined by a fine trio, the duo really rip into "Cherokee" and "Jumpin' at the Woodside" (listen to their blistering tradeoffs) and, even with a fine ballad medley, it is these torrid jams that make this a highly recommended disc. *—Scott Yanow*

★ **Hamp: The Legendary Decca Recordings** / May 26, 1942-Mar. 20, 1963 / GRP ✦✦✦✦✦
A very nice two-disc set indeed, with a wonderful cross-section of Hampton's career, with the focus rightfully on the pre-1950 stage, with the final few cuts taking Hampton as far as a 1963 club date with trumpeter Charlie Teagarden. The music here is often delicate, spun from silver, and it's doubtful you'll find a better compilation of jazz vibraphone work. One fascinating highlight: Hampton's 15-minute version of "Stardust." *—Steven McDonald*

1945-1946 / Jan. 22, 1945-Jan. 30, 1946 / Classics ✦✦✦✦✦
The sixth CD in Classics' series of Lionel Hampton records documents his music during a one-year period. Hampton's big band, riding high after "Flying Home," continued to grow in popularity during this era. The vibraphonist's showmanship and his sidemen's extroverted solos generated constant excitement, as can be heard throughout these 20 selections. With the exception of Dinah Washington's lone vocal on "Blow Top Blues" and the original version of "Hey! Ba-Ba-Re-Bop," most of the selections were formerly a bit rare, including a pair of rollicking V-disc performances ("Vibe Boogie" and "Screamin' Boogie"). Hampton is heard on 14 numbers with his big band (which included such key sidemen as trumpeter Joe Morris, tenorman Arnett Cobb, the eccentric Herbie Fields on alto and clarinet, and pianist Milt Buckner), four workouts with a septet, and two tunes (including a pair of vocals) with a rhythm quartet. Bing Crosby guests on so-so versions of "Pinetop's Boogie Woogie" and "On the Sunny Side of the Street" (sounding very much out of place), but otherwise, everything works. Stirring and accessible music. *—Scott Yanow*

The Complete Quartets & Quintets / Sep. 2, 1953-Sep. 1953 / Verve ✦✦✦✦

Slide Hampton (Locksley Wellington Hampton)

b. Apr. 21, 1932, Jeannette, PA
Trombone, Arranger / Hard Bop, Bop
Slide Hampton has been a fine trombonist and arranger since the mid-'50s, helping to keep the tradition of bop alive in both his playing and his writing. After working with Buddy Johnson (1955-56) and Lionel Hampton, he became an important force in Maynard Ferguson's excellent big band of 1957-59. He led octets in the 1960s with such sidemen as Freddie Hubbard and George Coleman. After traveling with Woody Herman to Europe in 1968, Hampton settled overseas where he stayed very active. Since returning to the U.S. in 1977, he has led his World of Trombones (which features nine trombonists), played in a cop-op quintet called Continuum and been involved in several Dizzy Gillespie tribute projects, recording in the 1990s for Telarc. *—Scott Yanow*

World of Trombones / Jan. 8, 1979-Jan. 9, 1979 / 1201 Music ✦✦✦✦
Ambitious project with nine trombonists merging their skills under the leadership of Slide Hampton. The list includes both established veterans like Curtis Fuller and Steve Turre and emerging newcomers Janice Robinson and Afro-Latin star Papo Vasquez. Hampton's arrangements are excellent, but there's more emphasis on performance style than real solo development. Pianist Albert Dailey and bassist Ray Drummond were also outstanding. *—Ron Wynn*

● **Roots** / Apr. 17, 1985 / Criss Cross ✦✦✦✦✦
Tremendous '85 quintet session with trombonist Slide Hampton heading a distinguished group and nicely teaming with tenor saxophonist Clifford Jordan in a first-rate hard bop frontline. The rhythm section's quality isn't far behind, especially pianist Cedar Walton and drummer Billy Higgins. *—Ron Wynn*

Herbie Hancock

b. Apr. 12, 1940, Chicago, IL
Piano (Electric), Keyboards, Piano, Synthesizer, Composer / Electro, Modal Music, Hard Bop, Post-Bop, Fusion, Jazz-Funk, Funk
Herbie Hancock will always be one of the most revered and controversial figures in jazz—just as his employer/mentor Miles Davis was when he was alive. Unlike Miles, who pressed ahead relentlessly and never looked back until near the very end, Hancock has cut a zigzagging forward path, shuttling between almost every development in electronic and acoustic jazz and R&B over the last third of the 20th century. Though grounded in Bill Evans and able to absorb blues, funk, gospel, and even modern classical influences, Hancock's piano and keyboard voices are entirely his own, with their own urbane harmonic and complex, earthy

rhythmic signatures—and young pianists cop his licks constantly. Having studied engineering and professing to love gadgets and buttons, Hancock was perfectly suited for the electronic age; he was one of the earliest champions of the Rhodes electric piano and Hohner clavinet and would field an ever-growing collection of synthesizers and computers on his electric dates. Yet his love for the grand piano never waned, and despite his peripatetic activities all around the musical map, his piano style continues to evolve into tougher, ever-more-complex forms. He is as much at home trading riffs with a smoking funk band as he is communing with a world-class post bop rhythm section—and that drives purists on both sides of the fence up the wall. *—Richard S. Ginell*

☆ **The Complete Blue Note Sixties Sessions** / May 28, 1962-Apr. 23, 1969 / Blue Note ✦✦✦✦✦
From the start of his solo recording career in 1962, when he was 22, Herbie Hancock was a very original pianist/composer. Strangely enough, despite the explorative nature of much of his music, Hancock was also quite accessible, recording the future hit "Watermelon Man" on his debut date. This six-CD set is a must for all jazz collectors who do not already own Hancock's Blue Note albums, for the box contains the complete contents of the pianist's albums *Takin' Off, My Point of View, Inventions & Dimensions, Empyrean Isles, Maiden Voyage, Speak Like a Child* and *The Prisoner.* In addition, there are a dozen alternate takes (seven not previously out), five selections taken from dates led by others (Donald Byrd, Jackie McLean, Wayne Shorter and Bobby Hutcherson) and an unissued R&B-ish number ("Don't Ever Go There") from an abandoned 1966 project. The title of the attractive 1998 package is not completely accurate, for although the program includes all of Hancock's Blue Note dates as a leader, it does not have all of his recordings as a sideman for the label (which would take a really huge box). There are many classics in this reissue, including "Watermelon Man," "Blind Man, Blind Man," "Cantaloupe Island," "Maiden Voyage" (including a second version from a Hutcherson date), "The Eye of the Hurricane," "Dolphin Dance," "The Prisoner" and the entire *Speak Like a Child* album. Among Hancock's sidemen are trumpeters Freddie Hubbard, Donald Byrd, Thad Jones and Johnny Coles, tenors Dexter Gordon, Hank Mobley and Joe Henderson, bassists Butch Warren, Chuck Israels, Paul Chambers, Ron Carter and Buster Williams and drummers Billy Higgins, Tony Williams, Willie Bobo, Mickey Roker and Albert "Tootie" Heath. Timeless music that is still quite undated and fresh. *—Scott Yanow*

Takin' Off / May 28, 1962 / Blue Note ✦✦✦✦✦
This CD reissues pianist Herbie Hancock's first album as a leader, a set best-known for introducing his catchy song "Watermelon Man." The release not only brings back the original hard bop-oriented program but adds three previously unissued alternate takes, including one of "Watermelon Man." The all-star quintet (which includes trumpeter Freddie Hubbard, tenor saxophonist Dexter Gordon, bassist Butch Warren and drummer Billy Higgins) sounds consistently inspired with Gordon just starting to be influenced by John Coltrane and Hubbard full of youthful fire. Even at this early stage, Herbie Hancock had his own original voice. *—Scott Yanow*

My Point of View / Mar. 19, 1963 / Blue Note ✦✦✦✦
Takin' Off was an impressive debut effort from Herbie Hancock, and his second record, *My Point of View,* proved that it was no fluke. Hancock took two risks with the album—his five original compositions covered more diverse stylistic ground than his debut, and he assembled a large septet for the sessions; the band features such stellar musicians as trumpeter Donald Byrd, tenor saxophonist Hank Mobley, drummer Tony Williams, guitarist Grant Green, bassist Chuck Israels, and trombonist Grachan Moncur III. It's a rare occasion that all seven musicians appear on the same track, which speaks well for the pianist's arranging capabilities. Hancock knows how to get the best out of his songs and musicians, which is one of the reasons why *My Point of View* is a captivating listen. The other is the sheer musicality of the record. Hard bop remains the foundation for Hancock's music, but he explores its limitations, finding its soulful side (the successful "Watermelon Man" rewrite "Blind Man, Blind Man"), its probing, adventurous leanings (the edgy "King Cobra"), and its ballad side. "The Pleasure Is Mine" is a lovely, simple ballad, while "A Tribute to Someone" takes the form to more challenging territory—it's lyrical, but it takes chances. The closer "And What if I Don't" finds the band working a relaxed, bluesy groove that gives them opportunities to spin out rich, tasteful solos. It's a little more relaxed than *Takin' Off,* but in its own way *My Point of View* is nearly as stunning. *—Stephen Thomas Erlewine*

Inventions and Dimensions / Aug. 30, 1963 / Blue Note ✦✦✦✦
For his third album, *Inventions and Dimensions,* Herbie Hancock changed course dramatically. Instead of recording another multi-faceted album like *My Point of View,* he explored a Latin-inflected variation of post-bop with a small quartet. Hancock is the main harmonic focus of the music—his three collegues are bassist Paul Chambers, drummer Willie Bobo and percussionist Osvaldo "Chihuahua" Martinez, who plays conga and bongo. It is true that the music is rhythm-intensive, but that doesn't mean it's dance music. Hancock has created an improvisatory atmosphere where the rhythms are fluid and the chords, harmonies and melodies are unexpected. On every song but one, the melodies and chords were improvised, with Hancock's harmonic ideas arising from the rhythms during the recording. The result is risky, unpredictable music that is intensely cerebral and quite satisfying. *Inventions and Dimensions* displays his willingness to experiment and illustrates that his playing is reaching new, idiosyncratic heights. Listening to this, the subsequent developments of Miles Davis' invitation to join his quartet and the challenging *Empyrean Isles* come as no surprise. *—Stephen Thomas Erlewine*

Empyrean Isles / Jun. 17, 1964 / Blue Note ✦✦✦✦✦
My Point of View and *Inventions and Dimensions* found Herbie Hancock exploring the fringes of hard bop, working with a big band and a Latin-flavored percussion section, respectively. On *Empyrean Isles,* he returns to hard bop, but the results are anything but conventional. Working with cornetist Freddie Hubbard, bassist Ron Carter and drummer Tony Williams—a trio just as young and adventurous as he was—Hancock pushes at the borders of hard bop, finding a brilliantly evocative balance between traditional bop, soul-injected grooves and experimental, post-modal jazz. Hancock's four original concepts are loosely based on the myths of the Empyrean Isles, and they are designed to push the limits of the band and of hard bop. Even "Cantaloupe Island," well known for its funky piano riff, takes chances and doesn't just ride the groove. "The Egg," with its minimal melody and extended solo improvisations, is the riskiest number on the record, but it works because each musician spins inventive, challenging solos that defy convention. In comparison, "One Finger Snap" and "Oliloqui Valley" (alternate takes of both tracks are included as bonuses on the CD reissue) adhere to hard bop conventions, but each song finds the quartet vigorously searching for new sonic territory with convincing fire. That passion informs all of *Empyrean Isles,* a record that officially established Hancock as a major artist in his own right. *—Stephen Thomas Erlewine*

★ **Maiden Voyage** / May 17, 1965 / Blue Note ✦✦✦✦✦
Less overtly adventurous than its predecessor, *Empyrean Isles, Maiden Voyage* nevertheless finds Herbie Hancock at a creative peak. In fact, it's arguably his finest record of the '60s, reaching a perfect balance between accessible, lyrical jazz and chance-taking hard bop. By this point, the pianist had been with Miles Davis for two years, and it's clear that Miles' subdued yet challenging modal experiments had been fully integrated by Hancock. Not only that, but through Davis, Hancock became part of the exceptional rhythm section of bassist Ron Carter and drummer Tony Williams, who are both featured on *Maiden Voyage,* along with trumpeter Freddie Hubbard and tenor saxophonist George Coleman. The quintet plays a selection of five Hancock originals, many of which are simply superb showcases for the group's provocative, unpredictable solos, tonal textures and harmonies. While the quintet takes risks, the music is lovely and accessible, thanks to Hancock's understated, melodic compositions and the tasteful group interplay. All of the elements blend together to make *Maiden Voyage* a shimmering, beautiful album that captures Hancock at his finest as a leader, soloist and composer. *—Stephen Thomas Erlewine*

Speak Like a Child / Mar. 6, 1968+Mar. 9, 1968 / Blue Note ✦✦✦✦✦
Between 1965's *Maiden Voyage* and 1968's *Speak Like a Child,* Herbie Hancock was consumed with his duties as part of the Miles Davis Quintet, who happened to be at their creative and popular peak during those three years. When Hancock did return to a leadership position on *Speak Like a Child,* it was clear that he had assimilated not only the group's experiments, but also many ideas Miles initially sketched out with Gil Evans. Like *Maiden Voyage,* the album is laidback, melodic and quite beautiful, but there are noticeable differences between the two records. Hancock's melodies and themes have become simpler and more memorable, particularly on the title track, but that hasn't cut out room for improvisation. Instead, he has found a balance between accessible themes and searching improvisations that work a middle ground between post-bop and rock. Similarly, the horns and reeds are unconventional. He has selected three parts—Thad Jones' flugelhorn, Peter Phillips' bass trombone, Jerry Dodgion's alto flute—with unusual voicings, and he uses them for tonal texture and melodic statements, not solos. The rhythm section of bassist Ron Carter and drummer Mickey Roker keeps things light, subtle, and forever shifting, emphasizing the hybrid nature of Hancock's original compositions. But the key to *Speak Like a Child* is in Hancock's graceful, lyrical playing and compositions, which are lovely on the surface and provocative and challenging upon closer listening. *—Stephen Thomas Erlewine*

The Prisoner / Apr. 18, 1969-Apr. 23, 1969 / Blue Note ✦✦✦
As one of the first albums Herbie Hancock recorded after departing Miles Davis' quintet in 1968, as well as his final album for Blue Note, *The Prisoner* is one of Hancock's most ambitious efforts. Assembling a nonet that features Joe Henderson (tenor sax, alto flute), Johnny Coles (flugelhorn), Garnett Brown (trombone), Buster Williams (bass), and Albert "Tootie" Heath (drums), he has created his grandest work since *My Point of View.* Unlike that effort, *The Prisoner* has a specific concept—it's a tribute to Dr. Martin Luther King, evoking his spirit and dreams through spacious, exploratory post-bop. Often, the music doesn't follow conventional patterns, but that doesn't mean that it's alienating or inaccessible. It is certainly challenging, but Hancock's compositions (and his arrangement of Charles Williams' "Firewater") have enough melody and space to allow listeners into the album. Throughout the record, Hancock, Coles, and Henderson exchange provocative, unpredictable solos that build upon the stark melodies and sober mood of the music. The tone is not of sorrow or celebration, but of reflection and contemplation, and on that level, *The Prisoner* succeeds handsomely, even if the music meanders a little too often to be judged a complete success. *—Stephen Thomas Erlewine*

Mwandishi: The Complete Warner Bros. Recordings / Oct. 4, 1969-Feb. 17, 1972 / Warner Archives ✦✦✦✦✦
This two-CD set reissues the complete contents of three LPs: *Fat Albert Rotunda, Mwandishi,* and *Crossings.* The earliest session (extensions of generally memorable funk themes used in a Bill Cosby cartoon) features the keyboardist in a sextet on most selections with tenor saxophonist Joe Henderson, trumpeter Johnny Coles, and trombonist Garnett Brown; two songs use a 15-piece group. However, the bulk of this set showcases Hancock's regular sextet of the era (which was comprised of trumpeter Eddie Henderson; Benny Maupin on bass clarinet, alto flute, and soprano; trombonist Julian Priester; bassist Buster Williams; and drummer Billy Hart); the later session also adds Patrick Gleeson's Moog synthesizer. *Mwandishi* and *Crossings* are explorative and loosely funky, avant-garde yet influenced by rock and funk. The results are often quite fascinating, but this group (which only recorded one further album for Columbia) was a commercial flop, which Hancock would eventually break up in favor of the Headhunters. *—Scott Yanow*

Sextant / 1972 / Columbia/Legacy ✦✦✦

★ **Head Hunters** / 1973 / Columbia/Legacy ✦✦✦✦✦
Head Hunters was a pivotal point in Herbie Hancock's career, bringing him into the vanguard of jazz fusion. Hancock had pushed avant-garde boundaries on his own albums and with Miles Davis, but he had never devoted himself to the groove as he did on *Head Hunters.* Drawing heavily from Sly Stone, Curtis Mayfield, and James Brown, Hancock developed deeply funky, even gritty, rhythms over which he soloed on electric synthesizers, bringing the instrument to the forefront in jazz. It had all of the sensibilities of jazz, particularly in the way it wound off into long improvisations, but its rhythms were firmly planted in funk, soul,

and R&B, giving it a mass appeal that made it the biggest-selling jazz album of all time (a record which was later broken). Jazz purists, of course, decried the experiments at the time, but *Head Hunters* still sounds fresh and vital two decades after its initial release, and its genre-bending proved vastly influential on not only jazz, but funk, soul, and hip-hop. —*Stephen Thomas Erlewine*

Thrust / 1974 / Columbia/Legacy ✦✦✦✦
The follow-up to the breakthrough Headhunters album was virtually as good as its wildly successful predecessor: an earthy, funky, yet often harmonically and rhythmically sophisticated tour de force. There is only one change in the Headhunters lineup—swapping drummer Harvey Mason for Mike Clark—and the switch results in grooves that are even more complex. Hancock continues to reach into the rapidly changing high-tech world for new sounds, most notably the metallic sheen of the then-new ARP string synthesizer which was already becoming a staple item on pop and jazz-rock records. Again, there are only four long tracks, three of which ("Palm Grease," "Actual Proof," "Spank-A-Lee") concentrate on the funk, with plenty of Hancock's wah-wah clavinet, synthesizer textures and effects, and electric piano ruminations that still venture beyond the outer limits of post-bop. The change-of-pace is one of Hancock's loveliest electric pieces, "Butterfly," a match for any tune he's written before or since, with shimmering synth textures and Bennie Maupin soaring on soprano (Hancock would re-record it 20 years later on *Dis Is Da Drum*, but this is the one to hear). This supertight jazz-funk quintet album still sounds invigorating a quarter of a century later. —*Richard S. Ginell*

Flood / Jun. 28, 1975-Jul. 1, 1975 / Columbia ✦✦✦✦
Herbie and the Headhunters take to the road in this live double album, recorded and released only in Japan. Contrary to the impression left by his American releases at this time, Hancock was still very much attached to the acoustic piano, as his erudite opening workout on "Maiden Voyage/Actual Proof" with his funk rhythm section makes clear. The electric keyboards, mostly Rhodes piano and clavinet, make their first appearances on Side 2, where Hancock now becomes more of a funky adjunct to the rhythm section, bumping along with a superb feeling for the groove while Bennie Maupin takes the high road above on a panoply of winds. Except for "Voyage," the tunes come from the *Head Hunters*, *Thrust* and *Man-Child* albums (another reason why this was not released in the U.S.). "Chameleon" comes with a lengthy outbreak of machine pink noise that attests to Hancock's wide-eyed love of gadgetry. In all, this was a great funk band, not all that danceable because of the rapid complexities of Mike Clark's drumming, and quite often, full of harmonic depth and adventure. —*Richard S. Ginell*

V.S.O.P.: The Quintet / Jul. 16, 1977-Jul. 18, 1977 / Columbia ✦✦✦✦
With the cheers and huzzahs from their 1976 one-off reunion still resounding, the reconstituted Miles Davis Quintet minus Miles went on the road in 1977, spreading their 1965-vintage gospel according to the Prince Of Darkness to audiences in Berkeley and San Diego, California. In doing so, Herbie Hancock, Wayne Shorter, Ron Carter, and Tony Williams, plus interloper Freddie Hubbard seem to pick up where they left off, with repertoire mostly new to the five collectively and developed from there. It isn't exactly the same—you miss Miles' brooding presence and sense of space in Hubbard's busy, fiery playing, and Hancock is a more harmonically daring, assertive player than he was with Miles—but the interlocking telepathy and individual virtuosity of the musicians is pretty amazing. This also isn't the best tape from the tour; they were even tighter and more volatile in Japan five days later on Sony's *Tempest in the Colosseum*. The *V.S.O.P.* tours amount to a pit stop in the general shape of Hancock's evolution but their influence upon the direction of jazz as a whole in the '80s and '90s would be staggering. —*Richard S. Ginell*

An Evening with Herbie Hancock and Chick Corea in Concert / Feb. 1978 / Columbia ✦✦✦✦

Future Shock / 1983 / Columbia/Legacy ✦✦✦
Herbie Hancock completely overhauled his sound and conquered MTV with his most radical step forward since the sextet days. He brought in Bill Laswell of Material as producer, along with Grand Mixer D.ST on turntables—and the immediate result was "Rockit," which makes quite a post-industrial metallic racket. Frankly, the whole record is an enigma; for all of its dehumanized, mechanized textures and rigid rhythms, it has a vitality and sense of humor that make it difficult to turn off. Moreover, Herbie can't help but inject a subversive funk element when he comps along to the techno beat—and yes, some real, honest-to-goodness jazz licks on a grand piano show up in the middle of "Auto Drive." —*Richard S. Ginell*

Sound-System / 1984 / Columbia/Legacy ✦✦✦
In the grand tradition of sequels, *Sound-System* picks up from where *Future Shock* left off—if anything, even louder and more bleakly industrial than before (indeed, "Hardrock" is "Rockit" with a heavier rock edge). Yet Hancock's experiments with techno-pop were leading him in the general direction of Africa, explicitly so with the addition of the Gambian multi-instrumentalist Foday Musa Suso on half of the tracks. "Junku," written for the 1984 Olympic Games with Suso's electrified kora in the lead, is the transition track that stands halfway between "Rockit" and Hancock's mid-'80s Afro-jazz fusions. Also, "Karabali" features an old cohort, the squealing Wayne Shorter on soprano sax. Despite succumbing a bit to the overwhelming demand for more "Rockits," Hancock's electric music still retained its adventurous edge. —*Richard S. Ginell*

Dis Is Da Drum / 1993-1994 / Mercury ✦✦✦✦

New Standard / 1995 / Verve ✦✦✦✦

Gershwin's World / Mar. 1998-Jun. 1998 / Verve ✦✦✦✦✦

The Best of Herbie Hancock: The Hits / Feb. 8, 2000 / Columbia/Legacy ✦✦✦✦

Roy Hargrove

b. Oct. 16, 1969, Waco, TX
Trumpet / M-Base, Hard Bop
Roy Hargrove is a hard bop-oriented Young Lion who has a great deal of potential. A fine straightahead player who does not sound overly influenced by any of his predecessors, Hargrove's fiery solos resulted in him winning the *Downbeat* Readers' Poll in 1995. He met Wynton Marsalis in 1987 when the trumpeter visited his high school and impressed Marsalis, who let him sit in with his band. With the help of Wynton, Hargrove was soon playing with major players including Bobby Watson, Ricky Ford, Carl Allen and in the group Superblue. Hargrove attended Berklee (1988-89) and in 1990 released his first of four recordings for Novus; he was 20 at the time. He has been touring ever since with his own group which for several years including Antonio Hart. In addition to Novus, Hargrove has recorded for Verve and as a sideman with quite a few notables including Sonny Rollins, James Clay, Frank Morgan and Jackie McLean plus the group Jazz Futures. His Verve album roster includes 1995's *Family* and *Parker's Mood*. *Moment To Moment* followed five years later. —*Scott Yanow*

• **With the Tenors of Our Time** / Dec. 18, 1993-Jan. 17, 1994 / Verve ✦✦✦✦✦
Trumpeter Roy Hargrove has the opportunity of a lifetime on this recording, sharing separate songs with five great tenors: Johnny Griffin, Joe Henderson, Branford Marsalis, Joshua Redman and Stanley Turrentine. Everyone fares well, including Hargrove's group (Ron Blake on tenor and soprano, pianist Cyrus Chestnut, bassist Rodney Whitaker and drummer Gregory Hutchinson). The young trumpeter (who is vying for Lee Morgan's unoccupied chair) keeps up with the saxophonists on this generally relaxed affair; recommended for hard bop fans. —*Scott Yanow*

Family / Jan. 26, 1995-Jan. 29, 1995 / Verve ✦✦✦✦

Parker's Mood / Apr. 12, 1995-Apr. 14, 1995 / Verve ✦✦✦✦
On this unusual album, Roy Hargrove (trumpet, flugelhorn), Christian McBride (bass) and Stephen Scott (piano) pay homage to the father of bebop with a generous set of (mostly) Charlie Parker compositions performed in trio, duet and solo arrangements. These three musicians, all of whom are part of the back-to-bop youth movement and all of whom have made names for themselves as session players and fledgling bandleaders, approach the tunes with a combination of reverence and iconoclastic innovation—how often do you think you'll hear "Red Cross" as a bass solo or "Chasin' the Bird" as a trumpet/bass duet? This approach has its limitations, of course; as revealing as Hargrove's solo take on "Dewey Square" is, sometimes the weight of rhythmic responsibility weighs too heavily on McBride's shoulders during the trio numbers, and the groove suffers. Unless you're listening on headphones or in a quiet room with very good speakers, the rhythmic thread of the bassline can easily get lost in the mix, leaving Scott's syncopated comping sounding disjointed. But it doesn't happen very often, and the overall effect of this album is one of new light being shed on an aging but beautiful art collection. Those who know these tunes already will enjoy the album most. Those who don't will find they have much to learn, and should be excited at the prospect. —*Rick Anderson*

Habana / Jan. 5, 1997+Jan. 6, 1997 / Verve ✦✦✦✦
At last, this highly touted, heretofore conservative Young Lion makes his move beyond neo-bop toward something new, fresh and potentially important. He had to go to Havana to find it, starting with some jam sessions with Cuba's Los Van Van dance band in February 1996, which led to the formation of an exciting ten-piece U.S./Cuban band called Crisol. True, this album is a somewhat subdued recorded debut; as heard at the Playboy Jazz Festival in June 1997, Crisol is obviously capable of real thermal combustion. But one can still hear the embryo of its complex fusion of Afro-Cuban rhythm, bop and progressive jazz impulses on this disc. Hargrove himself still seems dazzled by his new discovery, groping a bit for direction in his own solos. But challenged by the asymmetrical rhythms, he takes more chances and jaggedly strikes some fire. Irakere's Chucho Valdes, an awesome pianist and progressive-minded musician, is one of the anchors of the band, and Russell Malone contributes some of his meatiest, most driven guitar work. The tune that remains most indelibly in the memory is trombonist Frank Lacy's "O My Seh Yeh," which opens and closes the CD in neat, bookended fashion. But the most promising track is a smoking arrangement of Kenny Dorham's "Afrodisia," where the heat of this crosscultural exchange rises well above room temperature. One can only hope that U.S. and Cuban politicos will forego their usual roadblocks and allow these meetings to continue. —*Richard S. Ginell*

Joe Harriott

b. Jul. 15, 1928, Kingston, Jamaica, **d.** Jan. 2, 1973, London, England
Sax (Alto) / Avant-Garde Jazz, Post-Bop
Joe Harriott's music goes virtually unheard today, yet the alto saxophonist exerted a powerful influence on early free jazz in England. The Jamaican-born and raised Harriott played with his countrymen, trumpeter Dizzy Reece and tenor saxophonist Wilton "Bogey" Gaynair, before emigrating to England in 1951. In London, Harriott worked freelance and in the band of trumpeter Pete Pitterson. In 1954, he landed an important gig with drummer Tony Kinsey; the next year he played in saxophonist Ronnie Scott's big band. His first album as a leader was 1959's *Southern Horizon*. Originally a bop-oriented player, Harriott gradually grew away from the conventions of that style. During a 1960 hospital stay, Harriott envisaged a new method of improvisation that, to an extent, paralleled the innovations of Ornette Coleman. Harriott was initially branded a mere imitator of Coleman, but close listening to both men reveals distinct differences in their respective styles. Harriott manifested a more explicit philosophical connection with bebop, for one thing, and his music was more concerned with ensemble interaction than was Coleman's early work. The 1960 album *Free Form*, which included trumpeter Shake Keane, pianist Pat Smythe, bassist Coleridge Goode, and drummer Phil Seaman, illustrated Harriott's new techniques. Beginning in 1965, he began fusing jazz with various types of world folk musics. He collaborated with Indian musician John Mayer on a record—1967's *Indo-Jazz Suite*—that utilized modal and free jazz procedures. The album's traditional jazz quintet instrumentation was augmented by a violin, sitar, tambura, and tabla. Harriott's recorded output was scarce, and virtually none of it remains in print. —*Chris Kelsey*

• **Southern Horizons** / May 5, 1959-Apr. 21, 1960 / Jazzland ✦✦✦✦

Free Form / Nov. 1960 / Jazzland ✦✦✦✦
The few recordings of Jamaican born saxophonist Joe Harriott have been hard to come by

since they were initially released in the early '60s. One of the most famous is *Free Form,* recorded in London and released in 1960. Comparable to Ornette Coleman's recordings of the period, these eight pieces incorporate Harriott's hard bop influence, cutting through adventurous compositions including "Abstract," "Straight Lines," and "Impression." When listening to *Free Form* (or early Coleman for that matter) with a 21st century perspective, it's hard to imagine that this music was often considered intolerable upon release. It's unfortunate that Harriott and trumpeter/flügelhornist Shane Keane missed out on being as widely lauded as Coleman and Don Cherry finally became. In 1999 tenor saxophonist Ken Vandermark attempted to spotlight that ill-fated situation by releasing a disc of Harriott compositions, including three from *Free Form,* on his 1999 release *Straight Lines.* —*Al Campbell*

Abstract / Nov. 22, 1961-May 5, 1962 / Columbia ♦♦♦
Altoist Joe Harriott, whose fairly free jazz in the early '60s was sometimes a little reminiscent of both Ornette Coleman and Charles Mingus, was one of the most advanced jazz musicians then working in England. This out of print LP (none of Harriott's recordings are easily available in the 1990s) features Harriott and his quintet (which consists of trumpeter Shake Keane, pianist Pat Smythe, bassist Coleridge Goode, either Bobby Orr or Phil Seamen on drums, and, on a couple tunes, Frank Holder on bongos). They perform seven of the leader's originals and "Oleo," and the music is consistently unpredictable, although not afraid to swing hard in spots. A reappraisal and rediscovery of Joe Harriott is long overdue. —*Scott Yanow*

Indo-Jazz Suite / Oct. 10, 1966 / Atlantic ♦♦♦♦

Eddie Harris

b. Oct. 20, 1934, Chicago, IL, **d.** Nov. 5, 1996, Los Angeles, CA
Sax (Tenor) / Hard Bop, Soul-Jazz, Jazz-Funk
Eddie Harris had a diverse and erratic recording career, leading to many observers greatly underrating his jazz talents. Harris had his own sound on tenor since at least 1960, his improvisations range from bop to free, he was a pioneer with utilizing the electric sax (and was much more creative on it than most who followed), he introduced the reed trumpet, was a fine pianist (one of his first professional jobs was playing piano with Gene Ammons), composed the standard "Freedom Jazz Dance" and, although his vocals are definitely an acquired taste, he was a skilled comedian.

After getting out of the military, Eddie Harris's very first recording resulted in a hit version of "Exodus." His high-note tenor playing (which managed to sound comfortable in the range of an alto or even soprano) was well-featured on a series of strong selling Vee Jay releases (1961-63). After two outings for Columbia (1964), he switched to Atlantic for a decade. In 1966 Harris started utilizing an electric sax and he debuted the popular "Listen Here" (although the 1967 recording is better-known). At the 1969 Montreux Jazz Festival Harris and Les McCann made for a very appealing combination, recording such songs as "Compared to What" and "Cold Duck Time." Harris's later output for Atlantic was streaky, sometimes rock-oriented and occasionally pure comedy. Later in life he recorded generally recorded strong jazz sets for such labels as Impulse, Enja and SteepleChase while remaining a unique musical personality. —*Scott Yanow*

☆ **Exodus to Jazz** / Jan. 17, 1961 / Vee-Jay ♦♦♦♦♦
This reissue of tenor saxophonist Eddie Harris's debut as a leader brings back his hit recording of "Exodus" (here heard in both the single and the full-length versions) and a variety of appealing originals. Harris, whose impressive range often puts him in the alto (and even soprano) register, was distinctive from the start. Joined by a fine Chicago-based quintet that also features pianist Willie Pickens and guitarist Joe Diorio, Harris in top form on this classic session. —*Scott Yanow*

● **The Artist's Choice: The Eddie Harris Anthology** / Jan. 1961-Feb. 20, 1977 / Rhino ♦♦♦♦♦
Eddie Harris' tenure at Atlantic in the 1960s and '70s was his most productive, but until recently it was represented only by a pair of single album collections. Now, a fine two-disc anthology containing selections chosen by Harris and his comments fully cover his Atlantic years. The discs include his huge singles "Exodus" and "Love Theme From *The Sandpiper* (Shadow Of Your Smile)," plus soul/jazz numbers like "Get On Down," "Funkaroma" and "1974 Blues," his most famous single composition, "Freedom Jazz Dance," and his remakes of "Giant Steps" and "Love For Sale." Harris has creatively utilized the varitone attachment on his saxophone and the reed trumpet, while constructing and playing his blues, soul and funk solos with zest and a minimum of gimmickry. —*Ron Wynn*

For Bird to Bags / 1965 / Koch Jazz ♦♦♦♦
It is only right that tenor-saxophonist Eddie Harris recorded for the Exodus label at least on one occasion, since that was the name of his first hit. Most unusual among the selections is "Salute to Bird" (on which Harris quotes many Charlie Parker tunes) and "Salute to Bags" (during which the leader switches to piano). Harris plays with a Chicago-based quintet featuring Charles Stephney on vibes and piano; guitarist Roland Faulkner; pianist Willie Pickens; and guitarist Joe Diorio (the last two of which were on the artist's earlier records) make guest appearances. Throughout, Harris (whose mastery of the extreme upper register and immediately recognizable sound are both quite impressive) is in excellent form; pity that this music was last available on a long out-of-print LP. —*Scott Yanow*

The In Sound/Mean Greens / Aug. 9, 1965-Jun. 7, 1966 / Rhino ♦♦♦♦♦
This CD from Rhino's valuable Atlantic reissue program combines together two former LPs from thge 1965-67 period. *The In Sound* is among tenor-saxophonist Eddie Harris's most significant recordings, highlighted by the original version of his "Freedom Jazz Dance," and including a memorable rendition of "The Shadow of Your Smile," three standards and a blues. Harris is assisted by an all-star rhythm section (pianist Cedar Walton, bassist Ron Carter and drummer Billy Higgins) and, on three selections, trumpeter Roy Codrington. The lesser-known *Mean Greens* set (comprised entirely of originals except for Harris's high-note treatment of "It Was a Very Good Year") utilizes the same personnel on the first four numbers and is just as exciting with the calypso "Yeah Yeah Yeah" being a highpoint. The final three performances are more unusual for Harris switches to electric piano and jams with a Latin rhythm section; included is the original (and somewaht obscure) recording of "Listen Here" which predates his hit version by over a year. Overall this CD is a well-rounded and highly recommended set. —*Scott Yanow*

☆ **The "In" Sound** / Aug. 30, 1965 / Atlantic ♦♦♦♦♦
This is one of Eddie Harris' great records and fortunately all of the music from the LP has returned as part of a reissue in the Rhino/Atlantic CD series (combined with Harris' *Mean Greens* date). The underrated but popular tenor-saxophonist introduces his standard "Freedom Jazz Dance," plays one of the earlier versions of "The Shadow of Your Smile," romps on "Love for Sale" and "'S Wonderful," and also performs "Born to Be Blue" and his own "Cryin' Blues." Harris is heard in prime form in a quartet/quintet with pianist Cedar Walton, bassist Ron Carter, drummer Billy Higgins, and sometimes trumpeter Ray Codrington. A gem. —*Scott Yanow*

The Electrifying Eddie Harris/Plug Me In / Apr. 20, 1967-Mar. 15, 1968 / Rhino ♦♦♦♦♦
This CD combines two fine Harris dates from 1967 and 1968. *The Electrifying Eddie Harris* had bluesy, soulful examples of Harris on baritone sax. "Listen Here" ranked second only to "Freedom Jazz Dance" among his most popular compositions, while he stretched out on "Spanish Bull." "Theme In Search Of A Movie," "Sham Time" and "Judie's Theme" were good-time concessions to pop and jazz-soul audiences, yet still retained some fiber and spark. Once more, Harris found a good compromise between artistic and commercial concerns, although this date was more weighted toward funk and pop. —*Ron Wynn*

Second Movement / 1971 / Label M. ♦♦♦♦
Eddie Harris and Les McCann's *Second Movement* is the second and last duet recording by Harris and McCann, and the follow-up to their 1969 "live" recording *Swiss Movement.* It is among the series from Label M which launched its reissue series from the Atlantic Records' archives in November 2000. The tenor saxophonist and the vocalist and pianist display their brand of showmanship and musicality that rivaled such great pairings as Johnny Griffin and Eddie "Lockjaw" Davis, Shirley Scott and Stanley Turrentine, or Sonny Stitt and Gene Ammons. This CD is a \soul/jazz \funk workout and features great technology that emphasizes one of their best songs, "Shorty Rides Again."These technological enhancements add to the explosive chemistry of McCann and Harris as well as waking up the resonance and excitement inherent in the compositions, vocals of Cissy Houston, and the extended vamps ignited by Harris on electric sax. The original album released in 1971 was panned by critics for abandoning straight-ahead \jazz for commercial, experimental for self-indulgent purposes, however, when measured by 21st century standards, this CD is a gem that continues to inspire a new generation of \soul/jazz musicians. —*Paula Edelstein*

There Was a Time (Echo of Harlem) / May 9, 1990 / Enja ♦♦♦♦♦
Eddie Harris, famous as the master of the electrified sax and for his brand of funky jazz, sticks exclusively to acoustic straightahead music on this rewarding Enja CD. With assistance from pianist Kenny Barron, bassist Cecil McBee and drummer Ben Riley, Harris is heard in peak form on such songs as "Love Letters," "Autumn in New York," "The Song Is You" and a lengthy "Harlem Nocturne." Although Harris has maintained a fairly low profile during the past decade, he is still playing in his prime as this highly recommended CD demonstrates. —*Scott Yanow*

Gene Harris

b. Sep. 1, 1933, Benton Harbor, MI, **d.** Jan. 16, 2000
Piano / Hard Bop, Fusion, Soul-Jazz
One of the most accessible of all jazz pianists, Gene Harris's soulful style (influenced by Oscar Peterson and containing the bluesiness of a Junior Mance) was immediately likable and predictably excellent. After playing in an Army band (1951-54), he formed a trio with bassist Andy Simpkins and drummer Bill Dowdy which was by 1956 known as the Three Sounds. The group was quite popular and recorded regularly during 1956-70 for Blue Note and Verve. Although the personnel changed and the music became more R&B-oriented in the early '70s, Harris retained the Three Sounds name for his later Blue Note sets. He retired to Boise, ID, in 1977 and was largely forgotten when Ray Brown persuaded him to return to the spotlight in the early '80s. Harris worked for a time with the Ray Brown Trio and led his own quartets in the years to follow, recording regularly for Concord and heading the Phillip Morris Superband on a few tours; 1998's *Tribute to Count Basie* even earned a Grammy nomination. While awaiting a kidney transplant, he died January 16, 2000 at the age of 66. —*Scott Yanow*

● **Introducing the Three Sounds** / Sep. 16, 1958-Sep. 18, 1958 / Blue Note ♦♦♦♦♦

Live at the It Club / Mar. 6, 1970 / Blue Note ♦♦♦
Recorded in 1970 but not released until 1996, *Live At the "It Club"* shows the Three Sounds pulling out funky, gritty rhythms out of their basic bluesy hard-bop sound. The group's funky influences are most noticeable in the rhythm section of drummer Carl Burnette and bassist Henry Franklin, who had been playing with Harris for only a short time when this set was recorded. The rhythm section pushes Harris, making the music loose and swinging—the groove matters more than anything on the album. Occasionally, the energy of the Three Sounds lags, but *Live at the "It Club"* is an enjoyable piece of grooving soul-jazz. —*Stephen Thomas Erlewine*

In a Special Way / Mar. 29, 1976-Apr. 7, 1976 / Blue Note ♦♦

The Gene Harris Trio Plus One / Nov. 19, 1985-Dec. 1985 / Concord Jazz ♦♦♦

Tribute to Count Basie / Mar. 1987-Jun. 1987 / Concord Jazz ♦♦♦

Listen Here! / Mar. 1989 / Concord Jazz ♦♦♦♦♦
Although often associated with the blues, only one of the ten selections on this quartet set by pianist Gene Harris (who is joined by guitarist Ron Eschete, bassist Ray Brown and drummer Jeff Hamilton) is technically a blues. An excellent all-around showcase for the soulful pianist, Harris sounds in prime form exploring such tunes as "This Masquerade," "Don't Be That Way," Eddie Harris' "Listen Here" and "The Song Is Ended." This CD gives listeners a pretty definitive look at Gene Harris' accessible and swinging style. —*Scott Yanow*

At Last / May 1990 / Concord Jazz ✦✦✦✦✦
A wonderful teamup of Gene Harris with Scott Hamilton. *—Ron Wynn*

Black and Blue / Jun. 29, 1991 / Concord Jazz ✦✦✦✦
Although there are few actual blues on this CD, pianist Gene Harris gives all of the songs (whether complex standards, ballads or near-blues) a bluesy feel, adding soul and a church feeling to each of the melodies. With the assistance of guitarist Ron Eschete, bassist Luther Hughes and drummer Harold Jones, Harris is in typically fine form. *—Scott Yanow*

Brotherhood / Aug. 4, 1992-Aug. 5, 1992 / Concord Jazz ✦✦✦✦✦

In His Hands / Dec. 9, 1996+Dec. 10, 1996 / Concord Jazz ✦✦✦

Down Home Blues / Dec. 11, 1996-Dec. 12, 1996 / Concord Jazz ✦✦✦

Alley Cats / Oct. 12, 1999 / Concord Jazz ✦✦✦✦
Too many artists have gone their entire careers without providing any live albums, but that hasn't been a problem for Gene Harris whose live recordings from the 1980s and 1990s ranged from unaccompanied solo piano to big-band dates. Arguably, the best live album he gave listeners in the 1990s was *Alley Cats;* recorded live at *Jazz Alley* in Seattle on December 11-12, 1998, this CD finds Harris' working quintet (Harris on piano, Frank Potenza on guitar, Luther Hughes on bass, and Paul Kreibich on drums) joined by such accomplished soloists as Red Hollywood (tenor sax), Ernie Watts (alto and tenor sax), and Jack McDuff (organ). Many inspired moments occur, and a 65-year-old Harris really goes that extra mile on gems ranging from Nat Adderley's "Jive Samba" and Benny Golson's "Blues March" to Joe Sample's "Put It Where You Want It" (which, in the 1970s, was introduced by the Crusaders before being covered by the Average White Band). A talented but underexposed singer (underexposed in the 1990s, anyway) who has recorded R&B albums but is quite capable of handling jazz, Harris' daughter Niki Harris is featured on earthy performances of "You've Changed," "Please Give Me Someone to Love," and "Guess Who." McDuff, meanwhile, brings his gritty, down-home Hammond B-3 to two songs: Eddie Harris' "Listen Here" and Gene Harris' "Walkin' With Zach." Soul-jazz enthusiasts will definitely want this excellent CD. *—Alex Henderson*

Hampton Hawes

b. Nov. 13, 1928, Los Angeles, CA, **d.** May 22, 1977, Los Angeles, CA
Keyboards, Piano / Crossover Jazz, Hard Bop, Bop
Hampton Hawes was one of the finest jazz pianists of the 1950s, a fixture on the Los Angeles scene who brought his own interpretations to the dominant Bud Powell style. In the mid-to-late '40s he played with Sonny Criss, Dexter Gordon and Wardell Gray among others on Central Avenue. He was with Howard McGhee's band (1950-51), played with Shorty Rogers and the Lighthouse All-Stars, served in the Army (1952-54) and then led trios in the L.A. area, recording many albums for Contemporary. Arrested for heroin possession in 1958, Hawes spent five years in prison until he ws pardoned by President Kennedy. He led trios for the remainder of his life, using electric piano (which disturbed his longtime fans) for a period in the early-to-mid-'70s but returning to acoustic piano before dying from a stroke in 1977. Hampton Hawes's memoirs *Raise Up off Me* (1974) are both frank and memorable and most of his records (for Xanadu, Prestige, Savoy, Contemporary, Black Lion and Freedom) are currently available. *—Scott Yanow*

The Everybody Likes Hampton Hawes, Vols. 1-3: The Trio / Jun. 28, 1955-Jan. 25, 1956 / Contemporary/OJC ✦✦✦
An essential set of powerhouse mid-50s trio works with Hawes, Red Mitchell (b), and Chuck Thompson (d). *—Ron Wynn*

Hampton Hawes Trio, Vol. 1 / Jun. 28, 1955 / Contemporary/OJC ✦✦✦✦✦
The first of pianist Hampton Hawes' long string of Contemporary recordings (which, as with most of his output for that label, has been reissued on CD in the Original Jazz Classics series) features him in his early prime in a trio with bassist Red Mitchell and drummer Chuck Thompson. In addition to three of his basic originals, Hawes performs fresh and swinging versions of seven standards, making such overplayed tunes such as "I Got Rhythm," "What Is This Thing Called Love" and "All the Things You Are" really come alive. A gem, the first of many classic Hawes Contemporary dates. *—Scott Yanow*

All Night Session! Hampton Hawes Quartet, Vol. 2 / Dec. 3, 1955-Jan. 25, 1956 / Contemporary/OJC ✦✦✦✦
The second volume of mid-'50s trio sessions featuring pianist Hampton Hawes. He does moving ballads, reinterprets standards with elan, and pens originals that show his blues and gospel influence, while also exhibiting his voicings and fluidity. *—Ron Wynn*

All Night Session!, Vol. 1 / Nov. 12, 1956 / Contemporary/OJC ✦✦✦✦✦
The original recording of the first in a series of smashing 50s concerts. *—Ron Wynn*

★ **Four! Hampton Hawes!!!!** / Jan. 27, 1958 / Contemporary/OJC ✦✦✦✦✦
Pianist Hampton Hawes' 1950s recordings for the Contemporary label are at such a high level that they could all be given five stars. This outing with bassist Red Mitchell, drummer Shelly Manne and guitarist Barney Kessel (who is a slight wild card) is also quite successful. Two previously unreleased numbers ("Thou Swell" and "The Awful Truth") have been added to the CD reissue. Highlights of the exciting bop date include "Yardbird Suite," "There Will Never Be Another You" and "Love Is Just Around the Corner." *—Scott Yanow*

For Real! / Mar. 17, 1958 / Contemporary/OJC ✦✦✦✦
Although this was at least Hampton Hawes' 11th record as a leader, it was his first (and one of his relatively few) that included a horn player. The pianist matches quite well with the hard bop tenor of Harold Land (heard in his early prime), and the quartet outing, which also includes drummer Frank Butler, has an extra bonus in the playing of the brilliant bassist Scott LaFaro. Performing three bop standards (including "Crazeology") and three originals (two of which were co-written by Land), pianist Hawes sounds inspired by the other players and is in top form throughout the generally memorable outing. *—Scott Yanow*

The Green Leaves of Summer / Feb. 17, 1964 / Contemporary/OJC ✦✦✦✦✦
Pianist Hampton Hawes' first recording after serving five years in prison finds Hawes evolving a bit from a Bud Powell-influenced bop pianist to one familiar with more modern trends in jazz. Reissued on CD, this trio date finds Hawes interacting closely with bassist Monk Montgomery and drummer Steve Ellington (making his recording debut). Hawes had lost nothing of his swinging style while in prison, as can be heard on such numbers as "Vierd Blues," "St. Thomas" and "Secret Love," and he was just starting to hint at moving beyond bop. Recommended. *—Scott Yanow*

The Seance / Apr. 30, 1966-May 1, 1966 / Contemporary/OJC ✦✦✦✦✦
Hampton Hawes made many of his finest records for Lester Koenig's Contemporary label. His final sessions before choosing to freelance (he would rejoin Koenig during his last year) resulted in two live albums, both reissued on CD. Teamed up with bassist Red Mitchell and drummer Donald Bailey, Hawes displays the influence of the avant-garde in places, stretching out his improvisations a bit while still showing off his roots in bop. Both CDs are equal in value, and this particular set includes such highlights as "Oleo," "Easy Street" and "My Romance." *—Scott Yanow*

Coleman Hawkins

b. Nov. 21, 1904, St. Joseph, MO, **d.** May 19, 1969, New York, NY
Sax (Tenor) / Mainstream Jazz, Classic Jazz, Swing, Bop
Coleman Hawkins was the first important tenor saxophonist and he remains one of the greatest of all time. A consistently modern improviser whose knowledge of chords and harmonies was encyclopedic, Hawkins had a 40-year prime (1925-65) during which he could hold his own with any competitor. As a member of Fletcher Henderson's orchestra, Hawkins was already the top tenor in jazz by 1924, although his staccato runs and use of slap-tonguing sound quite dated today. However after Louis Armstrong joined Henderson later in the year, Hawkins learned from the cornetist's relaxed legato style and advanced quickly. By 1925 Hawkins was truly a major soloist and the following year his solo on "Stampede" became influential. Hawk (who doubled in early years on clarinet and bass sax) would be with Fletcher Henderson's Orchestra up to 1934 and during this time he was the obvious pacesetter among tenors. By 1934 Hawkins had moved to Europe, spending five years overseas and freelancing throughout the continent. Although by 1939 Lester Young had emerged with a totally new style on tenor, Hawkins showed that he was still a dominant force by winning a few heated jam sessions. His recording of "Body and Soul" that year became his most famous record. Some of his finest recordings were cut during the first half of the 1940s including a stunning quartet version of "The Man I Love." Although he was already a 20-year veteran, Hawkins encouraged the younger bop-oriented musicians and did not need to adjust his harmonically-advanced style in order to play with them. He used Thelonious Monk in his 1944 quartet, led the first official bop record session (which included Dizzy Gillespie and Don Byas), had Oscar Pettiford, Miles Davis and Max Roach as sidemen early in their careers, toured in California with a sextet featuring Howard McGhee and in 1946 utilized J.J. Johnson and Fats Navarro on record dates. By 1965 Hawkins was even showing the influence of John Coltrane in his explorative flights and seemed ageless. *—Scott Yanow*

★ **Body and Soul** / Oct. 11, 1939-Jul. 9, 1956 / RCA ✦✦✦✦✦
Ignoring past reissues (including a definitive two-CD set from 1995 that had 40 recordings), RCA came out with this 19-selection single CD in 1996; all of the performances were in the previous reissue. If found at a budget price, this CD can act as a fine introduction to the great tenor Coleman Hawkins. Among its highpoints are two very different versions of "Body and Soul," and classic renditions of "When Day Is Done," "The Sheik of Araby," and the modernistic "Half Step Down, Please," an appealing "I Love Paris" and a few numbers with strings and woodwinds. The music dates from 1939-40, 1946-47 and 1956 and is generally beyond criticism. *—Scott Yanow*

1939-1940 / Oct. 11, 1939-Aug. 9, 1940 / Classics ✦✦✦✦✦

☆ **Rainbow Mist** / Feb. 16, 1944-May 22, 1944 / Delmark ✦✦✦✦✦
Hawkins was always an open-minded musician. A very advanced player even when he first emerged with Fletcher Henderson's orchestra in the '20s, by the '40s he may have been technically middle-aged but remained a young thinker. For his recording session of February 16, 1944, the great tenor invited some of the most promising younger players (including trumpeter Dizzy Gillespie, bassist Oscar Pettiford and drummer Max Roach) and the result was the very first bebop on records. During their two sessions, the large ensemble recorded six selections including Gillespie's "Woody'n You," Hawk's "Disorder at the Border" and a new treatment of "Body and Soul" by the tenorman which he retitled "Rainbow Mist." Also on this highly recommended CD are four titles matching together the tenors of Hawkins, Ben Webster and Georgie Auld (with trumpeter Charlie Shavers included as a bonus) and a session from Auld's big band, highlighted by Sonny Berman's trumpet solo on "Taps Miller." *—Scott Yanow*

Bean and the Boys / Oct. 19, 1944-Dec. 21, 1949 / Prestige ✦✦✦✦✦
This LP (whose contents have been reissued in different settings on CD) features the always adventurous tenor saxophonist Coleman Hawkins with three different modern groups. The first four selections are the earliest studio recordings of pianist/composer Thelonious Monk, who was clearly happy to be performing in Hawkins' quartet. A date from Dec. 1946, matches Hawkins with such young modernists as trumpeter Fats Navarro, trombonist J.J. Johnson and vibraphonist Milt Jackson on intriguing versions of "I Mean You" and two versions of "Bean and the Boys," showing that Hawk was able to keep up with (and indeed master) the innovations of bebop. He is also heard on two ballad showcases and in a less memorable but still enjoyable 1949 date with a variety of French musicians, plus drummer Kenny Clarke, that is highlighted by a pair of blues. *—Scott Yanow*

Body and Soul Revisited / Oct. 19, 1951-Oct. 13, 1958 / Decca/GRP ✦✦✦
Hawkins had been the dominant tenor-saxophonist from the mid-'20s up until 1940, but even though he remained a major force, his influence was waning, due to the emergence of Lester Young and then Charlie Parker. By the early '50s he only recorded on an infrequent

basis. Fortunately a few years later (partly due to the rise of Sonny Rollins whose original hero was Hawk), his fortunes were on the rise again. This Decca CD contains quite a variety of music. There are ten selections of melodic "mood" music from 1951-53 in which Hawkins mostly sticks to the melody (an exception is an excellent version of "If I Could Be with You"). Then the great tenor is heard in an occasionally exciting session with Cozy Cole's All-Stars; cornetist Rex Stewart steals the show with a couple of colorful solos. The best music on this CD is taken from a 1955 radio broadcast in which Hawkins plays "Foolin' Around" (based on the chords of "Body and Soul") totally unaccompanied and roars on "The Man I Love." This set concludes with three selections (one previously unissued) from a fine session led by clarinetist Tony Scott. *—Scott Yanow*

The Hawk Flies High / Mar. 12, 1957-Mar. 15, 1957 / Riverside/OJC ♦♦♦♦♦
1957 was one of the great years for the veteran tenor-saxophonist (who was then 51); he suddenly became rediscovered, even though he had never suffered a period of decline. *The Hawk Flies High* found him playing mostly with bop-oriented musicians a couple decades his junior (including trombonist J.J. Johnson and trumpeter Idrees Sulieman) and more than holding his own. The memorable "Sanctity" has a particularly classic Hawkins solo but each of the six tracks are quite enjoyable. *—Scott Yanow*

Coleman Hawkins Encounters Ben Webster / Oct. 16, 1957 / Verve ♦♦♦♦
W/ Ben Webster. These aren't encounters in the confrontational sense, but a merger of great musical minds. *—Ron Wynn*

The Genius of Coleman Hawkins / Oct. 1957 / Verve ♦♦♦♦
Genius may not be the right word, but "brilliance" certainly fits. At the age of 51 in 1957 Hawkins had already been on records for 35 years and had been one of the leading tenors for nearly that long. This CD matches him with the Oscar Peterson Trio (plus drummer Alvin Stoller) for a fine runthrough on standards. Hawk plays quite well, although the excitement level does not reach the heights of his sessions with trumpeter Roy Eldridge. *—Scott Yanow*

Soul / Nov. 7, 1958 / Prestige/OJC ♦♦

Hawk Eyes / Apr. 3, 1959 / Prestige/OJC ♦♦♦♦
Tenor-great Coleman Hawkins tended to be at his best when challenged by another horn player. On this highly enjoyable CD, Hawkins is joined by the superb trumpeter Charlie Shavers and a strong rhythm section that includes guitarist Tiny Grimes and pianist Ray Bryant. With such superior songs as "Through for the Night," "I Never Knew" and "La Rosita," in addition to long jams, plenty of fireworks occur during this frequently exciting session. *—Scott Yanow*

With the Red Garland Trio / Aug. 12, 1959 / Swingville/OJC ♦♦♦

Coleman Hawkins All Stars / Jan. 8, 1960 / Prestige/OJC ♦♦♦

In a Mellow Tone / Dec. 30, 1960 / Prestige/OJC ♦♦♦♦♦
A superior session with Hawkins, Eddie "Lockjaw" Davis (ts), and others. *—Ron Wynn*

Night Hawk / Dec. 30, 1960 / Prestige/OJC ♦♦♦♦
Hawkins was one of the main inspirations of his fellow tenor Eddie "Lockjaw" Davis, so it was logical that they would one day meet up in the recording studio. This CD has many fine moments from these two highly competitive jazzmen, particularly the lengthy title cut and a heated tradeoff on "In a Mellow Tone," on which Davis goes higher but Hawkins wins on ideas. *—Scott Yanow*

Alive! / Aug. 13, 1962+Aug. 15, 1962 / Verve ♦♦♦♦♦
From the mid-'50s until Coleman Hawkins's death in 1969, the tenor-saxophonist frequently teamed up with trumpeter Roy Eldridge to form a potent team. However, Hawkins rarely met altoist Johnny Hodges on the bandstand, making this encounter a special event. Long versions of "Satin Doll," "Perdido" and "The Rabbit in Jazz" give these three classic jazzmen (who are ably assisted by the Tommy Flanagan Trio) chances to stretch out and inspire each other. The remainder of this CD has Eldridge and Hodges absent while Coleman Hawkins (on "new" versions of "Mack the Knife," "It's the Talk of the Town," "Bean and the Boys" and "Caravan") heads the quartet for some excellent playing. Timeless music played by some of the top veteran stylists of the swing era. *—Scott Yanow*

Duke Ellington Meets Coleman Hawkins / Aug. 18, 1962 / Impulse! ♦♦♦♦♦
This CD documents a historic occasion. Although Coleman Hawkins had been an admirer of Duke Ellington's music for at least 35 years at this point and Ellington had suggested they record together at least 20 years prior to their actual meeting in 1962, this was their first (and only) meeting on record. Although it would have been preferable to hear the great tenor performing with the full orchestra, his meeting with Ellington and an all-star group taken out of the big band does feature such greats as Ray Nance (on cornet and violin), trombonist Lawrence Brown, altoist Johnny Hodges, and baritonist Harry Carney. Highpoints include an exuberant "The Jeep Is Jumpin," an interesting remake of "Mood Indigo," and a few new Ellington pieces. This delightful music is recommended in one form or another. *—Scott Yanow*

Desafinado: Bossa Nova and Jazz Samba / Sep. 12, 1962+Sep. 17, 1962 / GRP/Impulse! ♦♦♦♦♦
This set seems to have the word "fad" written all over it, but surprisingly it is a major success. During the era when everyone was trying to cash in on the popularity of bossa nova, tenor-great Coleman Hawkins recorded eight selections with a group consisting of two guitars, bass and three percussionists. In addition to a classic version of "O Pato" and such typical songs as "Desafinado" and "One Note Samba," Hawkins and company even turn "I'm Looking over a Four Leaf Clover" into a strong bossa. *—Scott Yanow*

Tenor Giants / Nov. 10, 1938-Dec. 4, 1943 / GRP ♦♦♦♦♦
This reissue illustrates Hawkins' influence during the swing era by focusing on his work for Commodore in 1940 and 1943 as well as fellow tenor great Chu Berry's recordings for the same label in 1938 and 1941. (Berry certainly wasn't the only tenor man Hawkins influenced; his big, rugged tone had a direct or indirect influence on everyone from Illinois Jacquet, Ben Webster, and Willis Jackson to Sonny Rollins and Booker Ervin). Though Hawkins' influence on Berry is undeniable, Berry was quite recognizable himself—and his individuality shines through on this CD. Berry swings aggressively on "Sittin' In" and "46 West 52" in 1938 and "Blowin' Up a Breeze" on August 28, 1941 (only two months before he died in a car crash), while his ballad-playing on "Stardust" and "Body and Soul" is gorgeous and unapologetically romantic. Some jazz historians feel that Berry could be overly sentimental on ballads, but to this journalist, his playing was a soulful, lyrical delight. (Besides, there's no law stating that jazz has to be 100% intellect 100% of the time). Meanwhile, the Hawkins material comes from all-star sessions that Leonard Feather produced or co-produced; the 1943 session boasts such heavyweights as trumpeter Cootie Williams and pianist Art Tatum, while the 1940 date, billed as "Coleman Hawkins and the Chocolate Dandies," and finds trumpeter Roy Eldridge and alto saxophonist/clarinetist Benny Carter joining Hawkins on the front line. Hawkins and Carter were both part of the original Chocolate Dandies sessions of 1929-1930, and their rapport was equally strong in 1940. From the forceful to the romantic, *Tenor Giants* paints an impressive picture of both Hawkins and Berry. *—Alex Henderson*

Erskine Hawkins

b. Jul. 26, 1914, Birmingham, AL, **d.** Nov. 11, 1993, Willingboro, NJ
Trumpet / New York Blues, Jump Blues, Swing
A talented high-note trumpeter and a popular bandleader, Erskine Hawkins was nicknamed "The 20th Century Gabriel." He learned drums and trombone before switching to trumpet when he was 13. While attennding the Alabama State Teachers College, he became the leader of the college band, the 'Bama Street Collegians. They went to New York in 1934, became the Erskine Hawkins Orchestra, started making records in 1936 and by 1938 were quite successful. With Hawkins and Dud Bascomb sharing the trumpet solos, Paul Bascomb or Julian Dash heard on tenors, Haywood Henry on baritone and pianist Avery Parrish, this was a solidly swinging band that delighted dancers and jazz fans alike. Hawkins had three major hits ("Tuxedo Junction," "After Hours" and "Tippin' In") and was able to keep the big band together all the way until 1953; some of their later sessions were more R&B-oriented yet never without jazz interest. Hawkins led a smaller unit during his last few decades (the survivors of the big band had a recorded reunion in 1971) and the trumpeter kept on working into the 1980s. *—Scott Yanow*

1936-1938 / Jul. 20, 1936-Sep. 12, 1938 / Classics ♦♦♦♦♦
This excellent CD has the first 24 recordings by trumpeter Erskine Hawkins' Orchestra, which was originally known as the 'Bama State Collegians. From the start, Hawkins had his sound together, with such top soloists as Dud Bascomb and the leader on trumpets, either Paul Bascomb or Julian Dash on tenor, baritonist Haywood Henry, and pianist Avery Parrish. Although there are some vocals from James Morrison, Billie Daniels and Merle Turner, it is the many spirited instrumentals that made Hawkins' big band one of the most popular of the next decade. Among the highlights of this superior set are "Swinging In Harlem," "Uproar Shout," "I Found a New Baby" and "Rockin' Rollers' Jubilee." *—Scott Yanow*

1938-1939 / Sep. 12, 1938-Oct. 2, 1939 / Classics ♦♦♦♦♦
The second in the Classics label's reissuance of all of trumpeter/bandleader Erskine Hawkins' early recordings features the orchestra in its early prime. Although underrated in the history books, Hawkins led one of the finest big bands of the era. Among the more memorable selections in this consistently exciting set are "Weary Blues," "King Porter Stomp," "Swing Out," "Swingin' On Lenox Avenue," "Gin Mill Special," and the original version of "Tuxedo Junction." All of the CDs in the valuable series are highly recommended to swing collectors. *—Scott Yanow*

★ **The Original Tuxedo Junction** / Sep. 12, 1938-Jan. 10, 1945 / Bluebird/RCA ♦♦♦♦♦
This is an excellent one-CD sampler of the music of Erskine Hawkins' Orchestra. Although serious collectors will want to get the comprehensive Classics releases, this is a perfect place for more general listeners to begin. Hawkins' three biggest hits ("Tuxedo Junction," "After Hours," and "Tippin' In") lead off the set which otherwise has highlights from 1938-42. With the exception of 1945's "Tippin' In" (which features some memorable lead alto by Bobby Smith), all of Hawkins' key soloists are here, including the leader and Dud Bascomb on trumpets, either Paul Bascomb or Julian Dash on tenor, baritonist Haywood Henry, and pianist Avery Parrish (who made "After Hours" famous). Timeless swing. *—Scott Yanow*

Tuxedo Junction / Sep. 12, 1938-Jan. 10, 1945 / Bluebird/RCA ♦♦♦

1940-1941 / Nov. 6, 1940-Dec. 22, 1941 / Classics ♦♦♦♦♦
Although Erskine Hawkins' Orchestra was at its best on instrumentals, it did record a fair amount of vocal numbers during the swing era. The fourth Classics CD to chronologically reissue the trumpeter/bandleader's recordings has 13 vocals among the 22 selections, including six by the indifferent Jimmy Mitchelle, but there are also a bunch of swinging instrumentals (often arranged by Sammy Lowe), including "Soft Winds," "Riff Time," "Blackout" and "Shipyard Ramble," that feature tenors Julian Dash and Paul Bascomb along with trumpeters Dud Bascomb and Hawkins. *—Scott Yanow*

1941-1945 / Dec. 22, 1941-Nov. 21, 1945 / Classics ♦♦♦♦
All of the recordings cut by the always-underrated Erskine Hawkins Orchestra during a four-year period are reissued on this Classics CD. Actually there is only one cut from 1941 and seven songs from 1942 so the bulk of the set deals with the 1945 edition of the orchestra. In general the instrumentals are much more rewarding than the vocals, featuring solos by the trumpeter/leader, altoist Bobby Smith (who stars on the hit record of "Tippin' In") and tenor-saxophonist Julian Dash. The vocals by James Mitchelle, Ida James, Carol Tucker and Dolores Brown are harmless if forgettable; pianist Ace Harris fares best singing "Caldonia." In addition to "Tippin' In," highlights include "Lucky Seven," "Bear Mash Blues" (a near-classic by Sammy Lowe), "Caldonia," "Good Dip" and "Holiday for Swing." This is the fifth Erskine Hawkins CD from Classics and, due to the consistency of the band, all are recommended. *—Scott Yanow*

1946-1947 / Apr. 24, 1946-Dec. 20, 1947 / Classics ♦♦♦♦♦
Although by 1946 Erskine Hawkins no longer had any hit records in the future (1945's *Tippin' In* was his last one), his orchestra was still one of the best in jazz. Most of the 22 selec-

tions on this 1998 CD (the sixth in Classics' complete Hawkins series) are obscure but quite worthwhile. There are vocals on 13 of the songs (four by Jimmy Mitchelle, one from Ruth Christian, Ace Harris sounding spirited on "Well Natch," and seven easy-to-take vocals by Laura Washington) but it is the nine instrumentals that take honors. Although there are hints of bebop in the later records from 1947, most of the music on this CD is still very much in the swing vein. Taken as a whole, there is ample evidence here for the Erskine Hawkins Orchestra to be rated as one of the finest (and most underrated) big bands of the 1946-47 period. The key soloists in the orchestra are Hawkins and Sammy Lowe on trumpets, Matthew Gee on trombone, altoist Bobby Smith, Julian Dash on tenor, and baritonist Haywood Henry who is often heard on clarinet. Highlights include "Sneakin' Out," "Feelin' Low," "Needle Points," and "Lazy Blues." Recommended. *—Scott Yanow*

Jimmy Heath

b. Oct. 25, 1926, Philadelphia, PA
Sax (Tenor), Sax (Soprano), Flute, Arranger / Hard Bop
The middle of the three Heath Brothers, Jimmy Heath has a distinctive sound on tenor, is a fluid player on soprano and flute and a very talented arranger/composer whose originals include "C.T.A." and "Gingerbread Boy." He was originally an altoist, playing with Howard McGhee during 1947-48 and the Dizzy Gillespie big band (1949-50). Called "Little Bird" because of the similarity in his playing to Charlie Parker, Heath switched to tenor in the early '50s. Although out of action for a few years due to "personal problems," Heath wrote for Chet Baker and Art Blakey during 1956-57. Back in action in 1959, he worked with Miles Davis briefly that year in addition to Kenny Dorham and Gil Evans, and started a string of impressive recordings for Riverside. In the 1960s Heath frequently teamed up with Milt Jackson and Art Farmer and he also worked as an educator and a freelance arranger. During 1975-82 Jimmy Heath teamed up with Percy and Tootie in the Heath Brothers and since then has remained active as a saxophonist and writer. In addition to his earlier Riverside dates, Jimmy Heath has recorded as a leader for Cobblestone, Muse, Xanadu, Landmark and Verve. *—Scott Yanow*

The Thumper / Nov. 27, 1959-Dec. 7, 1959 / Riverside/OJC ✦✦✦✦
Jimmy Heath at age 33 made his recording debut as a leader on this Riverside session which has been reissued on CD in the OJC series. The hard bop tenor-saxophonist is in superior form, contributing five originals (of which "For Minors Only" is best known), jamming with an all-star sextet (including cornetist Nat Adderley, trombonist Curtis Fuller, pianist Wynton Kelly, bassist Paul Chambers and drummer Albert "Tootie" Heath) and taking two standards as ballad features. The excellent session of late '50s straightahead jazz is uplifted above the normal level by Heath's writing. *—Scott Yanow*

Really Big! / Jun. 24, 1960-Jun. 28, 1960 / Riverside/OJC ✦✦✦✦✦
Jimmy Heath's first chance to lead a fairly large group, an all-star ten-piece, found him well featured both on tenor and as an arranger/composer. With such colorful players as cornetist Nat Adderley, flugelhornist Clark Terry, altoist Cannonball Adderley, and either Cedar Walton or Tommy Flanagan on piano, Heath introduces a few originals (including "Big 'P' and "A Picture of Heath") and uplifts "Green Dolphin Street," "Dat Dere," and "My Ideal," among others. A well-conceived set that has been reissued on CD. *—Scott Yanow*

The Quota / Apr. 14, 1961+Apr. 20, 1961 / Riverside/OJC ✦✦✦✦
Jimmy Heath's considerable talents are very evident on this fine hard bop title. His supple, Dexter Gordon-inspired tenor work shines throughout the album's seven tracks, which range from the challenging yet fleet originals "Funny Time" and "The Quota" to attractive covers like "When Sunny Gets Blue" and Milt Jackson's "Bells and Horns." Heath also mixes it up stylistically with elements of both East Coast jazz (Philly native, vigorous ensemble work) and West Coast jazz (spry, vaporous arrangements), showing his flexibility amidst the music's healthy, bi-coastal rivalry of the late-'50s and early-'60s California stars Art Pepper and Chet Baker would cover several Heath numbers on their excellent 1956 collaboration *Playboys*. *The Quota* also benefits from stellar solo contributions by trumpeter Freddie Hubbard, French horn player Julius Watkins, and pianist Cedar Walton; brothers Percy and Albert Heath handle the bass and drums chores admirably, and they make a family reunion of it. *The Quota*'s strong material, tight arrangements, and thoughtful solos help make this Heath title one of the better hard bop releases available and a must for any jazz collection. *—Stephen Cook*

● **On the Trail** / 1964 / Riverside/OJC ✦✦✦✦✦
Unlike some of his other Riverside recordings, the accent on this Jimmy Heath CD reissue is very much on his tenor playing (rather than his arrangements). Heath is in excellent form with a quintet that also includes pianist Wynton Kelly, guitarist Kenny Burrell, bassist Paul Chambers and drummer Albert "Tootie" Heath. The instantly recognizable hard bop saxophonist performs four standards and three of his own compositions, including the original versions of "Gingerbread Boy" and "Project S." It's a good example of his playing talents. *—Scott Yanow*

Neal Hefti

b. Oct. 29, 1922, Hastings, NE
Trumpet, Composer, Arranger / Swing
One of the top jazz arranger/composers of the 1950s, Neal Hefti first wrote charts in the late 1930s for Nat Towles. He contributed arrangements to the Earl Hines big band, played trumpet with Charlie Barnet, Horace Heidt and Charlie Spivak (1942-43) and toured with Woody Herman's First Herd (1944-46), marrying Woody's singer Francis Wayne. It was with Herman that Hefti began to get a strong reputation, arranging an updated "Woodchopper's Ball" and "Blowin' up a Storm," and composing "The Good Earth" and "Wild Root." He also took a notable solo during a Lucky Thompson session on "From Dixieland to Bop." However Hefti soon relegated his trumpet playing to a secondary status (although he played it on an occasional basis into the 1960s) and concentrated on his writing. He contributed charts to the orchestras of Charlie Ventura (1946), Harry James (1948-49) and most notably Count Basie (1950-62). For Basie he wrote "Little Pony," "Cute," "Li'l Darling," "Whirlybird" and many other swinging songs, often utilizing Frank Wess's flute in inventive fashion. Neal Hefti also led his own bands off and on in the 1950s but in later years concentrated on writing for films while remaining influenced by his experiences in the jazz world. *—Scott Yanow*

● **Batman Theme & 19 Bat Songs** / Razor & Tie ✦✦✦✦✦
Batman Theme & 19 Bat Songs effectively acts as the soundtrack to the '60s television series *Batman*, since all of the 20 tracks were written and performed by Neal Hefti for use on the TV show. There's the familiar "Batman Theme," of course, as well as a number of rousing adventure and comical villainous themes. Anyone who appreciated the tongue-in-cheek, campy humor of the Adam West Batman will likely enjoy this collection. *—Stephen Thomas Erlewine*

Julius Hemphill

b. 1940, Fort Worth, TX, **d.** Apr. 2, 1995
Sax (Soprano), Sax (Alto), Flute, Composer / Avant-Garde Jazz, Free Jazz
Hemphill was best known for his work with the World Saxophone Quartet—he was arguably the band's most distinctive writer—but his work as an improvising saxophonist and composer encompassed a variety of other contexts over the course of his career. Hemphill worked with everything from big bands to duos; he especially excelled at composing for unusual instrumental combinations. His primary instrument was the alto; he got a huge, somewhat harsh tone and he possessed a formidable technique and a fertile imagination.

Hemphill's first instrument was the clarinet, and he studied with the renowned jazz clarinetist John Carter and played with local R&B bands in Fort Worth. After moving to St. Louis in 1968, he became involved with the Black Artists Group—a new music collective that also included Oliver Lake, Hamiet Bluiett and Joseph Bowie—and released the influential records *Dogon A.D.* and *Blue Boyé* on his own record label. Hemphill moved to New York in the mid-'70s, and in 1976 he formed the World Saxophone Quartet with Lake, Bluiett, and David Murray, which would prove to be the most commercially successful and long-lasting of his performing units. In the '70s and '80s Hemphill played and recorded fairly often for several labels, almost always under his own leadership. In the late '80s, Hemphill and the WSQ began an association with Elektra, which led to a number of well-distributed and aesthetically rewarding albums. Hemphill left the WSQ in the early '90s, thus weakening the ensemble from a conceptual standpoint. He went on to form his own all-sax group, which made a pair of albums—1991's *Fat Man and the Hard Blues* and 1993's *Five Chord Stud*. Hemphill's death in 1995 prematurely curtailed the career of one of free jazz's most visionary composers. *—Chris Kelsey*

★ **Dogon A.D.** / Feb. 1972 / Freedom ✦✦✦✦✦
This historic album features four then-unknowns on three lengthy avant-garde explorations that were quite influential not only in St. Louis (where they were recorded) but eventually on such diverse players as altoists Tim Berne and David Sanborn. Julius Hemphill (on alto and flute), trumpeter Baikida Carroll, cellist Abdul Wadud and drummer Philip Wilson are in superb form, both as soloists and in ensembles where they react instantly to each other. This important music is better to be heard than described. *—Scott Yanow*

Coon Bid'ness / Feb. 19, 1975 / Black Lion ✦✦✦✦✦
This historic LP includes a 20-minute performance with altoist Julius Hemphill, trumpeter Baikida Carroll, baritonist Hamiet Bluiett, cellist Abdul Wadud and drummer Philip Wilson ("The Hard Blues") taken from the same session that resulted in *Dogon A.D.* In addition, there are four briefer tracks that feature Hemphill, Bluiett, Wadud, altoist Arthur Blythe, drummer Barry Altschul and the congas of Daniel Zebulon. The music throughout is quite avant-garde but differs from the high-energy jams of the 1960s due to its emphasis on building improvisations as a logical outgrowth from advanced compositions. It's well worth several listens. *—Scott Yanow*

Blue Boyé / Jan. 1977 / Screwgun ✦✦✦

☆ **Fat Man and the Hard Blues** / Jul. 15, 1991+Jul. 16, 1991 / Black Saint ✦✦✦✦✦
After leaving The World Saxophone Quartet, the innovative altoist/composer Julius Hemphill recorded with an unaccompanied sax sextet. This CD features such great players as Marty Ehrlich, Carl Grubbs, the young James Carter, Andrew White and baritonist Sam Furnace along with the leader on 14 of Hemphill's compositions. These miniatures (all under seven minutes) are most notable for their fresh melodies, logical arrangements and spirited ensembles. *—Scott Yanow*

Five Chord Stud / Nov. 18, 1993-Nov. 19, 1993 / Black Saint ✦✦✦✦✦
Although altoist Julius Hemphill gets top billing on this CD, his heart surgery in 1993 forced him to stop playing. However, this saxophone sextet was his regular group; he contributed six of the eight compositions (the other two are free improvisations) and the chancetaking heard throughout this adventurous music definitely makes most of the performances sound like they came from a Julius Hemphill recording even if his alto is missed. The sextet has a very strong lineup (altoists Tim Berne, Marty Ehrlich and Sam Furnace, tenors James Carter and Andrew White and baritonist Fred Ho) and the resulting CD contains more than its share of variety. The music ranges from the soulful "Spiritual Chairs" and a boppish "Band Theme" to introspective ballads and wild passionate interplay. Other than Fred Ho (who is not heard from enough), each of the players has their chance to star. The generally fascinating music rewards repeated listenings but one has to have an open mind before putting it on. *—Scott Yanow*

At Dr. King's Table / 1997 / New World ✦✦✦

Fletcher Henderson

b. Dec. 18, 1897, Cuthbert, GA, **d.** Dec. 29, 1952, New York, NY
Piano, Arranger / Classic Jazz, Swing
Fletcher Henderson was very important to early jazz as leader of the first great jazz big band, as an arranger and composer in the 1930s and as a masterful talent scout. Between 1923-39 quite an all-star cast of top young Black jazz musicians passed through his orchestra including Louis Armstrong, Cootie Williams, Roy Eldridge, Coleman Hawkins Ben Webster, Lester

Young, Benny Carter and such arrangers as Don Redman and Edgar Sampson. And yet at the height of the swing era, Henderson's band was little-known.

A song demostrator and backing pianist during the early '20s, Henderson organized his first big band in 1924 and soon reached the top of his field, especially after Louis Armstrong joined up in late 1924 and Don Redman started contributing more swinging arrangements. After Redman's departure in 1927, Henderson himself developed into a top arranger by the early '30s, though the Depression took its toll on the band and it broke up by 1935. He had already begun contributing his better arrangements to Benny Goodman for well-known hits, and Henderson occasionally led bands during the late '30s and early '40s. In 1950 Henderson had a fine sextet with Lucky Thompson but a stroke ended his career and led to his death in 1952. *— Scott Yanow*

☆ **A Study in Frustration/Thesaurus of Classic Jazz** / Aug. 7, 1923-May 28, 1938 / Columbia ♦♦♦♦♦
This four-LP set, which is now also available as a three-CD box, is easily the definitive Fletcher Henderson package. Between 1923-38, Henderson's orchestra was one of the finest swing bands in the world, and during 1923-27 (until Duke Ellington's emergence) it was the first and the best. The arrangements of Don Redman in the early days set the pace for jazz; Benny Carter and Horace Henderson also wrote some important charts before Henderson himself finally developed into a major arranger in 1932. This Columbia set is not complete, but it includes 64 selections, at least 60 of them gems. This essential box (which contains three wonderful versions of "King Porter Stomp") belongs in everyone's jazz collection. *— Scott Yanow*

Fletcher Henderson and Louis Armstrong / Oct. 10, 1924-Oct. 21, 1925 / Timeless ♦♦♦
This rather unusual CD has 24 selections but most of them are shorter excerpts. The focus is on the brilliant solos that Louis Armstrong took while a member of the Fletcher Henderson Orchestra. Since his cornet flights were years ahead of some of the wheezing arrangements and the attempts by the other sidemen, the producers simply cut out the more dated segments and sometimes spliced in several of his solos from different takes of the same song. Where the producers erred was in not including every Armstrong solo with Henderson and, most importantly, programming the CD in complete chronological order so one could more easily trace the month-by-month growth of this innovative jazzman. Still, this is a historical curiosity and the music is consistently exciting. *— Scott Yanow*

1925-1926 / Nov. 23, 1925-Apr. 14, 1926 / Classics ♦♦♦♦♦
The Classics series has undergone the admirable task of reissuing on CD in chronological order every selection (although no alternate takes) of Fletcher Henderson's orchestra. This set finds the post-Armstrong edition of this pacesetting big band swinging hard on a variety of standards and obscurities. With cornetist Joe Smith, trombonist Charlie Green, clarinetist Buster Bailey and tenor great Coleman Hawkins contributing many fine solos and Don Redman's often-innovative arrangements inspiring the musicians, at this period Fletcher Henderson's orchestra had no close competitors among jazz-oriented big bands. Even the weaker pop tunes (like "I Want to See a Little More of What I Saw in Arkansas") have their strong moments. *— Scott Yanow*

● **1926-1927** / Apr. 14, 1926-Jan. 22, 1927 / Classics ♦♦♦♦♦
This CD, in Classics' chronological series, which captures the Fletcher Henderson Orchestra at its peak, is overloaded with classics: "Jackass Blues," "The Stampede" (which has a very influential tenor solo by Coleman Hawkins), "Clarinet Marmalade" "Snag It" and "Tozo" among others. In addition to Coleman Hawkins, Tommy Ladnier emerges as a major trumpeter and Fats Waller drops by for his "Henderson Stomp." Eight years before the official beginning of the swing era, Fletcher Henderson's orchestra was outswinging everyone. *— Scott Yanow*

1927 / Mar. 11, 1927-Oct. 24, 1927 / Classics ♦♦♦♦♦
Fletcher Henderson's orchestra was at the peak of its powers during this period, as can be heard on such torrid recordings as "Fidgety Feet," "Sensation," "St. Louis Shuffle," and "Hop Off"; even the overly complex Don Redman arrangement "Whiteman Stomp" (which Paul Whiteman's musicians apparently had trouble learning) is no problem for this brilliant orchestra. Classics' chronological reissue of Henderson's valuable recordings on this CD covers the many highpoints of the peak year of 1927; only Duke Ellington's orchestra was on the level of this pace-setting big band. *— Scott Yanow*

1927-1931 / Nov. 4, 1927-Feb. 5, 1931 / Classics ♦♦♦♦♦
With its high musicianship and many talented soloists (including trumpeters Rex Stewart and Bobby Stark, trombonist Jimmy Harrison, Coleman Hawkins on tenor and altoist Benny Carter), the Fletcher Henderson Orchestra should have prospered during this period, but unaccountably its leader (never a strong businessman) seemed to be losing interest in the band's fortunes and made several bad decisions. The result is that by 1931 Henderson's orchestra was struggling while Duke Ellington's was becoming a household name. This Classics CD, in covering over three years, demonstrates how few recordings this band made (only four songs apiece in both 1929 and 1930), although the quality largely makes up for the quantity. The original band version of "King Porter Stomp" and an explosive "Oh Baby" are the highpoints of this satisfying collection. *— Scott Yanow*

Tidal Wave / Apr. 10, 1931-Sep. 25, 1934 / GRP/Decca ♦♦♦♦♦
Fletcher Henderson's five Decca sessions are reissued in full on this fine CD. The 1931 and 1934 big bands are showcased. While the former group (heard on eight numbers) features such soloists as trumpeters Bobby Stark and Rex Stewart, trombonist Benny Morton and Coleman Hawkins on tenor, the later group showcases trumpeter Red Allen, trombonist Claude Jones, clarinetist Buster Bailey and tenor Ben Webster; altoist Benny Carter has a guest appearance on "Liza." Highlights of these early swing performances include "Sugar Foot Stomp," "Singin' the Blues" (which has Rex Stewart paying tribute to Bix Beiderbecke), the atmospheric "Radio Rhythm," "Big John's Special," "Down South Camp Meetin"' and "Rug Cutter's Swing." Excellent music that proves that swing did not begin with Benny Goodman in 1935. *— Scott Yanow*

1934-1937 / Sep. 25, 1934-Mar. 2, 1937 / Classics ♦♦♦♦♦
In early 1935 Fletcher Henderson broke up his classic orchestra but a year later, with the success of so many other big bands, he formed a new ensemble. This Classics CD includes four songs from 1934, Henderson's entire output from 1936 and his first recording of 1937. The main difference between the two units is that the later one boasted the trumpet of Roy Eldridge and tenor solos from Coleman Hawkins's potential successor, Chu Berry. "Christopher Columbus" became a hit as did the band's new theme song ("Stealin' Apples") but the brief bit of glory would not last. However, Henderson's brand of swing music still sounds fresh today and this CD is easily recommended. *— Scott Yanow*

Joe Henderson

b. Apr. 24, 1937, Lima, Ohio, **d.** Jun. 30, 2001
Sax (Tenor) / Hard Bop, Post-Bop
Joe Henderson is proof that jazz can sell without watering down the music; it just takes creative marketing. Although his sound and style are virtually unchanged from the mid-'60s, Henderson's signing with Verve in 1992 was treated as a major news event by the label (even though he had already recorded many memorable sessions for other companies), his Verve recordings had easy-to-market themes (tributes to Billy Strayhorn, Miles Davis and Antonio Carlos Jobim) and as a result he became a national celebrity and a constant pollwinner while still sounding the same as when he was in obscurity in the 1970s. The general feeling is that it couldn't happen to a more deserving jazz musician.Henderson appeared on many Blue Note sessions both as a leader and as a sideman, spent 1964-66 with Horace Silver's Quintet and during 1969-70 was in Herbie Hancock's band. From the start he had a very distinctive sound and style which, although influenced a bit by both Sonny Rollins and John Coltrane, also contained a lot of brand new phrases and ideas. Henderson has long been able to improvise in both inside and outside settings, from hard bop to free form. *— Scott Yanow*

★ **Page One** / Jun. 3, 1963 / Blue Note ♦♦♦♦♦
Tenor-saxophonist Joe Henderson's debut as a leader is a particularly strong and historic effort. With major contributions made by trumpeter Kenny Dorham, pianist McCoy Tyner, bassist Butch Warren and drummer Pete La Roca, Henderson (who already had a strikingly original sound and a viable inside/outside style) performs six generally memorable compositions on this CD reissue. Highlights include the original versions of Dorham's "Blue Bossa" and Henderson's "Recorda Me." It's highly recommended. *— Scott Yanow*

Our Thing / Sep. 9, 1963 / Blue Note ♦♦♦♦♦
Joe Henderson's second recording as a leader features a very strong supporting cast: trumpeter Kenny Dorham (one of Henderson's earliest supporters), pianist Andrew Hill, bassist Eddie Khan, and drummer Pete La Roca. Together they perform three Dorham and two Henderson originals, advanced music that was open to the influence of the avant-garde while remaining in the hard bop idiom. The up-tempo blues "Teeter Totter" contrasts with the four minor-toned pieces and, even if none of these songs became standards, the playing is consistently brilliant and unpredictable. Even at this relatively early stage, Joe Henderson showed his potential as a great tenorman. *— Scott Yanow*

In 'n Out / Apr. 10, 1964 / Blue Note ♦♦♦♦♦
Joe Henderson's third Blue Note release (which is here reissued on CD along with the addition of a previously unissued version of the title cut) matches the very distinctive tenor with the veteran trumpeter Kenny Dorham and an unbeatable rhythm section: pianist McCoy Tyner, bassist Richard Davis and drummer Elvin Jones. Henderson, who has always had the ability to make a routine bop piece sound complex and the most complicated free improvisation seem logical, and Dorham provided all of the material and the music still sounds fresh over three decades later. *— Scott Yanow*

Inner Urge / Nov. 30, 1964 / Blue Note ♦♦♦♦♦
The fourth of Joe Henderson's early Blue Note recordings is his first in a quartet setting without trumpeter Kenny Dorham. Henderson (who is accompanied by pianist McCoy Tyner, bassist Bob Cranshaw and drummer Elvin Jones) is in explorative form on three of his originals (including "Inner Urge" and the original version of "Isotope"), Duke Pearson's "You Know I Care" and the standard "Night and Day." The music straddles the boundaries between hard bop and the avant-garde and, while Henderson's improvisations are chordal-based, they are also quite unpredictable and prone to emotional outbursts. This colorful music is highly recommended. *— Scott Yanow*

Mode for Joe / Jan. 27, 1966 / Blue Note ♦♦♦♦♦
Tenor-saxophonist Joe Henderson's fifth and final early Blue Note album is his only one with a group larger than a quintet. Henderson welcomes quite an all-star band (trumpeter Lee Morgan, trombonist Curtis Fuller, vibraphonist Bobby Hutcherson, pianist Cedar Walton, bassist Ron Carter and drummer Joe Chambers) and together they perform originals by Henderson (including "A Shade of Jade"), Walton and Morgan ("Free Wheelin'"). The advanced music has plenty of exciting moments and all of the young talents play up to the level one would hope. *— Scott Yanow*

The Kicker / Aug. 10, 1967 / Milestone/OJC ♦♦♦♦♦
Joe Henderson's first recording for Milestone was very much a continuation of the adventurous acoustic music he had recorded previously for Blue Note. For those listeners who do not wish to invest in the tenor-saxophonist's "complete" eight-CD Milestone box set, this single-CD is a good place to start in investigating his "middle period" music. Henderson is featured in a sextet with trumpeter Mike Lawrence, trombonist Grachan Moncur III, pianist Kenny Barron, bassist Ron Carter and drummer Louis Hayes on a well-rounded set highlighted by "Mamacita," "Chelsea Bridge," "If," "Without a Song" and "Nardis." *— Scott Yanow*

☆ **The Milestone Years** / Aug. 10, 1967-Sep. 26, 1976 / Milestone ♦♦♦♦♦
Tenor-saxophonist Joe Henderson's most famous recordings are his early Blue Notes and his more recent Verves but in between he recorded exclusively for Milestone and, although he was in consistently fine form in the diverse settings, Henderson was somewhat neglected during his middle years. This massive eight-CD set contains all of the music from

Henderson's dozen Milestone LPs plus a duet with altoist Lee Konitz and his guest appearances with singer Flora Purim and cornetist Nat Adderley. The music ranges from Blue Note-style hard bop and modal explorations to fusion and '70s funk with important contributions made by trumpeters Mike Lawrence, Woody Shaw and Luis Gasca, trombonist Grachan Moncur and keyboardists Kenny Barron, Don Friedman, Joe Zawinul, Herbie Hancock, George Cables, Alice Coltrane, Mark Levine and George Duke among others. Not all of the music is classic (some of the later sets are unabashedly commercial) but none of the 82 selections are dull and the very distinctive Joe Henderson always gives his best. It's highly recommended. *—Scott Yanow*

Tetragon / Sep. 27, 1967-May 16, 1968 / Milestone/OJC ✦✦✦✦
Joe Henderson's second Milestone recording (which, as with all the others, is currently available on his massive "complete" eight-CD box set) features the great tenor with two separate rhythm sections: Kenny Barron or Don Friedman on piano, bassist Ron Carter and either Louis Hayes or Jack DeJohnette on drums. Highlights of this album include the title track, "I've Got You Under My Skin" and "Invitation." *—Scott Yanow*

Four / Apr. 21, 1968 / Verve ✦✦✦✦✦
Released for the first time on this CD in 1994, the previously unknown live session from 1968 features the great tenor Joe Henderson (who was then just a few days short of turning 31) playing for the first and possibly only time with the Wynton Kelly Trio. Henderson, pianist Kelly, bassist Paul Chambers and drummer Jimmy Cobb really stretch out on six standards (including a two-song medley), all of which clock in between 11:47 and 16:05 (except for a three-minute "Theme"). Henderson really pushes the rhythm section (which, although they had not played with the tenor previously, had been together for a decade) and he is certainly inspired by their presence. This is a frequently exciting performance by some of the modern bop greats of the era. *—Scott Yanow*

Straight, No Chaser / Apr. 28, 1968 / Verve ✦✦✦✦
Taken from the same live session that resulted in the Verve CD *Four,* this set (which was released for the first time in 1996) matches the great tenor Joe Henderson with the former Miles Davis rhythm section of pianist Wynton Kelly, bassist Paul Chambers and drummer Jimmy Cobb. Although Henderson had not played with the other musicians before, they blend together quite well and obviously inspired each other. In addition to a variety of standards, the quartet also performs a couple of then-recent songs ("Days Of Wine And Roses" and "On A Clear Day"), the ancient "Limehouse Blues" and Miles Davis' "Pfrancin." Recommended. *—Scott Yanow*

Joe Henderson in Japan / Aug. 4, 1971 / Milestone/OJC ✦✦✦✦✦
Tenor saxophonist Joe Henderson toured Japan in the summer of 1971 and performed in Tokyo with an all Japanese rhythm section (keyboardist Hideo Ichikawa, bassist Kunimitsu Inaba, and drummer Notohiko Hino). Henderson really stretches out on two of his compositions ("Out 'N' In" and "Junk Blues"), "'Round Midnight," and Kenny Dorham's "Blue Bossa." The trio gives him strong support and Henderson is heard throughout in top form. The frequently superb performances heard on this album have been reissued in Joe Henderson's eight-CD "complete" Milestone box set. *—Scott Yanow*

Canyon Lady / Oct. 1973 / Milestone/OJC ✦✦✦

Relaxin' at Camarillo / Aug. 20, 1979+Dec. 29, 1979 / Contemporary/OJC ✦✦✦

☆ **The State of the Tenor Live at the Village Vanguard** / Nov. 14, 1985-Nov. 16, 1985 / Blue Note ✦✦✦✦✦
Blue Note's Doubletime series combines live sessions previously issued in two single albums into one double CD. One of the first releases was Joe Henderson's brilliant tenor sax recital recorded live at the Village Vanguard in 1985. *The State Of The Tenor, Vols. 1 & 2* featured Henderson backed only by bass and drums in a setting that paid homage to his prime stylistic source, Sonny Rollins, while displaying his prime skills in an ideal forum. The 14 selections ranged from customary standards to Henderson originals, and included compositions by Sam Rivers, Thelonious Monk, Duke Ellington, Charlie Parker, Charles Mingus, and Horace Silver. It was not only a fine trio outing, but a series of performances in which Henderson stripped songs to their essence, turning them into his own vision. *—Ron Wynn*

★ **Lush Life: The Music of Billy Strayhorn** / Sep. 3, 1991-Sep. 8, 1991 / Verve ✦✦✦✦✦
With the release of this CD, the executives at Verve and their marketing staff proved that, yes indeed, jazz can sell. The veteran tenor Joe Henderson has had a distinctive sound and style of his own ever since he first entered the jazz major leagues yet he has spent long periods in relative obscurity before reaching his current status as a jazz superstar. As for the music on his "comeback" disc, it does deserve all of the hype. Henderson performs ten of Billy Strayhorn's most enduring compositions in a variety of settings ranging from a full quintet with trumpeter Wynton Marsalis and duets with pianist Stephen Scott, bassist Christian McBride and drummer Gregory Hutchinson to an unaccompanied solo exploration of "Lush Life." This memorable outing succeeded both artistically and commercially and is highly recommended. *—Scott Yanow*

Big Band / Mar. 16, 1992-Jun. 26, 1996 / Verve ✦✦✦✦
Big Band is a special record in Joe Henderson's catalog. As the first time he has recorded with a big band, it would be noteworthy, but what makes it truly exceptional is how Henderson effortlessly adapts to the setting, not only in the way he plays, but also in the way he can write. Every song on the album has been written and/or arranged by Henderson, and the quality of the music makes one wonder why he didn't venture into the genre earlier. It's a record that proves that big band music can still sound alive and vital, even in the '90s. *—Leo Stanley*

So Near, So Far (Musings for Miles) / Oct. 12, 1992-Oct. 14, 1992 / Verve ✦✦✦✦✦
Joe Henderson's follow-up to his hugely successful *Lush Life* disc is another concept album, this time involving ten songs (including many lesser-known ones) associated with Miles Davis. Henderson only actually played with Davis for a few weekends around 1967 but he shows a great deal of understanding for this potentially difficult music. With particularly strong assistance from guitarist John Scofield, bassist Dave Holland and drummer Al Foster, Henderson revives such forgotten songs as "Teo," "Swing Spring" and "Side Car" in addition to coming up with fresh interpretations of "Miles Ahead," "Milestones" and "No Blues." He is to be congratulated for not taking the easy way out and sticking to the simpler material of Davis's earlier years. *—Scott Yanow*

Double Rainbow: The Music of Antonio Carlos Jobim / Sep. 19, 1994-Nov. 6, 1994 / Verve ✦✦✦✦✦
The third of tenor-saxophonist Joe Henderson's tribute CDs on Verve was originally supposed to be a collaboration with the great bossa nova composer Antonio Carlos Jobim but Jobim's unexpected death turned this project into a memorial. Henderson performs a dozen of the composer's works with one of two separate groups: a Brazilian quartet starring pianist Eliane Elias and a jazz trio with pianist Herbie Hancock, bassist Christian McBride and drummer Jack DeJohnette. In general Henderson avoids Jobim's best-known songs in favor of some of his more obscure (but equally rewarding) melodies and in some cases (such as a very straightahead "No More Blues") the treatments are surprising. Highlights of this very accessible yet unpredictable CD include "Felicidade," "Triste," "Zingaro" and a duet with guitarist Oscar Castro-Neves on "Once I Loved" although all of the performances are quite enjoyable. Highly recommended. *—Scott Yanow*

Porgy and Bess / May 25, 1997-May 28, 1997 / Verve ✦✦✦✦

Scott Henderson

b. 1955
Guitar / Fusion
One of the finest fusion (as opposed to crossover) guitarists of the 1980s and '90s, Scott Henderson's explosive playing is often teamed up with electric bassist Gary Willis in their group Tribal Tech. Originally most influenced by rock, Henderson (who grew up in West Palm Beach, FL) played in local funk and rock bands. In 1980 he moved to Los Angeles to attend the Guitar Institute of Technology, studying with Joe Diorio. After graduating he became a teacher himself at GIT. Henderson played with Jeff Berlin and Jean-Luc Ponty and in 1985 toured with the original version of Chick Corea's Elektric Band. During 1987-89 he worked on and off with Joe Zawinul's Syndicate and since then Tribal Tech has been his main band. As a leader Scott Henderson has recorded for Passport, Relativity and Bluemoon. *—Scott Yanow*

Nomad / Apr. 1988 / Relativity ✦✦✦✦
Like its predecessors, Henderson's third date as a leader is a fine example of how creative and inspired genuine jazz-rock can be. Tough and aggressive yet full of appealing melodic and harmonic nuances, this CD contains not one iota of the type of lightweight smooth jazz or muzak for which Henderson has often voiced his contempt. With *Nomad,* Tribal Tech underwent a few personnel changes, and for the first time, recorded an entire album minus a sax. While electric bassist Gary Willis, drummer Steve Houghton and percussionist/mallet player Brad Dutz remained, saxman Bob Sheppard was gone, and keyboardist Pat Coil had been replaced by David Goldblatt. Despite these changes, Tribal Tech's sound (which was essentially guided by Henderson and Willis) remained easily recognizable. The '70s breakthroughs of Weather Report, Return to Forever and John McLaughlin, among others, still had an impact on Tribal Tech, but by 1988, it was even more evident that Henderson was a fine soloist and composer in his own right. *—Alex Henderson*

Tribal Tech / 1991 / Combat ✦✦✦✦✦
Guitarist Henderson once again displays his talents as a composer in the jazz-fusion idiom. Unlike his earlier releases, this album reveals a bluesier side to his playing. The interplay amongst the band members is superb and extremely satisfying! *—Paul Kohler*

● **Illicit** / Apr. 1992 / Blue Moon ✦✦✦✦✦

Tore Down House / Aug. 1996 / Atlantic ✦✦✦✦✦
This album resonates with sheer power. Like a steamroller tearing down a house, Scott Henderson and company comes shining through with *Tore Down House,* a gripping list of songs that beg the listener to truly appreciate the blues. Throughout the compilation, Henderson explores his diverse range of blues improvisation, using a plethora of pedals and effects, but not as so to diminish the full strength of the classic Fender Strat sound. "Dolemite" gets the jam going with a spontaneous free-for-all blues session. "I Hate You" is a romantic, witty ballad seemingly coming from the lost decade of the '50s. "Darling you ruined my life/so I hate you and I always will," sings guest Thelma Houston with chants of "You suck" in the background, granting a message of what one would feel about those who can't stand to be around that certain someone that's destroying their life. "Take this job and shove it./I'm going to guitar school," shouts the fiery Henderson in the rocking blues breaker, "Gittar School." With six other surprises featured on *Tore Down House,* it's a sure bet the first time listener of this artist's art will become a longtime fan. His band features a splendid group of experienced blues rockers, such as the likes of Pat O'Brien on harmonica, Dave Carpenter on bass, Kirk Covington on drums, Scott Kinsley on keyboards, and a host of sax, trumpet, and other brass players. This is a hands down classic blues album and a must for those who are crazy for the genre. *—Shawn Haney*

Thick / Jun. 1998-Jul. 1998 / Zebra ✦✦✦✦✦
Scott Henderson is a benchmark in the jazz fusion guitar world. He can just as easily lay down a mean blues lick or rock you hard, burning the frets like a wild man. Standing shoulder to shoulder, you have the creative genius and frenetic bounce of Gary Willis on bass with Scott Kinsey's inventive keyboard magic. Confidently, Kirk Covington pulls a polyrhythmic mixer out and drums away any doubts you may have about the power and grace of Tribal Tech. This band is never afraid to stretch, to totter along the edge, to wander into bizarre fugues, and then come rushing back at you, head on, 90 mph, with tight, intricate, jazz fusion solidity. And now with *Thick,* they have gone a step further and decided to abandon the charts, the maps, and the guidelines. This is their chance to have a good time, to do what musicians enjoy most—to spontaneously create in 100 percent freedom, seizing the moment to let the chemistry of who they are come through. *Thick* is essentially an in-studio jam session

where four skilled guys let it all hang out. Tribal Tech will surprise you with their fiery creativity. *—John Patterson*

Jon Hendricks (John Carl Hendricks)

b. Sep. 16, 1921, Newark, OH
Vocals, Lyricist / Vocal Jazz, Vocalese, Bop
The genius of vocalese, Jon Hendricks' ability to write coherent lyrics to the most complex recorded improvisations is quite notable as were his contributions to the classic jazz vocal group Lambert, Hendricks and Ross. In 1957 Hendricks made his recording debut (cutting "Four Brothers" and "Cloudburst" while backed by the Dave Lambert Singers). Soon he teamed up with fellow singers Dave Lambert and Annie Ross to form their vocal trio, starting off with a recreation of some of Count Basie's recordings. Lambert, Hendricks and Ross (after 1962 Yolande Bavan took Ross's place) stayed together up to 1964 and they have yet to be topped as a jazz vocal group, influencing those that would follow (including the Manhattan Transfer). In 1960 Hendricks wrote and directed the show *Evolution of the Blues* for the Monterey Jazz Festival; he would revive it several times during the next 20 years. *—Scott Yanow*

● **Evolution of the Blues Song** / Sep. 21, 1960 / Columbia ✦✦✦✦✦
Of the many projects Hendricks has been involved in, this is his crowning glory. It toured the country as a stage production, depicting the history of African-American roots music, from spirituals and field hollers to blues, gospel, and jazz. Hendricks recites signposts of the musical progression in rhyme, and singing here and there. Pony Poindexter plays a little tenor sax and talks about New Orleans, while Ike Isaacs' trio backs the singers. An intro by Hendricks postulates that adults "have their minds made up, don't confuse 'em with facts" and refers to musicians as "metaphysicians." This is one of several pieces where the chorus hums while Hendricks tells his tale. African drums, serving as a call-and-response device, inform "Amo." A slave story told in a Harry Belafonte style by Hendricks accents "Some Stopped on De Way," while a spiritual rap precedes "Swing Low Sweet Chariot." Big Miller digs into a personalized gospel blues, "If I Had My Share," and Witherspoon belts "Please Send Me Someone to Love" like only he can. A highlight is Miller's "Sufferin' Blues," followed by Hendricks' field holler "Aw, Gal" and Witherspoon's groovin' "C.C. (Circuit) Rider." Poindexter returns on "Jumpin' With Symphony Sid," which includes references to jazz and Lester Young. The program ends with Witherspoon's brilliant rendition of Big Bill Broonzy's "Sun Gonna Shine," Hendricks' downtrodden take on "W.P.A. Blues," and Big Miller's turn on "Motherless Child." If you'd like to get your children—or uninformed grown-ups—a quick, painless, enjoyable lesson in the last 100+ years of our American classical heritage, this is a perfect primer. *—Michael G. Nastos*

Jon Hendricks Recorded in Person at the Trident / 1963 / Smash ✦✦✦✦✦
One of singer Jon Hendricks' better post-Lambert, Hendricks & Ross recordings of the 1960s, this spirited live set has been reissued on CD by Polygram under the Smash subsidiary. Recorded in Sausalito, CA, with local musicians (the fine but obscure tenor Noel Jewkes, pianist Flip Nunez, bassist Fred Marshall, and drummer Jerry Granelli), the CD does an excellent job of summing up Hendricks' music of the era. He performs some hip bop ("Stockholm Sweetnin'"), revisits some of his previous group material ("Cloudburst" and "Shiny Stockings"), sings a couple of current tunes ("This Could Be the Start of Something Big" and "Watermelon Man"), performs a touching version of "Old Folks," breaks up the place with his humorous "Gimme That Wine," and revives the ancient ballad "I Wonder What's Become of Sally." Excellent music. *—Scott Yanow*

Freddie Freeloader / Jun. 7, 1989-Mar. 20, 1990 / Denon ✦✦✦✦✦
This CD would be highly recommended if it were only for Jon Hendricks' brilliant vocalese version of "Freddie Freeloader," twhich has Bobby McFerrin singing pianist Wynton Kelly's part, Al Jarreau as Miles Davis, George Benson as Cannonball Adderley, and Hendricks recreating John Coltrane. However, all 13 selections on the very memorable set have their strong moments, and the other guests include the Manhattan Transfer, the Count Basie Orchestra, Wynton Marsalis, Stanley Turrentine, Tommy Flanagan, Al Grey and the Jon Hendricks Vocalstra. "Jumpin' at the Woodside" recalls the Lambert, Hendricks & Ross version, Judith Hendricks sings Louis Armstrong's solos on "Stardust" and "Swing That Music," Turrentine helps to recreate "Sugar," there are a couple of Thelonious Monk tunes, and the exciting proceedings conclude with "Sing, Sing, Sing." Essential music. *—Scott Yanow*

Boppin' at the Blue Note / Dec. 23, 1993-Dec. 26, 1993 / Telarc ✦✦✦✦✦
Jon Hendricks, the genius of vocalese (writing words to fit the recorded solos of jazz greats) has long been one of the top lyricists in music. However the emphasis during the first seven songs of this live CD is on scatting and heated bop-oriented improvising. Hendricks, assisted by Michelle Hendricks, is joined by quite an all-star horn section: trumpeter Wynton Marsalis, trombonist Al Grey, altoist Red Holloway and tenor Benny Golson in addition to a supportive four-piece rhythm section. After a warmup on "Get Me to the Church on Time," Jon Hendricks sings some humorous lyrics on "Do You Call That a Buddy," swings hard on his original boppish "Good Ol' Lady" and gets a bit lowdown on "Contemporary Blues." The biggest surprise of the date is "Everybody's Boppin"' which features scatting by Jon Hendricks, Michele Henricks and Wynton Marsalis. Wynton is quite effective and typically virtuosic in a manner similar to Dizzy Gillespie. Michele is excellent on an uptempo "Almost Like Being in Love" and "Since I Fell for You," Jon sings the blues on "Roll 'Em Pete" and, together with Kevin Burke and Judith, Michele and Aria Hendricks, performs vocalese versions of three Count Basie charts long ago recorded by Lambert, Hendricks And Ross: recreations of recreations. This is Jon Hendricks's best all-round recording in several years and was one of the finest jazz vocal albums to be released in 1995. *—Scott Yanow*

Woody Herman (Woodrow Charles Herman)

b. May 16, 1913, Milwaukee, WI, **d.** Oct. 29, 1987, Los Angeles, CA
Sax (Soprano), Sax (Alto), Clarinet / Swing, Cool, Bop, Big Band
A fine swing clarinetist, an altoist whose sound was influenced by Johnny Hodges, a good soprano saxophonist and a spirited blues vocalist, Woody Herman's greatest significance to jazz was as the leader of a long line of big bands. He always encouraged young talent and more than practically any bandleader from the swing era, kept his repertoire quite modern. Although Herman was always stuck performing a few of his older hits (he played "Four Brothers" and "Early Autumn" nightly for nearly 40 years), he much preferred to play and create new music.

After playing with the Isham Jones orchestra for two years, Woody Herman formed one of his own in 1936, out of the remaining nucleus when Jones broke up the band. The great majority of the early Herman recordings feature the bandleader as a ballad vocalist but it was the instrumentals that caught on, leading to his group being known as "The Band That Plays the Blues." Herman's theme "At the Woodchopper's Ball" became his first hit (1939).

By the end of 1944, Woody Herman had what was essentially a brand new orchestra, the Herd (later renamed the First Herd). It was a wild goodtime band, with screaming ensembles and such Herman favorites entering the book as "Apple Honey," "Caldonia," "Northwest Pasage," "Bijou," and the nutty "Your Father's Mustache." Family troubles caused Herman to break up the big band at the height of its success in 1946, though by the following year he had a new orchestra. The Second Herd, also known as the Four Brothers band, featured the three cool-toned tenors of Stan Getz, Zoot Sims and Herbie Steward (later replaced by Al Cohn), plus baritonist Serge Chaloff. Still, the band struggled financially and collapsed in 1949.

After leading the Third Herd during much of 1950-56, Herman's New Thundering Herd became a hit at the 1959 Monterey Jazz Festival. Though his boppish unit gradually became more rock-oriented during the '60s and '70s, Herman returned to emphasizing straightahead jazz by the late '70s. He died in 1987, just one year after celebrating his 50th anniversary as a bandleader. *—Scott Yanow*

★ **Blues on Parade** / Apr. 26, 1937-Jul. 24, 1942 / GRP ✦✦✦✦✦
This single CD gives a definitive look at Woody Herman's first orchestra, the Decca ensemble he led during 1936-42 billed "the Band That Plays the Blues." Although he also recorded many vocal ballads during this era, the emphasis here is on hot swing with such highlights as the original version of "Woodchopper's Ball," "Blue Prelude," "Blue Flame," the humorous "Fan It" and two takes of "Blues on Parade." Also heard are performances by Herman's early small combos (the Woodchoppers and the Four Chips) along with a Dizzy Gillespie composition/arrangement ("Down Under") that hints at Woody Herman's future. *—Scott Yanow*

☆ **Thundering Herds 1945-1947** / Feb. 19, 1945-Dec. 27, 1947 / Columbia ✦✦✦✦✦
This three album box set is still the best compilation to date of Herman's First and Second Herds. These 48 selections (the cream of his Columbia recordings) include many classics such as "Apple Honey," "Caldonia," "Northwest Passage," "Biou," "Your Father's Moustache," eight numbers from Woody Herman's Woodchoppers, "Let It Snow," a new rendition of "Woodchopper's Ball," the four-part "Summer Sequence" and the original version of "Four Brothers." Even the lesser items on this set are memorable, making this the number one Herman release to own. *—Scott Yanow*

Second Herd—1948 / Mar. 12, 1948-May 12, 1948 / Storyville ✦✦✦✦
Woody Herman's Second Herd came of age during a year (1948) when, due to a recording strike, very few records were made. This CD contains three radio broadcasts and gives listeners a good idea of what it was like to see the big band live. With such major players as trumpeter/arranger Shorty Rogers, trombonist Earl Swope, guitarist Jimmy Raney, baritonist Serge Chaloff, and the tenors of Al Cohn, Stan Getz, and Zoot Sims, this was a powerhouse unit that was pretty modern for the time. Mary Ann McCall and Woody Herman take occasional vocals, and there are some dance numbers, but it is the jazz tunes (such as "Half Past Jumping Time," "Non Alcoholic," "Tiny's Blues," "The Goof and I," and "Four Brothers") that make this a fairly significant release. *—Scott Yanow*

★ **Keeper of the Flame: The Complete Capitol Recordings** / Dec. 29, 1948-Jul. 21, 1949 / Capitol ✦✦✦✦✦
Subtitled *The Complete Capitol Recordings of the Four Brothers Band*, this CD contains 19 selections from Herman's Second Herd, including three songs never before released. Top-heavy with major soloists (including trumpeters Red Rodney and Shorty Rogers, trombonist Bill Harris, tenors Al Cohn, Zoot Sims, Stan Getz and Gene Ammons and vibraphonist Terry Gibbs, not to mention Herman himself) this boppish band may have cost the leader a small fortune but they created timeless music. Highlights include "Early Autumn" (a ballad performance that made Stan Getz a star), the riotous "Lemon Drop" and Gene Ammons's strong solo on "More Moon." *—Scott Yanow*

The Herd Rides Again / Jul. 30, 1958-Aug. 1, 1958 / Evidence ✦✦✦
This CD contains a better-than-expected reunion of Herman's First Herd. Actually many of the key players from that classic band (such as tenorman Flip Phillips and trombonist Bill Harris) were not on this date while some of the musicians who did participate were Hermanites from a later era or (in the case of trombonist Bob Brookmeyer and tenor-saxophonist Sam Donahue) had never been a part of his bands before. Because the music was generally only a decade old, the results are quite satisfying, with fresh solos and spirited ensembles giving new life to such numbers as "Northwest Passage," "Caldonia" and "Blowin' up a Storm," among others. Certainly Brookmeyer's playing on "Bijou" will not remind anyone of Bill Harris. *—Scott Yanow*

Wild Root / Jul. 30, 1958-Dec. 26, 1958 / Vee-Jay ✦✦✦
Half of these 1958 sessions mix past members of the Herd with new ones, on remakes of old Herman charts. These swing pretty respectably, but more interesting are the four cuts from a December 26, 1958 session with Charlie Byrd as featured guitrarist. These have a Latin flavor that pushes the music into more exciting territory; "Bamba Samba" is a particularly lively effort in this direction. *—Richie Unterberger*

Herman's Heat & Puente's Beat / Sep. 1958 / Evidence ✦✦✦✦✦
Tito Puente and Woody Herman teamed in 1958 for a mutually satisfying meeting in the same way that Charlie Parker, Dizzy Gillespie, and Machito found commond ground in the late '40s. Puente's Latin rhythms and beats meshed with the swing and bebop of Herman's band on half of the disc's cuts, and the results were hot and delightful. With Puente heading

the rhythm section and playing timbales, Robert Rodriquez on bass, and assorted percussion from Gilbert Lopez, Raymond Rodriquez, and Ray Barretto, the band stays locked into the Latin groove while the saxophonists and trumpeters weave in, out, and around the beat. There are also more conventional Herman swing numbers such as "Blue Station" and "Woodchopper's Ball," where the standard Herman stomping sound is in effect. *—Ron Wynn*

Big New Herd at the Montery Jazz / Oct. 3, 1959 / Koch International ✦✦✦✦✦
At the 1959 *Monterey Jazz Festival*, Woody Herman headed an all-star orchestra that served as the house band for the weekend in addition to performing its own sets. The lineup is quite remarkable, including Herman on clarinet on alto, both Al Porcino and Bill Chase on first trumpets, Conte Candoli and Ray Linn taking trumpet solos, trombonist Urbie Green, Victor Feldman on piano and vibes, guitarist Charlie Byrd, bassist Monty Budwig, drummer Mel Lewis, baritonist Med Flory and the tenors of Zoot Sims, Don Lanphere, Bill Perkins and Richie Kamuca. Nearly every one of these players is featured in one spot or another. The saxes have a workout on "Four Brothers," "Monterey Apple Tree" is a renamed "Apple Honey," Urbie Green is in the spotlight on "Skylark," and the three other numbers keep the momentum flowing during a relatively brief program that does not quite reach 36 minutes. No less than 11 soloists are heard here, with Zoot Sims clearly inspiring the others. Exciting music. *—Scott Yanow*

The Raven Speaks / Aug. 28, 1972-Aug. 30, 1972 / Fantasy/OJC ✦✦✦✦✦
The best of his Fantasy releases of the '70s, this well-rounded CD is highlighted by a great jam on "Reunion at Newport" and strong soloing from Herman (on soprano and clarinet), pianist Harold Danko, trumpeter Bill Stapleton and the tenors of Gregory Herbert and Frank Tiberi. The Herman orchestra performs a couple of modern ballads ("Alone Again Naturally" and "Summer of '42"), some blues and a few swinging numbers, showing off their versatility with expertise and spirit. *—Scott Yanow*

Giant Steps / Apr. 9, 1973-Apr. 12, 1973 / Fantasy/OJC ✦✦✦✦
Woody Herman always went out of his way during his long career to encourage younger players, often persuading them to write arrangements of recent tunes for his orchestra. On this recording one gets to hear his band interpret such selections as Chick Corea's "La Fiesta," Leon Russell's "A Song for You," "Freedom Jazz Dance," "A Child Is Born" and "Giant Steps"; what other bandleader from the '30s would have performed such modern material— With strong solo work from tenors Gregory Herbert and Frank Tiberi, trumpeter Bill Stapleton and Herman himself, this is an impressive effort. *—Scott Yanow*

Thundering Herd / Jan. 2, 1974-Jan. 4, 1974 / Fantasy/OJC ✦✦✦
Of all the big-band leaders of the swing era, Woody Herman went the most out of his way to interpret current material and keep his orchestra young, enthusiastic and modern. For this Fantasy date (reissued on CD in the OJC series), Herman's band not only plays two John Coltrane songs, but material from Frank Zappa ("America Drinks and Goes Home"), Stanley Clarke ("Bass Folk Song") and even Carole King ("Corazon"). This is one of Herman's most successful efforts of the period, for the arrangements (by Alan Broadbent, Bill Stapleton and Tony Klatka) are inventive and generally swinging, with such soloists as Frank Tiberi on tenor, flugelhornist Klatka and electric keyboardist Andy Laverne keeping the music continually interesting. "Blues for Poland," "Lazy Bird" and the Zappa piece are high points. *—Scott Yanow*

Woody and Friends at the Monteray Jazz Festival / Sep. 15, 1979 / Concord Jazz ✦✦✦✦

Woody Herman Presents . . . , Vol. 2: Four Others / Jul. 1981 / Concord Jazz ✦✦✦✦

Fiftieth Anniversary Tour / Mar. 1986 / Concord Jazz ✦✦✦✦✦

Woody Herman Featuring Stan Getz / Nov. 20, 1976 / RCA ✦✦✦✦

Complete Capitol Recordings of Woody Herman / Mosaic ✦✦✦✦

Andrew Hill

b. Jun. 30, 1937, Chicago, IL
Piano / Avant-Garde Jazz, Modal Music, Post-Bop
Andrew Hill has long been a highly original pianist and composer. Never quite free form but too advanced to be accepted by bop fans, Hill's complex music has never really caught on although he is widely respected as an innovative jazz musician. He started on piano when he was 13, studied with the composer Paul Hindemith and throughout the 1950s freelanced in jazz and R&B settings in Chicago. In 1961 Hill moved to New York and became Dinah Washington's accompanist. After a stint with Rahsaan Roland Kirk in 1962, he has mostly worked as a leader. Hill's series of explorative and advanced Blue Note albums (1963-1966) have been reissued in a Mosaic box set; *Point of Departure* (1964) has such sidemen as Kenny Dorham, Eric Dolphy and Joe Henderson and other dates feature John Gilmore, Freddie Hubbard, Sam Rivers and Henderson. Hill also recorded for Blue Note during 1968-70, became an educator and by the mid-'70s was teaching in public schools in California. He has recorded less frequently during the past couple of decades for labels such as SteepleChase, Freedom, East Wind, Soul Note and Blue Note but remains a very viable performer who has stuck to his own singular musical vision. *—Scott Yanow*

☆ **Black Fire** / Nov. 8, 1963 / Blue Note ✦✦✦✦✦
Black Fire, Andrew Hill's debut record for Blue Note, was an impressive statement of purpose that retains much of its power decades after its initial release. Hill's music is quite original, building from a hard bop foundation and moving into uncharted harmonic and rhythmic territory. His compositions and technique take chances; he often sounds restless, searching relentlessly for provocative voicings, rhythms, and phrases. *Black Fire* borrows from the avant-garde, but it's not part of it—the structures remain quite similar to bop, and there are distinct melodies. Nevertheless, Hill and his band—comprised of tenor saxophonist Joe Henderson, bassist Richard Davis, and drummer Roy Haynes—are not content with the limitations of hard bop. Much of the music is informed by implied Afro-Cuban rhythms and modal harmonics, resulting in continually challenging and very rewarding music. Hill's complex chording is thoroughly impressive, and Henderson's bold solos are more adventurous than his previous bop outings would have suggested. Their expertise, along with the nimble, unpredictable rhythm section, help make *Black Fire* a modern jazz classic. *—Stephen Thomas Erlewine*

☆ **Complete Blue Note Andrew Hill Sessions (1963-66)** / Nov. 8, 1963-Mar. 7, 1966 / Mosaic ✦✦✦✦✦
Andrew Hill was one of the greatest pianists of the '60s, but he never quite received his due. Hill was a skillful, cerebral musician that consciously positioned his music between hard bop and free. He was at his peak in the mid-'60s, as his playing and composing continued to explore new territory. All of his seminal recordings for Blue Note between 1963 and 1966 are collected on the limited-edition, seven-disc box set *The Complete Blue Note Andrew Hill Sessions (1963-66)*. During those three years, he recorded with an astonishing array of talents, including Eric Dolphy, Freddie Hubbard, Sam Rivers, Joe Henderson, Roy Haynes, Elvin Jones, Tony Williams, Richard Davis, Joe Chambers, John Gilmore, and Kenny Dorham. The box features 15 alternate takes, including ten previously unreleased cuts and a composition that has never been released. The sheer scope of the set means that it's only of interest to serious jazz collectors, but it proves that Hill was one of the most adventurous and rewarding pianists of the '60s. *—Stephen Thomas Erlewine*

Smoke Stack / Dec. 13, 1963 / Blue Note ✦✦✦
Trimming away some of the overt Afro-Cuban rhythms that distinguished *Black Fire*, Andrew Hill turned in a dense, cerebral set of adventurous post-bop on his second Blue Note session, *Smoke Stack*. Comprised entirely of original Hill compositions, *Smoke Stack* is in the middle ground between hard bop and free jazz—it isn't as loose and dissonant as free, but with its long, winding modal improvisations and hazy song structures, it's a lot less accessible than bop. It also isn't as successful as *Black Fire*, which worked similar territory with edgier results. Part of the problem is that Hill simply meanders throughout most of *Smoke Stack*, wandering off into quietly discordant sections that turn in on themselves. It's subdued music that requires concentration, but doesn't necessarily reward such effort. Even with its faults, *Smoke Stack* is far from an unworthy record—Hill's insular, intellectual style may be occasionally frustrating, but his playing is frequently provocative and challenging, and his backing group of Richard Davis (bass), Eddie Khan (bass), and Roy Haynes (drums) offer sympathetic support. However, it's an album that promises more than it delivers. [Blue Note's CD reissue of *Smoke Stack* included four alternate takes as bonus tracks.] *—Stephen Thomas Erlewine*

Judgment! / Jan. 8, 1964 / Blue Note ✦✦✦✦✦
Augmenting his rhythm section of bassist Richard Davis and drummer Elvin Jones with vibraphonist Bobby Hutcherson, pianist Andrew Hill records an excellent set of subdued but adventurous post-bop with *Judgment*. Without any horns, the mood of the session is calmer than *Black Fire*, but Hill's compositions take more risks than before. Close listening reveals how he subverts hard bop structure and brings in rhythmic and harmonic elements from modal jazz and the avant-garde. The harmonic structure on each composition is quite complex, fluctuating between dissonant chords and nimble, melodic improvisations. Naturally, Hill's playing shines in this self-created context, but Hutcherson equals the pianist with his complex, provocative solos and unexpected melodic juxtapositions. Jones shifts the rhythms with style, and his solos are exceptionally musical, as is Davis' fluid bass. The combination of the band's intricate interplay and the stimulating compositions make *Judgment* another important release from Hill. It may require careful listening, but the results are worth it. *—Stephen Thomas Erlewine*

★ **Point of Departure** / Mar. 31, 1964 / Blue Note ✦✦✦✦✦
The most famous session that pianist Andrew Hill ever led, this avant-garde date matches his distinctive style with quite a cast of players: trumpeter Kenny Dorham, Eric Dolphy (on alto, flute and bass clarinet), tenor saxophonist Joe Henderson, bassist Richard Davis and drummer Tony Williams. The CD reissue adds two "new" alternate takes to the original five-song program, all Hill originals. The complex inside/outside music, which is full of surprising twists, is a classic in its own way and is essential for any representative jazz collection. *—Scott Yanow*

Andrew!!! / Jun. 25, 1964 / Blue Note ✦✦✦✦

Compulsion / Oct. 3, 1965 / Blue Note ✦✦✦✦

Grass Roots / Aug. 5, 1968 / Blue Note ✦✦✦✦
As the '60s drew to a close, Blue Note spent less time than ever with adventurous music, since it didn't sell as well as soul-jazz or mainstream hard bop. So, it may seem a little strange that the label invited Andrew Hill back to record in 1968, two years after he last cut a session for the label. Hill's work for the label stands among the most challenging cerebral post-bop of the '60s, but there was another side of Hill that wasn't showcased on those records: He also had a knack for groove and melody, as indicated by his composition "The Rumproller," a hard-grooving hard-bop classic made famous by trumpeter Lee Morgan. That was the side that Blue Note wanted to showcase on *Grass Roots*. Hill and his band were working from the basic template of making a commercial hard-bop album, but nevertheless pushed themselves to challenging territory. Blue Note sat on the session however, and Hill went back to the studio four months later with a new group of musicians: trumpeter Lee Morgan, tenor saxophonist Booker Ervin, bassist Ron Carter, and drummer Freddie Waits. This group was every bit as adventurous as the last, but they laid down a solid groove without compromising the music. The end result may not be as bracing as Hill's earlier works, but it's a pleasure to hear him in such a genial, welcoming mood. Furthermore, the record is hardly insubstantial musically—the songs have strong melodies, even hooks, to bring casual listeners in, but they give the musicians the freedom to find a distinctive voice in their solos. It's the best of both worlds, actually—accessible, just like Blue Note wanted, without compromising Hill's integrity. [Blue Note's 2000 CD reissue contains the entire first draft of the album as a bonus.] *—Stephen Thomas Erlewine*

Dance with Death / Oct. 11, 1968 / Blue Note ✦✦✦

One for One / Aug. 1, 1969-Jan. 23, 1970 / Blue Note ✦✦✦✦

Spiral / Dec. 20, 1974+Jan. 20, 1975 / Freedom ♦♦♦♦

Nefertiti / Jan. 25, 1976 / Inner City ♦♦♦♦

Shades / Jul. 3, 1986-Jul. 4, 1986 / Soul Note ♦♦♦♦

Verona Rag / Jul. 5, 1986 / Soul Note ♦♦♦♦♦

Eternal Spirit / Jan. 30, 1989-Jan. 31, 1989 / Blue Note ♦♦♦♦♦

But Not Farewell / Jul. 12, 1990-Sep. 1990 / Blue Note ♦♦♦♦

Dusk / Sep. 15, 1999 Sep. + 19 / Palmetto ♦♦♦♦♦

Earl Hines

b. Dec. 28, 1903, Dusquesne, PA, **d.** Apr. 22, 1983, Oakland, CA
Piano, Composer / Classic Jazz, Swing, Big Band

Once called "the first modern jazz pianist," Earl Hines differed from the stride pianists of the 1920s by breaking up the stride rhythms with unusual accents from his left hand. While his right hand often played octaves so as to ring clearly over ensembles, Hines had the trickiest left hand in the business, often suspending time recklessly but without ever losing the beat. First recorded in 1922, he moved to Chicago one year later and began teaming up with Louis Armstrong as early as 1926. In 1928, Hines recorded his first ten piano solos and worked on classic recordings by Jimmy Noone's Apex Club Orchestra and Louis Armstrong's Hot Five. Later that year he debuted his own big band, which lasted for more than 20 years. In 1940 Billy Eckstine became the band's popular singer and in 1943, Hines welcomed such modernists as Charlie Parker (on tenor), trumpeter Dizzy Gillespie and singer Sarah Vaughan in what was the first bebop orchestra.

Finally forced to break up the band in 1948, he played with the Louis Armstrong All-Stars and headed a Dixieland band throughout the 1950s, though he was largely forgotten in the jazz world by the early '60s. Then in 1964 he played three New York concerts; Hines's continuing creativity amazed critics, leading to a major comeback. Hines travelled the world with his quartet and recorded dozens of albums until his death at the age of 79. *—Scott Yanow*

1928-1932 / Dec. 8, 1929-Jun. 28, 1932 / Classics ♦♦♦♦♦

1932-1934 / Jul. 1932-Mar. 1934 / Classics ♦♦♦♦♦

1934-1937 / Sep. 12, 1934-Aug. 10, 1937 / Classics ♦♦♦♦♦

1937-1939 / Feb. 10, 1937-Oct. 6, 1939 / Classics ♦♦♦♦♦

The Father Jumps / Jul. 12, 1939-Jan. 12, 1945 / RCA ♦♦♦♦♦
This excellent two-LP set is much more comprehensive than the recent Bluebird CD. Included here are most of the best recordings by Earl Hines's big band during 1939-42 along with two selections from 1945. During most of this time, Hines featured such talented sidemen as trumpeter Walter Fuller, Omer Simeon on clarinet and alto, tenorman Budd Johnson and later Franz Jackson. A young Billy Eckstine takes a few vocals (most notably his first hit "Jelly, Jelly") and Hines' piano is a major factor on many of the recordings. Highlights include "Grand Terrace Shuffle," "Piano Man," "Boogie Woogie on St. Louis Blues," "The Father Jumps" and "The Earl." Pity that this set is out of print. *—Scott Yanow*

★ **Piano Man** / Jul. 12, 1939 Mar. 19, 1942 / Bluebird/RCA ♦♦♦♦♦
This sampler of Earl Hines's Bluebird recordings features five brilliant piano solos from the often-breathtaking pianist, "Blues in Thirds" by Sidney Bechet's Trio with Hines and 16 of the better performances from his big band of 1939-42. An excellent purchase for those not familiar with Hines's big-band days, this CD includes such classics as "Piano Man," "Boogie Woogie on St. Louis Blues" and "Jelly, Jelly" along with many hot swinging performances from this very underrated orchestra. *—Scott Yanow*

Another Monday Date / Nov. 1955-Dec. 1956 / Prestige ♦♦♦♦
Two of pianist Earl Hines's finest recordings sessions of the 1950s are included on this CD. One is a tribute to Fats Waller on which Hines (with guitarist Eddie Duran, bassist Dean Reilly and drummer Earl Watkins) explores songs associated with Waller. The other date is Hines's only solo session of the decade and features him playing his own compositions (including "Everything Depends on You," "You Can Depend on Me," "Piano Man" and "My Monday Date") along with "Am I Too Late?" During the 1950s, Hines was somewhat forgotten in jazz, reduced to playing Dixieland dates, so this two-fer is far superior to his other sessions prior to his "comeback" of 1964. *—Scott Yanow*

Earl Hines Plays Duke Ellington / Jun. 1, 1971-Dec. 10, 1971 / New World ♦♦♦♦♦
During a four-year period, pianist Earl Hines recorded enough of Duke Ellington's compositions to fill up four LPs. This double CD contains 20 of his better performances including both Ellington's better-known standards and a few obscurities (most notably lengthy versions of "The Shepherd" and "Black Butterfly"). The music is satisfying, although one wishes that New World had reissued all of the music from this extensive project on three CDs. *—Scott Yanow*

Hines Does Hoagy / Nov. 26, 1975+Oct. 1, 1984 / Audiophile ♦♦♦♦♦
Earl Hines pays tribute to composer Hoagy Carmichael on this inventive set of solo piano. Highpoints of this fine LP include a ten-minute version of "Stardust," "Skylark" and "Ole Buttermilk Sky." Pity that Hines did not tackle "Riverboat Shuffle" but he chose to mostly stick to Carmichael's classic ballads. One of three albums recorded by the great pianist in a two-day period, this is one of about fifty recommended Hines sets. *—Scott Yanow*

☆ **Tour de Force** / Nov. 22, 1972-Nov. 29, 1972 / 1201 Music ♦♦♦♦♦
Pianist Earl Hines is in top form on this brilliant set of solo piano. This CD (which has three previously unreleased performances along with five of the six numbers from its counterpart LP) and *Tour De Force Encore* greatly expand upon the original set. Whether it be "Mack the Knife," "Indian Summer" or "I Never Knew," Hines is near the peak of his creativity on this CD, taking wild chances with time and coming up with fresh new variations on these veteran standards. *—Scott Yanow*

☆ **Live at the New School** / Mar. 27, 1973 / Chiaroscuro ♦♦♦♦♦
This album features pianist Earl Hines at the absolute peak of his powers. Nine years after his renaissance began, Hines seemed to still be getting more daring in his playing. This version of "I've Got the World on a String" is somewhat miraculous (the chances he takes are breathtaking) and the Fats Waller medley (which features six songs) is definitive. The inclusion of "When the Saints Go Marching In" might not have been necessary, and "Boogie Woogie on the St. Louis Blues" is a bit exhibitionistic but those are minor complaints about a definitive and classic session by a true jazz master. *—Scott Yanow*

Earl Hines Plays Cole Porter / Apr. 16, 1974 / New World ♦♦♦♦
This CD reissue of an Earl Hines solo piano session originally made for the Australian Swaggie label is a bit unusual. Hines had apparently not played any of the seven songs (which include such standards as "Night And Day," "What Is This Thing Called Love" and "I Get A Kick Out Of You") previously, nor would they enter his repertoire after the session. No matter, Hines interprets the compositions as if he had been familiar with them for decades. His chancetaking improvisations have their hair raising moments (particularly when he suspends time) and are quite exciting. A superb effort by the immortal pianist who at 71 still seemed to be improving. *—Scott Yanow*

Way Down Yonder in New Orleans / 1975 / Biograph ♦♦♦♦♦

Milt Hinton

b. Jun. 23, 1910, Vicksburg, MS, **d.** Dec. 19, 2000, Queens, NY
Bass / Swing

Bassist Milt Hinton has probably appeared on more records than any other musician in the world and he remains a vital figure in jazz even at the age of 86. He grew up in Chicago and worked with many legendary figures from the late '20s to the mid-'30s including Freddie Keppard, Jabbo Smith and Tiny Parham (with whom he made his recording debut in 1930). He was with Cab Calloway's Orchestra and his later small group during 1936-51. Considered the best bassist before the rise of Jimmy Blanton in 1939, Hinton was an ally of Dizzy Gillespie in modernizing Calloway's music. After leaving Cab, Hinton worked in clubs with Joe Bushkin, had brief stints with Count Basie and Louis Armstrong's All-Stars and in 1954 became a staff musician at CBS, appearing on a countless number of recordings (jazz and otherwise) during the next 15 years; everything from Jackie Gleason mood music and polka bands to commercials and Buck Clayton jam sessions. By the 1970s Hinton was appearing regularly at jazz parties and festivals and his activities have not slowed down during the past two decades; in 1995 he toured with the Statesmen of Jazz. Although a modern soloist, Hinton has also kept the art of slap bass alive. *—Scott Yanow*

● **Basses Loaded** / Feb. 1, 1955 / Victor ♦♦♦♦♦

Back to Bass-ics / Sep. 3, 1984 / Progressive ♦♦♦♦
Bassist Milt Hinton, despite recording countless sessions during seven decades, has only led his own recording dates on a very infrequent basis. For this session, he heads a trio also including pianist Jane Jarvis and drummer Louie Bellson. While Bellson is mostly content to swing quietly in the background, Hinton and Jarvis split the solo space on a variety of standards (including "Undecided," "Fascinating Rhythm" and "Joshua Fit De Battle of Jericho") and three group originals. Hinton's charming personality constantly shines through, and the subtle yet passionate music is consistently delightful. This performance was reissued on a 1989 CD. *—Scott Yanow*

Old Man Time / Oct. 3, 1989-Mar. 2, 1989 / Chiaroscuro ♦♦♦♦♦
This double-CD set gave bassist Milt Hinton an opportunity to engage in reunions with many of his old friends from the 1930s. The seven sessions were compiled during a 12-month period and the results are often delightful. The opening "Old Man Time" is sung by Hinton himself, and it is both insightful and humorous. The other highlights include Joe Williams singing "Four or Five Times" (which features some very rare Flip Phillips clarinet), three bass guitar duets with Danny Barker, appearances by Dizzy Gillespie, Lionel Hampton, Clark Terry, Al Grey, Ralph Sutton, and the formation of a group called "The Survivors" that has guitarist Al Casey at age 75 being the youngest member; the latter band also includes 85-year-old trumpeter Doc Cheatham, Eddie Barefield, Buddy Tate and even Cab Calloway. A lot of storytelling takes place during the songs and, in addition to the 92Ω minutes of music, there are two "Jazzspeaks." The 13-minute one features Hinton, Calloway, Cheatham and Barefield reminiscing about their experiences in the early days, while a marvelous 45-minute monologue by the bassist covers most of his long and productive life and is consistently fascinating. Highly recommended. *—Scott Yanow*

Hiroshima

f. 1974, Los Angeles, CA
Group / Crossover Jazz, Contemporary Jazz, World Fusion

Hiroshima, a group whose music falls between r&b, pop, World Music and jazz, has long had its own niche. The band integrates traditional Japanese instruments into their musical blend and has generally been both commercial and creative within its genre. Hiroshima's founding members are keyboardist Dan Kuramoto (who also played shakuhachi), June Okida Kuramoto on koto (a key part of the group's sound), Johnny Mori on taiko drums and Danny Yamamoto on drums, percussion and taiko. Other additions including keyboardist Kimo Cornwell, bassist Dean Cortez and singer Teri Koide (who was later succeeded by Kimaya Seward). Some of the musicians were descendants of JapaneseAmericans held in U.S. detention camps during World War II. Hiroshima has recorded a series of best-selling albums for Arista, Epic and Qwest and, although they have evolved over time (moving further away from jazz), they have managed to not only retain but increase their popularity. *—Scott Yanow*

● **The Best of Hiroshima** / 1983-1989 / Epic ♦♦♦♦
The Best of Hiroshima is a ten-track collection that contains a good overview of the fusion group's Epic recordings, including such cuts as "San Say, " "One Wish, " "Thousand Cranes, " "Hawaiian Electric, " "Island World, " "I Do Remember" and "Time on the Nile." *—Stephen Thomas Erlewine*

Ongaku / 1988 / Arista ✦✦✦✦

Between Black and White / Aug. 10, 1999 / Windham Hill ✦✦✦✦
1999 marked 20 years since the band's unique combination of distinctively Japanese elements—June Kuramoto's classical-flavored koto, Johnny Mori's booming Taiko drum—with funky pop, urban, and jazz sensibilities first hit the instrumental music charts, and 25 years since saxophonist and East L.A. native Dan Kuramoto first formed the ensemble. Their Windham Hill Jazz debut (and 11th release overall) *Between Black and White* finds them once again blending contemporary root music, mystical Eastern exotica, and melodically rich smooth jazz that further deepens their larger commitment to global unity on the cusp of the new millennium. Hiroshima once again dares to push the envelope and engage diversity from track to track. The mix of dreamy koto and keyboard mysticism and thick hip-hop grooves and soulful sax on "Mix Plate" sets the tone for the whole project on the instrumental side. Hiroshima has worked with some great vocalists over the years, and Terry Steele—who wrote Luther Vandross' signature smash "Here and Now"—adds to the litany with his cool, romantic approach to "The Door Is Open." *—Jonathan Widran*

Al Hirt (Alois Maxwell Hirt)

b. Nov. 7, 1922, New Orleans, LA, **d.** Apr. 27, 1999
Trumpet / Dixieland Revival, Dixieland
A virtuoso on the trumpet, Al Hirt was often "overqualified" for the Dixieland and pop music that he performed. He studied classical trumpet at the Cincinnati Conservatory (1940-43) and was influenced by the playing of Harry James. He freelanced in swing bands (including both Tommy and Jimmy Dorsey and Ray McKinley) before returning to New Orleans in the late '40s and becoming involved in the Dixieland movement. He teamed up with clarinetist Pete Fountain on an occasional basis from 1955 on and became famous by the end of the decade. An outstanding technician with a wide range along with a propensity for playing far too many notes, Hirt had some instrumental pop hits in the 1960s and also recorded swing and country music but mostly stuck to Dixieland in his live performances. He remained a household name throughout his career, although one often feels that he could have done so much more with his talent. Hirt's early Audiofidelity recordings (1958-60) and collaborations with Fountain are the most rewarding of his long career; he died at his home in New Orleans on April 27, 1999. *—Scott Yanow*

☆ **The Very Best of Al Hirt & Pete Fountain** / 1957 / MGM ✦✦✦✦✦
This is an album that lives up to its name, for both trumpeter Al Hirt and clarinetist Pete Fountain rarely sounded better than they did on this collaboration. With the underrated trombonist Bob Havens, pianist Roy Zimmerman, bassist Bob Coquille, and drummer Paul Edwards completing the group, plenty of fireworks are felt. Fountain is very effective switching to tenor on a rollicking "Washington and Lee Swing"; Hirt is exuberant on "South Rampart Street Parade" and "Panama"; and each of the dozen selections is full of excitement. The musicians were clearly inspired and rarely sounded more creative. A classic encounter that unfortunately has yet to be reissued on CD. *—Scott Yanow*

That's a Plenty / Mar. 29, 1988-Mar. 31, 1988 / Pro Arte ✦✦✦✦
Trumpeter Al Hirt is represented on relatively few CDs. This particular release finds him heading a septet that also features veteran clarinetist Peanuts Hucko, trombonist James Huggan and keyboardist Dave Zoller. The repertoire is typical Dixieland, along with an occasional swing ballad and a version of Hirt's famous hit "Java." The virtuoso trumpeter, who was 65 at the time, was still in prime form, swinging his way through "That's A Plenty," "Royal Garden Blues," "Bourbon Street Parade" and "The Saints" with flash and excitement. *—Scott Yanow*

A Rainy Night in Georgia / 1993 / Sony Special Products ✦✦✦
Hirt lends his stunning trumpet prowess to renditions of favorites like "Dream Baby," "The Lonely Bull" and "Dream a Little Dream of Me" on *A Rainy Night in Georgia,* a solid budget-line offering. *—Raymond McKinney*

● **The Al Hirt Collection** / Oct. 21, 1997 / Razor & Tie ✦✦✦✦✦
The Al Hirt Collection is an outstanding introduction to the trumpeter's biggest hits from the mid-1960s, assembling instrumental favorites including "Java," "Cotton Candy," "Sugar Lips," "Up Above My Head (I Hear Music in the Air)" and "Fancy Pants." What makes the package so special, however, is the inclusion of the complete and much sought-after 1964 LP *Beauty and the Beard,* recorded with the young Ann-Margret; equally noteworthy is Hirt's blistering rendition of the "Green Hornet Theme," plainly one of the most memorable and exciting theme songs in the history of television. *—Jason Ankeny*

Honey in the Horn/Our Man in New Orleans / May 18, 1999 / RCA Victor ✦✦✦✦
Honey in the Horn/Our Man in New Orleans reissues and repackages two of Al Hirt's most popular albums for RCA. Part of this set comes from *Honey in the Horn,* a '60s pop album featuring a big Nashville sound and vocals by the Anita Kerr singers. The other half of the reissue comes from the original *Our Man in New Orleans,* which finds Hirt's regular band, supported by a big swing brass section, serving up Dixieland sounds with a twist. Though it's not the CD debut for these albums, the original covers and liner notes make it a wise choice for fans as well as novices to Hirt's style. *—Heather Phares*

Music to Watch Girls By / RCA Victor ✦✦✦✦✦

Art Hodes

b. Nov. 14, 1904, Nikoliev, Russia, **d.** Mar. 4, 1993, Harvey, IL
Piano / Dixieland
Throughout his long career, Art Hodes was a fighter for traditional jazz, whether through his distinctive piano playing, his writings or his work on radio and educational television. Renowned for the feeling he put into blues, Hodes was particularly effective on uptempo tunes where his on-the-beat chordings from his left hand could be quite exciting.Hodes had the opportunity to witness Chicago jazz during its prime years in the 1920s and he learned from other pianists. In 1928 he made his recording debut with Wingy Manone but spent most of the 1930s in obscurity in Chicago until he moved to New York in 1938. He played with Joe Marsala and Mezz Mezzrow before forming his own band in 1941. Hodes recorded frequently during the 1970s and '80s and was widely recognized as one of the last survivors of Chicago jazz. *—Scott Yanow*

★ **Complete Blue Note Art Hodes Sessions** / Mar. 18, 1944-Dec. 16, 1945 / Mosaic ✦✦✦✦✦
From 1944-45, pianist Art Hodes led nine sessions for Blue Note in addition to being a featured sideman on a quartet date headed by drummer Baby Dodds. This limited edition five-LP box set from Mosaic has all 70 selections, including ten that were previously unissued. Hodes, a veteran of 1920s Chicago who later received recognition for his blues playing, loved playing Dixieland and classic jazz. In settings ranging from a trio to a septet, Hodes inspires and interacts with some of the top trad jazz players of the mid-1940s, including trumpeters Max Kaminsky and (on one session) Wild Bill Davison; trombonists Ray Conniff, Sandy Williams, and Vic Dickenson; clarinetists Rod Cless, Edmond Hall, Mezz Mezzrow, Omer Simeon, and Albert Nicholas; the great soprano innovator Sidney Bechet; bassists Bob Haggart, Israel Crosby, Pops Foster, and Wellman Braud; and drummers Dodds, Danny Alvin, and Fred Moore, among others. The music overall is generally straightforward Dixieland with plenty of exciting ensembles and hot solos. A collector's item that (typically for Mosaic) was perfectly conceived. *—Scott Yanow*

Original Blue Note Jazz, Vol. 2 / Jun. 1, 1944 / Blue Note ✦✦✦✦✦

Hodes' Art / Oct. 22, 1968-Apr. 23, 1972 / Delmark ✦✦✦
Opportunities for pianist Art Hodes to record in the 1960s were quite rare. In fact, other than a record documenting a concert, Hodes' entire output from 1963-70 was three albums cut for Delmark in 1968; traditional jazz was definitely out of style. This particular Delmark CD has brief moments from a variety of veteran greats. "When My Sugar Walks Down the Street" matches Hodes and his rhythm section with trombonist George Brunis, trumpeter Nappy Trottier and clarinetist Volly De Faut; the clarinetist (a veteran of the early '20s) also plays on "Struttin' With Some Barbeque." In addition to three piano-bass-drums trio numbers, Hodes is heard on six relaxed selections in a trio with clarinetist Raymond Burke (in good form) and veteran bassist Pops Foster. This music is historic and enjoyable. *—Scott Yanow*

Up in Volly's Room / Mar. 15, 1972-Apr. 25, 1972 / Delmark ✦✦✦✦
Clarinetist Volly DeFaut made a few notable recordings during the first half of the 1920s, including some with Jelly Roll Morton, and then largely dropped out of music. Fortunately, he never completely gave up playing, and his contributions to these 1972 sessions (reissued on CD) are one of the main reasons to acquire this release. While seven numbers match DeFaut with pianist Art Hodes, bassist Truck Parham and drummer Barrett Deems, there are also four Hodes-Parham duets and versions of "Ja Da" and "Panama Rag" that add trumpeter Nappy Trottier and trombonist George Brunies to the full group. Hodes, who is really rollicking on the more uptempo material, adds a strong blues sensibility to each of the songs. Among the many highlights of the delightful set (mostly comprised of Dixieland standards) are "St. Louis Blues," "Struttin' With Some Barbeque," "After You've Gone" and "Volly's Room." *—Scott Yanow*

Pagin' Mr. Jelly / Nov. 4, 1988 / Candid ✦✦✦✦
Art Hodes was just ten days short of his 84th birthday at the time of this Candid solo piano CD. Hodes had his own style for quite a few decades by then. A masterful blues player, on the more up-tempo tunes, Art's left hand tended to state each beat in double-time, a very effective device. For this tribute to Jelly Roll Morton, Hodes performs 13 tunes recorded by Morton (eight of which Jelly Roll wrote) along with two of his own originals: a blues number and "Pagin' Mr. Jelly," which is partly based on Morton's "King Porter Stomp." The five faster performances really stomp, the three medium-tempo renditions swing, and the seven more introspective pieces are quite soulful. Recommended. *—Scott Yanow*

Final Sessions / Jul. 30, 1990-Aug. 19, 1990 / Music & Arts ✦✦✦✦
Pianist Art Hodes, one of the leading pianists during the revival years of classic jazz, is surprisingly strong during what would be his final recordings. Already in his mid-eighties, Hodes (three years before his death) explores 13 familiar themes ranging from "Alexander's Ragtime Band" and "Royal Garden Blues" to "America the Beautiful." Six songs are duets with Jim Galloway on soprano. Hodes also teams up with clarinetist Kenny Davern for "Summertime." There are four trios with both horns and also two unaccompanied piano solos. Hodes was a very consistent performer throughout his lengthy career and his last album (available as a 71-minute CD) is well worth hearing. *—Scott Yanow*

Johnny Hodges

b. Jul. 25, 1907, Cambridge, MA, **d.** May 11, 1970, New York, NY
Sax (Soprano), Sax (Alto) / Swing, Ballads
Possessor of the most beautiful tone ever heard in jazz, altoist Johnny Hodges formed his style early on and had little reason to change it through the decades. Although he could stomp with the best swing players and was masterful on the blues, Hodges's luscious playing on ballads has never been topped. Hodges' real career began in 1928 when he joined Duke Ellington's Orchestra. He quickly became one of the most important solo stars in the band and a real pacesetter on alto; Benny Carter was his only close competition in the 1930s. Hodges was featured on a countless number of performances with Ellington and also had many chances to lead recording dates with Duke's sidemen. Whether it was "Things Ain't What They Used to Be," "Come Sunday" or "Passion Flower," Hodges was an indispensable member of Ellington's Orchestra in the 1930s and '40s. It was therefore a shock in 1951 when he decided to leave Duke and lead a band of his own. He had a quick hit in "Castle Rock" but his combo ended up struggling and breaking up in 1955. Hodges's return to Ellington was a joyous occasion and he never really left again. *—Scott Yanow*

Passion Flower / Nov. 2, 1940-Jul. 9, 1946 / Bluebird/RCA ✦✦✦✦✦
For 42 years (with a four-year interruption), altoist Johnny Hodges was the top soloist in Duke Ellington's all-star Orchestra. This excellent CD reissue has the eight selections (plus an alternate take) from Hodges's two Bluebird sessions of 1940-41; among the sidemen on

such classics as "Day Dream," "Good Queen Bess," "Passion Flower" and "Things Ain't What They Used to Be" are either Cootie Williams or Ray Nance on trumpet, trombonist Lawrence Brown and Ellington himself. In addition there are 13 selections by the Duke Ellington Orchestra of 1940-46 that feature Hodges including "Don't Get Around Anymore," "In a Mellotone," "Warm Valley," "I Got It Bad" and "Come Sunday." This is classic music that has been intelligently repackaged. *—Scott Yanow*

Caravan: With the Duke Ellington All-Stars and the Billy Strayhorn All-Stars / Jun. 1947-Jun. 19, 1951 / Prestige ♦♦♦♦
This single CD, which reissues all of the music from a double-LP, has a variety of formerly rare sessions from 1947-51. Although the great altoist Johnny Hodges gets top billing, and he leads three sessions from 1947 (featuring such top Ellington stars as trombonist Lawrence Brown, tenorman Al Sears, baritonist Harry Carney and either Taft Jordan or Harold Baker on trumpet), he is actually absent on the second half of the release. With Billy Strayhorn and/or Duke Ellington as leader and Willie Smith on alto, these enthusiastic swing performances range in personnel from a three-trombone septet to a version of "Caravan" with Ellington on piano and Strayhorn making a rare appearance on organ. Although the music falls just short of classic, Ellington collectors will love these rarities. *—Scott Yanow*

☆ **The Complete Johnny Hodges Sessions (1951-1955)** / Jan. 15, 1951-Sep. 8, 1955 / Mosaic ♦♦♦♦♦
As is true of most Mosaic box sets, it would be very difficult to improve upon this reissue. After 22 years, altoist Johnny Hodges left Duke Ellington's orchestra in 1950 to try to make it on his own as a bandleader. Five years later, he returned to Ellington for the final 15 years of his life after having recorded the music heard on this six-LP set. Hodges's small group, a unit that emphasized blues, ballads, and riff-filled romps, was an extension of the Ellington band. Hodges had a big hit with "Castle Rock" (ironically a feature for tenor saxophonist Al Sears), but otherwise had trouble at the end making ends meet. Other notable sidemen on these enjoyable performances include trumpeters Emmett Berry and Harold "Shorty" Baker, trombonist Lawrence Brown, and tenors Flip Phillips, Ben Webster, and John Coltrane on one session (during which he unfortunately does not solo); the final session, from Sept. 8, 1955 (after Hodges had already returned to Ellington), also has trumpeter Clark Terry and pianist Billy Strayhorn. Most of this music had been long out of print at the time this 1989 box was released. A highly recommended gem of swinging jazz. *—Scott Yanow*

Masters of Jazz, Vol. 9 / Nov. 22, 1960-Mar. 14, 1961 / Storyville ♦♦♦♦♦
Here is a CD that is highly recommended for swing collectors. Altoist Johnny Hodges and tenor-saxophonist Ben Webster team up for a sextet set from 1960, a club appearance that was released for the first time on this set. Their six performances (all are basic Hodges originals) find the pair of veteran swing stylists in prime form. The remainder of the program (three standards plus Hodges' "Good Queen Bess") is played by a septet dominated by Ellington musicians including the leader/altoist, baritonist Harry Carney, trumpeter Ray Nance and trombonist Lawrence Brown. Excellent music that still has not dated. *—Scott Yanow*

At Sportpalast, Berlin / Mar. 1961 / Pablo ♦♦♦♦
This double-CD, a straight reissue of a Pablo double-LP, documents a fun set. Altoist Johnny Hodges and some fellow members of Duke Ellington's Orchestra (Ray Nance on cornet, violin and vocals, trombonist Lawrence Brown, baritonist Harry Carney, bassist Aaron Bell, drummer Sam Woodyard and guest pianist Al Williams) jam through a mostly typical set of standards and Ellington tunes. Everyone gets featured and, even if there are no real surprises, the musicians are consistently heard in top form. Superior small-group swing by some of the best. *—Scott Yanow*

Johnny Hodges with Billy Strayhorn and the Orchestra / Dec. 11, 1961-Dec. 12, 1961 / Verve ♦♦♦♦
Alto saxophonist Johnny Hodges recorded frequently for Verve in the 1950s and 1960s, although nearly all of the musicians on this CD are from the Ellington orchestra and the arrangements are by Billy Strayhorn. Hodges is never less than superb throughout this reissue, while Lawrence Brown, Harry Carney and non-Ellingtonians Howard McGhee on trumpet and pianist Jimmy Jones also deserve praise. Strayhorn's exotic chart of "Azure" and emotional scoring of "Your Love Has Faded" are especially striking. Recommended. *—Ken Dryden*

● **Everybody Knows** / Feb. 6, 1964+Mar. 8, 1965 / GRP/Impulse! ♦♦♦♦♦
This excellent single CD has the complete contents of two Impulse LPs: *Everybody Knows Johnny Hodges* and *Inspired Abandon,* which was actually a Lawrence Brown album featuring Hodges. The two similar and equally rewarding swing-oriented albums find Hodges joined by a variety of top Ellington stars, including trumpeters Cat Anderson and Ray Nance, either Harold Ashby or Paul Gonsalves on tenors and trombonist Brown, among others. The renditions of "310 Blues," "The Jeep Is Jumpin'," "Stompy Jones" and "Mood Indigo," in particular, sound quite fresh and inventive. Recommended. *—Scott Yanow*

In a Mellow Tone / Sep. 10, 1966-Sep. 11, 1966 / Bluebird/RCA ♦♦♦♦♦
Altoist Johnny Hodges and organist Wild Bill Davis teamed up successfully on quite a few albums in the 1960s. This set, reissued on CD, was their final one and quite possibly their most rewarding. With solo work provided not only by the co-leaders but trombonist Lawrence Brown, obscure tenor Bob Brown, and guitarist Dickie Thompson (drummer Bobby Durham helps out in support), this is a particularly interesting unit. Unlike most of their other collaborations, this outing by Hodges and Davis sticks mostly to better-known material, including a previously unissued version of Duke Ellington's "Squeeze Me But Please Don't Tease Me" and four Hodges originals. Highlights include "It's Only a Paper Moon," "Taffy," "Good Queen Bess," and "In a Mellotone." This release is recommended as a strong (and swinging) example of Johnny Hodges outside of the Duke Ellington Orchestra. *—Scott Yanow*

Triple Play / Jan. 9, 1967-Jan. 10, 1967 / Bluebird/RCA ♦♦♦♦
Altoist Johnny Hodges is heard in three different settings on this reissue CD. Such top swing stars as trumpeters Ray Nance, Cat Anderson and Roy Eldridge, trombonists Buster Cooper, Lawrence Brown and Benny Powell, tenors Paul Gonsalves and Jimmy Hamilton, baritonist Harry Carney, pianists Hank Jones and Jimmy Jones (the latter two sometimes together), guitarists Tiny Grimes, Les Spann and Billy Butler, bassists Milt Hinton, Aaron Bell and Joe Benjamin and drummers Gus Johnson, Rufus Jones and Oliver Jackson are heard in nonets with the great altoist. Despite the many changes in personnel, the music is pretty consistent, with basic swinging originals, blues and ballads all heard in equal proportion. As usual, Johnny Hodges ends up as the main star. *—Scott Yanow*

Dave Holland

b. Oct. 1, 1946, Wolverhampton, W. Midlands, England
Bass / Avant-Garde Jazz, Free Jazz, M-Base, Post-Bop
Dave Holland is of a generation of bassists that, in the '60s and '70s, built upon the innovations of slightly-older players like Scott LaFaro, Gary Peacock, and Barre Phillips, carrying the instrument to yet another new level of creativity. Holland helped refine and extend the melodic possibilities of the cumbersome double bass, though his sense of swing is unexcelled. Additionally, Holland is possibly the most accomplished pure jazz composer among bassists, after Charles Mingus. Holland's small groups in the '80s and '90s, while working firmly within the jazz idiom, presented a fresh alternative to the fusty recreations of the neo-boppers.

After playing ukelele, guitar, and bass guitar from an early age, Holland took up the double bass as a teenager and began playing professionally shortly thereafter. In 1966, he began playing with many of the musicians with whom he would collaborate over the next two decades: musicians like the trumpeter Kenny Wheeler, saxophonist John Surman, pianist John Taylor, who were well in-tune with the jazz innovations of the time. Holland played London clubs with England's top jazz musicians, and in 1968, Miles Davis asked him to join his band. Holland participated in the making of several classic Davis recordings, including *In A Silent Way* and *Bitches Brew.* In 1970 he co-founded (with Anthony Braxton, Chick Corea, and Barry Altschul) the group Circle, which embraced free jazz concepts. In 1975 he formed the Gateway trio—with Jack DeJohnette (drums) and John Abercrombie (guitar)—a group which would continue to record and tour intermittently for the next 25 years. In the '80s, Holland worked extensively with Sam Rivers, and began organizing his own small groups. Although the personnel would vary, the band would ultimately draw its identity from Holland's compositions. In the '80s and '90s, Holland also worked as an educator, at the Banff School in Canada and the New England Conservatory of Music. Aside from leading his own group, Holland's musical activities in the '90s included projects with DeJohnette, Gateway, and Herbie Hancock. *—Chris Kelsey*

Conference of the Birds / Nov. 30, 1972 / ECM ♦♦♦♦
This was one of bassist Dave Holland's most adventurous sets, an avant-garde outing with both Sam Rivers and Anthony Braxton on reeds, along with percussionist Barry Altschul. Braxton, Altschul and Holland had been members of Circle (with Chick Corea) and were soon to form a quartet that included trumpeter Kenny Wheeler. The contrast between the two masterful reed players on the six Holland originals is the main reason to acquire this minor classic. *—Scott Yanow*

Emerald Tears / Aug. 1977 / ECM ♦♦♦♦
As strong and inventive a player as Dave Holland is, he was unable to make this set of unaccompanied bass solos (which have been reissued on CD) of more than minor interest. Performing six of his originals, one by Anthony Braxton and Miles Davis' "Solar," Holland unfortunately avoids infusing the music with any humor or much variety, making this a sleepy session for most listeners. *—Scott Yanow*

● **Jumpin' In** / Oct. 1983 / ECM ♦♦♦♦♦
Bassist Dave Holland leads one of his most stimulating groups on this superlative quintet date. With the young Steve Coleman on alto and flute, trumpet great Kenny Wheeler, trombonist Julian Priester and drummer Steve Ellington in the band, Holland had a particularly creative group of musicians in which to interpret and stretch out his six originals; Coleman also contributed one composition. This set, which has plenty of variety in moods, tone, colors and styles, is one of Holland's better recordings. *—Scott Yanow*

The Razor's Edge / Feb. 1987 / ECM ♦♦♦♦♦
Dave Holland's mid-1980s band played inventive music that was between post-bop and the avant-garde. The group acted as a launching pad for altoist Steve Coleman, gave publicity to the always-underrated trumpeter Kenny Wheeler, and in 1987 also featured trombonist Robin Eubanks and drummer Marvin "Smitty" Smith. The group's three ECM releases are well worth exploring, and this set gives listeners a strong example of their work. *—Scott Yanow*

Extensions / Sep. 1989 / ECM ♦♦♦♦♦
Dave Holland Quartet. With Kevin Eubanks (g). This was the 1990 *Down Beat* Critic's Album of the Year. Very good band/album music. Percussionist Smitty Smith is unreal. Recommended. *—Michael G. Nastos*

Points of View / Sep. 25, 1997-Sep. 26, 1997 / ECM ♦♦♦♦
For *Points of View,* Holland expands his group into a quintet, shakes up the remaining personnel, and comes up with a marvelous example of thoughtful, dynamically shifting ECM chamber jazz. The new wrinkles in the sound are the return of Robin Eubanks on trombone, which gives the front line a richer, more balanced texture, and drummer Billy Kilson, who displays a wider, more animated range of rhythmic sympathies than did Gene Jackson on *Dream of the Elders.* Steve Nelson on vibes and marimba is the only returnee, and Steve Wilson contributes a dry tone on both alto and soprano saxes. The elegant textures so typical of ECM belie considerable stylistic variety here, including a gentle reversion to the progressively funky Holland band of the '80s on "Metamorphos"; a happy-go-lucky, easy-swinging tribute to Ray Brown, "Mr. B."; reflective, relaxed ballad work in "The Benevolent One," and Nelson's charming calypso/folk lullaby for marimba, "Serenade." Of course, Holland leaves himself a lot of solo space, which he fills with mobile eloquence. *—Richard S. Ginell*

Prime Directive / Dec. 10, 1998 Aug. 2, - 19 / ECM ✦✦✦✦✦
You may have to wait a while between Dave Holland-led releases, but it's always worth it. Tremendous taste prevents Holland from making unsatisfying music. He is a great leader in the truest senses of the word—he gives his team space, trusts their abilities and judgment, yet all the while remains firmly in command and infuses the results with his own style and personality. *Prime Directive* is a wonderful jazz album. These 77 minutes and nine tracks do not cheat or disappoint. The straight-ahead tunes—composed by double-bassist Holland and his talented band mates (one each)—all bear Holland's distinctive rhythmic patterns and harmonics. A fine example is the title track, on which Robin Eubanks on trombone and Chris Potter on saxophones hold a stimulating musical conversation over the rhythm section's driving groove. For listeners who prefer a more deliberate pace, there's the searching, contemplative "Make Believe," with Steve Nelson's lovely vibraphone work appointing the mood. On the hopeful, "A Seeking Spirit," fans will be tapping along to the rhythmic feast offered up by the leader and his pace-setting partner Billy Kilson on drums. The melancholy "Candlelight Vigil" presents Holland at his bowed best. Finally, "Wonders Never Cease" finds the entire band at the height of their collective, improvisational prowess. *Prime Directive* is recommended; a great leader is, indeed, hard to find. *—Brian Bartolini*

Red Holloway

b. May 31, 1927, Helena, AR
Sax (Tenor), Sax (Alto) / Soul-Jazz, Swing, Bop
An exuberant player with attractive tones on both tenor and alto, Red Holloway is also a humorous blues singer. Whether it be bop, blues or R&B, Holloway can hold his own with anyone. Holloway played in Chicago with Gene Wright's big band (1943-46), served in the Army and then played with Roosevelt Sykes (1948) and Nat Towles (1949-50) before leading his own quartet (1952-61) during an era when he also recorded with many blues and R&B acts. Holloway came to fame in 1963 while touring with Jack McDuff, making his first dates as a leader for Prestige (1963-65). Although he has cut many records in R&B settings, Red Holloway is a strong bop soloist at heart as he proved in the 1970s when he battled Sonny Stitt to a tie on their recorded collaboration. He has mostly worked as a leader since then but has also guested with Juggernaut and the Cheathams and played with Clark Terry on an occasional basis. *—Scott Yanow*

Cookin' Together / Feb. 2, 1964 / Prestige/OJC ✦✦✦✦✦
For this set, tenor saxophonist Red Holloway, who was a regular member of organist Jack McDuff's group, used McDuff's sidemen (who included guitarist George Benson) and the organist himself. This Prestige date has thus far only been reissued by the OJC series on LP. The material is comprised of Burt Bacharach's "Wives and Lovers," "This Can't Be Love," and five Holloway originals, which have more diversity than one might expect. An interesting aspect to the soulful and swinging set is that McDuff made his debut on piano for two songs. *—Scott Yanow*

Brother Red / Feb. 6, 1964-Feb. 7, 1964 / Prestige ✦✦✦✦

Red Holloway and Company / Jan. 1987 / Concord Jazz ✦✦✦✦

● **Locksmith Blues** / Jun. ??, 1989 / Concord Jazz ✦✦✦✦✦
This is a fun set, which is not surprising when one considers that two of jazz's most good-humored players (saxophonist Red Holloway and flugelhornist Clark Terry) are the co-leaders. The sextet (which also includes pianist Gerald Wiggins, guitarist Phil Upchurch, bassist Richard Reid and drummer Paul Humphrey) plays a colorful set of jazz standards, including "Red Top," "Come Sunday" and "Cotton Tail," and three basic Holloway originals, one of which ("Locksmith Blues") finds Holloway and C.T. clearly enjoying themselves while sharing the vocals. Everyone is heard in top form, making this straight-ahead CD an excellent example of the co-leaders' talents. *—Scott Yanow*

Live at the Floating Jazz Festival 95 / Nov. 5, 1995-Nov. 9, 1995 / Chiaroscuro ✦✦✦✦

Legends of Acid Jazz / Oct. 10, 1963+Aug. 27, 1963 / Prestige ✦✦✦✦
Red Holloway recorded four albums for Prestige during 1963-65, but did not have another opportunity to lead his own record date until 1982. This 1998 CD reissues his first (*The Burner*) and fourth (*Red Soul*) sets for Prestige. The earlier session is the most interesting of the two for; in addition to Holloway (who is heard throughout on tenor), there are fine solos from the bluesy guitarist Eric Gale and organist John Patton; two of the numbers ("Crib Theme" and "The Burner") are extended (over ten-minutes) workouts. The later album matches Holloway with guitarist George Benson (his associate at the time with Jack McDuff's combo) and either organist Dr. Lonnie Smith or pianist Norman Simmons. Although Red Holloway would continue to grow as a highly expressive blues-based soloist through the years, these performances (soul jazz that occasionally becomes hard bop) show that he was already a fairly distinctive and powerful soloist as early as 1963. *—Scott Yanow*

In the Red / Nov. 27, 1997 / High Note ✦✦✦✦

Richard "Groove" Holmes (Richard Arnold Holmes)

b. May 2, 1931, Camden, NJ, **d.** Jun. 29, 1991, St. Louis, MO
Organ (Hammond), Organ / Hard Bop, Soul-Jazz
Revered in soul-jazz circles, Richard "Groove" Holmes was an unapologetically swinging Jimmy Smith admirer who could effortlessly move from the grittiest of blues to the most sentimental of ballads. Holmes, a very accessible, straight-forward and warm player who was especially popular in the Black community, had been well respected on the Philadelphia/Southern New Jersey circuit by the time he signed with Pacific Jazz in the early 1960s and started receiving national attention by recording with such greats as Ben Webster and Gene Ammons. Holmes, best known for his hit 1965 version of "Misty," engaged in some inspired organ battles with Jimmy McGriff in the early 70s before turning to electric keyboards and fusion-ish material a few years later. The organ was Holmes' priority in the mid-to-late 80s, when he recorded for Muse. Holmes was still delivering high-quality soul-jazz for that label (often featuring tenor titan Houston Person) when a heart attack claimed his life at the age of 60 in 1991. *—Alex Henderson*

Groovin' with Jug / Aug. 15, 1961 / Pacific Jazz ✦✦✦✦✦
Ironically, Gene "Jug" Ammons tended to be critical of organists; he was quoted as saying that "organ players don't know any changes." However, as critical the Chicago tenor saxman might have been of organists—most of them, anyway—he did some of his best work in their presence. When you united Ammons with Jack McDuff, Johnny "Hammond" Smith and other B-3 masters in the '60s, the sparks would fly. They certainly fly on this excellent album, which finds Ammons and Richard "Groove" Holmes co-leading a soul-jazz/hard bop organ combo that also includes guitarist Gene Edwards and drummer Leroy Henderson. The quartet is heard in two settings on August 15, 1961—three of the eight selections were produced by Richard Bock in a Los Angeles studio in the afternoon, while the other five were recorded several hours later an L.A. club called *the Black Orchid*. Ammons and Holmes prove to be a strong combination in both settings, although their playing is somewhat looser at *the Orchid*, where the delights include some slow blues (Ammons' "Hittin' The Jug"), a smoky ballad ("Willow Weep For Me") and a lightning-fast barnburner (Ammons' "Juggin' Around"). However critical Ammons might have been of most organists, it's obvious that he and Holmes share a lot of common ground on *Groovin' With Jug*. *—Alex Henderson*

After Hours / 1962 / Pacific Jazz ✦✦✦✦✦
Richard "Groove" Holmes was one of the first jazz organists to emerge after the rise of Jimmy Smith (who would remain a lifelong influence). Holmes had a lighter tone on the more up-tempo pieces, but on the ballads (such as "Denise" on this set) his organ could give the impression of weighing a ton. This CD reissue combines together most of the music from Holmes' two early albums: *After Hours* and *Tell It like It 'Tis*. These trio renditions (with either Joe Pass or Gene Edwards on guitar and Larance Marable or Leroy Henderson on drums) give one a strong sampling of the organist's talents on a variety of blues, bop standards, and obscure originals. *—Scott Yanow*

Misty / Aug. 3, 1965-Aug. 12, 1966 / Prestige/OJC ✦✦✦✦
Organist Richard "Groove" Holmes in the mid-'60s had a hit with his medium-tempo rendition of "Misty." This CD reissue has the original short version (which was cut as a 45) plus other medium-tempo ballads performed in similar fashion. Holmes and his trio (featuring guitarist Gene Edwards and drummer George Randall) play enjoyable if not overly substantial versions of such songs as "The More I See You," "The Shadow of Your Smile," "What Now My Love" and "Strangers in the Night," trying unsuccessfully for another pop hit; the organist's sound is more appealing than some of the tunes. *—Scott Yanow*

Soul Message / Aug. 3, 1965 / Prestige/OJC ✦✦✦✦✦
Organist Richard "Groove" Holmes hit upon a successful formula on this Prestige session (reissued on CD in the OJC series), mixing together boogaloo rhythms with emotional solos. His doubletime version of "Misty" became a big hit, and the other selections, including Horace Silver's "Song for My Father" and a pair of soulful originals, are in a similar vein. The lone ballad of the set ("The Things We Did Last Summer") is a fine change of pace. With the assistance of guitarist Gene Edwards and drummer Jimmie Smith, Groove Holmes shows that it is possible to create music that is both worthwhile and commercially successful. *—Scott Yanow*

★ **Blue Groove** / Mar. 15, 1966-May 29, 1967 / Prestige ✦✦✦✦✦
This CD, which reissues two former LPs by Richard "Groove" Holmes (*Get Up & Get It* and *Soul Mist*), showcases the organist in a quintet featuring the tenor of Teddy Edwards and guitarist Pat Martino, with his trio, and (on two standards) with trumpeter Blue Mitchell and tenor-saxophonist Harold Vick. Overall, this 73-minute set has many fine solos, spirited ensembles and two well-rounded programs. *—Scott Yanow*

Spicy / Nov. 28, 1966 / Prestige ✦✦✦
Although this is dependable B-3 Hammond soul-jazz, some of the songs selected for this set, such as "If I Had a Hammer" and "Never on Sunday," are inappropriate for soul-jazz translation. On the other hand, the adaptation of Luiz Bonfa's "Manha de Carnaval" is good, and Nat Adderley's "Work Song" is a classic that's hard to mess up. Only one Holmes original, "Boo-D-Doo," on a session aided by guitarists Gene Edwards and Boogaloo Joe Jones. The 1999 Prestige CD reissue of *Spicy* (issued as part of Prestige's *Legends of Acid Jazz* series) adds the whole of a live 1966 LP, *Living Soul*, onto the same disc. *—Richie Unterberger*

Legends of Acid Jazz / Feb. 14, 1968-Aug. 26, 1968 / Prestige ✦✦✦✦
Other than the fact that it features Richard "Groove" Holmes' groovin' organ, the music on this 1997 CD reissue (which contains all of the selections from the LPs *The Groover* and *That Healin' Feelin'*) has little to do with acid-jazz, but certainly qualifies as superior soul-jazz. The last in a long string of Prestige recordings that Holmes had initiated in 1965 is a consistently hard-swinging set. The earlier date matches the organist with either George Freeman or Earl Maddox on guitar and drummer Billy Jackson, while the later date has notable playing by Rusty Bryant (on tenor and alto), the highly expressive guitar of Billy Butler and drummer Herbie Lovelle. More bop-oriented than normal, the reissue includes such numbers as "Speak Low," "Blue Moon," "Just Friends," "On a Clear Day" and the Johnny Hodges/Al Sears hit "Castle Rock." Recommended. *—Scott Yanow*

Groove's Groove / 1977-1988 / 32 Jazz ✦✦✦✦

Blues All Day Long / Feb. 24, 1988 / 32 Jazz ✦✦✦✦✦

Hot Tat / Sep. 5, 1989 / Muse ✦✦✦✦

George Howard

b. 1956, Philadelphia, PA, **d.** Mar. 20, 1998
Sax (Soprano), Producer / Smooth Jazz, Quiet Storm, Crossover Jazz, Jazz-Pop, Urban
George Howard's polished fusion of funk, jazz and urban soul helped the soprano saxophonist become one of the most popular contemporary jazz performers of the '80s and '90s. Since he concentrated on groove and overall sound instead of improvisation, Howard never

received much attention from jazz critics, but he retained a large audience well into his second decade of performing. In 1982 he released his debut album, *Asphalt Garden*, on Palo Alto. The record was a moderate hit, as was its follow-up, 1984's *Steppin' Out*. It wasn't until the 1985 release of *Dancing in the Sun* that Howard earned a large audience. The album reached number one on the contemporary jazz charts. Following the release of *Dancing In the Sun*, he moved to MCA, where he issued *A Nice Place to Be*, *Reflections*, *Personal* and *Love Will Follow*. In 1991, Howard signed to GRP; all of his recordings for the label were quite successful, confirming his place among the most popular contemporary jazz performers of the '90s. He died unexpectedly March 29, 1998. A few months later, his last recording—a version of Sly Stone's *There's A Riot Goin' On*, which was conceived as part of Blue Note's cover series—was released. *—Stephen Thomas Erlewine*

• **The Very Best of George Howard (& Then Some)** / 1985-1997 / GRP ✦✦✦✦
George Howard always said that his music was not jazz, even while he appeared at jazz festivals. A fine R&B-ish soprano saxophonist heavily influenced by Grover Washington, Jr., Howard's recordings tended to be steady sellers but artistically quite erratic, geared toward a dancing funk audience. This best-of collection puts the focus on Howard's playing (the majority of the pieces are instrumentals) and is one of the better sets for listeners who want to actually hear his saxophone. Nine songs are drawn from eight of George Howard's GRP CDs, and there are two previously unreleased numbers from 1997 (Midnight Mood" and "Find Your Way") that are among his final recordings. *—Scott Yanow*

Personal / 1989 / MCA ✦✦✦
The late Kenny G of R&B gave his personal best on these suave yet funky soul grooves, backing his very original soprano sax work with the likes of guitarist Paul Jackson Jr., keyboardist Preston Glass, and top R&B producer George Duke. Howard's horn is very agreeable, melodic and often exciting in its sense of playfulness, but a few less vocals would make it stand out even more. *Personal* is a must buy for sax lovers and instrumental fans who like to shake their booties. Before his death later in the decade, Howard released a slew of popular R&B sax albums that were even better than this. Top cuts include *Uptown* and *Imin Effect*. *—Jonathan Widran*

Do I Ever Cross Your Mind— / 1992 / GRP ✦✦✦✦
Unlike most of the soprano blowers out there in the pop-jazz market, Howard avoids the "Fuzak" plague, and keeps a stronghold on his R&B roots. At the same, time, Howard's 1992 CD stays away from the vocal-dominated tracks, which pop up all the more frequently in this genre. A solid, masterful set of funk/fusion. *—Steve Aldrich*

Love and Understanding / Jan. 13, 1992 / GRP ✦✦✦
After eight albums, the late soprano saxophonist George Howard found a comfortable and solid if slightly predictable niche in the intensifying realm of instrumental R&B. On *Love & Understanding*, his first original GRP outing (after a re-release of 1985's *Dancing in the Sun*), he sticks to the basic funk and romance formulas which made him one of the most consistent suppliers of sweet and nasty improvisational soul over the previous half decade. As always, his smooth yet bouncy lines and frequent circular breathing patterns stand out over the even most tried and true material, but he earns some kudos with "Talk to the Drum," an adventurous sax/percussion duet with masters Lenny Castro and Munyungo Jackson. *—Jonathan Widran*

Attitude Adjustment / 1995 / GRP ✦✦✦

Midnight Mood / Jan. 27, 1998 / GRP ✦✦✦
For George Howard, *Midnight Mood* is business as usual, and not in a good sense. This predictable CD found the saxophonist (who's heard mostly on soprano) once again resorting to the worn-out pop/urban contemporary/jazz formula that had grown incredibly tiresome by 1985 and wasn't sounding any better in 1998. From the vacuous, knee-jerk elevator music of "Still In Love" and "Within Your Eyes" to a robotic cover of D'Angelo's R&B hit "Smooth," Howard sees to it that every note is in place and is careful to avoid any type of spontaneity. The album does contain a few decent cuts, including the haunting "Africa" and the sexy "Find Your Way" (which features R&B singer Marva King). But on the whole, *Midnight Mood* is the work of someone much more interested in selling CDs than saying anything meaningful on his horn. *—Alex Henderson*

Freddie Hubbard (Frederick Dewayne Hubbard)

b. Apr. 7, 1938, Indianapolis, IN
Flugelhorn, Trumpet / Hard Bop, Post-Bop, Fusion, Jazz-Funk
One of the great jazz trumpeters of all time, Freddie Hubbard formed his sound out of the Clifford Brown/Lee Morgan tradition and by the early '70s was immediately distinctive and the pacesetter in jazz. However a string of blatantly commercial albums later in the decade damaged his reputation and, just when Hubbard in the early '90s seemed perfectly suited for the role of veteran master, his chops started causing him serious troubles. After moving to New York in 1958, Hubbard appeared on several landmark albums of the '60s including Eric Dolphy's *Out to Lunch*, John Coltrane's *Ascension*, Ornette Coleman's *Free Jazz*, Oliver Nelson's *Blues and the Abstract Truth* and Herbie Hancock's *Maiden Voyage*. He also started recording as a leader for Blue Note in 1960, and gained fame playing with Art Blakey's Jazz Messengers from 1961 to 1964. A blazing trumpeter with a beautiful tone on flugelhorn, Hubbard fared well in freer settings but was always essentially a hard bop stylist. In 1970, Freddie Hubbard recorded two of his finest albums (*Red Clay* and *Straight Life*) for CTI. But after the glory of the CTI years, he made the mistake of signing with Columbia and recording one dud after another. However, on his 1980s recordings for Pablo, Blue Note and Atlantic he showed that he could reach his former heights. By the late '80s, his once-mighty technique started to seriously falter. *—Scott Yanow*

Goin' Up / Nov. 6, 1960 / Blue Note ✦✦✦✦
For his second recording as a leader, trumpeter Freddie Hubbard (22 at the time) performs two compositions apiece by Kenny Dorham and Hank Mobley, the obscure "I Wished I Knew" and his own "Blues for Brenda." Hubbard (featured in a quintet with tenor-saxophonist Mobley, pianist McCoy Tyner, bassist Paul Chambers and drummer Philly Joe Jones) takes quite a few outstanding solos, playing lyrically on the ballads and building his own sound out of the Clifford Brown/Lee Morgan tradition. It's an excellent set of advanced hard bop that was reissued as a CD in 1997. *—Scott Yanow*

Here to Stay / Apr. 9, 1961-Dec. 27, 1962 / Blue Note ✦✦✦✦
This two-LP set, which was released in 1979 as part of United Artists' Blue Note reissue series, brought back trumpeter Freddie Hubbard's early album *Hub Cap*, a sextet session with tenor-saxophonist Jimmy Heath, trombonist Julian Priester, and pianist Cedar Walton. Although that session (comprised of four Hubbard compositions, one of Walton's songs, and Randy Weston's "Cry Me Not") is excellent, it is the full album of previously unreleased material from an all-star quintet that is of greatest interest. Hubbard teams up with fellow Jazz Messengers Wayne Shorter (on tenor), Walton, bassist Reggie Workman, and (in Blakey's spot) drummer Philly Joe Jones for some advanced hard bop. Highpoints include the fiery "Philly Mignon" and a strong version of "Body and Soul." *—Scott Yanow*

Hub Cap / Apr. 9, 1961 / Blue Note ✦✦✦
On *Hub Cap*, his third effort as a leader, Freddie Hubbard sticks to the tried-and-true hard bop formula, which is something of a mixed blessing. There's no question that much of this music is enjoyable, but it's not quite up to the standards of its two predecessors. Part of the problem is Hubbard's sextet, which features tenor saxophonist Jimmy Heath, trombonist Julian Priester, pianist Cedar Walton, bassist Larry Ridley, and drummer "Philly" Joe Jones. All of the musicians are talented, but only a few are inventive, and that becomes a problem, since it becomes clear that Hubbard is beginning to break free from his influences and develop his own style. In other words, he's capable of more adventurous music than this straight-ahead hard bop. That said, *Hub Cap* is a very good hard bop date. There is energy to the performances, and the artist's vigorous, inspired playing continues to impress, as do some of his original compositions. Only when compared to Hubbard's first two records, or what would come later, does *Hub Cap* seem like a lesser effort. *—Stephen Thomas Erlewine*

Minor Mishap / Aug. 2, 1961 / Black Lion ✦✦✦✦
This is one of Freddie Hubbard's more obscure sessions of the 1960s. Actually it was originally led by the forgotten trombonist Willie Wilson (who died in 1963) but has been reissued by Black Lion on CD under Hubbard's name. The 23-year-old trumpeter is teamed with Wilson, baritonist Pepper Adams and the Duke Pearson Trio (with bassist Thomas Howard and drummer Lex Humphries) for originals by Wilson, Pearson, Adams, Donald Byrd and Tommy Flanagan in addition to two standards that feature the trombonist; the reissue adds five alternate takes to the original seven-song program. Hubbard and Adams both have plenty of solos on this excellent hard bop date, one that is worth picking up by straightahead jazz fans. *—Scott Yanow*

☆ **Ready for Freddie** / Aug. 21, 1961 / Blue Note ✦✦✦✦✦
Trumpeter Freddie Hubbard really came into his own during this Blue Note session. He is matched with quite an all-star group (tenor-saxophonist Wayne Shorter, pianist McCoy Tyner, bassist Art Davis and drummer Elvin Jones in addition to Bernard McKinney on euphonium), introduces two of his finest compositions ("Birdlike" and "Crisis") and is quite lyrical on his ballad feature "Weaver of Dreams." Hubbard's sidemen all play up to par and this memorable session is highly recommended; it's one of the trumpeter's most rewarding Blue Note albums. *—Scott Yanow*

The Artistry of Freddie Hubbard / Jul. 2, 1962 / Impulse! ✦✦✦✦
Trumpeter Freddie Hubbard leads a particularly talented sextet (with trombonist Curtis Fuller, a rare outing away from Sun Ra for tenor-saxophonist John Gilmore, pianist Tommy Flanagan, bassist Art Davis and drummer Louis Hayes) on three of his originals and strong versions of "Summertime" and "Caravan." This advanced hard bop music was reissued on CD in 1996 with 20-bit mastering. *—Scott Yanow*

Hub-Tones / Oct. 10, 1962 / Blue Note ✦✦✦✦✦
Trumpeter Freddie Hubbard teams up on record with James Spaulding (who doubles on alto and flute) for the first time on this excellent set. With the assistance of pianist Herbie Hancock, bassist Reggie Workman and drummer Clifford Jarvis, the quintet performs four of the trumpeter's originals (including "Lament for Booker" and the title cut) plus an advanced version of the standard "You're My Everything." John Coltrane's modal music was starting to influence Hubbard's conception and his own playing was pushing ahead the modern mainstream without really entering the avant-garde. *—Scott Yanow*

The Body and Soul / Mar. 8, 1963-May 2, 1963 / Impulse! ✦✦✦✦
The second of trumpeter Freddie Hubbard's two Impulse albums features the 25-year old in three separate settings. He is heard along with tenor-saxophonist backed by with strings ("Skylark," "I Got It Bad" and "Chocolate Shake" are all given beautiful treatments), with a 16-piece band and in a septet with Eric Dolphy and Wayne Shorter. This well-rounded and highly recommended showcase shows why Freddie Hubbard was considered the top trumpeter to emerge during the early '60s. *—Scott Yanow*

Breaking Point / May 7, 1964 / Blue Note ✦✦✦✦✦
This CD reissue (which augments the original five-song program with alternate takes originally issued on 45s of "Blue Frenzy" and "Mirrors") brings back the first recording Hubbard cut with his own working band (as opposed to an all-star studio group). On these selections (particularly the memorable "Breaking Point"), Hubbard and his quintet (James Spaulding on alto and flute, pianist Ronnie Matthews, bassist Eddie Khan and drummer Joe Chambers) play music that falls in between hard bop and the avant-garde, stretching the boundaries of the jazz modern mainstream. Their explorative flights are still quite interesting more than three decades later and Hubbard, having broken away from his earlier Clifford Brown and Lee Morgan influences, really sounds very much like himself. *—Scott Yanow*

Backlash / Oct. 19, 1966+Oct. 24, 1966 / Koch International ✦✦✦✦
Trumpeter Freddie Hubbard led a particularly fine quintet in the mid-'60s that has long been underrated. The edition heard on this Atlantic LP features James Spaulding on alto and flute, pianist Albert Dailey, bassist Bob Cunningham, and drummer Otis Ray Appleton. This stu-

dio recording is most notable for debuting Hubbard's "Little Sunflower" and also has a good remake of "Up Jumped Spring," along with four other obscure pieces. The music straddles the boundaries between hard bop, soul, and the avant-garde, and has plenty of unpredictable moments. This is the strongest of Freddie Hubbard's three Atlantic records of the period. — *Scott Yanow*

High Blues Pressure / Nov. 1967 / Koch Jazz ✦✦✦
For this studio album, Freddie Hubbard expanded his quintet by adding tenor-saxophonist Bennie Maupin, Kiane Zawadi on euphonium and the tuba of Howard Johnson. The music is complex but swinging with fine solos from the trumpeter/leader, altoist James Spaulding, Maupin and pianist Kenny Barron. — *Scott Yanow*

☆ **Red Clay** / Jan. 27, 1970-Jan. 29, 1970 / Columbia ✦✦✦✦✦
Freddie Hubbard has long considered this recording to be his best, and with good reason. The trumpeter is heard at the peak of his powers performing five originals (one, "Cold Turkey," was released for the first time on this CD reissue) in a quintet with tenor-saxophonist Joe Henderson, keyboardist Herbie Hancock, bassist Ron Carter and drummer Lenny White. "Red Clay" is a classic and the other selections ("The Intreprid Fox," "Suite Sioux" and "Delphia") all feature Hubbard taking colorful solos in a style that blends together hard bop with subtle funky rhythms. Classic music of the early 1970s. — *Scott Yanow*

★ **Straight Life** / Nov. 16, 1970 / Columbia ✦✦✦✦✦
Recorded between trumpeter Freddie Hubbard's better-known classics *Red Clay* and *First Light*, *Straight Life* is actually arguably Hubbard's greatest recording. Hubbard, joined by an all-star group that includes tenor-saxophonist Joe Henderson, keyboardist Herbie Hancock, guitarist George Benson, bassist Ron Carter and drummer Jack DeJohnette, is frequently astounding on "Straight Life" (check out that introduction) and "Mr. Clean," constructing classic solos. The very memorable set is rounded off by the trumpeter's duet with Benson on a lyrical version of the ballad "Here's That Rainy Day." This exciting CD is essential for all serious jazz collections. — *Scott Yanow*

First Light / Sep. 14-16, 1971 / Columbia ✦✦✦✦✦
The third of Freddie Hubbard's "big three" recordings for CTI (it was preceded by *Red Clay* and *Straight Life*), *First Light* was probably the trumpeter's most popular album. The first of his recordings to utilize the string and woodwind arrangements of Don Sebesky, Hubbard sounds quite inspired by his accompaniment and plays at his best throughout, particularly on "First Light" and "Uncle Albert/Admiral Halsey." The CD reissue by Columbia adds one previously unissued selection ("Fantasy in D") to the original program. — *Scott Yanow*

Sky Dive / Oct. 4, 1972+Oct. 5, 1972 / Columbia ✦✦✦✦
Freddie Hubbard's fourth CTI recording (and the second one with Don Sebesky arrangements) certainly has a diverse repertoire. In addition to his originals "Povo" and "Sky Dive" (both of which are superior jam tunes), the trumpeter stretches out on the theme from *The Godfather* and Bix Beiderbecke's "In a Mist." The charts for the brass and woodwinds are colorful, there is a fine supporting cast that includes guitarist George Benson, Keith Jarrett on keyboards and flutist Hubert Laws and Hubbard takes several outstanding trumpet solos. — *Scott Yanow*

Keep Your Soul Together / Oct. 1973 / Columbia ✦✦✦✦
Trumpeter Freddie Hubbard's CTI recordings have long been underrated and a bit downgraded by writers who get them confused with his much commercial output for Columbia. For this LP (not yet reissued on CD) Hubbard is heard in fine form on four of his originals (highlighted by "Spirits of Trane") with a septet that includes tenor-saxophonist Junior Cook, keyboardist George Cables, guitarist Aurell Ray, either Kent Brinkley or Ron Carter on bass, drummer Ralph Penland and Juno Lewis on percussion. The music is sometimes funky but definitely creative jazz with Hubbard heard during his prime period. — *Scott Yanow*

Keystone Bop / Nov. 27, 1981+Nov. 29, 1981 / Fantasy ✦✦✦

Keystone Bop: Sunday Night / Nov. 29, 1981 / Prestige ✦✦✦

Born to Be Blue / Dec. 14, 1984 / Pablo/OJC ✦✦✦✦

Face to Face / May 24, 1982 / Pablo/OJC ✦✦✦✦✦

Sweet Return / Jun. 13, 1983-Jun. 14, 1983 / Atlantic ✦✦✦✦
One of Freddie Hubbard's best albums since the early '70's, this quintet date finds him joined by quite an all-star lineup: Lew Tabackin on tenor and flute, pianist Joanne Brackeen (who has many fine solos throughout the album), bassist Eddie Gomez and drummer Roy Haynes. Highpoints include Hubbard's tender version of "Misty" (at the time he had a particularly lovely tone on fluegelhorn), Brackeen's "Heidi-B" and the quintet's rendition of the standard "The Night Has a Thousand Eyes." — *Scott Yanow*

Above & Beyond / Jun. 17, 1982 / Metropolitan ✦✦✦✦✦

Bobbi Humphrey

b. Apr. 25, 1950, Dallas, TX
Flute / Crossover Jazz, Mainstream Jazz, Fusion, Soul-Jazz, Jazz-Funk
Bobbi Humphrey was a jazz flautist whose musical tastes leaned toward fusion and smooth jazz-pop. From the outset of her career, Humphrey was quite popular, winning a large crossover audience with her pop-oriented jazz-fusion. Throughout her career, her popularity exceeded her critical acclaim, although several critics did praise her technique and showmanship. Despite the lack of critical praise, audiences stayed with Humphrey for decades, buying her records and attending her concerts from the Montreux Festival to Carnegie Hall.

Although Bobbi Humphrey was born in Marlin, Texas, she was raised in Dallas. She began playing flute in high school and continued her studies at Texas Southern University and Southern Methodist University. Dizzy Gillespie saw Humphrey play at a talent contest at Southern Methodist, and impressed with what he had heard, he urged her to pursue a musical career in New York City. She followed through on his advice, getting her first big break performing at the Apollo Theatre on Amateur Night. Shortly afterward, she began playing regularly throughout the city, including a gig with Duke Ellington.

Humphrey signed with Blue Note in 1971. Her smooth blend of jazz, funk, pop and R&B fit in well with the new sound of Blue Note, and her six albums for the label—*Flute In, Dig This, Blacks and Blues, Satin Doll, Live at Montreux*, and *Fancy Dancer?* were all successes. In particular, 1973's *Blacks and Blues* was a rousing success, earning her a crossover pop and R&B audience. That same year, she played the Montreux Festival in Switzerland. In 1976, she was named Best Female Instrumentalist by *Billboard*. The following year, she switched record labels, signing with Epic and releasing *Tailor Made* that same year. She also played on Stevie Wonder's platinum album *Songs in the Key of Life* in 1977.

Tailor Made was the first of three albums on Epic Records—*Freestyle* followed in 1978, and *The Good Life* appeared about a year afterward. During the '80s, Humphrey continued to perform regularly, even if she didn't record often. She returned to recording in 1989, releasing *City Beat* on Malaco Records. Five years later, *Passion Flute* appeared on the Paradise Sounds label. — *Stephen Thomas Erlewine*

Flute In / Sep. 30, 1971-Oct. 1, 1971 / Blue Note ✦✦✦✦
A landmark signing, Humphrey's the first female ever signed by Blue Note Records. Bobbi's debut pays homage to songs popularized by others, no original material made it pass the drawing board. The petite flautist from Texas sticks to tradition on covers of "Ain't No Sunshine, " and "It's Too Late," her flute conveying the songs' sentiment, and sadness as convincingly as any voice in music. Jazz roots spar with funk and soul influences on Lee Morgan's "Sidewinder, " and Eddie Harris' "Set Me Free." The fight continues on Ben E. King's "Spanish Harlem, " and which has more bounce and rhythm than the original. Bobbi displays dexterity and power throughout her coming out, mainstream LP. — *Andrew Hamilton*

Blacks and Blues / Jun. 7, 1973+Jun. 8, 1973 / Blue Note ✦✦✦✦
An amazing collection from the diminutive female flautist/singer, Bobbi Humphrey, the first female artist signed by Blue Note Records. Producers Fonce Mizell and Freddie Perren made their mark as part of the Corporation, which crafted studio tracks that made the Jackson Five as American as apple pie, and as world renowned. This tight, six-song album explodes from the first cut with a torrid, fast, bebop groove called "Chicago Damn," which features chant vocals from Fonce, Freddie and Larry Mizell, and Humphrey's riveting, perky blows riding above a scintillating rhythm track. "Harlem River Drive" is laid-back, cool and relaxing, the ultimate cruising tune. "Just a Love Child" is sweet, innocent and will burrow in your heart and never leave. Bobbi sings the ballad in a youthful but stunning soprano. The title cut, "Black & Blues," is steeped in traditional jazz, a mid-tempo rambler with staid backing vocals. A heavy, pounding bottom drives and enhances "Jasper County Man," the earthiness of Humphrey's playing makes you shiver. "Baby's Gone" is the last cut on *Black & Blues*. Listen at your own risk; very few jazz oriented tunes can be classified as tear jerkers but this one fits the bill. Pain is evident in every note of the loping, instrumental instigated by Mizell's and Perren's morbid backing cries. — *Andrew Hamilton*

City Beat / Jul. 1989 / Malaco ✦✦✦✦✦
A representative effort by flutist Humphrey, who delivers a jazz-pop sound. — *David Szatmary*

● **Blue Break Beats** / Jul. 20, 1972-Aug. 5, 1975 / Blue Note ✦✦✦✦
It must be difficult for Blue Note to compile a best of Bobbi Humphrey CD, since nearly all of her Blue Note LPs sounded like greatest hits compilations. Somebody picked six from a field of plenty. Why not just reissue all of her Blue Note LPs on CD— Combine two albums on one CD, and blow our minds. These little, skimpy, six-track *Blue Break Beats*, while better than nothing, are far from nirvana. *Black and Blues* represents her critically acclaimed album of the same name, and is the most traditional jazz song on the set. The moody, cool, deftly executed "Smiling Faces Sometimes" is awesome. It's not as well known as some later cuts, it appeared on *Dig This*, the LP before *Black & Blues*, and suffered from promotion tantamount to a magic marker sign used to promote a lemonade stand. You get a taste of her vocal ability on "My Little Girl," a tender number inspired by the birth of her first child. On the jamming "Harlem River Drive," Bobbi displays dexterity and strength flowing with the beat like a salmon swimming upstream. Esoteric and mind-bending are two words that describe the glittering "San Francisco Lights," the beat is camouflage by shimmering effects and uncharacteristically lazy fluting from Bobbi, bending notes as naturally as one bends one's arm. Humphrey's sensitive, succulent phrasing is as identifiable as any voice in music. It's an indictment of the music industry that this fine talent hasn't achieved more, she gives her all every time out the chute. — *Andrew Hamilton*

Charlie Hunter

b. 1968, Rhode Island
Guitar / Jazz-Rock, Acid Jazz, Post-Bop, Fusion
Charlie Hunter, who plays an eight-string guitar, provides his own basslines and leads an otherwise bassless guitar-sax-drums trio. He grew up in Berkeley, CA, and began playing guitar when he was 12. Hunter played in rock bands until forming his trio with tenor saxophonist Dave Ellis and drummer Jay Lane. Although very much a jazz group, the group also displays their interests in funk and rock. In addition to recording for Blue Note with his trio, Hunter works with T.J. Kirk, a band playing the music of Thelonious Monk, James Brown and Rahsaan Roland Kirk that has recorded for Warner Bros. In 1997 Charlie Hunter toured with a two-horn quartet (his guitar not only filled in for a bass but sometimes sounded eerily like an organ) and recorded a suprisingly successful jazz transformation of Bob Marley's reggae classic *Natty Dread*. — *Scott Yanow*

Bing, Bing, Bing! / 1995 / Blue Note ✦✦✦✦
It is difficult not to be impressed with the playing of guitarist Charlie Hunter. By using an extra string, Hunter is able to create his own basslines and have a very self-sufficient bassless (and keyboardless) trio with tenor-saxophonist Dave Ellis and drummer Jay Lane that has all of the parts covered. The music on this CD (all originals) crosses over between straightahead jamming to '70s retro funk (a la Eddie Harris) that is infectious enough to fit into an acid jazz setting. However, even at its funkiest, the rhythms are subtle and the improvising

reasonably creative, making this a potentially popular group that should still interest jazz listeners. *—Scott Yanow*

Natty Dread / 1997 / Blue Note ♦♦♦♦
As part of Blue Note's developing Cover Series, where their artists cover an entire pop album as if they were jazz compositions, Charlie Hunter chose Bob Marley's milestone, *Natty Dread*. The concept of the Cover Series is undeniably gimmicky, but there's no discounting Marley's skills as a songwriter and the immense talents of Hunter and his quartets. Not content to simply replicate the original album, the guitarist twists it around, accentuating the rhythms and bluesy scales to varying degrees. Within the new arrangements, Hunter is able to spin off remarkably tasteful and fluid lines, and saxophonists Kenny Brooks (tenor) and Calder Spanier (alto) are equally graceful and provocative. Occasionally, the results are a little uneven, but overall Hunter's version of *Natty Dread* is an impressive interpretation. *—Stephen Thomas Erlewine*

Return of the Candyman / Mar. 10, 1998 / Blue Note ♦♦♦♦
After releasing *Natty Dread*, Charlie Hunter decided to form a new band, one without horns. The ensuing Pound For Pound features Hunter with a drummer, synthesizers, and vibraphonist Stefon Harris. Removing the horns puts Hunter's guitar in the spotlight, and he rises to the occasion, fulfilling the promise he's displayed on all of his previous releases. There's a stronger groove here than on any of Hunter's previous records, but what's remarkable about the album is the way he keeps the groove rolling while pushing the music into unpredictable, adventurous territory. That fusion of groove and challenging jazz makes *Return of the Candyman* a thoroughly rewarding listen. *—Stephen Thomas Erlewine*

● **Charlie Hunter** / Jan. 19, 2000 - 20 / Blue Note ♦♦♦♦
Charlie Hunter is a restless musician in a dilemma. The variety of players and settings on his first several albums are testament to his restless spirit. But as his technique and confidence grow, it seems that the best showcase for his talent would be in small groups with minimal accompaniment, due to his ability to play rhythm and melody simultaneously. Since his last album, *Duo*, was the epitome of minimal accompaniment, Hunter must have felt obliged to vary the sound somewhat. For this album, Hunter continues his collaboration with percussionist Leon Parker, as well as bringing Josh Roseman and Peter Apfelbaum on trombone and sax, respectively, plus a couple of Parker's students. But the show still belongs to Hunter; there is one solo cut and three duets with Parker. When the other percussionists join in, the rhythms remain lean, with each player utilizing only one or two items. This leaves plenty of space for Hunter, while providing nice counterpoint to his playing. The horns are used on only four of the nine tracks of the album, but do a lot to expand the overall sound. Apfelbaum and Roseman solo nicely, but just as exciting is hearing Hunter's comping behind them. His technique really is amazing, but always at the service of music, not virtuosity. The tunes themselves lay down a solid groove; never too far from soul-jazz or funk, but with a boppish vocabulary that says this is no ordinary groove band. *Charlie Hunter* is another fine offering from a uniquely talented player, demonstrating both a high degree of musical sensitivity and astonishing technical abilities. *—Sean Westergaard*

Bobby Hutcherson

b. Jan. 27, 1941, Los Angeles, CA
Vibraphone / Hard Bop, Post-Bop
Although when he first came up vibraphonist Bobby Hutcherson was associated with the avant-garde. He has since settled down into being "merely" a brilliant stylist whose playing falls between hard bop and post bop rather than becoming an innovator.

Hutcherson originally studied piano and then started concentrating on vibes as a teenager. He worked in the L.A. area with Curtis Amy and Charles Lloyd before joining the Al Grey-Billy Mitchell Quintet. Hutcherson moved to New York in 1961, made a big impression with his playing on Eric Dolphy's *Out to Lunch* (1964) and worked with everyone from Jackie McLean, Hank Mobley and Grachan Moncur III to Hank Mobley, Herbie Hancock, Andrew Hill, McCoy Tyner and Grant Green. Whenever an advanced vibraphonist was needed for a recording, Hutcherson got the call. He recorded a long series of albums as a leader for Blue Note (1965-77), co-led a quintet with Harold Land (1967-71) and has headed his own groups ever since other than his dates with the Timeless All Stars in the 1980s. In addition to Blue Note, Bobby Hutcherson has recorded as a leader for Cadet, Columbia, Timeless, Evidence, Contemporary and Landmark. *—Scott Yanow*

☆ **Dialogue** / Apr. 3, 1965 / Blue Note ♦♦♦♦♦
Vibraphonist Bobby Hutcherson's debut as a leader is still one of his most advanced recordings. Reissued on CD, the six-song program (including an Andrew Hill composition "Jasper" that was only previously out on an obscure 1979 LP) has an all-star group of young greats (trumpeter Freddie Hubbard; Sam Rivers on tenor, soprano, bass clarinet and flute; pianist Andrew Hill; bassist Richard Davis; and drummer Joe Chambers in addition to Hutcherson), complex originals by Hill and Chambers and plenty of dynamic solos. The adventurous music falls between post bop and the avant-garde and finds the musicians all sounding quite inspired and challenged. An underrated Blue Note classic. *—Scott Yanow*

Spiral / Apr. 3, 1965+Nov. 25, 1968 / Blue Note ♦♦♦
Not released initially until this 1979 LP, these fine advanced performances deserved a better fate. One song, "Jasper," features an all-star sextet (comprised of vibraphonist Bobby Hutcherson; Sam Rivers on tenor and bass clarinet; trumpeter Freddie Hubbard; pianist Andrew Hill; bassist Richard Davis; and drummer Joe Chambers) and has been reissued on CD. The other five selections (which have not yet returned) are more in the modal/hard bop vein, matching Hutcherson with his future co-leader, tenor-saxophonist Harold Land, and pianist Stanley Cowell, bassist Reggie Johnson, and drummer Chambers. All of the songs are originals by band members and have their unpredictable moments while not forgetting to swing. Intriguing music that hopefully will resurface someday. *—Scott Yanow*

● **Components** / Jun. 10, 1965 / Blue Note ♦♦♦♦♦
This CD reissue spans a wide variety of styles, from hard bop (Bobby Hutcherson's attractive "Little B's Poem") to mostly atonal sound explorations ("Air"). There are four compositions apiece by the vibraphonist/leader and drummer Joe Chambers with Chambers tending to be freer and more avant-garde. The talented young musicians (trumpeter Freddie Hubbard, James Spaulding on alto and flute, pianist Herbie Hancock, bassist Ron Carter, Chambers and Hutcherson) are up to the challenge and the results are always stimulating. Open-eared listeners are advised to pick up this CD, taken from a period when the versatile Bobby Hutcherson was considered one of the brightest new voices of what was called "the New Thing." *—Scott Yanow*

Happenings / Feb. 8, 1966 / Blue Note ♦♦♦♦
This is an excellent showcase for Bobby Hutcherson, who plays vibes and marimba in a quartet with pianist Herbie Hancock, bassist Bob Cranshaw, and drummer Joe Chambers. On the straight CD reissue of the original LP, Hutcherson performs six of his diverse originals (which range from advanced hard bop to the nearly free form "The Omen") plus Hancock's "Maiden Voyage." Hutcherson's outings on marimba are particularly interesting since they show the influence of modern classical music. His own style would become more conservative and predictable through the years, making Bobby Hutcherson's earlier records the ones to get for adventurous listeners. *—Scott Yanow*

Stick-Up! / Apr. 14, 1966 / Blue Note ♦♦♦♦♦
Just being notified as to this set's all-star lineup (vibraphonist Bobby Hutcherson, tenor-saxophonist Joe Henderson, pianist McCoy Tyner, bassist Herbie Lewis and drummer Billy Higgins) should cause most veteran jazz collectors to go out of their way to acquire the release. The quintet performs five of Hutcherson's little-known (but worthwhile) compositions plus Ornette Coleman's catchy "Una Muy Bonita." The advanced modal music (which sometimes hints at the avant-garde while holding on to its roots in hard bop) continually keeps one's interest. This excellent set was reissued in 1997 on CD. *—Scott Yanow*

Oblique / Jul. 21, 1967 / Blue Note ♦♦♦♦
There is a tension in this modern mainstream performance from 1967 that is often absent from today's music. While still playing music based on hard bop, vibraphonist Bobby Hutcherson and his quartet (which includes pianist Herbie Hancock, bassist Albert Stinson and drummer Joe Chambers) pulled at the chord structures and stretched the boundaries of the music during their improvisations. The two Chambers pieces ("Oblique" and "Bi-Sectional") are the freest and most fascinating recordings, but even Hancock's repetitive vamp ("Theme from Blow Up") is of interest. The four young masters on the CD reissue were quite capable of playing a variety of styles, and their versatility, creativity, and fire make this CD a standout. *—Scott Yanow*

Patterns / Mar. 14, 1968 / Blue Note ♦♦♦♦
This lesser-known Bobby Hutcherson CD (reissued in 1995) has concise but searching solos from the vibraphonist, James Spaudling (doubling on alto and flute), pianist Stanley Cowell, bassist Reggie Workman and drummer Joe Chambers on originals by Chambers (four), Cowell and Spaulding. All of the musicians worked together often during this period (Chambers is on nine of Hutcherson's ten Blue Note albums) and they make the complex music sound much simpler (and perhaps more logical) than it really is. None of the songs caught on although some (particularly Cowell's "Effi" and the drummer's "Patterns" which is heard in two versions) seem eerily familiar. A good example of advanced hard bop. *—Scott Yanow*

Total Eclipse / Jul. 12, 1967 / Blue Note ♦♦♦♦♦
Although thought of as an avant-garde vibraphonist when he first emerged, Bobby Hutcherson eventually became an important part of the modern mainstream. This set, with its modal originals, is somewhere in between where Hutcherson had been and where he was going. Joined by tenor-saxophonist Harold Land (with whom he had just started co-leading a quintet) and the up-and-coming pianist Chick Corea, Hutcherson is in excellent form on four of his originals and Corea's "Matrix." *—Scott Yanow*

Medina / Aug. 11, 1969 / Blue Note ♦♦♦♦
The Bobby Hutcherson-Harold Land Quintet was one of the main unsung groups of this era. Not avant-garde enough to be grouped with the free jazz innovators and owing nothing to fusion, vibraphonist Hutcherson and tenor-saxophonist Land seemed to fall between the cracks as bandleaders, if not as solo musicians. This 1969 recording, not released until 1980, teams the co-leaders with pianist Stanley Cowell, bassist Reggie Johnson, and drummer Joe Chambers for a variety of complex originals; two apiece by Hutcherson, Cowell, and Chambers. The modal music is between hard bop and the avant-garde, but can simply be called explorative and unpredictable. The CD reissue, which came out in 1998, augments the original six selections with five more numbers which originally (along with one earlier and unrelated cut not included here) comprised the LP *Spiral*. The personnel is the same as is the advanced hard bop/modal style and the reliance on originals (two by Chambers and one apiece by Cowell, Land, and Hutcherson), so this expanded reissue makes a great deal of sense. *—Scott Yanow*

San Francisco / Jul. 15, 1970 / Blue Note ♦♦♦♦♦
This CD reissue is an exact duplicate of the original LP. Vibraphonist Bobby Hutcherson and tenor-saxophonist Harold Land co-led a quintet on the West Coast for quite a few years. The remainder of the personnel was often open to change and on this particular release the duo is augmented by keyboardist Joe Sample (normally with The Jazz Crusaders at the time), bassist John Williams and drummer Mickey Roker. The music is often quite advanced yet more accessible than one would expect. There are hints of rock rhythms on a few tracks along with modal melodies influenced by John Coltrane and plenty of rewarding solos from the co-leaders. *—Scott Yanow*

Live at Montreux / Jul. 5, 1973 / Blue Note ♦♦♦♦♦
By 1973 Blue Note was pretty well a dead label and this often-brilliant advanced hard bop set was only released at the time in Europe and Japan. Now with the CD reissue, Americans can finally hear the mutually inspiring performance of vibraphonist Bobby Hutcherson and trumpeter Woody Shaw. Joined by a fine rhythm section, they create fiery solos on modal originals with Shaw in particular in prime form. Highly recommended. *—Scott Yanow*

Un Poco Loco / 1979 / Koch Jazz ♦♦♦♦

Solo/Quartet / Sep. 28, 1981-Mar. 1, 1982 / Contemporary/OJC ♦♦♦♦♦
This is one of vibraphonist Bobby Hutcherson's most unusual and interesting releases. The first half of the set features Hutcherson all by himself although, by utilizing overdubbing, he almost sounds like Max Roach's M'Boom ensemble. Hutcherson is heard on vibes, marimbas, bass marimba, chimes, xylophone and bells and these three selections are quite fun and energetic. The second half is more conventional, with Hutcherson welcoming pianist McCoy Tyner (in his first sideman appearance in a decade), bassist Herbie Lewis and drummer Billy Higgins for two standards and a pair of the vibist's originals. The quartet set is excellent but it is Bobby Hutcherson's solo performances that are most memorable and unique. *—Scott Yanow*

In the Vanguard / Dec. 5, 1986+Dec. 6, 1986 / 32 Jazz ♦♦♦♦♦

Skyline / Aug. 3, 1998-Aug. 5, 1998 / Verve ♦♦♦♦
Legendary vibist Bobby Hutcherson delivers an attractive collection on this, his first recording for the Verve label. Accompanied by an all-star lineup, it's Hutcherson himself who raises *Skyline* to a level above the average straight-ahead jazz jam, but he is obviously inspired by his young bandmates. Alto saxman Kenny Garrett is especially impressive here. Highlights include a "Delilah" played in a relaxed, slow groove; a beautiful reading of Herbie Hancock's "Chan's Song"; and a lovely piano/vibes duet on the Hutcherson original "Candle." In addition, the opening "Who's Got You" features fine interplay between Hutcherson and Garrett, and smokin' solos from the whole crew, while the arrangement of "I Only Have Eyes for You" takes that warhorse far beyond the mundane place where it usually resides. *—Jim Newsom*

Kicker / Dec. 29, 1963 / Blue Note ♦♦♦♦
Bobby Hutcherson recorded frequently for Blue Note in the 1960s, though this session remained unissued until 1999. The first half features the vibraphonist in a cooking hard bop session with Joe Henderson and Duke Pearson, starting with an energetic take on the normally slow ballad "If Ever I Would Leave You" and a sizzling Hutcherson original, "For Duke P." Guitarist Grant Green is added for the second half, beginning with the first recording of Henderson's "The Kicker," which became well known from it's later rendition on Horace Silver's highly successful release *Song for My Father.* Because this is part of Blue Note's limited-edition *Jazz Connoisseur* series, don't delay in picking it up. *—Ken Dryden*

Dick Hyman

b. Mar. 8, 1927, New York, NY
Piano / Spy Music, Lounge, Classic Jazz, Stride, Swing
A very versatile virtuoso, Dick Hyman once recorded an album on which he played "A Child Is Born" in the styles of 11 different pianists from Scott Joplin to Cecil Taylor. Hyman can clearly play anything he wants to and during the past two decades he has mostly concentrated on pre-bop swing and stride styles. Hyman worked with Red Norvo (1949-50) and Benny Goodman (1950) and then spent much of the 1950s and '60s as a studio musician. He appears on the one known sound film of Charlie Parker (*Hot House* from 1952), recorded honky tonk under pseudonyms, played organ and early synthesizers in addition to piano, was Arthur Godfrey's music director (1959-62), collaborated with Leonard Feather on some History of Jazz concerts (doubling on clarinet) and even performed rock and free jazz, but all of this was a prelude to his present-day work. In the 1970s Hyman played with the New York Jazz Repertory Company, formed the Perfect Jazz Repertory Quintet (1976) and started writing soundtracks for Woody Allen films. He has recorded frequently during the past 25 years (sometimes in duets with Ruby Braff) for Concord, Music Masters and Reference and ranks at the top of the classic jazz field. *—Scott Yanow*

Moog: The Electric Eclectics of Dick Hyman / 1969 / Varese ♦♦♦♦♦
In the late '60s, pianist Dick Hyman, famous for "Moritat, Theme from Threepenny Opera," aexperimented with various keyboard instruments, including Baldwin and Lowrey organs. This release was his first with what was then a completely newfangled machine, the Moog synthesizer. Hyman took the Moog by the horns and milked it for all it was worth on nine originals, including the monster hit single "The Minotaur" (which inspired Emerson, Lake and Palmer's "Lucky Man").

The first few tracks are in a pop-song mold, but they are pop songs composed as only a jazz musician with two decades of experience under his belt could. Hyman then hits the listener with a few spacier, improvised numbers that come off as very accessible avant-garde music. Following the "The Minotaur" are two improvised pieces. *Moog: The Electric Eclectics of Dick Hyman* ends with "Evening Thoughts," an impressionistic track reminiscent of "Ebb Tide" by Earl Grant, on which the sounds of the seashore are conjured up on various keyboard instruments. Hyman writes about his intentions for each track in the liner notes.

Aside from some other Moog tracks sprinkled throughout DCC Compact Classics' *Music for a Bachelor's Den* series, it's surprising that it's taken this long in the lounge reissue bonanza for the Moog to finally appear (not counting *The Moog Cookbook,* a fab spinning of modern rock nuggets into string cheese.) *Moog* features three bonus tracks from Hyman's next album *Age of Electronicus;* his recasting of James Brown's "Give It Up or Turn It Loose" is well worth the price of admission.

Though this album could easily be tossed into the novelty or "period piece" category, it was not originally intended as that. Hyman recorded a showcase what this new instrument could do, and in the process made an enjoyable album. *—Jim Powers*

★ **Jelly and James: Music of "Jelly Roll" Morton and James P. Johnson** / 1973-1975 / Sony Classical ♦♦♦♦♦
With the exception of a version of "Fickle Fay Creep," this single CD has all of the music recorded by Dick Hyman for tribute LPs for Jelly Roll Morton and James P. Johnson. By varying the instrumentation (which ranges from a piano solo and duets to a big band) and by picking musicians who really understand vintage jazz, Hyman put together two classic sets. The Morton date features such musicians as clarinetist Kenny Davern (doubling on soprano), violinist Joe Venuti, trumpeter Pee Wee Erwin, and trombonist Vic Dickenson (among others), and the highlights include Hyman's showcase on "Fingerbuster," "King Porter Stomp," "The Crave," and an exuberant "Black Bottom Stomp." The James P. Johnson project is most notable for three duets by Hyman (one on pipe organ) with cornetist Ruby Braff and for excellent orchestrations for both a theater orchestra and a jazz band. Essential music for any serious pre-bop collection. *—Scott Yanow*

Charleston / Apr. 29, 1975-May 29, 1975 / Columbia ♦♦♦♦♦
Dick Hyman is a modern day wonder; a pianist who can seemingly re-create the style of practically any jazz keyboardist. Since his favorite era is pre-swing, he has mostly concentrated on the jazz pioneers in recent years. This well-rounded set looks into the music of James P. Johnson, the king of stride pianists and an eminent composer of the 1920s. Hyman casts Johnson's music in several different settings. He takes "Caprice Rag" as a piano solo, joins in on three duets with cornetist Ruby Braff (including one outing on organ), uses a fairly straight dance band and an even less adventurous theater orchestra on some tracks, and for three selections features a jazz band that includes Braff, Bob Wilber on soprano, and trombonist Vic Dickenson. Although there is not a great deal of improvisation on this program, the expert transcriptions and colorful arrangements pay a glorious tribute to the great James P. Johnson. *—Scott Yanow*

☆ **The Music of Jelly Roll Morton** / Feb. 26, 1978 / Smithsonian ♦♦♦♦♦
Of all the Jelly Roll Morton tribute albums that have been recorded through the years, Dick Hyman's is one of the most rewarding. He utilizes a very suitable septet (with clarinetist Bob Wilber, trumpeter Warren Vache, trombonist Jack Gale, Marty Grosz on guitar and banjo, Major Holley doubling on bass and tuba, and Morton alumnus Tommy Benford on drums) on nine of Morton's best tunes, including two ("King Porter Stomp" and "Wolverine Blues") not recorded by Morton in this format. In addition, there is a close recreation of the quartet piece "Mournful Serenade," a couple of trios with Wilber and Benford, and two piano solos ("Fingerbreaker" and "The Pearls") that give Hyman an opportunity to do his Jelly Roll Morton impressions. This LP should satisfy all traditional jazz fans. *—Scott Yanow*

Live at Maybeck Recital Hall, Vol. 3: Music of 1937 / Feb. 14, 1989 / Concord Jazz ♦♦♦♦
Dick Hyman is such a versatile pianist that his own style has often been overshadowed by his interpretations of other pianist's work. *Music of 1937,* which features 11 diverse songs premiered in that year, finds Hyman at times hinting at Oscar Peterson (especially on "Where or When"), the stride piano masters, classical music and even the basslines of Dave McKenna, but mostly he plays in his own virtuosic yet very melodic and accessible style. "Loch Lomond" pays tribute to Benny Goodman's rendition, "Thanks for the Memory" is based a bit on Bob Hope's original recording and Art Tatum would have been proud to have cut this version of "In the Still of the Night." The wide range of emotions (from an exuberant "Bob White" to a somber "The Folks Who Live on the Hill") and Hyman's typically brilliant playing on the solo recital make this CD a particular standout. *—Scott Yanow*

Stride Piano Summit / Jun. 15, 1990 / Milestone ♦♦♦♦♦

Dick Hyman & Ralph Sutton / Nov. 12, 1993 / Concord Jazz ♦♦♦♦♦
Dick Hyman and Ralph Sutton are two warriors working in truly traditional genres and finding ways to rework, vary, extend, embellish and experiment with classic rhythms, never moving away from a recognizable base, but not repeating staid riffs and lines. This session is a joint recital, where they take turns working off each's leads, sometimes playing snappy unsion sections, sometimes matching ideas in equally jovial fashion, or each player taking a marvelous solo. The sound is magical, partly because they're in the sonic castle of Maybeck Recital Hall, and also because of their own skills. This will transport you back in time, then haul you firmly into the present, as neither Dick Hyman nor Ralph Sutton are doing nostalgia, just playing the songs they love. *—Ron Wynn*

Abdullah Ibrahim (Adolph Johannes Brand)

b. Oct. 9, 1934, Cape Town, South Africa
Piano / African Jazz, African Folk, Post-Bop
The melodic sounds of South Africa are fused with the improvisation of jazz and the technical proficiency of classical music by South Africa-born pianist Dollar Brand or, as he's called himself since converting to Islam in 1968, Abdullah Ibrahim. Since attracting international acclaim as a member of the Jazz Epistles, one of South Africa's first jazz bands, Brand has continued to explore new ground with his imaginative playing. Exposed to a variety of music as a youngster, including traditional African music, religious songs and jazz, Brand began studying piano at the age of seven. Becoming a professional musician in 1949, he performed with such South African groups as the Tuxedo Slickers and the Willie Max Big Band. Ten years later, he joined the Jazz Epistles, a group featuring trumpet player Hugh Masekela and alto saxophonist Kippi Moeketsi. The band, which had been formed in 1959 by American pianist John Mohegan for a recording session, "Jazz In Africa", had recorded the first jazz album by South African musicians.

In 1962, Brand left South Africa, with vocalist Sathima Bea Benjamin, who he married in 1965, and temporarily settled in Zurich. Performing with his trio, featuring bassist Johnny Gertze and drummer Makaya Ntshoko, Brand was overheard by Duke Ellington at the Africana Club. Ellington was so impressed by what he heard that he arranged a recording session for Brand and the trio. The resulting album, "Duke Ellington Presents The Dollar Brand Trio", was released on the Reprise label in 1963. Brand continued to be supported by Ellington following the album's release. In addition to being booked to play, at Ellington's urging, at the Newport Jazz Festival in 1965, Brand served as Ellington's substitute and performed five shows with the Ellington Orchestra the following year. Shortly afterwards, Brand disbanded the trio and accepted an invitation to join the Elvin Jones Quartet. The collaboration with Jones lasted six months. After leaving Jones' Quartet, Brand continued to be involved with a variety of projects Besides touring as a soloist in 1968, he worked with bands led by Don Cherry and Gato Barbieri. In 1983, Brand formed a septet, Ekaya.

Briefly returning to South Africa in 1976, Brand settled in New York the same year. Although he returned to South Africa to live in 1990, he continues to divide his time between his birthplace and his adopted home in New York.

In 1997, Brand collaborated on an album and tour with jazz drummer Max Roach. The following year, Swiss composer Daniel Schnyder arranged several of Brand's compositions for a twenty-two piece orchestra for a Swiss television production and for a world tour undertaken by the full-sized Munich Radio Philharmonic Orchestra, conducted by Barbara Yahr of the United States. Brand has composed the scores for such films as "Chocolat" and "No Fear No Die". *—Craig Harris*

Duke Ellington Presents the Dollar Band Trio / Feb. 1963 / Warner Brothers ♦♦♦

Fats Duke and the Monk / Feb. 18, 1973 / Sackville ♦♦♦♦
After a decade of generally intriguing recordings, pianist Abdullah Ibrahim really found his own voice by the early '70s. His lengthy solo set from February 18, 1973, originally released as a pair of Sackville LPs (*Sangoma* and *African Portraits*), has been reshuffled and expanded a bit upon the release of this CD and its companion *Ancient Africa*. One selection apiece from the two albums have been grouped with the previously unreleased "Salaam Peace" to form this disc. Ibrahim is heard on three lengthy medleys; best are "African Portraits" and "Fats, Duke & the Monk," although Fats Waller (who is only represented by a brief "Honeysuckle Rose") gets short shrift on the latter. Ibrahim's passionate solos (which are sometimes joined by his verbal cries) are picturesque, episodic, and utterly fascinating on this set even if *Ancient Africa* actually gets the edge. *—Scott Yanow*

The Banyana: Children of Africa / Jan. 27, 1976 / Enja ♦♦♦♦
Abdullah Ibrahim sings and plays soprano on "Ishmael" but otherwise sticks to piano on this trio set with bassist Cecil McBee and drummer Roy Brooks. As usual Ibrahim's folkish melodies (this CD has six of his originals plus a previously alternate take of "Ishmael") pay tribute to his South African heritage and Islam religion without becoming esoteric or inaccessible. Some of the unpredictable music gets a bit intense (Ibrahim is in consistently adventurous form) but his flights always return back to earth and have an air of optimism. An above average effort from a true individualist. *—Scott Yanow*

African Marketplace / Dec. 1979 / Discovery ♦♦♦♦♦
This is one of Abdullah Ibrahim's most colorful band recordings. With a 12-piece group that includes altoist Carlos Ward, trombonist Craig Harris and bassist Cecil McBee along with some lesser-known names, Ibrahim performs eight folklike originals that pay tribute to his life growing up in South Africa. "The Homecoming Song," "Anthem for the New Nation" and especially "The Wedding" (a beautiful hymn) are particularly memorable. *—Scott Yanow*

☆ **Live at Montreux** / Jun. 18, 1980 / Enja ♦♦♦♦♦
A 1990 reissue of a tremendous concert done in 1980. Carlos Ward and Craig Harris star alongside Ibrahim. *—Ron Wynn*

★ **Water from an Ancient Well** / Oct. 1985 / Tiptoe ♦♦♦♦♦
Also made available domestically at one time by the defunct Black-Hawk label, this superior Abdullah Ibrahim recording features the pianist/composer with a very strong septet. Such superior musicians as tenor-saxophonist Ricky Ford, altoist Carlos Ward, baritonist Charles Davis and trombonist Dick Griffin are heard at their most creative and emotional on these eight Ibrahim originals. Many of the melodies (particularly "Mandela," "Song for Sathima," "Water from an Ancient Well" and the beautiful "The Wedding" are among Ibrahim's finest compositions. *—Scott Yanow*

African River / Jun. 1, 1989 / Enja ♦♦♦♦
For this excellent date, pianist Abdullah Ibrahim performs eight of his compositions with a particularly strong group of players: trombonist Robin Eubanks, John Stubblefield on tenor and flute, Horace Alexander Young switching between soprano, alto and piccolo, Howard Johnson on tuba, baritone and trumpet, bassist Buster Williams and drummer Brian Abrahams. But more important than the individual players are the colorful ensembles and the frequently memorable compositions. Highlights include "African River," "Sweet Samba," "Duke 88" and a beautiful version of "The Wedding." *—Scott Yanow*

Yarona / Jan. 13, 1995-Jan. 14, 1995 / Tip Toe ♦♦♦♦
Having explored various African jazz themes on *Knysna Blue* in a solo setting, Ibrahim continued in this direction with his group Ekaya. The trio, rounded out by bassist Marcus McLaurine and drummer George Johnson allow the pianist to engross himself in his shifting ideas that range from bop, African pop, swing, and even hints of a Keith Jarrett influence. "Mannenberg" and "African Marketplace," two Ibrahim classics, are given brief but interesting updates. The remainder of the tracks are all excellent and most exceed six minutes long, allowing for the non-hurried development of ideas by this remarkable trio. Highly recommended for both performance and originality. *—Robert Taylor*

Cape Town Flowers / Aug. 15, 1996 / Tiptoe ♦♦♦♦
Cape Town Flowers is an enchanting effort from Abdullah Ibrahim, finding the pianist in a trio setting performing 11 original compositions. With the exception of the nine-minute title track and "Monk In Harlem," most of the album's songs clock in at under five minutes, many under four. Each of the pieces is understated, lovely, and nearly dreamlike. The length of the tracks may make *Cape Town Flowers* seem like a slight record, but the truth is, that very brevity and the way the songs form a sonic tapestry is exactly what makes the record a modest gem. *—Stephen Thomas Erlewine*

The African Suite / Nov. 12, 1997-Nov. 16, 1997 / Enja ♦♦♦♦
African Suite presents Abdullah Ibrahim's regular trio with bassist Belden Bullock and drummer George Gray along with a large string section drawn from the Youth Orchestra of the European Community. Daniel Schnyder crafted the arrangements, which are orchestral reworkings of some of Ibrahim's compositions roughly spanning a 25-year period. The strings serve to heighten the evocative globalism of Ibrahim's work, in which the pianist's South African origin, Islamic faith, longtime European residence, and jazz immersion are incorporated with a dazzling imaginative breadth.

Here perhaps more than ever before, Ibrahim's piano is a subtle tool, coaxing the spare, singable melodies into being and generally hovering over the proceedings like a wise, almost detached presence. Both the pianist and the orchestra get a chance to shine alone, Ibrahim on "Aspen" and the orchestra on "Blanton." The latter, dedicated to the late Ellington bassist Jimmy Blanton, sounds uncannily like a jazz bassist bowing an arco solo.

The rhythm section gets a bit busier on the slow-grooving "Ishmael," the rollicking "Tsakwe," the 6/4 sketch "Damara Blue," and the brooding funk piece "Tintinyana." For sheer eclecticism and catchiness, nothing beats the "All Blues"-style "Barakaat" and the African-soul-jazz finale "The Mountain of the Night." But the strings are integrated more effectively on the calmer numbers, especially "The Call" and an absolutely breathtaking arrangement of "The Wedding." One only wishes something could have been done about the audible hiss on parts of the recording. *—David R. Adler*

Cape Town Revisited / 1997 / Tiptoe ♦♦♦♦
Recorded live in Cape Town South Africa on December 13, 1997, South African born pianist Abdullah Ibrahim and his trio are heard in an uninterrupted performance where these original pieces morph together naturally. This is especially true on the three movements of "Cape Town to Congo Square," reflecting and encompassing the joy of carnival, jazz, street parades, and ancient spiritual rhythms. Ibrahim's trio includes Marcus Mclaurine on bass, George Gray on drums, and Feya Faku playing trumpet on four tracks. *—Al Campbell*

ICP Orchestra

Group / Avant-Garde Jazz, Modern Creative
The ICP Orchestra recorded relatively little, but achieved international acclaim for its sophisticated improvisations, creative interpretations of Duke Ellington and Thelonious Monk, and extraordinary level of musicianship. The Amsterdam-based group is a blend of European improvised music, jazz music and the Dutch irreverent attitude, in general, which all combine into a highly sophisticated yet enjoyable music that has astonished and impressed music lovers for several decades.

ICP (Instant Composers Pool) began as a label and group concept in the late '60s with Dutch musicians Willem Breuker (reeds), Han Bennink (drums, etc.), and Misha Mengelberg (piano), and quickly became an umbrella name for their various projects. Breuker and Mengelberg clashed, however, on various musical issues including use of pre-composed material vs. instant composing. So, each led their own ICP gigs, with Bennink in most. By 1973, the inevitable split came and musicians went with one or the other, resulting in the theatrical Willem Breuker Kollektief, and Mengelberg's ICP Orchestra, which changed line-ups for several years, with only Mengelberg, Bennink and American tubist Larry Fishkind as mainstays. Rotating members included Brotzmann, John Tchicai, and trombonist George Lewis. The ICP Orchestra first recorded in early 1977, yielding *ICP-Tentet in Berlin* (SAJ). By the time *Japan Japon* (DIW, 1982) was recorded, trombonist Wolter Wierbos and reeds player Michael Moore had joined, as had, violist Maurice Horsthuis (he eventually left). Horthuis was soon followed by his Amsterdam String Trio bandmates, bassist Ernst Glerum and cellist Ernst Reijseger (Reijseger, Moore and Bennink also formed the Clusone Trio together). Due to the large roster, Mengelberg's "instant composing" tenet shifted slightly to "conducted improvisation." By the mid-'90s, the band included saxophonist Ab Baars and trumpeter Thomas Heberer, and cellist Tristan Honsinger. ICP Orchestra recorded tributes to Thelonious Monk and Herbie Nichols in 1984 and 1986, respectively. Mengelberg has also led the group in many brilliant (but unrecorded) programs of Ellington's music. The group recorded two volumes of *Bodspaadje Konijnehol* ("Forest Path Rabbithole") in 1989-90, then didn't record again until 1997, resulting in the well-received *Jubilee Varia* on HatArt. By the time the group toured for the album's 1999 release, Reijseger had left the group permanently. *—Joslyn Layne*

● **Jubilee Varia** / 1999 / hatOLOGY ♦♦♦♦♦
Yes, there is a quality of mishmash to it all, but nonetheless, this long-awaited recording by the ICP Orchestra should satisfy those who enjoy the unique sounds that pianist Misha Mengelberg, drummer Han Bennink, and the other seven participants create. There are two suites, each divided into three distinct pieces, and not all feature the entire ensemble. For example, the opening section of "Jubilee Varia Suite" is a duo between Mengelberg and Bennink, which is followed by a trio of cellists Ernst Reijseger and Tristan Honsinger and bassist Ernst Glerum. Along the way, everyone glows, and there is choice sound from Walter Wierbos (on trombone), Thomas Heberer (on trumpet), and Michael Moore and Ab Baars (on clarinet and saxophones). Ultimately, it is the originality, the humor, and the wackiness of it all combined with the consummate musicianship, that entertain and impress. The excellent liners by Kevin Whitehead are a plus. *—Steve Loewy*

Mark Isham

Trumpet, Synthesizer / Original Score, Film Music, Soundtracks, Crossover Jazz, Post-Bop, Ambient, Progressive Electronic, Chamber Jazz
Born in New York but now based in San Francisco, this multi-instrumentalist and composer made his reputation early in the '70s while playing with progressive rock bands and jazz groups like Art Lande's Rubisa Patrol. He has performed or recorded with such artists as Van Morrison, Was (Not Was), and David Sylvian. His trumpet sound is reminiscent of Miles Davis with his use of a mute and his sparse phrasing, but his great talent as a composer lies in his ability to combine synthesizer and acoustic instruments into an effective whole; as a result, he is in big demand for film scores. Isham's stately and often dreamy music reveals his classical training while inventively exploring the sonic possibilities of electronic instruments. *—Scott Bultman*

★ **Vapor Drawings** / Apr. 1983-May 1983 / Windham Hill ♦♦♦♦♦
Crystalline synthesizer textures form the perfect atmosphere for Isham's melodic trumpet solos (with percussion from his Group 87 bandmate Peter Van Hooke). His talent for blending electronic and acoustic sounds produces beautiful and organic music, and this first album for Windham Hill cemented his reputation. *—Scott Bultman*

Film Music / 1987 / Windham Hill ♦♦♦♦♦
His scores for *Never Cry Wolf*, the Academy Award-winning documentary *The Times of Harvey Milk*, and the Mel Gibson/Diane Keaton film *Mrs. Soffel* showcase his musical depth and dreamy style. On the *Mrs. Soffel* score, Isham's blend of acoustic and synthesizer textures are haunting and deeply moving. *—Scott Bultman*

Blue Sun / 1995 / Columbia ♦♦♦♦
A fine album by this trumpeter better known for film scores and Windham Hill new age electronics than for jazz. However, on this outing, Mark Isham struts his jazz stuff. Although the instrumentation includes electric bass, occasional electric piano, and a sprinkling of atmospheric electronics, the feel here is of an acoustic recording of the cool jazz school. Isham's quintet includes Steve Tavaglione on tenor saxophone and David Goldblatt on piano, both of whom inform this music with elegance and grace. Isham himself has never sounded better on record, recalling the Miles Davis of the '50s at times, and the rhythm section of drummer Kurt Wortman and bassist Doug Lunn keeps the music moving at a relaxed pace. Isham's work in his Windham Hill days was, while interesting, easily identifiable and properly classified in the new age bin. Here, he has moved into a new, classy direction, proving he can write and perform well-crafted music of substance. *—Jim Newsom*

Education of Little Tree / Jan. 13, 1998 / Sony Classical ♦♦♦♦
Mark Isham's score for *The Education of Little Tree* is a surprisingly rich, full musical experience, avoiding many of the minimalistic, spare signatures of his other soundtracks. Instead, Isham has created a lush array of sounds that fits the family film perfectly, in addition to working splendidly as its own entity. *—Rodney Batdorf*

Afterglow / Feb. 3, 1998 / Columbia ♦♦♦♦
Isham's soundtrack to the Alan Rudolph drama *Afterglow* is typical of his film work, a moody and frequently moving record distinguished by his signature trumpet sound; his support unit includes saxophonist Charles Lloyd, vibist Gary Burton, violinist Sid Page, bassist Jeff Littleton, pianist Geri Allen and drummer Billy Higgins. *—Jason Ankeny*

Miles Remembered: The Silent Way Project / Jan. 1996-Oct. 1996 / Columbia ♦♦♦
In A Silent Way is one of the most celebrated albums in jazz history and it still sounds fresh decades after it was originally recorded. During the '90s, its evocative sonic textures and blends of acoustic and electric instruments could be heard throughout contemporary music, particularly in electronica artists who seized the more cerebral aspects of the album. Conversely, Mark Isham hears the space and atmosphere within the album, along with the rest of Miles Davis' electric fusion period. That's why his Davis tribute, *Miles Remembered: The Silent Way Project*, is so interesting. Even on edgier numbers, such as "Right Off" (the closest Davis ever got to metallic hard rock), Isham finds spacious sonic textures. It may be smoother than Davis fusion and have a different sense of purpose, but it's never boring, and it's often quite rewarding, standing as a testament to Davis' original vision and Isham's skills as an arranger and interpreter. *—Stephen Thomas Erlewine*

Milt Jackson

b. Jan. 1, 1923, Detroit, MI, **d.** Oct. 9, 1999
Vibraphone / Hard Bop, Bop
Before Milt Jackson there were only two major vibraphonists: Lionel Hampton and Red Norvo. He soon surpassed both of them in significance and, despite the rise of other players (including Bobby Hutcherson and Gary Burton), still wins the popularity polls. Jackson (or Bags as he has long been called) has been at the top of his field for 50 years, playing bop, blues and ballads with equal skill and sensitivity. After Dizzy Gillespie discovered him playing in Detroit, he offered him a job with his sextet and (shortly after) his innovative big band (1946). Jackson recorded with Dizzy and was soon in great demand. After playing with Gillespie's sextet (1950-52) which at one point included John Coltrane, Jackson recorded with a quartet comprised of John Lewis, Percy Heath and Kenny Clarke (1952) which soon became a regular group called the Modern Jazz Quartet. Although he recorded regularly as a leader (including dates in the 1950s with Miles Davis and/or Thelonious Monk, Coleman Hawkins, John Coltrane and Ray Charles), Jackson stayed with the MJQ through 1974, becoming an indispensable part of their sound. *—Scott Yanow*

In the Beginning / Apr. 1948 / Galaxy/OJC ♦♦♦
This is a very interesting CD, particularly for bop collectors, since it contains very rare early performances by altoist Sonny Stitt and vibraphonist Milt Jackson; some of the titles were originally under trumpeter Russell Jacquet's name. There are eight songs by a quintet with Stitt, Jacquet and pianist Sir Charles Thompson, what could be considered the first Modern Jazz Quartet records (actually a quintet with Milt Jackson, pianist John Lewis, drummer Kenny Clarke, bassist Al Jackson and Chano Pozo on congas) and five songs from a septet with Jacquet, Stitt, trombonist J.J. Johnson and baritonist Leo Parker. Recorded in Detroit for the tiny Galaxy label, these performances are not essential but they do give listeners an early glimpse at the future stars. *—Scott Yanow*

Milt Jackson / Jun. 1948-Apr. 1952 / Blue Note ♦♦♦♦♦

Opus De Funk / Jun. 16, 1954-Nov. 7, 1962 / Prestige ♦♦♦♦♦
This out-of-print two-LP set includes all of the music from a 1954 session with trumpeter Henry Boozier and pianist Horace Silver (highlighted by the original version of Silver's "Opus De Funk"), a quartet date with Silver in 1955 (later reissued on CD as simply *Milt Jackson Quartet*) and the 1962 album *Invitation* (a sextet set with trumpeter Kenny Dorham, tenor-saxophonist Jimmy Heath and pianist Tommy Flanagan). Throughout Milt Jackson is in typically consistent form and all of his illustrious sidemen play up to their usual level during these excellent straightahead sessions. *—Scott Yanow*

Milt Jackson Quartet / May 20, 1955 / Prestige/OJC ♦♦♦
The music on this quartet date (which features vibraphonist Milt Jackson, pianist Horace Silver, bassist Percy Heath and drummer Connie Kay) is excellent but the playing time (31 minutes) is pretty disgraceful, particularly when one considers that Jackson did a lot of recording for Prestige; certainly more selections could have been added to make this CD have a decent amount of music. Even the old two-LP set *Opus De Funk* added four selections to the album containing this otherwise enjoyable straightahead set. Quantity aside, Bags and Silver make for a good combination on five standards and Jackson's "Stonewall." *—Scott Yanow*

Jackson' Ville / Jan. 23, 1956 / Savoy Jazz ♦♦♦♦♦
This fine 1956 date features Jackson leading a session that moves with ease and authority through a relaxing eight-minute ride on Charlie Parker's "Now's the Time," an Ellington ballad medley, and a pair of the vibist's own blues-based, hard bop compositions. The real treat here is Lucky Thompson's tenor sax. The Don Byas-influenced Thompson has a sound that invites the listener to luxuriate in its grace and strength. Thompson solos on "Mood Indigo" with a sublime, breathy legato, adding bite and rougher edges—without sacrificing nuance or subtlety—on Jackson's "Minor Conception" and "Soul in 3/4." For his part, Jackson reels off a fluid stream of shifting, seamless, advanced blues—his time, phrasing, and execution all exquisite. In the rhythm section, Hank Jones (piano), Wendell Marshall (bass), and Kenny Clarke (drums) support with the ego-free artistry expected of the Savoy house band of the day. *Jackson's Ville* is one of four Savoy CDs that pair Jackson with Thompson. The others are *The Jazz Skyline, Roll ëem Bags,* and *Meet Milt Jackson.* Each on its own is short measure (*Jackson's Ville* clocks in at 30 minutes). As a collection, though, they comprise a vital document that sits nicely alongside Jackson's and Thompson's work with Miles Davis from this period. *—Jim Todd*

The Jazz Skyline / Jan. 23, 1956 / Savoy ♦♦♦♦
This session has interest as an example of Milt Jackson's mid-'50s work in a non-Modern Jazz Quartet context. And despite the many critical assertions that the vibist was restrained by pianist John Lewis' direction, his playing here revealed no marked changed. The overall feel of the group (Lucky Thompson, tenor sax; Hank Jones, piano; Wendell Marshall; bass, Kenny Clarke, drums; Jackson, vibes), however, was somewhat more dynamic than that of The MJQ, as Clarke and Jones generally achieved a greater sense of forward momentum than Connie Kay or Lewis. *—Bob Rusch, Cadence*

Plenty, Plenty Soul / Jan. 5, 1957+Jan. 7, 1957 / Atlantic ♦♦♦♦♦
This superior reissue combines together two sessions led by vibraphonist Milt Jackson. Actually, although Bags is in fine form (and contributed four of the seven selections), he is often overshadowed by rather inspired solos from his sidemen. The first side of this LP, which features a nine-piece group, is highlighted by the contributions of the exuberant altoist Cannonball Adderley while the flip side has a sextet that is not hurt by the solos of tenor-saxophonist Lucky Thompson. With pianist Horace Silver helping out on both dates, these all-star dates still sound fresh and enthusiastic decades later. *—Scott Yanow*

Bean Bags / Sep. 12, 1959 / Koch Jazz ♦♦♦♦
Many of vibraphonist Milt Jackson's Atlantic recordings are long overdue to appear on CD, and that certainly includes this album, a meeting with the great tenor Coleman Hawkins. Assisted by a top-notch quartet (pianist Tommy Flanagan, guitarist Kenny Burrell, bassist Eddie Jones and drummer Connie Kay), Bean and Bags romp through "Stuffy," "Get Happy," a pair of Jackson originals and two fine ballads, with "Don't Take Your Love from Me" being particularly memorable. *—Scott Yanow*

★ **Bags and Trane** / Jan. 15, 1959 / Atlantic ♦♦♦♦♦
Vibraphonist Milt Jackson and tenor-saxophonist John Coltrane make for a surprisingly complementary team on this 1959 studio session, their only joint recording. With fine backup by pianist Hank Jones, bassist Paul Chambers and drummer Connie Kay, Bags and Trane stretch out on two of Jackson's originals (including "The Late Late Blues") and three standards: a romping "Three Little Words," "The Night We Called It a Day" and the rapid "Be-Bop." This enjoyable music has been included as part of Rhino's *Heavyweight Champion: The Complete Atlantic Recordings* box. *—Scott Yanow*

Bags Meets Wes / Dec. 18, 1961+Dec. 19, 1961 / Riverside/OJC ♦♦♦♦♦
Milt Jackson was 38 when, in December 1961, he co-led this superb hard-bop date with the distinctive guitarist Wes Montgomery. A jazzman who was as opinionated as he was gifted, Jackson wouldn't hesitate to tell you exactly what he thought of a musician—so when he praised Montgomery, you knew his praise was genuine. Not surprisingly, the boppers prove to be quite compatible on *Bags Meets Wes*, which finds them co-leading an all star-quintet that also includes pianist Wynton Kelly, bassist Sam Jones, and drummer Philly Joe Jones (who shouldn't be confused with swing drummer Jo Jones). Although Jackson and Montgomery prove what lyrical ballad players they could be on the standard "Stairway to the Stars," ballads aren't a high priority on this album. Instead, the improvisers put more of their energy into the blues—and the 12-bar format serves them well on "Sam Sack," "Blue Roz," and "S.K.J." Equally strong are hard-swinging versions of Montgomery's "Jingles" and Benny Golson's "Stablemates."

Originally released on LP by Riverside in the early 1960s, *Bags Meets Wes* has been reissued several times over the years. When Fantasy reissued it on CD for the Original Jazz Classics (OJC) series, the label added alternate takes of "Jingles," "Stairway to the Stars," and "Delilah"—all of which are only slightly inferior to the master takes. *Bags Meets Wes* has also been reissued as a 24-karat gold audiophile CD by DCC Compact Classics. *—Alex Henderson*

Big Bags / Jun. 19, 1962-Jul. 1962 / Riverside/OJC ♦♦♦♦
Vibraphonist Milt Jackson is backed by a big band for this change-of-pace release, reissued on CD along with two alternate takes. The Ernie Wilkins and Tadd Dameron arrangements fit the high-quality standards well and Jackson (who contributed two originals) is in top form. There are short solos for cornetist Nat Adderley, trombonist Jimmy Cleveland and the tenors of James Moody and Jimmy Heath but Milt Jackson is the main voice throughout this melodic and always-swinging set. *—Scott Yanow*

Live at the Village Gate / Dec. 9, 1963 / Riverside/OJC ♦♦♦♦
Vibraphonist Milt Jackson's own sessions outside of The Modern Jazz Quartet tend to be hard-swinging jams through attractive chord changes, a mixture of boppish romps and thoughtful ballad statements. Jackson has frequently worked with tenors and Jimmy Heath, who is well-featured throughout this set (a CD reissue that brings back an earlier LP plus two "new" selections) became an occasional associate. With fine work by pianist Hank Jones, bassist Bob Cranshaw and drummer Al "Tootie" Heath, Milt Jackson is in typically swinging form on some blues, standards, ballads and Jimmy Heath's "Gemini." *—Scott Yanow*

Sunflower / Dec. 12, 1972-Dec. 13, 1972 / Columbia/Legacy ♦♦♦♦♦
Vibraphonist Milt Jackson recorded three albums for CTI in the early '70s; this album is the

best of the trio. The Don Sebesky arrangements for the strings showcase Jackson well, trumpeter Freddie Hubbard and pianist Herbie Hancock make impressions the four songs (highlighted by Hubbard's "Sunflower") receive fine treatment. *—Scott Yanow*

☆ **The Big 3** / Aug. 25, 1975 / Pablo/OJC ✦✦✦✦✦
This CD (a straight reissue of the original LP) features a rather notable pianoless combo: vibraphonist Milt Jackson, guitarist Joe Pass and bassist Ray Brown. During the Pablo years these three masterful players recorded together in many settings but only this once as a trio. The colorful repertoire (which ranges from "The Pink Panther" and "Blue Bossa" to "Nuages" and "Come Sunday") acts as a device for the musicians to construct some brilliant bop-based solos. *—Scott Yanow*

Soul Fusion / Jun. 1, 1977-Jun. 2, 1977 / Pablo/OJC ✦✦✦✦✦
Pianist Monty Alexander had first appeared on a Milt Jackson record in 1969. Eight years later the great vibraphonist used Alexander's trio (which included bassist John Clayton and drummer Jeff Hamilton, future big band co-leaders) for this spirited Pablo session which has been reissued on CD. Much of the material is obscure (including Jackson's three originals) with Stevie Wonder's "Isn't She Lovely" being the only standard. The music however is as straightahead as one would expect from these fine musicians and can be easily recommended to their fans. *—Scott Yanow*

Montreux '77 / Jul. 13, 1977 / Pablo/OJC ✦✦✦✦
This set from the 1977 Montreux Jazz Festival was very much a spontaneous jam session. Flugelhornist Clark Terry, who happened to be in town early, was added to vibraphonist Milt Jackson's group at the last moment. When players the caliber of Terry, tenor saxophonist Eddie "Lockjaw" Davis, pianist Monty Alexander, bassist Ray Brown, drummer Jimmie Smith and Jackson get together, one does not have to worry about the lack of rehearsal time. The sextet romps happily through Brown's "Slippery," "A Beautiful Friendship," "Mean to Me," "You Are My Sunshine," the CD's bonus cut "That's The Way It Is" and "C.M.J."; both Terry and Jackson have humorous vocals on the latter. *—Scott Yanow*

Night Mist / Apr. 14, 1980 / Pablo/OJC ✦✦✦✦✦
Most of vibraphonist Milt Jackson's recordings as a leader have been at the head of a quartet or quintet. This spirited set has a variety of "near blues" material being interpreted by an all-star septet featuring such unique voices as trumpeter Harry "Sweets" Edison, the tenor of Eddie "Lockjaw" Davis and altoist Eddie "Cleanhead" Vinson in addition to Jackson, pianist Art Hillery, bassist Ray Brown and drummer Larance Marable. There are plenty of magical moments created on this set by these classic jazzmen. *—Scott Yanow*

Mostly Duke / Apr. 23, 1982-Apr. 24, 1982 / Pablo/OJC ✦✦✦✦✦

Memories of Thelonious Sphere Monk / Apr. 28, 1982 / Pablo/OJC ✦✦✦✦✦
Milt Jackson and his quartet of 1982 (with pianist Monty Alexander, bassist Ray Brown and drummer Mickey Roker) recorded three albums of material during an engagement at Ronnie Scott's Club in London. Pianist/composer Thelonious Monk had passed away two months earlier and Jackson decided to pay tribute to his old associate. The vibraphonist is in excellent form on four of Monk's standards in addition to a lengthy "Django," his own "Think Positive" and Ray Brown's "Blues for Groundhog." *—Scott Yanow*

The Prophet Speaks / 1994 / Qwest ✦✦✦✦✦

Sa Va Bella (For Lady Legends) / 1997 / Warner Brothers ✦✦✦✦

Explosive! / Feb. 23, 1999 / Warner Brothers ✦✦✦✦
This is such a logical combination. When vibraphonist Milt Jackson and the Clayton-Hamilton Jazz Orchestra appeared together at the Jazz Bakery near Los Angeles during the same period as when this CD was recorded, Jackson (who usually frowns when he plays) could not stop smiling. He loved both John Clayton's arrangements and the sound of the 19-piece orchestra. Jackson, a major voice on his instrument since at least 1946, seemed as happy listening to the band as he did playing with it. And, although he has the most solos, he does not overshadow the mighty ensemble on this CD. Longtime fans of the big band are used to hearing the orchestra feature drummer Jeff Hamilton's brushes on a slow rendition of "Indiana" and both the bowed bass of John Clayton and the lyrical alto of Jeff Clayton on Johnny Mandel's classic "Emily." Both of those selections are give definitive treatment on the CD and some of the other better numbers are Jackson's trademark "Bags' Groove," Thelonious Monk's "Evidence," "Along Came Betty" and a few originals. Throughout, the swinging by the Clayton-Hamilton Orchestra is worthy of Count Basie, Milt Jackson often sounds exuberant, and together they have collaborated in creating an instant classic. *—Scott Yanow*

Ronald Shannon Jackson

b. Jan. 12, 1940, Fort Worth, TX
Drums / Free Funk, Free Jazz, Hard Bop, Fusion
Drummer Ronald Shannon Jackson and his Decoding Society of the 1980s learned from the example of Ornette Coleman's Prime Time and are a logical extension of the group. They featured colorful and noisy ensembles, were not afraid of the influence of rock and their rhythms were funky, loud and unpredictable. Jackson played professionally in Texas with James Clay when he was 15. He moved to New York in 1966 where he worked with Byard Lancaster, Charles Mingus, Betty Carter, Stanley Turrentine, Jackie McLean, McCoy Tyner, Kenny Dorham and most significantly Albert Ayler (1966-67) among others. He took time off of the scene and then joined Ornette Coleman's Prime Time (1975-79). Jackson also worked with Cecil Taylor (1978-79) and James "Blood" Ulmer (1979-80). The Decoding Society (formed in 1979) through the years featured many talented and advanced improvisers with the best-known ones being Vernon Reid, Zane Massey, Billy Bang and Byard Lancaster. Jackson also played with the explosive group Last Exit (starting in 1986) and in the early '90s with Power Tools. Ronald Shannon Jackson's music is not for easy-to-offend ears! *—Scott Yanow*

★ **Eye on You** / 1980 / About Time ✦✦✦✦✦
Drummer Roland Shannon Jackson's Decoding Society on this *About Time* LP is comprised of quite an all-star lineup: violinist Billy Bang, altoist Byard Lancaster, tenor-saxophonist Charles Brackeen, Vernon Reid and Bern Nix on guitars, bassist Melvin Gibbs, and percussionist Erasto Vasconcelos. The Decoding Society plays what could be called free funk, a combination of loud funky rhythms with free jazz and the harmolodics pioneered by Ornette Coleman's Prime Time. Everyone solos together constantly, leading to dense and exciting ensembles that are overflowing with passion. Although this style of jazz (a forerunner of Steve Coleman's groups) never really caught on, the music is quite stimulating and a logical extension of '70s fusion. *—Scott Yanow*

Mandance / Jun. 1982 / Antilles ✦✦✦✦✦
The ensemble-oriented "free funk" music of drummer Roland Shannon Jackson's Decoding Society never can be accused of being overly mellow or lacking in excitement. The 1982 version of his band features trumpeter Henry Scott, Zane Massey on reeds, guitarist Vernon Reid, and both Melvin Gibbs and Bruce Johnson on electric basses. The frenetic and intense ensembles (essentially everyone solos at once) would not be classified as relaxing background music. *—Scott Yanow*

Barbeque Dog / Mar. 1983-Apr. 1983 / Antilles ✦✦✦✦

Red Warrior / 1990 / Knitting Factory ✦✦✦✦✦
Forsaking the keyboard and saxophone lineups of many of his Decoding Society bands, composer/drummer Ronald Shannon Jackson uses a three-guitar and two-bass group on *Red Warrior,* creating a dense musical backdrop for his inspired arrangements. The "stripped down" band configuration is reflected in the loose, jam session feel of the record, which, unlike the earlier, more sonically varied album *Decode Yourself,* includes a good number of blues-based tracks ("Ashes," "Gates to Heaven," and "In Every Face"). This is not to say *Red Warrior* is a straightforward record, by any means. As is Jackson's inclination, the mix is expanded with plenty of jazz improvisation, weaves of effects-riddled guitar lines, complex head statements, and, of course, the drummer's pan-stylistic rhythmic support. The album also contains a variety of material, including the "Mahavishnu Orchestra meets Dr. John," New Orleans shuffle blues "Red Warrior" and the sprawling, free-form "Elders." Excellent contributions are made by the entire band, which includes guitarists Jef Lee Johnson, Steve Salas, and Jack DeSalvo and bassists Ramon Pooser and Conrad Mathieu. *Red Warrior* is just one of several, very impressive releases to be put out in the last two decades by Jackson, who, like contemporary composer Henry Threadgill, has unforgivably been overlooked and unsung all these years. *—Stephen Cook*

Earned Dreams / 1984 / Knitting Factory ✦✦✦✦
Drummer Ronald Shannon Jackson's Decoding Society sounded like a tighter version of Ornette Coleman's free funk band Prime Time, which originally included Jackson as a member. That influence remained prominent during this live performance at *Caravan of Dreams* in Fort Worth in 1984. *Earned Dreams* features Zane Massey on alto and tenor saxophones, Akbar Ali on violin, Henry Scott on trumpet, Vernon Reid on guitar, Melvin Gibbs on bass, and Bruce Johnson on electric bass. This ensemble maintained intense creative mayhem while sticking with tight funk structures. One of several out-of-print Jackson titles made available again by Knitting Factory's reissue label Knit Classics. *—Al Campbell*

Willis "Gator" Jackson

b. Apr. 25, 1932, Miami, FL, **d.** Oct. 25, 1987, New York, NY
Sax (Tenor) / Hard Bop, Jump Blues, Soul-Jazz
An exciting tenor saxophonist whose honking and squeals (although influenced by Illinois Jacquet) were quite distinctive, Willis Jackson was also a strong improviser who sounded perfectly at home with organ groups. He played locally in Florida early on until joining Cootie Williams (on and off during 1948-55). His two-sided honking feature "Gator Tail" with "Cootie" (which earned him a lifelong nickname) was a hit in 1948 and he started recording as a leader in 1950. Jackson was married to singer Ruth Brown for eight years and often appeared on her recordings during this era. His extensive series of Prestige recordings (1959-64) made him a big attraction on the organ circuit. Although generally overlooked by critics, Willis Jackson continued working steadily in the 1970s and '80s. In 1977 he recorded one of the finest albums of his career for Muse, *Bar Wars.* *—Scott Yanow*

● **Legends of Acid Jazz** / May 6, 1998 / Prestige ✦✦✦✦✦
Willis "Gator" Jackson's initial reputation was made as a honking and screaming tenor-saxophonist with Cootie Williams' late 1940's orchestra and on his own R&B-ish recordings. By 1959, Jackson had de-emphasized some of his more extroverted sounds (although they occasionally popped up) and had re-emerged as a solid swinger influenced by Gene Ammons and (on ballads) Ben Webster. This CD reissue from 1998 brings back in full two of Jackson's 1959-60 LPs: *Blue Gator* and *Cookin' Sherry.* Some of the music (which often falls into the soul jazz genre) is reminiscent of the funky groove music that would become popular in the late 1960's. Jackson sounds fine and is joined throughout by guitarist Bill Jennings, organist Jack McDuff, one of three bassists, one of two drummers and sometimes Buck Clarke on conga. The accessible music alternates between warm ballads and jump tunes. *—Scott Yanow*

Illinois Jacquet (Jean Baptiste Illinois Jacquet)

b. Oct. 31, 1922, Boussard, LA
Sax (Tenor), Sax (Alto), Bassoon / Jump Blues, Swing, Bop
One of the great tenors, Illinois Jacquet's 1942 "Flying Home" solo is considered the first R&B sax solo and spawned a full generation of younger tenors (including Joe Houston and Big Jay McNeely) who built their careers from his style and practically from that one song. He was the star of Lionel Hampton's 1942 big band ("Flying Home" became a signature song for Jacquet, Hampton and even Illinois's successor Arnett Cobb), and also was with Cab Calloway (1943-44) and well-featured with Count Basie (1945-46). Jacquet's playing at the first Jazz at the Philharmonic concert (1944) included a screaming solo on "Blues" that found him biting on his reed to achieve high register effects; the crowd went wild. In 1945 Jacquet put together his own band and both his recordings and live performances were quite exciting. He ap-

peared with JATP on several tours in the 1950's, recorded steadily and never really lost his popularity. *—Scott Yanow*

☆ **The Complete Illinois Jacquet Sessions 1945-50** / Jul. 1945-May 22, 1950 / Mosaic ♦♦♦♦♦
This four-CD set has all of the recordings made as a leader by tenor-saxophonist Illinois Jacquet during a period when he was at the height of his popularity. After his classic solo made "Flying Home" a major hit for Lionel Hampton in 1942, Jacquet spent time with Cab Calloway's band, was a sensation with Jazz at the Philharmonic, and was featured as a star soloist with Count Basie. In 1946, Jacquet went out on his own and his combo (ranging from six to eight pieces) was extremely popular, featuring its leader's hard-swinging solos which utilized a liberal amount of honks and screams. The first real R&B tenorman, Illinois Jacquet was always a much more well-rounded soloist than the specialists who followed him. The 17 sessions that are included on this essential box draws its material from the Aladdin, Apollo, ARA, Savoy, and Victor catalogues. Some of the music has been readily available in recent years, but this is the best way to acquire the swinging performances. Among Jacquet's most notable sidemen are trumpeters Joe Newman, Emmett Berry (who was actually the leader of one of these dates), Russell Jacquet (who also contributes some bluish vocals), and Fats Navarro (who solos on one song); trombonists Henry Coker, Trummy Young, and J.J. Johnson; baritonist Leo Parker; pianists Sir Charles Thompson, Bill Doggett, and John Lewis; bassist Charles Mingus; drummers Johnny Otis and Shadow Wilson; and (on two songs) singer Wynonie Harris. Fun music. *—Scott Yanow*

Flying Home / Dec. 1947-Jul. 1967 / Bluebird/RCA ♦♦♦
This is a great selection of Jacquet's late-'40s/early-'50s work, hot on the heels of his success with Jazz At The Philharmonic and his tenure with the Lionel Hampton Band. There's lots of honking and squealing coupled to Jacquet's patented abrasive tone, one of the most exciting in jazz, heard to good effect on "Jet Propulsion." Jacquet's brother Russell vocalizes on "Try Me One More Time," making himself a worthy foil, and stalwarts like Leo Parker, Shadow Wilson and J.J. Johnson are counted up in the mix. The closing track is somewhat of a ringer; recorded live in 1967 at the Newport Folk Festival, it's a high voltage take on the the title cut with Illinois' old boss Hampton making a guest appearance. *—Cub Koda*

Illinois Flies Again / 1966 / Chess ♦♦♦♦♦
The first seven tracks on this 13-track CD constitute what could be the best live album in the entire Chess Records library (and that's going some when one considers that *Bo Diddley's Beach Party* is part of that canon). If they appreciate music up in heaven, someone in high places must smile on Chess Records' management for having the presence of mind to record this show at Lennie's On The Turnpike in West Peabody, Mass. in March of 1966. Jacquet is part of a trio here with Milt Buckner on Hammond organ and Alan Dawson at the drums. To call this a seminal Jacquet release would be putting it mildly—the disc overflows with energy from the opening notes of an extended jam built around "On a Clear Day (You Can See Forever)." There's not a wrong note or a wasted bar of music on this extraordinary document of Jacquet's work. The producers have padded it out with six numbers cut in New York three years earlier, putting Jacquet in a more subdued septet featuring Kenny Burrell on guitar. The Charly Records CD reissue can be found, but the LP is long out of print. *—Bruce Eder*

Bottoms Up / Mar. 26, 1968 / Prestige/OJC ♦♦♦♦♦
Even in 1968 when the jazz avant-garde was becoming quite influential, tenor-saxophonist Illinois Jacquet played in his own timeless style, performing in an idiom little changed during the past 20 years. With the assistance of pianist Barry Harris, bassist Ben Tucker and drummer Alan Dawson, Jacquet is heard throughout this CD reissue (which adds a previously unissued "Don't Blame Me" to the original program) swinging hard and generally expressing himself in a typically extroverted fashion. "Bottoms Up" (a relative of "Flying Home"), "Jivin' with Jack the Bellboy" and Jacquet's excellent original ballad "You Left Me All Alone" are most memorable. *—Scott Yanow*

The Soul Explosion / Mar. 25, 1969 / Prestige/OJC ♦♦♦♦♦
The great tenor Illinois Jacquet is joined by a ten-piece group that includes trumpeter Joe Newman and Milt Buckner on piano and organ for this 1969 Prestige studio session which has been reissued on CD by the OJC series. Jacquet is in prime form, particularly on "The Soul Explosion" (which benefits from a Jimmy Mundy arrangement), a definitive "After Hours" and a previously unissued version of "Still King." This blues-based set is full of soul but often swings quite hard with the focus on Jacquet's exciting tenor throughout. *—Scott Yanow*

★ **The Blues: That's Me!** / Sep. 16, 1969 / Prestige/OJC ♦♦♦♦♦
Tenor-saxophonist Illinois Jacquet is heard in top form throughout this quintet set with pianist Wynton Kelly, guitarist Tiny Grimes, bassist Buster Williams and drummer Oliver Jackson. The music, which falls between swing, bop and early rhythm & blues, is generally quite exciting, especially "Still King," "Everyday I Have the Blues" and the lengthy title cut. A particular surprise is a moody version of "'Round Midnight" which features some surprisingly effective Illinois Jacquet, on bassoon. This CD reissue is highly recommended. *—Scott Yanow*

Blues from Louisiana / Jul. 7, 1973 / Classic Jazz ♦♦♦♦♦
This was an odd record, taken either from different live sessions or as part of a bigger all star bash... "On A Clear Day" was open, loose and swingingly pushed by Jacquet's big throaty vibrato on tenor; "Marlow's La. Blues" was a slow d-r-a-w-n out funky teaser climacitc and worried to death by organist Milt Buckner and Jacquet. *—Bob Rusch, Cadence*

Jazz at the Philharmonic: First Concert / Mar. 22, 1994 / Verve ♦♦♦♦

Ahmad Jamal (Frederick Russell Jones)

b. Jul. 2, 1930, Pittsburgh, PA
Piano / Post-Bop, Cool
One of the few pianists in the 1950s who did not sound like a close copy of Bud Powell, Ahmad Jamal's use of space, ability to gradually increase or decrease the volume with his trio and brilliant use of tension and release were quite original. He greatly impressed Miles Davis (who borrowed from his repertoire and insisted that Red Garland try to sound like him) and Jamal also cut some very popular records without altering his style.

Jamal began playing professionally in Pittsburgh when he was 11. In the late '40s he joined George Hudson's Orchestra. In 1951 he formed his first trio, the Three Strings, a group with guitarist Ray Crawford and bassist Eddie Calhoun. Israel Crosby took Calhoun's place in 1955. One of Jamal's recordings from that year was a version of "Pavanne" that at one point states the melody from John Coltrane's "Impressions," five years before 'Trane "wrote" the song! In 1956 Jamal switched to a piano-bass-drums trio with Walter Perkins replacing Crawford. With Vernell Fournier on drums by 1958, Jamal recorded his most popular album, *Ahmad Jamal at the Pershing,* and his version of "Poinciana" is still famous. The trio broke up in 1962 but Jamal continued growing as a pianist (sometimes doubling on electric piano in the 1970s) and he remains one of the most distinctive (and indirectly influential) pianists in jazz. Ahmad Jamal recorded through the years for Epic, Argo/Cadet, Impulse, Catalyst, 20th Century, Atlantic and Telarc. *—Scott Yanow*

Poinciana / Oct. 25, 1952-1955 / Portrait ♦♦♦♦♦
This fascinating 1989 reissue features pianist Ahmad Jamal at the beginning of his recording career. With guitarist Ray Crawford and either Eddie Calhoun or Israel Crosby on bass, Jamal showcases a style that would be a major influence on Miles Davis' music. Jamal's use of space and dynamics was very different than the style of any other jazz pianist of the era. His versions of "Old Devil Moon," "Will You Still Be Mine," "The Surrey With the Fringe On Top" and "A Gal In Calico" inspired Miles to record the songs in a similar fashion, and his "Billy Boy" became the basis of a performance by the Red Garland Trio. Most fascinating is Jamal's inventive interpretation of "Pavanne," for it has a section very reminiscent of "So What" (which was not "composed" by Davis until over two years later) and a melody statement that is exactly the same as John Coltrane's "Impressions." *—Scott Yanow*

★ **At the Pershing: But Not for Me** / Jan. 16, 1958 / Chess ♦♦♦♦♦
Recorded at Pershing Club, Chicago, IL. A two-fer. Third album (includes hit "Poinciana") was the turning point in his career. His liberal use of silence influenced many jazz musicians, including Miles Davis. *—Michael Erlewine*

Ahmad's Blues / Sep. 6, 1958 / Chess/GRP ♦♦♦♦♦
This CD reissues most of the music recorded on one night by the 1958 Ahmad Jamal Trio (which consisted of the pianist/leader, bassist Israel Crosby and drummer Vernel Fournier) during a live performance in Washington D.C. Originally released as the LP *Ahmad Jamal* plus part of *Portfolio of Ahmad Jamal,* these 16 selections display the uniqueness and tightness of this memorable unit. With great attention paid to dynamics and the use of space yet always swinging (at least lightly), the Ahmad Jamal Trio is heard at its best on such numbers as "It Could Happen to You," "Stompin' at the Savoy," "Squatty Roo," "A Gal in Calico" and "Let's Fall in Love." *—Scott Yanow*

Freeflight / Jun. 17, 1971 / GRP ♦♦♦♦♦
This CD reissue from the 1971 Montreux Jazz Festival has one of pianist Ahmad Jamal's finest recordings of the early '70s. Performing with bassist Jamil Sulieman Nasser and drummer Frank Gant, Jamal shows that his basic style has evolved since the 1950s but is still quite recognizable. He uses the electric piano as a double for color and stretches out on three numbers (including a remake of his hit "Poinciana") in addition to playing a five minute version of Herbie Hancock's "Dolphin Dance." An excellent effort. *—Scott Yanow*

Chicago Revisited: Live at Joe Segal's Jazz Showcase / Nov. 13, 1992-Nov. 14, 1992 / Telarc ♦♦♦♦♦
Although it had been more than 40 years since his debut recording, pianist Ahmad Jamal's playing was as viable as ever in the 1990s. Teamed up with bassist John Heard and drummer Yoron Israel for this live Telarc CD, Jamal plays a particularly inspired repertoire that includes "All the Things You Are," Clifford Brown's "Daahoud," John Handy's "Dance to the Lady" and "Be My Love" among its nine selections. Jamal's style had developed since his early days, but his basic approach was unchanged while still sounding quite fresh. This date is an excellent example of Ahmad Jamal's unique sound and highly appealing music in the 1990s. *—Scott Yanow*

I Remember Duke, Hoagy & Strayhorn / Jun. 2, 1994-Jun. 3, 1994 / Telarc ♦♦♦♦
Ahmad Jamal, in paying tribute to Duke Ellington, Billy Strayhorn and Hoagy Carmichael, performs nearly every selection on this CD at a very slow tempo. Or at least his sidemen do, since the pianist often plays doubletime lines, witty quotes from other songs and occasional violent outbursts. In general the music is quite thoughtful and subtle with plenty of surprising ideas and unusual turns. Carmichael gets stiffed a bit (just two songs counting the "Stardust"-inspired "I Remember Hoagy") and a couple of numbers are departures from the theme (including "My Flower," "Never Let Me Go" and "Goodbye") but most of the, melodies come from the Ellington/Strayhorn songbook. Throughout, Ahmad Jamal (with the assistance of bassist Ephriam Wolfolk and drummer Arti Dixson) shows that he can sound relaxed, alert and swinging at the slowest of paces, making this a set deserving (and perhaps needing) several listens to fully appreciate. *—Scott Yanow*

Big Byrd: the Essence, Part 2 / Oct. 30, 1994+Feb. 7, 1995 / Verve ♦♦♦♦♦
The elements that made *The Essence Part One* such a success—bright, crisp, rhythmically alive piano work often revolving around a tense bass ostinato and propulsive percussion—are abundantly present on *Part Two,* which was drawn from the same Paris and New York sessions but released a year after its predecessor. In no way is this a collection of leftovers; the quality level is so high that one can only conclude that marketing considerations alone prevented *The Essence* from being issued as a double album in the first place. Jamal fields two trios, anchored on bass by James Cammack in the Paris sessions and former colleague Jamil Nasser in the New York ones and by drummer Idris Muhammad on both. Everyone gets an extra jolt of momentum whenever the Afro-Latin percussion of Manolo Badrena goes into action, and violinist Joe Kennedy Jr. adds a potent, slightly raw-edged solo voice to "Manhattan Relfections." A muted, skittering Donald Byrd appears only on the title track—hence its name—which winds its way through several tempo changes and dramatically charged

sections over a vast 15-minute timespan. Into his mid-60s, Jamal remained as distinctive and inventive a pianist as ever, with delightful surprises lurking around every bend. *—Richard S. Ginell*

Cross Country Tour: 1958-1961 / Jan. 16, 1958-1961 / GRP ✦✦✦✦✦
This two-CD set has highlights from pianist Ahmad Jamal's famous trio dates for Argo, with selections drawn from *At the Pershing, At the Pershing Vol. 2, Portfolio of Ahmad Jamal, Alhambra,* and *At the Blackhawk,* plus one selection only out before in a sampler. It is a pity that the five valuable albums were not reissued in full on a three-CD set, for these were among the most important recordings of Jamal's career. His trio (with bassist Israel Crosby and drummer Vernel Fournier) had a unique sound, utilizing close communication and dynamics to an extraordinary degree. "Poinciana" was a huge hit, and other highlights included on this twofer include "But Not for Me," "Cherokee," "Billy Boy," "This Can't Be Love" and "Falling In Love With Love." Although easily recommended as an introduction to this classic group, the preferred complete sessions will hopefully appear on CD someday too. *—Scott Yanow*

Nature: The Essence, Pt. 3 / Jul. 23, 1997-Jan. 2, 1998 / Atlantic ✦✦✦✦
Still pursuing his own muse, Jamal is up to his usual tricks with his hypnotic vamps and and feverish runs, as ever refusing to toe the line and sound like everyone else. In this, the third installment of his Essence series, Jamal adds a different twist—a fine jazz steel drum player named Othello Molineaux—and he mixes a few transfigured standards ("The End of a Love Affair" is completely re-routed through his nervous system) with pieces of his own. The first version (for quartet) of "If I Find You Again" is a magnificent example of the tension Jamal can generate. "And We Were Lovers" and "Chaperon" are huge, borderline bombastic piano solos that ought to erase any doubts that Jamal continues to command one monster keyboard technique. As in the previous Essence entries, a guest horn player shows up briefly, tenorman Stanley Turrentine in epigrammic form on "Devil's in My Den," and the ultra-responsive rhythm section remains Idris Muhammad (drums) and James Cammack (bass). *—Richard S. Ginell*

Bob James

b. Dec. 25, 1939, Marshall, MO
Keyboards, Piano, Composer, Arranger / Smooth Jazz, Crossover Jazz, Jazz-Pop
Bob James's recordings have practically defined pop/jazz and crossover during the past two decades. Very influenced by pop and movie music, James has often featured R&Bish soloists (most notably Grover Washington, Jr.) who add a jazz touch to what is essentially an instrumental pop set. He actually started out music going in a much different direction. In 1962 Bob James recorded a boppish trio set for Mercury and three years later his album for ESP was quite avant-garde, with electronic tapes used for effects. After a period with Sarah Vaughan (1965-68), he became a studio musician and by 1973 was arranging and working as a producer for CTI. In 1974 James recorded his first purely commercial effort as a leader; he later made big-selling albums for his own Tappan Zee label, Columbia and Warner Bros. including collborations with Earl Klugh and David Sanborn. Listeners who prefer challenging jazz to background dance music will be consistently disappointed by Bob James's post-1965 albums. *—Scott Yanow*

One / Apr. 1974 / Warner Brothers/Tappan Zee ✦✦✦✦
Bob James's first recording for his Tappan Zee label, which has been reissued on CD along with virtually James's entire output by Warner Bros., is typically lightweight. Although Grover Washington, Jr., has two spots on soprano and trumpeter Jon Faddis is in the brass section, James's dated Fender Rhodes keyboard is the lead voice throughout the six pieces, which include two adaptations of classical works. Only a lightly funky version of "Feel Like Making Love" rises above the level of pleasant background music. *—Scott Yanow*

Two / 1975 / Warner Brothers/Tappan Zee ✦✦✦
Bob James largely defined pop/jazz crossover in the 1970s. This CD, reissued by Warner Brothers, is typical of his output. Mixing together aspects of pop, R&B and classical with just a touch of jazz, James (heard throughout on electric keyboards) put the emphasis on catchy melodies and lightly funky rhythms. The results range from insipid to pleasant, with a brass section, a string section and vocalists (including Patti Austin) utilized to create what is essentially background music. *—Scott Yanow*

Three / 1976 / Warner Brothers/Tappan Zee ✦✦✦
Virtually all of keyboardist/arranger Bob James's Tappan Zee catalog has been reissued by Warner Bros. on CD. Unfortunately, the lightweight crossover music has not dated well. James's keyboards often sound gimmicky, the arrangements are danceable but mundane, and, despite two spots for Grover Washington, Jr.'s tenor, little of significance occurs. *—Scott Yanow*

H / 1979 / Warner Brothers/Tappan Zee ✦✦✦
This CD reissue features some typical pop/jazz from keyboardist/arranger/composer Bob James. James often uses his musicians as a prop, adding some coloring by having short solos by Grover Washington, Jr.'s soprano (whose two appearances are easily this set's highpoints), and guitarists Hiram Bullock and Bruce Dunlap. An oversized rhythm section, a large horn section and strings fail to uplift the pleasant but lightweight music much. James plays well enough but no real chances are taken on this obviously commercial effort. *—Scott Yanow*

All Around the Town / Dec. 18, 1979-Dec. 22, 1979 / Warner Brothers/Tappan Zee ✦✦✦
Although Bob James has recorded more than his share of mindless throwaways over the years, he surprises us every now and then by coming out with something worthwhile. Recorded live at three New York venues (The Bottom Line, Carnegie Hall and Town Hall), *All Around the Town* was a definite improvement over tasteless studio projects like *Heads, Lucky Seven* and *Touchdown.* Pop-flavored jazz is dominant, although the keyboardist/pianist manages to get in a little straight-ahead jazz as well. James is especially inspired on his modal post-bop piece "The Golden Apple" and Benny Goodman's swing-era hit "Stompin' at the Savoy," but he also has some nice solos on pop-jazz offerings like "Angela (Theme From Taxi)" and "Westchester Lady." And on Boz Scaggs' "We're All Alone," James shows that a 1970s pop hit can be an appropriate vehicle for jazz blowing. The CD's weakest offering is the opener "Touchdown," which doesn't improve at all on stage and still sounds like corny 1970s movie music. But for the most part, this is an album James can be proud of. *—Alex Henderson*

Touchdown / 1979 / Warner Brothers/Tappan Zee ✦✦✦
Playing uninspired background "muzak" had brought Bob James commercial success, and financially, he certainly had no incentive to change. Despite employing such talent as David Sanborn (alto sax), Hubert Laws (flute), Ron Carter (bass) and Idris Muhammad (drums), *Touchdown* is a bland throwaway. Overproduction is the rule here, and their talents are largely smothered by James' excessive production and trite arrangements. This CD does contain James' likeable "Angela (Theme from Taxi')," but most of the songs on *Touchdown* are pure schlock. *—Alex Henderson*

Hands Down / 1982 / Warner Brothers/Tappan Zee ✦✦✦

Double Vision / 1986 / Warner Brothers ✦✦✦✦
This combination works quite well. Poppish keyboardist/arranger Bob James joins with electric bassist Marcus Miller, drummer Steve Gadd, guitarist Paul Jackson, percussionist Paulinho Da Costa and (on two songs) guitarist Eric Gale to accompany the distinctive and always soulful altoist David Sanborn. Sanborn caresses the strong melodies, mostly originals by James and Miller, and plays well with guest vocalist Al Jarreau on "Since I Fell for You." One of the best recordings ever released under Bob James' name (Sanborn gets co-billing) and a big seller. *—Scott Yanow*

Grand Piano Canyon / 1990 / Warner Brothers ✦✦✦✦
This CD is more jazz-oriented than most of Bob James' recordings and even takes chances in a few spots. The tunes, mostly by James, contain several strong melodies, including a tribute piece for Sarah Vaughan; among the sidemen are guitarist Lee Ritenour, Kirk Whalum on tenor and soprano, and (in a guest spot) tenor great Michael Brecker. The results overall are still poppish in places, but the diverse instrumentation, which changes from song to song, and the wide range of moods covered make this release of some interest. *—Scott Yanow*

● **Straight Up** / Dec. 20, 1995-Dec. 21, 1995 / Warner Brothers ✦✦✦✦✦
This record is an unexpected treat. Bob James has had a lucrative career writing and playing crossover pop/jazz. Although he had actually started his career with a straightahead trio date for Mercury in 1962 and also led a bizarre avant-garde session for ESP in 1965, his career since 1974 has offered very little of interest to consumers who prefer to hear inventive jazz as opposed to pleasant background music. But for this session Bob James returned to the roots few knew he had. Playing in an acoustic trio with bassist Christian McBride and drummer Brian Blade, James contributes five straightforward originals in addition to the standard "Lost April" and interprets tunes by Pat Metheny/Lyle Mays, Horace Silver ("The Jody Grind") and Denny Zeitlin. James plays quite well, takes plenty of chances and sounds influenced a bit by Bill Evans while not hinting at all at his usual pop material. With McBride and Blade contributing consistently stimulating interplay, Bob James has recorded what is certainly the finest jazz album of his career. *—Scott Yanow*

Joined at the Hip / 1996 / Warner Brothers ✦✦✦✦✦

Joy Ride / Aug. 10, 1999 / Warner Brothers ✦✦✦

Harry James

b. Mar. 15, 1916, Albany, GA, **d.** Jul. 5, 1983, Las Vegas, NV
Trumpet / Sweet Bands, Traditional Pop, Swing, Big Band
Harry James was the most famous trumpeter of the swing era and his big band was the most popular in the world during 1942-46 (after Glenn Miller went in the Army). A household name even today, James was a talented player with a wide range and impressive technique whose heart was always in jazz even when playing schmaltzy versions of pop melodies or flashy versions of classical themes. James was a star from the time he first joined Benny Goodman's Orchestra (1937-39) and he greatly overshadowed the band's former soloist Ziggy Elman. He had a few record sessions of his own while still with BG and when he formed his own big band in 1939 it was with Goodman's blessing. The Harry James Orchestra struggled for a time but in 1941 they had their first huge hit with an instrumental version of "You Made Me Love You." Other big sellers followed including "Strictly Instrumental," "Sleepy Lagoon," "I'll Get By," "I Had the Craziest Dream" (one of many Helen Forrest vocals) and the classic "It's Been a Long Long Time"; James's repertoire also always included his theme "Ciribiribin" and "Two O'Clock Jump." A celebrity who had speaking parts in several movies, he married Betty Grable, added a string section to his band for a few years and was flying high. Even with the end of the big-band era, James was able to keep his orchestra together (although he dropped the strings after 1947). *—Scott Yanow*

1937-1939 / Dec. 1, 1937-Mar. 6, 1939 / Classics ✦✦✦✦✦
Trumpeter Harry James was very consistent in his musical tastes throughout his career. This CD, which has the first 22 selections that James recorded as a leader, starts off with eight numbers in which the trumpeter (still a Benny Goodman sideman at the time) uses many of Count Basie's top sidemen (including trombonist-arranger Eddie Durham, tenor saxophonist Herschel Evans and singer Helen Humes) for swinging performances highlighted by "Life Goes to a Party" and "One O'Clock Jump"; James' bands (particularly from the 1950s on) would often sound like a duplicate of Basie's. In addition, this CD has four tunes from 1938 in which James mostly uses Goodman players (plus baritonist Harry Carney), and he is also heard on the first six numbers by his big band (including "Two O'Clock Jump" and his earliest recording of his theme "Ciribiribin"). However, the hottest performances are four numbers in which James is backed by a boogie-woogie trio featuring either Pete Johnson or Albert Ammons on piano. This enjoyable CD is full of many examples of James' hot swing trumpet and is easily recommended to swing fans. *—Scott Yanow*

Bandstand Memories: 1938 to 1948 / Apr. 2, 1938-Nov. 30, 1948 / Hindsight ✦✦✦✦✦
This very interesting three-CD set features trumpeter Harry James's Orchestra on a variety of previously unreleased radio broadcast performances. While there are many vocals from

Music Map

Jazz Innovators

Throughout the history of jazz there have been literally thousands of talented improvisers and hundreds who have developed their own individual voices and approaches. There are six, however, whose accomplishments, originality, innovations, and influence tower above the rest; each one of the six greatly altered the vocabulary of jazz and permanently changed the music:

Louis Armstrong (trumpet, vocals)
Duke Ellington (composer, arranger, bandleader, piano)
Charlie Parker (alto sax)
Dizzy Gillespie (trumpet)
Miles Davis (trumpet, bandleader)
John Coltrane (tenor sax, soprano sax)

Here is a list of the second level of jazz greats, artists whose music also greatly enhanced jazz. The categories are meant as a guide and do not necessarily sum up the musicians' entire careers:

New Orleans Jazz

Jelly Roll Morton (piano, composer)
King Oliver (cornet)
Red Allen (trumpet)
Kid Ory (trombone)
Johnny Dodds (clarinet)
Sidney Bechet (soprano, clarinet)

Classic Jazz

Bix Beiderbecke (cornet)
Jack Teagarden (trombone, vocals)
Pee Wee Russell (clarinet)
Bud Freeman (tenor)
James P. Johnson (piano)
Fats Waller (piano, composer, vocals)
Earl Hines (piano)
Joe Venuti (violin)
Bessie Smith (vocals)
Eddie Condon (bandleader)

Swing

Roy Eldridge (trumpet)
Bunny Berigan (trumpet)
Charlie Shavers (trumpet)
Clark Terry (flugelhorn)
Benny Goodman (clarinet, bandleader)
Artie Shaw (clarinet, bandleader)
Coleman Hawkins (tenor)
Lester Young (tenor)
Ben Webster (tenor)
Johnny Hodges (alto)
Benny Carter (alto, arranger)
Harry Carney (baritone)
Art Tatum (piano)

–Continued next column–

Teddy Wilson (piano)
Count Basie (piano, bandleader)
Nat King Cole (piano, vocals)
Django Reinhardt (guitar)
Charlie Christian (guitar)
Lionel Hampton (vibes)
Stephane Grappelli (violin)
Jimmy Blanton (bass)
Gene Krupa (drums)
Buddy Rich (drums)
Louis Bellson (drums)
Billie Holiday (vocals)
Ella Fitzgerald (vocals)

Bop

Howard McGhee (trumpet)
Fats Navarro (trumpet)
J.J. Johnson (trombone)
Buddy DeFranco (clarinet)
Dexter Gordon (tenor)
Bud Powell (piano)
Thelonious Monk (piano, composer)
Oscar Peterson (piano)
Erroll Garner (piano)
Milt Jackson (vibes)
Joe Pass (guitar)
Oscar Pettiford (bass)
Max Roach (drums, bandleader)
Sarah Vaughan (vocals)
Lambert, Hendricks & Ross (vocal group)

Cool Jazz

Gerry Mulligan (baritone)
Lennie Tristano (piano, bandleader)

Hard Bop

Clifford Brown (trumpet)
Lee Morgan (trumpet)
Freddie Hubbard (trumpet)
Cannonball Adderley (alto)
Phil Woods (alto)
Art Pepper (alto)
Sonny Rollins (tenor)
Rahsaan Roland Kirk (tenor, stritch, manzello, flutes)
Wes Montgomery (guitar)
Horace Silver (piano, composer)
Jimmy Smith (organ)
Art Blakey (drums, bandleader)

Avant-Garde

Charles Mingus (bass, bandleader)
Eric Dolphy (alto, bass clarinet, flute)
Ornette Coleman (alto, composer)
Anthony Braxton (alto, composer)
Cecil Taylor (piano)

–Continued next page–

Music Map

Jazz Innovators – *continued*

Post Bop
Woody Shaw (trumpet)
Jackie McLean (alto)
Joe Henderson (tenor)
Wayne Shorter (tenor, soprano, composer)
Bill Evans (piano)
McCoy Tyner (piano)
Elvin Jones (drums)
Tony Williams (drums)
Gil Evans (arranger)

Fusion
Chick Corea (piano, keyboards)
Herbie Hancock (piano, keyboards)
Joe Zawinul (keyboards)
Jaco Pastorius (electric bass)

Modern Mainstream/1990's Jazz
Wynton Marsalis (trumpet)
Eddie Daniels (clarinet, tenor)
Keith Jarrett (piano)
Pat Metheny (guitar)
John Scofield (guitar)
Bill Frisell (guitar)

Frank Sinatra (in his pre-Tommy Dorsey days), Helen Forrest and Kitty Kallen, it is the instrumentals that are of greatest interest, particularly the earliest tracks which date from the period before James really hit it big. Many of these songs were not recorded commercially by the trumpeter and this strong jazz-oriented set is highly recommended to swing fans. *— Scott Yanow*

1939 / Apr. 6, 1939-Oct. 13, 1939 / Classics ♦♦♦♦
The second Harry James CD put out by the Classics label, this set traces the trumpeter's recording career during a six-month period when his big band was struggling financially. It is surprising that James did not catch on immediately, considering how popular he had been with Benny Goodman and since his band at the time was pretty good. Other than the leader, there were no major soloists in the orchestra (altoist Dave Matthews was perhaps best-known), but the arrangements for the instrumentals (including "Indiana," "I Found a New Baby," a surprisingly cooking "Willow Weep for Me" and "Feet Draggin' Blues") were excellent. A little over half of the 23 selections on this reissue have vocals (eight are Frank Sinatra's first appearances on record, including the minor hit "All or Nothing at All"), but the high points are an interesting, unreleased version of "Flash" and "Sleepy Time Gal," which showcases James with just the rhythm section. Recommended for swing fans bored with the usual Harry James greatest-hits sets. *— Scott Yanow*

● **First-Team Player on the Jazz Varsity** / Feb. 12, 1940-Aug. 12, 1940 / Savoy ♦♦♦♦♦
This perfectly done two-LP set (which should be reissued in full on CD) was put out by Muse on their Savoy subsidiary in 1987. Included are all 31 of the recordings that Harry James and his orchestra recorded for the Varsity label during 1940; if only Columbia treated their recordings by the great swing trumpeter with as much wisdom. Recorded just prior to when James's orchestra caught on (it would be the most popular in the world during 1942-45), these sessions have short solos from altoist Dave Matthews, Vido Musso on tenor, and pianist Jack Gardner, along with vocals from Dick Haymes, but one's attention is consistently grabbed by the full ensemble, particularly James' colorful trumpet. Highly recommended if it can be found. *— Scott Yanow*

★ **Snooty Fruity** / Nov. 21, 1944-Feb. 15, 1955 / Columbia ♦♦♦♦♦
Although altoist Willie Smith is strangely enough given top billing, all 18 selections in this CD actually feature the great swing trumpeter Harry James and his popular bands (of which Smith was a key sideman). Many of James's most exciting jazz performances are on this set including the extended "Tuxedo Junction," "Moten Swing," the "New Two O' Clock Jump," "The Great Lie" and "Stompin' at the Savoy." This essential CD is especially recommended to detractors who think that Harry James was overrated. *— Scott Yanow*

Harry James with Dick Haymes 1940 / Feb. 1940-Jul. 1940 / Flyright ♦♦♦♦♦

1939-1940 / Nov. 8, 1939-Apr. 16, 1940 / Classics ♦♦♦

Feet Draggin' Blues, 1944-1947 / Nov. 21, 1944-Nov. 6, 1947 / HEP ♦♦♦
Feet Draggin' Blues, 1944-1947 showcases 20 songs by Harry James and his band. The band is occasionally accompanied by a large string section, and the album features several tracks recorded by his small groups. The strings and the accompanying heavy James vibrato is employed for such ballads as the hauntingly beautiful "Stella by Starlight." The hot stuff is seen mostly on tunes arranged and composed with Ray Conniff, like "Friar Rock" where the James vibrato is far less conspicuous. Conniff was doing the bulk of the arranging at this time and there is a hint of the style he later adopted when leading his own band, but fortunately for James, at this point in time, Conniff's arrangements were still interesting. The small group is heard on such numbers as "I'm Confessin." That James had at least a feel for the blues is shown on "East Coast Blues."

During this period, James' bands were, as usual, loaded with top-flight musicians and most of them are heard soloing. Willie Smith is not only heard on alto, but he sings on "Who's Sorry Now." Other outstanding individual efforts come from Corky Corcoran, Juan Tizol, Babe Russin, and a rare introduction by guitarist Allan Reuss on "I'm Beginning to See the Light", where Kitty Kallen is featured on vocals. Even in the early 40s there is a premonition of what was to come with the Basie-like "Easy." This album is an excellent cross section of what a very popular band was doing during the middle 1940s. *— Dave Nathan*

Trumpet Blues: The Best of Harry James / Jul. 18, 1955-Jul. 1, 1958 / Capitol Jazz ♦♦♦
Released to coincide with the publication of Peter Levinson's biography of the same name, Capitol Jazz's *Trumpet Blues: The Best of Harry James* is an excellent collection of 16 highlights from James' stint at Capitol between 1955 and 1958. These don't quite rank among James' very best recordings, which are generally considered to be his '30s and '40s work, but they're enjoyable latter-day waxings, finding him in a relaxed, generous mood. Among the highlights are the re-recorded title tracks and duets with Buddy Rich, Willie Smith, Corky Corcoran, and Helen Forrest. *Trumpet Blues* shouldn't be considered a definitive statement, but it's a nice addendum of latter-day recordings to a collection of James' classic recordings. *— Stephen Thomas Erlewine*

Complete Recordings / Jul. 13, 1939-Nov. 8, 1939 / Columbia/Legacy ♦♦♦♦♦

Joseph Jarman

b. Sep. 14, 1937, Pine Bluff, AR
Multi Instruments, Sax (Alto), Reeds / Avant-Garde Jazz, Free Jazz, Avant-Garde
Jarman was not so accomplished a saxophonist as his reed-playing partner in the Art Ensemble of Chicago, Roscoe Mitchell. But Jarman's sense of color was fine, his blunt-edged improvisations projected an emotionally immediacy of their own, and his interest in poetry and theatre informed the band's live performances. While attending high school in Chicago in the early '50s, Jarman took up the drums, under the tutelage of the famous music teacher Walter Dyett. He switched to saxophone and clarinet while in the army. Upon his discharge in 1958, he returned to Chicago. There, he joined pianist Muhal Richard Abrams' Experimental Band (formed in 1961), alongside alongside his future Art Ensemble compatriots Malachi Favors and Mitchell. Jarman played in a hard-bop sextet with Mitchell, and in 1965 became one of the first members of the Association for the Advancement of Creative Musicians. Starting around 1967, Jarman was one of the first saxophonists to perform solo, a tactic also embraced by other members of the AACM, notably Anthony Braxton. Jarman led his own group from 1966-8, which included bassist Charles Clark, drummer Thurman Barker, and pianist Christopher Gaddy, among others. Separate editions of that band recorded a pair of albums for Delmark: *Song for...* (1966), and *As if it were the Seasons* (1968). In 1967, Lester Bowie recorded a *Numbers 1 & 2* for Nessa; on "2", the four musicians who would become the Art Ensemble (Bowie, Mitchell, Favors, and Jarman) recorded together for the first time. In 1969, that band would become Jarman's primary creative outlet. By then, the untimely deaths of Gaddy and Clark had compelled Jarman to disband his own group. Jarman would continue with the Art Ensemble until 1993. In that time he also recorded under his own name, for the Black Saint, AECO, and India Navigation labels. Upon leaving the Art Ensemble, Jarman virtually retired from music, in order to devote himself more completely to spiritual matters. As the '90s progressed, however, he did continue to perform and record, often as a guest with such musicians as Marilyn Crispell, guitarist/composer Scott Fields, bassist Reggie Workman, and drummer Lou Grassi. *— Chris Kelsey*

● **Song For** / Oct. 20, 1966-Dec. 16, 1966 / Delmark ♦♦♦♦♦
This was one of the early classics of the AACM. Altoist Joseph Jarman, who would become a permanent member of The Art Ensemble of Chicago shortly after this recording, is heard in a sextet with trumpeter William Brimfield, the legendary tenor Fred Anderson, pianist Christopher Gaddy, bassist Charles Clark and either Steve McCall or Thurman Barker on drums. The four very diverse improvisations include one that showcases a Jarman recitation, a dirge, the intense "Little Fox Run" and the title cut which contrasts sounds and a creative use of silence. Overall this music was the next step in jazz after the high-energy passions of the earlier wave of the avant-garde started to run out of fresh ideas. It's recommended for open-eared listeners. The 1996 CD reissue adds an alternate take of "Little Fox Run" to the original program. *—Scott Yanow*

As If It Were the Seasons / Jun. 19, 1968-Jul. 17, 1968 / Delmark ♦♦♦♦
This set is one of the legendary early AACM releases. Joseph Jarman (heard on alto, bassoon and soprano in addition to fife and recorder) is featured shortly before he became a member of the Art Ensemble of Chicago. Some of his sidemen would become well-known (pianist Richard Abrams, tenors Fred Anderson and John Stubblefield), while others remained obscure or short-lived (bassist Charles Clark, drummer Thurman Barker, flutist Joel Brandon, trumpeter John Jackson and trombonist Lester Lashley). The two lengthy group improvisations (Sherri Scott adds her voice to "Song for Christopher") contrast sound and silence, noise with more conventional sounds, "little instruments" with powerful saxophones. Certainly not for everyone's taste, the truly open-eared will find the innovative results quite intriguing. *—Scott Yanow*

Magic Triangle / Jul. 24, 1979-Jul. 26, 1979 / Black Saint ♦♦♦♦♦

Pachinko Dream Track 10 / May 26, 1996 / Music & Arts ♦♦♦♦

Keith Jarrett

b. May 8, 1945, Allentown, PA
Piano (Electric), Piano / Avant-Garde Jazz, Contemporary Jazz, Post-Bop, Fusion
One of the most significant pianists to emerge since the 1960s, Keith Jarrett's career has gone through several phases. He gained international fame for his solo concerts which found him spontaneously improvising all of the music without any prior planning, but he has also led a couple of dynamic quartets/quintets, performed classical music and recently been playing explorative versions of standards with his longtime trio. Although his tendency to "sing along" with his piano now and then is distracting, Jarrett continues to grow as a powerful improviser after 30 years of important accomplishments. He has had an original and influential style of his own since the early '70s and remains a vital force in jazz. *—Scott Yanow*

Somewhere Before / Oct. 30, 1968-Oct. 31, 1968 / Atlantic ♦♦♦♦
While still a member of the Charles Lloyd Quartet, Keith Jarrett did some occasional moonlighting with a trio, anchored by two future members of Jarrett's classic quartet, Charlie Haden (bass) and Paul Motian (drums). On this CD, Jarrett turns in a very eclectic set at Shelly's Manne-Hole in Hollywood, careening through a variety of idioms where his emerging individuality comes through in flashes. He covers Bob Dylan's "My Back Pages"—which actually came out as a single on the Vortex label—in an attractive, semi-funky style reminiscent of Vince Guaraldi. "Pretty Ballad" delivers a strong reflective dose of Bill Evans, while "Moving Soon" is chaotic free jazz. By the time we reach "New Rag," we begin to hear the distinctive Jarrett idiom of the later trios, but then, "Old Rag" is knockabout stride without the stride. As an example of early, unfocused Jarrett, this is fascinating material. *—Richard S. Ginell*

Foundations: The Keith Jarrett Anthology / 1968-1971 / Rhino/Atlantic ♦♦♦♦
This two-disc anthology presents formative Jarrett material from the late '60s and early '70s; it doesn't have the depth, emotional intensity, imagination or charm of his Impulse or ECM releases, but still contains some fine tracks. These include two superb songs with Gary Burton, plus a cut with Blakey's Messengers and some odds and ends from unrelated dates. The second disc includes three 1971 tunes by The Jarrett unit with Haden, Motian and Redman. At this time, the foursome wasn't fully comfortable or used to each other, and there are uncertain, tentative stretches balanced by other periods with all four interacting smoothly. Jarrett is regarded now as an enigma by some and a genius by others; these songs are reminders of a less assured, but in some ways less predictable and wary pianist. *—Ron Wynn*

The Mourning of a Star / Jul. 9, 1971 / Wounded Bird ♦♦♦

Birth / Jul. 15, 1971-Jul. 16, 1971 / Wounded Bird ♦♦♦

Expectations / Oct. 1971 / Columbia/Legacy ♦♦♦♦
This was the first real indication to the world that Keith Jarrett was an ambitious, multi-talented threat to be reckoned with, an explosion of polystylistic music that sprawled over two LPs (now squeezed onto a single CD). Using his classic quartet (Dewey Redman, Charlie Haden, Paul Motian) as a base, Jarrett occasionally adds the biting rock-edged electric guitar of Sam Brown and always-intriguing percussionist Airto Moreira, and indulges in some pleasant string and brass arrangements of his own, along with some grinding organ smears and acceptable soprano sax. Jarrett again turns his early rampant eclecticism loose—from earthy gospel-tinged soul-jazz to the freewheeling atonal avant-garde—yet this time he does it with an exuberance and expansiveness that puts his previous solo work in the shade. "Common Mama," a spicy Latin workout with brass punctuations, "Take Me Back," driving soul jazz with streaks of electric jazz-rock, and the lengthy, nearly free "Nomads" are the most invigorating tracks. *—Richard S. Ginell*

Facing You / Nov. 10, 1971 / ECM ♦♦♦♦♦
Keith Jarrett's first solo acoustic piano recording remains one of his best. At this point in late 1971, Jarrett had just started improvising completely freely. That does not mean that his solos were necessarily atonal but simply that they were not planned in any way in advance. The music on these eight improvisations are often quite melodic, very rhythmic and bluesy. This set makes for a perfect introduction to Jarrett's many solo piano recordings. *—Scott Yanow*

Fort Yawuh / Feb. 24, 1973 / Impulse! ♦♦♦♦
On *Fort Yawuh*, Keith Jarrett is joined by Dewey Redman (tenor sax), Charlie Haden (bass), Paul Motian (drums), and Danny Johnson (percussion) to produce this set recorded live at the legendary *Village Vanguard* in New York City on February 24, 1973. About two minutes into "Fort Yawuh," Jarrett prepares the listener for a piano solo by announcing himself with quick and sharp keyboard jabs that evolve into spared and beautiful crescendos that before too long involve the soulful wails of Redman on the sax. The following song, "De Drums," is the one track that really swings on this album. Another long one, at 12 minutes in length, "De Drums" is much more focused on a steady and consistent rhythm that is established immediately by a smooth five-note bass line accented by the piano and shakers. Although describable as smooth and cool, this song has a palpable energy perhaps due to the construction of the bass line whose pauses give an enjoyable sense of suspense. A little more than five minutes into this song there is a thematic shift that speeds up the tempo and makes this title swing even more while involving Redman's sax and Motian's drum kit. Half past the eight-minute mark the tempo settles back down to its original drawl, and the song finishes with a lazy bop that makes this the standout track on the album. Fans of Jarrett's avant-garde liberalism will find "De Drums" to be the track most unlike the other four selections on this album. "Still Life, Still Life" is more like a ballad in that it's very slow, but it still maintains the structural freedom featured in the "Fort Yawuh," "(If the) Mysfits (Wear It)," and "Roads Traveled, Roads Veiled." *—Qa'id Jacobs*

The Impulse Years 1973-1974 / Feb. 24, 1973-Oct. 10, 1974 / Impulse! ♦♦♦♦♦
The Keith Jarrett American Quartet/Quintet of the 1970s was arguably his finest group, a post-bop unit featuring the pianist/leader, tenor saxophonist Dewey Redman, bassist Charlie Haden, drummer Paul Motian and sometimes Guilherme Franco and/or Danny Johnson on percussion. A highly recommended four-CD set traced the group's final Impulse recordings of 1975-1976. This five-CD box from 1997 reissues all of the music from the sessions that resulted in *Fort Yawuh* (which is expanded to two CDs), *Treasure Island, Death and the Flower* and *Backhand*. The 29 selections (some of which also include guitarist Sam Brown) include nine previously unreleased performances and three songs that are heard for the first time in expanded unedited versions. Although not reaching as many heights as the later Impulse box, there are many strong moments. The music performed by this underrated group (which is heard at its best on the 22Ω-minute "Death and the Flower" and "Inflight") is inside/outside, hinting at the avant-garde while not shy of using melodies and rhythms. Redman in particular was heard at his best with Jarrett's classic unit. *—Scott Yanow*

☆ **Solo Concerts: Bremen and Lausanne** / Mar. 20, 1973-Jul. 1, 1973 / ECM ♦♦♦♦♦
These are the recordings that made Keith Jarrett famous. Originally released as a three-LP set, the two solo piano recitals feature Jarrett freely improvising and never seeming to run out of ideas. A simple figure often develops through repetition and subtle variations into a rather complex sequence and eventually evolves into a new figure. One of the improvisations lasts for three LP sides (64 minutes), while the second concert has two long solos for 30 and 35 minutes respectively. Despite the length, the music never loses one's interest, making this an essential recording for all jazz collections. *—Scott Yanow*

Belonging / Apr. 24, 1974-Apr. 25, 1974 / ECM ♦♦♦♦♦
On Keith Jarrett's first recording with his "European" quartet—Jan Garbarek (sax), Palle Danielsson (bass), Jon Christiensen (drums)—he stakes out somewhat less abrasive territory than that which his "American" foursome was exploring at this time. Garbarek sports a neutral, vibratoless tone that occasionally reaches an emotional climax; the rhythm section is supportive and just loose enough. The record operates at its strongest level when Jarrett locks the quartet into his winning gospel mode on "'Long as You Know You're Living Yours" and the tense drive of "Spiral Dance"; the reflective numbers are less compelling. Still, this LP-turned-CD successfully bucked the powerful electric trends of its time and holds up well today. *—Richard S. Ginell*

Luminessence / Apr. 29, 1974-Apr. 30, 1974 / ECM ♦♦♦♦
Keith Jarrett does not actually play on this CD; rather, he composed three angst-ridden pieces of varying lengths for string orchestra, over which Jan Garbarek improvises on tenor and soprano saxes. The concept is not unlike that of Stan Getz's *Focus*, but this music is far more static, downcast, and free of the pulse of jazz. As was characteristic of his writing then, Jarrett's string parts are mostly turgid and thick-set, indulging in weird, sliding microtones on "Windsong," weighted down by some kind of emotional burden. Particularly when delivering piercing sustained notes on soprano, Garbarek often sounds like a native of the Middle East. The strings are from the Stuttgart Radio Symphony, led by Mladen Gutesha, who faithfully executes Jarrett's dolorous wishes. *—Richard S. Ginell*

★ **The Köln Concert** / Jan. 24, 1975 / ECM ♦♦♦♦♦
Many critics consider this to be Keith Jarrett's most rewarding solo recording although *Solo Concerts* from the previous year is on the same level. Originally released as a two-LP set, this music is best suited for CD because, while the first 26-minute improvisation fits on one LP side, the second of the two solos (which totals 41 minutes) was programmed over the remaining LP, with side four being only seven minutes long. Logistics aside, the music is quite brilliant with Jarrett (who was improvising freely without any prior planning) developing the most interesting and occasionally startling ideas. The strong fresh melodies and his bluesy feel make this a very enjoyable outing. *—Scott Yanow*

Death and the Flower / Oct. 9, 1974-Oct. 10, 1974 / GRP ♦♦♦

Mysteries: Impulse Years 1975-1977 / Dec. 1975-Sep. 9, 1977 / GRP ♦♦♦
At two marathon three-day recording sessions in December 1975 and October 1976, the finest group that pianist Keith Jarrett ever led (his quartet/quintet with tenor saxophonist Dewey Redman, bassist Charlie Haden, drummer Paul Motian and, on the first sessions, percussionist Guilherme Franco) recorded enough material for four memorable albums: *Shades, Mysteries, Byablue* and *Bop-Be*. This four-CD 1996 box set has the complete sessions, including 11 previously unreleased alternate takes. Jarrett's inside/outside music (his unisons with Redman had a unique sound) both held onto the tradition of chordal improvi-

sation and were reminiscent of Ornette Coleman's earlier acoustic groups. There are a few brief exotic sound explorations, but most of the music (best shown on the opening "Shades of Jazz") extends the swinging tradition into complex areas that have yet to be fully explored by others. Continually fascinating music. *—Scott Yanow*

☆ **The Survivor's Suite** / Apr. 1976 / ECM ✦✦✦✦✦
This is one of the finest recordings by pianist Keith Jarrett's mid-'70s group. Jarrett (on piano, soprano and bass recorder), tenor-saxophonist Dewey Redman, bassist Charlie Haden and drummer Paul Motian (no percussionist this time) by 1976 were thinking alike during the ensemble's improvisations. "The Survivor's Suite," a 49-minute two-part work, finds the group continually building up and then releasing tension together. There are strong individual solos but it is the interplay between the bandmembers that makes this a particularly memorable outing. *—Scott Yanow*

Staircase / May 1976 / ECM ✦✦✦✦
The fourth of Keith Jarrett's solo piano albums turns inward, away from the funky, pulsating melodic inventions of its predecessors toward a more reflective, scattered, never-despairing romanticism well removed from the pulse of jazz. As such, it is paradoxically his weakest solo piano album of the '70s and also the most influential, for here is the blueprint for sensitive meandering that the New Age piano crowd took off upon in the 1980s. A studio session, *Staircase* is actually only one of four separately titled improvisations on this double album (now on one CD)—the others are "Hourglass," "Sundial" and "Sand"—but their overall moods of repose are so similar that it hardly matters what they are called. One can always admire Jarrett's lovely tone and flexible touch, yet when he gets stuck for ideas, the repetitions finally begin to grate. Maybe he really needs the stimulus of a live audience in order to get the creative and rhythmic juices flowing when flying solo. *—Richard S. Ginell*

Sun Bear Concerts / Nov. 5, 1976-Nov. 18, 1976 / ECM ✦✦✦✦
This gargantuan package—a ten-LP set now compressed into a chunky six-CD box—once was derided as the ultimate ego trip, probably by many who didn't take the time to hear it all. You have to go back to Art Tatum's solo records for Norman Granz in the '50s to find another large single outpouring of solo jazz piano like this, all of it improvised on the wing before five Japanese audiences in Kyoto, Osaka, Nagoya, Tokyo and Sapporo. Yet the miracle is how consistently good much of this giant box is. In the opening Kyoto concert, Jarrett's gospel-driven muse is in full play, up to the level of his peak solo performances in Bremen and Koln, and the Osaka and Nagoya concerts have pockets of first-rate, often folk-like, even profound lyrical ideas. The Tokyo concert takes a while to get in gear, but when Jarrett finally locks into one of his grooving vamps, he carries us along, and there is a memorably melodic encore. In Sapporo, Jarrett breaks from a nicely flowing pattern into a jumpy rhythm that reminds one of C&W guitar fingerpicking, and there's some exuberant barrelhouse stuff and outbreaks of dissonance in Part II. Each concert is placed on a single CD, while the much briefer sixth disc is reserved for the encores from Nagoya, Tokyo and Sapporo. While *Sun Bear* breaks little ground that his earlier solo piano albums had not already covered, it is nevertheless richly inventive within Jarrett's personal parameter of idioms. If price is not a barrier, the Jarrett devotee need not hesitate. *—Richard S. Ginell*

Silence / Sep. 9, 1977 / GRP ✦✦✦✦
The 1992 CD reissue of the Keith Jarrett "American" Quartet's last recording session combines most of the contents of the LPs *Byablue* and *Bop-Be*, omitting "Yahllah" and "Konya" from the former and "Pyramids Moving" from the latter. (Tellingly, in keeping with conservative '90s tastes—never mind the time-limit excuse—the deleted tracks are the ones which have an experimental Middle Eastern flavor.) Still, this partial sampling of the session indicates that the quartet went out on a high note, still exciting and inventive, the old interplay very much in action, unrepentantly acoustic in an electric era. Like the LP of the same name, "Byablue" brackets the CD with a group version at the beginning and a solo piano benediction at the close, which under these conditions becomes an emotional elegy for the soon-to-be defunct quartet by its leader. *—Richard S. Ginell*

My Song / Nov. 1977 / ECM ✦✦✦✦✦

Nude Ants / May 1979 / ECM ✦✦✦✦✦

Changes / Jan. 1983 / ECM ✦✦✦✦

Standards, Vol. 1 / Jan. 1983 / ECM ✦✦✦✦

Standards, Vol. 2 / Jan. 1983 / ECM ✦✦✦✦

Standards Live / Jul. 2, 1985 / ECM ✦✦✦✦

Changeless / Oct. 9, 1987-Oct. 14, 1987 / ECM ✦✦✦✦

Tribute / Oct. 15, 1989 / ECM ✦✦✦✦✦
The Keith Jarrett Standards Trio gets back down to business with two CDs' worth of familiar and perhaps not-so-familiar tunes, recorded in one evening in Cologne, Germany. There is a concept this time, for all the standards carry a dedication to some jazz man or woman who performed them—and they are not predictable choices; Lee Konitz for "Lover Man," "It's Easy to Remember" for John Coltrane, "All of You" for Miles Davis, etc. Almost every number has a reflective solo piano introduction, with one of the notable exceptions being Jarrett's rolling, convoluted opening variations on "All the Things You Are" (Sonny Rollins). "Solar" (the Bill Evans tribute) has challenging, fractured interplay between Jarrett, Jack DeJohnette and Gary Peacock, and it directly segues into Jarrett's own obsessive "Sun Prayer," which seems to lose its way after a fine start. The other Jarrett composition, "U Dance," a carefree folk-like tune with a rhumba rhythm, closes the concert with a tribute to no one in particular. While the Standards Trio rarely takes anything for granted, transforming everything in its path, the results are not quite as inventive here as on other releases, though Disc Two is clearly more interesting overall than Disc One. Warning to the wary: Keith Jarrett, singer, is in rare groaning form on "I Hear a Rhapsody" and "Solar." *—Richard S. Ginell*

Paris Concert / Oct. 17, 1988 / ECM ✦✦✦✦
The self-imposed quarantine on solo concerts over, Keith Jarrett returned to the improvisatory format that he virtually invented, mellower and more devotional than ever. Indeed, within the 38 minutes of solo improvisation captured at Paris's Salle Pleyel, Jarrett pulls further away from the old rousing (and thoroughly American) gospel, blues and folk roots of earlier concerts toward a more abstract concept. Opening with a soaring, lyrical canonic melody, he rambles through his familiar obsessive hammering, grand tremolos, and the like before topping it off with an ethereal tune that turns somber. There are two encores—Russ Freeman's "The Wind," awhich begins with a brief swatch of Steve Reich-like minimalism but swiftly turns reflective the rest of the way, and "Blues," a welcome if brief return to one of the pianist's root sources. Again, Jarrett's virtuosic abilities are never in doubt, and he rarely flaunts his technique for its own sake, but one senses that the inspiration level is down; one doesn't come out of the CD all charged up as with many earlier solo concerts. *—Richard S. Ginell*

Vienna Concert / Jul. 13, 1991 / ECM ✦✦✦✦
Keith Jarrett feels that this is his finest solo concert; having "courted the flame for a very long time," he writes, this music speaks "the language of the flame itself." Perhaps playing in the European-tradition-encrusted Vienna Staatsoper had an overt influence, for never has a recorded Jarrett solo concert fallen into such a logical, even classical overall structure as this one—all on the wing, mind you. Part I develops in a majestic 41-minute arch, opening with a simple chorale, devotional and trenchant, and suddenly kicking into a daring, complex, agitated toccata without a key center, technically dazzling and darting. That coalesces into a grand tonal passage with inferences of the great European piano concertos before subsiding into a quietly affirmative finale. Part II is shorter and less rigorously structured, surging and ebbing around shimmering tremolos and a brief pulsating rhythm, alternately evoking the Middle East and the medieval Dies Irae. Jarrett's exalted judgment is close to the mark; though more Eurocentric than ever, these are his most impressive solo performances since *Sun Bear*. *—Richard S. Ginell*

Bye Bye Blackbird / Oct. 12, 1991 / ECM ✦✦✦✦✦
This is the Keith Jarrett/Gary Peacock/Jack DeJohnette Trio's elegy for their former employer Miles Davis, recorded only 13 days after the maestro's death. The lonely figure in shadow with a horn on the cover contrasts with the joyous spirit of many of the tracks on this CD, yet there is still a ghostly presence to deal with—and in keeping with Miles' credo, Jarrett's choice of notes is often more purposefully spare than usual. There is symmetry in the organization of the album, with "Bye Bye Blackbird" opening and the Trio's equally jaunty "Blackbird, Bye Bye" closing the album, and the interior tracks immediately following the former and preceding the latter are "You Won't Forget Me" and "I Thought About You." The centerpiece of the CD is an 18 1/2-minute group improvisation, "For Miles," which after some DeJohnette tumbling around becomes a dirge sometimes reminiscent of Miles' own elegy for Duke Ellington, "He Loved Him Madly." As an immediate response to a traumatic event, Jarrett and his colleagues strike the right emotional balance to create one of their more meaningful albums. *—Richard S. Ginell*

At the Deer Head Inn / Sep. 16, 1992 / ECM ✦✦✦✦

☆ **Keith Jarrett at the Blue Note: The Complete Recordings** / Jun. 3, 1994-Jun. 5, 1994 / ECM ✦✦✦✦✦
The six-CD box set *Keith Jarrett At The Blue Note* fully documents three nights (six complete sets from June 3-5, 1994) by his trio with bassist Gary Peacock and drummer Jack DeJohnette. Never mind that this same group has already had ten separate releases since 1983; this box is still well worth getting. The repertoire emphasizes (but is not exclusively) standards with such songs as "In Your Own Sweet Way," "Now's The Time" "Oleo," "Days Of Wine And Roses" and "My Romance" given colorful and at times surprising explorations. Some of the selections are quite lengthy (including a 26 1/2 minute version of "Autumn Leaves") and Jarrett's occasional originals are quite welcome; his 28 1/2 minute "Desert Sun" reminds one of the pianist's fully improvised "Solo Concerts" of the 1970's. Throughout the three nights at the Blue Note, the interplay between the musicians is consistently outstanding. Those listeners concerned about Jarrett's tendency to "sing along" with his piano have little to fear for, other than occasional shouts and sighs, he wisely lets his piano do the talking. *—Scott Yanow*

La Scala / Feb. 13, 1995 / ECM ✦✦✦✦

Tokyo '96 / Mar. 30, 1996 / ECM ✦✦✦✦✦
Recorded in Tokyo's Orchard Hall before Japanese royalty and a packed house—and released two years later while Jarrett was out of action suffering from chronic fatigue syndrome—the Standards Trio lives up to its formidable track record of consistency and then some. Jarrett and perennial cohorts Gary Peacock and Jack DeJohnette are, if anything, even sharper, swinging harder and more attuned to each other than ever. There was a stronger Latin subtext in Tokyo that night than usual; "I'll Remember April" opens with a long, spare drum solo and becomes a high-spirited calypso-flavored workout, and "Last Night When We Were Young" segues into a Jarrett boogaloo improv called "Caribbean Sky." Two bop standards touch off further electric sparks; there is a joyously funky "Billie's Bounce," and Jarrett really puts all of Bud Powell's imitators in the shade with his right-handed prowess on "John's Abbey." Even those who have assiduously collected all of the Standards Trio's voluminous output will find Jarrett, Peacock and DeJohnette speaking to them in fresh ways here. *—Richard S. Ginell*

Whisper Not / Jul. 5, 1999 / ECM ✦✦✦✦✦
For Keith Jarrett, this extremely satisfying concert with the Standards Trio on two CDs is a personal landmark, the first for-the-record sign that he had recovered from the chronic fatigue syndrome that laid him low for three years in the late 1990s. Indeed, by the time this Paris gig took place, he had come all the way back—his technical facilities intact (a handful of smeared notes aside), his inventiveness bubbling over. Old cohorts Gary Peacock (bass) and Jack DeJohnette (drums) are back, too, regenerating their propulsive, swinging, collective E.S.P. at will. Not too much has changed from the pre-illness days, though the focus is very much on classic bebop now—with Bud Powell getting a good deal of attention with an outstanding "Bouncing With Bud" and a terrific "Hallucinations" that has an atypically funny false ending. Jarrett's bebop runs on "Groovin' High" are astonishing, "Wrap Your Troubles

in Dreams" is appealingly jaunty and carefree, and ballads like "'Round Midnight" and "Prelude to a Kiss" revert to the melodic simplicity that was cultivated during Jarrett's down time. Even though the Standards Trio has been one of the most prolifically recorded groups of its era, only the final encore, "When I Fall in Love," had been recorded before by this group. So even those who think they have enough material by this group will be rightly tempted to invest in this document of Jarrett's resurrection. *—Richard Ginell*

Jazz at the Philharmonic

Group / Swing, Bop

In 1944 producer Norman Granz organized a concert billed as "Jazz at the Philharmonic" as a fundraiser in Los Angeles. The event, which was recorded, featured Illinois Jacquet, Jack McVea, J.J. Johnson, Shorty Sherock and a rhythm section with Nat King Cole and Les Paul; Jacquet's playing in particular caused a bit of a sensation. After a few more similar events, Granz in 1946 began organizing extensive annual tours using classic swing and bop musicians in a jam-session setting. Although some critics often complained that these events encouraged grandstanding (R&B honking was getting popular during the era), a great deal of rewarding and exciting music resulted and Granz recorded (and later released) much of it on his Verve label. He paid his musicians very well and did his best to fight racism every bit of the way. Among JATP's stars through the years were Coleman Hawkins, Lester Young, Stan Getz,Dizzy Gillespie, Charlie Parker, Oscar Peterson, Gene Krupa and Buddy Rich. Ella Fitzgerald started touring with JATP early on, usually having her own separate set and joining in on a finale.Granz kept the spirit of Jazz at the Philharmonic alive on his many jam session-type records for Pablo in the 1970s. *—Scott Yanow*

Best of the 1940s Concerts / Jul. 2, 1944-Sep. 18, 1949 / Verve ♦♦♦♦

In 1998 Verve came out with a ten-CD set that contained all of their *Jazz At The Philharmonic* recordings from the 1944-49 period. This single-disc sampler has nine performances drawn from those concerts and is more for the less fanatical and more budget-minded consumer. This sampler is better than most, for each of the performances has its classic moments, and taken as a whole, it does give one a strong overview of the classic series. Among the highlights are Charlie Parker's remarkable solo on "Oh, Lady Be Good," his equally creative two-chorus exploration of "Embraceable You," Flip Phillips' famous spot on "Perdido," features for Billie Holiday and Ella Fitzgerald ("Flying Home"), the Gene Krupa trio on "Idaho" and a superior version of "How High the Moon." Among the many all-stars heard from are trumpeters Roy Eldridge, Buck Clayton and Howard McGhee, Bird and Willie Smith on altos, trombonists Tommy Turk, Bill Harris and Trummy Young and the great tenors of Illinois Jacquet, Flip Phillips, Coleman Hawkins and Lester Young. Recommended to jazz fans not able to buy the more essential ten-CD box. *—Scott Yanow*

The First Concert / Jul. 2, 1944 / Verve ♦♦♦♦♦

This single CD contains the seven documented selections from the very first performance of Norman Granz' travelling jam session, Jazz at the Philharmonic. A pretty colorful cast of characters is heard from: trumpeter Shorty Sherock (on the last three numbers); trombonist J.J. Johnson (who is on the first four selections); Illinois Jacquet and Jack McVea on tenors; and a strong rhythm section that includes pianist Nat King Cole and guitarist Les Paul. Together they perform six standards and a blues number, with five of the seven selections being over nine-minutes long. Jacquet's screaming solos (he was the first real R&B tenor player) and the humorous and rather remarkable tradeoff between Cole and Paul on "Blues" are the highpoints of this historically significant and very enjoyable release which ranges from touches of Dixieland through swing, bop, and early R&B. *—Scott Yanow*

☆ **Historic Recordings** / 1944 1946 / Verve ♦♦♦♦♦

1944 & 1946. With Nat Cole (p) Trio, Les Paul (g), Illinois Jacquet (sax); plus lots of Billie Holiday. Recorded in Los Angeles. *—Michael G. Nastos*

☆ **Bird & Pres: The '46 Concerts** / Jan. 1946-Apr. 22, 1946 / Verve ♦♦♦♦♦

This double LP, which was released by Verve in 1977, contains nine lengthy performances, all taken from 1946 Jazz at the Philharmonic concerts. Altoist Charlie Parker is on all but the first two selections, and those seven numbers have been reissued on CD. The main problem with these recordings is that the rhythm section (particularly Lee Young's drumming) is over-recorded and very repetitive, and sometimes the mixture of bop and swing stylists (especially on the two numbers without Parker) leads to some uncomfortable ensembles. However this version of "Lady Be Good" is a classic (especially the solos of pianist Arnold Ross and Bird), and there are some good moments on the other selections by the likes of tenors Lester Young, Coleman Hawkins, and Charlie Ventura; altoist Willie Smith; trumpeters Dizzy Gillespie, Howard McGhee, Buck Clayton, and Al Killian; and pianists Mel Powell and Ken Kersey. *—Scott Yanow*

★ **Bird & Pres** / Sep. 18, 1949 / Verve ♦♦♦♦♦

Of the ten Jazz at the Philharmonic LPs released by Verve in the early '80s, this one has the most essential music, and its contents have since been reissued on CD. For those who do not have the latest reissue and run across this album, don't let it get away. Not only does this set feature altoist Charlie Parker and the tenors of Flip Phillips and Lester Young, but trumpeter Roy Eldridge, the forgotten but brilliant trombonist Tommy Turk, pianist Hank Jones, bassist Ray Brown, and drummer Buddy Rich. "The Opener" and "Lester Leaps In" (both over 12 minutes long) are quite exciting, but it is Charlie Parker's remarkable solo on "Embraceable You" that takes honors. The concluding blues (rightfully called "The Closer") is also quite memorable, for after Eldridge and Rich have a tradeoff, the performance ends temporarily until it is remembered that Bird had not had a chance to play yet. His second breath (which has a countless number of perfectly placed notes) cuts everyone. *—Scott Yanow*

Frankfurt, 1952 / Nov. 20, 1952 / Pablo ♦♦♦♦

This is a previously unreleased concert performance catching the J.A.T.P. troupe (this time featuring Lester Young, Flip Phillips, Roy Eldridge, Hank Jones, Ray Brown, Max Roach and an uncredited Irving Ashby on guitar) on the last night of their European tour of 1952. After Norman Granz' introductions to an enthusiastic Frankfurt audience, the group kicks off with a swinging version of "How High the Moon" that goes on for some 11 minutes. This is followed by "Undecided," taken at an even faster pace but still clocking in at almost 12 minutes and featuring an extraordinary solos by Eldridge and Young. A "Ballad Medley" is next, spotlighting four selections interpreted as solo turns. Flip Phillips starts thing off with a nice reading of "Deep Purple," segueing into Roy Eldridge's take on "Rockin' Chair." Next up is Hank Jones' nice, understated version of "This Is Always," which sets the stage for Lester Young's stunning "I Cover the Waterfront." The concert closes with an uptempo "Dre's Blues," which speeds up to an almost impossible tempo after Max Roach's drum solo. All in all, another classic entry in this long-standing series that languished in the vaults for far too long. *—Cub Koda*

Hartford, 1953 / May 1953 / Pablo ♦♦♦♦

This CD has some typically exciting performances from Norman Granz's traveling jam session Jazz at the Philharmonic. Actually the JATP All-Stars (trumpeters Charlie Shavers and Roy Eldridge, trombonist Bill Harris, Ben Webster and Flip Phillips on tenors, altoists Benny Carter and Willie Smith, the Oscar Peterson Trio and drummer Gene Krupa) only appear on one song, an enjoyable 15-minute version of "Cotton Tail." The Oscar Peterson Quartet (with guitarist Herb Ellis, bassist Ray Brown and drummer J.C. Heard) are in excellent form on four selections (including a burning "7 Come 11") and tenor-great Lester Young (accompanied by Peterson's group) shows on three numbers that he was still very much in his prime in 1953. Fans of swinging jazz will want this colorful music, which was released for the first time in 1984 on Pablo (and does not duplicate any of the Verve sets). *—Scott Yanow*

☆ **Tokyo: Live at the . . .** / Nov. 4, 1953-Nov. 8, 1953 / Pablo ♦♦♦♦♦

This two-CD set (originally out as three LPs) features the contents of a single Jazz at the Philharmonic concert held in Tokyo. There are mini-sets by the Oscar Peterson Trio, with guitarist Herb Ellis and bassist Ray Brown (which is highlighted by "Tenderly" and "Swingin' Till the Girls Come Home"), and Gene Krupa (in a trio with altoist Benny Carter and Peterson), along with ten numbers that feature Ella Fitgerald (who scats wildly on "Lady Be Good," "How High the Moon," and the closing "Perdido"). But the real reason to get this set is for the Jazz at the Philharmonic All-Stars (trumpeters Roy Eldridge and Charlie Shavers; trombonist Bill Harris; altoists Willie Smith and Benny Carter; tenors Ben Webster and Flip Phillips; the Oscar Peterson Trio; and drummer J.C. Heard) who, in addition to a seven-song ballad medley and a drum feature, stretch out on "Tokyo Blues" and "Cotton Tail." The latter has a witty and explosive trumpet battle by Shavers and Eldridge; Shavers comes out on top. This reissue is highly recommended as a fine example of the excitement of Jazz at the Philharmonic in the mid-'50s. *—Scott Yanow*

The Exciting Battle: Stockholm '55 / Feb. 2, 1955 / Pablo ♦♦♦♦♦

Frenetic jam session date done in 1955 in Stockholm with an all-out tenor battle between Illinois Jacquet, Flip Phillips, and many others. This has been reissued on CD. *—Ron Wynn*

In London 1969 / Mar. 1969 / Pablo ♦♦♦♦♦

By 1969 producer Norman Granz's Jazz at the Philharmonic was largely a thing of the past in the U.S., but he put together occasional European tours that resulted in the very interesting and consistently enjoyable music heard on this double CD. Trumpeters Dizzy Gillespie and Clark Terry, tenors Zoot Sims and James Moody, pianist Teddy Wilson, bassist Bob Cranshaw and drummer Louis Bellson form the core group and play two jams and a four-song ballad medley in addition to accompanying blues singer/guitarist T-Bone Walker on three numbers. Teddy Wilson's Trio with Cranshaw and Bellson is in typically flawless form on a few songs and then comes the biggest surprise of the two-fer. The great veteran tenor Coleman Hawkins was in sad shape during the last few years of his life (he would pass away two months after this concert) yet he manages to almost sound as if he were still in his prime, far exceeding any of his post-1965 recordings on "Blue Lou" and three ballads including a partly unaccompanied "September Song" and an emotional rendition of "Body and Soul." Altoist Benny Carter is also heard from and all of the horns join in for a finale, "What Is This Thing Called Love—" This is historic and frequently exciting music. *—Scott Yanow*

Jazz at the Philharmonic at the Montreux Jazz Festival 1975 / Jul. 16, 1975 / Pablo/OJC ♦♦♦♦

Norman Granz and Pablo Records took over a large segment of the 1975 Montreux Jazz Festival and many recordings resulted. This particular CD is a colorful reissue featuring trumpeters Roy Eldridge and Clark Terry, Zoot Sims on tenor, altoist Benny Carter, guitarist Joe Pass, pianist Tommy Flanagan, bassist Keter Betts, and drummer Bobby Durham performing four fairly lengthy renditions of standards. Everyone is in fine form, but it is the joyful playing of the two complementary but contrasting trumpeters (both of whom can be immediately recognized in a note or two) that makes this a recommended set for fans of straight-ahead jazz. *—Scott Yanow*

Jazz Passengers

f. 1987

Group / Contemporary Jazz, Post-Bop

The Jazz Passengers were founded in 1987 by Roy Nathanson and trombonist Curtis Fowlkes in order to bring lively humor and entertainment back into modern jazz. The name, a take-off on Art Blakey's Jazz Messengers, signifies that the musicians are merely along for a wild ride. The band also includes percussionist E.J. Rodriguez, bassist Brad Jones (a cohort of Elvin Jones and Muhal Richard Abrams), Steely Dan touring vibist Bill Ware and guitarist Marc Ribot, who has appeared on albums by noted singer/songwriters Elvis Costello and Tom Waits. Nathanson and Fowlkes met while playing in the pit band for the Big Apple Circus, which gave them the opportunity to play the Charles Mingus music they loved and pay the bills as well. The two joined John Lurie's Lounge Lizards and left after a short time to record a duet album together. They added more and more studio musicians until eventually, the Jazz Passengers were born. The group made a name for itself in the New York City avant-garde scene centering on the *Knitting Factory* with its hybrid of Mingus-influenced postbop, dance rhythms and original tunes complete with lyrics and/or entertaining stories. After five albums on small independent labels, the Passengers finally recorded their major-label debut, *Jazz Passengers in Love.* In 1994, rock singer Deborah Harry started touring and recording with the band. *—Steve Huey*

Implement Yourself / 1990 / New World ✦✦✦✦
Arguably the best group to emerge on the new music/avant-garde scene in many years, Roy Nathanson's Jazz Passengers suffer from both audience ignorance about their talents and meager album distribution due to being on a small label. But they make fine, constantly changing music that's reminiscent of The Art Ensemble in its early days. *—Ron Wynn*

• **Live at the Knitting Factory** / Jan. 7, 1991-Jan. 14, 1991 / Knitting Factory ✦✦✦✦✦
The Jazz Passengers blend collective improvisation, outside arrangements, free playing and cohesive intragroup interplay better than most hard bop and mainstream jazz groups. They also include other non-jazz elements into their music, from funk to rock and blues. This melange of styles and idioms was on display throughout the 1991 concert captured on this CD. Whether it was the African/Arabic flavor of "Jazz Passengers In Egypt Overture" or the offbeat pace of "Prozak" and "Tikkun," The Passengers don't content themselves with merely executing chord changes and ripping out solos. They take their followers on trips that seldom proceed smoothly, but always result in rewarding experiences. *—Ron Wynn*

Individually Twisted / 1996 / 32 Jazz ✦✦✦

Live in Spain / Jul. 1997 / 32 Jazz ✦✦✦✦
Artists ranging from Chaka Khan, Natalie Cole and Teena Marie to Sting have demonstrated that certain rock and R&B stars can successfully handle jazz-oriented or jazz-influenced situations if given the chance. Similarly, Deborah Harry made a radical departure from the type of pop-rock she was known for when, in the mid-'90s, she became the lead singer for an avant-garde jazz outfit known as the Jazz Passengers. Recorded live at Spain's Victoria Jazz Festival in 1997, this CD proves that the former lead singer of Blondie was definitely up for the challenge. In fact, Harry sounds quite inspired on such abstract inside/outside offerings as "Maybe I'm Lost," "Lady Butter" and "Samba Uber Alles." It's important to stress that as angular, quirky and cerebral as much of this music is, the band is actually very musical. Even at their most daring, Harry and fellow Passengers Roy Nathanson (alto, tenor and soprano sax), Rob Thomas (violin) and Curtis Hasselbring (trombone) remind us how focused avant-garde jazz can be. For Harry, making the transition from "In the Sun" and "Hanging on the Telephone" to the Passengers is comparable to an actress who'd made her mark in romantic comedies getting into film noir, or basketball icon Michael Jordan trying his hand at baseball. But while Jordan realized that he wasn't much of a baseball player, Harry makes an impressive and convincing jazz singer. *—Alex Henderson*

Eddie Jefferson (Edgar Jefferson)

b. Aug. 3, 1918, Pittsburgh, PA, **d.** May 9, 1979, Detroit, MI
Vocals, Lyricist / Vocal Jazz, Vocalese, Bop
The founder of vocalese (putting recorded solos to words), Eddie Jefferson did not have a great voice but he was one of the top jazz singers, getting the maximum out of what he had. He started out working as a tapdancer but by the late '40s was singing and writing lyrics. A live session from 1949 (released on Spotlite) finds him pioneering vocalese by singing his lyrics to "Parker's Mood" and Lester Young's solo on "I Cover the Waterfront." However, his classic lyrics to "Moody's Mood for Love" were recorded first by King Pleasure (1952) who also had a big hit with his version of "Parker's Mood." Jefferson had his first studio recording that year (which included Coleman Hawkins's solo on "Body and Soul") before working with James Moody (1953-57). Although he recorded on an occasional basis in the 1950s and '60s, his contributions to the idiom seemed to be mostly overlooked until the 1970s. Jefferson worked with Moody again (1968-73) and during his last few years often performed with Richie Cole. He was shot to death outside of a Detroit club in 1979. Eddie Jefferson, who also wrote memorable lyrics to "Jeannine," "Lady Be Good," "So What," "Freedom Jazz Dance" and even "Bitches' Brew," recorded for Savoy, Prestige, a single for Checker, Inner City and Muse; his final sides appeared in 1999 under the title *Vocal Ease*. *—Scott Yanow*

The Jazz Singer / Jan. 19, 1959-Oct. 29, 1965 / Evidence ✦✦✦✦✦
Eddie Jefferson, one of the great jazz singers and an important pioneer of vocalese, is heard in peak form on this Evidence CD which reissues an Inner City LP and adds six previously unissued selections to the program. The bulk of the music is from 1959-61 with Jefferson backed by several horns (including trumpeter Howard McGhee and tenor saxophonist James Moody and sometimes three other vocalists. There are many highlights including Jefferson's original classic versions of "Body and Soul" (a tribute to Coleman Hawkins, the "king of the saxophone") and "So What" (dedicated to Miles Davis), a remake of "Moody's Mood for Love" and vocalese adaptations of a few Lester Young and Charlie Parker solos. Most of the unissued tracks are from these sessions but there is also "Silly Little Cynthia" from 1964 (a duet with pianist Tommy Tucker) and a meeting with guitarist Louisiana Red on 1965's "Red's New Dream." When one considers that Jefferson otherwise did not record during 1963-67, it makes those two numbers not only enjoyable but historic. This CD is highly recommended for all jazz collections. *—Scott Yanow*

★ **Letter from Home** / Dec. 18, 1961-Feb. 8, 1962 / Riverside/OJC ✦✦✦✦✦
This CD (which augments the original LP program with two alternate takes) is a fine showcase for the vocalese master Eddie Jefferson. Backed by either a tentet or a quintet which gives solo space to altoist James Moody and the tenor of Johnny Griffin, Jefferson sings his lyrics to such numbers as "Take the 'A Train," "Billie's Bounce," "I Cover the Waterfront," "Parker's Mood" (the latter differs from the famous lines immortalized by King Pleasure), "A Night in Tunisia" and "Body and Soul" among others. Jefferson is in prime form and these boppish renditions as a whole form a near-classic. *—Scott Yanow*

Body and Soul / Sep. 27, 1968 / Prestige/OJC ✦✦✦✦✦
Eddie Jefferson had not been on record in quite a few years when he recorded this excellent set (reissued on CD) for Prestige. A few of the songs ("Mercy, Mercy, Mercy," "Psychedelic Sally" and "See If You Can Git to That") were attempts to update the singer's style in the mod idiom of the late '60s but the most memorable selections are "So What" (on which Jefferson recreates Miles Davis's famous solo), "Body and Soul", "Now's the Time," "Oh Gee" and "Filthy McNasty"; the latter has very effective lyrics by writer Ira Gitler. Tenorman James Moody, trumpeter Dave Burns and pianist Barry Harris are in the supporting cast of this excellent set. *—Scott Yanow*

Come Along with Me / Aug. 12, 1969 / Prestige/OJC ✦✦✦✦✦
Vocalist Eddie Jefferson (the founder of vocalese) is in top form throughout this outstanding set, a CD reissue of the original LP. There is a liberal amount of solo space for trumpeter Bill Hardman, altoist Charles McPherson and pianist Barry Harris but it is Jefferson's singing and his witty lyrics to such songs as Horace Silver's "The Preacher," "Yardbird Suite," "Dexter Digs In," "Baby Girl" (based on "These Foolish Things") and even "When You're Smiling" that are the main reasons to acquire this very enjoyable disc. *—Scott Yanow*

Vocal Ease / Mar. 5, 1974-Mar. 27, 1976 / 32 Jazz ✦✦✦
Vocal Ease is a compilation culled from three of Eddie Jefferson's '70s titles: *Things Are Getting Better, Still on the Planet,* and *The Live-Liest*. It features the late vocalese master toward the end of his career, sounding fantastic and making bold repertoire choices. The biggest surprise by far is Miles Davis's "Bitches Brew." To hear Davis's heady abstractions put to words is quite remarkable, even if the track pales in comparison to the original. Jefferson also tackles Sly Stone's "Thank You (Fallettinme Be Mice Elf Agin)," using it as an opportunity to say "thank you" to a pantheon of jazz greats. He delves deep into Adderley-style '70s soul-jazz with "Zap! Carnivorous," "Things Are Getting Better," and "I Got the Blues," a *Fat Albert*-like riff based on Lester Young's "Lester Leaps In." On the more straight-ahead front, there's Davis's "So What" (played quite fast), Dizzy Gillespie's "Night in Tunisia," and Charlie Parker's "Ornithology" and "Billie's Bounce." Jefferson sounds great, filtering bebop through a hip '70s lens and making clear his influence on younger singers like Miles Griffith and George V. Johnson, Jr. Instrumental highlights are provided by great players such as Richie Cole on alto sax, Mickey Tucker on keyboards, and Eddie Gladden on drums. *—David R. Adler*

Leroy Jenkins

b. Mar. 11, 1932, Chicago, IL
Violin / Avant-Garde Jazz, Free Jazz
Free jazz's leading violinist, Leroy Jenkins has greatly expanded the options and range of sounds and possibilities for stringed instruments in free music. His techniques have included sawing, string bending and plucking. Jenkins plays adventurous phrases and distorted solos, while including elements of blues, bebop and classical in his approach. Jenkins' often lists as influences a diverse group of violinists (Eddie South and Jascha Heifetz) and other instrumentalists (Charlie Parker, Ornette Coleman and John Coltrane among others). Jenkins began playing violin at eight, often at church in Chicago. He was another student of Walter Dyett at Du Sable High, where he also played alto sax. Jenkins graduated from Florida A&M, where he dropped alto and concentrated on violin. He spent about four years teaching stringed instruments in Mobile, Alabama. Jenkins returned to Chicago in the mid-'60s, and divided his time from 1965 to 1969 between teaching in the Chicago public school system and working with the Association for the Advancement of Creative Musicians (AACM). Jenkins was among the AACM musicians who left Chicago for Europe in the late '60s. While in Paris, Jenkins, Anthony Braxton, Leo Smith and Steve McCall founded The Creative Construction Company. He also played with Ornette Coleman there. Jenkins returned to Chicago in 1970, and moved to New York with Braxton shortly after, living and studying at Coleman's New York home for three months. After working briefly with Cecil Taylor and Braxton, Jenkins played with Archie Shepp, Alice Coltrane and Rahsaan Roland Kirk. But more importantly, in 1971 Jenkins, Sirone and Jerome Cooper founded The Revolutionary Ensemble, one of the decade's great trios. They were truly a co-operative venture, with each musician contributing compositions, and their performances often resembling works in progress. All three played several instruments during their concerts. The Ensemble maintained its integrity while making albums that were aesthetic triumphs and commercial flops for six years on various labels. After the trio disbanded, Jenkins made several tours of Europe, led a quintet and a trio featuring Anthony Davis and Andrew Cyrille. During the mid-'80s he served on the board of directors of the Composers' Forum, and was a member of Cecil Taylor's quintet in 1987. Jenkins has presented many free music performances and written numerous pieces for soloists, small groups and large ensembles. A few of his Black Saint and India Navigation sessions are available on CD. *—Ron Wynn*

Solo Concert / Jan. 11, 1977 / India Navigation ✦✦✦✦✦
About as adventurous and experimental as violin playing gets. Despite far-out tendencies, Jenkins knows when to come back in and how. *—Ron Wynn*

Space Minds / New Worlds / Survival America / Aug. 1978-Sep. 1978 / Tomato ✦✦✦✦
Space Minds, New Worlds, Survival of America. Music that is dynamic, and invigorating, far from hard bop, swing, or traditional styles. *—Ron Wynn*

Lifelong Ambitions / Mar. 11, 1977 / Black Saint ✦✦✦✦✦
Leroy Jenkins, free jazz's greatest violinist, has always worked best in intimate situations with equally talented partners. He certainly had the optimum conditions on this duet date pairing him with outstanding pianist, composer, arranger and conductor Muhal Richard Abrams. The duo played six Jenkins compositions for the session, which was recorded live. Abrams and Jenkins frequently alternated roles, letting each other set the pace, never colliding and forging a highly effective musical partnership. Jenkins' whiplash lines, percussive effects and seamless blend of free and blues influences was capably contrasted by Abrams' driving, soulful piano phrases and solos. *—Ron Wynn*

Urban Blues / Jan. 2, 1984 / Black Saint ✦✦✦✦
Violinist Leroy Jenkins was at the helm of Sting, which played funky and free, did originals and vintage spirituals, and would shift from stretches of collective improvisation to challenging solo exchanges. They were a unique, intriguing group, but sadly didn't last. This 1984 album, reissued on CD, presented them at their best, displaying the breadth of influences, genres, sources and styles that converged and resulted in the work of a great band. *—Ron Wynn*

Themes & Improvisations on the Blues / Apr. 9, 1992 / CRI ✦✦✦✦

● **Solo** / Oct. 24, 1992 / Lovely Music ♦♦♦♦♦
An extraordinary CD of solo violin and viola improvisations by the composer/performer who has been called "not only the father of extended improvisational string music, but also one of the guiding lights of creative music as a whole" (String Magazine.) In other words, "no violinist in the field can touch Leroy Jenkins" (The Village Voice). The selections on this CD cover a wide spectrum of expression and ideas in both Jenkins' original compositions and his reading of two modern classics by Gillespie and Coltrane: "Blues #1," "Um Cha Chi Chum," "Hipnosis," "Big Wood," "Folk Song," "Off the Top of My Head," "Wouldn't You" (D. Gillespie), "Dive for the Oyster, Dip for the Pearl," "Keep On Trucking Brother," "Festival Finale," and the famous "Giant Steps" (J. Coltrane). —"Blue" Gene Tyranny

Bunk Johnson (William Geary Johnson)

b. Dec. 27, 1889, New Orleans, LA, **d.** Jul. 7, 1949
Trumpet / New Orleans Jazz
Due to the difference of opinion between his followers (who claimed he was a brilliant stylist) and his detractors (who felt that his playing was worthless), Bunk Johnson was a controversial figure in the mid-'40s when he made a most unlikely comeback. The truth is somewhere in between. He did have a pretty tone and, although not an influence on Louis Armstrong (as he often stated), was a major player in New Orleans starting around 1910 when he joined the Eagle Band. Johnson was active in the South until the early '30s but did not record during that era. Discovered in the latter part of the decade by Bill Russell and Fred Ramsey, he was profiled in the 1939 book *Jazzmen*. A collection was taken up to get Bunk new teeth and a horn. An alcoholic, Johnson's playing tended to be erratic and when Sidney Bechet recruited him for a band in 1945, he essentially drank himself out of the group. In 1946 Bunk led a group that included the nucleus of the ensemble George Lewis would make famous a few years later but Johnson disliked the playing of the primitive New Orleans musicians. He was more comfortable the following year heading a unit filled with skilled swing players and his final album (Columbia's *The Last Testament of a Great Jazzman*) was one of his best recordings. *—Scott Yanow*

Bunk and Lu / Dec. 19, 1941-Feb. 1944 / Good Time Jazz ♦♦♦♦♦
Included on this historic CD are two rather significant sessions. Lu Watters' Yerba Buena Jazz Band was a major force in launching the Dixieland revival, and their first eight recordings, from their initial session, lead off the disc. Featured are trumpeters Lu Watters and Bob Scobey, trombonist Turk Murphy and clarinetist Ellis Horne on such numbers as "Irish Black Bottom," "Maple Leaf Rag" and "Muskrat Ramble"; pianist Wally Rose's feature on "Black & White Rag" helped start a mini ragtime revival. The second half of the CD has one of legendary trumpeter Bunk Johnson's finest recordings. He is heard leading the wartime version of the Yerba Buena band (which still included Murphy and Horne, in addition to pianist Burt Bales), and Bunk rarely sounded stronger; he is also perfectly in tune for a change. Sister Lottie Peavey takes a fair number of gospel-oriented vocals; Clancy Hayes sings definitive versions of "Ace In the Hole" and "219 Blues," and Johnson himself vocalizes on "Down By the Riverside." But it is for Bunk's trumpet that the latter part of the CD is most notable. *—Scott Yanow*

1944 / Jul. 29, 1944-Aug. 1944 / American Music ♦♦♦♦♦

King of the Blues / Jul. 1944-Aug. 1944 / American Music ♦♦♦♦

☆ **Bunk's Brass Band and Dance Band 1945** / May 14, 1945-May 18, 1945 / American Music ♦♦♦♦♦
This CD starts off with a potentially very interesting session, the first-ever recording of a New Orleans brass band. Bunk Johnson heads a group consisting of two trumpeters (the other is Kid Shots Madison), trombonist Jim Robinson, George Lewis on the eerie Eb clarinet, Isidore Barbarin on alto horn, the baritone horn of Adolphe Alexander, Joe Clark on bass horn, Baby Dodds on snare drum and Lawrence Marrero on bass drum. Unfortunately, the band (particularly Lewis) is generally out of tune, which—despite the power and sincerity of the music—reduces the effectiveness of the recording. The second half of the disc has more conventional performances by Bunk, Lewis and Robinson in a spirited New Orleans jazz sextet, playing numbers such as "Runnin' Wild," "Kentucky Home" and "The Sheik of Araby." *—Scott Yanow*

★ **Last Testament** / Dec. 23, 1947-Dec. 26, 1947 / Delmark ♦♦♦♦♦
Bunk Johnson had a rather unlikely career. Completely forgotten and out of music by the late 1930s, he was given a new set of teeth and a trumpet and hailed as a legend. Johnson made an impressive comeback, but excessive drinking resulted in an erratic and short-lived career. Both overpraised by some and dismissed by others, Bunk was actually a fine player when he was at his best. His final recording, reissued on this CD along with two alternate takes, was arguably his best. Utilizing more modern players than his usual New Orleans band (trombonist Ed Cuffee, clarinetist Garvin Bushell, pianist Don Kirkpatrick, guitarist Danny Barker, bassist Wellman Braud and drummer Alphonse Steele), Bunk Johnson performed a wide variety of music ranging from folk songs and swing standards (such as "Out of Nowhere" and "You're Driving Me Crazy") to some rags (most notably "The Entertainer"). Throughout, Bunk sounds at the top of his game, making this CD his definitive release. *—Scott Yanow*

J.J. Johnson (James Louis Johnson)

b. Jan. 22, 1924, Indianapolis, IN, **d.** Feb. 4, 2001, Indianapolis, IN
Trombone, Composer, Arranger / Third Stream, Hard Bop, Bop
Considered by many to be the finest jazz trombonist of all time, J.J. Johnson somehow transferred the innovations of Charlie Parker and Dizzy Gillespie to his more awkward instrument, playing with such speed and deceptive ease that at one time some listeners assumed he was playing valve (rather than slide) trombone. He made his recording debut with Benny Carter and played at the first JATP concert (1944). Johnson also had plenty of solo space during his stay with Count Basie's Orchestra (1945-46). During 1946-50 he played with all of the top bop musicians including Charlie Parker (with whom he recorded in 1947), the Dizzy Gillespie big band, Illinois Jacquet (1947-49) and the Miles Davis Birth of the Cool Nonet. His own recordings from the era included such sidemen as Bud Powell and a young Sonny Rollins. In August 1954 he formed a two-trombone quintet with Kai Winding that became known as Jay and Kai and was quite popular during its two years. He began to compose ambitious works starting with 1956's "Poem for Brass" and including "El Camino Real" and a feature for Dizzy Gillespie, "Perceptions;" his "Lament" became a standard. *—Scott Yanow*

Jazz Quintet / Jun. 26, 1946-May 11, 1949 / Savoy Jazz ♦♦♦♦♦
One can fault this CD for having brief playing time (a dozen selections totaling less than 33 minutes) and for not including the alternate takes, but the music is beyond criticism. When trombonist J.J. Johnson burst on the scene in the mid-1940s, his speed, fluency and quick ideas put him at the top of his field, where he remained for over a half century. This 1992 CD has the trombonist's first three sessions as a leader, music that qualifies as classic bebop. Johnson is matched with either altoist Cecil Payne, baritonist Leo Parker or tenor great Sonny Rollins (on one of his first dates) in quintets that also have Bud Powell, Hank Jones or John Lewis on piano; Leonard Gaskin, Al Lucas or Gene Ramey on bass; and Max Roach or Shadow Wilson on drums. Other than the ballads "Don't Blame Me" and "Yesterdays," the repertoire is comprised of originals (including Rollins' "Audobon") containing lots of tricky lines, concise but heated solos and virtuosic playing. Until a more complete reissue takes place, bop fans not owning the music (plus the alternates) on earlier LPs will definitely find this CD valuable. *—Scott Yanow*

Jay and Kai / Dec. 24, 1947-Aug. 26, 1954 / Savoy ♦♦♦

The Eminent Jay Jay Johnson, Vol. 1 / Jun. 20, 1953-Sep. 24, 1954 / Blue Note ♦♦♦♦♦
The CD reissue of the two volumes titled *The Eminent Jay Jay Johnson* straighten out his three Blue Note sessions of 1953-55 and add alternate takes. This particular CD concentrates exclusively on the trombonist's 1953 sextet date with the great trumpeter Clifford Brown, Jimmy Heath (who doubles on tenor and baritone), pianist John Lewis, bassist Percy Heath and drummer Kenny Clarke. The six titles (plus three alternates) are highlighted by "It Could Happen to You," "Turnpike" and a classic rendition of "Get Happy." Although Johnson has a couple of features, Clifford Brown largely steals the show. This CD is well worth getting by listeners who do not have the music on Brownie's own *Complete* Blue Note set. *—Scott Yanow*

The Eminent Jay Jay Johnson, Vol. 2 / Sep. 24, 1954-Jun. 6, 1955 / Blue Note ♦♦♦♦♦
The second of two Blue Note CDs (which differ in their content from the similarly titled LPs) contains two complete sessions that showcase trombonist J.J. Johnson. The first six titles (highlighted by "Old Devil Moon" and "Too Marvelous for Words") feature Johnson in a quintet with pianist Wynton Kelly, bassist Charles Mingus, drummer Kenny Clarke and the congas of Sabu. For the later session, there are also six titles (including "Pennies from Heaven" and "Portrait of Jennie") plus three alternate takes; Johnson is joined by Hank Mobley on tenor, pianist Horace Silver, bassist Paul Chambers and drummer Kenny Clarke. Both of these dates offer listeners excellent examples of the talents of the great trombonist who always played his instrument with the fluidity of a trumpet. Recommended. *—Scott Yanow*

The Complete J.J. Johnson Columbia Small Group Sessions / Jul. 24, 1956-Jan. 12, 1961 / Mosaic ♦♦♦♦♦
This seven-CD limited-edition box set from Mosaic is another mind-boggling collection. The masterful trombonist J.J. Johnson recorded steadily for Columbia during the 1956-61 period, heading groups that ranged from quartets to sextets that performed solid hard bop. Johnson is joined on various selections by tenors Bobby Jaspar (doubling on flute) and Clifford Jordan; cornetist Nat Adderley; the young trumpeter Freddie Hubbard; pianists Hank Jones, Tommy Flanagan, Cedar Walton, and Victor Feldman; bassists Percy Heath, Wilbur Little, Paul Chambers, Spanky DeBrest, Arthur Harper, and Sam Jones; and drummers Elvin Jones, Max Roach, Albert "Tootie" Heath, and Louis Hayes. The music was originally issued on nine LPs; plus, there are 21 previously unreleased selections. Johnson's high-quality and consistently inventive playing is quite impressive, making this box a true must for his greatest fans. *—Scott Yanow*

J.J. Inc. / Aug. 1, 1960-Aug. 3, 1960 / Columbia/Legacy ♦♦♦♦
Trombonist J.J. Johnson's 1960 sextet is featured on this Columbia CD. Most notable among the sidemen is a rather young trumpeter named Freddie Hubbard on one of his first sessions; also helping out are tenor saxophonist Clifford Jordan, pianist Cedar Walton, bassist Arthur Harper and drummer Albert "Tootle" Heath. Seven of the compositions (which are joined by Dizzy Gillespie's "Blue 'N' Boogie") are Johnson's and, although none caught on, "Mohawk," "In Walked Horace" and "Fatback" (which is heard in two versions) are all fairly memorable. The six songs on the original LP are joined by three others from the same dates, two of which were released slightly earlier for the first time on a J.J. Mosaic box set that includes all of this music. A fine straightahead set. *—Scott Yanow*

The Great Kai & J. J. / Nov. 4, 1960-Nov. 9, 1960 / Impulse! ♦♦♦♦♦
This Impulse set (which was given the catalog number of A-1 when it first came out) was the first recorded reunion of trombonists J.J. Johnson and Kai Winding. Given a straight reissue on CD (the original liner notes are reproduced so small as to be largely unreadable), the music still sounds fresh and lively. With pianist Bill Evans, either Paul Chambers or Tommy Williams on bass and Roy Haynes or Art Taylor on drums, the two trombonists are in melodic and witty form on such tunes as "This Could Be the Start of Something Big," "Blue Monk," "Side by Side" and the "Theme from Picnic." Recommended. *—Scott Yanow*

Proof Positive / May 1, 1964 / GRP/Impulse! ♦♦♦♦♦
This CD reissue finds trombonist J.J. Johnson in prime form. In fact, his melancholy minor-toned explorations often recall Miles Davis, whose group he had played with the year before). Backed on six of the seven tracks by pianist Harold Mabern, who at the time was heavily influenced by McCoy Tyner, bassist Arthur Harper and drummer Frank Gant, Johnson gets to really stretch out on "Neo," "Minor Blues" and "Blues Waltz"; "Gloria" was previously available only on an Impulse sampler. Manny Albam's "Lullaby of Jazzland," on which Johnson is joined by guitarist Toots Thielemans, pianist McCoy Tyner, bassist Richard Davis and drummer Elvin Jones, rounds out the excellent set. *—Scott Yanow*

Concepts in Blue / Sep. 23, 1980-Sep. 26, 1980 / Pablo/OJC ✦✦✦✦
This is a fun set of straightahead jazz. The colorful frontline (trombonist J.J. Johnson, flugelhornist Clark Terry, and Ernie Watts on tenor and alto) obviously enjoyed playing the blues-oriented repertoire and the solos are consistently rewarding. Nothing all that innovative occurs but the results are pleasing. *—Scott Yanow*

★ **Things Are Getting Better All the Time** / Nov. 28, 1983-Nov. 29, 1983 / Pablo/OJC ✦✦✦✦✦
J.J. Johnson teams up with fellow trombonist Al Grey for a variety of superior standards and obscurities in a quintet with pianist Kenny Barron, bassist Ray Brown and drummer Mickey Roker. Reissued on CD, this session has many joyful moments, and the interaction between the two very different-sounding trombonists (Grey is hot, while Johnson is cool) on such tunes as "Soft Winds," "It's Only a Paper Moon," "Boy Meets Horn" and the title cut is consistently memorable and enjoyable. Recommended. *—Scott Yanow*

Standards: Live at the Village / Jul. 1988 / Antilles ✦✦✦✦✦
The second of two CDs coming from the same engagement at the Village Vanguard (the first was *Quintergy*), this set features trombonist J.J. Johnson's quintet with Ralph Moore on tenor and soprano, pianist Stanley Cowell, bassist Rufus Reid and drummer Victor Lewis jamming on nine standards, plus the leader's "Shortcake." Johnson is in top form, particularly on "My Funny Valentine," "Just Friends," "Misterioso" and "Autumn Leaves." A good example of the ageless trombonist's talents. *—Scott Yanow*

Let's Hang Out / Dec. 7, 1992-Dec. 9, 1992 / Verve ✦✦✦✦

Brass Orchestra / Sep. 24, 1996-Sep. 27, 1996 / Verve ✦✦✦✦
J.J. Johnson finds himself at the helm of a dream band here—a full brass orchestra with French horns, euphoniums, tubas and a harp—and gets to exploit its possibilities wherever they might lead. The results are beyond category, where the veteran trombonist's writing has a feathery richness, urbanity, and a depth charge in the bass reminiscent of, but not really indebted to, Gil Evans. There is plenty of straight-ahead jazz grooving but also several episodes of formal, almost classical writing, as in the suitably joyous "If I Hit The Lottery," and rigorous combinations of both, like the angular tribute to Béla Bartók, "Canon for Bela." The generous Johnson doesn't even appear on a piece he commissioned from Robin Eubanks called "Cross Currents"—Eubanks performs the sputtering trombone solo—nor on Slide Hampton's blazing "Comfort Zone." He also revisits some of his early Third Stream experiments from the '50s and '60s; "Ballad for Joe" derives from his *Poem for Brass* and "Horn of Plenty" and "Ballade" from the *Perceptions* album (the latter two sound a bit staid under the current light). Johnson's own trombone solos are always imaginative, authoritative and irresistibly swinging; at 72, he plays as well here as he ever did. This is a must-buy for all J.J. fans and those who thought that the Third Stream could never rise again. *—Richard S. Ginell*

Heroes / Oct. 1, 1996-Oct. 4, 1996 / Verve ✦✦✦✦
A collection of mostly original material, J.J. Johnson's *Heroes* features an attractive blend of instruments and players. The two versions of "Carolyn" which bookend the album are positively gorgeous, while "Thelonious the Onliest" captures the quirky spirit of its namesake. The "Wayne" on "In Walked Wayne" is Wayne Shorter, who pushes his tenor sax over, under, around and through the tune. Miles' "Blue in Green" receives a classy interpretation, and Coltrane's "Blue Train" proves a fine vehicle for Johnson and friends. For the most part, this is a beautiful album on which the leader's trombone mixes nicely with Don Faulk's tenor and soprano saxophones, while Rufus Reid and Victor Lewis keep the rhythm low-key. Renee Rosnes' solo piano stroll through Johnson's "Vista" is especially nice. In fact, the one word which keeps coming to mind while listening to *Heroes* is "classy," and that it is. *—Jim Newsom*

James P. Johnson

b. Feb. 1, 1894, New Brunswick, NJ, **d.** Nov. 17, 1955, New York, NY
Piano, Composer / Classic Jazz, Stride, Ragtime
One of the great jazz pianists of all time, James P. Johnson was the king of stride pianists in the 1920s. He began working in New York clubs as early as 1913 and was quickly recognized as the pacesetter. In 1917 he began making piano rolls. Duke Ellington learned from these (by slowing them down to half-speed) and a few years later Johnson became Fats Waller's teacher and inspiration. During the 1920s he began to record, was the nightly star at Harlem rent parties (accompanied by Waller and Willie "The Lion" Smith) and he wrote some of his most famous compositions. For the 1923 Broadway show *Running Wild*, Johnson composed "The Charleston" and "Old Fashioned Love," while his earlier piano feature "Carolina Shout" became the test piece for other pianists. Ironically, Johnson—the most sophisticated pianist of the 1920s—was also an expert accompanist for blues singers and he starred on several memorable Bessie Smith and Ethel Waters recordings. Because he was very interested in writing longer works, Johnson spent much of the 1930s working on such pieces as "Harlem Symphony," "Symphony in Brown" and a blues opera. Unfortunately much of this music has been lost through the years. *—Scott Yanow*

Carolina Shout / May 1917-Jun. 1925 / Biograph ✦✦✦
This CD contains 14 of James P. Johnson's piano rolls (cut during an eight-year period) mostly for the QRS company. Although piano rolls generally sound somewhat mechanical (particularly rhythmically), this set is not without interest. There is a version of "Carolina Shout" that originally inspired Duke Ellington and a highlight is a song that few remember that Johnson wrote and he never otherwise recorded, "The Charleston." *—Scott Yanow*

Parlor Piano Solos from Rare Piano Rolls / May 1917-Jun. 1921 / Biograph ✦✦✦✦
The great stride pianist James P. Johnson recorded quite a few piano rolls, starting in 1917. Biograph has reissued a few CDs of this material, which was mostly recorded off of player pianos back in 1970 and 1972. As is usual with most piano rolls, one cannot always trust that the music was solely performed by just one pianist; some of the passages clearly sound like three or four hands playing at once. In addition, the rhythms can be rather mechanical, particularly compared to Johnson's recorded piano solos. However what is most intriguing about these piano rolls are the large number of selections that Johnson never recorded: songs such as "When It's Cherry Time in Tokio," "It Takes Love to Cure the Heart's Disease" and "Doctor Jazzes Raz-Ma-Taz!" In addition, the alternate versions of "Eccentricity," "Fascination" and particularly Johnson's signature piece "Carolina Shout" (the latter was an inspiration for Duke Ellington) are well worth hearing despite the idiom's limitations. *—Scott Yanow*

★ **Snowy Morning Blues** / Jan. 21, 1930-Sep. 22, 194 / GRP ✦✦✦✦✦
James P. Johnson was one of the greatest jazz pianists of all time and in the 1920s was considered the "king of the stride piano." This Decca reissue CD contains a great deal of valuable music. Johnson is first heard on four classic piano solos from 1930 ("You've Got to Be Modernistic" and "Jingles" are particularly memorable) and then on eight Fats Waller-associated tunes in duets with drummer Eddie Dougherty from 1944; the latter performances differ from the eight identical Waller songs that Johnson had recorded earlier in the same year as solos. Since Waller (who had passed away in 1943) was his close friend and former student, there is a lot of emotion in the tributes but also much joy. This highly recommended CD concludes with James P. Johnson romping on eight of his own timeless compositions including "Carolina Shout," "Old Fashioned Love" and "If I Could Be with You." *—Scott Yanow*

The Original James P. Johnson 1942-1945 / 1943-1945 / Smithsonian/Folkways ✦✦✦✦
The great stride pianist James P. Johnson is heard on 14 of the 16 selections included on this LP, taking memorable piano solos; two of the selections ("Memphis Blues" and the first take of "Sweet Lorraine") are actually by an uncredited Cliff Jackson. Despite that error, the music is recommended because Johnson is in top form throughout, particularly on such numbers as "Daintiness Rag," "Snowy Morning Blues," "Liza" and "The Dream." *—Scott Yanow*

Pete Johnson

b. Mar. 25, 1904, Kansas City, MO, **d.** Mar. 23, 1967, Buffalo, NY
Piano / Jazz Blues, Boogie-Woogie
Pete Johnson was one of the three great boogie-woogie pianists (along with Albert Ammons and Meade Lux Lewis) whose sudden prominence in the late '30s helped make the style very popular. Originally a drummer, Johnson switched to piano in 1922. He was part of the Kansas City scene in the 1920s and '30s, often accompanying singer Big Joe Turner. Producer John Hammond discovered him in 1936 and got him to play at the Famous Door in New York. After taking part at Hammond's 1938 *Spirituals to Swing* Carnegie Hall concert in 1938, Johnson started recording regularly and appeared on an occasional basis with Ammons and Lewis as the Boogie Woogie Trio. He also backed Turner on some classic records. Johnson recorded often in the 1940s and spent much of 1947-49 based in Los Angeles. He moved to Buffalo in 1950 and, other than an appearance at the 1958 Newport Jazz Festival, he was in obscurity for much of the decade. A stroke later in 1958 left him partly paralyzed. Johnson made one final appearance at John Hammond's January 1967 *Spirituals to Swing* concert, playing the right hand on a version of "Roll 'Em Pete" two months before his death. *—Scott Yanow*

● **1938-1939** / Dec. 30, 1938-Dec. 1938 / Classics ✦✦✦✦✦
This superlative CD reissue features boogie-woogie pianist Pete Johnson on two classic numbers with singer Big Joe Turner (the original versions of "Goin' Away Blues" and "Roll 'Em Pete"), with inspiring trumpeter Harry James ("Boo Woo" and "Home James"), with his Boogie Woogie Boys (a sextet that includes Turner and trumpeter Hot Lips Page), interacting with fellow pianists Albert Ammons and Meade Lux Lewis (joining Big Joe on "Café Society Rag"), and on a pair of trio numbers. However, it is Johnson's ten unaccompanied piano solos (mostly released previously by Solo Art) that are the rarest and most notable. Taken as a whole, this is Pete Johnson's definitive release, showing that he was much more than just a one-dimensional (although powerful) boogie-woogie specialist. *—Scott Yanow*

The Boogie Woogie Boys / Feb. 1939-Jan. 1953 / Storyville ✦✦✦✦✦

1944-1946 / Feb. 17, 1944-Jan. 31, 1946 / Classics ✦✦✦✦✦
The third "complete" Pete Johnson CD put out by the European Classics label features the great boogie-woogie pianist in three different settings. There are eight formerly rare piano solos from 1944 that cover a variety of moods, five selections with a hot Kansas City octet which includes trumpeter Hot Lips Page, tenorman Budd Johnson and two vocals from the young Etta Jones, and eight intriguing numbers in which Johnson is gradually joined by an additional musician on each track. "Page Mr. Trumpet" is an exciting outing for Hot Lips, and the other top players include clarinetist Albert Nicholas, trombonist J.C. Higginbotham and tenorman Ben Webster. A particularly exciting release. *—Scott Yanow*

1947-1949 / Apr. 18, 1947-Apr. 1949 / Melodie Jazz Classics ✦✦✦
Classics 1110 is the fourth installment chronicling 21 final key recordings of boogie woogie pianist Pete Johnson. 1947-1949 found Johnson leading three different quartets (the second with Al Mckibbon on bass and J.C. Heard on drums) for the Apollo, Modern, and French Jazz Selection labels, while the final session features a sextet on six tracks, blistering through the excellent "Rocket 88 Boogie, Parts 1 and 2" for the Down Beat/Swingtime label. These sessions have a common thread in the predominate use of guitar from Charles Norris, Carl Lynch, Johnny Rogers, and Herman Mitchell thoroughly featured alongside Johnson's piano throughout. Soon after these sessions Johnson left his West Coast home for Buffalo where he essentially retired, showing up occasionally at the odd live appearance or on other musicians' sessions. *—Al Campbell*

Elvin Jones

b. Sep. 9, 1927, Pontiac, MI
Drums / Avant-Garde Jazz, Hard Bop, Post-Bop
Elvin Jones will always be best-known for his association with the classic John Coltrane Quartet (1960-65) but he has also had a notable career as a bandleader and has continued being a major influence during the past 30 years. One of the all-time great drummers (bridging the gap between advanced hard bop and the avant-garde), Elvin is the younger brother of a remarkable musical family that also includes Hank and Thad Jones, and was a part of the very fertile Detroit jazz scene of the early '50s. He moved to New York in 1955, worked

with Teddy Charles and the Bud Powell Trio and recorded with Miles Davis and Sonny Rollins (the latter at his famous Village Vanguard session). After stints with J.J. Johnson (1956-57), Donald Byrd (1958), Tyree Glenn and Harry "Sweets" Edison, Jones became an important member of John Coltrane's Quartet, pushing the innovative saxophonist to remarkable heights and appearing on most of his best recordings. *—Scott Yanow*

Elvin! / Jul. 11, 1961-Jan. 3, 1962 / Riverside/OJC ♦♦♦♦
Drummer Elvin Jones' first full-length album as a leader (reissued on CD in the OJC series) is different than one would expect when it is taken into consideration that he was a member of the fiery John Coltrane Quartet at the time. This sextet session, which also includes his brothers Thad and Hank on cornet and piano in addition to flutist Frank Wess, Frank Foster on tenor, and bassist Art Davis, is straight-ahead with a strong Count Basie feel. Jones is still recognizable on the fairly obscure material (only "You Are Too Beautiful" qualifies as a standard) and shows that he can cook in the fairly conventional setting. All of the musicians are in fine form, and two selections feature the rhythm section as a trio. *—Scott Yanow*

Illumination! / Aug. 8, 1963 / Impulse! ♦♦♦♦
Until it was reissued in 1998, this was one of the more elusive Impulse sets of the 1960s. Recorded in 1963 and co-led by John Coltrane's drummer and bassist (Elvin Jones and Jimmy Garrison), the music is most significant for introducing Sonny Simmons (alto and English horn) and Prince Lasha (flute and clarinet), who are joined in the sextet by underrated baritonist Charles Davis and Trane's pianist McCoy Tyner. Each of the musicians except Jones contributed an original (there are two by Davis); the music ranges from advanced hard bop to freer sounds that still swing. While Garrison's contributions are conventional (this was his only opportunity to lead or co-lead a date), Jones is quite powerful. However, it is the playing of both Simmons, who tears it apart on English horn during "Nuttin' Out Jones," and Lasha (when is he going to be rediscovered and recorded again?) that make this early "New Thing" date of greatest interest. *—Scott Yanow*

Dear John C. / Feb. 23, 1965-Feb. 25, 1965 / GRP ♦♦♦♦
Drummer Elvin Jones may have been breaking down new rhythmic boundaries at the time with John Coltrane's Quartet but his own sessions as a leader were not all that innovative. This quartet set with altoist Charlie Mariano, bassist Richard Davis and either Roland Hanna or Hank Jones on piano is an example of how the avant-garde of the era was starting to influence the more mainstream players. The music is in general safe but enjoyable with the virtuosic bassist Richard Davis often taking solo honors on what was in reality a modern bop date. *—Scott Yanow*

Heavy Sounds / Jun. 19-20, 1967 / Impulse! ♦♦♦
For this CD reissue, an Impulse session co-led by drummer Elvin Jones and bassist Richard Davis was brought back by MCA. Tenor-saxophonist Frank Foster and pianist Billy Green complete the quartet which performs an erratic but generally interesting set of music including "Shiny Stockings," Foster's funky "Raunchy Rita" and "Elvin's Guitar Blues"; the latter briefly features Jones making his first and only appearance on guitar. The music is essentially advanced hard bop but is not all that essential. [The 1999 CD reissue is a 20-bit remaster.] *—Scott Yanow*

Puttin' It Together / Apr. 8, 1968 / Blue Note ♦♦♦♦
Joe Farrell (heard on this CD reissue on tenor, soprano and flute) did some of his finest playing while with drummer Elvin Jones' trio during 1968-69. Joined by bassist Jimmy Garrison (in one of his first post-Coltrane recordings), Farrell really digs into group originals, obscurities, "For Heaven's Sake," and Jimmy Heath's "Gingerbread Boy." With Jones pushing him and Garrison sounding quite advanced, Farrell was consistently inspired to play at the peak of his creativity. *—Scott Yanow*

☆ **Complete Blue Note Recordings** / Apr. -, 19681Jul. 973 / Mosaic ♦♦♦♦♦
This limited-edition eight-disc set combines all of Elvin Jones' Blue Note recordings from April 1968 through July 1973. This 65-track set contains the LPs *Puttin It Together, Ultimate Elvin Jones, Poly-Currents, Coalition, Genesis, Merry Go Round, Live at the Lighthouse, Mr. Jones,* and *The Prime Element.* Jones makes his presence as a band leader undeniable on these sessions allowing the musicians to stretch out while directing the evolution of the pieces. The closest comparison would be to Art Blakey; Jones was a band leader, drum master, and someone who knew instinctively who would fit in his bands, whether it was a wide range of established jazz veterans or some that would go on to achieve that status. Some of this is quite adventurous and, while certainly not taking the extreme direction of John Coltrane's group after Jones and McCoy Tyner left it, moments of this modal hard bop music approach that level of intensity. *—Al Campbell*

Poly-Currents / Sep. 26, 1969 / Blue Note ♦♦♦♦♦
Most of this CD reissue features drummer Elvin Jones leading a sextet full of notables, which also includes the underrated tenor great George Coleman, Joe Farrell on tenor, flute and English horn, baritonist Pepper Adams, bassist Wilbur Little, and Candid on congas. They stretch out on group originals highlighted by "Mr. Jones" and "Whew." In addition, flutist Fred Tompkins teams up with Farrell's flute, Little and Jones on his own "Yes." Advanced modal hard bop with all of the musicians playing in top form. *—Scott Yanow*

Live at the Lighthouse, Vol. 1 / Sep. 9, 1972 / Blue Note ♦♦♦♦
Drummer Elvin Jones' 45th birthday (September 9, 1972) was a good excuse to record his group of the period. The results were originally released as a double-LP and have been reissued as two CDs with over an hour of new music added. Jones' pianoless quartet features two masterful saxophonists (both doubling on tenor and soprano) who at the time sounded very close to John Coltrane. Dave Liebman and Steve Grossman were among the first young saxophonists not closely associated with Coltane who used his style as a starting point in their search for their own musical identities. Their high-powered and sometimes rowdy flights are consistently stimulating. With Gene Perla's alert, sensitive, and inventive bass holding the unit together, Elvin Jones was able to play as free as he desired. The first volume (taken from three sets at *the Lighthouse*) has six fiery selections, four of which were previously unreleased. *—Scott Yanow*

Live at the Lighthouse, Vol. 2 / Sep. 9, 1972 / Blue Note ♦♦♦♦
The second of two CDs featuring music recorded at *the Lighthouse* during a marathon session is the equal of the first. Greatly expanded from the original two-LP set, this disc has a pair of selections from the two-fer ("Sweet Mama" and "The Children, Save the Children") and three performances ("I'm a Fool to Want You," "Britt Piece," and the 28-and-a-half-minute "Children's Merry-Go-Round") that were previously unreleased at the time of this 1990 package. Dave Liebman (on tenor and soprano) is heard in one of his finest pre-Miles Davis recordings; the young tenor Steve Grossman keeps up with him, and bassist Gene Perla acts as a bridge between the fiery saxophonists and explosive drummer Elvin Jones. Exciting and adventurous music that stretches the boundaries of modal hard bop jazz. *—Scott Yanow*

Love & Peace / Apr. 8, 1978-Apr. 1, 1978 / Storyville ♦♦♦♦♦
With the exception of one number ("House That Love Built") from 1978 that matches drummer Elvin Jones with the reeds of Frank Foster and Pat LaBarbera, guitarist Roland Prince and bassist Andy McCloud, this CD reissue focuses on an unusual and generally successful reunion session. Drummer Jones and pianist McCoy Tyner have not recorded together that often since leaving John Coltrane's Quartet in late 1965. With Pharoah Sanders (who was part of the reason they departed) on tenor, bassist Richard Davis in the late Jimmy Garrison's spot, and guitarist Jean-Paul Bourelly an added wild card, the musicians avoid Coltrane tunes in favor of newer originals and the standard "Sweet and Lovely." Sanders sounds very much like late-1950s Coltrane; Bourelly is a bit out of place, and Tyner easily takes solo honors. An interesting but not overly memorable outing that was originally cut for the Japanese Trio label and made available in the U.S. by the now-defunct Black-Hawk company. *—Scott Yanow*

In Europe / Jun. 23, 1991 / Enja ♦♦♦♦♦
Recorded live at a jazz festival in Germany, *In Europe* represents a typical Jazz Machine live performance, three selections from the group's regular repertoire where the musicians get plenty of room to stretch out, fueled by Jones' propulsive polyrhythms. "Ray-El," written by Elvin's brother Thad Jones, is a medium tempo blues number featuring a fine flute solo by Sonny Fortune. The traditional Japanese folk song "Doll of the Bride" is a 32 minute tour-de-force beginning with Fortune's flute and a long Jones drum solo using mallets, then moving into a Latin-ish vamp with excellent solos from Fortune on tenor sax and Willie Pickens on piano. "Island Birdie," written by McCoy Tyner, is a happy calypso reminiscent of "St. Thomas" with a nice turn on soprano sax by Ravi Coltrane, the son of Elvin's former employer John Coltrane, and bassist Chip Jackson. This was Jones return to recording after a seven year hiatus. *—Greg Turner*

● **It Don't Mean a Thing** / Oct. 18, 1993-Oct. 19, 1993 / Enja ♦♦♦♦♦
Elvin Jones has participated in many recording sessions through the years but this CD is one of the most well-rounded sets he has ever led. The lineup of musicians is very impressive: trumpeter Nicholas Payton, Sonny Fortune on tenor and flute, trombonist Delfeayo Marsalis, pianist Willie Pickens, bassist Cecil McBee and vocalist Kevin Mahogany. Everyone plays up to their potential and the material has plenty of variety, ranging from Monk, Ellington and Strayhorn to a traditional Japanese folk song arranged by Elvin's wife Keiko ("A Lullaby of Itsugo Village"), two features for Mahogany (a touching version of "Lush Life" and his scat-filled "Bopsy") and some authentic-sounding R&B (Sam Cooke's "A Change Is Gonna Come"). Payton, Marsalis and Fortune are not on every selection but each have their chance to shine while pianist Willie Pickens is showcased with the trio on a medley of "A Flower Is a Lovesome Thing" and "Ask Me Now." And as for the drummer, there is still no one around who has captured the sound and spirit of Elvin Jones. *—Scott Yanow*

Hank Jones

b. Jul. 31, 1918, Vicksburg, MS
Piano / Swing, Bop
The oldest of the three illustrious Jones brothers (which include Thad and Elvin), Hank Jones was also the first of the great Detroit pianists to emerge after World War II, although by then he had long since left town. In 1944 he moved to New York to play with Hot Lips Page. He had stints with John Kirby, Howard McGhee, Coleman Hawkins, Andy Kirk and Billy Eckstine. Influenced by Teddy Wilson and Art Tatum, Jones' style was also open to bebop and his accessible playing was flexible enough to fit into many genres. He worked as accompanist for Ella Fitzgerald (1948-53) and recorded with Charlie Parker. In the 1950s Jones performed with Artie Shaw, Benny Goodman, Lester Young, Cannonball Adderley and many others. He was on the staff of CBS during 1959-1976 but always remained active in jazz. In the late '70s Jones was the pianist in the Broadway musical *Ain't Misbehavin'.* *—Scott Yanow*

● **The Trio** / Aug. 4, 1955 / Savoy ♦♦♦♦♦
This is a superb Hank Jones date; highly recommended for fans of piano trio music. In 1955, most jazz pianists were immersed in the school of Bud Powell. Jones is unique in that he developed his harmonic concept prior to Powell's ascendancy and the Bebop revolution, but went on to fully assimilate the melodic vocabulary of bop. He has synthesized important elements from many great players into his own recognizable style. His versatility is evident on these eight selections. Jones plays swinging bop lines on his original "We're All Together" and his blues head, "Odd Number," displays the Powell influence most clearly. Upon hearing the delicate touch and harmonic subtlety with which Jones plays ballads, including "We Could Make Such Beautiful Music Together," "Cyrano," "There's a Small Hotel" and "My Funny Valentine," one can imagine that a young Bill Evans was quite familiar with this recording. Jones' mastery of block chords is particularly impressive. Occasionally reissued under drummer Kenny Clarke's name, this important Savoy session also includes bassist Wendell Marshall, who had spent the previous seven years with Duke Ellington's band. *—Lee Bloom*

Hank Jones Quartet/Quintet / Nov. 1, 1955 / Savoy ♦♦♦

Great Jazz Trio at the Village Vanguard / Feb. 19, 1977-Feb. 20, 1977 / Inner City ♦♦♦♦♦
The name "Great Jazz Trio" is not an overstatement when being applied to a group comprised of pianist Hank Jones, bassist Ron Carter and drummer Tony Williams. The all-stars really dig into "Moose the Mooche," "Naima," Claus Ogerman's "Favors" and the Ron Carter

blues "12+12." It is a pleasure to hear Williams pushing Jones to come up with some of his most fiery recent playing. *—Scott Yanow*

Just for Fun / Jun. 27, 1977-Jun. 28, 1977 / Galaxy/OJC ♦♦♦♦
Pianist Hank Jones recorded many dates as a leader during the latter half of the 1970s. A superior transitional player whose two-handed style looks toward both swing and bop, Jones is mostly featured on this CD reissue of a Galaxy date in a trio with bassist Ray Brown and drummer Shelly Manne, although three numbers also welcome guitarist Howard Roberts. None of the seven compositions (by Jones, Brown, Pepper Adams, Thad Jones and J.J. Johnson, along with Sara Cassey's title cut) became well-known, but the fine interplay between the musicians and the concise and purposeful solos uplift the tunes. *—Scott Yanow*

Lazy Afternoon / Jul. 1989 / Concord Jazz ♦♦♦♦
Hank Jones, the father of Detroit's piano legacy (preceding Tommy Flanagan, Barry Harris and Roland Hanna) is teamed on this Concord CD with the typically superb bass of Dave Holland, the supportive drumming of Keith Copeland and (on half the songs) Ken Peplowski's alto (with just a touch of his clarinet). Jones performs a diverse yet unified set of standards and originals. His use of celeste on a moody "Lazy Afternoon," his Monkish "Intimidation" and a trio romp on "Speak Low" are among the highpoints of the excellent release by an ageless master. *—Scott Yanow*

Live at Maybeck Recital Hall, Vol. 16 / Nov. 11, 1991 / Concord Jazz ♦♦♦♦♦
Here, Concord persuaded a reigning giant of the piano to record at Maybeck's Yamaha keyboard—and the result is one of the most musical, and certainly one of the most enjoyable, concerts in the whole series. Recorded closely enough so that you can hear him grunting along with the music, Jones gives full vent to his melodic gifts in a brace of pop and jazz standards from several decades, never staying on any of them for more than five minutes, rarely falling back on the usual pianistic bop patterns. Starting out with very attractive stride work on "I'll Guess I Have to Change My Plan" and "It's the Talk of the Town," he always chooses his notes with care while rarely losing touch with the pulse of jazz, which is all too tempting in a solo format. Among the more touching moments are the treatments of "I Cover the Waterfront" and "Memories Of You"; "Blue Monk" and Joe Bushkin's "Oh, Look At Me Now" have the most wit. *—Richard S. Ginell*

A Handful of Keys: The Music of Hank Jones / Apr. 28, 1992-Apr. 29, 1992 / Verve ♦♦♦♦
There are a playfulness and charm underneath Jones' solos that repeatedly surface throughout his excellent renditions on this disc dedicated to Fats Waller's music. While 10 of the 16 songs are Waller compositions, those that aren't, like "How Come You Do Me Like You Do" and "Your Feet's Too Big," are closely identified with him. Jones' flourishes, expert handling of stride rhythms, and delicate but skillful reworkings not only capture the flavor Waller brought to such songs as "Ain't Misbehavin'," "Honeysuckle Rose" and the title track, but add his character to them with tricky phrases, quick melodies and nimble lines. *—Ron Wynn*

Sarala / Apr. 1995 / Verve ♦♦♦♦
This must surely be one of the most unusual items in Hank Jones' catalog. Few people would probably associate Jones—one of the finest pianists that jazz has ever known, and a man who has played with everyone from Charlie Parker to Tony Williams—with contemporary Afro-pop; yet this album is an infectiously grooving example of just that, featuring the remarkably versatile pianist alongside a stellar cast of musicians from the West African nation of Mali. At first glance, the Malian pop music that is featured on this cross-cultural outing would seem to be light-years from the kind of harmonically sophisticated jazz that Jones has played throughout most of his long and distinguished career. The chord changes that ordinarily undergird Jones' elegantly constructed solos are conspicuously absent from Malian music, which derives much of its unique flavor from the complex rhythmic interplay between electric guitars, keyboards, and traditional African instruments. Nonetheless, Jones plays this material as if he were born to it. His solos, while brief, beautifully straddle the line between his own personal style and the equally distinctive sound of his Malian bandmates; and his lines mesh perfectly with the mesmerizing rhythmic accompaniment provided by the rest of the ensemble. And quite an ensemble it is; some of the biggest names in Malian pop are featured on this album under the direction of leader Cheick-Tidiane Seck, and traditional instruments like the n'goni lute and balafon xylophone are given plenty of solo space. In addition, every track features a traditional Malian praise-song delivered by a powerful lead vocalist and a full complement of backup singers. An unlikely partnership, perhaps, but one that yields extraordinary results. *—Alexander Gelfand*

Master Class / Jan. 18, 1977-Jan. 25, 1978 / 32 Jazz ♦♦♦♦♦
The two LPs reissued on this 1998 CD (*Bop Redux* and *Groovin' High*), both originally put out by Muse, feature veteran pianist Hank Jones mostly playing bop-era standards. The former set matches Jones in a trio with bassist George Duvivier and drummer Ben Riley, while the latter is a quintet outing for Jones with bassist Sam Jones, drummer Mickey Roker, tenor saxophonist Charlie Rouse and Hank's brother cornetist Thad Jones. The pianist's swing-to-bop transitional style (which shares some characteristics in a more updated fashion with Teddy Wilson) was always versatile enough to sound quite at home in a bop format as he shows throughout the two excellent dates. Highlights include "Yardbird Suite," "Bloomdido," "Sippin' at Bells" and "Groovin' High." *—Scott Yanow*

Favors / May 18, 1996 / Verve ♦♦♦♦♦
Favors is a live recording from May 1996 of a Hank Jones recital in Osaka, Japan. Six cuts feature the trio work of pianist Jones, bassist George Mraz, and drummer Dennis Mackrel. The remaining five tracks augment the group with the Osaka College of Music's Winds Jazz Orchestra. Hank Jones' rich musical career has spanned over fifty years; his playing synthesizes important elements of many of the influential pianists in jazz history, from Art Tatum and Erroll Garner to Bud Powell and Bill Evans. Most significantly, Jones has fused these varied sources into a wholly personal style characterized by an almost orchestral approach to arrangement and harmony, a silvery touch, and masterful attention to detail. *Favors* is meticulously recorded and features thoughtful arrangements of six jazz standards, as well as two Hank Jones compositions. The performance of the title track, written by Claus Ogerman, is exemplary of trio playing at its most elegant. The larger ensemble arrangements by Katsuhiko Tanaka effectively frame the subtle piano work of this consummate jazz artist. Having actually experienced over half a century of the evolution of jazz piano, Jones beautifully consolidates qualities of stride, swing and bebop with more recent harmonic developments. Refined and enriched with time, the musicality of Hank Jones is a deeply fulfilling experience. *—Lee Bloom*

Jo Jones (Jonathan Jones)

b. Oct. 7, 1911, Chicago, IL, **d.** Sep. 3, 1985, New York, NY
Drums / Swing
Jo Jones shifted the timekeeping role of the drums from the bass drum to the hi-hat cymbal, greatly influencing all swing and bop drummers. Buddy Rich and Louie Bellson were just two who learned from his light but forceful playing, as Jones swung the Count Basie Orchestra with just the right accents and sounds. He joined Walter Page's Blue Devils in Oklahoma City in the late '20s. After a period with Lloyd Hunter's band in Nebraska, Jones moved to Kansas City in 1933, joining Count Basie's band the following year. He went with Basie to New York in 1936 and with Count, Freddie Green and Walter Page he formed one of the great rhythm sections. Jones was with the Basie band until 1948 and in later years he participated in many reunions with Basie alumni. He was on some Jazz at the Philharmonic tours and recorded in the 1950s with Illinois Jacquet, Billie Holiday, Teddy Wilson, Lester Young, Art Tatum and Duke Ellington among others. *—Scott Yanow*

★ **The Essential Jo Jones** / Aug. 11, 1955-Apr. 30, 1958 / Vanguard ♦♦♦♦♦
Jo Jones, one of the most influential drummers of the swing era, did not lead that many record sessions of his own during his career. Producer John Hammond gave him his first two dates when he was working for Vanguard and, with the exception of a second take of "Shoe Shine Boy," all of the music from the two LPs is on this single-CD reissue. The first session is very much in the spirit of Count Basie's band; in fact Basie himself makes a guest appearance on "Shoe Shine Boy." The other swing-oriented players include trumpeter Emmett Berry, trombonist Freddie Green, tenor saxophonist Lucky Thompson and (on one song apiece) trombonist Lawrence Brown and clarinetist Rudy Powell. The later date is quite a bit different, a trio session with pianist Ray Bryant and bassist Tommy Bryant. There are a liberal amount of drum solos but of greatest interest are the early versions of Ray Bryant's "Cubano Chant" and "Little Susie." *—Scott Yanow*

The Main Man / Nov. 29, 1976-Nov. 30, 1976 / Pablo/OJC ♦♦♦♦
65 at the time and still in fine form, drummer Jo Jones had a rare opportunity to lead his own album for Pablo in 1976; the music has since been reissued on an OJC CD. Jones jams through four swing standards and a couple of basic originals with an all-star group including both Harry "Sweets" Edison and Roy Eldridge on trumpets, trombonist Vic Dickenson, tenor saxophonist Eddie "Lockjaw" Davis, pianist Tommy Flanagan, rhythm guitarist Freddie Green and bassist Sam Jones. The music is very much in the Count Basie groove, with purposeful and concise solos, along with some good spots for the leader. *—Scott Yanow*

Our Man Papa Jo! / Dec. 12, 1977 / Denon ♦♦♦♦
The final session for a jazz legend. Drummer Jo Jones was nearing the end when he got together with his old friends, pianist Hank Jones and bassist Major Holley, for this 1982 session. He still managed to play with some degree of authority and anchor the rhythm section, while saxophonist Jimmy Oliver and Jones took care of solo responsibilites. This has been reissued on CD. *—Ron Wynn*

Philly Joe Jones (Joseph Rudolph Jones)

b. Jul. 15, 1923, Philadelphia, PA, **d.** Aug. 30, 1985, Philadelphia, PA
Drums / Hard Bop
A fiery drummer and a masterful accompanist, Philly Joe Jones came to fame as a key member with the first classic Miles Davis Quintet. After serving in the Army, he moved to New York in 1947, became the house drummer at Cafe Society and played with the who's who of bop (including Charlie Parker, Dizzy Gillespie and Fats Navarro). He worked regularly with Ben Webster, Joe Morris, Tiny Grimes, Lionel Hampton and Tadd Dameron (1953). Jones was with Miles Davis during 1955-58 including the quintet years (1955-56) with John Coltrane, Red Garland and Paul Chambers and the beginnings of the super sextet that also included Cannonball Adderley (recording the classic *Milestones* album). In 1958 he started leading his own groups, recording for Riverside (1958-59) and Atlantic (1960). Jones lived in London and Paris during 1967-72 (performing and recording with some avant-garde players including Archie Shepp). He eventually returned to Philadelphia where he led a fusion group Le Grand Prix, toured with Bill Evans during 1976, recorded for Galaxy in 1977 and 1979 and worked with Red Garland. Starting in 1981 he led the group Dameronia which revived Tadd Dameron's music. But in reality everything that Philly Joe Jones did after Miles Davis was anti-climatic. *—Scott Yanow*

Blues for Dracula / Sep. 17, 1958 / Riverside/OJC ♦♦♦♦
Drummer Philly Joe Jones' debut recording as a leader, made shortly after he left Miles Davis' Quintet, starts out with his amusing but overly long monologue on "Blues for Dracula," during which he does his best to imitate Bela Lugosi. The remainder of the set (which has been reissued on CD) is more conventional, with fine playing from cornetist Nat Adderley, trombonist Julian Priester, the great tenor Johnny Griffin, pianist Tommy Flanagan, bassist Jimmy Garrison, and the drummer/leader. Dizzy Gillespie's "Ow" and Cal Massey's "Fiesta" are heard in lengthy versions on the worthwhile but not overly essential release. *—Scott Yanow*

Drums Around the World: Philly Joe Jones Big Band Sounds / May 28, 1959-May 29, 1959 / Riverside/OJC ♦♦♦
Drummer Philly Joe Jones takes a lot of solo space (including an unaccompanied "The Tribal Message") throughout this CD reissue. He utilizes an all-star group with such soloists as trumpeter Lee Morgan and Blue Mitchell, trombonist Curtis Fuller, Herbie Mann on flute and piccolo, altoist Cannonball Adderley, Benny Golson on tenor, baritonist Sahib Shihab, pianist Wynton Kelly and either Sam Jones or Jimmy Garrison on bass. The music is supposed to

showcase styles from around the world including Latin America and the Far East but in general those references are somewhat superficial (including "Cherokee") and come out sounding like hard bop. There is some strong playing but this set is primarily recommended to fans of Philly Joe Jones's drum solos. *—Scott Yanow*

Showcase / Nov. 1959-Dec. 1959 / Riverside/OJC ✦✦✦✦
This is a particularly interesting hard bop-oriented set led by drummer Philly Joe Jones. Most unusual is "Gwen," a Jones ballad that has the leader on both piano and (via overdubbing) drums in a trio with bassist Jimmy Garrison. Otherwise, trumpeter Blue Mitchell, trombonist Julian Priester, tenor saxophonist Bill Barron, either Dolo Coker or Sonny Clark on piano, Garrison, and Jones form a sextet that performs modern tunes by Barron, Priester and Jones, in addition to "I'll Never Be the Same" and Philly Joe's feature on "Gone" (based on the Miles Davis/Gil Evans interpretation of "Porgy and Bess"). A well-conceived, diverse and recommended CD reissue. *—Scott Yanow*

Mean What You Say / Apr. 6, 1977-Apr. 7, 1977 / Sonet ✦✦✦✦✦
Philly Joe Jones led a quartet (pianist Mickey Tucker, Charles Bowen on soprano and tenor saxes, bassist Mickey Bass) and quintet (add trumpeter Tommy Turrentine) on an April 1977 date called *Mean What You Say*. This was a nice blowing date for Bowen, who at the time had an R&B background and had never before recorded a jazz album ... Mickey Tucker was very strong on this set and at times almost seemed to be the leader with Jones seemingly pushing to assert his position. Still, this was an enjoyable recording with just that little extra added personality to give it an extra edge. *—Bob Rusch, Cadence*

● **To Tadd with Love** / Jun. 28, 1982 / Uptown ✦✦✦✦✦
Drummer Philly Joe Jones led the group Dameronia during his last years, a band dedicated to performing the music of the great composer Tadd Dameron. Their debut disc for Uptown has Donald Sickler's transcriptions of six Dameron originals (including "Philly J.J.," "Soultrane," and "On a Misty Night"). The nonet is comprised of many fine veteran players: trumpeters Sickler and Johnny Coles, trombonist Britt Woodman, altoist Frank Wess, Charles Davis on tenor, baritonist Cecil Payne, pianist Walter Davis Jr., bassist Larry Ridley, and Jones himself. This loving tribute (which perfectly balances the arrangements with concise solo space) is highly recommended. *—Scott Yanow*

Quincy Jones

b. Mar. 14, 1933, Chicago, IL
Producer, Composer, Arranger / Traditional Pop, Crossover Jazz, Jazz-Pop, Swing, Bop, Urban, Big Band
Quincy Jones has had several very successful careers, largely leaving jazz altogether by the early '70s to make his money out of producing pop, R&B and even rap records. His first important job was playing trumpet and arranging for Lionel Hampton's Orchestra (1951-53), sitting in a trumpet section with Clifford Brown and Art Farmer. During the 1950s he started freelancing as an arranger, writing memorable charts for sessions led by Oscar Pettiford, Brown, Farmer, Gigi Gryce, Count Basie, Tommy Dorsey, Cannonball Adderley and Dinah Washington among others. He toured with Dizzy Gillespie's big band (1956), started recording as a leader for ABC-Paramount in 1956 and worked in Paris (1957-58) for the Barclay label as an arranger and producer. In 1959 Jones toured Europe with his all-star big band which was originally put together to play for Harold Arlen's show *Free and Easy*. He kept the orchestra together through 1960, recording for Mercury. In 1961 Jones returned to New York and became the head of Mercury's A&R department, becoming a vice-president in 1964. Although he kept on recording throughout the 1960's, Jones's focus shifted to writing for films and television. During 1969-81 he worked for A&M, founding Qwest Records in 1980, a label that has become more active in the 1990s. *—Scott Yanow*

★ **This Is How I Feel About Jazz** / Sep. 14, 1956-Feb. 1956 / GRP ✦✦✦✦✦
The music on this CD is from a period when arranger Quincy Jones was a major part of the jazz world, rather than being content just to take bows for it. Six high-quality selections from a 1956 album offer logical, swinging and often distinct arrangements with plenty of solos from the all-star cast (which includes Lucky Thompson on tenor, altoist Phil Woods and trumpeter Art Farmer); highlights include "Stockholm Sweetnin'," "Walkin'" and "Sermonette." The remainder of the CD reissues two-thirds of a slightly odd collection led and produced (but not arranged) by Jones. Originally titled *Go West, Man*, the LP was designed to show off the talents of West Coast arrangers Jimmy Giuffre, Lennie Niehaus and Charlie Mariano. Three selections have an alto summit featuring Benny Carter, Art Pepper, Herb Geller and Charlie Mariano and there are also some numbers with a sax section; three songs with a trumpet section had to be left out due to lack of space. Although these performances are enjoyable, it is the Quincy Jones charts that are most memorable, making one regret his decision in the early 1970s to leave jazz altogether. *—Scott Yanow*

☆ **The Birth of a Band, Vol. 1** / Jun. 16, 1959 / Mercury ✦✦✦✦✦
Although this particular big band changed its personnel quite a bit before touring Europe, Quincy Jones began 1959 with high hopes. On one of his finest jazz recordings, Jones' arrangements feature such top players as trumpeter Harry "Sweets" Edison, Zoot Sims and Sam "The Man" Taylor on tenors, altoist Phil Woods and flugelhornist Clark Terry. Highlights include the title cut, "The Midnight Sun Will Never Set," "Moanin'" and three Benny Golson tunes ("I Remember Clifford," "Along Came Betty" and "Whisper Not"). This music has been reissued on CD. *—Scott Yanow*

Q Live in Paris Circa 1960 / 1960 / Warner Brothers ✦✦✦✦
In late 1959, 26-year-old trumpeter/arranger Quincy Jones was engaged to conduct a jazz band for a musical called *Free and Easy*, the songs for which were written by Harold Arlen and Johnny Mercer. The unusual intention was to tour Europe before coming to Broadway, but the show never finished its engagement in Paris, closing down amid recriminations and stranding the cast and the orchestra. Though Arlen's biographer, Edward Jablonski, states that only Jones came out of the situation well, touring Europe successfully with the band, Jones remembers things differently, calling the experience one that brought him closer to contemplating suicide than any other. Eventually, Jones was forced to disband the group, but he first fulfilled the show's engagement at the Alhambra Theatre, and this album, originally issued as a bootleg disc, was recorded at the final performance. This is not the music from the abortive musical, but rather a set of Jones originals and jazz standards. The band, which features such notable figures as Clark Terry and Phil Woods, is accomplished, and the music is performed in the mold of the Ellington and Basie bands, albeit with the flair that Jones was even then showing as an arranger. This is not really the historic find Jones seems to think it is, but it isn't a vanity release either. It's a curio, with some fine blowing from a band that often seems directionless. *—William Ruhlmann*

The Quintessence / Nov. 29, 1961-Dec. 18, 1961 / GRP/Impulse! ✦✦✦
If it were not for this CD reissue's extreme brevity (under 31 minutes), it would receive a much higher rating. One of arranger/composer Quincy Jones' finest recordings, this 1961 set features such top players as trumpeters Clark Terry, Thad Jones and Freddie Hubbard, Julius Watkins on French horn, and most notably altoist Phil Woods in several big-band settings. Jones' three originals include "Quintessence" and "For Lena and Lennie"; plus, there are reworkings of "Invitation" and pieces by Benny Golson and Thelonious Monk, among others. The music swings, and the solos are logical outgrowths of the arrangements; if only more than one piece were over 4Ω minutes long. *—Scott Yanow*

The Best / Jun. 1969-1981 / A&M ✦✦✦
Quincy Jones' A&M recordings, which roam gradually from the maestro's old big-band base to smoothly polished assaults on the pop charts, are given a cursory glance here. Special attention is paid to 1974's *Body Heat*,—the big initial plunge into mainstream soul—and the later hit albums *Sounds... And Stuff like That* and *The Dude*, at the expense of the early Creed Taylor-produced albums ("Killer Joe" is the sole representative) and transition records like *Smackwater Jack* ("What's Going On," with its anemic vocal by Q, is not the best choice). One reason why this best-of collection does not do justice to its subject is that it barely touches upon the fascinating tracks from all of Jones' A&M phases that feature galaxies of jazzmen. It is decent entertainment, though, for casual listening. *—Richard S. Ginell*

☆ **Walking in Space** / Jun. 18, 1969-Jun. 19, 1969 / A&M ✦✦✦✦✦
The protean Quincy Jones returned to the recording studio as a leader after a long stretch in Hollywood with this triumphantly contemporary big band album. He re-established himself firmly with his big band jazz base while casting a keen eye on the pop scene and the world of electric instruments (even Ray Brown is caught playing superb electric bass here). The diplomat also unveils his uncanny ability to attract some of the biggest names in jazz as sidemen(Freddie Hubbard, Roland Kirk, Hubert Laws, J.J. Johnson, Kai Winding, etc.), a quality that will be put to use again and again in the following decades. For jazz buffs, the long, dramatic title track from the then-raging musical *Hair* is the highlight; Hubbard positively sizzles on muted trumpet, and the brash Kirk blasts through the grooving rhythm section under heavy reverb. You also get Jones' classic, swaggering arrangement of Benny Golson's "Killer Joe"—practically the definitive version—and a rendition of Edwin Hawkins' freak hit "Oh Happy Day" that bursts with wit and sheer joy. This is one of the great peaks of Creed Taylor's *AM* period, and it still sounds spectacular today. *—Richard S. Ginell*

Gula Matari / Mar. 25, 1970-May 1, 1970 / A&M ✦✦✦✦✦
With his second and last album under the Creed Taylor aegis, the complexities of Quincy Jones' catholic, evolving tastes start to reveal themselves. We hear signs of his gradual gravitation toward pop right off the bat with the churchy R&B cover of Paul Simon's mega-hit "Bridge Over Troubled Water," dominated by Valerie Simpson's florid soul vocal and a gospel choir. His roots fixation surfaces in the spell-like African groove of the title track, a dramatic tone poem that ebbs and flows masterfully over its 13-minute length. From this point on, it's all jazz; the roaring big band comes back with a vengeance in "Walkin'," where Milt Jackson, Herbie Hancock, Hubert Laws, and other jazzers take fine solo turns, and things really get rocking on Nat Adderley's "Hummin'." Major Holley is a riot with his grumble-scat routine on bass. The whole record sounds like they must have had a ball recording it. *—Richard S. Ginell*

Smackwater Jack / 1971 / A&M ✦✦✦✦✦
This is where a lot of serious jazz purists get off the train but for the rest of us, this is an exciting journey into Quincy Jones territory where labels are meaningless. Though Q takes us deep into Hollywood and TV with his themes to *Ironside, The Anderson Tapes* and the first *Bill Cosby Show* (with humorous vocals from the Cos' himself), his jazz base remains intact in these fascinating charts, and stellar friends like Freddie Hubbard, Milt Jackson, Toots Thielemans, and Jim Hall are left alone to shine. The centerpiece, "Guitar Blues Odyssey: From Roots to Fruits" is the first of many attempts by Q to summarize musical evolution in one fell swoop. Moreover, this ambitious collage actually works—and it's great fun to hear Thielemans, Hall, Eric Gale and Joe Beck try to mimic guitarists from Robert Johnson to Wes Montgomery to Jimi Hendrix. One can't be quite as enthusiastic about Q's rather weak-kneed vocals on two tracks, but that's about the only stumble in this hugely enjoyable project *—Richard S. Ginell*

Body Heat / 1974 / A&M ✦✦✦✦
At the time, this was a breathtaking leap for Quincy Jones, right into the very heart of mainstream commercial soul—and it turned out to be very lucrative, rising to number six on the pop album charts. Jazz per se has been left far behind but the same musical sensibility, the same brilliant production skills, and the same knack for what will appeal to a wider audience are still at work, and the result is a surprisingly pleasing album. Amazingly Q still draws a constellation of jazz stars into his studio bands (Herbie Hancock, Frank Rosolino, Hubert Laws, Jerome Richardson, Grady Tate, Bob James), plus soul names like Billy Preston, Bernard Purdie and the soon-to-be-ubiquitous guitarist Wah Wah Watson. The emphasis, though, is first on the honeyed soul vocals from a variety of newcomers, and second on the funky grooves laced with the buzz of now-prized analogue synthesizers and wah-wah guitars. There is one reminder of Q's big-band days, a busy electronic retrofitting of his classic chart of Benny Golson's "Along Came Betty," where one can hear Laws blow at some length. Otherwise, to paraphrase Q himself, if you check your jazz boots at the door, you might enjoy this. *—Richard S. Ginell*

Sounds & Stuff / 1978 / A&M ♦♦♦

The Dude / 1980-1981 / A&M ♦♦♦
Now running his own Qwest label and a thousand other things, Quincy Jones still owed one more album to A&M and he gave them a blockbuster, one that reached number ten, yielded three hit pop singles and made a star out of soul balladeer James Ingram. "Ai No Corrida," and the leadoff track, is the Quincy Jones hit method par excellence—great pacing, superb sound, a catchy tune, a hot Ernie Watts tenor sax solo and you can dance to it, too. Stevie Wonder's irresistible synthesizer hooks lift his "Betcha Wouldn't Hurt Me," and Q and omnipresent composer Rod Temperton are far-seeing enough on the title track to anticipate the rise of rap. But where does all of this pop wizardry, soon to assume mythic dimensions on Michael Jackson's *Thriller,* leave the jazz listener? Yes, Quincy has thought of you too, however briefly, on Ivan Lins' wistful "Velas," where perennial house jazzer Toots Thielemans eloquently returns, taping his part in Belgium. Obviously, though, the main purpose here is to make hit pop singles, and *The Dude* does a pretty good job of that. *—Richard S. Ginell*

Back on the Block / 1989 / Qwest ♦♦♦♦

Q's Jook Joint / Nov. 1994-1995 / Qwest ♦♦

Pure Delight: The Essence of Quincy Jones and His Orchestra (1953-1964) / May 27, 1956-Dec. 20, 1964 / Razor & Tie ♦♦♦♦♦
The Razor & Tie collection *Pure Delight* focuses on the Quincy Jones' Orchestra as one of the quintessential post-modern big bands, comfortable in any musical setting, location, or format, and including a retinue of excellent players with no regard for race, gender or nationality. Culling most of its tracks from Jones' solid—yet still long out of print—albums for Mercury of the early '60s (*The Birth of a Band, Jazz Abroad, I Dig Dancers, Big Band Bossa Nova*), the collection hits many highpoints with dozens of top-flight guests. Several of the best include a 1959 version of "I Remember Clifford" with Clark Terry on flugelhorn; "Tickle Toe" (from the same session) with Terry, Zoot Sims, and Joe Newman; "Comin' Home Baby" from 1963 with Terry, Burrell, and Roland Kirk; and last but not least "I Had a Ball" from 1964 with a truly killer lineup: Dizzy Gillespie, Milt Jackson, James Moody, Roland Kirk, and Art Blakey. In all, *Pure Delight* compiles some of the most elegantly swinging selections of Quincy Jones' entire career. *—John Bush*

From Q with Love / Feb. 9, 1999 / Warner Brothers ♦♦♦

Basie and Beyond / Oct. 3, 2000 / Warner Brothers ♦♦♦

Thad Jones (Thaddeus Joseph Jones)

b. Mar. 28, 1923, Pontiac, MI, **d.** Aug. 20, 1986, Copenhagen, Denmark
Flugelhorn, Cornet, Trumpet, Composer, Arranger / Hard Bop, Bop
A harmonically advanced trumpeter/cornetist with a distinctive sound and a talented arranger/composer, Thad Jones (the younger brother of Hank and older brother of Elvin) had a very productive career. Jones became well-known during his long period (1954-63) with Count Basie's Orchestra, taking a "Pop Goes the Weasel" chorus on "April in Paris" and sharing solo duties with Joe Newman. While with Basie, Jones had the opportunity to write some arrangements and he became a busy freelance writer after 1963. He joined the staff of CBS, co-led a quintet with Pepper Adams and near the end of 1965 organized a big band with drummer Mel Lewis that from February 1966 on played Monday nights at the Village Vanguard. During the next decade the orchestra (although always a part-time affair) became famous and gave Jones an outlet for his writing. He composed one standard ("A Child Is Born") along with many fine pieces including "Fingers," "Little Pixie" and "Tiptoe." In 1978 Jones surprised Lewis by suddenly leaving the band and moving to Denmark, an action he never explained. He wrote for a radio orchestra and led his own group called Eclipse. In late 1984 Jones took over the leadership of the Count Basie Orchestra but within a year bad health forced him to retire. *—Scott Yanow*

The Fabulous Thad Jones / Aug. 11, 1954-Mar. 10, 1955 / Debut/OJC ♦♦♦♦♦
Trumpeter Thad Jones made his debut as a leader for Charles Mingus' Debut label during 1954-55, music that has been reissued as a single CD in the OJC series and as part of a huge 12-CD Mingus Debut box set. The 12 performances (which include two alternate takes) really put the focus on Jones' accessible yet unpredictable style. Half of the music showcases Jones in a quartet with pianist John Dennis, bassist Mingus and drummer Max Roach. while the other six numbers are more in a Count Basie groove with Frank Wess on tenor and flute, pianist Hank Jones, Mingus and drummer Kenny Clarke. The originals tend to be tricky, and even such standards as "I'll Remember April," "You Don't Know What Love Is" and "Get Out of Town" have their surprising moments. *—Scott Yanow*

★ **The Magnificent Thad Jones** / Jul. 14, 1956 / Blue Note ♦♦♦♦♦
This CD reissue has one of trumpeter Thad Jones' finest small-group sessions of the 1950s; the music has also been reissued in full as part of a large Mosaic box set. Jones, who is matched with tenor saxophonist Billy Mitchell, pianist Barry Harris, bassist Percy Heath, and drummer Max Roach, performs a couple of his lesser-known but superior originals, two obscurities, and duets with guitarist Kenny Burrell on "Something to Remember You By," "I've Got a Crush on You" (which was not on the original LP), and "April In Paris." The latter in spots purposely recalls the Count Basie hit recording, in which Jones had played a major part. The music throughout is unpredictable and harmonically sophisticated bop. *—Scott Yanow*

After Hours / Jun. 21, 1957 / Prestige/OJC ♦♦♦♦
Although Thad Jones' name appears first on this CD reissue, pianist Mal Waldron is actually the session's main force. Waldron contributed all four selections (all of which are worthwhile, even if none caught on) and is a key soloist with the sextet, which also includes trumpeter Jones, Frank Wess on tenor and flute, guitarist Kenny Burrell, bassist Paul Chambers and drummer Art Taylor. Fine straight-ahead music, very much in the modern mainstream of 1957. *—Scott Yanow*

Mean What You Say / Apr. 26, 1966-May 9, 1966 / Mileston/OJC ♦♦♦♦♦
A classic set recorded for Milestone and reissued in the OJC series, this date is co-led by Thad Jones (heard throughout on flugelhorn) and baritonist Pepper Adams; pianist Duke Pearson, bassist Ron Carter and drummer Mel Lewis complete the band. The high-quality hard bop unit performs four of Jones' originals, a song apiece by Carter and Pearson, and Burt Bacharach's "Wives and Lovers" and "Yes Sir, That's My Baby." Jones and Adams always made for a potent team, but the rise of the Thad Jones/Mel Lewis Orchestra meant that this particular quintet only lasted a short time. *—Scott Yanow*

☆ **The Complete Solid State Recordings of the Thad Jones/Mel Lewis Orchestra** / May 4, 1966-May 25, 1970 / Mosaic ♦♦♦♦♦
The Thad Jones/Mel Lewis big band was one of the finest jazz orchestras of the late '60s, but its Solid State LPs had been long out of print for decades before Mosaic wisely reissued all of the music (plus seven previously unissued performances) on this deluxe but limited-edition five-CD set. With Jones' colorful and distinctive arrangements, soloists such as trumpeters Danny Stiles, Marvin Stamm, and Richard Williams; trombonists Bob Brookmeyer and Jimmy Knepper; the reeds of Jerome Richardson, Jerry Dodgion, Joe Farrell, Billy Harper, Eddie Daniels, and Pepper Adams; and pianists Hank Jones and Roland Hanna; plus a rhythm section driven by bassist Richard Davis and drummer Mel Lewis, this was a classic band. Highlights among the 42 performances include "Mean What You Say," "Don't Git Sassy," "Tiptoe," "Fingers," "Central Park North," and the original version of "A Child Is Born," but nearly every selection is memorable. *—Scott Yanow*

☆ **Thad Jones and the Mel Lewis Quartet** / Sep. 24, 1977 / A&M ♦♦♦♦♦
This is one of the finest small-group sessions of cornetist Thad Jones's career. With strong and very alert assistance from drummer Mel Lewis (his co-leader in their celebrated big band), pianist Harold Danko and bassist Rufus Reid, Jones plays at his peak on six standards, two of which were issued for the initial time on this CD reissue. Four of the songs are at least nine minutes long (two are over 15 minutes) yet Thad never loses his momentum. The musicians constantly surprise each other and there are many spontaneous moments during this often-brilliant outing. *—Scott Yanow*

Scott Joplin

b. Nov. 24, 1868, Bowie City, TX, **d.** Apr. 1, 1917, New York, NY
Piano, Composer / Ragtime
Ragtime was jazz's direct predecessor (differing from jazz in the absence of blues and improvisation) and Scott Joplin was ragtime's greatest composer. Joplin began having pieces published as early as 1895 and in 1899 his "Maple Leaf Rag" (published by his supporter John Stark) became ragtime's most popular number, selling over 75,000 copies of sheet music during its first year. Joplin soon had many other rags published that helped to make ragtime the pop music of its day, but the tragedy of his life was that his goals were beyond ragtime. He staged a ballet (*The Ragtime Dance*) and two ragtime operas (*The Guest of Honor* and *Treemonisha*) but none were successful, a fact that continually frustrated him. By 1910 Joplin was becoming ill with syphilis and at his death in 1917, ragtime was in the process of being replaced by jazz. Ironically, 57 years after his death, Scott Joplin finally became a household name because his music (most notably "The Entertainer") was used by Marvin Hamlisch in his score for the popular film *The Sting.* Although he never recorded, Scott Joplin's music has been fully documented with "Maple Leaf Rag" becoming a Dixieland jazz standard and pianist Richard Zimmerman (on an excellent five-LP set for Murray Hill) recording everything that Joplin ever wrote. *—Scott Yanow*

● **Piano Rags by Scott Joplin** / 1970 / Nonesuch ♦♦♦♦♦
A few years before the release of the movie "The Sting" launched a major revival of ragtime, Joshua Rifkin caused a stir with what would be the first of three albums of Scott Joplin piano solos. Although later criticized by some for playing the rags quite straight in a classical approach, Rifkin's straightforward renditions of eight Joplin rags (including "Maple Leaf Rag," "The Entertainer," "The Ragtime Dance" and "Euphonic Sounds") helped introduce these important pieces to a new generation of listeners. All three of his Nonesuch albums are worth picking up as perfect introductions to Scott Joplin's music. *—Scott Yanow*

King of the Ragtime Writers / Feb. 28, 1992 / Biograph ♦♦♦♦♦

The Elite Syncopations: Classic Ragtime from Rare Piano Rolls / 1899 / Biograph ♦♦♦♦♦
If you want to hear exactly how ragtime should be played, here's the real thing from a founding father. These vintage Scott Joplin rags were transferred to digital from piano rolls and are the way he wanted his rags to sound. *—Ron Wynn*

Clifford Jordan

b. Sep. 2, 1931, Chicago, IL, **d.** Mar. 27, 1993, New York, NY [Manhattan]
Sax (Tenor) / Hard Bop, Post-Bop
Clifford Jordan was a fine inside/outside player who somehow held his own with Eric Dolphy in the 1964 Charles Mingus Sextet. Jordan had his own sound on tenor almost from the start. He gigged around Chicago with Max Roach, Sonny Stitt and some R&B groups before moving to New York in 1957. Jordan immediately made a strong impression, leading three albums for Blue Note (including a meeting with fellow tenor John Gilmore) and touring with Horace Silver (1957-58), J.J. Johnson (1959-60), Kenny Dorham (1961-62) and Max Roach (1962-64). After performing in Europe with Mingus and Dolphy, Jordan worked mostly as a leader but tended to be overlooked since he was not overly influential or a pacesetter in the avant-garde. A reliable player, Clifford Jordan toured Europe several times, was in a quartet headed by Cedar Walton in 1974-75 and during his last years led a big band. He recorded as a leader for Blue Note, Riverside, Jazzland, Atlantic (a little-known album of Leadbelly tunes), Vortex, Strata-East, Muse, SteepleChase, Criss Cross, Bee Hive, DIW, Milestone and Mapleshade. *—Scott Yanow*

★ **Blowing in from Chicago** / Mar. 3, 1957 / Blue Note ♦♦♦♦♦
Clifford Jordan's first date as a leader actually found him sharing a heated jam session with fellow tenor John Gilmore. Backed by pianist Horace Silver, bassist Curly Russell and drummer Art Blakey, the two saxophonists square off mostly on obscurities (other than Gigi Gryce's "Blue Lights" and "Billie's Bounce"); the original six selections are joined by the pre-

viously unreleased "Let It Stand" on the CD reissue. This was one of Gilmore's few sessions outside of Sun Ra's orbit, and if anything, he slightly overshadows the cooler-toned Jordan. Recommended. *—Scott Yanow*

Cliff Craft / Nov. 10, 1957 / Blue Note ♦♦♦
Happily, Blue Note Records and Michael Cuscuna have reissued this wonderfully relaxed recording, which dates from a very fertile period of the renowned jazz label's history. Tenor saxman Jordan was influenced by and shares influences with Sonny Rollins, Dexter Gordon, John Coltrane and Hank Mobley; the early inspiration of Lester Young can also be heard. On this date, the selection of tunes is pleasantly balanced between three originals, two bebop standards, and Ellington's "Sophisticated Lady." Trumpeter Art Farmer's playing is up to his usual high standard—thoughtful, sensitive and technically brilliant. Pianist Sonny Clark is captured during the most prolific phase of his ten-year recording career; together with bassist George Tucker and drummer Louis Hayes, they create a solid, swinging and simpatico rhythm section. *—Lee Bloom*

Spellbound / Aug. 10, 1960 / Riverside/OJC ♦♦♦♦
Tenor-saxophonist Clifford Jordan was sponsored by Cannonball Adderley on this set for Riverside which has been reissued on CD in the OJC series. Jordan did not at this point quite have the distinctive sound that he would develop by his period with Charles Mingus but he was already a strong hard bop stylist. Assisted by pianist Cedar Walton, bassist Spanky DeBrest and drummer Albert "Tootie" Heath, Jordan performs four originals ("Toy" is best known), an unusual waltz version of "Lush Life," the ballad "Last Night When We Were Young" and the romping Charlie Parker blues "Au Privave." It's an excellent straightahead outing. *—Scott Yanow*

Bearcat / Oct. 1961-1962 / Jazzland/OJC ♦♦♦
This CD is a straight reissue of the original Jazzland LP. Tenor saxophonist Clifford Jordan, who is joined by pianist Cedar Walton, bassist Teddy Smith and drummer J.C. Moses, is heard in his early prime and displays an original tone while playing in the hard bop style. He stretches out on five of his swinging and fairly advanced originals, "How Deep Is the Ocean," and Tom McIntosh's "Malice Towards None." It would be 1973 before Jordan had another opportunity to be showcased in a quartet format, making this formerly rare set one of his best all-around recordings. *—Scott Yanow*

These Are My Roots: Clifford Jordan Plays Leadbelly / Feb. 1, 1965-Feb. 17, 1965 / Koch Jazz ♦♦♦♦
At first glance, this appears to be a very illogical album. Back in 1965, tenor saxophonist Clifford Jordan recorded a tribute to the late folk singer Leadbelly. The date, originally cut for Atlantic and reissued by Koch in 1999, is actually more successful than one might expect. Jordan performs nine of Leadbelly's originals (including the hit "Goodnight Irene"), turning the music into jazz without lessening the impact of the melodies or their folk roots. Trumpeter Roy Burrowes, trombonist Julian Priester, bassist Richard Davis and drummer Albert "Tootie" Heath are on most of the selections along with Jordan, while Chuck Wayne (on guitar and banjo) helps out on four tunes, and pianist Cedar Walton is on three. The fine young singer Sandra Douglass is excellent on "Take This Hammer" and "Black Girl," making one wonder whatever happened to her. Overall, this project is an unexpected success—one would not have thought that Clifford Jordan and Leadbelly had that much in common! *—Scott Yanow*

Glass Bead Game / Oct. 29, 1973-Oct. 29, 1973 / Strata East ♦♦♦♦♦

The Highest Mountain / Mar. 18, 1975 / Muse ♦♦♦♦
Tenor-saxophonist Clifford Jordan teams up with pianist Cedar Walton, bassist Sam Jones and drummer Billy Higgins for this excellent modern hard bop set which has been reissued on CD by Muse. Of the five compositions (which include an original apiece by Jordan, Walton, Jones and Bill Lee), only Thelonious Monk's "Blue Monk" and Jordan's title cut had much life beyond this set but the music is consistently memorable, including Walton's "Midnight Waltz." All of the musicians play up-to-par and Clifford Jordan (who was continually underrated throughout his life) is immediately recognizable as usual. *—Scott Yanow*

Night of the Mark 7 / Mar. 26, 1975 / 32 Jazz ♦♦♦♦
The late tenor saxophonist Clifford Jordan always had a distinctive tone and a flexible, swinging style. He never became overly famous as a leader (he is best remembered for his association with Charles Mingus), but his own record dates were consistently rewarding, including this one. Assisted and inspired by pianist Cedar Walton, bassist Sam Jones and drummer Billy Higgins, Jordan performs Thelonious Monk's "Blue Monk," Jones' blues "One for Amos," Walton's appealing "Midnight Waltz," the tenor's own title cut, and Bill Lee's "John Coltrane." The latter piece brings back some of Coltrane's intensity and hints at part of his *Love Supreme* suite. There are plenty of fine solos throughout the live date (recorded in Paris) by Jordan and Walton. Overall, this CD features high-quality hard bop from four of the greats of the idiom, so it is easily recommended to those not already owning the music. *—Scott Yanow*

The Adventurer / Feb. 9, 1978 / 32 Jazz ♦♦♦♦

Repetition / Feb. 9, 1984 / Soul Note ♦♦♦♦♦
Clifford Jordan was in top form for this marathon, noon-to-midnight quartet studio session with Barry Harris, Walter Booker, and Vernel Fournier. The veteran hard bopper brought three potent originals to the date, and the group collaborated on the driving up-tempo "Fun." Neal Hefti's "Repetition" could be subtitled "Relaxation" for its easygoing tempo. The short but effective rendition of Monk's "Evidence" packs plenty of punch, while the medley of Fats Navarro's "Nostalgia" and Tadd Dameron's "Casbah" is also a masterful performance. The only downside to this release is the self-serving liner notes by the enormously egocentric Stanley Crouch. *—Ken Dryden*

Two Tenor Winner! / Oct. 1, 1984 / Criss Cross ♦♦♦♦♦

Royal Ballads / Dec. 23, 1986 / Criss Cross ♦♦♦♦♦

Live at Ethell's / Oct. 16, 1987-Oct. 18, 1987 / Mapleshade ♦♦♦♦♦
Tenor saxophonist Clifford Jordan never seemed to record an uninspired record. This Mapleshade CD, cut live at a Baltimore club, matches Jordan with pianist Kevin O'Connell, bassist Ed Howard and drummer Vernel Fournier. In addition to four standards (including "Lush Life" and "'Round Midnight"), Jordan performs Stanley Cowell's "Cal Massey" and three of his own straight-ahead but diverse originals. Excellent advanced straight-ahead music from an underrated great. *—Scott Yanow*

Play What You Feel / Dec. 1990 / Mapleshade ♦♦♦♦

Live at Condon's, New York/Down Through the Years / Oct. 7, 1991 / Milestone ♦♦♦♦

Duke Jordan (Irving Sidney Jordan)

b. Apr. 1, 1922, New York, NY
Piano / Hard Bop, Bop
Although he has had a long career, Duke Jordan will always be best-known for being pianist with Charlie Parker's classic 1947 quintet. A little earlier he had worked with the Savoy Sultans, Coleman Hawkins and the Roy Eldridge big band (1946). After his year with Parker, (his piano introductions to such songs as "Embraceable You" were classic), Jordan worked with the Sonny Stitt-Gene Ammons quintet (1950-51) and Stan Getz (1949 and 1952-53). He started recording as a leader in 1954, debuting his most famous composition "Jor-du" the following year. Although he worked steadily during the next few decades (writing part of the soundtrack for the French film *Les Liaisons Dangereuses*), Jordan was in obscurity until he began recording on a regular basis for SteepleChase in 1973. Duke Jordan, who was married for a time to the talented jazz singer Sheila Jordan, has lived in Denmark since 1978 and has recorded through the years for Prestige, Savoy, Blue Note, Charlie Parker Records, Muse, Spotlite and Steeplechase. Still possessing an unchanged bop style, Jordan remained active throughout the '90s. *—Scott Yanow*

Jordu / Jul. 2, 1949-Jan. 28, 1954 / Prestige ♦♦♦♦
The music on this LP has not yet been reissued on CD in the United States. The first two titles ("Spider's Webb" and "Strike Up the Band") feature bebop pianist Duke Jordan as a sideman in a quartet with bassist Tubby Phillips and drummer Roy Hall, led by the talented tenor saxophonist Don Lanphere. The remaining eight selections are from Jordan's debut as a leader, originally cut for the French Vogue label, a 1954 trio set with bassist Gene Ramey and drummer Lee Abrams. The pianist's style changed very little through the years, and virtually all of his recordings are worth picking up for bop fans. This album is perhaps most notable for the inclusion of the initial version of Jordan's most famous original, "Jordu." *—Scott Yanow*

★ **Flight to Jordan** / Aug. 4, 1960 / Blue Note ♦♦♦♦♦
Duke Jordan, who played regularly with the Charlie Parker Quintet in 1947, has long been known as a superior bebop pianist whose style was touched by the genius of Bud Powell's innovations. This quintet album (which also features trumpeter Dizzy Reece and the young tenor Stanley Turrentine) gave Jordan an opportunity to record six of his originals and, although none became as well-known as his "Jordu," the music has plenty of strong melodies and variety. This is one of Duke Jordan's better recordings and is quite enjoyable. *—Scott Yanow*

Flight to Denmark / Nov. 25, 1973-Dec. 2, 1973 / Steeple Chase ♦♦♦♦♦
Pianist Duke Jordan has recorded a long series of sessions for the Danish SteepleChase label starting with this 1973 set which has been reissued on CD with four additional selections (three of which are alternate takes). Performing in a trio with bassist Mads Vinding and drummer Ed Thigpen, Jordan plays five of his originals (including "No Problem," "Flight to Denmark" and "Jordu") plus four standards. The pianist's style is easily recognizable (it had not changed much nor lost its enthusiasm since 1947 when he achieved fame playing with Charlie Parker) and this CD is a good example of his talents. *—Scott Yanow*

Two Loves / Nov. 25, 1973-Dec. 12, 1973 / Steeple Chase ♦♦♦♦♦
The companion piece to *Flight to Denmark*, Duke Jordan's *Two Loves* was compiled from the same two recording dates in late 1973. Although he had built a solid resume working with Charlie Parker, Coleman Hawkins, Roy Eldridge, Stan Getz, Gene Ammons, Art Farmer, and Oscar Pettiford, he fell into obscurity during the early '60s, leaving the jazz scene to spend over five years driving a cab in New York. In 1973, the pianist was invited to tour Denmark and, not having recorded since 1962, Jordan began doing sessions for SteepleChase records. These dates were the first products of what was to become a prolific relationship with the Danish label. Joined by drummer Ed Thigpen (Oscar Peterson, Bud Powell, Ella Fitzgerald) and Danish bassist Mads Vinding, Jordan performs five original compositions, three standards, and Thelonious Monk's "Blue Monk." Jordan's style is perhaps the most subdued of the first generation bebop pianists; his touch is gentle, his chords are simply constructed, and his preference for medium tempos is evident. Though not the most flashy of beboppers, Jordan is quite an excellent composer. (His "Jordu" remains a favorite of many contemporary players.) The bluesy original "Subway Inn" is reminiscent of Bobby Timmons' popular "Moanin'" with its call and response motif. Best on this date, though, is the bittersweet title track, "Two Loves," which Jordan performs on solo piano. The harmonic inspiration of Tadd Dameron and John Coltrane can be felt in this composition. Overall, an enjoyable session despite a piano with less than perfect intonation and an unfortunately dry drum sound. *—Lee Bloom*

Duke's Delight / Nov. 18, 1975 / Steeple Chase ♦♦♦♦♦
Starting in 1973, pianist Duke Jordan recorded a long series of excellent sets for the European SteepleChase label; all should be of interest to bop collectors. This CD reissue, which adds an alternate take of the title cut to the original LP program, has five quintet numbers—all Jordan originals—with trumpeter Richard Williams (in excellent form), tenor saxophonist Charlie Rouse, bassist Sam Jones and drummer Al Foster, plus a solo piano rendition of "Solitude." The date lives up to its potential. *—Scott Yanow*

One for the Library / Oct. 9, 1993 / Storyville ♦♦♦
Duke Jordan has long been one of the top bebop pianists, although living in Europe for many years has resulted in his often being overlooked. On this CD, he performs 18 unaccompa-

nied solos, all but one of which are under 4Ω minutes long. Jordan plays six originals and a dozen veteran standards (such as "All The Things You Are," "The Way You Look Tonight," "It's Only a Paper Moon" and "Three Little Words") quite well. The pianist strides and lays down basslines in spots; however, his strength has always been his single-note right-hand lines, and he actually sounds at his best in a trio format. *— Scott Yanow*

Louis Jordan

b. Jul. 8, 1908, Brinkley, AR, **d.** Feb. 4, 1975, Los Angeles, CA
Vocals, Sax (Alto), Saxophone / East Coast Blues, Jump Blues, Swing, Urban Blues
Effervescent saxophonist Louis Jordan was one of the chief architects and prime progenitors of the R&B idiom. His pioneering use of jumping shuffle rhythms in a small combo context was copied far and wide during the 1940s. Jordan's sensational hit-laden run with Decca Records contained a raft of seminal performances, featuring inevitably infectious backing by his band, the Tympany Five, and Jordan's own searing alto sax and street corner jive-loaded sense of humor. He was one of the first Black entertainers to sell appreciably in the pop sector; his Decca duet mates included Bing Crosby, Louis Armstrong, and Ella Fitzgerald. From 1942 to 1951, Jordan scored an astonishing 57 R&B chart hits (all on Decca), beginning with the humorous blues "I'm Gonna Leave You on the Outskirts of Town" and finishing with "Weak Minded Blues." In between, he drew up what amounted to an easily followed blueprint for the development of R&B (and for that matter, rock & roll—the accessibly swinging shuffles of Bill Haley & the Comets were directly descended from Jordan; Haley often pointed to his Decca labelmate as profoundly influencing his approach). "G.I. Jive," "Caldonia," "Buzz Me," "Choo Choo Ch' Boogie," "Ain't That Just like a Woman," "Ain't Nobody Here but Us Chickens," "Boogie Woogie Blue Plate," "Beans and Cornbread," "Saturday Night Fish Fry," and "Blue Light Boogie"—every one of those classics topped the R&B lists, and there were plenty more that did precisely the same thing. Black audiences coast-to-coast were breathlessly jitterbugging to Jordan's jumping jive (and one suspects, more than a few Whites kicked up their heels to those same platters as well). *— Bill Dahl*

☆ **Let the Good Times Roll: The Complete Decca Recordings 1938-54** / 1938-1954 / Bear Family ✦✦✦✦✦
The price of this multi-disc import boxed set is indeed a hefty one, but it contains every track the pioneering saxman waxed for Decca—the multitude of hits that inexorably influenced the future of R&B and eventually rock & roll. Bear Family's attention to detail in its presentation is always immaculate, and sound quality follows suit. *— Bill Dahl*

Five Guys Named Moe / Aug. 1943-1946 / Decca ✦✦✦✦✦
Included on this CD are 27 formerly rare performances by altoist/singer Louis Jordan and his famous Tympani Five. Consisting of radio appearances, plus specially recorded V-discs, the release has quite a few songs not otherwise recorded by Jordan, along with different versions of "Five Guys Named Moe," "Outskirts of Town" and "Caldonia." A special bonus is hearing clarinetist Barney Bigard jam "Rose Room" with the band. The front cover of the CD proclaims "The Father of Rock n' Roll," and in ways that is true, although ironically the rise of rock in the mid-1950s knocked Louis Jordan permanently off the pop charts. Recommended. *— Scott Yanow*

One Guy Named Louis / Jan. 1954-Apr. 1954 / Blue Note ✦✦✦
It is a strange fact that as rock & roll began to catch on, one of the artists who helped influence its birth was dropping rapidly in popularity. Singer/altoist Louis Jordan, who had had dozens of hits with his Tympani Five while on Decca, recorded 21 songs for Aladdin in 1954 (all of which are included on this CD) and none of them sold well. The strange part is that there is nothing wrong with the music. It compares quite well artistically with his earlier performances; it was just out of style. That fact should not trouble latter-day Jordan fans, for the formerly rare music on this set is witty, swinging and eternally hip. *— Scott Yanow*

No Moe!— *Greatest Hits / Oct. 22, 1956-Aug. 1956 / Verve* ✦✦✦
With the exception of four numbers taken from a 1957 set in which he heads a quintet co-starring organist Jackie Davis, this CD consists of a dozen songs taken from a 1956 date already reissued (with additional material) on the previously issued CD *Rock 'N' Roll*. Louis Jordan, who had not had a new hit since 1951 (and unfortunately none were in the future) is mostly heard remaking his earlier triumphs such as "Saturday Night Fish Fry," "Ain't Nobody Here but Us Chickens" and "Choo Choo Ch'Boogie." The music is spirited but the earlier CD is the better purchase. *— Scott Yanow*

★ **The Best of Louis Jordan** / 1977 / MCA ✦✦✦✦✦
This is a best-of CD collection that actually lives up to its name. Virtually all of Louis Jordan's hits, which musically bridged the gap between small-group swing, R&B and rock & roll, are on this single CD, including "Choo Choo Ch'Boogie," "Let the Good Times Roll," "Ain't Nobody Here But Us Chickens," "Saturday Night Fish Fry," "Caldonia," "Five Guys Named Moe" and "Don't Let the Sun Catch You Cryin'." Serious collectors will want to explore a more complete series, particularly the one put out by Classics, but for a single acquisition, this is the Louis Jordan set to get. Jordan's very likable and good-humored vocals, as well as his hot alto, and the playing of the Tympani Five belong in everyone's music collection. *— Scott Yanow*

☆ **Let the Good Times Roll: Anthology 1938-1953** / Dec. 20, 1938-May 28, 1953 / MCA ✦✦✦✦✦
It might seem like a stretch to say that Louis Jordan helped to pave the way for everyone from Led Zeppelin, U2 and the Beatles to James Brown, Marvin Gaye and Parliament/Funkadelic, but when you get down to it, that's a very fair and accurate assertion. The jump blues/swing/early R&B innovator definitely played a crucial role in the development of rock & roll and soul music, and it's been argued that he was the first rock & roller. To be sure, this two-CD set is full of seminal recordings that were primary listening for Little Richard, Etta James, Chuck Berry, Elvis Presley, James Brown, Bill Haley, Ruth Brown and so many others. Jordan and his Tympani Five swung hard, and the hard swinging of "Is You or Is You Ain't My Baby," "Saturday Night Fish Fry," "Choo Choo Ch'Boogie" and other recordings that Decca/MCA includes certainly did their part to make the rock explosion of the '50s possible. MCA's digital remastering is superb, and those who associate 78-era recordings with pops, ticks, etc. will be pleased to hear how good the pre-1950 material sounds. Was Jordan the first rock & roller— That's open to debate. But one thing's for certain: *Let the Good Times Roll* is a musical treasure chest that lovers of swing, rock, blues and R&B should make a point of obtaining. *— Alex Henderson*

Stanley Jordan

b. Jul. 31, 1959, Chicago, IL
Guitar / Contemporary Jazz, Jazz-Pop, Neo-Bop
Stanley Jordan's discovery in the early '80s rightfully earned a lot of headlines in the jazz world for he came up with a new way of playing guitar. Although he was not the first to use tapping, Jordan's extensive expertise gave him the ability to play two completely independent lines on the guitar (as if it were a keyboard) or, when he wanted, two guitars at a time. He had originally studied piano although he switched to guitar when he was 11. After graduating from Princeton in 1981, Jordan played for a time on the streets of New York. Soon he was discovered, had the opportunity to play with Benny Carter and Dizzy Gillespie and, after recording a solo album for his own Tangent label, signed with Blue Note. Since then his career has been surprisingly aimless. Stanley Jordan can play amazing jazz but he often wastes his talent on lesser material, so one has to be picky in deciding which of his recordings to acquire. *— Scott Yanow*

● **Stanley Jordan** / Sep. 1984-Oct. 1984 / Blue Note ✦✦✦✦✦
Other than a little-known independent release in 1982, this Blue Note set has guitarist Stanley Jordan's recording debut. Seven selections are unaccompanied solos, with percussionist Sammy Figueroa added on some of the numbers, and there are three cuts with a rhythm section. Jordan's remarkable tapping technique (which has surprisingly not been emulated much by later guitarists and bassists) allows him to play his instrument like a piano, making most other guitarists sound one-handed. Jordan's playing sounds quite miraculous on such numbers as "Eleanor Rigby," "Freddie Freeloader," his own "Fundance" and Jimi Hendrix's "Angel." *— Scott Yanow*

Magic Touch / Sep. 1984 / Blue Note ✦✦✦✦✦
This is the debut album by a musician who helped to redefine how a guitar is played. *— Paul Kohler*

Cornucopia / Aug. 21, 1986-Mar. 21, 1989 / Blue Note ✦✦✦✦✦
The first half of this CD by the remarkable guitarist Stanley Jordan is so strong that it is a pity that things decline during the latter half. Jordan is quite outstanding on "Impressions" and "Autumn Leaves," emulates B.B. King on "Still Got The Blues", interprets a thoughtful "Willow Weep For Me" and performs a dazzling tour-de-force on the uptempo blues "Fundance"; the latter two are unaccompanied solos that sound like duets or trios. However a couple of funk pieces (including an unimaginative rendition of "What's Going On") and a New Age synthesizer selection are on a lower level. The title cut clocks in at 21:45 and, although it finds Jordan creating "impossible" technical feats on solo guitar, it meanders on indefinitely and gets boring very quickly. This is a frustrating release; get it for the good half if you see it at a budget price. *— Scott Yanow*

Standards, Vol. 1 / Oct. 1986 / Blue Note ✦✦✦✦✦
Guitarist Stanley Jordan (the master of tapping, making his instrument sound like two or three at once) has a wide definition of standards, ranging beyond jazz. His second official Blue Note release therefore not only includes "Georgia On My Mind" and "My Favorite Things," but Paul Simon's "The Sounds of Silence," "Moon River," the Beatles' "Because," and "Silent Night." But no matter what the tune, the main reason to acquire this set of unaccompanied guitar solos is to hear how here remarkable and versatile Jordan's technique is. *— Scott Yanow*

Stolen Moments / Nov. 7, 1990-Nov. 9, 1990 / Somethin' Else ✦✦✦✦
This trio set with bassist Charnett Moffett and drummer Kenwood Dennard features the tapping guitarist Stanley Jordan during a typical live show from 1990 playing many songs that he had previously recorded. While "Stairway to Heaven" is treated as very credible rock and "Lady in My Life" gets funky, "Autumn Leaves" really cooks and Jordan fares well on "Stolen Moments" (during which he does a strong imitation of a keyboard) and "Impressions." Jordan's lone original, the rockish "Return Expedition" is at 15 minutes way too long and serves primarily as an opportunity for his two fine backup players to take lengthy solos. Jordan's unaccompeied display on the concluding "Over the Rainbow" compensates. An interesting program. *— Scott Yanow*

Live in New York / Mar. 21, 1989 / Blue Note ✦✦✦✦
This concert was originally intended to be a video release showcasing Stanley Jordan in acoustic, electric and solo settings. His tight rhythm section—including Jeff "Tain" Watts on drums, Kenny Kirkland on piano and Charnett Moffett on bass—drives his complex and moving guitar playing through the standout acoustic tracks "Impressions" and "Cousin Mary," both by John Coltrane. But concert highlights are Jordan's two solo pieces, the bluesy "Willow Weep for Me" and classic showtune "Over the Rainbow," where he performs with an exhilarating freedom and virtuosity. Jordan resists the temptation to slip into the then-ubiquitous "smooth jazz" sound, making this a timeless release. *— Ryan Randall Goble*

Wynton Kelly

b. Dec. 2, 1931, Jamaica, **d.** Apr. 12, 1971, Toronto, Ontario, Canada
Piano / Hard Bop
A superb accompanist loved by Miles Davis and Cannonball Adderley, Wynton Kelly was also a distinctive soloist who decades later would be a strong influence on Benny Green. He grew up in Brooklyn and early on played in R&B bands led by Eddie "Cleanhead" Vinson, Hal Singer and Eddie "Lockjaw" Davis. Kelly, who recorded 14 titles for Blue Note in a trio (1951), worked with Dinah Washington, Dizzy Gillespie and Lester Young during 1951-52. After serving in the military he made a strong impression with Washington (1955-57), Charles Mingus (1956-57) and the Dizzy Gillespie big band (1957) but he would be most famous for his stint with Miles Davis (1959-63), recording such albums with Miles as *Kind of Blue, At the Black-*

hawk and *Someday My Prince Will Come.* When he left Davis, Kelly took the rest of the rhythm section (bassist Paul Chambers and drummer Jimmy Cobb) with him to form his trio. The group actually sounded at its best backing Wes Montgomery. Before his early death, Kelly recorded as a leader for Blue Note, Riverside, Vee-Jay, Verve and Milestone. *—Scott Yanow*

Piano / Jan. 31, 1958 / Riverside/OJC ♦♦♦♦♦
With the exception of an album for Blue Note in 1951, this was pianist Wynton Kelly's first opportunity to record as a leader. At the time he was still a relative unknown but would soon get a certain amount of fame as Miles Davis's favorite accompanist. With guitarist Kenny Burrell, bassist Paul Chambers and (on three of the seven selections) drummer Philly Joe Jones, Kelly performs four jazz standards, Oscar Brown, Jr.'s "Strong Man" and two of his originals. Kelly became a major influence on pianists of the 1960s and '70s and one can hear the genesis of many other players in these swinging performances. The CD reissue adds an alternate take of "Dark Eyes" to the original program. *—Scott Yanow*

Kelly Blue / Feb. 19, 1959-Mar. 10, 1959 / Riverside/OJC ♦♦♦♦♦
Originally cut for Riverside, this set mostly features the influential pianist Wynton Kelly in a trio with his fellow rhythm section mates from the Miles Davis bands, bassist Paul Chambers and drummer Jimmy Cobb. "Kelly Blue" and "Keep It Moving" add cornetist Nat Adderley, flutist Bobby Jaspar and the tenor of Benny Golson to the band for some variety. The CD reissue augments the program with a previously unreleased "Do Nothin' Till You Hear From Me" and the alternate take of "Keep It Moving." Kelly was renowned as an accompanist, but as he shows on a set including three of his originals and four familiar standards (including "Softly As In a Morning Sunrise" and "Willow Weep for Me"), he was also a strong bop-based soloist too. A fine example of his talents. *—Scott Yanow*

Kelly Great / Aug. 12, 1959 / Vee-Jay ♦♦♦
Pianist Wynton Kelly teams up with trumpeter Lee Morgan, tenor saxophonist Wayne Shorter, bassist Paul Chambers and drummer Philly Joe Jones for a fine advanced hard bop date. There are four originals (all virtually forgotten decades later) by Kelly, Shorter and Morgan but it is the lone standard, a playful version of "June Night" (which has some puckish Morgan trumpet), that is the standout. At 35 minutes, this CD reissue of a former LP is pretty brief, but what is here on the formerly-rare session should satisfy collectors of the style. *—Scott Yanow*

★ **Someday My Prince Will Come** / Sep. 20, 1961-Sep. 21, 1961 / Vee-Jay ♦♦♦♦♦
Pianist Wynton Kelly is heard on this CD reissue (the ten songs from the original LP plus five "new" alternate takes) with either bassist Sam Jones and drummer Jimmy Cobb or bassist Paul Chambers and drummer Philly Joe Jones. His light touch and perfect taste are very much present along with a steady stream of purposeful single-note lines that are full of surprising twists. Trumpeter Lee Morgan and tenor-saxophonist Wayne Shorter drop by for one song (the blues "Wrinkles") but otherwise this recommended set (a definitive Wynton Kelly release) showcases magical trio performances. *—Scott Yanow*

Smokin' at the Half Note / Jun. 1965-Sep. 22, 1965 / Verve ♦♦♦♦♦
Some recorded Sept 22, 1965, at Englewood Cliffs, NJ. Wynton Kelly Trio w/ Wes Montgomery (g). Slow to mid-tempos—very listenable. Both Wynton and Wes are in fine form. A rare chance to hear Montgomery in a small-group setting. *—Michael Erlewine*

Stan Kenton

b. Dec. 15, 1911, Wichita, KS, **d.** Aug. 25, 1979, Los Angeles, CA
Piano, Composer, Arranger / Orchestral Jazz, Traditional Pop, Progressive Jazz, Progressive Big Band, Big Band
There have been few jazz musicians as consistently controversial as Stan Kenton. Dismissed by purists of various genres while loved by many others, Kenton ranks up there with Chet Baker and Sun Ra as jazz's top cult figure. He led a succession of highly original bands that often emphasized emotion, power and advanced harmonies over swing, and this upset listeners who felt that all big bands should aim to sound like Count Basie. Kenton always had a different vision. In 1941 he formed his first orchestra, which later was named after his theme song "Artistry in Rhythm." A decent Earl Hines-influenced pianist, Kenton was much more important in the early days as an arranger and inspiration for his loyal sidemen. By late 1943 with a Capitol contract, a popular record in "Eager Beaver" and growing recognition, the Stan Kenton Orchestra was gradually catching on. Its soloists during the war years included Art Pepper, briefly Stan Getz, altoist Boots Mussulli and singer Anita O'Day. By 1945 the band had evolved quite a bit as Pete Rugolo became the chief arranger and June Christy was Kenton's new singer; her popular hits made it possible for Kenton to finance his more ambitious projects. Calling his music "Progressive Jazz," Kenton sought to lead a concert orchestra as opposed to a dance band at a time when most big bands were starting to break up. In 1950 he put together his most advanced band, the 39-piece Innovations in Modern Music orchestra, but soon reverted to his usual 19-piece lineup. Then quite unexpectedly, Kenton went through a swinging period. His last successful experiment was his mellophonium band of 1960-63. *—Scott Yanow*

☆ **The Complete Capitol Studio Recordings of Stan Kenton 1943-1947** / Nov. 19, 1943-Dec. 22, 1947 / Mosaic ♦♦♦♦♦
Documenting Stan Kenton's always controversial but never sleepy music, the seven-CD *Complete Capitol Studio Recordings of Stan Kenton 1943-47* features the orchestra at a time when it was reaching its greatest popularity, evolving from using the artist's charts into the Pete Rugolo era. In addition to some unreleased tracks, there are also several rare sessions included that were recorded at the time strictly for radio airplay. Most of Kenton's biggest hits ("Artistry in Rhythm," "Eager Beaver," "And Her Tears Flowed Like Wine," "Tampico," "Southern Scandal," "Artistry Jumps," "Intermission Riff," "Across the Alley From the Alamo," and "The Peanut Vendor") are here, as are many concert works. A classic reissue. *—Scott Yanow*

☆ **Retrospective** / Nov. 19, 1943-Jul. 18, 1968 / Capitol ♦♦♦♦♦
This four-CD set has virtually all of Stan Kenton's most significant recordings from his prime years. Although Kenton completists will prefer to pick up dozens of his individual Creative World releases instead, all other jazz collectors are well-advised to get this very well-conceived release. Starting with the original version of "Artistry in Rhythm" from 1943 and continuing through all of the different editions of Kenton's orchestras up to 1968's "How Are Things in Glocca Morra," this set includes not only all of the band's most popular recordings but some of its most inventive and esoteric ones too. Whether it be "Tampico," "Concerto to End All Concertos," "Jolly Rogers," "Art Pepper," "Orange Colored Sky" (with guest Nat King Cole), "All About Ronnie," "Peanut Vendor," and "Maria" or a section of "City of Glass" and a number from the Kenton/Wagner album, the remarkable career of Stan Kenton is covered definitively on this package. It's highly recommended for all jazz collections. *—Scott Yanow*

City of Glass: Stan Kenton Plays Bob Graettinger / Dec. 6, 1947-May 28, 1953 / Capitol ♦♦♦♦♦
Bob Graettinger was arguably the most radical arranger to ever work in jazz. In fact, it is doubtful if any other big-band leader other than Stan Kenton (who always encouraged adventurous writers) would have used his very complex charts during this era. Graettinger's works, which were influenced by aspects of modern classical music (but were not at all derivative) are all included on this fascinating, if difficult, CD reissue. The four-part "City of Glass," the pieces that comprised "This-Modern World" and a variety of shorter works (including the remarkably dense "Thermopylae") make for some very stimulating listening. This is avant-garde music that still sounds futuristic 45 years later. *—Scott Yanow*

☆ **The Complete Capitol Recordings of Stan Kenton** / Feb. 3, 1950-Sep. 11, 1963 / Mosaic ♦♦♦♦♦
With Stan Kenton's sound having gone through so many changes, one must listen to this seven-CD set with a certain degree of suspense and awe, since almost none of it (or Kenton's other early work) is otherwise available on CD, making it even more unusual and essential. The vast majority of even the released material in this box was never on LP originally, though Kenton's own label released some of it on compilation LPs. Disc One, covering November 1943 to May 1945, shows off a bold, brash, very dexterous swing band. Entering new areas is the exquisite, impressionistic "Artistry in Rhythm," which packed a remarkable range of timbres and sounds (some very classically influenced) into its three minutes and change. Anita O'Day was added in 1944, and her sides are just about worth the price of this entire disc. Although her successor, June Christy, acquits herself well, the real highlights of Disc Two lie with the Capitol Transcription Services sides. Disc Three opens with more radio transcriptions, all of exceptional historical and musical value. This is the point where Pete Rugolo's arrangements begin to take over for Kenton's own. Disc Four moves into Kenton's increasingly progressive and experimental period. The set ends as Kenton was making his very first records with his new concert-oriented band, with the emphasis clearly on extending the boundaries of jazz—as much as any of Duke Ellington's extended concert numbers of the same era, this was the beginning of symphonic jazz, and it came without the sonic excesses that would mar future Kenton experiments in this direction. The material has been assembled in session/transcription order; the sound quality is generally excellent, and the notes, as always, are thoroughly detailed and very well researched. *—Bruce Eder*

★ **The Innovations Orchestra** / Feb. 3, 1950-Aug. 24, 1950 / Capitol ♦♦♦♦♦
During 1950-51, Stan Kenton did the unthinkable by putting together a 40-piece orchestra that included a full string section. The music was quite uncommercial, complex and advanced with the emphasis on the arrangements rather than the soloists (which include trumpeters Shorty Rogers and Maynard Ferguson, trombonist Milt Bernhart, altoist Art Pepper, tenor saxophonist Bob Cooper and guitarist Laurindo Almeida). This two-CD set has all of the music originally released on the albums *Innovations in Modern Music* and *Stan Kenton Presents* plus 14 other key selections by the forbidding but intriguing orchestra. Although there are two numbers by Bob Graettinge (the most radical of the Kenton arrangers), his main works have already been issued separately as *Stan Kenton Plays Bob Graettinger.* The primary arrangers on this twofer are Pete Rugolo (whose work is often quite serious although "Mardi Gras" is a definite contrast!), Bill Russo (including the memorable "Solitaire"), Johnny Richards and, for a few swinging numbers that are a major contrast, Shorty Rogers. Among the more famous selections on this definitive twofer are "Lonesome Road" (which has one of two June Christy vocals), "Soliloquy," and "Cuban Episode" . The last four selections on the reissue are taken from an Oct. 14, 1951 concert that was part of this very expensive ensemble's second and final tour. By 1952 Kenton was leading a more conventional big band, but the recordings of his Innovations Orchestra have since become legendary and stand apart from the other music of the 1950s. *—Scott Yanow*

● **New Concepts of Artistry in Rhythm** / Sep. 8, 1952-Sep. 16, 1952 / Capitol ♦♦♦♦♦
Stan Kenton's 1952 Orchestra was a very interesting transitional band, still performing some of the complex works of the prior Innovations orchestra but also starting to emphasize swing. This CD contains the rather pompous "Prologue" and Bill Holman's complex "Invention for Guitar and Trumpet" (starring guitarist Sal Salvador and trumpeter Maynard Ferguson) but also Gerry Mulligan's boppish "Young Blood" and Bill Russo's features for trumpeter Conte Candoli ("Portrait of a Count"), trombonist Frank Rosolino ("Frank Speaking") and altoist Lee Konitz ("My Lady"). *—Scott Yanow*

Kenton in Hi-Fi / Feb. 11, 1956-Feb. 12, 1956 / Capitol ♦♦♦♦
After years of big band experimentation, Stan Kenton seemed to settle into a more grounded groove on 1956's *In Hi-Fi.* To his credit, Kenton did keep things swinging before, even in the midst of high brow bombast like the string-laden, 39 piece Innovations in Modern Music orchestra and numerous jazz meets Stravinsky projects. This uncanny balance of flow and brains came out of Kenton's own tempered direction and fine contributions by the likes of arranger Pete Rugolo, trumpeter Shorty Rogers, alto saxophonist Art Pepper, and singers Anita O'Day and June Christy. Thanks to a seamless mix of dazzling charts and liberal doses of Lunceford and Ellington-inspired swing, the marriage certainly works on *Kenton in Hi-Fi.* Old hits like "Eager Beaver" and "Artistry In Boogie" sparkle in the warm glow of '50s stereo technology, while fiery renditions of "Lover" and "The Peanut Vendor" show the famous muscle of the Kenton band. With the stellar playing of tenor saxophonist Vido Musso, trumpeter Pete Candoli, and drummer Mel Lewis to look forward to, one can see why this

album was not only one of Kenton's most popular releases, but a critical success as well. —*Stephen Cook*

Cuban Fire, Vol. 1 / May 22, 1956-May 24, 1956 / Capitol ♦♦♦♦♦

West Side Story / Mar. 15, 1961-Apr. 11, 1961 / Blue Note ♦♦♦♦♦
When the producers of the film *West Side Story* heard a sampling of what the Stan Kenton Orchestra had done to their score, they were disappointed that they had not thought to ask the band to play on the soundtrack. Johnny Richards's arrangements of ten of the famous play's melodies are alternately dramatic and tender with plenty of the passion displayed by the characters in the story. Soloists include altoist Gabe Baltazar, veteran tenor Sam Donahue and trumpeter Conte Candoli, but it is the raging ensembles that are most memorable about the classic recording. This CD reissue is highly recommended. —*Scott Yanow*

Adventures in Blues / Dec. 7, 1961-Dec. 13, 1961 / Creative World ♦♦♦♦
Arranger Gene Roland composed nine blues-based originals for this LP, featuring himself on soprano and mellophonium along with altoist Gabe Baltazar and trumpeter Marvin Stamm. This is one of the finer recordings by the Mellophonium Band, arguably Stan Kenton's last great orchestra. With the use of 20 horns, Roland was able to get a surprising amount of variety out of the material, making this a Kenton recording well worth investigating. —*Scott Yanow*

Adventures in Jazz / Dec. 11, 1961-Dec. 14, 1961 / Blue Note ♦♦♦♦♦
This excellent outing by the 1961 edition of Stan Kenton's orchestra has one classic (Bill Holman's arrangement of "Malaguena"), a superior solo by altoist Gabe Baltazar on "Stairway to the Stars," a feature for Ray Starling's Mellophonium ("Misty"), a good workout by veteran tenor Sam Donahue on "Body and Soul," Holman's reworking of "Limehouse Blues," and two colorful Dee Barton composition/arrangements. This well-rounded LP (which also has some solos by trumpeter Marvin Stamm) is one of Kenton's best of the era. [A 1999 reissue by Blue Note added three bonus tracks and remixed sound.] —*Scott Yanow*

Mellophonium Moods / Mar. 1962 / Status ♦♦♦♦♦

☆ **50th Anniversary Celebration: The Best of Back to Balboa** / May 30, 1991-Jun. 2, 1991 / Mama ♦♦♦♦♦
During the 50th anniversary of Stan Kenton's debut at the Rendezvous Ballroom on Balboa Island in California (an engagement that served as a spectacular beginning to his career), a four-day convention was held to celebrate the late bandleader's legacy, filled with music by his alumni and very interesting panel discussions. The MAMA Foundation put out many of the highlights on this very impressive five-CD set. The first two CDs have 29 selections by an all-star orchestra (which includes among others, trumpeters Conte and Pete Candoli and saxophonists Bob Cooper, Gabe Baltazar, Bud Shank, Bill Perkins and Jack Nimitz) and such guests as Anita O'Day, Maynard Ferguson and Chris Connor; the original arrangers conducted their own work. The next two discs have individual selections for Bob Florence's Limited Edition (a particularly touching medley of "Artistry in Rhythm" and "All the Things You Are"), Maynard Ferguson's Big Bop Nouveau Band, the Lighthouse All-Stars, big bands led by Shorty Rogers, Buddy Childers, Bill Holman, Tom Talbert and Mark Masters and combos headed by Lee Konitz, Bob Cooper, Gabe Baltazar, Bill Perkins and Bud Shank along with The CSULB Vocal Jazz Ensemble. The performances are quite satisfying and pretty well cover Kenton's entire career. The final disc actually has over two hours taken from the informative, humorous and often-touching panel discussions; one hour is heard in each speaker simultaneously so one side has to be turned off at a time. This valuable set is essential for all listeners having at least a slight interest in Stan Kenton's music. —*Scott Yanow*

Barney Kessel

b. Oct. 17, 1923, Muskogee, OK
Guitar (Electric), Guitar / West Coast Jazz, Cool, Bop
One of the finest guitarists to emerge after the death of Charlie Christian, Barney Kessel was a reliable bop soloist throughout his career. He played with a big band fronted by Chico Marx (1943), was fortunate enough to appear in the classic jazz short *Jammin' the Blues* (1944) and then worked with the big bands of Charlie Barnet (1944-45) and Artie Shaw (1945); he also recorded with Shaw's Gramercy Five. Kessel became a busy studio musician in Los Angeles but was always in demand for jazz records. He toured with the Oscar Peterson Trio for one year (1952-53) and then, starting in 1953, led an impressive series of records for Contemporary that lasted until 1961 (including several with Ray Brown and Shelly Manne in a trio accurately called "The Poll Winners"). After touring Europe with George Wein's Newport All-Stars (1968) Kessel lived in London for a time (1969-70). In 1973 he began touring and recording with the Great Guitars, a group also including Herb Ellis and Charlie Byrd. A serious stroke in 1992 put Barney Kessel permanently out of action but many of his records (which include dates for Onyx, Black Lion, Sonet and Concord in addition to many of the Contemporaries) are currently available along with several video collections put out by Vestapol. —*Scott Yanow*

Easy Like, Vol. 1 / Nov. 14, 1953-Dec. 19, 1953 / Contemporary ♦♦♦♦♦
Other than four songs apiece released by Onyx and Verve, this CD reissue has guitarist Barney Kessel's first sessions as a leader, performances which launched his longtime association with the Contemporary label. Augmented by two "new" alternate takes, the set features Kessel in boppish form with quintets in 1953 and 1956 featuring either Bud Shank or Buddy Collette doubling on flute and alto. Kessel shows off the influence of Charlie Christian throughout the performances, with the highlights including "Easy Like," "Lullaby of Birdland," "North of the Border" and the accurately titled "Salute to Charlie Christian." —*Scott Yanow*

Kessel Plays Standards / Jun. 4, 1954-Sep. 12, 1955 / Contemporary/OJC ♦♦♦♦♦
Guitarist Barney Kessel teams up with Bob Cooper (mostly on oboe but also doubling a bit on tenor), either Claude Williamson or Hampton Hawes on piano, Monty Budwig or Red Mitchell on bass, and Shelly Manne or Chuck Thompson on drums. Other than his own "64 Bars on Wilshire" and "Barney's Blues," the repertoire on this CD reissue is comprised of jazz standards. Inventive frameworks and the utilization of Cooper's jazz oboe (a real rarity in jazz of the time) give the otherwise boppish reissue its own personality. —*Scott Yanow*

★ **Barney Kessel, Vol. 3: To Swing or Not to Swing** / Jul. 26, 1955 / Contemporary/OJC ♦♦♦♦♦
Guitarist Barney Kessel's string of recordings for Contemporary in the 1950s included some of the finest work of his career. The unusual repertoire on this set—which includes "Louisiana," "Indiana" and "12th Street Rag," along with four Kessel originals and more usual standards—would by itself make this bop/cool set noteworthy. Add to that a very interesting lineup of players (trumpeter Harry "Sweets" Edison, Georgie Auld or Bill Perkins on tenor, pianist Jimmy Rowles, the rhythm guitar of Al Hendrickson, bassist Red Mitchell, and Shelly Manne or Irv Cottler on drums) and some excellent showcases for Kessel, and the overall results are a CD highly recommended to fans of straight-ahead jazz. —*Scott Yanow*

Music to Listen to Barney Kessel By / Aug. 6, 1956-Dec. 4, 1956 / Contemporary/OJC ♦♦♦♦
Featured is Kessel's guitar with five woodwinds and a rhythm section. 12 songs were recorded with Buddy Collette (fl), Andre Previn (p), Shelly Manne (d), Jimmy Rowles (p), Red Mitchell (b), Buddy Clark (b), and others. —*AMG*

The Poll Winners with Ray Brown and Shelly Manne / Mar. 18, 1957-Mar. 19, 1957 / Contemporary ♦♦♦♦
Because guitarist Barney Kessel, bassist Ray Brown and drummer Shelly Manne all won the *Downbeat, Metronome* and *Playboy* jazz polls of 1956, it was decided to team the trio together for this and a few other future recordings. Kessel is generally the lead voice of the pianoless group although Brown and Manne also have plenty of solo space. Together they perform swinging yet quiet versions of a variety of standards (in addition to the guitarist's "Minor Mood") in a relaxed and thoughtful set, reissued on this CD. —*Scott Yanow*

Let's Cook / Aug. 6, 1957-Nov. 11, 1957 / Contemporary/OJC ♦♦♦♦
It is a pity that this excellent session from guitarist Barney Kessel has not yet been reissued on CD. Actually, there are two different sets on this LP. Kessel is matched with vibraphonist Victor Feldman, pianist Hampton Hawes, bassist Leroy Vinnegar, and drummer Shelly Manne for a blues-with-a-bridge (the 11-minute "Let's Cook"), Vernon Duke's ballad "Time Remembered," and "Just in Time." The second half of the album has modernized versions of "Tiger Rag" and "Jersey Bounce" as played by the guitarist, tenor saxophonist Ben Webster, trombonist Frank Rosolino, pianist Jimmie Rowles, Vinnegar, and Manne. Throughout, Kessel keeps with the other all-stars, swinging hard while paying tribute to the legacy of Charlie Christian. —*Scott Yanow*

The Poll Winners Ride Again / Aug. 19, 1958-Aug. 21, 1958 / Contemporary/OJC ♦♦♦♦
Guitarist Barney Kessel, bassist Ray Brown and drummer Shelly Manne were dubbed "the Poll Winners" when they swept the *Downbeat, Metronome* and *Playboy* polls during 1956-57. They recorded several albums together and this CD reissue features the pianoless trio playing a variety of material, some of it a little odd (including "Volare," "Custard Puff," "When the Red, Red Robin Comes Bob, Bob Bobbin' Along" and "The Merry Go Round Broke Down"). This is a good outing, particularly for bop guitarist Barney Kessel. —*Scott Yanow*

Some Like It Hot / Mar. 30, 1959-Apr. 3, 1959 / Contemporary/OJC ♦♦♦♦♦
This CD reissue brings back the original Barney Kessel LP of the same name and adds two alternate takes. The release of the movie *Some Like It Hot* served as a good excuse for guitarist Kessel to join together with Art Pepper (switching between alto, clarinet and tenor), trumpeter Joe Gordon, pianist Jimmie Rowles, rhythm guitarist Jack Marshall, bassist Monty Budwig and drummer Shelly Manne to interpret a variety of vintage numbers, most of which date from the 1920s. Such tunes as "I Wanna Be Loved By You," "Runnin' Wild," "Down Among the Sheltering Palms" and "By the Beautiful Sea" are given fairly modern arrangements but still retain the flavor of the 1920s, and it is particularly interesting to hear Gordon and Pepper soloing on these ancient songs. —*Scott Yanow*

Poll Winners Three! / Nov. 2, 1959 / Contemporary/OJC ♦♦♦♦
From 1956-59, it seemed as if guitarist Barney Kessel, bassist Ray Brown and drummer Shelly Manne won just about every jazz poll. For their third joint recording, which has been reissued on CD, the musicians contributed an original apiece and also performed seven standards. Highlights of the fairly typical but swinging straightahead set include "Soft Winds," "It's All Right With Me," "Mack the Knife" and "I'm Afraid the Masquerade Is Over." —*Scott Yanow*

Feeling Free / Feb. 13, 1969 / Contemporary/OJC ♦♦♦♦♦
From 1953-61, guitarist Barney Kessel recorded some of the finest albums of his career for the Contemporary label. In 1969, he came back to the company for this single effort, and in the mid-1980s he would return to Contemporary for his final sessions. The 1969 project, which has not yet been reissued on CD, lives up to its title, being one of Kessel's most adventurous dates. He utilized vibraphonist Bobby Hutcherson, bassist Chuck Domanico and drummer Elvin Jones for four fairly free originals, Paul Simon's "The Sounds of Silence," and the pop tune "This Guy's In Love With You." Throughout, Kessel shows that he was familiar with aspects of the avant-garde and that he had a willingness to really stretch himself. An intriguing set. —*Scott Yanow*

Limehouse Blues / Jun. 23, 1969-Jun. 24, 1969 / Black Lion ♦♦♦♦♦
Guitarist Barney Kessel and violinist Stephane Grappelli always made for a mutually complementary team. Kessel's background was in Charlie Christian rather than Django Reinhardt (although Django can be felt now and then in his style), but there was always a lot of common ground between him and Grappelli. This LP (whose music has been mostly reissued on CD) also has rhythm guitarist Nini Rosso, bassist Michel Gaudry, and drummer Jean-Louis Viale in the quintet. Other than the guitarist's bossa nova "Little Star," the group sticks to swing-era standards, with the highlights including "It Don't Mean a Thing," "Tea for Two," and "How High the Moon." Predictably swinging music. —*Scott Yanow*

☆ **Straight Ahead** / Jul. 12, 1975 / Contemporary ♦♦♦♦♦

King Oliver (Joe Oliver)

b. May 11, 1885, New Orleans, LA, **d.** Apr. 8, 1938, Savannah, GA
Cornet / New Orleans Jazz, Classic Jazz
Joe "King" Oliver was one of the great New Orleans legends, an early giant whose legacy is only partly on records. In 1923 he led one of the classic New Orleans jazz bands, the last significant group to emphasize collective improvisation over solos, but ironically his second cornetist (Louis Armstrong) would soon permanently change jazz. And while Armstrong never tired of praising his idol, he actually sounded very little like Oliver; the King's influence was more deeply felt by Muggsy Spanier and Tommy Ladnier. In 1919 Oliver left New Orleans for Chicago and one year later, began working as a leader. He soon sent for his protégé Louis Armstrong and with clarinetist Johnny Dodds, trombonist Honore Dutrey, pianist Lil Harden and drummer Baby Dodds as a core, Oliver had a remarkable band whose brilliance was only hinted at on records. After the band broke up in 1924, he took over Dave Peyton's group in 1925 and renamed it the Dixie Syncopators; new recordings resulted, including "Snag It" which has a famous eight-bar passage by Oliver. Dental problems made playing cornet increasingly painful and, on many of his later recordings, he is barely present. Although his last recordings (from 1931) are superior examples of hot dance music, he was quickly becoming a forgotten name. Unsuccessful tours in the South eventually left Oliver stranded there, working as a janitor in a poolroom before his death at age 52. *—Scott Yanow*

★ **King Oliver's Creole Jazzband 1923-1924** / Apr. 5, 1923-Dec. 6, 1924 / Retrieval ♦♦♦♦♦
The music on this 1997 two-CD import set has been reissued many times, but this is the most complete version yet. Cornetist King Oliver's Creole Jazz Band in 1923 was not only the finest jazz group on record, but the most exciting unit up to that point in time. Although it featured some short solos from the octet (particularly Oliver, 22-year old cornetist Louis Armstrong, trombonist Honore Dutrey, and the great clarinetist Johnny Dodds), the emphasis was on the ensembles. All 37 of the band's recordings are on this two-fer (including such classics as the two versions of "Dippermouth Blues," "Froggie Moore," the two renditions of "Snake Rag," "High Society," "Sobbin' Blues," "Chattanooga Stomp," "Buddy's Habits," and three versions of "Mabel's Dream"). In addition, Oliver is heard in 1924 backing the vaudeville team of Butterbeans & Susie and taking two duets with Jelly Roll Morton (including "King Porter Stomp"). This classic New Orleans music is essential for any comprehensive jazz collection. *—Scott Yanow*

☆ **King Oliver: Louis Armstrong** / 1923-1924 / Milestone ♦♦♦♦♦
Classic renditions (1923-24) of "Snake Rag," "Dippermouth Blues," and "Canal Street Blues" come from the hottest band of its day—Oliver's Creole Jazz Band. *—Bruce Boyd Raeburn*

1926-1928 / Mar. 1926-Jun. 1928 / Classics ♦♦♦♦♦

1928-1930 / Sep. 12, 1928-Jan. 28, 1930 / Classics ♦♦♦♦♦

☆ **King Oliver** / Jan. 16, 1929-Sep. 19, 1930 / RCA ♦♦♦♦♦
This double-CD set (part of the French RCA *Jazz Tribune* series) includes all of King Oliver's Victor recordings of 1929-30, except for a few alternate takes. The 32 selections are better than one might expect, considering that Oliver's playing abilities were rapidly fading (due to serious gum problems). The cornetist in fact takes a few memorable solos, particularly on "Too Late" and "Struggle Buggy." But it is the high musicianship of his sidemen that make this set so enjoyable, including trumpeters Dave Nelson, Red Allen, and Bubber Miley (who is outstanding on "St. James Infirmary"); trombonists J.C. Higginbottham and Jimmy Archey; clarinetist Omer Simeon; altoist Charlie Holmes; and, filling in for Oliver, cornetists Louis Metcalf and Punch Miller. *—Scott Yanow*

King Oliver and His Orchestra / Jan. 16, 1929-Sep. 19, 1930 / French RCA ♦♦♦♦♦
Much more complete than any domestic reissue, this double-CD from French RCA in their Jazz Tribune series (a straight duplication of the earlier two-LP set) features the influential cornetist King Oliver in many of his final recordings. Oliver was finding it increasingly painful to play during this era (in fact Louis Metcalf and Punch Miller substitute for him on the first seven selections), but ironically he had one of his finest bands at the time. He does take a particularly heroic solo on "Too Late" (one of the highpoints of his career) and on a few other tracks, but the main reason for the performances' success is the high-quality musicianship of Oliver's hot dance band. Such soloists as trumpeters Bubber Miley (featured on "St. James Infirmary") and Red Allen, trombonist Jimmy Archey, altoist Hilton Jefferson, and a variety of lesser-known but talented players make each of the 32 recordings well worth hearing. Recommended to fans of pre-swing big bands and classic jazz. *—Scott Yanow*

1930-1931 / Apr. 1930-Apr. 1931 / Classics ♦♦♦♦♦

Rahsaan Roland Kirk (Ronald T. Kirk)

b. Aug. 7, 1936, Columbus, OH, **d.** Dec. 5, 1977, Bloomington, IN
Manzello, Stritch, Multi Instruments, Sax (Tenor), Flute, Clarinet / Avant-Garde Jazz, Post-Bop
Arguably the most exciting saxophone soloist in jazz history, Kirk was a post-modernist before that term even existed. Kirk played the continuum of jazz tradition as an instrument unto itself; he felt little compunction about mixing and matching elements from the music's history, and his concoctions usually seemed natural, if not inevitable. When discussing Kirk, a great deal of attention is always paid to his eccentricities—playing several horns at once, making his own instruments, clowning on stage. However, Kirk was an immensely creative artist; perhaps no improvising saxophonist has ever possessed a more comprehensive technique—one that covered every aspect of jazz, from Dixie to free—and perhaps no other jazz musician has ever been more spontaneously inventive. His skills in constructing a solo are of particular note. Kirk had the ability to pace, shape, and elevate his improvisations to an extraordinary degree. During any given Kirk solo, just at the point in the course of his performance when it appeared he could not raise the intensity level any higher, he always seemed able to turn it up yet another notch. *—Chris Kelsey*

Introducing Roland Kirk / Jun. 7, 1960 / Chess ♦♦♦
Roland Kirk's second recording was his first to get noticed. Playing three horns at once got him some attention but those who listened closely realized that Kirk was a truly masterful player. Teamed with Ira Sullivan (who himself switched between trumpet and tenor) and a Chicago-based rhythm section, Kirk is in good form on these bop-oriented selections although his great sessions were in the near future. *—Scott Yanow*

☆ **Kirk's Work** / Jul. 11, 1961 / Prestige/OJC ♦♦♦♦♦
Roland Kirk is in excellent form on this CD reissue of a typically varied (and occasionally amazing) set with organist Jack McDuff, bassist Joe Benjamin and drummer Art Taylor. Kirk mostly sticks to playing tenor and manzello (with highlights including "Three for Dizzy" and "Makin' Whoopee") but takes "Funk Underneath" as a flute feature and tears into the ancient "Skater's Waltz" on both stritch and manzello. McDuff plays well but Roland Kirk dominates the set, displaying an encyclopediac knowledge of music and swinging up a storm. *—Scott Yanow*

☆ **Complete Recordings of Roland Kirk** / Aug. 16, 1961-Nov. 17, 1965 / Mercury ♦♦♦♦♦
This ten-CD set not only contains all of the music from Roland Kirk's nine albums for Mercury and Limelight and his guest appearances with Quincy Jones, Tubby Hayes and on one song with organist Eddie Baccus, but quite a few previously unreleased selections (especially from the *Kirk in Copehagen* sessions). Roland Kirk was a unique performer, not only able to play a variety of reed instruments at the same time (including the tenor, flute, clarinet, manzello and stritch) and 20-minute one-breath solos (via circular breathing) but a master of virtually every jazz style from bop and New Orleans to free. Some of his greatest recordings are on this remarkable set, including the entire albums originally titled *We Free Kings, Domino, Reeds and Deeds, Gifts and Messages, I Talk with the Spirits* and *Rip, Rig & Panic.* Such pianists as Richard Wyands, Wynton Kelly, Andrew Hill (including a previously unreleased three-song set from the 1962 Newport Jazz Festival), Harold Mabern, Tete Montoliu, Horace Parlan and Jaki Byard are heard from and the Tubby Hayes date matches together the three reeds of Kirk, Hayes and James Moody in memorable fashion. Although more general collectors may want to start off with a smaller Roland Kirk set, those in-the-know will go out of their way to grab this one before it disappears. *—Scott Yanow*

Talkin' Verve: Roots of Acid Jazz / Aug. 16, 1961-May 2, 1967 / Verve ♦♦♦
This hodgepodge collection has 15 selections mostly taken from Rahsaan Roland Kirk's Mercury recordings of the early 1960s (other than one selection apiece that originally appeared on Limelight or Verve). Although certainly not for completists, this sampling does give listeners a good inkling of Kirk's eclectic talents. Whether jamming in a quartet, playing commercial music with Quincy Jones or jiving around in his colorful and insightful way, Roland Kirk was always a vital force. Highlights include "Hip Chops," "You Did It, You Did It," "A Sack Full Of Soul," "Jive Elephant," "Blue Rol" and even "Theme From Peter Gunn." *—Scott Yanow*

We Free Kings / Aug. 16, 1961-Aug. 17, 1961 / Mercury ♦♦♦♦♦
This CD is one of Roland Kirk's finer recordings from his Mercury period. Accompanied by a rhythm section led by pianist Richard Wyands, Kirk on tenor, manzello and stritch (sometimes all three at once) and flute plays some typically miraculous music. Highlights include "Three for the Festival," "Moon Song," "Blues for Alice" and "We Free Kings" but all of the selections contain plenty of Kirk's magic. Twenty years after his death there is still no one around to replace Roland Kirk. This release is recommended to those listeners who do not already have his ten-CD complete Mercury set. *—Scott Yanow*

● **Does Your House Have Lions: The Rahsaan Roland Kirk Anthology** / Nov. 6, 1961-Mar. 1976 / Rhino ♦♦♦♦♦
The Atlantic/Rhino anthology line has delighted novices and angered purists who have balked at what they deem questionable inclusions and exclusions, plus non-chronological sequencing and liners with plenty of personal anecdotes but limited musical analysis. The 31 selections on this two-disc set range from 1961 to 1976 and cover Kirk originals, covers, straight jazz, pop/soul, gospel-backed and hard bop workouts, and feature both live and studio segments. While it is a bit jarring to hop from the early '60s to the '70s and back, series compiler Joel Dorn opted for stylistic organization rather than session exactness. Any hardcore Kirk fan will want the individual albums the label is reissuing. Otherwise, the anthology serves its purpose, which is to spotlight a brilliant player and make you want to hear more. *—Ron Wynn*

Domino / Apr. 17, 1962-Sep. 6, 1962 / Verve ♦♦♦♦♦
Early '60s Kirk vehicle in which his inspired blend of show business, hard bop and multi-horn/multiphonic solos hadn't yet jelled. It's conventional, straight-ahead material, well played but not as imaginative nor as transcendent as Kirk's music would become in the '70s. *—Ron Wynn*

Dog Years in the Fourth Ring / 1963-1975 / 32 Jazz ♦♦♦♦♦
Producer Joel Dorn has long championed the memory of the remarkable Rahsaan Roland Kirk. This three-CD set contains the long-out-of-print Atlantic album *Natural Black Inventions: Root Strata* and two CDs of previously unreleased concert performances. The former features Kirk playing unaccompanied solos (with the exception of a couple of guest percussionists on a few tracks) without any overdubbing. To give one an idea as to how remarkable the results are, Rahsaan is heard utilizing tenor, stritch, manzello, several clarinets, flutes, black mystery pipes, harmonium, piccolo, a music box, tympani, gong, bells, bird sounds and percussion. The music ranges from Dixieland to free and hints strongly at his tremendous talents. The "new" material on the other two CDs is taken from private tapes recorded in 1963 (with Tete Montoliu), 1964 (with the George Gruntz Trio), at a 1970 concert, in Paris and Boston in 1972, Berlin in 1973, and on two occasions in 1975. For those foolish enough to think of Rahsaan Roland Kirk as a gimmicky player, they should hear him do a very close impression of Lester Young on "Lester Leaps In," pay tribute to Sidney Bechet on "Petite Fleur," rip into "Giant Steps," and play pure bop on "Blues for Alice." One of the finest jazz releases of 1997. *—Scott Yanow*

I Talk to the Spirits / Sep. 16, 1964-Sep. 17, 1964 / Verve ♦♦♦♦♦
Multi-instrumentalist Roland Kirk leaves the stritch, manzello and other exotic instru-

ments at home for this all-flute outing from his pre-"Rahsaan" days. Consisting mostly of originals, with a couple of showtunes and a swinging take on John Lewis' "Django" thrown in, this recording provides the best sampling of Kirk's unique flute style. He hums along with himself as he plays, inserts pieces of lyrics when the mood hits, finds overtones and multi-part harmonies as he blows madly through the upper register and sails sweetly through the lower. Included here is the original version of "Serenade to a Cuckoo," a song later taken to rock audiences with its inclusion on the first Jethro Tull album. (In fact, for the Tull fan who wants to hear where Ian Anderson borrowed his style, *I Talk With the Spirits* is the place to go.) The playing on this outing is uniformly excellent, with Kirk ranging from his trademark uptempo overblowing on "A Quote From Clifford Brown" to bluesy growling on "The Business Ain't Nothing But the Blues" to placid beauty on the ballad "Trees." He guides Kurt Weill's "My Ship" on a five-minute voyage through calm seas and turbulent double-timed storms. Kirk's sense of whimsy and musical fun is evident throughout. *—Jim Newsom*

Rip, Rig and Panic/Now Please Don't You Cry, Beautiful Edith / Jan. 13, 1965-Apr. 1, 1967 / EmArcy ♦♦♦♦♦
Two of Roland Kirk's albums are combined together on this CD. *Rip, Rig & Panic* is one of the remarkable multi-instrumentalist's greatest recordings for it matches him with pianist Jaki Byard (along with bassist Richard Davis and drummer Elvin Jones) who also has the ability to play in virtually every jazz style. With such titles as "No Tonic Pres," "Once in a While", "From Bechet, Byas and Fats" and the electronic "Slippery, Hippery, Flippery," obviously this is an eclectic (and unique) set. While that session has also been included in the ten-CD complete Mercury box, *Now Please Don't You Cry, Beautiful Edith* is a lesser-known recording (originally on Verve) that has Kirk backed up by pianist Lonnie Smith, bassist Ronald Boykins and drummer Grady Tate. Highlights inclue "Stompin' Ground," "It's a Grand Night for Swinging," "Alfie" and the title cut. *—Scott Yanow*

Here Comes the Whistleman / Mar. 14, 1965 / Label M. ♦♦♦♦

★ **The Inflated Tear** / Nov. 27, 1967-Nov. 30, 1967 / Atlantic ♦♦♦♦♦
This is a fine all-around set by the remarkable Rahsaan Roland Kirk which has yet to be fully reissued on CD. The LP, from the Atlantic *Jazzlore* reissue series of the early '80s, features Kirk on tenor, manzello, stritch, clarinet, flute, English horn, flexafone and whistle performing a wide variety of colorful originals along with Duke Ellington's "Creole Love Call." Highlights include the memorable "The Black and Crazy Blues," "The Inflated Tear" and "A Handful of Fives." It's one of Kirk's better Atlantic sets. *—Scott Yanow*

Aces Back to Back / Jun. 18, 1968-1976 / 32 Jazz ♦♦♦♦♦
Rahsaan Roland Kirk was a true marvel who could play creatively in any style. This particular four-CD set (reissued in 1998) has four of Kirk's more underrated albums from his Atlantic period: *Left & Right,* which features his episodic "Expansions" and several featured numbers with strings; the eccentric but often memorable *Rahsaan Rahsaan,* which finds him at one point playing "Sentimental Journey" and "Going Home" simultaneously before cooking on "Lover"; *Prepare Thyself to Deal With a Miracle,* highlighted by a 21-minute, one-breath "Saxophone Concerto"; and *Other Folks Music.* Throughout the four colorful and diverse albums (which date from 1968-76), Kirk can be heard on tenor, flute, manzello, stritch, clarinet, reed trumpet, harmonica, nose flute, black mystery pipes, keyboards, and percussion, as well as giving a humorous but often insightful monologue. His backup groups (which include trumpeter Richard Williams, baritonist Pepper Adams, Howard Johnson on tuba, violinist Leroy Jenkins and pianist Hilton Ruiz, among many others) are impressive, but Rahsaan Roland Kirk was on a different level altogether; there has never been another one like him. Although some selections are stronger than others, there are enough miraculous moments to make this a highly recommended set, particularly to listeners not familiar with this truly remarkable musician. *—Scott Yanow*

Volunteered Slavery / Jul. 7, 1969-Jul. 23, 1969 / Rhino ♦♦♦♦
This recording has plenty of variety. Rahsaan Kirk (on tenor, flutes, manzello, stritch and even gong) performs three melodic originals (including the title cut) along with two pop tunes during which he is assisted by "the Roland Kirk Spirit Choir" on background vocals. However it is his performance at the 1969 Newport Jazz Festival (near-riotous versions of "One Ton" and "Three for the Festival" plus a remarkable John Coltrane three-song medley) that is most memorable. *—Scott Yanow*

Blacknuss / Aug. 31, 1971-Sep. 8, 1971 / Rhino ♦♦♦

I, Eye, Aye: Live at The Montreux Jazz Festival, 1972 / Jun. 24, 1972 / Rhino ♦♦♦♦
The amazing Rahsaan Roland Kirk was such a visual artist that sometimes his recordings only hinted at the events that were occuring during his performances. Kirk's appearance at the 1972 Montreux Jazz Festival (which is released on this 1996 CD for the first time) gave him the opportunity to show off some (but certainly not all) of his talents. On the opener "Seasons," Rahsaan plays two flutes together, getting a wide variety of highly expressive sounds while swinging. "Balm In Gilead" (a passionate tribute to Paul Robeson) features Kirk's often-overlooked clarinet, "Volunteered Slavery" (with its "Hey Jude" vamp) gets rather carried away and "Blue Rol No. 2" has Kirk making music on a nose flute. After showing off his circular breathing on "Satin Doll" and "Improvisation," Rahsaan's medley of "Serenade To A Cuckoo" and "Pedal Up" finds him coming up with close impressions of John Coltrane on soprano and Pharoah Sanders' screeching. Rahsaan Roland Kirk was both consistently entertaining and innovative while making music that still sounds fresh and unique. This previously unreleased set should delight Kirk's fans. *—Scott Yanow*

☆ **Bright Moments** / Jun. 8, 1973-Jun. 9, 1973 / Rhino ♦♦♦♦♦
This Rhino two-CD set (a straight reissue of an Atlantic two-LP release) is the closest one can come nowadays to hearing what it would be like to see Rahsaan Roland Kirk perform in a club. Kirk, who is joined by a fine four-piece rhythm section for this appearance at San Francisco's legendary Keystone Korner, has colorful (and sometimes very humorous) monologues between the songs and shows off his remarkable virtuosity. Whether it be his emotional renditions of "Prelude to a Kiss" and "If I Loved You," this demonstration of nose flutes on "Fly Town Nose Blues," some authentic New Orleans clarinet playing on "Dem Red Beans and Rice" or a memorable version of his theme "Bright Moments," the music is exciting and unpredictable. This is the definitive Rahsaan Roland Kirk recording of the 1970s and is essential for any serious jazz collection. *—Scott Yanow*

Simmer, Reduce, Garnish & Serve / 1976-1977 / Warner Archives ♦♦♦♦
This single CD has selections from Rahsaan Roland Kirk's final three albums. His work on his last record *Boogie-Woogie String Along for Real* was quite heroic and miraculous because he had suffered a major stroke that greatly limited his abilities; in fact Kirk had the use of only one of his hands so his playing was sadly restricted. There is a remarkable amount of variety plus a liberal dose of Kirk's humor on this retrospective, ranging from a "Bagpipe Medley" and "Sweet Georgia Brown" (complete with a whistler and Freddie Moore's washboard) to a warm "I'll Be Seeing You" and a tribute to Johnny Griffin, the main influence on Rahsaan's tenor sound. For those listeners who do not already have the three LPs, this is a strong best-of sampler of the saxophonist's final period although his earlier recordings are recommended first. This CD concludes with an emotional and rather touching collage that pays tribute to Kirk's genius and mourns his premature death. *—Scott Yanow*

Standing Eight / Sep. 15, 1998 / 32 Jazz ♦♦♦♦
In 1998, 32 Jazz reissued three albums from Rahsaan Roland Kirk's late period on the double CD *A Standing Eight.* Those albums were *The Return of the 5000lb. Man* and *Kirkatron*—both of which consisted of recordings made not long before the innovator suffered a debilitating stroke in 1975—and the post-stroke session *Boogie-Woogie String Along for Real.* Hearing the pre-stroke and post-stroke material on the same collection, one cannot help but notice the contrast. The pre-stroke Kirk of *Return* and *Kirkatron* is a risk-taking, unpredictable, fearless daredevil of a musician who dazzles with everything from a tender flute solo on Minnie Riperton's "Loving You" to some soul-bearing tenor playing on Lester Young's "Goodbye Pork Pie Hat," Leon Russell's "This Masquerade" and the hauntingly eccentric "Theme for the Eulipions." Meanwhile, the post-stroke Kirk of *Boogie-Woogie* is someone who manages to deliver a worthwhile album despite his obvious impairment and physical limitations. Because the stroke had left him paralyzed on one side, Kirk faced the challenge of playing tenor and flute with the use of only one hand. Though parts of the CD are melancholy (especially his tenor playing on "I Loves You, Porgie"), Kirk's fighting spirit comes through on the quirky "Make Me a Pallet on the Floor" and Percy Heath's humorous "Watergate Blues." Sadly, *Boogie-Woogie* would be the innovator's final album before his death on December 5, 1977 at the relatively young age of 41. *—Alex Henderson*

Left Hook, Right Cross / Jul. 13, 1999 / 32 Jazz ♦♦♦♦
32 Jazz's *Left Hook, Right Cross* is a double-disc set that features Rahsaan Roland's 1969 album *Volunteered Slavery* on the first disc and 1972's *Blacknuss* on the second. Although three years separate the two records, they share a similar sensibility in how they offer unpredictable, totally original interpretations of pop and soul songs next to adventurous originals and readings of contemporary jazz pieces. Overall, *Volunteered Slavery* is a stronger piece, but both are quality albums, making *Left Hook, Right Cross* an excellent bargain. *—Stephen Thomas Erlewine*

John Klemmer

b. Jul. 3, 1946, Chicago, IL
Kalimba, Vocals, Sax (Tenor), Sax (Soprano), Sax (Alto), Keyboards, Flute / Smooth Jazz, Jazz-Rock, Crossover Jazz, Hard Bop, Post-Bop, Fusion
Active composer, and innovator on the electrified saxophone, John Klemmer was a strong Coltrane-inspired tenor saxophonist. He began playing music early, and made his debut recording as a leader in 1967. After moving to L.A.in 1968, he worked in Don Ellis's big band for two years, and with artists including Oliver Nelson, with whom Klemmer toured West Africa. Klemmer led fusion groups through the early '70s, recorded albums for Cadet Records, Impulse, and others, and worked as a producer for pop, jazz, and R&B artists. From the mid-'70s through the late '80s, he recorded successful easy listening, pop albums for MCA and Elektra, featuring his electrified horn and an echoplex. After his own hit record, *Touch,* Klemmer recorded solo sax albums, including *Cry,* which preceded smooth jazz and his variety of projects earned him a great deal of crossover appeal. Klemmer alternated his pop-oriented projects with more fiery efforts; his finest jazz album was the two-LP set *Nexus.* After the 1989 release of *Music,* Klemmer went on sabbatical from touring and recording, to focus more on composing; rumors that this sabbatical was due to health problems were untrue. In addition to composing all of his own material, Klemmer co-wrote pop songs for other artists, including Manhattan Transfer's "Walk in Love," with David Batteau and Danny O'-Keefe. The late '90s found Klemmer returning to the stage (in the West Coast), and the studio, releasing the albums *Simpatico* and *Making Love, Vol. 1* (1998) on his own label, Touch Records, and guesting on albums by new age artists including 3rd Force, and David Arkenstone. Over the course of his career, Klemmer performed and recorded with a number of jazz and pop artists including Steely Dan, and John Lee Hooker, and was sampled by many more. By 2000, most of John Klemmer's earlier recordings were still awaiting CD issue. *—Scott Yanow and Joslyn Layne*

Waterfalls / Jun. 17, 1972 / Impulse! ♦♦♦♦♦
John Klemmer was (along with Eddie Harris) a pioneer and an innovator at utilizing electrical devices on his saxophone. For this live set, Klemmer used an Echoplex on his tenor and soprano and was joined by keyboardist Mike Nock, electric bassist Wilton Feldman, drummer Eddie Marshall, Victor Feldman on percussion, and (on two of the eight songs) vocalist Diana Lee. Recorded live on June 17, 1972 (with additional recording added five days later), this CD reissue gives one a good example of Klemmer's playing before his mood music records caught on. He certainly achieved some unusual effects at the time although he never became an influential force. Worth investigating by open-eared listeners. *—Scott Yanow*

Touch / Jul. 1975-Aug. 1975 / MCA ♦♦♦♦
Better solos and higher energy level than most of Klemmer's albums. This is the best-sounding version. *—Ron Wynn*

Arabesque / 1977 / MCA ♦♦♦♦
A light, pop-influenced effort much in the vein of his commercial breakthrough *Touch*, *Arabesque* possesses a creativity and feeling which allows it to rise above the standard lite-jazz fare—fans of Klemmer's more adventurous recordings need not bother, but listeners in search of inspired mood music will find much of value here. *—Raymond McKinney*

★ **Nexus for Duo and Trio** / 1979 / Jive/Novus ♦♦♦♦♦
At a period of time when John Klemmer had a pop hit with "Touch" and was becoming well-known for his electrified renditions of simple melodies, this double LP must have shocked some of his unsuspecting fans. The tenor-saxophonist is heard on five jazz standards with bassist Bob Magnusson and drummer Carl Burnett, and on four often-stunning tenor-drums duets with Burnett; four of the performances are over ten minutes long. Quite possibly John Klemmer's finest hour (or really two hours) on record. Five of the nine performances have been reissued on CD by Bluebird but, if you can, get the double LP (and the entire program) instead. *—Scott Yanow*

☆ **Nexus One (for Trane)** / 1979 / Bluebird/RCA ♦♦♦♦♦
This CD reissues five of the nine selections from what was arguably tenor-saxophonist John Klemmer's greatest recording session. In addition to forceful versions of "Mr. P.C." and "My One and Only Love" that feature the artist joined by bassist Bob Magnusson and drummer Carl Burnett, there are three lengthy explorations (of "Softly as in a Morning Sunrise," "Impressions," and his original "Nexus") that are taken as tenor-drum duets. The music is so powerful that listeners should search for the original double LP which includes three additional trios and a duet on "Four." Klemmer, who was becoming very popular as a melodic pop saxophonist, must have surprised many of his fans with this very explorative document. *—Scott Yanow*

Mosaic: The Best of John Klemmer / Jul. 1975-Aug. 1978 / GRP ♦♦♦
In the early 1970s, when John Klemmer left Don Ellis' Orchestra and went out on his own, he soon discovered a formula that worked. An innovator with the electric saxophone, Klemmer mostly caressed the melodies on his commercial recordings, letting his sound tell the story. These easy-listening sounds (which included the major hit "Touch") helped lead the way to today's pop/jazz scene. This 1996 CD sampler has selections from 1975's *Touch* (including the title cut), *Barefoot Ballet, Arabesque, Lifestyle (Living and Loving), Brazilia* and *Blowin' Gold* (which, dating from 1969, predates Klemmer's pop success). The lack of variety between the songs is a minus for those who listen closely, but may be a plus for others who use this CD mostly for romantic backgrounds. Klemmer is joined by oversized rhythm sections that sometimes utilize keyboardist Dave Grusin and guitarist Larry Carlton; he is purposely restrained and plays prettily throughout. *—Scott Yanow*

Earl Klugh

b. Sep. 16, 1954, Detroit, MI
Guitar / Crossover Jazz, Jazz-Pop
An acoustic guitarist with a very pretty tone, Earl Klugh does not consider himself a jazz player and thinks of Chet Atkins as being his most important influence. Klugh played on a Yusef Lateef album when he was 15 and gained recognition in 1971 for his contributions to George Benson's *White Rabbit* record. He played regularly with Benson in 1973, was a member of Return to Forever briefly in 1974 and then in the mid-'70s began recording as a leader. Klugh's popular recordings (for Blue Note, Capitol, Manhattan and Warner Bros.) tend to use light funk beats, stick closely to the melody and put the emphasis on his sound; little surprising ever occurs. *—Scott Yanow*

Heart String / Oct. 1978 Aug. 1, - 19 / Blue Note ♦♦♦
To dismiss an Earl Klugh recording as easy listening is unfair. Klugh is one of the most inventive and accomplished guitarists to emerge from the 1970s. His discography has been heavily criticized in jazz circles, and for the most part deservedly so, as not qualifying as true Jazz music (based on improvisation). The spirit of jazz has always been that of improvisation, which is why Klugh has argued against himself being labeled a "jazz" musician. Labels aside, Klugh's brilliance has been overlooked because his releases have been on the softer side. The music here is full of heavy strings, funky backbeats and that '70s sound, but that is the charm of this recording. Klugh's "Acoustic Lady" is an infectious song and showcases his harp-like sound on the guitar. While it may be classified as easy listening, it is certainly not easy playing. A very beautiful and warm recording with enough guitar playing to keep even the most advanced players baffled. *—Robert Taylor*

Two of a Kind / 1982 / Manhattan ♦♦♦♦
Keyboardist Bob James and acoustic guitarist Earl Klugh struck gold with this session, recently reissued on CD. The formula hasn't changed much in succeeding years. Both Klugh and James are capable musicians; they demonstrated on this collection of light, innocuous melodies and occasionally interesting backbeats a high degree of professionalism. Klugh is a first-rate guitarist whose solos are concise and nicely delivered, but frequently sound thin. James' piano and electric keyboard playing is a puzzling combination of flawlessness and lifelessness. *—Ron Wynn*

Soda Fountain Shuffle / 1984 / Warner Brothers ♦♦♦

● **Solo Guitar** / 1989 / Warner Brothers ♦♦♦♦
Earl Klugh's long-awaited solo album showcased his pretty sound on the acoustic guitar, giving two-to-three-three minute melodic readings of superior standards. Some of the pieces (notably "I'm Confessin'") found Klugh playing a relaxed "stride" similiar to some of the guitarists of the '30s. *—Scott Yanow*

The Earl Klugh Trio, Vol. 1 / 1991 / Warner Brothers ♦♦♦♦
A departure from the type of boring, innocuous elevator Muzak Earl Klugh is best known for, *Earl Klugh Trio, Vol. 1* gave listeners a rare chance to hear the guitarist playing straight-ahead jazz. Some bebop musicians contend that playing dull background music year after year means you can kiss your bebop chops goodbye, but there's no evidence of that on this rewarding CD. With Klugh sticking to acoustic guitar and employing Ralph Armstrong on upright bass and Gene Dunlap on drums, someone who is best known for recording schlock offers tasteful and lyrical interpretations of such well known standards as "I'll Remember April," "Night and Day" and "One Note Samba." Klugh also excels on "Lonely Girl" (a beautiful but underexposed Neal Hefti piece) and pleasantly surprises us by demonstrating that the theme from the 1960s sitcom "Bewitched" and the Aretha Franklin hit "I Say a Little Prayer" (written by Burt Bacharach & Hal David) can work in an acoustic bebop setting. Undeniably, this is the best album Klugh ever recorded—it's too bad it was a departure from his norm instead of a primary direction. *—Alex Henderson*

Late Night Guitar / 1979-1980 / One Way ♦♦♦
This is the perfect setting for acoustic guitarist Earl Klugh, playing strong melodies (including such standards as "Smoke Gets In Your Eyes," "Laura," "Mona Lisa" and "Two for the Road") while joined by strings and several horns in an orchestra arranged and conducted by Dave Mathews. As usual for a Klugh session (this one unfortunately has not yet been reissued on CD), the guitarist sticks mostly to the themes and does not improvise much, as he never considered himself a jazz player; but the overall effect is quite pleasing. *—Scott Yanow*

Peculiar Situation / Jul. 27, 1999 / Windham Hill ♦♦♦♦
Windham Hill's eagerness to become one of smooth jazz's top labels has led them to sign a handful of influential masters of the form. They couldn't have placed a surer bet than on Earl Klugh, whose snappy acoustic style first hit the airwaves in the mid-'70s. While he's experimented a few times in recent years with orchestral projects, his *Peculiar Situation* finds him for the most part mining familiar and friendly territory. The sharp crisp melody over a thick, rolling bass groove on the title cut (with the occasional synth flourish at the end of the chorus part) characterizes his overall funk approach, while the graceful high-toned melody that leads "Southern Dog" is classic Klugh balladry. One of his more unique traits is how he modulates his strings; the melody line on the title track features a high tone, and his solo improvisation delves into the lower registers. Klugh has long enjoyed sampling the worldbeat experience, getting his fill here with the galloping samba bass lines, vibes harmonies, conga line festivity, and call and response African-flavored vocals on "Desert Paradise." Roberta Flack is on board for his first ever vocal track, her easy honey voice all but melting upon his subtle string harmonies on "Now and Again." *—Jonathan Widran*

Lee Konitz

b. Oct. 13, 1927, Chicago, IL
Sax (Soprano), Sax (Alto) / Post-Bop, Cool
One of the most individual of all altoists (and one of the few in the 1950s who did not sound like a cousin of Charlie Parker), the cool-toned Lee Konitz has always had a strong musical curiosity that has led him to consistently take chances and stretch himself, usually quite successfully. Konitz gained some attention for his solos with Claude Thornhill's Orchestra (1947). He began studying with Lennie Tristano, who had a big influence on his conception and approach to improvising. Konitz was with Miles Davis's Birth of the Cool Nonet during their one gig and their Capitol recordings (1948-50) and recorded with Tristano's innovative sextet (1949), including the first two free improvisations ever documented. Konitz blended very well with Warne Marsh's tenor (their unisons on "Wow" are miraculous) and would have several reunions with both Tristano and Marsh through the years but he was also interested in finding his own way. Konitz toured Scandinavia (1951) where his cool sound was influential and he fit in surprisingly well with Stan Kenton's Orchestra (1952-54). He was primarily a leader from that point on. His recordings have ranged from cool bop to thoughtful free improvisations and his Milestone set of *Duets* (1967) is a classic. *—Scott Yanow*

Subconscious-Lee / Jan. 11, 1949-Apr. 7, 1950 / Prestige/OJC ♦♦♦♦♦
A debut for both Konitz and the Prestige label, *Subconscious-Lee* brings together many of the students who came through Lennie Tristano's idiosyncratic "school" of jazz during the immediate postwar years. Forging a heady approach to Charlie Parker's innovations, full of lithe and at times super fast solo lines, Tristano and his favorite pupil Konitz in particular nurtured an introverted, wan, yet still swinging alternative to the frenetic muscle of bebop. Other students like tenor saxophonist Warne Marsh, pianist Sal Mosca, and bassist Arnold Fishkin staked claims as well and show up prominently here. And while Tristano's "Judy" and "Retrospection" get mired in somewhat tired contemplation, Konitz' "Subconscious-Lee" and Marsh's "Marshmallow" stand out with brisk tempos, cascading horn lines, and fetching head statements. Avoiding the meandering course of his originals, Tristano shines at the piano with a bevy of exciting and substantial solos; Mosca and guitarist Billy Bauer keep up the good work with fine contributions of their own. Good for both mind and feet and chock full of groundbreaking work by Konitz and Marsh especially, this 1949-1950 recording makes for essential jazz listening. *—Stephen Cook*

Konitz Meets Mulligan / Jan. 30, 1953 / Pacific Jazz/Blue Note ♦♦♦♦♦
W/ Gerry Mulligan Quartet. A simply wonderful pairing of idiosyncratic talents. *—Ron Wynn*

Inside Hi-Fi / Sep. 26, 1956-Sep. 16, 1956 / Koch International ♦♦♦♦
This excellent recording (part of their 1987 *Jazzlore* series) features altoist Lee Konitz with two separate quartets during 1956. Either guitarist Billy Bauer or pianist Sal Mosca are the main supporting voices in groups also including either Arnold Fishkind or Peter Ind on bass and Dick Scott on drums. The most unusual aspect to the set is that on the four selections with Mosca, Konitz switches to tenor, playing quite effectively in a recognizable cool style. The overall highlights of this enjoyable album are "Everything Happens to Me," "All of Me," and "Star Eyes," but all eight performances are well played and swinging. *—Scott Yanow*

☆ **Live at the Half Note** / Feb. 24, 1959-Mar. 3, 1959 / Verve ♦♦♦♦♦
The music on this two-CD set has a strange history. Pianist Lennie Tristano had a rare reunion with altoist Lee Konitz and tenor-saxophonist Warne Marsh (his two greatest "students") during an extended stay at the Half Note in 1959. Tristano took Tuesday nights off to teach and Bill Evans was his substitute but the pianist had a couple of those performances recorded for posterity. Years later while listening to his tapes he was so impressed with Marsh's playing that he sent edited versions (comprised entirely of the tenor's solos) to Marsh

and somehow they ended up being released in that form by the Revelation label. Finally in 1994 the unedited music was issued by Verve; the consistently exciting playing by Konitz, Marsh and Evans (with backup by bassist Jimmy Garrison and drummer Paul Motian) makes one wonder what took so long. They perform a dozen extended standards (or "originals" based on the chord changes of familiar tunes) with creativity and inspiration. In fact, of all the Konitz-Marsh recordings, this set ranks near the top. *—Scott Yanow*

Lee Konitz Meets Jimmy Giuffre / May 12, 1959-May 13, 1959 / Verve ♦♦♦♦♦
This unusual two-CD set not only reissues the original LP of the same name but three other rare Verve LP's from the 1950's. Altoist Lee Konitz (on "An Image") is showcased during a set of adventurous Bill Russo arrangements for an orchestra and strings in 1958, pops up on half of Ralph Burns' underrated 1951 classic *Free Forms* (the most enjoyable of the four sets) and meets up with baritonist Jimmy Giuffre, whose arrangements for five saxes (including the great tenor Warne Marsh) and a trio led by pianist Bill Evans are sometimes equally influenced by classical music and bop. The least interesting date showcases Giuffre's clarinet with a string section on his five-part "Piece For Clarinet And String Orchestra" and the 16 brief movements of "Mobiles." Overall this third-stream two-fer contains music that is easier to respect and admire than to love although Lee Konitz fans will probably want to acquire the obscure performances. *—Scott Yanow*

★ **The Lee Konitz Duets** / Sep. 25, 1967 / Milestone/OJC ♦♦♦♦♦
This CD brings back one of altoist Lee Konitz's greatest sessions. In 1967 he recorded a series of very diverse duets, all of which succeed on their own terms. Konitz is matched with valve trombonist Marshall Brown on a delightful version of "Struttin' with Some Barbecue," matches wits with the tenor of Joe Henderson on "You Don't Know What Love Is," plays "Checkerboard" with pianist Dick Katz, "Erb" with guitarist Jim Hall, "Tickle Toe" with the tenor of Richie Kamuca (Konitz switches to tenor on that cut) and an adventurous and fairly free "Duplexity" with violinist Ray Nance, has three different duets on "Alone Together" and, on "Alphanumeric," welcomes practically everyone back for a final blowout. The music ranges from Dixieland to bop and free and is consistently fascinating. *—Scott Yanow*

Spirits / Mar. 3, 1971-Mar. 9, 1971 / Milestone/OJC ♦♦♦♦
Altoist Lee Konitz revisits his roots in pianist Lennie Tristano's music on this enjoyable recording from 1971. Four of the nine songs are duets with pianist Sal Mosca (who always sounded a lot like Tristano) while the five other pieces add bassist Ron Carter and drummer Mousie Alexander to the group. Konitz performs three of his own compositions, five by Tristano and one from tenor saxophonist Warne Marsh; typically all of these originals are based closely on the chord changes (and sometimes the melodies) of familiar standards. Despite that lack of originality, this is excellent music and finds altoist Lee Konitz in creative form. *—Scott Yanow*

Satori / Sep. 30, 1974 / Milestone/OJC ♦♦♦♦
This is an excellent release that is fairly typical of a Lee Konitz program from the 1970s and '80s. There are a few standards (such as "Just Friends," "Green Dolphin Street" and "What's New"), a few fairly advanced pieces ("Satori" and "Free Blues"), thoughtful improvisations and a bit of hard-swinging. Inspired by the presence of pianist Martial Solal, bassist David Holland and drummer Jack DeJohnette, Konitz stretches himself as usual and comes up with consistently fresh statements while generally playing at a low introspective volume. *—Scott Yanow*

☆ **The Lee Konitz Nonet** / Oct. 13, 1976-Oct. 18, 1976 / Roulette ♦♦♦♦♦
This is a group that should have been able to stay together but it was formed a few years too soon, at the height of the fusion era. Altoist Lee Konitz's nonet (featuring trumpeter Burt Collins, trombonist Jimmy Knepper and keyboardist Andy Laverne among others) reflected its leader's interest in a wide variety of jazz. The music on this out-of-print but valuable album ranges from swing classics ("If Dreams Come True" and "A Pretty Girl Is like a Melody") and bop ("Without a Song") to Wayne Shorter's "Nefertiti" and a pair of Chick Corea tunes ("Matrix" and "Times Lie"). Sy Johnson wrote most of the arrangements (including a full orchestration of six choruses from Chick Corea's piano solo on "Matrix"). This album is well worth a long search since it is one of Lee Konitz's finest recordings of the 1970s. *—Scott Yanow*

Figure and Spirit / Oct. 20, 1976 / Progressive ♦♦♦♦♦
Altoist Lee Konitz (who doubles on this CD on soprano) teams up with tenor-saxophonist Ted Brown, pianist Albert Dailey, bassist Rufus Reid and drummer Joe Chambers for this session. The six songs (originals based on standards by Konitz, Brown and Lennie Tristano) were all performed in one take and although there are a few minor mistakes, the music is quite exciting and spontaneous. Brown was the best possible substitute for Wayne Marsh (Konitz's original choice for the record) and sounds in prime form. It's worth acquiring by fans of straightahead jazz, Lennie Tristano and Lee Konitz. *—Scott Yanow*

And the Jazzpar All Star Nonet / Mar. 27, 1992-Mar. 29, 1992 / Storyville ♦♦♦♦♦
On this diverse and highly enjoyable set altoist Lee Konitz is heard in a variety of settings. Five songs (four of them recently composed) feature Konitz interacting with a fine Danish nonet and on "Subconscious Lee" he is showcased in a quintet with flugelhornist Allan Botchinsky and pianist Peggy Stern. However it is his six duets (with Stern, Botchinsky, bassist Jesper Lundgaard and fellow altoist Jens Sondergaard) that are most notable. Konitz, who can play as freely as any avant-gardist, somehow always sounds relaxed and thoughtful, turning these duets into comfortable dialogues. *—Scott Yanow*

Jazz Nocturne / Oct. 5, 1992 / Evidence ♦♦♦♦♦

Strings for Holiday / Mar. 18, 1996-Mar. 19, 1996 / Enja ♦♦♦♦

Alone Together / Nov. 21, 1996-Nov. 22, 1996 / Blue Note ♦♦♦♦♦

Another Shade of Blue / Dec. 21, 1997-Dec. 22, 1997 / Blue Note ♦♦♦♦
This follow up to an earlier CD (*Alone Together*) with Brad Mehldau and Charlie Haden took place exactly one year later at the same venue, L.A.'s *Jazz Bakery.* Like the first release, the trio takes their time exploring each tune, whether it's the leader's opening blues or a favorite ballad like "What's New" or "Body and Soul." This stimulating set is highly recommended! *—Ken Dryden*

Sound of Surprise / Apr. 21, 1999-Apr. 22, 1999 / RCA Victor ♦♦♦♦

Gene Krupa

b. Jan. 15, 1909, Chicago, IL, **d.** Oct. 16, 1973, Yonkers, NY
Drums / Swing, Dixieland, Big Band
The first drummer to be a superstar, Gene Krupa may not have been the most advanced drummer of the 1930s but he was in some ways the most significant. Prior to Krupa, drum solos were a real rarity and the drums were thought of as a merely supportive instrument. Krupa, who with his good lucks and colorful playing became a matinee idol, changed the image of drummers forever. Krupa made history with his first record—for a session in 1927 with the McKenzie-Condon Chicagoans, he became the first musician to use a full drum set on records. In December 1934 he joined Benny Goodman's new orchestra and for the next three years he was an important part of BG's pacesetting big band. Krupa, whose use of the bass drum was never too subtle, starred with Goodman's Trio and Quartet and his lengthy drum feature "Sing, Sing, Sing" in 1937 was historic. Gene soon departed to form his own orchestra. It took the drummer a while to realize with his band that drum solos were not required on every song. It was not until 1941 when he had Anita O'Day and Roy Eldridge that Krupa's big band really took off. Among his hits from 1941-42 were "Let Me Off Uptown," "After You've Gone," "Rockin' Chair" and "Thanks for the Boogie Ride." He put together another big band in mid-1944, one that had a string section. The strings only lasted a short time but Krupa was able to keep his band working into 1951, after which he generally worked with trios or quartets. *—Scott Yanow*

1935-1938 / Nov. 19, 1935-Jun. 18, 1938 / Classics ♦♦♦♦♦
The first CD in the European Classics label's "complete" Gene Krupa series starts off with two all-star sessions that preceded the drummer's first dates as a big-band leader. Krupa, Benny Goodman, bassist Israel Crosby (featured on "Blues of Israel") and several sideman from Goodman's 1935 band jam four songs, and from the following year, Krupa is joined by trumpeter Roy Eldridge, tenor saxophonist Chu Berry, pianist Jess Stacy, guitarist Allan Reuss, Crosby and (on two of the four songs) singer Helen Ward. The two instrumentals ("I Hope Gabriel Likes My Music" and "Swing Is Here") are near-classics that are quite heated. Otherwise, this CD has Krupa's first 15 numbers with his big band, a promising outfit which during 1938 also featured tenor saxophonist Vido Musso, pianist Milt Raskin and the vocals of Irene Daye and Helen Ward. Highlights include "Feeling High and Happy," "Wire Brush Stomp" and the previously unissued "The Madam Swings It." *—Scott Yanow*

1938 / Jul. 19, 1938-Dec. 12, 1938 / Classics ♦♦♦♦
The second Gene Krupa CD in Classics complete reissuance of his swing-era recordings has 22 titles from Krupa's Orchestra during the latter half of 1938. The big band did not yet have its own personality, but Irene Day was a fine pop/swing vocalist; Leo Watson is in typically eccentric form singing four goodtime numbers; the arrangements of Jimmy Mundy and Chappie Willett generally swing hard; Vido Musso and Sam Donahue get off some fine tenor solos; and the leader/drummer really drives the band. Well worth picking up by swing fans. *—Scott Yanow*

1939 / Feb. 26, 1939-Jul. 25, 1939 / Classics ♦♦♦♦
The European label's third Gene Krupa set reissues all of the recordings made by the drummer's big band during a five-month period in 1939. Although working steadily, Krupa's Orchestra had not broken through yet (it was still two years away from its prime period). With Irene Daye contributing ten pleasing vocals among the 22 selections and such soloists as trumpeter Nate Kazebier, trombonist Floyd O'Brien, tenor-saxophonist Sam Donahue and pianist Milt Raskin (along with the drummer/leader), the group was starting to show some strong potential, particularly on the instrumentals such as "The Madam Swings It" and "Hodge Podge." Well-played if not overly distinctive swing music. *—Scott Yanow*

1939-1940 / Jul. 24, 1939-Feb. 12, 1940 / Classics ♦♦♦
The fourth CD in the Classics label's "complete" Gene Krupa series contains 23 recordings recorded by the drummer with his big band during a seven-month period. Irene Daye does a generally fine job on her 14 vocals and singer Howard Dulany weighs down one ballad but naturally the instrumentals are of greatest interest. This period in Krupa's career is generally overlooked in favor of his famous performances with Anita O'Day and Roy Eldridge but there are several gems including a swinging rendition of "My Old Kentucky Home," "On the Beam," "Symphony in Riffs," the hit "Drummin' Man," "Three Little Words," the two part "Blue Rhythm Fantasy," "The Rumba Jumps" and "Boog It." The main soloists include trumpeter Corky Cornelius, the Artie Shaw-inspired clarinetist Sam Musiker and tenorman Sam Donahue in addition to the colorful leader. *—Scott Yanow*

Drum Boogie / Jan. 2, 1940-May 21, 1941 / Columbia ♦♦♦♦♦
Gene Krupa's best-known band was the one he led during 1941-42 which featured singer Anita O'Day and trumpeter Roy Eldridge. This fine CD has 16 selections from the orchestra that preceded that group, a big band almost on the same level. Although the programming is not in strict chronological order, the swinging music is consistently enjoyable. With Irene Day taking some vocals, and solo space for tenorman Sam Donahue and trumpeters Corky Cornelius and Shorty Sherock, many of the best recordings by this outfit are featured including the hit "Drum Boogie," "No Name Jive," "Rhumboogie" and "Blue Rhythm Fantasy." Well worth picking up. *—Scott Yanow*

1940, Vol. 1 / Feb. 19, 1940-Jun. 3, 1940 / Classics ♦♦♦♦
The fifth Gene Krupa CD in Classics' series (which reissues all of the drummer's swing-era studio recordings as a leader) documents Krupa's big band during a four-month period. Of the 22 selections (the majority of which have not been reissued elsewhere), seven have commercial ballad vocals by Howard Dulany, and six have reasonably enjoyable singing from Irene Daye. Of greatest interest are the nine instrumentals (including "Say Si Si," "Manhattan Transfer," "Tuxedo Junction," "Tiger Rag," "No Name Jive" and "Blues Krieg"), although

during this era Krupa's orchestra had few major soloists. Tenor saxophonist Sam Donahue plays well, as do trumpeters Shorty Sherock (before he departed in May) and Corky Cornelius, but the Krupa big band's great days were still in the future. Still, swing collectors will want this entire series. *—Scott Yanow*

★ **Uptown** / May 8, 1941-May 9, 1949 / Columbia ✦✦✦✦✦
Drummer Gene Krupa's most famous band was his 1941-42 orchestra which featured singer Anita O'Day and trumpeter Roy Eldridge. This definitive CD has 20 selections from that particular unit plus four tunes from Krupa in 1949 when Eldridge had briefly rejoined his band. Virtually all of Krupa's biggest hits are here including "Green Eyes," "Let Me Off Uptown," "After You've Gone," "Rockin' Chair," "Thanks for the Boogie Ride" and "That Drummer's Band." This was a classic band, so this is a highly recommended disc for all swing collections. *—Scott Yanow*

Krupa & Rich / May 16, 1955-Nov. 1, 1955 / Verve ✦✦✦✦
On this CD reissue, drummers Gene Krupa and Buddy Rich only actually play together on one of the seven songs, a lengthy rendition of "Bernie's Tune" that has a six-minute "drum battle." Krupa and Rich do perform two songs apiece with a remarkable all-star band consisting of trumpeters Dizzy Gillespie and Roy Eldridge, tenors Illinois Jacquet and Flip Phillips, pianist Oscar Peterson, guitarist Herb Ellis, and bassist Ray Brown. Each of the principals get some solo space, giving this release more variety than one might expect. In addition there are two bonus cuts from a Buddy Rich date that feature the drummer with trumpeters Thad Jones and Joe Newman, tenors Ben Webster and Frank Wess, Oscar Peterson, Ray Brown, and rhythm guitarist Freddie Green. Excellent music overall if not quite essential. *—Scott Yanow*

That Drummer's Band / Jun. 2, 1938-Sep. 26, 1945 / EPM Musique ✦✦✦✦✦
Anthology from 1988 featuring the biggest hits by drummer Gene Krupa heading his own band in 1940. This was period directly after Krupa left the Benny Goodman orchestra and formed his own big band that included tenor saxophonist Charlie Ventura, and used arrangements from a young baritone saxophonist named Gerry Mulligan. *—Ron Wynn*

Radio Years, 1940 / Jan. 31, 1940-Feb. 2, 1940 / Storyville ✦✦✦✦✦
This 1995 CD contains two jazz-oriented radio broadcasts by the early Gene Krupa Big Band. Superior in general to their studio recordings of the era, these performances have plenty of fine solo space for trumpeters Shorty Sherock and Corky Cornelius and tenorman Sam Donohue; the drummer/leader is prominent in the ensembles, and Irene Daye takes seven vocals (there are also nine instrumentals). The announcer (who constantly calls Krupa "America's Number One Drummer Boy") is a bit annoying, but the swinging music is consistently excellent, making this CD a definitive example of Gene Krupa's Orchestra before Anita O'Day and Roy Eldridge joined up. *—Scott Yanow*

1941 / Jan. 17, 1941-May 8, 1941 / Classics ✦✦✦
Gene Krupa's band was in a state of transition when these sides were cut in 1941. Vocalist Irene Day was leaving, the marvelous Anita O'Day and Roy Eldridge were coming aboard, and the band was finally coming up to their leader's fiery level of playing. You can hear the change on tracks like "Alreet," and Anita's and Roy's spirited exchange on "Let Me Off Uptown." Everything on here works just fine, grade-A swing propelled by Krupa's always explosive drumming and the spirited playing of his band. Transfers of the of the old Okeh 78s are a bit fusty but generally fine, and the enclosed information in the booklet make this a good buy worth tracking down. *—Cub Koda*

1942-1945 / 1942-1945 / Classics ✦✦✦✦
This volume catches Krupa at the end of his first band and the start of his much larger second edition of it. Featuring Anita O'Day and Roy Eldridge on vocals, the early tracks like "Knock Me A Kiss," and "Barrelhouse Bessie From basin street" have much to recommend them while "That Drummer's Band" swings effortlessly. The second version of the band features a full string section with far more emphasis on vocals with Krupa letting his jazz soul come up for air with his trio sides with Charlie Ventura ("Body and Soul" and "Stompin' At The Savoy" being prime examples). Another great volume in this set. *—Cub Koda*

Complete Capitol Recordings of Gene Krupa and Harry James / Mosaic ✦✦✦✦✦

Steve Lacy (Steven Morman Lackritz)

b. Jul. 23, 1934, New York, NY
Sopranino Saxophone, Sax (Soprano) / Avant-Garde Jazz, Free Jazz, Post-Bop
One of the great soprano saxophonists of all time (ranking up there with Sidney Bechet and John Coltrane), Steve Lacy's career was fascinating to watch develop. He debuted on record in a modernized Dixieland format with Dick Sutton in 1954. However Lacy soon jumped over several styles to play free jazz with Cecil Taylor during 1955-57. He recorded with Gil Evans in 1957 (they would work together on an irregular basis into the 1980s), was with Thelonious Monk's quintet in 1960 for four months and then formed a quartet with Roswell Rudd (1961-64) that exclusively played Monk's music. Lacy, who is considered the first "modern" musician to specialize on soprano (an instrument that was completely neglected during the bop era), began to turn towards avant-garde jazz in 1965. His music evolved from free form to improvising off of his scalar originals. *—Scott Yanow*

Soprano Sax / Nov. 1, 1957 / Prestige/OJC ✦✦✦✦✦
This was the first of three recordings soprano saxophonist Steve Lacy made for Prestige and this 11/1/57 session was his first as a leader... There was a controlled tension to this date, like everybody's trying to play, carefully, to a common goal. It's almost as if someone were present to make sure everybody stayed within obvious perimeters. *—Bob Rusch, Cadence*

Reflections: Steve Lacy Plays Thelonious Monk / Oct. 17, 1958 / New Jazz/OJC ✦✦✦✦✦
All of soprano saxophonist Steve Lacy's early recordings are quite fascinating, for during 1957-1964, aspects of his style at times hinted at Dixieland, swing, Monk, and Cecil Taylor, sometimes at the same time. For this CD reissue (a straight reproduction of the original *New Jazz* LP), Lacy teams up with pianist Mal Waldron, bassist Buell Neidlinger, and drummer Elvin Jones for seven Thelonious Monk compositions. The typical standbys (such as "'Round Midnight," "Straight No Chaser," and "Blue Monk") are avoided in favor of more complex works such as "Four in One," "Bye-Ya," and "Skippy"; the sweet ballad "Ask Me Now" is a highpoint. Lacy always had an affinity for Monk's music and, even nearly 40 years later, this set is a delight. *—Scott Yanow*

★ **The Straight Horn of Steve Lacy** / Sep. 1960 / Candid ✦✦✦✦✦
Some of soprano saxophonist Steve Lacy's most interesting recordings are his earliest ones. After spending periods of time playing with Dixieland groups and then with Cecil Taylor (which was quite a jump), Lacy made several recordings that displayed his love of Thelonious Monk's music plus his varied experiences. On this particular set, Lacy's soprano contrasts well with Charles Davis' baritone (they are backed by bassist John Ore and drummer Roy Haynes) on three of the most difficult Monk tunes ("Introspection," "Played Twice," and "Criss Cross") plus two Cecil Taylor compositions and Charlie Parker's (or is it Miles Davis'?) "Donna Lee." *—Scott Yanow*

Evidence / Nov. 14, 1961 / New Jazz/OJC ✦✦✦✦
Soprano saxophonist Steve Lacy continued his early exploration of Thelonious Monk's compositions on this 1961 Prestige date, *Evidence*. Lacy worked extensively with Monk, absorbing the pianist's intricate music and adding his individualist soprano saxophone mark to it. On this date, he employs the equally impressive Don Cherry on trumpet, who was playing with the Ornette Coleman quartet at the time, drummer Billy Higgins, who played with both Coleman and Monk, and bassist Carl Brown. Cherry proved capable of playing outside the jagged lines he formulated with Coleman, being just as complimentary and exciting in Monk's arena with Lacy. Out of the six tracks, four are Monk's compositions while the remaining are lesser known Ellington numbers: "The Mystery Song" and "Something to Live For" (co-written with Billy Strayhorn). *—Al Campbell*

School Days / Mar. 1963 / hatHUT ✦✦✦✦

Stamps / Aug. 27, 1977-Feb. 22, 1978 / hatHUT ✦✦✦✦✦

The Flame / Jan. 18, 1982-Jan. 19, 1982 / Soul Note ✦✦✦✦✦
The instrumentation on this set is comprised of soprano saxophonist Steve Lacy, pianist Bobby Few and drummer Dennis Charles, but the adventurous music certainly does not remind one of the Benny Goodman Trio. On four Lacy originals and one by Few, the musicians take wandering group improvisations that are rarely aimless. By having impressive technique and (just as importantly) open ears, the players constantly react to each other and come up with fresh ideas. An intriguing set. *—Scott Yanow*

Morning Joy: Live at Sunset Paris / Feb. 19, 1986 / hatART ✦✦✦✦✦
This disc makes for an intimate portrait of the working band soprano saxophonist Lacy had throughout most of '80s and '90s. Taken from a 1986 club date in Paris, *Morning Joy* features Lacy backed by alto saxophonist Steve Potts, bassist Jean-Jaques Avenel, and drummer Oliver Johnson (regular band members pianist Bobby Few and vocalist/violinist Irène Aebi were not present). The four stretch out on a typical set of Thelonious Monk covers and Lacy compositions, displaying the kind of sympathetic and almost telepathic ensemble playing the group was known for, especially on Lacy's "Prospectus." That number's buoyant mix of high-life rhythms and fluid horn solos is contrasted by the darker, avant-blues mood of originals like "Wicketts" and "As Usual." In addition to being two of Lacy's best pieces, these extended cuts nicely showcase the contrasting yet complimentary styles of the two horn soloists: Lacy mercurial, at times threatening to explode, and Potts more straightforward, energetically piping out staccato phrases. Avenel and Johnson contribute inspired solos of their own and anchor the proceedings with expansive rhythmic support. With relatively cheerful readings of Monk's "Epistrophy" and "In Walked Bud" rounding out the set, *Morning Joy* qualifies as both an essential Lacy title and the first disc to get for those interested in his live recordings. *—Stephen Cook*

Only Monk / Jul. 29, 1986-Jul. 31, 1986 / Soul Note ✦✦✦✦
Steve Lacy has long been one of the foremost interpreters of pianist Thelonious Monk's music. This set is a solo soprano saxophone recital in which Lacy digs into nine of Monk's compositions. Most of the interpretations are quite concise, with all but the seven-minute "Work" clocking in at under six minutes. As usual, Lacy shows great respect for the melodies, and his improvisations are built off of the themes rather than just the chord changes. The sparse setting allows the soprano master to utilize space effectively and to take his time. The overall results, which are certainly for selective tastes, are often fascinating. *—Scott Yanow*

Live at Sweet Basil / Jul. 6, 1991-Jul. 7, 1991 / Jive/Novus ✦✦✦✦✦

5 X Monk X Lacy / Mar. 26, 1994 / Silkheart ✦✦✦✦✦
No matter how many times Steve Lacy records the music of Thelonious Monk, his enthusiasm always makes it sound as if he is exploring the themes for the first time, although his mastery of Monk's music gives away the truth. Ever since the mid-1950s, the innovative soprano saxophonist has returned to Monk's pieces on a fairly regular basis. For this Stockholm concert, ana unaccompanied Lacy starts out with concise versions of five of Monk's numbers; only "Pannonica" exceeds four minutes. His interpretations are so self-sufficient that one does not miss the other instruments, although it is quite easy to "hear" the bass and drums behind the soprano. The remaining five performances are all Lacy originals, and although not overtly Monkish, his use of the themes as the basis for his improvising, thoughtful solos (often sounding as if he is thinking aloud), and highly original yet logical evolution of his improvisations (which often feature an inventive use of repetition) make the results continually fascinating. Highly recommended. *—Scott Yanow*

Solo: Live at Unity Temple / Nov. 6, 1997 / Wobbly Rail ✦✦✦✦
This third release on the Wobbly Rail label is a November, 1997 solo performance by Steve Lacy in a Chicago building designed for both worship and music by famed architect Frank Lloyd Wright. The acoustics of *Unity Temple* and Lacy's performance that day have an unusual warmth and spacious intimacy. Lacy's fluid lyricism is at full strength while he performs a very lovely "Monk Medley," as well as originals including "Revenue" (found on a 1993 Soul Note release of the same name) and "Art" (*Momentum*, 1987). *—Joslyn Layne*

Monk's Dream / Jun. 21, 1999-Jun. 22, 1999 / Verve ♦♦♦♦
Having played together off and on for over 40 years, Steve Lacy and Roswell Rudd are hardly strangers to each other. In the early 1960s, when they led a quartet devoted to Thelonious Monk's music, they could barely find anyone to record them (the exception being the Emanem LP *School Days*, reissued on CD as Hat Art 6140); today a Monk tribute album is a much more salable item. But despite its title and the presence of two Monk compositions, the title work and "Pannonica," that's not what this is. Rather, it is a kind of newly recorded Lacy sampler, adding to the Monk tunes: one by Duke Ellington ("Koko"), three Lacy works that have been recorded previously ("The Door," "The Bath," "The Rent"), and three new Lacy numbers ("A Bright Pearl," "Traces," "Grey Blue"). The familiarity of the players—who, in addition to Lacy and Rudd, include Lacy's regular rhythm section of Jean-Jacques Avenel and John Bestsch—is both good news and bad news. Certainly, they sound comfortable with each other, but also, given their long association and the mostly familiar material, they don't seem to have been greatly challenged. They sound most comfortable with the Monk tunes and take some chances with the Ellington, but on Lacy's tunes they sometimes stretch out pointlessly. This is particularly the case on the nearly 12-minute "The Bath," which Lacy wrote for a film about a bum who gets to take a bath for the first time in years. The song begins playfully, but it runs on and on until you'd think Rudd was trying to play every possible note on the trombone. *Monk's Dream* is a warm reunion of old friends, but those friends could have tried a little harder to come up with something fresh. *—William Ruhlmann*

Snips: Live at Environ / May 16, 1976 / Jazz Magnet ♦♦♦♦
Even the most experienced jazz listener might find the idea of over 80 minutes of unaccompanied soprano saxophone a bit daunting. But this is a vital historical document, as it captures the enigmatic Steve Lacy in a 1976 solo concert at *Environ*, a now-defunct Manhattan loft. Audience and ambient noises make it onto the recording, but these flaws make the loft concert atmosphere more vivid and distract only minimally from the focal point of Lacy's instrument.

Lacy breaks into vocalizations at certain points, as on the opening "Hooky" in which he repeatedly intones "don't go to school" and then uses the phrase as a basis for melodic invention. Similarly, he mouths a Buddhist chant intermittently during the course of the "Four Edges" suite, again using the rhythmic pattern of the phrase as a basis for improvisation.

Along with a six-movement "Tao" suite, Lacy performs "New York Duck," "Snips," "Pearl Street," and "Revolutionary Suicide" during the course of the two discs. Some may find the music, not to mention the solo format, difficult and inaccessible. But Lacy's playing is remarkable for its strong narrative quality and its inexhaustible flow of ideas. This is Lacy stretching to his limits. It's also a rare glimpse into the vibrant New York loft scene of the '60s and '70s. *—David R. Adler*

Hooky / Oct. 1, 2000 / Emanem ♦♦♦♦♦
March 24, 1976: Steve Lacy plays his first concert in Montreal, at *St.-Jean L'...vangéliste Church*. This solo appearance was recorded but only 25 minutes of the performance can be found on side one of the 1979 Quark LP *The Woe* (side two being "The Woe"). Over 20 years later, the label Emanem released the complete concert (minus an aborted piece and applause) on the CD *Hooky*. Good idea. The church's acoustics gave Lacy's soprano saxophone more body than usual—he also played with the room's possibilities on "The New Duck"—and compensated for poor sound quality (as the left channel on the recording is defective at times). The first set was comprised of a selection of short original compositions, including "The Crust," "Pearl Street," and "Hooky," the latter being only documented on this CD. In the second set, Lacy performed his suite "Tao" and came back for an encore ("Revolutionary Suicide"). Apart from "Hooky," all the material is well documented elsewhere, but the saxophonist was very inspired on this particular date. Lifted by an impressive sense of well-being (which becomes almost palpable on "Tao"), the music totally makes up for the small recording imperfections. Fans of Lacy will find him at his best on *Hooky*. *—François Couture*

Oliver Lake

b. Sep. 14, 1942, Marianna, AR
Sax (Soprano), Sax (Alto), Saxophone, Flute / Avant-Garde Jazz, Free Jazz
Oliver Lake is an explosively unpredictable soloist, somewhat akin to Eric Dolphy in the ultra-nimble manner in which he traverses the full range of his main horn, the alto. Lake's astringent saxophone sound is his trademark—piercing, bluesy, and biting in the manner of a Maceo Parker, it was a perfect lead voice for the World Saxophone Quartet, the band with which Lake has made his most enduring mark on jazz. From the late '60s to the early '70s he taught school, played in various contexts around St. Louis, and led—along with Julius Hemphill and Charles "Bobo" Shaw, among others—a musicians' collective, the Black Artist's Group (BAG). Lake lived in Paris from 1972-74, where he worked in a quintet comprised of fellow BAG members. By 1975, he had (along with most of his BAG colleagues) moved to New York, where he became active on what was called by some the "loft jazz" scene. In 1976, with Hemphill, Hamiet Bluiett, and David Murray, he founded the World Saxophone Quartet. Over the next two decades, that band reached a level of popularity perhaps unprecedented by a free jazz ensemble. Its late-'80s albums of Ellington works and R&B tunes attracted an audience that otherwise might never have found its way to such an esoteric style. *—Chris Kelsey*

Ntu: The Point from Which Freedom Begins / 1971 / Freedom ♦♦♦♦
Altoist Oliver Lake's debut recording features him with a ten-piece unit in St. Louis. The performances are quite avant-garde, often very loose and influenced by The Art Ensemble of Chicago; Don Moye sits in on congas. In addition to Lake, the other notable players include trumpeter Baikida E.J. Carroll, trombonist Joseph Bowie and drummer Bobo Shaw. Much of this music is hit and miss but it has its successful moments. *—Scott Yanow*

Heavy Spirits / Jan. 31, 1975-Feb. 3, 1975 / Black Lion ♦♦♦♦♦
This will be one of the least accessible of altoist Oliver Lake's recordings for most people but repeated listenings reveal a great deal of beauty. The avant-garde master is backed by three violinists on a trio of intense pieces, takes "Lonely Blacks" unaccompanied and performs "Rocket" in an unusual trio with trombonist Joseph Bowie and drummer Bobo Shaw. The other three selections have a more conventional instrumentation (a quintet with trumpeter Olu Dara and pianist Donald Smith) but are almost as challenging. It's worth investigating but listeners will have to have patience in order to fully appreciate this music. *—Scott Yanow*

The Prophet / Aug. 11, 1980-Aug. 12, 1980 / Black Saint ♦♦♦♦
Following the release of his advanced live trio recording *Zaki*, alto saxophonist Oliver Lake recorded a relatively straight-ahead date, *The Prophet*, a tribute to Eric Dolphy. Released on the Black Saint label in 1980, *The Prophet* combines Lake's (and Dolphy's) ability to blur the line between post-bop and avant-garde jazz on three Dolphy compositions ("Hat and Beard," "Something Sweet, Something Tender," and "Prophet") with three Lake originals. This is not the only tribute to Dolphy that Lake would record; 16 years later he issued *Tribute to Dolphy*, also on Black Saint, with a different band. *—Al Campbell*

● **Expandable Language** / Sep. 17, 1984-Sep. 20, 1984 / Black Saint ♦♦♦♦♦
This freebop session (which is often quite free but often has a strong pulse) is one of altoist Oliver Lake's more rewarding sessions. Guitarist Kevin Eubanks sometimes seems a bit out of place (generally he plays in more conservative settings) but pianist Geri Allen, bassist Fred Hopkins and drummer Pheeroan AkLaff are quite comfortable thinking on their feet during these spirited performances. *—Scott Yanow*

Gallery / Jul. 1986 / Gramavision ♦♦♦♦
Unlike some musicians associated with the avant-garde, altoist Oliver Lake often sounds at his strongest when backed by a piano-bass-drums rhythm section. This excellent set finds Lake switching between alto, tenor, soprano and flute on six of his stronger originals (including "Olla's Blues," "Sad Louis" and "Gallery") while assisted by pianist Geri Allen, bassist Fred Hopkins and drummer Pheeroan akLaff; trumpeter Rasul Siddik guests on "Le Sport Suite." Lake's playing is abstract yet related to the themes, and he is heard throughout in top form, making this an easily recommended set for open-eared listeners. *—Scott Yanow*

Dedicated to Dolphy / Nov. 1, 1994-Nov. 8, 1994 / Black Saint ♦♦♦♦
Alto saxophonist Oliver Lake doesn't have the multi-instrumental versatility or range of expression of the late Eric Dolphy, but he demonstrates the same controlled passion on this satisfying quintet date. His reworking of Dolphy's quirky "Hat and Beard" is actually brighter-sounding as a result of substituting alto sax for bass clarinet. Pianist Charles Eubanks' bluesy chords on "245" provide inspiration for the leader and the fine young trumpeter Russel Gunn. An excellent salute to Dolphy with a couple of strong Lake originals thrown in for good measure. *—Ken Dryden*

Movement, Turns & Switches / Jul. 10, 1996-Dec. 10, 1996 / Passin' Thru ♦♦♦♦♦
This is a consistently fascinating set by altoist Oliver Lake's String Project. Best known for his exploratory flights, Lake is an underrated arranger/composer. For the unusual but consistently fascinating effort, he utilizes a string quartet (violinist Ashley Horne and Sandra Billingslea, Ashley Horne on viola, and cellist Eileen Folson) for five of his six originals, occasionally adding bassist Belden Bullock and (on one song apiece) trumpeter Kenyatta Beasley (during the well-titled "Fan Fare Bop") and Neil Clarke on conga. The music is adventurous but quite coherent, often rhythmic and melodic but very open to advanced ideas. These string players can definitely stretch out; improvised sections coincide closely with written passages, so it is sometimes difficult to know which are which. Lake keeps his solo statements concise, tempering his fire with the desire to blend in with the strings. For variety, the leader is absent on the title cut, a fairly outside duet by violinist Regina Carter and pianist Donal Fox. Overall, this is a CD that rewards repeated listenings and is one of the highlights of Oliver Lake's productive career. *—Scott Yanow*

Lambert, Hendricks & Ross

f. 1957, **db.** 1964
Group / Vocal Jazz, Traditional Pop, Vocalese, Bop
The premier jazz vocal act of all time, Lambert, Hendricks & Ross revolutionized vocal music during the late '50s and early '60s by turning away from the increasingly crossover slant of the pop world to embrace the sheer musicianship inherent in vocal jazz. Applying the concepts of bop harmonies to swinging vocal music, the trio transformed dozens of instrumental jazz classics into their own songs, taking scat solos and trading off licks and riffs in precisely the same fashion of their favorite improvising musicians. Vocal arranger Dave Lambert wrote dense clusters of vocal lines for each voice that, while only distantly related, came together splendidly. Jon Hendricks wrote clever, witty lyrics to jazz standards like "Summertime," "Moanin'" and "Twisted," and Ross proved to be one of the strongest, most dexterous female voices in the history of jazz vocals. Together Lambert, Hendricks & Ross paved the way for vocal groups like Manhattan Transfer while earning respect from vocalists and jazz musicians alike.

The act grew out of apartment jam sessions and a few recordings by Lambert and Hendricks, who were mostly unsuccessful until a chance meeting with solo vocalist Annie Ross hit paydirt. The trio's first LP, 1957's *Sing a Song of Basie*, featured incredible vocal recreations of complete solos from an array of Basie classics. Next year's *Sing Along with Basie* featured the bandleader himself and his group in a supporting role. The trio then recruited a straight rhythm trio, began touring and recording that way, and jumped to Columbia in 1959 to record three albums, including a tribute to Duke Ellington. After constant touring began to wear her out, however, Ross left the group in 1962. Lambert and Hendricks understandably struggled to replace her, and called it quits in 1964 after recording three LPs with Yolande Bavan. Lambert was killed in a traffic accident just two years later, though both Hendricks and Ross continued to perform and record. *—John Bush*

☆ **Sing a Song of Basie** / Aug. 26, 1957-Nov. 26, 1957 / Verve ♦♦♦♦♦
The premiere jazz vocal group, Lambert, Hendricks and Ross, made their recording debut on this classic album which has been reissued on CD by GRP. After unsuccessfully searching for a dozen singers in 1957 who could sing vocalese in a recreation of some famous records by the Count Basie Orchestra, Dave Lambert, Jon Hendricks and Annie Ross decided to overdub their voices several times instead. Utilizing just a rhythm section, the vocalists in

note-for-note reproductions of ten Basie records sing the witty and inventive lyrics of Hendricks. Highlights include "It's Sand, Man," "One O'Clock Jump" the uptempo "Little Pony" and "Avenue C." This record was a sensation when it was released and it is still quite enjoyable and unique. *— Scott Yanow*

Twisted: The Best of Lambert, Hendricks & Ross / 1957-1961 / Rhino ✦✦✦✦✦
Good anthology showcasing hits from the premier jazz vocal trio of the '50s and '60s. The title track, "Sing A Song Of Basie, " and other anthems are included. This is an excellent introductory release and good sampler. *— Ron Wynn*

Everybody's Boppin' / Aug. 6, 1959-Mar. 14, 1961 / Columbia ✦✦✦✦✦
Lambert, Hendricks and Ross made their debut on Columbia in 1959, and this CD contains not only all of the music from their first CBS album, but five titles from two later records. This set has many memorable classics from the great singers Dave Lambert, Jon Hendricks (the top vocalese lyricist) and Annie Ross. Highlights include the upbeat "Charleston Alley," a remake of Ross' "Twisted," the heated "Cloudburst," Hendricks' humorous "Gimme That Wine," "Summertime" (a recreation of Miles Davis' version with Gil Evans), and "Come on Home." Although Lambert, Hendricks and Ross only lasted a few years, their influence on other vocal groups was enormous. This set is a perfect place for collectors to begin to explore their vocal magic. *— Scott Yanow*

★ **The Hottest New Group in Jazz** / Aug. 6, 1959-Mar. 9, 1962 / Columbia/Legacy ✦✦✦✦✦
The immortal jazz vocal group Lambert, Hendricks & Ross recorded five albums during its career: one apiece for Impulse and World Pacific, and three for Columbia. This two-CD set has all of the music from LHR's Columbia dates (*The Hottest Group In Jazz, Sing Ellington* and *High Flying*), plus four previously unissued and three very obscure selections. Dave Lambert, Jon Hendricks and Annie Ross were all very talented jazz singers as individuals and masters of vocalese. Virtually every performance of theirs together was special and in the long run influential. With assistance by the Gildo Mahones Trio, trumpeter Harry "Sweets" Edison (on the earlier album) and altoist Pony Poindexter (during the seven "bonus" tracks), the vocal group is heard in memorable form throughout the two-fer. Among the many highlights are "Twisted," "Cloudburst," Hendricks' hilarious "Gimme That Wine," "Everybody's Boppin'," "Cottontail," "All Too Soon," "Main Stem," "Farmer's Market," "Cookin' at the Continental," "Halloween Spooks" and "Popity Pop." Essential music for all serious jazz collections. *— Scott Yanow*

Eddie Lang

b. Oct. 25, 1902, Philadelphia, PA, **d.** Mar. 26, 1933, New York, NY
Guitar / Classic Jazz
The first jazz guitar virtuoso, Eddie Lang was everywhere in the late '20s; all of his fellow musicians knew that he was the best. In 1924 he debuted with the Mound City Blue Blowers and was soon in great demand for recording dates, both in the jazz world and in commercial settings. His sophisticated chord patterns made him a superior accompanist who uplifted everyone else's music and Lang was also a fine single-note soloist. He often teamed up with violinist Joe Venuti (including some classic duets) and played with Red Nichols's Five Pennies, Frankie Trumbauer and Bix Beiderbecke, the orchestras of Roger Wolfe Kahn, Jean Goldkette and Paul Whiteman and anyone else who could hire him. Lang, who led some dates of his own during 1927-29, also worked regularly with Bing Crosby during the early '30s. Tragically his premature death was caused by a botched operation on a tonsillectomy. *— Scott Yanow*

★ **Jazz Guitar** / Apr. 1, 1927-Jan. 15, 1932 / Yazoo ✦✦✦✦✦
Eddie Lang did not lead many sessions during his short life and the great majority are on this Yazoo collection. The most in-demand guitarist of 1925-33, Lang's rare opportunities to head his own dates put the focus on his single-note lines and gave him a chance to be in the spotlight rather than making other players sound good. This album has two unaccompanied solos (including Rachmaninoff's "Prelude"), duets with pianists Frank Signorelli, Arthur Schutt and Rube Bloom and three of his famous collaborations with fellow guitarist Lonnie Johnson. However the most memorable tracks are Lang's two exciting duets with guitarist Carl Kress: "Pickin' My Way" and an alternate take of "Feeling My Way." This is highly recommended music from the best jazz guitarist prior to the rise of Django Reinhardt. *— Scott Yanow*

☆ **Pioneers of Jazz Guitar 1927-1938** / Apr. 1, 1927-Aug. 8, 1939 / Challenge ✦✦✦✦✦
This 1998 CD has a great deal of timeless music. Guitar features were very rare in jazz prior to Django Reinhardt, and particularly before the guitar became amplified in the late 1930s. This essential reissue has all of Eddie Lang's guitar features (leaving out only a few numbers in which he led a bigger group), the two Lang/Carl Kress duets, the Kress/Dick McDonough duets, and all of Kress' unaccompanied solos. The Lang numbers (mostly duets with Arthur Schutt, Frank Signorelli or Rube Bloom offering quiet support on piano) were unprecedented in jazz at the time. Highlights include "Add a Little Wiggle," "I'll Never Be the Same" and "There'll Be Some Changes Made." Actually, the most memorable moments on this CD are the two Lang/Kress collaborations, classics from 1932 called "Pickin' My Way" and "Feelin' My Way." Lang's single-note lines work perfectly with Kress' advanced chords, and it is surprising that no arranger has transcribed these wonderful performances and orchestrated them for a larger group. Highly recommended, and proof that the jazz guitar did not begin with Charlie Christian. *— Scott Yanow*

Pete LaRoca (Peter Sims)

b. Apr. 7, 1938, New York, NY
Drums / Hard Bop, Latin Jazz
Pete La Roca's decision to leave music in 1968 and become an attorney (under his original name of Pete Sims) cut short a productive career. He started his career playing timbales in Latin bands, changing his name to Pete La Roca at the time. He played drums with Sonny Rollins (1957-early 1959) and had associations with Jackie McLean, Slide Hampton, the John Coltrane Quartet (where he was the original drummer in 1960) and Marian McPartland. La Roca led his own group (1961-62), was the house drummer at the Jazz Workshop in Boston (1963-64) and worked with Art Farmer (1964-65), Freddie Hubbard, Mose Allison, Charles Lloyd (1966), Paul Bley and Steve Kuhn among others. He led two impressive albums: the classic Blue Note record *Basra* with Joe Henderson and *Bliss*, a Douglas session (reissued on Muse) featuring Chick Corea and John Gilmore. La Roca started playing jazz again in 1979 and has performed on an occasional basis up to the present time. *— Scott Yanow*

● **Basra** / May 19, 1965 / Blue Note ✦✦✦✦✦
It is strange to realize that drummer Pete La Roca only led two albums during the prime years of his career, for this CD reissue of his initial date is a classic. La Roca's three originals ("Basra," which holds one's interest despite staying on one chord throughout, the blues "Candu," and the complex "Tears Come From Heaven") are stimulating but it is the other three songs that really bring out the best playing in the quartet (which is comprised of tenor saxophonist Joe Henderson, pianist Steve Kuhn, and bassist Steve Swallow in addition to La Roca). "Malaguena" is given a great deal of passion, Swallow's "Eiderdown" (heard in its initial recording) receives definitive treatment, and the ballad "Lazy Afternoon" is both haunting and very memorable; Henderson's tone perfectly fits that piece. *— Scott Yanow*

Turkish Women at the Bath / 1967 / 32 Jazz ✦✦✦✦

Swingtime / Feb. 8, 1997-Mar. 1, 1997 / Blue Note ✦✦✦✦✦
Drummer Pete La Roca (who has gone back to his original name of Pete Sims) had an opportunity in 1997 to lead his first record date in 30 years. Sims, who had become active in jazz again after a long period outside of music, put together a particularly strong band for this CD, utilizing both Dave Liebman and Lance Bryant on sopranos, trumpeter Jimmy Owens, tenor saxophonist Ricky Ford, pianist George Cables, and bassist Santi Debriano. Owens and Liebman, especially, sound inspired, while Ford displays a more original tone than he had had previously, although Dexter Gordon's influence can still be felt in some of his phrases. The music is essentially advanced hard bop with plenty of variety. Highlights include a version of "Body and Soul" based on the famous John Coltrane recording, "Susan's Waltz," "Nhon Bashi," and Chick Corea's "Amandas Song." Even a perky, if slightly out-of-place rendition of "The Candyman" works well. Highly recommended. *— Scott Yanow*

Last Exit

f. 1986, **db.** 1994
Group / Avant-Garde Jazz, Free Jazz
When it comes to avant-garde jazz/rock noise, few bands kicked out the jams better than did Last Exit. A who's-who of jazz players with punk-ass attitudes, Last Exit—guitarist Sonny Sharrock, bassist Bill Laswell, drummer Ronald Shannon Jackson, and saxophonist Peter Brotzmann—could swing, rock, and create an all-out free-jazz din all in the blink of an eye. More important, Last Exit was about was the thrill and danger of total improvisation; so much did they believe in this concept that their debut performance in Zurich in 1986 was completely improvised and unrehearsed. For a group so driven by improvisation, it is not surprising to find out that much of Last Exit's catalog consists of live recordings. Because of the reputations of the individual players, as well as Laswell's position as a big-shot producer (Motörhead, Iggy Pop, Herbie Hancock), Last Exit got a major-label shot with Virgin in 1988. They never became huge, but they continued on devoting touring time in between various solo projects until they called it a career after the tragic death of Sonny Sharrock in 1994. Thankfully, there is plenty of Last Exit to be heard, and, rumor has it, plenty of live recordings yet to be released. *— John Dougan*

Last Exit / Feb. 16, 1986 / Enemy ✦✦✦✦
Recorded live in Paris in 1986, Last Exit is in rare form here, rocketing through tracks like "Discharge," "Pig Freedom" and "Zulu Butter." Everybody gets in some good licks, but pay special attention to Laswell and Shannon Jackson, who play against each other creating a tense, brittle beat. When they lock into a groove it will take your breath away, as will the terrible beauty of Sonny Sharrock's brilliant guitar playing. *— John Dougan*

● **Iron Path** / 1988 / Venture/Virgin ✦✦✦✦
Their sole major-label release, their first studio recording, and a record that iconoclastic critic Chuck Eddy considers one of the 500 greatest heavy metal albums in the history of the universe. But that doesn't mean you should invite all your Deep Purple and Iron Maiden loving friends over for a listening party; they won't be amused. Using the studio to their advantage, Last Exit explores sonic texture on "Prayer" and "The Fire Drum," but never loses sight of the power and energy that makes their live recordings so memorable. If you were to have one Last Exit recording, this might well be the one. But any one of their live records would enhance your appreciation of this great record immeasurably. *— John Dougan*

Yusef Lateef (William Evans)

b. Oct. 9, 1920, Chattanooga, TN
Sax (Tenor), Oboe, Flute / Hard Bop, Post-Bop, Modern Creative
Yusef Lateef has long had an inquisitive spirit and he was never just a bop or hard bop soloist. Lateef, who does not care much for the name "jazz," has consistently created music that has stretched (and even broke through) boundaries. A superior tenor-saxophonist with a soulful sound and impressive technique, by the 1950s he was one of the top flutists around. He also developed into the best jazz soloist to date on oboe, an occasional bassoonist and introduced such instruments as the argol (a double clarinet that resembles a bassoon), shanai (a type of oboe) and different types of flutes. Lateef played "world music" before it had a name and his output was much more creative than much of the pop and folk music that passes under that label in the 1990s. *— Scott Yanow*

● **Every Village Has a Song: The Yusef Lateef Anthology** / May 6, 1949-Apr. 4, 1973 / Rhino/Atlantic ✦✦✦✦
This good two-disc set covers Lateef's tenure at Atlantic as well as featuring formative material from early sessions for Transition, Prestige/Moodsville, Riverside, Impulse, Blue Note and Savoy. The discs show Lateef honing a thick, bluesy, expressive tenor tone in the begin-

ning, evolving into a superior straight jazz player, then expanding his repertoire and choice of instruments and contexts. His flute playing became arguably superior to his tenor, while his solos on oboe, shenai and other previously little-known instruments enabled Lateef to create arresting, fresh and ultimately significant music. While the sampler approach can't fully document his contributions, it's a solid introduction for those unfamiliar with his output. *—Ron Wynn*

Jazz Moods / 1957 / Savoy ✦✦✦✦✦

Prayer to the East / Oct. 10, 1957 / Savoy ✦✦✦✦✦

Cry!/Tender / Oct. 11, 1957-Oct. 16, 1959 / New Jazz/OJC ✦✦✦✦
This well-rounded program, reissued on CD in the OJC program, features Yusef Lateef (tripling on tenor, flute and oboe) heading a quintet also including trumpeter Lonnie Hillyer, pianist Hugh Lawson, bassist Herman Wright and drummer Frank Gant. The music alternates between straightahead pieces and more atmospheric and exotic works. An earlier track ("Ecaps") features Lateef with a different quintet that also includes flugelhornist Wilbur Harden. *—Scott Yanow*

Other Sounds / Oct. 11, 1957 / New Jazz/OJC ✦✦✦✦
These recordings are among his early African/Middle Eastern fusion efforts, with many exotic instruments. *—Myles Boisen*

The Sounds of Yusef / Oct. 11, 1957 / Prestige/OJC ✦✦✦

The Many Faces of Yusef Lateef / May 9, 1960-Jun. 23, 1961 / Milestone ✦✦✦✦
All of the music on this out-of-print double LP from 1973 has since been reissued on CD. Yusef Lateef (on tenor, oboe, flute and argol) is heard throughout in superior form. On eight numbers (including "Goin' Home," "I'm Just a Lucky So and So" and "Ma, He's Makin' Eyes at Me") he leads a quintet with cellist Ron Carter and pianist Hugh Lawson; there are also seven numbers with a nonet including two trumpets and a bassoon, and two short pieces that feature Lateef with a rhythm section, two percussionists and background singers. These often-boppish but sometimes quite adventurous performances are well worth hearing. *—Scott Yanow*

The Three Faces of Yusef Lateef / May 9, 1960 / Riverside/OJC ✦✦✦✦✦
This is one of Yusef Lateef's most accessible sessions with such famous songs as "Goin' Home," "I'm Just a Lucky So and So" and the ancient standard "Ma He's Makin' Eyes at Me." Lateef (featured on tenor, flute and oboe) is teamed up with pianist Hugh Lawson, cellist Ron Carter, bassist Herman Wright and drummer Lex Humphries for a set of stimulating music which also includes a few of Lateef's thought-provoking originals. This CD reissue is recommended as are all of his recordings from the era. *—Scott Yanow*

The Centaur and the Phoenix / Oct. 4, 1960-Oct. 6, 1960 / Riverside/OJC ✦✦✦✦
For this CD reissue of a Riverside date, the great multi-reedist Yusef Lateef (who switches between tenor, flute, oboe, and the argol) is joined on most selections by five other horns (including a bassoonist) and a rhythm section headed by pianist Joe Zawinul. The music has a lot of diversity, from stomps and ballads to Eastern-influenced explorations; two bonus cuts from the same date match Lateef with a four-piece rhythm section that includes pianist Barry Harris and two percussionists. Highlights include "Everyday I Fall in Love," "Summer Song," "Jungle Fantasy," and "The Centaur and the Phoenix." Virtually everything that Yusef Lateef recorded during this era is well worth acquiring. *—Scott Yanow*

☆ **Eastern Sounds** / Sep. 5, 1961 / Prestige/OJC ✦✦✦✦✦
Although originally issued on the Moodsville label (a subsidiary of Prestige), this classic Yusef Lateef date is not all ballads. Accompanied by pianist Barry Harris, bassist Ernie Farrow and drummer Lex Humphries, Lateef (switching between tenor, oboe and flute) is quite memorable on such pieces as the "Love Theme from *Spartacus*," "Blues for the Orient," "Don't Blame Me" and "The Plum Blossom." He has long been a true original with an active musical curiosity and this set gives listeners a strong example of his work. *—Scott Yanow*

Into Something / Dec. 29, 1961 / Prestige/OJC ✦✦✦✦✦
This superior set (which has been reissued on CD) features Yusef Lateef on some straightahead tunes including "When You're Smiling," "I'll Remember April" and "You've Changed." In addition there are some more adventurous and exotic works too, making this a well-rounded program. Lateef is joined by pianist Barry Harris, bassist Herman Wright and drummer Elvin Jones for a particularly memorable performance. *—Scott Yanow*

★ **Live at Pep's** / Jun. 29, 1964 / Impulse! ✦✦✦✦✦
This mid-'60s concert was one of Lateef's finest, as it perfectly displayed his multiple influences and interests. There were hard bop originals, covers of jazz classics like Oscar Pettiford's "Oscarlypso" (a CD bonus track) and Leonard Feather's "Twelve Tone Blues," as well as an unorthodox but effective version of Ma Rainey's "See See Rider." On "Sister Mamie," "Number 7" and drummer James Black's "The Magnolia Triangle," Lateef moved away from strict jazz, although he retained his improvisational flair. Lateef played meaty tenor sax solos, entrancing flute and bamboo flute offerings, and also had impressive stints on oboe, shenai and argol. This was a pivotal date in his career, and those unaware of it will get a treat with this disc. *—Ron Wynn*

The Man with the Big Front Yard / May 31, 1967-1976 / 32 Jazz ✦✦✦
Unlike his earlier Riverside and Impulse recordings, multi-instrumentalist Yusef Lateef's work for Atlantic was quite streaky and erratic as he tried many experimental directions, seemingly all at once. This 1998 three-CD set reissues all of the music originally on four LPs: *The Complete Yusef Lateef, Yusef Lateef's Detroit, Hush 'N' Thunder* and *The Doctor Is In... And Out.* The strongest set is the first one (from 1967), which almost sounds like an Impulse date. Lateef is heard on tenor, alto, oboe (on a beautiful version of "In the Evening") and flutes while backed by pianist Hugh Lawson, bassist Cecil McBee and drummer Roy Brooks; only the leader's closing vocal on "You're Somewhere Thinking of Me" is a bit weak. The *Detroit* album has Lateef sticking to tenor and flute, and joined by a trumpet section, an expanded rhythm section and four strings for a variety of originals and "That Lucky Old Sun." *Hush 'N' Thunder* is strongest during a Lateef/Kermit Moore tenor-cello duet on "Come Sunday" and a quartet rendition of Kenny Barron's "Sunset," but it also has a few throwaway tracks. The 1976 recording *The Doctor Is In... And Out* shoots all over the place with sound effects, odd narration and Lateef playing along with a circa-1915 record of a vocal quartet on "In a Little Spanish Town." This is an interesting reissue, recommended with reservations to Lateef fans able to find it at a budget price, but the Riversides and Impulses should be acquired first. *—Scott Yanow*

☆ **Live at Pep's, Vol. 2** / Jun. 29, 1964 / Impulse! ✦✦✦✦✦
Thankfully Impulse had the good sense to complete the entire *Live at Pep's* evening by releasing *Volume 2* in 1999. Impulse has been notoriously slow to release any of Yusef Lateef's material that he recorded for them in the 1960s onto CD (shamefully, only the two *Live at Pep's* albums were domestically available in 1999). *Volume Two* is an extension of the material that had been previously available in that it is an incredible document of a live Yusef \hard bop date and is particularly incredible in its chops and recording quality. The selections and the energy that is put into each and every song is especially moving, but shines specifically bright on "P-Bouk" and "Yusef's Mood," both showcasing Yusef's highly personal and breathy approach to the flute. If you've got *Volume One, Volume Two* is an absolute, unquestionable must-have. If you don't have *Volume One* (or any Yusef Lateef recordings for that matter), buy them both. *—Jack LV Isles*

Last Savoy Sessions / Oct. 10, 1957 Sep. 6, - 19 / Savoy Jazz ✦✦✦✦✦
These pivotal sessions for Lateef and his Detroit based groups comprise some of his most important music recorded for the Savoy label. This double CD set consists of complete albums *The Dreamer* and *The Fabric of Jazz.* (1959) and *Jazz & The Sounds of Nature* and *Prayer to the East* (1957) as well as a bonus cut. CD one is from the 1959 date, and contains some true Lateef classics like the slow swing of "Oboe Blues" and the bright, uppity waltz of "Valse Bouk."

The 1957 dates on Disc Two show Lateef and Harden more focused and together or contrary and conversational. "8540 12th St." showcases the two horns mostly listening and spontaneously responding with some unison added on this classic hard bopper, Harden's poignant one note preludes on his solo are unique as an organist might play it. The *Prayer to the East* session includes the easy blues swing of the title cut, with Lateef's flute invoking Arabic inflections. Others from *The Sounds of Nature* are the Afro-Cuban to swing-beated "Check Blues" with unusual harmonics from overblown flute or stabbing flugelhorn notes, and the 6/8 one-note bass (or rabat) foundation for "Gypsy Arab," a flute/percussion processional with gong coda. This is a welcome reissue, as it puts the final stripe on Lateef's prolific music for Savoy prior to his more commercialized outings for Atlantic proper. It's some of his more profound, definitve work and is easily worthy of a hearty and universal high recommendation, especially a must buy for those new to Lateef's musings. *—Michael G. Nastos*

Hubert Laws

b. Nov. 10, 1939, Houston, TX
Piccolo, Flute / Crossover Jazz, Jazz-Pop, Hard Bop
A talented flutist whose musical interest was never exclusively straightahead jazz, Hubert Laws exceeded Herbie Mann in popularity in the 1970s when he recorded for CTI. He was a member of the early Jazz Crusaders while in Texas (1954-60) and he also played classical music during those years. In the 1960s Laws made his first recordings as a leader (Atlantic dates from 1964-66) and gigged with Mongo Santamaria, Benny Golson, Jim Hall, James Moody and Clark Terry among many others. His CTI recordings from the first half of the 1970s made Laws famous and were a highpoint, particularly compared to his generally wretched Columbia dates from the late '70s. He was less active in the 1980s but has come back with a pair of fine Music Masters sessions in the 1990s. Hubert Laws has the ability to play anything well but he does not always seem to have the desire to perform creative jazz. *—Scott Yanow*

The Laws of Jazz / Apr. 2, 1964-Apr. 22, 1964 / Rhino ✦✦✦✦
Flutist Hubert Laws began his solo career with two little-known LPs for Atlantic, of which this was the first. Joined by pianist Armando Corea (before he became known as Chick), bassist Richard Davis and either Jimmy Cobb or Bobby Thomas on drums, Laws is in fine form during what is essentially a straight-ahead jazz set. Some of the music is a little funky, but throughout, Laws (who plays piccolo on two of the seven numbers) is in excellent form. Highlights include "Miss Thing," "Bessie's Blues" and his own "Bimbe Blue." Neither of the Atlantic sets have been reissued in full on CD yet. *—Scott Yanow*

☆ **Afro Classic** / Dec. 1970 / Columbia ✦✦✦✦✦
Hubert Laws' second effort for CTI (following the lesser-known *Crying Song*) made him into a major star in the jazz world. Performing two melodies by Bach, one by Mozart, James Taylor's "Fire and Rain," and the theme from *Love Story,* the flutist plays quite beautifully throughout this classic outing. Don Sebesky's arrangements perfectly frame Laws' flute, and the backup group (an enlarged rhythm section plus bassoonist Fred Alston, Jr.) includes guitarist Gene Bertoncini, vibraphonist Dave Friedman and keyboardist Bob James. *—Scott Yanow*

Wild Flower / Jan. 27, 1972 / Atlantic ✦✦✦✦✦
A nice date from an earlier Laws period with a harder tone and more traditional jazz direction. *—Ron Wynn*

★ **In the Beginning** / Feb. 6, 1974-Feb. 11, 1974 / CTI ✦✦✦✦✦
This double album features flutist Hubert Laws at his finest. The music ranges from classical-oriented pieces to straightahead jazz with touches of '70s funk included in the mix. The supporting cast includes keyboardist Bob James on most tracks, guitarist Gene Bertoncini, bassist Ron Carter, drummer Steve Gadd, three strings and Hubert's brother Ronnie on tenor (his solo on John Coltrane's "Moment's Notice" is arguably Ronnie's best ever on record). Whether it be works by Satie or Sonny Rollins, this recording is one of the most rewarding of Hubert Laws's career. *—Scott Yanow*

George Lewis

b. Jul. 13, 1900, New Orleans, LA, **d.** Dec. 31, 1968, New Orleans, LA
Clarinet / New Orleans Jazz
George Lewis never tried to be a virtuoso soloist. He loved to play melodic ensembles where his distinctive clarinet was free to improvise as simply as he desired. When Lewis was inspired and in tune, he could hold his own with any of his contemporaries in New Orleans and he always sounded beautiful playing his "Burgundy Street Blues." To everyone's surprise (including himself), he became one of the most popular figures of the New Orleans revival movement of the 1950s. It took Lewis a long time to achieve fame. He played with Bunk Johnson in Evan Thomas's group in the early '30s but had a day job throughout most of the decade. When Bunk was discovered in 1942, Lewis became part of his band, playing with him on and off through 1945 and getting opportunities to lead his own sessions during 1943-45. In 1950 he was portrayed in an article for *Look.* That exposure led to him recording regularly and by 1952 Lewis was in such great demand that he was soon working before crowds in California and touring Europe and Japan. He became a symbol of what was right and wrong about the New Orleans revival movement, overpraised by his fans and overcritized by his detractors. At his best he was well worth hearing. *—Scott Yanow*

☆ **Complete Blue Note Recordings** / May 15, 1943-Apr. 11, 1955 / Mosaic ✦✦✦✦✦
A centerpiece for the dedicated New Orleans collector, it begins with Lewis's "Climax" session in 1943 and ranges through a variety of studio and concert performances over a twelve-year period—definitely some of the clarinetist's best work (1943-1944, 1954-1955). *—Bruce Boyd Raeburn*

George Lewis of New Orleans / Feb. 26, 1946-Feb. 27, 1946 / Riverside ✦✦✦✦
Some great New Orleans standards appear from The Original Zenith Brass Band and The Eclipse Alley Five, featuring Lewis in good company—Isidore Barbarin (Paul's father), Peter Bocage, Jim Robinson, Baby Dodds, and others. *—Bruce Boyd Raeburn*

At Herbert Otto's Party (1949) / Nov. 23, 1949 / American Music ✦✦✦✦✦
George Lewis at his peak is captured while performing for a private party in New Orleans. There's an excellent example of "Burgundy Street Blues," his signature piece. *—Bruce Boyd Raeburn*

The Beverly Caverns Sessions / May 26, 1953-May 27, 1953 / Good Time Jazz ✦✦✦✦✦
Clarinetist George Lewis and his usual band of this period (which consisted of trumpeter Kid Howard, trombonist Jim Robinson, pianist Alton Purnell, Lawrence Marrero on banjo, bassist Slow Drag Pavageau and drummer Joe Watkins) are in better-than-average form on this well-recorded live set. Lewis and his group emphasize ensembles on the dozen New Orleans standards and the clarinetist/leader is in surprisingly extroverted form, easily the most impressive soloist. Fans of traditional jazz should go out of their way to pick up this CD. These performances were released for the first time in 1994. *—Scott Yanow*

★ **Jazz Funeral in New Orleans** / Oct. 26, 1953 / Tradition ✦✦✦✦✦
This CD brings back a classic, one of the greatest sessions ever by clarinetist George Lewis. The title of the CD is actually quite inaccurate, for "Just a Closer Walk With Thee" is the only funeral song included on the date, and there is nothing somber about any of the joyful music. Trumpeter/vocalist Kid Howard, who was often very erratic during the era (particularly on radio broadcasts), sounds in top form; the consistent trombonist Jim Robinson is an asset in the ensembles as usual, the rhythm section really drives the group, and clarinetist Lewis often seems to be quite exuberant. Their version of "When the Saints Go Marching In" is definitive, and other highlights include "Ice Cream" and "Panama." This set of prime New Orleans jazz music (last available as a DCC audiophile CD) belongs in every serious jazz collection. *—Scott Yanow*

George Lewis with Guest Artist Red Allen / Aug. 6, 1951-Sep. 25, 1953 / Riverside ✦✦✦✦✦
In 1951, clarinetist George Lewis was on the brink of gaining fame beyond his wildest dreams and becoming a symbol of the New Orleans revival movement; however, he had not yet settled on a regular trumpeter for his group. Elmer Talbert had departed, Percy Humphrey would join up later in the year, and by 1953 Lewis would finally settle on the erratic but spirited Kid Howard. Lewis tended to adjust his style depending on who was the lead horn, so his playing on this particular CD is quite interesting. Ten songs find his group sounding a bit like the Kid Ory band; this was due to the solid and occasionally exciting trumpeter Alvin Alcorn. Alcorn and Lewis made for a fine team, making one wish that they had collaborated much more in the future (there would be a 1958 Verve LP). Highlights include "Dippermouth Blues," "Long Way to Tipperary," "Big Butter and Egg Man" and "Weary Blues." However, the main reason to acquire this CD are for five performances in which the group is joined by trombonist Jim Robinson and the great trumpeter Henry "Red" Allen. Allen had worked with Lewis back in the 1920s and he was a very different player for the band. Allen's powerful solos, dominant ensemble playing and pure brilliance uplifted the whole group, and Lewis rose to the occasion. There are two versions of "St. James Infirmary" (with Allen's vocals) but the high points are the rambunctious versions of "Darktown Strutters' Ball," "Hindustan" and "Some of These Days." Trad fans will definitely want to hear the intriguing Lewis/Allen band. *—Scott Yanow*

Jazz in the Classic New Orleans Tradition / Aug. 20, 1951-Sep. 25, 1953 / Riverside/OJC ✦✦✦✦✦

Classic New Orleans Jazz, Vol. 1 / Apr. 20, 1965-Mar. 16, 1966 / Biograph ✦✦✦✦
Some of clarinetist George Lewis' finest playing of the 1960s was done outside of the confines of his regular group. On 11 of the 12 numbers included on this CD reissue (two of the tunes were previously unissued), Lewis is joined by a New Orleans group called the Mustache Stompers, which consists of trumpeter George Blood, trombonist Jay Brackett and a three-piece pianoless rhythm section; the other number is with trumpeter De De Pierce. Although none of his sidemen are that distinctive, their musicianship and enthusiasm seem to inspire Lewis to play at his best. Most of the tunes are Dixieland and New Orleans standards (such as two versions of "I Can't Give You Anything but Love," "Rosetta" and "Jazz Me Blues"), but there are also a couple of ad-lib blues and an effective jam on "Stompin' at the Savoy." Recommended. *—Scott Yanow*

John Lewis

b. May 3, 1920, La Grange, IL, **d.** Mar. 29, 2001
Piano, Composer / Third Stream, Cool, Bop
The musical director of the Modern Jazz Quartet for its entire history, John Lewis found the perfect outlet for his interest in bop, blues and Bach. Possessor of a "cool" piano style that makes every note count, Lewis with the MJQ has long helpled make jazz look respectable to the classical music community without watering down his performances. After serving in the military, Lewis was in the Dizzy Gillespie big band (1946-48). He recorded with Charlie Parker during 1947-48 and played with Miles Davis's Birth of the Cool Nonet, arranging "Move" and "Rouge." He worked with Illinois Jacquet (1948-49) and Lester Young (1950-51) and appeared on many recordings during the era. In 1951 Lewis recorded with the Milt Jackson Quartet which by 1952 became the Modern Jazz Quartet. Lewis's musical vision was fulfilled with the MJQ and he composed many pieces with "Django" being the best-known. When the MJQ broke up in 1974, Lewis worked as an educator and occasionally recorded as a leader. With the MJQ's rebirth in 1981, he has resumed his former role as its guiding spirit. *—Scott Yanow*

★ **Grand Encounter** / Feb. 10, 1956 / Pacific Jazz ✦✦✦✦✦
Also reissued as *2 Degrees East, 3 Degrees West* and occasionally listed under tenor saxophonist Bill Perkins' name, this classic session is the ultimate in cool jazz. Perkins' mellow tone matches quite well with the quiet but inwardly passionate playing of pianist John Lewis, guitarist Jim Hall, bassist Percy Heath, and drummer Chico Hamilton. Lewis is featured with the rhythm section on "I Can't Get Started," Hall is added for "Skylark," and the full group plays three standards plus Lewis' memorable (and atmospheric) "2 Degrees East, 3 Degrees West." *—Scott Yanow*

Afternoon in Paris / Dec. 4, 1956-Dec. 7, 1956 / Koch Jazz ✦✦✦✦
It was in Paris that John Lewis co-led this 1956 date with Sacha Distel, a French guitarist who never became well-known in the U.S. but commanded a lot of respect in French jazz circles. The same can be said about the other French players employed on *Afternoon in Paris*?neither tenor saxophonist Barney Wilen nor bassist Pierre Michelot were huge names in the U.S., although both were well-known in European jazz circles. With Lewis on piano, Distel on guitar, Wilen on tenor, Michelot or Percy Heath on bass, and Kenny Clarke or Connie Kay on drums, the part-American, part-French group of improvisers provides an above-average bop album that ranges from "Willow Weep for Me," "All The Things You Are," and "I Cover the Waterfront" to Milt Jackson's "Bags' Groove" and Lewis' title song. The big-toned Wilen was only 19 when *Afternoon in Paris* was recorded, but as his lyrical yet hard-swinging solos demonstrate, he matured quickly as a saxman. It should be noted that all of the Americans on this album had been members of the Modern Jazz Quartet; the only MJQ member who isn't on board is vibist Jackson. Originally released by Atlantic, *Afternoon in Paris* was finally reissued on CD in 1999 after being out of print for many years. *—Alex Henderson*

Wonderful World of Jazz / Jul. 29, 1960-Sep. 9, 1960 / Atlantic ✦✦✦✦✦
This is one of pianist John Lewis' most rewarding albums outside of his work with the Modern Jazz Quartet. Three numbers (including a remake of "Two Degrees East, Three Degrees West") showcase his piano in a quartet with guitarist Jim Hall, bassist Geroge Duvivier and drummer Connie Kay. A 15-minute rendition of "Body and Soul" has one of tenor saxophonist Paul Gonsalves' finest solos while "Afternoon in Paris" features a diverse cast with trumpeter Herb Pomeroy, Gunther Schuller on French horn, tenorman Benny Golson, baritonist Jimmy Giuffre and guitarist Jim Hall; altoist Eric Dolphy cuts everyone. This set was reissued in 1988 as part of Atlantic's *Jazzlore* series. *—Scott Yanow*

John Lewis Presents Jazz Abstractions / Dec. 19, 1960-Dec. 20, 1960 / Atlantic ✦✦✦✦
Although John Lewis is listed as the leader (this album's alternate title is "John Lewis Presents Contemporary Music"), the pianist does not actually appear on this record and only contributed one piece ("Django"). On what is very much a Gunther Schuller project, Schuller composed "Abstraction" and was responsible for the adventurous three-part "Variants on a Theme of John Lewis (Django)" and the four-part "Variants on a Theme of Thelonious Monk (Criss-Cross)"; Jim Hall contributed "Piece for Guitar & Strings." One of the most successful third stream efforts, this LP combines avant-garde jazz with aspects of classical music. Among the more notable stars, altoist Ornette Coleman is on "Abstraction" and "Criss Cross" (both of which have been reissued in his Rhino CD box) and multi-instrumentalist Eric Dolphy is on both of the "Variants." Other musicians in the eclectic cast include guitarist Hall, bassist Scott LaFaro, pianist Bill Evans, and several classical string players. This is very interesting music. *—Scott Yanow*

Evolution / Jan. 12, 1999-Jan. 15, 1999 / Atlantic ✦✦✦✦
John Lewis, a founding member of the Modern Jazz Quartet (and architect, with Gunther Schuller, of the "Third Stream" movement that attempted a fusion of classical music and jazz), has always been known for the delicacy and refinement of his playing and for the quality of his compositions. This solo album will only add to his reputation in both regards. That he's able to make "Sweet Georgia Brown" sound like a recital piece is testament to his sophistication (and perhaps his sense of humor); that his own "Two Degrees East, Three Degrees West" manages to evoke New Orleans and Ravel simultaneously speaks to the depth of his musicianship. "Django," perhaps Lewis' most famous composition, is given a stop-action tango treatment here, and his "At the Horse Show" is as graceful as a colt. However, Lewis' voice is far too well-miked, which means he mutters and grunts in the left channel throughout the proceedings. Recommended nevertheless. *—Rick Anderson*

Meade "Lux" Lewis (Meade Anderson Lewis)

b. Sep. 4, 1905, Chicago, IL, **d.** Jun. 7, 1964, Minneapolis, MN
Piano / Boogie-Woogie, Piano Blues
One of the three great boogie-woogie pianists (along with Albert Ammons and Pete Johnson) whose appearance at John Hammond's 1938 *Spirituals to Swing* concert helped start the boogie-woogie craze, Meade Lux Lewis was a powerful if somewhat limited player. He

played regularly in Chicago in the late '20s and his one solo record of the time "Honky Tonk Train Blues" (1927) was considered a classic. However, other than a few sides backing little-known blues singers, Lewis gained little extra work and slipped into obscurity. John Hammond heard Lewis's record in 1935 and after a search found Lewis washing cars for a living in Chicago. Soon Meade Lux Lewis was back on records and after the 1938 concert he was able to work steadily, sometimes in duets or trios with Ammons and Johnson. He became the first jazz pianist to double on celeste (starting in 1936) and was featured on that instrument in a Blue Note quartet date with Edmond Hall and Charlie Christian; he also played harpsichord on a few records in 1941. After the boogie-woogie craze ended, Lewis continued working in Chicago and California, recording as late as 1962 although by then he was pretty much forgotten. Meade Lux Lewis led sessions through the years that have come out on MCA, Victor, Blue Note, Solo Art, Euphonic, Stinson, Atlantic, Storyville, Verve, Tops, ABC-Paramount, Riverside and Philips. *—Scott Yanow*

☆ **The Complete Blue Note Recordings** / Jan. 6, 1939-Aug. 22, 1944 / Mosaic ✦✦✦✦✦
Mosaic's *Complete Blue Note Recordings* contains all of the recordings Meade Lux Lewis made for the label between 1939 and 1944, making it the definitive statement on the influential boogie-woogie pianist. *—Leo Stanley*

Tidal Boogie / 1954 / Tradition ✦✦✦✦✦
The running time on these ten tracks, recorded in 1954 by Lewis with bassist Red Callendar and an unknown electric guitarist, is a paltry 27 minutes, but they're 27 delightful minutes. Lewis' work is captured in between his 1952 Atlantic sessions and his 1957 Verve recordings, playing an easy, rollicking set that includes "Basin Street Blues," "Darktown Strutters Ball," "Birth of the Blues," and the title track. Ironically, the unnamed guitarist almost dominates "Birth of the Blues" and "Tidal Boogie," and it's a shame his name hasn't been preserved or recorded, but Lewis gets to shine on this number as well. The audio restoration by Seth Winner puts the piano practically against the ear of the listener, so that one can actually feel the action of the keys, and the bass and guitar are a match. *—Bruce Eder*

● **The Blues Piano Artistry of Meade Lux Lewis** / Nov. 1, 1961 / Riverside/OJC ✦✦✦✦✦
Boogie-woogie pianist Meade Lux Lewis's next-to-last record was his first recording in five years and his final opportunity to stretch out unaccompanied. This solo Riverside set (reissued by OJC on CD) as usual finds Lewis generally sticking to the blues (with "You Were Meant for Me" and "Fate" being exceptions), mostly performing originals. On a few of the songs Lewis switches effectively to celeste. It apparently only took Meade Lux Lewis two hours to record the full set and the results are quite spontaneous yet well organized, a fine all-around portrait of the veteran pianist in his later period. *—Scott Yanow*

Ramsey Lewis (Ramsey Emmanuel Lewis, Jr.)

b. May 27, 1935, Chicago, IL
Keyboards, Piano / Pop-Soul, Northern Soul, Crossover Jazz, Jazz-Pop, Soul-Jazz
Ramsey Lewis has long straddled the boundary between bop-oriented jazz and pop music. Most of his recordings (particularly by the mid-'60s) were very accessible and attracted a large nonjazz audience. In 1956 he formed a trio with bassist Eldee Young and drummer Red Holt. From the start (1958) their records for Argo/Cadet were popular although in the early days they had a strong jazz content. In 1958 Lewis also recorded with Max Roach and Lem Winchester. On the 1965 albums *The In Crowd* and *Hang On*, Ramsey made the pianist into a major attraction and from that point on his records became much more predictable and pop-oriented. In 1966 his trio's personnel changed with bassist Cleveland Eaton and drummer Maurice White (later the founder of Earth, Wind and Fire) joining Lewis. In the 1970s Lewis often played electric piano although by later in the decade he was sticking to acoustic and hiring an additional keyboardist. He can still play melodic jazz when he wants to but Ramsey Lewis has mostly stuck to easy-listening pop music during the past 30 years. *—Scott Yanow*

Consider the Source / 1956-Apr. 1959 / Chess ✦✦✦✦
Long before he became a crossover star, Ramsey Lewis essentially played straight-ahead jazz. On this Chess reissue CD, 17 selections are taken from three former LPs dating from 1956-1959. Although one wishes that all of the music had been reissued complete on two CDs, this set with bassist Eldee Young and drummer Red Holt does give one a definitive look at Lewis in his early days. The pianist had a bluish and soulful yet swinging style, and among the highlights of the CD are "I'll Remember April," a memorable rendition of "Delilah," "Please Send Me Someone to Love," and "On the Street Where You Live." *—Scott Yanow*

Down to Earth / Nov. 6, 1958-Dec. 4, 1958 / Verve ✦✦✦✦
The Ramsey Lewis Trio were popular from the start, cutting four albums of material during 1958, only two years after Lewis began teaming up with bassist Eldee Young and drummer Red Holt. This recording (one of very few by the group in its early days that were not made for Argo or Cadet) has the trio emphasizing folk songs and traditional melodies such as "Dark Eyes," "Come Back to Sorrento," "John Henry," and "Billy Boy." Their concise interpretations (only two songs are longer than 3:15) feature swinging solos by Lewis and respect for the melodies. The music (if not essential) is quite accessible while still being jazz oriented. Worth picking up. *—Scott Yanow*

● **The In Crowd** / May 13, 1965-May 15, 1965 / Chess ✦✦✦✦✦
This is the record that put the legendary Ramsey Lewis on the map. Lewis is known as an incredible stylist on piano, comfortably adapting almost any kind of music into his own jazz fusion vision. Film scores, pop, light classical hall fit comfortably into his music, and this album is an excellent example of his vision. But, it's not only Lewis alone. His absolutely fabulous rhythm section of Red Holt (drums) and Eldee Young on (bass/cello) frame all of Ramsey's performances with funk and grace and a superior forward momentum. Aside from the groovin' hit "The in Crowd," the album contains fantastic readings of Duke Ellington's "Come Sunday" and the "Love Theme From Spartacus." This album is one of the places where Afro and funk-jazz started, and aside from it's historical significance, it's a stone groove. *—Matthew Greenwald*

Wade in the Water / May 23, 1966-Jun. 29, 1966 / Jazz Time ✦✦✦✦✦
With Cleveland Eaton II (bass) and Maurice White (drums) replacing Eldee Young and Red Holt in the trio, Ramsey Lewis alters course just a bit from his handclapping soul-jazz idiom that was so popular at the time. The two new sidemen are relegated more to the background, and some punchy big band charts by Chicago's Richard Evans share the spotlight with Lewis' gospel/blues-drenched piano. Nevertheless, the old swinging fervor is left intact this time, as Lewis and company purvey a set of ten pop hits with a few others worked in. They even got a large-scale hit (No. 19 on the pop charts) out of the old gospel tune "Wade in the Water" (the photo of the tall, pretty model doing so on the cover might have struck some as being sacrilegious). The best cut of the bunch is the hard-swinging, down-home treatment of the Stevie Wonder hit "Up Tight" that got almost as much airplay as the title track. Like "The 'In' Crowd," this record evokes its era indelibly. *—Richard S. Ginell*

Maiden Voyage / Apr. 1968-Dec. 1968 / Chess ✦✦✦

Sun Goddess / 1974 / Columbia ✦✦✦✦

We Meet Again / 1988-1989 / Columbia ✦✦✦✦

Dance of Your Soul / 1997 / GRP ✦✦✦

In Person: 1960-1967 / Apr. 30, 1960-Jul. 1967 / GRP ✦✦✦✦✦
Ramsey Lewis' 1965 hit "The 'In' Crowd" made him a major name in the pop world and resulted in some similar live sets that featured audience participation, singing and rhythmic handclapping. Actually, Lewis had had previous success in the pop/jazz world, and two of the five live albums that were skimmed for this 1998 two-CD set (none of the dates are reissued completely) predate "The 'In' Crowd." Lewis is teamed with bassist Eldee Young and drummer Red Holt for the first four dates; they are replaced by bassist Cleveland Eaton and drummer Maurice White on the last session. The music is taken from *The Ramsey Lewis Trio In Chicago, At the Bohemian Caverns, The 'In' Crowd, Hang On Ramsey* and *Dancing In the Street*, all originally Argo or Cadet LPs. Highlights include "Ole Devil Moon," "Carmen," "My Babe," "The 'In' Crowd," "Hang On Sloopy" and a "Black Orpheus Medley." A fine sampling of 1960s Ramsey Lewis. *—Scott Yanow*

Appassionata / May 13, 1999-Jul. 5, 1999 / Narada ✦✦✦✦
Milwaukee-based Narada Records has long been a powerhouse source of new age and global music, but the millennium also brought a commitment to solid jazz recordings, both straight-ahead and smooth. Who better to start both types with than Ramsey Lewis, who goes the funky, smooth route on his *Urban Knights III* project and returns to his trio roots on this multi-faceted overview of all of the musical loves of his life— Swinging both high and low with Chicago-based bassist Larry Gray and drummer Ernie Adams, Lewis brings the titular passion to tunes inspired by or taken from opera, classical, jazz, and gospel. The connecting thread is that all of the covers are of songs that Lewis played during his formative adolescent years when he was first discovering his voice on the piano. The key to his successful delivery is altering the mood, sometimes jarringly, within the context of a lengthy, slow-building thematic piece. "Pavane" begins with a cool, seductive trio invitation before Gray's bass starts throbbing and Lewis switches gear from lighthearted melodicism to hard-hitting percussive pounding. Anyone who has ever doubted that jazz and classical music have something in common should take a listen to "For the Love of Art," where Lewis blends the intense yet eloquent fingering of classical with some out-there improvisational sections. Gray also creates a great deal of melancholy drama by taking the bow to his bass (like a cello) on the opening section of the Pavarotti favorite "Nessun Dorma" and later on the punchier "Vesti La Giubba." The immensely ambitious project concludes with one of the simplest arrangements, a playful gospel/blues trio jam called "A Moment Spiritual." *—Jonathan Widran*

The Lighthouse All-Stars

f. 1949, Hermosa Beach, CA, **db.** 1962
Group / West Coast Jazz, Cool, Bop
Bassist Howard Rumsey initiated a jazz policy at the Lighthouse Cafe in Hermosa Beach, CA, in 1949. His Lighthouse All-Stars performed on a nightly basis and on Sundays there was traditionally a 12-hour jam session. The Contemporary label recorded Rumsey's groups on a fairly regular basis during 1952-57 and such major players as Shorty Rogers, Maynard Ferguson, Rolf Ericson, Stu Williamson, Conte Candoli, Milt Bernhart, Bob Enevoldsen, Frank Rosolino, Jimmy Giuffre, Bob Cooper, Bud Shank, Hampton Hawes, Marty Paich, Claude Williamson, Sonny Clark, Shelly Manne, Max Roach, Stan Levey and guests Miles Davis and Chet Baker were among the participants. The music was essentially bebop with some cooler-toned performances, particularly the ones starring Cooper on oboe or English horn and Shank on flute. The Lighthouse All-Stars only made one record after 1957 (an outing for Philips during 1961-62) before passing into history. In the 1980s the group was revived for some appearances and further Contemporary recordings; the last version featured Shorty Rogers, Cooper (after Coop's death Jack Nimitz took his place), Shank, Bill Perkins, Pete Jolly, Monty Budwig and Larance Marable. *—Scott Yanow*

● **Jazz Invention** / Feb. 12, 1989 / Contemporary ✦✦✦✦✦
To celebrate the 40th anniversary of the first music played at the legendary club the Lighthouse, the Lighthouse All-Stars were reunited for a special concert. Some of the personnel was a little different than in the old days. Howard Rumsey no longer played bass and both trombonist Frank Rosolino and drummer Shelly Manne were no longer around but the group was still filled with plenty of great talent: Tenorman Bob Cooper, altoist Bud Shank, trumpeter Conte Candoli, valve trombonist Bob Enevoldsen, pianist Claude Williamson, bassist Monty Budwig and drummer John Guerin. Together they perform eight songs from the period with spirit and creativity within the genre of cool jazz. As a result of this successful reunion, Shorty Rogers would be heading the group for the next few years. *—Scott Yanow*

Eight Brothers / Jan. 13, 1992-Jan. 14, 1992 / Candid ✦✦✦✦
The 1992 Lighthouse All-Stars, a reunion group of 1950s Los Angeles veterans, consisted of

flugelhornist Shorty Rogers, trumpeter Conte Candoli, altoist Bud Shank, tenor saxophonist Bob Cooper, Bill Perkins on baritone, tenor and soprano, pianist Pete Jolly, bassist Monty Budwig and drummer Larance Marable. Budwig passed away from cancer just a couple months after this recording, which may have been the last of his very productive career. Although one thinks of the Lighthouse All-Stars as being a cool jazz group, the music on their Candid date—eight then-new Rogers compositions and one apiece from Shank and Cooper along with a reworking of "Battle Hymn of the Republic"—is actually more in the hard bop and even post-bop vein. The CD is billed as being co-led by Shorty Rogers and Bud Shank—Rogers because of the writing and Shank since he had emerged into the band's most prominent soloist. All of the veteran musicians play up to par, and the results are quite enjoyable, even if none of the new songs became standards. *—Scott Yanow*

Abbey Lincoln (Anna Marie Wooldridge)

b. Aug. 6, 1930, Chicago, IL
Vocals / Avant-Garde Jazz, Vocal Jazz, Standards, Post-Bop
As with her hero Billie Holiday, Abbey Lincoln always means the lyrics she sings. A dramatic performer whose interpretations are full of truth and insight, Lincoln actually began her career as a fairly lightweight supper-club singer. Her first of three albums for Riverside (1957-59) had Max Roach on drums and he was a major influence on her; she began to be choosy about the songs she sang and to give words the proper emotional intensity. Lincoln held her own on her early dates with such sidemen as Kenny Dorham, Sonny Rollins, Wynton Kelly, Curtis Fuller and Benny Golson. Lincoln's Candid date *Straight Ahead* (1961) had among its players Roach, Booker Little, Eric Dolphy and Coleman Hawkins and she made some important appearances on Roach's Impulse album *Percussion Bitter Suite.* Lincoln and Roach were married in 1962, an association that lasted until 1970. They worked together for a while but Lincoln (who found it harder to get work in jazz due to the political nature of some of her music) became involved in acting and did not record as a leader during 1962-72. She finally recorded for Inner City in 1973 and gradually became more active in jazz. *—Scott Yanow*

That's Him / Oct. 28, 1957 / Riverside/OJC ♦♦♦♦
This CD reissue brings back singer Abbey Lincoln's second recording and first for Riverside, adding alternate takes of "I Must Have That Man" and "Porgy" to the original LP program. Lincoln is accompanied by quite an all-star roster (tenor saxophonist Sonny Rollins, trumpeter Kenny Dorham, pianist Wynton Kelly, bassist Paul Chambers and drummer Max Roach) and, even this early, she was already a major jazz singer with a style of her own. Abbey Lincoln was careful from this point on to only interpret lyrics that she believed in. Her repertoire has a few superior standards (including several songs such as "I Must Have That Man" and "Don't Explain" that are closely associated with Billie Holiday) plus Oscar Brown Jr.'s "Strong Man" and "Tender as a Rose"; she takes the latter unaccompanied. "Don't Explain" is slightly unusual in that Paul Chambers is absent and Wynton Kelly makes an extremely rare appearance on bass. All three of Abbey Lincoln's Riverside albums (each of which have been reissued in the OJC series) are well worth several listens. *—Scott Yanow*

It's Magic / Aug. 23, 1958 / Riverside/OJC ♦♦♦♦♦
Because Abbey Lincoln has always been careful to sing songs that have a deep meaning for her, all of her recordings through the years are memorable in their own way; there are no duds in her discography. Her second Riverside session (and her third recording) has been reissued on this CD in the Original Jazz Classics series. The backup musicians are among the best in jazz at the time (Kenny Dorham or Art Farmer on trumpet, trombonist Curtis Fuller, Benny Golson on tenor, Jerome Richardson or Sahib Shihab on reeds, pianist Wynton Kelly, Paul Chambers or Sam Jones on bass and drummer Philly Joe Jones) and they have opportunities to play short solos. Lincoln is heard at her early best on such numbers as "I Am in Love," "An Occasional Man," "Out of the Past" and Randy Weston's "Little Niles." Recommended. *—Scott Yanow*

Abbey Is Blue / Mar. 25, 1959-Mar. 26, 1959 / Riverside/OJC ♦♦♦♦♦
Abbey Lincoln's third of three Riverside albums (all of these recommended sets have been reissued on CD) directly precedes her more adventurous work with drummer (and then-husband) Max Roach. With fine backup from trumpeter Kenny Dorham, pianist Wynton Kelly, Les Spann (doubling on guitar and flute), bassist Sam Jones and drummer Philly Joe Jones) on seven of the ten numbers and by Roach's regular quintet of the time on the other three selections, Abbey Lincoln is quite emotional and distinctive during a particularly strong set. Highlights include the first vocal version ever of "Afro-Blue," "Come Sunday," Oscar Brown Jr.'s "Brother, Where Are You," "Softly, As in a Morning Sunrise," "Long as You're Living" and Lincoln's own "Let Up." A very memorable set. *— Scott Yanow*

☆ **Freedom Now Suite** / Aug. 31, 1960-Sep. 6, 1960 / Candid ♦♦♦♦♦
Definitive social protest and jazz. Lincoln and her then-husband Max Roach were a great team. *—Ron Wynn*

★ **Straight Ahead** / Feb. 22, 1961 / Barnaby ♦♦♦♦♦
Reissued several times since it originally came out on a Candid LP, this is one of Abbey Lincoln's greatest recordings. It is a testament to the credibility of her very honest music (and her talents) that Lincoln's sidemen on this date include the immortal tenor saxophonist Coleman Hawkins (who takes a memorable solo on "Blue Monk"), Eric Dolphy on flute and alto, trumpeter Booker Little (whose melancholy tone is very important in the ensembles), pianist Mal Waldron, and drummer Max Roach. Highpoints include "When Malindy Sings," "Blue Monk," Billie Holiday's "Left Alone," and "African Lady." *—Scott Yanow*

People in Me / Jun. 23, 1973-Jun. 27, 1973 / Polygram ♦♦♦♦
The music on this out-of-print LP from the defunct Inner City label was recorded in Japan and has been released by several other record companies since. Abbey Lincoln's first record in a decade, the set features the very original singer joined by a couple of Japanese players (pianist Hiromasa Suzuki and bassist Kunimitsu Inaba) plus drummer Al Foster, percussionist Mtume and the horns (soprano, tenor and flute) of Dave Liebman. Abbey Lincoln wrote or co-composed all eight selections, best-known of which is "People in Me." Every Abbey Lincoln recording is well worth picking up for her sincerity, credibility and talent make each of her dates memorable in their own way. *—Scott Yanow*

Abbey Sings Billie, Vol. 1 / Nov. 6, 1987-Nov. 7, 1987 / Enja ♦♦♦♦♦
Abbey Lincoln's idol has always been Billie Holiday. Although she has never really copied Lady Day and she has long had her own style and sound, the feeling and intensity that Lincoln gives the lyrics she interprets is reminiscent of late-period Holiday. A perfect person to pay tribute to Billie Holiday, Lincoln (on the first of two Enja CDs) is joined by the underrated tenor Harold Vick (who would pass away unexpectedly within a short time after this recording), pianist James Weidman, bassist Tarik Shaha and drummer Mark Johnson for fresh renditions of standards. Mal Waldron's "Soul Eyes" is taken as an instrumental feature for Vick and other highlights include "What a Little Moonlight Can Do," "Strange Fruit," an emotional "I'll Be Seeing You" and a song perfectly suited for Abbey Lincoln's voice: "Crazy He Calls Me." One of the singer's best recordings of the 1980s and a fine complement to the equally rewarding *Vol. 2. —Scott Yanow*

Abbey Sings Billie, Vol. 2 / Nov. 6, 1987-Nov. 7, 1987 / Enja ♦♦♦♦♦
Abbey Lincoln is the perfect person to pay tribute to Billie Holiday. She knew Lady Day during her last years and, like Holiday, Lincoln has always lived the words she sings and chosen to only intepret lyrics that have great meaning to her. Her expressive powers have been quite strong throughout her career and there are plenty of dramatic moments on this disc along with its first volume. Tenor-saxophonist Harold Vick, who would die suddenly within days of these sessions, is quite effective as is the supportive rhythm section. Abbey Lincoln shows off her versatility on such diverse numbers as "Gimme a Pigfoot," "Don't Explain" and "Please Don't Talk About Me When I'm Gone." *—Scott Yanow*

The World Is Falling Down / Feb. 21, 1990-Feb. 27, 1990 / Verve ♦♦♦♦♦
Abbey Lincoln's first in a series of impressive recordings for Verve matches her unique voice and very credible style with flugelhornist Clark Terry, the altos of Jackie McLean and Jerry Dodgion, bassist Charlie Haden, drummer Billy Higgins and French pianist Alain Jean-Marie. McLean has all of the alto solos and most of the instrumental arrangements were contributed by Ron Carter. Lincoln has always been expert at picking out superior material to record and all eight numbers on this CD are memorable in their own way, particularly Haden's classic "First Song," a French version of "How High the Moon," "Hi Fly," Michel Legrand's "You Must Believe in Spring" and Lincoln's two originals "The World Is Falling Down" and "I Got Thunder." *—Scott Yanow*

When There is Love / Oct. 4, 1992-Oct. 6, 1992 / Verve ♦♦♦♦
This CD is a change of pace for Abbey Lincoln. She interprets ten standards (plus four of her originals), all love songs performed as duets with pianist Hank Jones. Although there is some social comentary, the emphasis is on male-female relationships and Lincoln sounds more optimistic than usual. Among the more memorable selections are Duke Ellington's "Black Butterfly," "The Nearness of You," "You Came a Long Way from St. Louis," Fats Waller's "Jitterbug Waltz" and "You Won't Forget Me." *—Scott Yanow*

Over the Years / Mar. 18, 2000-Apr. 23, 2000 / Verve ♦♦♦♦
Recorded mostly in New York, *Over the Years* is aimed at summing up Abbey Lincoln's long career. Joining her are excellent, but not so well-known performers, plus the giant sax player Joe Lovano. But it is Lincoln's special interpretative powers that carry the day, as one would expect. The play list is rather unusual even for an iconoclast like Lincoln. There are tunes from the 1940s, traditional material, some romantic standards, and her own compositions. "Lucky to Be Me," from the musical On the Town, features some ear-catching work by the rhythm section of Brandon McCune, John Ormond, and Jaz Sawyer. Another fine track is the traditional "Blackberry Blossoms" to which Lincoln has added her own lyrics. She is ably supported on this cut by guest tenor player Joe Lovano and guest guitarist Kendra Shank, who is also a singer of note. The album's coda is appropriate as Lincoln sings "Tender As a Rose" a cappella, letting her vocal chords stand on their own without benefit of instrumental accompaniment as she ends it with "as that's the way the story goes." *—Dave Nathan*

Booker Little

b. Apr. 2, 1938, Memphis, TN, **d.** Oct. 5, 1961, New York, NY
Trumpet / Avant-Garde Jazz, Post-Bop
The first trumpeter emerging after Clifford Brown's death to gain his own sound, Booker Little had a tremendous amount of potential before his premature death. He began on trumpet when he was 12 and played with Johnny Griffin and the MJT -+3 while attending Chicago Conservatory. Little was with Max Roach (1958-59) and then freelanced in New York. He recorded with Roach and Abbey Lincoln, was on John Coltrane's *Africa/Brass* album and was well-documented during a July 1961 gig at the Five Spot with Eric Dolphy. Little had a memorable melancholy sound and his interval jumps looked towards the avant-garde but he also swung like a hard bopper. Booker Little led four sessions (one album apiece for United Artists, Time, Candid and Bethlehem) but died of uremia at the age of 23, a particularly tragic loss. *—Scott Yanow*

Booker Little 4 and Max Roach / Oct. 1958 / Blue Note ♦♦♦♦♦
This CD reissue features trumpeter Booker Little at the beginning of his tragically brief career. The first six selections find the distinctive soloist playing with a quintet also including the young tenor George Coleman, pianist Tommy Flanagan, bassist Art Davis and drummer Max Roach (who was his regular employer at the time). Little contributed three now-obscure originals and also plays two standards and an early version of Miles Davis' "Milestones." The remainder of the CD has lengthy versions of "Things Ain't What They Used to Be" and "Blue 'N Boogie" from a jam session that matched Little with fellow Memphis-based players including Coleman, altoist Frank Strozier, and the masterful pianist Phineas Newborn. Overall this forward-looking hard bop set is easily recommended. *—Scott Yanow*

☆ **Out Front** / Mar. 17, 1961-Apr. 4, 1961 / Candid ♦♦♦♦♦
Booker Little was the first trumpet soloist to emerge in jazz after the death of Clifford Brown to have his own sound. His tragically brief life (he died at age 23 later in 1961) cut short what

would have certainly been a major career. Little, on this sextet date with multi-reedist Eric Dolphy, trombonist Julian Priester, and drummer Max Roach, shows that his playing was really beyond bebop. His seven now-obscure originals (several of which deserve to be revived) are challenging for the soloists and there are many strong moments during these consistently challenging and satisfying performances. *—Scott Yanow*

Booker Little and Friend / Aug. 1961-Sep. 1961 / Bethlehem Archives/Avenue Jazz ✦✦✦✦✦
A CD reissue of trumpeter Booker Little's *Victory and Sorrow* album for Bethlehem, this release adds two previously unheard alternate takes of "Matilde" to the original program. Little's final recording before he died of uremia at the age of 23, the sextet session also features fine playing by trombonist Julian Priester, tenor saxophonist George Coleman, pianist Don Friedman, bassist Reggie Workman, and drummer Pete LaRoca. However, Booker Little is generally the top soloist on the harmonically advanced hard bop date and he is in peak form throughout although he would pass away on October 5 of that year. Of his six originals, "Molotone Music" and "Victory and Sorrow" are most memorable even if Little's beautiful playing on a quartet version of the date's one standard, "If I Should Lose You," is actually the highpoint. *—Scott Yanow*

★ **Victory and Sorrow** / Aug. 1961-Sep. 1961 / Affinity ✦✦✦✦✦
Although he only lived to be 23 and recorded for just a little over three years, Booker Little proved to be one of the top young trumpeters of his era. *Victory and Sorrow* was his fourth and final recording as a leader. Little's melancholy tone is heartbreaking on the date's lone standard "If I Should Lose You" and he contributed all of the other six selections. With fine playing from tenor-saxophonist George Coleman, trombonist Julian Priester, pianist Don Friedman, bassist Reggie Workman and drummer Pete LaRoca, this advanced session has many touching and hard-swinging moments. *—Scott Yanow*

Sounds of the Inner City / Jan. 25, 2000 / Collectables ✦✦✦
Two masters of hard bop, trumpeter Booker Little and tenor saxophonist Booker Ervin, square off on this 1960 session reissued by Collectables as *Sounds of the Inner City*. This date has been released under various titles over the years since its original inception as *Teddy Charles New Directions quartet featuring Booker Little and Booker Ervin*. Most of the material is straight-ahead bop under the leadership of vibraphonist Teddy Charles with Mal Waldron on piano, Addison Farmer on bass, and Ed Shauhnesssy on drums. This is a noteworthy reissue considering that there are so few instances of Little's lyrical trumpet style and Ervin's passionate tenor recorded together. Original compositions include Ervins's [illegible]oochie," Little's "The Confined Few" and "Witch Fire," Shauhnessy's "Blues de Tambour," [illegible]mad Jamal's "Cycles," plus the standard "Stardust" (receiving an especially melan- [illegible] The only complaint is the lack of liner notes, which excludes information on person[illegible]ion history. *—Al Campbell*

Charles Lloyd

b. Mar. 15, 1938, Memphis, TN
Sax (Tenor), Flute / Avant-Garde Jazz, Hard Bop
During 1966-69 Charles Lloyd led one of the most popular groups in jazz, a unit that played at the rock palace Fillmore West in San Francisco and toured the U.S.S.R. Lloyd's music, although generally a bit melodic, was not watered-down and managed to catch on for several years during a time when jazz was at its low point in popularity. In 1961 he joined the Chico Hamilton Quintet on flute and tenor, making his recording debut and gaining a strong reputation. During 1964-65 he was with the Cannonball Adderley Sextet and then in mid-1965 formed his own group. By 1966 the Charles Lloyd Quartet included Keith Jarrett, Cecil McBee and Jack DeJohnette, and the band was the hit of the 1966 Monterey Jazz Festival, recorded steadily, toured Europe six times and was remarkably popular. Lloyd, whose most famous composition is "Forest Flower," played tenor in a soft-toned version of John Coltrane while his lyrical flute playing is more original. *—Scott Yanow*

● **Forest Flower** / Sep. 8, 1966-Sep. 18, 1966 / Rhino ✦✦✦✦✦
This classic album is dominated by the Charles Lloyd Quartet's historic appearance at the 1966 Monterey Jazz Festival. In addition to "East of the Sun," Lloyd (on tenor and flute), pianist Keith Jarrett, bassist Cecil McBee and drummer Jack DeJohnette performed the 17Ω-minute, two-part "Forest Flower," which was the hit of the festival and helped make the group a sensation. Also included on this album are renditions of Jarrett's "Sorcery" and McBee's "Song of Her" that were recorded ten days earlier. This record, one of the high points of Charles Lloyd's career, should be much more widely available. *—Scott Yanow*

Charles Lloyd in Europe / Oct. 29, 1966 / Atlantic ✦✦✦

Notes from Big Sur / Nov. 1991 / ECM ✦✦✦✦

The Call / Jul. 1993 / ECM ✦✦✦✦

All My Relations / Jul. 1994 / ECM ✦✦✦✦✦
This CD by the Charles Lloyd Quartet avoids fitting into any of the stereotypes that one might have about ECM's recordings. Pianist Bobo Stenson has carved his own identity out of the styles of Bill Evans and Keith Jarrett, drummer Billy Hart is stimulating in support and Anders Jormin provides a walking bass on many of the tracks; a rarity for ECM sessions. As one might expect, the main focus is on Charles Lloyd whose playing during the past decade has been some of the finest of his career. He mostly sticks to tenor (just playing flute on "Little Peace" and Chinese oboe on the very brief "Milarepa"), and although traces of John Coltrane's sound will always be in his tone, Lloyd comes up with quite a few original ideas. He is best on "Thelonious Theonlyus" (which has a slight calypso feel to it), the episodic "Cape to Cairo Suite" (a tribute to Nelson Mandela), a long tenor/drums duet on "All My Relations" (which is a mix between "Chasin' the 'Trane" and "Bessie's Blues") and the brooding spiritual "Hymne to the Mother." A strong effort. *—Scott Yanow*

Canto / Dec. 1996 / ECM ✦✦✦✦✦
Although he has not had as high a profile in the 1990s as he did in the mid- to late '60s, when he was one of the best-known musicians in jazz, Charles Lloyd spent the decade playing at the peak of his powers. His underrated series of recordings for ECM has resulted in quite a few gems, including this 1997 release. Traces of John Coltrane will always be a part of Lloyd's sound, and a few of the selections on the date recall Trane-associated pieces ("How Can I Tell You" is not dissimilar to "I Want to Talk About You," and "Desolation Sound" recalls "Soul Eyes" a bit). However, Lloyd does sound pretty original most of the time, adding his own brand of spirituality to "Durga Durga," playing the Tibetan oboe on the atmospheric "Nachiketa's Lament" and emphasizing Arabic-sounding scales on the intriguing and well-constructed "Tales of Rumi," which at 16:40 is both the longest and the most memorable performance of the set. Led by Lloyd's longtime pianist Bobo Stenson and also including bassist Anders Jormin and drummer Billy Hart, the rhythm section is both sensitive and alert, fiery when called for and very aware of where the tenorman is heading. Highly recommended. *—Scott Yanow*

Just Before Sunrise: Dream Weaver & Love In / Apr. 6, 1999 / 32 Jazz ✦✦✦
The Charles Lloyd Quartet's first (*Dream Weaver*) and fifth (*Love-In*) recordings are reissued in full on this double-CD from 32 Jazz. In addition to Lloyd on tenor and flute (who is supported by either Cecil McBee or Ron McClure on bass and drummer Jack DeJohnette), the co-star is pianist Keith Jarrett, who was just becoming to come into his own after a stint with Art Blakey's Jazz Messengers. Although Coltrane was Lloyd's early influence (and sometimes here he sounds close to 'Trane), Lloyd always had something of his own personality on tenor, and of course his flute playing was unlike any obvious role model. The music on the two-fer ranges from a straightahead rendition of "Autumn Leaves" (which is framed by a pair of brief Lloyd originals) to freer post bop flights and a few that use boogaloo rhythms; nearly all of the songs were composed by Lloyd. It is hard to believe, listening to the explorative piano solo on "Tribal Dance," that *Love-In* was recorded at *the Fillmore West*. Among the other highlights are "Sombrero Sam," "Sunday Morning" and a medley of "Memphis Dues Again" and "Island Blues." The Charles Lloyd Quartet is proof that, every once in awhile, certain fortunate jazz musicians are successful both artistically and commercially. Highly recommended. *—Scott Yanow*

Soundtrack/Charles Lloyd in the Soviet Union / May 18, 1999 / Collectables ✦✦✦

Jeff Lorber

b. Nov. 4, 1952, Philadelphia, PA
Keyboards, Synthesizer, Composer / Smooth Jazz, Crossover Jazz, Jazz-Pop
With a smooth sound bringing together elements of funk, R&B, rock and electric jazz, keyboardist Jeff Lorber helped pioneer a genre of fusion later formatted under such names as NAC and Contemporary Jazz. Born in Philadelphia on November 4, 1952, he began playing the piano at the age of four, and as a teen performed with a variety of local R&B bands. Lorber's infatuation with jazz began during his stay at the Berklee College of Music, and after forming the Jeff Lorber Fusion he issued the group's self-titled debut in 1979. During the first half of the following decade, the band became one of the most popular jazz acts of the period, touring non-stop and even scoring a Best R&B Instrumental Grammy nomination for their radio hit "Pacific Coast Highway." 1984's *Step by Step* was their most successful outing yet, but at the Fusion's peak, Lorber disbanded the group, instead turning to production and session work. He did not issue his first proper solo LP until 1991's *Worth Waiting For*, remaining both a prolific performer and producer for the rest of the decade. *—Jason Ankeny*

State of Grace / Jun. 18, 1996 / Verve ✦✦✦✦
Also delving deep as ever into the retro, vibin, chillin' atmospheres is veteran keyboard funkateer Jeff Lorber, who was actually around playing and helping create the style in the first place. On the cool explosions of *State of Grace* (Verve Forecast), one of pop fusion's early forebears shuns the synthesizer effects and again pulls out his healthy, well-traveled rack of simmering memories—the Fender Rhodes, Hammond B-3, Hohner Clavinet, Wurlitzer electric piano, Mini-Moog, and, in keeping with the eloquence promised in the album title, the Steinway M grand piano. The result is a mostly hypnotic, marvelously organic ride through territory that is all at once familiar and uncharted. Percussive melodies are still the key to Lorber's *West Side Stories*, but this time he complements his trademark soul with the spiritual flute flutterings of Gary Meek, in addition to all-star contributions by Art Porter and Dave Koz. Koz and Lorber's recent trip to Indonesia for a songwriting symposium with Asian composers led to the most intriguing tune here, the mysterious and exotic "The Island of Temples." What luck that just as a guy like Lorber decides he never wants to leave the '70s, the mystical Me Decade is suddenly back, welcoming his likes again with open arms. *—Jonathan Widran*

Midnight / Mar. 17, 1998 / Zebra ✦✦✦✦
How's this for a definition of a smooth jazz elder statesman: one whose career spans an entire generation, whose hit album in 1999 uses the same instrumentation and stylistic approach as his first demo 24 years before, only now those old instruments and style are hip again as part of a retro movement— Listened to side by side, *Midnight* and his 1977 breakthrough *Water Sign* are like twin sons born to the same family years apart. In addition to the hypnotic clicking wah-wah guitar grooves, both albums focus on Fender Rhodes and Hammond B-3, the attractive one-two keyboard punch Lorber has favored for all of his career but the mid-'80s when he experimented with techno sounds. Lorber sets the tone on the hiss-and-pop LP effect before the music begins on "Down Low." The title of the second track, "The Simple Life," best reflects this old-school mentality. On that tune, Lorber experiments on the Rhodes by holding notes of the melody for different lengths of time, creating those unusual distortions; then he'll use those sounds alternately while improvising off the main melody and enhance certain lines with a brief B-3 wash or an acoustic piano flourish. The introduction to the title track is a wayward Rhodes line wandering in search of a groove, which Lorber helps create by providing the wah-wah-flavored rhythmic click himself. *—Jonathan Widran*

● **The Definitive Collection** / Feb. 22, 2000 / Arista ✦✦✦✦
Long before the coining of the radio-generated buzzwords "new adult contemporary" or "smooth jazz," the composer/keyboardist Jeff Lorber was riding a creative wave of pop/jazz fusion, building a loyal following for a synthesis of sound so fresh and distinctive that only one name could really define it—the Jeff Lorber Fusion. It was pop, it was soul, it was rock-

fusion, with dashes of jazz, blues and—dare it be mentioned, yet of its time—a dash of disco. The buoyant funk tune "Fusion Juice" sums up the spirit and percussive energy the band had, and which the keyboardist has carried on into his popular '90s work. The 16 tracks perfectly represent a time that postdates the hardcore jazz fusion of the early '70s and predates smooth jazz. (The Fusion was together from the mid-'70s through the early '80s, and that includes warts and all.) Despite the glorious melodies, beautiful keyboard passages, and irresistible funk, a few spacey synth solos would be conspicuously cornball if they were played today. While Lorber lovers and serious modern jazz collectors will no doubt thrill to get their hands on this wealth of classic material, fans of both smooth jazz and pop music who don't know Lorber from Count Basie may want to hear it for another reason—the early development of a then-obscure Seattle saxman known as Kenny Gorelick (later known as multi-million selling Kenny G). G's fans will immediately recognize his soprano tones on the dreamy "Tierra Verde" but will have a harder time picking his funkier style out of the slamming, discofied "Fusion Juice." This collection will also please audiophiles who have long desired to throw out their old scratched Lorber records and hear these classics remastered. *—Jonathan Widran*

Joe Lovano

b. Dec. 29, 1952, Cleveland, OH
Sax (Tenor), Sax (Soprano), Drums / Hard Bop, Post-Bop
Active during a period of jazz's history when it seems radical innovation is a thing of the past, Joe Lovano nevertheless coalesces various stylistic elements from disparate eras into a personal and forward-seeking style. While not an innovator in a macro sense, Lovano has unquestionably charted his own path. His playing contains not an ounce of glibness, but possesses in abundance the sense of spontaneity that's always characterized the music's finest improvisers. Lovano doesn't adopt influences—he absorbs them, so that when playing a standard, he exudes the same sense of abandon as when playing totally free (which, it should be pointed out, he does well, if infrequently). Lovano's most significant achievement is his incorporation of free and modal expressive devices into traditional chord-change improvisation.

Lovano is the son of the respected Cleveland saxophonist, Tony "Big T" Lovano. Joe started playing alto sax as a child, taught by his father, who also introduced him to jazz. In his youth, Joe would hear many of the prominent jazz artists who passed through town, including Dizzy Gillespie, James Moody, Sonny Stitt, and Rahsaan Roland Kirk. Joe began playing in jam sessions around Cleveland while still in his teens. Although thoroughly steeped in bebop, he also developed an interest in the jazz experimentalism of the 1960s, listening to such musicians as John Coltrane, Jimmy Giuffre, and Ornette Coleman. Following high school, Lovano moved to Boston and attended the Berklee School of Music. Fellow students included such future collaborators as John Scofield, Bill Frisell, and Kenny Werner. While at Berklee, Lovano discovered modal harmony and opened up to the broad areas of tonal freedom that he found so attractive in the music of John Coltrane, among others. After leaving Berklee, Lovano worked with the organists Lonnie Smith (with whom he made his recording debut) and Jack McDuff. He toured with Woody Herman from 1976-9. After leaving Herman, Lovano settled in New York City, where he quickly established himself. He joined drummer Mel Lewis' Orchestra in 1980; he played the band's regular Monday night gigs at the Village Vanguard until 1992. He also recorded several times with the band. Lovano would also work with, among others, Elvin Jones, Carla Bley, Lee Konitz, Charlie Haden, and Bob Brookmeyer. He joined drummer Paul Motian's band in 1981 (which also included his Berklee classmate Frisell), and played with guitarist John Scofield's quartet. Lovano began leading dates for Blue Note in the '90s, recording in a variety of contexts ranging from trios to larger woodwind and brass ensembles. Lovano received a number of Grammy nominations for his work on Blue Note. His 1996 album, *Quartets: Live at the Village Vanguard* (Blue Note), was named "Jazz Album of the Year" by readers of Downbeat Magazine. Lovano's wife is vocalist Judi Silvano. *—Chris Kelsey*

Tones, Shapes and Colors / Nov. 21, 1985 / Soul Note ✦✦✦✦
Joe Lovano's recorded debut as a leader features the tenor in a quartet with pianist Ken Werner, bassist Dennis Irwin and drummer Mel Lewis. Together, they perform three originals apiece by the leader and Werner. None of the tunes are simple or based on the chords of standards, but although they did not catch on, the interplay by the musicians, the excellent pacing of tempos and moods, and the consistently satisfying solos make this a set worth searching for. *—Scott Yanow*

Landmarks / Aug. 13, 1990-Aug. 14, 1990 / Blue Note ✦✦✦✦✦
Although the title of this CD makes it sound as if tenor-saxophonist Joe Lovano was performing veteran jazz classics on this date, all but one of the ten songs played by his quintet are actually Lovano originals. With strong assistance provided by guitarist John Abercrombie, pianist Ken Werner, bassist Marc Johnson and drummer Bill Stewart, Lovano often sounds like a mixture of Dewey Redman and early John Coltrane on his enjoyable set. His music has enough variety to hold one's interest, Abercrombie is in particularly strong form and Lovano is consistently creative during the modern mainstream music. *—Scott Yanow*

From the Soul / Dec. 28, 1991 / Blue Note ✦✦✦✦✦
Joe Lovano heads a lineup with pianist Michel Petrucciani, bassist Dave Holland, and late drummer Ed Blackwell. It's hard-edged, explosive playing all around, with Blackwell laying down his patented bombs while Petrucciani and Holland converge behind Lovano's dynamic solos. *—Ron Wynn*

Quartets: Live at the Village Vanguard / Mar. 12, 1994-Jan. 22, 1995 / Blue Note ✦✦✦✦✦
This double CD features tenor saxophonist Joe Lovano during two appearances at *the Village Vanguard* recorded ten months apart. Other than the leader, the pair of quartets are completely different and they bring out two sides of Lovano. The earlier session features the leader in a stimulating piano-less quartet, matching wits and creativity with flügelhornist Tom Harrell. While the music is closer to Ornette Coleman than to Gerry Mulligan (to name two famous pianoless groups), Harrell's tone more closely resembles Chuck Mangione than Don Cherry although fortunately he is much more inventive. The four Lovano originals are adventurous and all of the musicians sound as if they are stretching themselves. The second disc showcases Lovano in a more conventional quartet. The repertoire (just one original this time) covers John Coltrane, Thelonious Monk, Miles Davis, Charles Mingus, and Gordon Jenkins and finds the tenorman displaying his roots in Sonny Rollins. The rhythm section on the later date (pianist Mulgrew Miller, bassist Christian McBride, and drummer Lewis Nash) is excellent at accompanying (rather than challenging) Lovano. In both cases, Joe Lovano is heard in prime form, making this an easily recommended two-fer. *—Scott Yanow*

★ **Rush Hour** / Apr. 6, 1994-Jun. 12, 1994 / Blue Note ✦✦✦✦✦
This is one of the most exciting jazz releases of 1995. Joe Lovano is showcased on four songs backed by a string section, is accompanied by a stringless big band filled with woodwinds and brass during four other pieces, performs Ornette Coleman's "Kathline Gray" with a chamber group, takes two songs as duets with his wife Judi Silvano (who contributes wordless vocals), plays his own "Wildcat" as an overdubbed feature for his tenor and drums and does a straightforward version of "Chelsea Bridge" unaccompanied. Gunther Schuller's arrangements for the larger pieces (which include three of his own colorful originals: "Rush Hour on 23rd Street," "Lament for M" and "Headin' out, Movin' In") expertly blend together Gil Evans-type orchestrations with aspects of modern classical music and freer forms of jazz while allowing the music to swing. Silvano's voice is also an asset on three of the orchestra performances and trumpeter Jack Walrath briefly makes his presence felt. However this very well-conceived release would not have succeeded were it not for the talent, versatility and risktaking of Joe Lovano. His improvisations (mostly on tenor) push the boundaries of this already adventurous music, Lovano's sound (which occasionally hints a little at Clifford Jordan) is quite original and, on the basis of this date alone, he must rank as one of the top tenors of the 1990s. *—Scott Yanow*

Trio Fascination—*Edition One* */ Sep. 16, 1997-Sep. 17, 1997 / Blue Note* ✦✦✦✦
Whether embracing Gunther Schuller's arrangements or paying tribute to Frank Sinatra, Joe Lovano was as consistent as he was unpredictable in the 1990s. Most of his Blue Note output was excellent, and *Trio Fascination, Edition One* is no exception. This impressive inside/outside date finds Lovano forming a pianoless trio with bassist Dave Holland and drummer Elvin Jones, and the three are very much in sync on originals that range from the dusky "Sanctuary Park" and the haunting "Studio Rivbea" to the very angular "New York Fascination" and the difficult "Cymbalism." Meanwhile, "Impressionistic" is an eerie number with Middle Eastern overtones. The only song on the CD that isn't an original is a very personal interpretation of the standard "(I Don't Stand A) Ghost of a Chance." Heard on tenor, a[illegible] soprano, the saxophonist never fails to command our attention on this cons[illegible] and captivating release. *—Alex Henderson*

Friendly Fire / Dec. 15, 1998-Dec. 16, 1998 / Blue Note ✦✦✦✦
The teaming of Joe Lovano and Greg Osby, two of the most exciting saxophonists of the '90s, is kind of a dream come true, and it's a pleasure to say that *Friendly Fire* doesn't disappoint. True, it may not be as adventurous as some listeners may have hoped for, but it's undoubtedly vibrant hard-bop with an evident adventurous streak. Lovano and Osby are both first-class improvisers, and they turn in dynamic performances throughout the album, whether it's on originals or standards. They turn *Friendly Fire* into a compelling listen that's the musical equivalent of the title's promise. *—Stephen Thomas Erlewine*

52nd Street Themes / Nov. 3, 1999-Nov. 4, 1999 / Blue Note ✦✦✦✦
The latest CD by jazz saxophonist Joe Lovano blends New York attitude with Midwestern warmth in an homage to the Manhattan street where bebop ruled in the '50s and '60s. The music here, like that of such other thematic Lovano albums as *Rush Hour* (his 1995 celebration of third-stream music) and *Celebrating Sinatra*, evokes the past without being at all archival. Fronting a four-man sax section, Lovano blasts through such strong Dameronia as "The Scene Is Clean" and "Tadd's Delight," refreshes the indelible lyricism of Dameron's lovely "If You Could See Me Now," and, in an intimate duet with pianist John Hicks, velvetizes Billy Strayhorn's lush "Passion Flower." It also features Miles Davis' early "Sippin' at Bells"; Lovano's homage to Charlie Parker, the complex "Charlie Chan," a three-way saxophone conversation between Lovano and fellow tenormen George Garzone and Ralph Lalama that's punctuated by Lewis Nash's pinpoint drums; "Abstractions on 52nd Street," Lovano's extrapolation and embellishment of a Thelonious Monk line; and George Gershwin's "Embraceable You," plushly orchestrated by Willie "Face" Smith and lovingly performed by Lovano. Others contributing sax are Gary Smulyan (baritone) and Steve Slagle (alto); Tim Hagans and Conrad Herwig play trumpet and trombone, respectively, while Dennis Irwin handles bass. Like many other Lovano records, this hews close to tradition but updates it effectively. Besides the fervor of the playing—Smith says he would've played saxophone, but these New York players were much better prepared—the song selection is astute, Lovano's originals are solid, and Smith's sole compositional contribution, "Deal," is tasty indeed. *—Carlo Wolff*

Frank Lowe

b. Jun. 24, 1943, Memphis, TN
Sax (Tenor) / Avant-Garde Jazz, Free Jazz
A powerful tenor saxophonist whose roots in R&B and bop can often be felt even in his freer improvisations, Frank Lowe has stuck to his own singular musical path throughout his low-profile career. He started playing the tenor when he was 12 and spent some time at the University of Kansas and in San Francisco. He gigged regularly with Sun Ra in New York (1966-68) and worked with many of the top avant-garde players of the era, including Alice Coltrane, drummer Rashied Ali (they made a duo set for Survival in 1973), Archie Shepp and Don Cherry. Frank Lowe, who has recorded as a leader for ESP, Freedom, Black Saint, Marge, Palm, Kharma, Cadence and most recently CIMP, has headed his own bands on an irregular basis during the past two decades and remains an underrecognized free jazz master. *—Scott Yanow*

Black Beings / 1973 / ESP ✦✦✦
One of the later ESP blowouts, this CD reissue features the powerful tenor of Frank Lowe in-

teracting with Joseph Jarman (heard here on alto and soprano), violinist Leroy Jenkins (operating under the pseudonym of "The Wizard" but quite recognizable), bassist William Parker and drummer Rashid Sinan. Two of the three originals (which include the 25-minute "In Trane's Name") are lengthy and wander a bit, but the intense music is well worth hearing by free-jazz collectors. *—Scott Yanow*

Fresh / Sep. 1974-Mar. 7, 1975 / Black Lion ✦✦✦✦✦
The emphasis is on color and sound on this spirited avant-garde album. Four of the five selections feature the adventurous tenor of Frank Lowe with trumpeter Lester Bowie, trombonist Joseph Bowie, cellist Abdul Wadud and either Steve Reid or Bob Shaw on drums. They perform two Lowe originals and two pieces by Thelonious Monk; these renditions are full of surprises and contrasts. In addition, Lowe is heard with an unknown group of local musicians called "the Memphis Four" on "Chu's Blues" in 1974. Open-eared listeners should find this set to be quite stimulating. *—Scott Yanow*

The Flam / Oct. 20, 1975-Oct. 21, 1975 / Black Saint ✦✦✦✦✦
On this free jazz date the powerful tenor Frank Lowe teams up with trumpeter Leo Smith, trombonist Joseph Bowie, bassist Alex Blake and drummer Charles Bobo Shaw for five group originals including the collaboration "Third St. Stomp." The very explorative and rather emotional music holds one's interest throughout. These often heated performances are better heard than described. *—Scott Yanow*

Decision in Paradise / Sep. 24, 1984-Sep. 28, 1984 / Soul Note ✦✦✦✦
The all-star lineup (tenor-saxophonist Frank Lowe, trumpeter Don Cherry, trombonnist Grachan Moncur III, pianist Geri Allen, bassist Charnette Moffett and drummer Charles Moffett) practically guarantees that this music will be worth hearing. Although a touch more conservative than one might expect (more of an open-minded straightahead set than music emphasizing sound explorations), all six group originals are of interest including Lowe's unaccompanied performance on Butch Morris's "I'll Whistle Your Name" and Moncur's whimsical "You Dig." *—Scott Yanow*

● **Bodies and Soul** / Nov. 18, 1995-Nov. 19, 1995 / CIMP ✦✦✦✦✦
Frank Lowe led his first record date in 1975 but the explorative tenor saxophonist has never gained more than an underground reputation. A masterful improviser who has retained a free spirit through the years, Lowe's music is actually much more accessible than one might expect. On *Bodies and Soul*, Lowe's sound varies from the gruff roars of prime Archie Shepp to Sonny Rollins. Assisted by bassist Tim Flood (making his recording debut) and veteran drummer Charles Moffett, Lowe explores four originals plus music by John Coltrane ("Impressions"), Pharoah Sanders, Ornette Coleman, Phillip Watson, Don Cherry, and even a melodic and unaccompanied version of Johnny Green's "Body and Soul." The free bop music is often quite thoughtful but never predictable and is well worth an investigation. *—Scott Yanow*

Live from Soundscape / 1982 / DIW ✦✦✦

Jimmie Lunceford

b. Jun. 6, 1902, Fulton, MS, **d.** Jul. 12, 1947, Seaside, OR
Sax (Alto) / Swing
The Jimmie Lunceford Orchestra has always been a bit difficult to evaluate. Contemporary observers rated Lunceford's big band at the top with Duke Ellington and Count Basie but, when judging the music solely on their records (and not taking into account their visual show, appearance and showmanship), Lunceford's ensemble has to be placed on the second tier. His orchestra lacked any really classic soloists, and a large portion of the band's repertoire either featured dated vocals or were pleasant novelties. And yet, the well-rehearsed ensembles were very impressive, some of the arrangements (particularly those of Sy Oliver) were quite original and the use of glee-club vocalists and short concise solos were pleasing and often memorable. Plus Lunceford's was the first orchestra to feature high-note trumpeters and had a strong influence on the early Stan Kenton Orchestra. From a band organized by Lunceford in 1927, his orchestra broke through in 1934 with strong performances at New York's Cotton Club. Their tight ensembles and colorful shows made them a major attraction throughout the remainder of the swing era. Unfortunately, Lunceford underpaid most of his sidemen, and the orchestra gradually declined during the '40s until Lunceford's sudden death in 1947. After Lunceford's death, pianist/arranger Ed Wilcox and Joe Thomas tried to keep the orchestra together but in 1949 the band permanently broke up. *—Scott Yanow*

1930-1934 / Jun. 6, 1930-Nov. 7, 1934 / Classics ✦✦✦✦✦
The first in Classics' "complete" Jimmie Lunceford series has two titles apiece from 1930 (when the band was based in Tennessee) and 1933 along with its first six sessions for Decca in 1934. Lunceford's band had an immediately recognizable sound by 1934 and, despite the presence of such top soloists as altoist Willie Smith, tenor-saxophonist Joe Thomas and high-note trumpeter Tommy Stevenson, it was its arranged ensembles (particularly those of Sy Oliver) that gave the orchestra its musical identity. Among the better selections on this CD are "Flaming Reeds And Screaming Brass," "White Heat," "Swinging' Uptown," "Rose Room," "Miss Otis Regrets" and the band's fresh interpretations of Duke Ellington's "Black And Tan Fantasy" and "Mood Indigo." *—Scott Yanow*

☆ **The Complete Jimmie Lunceford** / May 15, 1933-Dec. 23, 1940 / Columbia ✦✦✦✦✦
The one fault to this magnificent four-LP box set is that it is out of print. Put out by French CBS in 1981, the definitive reissue has all of Jimmie Lunceford's recordings for Vocalion and Okeh, including two titles from 1933 and all of his 1939-1940 performances (which were cut between two long periods with Decca). The only two personnel changes that took place during 1939-1940 were important ones as trumpeters Snooky Young and Gerald Wilson joined Lunceford while arranger/trumpeter Sy Oliver (who was largely responsible for the big band's musical identity) left to join Tommy Dorsey. Lunceford's Orchestra was at its peak during this period, and highpoints of its stay with Vocalion include "Tain't What You Do," "What Is This Thing Called Swing," "Ain't She Sweet," "White Heat," "Well, All Right Then," "Belgium Stomp," "Wham," "Uptown Blues," "Lunceford Special," and "What's Your Story, Morning Glory—" In addition to Snooky Young, the main soloists are trombonist Trummy Young, altoist Willie Smith, and tenor saxophonist Joe Thomas, but the Lunceford sound was very much a group effort, dependent on high musicianship, surprising arrangements, and tight ensembles. Not every selection in this box is a classic (Dan Grissom's vocals are an acquired taste), but this is a perfectly conceived reissue. All of the music except for the nine alternate takes have been reissued on CD by the Classics label. *—Scott Yanow*

Rhythm Is Our Business / Sep. 4, 1934-May 29, 1935 / ASV/Living Era ✦✦✦✦✦
The first of six Lp's released by MCA in the early 1980's in their Jazz Heritage series that reissued highlights from Jimmie Lunceford's career is the strongest overall. Sticking to the 1934-35 period, such memorable numbers as "Dream Of You," "Stomp It Off," "Rhythm Is Our Business," "Sleepy Time Gal" (with its brilliant sax section chorus) and Duke Ellington's "Mood Indigo" and "Black And Tan Fantasy" are among the highlights. The arrangements of Willie Smith, Ed Wilcox, Eddie Durham and particularly Sy Oliver take precedent over the short solos, really showing off the band's consistently high musicianship. Fortunately all of this music has since been reissued on CD. *—Scott Yanow*

● **Stomp It Off** / Sep. 4, 1934-May 29, 1935 / GRP ✦✦✦✦✦
While European labels (most notably Classics and Masters of Jazz) reissue every Jimmie Lunceford recording, its domestic counterpart as usual only gives consumers best-of collections. This CD is actually quite good, consisting of highlights from Lunceford's first year with Decca and serving as a fine introduction to his orchestra's music. Nearly all of the 21 numbers are excellent, and among the more colorful selections are reworkings of three Duke Ellington tunes, "Miss Otis Regrets," "Dream of You," two versions of the bubbly "Rhythm Is Our Business," and "Sleepy-Time Gal," which has a remarkable sax section chorus. *—Scott Yanow*

★ **Big Bands** / Oct. 29, 1934-Dec. 22, 1941 / Time-Life Music ✦✦✦✦✦
The Jimmie Lunceford entry in Time-Life Music's *Big Bands* series goes a long way toward filling the gap in availability of the Lunceford band's best and most popular recordings of the 1930s and '40s. Leading off with the group's biggest hit, "Rhythm Is Our Business," it also includes their other best-known recordings ("Organ Grinder's Swing" and "Blues in the Night") as well as lesser hits ("For Dancers Only" and "T'ain't What You Do"). Good choices are made among the tracks Lunceford recorded for Decca and Columbia, including 16 Sy Oliver arrangements out of the 21 performances, among them such characteristic efforts as "Stomp It Off" and "Well All Right Then." For a band of its stature, the Lunceford outfit remains underrated, and the relatively small body of its work in print domestically has contributed to that injustice. This well-thought-out "best of" serves as a corrective. *—William Ruhlmann*

1934-1935 / Nov. 7, 1934-Sep. 30, 1935 / Classics ✦✦✦✦✦
The second of Classics' reissuance of all the master takes of Jimmie Lunceford's recordings finds the orchestra gaining in popularity and in power. Among the highlights (most of the songs were arranged by Sy Oliver or Ed Wilcox) are "Since My Beat Gal Turned Me Down," "Rhythm Is Our Business," "Shake Your Head," "Sleepy-Time Gal," "Four or Five Times" and "Swanee River." The high musicianship and clean ensembles (along with the showmanship) are most impressive and the concise solos (particularly from altoist Willie Smith, tenor saxophonist Joe Thomas and trumpeter Sy Oliver) are enjoyable and fit in logically as part of the arrangements. *—Scott Yanow*

1935-1937 / Sep. 30, 1935-Jun. 15, 1937 / Classics ✦✦✦✦✦
Although there have been a few GRP/Decca samplers released domestically, the best way for serious collectors to acquire the recordings of Jimmie Lunceford are by getting the reissue CDs put out by the European labels. On Classics' third Lunceford set, the personnel stays the same (except for one minor change) during the 15-month period that is covered. The well-rehearsed unit continued to grow and develop during this time. Among the highpoints of the CD are "My Blue Heaven," "Organ Grinder's Swing," "Harlem Shout" and "Slumming on Park Avenue." Although one can do without the occasional Dan Grissom vocals, the concise solos, tricky charts and hip singing of Sy Oliver make this music well worth investigating by fans of the swing era. *—Scott Yanow*

Jimmy Lyons

b. Dec. 1, 1933, Jersey City, NJ, **d.** May 19, 1986, New York, NY
Sax (Soprano), Sax (Alto) / Avant-Garde Jazz, Free Jazz
Imagine what Sonny Stitt might have sounded like had he embraced free jazz after mastering bebop, and you've probably conjured a pretty good mental impression of Jimmy Lyons. Like Stitt, Lyons was enamoured of Charlie Parker's style, particularly in terms of phrasing. Lyons' slippery, bop-derived rhythms and melodic contours lent his improvisations a Bird-like cast, even as his performance contexts were more harmonically free. Lyons made his reputation playing with the pianist Cecil Taylor, with whom he became inextricably linked. He was a near constant presence in Taylor's bands, from 1960 until the saxophonist's death in 1986. Lyons always lent an explicitly swinging element to the pianist's music, helping remind the listener most emphatically that—regardless of how much Taylor may have been influenced by European art music—this was unquestionably jazz.

A teen-aged Lyons was given an alto sax by the clarinetist Buster Bailey, an important member of Fletcher Henderson's band in the '20s and '30s. Lyons studied with the veteran big band saxophonist Rudy Rutherford, and at a young age made friends with such jazz luminaries as Elmo Hope, Bud Powell, and Thelonious Monk. Lyons came into its own as a professional upon his association with Taylor in 1960. With Taylor, Lyons recorded a number of landmark albums, including *Cecil Taylor Live at Café Montmartre* (1962), in a trio with the drummer Sunny Murray; and *Unit Structures* (1966), in a larger band that included significantly the drummer Andrew Cyrille. Lyons took his own bands into the studio infrequently. In 1969 he led his first session, an album entitled *Other Afternoons*, which was issued on the now-defunct BYG label. Beginning in 1978 he began leading record dates more often. In the years to come he would release several albums on the Hat Hut and Black Saint labels.

Like many jazz musicians, Lyons was compelled by circumstance to augment his performance income by teaching. In 1970-71 he taught music at Narcotic Addiction Control, a drug treatment center in New York City. From 1971-73 he served—with Taylor and Cyrille—as artist-in-residence at Antioch College, and in 1975 he directed the Black Music Ensemble at Bennington College. Perhaps Lyons' stature as a musician is best illustrated by the fact that Taylor essentially found him irreplaceable. After Lyons, Taylor never established a similar long-standing relationship with another musician. Jimmy Lyons' premature death at the age of 52 robbed Taylor—and the jazz avant-garde, in general— of a vital, swinging, eminently creative voice. *—Chris Kelsey*

Other Afternoons / Aug. 15, 1969 / Affinity ✦✦✦✦✦
Because he spent virtually his entire career as Cecil Taylor's altoist, Jimmy Lyons had relatively few chances to record as a leader. This Affinity LP was his first opportunity to head a session and Lyons picked a particularly superior group of sidemen: trumpeter Lester Bowie, bassist Alan Silva, and drummer Andrew Cyrille. Rather than sounding like the Art Ensemble of Chicago (Bowie's group) or Taylor's Unit, the all-star band comes closer at times to seeming like an updated version of Ornette Coleman's quartet. The renditions of four originals are quite adventurous and passionate yet thoughtful and logical. An excellent outing. *—Scott Yanow*

Riffs / Sep. 13, 1980-Sep. 14, 1980 / Hat Musics ✦✦✦✦
For one of his very infrequent recordings outside of the realm of Cecil Taylor, altoist Jimmy Lyons teams up with the talented jazz bassoonist Karen Borca, bassist Jay Oliver and drummer Paul Murphy for lengthy and rather adventurous versions of "Theme" and "Riffs *1/II*" plus the brief "Riffs *1/I*" which serves as a prelude to the longer "Riffs." It is always intriguing to hear Lyons stretching out without a piano and this set helped make listeners aware of Borca's brilliant playing on the rarely utilized bassoon. *—Scott Yanow*

● **Give It Up** / Mar. 6, 1985-Mar. 7, 1985 / Black Saint ✦✦✦✦
Altoist Jimmy Lyons spent most of his career as a member of Cecil Taylor's Units. For his own projects, it is not too surprising that he chose not to utilize a piano; who could fill in for C.T.— On these occasions, Lyons often teamed up with the adventurous bassoonist Karen Borca and for this set their quartet (with bassist Jay Oliver and drummer Paul Murphy) is joined by the lyrical trumpet of Enrico Rava. They stretch out on four of Lyons' emotional originals, the ensemble work is frequently exciting and the frontline boasts three distinctive and rather different (but complementary) solo voices. Highly recommended. *—Scott Yanow*

Machito (Frank Grillo)

b. Feb. 16, 1912, Havana, Cuba, **d.** Apr. 15, 1984, London, England
Vocals, Maraccas / Cuban Jazz, Afro-Cuban Jazz, Latin Jazz
Machito played a huge role in the history of Latin jazz, for his bands of the 1940s were probably the first to achieve a fusion of powerful Afro-Cuban rhythms and jazz improvisation. At its roaring best, the band had a hard-charging sound, loaded with jostling, hyperactive bongos and congas and razor-edged riffing brass. Machito was the front man, singing, conducting, shaking maracas, while his brother-in-law Mario Bauza was the innovator behind the scenes, getting Machito to hire jazz-oriented arrangers. He founded the Afro-Cubans in 1940, taking on Bauza the following year as music director where he remained for 35 years. After making some early 78s for Decca, the Afro-Cubans really began to catch on after the end of World War II, appearing with—and no doubt influencing—Stan Kenton's orchestra and recording some exciting sides for Mercury and Clef. Upon Bauza's urging, Machito's band featured a galaxy of American jazz soloists on its recordings from 1948 to 1960, including Charlie Parker, Dizzy Gillespie, Buddy Rich, Cannonball Adderley, Herbie Mann and Johnny Griffin. Playing regularly at New York's Palladium, Machito's band reached its peak of popularity during the mambo craze of the 1950s, survived the upheavals of the '60s and despite the loss of Bauza in 1976, continued to work frequently in the '70s and early '80s when the term "salsa" came into use. *—Richard S. Ginell*

Dizzy Gillespie/Charlie Parker / 1948 / Verve ✦✦✦✦✦
A selection of prime Latin jazz cuts w/ both Parker and Diz plus Machito. *—Ron Wynn*

★ **Mucho Macho Machito & His Afro** / 1948 / Pablo ✦✦✦✦✦
The most famous (and common) Machito performances feature his infectious Cuban band welcoming guests from the bebop world. This CD is different, for it has 24 selections from the 1948-49 period by Machito's Afro-Cuban Salseros without the assistance of famous names. Utilizing three trumpets (including Mario Bauza), four saxophones, piano, bass, four percussionists, and the vocals of the leader and Gracilea, the high-powered and always danceable band is heard throughout the CD in prime form. Whether playing originals, updated folk songs or jazz standards, Machito's mighty crew was the pacesetter in Latin jazz of the era. This important release gives listeners a strong example of how the Afro-Cuban jazz band probably sounded live in concert. *—Scott Yanow*

Machito at the Crescendo / 1960-1961 / GNP Crescendo ✦✦✦✦✦
Machito, one of the most revered artists in the history of Afro-Cuban music, lives up to his well-deserved reputation for giving 200 percent in concert on *At the Crescendo*. Captured live at Hollywood, CA's *Crescendo* (a legendary, long-gone Sunset Strip nightclub owned by record exec/producer/concert promoter Gene Norman), Machito and his orchestra swing hard and passionately on both fiery, rhythmic salsa like "Ven Conmigo Guajira," "No Tiene Telerana" and "El Columpio" and spirited Latin-jazz interpretations of Sonny Rollins' "Pent-Up House" (wrongly credited to Miles Davis in the CD's liner notes) and Ray Bryant's "Cuban Fantasy." No one with even a moderate interest in Afro-Cuban music should pass up this dynamic performance (reissued on CD in 1990). *—Alex Henderson*

Mahavishnu Orchestra

f. 1971
Group / Jazz-Rock, Fusion
One of the premiere fusion groups, the Mahavishnu Orchestra was considered by most observers during its prime to be a rock band but its sophisticated improvisations actually put its high-powered music between rock and jazz. Founder and leader John McLaughlin had recently played with Miles Davis and Tony Williams's Lifetime. The original lineup of the group was McLaughlin on electric guitar, violinist Jerry Goodman, keyboardist Jan Hammer, electric bassist Rick Laird and drummer Billy Cobham. They recorded three intense albums for Columbia during 1971-73 and then the personnel changed completely for the second version of the group. In 1974 the band consisted of violinist Jean-Luc Ponty, Gayle Moran on keyboards and vocals, electric bassist Ralphe Armstrong and drummer Michael Warden; by 1975 Stu Goldberg had replaced Moran and Ponty had left. John McLaughlin's dual interests in Eastern religion and playing acoustic guitar resulted in the band breaking up in 1975. Surprisingly an attempt to revive the Mahavishnu Orchestra in 1984 (using Cobham, saxophonist Bill Evans, keyboardist Mitchell Forman and electric bassist Jonas Hellborg and percussionist Danny Gottlieb) was unsuccessful; one Warner Bros. album resulted. However when one thinks of the Mahavishnu Orchestra, it is of the original lineup which was very influential throughout the 1970s. *—Scott Yanow*

★ **The Inner Mounting Flame** / Aug. 14, 1971 / Columbia/Legacy ✦✦✦✦✦
This is the album that made John McLaughlin a semi-household word, a furious, high-energy, yet rigorously figured-out meeting of virtuosos that, for all intents and purposes, defined the fusion of jazz and rock a year after Miles Davis' *Bitches Brew* breakthrough. It also inadvertently led to the derogatory connotation of the word fusion, for it paved the way for an army of imitators, many of whose excesses and commercial panderings devalued the entire movement. Though much was made of the influence of jazz-influenced improvisation in the Mahavishnu band, it is the rock element that predominates, stemming directly from the electronic innovations of Jimi Hendrix. The improvisations, particularly McLaughlin's post-Hendrix machine-gun assaults on double-necked electric guitar and Jerry Goodman's flights on electric violin, owe more to the freak-outs that had been circulating in progressive rock circles than to jazz, based as they often are on ostinatos on one chord. These still sound genuinely thrilling today on CD, as McLaughlin and Goodman battle Jan Hammer's keyboards, Rick Laird's bass and especially Billy Cobham's hard-charging drums, whose jazz-trained technique pushed the envelope for all rock drummers. What doesn't date so well are the composed medium- and high-velocity unison passages that are played in such tight lockstep that they can't breathe. There is also time out for quieter, reflective numbers that are drenched in studied spirituality ("A Lotus on Irish Streams") or irony ("You Know You Know"); McLaughlin was to do better in that department with less driven colleagues elsewhere in his career. Aimed with absolute precision at young rock fans, this record was wildly popular in its day, and it may have been the cause of more blown-out home amplifiers than any other record this side of Deep Purple. *—Richard S. Ginell*

☆ **Birds of Fire** / 1972 / Columbia/Legacy ✦✦✦✦✦
Emboldened by the popularity of *Inner Mounting Flame* among rock audiences, the first Mahavishnu Orchestra set out to further define and refine its blistering jazz-rock direction in its second—and, no thanks to internal feuding, last—studio album. Although it has much of the screaming rock energy and sometimes exaggerated competitive frenzy of its predecessor, *Birds of Fire* is audibly more varied in texture, even more tightly organized, and thankfully more musical in content. A remarkable example of precisely choreographed, high-speed solo trading—with John McLaughlin, Jerry Goodman and Jan Hammer all of one mind, supported by Billy Cobham's machine-gun drumming and Rick Laird's dancing bass—can be heard on the aptly named "One Word," and the title track is a defining moment of the group's nearly atonal fury. The band also takes time out for a brief bit of spaced-out electronic burbling and static called "Sapphire Bullets of Pure Love." Yet the most enticing pieces of music on the record are the gorgeous, almost pastoral opening and closing sections to "Open Country Joy," a relaxed, jocular bit of communal jamming that they ought to have pursued further. This album actually became a major crossover hit, rising to No. 15 on the pop album charts, and it remains the key item in the first Mahavishnu Orchestra's slim discography. *—Richard S. Ginell*

Love, Devotion and Surrender / 1972 / Columbia ✦✦✦✦✦
Mahavishnu John McLaughlin's and Devadip Carlos Santana came together under the influences of John Coltrane and Sri Chinmoy (the latter of whom McLaughlin would eventually renounce), cut their hair, and joined forces in probably the greatest guitar summit meeting of the jazz-rock era. Their rapport is obvious from the first track, Coltrane's "A Love Supreme"; both guitarists are on fire, flashing their stuff with extraordinary energy and remarkable arrhythmic placement of each note. From this point, the two fuse the high-octane virtuosity of the Mahavishnu Orchestra and Tony Williams' Lifetime (present are Billy Cobham and Jan Hammer—on drums!—from the former and Larry Young from the latter) with Santana's thundering Latin percussion team of Armando Peraza and James Mingo Lewis, without either element dominating. The music reaches an ecstatic peak on the lengthy jam "Let Us Go Into the House of the Lord" (based on the chords of Bobby Womack's "Breezin'"), where Santana's trademark ascending chromatic flurries give way to McLaughlin machine-gun volleys that make more coherent musical sense than anything he was recording with the first Mahavishnu group around this time. Whatever you may think of gurus and Indian religions, there must be something to it if the results of spiritual immersion are as spectacular and fulfilling as the music on this CD. *—Richard S. Ginell*

The Lost Trident Sessions / May 25, 1973 / Columbia/Legacy ✦✦✦
Recorded in London on June 25, 1973, these sessions for a planned third Mahavishnu Orchestra album were shelved when the band decided to put out the live *Between Nothingness and Eternity* instead. Bootlegged in the past, two-track mixes of the missing album were discovered in the vaults in the late 1990s, paving the way for its official release in 1999. It's thus the last of the three studio albums done by the original Mahavishnu lineup (with Cobham on drums, Goodman on violin, Hammer on keyboards and Laird on bass). Although McLaughlin had been the only composer on the first two Mahavishnu albums, he only penned half of the six tracks here, with Goodman, Hammer and Laird pitching in a song each. It's fiery, if perhaps over-busy at times, fusion, McLaughlin reaching his most feverish pitches in the frenetic concluding passage of the ten-minute "Trilogy." The numbers written

by other members than McLaughlin tend to be a little more subdued, and perhaps unsurprisingly less inclined toward burning guitar solos. *—Richie Unterberger*

Between Nothingness and Eternity / Aug. 1973 / Columbia ✦✦✦✦✦
The first Mahavishnu Orchestra's slim catalog is padded out somewhat by this live album, on which the five jazz/rock virtuosos can be heard stretching out at greater length than in the studio. There are only three selections on the disc, each developing organically through a number of sections, and there are fewer lockstep unison passages than on the earlier recordings. McLaughlin is as flashy and noisy as ever on double-necked electric guitar, and violinist Jerry Goodman and keyboardist Jan Hammer are a match for him in the speed department. Yet one really doesn't hear much music on this album; electricity and competitive empathy are clearly not enough. Beyond the personality conflicts that broke up the band, they seem to have been approaching, though not quite reaching, a musical dead end as well. *—Richard S. Ginell*

Apocalypse / Mar. 1974 / Columbia ✦✦✦✦✦
The first recording of the second Mahavishnu Orchestra was a real stretch for John McLaughlin, an encounter with Michael Tilson Thomas and the London Symphony Orchestra. The union wasn't taken seriously at the time, and it ended up harming the reputation of Thomas—a remarkably adventurous young conductor who defied the stuffy classical powers-that-be and thus probably delayed his eventual rise to the top—more than McLaughlin. But those with ears, then and now, beheld a remarkable series of pieces that neatly juxtapose and occasionally combine the combustion of McLaughlin's group with rich, tasteful symphonic statements orchestrated for McLaughlin by Michael Gibbs. The new Mahavishnu-ites, electric violinist Jeac-Luc Ponty and keyboardist/vocalist Gayle Moran, have their moments, but the real focus of this disc is the quality of the symphonic conceptions and how well McLaughlin blends his lyrical and fiery guitar into the mixture. The best stretch is the breathtakingly ethereal opening of "Hymn to Him"; the promise of fusing rock, jazz and classical elements had never been executed so alluringly before—and wouldn't you know, an old experienced hand at introducing classical textures into rock, the Beatles' George Martin, is the producer. Don't let old, outworn preconceptions on either side of the fence prevent you from checking out this beautiful record. *—Richard S. Ginell*

Visions of the Emerald Beyond / Dec. 4, 1974-Dec. 14, 1974 / Columbia ✦✦✦
As the second album to document the second Mahavishnu Orchestra, this one isn't as, well, apocalyptic as its predecessor, yet it does focus more intently on the band itself. Jean-Luc Ponty's curling electric violin lines help give this Mahavishnu band a more European sound than its predecessor, and some of the orchestral concepts of *Apocalypse* work their way into the picture via comments by a string trio and trumpet/sax duo. This band also had some interest in a bombastic funk direction that may have been borrowed from Mr. "Chameleon" Herbie Hancock, and would later be followed by Mahavishnu Two's drummer, Michael Walden. Gayle Moran's ethereal vocals don't date as badly as those on many jazz-rock records; at least she can sing. Overall, this Mahavishnu edition is more refined and not as aggressive as the first—although they could charge ahead pretty hard, as "Be Happy" and "On the Way Home to Earth" demonstrate—yet they were still capable of making memorable electric music. *—Richard S. Ginell*

Inner Worlds / 1975 / Columbia ✦✦✦✦✦
The state of the second Mahavishnu Orchestra continued to be volatile in 1975, with violinist Jean-Luc Ponty out, keyboardist Gayle Moran replaced by Stu Goldberg, and all string and horn backings removed, leaving just a steaming quartet and this lone remarkable album. The addition of Goldberg, a more interesting musician than Moran, is significant, but the biggest charge is provided by the leader who, in tandem with the latest electronic equipment, turns in some of his most passionately alive playing of the whole Mahavishnu series. The leadoff track "All in the Family" has fantastic energy and drive, pushed on by Narada Michael Walden's drums and marimba. "Miles Out" has McLaughlin doing some inspired jamming with his guitar hooked into a "360 Systems Frequency Shifter" (an electronic device with the wildly fluid sound of a ring-modulator), and he moves over to an early guitar synthesizer on "Morning Calls," "Lotus Feet" and the streaking title track. There is some funk residue from *Visions of the Emerald Beyond* on "Planetary Citizen" yet oddly enough, the so-so soul vocals from Walden on several tracks and one by bassist Ralphe Armstrong do not harm the cause, as the playing of the quartet is so fiery. But this somewhat overlooked album would be the last hurrah for the Mahavishnu concept for nearly a decade—and when it returned, the sounds it produced would bear little resemblance to this power-packed music. *—Richard S. Ginell*

Junior Mance (Julian Clifford Mance, Jr.)

b. Oct. 10, 1928, Chicago, IL
Piano / Soul-Jazz, Bop
Junior Mance is well-known for his soulful bluesy style but he is also expert at playing bop standards. He started playing professionally when he was ten. Mance worked with Gene Ammons in Chicago during 1947-49, played with Lester Young (1950) and was with the Ammons-Sonny Stitt group until he was drafted. He was the house pianist at Chicago's Bee Hive (1953-54), worked as Dinah Washington's accompanist (1954-55), was in the first Cannonball Adderley Quintet (1956-57) and then spent two years touring with Dizzy Gillespie (1958-60). After a few months with the Eddie "Lockjaw" Davis-Johnny Griffin group, Mance formed his own trio and has mostly been a leader ever since. He has led sessions for Verve, Jazzland, Riverside, Capitol, Atlantic, Milestone, Polydor, Inner City, JSP, Nilva, Sackville and Bee Hive among other labels. *—Scott Yanow*

Junior Mance Trio at the Village Vanguard / Feb. 22, 1961-Feb. 23, 1961 / Jazzland/OJC ✦✦✦✦✦
Pianist Junior Mance has long been typecast as a soulful blues player so, as if to confuse listeners, he starts off this live set with an uptempo "Looptown" on which he displays technique worthy of Oscar Peterson. Mance's many fans have no reason to despair though for, in addition to a boppish rendition of "Girl of My Dreams," the pianist does perform a generous amount of blues and soulful pieces. Bassist Larry Gales and drummer Ben Riley alsohelp out . *—Scott Yanow*

Junior's Blues / Feb. 14, 1962 / Riverside ✦✦✦
At age 33 for this one, Mance (piano), with Bob Cranshaw (bass) and Mickey Roker (drums), has all the jazz and blues bases covered, going back to boogie and stride, through swing and bop, with a couple of more modernistic numbers rounding out this complete overview of classic American soul-based black music. Mance evokes wonderfully patient, romantic notions on "Creole Love Call," with creamy, molasses-like melodicism stirred by Roker's expert brush work. "Yancey Special" has Mance digging in and getting down as Roker shuffles along. "In the Evening" is much more tinkling and upbeat here than Leroy Carr wrote it, whereas the hard-swinging "Jumpin' the Blues" is as much fun to hear as it must have been to play. At his most delicate on Ray Brown's "Gravy Waltz," Mance starts solo, staggering the melody, while a relaxed "Blue Monk" has Mance tossing in extra notes during the melody, Roker's intricate brush work personifying cool. Mance also wrote three originals for the date: "Down the Line" is a straight up-and-down 12-bar blues, replete with tinkles and head-nodding chords; "Rainy Mornin' Blues" evokes the falling precipitation's patterns in soulful tones; while "Cracklin'" is the most urgent swinger, with repeated chorus and gospel flavoring. In his liner notes, Dan Morgenstern depicts this music perfectly as "the basic spirit of jazz," and for the times that rings true. It's one of many consistently crafted works Mance would make over the years that mixed jazz and blues 50/50. Recommended. *—Michael G. Nastos*

Happy Time / 1962 / Original Jazz Classics ✦✦✦✦
Pianist Junior Mance was in excellent company on this inspired 1962 session with bassist Ron Carter and drummer Mickey Roker. Its unfortunate this trio only recorded together on this one date as their unity propels the blues, gospel, and bebop ideas Mance consistently feeds them. The program is highlighted by three Mance originals "Out South," "Taggie's Tune," and the torrid joy of the opening theme "Happy Time," along with versions of "Jitterbug Waltz," "Tin Tin Deo," and Mance at his soulful bluesy best on Clark Terry's "The Simple Waltz." *—Al Campbell*

• **Mance's Special** / Sep. 14, 1986-Nov. 30, 1988 / Sackville ✦✦✦✦✦
Fine '86 set with pianist Junior Mance running through romping blues, intricate originals, and moving standards and ballads in a solo set. While he's best at blues-tinged material, Mance shows the versatility necessary to do other material, and doesn't substitute cliches and gimmicks for ideas and substance. *—Ron Wynn*

At Town Hall, Vol. 1 / Mar. 30, 1995 / Enja ✦✦✦✦
The veteran pianist Junior Mance has long been known for his soulful take on bop and hard bop. For his Enja release, a live quartet set with tenor-saxophonist Houston Person, Mance is heard in top form on a pair of swing-era standards and three of his originals, all of which are at least 82 minutes long. Most memorable is "Jubilation" (which lives up to its name), "Small Fry" and a 15-minute version of "I Cried for You." Bassist Calvin Hill and drummer Alvin Queen are fine in support of the two lead voices and it is of little surprise that Mance and Person work together quite well for their styles have long been very complementary. This CD is easily recommended to their fans. *—Scott Yanow*

Joe Maneri

b. 1927, Brooklyn, NY
Sax (Tenor), Clarinet, Alto / Avant-Garde Jazz, Free Jazz
Microtonal innovator Joe Maneri was born in Brooklyn, NY in 1927, learning to play clarinet from a neighborhood shoemaker and making his professional debut on the Catskills society band circuit at age 17. Three years later, he was introduced to the work of Arnold Schoenberg, the famed inventor of the 12-tone system, and immediately thereafter formed his own 12-tone jazz ensemble, additionally performing in a number of ethnic music combos; a decade of study under composer Joseph Schmidt (himself a former Schoenberg student) followed before Maneri came to the attention of conductor Eric Leinsdorf, who commissioned him to compose a piano concerto. He made his first recordings for Atlantic in 1962; after the session went unreleased, Maneri was largely silent for the remainder of the decade, finally resurfacing in 1970 teaching theory and composition at the New England Conservatory of Music. Exploring microtones in his subsequent compositions and improvisations alike, Maneri's first officially-released recording, 1991's *Kavalinka*, found him joined by his violinist son Mat and percussionist Masashi Harada; two more efforts—the Leo Lab session *Get Ready to Receive Yourself* and *Three Men Walking*, an ECM date featuring guitarist Joe Morris—followed in 1995. Bassist Barre Phillips joined the Maneris for *Tales of Rohnlief*. *—Jason Ankeny*

Three Men Walking / Oct. 1995-Nov. 1995 / ECM ✦✦✦✦
Joe Maneri, 68 at the time of this intriguing ECM set, is an avant-garde explorer who has not mellowed with age. A master at playing microtonal music (notes between the 12 usual tones), Maneri is a thoughtful clarinetist and saxophonist capable of playing with great intensity at times while still leaving plenty of space. The fact that pianist Paul Bley (who has a similar musical philosophy) is a fan is not much of a surprise. On this CD, Maneri teams up with his son violinist Mat Maneri and guitarist Joe Morris for adventurous free improvisations plus an abstract but fairly melodic rendition of the standard "What's New." In addition to trio numbers, there are a few short solo explorations. During the best moments of the recommended release (such as occurs on "Deep Paths"), the music becomes a colorful and highly expressive (but never overcrowded) three-way conversation. *—Scott Yanow*

Paniots Nine / 1963 / Avant ✦✦✦✦✦
About 35 years before the current crop of downtown New York improvisers—such as Don Byron, Pachora, and John Zorn's Masada—were melding free jazz with world musics like Klezmer, and Greek, Eastern European, and Arabic modalities, there was Joe Maneri. *Paniots Nine* includes a demo made for Atlantic Records in 1963 by the saxophonist/clarinetist/composer and his working band at the time: pianist Don Burns, bassist John Beal, and drummer Pete Dolger, who were all interested in free jazz, and 20th century classical music

(Maneri had already been commissioned to write a piano concerto for the Boston Symphony, and all had played weddings, from Turkish to Jewish). The sound quality is not digital, but more than acceptable considering it was taken from a copy of a reel-to-reel tape.

This album is revelatory, capturing the use of weirdo time signatures like 9/8 in soloing and improvising, laced through with strange intervals and mode changes, and full of joy and drama. The boundaries blur between Eastern European wedding music and free jazz. The whirling clarinets and bowed bass played against a drummer who refused the traditional (in jazz, anyway) concept of rhythm in favor of counterrhythm atop the entire band, with the piano trailing in a rush. Of the eight pieces here, five are Maneri's, and he is the undisputed leader of this ensemble. His soloing shows not only a wealth of knowledge and a command of the instrument, but razor-sharp listening focus. Joe Maneri is a well-respected teacher who counts many creative musicians among his former students. He has in recent years resumed a performing career and commenced recording with the ECM label (those records smoke too). *Paniots Nine* provides the chance to hear his already well-developed ideas put into practice, and it is a delight. *—Thom Jurek*

• **Tales of Rohnlief** / 1998 / ECM ✦✦✦
Saxophonist, clarinetist, and pianist Joe Maneri engages here in a set of spirited improvisational dialogues with son Mat on electric six-string and baritone violin and Barre Phillips on five-string double bass. The two elder statesmen and the relative youngster are highly empathetic collaborators on these excursions, which fall somewhere between free jazz and experimental chamber music. While all three musicians are given equal prominence in the mix, Joe usually leads the way, with the violin and bass used to comment on or embellish the reedman's liquid phrases. Much of the improvisation floats freely in space, as slippery sax or clarinet lines intertwine with the moody arco of the unconventional strings. There is considerable variety as well, with squawks, smears, overtones, and percussive bowing all part of the expressive palette. At several points in the CD, Joe, the former street preacher, steps out with vocal recitations that flirt with the Phil Minton school of Dadaist absurdism. Joe's private language, delivered with disarming emotional directness, actually conceals allusions to artistic pioneers both musical and literary. Joe's piano ranges from Misha Mengelberg-styled fractured Monk-isms to (usually) a sparser and more atmospheric playing. "The Aftermath" features Phillips and Mat in a spacious duet, while "Elma My Dear," finds the bassist with Joe on tenor, a duet which begins calmly enough but moves through tension-filled episodes to a tentative reconciliation. *Tales of Rohnlief* is music for the adventurous listener with time to savor its subtleties. But those with ears tuned to more conventional musical rules should still find plenty of beauty, warmth, and even humor in this recording. *—Dave Lynch*

Albert Mangelsdorff

b. Sep. 5, 1928, Frankfurt, Germany
Trombone / Avant-Garde Jazz, Free Jazz
The master of multiphonics (playing more than one note at a time on a horn), Mangelsdorff has been a giant of the European avant-garde for the past 30 years. He originally studied violin and worked as a jazz guitarist before taking up the trombone in 1948. He played bop in the 1950s including with Hans Koller and local orchestras. In 1958 Mangelsdorff visited the United States to play with Marshall Brown's International Youth Band at the Newport Jazz Festival but his stays in America have always been fairly brief. By the time he recorded an album with John Lewis in 1962, Mangelsdorff was starting to lean towards the avant-garde. He has since recorded unaccompanied solo albums, been documented at a concert with Jaco Pastorius, led trios and worked with the Globe Unity Orchestra and the United Jazz & Rock Ensemble. Of his many records, the John Lewis set and his valuable MPS albums will be difficult to find but Albert Mangelsdorff's work for Enja and Sackville can be acquired. *—Scott Yanow*

• **Tromboneliness** / Jan. 1976-Mar. 1976 / Sackville ✦✦✦✦✦
A full album of unaccompanied solo trombone might seem a bit tedious but Albert Mangelsdorff is on a different level than most trombonists. For one thing he is a master of multiphonics (playing chords on a horn) and his use of a wa-wa mute is also quite expert. Although an avant-garde master, Mangelsdorff's version of "Creole Love Call" on this solo album is brilliant, as are his seven diverse originals. In addition, there is plenty of humor on these rambunctious performances. *—Scott Yanow*

Live at Montreux / Jul. 11, 1994 / Challenge ✦✦✦✦
Recorded live at the 1994 *Montreux Jazz Festival* in Switzerland and released by Challenge in 2000, this excellent performance unites trombonist Albert Mangelsdorff with drummer Reto Weber's Percussion Orchestra. *Live At Montreux* is an example of multiculturalism at its finest—you have jazz musicians from Germany (Mangelsdorff), and Switzerland (Weber), joining forces with a percussionist from Ghana (Nana Twum Nketia), and a zarb player from Iran (Keyvan Chemirani), at a Swiss jazz festival—and the label that released this CD is based in Holland. Mangelsdorff was 65 when *Live At Montreux* was recorded, and it's clear that the German improviser wasn't shying away from challenges in his old age. The music that Mangelsdorff, Weber and their allies provide is an intriguing, abstract blend of world music and avant-garde jazz. Mangelsdorff's trombone is the only wind instrument, and when he isn't blowing, all you hear are drums and percussion. Some will find the music too esoteric, but if you're a truly adventurous listener, the rewards are abundant. Sadly, Nana Twum Nketia died several months after *Live At Montreux* was recorded. *—Alex Henderson*

Chuck Mangione

b. Nov. 29, 1940, Rochester, NY
Piano (Electric), Flugelhorn, Trumpet, Producer / Crossover Jazz, Jazz-Pop, Neo-Bop
Throughout the 1970s, Chuck Mangione was a celebrity. His purposely lightweight music was melodic pop that was upbeat, optimistic and sometimes uplifting. Mangione's records were big sellers yet few of his fans from the era knew that his original goal was to be a bebopper. Mangione played with the big bands of Woody Herman and Maynard Ferguson (both in 1965) and Art Blakey's Jazz Messengers (1965-67). In 1968, now sticking mostly to his soft-toned flugelhorn, Mangione formed a quartet that also featured Gerry Niewood on tenor and soprano. They cut a fine set for Mercury in 1972 but otherwise Mangione's recordings in the 1970s generally used large orchestras and vocalists (including Esther Satterfield), putting the emphasis on lightweight melodies such as "Hill Where the Lord Hides," "Land of Make Believe," "Chase the Clouds Away" and the huge 1977 hit (featuring guitarist Grant Geissman) "Feels So Good." After a recorded 1978 Hollywood Bowl concert that summed up his pop years and a 1980 two-LP set that alternated pop and bop (with guest Dizzy Gillespie), Mangione gradually faded out of the music scene. *—Scott Yanow*

The Jazz Brothers / Aug. 8, 1960 / Milestone/OJC ✦✦✦

Hey Baby! / Mar. 8, 1961 / Riverside/OJC ✦✦✦

Recuerdo / Jul. 31, 1962 / Jazzland/OJC ✦✦✦✦
After three recordings co-leading the Jazz Brothers with pianist Gap Mangione, trumpeter Chuck Mangione headed his first solo record date. The CD reissue adds alternate takes of "Solar" and "The Little Prince" to the original LP program. Joined by an all-star rhythm section (pianist Wynton Kelly, bassist Sam Jones and drummer Louis Hayes) plus Joe Romano on tenor, flute and alto, Mangione mostly sticks to bebop on four jazz standards (including Charlie Parker's "Big Foot") and three of his originals. Although only 21 at the time, he holds his own with the illustrious rhythm section and was starting to display his own musical personality. His next recording as a leader would not take place until 1970, and by then he was starting to explore the pop-jazz formula that was to gain him great commercial success. *—Scott Yanow*

Friends and Love . . . A Chuck Mangione Concert / May 9, 1970 / Mercury ✦✦✦✦

Chuck Mangione Quartet / Mar. 1972 / Mercury ✦✦✦✦✦

Alive! / Aug. 1972 / Mercury ✦✦✦✦✦

• **Land of Make Believe** / 1973 / Mercury ✦✦✦✦✦
Though much less expansive than Mangione's other Mercury concerts (only 37 minutes on a single CD or LP), *Land of Make Believe* is the most successful of the lot, a winning combination of attractive tunes, big-thinking orchestrations, just enough jazz content, and a genuinely felt sense of idealism. Here there is no dead weight; all of the material is very engaging, and the combined forces of Mangione's quartet and the Hamilton (Ontario) Philharmonic are on fire. The performance of Mangione's "Legend of the One-Eyed Sailor" still exerts a ferocious jolt of life-affirming energy; "El Gato Triste" is an attractive Latin number; the buoyant "Gloria" from *The Mass of St. Bernard* with the Horsehead Chamber Singers makes one want to hear more. The child-like title tune has both a touching sense of naiveté and a lot of drive in key spots—credit expert drummer Joe LaBarbera with the latter—and Esther Satterfield's clear-eyed Nancy Wilson-like vocals made her famous for a time. This would be Mangione's most irresistible attempt to embrace the whole world of music—and for awhile, it was possible to believe that he would become a major unifying figure in American music. Alas, thus far, this would be the last full flowering of that promise. *—Richard S. Ginell*

Bellavia / 1975 / A&M ✦✦✦

Chase the Clouds Away / 1975 / A&M ✦✦✦

• **Feels So Good** / 1977 / A&M ✦✦✦✦
Due to the title cut, this was a huge seller when it originally came out. Reissued on CD, this set from flugelhornist Chuck Mangione (which helped give guitarist Grant Geissman some fame) is actually stronger from the jazz standpoint than Mangione's subsequent dates. The leader has some good solos as does Geissman and saxophonist Chris Vadala and the quintet's ensembles are generally both sparse and attractive. Pity that in ways this was Chuck Mangione's last worthwhile release to date; success did stunt his artistic growth. *—Scott Yanow*

An Evening of Magic, Live at the Hollywood Bowl / Jul. 16, 1978 / A&M ✦✦✦

Fun and Games / 1979 / A&M ✦✦✦

Tarantella / Dec. 27, 1980 / A&M ✦✦✦✦

Everything for Love / May 8, 2000-May 11, 2000 / Chesky ✦✦✦

Herbie Mann (Herbert Jay Solomon)

b. Apr. 16, 1930, Brooklyn, NY
Flute / Crossover Jazz, Afro-Cuban Jazz, Jazz-Pop, Soul-Jazz, Jazz-Funk
Herbie Mann has played a wide variety of music throughout his career. He became quite popular in the 1960s but in the '70s became so immersed in pop and various types of world music that he seemed lost to jazz. Fortunately Mann has never lost his ability to improvise creatively as he has shown in recent times. After serving in the Army, he was with Mat Mathews's Quintet (1953-54) and then started working and recording as a leader. During 1954-58 Mann stuck mostly to playing bop; he doubled on cool-toned tenor and was one of the few jazz musicians in the 1950s who recorded on bass clarinet. He also recorded in 1957 a full album (for Savoy) of unaccompanied flute. In 1959 Mann formed his Afro-Jazz Sextet, a group using several percussionists, vibes and the leader's flute.The most popular jazz flutist during the era, Mann explored bossa nova (even recording in Brazil in 1962), incorporated music from many cultures (plus current pop tunes) into his repertoire and had among his sidemen such top young musicians as Willie Bobo, Chick Corea, Attila Zoller and Roy Ayers. As the 1970s advanced, Mann became much more involved in rock, pop, reggae and even disco, but gradually came back to jazz. *—Scott Yanow*

Herbie Mann Plays / Dec. 1954 / Bethlehem Archives/Avenue Jazz ✦✦✦✦
Flutist Herbie Mann's first recording as a leader (seven selections from 1954 originally on a 10" LP plus four others cut in 1956) has been reissued on CD with three alternate takes added on. Even back in 1954, Mann (who doubles here on flute and alto flute) had his own sound. The music (featuring either Benny Weeks or Joe Puma on guitar in a piano-less quartet) is essentially straight-ahead bop and finds Mann playing quite melodically and with swing.

This set is a good example of Herbie Mann's early style before he started exploring various types of world musics. *—Scott Yanow*

Flute Souffle / Mar. 21, 1957-Mar. 27, 1957 / Prestige/OJC ♦♦♦♦♦
At the time of this Prestige set (reissued on CD), Herbie Mann was a flutist who occasionally played tenor and Bobby Jaspar a tenor-saxophonist who doubled on flute. Two of the four songs find them switching back and forth while the other two are strictly flute features. With pianist Tommy Flanagan, guitarist Joe Puma, bassist Wendell Marshall and drummer Bobby Donaldson contributing quiet support, the two lead voices constantly interact and trade off during this enjoyable performance. Highpoints are the haunting "Tel Aviv" and a delightful version of "Chasing the Bird." *—Scott Yanow*

Sultry Serenade / Apr. 1, 1957-Apr. 8, 1957 / Riverside ♦♦♦
For five of the eight cuts here, Mann has a sextet that sports an intriguing sonority—his flute stands alongside such underappreciated masters as the baritone saxophonist/bass clarinetist Jack Nimitz, trombonist Urbie Green and guitarist Joe Puma. No less a great bassist than Oscar Pettiford lays down the low-end law, while drummer Charlie Smith proves an expert with brushes on drums and cymbals. There are also three quartet dates sans Green and Nimitz. This is most definitely very fine post-bop modern jazz, with a harmonic twist or turn here and there. Mann has a pied-piper-like approach during his lone composition "Let Me Tell You," a head-nodding swing over an easy tempo. On Mann's spooky arrangement for the standard ballad "When the Sun Comes Out," the bass clarinet of Nimitz cues Smith's cymbal washes, with Green's trombone and Mann's whooshy flute making inquiring statements as the guitar embellishes with slightly wrought chords. Mann switches to bass clarinet on "Lazy Bones," paced as its title says. Nimitz is on a throaty Gerry Mulligan-esque bari with Green, collectively attaining a low-end growl, sounding like they're all ready to pounce, as Puma's snappy solo grounds the strike force. Mann (on flute) and Puma lead the easygoing Tyree Glenn-penned title track, with Nimitz's bass clarinet traipsing on eggshells for this dainty melody. The quartet tracks include "Swingin' 'Til the Girls Come Home," which proves the ultimate vehicle for Mann's lyricism, Puma's improvisational expertise, and those typical tall round notes from genius Pettiford. This date should not be forgotten as one of Herbie Mann's best. *—Michael G. Nastos*

Yardbird Suite / May 14, 1957 / Savoy ♦♦♦♦
Although flutist Herbie Mann's reputation suffered in the jazz world in later years due to his interest in other styles of music, during the 1954-58 period he stuck mostly to cool bebop and held his own with the best. This Savoy recording finds him matching ideas with the great altoist Phil Woods, along with vibraphonist Eddie Costa, guitarist Joe Puma, bassist Wendell Marshall and drummer Bobby Donaldson, and the results are quite enjoyable. In addition to his flute flights on three group originals and "Yardbird Suite," Mann fares quite well on tenor during the two other pieces. *—Scott Yanow*

Flute, Brass, Vibes and Percussion / 1960 / Verve ♦♦♦♦♦
In 1960, flutist Herbie Mann put together a very interesting band that was in its brief existence (before Mann's interests shifted elsewhere) one of the top in Afro-Cuban jazz. Utilizing four trumpets (including Doc Cheatham), up to three percussionists and a flute-vibes-bass-drums quartet, Mann performs four standards (including "Dearly Beloved," "I'll Remember April" and "Autumn Leaves") and two originals in a style that was beyond bop and much more African- and Cuban-oriented. This LP (long deserving of being reissued on CD) is quite underrated and is one of the finest of Mann's long career. *—Scott Yanow*

Herbie Mann Anthology / Aug. 3, 1960-Apr. 18, 1992 / Rhino ♦♦♦
This two-disc anthology doesn't cover Mann's bop or swing origins, instead concentrating on Mann's evolution from the 1960s to the 1990s. The first disc has more interest for jazz fans; it includes the influential "Memphis Underground" and "Coming Home Baby," showing his early flirtations with Latin and African music, as well as live workouts and Southern sessions. The second disc documents Mann's move into straight pop and light instrumentals, although near its conclusion he's returned to the groove-oriented Afro-Latin music of his earlier days. While there are questionable inclusions, especially the inferior live version of "Hold On I'm Comin'" rather than the definitive rendition from *Memphis Underground,* this set offers a good overview of a controversial but consistent musician. *—Ron Wynn*

The Best of Herbie Mann / 1960-1969 / Atlantic ♦♦♦

● **At the Village Gate** / Nov. 17, 1961 / Atlantic ♦♦♦♦♦
Remarkably few of flutist Herbie Mann's recordings are available on CD, but fortunately, this one did get reissued. Mann's hit version of "Comin' Home Baby" from this live set became his first big hit. The composer Ben Tucker plays second bass on that cut, and Mann's other sidemen include vibraphonist Hagood Hardy, bassist Ahmed Abdul-Malik, drummer Rudy Collins and Chief Bey and Ray Mantilla on percussion. In addition to "Comin' Home Baby," Mann and his men perform memorable versions of "Summertime" and "It Ain't Necessarily So"; the latter is 20 minutes long. Recommended. *—Scott Yanow*

Standing Ovation at Newport / May 24, 1965-Jul. 3, 1965 / Atlantic ♦♦♦♦
The performance by Herbie Mann's group was one of the high points of the 1965 *Newport Jazz Festival.* This album includes Mann's "Mushi Mushi" from an earlier date, but it is the lengthy versions of "Patato," "Stolen Moments," and particularly the encore "Comin' Home Baby" from Newport that are most memorable. During this period, the flutist's group included vibraphonist Dave Pike, two trombonists, the young Chick Corea on piano, bassist Earl May, drummer Bruno Carr, and Patato Valdes on conga. For "Comin' Home Baby," composer Ben Tucker, who had played earlier in the day as part of Billy Taylor's Trio, sits in on bass. *—Scott Yanow*

☆ **Concerto Grosso in D Blues** / Nov. 1968 / Wounded Bird ♦♦♦♦♦
Not only is this rare LP one of Herbie Mann's own favorites, it is one of the most moving classical/jazz fusions ever recorded. Right after the 1968 *Berlin Jazz Days* festival, Mann, his quintet, co-composer/conductor William Fischer, and a team of 80 Berlin musicians entered Teldec studios to record the huge, ambitious title piece, a concerto that successfully spans the decades from Tchaikovsky to Stockhausen, and from New Orleans to free jazz. With some stretches of group improvisation, the piece has structure, memorable yet surprisingly simple motifs, and holds together even when stretched to the limits of coherence by general outbreaks of freeform. To fill out the album, Mann and Fischer came up with three chamber pieces that if anything are even more successful than the main course. The best of the lot, the wistful "My Little Ones" (written for Mann's children), contains what is perhaps Mann's most haunting solo on record, at once loving and soaring, backed perfectly by Fischer's economical writing for double string quartet. *—Richard S. Ginell*

Memphis Underground / 1969 / Atlantic ♦♦♦

Push Push / Jul. 1, 1971 / Embryo ♦♦♦♦
Flutist Herbie Mann opened up his music on this date (and during the era) toward R&B, rock and funk music. The results were generally appealing, melodic and danceable. On such songs as "What's Going On," "Never Can Say Goodbye," "What'd I Say" and the title cut, Mann utilizes an impressive crew of musicians, which include guitarist Duane Allman and keyboardist Richard Tee. *—Scott Yanow*

Hold On, I'm Coming / 1972 / Atlantic ♦♦♦♦♦
This is one of the best Herbie Mann recordings and arguably his most rewarding of the 1970s. This long out of print LP features the leader/flutist, David Newman (on tenor and flute), the avant-garde guitarist Sonny Sharrock, and a fine backup rhythm section (electric pianist Pat Rebillot, bassist Andy Muson, and drummer Reggie Ferguson) stretching out on a variety of R&Bish material including "Respect Yourself," "Memphis Underground," and "Hold on, I'm Comin." The high quality of the solos and the spirited ensembles (which were inspired by the audience at the 1972 *New York Jazz Festival*) make this a generally memorable session. *—Scott Yanow*

65th Birthday Celebration: Live at the Blue Note in New York City / Apr. 25, 1995-Apr. 30, 1995 / Lightyear ♦♦♦♦♦
To celebrate his 65th birthday, the influential flutist Herbie Mann played for a week at *the Blue Note* in New York, along with some of his favorite musicians. Among the many guests on this CD are such notables as trumpeters Claudio Roditi and Randy Brecker, altoists David Newman, Paquito D'Rivera and Bobby Watson, fellow flutist Dave Valentin, Tito Puente on timbales and several rhythm sections. Alternating between Brazilian music, vintage funk jazz (such as "Memphis Underground"), a catchy boogaloo blues ("Dippermouth") and a few straight-ahead tracks ("Au Privave" and "Jeep's Blues"), the flutist sounds as if he had a great time. The diverse music is consistently infectious and joyful, with all eight selections well worth hearing. Highly recommended. *—Scott Yanow*

☆ **America/Brasil** / Apr. 25, 1995-Apr. 30, 1995 / Lightyear ♦♦♦♦♦
America/Brasil is a rollicking, celebratory album that keeps Herbie Mann on the winning streak he started with the release of *Peace Pieces* in 1995. Recorded during a week of concerts to mark his 65th birthday in April, 1995, this disc is much stronger than its immediate predecessor, *Celebration,* also taken from the same week of live concert performances at New York's *Blue Note* jazz club. The material here is superb, and the playing topnotch. As the title implies, the emphasis here is on Mann's Brazilian side, but there are touches of the non-Brazilian with Bill Evans' "Peri's Scope," and Miles Davis' "All Blues." "Summertime" is recast in an Afro-Cuban mode with Paquito D'Rivera sharing the solo space on alto sax. However, lengthy Brazilian showstoppers are placed at the beginning, middle and end of this wonderful disc. The opening "Keep the Spirits Singing" is propelled by the polyrhythmic pulse of percussionists Cyro Baptista and "Café," and the 17-minute title track finale features trumpeters Randy Brecker and Claudio Roditi, trombonist Jim Pugh and guitarist Romero Lubambo. Even with the all-star cast assembled for this special week of concerts, it's Herbie Mann himself whose playing shines the brightest throughout this recording, celebrating his past and affirming his place in the present as the finest flutist working in jazz. *—Jim Newsom*

Herbie Mann-Sam Most Quintet / Apr. 6, 1999 / Rhino ♦♦♦♦
This 1999 CD reissues an early Herbie Mann set that matches him with his fellow flutist, Sam Most. Originally, this date was known as *The Mann With the Most.* Recorded back during Mann's bebop period, the set teams the two flutists with guitarist Joe Puma, bassist Jimmy Gannon and drummer Lee Kleinman. The quintet performs nine standards plus an original apiece from Most and Puma. Highlights include "Fascinating Rhythm," "Let's Get Away from It All" and "Seven Come Eleven." Most was actually the better known of the two flutists at the time but, while he ended up in the Los Angeles studios, Mann's constant musical curiosity would result in him gaining worldwide fame. Their enjoyable music, brought back by Avenue Jazz, finds the flutists battling it out to a draw. *—Scott Yanow*

Shelly Manne

b. Jun. 11, 1920, New York, NY, **d.** Sep. 26, 1984, Los Angeles, CA
Drums / West Coast Jazz, Cool, Bop
Shelly Manne made a countless number of records from the 1940s into the 1980s but is best-known as a good-humored bandleader who never hogged the spotlight. He was with Joe Marsala's band (making his recording debut in 1941), played briefly in the big bands of Will Bradley, Raymond Scott and Les Brown and was on drums for Coleman Hawkins's classic "The Man I Love" session of late 1943. Manne worked on and off with Stan Kenton during 1946-52, then moved to Los Angeles where he became the most in-demand of all jazz drummers. He began recording as a leader on a regular basis starting in 1953 when he first put together the quintet Shelly Manne and His Men. Manne, who had the good fortune to be the leader of a date by the Andre Previn Trio that resulted in a major seller (jazz versions of tunes from *My Fair Lady*), always had an open musical mind and he recorded some fairly free pieces on *The Three and the Two* (trios with Shorty Rogers and Jimmy Giuffre that did not have a piano or bass along with duets with Russ Freeman) and enjoyed playing on an early session with Ornette Coleman. In addition to his jazz work, Manne appeared on many film soundtracks and even acted in *The Man with the Golden Arm.* *—Scott Yanow*

Shelly Manne and His Men / 1953 / Contemporary ♦♦♦♦♦

★ **Vol. 1: The West Coast Sound** / Apr. 6, 1953-Sep. 13, 1955 / Contemporary/OJC ♦♦♦♦♦
Drummer Shelly Manne's first sessions for Contemporary contain plenty of definitive examples of West Coast jazz. This CD has four titles apiece from a 1953 septet date with altoist Art Pepper, Bob Cooper on tenor, baritonist Jimmy Giuffre and valve trombonist Bob Enevoldsen, four from a few months later with Bud Shank in Pepper's place and four other songs from 1955 when Manne headed a septet with altoist Joe Maini and Bill Holman on tenor in addition to Giuffre and Enevoldsen. With arrangements by Marty Paich (who plays piano on the first two dates), Giuffre, Shorty Rogers, Bill Russo, Holman and Enevoldsen, the music has plenty of variety yet defines the era, ranging from Bill Russo's "Sweets" (a tribute to trumpeter Harry "Sweets" Edison), Giuffre's "Fugue," the Latin folk tune "La Mucura" and updated charts on older swing tunes. Highly recommended and proof (if any is really needed) that West Coast Jazz was far from bloodless. *—Scott Yanow*

New Works: Shelly Manne, Vol. 2 / Dec. 18, 1953-May 17, 1954 / Contemporary ♦♦♦♦♦

Shelly Manne & His Men, Vol. 2 / Dec. 18, 1953-Jun. 24, 1957 / Contemporary/OJC ♦♦♦

Shelly Manne, Vol. 3 / Sep. 10, 1954 / Contemporary ♦♦♦♦♦

The Three and "The Two" / Sep. 10, 1954-Sep. 14, 1954 / Contemporary/OJC ♦♦♦♦♦
These two sets for the Contemporary label (reissued on CD in the OJC label) are two of the more unusual sessions led by drummer Shelly Manne in the 1950s. "The Three" features trumpeter Shorty Rogers, Jimmy Giuffre alternating on clarinet, tenor and baritone, and Manne; no piano or bass. Some of the six performances (particularly the four originals) are quite free, particularly the completely improvised "Abstract No. 1." Although these selections were not influential, they rank second in chronological order (behind Lennie Tristano's performances of 1949) among free jazz records. The remainder of this set ("The Two") is a duet between pianist Russ Freeman and Manne and is also quite advanced in spots, although in general it is a more swinging session while still being unpredictable. Overall, a very interesting reissue. *—Scott Yanow*

Vol. 4: Swinging Sounds / Jan. 19, 1956-Feb. 2, 1956 / Contemporary/OJC ♦♦♦♦
This early edition of Shelly Manne & His Men is a well-integrated unit featuring the light-toned trumpet of Stu Williamson, the cool but hard-driving altoist Charlie Mariano, pianist Russ Freeman and bassist Leroy Vinnegar in addition to the drummer/leader. The excellent quintet plays one original apiece from each musician except Vinnegar in addition to Bud Powell's "Un Poco Loco," Sonny Rollins' "Doxy," the standard "Bernie's Tune" and their closing theme, Bill Holman's "A Gem from Tiffany." *—Scott Yanow*

More Swinging Sounds / Jul. 16, 1956-Aug. 16, 1956 / Contemporary/OJC ♦♦♦♦♦
Drummer Shelly Manne and his 1956 quintet (with trumpeter Stu Williamson, altoist Charlie Mariano, pianist Russ Freeman and bassist Leroy Vinnegar) perform some challenging material on this CD reissue. The longest piece is Bill Holman's 15 1/2 minute four-part suite "Quartet" which, despite its potential complexity, actually swings pretty well. In addition, Manne & His Men interpret Johnny Mandel's obscure "Tommyhawk," a Mariano blues number, Charlie Parker's "Moose the Mooche" and Russ Freeman's "The Wind." Shelly Manne deserves great credit for being continually open to new directions and fresh material while staying on his own singular path. *—Scott Yanow*

☆ **My Fair Lady** / Aug. 17, 1956 / Contemporary/OJC ♦♦♦♦♦
This trio set by "Shelly Manne & His Friends" (which consists of the drummer/leader, pianist Andre Previn and bassist Leroy Vinnegar) was a surprise best-seller and is now considered a classic. Previn (who is really the main voice) leads the group through eight themes from the famous play including "Get Me to the Church on Time," "I've Grown Accustomed to Her Face," "I Could Have Danced All Night" and "On the Street Where You Live." A very appealing set that is easily recommended; an audiophile version has also been released on CD by DCC Jazz. *—Scott Yanow*

At the Blackhawk, Vol. 1 / Sep. 22, 1959-Sep. 24, 1959 / Contemporary/OJC ♦♦♦

At the Blackhawk, Vol. 2 / Sep. 23, 1959-Sep. 24, 1959 / Contemporary/OJC ♦♦♦♦
Vol. 2 of the five CDs that document drummer Shelly Manne's Quintet at the *Black Hawk* club in San Francisco during a three-day period adds a new alternate take of Charlie Mariano's "Step Lightly" to the original program ("Step Lightly," "What's New," "Vamp's Blues"). These lengthy performances ("Vamp's Blues" is over 19 minutes long) give trumpeter Joe Gordon, the cool-toned tenor-saxophonist Richie Kamuca, pianist Victor Feldman, bassist Monty Budwig and the leader/drummer a chance to really stretch out. Fine 1950s bebop. *—Scott Yanow*

At the Blackhawk, Vol. 3 / Sep. 23, 1959-Sep. 24, 1959 / Contemporary/OJC ♦♦♦♦
Originally released as four LPs, the Shelly Manne Quintet's three days at San Francisco's *Black Hawk* club is now documented on five CDs. The third volume adds a second (and longer) version of "Whisper Not" to the original rendition, Cole Porter's "I Am in Love" and the spontaneous 18-minute "Black Hawk Blues." Considering how much music was documented, it is fortunate that trumpeter Joe Gordon, tenorman Richie Kamuca, pianist Victor Feldman, bassist Monty Budwig and drummer Shelly Manne were in top form for this enjoyable gig. The music is high-quality straightforward and uncomplicated bebop. *—Scott Yanow*

At the Blackhawk, Vol. 4 / Sep. 23, 1959-Sep. 24, 1959 / Contemporary/OJC ♦♦♦♦
Shelly Manne's 1959 Quintet (with trumpeter Joe Gordon, tenor-saxophonist Richie Kamuca, pianist Victor Feldman, bassist Monty Budwig and the drummer/leader) was not his most important but it was a hard-swinging unit well versed in bebop. Their three days at *the Black Hawk* (a popular San Francisco jazz club during this era) was almost completely documented, originally on four LPs and now expanded to five CDs. As with the first three sets, the fourth volume adds an alternate take (of "Cabu") to the original program ("Cabu," "Just Squeeze Me," "Nightingale" and a full-length version of their theme "A Gem from Tiffany"). The lengthy solos are consistently excellent, making this entire series recommended to straightahead fans. *—Scott Yanow*

At the Blackhawk, Vol. 5 / Sep. 23, 1959-Sep. 24, 1959 / Contemporary/OJC ♦♦♦♦
Unlike the first four volumes of this series, which included three or four selections previously released plus a "new" alternate take, the final CD of the extensive documentation of the Shelly Manne Quintet's stint at the *Black Hawk* club consists entirely of previously unreleased material. Fortunately, the performances by trumpeter Joe Gordon, tenor saxophonist Richie Kamuca, pianist Russ Freeman, bassist Monty Budwig, and the drummer/leader are the same high level as on the more familiar material. They perform obscure songs by Horace Silver (has anyone else ever recorded his "How Deep Are the Roots—") and Victor Feldman in addition to a trio feature on "Wonder Why," the ballad "This Is Always," and a new version of the band's theme song, "A Gem From Tiffany." *—Scott Yanow*

At the Manne-Hole, Vol. 1 / Mar. 3, 1961-Mar. 5, 1961 / Contemporary/OJC ♦♦♦♦♦
On the first of two CDs (both of which are straight reissues of the original LPs), Shelly Manne and His Men are heard in prime form performing live at their home base, Shelly's Manne-Hole. Trumpeter Conte Candoli was in particularly strong form throughout the stint, showing self-restraint yet playing with power. Tenor-saxophonist Richie Kamuca made for a complementary partner while pianist Russ Freeman and bassist Chuck Berghofer formed an excellent rhythm section with the leader/drummer. For *Vol. 1* they play "Love for Sale," Duke Ellington's fairly obscure "How Could It Happen to a Dream," "Softly as in a Morning Sunrise" and Dizzy Gillespie's uptempo blues "The Champ." This classic music falls between cool jazz and hard bop. *—Scott Yanow*

At the Manne-Hole, Vol. 2 / Mar. 3, 1961-Mar. 5, 1961 / Contemporary/OJC ♦♦♦♦♦
The second of two CDs featuring Shelly Manne's Quintet in superior form at the legendary *Shelly's Manne-Hole* club in Hollywood. Trumpeter Conte Candoli (in top form) and the cool-toned tenor Richie Kamuca work together very well while the contributions of the rhythm section (pianist Russ Freeman, bassist Chuck Berghofer and the drummer/leader) should not be overlooked. Together they perform four standards (highlighted by "On Green Dolphin Street" and "If I Were a Bell") plus their closing theme "A Gem from Tiffany." Both of the volumes are easily recommended. *—Scott Yanow*

Perk Up / Jun. 19, 1977-Jun. 20, 1977 / Concord Jazz ♦♦♦♦
This CD reissue brings back one of the oldest recordings ever issued by the Concord label, a set that was already nine years old when it debuted. Drummer Shelly Manne heads a strong quintet comprised of trumpeter Conte Candoli, altoist Frank Strozier (who doubles on flute), pianist Mike Wofford and bassist Monty Budwig. Although the musicians are all associated with the West Coast hard bop tradition, there are plenty of moments during this stimulating set when they make it obvious that they had been listening with some interest to some of the avant-garde players, allowing the new innovations to open up their styles a bit. The fresh material (two standards and a pair of originals apiece by Strozier, Wofford and pianist Jimmy Rowles) inspire the soloists and the music is not at all predictable. Worth investigating. *—Scott Yanow*

Branford Marsalis

b. Aug. 26, 1960, Breaux Bridge, LA
Sax (Tenor), Sax (Soprano), Sax (Alto) / New Orleans Jazz, M-Base, Hard Bop, Post-Bop
The oldest of the four musical Marsalis brothers, Branford Marsalis has already had an impressive career. He mostly played tenor and soprano while with Wynton Marsalis's influential group (1982-85), at first sounding most influenced by Wayne Shorter but leaning more towards John Coltrane at the end. The musical telepathy between the two brothers (who helped to revive the sound of the mid-'60s Miles Davis Quintet) was sometimes astounding. In 1985 when he left Wynton to join Sting's pop/rock group, it caused a major (if temporary) rift with his brother that made headlines. Marsalis enjoyed playing with Sting but did not let the association cause him to forget his musical priorities. By 1986 he was leading his own group; he became even more of a celebrity when he joined Jay Leno's *Tonight Show* as the musical director in 1992. However being cast in the role of Leno's sidekick rubbed against Marsalis's temperament and after two years he had had enough. Marsalis, who attempted to mix together hip-hop and jazz in his erratic *Buckshot LeFonque* project, has recorded steadily for Columbia ever since 1983 (including a classical set) and still seems to be searching for his niche. *—Scott Yanow*

Scenes in the City / Apr. 18, 1983-Nov. 29, 1983 / Columbia ♦♦♦♦♦
Branford Marsalis's debut as a leader is ambitious yet consistently successful. On "Scenes of the City," his narrative is in the same spirit of some of Charles Mingus's recordings of the 1950s. Otherwise the music is in the modern mainstream vein with Marsalis (on tenor and soprano) hinting strongly at Wayne Shorter and John Coltrane, along with a touch of Sonny Rollins. The backup crew includes such notable young lions as pianist Mulgrew Miller and Kenny Kirkland, bassist Charnett Moffett, and drummers Jeff "Tain" Watts and Marvin "Smitty" Smith in addition to bassist Ron Carter. It's an impressive start to a notable career. *—Scott Yanow*

Royal Garden Blues / Mar. 18, 1986-Jul. 2, 1986 / Columbia ♦♦♦♦
Branford Marsalis' second album as a leader followed his first by three years and he had grown a lot in the interim. He had switched permanently to tenor (doubling on soprano), left his brother Wynton's group, toured with Sting and begun heading his own group. Although using quartets on each of the seven selections, Marsalis varies the personnel quite a bit, utilizing pianists Ellia Marsalis, Kenny Kirkland, Larry Willis and Herbie Hancock, bassists Ron Carter, Charnett Moffett and Ira Coleman and drummers Ralph Peterson, Al Foster, Marvin "Smitty" Smith and Jeff Watts. One of Branford's more playful albums, the repertoire includes a tribute of sorts to his native New Orleans on "Royal Garden Blues" plus "Strike Up the Band" and recent originals. An excellent outing. *—Scott Yanow*

Renaissance / Dec. 31, 1986-Jan. 28, 1987 / Columbia ♦♦♦♦
The highpoint of Branford Marsalis' third Columbia release as a leader is a 15-minute version of Jimmy Rowles' "The Peacocks" played in a trio with pianist Herbie Hancock and bassist Buster Williams. The remainder of the program matches Marsalis with pianist Kenny Kirkland, bassist Bob Hurst and drummer Tony Williams on a pair of standards ("Just One of Those Things" and a live version of "St. Thomas"), J.J. Johnson's "Lament" and originals by Marsalis and Williams. Although he did not have an immediately recognizable sound on

tenor and soprano at this point, it was obvious from nearly the start that Branford Marsalis would have a very significant career. This is one of his better early efforts. *—Scott Yanow*

Random Abstract / Aug. 1987 / Columbia ✦✦✦✦✦
Branford Marsalis (on tenor and soprano) and his 1987 quartet (which also includes pianist Kenny Kirkland, bassist Delbert Felix and drummer Lewis Nash) stretch out on a wide repertoire during this generally fascinating set. Very much a chameleon for the date, Marsalis does close impressions of Wayne Shorter on "Yes and No," John Coltrane ("Crescent City"), Ben Webster (a warm version of "I Thought About You"), Ornette Coleman ("Broadway Falls") and even Jan Garbarek (on a long rendition of Coleman's "Lonely Woman"); the release also includes a jam on Kirkland's "LonJellis," a piece without chord changes. This is one of Branford Marsalis' most interesting (and somewhat unusual) recordings to date. *—Scott Yanow*

● **Trio Jeepy** / Jan. 3, 1988-Jan. 4, 1988 / Columbia ✦✦✦✦✦
Branford Marsalis clearly had a lot of fun during this set. On seven of the ten numbers included on the double-LP (the CD reissue actually has one less selection), Marsalis romps on tenor and soprano in a trio with veteran bassist Milt Hinton and drummer Jeff "Tain" Watts; the remaining three numbers have Delbert Felix in Hinton's place. The performances are quite spontaneous (the occasional mistakes were purposely left in) and Marsalis really romps on such tunes as "Three Little Words," "Makin' Whoopee" and "Doxy." On the joyful outing that is also one of Branford Marsalis' most accessible recordings, Milt Hinton often steals the show. *—Scott Yanow*

Crazy People Music / Jan. 10, 1990-Mar. 1, 1990 / Columbia ✦✦✦✦
Branford Marsalis (on tenor and soprano) performs four of his originals, Bob Hurst's "The Dark Knight," Keith Jarrett's obscure "Rose Petals" and "The Ballad of Chet Kincaid" (co-written by Bill Cosby and Quincy Jones) on this outing with his 1990 quartet, an impressive group that also includes pianist Kenny Kirkland, bassist Hurst and drummer Jeff "Tain" Watts. None of the songs would catch on but Marsalis is heard throughout in prime form, sounding more original than usual and really pushing himself. *—Scott Yanow*

The Beautyful Ones Are Not Yet Born / May 16, 1991-May 18, 1991 / Columbia ✦✦✦✦✦
This set is one of Branford Marsalis' strongest of the 1990s. Marsalis really stretches out on eight numbers including six of his originals (the other two songs are by bassist Bob Hurst). There is one guest appearance apiece from brother-trumpeter Wynton and tenor saxophonist Courtney Pine but otherwise Branford is accompanied only by Hurst and drummer Jeff "Tain" Watts. His playing is often reminiscent in style (but not really sound) of John Coltrane, he is more concise and disciplined than in some of his early-'90s concert appearances and Marsalis is at his most explorative on this inventive blowing session. *—Scott Yanow*

Bloomington / Sep. 23, 1991 / Columbia ✦✦

I Heard You Twice the First Time / 1992 / Columbia ✦✦✦
Branford Marsalis plays the blues on this interesting if erratic CD. Among his many guests are B.B. King (although there is surprisingly no interaction between Marsalis and King), John Lee Hooker, Russell Malone, Linda Hopkins (who comes across very well), Joe Louis Walker and brothers Wynton and Delfeayo. Ranging from hints of field hollers and New Orleans to country blues, a vignette ("Brother Trying to Catch a Cab (On the East Side) Blues") and a few more conventional burnouts, this is an intriguing set that is worth picking up. *—Scott Yanow*

Dark Keys / Jul. 31, 1996-Aug. 2, 1996 / Sony ✦✦✦
Dark Keys is Branford Marsalis' first major solo album since taking a leave from recording to be the musical director of *The Tonight Show* in 1993. Instead of following through with the hip-hop inclinations of Buckshot LeFonque, Marsalis has returned to traditional jazz, yet this is far from standard bop. Marsalis pushes at the borders of post-bop, adding elements of hip-hop and rock & roll, making for an adventurous and exciting listen. Occasionally, his experiments are unsuccessful, yet they are never less than intriguing. *—Leo Stanley*

Requiem / Aug. 17, 1998-Dec. 10, 1998 / Columbia ✦✦✦✦
Branford Marsalis' longtime pianist Kenny Kirkland died two months after the sessions for this album began—hence the title—and after a futile attempt to finish the recording in December 1998, Branford decided to leave the music as is, first takes and all. If there are any serious flaws in the playing, they will escape the vast majority of ears out there, for this is an uncompromising, well-played disc of acoustic jazz that leans a bit toward adventure at times. At first, Branford's foursome (Kirkland, Eric Revis on bass, and Jeff "Tain" Watts on drums) seems content to turn out a pretty good facsimile of the John Coltrane Quartet, with Kirkland playing brilliantly and reflectively in the McCoy Tyner manner. But with "Lykief"—a pun on Keith Jarrett's name—Branford takes up Jarrett's long unanswered challenge and pushes through a tumbling, nearly rhythmically free piece attractively anchored by Jarrett's gospel harmonies and melodic methods. "Bullworth" blasts off on a Watts hip-hop rhythm, with Branford going nuts in an angular bit of soloing, and "16th St. Baptist Church" apparently sends the CD home on a funky New Orleans street march, only to be followed by a touching, uncredited Marsalis/Kirkland benediction. Once again, the post-*Tonight Show,* post-Buckshot Marsalis makes a credibly serious jazz statement in what turned out to be the swan song for one of the neo-bop era's finest lineups. *—Richard S. Ginell*

Contemporary Jazz / Dec. 1, 1999-Dec. 4, 1999 / Columbia ✦✦✦✦
This album was much anticipated, for it would be Branford Marsalis's first since the death of his longtime pianist Kenny Kirkland. Happily, it is a knockout. While no one can entirely recreate the famed chemistry that existed between Kirkland and Marsalis, pianist Joey Calderazzo does a marvelous job handling the extraordinary complexity, energy, and beauty of Marsalis's music. Bassist Eric Revis and drummer Jeff "Tain" Watts, both of whom played on 1999's *Requiem* (which wound up being the last recording of Kirkland's life), carry on here in the spirit of their departed friend, fleshing out Marsalis's increasingly challenging ensemble concepts and—most importantly—swinging like men possessed.

"In the Crease" and "Tain Mutiny," with their unpredictable twists and turns, are indicative of the gravitas of Marsalis's work ever since he left his post at *The Tonight Show.* But the album's high point is a lengthy take of "Elysium," a tune that appeared on *Requiem* as a trio piece, an aesthetic choice necessitated by the sudden death of Kirkland who never had a chance to play on the track. Here the full quartet weighs in, deftly executing a dizzying series of tempo shifts and subtle cues, all seamlessly worked into a fabric of extended, burning improvisation.

Finally, "Sleepy Hollow," a slow blues tucked away at the end of the program as a hidden track, sounds as though the band just let the tape roll as they warmed down from the session. It's a delightfully unrehearsed moment, perhaps a closing homage to Kirkland, drawn from deep down in the tradition. *—David R. Adler*

Ellis Marsalis

b. Nov. 14, 1934, Gert Town, LA
Piano / Hard Bop, Post-Bop
It is a bit ironic that Ellis Marsalis had to wait for sons Wynton and Branford to get famous before he was able to record on a regular basis, but Ellis has finally received his long-overdue recognition. The father of six sons (including Wynton, Branford, Delfeayo and Jason), Ellis Marsalis's main importance to jazz may very well be as a jazz educator; his former pupils (in addition to his sons) include Terence Blanchard, Donald Harrison, Harry Connick, Jr., Nicholas Payton and Kent and Marlon Jordan among others. He started out as a tenor-saxophonist, switching to piano while in high school. Marsalis was one of the few New Orleans musicians of the era who did not specialize in Dixieland or rhythm & blues. He played with fellow modernists (including Ed Blackwell) in the late '50s with AFO, recorded with Cannonball and Nat Adderley in the 1960s, played with Al Hirt (1967-70) and was busy as a teacher. Marsalis freelanced in New Orleans during the 1970s and taught at the New Orleans Center for Creative Arts. He recorded with Wynton and Branford on *Father and Sons* in 1982, an album that they shared with Chico and Von Freeman. Since then Marsalis has recorded for ELM, Spindletop (a duet session with Eddie Harris), Rounder, Blue Note and Columbia, issuing *Twelve's It* on the latter in 1998. *Duke in Blue* followed a year later. *—Scott Yanow*

Father and Sons / 1982 / Columbia ✦✦✦✦✦
The side with sons Wynton and Branford is worth the price of admission. They swing very hard. *—Michael G. Nastos*

Piano in E-Solo Piano / Jul. 24, 1986 / Rounder ✦✦✦✦✦
Ellis Marsalis got his time in the spotlight with this fine solo piano session. His mix of swing, Afro-Latin, classical and bebop was spotlighted on superbly crafted versions of Horace Silver's "Nica's Dream" and John Lewis' "Django," as well as Bud Powell's "Hallucinations" and Fats Waller's "Jitterbug Waltz." Marsalis' own originals, "Fourth Autumn" and "Zee Blues" were also expertly written, with charming melodies and smooth, relaxed, yet impressive solos. While he'll probably never get as much publicity as sons Wynton and Branford, Ellis Marsalis certainly deserves high praise for his formidable piano skills. *—Ron Wynn*

Ellis Marsalis Trio / Mar. 18, 1990 / Blue Note ✦✦✦✦
Pianist Ellis Marsalis is in excellent form for this trio outing with bassist Bob Hurst and drummer Jeff "Tain" Watts. The performances fall generally into the medium-tempo range, with Ellis scattering some witty song quotes throughout the lightly swinging renditions. The high points include one of the more delightful versions ever of Johnny Mandel's "Emily," some close interplay during "Little Niles" and a tongue-in-cheek version of "Limehouse Blues" that includes slapped bass, parade rhythms and Marsalis trying in vain to sound Dixielandish. One programming error should be noted: there is no such song as "Just Squeeze Me" and, rather than the one performed being Fats Waller's "Squeeze Me," it is actually Duke Ellington's "Squeeze Me, But Please Don't Tease Me." *—Scott Yanow*

● **Whistle Stop** / Mar. 20, 1993-Jun. 6, 1993 / Columbia ✦✦✦✦✦
For this CD, veteran pianist Ellis Marsalis performs songs composed by some of the top modern New Orleans players of the 1960s including drummer James Black, tenor-saxophonist Nat Perrilliat, clarinetist Alvin Batiste, saxophonist Harold Battiste and himself. With the exception of Alvin Batiste's tunes (based on "Cherokee" and a Dixielandish blues), the originals have strong melodies, slightly tricky chord structures and sound quite fresh today. Marsalis utilizes his son Branford on tenor and soprano, bassist Robert Hurst and drummer Jeff "Tain" Watts; the young Jason Marsalis sits in on drums during two numbers. Ellis Marsalis is in particularly inventive form on this unusually obscure material. *—Scott Yanow*

Loved Ones / Aug. 14, 1995-Sep. 11, 1995 / Columbia ✦✦✦✦

Twelve's It / Mar. 1, 1996-Jan. 6, 1998 / Columbia ✦✦✦✦

Wynton Marsalis

b. Oct. 18, 1961, New Orleans, LA
Trumpet, Composer, Arranger / Contemporary Jazz, New Orleans Jazz, Post-Bop, Neo-Bop, Swing, Classical
The most famous jazz musician since 1980, Wynton Marsalis made a major impact on jazz almost from the start. In the early '80s it was major news that a young and very talented Black musician would choose to make a living playing acoustic jazz rather than fusion, funk or R&B. Marsalis's arrival on the scene started the "Young Lions" movement and resulted in major labels (most of whom had shown no interest in jazz during the previous decade) suddenly signing and promoting young players. There had been a major shortage of new trumpeters since 1970 but Marsalis' sudden prominence inspired an entire new crop of brass players. The music of the mid-'60s Miles Davis Quintet had been somewhat overshadowed when it was new but Marsalis's Quintet focused on extending the group's legacy and soon other "Young Lion" units were using Davis's late acoustic work as their starting point. During the past 15 years Marsalis has managed to be a controversial figure despite his obvious abilities. His trumpet playing has been both overcriticized and (at least early on) overpraised—he was so widely praised by the jazz press at the time (due to their relief that the future of jazz finally seemed safe) that there was an inevitable backlash. With the 1990 recording *Tune in Tomorrow,* Marsalis at last sounded like himself. He had found his own voice by exploring earlier styles of jazz (such as Louis Armstrong's playing), mastering the wa-wa mute and

studying Duke Ellington. From that point on, even when playing a Miles Davis standard, Marsalis has had his own sound and has finally taken his place as one of jazz's greats. *—Scott Yanow*

Wynton Marsalis / Aug. 1981 / Columbia ✦✦✦✦✦
Trumpeter Wynton Marsalis's debut on Columbia, recorded when he was only 19, made it clear from the start that he was going to be a major force in jazz. At the time Marsalis (who was originally a bit influenced by Freddie Hubbard) was starting to closely emulate Miles Davis of the mid-'60s and his slightly older brother Branford took Wayne Shorter as his role model. The inclusion of Davis's rhythm section from that era (pianist Herbie Hancock, bassist Ron Carter and drummer Tony Williams) on four of the seven selections reinforced the image. The three other numbers feature such up-and-coming talents as pianist Kenny Kirkland, Charles Fambrough or Clarence Seay on bass and drummer Jeff "Tain" Watts, helping to launch the rise of the Young Lions. But although not overly original, there is a great deal of outstanding playing on this set, including a definitive version of Tony Williams's "Sister Cheryl" and the long tradeoff between Wynton and Branford on "Hesitation." *—Scott Yanow*

Think of One / 1983 / Columbia ✦✦✦✦✦
Wynton Marsalis's second Columbia recording as a leader features his working band of 1983: brother Branford on tenor and soprano, pianist Kenny Kirkland, either Phil Bowler or Ray Drummond on bass and drummer Jeff "Tain" Watts. They perform the ballad "My Ideal," Duke Ellington's "Melancholia" and Thelonious Monk's "Think of One" along with some group originals. Wynton was deep in his Miles Davis period while Branford (who was still most influenced by Wayne Shorter) was just beginning to come into his own. Of course Wynton was already a remarkable virtuoso a few years earlier. All of his recordings are worth getting and this early document has more than its share of brilliant playing. *—Scott Yanow*

Hot House Flowers / May 30, 1984-May 31, 1984 / Columbia ✦✦✦

★ **Black Codes (From the Underground)** / Jan. 11, 1985-Jan. 14, 1985 / Columbia ✦✦✦✦✦
This is probably the best Wynton Marsalis recording from his Miles Davis period. With his brother Branford (who doubles here on tenor and soprano) often closely emulating Wayne Shorter and the rhythm section (pianist Kenny Kirkland, bassist Charnett Moffett and drummer Jeff Watts) sounding a bit like the famous Herbie Hancock-Ron Carter-Tony Williams trio, Wynton is heard at the head of what was essentially an updated version of the mid-to-late-'60s Miles Davis Quintet (despite Stanley Crouch's pronouncements in his typically absurd liner notes about Marsalis's individuality). The music is brilliantly played and displays what the "Young Lions" movement was really about; young musicians choosing to explore acoustic jazz and to extend the innovations of the pre-fusion modern mainstream style. Marsalis would develop his own sound a few years later but even at age 23 he had few close competitors. *—Scott Yanow*

J Mood / Dec. 17, 1985-Dec. 20, 1985 / Columbia ✦✦✦✦✦
When Branford Marsalis and Kenny Kirkland chose to leave Wynton Marsalis's group to make money with Sting, Wynton had to regroup fast. For this quartet recording with bassist Robert Hurst III and drummer Jeff "Tain" Watts, the trumpeter met up with pianist Marcus Roberts for the first time, performing originals by Wynton, Roberts, Ellis Marsalis and Donald Brown. Marsalis was still very much under Miles Davis's influence at the time but at age 24 he had rather remarkable technique. He stretches out in explorative and consistently creative fashion on these seven straightahead and generally unpredictable selections. *—Scott Yanow*

Standard Time, Vol. 1 / May 29, 1986-Sep. 25, 1986 / Columbia ✦✦✦✦
On the first of three volumes, Wynton Marsalis explores ten standards plus two of his originals with his quartet of the period (which consists of pianist Marcus Roberts, bassist Robert Hurst III and drummer Jeff "Tain" Watts). Marsalis's tone is quite beautiful on the well-balanced set; even the ballads have their unpredictable moments. Among the more memorable performances are his treatments of "Caravan," "April in Paris," "New Orleans," "Memories of You" and two versions of "Cherokee." *—Scott Yanow*

Live at Blues Alley / Dec. 19, 1986-Dec. 20, 1986 / Columbia ✦✦✦✦✦
This double album features the great trumpeter Wynton Marsalis and his 1986 quartet, a unit featuring pianist Marcus Roberts, bassist Robert Hurst and drummer Jeff "Tain" Watts. Although Marsalis during this period still hinted strongly at Miles Davis, his own musical personality was starting to finally shine through. With the versatile Marcus Roberts (who thus far has been the most significant graduate from Marsalis's groups), Wynton Marsalis was beginning to explore older material, including on this set "Just Friends," and "Do You Know What It Means to Miss New Orleans—" other highlights include lengthy workouts on "Au Privave" and Kenny Kirkland's "Chambers of Tain." This two-fer is recommended, as are virtually all of Wynton Marsalis's recordings. *—Scott Yanow*

Standard Time, Vol. 2: Intimacy Calling / Sep. 1987-Aug. 1990 / Columbia ✦✦✦✦
Wynton Marsalis's second of three standard albums was actually released after the third volume. On most of the selections, the brilliant trumpeter is heard in excellent form with his quartet (comprised of pianist Marcus Roberts, bassist Reginald Veal or Robert Hurst and either Herlin Riley or Jeff Watts on drums); tenorman Todd Williams helps out on "I'll Remember April" and altoist Wes Anderson is also added to "Crepuscule with Nellie." Marsalis's tone really makes the ballads worth hearing, and his unusual choice and placement of notes keeps the music stimulating. This mostly bop-oriented set is rounded off by a jaunty version of "Bourbon Street Parade." *—Scott Yanow*

Levee Low Moan: Soul Gestures in Southern Blue, Vol. 3 / 1988 / Columbia ✦✦✦

Thick in the South: Soul Gestures in Southern Blue, Vol. 1 / 1988 / Columbia ✦✦✦✦

Uptown Ruler: Soul Gestures in Southern Blue, Vol. 2 / 1988 / Columbia ✦✦✦

The Majesty of the Blues / Oct. 27, 1988-Oct. 28, 1988 / Columbia ✦✦✦

Standard Time, Vol. 3 / 1990 / Columbia ✦✦✦

Blue Interlude / 1991 / Columbia ✦✦✦✦✦
Wynton Marsalis's septet was the perfect outlet both for his playing and his writing. The impressive young personnel (pianist Marcus Roberts, altoist Wessell Anderson, Todd Williams on tenor, soprano and clarinet, trombonist Wycliffe Gordon, bassist Reginald Veal and drummer Herlin Riley) was flexible enough to sound like a New Orleans parade band or the David Murray Octet and Wynton's writing also made them occasionally appear to be a small group from the Duke Ellington Orchestra. On this CD the music is quite strong as are the solos and the colorful group is heard at their best on a wide variety of challenging material. *—Scott Yanow*

In This House, On This Morning / May 28, 1992-Mar. 21, 1993 / Columbia ✦✦✦✦✦
For this double CD trumpeter Wynton Marsalis musically depicts in three parts a lengthy Sunday church service with program music composed for each of the traditional activities. The set does take quite awhile to get going with much of the first two parts consisting of introductions and transitions to themes that never seem to arrive. There are some exceptions, particularly Marsalis's violent trumpet distortions on "Call to Prayer," a spirited New Orleans blues and Todd Williams's tenor solo on another blues. However it is the third section that is most notable. The 28-minute "In the Sweet Embrace of Life" instrumentally portrays a preacher giving a heated sermon, building up to a very feverish level. Marsalis's model in his writing is clearly Duke Ellington. Trombonist Wycliffe Gordon is an expert with mutes and Todd Williams is able to hint at both Paul Gonsalves on tenor and Dixieland clarinetists on soprano while altoist Wes Anderson and pianist Eric Reed are also major assets to the septet. Due to the memorable final section, this lengthy work is one of the highpoints of his career thus far. *—Scott Yanow*

☆ **Citi Movement** / Jul. 27, 1992-Jul. 28, 1992 / Columbia ✦✦✦✦✦
This double CD contains Wynton Marsalis's score for the modern ballet *Griot New York.* Even more than his trumpet playing, his writing skills had developed quickly during the five years prior to this set. Marsalis's superb septet (which included trombonist Wycliffe Gordon, altoist Wes Anderson, Todd Williams on tenor and soprano, pianist Eric Reed, bassist Reginald Veal and drummer Herlin Riley) performs the complex and consistently colorful music, which goes through a wide variety of styles (including New Orleans jazz, swing, bop, modal music and even some sections bordering on the avant-garde). The results are unpredictable, exciting and quite enjoyable. This is one of Wynton Marsalis's finest recordings to date. *—Scott Yanow*

Blood on the Fields / Jan. 22, 1995-Jan. 25, 1995 / Columbia ✦✦✦✦
The music on this three-CD set (released in 1997) won a Pulitzer Prize, but is not without its faults. Trumpeter Wynton Marsalis tells the story of two Africans (singers Miles Griffith and Cassandra Wilson) who are captured, brought to the United States and sold as slaves. Because the male had formerly been a prince while the female had been a commoner, he considers himself to be her superior. He asks for but then ignores the advice of a wise man (Jon Hendricks), gets caught trying to escape, discovers what "soul" is, finally accepts the female as his equal and eventually escapes with her to freedom. Marsalis wrote a dramatic, episodic and generally thought-provoking three-hour work, utilizing the three singers plus 15 other musicians (all of whom have significant musical parts to play) in a massive 27-part suite. Hendricks is delightful (and the star of the catchiest piece, "Juba and a O'Brown Squaw"), Wilson has rarely sounded better, and Griffith keeps up with the better-known singers, while the musicians (particularly trombonist Wycliffe Gordon, baritonist James Carter, pianist Eric Reed and, near the work's conclusion, violinist Michael Ward in addition to Marsalis) are quite superb. It should, however, be mentioned that the use of group narration to tell parts of the story does not work that well, the music could have used a stronger and more complicated story (the last hour has very little action), and few of the themes are at all memorable; Marsalis in the mid-1990s was a more talented arranger than composer (despite Stanley Crouch's absurd raving in the liner notes). But as is true of all of Wynton Marsalis's recordings, this one deserves several close listenings. *—Scott Yanow*

Jump Start and Jazz / Jan. 23, 1993-Aug. 18, 1995 / Columbia ✦✦✦

Standard Time, Vol. 5: The Midnight Blues / Sep. 15, 1997-Sep. 18, 1997 / Columbia ✦✦

Standard Time, Vol. 4: Marsalis Plays Monk / Sep. 17, 1993-Oct. 4, 1994 / Columbia ✦✦✦

Big Train / Dec. 20, 1998 / Columbia ✦✦✦✦

Standard Time, Vol. 6: Mr. Jelly Lord / 1993-Jan. 1999 / Columbia ✦✦✦✦✦
In this tribute to Jelly Roll Morton, at last there is a large sampling of the Wynton Marsalis who can get large crowds at outdoor jazz festivals like *the Playboy at Hollywood Bowl* to dance and wave white handkerchiefs. This is mostly gutbucket, stomping, swinging New Orleans jazz through the eyes and ears of avid students of old records—and they have absorbed a good deal of the original raffish, joyous feeling. Dedicated scholars as they are, the band even recreates the original zany dialogue that opens Morton's recordings of "Dead Man Blues" and "Sidewalk Blues" (with a small alteration in the latter for PC purposes), leading to swaggering performances of both. Marsalis by now is an absolute virtuoso of the plunger mute, and he gets ample room to growl and snarl, often alongside trombonist/co-arranger Wycliffe Gordon. Without the mute, he is often majestically commanding, totally in his element. As befitting the contrapuntal New Orleans ethos, Wynton is also generous with the spotlight, turning over an entire track to Danilo Perez's lurching solo piano rendition of "Mamanita," another to the thick-toned period clarinet of performing musicologist Michael White on "Big Lip Blues," and another, alas, to Harry Connick Jr.'s ham-handed solo treatment of "Billy Goat Stomp." The most startling performance—authenticity taken to its extreme—comes at the end as Wynton and pianist Eric Reed wander into *Thomas Edison Laboratories* (circa 1993) to record a cylinder of "Tom Cat Blues" with vintage acoustical equipment. The results are often hilarious, and certainly instructive (try this out as a blindfold test on friends who think that they don't make jazz records like they used to). *—Richard S. Ginell*

Reeltime / Oct. 5, 1999 / Sony Classical ✦✦✦✦

Live at the Village Vanguard / Mar. 1990-1994 / Columbia ✦✦✦✦
As if releasing eight single albums in 1999 weren't enough, Wynton Marsalis capped this deluge of material at the end of the year with a seven-CD mini-box of live recordings, taped over a five-year span at New York City's *Village Vanguard* club. Greed certainly wasn't the motive,

for Sony Music priced the set at an unbelievably low $39.98, so the issue is whether Marsalis is justified in feeling that his music is worth documenting in such exhaustive detail. Each disc is organized to simulate a different night of the week, with a different, often loosely defined, and not-always-followed theme for each disc. The box reflects the Marsalis septet in a joyous mood as it hit the *the Vanguard* stage each night, spurred on by a vocal, exuberant throng packed into the small, wedge-shaped joint. The well-drilled septet was capable of assimilating a varied, if selective, spectrum of jazz tradition, from the New Orleans funeral music and handkerchief-waving street sass of "Flee As a Bird to the Mountain/Happy Feet Blues" to the sizzling post-bop of "The Cat in the Hat Is Back." Their indefatigable trumpeter/leader is the most liberated, expressive player of the lot. Along with a selection of standards and originals, there are also full-length and excerpted live treatments of some of Marsalis' extended pieces. A number of the performances, particularly of some of his own material, are a bit too well drilled; the loosest contrapuntal New Orleans jams go over the best for the home listener. In the grand scheme of jazz history, this music won't rank with some other landmark sessions at *the Vanguard* in terms of influence or transcendence. Yet the music deserves a hearing as an extended souvenir of one of the most talented neo-conservative bands of the '90s. *—Richard S. Ginell*

The Marciac Suite / Feb. 1, 1999-Feb. 2, 1999 / Columbia ✦✦✦✦✦

Warne Marsh

b. Oct. 26, 1927, Los Angeles, CA, **d.** Dec. 18, 1987, Hollywood, CA
Sax (Tenor) / Cool

Along with Lee Konitz, Warne Marsh was the most successful "pupil" of Lennie Tristano and, unlike Konitz, Marsh spent most of his career exploring chordal improvisation the Tristano way. The cool-toned tenor played with Hoagy Carmichael's Teenagers during 1944-45 and then after the Army he was with Buddy Rich (1948) before working with Lennie Tristano (1949-52). His recordings with Tristano and Konitz still sound remarkable today with unisons that make the two horns sound like one. Marsh had occasional reunions with Konitz and Tristano through the years, spent periods outside of music, and stayed true to his musical goals. He moved to Los Angeles in 1966 and worked with Supersax during 1972-77, also filling in time teaching. Marsh, who collapsed and died on stage at the legendary Donte's club in 1987 while playing "Out of Nowhere," is now considered legendary. He recorded as a leader for Xanadu, Imperial, Kapp, Mode (reissued on V.S.O.P.), Atlantic, Wave, Storyville, Revelation, Interplay, Criss Cross and Hot Club. *—Scott Yanow*

Lee Konitz with Warne Marsh / 1955 / Atlantic ✦✦✦

Music for Prancing / Sep. 1957 / VSOP ✦✦✦✦
With a reputation as one of the originators of cool jazz, it's ironic that over the years tenor saxophonist Warne Marsh gained a following of musicians mainly associated with the avant-garde, spearheaded by multi-reedist Anthony Braxton. These musicians heard what this disc demonstrates: that cool didn't always mean smoothed out. Originally issued in 1957, *Music for Prancing* is Marsh's second session as a leader with pianist Ronnie Ball, Red Mitchell on bass, and Stan Levey on drums. The quartet performs four standards such as the usually subdued Rodgers & Hart ballad "You Are Too Beautiful," which they make swing, and two originals: Ball's "Ad Libido" and Marsh's "Playa del Ray." A strong CD reissue on the budget label VSOP. *—Al Campbell*

Ne Plus Ultra / Oct. 25, 1969-Sep. 14, 1969 / hatHUT ✦✦✦✦
This was tenor saxophonist Warne Marsh's first recording as a leader since 1960. Teamed up with complementary altoist Gary Foster (who was most influenced by Marsh's former musical partner Lee Konitz), bassist Dave Parlato and drummer John Tirabasso, Marsh runs through some of his favorite chord changes, including "Lennie's Pennies," "Subconscious-Lee" and "You Stepped Out of a Dream." In addition, there is a fairly free group improvisation (the 15-minute "Touch and Go") and a brief rendition of Bach's "Two-Part Inventions 13." A strong all-around CD reissue that was originally released by the Revelation label. *—Scott Yanow*

Live at the Montmartre Club: Jazz Exchange, Vol. 1 / Dec. 3, 1975-Dec. 27, 1975 / Storyville ✦✦✦✦
The first of three releases that document a European tour undertaken by tenor saxophonist Warne Marsh and altoist Lee Konitz finds the Lennie Tristano alumni in prime form. Marsh and Konitz often thought alike musically, and this set certainly has its exciting moments. Joined by pianist Ole Kock Hansen, bassist Niels-Henning Orsted Pedersen and either Alex Riel or Svend Erik Norregard on drums, the two classic saxophonists explore "originals" based closely on common chord changes (including "April" and "Background Music"), plus "You Stepped Out of a Dream" and Lester Young's "Pound Cake." Highly recommended, as are the two following volumes. *—Scott Yanow*

Warne Marsh & Lee Konitz (Live at Club Montmartre) / Dec. 3, 1975-Dec. 27, 1975 / Storyville ✦✦✦✦✦

Warne Marsh Quintet / Dec. 3, 1975-Dec. 5, 1975 / Storyville ✦✦✦✦✦

Unissued 1975 Copenhagen Studio Recordings / Dec. 28, 1975 / Storyville ✦✦✦✦
One of the great jazz improvisers and always vastly underrated, the late tenor saxophonist Warne Marsh had several previously unknown sessions released for the first time by Storyville on CD during 1996-97. This studio set matches Marsh with guitarist Dave Cliff, bassist Niels Pedersen and drummer Alan Levitt. His sidemen's tasteful yet stimulating support allows Marsh to be in the spotlight virtually the entire time, coming up with fresh statements on such pieces as "Blues in G Flat," "The Song Is You," "Without a Song" and even "Be My Love." Throughout, the unique tenorman's cool tone and harmonically advanced style are heard in superb form. *—Scott Yanow*

• **Star Highs** / Aug. 14, 1982 / Criss Cross ✦✦✦✦✦
Tenor saxophonist Warne Marsh and pianist Hank Jones had not performed together before they met up in the studio to make what would be the second release for the Criss Cross label. With bassist George Mraz and drummer Mel Lewis completing the quartet, plenty of sparks fly between the two lead soloists. Marsh plays with more fire than one would expect from the cool-toned tenor; the material (four lesser-known tunes by the leader, one by Jones, "Moose the Mooche," and "Victory Ball") is fresher than usual, and the album can be easily recommended to straight-ahead jazz collectors. *—Scott Yanow*

A Ballad Album / Apr. 7, 1983 / Criss Cross ✦✦✦✦✦
Although there is a certain amount of tempo variation, this is largely a ballad showcase CD for tenor saxophonist Warne Marsh. With fine support from pianist Lou Levy, bassist Jesper Lundgaard and drummer James Martin, Marsh sounds quite lyrical on eight veteran standards including "I Can't Give You Anything But Love, Baby," "The Nearness of You" and "Emily." The CD reissue adds three alternate takes to the original program. Fine music that is both relaxing and (thanks to Marsh) somewhat unsettling under the surface. *—Scott Yanow*

Pat Martino (Pat Azzara)

b. Aug. 25, 1944, Philadelphia, PA
Guitar / Post-Bop

One of the most original of the jazz-based guitarists to emerge in the 1960s, Pat Martino made a remarkable comeback after brain surgery in 1980 to correct an aneurysm caused him to lose his memory and completely forget how to play. It took years but he regained his ability, partly by listening to his older records! Martino began playing professionally when he was 15. He worked early on with groups led by Willis Jackson, Red Holloway and a series of organists including Don Patterson, Jimmy Smith, Jack McDuff, Richard "Groove" Holmes and Jimmy McGriff. After playing with John Handy (1966), he started leading his own bands and heading sessions for Prestige, Muse and Warner Bros. that found him welcoming the influences of avant-garde jazz, rock, pop and world music into his advanced hard bop style. After the operation, Martino did not resume playing until 1984, making his recording comeback with 1987's *The Return*. Although not as active as earlier, Pat Martino has regained his earlier form, recording again for Muse and Evidence; he later signed with Blue Note, issuing *All Sides Now* in 1996, followed two years later by *Stone Blue* and in 1999 by *Mission Accomplished*. *—Scott Yanow*

El Hombre / May 1, 1967 / Prestige/OJC ✦✦✦✦✦
Guitarist Pat Martino's debut as a leader finds the 22-year-old showing off his roots in soul-jazz organ groups while looking ahead at the same time. Joined by organist Trudy Pitts, flutist Danny Turner, drummer Mitch Fine, and both Abdu Johnson and Vance Anderson on percussion, Martino primarily plays a straight-ahead set (five of his originals, "Just Friends," and "Once I Loved"), but already displays a fairly distinctive sound. This CD reissue brings back Martino's impressive start to what would be a productive solo career. *—Scott Yanow*

• **East!** / Jan. 8, 1968 / Prestige/OJC ✦✦✦✦✦
Despite the title and the cover of this CD reissue (which makes it appear that the performances are greatly influenced by music of the Far East), the style played by guitarist Pat Martino's quartet is very much in the hard bop tradition. Martino was already developing his own sound and is in excellent form with pianist Eddie Green, drummer Lenny McBrowne and either Ben Tucker or Tyrone Brown on bass during two group originals, Benny Golson's "Park Avenue Petite," John Coltrane's "Lazy Bird" and the standard "Close Your Eyes." It's a good example of Pat Martino's playing in his early period. *—Scott Yanow*

Footprints / Mar. 24, 1972 / 32 Jazz ✦✦✦✦✦
Originally released by Cobblestone and later by Muse, this 1997 CD reissue from 32 Jazz features the distinctive and exploratory guitarist Pat Martino in a tribute to Wes Montgomery. Martino does not attempt to sound like Wes (although he uses octaves here and there), and only one of the six selections ("Road Song") was actually recorded by Montgomery; the tribute is more heartfelt than imitative. With the intuitive assistance of rhythm guitarist Bobby Rose, bassist Richard Davis and drummer Billy Higgins, Martino stretches out on six selections, including a bluesy original ("The Visit"), "Footprints," and "Alone Together," always sounding like himself and pushing the boundaries of straight-ahead jazz. *—Scott Yanow*

We'll Be Together Again / Feb. 13, 1976-Feb. 17, 1976 / 32 Jazz ✦✦✦✦✦
When *We'll Be Together Again* was recorded in 1976, a 31-year-old Pat Martino was four years away from being operated on for the brain aneurism that would wipe out his memory. The Philadelphia guitarist was also very much at the height of his creative powers—a fact that's hard to miss on this excellent session, which 32 Jazz reissued on CD in 1998. Forming an intimate duo with electric pianist Gil Goldstein, Martino is at his most introspective on sparse interpretations of the standards "You Don't Know What Love Is" and "Willow Weep for Me" as well as Henry Mancini's "Dreamsville," J.J. Johnson's "Lament" and Stephen Sondheim's "Send in the Clowns." Martino's lyricism was never more personal than it is on this album, which was first released by Muse and was out of print for many years. Thankfully, *We'll Be Together Again* finally came out on CD when 32 Jazz reissued it in 1998. *—Alex Henderson*

The Maker / Sep. 14, 1994 / Evidence ✦✦✦✦✦

All Sides Now / Jun. 1, 1996-Jan. 15, 1997 / Blue Note ✦✦✦✦
Veteran Pat Martino is teamed up with a variety of different fellow guitarists on this interesting if not quite essential release. Martino matches wits with guitarist Charlie Hunter (who on Stevie Wonder's "Too High" often sounds like an organist), Tuck Andress, Kevin Eubanks, Les Paul ("I'm Confessin'"), Mike Stern and Michael Hedges. In addition, Cassandra Wilson sings Joni Mitchell's "Both Sides Now" accompanied by Martino, and rock guitarist Joe Satriani tries to sit in on two numbers (with indifferent results). A decent effort, but not up to Pat Martino's most significant releases. *—Scott Yanow*

Stone Blue / Feb. 14, 1998-Feb. 22, 1998 / Blue Note ✦✦✦✦

Mission Accomplished / Mar. 1, 1994-May 27, 1994 / 32 Jazz ✦✦✦✦
32 Jazz's double disc set *Mission Accomplished* contains two complete albums Pat Martino recorded for Muse Records: *Night Wings* and *Interchange*. Both albums were slightly overlooked upon their original release, but this excellent release illustrates that they captured

him at the top of his game. Another predictably excellent release from 32 Jazz. *—Stephen Thomas Erlewine*

Hugh Masekela (Hugh Ramopolo Masekela)

b. Apr. 4, 1939, Witbank, South Africa
Vocals, Flugelhorn, Trumpet / African Jazz, Jazz-Pop, Soul-Jazz, World Fusion
Hugh Masekela has an extensive jazz background and credentials, but has enjoyed major success as one of the earliest leaders in the world fusion mode. Masekela's vibrant trumpet and flugelhorn solos have been featured in pop, R&B, disco, Afropop and jazz contexts. His style, especially on flugelhorn, is a charismatic blend of striking upper register lines, half valve effects, repetitive figures and phrases, with some note bending, slurs and tonal colors. Though he's often simplified his playing to fit into restrictive pop formulas, Masekela's capable of outstanding ballad and bebop work. He played with a variety of South African jazz bands before leaving the country in 1960 with his his wife at that time, Miriam Makeba. During the early '60s, Masekela recorded for MGM, Mercury and Verve, developing his hybrid African/pop/jazz style. He even started his own record label (Chisa), and cut several albums which expanded his style and scored pop success—the single "Grazing in the Grass" topped the charts in 1968. During the 1970s, Masekela moved in a more ethnic direction, playing with Nigerian Afrobeat great Fela Kuti, working on a session with Dudu Pukwana and others that resulted in his finest jazz/African album, *Home Is Where the Music Is.* In the '80s, he returned to South Africa and was part of Paul Simon's Graceland tour. Though the jazz content of his work has varied over the years, Hugh Masekela has far more material on the plus side than the negative. *—Ron Wynn*

Trumpet African / 1962 / Mercury ✦✦✦

● **The Lasting Impression of Ooga Booga** / 1965 / Verve ✦✦✦✦✦
In patching together a program of Hugh Masekela's MGM recordings onto a single overstuffed CD, Verve took the original *The Americanization of Ooga Booga* album, leapfrogged over its successor, *Next Album,* and coupled it with the third MGM LP, *The Lasting Impressions of Hugh Masekela.* That made good sense since the two albums originate from the same live date at *the Village Gate,* recorded when the trumpeter was still in the process of making an impression in the U.S. Masekela is full of wild, sputtering, high-rolling exuberance, developing some of his familiar signature trumpet riffs, freely exploring South African rhythms, harmonic sequences and chants, and mixing them with soul-jazz at a time when hardly anyone else would bother (the mixture of township jive and jazz works especially well on "U-Dwi"). He also ties into Brazil with a fine rendition of Jorge Ben's "Mas Que Nada" and assimilates Coltrane into his bloodstream with a tribute called "Mixolydia." In general, the *Americanization* tracks are the picks of the crop (*Impressions,* after all, had been compiled in 1968 to cash in on Masekela's surprise No. 1 single, "Grazing in the Grass"). With the rhythm section of Larry Willis on piano, Harold Dotson on bass, and Henry Jenkins on drums, this music still holds up marvelously today. *—Richard S. Ginell*

The Emancipation of Hugh Masekela / 1966 / Chisa ✦✦✦✦
South African expatriate Hugh Masekela was the architect of an extremely interesting and viable musical form, an audacious blending of South African rhythms, swing jazz, and rock & roll. *Emancipation* is the first American effort in this area, and it's a fantastic, soul-deep affair. With a crack band including Charlie Smalls on piano and two drummers (the original Big Black on percussion), Masekela's vocals and intense trumpet have the perfect platform from which to fly. One track in particular, "She Doesn't Write," is almost a template for "Grazing in the Grass," which was a huge hit the following year. Masekela was also involved with the Jim Dickson/Byrds/Peter Fonda crowd at the time, and that influence can be felt here as well. A perfect introduction to Hugh Masekela. *—Matthew Greenwald*

Masekela / 1968 / UNI ✦✦✦✦✦
It all comes together here, with a magic synthesis of trumpet-led African sounds, jazz, and R&B. *—Hank Davis*

Home Is Where the Music Is / Jan. 1972 / Blue Thumb ✦✦✦✦✦
An outstanding blend of Afro-pop and jazz with strong work by Dudu Pukwana. *—Ron Wynn*

Tomorrow / 1986-1987 / Warner Brothers ✦✦✦✦✦
Still in exile from his homeland, Hugh Masekela leaves no doubt where he would rather be in this carefully-produced, majestically swinging, techno-pop-jazz album that leans heavily in the direction of Soweto. Masekela often performs sophisticated takes on three-chord township jive, leading the massed vocals with his own coarse yet evocatively blunt voice, while leaving himself just enough room to peel off a few patented, repeated-note trumpet licks and double-tracked flugelhorn statements. Later on the record, the keys turn minor but the high-tech verve is still there. The key track is a fine version of Masekela's signature tune of the '80s, "Bring Him Back Home," which became prophetic in the next decade with the release of Nelson Mandela from prison (though the "walking hand in hand with Winnie Mandela" bit didn't last long). From the vantage point of London, Masekela expresses homesickness in "London Fog," celebrates the imminent fall of several of the world's petty dictators in "Everybody's Standing Up," and in general lets us know that he's gonna be back home soon. His backup band, Kalahari, and a quartet of vocalists share Masekela's passion—and the outcome of this chemistry is one of Masekela's best albums of the last 20 years. *—Richard S. Ginell*

Christian McBride

b. May 31, 1972, Philadelphia, PA
Bass / Hard Bop
Everyone's favorite young acoustic bassist of the 1990s, Christian McBride's large sound and expertise both with plucked and bowed solos recall Ray Brown and particularly Paul Chambers. He actually started on electric bass when he was eight and took R&B gigs in high school but by then he was getting more interested in jazz and playing the acoustic bass. McBride studied at Juilliard (starting in 1989) and then played briefly in the bands of Bobby Watson, Benny Golson, Roy Hargrove and Freddie Hubbard. He toured with the Benny Green Trio, played duets with Ray Brown at the 1994 Monterey Jazz Festival and recorded his debut as a leader for Verve before touring with his own group in 1995. *Family Affair* followed in 1998. In 2000, McBride released his most ambitious project to date, *Sci-Fi.* *—Scott Yanow*

● **Gettin' to It** / Aug. 30, 1994-Sep. 1, 1994 / Verve ✦✦✦✦
McBride had already made his name as an astounding bass sideman when he recorded his first album as a leader, which nailed him as another in the long line of mainstream-minded Young Lions. McBride would shed that tag within a few years when he brought forth his other interests, but for now, he headed a series of three-to-six-piece bands compromised mostly of somewhat older Young Lions similarly attached to tradition. They're in pretty good form, too—the tasty Cyrus Chestnut on piano, the growing trumpeter Roy Hargrove, big-toned tenorman Joshua Redman—and the more experienced trombonist Steve Turre and drummer Lewis Nash complete the personnel. McBride's big rock-solid tone and melodic agility give his playing the properties of a horn—at 22, he was a mature master—yet his ideas as a leader were not yet as imaginative as his bass playing. One exception—and easily the most entertaining and musical track on the CD is the birth on records of McBride's bass trio with mentor Ray Brown and veteran Milt Hinton in "Splanky"; you'd never guess that three unaccompanied bassists could make such sublimely enjoyable music. Another is the title track, whose funky tune and rhythm are audibly inspired by James Brown. Mostly, though, this is a promising but cautious debut. *—Richard S. Ginell*

A Family Affair / Jan. 27, 1998-Jan. 31, 1998 / Verve ✦✦✦✦
Hallelujah! Christian McBride is not one of those straitlaced, down-the-line neo-boppers after all. Here, the prodigiously talented young standup bassist proves that he is also an astoundingly gifted electric bassist, and that '70s-vintage funk and soul is every bit as close to his heart as '50s and '60s hard bop. On electric, McBride weaves inventive countermelodies around tenor sax Tim Warfield's lead lines, taking Jaco Pastorius' technique a step further in sheer speed and the ability to play really nasty funk patterns. The stylistic palette of the disc is much wider than anything McBride has done before as a leader, ranging from soul ballads (a lovely cover of Stevie Wonder's nearly forgotten "Summer Soft," Wonder-like vocals from Vesta on "...Or So You Thought") to powerful funk ("Brown Funk (for Ray)"), open-ended electric jazz-rock ("Wayne's World"), and yes, straight-ahead acoustic jazz grooving (on Sly Stone's "Family Affair"). Charles Craig excels on acoustic piano, Fender Rhodes and Wurlitzer electric pianos; drummer Gregory Hutchinson fearlessly handles any stylistic curveballs that McBride throws at him; and guitarist Russell Malone and percussionist Munyungo Jackson turn up now and then. As produced by fellow polystylist George Duke, this is a most encouraging step out of the trap of lockstep bop for McBride. *—Richard S. Ginell*

Sci-Fi / Sep. 12, 2000 / Verve ✦✦✦✦
On a large scale, there is no denying that music can move masses of people to assert themselves and establish a particular vision that will benefit many for years to come. With the release of *Sci-Fi,* the highly acclaimed bassist Christian McBride has established another great realm of music for his fans to explore. Accompanied by the dynamic Ron Blake on tenor and soprano sax, Shedrick Mitchell on piano and Fender Rhodes, the great Herbie Hancock on piano, Rodney Green on drums, David Gilmore on electric and acoustic guitar, Dianne Reeves giving great vocalese on "Lullaby for a Ladybug," James Carter on bass clarinet, and the exciting Toots Thielemans on harmonica, listeners will soon discover that the jazz galaxy will never be the same. The acoustic fusion and thematic sound concept for the CD settled in after McBride wrote "Science Fiction" and discovered it made a great nucleus for the CD. Featured selections include McBride's brilliant arrangements of masterworks by Stanley Clarke, Sting, Jaco Pastorius, and Steely Dan as well as seven original compositions by the versatile leader. Flawless piano grace from Herbie Hancock on "Xerxes" and "Lullaby for a Ladybug" and McBride's Fender Rhodes work throughout is a listen to behold. The conversation between McBride's double bass and Carter's bass clarinet on "Walking on the Moon" is one of the greatest moments in jazz and shouldn't be missed. *Sci-Fi* is a seminal work by seminal artists and should be considered one of the most essential jazz recordings of the 21st century. *—Paula Edelstein*

Les McCann

b. Sep. 23, 1935, Lexington, KY
Vocals, Keyboards, Piano / Hard Bop, Soul-Jazz
Les McCann reached the peak of his career at the 1968 Montreux Jazz Festival, recording "Compared to What" and "Cold Duck Time" for Atlantic. Although he has done some worthwhile work since then, much of it has been anti-climatic. McCann turned down an invitation to join the Cannonball Adderley Quintet so he could work on his own music. He signed a contract with Pacific Jazz and in 1960 gained some fame with his albums *Les McCann Plays the Truth* and *The Shout.* His soulful funk style on piano was influential and McCann's singing was largely secondary until the mid-'60s. He recorded many albums for Pacific Jazz during 1960-64, mostly with his trio but also featuring Ben Webster, Richard "Groove" Holmes, Blue Mitchell, Stanley Turrentine, Joe Pass, the Jazz Crusaders and the Gerald Wilson Orchestra. McCann switched to Limelight during 1965-67 and then signed with Atlantic in 1968. After the success of *Swiss Movement,* McCann emphasized his singing at the expense of his playing and he began to utilize electric keyboards. *—Scott Yanow*

● **Les McCann Anthology: Relationships** / Feb. 1960-Nov. 1972 / Rhino ✦✦✦✦✦
One of the many two-CD samplers of Atlantic jazz artists put together by Rhino Records, this retrospective has some of the highpoints of pianist-vocalist Les McCann's career but is far from perfect. The first CD is purely instrumental, showcasing McCann with several of his trios and in collaborations with organist Richard "Groove" Holmes, the tenors of Ben Webster and Stanley Turrentine, the Jazz Crusaders and Gerald Wilson's Orchestra. The second half of the two-fer has three selections on which McCann backs singer Lou Rawls (why were these included—) and just two vocals from the pianist. "Compared to What" and "Cold Duck Time" (from his famous meeting with Eddie Harris at the 1968 *Montreux Jazz Festival*) have been reissued several times, there are no selections from the 1973-95 period and the music

is not programmed in strictly chronological order. Taken as a whole, there is plenty of rewarding music on the collection (including "The Truth," "The Shampoo," "A Little 3/4 for God & Co." and "With These Hands"), but McCann's vocalizing and his post-1972 music should not have been neglected. *—Scott Yanow*

Les McCann Ltd. in New York / 1960-Dec. 28, 1961 / Capitol ♦♦♦♦♦

☆ **Much Les** / Jul. 22, 1968-Jul. 24, 1968 / Rhino ♦♦♦♦♦
This straight CD reissue of an Atlantic LP offers one a pretty definitive look at Les McCann in his prime. The pianist/singer develops long funky vamps that swing, sings "With These Hands" and, even with a string section added to four of the six numbers and three also having two percussionists, the emphasis is on McCann's trio with bassist Leroy Vinnegar and drummer Donald Dean. This is high-quality and intelligent groove music. *—Scott Yanow*

★ **Swiss Movement: Montreux 30th Anniversary Edition** / Jun. 22, 1969 / Rhino ♦♦♦♦♦
One of the most popular soul-jazz albums of all time, and one of the best, although Harris (and trumpeter Benny Bailey) had never played or rehearsed with the Les McCann Trio before, and indeed weren't even given the music. Perhaps that sparked the spontaneous funk that comes through clearly on the tape of this show, recorded at *the Montreux Festival* in 1969. It's actually much more of a showcase for McCann than Harris, although the tenor saxist's contributions are significant. The sole vocal, a version of Gene McDaniels' "Compared to What," aremains McCann's signature tune. It's worth picking up Rhino's "Montreux 30th Anniversary Edition," as it adds a nine-minute bonus track ("Kaftan") and historical liner notes. *—Richie Unterberger*

Live at Montreux / Jun. 1972 / Wounded Bird ♦♦♦♦
Having rocketed the *Montreux Jazz Festival* to prominence in 1968 with *Swiss Movement*, Atlantic naturally thought they could score again four years later with the super-funky electric edition of Les McCann Ltd. While there were no major hits this time, Atlantic got enough from McCann's set to put out a hot double album loaded with gritty vocals, gospel-drenched electric piano, cooking instrumentals, plenty of his popular protest songs, and a few new numbers such as the driving "Cochise." Backed with stone-tough grooves by Jimmy Rowser (bass), Buck Clarke (congas, percussion), and Donald Dean (drums), most of McCann's performances are at least the equal of his studio recordings, though the inevitable return of "Compared to What" falls short of the pacesetting version of 1968. Eddie Harris didn't turn up this time at *Montreux*, but Rahsaan Roland Kirk did, wandering in on the middle of "Get Yourself Together," doing a wailing thing like an air raid siren and a funky impromptu encore. For a vivid snapshot of Les McCann at the high noon of his career, this double-LP set is worth scouring the used racks for. *—Richard S. Ginell*

Layers / Nov. 1972 / Rhino ♦♦♦
On this studio session, Les McCann augments his piano with various keyboards and synthesizers, showing the influence of Miles Davis's music of the period. McCann sets solid grooves with his trio (plus two percussionists) but dilutes his sound to a large extent. The music is set up as two lengthy suites but unfortunately lacks any really catchy melodies. McCann does his best to stretch himself and there are moments of interest but this album is not all that essential. *—Scott Yanow*

How's Your Mother / Jul. 1967 / 32 Jazz ♦♦♦♦
Back at the time that the previously unissued music on this 1998 CD was performed, Les McCann was known as a funky jazz pianist who occasionally sang; his famous version of "Compared to What" was a year away. For a purely instrumental trio date recorded live at the Village Vanguard with bassist Leroy Vinnegar and drummer Frank Severino, McCann is heard throughout in prime form. He digs into his typical repertoire of the period, which includes "Love for Sale," "Sunny," "I Am in Love," "Goin' Out of My Head," Vinnegar's "Doing That Thing" and three of his originals (best known of which is "The Shampoo," which is heard here as a brief closing theme). Overall, this CD gives one a good example of how McCann sounded in his early days. *—Scott Yanow*

Jack McDuff (Eugene McDuffy)

b. Sep. 17, 1926, Champaign, IL, **d.** Jan. 23, 2001, Minneapolis, MN
Organ (Hammond), Organ / Hard Bop, Soul-Jazz, Jazz-Funk
A marvelous bandleader and organist as well as capable arranger, "Brother" Jack McDuff has one of the funkiest, most soulful styles of all time on the Hammond B-3. His rock-solid bass lines and blues-drenched solos are balanced by clever, almost pianistic melodies and interesting progressions and phrases. McDuff began gaining attention working with Willis Jackson in the late '50s and early '60s, cutting high caliber soul jazz dates for Prestige. McDuff made his recording debut as a leader for Prestige in 1960, playing in a studio pickup band with Jimmy Forrest. They made a pair of outstanding albums, *Tough Duff* and *The Honeydripper*. McDuff organized his own band the next year, featuring Harold Vick and drummer Joe Dukes. Things took off when McDuff hired a young guitarist named George Benson. They were among the most popular combos of the mid-'60s, and made several excellent albums. McDuff experimented with electronic keyboards and fusion during the '70s, then in the '80s got back in the groove with the Muse session *Cap'n Jack*. *—Ron Wynn and Bob Porter*

Tough 'Duff / Jul. 12, 1960 / Prestige/OJC ♦♦♦♦♦
Organist Jack McDuff's second set as a leader teams him with tenor saxophonist Jimmy Forrest, vibraphonist Lem Winchester (an unusual addition for this type of soul-jazz set), and drummer Bill Elliott. This CD reissue finds the group playing fairly basic material, including a pair of McDuff originals, "Smooth Sailing" and "Autumn Leaves." McDuff, Forrest and Winchester have no difficulty chewing up the chord changes, and although no real surprises occur, the results are typically swinging and groovin.' *—Scott Yanow*

The Honeydripper / Feb. 3, 1961 / Prestige/OJC ♦♦♦♦♦
This CD reissue is possibly most significant for being guitarist Grant Green's recording debut. Organist Jack McDuff, the tough-toned tenor Jimmy Forrest, Green and drummer Ben Dixon make for a potent and swinging combination. The repertoire (which has three standards and three originals, including "Whap") is comprised of blues, blues-oriented tunes (including "I Want a Little Girl") and Henry Mancini's "Mr. Lucky." Due to the high-quality solos, which are full of personality, this reissue is highly recommended to fans of the genre. *—Scott Yanow*

Brother Jack Meets the Boss / Jan. 23, 1962 / Prestige/OJC ♦♦♦♦
It is not too surprising that this is a very successful soul-jazz/hard bop outing, for it teams organist Brother Jack McDuff with the great tenor Gene Ammons. The quintet (which also includes the notable Harold Vick on second tenor, guitarist Eddie Diehl and drummer Joe Dukes) performs three basic McDuff tunes, Eddie "Cleanhead" Vinson's "Mr. Clean," Horace Silver's "Strollin'," and the still-viable swing standard "Christopher Columbus." Ammons, whose every note was always full of passion, fits in perfectly with McDuff's group; this accessible set has been reissued on CD. *—Scott Yanow*

Screamin' / Oct. 23, 1962 / Prestige/OJC ♦♦♦♦
Organist Jack McDuff teams up with his regular drummer Joe Dukes, altoist Leo Wright and guitarist Kenny Burrell for a spirited blues-oriented set which has been reissued on CD in the OJC series. "Soulful Drums," featuring Dukes's drum breaks, was a minor hit. Other selections on this generally fine organ date include spirited versions of "He's a Real Gone Guy," "After Hours" and "One O'Clock Jump" even if the title cut does not quite live up to its name. *—Scott Yanow*

Crash! / Jan. 8, 1963-Feb. 26, 1963 / Prestige ♦♦♦♦♦
Organist Jack McDuff has long had a powerful style and the two former LPs that are combined on this single CD offer some strong examples of his accessible playing. In both cases McDuff is joined by guitarist Kenny Burrell (in fact one of the two sets was originally under Burrell's name), drummer Joe Dukes and occasionally Ray Barretto on congas. In addition Harold Vick is on tenor for most selections and Eric Dixon guests on tenor and flute during three songs. Highlights include a driving "How High the Moon," "Love Walked In" and a pair of original blues: "Smut" and "Our Miss Brooks." McDuff and Burrell work together quite well. This 76-minute CD is easily recommended to fans of the jazz organ. *—Scott Yanow*

★ **Brother Jack McDuff Live!** / Jun. 5, 1963-Oct. 3, 1963 / Prestige ♦♦♦♦♦
Good as organist Jack McDuff's studio recordings are from the early '60s, it is his live sets that are truly exciting. This single CD combines together two former in-concert LPs and find McDuff leading a very strong group that features the young guitarist George Benson, tenorman Red Holloway, drummer Joe Dukes and on a few numbers the second tenor of Harold Vick. The material (cooking blues, standards, Latin numbers and originals) has plenty of variety and drive, McDuff really pushes Benson and Holloway, and the music is both accessible and creative. *—Scott Yanow*

Legends of Acid Jazz / Jul. 1964 / Prestige ♦♦♦♦
While these 12 selections were originally released on six different albums between 1965 and 1969, all of them were cut during July 1964: nine at a New York studio session, and three (embellished by Benny Golson big-band arrangements) live at Stockholm. Thus it makes for a thematically coherent compilation, every track featuring a young George Benson on guitar and Joe Dukes on drums; Red Holloway plays tenor sax on all but two songs. It's top-drawer soul-jazz, recommended to those who might find some of McDuff's other releases too homogenous, as his B-3 travels through diverse moods here: the uptempo blues of "Scufflin'," the slow-burning funk of "Our Miss Brooks," R&B/soul in the cover of "I Got a Woman." The closing "Lexington Avenue Line" is the oddest track, though quite a good one, sounding like a movie soundtrack theme with its dramatic strings. *—Richie Unterberger*

Silken Soul / Jul. 1964-1965 / Prestige ♦♦♦♦♦
This 13-track, 72-minute compilation is drawn from no less than seven albums Jack McDuff cut for Prestige, though all selections were recorded in 1965 and 1966. They must have been going 24-7 on soul-jazz sessions in their days; can you imagine comparably prolific studio activity on one label aimed toward the general record-buying market by a fairly though not hugely popular jazz artist in the 21st century? It's a good organ soul-jazz collection, above the average for discs of such mid-1960s material, the band almost always featuring tenor saxophonist Red Holloway and guitarist Pat Martino (though George Benson plays on a couple of songs, "How High the Moon" and "Silk'n'Soul"). The repertoire, too, is more varied than much similar stuff in the same groove, favoring the up-tempo mode, and getting into Latin beats and movie themes occasionally; "Stop It," with its periodic injections of shouts of the title phrase, could have fit into Ray Charles' instrumental set. Whether a shuffle or a near-frenetic tune, the funky organ-grounded riffs are consistently good, and the arrangements leave space for the sax and guitar to have their say. Considering how homogenous the soul-jazz organ style can sound over the course of half a dozen albums—not just by McDuff, but by anyone—this well-chosen condensation of his mid-'60s output is a recommended buy if you like, but don't love, the genre. *—Richie Unterberger*

Moon Rappin' / Dec. 3, 1969-Dec. 11, 1969 / Blue Note ♦♦♦

Down Home Style / Jun. 10, 1969 / Blue Note ♦♦♦♦

The Re-Entry / Mar. 25, 1988 / 32 Jazz ♦♦♦♦

Color Me Blue / May 1991-Mar. 1992 / Concord Jazz ♦♦♦♦♦
Recent cuts showing that organist Jack McDuff can still stomp through bluesy wailers, pound the bass pedals, and lead a hot combo through funky, exuberant numbers. He's heading a group with former band members like guitarist George Benson and drummer Joe Dukes, plus saxophonist Red Holloway, guitarist Ron Eschete and Phil Upchurch, among others. *—Ron Wynn*

That's the Way I Feel About It / Dec. 16, 1996-Jan. 23, 1997 / Concord Jazz ♦♦♦
At times, McDuff demonstrates how soul-jazz organ stars used to make albums back in their '60s heyday, playing then-current pop hits like "The Age of Aquarius" and the theme from *Mission: Impossible* (which, thanks to cinema, was a hit all over again in 1996 when this CD was made). We also hear McDuff trying out his vocal cords for the first time on Louis Jordan's "Saturday Night Fish Fry"; actually, he merely talks the lyrics over the rhythm section—

and at 70, he's entitled to this charming lark. Otherwise, this is another fine, home-cookin' soul-jazz session, with McDuff's Hammond B-3 burning at its usual low-intensity, high-blues-content level. Chris Potter dances around the organ on flutes, Andrew Beals and Jerry Weldon offer solid solos on alto and tenor respectively, and the rest of the Heatin' System runs the gamut from Latin to soul-deep grooves. Fans of the genre can buy with peace of mind. *—Richard S. Ginell*

Howard McGhee

b. Mar. 6, 1918, Tulsa, OK, **d.** Jul. 17, 1987, New York, NY

Trumpet / Hard Bop, Bop

During 1945-49 Howard McGhee was one of the finest trumpeters in jazz, an exciting performer with a sound of his own who among the young bop players ranked at the top with Dizzy Gillespie and Fats Navarro. McGhee participated in the fabled bop sessions at Minton's Playhouse and Monroe's Uptown House, modernizing his style away from Roy Eldridge and towards Dizzy Gillespie. He traveled to California with Coleman Hawkins in 1945; their concise recordings of swing-to-bop transitional music (including "Stuffy," "Rifftide" and "Hollywood Stampede") are classic. McGhee stayed in California into 1947, playing with Jazz at the Philharmonic, recording and gigging with Charlie Parker (including the ill-fated "Lover Man" date) and having an influence on young players out on the Coast. His Dial sessions were among the most exciting recordings of his career and back in New York he recorded for Savoy and had a historic meeting on record with Navarro (1948 on Blue Note). However drugs began to adversely affect McGhee's career, and he was inactive during much of the 1950s. *—Scott Yanow*

☆ **Trumpet at Tempo** / Sep. 4, 1945-Dec. 3, 1947 / Jazz Classics ♦♦♦♦♦

While the critical jury is still out on his overall contribution to the form, the indisputable fact remains that until the arrival of Dizzy Gillespie and Charlie Parker in California, Howard McGhee was the West Coast trail blazing bebopper in residence. These early sides show him in top form, straddling a bridge between Roy Eldridge and the new sound that was in the wind. Kicking off with a four-side 1945 date for Philo/Aladdin, Howard's bravura tone is well represented and his stratospheric runs on "Mop Mop" sit comfortably alongside his more reflective work on "Stardust." McGhee was also the trumpeter on the ill-fated Bird session that produced "Lover Man." After Parker left the studio, McGhee jammed two tunes with the remaining personnel, "Thermodynamics" and the title cut, his inspired improvisation on the chord changes to "Indiana." The first actual Dial label date with Howard as leader featured Dodo Marmarosa on piano, producing four classics of the idiom: "Midnight at Minton's," "High Wind in Hollywood," "Dialated Pupils," and "Up in Dodo's Room," alternates of which can be found on the companion Dodo Marmarosa collection, *Up in Dodo's Room.* But the bop motherlode comes with the inclusion of 11 tracks (two alternates) from McGhee's final date for the label, held in New York and featuring James Moody on tenor sax, Milt Jackson on vibes, Ray Brown on bass, Hank Jones on piano and J.C. Heard on drums, a classic lineup indeed. Although McGhee's later work could vacillate between brilliant and banal, the potency of these recordings in indisputable. *—Cub Koda*

● **Maggie's Back in Town** / Jun. 26, 1961 / Contemporary/OJC ♦♦♦♦♦

Trumpeter Howard McGhee, after spending much of the 1950s only partly active in music (due to drug problems), made a full-fledged comeback in the early '60s, only to find his bop-oriented music out-of-fashion. This Contemporary set (reissued on CD in the OJC series) was McGhee's finest recording of the period, a quartet outing with the brilliant pianist Phineas Newborn, bassist Leroy Vinnegar and drummer Shelly Manne. Although tenor saxophonist Teddy Edwards is not on the date, two of his compositions (his famous "Sunset Eyes" and a tribute to the trumpeter "Maggie's Back in Town") are fully explored by the quartet. Other titles include three standards plus McGhee's original blues "Demon Chase." This CD is a perfect starting point for listeners not familiar with the underrated (and often overlooked) Howard McGhee. *—Scott Yanow*

Introducing the Kenny Drew Trio / Jan. 23, 1950-Apr. 16, 1953 / Blue Note ♦♦♦♦

This 1998 CD has all of the music from two formerly scarce ten-inch Lps. Trumpeter Howard McGhee heads an all-star group that includes trombonist J.J. Johnson, tenor-saxophonist Brew Moore, pianist Kenny Drew, bassist Curly Russell and drummer Max Roach on "I'll Remember April," an original by the leader and four songs (plus an alternate take) by Drew who was making his recording debut. Because it was the tail-end of the 78 era, all of the performances are between 2:34 and 3:07 in length but the concise solos are generally quite strong. Although McGhee gets the top billing on this CD, the second half of this disc is actually by the Kenny Drew Trio (with Russell and drummer Art Blakey) from three years later, Drew's debut as a leader. Other than his "Gloria" and the basic "Drew's Blues," all of the music (which is augmented by two alternate takes) is standards including "Be My Love," "Yesterdays" and a surprisingly heated rendition of "It Might As Well Be Spring." Easily recommended to bebop collectors. *—Scott Yanow*

Complete Savoy & Dial Masters: Leader Sessions / Jul. 29, 1946-Feb. 1948 / Definitive Classics ♦♦♦

Howard McGhee was one of the main bebop trumpeters of the mid- to late '40s with Dizzy Gillespie and Fats Navarro. These 20 cuts are the complete master takes, originally made for the Savoy and Dial labels, and retain the vital energy that went along with the initial wave of beboppers. McGhee is heard at the peak of his powers, playing a few standards ("I'm in the Mood for Love," "The Man I Love") and many self-penned titles that provide a behind-the-scenes story of this music ("Dilated Pupils," "High Wind in Hollywood," "Trumpet at Tempo," "Midnight at Minton's," and "Sleepwalker Boogie"). The equally impressive sidemen on this disc include Teddy Edwards and James Moody on tenor saxophone, Jimmy Heath on alto saxophone, pianists Dodo Marmarosa and Hank Jones, vibraphonist Milt Jackson, Ray Brown on bass, and J.C. Heard and Roy Porter on drums. *—Al Campbell*

Jimmy McGriff (James Harrell McGriff, Jr.)

b. Apr. 3, 1936, Philadelphia, PA

Organ (Hammond), Organ / Hard Bop, Soul-Jazz

Jimmy McGriff calls himself a blues organ player—and that's the feeling he delivers in his best soul-jazz albums, with plenty of deep, in-the-pocket swing punctuated by grunting chords in the bass. Though both his parents were pianists, McGriff started on bass and sax, picking up drums, vibraphone and ultimately piano as a teenager. After studying at Combe College of Music in Philadelphia and Juilliard, McGriff became an MP in Korea and worked on the Philadelphia police force for 2 years. After deciding upon music as a career, he studied organ with Jimmy Smith, Richard "Groove" Holmes and Milt Buckner and scored a hit record "I Got a Woman" in 1963 (number 20 on the pop charts). This led to a string of R&B hit singles for Sue Records, followed by a prolific series of organ sessions for Solid State (where another substantial hit, "The Worm," emerged in 1969), Blue Note, Capitol, Groove Merchant and LRC. In the 1970s, following the trends of the time, McGriff began to turn toward pop and fusion, adopting electronic keyboards with mixed results. But when he signed with Milestone in 1983, McGriff returned to the Hammond B-3 organ and soul jazz, anticipating the organ jazz revival with a series of strong, gritty albums, some of which feature Hank Crawford as co-leader. After bouncing around on a number of labels and idioms in the '90s, McGriff returned to Milestone in late 1996 with the soulfully sophisticated *The Dream Team; The Dream Team* followed two years later, and in the spring of 2000 he resurfaced with *McGriff's House Party.* *—Richard S. Ginell*

At the Apollo / 1963 / Collectables ♦♦♦♦♦

The third album from McGriff on the Sue label was recorded live at New York's *Apollo Theater* in 1963. It features McGriff with Rudolph Johnson on tenor sax, Larry Frazier on guitar, and Willie Jenkins on drums. Contains a great version of "Red Sails in the Sunset" and "A Thing for Jug." *—Michael Erlewine*

● **Greatest Hits** / 1963-1971 / Blue Note ♦♦♦♦♦

Blue Note's *Greatest Hits* doesn't limit itself to the recordings Jimmy McGriff made for the label during the late '60s and early '70s. Instead, it culls from his Sue, Veep and Solid State recordings as well, making it a definitive overview of his career as a gritty, funky singles artist. And, as *Greatest Hits* demonstrates, McGriff could create a monster groove, making his singles intoxicating slices of funky jazz. All of his R&B hits—"I've Got a Woman," "All About My Girl," "Kiko," "The Worm"—are here, as are lesser-known singles and terrific album tracks, resulting in a compilation that isn't just a terrific introduction for neophytes, but also a useful retrospective for collectors. *—Stephen Thomas Erlewine*

I've Got a Woman / 1963 / Collectables ♦♦♦♦♦

McGriff's first album is great. The title cut was in the top 20 in 1962. Also on the same album is "M.G. Blues" and "All About My Girl." This session McGriff, Richard Easley on drums and Walter Miller on guitar. Hi-impact early McGriff is the still the best, and this is the album that started it all, on the Sue label. Three cuts available on the Collectable CD *A Toast to Jimmy McGriff's Golden Classics.* *—Michael Erlewine*

Jimmy McGriff at the Organ / 1963 / Sue ♦♦♦

Electric Funk / Sep. 1969 / Blue Note ♦♦♦

The title of *Electric Funk* may lead you to believe that it's a set of unrepentant, rampaging hard funk, but that's not quite the case. The record is laid-back but undeniably funky, with Jimmy McGriff and electric pianist Horace Ott leading an unnamed group through a set of soul workouts. It's not jazz, it's jazzy soul, and it's among the funkiest of any soul-jazz records from the late '60s, filled with stuttering drum breaks, lite fuzz guitars, elastic bass, smoldering organ and punchy, slightly incongruous horn charts. *—Stephen Thomas Erlewine*

Countdown / Apr. 27, 1983-Apr. 28, 1983 / Milestone ♦♦♦♦

Jimmy McGriff's Milestone debut, which has been reissued on CD, features the soulful organist heading a group of lesser-known players—including three horns and the fine guitarist Melvin Sparks—and doing his best to emulate the sound of a big band. The material ("I'm Walkin'," a couple of Frank Foster numbers including "Shiny Stockings," Benny Green's "Blow Your Horn," "Since I Fell for You" and a McGriff original) is strong and inspires the musicians to play funky, grease-filled solos. Few surprises occur, but the music is quite enjoyable and easily recommended to fans of this genre. *—Scott Yanow*

The Starting Five / Oct. 14, 1986-Oct. 15, 1986 / Milestone ♦♦♦♦♦

Due to the strong lineup and the basic but perfectly suitable material, this Jimmy McGriff CD is well worth picking up. The groovin' organist teams up with David "Fathead" Newman (heard on alto, tenor and flute), Rusty Bryant (doubling on tenor and alto), either Mel Brown or Wayne Body on guitar, and drummer Bernard Purdie. Basic originals alternate with such standbys as "I'm Getting Sentimental Over You" and "Georgia On My Mind," with everyone playing up to their potential. A fun and swinging session. *—Scott Yanow*

Blue to the 'Bone / Jul. 19, 1988-Jul. 20, 1988 / Milestone ♦♦♦♦

State of the Art / 198 / Milestone ♦♦♦♦

Right Turn on Blues / Jan. 22, 1994-Jan. 23, 1994 / Telarc ♦♦♦♦♦

Blues Groove / Jul. 21, 1995-Jul. 22, 1995 / Telarc ♦♦♦♦

The Dream Team / Aug. 19, 1996 / Milestone ♦♦♦♦♦

Straight Up / May 18, 1998-May 19, 1998 / Milestone ♦♦♦♦♦

McGriff's House Party / Sep. 28, 1999-Sep. 29, 1999 / Milestone ♦♦♦

This Milestone release continues in the soul groove that Jimmy McGriff helped create in the early '60s. McGriff's *House Party* took two days to complete and found the participants in a hard funk mood. The fine groove ensemble on this disc features Kenny Rampton's trumpet on four cuts, tenor saxophonists Eric Alexander or Bill Easley, Rodney Jones on guitar, and Bernard Purdie on drums. It's to McGriff's credit that he invited another organ legend, Dr. Lonnie Smith, along on four especially greasy cuts that will have fans of the genre in Hammond hysteria. Highlights include "Neckbones à la Carte," an up-tempo James Brown-style funk written by guitarist Rodney Jones. "Blues for Stitt" is Easley's tribute to the legendary tenor saxophonist. "Red Roses for a Blue Lady" trots along with an extra bite given to this standard from Alexander. Special guest guitarist George Benson doesn't actually play on this date but he does make his presence felt by contributing "Red Cadillac Boogaloo," which he composed while enjoying the session from the control booth. The slow closing blues "Dishin the Dirt" signals last call and winds up another enjoyable and recommended soul groove session from Jimmy McGriff. *—Al Campbell*

McKinney's Cotton Pickers

f. 1926, **db.** 1934

Big Band / Classic Jazz, Swing, Big Band

William McKinney was a drummer who by 1923 had retired from playing in favor of conducting and managing a big band. In 1926 his outfit became known as McKinney's Cotton Pickers and the following year they scored a major coup by hiring arranger/altoist/vocalist Don Redman away from Fletcher Henderson. As the band's musical director, Redman put together an outfit that competed successfully with Henderson and the up-and-coming Duke Ellington. It was the advanced arrangements, the tight ensembles and the high musicianship of the orchestra on a whole that was most impressive; among their more rewarding recordings overall were "Four or Five Times," "It's Tight like That," "It's a Precious Little Thing Called Love" and four future standards that Redman introduced: "Gee Baby Ain't I Good to You," "Baby Won't You Please Come Home," "I Want a Little Girl" and "Cherry." It was a major blow in 1931 when Redman departed to form his own band. Benny Carter took over as musical director but despite the presence of such fine players as Doc Cheatham and Hilton Jefferson, there would only be one final recording session. The Depression eventually did the band in and after much turnover in 1934 the classic group broke up. McKinney organized later versions of the Cotton Pickers but without making an impression. *—Scott Yanow*

● **1928-1929** / Jul. 11, 1928-Nov. 5, 1929 / Classics ✦✦✦✦✦
This is the first of three Classics CD's featuring all of the master takes by McKinney's Cotton Pickers, one of the finest big bands of the late 1920's. The inventive arrangements of leader Don Redman (who also plays alto and clarinet in addition to taking some vocals) are even better than the individual solos. Highlighted by such numbers as "Four Or Five Times," "Milenberg Joys," "Cherry," "Don't Be Like That," "There's A Rainbow 'Round My Shoulder" and a surprisingly hard-swinging version of "It's A Precious Little Thing Called Love," the Cotton Pickers feature tight ensembles, spirited vocals and concise hot solos. All three of their Classics CD's are well worth picking up. *—Scott Yanow*

● **The Band Don Redman Built** / Jul. 11, 1928-Nov. 3, 1930 / Bluebird/RCA ✦✦✦✦✦
While the European Classics label has reissued all of the recordings of McKinney's Cotton Pickers, the American Bluebird label has only come out with this best-of collection. The 22 selections on their lone CD are consistently excellent and on a whole does a fine job of summing up the legacy of this legendary early big band, but serious collectors will want the other performances, too. So this release is for general listeners; among the more memorable numbers (all of which were arranged by leader Don Redman) are "Four or Five Times," "Cherry," "It's Tight Like That," "I've Found a New Baby," "Gee Baby, Ain't I Good to You," and "I Want a Little Girl." *—Scott Yanow*

☆ **The Complete McKinney's Cotton Pickers, Vol. 1-2** / Jul. 11, 1928-Nov. 6, 1929 / RCA ✦✦✦✦✦
During 1979-1984 on three double LPs, French RCA (in their *Jazz Tribune* series) reissued the complete output of McKinney's Cotton Pickers (one of the great big bands of the 1928-1931 period). All of the master takes have since been reissued on CD by the Classics label but, due to the inclusion of the alternate takes, the LP series has yet to be equaled. For the first two-fer, there are six rare alternates plus 27 regular takes. Covering the Cotton Pickers' first (and best) year, this set has many highlights, including "Four or Five Times," "Milenberg Joys," "Cherry," "Nobody's Sweetheart," "Don't Be Like That," "There's a Rainbow 'Round My Shoulder," "I Found a New Baby," and the original version of Don Redman's "Gee Baby Ain't I Good to You." In addition to work with the regular band (which featured such fine players as trumpeters Langston Curl and John Nesbitt, tenorman/singer George Thomas, and Redman himself on alto, clarinet, and vocals), there are a few numbers on which Redman leads an integrated band that includes sidemen from Jean Goldkette's Orchestra along with an all-star date (continued on the second two-fer) that has such guests as altoist Benny Carter, tenor great Coleman Hawkins, and pianist Fats Waller. Essential music. *—Scott Yanow*

1929-1930 / Nov. 6, 1929-Nov. 5, 1930 / Classics ✦✦✦✦✦
On the second of three Classics CD's that releases the complete output of McKinney's Cotton Pickers (but without the alternate takes), there are many classic performances including "Wherever There's A Will There's A Way," "If I Could Be With You," "Honeysuckle Rose," "Baby Won't You Please Come Home" and "I Want A Little Girl." In addition to the band's regular soloists (trumpeters John Nesbitt, Joe Smith and Langston Curl, trombonist Ed Cuffee and tenorman George Thomas), some tunes also feature guests Coleman Hawkins on tenor, altoist Benny Carter and pianist Fats Waller. Timeless classic jazz. *—Scott Yanow*

1930-1931/1939-1940 / Nov. 4, 1930-Jan. 17, 1940 / Classics ✦✦✦✦
The Classics label's superb series of McKinney's Cotton Pickers releases continues with this set, which features recordings from the original group as well as performances from Don Redman's swing orchestra of the late 1930s. *—Jason Ankeny*

John McLaughlin

b. Jan. 4, 1942, Yorkshire, England

Guitar (Electric), Guitar / Post-Bop, Fusion

A household name since the early '70s, John McLaughlin was an innovative fusion guitarist when he led the Mahavishnu Orchestra and has continued living up to his reputation as a phenomenal and consistently inquisitive player through the years. His first album was a classic (1969's *Extrapolation*) and was followed by an obscurity for the Dawns label with John Surman, a quintet set with Larry Young (*Devotion*) and *My Goals Beyond* in 1970 which was half acoustic solos and half jams involving Indian musicians. In 1969 McLaughlin moved to New York to play with Tony Williams's Lifetime and he appeared on two classic Miles Davis records: *In a Silent Way* and *Bitches Brew*. In 1971 McLaughlin formed the Mahavishnu Orchestra, a very powerful group often thought of as rock but having the sophisticated improvisations of jazz. McLaughlin then surprised the music world by radicalliy shifting directions, switching to acoustic guitar and playing Indian music with his group Shakti. They made a strong impact on the world music scene (which was in its infancy) during their three years. Since then McLaughlin has gone back and forth between electric and acoustic guitars. *—Scott Yanow*

Extrapolation / Jan. 18, 1969 / Polydor ✦✦✦
John McLaughlin's first recording as a leader features the future innovator playing guitar in an English quartet. Although McLaughlin contributed all ten pieces, baritonist John Surman actually dominates this music, often swinging quite hard. The historically significant set, although a lesser-known item in McLaughlin's discography, is quite musical and enjoyable in its own right. *—Scott Yanow*

★ **My Goals Beyond** / Jun. 1970 / Rykodisc ✦✦✦✦✦
After bouncing around on a couple of labels, the CD reissue of this album ultimately ended up on Rykodisc. The startling thing about this record is that it points the way toward two directions McLaughlin would take in the future—exploring Indian music and the acoustic guitar—and this while he was in the thick of the burgeoning electronic jazz-rock movement. The first half is a John McLaughlin acoustic guitar *tour de force,* where he thwacks away with his energetic, single-minded intensity on three jazz standards and five originals (including one genuine self-penned classic, "Follow Your Heart") and adds a few percussion effects via overdubbing. The second half is devoted to a pair of marvelously intricate fusions of Indian rhythms and drones called "Peace One" and "Peace Two," with jazz flights from flutist/soprano saxophonist Dave Liebman, a simpatico encounter with future Mahavishnu cohorts Billy Cobham on drums and Jerry Goodman on violin, and Airto blending his sounds seamlessly with the Indian tambura and tabla. Throughout, McLaughlin's acoustic lines faultlessly straddle the line between the subcontinent and jazz, and the ethereal results still hold up beautifully today. *—Richard S. Ginell*

Devotion / Sep. 1970 / Douglas ✦✦✦✦✦
This often-exciting set, John McLaughlin's third as a leader and predating The Mahavishnu Orchestra by just a year, is actually more in the style of Tony Williams's Lifetime than McLaughlin's later groups. That fact is not all that surprising when one considers that Lifetime's organist Larry Young is an integral of this rockish but explorative set. None of the individual songs (which also feature bassist Billy Rich and drummer Buddy Miles) caught on but McLaughlin's guitar style was already becoming distinctive. *—Scott Yanow*

Electric Guitarist / 1978 / Columbia ✦✦✦✦
This is an album of reconciliation and penance, a series of reunions with several former colleagues from the early jazz-rock days, some of whom had parted on bitter terms with McLaughlin. But there are no egos out of control here; everyone has grown up, and partly as a result, there is a high level of musical inspiration devoid of pointless decibel wars. Jerry Goodman and Billy Cobham of the first Mahavishnu Orchestra show up first, then a genial reunion with Carlos Santana has some of the old fire. From this point, the CD undergoes a clever systematic reduction in numbers—first to five players, then four (the great combination of Chick Corea, Stanley Clarke and Jack DeJohnette), then three (a delightfully loose reunion of Lifetimers Tony Williams and Jack Bruce), then two (a fierce duel with Cobham), and finally just McLaughlin himself delivering the benediction on, of all things, "My Foolish Heart." Jazz is the dominant flavor in these fusions, often in a more restrained manner than the early-'70s sessions, and it pointed the way toward a new musical maturity for McLaughlin the electric guitarist. *—Richard S. Ginell*

Passion, Grace and Fire / Oct. 1982-Nov. 1982 / Columbia ✦✦✦✦
Two years after they recorded *Friday Night in San Francisco,* John McLaughlin, Al DiMeola and Paco De Lucia reunited for another set of acoustic guitar trios. If this can be considered a guitar "battle" (some of the playing is ferocious and these speed demons do not let up too often), then the result is a three-way tie. This guitar summit lives up to its title. *—Scott Yanow*

Friday Night in San Francisco / Dec. 5, 1986 / Columbia ✦✦✦✦✦

Que Alegria / Nov. 29, 1991-Dec. 3, 1991 / Verve ✦✦✦
The John McLaughlin Trio goes into the studio and broadens its stylistic range considerably in another musically satisfying, open-minded outing. Again, McLaughlin sounds rejuvenated and refreshed in this format, as he switches between acoustic guitar and a guitar synthesizer attachment that softens and rounds his attacks while creating some luminous timbres and textures. McLaughlin's on-again, off-again Indian kick rises prominently into view here as Trilok Gurtu's role broadens into that of an all-purpose percussionist, producing some amazing sounds as backdrops. Pastorius-influenced bassist Kai Eckhardt gets downright funky on "1 Nite Stand" but gives way to the equally accomplished Dominque Di Piazza on most tracks. Yes, there is even some fantastic straight-ahead blues grooving on "Hijacked"—if one may be permitted to use the terms guitar synthesizer and straight-ahead in the same sentence. *—Richard S. Ginell*

Time Remembered: John McLaughlin Plays Bill Evans / Mar. 25, 1993-Mar. 28, 1993 / Verve ✦✦

Tokyo Live / Dec. 16, 1993-Dec. 18, 1993 / Verve ✦✦✦✦
Although it is tempting to think that The Free Spirits (the trio featured on this CD), due to the similarity of the instrumentation (guitarist John McLaughlin, organist Joey DeFrancesco and drummer Dennis Chambers), would be an updating of Tony Williams's groundbreaking fusion group Lifetime, the reality is somewhat different. McLaughlin may get top billing but this music sounds very much like a Joey DeFrancesco-led Jimmy Smith revival date with most of the selections being blues-based. There are some introspective moments for the guitarist (who plays strictly electric here) but DeFrancesco dominates the ensembles and takes the lion's share of the solo space. The music is enjoyable enough although none of the compositions (all but Miles Davis's "No Blues" are by McLaughlin) are all that memorable. *—Scott Yanow*

After the Rain / Oct. 4, 1994-Oct. 5, 1994 / Verve ✦✦✦✦
In the early '70s John McLaughlin was 1/3 of the supergroup Lifetime with drummer Tony Williams and organist Larry Young. This particular CD from 1994 matches him with drummer Elvin Jones and organist Joey DeFrancesco but the music has little in common with Lifetime. Instead many of the tunes can be considered to be tributes to John Coltrane; Jones's participation certainly reinforces that connection. McLaughlin, back on electric guitar after sveral years sticking almost exclusively to acoustic, is in top form on such numbers as "Take the Coltrane," "My Favorite Things," "Crescent" and "Afro Blue." The improvising is advanced and colorful with DeFrancesco keeping the proceedings swinging and, even if the results are not quite classic, the collaboration is somewhat unique. *—Scott Yanow*

The Promise / 1995 / Verve ✦✦✦✦✦
John McLaughlin shoots out in many different directions during this very diverse release. He trades off with fellow guitarist Jeff Beck on "Django," jams his own "Thelonious Melodius" in a trio with organist Joey DeFrancesco and drummer Dennis Chambers, has a duet with DeFrancesco (who switches to trumpet) on "No Return," stretches out with tenor great Michael Brecker on the 14 1/2-minute "Jazz Jungle," collaborates on acoustic guitar with Paco De Lucia and Al DiMeola, plays Indian music with Zakir Hussain and Trilok Gurtu, and interacts with altoist David Sanborn—among others. A good introduction to latter-day John McLaughlin, this colorful set has plenty of surprises. *—Scott Yanow*

Paco de Lucia/John McLaughlin/Al Di Meola / May 1996-Jul. 1996 / Verve ✦✦✦✦
The acoustic guitar trio of John McLaughlin, Al DiMeola, and Paco DeLucia can always be relied upon to create quiet but fiery music. The three virtuosos always sound restrained and tasteful (yet inwardly explosive) when they play together. This 1996 effort has three originals apiece from McLaughlin and DiMeola, two by DeLucia and a beautiful McLaughlin-DiMeola duet on "Manha de Carnaval" that makes one wish they would more fully explore bossa nova. Most of the selections are thoughtful, but there are also plenty of explosive outbursts for contrast (along with the jubilant closer "Cardeosa") on the highly arranged yet spontaneous-sounding program. *—Scott Yanow*

Remember Shakti: The Believer / 1999 / Verve ✦✦✦✦
When Eastern classical musicians and Western jazz or pop musicians get together to jam, the result are always heartwarming; two wildly disparate traditions coming together to make music is such an irresistible gesture of human unity and cross-cultural cooperation. What's not to love— Frankly, what's not to love is often the music itself, which all too frequently is long on multicultural good intentions and short on things like coherence, interest, and hooks. The intermittently mystical jazz guitarist John McLaughlin, who has been nursing an India jones for decades now, is hardly innocent of such offenses. But on *The Believer,* a live set featuring McLaughlin, electric mandolinist U. Shrinivas, kanjira and ghatam player V. Selvaganesh, and legendary tabla player Zakir Hussain, he delivers a gloriously tight, rhythmically thrilling program of original compositions (as well as one contribution each from Shrinivas and Hussain). The group is called Remember Shakti in reference to Shakti, the similarly configured band that McLaughlin co-led in the mid-'70s. If anything, his playing has grown more exciting than it was then; listening to him negotiate the thorny rhythmic changes of this music in unison with Shrinivas and to both of them bouncing off the complexly woven rhythmic patterns laid out by Hussain and Slevaganesh is not only impressive, but uplifting as well. Highlights include the downright funky "Anna" and Shrinivas' composition "Maya." Very highly recommended. *—Rick Anderson*

Jackie McLean

b. May 17, 1932, New York, NY
Sax (Alto) / Hard Bop, Post-Bop
Jackie McLean has long had his own sound, played slightly sharp and with great intensity; he is recognizable within two notes. McLean was one of the few bop-oriented players of the early '50s who explored free jazz in the 1960s, widening his emotional range and drawing from the new music qualities that fit his musical personality. He made his recording debut with Miles Davis in 1951 and the rest of the decade could be considered his apprenticeship. McLean worked with George Wallington, Charles Mingus and Art Blakey's Jazz Messengers (1956-58). He recorded a classic series of 21 Blue Note albums from 1959-67; on sessions such as *One Step Beyond* and *Destination Out,* McLean really stretches and challenges himself—this music is quite original and intense yet logical. By 1968 however he was moving into the jazz education field and other than some SteepleChase records from 1972-74 (including two meetings with his early idol Dexter Gordon) and an unfortunate commercial outing for RCA (1978-79), McLean was less active as a player during the 1970s. However in the 1980s he returned to a more active playing schedule, recording with all of the intensity and passion of his earlier days. *—Scott Yanow*

Lights Out! / Jul. 27, 1956 / Prestige/OJC ✦✦✦✦
Altoist Jackie McLean's second session as a leader is reissued on this CD. The music that he makes with trumpeter Donald Byrd, pianist Elmo Hope, bassist Doug Watkins and drummer Art Taylor is essentially hard bop with fairly simple (or in some cases nonexistent) melody statements preceding two romps through the "I Got Rhythm" chord changes, a pair of blues, a thinly disguised "Embraceable You" and a straightforward version of "A Foggy Day." Enjoyable if not really essential music from the up-and-coming altoist. *—Scott Yanow*

4, 5 and 6 / Jul. 13, 1956-Jul. 20, 1956 / Prestige/OJC ✦✦✦✦
This is a well-rounded CD reissue that brings back altoist Jackie McLean's third recording as a leader. McLean has several fine ballad features ("Sentimental Journey," "Why Was I Born," "When I Fall in Love" and Mal Waldron's "Abstraction") welcomes trumpeter Donald Byrd to Kenny Drew's "Contour" and jams on a lengthy version of Charlie Parker's "Confirmation" with a sextet that includes Byrd and tenor saxophonist Hank Mobley. With pianist Waldron, bassist Doug Watkins and drummer Art Taylor offering fine support, this is a strong hard bop set that is tied to the tradition of bebop while looking forward. *—Scott Yanow*

McLean's Scene / Dec. 4, 1956-Feb. 15, 1957 / New Jazz/OJC ✦✦✦✦

Jackie McLean and Co. / Feb. 8, 1957 / Prestige/OJC ✦✦✦

Strange Blues / Feb. 15, 1957-Aug. 30, 1957 / Prestige/OJC ✦✦✦✦
The last of the Jackie McLean Prestige sessions, this CD reissue has material from two different sets, but fortunately, the music is on a higher level than one might expect of "leftovers." "Strange Blues" is from a marathon quartet set that McLean had with pianist Mal Waldron, bassist Arthur Phipps and drummer Art Taylor as is a rendition of "What's New" that is an alternate version to the one included on *Makin' the Changes.* In addition, "Disciples Love Affair" and "Millie's Pad" match McLean with the tuba of Ray Draper (who contributed both songs), trumpeter Webster Young, pianist John Meyers, bassist Bill Salter and drummer Larry Ritchie, while the incomplete "Not So Strange Blues" is all McLean on an explosive blues with the rhythm section. A generally strong set chiefly recommended to Jackie McLean completists. *—Scott Yanow*

Alto Madness / May 3, 1957 / Prestige/OJC ✦✦✦

A Long Drink of the Blues / Feb. 15, 1957-Aug. 30, 1957 / New Jazz/OJC ✦✦✦✦
This CD reissue begins with what is titled "Take 1" of "A Long Drink of the Blues." After a false start, the musicians argue for two minutes about the tempo; why was this ever released— "Take 2" is a much more successful 20-minute jam featuring Jackie McLean (doubling on alto and tenor), trombonist Curtis Fuller, trumpeter Webster Young, pianist Gil Coggins, bassist Paul Chambers and drummer Louis Hayes. The second half of this reissue is from a quartet session that showcases McLean on three standard ballads with pianist Mal Waldron, bassist Arthur Phipps and drummer Art Taylor. Although not quite as intense as McLean's later Blue Note dates, the ballad renditions show just how mature and original a soloist he was even at this early stage. Despite "Take 1," this CD is worth getting. *—Scott Yanow*

Jackie's Bag / Jan. 18, 1959-Sep. 1, 1960 / Blue Note ✦✦✦✦✦
This very interesting LP was a giant step forward for altoist Jackie McLean, although it was originally released after a couple of his other Blue Note albums. For the first time, McLean shows some of the influence of Ornette Coleman—not in his sound but in his improvising approach—and his freer style bridged the gap between hard bop and the avant-garde. Three of the songs, highlighted by "Quadrangle" and "Fidel," match McLean in 1959 with trumpeter Donald Byrd, pianist Sonny Clark, bassist Paul Chambers, and drummer Philly Joe Jones, while the other numbers, which include "Appointment in Ghana," showcase McLean in a sextet with trumpeter Blue Mitchell, Tina Brooks on tenor, pianist Kenny Drew, Chambers and drummer Art Taylor. Jackie McLean's Blue Note albums were the most significant of his career, and this LP is well worth searching for. *—Scott Yanow*

New Soil / May 2, 1959 / Blue Note ✦✦✦✦✦
This CD reissue adds "Formidable," which was first released on the 1980 LP *Vertigo,* to the original program. A quintet date with trumpeter Donald Byrd, pianist Walter Davis, Jr., bassist Paul Chambers and drummer Pete La Roca, this music is far superior to the jam session-oriented sets that altoist Jackie McLean made for Prestige a few years earlier. Rehearsal time gave the musicians an opportunity to learn the two McLean originals and the four songs contributed by Davis; the latter's "Davis Cup" is the best-known of the pieces. The music is funky but adventurous, beyond hard bop but still tied to chordal improvisation. Stimulating listening. *—Scott Yanow*

Vertigo / May 2, 1959-Feb. 11, 1963 / Blue Note ✦✦✦✦
This 1980 recording released for the first time—"Formidable" from a 1959 session and five numbers from a 1963 McLean set. While "Formidable" has a strong quintet (with altoist Jackie McLean, trumpeter Donald Byrd, pianist Walter Davis, bassist Paul Chambers, and drummer Pete La Roca), the 1963 session has the recording debut of drummer Tony Williams along with strong contributions from Byrd, pianist Herbie Hancock (then also near the beginning of his career), and bassist Butch Warren. The latter unit sticks to group originals by Byrd, Hancock, and McLean, and the music ranges from catchy funk and hard bop to strong hints of the avant-garde. *—Scott Yanow*

Swing, Swang, Swingin' / Oct. 2, 1959 / Blue Note ✦✦✦✦
This set (reissued on CD in 1997) is different from most Jackie McLean Blue Note sessions in that the altoist, other than an original blues, sticks to standards. McLean's quartet outing (with pianist Walter Bishop, Jr., bassist Jimmy Garrison and drummer Art Taylor) is actually more notable for the passion and intensity expressed in every note the leader plays than it is for the actual ideas. Even when performing at a relaxed pace, the instantly recognizable McLean turns up the heat on tunes such as "What's New," "I Remember You" and "I Love You," making every note count. Although not as essential as the Blue Note dates in which he explored new material, this formerly rare set is enjoyable and easily recommended to Jackie McLean fans. *—Scott Yanow*

Bluesnik / Jan. 8, 1961 / Blue Note ✦✦✦✦✦
This is one of the most accessible of altoist Jackie McLean's Blue Note sessions, for the six songs, which have been augmented on the CD reissue by "new" alternate versions of "Goin' Way Blues" and "Torchin'," are all blues. McLean teams up with the fiery young trumpeter Freddie Hubbard, pianist Kenny Drew, bassist Doug Watkins and drummer Pete La Roca for diverse originals by the leader, Drew and Hubbard that all have the feeling (if not always the exact structure) of the blues. The variety of tempos, moods and styles make this a highly recommended set. *—Scott Yanow*

☆ **Let Freedom Ring** / Mar. 19, 1962 / Blue Note ✦✦✦✦✦
This is one of altoist Jackie McLean's most significant recordings. A veteran of the hard bop scene of the 1950s, McLean was one of the few musicians from his generation to embrace aspects of the avant-garde without losing his own musical personality. McLean kept his own intense sound but opened up his playing to the point where he could improvise without using chord structures or even a steady tempo. His emotional style is heard at its prime on the four selections included on this CD reissue, a quartet date with pianist Walter Davis, bassist Herbie Lewis and drummer Billy Higgins. Although the music is not quite as free as Ornette Coleman's, it is nearly as innovative, particularly when one considers the expanded vocabu-

lary that McLean uses (with screams and honks being integrated logically into his solos). Even on Bud Powell's ballad "I'll Keep Loving You," McLean's playing is very advanced and, in its own way, free. This is a gem that still sounds quite modern. *—Scott Yanow*

Tippin' the Scales / Sep. 28, 1962 / Blue Note ♦♦♦♦
This fairly straightahead LP by altoist Jackie McLean was released for the first time in 1984. Due to its boppish nature, as opposed to his more adventurous recordings of the period, it languished in the vaults for over 20 years, but the music is actually quite enjoyable. With assistance from pianist Sonny Clark, bassist Butch Warren and drummer Art Taylor, McLean is in excellent form on two of his originals, three by Clark (including "Nursery Blues" and "Nicely") and the standard ballad "Cabin in the Sky." A fine hard bop session. *—Scott Yanow*

★ **One Step Beyond** / Apr. 30, 1963 / Blue Note ♦♦♦♦♦
One of the great Jackie McLean records, this album features the innovative altoist performing two of his originals plus a pair by trombonist Grachan Moncur III. With vibraphonist Bobby Hutcherson (on one of his earliest recordings), bassist Eddie Khan, and drummer Tony Williams (McLean's discovery) completing the quintet, this was a group that could play the most advanced material with creativity and improvise freely when it fit the music. The solos and ensembles on the "difficult" material are quite memorable, and it is to Jackie McLean's credit that he was not satisfied to spend his entire career playing hard bop; his musical curiosity led him to listening closely to the music of Ornette Coleman and to adapting aspects of free jazz that fit his distinctive sound. *—Scott Yanow*

Destination Out / Sep. 20, 1963 / Blue Note ♦♦♦♦♦
Five very talented and versatile jazzmen (altoist Jackie McLean, trombonist Grachan Moncur III, vibraphonist Bobby Hutcherson, bassist Larry Ridley and drummer Roy Haynes) explore three of Moncur's originals plus McLean's "Kahlil the Prophet" on this CD reissue of their 1963 Blue Note album. McLean was one of the few players of his generation to be influenced by the free jazz movement yet he never lost his musical personality or his distinctive sound. The improvisations by these musicians are both thoughtful and passionate, making expert use of space, tricky time changes and emotional intensity. *—Scott Yanow*

☆ **The Complete Blue Note 1964-1966** / Aug. 5, 1964-Apr. 18, 1966 / Mosaic ♦♦♦♦♦
Altoist Jackie McLean has recorded so many fine albums throughout his career, particularly in the '60s for Blue Note, that Mosaic could have reissued his complete output without any loss of quality. This four-CD limited-edition box set contains six complete LPs worth of material plus one "new" alternate take. The music (which also features trumpeters Charles Tolliver and Lee Morgan; pianists Herbie Hancock, Larry Willis, and Harold Mabern; vibraphonist Bobby Hutcherson; bassists Cecil McBee, Bob Cranshaw, Larry Ridley, Herbie Lewis, and Don Moore; and drummers Roy Haynes, Billy Higgins, Clifford Jarvis, Jack DeJohnette, and Billy Higgins) is explorative (showing the influence of Ornette Coleman) but without totally disregarding McLean's bebop roots. The performances straddle the boundaries between advanced hard bop and free jazz with Jackie McLean consistently emerging as the main star; his solos are consistently exciting and full of unexpected twists and turns. *—Scott Yanow*

It's Time / Aug. 5, 1964 / Blue Note ♦♦♦♦
Altoist Jackie McLean and his sidemen on this excellent quintet set (which also features trumpeter Charles Tolliver, pianist Herbie Hancock, bassist Cecil McBee, and drummer Roy Haynes) explore aspects of free jazz (particularly on "Cancellation") without letting go completely of the concepts of chordal improvisation. Strange as it seems, McLean's sound and highly expressive vocabulary are more advanced than his actual notes while Tolliver's notes are more unpredictable than his Clifford Brown-inspired tone. Ranging from "Cancellation" to the funky "Das' Dat," this is a stimulating LP that has been reissued as part of Mosaic's four-CD Jackie McLean box set. *—Scott Yanow*

Dr. Jackle / Dec. 18, 1966 / Steeple Chase ♦♦♦♦
Jackie McLean was one of the few hard bop stars (John Coltrane was another) who was greatly affected by the avant-garde innovations of the 1960s. His sound did not change but his solos became freer and much more emotional. By the time he played in Baltimore for the 1966 concert released on this CD, he had greatly opened up his style and had reconciled his roots with free jazz. With the strong assistance of pianist Lamont Johnson, bassist Scotty Holt and drummer Billy Higgins, McLean stretches out on five numbers (including a previously unreleased "Jossa Bossa") which clock in between 8 and over 14 1/2 minutes. From the start the music is quite intense and it may take listeners a few moments to get used to the altoist's abrasive and sharp tone. However his creative ideas and constant originality win one over fast and, by the time he finished the set with a blues ("Closing"), the logic of Jackie McLean's improvisations is more apparent. The recording quality is sometimes a little distorted but the power, color and pure courage of the music is memorable. *—Scott Yanow*

New and Old Gospel / Mar. 24, 1967 / Blue Note ♦♦♦♦
This set (which has been reissued on CD) should have been a classic but it has one fatal flaw. The only recorded meeting between Jackie McLean and Ornette Coleman (instead of matching the two altoists together) features Coleman exclusively on trumpet. Ornette, who had been playing trumpet for only three years at the time, is much weaker on that instrument than on alto and is simply no match for McLean. It is a pity that this set is so flawed because the originals are quite advanced, pianist Lamont Johnson (who is joined by bassist Scott Holt and drummer Billy Higgins) has what is probably his finest recorded performance and McLean (one of the few hard bop veterans to embrace Coleman's innovations) was in the middle of a peak period. But Ornette Coleman's colorful and unpredictable ideas are ill-served by his erratic trumpet technique, sinking this disappointing effort. *—Scott Yanow*

'Bout Soul / Sep. 8, 1967 / Blue Note ♦♦♦♦♦
'Bout Soul does not mean the same thing as soul-jazz, as the opening track "Soul" makes abundantly clear. Written by Grachan Moncur III and poet Barbara Simmons, "Soul" is a tonally free tone-poem that features Simmons' spoken recital. It's about what the concept of soul is, not what soul music is, and that should not come as a surprise to anyone acquainted with Jackie McLean's work. Even as his Blue Note contemporaries were working commercial soul-jazz grooves, McLean pushed the borders of jazz, embracing the avant-garde and free jazz. *'Bout Soul* is one of his most explicit free albums, finding the alto saxophonist pushing a quintet—trumpeter Woody Shaw (who sits out "Dear Nick, Dear John"), pianist Lamont Johnson, bassist Scotty Holt, drummer Rashied Ali—into uncompromising, tonally free territory. This is intensely cerebral music that is nevertheless played with a fiery passion. Although the music was all composed, it is played as if it was invented on the spot. Fans of McLean's straight-ahead hard bop, or even of his adventurous mid-'60s sessions, might find this a little off-putting at first, but *'Bout Soul* rewards close listening. It is one of McLean's best avant sessions. *—Stephen Thomas Erlewine*

Demon's Dance / Dec. 22, 1967 / Blue Note ♦♦♦♦♦
Altoist Jackie McLean's final Blue Note album preceded four and a half years of silence as he withdrew from the New York scene and started working as an educator. McLean was still very much in top form at the time of this hard-to-find LP. Teaming up with trumpeter Woody Shaw, pianist LaMont Johnson, bassist Scott Holt, and drummer Jack DeJohnette, McLean is quite passionate and typically intense on two of his originals plus a couple songs apiece from Cal Massey (including "Message From Trane") and Shaw. The modal-oriented music fit the styles of these advanced jazzmen and the results are quite stimulating and adventurous. *—Scott Yanow*

☆ **Dynasty** / Nov. 5, 1988 / Triloka ♦♦♦♦♦
This is one of the great Jackie McLean albums. After nearly a decade off of records, the veteran altoist teamed up with his son Rene (who triples on tenor, soprano and flute), pianist Hotep Idris Galeta, bassist Nat Reeves and drummer Carl Allen for a very passionate and high-powered live set. Whether it be originals by Rene McLean (including "J. Mac's Dynasty") or Galeta, a very intense version of "A House Is Not a Home" or Jackie's "Bird Lives," this is dynamic and consistently exciting music. The go-for-broke solos (which transcend any easy categories) and Jackie's unique sharp tone make this an essential CD, one of the top recordings to be released in 1990. *—Scott Yanow*

Rites of Passage / Jan. 29, 1991-Jan. 30, 1991 / Triloka ♦♦♦♦♦
Recorded over two years after his "comeback" album, *Dynasty,* but using the same personnel, altoist Jackie McLean once again sounds in prime form. His intensity and passion had not declined through the years and his sometimes-abrasive tone had, if anything, become even more distinctive. With this particularly strong group (which has son Rene on tenor, alto and soprano, pianist Hotep Idris Galeta, bassist Nat Reeves and drummer Carl Allen), McLean pours his heart out on two of his originals plus pieces by Rene And Galeta. Outstanding no-holds-barred music. *—Scott Yanow*

The Jackie Mac Attack Live / Nov. 2, 1992-Nov. 3, 1992 / Verve ♦♦♦♦♦
Veteran altoist Jackie McLean is in top form on this live quartet session with pianist Hotep Idris Galeta, bassist Nat Reeves and drummer Carl Allen. He performs two originals by Galeta, Rene McLean's "Dance Little Mandissa," "'Round Midnight" and his own "Minor March" and "Five." The amount of passion and intensity that McLean puts into his improvisations is quite impressive, and 40 years after his recording debut, he remains in prime form. This strong, advanced hard bop date gives listeners a good example of his abilities. *—Scott Yanow*

Marian McPartland (Marian Turner)

b. Mar. 20, 1918, Windsor, England
Piano / Post-Bop, Swing, Bop
Marian McPartland has become famous for hosting her *Piano Jazz* radio program since 1978 but she was a well-respected pianist decades before. She played in a four-piano vaudeville act in England and performed on the European continent for the troops during World War II. In Belgium in 1944 she met cornetist Jimmy McPartland and they soon married. Marian moved with her husband to the United States in 1946 where she sometimes played with him even though her style was more modern than his Dixieland-oriented groups. McPartland eventually had her own trio at the Embers (1950) and the Hickory House (1952-60) which until 1957 included drummer Joe Morello. She recorded regularly for Savoy and Capitol during the 1950s and also made sessions for Argo (1958), Time (1960 and 1963), Sesac and Dot. Although divorced eventually from Jimmy, they remained close friends, sometimes played together and remarried just weeks before his death. She formed her own Halycon label and recorded several fine albums between 1969-77. McPartland also made three albums for Tony Bennett's Improv label during 1976-77 before signing with Concord where she has been since 1978. The Jazz Alliance label has made available over 30 CD's worth of material from Marian McPartland's *Piano Jazz* show, some of which are quite fascinating and significant. *—Scott Yanow*

Jazz at the Hickory House / Apr. 21, 1952-Oct. 1953 / Savoy ♦♦♦♦

A Sentimental Journey / Nov. 1972-Jun. 1973 / Jazz Alliance ♦♦♦♦

Now's the Time / Jun. 30, 1977 / Halcyon ♦♦♦♦

● **Piano Jazz: McPartland/Evans** / Nov. 6, 1978 / Jazz Alliance ♦♦♦♦♦
This is one of the finest of all the Marian McPartland *Piano Jazz* radio shows. Bill Evans (less than two years before his death) not only plays in prime form and talks a little about his career but explains to McPartland in detail his approach to playing piano. One gets to know not only Bill Evans the musician but the man, too. Musically Evans performs a brief "Waltz for Debbie," "All of You," and "Reflections in D"; McPartland plays "While We're Young"; and they duet on five numbers, including "In Your Own Sweet Way," "Days of Wine and Roses," and "I Love You." This is a special show well worth hearing several times. *—Scott Yanow*

Portrait of Marian McPartland / May 1979 / Concord Jazz ♦♦♦♦
Although she was married to Dixieland trumpeter Jimmy McPartland and entered the jazz big leagues in the 1940s, pianist Marian McPartland has long been a harmonically sophisticated improviser, open to the influence of later stylists including Bill Evans. For this Concord release (which has been reissued on CD), McPartland teams up with the underrated Jerry Dodgion (who doubles on alto and flute), bassist Brian Torff and drummer Jake Hanna for a program that balances thoughtful ballads with a few faster pieces. Highlights include touch-

ing versions of "It Never Entered My Mind" and "Spring Can Really Hang You Up the Most" and spirited jams on "I Won't Dance" and Chick Corea's blues "Matrix." *—Scott Yanow*

At the Festival / Aug. 1979 / Concord Jazz ✦✦✦✦✦
One of Marian McPartland's better all-round sets for Concord, this date features the veteran pianist at the 1979 *Concord Jazz Festival.* Joined by bassist Brian Torff and drummer Jake Hanna, McPartland plays her own "In the Days of Our Love" plus five diverse standards that range from "Cotton Tail" to Chick Corea's "Windows." For the last three numbers ("Here's That Rainy Day," "On Green Dolphin Street" and "Oleo"), McPartland's trio is joined by the excellent but underrated altoist Mary Fettig Park; when is she going to record an album of her own— Recommended. *—Scott Yanow*

Live at Maybeck Recital Hall, Vol. 9 / Jan. 20, 1991 / Concord Jazz ✦✦✦✦✦
Marian McPartland has become a jazz legend over the past two decades and this captivating solo concert has something for everyone. Whether it's her jaunty opener "This Time the Dream's On Me," athe deliberate somber take of "Willow Weep for Me," or her thunderous performance of her "Theme From Piano Jazz" (usually heard only as an incomplete snippet on her long-running NPR series), her chops are never in question. Other highlights include Duke Ellington's "Clothed Woman," a piece rarely performed even by its composer; McPartland slowly unveils its shrouds, gliding through its maze of dramatic chords, joyous stride piano and repetitious vamps with a veteran's confidence (she played it with Ellington in the audience during her long run at *the Hickory House* in the 1950s). The CD closes with "I'll Be Around," a warm tribute to her good friend and the song's composer, the late Alec Wilder. It's a shame that this superb concert wasn't captured on video as well in order for the rest of us to catch her playfulness at the piano, her head thrown back with laughter, with her witty introductions to each piece (which are unfortunately edited out of the CD). This performance not only ranks with the best of the Maybeck solo series, but it should be considered as one of the best solo concerts ever to be released. *—Ken Dryden*

In My Life / Jan. 1993 / Concord Jazz ✦✦✦✦✦
Pianist Marian McPartland displays her versatility throughout this reflective and generally thoughtful CD on such selections as The Beatles "In My Life," John Coltrane's "Red Planet," Ivan Lins's "Velas" and Ornette Coleman's "Ramblin." Despite the diverse repertore, McPartland's own flexible style shines through and her individual musical personality is felt in each song. Altoist Chris Potter makes the trio a quartet on half of the selections and he uplifts the session a bit. McPartland's closing wistful solo piano version of "Singin' the Blues" (dedicated to her late husband cornetist Jimmy McPartland) should not be missed. *—Scott Yanow*

Plays the Music of Mary Lou Williams / Jan. 17, 1994-Jan. 18, 1994 / Concord Jazz ✦✦✦✦✦

Just Friends / Sep. 4, 1997-Jan. 26, 1998 / Concord Jazz ✦✦✦✦✦
Some jazz fans casually dismiss duo piano performances as mere novelties which all too often result in train wrecks. With hundreds of *Piano Jazz* sessions and a few additional multiple piano releases to her credit, plus an amazing ability to complement the style of any musical partner, Marian McPartland should have long since destroyed this musical myth. She's joined by six different pianists on this delightful date, who she has considered among her favorite *Piano Jazz* guests; however, these recordings were made specifically for Concord. Tommy Flanagan joins her for a joyous run through "Jeepers Creeper" and a lyrical take of "I've Got a Crush on You." Renee Rosnes sits in for a swinging version of "Some Time Ago" and a bossa nova treatment of "It's You or No One," while Geri Allen and Marian revive the forgotten chestnut "Lullaby of the Leaves" and also create an eerie duo improvisation, "Chrysalis." George Shearing and Marian amuse themselves with a jaunty arrangement of the title track, then play Shearing's chart of Marian's "Twilight World." But the cream of the duets are shared with old friend Dave Brubeck. Brubeck actually composed "Marian McPartland" on the way to his second *Piano Jazz* appearance; their wonderful improvisations around this catchy upbeat theme find both of them at the top of their game. Marian wraps the CD alone with the Dixieland standard "When the Saints Go Marching In," though her relaxed approach serves as an emotional elegy to her late husband Jimmy. Jazz piano just doesn't get any better than this. *—Ken Dryden*

The Single Petal of a Rose: The Essence of Duke Ellington / Apr. 17, 2000 / Concord Jazz ✦✦✦✦✦
The great American composer, Duke Ellington, is honored by the first lady of jazz piano, Marian McPartland, with *The Single Petal of a Rose: The Essence of Duke Ellington.* Recorded live at *Maybeck Studio for the Performing Arts,* this great program of solo and duet compositions features McPartland opening her spontaneous program with a vivid account of "Take the A Train." She follows it with a swinging performance of "Just Squeeze Me." Joined by Bill Douglas on acoustic bass, the duo's rapport is very fresh despite having collaborated for 15 years. Douglas' solos also make the musical concepts more interesting and keep the duo in good shape with creative reharmonizations. All songs were composed by Duke Ellington, except for McPartland's own "Cerulescence," a serene solo piano tribute to Duke and the opening track, which was composed by Billy Strayhorn. "Take the Coltrane," composed for Ellington's duo album with saxophonist John Coltrane, and her lovely rendition of "Single Petal of a Rose" are but two of the obscure but marvelous Ellington treasures portrayed in a new setting. McPartland concludes her program with a slow, sensitive, insightful rendition of "C Jam Blues" in what must be one of the most masterful arrangements of this great classic. *The Single Petal of a Rose: The Essence of Duke Ellington* is sure to become one of Marian McPartland's most remarkable accomplishments. *—Paula Edelstein*

Joe McPhee

b. Nov. 3, 1939, Miami, FL
Sax (Tenor), Sax (Soprano), Trumpet / Avant-Garde Jazz, Free Jazz
Since his emergence on the creative jazz and new music scene in the late '60s, Joe McPhee has recorded over 40 albums and shown that emotional content and theoretical underpinnings are a thoroughly compatible and important pairing in improvised music. He began on trumpet at age 8, and switched to the saxophone in his late 20s, eventually adding pocket trumpet, clarinet, valve trombone, and piano to his repertoire. His first recordings as a leader (including *Nation Time,* 1970) appeared on his CJR label, co-founded with painter Craig Johnson in 1969. By the mid-'70s the Swiss Hat Hut label was formed to release McPhee's recordings, starting with *Black Magic Man* (1970), and including the landmark solo recording *Tenor* (1976). McPhee's earliest recordings were often inspired by the revolutionary movements of the time, but his later endeavors were less driven by politics and more about sonic exploration. In the early '80s, exposure to composer Pauline Oliveros' "deep listening" theories, and his own readings, strengthened his interest in extended techniques. This led to his "Po Music" concept (a "Positive, Possible, Poetic Hypothesis"): a "process of provocation" that can be used to "move from one fixed set of ideas in an attempt to discover new ones." McPhee's application of Po principles to improvisation can be heard on several Hat recordings, including *Topology* and *Oleo/A Future Retrospective.* He went on hiatus in the '80s to care for his aging parents, and received some long-overdue notice from the U.S. jazz community upon his reemergence in the '90s. Twenty years after *Tenor,* Hatology released McPhee's second solo recording (this time on various instruments), *As Serious as Your Life.* McPhee also began a fruitful relationship with Chicago reedsman Ken Vandermark, resulting in recordings for Okkadisk, and in the late '90s, formed Trio X with bassist Dominic Duval and drummer Jay Rosen, and recorded for CIMP. *—Dave Lynch*

Nation Time / Dec. 12, 1970-Dec. 13, 1970 / Atavistic ✦✦✦✦
Tenor saxophonist Joe McPhee has been a cult figure in the jazz world despite a string of releases on the visible Hat Art label and vocal support from the likes of Ken Vandermark. *Nation Time* is good evidence why. Its three tracks were recorded live in December 1970 and released the following year on the tiny independent CjR Records. "Nation Time" and "Scorpio's Dance" feature McPhee with a quintet that mixes electric and acoustic instruments with dual percussionists. In a way, this is familiar territory, working Coltrane-inspired repetitions and a nearly reckless group interplay against a variety of musical textures. Here some electric piano or full-speed drumming, there roughly wailed sax or a trumpet pushing notes to a near drone. But no matter how familiar the approach, the end result is inventive and captivating as these two pieces shift from nearly conventional extended improvisations to less structured sound without ever sounding forced.

However, it's the 13-minute "Shakey Jake" that seems like the birth of a wonderful new style that unfortunately never went any further. With the quintet expanded by an alto sax, organist, and electric guitarist, McPhee gets busy marrying free jazz to James Brown funk or maybe creating a vision of what would have happened if early-'60s Coltrane had revisited his R&B youth. The band sets up a complex but danceable groove while the soloists surf along, twisting melodies and pushing the beat but never relying on repeated riffs. Despite their various ideas and overlapped solos, the effect is collaborative not competitive as if they realized what a rare experience this would be. *—Lang Thompson*

Survival Unit II: At WBAI's Free Music Store / Oct. 30, 1971 / hatART ✦✦✦✦
The Hat Art label was formed in the mid-'70s partly to document the music of multi-instrumentalist Joe McPhee. The tapes of this live concert, which was broadcast by the small New York radio station WBAI, were released for the first time on this 1996 CD. Doubling on tenor and trumpet, McPhee is joined by Clifford Thornton (heard on baritone horn and cornet), Byron Morris (on soprano and alto), pianist Mike Kull, and percussionist Harold E. Smith. Due to the passionate nature of much of this fairly free music and the use of Thornton's baritone horn, one does not really notice the absence of a string bass. The six lengthy pieces (which are sandwiched by somewhat stilted announcing) are full of fire but also have their quiet and lyrical moments. A strong all-around performance that should not have taken 25 years to release. *—Scott Yanow*

Tenor/Fallen Angels / Oct. 1977 / hatOLOGY ✦✦✦✦✦
This release adds a 15-minute track ("Fallen Angels") to the original LP issue of *Tenor,* which made a strong impact when released in the 1970s. Decades later, the music remains a tour de force, though in retrospect, it does not sound quite as revolutionary as it did when first released. Solo tenor is not an easy task, and the fact that McPhee can maintain the listener's interest for an hour of performance is astonishing. That he does so with an endless stream of creativity is remarkable. McPhee was (and is) a master of new sounds. He trailblazes paths, unafraid of consequences, devoid of cliches. His improvisations incorporate squeaks and squeals, but also bop-like stabs and outrageously radical runs that scream for attention. McPhee has come a long way since this major recording, but this still remains one of the best solo tenor albums of avant-garde jazz. *—Steven Loewy*

● **Visitation** / Nov. 6, 1983 / Sackville ✦✦✦✦✦
The versatile Joe McPhee (who on this set plays fluegelhorn, pocket trumpet, tenor and soprano) teams up with Bill Smith's Ensemble (Smith on soprano, sopranino and alto, violinist David Prentice and bassist David Lee) plus drummer Richard Bannard for a stimulating set of avant-garde music. The interplay between these masterful improvisers on group originals and Albert Ayler's classic "Ghosts" is consistently impressive and worthy of a close investigation by the more open-eared segment of the jazz audience. *—Scott Yanow*

A Meeting in Chicago / Feb. 14, 1996 / Okka Disk ✦✦✦✦
A Meeting in Chicago finds Ken Vandermark teamed up with one of his early personal influences, brass and reedsman Joe McPhee, with frequent Vandermark collaborator, bassist Kent Kessler, rounding out the date. The recording took place on Valentine's Day, 1996 and was originally issued on 8th Day Musics in the summer of 1997; Chicago jazz and improvised music label Okkadisk reissued it the following year. Both McPhee and Vandermark use a number of instruments from the reed and brass families throughout this varied recording of pairings, trio pieces, and solos. Of particular note are the soft beauty of the trio's "Matter of the Heart," Kessler's bowed solo piece "Central Wisconsin Double Wide," the aptly named McPhee and Vandermark duo "Hard Circles," and the suspenseful and heartfelt "Empty Bottle Blues." Ranging from fast and active to mellow and sparse, this recording session of truly excellent players holds many interesting moments for fans. *—Joslyn Layne*

Rapture / Dec. 28, 1998 / Cadence Jazz ✦✦✦✦✦
Joe McPhee has built up a remarkable discography, on a variety of instruments. Although he remains somewhat of a cult figure, his growing reputation and enormous talent mark him

as one of the major contributors to modern jazz improvisation. One of his striking characteristics is his ability to find new players and to pursue new directions. Here, he performs on saxophone with longtime colleagues, bassist Dominic Duval and drummer Jay Rosen, and adds the voice and violin of little-known Rosi Hertlein. Captured live at New York City's *Knitting Factory,* the group's highlight is clearly the lengthy (more than 47 minutes) "Lift Every Voice and Sing," the lovely spiritual by James Weldon Johnson. The piece slowly unfolds, revealing solo and group improvisations of major substance and incredible beauty, not to mention virtuosity. The violin, in particular, adds a new layer, and Hertlein's interaction with Duval is not to be missed. *—Steven A. Loewy*

The Dream Book / Aug. 27, 1998 / Cadence/CJR ✦✦✦✦✦
This might have been called "The Dream Duo." Joe McPhee on alto sax and pocket trumpet with Dominic Duval on acoustic string bass is an unbeatable combination, and one that produces free-style jazz improvisation of the highest order. In a way, this is a concept album of sorts. Recorded live at *the Knitting Factory* in New York City, the recording was inspired by the works of Ornette Coleman (as well as the artwork of modernist Helen Douglas), and each track is dedicated to a different player (Coleman, Dewey Redman, Charlie Haden, Charles Moffett, David Izenson, Scott La Faro, and Don Cherry). The music is a worthy tribute, as McPhee and Duval produce marvelous, generally subdued songs that merely hint at (and never ape) their namesakes. With total command of their instruments, and endless ideas, the duo produces expectantly stunning results. Wondrous and evocative. *—Steven Loewy*

No Greater Love / Mar. 17, 1999-Mar. 18, 1999 / CIMP ✦✦✦✦

Brass City / Oct. 3, 1997 / Okka Disk ✦✦✦

The Watermelon Suite / May 26, 1998-May 27, 1998 / CIMP ✦✦✦

Charles McPherson

b. Jul. 24, 1939, Joplin, MO
Sax (Alto) / Hard Bop, Bop
A Charlie Parker disciple who brings his own lyricism to the bebop language, Charles McPherson has been a reliable figure in modern mainstream jazz for the past 35 years. He played in the Detroit jazz scene of the mid-'50s, moved to New York in 1959 and within a year was working with Charles Mingus. McPherson and his friend Lonnie Hillyer succeeded Eric Dolphy and Ted Curson as regular members of Mingus's band in 1961 and he worked with the bassist off and on up until 1972. Although he and Hillyer had a short-lived quintet in 1966, McPherson was not a fulltime leader until 1972. In 1978 he moved to San Diego which has been his home ever since and sometimes he uses his son Chuck McPherson on drums. Charles McPherson, who helped out on the film *Bird* by playing some of the parts not taken from Charlie Parker records, has led dates through the years for Prestige (1964-69), Mainstream, Xanadu, Discovery and Arabesque. *—Scott Yanow*

Be-Bop Revisited / Nov. 20, 1964 / Prestige/OJC ✦✦✦✦✦
Bebop is the thing on this excellent outing as altoist Charles McPherson and pianist Barry Harris do their interpretations of Charlie Parker and Bud Powell. With trumpeter Carmell Jones, bassist Nelson Boyd and drummer Al "Tootie" Heath completing the quintet, the band romps through such bop classics as "Hot House," "Nostalgia," "Wail" and "Si Si" along with an original blues and "Embraceable You." A previously unissued "If I Love You" is added to the CD reissue. McPherson and Jones make for a potent frontline on these spirited performances, easily recommended to fans of straightahead jazz. *—Scott Yanow*

Con Alma / Aug. 4, 1964 / Prestige/OJC ✦✦✦✦
Altoist Charles McPherson teams up with distinctive tenor Clifford Jordan, pianist Barry Harris, bassist George Tucker and drummer Alan Dawson for jazz classics by Thelonious Monk, Duke Ellington, Charlie Parker, Dizzy Gillespie (a mysterious version of "Con Alma") and Dexter Gordon in addition to an original McPherson blues, "I Don't Know," which closely recalls "Parker's Mood." McPherson and Harris both have their share of fine solos, but Jordan generally takes honors on this set; he is the only musician who was looking beyond bop and playing in a more original style. *—Scott Yanow*

From This Moment On! / Jan. 31, 1968 / Prestige/OJC ✦✦✦

Live in Tokyo / Apr. 14, 1976 / Xanadu ✦✦✦✦✦

Free Bop! / Oct. 23, 1978 / Xanadu ✦✦✦✦✦
Entertaining hard-bop workout. This is perhaps his fiercest, most exciting playing as a leader. *—Ron Wynn*

First Flight Out / Jan. 25, 1994-Jan. 26, 1994 / Arabesque ✦✦✦✦

● **Come Play with Me** / Mar. 2, 1995 / Arabesque ✦✦✦✦✦
Charles McPherson, who will always be best-known for his roots in Charlie Parker's style and his period with Charles Mingus, proves on this CD to still be in his musical prime decades later. Although he had rarely played with any of the sidemen heard on his Arabesque release before, the quartet presents a unified sound, as if they were a regularly working group. McPherson performs three veteran standards and six originals with most of the latter being closely related to the blues; "Pretty Girl Blues" sounds like a mixture of a couple of Bird lines and "Fun House" is based on "Limehouse Blues" while the best of the new compositions is the hard bop boogaloo "Marionette." But no matter what the vehicle, McPherson is in top form throughout this fine date and he sounds clearly inspired by the presence of pianist Mulgrew Miller, bassist Santi Debriano and drummer Lewis Nash. *—Scott Yanow*

Manhattan Nocturne / Apr. 24, 1997-Apr. 25, 1997 / Arabesque ✦✦✦✦✦
Alto saxophonist/composer McPherson has been playing masterful bop and its extensions for several decades. He shows no signs of slowing down with this extraordinary set of eight compositions, half that he wrote, split into two bop or bop-informed standards, two low-key numbers, two in the mid-rhythmic range, and two modal ostinato-based figures as vehicles for improvising. All are spiced by the bubbling conga playing of Bobby Sanabria and solidly reinforced by the battleship dense musings of pianist Mulgrew Miller, bassist Ray Drummond, and drummer Victor Lewis, an undeniably brilliant backing ensemble. Listen to the fluidity of McPherson's on any of these cuts, and you'll know why he remains the eminent extension of Charlie Parker. McPherson concisely digs into "Blue'n'Boogie," then stands back and lets Miller, Drummond, and Lewis fly at about 200 mph. The Afro-Cuban cooker "Fire Dance" lets Sanabria loose, and the whole band really catches fire. The slower tunes are quite a contrast. The ten-plus-minute ballad "How Deep Is the Ocean—" features a ruminating refrain played in ultra dramatic proportions by the saxophonist. The dusky, sensual, black-hued title track and similarly shadowed "You're My Thrill," with Sanabria's skulking congas and Lewis's jungle rhythms transcending the obvious romantic notions, are outstanding examples of music that doesn't have to be burning to be compelling and sensational in its own way. This CD by McPherson is his best of the '70s, '80s, and '90s, and he's done some very good ones. The combination of seasoned, thinking musicians and excellent material, played to the hilt, is too good a combination for any jazz lover to resist. *—Michael G. Nastos*

Jay McShann (James Columbus McShann)

b. Jan. 12, 1909, Muskogee, OK
Vocals, Piano / Jump Blues, Swing, Piano Blues, Big Band
The great veteran pianist Jay McShann had a long career and it is unfair to primarily think of him as merely the leader of an orchestra that featured a young Charlie Parker. McShann formed his own sextet in 1937 and by 1939 had his own big band. In 1940 at a radio station in Wichita, KS, McShann and an octet out of his orchestra recorded eight songs that were not released commercially until the 1970s; those rank among the earliest of all Charlie Parker records (he is brilliant on "Honeysuckle Rose" and "Lady Be Good") and also feature the strong rhythm-section team McShann had with bassist Gene Ramey and drummer Gus Johnson. The full orchestra recorded for Decca on two occasions during 1941-42 but they were typecast as a blues band and did not get to record many of their more challenging charts. There was a final session in December 1943 without Parker but McShann was soon drafted and the band broke up. After being discharged later in 1944, he briefly reformed his group but soon moved to Los Angeles where he led combos for the next few years; his main attraction was the young singer Jimmy Witherspoon. McShann was in obscurity for the next two decades, but was rediscovered in 1969 and toured constantly, recorded frequently and appeared at many jazz festivals since then. *—Scott Yanow*

★ **Blues from Kansas City** / Apr. 30, 1941-Dec. 1, 1942 / GRP ✦✦✦✦✦
This CD surpasses all former collections of pianist Jay McShann's early recordings, for it is comprised of every commercial side made by McShann during 1941-1943, including 11 delightful, if rarely heard, trio and quartet numbers (featuring McShann, bassist Gene Ramey, and drummer Gus Johnson), along with four lesser-known vocals by the limited but talented Walter Brown that are normally skipped. The result is as complete a musical picture of Jay McShann's early piano style and his orchestra (at least how they sounded in the studios) as is possible. Altoist Charlie Parker has five influential if brief solos (best is "Sepian Bounce") and trumpeters Orville Minor and Buddy Anderson, altoist John Jackson, and Paul Quinichette on tenor also have their spots. However, McShann is clearly the main star of this definitive set by the last of the great Kansas City swing big bands. Highly recommended. *—Scott Yanow*

☆ **The Jazz Heritage: Early Bird Charlie Parker (1941-1943)** / Apr. 30, 1941-Dec. 1, 1943 / Spotlite ✦✦✦✦✦
Until the '92 release of another, better prepared reissue package, this single album reissue was the only domestic Jay McShann release covering his vital early '40s period in print. As such, if you can't find or don't want the more recent release, it's worth having. It was inexpensive and reasonably comprehensive for the times, although it's not as well engineered as the current material. *—Ron Wynn*

Going to Kansas City / Mar. 6, 1972 / New World ✦✦✦✦
This set, originally put out on Master Jazz and the Australian Swaggie label, features pianist Jay McShann at the peak of his powers. Teamed up with a couple of fine swing tenors (Buddy Tate, who doubles on clarinet, and Julian Dash), bassist Gene Ramey and drummer Gus Johnson, McShann romps through some forgotten numbers from the book of his 1940s big band ("Say Forward, I'll March" and "Four Day Rider"), a few Count Basie-associated tunes, and a couple of basic originals, taking two bluesy vocals. The set gives listeners a strong sampling of Jay McShann's accessible and swinging music. *—Scott Yanow*

The Last of the Blue Devils / Jun. 29, 1977-Jul. 1, 1977 / Koch Jazz ✦✦✦✦
When Charlie Parker first came to New York in 1942, he was a sideman in Jay McShann's big band. Every jazz fan knows what happened after that—Parker changed the world and McShann became a footnote in Parker's biography. That's too bad, and not just for him; if the 1978 session remastered and reissued on this disc is anything to go by, McShann had much more to offer the world than his role as caregiver to the inventor of bebop. Leading an all-star cast that includes saxophonist Paul Quinichette, the ubiquitous Milt Hinton on bass, and a young, up-and-coming guitarist named John Scofield, McShann teaches an entire course on the history of blues-based jazz, going from his own "Confessin' the Blues" through "Hootie Blues" (which he co-wrote with Parker and Walter Brown) and an intensely swinging version of Count Basie's "Jumpin' at the Woodside." He goes off on a welcome tangent with Pete Johnson's sweet stride ballad "Just for You" and comes on home with the boogie-woogie composition "'Fore Day Rider" and Leiber and Stoller's "Kansas City." Highly recommended. *—Rick Anderson*

1941-1943 / Nov. 19, 1996 / Classics ✦✦✦✦✦
Twenty-one sides cut by Jay McShann and His Orchestra and the Jay McShann Quartet for Decca Records between 1941 and 1943, with Charlie Parker on about half of what's here, and stretching out on a handful of cuts. The highlight is the group's recording of "Confessin' the Blues," which was a huge hit and resulted in their recording of more than half a dozen similar vocal blues numbers, featuring Walter Brown (who wrote "Confessin'") on vocals. The material here is pretty much weighted to jump blues and boogie-woogie-style numbers, all of it hot and extraordinarily well-played. The pity is, between Decca's insistence on more songs like "Confessin' the Blues" (which was later covered by Chuck Berry and the Rolling

Stones, among others) and the 1942 recordings band, not much of McShann's repertory or Parker's more outstanding material from the period was laid down. What is here, however, is extraordinary, some of the tighted, bluesiest jazz you'll ever here, all in excellent sound as well, and Parker does soar on a large handful of these tracks. *—Bruce Eder*

My Baby with the Black Dress On / Dec. 15, 1991-Dec. 20, 1991 / Chiaroscuro ✦✦✦✦
In the 20th Century, Jay McShann was documented in a variety of settings, everything from the big bands that made him famous in the 1940s to sextets and intimate trios. But the veteran pianist/singer has no band at all on *My Baby With the Black Dress On,* which finds an 82-year-old McShann playing unaccompanied solo piano aboard the S/S Norway (a cruise ship) in different parts of the Caribbean in December 1991. At 82, McShann didn't have the voice he once did, but his hands and fingers were still in great shape. His piano playing is as impressive as ever on inspired performances of "Stardust," "Body and Soul," and other well known standards. Because he doesn't have other musicians to worry about, McShann is all the more spontaneous and improvisatory, in fact, he didn't follow any lists of songs during his S/S Norway engagement of December 1991. If he decided to play "I'll See You in My Dreams" at a given moment, "I'll See You in My Dreams" is what the audience would hear. This CD falls short of essential, but it's a generally rewarding example of late period McShann. *—Alex Henderson*

Medeski, Martin & Wood

f. 1992

Organ (Hammond), Keyboards, Organ / Jam Bands, Post-Bop, Fusion, Soul-Jazz, Jazz-Funk
Organist John Medeski, percussionist Billy Martin, and bassist Chris Wood formed the band that bears their names in New York City in 1992. The members had previously played with such avant-garde jazz groups as the Lounge Lizards, the Mandala Octet, John Zorn's Masada, and Marc Ribot's Shrek. The band's funky version of jazz fusion and deep, improvisatory grooves earned them a stellar reputation on the club circuit as a live act, and their shows are frequently taped and traded by their steadily growing fan base, creating an almost Grateful Dead-like atmosphere. Their 1992 debut, *Notes from the Underground,* featured the band's reinvention of classics by jazzmen like Wayne Shorter and Duke Ellington, and 1994's *Friday Afternoon in the Universe* is the closest they have come to fully capturing the improvisational flair that fires their live performances. After releasing 1996's *Shack-man,* Medeski, Martin & Wood signed with Blue Note, releasing *Combustication* in 1998. A *Combustication Remix EP* was issued in April of 1999; *Tonic* followed a year later, marking both the group's first officially released live album and their first acoustic recording since *Notes from the Underground. Dropper* was released in fall 2000. *—Steve Huey*

Notes from the Underground / Dec. 15, 1991-Jan. 23, 1992 / Accurate Jazz ✦✦✦✦
Before they went electric and funky, John Medeski, Billy Martin and Chris Wood were acoustic and funky—and a lot of other things—on this exciting early CD. They ruminate like a conventional jazz piano trio when the whim hits them, or move outside when Medeski explodes into Don Pullen-esque clusters. Their metier, though, was clearly the neo-funk thing, for when Martin pulls off those crackling hip-hop and M-Base-related beats on tracks like "Uncle Chubbs" and "Orbits," the band really achieves liftoff. "Caravan" gets a rolling New Orleans funk treatment, and the finale "Querencia" is a lengthy excursion into dense avant-garde underbrush with a touch of the street in the beat. On several tracks, a three-brass, two reeds horn section add an extra level of excitement, and the trio tracks are recorded live to DAT (hence the exceptionally crisp sound). *—Richard S. Ginell*

It's a Jungle in Here / Aug. 2, 1993-Aug. 4, 1993 / Gramavision ✦✦✦✦✦

Friday Afternoon in the Universe / Jan. 1994-Jul. 26, 1994 / Gramavision ✦✦✦✦
Here, the MMW direction and loyalties become very clear; they're possessed and driven by the fatback funk and instruments of an earlier generation. John Medeski becomes one of the wave of keyboardists in the '90s who started dragging wonderful old Wurlitzer electric pianos, Hohner clavinets, Hammond organs, wah-wah pedals, and other devices out of mothballs and used them almost as quasi-percussion instruments at times. Chris Wood remains resolutely on standup bass, playing with a great feeling for Billy Martin's supremely funky drumming. Some of the results harken back to Miles Davis' jungle bands of the mid-'70s, picking up on the atonality and crosstalk over the JB's/Sly Stone beat ("We're So Happy"). Others are just happy to groove along on the rhythms of some of the most irresistible group chemistry of the 1990s. *—Richard S. Ginell*

Shack Man / Oct. 15, 1996 / Gramavision ✦✦✦✦
Medeski, Martin & Wood's *Shack Man* is the best example to date of the trio's cerebral fusion of soul-jazz, hip-hop and post-punk worldbeat. Relying on a laidback groove for most the album, the group just rolls along. *Shack Man* is the kind of album that will appeal most to soul-jazz beginners; for aficianados, the lack of grit in the groove makes it rather tedious. *—Leo Stanley*

Combustication / Aug. 11, 1998 / Blue Note ✦✦✦✦
As the only jazz band to be accepted by the neo-hippies of the *HORDE* '90s, Medeski, Martin & Wood pulled off the strange coup of being embraced by rock and jazz audiences, who both loved their endless improvisations. They managed to walk the fine line dividing between the two camps, as their funkified soul-jazz was self-referential and cerebral, not earthy and instinctual. That's part of the reason why some soul-jazz diehards didn't embrace MMW—the ingredients may be there, but it just didn't taste like a real Jimmy Smith record. Perhaps conscious of this, MMW makes no excuses about their heritage on their fifth album, *Combustication.* Perhaps because it is their first effort for a real jazz label (Blue Note), *Combustication* happens to be their most adventurous effort yet. Ironically, it's because the group embraces alt-rock and hip-hop conventions like turntable scratching. That ultimately turns out to be just window-dressing, however—beneath it all, MMW's music remains essentially the same, but the handful of curve balls makes *Combustication* worth close listening for those already on their side. *—Stephen Thomas Erlewine*

• **Last Chance to Dance Trance (perhaps): Best Of (1991-1996)** / Dec. 15, 1991-Jun. 1996 / Gramavision ✦✦✦✦✦
13 songs from the funk-jazz period of Medeski, Martin & Wood's career before their move from Grammavision to the Blue Note label, *Last Chance to Dance Trance* documents the period when the trio was building their fan base both in and out of the jazz world. Irresistibly catchy, this album is pure organ-bubble-jam-pop. John Medeski consistently steals the show with his frantic massaging of the Hammond B-3, while Billy Martin and Chris Wood give the whole thing some backbone. Though their later mixing of jazz and sampling on *Combustication* and other albums would boldly go where no one had gone before, this album may very well represent the best portion of their career. *—Stacia Proefrock*

The Dropper / 1999-2000 / Blue Note ✦✦✦✦
Drifting back closer to the avant-garde territory that they cut their teeth on, Medeski, Martin & Wood explore percolating sonic textures on *The Dropper.* Released by Blue Note in late 2000, the jazz trio's seventh album is a complex blend of Latin jazz, haunting soundscapes, hip-hop grooves, and John Medeski's trademark organ funk. The group is assisted on several tracks by guitarist Marc Ribot and the fourth instrument serves to add another layer to the eclectic mix, at times getting buried beneath the sampled loops and B-3 dirt.

Recorded in the band's Brooklyn studio, Shacklyn, and co-produced by acclaimed hip-hop engineer Scotty Hard (Wu-Tang Clan, P.M. Dawn, Kool Keith), *The Dropper* exudes a street-wise, gritty vibe almost like the Beastie Boys' *Paul's Boutique* without the clever references. In fact, several of the 13 tracks on this album ("Philly Cheese Blunt", "Big Time") could be slipped into *Check Your Head* or the second half of *Ill Communication* and nobody would know. The less immediately funky tracks, like the avant-rhumba "Partido Alto" or the chilling final track "Norah 6" (accompanied by a sighing string section) may not appeal to the baseball capped Ninja Tune aficionados or the groove-seeking neo-deadheads, but fans of their early works in the New York experimental jazz-fusion scene will find several points of interest. While *The Dropper* is less immediately accessible than many of their previous albums, it ends up being more sonically rewarding, continuing to blur the lines between jazz, rock, and funk. *—Zac Johnson*

Brad Mehldau

Piano / Contemporary Jazz, Post-Bop
Brad Mehldau is another of the plethora of young jazz pianists in the '90s who have adopted Bill Evans as their role model. Yet while the influence of Evans still thoroughly dominates Mehldau's introspective manner, harmonic constructions, and preferred format (the piano trio), he is one of the more absorbing and thoughtful practitioners within that idiom, and he is receptive to the idea of using material from the rock era (Paul McCartney's "Blackbird," for example). Though Mehldau's training is primarily classical, his interest in jazz began early. He played in the Hall High School jazz band of Hartford, Conn, winning Berklee College's Best All Around Musician award while still in his junior year at high school. He studied jazz at New York's New School for Social Research under Fred Hersch, Junior Mance, Kenny Werner and Jimmy Cobb. Cobb soon hired him to play in his band Cobb's Mob, and Mehldau also played and recorded with the Joshua Redman Quartet before forming his own trio in 1994 and recording his first Warner Bros. album *Introducing* in 1995. *Art of the Trio, Vol. 1* followed in 1997, with the next two volumes in the series appearing over the following months. Two years later, Mehldau returned with *Elegiac Cycle* as well as *Art of the Trio 4: Back at the Vanguard. Places* followed in 2000. *—Richard S. Ginell*

• **Introducing Bran Mehldau** / Mar. 13, 1995-Apr. 3, 1995 / Warner Brothers ✦✦✦✦
Pianist Brad Mehldau's debut as a leader features his straightahead style in trios with either Larry Grenadier or Christian McBride on bass and Jorge Rossy or Brian Blade on drums. The well-rounded set is highlighted by tasteful and swinging versions of five standards (including John Coltrane's "Countdown," "It Might as Well Be Spring" and "From This Moment On") and four of the pianist's originals. This CD (which is sometimes available at a budget price) serves as a fine start to what should be a productive career. *—Scott Yanow*

Art of the Trio, Vol. 1 / Sep. 4, 1966-May 9, 1966 / Warner Brothers ✦✦✦
At this point in time, pianist Brad Mehldau's style falls between Keith Jarrett and Bill Evans, being heavily influenced by the voicings of the latter and the free yet lyrical improvising of the former. With fine backup work by bassist Larry Grenadier and drummer Jorge Rossy, Mehldau explores five standards (including the Beatles' "Blackbird" and "Nobody Else But Me") and four originals, coming up with melodic yet adventurous ideas. Mehldau displays much potential for the future. *—Scott Yanow*

Art of the Trio, Vol. 2: Live at the Village Vanguard / Jul. 29, 1997-Aug. 3, 1997 / Warner Brothers ✦✦✦✦
It takes a certain nerve for a young jazz artist to call an album *Live at the Village Vanguard.* The title evokes some mighty powerful spirits from the jazz pantheon. John Coltrane, Sonny Rollins. Bill Evans. Joe Henderson. But pianist Brad Mehldau is more than up to this daunting challenge. On this set of standards by the likes of Cole Porter, Thelonious Monk and Henry Mancini, Mehldau exhibits a musical erudition and a technical prowess that belies his youth. Though the obvious comparisons are with Evans and Keith Jarrett, Mehldau has a highly individual style that draws heavily on his classical training. Along with bassist Larry Grenadier and drummer Jorge Rossy, he has made a stunning album of exploratory jazz that holds its own with the great "Live at the Village Vanguard" recordings of the past. *—Joel Roberts*

Art of the Trio, Vol. 3: Songs / May 27, 1998-May 28, 1998 / Warner Brothers ✦✦✦✦✦

Elegiac Cycle / Feb. 1, 1999-Feb. 2, 1999 / Warner Brothers ✦✦✦✦✦
Brad Mehldau's first solo piano album is not only his best record to date, it is one of the most searching, most inventive solo piano albums since Keith Jarrett's best solo concerts of the 1970s, and it throws virtually the whole *Maybeck* series into a cocked hat, too. For one thing, it is a truly unified cycle of mostly improvised reminiscences, starting from a Chopin prelude-like base on "Bard," peaking dynamically with "Trailer Park Ghost," and cycling right back to the "Bard" theme seamlessly, inevitably, at the close. It is also radically different from

so many jazz solo piano records because Mehldau's primary thrust is contrapuntal, with both hands playing independent single lines, not the usual bop runs with harmonies or stacked chords. Perhaps Mehldau's playing doesn't swing here as much as one would like, but it is always intelligent, often endearingly melodic, always technically resourceful ("Memory's Tricks," for example, turns into a two-part invention), and even when he breaks off some startling change, you always sense the shape and direction of each piece. Here, he throws off the shackles of the Bill Evans model once and, hopefully, for all, employing classical models other than impressionists (Bach, Brahms, Chopin, and Schumann come to mind), and in doing so, he makes a big mark on the future of jazz solo piano. And Mehldau is not only an unusually gifted pianist, he is also an intriguing thinker; his long, rambling, wide-ranging essay in the booklet is one of the most interesting artist-penned liner notes in memory. *—Richard S. Ginell*

Art of the Trio, Vol. 4: Back at the Vanguard / Jan. 5, 1999-Jan. 10, 1999 / Warner Brothers ✦✦✦✦✦
Appearing just three months after Brad Mehldau's elegant solo piano album *Elegiac Cycle, Art of the Trio, Vol. 4: Back to the Vanguard* provides a remarkable contrast to the refined, cerebral, hypnotic affair that was released before it. Not that the performances on *Back to the Vanguard* aren't hypnotic, since they're utterly captivating. The difference is that this live recording captures exactly how vital and impassioned Mehldau's playing is. Working with bassist Larry Grenadier and drummer Jorge Rossy, he turns these songs—including three originals, one Miles Davis number, two standards, and Radiohead's "Exit Music"—inside out, finding the heart of the song, and exploring a bewildering array of variations of the themes and chords. This music surges forward, unhinged and forceful, complex but completely accessible. Mehldau spends much of his liner notes on the defensive, explaining how many jazz critics have misread his music. He has a point—he has often been ghettoized as a jazz intellectual, but as this exceptional album proves, there is considerable emotion and feeling and plain excitement behind his music, even during the mesmerizing quiet sections. *—Stephen Thomas Erlewine*

Places / Jan. 24, 2000-Mar. 25, 2000 / Warner Brothers ✦✦✦✦✦
Brad Mehldau is becoming a more interesting, more thought-provoking, more individualistic musician with each release—breaking away from the same old models, finding new ones to integrate into his own personality. The 11 compositions on this CD were conceived on the road, and only midway through did Mehldau realize that they developed similar ideas. Which indeed they do, seizing upon repeated riffing and vamps that Keith Jarrett has explored and sending them in cogent directions. The designated theme is travel; each selection bears the name of a place or mood, and the catchy, contemplative "Los Angeles" serves as the album's bookends, as well as a solo pit stop in the center. Like *Elegiac Cycle, Places* works like a song cycle; a unified, beautifully proportioned conception, with lots of rambunctious, swinging outbreaks amidst the contemplation. The titles in themselves mean nothing as far as the content of the music is concerned—or so he writes in another lengthy, provocative liner note. Rather, the album is about the constancy of his personality and musical language, taking all of your personal mental baggage with you wherever you travel. This is an important album, one that anyone interested in piano jazz ought to check out. *—Richard Ginell*

Myra Melford

b. Jan. 5, 1957, Glencoe, IL
Piano, Composer / Avant-Garde Jazz, Post-Bop, Modern Creative
An ambitious composer/pianist with a taste for adventure, Melford emerged in the late '80s and early '90s as one of the more highly-acclaimed young jazz pianists of the day. Melford's early work reflected her primary musical mentors/influences: on piano, Don Pullen, whose percussive mannerisms she successively adapted; and, as a composer, Henry Threadgill, whose formal techniques she obviously studied. Melford professes an affinity to the blues styles she heard and studied as a youth in Chicago (she grew up in nearby Evanston, IL), which she incorporates into her avant-garde tinged musical sensibility. As a youth she studied boogie-woogie piano with Erwin Helfer. Melford attended college at Evergreen State in Washington State, where she studied with the pianist Art Lande and developed an interest in jazz. She went on to also attend the Cornish Institute in Seattle. In 1984 she moved to New York, where she would play in the bands of Threadgill, Leroy Jenkins, and Butch Morris, among others. She also studied privately with Pullen. In the mid-to-late '80s she performed and recorded in a duo with the flutist Marion Brandis. She formed a trio with bassist Lindsay Horner and drummer Reggie Nicholson, with which she recorded a pair of now-deleted albums—*Jump* (1990) and *Now and Now* (1991)—for the rock-oriented Enemy label, which helped establish her reputation. As the '90s progressed, Melford added horns to her sound; the trumpeter Dave Douglas is a member of her Same River, Twice band, which has recorded albums for the Gramavision and Arabesque labels. She has continued to perform with bands led by Jenkins and Threadgill; she is also a member of one of Douglas' many ensembles. In 2000 Melford received a Fulbright Scholarship to study North Indian music on the harmonium with Sohanlal Sharma in Calcutta. *—Chris Kelsey*

Eleven Ghosts / Feb. 11, 1994-Feb. 12, 1994 / hatOLOGY ✦✦✦✦
Supreme musicians Myra Melford and Han Bennink join together for a duo recording as blues progressions, boogie woogie, and Harlem stride become the trampoline from which they jump. It's free, free, but far less cryptic—and more accessible—than one might expect. Melford is a very accomplished pianist: straight and outside, serious and silly—she's done it, and done it well. Bennink has a wide repertoire of percussive creativity. He's a light-hearted master who can recreate the sounds of a kitchen's ride through an earthquake. Rising uniquely to any level of playing—abstract, straight, or wack—he can play like three drummers at once. These two musicians play musical strands that run parallel, complementing each other nicely. The piano softly twinkles up and down the scales; gossamer strings connect Melford's hands to old barrelhouse tunes. Meanwhile, the drums unravel any hope of 4/4 time and get happily tangled up in the string. Melford bangs cluster punches while Bennink scrambles up one side of a song, only to roll down the other side, arms flapping. Playful, they twirl around each other. Masterful, they create an off-the-wall pair who surprise and delight. The longest piece, "Which Way Is That?," twists its own focus lens, alternately smearing the tune's structure until it's all blurred together and putting it back into focus until it's explicitly restated. "Some Relief" is a brief intermission, a straight little ditty as respite. "And Now Some Blues" sometimes allows the piano blues to roll, but often deconstructs it, and their take on "The Maple Leaf Rag" is quite excellent and an appropriate closer for this album. Although grouped in the more avant-garde end of jazz, *Eleven Ghosts* won't scare the audience off. Even people who stiffen at the words "outside jazz" will relax their shoulders while listening to this album. *—Joslyn Layne*

Even the Sounds Shine / May 5, 1994-May 6, 1994 / hatART ✦✦✦✦✦

The Same River, Twice / Jan. 25, 1996-Jan. 26, 1996 / Gramavision ✦✦✦✦✦
Myra Melford's studies with avant-bop pianist Don Pullen and idiosyncratic jazz composer Henry Threadgill are reflected in the seamless combination of structure and free improvisation in both her writing and piano playing. Her only release on the Gramavision label, *The Same River, Twice* nicely exemplifies the mix with a selection of sprawling, exploratory numbers and shorter, more straightforward pieces. On relatively accessible cuts like "Bound Unbound" and "Changes I & II," Melford incorporates hints of boogie-woogie and soul into dense hard bop heads, providing plenty of room for a series of clever solo statements and boisterous unison stretches by members of her ensemble. Longer pieces like "Crush" and "The Large Ends the Way" are harder to penetrate, but repeated exposure reveals an ingenuous blend of frenetic, open-ended sections and slower, ethereal passages. The stellar backing is provided by trumpeter Dave Douglas, cellist Erik Friedlander, drummer Michael Sarin, and reed player Chris Speed. Melford's own impressive work at the piano finds her spanning the tumultuously free playing of Cecil Taylor and more blues-tinged, hard-bop keyboard terrain. A fine release by one of the brightest composers and players to appear on the jazz scene in the '90s. *—Stephen Cook*

● **Above Blue** / Mar. 31, 1998-Apr. 1, 1998 / Arabesque ✦✦✦✦✦
Melford, an original voice on piano if there ever was one, keeps on stretching. With her potent quintet The Same River, Twice, she is the fuse for explosions of deep group interaction, offering visceral harmonic statements while injecting her busy, dancing, at times pensive and occasionally cluster-laden outspoken style to the forefront, its territory mapped by very few. Featuring the sonorific combination of trumpet-sax/clarinet-cello via Dave Douglas, Chris Speed and Erik Friedlander, Melford molds her intricate modern music from highly concentrated elements, colored by an ingeniously rich palette. Melodies fly, splatter and land with thuds and whistles. Douglas is especially responsive, Speed works out and Friedlander fills in the cracks. Classical dynamics, jazz phrasing, sometimes swinging, themes occult and ethnic or funky and deep, guide the participants through these eight pieces. Drummer Michael Sarin impresses not only for his ability to play tastefully, but in keeping the band glued solidly together. Titles are typically Melford, cut-and-pasted with lower case "i"'s; the lingering, doleful "Here Is Only Moment," the more moody "Still in After's Shadow," the popping, danceable "Yet Can Spring" (for Don Pullen) and a northerner's fave, the blast furnace hot "Be Melting Snow." The shimmering but urgent, Balkan-like title track, as compelling as new music can be, might be a personal best for this gifted lady. It's easy to find the joy and brilliance in the music of Melford, not to mention the clarity. As she further asserts her muse in a quest to continually be unique and different, we all benefit, learning and growing as she does. This kind of music is indeed high art, rare, but unquestionably within reach. *—Michael G. Nastos*

Dance Beyond the Color / May 12, 1999-May 13, 1999 / Arabesque ✦✦✦

Yet Can Spring / Feb. 6, 2001 / Arabesque ✦✦✦

Gil Melle

b. Dec. 31, 1931, Jersey City, NJ
Sax (Baritone), Composer / Avant-Garde Jazz, Computer Music, Film Music, Hard Bop, Cool, Bop
A true renaissance man, Gil Melle began his career as a post-bop baritone saxophonist, later branching out into a wide variety of artistic and scientific fields. He abandoned jazz fairly early on, choosing to compose film and television scores and experiment with electronic music. Then again, Melle's music wasn't strictly jazz—it was a hybrid of jazz (drawn from Duke Ellington in particular) and classical music he called "primitive modern," which was displayed on a series of albums for Blue Note and Prestige in the late '50s. Born in New York City, Melle signed to Blue Note at the age of 19, becoming the first Caucasian on the label's roster. At Blue Note, he released five 10-inch records before recording his first full-length, 12-inch LP, *Patterns in Jazz*, in 1956. He left Blue Note shortly after; between 1956 and 1957, he recorded three albums for Prestige—*Primitive Modern, Gil's Guests*, and *Quadrama*—before deciding to halt his career as a traditional jazz bandleader. Melle moved to Los Angeles in the '60s, where he began to compose scores for film and television. He also began working with electronic music, building his own synthesizers—including (arguably) the first drum machine—and performing with the first all-electronic jazz band, the Electronauts. In 1967, he returned to recording with *Tome VI*, an all-electronic jazz album released on Verve. He wrote scores for *Night Gallery* and *The Andromeda Strain* entirely with synthesizers, which was unheard of at the time. Melle kept amazingly busy, composing scores, building specialized computers and synthesizers, painting, piloting, restoring automobiles and planes, and keeping an antiquarian microscopical instrumentation collection. As of the mid-'90s, Melle decided to concentrate on the visual arts, in particular his acclaimed computer-based digital painting. *—Stephen Thomas Erlewine*

Patterns in Jazz / Apr. 1, 1956 / Blue Note ✦✦✦✦✦
Like the modern art that stormed the art world in the '50s, *Patterns in Jazz*, Gil Melle's debut album for Blue Note, is filled with bright, bold colors and identifiable patterns that camouflage how adventurous the work actually is. On the surface, the music is cool and laid-back, but close listening reveals the invention in Melle's compositions and arrangements of the standards "Moonlight in Vermont" and "Long Ago and Far Away." Part of the charm of *Pat-*

terns in Jazz is the unusual instrumental balance of Melle's bari sax, Eddie Bert's trombone, Joe Cinderella's guitar, and Oscar Pettiford's bass. These low, throaty instruments sound surprisingly light and swinging. Compared to the two standards, Melle's original compositions are a little short on melody, but they give the musicians room to improvise, resulting in some dynamic music. Ultimately, *Patterns in Jazz* is cerebral music that swings—it's entertaining, but stimulating. *—Stephen Thomas Erlewine*

Primitive Modern/Quadrama / Apr. 1, 1956-Apr. 26, 1957 / Prestige/OJC ✦✦✦
2-fer. Here is an odd mix of jazz arrangements and pseudo-classical third-stream compositions, with the presence of musicians like Shadow Wilson, not usually found in such settings. It is ultimately a mixed message, for Melle fans only. *—Ron Wynn*

Gil's Guests / Aug. 10, 1956-Jan. 18, 1957 / Prestige/OJC ✦✦✦
Baritonist Gil Melle's recordings are usually a bit unusual and this CD reissue is no exception. Melle's nine compositions are performed by one of three sextet/septets featuring either Art Farmer, Kenny Dorham or Donald Byrd on trumpets, Hal McKusick or Phil Woods on alto, guitarist Joe Cinderella, bassist Vinnie Burke, drummer Ed Thigpen and sometimes either Julius Watkins on French horn or Don Butterfield on tuba. The charts are unpredictable and often dramatic, looking ahead toward a musical future that never occurred. Watkins takes solo honors during his three appearances. *—Scott Yanow*

● **Complete Blue Note 50s Sessions** / Mar. 2, 1952-Apr. 1, 1956 / Blue Note ✦✦✦✦✦
Blue Note raids the back of its vaults for all four of Mellé's long-out-of-print 10-inch LPs, plus the 12-inch *Patterns In Jazz,* in order to place back in circulation a musician who had been nearly invisible to the jazz world for a good three decades. Though Mellé's entertaining self-penned liner notes may be outrageously self-aggrandizing, this collection leaves little doubt that he was (and remains) a marvelous saxophonist and an intriguing composer who hasn't been given his due. On the early sides, Mellé plays an erudite, relaxed, always musical tenor sax, and "Transition" marks his recorded debut on baritone, which he uses in a thoughtful, even quizzical manner for the remainder of the set. As a composer, Mellé was very much the uncompromising cool bopper, but also equipped with a fascinating mind of his own. His first session is also the most startling: "Four Moons" is brilliant in its Kentonian harmonic way, with vibraphone striking the chords; so is his most famous jazz composition "The Gears," with its Monica Dell scat vocal lead doubled by vibraphone. Further on in the set, Mellé does away with the piano in the cool tradition, but gives the lineup an unorthodox twist by using a guitarist (Tal Farlow, Lou Mecca or Joe Cinderella) in the keyboard role, and a trombonist (Eddie Bert or the swinging, vastly underrated Urbie Green) or even a tuba (Don Butterfield) on the front line. He also employs consistently first-class rhythm sections, with Max Roach and a young Joe Morello among the drummers. For those super-collectors who may have the extremely rare originals (now worth hundreds of dollars each), there is one unreleased track, "The Nearness of You"; the digitally remastered sound, flaws in the master tapes aside, is excellent. *—Richard S. Ginell*

Misha Mengelberg

b. Jun. 5, 1935, Kiev, Ukraine
Piano, Composer, Arranger / Avant-Garde Jazz, Post-Bop, Avant-Garde
Pianist Misha Mengelberg leads the Dutch ensemble ICP Orchestra, and is known for his role in the development of creative music in 1960s Netherlands. Usually in groups with explosive drummer Han Bennink, Mengelberg has mixed composition and improvisation for decades, and during his long and full career, became one of the most distinctive pianists in avant-garde jazz.

He was born in Kiev, 1935, son of pianist/conductor, Karel Mengelberg and immigrated to Amsterdam during childhood. Mengelberg was entrenched in playing chess and the piano by his teens, and listening to his biggest jazz influences, namely Thelonious Monk. His compositions while studying classical music at the Royal Conservatory in the Hague were heavily conceptual, and hearing John Cage intensified his experimental leanings. Mengelberg won jazz competitions, and by the early '60s, led a quartet including drummer Han Bennink which became a trio that backed Johnny Griffin in 1963, and Eric Dolphy for a few gigs in 1964—including the concert released as *Last Date.* Mengelberg played the 1966 Newport Jazz Festival, and in the Dutch group that played with Cecil Taylor in 1967. Mengelberg won the Wessel Ilcken Prize, then he and Bennink met saxophonist Willem Breuker.

Out of these three arose the ICP (Instant Composers Pool) label and numerous projects, but a rift in the '70s sent Breuker in another direction, and led Mengelberg to form the ICP Orchestra. Mengelberg helped instigate arts funding reform to include improvisation, resulting in the BIMHuis venue and STEIM (Studio for Electro-Instrumental Music, begun with Louis Andriessen), serving as president of BIM and director of STEIM. He also performed with Wim T. Schippers from 1974-82. Mengelberg's ICP Orchestra had a shifting lineup before stabilizing in the '80s, including Bennink, Wolter Wierbos, Michael Moore, Ab Baars and more. Due to the group's size, Mengelberg's "instant composing" tenet shifted to "conducted improvisation," and ICP performed and recorded for the next few decades. Mengelberg has collaborated with many of the best in European and American avant-garde jazz, including Evan Parker, Peter Brötzmann and Ken Vandermark. He has recorded for labels including Hat, DIW, and Soul Note. *—Joslyn Layne*

★ **Change of Season: The Music of Herbie Nichols** / Jul. 2, 1984-Jul. 3, 1984 / Soul Note ✦✦✦✦✦
After recording an album (*Regeneration*) split between Herbie Nichols and Thelonious Monk compositions, pianist Misha Mengelberg decided to devote a full project to the unjustly neglected Nichols. As with the earlier set, this date also includes soprano saxophonist Steve Lacy and drummer Han Bennink, but this time with trombonist George Lewis and bassist Arjen Gorter. For the first time, seven of Nichols' songs (including "House Party Starting," "Hangover Triangle" and "Change of Season") were performed by a medium-size group, rather than just Nichols' trio, and one can appreciate the formerly unheard colors in the pianist's nearly lost music. It is also a particular pleasure hearing Lewis and Lacy improvising on these challenging, yet fairly straight-ahead pieces. A gem. *—Scott Yanow*

Dutch Masters / Mar. 25, 1987 / Soul Note ✦✦✦✦✦

● **Who's Bridge** / 19941-199 / Avant ✦✦✦✦✦
Dutch pianist Mengelberg is in full reverie with this trio. He is teamed with Americans Brad Jones (bass) and Joey Baron (drums), who pretty much act as Mengelberg's supporting cast, never getting too rhythmically flashy. The pianist's sound is a witty combination of modern harmonic invention and melodic improvisational forays into Cecil Taylor territory. Many tuneful compositions crop up during the 11 tracks, all Mengelberg originals. The title cut sounds like a newborn standard, a nice swinger that leads to a bridge with frantic Taylor-like flourishes. Mengelberg's main influence, Herbie Nichols, comes shining through during another nice swinger, "Gare Guillemans," which features soulful touches and advanced harmonic nuances. The opening track, "Rollo II," starts off raucously before merging into a quaint swing reminiscent of "Tea for Two." "Rollo III" is bluesier and more Nichols-like. "A Bit Nervous" has a skittish calypso beat accented by Sunny Murray-ish piano. The lone solo piano number, "Peer's Counting Song," evokes the elegance of Ellington, the angularity of Monk, and the dark, rambling harmonics of Mal Waldron. Most fun is "Elevator," with Jones' twittering bass, Baron's tom-tom beat, and Mengelberg's dynamic piano. Each composition is a great example of the pianist's enormous musicianship. This is Mengelberg's finest hour. *—Michael G. Nastos*

Instant Discoveries, Nr. 5, The Field Recordings: Live In Holland '97 / Mar. 1, 1997-Mar. 2, 1997 / X-OR ✦✦✦✦✦
Hearing pianist Misha Mengelberg with this free-improvisational trio is an eye-opener. This recording documents portions of two concerts with saxophone whiz Mats Gustafsson, and percussion phenom Gert-Jan Prins. There are two long tracks that let the musicians stretch, and one deconstruction of Jerome Kern's "I've Told Every Little Star." Mengelberg is, as usual, a delight, as he carefully chooses his notes much the way a child might select his Brussels sprouts: slowly and deliberately, even reluctantly. In contrast, Gustafsson alternates between little sounds and gusts of energy. Throw into the mix the raucous braying of Prins' percussion and his wild electronics, and the stew boils to near perfection. Unfortunately, the sound is less than perfect, detracting considerably, particularly on the first number, which takes up more than half the space. Still, the singular joy of hearing these three together is a rare treat. *—Steve Loewy*

No Idea / Jun. 27, 1996 / DIW ✦✦✦

● **Two Days in Chicago** / Oct. 11, 1998-Oct. 12, 1998 / hatHUT ✦✦✦✦✦
If Thelonious Monk had been born 20 years later, in Europe, he may indeed have been-Misha Mengelberg. No other player/composer/improviser with the exception of Steve Lacy has been able to so completely enter into the harmonic mindset of Monk (and for that matter, the technical genius of his counterpart Herbie Nichols). And as much as that would be enough for so many on the scene today, it is a compliment the iconoclastic Mr. Mengelberg would shun because it is only a part of what he does.

This glorious double CD represents literally the two days Mengelberg spent in Chicago in 1998. One CD is a studio session, the other a live date. Mengelberg wasted no time in exploiting the many talents of his collaborators that include: saxophonists Fred Anderson, Ken Vandermark and Ab Baars, cellist Fred Lonberg-Holm, bassists Kent Kessler and Wilbert de Joode and drummers Hamid Drake and Martin van Duyunhoven.

CD one is a wildly mixed bag. First there is the Megleberg reading of Monk's "Eronel." With Vandermark and Drake as his sidemen, without a bassist, Mengelberg has already changed the model. With the hollow spot in rhythm section apparent, he just lets it stand, an element that needs not be filled because of Vandermark's fine, swinging, soulful solo. Megelberg himself is dancing around with Drake, trading fours and comping just persuasively enough to give Vandermark the nod for another chorus or two. When he takes-his own solo you can see why trhere isn't a bassist: there's no room with Drake claiming all the space around the piano, and Mengelberg alternating lines from Nichols, Tatum and Monk while slipping his own extended 12ths!!!! Into an melodic interval framework that is just breathtaking. The same is true of the other Monk contribution here: "Off Minor." Here, It's all Mengelberg and his spooky, shaded, diminished 7ths that hold the tune while Vandermark blows under the authority of his piano.

The various quartets and trios that make up the remainder of disc one are truly beautiful examples of what Mengelberg does as an improviser: he sheds all preconceived notion of what music is supposed to be when made on the spot and spontaneously composes with his groups. There are shards of meaning in each phrase as these groups eke out a syntax and structural conception for each piece.

Disc Two, the live set is perhaps, even more remarkable. It begins with the nearly 30-minute "Chicago Solo." Mengelberg gives his audience a full on look into his method, madness and mind as a musician. He creates no less than 10 themes and their variations and moves them through strange configurations of Puccini and Beethoven before Tristano and Teddy Wilson appear as ghosts to carry them off. This flows seamlessly into a gorgeous reading of "'Round Midnight," and flows seamlessly into a duo, another solo and finally a nearly seven minute version of "Body and Soul with a sextet that is notable not only for the sensitivity of Mengelberg's adaption, but the empathy he coaxes from his musicians, andt the depth of emotion conveyed—even as Baars arm wrestles with his saxophone and his own stormy relationship to such a beautiful standard.

This is easily one of Mengelberg's finest recorded moments and shows him in all of his roles shining with rough-hewn elegance and finely crafted edges. *—Thom Jurek*

Solo / 2000 / Buzz ✦✦✦✦
Listening to Misha Mengelberg play solo piano is like eavesdropping on a highly subversive mind at work. Everything is laid bare. Unlike Keith Jarrett, who endeavors to find a flow in solo-improvising, Mengelberg sets up expectations, then delights in sabotaging them. What starts out as a jaunty folk song of the sort one finds in a child's piano method book, "Koekoek" suddenly sprouts "wrong" notes, then collapses into crunching thumps. "Bill Evans in Dán begins, appropriately, with an oceanic pull but devolves into scary fits of isolation. Difficult, knotty, contradictory, and disjunctive, Mengelberg is suspicious of any sort

of music making that creates or sustains illusions. Like an abstract painter, he wants you to see that a line is a line, not a figure or a face. Yet there is a passion—and playfulness—running beneath this often atonal and dissonant astringency that, if given the chance, inexorably draws the careful listener in. Technically, Mengelberg's blunt attack and clanging tone, as well as his teetering rhythmic hesistations, are inspired by Thelonious Monk. Yet he also has developed a lightly skittering, oblique keyboard approach all his own, one that suggests subconscious trains of thought rising to the surface or knocking on the side doors. *Solo* is one of Mengelberg's finest albums, and a grand introduction to one of the cleverest minds in jazz. *—Paul de Barros*

Pat Metheny (Patrick Bruce Metheny)

b. Aug. 12, 1954, Lee's Summit, MO

Guitar, Composer / Folk-Jazz, Contemporary Jazz, Post-Bop, Fusion

One of the most original guitarists of the past 20 years (he is instantly recognizable), Pat Metheny is a chancetaking player who has gained great popularity but also taken some wild left turns. His records with the Pat Metheny Group are difficult to describe (folk-jazz— mood music—) but managed to be both accessible and original, stretching the boundaries of jazz and making Metheny famous enough so he could perform whatever type of music he wants without losing his audience. While he was a teenager Metheny made his recording debut with Paul Bley and Jaco Pastorius in 1974. He spent an important period (1974-77) with Gary Burton's group, met keyboardist Lyle Mays and in 1978 formed his Group which originally featured Mays, bassist Mark Egan and drummer Dan Gottlieb. Within a short period he was ECM's top artist and one of the most popular of all jazzmen, selling out stadiums. *—Scott Yanow*

Bright Size Life / Dec. 1975 / ECM ✦✦✦✦✦

Pat Metheny's debut studio album is a good one, a trio date that finds him already laying down the distinctively cottony, slightly withdrawn tone and asymmetrical phrasing that would serve him well through most of the swerves in direction ahead. His original material, all of it lovely, bears the bracing air of his Midwestern upbringing, with titles like "Missouri Uncompromised," "Midwestern Nights Dream" and "Omaha Celebration." There is also a sole harbinger of radical matters way down the road with the inclusion of a loose-jointed treatment of Ornette Coleman's "Round Trip/Broadway Blues," proving that *Song X* did not come from totally out of the blue. Besides the debut of Metheny, this CD also features one of the earliest recordings of Jaco Pastorius, a fully formed, well-matched contrapuntal force on electric bass, though content to leave the spotlight mostly to Metheny. Bob Moses, who like Metheny played in the Gary Burton quintet at the time, is the drummer, and he can mix it up, too. *—Richard S. Ginell*

Watercolors / Feb. 1977 / ECM ✦✦✦✦

Pat Metheny emerges on his second album as an ECM impressionist, generally conforming to the label's overall sound while still asserting his own personality. As the title suggests, there are several mood pieces here that are suspended in the air without rhythmic underpinning, a harbinger for the new age invasion still in the future. Metheny's softly focused, asymmetrical guitar style, with echoes of apparent influences as disparate as Jim Hall, George Benson, Jerry Garcia, and various country guitarists, is quite distinctive even at this early juncture. Metheny's long-running partnership with keyboardist Lyle Mays also begins here, with Mays mostly on acoustic piano but also providing a few mild synthesizer washes. Danny Gottlieb is on drums and ECM regular Eberhard Weber handles the bass. This is essentially the first album by the Pat Metheny Group per se, although the band had yet to find its direction in this somewhat diffuse showing. *—Richard S. Ginell*

★ **Pat Metheny Group** / Jan. 1978 / ECM ✦✦✦✦✦

The first recording by Pat Metheny's "Group" features the innovative guitarist along with keyboardist Lyle Mays, bassist Mark Egan and drummer Dan Gottlieb. The music is quite distinctive, floating rather than swinging, electric but not rockish and full of folkish melodies. The best known of these six Metheny-Mays originals are "Phase Dance" and "Jaco." This music grows in interest with each listen. *—Scott Yanow*

New Chautauqua / Aug. 1978 / ECM ✦✦✦

Always exploring side routes even at this early stage, Metheny goes it all alone here, overdubbing himself on electric six- and 12-string guitars, acoustic guitar, electric bass, and 15-string harp guitar. Yet this record is basically an indulgence, one where Metheny spins his wheels within the context of the impressionistic ECM ambience, creating pretty sounds but only fleeting streaks of memorable music. The album gets off to a great start on the title track, where Metheny's folk influences come to the fore with a strummed acoustic guitar base and electric guitar overhead. But the lengthy "Long-Ago Child/Fallen Star" drifts aimlessly in a dreamy fashion that only a new age navelgazer could love, and he doesn't grab the listener by the lapels again until the lovely vamp of "Sueno Con Mexico" way down the line. Chalk it up to growing pains. *—Richard S. Ginell*

American Garage / Jun. 1979 / ECM ✦✦✦✦✦

The back liner photo gives the impression of a grungy Midwestern garage band, but no, that doesn't describe this sophisticated jazz-rock quartet, which was simultaneously breaking into mass-market acceptance and away from the contemplative ECM stereotype. The arrangements are more structured, the playing often more intense and searching, with a more pronounced rock influence. On the title track, Metheny digs in and displays some authoritative rock-oriented licks and intensity, and the rhythms on "The Search" have a slight, at times asymmetrical Latin feeling. The nearly 13-minute "The Epic" finds the Metheny group developing some real combustion in the improvised sections as Metheny, keyboardist Lyle Mays, bassist Mark Egan and drummer Danny Gottlieb grow tighter as a unit. In hindsight, some of the music seems a bit too tightly conceived to allow adequate breathing room, but this is still high-quality jazz-rock for its time. *—Richard S. Ginell*

80/81 / May 26, 1980-May 29, 1980 / ECM ✦✦✦✦✦

Pat Metheny's credibility with the jazz community went way up with the release of this package, a superb two-CD collaboration with a quartet of outstanding jazz musicians that dared to be uncompromising at a time when most artists would have merely continued pursuing their electric commercial successes. From the disbanded Keith Jarrett American quartet came bassist Charlie Haden and tenor Dewey Redman—who alternates with and occasionally plays alongside tenor Michael Brecker—and Jack DeJohnette provides more combustible drumming than Metheny had ever experienced on record before. Yet Metheny's off-kilter wandering on solo electric guitar is a comfortable fit for the post-bop rhythmic crosscurrents of this music. Indeed, Haden and Metheny are in total sympathy, perhaps celebrating their mutual Missouri roots, and Metheny's difficult "Pretty Scattered"—which he mockingly described as "Guitar Revenge!"—nearly manages to stump even Redman and Brecker. The first of the "Two Folk Songs" is a great example of the Metheny folk-jazz fusion, with furious strummed guitar underpinning Brecker's melodic line and excursions on the outside and DeJohnette's spectacular drums. Another remarkable track is "Open," a group improvisation that finds DeJohnette shaping the track's direction with a pushing solo and Metheny and the saxes emerging at the end. The two original LPs were organized so that the more distinctive Metheny fusions were on sides one and four and the overt jazz tracks occupied sides two and three. *—Richard S. Ginell*

Offramp / Oct. 1981 / ECM ✦✦✦✦✦

If 1980's *As Wichita Falls, So Falls Wichita Falls* was defined by Pat Metheny's charisma, its less accessible but certainly rewarding successor, *Offramp,* finds him leaning more toward the abstract. But as cerebral as Metheny gets on such atmospheric pieces as "Are You Going with Me" and "Au Lait," his playing remains decidedly lyrical and melodic. Clearly influenced by Jim Hall, the thoughtful Metheny makes excellent use of space—choosing his notes wisely and reminding us that while he has heavy-duty chops, he's not one to beat us over the head with them. Even when he picks up the tempo for the difficult and angular title song, he shuns empty musical aerobics. Throughout the CD, Metheny enjoys a powerful rapport with keyboardist Lyle Mays, who also avoids exploiting his technique and opts for meaningful storytelling. *—Alex Henderson*

Rejoicing / Nov. 29, 1983-Nov. 30, 1983 / ECM ✦✦✦✦✦

Pat Metheny takes a vacation from his "Group" and performs advanced material with bassist Charlie Haden and drummer Billy Higgins. In addition to Horace Silver's "Lonely Woman," Haden's "Blues for Pat" and three Ornette Coleman tunes, the guitarist plays three of his originals including "The Calling," a lengthy exploration of sounds with his guitar synthesizer. Throughout this excellent set, Metheny and his sidemen engage in close communication and create memorable and unpredictable music. *—Scott Yanow*

Song X / Dec. 1985 / Geffen ✦✦✦✦✦

W/ Ornette Coleman. Metheny pays tribute to a surprising influence, teaming with Ornette Coleman in a collaboration that shocked everyone with its musical effectiveness. *—Ron Wynn*

Still Life (Talking) / 1987 / Geffen ✦✦✦✦✦

While Brazilian music had captured Metheny's attention since the '70s, he placed an especially strong emphasis on Brazilian elements in the late '80s. A master of uniting seemingly disparate elements as a cohesive whole, the imaginative guitarist effectively combines Brazilian-influenced harmonies and rhythm with jazz, folk and pop elements on "So May It Secretly Begin," "Third Wind," "Minuano (Six Eight)" and other celebrated gems included on the CD *Still Life (Talking).* The Brazilian leanings are put aside on one of Metheny's most unique offerings ever, "Last Train Home," which boasts a charming Western theme that brings to mind a peaceful journey across the Arizona Desert. That may not sound like the description of a jazz piece, but then, making the unlikely a reality is among Metheny's many admirable qualities. *—Alex Henderson*

Letter from Home / 1989 / Geffen ✦✦✦✦✦

Picking up where *Still Life (Talking)* leaves off (instead of throwing us a curve ball like *Song X*), the equally triumphant *Letter from Home* stresses Brazilian elements with superb results. While a number of these treasures—including "Beat 70," "Have You Heard" and "Every Summer Night"—are light and accessible enough to have enjoyed exposure on some "smooth jazz" stations, *Letter* contains the type of depth and honesty that's sorely lacking in most "smooth jazz." Metheny has always known the difference between light and lightweight, and even at his most delicate, he avoids entering "muzak" territory. True to form, the improvisor doesn't shy away from making extensive use of technology, but is insightful enough to do so in a very warm and soulful fashion. Like *Still Life, Letter from Home* is a fine example of a CD that is both a commercial and an artistic success. *—Alex Henderson*

Question and Answer / Dec. 21, 1989 / Geffen ✦✦✦✦✦

Here we have three absolutely breathtaking jazz performers locked into a studio for a day or so. From this combination of guitar, standup bass, and acoustic drum kit, we've got nine tracks of sheer jazz joy—three guys just blowing for the hell of it, recorded on the fly. There's a strong sense here that engineer Rob Eaton probably tried to get everybody properly set up and balanced before the session started and just gave up when everybody started playing. It's a delight to hear, because everything has gone into the performance, which is spontaneous and graceful—no going back for the next take here. Metheny's playing is definitely modernistic, highly fluid, almost liquid lightning—no effects boxes here, though (he does play Synclavier on the last track, "Three Flights Up," but it's great anyway). Roy Haynes, likewise, should be heard by anybody wanting to get behind the traps: this man has a sense of humor, and he's a blur of motion. Dave Holland, on bass, is no slouch either, keeping pace with Metheny's guitar lines, and balancing up against Hayne's drums. Together, these guys are incredible. They get into both original material and standards (including an ecstatic version of Miles Davis' "Solar" that opens the album) with the same energy and feel for what they're doing. This is an album with serious crossover potential, and it should definitely be heard by anyone serious about music in any way. *—Steven McDonald*

I Can See Your House from Here / Dec. 1993 / Blue Note ✦✦✦✦

Guitar giants John Scofield and Pat Metheny teamed up for the first time on records for this CD. The collaboration does take awhile to get going and it is not until the fourth cut, the bluish "Everybody's Party," that the sparks begin to fly; fortunately the momentum does not let up much throughout the remainder of the CD. All of the selections (including two blues) are originals by either of the guitarists and, with the accompaniment of bassist Steve Swallow and drummer Bill Stewart, this varied set generally lives up to expectations. *—Scott Yanow*

Road to You-Live in Europe / 1993 / Geffen ✦✦✦✦✦
When Metheny celebrates his cerebral side, he usually follows up with something more accessible. After his difficult yet rewarding collaboration with John Scofield, *I Can See Your House from Here*, Metheny stresses accessibility with this captivating live album. The primary focus is on his Brazilian-influenced material from *Still Life (Talking)* and *Letter from Home*, and the very cohesive Metheny Group offers characteristically expressive versions of such favorites as "Have You Heard," "Beat 70" and "Better Days Ahead." While he could have offered a wider variety of material and perhaps revisited some of his early gems, everything he does include comes across as honest and heartfelt. Thankfully, Metheny's emphasis on accessibility and crowd-pleasing doesn't come at the expense of his artistic integrity. *—Alex Henderson*

We Live Here / 1994 / Geffen ✦✦✦✦✦
The first Pat Metheny Group recording in five years is a bit unusual in two ways. The band uses "contemporary" pop rhythms on many of their selections but in creative ways and without watering down the popular group's musical identity. In addition Metheny for the first time in his recording career sounds a bit like his early influence Wes Montgomery on a few of the songs. With his longtime sidemen (keyboardist Lyle Mays, bassist Steve Rodby and drummer Paul Wertico) all in top form, Metheny successfully reconciles his quartet's sound with that of the pop music world, using modern technology to expand the possibilities of his own unusual vision of creative improvised music. And as a bonus, some of the melodies are catchy. *—Scott Yanow*

Imaginary Day / 1997 / Warner Brothers ✦✦✦✦
More than ever, the Pat Metheny Group is into creating thick, exotic, electronic sonic landscapes, and *Imaginary Day* goes even further out on the cutting edges of technology and global influences than its predecessors. The floating Metheny group signature is often present, but with radically reworked textures, and Brazil seems to be off his international itinerary, replaced by whiffs of repetitive Iranian folk music, Balinese gamelan music and other global influences. Indeed, Metheny only sounds something like his familiar soft-focused self on "A Story Within the Story," tplaying what amounts to a fine hard bop solo, and the song-like "Across the Sky." At all other times, he expands his sonic palette on various guitar synthesizers and newly minted guitar mutations, at one point assigning an entire solo piece, "Into the Dream," to the 42-string "pikasso guitar," which sounds like a glittering African zither. "The Roots of Coincidence" is a total departure for the group, a gleefully hard-edged, out-and-out rock piece with thrash-metal and techno-pop episodes joined by abrupt jump cuts. Along with his core lineup of Lyle Mays, Steve Rodby and Paul Wertico, Metheny also includes the duo of multi-instrumentalists Mark Ledford and David Blamires adding various horns and things, and four top-line percussionists—Mino Cinelu, Dave Samuels, Glen Velez and Don Alias—replacing departing member Armando Marcal. Through all the experiments, the Metheny Group's music remains uplifting, intelligent, and always accessible to the casual and attentive ear in the late '90s, even as it becomes more portentous. The "words" on the cover art and booklet are written in some kind of strange Esperanto alphabet, with symbols and objects replacing each letter, but there are enough translations in plain English to get you through. *—Richard S. Ginell*

Trio 99>00 / 1999 / Warner Brothers ✦✦✦✦✦
Mixing up his pitches just to keep his fans off balance as always, Metheny returns to the strict jazz-guitar trio format for the first time in a decade, in league with a couple of combative, unintimidated partners. At the age of 45, Metheny leaves no doubt that he has become a masterful jazz player, thoroughly at home with even the most convoluted bebop licks ("What Od You Want?") yet still as open as ever to ideas outside the narrow mainstream, as illustrated in the country-western-tinged phrasing on "The Sun in Montreal." Bassist Larry Grenadier propels his own voice prominently into the texture, even when walking the fours, and drummer Bill Stewart does not hesitate to go against the grain of Metheny's ideas. There is a slow, almost bossa nova-like take on "Giant Steps" that works unexpectedly well; it actually becomes a lyrical, gliding thing. *Bye Bye Birdie*'s "Got a Lot of Livin' to Do" gets a rare contemporary cover, and why not— it's a good tune that holds up, even when fractured as creatively as it is here. There are also a few songs on acoustic guitar that sound like embryonic soundtrack material: "Just Like the Day," "We Had a Sister," and "Travels," the latter being Metheny's first studio recording of a tune that was recorded live 17 years before. Metheny's brigade of jazz buffs will savor this. *—Richard S. Ginell*

Mezz Mezzrow (Milton Mesirow)

b. Oct. 9, 1899, Chicago, IL, **d.** Aug. 5, 1972, Paris, France
Sax (Tenor), Clarinet, Clarinet / Dixieland
Mezz Mezzrow occupies an odd and unique place in jazz history. Although an enthusiastic clarinetist, he was never much of a player, sounding best on the blues. A passionate propagandist for Chicago and New Orleans jazz and the rights of Blacks (he meant well but tended to overstate his case), Mezzrow was actually most significant for writing his colorful and somewhat fanciful memoirs *Really the Blues* and for being a reliable supplier of marijuana in the 1930s and '40s. In the 1920s he was part of the Chicago jazz scene, at first helping the young White players and then annoying them with his inflexible musical opinions. Mezzrow recorded with the Jungle Kings, the Chicago Rhythm Kings and Eddie Condon during 1927-28, often on tenor. In the 1930s he led a few swing-oriented dates that featured all-star integrated bands in 1933-34 and 1936-37. The French critic Hugues Panassie was always a big supporter of Mezzrow's playing and Mezz was well-featured on sessions in 1938 with Tommy Ladnier and Sidney Bechet; "Really the Blues" is a near-classic. Mezzrow had his own King Jazz label during 1945-47, mostly documenting ensemble-oriented blues jams with Bechet and occasionally Hot Lips Page. After appearing at the 1948 Nice Jazz festival, Mezzrow eventually moved to France where he recorded fairly regularly during 1951-55 (including with Lee Collins and Buck Clayton) along with a final album in 1959. *—Scott Yanow*

● **1928-1936** / Apr. 6, 1928-Mar. 12, 1936 / Classics ✦✦✦✦✦
Mezz Mezzrow was never that strong a player. His technique was weak, and although he played with enthusiasm and was decent on the blues, he fumbled a lot. However, Mezz did appear on a lot of significant recordings through the years, and some are on this Classics CD. Playing tenor, Mezzrow is heard in 1928 with the Chicago Rhythm Kings, the Jungle Kings (the same group under a different name), Frank Teschemacher's Chicagoans and the Louisiana Rhythm Kings. Those six titles by overlapping bands feature such major players early in their careers as cornetist Muggsy Spanier, clarinetist Frank Teschemacher, pianist Joe Sullivan, Eddie Condon (on banjo) and drummer Gene Krupa; Red McKenzie takes a vocal on "There'll Be Some Changes Made." Also on this CD are eight swing-oriented numbers from 1933-34 by a big band headed by Mezzrow and including such top musicians as trumpeter Max Kaminsky, trombonist Floyd O'Brien, altoist Benny Carter, Bud Freeman on tenor and either Teddy Wilson or Willie "The Lion" Smith on piano. Despite the inclusion of such titles as "Free Love" and "Dissonance," the music is essentially no-nonsense swing. This CD is rounded off by four selections from Art Karle and His Boys (mainly showcases for the dated vocals of Chick Bullock, although trumpeter Frankie Newton is in the backup band) and two songs from Mezz's first 1936 session as a leader. The excellent and often essential music is obviously of greatest interest for the contributions of the many all-stars. *—Scott Yanow*

King Jazz Story, Vol. 1: Out of the Gallion / Mar. 27, 1945-Dec. 20, 1947 / Storyville ✦✦✦✦
The entire output of clarinetist Mezz Mezzrow's King Jazz label has been reissued over five CDs (the four volumes in this series and a Sidney Bechet set), although due to the many alternate takes and the similar sessions, the reissue producers decided not to program the material in strict chronological order. The first volume has three piano solos from Sammy Price, four numbers from a heated septet date with the great soprano Sidney Bechet and trumpeter Hot Lips Page, and 15 selections by various quintets featuring Mezzrow and Bechet. On five instances, Mezzrow is heard years later telling the story behind certain performances. There is a certain sameness to much of the material, but some selections stand out, particularly "Evil Gal Blues" (featuring a vocal by Coot Grant), a two-part "The Blues and Freud," "Ole Miss," "Blues of the Roaring Twenties," "The Sheik of Araby" and the romping "Perdido Street Stomp." *—Scott Yanow*

King Jazz Story, Vol. 2: Really the Blues / Mar. 27, 1945-Dec. 20, 1947 / Storyville ✦✦✦✦
On the second of five CDs (the four sets in this series plus a single Sidney Bechet release) all of the recordings made for Mezz Mezzrow's King Jazz label have been reissued although unfortunately not in chronological order. This CD contains three piano solos by Sammy Price, five selections from the Mezzrow-Bechet septet (featuring trumpeter Hot Lips Page) plus 14 blues-oriented performances that feature clarinetist Mezz and the great soprano Sidney Bechet in a quintet; Mezzrow also introduces five of the numbers. A pair of two-part jams ("Really the Blues" and "Revolutionary Blues") stand out from the 74 minutes of fairly similar material; Bechet is in typically explosive form throughout. *—Scott Yanow*

1944-1945 / Mar. 15, 1944-Aug. 30, 1945 / Melodie Jazz Classics ✦✦✦

1947 / Sep. 18, 1947-Dec. 19, 1947 / Classics ✦✦✦✦
Mezz Mezzrow was a jazz musician better known for writing his exaggerated autobiography *Really the Blues* in 1946 than for his clarinet playing. This Classics disc highlights the year 1947 when Mezzrow was recording for his own King Jazz label. Even on up-tempo hot numbers, a hazy laid back approach was consistently maintained, which may have had something to do with Mezzrow's fondness for marijuana. However, these are highly enjoyable recordings that feature vocalist Coot Grant on six of the discs 20 tracks along with top New Orleans jazzmen including Sidney Bechet, Pops Foster, and Baby Dodds. *—Al Campbell*

Glenn Miller (Alton Glenn Miller)

b. Mar. 1, 1904, Clarinda, IA, **d.** Dec. 15, 1944, English Channel
Trombone / Sweet Bands, Swing, Big Band
Glenn Miller led the most popular band in the world during 1939-42 and the most beloved of all the swing-era orchestras. His big band played a wide variety of melodic music (including swing, vocal ballads and novelties) and had tremendous success in every area. Jazz was only part of their music and Miller (like Stan Kenton) was just not interested in swinging like Count Basie. He employed some good horn soloists along the way but was most concerned in displaying strong musicianship, well-rehearsed ensembles, danceable tempoes and putting together an enjoyable and well-rounded show. In 1935 he led his first session but even by 1937, Glenn Miller was still obscure. He was inspired by the success of many new big bands and he put together an orchestra of his own. That venture started out promising with some fine recordings but it soon failed, partly because it did not have a personality of its own. In mid-1938 Miller tried again and although he had a recording contract with Bluebird, the first year was mostly a struggle. However this time around, by having a clarinet double the melody of the saxophones an octave higher, he had his own trademark. "Moonlight Serenade" (Miller's theme), "Sunrise Serenade" and particularly "Little Brown Jug" became hits and by the end of 1939 Glenn Miller was a household name and his band was considered a sensation. During 1939-42 there were many additional hits including "In the Mood," "At Last," "Stairway to the Stars," "Tuxedo Junction," "Pennsylvania 6-5000," "Chattanooga Choo Choo," "A String of Pearls," "Elmer's Tune," "Don't Sit Under the Apple Tree," "American Patrol," "I've Got a Gal in Kalamazoo," "Serenade in Blue" and "Jukebox Saturday Night." There was simply no competition. Only Miller's decision to enlist in the Army stopped his orchestra's success. He flew across the English Channel in December 1944 with plans of setting up engagements on the Continent. His plane was shot down (quite possibly in error by the Allies) and lost. *—Scott Yanow*

Best of the Big Bands: Evolution of a Band / Apr. 25, 1935-May 23, 1938 / Columbia ✦✦✦
The majority of Glenn Miller's early recordings as a bandleader are included on this CD which is subtitled "Evolution of a Band." Miller heads a studio group (which includes trum-

peter Bunny Berigan) on two numbers from 1935 (why weren't all four from that date included?) and on three complete sessions from 1937-38; if the liner notes are to be believed the final four performances are previously unissued alternate takes. All of the selections from 1937-38 are taken from a period when Miller was struggling to find his sound and, even by the time of "Dippermouth Blues" (from May 23, 1938), he had not found it yet. But although these recordings are not that distinctive, there are some good moments; the vocals by Kathleen Lane and Gail Reese are excellent. *—Scott Yanow*

On the Air / Jun. 25, 1938-Nov. 29, 1941 / RCA Victor ♦♦♦♦
Three LPs (which were originally available separately) are combined in this box set. The performances by Glenn Miller's Orchestra (dance music, vocal features and a bit of jazz) are taken from radio broadcasts and over half of the selections were not recorded by the band commercially. Since most of this music (released for the first time in 1963 and kept in-print for many years afterward) has not reappeared on CD, this is a set that Glenn Miller collectors will want to go out of their way to acquire although more general listeners should get the studio recordings first. *—Scott Yanow*

☆ **The Complete Glenn Miller, Vols. 1-13** / Sep. 27, 1938-Jul. 16, 1942 / Bluebird/RCA ♦♦♦♦♦
This 13-CD set (which is enclosed in an attractive and compact black box) completely reissues the contents of the nine double-LP series of the same name, all 277 studio recordings (including 20 alternate takes which have been placed on the 13th disc) that were made by Glenn Miller's extremely popular orchestra. In addition to all of the hits and the occasional jazz performances, the misses (and the many Ray Eberle vocals) are also on this set so general collectors just wanting a taste of Glenn Miller's music would be better off getting a less expensive greatest-hits set. However, true Glenn Miller fans should consider this remarkable reissue to be essential; it's all here. *—Scott Yanow*

★ **The Popular Recordings (1938-1942)** / Sep. 27, 1938-Jul. 15, 1942 / Bluebird/RCA ♦♦♦♦♦
Of the many compilations of Glenn Miller hits, this three-disc set strikes the best balance between comprehensiveness and economy. More casual listeners might want to try *Pure Gold,* while true scholars will have to have the *Complete Glenn Miller,* but this 60-track collection contains the best of the most popular bandleader of the last part of the swing era. *—William Ruhlmann*

★ **The Essential Glenn Miller** / Apr. 4, 1939-Jul. 15, 1942 / Bluebird/RCA ♦♦♦♦♦
Glenn Miller's 1939-42 Victor recordings have been reissued a countless number of times in many different ways through the years. This two-CD set does an excellent job of repackaging all of his hits plus a variety of vocal numbers in chronological order. The 47 selections sum up Miller's legacy quite well, making this a definitive set for listeners who do not desire everything that Glenn Miller recorded. *—Scott Yanow*

Legendary Performer / May 17, 1939-Sep. 24, 1942 / Bluebird/RCA ♦♦♦♦♦
On first glance, this CD may appear to be a greatest-hits package since many of the songs were recorded by Glenn Miller's Orchestra in the studios, but actually the set contains (in chronological order) many of Miller's most historic radio performances. Starting with his theme "Moonlight Serenade" from the band's opening appearance at the Glen Island Casino (when they were unknown), one can experience from song-to-song the quick rush to success, a New Year's Eve version of "In the Mood," and a classic rendition of "Chattanooga Choo Choo" (with Miller being awarded the first Gold record in history), all the way up to the announcement of Miller's entry into the Army, a surprise guest appearance by Harry James and Glenn Miller's emotional farewell to the audience. This is an essential release for anyone with an interest in Glenn Miller's music and life. *—Scott Yanow*

The Carnegie Hall Concert / Oct. 6, 1939 / Bluebird/RCA ♦♦♦♦♦
It took RCA-BMG until 1993 to get this performance out on CD, but the wait was worth it. Apart from its brief 35 minutes (Miller was sharing a program with Benny Goodman, Fred Waring, and Paul Whiteman, the self-proclaimed "King of Jazz," and who also introduces him), this is a choice release, capturing Glenn Miller and his orchestra in the midst of their first big flush of success—it was only a few months earlier that their gig at *the Glen Island Casino* and the resulting radio broadcasts transformed Miller into a household name. Miller had a reputation for stuffiness that has outlived him—he did, indeed, hold the jazzier impulses of his band members in check—but here the performance really jumps. The core of Miller's repertory is featured, including a swinging version of "Little Brown Jug," a bracing "Running Wild," a rocking "Bugle Call Rag," and a bouncing, soaring "One O'Clock Jump" (complete with a male chorus that works), all culminating in a cooking version of "In The Mood" (Miller's latest recording at the time of the show). The pop elements are restrained here, in contrast to many of Miller's most familiar recordings, with only one vocal number by Ray Eberle and three by Marion Hutton, one of which, "Jim Jam Jump," is pretty hot—one can even forgive the instrumental digression of "Danny Boy." The sound is surprisingly good given the age of the performance, and the digital remastering works wonders. *—Bruce Eder*

☆ **Major Glenn Miller & the Army Air Force Band (1943-1944)** / Oct. 29, 1943-Apr. 22, 1944 / Bluebird/RCA ♦♦♦♦♦
During the two years of its existence the Glenn Miller Army Air Force Band (the greatest orchestra he ever led) performed and recorded frequently although most of its sessions have been difficult to find ever since. The group was filled with talented jazz soloists (including trumpeters Bobby Nichols and Bernie Privin, clarinetist Peanuts Hucko and pianist Mel Powell), had fine singers in Ray McKinley, Johnny Desmond and the Crew Chiefs and even an occasional 21-piece string section. This CD has many of the best performances by the huge band including "St. Louis Blues March," "Tail-End Charlie," "Anvil Chorus," "Everybody Loves My Baby" and "It Must Be Jelly" and it is highly recommended to swing fans and jazz historians. *—Scott Yanow*

Secret Broadcasts / Mar. 10, 1944-Jun. 2, 1944 / RCA ♦♦♦♦♦
This superb three-CD set has highlights of the many radio broadcasts made by Glenn Miller's Army Air Force Band while in Great Britain. Miller had a dream orchestra that had a hard-swinging rhythm section (which included pianist Mel Powell and drummer Ray McKinley), top soloists in clarinetist Peanuts Hucko, trumpeters Bobby Nichols and Bernie Privin and some lesser-known saxophonists plus singer Johnny Desmond with the Crew Chiefs and a full string section arranged by Jerry Gray. Glenn Miller completists will prefer the first two volumes of the English Avid label's Miller series for that duplicates these three CDs while adding another full disc of material, but listeners wanting one definitive set are advised to pick up this release. The music ranges from heated swing (including some remakes of Miller's earlier hits) to mood music, ballad vocals and adventurous performances that hint at what Glenn Miller might have performed during the postwar years if he had lived. *—Scott Yanow*

Charles Mingus

b. Apr. 22, 1922, Nogales, AZ, **d.** Jan. 5, 1979, Cuernavaca, Mexico
Piano, Bass, Composer / Avant-Garde Jazz, Hard Bop, Post-Bop, Bop, Avant-Garde
Irascible, demanding, bullying, and probably a genius, Charles Mingus cut himself a uniquely iconoclastic path through jazz in the middle of the 20th century, creating a legacy that became universally lauded only after he was no longer around to bug people. As a bassist, he knew few peers, blessed with a powerful tone and pulsating sense of rhythm, capable of elevating the instrument into the front line of a band. But had he been just a string player, few would know his name today. Rather, he was the greatest bass-playing leader/composer jazz has ever known, one who always kept his ears and fingers on the pulse, spirit, spontaneity, and ferocious expressive power of jazz. Intensely ambitious yet often earthy in expression, simultaneously radical and deeply traditional, Mingus' music took elements from everything he had experienced—from gospel and blues through New Orleans jazz, swing, bop, Latin music, modern classical music, even the jazz avant-garde. His touchstone was Duke Ellington, but Mingus took the sonic blend and harmonies of Ellingtonia much further, throwing in abrasive dissonances and abrupt changes in meter and tempo, introducing tremendously exhilarating accelerations that generated a momentum of their own. While his early works were written out in a classical fashion, by the mid-1950s, he had worked out a new way of getting his unconventional visions across, dictating the parts to his musicians while allowing plenty of room for the players' own musical personalities and ideas. *—Richard S. Ginell*

☆ **The Complete Debut Recordings** / Apr. 1951-1958 / Debut ♦♦♦♦♦
This mammoth 12-CD box set may not contain Charles Mingus's most significant recordings (those would take place shortly after these sessions) but there is a remarkable amount of exciting and somewhat innovative music in this reissue of all of the dates recorded for Mingus's label Debut. There are duets and trios with pianist Spaulding Givens, a variety of odd third-stream originals (some with vocalist Jackie Paris and altoist Lee Konitz), the famous Massey Hall concert with Charlie Parker and Dizzy Gillespie (heard in two versions, one with Mingus's overdubbed bass), a four-trombone date with J.J. Johnson, Kai Winding, Bennie Green and Willie Dennis, trio sets with pianists Paul Bley, Hazel Scott and the obscure John Dennis, a quintet with trumpeter Thad Jones and Frank Wess on tenor and flute, Miles Davis's "Alone Together" session, a date led by trombonist Jimmy Knepper, a completely unissued 1957 sextet session and, most importantly, a greatly expanded live session with trombonist Eddie Bert and tenor-saxophonist George Barrow which found Mingus finally finding himself musically. Many of these performances are now also available in smaller sets but this attractive box (which has 64 previously unissued tracks among the 169 selections) is the best way to acquire this valuable music. *—Scott Yanow*

Thirteen Pictures: The Charles Mingus Anthology / Apr. 12, 1952-1977 / Rhino ♦♦
It is a thankless and impossible task to sum up the career of Charles Mingus on only two CDs; everyone knows that. But Rhino does have the advantage of being a licensing company, and they did roam far afield for material from most of the important sources, to Atlantic, Debut, Impulse!, United Artists, EmArcy, Mingus' custom Jazz Workshop label, even into the hard-to-crack vaults of Columbia. Instead of a sensible chronological approach though, Rhino scrambles the sequencing into something incomprehensible. Nevertheless the newcomer to Mingus will get a colorful, varied, even powerful portrait of the irascible composer/bandleader/bassist. In addition to famous signature numbers like "Haitian Fight Song," "Better Get It in Your Soul," Goodbye Pork Pie Hat" and "Pithecanthropus Erectus," there are a pair of extended works, and odd sidetrips like a trio date with Duke Ellington and Max Roach. It might have been an indulgence on co-producer Hal Willner's part to devote more than two-fifths of the space in what was supposed to be a Mingus primer to the huge 28-minute "Cumbia and Jazz Fusion" and a 25-minute live rendition of "Meditations on Integration." But it was a courageous indulgence, for "Cumbia's" kaleidoscope of Colombian rhythms, big-band flourishes, extended improvisation, and weird vocal humor makes for a bold entryway into Mingus' world, and "Meditations," despite the poor sound, receives a provocative performance. Oddly, for a label that distributes Atlantic's archival material, Rhino only includes four Atlantic cuts, but with the complete Mingus Atlantic sessions from 1956-1961 now available in another Rhino box, perhaps that was the plan all along. As such, this is about as useful a relatively affordable Mingus sampler as there is on CD, which isn't saying much, actually. *—Richard S. Ginell*

Jazz Composers Workshop / Oct. 31, 1954-Jan. 30, 1955 / Savoy ♦♦♦

Mingus at the Bohemia / Dec. 23, 1955 / Debut/OJC ♦♦♦♦♦

Plus Max Roach / Dec. 23, 1955 / Debut/OJC ♦♦♦♦

☆ **Pithecanthropus Erectus** / Jan. 30, 1956 / Atlantic ♦♦♦♦♦
This Atlantic set has the first truly classic Charles Mingus performance, the lengthy title cut which attempts to depict musically the rise and fall of man. Altoist Jackie McLean, tenor-saxophonist J.R. Monterose, pianist Mal Waldron and drummer Willie Jones join the bassist/leader for some stirring music with the humorous "A Foggy Day," (complete with sirens and horns honking like automobiles), "Profile of Jackie" and "Love Chant" completing the particularly strong program. *—Scott Yanow*

☆ **Passions of a Man: The Complete Atlantic Recordings (1956-1961)** / 1956-1961 / Rhino ♦♦♦♦♦
Passions of a Man: The Complete Atlantic Recordings (1956-1961) presents an interesting

problem. There's little arguing that the music on *Passions of a Man* is seminal, ranking among his very best recordings. The question is whether the six-disc set is indispensable, considering that it is low on unreleased material and boasts one full interview disc. All of Mingus' Atlantic recordings between 1956 and 1961 are included in session order, with alternate takes of "E's Flat Ah's Flat Too," "My Jelly Roll Soul," "Tensions" and "Wednesday Night Prayer Meeting" being added to disc three. The interview is interesting, yet most listeners will be content to hear it only once, so it simply adds weight and cost to the box. Still, the cost is justified—*Passions of a Man* is beautifully produced, sporting sparkling remastered sound, new liner notes as well as the original album liner notes, a complete Atlantic discography, and rare photos. For fans that have yet to purchase CD copies of *The Clown, Mingus At Antibes* or *Oh Yeah,* it's an essential purchase, but those who already own those discs might find too much repetition and not enough bonuses to make it worthwhile. *—Stephen Thomas Erlewine*

The Clown / Feb. 13, 1957-Mar. 12, 1957 / Rhino ✦✦✦✦✦
All of Charles Mingus's Atlantic sessions are well worth picking up, including this LP. "Haitian Fight Song" is a classic, "Reincarnation of a Lovebird" is close, "Blue Cee" gives the principals (which include trombonist Jimmy Knepper and Shafi Hadi on alto and tenor) a chance to stretch out and Jean Shepherd verbally improvises a memorable story on "The Clown." *—Scott Yanow*

Mingus Three / Jul. 9, 1957 / Blue Note ✦✦✦
A rather conventional Charles Mingus recording, this trio set mostly features pianist Hampton Hawes (along with drummer Danny Richmond) performing jazz standards and blues along with Mingus's "Dizzy Moods." The music is high-quality bop as one would expect from the talented musicians (Mingus has almost as much solo space as Hawes) and this 1997 CD's contents have been reissued several times through the years. *—Scott Yanow*

☆ **New Tijuana Moods** / Jul. 18, 1957-Aug. 6, 1957 / Bluebird/RCA ✦✦✦✦✦
Inspired by a somewhat riotous trip to Mexico, this set was one of bassist Charles Mingus' early classics. Virtually all of the musicians (trumpeter Clarence Shaw, trombonist Jimmy Knepper, altoist Shafi Hadi, pianist Bill Triglia and drummer Danny Richmond, plus percussionists Frankie Dunlop and Ysabel Morel) were inspired to play way above their heads by the volatile bandleader. This reissue of an earlier CD reissue appeared even earlier as a two-LP set with alternate takes to all five selections ("Dizzy Moods," the passionate "Ysabel's Table Dance, "Tijuana Gift Shop," "Los Mariachis" and "Flamingo"). This particular CD leaves out the lengthy alternate to "Los Mariachis" due to lack of space, but otherwise has the complete sessions. There are plenty of intense moments, some fairly free improvising in spots, and some of the best playing ever by these musicians. Recommended. *—Scott Yanow*

East Coasting / Aug. 1957 / Bethlehem Archives/Avenue Jazz ✦✦✦✦
One of Charles Mingus's lesser-known band sessions, this set of five of his originals (plus the standard "Memories of You") features his usual sidemen of the period (trombonist Jimmy Knepper, trumpeter Clarence Shaw, Shafi Hadi on tenor and alto and drummer Danny Richmond) along with pianist Bill Evans. The music stretches the boundaries of bop, is never predictable and, even if this is not one of Mingus's more acclaimed dates, it is well worth acquiring for the playing is quite stimulating. *—Scott Yanow*

☆ **Blues and Roots** / Feb. 4, 1959 / Rhino ✦✦✦✦✦
One of Charles Mingus's finest studio albums, this date finds the bassist utilizing a nonet (including altoists Jackie McLean and John Handy, Booker Ervin on tenor, baritonist Pepper Adams and the trombones of Jimmy Knepper and Willie Dennis) on six diverse but consistently stimulating originals. Highlights including "Wednesday Night Prayer Meeting," "Cryin' Blues," "E's Flat Ah's Flat Too" and especially "Moanin'." Although "My Jelly Roll Soul" does not really work, the other numbers find Mingus successfully looking both backwards (with group improvising, stop-time breaks and church-like harmonies) and forward (with advanced improvisations and a wider use of emotions than was being utilized in bop). *—Scott Yanow*

☆ **The Complete 1959 CBS Charles Mingus Sessions** / May 5, 1959-Nov. 13, 1959 / Columbia/Legacy ✦✦✦✦✦
In 1993, Mosaic released *The Complete 1959 CBS Charles Mingus Sessions,* a four-LP set that contained (nearly) everything Mingus recorded for the label during that pivotal year. All the music on the set was wonderful, but its strict adherence to chronological session order made it difficult for anyone outside academics to enjoy, especially since *Mingus Ah Um* and *Mingus Dynasty,* the two albums culled from these sessions, were among his best, tightest LPs. Five years after Mosaic's effort, Columbia/Legacy issued *The Complete 1959 Columbia Sessions,* a three-CD attempt to chronicle the same sessions, and their work is definitive. Instead of relying on chronological session order, they have devoted the first two discs to the original albums in their original running order. The label has restored all of the songs to their unedited forms, restoring "lost" solos to no less than ten of the 18 master takes. *Mingus Ah Um* and *Mingus Dynasty* also feature outtakes from the sessions which have only been available on the@ Mosaic box. The third disc is devoted to alternate takes, including a previously unreleased version of "Diane." This sequencing does justice to the albums, preserving their carefully considered running order while illuminating the original albums with valuable bonus tracks. Hardcore fans that already own the Mosaic box may find this set unnecessary, even if it does contain a couple of otherwise unavailable cuts, but any Mingus or jazz fan—including casual fans—who doesn't own the material on *The Complete 1959 Columbia Recordings* will find this box essential. *—Stephen Thomas Erlewine*

★ **Mingus Ah Um** / May 5, 1959-May 12, 1959 / Columbia/Legacy ✦✦✦✦✦
This LP from 1959 is one of Charles Mingus's classics, highlighted by the original versions of "Better Git It in Your Soul," "Goodbye Pork Pie Hat," "Boogie Stop Shuffle" and "Fables of Faubus." Such top-notch musicians as altoist John Handy, tenors Booker Ervin and Shafi Hadi, trombonists Jimmy Knepper and Willie Dennis, pianist Roland Hanna and drummer Danny Richmond gave bassist Mingus one of his strongest units. *—Scott Yanow*

Mingus Dynasty / Nov. 1, 1959-Nov. 13, 1959 / Columbia/Legacy ✦✦✦✦✦
This recording finds bassist Charles Mingus leading two overlapping but different nine and ten piece groups. Much of the music was written for soundtracks of the time but they easily stand out on their own with fine solos from trombonist Jimmy Knepper, Booker Ervin on tenor, altoist John Handy and pianist Roland Hanna uplifting such songs as "Slop," "Song with Orange," "Far Wells, Mill Valley" and two Duke Ellington-associated numbers. The music can also be heard in unedited form (with many solos added back in) on a Mosaic box set. *—Scott Yanow*

Shoes of the Fisherman's Wife.... / Nov. 1, 1959-Sep. 23, 1971 / Columbia ✦✦✦
Most of the *Mingus Dynasty,* which features the same lineup as *Mingus Ah Um* and has a similar feel but is less driving. Inexplicable inclusion of "Shoes of the...." from *Let My Children Hear Music,* recorded twelve years later. All great music. *—Michael Katz*

★ **Mingus at Antibes** / Jul. 13, 1960 / Atlantic ✦✦✦✦✦
During 1960 bassist Charles Mingus led one of his finest bands, a pianoless quartet with Eric Dolphy (on alto, flute and bass clarinet), trumpeter Ted Curson and drummer Danny Richmond. For this live concert, the band is augmented by the great tenor Booker Ervin for some stirring music. All of the music is memorable: "Wednesday Night Prayer Meeting," "Prayer for Passive Resistance," "What Love," "Folk Forms I," and "Better Git It in Your Soul." The immortal pianist Bud Powell sits in on a fine version of "I'll Remember April" and Dolphy and Ervin in particular generate a great deal of heat during some of their solos. *—Scott Yanow*

Charles Mingus Presents Charles Mingus / Oct. 20, 1960 / Candid ✦✦✦✦✦
Charles Mingus has a fascinating way of offering music that is grounded in tradition while remaining startlingly original. The freshness of a disc like *Charles Mingus Presents Charles Mingus,* has the effect of rendering much of what passes for jazz as tedious. The band is small for Mingus, and includes Eric Dolphy on alto saxophone and bass clarinet, Ted Curson on trumpet, and Dannie Richmond on drums. It would be one of Dolphy and Curson's last recording dates with the artist, and they seem determined to go all out for it. The leader's bass line kicks off "Folk Forms No. 1," followed by Dolphy outlining the melody, and then joined by Curson. A simple riff develops into a lively New Orleans funeral march that's developed for 12 minutes. "Original Faubus Fables" is serious in intent—a political attack on segregation governor Faubus—but Mingus and Richmond's singing is difficult to listen to with a straight face. Still, this doesn't distract from the wonderful music. Again and again, the elasticity of the sound is fascinating, at once spacious with the bass and drums balanced against the brass and then noisy, with the horns wailing and crying. The last two pieces, "What Love?" and the outrageously titled "All the Things You Could Be by Now if Sigmund Freud's Wife Was Your Mother," are much looser, bordering on free jazz. The album accomplishes what the best of Mingus accomplishes: the perfect tension between jazz played as an ensemble and jazz played as totally free. *—Ronnie Lankford, Jr.*

☆ **The Complete Candid Recordings** / Oct. 20, 1960-Nov. 11, 1960 / Mosaic ✦✦✦✦✦
Bassist/leader Charles Mingus cut some of his most exciting and rewarding recordings for Candid in 1960 and this superb four-LP set (which unfortunately is a limited edition) contains all of the music except for a couple of alternate takes that showed up later on. Five selections feature the brilliant piano-less quartet of Eric Dolphy (on alto, bass clarinet, and flute), trumpeter Ted Curson, Mingus, and drummer Dannie Richmond, and these are highlighted by the bass clarinet-bass conversation on "What Love" and the interplay between the four musicians on the very memorable "Folk Forms No. 1." Other musicians are added to six other selections (including the 19-minute jam "MDM") and five other numbers feature trumpeter Roy Eldridge who is teamed with altoist Dolphy on three of the songs; those pieces originally appeared on the Newport Rebels' LP. This is a highly recommended set. *—Scott Yanow*

☆ **Oh Yeah** / Nov. 6, 1961 / Rhino ✦✦✦✦✦
One of the great Charles Mingus CD's, this Atlantic reissue (which finds Mingus sticking exclusively to piano and vocal shouts throughout) not only features tenor-saxophonist Booker Ervin, trombonist Jimmy Knepper, bassist Doug Watkins and drummer Dannie Richmond but the amazing Rahsaan Roland Kirk on tenor, manzello, stritch, flute and siren. The music is quite emotional and passionate with "Hog Callin' Blues," "Wham Bam Thank You Ma'am" and the explosive "Ecclusiastics" being particularly memorable. *—Scott Yanow*

The Complete Town Hall Concert / Oct. 12, 1962 / Blue Note ✦✦✦
Charles Mingus's Town Hall Concert has long been considered a famous fiasco, and the original United Artists LP (which contained just 36 minutes of music and did not bother identifying the personnel) made matters worse. But this 1994 Blue Note CD does its best to clean up the mess. It contains over half an hour of previously unreleased music and programs the selections largely in the same order as the concert. There are still confusing moments, inconclusive performances and songs cut off prematurely; Mingus was not in a good temper that day. A highlight among the "new" material is an Eric Dolphy alto solo on the second version of "Epitaph." Blue Note is to be congratulated for doing what they could with what they had, but there are still at least a couple dozen Mingus recordings that would be recommended before this one. *—Scott Yanow*

☆ **The Black Saint and the Sinner Lady** / Jan. 20, 1963 / Impulse! ✦✦✦✦✦
One of Charles Mingus's most successful longer suites, the six-part "Black Saint and the Sinner Lady" is full of surprising moments with the 11-piece band exploring a wide variety of moods and colors. Of particular note are Quentin Jackson's wa-wa trombone (which lets Mingus hint strongly at Duke Ellington) and Charlie Mariano's passionate alto. *—Scott Yanow*

☆ **Mingus, Mingus, Mingus, Mingus, Mingus** / Jan. 1963-Sep. 20, 1963 / Impulse! ✦✦✦✦✦
This CD features two separate recording sessions with such top players as trumpeter Richard Williams, trombonists Quentin Jackson and Britt Woodman, Dick Hafer and Booker Ervin on tenors, the many reeds of Eric Dolphy and Jerome Richardson, altoist Charles Mariano and pianist Jaki Byard. Of the seven selections (all of which are memorable), highpoints include "Mood Indigo," the fiery "Hora Decubitus" and the definitive version of "Better Get Hit in Yo' Soul." *—Scott Yanow*

Mingus Plays Piano / Jul. 30, 1963 / Impulse! ✦✦✦✦
Bassist Charles Mingus would never qualify as a virtuoso on the piano but his technique was

reasonably impressive and his imagination quite brilliant. This unique solo piano CD (which was reissued in 1997) has a few standards ("Body and Soul," "Memories of You" and "I'm Getting Sentimental over You") along with some freely improvised originals, most of which are quite fascinating to hear, as if one were listening to Mingus think aloud. *—Scott Yanow*

Town Hall Concert / Oct. 12, 1962 / Jazz Workshop/OJC ✦✦✦✦

Revenge! / Apr. 17, 1964 / Revenge ✦✦✦✦

Mingus in Europe / Apr. 26, 1964 / Enja ✦✦✦✦✦

Right Now: Live at the Jazz Workshop / Jun. 2, 1964-Jun. 3, 1964 / Debut/OJC ✦✦✦
Soon after Charles Mingus finished touring Europe with his band (the unit that featured Eric Dolphy), he recorded this CD, performed live at The Jazz Workshop in San Francisco. With tenor-saxophonist Clifford Jordan and drummer Danny Richmond still in the group but Jane Getz replacing pianist Jaki Byard and altoist John Handy filling in for Dolphy on one song, the band performs excellent versions of "Meditations on Integration" and "New Fables," both of which are over 23 minutes long. Although not up to the passionate level of the Mingus-Dolphy Quintet, this underrated unit holds its own. *—Scott Yanow*

Let My Children Hear Music / Sep. 23, 1971-Nov. 18, 1971 / Columbia ✦✦✦✦
The CD reissue of the original LP adds one selection ("Taurus in the Arena of Life") to the program of original music. Mingus's unique compositions (mostly recent although one was written back in 1939) receive sympathetic treatment by a partly unidentified large orchestra and are full of interesting textures, sound explorations and surprises. It makes for a stimulating listen. *—Scott Yanow*

Charles Mingus and Friends in Concert / Feb. 4, 1972 / Columbia/Legacy ✦✦✦
Most of Charles Mingus's larger-group recordings, particularly in the later part of his career, tended to be unruly and somewhat undisciplined. This two-CD reissue set (which adds five selections to the original two-LP program), which celebrated Mingus's return to jazz after six years of little activity. Such great jazzmen as baritonist Gerry Mulligan, tenor saxophonist Gene Ammons, altoist Lee Konitz, pianist Randy Weston, James Moody (heard on flute) and a variety of Mingus regulars had a chance to play with the great bassist; even fellow bassist Milt Hinton and Bill Cosby (taking a humorous scat vocal) join in. Most of the music is overly loose but the overcrowded "E's Flat, Ah's Flat Too" and particularly the "Little Royal Suite" are memorable. The "Little Royal Suite," in addition to Ammons, Konitz, Mulligan, Charles McPherson and Bobby Jones, features an 18-year old Jon Faddis (who was sitting in for an ailing Roy Eldridge) stealing the show. *—Scott Yanow*

Mingus Moves / Oct. 29, 1973-Oct. 31, 1973 / Rhino ✦✦✦✦
On this Atlantic LP, Charles Mingus introduced his new group which at the time included trumpeter Ronald Hampton, tenor-saxophonist George Adams, pianist Don Pullen and his longtime drummer Dannie Richmond. Together this excellent quintet performed seven recent compositions including one ("Moves") that features the vocals of Honey Gordon and Doug Hammond. Only three of the pieces are by Mingus but all of the music is greatly influenced by his searching and unpredictable style. *—Scott Yanow*

Changes One / Dec. 27, 1974-Dec. 30, 1974 / Rhino ✦✦✦✦✦
Charles Mingus's finest recordings of his later period are *Changes One* and *Changes Two*, two Atlantic LPs that have been reissued on CD by Rhino. The first volume features four stimulating Mingus originals ("Remember Rockefeller at Attica," "Sue's Changes," "Devil Blues" and "Duke Ellington's Sound of Love") performed by a particularly talented quintet (tenor-saxophonist George Adams who also sings "Devil Blues," trumpeter Jack Walrath, pianist Don Pullen, drummer Dannie Richmond and the leader/bassist). The band has the adventurous spirit and chancetaking approach of Charles Mingus's best groups, making this an easily recommended example of the great bandleader's music. *—Scott Yanow*

Changes Two / Dec. 27, 1974-Dec. 30, 1974 / Rhino ✦✦✦✦✦
Along with its companion volume *Changes One*, this is one of the great sessions from one of the best working bands of the 1970s. Starting with the spirited "Free Cell Block F, 'Tis Nazi U.S.A," this volume also includes the vocal version of "Duke Ellington's Sound of Love" with guest singer (and acquired taste) Jackie Paris, a remake of the classic Mingus composition "Orange Was the Color of Her Dress, Then Silk Blue," Jack Walrath's "Black Bats and Poles," and Sy Johnson's "For Harry Carney." The challenging repertoire from these December 1974 dates sustained the Jazz Workshop for several years; these are the definitive performances. Rhino's reissue duplicates the original LP down to the layout. *—Stuart Kremsky*

Cumbia and Jazz Fusion / Mar. 31, 1976-May 1, 1977 / Rhino ✦✦✦✦
As Charles Mingus's career (and life) moved into its final phase, his recordings exclusively featured large (and often potentially unruly) ensembles. This CD, which contains two rather long performances originally recorded as soundtracks for films, is better than most of what followed. "Cumbia & Jazz Fusion" has a large percussion section and quite a few woodwinds along with trumpeter Jack Walrath, tenor-saxophonist Ricky Ford and trombonist Jimmy Knepper while "Music for 'Todo Modo"' adds five horns to Mingus's Quintet. The music is episodic but generally holds its own away from the film. *—Scott Yanow*

Epitaph / 1990 / Columbia ✦✦✦

Blue Mitchell (Richard Allen Mitchell)

b. Mar. 13, 1930, Miami, FL, **d.** May 21, 1979, Los Angeles, CA
Trumpet / Hard Bop

Owner of a direct, lightly swinging, somewhat plain-wrapped tone that fit right in with the Blue Note label's hard bop ethos of the 1960s, Blue Mitchell tends to be overlooked today perhaps because he never really stood out vividly from the crowd, despite his undeniable talent. He started touring in the early '50s with the R&B bands of Paul Williams, Earl Bostic and Chuck Willis before returning to jazz and attracting the attention of Cannonball Adderley, with whom he recorded for Riverside in 1958. That year, he joined the Horace Silver Quintet, with whom he played and recorded until the band's breakup in March 1964, polishing his hard bop skills. When Silver disbanded, Mitchell's spinoff quintet carried on with a young future star named Chick Corea in the piano chair. This group, with several personnel changes, continued until 1969, recording a string of albums for Blue Note. Probably aware that opportunities for playing straight-ahead jazz were dwindling, Mitchell became a prolific pop and soul sessionman in the late '60s. *—Richard S. Ginell*

☆ **Big 6** / Jul. 2, 1958-Jul. 3, 1958 / Riverside/OJC ✦✦✦✦✦
Trumpeter Blue Mitchell was a virtual unknown when he recorded this Riverside album, his first as a leader. Now reissued on CD in the *OJC* series, Mitchell is heard in excellent form in an all-star sextet with trombonist Curtis Fuller, tenor-great Johnny Griffin, pianist Wynton Kelly, bassist Wilbur Ware and drummer Philly Joe Jones. In addition to some group originals, obscurities and the standard "There Will Never Be Another You," the group also plays the earliest recorded version of Benny Golson's "Blues March," predating Art Blakey's famous recording. *—Scott Yanow*

Out of the Blue / 1958 / Riverside/OJC ✦✦✦✦
This early recording by Blue Mitchell finds the distinctive trumpeter in excellent form in a quintet also featuring tenor saxophonist Benny Golson (who contributed "Blues on My Mind"), either Wynton Kelly or Cedar Walton on piano, Paul Chambers or Sam Jones on bass and drummer Art Blakey. The consistently swinging repertoire includes a surprisingly effective version of "When the Saints Go Marching In." "Studio B," recorded in the same period but formerly available only in a sampler, has been added to the program. It's an enjoyable date of high-quality hard bop. *—Scott Yanow*

Blue Soul / Sep. 28, 1959 / Riverside/OJC ✦✦✦✦✦
This CD reissue bring back one of trumpeter Blue Mitchell's better sessions from his early period, his third recording as a leader for Riverside. Six of the selections also feature trombonist Curtis Fuller (in excellent form) and the tenor of Jimmy Heath in a sextet with pianist Wynton Kelly, bassist Sam Jones and drummer Philly Joe Jones; the arrangements were provided by Heath and Benny Golson. The other three numbers are more informal and showcase Mitchell in a quartet with Kelly and the two Joneses. Excellent hard bop with the repertoire consisting of "The Way You Look Tonight," "Polka Dots and Moonbeams," "Nica's Dream" and two originals apiece from Golson, Heath and Mitchell. *—Scott Yanow*

Blue's Moods / Aug. 24, 1960-Aug. 25, 1960 / Riverside/OJC ✦✦✦✦
Of trumpeter Blue Mitchell's seven Riverside recordings (all of which have been reissued as CDs in the Original Jazz Classics series), only this set (along with three numbers on *Blue Soul*) feature Mitchell as the only horn. Joined by pianist Wynton Kelly, bassist Sam Jones and drummer Roy Brooks, the trumpeter is typically distinctive, swinging and inventive within the hard bop genre. He performs four standards, Ronnell Bright's "Sweet Pumpkin," and the obscure "Avars," and a pair of originals in fine fashion. *—Scott Yanow*

Smooth As the Wind / Dec. 27, 1960-Mar. 30, 1961 / Riverside/OJC ✦✦✦✦
Trumpeter Blue Mitchell is in excellent form on this very interesting session which has been reissued on CD. Mitchell is accompanied by a brass section, a rhythm section and strings. The arrangements (seven by Tadd Dameron and three from Benny Golson) are generally quite stimulating, inspiring the trumpeter to come up with many fresh melodic solos. The repertoire includes two songs that Mitchell played regularly with Horace Silver's Quintet, a pair of superior Tadd Dameron tunes (including the title cut) and six standards. By varying tempoes and moods, Dameron and Golson helped create one of the better soloist-with-strings jazz dates. *—Scott Yanow*

A Sure Thing / Mar. 7, 1962-Mar. 28, 1962 / Riverside ✦✦✦✦
Trumpeter Blue Mitchell is well featured on this CD reissue with a nonet arranged by Jimmy Heath. The music is straightahead but, thanks to Heath's arrangements, sometimes unpredictable. Best is Mitchell's solo on "I Can't Get Started," "Hootie's Blues" and a quintet workout (with Heath, pianist Wynton Kelly bassist Sam Jones and drummer Albert "Tootie" Heath) on "Gone with the Wind." *—Scott Yanow*

The Cup Bearers / Aug. 28, 1962-Aug. 30, 1962 / Riverside ✦✦✦✦
Trumpeter Blue Mitchell and four-fifths of the Horace Silver Quintet (with Cedar Walton in Silver's place) perform a variety of superior songs on this CD reissue including Walton's "Turquoise," Tom McIntosh's "Cup Bearers," Thad Jones's "Tiger Lily" and a couple of standards. The music swings hard, mostly avoids sounding like a Horace Silver group, and has particularly strong solos from Mitchell, tenor-saxophonist Junior Cook and Walton; excellent hard bop. *—Scott Yanow*

The Complete Blue Note Sessions (1963-67) / Aug. 13, 1963-Nov. 17, 1967 / Mosaic ✦✦✦✦✦
Blue Mitchell was always a consistent, lyrical, and pleasing trumpeter. Although not as significant during the 1960s as Lee Morgan and Freddie Hubbard (much less Dizzy Gillespie and Miles Davis), Mitchell had his own appealing sound and was a major asset on many modern mainstream dates. This four-CD limited-edition Mosaic box set collects Mitchell's first six Blue Note dates as a leader: *Step Lightly, The Thing to Do, Down With It, Bring It Home to Me, Boss Horn,* and *Heads Up.* Three albums are by his quintet, which included tenor saxophonist Junior Cook and usually the young pianist Chick Corea and was formed shortly after he left Horace Silver, and the three others are with larger groups, two of which have arrangements by Duke Pearson. Among the other key sidemen are tenor great Joe Henderson, altoist Leo Wright, baritonist Pepper Adams, and pianists Herbie Hancock and McCoy Tyner. There are just two previously unreleased cuts (both alternate takes), but most of the sets have been somewhat rare for years, and taken as a whole, the swinging hard bop and boogaloo performances are Blue Mitchell's finest recordings as a leader. *—Scott Yanow*

★ **The Thing to Do** / Jul. 30, 1964 / Blue Note ✦✦✦✦✦
This Blue Mitchell date is a classic, particularly the opening "Fungii Mama," which is really catchy. The trumpeter's quintet of the period (which includes tenor saxophonist Junior Cook, the young pianist Chick Corea, bassist Gene Taylor and drummer Al Foster) also performs two Jimmy Heath tunes and a song apiece by Joe Henderson ("Step Lightly") and Corea. The record is prime Blue Note hard bop, containing inventive tunes, meaningful solos, and an enthusiastic but tight feel. Highly recommended. *—Scott Yanow*

Down with It / Jul. 14, 1965 / Blue Note ♦♦♦♦
Down With It is a fairly standard bop and soul-jazz session from Blue Mitchell. Leading a quintet that features a young Chick Corea on piano, tenor saxophonist Junior Cook, bassist Gene Taylor and drummer Al Foster, Mitchell creates a laid-back atmosphere which makes R&B covers like "Hi-Heel Sneakers" or the lite bossa nova of "Samba De Stacy" roll along nicely. Just as often, the record is so relaxed that it fails to generate much spark, but each the soloists have fine moments that makes the session worthwhile for jazz purists. *—Stephen Thoms Erlewine*

Red Mitchell (Keith Moore Mitchell)

b. Sep. 20, 1927, New York, NY, **d.** Nov. 8, 1992, Salem, OR
Bass / West Coast Jazz, Hard Bop, Cool
A talented bassist who was always in great demand, Red Mitchell was originally a pianist and he doubled on piano on an occasional basis throughout his career. He switched to bass when he was a member of an Army band in Germany. Mitchell played with Jackie Paris (1947-48), Mundell Lowe, Chubby Jackson's big band and Charlie Ventura (1949), toured with Woody Herman's Orchestra (1949-51) and was a member of the popular Red Norvo Trio (1952-54). He played with the Gerry Mulligan Quartet (1954) and then settled in Los Angeles where during 1954-68 he played with nearly everyone, from West Coast jazz stars (particularly Hampton Hawes) to recording with Ornette Coleman (1959) and being a member of the studio orchestra of MGM. He also co-led a quintet with Harold Land during 1961-62 that recorded for Atlantic. In 1968 Mitchell moved to Stockholm where he led groups, played with European jazzmen and accompanied visiting Americans including Dizzy Gillespie and Phil Woods. Mitchell made occasional visits to the U.S. and shortly before he died he moved to Oregon. In addition to the Atlantic date, Red Mitchell led albums for Bethlehem (1955), Contemporary, Pacific Jazz, Mercury, SteepleChase, Caprice, Gryphon, Phontastic, Enja and Capri in addition to a few smaller European labels. *—Scott Yanow*

Presenting Red Mitchell / Mar. 26, 1957 / Riverside/OJC ♦♦♦♦
Bassist Red Mitchell, who had led two fairly obscure sessions for Bethlehem in 1955, came up with a gem on his lone Contemporary set as a leader (which has been reissued as this CD). Based in Los Angeles at the time, Mitchell utilized pianist Lorraine Geller and two up-and-coming players: James Clay (who splits his time between tenor and flute) and, in one of his first recording sessions, drummer Billy Higgins. The quartet performs then-recent tunes by Miles Davis, Sonny Rollins and Clifford Brown ("Sandu"), a pair of Mitchell originals, "Scrapple From the Apple" and "Cheek to Cheek." Despite Higgins' and (to a lesser extent) Clay's connections with Ornette Coleman, the music is strictly high-quality modern mainstream bop of the era. Easily recommended to collectors of straight-ahead jazz. *—Scott Yanow*

● **Hear Ye!** / Oct. 14, 1961 / Koch International ♦♦♦♦♦
In the early '60s, bassist Red Mitchell and tenor saxophonist Harold Land co-led a quintet in Los Angeles. The group did not catch on but they did record one Atlantic set that has been reissued on CD. In addition to the co-leaders, the quintet included trumpeter Carmell Jones, pianist Frank Strazzeri, and drummer Leon Pettis, and, although their original program of six songs was comprised entirely of group originals, the music falls easily into the hard bop area with plenty of fine solos and swinging ensembles. The CD reissue adds two previously unreleased tracks including a lone standard, "I'm Old Fashioned." This is a fine effort from a group that deserved greater recognition at the time. *—Scott Yanow*

Red Mitchell-Warne Marsh Big Two, Vol. 2 / Apr. 18, 1980-Apr. 19, 1980 / Storyville ♦♦♦♦
Bassist Red Mitchell and tenor saxophonist Warne Marsh team up on this second of two CDs. Although tenor-bass duets have a limited range of sound, Mitchell's virtuosity and Marsh's ability to come up with endless melodic ideas over common chord changes results in this set holding one's interest. Two of the 11 selections ("Background Music" and "Scrapple From the Apple") were previously unissued. With the underrated cool-toned tenor in superior form, the date (which also includes "Hot House," "Tea for Two" and "Ornithology" among the top numbers) should greatly interest his fans. *—Scott Yanow*

Roscoe Mitchell

b. Aug. 3, 1940, Chicago, IL
Reeds (Multiple), Sax (Tenor), Sax (Soprano), Sax (Alto), Flute / Avant-Garde Jazz, Free Jazz, Avant-Garde
Saxophonist and flutist Roscoe Mitchell is a core member of the Art Ensemble of Chicago and AACM, and an influential composer and improviser. Starting out on saxophone and clarinet, Mitchell played with Albert Ayler while in Germany, in the Army. Upon returning to the U.S. in 1961, Mitchell played bop with local students Malachi Favors, Joseph Jarman, Henry Threadgill, and Anthony Braxton. Mitchell began listening to Ornette Coleman and John Coltrane, and studied with pianist/composer Muhal Richard Abrams. In 1962 he played in Abrams' Experimental Band, and became an early member of the Association for the Advancement of Creative Musicians (AACM) in 1965. In 1966, Mitchell's sextet recorded the first AACM album, *Sound* (Delmark). *Sound* examined the interaction between sound and silence, utilizing such unorthodox devices as spontaneous collective improvisation, and toy instruments. Mitchell also performed and recorded solo, and, by 1967, led the Roscoe Mitchell Art Ensemble with Favors, Lester Bowie, and Phillip Wilson. Jarman replaced Wilson, and the group moved to Paris in 1969. Renamed the Art Ensemble of Chicago, the group—now with drummer Famoudou Don Moye—recorded extensively. Returning to the U.S. in 1971, Mitchell played in St. Louis, then resettled in Chicago. Around 1974, he established the Creative Arts Collective in East Lansing, MI. The '70s brought other collaborations, and solo work, in addition to work with the Art Ensemble, which became one of the most highly-acclaimed jazz band of the next two decades. In the '80s and '90s, Mitchell also led The Sound Ensemble, which included members of his Creative Arts Collective. Branching out even more in the '90s, Mitchell collaborated with classical composer/performers including Pauline Oliveros and Thomas Buckner. A trio with Buckner and pianist Borah Bergman was an ongoing unit to the end of the millennium. As an improvising composer, Mitchell's use of unusual sonorities and his embrace of quiet sounds helped define an entire jazz sub-genre, and he continues to be a major figure. *—Chris Kelsey*

★ **Sound** / Aug. 10, 1966-Aug. 26, 1966 / Delmark ♦♦♦♦♦
This innovative set helped introduce the sound and music of the AACM to record, and it just preceded the formation of the Art Ensemble of Chicago. Altoist Roscoe Mitchell joined with trumpeter Lester Bowie, trombonist Lester Lashley, tenor saxophonist Maurice McIntyre, bassist Malachi Favors and drummer Alvin Fielder to perform five numbers (two released for the first time on this 1996 reissue CD) that were quite a bit different than most of the high energy avant-garde releases of the time. Utilizing silence as part of the music, sometimes playing "little instruments" (which ranged from toys to percussion devices), and sometimes hinting at earlier styles while improvising very freely, Mitchell performed music that was both fascinating and sometimes difficult to listen to. The two versions of "Ornette" on this set are fine examples of freebop, while the two lengthy versions of "Sound" ramble on in intriguing fashion. A classic of its kind. *—Scott Yanow*

Nonaah / Aug. 23, 1976-Feb. 22, 1977 / Nessa ♦♦♦♦♦
1976-1977. This is one of Mitchell's best solo statements. It includes a full-side treatment of the title cut, solo works, duos, and an incredible alto number with Mitchell, Henry Threadgill (as), Joseph Jarman (reeds), and the undervalued Wallace McMillan (b). *—Ron Wynn*

Snurdy McGurdy and Her Dancin' Shoes / Dec. 11, 1980-Dec. 12, 1980 / Nessa ♦♦♦♦
This album is more upbeat and humorous, less dense and intense than some past Mitchell dates, but the music's just as ferocious. *—Ron Wynn*

The Flow of Things / Jun. 29, 1986-Sep. 7, 1986 / Black Saint ♦♦♦
Sounding like a sour piece of gauzy metal set aflame, Roscoe Mitchell's soprano saxophone endlessly snakes its way through the three sections of "The Flow of Things" on this 1987 album of the same name. The piece forms the meat of this solo effort by the Art Ensemble of Chicago soloist, demonstrating Mitchell's knack for circular breathing as well as a long-standing love of full-throttle, free-wheeling group improvisation. It's not about swinging, but if you fancy being pinned to the wall by a barrage of high-end repartee by some of the best in the avant-garde jazz business, then this one's for you. Joining the fray are fellow AACM members pianist Jodie Christian and drummer Steve McCall, as well as Art Ensemble bassist Malachi Favors. Providing a break from the intensity, Mitchell offers up one of his engaging, mystically minimal sound sculptures, "Card for Quartet." The piece definitely gives one an idea of how the music of avant-garde classical composers like Varese, Cage, and Stockhausen can fit into a jazz context. *The Flow of Things* is probably not the best entrée into Mitchell's work, but after a few Art Ensemble of Chicago records and one of his earlier efforts, make sure to come back for a listen. *—Stephen Cook*

Hey Donald / May 23, 1994-May 25, 1994 / Delmark ♦♦♦♦♦
Since Roscoe Mitchell (who on this set made his return to the Delmark label after 28 years) is best known as a free jazz pioneer and a longtime member of the Art Ensemble of Chicago, the straightahead nature of a few of the selections will surprise some of his followers. "Walking in the Moonlight" is a sly and witty strut, "Jeremy" a melodic ballad for the leader's flute and "Hey Donald" could have come from the Sonny Rollins songbook. But Mitchell has not forsaken his innovative style. On "Dragons" his soprano playing (with its circular breathing) sounds very African, there are four free duets with bassist Malachi Favors and the blowouts on "Song for Rwanda" and "See You at the Fair" are pretty adventurous. In general Mitchell (who is joined by a versatile rhythm section comprised of pianist Jodie Christian, bassist Favors and drummer Tootie Heath) saves the more boppish pieces for his tenor while on soprano his intense sound creates a drone effect reminiscent a bit of bagpipes. All in all his release for Delmark should keep listeners guessing. *—Scott Yanow*

Sound Songs / Oct. 9, 1994 / Delmark ♦♦♦♦
Avant-garde pioneer Roscoe Mitchell performs all of the music on this two-CD set, some of it unaccompanied solos with about half of the selections using overdubbing. Mitchell is mostly heard on alto and soprano but also utilizes percussion and "little instruments" in addition to flutes. Some of the numbers are closely planned, programmed loosely with themes and plots, but there is also plenty of free-form improvising. Mitchell, a master at using silence and repetition, creates thoroughly unpredictable music that is generally quite logical in hindsight. Still, since these are sound explorations and there are plenty of violent moments, this is mostly for very open-eared listeners. *—Scott Yanow*

Nine to Get Ready / May 1997 / ECM ♦♦♦
An interesting but not essential set, this unusual date allowed Roscoe Mitchell (heard on soprano, alto, tenor and flute) to head a nonet also consisting of trumpeter Hugh Ragin, trombonist George Lewis, both Matthew Shipp and Craig Taborn on pianos, the twin basses of Jaribu Shahid and William Parker and both Tani Tabbel and Gerald Cleaver on drums. The performances are mostly concise, emphasize ensembles (it is difficult to believe that the two rhythm sections are playing simultaneously) and are sometimes surprisingly mellow although there are intense moments (such as on "Hop Hip Bip Bir Rip"). None of the original pieces are that memorable but the overall mood is haunting and at times jubilant. An intriguing addition to Roscoe Mitchell's discography. *—Scott Yanow*

In Walked Buckner / Jul. 13, 1998-Jul. 14, 1998 / Delmark ♦♦♦♦
Roscoe Mitchell once fronted perhaps his most daringly different trio with multi-instrumentalist Gerald Oshita and vocalist Thomas Buckner. This recording, dedicated to Buckner, captures the singing characteristics of Buckner in a purely instrumental way, and quite beautifully. Timbres are rare and off-kilter, free flowing, static, or flat-out swinging. In the middle is Mitchell, carrying the torch that has kept him a vital, adventurous American musician for three decades. Armed with a raft of woodwind instruments, Mitchell, with yeoman's help from bassist Reggie Workman, the judicious pianistics of Jody Christian and the masterful drumming of Al Heath, makes the quartet, when they play together, unstoppable. Substantive solo space is distributed, especially for the leader. Check out his saxophone on the self-explanatory "Squeaky." Smaller combinations are fashioned with a no-time policy.

Improvisations are stark and real. Spiritual evocations are evident. The bulk of the remainder of the eight-cut program, from the ethereally nautical "Off Shore," the lilting "Le Dreher Suite" and the haunting "Opposite Sides" emphatically showcase Mitchell's other worldly flute work. They are convincing exhibits of Mitchell's position as perhaps the premier and essential improvised musical voice in the avant garde of them all. In spirit, execution and intent, Mitchell succeeds on all levels, except perhaps as a hitmaker. Surely his fans like it that way. Highly recommended to appreciators of this style. *—Michael G. Nastos*

Hank Mobley

b. Jul. 7, 1930, Eastman, GA, **d.** May 30, 1986, Philadelphia, PA
Sax (Tenor) / Hard Bop
Accurately described by critic Leonard Feather as "the middleweight champion of the tenor" due to his sound (not as light as Lester Young's or as heavy as Sonny Rollins), Hank Mobley tended to be taken for granted during his career but recorded a long string of valuable albums for Blue Note. He first gained attention for his work with Max Roach (on and off during 1951-53) and Dizzy Gillespie (1954). An original member of the Jazz Messengers (1954-56), Mobley joined Horace Silver when the pianist broke away from Art Blakey to form his own group (1956-57). Mobley was back with Blakey for a bit in 1959 and spent an unhappy period with Miles Davis (1961-62) but mostly worked as a leader in the 1960s. He was in Europe during much of 1968-70 and recorded with Cedar Walton in 1972 but by the mid-'70s was largely retired due to bad health. Hank Mobley led isolated dates for Savoy, Prestige and Roulette but it is for his 25 Blue Note albums (recorded during 1955-70) with the who's who of hard bop (including such sidemen as Horace Silver, Art Blakey, Lee Morgan, Milt Jackson, Art Farmer, Donald Byrd, Bobby Timmons, Sonny Clark, Kenny Dorham, Pepper Adams, Wynton Kelly, Freddie Hubbard, Grant Green, Philly Joe Jones, Herbie Hancock, Andrew Hill, Barry Harris, Curtis Fuller, McCoy Tyner, Billy Higgins, James Spaulding, Jackie McLean, Blue Mitchell, Cedar Walton, Ron Carter and Woody Shaw) that he will be best-remembered. *—Scott Yanow*

☆ **The Complete Blue Note Hank Mobley Fifties Sessions** / Mar. 27, 1955-Feb. 9, 1958 / Mosaic ✦✦✦✦✦
This is a typically remarkable box set from Mosaic. The six-CD limited edition package has all of tenor saxophonist Hank Mobley's recordings as a leader for Blue Note from a three-year period, all of the music originally included in the albums titled *The Hank Mobley Quartet, Hank Mobley Sextet, Hank Mobley and His All-Stars, Hank Mobley Quintet, Hank, Hank Mobley, Curtain Call, Poppin'* and *Peckin' Time;* not a lot of imagination went into the these records' original titles. There is only one previously unissued selection (the alternate take of "Barrel of Funk"), but two of the albums were only out previously in Japan, and most of the others had not been previously available on CD. Mobley, an underrated player with a distinctive sound (influenced at times by Sonny Rollins), would continue to grow as an improviser and composer throughout the 1960s, but even on his earliest date here, he is a strong (if unsung) soloist. Featured along with the leader are a who's-who of 1950s hard bop, including trumpeters Donald Byrd, Lee Morgan, Bill Hardman, Kenny Dorham and Art Farmer, pianists Horace Silver, Bobby Timmons, Sonny Clark and Wynton Kelly, vibraphonist Milt Jackson, bassist Doug Watkins, Paul Chambers, Wilbur Ware and Jimmy Rowser and drummers Art Blakey, Charlie Persip, Philly Joe Jones and Art Taylor. A must for Hank Mobley and 1950s Blue Note fans, but this deluxe box (released in 1998) promises to go out of print quickly. *—Scott Yanow*

The Jazz Message of Hank Mobley, Vol. 1 / Jan. 30, 1956 / Savoy ✦✦✦

Messages / Jul. 20, 1956-Jul. 27, 1956 / Prestige ✦✦✦✦
With the exception of Hank Mobley's original "Alternating Current," which was left out due to lack of space, this single CD has all of the music from the two Prestige LPs *Mobley's Message* and *Hank Mobley's Second Message;* a two-LP set from 1976 which had the same *Messages* title and catalog number, but also the complete program, is actually the preferred acquisition, but will be difficult to locate. The first session mostly features the fine tenor Hank Mobley jamming on four superior bop standards, including "Bouncing with Bud," "52nd Street Theme" and "Au Privavem" and his own "Minor Disturbance" in a quintet with trumpeter Donald Byrd, pianist Barry Harris, bassist Doug Watkins and drummer Art Taylor; altoist Jackie McLean has a strong cameo on "Au Privave." The second set, recorded a week later, is less of a jam session, with Mobley, trumpeter Kenny Dorham, pianist Walter Bishop, bassist Doug Watkins and drummer Art Taylor essaying three of Mobley's now-obscure compositions, Benny Harris's "Crazeology" and the standards "These Are the Things I Love" and "I Should Care." The two dates give one a good example of Hank Mobley's playing prior to becoming a regular Blue Note artist, where he would create his greatest work. *—Scott Yanow*

The Jazz Message of Hank Mobley, Vol. 2 / Jul. 23, 1956-Nov. 7, 1956 / Savoy ✦✦✦

Tenor Conclave / Sep. 7, 1956 / Prestige/OJC ✦✦✦

Hank Mobley and His All-Stars / Jan. 13, 1957 / Blue Note ✦✦✦✦

Hank Mobley Quintet / Mar. 9, 1957 / Blue Note ✦✦✦✦✦

Poppin' / Oct. 20, 1961 / Blue Note ✦✦✦✦
Poppin' was one of many sessions tenor saxophonist Hank Mobley recorded in the late '50s and early '60s but remained unreleased until the late '70s and '80s. It's hard to say why this album sat on the shelves, since it as good as the other records he cut at the time. Leading a sextet featuring trumpeter Art Farmer, baritone saxophonist Pepper Adams, pianist Sonny Clark, bassist Paul Chambers, and drummer Philly Joe Jones, Mobley plays a selection of five originals and contemporary jazz songs with passion and vigor. All of the musicians turn in fine performances (Clark in particular stands out with his lithe solos and tasteful accompaniment), and the result is a winning collection of straight-ahead hard bop that ranks as another solid addition to Mobley's strong catalog. *—Stephen Thomas Erlewine*

Peckin' Time / Feb. 9, 1958 / Blue Note ✦✦✦✦✦
Tenor saxophonist Hank Mobley, who throughout his career was overshadowed by more influential tenors such as Sonny Rollins and John Coltrane, was himself a talented and fairly original player and a fine composer; many of his originals deserve to be revived. For this Blue Note session, which in its CD reissue includes three alternate takes, Mobley, trumpeter Lee Morgan, pianist Wynton Kelly, bassist Paul Chambers and drummer Charlie Persip interpret four of the tenor's songs, including "High and Flighty" and the 12-minute "Gil-Go Blues," along with the standard "Speak Low." The results are high-quality hard bop, the modern mainstream of the era. *—Scott Yanow*

★ **Soul Station** / Feb. 7, 1960 / Blue Note ✦✦✦✦✦
Other than his 1955 debut for Blue Note, this set (reissued on CD) was tenor saxophonist Hank Mobley's first opportunity to record as leader of a quartet without any other competing horns. With the stimulating support of pianist Wynton Kelly, bassist Paul Chambers and drummer Art Blakey, Mobley is in peak form on four of his originals (of which "This I Dig of You" is best-known), "Remember" and the ballad "If I Should Lose You." Mobley's improvisations are melodic and thoughtful, yet always swinging and full of inner fire. This CD serves as a perfect introduction to the playing and writing abilities of this underrated talent. *—Scott Yanow*

Roll Call / Nov. 13, 1960 / Blue Note ✦✦✦✦✦
This set, reissued on CD, differs from tenor saxophonist Hank Mobley's *Soul Station* release of nine months earlier in that although he uses the same impressive rhythm section (pianist Wynton Kelly, bassist Paul Chambers, and drummer Art Blakey), Mobley also welcomes young trumpeter Freddie Hubbard. Hubbard actually steals the show on a few of the numbers, but since five of the pieces are Mobley originals, including such forgotten gems as "Roll Call," "My Groove Your Move," and "A Baptist Beat," the tenorman obviously set up this date partly as a way of featuring the fiery Hubbard. Art Blakey took note of the trumpeter's talents and hired him to replace Lee Morgan with the Jazz Messengers a year later. Overall, this is an excellent hard bop date and, as is true of all of Hank Mobley's Blue Note albums, it is easily recommended to fans of straight-ahead jazz. *—Scott Yanow*

Workout / Mar. 26, 1961 / Blue Note ✦✦✦✦✦
This is one of the best-known Hank Mobley recordings, and for good reason. Although none of his four originals ("Workout," "Uh Huh," "Smokin'," "Greasin' Easy") caught on, the fine saxophonist is in top form. He jams on the four tunes, plus "The Best Things in Life Are Free," with an all-star quintet of young modernists—guitarist Grant Green, pianist Wynton Kelly, bassist Paul Chambers and drummer Philly Joe Jones—and shows that he was a much stronger player than his then-current boss Miles Davis seemed to think. This recommended CD reissue adds a version of "Three Coins in the Fountain" from the same date, originally released on *Another Workout*, to the original LP program. *—Scott Yanow*

No Room for Squares / Mar. 7, 1963-Oct. 2, 1963 / Blue Note ✦✦✦✦
By 1963, Hank Mobley, whose tenor tone perfectly fit the hard bop modern mainstream music of the late '50s and early '60s, had altered his sound slightly to get a harder tone, influenced to an extent by John Coltrane. This CD reissue differs quite a bit from the original LP program, adding alternate takes of "No Room for Squares" and "Carolyn," along with two previously unissued selections ("Comin' Back" and "Syrup and Biscuits") while dropping two songs from the LP which were cut at a slightly earlier session. Mobley leads a top-notch quintet with trumpeter Lee Morgan, pianist Andrew Hill, bassist John Ore and drummer Philly Joe Jones through a set of high-quality, if obscure, originals written by either the leader or Morgan. The music is as satisfying and adventurous, as one would expect. *—Scott Yanow*

Straight No Filter / Jul. 7, 1963-Feb. 4, 1965 / Blue Note ✦✦✦✦✦
Straight No Filter finds tenor Hank Mobley in several settings from the mid-'60s, each of them excellent. The overall roster is quite impressive, starting with the first set which features trumpeter Lee Morgan, pianist McCoy Tyner, bassist Bob Cranshaw, and drummer Billy Higgins. The upbeat title cut is given a loose, \post-bop feel by Tyner's comping, but things are brought back to earth by Mobley's emotional playing. A number of exchanges between Morgan and Mobley's horns give the piece an effective ending. "Chain Reaction" gives this group nearly 11 minutes to stretch things out, while "Soft Impressions" features a heavy \blues groove. A couple of other standouts on this album—"This Feelin's Good" and "Yes Indeed"—feature trumpeter Donald Byrd, pianist Herbie Hancock, bassist Butch Warren, and drummer Philly Joe Jones. Hancock provides a distinctive backdrop for Mobley and Morgan's solos while turning in some fine work himself. Mobley shines on Sy Oliver's "Yes Indeed," delivering a soulful solo, shot through with the \blues. His playing throughout *Straight No Filter* is warm, accessible, and inventive, and it is instructive to have these sessions side by side, giving the listener a chance to compare Mobley's work in different settings. It should be mentioned that he penned eight out of the nine of these fine compositions. Bob Blumenthal's liner notes are helpful, breaking down the individual sessions and providing a good overview of Mobley's career. *Straight No Filter* will be welcomed by Mobley's fans and lovers of \hard bop. It shouldn't be missed. *—Ronnie Lankford, Jr.*

The Turnaround / Mar. 7, 1963-Feb. 5, 1965 / Blue Note ✦✦✦✦
The CD reissue of Hank Mobley's *The Turnaround* is different from the original LP in that two songs from a March 7, 1963, date were dropped, while two previously unissued ones from February 4, 1965, were added. Most intriguing about this quintet set with trumpeter Freddie Hubbard, pianist Barry Harris, bassist Paul Chambers, and drummer Billy Higgins are the six likable but complex Mobley compositions. A very underrated writer, many of Hank Mobley's originals deserve to be revived, including these six ("Pat 'N Chat," "Third Time Around," "Hank's Waltz," "The Turnaround," "Straight Ahead," and "My Sin"). Rather than stick to the standard 32-bar format heard on most pre-1970 songs, Mobley's pieces utilize choruses of 44, 20, and 50 bars while still sounding logical. All of the musicians play up to par on these advanced hard bop tunes. *—Scott Yanow*

Dippin' / Jun. 18, 1965 / Blue Note ✦✦✦✦✦
All of tenor saxophonist Hank Mobley's Blue Note recordings are recommended for his harmonically advanced, tricky, yet logical originals, in addition to consistently fine soloing from some of the top modern mainstream players of the era; these albums helped define the Blue

Note sound of the 1960s. For this date, a straight CD reissue of the original LP, Mobley, trumpeter Lee Morgan, pianist Harold Mabern, bassist Larry Ridley and drummer Billy Higgins perform four of the tenorman's originals, the highly appealing "Recado Bossa Nova" and the standard ballad "I See Your Face Before Me." An excellent outing, even if no "hits" resulted. *—Scott Yanow*

A Caddy for Daddy / Dec. 18, 1965 / Blue Note ✦✦✦✦
Hank Mobley was a perfect artist for Blue Note in the 1960s. A distinctive but not dominant soloist, Mobley was also a very talented writer whose compositions avoided the predictable, yet could often be quite melodic and soulful; his tricky originals consistently inspired the young all-stars in Blue Note's stable. For this CD, which is a straight reissue of a 1965 session, Mobley is joined by trumpeter Lee Morgan, trombonist Curtis Fuller, pianist McCoy Tyner, bassist Bob Cranshaw and drummer Billy Higgins (a typically remarkable Blue Note lineup) for the infectious title cut, three other lesser-known but superior originals, plus Wayne Shorter's "Venus Di Mildew." Recommended. *—Scott Yanow*

A Slice of the Top / Mar. 18, 1966 / Blue Note ✦✦✦✦✦
This is one of tenor saxophonist Hank Mobley's more intriguing sessions, for the talented composer had an opportunity to have four of his originals, plus the standard "There's a Lull in My Life," performed by an octet in the cool-toned style of Miles Davis's "Birth of the Cool" nonet, arranged by Duke Pearson. Although recorded in 1966, this date was not released until 1979 and unfortunately has not yet been reissued on CD. Mobley, who continued to evolve into a more advanced player throughout the 1960s, fits right in with such adventurous players as altoist James Spaulding, trumpeter Lee Morgan (with whom Mobley recorded frequently), pianist McCoy Tyner, bassist Reggie Workman and drummer Billy Higgins. The inclusion of Kiane Zawadi on euphonium and Howard Johnson on tuba adds a lot of color to this memorable outing. *—Scott Yanow*

Hi Voltage / Oct. 9, 1967 / Blue Note ✦✦✦✦
This is a typically enjoyable Hank Mobley date from the last great year of music from Blue Note, 1967. The talented tenor, who contributed all six compositions, is teamed with trumpeter Blue Mitchell, altoist Jackie McLean, pianist John Hicks, bassist Bob Cranshaw and drummer Billy Higgins (all Blue Note veterans except Hicks), and everyone plays up to par. The music sticks to advanced hard bop with hints of funk, bossa nova and modal tunes. Strange that none of these selections, which include the ballad "No More Goodbys," "Bossa De Luxe" and "Flirty Gerty," caught on. *—Scott Yanow*

Third Season / Feb. 24, 1967 / Blue Note ✦✦✦✦

Far Away Lands / May 26, 1967 / Blue Note ✦✦✦✦

Reach Out / Jan. 19, 1968 / Blue Note ✦✦

Thinking of Home / Jul. 31, 1970 / Blue Note ✦✦✦✦✦

The Modern Jazz Quartet

f. 1952
Group / Third Stream, Cool
Pianist John Lewis, vibraphonist Milt Jackson, bassist Ray Brown and drummer Kenny Clarke first came together as the rhythm section of the 1946 Dizzy Gillespie Orchestra and they had occasional features that gave the overworked brass players a well-deserved rest. They next came together in 1951, recording as the Milt Jackson Quartet. In 1952 with Percy Heath taking Brown's place, the Modern Jazz Quartet became a permanent group. Other than Connie Kay succeeding Clarke in 1955, the band's personnel was set. In the early days Jackson and Lewis both were equally responsible for the group's musical direction but the pianist eventually took over as musical director. The MJQ has long displayed Lewis's musical vision, making jazz seem respectable by occasionally interacting with classical ensembles and playing concerts at prestigious venues, but always leaving plenty of space for bluesy and swinging improvising. Their repertoire, in addition to including veteran bop and swing pieces, introduced such originals as Lewis' "Django" and Jackson's "Bags' Groove." *—Scott Yanow*

MJQ / Dec. 22, 1952-Jun. 16, 1954 / Prestige/OJC ✦✦✦✦
Two different groups are heard from on this CD reissue. The original Modern Jazz Quartet (with vibraphonist Milt Jackson, pianist John Lewis, bassist Percy Heath and drummer Kenny Clarke) performs four numbers at the first recording session of The MJQ. In addition there are four selections from a pickup group led by Jackson that also includes pianist Horace Silver and trumpeter Henry Boozier; the latter date introduced Silver's "Opus De Funk." Overall this somewhat brief CD has swinging music that bop fans will want to get. *—Scott Yanow*

MJQ: 40 Years / Dec. 22, 1952-Feb. 3, 1988 / Atlantic ✦✦✦✦✦
To celebrate The Modern Jazz Quartet's 40th anniversary as a group, Atlantic came out with an attractive four-CD box set that has selections (programmed in chronological order) that cover the group's long career. Most of the selections come from the Atlantic catalog although they have leased a few numbers owned by other labels and, with the exception of four songs from a Japanese concert and one previously unissued performance, all of the music is readily available elsewhere. But this well-conceived set serves as a perfect introduction for new listeners and as a fine retrospective of this important group's legacy. All of the best-known compositions are included and they find vibraphonist Milt Jackson, pianist John Lewis, bassist Percy Heath and drummer Connie Kay (along with a few notable guests) playing at their peak. *—Scott Yanow*

The Modern Jazz Quartet Plays Jazz Classics / Dec. 22, 1952-Jan. 9, 1955 / Prestige ✦✦✦✦✦
An early work that laid out the essence of The Modern Jazz Quartet, a unit that brought both jazz sensibility and classical precision to anything they played. This time they performed classical material with an improvisational backdrop, something that pianist John Lewis particularly loved. Vibist Milt Jackson also executed his parts smoothly, while bassist Percy Heath and drummer Connie Kay were consistently supportive and steady. *—Ron Wynn*

☆ **Django** / Jun. 25, 1953-Jan. 9, 1955 / Prestige/OJC ✦✦✦✦✦
Although it had recorded one prior session, The Modern Jazz Quartet really came into its own during the three dates that comprise this CD reissue. Highlights include the original versions of John Lewis's "Django," "Milano," "Delauney's Dilemma" and the four-part "La Ronde Suite." In addition to vibraphonist Milt Jackson, pianist John Lewis and bassist Percy Heath, these performances have the last studio appearances of drummer Kenny Clarke with the group. *—Scott Yanow*

Concorde / Jul. 2, 1955 / Prestige/OJC ✦✦✦✦
This CD reissue is most significant for having the first recordings of drummer Connie Kay as a regular member of The Modern Jazz Quartet. His subtle style fit in perfectly with vibraphonist Milt Jackson, bassist Percy Heath and pianist John Lewis. Highlights of this rather brief (around 33 minutes) CD are a four-song "Gershwin Medley," "Softly as in a Morning Sunrise" and "Ralph's New Blues." Excellent and somewhat historic music although the brevity of this set makes one wish that it were combined on CD with Prestige's other MJQ sessions. *—Scott Yanow*

Fontessa / Jan. 22, 1956-Feb. 14, 1956 / Atlantic ✦✦✦✦✦
This LP has a particularly strong all-around set by The Modern Jazz Quartet. While John Lewis' "Versailles" and an 11-minute "Fontessa" show the seriousness of the group (and the influence of Western classical music), other pieces (such as "Bluesology," "Woody'n You" and a pair of ballads) look toward the group's roots in bop and permit the band to swing hard. *—Scott Yanow*

The Modern Jazz Quartet with Sonny Rollins / Aug. 3, 1958-Sep. 3, 1958 / Atlantic ✦✦✦✦✦

Pyramid / Aug. 22, 1959-Jan. 15, 1960 / Atlantic ✦✦✦✦✦
This is a strong recording from The Modern Jazz Quartet with inventive versions of John Lewis's "Vendome," and Ray Brown's "Pyramid," Jim Hall's "Romaine," Lewis's famous "Django," and cooking jams on "How High the Moon" and "It Don't Mean a Thing." The MJQ had become a jazz institution by this time, but they never lost their creative edge, and their performances (even on the remakes) are quite stimulating, enthusiastic and fresh. *—Scott Yanow*

Odds Against Tomorrow / Oct. 9, 1959 / Blue Note ✦✦✦✦✦
The Modern Jazz Quartet never actually recorded for Blue Note but their United Artists date was reissued on this Blue Note CD. The MJQ (vibraphonist Milt Jackson, pianist John Lewis, bassist Percy Heath and drummer Connie Kay) perform six of Lewis's compositions which were used in the film *Odds Against Tomorrow*. Best known is "Skating in Central Park" but all of the selections have their memorable moments and it is good to hear this classic unit playing such fresh material. *—Scott Yanow*

Dedicated to Connie / May 27, 1960 / Atlantic ✦✦✦✦✦
After drummer Connie Kay passed away, this previously unreleased concert, recorded in Slovenia in 1960, was issued on a double CD and dedicated to him. The Modern Jazz Quartet (which also includes pianist John Lewis, vibraphonist Milt Jackson and bassist Percy Heath) is heard in surprisingly inspired form playing their usual repertoire of the time. Highlights include a 23-minute medley of John Lewis compositions, "Bag's Groove," "It Don't Mean A Thing," "Django," "How High The Moon" and "Skating In Central Park." Lewis has stated that the group never played better than during this concert. Although that statement is debatable, the MJQ certainly sounds in prime form throughout the easily recommended release. *—Scott Yanow*

★ **Lonely Woman** / Jan. 24, 1962-Feb. 2, 1962 / Atlantic ✦✦✦✦✦
Having sponsored Ornette Coleman at the School of Jazz near Lennox, MA, pianist and composer John Lewis helped launch the controversial career of one of the last great innovators in jazz. Lewis' support of the ragtag Texas native was somewhat unique in jazz circles at the time and even surprising, especially considering the gulf between the classical jazz formality of his group the Modern Jazz Quartet and Coleman's radical notions of free improvisation. Nevertheless, Lewis not only saw in Coleman the first jazz genius since bebop's Parker, Gillespie, and Monk, but put pay to the praise with the MJQ's 1962 rendition of one of Coleman's most famous numbers, "Lonely Woman." (Along with Art Pepper's 1960 version of "Tears Inside," this was one of the earliest of Coleman covers done.) The 1962 Atlantic album of the same name turns out to be one of the band's best efforts. Lewis and fellow MJQ members Milt Jackson, Percy Heath, and Connie Kaye capitalize on the dramatic theme of "Lonely Woman" while adding a bit of chamber music complexity to the mix. The quartet doesn't take Coleman's free form harmolodic theory to heart with a round of quixotic solos, but the group does spotlight the often overlooked strength of his compositional ideas. And while the MJQ further plies its knack for involved pieces on Lewis originals like "Fugato" and "Trieste," the group also balances out the set with looser material more in tune with Jackson's blues and swing sensibilities. A great disc that's perfect for the curious jazz lover. *—Stephen Cook*

Blues on Bach / Nov. 26, 1973-Nov. 27, 1973 / Atlantic ✦✦✦✦
This album has an interesting concept, alternating four original blues with five adaptations of melodies from classical works by Bach. The Modern Jazz Quartet had long been quite adept in both areas and, despite a certain lack of variety on this set (alternating back and forth between the two styles somewhat predictably), the music is largely enjoyable. Vibraphonist Milt Jackson, pianist John Lewis (doubling here on harpsichord), bassist Percy Heath and drummer Connie Kay were still all very much in their musical prime during the 21st year of The MJQ's existence. *—Scott Yanow*

★ **The Last Concert** / Nov. 25, 1974 / Atlantic ✦✦✦✦✦
The Modern Jazz Quartet broke up after the concert documented on this double CD. It would be nearly seven years before the group got back together again but it certainly went out on top. Mostly revisiting their greatest hits, the MJQ is heard on this two-fer playing inspired versions of such songs as "Softly As in a Morning Sunrise," "Bags' Groove," "Skating in Central Park," "Confirmation," "The Golden Striker," and, of course, "Django." This set is a real gem (the music is essential for all serious jazz collections), featuring vibraphonist Milt Jackson, pianist John Lewis, bassist Percy Heath, and drummer Connie Kay at their very best. *—Scott Yanow*

Echoes / Mar. 6, 1984 / Pablo ♦♦♦♦♦
If proof were needed that The Modern Jazz Quartet was back together permanently after a seven-year hiatus (1974-81), it is this CD for the six selections were all fairly new (as opposed to more runthroughs of their earlier hits). Pianist John Lewis contributed three compositions (including the appealing "That Slavic Smile" and "Sacha's March"), vibraphonist Milt Jackson wrote two and bassist Percy Heath brought in his lighthearted "Watergate Blues." With drummer Connie Kay as usual rounding out the group, The MJQ's return was one of the happiest events in jazz of the 1980s. *— Scott Yanow*

Celebration / Jun. 17, 1992-Jul. 16, 1993 / Atlantic ♦♦♦♦♦
As part of their 40th anniversary, The Modern Jazz Quartet welcomed ten guest artists to their CD: Bobby McFerrin (brilliant on "Billie's Bounce"), Take Six, Phil Woods, Wynton Marsalis (who gets to show off his technique on "Cherokee"), Illinois Jacquet, Harry "Sweets" Edison, Branford Marsalis, Jimmy Heath, Freddie Hubbard and Nina Tempo. As usual vibraphonist Milt Jackson and pianist John Lewis also have plenty of solo space and bassist Percy Heath is perfect in support. Since drummer Connie Kay was ailing in 1992 (but back in action the following year), Mickey Roker fills in on seven of the 13 selections. With the exception of "Django" (which features Phil Woods), and "Bags' Groove," the music sticks to bop standards rather than MJQ standbys. It's an enjoyable and varied set. *— Scott Yanow*

Grachan Moncur III

b. Jun. 3, 1937, New York
Trombone / Avant-Garde Jazz, Free Jazz
One of the first trombonists to explore free jazz, Grachan Moncur III is still best-known for his pair of innovative Blue Note albums (1963-64) which also featured Lee Morgan and Jackie McLean on the first session and Wayne Shorter and Herbie Hancock on the later date. The son of bassist Grachan Moncur II who played with the Savoy Sultans during 1937-45, Grachan III started on trombone when he was 11. He toured with Ray Charles (1959-62) was with the Jazztet (1962) and in 1963 played advanced jazz with Jackie McLean. Moncur toured with Sonny Rollins (1964) and played and recorded with Marion Brown, Joe Henderson and Archie Shepp, matching up with fellow trombonist Roswell Rudd in the latter group. He also was part of the cooperative band 360 Degree Music Experience with Beaver Harris. Grachan Moncur, who has also recorded as a leader for BYG (1969) and JCOA (1974), has continued playing challenging music up to the present day and has been an educator. Some of his more recent associations have been with Frank Lowe (1984-85), Cassandra Wilson (1985) and the Paris Reunion Band. *— Scott Yanow*

Evolution / Nov. 21, 1963 / Blue Note ♦♦♦♦♦
Trombonist Grachan Moncur III's debut as a leader is a little ironic now, since he is no longer as well-known as his sidemen: trumpeter Lee Morgan, altoist Jackie McLean, vibraphonist Bobby Hutcherson, bassist Bob Cranshaw and drummer Tony Williams. However, Moncur contributed the four originals (including one called "Monk In Wonderland"), plays brilliantly, and sets the tone and moods for this often swinging but exploratory avant-garde set. Well worth several listens. *— Scott Yanow*

● **Some Other Stuff** / Jul. 6, 1964 / Blue Note ♦♦♦♦♦
Grachan Moncur III was one of the top trombonists of the jazz avant-garde in the 1960s although he had only a few chances to lead his own record sessions. This 1964 set (which has been reissued on CD) was one of his finest, a quintet outing with bassist Cecil McBee, two of the members of the Miles Davis Quintet (pianist Herbie Hancock and drummer Tony Williams), and tenor saxophonist Wayne Shorter just a brief time before he joined Miles. The group performs four of Moncur's challenging originals, including "Nomadic" (which is largely a drum solo) and "The Twins," which is built off of one chord. None of the compositions caught on but the strong and very individual improvising of the young musicians is enough of a reason to acquire the advanced music. *— Scott Yanow*

T.S. Monk (Thelonious Monk, Jr.)

b. Dec. 27, 1949, New York, NY
Drums / Hard Bop, Post-Bop
Although it took him a while before he decided to dedicate himself to playing jazz, T.S. Monk (Thelonious Monk, Jr.) has already accomplished a lot. He started out playing trumpet, and piano before switching to drums when he was 13, taking some lessons from Max Roach. His first public performance was with his father Thelonious Monk on a television show in 1970. He toured with his father's quartet during 1970-71 and then played with the fusion band Natural Essence, the Paul Jeffrey Big Band and had an R&B group called T.S. Monk that had a few hits. In 1986 he established the Thelonious Monk Institute of Jazz, an organization that not only celebrates Monk, Sr.'s music but has an annual competition that has resulted in fame for some of its winners. His work with the Institute inspired the drummer to return to jazz. He played in Clifford Jordan's big band and with Walter Davis before putting together his own sextet which has had stable personnel since the late '80s. Monk's group often performs obscure jazz originals from the 1960s hard bop era with accurate transcriptions contributed by its trumpeter/arranger Don Sickler. Monk himself is an excellent drummer who sounds a little reminiscent of Tony Williams. *— Scott Yanow*

● **The Charm** / 1995 / Blue Note ♦♦♦♦♦
T.S. Monk, by successfully keeping his sextet together as a regularly working outfit for several years, has been able to form a recognizable group sound in the hard bop tradition. Trumpeter Don Sickler's skills at transcribing charts from records has been a major asset and the band's emphasis of obscurities has resulted in a very fresh repertoire; certainly Buddy Montgomery's "Budini," Melba Liston's "Just Waiting," and even Walter Davis Jr.'s "Gypsy Folk Tales" would never qualify as standards. In addition to the older material (which includes an offbeat version of Thelonious Monk's "Bolivar Blues"), pianist Ronnie Mathews and altoist Bobby Porcelli have contributed newer pieces that fit the group's style. Although sometimes overlooked, T.S. Monk's sextet (which also includes Willie Williams on tenor and soprano and bassist Scott Colley) has no weak links and is one of the most consistently satisfying jazz groups from the mid-'90s. Their fine disc is easily recommended. *— Scott Yanow*

Monk on Monk / Feb. 6, 1997-Feb. 27, 1997 / N2K ♦♦♦♦♦
To celebrate what would have been his father Thelonious Monk's 80th birthday, drummer T.S. Monk put together an all-star group (an expanded version of his sextet) and toured, performing an all-Thelonious program. Just prior to the beginning of the live performances, T.S. and his band recorded this CD. The music is excellent, but there are so many guest artists making cameo appearances (including trumpeters Roy Hargrove, Clark Terry, Arturo Sandoval and Wallace Roney, Wayne Shorter on soprano, tenors Grover Washington Jr. and Jimmy Heath, pianists Herbie Hancock and Geri Allen, bassists Ron Carter, Christian McBride and Dave Holland and singers Dianne Reeves and Kevin Mahogany) that one never really gets to hear Monk's band very much. Considering that T.S.'s unit includes altoist Bobby Watson and singer Nnenna Freelon (both of whom are only heard from briefly), it is a pity that he opted for so many unnecessary guests. There are good versions of such tunes as "Little Rootie Tootie" (which has a very effective Grover Washington Jr. tenor solo), "Crepuscule With Nellie" (one of the few renditions of a band actually stretching out on this theme), and "Bright Mississippi," plus the debut of a recently discovered Monk composition ("Two Timer"), so this set is recommended. But one is left looking forward to hearing the actual T.S. Monk ensemble interpret the songs. *— Scott Yanow*

Cross Talk / May 18, 1999 / N2K ♦♦♦♦
Drummer Monk's follow-up to the 1998 Jazz CD of the Year *Monk on Monk* is a departure from both that album and his previous pop-funk efforts. Playing Roland V-10 electric drums and additional acoustic percussion, Monk and arranger Don Sickler are striving for a different sound, which they largely achieve. Diversity is the password, as the two avoid getting stuck in ruts or etched in stone, while using jazz foundations to create organs of woodwind- and brass-fired beauty, tastefully triggered by percussion. The middle of the CD really defines their sound; Donald Brown's "Smile of the Snake" has a broader, slyer grin than the original version, and is much faster and funkier. The James Williams piece "A Touching Affair" sports a tabla and funk-lite sound that would please Creed Taylor. (Note: ex-Jazz Messengers Brown and Williams are pianists—not on this session—from Memphis.) Highlights include the hard-bopping "Squeaky Clean" and the simply gorgeous horns on the aforementioned "Heart" and the Jazz Messenger-ish "A Chant for Bu." The CD goes out with a bang on the title track, inexorably funky but with as potent and punchy a horn chart as you'll hear—fully realized, deliberate, jazzy. Saxophonists Willie Williams and Bobby Porcelli are outstanding throughout, especially when they play together. Sickler, in his double duty as arranger and trumpeter, is quite innovative and dependable. Monk made a bold move in doing a recording such as this, and we should appreciate that he did it his way. *— Michael G. Nastos*

Thelonious Monk

b. Oct. 10, 1917, Rocky Mount, NC, **d.** Feb. 17, 1982, Weehawken, NJ
Piano, Composer / Modal Music, Hard Bop, Post-Bop, Bop
The most important jazz musicians are the ones who are successful in creating their own original world of music with its own rules, logic and surprises. Thelonious Monk, who was criticized by observers who failed to listen to his music on its own terms, suffered through a decade of neglect before he was suddenly acclaimed as a genius; his music had not changed one bit in the interim. In fact, one of the more remarkable aspects of Monk's music was that it was fully formed by 1947 and he saw no need to alter his playing or compositional style in the slightest during the next 25 years. It was when he became Coleman Hawkins's regular pianist that Monk was initially noticed. He cut a few titles with Hawkins (his recording debut) and, although some of Hawkins's fans complained about the eccentric pianist, the veteran tenor could sense the pianist's greatness.The 1945-54 period was very difficult for Monk. Because he left a lot of space in his rhythmic solos and had an unusual technique, many people thought that he was an inferior pianist. His compositions were so advanced that the lazier bebop players (although not Dizzy Gillespie and Charlie Parker) assumed that he was crazy. And Monk's name, appearance (he liked funny hats) and personality (an occasionally uncommunicative introvert) helped to brand him as some kind of nut. Fortunately Alfred Lion of Blue Note believed in him and recorded Monk extensively during 1947-48 and 1951-52. His fortunes slowly began to improve. In 1955 he signed with Riverside and producer Orrin Keepnews persuaded him to record an album of Duke Ellington tunes and one of standards so his music would appear to be more accessible to the average jazz fan. In 1956 came the classic *Brilliant Corners* album but it was the following year when the situation permanently changed. Monk was booked into the Five Spot for a long engagement and he used a quartet that featured tenor-saxophonist John Coltrane. Finally the critics and then the jazz public recognized Thelonious Monk's greatness during this important gig. *— Scott Yanow*

☆ **The Complete Blue Note Recordings** / Oct. 15, 1947-Apr. 14, 1957 / Mosaic ♦♦♦♦♦
Shortly after Mosaic's limited-edition four-LP box set of pianist/composer Thelonious Monk's Blue Note recordings ran out of stock, Blue Note reissued Monk's entire output plus his recently discovered 1958 live performance with John Coltrane on this four-CD package. The music is unique, highly influential and timeless. Monk did not record all that often for Blue Note during 1947-52 (six sessions) but the number of classics is quite impressive: "Ruby My Dear," "Well You Needn't," "Off Minor," "In Walked Bud," "'Round Midnight," "Evidence," "Misterioso," "Epistrophy," "I Mean You," "Four in One," "Criss Cross," "Straight No Chaser," and "Ask Me Now." Add to that his two appearances on a 1957 Sonny Rollins date along with the remarkable Coltrane session and the result is a set that should be in every jazz collection. *— Scott Yanow*

Genius of Modern Music, Vol. 1 / Oct. 15, 1947-Nov. 21, 1947 / Blue Note ♦♦♦♦♦

Genius of Modern Music, Vol. 2 / Jul. 23, 1951-May 30, 1952 / Blue Note ♦♦♦♦♦

Thelonious Monk Trio / Oct. 15, 1952-Sep. 22, 1954 / Prestige/OJC ♦♦♦♦♦
Half of Thelonious Monk's Prestige recordings are reissued on this CD in the Original Jazz

Classics series. With either Percy Heath or Gary Mapp on bass and Art Blakey or Max Roach on drums, Monk introduces such compositions as "Little Rootie Tootie," "Bye-Ya," "Monk's Dream," "Twinkle Tinkle," "Bemsha Swing" and "Reflections." Although Monk was suffering from lack of work and a complete lack of recognition from the public, his music was virtually the same as it would be five years later when he was suddenly "discovered." Brilliant performances. *— Scott Yanow*

Monk / Nov. 13, 1953-May 11, 1954 / Prestige/OJC ♦♦♦♦
Thelonious Monk's Prestige recordings (reissued on three LP-length CDs) have been somewhat neglected through the years but, with the exception of a date for Vogue, they are the only documentation that exists of the unique pianist-composer's work as a leader during the latter half of 1952 through 1954. This set has four numbers (including Monk's originals "Wee See," "Locomotive" and the catchy "Hackensack") featuring Monk with trumpeter Ray Copeland (an underrated player), tenor saxophonist Frank Foster, bassist Curly Russell and drummer Art Blakey. However it is "Let's Call This" and the two versions of "Think of One" that are best-known, for Monk teams up with the French horn wizard Julius Watkins, bassist Percy Heath, drummer Willie Jones and the great tenor Sonny Rollins. Every Thelonious Monk recording is well worth getting although this one is not quite essential. *— Scott Yanow*

Thelonious Monk & Sonny Rollins / Nov. 13, 1953-Oct. 25, 1954 / Prestige/OJC ♦♦♦♦
This CD wraps up Thelonious Monk's recordings for Prestige and makes a fine complement to the OJC CDs *Monk* and *Thelonious Monk Trio*. Tenor saxophonist Sonny Rollins (in exuberant form) gets co-billing, and two of the songs ("The Way You Look Tonight" and "I Want to Be Happy") are actually from his own Prestige date; Monk was not a sideman for just anyone. The original version of "Friday the 13th" (which features Rollins and the French horn of Julius Watkins) and trio renditions (with bassist Percy Heath and drummer Art Blakey) of Monk's compositions "Work" and "Nutty" are also included on this excellent release. [A 20-bit remaster of *Thelonious Monk & Sonny Rollins* was released in October 1999.] *— Scott Yanow*

☆ **Complete Black Lion and Vogue** / Jun. 7, 1954-Nov. 15, 1971 / Mosaic ♦♦♦♦♦
This four-LP limited-edition box set from Mosaic contains the nine piano solos recorded by Thelonious Monk while in Paris on June 7, 1954 (most of which have also been issued by GNP Crescendo), and, more importantly, his complete marathon London session of November 15, 1971. The latter, split between solo and trio performances (with bassist Al McKibbon and drummer Art Blakey), was (other than a record with the Giants of Jazz) Monk's final recording and found the unique pianist in brilliant form, really romping on some of his solos. Although the majority of the songs are his originals, the emphasis on this essential music is on the piano playing. Those critics and listeners who feel that Monk was a limited musician should give these final performances a very close listen. *— Scott Yanow*

☆ **The Complete Riverside Recordings** / Jul. 21, 1955-Apr. 21, 1961 / Riverside ♦♦♦♦♦
Although this 15-CD box set is not inexpensive, this is the most essential of all of Thelonious Monk's releases. It was during his years with Riverside that Monk achieved the fame he had long deserved. Producer Orrin Keepnews was wise enough to feature the unique pianist/composer in a wide variety of settings and they are all here: separate trio sessions comprised of Duke Ellington songs and standards, meetings on record with Sonny Rollins (including "Brilliant Corners"), John Coltrane, Coleman Hawkins, Gerry Mulligan and Johnny Griffin, the beginnings of Monk's Quartet with Charlie Rouse, a truncated (and previously unissued) session with Shelly Manne, Monk's famous Town Hall concert of 1959 and a full date of unaccompanied piano solos. Most of this music has also been made available on Milestone two-LP sets and single CDs but this is the best (and most complete) way to acquire these classics. *— Scott Yanow*

Plays Duke Ellington / Jul. 21, 1955-Jul. 27, 1955 / Riverside/OJC ♦♦♦♦♦
For Thelonious Monk's Riverside debut, producer Orrin Keepnews decided that it would be best to make the somewhat forbidding pianist-composer seem a bit more accessible to the jazz world. Rather than have Monk play his own complex originals, this time around the pianist (in a trio with bassist Oscar Pettiford and drummer Kenny Clarke) interpreted eight Duke Ellington compositions. The results are very interesting with Monk bringing out new angles and ideas to such songs as "Mood Indigo," "Caravan," "It Don't Mean a Thing" and "Sophisticated Lady." A special highlight is an eerie investigation of "Black and Tan Fantasy." This CD reissue (whose music is also on Thelonious Monk's huge Riverside box) is recommended. *— Scott Yanow*

Straight, No Chaser: Thelonious Monk / Sep. 1956-1968 / Columbia ♦♦♦♦

★ **Brilliant Corners** / Dec. 17, 1956-Dec. 23, 1956 / Riverside/OJC ♦♦♦♦♦
Thelonious Monk's classic third recording for Riverside (which has been reissued on CD in the OJC series) features five of his originals. The impossible-to-play "Brilliant Corners" finds the pianist in an all-star quintet with tenor saxophonist Sonny Rollins (who co-stars), altoist Ernie Henry, bassist Oscar Pettiford and drummer Max Roach. They also investigate Monk's "Pannonica" (which has the pianist doubling on celeste) and the eccentric "Ba-lu Bolivar Ba-Lues-Are." In addition, Monk plays "I Surrender Dear" unaccompanied, and there is a swinging version of "Bemsha Swing" from the earlier session with Rollins, Roach, bassist Paul Chambers and the pleasant trumpet of Clark Terry. All of the music on this LP-length CD is also available as part of Thelonious Monk's huge *Complete on Riverside* box set. *— Scott Yanow*

Thelonious Himself / Apr. 5, 1957-Apr. 16, 1957 / Riverside/OJC ♦♦♦♦
This OJC CD reissues a mostly-solo set by pianist Thelonious Monk. Monk's hesitant stride and thoughtful yet very unpredictable flights are always a joy to hear. He performs a variety of swing standards (including "April in Paris" and "I'm Getting Sentimental over You"), his blues "Functional" and as a "bonus" track there is an alternate take of "'Round Midnight" from the earlier date. The one non-solo track is "Monk's Mood," a ballad that finds Monk joined by tenor saxophonist John Coltrane and bassist Wilbur Ware. The overall results are not quite essential but they should greatly interest Thelonious Monk fans who do not have his huge Riverside box set. *— Scott Yanow*

Art Blakey's Jazz Messengers with Thelonious Monk / May 14, 1957-May 15, 1957 / Atlantic ♦♦♦♦♦
Thelonious Monk rarely performed or recorded as a sideman, making this Atlantic CD reissue on which he shares co-billing with drummer Art Blakey a rare event. Monk sounds quite comfortable sitting in with the 1957 version of The Jazz Messengers; in fact tenor-saxophonist Johnny Griffin would soon join his own quartet. The Messengers (which also includes trumpeter Bill Hardman and bassist Spanky DeBrest) perform fine versions of five Monk compositions and Griffin's "Purple Shades." *— Scott Yanow*

☆ **Monk's Music** / Jun. 25, 1957-Jun. 26, 1957 / Riverside/OJC ♦♦♦♦♦
This CD reissue has a unique session in which pianist Thelonious Monk heads quite an all-star group: tenors John Coltrane and Coleman Hawkins, altoist Gigi Gryce, trumpeter Ray Copeland, bassist Wilbur Ware and drummer Art Blakey. The only time that Coltrane and Hawkins recorded together, the date is highlighted by a lengthy version of "Well You Needn't" that finds both tenors in top form (even if Monk has to shout out Coltrane's name at one point to get his attention). Hawkins is showcased on a tender rendition of "Ruby, My Dear" and three alternate takes help extend the time of the CD. *— Scott Yanow*

☆ **Thelonious with John Coltrane** / Jun. 25, 1957-Jul. 1957 / Riverside/OJC ♦♦♦♦♦
Thelonious Monk finally came to fame in the summer of 1957 when he performed regularly with his quartet (featuring the tenor of John Coltrane) at the Five Spot. Unfortunately the Monk-Coltrane musical partnership was not extensively documented but this CD reissue includes three brilliant recordings with a quartet also including bassist Wilbur Ware and drummer Shadow Wilson: "Ruby My Dear," "Trinkle Tinkle" and "Nutty." Trane perfectly fit into Monk's music and it was a mutually beneficial relationship. Also on the CD is a Monk piano solo on "Functional" and alternate takes of "Off Minor" and "Epistrophy" that match together Monk, Coltrane, the veteran tenor Coleman Hawkins, altoist Gigi Gryce and trumpeter Ray Copeland. Highly recommended, particularly for the quartet tracks, although true Monk collectors should acquire his huge Riverside box set instead. *— Scott Yanow*

Discovery! Live at the Five Spot / 1957 / Blue Note ♦♦♦♦♦
The collaboration between pianist Thelonious Monk and tenor saxophonist John Coltrane was considered (along with the 1943 Earl Hines big band with Charlie Parker and Dizzy Gillespie and the music of the pioneering jazz cornetist Buddy Bolden) to be one of the three lost wonders of jazz history. Although they recorded a trio of quartet numbers in the studios (which are included in various Milestone and Riverside reissues), there was apparently no documentation of their lengthy gig at *the Five Spot* in 1957, until a tape that Coltrane's wife had recorded was recently discovered. This CD has the results, five songs performed by Monk, Coltrane, bassist Ahmed Abdul-Malik and drummer Roy Haynes at *the Five Spot*. High points of this somewhat miraculous find include "Trinkle Tinkle," "In Walked Bud" and "I Mean You"; there are also shorter versions of "Epistrophy" and "Crepuscule With Nellie." *— Scott Yanow*

Misterioso / Aug. 7, 1958 / Riverside/OJC ♦♦♦♦♦
Tenor saxophonist Johnny Griffin's hard-driving style perfectly fit pianist-composer Thelonious Monk's music and their 1958 quartet (with bassist Ahmed Abdul-Malik and drummer Roy Haynes) was well documented during one night at the Five Spot Cafe; a second CD (*Thelonious in Action*) is taken from the same evening. Of the two releases, this one gets the edge due to Griffin's memorable improvising on a heated version of "In Walked Bud." Other highpoints include "Nutty," "Let's Cool One" and "Evidence." *— Scott Yanow*

Thelonious in Action: Recorded at the Five Spot Cafe / Aug. 7, 1958 / Riverside/OJC ♦♦♦♦♦
One of the most exciting groups that pianist-composer Thelonious Monk ever led was his 1958 quartet with tenor saxophonist Johnny Griffin, bassist Ahmed Abdul-Malik and drummer Roy Haynes. During one night at *the Five Spot Cafe* they recorded enough music to fill up two CDs; all of the performances are also on Monk's large Riverside box set. *In Action*, a companion to *Misterioso*, shows that Griffin was possibly even a more perfect sideman for Monk than John Coltrane had been the year before. Highlights include "Rhythm-A-Ning," "Blue Monk," "Evidence" and "Blues Five Spot." *— Scott Yanow*

☆ **The Thelonious Monk Orchestra at Town Hall** / Feb. 28, 1959 / Riverside/OJC ♦♦♦♦♦
Pianist Thelonious Monk's appearance with a tentet at a 1959 Town Hall concert was a major success. With Hal Overton contributing arrangements of Monk's tunes (including a remarkable transcription of Monk's original piano solo on "Little Rootie Tootie") and solos provided by trumpeter Donald Byrd, trombonist Eddie Bert, altoist Phil Woods, Charlie Rouse on tenor and baritonist Pepper Adams, this date was a real standout. The program (plus three additional numbers) has also been included in Monk's huge Riverside box set but, for more budget-minded consumers, this CD is a must. There would only be one other recorded occasion (Thelonious Monk's 1963 Philharmonic Hall concert) when the unique pianist was as successfully featured with a larger ensemble. *— Scott Yanow*

Five by Monk by Five / Jun. 1, 1959-Jun. 2, 1959 / Riverside/OJC ♦♦♦♦
The title on this CD reissue refers to the fact that five musicians perform five Thelonious Monk compositions. In addition to the five titles ("Straight No Chaser," "Jackie-ing," "Played Twice," "I Mean You" and "Ask Me Now") there are two "bonus cuts" (alternate versions of "Played Twice." This was one of tenor saxophonist Charlie Rouse's first sessions with Monk (he would be his regular tenor soloists for the next decade) and gave cornetist Thad Jones a rare chance to play with the unique pianist-composer; his style fit right in. *— Scott Yanow*

Alone in San Francisco / Oct. 21, 1959-Oct. 22, 1959 / Riverside/OJC ♦♦♦♦♦
This CD reissue brings back one of Thelonious Monk's best solo piano sessions. Monk's sparse style and hesitating stride were quite distinctive and his chord voicings (even when playing a conventional triad) always sounded quite unique. In addition to such originals as "Pannonica," "Ruby, My Dear" and "Blue Monk," Monk has off-the-wall interpretations of "You Took the Words Right Out of My Heart" and two versions of the obscure "There's Danger in Your Eyes, Cherie." Recommended. *— Scott Yanow*

At the Blackhawk / Apr. 29, 1960 / Riverside/OJC ♦♦♦♦
Thelonious Monk's 1960 quartet (which also includes tenor saxophonist Charlie Rouse,

bassist John Ore and (for a brief period) drummer Billy Higgins is augmented on this live session by two guests: trumpeter Joe Gordon and the tenor of Harold Land. The extra horns uplift the date and add some surprising moments to what otherwise might have been a conventional but still spirited live session. Highlights include "Let's Call This," "Four in One" and a swinging version of "I'm Getting Sentimental over You." *—Scott Yanow*

★ **Monk's Dream** / Oct. 31, 1962-Nov. 6, 1962 / Columbia ✦✦✦✦✦
Most of Thelonious Monk's recordings for Columbia featured his regular working quartet which at the time of his debut consisted of tenor-saxophonist Charlie Rouse, bassist John Ore and drummer Frankie Dunlop. The music on this recording is fairly typical of his repertoire of the period, five originals (only "Bright Mississippi" had not been recorded before) and three standards, two of which are taken as brief piano solos. However despite a certain amount of predictability, the playing is consistently excellent and enthusiastic; even if the jazz world was starting to catch up to Monk, his highly original music stood on its own merits. *—Scott Yanow*

The Composer / Nov. 6, 1962-Nov. 20, 1968 / Columbia ✦✦✦

Criss-Cross / Nov. 6, 1962-Mar. 29, 1963 / Columbia ✦✦✦✦✦
This CD reissue of the Columbia LP adds a previously unissued version of "Pannonica" to the original program along with updated liner notes. The high-quality repertoire (which includes "Hackensack," "Tea for Two," "Criss-Cross" and "Rhythm-A-Ning") and some consistent solos from the leader/pianist and tenor-saxophonist Charlie Rouse make this a CD worth picking up. *—Scott Yanow*

☆ **Big Band and Quartet in Concert** / Dec. 30, 1963 / Columbia ✦✦✦✦✦
This is one of pianist-composer Thelonious Monk's greatest recordings and represents a highpoint in his career. Performing at *Philharmonic Hall* in New York, Monk is heard taking an unaccompanied solo on "Darkness on the Delta" and jamming with his quartet (which had Charlie Rouse on tenor, bassist Butch Warren and drummer Frank Dunlop) on fine versions of "Played Twice" and a previously unreleased rendition of "Misterioso." However this two-CD set has its most memorable moments during the six full-length performances by a ten-piece group. Monk's quartet was joined by cornetist Thad Jones, trumpeter Nick Travis, Steve Lacy on soprano, altoist Phil Woods, baritonist Gene Allen and trombonist Eddie Bert. Jones and Woods have plenty of solos and, although Lacy surprisingly does not have any individual spots, his soprano is a major part of some of the ensembles. Most remarkable is "Four in One" which after one of Monk's happiest (and very rhythmic) solos features the orchestra playing a Hal Overton transcription of a complex and rather exuberant Monk solo taken from his original record. This two-CD set is a gem and can be considered essential for all jazz collections. *—Scott Yanow*

Solo Monk / Oct. 31, 1964-Feb. 23, 1965 / Columbia ✦✦✦✦✦
One of Thelonious Monk's more delightful solo piano sets, this CD reissue (which adds a previously unreleased version of "Introspection" to the original twelve-song program) has many memorable moments. "Dinah" is given a heated yet sparse stride, "I'm Confessin'" is heard in a charming version and Monk originals "Ruby, My Dear" and the beautiful "Ask Me Now" hold their own with such veteran tunes as "I Surrender Dear" and "I Hadn't Anyone Till You." A highly enjoyable yet thought-provoking set of music that was performed with a liberal dose of humor. *—Scott Yanow*

Straight, No Chaser / Nov. 14, 1966-Jan. 10, 1967 / Columbia/Legacy ✦✦✦✦
By 1967, Thelonious Monk was being criticized by the jazz press for getting a bit stale, using the same personnel and performing the same songs as he had for the past few years. In reality, Monk was still able to bring vitality to his performances despite some predictability. This album includes some warhorses ("Straight, No Chaser," "I Didn't Know About You," and a solo piano version of "Between the Devil and the Deep Blue Sea") along with "Japanese Folk Song" and the pianist's lesser-played originals "Locomotive" and "We See." Monk and tenor saxophonist Charlie Rouse (who are ably supported by bassist Larry Gales and drummer Ben Riley) take consistently fine solos throughout the Columbia set. *—Scott Yanow*

Underground / Dec. 14, 1967-Feb. 14, 1968 / Columbia ✦✦✦✦✦
This album has a remarkable photo of Thelonious Monk on its cover in which the eccentric pianist-composer is depicted in a colorful setting as a French resistance fighter circa World War II; it has to be seen to be fully appreciated. On his next-to-last Columbia album (and final quartet album with his longtime tenor Charlie Rouse) Monk plays some very interesting material including such originals as "Ugly Beauty," "Green Chimneys," "Raised Fourth" and "Boo Boo's Birthday." A special treat is vocalist Jon Hendricks' guest spot singing his own words to "In Walked Bud." *—Scott Yanow*

Monk's Blues / Nov. 19, 1968-Nov. 20, 1968 / Columbia ✦✦

Live at the It Club: Complete / Oct. 31, 1964-Nov. 1, 1964 / Columbia/Legacy ✦✦✦✦✦
In 1998, Columbia/Legacy reissued Thelonious Monk's 1964 album *Live at the It Club* as a double-disc set that contained all of his performances from that night. In many respects, the set was an entirely new album. Three songs—"Teo," "Bright Mississippi," "Just You, Just Me"—were previously unreleased, and nine others were restored to their full length after previously being released in edited forms ("Blue Monk," "Well, You Needn't," "Rhythm-a-Ning," "Blues Five Spot," "Bemsha Swing," "Evidence," "Nutty," "Epistrophy [Theme]," "Straight, No Chaser," "I'm Getting Sentimental Over You," "Ba-lue Bolivar Ba-lues-are"). Although the set isn't exactly seminal, it nevertheless is highly enjoyable, capturing Monk in a relaxed small-group setting with Charlie Rouse, Larry Gales, and Ben Riley. *—Stephen Thomas Erlewine*

Monk Alone: The Complete Columbia Solo Studio Recordings: 1962-1968 / Nov. 1, 1962-Nov. 19, 1968 / Columbia/Legacy ✦✦✦✦✦
As any Monk aficionado knows, his solo piano performances were wonderful, idiosyncratic, living works of art that often wound up in completely different territory from where they began. Sometimes the results would be a little shakey; often they would be inspiring. Regardless, these solo performances were adventures, and that quality makes the double disc *Monk Alone: The Complete Columbia Solo Studio Recordings, 1962-1968* irresistable. Much of this music was released on such Columbia albums as *Monk's Dream* and *Underground* over the course of the '60s, but this is the first time all the material has been collected in one place and the results are frequently stunning. The first disc, plus the first two tracks on disc two, contain the master takes. The second disc is largely comprised of alternate takes—four have been released, the remaining 14 make their debut here. That's nearly a full album of "new" material and almost all of it is as compelling as the master takes. Certainly, the collection is designed for Monk completists, but even casual fans will find something to marvel at here. *—Stephen Thomas Erlewine*

Complete Prestige Recordings / Oct. 19, 1944-Oct. 25, 1954 / Prestige ✦✦✦✦
Thelonious Monk was only with Prestige from 1952-1954, which explains why Fantasy's *The Complete Prestige Recordings* contains only three CDs. But Monk's Prestige output is noteworthy and generally rewarding, if imperfect at times. Not everything on *The Complete Prestige Recordings* is essential, but for the serious Monk collector, its rewards are great. The set gets off to an interesting start with four 1944 recordings from a Coleman Hawkins session. The material originally came out on the small Joe Davis label, but these performances are historically important because they marked the first time Monk was recorded as a sideman, and the first time that Prestige founder Bob Weinstock was exposed to Monk. The set then fast forwards to Monk's Prestige period, when he led various trios and quintets and was employed as a sideman by Sonny Rollins and Miles Davis. All of disc three is devoted to 1954's historic Davis/Monk encounter; unfortunately, Davis and Monk's egos clashed, but that didn't prevent them from delivering memorable performances. *The Complete Prestige Recordings* isn't for casual listeners, but it has a lot more ups than downs, and is enthusiastically recommended to serious jazz collectors. *—Alex Henderson*

Wes Montgomery (John Leslie Montgomery)

b. Mar. 6, 1925, Indianapolis, IN, **d.** Jun. 15, 1968, Indianapolis, IN
Guitar (Electric), Guitar / Crossover Jazz, Hard Bop
Wes Montgomery was one of the great jazz guitarists, a natural extension of Charlie Christian whose appealing use of octaves became influential and his trademark. He achieved great commercial success during his last few years, only to die prematurely. He recorded with his brothers, vibraphonist Buddy and electric bassist Monk, during 1957-59 and made his first Riverside album (1959) in a trio with organist Melvin Rhyne. In 1960 the release of his album *The Incredible Jazz Guitar of Wes Montgomery* made him famous in the jazz world. Other than a brief time playing with the John Coltrane Sextet (which also included Eric Dolphy) later in the year, Wes would be a leader for the rest of his life. Montgomery's recordings can be easily divided into three periods. His Riverside dates (1959-63) are small-group sessions and his most spontaneous jazz outings. With the collapse of Riverside, Montgomery moved over to Verve where during 1964-66 he recorded an interesting series of mostly orchestral dates with arranger Don Sebesky and producer Creed Taylor. In 1967 Wes signed with A&M and during 1967-68 he recorded three best-selling albums that found him merely stating simple pop melodies while backed by strings and woodwinds. His jazz fans were upset but Montgomery's albums were played on AM radio during the period, he helped introduce listeners to jazz and his live performances were as freewheeling as his earlier Riverside dates. *—Scott Yanow*

Fingerpickin' / Dec. 30, 1957-Apr. 22, 1958 / Pacific Jazz ✦✦✦
Guitarist Wes Montgomery first recorded in the late '40s during his brief period with Lionel Hampton before returning to Indianapolis. He next emerged on record on December 30, 1957, for a Pacific Jazz set with local musicians including his two brothers, vibraphonist Buddy and electric bassist Monk. This CD reissues the complete album (which usually has appeared in piecemeal fashion) and finds Wes already quite recognizable. The pretty standard hard bop music (which usually features Buddy's vibes as the lead voice) is also of interest due to the presence of trumpeter Freddie Hubbard who at age 17 was making his recording debut; he sounds a bit nervous. In addition to this set, the CD has three songs from the one session that Wes made with his brothers' popular group, the Mastersounds. He actually appeared on the full album (a set of music taken from the film *Kismet*) but these are the only titles that include guitar solos. Although this reissue on a whole is not essential, the music is generally enjoyable and the CD will fill some gaps in one's Wes Montgomery collection. *—Scott Yanow*

Far Wes / Apr. 1958-Oct. 1959 / Pacific Jazz ✦✦✦✦✦
This historical CD contains some of guitarist Wes Montgomery's first recordings; in fact only three small-group songs predate these performances. The then-obscure guitarist is heard in two different quintets, both of which include his brothers Buddy (on piano) and Monk (playing electric bass). The earlier set has Harold Land's tenor as a lead voice while altoist Pony Poindexter takes his place on the later date, Wes's sound was already quite recognizable and he contributes six originals which alternate with Harold Land's "Hymn for Carl" and four standards. *—Scott Yanow*

☆ **The Complete Riverside Recordings** / Oct. 5, 1959-Nov. 27, 1963 / Riverside ✦✦✦✦✦
Wes Montgomery recorded exclusively for the Riverside label during the four years covered by this massive 12-CD box set and, although his later albums for Verve and particularly the pop/jazz *AM* dates sold many more copies, it is for his Riverside dates that his legacy was primarily formed. Virtually unknown at the time of his debut on Riverside, Montgomery soon became a major influence whose style is still copied in the 1990s. The guitarist is heard in quite a few different settings on this box including in trios with organist Melvin Rhynbe, a quartet with pianist Tommy Flanagan, as a sideman on different sessions with Nat Adderley, Harold Land and Cannonball Adderley, performing with his brothers Buddy and Monk, holding his own with pianist George Shearing, vibraphonist Milt Jackson and tenor great Johnny Griffin and (for an album ironically titled *Fusion*) playing with strings for the first time. All in all there are a tremendous amount of rewarding performances included in this essential set, most of which show why Wes Montgomery is still considered one of the all-time great jazz guitarists. *—Scott Yanow*

A Dynamic New Sound / Oct. 5, 1959-Oct. 6, 1959 / Riverside/OJC ✦✦✦
Wes Montgomery's first of many sessions for Riverside matched his guitar with organist Melvin Rhyne and drummer Paul Parker for some straightahead swinging. Highlights in-

clude "Yesterdays," "'Round Midnight" and Montgomery's originals "Missile Blues" and "Jingles." This CD reissue adds two alternate takes to the original program. *—Scott Yanow*

★ **The Incredible Jazz Guitar of Wes Montgomery** / Jan. 26, 1960-Jan. 28, 1960 / Riverside/OJC ✦✦✦✦✦
This is one of Wes Montgomery's greatest recordings, a classic that really alerted the world about the talents of the guitarist. In a quartet with pianist Tommy Flanagan, bassist Percy Heath and drummer Albert Heath, Wes introduced his originals "West Coast Blues," "Four on Six," and "D-Natural Blues," performed his "Mister Walker" and stretched out on "Airegin," the ballad "Polka Dots and Moonbeams," "In Your Own Sweet Way" and "Gone with the Wind." All of the unique qualities of Wes Montgomery's style are on display on this essential CD reissue which is also available as part of his 12-CD Riverside boxed set. *—Scott Yanow*

Groove Brothers / Jul. 1960-Dec. 1961 / Milestone ✦✦✦✦
Although this is billed to Wes Montgomery, it is in fact a combination of two early-'60s LPs by the Montgomery Brothers—*The Montgomery Brothers* and *The Montgomery Brothers in Canada*?onto one disc. (Also note that it's almost entirely different from the Montgomery Brothers' Milestone double LP that also bears the name *Groove Brothers*, which mostly features material from their Riverside LP *Groove Yard*.) With Wes on guitar, Monk on bass, and Buddy on piano (Larance Marable fills out the quartet on drums), *The Montgomery Brothers* (1960) is a boppish set of five lengthy tracks, divided between both originals (penned by either Wes or Buddy) and standards. "June in January" is a particularly good vehicle for Wes' fluid single-note runs, while "D-Natural Blues" is one of his more enduring and good-natured compositions from the period. Buddy Montgomery, who often played the piano with the Montgomery Brothers, sticks exclusively to vibes on *The Montgomery Brothers in Canada*, which in addition to Wes and Monk has Paul Humphrey on drums. This club date (which on this CD reissue has been presented without the overdubbed applause on the original LP) is a solid set of cool but not cold bop, with a low-key mood and uniformly tasteful playing. Only one original on here (by Buddy), but it's a beaut: the buoyant "Beaux Arts" has gorgeous alternations of single-note solos and chording by Wes. In a different vein, "Angel Eyes," which begins with a long drumless passage, shows Wes' skill with a delicate slow ballad. *—Richie Unterberger*

Movin' Along / Oct. 11, 1960-Oct. 12, 1960 / Riverside/OJC ✦✦✦✦✦
Because it was recorded between two of Wes Montgomery's best-known albums (*Incredible Jazz Guitar* and *So Much Guitar*), this particular CD is a bit underrated. The great guitarist is teamed with flutist James Clay (who switches to tenor on Wes's "So Do It"), pianist Victor Feldman, bassist Sam Jones and drummer Louis Hayes for four standards (highlighted by Clifford Brown's "Sandull" and "Body and Soul"), Sam Jones's "Says You" and two Montgomery originals. The reissue also adds a pair of alternate takes to the fine program. Wes Montgomery made many of his finest jazz recordings originally for Riverside and this is an often-overlooked gem. *—Scott Yanow*

So Much Guitar / Aug. 4, 1961 / Riverside/OJC ✦✦✦✦✦
This CD contains one of Wes Montgomery's finest recordings, a Riverside date that showcases the influential guitarist in a quintet with pianist Hank Jones, bassist Ron Carter, drummer Lex Humphries and the congas of Ray Barretto. All eight performances are memorable in their own way with "Cottontail," "I'm Just a Lucky So and So" and a brief unaccompanied "While We're Young" being highpoints. *—Scott Yanow*

★ **Full House** / Jun. 25, 1962 / Riverside/OJC ✦✦✦✦✦
An audiophile reissue of an Original Jazz Classics CD also currently available, this live set is notable for teaming guitarist Wes Montgomery and the Wynton Kelly Trio (comprised of pianist Kelly, bassist Paul Chambers and drummer Jimmy Cobb) with the fiery tenor Johnny Griffin. As with the OJC release, six selections (highlighted by "Blue 'N' Boogie" and Wes' "S.O.S.") are augmented by "Born To Be Blue" and a pair of alternate takes. *—Scott Yanow*

Fusion! Wes Montgomery with Strings / Apr. 18, 1963-Apr. 19, 1963 / Riverside/OJC ✦✦✦✦
Although most Wes Montgomery fans associate his playing with strings with his later A&M and Verve recordings, the influential guitarist actually fronted a string section for the first time on this Riverside date from 1963 which had the ironic name of *Fusion*. As with his later albums, Montgomery's guitar solos here are brief and melodic but the jazz content is fairly high even if the emphasis is (with the exception of "Tune-Up") on ballads. This CD has three additional performances than the original LP and is worth picking up; the music is quite pretty and pleasing. *—Scott Yanow*

Portrait of Wes / Oct. 10, 1963-Nov. 27, 1963 / Riverside/OJC ✦✦✦✦
Wes Montgomery's first recordings for Riverside were in a trio with organist Mel Rhyne and ironically his final albums for the struggling (and soon to be bankrupt) label were with Rhyne again. The brilliant guitarist is in fine form on these appealing tunes with the highlights including "Freddie the Freeloader," "Blues Riff" and "Moanin'." As is true with most of Montgomery's CD reissues, there are a couple of "bonus" cuts (alternates of "Blues Riff" and "Moanin'") added to bring the playing time up a bit. All of this music is also available as part of Wes Montgomery's 12-CD Riverside box set. *—Scott Yanow*

Movin' Wes / Nov. 11, 1964-Nov. 16, 1964 / Verve ✦✦✦
Wes Montgomery's debut for Verve, although better from a jazz standpoint than his later A&M releases, is certainly in the same vein. The emphasis is on his tone, his distinctive octaves and melody statements. Some of the material (such as "People" and "Matchmaker") are pop tunes of the era and the brass orchestra (arranged by Johnny Pate) is purely in the background but there are some worthy performances; chiefly the two-part "Movin' Wes," "Born to Be Blue" and "West Coast Blues." *—Scott Yanow*

Talkin' Verve: Roots of Acid Jazz / Nov. 18, 1964-Sep. 23, 1966 / Verve ✦✦

Impressions: The Verve Jazz Sides / Jan. 1, 1965-Sep. 16, 1966 / Verve ✦✦✦✦✦
The two-CD set *Impressions: The Verve Jazz Sessions* salvages Wes Montgomery's straight jazz sessions for Verve, leaving the pop-oriented covers and orchestral sessions to the original albums. There are selected numbers from albums like *Movin' Wes*, *Goin' Out of My Head* and *California Dreaming*, illustrating that those albums were hardly worthless—each track proves that Montgomery's touch remained elegant and supremely tasteful. The second disc is devoted to the complete sessions for *Smokin' at the Half Note*, the legendary recording Montgomery made at Van Gelder Studios in 1965 with bassist Paul Chambers, pianist Wynton Kelly and drummer Jimmy Cobb. The music on the record is easily among Montgomery's finest, and this is the first time that all the music from the sessions has been collected in one place. That alone makes it worthwhile for hardcore collectors, but the set also makes an excellent summation of his Verve years for less dedicated fans, since it rounds up his very best work on one attractive set. *—Stephen Thomas Erlewine*

Bumpin' / May 1967 / Verve ✦✦✦✦✦
Wes Montgomery's second Verve album was the best of his orchestral performances. With arrangements by Don Sebesky, Montgomery had opportunities to stretch out on a couple of the selections (most notably on the title cut and "Here's That Rainy Day") and, even though the jazz is not up to the level of his freewheeling Riverside performances, this set is a good compromise between the demands of the jazz and pop worlds. Plus some of the melodies are quite memorable. *—Scott Yanow*

★ **Smokin' at the Half Note** / May 1965-Sep. 22, 1965 / Verve ✦✦✦✦✦
Smokin' at the Half Note is essential listening for anyone who wants to hear why Montgomery's dynamic live shows were considered the pinnacle of his brilliant and incredibly influential guitar playing. Pat Metheny calls this "the absolute greatest jazz guitar album ever made," and with performances of this caliber ("Unit 7" boasts one of the greatest guitar solos ever recorded) his statement is easily validated. Montgomery never played with more drive and confidence, and he's supported every step of the way by a genuinely smokin' Wynton Kelly Trio. In 1998, Verve reissued the complete show on disc two of *Impressions: The Verve Jazz Sides*, although the scrambled track order and some non-essential cuts don't diminish the appeal of the original album. *—Jim Smith*

California Dreaming / Sep. 14, 1966-Sep. 16, 1966 / Verve ✦✦

A Day in the Life / Jun. 6, 1967-Jun. 26, 1967 / A&M ✦✦✦

James Moody

b. Mar. 26, 1925, Savannah, GA
Sax (Tenor), Sax (Alto), Flute / Hard Bop, Bop
James Moody has been an institution in jazz since the late '40s, whether on tenor, flute, occasional alto or yodelling his way through his "Moody's Mood for Love." After serving in the Air Force (1943-46), he joined Dizzy Gillespie's bebop orchestra and began a lifelong friendship with the trumpeter. Moody toured Europe with Gillespie and then stayed overseas for several years, working with Miles Davis, Max Roach and top European players. His 1949 recording of "I'm in the Mood for Love" in 1952 became a hit under the title of "Moody's Mood for Love" with classic vocalese lyrics written by Eddie Jefferson and a best-selling recording by King Pleasure. After returning to the U.S., Moody formed a septet that lasted for five years, recorded extensively for Prestige and Argo, took up the flute and then from 1963-68 was a member of Dizzy Gillespie's quintet. He worked in Las Vegas show bands during much of the 1970s before returning to jazz, playing occasionally with Dizzy, mostly working as a leader and recording with Lionel Hampton's Golden Men of Jazz. Moody, who has alternated between tenor (which he prefers) and alto throughout his career, has an original sound on both horns. He is also one of the best flutists in jazz. James Moody has recorded as a leader for Blue Note, Xanadu, Vogue, Prestige, EmArcy, Mercury, Argo, DJM, Milestone, Perception, MPS, Muse, Vanguard and Novus. *—Scott Yanow*

New Sounds / 1948 / Blue Note ✦✦✦✦✦

● **James Moody & the Swedish All-Stars' Greatest Hits** / Oct. 12, 1949-Jan. 25, 1951 / Prestige ✦✦✦✦✦
In 1999, Fantasy combined the Prestige LPs *James Moody's Greatest Hits* and *More of James Moody's Greatest Hits* onto the 71-minute CD *James Moody and the Swedish All-Stars' Greatest Hits*. This superb collection boasts 24 selections that were recorded in Stockholm between 1949 and 1951, when the American saxman was living in Sweden and was earning a reputation for being one of bebop's more accessible players. The CD's best-known track is Moody's 1949 interpretation of "I'm in the Mood for Love," which was the basis for King Pleasure's 1952 vocalese hit "Moody's Mood for Love." Equally essential are Moody's lyrical interpretations of "Body and Soul," "Embraceable You," "These Foolish Things," and "Out of Nowhere," all of which find him joined by Swedish beboppers of the day. Though some of the musicians are obscure, listeners with a serious knowledge of Sweden's contributions to jazz will recognize such names as Lars Gullin (baritone sax), Arne Domnerus (alto sax), Rolf Ericson (trumpet), and Jack Noren (drums). The sound is mildly scratchy, but Moody's performances on both tenor and alto are first-rate. For those who are exploring Moody's music for the first time, this CD is among the places to start. *—Alex Henderson*

Moody's Mood for Blues / Jan. 8, 1955-Jan. 28, 1955 / Prestige/OJC ✦✦✦
In the mid-'50s James Moody led a four-horn septet that played music falling somewhere between bop and rhythm & blues. The danceable rhythms and riffing made its recordings somewhat accessible but the solos of Moody (on tenor and alto) and trumpeter Dave Burns also held listener's interests. Vocalese master Eddie Jefferson has two guest appearances (on "Workshop" and "I Got the Blue") and Iona Wade sings "That Man O' Mine" in a Dinah Washington-influenced style but the emphasis is on Moody's solos and the ensembles; the leader's two versions of "It Might as Well Be Spring" (one on tenor, the other on alto) are highlights of this enjoyable CD reissue. *—Scott Yanow*

Hi-Fi Party / Aug. 23, 1955-Aug. 24, 1955 / Prestige/OJC ✦✦✦✦✦
For a period in the mid-'50s, tenor saxophonist James Moody (who doubled on alto) was able to keep together a swinging septet that played bop in a fairly accessible way. On this CD reissue of two 1955 sessions, Moody and his group (which includes the fine trumpeter Dave Burns, trombonist William Shepherd, baritone Pee Wee Moore, pianist Jimmy Boyd, bassist John Lathan, and drummer Clarence Johnson) perform swinging versions of fairly obscure

originals including the lengthy "Jammin' With James" (which has a long tradeoff between Moody and Burns), Benny Golson's "Big Ben," and "There Will Never Be Another You." The highpoint is Eddie Jefferson's one appearance, singing his alternate lyrics to Charlie Parker's famous solo on "Lady Be Good" which he renamed "Disappointed." *—Scott Yanow*

Wail, Moody, Wail / Dec. 12, 1955 / Prestige/OJC ♦♦♦♦
James Moody's mid-'50s band was a septet featuring four horns including the leader's tenor and alto. The bop-based group had plenty of spirit (as best shown here on the 14-minute title cut) if not necessarily a strong personality of its own. This CD (a straight reissue of the original LP plus two additional titles from the same session) is accessible, melodic and swinging; trumpeter Dave Burns is the best soloist among the sidemen. *—Scott Yanow*

Moody's Mood for Love / Dec. 14, 1956-Jan. 13, 1957 / GRP ♦♦♦♦
A strong version of the "Moody's Mood for Love", with a vocal by the late Eddie Jefferson (v). *—Ron Wynn*

Don't Look Away Now / Feb. 14, 1969 / Prestige/OJC ♦♦♦♦♦

The Blues and Other Colors / Aug. 14, 1968-Feb. 11, 1969 / Milestone/OJC ♦♦♦♦
This CD reissues a rather unusual James Moody date. Best known for his tenor and alto playing (although he is also recognized as a talented flutist), Moody is here heard exclusively on soprano and flute. Trombonist Tom McIntosh contributed a tune and arranged all eight pieces (which also include four Moody originals). Five of the numbers feature Moody in a nonet, including an emotional "Old Folks" and an advanced reworking of Duke Ellington's "Main Step." The other three numbers find Moody's flute joined by trombone, French horn, three strings, a rhythm section and Linda November's wordless vocalizing; of these, "Gone Are the Days" is quite eccentric, being turned into a protest piece with quite a few quotes from other songs. Throughout the CD, Moody plays quite well and sounds surprisingly effective on soprano, an instrument he would rarely return to in the future. *—Scott Yanow*

Young at Heart / 1996 / Warner Brothers ♦♦♦♦
With *Young At Heart*, James Moody interprets the core songs of Frank Sinatra's repertoire as if it were a songbook itself. The results are surprisingly effective, demonstrating the wonderful, lucid tones of Moody's saxophone, as well as the flexibility and depth of the songs themselves. On the album, Moody is supported by a small band, which is occasionally augmented by a full orchestra. *—Thom Owens*

Moody Plays Mancini / Feb. 4, 1997-Feb. 5, 1997 / Warner Brothers ♦♦♦♦
As popular and well-known as Henry Mancini was when he was alive, only after his death in 1994 have the substantial musical tributes been coming—and the tunes included on this graceful disc were suggested by the composer himself. Mancini was, of course, a product of the big band era—and thus, steeped in jazz—and his movie themes often make gratifying basic material for ballad improvisations. With only Gil Goldstein's electronic keyboards (used sparingly and strictly in a jazz context), Todd Coolman's bass, and Terri Lyne Carrington's drums to back him up, Moody's tenor, alto and soprano solos are consistently warm, melodic, and easy to assimilate, with a few nudges outside the changes on "Charade." Appropriately he also chooses to use the flute on the sly, sauntering *Pink Panther* theme and "Soldier In the Rain." The sentimental "Moon River" was the only tune Mancini did not recommend, but it was from Moody's wife's favorite film, and it gives Moody a chance to exercise his deep, endearingly rusty bass voice. *—Richard S. Ginell*

At the Jazz Workshop / Jun. 1961 / GRP ♦♦♦♦♦
This 1998 CD reissues the recording *Cookin' the Blues* and adds one selection only previously available on a sampler, plus three unissued cuts from the same date. Although James Moody, who is heard here on tenor, flute and alto, utilizes a septet that includes trumpeter Howard McGhee, he is the main soloist throughout. The live set finds Moody mostly emphasizing the blues at a variety of tempos, in addition to playing particularly memorable versions of "It Might as Well Be Spring," "'Round Midnight" and "Stablemates." Moody's friend singer Eddie Jefferson has three features: "Disappointed" (based on "Lady Be Good"), Horace Silver's "Sister Sadie," and a fine remake of "Moody's Mood for Love." Throughout the date, James Moody is heard in prime form on all three of his instruments; overall, this is one of his strongest sets. *—Scott Yanow*

1948-1949 / Sep. 12, 2000 / Melodie Jazz Classics ♦♦♦
These earliest sessions recorded by saxophonist James Moody under his own leadership, follow his initial years with Dizzy Gillespie, an association that would be maintained off and on throughout Dizzy's life. The disc starts in chronological order with eight sides recorded for Blue Note in October 1948. Arranged by composer Gil Fuller and backed by Moody's Modernists, which were, in essence, musicians comprised of Dizzy Gillespie's band including baritone saxophonist Cecil Payne, alto saxophonist Ernie Henry, Chano Pozo, and Art Blakey. These sessions were recorded in New York before Moody left for Europe, not to return to the states until years later. The remaining 14 tracks find him jamming with European musicians and fellow American expatriates including fellow tenor saxophonist Don Byas, mixing bebop and standards recorded in Zurich, Paris, Lausanne, and Stockholm for Vogue, Blue Star, and Prestige. *—Al Campbell*

Airto Moreira (Airto Guimorva Moreira)

b. Aug. 5, 1941, Itaiopolis, Brazil
Drums, Percussion / Afro-Brazilian, Crossover Jazz, Brazilian Jazz, Brazilian Pop, Latin Jazz, Fusion, Worldbeat
The most high-profile percussionist of the 1970s and still among the most famous, Airto Moreira (often simply known by his first name) helped make percussion an essential part of many modern jazz groups; his tambourine solos can border on the amazing! Airto originally studied guitar and piano before becoming a percussionist. He played locally in Brazil, collected and studied over 120 different percussion instruments and in 1968 moved to the U.S. with his wife, singer Flora Purim. Airto played with Miles Davis during part of 1969-70, appearing on several records (most notably *Live Evil*). He worked with Lee Morgan for a bit in 1971, was an original memeber of Weather Report and in 1972 was part of Chick Corea's initial version of Return to Forever with Flora Purim; he and Corea also recorded the classic *Captain Marvel* with Stan Getz. By 1973 Airto was famous enough to have his own group, signed to CTI and appearing on Purim's sessions. Since then he has stayed busy, mostly co-leading bands with his wife and recording as a leader for many labels including Buddah, CTI, Arista, Warner Bros, Caroline, Rykodisc, In & Out and B&W. Not all of his music as a leader would be called jazz but Airto remains a very impressive player. *—Scott Yanow*

● **Free** / Mar. 23, 1972-Apr. 12, 1972 / CTI ♦♦♦♦♦
Other than a couple of obscure efforts for Buddah in 1970, this was percussionist Airto's debut as a leader, and this is still his most famous record. A brass section arranged by Don Sebesky is heard on two tracks, and such all-stars as keyboardist Chick Corea, flutist Hubert Laws, the reeds of Joe Farrell and even pianist Keith Jarrett and guitarist George Benson make worthwhile appearances. Flora Purim joins Airto in the one vocal piece ("Free"), and "Return to Forever" receives an early recording. The music combines together jazz, Brazilian music and aspects of fusion and funk quite successfully. *—Scott Yanow*

Fingers / Apr. 1973 / CTI ♦♦♦♦♦
The 1970s were banner years for Airto Moreira—not only because of his association with Chick Corea's Return to Forever and his work on wife Flora Purim's *Milestone* dates, but also, because of the generally superb work he did under Creed Taylor's supervision at CTI from 1972-74. One of the five-star gems that the Brazilian percussionist recorded for CTI was *Fingers*, which employs Purim on percussion and vocals, David Amaro on guitar, Hugo Fattoruso on keyboards and harmonica, Jorge Fattoruso on drums and Ringo Thielmann on electric bass. Produced by Taylor and recorded at Rudy Van Gelder's famous New Jersey studio, this LP demonstrates just how exciting and creative 1970s fusion could be. When Moreira and his colleagues blend jazz with Brazilian music, rock and funk on such cuts as "Wind Chant," "Tombo in 7/4" and "Romance of Death," the results are consistently enriching. *Fingers* is an album to savor. *—Alex Henderson*

Virgin Land / Jun. 1974 / CTI ♦♦♦♦
An all-star cast accompanies Brazilian percussion master Airto Moreira on this percolating collection of jazz fusion pieces. Produced by drummer extraordinaire Billy Cobham, the album locks into a steamy groove on Stanley Clarke's "Stanley's Tune" and never lets up. The Middle Eastern flavor of some of the melodies, Moreira and wife Flora Purim's unique vocalizations, and the use of unusual instrumentation on several cuts help make this recording a unique highlight of the electric fusion era. Standout soloists include Eddie Daniels on clarinet and guitarists David Amaro and Gabriel DeLorme, while bassist Clarke provides his usual stellar performance. *—Jim Newsom*

The Other Side of This / 1988 / Rykodisc ♦♦♦♦♦
Using voice, drum, whistle, chime, shakers, rattle, tambourine, and digeridoo, Airto and company make music that comes from all regions and belongs to none. These are songs for ritual and healing, based on many cultures. The mood is ethereal, yet because of the predominance of percussion, also powerful. New age music with punch. *—Steven McDonald*

Lee Morgan

b. Jul. 10, 1938, Philadelphia, PA, **d.** Feb. 19, 1972, New York, NY
Trumpet / Hard Bop
One of the great jazz trumpeters of the 1960s, Lee Morgan was the natural successor to Clifford Brown, making an impact on the scene shortly after Brownie's death and at first playing in a very similar style. He was a bit of a prodigy, working professionally in Philadelphia when he was 15 and joining Dizzy Gillespie's orchestra when he was barely 18. Morgan led his first Blue Note session later that year and he would record his first two classic albums for the label during 1957-58: *The Cooker* and *Candy*. Morgan was with Gillespie's band into 1958 when he became a member of Art Blakey's Jazz Messengers (1958-61), touring and recording extensively with the group and sharing the frontline with Benny Golson, Hank Mobley and finally Wayne Shorter. After recording his biggest hit, "The Sidewinder," he entered his greatest period, recording one memorable album after another, writing "Ceora" and "Speedball" and spending a second period with Blakey (1964-65). Morgan's playing became more adventurous and by the end of the decade he was exploring modal music, using some avant-garde elements and opening his playing to the influence of funk. *—Scott Yanow*

Complete Blue Note Lee Morgan Fifties Sessions / Nov. 4, 1956-Feb. 2, 1958 / Mosaic ♦♦♦♦♦
Lee Morgan recorded for Blue Note in the late '50s, playing seven dates between 1956 and 1958. Morgan was still in his teens at the time and half of the joy of *The Complete Blue Note Lee Morgan Fifties Sessions* is hearing the trumpeter develop at a rapid rate. The four-disc box set *The Complete Blue Note* encompasses sessions with Horace Silver, Paul Chambers, Benny Golson, Wynton Kelly, Sonny Clarke, Doug Watkins, and Art Taylor. Morgan may have been young at the time these were recorded, but he was impressive even at the beginning, playing blistering hard bop and lyrical ballads with equal ease. He may have gone on to record greater, more influential albums but this music remains exciting, vital, and simply joyous. *—Stephen Thomas Erlewine*

Presenting Lee Morgan / Nov. 4, 1956 / Blue Note ♦♦♦

A-1—*The Savoy Sessions* / *Nov. 5, 1956-Nov. 7, 1956* / *Savoy* ♦♦♦

Dizzy Atmosphere / Feb. 18, 1957 / Specialty/OJC ♦♦♦♦
This somewhat obscure Lee Morgan set (originally cut for Specialty and made available on CD in the OJC series) features the trumpeter with other then-current members of the Dizzy Gillespie big band: trombonist Al Grey, tenor saxophonist Billy Mitchell, baritonist Billy Root, pianist Wynton Kelly, bassist Paul West and drummer Charlie Persip. With arrangements provided by Benny Golson and Roger Spotts, the music is modern bop for the period. Highlights include the 10 1/2-minute "Dishwater," "Over the Rainbow" and what was probably the first-ever version of Golson's "Whisper Not." Morgan plays extremely well throughout the spirited set, and he was just 18 at the time. *—Scott Yanow*

The Cooker / Sep. 29, 1957 / Blue Note ✦✦✦✦✦
The trumpeter, then just 19, teams up with baritonist Pepper Adams, pianist Bobby Timmons, bassist Paul Chambers and drummer Philly Joe Jones for a particularly strong set that is highlighted by a lengthy and fiery "Night in Tunisia," "Lover Man" and a rapid rendition of "Just One of Those Things." Morgan plays remarkably well for his age (already ranking just below Dizzy Gillespie and Miles Davis), making this an essential acquisition. *—Scott Yanow*

☆ **Candy** / Nov. 18, 1957-Feb. 2, 1958 / Blue Note ✦✦✦✦✦
Lee Morgan's only quartet album is one of his best. Although only 19 at the time, Morgan already had a mature style, a sound influenced by Clifford Brown and a near-complete mastery of the bop vocabulary. With the strong assistance of pianist Sonny Clark, bassist Doug Watkins and drummer Art Taylor, Morgan is very expressive and creative on this CD reissue, particularly on such songs as "Candy," "Since I Fell for You," "All the Way" and even "Personality." *—Scott Yanow*

Here's Lee Morgan / Feb. 2, 1960-Feb. 8, 1960 / Vee-Jay ✦✦✦✦
This CD reissue has its original six songs expanded to 11 with the inclusion of five alternate takes. The music is good solid hard bop that finds Lee Morgan (already a veteran at age 21) coming out of the Clifford Brown tradition to display his own rapidly developing style. Matched with Clifford Jordan on tenor, pianist Wynton Kelly, bassist Paul Chambers and drummer Art Blakey, Morgan's album could pass for a Jazz Messengers set. *—Scott Yanow*

Leeway / Apr. 28, 1960 / Blue Note ✦✦✦✦
This date was one of trumpeter Lee Morgan's more obscure Blue Note sessions, but fortunately, it has been reissued on CD. Matched with altoist Jackie McLean, pianist Bobby Timmons, bassist Paul Chambers and drummer Art Blakey, Morgan interprets two of Calvin Massey's compositions, McLean's "Midtown Blues" and his own blues "The Lion and the Wolff." The music is essentially hard bop with a strong dose of soul; the very distinctive styles of the principals are the main reasons to acquire this enjoyable music. *—Scott Yanow*

Expoobident / Oct. 14, 1960 / Vee-Jay ✦✦✦✦
Recorded late in the trumpeter's short career, this fine release originally issued by Vee-Jay Records has been given new life over the years through at least a couple of reissues. This one includes four previously released alternate takes from the seven tracks, each of which features a strong hard bop quintet, with Art Blakey on drums, Eddie Higgins on piano, Art Davis on bass, and Clifford Jordan on tenor saxophone. The set is a tad more laid-back than the earlier classic Blue Note sessions. Nonetheless, this one offers its rewards, including a rare chance to hear Eddie Higgins in full force, a late view of Blakey as a sideman, and a stunning front line with unsung giant, Clifford Jordan. Morgan is in good form, swinging and blowing passionately, and his interpretations of "Easy Living" and "Just in Time" are among his best. The Koch release retains the original liner notes by Nat Hentoff, as well as the attractive artwork on the initial issue. *—Steven Loewy*

★ **The Sidewinder** / Dec. 21, 1963 / Blue Note ✦✦✦✦✦
This album is trumpeter Lee Morgan's best-known recording; the catchy title cut became a hit, launched the boogaloo fad and is still performed decades later. The CD reissue (which adds an alternate take of "Totem Pole" to the original set) finds Morgan at the peak of his powers (where he would remain for the next four or five years) as the leading trumpeter in hard bop. The young (and already immediately recognizable) tenor Joe Henderson, pianist Barry Harris, bassist Bob Cranshaw and drummer Billy Higgins also make strong contributions to this well-rounded program which includes four other memorable Morgan originals: "Totem Pole," "Gary's Notebook," "Boy, What a Night" and "Hocus-Pocus." *—Scott Yanow*

☆ **Search for the New Land** / Feb. 15, 1964 / Blue Note ✦✦✦✦✦
This set (the CD reissue is a duplicate of the original LP) is one of the finest Lee Morgan records. The great trumpeter contributes five challenging compositions ("Search for the New Land," "The Joker," "Mr. Kenyatta," "Melancholee" and "Morgan the Pirate"); songs that deserve to be revived. Morgan, tenor-saxophonist Wayne Shorter, guitarist Grant Green, pianist Herbie Hancock, bassist Reggie Workman and drummer Billy Higgins are all in particularly creative form on the fresh material and they stretch the boundaries of hard bop (the modern mainstream jazz of the period). The result is a consistently stimulating set that rewards repeated listenings. *—Scott Yanow*

Tom Cat / Aug. 11, 1964 / Blue Note ✦✦✦✦
It seems strange that the music on this CD was not released initially until 1980. Trumpeter Lee Morgan had had an unexpected hit with "The Sidewinder" so his more challenging recordings were temporarily put aside. As it turns out, this was one of Morgan's better sets from the 1960s and he had gathered together quite an all-star cast: altoist Jackie McLean, trombonist Curtis Fuller, pianist McCoy Tyner, bassist Bob Cranshaw and drummer Art Blakey. They perform "Rigormortis," McCoy Tyner's "Twilight Mist" and three of the trumpeter's originals including the title cut. The advanced hard bop music still sounds fresh decades later despite its initial neglect. *—Scott Yanow*

The Rumproller / Apr. 21, 1965 / Blue Note ✦✦✦
To follow up on his unexpected boogaloo hit "The Sidewinder," Lee Morgan recorded Andrew Hill's somewhat similar "The Rumproller" but this time the commercial magic was not there. However the trumpeter, tenor-saxophonist Joe Henderson, pianist Ronnie Mathews, bassist Victor Sproles and drummer Billy Higgins all play quite well on the title cut, two of Morgan's songs (the bossa nova "Eclipso" is somewhat memorable), a ballad tribute to Billie Holiday and Wayne Shorter's "Edda." This album is worth picking up but it is not essential. *—Scott Yanow*

The Gigolo / Jun. 25, 1965-Jul. 1, 1965 / Blue Note ✦✦✦✦✦
Lee Morgan was the leading trumpeter in hard bop during the 1960s and he recorded quite a few classic albums for Blue Note. This is one of them. The CD reissue (which adds an alternate take of the title cut to the original five-song program) features Morgan at his best, whether playing his memorable blues "Speed Ball," an explorative ballad version of "You Go to My Head," a lengthy "The Gigolo" or his other two originals ("Yes I Can, No You Can't" and "Trapped"). There are no weak selections on this set and the playing by the leader, Wayne Shorter on tenor, pianist Harold Mabern, bassist Bob Cranshaw and drummer Billy Higgins is beyond any serious criticism. *—Scott Yanow*

☆ **Cornbread** / Sep. 18, 1965 / Blue Note ✦✦✦✦✦
This session (reissued on CD by Blue Note) is best known for introducing Lee Morgan's beautiful ballad "Ceora" but actually all five selections (which include Morgan's "Cornbread," "Our Man Higgins," "Most like Lee" and the standard "Ill Wind") are quite memorable. The trumpeter/leader performs with a perfectly complementary group of open-minded and talented hard bop stylists (altoist Jackie McLean, Hank Mobley on tenor, pianist Herbie Hancock, bassist Larry Ridley and drummer Billy Higgins) and creates a Blue Note classic that is heartily recommended. *—Scott Yanow*

Delightfulee / Apr. 8, 1966-May 27, 1966 / Blue Note ✦✦✦✦✦
This classic set by trumpeter Lee Morgan was reissued on LP in 1984. Of the four quintet numbers with tenor saxophonist Joe Henderson, pianist McCoy Tyner, bassist Bob Cranshaw, and drummer Billy Higgins, the instantly likable "Ca-Lee-So" is the most memorable, although the other three Morgan originals ("Zambia," "Nite Flite," and "The Delightful Deggie") also find the trumpeter in excellent form. An unusual aspect to this collection is that there are also two ballads ("Yesterday" and "Sunrise Sunset") that have a nonet playing Oliver Nelson arrangements behind Morgan's lyrical horn; Tyner and tenor saxophonist Wayne Shorter have opportunities to take concise solos. *—Scott Yanow*

Charisma / Sep. 29, 1966 / Blue Note ✦✦✦✦
This set (reissued on CD in 1997) was one of trumpeter Lee Morgan's lesser-known Blue Notes but it is quite rewarding. The notable sextet (which also includes altoist Jackie McLean, Hank Mobley on tenor, pianist Cedar Walton, bassist Paul Chambers and drummer Billy Higgins) performs originals by Morgan, Walton and Duke Pearson, including particularly catchy versions of the funky "Hey Chico" and Pearson's memorable "Sweet Honey Bee" (which should have become a hit). The three horns, all of whom sound quite individual, each have their exciting moments, and the results are quintessential mid-1960s hard bop. *—Scott Yanow*

The Procrastinator / Jul. 14, 1967-Oct. 10, 1969 / Blue Note ✦✦✦✦✦
It is surprising that Lee Morgan's *The Procrastinator* was not released when it was recorded in 1967 for the sextet (which includes Wayne Shorter, vibraphonist Bobby Hutcherson, pianist Herbie Hancock, bassist Ron Carter and drummer Billy Higgins) lives up to their potential on a well-rounded set of originals by Morgan and Shorter. The music ranges from the funky "Party Time" (which sounds like it could have been written by Horace Silver) to more explorative pieces. *—Scott Yanow*

The Sixth Sense / Nov. 10, 1967 / Blue Note ✦✦✦
For this lesser-known Lee Morgan LP, the trumpeter was starting to stretch beyond hard bop into more modal areas while retaining his easily recognizable sound. None of Morgan's originals (which are performed along with pianist Cedar Walton's "Afreaka" and Cal Massey's "The Cry of My People") caught on but the music is creatively performed by the trumpeter, altoist Jackie McLean (who was always a perfect musical partner), the obscure tenor Frank Mitchell, Walton, bassist Victor Sproles and drummer Billy Higgins. *—Scott Yanow*

Taru / Feb. 15, 1968 / Blue Note ✦✦✦✦
Trumpeter Lee Morgan performs two funky boogaloos, a ballad and three complex group originals on this album whose music was first released in 1980. This is a transitional date with the hard bop stylist leaning in the direction of modal music and even anticipating aspects of fusion. His sextet (which includes Bennie Maupin on tenor, guitarist George Benson, pianist John Hicks, bassist Reggie Workman and drummer Billy Higgins) is quite advanced for the period and inspires Morgan to some fiery and explorative playing. *—Scott Yanow*

Caramba / May 3, 1968 / Blue Note ✦✦✦
Until its 1996 reissue, this was one of the most obscure of all Lee Morgan Blue Note albums. A transitional effort that finds the trumpeter gradually moving beyond hard bop into more modal music, the date starts out with the surprisingly derivative title cut which is very similar to Eddie Harris' "Listen Here." Of the other selections, "Soulita" has the catchiest melody while Cal Massey's slow ballad "A Baby's Smile" was previously unreleased. While Morgan and his fine rhythm section (pianist Cedar Walton, bassist Reggie Workman and drummer Billy Higgins) are in typically swinging form, *Caramba* is most notable for featuring the young Bennie Maupin. Sticking exclusively to tenor, Maupin (who would be much more distinctive within a year) mixes together Joe Henderson and Wayne Shorter in winning fashion. Although not essential, this CD is a welcome reissue. *—Scott Yanow*

Live at the Lighthouse / Jul. 10, 1970-Jul. 12, 1970 / Blue Note ✦✦✦✦✦
This double LP, which was trumpeter Lee Morgan's next-to-last recording, contains four lengthy side-long explorations by the trumpeter's regular quintet of the period (with Bennie Maupin on tenor, flute and bass clarinet, pianist Harold Mabern, bassist Jymie Merritt and drummer Mickey Roker). The music is very modal-oriented and probably disappointed many of Morgan's longtime fans but he had gotten tired of playing the same hard bop-styled music that he had excelled at during the past decade and was searching for newer sounds. The influence of the avant-garde and early fusion is also felt in spots but the trumpeter's sound was still very much intact and he takes some fiery solos that still sound lively decades later. *—Scott Yanow*

Jelly Roll Morton (Ferdinand Joseph Lemott)

b. Oct. 20, 1890, New Orleans, LA, **d.** Jul. 10, 1941, Los Angeles, CA
Piano, Composer / New Orleans Jazz, Classic Jazz
One of the very first giants of jazz, Jelly Roll Morton did himself a lot of harm posthumously by exaggerating his worth, claiming to have invented jazz in 1902. Morton's accomplishments as an early innovator are so vast that he did not really need to stretch the truth. Morton was jazz's first great composer, writing such songs as "King Porter Stomp," "Grandpa's Spells," "Wolverine Blues," "The Pearls," "Mr. Jelly Roll," "Shreveport Stomp," "Milenburg

Joys," "Black Bottom Stomp," "The Chant," "Original Jelly Roll Blues," "Doctor Jazz," "Wild Man Blues," "Winin' Boy Blues," "I Thought I Heard Buddy Bolden Say," "Don't You Leave Me Here," and "Sweet Substitute." He was a talented arranger (1926's "Black Bottom Stomp" is remarkable), getting the most out of the three-minute limitations of the 78 record by emphasizing changing instrumentation, concise solos and dynamics. He was a greatly underrated pianist who had his own individual style. Although he only took one vocal on records in the 1920s ("Doctor Jazz"), Morton in his late-'30s recordings proved to be an effective vocalist. And he was a true character. *—Scott Yanow*

1923-1924 [Classics] / Jun. 1923-Jun. 9, 1924 / Classics ♦♦♦♦
Part of Classics' excellent chronological series, this examines Jelly Roll's recordings from 1923 to 1924, beginning with a Paramount single with his orchestra, "Big Fat Ham," followed by "Muddy Water Blues." Next up are the first six issued Gennett piano solos, then stray singles by Morton's Jazz Band, Steamboat Four, and Stomp Kings. These are proceeded by four more piano solo sides, which were cut for Paramount, before finishing out with a marathon piano solo session for Gennett in 1924. *—Cub Koda*

★ **1923-1924 [Milestone]** / 1923-1924 / Milestone ♦♦♦♦♦
Here are all of Jelly Roll's classic Gennett piano solos, including the only known alternate take of "New Orleans Joys," presented in the sequence in which they were recorded. The No Noise system used to clean these old 78s up does a decent enough job, considering when these sides were cut and their rarity. Also on tap are four more solo piano sides cut in Chicago in 1924, four band sides with various personnel, topped off with two piano/cornet duets with King Oliver. A large chunk of this man's genius in one very digestible package. *—Cub Koda*

1924-1926 / Sep. 1924-Dec. 1926 / Classics ♦♦♦♦♦

Piano Rolls / Sep. 1924-Dec. 1924 / Elektra ♦♦♦♦♦
Piano rolls generally sound rather wooden, with square rhythms and a honky-tonk feel; the displays of virtuosity are sometimes are impossible for one pianist to perform due to excessive hole punching. Jelly Roll Morton's 11 piano rolls of 1924 (which had previously been put out on LP by Biograph and Everest) often had more life than others of the period, but still sounded a bit mechanical. Using modern techniques during 1996-97 (including the Yamaha Disklavier), producer Artis Wodehouse was able to make Morton's piano rolls sound much more alive than they had previously for this CD. The interpretations almost pass for 1920s piano recordings, and Morton's feel comes across better than in previous versions of the rolls. Of the 11 selections, it is possible that "Sweet Man" was not performed by Jelly Roll (although his name was on the original roll), for the style sounds a bit different. But the other numbers (highlighted by "Shreveport Stomps," "Grandpa's Spells," "King Porter Stomp" and "Mr. Jelly Lord") definitely bring back the spirit of Jelly Roll Morton. *—Scott Yanow*

☆ **Jelly Roll Morton Centennial: His Complete Victor Recording** / Sep. 15, 1926-Sep. 28, 1939 / Bluebird/RCA ♦♦♦♦♦
This five-CD set contains the very best band recordings of Jelly Roll Morton's career. There are 111 performances in this reissue including all of the alternate takes. Bypassed are the pianist's recordings with the vaudevillian clarinetist Wilton Crawley, singers Lizzie Miles and Billie Young and two songs he performed on a radio broadcast in 1940; otherwise all of his Victor recordings are here. The classics (most from the 1926-28 period) include the remarkable "Black Bottom Stomp," "Grandpa's Spells," "The Pearls," "Wolverine Blues" (a trio with clarinetist Johnny Dodds and drummer Baby Dodds), "Shreveport Stomp," "Low Gravy," "Strokin' Away" and "I Thought I Heard Buddy Bolden Say" but listeners will have their own favorites. In general this is New Orleans jazz at its best with Jelly Roll Morton (as with the best jazz composer/bandleaders) creating his own world of music. *—Scott Yanow*

1926-1928 / Dec. 1926-Jun. 1928 / Classics ♦♦♦♦♦

1928-1929 / Dec. 6, 1928-Dec. 2, 1929 / Classics ♦♦♦♦♦

Kansas City Stomp: The Library of Congress Recordings, Vol. 1 / May 23, 1938-Jun. 7, 1938 / Rounder ♦♦♦♦♦
Pianist/composer Jelly Roll Morton, one of the pioneers of New Orleans jazz, was down and out in 1938 when Alan Lomax found him playing in a Washington D.C. dive. Lomax, realizing that Morton had seen and heard many timeless incidents that would otherwise be forgotten, started interviewing him for the Library of Congress on a wire recorder. Released originally on eight LPs, these discussions found Morton talking about the old days and peppering his talk with piano solos. Rounder has reissued all of the music (and done a fine job of correcting the speed) on four CDs but unfortunately decided to leave out Morton's often-fascinating monologues. This first CD has many strong moments including Morton's demonstration of the piano styles of many forgotten players, his depiction of a New Orleans funeral, his famous demonstration of how "Tiger Rag" evolved from being a quadrille into becoming jazz and comparisons of "Maple Leaf Rag" as played as ragtime and the way Morton preferred it. *—Scott Yanow*

The Library of Congress Recordings, Vol. 1 / May 23, 1938-Jun. 12, 1938 / Solo Art ♦♦♦♦♦
There are two different ways to acquire pianist/composer Jelly Roll Morton's famed *Library of Congress* recordings. Classic Jazz and the Australian label Swaggie on eight LPs have reissued virtually all of Morton's monologues and music; Jazzology is currently working on making these important recordings available on CD. The alternative method is to acquire Rounder's four-CD series. Rounder has pitch corrected all of the music but unfortunately decided to leave out most of Morton's storytelling, lessening the impact of these unique sessions. *Vol. 1* in the Classic Jazz series (all eight are recommended to true early jazz historians) finds Morton talking about his childhood, discussing the origin of his "Jelly Roll Blues," performing "King Porter Stomp" and "Panama" and, most interesting of all, doing his famous transformation of "Tiger Rag" from a quadrille into jazz. *—Scott Yanow*

The Pearls / May 23, 1938-Jun. 7, 1938 / Rounder ♦♦♦♦♦
This astounding 23-track compilation deserves a place in everybody's jazz collection—it's that important, that listenable, and that essential. It takes the cream of Morton's sessions from his legendary 1926 *Red Hot Peppers* to his 1939 dates leading a small New Orleans band, with all the essential stops along the way, including a 1927 trio with the Dodds brothers in Chicago. This is hot jazz nearing the apex of sophistication, just before Duke Ellington took it even more uptown. *—Cub Koda*

Winin Boy Blues / Jun. 7, 1938-Dec. 14, 1938 / Rounder ♦♦♦♦♦
The fourth and final CD in Rounder's *Library of Congress* series has the later recordings from this extensive program, including two numbers from six months after the original discussions had concluded. Morton, who is heard very briefly on guitar on "L'il Liza Jane," takes fine piano solos on such numbers as "Freakish," "Pep," "Ain't Misbehavin'" and a medley of "Spanish tinge" songs including "The Crave." This facinating series (which Rounder pitch corrected) is recommended to collectors of early jazz. *—Scott Yanow*

Bennie Moten

b. Nov. 13, 1894, Kansas City, MO, **d.** Apr. 2, 1935, Kansas City, MO
Piano / Classic Jazz, Big Band
Bennie Moten is today best-remembered as the leader of a band that partly became the nucelus of the original Count Basie Orchestra, but Moten deserves better. He was a fine ragtime-oriented pianist who led the top territory band of the 1920s, an orchestra that really set the standard for Kansas City jazz. In fact it was so dominant that Moten was able to swallow up some of his competitors' groups including Walter Page's Blue Devils, most of whom eventually became members of Moten's big band. Moten formed his group in 1922 and the following year they made their first recordings. Among Moten's 1923-25 sides for Okeh was the original version of his greatest hit "South." During 1926-32 Moten's Orchestra recorded for Victor and, although none of his original musicians became famous, the later additions included his brother Buster on occasional jazz accordion, Harlan Leonard, Jack Washington, Eddie Durham, Jimmy Rushing, Hot Lips Page and (starting in 1929) Count Basie. The most famous Bennie Moten recording session was also his last, ten songs cut on December 13, 1932 that find the ensemble strongly resembling Basie's five years later. *—Scott Yanow*

1923-1927 / Sep. 1923-Jun. 11, 1927 / Classics ♦♦♦♦♦

1927-1929 / Jun. 11, 1927-Jun. 17, 1929 / Classics ♦♦♦♦♦

1929-1930 / Jul. 18, 1929-Oct. 29, 1930 / Classics ♦♦♦♦♦

★ **Basie Beginnings (1929-1932)** / Oct. 23, 1929-Dec. 13, 1932 / Bluebird ♦♦♦♦♦
Bennie Moten's orchestra, arguably the top territory band at the time Count Basie joined as second pianist in 1929, had been reasonably well-represented on records since 1923. This does have the cream of Moten's 1929 and 1930 sessions, plus seven of the ten songs cut at their superb Dec. 13, 1932 date. Moten himself never again appeared on records after Basie joined. *—Scott Yanow*

1930-1932 / Oct. 29, 1930-Dec. 13, 1932 / Classics ♦♦♦♦♦

Paul Motian (Stephen Paul Motian)

b. Mar. 25, 1931, Philadelphia, PA
Drums, Percussion / Avant-Garde Jazz, Post-Bop
Paul Motian is a subtle drummer who is equally important as the leader of several rather stimulating bands and quite a few colorful recording sessions. Born in Philadelphia, Motian grew up in Providence, RI. After moving to New York in 1955 he played with many top jazz musicians from a wide variety of styles including Tony Scott, Gil Evans, Art Farmer, Lee Konitz, George Russell, Stan Getz, Lennie Tristano, Thelonious Monk, Coleman Hawkins and Roy Eldridge. As a member of Bill Evans's most famous trio (the one with Scott LaFaro), Motian helped define the role of the modern drummer in that type of intimate setting. He remained with Evans after LaFaro's death (Chuck Israels took over as bassist) until 1963. Motian then played with Paul Bley's Trio (1963-64) and he later had a longterm musical relationship with Keith Jarrett, starting in 1966 and including work with Jarrett's quintet in the 1970s. Motian also freelanced and among the many musicians that he worked with were Mose Allison, Charles Lloyd, Charlie Haden's Liberation Music Ensemble and Carla Bley. Motian began leading his own groups in 1977 and these included a trio with Joe Lovano and Bill Frisell and the Electric Bebop Band in the 1990's with Joshua Redman and two guitarists. He has recorded many albums as a leader (starting in 1972) for ECM, GM, Soul Note and JMT including collaborations with Lee Konitz. *—Scott Yanow*

Jack of Clubs / Mar. 26, 1984-Mar. 28, 1984 / Soul Note ♦♦♦♦
Starting in the early '80s, drummer Paul Motian led a series of fascinating bands, usually pianoless and featuring the highly original guitarist Bill Frisell. For this outing, Motian and Frisell are teamed with the tenors of Jim Pepper and Joe Lovano plus bassist Ed Schuller. The drummer's seven originals feature lots of variety in moods, ranging from witty to introspective and showcasing the colorful players at their best. Frisell (who is featured on "Lament") in particular sounds perfectly at home with Motian's group. *—Scott Yanow*

One Time Out / Sep. 21, 1987-Sep. 22, 1987 / Soul Note ♦♦♦♦
The key to this unusual trio is not the muscular tenor of Joe Lovano or the propulsive timekeeping of the drummer/leader but the remarkable guitarist Bill Frisell. Able to somehow produce sounds from this guitar that could be mistaken for a keyboard or a steel guitar, in styles ranging from heavy metal and avant-garde jazz to country music, Frisell is the reason that the trio can sound like a full band despite not having a keyboardist or a bassist. The music, which includes seven Motian originals along with "Monk's Mood" and "If You Could See Me Now," features both intense three-way free improvisations and introspective spacey ballads. Few of the tunes themselves will stick in one's mind (although "Morpion" could be an imaginary meeting betwee 1966 John Coltrane and Jimi Hendrix) but it is the basic sound of the unique group that makes the CD of great interest. *—Scott Yanow*

● **Monk in Motian** / Mar. 1988 / JMT ♦♦♦♦♦
This is an utterly fascinating tribute to the music of Thelonious Monk. Most of the selections feature the unusual trio of tenor saxophonist Joe Lovano, guitarist Bill Frisell (who with his wide range of original sounds is really a one-band band) and drummer Paul Motian. Tenor saxophonist Dewey Redman and pianist Geri Allen are guests on two songs apiece and fit in

quite well with the sparse but very complete trio. Among the ten Monk songs explored, taken apart and given surprising treatment are "Evidence," "Bye-Ya," "Ugly Beauty" and "Trinkle Tinkle." Recommended to open-eared listeners. *— Scott Yanow*

Paul Motian on Broadway, Vol. 1 (with Bill Frisell, Charlie Haden, Joe Lovano & Paul M / Nov. 1988 / JMT ✦✦✦✦✦
The quartet of tenorman Joe Lovano, guitarist Bill Frisell, bassist Charlie Haden and drummer Paul Motian digs into nine show tunes from the 1930s and 40s, reinventing them in colorful fashion. The key to the rewarding project is Frisell, whose versatility and wide range of highly original sounds make the overall results sound quite unique. Among the highlights of the memorable set are unusual versions of "Liza," "They Didn't Believe Me" and "Last Night When We Were Young." *— Scott Yanow*

Paul Motian on Broadway, Vol. 2 / Sep. 1989 / JMT ✦✦✦✦✦
The second of three Paul Motian records that spotlight jazz standards, *On Broadway, Vol. 2* includes innovative but respectful readings of tin pan alley nuggets by George Gershwin, Jerome Kern, Richard Rogers, and others. Motian's working band (guitarist Bill Frisell and tenor saxophonist Joe Lovano) and guest bassist Charlie Haden are in top form on both ballads ("Moonlight Becomes You" and "Good Morning Heartache") and up-tempo material ("I Got Rhythm" and "Nice Work If You Can Get It"). Frisell, in particular, stands out with his mercurial yet mindful solos, while Lovano impresses with vigorously fluid tenor work. Motian keeps things lively with his jaunty rhythmic sense and Haden anchors it all in typically unpredictable fashion. *On Broadway, Vol. 2* is not only one of many fine Motian recordings on the Swiss label JMT (later to morph into Motian's current label, Winter & Winter), but it also is a showcase of some of the smartest, most rewarding jazz improvisation of the last couple decades. *— Stephen Cook*

Sound of Love / Jan. 7, 1995-Jan. 10, 1995 / Winter & Winter ✦✦✦✦✦
This live 1995 recording from New York's *Village Vanguard* club features drummer Paul Motian, guitarist Bill Frisell, and tenor saxophonist Joe Lovano turning in a stellar set of jazz covers and Motian originals (this is the same trio the drummer led in the late '80s and recorded high-profile tributes to Bill Evans, Thelonious Monk, and Tin Pan Alley with). As the premium sound quality of the recording makes clear, this trio had an almost telepathic rapport on stage, inspiring each other in both ensemble playing and solo flights. This kind of hand-in-glove chemistry is certainly due in part to the group's many stints on the road, but also comes from the individual player's complimentary styles: Frisell and Lovano (albeit less subtly) both dig into the structure of the songs, producing clever and dynamic statements, while Motian contains the proceedings with his steady, yet elastic time keeping and provocative accents. The covers here include extended readings of Monk's "Misterioso" and Charles Mingus' beautiful ballad "Duke Ellington's Sound of Love," in addition to a loose and bittersweet rendition of the jazz standard "Good Morning Heartache." Motian balances out the set with originals like the thorny, Latin rhythms-based "Mumbo Jumbo," the lightly swinging waltz number "Once Around the Park," and the dark-hewn, yet beguiling closer "Play." This is a great recording of some of the best jazz combo playing from the '80s to 2000. For Motian newcomers, though, the best bet is to first get one of this group's studio-recorded repertoire titles (*Monk in Motian, Bill Evans, On Broadway*) before checking out this sprawling live release. *— Stephen Cook*

Flight of the Bluejay / Aug. 20, 1996-Aug. 21, 1996 / Winter & Winter ✦✦✦
During the 20 years that preceded this set, Paul Motian had led some of the most intriguing jazz groups around. For this project, his "Electric Bebop Band" consists of two tenors (Chris Potter and Chris Cheek), two guitars (Kurt Rosenwinkel and Brad Schoeppach), bassist Steve Swallow, and the leader himself on drums. With the exception of Motian's opening selection and a pair of originals by Rosenwinkel, the repertoire consists of three songs by Thelonious Monk and one tune apiece from Bud Powell, Miles Davis, George Shearing, Charlie Parker, and Rodgers & Hart. Essentially a straight-ahead bebop date, the most unusual aspect of the set (which unfortunately has no liner notes, so individual soloists are not identified) is that there are many sections where two different players solo together. Usually it is the two tenors or both of the guitarists, but occasionally it's a tenor and a guitarist. Everyone plays well, but nothing really that unexpected occurs. The songs are superior; the highlights include Powell's "Celia," a medium-slow "Blue Room," "Milestones" (the 1947 song), and Monk's "Work." But overall, this date falls short of being memorable. *— Scott Yanow*

Play Monk & Powell / Nov. 28, 1998-Nov. 29, 1999 / Winter & Winter ✦✦✦✦✦
Drummer Paul Motian has made a number of delightful albums with his unusually configured Electric Bebop Band, and the latest, focusing on compositions by bop legends Thelonious Monk and Bud Powell, may be his best. Guitarists Kurt Rosenwinkel and Steve Cardenas interact beautifully with saxophonists Chris Potter and Chris Cheek. The program opens with a sprightly run through Monk's "We See" before sliding smoothly into Powell's beautiful ballad "I'll Keep Loving You." The album's centerpiece, though, comes next: a loose-limbed but scrupulously accurate rendition of Monk's "Brilliant Corners," a composition so difficult that its first commercial release was pieced together from 27 unsuccessful takes. After that, the downright weird but structurally straightforward "Little Rootie Tootie" sounds like a five-minute vacation. Powell's "Blue Pearl" and anarchic "Parisian Thoroughfare" are given equally sympathetic performances. Purists may scoff at the sextet's configuration, but this album is a joy from beginning to end. (The disc's opulent packaging is also worth noting.) *— Rick Anderson*

Gerry Mulligan

b. Apr. 6, 1927, New York, NY, **d.** Jan. 20, 1996, Darien, CT
Sax (Baritone), Piano, Composer, Arranger / West Coast Jazz, Cool
The most famous and probably greatest jazz baritonist of all time, Gerry Mulligan was a giant. A flexible soloist who was always ready to jam with anyone from Dixielanders to the most advanced boppers, Mulligan brought a somewhat revolutionary light sound to his potentially awkward and brutal horn and played with the speed and dexterity of an altoist. His first notable recorded work on baritone was with Miles Davis's *Birth of the Cool* nonet (1948-50) but his arrangements ("Godchild," "Darn That Dream" and three of his originals "Jeru," "Rocker" and "Venus De Milo") were more significant than his short solos. It was not until 1951 that he began to get a bit of attention for his work on baritone. Mulligan recorded with his own nonet for Prestige, displaying an already recognizable sound. After he traveled to Los Angeles, he wrote some arrangements for Stan Kenton (including "Youngblood," "Swing House" and "Walking Shoes"), worked at the Lighthouse and then gained a regular Monday night engagement at the Haig. Around this time Mulligan realized that he enjoyed the extra freedom of soloing without a pianist. He jammed with trumpeter Chet Baker and soon their magical rapport was featured in his pianoless quartet. The group caught on quickly in 1952 and made both Mulligan and Baker into stars. A drug bust put Mulligan out of action and ended that Quartet but, when he was released from jail in 1954, Mulligan began a new musical partnership with valve trombonist Bob Brookmeyer that was just as successful. Being a very flexible player with respect for other stylists, Mulligan went out of his way to record with some of the great musicians he admired. At the 1958 Newport Jazz Fetival he traded off with baritonist Harry Carney on "Prima Bara Dubla" while backed by the Duke Ellington Orchestra, and during 1957-60 he recorded separate albums with Thelonious Monk, Paul Desmond, Stan Getz, Ben Webster and Johnny Hodges. *— Scott Yanow*

Mulligan Plays Mulligan / Aug. 27, 1951 / Prestige/OJC ✦✦✦✦
Gerry Mulligan's first session as a leader and one of the first to showcase his baritone was recorded in New York shortly before he relocated to Los Angeles and formed his famous pianoless quartet with Chet Baker. There is a piano on this set (George Wallington) but Mulligan's writing (all seven selections are his) for a two-baritone nonet that also features trumpeter Nick Travis and tenor-saxophonist Allan Eager is already in his influential "cool style"; best-known among the originals is "Bweebida Bwobbida." Two numbers on the CD reissue feature a smaller unit out of the group with "Mulligan's Too" being an extended workout for the leader and Eager. *— Scott Yanow*

☆ **Pacific Jazz and Capitol Recordings** / Jun. 10, 1952-Jun. 10, 1953 / Mosaic ✦✦✦✦✦
This five-LP box set, as its title states, contains all of the Gerry Mulligan Quartet's recordings for Pacific Jazz and Capitol, everything that that classic group ever recorded other than the material issued by Prestige and a half record recorded for GNP Crescendo. Unfortunately, this is a limited-edition set that is now out of print but it is well worth bidding on in auctions, for not only does it have all of the Mulligan Quartet's other recordings but also 15 previously unissued performances, all of the sides on which altoist Lee Konitz sat in with the quartet and the eight recordings by the 1953 Gerry Mulligan Tentette. These highly influential performances set the standard for West Coast cool jazz, made trumpeter Chet Baker a star, and remain some of the high points of Gerry Mulligan's very productive career. *— Scott Yanow*

Gerry Mulligan in Paris / Jun. 3, 1954-Jun. 7, 1954 / Vogue ✦✦✦✦✦
In June 1954, the Gerry Mulligan Quartet (with the leader/baritonist, valve trombonist Bob Brookmeyer, bassist Red Mitchell and drummer Frank Isola) performed at five all-star concerts, four of which were recorded. Only previously available in fragmented form, the very accessible yet chance-taking music has now been reissued in full on two CDs by the French Vogue label. The second volume is highlighted by "Laura," "Five Brothers," "Love Me or Leave Me," "Line for Lyons" and "Motel," but it is no exaggeration to say that every performance is well worth hearing. Both sets are highly recommended, for this cool-toned but witty and hard-swinging music is very enjoyable. *— Scott Yanow*

California Concerts, Vols. 1 & 2 / Nov. 12, 1954 / Pacific Jazz ✦✦✦

At Storyville / Dec. 6, 1956 / Pacific Jazz ✦✦✦✦✦
This live concert from the Storyville Club in Boston features Gerry Mulligan's Quartet in late 1956. Baritonist Mulligan had found a perfect partner in valve trombonist Bob Brookmeyer and (with the sympathetic support of bassist Bill Crow and drummer Dave Bailey) they romp through a variety of standards and group originals including such odd titles as "Bweebida Bwobbida," "Utter Chaos" (their theme song) and "Bike up the Strand." A fine all-round performance from this cool-toned bop unit. *— Scott Yanow*

Reunion with Chet Baker / Dec. 3, 1957-Dec. 17, 1957 / EMI-Manhattan ✦✦✦✦
The Gerry Mulligan Quartet of 1952-53 was one of the best-loved jazz groups of the decade and it made stars out of both the leader and trumpeter Chet Baker. Mulligan and Baker had very few reunions after 1953 but this particular CD from 1957 is an exception. Although not quite possessing the magic of the earlier group, the music is quite enjoyable and the interplay between the two horns is still special. With expert backup by bassist Henry Grimes and drummer Dave Bailey, these 13 selections (plus two new alternate takes) should please fans of both Mulligan and Baker. *— Scott Yanow*

Songbook / Dec. 4, 1957-Dec. 5, 1957 / Blue Note ✦✦✦✦✦
Until it was reissued on CD, this was one of the rarer Gerry Mulligan albums. The original program consisted of seven Mulligan compositions played by a five-sax octet (including the leader on baritone, altoist Lee Konitz, Allen Eager and Zoot Sims doubling on tenor and alto, Al Cohn on tenor and baritone and a rhythm section consisting of guitarist Freddie Green, bassist Henry Grimes, and drummer Dave Bailey). The session has a few surprise touches, giving listeners the rare opportunity to hear Eager and Sims soloing on alto and Cohn doubling on baritone. This was Allen Eager's first recording in several years and would be the last one of his prime (Eager's next album would be for Uptown in 1982); he had other interests outside of music. Perhaps the biggest surprise of the date is that the clever, witty and swinging arrangements are not by Mulligan but by Bill Holman. The CD reissue is rounded off by four selections from a largely unissued ("The Preacher" came out as an edited sampler) session featuring Mulligan with drummer Dave Bailey and a string quartet led by bassist Vinnie Burke. The performances are not chamber music but fairly conventional if spirited bop. Cellist Calo Scott trades off a bit with Jeru and guitarist Remo Palmieri makes one wonder what ever happened to him. Highly recommended for Gerry Mulligan fans. *— Scott Yanow*

☆ **What Is There to Say—** / Dec. 17, 1958-Jan. 15, 1959 / Sony ✦✦✦✦✦
The last of the pianoless quartet albums that Gerry Mulligan recorded in the 1950s is one of

the best, featuring the complementary trumpet of Art Farmer, bassist Bill Crow and drummer Dave Bailey along with the baritonist/leader. This recording is a little skimpy on playing time but makes every moment count. Virtually every selection is memorable with "What Is There to Say," "Just in Time," "Festive Minor," "My Funny Valentine" and "Utter Chaos" being the highpoints. Highly recommended both to Mulligan collectors and to jazz listeners who are just discovering the great baritonist. *—Scott Yanow*

★ **The Complete Gerry Mulligan Meets Ben Webster Sessions** / Nov. 3, 1959-Dec. 2, 1959 / Verve ♦♦♦♦♦

Although an earlier CD added five previously unissued tracks to the original LP *Gerry Mulligan Meets Ben Webster,* this Verve Master Edition two-CD set adds just about everything else recorded during the two sessions that produced the original record, and also features 20-bit sound. Even though Gerry Mulligan was outspoken against issuing material omitted from his original recordings, it is a treat to hear how the songs evolved in the studio. Webster and Mulligan seem mutually inspired throughout the sessions, and strong performances by pianist Jimmy Rowles, bassist Leroy Vinnegar, and drummer Mel Lewis are of considerable help. The music is presented in the order in which it was recorded, with each CD devoted to a separate session. In both cases it is clear that the initial takes of music from the Ellington songbook ("In a Mellotone" and "Chelsea Bridge") are more focused than the follow-up versions. They only needed one try to nail "What Is This Thing Called Love—" (also left off the LP), in an understated setting that shows off their beautiful interplay. Their barely disguised reworking of "I Got Rhythm," called "Who's Got Rhythm," was likely an effortless performance, though Webster seems to briefly laugh in the middle of his solo. Webster's swinging "Fajista" opens the second date, followed by two takes of Mulligan's beautiful ballad "Tell Me When." Webster's "Blues in B-Flat" is another fine swinger inexplicably left off the LP, and Rowles kicks off the oldie "Sunday" with a brief stride piano introduction (something Webster played himself but rarely in a recording studio). Fans on a budget can probably make due with the earlier CD reissue but serious fans of Mulligan and/or Webster should invest in this very rewarding set instead. *—Ken Dryden*

★ **Gerry Mulligan Meets Ben Webster** / Nov. 3, 1959-Dec. 2, 1959 / Verve ♦♦♦♦♦

The swing and bop start right here on this legendary 1959 session between baritone saxophonist Gerry Mulligan and tenor man Ben Webster. The opening track, Billy Strayhorn's "Chelsea Bridge" is lush and emotional and truly sets the tone for this album. With Jimmy Rowles on piano (his intro on "Sunday" sounds like a ragtimer like Willie "The Lion" Smith just pushed him off the stool before the band came in), Mel Lewis on drums and always superb Leroy Vinegar on bass present and accounted for, the rhythm section is superbly swinging with just the right amount of bop lines and chords in the mix to spice things up. The ghost of Duke Ellington hovers over every note on this record (Billy Strayhorn was one of his main arrangers) and that is a very good thing, indeed. There's a beautiful understated quality to the music on this session that makes it the perfect relaxing around the house on a rainy day disc to pop in the player. File this one under cool, very smooth and supple. *—Cub Koda*

☆ **Gerry Mulligan and the Concert Jazz Band at the Village Vanguard** / Dec. 1960 / Verve ♦♦♦♦♦

Carnegie Hall Concert / Nov. 24, 1974 / Columbia ♦♦♦♦

At this 1974 concert baritonist Gerry Mulligan and trumpeter Chet Baker had one of their very rare reunions; it would be only the second and final time that they recorded together after Mulligan's original quartet broke up in 1953. Oddly enough a fairly contemporary rhythm section was used (keyboardist Bob James, vibraphonist Dave Samuels, bassist Ron Carter, drummer Harvey Mason and, in one of his first recordings, guitarist John Scofield. However some of the old magic was still there between the horns and, in addition to two of Mulligan's newer tunes, this set (the first of two volumes) also includes fresh versions of "Line for Lyons" and "My Funny Valentine." *—Scott Yanow*

Gerry Mulligan Meets Scott Hamilton: Soft Lights and Sweet Music / Jan. 1986 / Concord Jazz ♦♦♦♦

Starting in the late '50s, Gerry Mulligan recorded a series of encounters with fellow saxophonists that included such immortals as Stan Getz, Paul Desmond, Johnny Hodges and Ben Webster. In 1986 he resumed the practice for this one date on which his baritone is matched with the tenor of the young great Scott Hamilton. The music, which includes warm ballads and fairly hot romps (five of the seven songs are Mulligan originals), consistently swing and are quite enjoyable. *—Scott Yanow*

Gerry Mulligan & Paul Desmond Quartet / Aug. 2, 1957-Aug. 27, 1957 / Verve ♦♦♦♦♦

This is the first recorded collaboration of baritone saxophone great Gerry Mulligan and the witty alto saxophonist Paul Desmond. Despite hardly any preparation for these recording sessions, the two men complement one another's playing beautifully, as both of them were highly melodic improvisers. Desmond brought three originals to the sessions: the driving "Blues in Time," the soft ballad "Wintersong" (which is based on the chord changes to "These Foolish Things"), and "Battle Hymn of the Republican" (which is actually a complex reworking of "Tea for Two"). Mulligan's contributions include his earlier hit "Line for Lyons," "Stand Still" (based on "My Heart Stood Still"), and the Latin-tinged "Fall Out" (taken from "Let's Fall in Love"). Mulligan was clearly annoyed when told that three unissued tracks ("Tea for Two," "Lover," and an alternate take of "Wintersong") had been added to the CD reissue, but was clearly amused at the accidental and unlisted first take of "Lover", which falls apart after a minute-and-a-half and is followed by some discussion. Bassist Joe Benjamin and drummer Dave Bailey provide excellent rhythmic support throughout this highly recommended CD. *—Ken Dryden*

The Art of Gerry Mulligan: The Final Recordings / Jul. 5, 1993-Jun. 27, 1995 / Telarc ♦♦♦♦♦

As one of the most famous baritone sax players in jazz, Gerry Mulligan is an icon from the 1950s cool jazz era. Known for his light, airy tone, he was also an excellent composer, arranger, and bandleader and an important figure in the development of cool jazz. On this CD, *The Art of Gerry Mulligan: The Final Recordings,* Telarc Jazz has compiled selections from three of Mulligan's recordings for the label during those years: *Paraiso-Jazz Brazil* with Jane Duboc on vocals; *Dream a Little Dream* a quartet recording; and *Dragonfly,* also by Mulligan's quartet but featuring special guests guitarist John Scofield, saxophonist Grover Washington Jr., and pianist Dave Grusin. Each of these creative periods produced an exceptional output of compositions including "O Bom Alvinho," & "Song for Strayhorn," and the ever-popular "Dragonfly." While this compilation represents only the latter part of his great career from 1993-1995, it is an exceptional preservation of the cool jazz legacy of Gerry Mulligan. *—Paula Edelstein*

David Murray (David Keith Murray)

b. Feb. 19, 1955, Berkeley, CA

Sax (Tenor), Clarinet (Bass) / Avant-Garde Jazz, Free Jazz, M-Base, Post-Bop, Progressive Big Band

Initially a free player in the vein of Albert Ayler and Archie Shepp, David Murray evolved into something of a mainstream tenorist, playing standards with conventional rhythm sections. But his readings of the old chestnuts veer from standard interpretations with a unique approach to chord changes and his deep sound, furry with a wide vibrato, reminiscent of Ben Webster and Coleman Hawkins. Murray adapted the expressive techniques of his former free-jazz self to his straight-ahead playing, with good results, recording over 50 albums during the '80s and '90s..

In his youth, Murray played music in church with his family. He was introduced to jazz while a student in Berkeley, playing alto sax in school band, and in the local group Notations of Soul. Hearing Sonny Rollins inspired Murray's switch from alto to tenor. He studied with trumpeter Bobby Bradford at Pomona College, where he met writer Stanley Crouch. Murray and Crouch moved to NYC in the mid-'70s, during the "loft jazz" era, and opened their own loft space, Studio Infinity. Murray quickly acquired a promising reputation, with Crouch as unofficial publicity agent and part-time drummer. Murray's early work was raw and shared Ayler's penchant for multiphonics, distorted timbres, and extreme volumes. Murray's first albums were *Flowers for Albert* and *Low Class Conspiracy* (both 1976). That year, Murray also co-founded the World Saxophone Quartet with Julius Hemphill, Oliver Lake, and Hamiet Bluiett.

His other groups include a big band, an octet, and various small bands. His octet records (mostly on Black Saint) document the evolution of Murray as a composer. As he got older, the influence of his swing and bop elders strengthened and the wilder elements of his playing toned down. By the mid-'90s, the relative predictability of his soloing was offset by his increased skill as a composer. *—Chris Kelsey*

Flowers for Albert / Jun. 16, 1976 / India Navigation ♦♦♦♦

David Murray, who was 21 at the time, shows a lot of promise on this early recording. The explorative tenor saxophonist joins with trumpeter Olu Dara, bassist Fred Hopkins and drummer Phillip Wilson for five adventurous pieces (three were released for the first time on this 1997 double-CD). In addition, Murray duets with Hopkins on "Ballad for a Decomposed Beauty" and collaborates with Wilson on their duet "Roscoe." The music is often quite free but it also takes its time, showing high energy in well-chosen spots. Since this period David Murray has lived up to his great potential. *—Scott Yanow*

☆ **Ming** / Jul. 25, 1980-Jul. 28, 1980 / Black Saint ♦♦♦♦♦

His octet was always the perfect setting for tenor saxophonist David Murray, large enough to generate power but not as out of control as many of his big band performances. Murray contributed all five originals (including "Ming" and "Dewey's Circle") and arrangements, and is in superior form on both tenor and bass clarinet. The "backup crew" is also quite notable: altoist Henry Threadgill, trumpeter Olu Dara, cornetist Butch Morris, trombonist George Lewis, pianist Anthony Davis, bassist Wilbur Morris and drummer Steve McCall. These avant-garde performances (reissued on CD) are often rhythmic enough to reach a slightly larger audience than usual, and the individuality shown by each of these major players is quite impressive. Recommended. *—Scott Yanow*

Home / Oct. 31, 1981-Nov. 1, 1981 / Black Saint ♦♦♦♦♦

Although David Murray has recorded in many different settings throughout his busy career, his octet has always been perfect for his talents. More disciplined than his big band, yet containing more tone colors than his smaller combos, the octet allowed Murray to be exploratory yet occasionally look backwards. This set, his second with the band, has quite an all-star lineup: Murray on tenor and bass clarinet, altoist Henry Threadgill, trumpeter Olu Dara, cornetist Butch Morris, trombonist George Lewis, pianist Anthony Davis, bassist Wilber Morris and drummer Steve McCall. All of the brilliant players have their opportunities to make strong contributions to Murray's five originals (best known of which is "3-D Family"), and the leader's writing is consistently colorful and unpredictable. Recommended. *—Scott Yanow*

★ **Murray's Steps** / Jul. 14, 1982-Jul. 19, 1982 / Black Saint ♦♦♦♦♦

The octet is the perfect vehicle for David Murray as an outlet for his writing, a showcase for his compositions and as an inspiring vehicle for his tenor and bass clarinet solos. For the third octet album (all are highly recommended) Murray meets up with altoist Henry Threadgill, trumpeter Bobby Bradford, cornetist Butch Morris, trombonist Craig Harris, pianist Curtis Clark, bassist Wilber Morris and drummer Steve McCall; quite a talented group of individuals. Their interpretations of four of Murray's originals ("Murray's Steps," "Sweet Lovely," "Sing Song" and "Flowers for Albert") are emotional, adventurous and exquisite; sometimes all three at the same time. *—Scott Yanow*

Live at Sweet Basil, Vol. 1 / Aug. 24, 1984-Aug. 26, 1984 / Black Saint ♦♦♦

The David Murray Big Band tends to be a bit undisciplined, with plenty of rambunctious and overcrowded ensembles. The high point of this first of two releases is easily the 12-minute "Bechet's Bounce," an often nutty and frequently hilarious "tribute" to Sidney Bechet that improves the longer it is played. The Dixieland-esque structures are better understood by some of the musicians than others, and this performance is quite erratic but certainly memorable.

Otherwise, the big band (which includes in its all-star cast cornetist Olu Dara, trombonist Craig Harris, altoist Steve Coleman and drummer Billy Higgins, plus Murray on tenor and bass clarinet) digs into Murray's "Lovers," "Silence" and "Duet for Big Band." *—Scott Yanow*

Live at Sweet Basil, Vol. 2 / Aug. 24, 1984-Aug. 26, 1984 / Black Saint ✦✦✦
The David Murray Big Band tends to be both erratic and colorful. Their second of two sets has the 11-piece all-star crew (conducted by Butch Morris) performing five of the leader's originals, including "Dewey's Circle." There are some strong moments, plenty of dense ensembles, and a strong group spirit that makes one wish that the group had recorded a little more coherently in the studios during this period. *—Scott Yanow*

Hope Scope / May 12, 1987 / Black Saint ✦✦✦✦✦
The perfect setting for the innovative David Murray is the octet that he leads on an irregular basis. This spirited set has tributes to Ben Webster and Lester Young but is at its best when the full ensemble (trumpeters Hugh Ragin and Rasul Siddik, trombonist Craig Harris, altoist James Spaulding, pianist Dave Burrell, bassist Wilber Morris and drummer Ralph Peterson, Jr., along with the leader on tenor and bass clarinet) get to improvise together. This is one of their strongest all-round recordings with "Hope Scope" being a particular highpoint. *—Scott Yanow*

☆ **Special Quartet** / Mar. 26, 1990 / Columbia ✦✦✦✦✦
When one reads the personnel on this CD, the potential seems enormous: tenor saxophonist David Murray, pianist McCoy Tyner, bassist Fred Hopkins and drummer Elvin Jones. Murray was a good choice for the tenor slot, because, although influenced by John Coltrane's adventurous spirit, he has never sounded like Coltrane, coming closer to the Ben Webster/Paul Gonsalves tradition but with a style of his own. In addition to Trane's "Cousin Mary" and "In a Sentimental Mood" (which Coltrane had recorded with Duke Ellington, and Murray takes as a duet with Tyner), the music includes three of the tenor's originals, including "3D Family") and a Butch Morris song. The fresh material really pushes Tyner, who mostly sticks to standards with his own trio, while Jones sounds as passionate as usual. A successful outing full of mutual inspiration; easily recommended. *—Scott Yanow*

The Sanctuary Within / Dec. 14, 1991-Dec. 14, 1991 / Black Saint ✦✦✦✦✦

David Murray Big Band, Conducted by Lawrence "Butch" Morris / Mar. 5, 1991-Mar. 6, 1991 / Columbia ✦✦✦✦
The David Murray big band, which can be undisciplined and even a bit out of control, is never dull. This generally brilliant effort has quite a few highpoints. "Paul Gonsalves" recreates the tenor's famous 1956 *Newport Jazz Festival* solo and has some heated playing from the ensemble. While "Lester" does not really capture the style of Lester Young, "Ben" does bring back the spirit of Ben Webster. "Calling Steve McCall" is a heartfelt tribute to the late drummer (although the poetry does not need to be heard twice) and trombonist Craig Harris' singing on "Let the Music Take You" is so-so, but the colorful "David's Tune" and the eerie "Istanbul" are more memorable. This disc is easily recommended to listeners with open ears. *—Scott Yanow*

Body and Soul / Feb. 11, 1993-Feb. 12, 1993 / Black Saint ✦✦✦✦✦
No matter how many albums Murray issues, he never coasts or goes through the motions. This is mainly a quartet date, although Murray shows on the title track his ability to back a singer as Taana Running gives a moving vocal, complete with her original lyrics. Otherwise, these are either spirited uptempo numbers or equally energized ballads. Murray's sweeping tenor sound remains a marvel, and few can match him in controlling drive, pitch and volume. Drummer Rashied Ali has not lost the rippling intensity from his days with John Coltrane; he and Murray conclude things in a dazzling duo performance on "Cuttin' Corners" deliberately intended to evoke memories of the Coltrane/Ali album *Interstellar Space*. *—Ron Wynn*

Picasso / Sep. 1, 1992-Sep. 11, 1992 / DIW ✦✦✦

South of the Border / May 23, 1992-May 25, 1992 / DIW ✦✦✦✦

For Aunt Louise / 1993 / DIW ✦✦✦
On these seven mainly up-tempo compositions, David Murray doubles on tenor saxophone and bass clarinet featuring the rhythm section of pianist John Hicks, bassist Fred Hopkins, and drummer Idris Muhammad. While Murray still produces exciting flashes of furious free jazz tenor, he reins in his avant garde leanings, playing in an overall melodic yet bluesy style. Amongst the variety of moods captured on this Japanese DIW release are the free funk sensibilities of "Fantasy Rainbow," hard bop on the John Hicks composition "Hicks Time," Kenny Dorham's "Asiatic Raes," and the Latin tinged "Concion de Amor." The centerpiece of the disc is the heartfelt waltz "Fishin' and Missin' You (For Aunt Louise)," in which Murray plays delicate but emotional bass clarinet. *—Al Campbell*

Creole / Oct. 19, 1997-Oct. 20, 1997 / Justin Time ✦✦✦

Speaking in Tongues / Dec. 5, 1997 / Justin Time ✦✦✦
Speaking in Tongues features more intuitive, forward-thinking work from this challenging saxophonist and his band. *—Heather Phares*

Octet Plays Trane / Apr. 30, 1999-May 1999 / Justin Time ✦✦✦✦✦
Tenor saxophonist David Murray and his octet rise to the challenge of performing five classic John Coltrane compositions not by playing note-for-note recreations but by allowing Trane's searching spirit to dominate the proceedings. Murray shines on all tracks, switching between tenor and bass clarinet. The octet featuring pianist D.D. Jackson, trombonist Craig Harris, trumpeters Ravi Best and Rasul Siddik, alto saxophonist and flutist James Spaulding, bassist Jaribu Shahid, and drummer Mark Johnson sound like twice the number of musicians throughout this disc. This is especially true on the raucous big band versions of "Giant Steps" and "Lazy Bird." However, they can achieve a complete turnaround when playing the ballad "Naima" or "India," which becomes an ethereal, haunting mix (complete with tabla) sounding more like electric period Miles Davis unplugged than Coltrane's arrangement. Murray's "The Crossing" is a bit of a puzzling inclusion, since it is the only non-Trane composition performed, somewhat defeating the intention of the disc. The proceedings wind down with an engaging 15-minute version of "A Love Supreme: Part 1: Acknowledgment" proving Murray has studied not only the music of John Coltrane, but like him insists on applying his individuality through his horn. *—Al Campbell*

Sunny Murray (James Marcellus Arthur Murray)

b. Sep. 21, 1937, Idabel, OK
Drums / Avant-Garde Jazz, Free Jazz
An important early free drummer, Sunny Murray was one of the first to play without keeping a steady rhythm or pulse (interacting directly with the lead voices) although he was always perfectly capable of playing more conventionally. He started on drums when he was nine and in 1956 moved to New York. Murray picked up early experience gigging with Red Allen, Willie "The Lion" Smith, Jackie McLean and Ted Curson. He made a giant stylistic leap when he started playing with Cecil Taylor (1959-64) and was the perfect "accompanist" for Albert Ayler (1964-67). Murray also worked with Don Cherry, Ornette Coleman and John Tchicai during the period. He spent 1968-71 in France, playing and recording with Archie Shepp and freelancing. In the 1970s Murray moved to Philadelphia and led bands usually called the Untouchable Factor. For a time in the 1980s his quintet included Steve Coleman, Grachan Moncur III, pianist Curtis Clark and bassist William Parker and he had a recorded reunion with Taylor in 1980. Sunny Murray has led dates for Jihad (a 1965 session with Albert Ayler as a sideman), ESP, Shandar, Pathe, BYG, Kharma, Philly Jazz, Marge, Moers Music and Circle although he has maintained a lower profile during the past decade. *—Scott Yanow*

Sunny's Time Now / Nov. 1965 / DIW ✦✦✦

Sunny Murray Quintet / Jul. 23, 1966 / ESP ✦✦✦✦
Drummer Sunny Murray's second date as a leader (following by eight months an almost-unknown set for Jihad that featured Don Cherry and Albert Ayler as sidemen) finds Murray leading a high-powered free jazz quintet. Best known among the sidemen are altoist Byard Lancaster and bassist Al Silva, although second altoist Jack Graham and trumpeter Jacques Coursil also play important roles in the music. Performing lengthy versions of three Murray originals and one by Graham, the band is fairly coherent but also full of fire and chance-taking solos. In ways, this is a typical ESP free-form blowing session, and certainly will be most enjoyed by open-eared listeners. *—Scott Yanow*

● **Never Give a Sucker an Even Break** / Nov. 22, 1969 / Affinity ✦✦✦✦✦
Free rhythm, resuscitations, and spiritual quaverings made up an LP of music which sprang directly from the Albert Ayler/John Coltrane roots. It was a solid effort in structured freedom, rather even-handed and with no great peaks or insights revealed. *—Bob Rusch, Cadence*

Najee

b. New York, NY
Sax (Tenor), Sax (Soprano) / Smooth Jazz, Quiet Storm, Crossover Jazz, Urban
One of the best selling instrumentalists of the late 1980s and early-to-mid 1990s, Najee has been a consistent favorite in the "quiet storm" and so-called "smooth jazz" markets. Often compared to Kenny G, George Howard and Dave Koz, the New Yorker has been greatly influenced by Grover Washington, Jr.—although he hasn't been nearly as adventurous. Heavily produced and quite formulaic, Najee's albums have tended to avoid improvisation and strive for commercial radio airplay above all else. Debuting in 1987 with *Najee's Theme*, Najee was an immediate hit in the new adult contemporary (NAC) market. Similiar pop/urban/jazz dates like 1988's *Day By Day* and 1990's *Tokyo Blue* did nothing to jeopardize his niche on "smooth jazz" radio. On stage, Najee takes some risks and stretches out more—in fact, he has been quoted as saying he'd like to record a straight-ahead jazz or hard bop album eventually. But financially, Najee has had little incentive to pursue such a project. *Morning Tenderness* followed in 1998. *—Alex Henderson*

● **Songs from the Key of Life** / Nov. 7, 1995 / EMI ✦✦✦✦✦
Throughout his career, saxophonist Najee has generally performed crossover music that mixes R&B, jazz and pop. This particular date is one of his strongest and most jazz-oriented, a well-conceived tribute to Stevie Wonder. Najee (heard on soprano, flute, alto and tenor) plays instrumental versions of the music from Wonder's famous *Songs From the Key of Life* album plus several other notable Wonder songs. Assisted by such players as keyboardists George Duke, Ronnie Foster and Herbie Hancock, guitarist Phil Upchurch and a top-notch horn section, Najee creates fresh renditions of 21 Stevie Wonder tunes. Highlights include "Love's in Need of Love Today," "Sir Duke," "Knocks Me Off My Feet," "If It's Magic" and a medley of "All Day Sucker" and "Easy Goin' Evening." Throughout the memorable set, Najee shows that he can be a strong jazz improviser while still remaining accessible. Recommended. *—Scott Yanow*

The Best of Najee / Nov. 17, 1998 / Blue Note ✦✦✦✦
The Best of Najee contains a selection of 11 highlights from the smooth saxophonist's late-'80s and '90s recordings for EMI/Capitol. There may be a few fan favorites missing, but Najee's career lends itself better to an anthology than most musicians, mainly because it is oriented toward songs, not performances. Consequently, this disc offers a good overview of his career, since it captures not only many of the best-known songs—"For the Love of You," "Tokyo Blue," "Can't Hide Love," "Day By Day," "Betcha Don't Know," "Najee's Theme"—it also gives a good sense of what his albums sound like. An excellent choice for the curious and casual fan. *—Stephen Thomas Erlewine*

Fats Navarro (Theodore Navarro)

b. Sep. 24, 1923, Key West, FL, **d.** Jul. 7, 1950, New York, NY
Trumpet / Bop
One of the greatest jazz trumpeters of all time, Fats Navarro had a tragically brief career yet his influence is still being felt. His fat sound combined aspects of Howard McGhee, Roy Eldridge and Dizzy Gillespie, became the main inspiration for Clifford Brown and through Brownie greatly affected the tones and styles of Lee Morgan, Freddie Hubbard and Woody Shaw.

Navarro originally played piano and tenor before switching to trumpet. He started gigging with dance bands when he was 17, was with Andy Kirk during 1943-44 and replaced Dizzy Gillespie with the Billy Eckstine big band during 1945-46. During the next three years Fats was second to only Dizzy among bop trumpeters. Navarro recorded with Kenny Clarke's Bebop Boys, Coleman Hawkins, Eddie "Lockjaw" Davis, Illinois Jacquet, and most significantly Tadd Dameron during 1946-47. He had short stints with the big bands of Lionel Hampton and Benny Goodman, continued working with Dameron, made classic recordings with Bud Powell (in a quintet with a young Sonny Rollins) and the Metronome All-Stars, and a 1950 Birdland appearance with Charlie Parker was privately recorded. However Navarro was a heroin addict and that affliction certainly did not help him in what would be a fatal bout with tuberculosis that ended his life at age 26. He was well-documented during the 1946-49 period and most of his sessions are currently available on CD but Fats Navarro (who would have turned 72 in 1995) could have done so much more! *—Scott Yanow*

☆ **Fat Girl** / Sep. 6, 1946-Dec. 5, 1947 / Savoy ♦♦♦♦♦
This out of print two-LP set features trumpeter Fats Navarro's Savoy recordings which have thus far only been reissued on CD in piecemeal fashion. The ill-fated Navarro is heard at the peak of his powers, whether teamed with trumpeter Kenny Dorham, altoist Sonny Stitt, and pianist Bud Powell in an octet, interacting with the equally fiery tenor saxophonist Eddie "Lockjaw" Davis, or jamming with pianist Tadd Dameron in quintets featuring baritonist Leo Parker, altoist Ernie Henry, or tenor saxophonist Charlie Rouse. Among the classic bebop recordings included on this hard-to-find but essential two-fer are "Webb City," the well-titled "Hollerin' and Screamin'," "Fat Girl," "Ef Pop," "A Bebop Carol," "Nostalgia," and "Fats Blows." *—Scott Yanow*

The Fabulous Fats Navarro, Vol. 1 / Jan. 29, 1947-Nov. 29, 1948 / Blue Note ♦♦♦♦♦
Primarily comprised of recordings made with pianist Tadd Dameron, *The Fabulous Fats Navarro, Vol. 1* spotlights the fluid and inventive bebop trumpeter on nine master takes and several alternate versions. (The impressive bonus cuts will not only excite completists, but should please the casual fan as well.) From the two Dameron-led dates in 1947 and 1948, we have classic Navarro performances like "The Chase," "Our Delight," "The Squirrel," and "Lady Bird." Navarro's stellar solos here (both muted and not) are complimented by equally impressive statements from alto saxophonist Ernie Henry and tenor saxophonists Wardell Gray and Charlie Rouse. And while drummers Shadow Wilson and Kenny Clarke provide fine rhythmic support throughout, conga player Chino Pozo (cousin of Chano Pozo) provides some nice additional texture on a few numbers. Also included on this disc are excellent tracks from a 1948 date with trumpeter Howard McGhee. Covering McGhee and Navarro originals like "Boperation" and "Double Talk," this session features more stellar solo work from Henry as well as some fine contributions by vibraphonist Milt Jackson (who actually plays piano on most of the cuts). And rounding out things are a few alternate takes from a date with pianist Bud Powell, including worthwhile versions of "Wail" and "Bouncing With Bud." This is an essential title for jazz enthusiasts, but one that seems to go in and out of print quite often. Luckily, all the tracks on both volumes of *The Fabulous Fats Navarro,* plus some additional Dameron cuts, can be heard on Blue Note's *Fats Navarro and Tadd Dameron: The Complete Blue Note and Capitol Recordings. —Stephen Cook*

★ **Fats Navarro and Tadd Dameron: The Complete Blue Note and Capitol Recordings** / Sep. 26, 1947-Aug. 8, 1949 / Blue Note ♦♦♦♦♦
Many valuable performances from the height of the bop era are included on this double CD. Subtitled "The Complete Blue Note and Capitol Recordings" and comprised of 23 songs and 13 alternate takes, the reissue features the great trumpeter Fats Navarro in peak form with three groups headed by pianist/arranger Tadd Dameron, in trumpet battles with one of his major influences, Howard McGhee, and on a remarkable all-star quintet with pianist Bud Powell and the young tenor Sonny Rollins; among the other sidemen are altoist Ernie Henry; tenors Charlie Rouse, Allen Eager, Wardell Gray, and Dexter Gordon; and vibraphonist Milt Jackson. In addition to such gems as "Our Delight," "Lady Bird," "Double Talk," "Bouncing With Bud," "Dance of the Infidels," and "52nd Street Theme," Fats is heard with the 1948 Benny Goodman septet ("Stealin' Apples") and Dameron leads a group with the 22-year-old Miles Davis. On a whole, this double CD has more than its share of essential music that belongs in all historical jazz collections. *—Scott Yanow*

The Fabulous Fats Navarro, Vol. 2 / Sep. 26, 1947-Aug. 8, 1949 / Blue Note ♦♦♦♦♦
Picking up some of the slack from the first volume, *The Fabulous Fats Navarro, Vol. 2* takes in two fine 1948 sessions featuring the bebop trumpeter. The first three cuts come from a Tadd Dameron-led date featuring top players like Dexter Gordon, Cecil Payne, Kai Winding, Sahib Shihab, and Kenny Clarke. The group avails itself nicely on Dameron originals like the mercurial Latin cut "Jahbero" (including congas and bongos), the classic "Lady Bird," and the predictably complex "Symphonette." Navarro runs the gamut here, turning in both high-flying solos and gracefully cool statements. And with enough in the way of engaging solo work, the alternate takes of all three of these tracks prove to be more than just filler. The remainder is culled from a session Navarro co-led with trumpeter Howard McGhee, and includes collaborative numbers like "The Skunk," "Boperation," and an alternate take of "Double Talk." The group also features Ernie Henry, Milt Jackson, Curly Russell, and Kenny Clarke. Now, plaudits aside, these two volumes of Blue Note Navarro recordings are not only hard to find (they've primarily been available only as an import), but seem to have come out with varying track listings over time. So, the best option is to pick up Blue Note's very welcome *Fats Navarro and Tadd Dameron: The Complete Blue Note and Capitol Recordings,* which not only has all the *Fabulous* material, but includes a Dameron date with Miles Davis, as well as a cover of Fats Waller's "Stealin' Apples" featuring Navarro, Benny Goodman, and Wardell Gray. *—Stephen Cook*

Nostalgia / Dec. 5, 1947-Oct. 28, 1947 / Savoy Jazz ♦♦♦♦♦
Taken from three different, late-'40s sessions, *Nostalgia* features Navarro in the fine company of bebop stars like Dexter Gordon, Tadd Dameron, and Art Blakey. While looser sounding than the legendary sides the trumpeter cut for Blue Note, the tracks here still include the usual bevy of sharp Navarro solos, plus stellar contributions by all involved. The first session with tenor saxophonist Charlie Rouse (one of the earliest recordings of the future Monk sideman), Dameron, and Blakey, finds Navarro mixing poised and fluid solo work with more intense high-note statements, demonstrating his masterful blend of both Miles Davis' cool approach and Dizzy Gillespie's incendiary technique. The highlights continue with four more cuts from a Dexter Gordon-led session from 1947, which adheres to the brief head statement and round of solos mode used on the earlier cuts. Dameron returns on piano, nicely comping behind Gordon's already distinct solo work and more of Navarro's pearl-like horn lines (these numbers have also been released on various Gordon titles on Savoy). The disc ends with a date led by honking tenor man Eddie "Lockjaw" Davis, which, while less intriguing than the other sessions, stills swings mightily with a mix of bebop and R&B flavored tunes. Benefiting from nicely remastered sound and some worthwhile alternate takes, *Nostalgia* is worthy of any jazz collection and certainly is an essential title from the bebop era. *—Stephen Cook*

Fats Navarro with Tadd Dameron / 1948 / Milestone ♦♦♦♦
On this CD reissue are all of the contents of a former two-LP set. Trumpeter Fats Navarro is featured on ten of the thirteen selections with pianist-arranger Tadd Dameron's Orchestra; the other three songs have trombonist Kai Winding in his place. With tenor saxophonist Allan Eager and (on six of the numbers) altoist Rudy Williams as the other key soloists, the boppish music is quite enjoyable. The recording quality of the live performances is decent for the time and the material (all but five are Dameron originals) is consistently of high quality. This valuable CD is easily recommended for bop collectors as is virtually every record that Fats Navarro made in his brief life. *—Scott Yanow*

1947-1949 / Jul. 11, 2000 / Melodie Jazz Classics ♦♦♦
Trumpeter Fats Navarro's reign in jazz was short lived. He died in 1950 at a young age due to living the Charlie Parker lifestyle. In the short period that he made records as a leader in the late '40s, it was obvious had he not burned out, he was on his way to legendary status. Along with Dizzy Gillespie, Navarro was the premiere bebop trumpet innovator, influencing Clifford Brown and everyone who followed him. These recordings captured on Classics *1108 from 1947-1949 highlight $Navarro* (or Fat Girl as he was often referred) at his height. Navarro leads combos on these sessions (some live) that include Tadd Dameron, Charlie Ventura, Charlie Rouse, Buddy Rich, and Art Blakey. Navarro is also heard on four cuts backing up vocalist Earl Coleman and his all-stars with drummer Max Roach. *—Al Campbell*

Oliver Nelson

b. Jun. 4, 1932, St. Louis, MO, **d.** Oct. 27, 1975, Los Angeles, CA
Sax (Tenor), Sax (Alto), Composer, Arranger / Hard Bop, Post-Bop
Oliver Nelson was a distinctive soloist on alto, tenor and even soprano but his writing eventually overshadowed his playing skills. He became a professional early on in 1947, playing with the Jeter-Pillars Orchestra and with St. Louis big bands headed by George Hudson and Nat Towles. In 1951 he arranged and played second alto for Louis Jordan's big band and followed with a period in the Navy and four years at a university. After moving to New York, Nelson worked briefly with Erskine Hawkins, Wild Bill Davis and Louie Bellson (the latter on the West Coast). In addition to playing with Quincy Jones' Orchestra (1960-61), between 1959-61 Nelson recorded six small-group albums and a big-band date; those gave him a lot of recognition and respect in the jazz world. *Blues and the Abstract Truth* (from 1961) is considered a classic and helped to popularize a song that Nelson had included on a slightly earlier Eddie "Lockjaw" Davis session, "Stolen Moments." He also fearlessly matched wits effectively with the explosive Eric Dolphy on a pair of quintet sessions. But good as his playing was, Nelson was in greater demand as an arranger, writing for big-band dates of Jimmy Smith, Wes Montgomery and Billy Taylor among others. Nelson was largely lost to jazz a few years before his unexpected death at age 43 from a heart attack. *—Scott Yanow*

Takin' Care of Business / Mar. 22, 1960 / New Jazz/OJC ♦♦♦♦♦
Oliver Nelson would gain his greatest fame later in his short life as an arranger/composer but this superior session puts the emphasis on his distinctive tenor and alto playing. In a slightly unusual group (with vibraphonist Lem Winchester, organist Johnny "Hammond" Smith, bassist George Tucker and drummer Roy Haynes), Nelson improvises a variety of well-constructed but spontaneous solos; his unaccompanied spots on "All the Way" and his hard-charging playing on the medium-tempo blues "Groove" are two of the many high-points. Nelson remains a vastly underrated saxophonist and all six performances on this recommended CD reissue (four of them his originals) are excellent. *—Scott Yanow*

Screamin' the Blues / May 27, 1960 / New Jazz/OJC ♦♦♦♦♦
Oliver Nelson (on tenor and alto meets Eric Dolphy (alto, bass clarinet and flute) on this frequently exciting sextet session with trumpeter Richard Williams, pianist Richard Wyands, bassist George Duvivier and drummer Roy Haynes. Although Dolphy is too unique and skilled to be overshadowed in a setting such as this, Nelson holds his own. He contributed five of the six compositions (including "Screamin' yhe Blues," "The Meetin"' and "Altoitis") and effectively matches wits and creative ideas with Dolphy. This CD reissue (also available as part of a huge Eric Dolphy box set) is recommended, as is the follow-up record *Straight Ahead. —Scott Yanow*

Soul Battle / Sep. 9, 1960 / Prestige/OJC ♦♦♦♦♦
This intriguing session matches together three powerful tenor players: Oliver Nelson, King Curtis (in a rare jazz outing) and Jimmy Forrest. With fine backup work by pianist Gene Casey, bassist George Duvivier and drummer Roy Haynes, the tenors battle to a draw on a set of blues and basic material (including a fine version of "Perdido"). This CD reissue adds one selection ("Soul Street") from the same date to the original LP program and is easily recommended to fans of big-toned tenors and straightahead swinging. *—Scott Yanow*

★ **The Blues and the Abstract Truth** / Feb. 23, 1961 / Impulse! ♦♦♦♦♦
This was Oliver Nelson's finest recording and one of the top jazz albums of 1961, a true classic. The lineup is an inspired one: Nelson on tenor and alto, Eric Dolphy doubling on alto and flute, a young trumpeter named Freddie Hubbard, baritonist George Barrow for section parts,

pianist Bill Evans, bassist Paul Chambers and drummer Roy Haynes. The contrasting voices of the soloists really uplift these superior compositions which are highlighted by "Stolen Moments" (a future standard), the fun "Hoe-Down" and "Yearnin." Dolphy cuts everyone but Nelson and Hubbard are also in top form. *—Scott Yanow*

Straight Ahead / Mar. 1, 1961 / New Jazz/OJC ✦✦✦✦✦
This CD reissue brings back a very interesting quintet set matching together Oliver Nelson (on alto and tenor) and Eric Dolphy (tripling on alto, flute and bass clarinet). With the assistance of pianist Richard Wyands, bassist George Duvivier and drummer Roy Haynes, the two reedmen battle it out on six compositions (five of Nelson's originals plus Milt Jackson's "Ralph's New Blues." Although none of Nelson's tunes caught on, this is a pretty memorable date. It certainly took a lot of courage for Oliver Nelson to share the frontline with the colorful Eric Dolphy but his own strong musical personality holds its own on this straightahead date. *—Scott Yanow*

More Blues & the Abstract Truth / Nov. 10, 1964-Nov. 11, 1964 / Impulse! ✦✦✦
Unlike the original classic *Blues and the Abstract Truth* set from three years earlier, Oliver Nelson does not play on this album. He did contribute three of the eight originals and all of the arrangements but his decision not to play is disappointing. However there are some strong moments from such all-stars as trumpeter Thad Jones, altoist Phil Woods, baritonist Pepper Adams, pianist Roger Kellaway and guest tenor Ben Webster (who is on two songs). The emphasis is on blues-based pieces and there are some strong moments even if the date falls short of its predecessor. *—Scott Yanow*

Sound Pieces / 1966 / Impulse! ✦✦✦✦
This CD reissue features Oliver Nelson in two very different settings. Although best-known as an altoist and a tenor-saxophonist, Nelson sticks exclusively to soprano throughout the set. He leads a 20-piece big band on three of his compositions which, although interesting, are not overly memorable. Best are five other numbers (two of which were originally issued on the record *Three Dimensions*) that showcase Nelson's soprano playing with a quartet also includes pianist Steve Kuhn, bassist Ron Carter and drumer Grady Tate. Although one would not think of Nelson as a soprano stylist, his strong playing actually put him near the top of his field on such numbers as "The Shadow Of Your Smile," "Straight No Chaser" and his own "Patterns." *—Scott Yanow*

Stolen Moments / Mar. 6, 1975 / Jamey Aebersold ✦✦✦✦✦
A beautiful swan song from the immensely talented Oliver Nelson featuring his terrific alto. Features an excellent West Coast small group with Bobby Bryant, Jerome Richardson, Buddy Collette, Bobby Bryant Jr., Jack Nimitz, Mike Wofford, Chuck Domanico amd Shelly Manne (d). *—Douglas Payne*

New Orleans Rhythm Kings

f. 1922, **db.** 1925
Group / Classic Jazz
The New Orleans Rhythm Kings were the finest jazz group to be on record in 1922 and the White band has served as proof that, even that early, Blacks were not the only ones that could play jazz with individuality and integrity. The key members of the group (leader-cornetist Paul Mares, trombonist George Brunis and clarinetist Leon Roppolo) were childhood friends from New Orleans. Roppolo was the first significant soloist on record while Brunis would have a long career playing Dixieland. The changing rhythm sections sometimes included the first great jazz bassist Steve Brown (although largely inaudible on his early session), drummer Ben Pollack (a future bandleader) and, on a pair of memorable sessions in 1923, pianist Jelly Roll Morton. Among the future standards introduced by the NORK were "Farewell Blues," "Panama," "That's a Plenty" and "Tin Roof Blues." The band broke up in 1924. *—Scott Yanow*

● **New Orleans Rhythm Kings and Jelly Roll Morton** / Aug. 29, 1922-Jul. 18, 1923 / Milestone ✦✦✦✦✦
This single-CD reissues all of the music on the earlier double-Lp of the same title (and catalog number) except for some alternate takes although it confuses matters a bit by adding a "new" alternate of "Milenberg Joys." The New Orleans Rhythm Kings were the best group on record during 1922 and all of its earliest recordings are on this essential release. With the solid cornet of Paul Mares, the excellent ensemble playing of trombonist George Brunies and the superb soloing of clarinetist Leon Ropollo, the NORK was the most advanced jazz band of its time. The recordings on the CD include sessions as an octet, a quintet and a tentet; some of the latter performances showcase the innovative pianist-composer Jelly Roll Morton. Highlights include "Tiger Rag," "Maple Leaf Rag," the original versions of "Farewell Blues," "That's A Plenty," "Bugle Call Rag" and "Tin Roof Blues" (the latter having Brunies' most famous trombone solo) plus the Morton sides (including "Clarinet Marmalade," "Mr. Jelly Lord" and "Milenberg Joys"). Classic and historic music. *—Scott Yanow*

Phineas Newborn

b. Dec. 14, 1931, Whiteville, TN, **d.** May 26, 1989, Memphis, TN
Piano / Hard Bop
One of the most technically skilled and brilliant pianists in jazz during his prime, Phineas Newborn remains a bit of a mystery. Plagued by mental and physical problems of unknown origin, Newborn faded from the scene in the mid-1960s, only to re-emerge at irregular intervals throughout his life. Newborn could be compared to Oscar Peterson in that his bop-based style was largely unclassifiable, his technique was phenomenal, and he was very capable of enthralling an audience playing a full song with just his left hand. He started out working in Memphis R&B bands with his brother, guitarist Calvin Newborn, and recorded with local players including B.B. King in the early 1950s. After moving to New York in 1956, Newborn astounded fans and critics alike. Although he worked briefly with Charles Mingus (1958) and Roy Haynes, Newborn usually performed at the head of a trio or quartet. His early recordings are quite outstanding. Unfortunately, after the mid-'60s, Newborn's profile dropped sharply, and although there were further recordings—and although he still sounded strong when appearing in public—the pianist was in danger of being forgotten by most of the jazz world during his last decade. *—Scott Yanow*

★ **Here Is Phineas** / May 3, 1956-May 4, 1956 / Koch International ✦✦✦✦✦
Other than two numbers cut for the Progressive label in Houston a couple years earlier (and thus far never reissued), this Atlantic session (put out as a Koch CD in 1999) was the recording debut for the remarkable Phineas Newborn. The 24-year-old pianist's playing on this trio/quartet date with bassist Oscar Pettiford and drummer Kenny Clarke (and occasionally guitarist Calvin Newborn) is virtuosic to say the least, on Oscar Peterson's level if not Art Tatum's. Newborn rips through the repertoire (which is highlighted by "Barbados," "Celia," "Dahooud" and "Afternoon in Paris"); try to tap your foot to "Celia" without breaking your ankle! George Wein in the liner notes faults Newborn's tendency to double time the ballads and some listeners may shake their heads at his constant outpouring of technically impossible runs (those speedy octaves are ridiculous), but if one has chops on this level, one should feel free to display them. This is a dazzling debut from an ill-fated but classic pianist, and this CD is a gem. *—Scott Yanow*

While My Lady Sleeps / Apr. 23, 1957-Apr. 3, 1958 / Bluebird/RCA ✦✦✦✦
This CD reissue is mostly comprised of a 1957 set featuring the virtuosic pianist Phineas Newborn backed by a string orchestra led by Dennis Farnon. Although not as vital as his usual trio dates and Farnon's string arrangements are not too inspiring, the music is pleasing and finds Newborn in his early prime. Particularly noteworthy are his versions of Eddie Miller's "Lazy Mood," "While My Lady Sleeps" and "Bali Hati." Also on this set are three quartet numbers and an unaccompanied rendition of "What's New" from the RCA album *Fabulous Phineas*. *—Scott Yanow*

☆ **A World of Piano** / Oct. 16, 1961-Nov. 21, 1961 / Contemporary/OJC ✦✦✦✦✦
Phineas Newborn's Contemporary debut (he would record six albums over a 15-year period for that label) was made just before physical problems began to interrupt his career. This CD reissue has two trio sessions and finds Newborn joined by either bassist Paul Chambers and drummer Philly Joe Jones or bassist Sam Jones and drummer Louis Hayes. Actually, the accompaniment is not that significant, for the virtuosic Newborn is essentially the whole show anyway. He performs five jazz standards and three obscurities by jazz composers on this superb recital; highlights include "Cheryl," "Manteca," "Daahoud" and "Oleo." *—Scott Yanow*

☆ **The Great Jazz Piano of Phineas Newborn Jr.** / Nov. 21, 1961-Sep. 12, 1962 / Contemporary/OJC ✦✦✦✦✦
This recording lives up to its title. Phineas Newborn at his prime had phenomenal technique (on the level of an Oscar Peterson), a creative imagination and plenty of energy. These trio sessions (with Leroy Vinnegar or Sam Jones on bass and either Milt Turner or Louis Hayes on drums) feature Newborn displaying plenty of heat and fresh ideas on compositions by Bud Powell, Bobby Timmons, Benny Golson, Duke Ellington, Thelonious Monk, Sonny Rollins and Miles Davis and two of his own. This is piano jazz at its highest level. *—Scott Yanow*

The Newborn Touch / Apr. 1, 1964 / Contemporary/OJC ✦✦✦✦✦
This CD reissue adds an alternate take and an unissued selection to the original program. Pianist Phineas Newborn's only recording of the 1963-68 period, the trio outing with bassist Leroy Vinnegar and drummer Frank Butler, finds Newborn's virtuosic style unchanged from the late '50s. As is usual on his Contemporary recordings, the pianist explores superior jazz compositions, in this case interpreting a song apiece by Benny Carter, Russ Freeman, Hampton Hawes, Art Pepper, Ornette Coleman ("The Blessing"), Carl Perkins, Frank Rosolino, Leroy Vinnegar, Jimmy Woods and Barney Kessel. Newborn's remarkable control of the piano was still unimpaired, and he is heard giving Oscar Peterson a run for his money. *—Scott Yanow*

Harlem Blues / Feb. 12, 1969-Feb. 13, 1969 / Contemporary/OJC ✦✦✦✦
The superb trio (pianist Phineas Newborn, bassist Ray Brown and drummer Elvin Jones) had never played together before but it didn't matter. They had little trouble finding common ground. The virtuosic pianist (still in peak form) leads the way on such pieces as his "Harlem Blues," "Ray's Idea" (composed decades earlier by Brown) and Horace Silver's "Cookin' at the Continental." *—Scott Yanow*

Look Out: Phineas Is Back / Dec. 7, 1976-Dec. 8, 1976 / Pablo/OJC ✦✦✦✦✦
Phineas Newborn was one of the great jazz pianists, possessing phenominal technique and mastery of the bebop vocabulary, but various illnesses plagued him throughout the 1960s and '70s. On what would be one of his final sessions, Newborn is in surprisingly strong form playing in a trio with bassist Ray Brown and drummer Jimmie Smith. Highlights include "Abbers Song" (a rapid runthrough on "I've Got Rhythm" chord changes), "A Night in Tunisia," a previously unreleased version of "Just in Time" that appeared for the first time on this CD reissue and a creative version of Stevie Wonder's "You Are the Sunshine of My Life." *—Scott Yanow*

David "Fathead" Newman

b. Feb. 24, 1933, Dallas, TX
Sax (Tenor), Sax (Soprano), Sax (Alto), Flute / Hard Bop, Soul-Jazz
As a teenager, David Newman played professionally around Dallas and Fort Worth with Charlie Parker's mentor, Buster Smith, and also with Ornette Coleman in a band led by tenor saxophonist Red Connors. In the early '50s, Newman worked locally with such R&B musicians as Lowell Fulson and T-Bone Walker. In 1952, Newman formed his longest-lasting and most important musical association with Ray Charles, who had played piano in Fulson's group. Newman stayed with Charles' band from 1954-64, while concurrently recording as a leader and a sideman with, among others, his hometown associate, tenor saxophonist James Clay. Upon leaving Charles, Newman stayed in Dallas for two years. He then moved to New York, where he recorded under King Curtis and Eddie Harris; he also played many commercial and soul dates. Newman returned to Charles for a brief time in 1970-71; from 1972-4 he played with Red Garland and Herbie Mann. Newman parlayed the renown he gained

from his experience with Charles into a fairly successful recording career. In the '60s and '70s, he recorded a series of heavily orchestrated, pop-oriented sides for Atlantic, and in the '80s he led the occasional hard bop session, but Newman's metier was as an ace accompanist. Throughout his career he recorded with a variety of non-jazz artists; Newman's brawny, arrogant tenor sound graced the albums of Aretha Franklin, Dr. John, and many others. It is, in fact, Newman's terse, earthy improvisations with Charles that remain his most characteristic work. *—Chris Kelsey*

★ **House of David: The David "Fathead" Newman Anthology** / 1952-1989 / Rhino ♦♦♦♦♦
There have not been many saxophonists and flutists more naturally soulful than David "Fathead" Newman. This two-disc set captures Newman at his best. He never really was an album artist; each album has had its nuggets, and that's what this captures. It has Newman wailing the blues, then stretching out in the Ray Charles band. He covers a Beatles tune, then an Aaron Neville number. He backs Aretha Franklin and pays homage to the great Buster Cooper. This is one anthology that can be recommended without hesitation, because there aren't going to be many complete Newman albums coming down the reissue pike. *—Ron Wynn*

Fathead: Ray Charles Presents David Newman / Nov. 5, 1958 / Atlantic ♦♦♦♦
The talented David Newman, who alternates on this album between tenor and alto, made his debut as a leader at this session. Since he was in Ray Charles' band at the time, Newman was able to use Charles on piano along with Hank Crawford (here called Bennie Crawford) on baritone, trumpeter Marcus Belgrave, bassist Edgar Willis and drummer Milton Turner. The music is essentially soulful bebop with the highlights including "Hard Times," "Fathead," "Mean To Me" and "Tin Tin Deo." Everyone plays well and this was a fine start to David "Fathead" Newman's career. *—Scott Yanow*

★ **It's Mister Fathead** / Nov. 5, 1958-Mar. 4, 1964 / 32 Jazz ♦♦♦♦♦
Although best-known as a tenor saxophonist, David "Fathead" Newman is an equally talented altoist and flutist. This 1998 double-CD brings back Fathead's first four sets as a leader (originally made for the Atlantic label) and the dates give one a definitive portrait of Newman in a variety of jazz settings. *Ray Charles Presents David Newman* (which is highlighted by "Hard Times," "Weird Beard," "Sweet Eyes" and "Mean to Me") teams the leader with trumpeter Marcus Belgrave, Hank Crawford (who sticks to baritone) and pianist Ray Charles in a sextet. "Straight Ahead" has Newman joined by pianist Wynton Kelly, bassist Paul Chambers and drummer Charlie Persip. The 1960 date starts off with "Batista's Groove" (which borrows some of its ideas from "Giant Steps") and sometimes has Newman showing off the influence of John Coltrane on tenor. However his flute playing on "Night of Nisan" is quite original and Newman holds his own with the rather illustrious rhythm section. "Fathead Comes On," performed by a quintet, is most notable for trumpeter Belgrave's consistently inventive playing while "House of David" (from 1967) finds the leader recalling Stanley Turrentine a bit with a quartet also featuring organist Kossie Gardner and guitarist Ted Dunbar. Even with a few lightweight tracks on the latter session, the music overall is rewarding with "The Holy Land" being a highlight. Highly recommended. *—Scott Yanow*

Captain Buckles / Nov. 3, 1970-Nov. 5, 1970 / Label M. ♦♦♦♦
An improvement over David Newman's preceding projects, this soulful but relatively straight-ahead effort teams him with trumpeter Blue Mitchell, guitarist Eric Gale, bassist Steve Novosel and drummer Bernard Purdie in a pianoless quintet. Switching between tenor, alto and flute, Newman performs four originals, a song by Mitchell, George Harrison's "Something," and the standard "I Didn't Know What Time It Was." *Captain Buckles* was reissued on CD in 2000 on Label M. *—Scott Yanow*

Mr. Gentle Mr. Cool (Tribute) / 1994 / Kokopelli ♦♦♦♦♦
David "Fathead" Newman is in excellent form on this tasteful program of 11 Duke Ellington compositions. Performing in a sextet with trombonist Jim Pugh, pianist David Leonhardt, bassist Peter Washington, Ron Carter on piccolo bass and drummer Lewis Nash, Newman splits his time between tenor and alto and takes a flute solo on "Azure." The music contains few real surprises (other than the utilization of both bass and piccolo bass) but swings nicely and has fine melodic solos. *—Scott Yanow*

Lone Star Legend / Sep. 23, 1980-Apr. 14, 1982 / 32 Jazz ♦♦♦♦♦
David "Fathead" Newman has such a strong reputation as a soulful saxophonist that sometimes people forget how creative a straight-ahead improviser he can be. His two Muse LPs, *Resurgence* and *Still Hard Times,* have been reissued in full on this deluxe single CD. Whether playing tenor, flute, soprano or alto, Newman's solos are full of personality and logical ideas. On one of the sets he is teamed with trumpeter Marcus Belgrave in a sextet (along with guitarist Ted Dunbar, pianist Cedar Walton, bassist Buster Williams and drummer Louis Hayes). The other date has Newman as part of an octet also including his old bandmate from his Ray Charles days, altoist Hank Crawford; baritonist Howard Johnson; trumpeter Charlie Miller; pianist Larry Willis; bassist Walter Booker; drummer Jimmy Cobb; and vibraphonist Steve Nelson, who has two features of his own. On both sets, Newman is heard in top form and he gets to show off his talents on all of his four axes. The highlights include "Everything Must Change," Walton's "To the Holy Land," "One for My Baby" and "Please Send Me Someone to Love" but all dozen performances are colorful and well-played. Prime Fathead. *—Scott Yanow*

James Newton

b. May 1, 1953, Los Angeles, CA
Flute / Avant-Garde Jazz, Third Stream, Post-Bop
Newton is a thoroughly contemporary artist, making elegant, sometimes eccentric, always high-minded albums that reflect a wide variety of jazz and classical influences without giving a fig about what happens to be popular at a given time. Besides producing a lovely tone quality, his flute work is highly resourceful, making use of flutter-tonguing, birdlike effects and simultaneous vocal/flute lines, trying to push the envelope of his instrument. As a composer, Newton finds wellsprings of inspiration in John Coltrane, Charles Mingus and Duke Ellington—the latter whose music he transformed completely on the adventurous *The African Flower* album—and he writes charts for all kinds of combinations of instruments. *—Richard S. Ginell*

Paseo Del Mar / 1978 / India Navigation ♦♦♦♦
James Newton's first American date as a leader finds him paying some tribute to Eric Dolphy, Thelonious Monk ("Monk's Notice") and Duke Ellington (on the one non-original, Duke's "Heaven") while also stretching jazz forward. Matched up with pianist Anthony Davis, cellist Abdul Wadud (who often functions in the role of a bass) and drummer Phillip Wilson, Newton is at his most adventurous on lengthy renditions of "Lake" and "San Pedro Sketches." It was obvious at the time that James Newton would be an important force in jazz for many years to come. *—Scott Yanow*

Mystery School / 1979 / India Navigation ♦♦♦♦♦
James Newton explores many moods and tone colors with this unusual album. The instrumentation (flutist Newton, clarinetist John Carter, bassoonist John Nunez, Charles Owens on oboe and English horn and the veteran Red Callender on tuba) by itself would give Newton's originals a sound of its own but the complex arrangements (which give more than adequate space for improvisations) display the influences of both modern classical music and jazz. *—Scott Yanow*

James Newton / Oct. 1982 / Gramavision ♦♦♦♦♦
Flutist James Newton teams up with six distinctive players on this continually interesting set: violinist John Blake, trombonist Slide Hampton, vibraphonist Jay Hoggard, pianist Anthony Davis, bassist Cecil McBee and drummer Billy Hart. The five selections include Billy Strayhorn's beautiful "Daydream," Davis' "Persephone" (a 17-bar piece), and three of the flutist's originals. The variety in the music ranges from an atonal "The Crips" to "Budapest," which recalls Charles Mingus, and the high quality of the players makes this thoughtful presentation a recommended set. *—Scott Yanow*

Luella / 1983 / Gramavision ♦♦♦♦♦
Most recordings by flutist James Newton are quite spontaneous in their improvising, but well-planned as a whole. This outing features Newton with three string players (violinists John Blake and Gayle Dixon and cellist Abdul Wadud) and a four-piece rhythm section (vibraphonist Jay Hoggard, pianist Kenny Kirkland, bassist Cecil McBee and drummer Billy Hart). Each of the five numbers has its purpose, including "Mr. Dolphy" (a tribute to Eric Dolphy), Wayne Shorter's moody "Anna Maria," and a three-part suite about South Africa ("Diamonds Are for Freedom"). Well worth several listens. *—Scott Yanow*

Echo Canyon / Sep. 5, 1984-Sep. 7, 1984 / Celestial Harmonies ♦♦♦

★ **The African Flower** / Jun. 24, 1985-Jun. 25, 1985 / Blue Note ♦♦♦♦♦
This wonderful set finds flutist James Newton creating fresh interpretations of seven songs written by Duke Ellington and/or Billy Strayhorn. His ensembles include violinist John Blake, altoist Arthur Blythe, cornetist Olu Dara, vibraphonist Jay Hoggard, pianist Roland Hanna (who has long had the ability to emulate Ellington's chord voicings and touch), bassist Rick Rozie, percussionist Anthony Brown, and either Pheeroan Ak Laff or Billy Hart on drums. In addition, Milt Grayson (who had sung with Ellington) takes a guest vocal on "Strange Feeling." Whether romping through "Cottontail," reviving "Virgin Jungle" (heard in an 11-minute version), or taking an unaccompanied flute flight on "Sophisticated Lady," James Newton's tribute set is quite memorable and a real gem. *—Scott Yanow*

Romance and Revolution / Aug. 20, 1986-Aug. 21, 1986 / Blue Note ♦♦♦♦♦
The great flutist James Newton pays tribute to Charles Mingus and (more indirectly) Eric Dolphy on his "Forever Charles" and a rare remake of Mingus' "Meditations On Integration." Newton interacts with both Steve Turre and Robin Eubanks on trombones, along with pianist Geri Allen, bassist Rick Rozie and drummer Pheeroan akLaff, bringing back the spirit of Mingus. In addition, there is a rendition of Ornette Coleman's "Peace" played with cellist Abdul Wadud, Rozie and akLaff, and a lengthy original ("The Evening Leans Toward You") that covers a wide range of moods. A stimulating set. *—Scott Yanow*

Herbie Nichols

b. Jan. 3, 1919, New York, NY, **d.** Apr. 12, 1963, New York, NY
Piano, Composer / Dixieland Revival, Swing, Bop
Although he was involved in bebop's beginnings, pianist/composer Herbie Nichols shied away from the attendant scene and spent his time in the '40s and mid-'50s playing swing and dixieland. He made only a handful of recording sessions in his complete lifetime. Nichols' music was enticing, enjoyable and listenable, yet also abstract, penetrating and echoed both Thelonious Monk and modern European classical artists like Erik Satie. Nichols utilized unusual rhythms and voicings, and borrowed freely from swing and dixieland. A highly intelligent player and composer whose occasional writings on jazz were concise, analytical and critical without being petty or personal, Nichols simply couldn't accept the nonsense that came with "the jazz scene" of his (or anyone else's) day. He preferred instead to play with musicians he felt didn't fear or distrust him for non-musical reasons; it's impossible to judge whether Nichols fears were accurate or based on perceptions that themselves may have been as questionable as the prejudices he felt were directed at him. *—Ron Wynn and Michael Erlewine*

The Art of Herbie Nichols / May 6, 1955-Apr. 19, 1956 / Blue Note ♦♦♦♦♦
An anthology collecting some pieces by neglected and overlooked pianist Herbie Nichols. Nichols had one of the truly unique styles in all of jazz piano history and didn't really borrow from or imitate anyone. This single disc doesn't match either an earlier Blue Note two-record set, now deleted, or the outstanding Mosaic set, but it's a fine introduction to Nichols' music. *—Ron Wynn*

☆ **The Complete Blue Note Recordings** / May 6, 1955-Apr. 19, 1956 / Mosaic ♦♦♦♦♦
A reissue of the 48 Herbie Nichols recordings formerly out on the limited edition five-LP Mosaic box set, this three-CD package from 1997 has the pianist/composer's greatest work. Nichols was largely neglected during his lifetime; only in the late '90s did the highly original musician start receiving some of the recognition he deserved. Although his originals were

often quite orchestral in nature, Nichols only had the opportunity to record in a trio format; the five sessions on this box (30 songs plus 18 alternate takes) feature either Al McKibbon or Teddy Kotick on bass and Art Blakey or Max Roach on drums. The music (all originals except George Gershwin's "Mine") is virtually unclassifiable, and although largely straight-ahead, sounds unlike anything produced by Herbie Nichols' contemporaries. Essential music. *—Scott Yanow*

● **The Bethlehem Session** / Nov. 1957 / Affinity ♦♦♦♦♦
Herbie Nichols was one of the tragedies of jazz, a very original pianist and composer who could not find regular employment for his thought-provoking music and ended up playing in anonymous Dixieland bands. He only recorded three complete albums as a leader and his *Bethlehem* date was his last. With perfectly suitable accompaniment from bassist George Duvivier and bassist Danny Richmond, Nichols introduces nine of his originals in addition to performing the standard "Too Close for Comfort." *—Scott Yanow*

Lennie Niehaus

b. Jun. 11, 1929, St. Louis, MO
Sax (Alto), Arranger / Film Music, Cool, Bop
An excellent altoist and jazz arranger in the 1950s (most notably for Stan Kenton), Lennie Niehaus in more recent times has won fame for his work scoring the music for Clint Eastwood films. After graduating from college, Niehaus played alto and occasionally wrote for Kenton (1951-52) before being drafted for the Army (1952-54). Upon his discharge Kenton welcomed Niehaus back and he worked for the bandleader on-and-off for the rest of the decade. Niehaus, who led and played alto on six albums between 1954-57 (five for Contemporary) had a cool tone a bit reminiscent of Lee Konitz. By the 1960s his playing had gone by the wayside as Niehaus concentrated on writing for films. Although he largely left jazz at that time, his work on *Play Misty for Me* and particularly *Bird* for Clint Eastwood allowed one to once again admire his jazz writing. *—Scott Yanow*

☆ **The Lennie Niehaus, Vol. 1: The Quintets** / Jul. 2, 1954-Jul. 9, 1954 / Contemporary/OJC ♦♦♦♦♦
Alto saxophonist Lennie Niehaus is better known as the arranger for Clint Eastwood's films, but he has long been familiar to jazz fans as a respected bandleader, composer, arranger, and soloist. This limited-edition audiophile reissue of his first solo recordings (following stints with Stan Kenton and Shorty Rogers) is a stunner. Included is the first 10" LP he recorded with a three-saxophone front line—in this case, with Jack Montrose (tenor), and Bob Gordon (baritone)—and other quintet sessions with musicians including pianist Hampton Hawes, and fellow Kentonite Shelly Manne (who was responsible for Niehaus' record deal with Contemporary's Lester Koenig in the first place). The involvement of Kenton bandmembers familiar with one another lends an ease and excitement to the proceedings. These quintet sessions are West Coast jazz at its finest. Melodic tunes give plenty of air to the lyrical yet complex nature of much of the music coming from that region at the time, with no remnants of the cool jazz period. These 1954 sides stomp with swing, color, and style. Bebop is called upon for tempo and pace, while swing and hard bop are referenced as checkpoints. There is a genuine glee in Niehaus' playing on "I Can't Believe You're in Love With Me," when he trades solos with Stu Williamson, while he paces the slightly faster take on "I Remember You," until slipping into one of those long, melodically sophisticated solos of his, just when you expected another chorus. Listening to this, it's hard to believe West Coast jazz ever got a bad rap. This set sounds as fresh today as it did then. *—Thom Jurek*

★ **Lennie Niehaus, Vol. 4: The Quintets and Strings** / Mar. 16, 1955-Apr. 25, 1955 / Contemporary/OJC ♦♦♦♦♦
This CD reissue brings back one of Lennie Niehaus's finest recordings of the 1950s. His alto is featured throughout the dozen selections and the varied settings (Niehaus is backed by a string quartet, a standard rhythm section and sometimes two other saxophonists in addition to performing four numbers with a standard quintet) gives him an opportunity to show off his writing abilities. Niehuas varies tempos a lot (the strings are often heard on faster material), there is solo space for the tenor of Bill Perkins, baritonist Bob Gordon and Stu Williamson on trumpet and valve trombone, and the leader's boppish alto is heard at the peak of his playing powers. Bop collectors can consider this disc to be essential. *—Scott Yanow*

Patterns / Aug. 2, 1989-Aug. 3, 1989 / Fresh Sound ♦♦♦♦♦
Lennie Niehaus, an excellent 1950s bop altoist, became so busy with arranging that he largely stopped playing in the early '60s. More than a quarter-century later, he made this "comeback" record, playing alto in a quintet also including Bill Perkins (on tenor, soprano, baritone and bass clarinet), pianist Frank Strazzeri, bassist Tom Warrington and drummer Joe LaBarbera. Niehaus had not declined one bit, and his playing throughout is quite exuberant. The group performs seven Niehaus originals, most of which are based on fairly common chord changes, plus three standards: "Polka Dots and Moonbeams," "But Not for Me" and the obscure "He Ain't Got Rhythm." Niehaus the arranger is not absent either; every song has colorful frameworks despite this being a quintet outing. Niehaus is backed only by Perkins' bass clarinet on parts of "But Not For Me"; arranged ensembles alternate with all-out jams; there are constant surprises in the solo order and length of the improvisations. Highly recommended to straight-ahead jazz fans, this is one of the strongest outings from Lennie Niehaus' playing career. *—Scott Yanow*

Zounds! / Aug. 23, 1954-Dec. 10, 1956 / Contemporary/OJC ♦♦♦♦
This formerly rare Contemporary set was reissued on a 1997 OJC CD. Lennie Niehaus, best known for his scores for Clint Eastwood films in the 1980s and '90s, was an excellent cool-toned bop altoist back in the 1950s who spent time working with Stan Kenton. For this album, he is heard on two different occasions providing arrangements and alto solos for octets. With such fine players as either Jack Montrose or Bill Perkins on tenor, Bob Gordon or Pepper Adams on baritone, and other top West Coast jazz musicians, Niehaus primarily performs cool jazz. The inventive charts (which on the later date utilize a French horn and a tuba) and the superior, concise solos make this a set well worth acquiring by fans of the West Coast jazz sound of the 1950s. *—Scott Yanow*

Jimmie Noone

b. Apr. 23, 1895, New Orleans, LA, **d.** Apr. 19, 1944, Los Angeles, CA
Clarinet / New Orleans Jazz
Considered one of the three top New Orleans clarinetists of the 1920s (with Johnny Dodds and Sidney Bechet), Jimmie Noone had a smoother tone than his contemporaries that appealed to players of the swing era (including Benny Goodman). Noone developed quickly and he played with Freddie Keppard (1913-14), Buddy Petit and the Young Olympia Band (1916) which he led. In 1917 he went to Chicago to join Keppard's Creole Band. After it broke up the following year he became a member of King Oliver's band, staying until he joined Doc Cook's Dreamland Orchestra (1920-26). Although Noone recorded with Cook, it was when he started leading a band at the Apex Club that he hit his stride. By 1928 he was recording for Vocalion, creating classic music including an early version of "Sweet Lorraine" (his theme song) and "Four or Five Times." Noone worked steadily in Chicago throughout the 1930s (although he received less attention from the jazz world), he used Charlie Shavers on some of his late-'30s recordings and welcomed the young singer Joe Williams to the bandstand. In 1944 Noone was in Kid Ory's band on the West Coast and seemed on the brink of greater fame when he unexpectedly died. *—Scott Yanow*

★ **Apex Blues** / May 16, 1928-Jul. 1, 1930 / Decca/GRP ♦♦♦♦♦
This CD reissues the first dozen selections from clarinetist Jimmie Noone's Apex Club Orchestra (all of the numbers with pianist Earl Hines although not the four alternate takes) plus eight slightly later numbers. Noone had an unusual quintet/sextet in which altoist Joe Poston constantly stated the melody (but never actually had any solos), giving the band an unique sound for the period. Many of Noone's greatest recordings are on this CD (including "I Know That You Know," "Four or Five Times," "Apex Blues," "My Monday Date," "Sweet Lorraine" and "My Daddy Rocks Me with One Steady Roll") although serious collectors will prefer to get the more complete two CDs from the Classics label instead. *—Scott Yanow*

The Jimmie Noone Collection, Vol. 1 (1928) / May 16, 1928-Dec. 27, 1928 / Collector's Classics ♦♦♦♦♦

1930-1934 / May 16, 1930-Nov. 23, 1934 / Classics ♦♦♦♦♦
The fourth of five CDs that reissue all of clarinetist Jimmie Noone's recordings as a leader (but not all of his alternate takes) covers a four-year period with 13 numbers from 1930, six from 1931, four from 1933 and the final two dating from 1934. The performances generally find Noone backed by multireedist Eddie Pollack (who stuck mostly to the melody) and challenged by Zinky Cohn whose style sounds remarkably close to Earl Hines. There are a lot of vocals on these sides which are surprisingly rewarding including Georgia White's debut ("When You're Smiling"), Elmo Tanner (best-known for his later work with Ted Weems), Pollack (who is joined by Noone on "You Rascal You"), May Alix, Art Jarrett and two early numbers from Mildred Bailey. Earl Hines makes a surprise guest appearance on one of the 1931 sessions. Recommended to early jazz collectors. *—Scott Yanow*

1934-1940 / Nov. 23, 1934-Dec. 11, 1940 / Classics ♦♦♦♦♦
On the fifth of Jimmie Noone's five CDs on the Classics label, the New Orleans clarinetist is heard on his final 24 selections as a leader (with the exception of a slightly later live session). The first six numbers close the book on his Apex Club Orchestra, featuring Eddie Pollack (in Joe Poston's old place) playing the melody on alto and sometimes baritone behind Noone's solos; trumpeter Jimmy Cobb and pianist Zinky Cohn get some solo space. Noone is also heard in 1936 with a freewheeling New Orleans group featuring trumpeter Guy Kelly and trombonist Preston Jackson, holding his own the following year with the dynamic young trumpeter Charlie Shavers and altoist Pete Brown, and doing his best in 1940 to overcome the weak cornet playing of Natty Dominique. The final four numbers (also from 1940) are dominated by Ed Thompson's dated vocals. No matter what the setting, Noone (who passed away in 1944) is heard in prime form. *—Scott Yanow*

Ken Nordine

Vocals / Beat Poetry, Free Jazz, Bop
Most Americans are probably familiar with Ken Nordine, even if they don't know it. His rich, deep baritone graces numerous television and radio ads. His most creative work, however, is reserved for his "word jazz," which marries liquid, free-association ruminations with jazzy instrumental backing. Active in radio since the 1950s, he's recorded numerous albums and syndicated broadcasts, and has even collaborated with the Grateful Dead.

Nordine got his start as a radio and television personality in Chicago, were he would sometimes do his raps over jazz records on his poetry show. His first *Word Jazz* album, from 1957, utilized the Chico Hamilton band (working under the alias of the Fred Katz group). This led to a series of *Word Jazz* recordings, which—like the beat poetry from the same era—looked beyond the conformity of the 1950s to more imaginative and colorful worlds, ones that had room for fantasy and irrationality, and not just mundane reality. He's recorded sporadically ever since, although he does studio recordings as a sideline to his work in radio and commercials. Nordine's soundscapes are best experienced not on his relatively few commercial recordings, but on his syndicated radio shows, 375 of which are available on cassette from Snail Records, Box 285-8C2, Florence, WI 54121. *—Richie Unterberger*

Colors / 1966 / Asphodel ♦♦♦♦♦
Twenty-four 90-second tone colors. *—Michael G. Nastos*

How Are Things in Your Town— / 1972 / Blue Thumb ♦♦♦♦
Two-fer compilation for "Mr. Word Jazz." Late-'50s/early-'60s poetry with social commentary. An utter delight. *—Michael G. Nastos*

● **The Best of Word Jazz, Vol. 1** / 1990 / Rhino ♦♦♦♦♦
Nordine is far better known for his voiceover work than for his albums, but those who do know the albums know the *Word Jazz* series best. This 1990 compilation gathers together a good selection of the earlier material, recorded between 1957 and 1960. It has a beatnik sensibility, with rhythmic poetic lines underpinned by hip cool jazz backing. It would be a fruitless pairing if it wasn't for two key things: First, Nordine's voice is amazing, polished by years

of professional work behind the microphone. Secondly, Nordine's storytelling is solid, and you find yourself being pulled into his world despite the offbeat nature of the material. When you are offered a tour of his brain, as in the CD-only "Looks Like It's Going to Rain," you're glad for the chance to go. A great overview of the crucial formative years. *—Sean Carruthers*

Red Norvo (Kenneth Norville)

b. Mar. 31, 1908, Beardstown, IL, **d.** Apr. 6, 1999
Vibraphone, Xylophone / Swing, Cool
Red Norvo was an unusual star during the swing era, playing jazz xylophone. After he switched to vibes in 1943 he had a quieter yet no less fluent style than Lionel Hampton. Although no match for Hamp popularity-wise, Norvo and his wife, singer Mildred Bailey, did become known as Mr. and Mrs. Swing. He recorded some extraordinary sides in the early-to-mid-'30s that showed off his virtuosity and imagination; two numbers (the atmospheric "Dance of the Octopus" and "In a Mist") had Benny Goodman playing bass clarinet! Norvo led his own bands during 1936-44 which, with its Eddie Sauter arrangements (particularly in the early days), had a unique ensemble sound that made it possible for one to hear the leader's xylophone. In 1944 Norvo (who by then had switched permanently to vibes) broke up his band and joined Goodman's Sextet. Through recordings and appearances, he showed that his style was quite adaptable and open to bop. At the beginning of the 1950s Norvo put together an unusual trio with guitarist Tal Farlow (later Jimmy Raney) and bassist Charles Mingus (later Red Mitchell). The light yet often speedy unisons and telepathic interplay by the musicians was quite memorable. *—Scott Yanow*

★ **Dance of the Octopus** / Apr. 18, 1933-Mar. 16, 1936 / HEP ✦✦✦✦✦
The first 26 selections that xylophonist Red Norvo ever led are on this essential (and generous) CD. Among the many illustrious sidemen are future bandleaders Benny Goodman (heard on bass clarinet during memorable versions of "In a Mist" and "Dance of the Octopus"), Jimmy Dorsey, Artie Shaw, Jack Jenney, Charlie Barnet and Bunny Berigan in addition to Chu Berry, Teddy Wilson and Gene Krupa. While the first half of the program features all-star groups, the later tracks are prime examples of small-group swing with arranger Eddie Sauter's mellophone, trumpeter Stew Pletcher and Herbie Haymer's tenor playing key roles. This readily available CD from the Scottish label Hep contains more than its share of classic performances and is essential. *—Scott Yanow*

Legendary Trio, Vol. 2: The Norvo-Mingus-Farlow Trio / Oct. 28, 1943-1950 / Vintage Jazz Classic ✦✦✦✦✦
With the exception of two titles and an alternate take featuring singer Helen Ward that were left over from Red Norvo's V-Disc sessions of 1943 (which were otherwise reissued in full on *Volume One*), this CD is comprised of 30 concise performances by Red Norvo's brilliant 1949-50 trio which, in addition to the vibraphonist/leader, also includes guitarist Tal Farlow and bassist Charles Mingus. These radio transcriptions (which do not duplicate the group's studio recordings) contain melodic but often-speedy versions of standards. The near-telepathic communication between the three brilliant players and the very appealing sound of the group make this an easily-recommended disc for lovers of straightahead jazz and vibes. *—Scott Yanow*

Improvisations on Keynote / Jul. 27, 1944-Oct. 10, 1944 / Mercury ✦✦✦✦✦
Volume Eight of Mercury's partial transfer onto CDs of its mighty *Complete Keynote Collection* LP set contains some wonderful Red Norvo small combo swing sessions. "Subtle Sextology," "Blues a la Red," "The Man I Love," and "Seven Come Eleven" come from some sextet sessions that sound very much like the sextet 78s that Benny Goodman was putting out around then. That figures, because Norvo participated on many of the BG sides—and so did pianist Teddy Wilson and bassist Slam Stewart; the latter gets plenty of humorous hum-scat time on these sides, too. For "Russian Lullaby," "I Got Rhythm," and "Sing Something Simple," the personnel shuffles (Wilson and Stewart remain) and expands to a septet for which Johnny Thompson writes some creative charts. Norvo plays xylophone on "Lullaby" and delivers unquenchably swinging vibraphone solos at all times. All but "Subtle Sextology" and "The Man I Love" are appended with outtakes—indeed, eight of the 14 tracks here were previously unissued—and "Sing Something Simple" never appeared on 78s at all. The remastered sound is all right, with a touch of distortion on occasional peaks. *—Richard S. Ginell*

☆ **Red Norvo Trio with Tal Farlow and Charles Mingus at the Savoy** / May 3, 1950-Apr. 13, 1951 / Savoy ✦✦✦✦✦
Although vibraphonist Red Norvo had been on records for nearly 20 years and had been a pacesetter in both swing and bop, it was when he formed his trio with guitarist Tal Farlow and bassist Charles Mingus in 1950 that he found the perfect setting for his vibes. The interplay between the three masterful musicians on the 25 performances included on this Savoy double-LP (issued by Arista in 1976) is quite memorable with many classic performances. Highlights include "Little White Lies," "Swedish Pastry," "Godchild," "Move," and "Deed I Do," among many others. This two-fer is highly recommended, particularly since Savoy has not yet released all of the music on CD. *—Scott Yanow*

The Red Norvo Trios / Sep. 1953-Oct. 1955 / Prestige ✦✦✦✦✦
Although the most famous of Red Norvo's vibes/guitar/bass trios featured guitarist Tal Farlow and bassist Charles Mingus, he continued the appealing format for a few years after his sidemen departed. This CD features Norvo with guitarist Jimmy Raney and bassist Red Mitchell on 15 enjoyable performances from 1953-54 and is rounded off by four songs from 1955 when Farlow rejoined Norvo and Mitchell. *—Scott Yanow*

Red Norvo, Jimmy Raney, Red Mitchell / Mar. 1954 / Fantasy/OJC ✦✦✦
This CD reissues an album by the 1954 version of the Red Norvo Trio which consists of vibraphonist Red Norvo, guitarist Jimmy Raney and bassist Red Mitchell. Although not quite reaching the heights of the earlier version with Tal Farlow and Charles Mingus, the close interplay between the musicians on cool-toned bop versions of such songs as "Just One of Those Things," "Crazy Rhythm" and "Bernie's Tune" is consistently hard-swinging yet light, adventurous yet accessible. An enjoyable set. *—Scott Yanow*

Music to Listen to Red Norvo By / Jan. 26, 1957-Mar. 2, 1957 / Contemporary/OJC ✦✦✦
Although vibraphonist Red Norvo is the leader of this sextet date, clarinetist Bill Smith (who contributed the 20-minute four-movement "Divertimento") often sets the tone for the music. His work has classical elements to it, but the five shorter pieces (by Jack Montrose, Barney Kessel, Lennie Niehaus, Duane Tatro, and Norvo) are much more jazz oriented. Norvo's light-toned sextet (which consists of his vibes, flutist Buddy Collette, clarinetist Bill Smith, guitarist Barney Kessel, bassist Red Mitchell, and drummer Shelly Manne) was not a regularly working unit, but it sounds well-integrated and tight during the complex, but generally swinging, music. *—Scott Yanow*

Chico O'Farrill (Arturo O'Farrill)

b. Oct. 28, 1921, Havana, Cuba, **d.** Jun. 27, 2001
Arranger / Afro-Cuban Jazz, Latin Jazz, Bop
Chico O'Farrill was right in the thick of the Afro-Cuban and Latin waves that hit jazz in the late '40s and '50s. His sophisticated writing for Latin big bands of the early '50s was often bold, brassy and tense, yet he could also achieve a delicate, almost classical ambience in such pieces as "Angels' Flight" and work capably in larger forms (the groundbreaking *Afro-Cuban Jazz Suites*).

O'Farrill took up the trumpet while in military school in Georgia, returning to Cuba as a full-fledged jazz fan after hearing the top American big bands. He studied composition in his native Havana and led his own band there before moving to New York City in 1948, where he soon made a name for himself writing music for Benny Goodman ("Undercurrent Blues"), Stan Kenton ("Cuban Episode") and Machito (*Afro-Cuban Jazz Suite*). From 1951 to 1954, O'Farrill made six fiery 10" albums of Latin and American big band jazz for Clef and Norgran, all of which have been reissued on a Verve 2-CD set, *Cuban Blues*. He also appeared with his own band at Birdland and toured the U.S. Toward the end of the decade, he moved to Mexico City, returning to New York in 1965 to work as arranger and music director of the TV series *Festival Of The Lively Arts* and to write arrangements for Count Basie. Though he continued to write pieces for Machito, Kenton, Gato Barbieri and Dizzy Gillespie into the '70s, there were no recording sessions under O'Farrill's name from 1966 until 1995, when he came roaring back on the scene, his imagination and vigor miraculously intact, with the outstanding *Pure Emotion* CD (Milestone). O'Farrill has also put his classical training to use by writing pieces for symphony orchestra like *Three Cuban Dances* and *Symphony No. 1*. *—Richard S. Ginell*

● **Cuban Blues: The Chico O'Farrill Sessions** / Dec. 21, 1950-Apr. 16, 1954 / Verve ✦✦✦✦✦
For any and all Latin jazz collectors, casual or serious, this is a fabulous deal, for it gathers together no less than six exceedingly rare Chico O'Farrill Clef and Norgran 10-inch albums, plus one under Machito's name, onto a slimline two-CD set. It will also come as a revelation to anyone who might scoff at anything associated with the 1950s mambo craze, for these discs reveal O'Farrill as a sophisticated, even daring arranger/composer who reached beyond merely providing a beat for dancers. Many of these charts—whether for the brief, dance-oriented Latin numbers, ultra-familiar standards like "Malaguena" and "The Peanut Vendor," or jazz tunes—are loaded with intricate figures and striking harmonies obviously gleaned from classical study, all crisply executed with a brash, shiny edge by his Afro-Cuban groups and bands staffed by American jazzmen. Occasionally, he even conjures a delicate, classical ambience from a number like "Angels' Flight" (named after Los Angeles' legendary downtown funicular). The apotheosis of O'Farrill's experiments are his two full-blown, groundbreaking Afro-Cuban Jazz Suites. The first features Flip Phillips and the redoubtable Charlie Parker as soloists within the Machito band, and the second is even bolder in its zigzag journey through the classical, Latin and jazz camps. Yet for all of his erudition, O'Farrill never forgets to ask for madly percolating Afro-Cuban grooves from his rhythm teams—which clinches the deal for any Latin music fan. *—Richard S. Ginell*

Pure Emotion / Feb. 1995 / Milestone ✦✦✦✦✦
After not having led a recording session under his own name in 29 years, O'Farrill came from seemingly out of nowhere to lead a terrific Afro-Cuban big band date on this CD. O'Farrill claims that he turned down offers to lead standard seven or eight-piece salsa bands on records over the years, preferring to wait until a big band opportunity came along—and clearly, he was bursting with accumulated charts dating from the 1960s through the 1990s. Not too much has changed since O'Farrill's exciting string of albums for Clef in the 1950s; if anything, his arranging hand has become surer, more sophisticated, thoroughly in touch as ever with a wide variety of influences. Most striking of all is how O'Farrill was able to build a fire underneath the musicians in the band, which includes leaders in their own right like trombonist Robin Eubanks, conguero Jerry Gonzalez and drummer Steve Berrios, as well as Tito Puente's tenor sax/flute player Mario Rivera and O'Farrill's son Arturo Jr. on piano. The most ambitious track is also the most entertaining one, an extended 1964 O'Farrill composition called "Variations on a Well-Known Theme" ("La Cucaracha"!) that deftly welds together various big band idioms, near-parodies of Muzak and television writing, and Afro-Cuban percussion workouts. Latin jazz fans will be pulverized and delighted by this recording. *—Richard S. Ginell*

The Heart of a Legend / Aug. 17, 1999 / Milestone ✦✦✦✦
The campaign to punch Chico O'Farrill into the general consciousness continues with what amounts to an anthology of his work, all freshly and brilliantly played by the Chico O'Farrill Afro-Cuban Jazz Big Band directed by his pianist son Arturo. The material on hand goes back to a 1956 cha-cha written on a plane ride to Havana, but the unifying thread is a suite from the film *Guaguasi* scattered in pieces throughout the album. It is an often astonishingly diverse portrait of O'Farrill, reflecting not only his percolating Afro-Cuban rhythmic base but also some of his other musical directions. There is a Basie-style big-band blues, "Sing Your Blues Away," with Freddie Cole doing a credible job as velvety blues shouter; a lightweight, fluffy thing called "Te Quiero" with flute/female choruses and a lascivious Gato Barbieri on tenor; and a recent Latin jazz suite of relatively modest proportions, "Trumpet Fantasy (For Wynton)." The best stuff comes early on: the marvelous "Theme From Guaguasi," a heartfelt

Afro-Cuban workout in 6/8 time called "Momentum," which is really a renamed piece inspired by the 1962 Cuban missile crisis ("Cuban Conflagration") that was rescued from oblivion for this album. Several other famous Latin jazz names turn up in fine form: Paquito D'Rivera, Cachao, Candido, Alfredo "Chocolate" Armenteros, Carlos "Patato" Valdes, and, in a closing duet, Arturo O'Farrill and Arturo Sandoval. There are a lot of board fades on these tracks, a highly unusual practice in the '90s on a jazz album. Though not as essential as *Pure Emotion*, this CD confirms the continued vitality of this 77-year-old master. *—Richard S. Ginell*

Carambola / Oct. 10, 2000 / Milestone ✦✦✦✦✦
The astounding comeback of Chico O'Farrill, at age 79 (perhaps age 29 in spirit), continued with this terrific collection of mostly Afro-Cuban styled compositions—some brand-new, some more than half a century old. Originally written for Dizzy Gillespie, the swinging title tune takes on a more complex Afro-Cuban treatment this time, with Michael Mossman capably taking on the trumpet work. "The Aztec Suite," written for Art Farmer, comes together smoothly and cohesively, with even more spectacular work by Mossman—and "Crazy City (... But I Love It)" is "Gone City" (recorded by Machito in 1949) in a more refined, shipshape, somewhat less frantic performance. The oldest piece, "Oye Mi Rumba" (1945), lures singer Graciela out of retirement for some endearingly authentic atmosphere. Don't overlook newer material like O'Farrill's treatment of "Delirio"—a beautiful bolero, very sophisticated in harmony—and "Rhapsody for Two Islands," a flamboyant little piece designed to evoke Cuba and Manhattan with a sudden, broadly-paced solo piano break that explicitly quotes "Rhapsody in Blue." Yet the highlight of the CD is undoubtedly the amazingly successful re-recording of O'Farrill's visionary "Afro-Cuban Jazz Suite," 50 years after the original Machito version was cut. His crisply executing 21st Century orchestra makes the material seem even more emotionally moving than before, although you do miss the impossibly fluid alto of Charlie Parker (guest soloist Mario Rivera makes an honorable stab at Bird's part) and irreplaceably wild Buddy Rich drums from the Machito record. This is a must-hear for Latin jazz lovers. *—Richard Ginell*

Oregon

f. 1970

Group / Folk-Jazz, Post-Bop, Fusion, World Fusion

One of the earliest and finest exponents of world jazz, Oregon began life in 1970 as an offshoot of the Paul Winter Consort, in which the group's original members had played. From the beginning, the band eschewed most jazz conventions. Percussionist Collin Walcott played tabla, sitar, and dulcimer, among other instruments, but did not use a trap set; bassist Glen Moore doubled on clarinet, viola, and piano, and its front line was formed by a double-reedist (Paul McCandless) and an acoustic guitarist (Ralph Towner). The band's music differed from much of what had heretofore been considered jazz. The concept of blues and swing was given a much-reduced prominence in favor of other, less literal forms of tonal and rhythmic organization. For example, Indian ragas would occasionally replace chord changes, and talas would supplant swing time. The group's dynamic approach was quieter than typical by jazz standards, and their overall aesthetic somewhat introspective. Improvisation was central to the band's work, however, and in this sense their music is most firmly in the jazz tradition. Oregon's music is characterized by a heightened method of ensemble interaction, a rapt attention to timbral contrast, and an openness to any and all cultural influences. After Walcott's death in a car accident in 1984, the group disbanded for a time, before eventually replacing him with the percussionist Trilok Gurtu. *—Chris Kelsey*

Music of Another Present Era / 1973 / Vanguard ✦✦✦✦✦
A 1989 reissue of an outstanding release that blows most similar ECM albums out of the water. *—Ron Wynn*

Distant Hills / Jul. 2, 1973-Jul. 5, 1973 / Vanguard ✦✦✦✦
This is one of the first releases to click from this group that knows how to make soothing, acoustic fare without becoming boring or wimpy. *—Ron Wynn*

Winter Light / Jul. 16, 1974-Aug. 7, 1974 / Vanguard ✦✦✦✦
Here are some simply brilliant, feathery compositions. Marvelous playing. *—Ron Wynn*

Out of the Woods / Apr. 1978 / Musicraft ✦✦✦✦

● **Roots in the Sky** / Dec. 1978-Apr. 1979 / Discovery ✦✦✦✦✦
A '92 CD reissue of their '79 album, among their only releases ever issued by a major label. It was characteristically free-wheeling and eclectic, with long stretches of classical, Asian, African, and jazz coming together, and the group mixing structured ensemble work with surging free solos. *—Ron Wynn*

Moon and Mind / 1978 / Vanguard ✦✦✦✦

Beyond Words / Mar. 20, 1995-Mar. 23, 1995 / Chesky ✦✦✦✦✦
With its combination of simple beauty and elegant intricacy, *Beyond Words* truly is. This time out, the three surviving original members of Oregon perform as a drummerless trio, handling a variety of compositions old and new, primarily from the pen of Ralph Towner. Towner's multi-instrumental versatility highlights and undergirds the proceedings, with his beautiful classical and 12-string guitar work especially satisfying. Paul McCandless delivers his usual flawless performance on an amazing variety of woodwinds. The interplay between his bass clarinet and Glen Moore's restored 1715 Klotz bass is superb on "Pepe Linque" and "Sicilian Walk." Towner's classic "The Silence of a Candle," first recorded on the landmark *Icarus* with the Paul Winter Consort, is reprised here, as are several other Oregon standards, including "Witchi-Tai-To." The only weak moments come in the set-closing "Silver Suite," which meanders aimlessly at times. Other than that, this is an album filled with gorgeous, multi-dimensional music played by a trio of inspired virtuosos. *—Jim Newsom*

Northwest Passage / Sep. 1996-Oct. 1996 / Intuition ✦✦✦✦
Oregon's first recording in a while features the three surviving original members (Ralph Towner on guitar and keyboards, bassist Glen Moore, and Paul McCandless, who switches between soprano, English horn, sopranino, oboe and bass clarinet) with either Arto Tuncboyaciyan or Mark Walker on percussion. They perform 14 originals that usually avoid blue notes, making the music sound very folk-oriented. There is plenty of variety in the atmospheres, and the consistently intriguing music should appeal to many listeners, including those who are into mood music, world music or folk songs in addition to jazz. *—Scott Yanow*

Original Dixieland Jazz Band

f. 1917, **db.** 1923

Group / New Orleans Jazz, Classic Jazz, Dixieland

The first jazz group to ever record, the Original Dixieland Jazz Band made history in 1917. They were not the first group to ever play jazz, nor was this White quintet necessarily the best band of the time, but during 1917-23 they did a great deal to popularize jazz. Comprised of drummer Tony Sbarbaro, cornetist Nick LaRocca, trombonist Eddie Edwards, pianist Henry Ragas and clarinetist Larry Shields, the group caused a major sensation after their first appearance in New York. Columbia quickly recorded the ODJB ("Darktown Strutters Ball" and "Indiana"), but the label was afraid to put out the records until Victor's recording of the novelty "Livery Stable Blues" became a huge hit and really launched the jazz age. During the next few years the ODJB would introduce such future standards as "Tiger Rag," "At the Jazz Band Ball," "Clarinet Marmalade" and many others. After introducing jazz to Europe during 1919-20, the group became a bit out of fashion in the US after the rise of Paul Whiteman and the New Orleans Rhythm Kings. After breaking up in the mid-'20s, a 1936 reunion brought a few final recordings. The Original Dixieland Jazz Band did make a strong contribution to early jazz, helped supply the repertoire of many later Dixieland bands, and were an influence on Bix Beiderbecke and Red Nichols. *—Scott Yanow*

★ **75th Anniversary** / Feb. 26, 1917-Jun. 7, 1921 / Bluebird/RCA ✦✦✦✦✦
The Original Dixieland Jazz Band was the first jazz group to record. Although their two earliest titles for Columbia ("Darktown Strutters Ball" and "Indiana") has not been reissued in a long time. All of The ODJB's output for Victor (including "Livery Stable Blues" which was the first jazz recording to ever be released) is on this definitive CD. This colorful group, which stuck exclusively to ensembles with no solos, introduced such standard tunes as "Original Dixieland One Step," "At the Jazz Band," "Fidgety Feet," "Sensation," "Clarinet Marmalade," "Margie," "Jazz Me Blues," "Royal Garden Blues" and "Tiger Rag," all of which are included on this release. It's an essential acquisition for any serious jazz library. *—Scott Yanow*

The Complete Original Dixieland Jazz Band / Feb. 26, 1917-Sep. 25, 1936 / RCA ✦✦✦✦✦
This double-CD has all of the Victor recordings of the first jazz group to record, The Original Dixieland Jazz Band. The five-piece New Orleans band, which essentially stuck exclusively to ensembles, set the standard for 1917-21 jazz. Their "Livery Stable Blues" (which found the horns imitating barnyard animals) was a big hit and The ODJB introduced such future Dixieland standards as "Original Dixieland One-Step," "At the Jazz Band Ball," "Fidgety Feet," "Sensation," "Clarinet Marmalade," "Jazz Me Blues," "Royal Garden Blues" and "Tiger Rag." The 23 numbers from 1917-21 (which are rounded out by the humorous "Bow Wow Blues (My Mama Treats Me like a Dog)" were reissued in a single CD by Bluebird but this two-fer also has The ODJB's "comeback" recordings of 1936; six titles by the original five plus eight very rare titles which find The ODJB forming the nucleus of a musical if not too distinctive big band. Important historical music. *—Scott Yanow*

Sensation! / Feb. 26, 1917-Nov. 24, 1920 / ASV/Living Era ✦✦✦✦
This set reissues 18 of The Original Dixieland Jazz Band's recordings. A cross-section of their output (rather than a complete set), the release starts off with their hit version of "Livery Stable Blues," and includes such classics as "Tiger Rag" and "Sensation," reissues some of the superior performances that were cut in London during 1919-1920 including "I've Lost My Heart in Dixieland," and concludes with "Margie." It's a fine introduction to this pioneering jazz band. *—Scott Yanow*

The Original Memphis Five

f. 1917, **db.** 1931

Group / New Orleans Jazz, Classic Jazz

Founded in 1917 by trumpeter Phil Napoleon and pianist Frank Signorelli, this excellent New Orleans jazz quintet made a ton of records between 1921-31, including many under different names (such as Ladd's Black Aces and the Carolina Cotton Pickers). Napoleon, trombonist Miff Mole (who in 1922 was succeeded by Charles Panelli), clarinetist Jimmy Lytell, Signorelli and drummer Jack Roth were regular fixtures in the early days; starting in 1926 the personnel changed fairly frequently with cornetist Red Nichols, drummer Ray Bauduc, Mole and (during one session apiece in 1928, 1929 and 1931), Tommy and Jimmy Dorsey making appearances. The original Memphis Five's music was melodic, swinging and very jazz-oriented. Unfortunately most of their hundreds of recordings have not been reissued on CD yet. *—Scott Yanow*

★ **Collection, Vol. 1: 1922-1923** / Apr. 22, 1922-Dec. 10, 1923 / Collector's Classics ✦✦✦✦✦
Phil Napoleon was arguably the best trumpeter on record during 1921-22 and one of the first jazz musicians to swing. Possessor of an attractive and clear tone along with impressive technique, Napoleon's melodic lead was heard on a countless number of sides by the original Memphis Five and other groups with similar personnel. Despite its title, this CD actually starts out with the nine selections recorded by Jazzbo's Carolina Serenaders, a quintet with Napoleon, trombonist Miff Mole, several different clarinetists, pianist Frank Signorelli and drummer Jack Roth. The set also has two numbers from the Southland Six (a similar group with Napoleon, trombonist Charles Panelli and clarinetist Jimmy Lytell) in addition to five sessions from the original Memphis Five. Throughout, Napoleon and his musicians sound as if they have evolved way ahead of the original Dixieland Jazz Band and show the influence of the New Orleans Rhythm Kings, but do not sound like a copy of either. This ensemble-oriented music does not include dated vocals, novelties (other than the weak "barking" on "That Barking Dog—*Woof! Woof!"), military staccato phrasing or doo-wacka-doo nonsense, and this CD fills an often overlooked gap in jazz history.* —Scott Yanow

Kid Ory (Edward Ory)

b. Dec. 25, 1886, La Place, LA, **d.** Jan. 23, 1973, Honolulu, HI
Trombone / New Orleans Jazz, Dixieland
Kid Ory was one of the great New Orleans pioneers, an early trombonist who virtually defined the "tailgate" style (using his horn to play rhythmic bass lines in the front line behind the trumpet and clarinet) and who was fortunate enough to last through the lean years so he could make a major comeback in the mid-'40s. In 1919 Ory moved to California and in 1922 (possibly 1921) recorded the first two titles by a Black New Orleans jazz band ("Ory's Creole Trombone" and "Society Blues") under the band title of "Spike's Seven Pods of Pepper Orchestra." In 1925 he moved to Chicago, played regularly with King Oliver and recorded many classic sides with Oliver, Louis Armstrong (in his *Hot Five and Seven*) and Jelly Roll Morton among others. The definitive New Orleans trombonist of the 1920s, Ory (whose "Muskrat Ramble" became a standard) was mostly out of music after 1930, running a chicken ranch with his brother. However in 1942 he was persuaded to return, and after a stint with Barney Bigard's group, he formed his own band. Ory's group was featured on Orson Welles's radio show in 1944 and the publicity made it possible for the band to catch on. The New Orleans revival was in full swing and Ory was still in prime form. *—Scott Yanow*

King of the Tailgate Trombone / 1948-1949 / American Music ♦♦♦♦
Consisting of previously unissued live performances from two editions of Kid Ory's Creole Jazz Bands, these relatively well-recorded jams should satisfy any lover of New Orleans jazz. Clarinetist Joe Darensbourg (who is on all of the selections) is in good form, trumpeter Andrew Blakeney (heard on 11 of the 15 numbers) has rarely sounded better and trumpeter Teddy Buckner (who stars during the last four songs), although not as expert an ensemble player as some of Ory's sidemen have been, takes some outstanding solos. The Dixieland standards that Ory performs include romping versions of "Panama," "Mahogany Hall Stomp," "Sugar Foot Stomp," "High Society" and "Sweet Georgia Brown." *—Scott Yanow*

This Kid's the Greatest! / Jul. 17, 1953-Jun. 18, 1956 / Good Time Jazz ♦♦♦♦♦
These lively and spirited sessions from 1953, 1954, and 1956 show that Ory still had plenty of gas left in the tank and could play tailgate 'bone in the New Orleans style better than anyone. Bouncy and lively, Ory leads three different configurations, pulling in players from all different musical strata (modern jazzers like Barney Kessel and jump blues pianist Lloyd Glenn work comfortably with old-timers like Minor Hall and Wellman Braud), making it all work seamlessly. Highlights include nice takes on old warhorses like "South Rampart Street Parade," "Bill Bailey," "Creole Love Call," "Milenberg Joys," "Ballin' the Jack," and "Four or Five Times," but the real treat is the Kid's vocal on his own "The Girls Go Crazy." Highly recommended. *—Cub Koda*

Kid Ory Plays the Blues / Oct. 3, 1953-Feb. 5, 1955 / Storyville ♦♦♦♦
During the 1950s trombonist Kid Ory, who would turn 70 in 1956, led his finest bands. Among the pacesetters in the New Orleans revival, Ory's groups were always in tune and featured both colorful ensembles and strong soloists. This Storyville recording has strong solos from either Teddy Buckner or Alvin Alcorn on trumpet and Bob McCracken, George Probert or Phil Gomez on clarinet. The rhythm section of pianist Don Ewell, bassist Ed Garland and drummer Minor Hall was one of the best in the idiom. Most of the songs in this series of live broadcasts from *Club Hangover* in San Francisco are blues (some just have "blues" in the title) but there is enough variety to make this a recommended set. *—Scott Yanow*

☆ **Kid Ory's Creole Jazz Band (1954)** / Aug. 9, 1954-Aug. 10, 1954 / Good Time Jazz ♦♦♦♦♦
Although some Kid Ory fans might disagree, the veteran trombonist led his finest bands (at least the ones that recorded) in the 1950s. The one heard on this CD is really quite definitive, featuring the brilliant ensemble player (and distinctive soloist) Alvin Alcorn on trumpet, the talented clarinetist George Probert and an excellent rhythm section (pianist Don Ewell, guitarist Bill Newman, bassist Ed Garland and drummer Minor Hall). Their versions on this set of "That's a Plenty," "Gettysburg March," "Clarinet Marmalade" and even "When the Saints Go Marching In" are true classics of New Orleans jazz. This joyous and exciting music is essential for all serious jazz collections. *—Scott Yanow*

Creole Jazz Band / Nov. 30, 1954-Dec. 2, 1954 / Good Time Jazz ♦♦♦♦♦
Trombonist Kid Ory, already 68 at the time of this recording, was at the peak of his powers in the mid-'50s. This particular version of his Creole Jazz Band was one of the finest, featuring trumpeter Alvin Alcorn and clarinetist George Probert, talented soloists who were also superb group players. Alcorn generated a lot of excitement perfectly placing long notes near the end of each ensemble chorus. This Good Time Jazz CD is almost up to the level of its 1954 and 1956 counterparts, highlighted by torrid versions of "Shake That Thing," "Royal Garden Blues" and "Indiana." *—Scott Yanow*

★ **Legendary Kid** / Nov. 22, 1955-Nov. 25, 1955 / Good Time Jazz ♦♦♦♦♦
One of trombonist Kid Ory's greatest recordings, this consistently exciting CD features trumpeter Alvin Alcorn, clarinetist Phil Gomez and a strong rhythm section that includes bassist Wellman Braud and Ory's longtime drummer Minor Hall. These versions of "Mahogany Hall Stomp," "There'll Be Some Changes Made," "At the Jazz Band Ball" and "Shine" are all gems, giving listeners some of the very best in New Orleans jazz, and showing that the music need not be played haltingly by over-the-hill musicians; one can capture its spirit and joy without sacrificing musicianship. Every jazz collection should have this music. *—Scott Yanow*

Kid Ory Favorites! / Jun. 1956-Jul. 1956 / Good Time Jazz ♦♦♦♦♦
Trombonist Kid Ory recorded what were arguably his finest recording sessions for Good Time Jazz. This double LP features Ory, trumpeter Alvin Alcorn and clarinetist Phil Gomez (one of his strongest frontlines) on 17 selections that epitomize the best in New Orleans jazz. Highlights include "Do What Ory Says," "Jazz Me Blues," "Original Dixieland One-Step," "Panama," "Maryland, My Maryland," "1919 Rag" and "Bugle Call Rag." Two selections ("Mood Indigo" and "Toot, Toot, Tootsie") have been left off the single-CD reissue. *—Scott Yanow*

Sunshine Exner Decca Recordings (1922-1947) / 1922-1947 / Document ♦♦♦
This CD, one of the very few put out by the blues label, Document, that is actually jazz rather than blues, is a historic gapfiller. Trombonist Kid Ory's Sunshine Orchestra (also sometimes called Spikes' Seven Pods of Pepper Orchestra!) was the first black band from New Orleans to make it onto records. Its two instrumentals from 1922 ("Ory's Creole Trombone" and "Society Blues") feature some primitive but lively playing by Ory, cornetist Mutt Carey, clarinetist Dink Johnson, pianist Fred Washington, drummer Ben Borders and the inaudible bass of Ed Garland. The same band backs a pair of dated vocals apiece by singers Roberta Dudley and Ruth Lee. Jumping to 1944, this CD has a broadcast version of "Mutt's Blues" by Kid Ory's Creole Jazz Band (with trumpeter Mutt Carey and clarinetist Jimmie Noone), a pair of obscure foursong sessions by the same group (with Joe Darensbourg taking the spot of the deceased Noone) cut for Exner and Decca and rarely reissued, and Ory's appearance with his band on Ruby Blesh's "This Is Jazz" radio program of August 9, 1947. The latter lasts a half-hour and features Ory, Darensbourg, trumpeter Andrew Blakeney, pianist Buster Wilson, guitarist Bud Scott, bassist Ed Garland and drummer Minor Hall performing seven numbers including "Oh Didn't He Ramble," "Maryland, My Maryland" and "Savoy Blues." Kid Ory's mid-'50s group would actually be more powerful than this early version but the music is full of infectious spirit. *—Scott Yanow*

Complete Kid Ory Verve Sessions / Mosaic ♦♦♦♦♦

Greg Osby

b. Aug. 3, 1960, St. Louis, MO
Sax (Soprano), Sax (Alto) / Avant-Garde Jazz, Free Funk, M-Base, Post-Bop
Post-bop saxophonist Greg Osby was born April 3, 1960 in St. Louis, playing in a series of R&B, funk, and blues units throughout his teen years before attending Howard University. Upon graduating from the Berkley School of Music, he settled in New York City and went on to play behind Jack DeJohnette, Andrew Hill, Herbie Hancock, and Muhal Richard Abrams; during the mid-'80s, Osby also served alongside Steve Coleman, Geri Allen, Gary Thomas, and Cassandra Wilson as a member of the renowned M-Base Collective. Making his solo debut with 1987's *Sound Theatre*, Osby went on to record several sets for the JMT label, also earning notice for his impressive contributions to Hill's 1989 date, *Eternal Spirit*, and its follow-up *But Not Farewell;* with 1990's *Man-Talk for Moderns, Vol. X*, he cut his first headling session for Blue Note, with subsequent efforts for the company (including 1993's *3-D Lifestyles* and 1995's *Black Book*), pioneering a distinctive fusion of jazz and hip-hop. While 1996's *Art Forum* captured the saxophonist in an acoustic setting, Osby continues exploring new avenues with each successive release, capturing the improvisational intensity of his live dates with 1999's *Banned in New York* and reuniting with Hill and fellow elder statesman Jim Hill for the following year's *The Invisible Hand*. *—Jason Ankeny*

● **Greg Osby and Sound Theater** / May 1987-Jun. 1987 / JMT ♦♦♦♦♦
This early effort by altoist Greg Osby (who doubles on soprano) matches him with pianist Michele Rosewoman, guitarist Kevin McNeal, bassist Lonnie Plaxico and either Terri Lyne Carrington or Paul Samuels on drums; two songs add Fusako Yoshikda on koto. The performances (mostly Osby originals) are complex, somewhat abrasive, and in the M-Base genre, swinging in their own funky fashion and following a different logic than bebop. Osby plays quite well, and the music grows in interest with each listen. *—Scott Yanow*

Zero / Jan. 9, 1998-Jan. 11, 1998 / Blue Note ♦♦♦♦

Banned in New York / Dec. 1, 1998 / Blue Note ♦♦♦♦♦
Hoping to capture the immediacy and raw energy of one of his live performances, Osby simply placed a mini-disc recorder on a table in front of the bandstand at New York City's *Sweet Basil* nightclub. Then he and his explosive young band—and I do mean young; drummer Rodney Green is just 19—launched into an hour-long set of nonstop music. One microphone, no breaks between songs, no stage announcements—just a solid hour of seamless, high-octane jazz. One of the most exciting improvisers around, Osby stretches out here on a set of standards by Ellington, Monk, Rollins, and Parker, plus one original. But don't expect to hear much that's familiar. The tunes are merely seeds for Osby's fast and furious improvisation. The young-gun rhythm section of Jason Moran on piano, Atsushi Osada on bass, and Green on drums keep things rolling at a full-throttle pace. This is jazz in its purest form: spontaneous, direct, and unfiltered. *—Joel Roberts*

Invisible Hand / Sep. 8, 1999-Sep. 9, 1999 / Blue Note ♦♦♦
Though chock full of Osby's signature brand of dissonance, *The Invisible Hand* is one of the altoist's mellower, more contemplative offerings. Its most novel aspect is the inclusion of pianist Andrew Hill and guitarist Jim Hall, two of jazz's fascinating elder statesmen. Hill's piano style is fractured and fragmented, yet suffused with its own ornamental beauty. Hall is a master of the understated, perfectly chosen phrase. Both have worked with Osby on more than one occasion. But *The Invisible Hand* is an historic first: prior to its recording, Hill and Hall had never played together. Disappointingly, the two are paired only on Hill's "Ashes" and Hall's "Sanctus"; otherwise, they appear separately. In fact, Hall is present only on three of the album's ten tracks, giving listeners only the briefest glimpse of his talents. Hill, appearing on six numbers, is utilized more effectively; the pianist is especially brilliant on Fats Waller's "Jitterbug Waltz." Gary Thomas, an Osby contemporary, overdubs multiple woodwinds to create thick orchestration on "Nature Boy," "With Son," and a couple of others. Bassist Scott Colley and drummer Terri Lynne Carrington provide reliable rhythmic support throughout. But overall the record suffers from a discontinuity brought about by repeated personnel shifts. In a sense, *The Invisible Hand* sounds like three different albums, and Osby's production seems unnecessarily convoluted. *—David R. Adler*

Hot Lips Page (Oran Thaddeus Page)

b. Jan. 27, 1908, Dallas, TX, **d.** Nov. 5, 1954, New York, NY
Vocals, Trumpet / Jazz Blues, Swing, Dixieland
One of the great swing trumpeters in addition to being a talented blues vocalist, Hot Lips Page's premature passing left a large hole in the jazz world; virtually all musicians (no matter their style) loved him. Page gained early experience in the 1920s performing in Texas, playing in Ma Rainey's backup band. He was with Walter Page's Blue Devils during 1928-31

and then joined Bennie Moten's band in Kansas City in time to take part in a brilliant 1932 recording session. Page freelanced in Kansas City and in 1936 was one of the stars in Count Basie's orchestra but, shortly before Basie was discovered, Joe Glaser signed Hot Lips as a solo artist. Although Page's big band did alright in the late '30s (recording for Victor), if he had come east with Basie he would have become much more famous. Page was one of the top sidemen with Artie Shaw's Orchestra during 1941-42 and then mainly freelanced throughout the remainder of his career, recording with many all-star groups and always being a welcome fixture at jam sessions. *—Scott Yanow*

• **The 1938-1940** / Mar. 10, 1938-Dec. 3, 1940 / Classics ♦♦♦♦♦

Dr. Jazz Series, Vol. 6 / Dec. 21, 1951-Mar. 7, 1952 / Storyville ♦♦♦♦♦
There are not that many recordings from the later part of Page's career, which makes this CD (comprised of radio broadcasts) of great interest. Page is heard on a variety of Dixieland and swing standards with quite an assortment of all-stars including cornetist Wild Bill Davison, trombonists Lou McGarity and Sandy Williams, clarinetists Pee Wee Russell, Bob Wilber, Eddie Barefield, Cecil Scott and Peanuts Hucko, pianists Red Richards, Dick Cary, Joe Sullivan and Charlie Queener and drummer George Wettling (who was actually the leader of these groups). Page is in exuberant form whether singing tunes such as "When My Sugar Walks down the Street" and a riotous "St. Louis Blues" or leading the ensembles. This is one of his best recordings currently available and is often quite exciting. *—Scott Yanow*

1940-1944 / 1995 / Classics ♦♦♦♦

1944-1946 / Nov. 30, 1944-Oct. 1946 / Classics ♦♦♦

Charlie Parker

b. Aug. 29, 1920, Kansas City, KS, **d.** Mar. 12, 1955, New York, NY
Sax (Alto) / Bop, Big Band
One of a handful of musicians who can be said to have permanently changed jazz, Charlie Parker was arguably the greatest saxophonist of all time. He could play remarkably fast lines that, if slowed down to half speed, would reveal that every note made sense. Bird, along with his contemporaries Dizzy Gillespie and Bud Powell, is considered a founder of bebop; in reality he was an intuitive player who simply was expressing himself. Rather than basing his improvisations closely on the melody as was done in swing, he was a master of chordal improvising, creating new melodies that were based on the structure of a song. In fact Bird wrote several future standards (such as "Anthropology," "Ornithology," "Scrapple from the Apple," and "Ko Ko" along with such blues as "Now's the Time" and "Parker's Mood") that "borrowed" and modernized the chord structures of older tunes. Parker's remarkable technique, fairly original sound and ability to come up with harmonically advanced phrases that could be both logical and whimsical were highly influential. By 1950 it was impossible to play "modern jazz" with credibility without closely studying Charlie Parker. *—Scott Yanow*

• **Yardbird Suite: The Ultimate Collection** / Jan. 1945-Sep. 26, 1952 / Rhino ♦♦♦♦♦
This nicely priced and packaged two-disc set is a convenient, introductory primer compilation to Parker's music for the average listener. What we have here are 38 tracks spread over two discs that touch on Parker's greatest musical achievements; the sides that are considered—in most cases—his groundbreaking work; his greatest compositions and arrangements in what are generally considered the best-known or most representative versions. What is very important about this box set is that it's the first multi-label best-of view retrospective. Up until this, any such compilations were single-label-driven affairs, but with this, the average listener—indeed, the novice coming to Parker's music for the first time, having heard the legend but not the message—has all the important stop-off points. The first disc features all the Guild and Musicraft sides with Dizzy Gillespie collected here, followed by the groundbreaking Dial and Savoy singles. The second disc continues Bird's seminal recordings for Dial and Savoy, plus a brace of important sides cut for Granz' Clef label are here. Following those are the inclusion of three performances from *Summit Meeting At Birdland*, taken from a live radio broadcast of an all-star lineup featuring Bird, Dizzy Gillespie and Bud Powell. While the Bird-with-strings sessions are Parker's all-time best-selling recordings, it's no small surprise that these tracks were also the licensing glitch that keeps this project from being truly complete. But certainly the next best thing are the live recordings of Bird's quintet with strings and oboe from the *Legendary Rockland Palace Concert*, selections of which close out the second disc and this compilation. While naysayers will carp about what *isn't* here, the fact remains that this is simply the best introduction to Bird's music. *—Cub Koda*

☆ **The Complete Savoy Studio Sessions** / 1945-1948 / Savoy ♦♦♦♦♦
This three-CD box set contains all of the recordings Charlie Parker made for the Savoy label and it is overflowing with gems and an almost countless number of alternate takes. Bird was one of the most important jazzmen of all time and nearly every note he recorded (in the studios if not live) is well worth hearing. This box starts off with his sideman date with Tiny Grimes in 1944, contains Parker's famous "Ko Ko" session of 1945 (with a young Miles Davis on trumpet and highlighted by "Now's the Time" and "Billie's Bounce"), and continues through his 1947-1948 quintet sessions with a more mature Miles Davis; either Bud Powell, John Lewis, or Duke Jordan on piano; bassists Tommy Potter, Curly Russell, or Nelson Boyd; and drummer Max Roach. Together they recorded such classics as "Donna Lee," "Chasin' the Bird," "Milestones," and "Parker's Mood." Every scrap that the great altoist cut for Savoy is in this box. *—Scott Yanow*

☆ **Bird: Complete on Verve** / Jan. 28, 1946-Dec. 10, 1954 / Verve ♦♦♦♦♦
As a leader, Charlie Parker recorded for Savoy and Dial during 1945-48 and then for Verve exclusively (at least in the studios) during 1949-54. This remarkable ten-CD box set, which adds quite a bit of material to an earlier ten-LP set, contains all of these recordings plus Bird's earlier appearances with Jazz at the Philharmonic. The JATP jams are highlighted by Parker's perfect solo on "Lady Be Good," a ferocious improvisation on "The Closer" and a solo on "Embraceable You" that tops his more famous studio recording. In addition, this box has all of the "Bird and Strings" sides, his meetings with Machito's Cuban orchestra, the 1950 session with Dizzy Gillespie and Thelonious Monk, small-group dates (including a 1951 meeting with Miles Davis), odd encounters with voices and studio bands, the famous "Jam Blues" with fellow altoists Johnny Hodges and Benny Carter and his final recordings, a set of Cole Porter tunes. The fact-filled 34 page booklet is also indispensable. Highly recommended. *—Scott Yanow*

Confirmation: The Best of the Verve Years / Jan. 28, 1946-Dec. 10, 1954 / Verve ♦♦♦♦♦
Anyone daunted by the expense of acquiring the 10-disc *The Complete Charlie Parker On Verve* may well have their prayers answered by this 2-CD distillation of the big box. It covers a wide stretch of material from Parker's career, going back to the first JATP concert in 1946 and stretching almost to the end of his Norman Granz period. One might prefer a chronological approach—which the box takes—to the wild skipping around from session to session and idiom to idiom that occurs here. But the set does touch all of the bases of the Verve catalogue—the JATP concerts, the string sessions, the Afro-Cuban experiments, the big band treatments, the botched Gil Evans session, and of course, the small combo formats that Parker usually worked within. As part of a basic Charlie Parker collection, which would also include samplings from the Dial and Savoy periods, these CDs are essential as an overview of the diverse formats that Parker explored while recording for Granz. *—Richard S. Ginell*

☆ **Complete Dial Sessions** / Feb. 5, 1946-Dec. 17, 1947 / Stash ♦♦♦♦♦
Charlie Parker recorded for Dial during the same period he was cutting his better-known sides for Savoy. This four-CD set contains his 89 Dial recordings including all of the alternate takes. The innovative altoist is heard with Dizzy Gillespie on "Diggin' Diz" and playing definitive versions of "Moose the Mooche," "Yardbird Suite," and "Ornithology" in a septet, struggling during his tragic "Lover Man" date; on excerpts from a poorly recorded live session, backing singer Earl Coleman, and interacting with the Erroll Garner Trio; playing his classic "Relaxin' at Camarillo" (four versions); and finally leading several sessions with his classic quintet (which included trumpeter Miles Davis, pianist Duke Jordan, bassist Tommy Potter, and drummer Max Roach) recording such gems as "Dewey Square," "Embraceable You," and "Scrapple From the Apple," the final session adds the great trombonist J.J. Johnson to the group for more classic music. Essential music, highly recommended for all jazz collections. *—Scott Yanow*

Bebop and Bird, Vols. 1 & 2 / 1946 1952 / Rhino ♦♦♦♦
Here's an intriguing concept, the first of two volumes that collect various cuts from 1946-1952 with Bird and bop elders Miles Davis (tpt), Max Roach (d), Errol Garner (p), and more. Great mastering and good selection. 1988 reissue. *—Ron Wynn*

The Complete Dean Benedetti Recordings of Charlie Parker / Mar. 1, 1947-Jul. 1, 1948 / Mosaic ♦♦

Diz 'N Bird at Carnegie Hall / Sep. 29, 1947 / Blue Note ♦♦♦♦
Nine years after Benny Goodman's groundbreaking concert, bebop finally came to *Carnegie Hall.* Most notable on this 1997 CD (which contains music that has been reissued many times, often incoherently) is the meeting between altoist Charlie Parker and trumpeter Dizzy Gillespie. Joined by the underrecorded piano of John Lewis, bassist Al McKibbon and the slightly overrecorded drums of Joe Harris, Bird and Diz generate some real fireworks on five songs, and Parker's rendition of "Confirmation," and the CD's high point, is definitive and memorable. The remainder of the set (ten selections including "Cool Breeze," "One Bass Hit," "Cubano-Be, Cubano-Bop" and "Things to Come") features the Gillespie big band in typically spirited form. Of particular interest are a few numbers ("Relaxin' at Camarillo," which was arranged by George Russell, "Hot House," and "Toccata for Trumpet") that were never recorded in the studio by the big band. Classic bebop. *—Scott Yanow*

Charlie Parker / Dec. 1947-Jul. 30, 1953 / Polygram ♦♦♦♦♦
If you have the original 10" LP issue of this album with the '50s David Stone Martin cover art, hang on to it (it's worth anywhere from $240 to 400!) but also acquire this greatly expanded CD version on the Verve Master Series. In addition to the original eight selections, recorded in 1953 with Al Haig or Hank Jones (piano), Percy Heath or Teddy Kotick (bass) and Max Roach (drums), you get an awesome variety of other Parker quartet, quintet and septet sessions, plus extensive outtakes and false starts (grouped at the end of the disc) from the 10" LP sessions. Bird was still in marvelously inventive form in 1953, hardly ever repeating the same idea twice, clearly inspired by the propulsive Roach groove. The spectacular Buddy Rich is the disruptive drummer on "Blues (fast)," "Celebrity" and three other cuts, one of which ("Ballade") features Coleman Hawkins. "The Bird" (1947) is lifted from *The Jazz Scene* anthology, and the septet tracks from 1949 have a light Afro-Cuban flavor. All of this had been previously revealed on the ten-CD *Complete Charlie Parker on Verve* in similarly good sound, so completists needn't bother. The sharpies at Verve do correct one egregious error from the original collector's item; the track perhaps understandably misidentified as Frank Loesser's "I Hear Music" on the LP is really Jerome Kern's "The Song Is You." Just thought we'd mention it... *—Richard S. Ginell*

South of the Border: The Verve Latin-Jazz Sides / Jan. 1948-Jan. 23, 1952 / Verve ♦♦♦♦♦
Verve gathers together all of the master takes of Charlie Parker's recordings with the swinging band of Afro-Cuban jazz pioneer Machito, along with ten other Latinized numbers that he cut in 1951-52. Besides illustrating the willingness of producer Norman Granz to experiment and take Parker out of a small-group bebop straitjacket, this CD shows that Bird's improvisational style changed hardly at all in a Latin setting. He continued to run off his patented lightning bop licks over the congas and bongos and they just happened to interlock with the grooves quite snugly, although he did adapt his phrasing of the tunes themselves to suit their rhythmic lines. Included here is the spectacular "No Noise" that he cut as a guest with Machito and tenorman Flip Phillips in 1948, as well as Chico O'Farrill's epic *Afro-Cuban Jazz Suite* (also with Machito). For those who do not have the 10-CD *The Complete Charlie Parker On Verve*?where all 14 selections can be found—this is an inexpensive way to hear Parker in a refreshingly different context at very nearly the top of his form. *—Richard S. Ginell*

Jazz at the Philharmonic, 1949 / Sep. 8, 1949 / Verve ♦♦♦♦♦

☆ **Charlie Parker with Strings: The Master Takes** / Nov. 30, 1949-May 22, 1953 / Verve ♦♦♦♦♦
When producer Norman Granz decided to let Parker record standards with a full string section (featuring Mitch Miller on oboe!), the purists cried sellout, but nothing could be further from the truth. There's a real sense of involvement from Bird on these sides, which collects up all the master takes and also includes some live tracks from *Carnegie Hall* which—judging from the sometimes uneasy murmurings of the crowd—amply illustrates just how weirdly this mixture of bop lines against "legit" arrangements was perceived. The music on this collection is lush, poetic, romantic as hell and the perfect antidote to a surfeit of jazz records featuring undisciplined blowing. There's lots of jazz, but there's only one Bird. *—Cub Koda*

Bird and Diz / Jun. 6, 1950 / Verve ♦♦♦♦♦
This session features quite a group: Charlie Parker on alto, trumpeter Dizzy Gillespie, pianist Thelonious Monk, bassist Curly Russell and drummer Buddy Rich. They perform five Bird originals along with "My Melancholy Baby" and there are also seven alternate takes included on this CD. This music is available as part of the Verve ten-CD box but this particular release is quite enjoyable by itself. Bird and Monk never recorded together otherwise. *—Scott Yanow*

The Complete Legendary Rockland Palace Concert 1952 / Sep. 26, 1952 / Jazz Classics ♦♦♦♦
There aren't many live recordings of Bird during his string-section period, which would usually feature his regular quintet as the rhythm section. Aside from the famous *Carnegie Hall* concert of 1950, much of what exists boasts atrocious sound quality. One of those was Parker's performance at a dance with both his quintet and a string section at New York City's *Rockland Palace* in 1952. With Walter Bishop on piano, Teddy Kotick on bass, Mundell Lowe on guitar (replacing the trumpet that would normally spell Bird on solos), and Max Roach on drums, the string section works the same charts as the studio versions, but Parker's solos are—as always—inventive and often differ from their better known incarnations. For years, part of this show was documented on several vinyl LPs taken from an audience recording off a wobbly sounding wire recorder. This new issue boasts the major find of a second tape recorded that night by far more professional means. The second tape had superior sound, plus several performances that didn't exist on the earlier version. The new tape had one major drawback; it contained almost no solos by musicians other than Bird. So the restoration on this two-disc set is painstakingly pieced together from the two existing tapes. While certain edits are noticeable, this audio restoration not only gives us a fuller picture of some of the music Parker played that evening, but in the best sound we can expect until future audio miracles are invented. As an added bonus, one track (a blisteringly fast take of "Lester Leaps In") was synched up between both tapes, resulting in a kind of 'surround sound stereo' that makes for interesting listening. An important chapter in Parker's musical history, now preserved in the best audio shape possible. *—Cub Koda*

Charlie Parker at Storyville / Mar. 10, 1953-Sep. 22, 1953 / Blue Note ♦♦♦
This LP contains two broadcasts featuring Charlie Parker at Boston's *Storyville* club in 1953. one set finds him accompanied by the Red Garland Trio (two years before Garland became famous playing with Miles Davis) while the other one also features trumpeter Herb Pomeroy and a trio led by pianist Sir Charles Thompson. The recording quality is just so-so but Bird was in fine form for these sessions, playing hot versions of his usual repertoire. *—Scott Yanow*

★ **Jazz at Massey Hall** / May 15, 1953 / Debut/OJC ♦♦♦♦♦
The music on this CD features the famous *Massey Hall* Concert which teamed together (for the last time on records) the unbeatable team of altoist Charlie Parker and trumpeter Dizzy Gillespie along with pianist Bud Powell, bassist Charles Mingus and drummer Max Roach. The full quintet performs six of their standards; listen to Bird burn on "Salt Peanuts" as a reaction to Gillespie's clowning. This is timeless and highly recommended music. *—Scott Yanow*

★ **Legendary Dial Masters, Vols. 1 & 2** / Feb. 5, 1946-Nov. 17, 1947 / Jazz Classics ♦♦♦♦♦

☆ **Complete Savoy Live Performances: Sept. 29, 1947-Oct. 25, 1950** / 1947-1950 / Savoy Jazz ♦♦♦♦♦
This four-CD set contains a somewhat streamlined presentation of Parker's complete known live broadcasts from New York's *Royal Roost*, dating during 1948 and 1949, augmented with five of the live September 29, 1947, *Carnegie Hall* recordings and one lower-quality tape made in Chicago during 1950. The vitality of these performances still radiates off the tapes in whatever format they're reproduced 50-plus years later—the interaction between the bandmembers, which include Miles Davis (or Kenny Dorham) on trumpet and Max Roach at the drums, and Tadd Dameron or Al Haig at the ivories, is spellbinding. The difference between these performances and Parker's studio work of the period is that he was always "on" for the broadcasts, and had already achieved something of a peak that he still missed in his studio work of the era—those along with him rose to the occasion, as witnessed by Kenny Dorham's playing on Miles Davis' "Half Nelson" in December of 1947. On the other hand, nobody could touch Parker when he was at his peak on stage, which he ascends easily on a jam set to Irving Berlin's "White Christmas." The Chicago material, which exists on a separate CD from Savoy (*One Night in Chicago*), isn't as well recorded—the rhythm section is muted, and the balances are off, but Parker is certainly audible, and hearing his improvisations on material like Rodgers & Hart's "There's a Small Hotel" is worth the price of the disc, even on what amounts to a good audience tape. The source material has been very carefully mastered, striking a good balance between clean playback and fidelity to the original performance, and the dozens of pages of notes represent virtually a separate, free-standing book on Parker during this period in his career. *—Bruce Eder*

☆ **The Complete Savoy and Dial Studio Recordings 1944-1948** / 1944-1948 / Atlantic ♦♦♦♦♦
Words can hardly describe the revolutionary effect of these seminal recordings—collected here on eight full-length CDs, with a comprehensive 93-page booklet with original essays, photos, and detailed discographical information—when first released. Charlie Parker's vision, spectacular technique, and style helped to transform the world of jazz in the 1940s, and it has never been the same. As with the efforts of creative visionaries, his early innovations were at first resisted by some as too radical, but with time, Bird became universally recognized for the genius he was. It is impossible to imagine any serious collection of 20th century music not containing at least some of the tracks collected on this splendid compilation. These disks collect all of Parker's studio sessions on Dial and Savoy, the two labels that assiduously chronicled his career during the decade. The set excludes four CDs of live material and most sessions recorded by amateurs, but includes outtakes, Bird's recordings as a sideman, and tracks cut or issued under the Savoy and Dial labels, including the Spotlite, Stash, Guild, Musicraft, Bel-Tone, and the Comet lines. So many great musicians performed with Bird that part of the thrill is not only the scintillating work of Parker, but also the opportunity to revisit seminal performances by Miles Davis, Dizzy Gillespie, Max Roach, Bud Powell, and a host of others. The sound is, for the most part, remarkably good, making this an indispensable collection for any lover of jazz. *—Steven Loewy*

Evan Parker

b. Apr. 5, 1944, Bristol, England
Sax (Tenor), Sax (Soprano) / Avant-Garde Jazz, Free Jazz
Among Europe's most innovative and intriguing saxophonists, Evan Parker's solos and playing style are distinguished by his creative use of circular breathing and false fingering. Parker can generate furious bursts, screeches, bleats, honks and spiraling lines and phrases and his solo sax work isn't for the squeamish. He's one of the few players not only willing but anxious to demonstrate his affinity for late-period John Coltrane. Parker worked with a Coltrane-influenced quartet in Birmingham in the early '60s. Upon resettling in London in 1965, Parker began playing with Spontaneous Music Ensemble. He joined them in 1967 and remained until 1969. Parker met guitarist Derek Bailey while in the group, and the duo formed The Music Improvisation Company in 1968. Parker played with them until 1971, and also began working with the Tony Oxley Sextet in the late '60s. Parker started playing extensively with other European free music groups in the '70s, notably The Globe Unity Orchestra as well as its founder Alexander von Schlippenbach's trio and quartet. Parker, Bailey and Oxley co-formed Incus Records in 1970 and continued operating it through the '80s. Parker also played with Chris McGregor's Brotherhood of Breath, other groups with Bailey and did duet sessions with John Stevens and Paul Lytton as well as giving several solo concerts. Parker's albums as a leader and his collaborations are all for various foreign labels; they can be obtained through diligent effort and mail order catalogs. *—Ron Wynn*

50th Birthday Concert / Apr. 10, 1994 / Leo ♦♦♦♦♦
This splendidly produced twofer features Parker on disc one with Alex von Schlippenbach and percussionist Paul Lovens, and on disc two with his usual trio of bassist Barry Guy and percussionist Paul Lytton. What a splendid birthday celebration this was! Parker is clearly at the peak of his form, and he is enjoying the interaction with these two splendid groups. Schlippenbach's angular, dense, and wild acrobatics blend well with Parker's energized super technique. The saxophonist is all over his horn, doubling himself, jabbing and darting, but always in control. The second disc displays Barry Guy and Paul Lytton interacting like clockwork, the moods changing, and the energy unrelenting. Lytton shows why he is Parker's drummer of choice: not only does he sport great technique, but he is always fascinating to hear. The six pages of photos and reminiscences by Parker in the liner notes are icing on the cake. Not to be missed, this is great Evan Parker all the way. *—Steve Loewy*

At the Vortex (1996) / 1996 / Emanem ♦♦♦♦♦
What a splendid summer night it must have been when Evan Parker, bassist Barry Guy, and percussionist Paul Lytton performed live at the small, but packed, *Vortex* club in London. Thanks to Emanem, the concert was recorded in its entirety, the two sets lasting almost eighty minutes. The totally improvised pieces unfold organically, with each player in top form, stretching out, with plenty of intense, exciting interaction. This is music of the first order, inspiring and uplifting. Parker blows at full throttle on both the tenor and soprano saxophones. His extended a cappella performance on soprano in the second set is nothing short of amazing. But don't forget Guy and Lytton, each of whom thrives in the club atmosphere. Whether as a duo, or performing solo, or as part of the trio, the bassist and percussionist dance, wrestle, and charge through extended forms. As a group, the three seasoned virtuosi are a tight, disciplined, unit, and the product of close listening and extraordinary musicianship. *—Steve Loewy*

● **Toward the Margins** / May 1996 / ECM ♦♦♦♦
Founded in 1992, Evan Parker's Electro-Acoustic Ensemble is a highly sophisticated grouping, which for this recording conceptually pairs three acoustic musicians with electronic tone manipulators. What keeps it so interesting is the different approaches to electronics, with Walter Prati transforming Parker's sounds, Marco Vecchi reformulating Paul Lytton's percussion, and violinist Philipp Wachsmann processing his own acoustic sounds and those of bassist Barry Guy. It is all fascinating stuff, and if it does not swing or fit into any easy definitions of "jazz," it takes the concept of improvisation to a new level. There is sometimes an aimlessness to it all that can be off-putting, but concentrated listening can produce wonderful rewards for the patient consumer. Parker's role seems less that of a leader than an instigator. He does, nonetheless, afford himself the opportunity to press his revolutionary technique to action. The detailed 20-page bookle, with extensive liner notes by Steve Lake is a real plus. *—Steven Loewy*

New Excursions / Jun. 19, 1998 / Ninth World ♦♦♦♦♦
Parker is joined by the outstanding Danish group Ghost in the Machine, and Master of Little Sounds, Martin Klapper for an exquisite set recorded live at *the Copenhagen International Experimental Festival.* While this is not Parker's first recording with the group, it is distinguished by excellent sound quality and a synergy that comes from familiar interaction. A remarkable quality in Parker is his ability to perform naturally in varied contexts. Here, he comfortably immerses himself in the noise element and alters his technique accordingly. The

results are totally compelling, as Peter Friis Nielsen's electric bass guitar and Klapper's "toys, tapes, and amplified objects" provide enough diversity to keep the listener consistently on edge. Ghost in the Machine are likely a blast to watch in person, and the concept somehow translates incredibly well to disc. *—Steven Loewy*

Drawn Inward / Dec. 1998 / ECM ✦✦✦✦
Evan Parker has performed in so many contexts, but he seems to have hit a particular stride with his Electro-Acoustic Ensemble, a strange combination of saxophones, strings, and electronics. What makes this so exceedingly attractive is the continuous wonder that permeates throughout. Parker is no means the standout performer; his soprano and tenor sometimes meld, at others lead, but it is his remarkable companions, Philipp Wachsmann (on violin, viola, and electronics), Barry Guy (on acoustic bass), Paul Lytton (on percussion and electronics), plus three very different electronic sound manipulators, Lawrence Casserly, Walter Prati, and Marco Vecchi, who combine to produce some electrifying and starkly delightful music. Parker fans that have not heard this group before may be surprised at the results. Although the saxophonist embraces his now well-known advanced techniques, they are clearly subordinate to the project. At times there is a busy intensity to it all, at others a serene quality. Highly complex strokes for an increasingly intricate society, perhaps, where moods change and so do their contexts. Don't file under easy listening. *—Steven Loewy*

Foxes Fox / Jul. 21, 1999 / Emanem ✦✦✦✦✦
This is apparently the first recording of the quartet consisting of Parker on both tenor and soprano saxes, Steve Beresford on piano, Louis Moholo on drums, and John Edwards on bass. It is a stunning document all the way around. Parker plays on only five of the nine tracks, but the members of the rhythm trio perform magnificently on their features. Beresford is an original improviser form the Cecil Taylor school, while Moholo adds a sophisticated air, and Edwards continues to show himself as one of the leading free-style bassists. Still, it is largely Parker's show, and although the saxophonist does not mine any new ground, he is in superb form. He plays mostly tenor, on which he blows more conventionally, though no less thrillingly than on soprano. A generous recording time just over 77 minutes is an extra bonus. *—Steven Loewy*

Monkey Puzzle / May 17, 1997 / Leo ✦✦✦✦

Synergetics: Phonomanie III / Sep. 18, 1993-Sep. 19, 1993 / Leo ✦✦✦✦

After Appleby / Jun. 28, 1999-Jun. 29, 1999 / Leo ✦✦✦✦✦
Evan Parker continues to record session after session of outstanding music. This two-CD set features a splendid quartet with Parker alternating between soprano and tenor saxophones, Barry Guy on bass, Marilyn Crispell on piano, and Paul Lytton on percussion. The first disc is taken from a studio recording just one day before the live club recording captured on the second disk. Lytton and Guy, in particular, are longtime collaborators with Parker, but the addition of the pianist is a welcome addition to the mix, giving the proceedings an extra depth. Crispell can spurt fleetingly across the keyboard with clusters of notes, but she also shows a lyrical side that displays considerable depth. The longer tracks feature the quartet, while the others alternate between different combinations of the musicians. All are in perfect form, and the clear recording quality and lengthy recording time (more than two hours) commend this double-disc set to admirers of Evan Parker and freely improvised music. *—Steven Loewy*

William Parker

Bass / Improvisation, Avant-Garde Jazz, Free Jazz, Avant-Garde, Modern Creative
In the early '90s, the direct musical heirs of Taylor, Ayler, and Coleman were mostly ignored by New York jazz critics, who found more to like about the hard bop revivalists who dominated major-label recording. Hence, the public visibility of musicians devoted to an "energy music" aesthetic was minimal. Despite its low profile, however, that strain of free jazz was kept alive by a fairly large group of Lower East Side musicians, many of whom gathered around the music's pre-eminent bassist, William Parker. Parker co-founded the Improvisers Collective, an organization that presented free jazz in combination with other types of spontaneous performance. He excels at the creation of dense, hyperactive streaks of color, gleaned from the inherent harmonic properties of the instrument. At bottom, he is a textural player. Lyricism plays a secondary role in his work, with or without the bow. His pizzicato style is overwhelmingly percussive, in intent and effect. Though he does, to an extent, serve as a harmonic anchor in his groups, his more important role is as a source of energy.

Parker was not formally trained as a classical player, though he did study with Jimmy Garrison, Richard Davis, and Wilbur Ware. Very early in his career he formed an association with Cecil Taylor, and he became Taylor's regular bassist in the '80s. Parker finally left Taylor in the early '90s and began working more often as a leader. He recorded a big-band record for his own label, then began releasing a series of CDs for other companies, significantly Black Saint. Besides his activities as a leader and community organizer, Parker would continue to work as a sideman through the mid-'90s; he remained the bassist of choice for downtown free players like David S. Ware, Matthew Shipp, and Rob Brown. *—Chris Kelsey*

Through Acceptance of the Mystery Peace / Feb. 1974-Jan. 21, 1979 / Eremite ✦✦✦✦
This recording is an important part of bassist William Parker's early discography. The CD collects the four ensemble pieces issued on the original LP, but adds one number and includes the complete version of another that was clipped. The sound quality is slightly subpar, but the raw, 1960s feel of this album should appeal to those who appreciate the unassuming brilliance of this giant of the string bass. Each of the five tracks features different groups, with Parker composing all pieces and appearing on four. The two larger ensembles presage some of the large bands Parker was to lead in the 1990s. Here, he features soloists on the level of Toshinori Kondo on alto horn, Daniel Carter on saxophones and trumpet, and Charles Brackeen on tenor saxophone. The chamber-like smaller groups stun with shimmering beauty, and string players Billy Bang, Tristan Honsinger, Ramsey Ameen, and Jason Hwang each contribute nicely. Some may not completely appreciate Parker's heartfelt recitation on the closing number, but there is plenty here to satisfy those who enjoy the bassist's style of new music. *—Steve Loewy*

In Order to Survive / Apr. 11, 1993-Jun. 28, 1993 / Black Saint ✦✦✦✦
Bassist William Parker's survival techniques demand liberty and solos for all. The members of this sextet feed off one another's energy, filling their collective plate with counterpoint, and expressing music in colors and feelings spontaneously derived from thematic motifs. Parker, a phenomenal theoretical and technical improvisor, has pianist Cooper Moore, drummer Denis Charles, trumpeter Lewis Barnes, trombonist Grachan Moncur III, and alto saxophonist Rob Brown in tow. Three of these pieces were recorded live at *Club Roulette* in NYC, the fourth at the *Knitting Factory*. Clocking in at nearly 40 minutes, "Testimony of No Future" develops from the piano-bass-drums trio's bop swing rhythms that set up a three note pattern that the horns then state and extrapolate on with counterpoint. This leads into extended solo fare from everyone—simple and direct, easy to follow, yet dense and saturated. The beautiful "Anast in Crisis, Mouth Full of Fresh Cut Flowers" has Moore's spiritual lines influencing Brown's alto greatly, with Moncur chiming in for a lucid, free association for seven minutes, again based on three notes. "Testimony of the Stir Pot" has thematic nuances that grow subtler over 20 minutes while horn lines flow parallel to Moore's lightning-quick runs. "The Square Sun," from the *Knitting Factory* session, features Barnes' rubato-style trumpet (which shows his unique blend of jazz past and present), Moore's haunting, dancing figures, percussionist Jackson Krall's wisp-of-smoke accents, and Parker's mouse-squeak bowed bass. Some tour-de-force music is found here, which makes one wonder if these performances wouldn't have yielded another CD or three from this band of extraordinary avant-gardists. Highly recommended for those who take their freedoms seriously. *—Michael G. Nastos*

Peach Orchard / Feb. 7, 1997-Mar. 21, 1998 / Aum Fidelity ✦✦✦✦✦
The Peach Orchard is a two-CD set showcasing bassist William Parker's work with an ensemble consisting of composer/instrument maker/pianist Cooper-Moore (who limits his involvement in music to Parker's groups), improvisational saxophonist, Rob Brown and percussionist extraordinaire Susie Ibarra (Assif Tsahar, Matthew Shipp Trio, Davis S. Ware Quartet, One World Ensemble). This cream of the New York, contemporary, free jazz scene veers from such challenging, busy compositions as the explosive first track "Thoth" to such reflective pieces as "Moholo," basically a study in rhythmic intricacy featuring a five-minute introduction led by Ibarra to the 19-minute piece. Brown is eloquent and lyrical as he sails up and down scales through "Three Clay Pots." The title track is inspired by the devastation of a cherished Navaho orchard by an oppressive U.S. Army. The lengthy piece (20:45) is the quartet's collage of hostility and deep sadness. Disc Two opens with the profound and eerie "Posium Pendasem 3." Assif Tsahar joins the group on bass clarinet for the melancholy, piano-led piece. The beautiful mystery of autumnal changes are explored in "Leaf Dance," at once both bittersweet (Brown's lines) and playful (Cooper-Brown). A traditional jazz melody acts as bookends for a series of Latin, common-time, and extemporaneous, thematic variations in "Theme For Pelikan." The band's theme, "In Order to Survive," a lively, rollicking and urgent composition fueled by the growing intricacy of Cooper-Brown's part closes this two-disc set that offers new discoveries upon every listen. *—Thomas Schulte*

Mayor of Punkville / Jul. 10, 1999-Nov. 27, 1999 / Aum Fidelity ✦✦✦✦✦
This is for all fans of such amazing big bands as the Sun Ra Arkestra, Charles Mingus' Big Band, the Italian Instabile Orchestra, Willem Breuker Kollektief, and other thrilling jazz groups of the larger variety. It is a terrific proof of bassist William Parker's strength as a leader and is one of his most engaging releases to date. *The Mayor of Punkville* compiles selections from Little Huey Creative Music Orchestra's performances at NYC's *Tonic* from July through November, 1999 onto two discs. The first opens rather appropriately with a short piece of drawn-out phrases overall reminiscent of an orchestra warm-up. The only number featuring vocals, "James Baldwin to the Rescue," comes next and vocalist Aleta Hayes comes across strong. This piece stays more scattered and more atmospheric, making it possible to get a bit lost in the longer instrumental sections. The highlight of the first disc, "Oglala Eclipse," follows and the orchestra really kicks and moves together as Arkestra notions rise up again in the back of the mind. Starting the second disc is "Interlude *7 (Huey's Blues)*" and, as with the other two interludes, the orchestra is found to be calm and steady. Little Huey is at its most shining during disc two, including the spitfire, shout-inducing, epic title track (which clocks in at just over 30 minutes), as well as the three-part "Steps to Noh Mountain." It's a great pleasure to hear three trumpets, four trombones, and six saxophones (all well-played) provide the body of a piece that has a lovely melody and great groove, working along with the strong rhythm section of drummer Andrew Baker and Parker on bass. It's loose, it's off-the-cuff, it's rebellious, and slightly minor(-keyed)—The Little Huey Creative Music Orchestra offer much enjoyment with the wonderful, beautiful *Mayor of Punkville*. *—Joslyn Layne*

● **Painter's Spring** / Apr. 2, 2000 / Thirsty Ear ✦✦✦✦✦
As the second release in the acclaimed *Blue Series* from Thirsty Ear Recordings, *Painter's Spring* by the William Parker Trio sustains the living bolt of energy infused in the free and avant-garde jazz genres by the debut of Matt Shipp's *Pastoral Composure*. Bassist William Parker wrote all of the compositions except the traditional "There Is a Balm in Gilead" and "Come Sunday," and together with Daniel Carter on alto and tenor sax, flute, and clarinet and Hamid Drake on drums, the trio lifts the program to the listener's attention with the melding of individual talents into one powerful musical force. The CD features a three-song suite—"Foundation *1,*" "Foundation *2,*" and "Foundation *4*"?and all are pure Parker with their wicked, loosely defined vamps full of buzzing, open drones, and short jabs. His spontaneous feelings and subtle variations that on "Come Sunday," complete with ample blocks of rhythm and melody, allow one to experience another level of sound through his masterful musician dimensions. As a master of the acoustic bass, Parker's techniques on *Painter's Spring* range from playing the bass in a percussive-like mode to using a mixture to staffed notation and diagrams in order to achieve an orchestral fidelity. Daniel Carter's performances are never the same and he blows an amazing set from beginning to end. Hamid Drake improvises his visions within the setting provided by Parker and Carter, drums an astounding solo on "Flash," and through this dynamic trio, this program pierces the veil of avant-garde and free jazz mystery. *—Paula Edelstein*

Horace Parlan

b. Jan. 19, 1931, Pittsburgh, PA
Piano / Hard Bop
Horace Parlan has overcome physical disability and thrived as a pianist despite it. His right hand was partially crippled by polio in his childhood, but Parlan's made frenetic, highly rhythmic right-hand phrases part of his characteristic style, contrasting them with striking left hand chords. He's also infused blues and R&B influences into his style, playing in a stark, sometimes somber fashion. Parlan has always cited Ahmad Jamal and Bud Powell as prime influences. He began playing in R&B bands during the '50s, joining Charles Mingus' group from 1957 to 1959 following a move from Pittsburgh to New York. Mingus aided his career enormously, both through his recordings and his influence. Parlan played with Booker Ervin in 1960 and 1961, then in the Eddie "Lockjaw" Davis-Johnny Griffin quintet in 1962. Parlan played with Rahsaan Roland Kirk from 1963 to 1966, and had a strong series of Blue Note recordings in the '60s. He left America for Copenhagen in 1973, and gained international recognition for some stunning albums on Steeplechase, including a pair of superb duet sessions with Archie Shepp. He also recorded with Dexter Gordon, Red Mitchell, and in the '80s Frank Foster and Michal Urbaniak. He also has recorded extensively for SteepleChase, Enja and Timeless. *—Ron Wynn*

Movin' and Groovin' / Feb. 29, 1960 / Blue Note ✦✦✦✦
Horace Parlan's debut album for Blue Note, *Movin' and Groovin',* is a thoroughly impressive affair, establishing Parlan as a distinctive hard bop stylist. Working with bassist Sam Jones and drummer Al Harewood, Parlan steals the show, playing hard-driving, bluesy bop and lyrical ballads. If it weren't for the inventive chord voicings and percussive right-hand attack, it would be impossible to tell that he was missing two fingers on his right hand, since his playing is remarkably agile and fluid. Parlan sounds vital on swinging blues, slow ballads, and straight-ahead bop, and Jones and Harewood provide appropriately empathetic support on this collection of standards, blues, bop, jazz, and originals. Everything swings, no matter the tempo, and the end result is a fine debut from a distinctive pianist. *—Stephen Thomas Erlewine*

Us Three / Apr. 20, 1960 / Blue Note ✦✦✦✦
The second of Horace Parlan's seven Blue Note recordings of 1960-63, this set (reissued on CD in 1997) features the pianist in a trio with bassist George Tucker and drummer Al Harewood. Parlan's chordal boppish style is heard in fine form on three originals (most notably the catchy "Wadin'") and four standards, including "I Want To Be Loved" and "The Lady Is a Tramp." An excellent outing for the pianist (who was then 29), and one of his best early showcases. *—Scott Yanow*

Headin' South / Dec. 4, 1960 / Blue Note ✦✦✦✦
On the surface, *Headin' South* is another set of bluesy soul-jazz, but it actually finds the Horace Parlan trio stretching out a little. Adding conga player Ray Barretto to his usual rhythm section of bassist George Tucker and drummer Al Harewood, Parlan decides to take chances with his standard-heavy repertoire. "Summertime" features some evocative bowing from Tucker, and the solo sections on "The Song Is Ended," "Prelude to a Kiss," and "My Mother's Eyes" offer probing, intriguing tonal textures that make the selection of Ahmad Jamal's "Jim Loves Sue" understandable. Barretto's "Congalegre" is a fun, Latin-inflected number, and Parlan's "Headin' South" is a strong, swinging blues, but the slow blues "Low Down" is nearly undone by his incessant circular arpeggio, which lasts for over a minute. Still, that's not nearly enough to sink the record, which is another understated but solid effort from Horace Parlan. *—Stephen Thomas Erlewine*

On the Spur of the Moment / Mar. 18, 1961 / Blue Note ✦✦✦✦
Again working with his longtime rhythm section of George Tucker (bass) and Al Harewood (drums), Horace Parlan manages to *On the Spur of the Moment* make distinctive by emphasizing the rhythmic side of his hard bop. Tenor saxophonist Stanley Turrentine and trumpeter Tommy Turrentine help give the quintet a bluesy edge, which the band exploits to an appealing effect throughout these six, mostly original, compositions. There are a few ballads, and even when things are at their hottest, Parlan's understated playing is a cue for the group to keep it tasteful, but that relaxed atmosphere is part of the reason why *On the Spur of the Moment* is another winning effort from the underrated pianist. *—Stephen Thomas Erlewine*

Up and Down / Jun. 81, 1961 / Blue Note ✦✦✦✦✦
By adding guitarist Grant Green and tenor saxophonist Booker Ervin to his standard rhythm section of bassist George Tucker and drummer Al Harewood, pianist Horace Parlan opens up his sound and brings it closer to soul-jazz on *Up and Down.* Green's clean, graceful style meshes well with Parlan's relaxed technique, while Ervin's robust tone and virile attack provides a good contrast to the laid-back groove the rhythm section lays down. Stylistically, the music is balanced between hard bop and soul-jazz, which are tied together by the bluesy tint in the three soloists' playing. All of the six original compositions give the band room to stretch out and to not only show off their chops, but move the music somewhat away from generic conventions and find new territory. In other words, it finds Parlan at a peak, and in many ways, coming into his own as a pianist and a leader. *—Stephen Thomas Erlewine*

Back from the Gig / Feb. 15, 1963 / Blue Note ✦✦✦✦✦
When the session that comprised the *Happy Frame of Mind* record was released as a Booker Ervin album, it was titled *Back From the Gig.* Horace Parlan, however, was the leader for the session, and the album was originally scheduled to be released in the mid-'60s by Blue Note as *Happy Frame of Mind.* After remaining unreleased for over a decade, it was issued as *Back From the Gig,* but once the CD revolution struck in the '80s, the music was reissued as it originally was intended—that is, the *Happy Frame of Mind* album. *Happy Frame of Mind/Back From the Gig* finds Horace Parlan breaking away from the soul-inflected hard bop that had become his trademark, moving his music into more adventurous, post-bop territory. Aided by a first-rate quintet—trumpeter Johnny Coles, tenor saxophonist Booker Ervin, guitarist Grant Green, bassist Butch Warren, drummer Billy Higgins—Parlan produces a provocative set that is grounded in soul and blues but stretches out into challenging improvisations. None of the musicians completely embrace the avant-garde, but there are shifting tonal textures and unpredictable turns in the solos which have been previously unheard in Parlan's music. Perhaps that's the reason the session sat unissued in Blue Note's vaults until 1976, when it was released as part of a double-record Booker Ervin set, but the fact of the matter is, it's one of Parlan's most successful efforts, finding the perfect middle ground between accessible, entertaining jazz and more adventurous music. *—Stephen Thomas Erlewine*

● **Happy Frame of Mind** / Feb. 15, 1963 / Blue Note ✦✦✦✦✦
Happy Frame of Mind finds Horace Parlan breaking away from the soul-inflected hard bop that had become his trademark, moving his music into more adventurous, post-bop territory. Aided by a first-rate quintet—trumpeter Johnny Coles, tenor saxophonist Booker Ervin, guitarist Grant Green, bassist Butch Warren, drummer Billy Higgins—Parlan produces a provocative set that is grounded in soul and blues but stretches out into challenging improvisations. None of the musicians completely embrace the avant-garde, but there are shifting tonal textures and unpredictable turns in the solos which have been previously unheard in Parlan's music. Perhaps that's the reason why *Happy Frame of Mind* sat unissued in Blue Note's vaults until 1976, when it was released as part of a double-record Booker Ervin set, but the fact of the matter is, it's one of Parlan's most successful efforts, finding the perfect middle ground between accessible, entertaining jazz and more adventurous music. *—Stephen Thomas Erlewine*

Glad I Found You / Jul. 30, 1984 / Steeple Chase ✦✦✦✦✦
Expatriate pianist Horace Parlan and a couple of fine Scandinavians (bassist Jesper Lundgaard and drummer Aage Tanggaard) welcome Thad Jones (heard exclusively here on flugelhorn) and the great tenor Eddie Harris to this spirited set. Jones was making a successful, if short-lived comeback, and at two years before his death, this was one of his final high-quality small-group recordings. Harris is heard throughout in top form. The quintet performs two Parlan originals (including "Something for Silver"), a couple of obscurities, John Lewis' "Afternoon In Paris" and Bud Powell's "Oblivion." Parlan sounds inspired by the other musicians on this spirited hard bop set. *—Scott Yanow*

The Complete Blue Note Horace Parlan Sessions / 2000 / Mosaic ✦✦✦✦✦

Joe Pass (Joseph Anthony Passalaqua)

b. Jan. 13, 1929, New Brunswick, NJ, **d.** May 23, 1994, Los Angeles, CA
Guitar / Jazz Blues, Hard Bop, Bop
Joe Pass did the near-impossible. He was able to play uptempo versions of bop tunes such as "Cherokee" and "How High the Moon" unaccompanied on the guitar. Unlike Stanley Jordan, Pass used conventional (but superb) technique, and his *Virtuoso* series on Pablo still sounds remarkable two decades later.

Joe Pass had a false start in his career. He played in a few swing bands (including Tony Pastor's) before graduating from high school and was with Charlie Barnet for a time in 1947. But after serving in the military, Pass became a drug addict, serving time in prison and essentially wasting a decade. He emerged in 1962 with a record cut at Synanon, made a bit of a stir with his *For Django* set, recorded several other albums for Pacific Jazz and World Pacific and performed with Gerald Wilson, Les McCann, George Shearing and Benny Goodman (1973).

However in general Pass maintained a low profile in Los Angeles until he was signed by Norman Granz to his Pablo label. 1973's *Virtuoso* made him a star and he recorded very prolifically for Pablo, unaccompanied, with small groups, on duo albums with Ella Fitzgerald and with such masters as Count Basie, Duke Ellington, Oscar Peterson, Milt Jackson and Dizzy Gillespie. Pass remained very active up until his death from cancer. *—Scott Yanow*

Joy Spring / Feb. 6, 1964 / Blue Note ✦✦✦✦
Joe Pass was near the beginning of his career (after a decade of fighting drug addiction) when he recorded the live quartet session included on this CD reissue. The great guitarist was in his early prime, nine years before he started recording for Pablo. Pass is immediately recognizable on the straightahead bebop date and is supported by a fine rhythm section that includes pianist Mike Wofford, bassist Jim Hughart and drummer Colin Bailey. The group stretches out on five standards (the renditions are 6 1/2-10 1/2 minutes apiece) but never runs out of inventive ideas. Easily recommended. *—Scott Yanow*

For Django / Oct. 1964 / BGO ✦✦✦✦✦
Long considered a classic, guitarist Joe Pass' fourth date as a leader (not yet available on CD) finds him performing music that was composed by Django Reinhardt, was part of his repertoire, or is one of two more recent tributes (John Lewis' "Django" and Pass' "For Django"). Pass is joined by the rhythm guitar of John Pisano, bassist Jim Hughart, and drummer Colin Bailey; the quartet would reunite in the 1980s. Although Pass was actually more strongly influenced by Charlie Christian than by Reinhardt and he had already formed his own style, he has no difficulty fitting into the music. Highlights include "Rosetta," "Nuages," and "Limehouse Blues." *—Scott Yanow*

Guitar Virtuoso / Jan. 30, 1973-Aug. 12, 1992 / Pablo ✦✦✦✦✦
As this lavishly boxed, four-CD distillation of his Pablo sessions proves, Joe Pass was probably the guitar-playing equivalent of Art Tatum on the Norman Granz roster—not only for his vast output, but also for the all-encompassing, almost orchestral way in which he got around his instrument. The set is divided equally into four sections—Disc One for his astounding solo electric and acoustic guitar sides, Disc Two for studio recordings with various groups, Disc Three for various live recordings solo and with groups, Disc Four the delicate Ella Fitzgerald and other duo partner sessions and quartet pieces backing Sarah Vaughan. Though the box is not in chronological order—which is not necessary here, since Pass was essentially a finished, non-evolving artist when he joined Pablo—Jim Ferguson's helpful commentary on the sessions is chronologically organized, balancing out Benny Green's personalized disc-by-disc analysis of the tracks. A couple of tracks with a modern Brazilian rhythm section also stand out, as does the supercharged "Sweet Georgia Brown" with Oscar Peterson and Niels-Henning Orsted Pedersen, and the set's lengthiest item, a fond 10-minute take out on "Stompin' at the Savoy" live at *Donte's* club in North Hollywood, CA. The latter track

and a scant two others are the only ones new to CD, and there are no unreleased goods to be heard, but with five hours of Pass taken a little at a time, this box will wear very well over the years. *—Richard S. Ginell*

★ **Virtuoso, Vol. 1** / Dec. 1973 / Pablo ✦✦✦✦✦
This is the album that made Joe Pass famous. On what was actually his second set of unaccompanied guitar solos ("Virtuoso *4*" from a month earlier was released years later), Pass shows that it is possible to play unaccompanied versions of such uptempo tunes as "How High the Moon," "Cherokee" and "The Song Is You" on guitar. Pass not only performs the melodies and heated solos, but provides bass lines and harmonies while using a conventional technique (unlike Stanley Jordan's later tapping). Pass would record many unaccompanied recordings and perform at numerous solo concerts during the next 20 years; this is the set that started it all, and it is a certified classic. An essential CD. *—Scott Yanow*

Portraits of Duke Ellington / Jun. 21, 1974 / Pablo ✦✦✦✦✦
Recorded just a month after Duke Ellington's death, this tribute album (reissued on CD) features guitarist Joe Pass (just beginning to become famous), bassist Ray Brown and drummer Bobby Durham jamming on eight Ellington tunes and "Caravan" (which was penned by one of Duke's key sidemen, Juan Tizol). The interplay between the three musicians is quite impressive, and Pass' mastery of the guitar is obvious (he didn't really need the other sidemen). Highlights include "In a Mellotone," "Don't Get Around Much Anymore" and "I Got It Bad." Recommended. *—Scott Yanow*

Joe Pass at the Montreux Jazz Festival 1975 / Jul. 17, 1975-Jul. 18, 1975 / Pablo ✦✦✦✦✦
Outstanding solo guitar by Joe Pass, done at the '75 *Montreux Festival* to an appreciative audience. Pass plays with more energy than on his studio works, doing the usual standards, ballads, and mainstream fare, but also demonstrating an exuberance and joyful flair that's more understated on most occasions. *—Ron Wynn*

Chops / Nov. 19, 1978 / Pablo/OJC ✦✦✦✦✦
The word "chops" is a major understatement when describing the talents of guitarist Joe Pass and bassist Niels-Henning Orsted Pedersen. Their duo Pablo date (which has been reissued as a CD in the OJC series) is as exciting and full of inventive interplay as one would hope. Pass and Pedersen play an ad-lib blues, nine jazz standards including a æ version of "Lover Man," plus "Oleo," "Quiet Nights," "Tricrotism" and "Yardbird Suite." Pass in particular sounds stimulated during this session and comes up with some of his hottest playing. *—Scott Yanow*

We'll Be Together Again / 1984-1985 / Pablo/OJC ✦✦✦✦✦
Few would argue with the statement that there are not an excess of guitar-trombone duet albums. In fact, this date (which has been reissued on CD) may very well be somewhat unique instrumentation-wise in jazz history. Trombonist J.J. Johnson had already been the pacesetter on his instrument for nearly 40 years at the time, while guitarist Joe Pass proved in the 1970s that he could make his axe fulfill all the roles of an orchestra. Still, the strong success of this inspired outing is a bit of a surprise. While Pass often adds walking lines behind J.J., Johnson sometimes plays long tones behind the guitarist's solos. Most exciting are the spots where the two share the lead equally. Other than Bud Powell's "Bud's Blues" and J.J.'s "Naked as a Jaybird," the duo sticks to standards. But obviously, these versions sound quite a bit different than usual. Highlights include "Wave," "Limehouse Blues," "Nature Boy" and "When Lights Are Low." Highly recommended. *—Scott Yanow*

Live at Yoshi's / Jan. 30, 1992-Feb. 1, 1992 / Pablo ✦✦✦✦✦
An inspired and exciting set by jazz's guitarist nonpareil, it ranges from a blistering race through Sonny Rollins' "Oleo" to the gentle duet with Pass's longtime partner Pisano on "Alone Together." "Swingin' Till the Girls Come Home" is a feature for Budwig, the great West Coast bass player who died shortly after this set. It's one of the best of the many Joe Pass albums. *—Les Line*

Songs for Ellen / Aug. 7, 1992-Aug. 20, 1992 / Pablo ✦✦✦✦✦
This posthumous CD is novel because it features Joe Pass exclusively on acoustic guitar, and it is obvious that he enjoyed every minute of these sessions. "The Shadow of Your Smile" is no longer easy listening fodder, as Pass turns it into a miniature master class in swing. "Star Eyes" is accented by the soft squeaks of Pass' fingers gently weaving their intricate magic. Most of the works of Joe Pass tended to be improvised blues, so the title track is an exception—a simple yet elegant ballad written for his wife. "Blues for Angel" highlights his matchless mastery of slow blues. The boppish blues "Satellite Village" is a perfect closer. The good news is that there are several more unreleased sessions by Joe Pass that will follow this superb collection. *—Ken Dryden*

Resonance / Dec. 1974 / Pablo ✦✦✦✦✦
Joe Pass thrived on intimate settings. The late improviser had no problem doing without a pianist, and many of his Pablo recordings of the 1970s, 1980s, and early 1990s found him leading small guitar trios or performing as an unaccompanied solo guitarist. That type of intimate setting serves him impressively well on *Resonance*, which was recorded live at *Donte's* in North Hollywood, CA (a suburb of Los Angeles) in December 1974 and finds him leading a trio that includes Jim Hughart on electric bass and Frank Severino on drums. Pass doesn't have a pianist or any horn players to share the spotlight with, and that's just as well because the guitarist has a lot to say. He is in fine form on lyrical performances of "Misty," "Corcovado," and "Come Rain or Come Shine," and is equally impressive on unusually fast versions of "It Could Happen to You" and "The Lamp Is Low." Those who think of the former as a sentimental ballad will find that the hard bopper has a very different take on the standard. During his career, Pass was a very consistent player—he rarely recorded a bad album, and *Resonance* is among the many releases that is well worth hearing. *—Alex Henderson*

Jaco Pastorius (John Francis Pastorius)

b. Dec. 1, 1951, Norristown, PA, **d.** Sep. 21, 1987, Fort Lauderdale, FL
Bass / Post-Bop, Fusion
Jaco Pastorius was a meteor who blazed onto the scene in the 1970s, only to flame out tragically in the 1980s. With a brilliantly fleet technique and fertile melodic imagination, Pastorius made his fretless electric bass leap out from the depths of the rhythm section into the front line with fluid machine-gun-like passages that demanded attention. He also sported a strutting, dancing, flamboyant performing style and posed a further triple-threat as a talented composer, arranger and producer. He and Stanley Clarke were the towering influences on their instrument in the 1970s. Everything started to come together for him quickly once he started playing with another rookie fusionmeister, Pat Metheny, around 1974. By 1976, he had been invited to join Weather Report, where he remained until 1981; he also found himself in constant demand as a sessionman and producer, and his first eponymous solo album for Epic in 1976 was hailed as a tour de force. Alas, Pastorius became overwhelmed by mental problems, exacerbated by drugs and alcohol, in the mid-'80s, leading to several embarrassing public incidents (one was a violent crackup onstage at Hollywood Bowl in mid-set at the 1984 Playboy Jazz Festival). Such episodes made him a pariah in the music business and toward the end of his life, he had become a street person, reportedly sighted in drug-infested inner-city hangouts. He died in 1987 from a physical beating sustained while trying to break into the Midnight Club in Fort Lauderdale. *—Richard S. Ginell*

★ **Jaco Pastorius** / Aug. 1976 / Epic/Legacy ✦✦✦✦✦
It's impossible to hear Jaco Pastorious' debut album today as it sounded when it was first released in 1976. The opening track—his transcription for fretless electric bass of the bebop standard "Donna Lee"—was a manifesto of virtuosity; the next track, the funk-soul celebration "Come On, Come Over" was a poke in the eye to jazz snobs and a love letter to the R&B greats of the previous decade (two of whom, Sam & Dave, sing on that track); "Continuum" was a spacey, chorus-drenched look forward to the years he was about to spend playing with Weather Report. The program continues like that for three-quarters of an hour, each track heading off in a different direction—each one a masterpiece that would have been a proud achievement for any musician. What made Jaco so exceptional was that he was responsible for all of them, and this was his debut album. Beyond his phenomenal bass technique and his surprisingly mature compositional chops (he was 24 when this album was released), there was the breathtaking audacity of his arrangements: "Okonkole Y Trompa" is scored for electric bass, French horn, and percussion, and "Speak Like a Child," which Pastorious composed in collaboration with pianist Herbie Hancock, features a string arrangement by Pastorious that merits serious attention in its own right. For a man with this sort of kaleidoscopic creativity to remain sane was perhaps too much to ask; his gradual descent into madness and eventual tragic death are now a familiar story, one which makes the bright promise of this glorious debut album all the more bittersweet. (This remastered reissue adds two tracks to the original program: alternate takes of "(Used to Be a) Cha Cha" and "6/4 Jam"). *—Rick Anderson*

The Birthday Concert / Dec. 1, 1981 / Warner Brothers ✦✦✦✦
On an irregular basis in the early 1980s, the innovative electric bassist Jaco Pastorius led a big band that he called Word of Mouth. This excellent CD documents Pastorius' 30th birthday party, a concert ar which he was joined by the Peter Graves Orchestra (consisting of 14 horns, two steel drums and two percussionists) plus drummer Peter Erskine, Don Alias on conga, and both Michael Brecker and Bob Mintzer on tenors. Brecker co-stars with Pastorius on a strong program that is highlighted by "The Chicken," and a burning rendition of "Invitation," and "Liberty City." The music is full of spirit and joy, featuring Pastorius at the peak of his powers just before his tragic decline. *—Scott Yanow*

Word of Mouth / Dec. 1981 / Warner Brothers ✦✦✦✦
Bassist Jaco Pastorius's Word of Mouth orchestra was an unfulfilled dream, a worthy concept that did not last long enough to live up to its potential. Its debut album was released without a listing of the personnel, so here it is: Wayne Shorter, Michael Brecker and Tom Scott on reeds, trumpeter Chuck Findley, the easily recognizable Toots Thielemans on harmonica, Howard Johnson on tuba, drummers Jack DeJohnette and Peter Erskine and percussionist Don Alias. The music ranges from The Beatles' "Blackbird" and some Bach to Jaco originals that cover straightahead jazz, Coltranish vamps and fusion. Next to the bassist/leader, Thielemans emerges as the main voice. It's worth checking out but not essential. *—Scott Yanow*

Invitation / Dec. 1983 / Warner Brothers ✦✦✦✦✦
Electric bassist Jaco Pastorius' Word of Mouth big band made two recordings for Warner Bros. during its short life, of which is this is the superior one. The large ensemble (five trumpets including Randy Brecker, five reeds with solo space for Bobby Mintzer on tenor and soprano, four trombones, two French horns, Toots Thielemans on harmonica, drummer Peter Erskine, percussionist Don Alias and Othello on steel drum) performs a variety of superior material. Although Pastorius takes his share of solo space, and the sound of a big band backing a bass soloist is rather unusual, he does not excessively dominate the music. Pastorius contributed some of the pieces (most notably "Liberty City"), is showcased on "Amerika," and also plays such tunes as "Invitation," "The Chicken," "Sophisticated Lady," "Giant Steps" and Gil Evans' "Eleven." Surprisingly, this important recording has not yet been reissued on CD. *—Scott Yanow*

Heavy 'n Jazz / Dec. 1986 / Jazzpoint ✦✦✦✦✦
Heavy 'n Jazz is the last live Jaco Pastorius performance currently available to the public, and is one of the most truly satisfying of his trio recordings. The album is heavy, as the title suggests, thanks to a powerful trio fronted by guitarist extraordinaire Bireli Lagrene displaying his fiercest rock chops. A fast-paced outing with more rock inflection than usual, the compact disc boasts very good sound quality. The performances contrast nicely with Pastorius' live jazz recordings with the Word of Mouth big band (*Invitation, The Birthday Concert*), particularly the cooker "Reza" which appears on all three CDs in vastly different presentations. Every cut on *Heavy 'n Jazz* is a gem. Of particular interest are Lagrene's solo piece, "Bluma," and his aggressive guitar work on the exciting, soaring "Medley," featuring "Teen Town." Pastorius' playing on "Star Spangled Banner" is at once terrifying and beautiful, while "Honestly" affords him a chance to play the hits—a collage of some of his oft-played riffs from well known Pastorius/Weather Report compositions. Heavy 'N Jazz is a must for Jaco-philes, however, jazz purists be warned. *—David Ross Smith*

Live in New York City, Vol. 1: Punk Jazz / 1990 / Big World ✦✦✦
The first in a three-volume series spotlighting the great electric bassist Jaco Pastorius head-

ing his Punk Jazz combo through fusion, jazz-rock, and even some blues and mainstream sets. This band provided Pastorius an outlet for all his musical loves, among them Caribbean, and also had enough instruments, colors, and textures to let him interact with the rhythm section sometimes, then take the spotlight himself on other occasions. *—Ron Wynn*

John Patitucci

b. Dec. 22, 1959, Brooklyn, NY
Bass / Post-Bop, Fusion
One of the top bassists of the 1990s (on both acoustic and electric), Patitucci's speed, very clear tone and versatility are quite impressive. He started playing bass when he was 11, grew up in Northern California and in 1978 moved south near Los Angeles. He played with Gap Mangione (1979) while going to college and during 1982-85 worked in Los Angeles with Tom Scott, Robben Ford, Stan Getz, Larry Carlton, Dave Grusin, Ernie Watts, Freddie Hubbard and others in addition to becoming a studio musician. In 1985 he gained a high profile when he joined Chick Corea as a regular member of both the Elektric and Akoustic bands. Patitucci toured and recorded extensively with Corea and has made a series of his own diverse sessions for GRP and Stretch (although he is not as strong a composer as he is a bassist). John Patitucci left the Elektric Band in the early '90s but has continued working with Corea on an occasional basis. *—Scott Yanow*

• **Heart of the Bass** / 1991 / Stretch ✦✦✦✦✦
Fusion standout John Patitucci flashes the speed, facility, and flash that's made him the darling of the contemporary jazz set. He's joined by the man whose band has showcased him, pianist Chick Corea, plus percussionist Alex Acuna and other guest stars. The songs are pretty routine, but Patitucci and Corea's performances elevate them. *—Ron Wynn*

Another World / 1993 / GRP ✦✦✦✦
John Patitucci has quickly developed into one of the world's great bassists, both on acoustic and electric. He is not on the same level as a composer, but is steadily improving, as witnessed by the music on this fine release. There are many bass solos as one would expect (Patitucci's high-note flights often sound like a guitar), but he does leave space for his sidemen, most notably keyboardist John Beasley (who has two numbers without the bassist), trumpeter Jeff Beal, and one selection apiece for the steel drums of Andy Narell and Mike Brecker's tenor. A few tracks are throwaway funk, but there are enough surprise twists and unusual improvisations to make this a recommended disc even for adventurous listeners. *—Scott Yanow*

Now / Jan. 14, 1998-Jan. 17, 1998 / Concord Jazz ✦✦✦✦
John Patitucci's creativity soared on *One More Angel,* an introspective and deeply personal effort that found him using music to reflect on events in his life (including a tragic miscarriage his wife Sashi had suffered). *One More Angel* was a darn tough act to follow, but the bassist provided a respectable follow-up with the very different *Now.* This time, Patitucci emphasizes the cerebral and the angular, and the native New Yorker (who plays acoustic bass on seven selections and electric bass on three) does it with the help of a pianoless team that includes Michael Brecker or Chris Potter on tenor sax, John Scofield on guitar and Bill Stewart on drums. Patitucci clearly enjoys a strong rapport with his sidemen on intellectual originals like "Espresso," "Out of the Mouths of Babes" and "Forgotten But Not Gone" as well as interpretations of McCoy Tyner's "Search for Peace" and John Coltrane's "Giant Steps" (an electric bass/drums duet with Stewart). Overall, *Now* isn't as accessible or as consistently lyrical as *One More Angel, Mistura Fina* or *Heart of the Bass?*this is a complex, cerebral offering that demands more of the listener than any of Patitucci's previous releases. But those who don't shy away from *Now* because of its complexity will find that the album has a lot going for it. *—Alex Henderson*

Imprint / Aug. 1999 / Concord Jazz ✦✦✦✦
When GRP dropped John Patitucci in 1996, it turned out to be a blessing in disguise. The bassist found a supportive new home in Concord Jazz, where his creativity was encouraged and he was able to take his share of chances. Just as 1998's cerebral *Now* was a departure from 1996's introspective, deeply personal *One More Angel, Imprint* finds Patitucci surprising his followers once again by emphasizing Latin elements. Employing drummer Jack DeJohnette and saxman Chris Potter, as well as Latino improvisers, pianist Danilo Perez and drummer/percussionist Horacio "El Negro" Hernandez, *Imprint* is the most Latin-minded album that he recorded in the 1990s. However, *Imprint* isn't Latin jazz in the sense that Poncho Sanchez is Latin jazz—it is more intellectual and less direct, and it's not as accessible. While Sanchez's releases tend to favor immediacy and take an extroverted, party-time approach, that's hardly what Patitucci is going for on this acoustic post-post-jazz effort. Sticking to the upright bass, Patitucci delivers an album that is almost as intellectual as *Now,* but with an emphasis on Latin rhythms. For those who aren't afraid of being challenged, *Imprint* is a welcome addition to the bassist's catalogue. *—Alex Henderson*

Don Patterson (Donald B. Patterson)

b. Jul. 22, 1936, Columbus, OH, **d.** Feb. 10, 1988, Philadelphia, PA
Organ (Hammond), Organ / Hard Bop, Soul-Jazz
Columbus Ohio born Don Patterson began his musical career as a pianist, inspired by Erroll Garner. A solid soul jazz, blues and hard bop organist with a pianistic background, Patterson didn't utilize the pedals or play with as much rhythmic drive as some other stylists, but developed a satisfactory alternative approach. Patterson's organ solos were smartly played, and more melodic than explosive. He switched from piano in 1956 after hearing Jimmy Smith. Patterson made his organ debut in 1959, and worked with Sonny Stitt, Eddie "Lockjaw" Davis, Gene Ammons and Wes Montgomery in the early '60s. He recorded with Ammons, Stitt and Eric Kloss in the early and mid-'60s. Patterson worked often in a duo with Billy James and made several recordings in the '60s and '70s as a leader. He and Al Grey worked together extensively in the '80s. Patterson recorded as a leader for Prestige and Muse. *—Ron Wynn and Michael G. Nastos*

Legends of Acid Jazz, Vol. 2 / Jul. 25, 1967 / Prestige ✦✦✦✦

Legends of Acid Jazz / May 12, 1964 / Prestige ✦✦✦✦
Among all the practitioners of soul-jazz during the genre heyday of the late 1960s into the 1970s, Hammond B-3 organ groovemeister Don Patterson and modern Texas tenor Booker Ervin (also a veteran of jazz ensembles led by Randy Weston and Charles Mingus) are among those usually overlooked. Yet the pair teamed up to release several albums during that time that were, if not standards of the genre precisely, full of vitality and fever—Ervin's playing, especially, often sounded so emotional and combustible that it seemed like he was suffering a nervous breakdown through his horn, perhaps a residue of his time with Mingus. *Legends of Acid Jazz: Don Patterson / Booker Ervin* surfs the cream of three mid-'60s recording sessions: in a trio setting with drummer Billy James, all five selections from *The Exciting New Organ of Don Patterson,* including one of Miles Davis' early signature tunes, "Oleo" (actually a Sonny Rollins composition); the title track from *Hip Cake Walk,* a 17-minute monument to the soulful power of organ that endured as Patterson's most-beloved hip-swiveler (featuring Leonard Houston on alto sax); and "Love Me With All Your Heart" from *Patterson's People. Legends of Acid Jazz: Don Patterson / Booker Ervin* suffers only slightly from a program that leans heavily toward the mainstream—"Love Me With..." goes more than six minutes, and "When Johnny Comes Marching Home" nearly eleven. *—Chris Slawecki*

Boppin' and Burnin' / Feb. 22, 1968 / Prestige/OJC ✦✦✦✦✦
Although organist Don Patterson is the leader of this set that in 1998 was reissued on a CD, the quintet date is most notable for the playing of trumpeter Howard McGhee. McGhee, who had not been heard from much on record for a few years, proves to still be in prime form. Altoist Charles McPherson, the young guitarist Pat Martino and drummer Billy James complete the group. The repertoire is particularly strong with two McGhee originals (including the memorable and haunting "Island Fantasy"), "Epistrophy," "Now's The Time" and a trumpet feature on "Donna Lee." Highly recommended. *—Scott Yanow*

• **Dem New York Blues** / Jun. 5, 1968-Jun. 2, 1969 / Prestige ✦✦✦✦✦
Despite claims to the contrary, organist Don Patterson was very much of the Jimmy Smith school, a hard-driving player with fine improvising skills but lacking a distinctive sound of his own. This CD (which reissues two complete LPs) features Patterson in prime form in a quintet with trumpeter Blue Mitchell, Junior Cook on tenor and guitarist Pat Martino, and with a separate group that features trumpeter Virgil Jones and both George Coleman and Houston Person on tenors. Although "Oh Happy Day" is a throwaway, Patterson's spirited renditions of the blues and standards make this a fairly definitive example of his talents. *—Scott Yanow*

Legends of Acid Jazz: Sonny Stitt/Don Patterson, Vol. 2 / Sep. 23, 1968-Sep. 24, 1968 / Prestige ✦✦✦
Two-for-one CD reissue combines two 1968 sessions, both featuring Stitt and Patterson, that were recorded on consecutive days (September 23-24, 1968), although one was issued under Patterson's name and the other under Stitt's. The first six songs were issued as the Patterson LP *Funk You!,* on which Patterson leads a date that also has Sonny Stitt and Charles McPherson on saxes, and Pat Martino on guitar. The other players get about as much space as Patterson, and as 1960s jazz with organ goes, this is pretty straight-ahead and boppish, rather than soul-jazz (as so much organ jazz from that decade was). For the bop factor, listen especially to the cover of Sonny Rollins' "Airegin," and on which Martino in particular shines. Patterson does get in a more soulful mood on his composition "Little Angie," which has an elegiac mood somewhat similar to occasional slow instrumentals cut by Booker T. & the MG's during that period. The other eight songs were issued as the Stitt LP *Soul Electricity!,* an album that got its name because for this session, Stitt plugged his alto and tenor saxophones into a Varitone attachment. What came out, though, was not fusion by any means, but a pretty straight-ahead session that found Sonny his usual competent self. The program is actually on the conservative side, leaning toward standards. Stitt's quartet is rounded out by Don Patterson on organ, Billy Butler on guitar, and Billy James on drums. This isn't the most logical package—Stitt's half is more straight-ahead in flavor and, more importantly, neither album fits too well into the soul-jazz or acid-jazz category—but for fans of either artist, the material is worth hearing. *—Richie Unterberger*

Steady Comin' at Ya / Oct. 30, 1972-Jan. 31, 1977 / 32 Jazz ✦✦✦

Big John Patton

b. Jul. 12, 1935, Kansas City, MO
Organ (Hammond), Organ / Hard Bop, Soul-Jazz
Big John Patton was not nearly as well-known as other warriors in the organ jazz field of the 1960s, yet he could be counted upon for a reliable, even fervent collection of blues and bop-saturated licks and steady bass lines on the Hammond B-3. Mostly self-taught with some rudimentary instruction from his mother, Patton started playing piano in 1948, eventually landing a gig with the Lloyd Price touring band from 1954 to 1959 before moving to New York. Once there, he began to make the transition from piano to organ, learning a lot from future two recording mates, drummer Ben Dixon and guitarist Grant Green. He recorded with Lou Donaldson for Blue Note from 1962 to 1964 and, after impressing Blue Note founder Alfred Lion, made the first of a string of albums as a leader for the label in 1963. Interestingly, many of his albums, though scheduled for release, never saw the light of day until after Blue Note's resurrection in 1985. When the Hammond B-3 and soul-jazz went out of fashion in the 1970s, Patton's career went into eclipse as well, and he settled in East Orange, NJ. But shortly after he started recording again in 1983, Patton was rediscovered by a younger generation, particularly the avant-garde figure John Zorn, who began using his sound out of its usual context on recordings like *The Big Gundown* and *Spillane's* "Two-Lane Highway." *—Richard S. Ginell*

Along Came John / Apr. 5, 1963 / Blue Note ✦✦✦✦
By the time John Patton recorded *Along Came John,* his debut as a leader, he had already become a familiar name around the Blue Note studios. He, guitarist Grant Green, and drummer Ben Dixon had become the label's regular soul-jazz rhythm section, playing on sessions by Lou Donaldson, Don Wilkerson, and Harold Vick, among others. They had developed an

intuitive, empathetic interplay that elevated many of their sessions to near-greatness, at least in the realm of soul-jazz. That's one of the reasons why *Along Came John* is so successful—the three know each other so well that their grooves are totally natural, which makes them quite appealing. These original compositions may not all be memorable, but the band's interaction, improvisation, and solos are. Tenor saxophonists Fred Jackson and Harold Vick provide good support, as well, but the show belongs to Patton, Green, and Dixon, who once again prove they are one of the finest soul-jazz combos of their era. *—Stephen Thomas Erlewine*

Blue John / Jul. 11, 1963-Aug. 2, 1963 / Blue Note ✦✦✦✦✦
Here we have another of those phantom John Patton albums, one that was pictured and even written about on Blue Note releases of the early '60s but not released until 1986, catalog number intact. As such, it is merely a fairly ordinary session of blues-based organ quintet jazz of the period which manages to keep up a series of steady, satisfying grooves laced with steady, unspectacular solos. "Country Girl" is the most stupefyingly ordinary tune of the lot, but the others aren't terribly catchy either. As the principal diverting novelty of the CD, George Braith pulls a Roland Kirk by playing the soprano sax and stritch simultaneously, mostly in reedy harmony. Otherwise, guitarist Grant Green is the most substantial player on the session; the other musicians are Tommy Turrentine on trumpet and Ben Dixon on drums. *—Richard S. Ginell*

The Way I Feel / Jun. 19, 1964 / Blue Note ✦✦✦
For his third album, Big John Patton decided to expand his band to quintet. Retaining the services of his longtime colleagues, guitarist Grant Green and drummer Ben Dixon, he hired tenor saxophonist Fred Jackson (who also played on *Along Came John*) and trumpeter Richard Williams. The combination of two horns can occasionally overshadow the groove Patton, Green, and Dixon lay down, but for the most part the musicians augment the music instead of detracting from it. Nevertheless, the combo never manages to match the peaks of *Along Came John* and *Blue John*. There are several fine moments on the record, and Green and Patton are typically enjoyable, but the record overall is a slight disappointment after its two predecessors. *—Stephen Thomas Erlewine*

Oh Baby / Mar. 8, 1965 / Blue Note ✦✦✦✦
Patton's fourth album for Blue Note. Big John Patton with Grant Green on guitar and Harold Vick on tenor sax. With tunes like "Fat Judy" and "Good Juice," there is no worry about there being a groove. The addition of a trumpet (Blue Mitchell) means you have a horn section, and this tends to be a little much now and again. Although a little on the light side, thanks to Patton and Green, the groove does go down. *—Michael Erlewine*

★ **Let 'em Roll** / Dec. 11, 1965 / Blue Note ✦✦✦✦✦
Patton with Grant Green (guitar), Otis Finch (drums) and Bobby Hutcherson (vibes). Grant Green provides just superb assistance. While vibes is not a usual instrument for soul jazz sessions, this album works anyway and the groove is established. Grant Green and Patton are just a great combination. *—Michael Erlewine*

Got a Good Thing Goin' / Apr. 29, 1966 / Blue Note ✦✦✦✦✦
Grant Green always brought out the best in Big John Patton. Almost any record that featured the guitarist and organist was dominated by their scintillating interplay, and it always sounded like they were trying to top each other's blistering, funky solos. Patton and Green rarely sounded better than they did on *Got a Good Thing Goin'*, a 1966 session that functioned as a showcase for the pair's dynamic interaction and exciting, invigorating solos. In particular, the duo's mastery is evident because there are no horns to stand in the way—only drummer Hugh Walker and conga player Richard Landrum provide support, leaving plenty of room for Green and Patton to run wild. All five numbers—two originals by Patton and Green, two pop covers ("Ain't That Peculiar," "Shake"), and Duke Pearson's "Amanda"—are simple blues and soul-jazz songs that provide ample space for the guitarist and organist to stretch out. And they do stretch out—as a pair, they have never sounded so fiery or intoxicating. Fans of hard bop may find the songs a little too simple, but hot, up-tempo soul-jazz rarely comes any better than it does on *Got a Good Thing Goin'*. *—Stephen Thomas Erlewine*

Memphis to New York Spirit / Jun. 9, 1969-Oct. 2, 1970 / Blue Note ✦✦✦
Although it was scheduled for release two times, *Memphis to New York Spirit* didn't appear until 1996, over 25 years after it was recorded. The album comprises the contents of two separate sessions—one recorded in 1970 with guitarist James "Blood" Ulmer, drummer Leroy Williams and saxophonist/flautist Marvin Cabell; the other recorded in 1969 with Cabell, Williams, and saxophonist George Coleman—that were very similiar in concept and execution. Patton leads his combo through a selection of originals and covers that range from Wayne Shorter and McCoy Tyner to the Meters. Though the group is rooted in soul-jazz, they stretch the limits of the genre on these sessions, showing a willingness to experiment, while still dipping into the more traditional blues and funk reserves. Consequently, *Memphis to New York Spirit* doesn't have a consistent groove like some other Patton records, but when it does click, the results are remarkable; it's a non-essential but worthy addition to a funky soul-jazz collection. *—Stephen Thomas Erlewine*

Blue Planet Man / Apr. 12, 1993-Apr. 13, 1993 / Evidence ✦✦✦
Though Big John Patton isn't the innovator that Larry Young was, it would be a mistake to think of him as being strictly a soul-jazz player. Patton can get funky, to be sure, but he hasn't been afraid to venture into post-bop territory and take the Hammond B-3 away from traditional soul-jazz settings. Recorded when the organist was 57, *Blue Planet Man* is an unpredictable set that ranges from grits-and-gravy soul-jazz to more intellectual post-bop. Patton gets into a funky, down-home soul-jazz groove on "Funky Mama," and vocalist Rorie Nichols has a very R&B-minded cameo on "What's Your Name—". Yet Patton is very Thelonious Monk-ish on the angular "Popeye" and is just as cerebral on "Bama" and Archie Shepp's "U-Jaama." In fact, one of the CD's main soloists is alto saxman John Zorn, who is primarily known for playing avant-garde and free jazz. Not one of Patton's essential releases, *Blue Planet Man* is definitely enjoyable and well-intended—the album reminds us that Patton can hardly be considered one-dimensional. *—Alex Henderson*

Minor Swing / Dec. 21, 1994 / DIW ✦✦✦
An organ trio fronted by an avant-garde alto saxophonist like John Zorn isn't usually a combination associated with groove oriented soul-jazz. Luckily, on *Minor Swing*, organist Big John Patton and John Zorn encourage taking chances and opening the music up, while not going so far out as to overwhelm the intended fundamental groove. Zorn sounds comfortable and content, always maintaining his individuality, taking a cue from tenor saxophonist Harold Alexander who played in a similar "out" style on Patton's 1968 session for Blue Note, *Boogaloo*. Patton's second comeback date of the '90s features Zorn with Ed Cherry (guitar) and Kenny Wollesen (drums) on six originals and Larry Young's "Tyrone." Patton and Zorn embrace Young's influence by employing elements of harder edged post bop that a large portion of groove-soul organ players tend to avoid. Although these sessions may be harder to obtain than his Blue Note dates, the '90s DIW and Evidence releases are highly recommended. *—Al Campbell*

This One's for J.A. / Dec. 26, 1996 / DIW ✦✦✦
On the third album of his '90s comeback, Big John Patton chooses to create a relaxed vibe, smoothly grooving through a surprising choice of material. Most of the record consists of challenging songs like Coltrane's "Syeeda's Song Flute" and Grachan Moncur III's "Sonny's Back," which gives Patton—as well as his supporting band, featuring guitarist Ed Cherry and tenor saxophonist Dave Hubbard—the chance to create intricate yet accessible music. This is music that can be heard as simply a good groove yet it rewards careful listening. *This One's for J.A.* again confirms that Patton has made one of the rare comebacks in jazz, one that does justice to his earlier work. *—Stephen Thomas Erlewine*

Nicholas Payton

b. 1973, New Orleans, LA
Trumpet / New Orleans Jazz, Hard Bop
One of the brightest new trumpet stars of the 1990s, Nicholas Payton combines references to his New Orleans heritage with the Young Lions' brand of hard bop and a warm sound. His father Walter Payton, a top bassist, and his mother (a classical pianist) encouraged his interest in music and he received his first trumpet when he was four. Payton developed quickly and at age nine he had opportunities to sit in with the Young Tuxedo Brass Band. One day when Payton was 12, Wynton Marsalis called to speak to his father; Nicholas spontaneously played his trumpet over the phone, impressing Marsalis who in the future would recommend him to other bandleaders. Payton worked steadily in New Orleans while in high school, he graduated from the New Orleans Center for Creative Arts and studied with Ellis Marsalis. In 1992 he toured with Marcus Roberts, in 1994 he toured Europe with Jazz Futures II and in addition Payton toured with Elvin Jones and worked with the Jazz at Lincoln Center program. He has recorded with Jones, as a leader on Verve and with the New Orleans Collective on Evidence. *Payton's Place*, which featured cameos by Wynton Marsalis and Roy Hargrove, appeared on Verve in 1998; *Nick@Night* followed two years later. *—Scott Yanow*

From This Moment / Sep. 11, 1994-Sep. 12, 1994 / Verve ✦✦✦✦
The young trumpeter Nicholas Payton is featured on this CD as the only horn in a sextet also including guitarist Mark Whitfield, pianist Mulgrew Miller and vibraphonist Monte Croft. Best are Payton's melodic and very mature statements on the veteran standards "You Stepped Out of a Dream," "It Could Happen to You," "From This Moment On" and "Taking a Chance on Love." His six originals are less memorable, but overall, this is a pleasing date that finds the trumpeter showing a great deal of potential. Payton's tone, mixing aspects of Freddie Hubbard, Wynton Marsalis and New Orleans jazz in a post-bop setting, is quite appealing. *—Scott Yanow*

● **Gumbo Nouveau** / Nov. 28, 1995-Nov. 30, 1995 / Verve ✦✦✦✦✦
Only 22 at the time of this CD, Nicholas Payton had already quickly developed into a major trumpeter. Possessing a fat tone that is sometimes reminiscent of Freddie Hubbard, Payton by the mid-1990's had become New Orleans' latest significant contribution to jazz. On his second Verve release, Payton interprets and modernizes ten songs associated with his hometown and/or Louis Armstrong. Fortunately Payton generally retains the flavor and joy of the original versions even while he transforms much of the music into hard bop. To cite a few examples, "Whoopin' Blues" has parade rhythms, sendoffs worthy of Lionel Hampton and beboppish solos, "Way Down Yonder In New Orleans" is taken as a slow and lightly swinging ballad and "I Gotta Right To Sing The Blues" is turned into a jazz waltz. "Li'l Liza Jane" becomes a largely unrecognizable hard bop romp and this version of the "Saints" is a bit melancholy but "Wild Man Blues" is a real tour-de-force for the trumpeter and the duet between Payton and pianist Anthony Wonsey on "Weather Bird" has the leader liberally quoting from Louis Armstrong's classic version. Throughout the date Nicholas Payton is the lead voice, pianist Wonsey is the main supporting player and there are occasional solos from altoist Jesse Davis and tenor-saxophonist Tim Warfield. New Orleans jazz purists may not care for all of the updating but the overall results are fresh and quite likable. Recommended. *—Scott Yanow*

Payton's Place / Sep. 29, 1997-Jan. 6, 1998 / Verve ✦✦✦
Payton's third album as a leader is assuredly more commanding than his previous projects, and his technically flawless trumpet is right among the leaders in the neo-bop field. Yet he remains essentially a preservationist, a throwback to the hard bopping '50s and '60s and a staunch believer in the orthodoxies and rituals involved. There are exceptions—a nice '60s Blue Note-style boogaloo for starters ("Zigaboogaloo"), a probing, driving, tempo-shifting workout on Wayne Shorter's "Paraphernalia" from *Miles In the Sky* (which is about as progressive as the record gets)—but conservatism prevails elsewhere, even in the mild-mannered cover of the Stylistics' "People Make the World Go Round." In a takeoff on the Three Tenors, "The Three Trumpeteers" finds Payton joyously uniting and dueling with Wynton Marsalis and the ubiquitous Roy Hargrove; thankfully, one can tell them apart by ear despite the orthodox hard bop format. Pianist Anthony Wonsey, hardnosed tenor saxman Timothy Warfield, bassist Reuben Rogers and drummer Adonis Rose expertly do what is expected of them, joined now and then by the above two guest trumpeters and another stock member of the Young Lions cast, tenor Joshua Redman. *—Richard S. Ginell*

NickNight / 1999 / Verve ♦♦♦
By the last years of the 1990s, Nicholas Payton's trumpet-playing and leadership abilities were growing in leaps and bounds in live performance. However, the valedictory record of that decade displays growth only in the former and mostly caution in the latter, for Payton remains staunchly committed to the neo-bop verities and ceremonies. Part of the problem is that Payton's material—he contributes ten of the 13 tracks—is still not terribly memorable by and large, although he may be developing a distinctive talent for naming tunes. You gotta love titles like "Captain Crunch (Meets the Cereal Killer)" and "NickNight," but the music is strictly traditional stuff, refusing to transcend the ordinary. There are exceptions early and late on the disc when touches of instrumental enterprise peek through; "Beyond the Stars" would sound like an ordinary slice of post-bop were it not for the fact that Anthony Wonsey (and Payton!) are playing harpsichords, adding a sting from an instrument not explored much in jazz since the swing era. The multi-sectioned "Faith" also has its best moments when backed by harpsichord and celeste, and "Sun Goddess," a tune done by Ramsey Lewis in the '70s, has a striking harpsichord-backed opening. There is no doubt that Payton's choice of notes and use of space continues to mature, and his quintet—with Wonsey on piano, Tim Warfield on saxophones, Reuben Rogers on bass, and Adonis Rose on drums—just gets tighter and more intuitively interactive. *—Richard S. Ginell*

Gary Peacock

b. May 12, 1935, Burley, ID
Bass / Avant-Garde Jazz, Free Jazz, Post-Bop
A subtle but adventurous bassist, Gary Peacock's flexibility and consistently creative ideas have been an asset to several important groups. He was originally a pianist, playing in an Army band while stationed in Germany in the late '50s. Peacock switched to bass in 1956, staying on in Germany after his discharge to play with Hans Koller, Attila Zoller, Tony Scott and Bud Shank. In 1958 he moved to Los Angeles where he performed with Barney Kessel, Don Ellis, Terry Gibbs and Shorty Rogers and (most importantly) Paul Bley among others. After moving to New York in 1962, Peacock worked with Bill Evans (1962-63), the Paul Bley trio, Jimmy Giuffre, Roland Kirk and George Russell. In 1964 after a brief stint with Miles Davis, Peacock started an assocation with Albert Ayler in Europe, also playing with Roswell Rudd and Steve Lacy. Peacock alternated between Ayler and Paul Bley for a time and returned briefly to Miles Davis in the late '60s. After a period in Japan (1969-72), Peacock studied biology (1972-76), worked with Bley, and off and on from the late '70s has played (and recorded) in a trio with Keith Jarrett and Jack DeJohnette. *—Scott Yanow*

Tales of Another / Feb. 2, 1977 / ECM ♦♦♦♦
Bassist Gary Peacock contributed all six originals to this set which also features pianist Keith Jarrett and drummer Jack DeJohnette. These musicians (who are equals) have played together many times through the years and their support of each other and close communication during these advanced improvisations is quite impressive. It's a good example of Peacock's music. *—Scott Yanow*

Shift in the Wind / Feb. 1980 / ECM ♦♦♦♦
Bassist Gary Peacock teams up with the underrated pianist Art Lande and drummer Eliot Zigmund for a set of group originals that emphasize close communication between the trio members, really an extension on the innovations of Bill Evans. The interplay between these masterful musicians is more significant than the actual compositions and rewards repeats listenings. *—Scott Yanow*

Tethered Moon / Nov. 16, 1991-Nov. 18, 1991 / Evidence ♦♦♦♦

● **Oracle** / May 1993 / ECM ♦♦♦♦♦
This set of duets by bassist Gary Peacock and guitarist Ralph Towner, as one might expect from an ECM album, makes expert use of space and has its quiet moments. But there is a surprising amount of ferocious interplay between the two musicians. They may play at a consistently low volume but the set of originals has a few rather passionate grooves and a little more energy than one would have predicted. *—Scott Yanow*

Just So Happens / Oct. 19, 1994 / Postcards ♦♦♦
Gary Peacock's duo album with Bill Frisell is rewarding, though a bit repetitive. Most interesting is the sonic contrast between Peacock's imposing upright bass and Frisell's quirky electric guitar. After eight tracks, however, the appearance of Frisell's acoustic guitar—on the standard "Good Morning, Heartache"—comes as a welcome change. Most of the pieces are free improvisations, and while they all have their moments, some wind up treading water. "In Walked Po," an oblique take on the blues, is an exception. "Reciprocity" and "N.O.M.B." are the only originals credited solely to Peacock, leading one to believe they were written before the session. Perhaps not surprisingly, these two tracks are the most coherent on the record. The duo also plays two versions of "Home on the Range" (one would have sufficed), and Peacock renders "Red River Valley" as an unaccompanied solo. For Frisell, at least, this could have been a sign of things soon to come: His *Nashville* album was released about a year later. *—David R. Adler*

Duke Pearson (Columbus Calvin Pearson, Jr.)

b. Aug. 17, 1932, Atlanta, GA, **d.** Aug. 4, 1980, Atlanta, GA
Piano, Producer, Arranger / Hard Bop
Duke Pearson was an accomplished, lyrical, and logical, if rather cautious, pianist who played a big part in shaping the Blue Note label's hard bop direction in the 1960s as a producer. He will probably be best remembered for writing several attractive, catchy pieces, the most memorable being the moody "Cristo Redentor" for Donald Byrd, "Sweet Honey Bee" for himself and Lee Morgan, and "Jeannine," which has become a much-covered jazz standard. He worked as a pianist in Atlanta and elsewhere in Georgia and Florida before moving to New York in 1959. There, he joined Donald Byrd's band, the Art Farmer/Benny Golson Sextet, and served as Nancy Wilson's accompanist. In 1963, he arranged four numbers for jazz septet and eight-voice choir on Byrd's innovative *A New Perspective* album; one of the tunes was "Cristo Redentor," which became a jazz hit. From 1963 to 1970, Pearson was in charge of several recording sessions for Blue Note, while also recording most of his albums as a leader. He also led a big band from 1967 to 1970 and again in 1972, hiring players like Pepper Adams, Chick Corea, Lew Tabackin, Randy Brecker and Garnett Brown. Pearson continued to accompany vocalists in the 1970s, but he spent a good deal of the latter half of the decade fighting the ravages of multiple sclerosis. *—Richard S. Ginell*

Tender Feelin's / Dec. 6, 1959 / Blue Note ♦♦♦
Tender Feelin's is an appropriate title for Duke Pearson's second album for Blue Note. The record is a lovely, relaxed collection of ballads, standards, and jazz staples, with a few originals thrown in for good measure. Since Pearson sticks to the trio format, supported by bassist Gene Taylor and drummer Lex Humphries, the mood of the album remains intimate and low-key. Pearson flourishes in this setting, whether he's playing blues, romantic ballads, or surprisingly lyrical improvised solos. Pearson would later explore more adventurous territory, as well as funkier grooves, but *Tender Feelin's* remains a wonderfully understated, romantic mainstream jazz record. *—Stephen Thomas Erlewine*

Dedication! / Aug. 2, 1961 / Prestige/OJC ♦♦♦♦

★ **Wahoo** / Nov. 24, 1964 / Blue Note ♦♦♦♦♦
A truly wonderful advanced hard bop date, *Wahoo* captures pianist Duke Pearson at his most adventurous and creative. With the exception of Donald Byrd's closing "Fly Little Bird Fly," Pearson wrote all of the material on this six-song album, and his compositions are clever, melodic, and unpredictable without being cloying or inaccessible. He has assembled a first-rate sextet to perform the material, enlisting trumpeter Byrd, tenor saxophonist Joe Henderson, bassist Bob Cranshaw, alto saxophonist/flautist James Spaulding, and drummer Mickey Roker. Even the subdued "Wahoo" and "ESP" search out new territory with their subtle themes and exploratory solo sections. The key to the success of *Wahoo* is that Duke Pearson is a gifted arranger, creating nimble, challenging arrangements that are accessible, but reveal more details upon each listen. As a pianist, he has moved beyond his initial Bud Powell influence and reveals new aspects of his technique. Henderson, Byrd, and Spaulding are equally impressive, helping elevate *Wahoo* to one of the finest sophisticated hard bop dates Blue Note released in the mid-'60s. *—Stephen Thomas Erlewine*

Honeybuns / May 25, 1965-May 26, 1965 / Koch Jazz ♦♦♦
This 1998 Koch CD reissues a Duke Pearson LP from 1966, containing music from the previous year. Other than "Our Love" (a familiar classical theme adapted to American pop music by Larry Clinton), all six selections are originals by the pianist. Utilizing a nonet that includes trumpeter Johnny Coles (who does his best to be soulful on "Honeybuns"), trombonist Garnett Brown, flutist Les Spann, altoist James Spaulding, tenor saxophonist George Coleman, baritonist Pepper Adams, bassist Bob Cranshaw and drummer Mickey Roker, Pearson performs music in a style that would have fit in quite well on Blue Note. Most memorable among his originals is "Is That So." This is not an essential date, but it is nice to have this rarity back in print again. *—Scott Yanow*

Sweet Honey Bee / Dec. 7, 1966 / Blue Note ♦♦♦♦
Pianist/composer Duke Pearson leads an all-star group on this runthrough of seven of his compositions. The musicians (trumpeter Freddie Hubbard, altoist James Spaulding, tenorman Joe Henderson on tenor, bassist Ron Carter, drummer Mickey Roker and the pianist/leader) are actually more impressive than many of the compositions, although the swinging minor-toned "Big Bertha" deserved to become a standard. The frameworks are quite intelligent, with everyone not soloing on each selection and the improvisations are concise and clearly related to each tune's melody and mood. Although not quite essential, this CD reissue has some rewarding music. *—Scott Yanow*

☆ **The Right Touch** / Sep. 13, 1967 / Blue Note ♦♦♦♦♦
Duke Pearson rises to the challenge of writing for an all-star octet (with trumpeter Freddie Hubbard, trombonist Garnett Brown, altoist James Spaulding, Jerry Dodgion on alto and flute, Stanley Turrentine heard on tenor, bassist Gene Taylor, drummer Grady Tate and the leader/pianist), contributing colorful frameworks and consistently challenging compositions. The set is full of diverse melodies (the CD reissue has a previously unissued take of "Los Malos Hombres") played by a variety of distinctive soloists; many of these songs deserve to be revived. This is one of the finest recordings of Duke Pearson's career. *—Scott Yanow*

Introducing Duke Pearson's Big Band / Dec. 15, 1967-Dec. 3, 1968 / Blue Note ♦♦♦♦
Duke Pearson had always displayed a flair for arranging, even on small combo albums, so it shouldn't have come as a surprise that he would attempt his own big band record. What is a surprise is how successful *Introducing Duke Pearson's Big Band* actually is. Pearson leads 13 other musicians through a selection of nine songs, including four originals, two contemporary jazz tunes by Chick Corea and Joe Sample, and three standards. His originals are continually unpredictable and memorable, and his arrangements, especially of the standards, are provocative and intriguing. While it might not appeal to fans of Pearson's wonderful small-group hard bop sessions, it is unquestionably an experiment that works, and one that confirms his remarkable skills and talents. *—Stephen Thomas Erlewine*

I Don't Care Who Knows It / Jun. 24, 1968-Feb. 13, 1970 / Blue Note ♦♦♦♦
The sessions that comprise *I Don't Care Who Knows It* date from 1969 and 1970 (with one stray track from a 1968 session with Bobby Hutcherson), when Duke Pearson was experimenting with Latin jazz, soul-jazz, and funk; they are also the second-to-last dates the pianist ever recorded for Blue Note. Working with a fairly large group that included bassist Ron Carter, drummer Micey Roker, saxophonists Jerry Dodgion, Frank Foster, Lew Tabackin, trumpeter Burt Collins, trombonist Kenny Rupp, and occasionally vocalist Andy Bey, Pearson plays the electric piano throughout the majority of the album. As expected, the music swings with an understated funk, with the band alternating between standard hard-bop and mellow, soulful grooves. On the whole, *I Don't Care Who Knows It* is fairly uneven—the sessions don't set well together, but work well as individual sets. Nevertheless, there is enough good material here to make it worthwhile for soul-jazz, Latin-jazz and, especially, Pearson aficionados. *—Stephen Thomas Erlewine*

Now Hear This! / Dec. 2, 1968-Dec. 3, 1968 / Blue Note ♦♦♦♦♦
Duke Pearson returned to a big band setting for *Now Hear This!,* once again proving his

agility and inventiveness as an arranger and leader. Working with a larger band than before—the total number of musicians weighs in at 17—Pearson nevertheless keeps things clean and uncluttered. His compositions, as well as the songs he covers, cover a broad range of emotions, styles, and tonal colors, with lush ballads taking the center stage. Even if much of this music is beautiful, Pearson's arrangements take chances and are unconventional, which means it rewards close listening as well. *—Stephen Thomas Erlewine*

How Insensitive / Apr. 11, 1969-Apr. 14, 1969 / Blue Note ✦✦

Art Pepper

b. Sep. 1, 1925, Gardena, CA, **d.** Jun. 1, 1982, Panorama City, CA

Sax (Alto), Clarinet / Hard Bop, Cool, Bop

Despite a remarkably colorful and difficult life, Art Pepper was quite consistent in the recording studios; virtually every recording he made is well worth getting. In the 1950s he was one of the few altoists (along with Lee Konitz and Paul Desmond) that was able to develop his own sound despite the dominant influence of Charlie Parker. Some of his happiest days were during his years with Stan Kenton (1947-52) although he became a heroin addict in that period. The 1950s found the altoist recording frequently both as a leader and a sideman resulting in at least two classics (*Plays Modern Jazz Classics* and *Meets the Rhythm Section*) but he also spent two periods in jail due to drug offenses during 1953-56. Pepper was in top form during his Contemporary recordings of 1957-60 but the first half of his career ended abruptly with long prison sentences that dominated the 1960s. Pepper began his serious comeback in 1975 and the unthinkable happened. Under the guidance and inspiration of his wife Laurie, he not only recovered his former form but topped himself with intense solos that were quite unique; he also enjoyed occasionally playing clarinet. His recordings for Contemporary and Galaxy rank with the greatest work of his career. When Pepper died at the age of 56, he had attained his goal of becoming the world's great altoist. *—Scott Yanow*

☆ **The Complete Pacific Jazz Small Group Recordings of Art Pepper** / Jul. 26, 1956-Aug. 12, 1957 / Mosaic ✦✦✦✦✦

This superior three-LP box set reissues all of altoist Art Pepper's small-group dates for the Pacific Jazz label. Virtually all of the music has since been reissued on CD (part of it as *The Artistry of Pepper* and part of it under trumpeter Chet Baker's name), but the Mosaic box, which has an attractive booklet, is the definitive treatment of this chapter in Pepper's musical story. The great altoist is heard in a sextet with Baker and tenor saxophonist Richie Kamuca, on a version of "Tenderly" with Chet Baker's big band, with Baker and tenor Phil Urso in a different sextet, sharing the spotlight with tenor saxophonist Bill Perkins in a quintet, and heading a nonet playing arrangements by Shorty Rogers. The music is very much in the cool/bop tradition, but Pepper is instantly recognizable (he never sounded that much like Charlie Parker) and even at this early stage, he was at the top of his form. All 26 performances are quite enjoyable and swinging, making this hard-to-find set worth the search. *—Scott Yanow*

The Way It Was / Nov. 26, 1956-Nov. 23, 1960 / Contemporary/OJC ✦✦✦✦✦

Despite his very erratic lifestyle, altoist Art Pepper never made a bad record. This collection is better than most. The first four titles team together Pepper with tenor-saxophonist Warne Marsh, pianist Ronnie Ball, bassist Ben Tucker and drummer Gary Frommer for generally intriguing explorations of four standards. One can feel the influence of Lennie Tristano (with Pepper in Lee Konitz's place) although Pepper had his own sound and a more hard-swinging style. The success of the Pepper-Marsh frontline makes one wish that they had recorded together again. The other three selections are leftovers from a trio of classic Pepper albums and all are quite worthwhile. Pepper is heard backed by three separate rhythm sections which include pianists Red Garland, Dolo Coker or Wynton Kelly, either Paul Chambers or Jimmy Bond on bass and Philly Joe Jones, Frank Butler or Jimmy Cobb on drums. Overall this album sticks to bop standards and finds Art Pepper in top form. *—Scott Yanow*

The Artistry of Pepper / Dec. 11, 1956-Aug. 12, 1957 / Pacific Jazz ✦✦✦✦✦

This CD starts off with four selections from a date led by tenor saxophonist Bill Perkins that features altoist Art Pepper; the remainder of the quintet is comprised of pianist Jimmy Rowles, bassist Ben Tucker and Mel Lewis. While they perform boppish versions of two standards and a pair of Pepper originals, the remainder of the CD has a particularly strong set that showcases Pepper in a nonet arranged by Shorty Rogers. The music in the latter date are all Rogers originals and there are alternate takes of "Diablo's Dance" and "Popo" to round out the program. The other soloists include trumpeter Don Fagerquist, Bill Holman on tenor, baritonist Bud Shank, valve trombonist Stu Williamson and pianist Russ Freeman. Highly recommended to fans of Art Pepper and West Coast jazz. *—Scott Yanow*

★ **Meets the Rhythm Section** / Jan. 19, 1957 / Contemporary/OJC ✦✦✦✦✦

Packing a dried-out cork taped to his sax with a Band-Aid, Art Pepper appeared at L.A.'s *Contemporary Studios* to jam with guys he idolized, had never met, and had no idea he'd meet until that morning in January of 1957. No one had discussed which songs to play, but as soon as Art arrived (late), Philly Joe Jones of the Miles Davis rhythm section suggested Cole Porter's "You'd Be So Nice to Come Home To." No one objected, and after a single rehearsal, the historic collaboration was in swing. Widely accepted as a singular landmark in a career built of singular landmarks, Art said he felt as though this recording convinced him that emotion was the paramount impulse of jazz performance. Working "fresh" with Philly Joe, Paul Chambers, and Red Garland, Art forgave his own occasional "squawking," saying that in the studio he "…finally realized that in playing I've got to play exactly as I feel it. I want the emotion to come out rather than try to make everything perfect." The unpredictably stunning "Imagination" and Art's signature "Straight Life" are testament to such commitments to impulse, and the stark dynamics of the battery of percussion in congress with his saxophone is breathtaking. The knowledge that they play all the songs for the first and only time together in the order you hear them on the record, suggests a kind of jazz-narrative genius on behalf of the man behind the plan, Contemporary president Les Koenig. A diamond of recorded jazz history. *—Becky Byrkit*

☆ **Art Pepper - Eleven: Modern Jazz Classics** / Mar. 14, 1959-May 11, 1959 / Contemporary/OJC ✦✦✦✦✦

This is a true classic. Altoist Art Pepper is joined by an 11-piece band playing Marty Paich arrangements of a dozen jazz standards from the bop and cool jazz era. Trumpeter Jack Sheldon has a few solos, but the focus is very much on the altoist who is in peak form for this period. The CD reissue adds two additional versions of "Walkin'" and one of "Donna Lee" to the original program. Throughout, Pepper sounds quite inspired by Paich's charts which feature the band as an active part of the music rather than just in the background. Highlights of this highly enjoyable set include "Move," "Four Brothers," "Shaw Nuff," "Anthropology," and "Donna Lee," but there is not a single throwaway track to be heard. Essential music for all serious jazz collections. *—Scott Yanow*

Gettin' Together / Feb. 29, 1960 / Contemporary/OJC ✦✦✦✦✦

As a sort of follow-up to Art Pepper's matchup with Miles Davis's trio in the 1957 classic *Art Pepper Meets the Rhythm Section*, Pepper utilizes Davis's sidemen on this 1960 near-classic. In addition to pianist Wynton Kelly, bassist Paul Chambers and drummer Jimmy Cobb, trumpeter Conte Candoli makes the group a quintet on four of the eight numbers. The CD reissue adds "The Way You Look Tonight" (formerly only available on another LP) and an alternate take of the title cut to the original repertoire. This time around, rather than emphasizing standards, Pepper performs just three ("Softly, As in a Morning Sunrise," Thelonious Monk's "Rhythm-A-Ning" and "The Way You Look Tonight") and includes three originals of his own: "Diane," "Bijou the Poodle" and "Gettin' Together." The music is all very straightahead and bop-oriented, but as usual, Pepper brings something very personal and unique to his playing; he sounds like no one else. *—Scott Yanow*

Smack Up / Oct. 24, 1960-Oct. 25, 1960 / Contemporary/OJC ✦✦✦✦✦

The title of this recording (which has been reissued on CD with two takes of the otherwise unknown "Solid Citizens" added) is ironic and inadvertently truthful. Within a short period, Art Pepper would begin spending many years in jail due to his heroin addiction; this was his next-to-last album of this period. Despite the bleak future, the great altoist (who never seemed to make an uninspired record during his unstable life) is in excellent form in a quintet with trumpeter Jack Sheldon, pianist Pete Jolly, bassist Jimmy Bond and drummer Frank Butler. Highlights of this fine album include Harold Land's title cut, the 5/4 blues "Las Cuevas De Mario" and Ornette Coleman's "Tears Inside." *—Scott Yanow*

Intensity / Nov. 23, 1960-Nov. 25, 1960 / Contemporary/OJC ✦✦✦✦✦

This album, reissued on CD with an additional song, "Fine Points," was altoist Art Pepper's final one of his early period and was released when he was already serving a long prison sentence due to his addiction to heroin. Assisted by pianist Dolo Coker, bassist Jimmy Bond and drummer Frank Butler, Pepper was just starting to show the influence of John Coltrane and Ornette Coleman in his style, freeing up his playing and displaying a greater intensity during his improvisations. Ironically, Pepper sticks to swinging standards such as "I Can't Believe That You're in Love with Me," "Gone with the Wind" and "I Wished on the Moon" as points of departure on the interesting and largely enjoyable set. Excluding a 1973 recording with Mike Vax's big band, it would be 15 years before Art Pepper led another record date in the studios. *—Scott Yanow*

The Trip / Sep. 15, 1976-Sep. 16, 1976 / Contemporary/OJC ✦✦✦✦✦

Although some listeners prefer altoist Art Pepper's playing of the 1950s, when he re-emerged in 1975, there was a much greater emotional intensity to his improvisations, and his solos used a wider vocabulary with nonmusical and emotional sounds being added to his ideas as punctuations. This strong quartet date (with pianist George Cables, bassist David Williams and drummer Elvin Jones) finds Pepper performing Michel Legrand's "The Summer Knows," lesser-known tunes by Woody Shaw and Joe Gordon and three originals of his own; the CD reissue also has an alternate take of "The Trip." Powerful music. *—Scott Yanow*

No Limit / Mar. 26, 1977 / Contemporary/OJC ✦✦✦✦✦

Art Pepper's third recording in his comeback years was recorded in a studio but has the emotional intensity and chance-taking improvisations of his live concerts of the period. Joined by his regular group (pianist George Cables, bassist Tony Dumas and drummer Carl Burnett), Pepper performs lengthy versions of three of his originals (including the modal "My Laurie") and "Ballad of the Sad Young Men." "Mambo de la Pinta" is a little unusual because Pepper overdubbed himself on tenor to join his alto in the ensembles. Throughout this album (and during his final ten years), Art Pepper played every note as if it might be his last one. The passion displayed on this particular album is enough of a reason by itself to acquire it. *—Scott Yanow*

☆ **The Complete Village Vanguard Sessions** / Jul. 28, 1977-Jul. 30, 1977 / Contemporary ✦✦✦✦✦

The Complete Village Vanguard Sessions is an exhaustive box set that contains all 45 takes from Art Pepper's legendary stay at *the Village Vanguard*. Any serious Pepper fan will find a lot to treasure here, but the sheer size of the set makes it intimidating for less dedicated listeners. *—Leo Stanley*

Thursday Night at the Village Vanguard / Jul. 28, 1977 / Contemporary/OJC ✦✦✦✦✦

Art Pepper's appearances at *the Village Vanguard* in 1977 were a major success, making the brilliance of the West Coast-based altoist obvious to the New York critics. His historical stint at *the Vanguard* was originally made available on four LPs (all reissued as CDs with one additional selection added on each disc) and more recently in more expanded form as a nine-CD boxed set. The single CD reissue of the Thursday night portion features the great altoist on lengthy versions of "Valse Triste," a particularly passionate version of "Goodbye," "Blues for Les," "My Friend John" and "Blues for Heard." In addition to Pepper, his trio—pianist George Cables, bassist George Mraz and drummer Elvin Jones—is also in top form, and the music is consistently stimulating and emotional. *—Scott Yanow*

Friday Night at the Village Vanguard / Jul. 28, 1977-Jul. 30, 1977 / Contemporary/OJC ✦✦✦✦✦

The second of four releases taken from altoist Art Pepper's very successful stint at *the Village Vanguard* in July 1977 has been reissued on CD with one extra track, "A Night in Tunisia." Pepper, who is greatly assisted by a highly sympathetic rhythm section (pianist George Cables, bassist George Mraz and drummer Elvin Jones) is at his best on "Caravan," which finds him doubling on tenor, and on an intense rendition of "But Beautiful." All of this music is currently available as part of a massive nine-CD box set that really documents the historic engagement. *— Scott Yanow*

Saturday Night at the Village Vanguard / Jul. 28, 1977-Jul. 30, 1977 / Contemporary/OJC ♦♦♦♦♦
The CD reissue of this release, the third of four single sets that document Art Pepper's well-received engagement at *the Village Vanguard,* adds "For Freddie" to the original three-song program. The other selections, which feature pianist George Cables, bassist George Mraz and drummer Elvin Jones in addition to the altoist/leader, are intense interpretations of "You Go to My Head," Pepper's "The Trip" and a 16-minute version of "Cherokee." The altoist was entering his peak period and the entire gig has also been fully documented on a massive nine-CD box set. *— Scott Yanow*

☆ **Complete Galaxy Recordings** / Dec. 1, 1978-Apr. 14, 1982 / Galaxy ♦♦♦♦♦
Altoist Art Pepper was at the height of his career during his final five years. A brilliant improviser in the 1950s, by the late '70s the many dark experiences he had had in life were reflected in a deep emotional intensity in his playing. He played each solo as if it might be his last and his passion was brutally honest. This giant 16-CD Galaxy set features Pepper at the peak of his powers. Most of the performances are in a quartet setting although there is a session with strings, five unaccompanied alto solos (he also plays clarinet on a few tracks) and a pair of CDs in which Pepper duets with pianist George Cables. Although more general collectors may want to acquire some of the individual sessions first (most of which are available separately on CD), the more dedicated jazz fans are advised to save their money and acquire this essential package. *— Scott Yanow*

Landscape / Jul. 1979 / Galaxy/OJC ♦♦♦♦♦
Altoist Art Pepper was in inspired form during this Tokyo concert, which has also been reissued as part of a huge "complete" Galaxy box set. This particular single-CD features Pepper (along with pianist George Cables, bassist Tony Dumas and drummer Billy Higgins) on memorable versions of "True Blues," "Sometime" (during which Pepper switches to clarinet), "Landscape," "Avalon," "Over the Rainbow," "Straight Life" and the CD "bonus" cut "Mambo De La Pinta." Throughout, Pepper's intensity and go-for-broke style are exhilarating. *— Scott Yanow*

☆ **Straight Life** / Sep. 21, 1979 / Galaxy/OJC ♦♦♦♦♦
Altoist Art Pepper recorded many albums for the Galaxy label during 1979-82, all of which have been reissued in a massive 16-CD "complete" box set. This single CD is pretty definitive and serves as a perfect introduction to Pepper's second (and most rewarding) period. Not only is there a superior version of Pepper's famous title cut but very emotional (and explorative) renditions of "September Song" and "Nature Boy." Filling out this quartet set (which also features pianist Tommy Flanagan, bassist Red Mitchell and drummer Billy Higgins) are "Surf Ride," "Make a List" and "Long Ago and Far Away." Brilliant music. *— Scott Yanow*

Roadgame / Aug. 15, 1981 / Galaxy/OJC ♦♦♦♦♦
Altoist Art Pepper's 1981 appearances at Los Angeles' now-obsolete *Maiden Voyage* club were fully documented, resulting in three LPs and a greatly expanded program that is included on Pepper's massive "complete" Galaxy box set. This particular release, the only one thus far to be made available as a single CD, has Pepper and his quartet (with pianist George Cables, bassist David Williams and drummer Carl Burnett) performing "Roadgame" (an alternate take has been added to the CD reissue), "Road Waltz," an intense "Everything Happens to Me" and "When You're Smiling"; on the latter, Pepper switches to clarinet. Although only a year away from his death, the great Art Pepper was still very much in his prime for this memorable outing. *— Scott Yanow*

Oscar Peterson

b. Aug. 15, 1925, Montreal, Quebec, Canada
Piano / Swing, Bop
Oscar Peterson is one of the greatest piano players of all time. A pianist with phenomenal technique on the level of his idol, Art Tatum, Peterson's speed, dexterity and ability to swing at any tempo have long been amazing. Very effective in small groups, jam sessions and in accompanying singers, O.P. is at his absolute best when performing unaccompanied solos. His original style does not fall into any specific idiom. Like Erroll Garner and George Shearing, Peterson's distinctive playing formed during the mid- to late '40s and fell somewhere between swing and bop. Peterson has been criticized through the years because he uses so many notes, has not evolved much since the 1950s, and has recorded a remarkable number of albums. Perhaps it is because critics ran out of favorable adjectives to use early in his career; certainly it can be said that Peterson plays 100 notes when other pianists might use ten, but all 100 usually fit, and there is nothing wrong with showing off technique when it serves the music. As with Johnny Hodges and Thelonious Monk, to name two, Peterson spent his career growing within his style rather than making any major changes once his approach was set, certainly an acceptable way to handle one's career. Because he was Norman Granz's favorite pianist (along with Tatum) and the producer tended to record some of his artists excessively, Peterson has made an incredible number of albums. Not all are essential, and a few are routine, but the great majority are quite excellent, and there are dozens of classics. *— Scott Yanow*

The Complete Young Oscar Peterson / Apr. 30, 1945-Nov. 14, 1949 / RCA ♦♦♦♦♦
This double CD reissues the complete contents of two valuable LPs, the first 32 studio recordings of the great pianist Oscar Peterson. Recorded in Montreal, Canada, with local musicians during 1945-49 before his fame spread worldwide, these trio performances let one hear how Peterson sounded before he fully discovered bop and formed his own distinctive sound; the pianist already had his remarkable virtuosity, along with a taste for boogie-woogie that he later lost. Sticking mostly to swing standards and rollicking blues, Peterson sounds more touched by the style of Teddy Wilson than he would later on. Fascinating and enjoyable music, highly recommended for all serious jazz collections. *— Scott Yanow*

☆ **At Zardis'** / Nov. 8, 1955 / Pablo ♦♦♦♦♦
The group that Oscar Peterson led between 1953-58 with guitarist Herb Ellis and bassist Ray Brown was one of the great piano trios of all time. It was never so much a matter of Peterson having two other musicians accompany him as it was that they could meet the pianist as near-equals and consistently inspire him. And unlike most trios, Peterson's had many arranged sections that constantly needed rehearsals and were often quite dazzling. This live double-CD from 1955 has previously unreleased (and unknown) performances of 31 songs (28 standards plus three of Peterson's originals) that were released for the first time in 1994. The pianist is often in typically miraculous form, Ellis (whether playing harmonies, offering short solos or getting his guitar to sound like a conga by tapping it percussively) proves to be a perfect partner, and Brown's subtle but sometimes telepathic contributions should not be overlooked either. *— Scott Yanow*

☆ **At the Stratford Shakesperean Festival** / Aug. 8, 1956 / Verve ♦♦♦♦♦
This CD contains what is considered by most listeners to be the finest recording of the Oscar Peterson-Herb Ellis-Ray Brown trio, a group that lasted from 1953-58. Although the soloing was always quite passionate and spontaneous, it was the very complex arrangements that really made this unit sound unique. The live CD adds two selections ("Nuages" and the 13-minute "Daisy's Dream") to the original program and contains particularly memorable renditions of "Falling in Love with Love," "How About You," "Swinging on a Star," "How High the Moon" and "52nd Street Theme." Essential music from a classic band. *— Scott Yanow*

☆ **At the Concertgebouw** / Sep. 29, 1957-Oct. 9, 1957 / Verve ♦♦♦♦♦
Although the music on this CD was originally said to be recorded in Europe, it actually comes from a Chicago concert, and the five additional selections (last issued on an LP shared with The Modern Jazz Quartet), supposedly performed in Chicago, are from an appearance in Los Angeles. But, despite the geographical mixups, the music is consistently brilliant and often wondrous. The Oscar Peterson-Herb Ellis-Ray Brown Trio had been together for over four years and these would be among their last (and finest) recordings. The very tricky arrangements sandwiched remarkable solos with pianist Peterson sounding especially inspired. Together with their *Stratford Shakespearean* CD of the previous year, this set features the Trio at the peak of their powers. Highlights include "The Lady Is a Tramp," "Budo," "Daahoud," "Indiana" and "Joy Spring." *— Scott Yanow*

Oscar Peterson Plays the Cole Porter Songbook / Jul. 14, 1959-Aug. 9, 1959 / Verve ♦♦♦♦♦
Peterson reworks Cole Porter and says something original and distinctive. *— Ron Wynn*

Oscar Peterson Plays the Duke Ellington Song Book / Jul. 14, 1959-Aug. 9, 1959 / Verve ♦♦♦♦
Twice in the 1950s, pianist Oscar Peterson recorded an extensive series of songbooks devoted to one composer. From 1952-53, Peterson, guitarist Barney Kessel and bassist Ray Brown were extensively documented; in 1959, the pianist joined up with Brown and drummer Ed Thigpen to repeat many of the programs (since the group had changed and the music could now be cut in stereo) plus additional songbooks. This 1999 CD brings together both of Peterson's Duke Ellington tributes; the same dozen songs were recorded with each of the two groups. The Duke Ellington-associated material—which includes two songs by Mercer Ellington and Billy Strayhorn's "Take the 'A' Train"—mostly consist of familiar songs, except for Mercer Ellington's "John Hardy's Wife." While the earlier session has a fair amount of variety in tempo and mood, with Kessel offering a competing and complementary solo voice to the pianist, the 1959 album was obviously put together very quickly during a two-month period when Peterson was being recorded constantly. Most of the latter songs are taken at slower and relaxed tempos that make the playing close to easy-listening background music. A comparison of the different versions of most of the songs shows the difference. However, due to the generosity of this reissue (24 concise selections that almost total 73 minutes) and the former rarity of the material (especially the Kessel date), Peterson fans will want to acquire this. *— Scott Yanow*

Jazz Soul of Oscar Peterson/Affinity / Jul. 21, 1959-Sep. 27, 1962 / Verve ♦♦♦♦♦
This 1996 single-CD reissues the complete contents of two former LPs by the Oscar Peterson Trio (consisting of pianist Peterson, bassist Ray Brown and drummer Ed Thigpen) in 1959 and 1962. Although the pianist is virtually always the lead voice, Brown and Thigpen both make strong (if subtle) contributions to the music. Highlights include "Liza," "Con Alma," "Waltz for Debby," Brown's "The Gravy Waltz" and "Yours Is My Heart Alone." An above-average release (and rather generous at 74 minutes) from the much-recorded Oscar Peterson. *— Scott Yanow*

The Trio [Verve] / Sep. 1961-Oct. 1961 / Verve ♦♦♦♦
Oscar Peterson's Trio with bassist Ray Brown and drummer Ed Thigpen lacked the competitiveness of his earlier group with Brown and guitarist Herb Ellis and the later daring of his solo performances, but the pianist was generally in peak form during this era. He sticks to standards on this live CD (a good example of the Trio's playing), stretching out "Sometimes I'm Happy" creatively for over 11 minutes and uplifting such songs as "In the Wee Small Hours of the Morning," "Chicago" and "The Night We Called It a Day." Few surprises occur, but Peterson plays at such a consistently high level that one doesn't mind. *— Scott Yanow*

West Side Story / Jan. 24, 1962-Jan. 25, 1962 / Verve ♦♦♦
The Oscar Peterson Trio (comprised of pianist Peterson, bassist Ray Brown and drummer Ed Thigpen) do a fine job of interpreting six melodies from *West Side Story* in addition to a closing reprise of the themes. Originally recorded for Verve, this well-recorded reissue is brief on time (31 minutes) and not all that essential but it swings nicely and is quite enjoyable. *— Scott Yanow*

Night Train / 1962 / Verve ♦♦♦♦
Verve's Master Edition of the Oscar Peterson Trio date released as *Night Train* includes stately covers of blues and R&B standards like "The Honeydripper," "C-Jam Blues," "Georgia on My Mind," "Bags' Groove," "Moten Swing" and "Things Ain't What They Used to Be." Ray Brown and Ed Thigpen provide tight accompaniment, and there are six pereviously unavailable tracks recorded the same day, including "My Heart Belongs to Daddy" and "Volare," as well as alternate takes of "Happy-Go-Lucky Local" and "Moten Swing." *— John Bush*

☆ **Oscar Peterson Trio Plus One** / Feb. 26, 1964 / Verve ✦✦✦✦✦
This is a true classic. Flugelhornist Clark Terry, who long has had the happiest sound in jazz, performs ten enthusiastic and generally hard-swinging songs with the Oscar Peterson Trio (which at the time included bassist Ray Brown and drummer Ed Thigpen). Terry is quite exuberant on such pieces as "Brotherhood of Man" and "Mack the Knife" and even the ballads ("They Didn't Believe Me" and "I Want a Little Girl" among them) are full of excitement. This session, though, is best known for having introduced Clark Terry's humorous "Mumbles" vocals which can be heard on that piece and "Incoherent Blues." This delightful and essential release has fortunately been reissued on CD. *—Scott Yanow*

With Respect to Nat / Oct. 28, 1965-Nov. 13, 1965 / Verve ✦✦✦✦✦
This album is quite unusual. Recorded shortly after Nat King Cole's death, pianist Oscar Peterson takes vocals on all but one of the dozen selections, sounding almost exactly like Cole. Peterson, who rarely ever sang, is very effective on the well-rounded program whether being backed by a big band (arranged by Manny Albam) on half of the selections, or recreating both the spirit of the Nat King Cole Trio and his own group of the late '50s during a reunion with guitarist Herb Ellis and basssist Ray Brown. *—Scott Yanow*

☆ **My Favorite Instrument** / Apr. 1968 / Verve ✦✦✦✦✦
Oscar Peterson recorded a remarkable amount of albums during his career but surprisingly this was his first full record of unaccompanied piano solos. Some observers consider his MPS recordings to be his best (quite a few are collected in the four-CD reissue *Exclusively for My Friends* including this one). The solo album features Peterson (freed from the constraints of his trio) stretching out on nine familiar standards, really tearing into a few of them including "Perdido," "Bye Bye Blackbird," "Lulu's Back in Town" while giving "Little Girl Blue" a beautiful lyrical treatment. A prelude to his outstanding Pablo recordings, *My Favourite Instrument* is one of Peterson's top albums of the 1960s. *—Scott Yanow*

☆ **Tracks** / Nov. 1970 / Verve ✦✦✦✦✦
Pianist Oscar Peterson is frequently astounding on this solo set. After nearly 20 years of mostly performing with trios, O.P. sounds quite liberated in this setting, throwing in some hot stride, unexpected changes in tempoes and keys, and surprises whenever he thinks of it. "Give Me the Simple Life," "Honeysuckle Rose" and the ironically titled "A Little Jazz Exercise" are quite remarkable yet Peterson also leaves space for some sensitive ballads. *—Scott Yanow*

★ **The Trio [Pablo]** / May 16, 1973-May 19, 1973 / Pablo/OJC ✦✦✦✦✦
Guitarist Joe Pass and bassist Niels Pedersen both play well on these live performances but the reason to acquire this set is for the remarkable Oscar Peterson. The pianist investigates several jazz styles brilliantly on "Blues Etude" (including stride and boogie-woogie), plays exciting versions of his "Chicago Blues" and "Easy Listening Blues," tears into "Secret Love" and shows honest emotion on "Come Sunday." Peterson really flourished during his years with Norman Granz's Pablo label and this was one of his finest recordings of the period. *—Scott Yanow*

Oscar Peterson & Roy Eldridge / Dec. 8, 1974 / Pablo/OJC ✦✦✦✦✦
Part of his five sessions that featured duets with different trumpeters, pianist Oscar Peterson's matchup with trumpeter Roy Eldridge (reissued on CD) has its strong moments. Eldridge did not quite have the range of his earlier years but his competitive streak had not mellowed with age. Peterson pushes Eldridge to his limit and the music is generally quite exciting. Highlights include "Little Jazz," "Sunday" and "Between the Devil and the Deep Blue Sea." *—Scott Yanow*

Oscar Peterson & Harry Edison / Dec. 21, 1974 / Pablo/OJC ✦✦✦✦✦
The third of Oscar Peterson's five duet albums with great trumpeters (the other encounters feature Dizzy Gillespie, Roy Eldridge, Clark Terry and Jon Faddis) teams the masterful pianist with the great swing stylist Harry "Sweets" Edison. The trumpeter, who uses repetition to great degree and had pared his style down to a relatively few notes, matches well with the virtuosic Peterson on these seven standards and their two simple originals "Basie" and "Signify." Together Edison and O.P. give the impression that their chancetaking improvisations are completely logical and a lot easier to play than they really are. *—Scott Yanow*

Live at the North Sea Jazz Festival / Jul. 13, 1980 / Pablo ✦✦✦✦✦
This double album matches and mixes together four masterful musicians: pianist Oscar Peterson, guitarist Joe Pass, bassist Niels Pedersen and harmonica great Toots Thielemans. Together they perform O.P.'s "City Lights" and ten veteran standards with creativity, wit and solid swing. There are a few miraculous moments as one would expect from musicians of this caliber and the results are generally quite memorable. *—Scott Yanow*

Two of the Few / Jan. 20, 1983 / Pablo/OJC ✦✦✦✦✦
This CD reissue brings back a unique duet recording featuring pianist Oscar Peterson and vibraphonist Milt Jackson. One would expect the instrumentation to feature mostly ballads but the opposite is true as O.P. and Bags romp through quite a few uptempo pieces. Highlights include "Lady Be Good," "Limehouse Blues," "Reunion Blues" and "Just You, Just Me." This is a successful and highly enjoyable outing. *—Scott Yanow*

Oscar Peterson with Harry Edison & Eddie Vinson / Nov. 12, 1986 / Pablo ✦✦✦✦✦
During Nov. 12-14, 1986, pianist Oscar Peterson recorded three albums worth of material for Norman Granz's Pablo label. This particular CD features the great pianist with his quartet (bassist Dave Young, drummer Martin Drew and guest guitarist Joe Pass) along with trumpeter Harry "Sweets" Edison and altoist Eddie "Cleanhead" Vinson. The strictly instrumental set has many fine solos on appealing tunes such as "Stuffy," "Broadway" and the lengthy blues "Slooow Drag." This boppish session gave Vinson a rare chance to really stretch out and he was up for the challenge. *—Scott Yanow*

The More I See You / Jan. 15, 1995-Jan. 16, 1995 / Telarc ✦✦✦✦✦
After Oscar Peterson suffered a severe stroke in the spring of 1993, it was feared that he would never again play on a professional level, but two years of intense therapy resulted in the masterful pianist returning to what sounds on this Telarc CD like near-prime form. For the all-star date, Peterson tears into seven standards and two blues and outswings all potential competitors. Altoist Benny Carter at 87 sounds like he is 47 (if Carter had retired back in 1940 he would still be a legend) and flugelhornist Clark Terry (now 74) proves to be not only (along with the remarkable 90-year old Doc Cheatham) the finest trumpeter over 70 but one of the top brassmen of any age. The cool-toned guitarist Lorne Lofsky and drummer Lewis Nash are also strong assets while bassist Ray Brown (a year younger than Peterson at a mere 68) displays his typical limitless energy. on appealing tunes such as "In a Mellow Tone," "When My Dream Boat Comes Home" and a medium-up version of "For All We Know," the musicians all play up to their usual high level, making this a joyous comeback album for the great Oscar Peterson. *—Scott Yanow*

Live at the Blue Note / Nov. 24, 1998-Nov. 26, 1998 / Telarc ✦✦✦✦✦
Oscar Peterson's landmark meeting with Milt Jackson in the mid-'60s produced the very successful studio date *Very Tall*. They've played and recorded together on a number of occasions since then, joined by Ray Brown more often than not, but these live tracks recorded at *the Blue Note* are among their most satisfying sessions. Peterson continues his strong comeback from the serious stroke that he suffered in 1993, replacing his once ferocious tempos with an uncanny lyricism. Brown's introduction to "Blues for JR" and his bass solo medley are superb, while Jackson remains a master of the blues. The finale of "Caravan" features drummer Karriem Riggins and brings the session to a thunderous climax. Highly recommended. *—Ken Dryden*

Michel Petrucciani

b. Dec. 28, 1962, Orange, France, **d.** Jan. 6, 1999, Paris, France
Piano / Contemporary Jazz, Post-Bop
Michel Petrucciani overcame the effects of osteogenensis imperfecta (a bone disease that greatly stunted his growth) to become a powerful pianist. Originally greatly influenced by Bill Evans and to a lesser extent Keith Jarrett, Petrucciani since developed his own individual voice. He started by playing in the family band with his guitarist father and bassist brother. At the age of 15 he had the opportunity to play with Kenny Clarke and Clark Terry and at 17 he made his first recording. Petrucciani toured France with Lee Konitz in a duo (1980) and moved to the U.S. in 1982. At that time he coaxed Charles Lloyd out of retirement and toured with his quartet, a mutually beneficial relationship. Petrucciani was a strong attraction in the U.S., usually playing with a quartet (sometimes featuring Adam Holzman's synthesizer for color) or as a soloist; in 1986 he recorded at Montreux with Jim Hall and Wayne Shorter. Although Petrucciani's ability to overcome his affliction was admirable, his impressive playing stood by itself; he died of a pulmonary infection on January 6, 1999. *—Scott Yanow*

100 Hearts / Jun. 1983 / Concord Jazz ✦✦✦✦✦
If it were not for Michel Petrucciani's good taste, it is likely that his very impressive technique would dominate his solos. As it is, the pianist has been able to use his technique in surprising ways, avoiding the obvious and showing self-restraint while coming up with ingenious ideas in his improvisations. This solo album, his first for an American label, finds Petrucciani exploring pieces by Ornette Coleman, Charlie Haden, and Sonny Rollins, in addition to two of his own songs and a lengthy wandering medley that somehow incorporates "Someday My Prince Will Come," "All the Things You Are," "A Child Is Born," and Bill Evans' "Very Early" into a collage. A very impressive outing. *—Scott Yanow*

The Best of the Blue Note Years / 1985-1991 / Blue Note ✦✦✦✦
The single-disc *Best Of* outing is a mixed blessing. The 12 performances include the wonderful "Bimini" from *Power Of Three*, as well as trio and quartet takes from arguably his best release, *Pianism*, and six cuts with him playing acoustic and electric keyboards on the same composition. But the disc gives a grab-bag feel for Petrucciani the composer and improviser; we can't tell how his approach evolved, nor chart his growth or stagnation. In addition, the company doesn't even provide complete recording information, omitting the dates for the tracks. A final insult are the ridiculously exaggerated, incomplete liner notes in which Petrucciani is placed in the company of Louis Armstrong, Duke Ellington and Count Basie, an absurd comparison. This isn't the way to celebrate or document a musician's contributions to a label. *—Ron Wynn*

● **Power of Three** / Jul. 14, 1987 / Blue Note ✦✦✦✦✦
This is an all-star summit that works quite well. Pianist Michel Petrucciani, a major jazz musician who had already led 11 record dates by this time (despite still being only 23), teams up with guitarist Jim Hall at the 1986 *Montreux Jazz Festival* for two lyrical duets: the altered blues "Careful," and in which they comp exquisitely behind each other's solos, and "In a Sentimental Mood." Petrucciani and Hall are joined by Wayne Shorter on soprano and tenor for "Limbo," "Morning Blues" and the calypso "Bimini," and these songs feature some of Shorter's finest jazz playing of the era. Highly recommended. *—Scott Yanow*

Promenade with Duke / 1993 / Blue Note ✦✦✦✦
In an interview, Michel Petrucciani said ".. my biggest inspiration is Duke Ellington, because in my very early age he gave [me] the inspiration to play the piano." With *Promenade with Duke* Petrucciani not only honors music Ellington composed, but music with which he was associated. There's some Billy Strayhorn pieces and other songs where Ellington's compositional contributions are arguably marginal. That the album offers an adventure in harmony is predicted by the first cut, "Caravan." Stretching over seven minutes in length, it explores, in-depth, virtually every nuance of this 1936 hit which Ellington wrote with trombonist Juan Tizol. Bold approaches to harmonies notwithstanding, Petrucciani does not desert his basic let-it-all-hang-out romanticism which he celebrates on "Lush Life." Petrucciani emphasizes feelings of sentimentality in his rendition of "In a Sentimental Mood." His interpretation is brooding and introspective, but every now and then some bright chords hold out the hope that the somber climate may be passing. Petrucciani is a master at clarifying the mood he is trying to create with his piano. Not all the music on the album is familiar Ellington, as shown

in the presence of two rarely performed pieces, "Hidden Joy" and "One Night in the Hotel." It is on the well-known "Take the A Train," however, that Petrucciani expresses best the joy he experiences with Ellington's music and the influence it has had on him. His is a rousing, twisting rendition of the Duke's signature tune. *Promenade with Duke* is one of the more innovative and stimulating sets of solo piano performances of Ellington's music on disc. *—Dave Nathan*

Au Theatre Des Champs-Elysees / Nov. 14, 1994 / Dreyfus ♦♦♦♦
Michel Petrucciani worked long and hard to come up with some of the extensive medleys heard in this brilliant solo piano concert. Much like the intriguing medley "Potpourri" heard on his American debut (*100 Hearts*), Petrucciani blends a number of recurring themes into a smoldering performance; the 40-plus-minute opening medley includes numerous songs, including "Maiden Voyage," "On Green Dolphin Street" and more. A breakaway run through Monk's "I Mean You" unfolds into a very dramatic arrangement of "'Round Midnight." His original waltz "Even Mice Dance" is segued into a startling virtuoso adaptation of "Caravan." Two original ballads, "Night Sun In Blois" and "Love Letter," add to the rich texture of this live date. The two-CD set closes with a dazzling rendition of "Besame Mucho," which he restores to grace by bringing out the lyricism of this very sad ballad, which is often destroyed when played by less talented musicians. *—Ken Dryden*

Solo Live / Feb. 27, 1999 / Dreyfus ♦♦♦♦♦
Solo Live, released shortly after his death, marks pianist Michel Petrucciani's lasting solo gift to the jazz world. Though clearly a virtuoso on his instrument, his playing always seemed to reflect as much respect for the audience as it did for his own talent. At its essence, Petrucciani's music is remarkably buoyant, decidedly joyful, improvisationally aggressive, and, above all, intended to evoke an emotional response on the part of the listener. His amazing reading of Ellington's "Caravan" is characteristic of this unique style. However, the pianist may best be remembered for his original compositions and three of his most memorable are included here. "Looking Up, " as the title would suggest, is overtly optimistic and inherently hopeful. "Home" is a clearly enunciated statement of warmth and comfort. "Brazilian Like" is orchestral and melodic to the point at which the tune remains in one's head long after its conclusion. Petrucciani closes the album with the medley of "She Did It Again/Take the A Train/She Did It Again"—his original sandwiched around Strayhorn's classic. A befitting set-closer for this extraordinary musician. *—Brian Bartolini*

Oscar Pettiford

b. Sep. 30, 1922, Okmulgee, OK, **d.** Sep. 8, 1960, Copenhagen, Denmark
Cello, Bass / Bop
Oscar Pettiford was (along with Charles Mingus) the top bassist of the 1945-60 period and the successor to the late Jimmy Blanton. In addition, he was the first major jazz soloist on the cello. A bop pioneer, it would have been very interesting to hear what Pettiford would have done during the avant-garde '60s if he had not died unexpectedly in 1960. He hit the big time in 1943 participating on Coleman Hawkins's famous "The Man I Love" session; he also recorded with Earl Hines and Ben Webster during this period. Pettiford co-led an early bop group with Dizzy Gillespie in 1944 and in 1945 went with Hawkins to the West Coast. Pettiford was part of Duke Ellington's Orchestra during much of 1945-48 (fulfilling his role as the next step beyond Jimmy Blanton) and worked with Woody Herman in 1949. Throughout the 1950s he mostly worked as a leader, although he appeared on many records both as a sideman and a leader, including with Thelonious Monk in 1955-56. Among Pettiford's better-known compositions are "Tricotism," "Laverne Walk," "Bohemia After Dark" and "Swingin' Till the Girls Come Home." *—Scott Yanow*

First Bass / Jun. 1953-Jul. 5, 1960 / IAJRC ♦♦♦♦♦
The remarkable Oscar Pettiford, arguably the top bassist in jazz during 1945-60 (Charles Mingus was his closest competitor) and the first great jazz cellist (preceded only by Harry Babasin), is showcased on 14 formerly rare titles on this CD from the collectors' IAJRC label. Pettiford is heard on four fascinating titles with Babasin, in which the two cellists are backed by a rhythm section, as part of a small group with vibraphonist Lionel Hampton, in a trio with guitarist Attila Zoller, jamming with pianist Phineas Newborn in 1958 (on "Yardbird Suite," where they are also joined by altoist Lee Konitz and tenorman Zoot Sims), and with top European players on three numbers from 1960. Whether playing bass or cello, Oscar Pettiford is well-featured on each selection, yet his strong soloing and creative ideas keep the music from ever becoming dull or predictable. Highly recommended for bop collectors. *—Scott Yanow*

The New Oscar Pettiford Sextet / Dec. 19, 1953-Aug. 22, 1959 / Debut/OJC ♦♦♦♦♦
One of the earliest bassists on the bebop scene in 1940s New York, Oscar Pettiford was also an unusually intrepid experimenter when it came to instrumentation. His cello playing is justly famous, and on the seven tracks that form the core of this reissue CD Pettiford includes a French horn (played by Julian Watkins) in the sextet. But most noteworthy of all is the quality of his compositions. "Pendulum at Falcon's Lair" is a piece of world-class bebop writing, while "Tamalpais Love Song" is almost classical in its structure, achieving a counterintuitive combination of complexity and simple beauty. In addition to the seven tracks from Pettiford's original 1953 session, this reissue includes four more that he recorded as sideman to saxophonist Serge Chaloff in 1949—the four are more strictly in the bop tradition and are, unfortunately, not recorded quite as well, but they demonstrate Pettiford's exceptional skill as an accompanist. *—Rick Anderson*

Another One / Aug. 12, 1955 / Bethlehem Archives/Avenue Jazz ♦♦♦♦
Oscar Pettiford became a major influence on a number of jazz artists along with fellow bassists Jimmy Blanton and Charles Mingus. *Another One,* Pettiford's third album as a leader for the Bethlehem label, was recorded in 1955. This exceptional date features the horns of Donald Byrd, Ernie Royal, Bob Brookmeyer, Gigi Gryce, and Jerome Richardson. Highlights include the Pettiford-penned "Bohemia After Dark," named after the club in Greenwich Village and acknowledged as a jazz standard, "Stardust," featuring Pettiford's poetic bass faintly accompanied by pianist Don Abney, and "Minor Seventh Heaven," with Pettiford switching to cello. This is not just a bebop date; Pettiford had the range to incorporate influences like Duke Ellington and calypso, creating a full, lyrical band sound that matched his bass playing. Pettiford's legacy was cut short after he passed away suddenly in 1958 in Copenhagen at the age of 37. *—Al Campbell*

★ **Deep Passion** / Jun. 11, 1956-Sep. 6, 1957 / Impulse! ♦♦♦♦♦
Two former Lp's by big bands led by bassist Oscar Pettiford (who doubles on cello) are reissued in full on this single CD. The arrangements by Gigi Gryce, Lucky Thompson and Benny Golson feature a lot of concise solos, an inventive use of the harp (either by Janet Putnam or Betty Glamann) and colorful ensembles. Among the many soloists are trumpeter Art Farmer, trombonists Jimmy Cleveland and Al Grey, the French horn of Julius Watkins, the tenors of Thompson or Golson and the bassist-leader. This formerly rare music is highly recommended to straightahead jazz fans for it is full of fresh material and subtle surprises. *—Scott Yanow*

Barre Phillips

b. Oct. 27, 1934, San Francisco, CA
Bass / Improvisation, Avant-Garde Jazz, Modern Creative
This adventurous and talented bassist and composer for bass is largely known for an extraordinary album produced in the early days of Opus One (#2) called *Journal Violone;* in this wide-ranging and always interesting 40-minute work Phillips explored many fresh pathways in the possibilities of experimental music for contrabass. Mr. Phillips was born in 1934 in San Francisco and Received a B.A. in Spanish in 1958. The original *Journal Violone* was recorded in the parish church of St. James' Norlands, in London, in November of 1968.

Ten years later Mr. Phillips recorded a *Journal Violone #2* for ECM (-1-1149) with reedman John Surman and singer Aina Kemanis which, in the opinion of at least one critic at the time, in no way achieved the honesty and creativity of the first *Journal.* Jurgen Gothe in the 1981 record-review publication *Pop Corner* said that Phillips had "succumbed to the ECM Osterizer, that massive musical mush-making machine run by Manfred Eicher whose avowed purpose is to turn us all in blanc-mange" and that the *Journal Vol. 2* was "as bland as a Ford Pinto full of Cream of Wheat."

Vol. One, however, is still available from the excellent Opus One Label; the record review *Coda* called it "perhaps the best music of its kind yet recorded." *—Philip Krumm*

● **Camouflage** / May 12, 1989 / Victo ♦♦♦♦
Recorded live at Vancouver's *Western Front* in 1990, this solo recording by bassist extraordinaire Barre Phillips is a set of improvisations. They explore not only Mr. Phillips' more than considerable abilities as a musician, but the limits of the instrument itself as a method of expression. Over six tracks and nearly one hour, Phillips bows, plucks, strums, bangs on, and beats his double bass, wrenching from it every possible emotion and tone that he was capable of revealing at the time. The title track, completely bowed, opens the record. Beginning as somber reflection, it gradually builds in tension using the D and A strings as elemental forces against the bottom C and G. About midway, that taught wire snaps and a cacophony of textures and timbres emerge, offering new rhythmic possibilities and sonic architectures. "Covered," which follows at ten minutes, is Phillips' solo playing as evidenced on his solo recording for ECM. While played traditionally, the harmonic ideas are anything but. There is a complexity here that reveals how drones, when played against various rhythmic figures, accentuate dynamics and create chordal backdrops for other melodic frameworks that in turn create a framework for new drones. The recording closes with the meditative "Around Again." This is Mr. Phillips making his bass "sing" reflectively, creating the manner and syntax of a sung ballad by using the instrument's "traditional" voice and stretching its tonality over three-and-a-half octaves. Longer lines give way to short staccato bursts that are deeply expressive and sonorous. *Camouflage* is a recording of seeming disguises for an instrument thought to be merely a rhythmic tool to anchor soloists to a structure. In the hands of a master musician like Mr. Phillips, his 40 years as a professional have taught him that appearances in vision and sound can be deceiving. *—Thom Jurek*

Trignition / 1998-1999 / Nine Winds ♦♦♦
Here's yet another interesting juxtaposition for multi-woodwindist Vinny Golia in this go-round between two bassists. Veteran creative improviser Barre Phillips and 20th century pioneer Bertram Turetzky do not even remotely approach time frames, swing or groove, but explore various sonic languages while Golia prompts them on his variety of clarinets and saxophones.

The nine selections claim no writer's credits; they are collective, spontaneous compositions. The two shorties, "Inconabular" and "Saylaa," have octave-leaping bassists, with a fluttering clarinet on the former and Golia's East Indian overdubbed sudnas in chaotic form on the latter. "The Incomplete Touching of the Ground" is free and flowing in no time, with Golia's clarinet again fluttering over strident, soaring, and pounding bass incursions. "Spherics & Whistles" is mostly mezzo forte range, with bass clarinet leading the bassists through alternating hole-boring, open-ended longer tones, and counterpointed lines. There are three takes, 11 to 13 minutes each, on the implications of space travel. Golia's bleeping, probing bari on "Bigman, Hugeman!" buoys nebulous chit-chat from Phillips and Turetzky; this leads to free gliding, and a reverent, peaceful section which precedes a scratchy, virulent ending. "It Was Probably the Last One to Be Named" starts with Golia's deeply squawky bass clarinet with reverberating, then percussionistic basses, and a fine duet between the two, with Golia laying out for the most part, but also seeping in from underneath in spooky, lugubrious, labyrinth undertones. "Anodyne" streaks to a galaxy that's farther out, with endless, vast, choppy nuances and Golia's clarinet navigating upfront.

The avant maven will find much here to appreciate, for it is a heavy wellspring of expression that bears close listening. *—Michael G. Nastos*

Flip Phillips (Joseph Edward Filipelli)

b. Feb. 26, 1915, Brooklyn, NY, **d.** Aug. 17, 2001
Sax (Tenor) / East Coast Blues, Jump Blues, Swing, Bop
Flip Phillips, who angered some critics early on because he gained riotous applause for his exciting solos during Jazz at the Philharmonic concerts, has for over 50 years been an excellent tenor saxophonist equally gifted on stomps, ballads and standards. He played clarinet regularly in a Brooklyn restaurant during 1934-39, was in Frankie Newton's group (1940-41) and spent time in the bands of Benny Goodman, Wingy Manone and Red Norvo. However it was in 1944 that he had his breakthrough. As a well-featured soloist with Woody Herman's Herd (1944-46), Phillips became a big star. His warm tenor was most influenced by Ben Webster but sounded distinctive even at that early stage. He toured regularly with Jazz at the Philharmonic during 1946-57, scoring a bit of a sensation with his honking solo on "Perdido" and holding his own with heavy competition (including Charlie Parker and Lester Young). He occasionally co-led a group with Bill Harris and that band was the nucleus of the ensemble that Benny Goodman used in 1959. Phillips then retired to Florida for 15 years, playing on just an occasional basis, taking up the bass clarinet as a double and making only a sporadic record date. But by 1975 he was back in music full-time making quite a few records and playing at festivals and jazz parties. Even as he passed his 80th birthday, Flip Phillips had lost none of the enthusiasm or ability that he had a half-century earlier. *—Scott Yanow*

★ **A Melody from the Sky** / Sep. 1944-Nov. 1945 / Doctor Jazz ✦✦✦✦✦
This CD is a straight reissue of a Flying Dutchman LP and has all four of tenor-saxophonist Flip Phillips's recording sessions as a leader prior to 1949. At the time he was a key member of Woody Herman's First Herd and these performances have short solos from other Herman sidemen (including trombonist Bill Harris and Neal Hefti on trumpet) although Phillips is the main star. His jumping tenor was already quite distinctive whether on romps or ballads. "Sweet and Lovely" and "Stompin' at the Savoy" are highpoints of this definitive early Flip Phillips set. *—Scott Yanow*

A Sound Investment / Feb. 16, 1971-Feb. 9, 1973 / Concord Jazz ✦✦✦✦✦
By sheer coincidence, this album was recorded a few months before and released just one month after the 1987 stock market crash; hence the upticking curve on the graph depicted on the jacket became a positive antidote of sorts to the financial screwups of the time. But without even seeing the jacket, one is always aware of the good vibes these tenor players generate in these small-combo contemporary swing sessions. Already in his 70s, Flip still plays with mature, husky soul, a slightly wailing upper register, and a feeling for space, while Hamilton's busier, directly booming tone becomes a neutral foil. Of the eight tunes, five of them are by Phillips, and the two rarely miss an opportunity to trade riffs good-naturedly in a friendly JATP manner. Good supporting cast, too, with guitarist Chris Flory making his mark as the ghost of Charlie Christian peers over the music stand. *—Richard S. Ginell*

● **Real Swinger** / May 1988-Jun. 1988 / Concord Jazz ✦✦✦✦✦
The great tenor saxophonist Flip Phillips (73 at the time) is heard in prime form throughout this exciting CD. Assisted by guitarists Howard Alden and Wayne Wright, pianist Dick Hyman, bassist Jack Lesberg and drummer Butch Miles, Phillips alternately roars and purrs throughout the set. His two originals ("Hashimoto's Blues" and "Christian Scientist") are excellent, and the choice of songs (which include Slim Gaillard's "Vol Vitu Gailey Star," "Tricotism" and "Cotton Tail") is inspired. With Alden and Hyman also contributing plenty of solos and Phillips making two appearances on bass clarinet (for "I Got a Right to Sing the Blues" and "Poor Butterfly"), this is a memorable outing that is highly recommended to fans of straight-ahead jazz. *—Scott Yanow*

Live at the 1993 Floating Jazz Festival / Nov. 1, 1993-Nov. 3, 1993 / Chiaroscuro ✦✦✦✦
Flip Phillips was 79 at the time of this live performance but proves to still be very much in his musical prime. Joined by a rhythm section comprised of fellow veterans (pianist Derek Smith, guitarist Bucky Pizzarelli, bassist Milt Hinton and drummer Ray Mosca), Phillips gives standards and riff tunes warm and often hard-swinging treatment. Other than a few tasteless (if humorous) jokes, this is a flawless release that serves as a definitive portrait of Flip Phillips in his later years. *—Scott Yanow*

Flip Wails: The Best of the Verve Years / Oct. 1947-Dec. 1957 / Verve ✦✦✦✦✦
Although Flip Phillips was a mainstay of Norman Granz' Jazz At The Philharmonic tours and recordings, Granz seldom put sessions around him, preferring to use him as a core group mainstay. This single-disc collection puts together a variety of performances beginning with a Howard McGhee session from 1947, and traveling throughout the 1950s showing Phillips at his romping best. Highlights include "Three Little Words," "Singing the Blues," a bebopping "Znarg's Blues" and a stately "If I Had You." Great playing from everyone aboard but Phillips sounds best in the company of Bill Harris on several tracks, and on a Buddy Rich Quartet session that closes out the disc. *—Cub Koda*

Swing Is the Thing! / Oct. 12, 1999-Oct. 13, 1999 / Verve ✦✦✦✦✦
Amazingly enough, this is 85-year-old Flip Phillips' first major-label recording as a leader, as well as one of the few albums he's ever released as a leader. You'd have to say that the old man still has plenty of wind in him, because this is a blowing session from start to finish, especially on tracks like "The Mark of Zorro" (versions of which open and close the album), "Where or When," and "Flip the Whip," when Phillips is joined by one or both of two fellow tenor men, James Carter and Joe Lovano. The rest of the time, he sticks with a rhythm section consisting of Howard Alden, Benny Green, Christian McBride, and Kenny Washington, though Duke Ellington's "In a Mellow Tune" is a duet with bassist McBride and "This Is All I Ask" pairs him with guitarist Alden. Alden especially also gets plenty of solo time in on what are really group performances. But that takes nothing away from the spry leader, who can roar on such numbers as the title tune and whisper with a husky tone on slow burners like "For All We Know." His playing is an inspiration. *—William Ruhlmann*

Courtney Pine

b. Mar. 18, 1964, London, England
Sax (Tenor), Sax (Soprano) / Post-Bop
For a while Courtney Pine appeared as if he were going to be the next Wynton Marsalis. While Marsalis in the mid-'80s was doing close impressions of mid-'60s Miles Davis, Pine's impressive playing was nearly identical to John Coltrane's of the same era. Since then Pine has received less publicity (at least in the U.S.) and his importance has diminished a bit. He played with reggae and funk bands while in school and has always had a strong interest in several forms of music outside of jazz. He played with John Stevens in the early '80s, formed the Jazz Warriors (an open-minded big band) a few years later and started leading his own small groups. In 1986 he toured with George Russell's Orchestra and sat in with Art Blakey's Jazz Messengers but since then, despite some fine records for Antilles, Pine's career has seemed a bit directionless. *—Scott Yanow*

● **Journey to the Urge Within** / Jul. 21, 1986-Jul. 23, 1986 / Antilles ✦✦✦✦✦
This early Courtney Pine recording (the tenor-saxophonist was 22 at the time), features some of the most promising Black English jazz musicians of the time including Pine (who also plays some bass clarinet and soprano), singer Cleveland Watkiss (who often is reminiscent of Bobby McFerrin), vibraphonist Orphy Robinson and pianist Julian Joseph. While most of these players have not yet lived up to their potential (Pine remains an expert Coltrane imitator), this disc has its share of strong music. The emphasis is on Courtney Pine's originals which cover a wide span of emotions and grooves. *—Scott Yanow*

Modern Day Jazz Stories / 1995 / Verve ✦✦✦✦✦

Underground / 1997 / Verve ✦✦✦✦

Jean-Luc Ponty

b. Sep. 29, 1942, Avranches, France
Violin / Crossover Jazz, Post-Bop, Fusion
It has been a long, fascinating odyssey for Jean-Luc Ponty, who started out as a straight jazz violinist only to become a pioneer of the electric violin in jazz-rock in the '70s and an inspired manipulator of sequencers and synthesizers in the '80s. At first merely amplifying his violin in order to be heard, he switched over to electric violin and augmented it with devices that were associated with electric guitarists and keyboardists, like Echoplex machines, distortion boxes, phase shifters, and wah-wah pedals. Classically trained, with an unquenchable ability to swing when he wants to, Ponty is often consumed by a passion for tight structures and repeating ostinatos. Undoubtedly, he rivals Stephane Grappelli for the title of the most prominent and influential European jazz violinist. After many years of classical training and performance, Ponty went completely over to jazz in the mid-'60s, recording with Stephane Grappelli, Stuff Smith and Svrend Asmussen on *Violin Summit*. In America by 1969, he played with Frank Zappa, the George Duke Trio and the Mahavishnu Orchestra. His solo albums of the '70s pulled away from the more volcanic aspects of fusion toward a more lyrical, European extension of Mahavishnu's idioms. In 1983, Ponty switched gears and recharged his creative batteries on the synthesizer. By 1991's *Tchokola* though, Ponty was on the move again, recording with West African musicians. *—Richard S. Ginell*

King Kong: Ponty Plays Zappa / Mar. 14, 1969-Mar. 15, 1969 / Blue Note ✦✦✦✦
Jean-Luc Ponty, whose violin playing always seemed in its own category and certainly far ahead of the usual straight-ahead format, was heard in a rock-oriented setting for the first time on this important LP. Ponty performs five Frank Zappa pieces, plus his own "How Would You Like to Have a Head Like That." Zappa arranged all of the music with the sidemen including keyboardist George Duke, either Buell Neidlinger or Wilton Felder on bass and Ernie Watts on tenor and alto. "Music for Electric Violin and Low Budget Orchestra" utilizes an odd instrumentation, including bassoon, oboe, two French horns, flute, viola and cello in addition to the usual rhythm section. The electric music (available on a 1993 CD reissue) still sounds fresh and unpredictable. *—Scott Yanow*

Live at Donte's / Mar. 1969 / Blue Note ✦✦✦✦✦
In October 1969 violinist Jean-Luc Ponty recorded a notable live set with keyboardist George Duke, bassist John Heard and drummer Dick Berk that gained him a lot of exposure in the U.S. He had actually played at *Donte's* in Los Angeles with Duke (on acoustic piano), Heard and drummer Al Cecchi the previous March. Four of the songs came out on a 1981 LP. This CD reissues that program and then doubles it with four more songs from the same engagement. This is a release that is particularly recommended to listeners who are not interested in Ponty's many fusion projects for his playing here is relatively straightahead and sounds influenced by the work of the mid-1960's Miles Davis Quintet, and not just because he performs Ron Carter's "Eighty-One." Also of great interest are the solos of Duke, who would eventually become a funk keyboardist and then a pop producer. In this context he sounds like a mixture of McCoy Tyner and Herbie Hancock. *—Scott Yanow*

Upon the Wings of Music / Jan. 1975 / Atlantic ✦✦✦✦✦
Jean-Luc Ponty, who at the time was still with the second version of The Mahavishnu Orchestra, is heard playing his own brand of fusion on this excellent recording which set the standard for his music of the next decade. With keyboardist Patrice Rushen, Dan Sawyer or Ray Parker on guitars, bassist Ralphe Armstrong and drummer Ndugu, the violinist performs eight of his highly arranged but spirited originals. His early Atlantic recordings (of which this is the first) remain underrated for their important contributions to the history of fusion. *—Scott Yanow*

Le Voyage: The Jean-Luc Ponty Anthology / May 25, 1975-Mar. 1993 / Rhino ✦✦✦✦✦
Ponty has worked with Frank Zappa and John McLaughlin, provided brilliant violin work as a session player, and has had a terrific run as a bandleader. This two-disc set dips into Ponty's Atlantic Records releases, tracing the development of Ponty's particular brand of jazz fusion and providing a very nice look at his career as a bandleader. A few of the cuts seem a bit watery and thin, but this is more to do with the original recording and mixing than the performance or mastering—Rhino's mastering department has provided the usual quality of pro-

duction here. Jean-Luc Ponty is a notable performer in the jazz arena, one who has a clear vision and strong ideals when it comes to his music—he likes to test his boundaries and explore new possibilities. A notable collection. —Steven McDonald

Enigmatic Ocean / Jun. 1977-Jul. 1977 / Atlantic ♦♦♦♦♦
Consistently imaginative, *Enigmatic Ocean* is one of Jean-Luc Ponty's finest accomplishments. The French violinist recorded his share of fusion gems during the 1970s, and this album is at the top of the list. Often aggressive but sometimes reflective and moody, this CD is as unpredictable as it is adventurous. Ponty has plenty of room to stretch out, let loose and blow, and electric guitarists Allan Holdsworth and Daryl Stuermer contribute some inspired solos as well. Also quite impressive is the insightful and passionate drumming of Steve Smith, who went on to lead the superb fusion band Vital Information. Ponty takes one risk after another, and all of them pay off beautifully. *—Alex Henderson*

Storytelling / 1989 / Columbia ♦♦♦♦
When this CD came out, it was violinist Jean-Luc Ponty's strongest in several years. Most of the originals have dense ensembles full of rhythmic patterns set by the keyboards for Ponty to play over. With the exception of "Chopin Prelude No. 20" (a violin improvisation in which the violinist is backed by just Clara Ponty's sober chordal piano), this date falls into the funky fusion area. The enthusiastic high energy playing, colorful solos (Ponty is in splendid form) and catchy melodies make this a very worthwhile session; Grover Washington (on soprano) and keyboardist Patrice Rushen make guest appearances. *—Scott Yanow*

● **The Very Best of Jean-Luc Ponty** / Jan. 1975-Aug. 1985 / Rhino ♦♦♦♦
This 2000 release should have been titled *The Very Best of Jean-Luc Ponty's Atlantic Years* because it contains some of the best recordings that he made during his stay at Atlantic from 1975-1985. The CD doesn't get into Ponty's pre-Atlantic work, some of which is essentially straight-ahead jazz; nor does it get into his Columbia or Epic output of the late '80s and early '90s. Although Ponty's pre-Atlantic and post-Atlantic recordings are noteworthy, it was during his stay at Atlantic that the French violinist did his most important, innovative, and essential work. *The Very Best of Jean-Luc Ponty* doesn't take as comprehensive a look at his Atlantic years as Rhino's two-CD set, *Le Voyage: The Jean-Luc Ponty Anthology*?this collection is more concise, making it the most logical choice if you're exploring his music for the first time. To its credit, Rhino presents the material in chronological order; so one hears how much Ponty evolved during his Atlantic years. While gems from '70s albums like *Upon the Wings of Music, Aurora, Voyage,* and *Enigmatic Ocean* are characterized by their spontaneity and their improvisatory spirit, tracks from 1983's *Individual Choice* and 1985's *Fables* are more high-tech and heavily produced. Ordinarily, it's disappointing to see a great improviser offering less improvisation, but the composing on those albums is so strong that you're inclined to be forgiving. From a compositional standpoint, high-tech '80s pieces like "Infinite Pursuit" and *Individual Choice*'s title track are excellent—even if they lack the spontaneity of Ponty's '70s treasures. All of Ponty's Atlantic albums are worth hearing, and some of them are truly essential. But for beginners, *The Very Best of Jean-Luc Ponty* would be the best starting point. *—Alex Henderson*

Bud Powell (Earl Powell)

b. Sep. 27, 1924, New York, NY, **d.** Jul. 31, 1966, New York, NY
Piano, Composer / Bop
One of the giants of the jazz piano, Bud Powell changed the way that virtually all post-swing pianists play their instruments. He did away with the left hand striding that had been considered essential earlier and used his left hand to state chords on an irregular basis. His right often played speedy single-note lines, essentially transforming Charlie Parker's vocabulary to the piano (although he developed parallel to Bird). Tragically Powell was a seriously ill genius—in a racial incident he was beaten on the head by police, never fully recovering and suffering from bad headaches and mental breakdowns throughout the remainder of his life. Despite this, he recorded some true gems during 1947-51 for Roost, Blue Note and Verve, composing such major works as "Dance of the Infidels, "Hallucinations," "Un Poco Loco," "Bouncing with Bud," and "Tempus Fugit." Even early on his erratic behavior resulted in lost opportunities but Powell's playing during this period was often miraculous. A breakdown in 1951 and hospitalization that resulted in electroshock treatments weakened him but Powell was still capable of playing at his best now and then. Generally in the 1950s his Blue Notes find him in excellent form while he is much more erratic on his Verve recordings.In later years Powell's recordings and performances could be so intense as to be scary, but other times he sounded quite sad. However his influence on jazz (particularly up until the rise of McCoy Tyner and Bill Evans in the 1960s) was very strong and he remains one of the greatest jazz pianists of all time. *—Scott Yanow*

● **Early Years of a Genius (1944-1948)** / Jan. 1944-Dec. 19, 1948 / Mythic Sound ♦♦♦♦♦
This set is the first of ten CDs consisting of privately recorded tracks owned by Powell's friend Francis Paudras. All of the releases will be wanted by the artist's greatest fans, but some are better than others. *Vol. 1* is the most historic, for ten selections feature the innovative pianist at age 20 in 1944 as a sideman with trumpeter Cootie Williams's Orchestra. There are some unique moments. Powell plays a duet with Williams on "West End Blues," joins in with Williams's sextet (which also includes altoist Eddie "Cleanhead" Vinson and tenorman Eddie "Lockjaw" Davis) on "Smack Me," and backs guest Ella Fitzgerald on two numbers, in addition to playing six songs with the full big band. This valuable set concludes with versions of "Perdido" and "Indiana" that Powell performed at *the Royal Roost* on Dec. 19, 1948, with an all-star group including trumpeter Benny Harris, trombonist J.J. Johnson, altoist Lee Konitz, and clarinetist Buddy DeFranco among others. Bop collectors will have to get this one. — *Scott Yanow*

☆ **Complete Blue Note and Roost Recordings** / Jan. 10, 1947-Dec. 29, 1958 / Blue Note ♦♦♦♦♦
Although pianist Bud Powell recorded some great albums elsewhere (most notably his first couple of sessions for Verve), on a whole his Blue Note records were his most significant and definitive. This four-CD set has all of the music from his five Blue Note albums, his two sessions for the Roost label and all known alternate takes. Powell literally changed the way that the piano is played in jazz and this magnificent set has more than its share of classics. In addition to the many trio performances, trombonist Curtis Fuller sits in on three numbers, there are a few solo cuts and one date features Powell at the head of a quintet with trumpeter Fats Navarro and the young tenor Sonny Rollins. Although there are a few faltering moments in the later dates, this essential release (unlike the similar Verve reissue) is quite consistent. *—Scott Yanow*

Complete Bud Powell on Verve / Jan. 1949-Sep. 13, 1956 / Verve ♦♦♦♦♦
This five-CD deluxe set contains an impressive 150-page booklet and reissues every scrap of music that the innovative pianist Bud Powell recorded for Verve. The first disc has the best music, four truly outstanding sessions from 1949-51. The other performances (trio sides from 1954-56) are much more erratic, particularly the alternate takes, with gems followed by completely lost solos. Bop fans will want this set but more general collectors are advised to pick up the Blue Notes first. *—Scott Yanow*

☆ **The Genius of Bud Powell, Vol. 1** / May 1949-Feb. 1951 / Verve ♦♦♦♦♦
This double LP, whose contents have since been reissued as part of a Verve CD box set, contains the cream of pianist Bud Powell's Verve recordings. The innovative pianist rarely sounded more creative and exciting than on the six titles that comprise his May 1949 Verve trio session: "Tempus Fugit," "Celia," "Cherokee," "I'll Keep Loving You," "Strictly Confidential" and "All God's Chillun Got Rhythm." The Feb. 1950 output (highlighted by a raging "Get Happy") and two numbers from July 1950 are also quite rewarding. The final date on this two-fer has eight piano solos from Feb. 1951, and this too is at a high level—particularly "Parisian Thoroughfare" and "Hallucinations," although one does miss the bass and drums. It is a pity that this set is out of print, for it is quite appealing, has excellent liner notes, and gives one a long look at Bud Powell at the peak of his powers. *—Scott Yanow*

★ **The Amazing Bud Powell, Vol. 1** / Aug. 8, 1949-May 1, 1951 / Blue Note ♦♦♦♦♦
The CD reissue of the two albums titled *The Amazing Bud Powell* puts the important recordings in chronological order (which it wasn't in the LP version) and adds some alternate takes; all of the music has also been included in a definitive four-CD box set. Although the latter is the best way to acquire the important performances, this CD gives one a strong sampling of pianist Bud Powell at his best. Powell is heard on a classic session with trumpeter Fats Navarro and tenor-saxophonist Sonny Rollins (which is highlighted by exciting versions of "Dance of the Infidels," "52nd Street Theme" and "Bouncing with Bud") and in a trio for "Over the Rainbow" and three versions of his intense "Un Poco Loco." *—Scott Yanow*

The Complete Bud Powell Blue Note Recordings (1949-1958) / Aug. 8, 1949-Dec. 29, 1958 / Mosaic ♦♦♦♦♦

The Amazing Bud Powell, Vol. 2 / May 1, 1951-Aug. 14, 1953 / Blue Note ♦♦♦♦
These two CD volumes (all of the music has also been reissued on a definitive, "complete" Blue Note Bud Powell four-CD set) differ from the original two LPs in that, in addition to the inclusion of some alternate takes, they are programmed in strict chronological order. The influential bebop pioneer (who not only set the standard for bop pianists but largely invented the style) is heard on fine trio performances from 1951 (with bassist Curly Russell and drummer Max Roach) and 1953 (during which he is matched with bassist George Duvivier and drummer Art Taylor). Highlights include "A Night in Tunisia," "Reets and I," "I Want to Be Happy" and "Glass Enclosure." *—Scott Yanow*

Bud Plays Bird / Oct. 14, 1957-Jan. 30, 1958 / Roulette ♦♦♦♦
Previously unissued until 1996, this trio session by pianist Bud Powell with bassist George Duvivier and drummer Art Taylor is better than his Verve recordings of the period if not quite up to the level of his earlier classic Blue Note dates. Actually it is a mystery how such excellent music could be unknown and go unreleased for so long. Powell performs 13 Charlie Parker compositions (including two versions of "Big Foot") and Dizzy Gillespie's "Salt Peanuts." Although there are some minor missteps, the music is quite enjoyable and generally hard-swinging with the more memorable performances including "Straw 'Nuff," "Yardbird Suite," "Confirmation" and "Ko Ko." *—Scott Yanow*

Time Waits: The Amazing Bud Powell, Vol. 4 / May 28, 1958 / Blue Note ♦♦♦♦♦
This set from pianist Bud Powell (which has been reissued on CD in a "complete" four-CD set) is most notable for having the debut versions of seven of Powell's compositions; most memorable are "Time Waits," "Monopoly" and especially "John's Abbey." With bassist Sam Jones and drummer Philly Joe Jones completing the trio, Powell is in surprisingly fine form throughout the enjoyable session, creating music that is far superior to his later Verve recordings. *—Scott Yanow*

A Portrait of Thelonious / Dec. 17, 1961 / Sony France ♦♦♦♦
This CD reissue is one of the most rewarding Bud Powell recordings to come from his period in France. Powell (along with bassist Pierre Michelot and drummer Kenny Clarke) explores four of Thelonious Monk's tunes, Earl Bostic's "No Name Blues" and the standard "There Will Never Be Another You" but it is the final two numbers ("I Ain't Foolin'" and "Squatty") which really find the bop master at his most spirited and swinging. This very rewarding CD releases for the first time the alternate take (a faster rendition without a clear melody) of "Squatty," a song that (based on its original version) deserves to be revived. One oddity: the applause heard throughout this release was added on later because this was actually a studio album. *—Scott Yanow*

Bouncing with Bud / Apr. 26, 1962 / Delmark ♦♦♦♦♦
This Delmark recording is an excellent set by the great pianist Bud Powell in a trio with the teenage bassist Niels Pederson and drummer William Shiopffe. Recored in Copenhagen, the session features Powell exploring seven bop standards (including his own "Bouncing with Bud") and "The Best Thing for You." All eight selections (which put the emphasis on faster material other than "I Remember Clifford") showcase Bud Powell during his European renaissance period, giving pianists a definitive lesson in playing bop. *—Scott Yanow*

Bud Powell in Paris / Feb. 1963 / Reprise ♦♦♦♦
Considering how late it was in his career, Bud Powell was in surprisingly good spirits at this

live session with bassist Gilbert Rovere and drummer Kansas Fields. The innovative pianist stretches out on nine bop standards including two he had written ("Reets and I" and "Parisian Thoroughfare"); in addition there are previously unreleased versions of "Indiana" and "B-Flat Blues." Far superior to most of his 1955-58 sessions, this was one of Powell's best late-period recordings; he is in near-prime form throughout. *—Scott Yanow*

Pérez Prado (Dámaso Pérez Prado)

b. Dec. 11, 1916, Mantanzas, Cuba, **d.** Sep. 14, 1989, Mexico City, Mexico
Piano, Composer, Arranger / Big Band Latino, Tropical, Mambo, Salsa, Big Band
Dubbed the King of Mambo at the height of his fame, Cuban bandleader/arranger Perez Prado was instrumental in creating the sound. Starting in the 1940s, he blended the music of his native country with elements of big band jazz to form an infectious and extremely danceable hybrid. First coming to notice as the pianist/arranger in the Cuban big band Orquesta Casino de la Playa, Prado's popularity spread to Mexico, Latin America and, in the 1950s, the United States. Because his two no. 1 hits, "Cherry Pink and Apple Blossom White" and "Patricia," were as much (or more) pop as mambo, Prado is sometimes unfairly remembered as an easy listening instrumentalist. In fact, the bulk of his material was comprised of hot dance tunes highlighting bursts of shrill horns, busy bongoes and, at times, ghostly organ. His irresistible, propulsive rhythms swung with great verve and humor, punctuated by shouts and grunts from various bandmembers. One of the most popular Latin musicians and bandleaders of his time, both in Latin America and the U.S., his innovations were also widely appreciated by jazz fans and musicians. He was largely forgotten by the American audience after 1960, but remained active until his death in 1989. *—Richie Unterberger*

Havana 3 A.M. / 1956 / RCA Victor ✦✦✦✦✦
Following the successes of his previous albums, mostly reissues of proven hits in Mexico, Prado was entitled to do his own, progressive thing at least for one album. *Havana, 3 a.m.* sneaked past the dance-music censors at RCA and kicked down the doors for acceptance of authentic Latin music in the U.S. Immediately into the first track, "La Comparsa," we hear the full flowering of the Prado sound: searing, blaring trumpet over heavy rhythm in very spare arrangements. "Freeway Mambo" is definitive, one of Prado's unsung best. That the music also is suitable for dancing seems irrelevant. This is the sound of the dancer on the jacket, of pre-Castro Cuba at night, of Spanish-influenced cities and African-influenced hill country. It is louder than bullfight music (even the ballads), absolutely direct and brash, yet so deftly and compellingly arranged that it never tires. A timeless classic, *Havana, 3 a.m.* is worth obtaining in both its original form and the simulated-stereo reissue on Arcano Records (DKL1-3173). *—Tony Wilds*

Mambo Mania/Havana 3 A.M. / 1949-Mar. 7, 1956 / Bear Family ✦✦✦✦✦
Bear Family's *Mambo Mania/Havana 3 A.M.* combines two albums Perez Prado originally released on RCA during the '50s on one compact disc. *Mambo Mania* was a delightful collection, boasting the hit single "Cherry Pink and Apple Blossom White," as well as tongue-in-cheek tributes to a number of popular musicians and songs from the era—"Mambo A La Kenton," "Marilyn Monroe Mambo," "St. Louis Blues Mambo," "Mambo a Billy May," "April in Portugal" and "Mambo de Chattanooga" (a mambo version of "The Chattanooga Shoe Shine Boy"). *Havana, 3 A.M.* offers more of the same, which is no problem at all. Prado leads his big band through a number of infectious, danceable originals and versions of "Besame Mucho" and "Granada" that are terribly entertaining. Rhino's *Mondo Mambo* remains the best way to become acquainted with the wonders of Prado, but if you want to dig deeper, this is the place to start expanding your collection. *—Stephen Thomas Erlewine*

Voodoo Suite/Exotic Suite / Apr. 8, 1954-Apr. 17, 1962 / Bear Family ✦✦✦

★ **Mondo Mambo: The Best of Perez Prado** / 1995 / Rhino ✦✦✦✦✦
20 tracks from the 1950s and early '60s. Includes the chart-toppers "Cherry Pink And Apple Blossom White" and "Patricia," but most of the album is given over to sassy, even frenetic at times, mambo dance tunes that rank among the most popular and infectious Cuban pop ever produced. *—Richie Unterberger*

Andre Previn (Andreas Ludwig Priwin)

b. Apr. 6, 1929, Berlin, Germany
Piano / West Coast Jazz, Cool, Bop
One of the most versatile musicians on the planet, Andre Previn has amassed considerable credentials as a jazz pianist, despite carving out separate lives first as a Hollywood arranger and composer, and then a world-class classical conductor, pianist and composer. Always fluid, melodic and swinging, with elements of Bud Powell, Oscar Peterson and Horace Silver mixed with a faultless technique, Previn hasn't changed much over the decades but can always be counted upon for polished, reliable performances at the drop of a hat. Originally swing-oriented, Previn discovered bop in 1950 just before his induction into the Army. Upon returning to Los Angeles, he went into overdrive, gigging as a jazz pianist, scoring films and playing chamber music. Previn scored a huge crossover hit with an album of jazz interpretations of *My Fair Lady,* which in turn led to a series of like-minded albums of Broadway scores and kicked off an industry trend. By 1962, he started to make the transition away from Hollywood toward becoming a full-time classical conductor, dropping his jazz activities entirely. In March 1989, shortly before resigning from the Los Angeles Philharmonic in a dispute with management, Previn returned to jazz with a trio album for Telarc with Ray Brown and Joe Pass, showing that he had not lost an iota of his abilities. *—Richard S. Ginell*

Pal Joey / Oct. 28, 1957-Oct. 29, 1957 / Contemporary/OJC ✦✦✦✦
For this CD reissue, pianist Andre Previn, bassist Red Mitchell and drummer Shelly Manne perform eight songs that debuted in the show *Pal Joey.* Best known is "I Could Write a Book," which quickly became a standard, but the other, more obscure songs such as "Take Him," "Zip" and "Do It the Hard Way" are also generally good devices for jazz improvising. An enjoyable set of straight-ahead trio music. *—Scott Yanow*

Gigi / Apr. 7, 1958-Apr. 8, 1958 / Contemporary/OJC ✦✦✦✦
Andre Previn's ten records for Contemporary during 1957-60 were among the finest jazz recordings of his career. Several of the albums were jazz interpretations of scores from Broadway shows although, ironically, the best-known one, *My Fair Lady,* came out under drummer Shelly Manne's name. For this particular CD reissue, Previn, Manne and bassist Red Mitchell perform eight songs from the Lerner and Lowe show *Gigi.* Previn had won an Oscar for his adaptation of the score, so he knew this music quite well. Best known among the songs are "I Remember It Well" and "Thank Heaven for Little Girls" but the trio also uplifts and swings the other lesser-known tunes. *—Scott Yanow*

Andre Previn Plays Vernon Duke / Aug. 12, 1958-Aug. 30, 1958 / Contemporary/OJC ✦✦✦✦✦
A measure of how respected Andre Previn has long been in many musical fields is that this set of unaccompanied jazz piano solos has liner notes by the composer of the ten songs, Vernon Duke. Previn alternates well-known Duke pieces such as "Autumn In New York," "Taking a Chance on Love," "What Is There to Say," and "I Can't Get Started" with a few obscure numbers including "The Love I Long For," "Ages Ago" and "I Like the Likes of You." This CD reissue finds Previn at the peak of his jazz powers, displaying an original yet accessible style that falls between swing and bop. Recommended. *—Scott Yanow*

● **King Size!** / Nov. 26, 1958 / Contemporary/OJC ✦✦✦✦✦
The multitalented Andre Previn is heard on this recording as the leader of a trio with bassist Red Mitchell and drummer Frankie Capp. Previn always had his own swing/bop piano style and he is in top form on two of his originals (including the bluish "Much Too Late") and four superior standards. This fine release gives one an excellent example of Previn's skills as a jazz pianist. *—Scott Yanow*

Andre Previn Plays Jerome Kern / Feb. 26, 1959-Mar. 10, 1959 / Contemporary/OJC ✦✦✦✦✦
For this solo piano session (a Contemporary date which has been reissued on CD), the remarkably versatile Andre Previn interprets ten Jerome Kern songs including several ("Sure Thing," "WhipPoor-Will," "Go Little Boat" and "Put Me to the Test") that are quite obscure. Sometimes he treats the melodies with great respect while other performances find him stretching the themes and coming up with fresh variations; "They Didn't Believe Me" is a highpoint. This is a well-rounded set with plenty of surprises along with consistently tasteful playing, one of Previn's better jazz efforts. *—Scott Yanow*

West Side Story / Aug. 24, 1959-Aug. 25, 1959 / Contemporary/OJC ✦✦✦✦
The last of a series of showtune albums recorded by the trio of pianist Andre Previn, bassist Red Mitchell and drummer Shelly Manne finds the all-star group focusing on the music of *West Side Story* (Previn and Manne alternated leadership, and it was the drummer's good fortune to have the famous *My Fair Lady* album under his own name). This CD reissue has eight of the main themes from the famous musical, including "I Feel Pretty," "Maria" and "America." As usual, the melodies are treated respectfully yet swingingly, and Andre Previn in particular excels in this setting. Recommended. *—Scott Yanow*

Like Previn! / Feb. 20, 1960-Mar. 1, 1960 / Contemporary/OJC ✦✦✦✦
This trio set for Contemporary (reissued on CD in the OJC series) differs from other Andre Previn sessions in that all eight of the selections were composed by the pianist. With fine assistance from bassist Red Mitchell and drummer Frankie Capp, Previn is in consistently swinging form on his originals and, even if none of the songs caught on, they make for a solid and varied set of bop-oriented music. *—Scott Yanow*

Give My Regards to Broadway / May 27, 1960-May 31, 1960 / Collectables ✦✦✦✦
One of pianist Andre Previn's first recordings after leaving the Contemporary label, this trio workout with bassist Red Mitchell and drummer Frank Capp is very much in the same straight-ahead genre. Previn's trio performs ten show tunes from ten different productions. Virtually all of the songs are still quite well known, including "Almost Like Being In Love," "The Sound of Music," "Too Close for Comfort" and "Diamond's Are a Girl's Best Friend." Previn really digs into the material (some of which is rarely played in a jazz setting), and, by adding swing and some subtle reharmonizations, turns the songs into straight-ahead jazz. This out-of-print LP is well worth picking up if found in bargain bins. *—Scott Yanow*

After Hours / Mar. 29, 1989 / Telarc ✦✦✦✦✦
Although Andre Previn had not recorded a regular jazz album in 27 years at this point in time (discounting a pair of Itzhak Perlman sessions featuring Previn's compositions), the great majority of the performances on this trio set with guitarist Joe Pass and bassist Ray Brown are first takes. Previn took time off from his busy schedule in the classical music world to return briefly to jazz, his first love. The results are often magical. Previn, Pass and Brown play together as if they had been touring as a group for years. The pianist is generous with solo space and Pass' solos are sometimes exhilarating. For Previn, it is as if the previous three decades did not occur for he plays in a style little changed from 1960, displaying an Oscar Peterson influence mixed in with touches of Lennie Tristano and Bill Evans' chording, performing ten standards and his own "One For Bunz." Highly recommended. *—Scott Yanow*

Uptown / Mar. 9, 1990-Mar. 10, 1990 / Telarc ✦✦✦✦
This was Andre Previn's second album after his long, symphonically enforced absence from jazz, and it sounds noticeably more fluid and relaxed than his first. No longer apprehensive about dusting off his old skills, Previn is delightfully confident and breezy (dig his sly turns on "Come Rain or Come Shine" and "C Jam Blues"), taking some chances as he rephrases and paraphrases a collection of revivified standards, mostly Arlen and assorted Ellingtonia. Even if Previn, that noted wit, sometimes sounds as if he is kidding the pants off these old tunes, it's great to hear him having such a good time playing jazz again. Mundell Lowe is Previn's new guitar partner, and Ray Brown returns on bass; both are right at home in this refined brand of chamber jazz grooving. Adding to the CD's appeal are some marvelously (and typically) graceful liner notes by Mel Powell, an old pal of Andre's and a lively fellow defector from the jazz piano ranks to the classical world. *—Richard S. Ginell*

Gigi / Apr. 7, 1958-Apr. 8, 1958 / Contemporary/OJC ✦✦✦✦
Andre Previn's ten records for Contemporary during 1957-60 were among the finest jazz recordings of his career. Several of the albums were jazz interpretations of scores from Broadway shows although, ironically, the best-known one, *My Fair Lady,* came out under

drummer Shelly Manne's name. For this particular CD reissue, Previn, Manne and bassist Red Mitchell perform eight songs from the Lerner and Lowe show *Gigi*. Previn had won an Oscar for his adaptation of the score, so he knew this music quite well. Best known among the songs are "I Remember It Well" and "Thank Heaven for Little Girls" but the trio also uplifts and swings the other lesser-known tunes. *—Scott Yanow*

Julian Priester

b. Jun. 29, 1935, Chicago, IL

Trombone / Avant-Garde Jazz, Post-Bop

Julian Priester has long been a flexible and adventurous trombonist who has not yet achieved the fame he deserved. He originally studied piano, baritone horn and finally trombone. Prior to moving to New York in 1958 he worked with Muddy Waters, Bo Diddley, Sun Ra (1954-56), Lionel Hampton and Dinah Washington (1957). Priester gained recognition for his playing with Max Roach (1958-61) during a period when the drummer often used Booker Little and Eric Dolphy. He played in a wide variety of settings throughout the 1960s including six months with Duke Ellington (1969-70). Priester's highest profile gig was with Herbie Hancock's sextet during 1970-73 with whom he toured and recorded. Moving to San Francisco in the mid-'70s, he experimented with electronic music while still playing trombone, recording with Stanley Cowell and Red Garland. Most of the first half of the 1990s was spent with Dave Holland's quintet and later in the decade he worked with George Gruntz and Sun Ra. *—Scott Yanow*

● **Keep Swingin'** / Jan. 11, 1960 / Riverside/OJC ♦♦♦♦

Trombonist Julian Priester sounds very much under the influence of J.J. Johnson during his debut as a leader, a Riverside date reissued on CD in the Original Jazz Classics series. The repertoire is comprised of four Priester originals, one apiece by Jimmy Heath (whose tenor makes the group a quintet on five of the eight songs) and baritonist Charles Davis, and two standards. Priester is heard in his early prime on a warm version of "Once in a While" and plays solid hard bop with pianist Tommy Flanagan, bassist Sam Jones, drummer Elvin Jones and sometimes Heath on this swinging modern mainstream session. *—Scott Yanow*

Love, Love / Jun. 28, 1974-Sep. 12, 1974 / ECM ♦♦♦♦

Trombonist Priester is electrified; setting is extended. Hard-hitting. *—Michael G. Nastos*

Hints on Light and Shadow / Nov. 14, 1996-Nov. 15, 1996 / Postcards ♦♦♦

This is an unusual set. Trombonist Julian Priester and Sam Rivers (alternating between tenor, soprano, flute and piano) perform a set of duets that also sometimes include the oddball electronics of Tucker Martine. The nine originals are mostly freely improvised; some strong themes do emerge, and there is some excellent interaction between Priester and Rivers (two underrated giants). However, Martine's electronics are occasionally so bizarre as to be distracting. *—Scott Yanow*

Tito Puente (Ernest Anthony Puente, Jr.)

b. Apr. 20, 1923, New York, NY, **d.** May 31, 2000, New York, NY

Vibraphone, Timbales, Percussion / Cuban Jazz, Big Band Latino, Afro-Cuban Jazz, Mambo, Latin Jazz, Salsa, Latin Pop

By virtue of his warm, flamboyant stage manner, longevity, constant touring, and appearances in the mass media, Tito Puente is probably the most beloved symbol of Latin jazz. As a timbales virtuoso, he combines mastery over every rhythmic nuance with old-fashioned showmanship—watching his eyes bug out when taking a dynamic solo is one of the great treats for fans. A trained musician, he is also a fine, lyrical vibraphonist, a gifted arranger, and plays piano, congas, bongos and saxophone. His appeal continues to cut across all ages and ethnic groups, helped no doubt by Santana's best-selling cover versions of "Oye Como Va" and "Para Los Rumberos" in 1970-71, cameo appearances on *The Cosby Show* in the 1980s, and the film *The Mambo Kings* in 1992. He debuted as a big-band drummer at the age of 13, and later studied composition, orchestration and piano at Juilliard and the the New York School of Music. More importantly, he played with and absorbed the influence of Machito, who was successfully fusing Latin rhythms with progressive jazz. After debuting a full orchestra in 1949, Puente helped fuel the mambo craze that gave him the unofficial—and ultimately lifelong—title "King of the Mambo," or just "El Rey." Puente never painted himself into a tight Latin music corner, though; his range extended to big band jazz (*Puente Goes Jazz*), bossa nova tunes, Broadway hits, boogaloos, and pop music—although in later years he tended to stick with older Latin jazz styles that became popularly known as salsa. An indefatigable visitor to the recording studios, Puente recorded his 100th album *The Mambo King* in 1991 amidst much ceremony and affection. Just months after accepting his fifth Grammy award, he died on June 1, 2000. *—Richard S. Ginell*

50 Years of Swing: 50 Great Years & Tracks / 1946-1995 / RMM ♦♦♦♦♦

50 Years of Swing: 50 Great Years & Tracks is a three-disc, 50-song collection chronicling Tito Puente's immensely popular and influential career. Over the course of the collection, Puente's groundbreaking fusions of Latin rhythms and bebop can be heard, as well as his forays into straight jazz and worldbeat, making *50 Years of Swing* a box set of enormous worth. It's one of the rare samplers that educates as it entertains. *—Stephen Thomas Erlewine*

★ **Best of Tito Puente: El Rey del Timbal!** / Nov. 23, 1949-Jan. 28, 1989 / Rhino ♦♦♦♦♦

Summarizing Tito Puente's numerous accomplishments on a single CD would be impossible. *El Rey De Timbal!*, a 1997 disc spanning 1949-87, barely scratches the surface—but for Puente, a five-CD box set would also only scratch the surface. But this gem-laden collection does illustrate just how remarkably consistent the salsa legend was during the course of 38 years. *El Rey De Timbal* kicks into high gear with 1949's "Ran-Kan-Kan" before treating us to such essential 1950s recordings as "Cao-Cao Mani Picao," "Cual Es Tu Idea," "Agua Limpia Todo" and "Oye Mi Guaguanco." Live versions of "Separala Tambien" and "A Gozar Timbero" from 1960 are superb, as is 1961's exuberant "T.P. On the Strip." Though salsa dominates the disc, Puente's Latin jazz output for Concord Picante in the 1980s is well represented by "El Rey De Timbal" and "Machito Forever." Diehard Puente fans will notice that "Ban Ban Quiere," "Oye Como Va" and other essential hits are missing, but then, no one said *El Rey De Timbal* was all-inclusive. Again, it barely scratches the surface, but what a marvelous surface it is. *—Alex Henderson*

Cuban Carnival / 1955-1956 / BMG ♦♦♦♦♦

While the music that came to be termed "salsa" originated in Cuba, Puerto Ricans have been among its strongest supporters. One New York-reared puertoriqueno who soared to the top of the salsa world in the 1950s was timbale player/vibist Tito Puente. Boasting such early Puente gems as "Cual Es La Idea," "Oye Mi Guanguanco" and "Yambecua," the exuberant, infectious *Cuban Carnival* is essential listening for anyone with even a casual interest in Afro-Cuban music. Many of the players Puente employs in his driving orchestra—including Mongo Santamaria, Willie Bobo and Carlos "Patato" Valdez—would become among the most celebrated percussionists in Latin music. Whether the style is mambo, son, cha-cha or rhumba, *Cuban Carnival* is outstanding from start to finish. *—Alex Henderson*

Top Percussion / 1957 / BMG ♦♦♦♦♦

A stunner from Puente's golden age, this 1957 recording brought together Tito, Mongo, Willie Bobo, Aguabella, and Julito Collazo on percussion with vocalists that included Mercedita Valdez, in seven wonderful cuts of traditional and (then) contemporary Afro-Cuban skin-on-skin. Then as an unexpected gift, there is a seven-minute Latin-jazz suite featuring Puente's considerable jazz-arranger head and a powerful band with Doc Severinson on lead trumpet. *—John Storm Roberts*

☆ **Dance Mania** / Nov. 1957-Dec. 1957 / RCA International ♦♦♦♦♦

Dance Mania is probably Puente's best-known album, appearing as it does in several reissue forms and having inspired subsequent *More Dance Mania* and *Dance Mania '80s* titles. Part of the reason is that it's his first major album of dance music, in stereo, on RCA. As with most of the rest of his work for the label, it more than lives up to expectations. Seven of its twelve tracks are Puente's own, and of the rest, two are from legendary conga star Francisco Aguabella. There isn't a weak track in the bunch, and most feature singing and instrumental solos. *Dance Mania* is a cohesive collection of mambo, guaguanco, guaracha, and son montuno, plus some equally lively cha cha cha and bolero tracks. While it probably does not deserve all of its reputation (unless one gives similar credit to some other Puente albums), it is essential. *—Tony Wilds*

On Broadway / Jul. 1982 / Concord Picante ♦♦♦♦♦

The great Latin bandleader Tito Puente has long been one of the pioneers in fusing bebop with very danceable Latin music. On this Concord disc, Puente plays vibes and timbales and utilizes an 11-piece band featuring trumpeter Jimmy Frisaura, Mario Rivera on tenor, soprano and flute, pianist Jorge Dalto and an infectious rhythm section. Jazz standards (including "Sophisticated Lady," "Bluesette" and even Freddie Hubbard's "First Light") alternate with Latin numbers. *—Scott Yanow*

☆ **El Rey (The King)** / May 1984 / Concord Picante ♦♦♦♦♦

With a title like *The King*, you can expect ten great tracks. With superb material and performances by Santos Colon, Andy Senatore, and Rudy Calzado, as well as one top instrumental ("Safari"), *El Rey* is possibly the king of Puente albums on Tico. Three are originals, and two are by Bobby Marin, but all feature the great arranging talent of Puente. "It Was Love" is a swinging ballad, and the mod excursion "Safari" is topped off by a sax-anticipating *Harlem River Drive*. "T.P. Treat," the second great Senatore song, is a wild "scat" boogaloo, and, of course, "Pata Pata" was obligatory in the boogaloo era. "Erasmo el Loco" keeps the crazy party going while taking a brief step back from the mainstream. "Shing-a-Tin Tin" is final proof that Puente can cut as good a boogaloo album as anyone. That may not be saying much, and indeed *El Rey* does not say much, but it sure feels good, and that's the point. *—Tony Wilds*

Mambo Diablo / May 1985 / Concord Picante ♦♦♦♦♦

Although he was never inactive, the 1980s found Tito Puente in a bit of a renaissance. His exciting Afro-Cuban jazz band had found a home on the Concord Picante label, and his music was increasing in popularity again. This particular CD has a stronger than usual repertoire, including "Take Five," "Lush Life" (done as Latin jazz), "Pick Yourself Up" and "Lullaby of Birdland"; the latter song has its composer George Shearing guesting on piano. Puente wrote half of the arrangements, contributed some excellent playing on timbales and vibes, and is heard heading a spirited three-horn, three-percussion octet. Very enjoyable music. *—Scott Yanow*

Sensacion / 1987 / Concord Picante ♦♦♦♦♦

Tito Puente's Latin ensemble always seems to play sensational music. Puente's Afro-Cuban jazz octet in 1985 featured pianist Sonny Bravo, trumpeter Ray Gonzalez and saxophonist Mario Rivera as the main soloists, along with the leaders' timbales and vibes. For this outing, vibraphonist Terry Gibbs sits in on "Jordu" and plays second vibes to Puente on "Guajira for Cal (Tjader)." Other highlights include "Fiesta A La King," "'Round Midnight," Clare Fischer's "Morning" and Chick Corea's "Spain." Recommended. *—Scott Yanow*

Special Delivery / Jun. 11, 1996-Jul. 13, 1996 / Concord Picante ♦♦♦♦♦

Tito Puente, the godfather of Latin jazz, celebrated 50 years in music with this sizzling CD. "Be-Bop" is launched with a duel between trumpeters Bobby Shew and Maynard Ferguson. Underrated alto saxophonist Bobby Porcelli and tenorman Mario Rivera make this version of "Stablemates" a keeper. The rarely heard "Venus De Milo" is revived with a warm tribute to composer Gerry Mulligan by baritone saxophonist Mitch Forman. *Special Delivery* is big-band Latin jazz at its best. *—Ken Dryden*

Don Pullen

b. Dec. 25, 1941, Roanoke, VA, **d.** Apr. 22, 1995, East Orange, NJ

Organ (Hammond), Piano, Organ / Avant-Garde Jazz, Free Jazz, Post-Bop

Don Pullen developed a surprisingly accessible way of performing avant-garde jazz. Although he could be quite free harmonically, with dense, dissonant chords, Pullen also utilized catchy rhythms, so even his freest flights generally had a handle for listeners to hang on to. The combination of freedom and rhythm gave him his own unique musical personality.

Pullen, who came from a musical family, studied with Muhal Richard Abrams (with whom he played in the Experimental Band) and in 1964 made his recording debut with Giuseppi Logan. In the 1960s, he recorded free duets with Milford Graves, led his own bands, and played organ with R&B groups, backing Big Maybelle and Ruth Brown, among others. Although he worked with Nina Simone (1970-71) and Art Blakey's Jazz Messengers (1974), Pullen became famous as the pianist with Charles Mingus' last great group (1973-75). From 1979-88, he co-led a notable inside/outside quartet with tenor saxophonist George Adams that was in some ways an extension of Mingus' band. In later years, Pullen led his African-Brazilian Connection and recorded with Kip Hanrahan, Roots, John Scofield, David Murray, Mingus Dynasty and Jane Bunnett, among others. His last project found the always-searching pianist seeking to fuse jazz with traditional native American music. Although his life was too short, Don Pullen fortunately did make a fair amount of recordings as a leader including for Sackville (1974), Horo, Black Saint, Atlantic (his funky "Big Alice" became a near-standard) and Blue Note. *—Scott Yanow*

Capricorn Rising / Oct. 16, 1975-Oct. 17, 1975 / Black Saint ✦✦✦✦✦

Tomorrow's Promises / 1976-1977 / Koch International ✦✦✦✦✦
This early Don Pullen recording helped introduce him to jazz listeners. The pianist is heard in a variety of settings including a duet with multireedist George Adams on "Last Year's Lies and Tomorrow's Promises," and in two groups with Adams and trumpeter Hannibal Marvin Peterson. Actually the most accessible and memorable piece is the rollicking "Big Alice" which also features violinist Michal Urbaniak and trumpeter Randy Brecker. Pullen, a very rhythmic avant-gardist who can play inside or outside, was well-served by this release. *—Scott Yanow*

Montreux Concert / Jul. 12, 1977 / Koch International ✦✦✦✦
A masterful inside/outside pianist whose percussive solos often made his music sound more accessible than one would expect (considering the fact that he often played atonally), Don Pullen is heard on two extensive side-long explorations on this LP: "Richard's Tune" and "Dialogue Between Malcolm and Betty." Pullen is assisted by electric bassist Jeff Berlin, drummer Steve Jordan, and on the latter piece, both Raphael Cruz and Sammy Figueroa on percussion. This album will be a difficult one to find, and the music has not yet been reissued on CD. *—Scott Yanow*

The Sixth Sense / Jun. 1985 / Black Saint ✦✦✦✦✦
Studio date with quintet. Another great Pullen album. *—Michael G. Nastos*

● **Breakthrough** / Apr. 30, 1986 / Blue Note ✦✦✦✦✦
Yes, this is a career breakthrough in a sense, for the Don Pullen/George Adams Quartet finally got a chance to record for a major American label after several Europe-only opuses. They seemed genuinely thrilled about it, for the supercharged leadoff track "Mr. Smoothie" sure sounds like a breakthrough with its ebullient mood. While grounded in hard-swinging post-bop, soul-jazz, and the blues, Adams and Pullen use the mainstream as a base for taking off into free regions at times, Adams with his gritty, combustible tenor, Pullen his trademark piano clusters. They can also groove in a melodic yet highly charged fashion on "Song From the Old Country" and reflect yearningly in the opening bars of "A Time for Sobriety." Drummer Dannie Richmond adds his Mingus-trained flexibility and drive, fluidly teamed with bassist Cameron Brown. Throughout the record, the band's creativity burns at white heat, making this disc a good first choice for newcomers to Pullen. *—Richard S. Ginell*

Random Thoughts / Mar. 23, 1990 / Blue Note ✦✦✦✦✦
As bent upon pianistic mayhem as Don Pullen often seemed, this was one of his more user-friendly discs, despite having only a bass and drums between himself and tender-eared listeners. Quite often, Pullen starts a piece as if it were a conventional piano trio number, but before long, he's piling up his trademark keyboard-shuffling glissandos, playing the instrument as if it was a big, glittering, percussive crashing board. Yet everything always swings, thanks to Pullen's own early gospel leanings, Lewis Nash's loosey-goosey traps work and James Genus' flexible bass. Among the more ingratiating pieces is "Indio Gitano," a mesmerizing series of Spanish Phrygian couplets that groove irresistibly in 5/4 time, and "626 Fairfax" is notable for the way Pullen's glissandos fit seamlessly into the piece's swinging and harmonic contexts. Don't his identification with the avant-garde scare you away from this engaging CD, for Pullen manages to make even fearsome things seem approachable. *—Richard S. Ginell*

Kele Mou Bana / Sep. 25, 1991-Sep. 26, 1991 / Blue Note ✦✦✦✦✦
This CD features pianist Don Pullen's "African-Brazilian Connection." Always a very percussive player, Pullen gets to romp with two percussionists on this date while altoist Carlos Ward flies over the top and bassist Nilson Matta keeps the foundation solid. The repertoire is comprised of originals and, even in its freer moments, the rhythms keep the music quite accessible. *—Scott Yanow*

Ike Quebec

b. Aug. 17, 1918, Newark, NJ, **d.** Jan. 16, 1963, New York, NY
Sax (Tenor) / Hard Bop, Jump Blues, Soul-Jazz, Swing
Influenced by Coleman Hawkins and Ben Webster but definitely his own person, Ike Quebec was one of the finest swing-oriented tenor saxman of the 1940s and '50s. Though he was never an innovator, Quebec had a big, breathy sound that was distinctive and easily recognizable, and he was quite consistent when it came to came to down-home blues, sexy ballads and uptempo aggression. Originally a pianist, Quebec switched to tenor in the early 1940s and showed that he had made the right decision on excellent 78s for Blue Note and Savoy (including his hit "Blue Harlem"). As a sideman, he worked with Benny Carter, Kenny Clarke, Roy Eldridge and Cab Calloway. In the late '40s, the saxman did a bit of freelancing behind the scenes as a Blue Note A*R man and brought $Thelonious Monk* and Bud Powell to the label. Drug problems kept Quebec from recording for most of the 1950s, but he made a triumphant comeback in the early 1960s and was once again recording for Blue Note and doing freelance A&R for the company. Quebec was playing as authoritatively as ever well into 1962, giving no indication that he was suffering from lung cancer, which claimed his life at the age of 44 in 1963. *—Alex Henderson*

☆ **Complete Blue Note Recordings** / Jul. 18, 1944-Sep. 23, 1946 / Mosaic ✦✦✦✦✦
This limited-edition four-LP box set from Mosaic has all of the early Blue Note recordings of tenors John Hardee and Ike Quebec. The little-known three sessions from Hardee are all from 1946 (one is under the leadership of guitarist Tiny Grimes) and find him in top form on a variety of swing-based originals, along with a few standards. In addition to Grimes, the sidemen include trombonist Trummy Young, guitarist Jimmy Shirley, and pianists Marlowe Morris and Sammy Benskin. Hardee would eventually settle in Texas as a full-time educator. In contrast, Ike Quebec, who is showcased on five dates (including 11 previously unissued performances), would achieve a bit of fame (his recordings of "Blue Harlem" and "If I Had You" gained some attention) before drugs forced him off the scene in the 1950s; he would make a brief comeback in the early '60s prior to his premature death. Quebec's early Blue Note dates are superior examples of small-group swing and have solo space for some notable stars: guitarist Tiny Grimes; pianist Ram Ramirez; trumpeters Jonah Jones, Buck Clayton, and Shad Collins; and trombonists Tyree Glenn and Keg Johnson. This 1984 box is certainly definitive but promises to be difficult to find. *—Scott Yanow*

☆ **Complete Blue Note 45 Sessions** / Jul. 1, 1959-Feb. 13, 1962 / Mosaic ✦✦✦✦✦
During his comeback years (1959-62) after a decade mostly off the scene, tenor saxophonist Ike Quebec recorded frequently for Blue Note. He started off with a session aimed at the 45 jukebox market and, although he eventually made a few full-length albums for the label, Quebec cut four 45 dates over a two-and-a-half-year period. This limited-edition (and now out of print) three-LP Mosaic box set has all of the jukebox sessions. Most of the 26 selections clock in between four and seven minutes and have long melody statements in addition to concise and soulful solos. Quebec, who was in consistently prime form during his last period, is joined by groups featuring either Skeeter Best or Willie Jones on guitar and Edwin Swanston, Sir Charles Thompson, or Earl Van Dyke on organ. Fun and generally danceable music. *—Scott Yanow*

Heavy Soul / Nov. 26, 1961 / Blue Note ✦✦✦✦
Thick-toned tenor Ike Quebec is in excellent form on this CD reissue of a 1961 Blue Note date. His ballad statements are quite warm, and he swings nicely on a variety of medium-tempo material. Unfortunately, organist Freddie Roach has a rather dated sound, which weakens this session a bit; bassist Milt Hinton and drummer Al Harewood are typically fine in support. Originals alternate with standards, with "Just One More Chance," "The Man I Love" and "Nature Boy" (the latter an emotional tenor-bass duet) being among the highlights. *—Scott Yanow*

It Might as Well Be Spring / Dec. 9, 1961 / Blue Note ✦✦✦
Working with the same quartet that cut *Heavy Soul?*organist Freddie Roach, bassist Milt Hinton and drummer Al Harewood—Ike Quebec recorded another winning hard bop album with *It Might As Well Be Spring*. In many ways, the record is a companion piece to *Heavy Soul*. Since the two albums were recorded so close together, it's not surprising that there a number of stylistic similarities, but there are subtle differences to savor. The main distinction between the two dates is that *It Might As Well Be Spring* is a relaxed, romantic date comprised of standards. It provides Quebec with ample opportunity to showcase his rich, lyrical ballad style, and he shines throughout the album. Similarly, Roach has a tasteful, understated technique, whether he's soloing or providing support for Quebec. The pair have a terrific, sympathetic interplay that makes *It Might As Well Be Spring* a joyous listen. *—Stephen Thomas Erlewine*

● **Blue & Sentimental** / Dec. 16, 1961-Dec. 23, 1961 / Blue Note ✦✦✦✦✦
Of tenor saxophonist Ike Quebec's six Blue Note albums from the 1961-62 period, this is the definitive one. The CD reissue (which adds "new" versions of "That Old Black Magic" and "It's All Right With Me" to the original LP program) mostly features Quebec in a quartet with guitarist Grant Green, bassist Paul Chambers and drummer Philly Joe Jones; "Count Every Star" has Quebec joined by Green, pianist Sonny Clark, bassist Sam Jones and drummer Louis Hayes. Although some of the renditions are medium-tempo swingers, it is the soulful ballad versions of "Blue and Sentimental" and "Don't Take Your Love from Me" that are most memorable. Recommended. *—Scott Yanow*

Easy Living / Jan. 20, 1962 / Blue Note ✦✦✦✦✦
This CD reissue (which adds three songs to the original LP) is really two sets in one. The first five selections are a blues-oriented jam session that matches together the contrasting tenors of Ike Quebec and Stanley Turrentine with trombonist Bennie Green, pianist Sonny Clark, bassist Milt Hinton and drummer Art Blakey. However it is the last three numbers ("I've Got a Crush on You, " "Nancy with the Laughing Face" and "Easy Living") that are most memorable; ballad features for Quebec's warm tenor. All in all this set gives one a definitive look at late-period Ike Quebec. *—Scott Yanow*

Soul Samba / Oct. 5, 1962 / Blue Note ✦✦✦
This CD reissues veteran tenor saxophonist Ike Quebec's final recording as a leader, cut a little more than three months before his death. Recorded during a period when seemingly everyone was making a bossa-nova record, Quebec's effort is a bit unusual in that none of the musicians (guitarist Kenny Burrell, bassist Wendell Marshall, drummer Willie Bobo and percussionist Garvin Masseaux) were associated with Brazilian (as opposed to Afro-Cuban) jazz. While Quebec emphasizes warm long tones (reminiscent of Coleman Hawkins in a romantic fashion, his sidemen play light and appealing bossa rhythms. The result is high-quality melodic Brazilian dance music (despite the lack of any Jobim songs) with Burrell in

particular being quite effective; the pleasing program concludes with three previously unissued alternate takes. *—Scott Yanow*

Sun Ra (Herman Sonny Blount)

b. May 22, 1914, Birmingham, AL, **d.** May 30, 1993

Organ (Hammond), Keyboards, Piano, Organ / Experimental Big Band, Multimedia, Avant-Garde Jazz, Free Jazz, Progressive Big Band, Avant-Garde

A jazz explorer who inextricably linked the otherworldliness of the African-American experience with ancient Egyptian mythology and the futurist possibilities of science-fiction, Sun Ra claimed astral lineage and backed up the fact with out-of-this-world recordings, hundreds of them, for obscure labels like ESP-Disk, Saturn, Delmark and the comparatively above-ground Impulse! Records. An early electric instrument user as well as a synth pioneer virtually without precedent in the non-academic community, Ra and his interstellar big band—variously credited as the Solar Arkestra, the Omniverse Arkestra, the Cosmo Discipline Arkestra, the Astro Infinity Arkestra and the Myth Science Arkestra—stood miles away from even the jazz avant-garde during the increasingly cosmic-conscious 1960s, so hopelessly removed from a position of influence that it would take decades for the leader and pianist's inspiration to seep into the broader music world. Years before his became the hip name for aspiring philosopher/producers to drop, Sun Ra was an outsider whose astro-philosophical musings and focus on numerology marked every LP he recorded, while his Afrocentric wardrobe and commune approach to running a big band reflected itself on live dates. *—Scott Yanow and John Bush*

Sound Sun Pleasure / 1953-1958 / Evidence ♦♦♦♦♦

Sun Ra's kaleidoscope of sounds was just taking shape in the 1950s and early '60s when the 13 tracks comprising this CD were recorded. His Astro-Infinity Arkestra included several emerging musicians who would later become major stars, like baritone saxophonist Charles Davis, Bob Northern on flugelhorn and James Spaulding, who is featured on various reeds. The great jazz violinist Stuff Smith is even along on "Deep Purple," providing a dazzling, bluesy solo right at home in The Ra mix. *—Ron Wynn*

The Singles / Sep. 1954-1982 / Evidence ♦♦♦♦♦

Back in the mid-'50s, bandleader Sun Ra decided to get his music to his audience through a more direct process by starting his own label, Saturn Records. Equal parts creative futuristic vision and small-time Southern R&B bandstand hustle, these 45s were pressed in unbelievably small quantities (sometimes in runs of only 50 copies), making them the holy grail of Sun Ra collectibles. The collection of singles runs a neat 30-year time-frame and features everything from Sun Ra with an embryonic form of his Arkestra doing backup duties behind doo-wop groups and R&B slopbucket singers like 'Space Age Vocalist' Yochannon to wild-ass sonic experiements from the late '70s into the early '80s that would have atmospherically fit on any of his avant-garde albums. Pieced together for this release from the contributions of private collectors around the world—and sonically cleaned up far beyond the audio capabilities of the original vinyl they were pressed on—these 49 three-minute opuses will alternately confuse, astound, confound, delight, and illuminate Sun Ra fans of all stratas of involvement. A major piece of puzzle that is the man, now in place. *—Cub Koda*

Sun Song / Jul. 12, 1956 / Delmark ♦♦♦♦

Other than the title cut (a spacey electronic fantasy which concludes this CD reissue), the music on the early effort from Sun Ra and his Arkestra is mostly pretty conventional. Although the leader offers some slightly left-of-center piano, Robert Herndon has a couple of colorful tympani solos, and there are some futuristic songtitles (such as "Call for All Demons," "Street Named Hell" and "Brainville"), the music could otherwise pass for a typical "territory band" of the mid-'50s. Most notable among the soloists are tenor saxophonist John Gilmore (an influence on John Coltrane), baritonist Pat Patrick and trombonist Julian Priester. This is a historic set that only hints in spots at Ra's upcoming innovations. *—Scott Yanow*

Angels & Demons at Play/The Nubians of Plutonia / 1956-1960 / Evidence ♦♦♦♦♦

Sun Ra ambles between vigorous hard bop, ambitious, adventurous free jazz, and African and Afro-Latin material on the 15 selections featured on this set of '50s and early '60s tracks. The first half was recorded in 1956 and 1960 and includes originals from Ronnie Boykins and Julian Priester, plus futuristic organ from Ra on "Music From the World Tomorrow" and hard-blowing solos from John Gilmore and Marshall Allen. The second half consists of rehearsal tapes from 1960 with The Arkestra steadily progressing and moving beyond conventional jazz modes into multiple rhythms, chants, and twisting, roaring arrangements spiced by vividly expressive solos. Plus, like every other disc in the series, it is superbly remastered. *—Ron Wynn*

We Travel the Spaceways/Bad and Beautiful / 1956-1961 / Evidence ♦♦♦♦♦

The opening numbers range from the humorous and futuristic bent of "Interplanetary Music" and "We Travel The Spaceways" to the more musically expansive "New Horizons" and "Space Loneliness." Trumpeter Phil Cochran and the superb horn section of Marshall Allen, John Gilmore and Pat Patrick sometimes remain in the maze and sometimes explode with short but peppery solos. The other songs mix bop and swing tunes with more experimental fare like "Ankh" and "Exotic Two," where Patrick, Gilmore, Ra and Allen soar while bassist Ronnie Boykins and drummer Tommy Hunter maintain the rhythmic center. *—Ron Wynn*

Sound of Joy / Nov. 1957 / Delmark ♦♦♦♦

This reissue, prior to the release of many of Sun Ra's Saturn albums on Evidence CDs, was often thought of as Ra's second recording although now several earlier dates have appeared. The music from Sun Ra's Chicago-based band of the 1950s (some of the same tunes, but different performances, also appear on Evidence's *Planet Earth/Low Ways*) is quite interesting for its ties to the bop and swing traditions are much more obvious than it would be in the near future. Ra's eccentric piano and occasional electric keyboard look forward as do some of the harmonies and Jim Herndon's colorful tympani. Two previously unissued cuts (which have also surfaced on an Evidence set) augment the original LP program. *—Scott Yanow*

Visits Planet Earth/Interstellar Low Ways / Nov. 1, 1958-1960 / Evidence ♦♦♦♦♦

This Evidence CD reissues two rare albums originally put out by bandleader Sun Ra on his Saturn label. Taken as a whole, it shows Ra's Arkestra evolving from its roots in bop and swing into a unique entity of its own. The first four titles (from 1956), despite Ra doubling on electric keyboards, are fairly conventional. Art Hoyle has a few fine trumpet solos and the twin baritones of Pat Patrick and Charles Davis battle it out on the boppish "Two Tones." The three numbers from 1958 are much more advanced, utilizing some modal vamps, and the final seven selections (from 1960) are generally avant-garde. The group has "vocals" on a couple of pieces, most successfully on the memorable "Rocket Number Nine Take Off for the Planet Venus," which also contains an explosive John Gilmore tenor solo. This excellent CD can be used as a way to get bebop fans interested in Sun Ra's exploratory music. *—Scott Yanow*

Holiday for Soul Dance / 1968-1969 / Evidence ♦♦♦♦

Sun Ra never concerned himself with the issues of innovation vs. preservation that seem to be the rage in current jazz circles. Instead, his music was both futuristic and classic, embracing the past and anticipating the future. A prime example is this fine eight-track collection of pre-rock standards done in 1968 and 1969. Of course, Ra didn't simply cover these numbers in a reverential manner; instead, he and The Astro-Infinity Arkestra stomp, romp, twist, strut and cut through a collection ranging from "But Not For Me" to "Early Autumn" and "Body and Soul." *—Ron Wynn*

The Magic City / 1965 / Evidence ♦♦♦♦

One's appreciation of Sun Ra's "The Magic City" (which takes up over 27 minutes of this 1993 CD) depends on how much one likes free jazz. Certainly it is doubtful that too many residents of Birmingham, Alabama (Ra's hometown, which had "The Magic City" as its motto) would have appreciated this music. Freely improvised and putting the emphasis on Ra's piano and clavioline, plus some torrid work by Marshall Allen on piccolo, this work may test one's tolerance, but it has become a cult favorite. Also on the set is the nearly 11-minute "The Shadow World" and a couple brief versions of an original ("Abstract Eye" and "Abstract 'I'"). As usual, Ra's band (which on these numbers was either 11 or 12 pieces) mixes some famous players (tenorman John Gilmore, baritonist Pat Patrick and altoist Marshall Allen) with a few unknowns, all doing their best to serve the leader's music as best they could. The results are sometimes ragged, but certainly intriguing. *—Scott Yanow*

☆ **The Heliocentric Worlds of Sun Ra, Vol. 1** / Apr. 20, 1965 / Calibre ♦♦♦♦♦

The Heliocentric Worlds of Sun Ra, Vol. 2 / Nov. 16, 1965 / Calibre ♦♦♦

Nothing Is / May 1966 / Get Back ♦♦♦♦

This ESP date was recorded in the middle of the free jazz revolution, but Sun Ra shows that he stood apart, having played some free music in his own style years before. The live performances have solos from tenorman John Gilmore, Marshall Allen (on oboe), baritonist Pat Patrick, bassist Ronnie Boykins and Ra on piano and his spooky-sounding clavoline, along with many ragged and boisterous ensembles. Among the pieces are "Exotic Forest," "Shadow World," "Theme of the Stargazers" and "Next Stop Mars." Both in music and song titles, Sun Ra was certainly ahead of his time. *—Scott Yanow*

★ **Atlantis** / 1967-1969 / Saturn ♦♦♦♦♦

This 1993 CD reissue brings back Sun Ra's monumental 22-minute work, "Atlantis." Ra's electronic keyboards (his highly original-sounding Solar Sound organ and a clavioline) dominate the piece, along with the playing of three drummers. The music is quite emotional, tense, and sometimes explosive. Ra is joined by two trumpets, two trombones, Robert Northern on French horn, three altoists (including Marshall Allen), John Gilmore on tenor, baritonist Pat Patrick, and bass clarinetist Robert Cummings, plus the three drummers; there is no bass. There are also five shorter pieces which are quite odd as well, featuring Ra (on a clavinet) joined by up to five percussionists and (on two numbers) Gilmore's tenor. The latter music is oddly funky, eccentric, and catchy in its own way. Sun Ra fans can consider the acquisition of this innovative set to be a must. *—Scott Yanow*

Space Is the Place [Blue Thumb] / Oct. 19, 1972-Oct. 20, 1972 / GRP ♦♦♦♦♦

Space Is the Place provides an excellent introduction to Sun Ra's vast and free-form jazz catalog. Typical of many Sun Ra recordings, the program is varied; earthbound songs, like the swing number "Images" and Egyptian exotica piece "Discipline 33," fit right in with more space-age cuts, like the tumultuous "Sea of Sound" and the humorous "Rocket Number Nine." Sun Ra fuses many of these styles on the sprawling title cut, as interlocking harmonies, African percussion, manic synthesizer lines, and joyous ensemble blowing all jell into some sort of church revival of the cosmos. Throughout the recording, Sun Ra displays his typically wide-ranging talents on space organ and piano, reed players John Gilmore and Marshall Allen contribute incisive and intense solos, and June Tyson masterfully leads the Space Ethnic Voices on dreamy vocal flights. This is a fine recording and a must for Sun Ra fans. *—Stephen Cook*

Sun Ra and His Orkestra Live at Montreux / Jul. 1976 / Inner City ♦♦♦♦♦

Lanquidity / Jul. 17, 1978 / Evidence ♦♦♦♦

While one can't quite call it the Sun Ra dance album, this 1978 recording, made for a tiny Philadelphia record label, finds the Sun Ra Arkestra's rhythm section settling into a steady groove on each of the lengthy tracks, while horns, reeds, guitars, and Sun Ra's keyboards solo in overlapping patterns on top. The title number recalls Charles Mingus' "Goodbye Porkpie Hat" in its slow pace and elegiac tone, while the middle three tracks have livelier beats with playing that often answers to the style of fusion played by many jazz groups in the late '70s. "There Are Other Worlds (They Have Not Told You Of)," the nearly 11-minute concluding tune, is the closest to more familiar 1960s and early-'70s Sun Ra, with its less cohesive lead work and the "ethnic voices" that speak, sing, and whisper about outer space. *Lanquidity* was extremely rare in its original vinyl pressing. It was reissued by Evidence Music on September 26, 2000, with liner notes in which John Dilberto discussed Sun Ra's 25-year residence in Philadelphia and Tom Buchler, who organized the recording session, discussed the making of the album. *—William Ruhlmann*

Sunrise in Different Dimensions / Feb. 24, 1980 / hatHUT ✦✦✦✦✦
This double LP features a live concert by Sun Ra & the Arkestra in Switzerland. The only fault to the set is that the two drummers (Chris Henderson and Eric Walker) fail to swing and often sound wooden on the vintage standards, which might be due to the lack of a bassist. However, the nonet (which also includes Ra on piano and organ, tenor great John Gilmore, altoist Marshall Allen, baritonist Danny Thompson, the reeds of Kenneth Williams and Noel Scott, and trumpeter Michael Ray), despite its slightly odd instrumentation, is heard throughout in excellent form. In addition to eight diverse and generally adventurous untitled originals by Ra, the ensemble performs ragged and eccentric versions of such 1930s pieces as "Big John's Special," "Yeah Man," "Queer Notions," "Limehouse Blues," and "King Porter Stomp." For the remainder of his life, Sun Ra would alternate between reinventions of swing tunes and his outer space originals; despite the drummers, this was one of the better examples of his late-period band. *—Scott Yanow*

Hours After / Dec. 18, 1986-Dec. 19, 1986 / Black Saint ✦✦✦✦
On this continually interesting program, Sun Ra and his Arkestra perform typically odd versions of a couple of standards ("But Not for Me" and "Beautiful Love"), a swinging original ("Hours After") and two outside pieces ("Dance of the Extra Terrestrains" and "Love on a Far Away Planet"). Almost up to the level of *Reflections In Blue* (recorded during the same two-day period), this date features one of the stronger versions of Ra's band. The 14-piece orchestra consists of trumpeter Randall Murray, trombonist Tyrone Hill, seven reeds (including the perennials: tenorman John Gilmore, altoist Marshall Allen and Pat Patrick on alto), guitarist Carl LeBlanc and a four-piece rhythm section that includes two drummers. Recommended. *—Scott Yanow*

Reflections in Blue / Dec. 18, 1986-Dec. 19, 1986 / Black Saint ✦✦✦✦✦
By the 1980s, Sun Ra was often revisiting the past in eccentric fashion. He had become interested again in the music of Fletcher Henderson and early Duke Ellington, and was playing occasional standards in concert, although in very much his own way. His 14-piece Arkestra of 1986 on this date not only performs demented renditions of "Say It Isn't So" and "Yesterdays" (hinting at swing while often including borderline outside solos), but originals that sound like crazy swing tunes, most notably the heated "Reflections In Blue" and "Nothin' From Nothin'." Certainly this studio set is not recommended for swing purists who take life too seriously, but the creative and often crazy music should delight many listeners. The follow-up album, *Hours After,* was recorded during the same two days. *—Scott Yanow*

Mayan Temples / Jul. 24, 1990-Jul. 25, 1990 / Black Saint ✦✦✦✦✦
One of the finest Sun Ra recordings from his final years, this effort is particularly recommended due to the many Ra keyboard solos and John Gilmore features, the latter of which include a tenor showcase on "Opus In Springtime." Trumpeters Michael Ray and Ahmed Abdullah, altoist Marshall Allen and singer June Tyson also have their spots, and the repertoire consists of ten Ra originals (including a remake of "El Is the Sound of Joy") and three standard ballads. Overall, this is a fine all-around studio set that avoids some of the excesses of Sun Ra's concerts of the period. Recommended. *—Scott Yanow*

Black Myth/Out in Space / Oct. 17, 1970-Nov. 7, 1970 / UNI/Mercury ✦✦✦✦
Although portions of the *Black Myth/Out in Space* were previously issued as *It's After the End of the World,* this two-disc set is far and away the definitive release of the material in question, compiling two 1970 festival appearances documenting Sun Ra at the peak of his considerable creative powers. *Black Myth,* recorded at *the Donaueschingen Music Festival,* is the real find here, with a series of compositions and solos written specifically for performance on that evening—the Arkestra, including John Gilmore and Pat Patrick, is in excellent form throughout, and the music is consistently inventive and galvanizing. The same sentiments apply to *Out in Space* as well—a set comprised primarily of cosmic journeys like "Walkin' on the Moon," "Outer Space Where I Came From" and "Theme of the Stargazers," it climaxes with a powerful rendition of "We Travel the Spaceways." *—Jason Ankeny*

Life Is Splendid / 1972 / Total Energy ✦✦✦

Great Lost Sun Ra Albums: Cymbals & Crystal Spears / 1973 / Evidence ✦✦✦
Sun Ra entered into an licensing agreement with Impulse! in the early '70s to distribute both old and new LPs from his own Saturn label. This was his first association with something like a major record company, and though it resulted in ten actual releases, it didn't last long; another 12 planned releases were cancelled. Among these were two newly recorded albums, *Cymbals* and *Crystal Spears,* both of which were shelved (though three tracks from the former were later released on the Saturn LP *Deep Purple*). The Evidence label's extensive Sun Ra reissue program brought these two albums into release for the first time in 2000 as the double CD *The Great Lost Sun Ra Albums: Cymbals & Spears,* a mere 27 years after they were recorded. *Cymbals* turns out to be a small band session on which no more than six and usually only four musicians are playing on any one selection. Sun Ra is mostly heard on organ, and his understated playing sets the tone for a group of moody, low-key tracks. No matter who is soloing, this is mostly a quiet, introspective session. It's last-set-of-the-night stuff. From the opening miniMoog solo by Sun Ra, *Crystal Spears* is something else again: a full band album. Its tunes feature as many as seven horn players on a track, with most of them contributing percussion when they're not blowing. The stretched-out arrangements allow plenty of room for solos, duos, and even periods of near-cacophony. It's doubtful that *Cymbals* and *Crystal Spears* would have altered Sun Ra's overall career had they been issued by Impulse! in 1973 as intended, but his work is so extensive and so varied that each individual record provides another valuable piece in the puzzle; here are two more. *—William Ruhlmann*

● **Greatest Hits: Easy Listening for Intergalactic Travel** / 1956-1973 / Evidence ✦✦✦✦✦
"Those wondering where to begin when buying their first Sun Ra album, this is it!," declares an Evidence Music press release on their Sun Ra anthology *Greatest Hits: Easy Listening for Intergalactic Travel.* It also notes that, since Sun Ra never had any actual "hits," the 18 tracks from 15 Sun Ra albums, plus two singles and a soundtrack excerpt, were chosen because they were fan favorites, because they displayed the artist's development over the years 1956-73, and because of "their musical 'accessibility'—relatively speaking of course." True enough. Proceeding chronologically, the album finds a bebop-influenced big band on its earliest tracks, which include the familiar jazz covers "'Round Midnight" and "I Loves You, Porgy." As early as 1960's "Rocket Number Nine Take Off for the Planet Venus," however, the band is beginning to exhibit its interest in space travel and equally spacy music, including chanting and an odd bass solo. From here on out, things get strange, but most of the tracks are low-key and at least somewhat composed. Within those "easy listening" parameters, however, there is room for everything from the outside saxophone work on the ballad "When Angels Speak of Love" to the heavily percussive "Yucatan" and the set-closing fractured pop of "The Perfect Man." If the album succeeds in its mission, it's because it does treat accessibility as a relative term that includes tracks like "Thither and Yon," with its wild reed solo, as well as fairly straight-ahead performances. Listeners looking for clues to the rest of Sun Ra's catalog in this compilation should be warned that there is more of the experimental stuff proportionally than is found here, but they can be eased into Sun Ra's cock-eyed vision by starting here. *—William Ruhlmann*

Pathways to Unknown Worlds/Friendly Love / 1973 / Evidence ✦✦✦

When Angels Speak of Love / 1963 / Evidence ✦✦✦

Jimmy Raney

b. Aug. 20, 1927, Louisville, KY, **d.** May 10, 1995, Louisville, KY
Guitar / Cool
Jimmy Raney was the definitive cool jazz guitarist, a fluid bop soloist with a quiet sound who had a great deal of inner fire. He worked with local groups in Chicago before spending nine months with Woody Herman in 1948. From then on he was in the major leagues, having associations with Al Haig, Buddy DeFranco, Artie Shaw and Terry Gibbs. His work with Stan Getz (1951-52) was historic as the pair made for a classic musical partnership. Raney was also very much at home in the Red Norvo Trio (1953-54) before spending six years primarily working in a supper club with pianist Jimmy Lyon (1954-60). After playing with Getz during 1962-63, he returned to Louisville and was outside of music until resurfacing in the early '70s. During the 1970s Raney recorded often for Xanadu. He worked frequently with his son Doug Raney (who has a very similar sound on guitar) and was less active in the late '80s and '90s up until his 1995 death. *—Scott Yanow*

Jimmy Raney: A / May 28, 1954-Feb. 18, 1955 / Prestige/OJC ✦✦✦✦✦
1954-1955. Incredibly talented guitarist on A+ record. Near essential. With Teddy Kotick (b) and Hall Overton (p). *—Michael G. Nastos*

★ **Live in Tokyo** / Apr. 12, 1976-Apr. 14, 1976 / Xanadu ✦✦✦✦✦
This album features the great guitarist Jimmy Raney in a trio with bassist Sam Jones and drummer Leroy Williams, all regulars for the Xanadu label in the 1970s. The boppish performances (which Raney considers among his very best) are subtle with lots of interplay between the players. Highpoints include "Anthropology," "A Burning Cherokee" and Raney's unaccompanied playing on "Stella by Starlight." *—Scott Yanow*

Raney (1981) / Feb. 27, 1981 / Criss Cross ✦✦✦✦✦
This was the first release by Criss Cross, one of the top bop-based labels in Europe. The CD reissue adds six alternate takes to the original seven-song program. The cool-toned guitarist Jimmy Raney is teamed with his son Doug (who has a very similar style on guitar) along with bassist Jesper Lundgaard and drummer Eric Ineke. Together they perform one original and six standards in light but forcefully swinging style. The interplay between the two guitarists is a major plus. *—Scott Yanow*

Freddie Redd

b. May 29, 1928, New York, NY
Piano, Composer / Hard Bop
A classic bop pianist and a composer of haunting melodies, Freddie Redd has had an episodic career, with high points followed by periods in which he maintained a low profile.Redd, who appeared with both jazz and early R&B groups, recorded his debut as a leader for Prestige in 1955, appeared on dates led by Gene Ammons and Art Farmer, and toured Sweden in 1956 with Ernestine Anderson and Rolf Ericson. When he returned to the U.S., Redd settled for a time in San Francisco, where he worked as the house pianist at Bop City and recorded for Riverside. He found his greatest fame when he wrote the music for the play *The Connection.* He acted and played in the landmark show in New York, London and Paris, was in the film, and recorded the music for Blue Note, the first of his three sessions for the label. Unfortunately, there were no encore writing assignments, and Redd soon moved to Europe, where he performed regularly but became quite obscure in the U.S. In 1974, he moved to Los Angeles, but despite worthy sessions for Interplay (1977), Uptown (1985), Triloka (1988) and Milestone (1990), Freddie Redd remains an underrated great, still playing in his prime without gaining much recognition. *—Scott Yanow*

San Francisco Suite for Jazz Trio / Oct. 2, 1957 / Riverside/OJC ✦✦✦✦✦
This early recording by pianist Freddie Redd (a straight CD reissue of the original Riverside LP) features Redd's trio of the time, with bassist George Tucker and drummer All Dreares. The CD reissue is highlighted by the 13-minute title piece, a suite that in its five melodies depicts the jazz life in San Francisco during the era. Redd shows potential both in his writing and his boppish playing. The remainder of the fine set has the group's interpretations of three other Redd originals and a trio of standards. An excellent effort. *—Scott Yanow*

★ **The Complete Blue Note Freddie Redd** / Feb. 15, 1960-Jan. 17, 1961 / Mosaic ✦✦✦✦✦
Available in a box set as either three LPs or two CDs, this limited-edition release has all of the music recorded at pianist Freddie Redd's three Blue Note sessions. In addition to the selections originally included on the LPs *Music From the Connection* and *Shades of Redd,* there is a completely unissued date that adds to the fairly slim Freddie Redd discography. Altoist Jackie McLean (who is on all three sets) and tenor saxophonist Tina Brooks (a key soloist on two) co-star with the pianist; trumpeter Benny Bailey is also heard from the later date. The

music is comprised mostly of Redd's originals (including seven songs written for the stage play *The Connection*) and fits into the style of the mainstream hard bop of the day, although with a few personal touches. Straight-ahead fans and Blue Note collectors can consider this set to be essential. *—Scott Yanow*

The Music from The Connection / Jun. 13, 1960 / Blue Note ✦✦✦✦✦
Freddie Redd composed the music for Jack Gelber's *The Connection*, a gritty play about musician junkies. Gelber had originally thought that the play would feature real musicians—who would also double as actors in minor roles—improvising on blues and jazz standards in the tradition of Charlie Parker, but Redd convinced him to use an original score. The two weaved Redd's original compositions into the score, making it an integral part of the play, but the music holds up superbly on its own. Using the direction "in the tradition of Charlie Parker" as a starting point, the pianist wrote seven pieces of straight-ahead bop, wide open for improvisations, and then assembled a sterling quartet featuring himself, alto saxophonist Jackie McLean, bassist Michael Mattos, and drummer Larry Ritchie. The end result was a set of dynamic straight-ahead bop. While both Redd and McLean show signs of their influences—the pianist blends Monk and Powell, while the saxophonist has built off of Bird's twisting lines—they have developed their own voices, which gives the driving, bluesy bop on *Music From the Connection* an edge. McLean's full, robust tone often dominates, but he never overshadows Redd's complex, intricate playing, and both musicians, as well as Mattos and Ritchie, effortlessly keep up with the changes from hard-hitting, up-tempo bop numbers to lyrical, reflective ballads. Musically, *Music From the Connection* might not offer anything unexpected, but whenever straight-ahead bop is done this well, it should be celebrated. *—Stephen Thomas Erlewine*

☆ **Shades of Redd** / Aug. 13, 1960 / Blue Note ✦✦✦✦✦
Quintet with Tina Brooks on tenor sax and Jackie McLean on alto sax plays all Redd originals with flair and bluesy poignancy. *—Michael G. Nastos*

Dewey Redman (Walter Dewey Redman)

b. May 17, 1931, Fort Worth, TX
Sax (Tenor) / Avant-Garde Jazz, Free Jazz, Post-Bop
One of the great avant-garde tenors, Dewey Redman has never received anywhere near the acclaim that his son Joshua Redman gained in the 1990s but ironically Dewey is much more of an innovative player. He began on clarinet when he was 13 and played in his high school marching band, a group that also included Ornette Coleman, Charles Moffett and Prince Lasha. Redman was a public school teacher during 1956-59 but, after getting his master's degree in education from North Texas State, he moved to San Francisco where he freelanced as a musician for seven years; Pharoah Sanders was among his sidemen. All of this was a prelude to his impressive association with the Ornette Coleman Quartet (1967-74) during which Redman's tenor playing was a perfect match for Ornette's alto. Redman could play as free as the leader but his appealing tone made the music seem a little more accessible. He also worked with Charlie Haden's Liberation Music Orchestra and was an important part of Keith Jarrett's greatest group, his quintet of the mid-'70s. Redman guested on Pat Metheny's notable *80/81* album and teamed up with Don Cherry, Charlie Haden and Ed Blackwell in the Ornette Coleman reunion band called Old and New Dreams. Despite all of this activity and plenty of recordings (including occasional ones as a leader), Dewey Redman has yet to be fully recognized for his innovative talents. *—Scott Yanow*

Look for the Black Star / Jan. 4, 1966 / Freedom ✦✦✦✦✦
Although always a bit under-recognized and overshadowed by his contemporaries, tenor-saxophonist Dewey Redman has long been one of the giants of the avant-garde and free bop. This early recording finds Redman discovering his own individual voice on five of his frequently emotional originals. Assisted by pianist Jym Young, bassist Donald Raphael Gareet and drummer Eddie Moore, this San Francisco date is quite adventurous and holds one's interest throughout. *—Scott Yanow*

The Ear of the Behearer / Jun. 8, 1973-Jun. 9, 1973 / Impulse! ✦✦✦✦
This 1998 CD reissues Dewey Redman's entire *The Ear of the Behearer* album (although it leaves out an alternate take of "Interconnection" that was released on a different set), plus four of the seven selections from his *Coincide* record of a year later. Some of the music is quite adventurous and free, while other tracks include some freebop, a struttin' blues ("Boody"), and quieter ballads. Redman, a distinctive tenor saxophonist, actually plays alto on five of the first six selections; he is less memorable (although no less exploratory) on the smaller horn. Redman is joined on most cuts by trumpeter Ted Daniel, throughout the *Behearer* date by cellist Jane Robertson, and on the full set by bassist Sirone and drummer Eddie Moore; violinist Leroy Jenkins and percussionist Danny Johnson also make guest appearances. These two albums were Redman's only sets as a leader for Impulse. Intriguing music. *—Scott Yanow*

In Willisau / Aug. 31, 1980 / Black Saint ✦✦✦✦
Tenor saxophonist Dewey Redman and drummer Ed Blackwell had first met up in the late '60s in Ornette Coleman's band and later on as half of Old And New Dreams. This set of live duets from *the Willisau '80 Jazz Festival* succeeds due to Redman's huge sound, Blackwell's colorful rhythms, and the close interplay between the two. Redman's musette playing on "We Hope" is an acquired taste, but otherwise, his tenor playing is heard in top form on his originals, particularly "Communication" and "Willisee," which clock in at just over 14 minutes apiece. Although some listeners will miss the usual chordal instruments (and particularly the bass), this combination works. *—Scott Yanow*

● **The Struggle Continues** / Jan. 1982 / ECM ✦✦✦✦
Tenor saxophonist Dewey Redman is joined by a standard rhythm trio on this date that consists of three very flexible and open musicians: pianist Charles Eubanks, bassist Mark Helias and drummer Ed Blackwell. Redman's five originals range from sonic explorations to freebop (mostly the latter) and find Redman in strong form. To wrap up the date, the quartet performs a bebop standard, Miles Davis' "Dewey Square." A fine outing. *—Scott Yanow*

Living on the Edge / Sep. 13, 1989-Sep. 14, 1989 / Black Saint ✦✦✦✦
The great tenor Dewey Redman has always been a versatile player and he really gets a chance to show off his individuality on this set, whether it is some freebop a la early Ornette Coleman, "Mirror Windows" (which is an explosion of sound and pure energy), the soulful "Blues for J.A.M.—Part 1," a free and speechlike tenor-piano duet with Geri Allen on "As One" and a boppish "Lazy Bird." On "If I Should Lose You," Redman has a rare chance to play some conventional but cliché-free alto. With bassist Cameron Brown and drummer Eddie Moore forming a solid team, this is an easily recommended set of inside/outside music. *—Scott Yanow*

Musics / Oct. 17, 1978-Oct. 19, 1978 / Galaxy/OJC ✦✦✦✦✦

In London / Oct. 1996 / Palmetto ✦✦✦✦
Accompanied by pianist Rita Marcotulli, bassist Cameron Brown and drummer Matt Wilson, veteran tenor saxophonist Dewey Redman puts on a well-rounded program. On "I Should Care," "The Very Thought of You" (a tribute to Dexter Gordon) and the bossa nova "Portrait In Black & White," he shows that, although his roots are in avant-garde jazz, Redman is quite capable of caressing a melody. In contrast, his renditions of "I-Pimp," "Tu-inns" and "Eleven" emphasize freer improvising and plenty of fire. In both contexts, Dewey Redman emerges as an underrated giant. *—Scott Yanow*

Don Redman

b. Jul. 29, 1900, Piedmont, WV, **d.** Nov. 30, 1964, New York, NY
Vocals, Sax (Alto), Clarinet, Composer, Arranger / Classic Jazz, Swing
The first great arranger in jazz history, Don Redman's innovations as a writer essentially invented the jazz-oriented big band with arrangements that developed yet left room for solo improvisations. Redman initially became Fletcher Henderson's chief arranger (although Fletcher was often later on mistakenly given credit for the innovative charts) in addition to playing clarinet, alto and (on at least one occasion) oboe. Redman, whose largely-spoken vocals were charming, recorded the first ever scat vocal on "My Papa Doesn't Two Time" in early 1924, predating Louis Armstrong. Although his early arrangements were futuristic, they could be a bit stiff and it was not until Armstrong joined Henderson's Orchestra that Redman (learning from the brilliant cornetist) began to really swing in his writing; "Sugar Foot Stomp" and "The Stampede" are two of his many classic charts. It was a shock to Henderson when Redman was persuaded in 1927 by Jean Goldkette to direct McKinney's Cotton Pickers. Redman soon turned the previously unknown group into a strong competitor of Henderson's, composing such future standards as "Gee Baby, Ain't I Good to You" and "Cherry." In 1931 Redman put together his own big band which lasted (if not prospered) up until 1941. After that he freelanced as an arranger for the remainder of the swing era and led an all-star orchestra in 1946 that became the first band to visit postwar Europe. *—Scott Yanow*

● **1931-1933** / Sep. 24, 1931-Feb. 2, 1933 / Classics ✦✦✦✦✦
The first of three Don Redman Classics CDs consists of his orchestra's earliest sessions. Although Redman's big band never hit it as big as his former employers (Fletcher Henderson and McKinney's Cotton Pickers), it was an impressive outfit thanks to the leader's advanced arrangements. Among the key sidemen on these performances are trumpeters Red Allen (who is on the first two sessions) and Sidney DeParis, tenor saxophonist Robert Carroll and pianist Horace Henderson. Highlights include "Chant of the Weed" (Redman's atmospheric theme song), "I Heard," "How'm I Doin'," and "Hot and Anxious." The main Don Redman CD to get. *—Scott Yanow*

1933-1936 / Feb. 2, 1933-May 7, 1936 / Classics ✦✦✦✦✦
The great arranger Don Redman made Fletcher Henderson's Orchestra in the mid-1920s the first real swing band, but during the swing era itself, Redman was little known to the general public. His big band (heard here on the second of three "complete" Classics CDs) failed to really catch on, although it stayed together throughout the 1930s. After recording a bunch of sessions in 1933, Redman's orchestra only cut two sides in Jan. 1934 and then none until May 1936. There are vocals on 22 of the 25 selections on this CD; of the three instrumentals, this version of "Christopher Columbus" might not be by Redman. The leader's charming vocals are fine, but the nine by Harlan Lattimore are of lesser interest, and Chick Bullock dominates a six-song session. There are some good solos along the way, particularly by trumpeter Sidney DeParis, trombonists Benny Morton and Claude Jones and the forgotten tenor Robert Carroll, but this CD is primarily for completists. *—Scott Yanow*

1936-1939 / May 7, 1936-Mar. 23, 1939 / Classics ✦✦✦✦✦
The third in the series of Don Redman Classics CDs finds the innovative arranger adjusting to the swing era. His big band is heard on sessions cut for ARC in 1936 ("Bugle Call Rag" is excellent), Variety in 1937 (including a previously unreleased "Swingin' With the Fat Man"), and Bluebird during 1938-39 (including "I Got Ya," "Down Home Rag" and "Milenberg Joys"). A lot of interesting names passed through the band during this era, including trumpeter Sidney DeParis, trombonist Quentin Jackson and singer Laurel Watson, and there is some pleasing music despite a fair amount of vocals. This series ended before Redman's last two big band sessions, but those have often been made available by RCA/Bluebird. The first CD in Classics' Redman series is the most essential. *—Scott Yanow*

Joshua Redman

b. Feb. 1, 1969, Berkeley, CA
Sax (Tenor) / Hard Bop, Post-Bop
Every few years it seems as if the jazz media goes out of its way to hype one young artist, overpraising him to such an extent that it is easy to tear him down when the next season arrives. In the early '90s Joshua Redman briefly became a media darling, but in his case he largely deserved the attention. A talented bop-based tenorman, Redman (who will probably never be an innovator) is a throwback to the styles of Red Holloway and Gene Ammons but also has an inquisitive spirit and can play intriguing music when inspired.

The son of the great tenor saxophonist Dewey Redman, Joshua graduated from Harvard and (after debating about whether to become a doctor) he seemed headed towards studying law at Yale. However Redman came in first place at the 1991 Thelonious Monk competition, landed a recording contract with Warner Bros. and was soon on the cover of most jazz magazines. Pat Metheny was a guest on one of his albums (the Redman-Metheny interplay during their engagements was quite memorable) and, although Redman has had success constantly touring with his own group, it is a pity that his apprentice period as a sideman was so brief. In 1996 Joshua Redman recorded and briefly toured with Chick Corea's "Tribute to Bud Powell" sextet; the solo *Timeless Tales (For Changing Times)* followed in 1998, and in 2000 he returned with *Beyond. Passage of Time* appeared in early 2001. *—Scott Yanow*

Joshua Redman / 1993 / Warner Brothers ✦✦✦

• **Wish** / 1993 / Warner Brothers ✦✦✦✦✦
Joshua Redman's sophomore effort found him leading a piano-less quartet that also included guitar great Pat Metheny and half of Ornette Coleman's trailblazing late-'50s/early-'60s quartet: acoustic bassist Charlie Haden and drummer Billy Higgins. With such company, Redman could have delivered a strong avant-garde or free jazz album; Haden and Higgins had played an important role in jazz's avant-garde because of their association with Coleman, and Metheny had himself joined forces with Coleman on their thrilling *Song X* session of 1985. But *Wish* isn't avant-garde; instead, it's a mostly inside post-bop date that emphasizes the lyrical and the introspective. The musicians swing hard and fast on Charlie Parker's "Moose the Mooche," but things become very reflective on pieces like Redman's "The Undeserving Many" and Metheny's "We Had a Sister." One of the nice things about Redman is his ability to provide jazz interpretations of rock and R&B songs. While neo-conservatives ignore them and many NAC artists simply provide boring, predictable, note-for-note covers, Redman isn't afraid to dig into them and show their jazz potential. In Redman's hands, Stevie Wonder's "Make Sure You're Sure" becomes a haunting jazz-noir statement, while Eric Clapton's ballad "Tears in Heaven" is changed from moving pop/rock to moving pop-jazz. The latter, in fact, could be called "smooth jazz with substance." Some of bop's neo-conservatives disliked the fact that Redman was playing with two of Coleman's former sidemen and a fusion icon like Metheny, but then, Redman never claimed to be a purist. Although *Wish* isn't innovative, it's an appealing CD from an improviser who is willing to enter a variety of musical situations. *—Alex Henderson*

MoodSwing / Mar. 8, 1994-Mar. 10, 1994 / Warner Brothers ✦✦✦✦
In the extensive liner notes of this CD, tenor saxophonist Joshua Redman writes that the main problem with jazz at the time was not the music but the public perception of it as forbidding and overly intellectual; that in reality jazz is quite fun and emotional. Those descriptions can certainly be applied to Redman's music, which, while pulling at the boundaries of modern hard bop, is also fairly easy to grab on to. Joined by his regular band members of the period (pianist Brad Mehldau, bassist Christian McBride and drummer Brian Blade), Redman performs a full set of originals which, although not derivative, do fit into the straight-ahead tradition. At this point in time, Redman was growing from album to album, having already started at a high level. A fine outing. *—Scott Yanow*

Spirit of the Moment: Live at the Village Vanguard / Mar. 21, 1995-Mar. 26, 1995 / Warner Brothers ✦✦✦✦✦
This double-CD gives one a definitive look at how the much-acclaimed tenor-saxophonist Joshua Redman sounded in the mid-'90s. Joined by pianist Peter Martin, bassist Christopher Thomas and drummer Brian Blade, Redman stretches from Gene Ammons (who is saluted on "Jig-A-Jug") to late period John Coltrane, showing off both his wide range and his lyricism. Redman is heard at his best on the four-minute cadenza that opens "St. Thomas," digging into "My One and Only Love" and playing almost outside on "Lyric." Of the 14 songs, nine are his originals and, although Redman was not at this point an innovator, he was well on his way to forming his own personal style. Recommended. *—Scott Yanow*

Freedom in the Groove / Apr. 10, 1996-Apr. 13, 1996 / Warner Brothers ✦✦✦✦
As the title suggests, Joshua Redman explores new rhythmic territory on *Freedom in the Groove.* Abandoning the traditional hard bop that has dominated his past recordings, Redman attempts to work himself into hip-hop and urban dance rhythms, which results in an occasionally intriguing but often frustrating album. Occasionally, the fusions work, with Redman contributing sympathetic, graceful licks to the gently insistent rhythms. Too often, the record sounds forced and stilted, which is unfortunate, since jazz/hip-hop fusions need a musician of Redman's caliber to make it credible in the jazz world. *—Leo Stanley*

Timeless Tales (For Changing Times) / Sep. 22, 1998 / Warner Brothers ✦✦✦

Beyond / May 1999 / Warner Brothers ✦✦✦
In his short career, Joshua Redman has been praised for his technical abilities and criticized for his lack of innovation—not surprising responses to the work of a talented young artist. On *Beyond,* his seventh album which was recorded a few months after his 30th birthday, he attempts, as the title suggests, to try some new things. Employing an all new group consisting of pianist Aaron Goldberg, bass player Reuben Rogers, and drummer Gregory Hutchinson, he presents an album of original tunes to follow *Timeless Tales (For Changing Times),* an album of cover material. Eschewing the pat jazz formula of a head followed by improvisations, he adopts a more free-flowing structure for his compositions in which anyone can start and the tune can develop in an open-ended fashion. He also experiments with time signatures: "A Life—," the closing track, is in 5/4 time; "Stoic Revolutions" is in 6/4; "Belonging (Lopsided Lullaby)" is in 9/4; "Suspended Emanations" is in 10/4; and the lead-off track, "Courage (Asymmetric Aria)," is in 13/4. While no doubt hard to play, the tunes don' t sound all that complicated, perhaps because Redman's saxophone floats over the rhythm section, taking its time to make its statements. As the song titles imply, this is a contemplative album full of small, introspective pleasures, such as the exploratory "Leap of Faith," on which Redman and Mark Turner engage in a tenor conversation. It's not clear that the technical challenges Redman presents himself and his sidemen with ultimately force them to do anything new, but *Beyond* represents a gifted musician tinkering with his musical approach with often satisfying results. *— William Ruhlmann*

Dizzy Reece (Alphonso Son Reece)

b. Jan. 5, 1931, Kingston, Jamaica
Trumpet / Hard Bop
Dizzy Reece is a fine hard-bop trumpeter who has been overshadowed by the innovators of the style. He started on trumpet when he was 14 and moved to Europe in 1949. It was while he was based in England (1954-59) that he achieved some recognition through a series of recordings with top English musicians plus a 1958 date with Donald Byrd. He moved to New York in 1959 but, after a few notable recordings and a bit of publicity, Reece seemed to largely fade away despite remaining active. He was with the Dizzy Gillespie's Orchestra in 1968 and the Paris Reunion Band in 1985. *—Scott Yanow*

Blues in Trinity / Aug. 24, 1958 / Blue Note ✦✦✦✦✦
As Dizzy Reece's first album for Blue Note, *Blues in Trinity* goes a long way to establish the trumpeter's signature sound. Reece doesn't take chances stylistically; he prefers to stay within the confines of hard bop. Nevertheless, he has a bold, forceful sound that simply burns with passion. Even on slower numbers, there's a fire to his playing that keeps *Blues in Trinity* from being predictable. The high quality of the album is even more impressive given the recording circumstances. The English-based Reece was playing in Paris at the time, and he assembled a sextet featuring the vacationing British musicians Tubby Hayes (tenor saxophone) and Terry Shannon (piano), visiting American stars Donald Byrd (trumpet) and Art Taylor (drums), and Canadian bassist Lloyd Thompson, who was playing in Paris with Zoot Sims. Although the band was thrown together, there's a definite spark to this combo, which interacts as if it had been playing together for a long time. Throughout it all, Reece steals the show with his robust playing, and that's why *Blues in Trinity* rises above the level of standard-issue hard bop and becomes something special. *—Stephen Thomas Erlewine*

Comin' On! / Apr. 3, 1960-Jul. 17, 1960 / Blue Note ✦✦✦✦
For a short time in the late '50s trumpeter Dizzy Reece was an up-and-coming jazz artist. However, success eluded him and he quietly faded into obscurity, only occasionally releasing material after the early '60s. As a matter of fact, the sessions that became *Comin' On!* languished in the Blue Note vaults for almost four decades. Rediscovered in 1999, these dates feature six well-rounded hard bop compositions by Reece along with three standards. The tracks from April 3, 1960, not only document the Blue Note debut of tenor saxophonist Stanley Turrentine but also employ the talents of the Jazz Messengers' rhythm section of the time, pianist Bobby Timmons, bassist Jymie Merritt, and drummer Art Blakey. By July 17, 1960, the only musician remaining from the previous date was Turrentine, sharing tenor duties with Musa Kaleem, who is also heard on flute. (The later session's rhythm section had changed to pianist Duke Jordan, bassist Sam Jones, and drummer Al Harewood.) Neglected, although spirited, sessions from an underrated trumpeter and composer. *—Al Campbell*

• **Asia Minor** / Mar. 13, 1962 / New Jazz/OJC ✦✦✦✦✦
This is one of trumpeter Dizzy Reece's finest recordings, a well-planned sextet date (reissued on CD) with baritonist Cecil Payne, Joe Farrell on tenor and flute, pianist Hank Jones, bassist Ron Carter and drummer Charlie Persip that is on the level of a Blue Note album. Reece (who contributed three diverse originals) performs mostly minor-toned songs that seem to really inspire the musicians. The solos tend to be concise but quite meaningful and overall this hard bop but occasionally surprising session is quite memorable. Strange that Reece would not get another opportunity to lead a record date until 1970. *—Scott Yanow*

Django Reinhardt (Jean Baptiste Reinhardt)

b. Jan. 23, 1910, Liverchies, Belgium, **d.** May 16, 1953, Fontainebleau, France
Guitar (Electric), Guitar, Guitar (Acoustic) / Swing
Django Reinhardt was the first hugely influential jazz figure to emerge from Europe—and he remains the most influential European to this day, with possible competition from Joe Zawinul, George Shearing, John McLaughlin, his old cohort Stephane Grappelli and a bare handful of others. A free-spirited gypsy, Reinhardt wasn't the most reliable person in the world, frequently wandering off into the countryside on a whim. Yet Reinhardt came up with a unique way of propelling the humble acoustic guitar into the front line of a jazz combo in the days before amplification became widespread. He would spin joyous, arcing, marvelously inflected solos above the thrumming base of two rhythm guitars and a bass, with Grappelli's elegantly gliding violin serving as the perfect foil. His harmonic concepts were startling for their time—making a direct impression upon Charlie Christian and Les Paul, among others—and he was an energizing rhythm guitarist behind Grappelli, pushing their groups into a higher gear. Not only did Reinhardt put his stamp upon jazz, his string-band music also had an impact upon the parallel development of Western swing, which eventually fed into the wellspring of what is now called country music. Although he could not read music, with Grappelli and on his own, Reinhardt composed several winsome, highly original tunes like "Daphne," "Nuages" and "Manoir de mes reves," as well as mad swingers like "Minor Swing" and the ode to his record label of the '30s, "Stomping at Decca." As the late Ralph Gleason said about Django's recordings, "They were European and they were French and they were still jazz." *—Richard S. Ginell*

First Recordings / Dec. 1934-Sep. 1935 / Prestige/OJC ✦✦✦✦✦
The dozen recordings on this CD (a straight reissue of an earlier Prestige LP) are not Django Reinhardt's very first recordings, nor are these all of the early selections by the Quintet of the Hot Club of France. Actually included are 11 of the classic string group's first 20 numbers, plus a version of "The Sheik of Araby" from a date led by Alix Combelle (doubling on clarinet and tenor). But although this CD is not for completists, there are many memorable and highly enjoyable performances. Guitarist Django Reinhardt and violinist Stephane Grappelli (backed by two rhythm guitars and bassist Louis Vola) made for a perfect team from the start, as can be heard on such numbers as "Tiger Rag," "Dinah" "Avalon" and even "Swanee River." A four-piece brass section (including trumpeter soloist Arthur Briggs) joins the quintet on "Avalon" and "Smoke Rings." An excellent introduction to early Reinhardt and Grappelli. *—Scott Yanow*

Swing from Paris / Sep. 1935-Aug. 1939 / ASV/Living Era ✦✦✦

Tremendous, exuberant material matching guitarist Django Reinhardt with violinist Stephane Grappelli. Both are playing aggressively, yet complementary. It's wonderful playing, and among the finest jazz ever made outside America. *—Ron Wynn*

☆ **Djangology** / May 4, 1936-Mar. 10, 1948 / EMI ✦✦✦✦✦
This massive ten-CD set of Django Reinhardt's recordings covers some of the same ground as the earlier 20-LP *Djangology* EMI series, duplicating the music on *Vols. 2-15* along with three tracks from the first LP and ten from *Vol. 16*. However, there are 34 additional selections that were formerly overlooked (on some of those songs Reinhardt only plays a minor role). This essential box contains 243 performances taken from a 12-year period, tracing Reinhardt's career from his performances with the Quintet of the Hot Club of France (which co-starred violinist Stephane Grappelli) through the war years (with the guitarist heard in a wide variety of settings) and the formation of his postwar quintet with clarinetist Hubert Rostaing before concluding with a reunion with Grappelli. Recommended to all serious Django Reinhardt collectors. *—Scott Yanow*

Vol. 3 / Mar. 14, 1938-May 17, 1939 / JSP ✦✦✦✦✦
This CD from the English label JSP will fill some major gaps even for veteran Django Reinhardt collectors for the 24 selections (which include five alternate takes) are among the rarest in Django's discography. The remarkable guitarist is teamed with violinist Stephane Grappelli and The Quintet of the Hot Club of France for consistently exciting and heated swing performances. Highlights include "Swing from Paris," "Swing '39," "Tea for Two" and "My Melancholy Baby." *—Scott Yanow*

★ **Peche a La Mouche** / Apr. 16, 1947-Mar. 10, 1953 / Verve ✦✦✦✦✦
Legend has it that guitarist Django Reinhardt was at his absolute peak in the 1930s during his recordings with violinist Stephane Grappelli and that when he switched from acoustic to electric guitar after World War II, he lost a bit of his musical personality. Wrong on both counts. This double CD documents his Blue Star recordings of 1947 and 1953 and Reinhardt (on electric guitar) takes inventive boppish solos that put him at the top of the list of jazz guitarists who were active during the era. Most of the earlier tracks feature Reinhardt in The Quintet of the Hot Club of France with clarinetist Hubert Rostaing but it is the eight later selections in which he is backed by a standard rhythm section that are most interesting. These well-recorded performances hint at what Django Reinhardt might have accomplished in the 1950s had he lived longer. Highly recommended. *—Scott Yanow*

Djangology 49 / Jan. 1949-Feb. 1949 / Novus ✦✦✦✦✦
In 1949, guitarist Django Reinhardt and violinist Stephane Grappelli met up in Italy, playing several engagements with Italian rhythm sections and recording an extensive series of songs. This Bluebird CD contains 20 of the best performances and, even if the rhythm section is fairly irrelevant, Django and Grappelli constantly challenge each other to play at their most creative. These recordings do not duplicate the ones reissued by EMI. *—Scott Yanow*

The Indispensable 1949-1950 / Jan. 1949-May 1950 / RCA ✦✦✦✦✦
This attractive two-LP set from French RCA in their *Jazz Tribune* series has 22 of the titles that guitarist Django Reinhardt and violinist Stephane Grappelli recorded together in Italy in 1949 during their final reunion on records. The two-fer overlaps the Bluebird CD to an extent but also has nine songs played in a 1950 quintet with altoist Andre Ekyan. These superlative performances demonstrate that Django Reinhardt, although not as popular in this late stage of his life, never really declined and was very open to the innovations of bop. *—Scott Yanow*

Nuages / May 4, 1936-Dec. 13, 1940 / Arkadia Jazz ✦✦✦✦
That Django Reinhardt was an original and a virtuoso was impressive enough. But what is astounding about his playing is that it was accomplished by someone who only had the use of two fingers on his left hand; he had been severely burned as a young man and lost the use of his ring and pinkie fingers. 45 years after his death there are still French guitarists who, in an attempt to get the same sound that Django had, will only use two fingers when they play. *Nuages* is a collection of recordings from the late '30s featuring Reinhardt's Quintet du Hot Club de France at its peak. The standards are all here: "Minor Swing" (in a statelier, more deliberate version than one normally hears, but one which still swings solidly), "Sweet Georgia Brown," "Swing Guitars." But there are also some unusual treats: a couple of novelty tunes featuring singer Freddy Taylor, a lovely version of "Farewell Blues" on which Django is accompanied by the Benny Carter orchestra, and two tracks with the legendary tenor saxophonist Coleman Hawkins. Essential. *—Rick Anderson*

☆ **With His American Friends** / Mar. 2, 1935-Nov. 6, 1945 / DRG ✦✦✦✦✦
The brilliant gypsy swing guitarist Django Reinhardt is most famous for his work with the Quintet of the Hot Club of France, an all-string group also including violinist Stephane Grappelli, two rhythm guitarists and a bassist. However, through the years, he also had opportunities to record with American stars. In some cases, they were added to a Quintet date, and in others, he was part of an all-star group. This three-CD set, released in 1998, has 57 performances; all but the final four numbers are from 1935-40, with quite a few cut in 1937. The value of this wonderful set to collectors depends on how much Django Reinhardt one already has in their collection, for every performance has been reissued in the past. For those listeners who do not own many of these sessions, the selections are essential, since Django and his guests are consistently inspired by each other's presence. Among the American stars who are featured along with Reinhardt and frequently Grappelli are Coleman Hawkins, Frank "Big Boy" Goudie, Bill Coleman, Freddy Taylor, Benny Carter, Dicky Wells, Eddie South, Larry Adler, Rex Stewart, Barney Bigard and Arthur Briggs. The selections are fortunately in chronological order, and each of the 17 recording session are reissued in complete form. An extremely well done reissue. *—Scott Yanow*

Return to Forever

Group / Fusion
Early jazz/rock fusion group of the '70s. Initially featuring Airto and Flora Purim, shifted focus to more electric guitar with Earl Klugh, Bill Connors, and Al Di Meola. Eventually added horns. Feature vehicle for electric pianist Chick Corea, bassist Stanley Clarke, and drummer Lenny White. See Chick Corea for album listings. *—Michael G. Nastos*

☆ **Return to Forever** / Feb. 2, 1972-Feb. 3, 1972 / ECM ✦✦✦✦✦
The first and by far the best and most appealing edition. Flora Purim sings wistfully; Stanley Clarke dominates on bass; Corea is a sharp, creative pianist. *—Ron Wynn*

Light as a Feather / Aug. 1972 / Polydor ✦✦✦✦✦
This is good; close to retaining the spirit of the original. *—Ron Wynn*

● **Hymn of the Seventh Galaxy** / Aug. 1973 / Polydor ✦✦✦✦✦
The second (and most popular) version of Return to Forever debuted with this strong fusion effort. This was guitarist Bill Connors's only recording with the group, and he is particularly fiery on "Captain Senor Mouse" and "Hymn of the Seventh Galaxy." With Chick Corea on keyboards, Stanley Clarke on electric bass and drummer Lenny White, this was one of the top fusion bands, mixing together the power and sound of rock with the sophisticated improvisations of jazz. Fans of late-'60s rock were able to enter the world of jazz through albums such as this near-classic. *—Scott Yanow*

Where Have I Known You Before / Jul. 1974-Aug. 1974 / Polydor ✦✦✦✦
This Return to Forever set finds guitarist Al DiMeola debuting with the pacesetting fusion quartet, an influential unit that also featured keyboardist Chick Corea, electric bassist Stanley Clarke and drummer Lenny White. On this high energy set, short interludes separate the main pieces: "Vulcan Worlds," "The Shadow of Lo," "Beyond the Seventh Galaxy," "Earth Juice" and the lengthy "Song to the Pharoah Kings." Acoustic purists are advised to avoid this music, but listeners who grew up on rock and wish to explore jazz will find this stimulating music quite accessible. *—Scott Yanow*

Romantic Warrior / Feb. 1976 / Columbia/Legacy ✦✦✦
The final, least successful edition of Return to Forever cut this session in the mid-'70s. They moved completely away from the Afro-Latin and jazz influences that marked their first record, and even modified the electric jazz-rock of the second. *Romantic Warrior* was more New Age with some light rock and fusion thrown in. *—Ron Wynn*

Buddy Rich (Bernard Rich)

b. Sep. 30, 1917, New York, NY, **d.** Apr. 2, 1987, Los Angeles, CA
Drums / Modern Big Band, Swing, Bop, Big Band
When it came to technique, speed, power and the ability to put together incredible drum solos, Buddy Rich lived up to the billing of "the world's greatest drummer." Although some other drummers were more innovative, in reality none were in his league even during the early days. A genius, Buddy Rich started playing drums in vaudeville as "Traps, the Drum Wonder" when he was only 18 months old; he was completely self-taught. By 1938 he had discovered jazz and was playing with Joe Marsala's combo. Rich was soon propelling Bunny Berigan's Orchestra, he spent most of 1939 with Artie Shaw (at a time when the clarinetist had the most popular band in swing) and then from 1939-45 (except for a stint in the military) he was making history with Tommy Dorsey. During this era it became obvious that Rich was the king of drummers, easily dethroning his friend Gene Krupa. In 1966 he beat the odds and put together a successful big band that would be his main outlet for his final 20 years. *—Scott Yanow*

This One's for Basie / Aug. 24, 1956-Aug. 25, 1956 / Verve ✦✦✦✦✦
Drummer Buddy Rich put together an interesting 11-piece group for this tribute to Count Basie. The only Basie alumnus present is trumpeter Harry "Sweets" Edison but the other soloists (trombonist Frank Rosolino and Bob Enevoldsen, Bob Cooper on tenor and pianist Jimmy Rowles) easily fit into the setting. Marty Paich contributed the arrangements, there are plenty of drum solos and the music, if not all that memorable, can easily be enjoyed by straightahead jazz fans. *—Scott Yanow*

Swingin' New Big Band / Sep. 29, 1966-Oct. 10, 1966 / Blue Note ✦✦✦✦
1966 was a most illogical time for anyone to try forming a new big band but Buddy Rich beat the odds. This CD reissues the first album by the Buddy Rich Orchestra, augmenting the original Lp program with nine previously unissued performances from the same sessions. The arrangements (eight by Oliver Nelson along with charts by Bill Holman, Phil Wilson, Jay Corre, Don Rader and others) swing, put the emphasis on the ensembles and primarily feature Corre's tenor although trumpeter Bobby Shew, altoist Pete Yellin, pianist John Bunch and guitarist Barry Zweig are also heard from. Most of the songs did not stay in the drummer's repertoire long (other than Bill Reddie's adaptation of "West Side Story" and "Sister Sadie") and in fact only three members of the 17-piece orchestra would still be working for Rich a year later. An enjoyable and somewhat historic set. *—Scott Yanow*

The New One! / Jun. 15, 1967-Nov. 30, 1967 / Pacific Jazz ✦✦✦✦
Despite its title, this was actually the third album by Buddy Rich's still-new big band. The recording is taken from two different periods that, although only five months apart, find the band undergoing some major turnover; only six of the 15 sidemen are the same. With such players as altoist Ernie Watts, trumpeter Chuck Findley, and usually Jay Corre on tenor, this was a strong outfit. Most of the material (other than "Chicago" and "I Can't Get Started") was new; among the high points are "The Rotten Kid," "New Blues" and the complex "Diabolus." *—Scott Yanow*

● **Mercy, Mercy** / 1968 / World Pacific ✦✦✦✦✦
This CD reissue brings back the finest all-round recording by Buddy Rich's big band. The original version of "Channel 1 Suite" is a classic and contains tenor saxophonist Don Menza's most memorable solo, plus a couple of brilliant improvisations from the explosive drummer/leader. Another highlight is an inventive Phil Wilson arrangement of "Mercy, Mercy, Mercy," and even "Alfie" (a melodic feature for altoist Art Pepper) and "Ode to Billie Joe" come across well. In addition to the original LP program, three selections were released for the first

time on this CD. "Chelsea Bridge" is particularly significant, for it showcases Pepper, who was making a brief (and unsuccessful) comeback seven years before he finally returned to the scene. This spirited and often-exciting set is a real gem and is essential. *—Scott Yanow*

Time Being / Aug. 13, 1971-Aug. 10, 1972 / Bluebird/RCA ✦✦✦✦✦
This 1987 sampler CD has some of the best selections recorded by the Buddy Rich big band for the LPs *A Different Drummer, Rich In London* and *Stick It.* The selection of tunes was well done, although the complete *Rich In London* (not yet out on CD) is also well worth getting. Among the key soloists are Pat LaBarbera on tenor and soprano, trombonist Bruce Paulson and altoists Jimmy Mosher (showcased on "Chelsea Bridge") and Joe Romano. Excellent fairly modern big-band music. *—Scott Yanow*

Stick It / Aug. 10, 1972 / RCA ✦✦✦✦
Three of the eight selections on this LP have been reissued on the sampler CD *Time Being,* but since the program is quite strong, the album is also recommended. One of the better recordings by Buddy Rich & His Big Band, this has more than its share of highlights, including a ballad feature for altoist Joe Romano ("God Bless the Child"), several notable spots for Pat LaBarbera (on tenor and soprano), some high-note trumpet by Lin Biviano on "Something," a strong rendition of "Uncle Albert/Admiral Halsey," and a surprise: a version of the Muppets' "Bein' Green" with Rich taking a surprisingly charming vocal while backed only by guitarist Walt Namuth. *—Scott Yanow*

The Best Band I Ever Had / Oct. 1977 / DCC ✦✦✦✦✦
This is a great direct-to-disc recording of an exciting, driving, contemporary big band, with no drum solos. *—Buz Overbeck*

1946-1948 / 1946 / Classics ✦✦✦✦
These recordings cover the first releases of Buddy Rich's first band, recording at the end of World War II. As such, the bulk of the recordings are Armed Forces V-Discs, accounting for all but 12 of the 22 selections aboard (the rest commercially released on the fledgling Mercury label). Rich had great players and good charts, but the times for big bands was on the wane, and soon Buddy joined up with Norman Granz and Jazz at the Philharmonic. But these first recordings as a leader show that Rich had a definite musical agenda, as the charts are chock full of fine ensemble playing with occasional solo outbursts from the leader. The V-Discs, many of them pickup dates, illuminate a more casual Rich still working in a big band mode on tracks like "Quiet Riot," "Nellie's Nightmare," and "Four Rich Brothers." A missing chapter in this artist's vast discography. *—Cub Koda*

The Rippingtons

f. 1987
Group / Smooth Jazz, Crossover Jazz, Jazz-Pop
One of the most popular groups in what is loosely termed "contemporary jazz," the Rippingtons were formed (and have been led ever since) by guitarist/keyboardist Russ Freeman (no relation to the veteran West Coast bop pianist of the same name). Freeman (b. Feb. 11, 1960 in Nashville) studied at Cal Arts and UCLA, and recorded *Nocturnal Playground* as a leader in 1985 for the Brainchild label, a one-man project. In 1987 he was approached to record for the Japanese Alfa label and came up with the Rippingtons name for the all-star group he used on the disc (*Moonlighting*), an ensemble featuring David Benoit, Kenny G. and Brandon Fields. Their album was released domestically by Passport and became a hit. Freeman soon formed a regular touring band (usually including saxophonist Jeff Kashiwa, bassist Kim Stone, drummer Tony Morales and percussionist Steve Reid), cut a second disc for Passport and the group has since recorded regularly for GRP. Russ Freeman writes all of the music for the Rippingtons, much of which falls in the pop/R&B genre. In the late '90s, the group moved over to the Windham Hill label, recording such albums as *Black Diamond* (1997), *Topaz* (1999), *Live! Across America,* and *Life in the Tropics* (2000). *—Scott Yanow*

Moonlighting / 1987 / GRP ✦✦✦✦✦
Released in 1986, this album not only stands as a genre-defining primer on what has become known as smooth jazz, but it also helped launch the careers of various artists whose music has been crucial to the genre's vitality. In addition to composer/guitarist/producer Russ Freeman and the Ripps, there's David Benoit (playing a gorgeous piano melody on "Mirage"), keyboardist Gregg Karukas, bassist Jimmy Johnson (who scored hits with Flim & the BBs), saxmen Brandon Fields and Dave Koz (whose floating Electronic Wind Instrument melody guides the silky "Dreams"), and some soprano-wielding guy named Kenny G. One of the G-man's least cloying—and indeed, most engaging—performances can be heard on the lilting, Calypso-influenced "She Likes to Watch." (One of Freeman's best tunes, it continues to get heavy airplay.) The opening, six-minute title track—a guitar-driven, light funk tune that weaves percussionist Steve Reid's nature soundscaping and exotic sound effects with a hypnotic synth melody—epitomizes the kind of smooth texturing for which the Rippingtons became famous. While the band's personnel has evolved, the best tunes on the Ripps' more recent recordings still feature Freeman jamming on guitars and Reid brewing up just the right amount of aggression and subtlety with his toys. The all-star personnel alone makes this a must-hear all these years later. The fact that it still holds up melodically, rhythmically, and production-wise makes it one of smooth jazz's most important and enjoyable recordings. *—Jonathan Widran*

• **The Best of the Rippingtons** / 1987-1993 / GRP ✦✦✦✦
Under the direction of Russ Freeman (equally skilled as a guitarist and as a keyboardist), the Rippingtons succeeded in combining jazz-influenced solos with light, funky rhythms and pop sensibilities. This particular CD has selections from eight of the group's GRP recordings, plus a pair of previously unreleased tracks ("Garden of Babylon" and "Sapphire Island") newly created for the sampler. With notable contributions from Freeman's longtime rhythm section and such saxophonists as Kenny G. (heard on "She Likes to Watch"), Brandon Fields, Eric Marienthal, Kirk Whalum and Jeff Kashiwa, the CD acts as both a definitive sampling of the band's history and as an introduction to their accessible music. The results overall are typically lightweight but reasonably enjoyable, with some fiery moments giving variety to the high-quality pop music. *—Scott Yanow*

Tourist in Paradise / May 1989 / GRP ✦✦✦✦
The ultimate contemporary jazz hyphenate Russ Freeman (guitarist/arranger/producer/keyboardist/composer) became one of smooth jazz's most influential artists through magnificent projects like this one, chosen by *Jazziz* as the best contemporary jazz album of all time. This third Ripps release is a masterpiece of mouthwatering pop-jazz tunes, featuring strong hooks, gorgeous texturing, and styles ranging from tropical (the sunny "Aruba" featuring Rob Mullins on keys and Carl Anderson scatting away) and Brazilian ("One Summer Night in Brazil," Freeman's lush centerpiece) to soulful (a cover of Al Green's "Let's Stay Together") and rockin' (the locomotive "Earthbound," which shows Freeman's strings at their frenzied peak). But there's more to the tourist story—there's also the bounce of bassist Steve Bailey, the boom of drummer Tony Morales, and the light exoticism of Steve Reid's soundscapes. The Rippingtons hit more peaks than valleys as the '90s unfolded, and Freeman expanded his scope beyond simple pop-jazz, but this one still sets the standard for smooth jazz. *—Jonathan Widran*

Curves Ahead / Aug. 1991 / GRP ✦✦✦✦✦
For a number of years, Rippingtons mastermind Russ Freeman had a hard time approaching the inspirational pop jazz perfection of 1989's *Tourist in Paradise,* but this fifth group album came close with its hummable compositions, eclectic blend of tempor, emphasis on acoustic piano and guitar, and wondrous musicianship. As a composer, Freeman has a distinctive knack for conjuring up exotic images ("Nature of the Beast" takes the listener to Africa, while "Aspen" travels high up into ski country) and for remembering past gems in his lush, unrivaled catalog. As such, the lovely "Morning Song" recalls "Oceansong," and "Aspen" looks back to "She Likes to Watch." Yet there are always enough new twists to keep listeners on their toes—for the first time, Freeman uses a horn section (featuring labelmate Nelson Rangell) which lights a fire under "Santa Fe Trail" and the title track. Rangell, who shares sax duties with Jeff Kashiwa and the soulful Kirk Whalum, is also allowed a few peppery flute runs. And no Ripps release would be complete without the marvelously original soundscaping of Steve Reid. Cameos by pianist Mark Portman, trombonist Bruce Fowler, Omar Hakim, and Dave Grusin round out yet another genre classic by Freeman. *—Jonathan Widran*

Live in L.A. / Sep. 25, 1992-Sep. 26, 1992 / GRP ✦✦✦✦
Any truehearted devotee of the Rippingtons Featuring Russ Freeman knows the two secrets of their unparalleled success in the contemporary jazz world over the course of numerous releases since 1986. First and foremost, it's those lush, ultra-melodic Freeman compositions, many of which have become genre classics. Beyond those, the band has attracted fans the world over with one of the most exciting and dynamic live shows in instrumental music. It seems wholly appropriate, then, to take stock of the wealth of Freeman's catalog not with a mere greatest-hits collection, but with the fun-filled CD and video package, *Live in L.A.* Recorded September 25 and 26, 1992, at *the Ventura Theatre* in Ventura and Los Angeles' famed *Greek Theatre,* this is first and foremost a project for an inspired by the Ripps' loyal fan base. The band's commitment to an always high intensity live set, with an ever evolving repertoire of old favorites and new gems, probably made the process of editing their normal 90-minute set down to the 60-minute length somewhat difficult. Nonetheless, the ten tunes here are indicative of all aspects of Freeman's composing talents as well as the Rippingtons' energetic interaction on stage. The core group of Freeman (guitar), Jeff Kashiwa (sax and EWI), Kim Stone (bass), Mark Portmann (keyboards), Steve Reid (percussion), and Tony Morales (drums) is complemented by the sassy textures of a three-piece horn section and cameos by GRP labelmates David Benoit and singer Carl Anderson. Highlights include "Indian Summer," "Weekend in Monaco," the lush "One Summer Night in Brazil," and the explosive jam "Highroller." *—Jonathan Widran*

Black Diamond / 1997 / Windham Hill ✦✦✦✦✦
After nearly a decade at GRP Records, smooth jazz's premier ensemble made a very successful switch to Windham Hill with this recording inspired by leader Russ Freeman's ski adventures in his adopted home of Colorado. Their tenth album continues the band's recent successful ventures into urban-flavored music while also showcasing Freeman's amazing talents for jazz and flamenco guitar playing, in addition to his trademark classical guitar-influenced pop/rock sound. The collection is also a celebration of ten years of the smooth jazz format and the Rippingtons' instrumental role in creating music that helps define the genre's sound. The band weaves through the title track with a soaring, echoing guitar melody over a cool, shuffling hip-hop groove. Mark Williamson's spiritual-flavored chanting enhances the moody textures and funky, retro-soul vibe of the electric guitar-driven "Deep Powder," while the steamy, classical guitar-led "Seven Nights in Rome" finds the band looking down from the mountaintop, thoughtfully recounting the romantic ambience of a recent concert trip to Italy. "North Peak"'s slamming percussion approximates a speedy downhill race, but all that chill is more than balanced by the daring and exotic "Angelfire," which blends Freeman's colorful flamenco stylings and Arturo Sandoval's crackling trumpet. *—Jonathan Widran*

Lee Ritenour

b. Jan. 11, 1952, Hollywood, CA
Guitar / Crossover Jazz, Jazz-Pop
Lee Ritenour has long been the perfect studio musician, one who can melt into the background without making any impact. While he possesses impresive technique, Ritenour has mostly played instrumental pop throughout his career, sometimes with a Brazilian flavor. His few jazz efforts have found him essentially imitating Wes Montgomery, but despite that he has been consistently popular since the mid-'70s. After touring with Sergio Mendes' Brasil '77 in 1973, Ritenour became a very busy studio guitarist in Los Angeles, taking time off for occasional tours with his groups and in the mid-'90s with Bob James in Fourplay. He also recorded many albums as a leader. *—Scott Yanow*

Festival / May 16, 1988-May 20, 1988 / GRP ✦✦✦✦
Ritenour's second acoustic album, like his first, has an overall Brazilian theme but this time, he recorded his ensemble of New York, L.A. and Brazilian musicians in one locale, New York City. This is a superior record to *Rio,* though, because there is a deeper Brazilian feeling to the arrangements, and Lee's own playing is even more refined and meaningful. "Waiting For

You," a solo track on an acoustic guitar synthesizer, is especially attractive. The core crew consists of a collection of pro's pros—Ernie Watts on alto and tenor, Dave Grusin or Bob James on keyboards, Marcus Miller or Anthony Jackson on bass, Omar Hakim on drums, Paulinho Da Costa and Carlinhos Brown on percussion—who lay down smooth yet gently grooving backdrops for Rit to ride. Joao Bosco and Gracinha Leporace contribute fascinating Portuguese vocals to the album's two most appealing and thoroughly Brazilian-flavored tracks, "Latin Lovers" and "Odile, Odila"—and Caetano Veloso brings a softer-focused vocal style to "Linda." *—Richard S. Ginell*

Wes Bound / Sep. 1992-Oct. 1992 / GRP ♦♦♦♦
Lee Ritenour, a superior studio guitarist, has recorded very few jazz albums throughout his career, preferring to play melodic pop and light funk. On the rare occasions when he has had an urge to perform jazz, Ritenour has been more than happy to show off the influence of Wes Montgomery; therefore, this tribute is a logical move, even if the results are not all that exciting. Ritenour mostly plays pieces from the later (and more commercial) half of Montgomery's career, along with four of his own originals that are sort of in the tradition. He also hedges his bet a little by throwing in a Bob Marley reggae tune. For jazz listeners who wish to sample some Lee Ritenour, this is one of his better recordings, but why purchase *Wes Bound* when there are so many more significant Wes Montgomery albums currently in print— *—Scott Yanow*

● **Larry & Lee** / Jun. 1994-Jan. 1995 / GRP ♦♦♦♦♦
Larry Carlton and Lee Ritenour have had parallel careers but this CD is their first joint meeting on records. The two guitarists complement each other well and there are hints of Wes Montgomery along with a tribute to Joe Pass ("Remembering J.P."), but the songs (all of them their originals) are little more than rhythmic grooves most of the time with the usual fade-outs. The consistently lightweight music is reasonably pleasing but never too stimulating. *—Scott Yanow*

Alive in L.A. / Jan. 23, 1997-Jan. 25, 1997 / GRP ♦♦♦♦♦
Jazz being the most spontaneous and improvisational of all musical forms, it's often best appreciated in a live setting, where artistry can take over for commercial considerations and jamming for minutes on end is encouraged. Lee Ritenour has enhanced his pop-jazz catalog in recent years with projects featuring tunes that would lend themselves to such creative stretching, and so wraps up his long run at GRP with *Alive in L.A.*, a brilliantly realized, no-overdubs-allowed ensemble date that delves into his diverse interests, from Brazilian to straight-ahead trio jazz and blues. Fans who know him best from his lighthearted radio fare may just be astounded at his chops, which do proud the grand traditions of his idol Wes Montgomery, and even try to reach a bit beyond. Recorded over three nights at the *Ash Grove* in Santa Monica, CA, Ritenour finds a gang of musicians even more explosive than his Fourplay pals in saxman Bill Evans (who wails heartily on Wes Montgomery's odd metered "4 on 6"), keyboardists Alan Pasqua and Barnaby Finch, and drummer Sonny Emory. Rit's clearly in charge, but it's the energetic company he keeps that makes this a hard-grooving, unforgettable date. *—Jonathan Widran*

This Is Love / 1997-1998 / i.e. Music/Polygram ♦♦♦♦♦
Ritenour's first solo album for his new i.e. music label is a good one, one of his best actually, whether staying in the strict jazz-lite format that marks a lot of his previous work or straying into the other idioms that pop up here. Whether emulating Wes Montgomery's octaves or curling around in single-string fashion, Ritenour's playing is irresistibly tasty and swinging, perhaps more so than ever, and the material has real melodic interest—more so than anything his former group Fourplay was performing around this time. Among the most interesting swerves off the track are the title tune, which mixes reggae with Montgomery in a very appealing way, and a surprisingly effective closing take on Faure's "Pavanne." There are extended samples from Sonny Rollins' *Alfie* score, with "Alfie's Theme" grooving away in a cool, soulful, organ-jazz seam and "Street Runner" tracking Rollins' recording, its quicksilver post-bop clip juxtaposed with repose. On both tracks, Ronnie Foster supplies authentic Hammond B-3—perhaps fulfilling a Jimmy Smith-meets-Wes Montgomery fantasy. Bill Evans and Ernie Watts take guest turns on tenor on a few cuts; Bob James chips on agreeably on Rhodes electric piano on "Can You Feel It—"; and Ritenour often takes matters into his own hands, programming electronic drums and performing on synthesizers. Hardcore jazzers who wrote Ritenour off as a lightweight ought to hear how he has grown as a mature jazz guitarist on this album. *—Richard S. Ginell*

Sam Rivers

b. Sep. 25, 1923, El Reno, OK
Sax (Tenor), Sax (Soprano), Flute, Composer, Arranger / Experimental Big Band, Improvisation, Avant-Garde Jazz, Free Jazz, Post-Bop, Progressive Big Band, Avant-Garde
Although often overlooked, Sam Rivers has long been one of the most original voices of the avant-garde, equally skilled on tenor, soprano and flute. In 1964 Tony Williams (who had played with Rivers when he was a teenager) recommended him for the tenor opening with Miles Davis' Quintet. Although Rivers' playing was too advanced for Davis at the time, he did last through a tour of Japan that was recorded. Rivers made a few records for Blue Note before becoming a member of Cecil Taylor's Unit during 1968-73. With his wife Bea, he opened Studio Rivbea as a jazz loft in New York in 1971 and became involved in teaching in addition to presenting concerts. Other than a late-'80s association with Dizzy Gillespie (where he good-naturedly played bebop and even took an occasional scat vocal), Sam Rivers has mostly been a leader during the past 25 years in a wide variety of settings. In the late 1990's he has been active in Florida, forming his own record label and acting as the inspiration and teacher for a jazz youth movement. *—Scott Yanow*

☆ **The Complete Blue Note Sam Rivers Sessions** / Dec. 11, 1964-Mar. 17, 1967 / Mosaic ♦♦♦♦♦
This three-CD limited-edition box set from Mosaic features the underrated avant-gardist Sam Rivers (who plays tenor, soprano, and flute) on his four Blue Note albums as a leader: *Fuschia Swing Song* (a quartet date with pianist Jaki Byard, bassist Ron Carter, and drummer Tony Williams), *Contours* (which features trumpeter Freddie Hubbard, pianist Herbie Hancock, Carter, and drummer Joe Chambers), *A New Conception* (which has pianist Hal Galper leading the rhythm section), and *Involution* (a sextet outing with altoist James Spaulding, trumpeter Donald Byrd, and trombonist Julian Priester), plus three previously unreleased selections. The earliest set shows off Rivers' roots, *A New Conception* has his adventurous (yet often tasteful) renditions of standards, and *Involution* (a 1967 set not released until 1977) has the most advanced music. A perfectly done reissue. *—Scott Yanow*

Fuschia Swing Song / May 21, 1965 / Blue Note ♦♦♦♦♦
For Sam Rivers' debut, *Fuchsia Swing Song*, the tenor saxophonist lined up a fine quartet—featuring pianist Jaki Byard, bassist Ron Carter, and drummer Tony Williams—and pursued a refreshing, unpredictable spin on the avant-garde. Rivers has a hard bop foundation, but he incorporated the developments of Coltrane and Coleman into his music, resulting in an adventurous and quite rewarding debut. His original compositions aren't always memorable, but his playing is always startling, as is the interaction between Carter, Williams, and Byard. Rivers would take his music further into uncharted territory within just a few months, but *Fuchsia Swing Song* remains a fresh debut. *—Stephen Thomas Erlewine*

★ **Contours** / May 21, 1965 / Blue Note ♦♦♦♦♦
On *Contours*, his second Blue Note album, tenor saxophonist Sam Rivers fully embraced the avant-garde, but presented his music in a way that wouldn't be upsetting or confusing to hard bop loyalists. Rivers leads a quintet featuring trumpeter Freddie Hubbard, pianist Herbie Hancock, bassist Ron Carter, and drummer Joe Chambers through a set of originals that walk a fine line between probing, contemplative post-bop and densely dissonant avant-jazz. Each musician is able to play the extremes equally well while remaining sensitive to the compositional subtleties. Rarely is *Contours* anything less than enthralling, and it remains one of the high watermarks of the mid-'60s avant-garde movement. *—Stephen Thomas Erlewine*

☆ **Involution** / Mar. 7, 1966-Mar. 17, 1967 / Blue Note ♦♦♦♦♦
This double LP, which came out in 1975, contains two superior (and previously unissued) sessions featuring the great tenor saxophonist Sam Rivers. Actually, one of the dates was originally led by pianist Andrew Hill, who performs in a quartet with Rivers, bassist Walter Booker, and drummer J.C. Moses. While that set has six of Hill's provocative originals, the other album (which teams Rivers with altoist James Spaulding, trumpeter Donald Byrd, trombonist Julian Priester, bassist Cecil McBee, and drummer Steve Ellington) features six of the tenor saxophonist's compositions. These very adventurous performances (some of Blue Note's finest avant-garde dates) are often intense and always adventurous. This stimulating music ranks with Sam Rivers' most significant recordings. *—Scott Yanow*

A New Conception / Oct. 11, 1966 / Blue Note ♦♦♦♦
The title of *A New Conception* refers to Sam Rivers' ingenious interpretations of standards on this record. Rivers treats the songs—such familiar items as "When I Fall in Love," "I'll Never Smile Again," "That's All," "What a Difference a Day Makes," and "Secret Love"—with respect, but he doesn't treat them as museum pieces. He knows that if the songs are to remain fresh, they need to be heard in different ways, and he skillfully opens up each composition to contemporary avant-garde techniques. Rivers and his supporting trio of pianist Hal Galper, bassist Herbert Lewis, and drummer Steve Ellington gradually ease each number into more adventurous territory, slowly shifting into exploratory instrumental sections, slyly varying the melodic themes, or adding shaded dissonant textures. It's challenging music that remains accessible, since it reconfigures familiar items in new, intriguing ways. The sheer skill in Rivers' arrangements once again confirms his large, unfortunately underappreciated, talent. *—Stephen Thomas Erlewine*

☆ **Dimensions and Extensions** / Mar. 17, 1967 / Blue Note ♦♦♦♦♦
Ambitious, atonal, challenging—all are accurate descriptions of *Dimensions and Extensions*, Sam Rivers' fourth album for Blue Note. Rivers remains grounded in hard bop structure, working with a sextet featuring Donald Byrd (trumpet), James Spaulding (alto saxophone, flute), Julian Priester (trombone), Cecil McBee (bass), and Steve Ellington (drums), but he explodes the boundaries of the form with difficult, dissonant compositions. With his unique, mercurial tone and edgy solos, he keeps pushing the sextet in different directions. It's intense, cerebral music, but since it has distinct themes and strong rhythms, the forays into free jazz, dissonant harmonies, and unpredictable tonal textures are actually quite accessible. Rivers simply burns on each track, whether playing tenor, soprano, or flute. Byrd doesn't display the wild imagination of Rivers, yet he keeps the pace with alternately languid and biting solos. Similarly, each of the remaining musicians makes a lasting impression with his individual time in the spotlight. With music as risky at this, it's forgivable that it occasionally meanders (especially on the slower numbers) but, overall, *Dimensions and Extensions* offers more proof that Sam Rivers was one of the early giants of the avant-garde. *—Stephen Thomas Erlewine*

Hues / Feb. 13, 1971-Nov. 10, 1973 / Impulse! ♦♦♦♦

Live / Aug. 3, 1973-Nov. 10, 1973 / Impulse! ♦♦♦♦
The music on this 1998 CD reissue was originally scattered over several releases until it was finally grouped together in 1978 for the double-LP *The Live Trio Sessions* (along with another eight minutes of related material not brought back here). The bulk of the music ("Hues Of Melanin") is from a Nov. 10, 1973 Yale University concert that features Rivers with both Cecil McBee and Lewis Worrell on basses along with drummer Barry Altschul. The continuous free improvisation has Rivers stretching out with great length on soprano, flute (complete with very odd vocal sounds), piano and then (during the final 5Ω minutes of the 44-minute performance) tenor. It is a pity that Rivers chose to feature his main ax so sparingly, for this piece would have been much stronger if he had played tenor for 35 minutes rather than just five. The latter part of the CD is from a Norway concert on Aug. 3, 1973 ("Suite for Molde"), with Arild Anderson taking McBee's place. Rivers plays soprano and flute for eight minutes and then tenor for 11 minutes; the latter section is the strongest section of the entire disc. Sam Rivers' longtime fans may think of this collection as bordering on the classic, and there are certainly some emotional moments, but Rivers has sounded more consistent elsewhere. *—Scott Yanow*

☆ **Streams: Live at Montreux** / Jul. 6, 1973 / Impulse! ♦♦♦♦♦

Streams featured Sam Rivers as the lead voice on the album-long "Streams," a lengthy multisectioned free improvisation recorded at *the Montreux Jazz Festival* (7/6/73). With support from the brillant bassist Cecil McBee and subtle drumming from the pre-disco Norman Connors, Rivers took a powerful solo on tenor, sung through his flute, rambled a bit on piano and concluded with a strong dosage of his soprano.... *Streams* remains one of Sam Rivers's strongest recordings. *—Scott Yanow*

Crystals / 1974 / Impulse! ♦♦♦♦
This LP is a rare big-band date led by tenor saxophonist Sam Rivers, who is also heard on soprano and flute. The large ensemble includes such notables as trumpeters Ted Daniel and Richard Williams, Joe Daley on trombone and tuba, and the tenors of Paul Jeffrey and Roland Alexander. The six Rivers originals are quite complex, often atonal and with short solos that are sometimes written out. In fact, some of the performances almost sound like modern classical music, except for the sense of swing and the improvising. This is a stimulating and difficult set well worth several listens, but unfortunately the album is currently quite scarce. *—Scott Yanow*

Sam Rivers/Dave Holland, Vols. 1-2 / Feb. 18, 1976 / Improvising Artists ♦♦♦♦

Colours / Sep. 13, 1982 / Black Saint ♦♦♦

Lazuli / Oct. 9, 1989-Oct. 10, 1989 / Timeless ♦♦♦

Portrait / Jun. 17, 1995 May 6, - 19 / FMP ♦♦♦♦

☆ **Inspiration** / Sep. 28, 1998-Sep. 29, 1998 / RCA ♦♦♦♦♦
Prior to *Inspiration*, Sam Rivers hadn't recorded for a major label in nearly 20 years, and he hadn't cut a studio session in two decades. That doesn't mean he was inactive; he was teaching, playing, and giving concerts but never recording. Aware that many of Rivers' big-band compositions—not only his recent material, but some earlier works as well—had never been given the proper treatment, saxophonist Steve Coleman helped arrange a recording contract with BMG, with the end result being the astonishing *Inspiration* album. The compositions on *Inspiration* are as old as 1968's "Beatrice" and as new as 1995's "Solace" (incidentally, both of those pieces are tributes to his wife Beatrice, who also provides half of the name of the featured big band, the Rivbea All-Star Orchestra). Remarkably, all of the compositions not only sound fresh, they sound visionary—still ahead of their time. It's not only because the stellar musicians give vibrant, unpredictable performances, although that undeniably helps; Rivers' writing is the real key. His writing for big band is utterly original, blending big-band, bop, and avant-garde traditions together in unique, surprising ways. The dissonance never sounds irritating—it sounds melodic—and the complex themes are strangely inviting. Similarly, Rivers' playing is robust, swinging between intense bursts of sound and beautiful lyricism, and sometimes combining it all at once. His 16 colleagues—including such luminaries as Steve Coleman, Greg Osby, Chico Freeman, and Ray Anderson—follow suit, delivering wonderfully shaded, invigorating performances. *Inspiration* truly is a revelation, proving not only that Rivers retains all his creative power at the age of 75, but that avant-garde jazz can be as inviting as any other style without sacrificing any of its depth or daring. *—Stephen Thomas Erlewine*

Culmination / Oct. 28, 1998-Dec. 1, 1998 / RCA ♦♦♦♦

Freddie Roach

b. May 11, 1931, New York, NY [The Bronx]
Organ / Soul-Jazz
One of the more underrated soul-jazz organists of the '60s, Freddie Roach recorded a series of seven albums for Blue Note and Prestige. Where his contemporaries played hard-driving, bluesy soul-jazz, Roach's approach was more textured and shaded. He was capable of blistering leads, but he was more interested in dynamics, harmonics and tonal color. As his career progressed, he became more interested in funky grooves, but his knack for tasteful, shaded solos and support never subsided. Roach, who had been playing organ since the age of eight, played both piano and organ with Chris Columbus, Cootie Williams and Lou Donaldson during the mid-'50s. But the key musical association for Roach was tenor saxophonist Ike Quebec, who asked the organist to join his band in the early '60s. His playing on two records for Blue Note (*Heavy Soul, It Might as Well Be Spring*) gained him his own contract with Blue Note for 1962's *Down to Earth,* his debut full-length. Over the next two years, Roach recorded four more albums for the label but departed in 1965. He reappeared one year later with albums for Prestige that were funkier efforts than any of his Blue Note recordings. Over the next three decades, Roach emerged as a cult figure of sorts, appealing to soul-jazz fans who became introduced to the genre through acid jazz. *—Stephen Thomas Erlewine*

● **Down to Earth** / Aug. 23, 1962 / Blue Note ♦♦♦♦♦
Freddie Roach differentiated himself from the legions of soul-jazz organists on his debut album, *Down to Earth.* Many jazz organists played the instrument down and dirty, and while there's funk in Roach's playing, his style is ultimately lighter than many of his peers, with clean, concise solos and chords. His backing trio—guitarist Kenny Burrell, tenor saxophonist Percy France, and drummer Clarence Johnston—follows his lead, providing supple instrumental support that never loses sight of the groove. Furthermore, Burrell and France both have their chances to shine, contributing some nicely understated solos. Nevertheless, *Down to Earth* remains Roach's show; he wrote five of the six songs and his organ is at center stage on each number. The legato blues of "De Bug" is a terrific showcase for Roach's elegantly funky style, while the sprightlier "Ahm Miz" proves that he can get gritty if he so chooses. But the signature of *Down to Earth* is Roach's tasteful bluesy grooves, which prove to be just as entertaining as the hotter styles of his Blue Note peers Jimmy Smith and John Patton. *—Stephen Thomas Erlewine*

Mo' Greens Please / Jan. 21, 1963-Mar. 11, 1963 / Blue Note ♦♦♦♦
Housed in one of Blue Note house graphic designer Reid Miles' most delightful covers—a powder-blue image featuring a nattily-dressed Freddie Roach receiving a heaping helping of the soul food in question— the outstanding *Mo' Greens Please* serves as a stepping stone between the more studied soul-jazz of the organist's label debut *Down to Earth* and the looser, deeper grooves of the following *Good Move!* In his liner notes, Roach credits contemporary dance crazes like the Twist, the Hully Gully, and the Bird for inspiring the tempos and moods of *Mo' Greens Please*'s ten cuts, while the titular promises of moments like "Party Time," "Nada Bossa," and the blistering "Blues in the Front Room" serve further notice of the eclectic menu in store. Though the product of two separate studio sessions, the first featuring the great Kenny Burrell on guitar, for all its stylistic detours the album hangs together beautifully—each of the players is at the top of his respective game, and in particular Roach attacks the organ with all the passion and flair of his most incendiary outings. *—Jason Ankeny*

Good Move! / Nov. 29, 1963-Dec. 9, 1963 / Blue Note ♦♦♦♦
Laid-back and loosely swinging, *Good Move* captures organist Freddie Roach near the peak of his form. Roach never leans too heavily on his instrument, preferring a calmer, tasteful attack, yet he is never boring because he has a strong sense of groove. He keeps things moving on slower numbers like Erroll Garner's "Pastel" and Gershwin's "It Ain't Necessarily So," but the true highlights are on originals like "Wine, Wine, Wine" and "On Our Way Up," where the bluesy structures and fluid rhythms give Roach a chance to stretch out. Throughout the record, he is capably supported by guitarist Eddie Wright and drummer Clarence Johnston, as well as trumpeter Blue Mitchell and tenor saxophonist Hank Mobley, who both contribute fine solos. *—Stephen Thomas Erlewine*

Brown Sugar / Mar. 18, 1964-Mar. 19, 1964 / Blue Note ♦♦♦♦♦
Brown Sugar marks a turning point for Freddie Roach: It's the moment he decided to get dirty, funky, and soulful. Previously, he had plenty of funk in his playing, but he was tasteful, at times a little bit too tasteful. On *Brown Sugar,* he simply burns. The album is devoted to blues, R&B, and soul, with the title track (the lone original on the album) functioning as a rallying cry of sorts. Roach is hotter than ever, but he never overplays or overloads the organ; whether it's slow blues or smoking R&B, he gets deep into the groove and works it hard, without neglecting to contribute compelling solos. And if you're looking for compelling solos, tenor saxophonist Joe Henderson proves that he is as exceptional with R&B and soul-jazz as he is with hard bop. Clarence Johnston, Roach's longtime drummer, provides stable support and guitarist Eddie Wright has his moments as well, helping make *Brown Sugar* the standout item in Roach's catalog. *—Stephen Thomas Erlewine*

All That's Good / Oct. 16, 1964 / Blue Note ♦♦

Max Roach

b. Jan. 10, 1924, New Land, NC
Drums / Avant-Garde Jazz, Hard Bop, Post-Bop, Bop
In a profession star-crossed by early deaths—especially the bebop division—Max Roach at this writing is a shining survivor, one of the last living giants from the birth of bebop. He and Kenny Clarke instigated a revolution in jazz drumming that persists to this day; instead of the swing approach of spelling out the pulse with the bass drum, Roach shifted the emphasis to the ride cymbal. The result was a lighter, far more flexible texture, giving drummers more freedom to explore the possibilities of their drum kits and drop random "bombs" on the snare drum, while allowing bop virtuosos on the front lines to play at faster speeds. To this base, Roach added sterling qualities of his own—a ferocious drive, the ability to play a solo with a definite storyline, mixing up pitches and timbres, the deft use of silence, the dexterity to use the brushes as brilliantly as the sticks. He would use cymbals as gongs and play mesmerizing solos on the tom-toms, creating atmosphere as well as keeping the groove pushing forward. But Roach didn't stop there, unlike other jazz pioneers who changed the world when they were young yet became set in their ways as they grew older. He has always had the curiosity and the willingness to grow as a musician and as a man, moving beyond bop into new compositional structures, unusual instrument lineups, unusual time signatures, atonality, music for Broadway musicals, television, film and the symphony hall, even working with a rapper well ahead of the jazz/hip-hop merger. *—Richard S. Ginell*

New Sounds: Max Roach Quintet / Art Blakey & His Band / Dec. 22, 1947-May 15, 1949 / Blue Note ♦♦♦♦♦

The Max Roach Quartet, Featuring Hank Mobley / Apr. 10, 1953-Apr. 21, 1953 / Debut/OJC ♦♦♦

Max Roach Plus Four / Sep. 17, 1956-Mar. 20, 1957 / EmArcy ♦♦♦♦♦
After the tragic deaths of trumpeter Clifford Brown and pianist Richie Powell in a car accident a few months earlier, drummer Max Roach regrouped with trumpeter Kenny Dorham and pianist Ray Bryant filling in the unfillable holes; tenor great Sonny Rollins and bassist George Morrow remained from the earlier band. This EmArcy CD finds Roach taking plenty of solo space including almost all of "Dr. Free-zee" and the climaxes of "Just One of Those Things" and "Woody'n You." The horns have plenty of good spots and other highlights of this worthy set includes George Russell's "Ezz-thetic" and a warm rendition of "Body and Soul." *—Scott Yanow*

Max Roach 4 Plays Charlie Parker / Dec. 20, 1957-Apr. 11, 1958 / EmArcy ♦♦♦♦
The music on this CD finds drummer Max Roach for the first time dropping the piano out of his quintet and performing with a pianoless quartet. With the departure of Sonny Rollins (who is replaced on three songs apiece by either Hank Mobley or George Coleman), Roach's group (which also featured trumpeter Kenny Dorham and either George Morrow or Nelson Boyd on bass) was temporarily without any major innovators (outside of the leader). So it was perfectly fitting that Roach would look backwards and perform six of Charlie Parker's compositions. Highlighted by "Yardbird Suite," "Confirmation" and "Ko Ko," this set is generally fine although the lack of a piano is really felt on some of this material. *—Scott Yanow*

Deeds, Not Words / Sep. 4, 1958 / Riverside/OJC ♦♦♦♦♦
This CD reissue of a Max Roach Riverside date is notable for featuring the great young trumpeter Booker Little and for utilizing Ray Draper's tuba as a melody instrument; tenor saxophonist George Coleman and bassist Art Davis complete the excellent quintet. Highlights include "It's You or No One," "You Stepped out of a Dream" and Roach's unaccompanied drum

piece "Conversation." This is fine music from a group that was trying to stretch themselves beyond hard bop. *—Scott Yanow*

☆ **Freedom Now Suite** / Aug. 31, 1960-Sep. 6, 1960 / Columbia ♦♦♦♦♦
This is a classic. At a time when the civil rights movement was starting to heat up, drummer Max Roach performed and recorded a seven-part suite dealing with black history (particularly slavery) and racism. "Driva' Man" has a powerful statement by veteran tenor Coleman Hawkins and there is valuable solo space elsewhere for trumpeter Booker Little and trombonist Julian Priester, but it is the overall performance of Abbey Lincoln that is most notable. Formerly a nightclub singer, Lincoln really came into her own under Roach's tutelage and she is a strong force throughout this intense set. On "Tryptich: Prayer/Protest/Peace," Lincoln is heard in duets with the drummer and her wrenching screams of rage are quite memorable. This timeless protest record is a gem. *—Scott Yanow*

We Insist! Freedom Now Suite / Aug. 31, 1960-Sep. 6, 1960 / Candid ♦♦♦♦♦
Booker Little, Ray Draper, George Coleman, and Art Davis appeared on this. *—AMG*

★ **Percussion Bitter Sweet** / Aug. 1961 / Impulse! ♦♦♦♦♦
This CD reissue brings back a classic album, one of the finest of drummer Max Roach's very productive career. The illustrious sidemen (trumpeter Booker Little, trombonist Julian Priester, Eric Dolphy on alto, bass clarinet and flute, tenorman Clifford Jordan, pianist Mal Waldron and bassist Art Davis in addition to some guest percussionists) all have opportunitites to make strong contributions and Dolphy's pleading alto solo on "Mendacity" is particularly memorable. Abbey Lincoln has two emotional and very effective vocals, but it is the overall sound of the ensembles and the political nature of the music that make this set (along with Roach's *Freedom Now Suite*) quite unique in jazz history. *—Scott Yanow*

It's Time / Feb. 15, 1962-Feb. 27, 1962 / Impulse! ♦♦♦♦
This Max Roach date had been out-of-print for around 30 years when it was finally reissued on CD by Impulse in 1996. An unusual set, this outing featured the drummer's all-star sextet (which consisted of trumpeter Richard Williams, tenor-saxophonist Clifford Jordan, trombonist Julian Priester, pianist Mal Waldron and bassist Art Davis) joined by a vocal choir conducted by Coleridge Perkinson and orchestrated by Roach (who contributed all six originals). Unlike most other collaborations, the choir was not overly gospel-oriented and was utilized as a sort-of jazz ensemble. Each of the horns has a feature or two and singer Abbey Lincoln stars on "Lonesome Lover." But despite the sincerity of this effort, there are times when one wishes the choir would leave altogether and let the quintet really stretch out. *—Scott Yanow*

Speak, Brother, Speak / Oct. 27, 1962 / Fantasy/OJC ♦♦♦

Birth and Rebirth / Sep. 1978 / Black Saint ♦♦♦♦♦
The first of drummer Max Roach's two duet sets with multireedist Anthony Braxton consists of seven fairly free improvisations that they created in the studio. Each of the selections (particularly "Birth" which builds gradually in intensity to a ferocious level, the waltz time of "Magic and Music," the atmospheric "Tropical Forest" and "Softshoe") have their own plot and purpose. Braxton (who performs on alto, soprano, sopranino and clarinet) and Roach continually inspire each other, which is probably why they would record a second set the following year. Stimulating avant-garde music. *—Scott Yanow*

M'Boom / Jul. 25, 1979-Jul. 27, 1979 / Columbia/Legacy ♦♦♦♦♦
In 1979 Max Roach founded M'Boom, a group consisting of eight percussionists. Their debut recording (which has been reissued on this Columbia CD) is far from being a monotonous drum battle. In fact, through the utilization of a wide range of instruments that include chimes, timbales, marimba, vibes, xylophone, tympani, various bells and steel drums, there are quite a lot of melodies to be heard during these nine performances (which are all group originals other than Thelonious Monk's "Epistrophy"). This is a particularly colorful set that is easily recommended not only to jazz and percussion fans but to followers of World music. *—Scott Yanow*

☆ **One in Two, Two in One** / Aug. 31, 1979 / hatHUT ♦♦♦♦♦
The second of two duet albums by drummer Max Roach and multireedist Anthony Braxton was recorded live and released on this two-LP set; this is the more interesting of the two projects since it is a nearly 78-minute continual improvisation. Braxton gets to stretch out on alto, soprano, sopranino, contra bass clarinet (which really gets a monstrous sound), clarinet and flute. With Roach pushing Braxton, the results are quite adventurous, yet full of joy. Followers of avant-garde jazz can consider this set to be essential. *—Scott Yanow*

Bright Moments / Oct. 1, 1986-Oct. 2, 1986 / Soul Note ♦♦♦♦♦
The combination of drummer Max Roach's regular group (which includes trumpeter Cecil Bridgewater, tenor saxophonist Odean Pope and electric bassist Tyrone Brown) with the Uptown String Quartet to form his Double Quartet works extremely well. Because the strings get to improvise and are not restricted to the background, the interplay between the two groups is a special highlight of this particularly strong outing. In addition to works by Pope and Brown (the latter contributed "Tribute to Duke and Mingus"), The Double Quartet interprets Steve Turre's "Double Delight," Randy Weston's "Hi Fly" and Roland Kirk's happy "Bright Moments." A frequently exquisite yet adventurous album, highly recommended. *—Scott Yanow*

The Max Roach Trio, Featuring the Legendary Hasaan/Drums Unlimited / Sep. 28, 1999 / Collectables ♦♦♦♦
This is a reissue of two classic Max Roach sessions recorded for Atlantic in the mid-'60s. *Featuring the Legendary Hasaan* (Hasaan Ibn Ali) is from 1965, and is the only recording ever made by this sadly neglected pianist. *Drums Unlimited* followed in 1966 with a stellar lineup of James Spaulding on alto sax, Freddie Hubbard on trumpet, Ronnie Mathews on piano, and Jymie Merritt on bass. Both are essential recordings under the leadership of this influential drummer, reissued together at a budget price from the Collectables label. *—Al Campbell*

Members, Don't Get Weary / Jun. 25, 1968-Jul. 1968 / Atlantic ♦♦♦♦♦
Although Max Roach was very much a product of the be-bop revolution of the 1940s, he proved to be quite receptive to modal post-bop and avant-garde jazz in the 1960s. One of the finest post-bop dates Roach recorded during that decade was 1968's *Members, Don't Git Weary,* which finds the drummer leading a cohesive modal quintet that employs Gary Bartz on alto sax, Charles Tolliver on trumpet, Stanley Cowell on acoustic and electric piano, and Jymie Merritt on electric bass. Despite the use of electric instruments, this isn't an album that emphasizes rock or funk elements or predicts the fusion explosion that was just around the corner—*Members, Don't Git Weary* is very much a straight-ahead effort, and the harmonic richness of modal playing is illustrated by such gems as Cowell's "Equipoise," Bartz's "Libra," and Merritt's "Absolutions." Roach's title song boasts a memorable, gospel-influenced vocal by Andy Bey, but all of the other selections are instrumental. Originally released on LP by Atlantic in 1968, this superb album was out of print for many years before finally being reissued on CD by Koch Jazz in 1999. *—Alex Henderson*

Marcus Roberts

b. Sep. 7, 1963, Jacksonville, FL
Piano, Composer / Contemporary Jazz, Hard Bop, Post-Bop
Marcus Roberts is a very talented—if very raw—young musician, whose good fortune it was to capture the attention and goodwill of the all-powerful Wynton Marsalis. Roberts is one of the generation of young African-American jazz musicians who seems bent on forging the future by reinventing the past; his infatuation with older forms renders his music a pastiche of obsolete styles. Roberts is a gifted mimic, though his adoption of his idols' surface mannerisms does not penetrate to the essence of their art. He replaced Kenny Kirkland as Marsalis's pianist in 1985, and recorded as a sideman with the trumpeter through the rest of the decade and into the '90s, while at the same time making records under his own name for Columbia. His lack of interest in expanding jazz's creative possibilities causes his music to have a hermetic quality, which is unfortunate, because one gets the feeling by listening to his recent compositions that, were Roberts to broaden his horizons a bit, he might be capable of doing excellent work. *—Chris Kelsey*

Alone with Three Giants / Jun. 3, 1990-Sep. 22, 1990 / Jive/Novus ♦♦♦♦♦
This set of unaccompanied piano solos features Marcus Roberts interpreting three Jelly Roll Morton, six Duke Ellington and six Thelonious Monk songs. Morton gets a bit shortchanged, with "Jungle Blues," "New Orleans Blues" and "The Crave" emphasizing the Spanish tinge in his music, but only certain aspects of his style. However, Roberts has Ellington (best is "Shout 'Em Aunt Tillie") and Monk (mostly lesser-known songs) down quite well. Already at this early stage, Marcus Roberts had a fairly encyclopedic style, updating older idioms with his own voice, displaying an eccentric stride style and using some modern harmonies. Excellent music. *—Scott Yanow*

● **If I Could Be with You** / 1993 / Jive/Novus ♦♦♦♦♦
This is one of Marcus Roberts' finest all-around recordings. The set of solo piano improvisations features Roberts performing many older tunes (including "Maple Leaf Rag" and four James P. Johnson tunes) plus some of his originals, showing off his stride technique. Roberts' right hand borders on the miraculous, while his left often breaks up rhythms, jumping one beat ahead or behind purposely for short stretches and adding tension to the performance. Among the CD's highlights are "Just a Closer Walk With Thee," "Carolina Shout," "Keep Off the Grass," "What Is This Thing Called Love" and Roberts' "Preach, Reverend, Preach." *—Scott Yanow*

Gershwin for Lovers / 1994 / Columbia ♦♦♦♦
This trio date (which features pianist Marcus Roberts, bassist Reginald Veal and drummer Herlin Riley) is a bit unusual in that Roberts, although he is heard interpreting vintage George Gershwin songs, gives the tunes fairly modern interpretations. There is no striding or James P. Johnson licks. Instead, the talented pianist transforms such songs as "A Foggy Day," "Our Love Is Here to Stay," "It Ain't Necessarily So" and "But Not for Me" into modern hard bop. A typically excellent effort. *—Scott Yanow*

Plays Ellington / 1995 / Novus ♦♦♦♦

Portraits in Blue / Jun. 2, 1995-Jul. 13, 1995 / Columbia ♦♦♦♦

Blues for the New Millennium / Oct. 20, 1996-May 31, 1997 / Columbia ♦♦♦♦

In Honor of Duke / Apr. 1, 1999-Apr. 3, 1999 / Columbia ♦♦♦♦♦

Shorty Rogers (Milton M. Rajonsky)

b. Apr. 14, 1924, Great Barrington, MA, **d.** Nov. 7, 1994, Van Nuys, CA
Trumpet, Arranger / West Coast Jazz, Cool
A fine middle-register trumpeter whose style seemed to practically define "cool jazz," Shorty Rogers was actually more significant for his arranging, both in jazz and in the movie studios. After gaining early experience with Will Bradley and Red Norvo and serving in the military, Rogers rose to fame as a member of Woody Herman's First and Second Herds (1945-46 and 1947-49), and somehow he managed to bring some swing to the Stan Kenton Innovations Orchestra (1950-51), clearly enjoying writing for the stratospheric flights of Maynard Ferguson. After that association ran its course, Rogers settled in Los Angeles where he led his Giants (which ranged from a quintet to a nonet and a big band) on a series of rewarding West Coast jazz-styled recordings and wrote for the studios, helping greatly to bring jazz into the movies; his scores for *The Wild One* and *The Man with the Golden Arm* are particularly memorable. After 1962, Rogers stuck almost exclusively to writing for television and films but in 1982 he began a comeback in jazz. Rogers reorganized and headed the Lighthouse All-Stars and, although his own playing was not quite as strong as previously, he remained a welcome presence both in clubs and recordings. *—Scott Yanow*

☆ **The Complete Atlantic and EMI Jazz Recordings** / Oct. 8, 1951-Mar. 30, 1956 / Mosaic ♦♦♦♦♦
This four-CD limited-edition box set from Mosaic (which was also made available as six LPs) features all of the recordings that trumpeter-arranger Shorty Rogers made for the Atlantic and EMI labels. Six titles from 1951 find Rogers leading an octet based on Miles Davis' *Birth of the Cool* nonet and featuring solos from altoist Art Pepper, the tenor of Jimmy Giuffre, and pi-

anist Hampton Hawes. Rogers also heads a quintet with altoist Bud Shank in 1954, a quintet with Giuffre (tripling on clarinet, tenor, and baritone) in 1955, and some slightly larger groups (with such sidemen as the Candoli Brothers, trumpeter Harry "Sweets" Edison, altoists Herb Geller and Shank, pianists Lou Levy and Pete Jolly, and drummer Shelly Manne, among others). Although West Coast jazz has received a bad rap by East Coast writers through the years, Rogers shows that his recordings actually contained plenty of fire and swing, looking back toward the swing era and ahead simultaneously. Among the many highlights of this essential set are "Popo," "Lotus Bud," "Not Really the Blues," "Trickleydidlier," "Martians Go Home," "Martians Come Back," "March of the Martians," and "Martians Stay Home." *—Scott Yanow*

● **Short Stops** / Jan. 12, 1953-Mar. 3, 1954 / Bluebird/RCA ✦✦✦✦✦
This double LP offers listeners a strong introduction to the trumpet playing and arrangements of Shorty Rogers, but unfortunately it has gone out of print and was the first and last in its series. The 32 selections feature six different groups headed by Rogers during 1953-1954, ranging from an octet to a big band; all of the bands feature sidemen who essentially formed a who's who of West Coast jazz. Among the other soloists are altoist Art Pepper; tenors Bill Holman, Bill Perkins, Zoot Sims, Bob Cooper, and Jimmy Giuffre; trumpeter Harry "Sweets" Edison; pianist Hampton Hawes; and altoists Herb Geller and Bud Shank. The majority of the selections are Rogers originals; there is music from the Marlon Brando film *The Wild One* and a Count Basie tribute set. Swinging and surprisingly fiery "cool jazz" that deserves to be reissued on CD in full. *—Scott Yanow*

Chances Are It Swings / Dec. 8, 1958-Dec. 20, 1958 / RCA ✦✦✦✦

Yesterday, Today and Forever / Jun. 1983 / Concord Jazz ✦✦✦✦✦
Other than an album cut for the Japanese Atlas album the previous month, this was trumpeter Shorty Rogers' first jazz record in 20 years; he had worked in the interim as a fulltime studio arranger. Rogers is in pretty good form on the quintet date although occasionally overshadowed by altoist Bud Shank (who doubles on flute). The rhythm section (pianist George Cables, bassist Bob Magnusson and drummer Roy McCurdy) is excellent, the repertoire (highlighted by "Budo," Tiny Kahn's "TNT," "Wagon Wheels" and Shorty's "Have You Hugged A Martian Today") is full of vehicles for swinging improvisations and the musicians sound fairly inspired. Recommended. *—Scott Yanow*

Sonny Rollins

b. Sep. 7, 1930, New York, NY
Sax (Tenor), Composer / Hard Bop, Post-Bop, Bop
Sonny Rollins has for over 40 years been one of the true jazz giants, ranking up there with Coleman Hawkins, Lester Young and John Coltrane as one of the all time great tenor saxophonists. Rollins' abilities were obvious to the jazz world from the start and he started recording with Miles Davis in 1951 and with Thelonious Monk two years later. After a period out of music, Rollins joined the Max Roach-Clifford Brown Quintet in late 1955, continuing after Brownie's death until 1957. From then on he was always a leader. Sonny Rollins' series of brilliant recordings for Prestige, Blue Note, Contemporary and Riverside in the 1950s found him in peak form and he was acclaimed the top tenor saxophonist of the time, at least until John Coltrane rose to prominence. His skill at turning unlikely material into jazz, his unaccompanied flights and his rhythmic freedom and tonal distortions kept Rollins one of the masters of jazz into the 90s. *—Scott Yanow*

☆ **The Complete Prestige Recordings** / May 26, 1949-Dec. 7, 1956 / Prestige ✦✦✦✦✦
This seven-CD box set lives up to its title, reissuing in chronological order all of tenor-saxophonist Sonny Rollins's recordings for Prestige. Dating mostly from 1951-56, these valuable performances find Rollins developing from a promising player to a potential giant; many of his best recordings would take place a year or two after this program ends. In addition to his own sessions, Rollins is featured with trombonist J.J. Johnson, on four dates with Miles Davis and on sessions led by Thelonious Monk and trumpeter Art Farmer. Among the other musicians participating are trumpeters Kenny Dorham and Clifford Brown, pianists John Lewis, Kenny Drew, Horace Silver, Elmo Hope, Ray Bryant, Red Garland and Tommy Flanagan, drummers Max Roach, Roy Haynes, Art Blakey and Philly Joe Jones, the Modern Jazz Quartet, Julius Watkins on french horn, altoist Jackie McLean and even Charlie Parker. Among the many highlights are the original versions of Rollins' compositions "Airegin," "Oleo," "Doxy," "St. Thomas" and "Blue 7" and his one recorded meeting with John Coltrane ("Tenor Madness"). Essential music that is treated as it should be. The attractive booklet is a major plus too. *—Scott Yanow*

Sonny Rollins with the Modern Jazz Quartet / Jan. 17, 1951-Oct. 7, 1953 / Prestige/OJC ✦✦✦✦
This CD reissue has tenor saxophonist Sonny Rollins' first recording sessions as a leader. The initial selection, "I Know," was recorded at the tail end of a Miles Davis date and it finds Davis switching to piano to back Rollins' solo on the "Confirmation" chord changes. Eight selections showcase Rollins with the rhythm section of pianist Kenny Drew, bassist Percy Heath and drummer Art Blakey, mixing together standards and originals and also somehow making worthwhile music out of "Shadrack." The Modern Jazz Quartet (vibraphonist Milt Jackson, pianist John Lewis, bassist Percy Heath and drummer Kenny Clarke) is actually only on four numbers (despite the release's title) including "Almost like Being in Love" and Rollins' original "No Moe." The program overall shows that, even in his formative stage, Sonny Rollins was near the top of his field. *—Scott Yanow*

Moving Out / Aug. 18, 1954-Oct. 25, 1954 / Prestige/OJC ✦✦✦✦

Work Time / Dec. 2, 1955 / Prestige/OJC ✦✦✦✦
For this LP-length CD reissue, tenor great Sonny Rollins plays five songs (including the unlikely "There's No Business like Show Business") in a quartet with pianist Ray Bryant, bassist George Morrow and his then-current employer drummer Max Roach. Rollins was an original stylist from the start and in late 1955 he was ready to take his place among the greats. The enjoyable outing (which is included in Rollins' huge Prestige box set) may not be essential but it is a strong effort. *—Scott Yanow*

★ **Saxophone Colossus** / Mar. 22, 1956-Oct. 5, 1956 / Prestige/OJC ✦✦✦✦✦
This two-LP set finds Sonny Rollins entering his prime years and quickly developing into the most influential tenor-saxophonist in jazz (at least until John Coltrane fully emerged). Three selections from the *Sonny Rollins Plus 4* session with Clifford Brown (which is highlighted by "Pent-Up House") and most of *Sonny Rollins Plays for Bird* (including a strong version of "Star Eyes") are here, but it is the inclusion of the entire *Saxophone Colossus* that makes this two-fer so highly recommended. One of his greatest sessions, all five numbers are classics: "Moritat" (which would serve as the basis for "Mack the Knife"), "Strode Rode," "You Don't Know What Love Is" and especialy the original versions of "Blue Seven" and "St. Thomas." With pianist Tommy Flanagan, bassist Doug Watkins and drummer Max Roach giving him stimulating backup, Rollins is in brilliant form on this essential music, all of which is also included in his Prestige seven-CD box set. [A 20-bit remaster of *Saxophone Colossus* was released in October 1999.] *—Scott Yanow*

Sonny Rollins Plus Four / Mar. 22, 1956 / Prestige/OJC ✦✦✦✦✦
In 1956 Sonny Rollins used the Clifford Brown-Max Roach Quintet (of which he was a member) as his sidemen for this Prestige set. The highpoints of this particularly strong hard bop set include "Valse Hot" (an early jazz waltz), a rapid rendition of "I Feel a Song Coming On" and Rollins's classic "Pent-Up House." Trumpeter Brown (heard on one of his final sessions) is in excellent form as is the strong rhythm section and the young tenor-leader himself. This excellent music is also included as part of Rollins's seven-CD box set for Prestige. *—Scott Yanow*

Tenor Madness / May 24, 1956 / Prestige/OJC ✦✦✦✦✦
This CD (whose contents have since been reissued many times) is highlighted by the one meeting on records between Sonny Rollins and John Coltrane, an exciting battle on "Tenor Madness." Otherwise this is a more conventional but no less worthy Rollins quartet session with him turning such odd material as "My Reverie" and "The Most Beautiful Girl in the World" into creative jazz. *—Scott Yanow*

Rollins Plays for Bird / Oct. 5, 1956 / Prestige/OJC ✦✦✦✦
Sonny Rollins, heard in his early prime, performs "I've Grown Accustomed to Your Face," "Kids Know" and a seven-song "Bird Medley" on this CD reissue of a Prestige LP. Actually Rollins is only on four of the tunes in the medley and not all of the songs have a close connection with Charlie Parker. Featured in a quintet with trumpeter Kenny Dorham, pianist Wade Legge, bassist George Morrow and drummer Max Roach, Rollins is in fine form although the hard bop music falls slightly short of being essential. *—Scott Yanow*

The Complete Blue Note Recordings / Dec. 16, 1956-Nov. 3, 1957 / Blue Note ✦✦✦✦✦
The Complete Blue Note Records is a five-disc box set that contains everything Sonny Rollins recorded for the label between 1956 and 1957. Each disc has been previously released individually—this set simply collects *Sonny Rollins, Vols. 1 & 2, Newk's Time* and *A Night at the Village Vanguard, Vols. 1 & 2* in one slipcase, with no new remastering. For anyone intending to replace their Rollins Blue Note collection, or wishing to acquire all of this music at the same time, this set is essential, but anyone that already owns the individual discs needn't bother with this set. *—Stephen Thomas Erlewine*

Sonny Rollins, Vol. 1 / Dec. 16, 1956 / Blue Note ✦✦✦
Compared to Sonny Rollins's other classics of this era, this Blue Note recording usually gets lost in the shuffle but the music is actually quite good. The great tenor is teamed with trumpeter Donald Byrd, pianist Wynton Kelly, bassist Gene Ramey and drummer Max Roach for four of his originals (none of which caught on) and an interesting transformation of "How Are Things in Glocca Morra—" *—Scott Yanow*

☆ **The Freelance Years: The Complete Riverside and Contemporary Recordings** / Dec. 17, 1956-Oct. 22, 1958 / Riverside ✦✦✦✦✦
Picking up only ten days after Fantasy's *Complete Prestige Recordings* box leaves off, these five discs run through one of Rollins' most fertile (some insist, *the* most fertile) periods. Not only are Rollins' Riverside and Contemporary sessions as a leader and sideman collected in toto; Fantasy also includes three tracks recorded for Period in 1957, which can finally be heard within the context of Rollins' late-'50s hot streak. The box kicks off at the end of 1956 with almost all of Thelonious Monk's *Brilliant Corners* album, where Rollins alternates with alto saxophonist Ernie Henry. Then comes a quantum leap in inspiration, *Way Out West*, which is just bursting with invention and wry humor as well as cyclical references to previously played tunes; it relies only upon bassist Ray Brown and drummer Shelly Manne for support without needing anything more. Four tracks from Kenny Dorham's *Jazz Contrasts* find Rollins taking a subdued or conventionally frenetic bop backseat, while *The Sound of Sonny* approaches *Way Out West*'s level as Rollins operates with piano trio backing and alone. Sonny appears only in flashes on Abbey Lincoln's sometimes melodramatic *That's Him*. Following the Period tracks, where Rollins' tone is especially grandiose in the Ben Webster tradition, Rollins, bassist Oscar Petitford, and drummer Max Roach extend themselves astonishingly well through the colossal, nearly 20-minute title track of *The Freedom Suite*. The odyssey concludes on the West Coast with another great session, the unquenchably swinging *Sonny Rollins Meets the Contemporary Leaders*—Rollins' last before his first "retirement"—where various combinations of sidemen provoke some especially creative playing from Sonny. All previously released alternate takes are included, but there is only one unreleased track—a rip-roaring alternate of "You" from the *Contemporary Leaders* sessions—which will drive Rollins completists entirely mad. If the budget allows, it's worth the splurge. *—Richard S. Ginell*

★ **Way Out West** / Mar. 7, 1957 / Contemporary/OJC ✦✦✦✦✦
This timeless recording established Sonny Rollins as jazz's top tenor-saxophonist (at least until John Coltrane surpassed him the following year). Joined by bassist Ray Brown and drummer Shelly Manne, Rollins is heard at one of his peaks on such pieces as "I'm an Old Cowhand," his own "Way out West," "There Is No Greater Love" and "Come, Gone" (a fast stomp based on "After You've Gone"). The William Claxton photo of Rollins wearing Western gear (and holding his tenor) in the desert is also a classic. *—Scott Yanow*

Sonny Rollins, Vol. 2 / Apr. 14, 1957 / Blue Note ♦♦♦
Compared to his Prestige, Riverside and Contemporary recordings of the 1950s, some of Rollins's appearances on Blue Note seemed anticlimactic but none should be overlooked. This unusual album mostly has Rollins in an all-star quintet with trombonist J.J. Johnson, pianist Horace Silver, bassist Paul Chambers and drummer Art Blakey but Thelonious Monk sits in on his ballad "Reflections" and on "Misterioso" both Silver and Monk get to take contrasting solos. Of the other selections, Rollins's two originals ("Why Don't I" and "Wail March") are worth reviving and he finds something new to say on "Poor Butterfly" and an uptempo "You Stepped out of a Dream." *—Scott Yanow*

☆ **The Freedom Suite Plus** / Jun. 11, 1957-Feb. 27, 1958 / Milestone ♦♦♦♦♦
Sonny Rollins was at one of the peaks of his career during 1956-1958, recording one classic after another. This two-LP set is highlighted by the great tenor's monumental 19-minute "The Freedom Suite," an exploration with bassist Oscar Pettiford and drummer Max Roach that hints at free jazz and Ornette Coleman (who had not yet emerged) even within its tight structure. The trio also digs into four unusual standards (including Noel Coward's "Someday I'll Find You" and "Shadow Waltz"). The latter half of this two-fer has Rollins (along with pianist Sonny Clark, either Percy Heath or Paul Chambers on bass, and drummer Roy Haynes) improvising on a wide variety of material including "Ev'ry Time We Say Goodbye," "Just in Time" (a classic if eccentric version), and even "Toot, Toot, Tootsie." In addition, Rollins takes "It Could Happen to You" as an unaccompanied tenor solo, the first time he had recorded in that format. Highly recommended music. *—Scott Yanow*

The Sound of Sonny / Jun. 11, 1957-Jun. 19, 1957 / Riverside/OJC ♦♦♦♦♦
All of the music on this audiophile DCC Classics CD (which was originally put out by Riverside) has also been reissued on a CD in the Original Jazz Classics series. Tenor-saxophonist Sonny Rollins, who was in one of his prime periods at the time, takes "It Could Happen to You" as an unaccompanied solo, performs six numbers (including the rather unlikely "Toot, Toot, Tootsie" and an intense "Just in Time") with pianist Sonny Clark, bassist Percy Heath and drummer Roy Haynes, and improvises the "Funky Hotel Blues" (which made its debut on a sampler) with Clark, Haynes and bassist Paul Chambers. This is an excellent if not quite essential release from the masterful tenorman. *—Scott Yanow*

Newk's Time / Sep. 22, 1957 / Blue Note ♦♦♦♦
This fairly conventional but frequently exciting quartet session finds Sonny Rollins in top form on material ranging from "Tune Up" and "The Surrey with the Fringe on Top" to his own "Blues for Philly Joe." With pianist Wynton Kelly, bassist Doug Watkins and drummer Philly Joe Jones, Rollins shows on the CD that even his less-acclaimed sessions from this era are brilliant. *—Scott Yanow*

Freedom Suite / Feb. 11, 1958-Mar. 7, 1958 / Riverside/OJC ♦♦♦♦♦
Tenor saxophonist Sonny Rollins' last Riverside album has been reissued on this Original Jazz Classics CD. Jamming in a pianoless trio with bassist Oscar Pettiford and drummer Max Roach, Rollins is very creative, stretching out on his lengthy "Freedom Suite," tclearly enjoying investigating the obscure Noel Coward melody "Someday I'll Find You," turning the showtune "Till There Was You" into jazz and finding beauty in "Shadow Waltz" and "Will You Still Be Mine." A near-masterpiece. *—Scott Yanow*

Sonny Rollins and the Big Brass / Jul. 10, 1958-Aug. 3, 1958 / Verve ♦♦♦♦
Big Brass is an appopriate name for the large ensemble arranged and conducted by Ernie Wilkins that accompanies the huge sound of Sonny Rollins. The energy within the leader's gospel-flavored shout "Grand Street" is considerable, while a swinging but no less powerful version of George & Ira Gershwin's "Who Cares" features a choice solo by guitarist Rene Thomas. Also added to this compilation are trio recordings with bassist Henry Grimes and drummer Specs Wright, including a brilliant leisurely stroll through "Manhattan," along with Rollins' *tour de force* unaccompanied tenor sax on "Body and Soul." Another bonus is the presence of four tracks recorded at the *Music Inn* with three-quarters of the Modern Jazz Quartet (without Milt Jackson); an easygoing version of Rollins' well-known "Doxy" and a tense "Limehouse Blues" are especially noteworthy. The alternate endings to "Grand Street" from the mono version of the original LP and a later reissue LP are included only for the most fanatic completists. *—Ken Dryden*

The Bridge / Jan. 30, 1962-Feb. 14, 1962 / Bluebird/RCA ♦♦♦♦♦
The music on this 1996 CD has been reissued many times including in the Bluebird series. Tenor-saxophonist Sonny Rollins' first recording after ending a surprising three-year retirement found the great saxophonist sounding very similar to how he had played in 1959 although he would soon start investigating freer forms. In a pianoless quartet with guitarist Jim Hall, bassist Bob Cranshaw and drummer Ben Riley, Rollins explores four standards (including "Without A Song" and "God Bless The Child") plus two fiery originals (highlighted by the title cut). The interplay between Rollins and Hall is consistently impressive, making this CD a near-classic and a very successful comeback. *—Scott Yanow*

What's New? / Apr. 5, 1962-May 14, 1962 / Bluebird/RCA ♦♦♦♦♦
This excellent album deserves to be reissued in full on CD but some of its music remains out-of-print. Many of these songs find Sonny Rollins utilizing the Latin rhythms of Candido in addition to his regular quartet members (guitarist Jim Hall, bassist Bob Cranshaw and drummer Ben Riley) and, on the calypso "Brownskin Girl," a vocal chorus interacts with the group. The highpoint is a lengthy "If Ever I Would Leave You" that is quite exciting. This underrated music is well worth an extensive search. *—Scott Yanow*

All the Things You Are / Jul. 15, 1963-Jul. 2, 1964 / Bluebird/RCA ♦♦♦♦

Sonny Rollins & Co. 1964 / Jan. 24, 1964-Jul. 9, 1964 / Bluebird/RCA ♦♦♦♦
This CD from the Bluebird reissue series fills a lot of gaps in Sonny Rollins' discography. The 13 selections are taken from six different sessions from 1964. The personnel changes from date to date, with either Ron Carter or Bob Cranshaw on bass and Roy McCurdy or Mickey Roker on drums, along with pianist Herbie Hancock on five songs and guitarist Jim Hall on three others. Some of the music is actually alternate takes, and in contrast to a rambling 16-minute version of "Now's the Time," a few of the briefer songs (seven are under 31 minutes) shut down prematurely. However, the great tenor's improvisations are consistently fascinating, as he reconciles his avant-garde flights to the standards he is performing; "Autumn Nocturne" is a high point. *—Scott Yanow*

Sonny Rollins on Impulse! / Jul. 8, 1965 / Impulse! ♦♦♦♦
The first of three studio albums that tenor-saxophonist Sonny Rollins recorded for Impulse contains the joyous calypso "Hold 'Em Joe" and four unusual versions of standards in which the rhythms he plays are more important than the actual melodies. Joined by pianist Ray Bryant, bassist Walter Booker and drummer Mickey Roker, Rollins sounds quite distinctive on this brief but enjoyable set. This enjoyable outing (which has among its highlights eccentric versions of "Blue Room" and "Three Little Words") was reissued on CD in 1997. *—Scott Yanow*

Alfie / Jan. 26, 1966 / Impulse! ♦♦♦♦♦
Sonny Rollins compositions for the film *Alfie* (which benefited greatly from Oliver Nelson's arrangements) are heard on this CD as played by Rollins and a ten-piece band. The music easily stands by itself without the movie and Rollins is in fine form on these generally memorable themes, particularly "On Impulse" and "Alfie's Theme." This superlative effort was most recently reissued on an Impulse CD in 1997. *—Scott Yanow*

☆ **East Broadway Rundown** / May 9, 1966 / Impulse! ♦♦♦♦♦
Around the ten-minute mark of the title track, things get very interesting indeed—moody and spooky as Jimmy Garrison hangs on a single note, making his bass throb along while Elvin Jones widens the space and fires drum and cymbal hits in all directions. Coming off of bass and drum solos that never seem to fit anywhere in the piece, it's a supreme moment of tension-building, one that gets repeated after Rollins and trumpeter Freddie Hubbard restate the theme in unison. This is the sound of Rollins' group working in unity. For much of "East Broadway Run Down," though, the rhythm section is off doing their thing, usually together, while Rollins meanders about in limbo, seemingly trying to figure out what it is that he should be doing. That Rollins was having an off day for this recording is a suspicion that's strengthened by Hubbard's part—where Rollins is wandering, Hubbard is charging ahead, focused and tight, fitting with the rhythm section, keeping the tension up. The remainder of the album is more on the mark, with "Blessing In Disguise" being quite enjoyable—it starts out in a cheerfully traditional vein and gradually, subtly, starts to slide off into an improvisational area only to come back again to the traditional, and so back and forth. Rollins floats his sax line around the melody with only occasional excursions toward the outer regions. "We Kiss in a Shadow," though, is charmingly straightforward, a ballad rendering supported by Jones and Garrison locking together on a nice rhythm construction that lets Rollins float around the melody. *—Steven McDonald*

Next Album / Jul. 1972 / Milestone/OJC ♦♦♦♦♦
Sonny Rollins first album after ending his six-year retirement is a particularly strong effort. The highpoint is a ten-minute version of "Skylark" that has a long unaccompanied section by the great tenor. Other memorable selections include "The Everywhere Calypso" and "Playing in the Yard." Rollins plays soprano on "Poinciana" and is heard using electronics (George Cables' electric piano) for the first time but this music is not all that different from what he was playing prior to his retirement. *—Scott Yanow*

Old Flames / Jul. 1993-Aug. 1993 / Milestone ♦♦♦♦

Sonny Rollins Plus Three / 1996 / Milestone ♦♦♦♦♦

Global Warming / Jan. 7, 1998-Feb. 28, 1998 / Milestone ♦♦♦♦

☆ **A Night at the Village Vanguard** / Nov. 3, 1957 / Blue Note ♦♦♦♦♦
This CD is often magical. Sonny Rollins, one of jazz's great tenors, is heard at his peak with a pair of piano-less trios (either Wilbur Ware or Donald Bailey on bass and Elvin Jones or Pete La Roca on drums) stretching out on particularly creative versions of "Old Devil Moon," "Softly As in a Morning Sunrise," "Sonnymoon for Two," and "A Night in Tunisia," among others. Not only did Rollins have a very distinctive sound but his use of time, his sly wit, and his boppish but unpredictable style were completely his own by 1957. [Originally released as two separate albums, *A Night at the Village Vanguard* was reissued in its entirety, complete with alternate takes, as a two-disc set in 1999; it was part of Blue Note's acclaimed Rudy Van-Gelder reissue series.] *—Scott Yanow*

The Complete RCA Victor Recordings / RCA ♦♦♦♦♦
This six-CD set has all of tenor saxophonist Sonny Rollins' recordings for RCA, including the complete contents of *The Bridge, What's New, Our Man In Jazz, Sonny Meets Hawk, Now's the Time* and *The Standard Sonny Rollins*, the three selections originally included in the sampler *3 for Jazz*, and 11 alternate takes only previously released on the French album *The Alternative Rollins*. Less known than Rollins' earlier Prestige and Riverside records and slightly later Impulse albums, his output for RCA was recorded right after the great tenor came back from an extended sabbatical. The music on *The Bridge* (which co-stars guitarist Jim Hall) is the most famous of these dates. Rollins became increasingly interested in the avant-garde during the era, and he used two of Ornette Coleman's sidemen (trumpeter Don Cherry and drummer Billy Higgins) in his group for a period. On *Sonny Meets Hawk*, Rollins challenged his idol Coleman Hawkins by playing as outside as possible (Hawkins responded well). Other musicians heard on the recordings include bassists Bob Cranshaw, Ron Carter and Henry Grimes, drummers Ben Riley and Mickey Roker, pianists Paul Bley and Herbie Hancock and (on a couple of numbers) cornetist Thad Jones. However, Rollins is the main star throughout the adventurous and sometimes eccentric performances, coming up with many remarkable ideas, often rollicking with a pianoless rhythm section and in two cases taking duets with the congas of Candido. Serious Sonny Rollins collectors will have to have this valuable set, although since most of the selections have also been reissued on individual CDs, more casual jazz fans may be satisfied with one or two of the smaller reissues. *—Scott Yanow*

ROVA

f. 1977

Saxophone / Avant-Garde Jazz, Free Jazz

The most advanced of the saxophone quartets, Rova (consisting of Jon Raskin, Larry Ochs, Andrew Voigt and Bruce Ackley) was formed in 1977. Since then this adventurous unit has recorded extensively for many labels (including Metalanguage, Moers, Ictus, New Albion, Sound Aspects, Hat Art and Black Saint), toured Europe and the Soviet Union (the latter twice) and put out sets of Steve Lacy and Anthony Braxton tunes in addition to many originals. In 1988 Steve Adams took Voigt's place. *—Scott Yanow*

Saxophone Diplomacy: Live in Russia, Latvia, Romania / Jun. 1983 / hatART ✦✦✦✦✦
The Rova saxophone quartet's 1983 tour of three countries behind the then still very erect Iron Curtain was indeed historic. The Eastern Europeans and the Californians had been exchanging not only music but literature (Larry Ochs' wife is poet, teacher and publisher Lyn Hejinian). The sounds Rova were making at this time in their history-Bruce Ackley was still a member-connected deeply with the Eastern Europeans who were still soaking up Albert Ayler, Ornette, Cecil Taylor and Coltrane. Rova were also in the stage of defining themselves as an entity, creating the first of their long structured group improvisations for performance and recording.

The result of the tour, as we get it here, is nothing less than awe-inspiring. From the near gospel call and response of Jon Raskin's "Flamingo Horizons" which becomes nearly hypnotic in its repetitive rhythmic structure, to Ochs' harmonic experiments in modalism in "Paint Another Take of the Shootpop," to his arrangement of vanguard jazz great Steve Lacy's "The Throes," all members were playing with an intensity and verve that could only come from being not only rehearsed, but nurtured by an audience. And they were. The applause sounds that come through are only rivaled by those Moscow's Ganelin Trio received in its homeland.

As an introduction to Rova, this is an excellent venture, as a moment of pinpointing when their early, loose-operation freestyle improvising ended and real compositional pieces for group improvisation began, this is also the recording to begin with. Indeed, were it not for *Saxophone Diplomacy,* Rova's classic, "The Crowd," may never have been written, and the original Ganelin Trio may never have come to America; a very important record. *—Thom Jurek*

Beat Kennel / Apr. 13, 1987-Apr. 15, 1987 / Black Saint ✦✦✦✦

● **This Time We Are Both** / Nov. 1989 / New Albion ✦✦✦✦✦
Recorded during their second tour of the Soviet Union, these six performances by ROVA (Larry Ochs on tenor and sopranino, Bruce Ackley on soprano, Steve Adams on alto and sopranino, and baritonist Jon Raskin) are consistently exciting and inventive. In general, the four masterful saxophonists start off with fairly accessible and rhythmic patterns before venturing into loose but controlled freedom. The sound explorations cover a great deal of emotional ground and usually change or conclude shortly after reaching their optimal length; there is no self-indulgent screaming or aimless wandering. One of ROVA's finest recordings. *—Scott Yanow*

Pipe Dreams / Jan. 1994 / Black Saint ✦✦✦✦✦
The Rova Saxophone Quartet doubled in size for this passionate set with the addition of Vinny Golia, Tim Berne, Glenn Spearman and Dave Barrett. By coming up with creative frameworks that utilize rhythmic motifs, preplanned sections, individual solos, duets and group improvising, Larry Ochs (who composed all five selections) was able to make use of the wide variety of sounds and tones that could be produced by this high-powered saxophone octet. The originals range from an Albert Aylerish march and a transcription of a Crotian song (made to sound as if two drunken choirs were singing at the same time) to the often scary "Triceratops." The constant changing of instrumentation and the use of contrast keep the music from ever losing momentum; there are no slow moments. The improvising is consistently free but with a purpose. Open-eared listeners will benefit from giving this stimulating release a close study. *—Scott Yanow*

John Coltrane's Ascension / Dec. 6, 1995 / Black Saint ✦✦✦✦

Gonzalo Rubalcaba

b. May 27, 1963, Havana, Cuba

Piano / Cuban Jazz, Afro-Cuban Jazz, Latin Jazz

One of the great Cuban jazz musicians, only in recent times has Gonzalo Rubalcaba been able to freely travel in the United States. He studied classical piano from 1971-83, toured France and Africa with the Orquesta Aragon in 1983 and formed the Grupo Proyecto in 1985, touring Europe frequently. In 1986 he met Charlie Haden who sang his praises and helped arrange his appearances at the Montreal and Montreux festivals. By 1990 Gonzalo Rubalcaba had been discovered by the jazz world and his records began to be released on Blue Note. An advanced improviser with a dense style, Rubalcaba has unlimited potential. *—Scott Yanow*

Discovery: Live at Montreux / Jul. 15, 1990 / Blue Note ✦✦✦✦✦
A very good Cuban pianist. His best is yet to come. *—Michael G. Nastos*

★ **The Blessing** / May 12, 1991-May 15, 1991 / Blue Note ✦✦✦✦✦
The virtuosic Cuban pianist Gonzalo Rubalcaba's first recording to be issued in the U.S. is still one of his best. With strong accompaniment from bassist Charlie Haden (one of his early champions) and drummer Jack DeJohnette, Rubalcaba is in frequently exciting form throughout these performances. Highlights include an outstanding investigation of "Besame Mucho," "Giant Steps," Ornette Coleman's beautiful "The Blessing" and an unusual treatment given Bill Evans's "Blue in Green." *—Scott Yanow*

Images / Aug. 24, 1991-Aug. 25, 1991 / Blue Note ✦✦✦✦✦
The high-powered yet sensitive Cuban pianist Gonzalo Rubalcaba teams up with the brilliant, strangely underrated bassist John Patitucci (who sticks to acoustic bass) and drummer Jack DeJohnette on this superior live set from the 1991 Mt. Fuji Jazz Festival. The repertoire is wide-ranging, with originals from each of the musicians, John Lennon's "Imagine," and a powerhouse version of "Autumn Leaves," and "Giant Steps." A particularly strong effort from Rubalcaba, who by the early '90s had emerged as one of the top pianists in jazz. *—Scott Yanow*

Rapsodia / Nov. 15, 1992-Nov. 21, 1992 / Blue Note ✦✦✦✦✦
Pianist Gonzalo Rubalcaba has such impressive technique that he has the potential of completely overwhelming any song he plays but Rubalcaba shows admirable restraint throughout much of this quartet date. Influenced to a degree by Chick Corea and Herbie Hancock, Rubalcaba still shows a fresh personality when he utilizes an electric keyboard on a few of the selections. His quartet (which includes trumpeter Reynaldo Melian, bassist Felipe Cabrera and drummer Julio Barreto), in addition to fine support, offers a contrasting solo voice in its virtuosic trumpeter. This is a well-rounded set of complex but fairly accessible music. *—Scott Yanow*

Imagine / May 14, 1993-Jun. 24, 1994 / Blue Note ✦✦✦✦✦
Gonzalo Rubalcaba, a Cuban jazz treasure, is heard on his CD from three separate occasions. Although Howard Mandel's odd liner notes make it sound like most of the music originated from Rubalcaba's 1993 New York concert at Alice Tully Hall (he even refers to a duet Rubalcaba had with singer Dianne Reeves as if it were included on this release), only the searching version of "First Song" with bassist Charlie Haden and drummer Jack DeJohnette is actually from that appearance. "Imagine" and "Circuito II." (both taken solo) were recorded in a Hollywood studio a year later and the remaining four songs (three with a Cuban quartet) are taken from a 1994 Westwood concert. Rubalcaba has limitless technique and (even with its touches of Herbie Hancock and Chick Corea) a sound of his own. His lyrical rendition of "Imagine" is a highlight as is the eccentric "Contagio" and a melancholy exploration of "Perfidia." Of Rubalcaba's sidemen, electric bassist Felipe Cabrera's very active accompaniment recalls Jaco Pastorius, drummer Julio Barreto is fine in support and trumpeter Reynaldo Melian is a virtuoso with a rather cold sound. All in all, this is a fine allround set by Gonzalo Rubalcaba that is full of complex ideas and subtle surprises. *—Scott Yanow*

Diz / Dec. 14, 1993-Dec. 15, 1993 / Blue Note ✦✦✦
Although one might assume that having the title of "Diz" means that this set would be a tribute to Dizzy Gillespie, only four of the nine selections were actually associated with the great trumpeter; the other numbers range from Bird and Bud Powell to Benny Golson and Charles Mingus ("Smooch"). Gonzalo Rubalcaba makes each of the jazz standards his own by reharmonizing the chord structures, playing in his own dense style and coming up with fresh new statements rather than just re-creating bebop. He is quite lyrical and somber on the ballads, makes "Donna Lee" unrecognizable, and (with the assistance of bassist Ron Carter and drummer Julio Barreto) modernizes all of the potential warhorses. This is a very interesting workout. *—Scott Yanow*

Inner Voyage / Nov. 23, 1998-Nov. 25, 1998 / Blue Note ✦✦✦✦✦
After taking the jazz world by storm with his exciting debut CD on Blue Note in 1991, Rubalcaba continued to delight his fans throughout the decade with one great recording after another. "Yolanda Anas," "Joan," and "Joao," each one a tribute to one of his children, are intimate musical portraits that have a childlike simplicity but also memorable melodies that linger in the mind. A salute to Blue Note president Bruce Lundvall is a complex post-bop blues featuring fierce solos by tenor saxophonist Michael Brecker and bassist Jeff Chambers. His breathtaking arrangement of "Here's That Rainy Day" is one of the most intimate ever recorded, played with an almost hushed tone. The pianist's introduction to "Caravan" has a swinging Latin flavor, though the body of the song is much looser and less thunderous than one might expect. Highly recommended. *—Ken Dryden*

Roswell Rudd

b. Nov. 17, 1935, Sharon, CT

Trombone / Avant-Garde Jazz, Free Jazz

It's no coincidence that free jazz's most acclaimed trombonist, Roswell Rudd, mostly bypassed bop, going straight from being a tailgate trombonist in a Dixieland band to cofounding the ultra avant-garde New York Art Quartet, with very few stops in-between. Bebop was spoken most naturally by players of keyed instruments. In Rudd's hands, the horn became less a note-playing machine than a kind of human-powered analog synthesizer, leading him to jump whole-heartedly into free jazz.

After playing the French horn, and learning about jazz from his father, Rudd began teaching himself the trombone as a teenager—Woody Herman's trombonist, Bill Harris, was an early favorite. Rudd played dixieland while attending Yale, then worked with legendary pianist Herbie Nichols (1960-62). From 1961-63, Rudd played Monk tunes in a band with soprano saxophonist Steve Lacy and drummer Dennis Charles, later informally known as the *School Days* quartet, after their 1963 album. In 1962 Rudd joined Bill Dixon's free jazz group with Archie Shepp. In 1964 he co-led the New York Art Quartet (with saxophonist John Tchicai) and participated in the October Revolution in Jazz festival. The latter half of the '60s, he played with Archie Shepp, Charlie Haden's Liberation Music Orchestra, and Gato Barbieri, and in the Primordial Quartet (with Lee Konitz) from 1968-70.

Other than recording some with Lacy, Rudd faded from visibility during the '70s & '80s, working non-musical jobs and teaching in colleges. After leaving the University of Maine, he moved to the Catskills, working in a hotel resort band. In the mid-'90s he was back, recording for the C.I.M.P. label. In 2000, Rudd and Lacy reunited to record *Monk's Dream* for Verve, and tour. At the turn of the millennium, Rudd was performing with some frequency in Europe and New York, regaining his reputation as the father of free jazz trombone. *—Chris Kelsey*

Flexible Flyer / Mar. 1974 / Black Lion ✦✦✦✦
For this set, trombonist Roswell Rudd (who doubles on French horn) heads a quintet that also includes pianist Hod O'Brien, bassist Arild Anderson, drummer Barry Altschul and,

most interestingly, singer Sheila Jordan. The repertoire includes "What Are You Doing the Rest of Your Life," Herbie Hancock's "Maiden Voyage" and a few originals, including three Rudd tunes that are played as a medley. The trombonist plays quite well; the rhythm section is tight yet adventurous; and the use of Jordan (who also has some individual spots) as part of some of the ensembles helps make the date something special. Recommended. *—Scott Yanow*

Inside Job / May 21, 1976 / Arista ✦✦✦
Solid quintet date w/ intense Dave Burrell on piano. *—Ron Wynn*

● **Regeneration** / Jun. 25, 1982-Jun. 26, 1982 / Soul Note ✦✦✦✦✦
The consensus album of the year in 1983, it includes one side of Monk and the other of Herbie Nichols's music. Includes Roswell Rudd (tb), Misha Mengleberg (p), Kent Carter (b), and Hans Bennik (d). *—Michael G. Nastos*

Broad Strokes / Mar. 15, 1999-Jan. 7, 2000 / Knitting Factory ✦✦✦✦
For those of us who recall fondly Roswell Rudd's outstanding work in the '60s and '70s, this latest effort may come as a bit of a disappointment. It is a mixed bag, an odd-ball collection of Rudd-led sessions over a nearly a year. The track with Steve Lacy and Elton Dean performing Monk's "Coming on the Hudson" is terrific, with Rudd in top form and the saxophonists adding considerably. Similarly, the tentet, with three trombones (Steve Swell and Josh Roseman, in addition to Rudd) performs a meaty version of Herbie Nichols' "Change of Season"; a less compelling rendition of Rudd's "Stokey" (which features less-than-exemplary lyrics sung by Steve Ruddick); and a fascinating take of Ellington's "All Too Soon/Way Low." Roswell's words to his "Sassy & Dolphy" miss the mark (and are sung by a rather sterile-sounding Christopher Rudd), and the trombonist's recitation on his own "God had a Girlfriend" just doesn't make it. On the other hand, who can resist Rudd and Sonic Youth guitarist Thurston Moore playing an excerpt from Saint-Saens' *Symphony No. 3* or a reunion of Roswell and Sheila Jordan. Rudd fans will not wish to pass this recording up, although it is much more an oddity than anything definitive or enduring. *—Steven Loewy*

Jimmy Rushing

b. Aug. 26, 1903, Oklahoma City, OK, **d.** Jun. 8, 1972, New York, NY
Vocals / Vocal Jazz, East Coast Blues, Jazz Blues, Jump Blues, Swing
He was known as "Mister Five-By-Five"—an affectionate reference to his height and girth—a blues shouter who defined and then transcended the form. The owner of a booming voice that radiated sheer joy in whatever material he sang, Jimmy Rushing could swing with anyone and dominate even the loudest of big bands. Rushing achieved his greatest fame in front of the Count Basie band from 1935 to 1950, yet unlike many band singers closely associated with one organization, he was able to carry on afterwards with a series of solo recordings that further enhanced his reputation as a first-class jazz singer. The unquenchably swinging Basie rhythm section was a perfect match for Rushing, making their earliest showing together on a 1936 recording of "Boogie Woogie" that stamped not only Rushing's presence onto the national scene but also that of Lester Young. After the Basie ensemble broke up in 1950, a victim of hard times for big bands, Rushing briefly retired, then formed his own septet. He started a series of solo albums for Vanguard in the mid-1950s, then turned in several distinguished recordings for Columbia in league with such luminaries as Dave Brubeck, Coleman Hawkins and Benny Goodman. *—Richard S. Ginell*

● **The Essential Jimmy Rushing** / Dec. 1, 1954-Mar. 5, 1957 / Vanguard ✦✦✦✦✦
This single CD reissues an earlier Jimmy Rushing two-LP set, leaving off two cuts due to lack of space. Jimmy Rushing, who may very well have been the definitive male big-band singer, sticks mostly to blues and Kansas City swing on the release and is backed by a variety of top swing all-stars including most notably tenor-saxophonist Buddy Tate, trumpeter Emmett Berry and trombonists Lawrence Brown and Vic Dickenson. The sidemen receive plenty of space for concise solos, particularly pianists Pete Johnson and Sammy Price. The performances (plus the 11 other songs that are awaiting reissue someday) are among the most rewarding of Jimmy Rushing's post-Basie career and are full of joy and timeless swing. *—Scott Yanow*

Everyday I Have the Blues / Feb. 9, 1967-Feb. 10, 1967 / Bluesway ✦✦✦✦✦
A CD reissue of the great blues shouter Jimmy Rushing singing recreated versions of his classics with the Basie band. This originally came out in the mid-'50s, when Rushing had left Basie and was heading his own band. While these versions aren't the definitive ones, they're far from bad. *—Ron Wynn*

The You and Me That Used to Be / Oct. 1971 / Bluebird/RCA ✦✦✦✦✦
On this straight CD reissue of Jimmy Rushing's final recording sessions, the singer is in spirited form despite being little more than a year from his death. On the ten swing standards and a lone blues ("Fine and Mellow"), Rushing is joined by pianist Dave Frishberg (also responsible for the arrangements), bassist Milt Hinton, and drummer Mel Lewis, plus either Ray Nance on cornet and violin and tenor saxophonist Zoot Sims, or Budd Johnson (on soprano) and Al Cohn (on tenor). Touching renditions of "I Surrender Dear" and "More Than You Know" find Rushing backed only by Frishberg's very able piano. This recommended CD is proof that "Mr. Five by Five" (whose career spanned more than 40 years) went out on top. *—Scott Yanow*

Rushing Lullabies: Little Jimmy Rushing and the Big Brass / Feb. 20, 1958-Jun. 19, 1959 / Columbia ✦✦✦✦
Although named after a former LP, this CD actually contains the complete contents of two albums (the other one was called *Little Jimmy Rushing and the Big Brass*), plus a brief previously unreleased number. Known for his renditions of swing-oriented blues, but also quite effective on ballads and jumping standards, the great singer is featured with a big band (which has solo space for many musicians, including tenors Buddy Tate and Coleman Hawkins, trumpeter Buck Clayton, and trombonist Dicky Wells) and a sextet with Tate, organist Sir Charles Thompson and pianist Ray Bryant. These were two of Rushing's better sets from the 1950s, and he is heard throughout the mostly veteran tunes in top form. Highlights include "I'm Coming Virginia," "Mister Five by Five," "When You're Smiling," "Good Rockin' Tonight" and "Russian Lullaby." *—Scott Yanow*

Oh Love / Jul. 7, 1999 / Vanguard ✦✦✦✦✦
Although Jimmy Rushing parted company with Count Basie in 1950, Basie's influence stayed with him right up until his death in 1972. Similarly, Basie didn't forget about Rushing either; the fact that Joe Williams, Basie's male vocalist from 1954-1961, was greatly influenced by Rushing certainly wasn't lost on the Count. Basie's influence is impossible to miss on *Oh Love*, a superb CD focusing on Rushing's John Hammond-produced work for Vanguard in the 1950s. Spanning 1955-1958, this collection of Kansas City swing, jump blues, and jazz/blues draws on three of the singer's old Vanguard LPs (*Listen to the Blues, If This Ain't the Blues*, and *Goin' to Chicago*), and finds him joined by such hard-swinging improvisers as tenor saxman Buddy Tate, trombonist Lawrence Brown, pianist Pete Johnson, and drummer Jo Jones (not to be confused with Philly Joe Jones). Rushing revisits many classics from his Basie years, including "Going to Chicago Blues," "Pennies From Heaven," "Gee Baby, Ain't I Good to You," and "Dinah," and he sings them with as much conviction as ever. These are essential recordings that have withstood the test of time quite nicely. *—Alex Henderson*

Every Day / Sep. 28, 1999 / Vanguard ✦✦✦✦✦
This CD compiles tracks from three separate LPs of the always swinging blues shouter Jimmy Rushing, produced by John Hammond in the 1950s. Most of the music comes from the best date, *Listen to the Blues;* highlights include a spirited "Evenin'," the classic "See See Rider" with a fine trumpet solo by Emmett Berry, and "Roll 'Em Pete," a popular boogie-woogie tune that finds the leader on the sidelines except for shouting encouragement. The three selections from *Listen to the Blues* are badly dated by the questionable addition of organist Marlowe Morris, while only the oft-requested "Sent for You Yesterday" is included from the far superior album *Goin' to Chicago.* It's good to see some of this important music become available once again, though Rushing fans would have preferred intact reissues of the original albums. *—Ken Dryden*

George Russell

b. Jun. 23, 1923, Cincinnati, OH
Drums, Piano, Composer, Arranger / Avant-Garde Jazz, Third Stream, Post-Bop
While George Russell has been very active as a free-thinking composer, arranger and bandleader, his biggest effect upon jazz has been that of the quieter role of theorist. His great contribution, apparently the first by a jazz musician to general music theory, was a book with the intimidating title *The Lydian Chromatic Concept of Tonal Organization*, where he concocted a concept of playing jazz based on scales rather than chord changes. Published in 1953, Russell's theories directly paved the way for the modal revolutions of Miles Davis and John Coltrane—and Russell even took credit for the theory behind Michael Jackson's huge hit "Wanna Be Startin' Somethin,'" which uses the Lydian scale (no, he didn't ask for royalties). Russell's stylistic reach in his own compositions eventually became omnivorous, embracing bop, gospel, blues, rock, funk, contemporary classical elements, electronic music and African rhythms in his recent, ambitious extended works—most apparent in his large-scale 1983 suite for an enlarged big band, *The African Game.* Like his colleague Gil Evans, Russell never stopped growing, but his work is not nearly as well-known that that of Evans, being more difficult to grasp and, in any case, not as well-documented by U.S. record labels. *—Richard S. Ginell*

Jazz Workshop / Mar. 31, 1956-Dec. 21, 1956 / Bluebird/RCA ✦✦✦✦✦
Reissued as a Koch CD, this set (originally cut for RCA) was composer/arranger George Russell's debut as a leader. The original program (which includes such numbers as "Ye Hypocrite, Ye Beelzebub," "Livingstone I Presume," "Ezz-thetic" and "Knights of the Steamtable") has been joined by alternate second versions of "Ballad of Hix Blewitt" and "Concerto for Billy the Kid." Listening to the music, it is hard to believe that Russell only utilized a sextet (comprised of trumpeter Art Farmer, altoist Hal McKusick, guitarist Barry Galbraith, pianist Bill Evans, one of two bassists and one of three drummers). The ensembles are frequently dense, the harmonies quite original and there are often several events occurring at the same time; one would swear there were at least four or five horns being heard in spots. "Fellow Delegates" is particularly intriguing for it finds Russell playing chromatic drums while joined by Osie Johnson on wood drums; the otherwordly effect is worthy of Sun Ra. Even the more conventional pieces such as "Ezz-thetic" (based on the chords of "Love for Sale" but here almost resembling a Lennie Tristano line played backwards) sound quite advanced. Russell was able to utilize some of the more versatile and technically skilled players of the era, several of whom worked regularly in the studios. Recommended. *—Scott Yanow*

New York, New York / Sep. 12, 1958-Mar. 25, 1959 / Impulse! ✦✦✦✦✦
This is a landmark of conceptual, arranging, production, and playing magnificence. John Coltrane (ts), Max Roach (d), Bill Evans (p), Jon Hendricks (v) all soar. *—Ron Wynn*

Jazz in the Space Age / May 1960-Aug. 1, 1960 / Decca/GRP ✦✦✦✦

George Russell Sextet at the Five Spot / Sep. 20, 1960 / Decca ✦✦✦✦
This limited-edition CD reissue covers six tracks recorded in the studio (since they obviously omit any of the background noise, and the usual out-of-tune piano heard on live dates recorded at the long defunct New York City nightclub is missing). The band includes trumpeter Al Kiger, trombonist David Baker, tenor saxophonist Dave Young, bassist Chuck Israels, and drummer Joe Hunt, along with Russell's sparse piano. Things kick off with a driving take of Miles Davis' "Sippin' at Bells," which features great interaction among the horns. Carla Bley's "Dance Class" is choppy, dissonant, and very humorous; she also wrote "Beast Blues," which features Kiger's muted horn, an energetic solo by Young, and a very understated solo by Baker. Baker contributed "121 Bank Street," a roller coaster post-bop vehicle. John Coltrane's "Moment's Notice," which had only been recorded three years earlier by its composer, is re-scored with a very spacious Russell arrangement that provides minimal accompaniment for the soloists. Unlike many of Russell's releases, this one has only one of his originals, "Swingdom Come," with a jagged angular theme that defies predictable paths.

Although Russell plays more of a composer/arranger style of piano, his very challenging arrangements are very attractive. Anyone who enjoys his releases for RCA, Riverside, and Decca from around this period in his career should definitely acquire this sure-to-be-collectable CD. *—Ken Dryden*

★ **Ezz-Thetics** / Jul. 8, 1961 / Riverside/OJC ♦♦♦♦♦
This is a true classic. Composer/pianist George Russell gathered together a very versatile group of talents (trumpeter Don Ellis, trombonist Dave Baker, Eric Dolphy on alto and bass clarinet, bassist Steve Swallow and drummer Joe Hunt) to explore three of his originals, "'Round Midnight" (which is given an extraordinary treatment by Dolphy), Miles Davis's "Nardis" and David Baker's "Honesty." The music is post-bop and although using ideas from avant-garde jazz, it does not fall into any simple category. The improvising is at a very high level and the frameworks (which include free and stoptime sections) really inspire the players. Highly recommended. *—Scott Yanow*

The Stratus Seekers / Jan. 31, 1962 / Riverside/OJC ♦♦♦♦♦
In 1962, the George Russell Septet included both obscure names (altoist John Pierce, tenor saxophonist Paul Plummer and drummer Joe Hunt, who would later work with Bill Evans) and future stars (trumpeter Don Ellis, trombonist Dave Baker, who would become a significant jazz educator, and bassist Steve Swallow). The six selections (plus a "new" alternate) heard on the CD reissue are highlighted by "Blues In Orbit" (later recorded by Gil Evans) and the title cut; two other numbers were written by the sidemen. It is particularly interesting to hear the young Ellis in this setting. The music has its own logic and is difficult to classify, and deserves further attention by jazz historians and analysts. *—Scott Yanow*

The Outer View / Aug. 27, 1962 / Riverside/OJC ♦♦♦♦♦
Composer George Russell's early-'60s Riverside recordings are among his most accessible. For this set (the CD reissue adds an alternate take of the title cut to the original program), Russell and his very impressive sextet (which is comprised of trumpeter Don Ellis, trombonist Garnett Brown, Paul Plummer on tenor, bassist Steve Swallow and drummer Pete La Roca) are challenged by the complex material; even Charlie Parker's blues "Au Privave" is transformed into something new. It is particularly interesting to hear Don Ellis this early in his career. The most famous selection, a very haunting version of "You Are My Sunshine," was singer Sheila Jordan's debut on records. *—Scott Yanow*

Vertical Form 6 / Mar. 10, 1977 / Soul Note ♦♦♦♦
A magnificent and critically acclaimed large band recording with arrangements by George Russell, who also conducted. His compositions, with their intricate, unpredictable, and keenly structured pace, textures, and layers, are expertly played by an international orchestra. This '77 release was unfortunately poorly distributed in America, since it was on a foreign label. *—Ron Wynn*

New York Big Band / Aug. 16, 1978-Mar. 77, 1977 / Soul Note ♦♦♦♦♦

☆ **Electronic Sonata for Souls Loved by Nature 1980** / Jun. 9, 1980-Jun. 10, 1980 / Strata East ♦♦♦♦♦
Composer, theorist, arranger, and pianist George Russell debuted his 14-part master composition "Electronic Sonata for Souls Loved By Nature" on April 28, 1969, at a concert in Norway. The ambitious, elaborate work blended bebop, free, Asian, and blues elements, as well as electronic effects, and mixed live performance with tape and vocal segments. It was a testimony to the prowess of trumpeter Manfred Schoof, tenor saxophonist Jan Garbarek, guitarist Terje Rypdal, bassist Red Mitchell, and drummer John Christensen that they weren't overwhelmed by the sheer weight of the experience. The digital mastering enables listeners to fully hear the disparate styles converging, and understand just how advanced Russell's concepts were, particularly for the time. While not everything worked, the composition ranks alongside Ornette Coleman's "Free Jazz" as one of jazz's finest, most adventurous pieces. *—Ron Wynn*

Pee Wee Russell (Charles Ellsworth Russell)

b. Mar. 27, 1906, St. Louis, MO, **d.** Feb. 15, 1969, Alexandria, VA
Clarinet / Dixieland
Pee Wee Russell, although never a virtuoso, was one of the giants of jazz. A highly expressive and unpredictable clarinetist, Russell was usually grouped in Dixieland-type groups throughout his career but his advanced and spontaneous solos (which often sounded as if he were thinking aloud) defied classification. A professional by the time he was 15, by 1925 he was in St. Louis jamming with Bix Beiderbecke. Russell moved to New York in 1927 and gained some attention for his playing with Red Nichols' Five Pennies. He played clarinet and tenor with Louis Prima during 1935-37, appearing on many records and enjoying the association. He then started working with Eddie Condon's freewheeling groups and would remain in Condon's orbit on and off for the next 30 years. Pee Wee's recordings with Condon in 1938 made him a star in the trad Chicago jazz world. Heavy drinking almost killed him in 1950 but Russell made an unlikely comeback and became more assertive in running his career. He started leading his own groups (which were more swing- than Dixieland-oriented), and by the early '60s was playing in a pianoless quartet with valve trombonist Marshall Brown. *—Scott Yanow*

☆ **Big Eight: Jack Teagarden / Pee Wee Russell** / Aug. 31, 1938-Dec. 15, 1940 / Riverside/OJC ♦♦♦♦♦
This classic set reissues a couple of important sessions that were made for the H.R.S. label and later acquired by Riverside. The great trombonist Jack Teagarden is heard in 1940 with an octet dominated by Duke Ellington sidemen (including cornetist Rex Stewart, clarinetist Barney Bigard, and tenor saxophonist Ben Webster). Recorded during a period when Teagarden was struggling with his big band, it was a rare treat for him to stretch out with a combo and the results (which include a superior version of "St. James Infirmary") are memorable. In addition, clarinetist Pee Wee Russell is heard with an all-star octet of his own that co-stars trumpeter Max Kaminsky, trombonist Dicky Wells, and pianist James P. Johnson in 1938; the final two numbers feature the unique trio of Russell, Johnson, and drummer Zutty Singleton. The musicians seem quite inspired and both trad and swing fans are advised to get this excellent reissue. *—Scott Yanow*

The Pied Piper of Jazz / Sep. 30, 1944 / Commodore ♦♦♦♦♦
Now here's some cooking music. I'd recommend this record just for the seven trio tracks; the added quartet tracks are a good bonus, but clearly of a more common cloth, though Pee Wee Russell was never really common—as in average. Surprisingly, to me, these sessions were rather overlooked by annotations of Russell's music, but then again Zutty Singleton (drums) and Joe Sullivan (piano) are often overlooked in favor of derivative or lesser talent. Sullivan was a great two-fisted pianist, and Singleton, along with Baby Dodds, a great stylist and father of traditional jazz whose influence could probably be traced right up to Ed Blackwell through Gene Krupa and Art Blakey. And it was absolutely fitting that he be the drummer on this trio date, because with Singleton at the drums you really never need a bass. On this record one gets to hear some prime playing from the clarinetist, but pay attention to the rhythm, particularly Sullivan and Singleton. *—Bob Rusch, Cadence*

Jazz Reunion / Feb. 23, 1961-Mar. 8, 1961 / Candid ♦♦♦♦♦
The reunion that took place in this 1961 session was between Russell and tenor-great Coleman Hawkins; they had first recorded one of the songs, ("If I Could Be with You") back in 1929. Both Hawk and Russell had remained modern soloists and on this unusual but very satisfying date (which also features trumpeter Emmett Berry and trombonist Bob Brookmeyer) they explore such numers as a pair of Ellington classics ("All Too Soon" and "What Am I Here For—"), two Russell originals, and even the boppish "Tin Tin Deo." *—Scott Yanow*

★ **Swingin' with Pee Wee** / Mar. 29, 1960 / Swingville ♦♦♦♦♦
During the last dozen years of his life before passing away in 1969, clarinetist Pee Wee Russell recorded and performed in a variety of surprisingly modern settings. It was not that Russell was not modern himself, for his eccentric style had long been quite distinctive, but he had previously been content to mostly play in freewheeling Dixieland bands. His encounters with valve trombonist Marshall Brown (who provided him with an advanced repertoire and arrangements) and a 1963 *Newport Jazz Festival* appearance with Thelonious Monk found Russell stretching himself. The two albums that are reissued in full on this 1999 CD are not quite as adventurous, being essentially small-group swing, which was still a bit ahead of Eddie Condon's bands. Russell and trumpeter Buck Clayton make for a perfectly compatible team on the 1960 date, a relaxed and swinging quintet session with pianist Tommy Flanagan, bassist Wendell Marshall and drummer Osie Johnson. The other set has basic arrangements from pianist Nat Pierce, quiet support from bassist Tommy Potter and drummer Karl Kiffe, and Russell joined by three of his favorite horn players (trumpeter Ruby Braff, trombonist Vic Dickenson and tenor saxophonist Bud Freeman). One can fully understand why the clarinetist was quite pleased with both of these albums. His playing is much more consistent and comfortable on the midtempo material than usual and he mostly gets to avoid the overly hyper Dixieland warhorses. A gem. *—Scott Yanow*

☆ **Ask Me Now!** / 1965 / Impulse! ♦♦♦♦♦
After a lifetime spent playing unusual and unpredictable clarinet solos in Dixieland settings, Russell late in life broke out of the stereotype and played in more modern settings. This Impulse LP (begging to be reissued on CD) has his clarinet placed in a pianoless quartet with valve-trombonist Marshall Brown, playing tunes by John Coltrane, Thelonious Monk, and Ornette Coleman, along with some classic ballads. It is a remarkable and very lyrical date that briefly rejuvenated the career of this veteran individualist. *—Scott Yanow*

Terje Rypdal

b. Aug. 23, 1947, Oslo, Norway
Guitar / Avant-Garde Jazz, Post-Bop, Fusion
Terje Rypdal has long had an unusual style, mixing together elements more commonly found in new age and rock than in jazz; yet he is also an adventurous improviser. Associated with the ECM label since the early '70s, Rypdal's playing is definitely an acquired taste, using space and dense sounds in an unusual manner. Classically trained as a pianist, Rypdal was largely self-taught on guitar and originally most influenced by Jimi Hendrix. He attended Oslo University, where he was taught the Lydian chromatic concept of tonal organization by its author, George Russell. Rypdal played with Russell for a time and started an association with Jan Garbarek in the late '60s. He formed the group Odyssey in 1972 and has led various small groups during the past two decades. An important guitarist and composer in Norway, Terje Rypdal has gained a cult following in the United States. He has recorded steadily for ECM since 1972 (using such sidemen at times as Garbarek, pianist Bobo Stenson, trumpeter Palle Mikkelborg, bassist Miroslav Vitous, drummer Jack DeJohnette and cellist David Darling). His two earlier sessions (for the Karusell label in 1968 and a notable 1969 Baden-Baden concert put out by MPS) are more difficult to find. *—Scott Yanow*

● **Works** / 1974-1981 / ECM ♦♦♦♦♦
An excellent sampler of Rypdal's music, it includes two cuts from his superb (but currently unavailable) early-'70s albums. *—Michael P. Dawson*

Odyssey / Aug. 1975 / ECM ♦♦♦♦♦
A magnificant effort that combines crushingly powerful rock/jazz ("Over Bierkerot" is a killer) with long, brooding electric ruminations, it was originally a double album; one track has been left off the CD. *—Michael P. Dawson*

Rypdal, Vitous, DeJohnette / Jun. 1978 / ECM ♦♦♦♦♦
An otherworldly soundscape of aching beauty, this album is a must-have for aficionados of any member of this trio. Rypdal's guitar is hauntingly reverbed and distant throughout, though occasionally on "Seasons" he becomes too fond of caterwauling guitar synth. But this is truly an effort of trio fusion, with ineffable pieces like "Den Forste Sne" ("The First Snow") appearing and melting away without any tangible solos or structure. From the opening cymbal strikes of "Sunrise," this album is marked by DeJohnette's best drumming on record; his cymbal sound, pushed to the front and recorded with mikes both above and below the cymbal's bell—"because that's how the drummer hears it"—is nothing short of revelatory. Vitous'

bass steadies Rypdal's flights of fancy, while his subtle electric piano lines float above. These elements combine most powerfully in "Believer," which builds from atmospheric shimmers of electric piano into a whorl of bass and plaintive guitar set against the dry rasp of resonating cymbals. *—Paul Collins*

Blue / Nov. 1986 / ECM ♦♦♦♦♦
Terje Rypdal's all too short-lived rock band the Chasers played like a jazz trio—a jazz trio that always pushed the barrier to achieve the visceral punch of rock. They could be funky as hell (note the dirtyass slow groove on "Kompet Gär"), terrifyingly experimental ("Og Hva Synes Vi Om Det"), cinematically bold ("Om Bare"), or wonderfully meditative and tender ("Blue"). That they could do all these things on recording and still seek the sound barrier as a band was an achievement equaled by few. One of the primary attributes of *Blue* is its sequencing; the entire recording seems to unfold endlessly and seamlessly. Nothing is rushed, and all parts and players contribute economically. The band establishes a textural point of view to improvise from in every selection, and doesn't seem to be hindered by the guitar-bass-drums limitation. Each track appears to reveal itself as a sound world, full of possibility and limitless space, giving the band a chance to offer itself to these compositions rather than just play them. Again, as evidenced by *Blue*, it's a shame this band didn't hang together longer in order to explore the full potential of its range of possibilities and sonic palettes. *—Thom Jurek*

Q.E.D. / Aug. 1991-Jan. 199 / ECM ♦♦♦
Q.E.D. (or opus 54, for Rypdal archivists) is a composition in five movements for electric guitar, string ensemble, and woodwinds, and in it Rypdal often alternates sections of great dissonance with near silence, or lonely sustained notes by just one or two instruments. It can have the sweeping starkness of a tracking shot over a fjord, but there's a certain coldness to it as well, and even confirmed fans of his jazz work may take a while to warm up to it. The second movement, with its needling backwards guitar over the string ensemble, is at times reminiscent of *Red*-era Frippertronics; the most dramatic and broodingly gorgeous playing arises in the fourth movement, though, with Rypdal's aching solos over ominous near-subsonic rumbling. *—Paul Collins*

Joe Sample

b. Feb. 1, 1939, Houston, TX
Keyboards, Piano / Crossover Jazz, Hard Bop, Fusion, Soul-Jazz
One of the many jazzmen who started out playing hard bop but went electric during the Fusion Era, Joe Sample was, in the late 1950s, a founding member of the Jazz Crusaders along with trombonist Wayne Henderson, tenor saxman Wilton Felder and drummer Stix Hooper. The Crusaders' debt to Art Blakey's Jazz Messengers was hard to miss—except that the L.A.-based unit had no trumpeter, and became known for its unique tenor/trombone front line. Sample, a hard-swinging player who could handle chordal and modal/scalar improvistion equally well, stuck to the acoustic piano during the Crusaders' early years—but would place greater emphasis on electric keyboards when the band turned to jazz/funk in the early 70s and dropped "Jazz" from its name. Though he'd recorded as a trio pianist on 1969's obscure *Fancy Dance*, 1978's *Rainbow Seeker* was often described as his first album as a leader. In contrast to the gritty music the Crusaders became known for, Sample's own albums on MCA and later, Warner Bros., have generally favored a very lyrical and introspective jazz/pop approach. *—Alex Henderson*

Fancy Dance / Apr. 20, 1969 / Gazell ♦♦♦♦
This recording (a reissue of a project for Sonet) was pianist Joe Sample's first solo set, although he was already well-known for his nine high-profile years with the Jazz Crusaders. Teamed with bassist Red Mitchell and drummer J.C. Moses, Sample plays mostly adventurous straight-ahead jazz on his date. There are some funky moments (particularly on the two blues), but all six of his originals have their challenging moments and Sample is heard stretching himself way beyond the predictable. *—Scott Yanow*

● **Carmel** / 1978 / Blue Thumb ♦♦♦♦♦
Pianist Joe Sample was a pioneer at creating melodic and accessible pop jazz. His recordings of the 1970s and '80s were consistently popular, especially this best-seller. Sample is joined on most selections by fellow Crusader Stix Hooper on drums, electric bassist Abraham Laboriel, percussionist Paulinho Da Costa and often guitarist Dean Parks; flutist Hubert Laws guests on "Midnight and Mist." Although it would not be considered creative jazz, the catchy and often-memorable melodies, and Sample's fine playing makes this CD reissue a pretty definitive example of his solo recordings. *—Scott Yanow*

Invitation / 1993 / Warner Brothers ♦♦♦♦
A luscious outing from piano great Joe Sample, this disc includes beautiful interpretations of ten standards and near-standards. Featuring plush orchestral arrangements by Dale Oehler wrapped over and around Sample's piano trio, *Invitation* is simply one of the loveliest recordings of Sample's career. With a rhythm section made up of bassist Cecil McBee and drummer Victor Lewis, augmented by Lenny Castro on percussion, the music is of a piece from start to finish. Producer Tommy Lipuma has found a wonderful setting for Sample to show his gorgeous, acoustic piano stylings, and the orchestra feels like part of the trio instead of an add-on. When Sample uses synths, they are indistinguishable from the orchestra. Overall, a smooth, romantic, highly recommended recording. *—Jim Newsom*

Did You Feel That— / 1994 / Warner Brothers ♦♦♦♦♦
There is some serious shaking going on in the studio here, and it appears the veteran Sample has found a great situation to let out his more aggressive edges. What must it be like to be a legend and try to somehow uncover a path you haven't driven on before— How can a cat like Sample top himself— It's always rewarding when a veteran artist twists expectations with a brand new sound, even if reaching into his past for the germ of the idea. Sample darts at the listener with a whole new, nonstop brass funk approach, allowing his all-star Soul Committee to lay down the grooves beneath his still plucky ivory spirit. Though *Did You Feel That?* cooks from start to finish, employing inventive rhythmic touches, simmering cool, and a flashy retro production style, it's sometimes too easy to compare the wild horn tandem of Oscar Brashear and Joel Peskin with old Sample cohorts Wilton Felder and Wayne Henderson. Sort of a Crusaders for the modern age. What shines through, however, is Sample's successful execution as a leader of a true ensemble, rather than just a slew of sessionaires. He takes some tasty solos, but makes sure that members of the Committee are allowed their own voices as they chime in with the Chairman of the Board. And just for the record, the other Committee members include drummer Steve Gadd, bassist Freddie Washington, guitarists Michael Landau and Arthur Adams, plus percussionist Lenny Castro. An added treat is the funky historical artwork, an Aaron Douglas painting called "Aspects of Negro Life" from "Slavery Through Reconstruction." It shows the joy of the culture, perfectly mirroring the excitement found on the album. *—Jonathan Widran*

The Song Lives On / Apr. 20, 1999 / GRP ♦♦♦♦
The daughter of the popular late R&B singer Donny, husky voiced Lalah Hathaway is the perfect foil for Joe Sample's compelling notion that *The Song Lives On*. Finding a happy medium between the graceful straight-ahead jazz trio vibe of his *Invitation* album and the plucky pop energy of *Spellbound*, Sample provides Hathaway on seven of the 11 tunes with a showcase for her sultry approach.

His and Bill Shnee's production approach is generally sparse, not much more than piano and bass, enhanced on occasion by Fender Rhodes and the occasional smoky input of Kirk Whalum. Sample doesn't seem to mind playing second fiddle most of the time, his trademark mix of dark chords and dancing, optimistic improvisations forming harmony lines behind her; often, though, his itchiness to step higher into the mix comes clear and he breaks into extended upbeat improvisations. On a cover of his Crusaders hit "Street Life," Hathaway turns the title into a mantra and Sample echoes her sentiments with sharp, percussive reiterations of the song's main melody. Then Hathaway stops and Michael Thompson steps in with some edgy electric guitar lines. Other song choices range from reverent takes on standards like "Fever" and "For All We Know" to vocal versions of older, well-known Sample instrumental hits; for example, with Norman Gimbel's cheery lyrics, Hathaway turns the once moody "All God's Children" into a life-affirming love song. The point seeming to be, in finding new life for both his old material and the classics, Sample is bringing a form of immortality to favorite songs. *—Jonathan Widran*

David Sanborn (David William Sanborn)

b. Jul. 30, 1945, Tampa, FL
Sax (Alto) / Smooth Jazz, Crossover Jazz, Jazz-Pop, Soul-Jazz
David Sanborn has been the most influential saxophonist on pop, R&B and crossover players of the past 20 years. Most of his recordings have been in the dance music/R&B vein although Sanborn is a capable jazz player. His greatest contributions to music have been his passionate sound (with its crying and squealing high notes) and his emotional interpretations of melodies which generally uplift any record he is on. Unlike his countless number of imitators, Sanborn is immediately recognizable within two notes. Sanborn began recording as a leader in the mid-'70s and he racked up a string of pop successes. Over the years he has worked with many pop players but he has made his biggest impact leading his own danceable bands. For a couple years in the early '90s, Sanborn was the host of the syndicated television series *Night Music* which had a very eclectic lineup of musicians (from Sonny Rollins and Sun Ra to James Taylor and heavy metal players), most of whom were given the unique opportunity to play together. It displayed David Sanborn's wide interest and musical curiosity even if many of his own recordings remain quite predictable. *—Scott Yanow*

Taking Off / 1975 / Warner Brothers ♦♦♦
Altoist David Sanborn has long been one of the leaders of what could be called rhythm & jazz (R&B-oriented jazz). His debut for Warner Brothers was a major commercial success and helped make him into a major name. The music is fairly commercial but certainly danceable and melodic. Even at that point in time, Sanborn's alto cries were immediately recognizable; the Brecker Brothers, guitarist Steve Khan and Howard Johnson on baritone and tuba are prominent in support. *—Scott Yanow*

The Best of David Sanborn / 1975-1987 / Warner Brothers ♦♦♦♦♦
During the 13 years he spent recording for Warner Bros., David Sanborn had more than his share of artistic triumphs, but at times wasted his considerable talents on radio-friendly schlock. Containing more pluses than minuses, *The Best of David Sanborn* paints an honest picture of his jazz/R&B/pop work for that label. Sanborn's distinctive alto is a joy on both rugged, gritty jazz/R&B like "Slam" and "Anything You Want" and such lyrical and heartfelt ballads as "Rain on Christmas," "A Tear for Crystal" and "Lisa." Meanwhile, a mindless, note-for-note cover of Gladys Knight & the Pips' "Neither One of Us" exemplifies Sanborn at his radio-friendly worst. But despite the inclusion of a few stinkers, this 16-song CD isn't a bad introduction to his Warner Bros. output. *—Alex Henderson*

Sanborn / Feb. 1976 / Warner Brothers ♦♦♦
This album is one of David Sanborn's better early recordings. Although the record is perhaps best known for the altoist's version of Paul Simon's "I Do It For Your Love," Sanborn's playing on some of the other cuts (most notably "Mamacita" and "7th Avenue") finds him really stretching within the R&B/crossover genre. Only "Smile" (which has some mundane vocalizing) is a minus, and it is more than compensated for by Sanborn's passionate improvising elsewhere. *—Scott Yanow*

Heart to Heart / Jan. 1978 / Warner Brothers ♦♦♦♦
By the time of his third album, altoist David Sanborn's popularity and influence was growing month by month. Most of these numbers feature Sanborn with an enlarged rhythm section (with such studio vets as guitarists Hugh McCracken and David Spinozza, Don Grolnick or Richard Tee on keyboards, vibraphonist Mike Mainieri, bassist Herb Bushler and drummer Steve Gadd). However, "Short Visit" is something special, for Sanborn was joined by what was mostly the Gil Evans Orchestra; Evans even wrote the chart. Otherwise, this is a

typical Sanborn release with plenty of danceable rhythms and the focus on his passionate alto. *—Scott Yanow*

Hideaway / 1979 / Warner Brothers ♦♦♦♦

● **Voyeur** / 1980 / Warner Brothers ♦♦♦♦♦
This 1980 recording is an excellent example of David Sanborn's music. The highly influential altoist is joined by familiar studio veterans (including guitarist Hiram Bullock and drummer Steve Gadd) with bassist/composer Marcus Miller being a key figure in creating the funky rhythms and colorful backgrounds. Miller, who shared the writing chores with Sanborn, not only contributed his powerful bass but backed the altoist during a duet version of "Just For You" on piano. Easily recommended to fans of R&B-ish jazz. *—Scott Yanow*

Straight to the Heart / 1984 / Warner Brothers ♦♦♦♦
With bassist Marcus Miller acting as producer and some memorable tunes being performed (most notably "Hideaway" and "Straight To the Heart"), this is one of altoist David Sanborn's better R&B-ish recordings. Joined by keyboardist Don Grolnick, guitarist Hiram Bullock, bassist Miller, drummer Buddy Williams and various guest musicians, Sanborn sounds fairly inspired and is in top form. *—Scott Yanow*

A Change of Heart / 1987 / Warner Brothers ♦♦♦
This is a fairly typical 1980s outing by the popular R&B-ish altoist David Sanborn. The main difference from the past is that the music often uses synthesizers and electronic rhythms to a greater degree than previously, but Sanborn's distinctive crying sound was still very much intact. The music is produced by Marcus Miller ("Chicago Song" and "Imogene"), Michael Colina, Ronnie Foster or Philippe Saisse; each of the producers plays keyboards and is responsible for the backgrounds behind the leader. Funky and danceable but no real surprises occur. *—Scott Yanow*

Another Hand / 1991 / Elektra ♦♦♦♦♦
When David Sanborn debuted on Elektra with *Another Hand* after a 13-year stay at Warner Bros., the altoist swore off formulaic, radio-oriented muzak and vowed to make artistic considerations his main priority. There's nothing shallow or contrived about the album, an exploratory, heartfelt effort generally defined by his introspective, soulsearching improvisations. Sanborn tends to be reflective rather than extroverted—an exception being the soul-jazz gem "Hobbies." Instead of avoiding complexity as some of his more commercial recordings did, *Another Hand* often thrives on it. The album's main flaw lies in the fact that too often, the sidemen tend to serve as a backdrop for Sanborn instead of being active soloists. But given the depth and overall excellence of Sanborn's playing, one tends to overlook that shortcoming. *—Alex Henderson*

Upfront / 1992 / Elektra ♦♦♦♦
Directly following his adventurous *Another Hand*, some listeners were disappointed with the fact that David Sanborn did not permanently switch from R&B/crossover to creative jazz. However, this CD is generally quite appealing and takes some chances within its genre. Although bassist Marcus Miller is once again an important collaborator, the emphasis is on "real" instruments, most notably the organ of Ricky Peterson; other musicians in the backup groups include John Purcell on various reeds, trumpeter Randy Brecker, drummer Steve Jordan and guest Eric Clapton, who takes a guitar solo on "Full House." The most unusual selection is the final cut, a version of Ornette Coleman's "Ramblin'" that finds Sanborn, Miller, Peterson and Jordan joined by the avant-garde trumpeter Herb Robertson. Overall, this is an above-average effort from the highly influential altoist. *—Scott Yanow*

Pearls / Mar. 28, 1995 / Elektra ♦♦♦♦♦
David Sanborn is joined on this CD by an orchestra arranged by Johnny Mandel for a set of music dominated by melodic versions of standards. Sanborn does not get all that far away from the themes (which include "Try a Little Tenderness," "Smoke Gets in Your Eyes," "For All We Know," "This Masquerade" and a very emotional "Everything Must Change" in addition to a few newer songs) but his sound is so soulful and full of passion that he does not really need to improvise much to make his point. It's a fine change of pace for the highly influential altoist. *—Scott Yanow*

Songs from the Night Before / 1996 / Elektra ♦♦♦
David Sanborn's distinctive alto is all over this set, caressing the melodies and playing short soulful solos in typical fashion. Joined by an electronic quartet that features prominent work by Ricky Peterson on keyboards (including bass and drum programming). plus a horn section, Sanborn gives humanity and honest feeling to what could have been an anonymous effort. In addition to the many originals, the influential altoist plays tasteful versions of Wayne Shorter's "Infant Eyes" and Eddie Harris' catchy "Listen Here." *—Scott Yanow*

Inside / Mar. 23, 1999 / Elektra ♦♦♦
As a rule, David Sanborn's Elektra output of the '90s had integrity. Whether he was being exploratory and introspective on *Another Hand* or taking a more commercial, R&B-minded approach on *Inside*, Sanborn avoided recording outright schlock during that decade. Make no mistake: *Inside* is far from straight-ahead acoustic jazz. Produced by Marcus Miller and boasting such guest vocalists as Sting, Cassandra Wilson and Lelah Hathaway, *Inside* is definitely a commercial album. But commercial isn't necessarily a bad thing, and most of the material is tasteful. Whether he's getting into instrumental funk-jazz grooves on "Brother Ray," "Corners" and "Trance" or featuring Wilson on a likable remake of Aretha Franklin's "Daydreaming," this CD is certainly not without its pleasures. The high point of the album, however, is Sting's haunting cameo on a cover of Bill Withers' "Ain't No Sunshine." Some of Sanborn's solos could have been longer, but all things considered, *Inside* is pleasing, if less than essential. *—Alex Henderson*

Pharoah Sanders (Farrell Sanders)

b. Oct. 13, 1940, Little Rock, AR
Multi Instruments, Sax (Tenor) / Avant-Garde Jazz, Free Jazz, Hard Bop, Post-Bop
Pharoah Sanders has had a rather unique career. He came to fame when he made the John Coltrane Quartet a Quintet, taking ferocious, emotional and atonal solos that started where Coltrane's left off. After Coltrane's death, for a period Sanders came close to making the avant-garde popular as his alternately intense and peaceful solos proved to be a perfect team with singer Leon Thomas. Unfortunately most of Sanders' output since the late '70s has been quite derivative of Coltrane's hard bop-oriented music circa 1959, years before he joined 'Trane. Sanders' decision in the early '80s to explore standards melodically pleased the bebop purists but resulted in many of his followers being disappointed by the absence of his own musical personality. Since that time Sanders (now a legend) has largely continued in that direction although occasionally (such as on drummer Franklin Kiermyer's very intense Evidence CD) the real Pharoah Sanders shows up and reminds the jazz world of his significance. *—Scott Yanow*

Pharoah's First / Sep. 10, 1964 / Calibre ♦♦♦♦♦
Pharoah Sanders's debut as a leader has been reissued on this ESP CD. Sanders, who is joined by trumpeter Stan Foster, pianist Jane Getz, bassist William Bennett and drummer Marvin Pattillo, sounds remarkably like John Coltrane on "Seven by Seven"; he had not found his own musical personality yet. "Bethera" is a bit more distinctive and overall this historic set should greatly interest fans of both Coltrane and Sanders. *—Scott Yanow*

Tauhid / Nov. 15, 1966 / Impulse! ♦♦♦
Tauhid marks the 1966 Impulse debut of tenor saxophonist Pharoah Sanders, who had already gained fame as a flame-throwing saxophonist of the "new thing" playing with John Coltrane. However, Sanders' tenor appearance doesn't saturate the atmosphere on this session; far from it. Sanders is content to patiently let the moods of these three pieces develop, whether it be through the percussion of Roger Blank and Nat Bettis, guitarist Sonny Sharrock, or his own piccolo. For those looking for Sanders' patented screeching tenor throughout, *Tauhid* will disappoint. *—Al Campbell*

Izipho Zam / Jan. 14, 1969 / Strata East ♦♦♦♦
Wild, crazy, and frenzied. Sanders and Sonny Sharrock (g) explore. *—Ron Wynn*

★ **Karma** / Feb. 14, 1969-Oct. 20, 1969 / Impulse! ♦♦♦♦♦
Many think this particular Sanders record is self-indulgent and rambling, and it's hard to argue with either point. That's not such a bad thing, however; in the case of the 33-minute "The Creator Has a Master Plan" it would seem to be a good thing, as Sanders and his group wander effortlessly from free playing to structured playing and back again, accommodating Leon Thomas' peace-and-love lyrics as well as a spirited scatting performance that incorporates Middle Eastern, Indian, and African vocal techniques. There are times when things blow into bursts of frantic noise, but the distinctly sectional nature of the piece means that the noise always forms back into something more peaceful and pulsing. Sanders is present throughout, squealing and snarling, cajoling, cagily floating back into the mix at times, then charging ahead like a rogue elephant. The second cut, the languid "Colors," might have benefited from a lengthier exploration; at a touch over five and a half minutes, the long, slow passages seem to be just starting development when the number ends. The reissue on GRP/Impulse! is a 20-bit remaster, and certainly benefits from the process with a nice soundstage and a firm, full sound; the percussion benefits greatly from this, surrounding the listener. Alas, the reissues continue to arrive in Eco-Paks, a format that's far harder to protect than old LP sleeves. *—Steven McDonald*

Jewels of Thought / Oct. 20, 1969 / Impulse! ♦♦♦♦
The follow-up to Pharoah Sanders's surprisingly popular *Karma*, this album consists of the 15-minute "Hum-Allah-Hum-Allah-Hum Allah" (featuring singer Leon Thomas) and the two-part 28Ω minute "Sun in Aquarius." In addition to Sanders (who is in intense form) and Thomas, the group includes pianist Lonnie Liston Smith, bassists Richard Davis and Cecil McBee and drummers Idris Muhammad and Roy Haynes. *—Scott Yanow*

Deaf Dumb Blind (Summun Bukmun Umyun) / Jul. 1, 1970 / Impulse! ♦♦♦♦
The supporting cast is particularly strong on this Pharoah Sanders recording (trumpeter Woody Shaw, altoist Gary Bartz, pianist Lonnie Liston Smith, bassist Cecil McBee, drummer Clifford Jarvis and two percussionists) but unfortunately Pharoah Sanders does not play any of his passionate tenor. Instead he sticks to soprano, which keeps this album from being essential. However the sidelong versions of "Summun, Bukmun, Umyun" and "Let Us Go into the House of the Lord" certainly have plenty of atmosphere and passion. *—Scott Yanow*

Thembi / Nov. 25, 1970-Jan. 12, 1971 / Impulse! ♦♦♦♦
The music on this Impulse recording is taken from two different sessions. Pharoah Sanders (on tenor, soprano, alto flute and percussion) is teamed with violinist Michael White on the first date while the second has drummer Roy Haynes and four African percussionists; in addition keyboardist Lonnie Liston Smith and bassist Cecil McBee are on both sets. Although the performances are fairly concise (only two numbers are over seven minutes), Sanders has plenty of typically fiery spots and certainly gets his message of musical freedom across. *—Scott Yanow*

Black Unity / Nov. 24, 1971 / Impulse! ♦♦♦
This CD consists only of the 37 1/2-minute "Black Unity." The piece starts out logically for its first ten minutes, building from a drone and a simple rhythmic melody up to an intense Pharoah Sanders tenor solo. But its final 20 or so minutes ramble on endlessly, with a lot of aimless and purposeless playing from the oversized rhythm section (which includes pianist Joe Bonner, both Cecil McBee and Stanley Clarke on basses and the two drummers Norman Connors and Billy Hart). Very little happens of any real substance, making the CD reissue a disappointment. *—Scott Yanow*

Elevation / Sep. 7, 1973-Sep. 13, 1973 / Impulse! ♦♦♦♦♦
Elevation, much like his previous Impulse! LP *Black Unity*, finds Sanders and his group less mindful of clear solos than creating sonic wallpaper in front of which occasional members peak out. The occasional presence of a male vocal chorus threatens to turn the entire effort into new age music, but, as on his breakout *Karma*, Sanders' whole is better than the sum of its parts. *—John Bush*

Journey to the One / Dec. 1979 / Evidence ✦✦✦✦✦
Formerly a Theresa double LP, this single CD contains all ten of Pharoah Sanders's performances from the sessions. As usual, Sanders shifts between spiritual peace and violent outbursts in his tenor solos. The backup group changes from track to track but often includes pianist John Hicks, bassist Ray Drummond and drummer Idris Muhammad. Sanders really recalls his former boss John Coltrane on "After the Rain" (taken as a duet with pianist Joe Bonner) and a romantic "Easy to Remember"; other highpoints include "You've Got to Have Freedom" (which has Bobby McFerrin as one of the background singers) and the exotic "Kazuko" on which Sanders is accompanied by kato, harmonium and wind chimes. *—Scott Yanow*

Rejoice / 1981 / Evidence ✦✦✦✦✦

Moonchild / Oct. 12, 1989-Oct. 13, 1989 / Timeless ✦✦✦✦

Welcome to Love / Jul. 17, 1990-Jul. 19, 1990 / Timeless ✦✦✦✦✦

Crescent with Love / Oct. 19, 1992-Oct. 20, 1992 / Evidence ✦✦✦✦

Save Our Children / Feb. 2, 1999 / Verve ✦✦

Spirits / 1998 / Meta ✦✦✦

Arturo Sandoval

b. Nov. 6, 1949, Artemisa, Cuba
Timbales, Flugelhorn, Trumpet / Cuban Jazz, Afro-Cuban Jazz, Latin Jazz
A blazing, technically flawless trumpeter from Cuba, Arturo Sandoval has been dazzling audiences all over the world with his supercharged tone and bop-flavored flurries way up in the trumpet's highest register. In slower numbers, he sports a golden, mellow tone on the flugelhorn, marked with a sure, subtle sense of swing. Apparently he is capable of playing anything, proving it more than once by tackling classical repertoire as well as jazz in the same concert, and he has enough curiosity to search far beyond his Cubop base for repertory. Yet he often lets his desire to please the crowd with high-note displays get in the way of musical values, and he has yet to make a great record that can stand with those trumpet giants that have preceded him. *—Richard S. Ginell*

To a Finland Station / Sep. 9, 1982 / Pablo ✦✦✦✦✦
With Dizzy Gillespie (tpt) in Helsinki. Excellent interplay. Lots of good feeling on this session. *—Michael G. Nastos*

★ **Straight Ahead** / Aug. 1988 / Ronnie Scott's Jazz House ✦✦✦✦✦
With his remarkable range and phenomenal technique, Arturo Sandoval is one of the world's great trumpeters; he can do virtually anything he wants on his instrument. Some detractors have claimed that he has too much technique (is such a thing possible—) and that his recordings thus far for GRP are a bit erratic. The latter criticism cannot be applied to this 1988 release. Sandoval is heard with a standard quartet comprised of the great pianist Chucho Valdes (the leader of Irakere), bassist Ron Matthewson and drummer Martin Drew. Recorded in England before Sandoval broke ties with Cuba, Arturo is in nearmiraculous form on some blues, a lyrical "My Funny Valentine" and a few basic originals. Just listen to him tear through "Blue Monk," playing in the low register with the speed of an Al Hirt before jumping into the stratosphere like Maynard Ferguson. This CD serves as an excellent introduction for the bop lover to the very talented Arturo Sandoval. *—Scott Yanow*

Flight to Freedom / 1991 / GRP ✦✦✦✦
In July 1990 after playing trumpet in his native Cuba for 28 of his 41 years, Arturo Sandoval had the opportunity to defect from Cuba along with his family. A brilliant virtuoso, Sandoval finally was able to play whatever music he wanted without having to satisfy a dictator and his potential was enormous. On his American debut, Sandoval mostly performs boppish jazz (other than the dull "Marianela") with slight touches of rock and spiced with Latin percussion. The trumpeter shows restraint on the ballads (including a tasty "Body and Soul") and displays plenty of fire on the often-funky uptempo romps, not overdoing the effortless high notes. With the assistance of the high-powered tenor of Ed Calle, the versatile guitarist Rene Luis Toledo and a variety of talented sidemen (including guest Chick Corea on three songs), Arturo Sandoval's long overdue debut is well-rounded, exciting and highlighted by a fast rendition of Dizzy Gillespie's "Tanga." *—Scott Yanow*

I Remember Clifford / 1992 / GRP ✦✦✦✦✦
Due to the straight-ahead nature of the music on this CD, plus trumpeter Arturo Sandoval's self-restraint, the release has thus far been most jazz purists' favorite among the trumpeter's releases. Sandoval, who is joined by pianist Kenny Kirkland, bassist Charnett Moffett, drummer Kenny Washington and either Ernie Watts, David Sanchez or Ed Calle on tenor, pays tribute to the great Clifford Brown by performing ten selections previously recorded by Brown, plus his original "I Left This Space For You." The emphasis is on bebop (no Latin or Cuban rhythms on this date) with the highlights including "Daahoud," "Joy Spring," "Cherokee" and an emotional "I Remember Clifford." *—Scott Yanow*

Arturo Sandoval & The Latin Train / Jan. 6, 1995-Jan. 11, 1995 / GRP ✦✦✦✦✦

Swingin' / Jan. 6, 1996-Jan. 9, 1996 / GRP ✦✦✦✦✦
It seems remarkable that Arturo Sandoval never seems to win any jazz polls for few trumpeters can come close to equaling his technique, jazz chops and warm sound. On this advanced hard bop date, the music is strictly straightahead without any Latin rhythms. Sandoval matches wits quite successfully with clarinetist Eddie Daniels on two songs, tenor great Michael Brecker on three (including a memorable rendition of "Moment's Notice") and veteran flugelhornist Clark Terry on a joyous "Mack The Knife." In addition, Sandoval pays tribute to Woody Shaw, John Coltrane and Dizzy Gillespie. Other highlights include the moody "Streets Of Desire" (on which Sandoval plays piano), the racehorse tempo of "Real McBop" (which has an impossible but impeccably played melody chorus) and Arturo's humorous use of the plunger mute on "It Never Gets Old." All in all, this is one of Arturo Sandoval's finest recordings to date. *—Scott Yanow*

The Best of Arturo Sandoval / Jun. 3, 1997 / Milan ✦✦✦✦✦
The skimpy booklet to this compilation is of no help whatsoever—no personnel, no dates, no sources—and one can only presume from some of the vintage instruments and rhythms that these tracks were probably recorded in the early '80s before Sandoval's defection and subsequent GRP contract. But regardless, they do present the Cuban trumpeter at his most charismatic, with his golden tone and fearless technique reaching high into the stratosphere at the slightest provocation. The collection runs blithely through a gamut of idioms—electronic semi-reggae ("Reggae Mi Lugar"), sheer MOR lounge pap ("My Way"), show tunes (*West Side Story*'s "Maria"), Sandoval-penned pieces in an electric jazz-lite format, and even a nifty small-group blues eventually scuttled by Sandoval's overreaching. The most ambitious cut by far is a 15-minute live workout with an electric band on "A Night In Tunisia," in which Sandoval trumpets and showboats at supersonic speeds in an awesome display of ego and lip strength. Again, Sandoval comes off as an irresistible force of nature with eclectic tastes and questionable taste. *—Richard S. Ginell*

Mongo Santamaria (Ramon Santamaria)

b. Apr. 7, 1922, Havana, Cuba [Jesus Maria]
Conga, Percussion / Boogaloo, Cuban Jazz, Afro-Cuban Jazz, Latin Jazz, Salsa
A Mongo Santamaria concert is a mesmerizing spectacle for both eyes and ears, and even in his 70s, this seemingly ageless Cuban percussionist/bandleader could energize packed behemoth arenas such as the Hollywood Bowl. A master conguero, Santamaria at his best creates an incantory spell rooted in Cuban religious rituals, quietly seating himself before his congas and soloing with total command over the rhythmic spaces between the beats while his band pumps out an endless vamp. He has been hugely influential as a leader, running durable bands that combine the traditional charanga with jazz-oriented brass, wind and piano solos. He also reached out into R&B, rock and electric jazz at times in his long career. No Cuban percussionist, with the possible exception of Santana's Armando Peraza (and let's not count Desi Arnaz!), has reached more listeners than him. Santamaria moved to New York in 1950, and spent six years performind and recording with Tito Puente and Cal Tjader. After his mass-market breakthrough, the 1963 Top Ten single "Watermelon Man," Santamaria's cross-pollenization of jazz, R&B and Latin music led to a high-profile contract with Columbia that resulted in a wave of hot, danceable albums between 1965 and 1970. He later returned to his Afro-Cuban base, recording for Vaya, Concord Picante and the Fantasy subsidiary Milestone. *—Richard S. Ginell*

★ **Mongo's Greatest Hits** / 1958-1963 / Fantasy ✦✦✦✦✦
This is a excellent single-disc sampler of what Mongo Santamaria was like before "Watermelon Man" catapulted him into the charts. Some of the Fantasy tracks sound like the musicians were just off the boat from Havana, and are a bit primitive in contrast to the brassy Santamaria of the mid- to late '60s, but they have overwhelming charm. The revered "Afro-Blue" can be heard in its original, spooky, stripped-down form, and it would be hard for anyone to resist the voodoo spell that the ten-plus minute "Mazacote" conveys. Besides Santamaria himself, included among the world-class percussionists on this record are Willie Bobo and Armando Peraza. The CD version adds four tracks, including "Watermelon Man" from the Battle/Riverside period and an alternate take of "Para Ti." *—Richard S. Ginell*

Sabroso / May 1959 / Fantasy/OJC ✦✦✦✦
1987 reissue of a wonderful album with Willie Bobo (per) and Pete Escovedo. *—Ron Wynn*

At the Black Hawk / 1962 / Fantasy ✦✦✦✦✦
Applying their famous two-fer philosophy to the digital era, Fantasy combines *Mighty Mongo* and *Viva Mongo!* on a single CD, showcasing two somewhat different slants on Mongo Santamaria's music during a period of exploration. *Mighty Mongo* leans more to Mongo's jazz side without sacrificing his Afro-Cuban rhythmic base, while *Viva Mongo* has a more distinctly ethnic Cuban sound with Rudy Calzado's solo vocals and the band's group chanting, Rolando Lozano's wooden flute riding playfully above the ensemble, and the traditional Cuban use of string counterlines. On *Mighty Mongo,* "Descarga at the Black Hawk" sets an especially tasty groove, with some timbales/congas/cymbals action on an extended vamp. Lozano shines in an extended flute solo on "Bacoso" before a scorcher of a percussion battle develops, while composer/pianist Joao Donato also doubles on trombone on "Sabor." *Viva Mongo*'s highlights include "Las Guajiras," a relaxed spellbinder at a guajira tempo; "Merengue Changa," a stupefying merger of two different rhythmic feelings; and the appropriately titled "Mambo Terrifico." Jose "Chombo" Silva, the Cuban Stan Getz worshipper who also evokes Coleman Hawkins on occasion, careens pleasingly on both albums. Of the two, *Viva Mongo* is perhaps the more vital record, but it's a close call; both are vibrant expressions of Mongo's art. *—Richard S. Ginell*

★ **Skins** / Jul. 9, 1962-1964 / Milestone ✦✦✦✦✦
This single CD has all of the contents of the two Mongo Santamaria Riverside albums originally titled *Mongo Explodes* and *Go, Mongo!* The music was last available as a two-LP set also titled *Skins.* The 1964 session, oddly programmed first, finds Santamaria on conga and bongos at the head of a ten-piece band also including trumpeter Marty Sheller, then-unknown flutist Hubert Laws (also featured on piccolo and tenor), Bobby Capers on alto and baritone, and a seven-piece rhythm section with five percussionists. Cornetist Nat Adderley guests on three of the ten numbers, which are all group originals, including four songs from Sheller. The early dates (Mongo's first as the leader of a fairly jazz-oriented Latin group) have Santamaria leading a completely different band, a nonet with just three percussionists. Most notable among the personnel are the young Chick Corea on piano and Pat Patrick, on leave from Sun Ra's band, as one of the two saxophonists. This time around, Mongo contributed four of the nine fairly obscure numbers. Although some of the songs on the 1964 date were put together in hopes of duplicating the commercial success of "Watermelon Man" (none succeeded), the music still sounds fairly fresh and lively. An excellent introduction to Mongo Santamaria's viable brand of Afro-Cuban jazz. *—Scott Yanow*

Watermelon Man / Dec. 17, 1962-Sep. 2, 1963 / Milestone ✦✦✦✦✦
Herbie Hancock's "Watermelon Man" was a gigantic hit for Mongo Santamaria in 1963, doing for him in the '60s what Perez Prado's big mambo hits did for him in the '50s. Naturally,

then, the follow-up LP to the single is devoted to twelve airplay-length tracks loaded with bright, swinging Latin cha-chas and mambo rhythms mixed with blues, soul and jazz, presumably suitable for twisting the night away. Rodgers Grant's piano supplies a good deal of the harmonic foundation of jazz, with the help of an occasional jazz solo from saxes Pat Patrick and Bobby Capers, while Marty Sheller's commanding party-time trumpet rides above the thundering congas of Mongo. In this setting, even the venerable "The Peanut Vendor" is brought right up to date. The 1998 CD reissue on Milestone adds six previously unissued tracks from a live San Francisco date in 1962. As all but one are between six and eight minutes, they allow the band to stretch out more than they did in the studio. In fact, the personnel is almost totally different than it is on the *Watermelon Man* album. Notable components of the live lineup are Willie Bobo is on timbales and Felix "Pupi" Legaretta on violin; only bassist Victor Venegas is on both the studio and live material. *—Richard S. Ginell*

Mongo at the Village Gate / Sep. 2, 1963 / Riverside/OJC ✦✦✦✦✦
This is a nonet with Pat Patrick, Bobby Capers, Marty Sheller and Chihuahua Martinez—a latin, jazz, and soul combo. MC'd by Symphony Sid, it is startlingly fresh for its era. It still sounds fresh. *—Michael G. Nastos*

Soy Yo / 1987 / Concord Jazz ✦✦✦✦

Soca Me Nice / May 1988 / Concord Jazz ✦✦✦✦

Live at Jazz Alley / Mar. 1990 / Concord Jazz ✦✦✦✦✦

Mongo Returns / Jun. 28, 1995-Jun. 29, 1995 / Milestone ✦✦✦✦

● **Skin on Skin: The Mongo Santamaria Anthology 1958-1995** / Oct. 1957-Jun. 29, 1995 / Rhino ✦✦✦✦✦
Licensing power makes Rhino's two-CD Mongo anthology a good choice for the newcomer, for it gathers together 34 tracks from 23 albums on seven labels, covering most of Mongo's long career. Even if you already have the Mongo collections issued by Fantasy, Columbia and Concord Picante, this one duplicates surprisingly little of the music on those albums. Indeed, many of the choices in all periods gravitate toward obscure album cuts, with just a handful of obvious Mongo classics like "Afro Blue," "Watermelon Man" and "Para Ti." The compilers seem to place their emphasis on how Mongo influenced the traditional Latin jazz performers of the '80s and '90s (his chief beneficiary, Poncho Sanchez, contributes a loving reminiscence in the booklet). While this philosophy serves the collection well from the early Fantasy through Riverside years, as well as the late Concord and Milestone stuff, it doesn't quite reveal how far-reaching Mongo's legacy really is. For example, they opt for atypically conservative Latin jazz material from the Columbia years and shortchange the charged-up boogaloos that give this period its zesty flavor; this is an example of '90s revisionism that doesn't tell it like it was. There is a lot of material from Mongo's brief, now-neglected Atlantic tenure (1969-72), especially the *Up from the Roots* album—after all, Rhino is the current custodian of that catalogue—and there is one decent unreleased selection from *Mongo '70*, "Panamanian Aire." Licensing restrictions beyond Rhino's control create a 15-year gap (1972-87), and it might have been nice to hear something from his obscure 1955 solo debut. But all things considered, no other collection does as well in summing up the career of this magnificent conguero/bandleader. *—Richard S. Ginell*

Afro-American Latin / Oct. 25, 1968-Mar. 5, 1969 / Columbia/Legacy ✦✦✦
Santamaria recorded an entire album in March 1969 that was inspired by the Afro-Cuban religion Santeria with encouragement from producer David Rubinson. It was done, however, in an era when Santamaria was being marketed by Columbia as a jazz-pop-soul crossover artist. The label rejected the album and it was shelved until 2000, when it finally appeared as a CD. While it's a solid record, and certainly closer to Santamaria's roots than much of his Columbia work was, one would be hard-pressed to say that its failure to appear when it was first made was a tragedy. Really, it's not too much different than the less soul-pop-oriented Latin jazz Santamaria has done throughout his career. Perhaps it's at times a little looser and bolder than Santamaria was wont to be, as with Sonny Fortune's squealing alto sax lines on "Mambo Leah" or the ten-minute "Obatala," a rave-up that moves from an opening conga/bata duet through several sections into a hyper-tempo charanga. But it's not all along these lines: "Sheila" is just a mellow jazz ballad (not that there's anything wrong with that) while "Me and You Baby" and "Boogaloo Wow" are more in line with the boogaloo that was raking in the sales for Mongo and Columbia. It's nice that Mongo fans have an opportunity to hear it after the passage of 30 years, but it's difficult to say that it would have made any difference to the trajectory of his career had it appeared as Santamaria and Rubinson intended, although the success of Santana right after its cancellation might have helped draw attention to it. One of the songs, the aforementioned "Me and You Baby," did appear on the 1970 album *All Strung Out;* otherwise, everything else was previously unreleased. In addition, there are five bonus live tracks recorded in 1968. *—Richie Unterberger*

Lalo Schifrin

b. Jun. 21, 1932, Buenos Aires, Argentina
Piano, Composer, Arranger / Spy Music, Original Score, Film Music, Soundtracks, Bop
Lalo Schifrin has spent much of his career outside of jazz but he has made his contributions to creative music. He studied at the Paris Conservatoire and was equally versed in classical and jazz in Argentina. In 1958, he moved to New York and gained fame for playing with Dizzy Gillespie's Quintet (1960-62); Dizzy recorded his lengthy works *Gillespiana* and *The New Continent.* After 1962, Schifrin mostly worked as a composer and arranger for films although his 1965 *Jazz Mass* received good notices and he recorded a quintet date for Palo Alto in 1982. In the early '90s his *Jazz Meets the Symphony* series featured tributes to many of his jazz idols, emphasizing lengthy medleys. Schifrin on an occasional basis returns to jazz to demonstrate how strong a pianist he remains. *—Scott Yanow*

Black Widow / Mar. 29, 1976-Mar. 30, 1976 / Columbia ✦✦✦✦
Soundtrack composer Lalo Schifrin began recording his first album for CTI in March 1976 (although he had worked with in-house producer Creed Taylor before, while both were at Verve). After some discussion between the two, *Black Widow* was diverted from being a funk album and instead attempted to cash in on the emerging disco phenomenon. While this may make jazz fans cringe (not to mention the eight violinists present), Schifrin's skill at arranging saves the day, as does the inclusion of a talented cast including trumpeter Jon Faddis, bassist Anthony Jackson and Pepper Adams on baritone sax. *Black Widow* also includes an interesting array of electronic effects which might deter jazz fans but intrigue musical adventurers. Although the sounds are contemporary, interesting takes on the theme from *Jaws,* Les Baxter's "Quiet Village" and "Moonglow & Theme from 'Picnic'" make the album an interesting listen. *—John Bush*

Jazz Meets the Symphony / Nov. 1992 / Atlantic ✦✦✦✦
On this third-stream effort, pianist/composer Lalo Schifrin, bassist Ray Brown and drummer Grady Tate swing while joined by the London Philharmonic. Most intriguing among Schifrin's arrangements are "Echoes of Duke Ellington" and "Dizzy Gillespie Fireworks," which are really medleys of Duke's and Dizzy's songs. Not all of the shorter pieces (particularly "Battle Hymn of the Republic" and "As Time Goes By") are too essential, and, on the whole, Schifrin's follow-up project (*More Jazz Meets the Symphony*) would result in a stronger record. However, this generally interesting set is still worth exploring; it was good to hear Lalo Schifrin in a jazz setting again. *—Scott Yanow*

Mission: Anthology / 1994 / One Way ✦✦✦✦✦
This One Way compilation reissues the complete contents of *Music from Mission: Impossible* and its follow-up, *More Mission: Impossible.* For fans of Lalo Schifrin's seminal score music for the television series, this is no less than a treasure. The set includes 22 tracks, beginning with the familiar theme but also featuring a host of influential titles such as "The Danube Incident," "Intrigue," "Jim on the Move," "Affair in Madrid," and "The Chelsea Memorandum." Not just a collection of familiar TV themes, *Mission: Anthology* is the best look at one of the foremost Hollywood composers of the era. *—John Bush*

● **Firebird: Jazz Meets the Symphony No. 3** / Jan. 1995 / Four Winds ✦✦✦✦✦
The third in Lalo Schifrin's series of grand fusions between the London Philharmonic and an all-star jazz combo is the most successful one yet. The immovable objects of symphony orchestra and jazz group are getting more closely in sync, thanks to the irresistible forces of Schifrin's long experience in both camps and his own luscious personal orchestral signatures. Ray Brown, Grady Tate, Jon Faddis (in particularly prime form), James Morrison and Paquito D'Rivera return from *Vol. 2,* as does the Schifrin method of juxtaposing tribute medleys to deceased giants with classical pastiches, standards and some of Schifrin's new pieces and greatest hits. Joe Zawinul's "Birdland," the leadoff track, has the most energy and fire from both quarters, while the inclusion of the most lucrative eight notes Lalo ever wrote, the theme from *Mission: Impossible,* was fortuitous timing (the hugely successful movie came out at about the same time). The idea of "Firebird" stems from an imaginary conversation between Charlie Parker and Stravinsky (not a new idea), but the concept doesn't quite come off, for they seem to be talking past each other in separate tongues. Much better is Schifrin's suave, swinging fusion of Gershwin's "An American in Paris" and Bud Powell's "Parisian Thoroughfare"; these two have plenty to say to each other. The whole thing is gorgeously and spaciously recorded; this should be a demonstration disc for hi-fi shows. *—Richard S. Ginell*

Gillespiana / Nov. 30, 1996 / Aleph ✦✦✦✦
For the first jazz release on his self-run Aleph label, Schifrin flew to Cologne, Germany to record this solid remake of *Gillespiana,* his 1960 five-movement concerto for Dizzy Gillespie with which Schifrin had been touring earlier in 1996. Designed to illustrate the sources that inspired Gillespie's music, the work remains one of the chameleonic Schifrin's best in a big-band idiom, particularly the dynamic Afro-Cuban-flavored blues "Toccata" that closes the concerto. The choice of Jon Faddis as Gillespie's stand-in was, of course, a no-brainer, for Faddis is the foremost Gillespie disciple on the scene, and his high-wire performance here captures both the stratospheric Gillespie of his youth and the mellower, slyer, muted Gillespie of later years. Fellow Jazz Meets The Symphony regular Paquito D'Rivera has some hot solo passages on alto; Alex Acuna and Marcio Doctor are given percussion showcases; Schifrin himself remains a persuasive jazz pianist, and Cologne's WDR Big Band almost matches the electricity that Schifrin's American bands generated on tour with this piece.

As an encore, Schifrin tacks on his pleasing bossa nova arrangement of Villa-Lobos' "Bachianas Brasileiras No. 5," with trumpeter Markus Stockhausen (son of composer Karlheinz Stockhausen) playing the tune nice and mellow. Currently, this album is being sold only through the Internet at www.schifrin.com. *—Richard S. Ginell*

Film Classics / Dec. 7, 1995-Dec. 8, 1995 / Aleph ✦✦✦✦
For the first release on his Aleph Records label, Lalo Schifrin conducts a concert of familiar movie themes. "Lalo Schifrin presents 100 Years of Cinema" is the subtitle, and it's not entirely accurate, since the earliest music here comes from 1939's *Gone With the Wind* and *The Wizard of Oz,* but after that it's an interesting mixture of genres ("Western Medley," "Classics Medley," "Movie Songs Medley") and well-known tunes like "As Time Goes By," "The Shadow of Your Smile," and "The Entertainer." Schifrin, who often sits in for some jazzy piano work, is joined by Dee Dee Bridgewater and Julia Migenes for occasional vocals. But the spotlight is mostly on the Philharmonic Orchestra of Marseilles, which sounds especially effective on orchestral showcases like "The Theme From James Bond," "Raiders of the Lost Ark March," and "Homage to Nino Rota." In some cases, when he's taking on fellow composers like John Williams or John Barry, Schifrin uses the standard orchestrations; otherwise, he supplies his own, often resulting in versions that are livelier and more rhythmic than the originals *— William Ruhlmann*

Metamorphosis: Jazz Meets the Symphony, #4 / May 1998 / Aleph ✦✦✦✦✦
Lalo Schifrin's fourth attempt to merge symphonic and jazz conceptions takes a turn into dangerous waters, venturing into 20th century classical techniques and some of jazz's most challenging composers. It was a gutsy move to confront the mantle of Gil Evans by rearranging "La Nevada," ayet Schifrin spoons on the added orchestral weight carefully, retaining and deepening Evans' mauve colors and dissonance—and it becomes a swinging delight. Moreover, Evans' sonorities become the dominant colors in the succeeding pieces "Sanctu-

ary," a suave, moody piece of work balancing both camps with assurance, and the "Tosca Variations," where the aria "E lucevan le stelle" is cleverly launched by Beethoven's *Moonlight Sonata.* Schifrin makes complex, appropriately quirky, even forbidding music out of a string of Thelonious Monk tunes in "Miraculous Monk" and continues the disturbing intensity on "Invisible City" before relaxing expansively in "Rhapsody For Bix"; the latter features a splashy, un-Bix-like soloist in trumpeter James Morrison. The cast of players changes considerably from previous albums; Morrison and Ray Brown remain in place, now joined by the London Symphony Orchestra, violinist/guitarist Markus Wienstroer, drummer Jeff Hamilton and conguero Francisco Aguabella—not to mention Schifrin himself on piano. Though one shouldn't use this disc as an entryway into the *Jazz Meets the Symphony* series, it is the boldest CD of the lot so far, unleashing the full resources of contemporary classical music and welding it firmly onto a jazz chassis. *—Richard S. Ginell*

The Eagle Has Landed / 1977 / Aleph ✦✦✦✦
Lalo Schifrin has done some of his best work as a film and television score composer with action/adventure stories and thrillers, so it's no surprise that his work on the war drama *The Eagle Has Landed* (which concerns a fictional plot to kidnap Winston Churchill) was one of his better efforts, full of tense, rhythmic music that complemented the suspense plot. Schifrin released some of the music on a 1978 soundtrack album on Entr'acte Records along with music from his score for *The Four Musketeers,* but now that he had his own record label, he was able to put a more complete version on disc. Apparently this is the score as originally recorded in 1977, most of which sat on the shelf for 22 years. Schifrin was right to resurrect it, since it shows off his strengths as a score composer. By itself, it makes for an anxious listening experience. *—William Ruhlmann*

Latin Jazz Suite / Jun. 1999 / Aleph ✦✦✦✦
Sprawling Latin jazz concert suites are nothing new; ask Chico O'Farrill, who pioneered that feat nearly a half-century before the chameleonic, prolific Lalo Schifrin got to it. But it isn't done very often and, when it is, the results usually are quite good. Each movement in Schifrin's project bears a title referring to some influential region—"Montuno" (Cuba), "Martinique" (Caribbean), "Pampas" (Argentina), "Fiesta" (Spain), "Ritual" (Africa), and "Manaos" (Brazil)—though they do not necessarily use the styles associated with those places. Clocking in at a staggering 65 minutes, the suite makes prudent use of all that space by turning over a lot of room to two star soloists, trumpeter Jon Faddis and saxophonist David Sanchez, not to mention the composer himself on piano. Faddis, a perennial guest on earlier Schifrin projects, is especially fiery and eloquent (perhaps Schifrin sees him as a reasonable facsimile of his late beloved sponsor, Dizzy Gillespie), and Sanchez can also be heard at his best on soprano and tenor. Much of this suite has a great deal of vitality—especially the last three movements, "Fiesta, " "Ritual," and "Manaos"—no doubt boosted by recording Cologne's participating WDR Big Band, the soloists, and a fine imported Latin percussion section (including Alex Acuna) in a live performance. Still, there are stretches where you wonder whether Schifrin, despite his enormous capacity for outside projects, has spent too much time scoring films; most of "Pampas," from the tune to the percussion effects, sounds just like something he would write for the latest celluloid thriller—and it seems a bit stale. Yet this has to be counted as a success overall, for the best passages ride quite high. *—Richard S. Ginell*

Irène Schweizer

b. Jun. 2, 1941, Schaffhausen, Switzerland
Piano / Improvisation, Avant-Garde Jazz, Early Creative, Modern Creative
Pianist Irène Schweizer performed and recorded with leading European improvisers and free jazz musicians since the 1960s, including female improvising groups starting in the late 1970s, is one of the initial organizers of *the Taktlos and Canaille music festivals,* and is a founding member of the Intakt label. Born in Schaffhausen, Switzerland in 1941, Schweizer grew up hearing dance bands in her father's restaurant. When she was about 12 years old, she started playing on the piano, and a couple of years later picked up the drums as well. At the age of 17, Schweizer's interest moved away from early jazz styles toward modern jazz, leading to her entry in a Zurich amateur festival in 1960. From 1961 to 1962, the aspiring pianist lived in England, working as an au pair, and taking piano lessons primarily with Eddie Thompson, who taught her stride, bebop and more. When Schweizer returned to Switzerland, she was playing soul jazz and hard bop, and started up a trio with drummer Mani Neumeier and Uli Trepte. Her playing was soon influenced by the South African players she heard at Zurich's *African Jazz Cafe.* Her exposure to Johnny Dyani, Dollar Brand and others also came around the same time Schweizer heard Ornette Coleman's *Free Jazz.* In addition to these influences, Schweizer was heavily affected by the recordings of Cecil Taylor. Her trio became known outside of Switzerland, and was invited to play *the Frankfurt Jazz Festival* in 1966. While there, Schweizer heard such German improvisers as saxophonist Peter Brotzmann and bassist Peter Kowald. The same year, she finally heard Cecil Taylor live, and as sometimes happens when musicians witness one they revere, she considered giving up the piano as a result. Lucky for music fans, Schweizer instead turned to developing her individual style and technique. During the late '60s, she was active in a trio with Kowald and Pierre Favre which Evan Parker eventually joined. This group disbanded a few years before her collaborations with Rüdiger Carl began in 1973 (Schweizer and Carl continued to work together off and on throughout their careers). Schweizer began giving solo performances starting in 1976, at *the Willisau Jazz Festival.* Schweizer also became involved in the Feminist Improvising Group, joining Maggie Nichols, Lindsay Cooper and more. The group changed its name in 1983 to one with less political connotations: the European Women's Improvising Group. Out of this large group arose an intermittent trio of Schwiezer, Nichols and Joëlle Léandre, called Les Diaboliques, formed in the early 1990s. Schweizer has recorded with amazing musicians from around the world including pianist Marilyn Crispell, and leading percussionists Han Bennink, Andrew Cyrille, Günter Sommer and more. *—Joslyn Layne*

● **Les Diaboliques** / 1993 / Intakt ✦✦✦✦
This is about as fine an example you are likely to find of these three "crazy" (meant affectionately) women pushing the limits. Recorded live at a European jazz festival, the trio of vocalist Maggie Nichols, bassist Joelle Leandre, and pianist Irene Schweizer never lets up, shooting fireworks of offbeat rhythms, screwball melodic lines, and distortions. Nichols often seems to take the lead, with her nonsense syllables, occasional warped commentary, Louis Armstrong scatting, and bent warbles bouncing off the walls. Leandre is in full force, too, as she stretches the strings with her patented technical bravado. In this company, Schweizer is the conservative one, her piano the glue that holds it all together, but her improvisational prowess is in full throttle, as shown particularly on her solo piece, "Rheingefallen." The three seem to be having fun, without sacrificing quality, and that, of course, gives the performance its special tenor. A coherent whole, there is a vivacious, wily spirit that never lets up, and never leaves the listener empty-handed. *Les Diaboliques,* indeed! *—Steven Loewy*

The Storming of the Winter Palace / May 18, 1985 / Intakt ✦✦✦
Recorded during a period when Schweizer was still immersed in her intense slash and burn style, she leads a quintet comprised of an all-star roster of free improvisers: vocalist Maggie Nicols, trombonist George Lewis, bassist Joelle Leandre, and percussionist Günter Sommer. The results are near perfect, with each musician given ample space to solo, and with tremendous, exciting interaction among the players. Three long pieces comprise the session, which was recorded at *the International-New-Jazz-Festival-Moers* to great fanfare. There are constantly expanding and contracting lines producing quick changes while the soloists jab and dart in and out. Schweizer is brilliant, one of the most underrated piano players of the late 20th century. Her command of the keyboard is complete and she uses it in its entirety with great taste and bravado. Maggie Nichols is another standout, as her mostly nonsense syllables complement the horns. George Lewis, too, is a wonder on trombone, his rapidly slinking blasts adding color and panache. In fact, there are no moments that lapse. Leandre and Sommer strike a solid chord throughout with remarkable contributions from each. *—Steven Loewy*

John Scofield

b. Dec. 26, 1951, Dayton, OH
Guitar / Contemporary Jazz, Post-Bop, Fusion
One of the "big three" of current jazz guitarists (along with Pat Metheny and Bill Frisell), Scofield's influence has been growing in recent years. Possessor of a very distinctive rock-oriented sound that is often a bit distorted, Scofield is a masterfu1 jazz improviser whose music generally falls somewhere between post bop, fusion and soul jazz. He started on guitar while at high school in Connecticut and from 1970-73 Scofield studied at Berklee and played in the Boston area. After recording with Gerry Mulligan and Chet Baker at Carnegie Hall, Scofield was a member of the Billy Cobham-George Duke band for two years. In 1977 he recorded with Charles Mingus and later joined the Gary Burton quartet and Dave Liebman's quintet. His own early sessions as a leader were funk-oriented. During 1982-85 Scofield toured the world and recorded with Miles Davis. Since that time he has led his own groups, played with Bass Desires and recorded frquently as a leader for Gramavision and Blue Note, using such major players as Charlie Haden, Jack DeJohnette, Joe Lovano and Eddie Harris. *—Scott Yanow*

Rough House / Nov. 27, 1978 / Enja ✦✦✦

Who's Who— / 1979-Aug. 1980 / One Way ✦✦✦

Electric Outlet / Apr. 1984-May 1984 / Gramavision ✦✦✦

Still Warm / Jun. 1986 / Gramavision ✦✦✦

Blue Matter / Sep. 1986 / Gramavision ✦✦✦✦
One of the top jazz guitarists from the mid-1980s on, John Scofield has always had a very recognizable sound and the ability to combine together R&B/funk with advanced jazz. He is the lead voice throughout most of this release, performing eight of his originals with a group also including keyboardist Mitchel Forman, electric bassist Gary Grainger, drummer Dennis Chambers, percussionist Don Alias and (on three of the numbers) Hiram Bullock on rhythm guitar. Although not for jazz purists, who should get his slightly later Blue Note releases instead, this set should interest guitar freaks. *—Scott Yanow*

Pick Hits Live / Oct. 7, 1987 / Gramavision ✦✦✦✦✦
One of guitarist John Scofield's best sessions for Gramavision, this live date features his regular band of the period, a quartet with keyboardist Robert Aries, electric bassist Gary Grainger and drummer Dennis Chambers, who had been playing together regularly for a year at that point. The close communication between the musicians on such numbers as "Pick Hits," "Protocol" and "Blue Matter" could only come from the players fully understanding each other's musical personalities. The music, electric but adventurous, funky but definitely exploratory jazz, is difficult to describe, but easier for Scofield's fans to enjoy. *—Scott Yanow*

Loud Jazz / Dec. 1987 / Gramavision ✦✦✦✦✦
There are "loud" moments on this studio set, but the title cut's name is more a humorous attempt to describe the John Scofield Quartet's music than an accurate depiction of their style. The leader/guitarist, who sounds typically distinctive, welcomes guest keyboardist George Duke to five of his nine originals. Scofield's regular group of the era consisted of keyboardist Robert Aries, electric bassist Gary Grainger and drummer Dennis Chambers and they are also joined here by percussionist Don Alias. The music (which includes such numbers as "Tell You What," "Dirty Rice," "Wabash" and "Spy Vs. Spy") has few memorable melodies but plenty of dynamic playing by Scofield, who at this point was growing as a major stylist from album to album. A strong effort. *—Scott Yanow*

Flat Out / Dec. 1988 / Gramavision ✦✦✦✦
Guitarist John Scofield's final in a long series of releases for Gramavision (he would soon sign with Blue Note) finds him looking ahead toward his future directions. His sidemen—organist Don Grolnick, acoustic bassist Anthony Cox and either Johnny Vidacovich or Terri Lyne Carrington—join him for standards including "Secret Love" and "All the Things You Are," some New Orleans R&B grooves (most notably on "Rockin' Pneumonia"), and a vari-

ety of Scofield's originals. The funk element heard on most of his earlier recordings is downgraded in favor of swinging in spots, and despite his trademark distorted tone, Scofield plays some solos that are almost boppish. *—Scott Yanow*

Time on My Hands / Nov. 19, 1989-Nov. 21, 1989 / Blue Note ✦✦✦✦
John Scofield's airy and instantly recognizable guitar is featured in a sparse quartet on this Blue Note CD. He performs 11 of his quirky compositions which, although occasionally hinting at Charles Mingus or Ornette Coleman, are true originals with new chord changes and sly unpredictable melodies. Bassist Charlie Haden and drummer Jack DeJohnette, both experts at utilizing space as part of the music, fit in perfectly with Scofield and display fire and swing in the appropriate spots. Joe Lovano's tenor also has its own sound and his stimulating solos consistently inspire Scofield. Recommended. *—Scott Yanow*

Grace Under Pressure / Dec. 1991 / Blue Note ✦✦✦✦
Two of the most distinctive guitarists of the 1990s team up on this quartet date with bassist Charlie Haden and drummer Joey Baron: John Scofield and Bill Frisell. While Scofield contributed all ten originals, Frisell with his wide variety of sounds and eccentric solos often comes close to stealing the show altogether. Five of the ten numbers add a three-piece brass section for color. None of the individual tunes would catch on, but the interplay between the two very different yet complementary guitarists is notable. *—Scott Yanow*

● **Hand Jive** / Oct. 1993-Nov. 1993 / Blue Note ✦✦✦✦✦
Guitarist John Scofield and tenor-saxophonist Eddie Harris make a very complementary team on this upbeat set of funky jazz for both have immediately identifiable sounds and adventurous spirits. Along with a fine rhythm section that includes Larry Goldings on piano and organ, Scofield and Harris interact joyfully on ten of the guitarist's originals. *—Scott Yanow*

Groove Elation / 1995 / Blue Note ✦✦✦✦✦
John Scofield has continued to grow and evolve year-by-year. This 1995 set is quite blues-oriented, sometimes boppish and fairly laidback, almost sounding like a Jimmy Smith or Groove Holmes date from the 1960s. Larry Goldings (who doubles occasionally on piano) is almost as significant in the ensembles as the leader/guitarist and has become the most important arrival on organ since Joey DeFrancesco and Barbara Dennerlein. Many of the tunes (all Scofield originals) use parade-like rhythms propelled by Idris Muhammad and Dennis Irwin (particularly the eccentric "Peculiar" and "Groove Elation") and the interplay between the two lead voices is quite appealing. Scofield is quite unselfish as far as taking solo space goes (he clearly enjoys the light funky grooves set by Goldings) and the results are quite appealing. *—Scott Yanow*

A Go Go / 1997 / Verve ✦✦✦✦✦
Out once again to stretch his considerable funk chops, Scofield returns joyously to the groove in tandem with a young, hard-swinging band out of time, Medeski, Martin and Wood. With their hip-hop grooves and retro keyboards—the funky old Wurlitzer electric piano, Hohner clavinet and organ—MMW's testament on the Gospel derived from James Brown comes on like a custom-tailored engine behind Scofield's jagged guitar. In his deceptively offhand way, Scofield locks right into the grooves, matching John Medeski's shafts of keyboards, Chris Wood's popping bass and Billy Martin's crazy rhythms with unpredictable accents and musical sidetrips. They really bear down on the home stretch of "Boozer"—the groove is at its most irresistible here—and they also change the pace a bit with a mood piece like "Kubrick." Scofield's tunes are often very catchy, occasionally reminding us that he has been listening to a lot of records by the Meters (dig "Jeep On 35"). This is one of the most viscerably enjoyable releases of 1998; in other words, this group gets down! *—Richard S. Ginell*

Bump / Mar. 14, 2000 / Verve ✦✦✦
John Scofield continued to use his Verve Records contract for unusual outings—like this one, his third release for the label, following the acoustic disc *Quiet* and *A Go Go* (which featured Medeski, Martin, and Wood). On *Bump,* he retained bassist Chris Wood and added Tony Scherr and Kenny Wollesen (the rhythm section from Sex Mob), keyboardist Mark De Gli Antoni from Soul Coughing, and drummer Eric Kalb and conga player Johnny Durkin from Deep Banana Blackout. Such sidemen allowed him to delve even more deeply into the second-line funk he had explored earlier in his career; indeed, "Three Sisters," the leadoff track, sounded like something Allen Toussaint might have produced for the Meters in the early '70s. The focus was always on the guitarist, and Scofield could remind you of Carlos Santana (on "Swinganova") or evoke Jeff Beck (on "Fez"). For the most part, however, he sounded like himself back in his days with Miles Davis, though by now, his playing was less busy and more fluid. *—William Ruhlmann*

Steady Groovin' / 1995 / Blue Note ✦✦✦✦

Works for Me / Jan. 30, 2001 / Verve ✦✦✦✦✦
Guitarist John Scofield takes the traditional jazz route on *Works for Me,* an excellent collection of 11 compositions that feature the all-star lineup of Christian McBride on acoustic bass, Kenny Garrett on alto saxophone, Brad Mehldau on acoustic piano, and the dynamic Billy Higgins on drums. This CD is unlike the alternative rock and funk jazz fusion on his previous efforts *A Go Go* and *Bump.* On this offering, John Scofield gives a great reassessment of straight-ahead post-bop jazz that is distinguished and stimulating. On "Big J," Scofield and saxophonist Kenny Garrett make a great team as they reach out with a call and response improvisation that engrosses the listener throughout its development. On "Loose Cannon," Garret means business as he launches into some great straight-ahead hard blowing. The ensemble changes the mood on "Love You a Long Time" with a soft approach to this resonant, melodic ballad. Drummer Billy Higgins is impossible to miss on "Freepie" and Christian McBride performs his stellar top to bottom command of acoustic bass techniques throughout this great program. Christian McBride plays a great solo on "Heel to Toe." From the hard swinging "Do I Crazy?" to the tranquil "Mrs. Scofield's Waltz," the versatility of John Scofield shows why he is one of the "Big 3" of current jazz guitarists. *—Paula Edelstein*

Raymond Scott (Harry Warnow)

b. Sep. 10, 1908, Brooklyn, NY, **d.** Feb. 8, 1994, North Hills, CA
Drums, Piano, Composer / Obscuro, Cartoon Music, Computer Music, Space Age Pop, Swing, Electronic, Novelty
Composer, bandleader and inventor Raymond Scott was among the unheralded pioneers of contemporary experimental music, a figure whose genius and influence have seeped almost subliminally into the mass cultural consciousness. As a visionary whose name is largely unknown but whose music is immediately recognizable, Scott's was a career stuffed with contradictions: though his early work anticipated the breathless invention of bebop, his obsession with perfectionism and memorization was the very antithesis of jazz's improvisational ethos; though his best-known compositions remain at large thanks to their endless recycling as soundtracks for cartoons, he never once wrote a note expressly for animated use; and though his later experiments with electronic music pioneered the ambient aesthetic, the ambient concept itself was not introduced until a decade after the release of his original recordings. *—Jason Ankeny*

Powerhouse, Vol. 1 / Mar. 11, 1935-Nov. 11, 1939 / Stash ✦✦✦✦✦
Between 1937-39 composer-pianist Raymond Scott and his six-piece "Quintette" recorded 24 originals that were most notable for their hilarious titles, somewhat bizarre but somehow logical arrangements and tight ensembles. To Scott's surprise, the group caught on for awhile and such numbers as "Powerhouse" and "The Toy Trumpet" became hits. This CD gathers together tapes from Scott's own library of radio broadcasts and rehearsals, all of it previously unissued and two of the performances predating the formation of the Quintette. Certainly occupying their own unique niche, the colorful arrangements somehow fit the titles (which include "Dinner Music for a Pack of Hungry Cannibals," "New Year's Eve in a Haunted House," "Oil Gusher," "Reckless Night on Board an Ocean Liner" and "Bumpy Weather Over Newark!") and one can understand why Carl Stalling was inspired to utilize many of these pieces in Warner Bros. cartoons. *—Scott Yanow*

● **The Music of Raymond Scott: Reckless Nights & Turkish Twilights** / Feb. 20, 1937-Jun. 17, 1940 / Columbia/Legacy ✦✦✦✦✦
The name may not be immediately familiar, but the music itself certainly is; to anyone weaned on the legendary Warner Bros. cartoons of the 1940s and 1950s, Raymond Scott's deliriously inventive freak jazz is the soundtrack of childhood, with each and every note capable of conjuring up indelible images of such immortal characters as Bugs Bunny, Porky Pig, and Daffy Duck. The WB connection is both Scott's greatest legacy and his greatest curse, however; he never composed a note specifically for cartoons, and his most memorable and distinctive melodies were actually co-opted for animated use by Warner's brilliant music director, Carl Stalling. *Reckless Nights and Turkish Twilights,* then, restores Scott's work to its original, stand-alone setting, confirming his cult reputation as one of the most innovative and original musical thinkers of his era. Even free of cartoon mayhem, his music is remarkably visual and colorful, perfectly evocative of such surreal titles as "Dinner Music for a Pack of Hungry Cannibals" and "War Dance for Wooden Indians"; probably the best-known cut here is the opening "Powerhouse," a uniquely mechanized piece used in any number of cartoons and television commercials and a perfect summation of Scott's intricate arrangments, complex shifting rhythms, and formal lunacy. Recommended for listeners ages eight to 80. *—Jason Ankeny*

Shirley Scott

b. Mar. 14, 1934, Philadelphia, PA
Organ (Hammond), Organ / Hard Bop, Soul-Jazz
An admirer of the seminal Jimmy Smith, Shirley Scott has been one of the organ's most appealing representatives since the late 1950s. Scott, a very melodic and accessible player, started out on piano and played trumpet in high school before taking up the Hammond B-3 and enjoying national recognition in the late '50s with her superb Prestige dates with tenor sax great Eddie "Lockjaw" Davis. Especially popular was their 1958 hit "In the Kitchen." Her reputation was cemented during the '60s on several superb, soulful organ/soul jazz dates where she demonstrated an aggressive, highly rhythmic attack blending intricate bebop harmonies with bluesy melodies and a gospel influence, punctuating everything with great use of the bass pedals. Scott married soul-jazz tenor man Stanley Turrentine, with whom she often recorded in the '60s. The Scott/Turrentine union lasted until the early '70s, and their musical collaborations in the '60s were among the finest in the field. Scott wasn't as visible the following decade, when the popularity of organ combos decreased and labels were more interested in fusion and pop-jazz (though she did record some albums for Chess/Cadet and Strata East). But organists regained their popularity in the late '80s, which found her recording for Muse. Though known primarily for her organ playing, Scott is also a superb pianist—in the 1990s, she has played piano exclusively on some trio recordings for Candid, and embraced the instrument consistently in Philly jazz venues. *—Alex Henderson and Ron Wynn*

Workin' / May 27, 1958-Mar. 24, 1960 / Prestige ✦✦✦
One of several trio and/or combo works that organist Shirley Scott recorded for Prestige in the late '50s and early '60s. Her swirling, driving lines, intense bass pedal support, and bluesy fervor were ideal for the soul jazz format, and this is a typical example. *—Ron Wynn*

Soul Sister / Jun. 23, 1960 / Prestige ✦✦✦
The one thing that makes this 1960 session stand out from much of Scott's other work is the prominence of Lem Winchester's vibes as the chief counterpoint to her organ. While this quartet date also has George Duvivier on bass and Arthur Edgehill on drums, there is no saxophone or guitar. It swings along nicely for the most part, though "Get Me to the Church on Time" (from *My Fair Lady*) was perhaps not the most inspired choice of cover material. There's only one Scott original on the program: the ten-minute "Blues for Tyrone" is, by a comfortable margin, the most smoldering, funky groove she dives into on the album. The record would have benefited from more outings of the sort, but the interpretation of Sonny Rollins' "Sonnymoon for Two" is solid. Prestige's 1999 CD reissue of *Soul Sister* has added

the entirety of her 1964 LP *Travelin' Light* onto the same disc, with the addition of the title cut recorded at the same session as *Soul Sister* from her album *Now's the Time.* —*Richie Unterberger*

Blue Seven / Aug. 22, 1961 / Prestige/OJC ✦✦✦
A quintet with Roy Brooks (d), Oliver Nelson (ts) and Joe Newman (tpt) plays one Scott original, the title song by Sonny Rollins, and an excellent "Wagon Wheels." —*Michael G. Nastos*

Shirley Scott Plays Horace Silver / Nov. 17, 1961 / Prestige ✦✦✦✦✦
Just what it says. The queen of the Hammond organ (along with Henry Grimes (b) and Otis Finch (d)) plays compositions by the funk-master himself, Horace Silver. Included are "Senor Blues" and "The Preacher." —*Michael Erlewine*

Sweet Soul / Dec. 5, 1962 / Prestige ✦✦✦✦✦
Reissued from the "Happy Talk" session this features Earl May on bass and Roy Brooks on drums. It includes a nice "Jitterbug Waltz." All are standards. —*Michael G. Nastos*

Soul Is Willing / Jan. 10, 1963 / Prestige ✦✦✦✦✦
This is a good album that shows the husband and wife team of Shirley Scott and Stanley Turrentine in their usual, excellent form—a fine example of organ combo soul jazz. Now part of the Prestige two-fer called *Soul Shoutin'.* —*Michael Erlewine*

★ **Soul Shoutin'** / Jan. 10, 1963-Oct. 15, 1963 / Prestige ✦✦✦✦✦
Organist Shirley Scott and her then-husband tenor great Stanley Turrentine always made potent music together. This CD, which combines together the former Prestige LPs *The Soul Is Willing* and *Soul Shoutin',* finds "Mr. T." at his early peak, playing some intense yet always soulful solos on such pieces as Sy Oliver's "Yes Indeed," "Secret Love" and his memorable originals "The Soul Is Willing" and "Deep Down Soul." Scott, who found her own niche within the dominant Jimmy Smith style, swings hard throughout the set and (together with drummer Crassella Oliphant and either Major Holley or Earl May on bass) the lead voices play with such consistent enthusiasm that one would think these were club performances. Highly recommended. —*Scott Yanow*

For Members Only/Great Scott! / Aug. 22, 1963-May 20, 1964 / MCA ✦✦✦✦✦
During the 1960's, Shirley Scott's Impulse albums were often split between big band selections (with orchestras arranged by Oliver Nelson) and trio features. This CD reissue from 1989 includes all of the contents from two of Scott's better Impulse albums, *Great Scott* and *For Members Only.* In general the eight trio numbers are the most rewarding performances on the disc since the material is fairly superior while the big band tracks emphasize then-current show and movie tunes. Overall this generous CD gives one a good overview of Shirley Scott's playing talents. —*Scott Yanow*

The Great Live Sessions / Sep. 23, 1964 / ABC/Impulse! ✦✦✦✦✦
Recorded live at the Front Room in Newark, NJ, the album includes ten tracks with a quartet including Stanley Turrentine (ts). On a rare night for music, the band delivered on all counts. You can't go wrong here. —*Michael G. Nastos*

Queen of the Organ / Sep. 23, 1964 / Impulse! ✦✦✦✦✦
This CD reissue brings back all of the music previously put out on the two-LP set *The Great Live Sessions* with the exception of one number ("Shirley's Shuffle") left out due to lack of space; with over 70 minutes of music, one cannot complain too much about the omission. Overall, this is a pretty definitive live set featuring organist Shirley Scott, tenor saxophonist Stanley Turrentine, bassist Bob Cranshaw and drummer Otis "Candy" Finch, one of the great soul-jazz combos of the 1960s. In addition to a swinging "Just In Time" and Duke Ellington's "Squeeze Me, But Please Don't Tease Me," the set mostly features obscurities and originals, plus a surprisingly effective version of the Beatles' "Can't Buy Me Love." The musicians sound quite heated and consistently inspired. Highly recommended. —*Scott Yanow*

Roll 'em / Apr. 15, 1966-Apr. 19, 1966 / Impulse! ✦✦✦
Organist Shirley Scott focuses on swing-era tunes throughout this enjoyable CD reissue. Four songs showcase her organ accompanied by a 17-piece big band arranged by Oliver Nelson while the remaining six numbers find her jamming with a trio that also includes either George Duvivier or Richard Davis on bass and Grady Tate or Ed Shaughnessy on drums. Although nothing all that unexpected occurs, it is fun to hear an organ performing such numbers as "For Dancers Only," "Little Brown Jug" and "Stompin' At The Savoy." —*Scott Yanow*

Shirley Scott and the Soul Saxes / Sep. 10, 1968-Jul. 10, 1969 / Atlantic ✦✦✦
Steamy workout with Scott, Hank Crawford (as), King Curtis (ts), and David Newman (ts). —*Ron Wynn*

Oasis / Aug. 28, 1989 / Muse ✦✦✦✦✦
In an ideal world, Shirley Scott would have made as many trips to the studio in the 1970s and 1980s as she did in the 1960s. But regrettably, she did very little recording in the 1970s and 1980s. After 1974's *One for Me* on Strata East, the Philadelphia organist/pianist stayed away from the recording scene for 15 years before making an impressive return to the studio with 1989's *Oasis.* Produced by tenor titan Houston Person, this solid hard-bop/soul-jazz effort finds a 55-year-old Scott leading a combo that employs Charles Davis on tenor sax, Virgil Jones on trumpet, Arthur Harper on bass, and Mickey Roker on drums. While Davis is the main pianist, Person is featured on Scott's relaxed 12-bar number "Blues Everywhere." Scott is in fine form throughout the album, playing with plenty of warmth and feeling on original material as well as soulful interpretations of "Alone Together," J.J. Johnson's "Lament," and "Nature Boy" (which has been performed as a ballad by Nat "King" Cole and others but gets a surprisingly uptempo treatment from Scott). In 1989, it was nice to know that Scott was recording again—and thankfully, she wouldn't neglect the studio in the 1990s. —*Alex Henderson*

Legends of Acid Jazz / Jun. 2, 1961-Nov. 17, 1961 / Prestige ✦✦✦✦
A smart combination of two 1961 albums, *Hip Soul* and *Hip Twist,* both of which featured Stanley Turrentine on sax. *Hip Soul* is the smokier and livelier of the pair, especially on "Stanley's Time" and the Turrentine-composed title track; the material is delivered with a taut intelligence. *Hip Twist* doesn't suffer much in comparison, though, and gives Scott a bit more presence, as she introduces several themes with impassioned swirls; unlike *Hip Soul,* it has a couple of tunes from her own pen. —*Richie Unterberger*

Doc Severinsen

b. Jul. 7, 1927, Arlington, OR
Trumpet / Swing, Instrumental Pop, Big Band
Though faithful watchers of *The Tonight Show with Johnny Carson* and most of the '70s and beyond generation identify Doc Severinsen as a garish dresser and pseudo-hip bandleader with minimial ability, Severinsen has a substantial bebop heritage. He's also a much better trumpeter than he usually showed during his television years, gifted with great range and excellent timbre and tone. He was a soloist in Tommy Dorsey's big band in the late '40s and early '50s, and had brief stints with Charlie Barnet and Benny Goodman. Severinsen joined NBC in 1949, and 13 years later was assistant leader of the orchestra, with Skitch Henderson running the band. Henderson left in 1967, and Severinsen took over. He lasted until 1992, when Carson retired and Jay Leno brought in a new band. He has many sessions available on CD, but you'd be better off getting Barnet and Dorsey reissues from the late '40s. His own albums have mininal jazz content at best. —*Ron Wynn*

● **Once More, With Feeling!** / 1991 / Amherst ✦✦✦✦
Of the Tonight Show Band's three Amherst CDs, this is the most highly recommended one. The repertoire is fresher than the songs featured on the two earlier releases and, in addition to the usual swing-era standards, such tunes as Tommy Newsom's "Three Shades Of Blue" and Stevie Wonder's "Isn't She Lovely" are included. Guest appearances by trumpeter Wynton Marsalis ("Avalon") and singer Tony Bennett ("I Can't Get Started") add some variety, the arrangements (mostly by the innovative Bill Holman and Tommy Newsom) are generally colorful, and the band (featuring such soloists as trumpeters Doc Severinsen, Snooky Young and Conte Candoli, tenor saxophonist Pete Christlieb and pianist Ross Tompkins) sounds in prime form. Recommended. —*Scott Yanow*

The Very Best of Doc Severinsen / Amherst ✦✦✦✦

Bud Shank (Clifford Everett Shank, Jr.)

b. May 27, 1926, Dayton, OH
Sax (Alto), Flute / West Coast Jazz, Hard Bop, Cool
Bud Shank began his career pigeonholed as a cool-schooler, but those who have listened to the altoist progress over the long haul know that he has become one of the hottest, most original players of the immediate post-Parker generation. Lumped in with the limpid-toned West Coast crowd in the '50s, Shank never ceased to evolve; in the '90s, he has more in common with Jackie McLean or Phil Woods than with Paul Desmond or Lee Konitz. Shank's keening, blithely melodic, and tonally expressive style is one of the more genuinely distinctive approaches to have grown out of the bebop idiom. Shank made a name for himself in the '50s as a central member of the West Coast jazz scene, and made a series of albums as a leader for World Pacific in the late '50s and early '60s. Shank ensconced himself in the L.A. studios during the '60s, emerging occasionally to record jazz and bossa nova albums with the likes of Chet Baker and Sergio Mendes. Shank's 1966 album with Baker, *Michelle,* was something of a popular success, reaching number 56 on the charts. Shank had been one of the earliest jazz flutists, but in the mid-'80s, he dropped the instrument in order to concentrate on alto full-time. —*Chris Kelsey*

The Pacific Jazz Bud Shank Studio Sessions / Jan. 25, 1956-Nov. 1961 / Mosaic ✦✦✦✦
When one thinks of altoist/flutist Bud Shank's recordings of the 1950s, it is normally of his work with Stan Kenton's orchestra or collaborations with Laurindo Almeida or Bob Cooper. However, Shank led a superior quartet from 1956-58 that also included pianist Claude Williamson, bassist Don Prell and either Chuck Flores or Jimmy Pratt on drums. This typically magnificent six-CD limited-edition box set from Mosaic has the quartet's four albums (including a set that was recorded in Johannesburg, South Africa), a selection by Shank with a sextet that includes vibraphonist Larry Bunker, and three slightly later sets. The latter feature either Billy Bean or Dennis Budimir on guitar, bassist Gary Peacock and Chuck Flores, Mel Lewis or Shelly Manne on drums; one set adds trumpeter Carmell Jones, and the other has both Jones and tenor saxophonist Bob Cooper. All of this music was fairly obscure but has dated quite well. In addition to alto and occasional flute, Shank took one of the quartet sets exclusively on tenor, which he has rarely played since; the two Carmell Jones dates find Shank doubling on alto and baritone. The music is consistently straight-ahead, featuring cool tones but hard swinging. Bud Shank and West Coast jazz fans are advised to order this 1998 set before it goes out of print. —*Scott Yanow*

Crystal Comments / Oct. 1979 / Concord Jazz ✦✦✦✦
Although Bud Shank has since given up the flute, his playing on the instrument was at its peak in the late 1970s. On this unusual trio set, he sticks to flute while joined by both pianist Bill Mays and Alan Broadbent on electric piano; the keyboardists switch instruments on "How Are Things In Glocca Morra." Despite the odd instrumentation, the music is essentially advanced hard bop, with the talented players exploring six standards including "Scrapple From The Apple," "Body And Soul" and "On Green Dolphin Street." An offbeat success that is a good companion to the classical-oriented Shank-Mays duets of *Explorations: 1980* recorded at the same sessions. —*Scott Yanow*

● **This Bud's for You** / Nov. 14, 1984 / 32 Jazz ✦✦✦✦✦
Originally known as a cool-toned altoist and occasional flutist, Bud Shank's playing from this recording forward surprised many listeners. There was a forcefulness and a passion to his alto solos (he had given up the flute) that had not been heard that much from him previously. Assisted by pianist Kenny Barron, bassist Ron Carter and drummer Al Foster, Shank rips into five bop standards, his own "Cotton Blossom" and Walter Norris' "Space Maker" with plenty of intensity, stretching himself and inspiring his sidemen. Highly recommended. —*Scott Yanow*

California Concert / May 19, 1985 / Contemporary/OJC ♦♦♦♦
Altoist Bud Shank and flugelhornist Shorty Rogers worked together on a fairly regular basis after Rogers returned to active playing in 1982. While Shank had advanced as an improviser (developing a wider range of expression and playing with more intensity than previously), Rogers' cool-toned style was largely unchanged. With pianist George Cables, bassist Monty Budwig and drummer Sherman Ferguson completing the quintet, Shank and Shorty perform three of Rogers' originals plus inventive reworkings of four swing and bop standards arranged by the flugelhornist. A fine outing. *—Scott Yanow*

Plays the Music of Bill Evans / Mar. 13, 1996-Mar. 14, 1996 / Fresh Sound ♦♦♦♦♦
Although they had parallel careers, altoist Bud Shank and pianist Bill Evans only met once—in 1980, when they played a concert opposite each other. Shank and Evans were supposed to record a duet album of the pianist's compositions for Pacific Jazz in the early '60s, but even though Shank was sent the tunes they were to perform, the project never materialized. In recent times, the discovery of the music resulted in this memorable CD. Joined by what he calls his favorite rhythm section (pianist Mike Wofford, bassist Bob Magnusson, and drummer Joe La Barbera), Shank performs eight of Evans' originals, plus Wofford's "Bill's Vane" and his own "Evanescent." The altoist has grown as a soloist through the decades, and the harmonically sophisticated and often complex music inspires him to consistently satisfying improvisations. Although Bill Evans was never that famous as a composer (other than his hit "Waltz for Debby," which is included here), his tricky and unpredictable originals are well worth exploring. Among the highlights of the set are "Peri's Scope," "Funkallero," "My Bells," and "No Cover, No Minimum." This easily recommended concept album works quite well, putting the focus on Bud Shank's continued excellence as a soloist and on the underrated compositional talents of Bill Evans. *—Scott Yanow*

Bud Shank and Bill Perkins / May 2, 1955-Dec. 11, 1958 / Blue Note ♦♦♦♦
Two of the stars of cool jazz (both of whom had long careers), Bud Shank and Bill Perkins, are featured to various degrees throughout this 1998 CD reissue. Shank, who during the 1980's and 90's stuck exclusively to his increasingly passionate alto, in the 1950's was practically the epitome of West Coast jazz. His cool tones on alto and his fluid flute were utilized on many dates; the main set on this CD also finds him switching in spots to tenor and baritone. Perkins, always a versatile reed soloist, is best-known for his tenor playing but during that date he also plays alto and (on two versions of "Fluted Columns) there are some rare examples of his flute. Shank and Perkins team up quite effectively with pianist Hampton Hawes, bassist Red Mitchell and drummer Mel Lewis for the May 2, 1955 session which includes a trio feature for Hawes ("I Hear Music"). Four numbers from Feb. 19, 1956 (with Shank on flute and alto, pianist Russ Freeman, bassist Carson Smith, drummer Shelly Manne and, on "Brother, Can You Spare A Dime," Perkins on tenor) are actually from a session led by Freeman but never completed and were only put out previously on samplers. "Angel Eyes" (by a quartet with Perkins and pianist Jimmy Rowles) is a leftover track from a later date as is "Sonny Speaks" which showcases Rowles in a trio without Perkins. This CD concludes with the one surviving number ("Ain't Got A Dime To My Name") surviving from a truncated Perkins quartet set from 1958. Taken as a whole, there are many rewarding solos to be heard by Shank, Perkins and the piano players on these formerly rare selections even if the CD falls short of being classic. *—Scott Yanow*

A Flower Is a Lovesome Thing / Sep. 15, 1998 / Koch ♦♦♦♦
Although Bud Shank and Bob Cooper played together many times through the years, they are heard on this CD on five separate selections apiece and never do meet up. In both cases, they are accompanied by the large Netherlands Metropole Orchestra. The recording dates have unfortunately been left off, but the music probably dates from the late 1980s. Shank is not only heard on alto, but switches to flute on two of the five numbers (he eventually gave up that instrument altogether). Shank sounds fine during his half (particularly during an inventive "Like Someone In Love" and the pretty "Never Never Land"), but Cooper generally steals the show. His rendition of "Speak Low" tops Shank's, and he is showcased throughout the second part of the CD in prime form. It was such a major loss when Bob Cooper (underrated through the years due to his decision to live in Los Angeles) passed away in 1997. He plays with plenty of exuberance during his features (check out his double-timing on "Stella By Starlight"), and his solos alone would make this CD highly recommended. *—Scott Yanow*

Sonny Sharrock (Warren Harding Sharrock)

b. Aug. 27, 1940, Ossining, NY, **d.** May 25, 1994, Ossining, NY
Guitar (Electric), Guitar / Avant-Garde Jazz, Free Jazz
Along with Derek Bailey (whose free-form explorations went in a different direction), Sonny Sharrock was the top avant-garde guitarist. His sonic explorations mixed together Jimi Hendrix with Pharoah Sanders and were often quite ferocious. From 1953-60 Sharrock was a singer in a doo wop group then in 1960 he started playing guitar. He studied composition at Berklee in 1961 (although he was thrown out of the guitar class!). Sharrock worked with Byard Lancaster (1966), was with Pharoah Sanders during 1967-68, participated (uncredited) on Miles Davis' *Jack Johnson* album and had his most high-profile job as a member of Herbie Mann's popular group where his adventurous guitar contrasted with Mann's flute and David Newman's soulful tenor. A long period of obscurity occurred after leaving Mann but by the 1980s Sharrock was being rediscovered, recording with Material in 1982 and Last Exit (a quartet with saxophonist Peter Brotzmann) later in the decade. 1991's *Ask the Ages* teamed Sharrock with Sanders, bassist Charnett Moffett and Elvin Jones. But just when he seemed on the brink of a potential commercial breakthrough, Sonny Sharrock died unexpectedly at the age of 53. *—Scott Yanow*

Black Woman / May 16, 1969 / Vortex ♦♦♦
Black Woman documents Sonny Sharrock's temporary departure from the confines of Herbie Mann's always invaluable patronage. Around the time of recording, Sharrock was struggling to express his own musical ideas within the rigid framework of the successful Mann bands. Black Woman marks an early opportunity for Sharrock's own voice to be heard; he composed all the songs except "Bailero" and personally chose the band to reflect his own interests. The music is full of Sharrock's skittering, trademark clusters of notes and remains at a consistently high-intensity level with Linda Sharrock, Milford Graves, and Teddy Daniel on board. At times the music reaches for the sublime as on "Peanut" with its mandolin-like, vibrato theme and otherworldly improvisations; can music evoke visions like Dante's Rings of Hell— The beauteous "Bialero" with piano and bass figures oscillating around Linda's lilting yet unpredictable voice and "Portrait of Linda in Three Colors, All Black" are Sonny Sharrock in glory. Linda Sharrock's vocals could be alarming to the uninitiated; she doesn't enunciate a single word throughout, except on the traditional "Bialero," instead using her instrument, her voice to express, like her husband does, the inexpressible: those emotions, passions, or exaltations that cannot be rationally shared, only referred to comparatively vaguely by the "knower." The results in this instance were later dubbed "energy music" by some well-intentioned critic. This album is not for everyone, even Sonny Sharrock fans may find the music beyond their wildest expectations. Black Woman has been successfully remastered and reissued only in Japan so far. *—Wilson McCloy*

Guitar / 1986 / Enemy ♦♦♦♦♦
This is pure, undiluted Sonny Sharrock. Taking advantage of the overdubbing process, Sharrock accompanies himself in a series of duets that demonstrate the range of his playing, from menacing to tender. The songs are fairly simple; a brief introduction and chord statement lays the foundation, then Sharrock flies about on top of it. The purity of his tone is both powerful and beautiful. "Broken Toys" is almost like a lullaby after the flying shrapnel of "Devils Doll Baby," where Sharrock shows off his dizzying, visceral slide guitar technique. "Black Bottom" is his take on the blues. "Princess Sonata" is a beautiful suite that encompasses all these aspects of his playing. *Guitar* makes a nice counterpoint to both *Seize the Rainbow*, a more rock-oriented release, and *Ask the Ages*, his reunion with Pharoah Sanders. Bill Laswell deserves some credit for revitalizing Sharrock's career in the '80s, and for sympathetic production on all three of these recordings. *Guitar* is a beautiful statement by one of jazz music's most unique voices. *—Sean Westergaard*

Seize the Rainbow / May 1987 / Enemy ♦♦♦
After some years off the scene, the avant-garde guitarist Sonny Sharrock started to record regularly again in the mid-1980s. This album from Enemy has him joined by bassist Melvin Gibbs and both Abe Speller and Pheeroan AkLaff on drums for seven intense originals in which Sharrock shows off the wide range of sounds he could create on his instrument. An interesting set, but definitely for specialized tastes. *—Scott Yanow*

Faith Moves / 1989-1990 / CMP ♦♦♦
One would think that, considering his power and often violent attack, the last thing Sonny Sharrock needs in a duet session is another guitarist. Actually this CD, which matches Sharrock with Nicky Skopelitis (who also plays the Greek baglama, a Turkish sax, the Carol sitar, an Iranian tar and an electric bass) is a set of passionate music that is more melodic than expected but still full of Sharrock's avant-rock explorations and explosions. *—Scott Yanow*

Highlife / Oct. 1990 / Enemy ♦♦♦
More rock, pop, and blues elements, but superbly crafted and employed. *—Ron Wynn*

★ **Ask the Ages** / 1991 / Axiom ♦♦♦♦♦
Sonny Sharrock was often thought of as the "Pharoah Sanders of the guitar," so it was quite fitting that one of his finest recordings is this matchup with Sanders, bassist Charnett Moffett and drummer Elvin Jones. This fiery outing was also very good for Sanders who, after many years of recording more lyrical material in the John Coltrane vein, returned to his prime early form with ferocious solos that match the intensity of Sharrock's. *—Scott Yanow*

Artie Shaw (Arthur Jacob Arshawsky)

b. May 23, 1910, New York, NY
Clarinet / Swing
One of jazz's finest clarinetists, Artie Shaw never seemed fully satisfied with his musical life, constantly breaking up successful bands and running away from success. While Count Basie and Duke Ellington were satisfied to lead just one orchestra during the swing era and Benny Goodman (due to illness) had two, Shaw led five, all of them distinctive and memorable. After moving to New York, Shaw became a close associate of Willie "the Lion" Smith at jam sessions and by 1931 was a busy studio musician. A major turning point occurred when he performed at an all-star big band concert at the Imperial Theatre in May 1936, surprising the audience by performing with a string quartet and a rhythm section. He used a similar concept in putting together his first orchestra, adding a dixieland-type frontline and a vocalist while retaining the strings. Shaw then put together a more conventional big band. The surprise success of his 1938 recording of "Begin the Beguine" made the clarinetist into a superstar and his orchestra into one of the most popular in the world. Shaw found the pressure of the band business difficult to deal with and in November 1939 he suddenly left the bandstand and moved to Mexico for two months. When Shaw returned his first session, one utilizing a large string section, resulted in another major hit "Frenesi"; it seemed that no matter what he did he could not escape from success. Shaw's third regular orchestra, which had a string section and such star soloists as trumpeter Billy Butterfield and pianist Johnny Guarnieri, was one of his finest, waxing perhaps the greatest version of "Stardust" along with the memorable "Concerto For Clarinet." Despite all this, Shaw broke up the orchestra in 1941, only to reform an even larger one later in the year. But, with the end of the swing era, Shaw again broke up his band in early-1946 and was semi-retired for several years, playing classical music as much as jazz. His last attempt at a big band was a short-lived one, a bop-pish unit that lasted for a few months in 1949; its modern music was a commercial flop. *—Scott Yanow*

● **Begin the Beguine** / Jul. 24, 1938-Jul. 23, 1941 / Bluebird/RCA ♦♦♦♦♦
Since Artie Shaw's Victor recordings have not been reissued in full on CD, this sampler serves as a fine place for swing beginners to start. Featured are many of the more popular recordings of his second and third orchestras including the title cut, "Frenesi," "Star Dust"

and "Summit Ridge Drive," giving one a good idea as to why Artie Shaw was so popular and still remains highly rated as a clarinetist today, decades after his retirement. *— Scott Yanow*

★ **Big Bands** / Jul. 24, 1938-Jan. 23, 1941 / Time-Life Music ♦♦♦♦♦
Time-Life Music's Artie Shaw entry in its *Big Bands* series is the best single-disc compilation of Shaw's most successful period as a bandleader, its selections licensed from RCA Victor. The 21-track album, four of whose tracks are Airchecks, contains most of his most important recordings, including "Begin the Beguine," "Frenesi," and "Star Dust." It is not, strictly speaking, a greatest-hits set, since it does not include such major hits as "They Say" and "Thanks for Ev'rything," but the selection manages an intelligent balance between Shaw's most popular performances and his most accomplished swing sides. The only real drawbacks to the album are its price (you can find cheaper, if less impressive, Shaw compilations in your local record store) and its availability (it's generally sold as part of the Time-Life mail order *Big Bands* series, though you can order it as a separate item by calling customer service at 1-800-621-7026). *— William Ruhlmann*

☆ **The Complete Gramercy Five Sessions** / Sep. 3, 1940-Aug. 2, 1945 / Bluebird/RCA ♦♦♦♦♦
Many swing big-band leaders featured small groups out of their orchestra as added attractions, particularly Benny Goodman, Tommy Dorsey with his Clambake Seven and Bob Crosby's Bobcats. In contrast, Artie Shaw recorded relatively few sides with his Gramercy Five. His original unit from 1940 found the great pianist Johnny Guarnieri playing harpsichord exclusively and matched Shaw's clarinet with trumpeter Billy Butterfield. Their eight recordings include "My Blue Heaven," "Smoke Gets in Your Eyes" and a million-seller, "Summit Ridge Drive." The remainder of this CD is from 1945 and features Shaw, trumpeter Roy Eldridge and the two young modernists pianist Dodo Marmarosa (on piano!) and guitarist Barney Kessel. Shaw would lead a few other Gramercy Fives in the future, but these are his two most famous. The music is consistently brilliant with every note counting. *— Scott Yanow*

Artie Shaw at the Hollywood Palladium / Oct. 26, 1940-Sep. 6, 1941 / HEP ♦♦♦♦
Although there are many releases featuring radio broadcasts from Artie Shaw's very popular 1939 orchestra, relatively few exist from his next two bands, the outfits from 1940 and 1941. This particular recording shows just how creative the writing was for his string orchestras. Billy Butterfield, Hot Lips Page, Jack Jenney and Georgie Auld are among the many soloists, and there is one rare small-group live version of "Dr. Livingstone I Presume." *— Scott Yanow*

1949 / 1949 / Music Masters ♦♦♦♦♦
In 1949 the swing era was already in the past and the public's enthusiasm for bebop was quickly receding. No matter, Artie Shaw decided that it was time to put together a modern big band. The venture only lasted three months, but the largely forgotten music that it performed was quite rewarding. This Music Masters CD consists of private recordings of the barely documented orchestra, valuable performances that feature the always-modern clarinetist with an outfit that included trumpeter Don Fagerquist, a great saxophone section with the tenors of Al Cohn and Zoot Sims, and guitarist Jimmy Raney. It is a real pleasure to hear Artie Shaw stretching out in this setting, and a real pity that this band could not have lasted. *— Scott Yanow*

Last Recordings: Rare and Unreleased / Feb. ??, 1954-Jun. ??, 1954 / Music Masters ♦♦♦♦♦
The first of two double-CD sets contains a healthy share of the recordings the clarinetist made with his final Gramercy Five, a unit that included pianist Hank Jones, either Tal Farlow or Joe Puma on guitar and usually Joe Roland's vibes. Unlike his longtime competitor Benny Goodman, Shaw felt perfectly comfortable with younger modernists. In fact his own clarinet playing had evolved through the years and sometimes he hints strongly at Buddy DeFranco without losing his own musical personality during these 20 performances. This is very rewarding music that makes one especially regret that Artie Shaw chose to give up the clarinet after this band ran its course. *— Scott Yanow*

Woody Shaw

b. Dec. 24, 1944, Laurinburg, NC, **d.** May 10, 1989, New York, NY
Flugelhorn, Trumpet / Hard Bop, Post-Bop
Woody Shaw was one of the top trumpeters of the 1970s and '80s, a major soloist influenced by Freddie Hubbard but more advanced harmonically who bridged the gap between hard bop and the avant-garde. Unfortunately he never broke through to greater stardom and his premature death from injuries incurred after being hit by a train was a major loss. Shaw left home for a tour with Rufus Jones when he was 18 and then joined Willie Bobo at a time when Bobo's band included Chick Corea. Shaw next played and recorded with Eric Dolphy; periods in the groups of Horace Silver (1965-66), Max Roach (1968-69) and Art Blakey (1973) followed in addition to making many recordings (some as a sideman for Blue Note) with such players as Jackie McLean, Andrew Hill and McCoy Tyner. Other than playing with Dexter Gordon in 1976, Shaw was primarily a leader from this point on. But overshadowed throughout his career by Hubbard, Miles Davis, Dizzy Gillespie and later on Wynton Marsalis, Shaw would never find much fame or fortune. *— Scott Yanow*

The Moontrane / Dec. 11, 1974-Dec. 18, 1974 / 32 Jazz ♦♦♦♦♦
Although he never received the notoriety of Freddie Hubbard or (at the time) Chuck Mangione, Woody Shaw was one of the leading trumpeters of the 1970s. This CD reissue brings back a strong date by one of Shaw's finest units, a band including Azar Lawrence on tenor and soprano, the up-and-coming trombonist Steve Turre, keyboardist Onaje Allen Gumbs, either Buster Williams or Cecil McBee on bass, drummer Victor Lewis, Tony Waters on congas and percussionist Guilherme Franco. Although none of the group originals (best known is the leader's "Moontrane") caught on, the adventurous music still sounds stimulating more than two decades later. Recommended. *— Scott Yanow*

Little Red's Fantasy / Jun. 29, 1976 / 32 Jazz ♦♦♦♦♦
Woody Shaw was one of the great trumpeters of the 1970s. Although influenced soundwise by Freddie Hubbard, Shaw's more advanced improvisations on his modal originals were quite original and fiery. This Muse set has three of his compositions (including "I Case You Haven't Heard") and a song apiece from pianist Ronnie Mathews and bassist Stafford James; altoist Frank Strozier and drummer Eddie Moore complete the quintet. The varied originals give the musicians strong foundations for their freewheeling and spontaneous solos, making this one of Woody Shaw's better recordings. *— Scott Yanow*

☆ **The Complete CBS Studio Recordings of Woody Shaw** / Dec. 15, 1977-Mar. 17, 1981 / Mosaic ♦♦♦♦♦
The bulk of Shaw's great sessions were recorded for small jazz independents, ensuring them widespread critical evaluation but little audience except with the hardcore faithful. Things seemed about to change in the late '70s when Miles Davis suggested to Columbia that they record Shaw's group. They actually took his suggestion and signed Shaw. He issued a string of remarkable but low-selling records, and Columbia cut him loose after four years and four albums. They compounded the crime by deleting the records shortly after Shaw departed. Mosaic has corrected that slight with another of their marvelously produced and comprehensively notated and packaged box sets. This three-disc collection covers Shaw's Columbia sessions. While it is sad that Shaw's stay at Columbia was not more personally beneficial, it was quite musically productive. *— Ron Wynn*

★ **Rosewood** / Dec. 15, 1977-Dec. 19, 1977 / Columbia/Legacy ♦♦♦♦♦
This album, Woody Shaw's first for a major label, has been reissued as part of his Mosaic box set. Shaw, one of the top trumpeters of the late '60s and throughout the next decade, is heard with a sextet (either Joe Henderson or Carter Jefferson on tenor, pianist Onaje Allan Gumbs, bassist Clint Houston and drummer Victor Lewis) on two numbers and with a "concert ensemble" (which reaches as many as 14 pieces) on the other four selections. Shaw is in top form throughout, particularly on "Rosewood," "Rahsaan's Run" and "Theme for Maxine." This modal music ranks with his best work, making the Mosaic box particularly essential. *— Scott Yanow*

Woody III / 1978 / Columbia ♦♦♦♦♦

Lotus Flower / Jan. 7, 1982 / Enja ♦♦♦♦♦

Bemsha Swing / Feb. 26, 1986-Feb. 27, 1986 / Blue Note ♦♦♦♦
Woody Shaw's premature and tragic death in 1989 robbed the jazz world of one of its most important trumpeters. Despite worsening health and terrible eyesight, he was still in very good playing form in 1986 when he performed the music (recorded at Baker's Keyboard Lounge in Detroit) that resulted in this previously unissued double-CD from 1997. Pianist Geri Allen was already a young giant at the time, sounding quite original with touches of Herbie Nichols in her voicings, and bassist Robert Hurst was just starting to become known, while veteran drummer Roy Brooks (who recorded the date) was a familiar name. The adventurous post-bop music includes three of Thelonious Monk's more joyful tunes, the standard "Star Eyes," two Shaw pieces ("Ginseng People" and "In a Capricornian Way"), and an original by Wayne Shorter. Allen's "Eric" and Brooks' "Theloniously Speaking" serve as features for the rhythm section. Although one would not associate Shaw with Allen, they prove a mutually inspiring team. There is no feeling of decline or even world weariness in the trumpeter's playing, and his solos are full of constant invention and enthusiastic ideas. This highly recommended set was one of Woody Shaw's last great recordings. *— Scott Yanow*

Solid / Mar. 24, 1986 / 32 Jazz ♦♦♦♦♦
This CD serves as a perfect introduction to the memorable but always underrated trumpeter Woody Shaw, who tragically had only three years left to live. Sticking to jazz standards (including "There Will Never Be Another You," a ten-minute rendition of "It Might as Well Be Spring," and a surprisingly effective up-tempo romp through "The Woody Woodpecker Song"), Shaw is heard in a quartet with pianist Kenny Barron, bassist Neil Swainson, and drummer Victor Jones, leading a quintet on two numbers with the up-and-coming altoist Kenny Garrett, and welcoming guest guitarist Peter Leitch to a sextet rendition of Sonny Rollins' "Solid." A gem. *— Scott Yanow*

Imagination / Jun. 24, 1987 / 32 Jazz ♦♦♦♦
Trumpeter Woody Shaw's final album as a leader (cut less than two years before his passing) is surprisingly upbeat. Although his health became shaky, Shaw never declined as a player, as he shows throughout the spirited quintet outing with his longtime trombonist Steve Turre, pianist Kirk Lightsey, bassist Ray Drummond and drummer Carl Allen. Other than Turre's "Steve's Blues," all of the pieces are veteran standards (including "If I Were A Bell," "Imagination" and "You And The Night And The Music"), yet they sound quite fresh and contain more than their share of subtle surprises. Recommended. *— Scott Yanow*

Last of the Line / Dec. 1965-Nov. 1975 / 32 Jazz ♦♦♦♦
All of the music from two Woody Shaw Muse albums (*Cassandranite* and *Love Dance*) and one selection from a 1971 date led by drummer Joe Chambers ("Medina") are reissued on this 1997 two-CD set. Trumpeter Shaw is heard near the beginning of his career on the former session, a 1965 outing with tenor saxophonist Joe Henderson and two different rhythm section (featuring either Larry Young or Herbie Hancock on piano). Although more influenced by Freddie Hubbard at that time then he would be, Shaw's harmonically advanced style was already quite recognizable. The *Love Dance* set (from 1975) has the trumpeter joined by other forward-thinking players, including altoist Rene McLean, Billy Harper on tenor and pianist Joe Bonner. The emphasis throughout is on original material, and the music is modal-oriented while looking toward the avant-garde. A logical pairing of advanced music by one of the great jazz trumpeters. *— Scott Yanow*

Two More Pieces of the Puzzle / Nov. 6, 1976-Apr. 13, 1977 / 32 Jazz ♦♦♦♦♦
This 1998 single CD combines all of the music from two of Woody Shaw's Muse albums: *The Woody Shaw Concert Ensemble* and *The Iron Men*. The former date matches the great trumpeter and his regular group of the period (altoist Rene McLean, pianist Ronnie Mathews, bassist Stafford James and drummer Louis Hayes) with tenor saxophonist Frank Foster and trombonist Slide Hampton for a frequently exciting Berlin concert. There are no slow moments, and although some of the obscure originals are quite lengthy (with Joe Chambers'

"Hello to the Wind" reaching nearly 17 minutes), the solos are consistently creative and often quite explorative. *The Iron Men* is particularly intriguing, for it teams Shaw (who is in prime form on both dates) with such advanced players as altoist Arthur Blythe, Anthony Braxton (on alto and soprano), pianist Muhal Richard Abrams, bassist Cecil McBee and either Joe Chambers or Victor Lewis on drums. The personnel and instrumentation differ from track to track, with the highlights includes Eric Dolphy's "Iron Man" and Fats Waller's "Jitterbug Waltz"; the latter has Braxton playing clarinet. A couple of brief free improvisations by the trio of Shaw, Abrams and McBee, in addition to Andrew Hill's "Symmetry" and the leader's "Song of Songs," round out this fascinating set. A generous and highly recommended CD. *—Scott Yanow*

Woody Shaw: Live, Vol. 1 / Jun. 6, 2000 / High Note ✦✦✦✦
Woody Shaw's *Live Volume One* contains four previously unissued live tracks cut in 1977. These are extraordinary post bop, up-tempo pieces with plenty of improvising solo space shared between Shaw and tenor/soprano saxophonist Carter Jefferson, admirably backed up by Larry Willis on piano, Stafford James on bass, and Victor Lewis drums. Included is Joe Bonner's composition "Love Dance," Willis's "Light Valley," Lewis's "Why," and Shaw's original "Stepping Stone," none clocking in under ten minutes. Just about any Woody Shaw session stands the test of time and this HighNote live date is no exception. *—Al Campbell*

George Shearing

b. Aug. 13, 1919, London, England
Piano / Latin Jazz, Cool, Bop
For a long stretch of time in the '50s and early '60s, George Shearing had one of the most popular jazz combos on the planet—so much so that, in the usual jazz tradition of distrusting popular success, he tends to be underappreciated. Shearing's main claim to fame was the invention of a unique quintet sound, derived from a combination of piano, vibraphone, electric guitar, bass and drums. Within this context, Shearing would play in a style he called "locked hands," which he picked up and refined from Milt Buckner's early-'40s work with the Lionel Hampton band, as well as Glenn Miller's sax section and the King Cole Trio. Stating the melody on the piano with closely knit, harmonized block chords, with the vibes and guitar tripling the melody in unison, Shearing sold tons of records for MGM and Capitol in his heyday. The wild success of this urbane sound obscures Shearing's other great contribution during this time, for he was also a pioneer of exciting, small-combo Afro-Cuban jazz in the 1950s. Indeed, Cal Tjader first caught the Latin jazz bug while playing with Shearing, and the English bandleader also employed such esteemed congueros as Mongo Santamaria, Willie Bobo and Armando Peraza. As a composer, Shearing is best known for the imperishable, uniquely constructed bop standard "Lullaby of Birdland," as well as "Conception" and "Consternation." His solo style, though all his own, reflects the influences of the great boogie-woogie pianists and classical players, as well as those of Fats Waller, Earl Hines, Teddy Wilson, Erroll Garner, Art Tatum and Bud Powell—and fellow pianists have long admired his light, refined touch. *—Richard S. Ginell*

The London Years 1939-1943 / Mar. 2, 1939-Dec. 21, 1943 / HEP ✦✦✦✦✦
Most of pianist George Shearing's earliest recordings are included on this enjoyable swing-oriented CD. During the war years, when he was in his early 20s, Shearing was most influenced by Teddy Wilson, Earl Hines and Art Tatum, but even at that early stage, he was developing his own musical personality. A virtuoso from the start, Shearing is in consistently brilliant form on these standards, originals, and a few interesting boogie-woogie stomps. Of the 25 selections, 22 are piano solos, two are duets with drummer Carlo Krahmer, and one song ("Squeezin' the Blues") is a rare outing for Shearing on accordion; his backup group consists of Krahmer and Leonard Feather on piano. Highly recommended. *—Scott Yanow*

Lullaby of Birdland / Feb. 17, 1949-Mar. 28, 1954 / Verve ✦✦✦✦✦
This double LP from 1986, although not "complete," does a fine job of summing up the MGM recordings of the George Shearing Quintet. The popular group is heard at its best on such songs as "September in the Rain," "East of the Sun," "Conception," "Tenderly," "Pick Yourself Up," and the original version of "Lullaby of Birdland." With such sidemen as Marjorie Hyams, Don Elliott, Joe Roland, Cal Tjader or George Devins on vibes, and Chuck Wayne, Dick Evans, or Toots Thielemans on guitar (and assistance on the final three of the 28 selections by either Candido or Armando Peraza on bongos), Shearing's groups were quite exciting during this era, showing stronger solo strength than they would in the 1960s, although the pianist/leader was clearly the main star. This definitive collection will hopefully resurface on CD eventually. *—Scott Yanow*

The Complete Capitol Live Recordings / Mar. 8, 1958-Jul. 6, 1963 / Mosaic ✦✦✦✦✦
Pianist George Shearing, whose vibes-guitar-piano-bass-drums quintet was one of the most popular in jazz throughout the '50s and '60s, seemed to have had a dual career while signed to Capitol. While his studio recordings often found his quintet augmented by strings, voices, brass, and/or Latin percussion in performances closer to mood music (or even Muzak) than jazz, his live engagements were definitely in the cool/bop vein. This Mosaic five-CD limited-edition box set brings back his five in-concert recordings, two of which are now double in length thanks to the inclusion of 13 previously unissued selections. There is more variety than expected to this program, with the full quintet featured on most numbers but space also set aside for showcases by the trio, Shearing's solo piano, and his regular "guest" Armando Peraza on congas. Shearing is the star throughout, although the sidemen include such fine players as vibraphonists Gary Burton, Emil Richards, and Warren Chiasson; guitarists Toots Thielemans (who plays harmonica on "Caravan"), Dick Garcia, John Gray, and Ron Anthony; bassists Al McKibbon, Ralph Pena, Bill Yancey, and Gene Cherico; and drummers Percy Brice and Vernel Fournier. Shearing's funny comments to the audience have also been included, and the result is a classy show filled with accessible but surprisingly inventive bop-based music. *—Scott Yanow*

The Swinging's Mutual / Jun. 29, 1960-Jan. 7, 1961 / Blue Note ✦✦✦

George Shearing and the Montgomery Brothers / Oct. 9, 1961-Oct. 10, 1961 / Jazzland/OJC ✦✦✦✦
Pianist George Shearing meets up with guitarist Wes, vibraphonist Buddy and bassist Monk Montgomery on this enjoyable if slightly lightweight outing. The performances are a bit too concise at times but the CD reissue does add three extra takes to the original 11-song program and has some fine soloing by the principals. Highlights include "Love Walked In," "Love for Sale" and "The Lamp Is Low." *—Scott Yanow*

Nat King Cole Sings/George Shearing Plays / 1961 / Capitol ✦✦✦✦✦

Jazz Moments / Jun. 20, 1962-Jun. 21, 1962 / Blue Note ✦✦✦✦
This album freed pianist George Shearing from the confines of his popular Quintet and showcases him in a trio with Ahmad Jamal's former sidemen (bassist Israel Crosby and drummer Vernel Fournier). Crosby, heard in his final recording, is in excellent form during these performances and receives some rare opportunities to solo. The main star as usual is the pianist, whose style was perfectly suited to the material heard on this album. Highlights include "Makin' Whoopee," "Like Someone in Love," "Symphony," "When Sunny Gets Blue" and "It Could Happen to You." *—Scott Yanow*

My Ship / Jun. 25, 1974 / Polydor ✦✦✦✦
This solo piano set by George Shearing (which has been reissued on CD through Polygram) is quite eccentric and unpredictable. Freed from the constraints of his popular Quintet, Shearing lets his imagination loose on songs ranging from "My Ship," "Happy Days Are Here Again," "The Entertainer" (which is turned into jazz after a rag beginning), "Londonberry Air," and unfortunately "Send In the Clowns," on which he makes the mistake of singing. Some of the classical allusions are a bit too cute, but Shearing's wit and charm eventually win one over. *—Scott Yanow*

Blues Alley and Jazz / Oct. 1979 / Concord Jazz ✦✦✦✦✦
Pianist George Shearing started a productive ten-year association with the Concord label with this live set, a duo outing matching him with the brilliant bassist Brian Torff. Their performances are virtuosic, intuitive, full of sly wit and always swinging; it is surprising that Torff did not become more famous. The close interaction between the two masterful musicians on such numbers as Billy Taylor's "One for the Woofer," "The Masquerade Is Over" and a humorous "Lazy River" are quite impressive as is Shearing's surprisingly effective vocal on "This Couldn't Be the Real Thing." This CD is recommended. *—Scott Yanow*

On a Clear Day / Aug. 1980 / Concord Jazz ✦✦✦✦✦
George Shearing's second Concord album, a set of duets with bassist Brian Torff like the previous *Blues Alley Jazz*, is the equal of the first. The close communication between the duo, and their ability to think fast and react to each other immediately, makes it possible for them to uplift such songs as "Love for Sale," "On a Clear Day," "Lullaby of Birdland" and even "Happy Days Are Here Again." Brilliant music. *—Scott Yanow*

First Edition / Sep. 1981 / Concord Jazz ✦✦✦✦
This tasteful set matches together pianist George Shearing and guitarist Jim Hall in a program of duets. The fresh material (two originals apiece by Shearing and Hall, the obscure "I See Nothing to Laugh About" and just three standards challenge the pair and their quiet and subtle styles match together well. The pianist's tributes to Antonio Carlos Jobim and Tommy Flanagan are among the more memorable pieces in this interesting and somewhat unexpected musical collaboration. *—Scott Yanow*

Evening with George Shearing and Mel Tormé / Apr. 15, 1982 / Concord Jazz ✦✦✦✦✦
Pianist George Shearing and singer Mel Tormé would match together perfectly every time they shared the stage; the mutual respect they had for each other was as obvious as the fact that they had very complementary styles. This CD, their first joint recording, is consistently exciting. With bassist Brian Torff making the group a trio, Shearing and Tormé swing hard on such tunes as "All God's Chillun Got Rhythm," "Give Me the Simple Life," "Love," and "Lullaby of Birdland" (which starts off with Shearing singing). In addition, there are a pair of instrumentals including "Manhattan Hoedown," which is a feature for Torff. Tormé's touching rendition of "A Nightingale Sang in Berkeley Square" by itself would be enough reason to acquire this highly enjoyable set. *—Scott Yanow*

Top Drawer / Mar. 1983 / Concord Jazz ✦✦✦✦

Dexterity / Nov. 1987 / Concord Jazz ✦✦✦✦

I Hear a Rhapsody: Live at the Blue Note / Feb. 27, 1992-Feb. 29, 1992 / Telarc ✦✦✦✦

Walkin'-Live at the Blue Note / Feb. 27, 1992-Feb. 29, 1992 / Telarc ✦✦✦✦

● **Reflections:The Best of George Shearing, 1992-1998** / Aug. 22, 2000 / Telarc ✦✦✦✦✦
Subtitled *The Best of George Shearing (1992-1998)*, *Reflections* truly is just that. This excellent compilation culls tracks from seven discs recorded while Shearing was in his seventies, placing him in different contexts performing a variety of mostly familiar material. His solo take on Dave Brubeck's "Summer Song" is especially beautiful, and the trio arrangements of "Straighten Up and Fly Right" and "Gee Baby, Ain't I Good to You" are standouts. However, it's the varied instrumentation that keeps the listener tuned in. The gorgeous accompaniment of the Robert Farnon Orchestra elevates and enriches "Oh, Lady Be Good!" without diminishing its inherent swing and gives "How Beautiful is the Night" a texturally shimmering glow. Vibist Steve Nelson and guitarist Louis Stewart are especially effective on the quintet version of Shearing's own "Conception" and add quiet depth to the Horace Silver composition, "Peace." *Reflections* provides a tasty re-introduction to some fine music from a very classy gentleman. *—Jim Newsom*

Archie Shepp

b. May 24, 1937, Fort Lauderdale, FL
Sax (Tenor), Sax (Soprano) / Avant-Garde Jazz, Free Jazz, Hard Bop
Archie Shepp has been at various times a feared firebrand and radical, soulful throwback and contemplative veteran. He was viewed in the '60s as perhaps the most articulate and disturbing member of the free generation, a published playwright willing to speak on the record in unsparing, explict fashion about social injustice and the anger and rage he felt. His tenor sax solos were searing, harsh and unrelenting, played with a vivid intensity. But in the '70s,

Shepp employed a fatback/swing-based R&B approach, and in the '80s he mixed straight bebop, ballads and blues pieces displaying little of the fury and fire from his earlier days. His Impulse albums included poetry readings and quotes from James Baldwin and Malcolm X. Shepp's releases sought to paint an aural picture of African-American life, and included compositions based on incidents like Attica or folk sayings. But starting in the late '60s, the rhetoric was toned down and the anger began to disappear from Shepp's albums. He substituted a more celebratory, and at times reflective attitude. Unfortunately his tone declined from the mid-1980's on (his highly original sound was his most important contribution to jazz) and Shepp is a less significant figure in the 1990's than one might hope. *—Ron Wynn and Scott Yanow*

The New York Contemporary Five / Nov. 11, 1963 / Storyville ✦✦✦✦✦
This historically significant CD has ten of the 11 selections recorded by The New York Contemporary Five (and originally issued on two separate LPs) on November 11, 1963. The short-lived group, which consists of cornetist Don Cherry, altoist John Tchicai, Archie Shepp on tenor, bassist Don Moore and drummer J.C. Moses, was avant-garde for the period, influenced most by Ornette Coleman's Quartet; the participation of Coleman's cornetist certainly helped. However Tchicai (although sometimes hinting at Coleman) had a different approach than Ornette Coleman and it was obvious that Shepp had already developed his own original voice and was the group's most passionate soloist. Together this very interesting quintet (which would soon break up) performs pieces by Ornette Coleman, Thelonious Monk (short melodic renditions of "Monk's Mood" and "Crepescule with Nellie"), Bill Dixon, Tchicai, Shepp and Cherry. *—Scott Yanow*

★ **Four for Trane** / Aug. 10, 1964 / Impulse! ✦✦✦✦✦
Tenor saxophonist Archie Shepp's debut for Impulse is a classic. This recording features the avant-garde innovator playing four of John Coltrane's compositions, including "Cousin Mary" and "Naima," along with his own "Rufus." To his great credit, Shepp never sounded like Coltrane—his raspy tone was much closer to a free version of Ben Webster—and he is heard in top form on this studio date with a sextet also including flugelhornist Alan Shorter, trombonist Roswell Rudd, altoist John Tchicai, bassist Reggie Workman and drummer Charles Moffett. Shepp's interpretations of the Coltrane tunes are quite fresh and original. Highly recommended to open-eared listeners. *—Scott Yanow*

Fire Music / Feb. 16, 1965-Mar. 28, 1965 / Impulse! ✦✦✦✦
This particular early Archie Shepp recording has its strong moments, although it is a bit erratic. Four selections utilize an advanced sextet. Of these songs, "Hambone" has overly repetitive and rather monotonous riffing by the horns behind the soloists, and Shepp's bizarre exploration of "The Girl from Ipanema" gets tedious, but the episodic "Los Olvidaos" is quite colorful, and the tenorman sounds fine on a spacey rendition of "Prelude to a Kiss." "Malcolm, Malcolm-Semper Malcolm" has Shepp reading a brief poem for the fallen Malcolm X before he jams effectively on tenor in a trio with bassist David Izenzon and drummer J.C. Moses. The CD is rounded out by a "bonus" cut not on the original LP—a live version of "Hambone" that is much more interesting than the earlier rendition. Overall, this set, even with its faults, is recommended. *—Scott Yanow*

On This Night / Mar. 9, 1965-Aug. 12, 1965 / Impulse! ✦✦✦✦✦
Tenor saxophonist Archie Shepp's third release for the Impulse label collects valuable loose ends recorded between March and August 1965. Among the highlights are a passionate reading of Duke Ellington's "In a Sentimental Mood" and the title piece, a moving tribute to WEB DuBois, featuring the haunting soprano vocalist Christine Spencer employing a distinct 20th century \classical influence, with Shepp on piano. The CD version of *On This Night* includes an alternate take of "The Mac Man," three of "The Chased," and a reading of his poem "Malcolm, Malcolm, Semper Malcolm." Shepp is the solo horn on these dates, playing at peak form with contributions from vibraphonist Bobby Hutcherson early in his career, David Izenzon or Henry Grimes on bass, and four rotating drummers, including Rashied Ali, J.C. Moses, Joe Chambers, and Ed Blackwell, playing a variety of percussion. *—Al Campbell*

New Thing at Newport / Jul. 2, 1965 / Impulse! ✦✦✦

Live in San Francisco / Feb. 19, 1966 / Impulse! ✦✦✦✦
This Impulse recording features the fiery tenor Archie Shepp with his regularly working group of the period, a quintet also featuring trombonist Roswell Rudd, drummer Beaver Harris and both Donald Garrett and Lewis Worrell on basses. Although two pieces (Shepp's workout on piano on the ballad "Sylvia" and his recitation on "The Wedding") are departures, the quintet sounds particularly strong on Herbie Nichols' "The Lady Sings the Blues" and "Wherever June Bugs Go" while Shepp's ballad statement on "In a Sentimental Mood" is both reverential and eccentric. *—Scott Yanow*

Mama Too Tight / Aug. 19, 1996 / Impulse! ✦✦✦✦✦
Tenor saxophonist Archie Shepp's Impulse recordings are among the most rewarding of his career. This album matches his raspy, explorative tenor with trumpeter Tommy Turrentine, trombonists Roswell Rudd and Grachan Moncur, clarinetist Perry Robinson, Howard Johnson on tuba, bassist Charlie Haden and drummer Beaver Harris. Although three of the four songs (including the nearly 19-minute "A Portrait of Robert Thompson," which uses a section of "Prelude to a Kiss") are eulogies for fallen heroes, the music goes through a wide variety of emotions, makes strong use of the blues, and is both adventurous and often surprisingly accessible. *—Scott Yanow*

The Magic of Ju-Ju / Apr. 26, 1967 / Impulse! ✦✦✦✦✦
On this 1966 Impulse release, tenor saxophonist Archie Shepp unleashed his 18-minute *tour de force* "The Magic of Ju-Ju," combining free jazz tenor with steady frenetic African drumming. Shepp's emotional and fiery tenor takes off immediately, gradually morphing with the five percussionists—Beaver Harris, Norman Connor, Ed Blackwell, Frank Charles, and Dennis Charles—who perform on instruments including rhythm logs and talking drums. Shepp never loses the initial energy, moving forward like a man possessed as the drumming simultaneously builds into a fury. Upon the final three minutes, the trumpets of Martin Banks and Michael Zwerin make an abrupt brief appearance, apparently to ground the piece to a halt. This is one of Shepp's most chaotic yet rhythmically hypnotic pieces. The three remaining tracks, somewhat overshadowed by the title piece, are quick flourishes of free bop on "Shazam," "Sorry Bout That," and the slower, waltz-paced "You're What This Day Is All About." *—Al Campbell*

The Way Ahead / Jan. 29, 1968-Feb. 26, 1969 / Impulse! ✦✦✦✦
Reissued on this 1998 CD are the elusive Archie Shepp four-song set *The Way Ahead*, plus two of the five selections that were originally part of his *Kwanza* album. In both cases the fiery tenor is joined by trumpeter Jimmy Owens and trombonist Grachan Moncur III. *The Way Ahead* also includes pianist Walter Davis Jr., bassist Ron Carter and either Beaver Harris or Roy Haynes on drums, while *Kwanza* has baritonist Charles Davis, pianist Dave Burrell, bassist Walter Booker and drummer Harris. Ironically enough, the leadoff piece "Damn If I Know" does not point to the way ahead, but backwards in time to a certain extent. For the first time in seven years, Shepp is heard on record using a pianist, and the tune itself is a blues. However, the tenor's ferocious sound and fairly free solos on that piece, a lengthy rendition of Moncur's "Frankenstein," "Fiesta," and an exploratory yet respectful version of Duke Ellington's "Sophisticated Lady" show that Shepp really had his approach during this period, owing little (other than inspiration) to John Coltrane. The two *Kwanza* pieces ("New Africa" and "Bakai") are, if anything, more emotional, as Shepp lets out some vocal cries during the former piece. The music overall, despite the passing of decades, still sounds quite advanced and relevant. *—Scott Yanow*

☆ **Live at the Donaueschingen Music Festival** / Oct. 21, 1967 / MPS ✦✦✦✦✦
This is an exciting album. The important tenor Archie Shepp and his 1967 group—with both Roswell Rudd and Grachan Moncur on trombones, bassist Jimmy Garrison, and drummer Beaver Harris—romp through the continuous 43-and-a-half-minute "One for the Trane" before an enthusiastic audience at a German music festival. Although he improvises very freely and with great intensity, Shepp surprised the crowd by suddenly bursting into a spaced-out version of "The Shadow of Your Smile" near the end of this memorable performance. On the whole, this very spirited set represents avant-garde jazz at its peak and Archie Shepp at his finest. *—Scott Yanow*

Yasmina, A Black Woman / Aug. 12, 1969 / Affinity ✦✦✦✦
There is some intriguing music on this Affinity recording. Tenor saxophonist Archie Shepp met up with members of the Chicago avant-garde school for the first time, including Art Ensemble of Chicago members Lester Bowie, Roscoe Mitchell and Malachi Favors, on the lengthy "Yasmina," a track that also includes drummers Philly Joe Jones, Art Taylor and Sunny Murray. On "Sonny's Back," there is an unlikely tenor tradeoff between Shepp and Hank Mobley, while "Body and Soul" gives Shepp a showcase opportunity. Although this set is not essential, it is unique enough to be recommended to avant-garde collectors. *—Scott Yanow*

Blase / Aug. 16, 1969 / Charly ✦✦✦

Things Have Got to Change / May 17, 1971 / Impulse! ✦✦✦

Attica Blues / Jan. 24, 1972-Jan. 26, 1972 / Impulse! ✦✦✦

The Cry of My People / Sep. 25, 1972-Sep. 27, 1972 / ABC/Impulse! ✦✦✦

Kwanza / 1974 / Impulse! ✦✦✦✦✦
Important document musically and for people who need information about the traditional African Holy Week. Twenty-four major names make appearances. *—Michael G. Nastos*

Montreux, Vol. 1 / Jul. 18, 1975 / Arista/Freedom ✦✦✦✦

Montreux, Vol. 2 / Jul. 18, 1975 / Arista/Freedom ✦✦✦✦✦

Steam / May 14, 1976 / Enja ✦✦✦✦
This colorful live LP features Archie Shepp on tenor, and a bit of his more basic piano, playing three lengthy compositions (Duke Ellington's "Solitude," Cal Massey's "A Message from Trane" and Shepp's own "Steam") in a sparse trio with bassist Cameron Brown and drummer Beaver Harris. The avant-garde innovator Shepp still sounds pretty strong at what was for him a fairly late period, displaying his distinctive raspy tone and what were for him some typically emotional ideas. *—Scott Yanow*

Attica Big Band / Oct. 24, 1979 / Inner City ✦✦✦✦✦
Live in Paris. 16 excellent tracks: loaded. A must-buy. *—Michael G. Nastos*

Conversations / Jan. 23, 1999-Jan. 24, 1999 / Delmark ✦✦✦✦
In a dedication to the late bassist Fred Hopkins, Shepp returns to the recording studio armed with his no-compromise, no-nonsense way of playing the tenor saxophone. It's still as cutting-edge dour as ever, supported by the beautiful underpinnings of the trio, with Ari Brown mostly on piano instead of saxophone as he is more widely heard, the peerless bassist Malachi Favors Maghostut, and Afrocentric drummer/percussionist/leader Kahil El'Zabar. As dictated by the art of improvisors, much ground is covered, and a track-by-track rundown is warranted. The introductory "Conversations" is based on a floating piano, free-time excursion rife for Shepp's tenor to express itself. "Kari" is a rambling swinger with Brown back to his tenor sax and Shepp on piano, the latter embellishing the melody with some Erroll Garner-like flourishes. "Whenever I Think of You" is a drop-dead gorgeous, mid-tempo meditative piece, sans Shepp, showcasing Brown's piano stylings. The 7/4 chant "Brother Malcolm," with Brown on tenor sax plus bass and conga, has the collective group vocally echoing Harlem nocturnes about Malcolm X, and the closer "Revelations" is a definitive workout for Shepp, a robust swinger where his more melodic but still pungent sax sound revels in its own free-spirited, outspoken glory. To say Shepp is back would be shortsighted; he's always been around, especially as a teacher at the University of Massachusetts-Amherst. This is a resolute affirmation of his powers, punctuating that he's still a vital force in the new music, as are his backup constituents on this very fine CD, a perfect introduction for the uninitiated and a must-buy for longtime fans. *—Michael G. Nastos*

Lover Man / Jan. 27, 1988 / Timeless ✦✦✦✦
Shepp has been criticized for his more commercial ventures such as this, but many will en-

joy its accessibly light charm. Most of the numbers are standards, including "My Funny Valentine," "Lover Man," and "Lush Life," and are performed by the saxophonist backed by a solid rhythm section. Dave Burrell is wonderfully deft on piano, and he is given ample opportunity to interact with Shepp. Annette Lowman sings on several numbers, and she adds just the right touch and phrasing. Shepp is in somewhat less than perfect form, but he is clearly enjoying himself. There is a touch of a blues and R&B feel that adds to the ambiance. Unlike some of Shepp's other ventures, there are no attempted serious statements made—only relaxing, good, swinging jazz that lifts the spirits or touches the soul, if only just a bit. *—Steven Loewy*

Matthew Shipp

b. Dec. 7, 1960, Wilmington, DE

Piano / Improvisation, Avant-Garde Jazz, Free Jazz, 20th Century Classical/Modern Composition, Avant-Garde

With his unique and recognizable style, pianist Matthew Shipp worked and recorded vigorously during the '90s, creating music in which free jazz and modern classical intertwine. He first became known in the early '90s as the pianist in the David S. Ware Quartet, and soon began leading his own dates—most often including Ware bandmate, leading bassist William Parker—and recording a number of duets with a variety of musicians, from the legendary Roscoe Mitchell to violinist Mat Maneri, who began appearing on recordings in the 1990s. Through his range of live and recorded performances and unswerving individual development, Shipp came to be regarded as a prolific and respected voice in creative music by the decade's close.

Born in the '60s and raised in Wilmington, Delaware, Matthew Shipp grew up around '50's jazz recordings. He began playing piano at the young age of five and decided to focus on jazz by the time he was 12. Shipp played on a Fender Rhodes in rock bands while privately devouring recordings by a variety of jazz players. His first mentor was a man in his hometown named Sunyata, who had an enthusiasm for a variety of studies in addition to music. Shipp later studied music theory and improvisation under Clifford Brown's teacher Robert "Boisey" Lawrey, as well as classical piano and bass clarinet for the school band. After one year at the University of Delaware, Shipp left and took lessons with Dennis Sandole for a short time, after which he attended the New England Conservatory of Music for two years.

Shipp moved to NYC in 1984 and soon met bassist William Parker, among others. Both were playing with tenor saxophonist Ware by 1989, and debuted as a recording artist in a duo with alto player Rob Brown. He married singer Delia Scaife around 1990. Shipp then went on to lead his own trio with Parker and drummers Whit Dickey and Susie Ibarra. Shipp has led dates for a number of labels, including FMP, No More, Eremite, Thirsty Ear, Silkheart and more. *—Joslyn Layne*

Prism / Mar. 26, 1993 / Brinkman ♦♦♦♦

Critical Mass / Sep. 23, 1994 / Thirsty Ear ♦♦♦♦

Matthew Shipp Duo with Roscoe Mitchell / Oct. 8, 1996 / Thirsty Ear ♦♦♦♦

The adventurous yet usually thoughtful pianist Matthew Shipp meets up with Roscoe Mitchell (doubling on alto and soprano) for 11 generally concise free improvisations. The unpredictable music moves logically, contains a fair share of variety and a good use of space, and covers a wide range of emotions. It is particular rewarding to hear Mitchell stretching out in this type of sparse setting. *—Scott Yanow*

☆ **Gravitational Systems** / May 10, 1998 / hatOLOGY ♦♦♦♦♦

This is pianist Matthew Shipp's fifth recording for hatOLOGY and its affiliated hat ART labels, and each disk has displayed a slightly different side to Shipp's way of playing. For sheer beauty and creative intensity, this one may be his best yet, which, considering the uniformly high level of his performances, is a mighty complement. As with most of his outings, virtually all the "compositions" are freely improvised, the exceptions being a startling version of "Greensleeves" that starts traditionally and slowly implodes, and John Coltrane's "Naima," which is barely recognizable in Shipp's hands. Shipp is joined throughout by long-time collaborator, violinist Mat Maneri, whose perky and celebratory virtuosic runs are a perfect foil to the pianist's dense, sometimes morose underpinnings. Maneri bounces deliciously off Shipp and the pianist responds orchestrally. A treat. *—Steven Loewy*

Multiplication Table / Jul. 17, 1997 / hatHUT ♦♦♦♦

DNA / Jan. 6, 1999 / Thirsty Ear ♦♦♦♦

The very adventurous pianist Matthew Shipp performs a set of duets with one of his main inspirations, bassist William Parker. They start off with a dark rendition of "When Johnny Comes Marching Home," play five spontaneous improvisations (three of which are concise) and close off the recital with a brief "Amazing Grace." Shipp's dense chords and atonal playing will remind some listeners of Cecil Taylor although there is a lyricism in his music (and an occasional use of space) that is very much his own. As usual, Parker plays in a driving fashion yet creates a wide variety of often other-worldly sounds. This CD will not convert any conservative listeners but it is up to Shipp's usual level. *—Scott Yanow*

Magnetism / Jan. 26, 1999 / Bleu Regard ♦♦♦♦♦

● **Pastoral Composure** / Jan. 6, 2000 / Thirsty Ear ♦♦♦♦♦

Pastoral Composure is a rich and moving album that is one of the highlights of Matthew Shipp's array of recent releases. The pianist and composer is joined by trumpeter and flugelhorn player Roy Campbell, leading bassist William Parker, and drummer Gerald Cleaver, who are all strong contributors to this January, 2000, session. The album doesn't lose momentum from the dramatic opener, "Gesture," through the solo piano exposition—the shortest number and closer—"XTU." The first cut opens with Cleaver's unexpected military-like rolls on a loose snare that remain an integral sound throughout the piece. Cleaver is soon joined by Shipp and Parker who stir up a thunderstorm with dark, tense chords and percussive left-hand work on the piano and a constant buzzing from the bass. Campbell soon enters on trumpet to make this one of the quartet numbers on this album. The album's second piece, "Visions," will surprise naysayers with its straight-ahead seams on a jaunty form, and restrained (yet discernible) Shipp attitude. His fluid solo take on Ellington's The stormy feel of "Gesture" returns with the title track, featuring Campbell's trumpet singing atop the churning waves of Cleaver and Parker, with Shipp providing a percussive counter-melody. Two tracks later comes the dark take on "Frère Jacques" that has some near-maddening sections, as well as boggling chordal work by Shipp and interesting soloing from Campbell. While Matthew Shipp has come out with numerous releases these past several years, resulting in a slightly overwhelming catalogue, *Pastoral Composure* is a necessary listen for fans. It is also one of Shipp's more accessible albums, making it great place to start for those interested in checking out this important modern jazz pianist. *—Joslyn Layne*

Matthew Shipp's New Orbit / Jan. 16, 2001 / Thirsty Ear ♦♦♦♦

As one of the most daring and original pianists in jazz, Matt Shipp continues to cover a wide spectrum of musical concepts and methods as artistic director of the *Blue Series* for Thirsty Ear Recordings. From avant-garde atonal textures to classical music textures and reams of cosmic consciousness and free expressionism, Shipp has been positioned in a lineage between Thelonious Monk and Cecil Taylor. As the fourth release in Thirsty Ear Recording's *Blue Series, New Orbit* finds Matthew Shipp at peace with himself in his attempt to unite the many experiences he has had as an Afro-American composer and the "various strands of the modern music world that are relevant to him." Shipp is joined on *New Orbit* by a great ensemble that includes Wadada Leo Smith on trumpet, bassist extraordinaire William Parker, and the dynamic Gerald Cleaver on drums. Shipp retains his distinctive sonics and musical lexicons on such songs as "Paradox X" and "U Feature" but raises the bar on the previous series' releases with the inclusion of a four-part suite consisting of the title track, "Orbit 2," "Orbit 3," and & "Orbit 4." By virtue of Shipp's creative powers, the suite strips away conventional interpretations and immerses the talents of his ensemble in new imagining and jazz abstracts. *New Orbit* is an excellent delivery of avant-garde and free jazz that remains uncompromising, unrelenting, and totally individual. *—Paula Edelstein*

Wayne Shorter

b. Aug. 25, 1933, Newark, NJ

Sax (Tenor), Sax (Soprano), Composer / Modal Music, Hard Bop, Post-Bop, Fusion

Though some will argue about whether Wayne Shorter's primary impact on jazz has been as a composer or as a saxophonist, hardly anyone will dispute his overall importance as one of jazz's leading figures over a long span of time. Though indebted to a great extent to John Coltrane, with whom he practiced in the mid-'50s while still an undergraduate, Shorter eventually developed his own more succinct manner on tenor sax, retaining the tough tone quality and intensity and in later years, adding an element of funk. On soprano, Shorter is almost another player entirely, his lovely tone shining like a light beam, his sensibilities attuned more to lyrical thoughts, his choice of notes becoming more spare as his career unfolded. Shorter's influence as a player, stemming mainly from his achievements in the 1960s and '70s, has been tremendous upon the neo-bop brigade who emerged in the early '80s, most notably Branford Marsalis. As a composer, he is best known for carefully conceived, complex, long-limbed, endlessly winding tunes, many of which have become jazz standards yet have spawned few imitators. *—Richard S. Ginell*

Second Genesis / Oct. 11, 1960 / Vee-Jay ♦♦♦♦

Wayning Moments / 1962 / Vee-Jay ♦♦♦♦

The liner notes, the originals of which are included with this reissue, reflect that "this is not experimental jazz." It isn't. It is finely performed mainstream jazz of the era in which it was made. While this recording does not equal the quality of the sessions to be recorded by Shorter later in the decade for Blue Note, it is pleasantly played bop. Shorter's tenor saxophone shows a conservative side, to be sure, and a young Freddie Hubbard hardly takes any chances. Still, the rhythm section anchored by pianist Eddie Higgins and including bassist Jymie Merritt and drummer Marshall Thompson, keeps a solid beat and the results are pleasant enough. Double takes of all but one of the eight charts is included, though there are really not any important substantive differences from the originals. The short recording times of each track limits the solos, but there is nonetheless an attractive simplicity infusing the set. Overall, this does not represent the best work of either Shorter or Hubbard, but it is still an interesting, if non-essential part of the discography of each of them. *—Steven Loewy*

Night Dreamer / Apr. 29, 1964 / Blue Note ♦♦♦♦♦

Tenor-saxophonist Wayne Shorter's Blue Note debut found him well prepared to enter the big time. With an impressive quintet that includes trumpeter Lee Morgan, pianist McCoy Tyner, bassist Reggie Workman and drummer Elvin Jones, Shorter performed a well-rounded program consisting of five of his originals (this CD reissue adds an alternate take of "Virgo") plus an adaptation of an "Oriental Folk Song." Whether it be the brooding title cut, the Coltranish ballad "Virgo" or the jams on "Black Nile" and "Charcoal Blues," this is a memorable set of high-quality and still fresh music. *—Scott Yanow*

☆ **JuJu** / Aug. 3, 1964 / Blue Note ♦♦♦♦♦

On this CD reissue, which adds "new" takes of "JuJu" and "House of Jade" to the original six-song LP program, tenor saxophonist Wayne Shorter has an opportunity to play with two then-current members of the John Coltrane Quartet (pianist McCoy Tyner and drummer Elvin Jones) and an alumnus (bassist Reggie Workman). There are times during these performances that Shorter recalls 'Trane but his brooding sound, relaxed approach and his ability to compose quirky originals set him apart even then. Of the repertoire on this quartet date, none were destined to become standards although "Yes or No," "Twelve More Bars to Go" and "JuJu" were all somewhat memorable. With the rhythm section sounding quite advanced if not as passionate as they usually played with Coltrane, Shorter has the perfect accompaniment for his melancholy and introverted flights. This CD is a fine example of his early work. *—Scott Yanow*

★ **Speak No Evil** / Dec. 24, 1964 / Blue Note ♦♦♦♦♦

This CD reissue brings back one of the classic Wayne Shorter albums. The highly original tenor, who had joined Miles Davis' Quintet a few months earlier, utilizes pianist Herbie Hancock and bassist Ron Carter from the group along with trumpeter Freddie Hubbard and drummer Elvin Jones. The masterful players help introduce six of Shorter's unusual originals including "Fee-Fi-Fo-Fum," "Speak No Evil" and "Infant Eyes." The music is often quite complex but also memorable and the style falls between advanced hard bop/modal jazz and the avant-garde. Well worth numerous listens. *—Scott Yanow*

The Soothsayer / Mar. 4, 1965 / Blue Note ♦♦♦♦♦
It seems odd that this set was originally not released until the late 1970's for the music holds its own with tenor-saxophonist Wayne Shorter's best albums of the 1960's. The CD reissue (from 1990) adds an alternate take of "Angola" to the six-song program. All but the adaptation of Jean Sibelius' "Valse Triste" were Shorter originals with "Lady Day" being perhaps the best-known. The utilization of an impressive sextet (which includes altoist James Spaulding, trumpeter Freddie Hubbard, pianist McCoy Tyner, bassist Ron Carter and drummer Tony Williams) gave Wayne Shorter the rare opportunity to write for three horns. This is stimulating and thought-provoking music that was way beyond the usual hard bop of the period. *—Scott Yanow*

Et Cetera / Jun. 14, 1965 / Blue Note ♦♦♦♦♦
It is strange that this classic Blue Note album was not released for the first time until 1980 for it finds tenor-saxophonist Wayne Shorter in prime form, his four originals (along with Gil Evans's "Barracudas") are quite inventive and the rhythm section (pianist Herbie Hancock, bassist Cecil McBee and drummer Joe Chambers) is state of the art for 1965. These challenging performances find the musicians really listening closely to each other and pushing themselves. Although advanced, the music should not be labelled "avant-garde" or "free jazz" as much as just simply being called "original." *—Scott Yanow*

The All Seeing Eye / Oct. 15, 1965 / Blue Note ♦♦♦♦♦
With such titles as "The All Seeing Eye," "Genesis," "Chaos," "Face of the Deep," and "Mephistopheles," it is clear from the start that the music on this CD reissue is not basic bop and blues. Wayne Shorter (who composed four of the five originals) picked an all-star cast (trumpeter Freddie Hubbard, altoist James Spaulding, trombonist Grachan Moncur III, pianist Herbie Hancock, bassist Ron Carter, and drummer Joe Chambers, along with brother Alan Shorter on flügelhorn for the final song) to perform and interpret the dramatic selections, and their brand of controlled freedom has plenty of subtle surprises. This is stimulating music that still sounds fresh over three decades later. *—Scott Yanow*

☆ **Adam's Apple** / Feb. 3, 1966-Feb. 14, 1966 / Blue Note ♦♦♦♦♦
This Wayne Shorter quartet session (with pianist Herbie Hancock, bassist Reggie Workman and drummer Joe Chambers) is perhaps most notable for the introduction of Shorter's famous blues "Footprints," recorded a few months before Miles Davis' renowned version. In addition to Jimmy Rowles' "502 Blues," the CD reissue has four other Shorter originals including "Adam's Apple" and "El Gaucho." Wayne Shorter was at the peak of his creativity during this period and all of his Blue Note albums from the 1960's are well worth acquiring by adventurous listeners. *—Scott Yanow*

Schizophrenia / Mar. 10, 1967 / Blue Note ♦♦♦♦♦
Wayne Shorter was at the peak of his creative powers when he recorded *Schizophrenia* in the spring of 1967. Assembling a sextet that featured two of his Miles Davis bandmates (pianist Herbie Hancock and bassist Ron Carter), trombonist Curtis Fuller, alto saxophonist/flautist James Spaulding and drummer Joe Chambers, Shorter found a band that was capable of conveying his musical "schizophrenia," which means that this is a band that can play straight just as well as they can stretch the limits of jazz. At their best, they do this simultaneously, as they do on the opener "Tom Thumb." The beat and theme of the song are straightforward, but the musical interplay and solos take chances that result in unpredictable music. And "unpredictable" is the operative phrase for this set of edgy post-bop. Shorter's compositions (as well as Spaulding's lone contribution, "Kryptonite") have strong themes, but they lead into uncharted territory, constantly challenging the musicians and the listener. This music exists at the border between post-bop and free—it's grounded in post-bop, but it knows what is happening across the border. Within a few years, he would cross that line, but *Schizophrenia* crackles with the excitement of Shorter and his colleagues trying to balance the two extremes. *—Stephen Thomas Erlewine*

Super Nova / Aug. 29, 1969-Aug. 2, 1969 / Blue Note ♦♦♦♦
This CD reissue brings back an important transitional album for tenor-saxophonist Wayne Shorter. Doubling on soprano (which he had recently begun playing), Shorter interprets five of his originals (including "Water Babies" which had been recorded previously by Miles Davis) and Antonio Carlos Jobim's "Dindi." He definitely used a forward-looking group of sidemen for his "backup band" includes guitarists John McLaughlin and Sonny Sharrock, Walter Booker (normally a bassist) on classical guitar for "Dindi," bassist Miroslav Vitous, both Jack DeJohnette and Chick Corea (!) on drums and percussionist Airto; Maria Booker takes a vocal on the touching version of "Dindi." The influence of Miles Davis' early fusion period is felt throughout the music but there is nothing derivative about the often-surprising results. As with Wayne Shorter's best albums, this set rewards repeated listenings. *—Scott Yanow*

Odyssey of Iska / Aug. 26, 1970 / Blue Note ♦♦♦

Native Dancer / Sep. 12, 1974 / Columbia/Legacy ♦♦♦♦
Some jazz purists would say that Wayne Shorter went downhill in the 1970s, when he passionately embraced electric jazz-fusion and co-led the innovative Weather Report with Joe Zawinul. But remember: Those are the same people who also claim that Miles Davis' stunning *Bitches Brew* has no value and that Chick Corea's visionary Return to Forever was a complete waste—so it's hard to take their opinions seriously. The fact is that the 1970s were a highly productive time for Shorter, and it wasn't until the 1980s that the tenor and soprano saxophonist really declined creatively. One of Shorter's best-selling albums from the 1970s was *Native Dancer,* a Brazilian-oriented jazz-fusion masterpiece that boasts Herbie Hancock on acoustic piano and electric keyboards, and employs such Brazilian talent as singer Milton Nascimento (a superstar in Brazil) and percussionist Airto Moreira. Everything on this melodic, consistently lyrical effort is a jewel, and that includes Hancock's "Joanna's Theme" as well as pieces by Nascimento ("From the Lonely Afternoons," "Ponta de Areia," "Tarde," "Lilia," and "Miracle of the Fishes") and by Shorter himself ("Ana Maria," "Beauty and the Beast," and "Diana"). Reissued on CD by Columbia in 1990, *Native Dancer* is clearly among Shorter's most essential albums. *—Alex Henderson*

High Life / 1994-1995 / Verve ♦♦♦♦

Dan Siegel

Keyboards, Piano, Synthesizer / Smooth Jazz, Crossover Jazz, Fusion, Jazz-Funk
Smooth jazz keyboardist Dan Siegel has been helping to shape the genre since his recording debut in 1980. Born in Seattle and raised in Eugene, OR, Siegel started taking piano lessons at age eight and was fronting a rock band at 12. After attending the Berklee College of Music in Boston, he received a degree in composition from the University of Oregon and began recording his own works. Soon thereafter, well-known independent jazz label Inner City Records signed the young keyboardist, releasing 1980's *Nite Ride,* which featured guitarist Lee Ritenour. Siegel's second album for Inner City, 1981's *The Hot Spot,* was more successful and spent ten weeks in the Top Ten of Billboard's jazz chart. In 1983, he moved to Los Angeles to pursue film and television work, as well as a more active recording career.

Spending half of the decade composing TV and film scores as well as releasing several albums of varying interest, he signed with Epic in 1986 and began moving away from the ailing jazz fusion scene and into the adult contemporary jazz sound that he had been toying with all along. Highlights of this era include 1994's worldbeat-influenced *Hemispheres* and the urban-flavored *Clairvoyance,* released in 1998. Siegel spent the 1990s recording for a variety of labels, working with some of the bigger names in smooth jazz (Boney James, Larry Carlton, John Patitucci), and leading the hard bop combo Birds of a Feather. In 2000, Legacy Recordings released a greatest hits compilation called *Along the Way: The Best of Dan Siegel.* *—Zac Johnson*

Hempispheres / Sep. 1994-Jan. 1995 / Playfull/Sunset Blvd. ♦♦♦♦♦
Since the advent of adult contemporary music, no single release defines the genre's sugary joys better than Dan Siegel's 1987 classic *Northern Nights.* Gems like "Rhapsody" pretty much set the tone for what pop instrumental music and contemporary jazz are all about, and still get airplay on the diet jazz stations years later. Siegel, who started doing this type of music long before it was en vogue (circa 1980), has felt somewhat constrained by all the expectations. Over the years, he's grown disillusioned with the limits of the adult contemporary format, and has longed to expand beyond the fluff and into some true exotica. The result is *Hemispheres,* one of his most original and intriguing discs. A smorgasbord of worldbeat sounds, beats, and textures, the collection allows the composer to keep a lower profile on the keyboard and keep the focus on some very unique all-star instrumental collaborations, including the title cut's violin (Charlie Bisharat), koto (Osamu Kitajima), Sitar, and shakuhachi. The smooth, tropical Homeland features steel pan (Andy Narell), banjo (Bela Fleck), and harmonica. Dori Caymmi's Sitar, Peter White's accordion, Rick Braun's trumpet, Boney James' sax, and the koto combine on the hypnotic "Ancient Footsteps." "Stix & Stones" finds Siegel in a percussive groove under Narell, Fleck, and Bisharat. There's also an explosive acoustic meets electric string fusion with Richard Smith, Ottmar Liebert, and a mandolin; and finally, a flute and bagpipe extravaganza. And that doesn't even cover the pleasant vocal track, sung by Kelly Coleman. *—Jonathan Widran*

● **Along the Way: The Best of Dan Siegel** / Oct. 24, 2000 / Epic/Legacy ♦♦♦♦♦

Horace Silver

b. Sep. 2, 1928, Norwalk, CT
Piano, Composer / Hard Bop, Fusion, Soul-Jazz
From the perspective of the late '90s, it is clear that few jazz musicians have had a greater impact on the contemporary mainstream than Horace Silver. The hard bop style that Silver pioneered in the '50s is now dominant, played not only by holdovers from an earlier generation, but also by fuzzy-cheeked musicians who had yet to be born when the music fell out of critical favor in the '60s and '70s. After Stan Getz played a concert in 1950 with a pickup rhythm section including Silver, he was so impressed he hired the whole trio. He worked with Getz for a year, and first recorded for Blue Note in 1952 with Lou Donaldson. One year later, joined forces with Art Blakey to form a cooperative under their joint leadership. The band's first album, *Horace Silver and the Jazz Messengers,* was a milestone in the development of the genre that came to be known as hard bop. By 1956, Silver had left the Messengers to record on his own. The series of Blue Note albums that followed established Silver for all time as one of jazz's major composer/pianists, featuring harmonically sophisticated and formally distinctive compositions for small jazz ensemble. His piano style—terse, imaginative, and utterly funky—became a model for subsequent mainstream pianists to emulate. After Blue Note's eclipse in the late '70s, he started his own label Silveto but abandoned his label venture in the '90s to record for Columbia. *—Chris Kelsey*

Horace Silver Trio, Vol. 1: Spotlight on Drums / Oct. 9, 1952-Nov. 23, 1953 / Blue Note ♦♦♦♦
This CD reissue has pianist Horace Silver's first sessions as a leader, trios with drummer Art Blakey and either Gene Ramey, Curly Russell or Percy Heath on bass. Silver already had his funky style pretty well together by 1952 (two years after being discovered by Stan Getz), and the program is most notable for introducing his compositions "Ecaroh" and "Opus De Funk." In addition, there are two percussion features: a drum solo by Blakey on "Nothing But Soul" and "Message From Kenya," a duet by the drummer with the percussion and vocals of Sabu Martinez. *—Scott Yanow*

☆ **Horace Silver and the Jazz Messengers** / Nov. 13, 1954-Feb. 6, 1955 / Blue Note ♦♦♦♦♦
A true classic, this CD found pianist Horace Silver and drummer Art Blakey co-leading the Jazz Messengers; Silver would leave a year later to form his own group. Also featuring trumpeter Kenny Dorham, Hank Mobley on tenor and bassist Doug Watkins, this set is most notable for the original versions of Silver's "The Preacher" and "Doodlin'," funky standards that

helped launch hard bop and both the Jazz Messengers and Silver's quintet. Essential music. *—Scott Yanow*

Six Pieces of Silver / Nov. 10, 1956 / Blue Note ✦✦✦✦✦
The first classic album by the Horace Silver Quintet, this CD is highlighted by "Senor Blues" (heard in three versions including a later vocal rendition by Bill Henderson) and "Cool Eyes." The early Silver quintet was essentially The Jazz Messengers of the year before (with trumpeter Donald Byrd, tenor-saxophonist Hank Mobley and bassist Doug Watkins while drummer Louis Hayes was in Blakey's place) but already the band was starting to develop a sound of its own. "Senor Blues" officially put Horace Silver on the map. *—Scott Yanow*

The Stylings of Silver / May 8, 1957 / Blue Note ✦✦✦

Further Explorations by the Horace Silver Quintet / Jan. 13, 1958 / Blue Note ✦✦✦✦
For a brief time, tenor saxophonist Clifford Jordan and trumpeter Art Farmer were the frontline of the Horace Silver Quintet. This 1997 CD reissue finds the group (which also includes bassist Teddy Kotick and drummer Louis Hayes) performing five of Silver's lesser-known originals and the standard "Ill Wind." The lyrical Farmer and the up-and-coming Jordan have plenty of fine solos, as does the influential Silver, whose funky, witty style stood apart from the prevailing Bud Powell influence of the era. Although none of the newer songs caught on as standards, this set (which has plenty of mood and groove variation) holds together very well and still sounds fresh 40 years later. *—Scott Yanow*

☆ **Finger Poppin' with the Horace Silver Quintet** / Feb. 1, 1959 / Blue Note ✦✦✦✦✦
The first recording by the most famous version of the Horace Silver Quintet is also one of the highpoints of the pianist/composer's career. Among the more memorable tracks of this classic set are "Juicy Lucy" (the epitome of funky jazz), "Cookin' at the Continental" and "Come on Home" but all eight performances are superlative. With trumpeter Blue Mitchell, Junior Cook's tenor, bassist Eugene Taylor and drummer Louis Hayes, Horace Silver had found the perfect forum for his piano and his highly accessible songs. Essential music. *—Scott Yanow*

Blowin' the Blues Away / Aug. 29, 1959-Sep. 13, 1959 / Blue Note ✦✦✦✦✦
The second recording by the classic version of the Horace Silver Quintet (with trumpeter Blue Mitchell, tenor-saxophonist Junior Cook, bassist Eugene Taylor and drummer Louis Hayes) introduced Silver's compositions "Sister Sadie" and "Peace" (both of which became jazz standards) in addition to the title track. No jazz library is complete without at least three or four Horace Silver albums. *—Scott Yanow*

Horace-Scope / Jul. 9, 1960 / Blue Note ✦✦✦✦
The most famous version of the Horace Silver Quintet lasted five years (1959-64) and resulted in six albums of which *HoraceScope* was the third. "Strollin'" is the best known of the new Silver compositions introduced on this set although his "Nica's Dream" (which was already a few years old) is the only standard. With trumpeter Blue Mitchell, tenor-saxophonist Junior Cook, bassist Gene Taylor and his new drummer Roy Brooks, this was the perfect group for Horace Silver's music. *—Scott Yanow*

Doin' the Thing (At the Village Gate) / May 19, 1961-May 20, 1961 / Blue Note ✦✦✦✦✦
This live set (recorded at the Village Gate) finds pianist/composer Horace Silver and his most acclaimed quintet (the one with trumpeter Blue Mitchell, tenor saxophonist Junior Cook, bassist Gene Taylor and drummer Roy Brooks) stretching out on four selections, including his new song "Filthy McNasty." Two shorter performances were added to the CD version of this enjoyable and always funky hard bop session. *—Scott Yanow*

The Tokyo Blues / Jul. 13, 1962-Jul. 14, 1962 / Blue Note ✦✦✦✦
Pianist Horace Silver had his most stable group during 1960-64 when his sidemen were trumpeter Blue Mitchell, tenor saxophonist Junior Cook, bassist Gene Taylor and drummer Roy Brooks. For this set (a straight CD reissue of the original LP), Joe Harris (listed as John Harris, Jr.) is in Brooks' place. The quintet performs four Silver originals (best known is the title cut) plus Ronnell Bright's obscure ballad "Cherry Blossom" which is well worth reviving. Although the five songs are dedicated to Japan and the Orient, this is nothing inherently Asian about the music; it is a typically funky Horace Silver hard bop date, one of his many recommended Blue Note sets. *—Scott Yanow*

Silver's Serenade / Apr. 11, 1963-Apr. 12, 1963 / Blue Note ✦✦✦✦
The sixth and final recording session by the most famous of Horace Silver's quintets (the version with trumpeter Blue Mitchell and tenor-saxophonist Junior Cook) did not introduce any new classic tunes ("Silver's Serenade" is the best known) but, as with the previous sets, the results are swinging, funky and quite creative within the idiom. All of Silver's Blue Note quintet recordings are quite enjoyable. *—Scott Yanow*

★ **Song for My Father** / Oct. 31, 1963-Oct. 26, 1964 / Blue Note ✦✦✦✦✦
Horace Silver's most famous album includes the memorable title cut, four of his other recent compositions (including "Calcutta Cutie" and "Lonely Woman") and Joe Henderson's "The Kicker." Although trumpeter Blue Mitchell and tenor-saxophonist Junior Cook reunited for "Calcutta Cutie," the remainder of this classic set features Henderson's tenor and trumpeter Carmell Jones. Funky hard bop at its best, this is essential music for any jazz collection. *—Scott Yanow*

The Cape Verdean Blues / Oct. 1, 1965-Oct. 22, 1965 / Blue Note ✦✦✦✦
By late 1965 Horace Silver's Quintet featured trumpeter Woody Shaw and tenor-saxophonist Joe Henderson and, on half of this set, the great trombonist J.J. Johnson sits in. "The Cape Verdean Blues," "Pretty Eyes" and Henderson's "Mo' Joe" are among the highlights of this high-quality set of funky hard bop by one of the pacesetting groups. *—Scott Yanow*

The Jody Grind / Nov. 2, 1966-Nov. 23, 1966 / Blue Note ✦✦✦✦
This excellent set finds Horace Silver fronting a particularly advanced edition of his quintet. This band featured trumpeter Woody Shaw, tenor-saxophonist Tyrone Washington and, on half of the six tracks (all Silver compositions) the alto and flute of James Spaulding. "The Jody Grind" and "Dimples" are the closest any of these songs came to becoming standards but Silver fans will find much to enjoy here. *—Scott Yanow*

Serenade to a Soul Sister / Mar. 25, 1968-Mar. 25, 1968 / Blue Note ✦✦✦✦✦
One of the final classic albums by the Horace Silver Quintet, this set finds Silver using such sidemen as trumpeter Charles Tolliver, either Stanley Turrentine or Bennie Maupin on tenors and, on half of the tracks, the young drummer Billy Cobham. The six Silver compositions include "Psychedelic Sally" and "Serenade to a Soul Sister." This music is both timeless and very much of the period. *—Scott Yanow*

Total Response (Phase I) / Jan. 29, 1971-Nov. 15, 1971 / Blue Note ✦✦

Silver 'n Brass / Jan. 10, 1975-Jan. 17, 1975 / Blue Note ✦✦✦

Silver 'n Wood / Nov. 7, 1975-Jan. 3, 1976 / Blue Note ✦✦✦

Hard Bop Grandpop / Feb. 29, 1996-Mar. 1, 1996 / GRP ✦✦✦✦✦
Pianist Horace Silver's 1996 CD introduced ten new compositions and, although none of the originals will probably become standards, they are consistently catchy, full of the infectious Silver personality and very viable vehicles for improvisation. The instrumental set matches Silver with quite an all-star group comprised of trumpeter Claudio Roditi, tenor saxophonist Michael Brecker (an alumnus), trombonist Steve Turre, baritonist Ronnie Cuber, bassist Ron Carter and drummer Lewis Nash. Most of the selections feature solo space for one or two of the horn players (all get their spots), and the results live up to the great potential. One of Horace Silver's finest recordings in his post-Blue Note era. *—Scott Yanow*

A Prescription for the Blues / 1997 / Impulse! ✦✦✦

Jazz Has a Sense of Humor / Dec. 17, 1998-Dec. 18, 1998 / GRP ✦✦✦✦

Retrospective / Oct. 9, 1952-Nov. 3, 1978 / Blue Note ✦✦✦✦✦
Career-spanning retrospectives are always difficult to pull off in jazz, since the music is often about the moment. An artist can peak for a few years, and that's what's worth hearing—the rest is interesting, but not quite as compelling, as a lengthy four-disc box set can prove. That certainly isn't the case with the four-disc Horace Silver *Retrospective*, an excellent, involving trawl through the pianist's seminal stay at Blue Note. Apart from the fourth disc, which is filled with his trippy late-'60s/early-'70s recordings that are largely unavailable in the U.S., there's not too much here for collectors, but it's an ideal set for any listener that wants to hear Silver's hard, funky style evolve. At the end of the set, it's hard not to be impressed with the scope and evolution of his music. *—Stephen Thomas Erlewine*

Zoot Sims (John Haley Sims)

b. Oct. 29, 1925, Inglewood, CA, **d.** Mar. 23, 1985, New York, NY
Sax (Tenor), Sax (Soprano) / Cool, Bop
Throughout his career, Zoot Sims was famous for epitomizing the swinging musician, never playing an inappropriate phrase. He always sounded inspired, and although his style did not change much after the early 1950s, Zoot's enthusiasm and creativity never wavered. He was a professional by the age of 15, landing his first important job with Bobby Sherwood's Orchestra, and joined Benny Goodman's big band for the first time in 1943; he would be one of BG's favorite tenormen for the next 30 years. He recorded with Joe Bushkin in 1944, and even at that early stage, his style was largely set. Sims gained his initial fame as one of Woody Herman's "Four Brothers" during his time with the Second Herd (1947-49). A freelancer throughout most of his career, he often led his own combos or co-led bands with his friend Al Cohn; the two tenors had very similar sounds and styles. Zoot started doubling on soprano quite effectively in the 1970s. Through the years, he appeared in countless situations, and always seemed to come out ahead. *—Scott Yanow*

Zoot Sims Quartets / Dec. 16, 1950-Aug. 14, 1951 / Prestige/OJC ✦✦✦✦
This CD reissue features the great tenor-saxophonist Zoot Sims (who was then 25) leading his first American recording dates. He is heard with two quartets, the team of pianist John Lewis, bassist Curly Russell and drummer Don Lamond and with pianist Harry Biss, bassist Clyde Lombardi and drummer Art Blakey. All but two numbers clock in around the three-minute mark: an over eight-minute alternate version of "Zoot Swings the Blues" and an 11-minute "East of the Sun." Sims is in fine form throughout these cool-toned but hard-swinging sets. *—Scott Yanow*

Tonite's Music Today / Feb. 1956 / Black Lion ✦✦✦✦✦
Valve trombonist Bob Brookmeyer's musical partnerships in the 1950s with Stan Getz and especially Gerry Mulligan were celebrated but he also recorded three fine albums with tenor-saxophonist Zoot Sims in 1956 that are quite enjoyable, feature colorful jammed ensembles and hard-swinging yet cool-toned solos that owe as much to the swing tradition as to the innovations of bebop. This Storyville CD finds Zoot and Brookmeyer accompanied by pianist Hank Jones, bassist Wyatt Reuther and drummer Gus Johnson. Highlights include "I Hear a Rhapsody," "Blue Skies" and Sims's first ever recorded vocal on a "Blues." This release is easily recommended as is its companion Storyville CD Morning Fun. *—Scott Yanow*

Morning Fun / Feb. 1956 / Black Lion ✦✦✦✦✦
Although it claims on the back of this CD that the music was recorded in August 1956, discographies state February and that seems more logical since valve trombonist Bob Brookmeyer and tenor-saxophonist Zoot Sims did not team up for a very long period (although three records resulted from their valuable collaboration). With assistance from pianist John Williams, bassist Bill Crow and drummer Jo Jones, Sims and Brookmeyer are in fine form on such selections as a rollicking "The King," "Lullaby of the Leaves," a brief two-song ballad medley and Brookmeyer's "Whooeeeee!" Sims takes a rare (and fairly effective) vocal on "I Can't Get Started." Recommended, as is the other Black Lion Zoot Sims CD from the same period, *Tonite's Music Today*. *—Scott Yanow*

That Old Feeling / Oct. 12, 1956-Nov. 9, 1956 / Chess ✦✦✦✦
That Old Feeling compiles 14 songs cut at two 1956 dates, which were released on Argo and ABC-Paramount. At the sessions, Sims not only played tenor, but cut a few songs on alto and baritone sax as well. *—AMG*

Zoot! / Dec. 13, 1956-Dec. 18, 1956 / Riverside/OJC ✦✦✦
For a little while in the mid-'50s, Zoot Sims occasionally doubled on alto although he soon switched back exclusively to tenor where he had a stronger musical personality. On this CD

reissue of a Riverside set from 1956, Sims plays alto on two of the seven tracks and works well with trumpeter Nick Travis. Actually pianist George Handy, who contributed four originals (two standards and drummer Osie Johnson's "Osmosis" complete the program) and did all of the arranging, comes across as the key supporting player; bassist Wilbur Ware and Johnson are fine in quiet support. Although Handy's arrangements are a bit modern, this is still a typically hard-swinging and melodic Zoot Sims date. *—Scott Yanow*

Jazz Alive: A Night at the Half Note / Feb. 6, 1959-Feb. 7, 1959 / United Artists ✦✦✦✦✦

Zoot at Ease / May 30, 1973-Aug. 9, 1973 / Progressive ✦✦✦✦
This Mobile Fidelity audiophile CD reissues a long out-of-print and rare Zoot Sims set originally made for the defunct Famous Door label. Accompanied by pianist Hank Jones, bassist Milt Hinton and either Louie Bellson or Grady Tate on drums, Zoot (who doubles on tenor and soprano) is in typically swinging form. In addition to a few standards, Sims explores some obscurities (including "Alabamy Home" and "In The Middle Of A Kiss") and even turns the theme of "Rosemary's Baby" into jazz. A slightly above-average set from a saxophonist who always sounded inspired. *—Scott Yanow*

★ **Zoot Sims and the Gershwin Brothers** / Jun. 6, 1975 / Pablo/OJC ✦✦✦✦✦
Along with his album with Count Basie (*Basie and Zoot*) during the same period, this is one of Sims's most exciting recordings of his career. Greatly assisted by pianist Oscar Peterson, guitarist Joe Pass, bassist George Mraz and drummer Grady Tate, he explores ten songs written by George and Ira Gershwin. Somehow the magic was definitely present and, whether it be stomps such as "The Man I Love," "Lady Be Good" and "I Got Rhythm" or warm ballads (including "I've Got a Crush on You" and "Embraceable You"), Zoot Sims is heard at the peak of his powers. A true gem. *—Scott Yanow*

Hawthorne Nights / Sep. 20, 1976-Sep. 21, 1976 / Pablo/OJC ✦✦✦✦
Unlike most of his Pablo sessions, this Zoot Sims CD is not a quartet outing but an opportunity for his tenor to be showcased while joined by a nine-piece group that includes six horns (three reeds among them). Bill Holman's inventive arrangements are a large part as to why the date is successful but Sims's playing on the five standards, two Holman pieces and his own "Dark Cloud" should not be overlooked. Fortunately there is also some solo space saved for the talented sidemen (which include Oscar Brashear and Snooky Young on trumpets, trombonist Frank Rosolino and the woodwinds and reeds of Jerome Richardson, Richie Kamuca and Bill Hood). A well-rounded set of swinging jazz. *—Scott Yanow*

If I'm Lucky / Oct. 27, 1977-Oct. 28, 1977 / Pablo/OJC ✦✦✦✦
Tenor saxophonist Zoot Sims recorded quite a few albums with pianist Jimmy Rowles during his Pablo years; all are recommended. Rowles assisted Sims in coming up with obscurities to interpret, and this CD reissue is highlighted by such little-performed songs as "If I'm Lucky," "Shadow Waltz," "Gypsy Sweetheart" and "I Wonder Where Our Love Has Gone." The lead voices are backed ably by bassist George Mraz and drummer Mousey Alexander on this enjoyable straight-ahead date. *—Scott Yanow*

For Lady Day / Apr. 10, 1978-Apr. 11, 1978 / Pablo ✦✦✦✦✦
It is strange that this album was not released until the CD came out in 1990 for tenor-saxophonist Zoot Sims and pianist Jimmy Rowles's tribute to Billie Holiday is melodic, tasteful and largely memorable. Together with bassist George Mraz and drummer Jackie Williams back in 1978, they perform 11 songs associated with Billie Holiday including quite a few that would have been lost in obscurity if Lady Day had not uplifted them with her recordings. Highlights include "Easy Living," "Some Other Spring," "I Cried for You," "Body and Soul" and "You're My Thrill." A lyrical and heartfelt tribute. *—Scott Yanow*

Zoot Sims in Copenhagen / Aug. 24, 1978 / Storyville ✦✦✦✦
Formerly put out by Storyville, this audiophile CD reissue features the great Zoot Sims performing in a quartet with bassist Niels Pedersen and two notable expatriates: pianist Kenny Drew and drummer Ed Thigpen. Sims, who doubles here on soprano, is in typically swinging form on such numbers as "Too Close for Comfort," "In a Mellowtone," an extended, nearly ten-minute rendition of "All the Things You Are," and "It's All Right With Me." The supporting rhythm section is perfect for this style of music, and Zoot is heard throughout in prime form. *—Scott Yanow*

Warm Tenor / Sep. 18, 1978-Sep. 19, 1978 / Pablo ✦✦✦✦
The Pablo label was a perfect home for Zoot Sims during the second half of the 1970s for the cool-toned tenor always sounded at his best in informal settings with small groups where he had the opportunity to stretch out. This quartet set with pianist Jimmy Rowles, bassist George Mraz and drummer Mousey Alexander (which has been reissued on CD) gives Zoot a chance to interpret a variety of mostly underplayed standards along with a duet with Mraz on an ad-lib "Blues for Louise." Highlights include "Old Devil Moon," "You Go to My Head," "Blue Prelude" and "You're My Thrill." *—Scott Yanow*

Blues for Two / Mar. 6, 1982-Jun. 23, 1982 / Pablo/OJC ✦✦✦✦✦
Although guitarist Joe Pass recorded many unaccompanied solo albums, he made relatively few dates as part of a duo. This CD reissue of a session with tenor-saxophonist Joe Pass works quite well because Zoot Sims was a natural swinger who did not need a full rhythm section to push him. His playing on the selections (mainly standards including "Dindi," "Poor Butterfly," "Pennies From Heaven" and "I Hadn't Anyone Till You") is as heated and lyrical as usual. Pass also warms up quickly to the situation (Sims must have been easy to accompany) and takes many fine solos of his own. The pair collaborated on the opening "Blues for 2" and "Takeoff" which wraps up the highly enjoyable set. *—Scott Yanow*

On the Korner / Mar. 20, 1983 / Pablo ✦✦✦✦✦
Just two years and three days away from his death at age 59, the great tenor Zoot Sims is heard in prime form on this live session from San Francisco's legendary club Keystone Korner. The music was not initially released until this 1994 CD but it was worth the wait. The hard-swinging tenor (who plays equally effective soprano on Duke Ellington's "Tonight I Shall Sleep" and "Pennies from Heaven") is ably supported by the fine pianist Frank Collett, bassist Monty Budwig and drummer Shelly Manne. Sims plays his usual repertoire from the period (including "I Hear a Rhapsody," "If You Could See Me Now" and "Dream Dancing") but, although he had previously recorded virtually all of these selections, the "new" versions are well worth hearing. This late date gives one a definitive look into Zoot Sims's playing of his last decade, when he interpreted standards in a timeless style that had grown but not really changed since the 1950s. Recommended. *—Scott Yanow*

Live in Philly / Apr. 7, 1998 / 32 Jazz ✦✦✦✦
Released for the first time on this 1998 CD, this excellent live set dates from the early 1970s (1973 is an educated guess) and features the always-swinging tenorman Zoot Sims in a quartet with pianist Benny Aronov, bassist Major Holley and drummer Mickey Roker. Zoot is in top form on a variety of veteran standards, including "In a Mellotone" and a lengthy "Do Nothing Till You Hear From Me." Holley's bowing and singing combination is showcased on "Polka Dots And Moonbeams," and Aronov shows plenty of fire and potential. Easily recommended to bop and Zoot Sims fans. *—Scott Yanow*

Jimmy Smith (James Oscar Smith)

b. Dec. 8, 1925, Norristown, PA
Organ (Hammond), Organ / Hard Bop, Soul-Jazz
Though he never received any exaggerated title like the king of soul jazz, Jimmy Smith certainly ruled the Hammond organ in the '50s and '60s. He revolutionized the instrument, showing it could be creatively used in a jazz context and popularized in the process. His Blue Note sessions from 1956 to 1963 were extremely influential and are highly recommended. Smith turned the organ into almost an ensemble itself. He provided walking bass lines with his feet, left hand chordal accompaniment, solo lines in the right and a booming, funky presence that punctuated every song, particulary the uptempo cuts. Smith turned the fusion of R&B, blues and gospel influences with bebop references and devices into a jubilant, attractive sound that many others immediately absorbed before following in his footsteps. A Birdland date and 1957 Newport Jazz Festival appearance launched Smith's career. He toured extensively through the '60s and '70s. His Blue Note recordings included superb collaborations with Kenny Burrell, Lee Morgan, Lou Donaldson, Tina Brooks, Jackie McLean, Ike Quebec and Stanley Turrentine among others. He also did several trio recordings, some which were a little bogged down by the excess length of some selections. Smith scored more hit albums on Verve from 1963 to 1972, many of them featuring big bands and using fine arrangements from Oliver Nelson. But Verve went to the well once too often seeking crossover dollars, loading down Smith's late '60s album with hack rock covers. His '70s output was quite spotty. *—Ron Wynn and Bob Porter*

A New Sound, A New Star: Jimmy Smith at the Organ, Vol. 1 / Feb. 13, 1956-Feb. 18, 1956 / Blue Note ✦✦✦✦✦
The debut of organist Jimmy Smith on records (he was already 30) was a major event, for he introduced a completely new and very influential style on the organ, one that virtually changed the way the instrument is played. This LP features the already-recognizable organist in a trio with guitarist Thornel Schwartz and Bay Perry on drums. Highlights of this very impressive debut include "The Way You Look Tonight," "Lady Be Good" and Horace Silver's "The Preacher." [Volume 1 and Volume 2 were packaged together and issued by Blue Note in 1997] *—Scott Yanow*

The Champ / Mar. 11, 1956 / Blue Note ✦✦✦✦✦

☆ **The Complete February 1957 Jimmy Smith Blue Note Sessions** / Feb. 11, 1957-Feb. 13, 1957 / Mosaic ✦✦✦✦✦
It would not be an overstatement to say that organist Jimmy Smith was busy during February 11-13, 1957, for he recorded enough material for these three CDs, 21 often lengthy performances that originally appeared on five LPs plus three others that had been previously unissued. Smith is not only heard early in his career with his regular trio but in a sextet with trumpeter Donald Byrd, altoist Lou Donaldson, tenor-saxophonist Hank Mobley, and drummer Art Blakey, in duets with Donaldson and with a quartet that also stars guitarist Kenny Burrell. These jam sessions feature plenty of exciting solos over fairly common chord changes, and despite the heavy competition, Jimmy Smith (who is still the king of the jazz organ) is the dominant force. Recommended. *—Scott Yanow*

The Sounds of Jimmy Smith / Feb. 11, 1957-Feb. 13, 1957 / Blue Note ✦✦✦

Jimmy Smith at the Organ, Vol. 1 / Feb. 12, 1957 / Blue Note ✦✦✦

Jimmy Smith at the Organ, Vol. 2 / Feb. 12, 1957-Feb. 13, 1957 / Blue Note ✦✦✦

Jimmy Smith Trio + LD / Jul. 4, 1957 / Blue Note ✦✦✦

Confirmation / Aug. 25, 1957-Feb. 25, 1958 / Blue Note ✦✦✦✦

House Party / Aug. 25, 1957-Feb. 25, 1958 / Blue Note ✦✦✦✦✦
Music from two different sessions are included on this enjoyable LP. All of organist Jimmy Smith's jam sessions are worth acquiring although several (such as this one) have been long out of print. Lengthy versions of "Au Privave" and "Just Friends" and more concise renditions of "Lover Man" and "Blues After All" match Smith with quite a variety of all-stars: trumpeter Lee Morgan, trombonist Curtis Fuller, Lou Donaldson or George Coleman on altos, Tina Brooks on tenor, guitarists Kenny Burrell or Eddie McFadden, and Art Blakey or Donald Bailey on drums. Everyone plays up to par, and the passionate solos (and Smith's heated background riffing) keep the proceedings continually exciting. *—Scott Yanow*

The Sermon / Aug. 25, 1957-Feb. 25, 1958 / Blue Note ✦✦✦✦✦
This CD reissue has two of the three selections (the 20-minute "The Sermon" and "Flamingo") from the original LP, adding five additional selections that are related. With such soloists as trumpeter Lee Morgan, trombonist Curtis Fuller, altoist Lou Donaldson, Tina Brooks on tenor, either Eddie McFadden or Kenny Burrell on guitar and Art Blakey or Donald Bailey on drums. The straightahead music is as good as one would expect (with the lengthy title cut being the obvious highpoint), and the CD overall offers listeners a strong dose of Jimmy Smith's Blue Note period. *—Scott Yanow*

Cool Blues / Apr. 7, 1958 / Blue Note ✦✦✦✦✦

Home Cookin' / Jul. 15, 1958-Jun. 16, 1959 / Blue Note ♦♦♦♦
Organist Jimmy Smith and guitarist Kenny Burrell always had a close musical relationship, making each of their joint recordings quite special. This album features the pair along with drummer Donald Bailey and (on four of the seven songs) the obscure but talented tenor saxophonist Percy France. The emphasis is on blues and basic material including versions of "See See Rider," Ray Charles's "I Got a Woman" and several groups originals, and as usual, the performances are swinging and soulful. The CD reissue adds five "new" performances to the original seven. *—Scott Yanow*

On the Sunny Side / Jul. 15, 1958 / Blue Note ♦♦♦♦

☆ **Crazy! Baby** / Jan. 4, 1960 / Blue Note ♦♦♦♦♦
Unlike most of the Jimmy Smith recordings from the era, this CD reissue (which adds "If I Should Lose You" and "When Lights Are Low" to the original LP program) features organist Jimmy Smith's regular group (rather than an all-star band). With guitarist Quentin Warren and drummer Donald Bailey completing the trio, Smith is heard in peak form on swinging and soulful versions of such tunes as "When Johnny Comes Marching Home," "Makin' Whoopee," "Sonnymoon for Two" and "Mack the Knife." Despite claims and some strong challenges by others, there has never been a jazz organist on the level of Jimmy Smith. *—Scott Yanow*

Open House/Plain Talk / Mar. 22, 1960 / Blue Note ♦♦♦♦♦
On March 22, 1960, Jimmy Smith, his trio (with guitarist Quentin Warren and drummer Donald Bailey), and three notable guests (tenor saxophonist Ike Quebec, altoist Jackie McLean, and trumpeter Blue Mitchell) recorded enough material for two LPs which were released as *Open House* and *Plain Talk*. This single CD reissues the complete contents of the marathon session. Four songs feature the full group while the remaining four ballads are showcases for Quebec ("Old Folks" and "Time After Time"), McLean ("Embraceable You"), and Mitchell ("My One and Only Love"). Although not essential, this well-rounded set has plenty of variety and strong moments, making it recommended to fans of the jazz organ and straight-ahead swinging. *—Scott Yanow*

★ **Back at the Chicken Shack** / Apr. 25, 1960 / Blue Note ♦♦♦♦♦
This may be the quintessential funky soul-jazz album. Period. I know of no better single recording and this is the one I would have to take to that desert island when I go. The term "all star" was coined for this group. Jimmy Smith is as hot as he gets and so is Stanley Turrentine on tenor sax. Just hot! Kenny Burrell is in top form too and Donald Bailey keeps the beat tight. Every jazz fan should hear it and every groove fan must own it. Also see the Smith album *Midnight Special*, which was recorded at the same session. *—Michael Erlewine*

☆ **Midnight Special** / Apr. 25, 1960 / Blue Note ♦♦♦♦♦
A perfect complement to *Back At the Chicken Shack*, which was recorded the same day. Organist Jimmy Smith, tenor saxophonist Stanley Turrentine and guitarist Kenny Burrell always make for a potent team, and with drummer Donald Bailey completing the group, the quartet digs soulfully into such numbers as the groovin' "Midnight Special," "Jumpin' the Blues" and "One O'Clock Jump." Highly recommended. *—Scott Yanow*

Prayer Meetin' / Jun. 13, 1960-Feb. 8, 1963 / Blue Note ♦♦♦♦♦
Prayer Meeting was organist Jimmy Smith's final Blue Note recording until 1986. On this CD reissue two earlier selections featuring Smith, tenor saxophonist Stanley Turrentine, guitarist Quentin Warren, bassist Sam Jones (the only time on Blue Note that Smith used a bassist), and drummer Donald Bailey jam on versions of "Lonesome Road" and the original "Smith Walk"; both selections went unreleased until popping up on a 1984 Japanese CD. The bulk of this set is from February 8, 1963, featuring the same personnel without Jones. Highlights include the title cut, a soulful version of "When the Saints Go Marching In," and the Gene Ammons blues "Red Top." Excellent music. *—Scott Yanow*

Jimmy Smith Plays Fats Waller / Jan. 23, 1962 / Blue Note ♦♦♦♦

☆ **Bashin': The Unpredictable Jimmy Smith** / Mar. 26, 1962-Mar. 28, 1962 / Verve ♦♦♦♦♦
Although still a regular Blue Note artist (he would make four more albums for the company within the next year), *Bashin'* was organist Jimmy Smith's debut for Verve, a label that he would record extensively for during 1963-72. On the first half of the program (reissued in full on this CD), Smith was for the first time joined by a big band. Oliver Nelson provided the arrangements, trumpeter Joe Newman and altoist Phil Woods have a solo apiece and "Walk on the Wild Side" became Smith's biggest hit up to that point. The final three numbers feature Smith's regular trio with guitarist Quentin Warren and drummer Donald Bailey swinging with soul as usual. The historical set (a bit of a turning point for Jimmy Smith's career) has its strong moments although it is not all that essential. *—Scott Yanow*

Walk on the Wild Side: The Best of the Verve Years / 1962-1973 / Verve ♦♦♦♦♦
Smith recorded most of his most popular sides for Verve, and this double CD contains 25 tracks taken from his recordings for the label between 1962 and 1973, in both small combo and big band settings. There are a few Jimmy Smith compilations out there, and this isn't necessarily the best; anthologies which focus on his early and mid-'60s prime might be better values overall. It does have his most famous performances—"Walk On The Wild Side," "Got My Mojo Workin'," and a couple of his great duets with guitarist Wes Montgomery. It's a decent enough pickup if you just want one or two Smith albums for your library, though not so definitive that it's worth getting if you already have some Smith compilations that cover the Verve era. *—Richie Unterberger*

I'm Movin' On / Dec. 31, 1963 / Blue Note ♦♦♦
This CD reissue of a formerly rare date has a perfectly suitable title for it is the first of four albums that organist Jimmy Smith made within an eight-day period for Blue Note before permanently leaving the label for Verve. Although notable for matching Smith with guitarist Grant Green in what would be their only joint recording (drummer Donald Bailey completes the trio), the music is fairly typical of a Jimmy Smith session with the repertoire including blues, a couple of standards and ballads. The solos are well-played but nothing too surprising occurs (except perhaps for the sappiness of "What Kind of Fool Am I"); the original LP program is expanded by the inclusion of two other selections from the same date. *—Scott Yanow*

Bucket! / Feb. 1, 1962 / Blue Note ♦♦♦
Recorded the first day of February in 1963, but not released for a few years, *Bucket!* is a fairly typical Jimmy Smith session, featuring the organist running through a selection of originals and standards with guitarist Quentin Warren and drummer Donald Bailey in tow. The vibe is relaxed, not too laid-back but hardly energetic, as the trio easily strolls through bluesy ballads and lightly swinging soulful ballads. It's damning with faint praise to say that nothing exceptional ever happens but it doesn't *need* to happen, but that is truly the case here. *Bucket!* is simply a middle-of-the-road affair, not quite boring but never quite compelling either. It's good easy-listening music, finding an organ master kicking out seven tunes (the 2000 CD reissue contains nine cuts, including the previously unreleased "Trouble in Mind" and an alternate take of "Sassy Mae") without any pressure and with a minimal sense of style. That makes for a pretty good record, one that hardcore fans will find satisfying after they've exhausted the greater Smith sessions, but not one that will captivate the attentions of anyone who isn't a dyed-in-the-wool Jimmy Smith aficionado. *—Stephen Thomas Erlewine*

The Cat / Apr. 27, 1964-Apr. 29, 1964 / Verve ♦♦♦♦

Got My Mojo Workin'/Hoochie Cooche Man / Dec. 16, 1965-Jun. 14, 1966 / Verve ♦♦♦♦
After leading a series of notable jam sessions for Blue Note, organist Jimmy Smith signed a lucrative contract with Verve in 1962. Throughout the remainder of the decade, he recorded songs that ranged from treasures to trash, turning most of the music into bluesy vamps. On this CD, a reissue of the LPs *Got My Mojo Workin'* and *Hoochie Cooche Man*, Smith's repertoire ranges from Billy Strayhorn's "Johnny Come Lately" and Oliver Nelson's "Blues and the Abstract Truth" to "I'm Your Hoochie Coochie Man" and "I Can't Get No Satisfaction." In most cases, Smith's versions bear little resemblance to the original recordings. The earlier set has Smith featured with both a quartet and an octet arranged by Oliver Nelson. The remainder of the CD is a big band with Nelson's charts making the orchestra as exuberant as Smith's solos. Overall, the CD is not as essential as Jimmy Smith's better Blue Note dates, but is a worthwhile acquisition for fans of the jazz organ due to his enthusiasm and his ability to uplift the material. *—Scott Yanow*

Peter and the Wolf / May 11, 1966-May 12, 1966 / Verve ♦♦♦♦♦
Of all of organist Jimmy Smith's big-band albums recorded for Verve, this is one of the most imaginative ones. Oliver Nelson arranged a variety of themes from Prokofiev's *Peter & the Wolf* into a swinging suite featuring the great organist Jimmy Smith. Although there is no verbal narrative on this LP, Nelson's liner notes tell the story (which can actually be followed through the music) and Smith pays respect to the original melodies while making strong statements of his own. A classic of its kind. *—Scott Yanow*

☆ **The Dynamic Duo** / Sep. 21, 1966-Sep. 28, 1966 / Verve ♦♦♦♦♦
Creed Taylor matched two of his most famous artists, Wes Mongomery and Jimmy Smith, on this session (Montgomery's last for Verve), and the results are incendiary—a near-ideal meeting of yin and yang. Smith comes at your throat with his big attacks and blues runs while Montgomery responds with rounder, smoother octaves and single notes that still convey much heat. They are an amazing pair, complementing each other, driving each other, using their bop and blues taproots to fuse together a sound. The romping, aggressive big band charts—Oliver Nelson at his best—on "Down by the Riverside" and "Night Train," and the pungently haunting chart for Gary McFarland's "13" (Death March)" still leave plenty of room for the soloists to stretch out. "James And Wes" and "Baby, It's Cold Outside" include drummer Grady Tate and conguero Ray Barretto, with Smith's own feet working the organ pedals. The *Verve Master Edition* reissue also includes an alternate take of "O.G.D." with Tate and Barretto, a track previously surfacing on a long-gone *Encyclopedia of Jazz* anthology LP from the '60s—a neat bonus that makes this the preferred version. *—Richard S. Ginell*

The Further Adventures of Jimmy and Wes / Sep. 21, 1966-Sep. 28, 1966 / Verve ♦♦♦♦

☆ **Root Down** / Feb. 8, 1972 / Verve ♦♦♦♦♦
Toward the end of his stint with Blue Note, Jimmy Smith's albums became predictable. Moving to Verve in the mid-'60s helped matters considerably, since he started playing with new musicians (most notably nice duets with Wes Montgomery) and new settings, but he never really got loose, as he did on select early Blue Note sessions. Part of the problem was that Smith's soul-jazz was organic and laid-back, *relaxed* and funky instead of down and dirty. For latter-day listeners, aware of his reputation as the godfather of modern soul-jazz organ (and certainly aware of the Beastie Boys' name drop), that may mean that Smith's actual albums all seem a bit tame and restrained, classy, not funky. That's true of the bulk of Smith's catalog, with the notable exception of *Root Down*. Not coincidentally, the title track is the song the Beasties sampled on their 1994 song of the same name, since this is one of the only sessions that Smith cut where his playing his raw, vital, and earthy. Recorded live in Los Angeles in February 1972, the album captures a performance Smith gave with a relatively young supporting band who were clearly influenced by modern funk and rock. They push Smith to playing low-down grooves that truly cook: "Sagg Shootin' His Arrow" and "Root Down (And Get It)" are among the hottest tracks he ever cut, especially in the restored full-length versions showcased on the 2000 Verve *By Request* reissue. There are times where the pace slows, but the tension never sags, and the result is one of the finest, most exciting records in Smith's catalog. If you think you know everything about Jimmy Smith, this is the album for you. *—Stephen Thomas Erlewine*

Off the Top / Jun. 7, 1982 / Elektra ♦♦♦♦

Go for Whatcha' Know / Jan. 2, 1986-Jan. 3, 1986 / Blue Note ♦♦♦♦

Fourmost / Nov. 16, 1990-Nov. 17, 1990 / Milestone ♦♦♦♦

Damn! / Jan. 24, 1995-Jan. 25, 1995 / Verve ♦♦♦♦

Dot Com Blues / Jan. 9, 2001 / Blue Thumb ♦♦♦

Lonnie Liston Smith

b. Dec. 28, 1940, Richmond, VA

Keyboards, Piano / Crossover Jazz, Post-Bop, Fusion, Jazz-Funk, Urban

Not to be confused with organist Dr. Lonnie Smith, keyboardist/pianist Lonnie Liston Smith started out playing straight-ahead acoustic jazz before becoming better known for embracing fusion, crossover, soul and funk with his 1970s band the Cosmic Echoes. Smith was born in Richmond, VA, but it was in New York that Smith started getting a lot of work as a jazz pianist in the 1960s. Greatly influenced by McCoy Tyner but quite distinctive himself, Smith played acoustic piano as a sideman for Pharoah Sanders, Rahsaan Roland Kirk, Betty Carter and Gato Barbieri but turned to fusion when Miles Davis hired him as an electric keyboardist in the early 1970s. By 1973, Smith was ready to lead a band of his own and formed the Cosmic Echoes with his brother, singer Donald Smith. The improviser made his recording debut as a leader with 1973's *Astral Traveling* and continued to fare well in the fusion/crossover realm with such imaginative gems as 1974's *Cosmic Funk* and 1975's *Expansions*. The atmospheric fusion, crossover, soul and funk that Smith played on his Cosmic Echoes dates of the 1970s had a very spiritual, mystic bent—if anyone bridged the gap between John Coltrane and Earth, Wind & Fire, it was Smith. He moved from RCA to Columbia with 1978's *Loveland*, and the 1980s found Smith recording for Doctor Jazz. In 1986, Smith surprised his followers with *Make Someone Happy*, an excellent acoustic trio date that found him returning to straight-ahead post-bop and interpreting standards. Unfortunately, the early 1990s weren't great years for Smith, who recorded some radio-oriented, formulaic NAC sessions that left much to be desired creatively. In fact, one could say that from a creative standpoint, he reached an all time low with 1991's *Magic Lady*. But Smith returned to a Cosmic Echoes-type sound on 1998's *Transformation*, which reunited him with his brother Donald. *—Alex Henderson*

Astral Travelling / 1973 / Flying Dutchman ♦♦♦♦♦

Lonnie Liston Smith was 32 when, in 1973, he finally got around to recording his first album as a leader, *Astral Traveling*. By that time, the pianist/keyboardist had a great deal of sideman experience under his belt, and this superb debut made it clear that former employers like Pharoah Sanders, Rahsaan Roland Kirk, Gato Barbieri, and Betty Carter had taught him well. One hears a lot of Sanders, John Coltrane, and McCoy Tyner influence on *Astral Traveling;* Smith obviously shares their passion for all things spiritual. Nonetheless, this LP leaves no doubt that the improviser is very much his own man and has a wealth of brilliant ideas of his own; thankfully, he has a cohesive band to help him carry them out. On *Astral Traveling*, Smith's 1973 edition of the Cosmic Echoes includes George Barron on soprano and tenor sax, Joe Beck on guitar, Cecil McBee on bass, David Lee Jr. on drums, James Mtume and Sonny Morgan on percussion, Badal Roy on Indian tabla drums, and Geeta Vashi on the Indian tamboura. An impressive lineup, and one that shows a great understanding of Smith's spiritual nature. Ninety-five percent of the time, *Astral Traveling* is serene and tranquil; but on "I Mani (Faith)," the unexpected interesting happens when Barron goes outside during his sax solo and gets into the type of dissonant, forceful screaming one would expect from Albert Ayler or late-period Coltrane. "I Mani (Faith)" has a hauntingly peaceful melody, but Barron's out-of-left-field solo makes it the most avant-garde track that Smith ever recorded as a leader. Produced by the late Bob Thiele—an eclectic heavyweight who worked with everyone from Coltrane, Ayler, and Charles Mingus to Coleman Hawkins, Count Basie, and Louis Armstrong—*Astral Traveling* is among Smith's most essential and rewarding albums. *—Alex Henderson*

● **Golden Dreams** / 1973-1976 / Bluebird/RCA ♦♦♦♦♦

This CD reissue has all ten selections from keyboardist Lonnie Liston's Smith album *Reflections of a Golden Dream*, plus four of the six cuts from his 1973 debut as a leader. The performances are essentially high-quality mood music, funky and a bit fusion-oriented, yet with moments of creativity. The personnel differs on most selections, with such supporting players as (on the 1973 set) bassist Cecil McBee and guitarist Joe Beck and in 1976 Donald Smith on flute and vocals, the reeds of David Hubbard and some background singers. A good introduction to Lonnie Liston Smith's early recordings. *—Scott Yanow*

Live / May 19, 1977-May 21, 1977 / RCA ♦♦♦♦♦

Recorded live at *Smucker's Cabaret* in Brooklyn, NY, in 1976, this superb LP is the only live album that Lonnie Liston Smith provided in the 1970s. It's also one of the most essential and improvisatory recordings he ever came out with. Smith and his band, the Cosmic Echoes, don't hesitate to let loose during this performance, which finds them bringing a very adventurous spirit to gems like "Watercolors" and "Sorcercess." Vocalist Donald Smith is in excellent form on "Expansions," "Visions of a New World," and "My Love," and there are many inspired solos by keyboardist/pianist Smith as well as saxman Dave Hubbard and guitarist Ronald Dean Miller. Though the Cosmic Echoes maintain their ethereal qualities, their playing definitely has a tougher edge on stage. *—Alex Henderson*

Watercolors / 1991 / Jive/Novus ♦♦♦♦♦

Dr. Lonnie Smith

Organ (Hammond), Organ / Hard Bop, Soul-Jazz, Jazz-Funk

Organist Lonnie Smith has often been confused with keyboardist/pianist Lonnie Liston Smith—and, in fact, more than a few retailers have wrongly assumed that they're one and the same. In the mid-1960s, the Hammond hero earned recognition for his membership in George Benson's classic quartet before going on to play with Lou Donaldson (contributing some memorable solos to the alto saxman's hit 1967 album *Alligator Boogaloo*) and recording enjoyable dates of his own for Blue Note. For all their accessibility and commercial appeal, funk-influenced Smith sessions like 1968's *Think* and 1970's *Drives* showed that he could be quite imaginative. Smith, who later entered academia and became Dr. Lonnie Smith, remained an inspired representative of soul-jazz and did some solid work with Donaldson in the '90s. *—Alex Henderson*

● **Think!** / Jul. 23, 1968 / Blue Note ♦♦♦♦♦

Organist Lonnie Smith's second recording as a leader and first of two for Blue Note is one of his strongest dates. Teamed up with trumpeter Lee Morgan, tenor saxophonist David Newman, guitarist Melvin Sparks, drummer Marion Booker, Jr. and three percussionists, Smith performs R&B-ish material in a soul-jazz vein. With Morgan and Newman playing stimulating solos and the leader keeping the performances grooving, the music is both accessible and challenging. This CD reissue is well worth picking up. *—Scott Yanow*

Move Your Hand / Aug. 9, 1969 / Blue Note ♦♦♦♦

Move Your Hand was recorded live at *Club Harlem* in Atlantic City on August 9, 1969. Organist Lonnie Smith led a small combo—featuring guitarist Larry McGee, tenor saxist Rudy Jones, bari saxist Ronnie Cuber, and drummer Sylvester Goshay—through a set that alternated originals with two pop covers, the Coasters' "Charlie Brown" and Donovan's "Sunshine Superman." Throughout, the band works a relaxed, bluesy, and, above all, funky rhythm; they abandon improvisation and melody for a steady groove, so much that the hooks of the two pop hits aren't recognizable until a few minutes into the track. No one player stands out, but *Move Your Hand* is thoroughly enjoyable, primarily because the group never lets their momentum sag throughout the session. Though the sound of the record might be somewhat dated, the essential funk of the album remains vital. *—Stephen Thomas Erlewine*

Drives / Jan. 2, 1970 / Blue Note ♦♦♦

Lonnie Smith had the raw skills, imagination, and versatility to play burning originals, bluesy covers of R&B and pop, or skillful adaptations of conventional jazz pieces and show tunes. Why he never established himself as a consistent performer remains a mystery, but this 1970 reissue shows why he excited so many people during his rise. Smith's solos on "Spinning Wheel" and his own composition, "Psychedelic PI," are fleet and furious, boosting the songs from interesting to arresting. He's also impressive on "Seven Steps to Heaven," while the array of phrases, rhythms, and voicings on "Who's Afraid of Virginia Woolf?" demonstrate a mastery of the organ's pedals and keys rivaling that of the instrument's king, Jimmy Smith. *—Ron Wynn*

Live at Club Mozambique / May 21, 1970 / Blue Note ♦♦♦♦♦

Recorded on May 21, 1970, at Detroit's Club Mozambique, this was shelved and remained unreleased until it was retrieved for CD issue in 1995. It's odd that Blue Note decided to sit on it for so long, because it ranks as one of Lonnie's better sets. The band, featuring George Benson on guitar, is relaxed and funky without being in your face about it, and unlike much soul-jazz of the time, most of the material is original, Smith having penned six of the eight numbers. Although the riffs often owe a lot to James Brown, this is definitely at least as much jazz as soul, with Lonnie taking a rare vocal turn on "Peace of Mind." *—Richie Unterberger*

Afro Blue / Jun. 17, 1993 / Music Masters ♦♦♦

The Turbanator / Jun. 9, 1991 / 32 Jazz ♦♦♦

Stuff Smith (Leroy Smith)

b. Aug. 14, 1909, Portsmouth, OH, **d.** Sep. 25, 1967, Munich, Germany

Violin / Swing

Stuff Smith was one of the big three of pre-bop violinists along with Joe Venuti and Stephane Grappelli. Many of his fans said that he could outswing all of his competitors and certainly Stuff was a major force on the bandstand. Smith, who cited Louis Armstrong as his main influence, studied music with his father and played with the family band as a child. His first major job and recordings were with Alphonse Trent's territory band in the 1920s but it was not until 1936 that he had his breakthrough. Leading a quintet at the Onyx Club with trumpeter Jonah Jones, Smith's comedy vocals and hard-swinging approach made the group a hit on 52nd Street for several years; his novelty "I'se a Muggin'" became a hit. Smith worked regularly with his trios in the 1940s but was in danger of being forgotten in the '50s when Norman Granz recorded him fairly extensively for Verve; Stuff also participated in Nat King Cole's After Midnight sessions for Capitol. The violinist moved to Copenhagen in 1965 and was active until his death two years later. *—Scott Yanow*

☆ **Stuff Smith (1936-1939)** / Feb. 11, 1936-Dec. 1939 / Classics ♦♦♦♦♦

This delightful CD has the first 24 titles ever led by violinist Stuff Smith, virtually all of Smith's prewar recordings and the complete output of the violinist's Onyx Club Boys (other than four songs from 1940). With trumpeter Jonah Jones and sometimes drummer Cozy Cole the stars of the supporting cast, this was one of the top swing combos of the era. Smith's hard-swinging violin, his enthusiastic vocals and his interplay with Jones made this a particularly hot unit. In addition to the hit "I'se A Muggin," highlights of the disc include "I Hope Gabriel Likes My Music," "After You've Gone," "You'se a Viper," "Old Joe's Hittin' The Jug," "Twilight In Turkey" and the classic "Here Comes the Man With the Jive." Highly recommended. *—Scott Yanow*

Stuff Smith-Dizzy Gillespie-Oscar Peterson / Jan. 21, 1957-Apr. 17, 1957 / Verve ♦♦♦♦♦

The great swing violinist Stuff Smith had not recorded as a leader since 1945 when producer Norman Granz got him to make three albums for Verve during a three-month period. Smith, who was still very much in his prime, recorded 11 selections (one previously unissued) with pianist Carl Perkins, either Red Callender or Curtis Counce on bass and Oscar Bradley or Frank Butler on drums (*Have Violin Will Swing*), jammed nine numbers (three released for the first time here) with the Oscar Peterson Trio (for the album titled *Stuff Smith*), and on five tunes teamed up with trumpeter Dizzy Gillespie and a rhythm section (*Dizzy Gillespie-Stuff Smith*); all are reissued in full on this generous two-CD set from 1994. In each of the settings, the violinist excels, making this an easily recommended and very satisfying release. *—Scott Yanow*

● **Live at the Montmartre** / Mar. 18, 1965 / Storyville ♦♦♦♦♦

Although he passed away in 1967, violinist Stuff Smith (who moved to Europe in 1965) did a fair amount of recording during his final two years. His CD reissue has an exciting concert from Copenhagen's Montmartre featuring Smith with pianist Kenny Drew, bassist Niels Pedersen and drummer Alex Riel. Stuff Smith never did decline, as he shows on hard-swinging versions of such songs as his "Skip It," "Take The 'A' Train," "Bugle Blues" and "Mack the Knife." *—Scott Yanow*

The Complete Verve Stuff Smith Sessions / Oct. 25, 1956-Oct. 22, 1959 / Mosaic ✦✦✦✦✦

Wadada Leo Smith

b. Dec. 18, 1941, Leland, MS

Trumpet / Avant-Garde Jazz, Avant-Garde Jazz, Free Jazz

A consistently adventurous trumpeter who has stuck to playing avant-garde jazz throughout his career, Leo Smith's dry, introverted style (which makes extensive use of space) is a strong contrast to the more jubilant flights of Lester Bowie. Smith originally played drums, mellophone and French horn before settling on trumpet. He gained early experience performing in R&B groups and played in an Army band while serving in the military. By 1967, Leo Smith was a member of Chicago's AACM. He soon helped to found the Creative Construction Company, an innovative trio with violinist Leroy Jenkins and multi-instrumentalist Anthony Braxton that toured Europe in the late 1960s. Smith, who was involved in making the documentary film *See the Music* in 1970, formed the New Dalta Ahkri in New Haven, Connecticut, an influential if underdocumented band that at times included Henry Threadgill, Anthony Davis and Oliver Lake. Smith studied ethnomusicology in the mid-'70s at Wesleyan, played with Braxton in 1976 and recorded with Derek Bailey's Company; has freelanced with his own diverse groups during the past 20 years. After becoming a Rastafarian in the 1980s, he changed his name to Wadada Leo Smith. He has been teaching at Cal Arts since 1993. Leo Smith, who founded the Kabell label in 1971, has also recorded for Freedom, Moers, ECM, Nesssa, FMP, Black Saint, Nessa and Sackville in settings ranging from unaccompanied solos to a big band. *—Scott Yanow*

Mass on the World / May 1978 / Moers ✦✦✦✦✦

Go in Numbers / Jan. 19, 1980 / Black Saint ✦✦✦✦✦

● **Rastafari** / Jun. 12, 1983 / Sackville ✦✦✦✦✦
Few of trumpeter Leo Smith's recordings are readily available, making this introspective but very interesting collaboration with soprano saxophonist Bill Smith, violinist David Prentice, bassist David Lee and vibraphonist Larry Potter an important release. The playing by these adventurous musicians is advanced and quite free on the four group originals, and all five players share equally in the creation of these fresh explorations. *—Scott Yanow*

Tao-Njia / May 7, 1996 / Tzadik ✦✦✦✦
Tao-Njia is a good album that's interesting, if not very active. Wadada Leo Smith's group Nda-Kulture performs the opening piece, "Another Wave More Waves," on an unusual instrumentation that works wonderfully: Smith switches between trumpet and flugelhorn while David Philipson plays two low drums and a frame drum, and Mika Noda performs on vibraphone, timpani, and tubular bells. The second piece, "Double Thunderbolt," is a composition in six parts composed as a memorial for Don Cherry. It begins with Smith playing bamboo flute, adding a Far Eastern meditative quality. A variety of Eastern bells and other instruments are rung as Harumi Makino Smith reads her poetry for two of the sections, followed each time by Smith soloing on trumpet. The final piece, and title track, is performed by the California EAR Unit and guests. Incorporating personal philosophy and beliefs into his compositions through mood and accompanying texts, Smith creates a warm album of spiritual instrumental music. *—Joslyn Layne*

Light upon Light / Jul. 20, 1999 / Tzadik ✦✦✦
Wadada Leo Smith's second recording for the Tzadik label, *Light Upon Light*, is more spacious and a little colder than his first, *Tao-Njia*. It consists of five compositions performed by varying lineups, including his group N'Da Kulture. The opening composition is performed by California's EAR Unit, who are also heard on *Tao-Njia*. "Moths, Flames, and the Giant Sequoia Redwood Trees" is a slightly atmospheric, scenic piece that includes the welcome presence of Vicki Ray's piano playing. Following this is a rather dramatic solo viola composition, on which high vibratos hint at the lower harmonic and melodic modes that the heard notes are only a variant of, or harmony to. Next comes "MultiAmerica," a work of sound effects, spoken word, and Smith's trumpet. "Nur," performed by New Century Players, was composed for the bassist Bertram Turetzky. It starts out minimal, with bass clusters, until celesta and harmonium toll in more activity and the composition gradually swells toward crescendo, then drops into a fast dwindle before actually peaking. During "A Thousand Cranes: A Memorial for Amir Hamzehi," Mark Trayle achieves accordion-like effects through electronics, while Smith provides slow trumpet statements that reverb and fade. *—Joslyn Layne*

Golden Quartet / Jan. 3, 2000 / Tzadik ✦✦✦✦✦
Wadada Leo Smith's third Tzadik release finds him in a modern jazz quartet of seasoned jazz cats and legendary improvisers. Pianist Anthony Davis, bassist Malachi Favors Magoustous, and drummer Jack DeJohnette join Smith in creating an unhurried, mature and, frankly, atypical Tzadik release in that even though it may sound somewhat free to more conservative ears, it is hardly antagonistic and is unmistakably a piano jazz quartet. Regardless of classification, this is an album of excellent jazz that is so fresh and well executed as to define and remind what's great about listening to the music. It's a pleasant surprise that such an incredible lineup of musicians can come together and yield a musical sum still greater than what you would expect, when considering the individual "parts." The opening cut, "DeJohnette," is dedicated to the drummer and offers him a space to romp and roll during a busy solo. In fact, all of the musicians take quite active solos during this piece, which is followed by a tender and softly played number dedicated, appropriately, to Smith's wife Harumi Makino Smith. Following this comes the upswing of "Celestial Sky . . . ," which begins with Smith's muted trumpet that is soon joined by anticipatory drums and bass that seem to barely reign in their excitement and need to run ahead, with Davis taking a mind-filling piano solo that crowns him the standout of this song's performance. The closing track, a hot, fast-moving piece named "America's Third Century Spiritual Awakening," is another highlight of this impressive album. *Golden Quartet* is Wadada Leo Smith's strongest date as a leader in quite some time and certainly is his best among Tzadik's catalogue. *—Joslyn Layne*

Willie "The Lion" Smith

b. Nov. 25, 1897, Goshen, NY, **d.** Apr. 18, 1973, New York, NY

Piano / Classic Jazz, Stride, Piano Blues

Willie "The Lion" Smith in the 1920s was considered one of the big three of stride piano (along with James P. Johnson and Fats Waller) even though he made almost no recordings until the mid-'30s. His mother was an organist and pianist and Smith started playing piano when he was six. He earned a living playing piano as a teenager, gained his nickname "the Lion" for his heroism in World War I and after his discharge he became one of the star attractions at Harlem's nightly rent parties. Although he toured with Mamie Smith (and played piano on her pioneering 1920 blues record "Crazy Blues"), Smith mostly freelanced throughout his life. He was an influence on the young Duke Ellington (who would later write "Portrait of the Lion") and most younger New York-based pianists of the 1920s and '30s. Although he was a braggart and (with his cigar and trademark derby hat) appeared to be a rough character, Smith was actually more colorful than menacing and a very sophisticated pianist with a light touch. His recordings with his Cubs (starting in 1935) and particularly his 1939 piano solos for Commodore (highlighted by "Echoes of Spring") cemented his place in history. Because he remained very active into the early '70s (writing his memoirs *Music on My Mind* in 1965), for quite a few decades Willie "the Lion" Smith was considered a living link to the glory days of early jazz. *—Scott Yanow*

1925-1937 / Nov. 5, 1925-Sep. 15, 1937 / Classics ✦✦✦✦✦
Willie "The Lion" Smith, one of stride piano's Big Three of the 1920s (along with James P. Johnson and Fats Waller), recorded a lot less than his two friends. In fact, with the exception of two selections apiece with the Gulf Coast Seven in 1925 (which features trombonist Jimmy Harrison and clarinetist Buster Bailey) and 1927's Georgia Strutters (starring singer Perry Bradford, Harrison, and cornetist Jabbo Smith), along with the rare and originally unreleased 1934 solo piano showcase "Finger Buster," this CD does not get started until 1935. Smith's Decca recordings of 1935 and 1937 were formerly quite obscure, showcasing his piano with three different versions of "His Cubs." The Lion is heard with a Clarence Williams-type quartet which includes cornetist Ed Allen and clarinetist Cecil Scott, matched up with trumpeter Dave Nelson and clarinetist Buster Bailey in a septet; and temporarily heading an early version of the John Kirby Sextet on a session dominated by drummer O'Neil Spencer's vocals. Highlights of this historic and enjoyable CD include "Santa Claus Blues," "Keep Your Temper," "Blues, Why Don't You Let Me Alone," and the earliest recording of the Lion's most famous composition, "Echo of Spring." *—Scott Yanow*

★ **1938-1940** / Nov. 30, 1938-Feb. 17, 1940 / Classics ✦✦✦✦✦
This is the one Willie "The Lion" Smith CD to get. The bulk of the release features Smith on 14 piano solos from Jan. 10, 1939 performing six standards and eight of his finest compositions. Although Smith (with his derby hat and cigar) could look quite tough, he was actually a sensitive player whose chord structures were very original and impressionistic. On such numbers as "Echoes of Spring" (his most famous work), "Passionette," "Rippling Waters" and "Morning Air," Smith was at his most expressive. In addition, this CD has a couple of collaborations with fellow pianists Joe Bushkin and Jess Stacy and a four-song 1940 swing/dixieland 1940 session with an octet featuring trumpeter Sidney DeParis. Because of the classic piano solos, this memorable set is quite essential. *—Scott Yanow*

Lucky Roberts and Willie The Lion Smith: Harlem Piano Solos / Good Time Jazz ✦✦✦
Vintage stride and boogie solos from the great pianist Willie "The Lion" Smith, as well as some answering and complementing playing from his longtime friend and friendly rival Luckey Roberts. *—Ron Wynn*

Muggsy Spanier (Francis Joseph Spanier)

b. Nov. 9, 1906, Chicago, IL, **d.** Feb. 12, 1967, Sausalito, CA

Cornet / Dixieland

Muggsy Spanier was a predictable but forceful cornetist who rarely strayed far from the melody. Perfectly at home in Dixieland ensembles, Spanier was also an emotional soloist (equally influenced by King Oliver and Louis Armstrong) who was an expert at using the plunger mute. He started on cornet when he was 13, played with Elmer Schoebel's band in 1921 and first recorded in 1924. Spanier was a fixture in Chicago throughout the decade (appearing on several important early records) before joining Ted Lewis in 1929. Although Lewis was essentially a corny showman, Spanier's solos gave his band some validity during the next seven years. After a stint with Ben Pollack's orchestra (1936-38), Spanier became seriously ill and was hospitalized for three months. After he recovered, the cornetist formed his famous eight-piece "Ragtime Band" and recorded 16 Dixieland performances for Bluebird (later dubbed "the Great 16") that virtually defined the music of the Dixieland revival movement. But because his group actually preceded the revival by a couple years, it soon had to break up due to lack of work! Muggsy joined Bob Crosby for a time, had his own short-lived big band, freelanced with Dixieland bands in New York and starting in 1950 he gradually relocated to the West Coast. During 1957-59 Spanier worked with Earl Hines' band and he continued playing up until his retirement in 1964, touring Europe in 1960 and always retaining his popularity in the Dixieland world. *—Scott Yanow*

☆ **The Great Sixteen** / Jul. 7, 1939-Dec. 12, 1939 / Bluebird ✦✦✦✦✦
During four sessions in 1939 cornetist Muggsy Spanier performed definitive versions of 16 Dixieland standards that, due to the joy of the music and its huge influence on the future revival movement, would later be dubbed "The Great 16." This CD, which adds eight alternate takes, could have been subtitled "The Great 24." Spanier and his octet (which includes trombonist George Brunies, clarinetist Rod Cless, usually pianist Joe Bushkin, and several different tenors) roar their way through such songs as "Big Butter and Egg Man," "That Da Da Strain," "I Wish I Could Shimmy Like My Sister Kate," "Dinah," and "Mandy, Make up Your Mind." Classic music. *—Scott Yanow*

Muggsy Spanier 1939-1942 / 1993 / Classics ✦✦✦✦✦

The Complete V-Disc Sessions 1944-1945 / Oct. 17, 1944-Oct. 22, 1945 / Storyville ✦✦✦✦✦
This 1997 reissue CD has all of the music (with one unfortunate exception) from three very

interesting and generally heated V-Disc sessions of 1944-45. Cornetist Muggsy Spanier leads an impressive octet (with trombonist Lou McGarity, clarinetist Pee Wee Russell and tenorman Boomie Richman) on five numbers including "That's A Plenty" and "Pee Wee Speaks," which has an eccentric "vocal" by the clarinetist. He also heads a slightly later octet that includes McGarity, clarinetist Peanuts Hucko and Bud Freeman on tenor. In addition to the master takes of five selections, there are also seven breakdowns and three full-length alternate takes. The final set is Freeman's famous V-Disc session with trumpeter Yank Lawson, trombonist Bill Mustarde and Hucko. While "Love Is Just Around the Corner" and "Coquette" are excellent performances, "For Musicians Only" and "The Latest Thing In Hot Jazz" are famous satires with Freeman making fun of various then-current musical trends. But unfortunately, his often-hilarious, two-minute verbal introduction of the former is unaccountably missing. Other than that flaw, this is a CD that all trad jazz fans will enjoy. Freeman (particularly on the various versions of "You Took Advantage of Me") is the main star. *—Scott Yanow*

★ **Manhattan Masters** / Mar. 1, 1945-Mar. 2, 1945 / Storyville ♦♦♦♦♦
When one thinks of the year 1945 in relationship to jazz history, the bebop revolution comes quickly to mind for some listeners, while others may think of the end of the big band era. However, at that point in time, the Dixieland revival was also gaining momentum. Many of the top classic jazz musicians who came to maturity in the 1920s were still only in their forties at the most, and, if anything, had grown as players through the years even while the continual evolution of jazz was in danger of passing them by. Certainly cornetist Muggsy Spanier, a basic but sincere and heartfelt improviser, and the eccentric and highly original clarinetist Pee Wee Russell were in peak form in 1945, as shown on the 18 selections that comprise this consistently exciting CD. With a supporting cast that includes Lou McGarity or Miff Mole on trombone, sometimes Ernie Caceres on baritone and rhythm sections headed by pianist Gene Schroeder, Spanier and Russell romp their way through a variety of Dixieland warhorses and a few original blues. Among the many highlights are "I Can't Give You Anything But Love," "I'm Sorry I Made You Cry," "That's A Plenty," "You're Lucky to Me" and "My Honey's Lovin' Arms." Although some Dixieland dates by the mid-1950s could be a bit tired and predictable, the music in the 1940s usually had a fresh excitement and a joy that is difficult to resist; both Spanier and Russell rarely sounded better. Dixieland fans can consider this 1998 CD reissue to be essential. *—Scott Yanow*

James Spaulding

b. Jul. 30, 1937, Indianapolis, IN
Sax (Alto), Flute / Hard Bop, Post-Bop
A superior alto saxophonist and flutist who can shift from bop and hard bop to very adventurous flights, James Spaulding gained his greatest recognition while a member of Freddie Hubbard's Quintet in the mid-1960's. He studied at the Chicago Cosmopolitan School of Music and then gigged and recorded regularly with Sun Ra during 1957-61. During the 1960s, Spaulding (who worked with Max Roach and Randy Weston) was in demand not only by Hubbard, but for Blue Note recordings by Joe Henderson, Wayne Shorter, Stanley Turrentine and Larry Young, among others. He had stints during the next couple of decades with a wide variety of top artists, including Charles Tolliver, Bobby Hutcherson, David Murray and (for a brief period) the World Saxophone Quartet, but is still vastly underrated. James Spaulding has recorded as a leader for Storyville (a Duke Ellington tribute set in 1976) and several dates for Muse (1988-93). *—Scott Yanow*

● **Brilliant Corners** / Nov. 25, 1988 / 32 Jazz ♦♦♦♦♦
James Spaulding is a very distinctive altoist and flutist whose inside/outside playing can cover anything from bop to freer improvisations. On what was surprisingly only his third recording as a leader, Spaulding is heard at the peak of his powers, leading a quartet/quintet also including pianist Mulgrew Miller, bassist Ron Carter, drummer Kenny Washington, and (on half of the selections) trumpeter Wallace Roney. They perform six Thelonious Monk tunes (including the complex title cut, the lyrical "Ask Me Now," and "Little Rootie Tootie") plus Bud Powell's "Down With It" and Miles Davis' "Little Willie Leaps." Spaulding takes four songs apiece on alto and flute, and this is his definitive recording. *—Scott Yanow*

Smile of the Snake / Dec. 3, 1996-Dec. 4, 1996 / High Note ♦♦♦♦♦
One of the most underrated saxophonists of the post-1960 era, James Spaulding has long been a passionate postbop altoist and a warm flutist. On this superior outing he is heard in top form on both of his axes (plus two appearances on bass flute) in a quartet with pianist Richard Wyands, bassist Ron McClure and drummer Tony Reedus. Producer Donald Sickler helped advise Spaulding on the material and the result is a high-quality set of obscurities by Wyands, McClure, Clifford Jordan, Donald Brown, Geoff Keezer and Idrees Sulieman. Spaulding digs into the songs, displays a great deal of versatility and certainly has his fiery moments. One of James Spaulding's finest allround recordings. *—Scott Yanow*

Escapade / Apr. 28, 1999 / High Note ♦♦♦♦
Well-swung standards and compositions of Kenny Dorham, Dexter Gordon, Grant Green and Hank Mobley are tapped for revision. Don Sickler (trumpet/flugelhorn) joins Spaulding for eight of the ten tracks, with the immaculate trio of pianist John Hicks, bassist Ray Drummond and drummer Kenny Washington as support. Spaulding's tart-sweet alto sax has never sounded better, while his pristine flute playing is easily in the top ten of late-'90s jazz performers. The CD is bookended by Dorham's music, the opening title track a flute/flugelhorn traipse through classic Blue Notesville in a light Afro-Cuban beat, the closer "La Mesha" a flute/flugel ballad. Mobley's music comes back to back, as jungle toms and light bluesy swing signify the easy mood of "High Modes," with flute and muted trumpet in unison, while the classic post-bop vehicle "The Breakthrough" has alto and trumpet strutting their stuff and puffing their chests. Gordon's similarly classic bopper "Cheesecake" has Sickler's flugelhorn playing a countermelody *vis a vis* Spaulding's standard alto line, and they do the same for the hip, churning melody of Grant Green's "Grant's Tune," except that Spaulding changes up on the tenor-led original by using his flute. The three numbers without Sickler are the scorching bop of "Just One of Those Things," the easy bossa beat of Duke Ellington's "Warm Valley," and the ballad treatment, on flute, of the final Mobley piece "Madeline." Spaulding shows a consistency within mainstream parameters, a real sense of teamwork with these worthy session mates, and a willingness to take chances. *—Michael G. Nastos*

Spyro Gyra

f. 1974, Buffalo, NY
Group / Smooth Jazz, Crossover Jazz, Jazz-Pop, Fusion
Founded in 1974 by altoist Jay Beckenstein, Spyro Gyra has consistently been one of the commercially successfully pop-jazz groups of the past 20 years. Although originally a studio group, the band became a full-time venture in 1979 and has been touring ever since. Critics love to attack this band's lightweight and rarely changing music, which combines R&B and elements of pop and Caribbean music with jazz, but its live performances are often stimulating—unlike many of its records, which emphasize the danceable melodies at the expense of improvising. Spyro Gyra independently recorded their debut album, releasing the record on the local independent label Amherst in 1976. The record slowly became a success and Amherst sold the rights to the band to Infinity Records, a division of MCA. *Morning Dance*, their first album for Infinity, was released in 1979. The record became a major hit, spawning a Top 40 single with "Morning Dance" and going platinum. *Morning Dance* firmly placed Spyro Gyra as one of the most popular artists in contemporary jazz, and throughout the '80s, their popularity continued growing. In 1990, Spyro Gyra moved to GRP and released *Fast Forward*, their first of six studio albums for GRP. *—Scott Yanow & Stephen Thomas Erlewine*

Catching the Sun / 1980 / Amherst ♦♦♦♦
One among many similar-sounding but highly popular albums by premier fusion ensemble Spyro Gyra. The group's songs usually contained catchy melodies, prominent backbeats, and some room for improvisational expression, although it was limited and required quick bursts rather than expansive statements. They were and still are near the top in the light jazz and fusion field. *—Ron Wynn*

Incognito / 1982 / Amherst ♦♦♦♦♦

● **Access All Areas** / Nov. 17, 1983-Nov. 19, 1983 / Amherst ♦♦♦♦♦
An excellent live double album, it includes live versions of songs from early albums. *—Paul Kohler*

City Kids / 1983 / Amherst ♦♦♦♦

Alternating Currents / 1985 / Amherst ♦♦♦♦
Featured is great songwriting and playing, and nice work by keyboardist Tom Schuman. *—Paul Kohler*

Breakout / 1986 / Amherst ♦♦♦♦♦
An album with more midtempo jazz-style tunes and nice arrangements, it features Julio Fernandez and synth programming by Eddie Jobson. *—Paul Kohler*

Dreams Beyond Control / 1993 / GRP ♦♦♦♦♦
Spyro Gyra mostly sticks to their formula of danceable melodic music on this GRP release but there are a few temporary departures. The harmonica of the talented Howard Levy is used prominently on "Breakfast at Igor's," two different horn sections pop up on a few songs and there are a pair of throwaway pop vocals from Alex Ligertwood. However, longtime Spyro Gyra fans have little to fear for the solos of saxophonist Jay Beckenstein and vibraphonist Dave Samuels are predictably pleasant, the light funk rhythms push the ensembles and the band's sound remains distinctive, familiar and comfortable. *—Scott Yanow*

Road Scholars / 1997 / GRP ♦♦♦♦♦
As boring and formula-driven as Spyro Gyra has often been in the studio, the band's live shows of the 1980s and 1990s could be just the opposite—exciting, loose and spontaneous. This stems from the fact that on stage, Spyro wasn't catering to commercial radio's rigid formats, and was much more inclined to take risks, improvise and gamble with inspiration. Undeniably Spyro's best release of the 1990s, *Road Scholars* documents its 1997 tour and finds saxman/leader Jay Beckenstein, keyboardist Tom Schuman, guitarist Julio Fernandez and others in generally good form. Spyro sounds inspired rather than calculated on familar material like "Morning Dance" and "Shaker Song," and meaty solos are the rule. *Road Scholars'* only studio offering is "Best Friends," a routine, pedestrian number with a Najee-meets-George Howard flavor. But on the whole, the release of this CD proved to be a pleasant surprise. *—Alex Henderson*

Mike Stern

b. Jan. 10, 1953, Boston, MA
Guitar / Post-Bop, Fusion
A rocking, experimental guitarist who rose to fame playing in a pair of Miles Davis's bands, Mike Stern's a competent bebop and hard bop player, but excellent fusion and jazz-rock musician. He's provided some wondrous riffs, blistering lines, complex voicings and dynamite phrases doing fusion, playing with much more force and vigor than on more conventional jazz. Stern attended Berklee in the early '70s, where he studied with Pat Metheny and Mick Goodrick. Metheny recommended him for a vacancy with Blood, Sweat And Tears, and Stern played with them two years. He later worked with Billy Cobham, then joined Davis' band in 1981. Stern stayed with him two years, then played with Jaco Pastorius' group "Word Of Mouth." Stern made his recording debut as a leader in 1985; He later toured with Davis again, played with Steps Ahead, and worked in bands led by Mike Brecker and Harvie Swartz. Stern's recorded as a leader for Atlantic in the '80s and '90s. He has several sessions available as a leader. *—Ron Wynn and Michael G. Nastos*

Upside Downside / Mar. 1986-Apr. 1986 / Atlantic ♦♦♦♦
Mike Stern's debut as a leader mostly features the high-powered guitarist heading a sextet also including tenor saxophonist Bob Berg, keyboardist Mitch Forman, bassist Mark Egan, drummer Dave Weckl and percussionist Dr. Gibbs. Altoist David Sanborn makes a guest appearance on "Goodbye Again," while "Mood Swings" features the quartet of Stern, Berg, electric bassist Jaco Pastorius (with whom Stern had worked in the Word of Mouth Orchestra)

and drummer Steve Jordan. The guitarist wrote or co-wrote all six selections, which generally have viable chord changes. The playing mostly fits into the genre of funky fusion, with Stern's passionate guitar heard throughout in fine form. *—Scott Yanow*

Time in Place / Dec. 1987 / Atlantic ✦✦✦✦
Guitarist Mike Stern's music has often been a little difficult to classify, featuring strong improvisations, the sound and power of rock, and elements of funk, R&B and sometimes pop. For his second recording as a leader, Stern is joined by either Bob Berg or Michael Brecker on tenor, keyboardist Jim Beard, electric bassist Jeff Andrews, drummer Peter Erskine and percussionist Don Alias; Don Grolnick sits in on organ during "No Notice." The music (seven Stern originals) ranges from the rhythmic to the more sophisticated and features plenty of the leader's high-powered guitar. *—Scott Yanow*

● **Standards (and Other Songs)** / 1992 / Atlantic ✦✦✦✦✦
Guitarist Mike Stern, best-known for playing rock-oriented fusion and in more commercial settings, surprised many listeners by recording an album dominated by standards. Actually there are three originals included among the 11 pieces but Stern also digs into such songs as "Like Someone in Love," "Moment's Notice," Chick Corea's "Windows" and "Straight No Chaser." Among Stern's sidemen on this fairly straightahead but adventurous set are trumpeter Randy Brecker, Bob Berg on tenor, and keyboardist Gil Goldstein. This little-known release is well worth acquiring before it inevitably goes out of print. *—Scott Yanow*

Play / Dec. 1998-Jan. 1999 / Atlantic ✦✦✦✦
Mike Stern is a preeminent guitarist for two key reasons: One, he can play all styles very well and with equal command; and two, he plays very well with all other players. He always shows great respect for those with whom he is playing and gives them each the time and space to develop their musical ideas. Stern displays these two qualities in abundance on *Play*. Several notable guests join Stern and his core band for this release. Guitarists John Scofield and Bill Frisell and drummer Dennis Chambers each team with Stern on several tracks. If you enjoy straight-ahead jazz, listen to Stern and Scofield on the title track, or mix in Bob Malach's tenor sax on "Outta Town." If you like your guitar music slightly more spacious and lyrical, try Stern and Frisell on the hypnotic "Blue Tone" or the pensive "All Heart." Finally, if you want to turn up the heat and move into some rock/funk-influenced fusion, then check out the groovy "Tipatina's," the bold rocker "Link," or the intensely funky "Big Kids." It is no surprise, based on his other work, that Chambers, in particular, gives the band a kick in the musical pants inspiring bassist Lincoln Goines to enjoy the ride. *Play* is an outstanding guitar album from the highly accomplished and incredibly versatile Mike Stern. It is highly recommended. *—Brian Bartolini*

Sonny Stitt (Edward Stitt)

b. Feb. 2, 1924, Boston, MA, **d.** Jul. 22, 1982, Washington, D.C.
Sax (Tenor), Sax (Alto) / Bop
Charlie Parker has had many admirers and his influence can be detected in numerous styles, but few have been as avid a disciple as Sonny Sitt. There was almost note-for-note imitation in several early Stitt solos, and the closeness remained until he began de-emphasizing the alto in favor of the tenor, on which he artfully combined the influences of Parker and Lester Young. Stitt gradually developed his own sound and style, though he was never far from Parker on any alto solo. A wonderful blues and ballad player whose approach was one of the influences on John Coltrane, he could rip through an uptempo bebop stanza, then turn around and play a shivering, captivating ballad. *—Ron Wynn and Bob Porter*

Sonny Stitt with Bud Powell and J.J. Johnson / Oct. 17, 1949-Jan. 26, 1950 / Prestige/OJC ✦✦✦✦✦
This superb CD reissues the complete output of three classic bop sessions including five "new" alternate takes. Sonny Stitt (who plays tenor throughout) is heard in a quintet with trombonist J.J. Johnson, pianist John Lewis, bassist Nelson Boyd and drummer Max Roach (playing three Johnson compositions and the original version of John Lewis's "Afternoon in Paris") and in a quartet with the great pianist Bud Powell, bassist Curly Russell and Max Roach. The latter two sessions are highlighted by rapid versions of "All God's Chillun Got Rhythm," "Strike up the Band" and "Fine and Dandy." Highly recommended music. *—Scott Yanow*

Prestige First Sessions, Vol. 2 / Feb. 17, 1950-Aug. 14, 1951 / Prestige ✦✦✦✦✦
Sonny Stitt is heard in his early prime throughout this CD, sticking to tenor on all but two of the 24 selections. Few could play bebop with Stitt's sincerity, quick reflexes and large vocabulary. He swings hard throughout the performances, most of which feature him as the only soloist. Three dull vocals aside (by the forgotten Teddy Williams and Larry Townsend), this gapfilling CD is highly recommended to fans of classic bebop. *—Scott Yanow*

Kaleidoscope / Oct. 8, 1950-Feb. 25, 1952 / Prestige/OJC ✦✦✦✦✦
Some of Sonny Stitt's better early sessions are collected together on this excellent CD. Stitt (switching between tenor, alto and on two numbers baritone) is heard with a variety of small groups ranging from quartets to an octet with three trumpeters and is the main star throughout these boppish performances. Highlights include "Cherokee," "Liza," "This Can't Be Love" and "Stitt's It." Recommended. *—Scott Yanow*

New York Jazz / Sep. 14, 1956 / Verve ✦✦✦✦
When Sonny Stitt was hot, and had a mind to, he could play most inspired music. *New York Jazz* was recorded in 1956 with Jimmy Jones (piano), Ray Brown (bass) and Jo Jones (drums), and it was a serious, but average (good) session. *—Bob Rusch, Cadence*

Sits in with the Oscar Peterson Trio / Oct. 10, 1957-May 18, 1959 / Verve ✦✦✦✦✦
This CD combines together a complete session that Sonny Stitt (doubling on alto and tenor) did with the 1959 Oscar Peterson Trio (which includes the pianist/leader, bassist Ray Brown and drummer Ed Thigpen) and three titles from 1957 with Peterson, Brown, guitarist Herb Ellis and drummer Stan Levey. The music very much has the feel of a jam session and, other than a themeless blues, all of the songs are veteran standards. Highlights of this fine effort include "I Can't Give You Anything but Love," "The Gypsy," "Scrapple from the Apple," "Easy Does It" and "I Remember You." Lots of cooking music. *—Scott Yanow*

Stitt Meets Brother Jack / Feb. 16, 1962 / Prestige/OJC ✦✦✦✦
Sonny Stitt (who sticks on this CD reissue to tenor) meets up with organist Brother Jack McDuff (along with guitarist Eddie Diehl, drummer Art Taylor and Ray Barretto on congas) for a spirited outing. Two standards ("All of Me" and "Time After Time") are performed with a variety of blues-based originals and the music always swings in a soulful boppish way. Worth picking up although not essential. *—Scott Yanow*

Boss Tenors in Orbit / Feb. 1962 / Verve ✦✦✦✦✦

Autumn in New York / 1962-Oct. 18, 1967 / 1201 Music ✦✦✦
This Black Lion CD combines together four selections from a quintet session featuring altoist Sonny Stitt, trumpeter Howard McGhee, pianist Walter Bishop, bassist Tommy Potter and drummer Kenny Clarke (three boppish blues and a Stitt feature on "Lover Man") with four selections showcasing Stitt with unknown accompaniment from a 1962 date at *Birdland*. The saxophonist recorded so many sessions that it is not necesssary to acquire them all to get a good sampling of his playing (particularly since his style was virtually unchanged after the mid-'50s), but the CD has its heated moments. *—Scott Yanow*

Stitt Plays Bird / Jan. 29, 1963 / Atlantic ✦✦✦✦✦
Sonny Stitt forged his own approach to playing bebop out of the sound and style of Charlie Parker, so this tribute album (reissued through Rhino on CD) was a very logical project. With fine support from guitarist Jim Hall, pianist John Lewis, bassist Richard Davis and drummer Connie Kay, Stitt performs ten Charlie Parker compositions, plus Jay McShann's "Hootie Blues"; these renditions of "Now's The Time" and "Yardbird Suite" were previously unreleased. Stitt, who mastered bebop and could play hot licks in his sleep, is in top form on such numbers as "Constellation," "Confirmation" and "Ko-Ko," making this an essential item for straight-ahead jazz fans (although the prolific altoist would record eight other albums in 1963 alone). *—Scott Yanow*

Salt and Pepper / Jun. 10, 1963-Sep. 5, 1963 / GRP/Impulse! ✦✦✦✦✦
This 72-minute CD starts off with one of the underrated gems of the 1960s, an exciting matchup by tenors Sonny Stitt and Paul Gonsalves. Other than the brief throwaway "Theme From Lord of the Flies" (producer Bob Thiele's idea), this is very much a jam session set, with "Salt and Pepper" being a heated medium-tempo blues and the two competitive tenors stretching out on "S'posin'" and a lengthy "Perdido." Actually, the most memorable selection from the date is the one on which Stitt switches to alto, "Stardust." His beautiful playing behind Gonsalves' warm melody statement raises the session to the classic level. Also included on this consistently exciting CD is a Sonny Stitt quartet set originally titled *Now*. Although Stitt (doubling on alto and tenor) recorded scores of quartet sessions, he sounds particularly inspired here, especially on such offbeat material as "Estralita," the Dixieland standard "Please Don't Talk About Me When I'm Gone," and "My Mother's Eyes." Highly recommended to bebop and straight-ahead jazz fans. *—Scott Yanow*

Soul People / Aug. 25, 1964-1966 / Prestige ✦✦✦✦✦
There are dozens of Sonny Stitt records available at any particular time; this CD reissue is one of the better ones. Mostly sticking to tenor, Stitt battles fellow tenor Booker Ervin with assistance from the fine organist Don Patterson and drummer Billy James on five selections and a ballad medley from 1964. Because both Stitt and Ervin always had very individual sounds, their tradeoffs are quite exciting and end up a draw. Among the "bonus" cuts of this CD are a feature for Patterson with a trio in 1966 ("There Will Never Be Another You") and a collaboration between Stitt, Patterson, James and guitarist Grant Green on a 1966 version of "Tune Up." Enjoyable and generally hard-swinging music. *—Scott Yanow*

Sonny Stitt . . . Pow! / Sep. 10, 1965 / Prestige ✦✦✦✦
Altoist Sonny Stitt and trombonist Benny Green make for a potent team on this spirited quintet set. With the exception of the lone standard "I Want to Be Happy," all of the material is obscure. However, the two distinctive horns (along with pianist Kirk Lightsey, bassist Herman Wright and drummer Roy Brooks) have little difficulty essaying these bop pieces, blues and ballads, and their personable styles match well together. This LP has been out of print for quite awhile, so grab it if you see it. *—Scott Yanow*

Legends of Acid Jazz / Jan. 4, 1971-Jul. 9, 1971 / Prestige ✦✦✦
This CD reissues the complete contents of two former Lp's by saxophonist Sonny Stitt: *Turn It On* and *Black Vibrations*. These are rather unusual entries in Stitt's huge discography in that Sonny often sounds like a guest performer on his own sessions rather than the leader. During the earlier date, Stitt uses an electrical device (a Varitone) on his tenor that waters down his tone a bit. With organist Leon Spencer, guitarist Melvin Sparks and drummer Idris Muhammad setting down unrelenting grooves on most of the five numbers (including the 11-minute title cut), Stitt only seems to be making cameo appearances although trumpeter Virgil Jones gets in a few good solos on three of the numbers. The later date (which also has some good Jones trumpet) finds Stitt playing acoustically and switching to alto on two of the six jams, but once again it is the nonstop chugging of Sparks, Muhammad and either Leon Spencer or guest organist Don Patterson that fuels the fire. It is silly to call these soul jazz outings "acid jazz" since Sonny Stitt's solos are essentially bebop, but the grooves are danceable and funky. *—Scott Yanow*

★ **Endgame Brilliance: Constellation & Tune-Up** / Feb. 8, 1972-Jun. 27, 1972 / 32 Jazz ✦✦✦✦✦
Although the "endgame" part of this CD's title is not quite accurate (the sets from 1972 were made a decade before Sonny Stitt's passing), the "brilliance" definitely fits. Two of the prolific saxophonist's most exciting sessions ever were his Muse albums *Constellation* and *Tune-Up*. This essential single CD reissues the complete contents of both dates. Strangely enough, *Constellation* is listed in this set as having been recorded June 27, 1971 (it is actually from 1972) and thus cut earlier, so it takes up the first (rather than the second) half of this CD. On both dates, Stitt (doubling on tenor and alto) is joined by the superb bop pianist Barry Harris and bassist Sam Jones with either Roy Brooks or Alan Dawson on drums. Stitt, who recorded many quartet sets through the years, was very inspired on both of these occasions.

His renditions of "Constellation," "Webb City," "Just Friends" and "Groovin' High" in particular are quite memorable. The high point is a 9 1/2-minute version of "I Got Rhythm" that features the classic saxophonist first taking a long solo on tenor and then following it up with an equally stunning flight on alto. A master of the bebop vocabulary, the competitive Sonny Stitt would have deserved fame if he had only recorded these two sessions and not bothered with the other 150 albums he led. This CD is essential for all bebop collections. *—Scott Yanow*

☆ **Tune-Up!** / Feb. 8, 1972 / Muse ♦♦♦♦♦
Sonny Stitt recorded over 100 albums as a leader and several dozen in a quartet setting in his productive career but this one ranks at the top. The bebop tenor and alto stylist is very inspired by the top-notch rhythm section (pianist Barry Harris, bassist Sam Jones and drummer Alan Dawson) and has rarely sounded more heated than on "Tune Up," "Idaho," "Just Friends" and "Groovin' High." However it is his nine-minute jam on "I Got Rhythm" (which finds Stitt taking blazing solos on both tenor and alto) that is the highpoint of this essential set. *—Scott Yanow*

12! / Dec. 12, 1972 / 32 Jazz ♦♦♦♦♦
Sonny Stitt was in prime form in the early '70s when he recorded two classics: *Tune Up* and *Constellation. 12!* from a year later tends to get overlooked but this album is also one of the saxophonist's most rewarding recordings. Assisted by pianist Barry Harris, bassist Sam Jones and drummer Louis Hayes, Stitt (switching between alto and tenor) is in superb form on five standards and two blues; highlights include "I Got It Bad," "Every Tub" and "Our Delight." *—Scott Yanow*

In Walked Sonny / May 16, 1975 / Sonet ♦♦♦♦♦
Stitt joined Art Blakey's Jazz Messengers for this hard-swinging LP, and he fits quite comfortably with the quintet (which includes the leader/drummer, trumpeter Bill Hardman, Dave Schnitter on tenor, pianist Walter Davis, Jr, and bassist Chin Suzuki). In addition to the title cut (a Sonny Stitt original), Stitt is in top form on "Blues March," "It Might as Well Be Spring," Freddie Hubbard's "Birdlike," and "I Can't Get Started"; he sits out on Davis' "Ronnie's a Dynamite Lady." The members of the Messengers sound inspired by Stitt's presence, and everyone is in fine form on this excellent hard bop session. *—Scott Yanow*

My Buder Bird / 1977 / Catalyst ♦♦♦♦

In Style / Mar. 18, 1981 / 32 Jazz ♦♦♦♦
Sonny Stitt (heard on both alto and tenor) is in excellent form for this CD reissue, yet another quartet date; he led over 100 sessions through the years. With pianist Barry Harris, bassist George Duvivier and drummer Jimmy Cobb inspiring him, Stitt is creative within the boundaries of bebop on such songs as "Just You, Just Me," "Is You Is or Is You Ain't My Baby," "Yesterdays" and a pair of his basic originals which he titled "Western Style" and "Eastern Style." *—Scott Yanow*

Just in Case You Forgot How Bad He Really Was / Sep. 1981 / 32 Jazz ♦♦♦♦
Although Joel Dorn's 32 Jazz label mostly concentrates on repackaging reissues from the Muse catalog, there have been some important discoveries. This 1997 CD has a previously unreleased Sonny Stitt club appearance that took place in San Francisco's *Keystone Korner* in Sept. 1981. It is a special all-star concert in which Stitt splits his time between tenor and alto and is joined by pianist Cedar Walton, bassist Herbie Lewis, drummer Billy Higgins and (on a few numbers) vibraphonist Bobby Hutcherson, altoist Richie Cole, and John Handy on alto and tenor. Stitt, a master of the bebop vocabulary, was not an innovator, but he was a fiery competitor who could blow most musicians off the stand when he chose to. In this case, he had a lot of respect for Cole and Handy, but still played at his best, just in case. The CD is mostly a showcase for the leader, who is well featured on the ad-lib "Dig Dr. Woody's Blues," "Everything Happens to Me" and "Laura." Other than a five-song ballad medley that features each of the saxophonists plus Walton and Hutcherson, not that much is heard from Handy, while Cole (who gets in a few good licks) is generally overshadowed by Stitt. Other highlights include lengthy renditions of "Lover Man" and "Wee." Sonny Stitt recorded scores and scores of bop-oriented sessions throughout his productive career, but his fans will still be happy that 32 Jazz has added such a strong date to his discography. Recommended. *—Scott Yanow*

Last Stitt Sessions, Vols. 1 & 2 / Jun. 8, 1982-Jun. 9, 1982 / 32 Jazz ♦♦♦♦♦
It is difficult to believe after listening to this two-CD set, that Sonny Stitt only had six weeks left in his life; he already had cancer but did not know it. Switching between tenor and alto, Stitt on the first disc is heard in top form with pianist Junior Mance, bassist George Duvivier, and drummer Jimmy Cobb while the second CD (recorded the following day) adds trumpeter Bill Hardman and has Walter Davis in Mance's place. As was typical of Stitt's career, the music throughout is high-quality bebop with the saxophonist stretching out creatively over common chord changes. This double CD (a straight reissue of two single LPs) shows that Sonny Stitt went out on top. *—Scott Yanow*

Legends of Acid Jazz: Sonny Stitt/Don Patterson, Vol. 2 / Sep. 23, 1968-Sep. 24, 1968 / Prestige ♦♦♦
Two-for-one CD reissue combines two 1968 sessions, both featuring Stitt and Patterson, that were recorded on consecutive days (September 23-24, 1968), although one was issued under Patterson's name and the other under Stitt's. The first six songs were issued as the Patterson LP *Funk You!*, on which Patterson leads a date that also has Sonny Stitt and Charles McPherson on saxes, and Pat Martino on guitar. The other players get about as much space as Patterson, and as 1960s jazz with organ goes, this is pretty straight-ahead and boppish, rather than soul-jazz (as so much organ jazz from that decade was). For the bop factor, listen especially to the cover of Sonny Rollins' "Airegin," and on which Martino in particular shines. Patterson does get in a more soulful mood on his composition "Little Angie," which has an elegiac mood somewhat similar to occasional slow instrumentals cut by Booker T. & the MG's during that period. The other eight songs were issued as the Stitt LP *Soul Electricity!*, an album that got its name because for this session, Stitt plugged his alto and tenor saxophones into a Varitone attachment. What came out, though, was not fusion by any means, but a pretty straight-ahead session that found Sonny his usual competent self. The program is actually on the conservative side, leaning toward standards. Stitt's quartet is rounded out by Don Patterson on organ, Billy Butler on guitar, and Billy James on drums. This isn't the most logical package—Stitt's half is more straight-ahead in flavor and, more importantly, neither album fits too well into the soul-jazz or acid-jazz category—but for fans of either artist, the material is worth hearing. *—Richie Unterberger*

Just the Way It Was: Live at the Left Bank / Sep. 26, 2000 / Label M. ♦♦♦
The second of two premier releases from Label M and the archives of The Left Bank Jazz Society of Baltimore, MD (along with *My Foolish Heart* from Stan Getz). One of Sonny Stitt's many performances for The Left Bank was recorded in March 1971 and is the source of this set. Stitt's electric saxophone, of course, is the main attraction. And while the treatment of the instrument scuttles some of its tone, with Stitt at the mouthpiece (he was the first to record the instrument, back in 1966), the electric tenor sax is more than just a novelty. The traditional "John Brown's Body" proves to be the set's highlight. *—John Duffy*

Billy Strayhorn

b. Nov. 29, 1915, Dayton, OH, **d.** May 31, 1967, New York, NY
Piano, Composer, Arranger / Swing
An extravagantly gifted composer, arranger and pianist—some considered him a genius—Billy Strayhorn toiled throughout most of his maturity in the gaudy shadow of his employer, collaborator and friend, Duke Ellington. Only in the last decade has Strayhorn's profile been lifted to a level approaching that of Ellington, where diligent searching of the Strayhorn archives (mainly by David Hajdu, author of the excellent Strayhorn bio *Lush Life*) revealed that Strayhorn's contribution to the Ellington legacy was far more extensive and complex than once thought. There are several instances where Strayhorn compositions were registered as Ellington/Strayhorn pieces ("Day Dream," "Something to Live For"), where collaborations between the two were listed only under Duke's name ("Satin Doll," "Sugar Hill Penthouse," "C-Jam Blues"), where Strayhorn pieces were copyrighted under Ellington's name or no name at all. Even tunes that were listed as Strayhorn's alone have suffered; the proverbial man on the street is likely to tell you that "Take the 'A' Train"—perhaps Strayhorn's most famous tune—is a Duke Ellington song. Still, among musicians and jazz fans, Strayhorn is renowned for acknowledged classics like "Lotus Blossom," "Lush Life," "Rain Check," "A Flower Is a Lovesome Thing" and "Mid-Riff." While tailored for the Ellington idiom, Strayhorn's pieces often have their own bittersweet flavor, and his larger works have coherent, classically influenced designs quite apart from those of Ellington. *—Richard S. Ginell*

Billy Strayhorn Trio / Oct. 3, 1950-Nov. 1950 / Mercer ♦♦♦

The Peaceful Side / May 1961 / United Artists ♦♦♦♦
This is a little-known and rather melancholy set, virtually Billy Strayhorn's only recording away from the world of Duke Ellington. The focus is totally on Strayhorn's piano throughout his interpretations of ten of his compositions (including "Lush Life," "Take the 'A' Train," and "Something to Live For"). Three selections have the Paris Blue Notes adding sparse wordless vocals, two other numbers add some quiet playing by the Paris String Quartet, and bassist Michel Goudret is on five of the ten selections (including one apiece with the strings and the voices). "Strange Feeling" and "Chelsea Bridge" are taken as unaccompanied piano solos. Of the ten songs, only "Just A-Sittin' and A-Rockin'" hints at happiness; otherwise, Strayhorn's melodic and concise playing is quite somber, peaceful in volume but filled with inner tension. *—Scott Yanow*

● **Lush Life** / Jan. 14, 1964-Aug. 14, 1965 / Red Baron ♦♦♦♦♦
Although not initially released until 1992, 25 years after composer Billy Strayhorn's death, this is his definitive CD. Strayhorn is heard singing "Lush Life" while backed by the Duke Ellington Orchestra in 1964 (his voice is not strong but his phrasing is quite sincere), jamming on piano with flugelhornist Clark Terry and Bob Wilbur (on clarinet and soprano) in a quintet, backing singer Ozzie Bailey and taking a pair of piano solos ("Love Came" and "Baby Clementine"). These are very valuable and intriguing recordings, shedding some new light on a nearly invisible genius. *—Scott Yanow*

String Trio of New York

f. 1979
Group / Avant-Garde Jazz, Post-Bop
The String Trio of New York has long been one of the more accessible avant-garde jazz units, not afraid to use melodies and swing even during its more advanced group improvisations. Formed in 1979, the band originally consisted of violinist Billy Bang, guitarist James Emery and bassist John Lindberg. In the late 1980s Bang departed and was replaced by Charles Burnham, and then in 1993 Regina Carter became the group's regular violinist. The trio has recorded rewarding sets for Black Saint, ITM (an obscure effort with singer Jay Clayton), Stash and Arabesque. *—Scott Yanow*

Rebirth of a Feeling / Nov. 25, 1983-Nov. 26, 1983 / Black Saint ♦♦♦♦♦
The String Trio of New York's strongest lineup was arguably the edition that included violinist Billy Bang, guitarist James Emery and bassist John Lindberg. That unit was at its best here; the threesome played adventurous unison lines and offered wide-ranging solos. The best example of their interactive/reactive mode was the 14-minute "Utility Grey," with its array of textures, colors, moods and voicings. Emery wrote two selections, Bang a pair, and Lindberg the finale, but this was a unified effort. The String Trio of New York ranks as a premier outside group of the 1970s and '80s. *—Ron Wynn*

● **Intermobility** / Jul. 1, 1992-Jul. 2, 1992 / Arabesque ♦♦♦♦♦
The 1992 edition of the String Trio of New York consisted of original members James Emery on guitar and bassist John Lindberg plus the great violinist Regina Carter. In addition to two originals apiece by Emery and Lindberg and one by Carter, the unique inside/outside group performs Wayne Shorter's "Ju-Ju," Ornette Coleman's "Peace," Eric Dolphy's "17 West," Th-

elonious Monk's "Ruby My Dear," Herbie Nichols' rarely played "House Party Starting" and a bop medley on this well-rounded CD. Due to the diversity of material, the adventurous improvisations and the high musicianship, this release serves as a perfect introduction to the music of the String Trio of New York. *— Scott Yanow*

Blues . . . ? / Oct. 6, 1993-Oct. 6, 1993 / Black Saint ✦✦✦✦
The String Trio of New York, which since 1991 has consisted of violinist Regina Carter, guitarist James Emery and bassist John Lindberg (the latter two were founding members in 1979), is often classified as an avant-garde group due to its unusual instrumentation and chancetaking improvisations. However this Black Saint release is among their most accessible. Although not all of the nine performances are blues (Duke Ellington's obscure "I'm Afraid" is a ballad and calling "Hurry Up and Wait" a reggae blues is stretching the point a bit), all of the selections are given blues feeling. In addition to five diverse originals (including an eccentric country blues "Bellyachin' Blues"), the group performs the Ellington piece (which was apparently never recorded by Duke), Lee Morgan's "Speedball," a mournful version of "Freddie Freeloader" and a six-song Charlie Parker blues suite which purposely slows down and speeds up in spots to jarring effect. With the exception of the latter (which ends inconclusively), this is a successful effort, well worth seeking out by adventurous listeners. *— Scott Yanow*

Faze Four: A Twenty Year Retrospective / Nov. 16, 1997-Nov. 17, 1997 / Black Saint ✦✦✦✦
Although sometimes classified as "avant-garde," much of the music on this outing by the String Trio of New York is fairly straightforward, at least until the final two selections. The group's new violinist, Diane Monroe, fits into the intuitive and fairly explorative music quite well, and she swings hard in spots. Melodic originals alternate with classics by Thelonious Monk, Duke Ellington and Charles Mingus. Mingus' rarely recorded "Pithecanthropus Erectus" is a high point, while the violinist's "Groovin' Roots" finds the trio sounding like a very advanced folk music group. The last two numbers, a concise free improvisation ("Introspections") and bassist John Lindberg's episodic "Circular Views," inspire the String Trio to really push itself. The communication is so strong between the players (Lindberg and guitarist James Emery have been playing together regularly since 1977) that one gets the feeling they could stretch their music a lot more in the future. Although this CD is really not a "20-year retrospective" (there are no compositions from the band's earlier violinists, nor any renditions of "greatest hits"), it does serve as a good excuse to celebrate the unique band's longevity. *— Scott Yanow*

Steve Swallow

b. Oct. 4, 1940, Fair Lawn, NJ
Bass / Post-Bop
Steve Swallow has long been many jazz critics' favorite electric bassist for, rather than playing his instrument in a rock-oriented manner, Swallow emphasizes the high notes and approaches the electric bass to an extent as if it were a guitar. He originally started on piano and trumpet before settling on the acoustic bass as a teenager. Swallow joined the Paul Bley trio in 1960 and with Bley was a part of an avant-garde version of the Jimmy Giuffre 3 during 1960-62. Swallow recorded with George Russell and was a member of Art Farmer's quartet (1962-65), Stan Getz's band (1965-67) and an important edition of Gary Burton's quartet (1967-70). The latter group (starting with the addition of guitarist Larry Coryell) was actually one of the first fusion groups and it was during that time that Swallow began playing electric bass; within a few years he stopped playing acoustic altogether. Swallow spent a few years in the early '70s living in Northern California during which he mostly playing locally. Since the late '70s he has been closely associated with Carla Bley's groups although he occasionally works on other projects (including a reunion of the Jimmy Giuffre 3). Steve Swallow has also proved to be a talented composer with "Eiderdown," "Falling Grace," "General Mojo's Well Laid Plan" and "Hotel Hello" being among his better-known pieces. *— Scott Yanow*

Swallow / Sep. 1991-Nov. 1991 / ECM ✦✦✦✦✦
All nine cuts were written by this premier electric bass guitarist and performed by a sextet with guests Gary Burton (vib) and John Scofield (g). *— Michael G. Nastos*

Real Book / Dec. 1993 / ECM ✦✦✦✦
If Steve Swallow is known primarily as an ace session bassist, it's not because his compositions are less than top-notch. This program finds him showing off his considerable writing chops with the help of an all-star group: trumpeter Tom Harrell, saxophonist Joe Lovano, pianist Mulgrew Miller and drummer Jack DeJohnette. His focus on the upper registers and the polyester tone of his five-string bass guitar will continue to annoy those who prefer to hear the bass played dark, low and woody, but there's no denying the consistent inventiveness of his playing or the charm of these compositions. *— Rick Anderson*

● **Deconstructed** / Dec. 1996 / ECM ✦✦✦✦✦
This CD by electric bassist Steve Swallow is a major surprise, for his ten originals are essentially bebop, often using chord changes that sound familiar; for example, the opening "Running in the Family" uses the chords of "Basin Street Blues." The song titles tend to be humorous if inscrutable (including "Another Fine Mess," "I Think My Wife Is a Hat," and "Name That Tune"), but the spirited playing is quite serious. Tenor saxophonist Chris Potter (on his way to becoming one of the greats) and trumpeter Ryan Kisor have plenty of solo space, guitarist Mick Goodrick makes his presence felt, and drummer Adam Nussbaum offers stimulating support. This rare straight-ahead outing by Steve Swallow sounds fresh, lively and creative, and it is one of his most rewarding recordings as a leader. *— Scott Yanow*

Lew Tabackin

b. May 26, 1940, Philadelphia, PA
Sax (Tenor), Flute / Hard Bop
Lew Tabackin is one of the few jazz musicians who has been able to develop completely different musical personalities on two instruments. As a tenor saxophonist, he is a hard-driving, tough-toned player reminiscent of Sonny Rollins, Don Byas, and sometimes, tone-wise, Ben Webster. But as a flutist, he sounds like a highly expressive master of Asian classical music. Whether heard as the main soloist with his wife Toshiko Akiyoshi's Jazz Orchestra or jamming with a small group, Tabackin has been a masterful player for the past 30 years.

Tabackin studied at the Philadelphia Conservatory from 1958-62 as a flute major. After serving in the Army and moving to New York in 1965, he worked with Maynard Ferguson, the Thad Jones-Mel Lewis Orchestra, Joe Henderson, Elvin Jones, and the Tonight Show Band, among others. From 1968-69, he was a main soloist with the Danish Radio Orchestra. After marrying Toshiko Akiyoshi, he toured Japan with her (1970-71). When they moved to Los Angeles in 1972, they formed her orchestra, which, thanks to Akiyoshi's arrangements and Tabackin's solo talents, became one of the top jazz big bands. In 1982, they relocated to New York, where the orchestra has continued on a part-time basis. Lew Tabackin has since played in many different small groups, remaining a brilliant improviser. He has recorded as a leader on an occasional basis through the years, most notably for Inner City (1974-77), Ascent (1979) and Concord (starting in 1989). *— Scott Yanow*

● **Desert Lady** / Dec. 1989 / Concord Jazz ✦✦✦✦✦
The great tenor-saxophonist and flutist Lew Tabackin is joined by pianist Hank Jones, bassist Dave Holland and drummer Victor Lewis on this well-rounded program. The Concord CD has many highlights including "Hot House," Duke Ellington's "Serenade To Sweden," Tabackin's "A Bit Byas'd" and "You Leave Me Breathless"; the leader's tenor in particular is in top form. Highly recommended to fans of straightahead jazz, this release gives one a strong sampling of Lew Tabackin's talents. *— Scott Yanow*

I'll Be Seeing You / Apr. 16, 1992-Apr. 17, 1992 / Concord Jazz ✦✦✦✦✦
Lew Tabackin, whose extroverted tone on tenor (influenced most by Don Byas and Ben Webster) contrasts with the Eastern sound that he gets on flute, is teamed quite successfully with pianist Benny Green, bassist Peter Washington and drummer Lewis Nash on this Concord CD. The repertoire, mostly lesser-known standards like John Coltrane's "Wise One" and Thelonious Monk's "In Walked Bud," is well-treated by these masterful musicians. *— Scott Yanow*

What a Little Moonlight Can Do / Apr. 4, 1994-Apr. 5, 1994 / Concord Jazz ✦✦✦✦
The deep, smooth tenor sax tones of Ben Webster and Coleman Hawkins are clearly the models that Lew Tabackin patterns his playing after on this album featuring his quartet. The sax giants' influence can clearly be seen on "What a Little Moonlight Can Do," on which Tabackin plays above the melody, concluding with Webster's patented fluttering, whispering tone. Tabackin's playing throughout this session, irrespective of the tempo, is contemplative, exploring every nook and cranny, every nuance, every subtlety of each tune. He and his quartet travel winding roads of complex and interesting improvisations, always managing to return to the basic melody unscathed. He gives himself plenty of time for each journey, with most of the tunes running more than six minutes in length but never becoming boring or repetitive. Tabackin and his quartet caress "Easy Living," with Benny Green's piano getting significant exposure. "I Wished on the Moon," made famous by Billie Holiday, is done more like a tango than the swinging number it became in the hands of Lady Day. There are two non-standards on the album. Jimmy Knepper's "Leave of Absinthe," based on the chord changes to "Lullaby of the Leaves," is a vehicle for Tabackin's flute playing, while Tabackin's "Broken Dreams," commissioned by his wife, bandleader Toshiko Akiyoshi, is a lovely ballad, again with Green's piano in the vanguard. The rhythm section backing Tabackin is world-class, with Green, Peter Washington on bass, and Lewis Nash on drums. Playing professionally since the 1960s, Tabackin shows that almost 30 years later, he hasn't lost any of his passion for the music. *— Dave Nathan*

Pyramid / Jul. 20, 1999 / Koch ✦✦✦✦
Lew Tabackin's guest appearance with the Netherlands Metropole Orchestra is one of the most enjoyable in their series of collaborations with jazz soloists. Tabackin is a swinging tenor saxophonist and a top notch flute player as well, playing both on the exciting opener by Duke Ellington, "Battle Royal" and showcasing his lyrical flute on "Speak Low." In addition to his outstanding playing throughout the CD, he composed the haunting bittersweet ballad "Broken Dreams." Most of the arrangements by conductor Rob Pronk complement Tabackin's playing without overwhelming him with excessive strings. This is a very well-crafted release worth purchasing. *— Ken Dryden*

Horace Tapscott

b. Apr. 6, 1934, Houston, TX
Piano / Avant-Garde Jazz, Post-Bop
Horace Tapscott has long been Los Angeles's top undiscovered legend, a brilliant pianist who has thus far only recorded for the tiniest (and most obscure) of labels. A powerful player perfectly able to interpret bop but heard at his best playing his own rhythmic originals with his quartet, Tapscott has had an original style for 30 years but his music is surprisingly accessible even at its most passionate. Tapscott caught the tail end of the legendary Central Avenue Scene (his early associates included Eric Dolphy and Don Cherry) and played with Gerald Wilson's Orchestra during 1950-51. He returned to Los Angeles in 1961, formed the Pan Afrikan Peoples Arkestra and has been a major part of the local jazz community ever since. Tapscott's recordings have mostly been made for Nimbus along with a pair of live sessions for Hat Art and one release for Arabesque. *— Scott Yanow*

The Giant Is Awakened / Apr. 1, 1969-Apr. 3, 1969 / Flying Dutchman ✦✦✦✦✦

West Coast Hot / Apr. 1969 / Jive/Novus ✦✦✦✦✦

Flight 17 / 1978 / Nimbus ✦✦✦✦
Other than half an album cut in 1969 for Flying Dutchman (which was shared with the John Carter/Bobby Bradford group), this release was pianist Horace Tapscott's recording debut as a leader. Tapscott's Pan-Afrikan Peoples Arkestra (consisting of two pianos, six reeds, two trombones, Red Callender on tuba, cello, two basses, a drummer, and a percussionist) had an unusual sound and made three records during 1978-1979. The band performs five group originals; surprisingly none were written by the leader. While there are some individual solos

(particularly by Tapscott), it is the dense and frequently exciting ensembles that are most notable in this avant-garde but rhythmic music. *—Scott Yanow*

Live at Lobero, Vol. 1 / Nov. 12, 1981 / Nimbus ✦✦✦✦✦
Pianist Horace Tapscott is always at his best when he is leading a trio. This rare outing features Tapscott with his longtime bassist Roberto Miranda and drummer Sonship on three extended performances including Tapscott's colorful "Sketches Of Drunken Mary" and a 21-minute version of "The Dark Tree." Hopefully this valuable Lp will someday be reissued on CD for Tapscott has made too few recordings during his long career. *—Scott Yanow*

● **The Dark Tree, Vol 1/Dark Tree, Vol. 2** / Dec. 14, 1989-Dec. 17, 1989 / hatOLOGY ✦✦✦✦✦
The under-recorded pianist/composer/arranger Horace Tapscott was a sort of legendary figure in jazz circles, a function of his genius combined with the paucity of recordings available that feature his playing. The double CD, *The Dark Tree*, is one of the best examples of his work, capturing him live at a local club with a quartet featuring clarinetist John Carter, another equally great West Coast jazz musician whom fame somehow eluded. (Other members of the quartet are long-time collaborator, drummer Andrew Cyrille, and bassist Cecil McBee.) The pianist shows his feathers on piece after piece (most of which were written by him), in which he is as comfortable with post-bop runs as he is with their avant-garde implications. Through it all, you can hear his blues-drenched roots. This one has been out-of-print as often as not, so it probably makes sense to get it while you can. *—Steven Loewy*

Aiee! the Phantom / Jun. 1995 / Arabesque ✦✦✦✦✦
Pianist-composer Horace Tapscott has long been Los Angeles' great local legend. He has had his own sound and style since the mid-1960's but, due to his relatively few recordings (mostly for Nimbus) and his desire to live in L.A. rather than New York, he has long been underrated if not completely overlooked. Falling between post bop and the avant-garde, Tapscott plays locally with a blazing (if thus far undocumented) quartet that includes saxophonist Michael Sessions. Recently he recorded *Aiee! The Phantom* with an all-star quintet including trumpeter Marcus Belgrave, altoist Abraham Burton, bassist Reggie Workman and drummer Andrew Cyrille. Tapscott performs four of his modal-based originals and a pair of obscurities quite freely but with attention paid to the moods of the compositions. Highlights include "Drunk Mary/Mary On Sunday," "To The Great House" and the adventurous "Mothership." Perhaps this recording (available from Arabesque, 10 West 37th Street, New York, NY 10018) will alert the rest of the jazz world as to the strong talents of the great veteran Horace Tapscott. *—Scott Yanow*

Thoughts of Dar Es Salaam / Jun. 30, 1996-Jul. 1, 1996 / Arabesque ✦✦✦✦

Buddy Tate (George Holmes Tate)

b. Feb. 22, 1913, Sherman, TX, **d.** Feb. 10, 2001, Chandler, AZ
Sax (Tenor), Clarinet / Swing
One of the more individual tenors to emerge from the swing era, the distinctive Buddy Tate came to fame as Herschel Evans' replacement with Count Basie's Orchestra. Earlier he had picked up valuable experience playing with Terrence Holder (1930-33), Count Basie's original Kansas City band (1934), Andy Kirk (1934-35) and Nat Towles (1935-39). With Basie a second time during 1939-48, Tate held his own with such major tenors as Lester Young, Don Byas, Illinois Jacquet, Lucky Thompson and Paul Gonsalves. After a period freelancing with the likes of Hot Lips Page, Lucky Millinder and Jimmy Rushing (1950-52), Tate led his own crowd-pleasing group for 21 years (1953-74) at Harlem's Celebrity Club. During this period Tate also took time out to record in a variety of setting (including with Buck Clayton and Milt Buckner) and he was the one of the star of John Hammond's Spirituals to Swing concert of 1967. Tate has kept busy since the Celebrity Club association ended, recording frequently, co-leading a band with Paul Quinichette in 1975, playing and recording in Canada with Jay McShann and Jim Galloway, visiting Europe many times and performing at jazz parties; he was also a favorite sideman of Benny Goodman's in the late '70s. Although age had taken its toll, in the mid-'90s Buddy Tate played and recorded with both Lionel Hampton and the Statesmen of Jazz. Tate lived in N.Y. until January, 2001, when he moved to Phoenix, AZ to live with his daughter. Buddy Tate died a few weeks later, on February 10. *—Scott Yanow*

Groovin' with Buddy Tate / Dec. 18, 1959-Feb. 17, 1961 / Swingville ✦✦✦✦

Tate-A-Tate / Oct. 18, 1960 / Swingville/OJC ✦✦✦✦
This LP reissue of a Storyville set (which has not yet been put out on CD) matches the distinctive tenor Buddy Tate with trumpeter Clark Terry and a fine rhythm section (pianist Tommy Flanagan, bassist Larry Gales and drummer Art Taylor). The swinging unit performs three C.T. originals, Tate's *"20 Ladbroke Square"* and two standards ("Take the 'A' Train" and "All Too Soon"). The music is enjoyable and practically defines mainstream jazz of the era. *—Scott Yanow*

Jive at Five / Jul. 23, 1975 / Storyville ✦✦✦✦
During an era when mainstream jam sessions were fairly rare and fusion reigned, Storyville documented an all-star group mostly comprised of swing era veterans. Tenor-saxophonist Buddy Tate, trombonist Vic Dickenson and trumpeter Doc Cheatham (who was 70 at the time and just beginning to emerge as a soloist) make for a potent frontline, pianist Johnny Guarnieri is heard in prime form and bassist George Duvivier and drummer Oliver Jackson are typically tasteful in support. Two alternate takes were added to the original seven-song program for this CD reissue and there are features for Dickenson (who sings and plays his own "Constantly"), Cheatham ("I've Got A Right To Sing The Blues") and Tate ("There Goes My Heart"). However it is the four group jams that are most exciting. Easily recommended to mainstream jazz fans. *—Scott Yanow*

Tate a Tete at La Fontaine, Copenhagen / Sep. 23, 1975-Sep. 24, 1975 / Storyville ✦✦✦✦
Tenor-saxophonist Buddy Tate meets up with pianist Tete Montoliu on this enjoyable blowing date. Other than "Buddy's Blues" (which has a Tate vocal), all of the songs are swing standards with "In A Mellow Tone" clocking in at 17 1/2 minutes. Violinist Finn Ziegler makes worthwhile guest appearances on two of the five selections and the group is completed by bassist Bo Stief and drummer Svend Erik Norregard. Easily recommended for swing fans, this album finds Buddy Tate still very much in prime form. *—Scott Yanow*

● **Hard Blowin'** / Aug. 25, 1978-Aug. 26, 1978 / Muse ✦✦✦✦✦
Muse has released at least six albums of material recorded at *Sandy's Jazz Revival* in Massachusetts during a week in 1978. This is veteran tenor Buddy Tate's most rewarding album from the engagement and a fine all-around showcase. Accompanied by pianist Ray Bryant, bassist George Duvivier and drummer Alan Dawson, Tate stretches out on four familiar standards and shows listeners that he really had one of the more distinctive tenor sounds of the swing era. Recommended. *—Scott Yanow*

Just Jazz / Apr. 28, 1984 / Reservoir ✦✦✦✦
Tenor-saxophonist Buddy Tate (who also contributes a bit of clarinet) blends in perfectly with trombonist Al Grey on this swinging quintet session. With pianist Richard Wyands, bassist Major Holley and drummer Al Harewood completing the group, Tate and Grey perform on original apiece and four veteran standards; the CD reissue adds two alternate takes. Both Tate and Grey were in their late prime at the time and the highpoints include Grey's title cut, "Straight Up And Fly Right," "Topsy" and "Tangerine." *—Scott Yanow*

Buddy & Claude / Nov. 23, 1999 / Prestige ✦✦✦✦
Buddy and Claude combines two 1960 sessions on a single 74-minute CD. The first is *Yes Indeed!*, a Claude Hopkins date that features Buddy Tate prominently and also employs trumpeter Emmett Berry, bassist Wendell Marshall, and drummer Osie Johnson. The other is Tate's *Tate-A-Tate*, which doesn't employ pianist Hopkins at all, but boasts Clark Terry on trumpet and flügelhorn, Tommy Flanagan on piano, Larry Gales on bass, and Art Taylor on drums. When these swing-to-bop sessions were recorded, Tate was in his late 40s, and his breathy tenor playing continued to reflect his years in the Count Basie Orchestra. Indeed, Basie's influence is prominent on both sessions, and it comes through whether Tate is swinging passionately on Duke Ellington's "It Don't Mean a Thing" and Billy Strayhorn's "Take the A Train," blowing the blues on "Empty Bed Blues," or favoring smoky, sentimental ballad playing on "What Is This Thing Called Love," "All Too Soon," and "Willow Weep for Me." It's interesting to note that Hopkins and Flanagan interact with Tate equally well—even though they were two very different pianists. Hopkins started out as a stride pianist, whereas Flanagan (who was 27 years younger) became well known in the 1950s and was primarily a hard bopper. Both pianists enjoy a strong rapport with Tate, and both of them do their part to make *Buddy and Claude* the rewarding reissue that it is. *—Alex Henderson*

Art Tatum

b. Oct. 13, 1909, Toledo, OH, **d.** Nov. 5, 1956, Los Angeles, CA
Piano / Swing
Art Tatum was among the most extraordinary of all jazz musicians, a pianist with wondrous technique who could not only play ridiculously rapid lines with both hands (his 1933 solo version of "Tiger Rag" sounds as if there were three pianists jamming together!) but was harmonically 30 years ahead of his time; all pianists have to deal to a certain extent with Tatum's innovations in order to be taken seriously. Able to play stride, swing and boogie-woogie with speed and complexity that could only previously be imagined, Tatum's quick reflexes and boundless imagination kept his improvisations filled with fresh (and sometimes futuristic) ideas that put him way ahead of his contemporaries. Born nearly blind, Tatum was largely self-taught. After making his recording debut in 1932, his solos of 1933 (including "Tiger Rag") announced the arrival of a truly major talent. Some observers criticized him for having too much technique (is such a thing possible?), working out and then keeping the same arrangements for particular songs and for using too many notes, but those minor reservations pale when compared to Tatum's reworkings of such tunes as "Yesterdays," "Begin the Beguine" and even "Humoresque." He recorded for Decca throughout the 1930s and Capitol in the late '40s, then worked extensively for Norman Granz near the end of his life in the 1950s, both solo and with all-star groups. His premature death from uremia has not resulted in any loss of fame, for Art Tatum's recordings still have the ability to scare modern pianists! *—Scott Yanow*

☆ **Piano Starts Here** / Mar. 21, 1933-1949 / Columbia/Legacy ✦✦✦✦✦
There are many Art Tatum records currently available, but this is the one to pull out to amaze friends, particularly with Tatum's wondrous version of "Tiger Rag," and during which he sounds like three pianists jamming together. This CD consists of Tatum's first studio session as a leader (which resulted in "Tea for Two," "St. Louis Blues," "Tiger Rag" and "Sophisticated Lady") and a remarkable solo concert performance from the spring of 1949. While "Tiger Rag" dwarfs everything else, the live set is highlighted by a very adventurous, yet seemingly effortless exploration of "Yesterdays," a ridiculously rapid "I Know That You Know," and the hard-cooking "Tatum Pole Boogie." This is an essential set of miraculous music that cannot be praised highly enough. *—Scott Yanow*

● **1932-1934** / Aug. 5, 1932-Oct. 9, 1934 / Classics ✦✦✦✦✦
This comprehensive CD contains Art Tatum's very first recording (a broadcast version of "Tiger Rag") four selections in which he accompanies singer Adelaide Hall (along with a second pianist) and then his first 20 solo sides. To call his virtuosic piano style remarkable would be a major understatement; he has to be heard to be believed. His studio version of "Tiger Rag" may very well be his most incredible recording; he sounds like three pianists at once. *—Scott Yanow*

1934-1940 / Oct. 9, 1934-Jul. 26, 1940 / Classics ✦✦✦✦✦
The second CD in Classics' Art Tatum series features the remarkable pianist as a soloist for many gems recorded for Decca and with a sextet on four numbers. Although alternate takes are bypassed, making the Decca CDs preferable, the set is overflowing with classics. Highlights include Tatum's interpretations of "Chloe," "The Sheik of Araby," "Elegie," "Humoresque," "Get Happy" and "Begin the Beguine." *—Scott Yanow*

☆ **Classic Piano Solos (1934-1939)** / 1934-1939 / GRP ✦✦✦✦✦

Classic Early Solos (1934-37) contains solo performances of 20 songs Art Tatum recorded in the beginning days of his career. These invigorating performances demonstrate that Tatum was already considerably accomplished at this early stage, and the performances are continually breathtaking. This disc should be heard by any serious fan of Tatum or jazz piano. *—Leo Stanley*

I Got Rhythm: Art Tatum, Vol. 3 (1935-1944) / Dec. 21, 1935-Jan. 5, 1944 / GRP ✦✦✦✦✦
This third Decca CD wraps up GRP's Art Tatum reissue series. There are two piano solos ("Tea For Two" and "Deep Purple"), an obscure 1935 version of "Take Me Back To My Boots And Saddle" with an unidentified group, the full session (including two alternate takes) by Art Tatum's "Swingsters" in 1937, two instrumentals from 1940 with a sextet including trumpeter Joe Thomas and clarinetist Edmond Hall and ten performances by Tatum's famous 1944 trio with guitarist Tiny Grimes and bassist Slam Stewart. Tatum's playing throughout is typically miraculous and this CD offers ample proof that he could play with other musicians, providing they were flexible and strong themselves. Highly recommended. *—Scott Yanow*

God Is in the House / Nov. 11, 1940-Sep. 16, 1941 / High Note ✦✦✦✦✦
This 1998 HighNote CD reissues a long-out-of-print Art Tatum LP that was put out by the defunct Onyx label in 1973. The live performances are from the Jerry Newman collection of acetate discs and are fortunately in better technical quality than most of the music from Newman's archives. The remarkable Art Tatum is heard playing three brief unaccompanied piano solos in 1940, three other numbers in which he is accompanied by Reuben Harris (beating out some quiet rhythms with whiskbrooms on a suitcase), and four duets with bassist-vocalist Chocolate Williams; Tatum has a brief vocal on "Knockin' Myself Out" and a more extensive one on "Toledo Blues," the only times he ever sang on record. In addition, Tatum and Williams back Ollie Potter (a pretty good if completely unknown singer) on "There'll Be Some Changes Made." Best of all are a pair of exciting trio numbers ("Lady Be Good" and a very memorable "Sweet Georgia Brown") in which Tatum stretches out with bassist Ebenezer Paul and the great, underrated trumpeter Frank Newton. It is fascinating to hear Newton's playing on "Sweet Georgia Brown," which is fairly simple and calm, while Tatum sounds like a volcano behind him. Highly recommended. *—Scott Yanow*

● **The Complete Capitol Recordings, Vol. 1** / Jul. 13, 1949-Dec. 20, 1952 / Capitol ✦✦✦✦✦
Tatum recorded 20 piano solos in 1949 and eight selections with his 1952 trio (which included guitarist Everett Barksdale and bassist Slam Stewart) for Capitol. Ten solos and four trios are included on each of the two CDs in this "complete" series; he can be heard here at the height of his powers. (He never did decline, creating miraculous variations of standards that still amaze today's pianists.) *—Scott Yanow*

The Complete Capitol Recordings, Vol. 2 / Sep. 29, 1949-Dec. 20, 1952 / Capitol ✦✦✦✦✦
On the second of two CDs, Art Tatum is heard playing solo in 1949 on ten standards and interacting with his 1952 trio (which included guitarist Everett Barksdale and bassist Slam Stewart) during four numbers. Tatum always had the ability to amaze fellow pianists (not to mention fans) and there are plenty of remarkable moments in this fine set. *—Scott Yanow*

The Complete Capitol Recordings / 1949-1952 / Blue Note ✦✦✦✦✦
Previously released as two separate volumes, *The Complete Capitol Recordings of Art Tatum* is a two-disc collection that presents everything the pianist recorded for Capitol Records in chronlogical order. There's 20 solo sides from 1949 and a 1952 session with a trio of guitarist Everett Barksdale and bassist Slam Stewart. Throughout the collection, Tatum sounds wonderful—he was a rare player that was extremely technically advanced and also very lyrical. For any Tatum fan, this set is a necessity. *—Leo Stanley*

20th Century Piano Genius / Apr. 16, 1950-Jul. 3, 1955 / Verve ✦✦✦✦
This double album was taped at a private party in 1956, featuring the amazing Art Tatum on solo piano. Tatum, who died the following year, never did decline, and he is in prime form throughout this highly enjoyable and frequently exciting set of standards. There are no real romps a la "Tiger Rag" but the 27 performances contain plenty of remarkable moments. *—Scott Yanow*

The Art Tatum Solo Masterpieces, Vol. 2 / Dec. 28, 1953-Jan. 19, 1955 / Pablo ✦✦✦✦
The second of eight CDs in this series of solo performances taken from four marathon record sessions has among its highlights "Elegy," "This Can't Be Love" and "Tea for Two," but in qeneral this series lacks the excitement of Tatum's earliest recordings. Excellent but somewhat predictable performances by the classic virtuoso. *—Scott Yanow*

The Art Tatum Solo Masterpieces, Vol. 3 / Dec. 28, 1953-Jan. 19, 1955 / Pablo ✦✦✦✦
The third of eight CDs in the Norman Granz series of Tatum piano solos is highlighted by "Yesterdays," "Prisoner of Love" and "Begin the Beguine" among others. He did little prior preparation for the four marathon sessions that resulted in a dozen LPs (now reissued as eight CDs), so this series lacks the excitement and adventure of his earliest recordings although it is still enjoyable in its own right. *—Scott Yanow*

The Complete Pablo Solo Masterpieces / Dec. 28, 1953-Jan. 19, 1955 / Pablo ✦✦✦✦
During four marathon recording sessions in 1953-55, Norman Granz recorded Art Tatum playing 119 standards, enough music for a dozen LPs. The results have been recently reissued separately on eight CDs and on this very full seven-CD box set. Frankly, Tatum did no real advance preparation for this massive project, sticking mosty to concise melodic variations of standards, some of them virtual set pieces formed over the past two decades. Since there are few uptempo performances, the music in this series has a certain sameness after awhile but, heard in small doses, it is quite enjoyable. A special bonus on this box (and not on the individual volumes) are four numbers taken from a 1956 *Hollywood Bowl* concert. *—Scott Yanow*

The Tatum Solo Masterpieces, Vol. 1 / Dec. 28, 1953-Jan. 19, 1955 / Pablo ✦✦✦✦
The first of eight CDs reissuing the 119 piano solo performances that Art Tatum recorded for Norman Granz during four marathon record sessions has its moments, although in general this series lacks the excitement of Tatum's earliest recordings. The pianist interprets such standards an this first volume as "Body and Soul," "It's Only a Paper Moon" and "Willow Weep for Me." *—Scott Yanow*

☆ **The Complete Pablo Group Masterpieces** / Jun. 25, 1954-Sep. 11, 1956 / Pablo ✦✦✦✦✦
Tatum spent most of his career as a solo pianist; in fact it was often said that he was such an unpredictable virtuoso that it would be difficult for other musicians to play with him. Producer Norman Granz sought to prove that the theory was false, so between 1954 and 1956 he extensively recorded Tatum with a variety of other classic jazzmen, resulting originally in nine LPs of material that is now available separately as eight CDs and on this very full six-CD box set. In contrast to the massive solo Tatum sessions that Granz also recorded during this period, the group sides have plenty of variety and exciting moments, which is not too surprising when one considers that Tatum was teamed in a trio with altoist Benny Carter and drummer Louie Bellson with trumpeter Roy Eldridge, clarinetist Buddy DeFranco and tenor-saxophonist Hen Webster in separate quartets, in an explosive trio with vibraphonist Lionel Hampton and drummer Buddy Rich, with a sextet including Hampton, Rich and trumpeter Harry "Sweets" Edison, and on a standard trio session. *—Scott Yanow*

The Tatum Group Masterpieces, Vol. 1 / Jun. 25, 1954 / Pablo ✦✦✦✦
During 1954-56 Norman Granz recorded the remarkable pianist Art Tatum with a variety of classic jazz masters, resulting in quite a bit of musical magic. This first of eight volumes finds Tatum matching wits with the classy alto of Benny Carter and drummer Louie Bellson—the results are both tasteful and frequently hard-swinging. *—Scott Yanow*

The Tatum Group Masterpieces, Vol. 2 / Mar. 23, 1955-Mar. 29, 1955 / Pablo ✦✦✦✦✦
The second of eight CDs teaming the amazing pianist with a variety of his contemporaries finds Tatum sharing the stage with trumpeter Roy Eldridge, bassist John Simmons and drummer Alvin Stoller. Eldridge, normally a very combative player, knows better than to directly challenge Tatum and instead is surprisingly restrained and muted on this enjoyable set of swing standards. *—Scott Yanow*

The Tatum Group Masterpieces, Vol. 3 / Aug. 1, 1955 / Pablo ✦✦✦✦✦
The third of eight CDs matching the great pianist with a variety of classic jazzmen is the first of two that finds him in a trio with vibraphonist Lionel Hampton and drummer Buddy Rich; no weak spots in that group. Much of this music really burns. *—Scott Yanow*

Art Taylor

b. Apr. 6, 1929, New York, NY, **d.** Feb. 6, 1995
Drums / Hard Bop, Bop
One of the great drummers of the 'ß50s, Art Taylor was on a countless number of hard bop and jam session-styled sessions. His first important gig was with Howard McGhee in 1948 and this was followed by associations with Coleman Hawkins (1950-51), Buddy DeFranco (1952), Bud Powell (1953 and 1955-7) and George Wallington (1954-56). Taylor seemed to live in Prestige's studios during the second half of the 1950s although he found time to lead his Wailers, visit Europe with Donald Byrd in 1958, gig and record with Miles Davis and play with Thelonious Monk (including his acclaimed Town Hall concert) in 1959. In 1963 Taylor moved to Europe where he spent most of the next 20 years (mostly living in France and Belgium), playing with Europeans and such Americans as Dexter Gordon and Johnny Griffin. He interviewed scores of his colleagues and collected many of the insightful discussions in his very readable book *Notes and Tones* (which was re-released in 1993). After returning to the U.S., Taylor resumed his freelancing and in the early '90s he organized a new version of the Wailers which, during its short existence prior to his death, temporarily filled the gap left by the end of the Jazz Messengers. *—Scott Yanow*

● **Taylor's Wailers** / Feb. 25, 1956-Mar. 22, 1957 / Prestige/OJC ✦✦✦✦✦
Five of the six selections on this CD reissue feature drummer Art Taylor in an all-star sextet of mostly young players comprised of trumpeter Donald Byrd, altoist Jackie McLean, Charlie Rouse on tenor, pianist Ray Bryant, and bassist Wendell Marshall. Among the highpoints of the 1957 hard bop date are the original version of Bryant's popular "Cubano Chant" and strong renditions of two Thelonious Monk tunes ("Off Minor" and "Well, You Needn't") cut just prior to the pianist/composer's discovery by the jazz public. Bryant is the most mature of the soloists, but the three horn players were already starting to develop their own highly individual sounds. The remaining track (a version of Jimmy Heath's "C.T.A.") is played by the quartet of Taylor, tenor saxophonist John Coltrane, pianist Red Garland, and bassist Paul Chambers and is a leftover (although a good one) from another session. *—Scott Yanow*

Taylor's Tenors / Jun. 3, 1959 / New Jazz/OJC ✦✦✦✦
Legendary drummer Art Taylor played on a multitude of classic jazz sessions, but only managed to release a few dates as a leader before he passed away in 1995. His second, *Taylor's Tenors*, from mid-1959, features two straight-ahead tenor saxophonists, Charlie Rouse and Frank Foster, engaging in an insightful yet swinging hard bop conversation. Rouse would shortly become Thelonious Monk's tenor of choice, while Foster continued his tenure with Count Basie's band for another five years. These six hard bop pieces include two by Monk, Jackie McLean's "Fidel," and originals each from Rouse, pianist Walter Davis, and Taylor. *—Al Campbell*

Art Taylor's Delight / Aug. 6, 1960 / Blue Note ✦✦✦✦
Drummer Art Taylor was on many sessions as a sideman in the 1950s but he only led three albums during the period, and this was his only one for Blue Note. Heading a quintet/sextet also including the underrated bop trumpeter Dave Burns, the up-and-coming tenorman Stanley Turrentine, pianist Wynton Kelly, bassist Paul Chambers, and (on three of the six songs) Potato Valdez on conga, Taylor performs a pair of Kenny Dorham tunes plus a song apiece by John Coltrane (the obscure "Syeeda's Song Flute"), Thelonious Monk, Denzil Best, and his own calypso "Cookoo and Fungi." This well-rounded hard bop date was last available as a reissue LP in 1985. *—Scott Yanow*

Wailin' at the Vanguard / Aug. 29, 1992-Aug. 30, 1992 / Verve ✦✦✦✦
Following the successful *Mr. A.T.*, drummer Art Taylor found himself to be a modern-day Art Blakey by leading a youthful group known as Taylor's Wailers. Pianist Jacky Terrason is a versatile player with a distinct voice, who along with Taylor is the heart and soul of this band. Going back to the '50s, the leader fancied the dynamics of two saxophonists playing off of each

other, which Abraham Burton and Willie Williams do exceedingly well here. Walter Bolden's compositions make for the most interesting moments here, in particular the "Bridge Theme" which is restated throughout. This is excellent hard bop played by a true master, and it's a shame that "Mr. A.T." passed away shortly after this recording was made. *—Robert Taylor*

Billy Taylor

b. Jul. 24, 1921, Greenville, NC
Piano / Hard Bop, Swing, Bop
Billy Taylor has been such an articulate spokesman for jazz and his profiles on CBS' *Sunday Morning* television program (where he has been a regular since 1981) are so successful at introducing jazz to a wider audience that sometimes one can forget how talented a pianist he has been for the past half-century. While not an innovator, Taylor has been flexible enough to play swing, bop and more advanced styles while always retaining his own musical personality. After graduating from Virginia State College in 1942, he moved to New York and played with such major musicians as Ben Webster, Eddie South, Stuff Smith (with whom he recorded in 1944) and Slam Stewart among others. In 1951 he was the house pianist at Birdland and soon afterward Taylor formed his first of many trios. He helped found the Jazzmobile in 1965, in 1969 became the first Black band director for a network television series (*The David Frost Show*), in 1975 he earned his doctorate at the University of Massachusetts and he both founded and served as director for the popular radio program *Jazz Alive*. But despite his activities in jazz education, Taylor has rarely gone long between performances and recordings, always keeping his bop-based style consistently swinging and fresh. *—Scott Yanow*

Billy Taylor Trio / Nov. 18, 1952-Dec. 29, 1953 / Prestige ✦✦✦✦
Two albums by pianist Billy Taylor are combined on this single CD reissue. With fine backing from bassist Earl May and drummer Charlie Smith, Taylor is tasteful, swinging and creative within the boundaries of bop and swing on this early set, among his first dates as a leader and excellent examples of his already individual style. *—Scott Yanow*

Cross Section / May 7, 1953-Jul. 30, 1954 / Prestige/OJC ✦✦✦✦
For this CD reissue, pianist Billy Taylor is features on eight songs with his trio of 1954 (which included bassist Earl May and drummer Percy Brice); the four originals (which alternate with standards) were all dedicated to disc jockeys of the time. The trio was pretty tight with Taylor in the lead and, although boppish, it also looked back toward the swing era. The remaining four numbers match Taylor and May with what was dubbed "Machito's Rhythm Section": Charlie Smith on conga, Joe Mangual on bongos, Uba Nieto playing timbales and Machito himself on maracas. The four mambos are ideal both for listening and for dance music. An enjoyable set. *—Scott Yanow*

The Billy Taylor Trio with Candido / Sep. 7, 1954 / Prestige/OJC ✦✦✦✦
Having already dedicated half of 1953's *Cross Section* to numbers with Machito's band, it was no surprise that Bill Taylor's 1954 follow-up, *Trio with Candido*, would feature more Latin touches—this time with star Cuban conga player Candido. In line with fellow jazz pianists George Shearing and Red Garland, Taylor doesn't incorporate the Cuban clavé beat so much as he includes the percussion for accentuation. In spite of this, Candido offers up some provocative solos, especially on the fast-paced Taylor original "A Live One," which features the pianist and percussionist trading an energetic set of fours. Medium to slow-tempo Taylor originals, though, dominate the program, including "Bit of Bedlam," where the chaos is decidedly cool. Throughout the album, Taylor uses his fleet, Teddy Wilson-informed solo chops to pleasant effect, even stretching out a bit on "Mambo Inn" to complement Candido's own lengthy workout. A very nice program of Latin-tinged bop numbers which unfortunately has not found its way to CD, but occasionally can be found on LP. For at least some of Taylor's Latin forays, there is the CD reissue of *Cross Section*. *—Stephen Cook*

● **My Fair Lady Loves Jazz** / Jan. 8, 1957-Feb. 5, 1957 / GRP ✦✦✦✦✦
Recorded at a time when *My Fair Lady* was a big Broadway hit (but a few years before it became a film), this CD reissue brings back one of the very best jazz interpretations of the classic score. The focus throughout is on the Billy Taylor trio (which included bassist Earl May and drummer Ed Thigpen) but Quincy Jones' arrangements for the seven horns are quite memorable. There is room for short solos from such players as trumpeter Ernie Royal, trombonist Jimmy Cleveland, altoist Anthony Ortega and baritonist Gerry Mulligan, and their presence clearly inspires pianist Taylor to some of his finest playing. Highly recommended. *—Scott Yanow*

Billy Taylor with Four Flutes / Jul. 20, 1959-Jul. 24, 1959 / Riverside ✦✦✦✦
In the 1950s, pianist Billy Taylor was best known for his work with his trios. For this Riverside set (reissued on CD in the OJC series) Taylor tried something different, writing arrangements for four flutists (including Frank Wess, Herbie Mann, and Jerome Richardson), his rhythm section, and the congas of Chino Pozo. The flutists get their opportunities to solo, and the music (which includes "The Song Is Ended," "St. Thomas," "Oh Lady Be Good," "How About You," and four of Taylor's originals) is essentially bop, but the unusual instrumentation gives the set its own personality. Enjoyable music that certainly stands out from the crowd. *—Scott Yanow*

You Tempt Me / Jun. 24, 1985 / Taylor Made ✦✦✦✦✦
In 1989 pianist Billy Taylor, who was between record contracts, started his own "Taylor Made" label to document his own music. On this excellent set with his trio (which also includes bassist Victor Gaskin and drummer Curtis Boyd), Taylor starts off with a slower than usual rendition of "Take the 'A' Train," performs two originals, and then concludes the program with five selections from his jazz suite "Let Us Make a Joyful Noise." Several of the latter pieces could stand on their own if played separately for they are excellent vehicles for chordal improvisation. The CD overall finds Billy Taylor in top form. *—Scott Yanow*

White Nights and Jazz in Leningrad / Jun. 13, 1988-Jun. 14, 1988 / Taylor Made ✦✦✦✦✦
For this well-rounded set, the debut release from his Taylor-Made label, pianist Billy Taylor and his trio (with bassist Victor Gaskin and drummer Bobby Thomas) are featured performing live from Leningrad in the Soviet Union. The music is typically straightahead and surprisingly only one of the nine numbers ("C-A-G") is a Taylor original. Highlights include a pair of Clare Fischer's better-known songs ("Pensativa" and "Morning"), "Secret Love," Wes Montgomery's "Jingles" and a touching version of "A Child Is Born." One of the better Billy Taylor CDs currently available. *—Scott Yanow*

Solo / Aug. 1, 1988-Aug. 2, 1988 / Taylor Made ✦✦✦✦✦
Other than a pair of obscure albums from 1956, this was Billy Taylor's first solo piano recording. Released by his Taylor-Made label, the music on this CD is consistently colorful. On the opener "All the Things You Are," Taylor plays the first three choruses quite successfully with just his left hand. Other highlights of this straightahead set include the pianist's "A Bit of Bedlam" (one of seven originals among the 13 songs), "More than You Know," "For Undine" and "Billy's Beat." Well worth checking out. *—Scott Yanow*

It's a Matter of Pride / 1993 / GRP ✦✦✦✦✦
This is a particularly well-constructed session by pianist Billy Taylor who is featured in a combo with bassist Christian McBride, drummer Marvin "Smitty" Smith, the congas of Ray Mantilla and, on three songs, tenor-saxophonist Stanley Turrentine; Grady Tate also contributes two warm ballad vocals. All nine songs were composed by Taylor (including three pieces taken from a more extended work in tribute to Martin Luther King) and the results are melodic, boppish and swinging. *—Scott Yanow*

Cecil Taylor

b. Mar. 15, 1929, New York, NY
Piano / Avant-Garde Jazz, Free Jazz
Soon after he first emerged in the mid-'50s, pianist Cecil Taylor was the most advanced improviser in jazz; four decades later he is still the most radical. Although in his early days he used some standards as vehicles for improvisation, since the early '60s Taylor has stuck exclusively to originals. To simplify describing his style, one could say that Taylor's intense atonal percussive approach involves playing the piano as if it were a set of drums. He generally emphasizes dense clusters of sound played with remarkable technique and endurance, often during marathon performances. Early gigs included work with groups led by Johnny Hodges and Hot Lips Page but, after forming his quartet in the mid-'50s, Taylor was never a sideman again. Despite occasional records, work was scarce. By 1962 Taylor's quartet featured his longtime associate Jimmy Lyons on alto and drummer Sunny Murray. Even with the rise of free jazz, his music was considered too advanced. In the mid-'60s Taylor recorded two very advanced sets for Blue Note but it was generally a lean decade. Things greatly improved starting in the '70s. Taylor taught at several universities, recorded more frequently, toured Europe and was awarded a Guggenheim Fellowship. Taylor later began incorporating some of his eccentric poetry into his performances and, unlike most musicians, hasn't mellowed with age. *—Scott Yanow*

Jazz Advance / 1956 / Blue Note ✦✦✦✦✦
This CD reissues Cecil Taylor's very first recording session. Although the album states that it is from Sept. 1956, all previous discographies state Dec. 10, 1955. Even at this early stage, the 26-year old pianist was extremely advanced in his playing. One can hear Taylor's roots in Duke Ellington and Thelonious Monk but his comping and chord voicings were already far ahead of most of his contemporaries. He takes "You'd Be So Nice to Come Home To" solo, has four trio numbers with bassist Buell Neidlinger and drummer Dennis Charles and, on C.T.'s "Charge 'Em Blues" and "Song," soprano saxophonist Steve Lacy makes the group a quartet. This is utterly fascinating music that hints strongly at what was to come. *—Scott Yanow*

Looking Ahead / Jun. 9, 1958 / Contemporary/OJC ✦✦✦✦
Due to the occasionally quiet ensembles, this CD reissue is one of the more accessible Cecil Taylor records despite the use of atonality in much of the music. Taylor, vibraphonist Earl Griffith, bassist Buell Neidlinger and drummer Dennis Charles explore six of Taylor's originals including "Wallering" (written in tribute to but not in the style of Fats Waller) and the explosive "Excursion on a Wobbly Rail." *—Scott Yanow*

Love for Sale / Apr. 15, 1959 / United Artists ✦✦✦✦
This is an utterly fascinating set (reissued on a 1998 CD) featuring the avant-garde pianist Cecil Taylor early in his career. He first performs three Cole Porter songs (!) in a trio with bassist Buell Neidlinger and drummer Dennis Charles. Because Taylor apparently wanted Neidlinger to walk conventionally and Charles to keep a pulse going, the music is more accessible than what was to come. However, Taylor's own lines, while sometimes hinting at the melody (most notably on "Love for Sale"), are generally atonal and percussive, lighter than they would be but still far ahead of their time. The second half of the disc adds trumpeter Ted Curson and tenor saxophonist Bill Barron to the group as the quintet performs three Taylor originals, none of which are half as radical as the pianist's playing. Curson and Barron were fairly advanced improvisers, but they still sound a decade behind Taylor. Well worth checking out. *—Scott Yanow*

☆ **Complete Candid Recordings of Cecil Taylor** / Oct. 12, 1960-Jan. 10, 1961 / Mosaic ✦✦✦✦✦
The sessions that comprise the four discs on this first-rate Mosaic boxed set were done in 1960 and 1961 for the short-lived Candid label. Taylor's concept had not yet evolved into a finished package; he wasn't always sure where he was going. There are solos that begin in one direction, break in the middle and conclude in another. Tenor saxophonist Archie Shepp often sounds unsure about what to play and whether to try and interact or establish his own direction. At the same time, there is plenty of exceptional playing from Taylor, Shepp and the drum/bass combination of Buell Neidlinger and Dennis Charles. You cannot honestly say everything works on these four discs, but there is never a dull moment. It won't please everyone, but listeners ready for a challenge should step right up. *—Ron Wynn*

Jumpin' Punkins / Jan. 9, 1961-Jan. 10, 1961 / Artists Only ✦✦✦✦
This single CD has some of the music formerly released on a limited-edition Cecil Taylor Mo-

saic box set. The two most intriguing performances are versions of Mercer Ellington's "Jumpin' Punkins" and "Things Ain't What They Used to Be" which feature the avant-garde pianist with trumpeter Clark Terry, trombonist Roswell Rudd, soprano saxophonist Steve Lacy, baritonist Charles Davis, tenor Archie Shepp, bassist Buell Neidlinger, and drummer Billy Higgins. Taylor's jarring comping behind the other soloists is quite interesting and somehow works. "O.P." and "I Forgot" feature Taylor with Neidlinger, drummer Dennis Charles, and (on the latter song) the young Archie Shepp. A good sampler of Cecil Taylor's marathon Candid sessions. *—Scott Yanow*

Nefertiti, the Beautiful One Has Come / Oct. 23, 1962 / Revenant ✦✦✦✦✦
This double-LP is the only recording that exists of Cecil Taylor and his group (other than two songs on the bootleg Ingo label) during 1962-65. Taylor's new altoist Jimmy Lyons (who occasionally hints at Charlie Parker) and the first truly "free" drummer Sonny Murray join the avant-garde pianist in some stunning trio performances recorded live at *the Cafe Montmartre* in Copenhagen. With the exception of an interesting version of "What's New" (which finds Lyons showing off his roots), the music is comprised entirely of Taylor originals and is atonal and full of power. *—Scott Yanow*

Great Paris Concert / Jul. 29, 1964 / Black Lion ✦✦✦✦
This three-LP set is a real blowout. Pianist Cecil Taylor, altoist Jimmy Lyons, Sam Rivers on tenor and soprano, and drummer Andrew Cyrille (there is no bass but it couldn't have been heard anyway) perform a 90-minute work followed by a 20-minute encore. The music is unrelentingly intense and Taylor does not let up for a moment. His fans are advised to pick up this major release but those listeners new to Taylor's music should investigate his solo piano works first. *—Scott Yanow*

★ **Unit Structures** / May 19, 1966 / Blue Note ✦✦✦✦✦
After several years off records, pianist Cecil Taylor finally had an opportunity to document his music of the mid-'60s on two Blue Note albums (the other one was *Conquistador*). Taylor's high-energy atonalism fit in well with the free jazz of the period but he was actually leading the way rather than being part of a movement. In fact this septet outing with trumpeter Eddie Gale, altoist Jimmy Lyons, Ken McIntyre (alternating between alto, oboe and bass clarinet), both Henry Grimes and Alan Silva on basses and drummer Andrew Cyrille is quite stunning and very intense. In fact it could be safely argued that no jazz music of the era approached the ferocity and intensity of Cecil Taylor's. *—Scott Yanow*

Conquistador / Oct. 6, 1966 / Blue Note ✦✦✦✦✦
For the second of Cecil Taylor's two Blue Note albums (following *Unit Structures*), the innovative pianist utilized a sextet comprised of trumpeter Bill Dixon, altoist Jimmy Lyons, both Henry Grimes and Alan Silva on basses and drummer Andrew Cyrille. During the two lengthy pieces, Lyons' passionate solos contrast with Dixon's quieter ruminations while the music in general is unremittingly intense. Both of the Taylor Blue Notes are quite historic and near-classics but, despite this important documentation, Cecil Taylor (other than a pair of Paris concerts) would not appear on records again until 1973. *—Scott Yanow*

☆ **The Great Concert** / Jul. 29, 1969 / Prestige ✦✦✦✦✦
Boxed set with Taylor in searing live concert alongside Sam Rivers (sax) and Jimmy Lyons (as). Three discs of amazing playing. *—Ron Wynn*

★ **Silent Tongues** / Jul. 2, 1974 / 1201 Music ✦✦✦✦✦
This is a classic Cecil Taylor solo concert, performed at the 1974 *Montreux Jazz Festival.* Taylor plays his five-movement work "Silent Tongues" along with a couple of brief encores. To simplify in explaining what he was doing at this point of time, it can be said that Taylor essentially plays the piano like a drum set, creating percussive and thunderous sounds that are other worldly and full of an impressive amount of energy and atonal ideas. Many listeners will find these performances to be quite difficult but it is worth the struggle to open up one's perceptions as to what music can be. *—Scott Yanow*

Dark Unto Themselves / Jan. 18, 1976 / Enja ✦✦✦✦✦
This CD reissue has a continuous 61æ-minute performance by pianist Cecil Taylor and his 1976 quintet (which also includes such fiery players as trumpeter Raphe Malik, his longtime altoist Jimmy Lyons, tenor saxophonist David Ware and drummer Marc Edwards). There is a quick theme along with brief transitions that form the composition "Streams and Chorus of Seed" but the bulk of the passionate performance is taken up by spontaneous and intense solos. Listeners with very open ears and longtime fans of Cecil Taylor can consider this explosive performance to be essential. *—Scott Yanow*

● **Cecil Taylor Unit** / Apr. 3, 1978-Apr. 6, 1978 / New World ✦✦✦✦✦
A sextet, this is as close to as definitive an ensemble as Taylor has launched. With Jimmy Lyons (sax), Raphe Malik (tpt), Ramsey Ameen (violin), Sirone (b), and R. Shannon Jackson (d). This runs 60 minutes on vinyl, including a 30-minute "Holiday en Masque." *—Michael G. Nastos*

It Is in the Brewing Luminous / Feb. 8, 1980-Feb. 9, 1980 / hatART ✦✦✦✦✦
Originally released as a double-LP and then reissued as a single CD, this continuous 71-minute live performance from 1980 features pianist Cecil Taylor with a particularly intriguing sextet comprised of his longtime altoist Jimmy Lyons, violinist Ramsey Ameen, Alan Silva on bass and cello and both Jerome Cooper and Sunny Murray on drums. Not too surprisingly, the playing is quite intense and dense with only a few moments of lyricism popping through. Taylor sounds very much like a human dynamo while Lyons' solos are full of fragile beauty. This is brilliant music that will not sound "safe" or "easy listening" even a century from now. *—Scott Yanow*

Winged Serpent (Sliding Quadrants) / Oct. 22, 1984-Oct. 24, 1984 / Soul Note ✦✦✦✦
Utilizing what was called an "Orchestra of Two Continents," pianist Cecil Taylor has a larger orchestra for this Soul Note release than usual. The 11-piece group is filled with brilliant and adventurous players: trumpeters Enrico Rava and Tomasz Stanko, altoist Jimmy Lyons, Frank Wright and John Tchicai on tenors, baritonist Gunter Hampel, bassoonist Karen Borca, bassist William Parker and both Rashied Bakr and Andre Martinez on drums. On the four Taylor originals, the colorful ensembles are quite dense although there is room for individual solos and heroics. Not too surprisingly Cecil Taylor is very much in control of the music. Incidentally this was probably Jimmy Lyons' last record with Taylor; he passed away in 1986. *—Scott Yanow*

For Olim / Apr. 9, 1986 / Soul Note ✦✦✦✦✦
One of Cecil Taylor's most satisfying solo concerts, this date features the always uncompromising and adventurous pianist exploring eight of his compositions, including a few that are quite brief (two are under two minutes). The difficult but lyrical live set rewards repeated listenings. *—Scott Yanow*

Olu Iwa / Apr. 1986 / Soul Note ✦✦✦✦✦
This session presented Taylor working alternately with a large group and intimate unit, recording two pieces on April 12. The opening 48-minute dialogue included the high-register wailing of tenor saxophonists Peter Brotzmann and Frank Wright and Taylor's undulating answering lines and sprawling solos. The second piece was a bit shorter (27 minutes), but no less ambitious, with shifting moods, themes and tempos. As usual, Taylor's music wasn't for the squeamish or those who desire nicely ordered, predictable material. It required intense concentration and attention from both performers and audience. *—Ron Wynn*

Live in Bologna / Nov. 1987 / Leo ✦✦✦✦✦
Having suffered the passing of longtime musical partner Jimmy Lyons just a year prior, pianist Cecil Taylor enlisted alto saxophonist and flute player Carlos Ward as a replacement for a series of European dates in 1987. Filling out the group were percussionist Thurman Barker and violinist Leroy Jenkins (both veterans of Chicago's trailblazing AACM free jazz collective), as well as bassist William Parker. The new group members proved to be up to Taylor's capricious and galvanizing ways on this Bologna concert recording, not only providing sympathetic support for the pianist's expansive explorations, but also creating uniquely improvised statements of their own. They maintain a high standard throughout the 90-minute concert (the CD version has been edited down for time limitations), shifting from frenetic, full-ensemble runs to slow, primordial stretches of music-making. Barker particularly stands out, adding a multitude of textures and colors on marimba and a variety of other percussion instruments, while Jenkins also impresses with violin work that matches Taylor's own protean playing. For his part, Ward might not be up to the incisive work Lyons produced during his 20-year tenure with Taylor, but he turns in enough engaging statements to blend in nicely with the others. Although this is a great Taylor release, certainly essential for fans, *Live in Bologna* might not be the best disc for newcomers. Curious listeners should start with either of Taylor's mid-'60s Blue Note discs (*Unit Structures* and *Conquistador*), or check out later titles like 1986's live solo piano recording *For Olim* and his A&M trio date *In Florescence.* *—Stephen Cook*

Sam "The Man" Taylor (Samuel L. Taylor)

b. Jul. 12, 1916, Lexington, TN
Sax (Tenor) / Jazz Blues, Jump Blues, Soul-Jazz, Swing, R&B
A certified honking sax legend, Sam "The Man" Taylor's non-stop drive and power worked perfectly in swing, blues and R&B sessions. He had a huge tone, perfect timing and sense of drama, as well as relentless energy and spirit. Taylor began working with Scat Man Crothers and the Sunset Royal Orchestra in the late '30s. He played with Cootie Williams and Lucky Millinder in the early '40s, then worked six years with Cab Calloway. Taylor toured South America and the Caribbean during his tenure with Calloway. Then Taylor became the saxophonist of choice for many R&B dates through the '50s, recording with Ray Charles, Buddy Johnson, Louis Jordan, and Big Joe Turner among others. He also did sessions with Ella Fitzgerald and Sy Oliver. During the '60s, Taylor led his own bands and recorded in a quintet called The Blues Chasers. He currently has one session available on CD recorded in the late '50s with Charlie Shavers and Urbie Green. *—Ron Wynn*

● **The Bad and the Beautiful** / Feb. 20, 1962 / Prestige ✦✦✦✦

Swingstation / Nov. 30, 1954-Jun. 4, 1956 / Verve ✦✦✦
Like fellow saxophone player Hal Singer, Sam "The Man" Taylor" moved easily between jazz and Rhythm and Blues (with early rock and roll overtones), although his rough, hard driving way with the horn usually finds him classified as an R&B icon. This bargain-priced album goes a long way to support the R&B labeling. Joined by another sax player who often found himself moving between jazz and R&B, baritone Haywood Henry, this album catches Taylor in three sessions he made for MGM Records in March of 1955 and November of 1956. In addition to Henry he is joined by other habitues of the R&B world like Lloyd Trotman on bass and Freddie Washington on piano. Among the tracks which show off Taylor's unique ways with the sax are "Ride, Sammy, Ride" where Taylor is urged on by the band shouting the title line, and a blues dripping "Sam's Blues". There's some yakety—yak *al la* Boots Randolph on "High Winds" which also features a rousing give and take between Taylor and Henry. With the exception of Henry and some occasional choruses by Freddie Washington, this album is pretty much Taylor's show. Little room is made for any of the other participants to solo. While this album is an excellent vehicle to show off the talents of a foremost R&B sax player, it also demonstrates that this sax style with its one-dimensional approach to the art of the sax wears thin very quickly. This is an interesting, but not a major reissue. However, it shows Taylor as he was before he started making romantic albums in the 1960's like *The Bad and the Beautiful.* *—Dave Nathan*

Jack Teagarden (Weldon Leo Teagarden)

b. Aug. 29, 1905, Vernon, TX, **d.** Jan. 15, 1964, New Orleans, LA
Vocals, Trombone / Swing, Dixieland
One of the classic giants of jazz, Jack Teagarden was not only the top pre-bop trombonist (playing his instrument with the ease of a trumpeter) but one of the best jazz singers too. After coming to New York in 1928, "Mr. T." caused a sensation with his daring solos. He would have been a logical candidate for fame in the swing era but he made a strategic error and signed a five-year sideman contract with Paul Whiteman. Teagarden finally put together a

big band in 1939 that lasted for seven years, though he faced bankruptcy during the mid-'40s. Bing Crosby helped Teagarden straighten out his financial problems and from 1947-51 he was a star sideman with Louis Armstrong's All-Stars. After leaving Armstrong, Teagarden was a leader of a steadily working sextet throughout the remainder of his career, playing Dixieland with such talented musicians as brother Charlie, trumpeters Jimmy McPartland, Don Goldie and Max Kaminsky and pianist Earl Hines. He died from a heart attack in 1964 and has yet to be replaced. *—Scott Yanow*

☆ **The Indispensable** / Mar. 14, 1928-Jul. 8, 1957 / RCA ♦♦♦♦♦
Much more complete than the Bluebird CD, this two CD set has trombonist Jack Teagarden featured with Roger Wolfe Kahn's orchestra (two takes of "She's a Great, Great Girl"), Eddie Condon's Hot Shots, the Mound City Blue Blowers, eight numbers with Ben Pollack, his better recordings with Paul Whiteman's Orchestra and a complete session under his own leadership in 1947, in addition to three numbers with Bud Freeman in 1957. This set is highly recommended to those who can locate it. *—Scott Yanow*

● **That's a Serious Thing** / Mar. 14, 1928-Jul. 8, 1957 / Bluebird/RCA ♦♦♦♦♦
This readily available Bluebird CD gives one an excellent overview of the talents of trombonist/singer Jack Teagarden. "Mr. T." is featured with Eddie Condon on a pair of classic 1929 selections and also with Roger Wolfe Kahn's orchestra ("She's a Great Great Girl"), Ben Pollack, the Mound City Blue Blowers, Fats Waller, Benny Goodman, Paul Whiteman, the Three T's, the Metronome All-Stars, Louis Armstrong (the exciting "Jack-Armstrong Blues"), and with Bud Freeman, in addition to a version of "St. Louis Blues" with Teagarden's group in 1947. Quite a few of these performances are famous, and although this is not a "complete" set, the consistent high quality of these recordings makes this CD highly recommended to all. *—Scott Yanow*

King of the Blues Trombone / Nov. 27, 1928-Jul. 23, 1940 / Epic ♦♦♦♦♦
This deluxe three-LP set (which will hopefully be reissued on CD eventually) features the great trombonist and vocalist Jack Teagarden in a variety of settings. These often-rare recordings showcase Teagarden as a sideman with Jimmy McHugh's Bostonians, Mills Merry Makers, the Whoopee Makers, Jack Pettis, Goody and His Good Timers, Joe Venuti, Ben Pollack, Benny Goodman, Frankie Trumbauer and Teagarden's own big band; the supporting cast includes Goodman, Jimmy McPartland, Artie Shaw, Jimmy Dorsey, Bud Freeman, Fats Waller and many other classic jazz artists. If you are fortunate enough to run across this collection, don't let it out of your sight. *—Scott Yanow*

1930-1934 / Oct. 1, 1930-Mar. 2, 1934 / Classics ♦♦♦♦
This Classics CD has the first 23 titles ever issued under the leadership of trombonist Jack Teagarden. Many of these selections were formerly rare, particularly the earlier titles on Domino, Banner and Crown. Best is the session that co-starred pianist/vocalist Fats Waller and, while some of the titles are a bit commercial, Teagarden's playing (and that of his better sidemen) uplift the music; "A Hundred Years from Today" is a classic. *—Scott Yanow*

1939-1940 / Aug. 23, 1939-Feb. 1940 / Classics ♦♦♦♦
The third in Classics' *Complete* Jack Teagarden series traces the trombonist's big-band recordings during his Columbia period. There were no great soloists among Teagarden's sidemen and some of these tunes (particularly the nine with Kitty Kallen vocals) are throwaways but Teagarden's own singing on six songs (including "Beale Street Blues" and "If I Could Be with You") and distinctive trombone give listeners strong reasons to acquire this entry in the worthy series. Other highlights include "Peg of My Heart," "Wolverine Blues," "Swinging' on the Teagarden Gate" and "The Blues." *—Scott Yanow*

Big Eight: Jack Teagarden / Pee Wee Russell / Aug. 31, 1938-Dec. 15, 1940 / Riverside/OJC ♦♦♦♦♦

1941-1943 / Jan. 31, 1941-Nov. 16, 1943 / Classics ♦♦♦♦♦
The fifth Classics CD to reissue all of trombonist/vocalist Jack Teagarden's early recordings as a leader has more than its share of gems. A dozen selections feature his 1941 big band, and unlike earlier sessions, there are no indifferent vocals or unnecessary pop baggage. Teagarden is heard in prime form on "Chicks Is Wonderful" (which strangely enough is an instrumental), "St. James Infirmary," "A Hundred Years From Today" and "Nobody Knows the Trouble I've Seen." There are also two selections that Teagarden performed in the movie *Birth of the Blues* with Bing Crosby: the classic title cut (sung by Crosby) and "The Waiter and the Porter and the Upstairs Maid" which finds Teagarden, Bing and Mary Martin all interacting in cheerful form. The last seven numbers on this highly enjoyable CD feature Teagarden jamming with the Capitol International Jazzmen in 1943. Teagarden takes three vocals (including "Stars Fell On Alabama") and is well showcased on a previously unissued "Mighty Lak' a Rose." In addition, tenor saxophonist Dave Matthews takes his greatest solo on "In My Solitude"; Billy May takes his hottest trumpet solos throughout the date; pianist Joe Sullivan is a strong asset; and the clarinet spot is taken by either Jimmie Noone or Heinie Beau. "I'm Sorry I Made You Cry" and "'Deed I Do" are both quite hot. Recommended. *—Scott Yanow*

Club Hangover Broadcasts with Jackie Coon / Apr. 3, 1954-Apr. 24, 1954 / Arbors ♦♦♦♦
This double-CD from Arbors contains four half-hour broadcasts by the Jack Teagarden sextet during its stay at *the Club Hangover* in San Francisco. At the time the trombonist's band featured trumpeter Jackie Coon, the obscure but talented clarinetist Jay St. John, Jack's sister Norma Teagarden on piano, bassist Kas Malone and drummer Ray Bauduc. Because of some odd regulations, Jack Teagarden was not allowed to sing at these engagements (because otherwise the music would be classified as "entertainment" and the club-owner would be subject to an additional tax) so the performances are strictly instrumentals. In addition to the band numbers, on each broadcast the intermission pianist had a chance to play one number; Lil Armstrong and Don Ewell are both heard from twice. Although the talking by the announcer is a bit annoying at times (he knew nothing about jazz), the Dixieland music is generally quite spirited if predictable and the three horns all get in their fair share of heated solos on the familiar warhorses. *—Scott Yanow*

The Complete Capitol Fifties Jack Teagarden Sessions / Oct. 18, 1955-Apr. 14, 1958 / Mosaic ♦♦♦♦♦
Jack Teagarden was the top jazz trombonist to emerge before World War II. While his most innovative days were in the late '20s and '30s, he remained a viable and highly enjoyable jazzman (and a popular attraction on the Dixieland circuit) up until his death in 1964. In the 1950s, he recorded six albums for Capitol, and they are reissued in full (plus some alternate takes and a "new" version of "St. James Infirmary") on Mosaic's four-CD box set. Teagarden is heard on two hot Dixieland dates (*Coast Concert* and *Jazz Ultimate*) with cornetist Bobby Hackett and either Matty Matlock or Peanuts Hucko on clarinet. An outing by his own working group (Big T's Dixieland Band) is a surprising disappointment, for the sextet is hamstrung by dully arranged ensembles instead of getting a chance to really stretch out. However, Teagarden's three albums with larger groups are all better than expected. *This Is Teagarden* revisits some older material, *Swing Low, Sweet Spiritual* (even with the dumb background singers) is generally successful, and the instrumental mood record *Shades of Night* has some beautiful trombone playing on the ballads. Although Teagarden was no longer a pacesetter in the 1950s, he is heard throughout in prime form. Dixieland collectors can consider this box to be essential. *—Scott Yanow*

100 Years from Today / Sep. 20, 1963-Sep. 21, 1963 / Memphis Archives ♦♦♦♦♦
Jack Teagarden's final recording, performed less than four months before his death, finds the trombonist/vocalist in particularly high spirits at *the Monterey Jazz Festival*. Mr. T. was reunited not only with his brother (trumpeter Charlie) and sister (pianist Norma), but his mother, who performs a couple of ragtime piano solos. The strong supporting cast, in addition to the many Teagardens, features clarinetist Pee Wee Russell, baritonist Gerry Mulligan, and pianist Joe Sullivan. The two sets included on this historical CD are filled with blues, standards, and Dixieland, the results of Jack Teagarden's two sets at *Monterey*. This important and enjoyable music is proof that the great trombonist went out on top. *—Scott Yanow*

Jacky Terrasson

b. Nov. 27, 1966, Berlin, Germany
Piano / Post-Bop
By the mid-'90s, pianist Jacky Terrasson was being hailed as one of the bright young lions on the traditional jazz scene. His self-titled 1995 debut for Blue Note Records drew high praise from all corners of the jazz world. His feathery keyboard touch is coupled with a lot of power and passion, a complete understanding of the blues and improvisation, and Terrasson is also a gifted arranger, putting his own personal stamp on well known tunes. He's been one of the jazz world's most talked about piano player/composers since he captured everyone's attention when he won the Thelonious Monk Competition in 1993. He's also one of the most sought-after sidemen in jazz, constantly in demand for touring jazz bands and recording dates. On his 1996 sophomore effort, *Reach*, he's ably backed by the same musicians who accompanied him on his debut: bassist Ugonna Okegwo and drummer Leon Parker. 1999's *What It Is* emphasized Terrasson's compositional skills as well as technique. *—Richard Skelly*

Jacky Terrasson / Jun. 1994-Aug. 1994 / Blue Note ♦♦♦♦
Jacky Terrasson delights in turning standards inside out. On his CD he gives odd rhythms to "I Love Paris," tpurposely speeds up and slows down the tempo on "Bye Bye Blackbird," takes "I Fall in Love Too Easily" very slow, does his best to disguise "Bye Bye Blackbird" and shows a graps of dynamics worthy of Ahmad Jamal. It is fortunate that bassist Ugonna Okegwo and drummer Leon Parker are very alert (or perhaps well-rehearsed) because to the uninitiated listener, these eccentric and rather quirky performances are often quite unpredictable and occasionally jarring. Well worth checking out. *—Scott Yanow*

● **Reach** / Feb. 20, 1996 / Blue Note ♦♦♦♦♦
The talented young pianist Jacky Terrasson and his trio (with bassist Ugonna Okegwo and drummer Leon Parker) find something new to say on a few standards (including a rare uptempo version of "For Sentimental Reasons") and introduce five of Terrasson's originals. Although he has does not have an original style yet, Terrasson displays a great deal of potential for the future. Highlights include "I Should Care," "Just One of Those Things" and a medley of his "Reach" with "Smoke Gets in Your Eyes." *—Scott Yanow*

What It Is / May 18, 1999 / Blue Note ♦♦♦♦
This set is a bit of a departure for pianist Jacky Terrasson who has generally been heard in acoustic trio formats. Terrasson utilizes a variety of other musicians in larger ensembles for mostly original works (other than Ravel's "Bolero"). Among his sidemen are tenor-saxophonist Michael Brecker (who gets off a couple intense solos), flutist Jay Collins, Mino Cinelu on percussion and guitarist Adam Rodgers, among others; Xiomara Laugarts sings on "Better World," and on a few numbers, Terrasson plays a bit of electric piano. Overall, this set is open to the influences of world music and more funk-oriented jazz, yet Jacky Terrasson still sounds quite creative, explorative and individual. An intriguing program. *—Scott Yanow*

Clark Terry

b. Dec. 14, 1920, St. Louis, MO
Vocals, Flugelhorn, Trumpet / Swing, Bop
Possessor of the happiest sound in jazz, flugelhornist Clark Terry always plays music that is exuberant, swinging and fun. A brilliant (and very distinctive) soloist, C.T. gained fame for his "Mumbles" vocals (which started as a satire of the less intelligible ancient blues singers) and is also an enthusiastic educator. He gained early experience playing trumpet in the viable St. Louis jazz scene of the early '40s (where he was an inspiration for Miles Davis), gaining a strong reputation playing with the big band of Charlie Barnet (1947-48), the orchestra and small groups of Count Basie (1948-51) and particularly with Duke Ellington (1951-59). Terry, a versatile swing/bop soloist who started specializing on flugelhorn in the mid-'50s, had many features with Ellington (including "Perdido") and started leading his own record dates during that era. He then joined the staff of NBC where he was a regular member of the Tonight Show Orchestra, and recorded regularly in the 1960s including a classic set with the Oscar Peterson Trio and several dates with the quintet he co-led with valve trombonist Bob

Brookmeyer. Throughout the 1970s,'80s and '90s C.T. has remained a major force, recording and performing in a wide variety of settings. *—Scott Yanow*

Serenade to a Bus Seat / Apr. 27, 1957 / Riverside/OJC ✦✦✦✦
This CD reissue matches together trumpeter Clark Terry (before he switched to flugelhorn) with tenor saxophonist Johnny Griffin, pianist Wynton Kelly, bassist Paul Chambers and drummer Philly Joe Jones. Most notable about the music is that Terry wrote five of the eight selections (including the colorful title cut which pays tribute to life on the road with Duke Ellington); the other numbers are "Donna Lee," a pretty version of "Stardust" and a slightly Latinized "That Old Black Magic." Terry and Griffin were a potent team, making one regret that they did not record together much through the years. This set contains excellent straightahead jazz performed with plenty of spirit. *—Scott Yanow*

Duke with a Difference / Jul. 29, 1957-Sep. 6, 1957 / Riverside/OJC ✦✦✦✦
For this CD reissue of a Riverside set, trumpeter Clark Terry and some of the top Ellington sidemen of the period (trombonist Britt Woodman, altoist Johnny Hodges, tenor-saxophonist Paul Gonsalves, Tyree Glenn on vibes, bassist Jimmy Woode and drummer Sam Woodyard) perform eight songs associated with Duke, but with fresh arrangements. There is plenty of solo space for C.T., Gonsalves and Hodges, and the arrangements by Terry and Mercer Ellington cast a new light on some of the warhorses; highlights include "C-Jam Blues," "Cottontail," "Mood Indigo" and "Come Sunday." *—Scott Yanow*

In Orbit / May 7, 1958-May 12, 1958 / Riverside/OJC ✦✦✦✦✦
One of Thelonious Monk's rare appearances as a sideman is on this quartet set led by flugelhornist Clark Terry. With bassist Sam Jones and drummer Philly Joe Jones, Terry and pianist Monk perform a set that surprisingly has only one Thelonious Monk song ("Let's Cool One"). Among the high points of this spirited, boppish date are C.T.'s "One Foot in the Gutter" and "Argentia." *—Scott Yanow*

Top and Bottom Brass / Feb. 24, 1959-Feb. 26, 1959 / Riverside/OJC ✦✦✦✦
This lesser-known Clark Terry session (reissued on CD in the *OJC* series) has an unusual lineup with the flugelhornist joined by Don Butterfield on tuba, pianist Jimmy Jones, bassist Sam Jones and drummer Art Taylor. Butterfield has nearly as much solo space as C.T. (and is given a prominent role in the ensembles) while Jimmy Jones's chordal solos are somewhat eccentric. Terry is in fine form on a variety of blues, originals and obscurities along with the interesting versions of "My Heart Belongs to Daddy" and "A Sunday Kind of Love" but the results overall are not all that significant. *—Scott Yanow*

★ **Color Changes** / Nov. 19, 1960 / Candid ✦✦✦✦✦
This is one of flügelhornist Clark Terry's finest albums. Terry had complete control over the music and, rather than have the usual jam session, he utilized an octet and arrangements by Yusef Lateef, Budd Johnson, and Al Cohn. The lineup of musicians (C.T., trombonist Jimmy Knepper, Julius Watkins on French horn, Yusef Lateef on tenor, flute, oboe, and English horn, Seldon Powell doubling on tenor and flute, pianist Tommy Flanagan, bassist Joe Benjamin, and drummer Ed Shaughnessy) lives up to its potential, and the charts make good use of the sounds of these very individual stylists. The material, which consists of originals by Terry, Duke Jordan, Lateef, and Bob Wilber, is both rare and fresh, and the interpretations always swing. Highly recommended. *—Scott Yanow*

Mellow Moods / Jul. 21, 1961-May 15, 1962 / Prestige ✦✦✦✦
This CD combines together two former LPs by flugelhornist Clark Terry: *Everything's Mellow* and *All American.* Since those two sessions were cut for the Moodsville label (where all of the sets were supposed to be emphasizing quiet ballads) and the second date has songs from a forgotten musical, this CD would not seem to have much potential. However Terry is highly expressive on the former date (a quartet outing with pianist Junior Mance, bassist Joe Benjamin and drummer Charlie Persip) and does not stick only to ballads, throwing in some blues and obscure melodies. As for the *All American* score, Oliver Nelson was enlisted to write arrangements for Terry's septet (which is comprised of Budd Johnson on tenor, trombonist Lester Robertson, baritonist George Barrow, pianist Eddie Costa in one of his final recordings, bassist Art Davis and drummer Ed Shaughnessy) and, except for a couple of purposely corny moments, the music is greatly uplifted; in fact a few of the songs deserve to be revived. C.T. and Budd are in great form throughout. This surprising CD is recommended. *—Scott Yanow*

☆ **Oscar Peterson Trio with Clark Terry** / 1964 / Mercury ✦✦✦✦✦
The Oscar Peterson Trio, with bassist Ray Brown and drummer Ed Thigpen, welcomed flugelhornist Clark Terry to this very memorable studio session. Whether on "Brotherhood of Man," "Mack the Knife" or "They Didn't Believe Me," all of the players are mutually inspired, and the results are not only joyful, but explosively exuberant. However, this album (reissued on CD) will be best remembered for Clark Terry's introduction of his unique vocal style on "Mumbles" and "Incoherent Blues"; those spontaneous performances still sound funny. A gem. *—Scott Yanow*

The Happy Horns of Clark Terry / Mar. 13, 1964 / GRP/Impulse! ✦✦✦✦
This all-star CD has plenty of memorable moments. Flugelhornist Clark Terry teams up with altoist Phil Woods (who doubles on clarinet), tenor great Ben Webster, pianist Roger Kellaway, bassist Milt Hinton and drummer Walter Perkins for a varied program that includes a rollicking version of "Rockin' in Rhythm," Bix Beiderbecke's "In a Mist," a Duke Ellington medley and "Return to Swahili" which is mostly a flugelhorn-drums duet. The lively music is quite enjoyable. *—Scott Yanow*

Memories of Duke / Mar. 11, 1980 / Pablo Today/OJC ✦✦✦✦
Flugelhornist Clark Terry and a strong quartet (pianist Jack Wilson, guitarist Joe Pass, bassist Ray Brown and drummer Frank Severino) perform nine songs associated with Duke Ellington, including seven of Ellington's compositions, plus a tune apiece from Billy Strayhorn ("Passion Flower") and Mercer Ellington ("Things Ain't What They Used to Be"). Terry knows these songs, which include "Cottontail," "Come Sunday" and "Sophisticated Lady," backwards, but he infuses each of his renditions with enthusiasm and melodic creativity. Recommended. *—Scott Yanow*

Yes, the Blues / Jan. 19, 1981 / Pablo/OJC ✦✦✦✦✦
This blues-oriented Pablo recording has an ideal matchup: flugelhornist Clark Terry and altoist Eddie "Cleanhead" Vinson. Both musicians take a good-humored vocal apiece, but the emphasis is on their playing. The complementary stylists, backed by pianist Art Hillery, bassist John Heard and drummer Roy McCurdy, work together very well on their originals, plus "Swingin' the Blues," and create some memorable, if fairly basic, music straddling the boundaries between swing, bop and early R&B. *—Scott Yanow*

To Duke and Basie / Jan. 28, 1986 / Rhino ✦✦✦✦✦
Flugelhornist Clark Terry and bassist Red Mitchell play a full program of duets, with most of the music being associated with either Count Basie or Duke Ellington. Actually, the most remembered selection of the date is C.T.'s humorous "Hey Mr. Mumbles, What Did You Say—," which has a call-and-response vocal by the two masterful musicians. Overall, this is a particularly delightful set, with plenty of wit displayed along with the hard swinging. *—Scott Yanow*

Live at the Village Gate / Nov. 19, 1990-Nov. 20, 1990 / Chesky ✦✦✦✦
Flugelhornist Clark Terry, three weeks shy of his 70th birthday at the time of this live performance, sounds very much at the peak of his powers throughout the date. Teamed up with old friend Jimmy Heath, who doubles on tenor and soprano, pianist Don Friedman, bassist Marcus McLauren and drummer Kenny Washington (altoist Paquito D'Rivera guests on "Silly Samba"), C.T. performs eight little-known originals. The tunes are all fairly basic, but they inspire these talented musicians to some of their best playing. The hard-swinging music, which includes a trumpet-drums duet on "Brushes & Brass" and some singing from the audience on "Hey Mr. Mumbles," is quite enjoyable, among the most accessible type of jazz. *—Scott Yanow*

Daylight Express / Jul. 26, 1957-Aug. 6, 1957 / GRP ✦✦✦✦✦
Two obscure but very enjoyable and complementary former Lps are reissued in full on this generous CD. The first half of the disc is primarily a showcase for trumpeter Clark Terry who is joined by Mike Simpson (on tenor and flute) in a sextet. C.T. sounds a bit more influenced by Dizzy Gillespie at this time than he would but he was already quite distinctive on such numbers as "Candy," "Blues For Daddy O's Jazz Patio Blues" and "Basin Street Blues." "Phalanges" is a hot bop line (by Louie Bellson) that deserves to be revived while "Trumpet Mouthpiece Blues" sounds like an ancestor of "Mumbles." The second half of the album matches Terry with tenor-saxophonist Paul Gonsalves (who is actually the leader) and a rhythm section that features some surprisingly advanced piano from Willie Jones that sometimes hints strongly at both Cecil Taylor and Sun Ra! Terry and Gonsalves (who were both with Duke Ellington at the time) always made for a good team. The tenor revisits the 1956 *Newport Jazz Festival* with his long solo on "Festival" and other tunes (all originals by one of the horn players) are basic and swinging; a previously unissued ballad, "The Girl I Call Baby" closes the rewarding and memorable set. Highly recommended. *—Scott Yanow*

Toots Thielemans (Jean Baptiste Thielemans)

b. Apr. 29, 1922, Brussels, Belgium
Harmonica, Guitar / Brazilian Jazz, Mainstream Jazz, Contemporary Jazz, Latin Jazz, Swing, Bop

Although preceded by Larry Adler (who has actually spent much of his career playing popular and classical music), Toots Thielemans virtually introduced the chromatic harmonica as a jazz instrument. In fact ever since the mid-'50s he has had no close competitors. Toots simply plays the harmonica with the dexterity of a saxophonist and has even successfully traded off with the likes of Oscar Peterson.

Toots Thielemans' first instrument was the accordion which he started when he was three. Although he started playing the harmonica when he was 17, Thielemans' original reputation was made as a guitarist who was influenced by Django Reinhardt. Very much open to bop, Thielemans played in American GI clubs in Europe, visited the U.S. for the first time in 1947 and shared the bandstand with Charlie Parker at the Paris Jazz Festival of 1949. He toured Europe as a guitarist with the Benny Goodman Sextet in 1950 and the following year moved to the U.S. During 1953-59 Toots was a member of the George Shearing quintet (mostly as a guitarist) and has freelanced ever since. He first recorded his big hit "Bluesette" (which featured his expert whistling and guitar) in 1961 and ever since has been greatly in-demand (particularly for his harmonica and his whistling) on pop records (including many dates with Quincy Jones) and as a jazz soloist. Toots' two-volume *Brasil Project* was popular in the 1990s and found him smoothly interacting on harmonica with top Brazilian musicians. *—Scott Yanow*

Man Bites Harmonica / Dec. 30, 1957-Jan. 7, 1958 / Riverside/OJC ✦✦✦✦✦
Although he plays guitar exclusively on two of the eight selections included on this CD reissue, it is Toots Thielemans' harmonica playing that is most unique. He holds his own on a hard bop blowing date with baritonist Pepper Adams, pianist Kenny Drew, bassist Wilbur Ware and drummer Art Taylor, jamming on such songs as "East of the Sun," "Struttin' with Some Barbeque" and "Isn't It Romantic." Even four decades later, no jazz harmonica player has dethroned the great Toots. *—Scott Yanow*

Images / Sep. 16, 1974 / Candid ✦✦✦✦✦
This 1997 CD reissues harmonica great Toots Thielemans' Choice LP *Captured Alive* and adds previously unreleased versions of "Stella By Starlight" and Toots' "Revol" from the same session. Thielemans, who single-handedly turned the chromatic harmonica into a jazz instrument (his only predecessor was Larry Adler, who legitimized the instrument by often playing classical music), shows on such numbers as "Giant Steps," "Airegin," and "Days of Wine and Roses" that the harmonica is a viable device for jazz improvising. Toots is assisted by the great pianist Joanne Brackeen (who contributed "Images" and "Snooze"), bassist Cecil McBee, and drummer Freddie Waits. A particularly strong outing that can serve as a perfect introduction to the harmonica wizard. *—Scott Yanow*

Live in the Netherlands / Jul. 13, 1980 / Pablo/OJC ✦✦✦✦

This rather memorable Pablo recording, his only album as a leader for Norman Granz's label (although he made several notable appearances as a sideman), features the great jazz harmonica player Toots Thielemans in a sparse trio with guitarist Joe Pass and bassist Niels Pedersen. The four main numbers ("Blues in the Closet," "Thriving from a Riff," "Autumn Leaves" and "Someday My Prince Will Come") are pure bebop and Thielemans' solo guitar rendition of "The Mooche" is also a highlight. *—Scott Yanow*

● **Only Trust Your Heart** / Apr. 1988-May 1988 / Concord Jazz ♦♦♦♦♦
Although the liner notes claim that this Concord release was Toots Thielemans' first recording as a leader in more than a dozen years, somehow the harmonica great's 14 European dates (not to mention sets released by Stash and Pablo) were overlooked. In any case, this is a pretty definitive session by the harmonica virtuoso who is joined by pianist Fred Hersch, either Marc Johnson or Harvie Swartz on bass and drummer Joey Baron. The material is filled with challenging and generally underplayed standards (including Wayne Shorter's "Speak No Evil," Thad Jones' "Three and One," Benny Carter's lyrical "Only Trust Your Heart" and Thelonious Monk's "Little Rootie Tootie") plus two fine Hersch originals. Ranging from hard bop to Brazilian music and post bop, this is a consistently enjoyable and highly recommended outing. *—Scott Yanow*

For My Lady / Apr. 3, 1991-Apr. 4, 1991 / EmArcy ♦♦♦♦
The emphasis is on ballads for harmonica player Toots Thielemans' outing with the Shirley Horn Trio. Horn, in addition to contributing some tastefully supportive piano and occasional solos, takes a vocal on "Someone to Watch Over Me." Toots sounds quite relaxed performing 11 standards (only "Blues in the Closet" generates much heat) plus his original "For My Lady" with such comfortable backing. *—Scott Yanow*

The Brasil Project, Vol. 2 / 1993 / Private Music ♦♦♦♦
Guitarist, harmonica player, and whistler Toots Thielemans' followup to the critically acclaimed *Brasil Project* doesn't stray far from its predecessor's path. There are 13 nice Afro-Latin selections with Thielemans backing such top Brazilian vocalists as Milton Nascimento, Gilberto Gil, Ivan Lins, Caetano Veloso, and Dori Caymmi, among others, and guitarists Oscar Castro-Nieves and Lee Ritenour assisting Thielemans with delicate shadings and accompaniment. *—Ron Wynn*

Chez Toots / Apr. 28, 1998 / Private Music ♦♦♦♦
On this unusual CD, the remarkable harmonica player Toots Thielemans explores a variety of mostly French melodies. The music is often nostalgic and wistful but generally swinging, with enough different tempos to hold one's interest throughout. The oddest aspect of the set is that there is an overdubbed vocal apiece by Diana Krall ("La Vie En Rose"), Dianne Reeves, Johnny Mathis, Shirley Horn and a promising newcomer known here only as Chip; Krall, Reeves and Chip sing in French. Thielemans plays beautifully throughout the relaxed date, which includes "I Wish You Love." "The Windmills of Your Mind," "Once Upon a Summertime" and "Moulin Rouge"; easily recommended. *—Scott Yanow*

Lucky Thompson (Eli Thompson)

b. Jun. 16, 1924, Columbia, SC
Sax (Tenor), Sax (Soprano) / Hard Bop, Bop
Lucky Thompson was one of the great tenors to emerge during the 1940s and one of the first "modern" soprano saxophonists (taking up the instrument prior to John Coltrane and around the same time as Steve Lacy) but he was always a bit overshadowed by more spectacular players. During 1944-45 he gained some attention with Count Basie (where Thompson had succeeded his main influence, Don Byas). Although his large tone looked towards the swing era, Thompson's advanced improvising fit in well with bop players. He settled on the West Coast after leaving Basie, was hired as "insurance" by Dizzy Gillespie in case Charlie Parker did not show up (he recorded with both) and cut many sessions (his solo on "Just One More Chance" was a personal favorite) during his stay in Los Angeles, performing with Boyd Raeburn and the short-lived Stars of Swing. He led a band regularly at the Savoy during 1951-53 and in 1954 starred on Miles Davis' famous *Walkin'* session. In 1956 Thompson was a top soloist with Stan Kenton (appearing on *Cuban Fire*) and during the next two years he cut many sessions both as a leader and as a sideman. *—Scott Yanow*

The Beginning Years / Nov. 1945-Jul. 7, 1947 / IAJRC ♦♦♦♦♦
The first CD put out by the collectors IAJRC label was a big success, a collection of some of tenor saxophonist Lucky Thompson's mid-'40s West Coast recordings. Thompson cut an enormous amount of sides while in Los Angeles during 1945-47 and some of the cream is on this CD. The skilled tenor (whose transitional style fell between swing and bop) is featured with ten different recording groups (many quite obscure) and among the other musicians are trumpeter Karl George, trombonist J.J. Johnson, clarinetist Rudy Rutherford, altoist Marshall Royal, pianists Bill Doggett and Dodo Marmarosa, bassists Oscar Pettiford and Charles Mingus, drummer Shadow Wilson, singers David Allyn and Ernie Andrews and the Mills Blue Rhythm Band. All of the 23 selections (which are of a consistently high quality) were formerly quite rare, making this CD a must for bop collectors. *—Scott Yanow*

☆ **Tricotism** / Jan. 24, 1956-Dec. 12, 1956 / GRP ♦♦♦♦♦
Thompson created a host of spectacular improvisations on the 16 songs on this wonderful CD reissue. It is comprised of two 1956 sessions; one featured Thompson heading a trio backed by bassist Oscar Pettiford and guitarist Skeeter Best, and the other has him heading either a quartet or quintet that included the great trombonist Jimmy Cleveland. Cleveland's smooth, superbly-articulated phrases and statements rank alongside Thompson's gliding lines in their brilliance, and pianist Hank Jones (on three cuts) also sparkles with some marvelous solos. But Lucky Thompson is the star on this date; his elegant, yet robust and exuberant playing demonstrated again what a loss his voluntary departure from the scene constitutes. *—Ron Wynn*

Happy Days / Mar. 8, 1963-Feb. 16, 1965 / Prestige ♦♦♦♦
This CD has the full contents of two of Lucky Thompson's LPs. The earlier session, since it was originally released on the Prestige subsidiary Moodsville, emphasizes ballads, as Thompson interprets eight Jerome Kern melodies (none of the obvious ones) plus his own moody original "No More." One of the first "modern" jazz musicians to start doubling on soprano (actually predating John Coltrane), Lucky Thompson displays a light but forceful tone on both soprano and tenor; his versions of "Look for the Silver Lining," "Who" and "They Didn't Believe Me" are particularly memorable. The second date was a six-song tribute to a new singer of the period, Barbra Streisand. Other than "People" (this version is harmless enough) and Thompson's "Safari," the other tunes are veteran standards, including "Happy Days Are Here Again" and a rare medium-tempo rendition of "As Time Goes By." Overall, this CD is full of excellent music by the always underrated Lucky Thompson. *—Scott Yanow*

● **Lucky Strikes** / Sep. 15, 1964 / Prestige/OJC ♦♦♦♦♦
This CD reissue serves as a perfect introduction to the talents of the underrated saxophonist Lucky Thompson. Heard on four songs apiece on tenor and soprano (he was one of the first bop-oriented soprano players), Thompson plays two standards and six originals in a quartet with pianist Hank Jones, bassist Richard Davis and drummer Connie Kay. The playing time on this straight reissue of an earlier LP is a bit brief (just over 38 minutes) the quality is quite high. Thompson's soprano solos in particular are quite memorable. *—Scott Yanow*

Lucky in Paris / Jan. 14, 1959-Jan. 15, 1959 / High Note ♦♦♦♦♦
Saxophonist Lucky Thompson deserves more credit for not only being an original jazz stylist, but one who also played with soul, passion and verve. This recording is as finely crafted as anything Thompson recorded, and maybe moreso because the empathy and interaction between him and his bandmates, especially the brilliant Algerian pianist Martial Solal, comes through on this date with alarming consistency. Though mostly known as a tenor man, Thompson's soprano playing is quite arresting. His primarily eighth-note phrasings have a distinct Parisian quality, more reminiscent of a harmonica or clarinet. The first two cuts, "How About You" and "Midnight Sun," display this attitude, and makes you wonder if maybe John Coltrane or Steve Lacy were listening and absorbing in the wings. It's quite different than any other approach to soprano heard thereafter. Of course, Thompson's throaty, lugubrious, soulful sound on tenor is irresistible, especially on a ballad like "Solitude." It's a treat to hear Thompson not only in such a sympathetic and well-recorded setting, but as relaxed yet freewheeling as you want with respect to the tricky science of improvising. There are two cuts with just Lucky and percussionist Gana M'bow, and they hint at a pre-eminent world music asethetic, but most are swingers, featuring the underrated French drummer Dave Pochonet, who shines as brightly as Solal. Vibist Michel Hausser gets little solo space, but there's some nice unison dealings on Dizzy Gillespie's "Ow." Overall, this is an extraordinary session, with ten cuts clocking in just shy of 44 minutes of sheer jazz delight. Lucky Thompson is as precious as gold, and any fortunate opportunity to hear him in such a positive setting has to be worth the price. This might very well be his best recording. Highly recommended. *—Michael G. Nastos*

Henry Threadgill (Henry Luther Threadgill)

b. Feb. 15, 1944, Chicago, IL
Sax (Alto), Flute, Composer / Avant-Garde Jazz
Although his music can be somewhat forbidding, Henry Threadgill has been one of the most respected members of the avant-garde for the past 20 years. As an altoist and flutist, he has long had an original tone but it his work as an innovative composer that is most impressive. He played percussion in marching bands while a child, learned baritone and clarinet in high school, studied at the American Conservatory of Music and played gospel music for traveling evangelists. In 1962-63 Threadgill was a part of Richard Abrams' Experimental Band and he became a member of the AACM. After a period in the Army, he worked in the house band at a Chicago blues club and recorded with Abrams. In 1971 Threadgill first teamed up with Steve McCall and Fred Hopkins in a trio and in 1975 the group became known as Air. Threadgill recorded and performed extensively with Air (and its successor New Air) and later led several unique ensembles including X75 (which had four bassists), his Sextett and Very Very Circus. His signing to Sony in 1994 was a big surprise, for Threadgill's compositions and improvisations are far from accessible; happily his Sony recordings show no sign of being watered-down. *—Scott Yanow*

Just the Facts and Pass the Bucket / 1983 / About Time ♦♦♦♦♦
Sextet (actually seven pieces). Dynamite open-ended compositions especially surly "Black Blues" and the determined "Man Called Trinity Deliverance." Features Olu Dara, Pheeroan Aklaff, and John Betsch and bassist Fred Hopkins. All pungently original material. *—Michael G. Nastos*

You Know the Number / Oct. 12, 1986-Oct. 13, 1986 / Jive/Novus ♦♦♦♦♦
You Know the Number is another outstanding record from the Henry Threadgill Sextet. Over the course of six originals, Threadgill and the band fuse complex and spirited arrangements with incisive solo work. The material includes the calypso-inspired numbers "To Be Announced" and "Bermuda Blues" (one of Threadgill's most straightforward compositions), as well as the bittersweet ballad "Silver and Gold Baby, Silver and Gold." Other songs, like "Theme From Thomas Cole" and "Those Who Eat Cookies," feature the kind of buoyant, march-like rhythms and spastic, cartoon soundtrack horn arrangements Threadgill favored. Throughout the set, the band revels in some lively New Orleans-style unison playing and contributes excellent solos (special mention should go to trumpeter Rasul Saddik for his adept and blazing solos, and also to drummers Pheeroan Aklaff and Reggie Nicholson for their propulsive and tight rhythmic support). As usual, Threadgill's solos include an intriguing mix of dark pathos and intensity, while bassist Fred Hopkins and trombonist Frank Lacy follow suit with intriguing contributions of their own. This title is a must for Threadgill fans and also worthwhile for those interested in the experimental side of jazz. *—Stephen Cook*

● **Rag, Bush and All** / Dec. 1988 / Jive/Novus ♦♦♦♦♦
This CD from altoist Henry Threadgill is a perfect mixture of improvisation and composition, hanging onto devices of the past while creating new music. Some of the ensembles (which match Threadgill with trumpeter Ted Daniels, bass trombonist Bill Lowe, cellist Diedre Murray, bassist Fred Hopkins, and both Newman Baker and Reggie Nicholson on

drums) recall Ornette Coleman's *Free Jazz* with the cello-bass interplay inspired by the one-time team of Scott LaFaro and Charlie Haden. The organized horn parts and the riffs behind the lead voices are quite original and sometimes more interesting than the solos themselves. Of the four songs, "Off the Rag" at first dispenses with the melody quickly but the theme constantly pops up in surprising places. "The Devil" is highlighted by Murray's double-time cello runs behind Threadgill's alto while "Gift" contrasts colorful percussion with solemn long tones from the ensemble. "Sweet Holy Rag" has several sections including a pretty classical-like melody, a danceable rumba, a drum feature, and a fairly violent trumpet solo. However, the more one describes this music, the more seems to be left out. Highly recommended to open-eared listeners. *—Scott Yanow*

Spirit of Nuff... Nuff / Nov. 19, 1990-Nov. 21, 1990 / Black Saint ✦✦✦✦✦
After trailblazing stints with the avant-garde jazz trio Air in the '70s and his seven-piece sextet in the '80s, Henry Threadgill changes direction once again with a two tuba, two guitar, trombone, and drums outfit he calls Very Very Circus. Threadgill's layered, idiosyncratic compositions still abound, but as one would expect from a front line like this, the sound is darker and more dense than on prior releases. The new approach is especially evident in the thick mix of reverb-riddled guitar notes, rumbling tuba phrases, and march rhythms heard on numbers like "Drivin' You Slow and Crazy," "Bee Dee Aff," and "Unrealistic Love." Threadgil does lighten the tone, though, by including the Calypso-inspired number "Hope a Hope A" and intricately buoyant themes like "Exacto" and "In the Ring." Standout contributions include Masujaa's mercurial guitar solo on "Unrealistic Love," Threadgill's haunting flute work on "First Church of This," and drummer Gene Lake's supple and tight rhythmic support throughout. Another excellent title from one of jazz's most progressive and original artists. *—Stephen Cook*

Too Much Sugar for a Dime / 1993 / Axiom ✦✦✦✦
Imagine writing for an instrumentation of two electric guitars, two tubas, French horn, drums and Henry Threadgill's alto. Threadgill was up to the challenge and his four avant-garde originals utilize the odd combination of tones to great advantage. Two additional songs feature Threadgill, just one tuba, drums, a few exotic instruments and three strings to create some particularly unusual music. It's for the open-eared listener only. *—Scott Yanow*

Song out of My Trees / Aug. 17, 1993-Aug. 19, 1993 / Black Saint ✦✦✦
Even longtime Threadgill fans may be surprised at the direction and content on his most recent session. The five tunes include three pieces where Threadgill is absent, and one ("Over The River Club") is a nine-minute-plus opus dominated by three guitars colliding, intersecting, and dueling. The title track showcases Threadgill's blues and gospel roots, with some wonderful organ by Amina Claudine Myers. Only "Crea" and "Gateway" are similar to past Threadgill works, with "Crea" featuring the unusual sound of Ted Daniel on hunting horns. Even a champion of the unorthodox like Threadgill may have some people scratching their heads after they hear this, but it's a signal that he'll never settle for doing what's expected. *—Ron Wynn*

Carry the Day / 1994 / Columbia ✦✦✦✦✦
It seems that every five years or so Columbia signs a token avant-garde musician. Arthur Blythe and Tim Berne emerged from their experiences as major-label artists relatively unscathed and, on evidence of Henry Threagill's somewhat forbidding Columbia debut, it would not be surprising if the altoist survived his stint with his priorities straight. There is certainly nothing commercial or watered down about this CD. The music ranges from "Come Carry the Day" (which builds from a group chart to some very dense ensembles) and Threadgill's Dolphyish alto on "Between Orchids" to a couple of very odd vocals and the intense group improv "Jenkins Boys." The group sound (with its accordions, tubas and Mark Taylor's french horn) is attractive in its own way even if the originals do little more than set mysterious moods. This unique music takes several listens to absorb and even then it still might be somewhat incomprehensible. At 37 minutes, it is all over too soon. *—Scott Yanow*

Where's Your Cup / Aug. 1996 / Columbia ✦✦✦✦

The Three Sounds

f. 1957, **db.** 1970
Group / Hard Bop, Soul-Jazz, Ballads
The Three Sounds were one of the most popular artists on Blue Note Records during the late '50s and '60s, thanks to their nimble, swinging, blues-inflected mainstream jazz. Since their records sounded interchangeable and their warm, friendly jazz was instantly accessible, many critics dismissed the group at the time as lounge-jazz, but in the '90s, critical consensus agreed that the group's leader, pianist Gene Harris, was an accomplished, unique stylist whose very ease of playing disguised his technical skill. Similarly, his colleagues, bassist Andrew Simpkins and drummer Bill Dowdy, were a deft, capable rhythm section that kept the group in an appealing, bluesy groove. That groove was so appealing that the Three Sounds maintained a large fan following into the late '60s. During the group's prime period—from their 1958 debut for Blue Note to the departure of Dowdy in 1967—the Three Sounds cut an enormous number of records. Many records hit the shelves, while others stayed in the vaults, to be issued at a later date. Throughout it all, the trio's sound remained essentially the same, with no real dip in quality until the group began to splinter in the late '60s. *—Stephen Thomas Erlewine*

☆ **Introducing the 3 Sounds** / Sep. 16, 1958-Sep. 18, 1958 / Blue Note ✦✦✦✦✦
What's remarkable about *Introducing the Three Sounds* is how the trio's lightly swinging sound arrived fully intact. From the basis of this album, it sounds as if pianist Gene Harris, bassist Andrew Simpkins, and drummer William Dowdy have been playing together for years. There's empathetic, nearly intuitive interplay between the three musicians, and Harris's deft style already sounds mature and entirely distinctive. There's no question that this music is easy to listen to, but dismissing it because of that would be wrong—there's genuine style in their light touch and in Harris' bluesy compositions. The Three Sounds never really deviated from the sound they established on *Introducing,* but that's one of the things that is so remarkable—they were fully formed on their very first album. Even if it was a peak, it wasn't the only peak in their career. They would often match the heights of this album, but this debut remains a shining jewel in their catalog, and the way to become acquainted with their sound. [The CD reissue of *Introducing the Three Sounds* contains the five outtakes plus the alternate take of "Goin' Home" that originally comprised the Japanese album, *Introducing the Three Sounds, Vol. 2.*] *—Stephen Thomas Erlewine*

● **The Best of the Three Sounds** / 1958-1970 / Blue Note ✦✦✦✦✦
The Best of the Three Sounds is a good overview of the trio's original stint at Blue Note. A handful of songs on this 13-song collection date from their late-'60s return to the label, when they played everything a little funkier than they did in their earlier days, but the bulk of the disc is comprised of their classic late-'50s and early-'60s records. Since all of the Three Sounds' albums sound quite similar and are of a consistently high quality, a novice could pick up any album and have a satisfactory introduction, but this nevertheless does a good job of picking up highlights like "Bobby," "Willow Weep for Me," "On Green Dolphin Street," "Poinciana," "Stompin' at the Savoy" and "At Last." It's a nice introduction to one of the most consistently entertaining and accessible artists on Blue Note's roster. *—Stephen Thomas Erlewine*

Standards / Oct. 10, 1959-Jun. 28, 1962 / Blue Note ✦✦✦
During the prime Blue Note years (1958-1962) of the Three Sounds (a trio comprised of pianist Gene Harris, bassist Andy Simpkins and drummer Bill Dowdy), the group did an awful lot of recording for the label. This 1998 CD has a dozen titles that had never been released previously from four sessions in 1959 and 1962. The standards (only "Lights Out" is actually a blues) are made bluesy by the trio. Strangely enough, Harris often sounds closer here to Red Garland (especially in his chord voicings) than to his own style. The fact that the music is not in general as funky as usual may be why producer Alfred Lion did not release with the sessions when they were recorded. However, although not essential, the playing is enjoyable on its own terms, with highlights including "Makin' Whoopee, "' "Witchcraft," "Sometimes I'm Happy," "Red Sails In The Sunset" and "Lights Out." *—Scott Yanow*

Black Orchid / Mar. 7, 1962-Mar. 8, 1962 / Blue Note ✦✦✦✦
Between 1958 and 1962, the Three Sounds were one of the most prolific artists on Blue Note, recording over ten albums worth of material during those four years. During all that time, the group never changed their style much, concentrating on lightly swinging, lightly soulful mainstream jazz that balanced jazz and pop standards with bluesy originals. As time progressed, they veered closer to soul-jazz, but each of their records sounded quite similiar and were equally satisfying. *Black Orchid,* their last album for Blue Note in the early '60s (they would rejoin the label in another four years), was no exception to the rule. It displays their knack for deftly swinging uptempo numbers, light blues and sensitive standards. If anything, it swings a little harder and is a little more soulful than some of its predecessors. Again, the very fact that the music is instantly enjoyable and accessible makes some jazz critics write the Three Sounds off, but Gene Harris, Andrew Simpkins and Bill Dowdy are genuine stylists with prodigious technique. It's difficult to make music this consistently enjoyable, and the Three Sounds illustrate that they have the knack once again on *Black Orchid.* *—Stephen Thomas Erlewine*

Live at the Lighthouse / Jul. 1967 / Blue Note ✦✦✦✦
Shortly after the *Vibrations* sessions, the Three Sounds had their first major personnel shakeup when William Dowdy left the group. Donald Bailey replaced the drummer, and the group played a number of live dates over the course of 1967. During that summer, their concerts at the famed Los Angeles venue *the Lighthouse* were recorded and released as *Live at the Lighthouse.* The selection of nine Three Sounds staples gives the group a chance to stretch out and prove that they could survive without Dowdy. Not only do they prove that they can carry on without him, they flourish. The music on *Live at the Lighthouse* is hotter than some of their studio recordings, pulsating with energy and good feelings, demonstrating that they had worked out any of the problems that hampered *Vibrations.* It's their finest set since *Black Orchid.* *—Stephen Thomas Erlewine*

Coldwater Flat / Apr. 11, 1968 / Blue Note ✦✦✦

Bobby Timmons

b. Dec. 19, 1935, Philadelphia, PA, **d.** Mar. 1, 1974, New York, NY
Piano, Composer / Hard Bop, Soul-Jazz
Bobby Timmons became so famous for the gospel and funky blues cliches in his solos and compositions that his skills as a Bud Powell-inspired bebop player have been long forgotten. After emerging from the Philadelphia jazz scene, Timmons worked with Kenny Dorham (1956), Chet Baker, Sonny Stitt and the Maynard Ferguson Big Band. He was partly responsible for the commercial success of both Art Blakey's Jazz Messengers and Cannonball Adderley's Quintet. For Blakey (who he was with during 1958-9), Timmons wrote the classic "Moanin'" and, after joining Adderley in 1959, his song "This Here" (followed later by "Dat Dere") became a big hit; it is little wonder that Adderley was distressed when Timmons in 1960 decided to return to the Jazz Messengers. "Dat Dere" particularly caught on when Oscar Brown, Jr. wrote and recorded lyrics that colorfully depicted his curious son. Timmons, who was already recording as a leader for Riverside, soon formed his own trio but was never able to gain the commercial success that his former bosses enjoyed. Stereotyped as a funky pianist (although an influence on many players including Les McCann, Ramsey Lewis and much later on Benny Green), Timmons' career gradually declined. He continued working until his death at age 38 from cirrhosis of the liver. *—Scott Yanow*

Moanin' Blues / Jan. 13, 1960-Oct. 21, 1964 / Prestige ✦✦✦✦
As an all-on-one-disc survey of the young composer-laureate of the funky school, this compilation will do very nicely. Drawing from four of Timmons' Riverside albums and one on Prestige, all the tunes are by Timmons save "Bags' Groove" and "Born To Be Blue"; the former takes us into the more advanced harmonic territory that Timmons was starting to explore in 1964. All three of his signature pieces, "Moanin," "This Here" and "Dat Dere," from Timmons' first recording as a leader, are here—good tunes all, done with as much unself-

conscious soul and élan as the far-better-known hit versions by former employers Art Blakey and Cannonball Adderley. Not only does the collection spotlight some instantly memorable gems that did not become well-known—with apologies to Brando, "So Tired" shoulda been a contender—it presents Timmons as a very likable pianist in the funk and bop idioms, with an emphatic touch and a penchant for not overplaying his hand with too many notes. And as for anyone who persists upon condemning this swinging musician as "just a funky piano player," the obvious riposte is, "And what's wrong with that—" *—Richard S. Ginell*

★ **This Here Is Bobby Timmons** / Jan. 13, 1960-Jan. 14, 1960 / Riverside/OJC ✦✦✦✦✦
This is a classic Riverside set that has been reissued on CD in the Original Jazz Classics series. Pianist Bobby Timmons by early 1960 had already had successful stints with Art Blakey (where he contributed "Moanin'") and Cannonball Adderley (writing "This Here" and "Date Dere"). For his first recording as a leader, Timmons (whose "funky" style was beginning to become very influential) performs those three hits along with his own "Joy Ride" and five standards in a trio with bassist Sam Jones and drummer Jimmy Cobb. Always more than just a soul jazz pianist, Timmons (who effectively takes "Lush Life" unaccompanied) became a bit stereotyped later in his career but at this early stage was at the peak of his creativity. Essential music. *—Scott Yanow*

Moanin' / Aug. 12, 1960-Sep. 10, 1963 / Milestone ✦✦✦✦✦
Compilation of five different albums 1960-1963. Great collection and collectable. *—Michael G. Nastos*

Soul Time / Aug. 12, 1960-Aug. 17, 1960 / Riverside ✦✦✦✦
Pianist Bobby Timmons, best known for his sanctified and funky playing and composing, is mostly heard in a straightahead vein on this CD reissue of a Riverside session. Timmons's four originals ("So Tired" is most memorable) alternate with three standards and are interpreted by a quartet with trumpeter Blue Mitchell, bassist Sam Jones and drummer Art Blakey. The swinging music is well-played, making this a good example of Bobby Timmons playing in a boppish (as opposed to funky) setting. *—Scott Yanow*

Easy Does It / Mar. 13, 1961 / Riverside/OJC ✦✦✦✦
Pianist Bobby Timmons, who became famous for his funky originals and soulful playing, mostly sticks to more bop-oriented jazz on this trio set with bassist Sam Jones and drummer Jimmy Cobb. He provides three originals (none of which really caught on) and is in excellent form on the five standards with highlights including "Old Devil Moon," "I Thought About You" and "Groovin' High." The Riverside CD reissue shows that Timmons was a bit more versatile than his stereotype; in any case the music is excellent. *—Scott Yanow*

Bobby Timmons Trio In Person: Recorded Live at the Village Vanguard / Oct. 1, 1961 / Riverside/OJC ✦✦✦✦
For this excellent live set (recorded at the Village Vanguard), pianist Bobby Timmons, bassist Ron Carter and drummer Albert "Tootie" Heath perform a couple of the pianist's originals ("So Tired" and "Popsy") along with some standards. The funky bop-oriented music is quite enjoyable and was very popular during the early '60s. The CD reissue adds previously unreleased versions of "They Didn't Believe Me" and "Dat Dere" to the original program. Easily recommended. *—Scott Yanow*

Born to Be Blue / Aug. 12, 1963 / Riverside/OJC ✦✦✦✦
Throughout his career, Bobby Timmons was typecast as a soulful and blues-oriented pianist due to his hits ("Moanin'," "This Here" and "Dis Dat"). But as he shows on this 1963 trio date (with either Sam Jones or Ron Carter on bass and drummer Connie Kay), Timmons was actually a well-rounded player when inspired. The repertoire on his CD ranges from bop to spirituals, from three diverse originals to "Born to Be Blue." This is excellent music but unfortunately Timmons would not grow much musically after this period. His CD is worth picking up. *—Scott Yanow*

Workin' Out / Oct. 21, 1964-Jan. 20, 1966 / Prestige ✦✦✦✦✦
This CD reissues the contents of two of pianist Bobby Timmons most advanced recordings of the 1960s. For an example of how the popular pianist had continued to evolve after his early funk hits, listen to his often-bitonal solo on "Bags' Groove" from 1964. That session features Timmons in a quartet with vibraphonist Johnny Lytle, bassist Keter Betts and drummer William "Peppy" Hinnant and is filled with subtle surprises. The second recording is even more interesting for Timmons is teamed with tenor-saxophonist Wayne Shorter, bassist Ron Carter and drummer Jimmy Cobb in 1966. The immediately recognizable Shorter in particular plays very well (this version of his "Tom Thumb" is its earliest recording) and the very modern playing of Carter pushes Timmons to really stretch himself. Both of these generally overlooked sessions (even Shorter's best fans may not know about his collaboration with Timmons) were formerly rare and are quite adventurous, making this a highly recommended acquisition that falls somewhere between hard bop and the early avant-garde. *—Scott Yanow*

Cal Tjader (Callen Radcliffe Tjader, Jr.)

b. Jul. 16, 1925, St. Louis, MO, **d.** May 5, 1982, Manila, Philippines
Vibraphone / Afro-Cuban Jazz, West Coast Jazz, Latin Jazz, Cool
Cal Tjader was undoubtedly the most famous non-Latino leader of Latin jazz bands, an extraordinary distinction. From the 1950s until his death, he was practically the point man between the worlds of Latin jazz and mainstream bop; his light, rhythmic, joyous vibraphone manner could comfortably embrace both styles. His numerous recordings for Fantasy and Verve and long-standing presence in the San Francisco Bay Area eventually had a profound influence upon Carlos Santana, and thus Latin rock. It was in George Shearing's band that Tjader's love affair with Latin music began, ignited by Shearing's bassist Al McKibbon, nurtured by contact with Willie Bobo, Mongo Santamaria and Armando Peraza, and galvanized by the '50s mambo craze. When he left Shearing the following year, Tjader promptly formed his own band that emphasized the Latin element yet also played mainstream jazz. Tjader recorded a long series of mostly Latin jazz albums for Fantasy from the mid-'50s through the early-'60s, switching to Verve in 1961 where under Creed Taylor's aegis, he expanded his stylistic palette and was teamed with artists like Lalo Schifrin, Anita O'Day, Kenny Burrell and Donald Byrd. *—Richard S. Ginell*

Good Vibes / Aug. 28, 1951-Mar. 2, 1954 / Concord Jazz ✦✦✦
This CD reissue brings back one of vibraphonist Cal Tjader's final recordings. The Latin jazz pacesetter is in typically fine form, alternating rhythmic pieces with some standards and taking "Doxy" in straightforward fashion without the percussionists. Tjader's final regular group featured pianist Mark Levine, bassist Rob Fisher, Vince Lateano on drums and timbales, future bandleader Poncho Sanchez on congas and either flutist Roger Glenn or Gary Foster (on flute, soprano and alto). Playing time is just 43 minutes (since this is a straight reissue of the original LP), but the quality is high, with the better tracks including "Guachi Guaro," "Speak Low," "Broadway" and "Doxy." *—Scott Yanow*

Los Ritmos Calientes / May 6, 1954-Oct. 11, 1957 / Fantasy ✦✦✦
Vibraphonist Cal Tjader's 1950s recordings for Fantasy did a great deal to popularize Latin jazz and solidify its innovations. This CD has the complete contents of the two LPs *Ritmo Caliente* and *Mas Ritmo Caliente*. With such fine sidemen as flutist Jerome Richardson, pianists Richard Wyands, Eddie Cano, Manuel Duran and Vince Guaraldi, bassists Al McKibbon, Boby Rodriguez and Eugene Wright, and quite a few percussionists (most notably Armando Peraza and, on three songs, Mongo Santamaria and Willie Bobo), the fusion of bop and Latin music results in some exciting playing. In addition to group originals, tunes such as Ray Bryant's "Cubano Chant," "Mambo Inn," "Bernie's Tune," "Perdido" and even "Big Noise From Winnetka" receive lively treatment. *—Scott Yanow*

Tjader Plays Mambo / Sep. 11, 1954-Feb. 21, 1956 / Fantasy/OJC ✦✦✦✦✦
Having finished his tenure with George Shearing in 1954, a thoroughly Latin-inoculated Cal Tjader took off on his own, recording several short slices of infectious Latin jazz, from which a dozen were selected for this album. Many of the selections are standards retrofitted with percolating Latin rhythms, cut and shaped to fit the old three-minute limit of 45 or 78 rpm singles. Tjader's crystalline vibes are teamed with a San Francisco Latin percussion section that lays down the grooves crisply and succinctly, with an occasional emulation of the more laid-back Shearing Latin sound ("East of the Sun"). Elsewhere, Cal experiments with a hot four-man trumpet section on four of the tracks, the best of which is a rhumba version of "Fascinating Rhythm." The earliest Tjader-led recording of "Guarachi Guaro" (later known as "Soul Sauce") is also included here. These seminal tracks helped launch the Cal Tjader Latin jazz style, and they still sound fresher than many other such historical landmarks. *—Richard S. Ginell*

Mambo with Tjader / 1954 / Fantasy/OJC ✦✦✦✦
Vibraphonist Cal Tjader was quickly becoming one of the most important forces in Latin-jazz when he recorded the infectious music on this CD reissue. Joined by pianist Manuel Duran, bassist Carlos Duran and a couple of percussionists, Tjader performes Latinized versions of such standards as "Cherry," "This Can't Be Love," "I'll Remember April," "Autumn Leaves" and even "Sonny Boy." Even over four decades later, the highly rhythmic music (which helped lay the groundwork for Latin-jazz in general) still sounds fresh and lively. *—Scott Yanow*

Tjader Plays Tjazz / Dec. 4, 1954 / Fantasy/OJC ✦✦✦✦
In a change of pace, for this recording vibraphonist Cal Tjader recorded cool-toned bop without a Latin rhythm section. Half of the ten songs (mostly jazz standards) feature Tjader switching to drums (his original instrument) in a quartet also including the obscure trombonist Bob Collins, guitarist Eddie Duran and bassist Al McKibbon. Tjader is back on vibes for the quintet selections with tenor saxophonist Brew Moore, pianist Sonny Clark, bassist Eugene Wright and drummer Bobby White. He sounds right at home in both formats and the swinging quintet numbers in particular are a good reason to search for this valuable album. *—Scott Yanow*

Cal Tjader Quartet / May 24, 1956 / Fantasy/OJC ✦✦✦✦
Vibraphonist Cal Tjader took a brief vacation from playing Afro-Cuban jazz to record this fine straight-ahead bop set. The 1997 CD reissue matches Tjader with the underrated but always swinging pianist Gerald Wiggins, bassist Eugene Wright (shortly before he joined Dave Brubeck's Quartet) and drummer Bill Douglass. They perform four basic originals (two apiece by Wig and Wright) and five standards, including a swinging "Battle Hymn of the Republic" and "Our Love Is Here to Stay." On this date, more than almost any other one, Tjader displays his debt to Milt Jackson's style. *—Scott Yanow*

Latin Kick / Nov. 1956 / Fantasy/OJC ✦✦✦✦✦
Cal Tjader's era-defining mixture of Afro-Cuban rhythms and mainstream jazz solos undergoes a bit of a horizontal expansion in these 1956 sessions. The tracks are often longer than on previous albums, finally taking advantage of the logistics of the LP, and as a result, both the Latin and jazz elements benefit. Tenor saxophonist Brew Moore gets extended chances to blow in an easy-grooving Getz-like manner on several tracks, and on "I Love Paris," Luis Miranda (congas) and Bayardo Velarde (timbales) engage in some spirited percussion battles over the vamping of the brothers Duran (Manuel on piano and Carlos on bass). Everything cooks in a bright yet disciplined manner, and Tjader's elliptical, swinging vibes preside genially over the ensemble. *—Richard S. Ginell*

☆ **Black Orchid** / 1956-1959 / Fantasy/OJC ✦✦✦✦✦
This CD has all of the music originally on the two LPs *Cal Tjader Goes Latin* and *The Cal Tjader Quintet*. Since each album had two sessions apiece, the CD does a fine job of giving one a sampling of the influential vibraphonist's popular Latin jazz groups of the era. Among the key sideman are flutist Paul Horn, Jose "Chombo" Silva on tenor, pianists Lonnie Hewitt, Vince Guaraldi and Manuel Duran, and Mongo Santamaria and Willie Bobo on percussion. The music (a mixture of Latinized standards and newer originals) is quite appealing, showing why this infectious blending of bop with Latin rhythms has always been one of the most accessible styles of jazz. *—Scott Yanow*

Jazz at the Blackhawk / Jan. 20, 1957 / Fantasy/OJC ✦✦✦✦
Latin jazz collectors note: the title emphatically is *Jazz at the Blackhawk*, and even the most determined listener will not find an iota of Cal Tjader's explorations of Latin rhythms here.

In its place, we get a sturdy set of bop-flavored workouts by Tjader's expert quartet, recorded live in San Francisco's famous long-defunct nightspot. Tjader himself often sounds like Milt Jackson as he handles the mallets fluidly through a set of standards, a pair of originals by himself and his wife, and—appropriately enough—a witty Baroque-like tune by his pianist Vince Guaraldi called "Thinking of You, MJQ." Eugene "The Senator" Wright (bass) and Al Torre (piano) make up the bop rhythm section, and as long as you know what you're getting, a good time can be had. *—Richard S. Ginell*

The Cal Tjader-Stan Getz Sextet / Feb. 8, 1958 / Fantasy ✦✦✦✦✦
An amazing ad-hoc session, thrown together in a San Francisco studio with now legendary personnel from two different groups. The lineup says it all—a meeting of the Latin jazz maestro and the future champion of Brazilian jazz, plus, from Tjader's group, Vince Guaraldi on piano and guitarist Eddie Duran, and from Getz's band, the then unknown teenager Scott LaFaro on bass and Billy Higgins on drums. A moment for the history books is an 11-minute workout on Guaraldi's pentatonic souvenir of Tokyo, "Ginza Samba," where the fast-samba theme finds Getz blowing to a Brazilian rhythm four years before "Desafinado." The jamming, though, is in a straight-ahead bebop groove where Getz's eloquence unfolds with almost unearthly ease. The rest of the album alternates between lyric ballads and solid, though non-Latin, swinging where Tjader, Guaraldi, and Duran graft onto the great Getz rhythm section like they've been playing together for decades (check out the funky combustion on "Crow's Nest"). Collectors' note: when Getz became a bossa nova star, this album was reissued in 1963 as *Stan Getz With Cal Tjader* with a different set of liner notes and remains available on LP and cassette in this form. *—Richard S. Ginell*

Cal Tjader's Latin Concert / Sep. 1958 / Fantasy/OJC ✦✦✦✦✦
This CD reissue gives one a pretty good sampling of vibraphonist Cal Tjader's influential Latin-jazz of the 1950s. With pianist Vince Guaraldi, bassist Al McKibbon, Willie Bobo on timbales and drums and the congas of Mongo Santamaria, Tjader's impressive unit performs four of his catchy originals and two by Santamaria in addition to Latinized versions of "The Continental" and Ray Bryant's "Cubano Chant." This highly rhythmic music is difficult to dislike. *—Scott Yanow*

★ **Monterey Concerts** / Apr. 20, 1959 / Prestige ✦✦✦✦✦
This CD (which reissues all of the music from the two LP's *Concert by the Sea* and *Vol. 2*) is the definitive early Cal Tjader album and one of the highpoints of his career. For a Carmel concert that was considered a preview concert for the 1959 *Monterey Jazz Festival*, Tjader was teamed up with flutist and altoist Paul Horn, pianist Lonnie Hewitt, bassist Al McKibbon, Willie Bobo (on drums and timbales) and percussionist Mongo Santamaria. Their renditions of Latinized jazz tunes along with a few Latin originals practically define the idiom. Highlights include "Doxy," one of the earliest versions of Santamaria's "Afro Blue" (predating John Coltrane's famous rendition by four years), "Love Me or Leave Me" and "A Night in Tunisia." Essential music for everyone's Latin-jazz collection. *—Scott Yanow*

☆ **Night at the Black Hawk** / 1959 / Fantasy/OJC ✦✦✦✦✦
Recording during a long holiday season gig at San Francisco's *Black Hawk* club, Tjader patched together a superb program split between straight-ahead jazz and Afro-Cuban workouts. At the time, Tjader had both Willie Bobo and Mongo Santamaria in his rhythm section; Bobo handles the trap drums during the bop numbers, while the Latin tunes find Willie and Mongo creating even more heat on the timbales and congas. Pianist Vince Guaraldi swings like a madman on "A Night in Tunisia" (though the piano is out of tune), comping and soloing elsewhere with his usual light-hearted assurance, if not the individuality that he would later bring to his own music. For this gig, Tjader adds the Cuban tenor saxophonist Jose "Chombo" Silva, who strikes the right husky Ike Quebec tone in "Blue and Sentimental" and elsewhere had been clearly listening to lots of Stan Getz. The *Black Hawk* was breaking in some excellent new stereo recording equipment at the time of this gig; hence the clear, sharp sound. This album was combined with all but one song from another album Tjader recorded at *the Black Hawk* in the late '50s, *Live and Direct*, on the single-disc Fantasy CD reissue *Black Hawk Nights* in 2000. *—Richard S. Ginell*

Latino / 1960 / Fantasy ✦✦✦✦✦
Vibraphonist Cal Tjader is heard leading five different groups throughout this CD but the identities of the flutists, bassists and pianists are less important than knowing that Tjader, Willie Bobo (on drums and timbales) and the great conga player Mongo Santamaria are on every selection. The music really cooks with torrid percussion, inspired ensembles and occasional solos from the sidemen (which sometimes include pianists Lonnie Hewitt or Vince Guaraldi, bassist Al McKibbon and flutist Paul Horn). Highlights include Latinized versions of "Key Largo" and "September Song," "Night in Tunisia," "The Continental" and a definitive version of Santamaria's "Afro Blue." This is Latin-jazz at its finest. *—Scott Yanow*

Talkin' Verve: Roots of Acid Jazz / Aug. 28, 1961-Sep. 19, 1967 / Polygram ✦✦✦
In apparent response to the sampling of old Latin jazz records by hip-hop artists, Verve raided its Cal Tjader archive to come up with this fiercely grooving collection drawn from nine of his Verve albums. For all of producer Creed Taylor's '60s penchant for fashioning two- to four-minute cuts aimed at airplay, he allowed Tjader's groups considerable room to stretch out on several of the tracks included here, particularly on the live "Los Bandidos" and the hypnotic collaboration with pianist Eddie Palmieri, "Picadillo." More importantly, Tjader's records with Taylor were more varied in texture than his earlier discs, venturing now and then from his solid Afro-Cuban base into Brazilian rhythms, soul, big-band backings, and '60s pop touches. Among the best cuts included here are "Sambo Do Suenho"—which has a killer bossa/Afro-Cuban rhythm stoked by Grady Tate, Armando Peraza and Ray Barretto working in terrific symmetry—Peraza's fast, hard-swinging "Maramoor Mambo," and Horace Silver's "Tokyo Blues," as spearheaded by Lalo Schifrin's driving big band. *—Richard S. Ginell*

Soul Sauce / Nov. 19, 1964-Nov. 20, 1964 / Verve ✦✦✦✦✦
Soul Sauce is one of the highlights from Tjader's catalog with its appealing mixture of mambo, samba, bolero, and boogaloo styles. Tjader's core band—long-time piano player Lonnie Hewitt, drummer Johnny Rae and percussionist's Willie Bobo and Armanda Peraza—starts things off with a cooled down version of Dizzy Gillespie and Chano Pozo's latin jazz classic "Guachi Guaro (Soul Sauce)". With the help of guitarist Kenny Burrell, trumpeter Donald Byrd, and tenor saxophonist Jimmy Heath they offer up a lively version of Mongo Santamaria's "Afro Blue." Sticking to his music's "Mambo Without a Migraine" reputation, though, Tjader's musicians keep things fairly calm, especially on Latinized ballads such as Billy May's "Somewhere In the Night" and on midtempo swingers like "Tanya." On *Soul Sauce* Tjader had perfected a middle ground between the brisk, collegiate mambo of his early Fantasy records and the mood-heavy sound of Asian themed albums like *Breeze From the East*. In the process, he dodged the "Latin lounge" label with an album full of smart arrangements, subtly provocative vibe solos, and intricate percussion backing. *—Stephen Cook*

Soul Burst / Feb. 9, 1966-Feb. 11, 1966 / Verve ✦✦✦
By the mid '60s, vibraphonist Cal Tjader was recording regularly for Verve in a wide variety of settings but with pretty consistent success. For this popular outing (reissued on CD in 1998), Tjader plays a few then-current Latin numbers (including Clare Fischer's famous "Morning"), revives "Manteca" and performs a pair of Kurt Weill standards ("My Ship" and "The Bilbao Song"). With Jerome Richardson, Seldon Powell and/or Jerry Dodgion prominent on flutes, such sidemen as the young pianist Chick Corea, guitarist Attila Zoller, bassist Richard Davis, drummer Grady Tate and some fine charts written by Oliver Nelson, the music is quite catchy and accessible, commercial but still creative within the genre. *—Scott Yanow.*

Primo / Feb. 8, 1973-Feb. 9, 1973 / Fantasy/OJC ✦✦✦✦
This CD brings back one of Cal Tjader's best late-period recordings and finds the vibraphonist adapting his 1950s Latin jazz concept to the 1970s without losing any vitality. Tjader is joined by four horns, the legendary keyboardist Charlie Palmieri, electric bassist Bobby Rodriguez, and six percussionists; Tito Puente (who plays timbales on Mario Bauza's "Tanga") and Palmieri provided the heated arrangements. A previously unreleased alternate take of "Bang Bang" is added to the CD reissue. Highly recommended to collectors of Latin jazz. *—Scott Yanow*

Black Hawk Nights / Dec. 1958-1959 / Fantasy ✦✦✦✦✦
In the late '50s, Cal Tjader and his bands played lengthy engagements at the *Black Hawk* jazz club in San Francisco. This CD combines almost everything from two albums he recorded there in the late '50s: the entirety of *A Night at the Blackhawk*, and all songs save one from *Live and Direct*. This is on the mellow side for Tjader, even by the vibraphonist's standards; if *A Night at the Blackhawk* is low-energy, *Live and Direct* is positively sleepy. *A Night at the Blackhawk* employs an all-star sextet including Willie Bobo on drums, Mongo Santamaria on congas, and Vince Guaraldi on piano. Despite the presence of Bobo and Santamaria though, it's only in the Latin-Afro-Cuban mood about half the time. That's heard on the mambo version of "Stompin' at the Savoy," "I Love Paris," and Dizzy Gillespie's "A Night in Tunisia," the last of which is of course a natural for the Latin-jazz treatment; otherwise it's pretty inside, straight-ahead stuff. Although *Live and Direct* was billed to the Cal Tjader Quintet, it in fact usually features just a quartet of Tjader, Lonnie Hewitt on piano, Victor Venegas on bass, and Willie Bobo on drums. The leader doesn't even play on "My Romance," a showcase for Hewitt. Latin-Afro-Cuban-jazz fusion is barely evident on the laidback *Live and Direct* session, except for the high-spirited finale. Actually, the *Live and Direct* set is rather too much on the polite, even sleepy side: the kind of thing you'd put on to fall asleep to in the wee hours. The pace does pick up for *Live and Direct*'s only Tjader original, "Raccoon Straits," and "Mambo Terrifico," the number that has Santamaria and Lozano on board. *—Richie Unterberger*

Ralph Towner

b. Mar. 1, 1940, Chehalis, WA
Guitar / Folk-Jazz, Post-Bop
One of the founders of Oregon, Ralph Towner is one of the few modern jazz musicians to specialize on acoustic guitar. His playing often stretches beyond the boundaries of conventional jazz into world music and is quite distinctive. He started playing piano when he was three and trumpet at five, performing in a dance band when he was 13. Towner studied classical guitar in Vienna and played with classical chamber groups in the mid-'60s. After moving to New York in 1969, Towner worked with Jimmy Garrison, Jeremy Steig and Paul Winter's Winter Consort (1970-71). In the latter group Towner first met up with Collin Walcott, Glen Moore and Paul McCandless and in 1971 they broke away to form Oregon, a highly versatile group that ranges from jazz and free improvisations to folk music. Towner (who guested with Weather Report in 1971 and played with Gary Burton a bit during 1974-75) has performed and recorded with Oregon extensively since its formation in addition to recording as a leader and with many other artists on the ECM label. *—Scott Yanow*

Solstice / Dec. 1974 / ECM ✦✦✦✦
Not only sounds wonderful, it has Jan Garbarek (ts). *—Ron Wynn*

Old Friends, New Friends / Jul. 1979 / ECM ✦✦✦✦
Due to the very interesting grouping of players—guitarist Ralph Towner, who also performs on piano and French horn; trumpeter Kenny Wheeler, cellist David Darling, bassist Eddie Gomez and drummer Michael Di Pasqua—and six of Towner's better originals, this is one of the guitarist's best in a long string of ECM recordings. Wheeler adds fire to the music that is tempered a bit by Darling's mellow cello. An intriguing set well worth several listens. *—Scott Yanow*

● **Solo Concert** / Oct. 1979 / ECM ✦✦✦✦
This very well-recorded album features Ralph Towner playing 12-string and classical guitar on "Nardis," two pieces by John Abercrombie and four of his own originals. The interpretations are typically sensitive, thoughtful and often introspective but also show off Towner's impressive technique. *—Scott Yanow*

Lennie Tristano

b. Mar. 19, 1919, Chicago, IL, **d.** Nov. 18, 1978, New York, NY

Piano, Teacher/Educator, Composer / Avant-Garde Jazz, Cool, Bop

The history of jazz is written as a recounting of the lives of its most famous (and presumably, most influential) artists. Reality is not so simple, however. Certainly the very most important of the music's innovators are those whose names are known by all—Armstrong, Parker, Young, Coltrane. Unfortunately, the jazz critic's tendency to inflate the major figures' status often comes at the expense of other musicians' reputations—men and women who have made significant, even essential, contributions of their own, are, for whatever reason, overlooked in the mad rush to canonize a select few. Lennie Tristano is one of those who have not yet received their critical due. In the mid-'40s, the Chicago-born pianist arrived on the scene with a concept that genuinely expanded the prevailing bop aesthetic. Tristano brought to the music of Charlie Parker and Bud Powell a harmonic language that adapted the practices of contemporary classical music; his use of polytonal effects in tunes like "Out on a Limb" was almost Stravinsky-esque, and his extensive use of counterpoint was (whether or not he was conscious of it at the time) in keeping with the trends being set in mid-century art music. Until relatively recently, it had seldom been acknowledged that Tristano had been the first to perform and record a type of music that came to be called "free jazz." In 1949—almost a decade before the making of Ornette Coleman's first records—Tristano's group cut the first recorded example of freely improvised music in the history of jazz. The two cuts, "Intuition" and "Digression," were created spontaneously, without any pre-ordained reference to time, tonality, or melody. The resultant work was an outgrowth of Tristano's preoccupation with feeling and spontaneity in the creation of music. It influenced, among others, Charles Mingus, whose earliest records sound eerily similar to those of Tristano in terms of style and compositional technique. *—Chris Kelsey*

Lennie Tristano Quintet: Live at Birdland 1949 / 1945-1949 / Jazz ✦✦✦✦

The Jazz label has made available several previously unknown Lennie Tristano sessions. The bulk of this LP features the pianist with tenor-saxophonist Warne Marsh, guitarist Billy Bauer, bassist Arnold Fishkin, and drummer Jeff Morton, performing five selections that utilize common chord changes. Tristano and Marsh in particular are in creative form. The final four numbers must rank as among Lennie Tristano's earliest recordings for those unaccompanied solos were cut in 1945. Even at that early date, the pianist had his very unique style together. Although not as boppish as his playing would become, the basic principles are in place with long melodic lines and constant improvising being emphasized. *—Scott Yanow*

☆ **Crosscurrents** / Mar. 4, 1949-Nov. 2, 1949 / Capitol ✦✦✦✦✦

Even though the music on this LP has yet to be made available on CD, it gets the highest rating because the performances are so unique. Pianist Lennie Tristano is heard with his finest group, a sextet with altoist Lee Konitz, tenor-saxophonist Warne Marsh, guitarist Billy Bauer, bassist Arnold Fishkin, and either Harold Granowsky or Denzil Best on drums. Their seven selections include some truly remarkable unisons on "Wow," memorable interplay by the horns on "Sax of a Kind," and the earliest examples of free improvisation in jazz: "Intuition" and "Digression." In addition, the set features clarinetist Buddy DeFranco with vibraphonist Teddy Charles in a sextet on three numbers and backed by a big band for two others; the radical "A Bird in Igor's Yard" was composed and arranged by George Russell. This essential LP (which is subtitled *Capitol Jazz Classics Vol. 14*) concludes with a feature for trombonist Bill Harris on Neal Hefti's "Opus 96." Consistently brilliant and advanced music. *—Scott Yanow*

★ **Intuition** / Mar. 4, 1949-Oct. 11, 1956 / Blue Note ✦✦✦✦✦

This CD brings back a formerly rare set by Warne Marsh, plus seven classic performances that serve as the high point of Lennie Tristano's career. Oddly enough, the Tristano date is programmed second. First is a full-length album which matches Warne Marsh with the cooler but complementary tone of fellow tenor Ted Brown (plus pianist Robbie Ball, bassist George Tucker and drummer Jeff Morton). The original eight selections are joined by four alternate takes recorded in mono. Marsh and Brown blend together well, Ball has several creative solos, and most of the "originals" are based closely on familiar standards. However, the main reason to acquire this CD is for the seven remarkable Tristano tracks which feature his finest group (consisting of the pianist/leader, altoist Lee Konitz, Marsh on tenor, guitarist Billy Bauer, bassist Arnold Fishkin and either Harold Granowsky or Denzil Best on drums). Tristano's music was unique and even more advanced than most bop of the late '40s. While he confined the rhythm section to very quiet timekeeping, the vibrato-less horns and Tristano himself played very long melodic lines, constantly improvising. The stunning unisons performed by Konitz and Marsh (particularly on "Wow") still sound remarkable today, as does the interplay of the two horns on "Sax of a Kind." "Intuition" and "Digression" were the first recorded free improvisations in jazz, but are quite coherent due to the musicians' familiarity with each other. Due to the Lennie Tristano performances, this CD reissue (which has over 75 minutes of music) is essential for all jazz collections. *—Scott Yanow*

Wow / 1950 / Jazz ✦✦✦✦✦

As is true of the Jazz label's CDs, there are no liner notes on this release and the total time falls into the range of an LP, but this is a rare live performance by pianist Lennie Tristano's finest group. The identities of the bassist and drummer (who are both relegated to quiet time-keeping) are unknown but the other musicians are quite distinctive. With altoist Lee Konitz, tenor-saxophonist Warne Marsh and guitarist Billy Bauer contributing their voices, Tristano explores a variety of common chord changes, a brief Fugue by Bach and his remarkable title cut. Well worth acquiring. *—Scott Yanow*

Live in Toronto (1952) / Jul. 17, 1952 / Jazz ✦✦✦✦

By 1952, pianist Lennie Tristano was starting to withdraw from public performances, spending most of his time teaching. This formerly unknown recording matches him with four of his best students: altoist Lee Konitz, tenor-saxophonist Warne Marsh, bassist Peter Ind and drummer Al Levitt. Together they explore six common chord changes, five of them given new titles. Although not essential, this music is quite enjoyable and a good example of Lennie Tristano's unique approach to jazz improvisation. *—Scott Yanow*

Continuity / Oct. 1958-Jun. 1964 / Jazz ✦✦✦✦

These valuable recordings document the great pianist Lennie Tristano during his later years, when public appearances were rare and recordings only an infrequent event. Tristano is heard playing at *the Half Note* on two separate occasions. Warne Marsh is on tenor, altoist Lee Konitz is a major asset to the selections from 1964, and the rhythm sections include either Henry Grimes or Sonny Dallas on bass and Paul Motian or Nick Stabulas on drums. The recording quality is decent if not admirable, but it is the music (six explorations of common chord changes and a 50-second "Everything Happens to Me") that is wonderful. Tristano, Marsh, and Konitz constantly create new melody lines and make highly original music. *—Scott Yanow*

Lennie Tristano/The New Tristano / 1955-1962 / Rhino ✦✦✦

This anthology combines two major Tristano albums; the first nine cuts were done in 1955 and include two trio and two solo numbers, plus five quartet pieces. The quartet tunes include alto saxophonist Lee Konitz and drummer Art Taylor. Tristano's piano solos are more challenging and ambitious on the disc's other six numbers, however; these are unaccompanied solo works recorded between 1960 and 1962, all except "You Don't Know What Love Is" Tristano originals. The variety and sheer amount of ideas, plus the facility of the lines and the overall performances, are impressive. Only the absence of the cut "C Minor Complex" (explained by time restrictions) mars things slightly, but this is a superb presentation of Lennie Tristano's work. *—Ron Wynn*

Stanley Turrentine

b. Apr. 5, 1934, Pittsburgh, PA, **d.** Sep. 12, 2000, New York, NY

Sax (Tenor) / Hard Bop, Fusion, Soul-Jazz

One of soul-jazz's finest tenor saxmen and a major influence on Grover Washington, Jr., Stanley Turrentine is a distinctive, highly expressive, soloist who seldom forgets jazz's blues roots. Always a lover of R&B and blues, Turrentine played with Ray Charles, Earl Bostic (for whom he replaced John Coltrane) and Lowell Fulson in the early '50s. By the end of the decade, he was enjoying a lucrative association with Jimmy Smith and recording as a leader for Blue Note (where he remained until the late '60s). In the '70s, he recorded several classic dates for CTI before delivering overproduced commercial dates for Fantasy that offered little evidence of his strong improvatory skills. But he successfully returned to soul-jazz and hard bop in the '80s and was still playing with plenty of warmth and passion on his MusicMasters CDs of the early-to-mid-'90s. *—Alex Henderson*

Blue Hour / Dec. 16, 1960 / Blue Note ✦✦✦✦✦

With the Three Sounds—Gene Harris (p), Andrew Simpkinds (b), and William Dowdy (d). Recorded in Englewood Cliffs, NJ. A small group setting. This is a beautiful album of relaxed, bluesy sound. *—Michael Erlewine*

Comin' Your Way / Jan. 20, 1961 / Blue Note ✦✦✦✦

With Tommy Turrentine (tp), Horace Parlan (p) George Tucker (b), and Al Harewood (d). Recorded at Englewood Cliffs, NJ. Small group. 1988 reissue of a sumptuous '60s soul-jazz date. Horace Parlan at his bluesy best. *—Ron Wynn*

Up at Minton's / Feb. 23, 1961 / Blue Note ✦✦✦✦✦

This is a particularly solid double CD featuring tenor-saxophonist Stanley Turrentine, guitarist Grant Green, pianist Horace Parlan, bassist George Tucker and drummer Al Harewood during a frequently exciting live set. Although recorded early in the careers of Turrentine and Green, both lead voices are easily recognizable with Green actually taking solo honors on several of the pieces. Standards and a couple of blues make up the repertoire, giving listeners a definitive look at the soulful Mr. T. near the beginning of his productive musical life. *—Scott Yanow*

Z.T.'s Blues / Sep. 13, 1961 / Blue Note ✦✦✦✦✦

An all-star lineup has Turrentine with Grant Green on guitar and Tommy Flanagan on piano. The rhythm section has Paul Chambers on bass and Art Taylor on drums. Green and Turrentine made few albums together, but the combination is a natural—the two greatest groove masters, bar none. Flanagan seldom appears in this type of setting and his playing is very tasteful. A studio recording by Rudy Van Gelder at Englewood Cliffs, NJ. If you can find a copy of this, it is a keeper. *—Michael Erlewine*

Ballads / 1961-1992 / Blue Note ✦✦✦

Although he's a monster tenor soloist on funky, exuberant, bluesy soul-jazz, Stanley Turrentine is even more awesome on ballads. His rich, steamy sound, full tone, and ability to pace and develop moods is ideal for show tunes and sentimental love songs. This nine-track set begins with Turrentine nicely caressing the melody and turning in a standout treatment on "Willow Weep For Me," continuing through tearjerkers ("Since I Fell For You") and blues anthems ("God Bless The Child"), and closing with Thad Jones' beautiful "A Child Is Born." Turrentine is matched with numerous premier players, and pianist McCoy Tyner, guitarist Jimmy Smith, and even Turrentine's brother Tommy (trumpet) gently support and complement the main soloist. One of the best Blue Note special discs, featuring moving, frequently hypnotic playing from a true tenor great. *—Ron Wynn*

☆ **That's Where It's at** / Jan. 2, 1962 / Blue Note ✦✦✦✦✦

A Blue Note release with Les McCann on piano, Herbie Lewis on bass, and Otis Finch on drums. Small group format. Excellent (and exciting) soul-jazz session with Turrentine blowing hot. *—Ron Wynn & Michael Erlewine*

Jubilee Shout / Jan. 20, 1961-Oct. 18, 1962 / Blue Note ✦✦✦✦

Featuring Turrentine with Sonny Clark on piano and Kenny Burrell on guitar. Also including Tommy Turrentine (tp), Butch Warren (b), and Al Harewood (d). Recorded at Englewood Cliffs, NJ, by Rudy Van Gelder. Here is classic funky soul-jazz groove, three up-tempo, three slow. Sonny Clark (p) soars, Turrentine red-hot. *—Ron Wynn & Michael Erlewine*

A Chip off the Old Block / Oct. 21, 1963 / Blue Note ✦✦✦✦

★ **Let It Go** / Sep. 21, 1964-Apr. 15, 1966 / Impulse! ✦✦✦✦✦

This is vital Turrentine with Shirley Scott on Hammond organ, Ron Carter on bass, and Mack Simpkins on drums. This album includes some additional tracks that were originally released on the Shirley Scott album *Everybody Loves a Lover.* Recorded in Englewood Cliffs, NJ. Husband and wife team Turrentine and Shirley Scott (organ) produce one classic soul-jazz groove album. *—Michael Erlewine*

Joyride / Apr. 14, 1965 / Blue Note ✦✦✦✦✦
Recorded at Englewood Cliffs, NJ, with a very large group that includes all kinds of horns plus Herbie Hancock (p) and Kenny Burrell (g). Arranged by Oliver Nelson. Throbbing tenor solos, with big-band backing. *—Ron Wynn*

Rough 'n' Tumble / Jul. 1, 1966 / Blue Note ✦✦✦✦
A somewhat larger group (eight pieces) with Grant Green (g), Blue Mitchell (tp), James Spaulding (as), Pepper Adams (bar), and McCoy Tyner on piano. Recorded at NYC. One of his most popular, tightest soul-jazz releases. *—Ron Wynn*

The Spoiler / Sep. 22, 1966 / Blue Note ✦✦✦✦✦
Other than a few short spots, Stanley Turrentine is the only significant soloist on this CD reissue which features a diverse program including "When the Sun Comes Out," "Maybe September," "You're Gonna Hear from Me" and a previously unreleased rendition of Max Roach's jazz waltz "Lonesome Lover." Although he is accompanied by an all-star group that includes trumpeter Blue Mitchell, altoist James Spaulding, baritonist Pepper Adams and pianist McCoy Tyner, Turrentine's sidemen could almost have been anonymous studio players for the tenor is the dominant voice throughout. It is surprising that Pearson did not make more extensive use of the other musicians' unique talents, particularly Tyner. However, despite some potentially indifferent material, Turrentine is in fine form throughout the date, even finding something to say on "Sunny." "La Fiesta" (no relation to the later Chick Corea tune) is the highpoint of a largely enjoyable set. *—Scott Yanow*

Sugar / Nov. 1970 / CTI ✦✦✦✦✦
First album after Turrentine switched to the CTI label and producer Creed Taylor. Recorded at Englewood Cliffs, NJ. Larger group with arrangements. By far the best thing he ever made on CTI. Among the handful of genuine jazz albums that were cut on that label. Includes George Benson (g), Ron Carter (b), Curtis Fuller (tb), and many more. *—Ron Wynn*

Cherry / May 1972 / Columbia ✦✦✦✦
Produced by Creed Taylor on CTI. Recorded at Englewood Cliffs, NJ. Small Group. Lush, wonderful playing by Turrentine, Jackson, despite very uneven material. *—Ron Wynn*

Don't Mess with Mister T. / Jun. 7, 1973 / Columbia ✦✦✦✦✦
Produced by Creed Taylor on CTI. Recorded at Englewood Cliffs, NJ. CD version, 1988 reissue. *—Ron Wynn*

McCoy Tyner (Alfred McCoy Tyner)

b. Dec. 11, 1938, Philadelphia, PA
Piano / Hard Bop, Post-Bop
It is to McCoy Tyner's great credit that his career after John Coltrane has been far from anticlimatic. Along with Bill Evans, Tyner has been the most influential pianist in jazz of the past 40 years with his chord voicings being adopted and utilized by virtually every younger pianist. A powerful virtuoso and a true original (compare his playing in the early '60s with anyone else from the time), Tyner (like Thelonious Monk) has not altered his style all that much from his early days but he has continued to grow and become even stronger. He made his recording debut with the Art Farmer-Benny Golson Jazztet but after six months left the group to join Coltrane in what (with bassist Jimmy Garrison and drummer Elvin Jones) would become the classic quartet. Few other pianists of the period had both the power and the complementary open-minded style to inspire Coltrane but Tyner was never overshadowed by the innovative saxophonist. During the Coltrane years (1960-65), the pianist also led his own record dates for Impulse. After leaving Coltrane, McCoy Tyner struggled for a period, working as a sideman (with Ike and Tina Turner!) and leading his own small groups; his recordings were consistently stimulating even during the lean years. *—Scott Yanow*

Inception / Jan. 10, 1962 / Impulse! ✦✦✦✦
Those familiar with the dense, percussive style that pianist McCoy Tyner has cultivated since the 1970s onwards may be surprised by what they hear on *Inception.* Like *Reaching Fourth* and *Nights of Ballads and Blues,* this album gives listeners the chance to hear what a very young Tyner sounded like outside the confines of the classic John Coltrane quartet of the early '60s; it reveals a lyrical approach to jazz piano that seems a far cry from Tyner's mature style. The choice of material is fairly evenly split between modal pieces like "Inception" and more harmonically involved tunes like "Speak Low," and the pianist's treatment of both demonstrates the extent to which his early work was rooted in bebop. Tyner had yet to develop the massive orchestral sound and highly distinctive vocabulary of modal licks that would mark his later style, and throughout this album he spins dizzyingly long and singing lines with an exquisitely light touch. The irresistible rush of forward momentum that he maintains on tracks like "Effendi" and "Blues for Gwen" is breathtaking, and there is an exuberant, almost athletic quality to much of his solo work. Bassist Art Davis and drummer Elvin Jones provide superb accompaniment throughout, and they lay a solid rhythmic foundation for Tyner's sparkling melodic flights. The pianist's penchant for drama, which asserts itself more strongly in his later work, is on brief display in the original ballad "Sunset"; his skills as an arranger, though evident on several tracks, are perhaps best illustrated by the intricate contrapuntal treatment of "There Is No Greater Love." *—Alexander Gelfand*

Nights of Ballads and Blues / Mar. 4, 1963 / Impulse! ✦✦✦

Today and Tomorrow / Jun. 4, 1963-Feb. 4, 1964 / GRP/Impulse! ✦✦✦✦
The great pianist McCoy Tyner teams up with trumpeter Thad Jones, altoist Frank Strozier, tenor-saxophonist John Gilmore (on vacation from Sun Ra), bassist Butch Warren and drummer Elvin Jones on the first three selections of this reissue CD; it is a pity that the potentially exciting group did not have more of an opportunity to play together for these three numbers are excellent. For the remainder of the set (three numbers from the original Lp plus three others taken from samplers), Tyner is showcased in a trio primarily on standards with bassist Jimmy Garrison and drummer Albert "Tootie" Heath. Virtually all of McCoy Tyner's recordings are easily recommended and this CD has more variety than most of his Impulses. *—Scott Yanow*

Live at Newport / Jul. 5, 1963 / Impulse! ✦✦✦✦✦
Live at Newport was the first live recording McCoy Tyner led, and it happened to be among his most memorable dates for Impulse, but like many memorable sessions, it was the end result of equal parts planning, spontaneity, and talent. According to Willis Conover's original liner notes, Tyner was worn out from playing Montreal the night before, and he was paired with three musicians he'd never played with before (trumpeter Clark Terry, alto saxophonist Charlie Mariano, and bassist Bob Cranshaw), two of who were using borrowed instruments. Given such chaotic circumstances, it's not surprising that the quintet (also featuring drummer Mickey Roker, a former colleague of Tyner's) chose to play two standards, plus Tyner's "Monk's Blues," Dizzy Gillespie's "Woody 'n' You," and the improvised opening jam, "Newport Romp." What is a surprise is that not only does the group hold together, but they excel. They sound empathetic, as if they've played many times before, yet there are enough sparks to signal that they're still unsure of what the other will play. The results are thoroughly compelling and unpredictable, even when it's just a Tyner showcase, like "Monk's Blues." Essentially a solo showcase with support from Cranshaw and Roker, Tyner really pushes on this number, beginning it as a Monk homage and pushing it to continually inventive territory. It's the riskiest playing on the record from Tyner, but just because *Live at Newport* isn't as risky as his work with Coltrane during the early '60s doesn't mean it's limp or complacent. It's straight-ahead hard bop in the best possible sense—accessible but stimulating, engaging and vibrant from beginning to end. *—Stephen Thomas Erlewine*

Reaching Fourth / Nov. 14, 1962 / Impulse! ✦✦✦✦✦
Pianist McCoy Tyner's second set as a leader has as of 1996 not been reissued on CD. Featured in a trio with bassist Henry Grimes and drummer Roy Haynes, Tyner performs two of his originals ("Reaching Fourth" and "Blues Back") plus three standards and "Theme For Ernie." One of the two most original and influential pianists to fully emerge in the 1960s (along with Bill Evans), McCoy Tyner's unique chord voicings and ease at playing creatively over vamps pushed the evolution of jazz piano forward quite a bit. This outing, although not as intense as his work with the John Coltrane Quartet, is generally memorable and still sounds quite viable 35 years later. *—Scott Yanow*

McCoy Tyner Plays Ellington / Dec. 7, 1964-Dec. 8, 1964 / GRP/Impulse! ✦✦✦✦
This is an interesting project (reissued on CD) that works quite well. The already distinctive pianist McCoy Tyner utilized bassist Jimmy Garrison, drummer Elvin Jones and two Latin percussionists to interpret a full set of Duke Ellington songs (although "Caravan" was actually composed by Juan Tizol). For this CD the original seven tunes are joined by a "new" alternate take of "Gypsy Without A Song" and previously unreleased renditions of "It Don't Mean A Thing" and "I Got It Bad." In addition to some well-known standards, Tyner debuted an unrecorded Ellington piece "Searchin'" and revived "Mr. Gentle & Mr. Cool." This is an excellent outing that displays both Tyner's debt to the jazz tradition and his increasingly original style. This fine set was reissued on CD by Impulse in 1997. *—Scott Yanow*

The Real McCoy / Apr. 21, 1967 / Blue Note ✦✦✦✦✦
2 1/2 years after his last recording as a leader for Impulse, pianist McCoy Tyner emerged to start a period on Blue Note that would result in seven albums. Having left John Coltrane's Quartet in late-1965, Tyner was entering a period of struggle although artistically his playing grew quite a bit in the late 1960's. For this release, the pianist is teamed with tenor-saxophonist Joe Henderson, bassist Ron Carter and drummer Elvin Jones for five of his originals. Highlights of the easily recommended CD reissue include "Passion Dance," "Four By Five" and "Blues On The Corner." *—Scott Yanow*

Tender Moments / Dec. 1, 1967 / Blue Note ✦✦✦✦✦
On this excellent set (reissued on CD by Blue Note), McCoy Tyner had the opportunity for the first time to head a larger group. His nonet is an all-star aggregation comprised of trumpeter Lee Morgan, trombonist Julian Priester, altoist James Spaulding, Bennie Maupin on tenor, the french horn of Bob Northern, Howard Johnson on tuba, bassist Herbie Lewis, and drummer Joe Chambers in addition to the pianist-leader. Tyner debuted six of his originals, and although none became standards (perhaps the best known are "The High Priest" and "All My Yesterdays"), the music is quite colorful and advanced for the period. Well worth investigating. *—Scott Yanow*

Time for Tyner / May 17, 1968 / Blue Note ✦✦✦✦
This CD reissue draws its music from two separate concerts nearly a year apart but utilizing the same personnel: pianist McCoy Tyner, vibraphonist Bobby Hutcherson, bassist Herbie Lewis, and drummer Freddie Waits. Although three numbers were performed at a John Coltrane Memorial Concert, they are all Tyner originals; the pianist and Hutcherson blend together quite well and both are experts at coming up with inventive ideas over modal vamps. The other three selections are veteran standards. "I Didn't Know What Time It Was" is taken by the full quartet, Hutcherson sits out on "Surrey With the Fringe on Top," and a rhapsodic "I've Grown Accustomed to Your Face" is a piano solo. A fine all-round showcase for McCoy Tyner in the late '60s. *—Scott Yanow*

● **Expansions** / Aug. 23, 1968 / Blue Note ✦✦✦✦✦
Of pianist McCoy Tyner's seven Blue Note albums of the 1967-70 period, *Expansions* is the most definitive. Tyner's group (comprised of trumpeter Woody Shaw, altoist Gary Bartz, tenor-saxophonist Wayne Shorter, Ron Carter on cello, bassist Herbie Lewis and drumemr Freddie Waits) is particularly strong, the compositions (four Tyner originals plus Calvin Massey's "I Thought I'd Let You Know") are challenging and the musicians seem quite inspired by each other's presence. The stimulating music falls between advanced hard bop and the avant-garde, pushing and pulling at the boundaries of modern mainstream jazz. *—Scott Yanow*

Extensions / Feb. 9, 1970 / Blue Note ✦✦✦✦✦
This CD has an interesting combination of players. It may be the only recording to include

both pianist McCoy Tyner and his successor with the John Coltrane Quartet, Alice Coltrane (who adds atmosphere with her harp). This set also matches the young altoist Gary Bartz with Wayne Shorter (doubling on tenor and soprano) who he succeeded in Miles Davis' group and has reunions between Shorter and bassist Ron Carter and by Tyner and drummer Elvin Jones. The all-star sextet stretches out on lengthy renditions of four of Tyner's modal originals and there is strong solo space for the leader and the two saxophonists. Wayne Shorter in particular is often quite intense. Stimulating music. *—Scott Yanow*

Asante / Jul. 21, 1970-Sep. 10, 1970 / Blue Note ♦♦♦♦
The final McCoy Tyner Blue Note album found the innovative pianist during a lowpoint in his career. His records were not selling that well, his mentor John Coltrane had passed away three years earlier and it was not obvious that Tyner would be able to continue struggling successfully to make a living out of music. Fortunately his fortunes would soon rise when he signed with Milestone in 1972 and the critics began to rediscover him. *Asante* is a bit unusual for the emphasis is on group interplay rather than individual solos. The four originals feature Tyner with altoist Andrew White, guitarist Ted Dunbar, bassist Buster Williams, drummer Billy Hart, Mtume on congas and two spots for the voice of Songai. Worth investigating. *—Scott Yanow*

☆ **Sahara** / Jan. 1972 / Milestone/OJC ♦♦♦♦♦
Pianist McCoy Tyner had three long-time associations with record labels: Impulse (1962-64), Blue Note (1967-70) and Milestone (1972-81). *Sahara* was his debut for Milestone, a quartet outing with altoist Sonny Fortune (who also plays soprano and flute), bassist Calvin Hill and drummer Alphonze Mouzon. This CD reissue is highlighted by the 23 1/2 minute title cut which finds Tyner making a rare (and brief) appearance on flute and his piano solo feature "A Prayer For My Family." *—Scott Yanow*

Song for My Lady / Sep. 6, 1972-Nov. 27, 1972 / Milestone/OJC ♦♦♦♦
It was during his years with Milestone (1972-81) that McCoy Tyner finally received recognition for his highly original and influential piano style. In general Tyner's Milestone records (most of which had their own personality) feautred plenty of diversity and a strong purpose. This 1972 CD reissue is highlighted by "The Night Has A Thousand Eyes," "A Silent Tear" (a piano solo) and the title cut. Two of the five selections showcase Tyner in a quartet with the reeds of Sonny Fortune, bassist Calvin Hill and drummer Alphonse Mouzon while "Native Song" and "Essence" add flugelhornist Charles Tolliver, violinist Michael White and the percussion of Mtume. Recommended. *—Scott Yanow*

☆ **Echoes of a Friend** / Nov. 11, 1972 / Milestone/OJC ♦♦♦♦♦
An obvious classic, this piano solo record (reissued on CD in the OJC series) features McCoy Tyner paying tribute to John Coltrane. Tyner not only plays three of Coltrane's songs ("Naima," "Promise" and "My Favorite Things") but two of his originals (a lengthy "The Discovery" and "Folks") which display how much the pianist had grown since leaving the saxophonist's group in late-1965. Few McCoy Tyner records are not easily recommended but this one even ranks above most. *—Scott Yanow*

Song of the New World / Apr. 6, 1973-Apr. 9, 1973 / Milestone/OJC ♦♦♦♦
This set gave pianist McCoy Tyner his first opportunity to write music for a larger group that included brass, flutes and on two of the five songs, a string section. The powerful pianist is in fine form and the main soloist throughout (although there are spots for trumpeter Virgil Jones and the flute of Sonny Fortune). Most memorable is the title cut and a reworking of "Afro Blue." *—Scott Yanow*

☆ **Enlightenment** / Jul. 7, 1973 / Milestone ♦♦♦♦♦
This is one of the great McCoy Tyner recordings. The powerful, percussive and highly influential pianist sounds quite inspired throughout his appearance at the 1973 *Montreux Jazz Festival.* Azar Lawrence (on tenor and soprano) is also quite noteworthy (why didn't he ever become famous—) and there is plenty of interplay with bassist Juney Booth and drummer Alphonse Mouzon. But Tyner is the main star, whether it be on his three-part "Enlightenment Suite," "Presence," "Nebula" or the 25-minute "Walk Spirit, Talk Spirit." *—Scott Yanow*

Sama Layuca / Mar. 26, 1974-Mar. 28, 1974 / Milestone ♦♦♦♦♦
Pianist McCoy Tyner is heard at the height of his powers throughout this rewarding set. He contributed all five compositions and has a colorful and diverse group of major players at his disposal to interpret them: vibraphonist Bobby Hutcherson, altoist Gary Bartz, Azar Lawrence on tenor and soprano, John Stubblefield doubling on oboe and flute, bassist Buster Williams, drummer Billy Hart and both Mtume and Guillherme Franco on percussion. The results (which include a brief Tyner-Hutcherson duet on "Above The Rainbow") are quite rewarding and serve as a strong example of McCoy Tyner's music. *—Scott Yanow*

Atlantis / Aug. 31, 1974-Sep. 1, 1974 / Milestone ♦♦♦♦
This single CD reissues all of the music from a former two-Lp set. Pianist McCoy Tyner's 1974 quintet consisted of the talented youngster Azar Lawrence on tenor and soprano (who strangely enough never became more famous than he was at the time), bassist Joony Booth, drummer Wilby Fletcher and percussionist Guilherme Franco. As is accurately stated in the new liner notes by Neil Tesser, *Atlantis* was the final recording from Tyner's last band to be based on the music of his former boss John Coltrane. While Lawrence (who was only 20 at the time) derived his style partly from aspects of Coltrane and the rhythm section is fiery, McCoy Tyner creates some very powerful and highly original solos, really tearing into some of the more extended pieces. Recorded live at San Francisco's legendary *Keystone Korner,* this set has four of Tyner's modal originals played by the full group, a rendition of "My One And Only Love" performed by the leader, Lawrence and Franco as a trio, and a solo piano version of "In A Sentimental Mood." Essential music that still sounds fresh and adventurous. *—Scott Yanow*

Trident / Feb. 18, 1975-Feb. 19, 1975 / Milestone/OJC ♦♦♦♦♦
Pianist McCoy Tyner's first full-length trio album since 1964 was one of his most popular. Accompanied by bassist Ron Carter and Elvin Jones, Tyner (who uses harpsichord and/or celeste for flavoring on three of the six pieces) shows why he was considered the most influential acoustic pianist of the era (before Bill Evans began to surpass him in that category). Whether it be Jobim's "Once I Loved," "Impressions," "Ruby, My Dear" or Tyner's three powerful originals, this set finds Tyner in peak form. *—Scott Yanow*

Fly with the Wind / Jan. 19, 1976-Jan. 21, 1976 / Milestone/OJC ♦♦♦♦

Supertrios / Apr. 9, 1977-Apr. 12, 1977 / Milestone ♦♦♦♦♦
This album features the great pianist McCoy Tyner with two separate trios, either bassist Ron Carter and drummer Tony Williams or bassist Eddie Gomez and drummer Jack DeJohnette. The former session, which has a Tyner/Williams duet on "I Mean You" and a collaboration between Tyner and Carter on "Prelude to a Kiss," is the more interesting of the two, with the pianist interacting with Miles Davis's former rhythm section on six highquality songs. But the Gomez-DeJohnette date (which includes four Tyner compositions plus "Stella by Starlight" and "Lush Life") also has its classic moments. Throughout, the percussive and highly influential pianist sounds inspired by the opportunity to create music with his peers. Recommended. *—Scott Yanow*

Four Times Four / Mar. 3, 1980-May 29, 1980 / Milestone ♦♦♦♦♦

Uptown/Downtown / Nov. 25, 1988-Nov. 26, 1988 / Milestone ♦♦♦♦♦

Live at Sweet Basil / May 19, 1989-May 20, 1989 / Evidence ♦♦♦♦♦

The Turning Point / Nov. 19, 1991-Nov. 20, 1991 / Verve ♦♦♦♦♦
This recording may not have been an actual "turning point" in pianist McCoy Tyner's productive career but its success gave momentum to his big band. Although only a part-time affair, Tyner's orchestra (seven brass, four reeds and a four-piece rhythm section) is considered one of the major jazz big bands of the 1990s, a perfect outlet for the leader's percussive and modal-oriented piano. With arrangements by Tyner, Dennis Mackrel, Slide Hampton, Steve Turre and Howard Johnson, many of these performances are quite powerful. It is a pity though that the liners do not identify the soloists since there are several that are quite colorful. Recommended. *—Scott Yanow*

Manhattan Moods / Dec. 3, 1993-Dec. 4, 1993 / Blue Note ♦♦♦♦

Infinity / Apr. 12, 1995-Apr. 14, 1995 / Impulse! ♦♦♦♦♦

McCoy Tyner & the Latin All-Stars / Jul. 29, 1998-Jul. 30, 1998 / Telarc ♦♦♦♦

James Blood Ulmer

b. Feb. 2, 1942, St. Matthews, SC
Vocals, Guitar / Avant-Garde Jazz, Free Funk, Crossover Jazz, Free Jazz
Free jazz has not produced many notable guitarists. Experimental musicians drawn to the guitar have had few jazz role models; consequently, they've typically looked to rock-based players for inspiration. James "Blood" Ulmer is one of the few exceptions—an "outside" guitarist who's forged a style based largely on the traditions of African-American vernacular music. Ulmer is an adherent of saxophonist/composer Ornette Coleman's vaguely-defined "Harmolodic" theory, which essentially subverts jazz's harmonic component in favor of freely improvised, non-tonal or quasi-modal counterpoint. Ulmer plays with a stuttering, vocalic attack; his lines are frequently texturally- and chordally-based, inflected with the accent of a soul-jazz tenor saxophonist. That's not to say his sound is untouched by the rock tradition—the influence of Jimi Hendrix on Ulmer is strong—but it's mixed with blues, funk, and free jazz elements. The resultant music is an expressive, hard-edged, loudly-amplified hybrid that is, at its best, on a level with the finest of the "Harmolodic" school.

Ulmer began his career playing in funk bands, first in Pittsburgh (1959-64) and later around Columbus, Ohio (1964-7). Ulmer spent four years in Detroit before moving to New York in 1971. He landed a nine-month gig at the famed "birthplace of bop", Minton's Playhouse, and played very briefly with Art Blakey. In 1973 he recorded *Rashied Ali Quintet* with the ex-John Coltrane drummer, on the Survival label. That same year he hooked up with Ornette Coleman, whose concept affected Ulmer's music thereafter. The guitarist's recordings from the late-'70s and early-'80s exhibit a unique take on his mentor's aesthetic. His blues and rock-tinged art was, if anything, more raw and aggressive than Coleman's free jazz and funk-derived music (a reflection, no doubt, of Ulmer's chosen instrument), but no less compelling from either an intellectual or a emotional standpoint. In 1981 Ulmer led the first of three record dates for Columbia, which helped to expose his music to a wider public. Around this time Ulmer began an association with tenor saxophonist David Murray, violinist Amin Ali, and drummer Ronald Shannon Jackson. As the Music Revelation Ensemble this intermittent assemblage (with various other members added and subtracted) would produce a number of intense, free-blowing albums over a span of almost two decades.

Ulmer's work has varied in quality over the years. In 1987, with the cooperative group Phalanx (George Adams, tenor sax; Sirone, bass; Rashied Ali, drums), Ulmer drew successfully on the free jazz expressionism that made his name. Generally, however, Ulmer's interest in "out" jazz waned in the '80s and '90s, to the extent that his music became progressively more structured, rhythmically regular, and (arguably) less inventive. Much of his later work bears scant resemblance to the edgy free jazz he played earlier. Nevertheless, '90s recordings with the Music Revelation Ensemble showed him still capable of playing convincingly in that vein. *—Chris Kelsey*

★ **Tales of Captain Black** / Dec. 5, 1978 / DIW ♦♦♦♦♦
1999's re-issue of James "Blood" Ulmer's *Tales of Captain Black* marks the first time this 1978 album was released on CD. *Tales of Captain Black* features Ulmer's first work as a bandleader; that the band he leads includes his mentor Ornette Coleman adds to the work's significance. The band performs fierce, kinetic Ulmer originals like "Moon Shine," "Revelation March" and "Revealing," under the production helm of Coleman and John Snyder. *—Heather Phares*

Are You Glad to Be in America— / Jan. 17, 1980 / Rough Trade ♦♦♦♦
In 1972, Ornette Coleman took guitarist James Blood Ulmer under his wing and taught Ulmer the principles of harmolodics, a musical system that treats the elements of harmony, rhythm, and melody equally. On *Are You Glad to Be in America?,* it drives a series of group improvisations that are simultaneously complex and direct. The sound of *Are You Glad?* is

largely defined by its rhythm section: G. Calvin Weston and Ronald Shannon Jackson's propulsive drumming, Amin Ali's kinetic bass, and Ulmer's tightly wound guitar. The two drummers lay down persistent, tense rhythms that establish the album's nervous energy. Leaving little space to explore a conventional groove (to push and pull at the rhythm), Amin aims his bass at the jittery pulse like everyone else. Yet his playing remains rooted in funk and his edgy, spiked tone is a defining texture. The three musicians construct multiple layers around Ulmer, like a more frantic version of the band in Miles Davis' *On the Corner* (1972). Shards of jazz, rock, funk, and surf guitar are shuffled together and unfurl in frenetic lines. At times the rhythms are too rigid and the results sound like an experiment from which the musicians are trying to break free. At best, the individuals lose themselves in a highly charged dialogue. On "Time Out," they create a chattering mass so dense it's difficult to discern where one instrument ends and another begins. Building steam from the taut structures, the individual voices of harmony, rhythm, and melody are found in dizzying group improvisations. *—Nathan Bush*

Freelancing / 1981 / Columbia ✦✦✦✦

Black Rock / 1982 / Columbia ✦✦✦✦✦

Odyssey / Mar. 1983-May 1983 / Columbia ✦✦✦✦✦
Odyssey is one of James Blood Ulmer's most adventerous and complex releases. Drawing equally from jazz, free-form noise, funk, and punk, *Odyssey* is dense with musical themes and sonic textures. Though the compositions often require some work in order to understand what Ulmer is trying to say, there is no mistaking that his guitar playing is bold and innovative, slamming together seemingly disperate and unagreeable genres and creating something gnarled, urban and new. It's one of his defining records. *—Leo Stanley*

Ken Vandermark

b. Sep. 22, 1964
Sax (Tenor), Clarinet (Bass), Clarinet / Avant-Garde Jazz, Experimental, Free Jazz
The catalyst behind the modern resurgence of the Chicago avant-garde community, reedist Ken Vandermark was born September 22, 1964 in Rhode Island and raised in Boston. Exposed to the music of Charlie Parker, Thelonious Monk and numerous others through his father, an avid jazz buff, Vandermark's first instrument was the tenor saxophone, although he later adopted the bass clarinet and clarinet as well. After attending film school, he relocated to Chicago in 1989—a nadir in the history of the city's improvised music scene—but in 1992 his free jazz ensemble the Vandermark Quartet (also featuring violinist/guitarist Daniel Scanlan, bassist Kent Kessler, and percussionist Michael Zerang) landed a weekly gig at the local *HotHouse* club which began drawing larger crowds seemingly each time out. By the time *HotHouse* lost its lease in 1995, the Chicago improvisational community was experiencing a full-blown renaissance, with Vandermark the scene's linchpin thanks to his tireless work in a series of projects including the NRG Ensemble, the Flying Luttenbachers, Caffeine, Cinghiale, Signal to Noise Unit, the Steel Wool Trio, Witches & Devils, Barrage Double Trio, and the Crown Royals; by 1997, however, he vowed to cut back his schedule to focus his energies into just three outlets—the Vandermark 5 (founded in 1996 with saxophonist Mars Williams, trombonist Jeb Bishop, bassist Kent Kessler and drummer Tim Mulvenna), the DKV Trio (with Kessler and percussionist Hamid Drake), and Steam (again with Kessler, Mulvenna, and pianist Jim Baker). Renowned for a powerful sound embracing bop, free-jazz and even R&B, Vandermark also collaborated with visiting musicians including German reedist Peter Brotzmann, French bassist Joelle Leandre, and Swedish saxophonist Mats Gustafsson, and was in 1999 the recipient of a MacArthur Foundation Genius grant. Mid-2000 saw the release of *Burn the Incline*. *—Jason Ankeny*

● **Simpatico** / Jun. 8, 1999 / Atavistic ✦✦✦✦✦

Burn the Incline / Dec. 9, 1999-Dec. 10, 1999 / Atavistic ✦✦✦✦✦
The fourth CD by the Vandermark 5 doesn't blast out of the gate with full-bore skronk the way *Simpatico* did, but rather insinuates itself with the listener in a more gradual fashion. "Distance," the leadoff track, starts with a bass solo from Kent Kessler, somewhat giving the impression that the band's performance has been caught in mid-stride. The tune does, in fact, burn its way up the incline—the band moves from a somewhat plaintive Ornette-ish theme through a chunky modal vamp into emphatic blues-funk riffing, with scorched-earth sax and guitar solos blasting away as the band gathers steam. "Distance" is almost a summary of everything that *Burn the Incline* offers aside from outright swing and free jazz. Swing enters the picture with "The Cooler", which like all else on the CD is filled with stellar soloing; there are wonderful turns by Jeb Bishop on trombone, Vandermark on bass clarinet, and Dave Rempis on tenor. The waiting around ends with "Roulette," a dose of blistering up-tempo funk with a dedication to bassist Nate McBride. The band remains relaxed during the lovely ballad "The Trouble Is"; this tune, with its beautiful alto solo from Rempis, proves that the Vandermark 5 can be compelling even when in a reflective mood. The CD closes with the rhythmically open "Ground", a piece that is multifaceted in the manner of "Distance" but with a pronounced tilt toward free jazz explosiveness. With this track, the apex has indeed been reached and the incline leading to it left smoldering in the Vandermark 5 's path. *—Dave Lynch*

Straight Lines / Jun. 1999 / Atavistic ✦✦✦✦

★ **Design in Time** / Jul. 6, 1999-Jul. 7, 1999 / Delmark ✦✦✦✦✦
An excellent recording from Chicago jazzmen Ken Vandermark, Tim Mulvenna, and Robert Barry. The trio takes classic "out" tunes and originals and makes them sparkle, giving each a clean execution that's as much inspired energy as it is technique and craft. Barry interlaces with Mulvenna, achieving a complementary and balanced percussion section that sometimes acts as foil, sometimes impetus, for the directions of the reed playing. Easily one of Vandermark's best recorded dates yet (it's a treat to hear his clarinet work here, too), *Design in Time* is filled with that certain something that's sometimes missing from his studio recordings, but never from his live shows. Particularly hot tracks include the trio's takes on Thelonious Monk's "Green Chimneys" and Ornette Coleman's "Feet Music." Vandermark's piece for Billy Higgins, "Well Suited," is a lovely ballad, featuring warm saxophone and summer-shower drum solos. *Design in Time* is a very strong jazz release that becomes more wowing and impressive with each listen. *—Joslyn Layne*

Nana Vasconcelos

b. Aug. 2, 1944, Recife, Brazil
Percussion, Composer / Soundtracks, Brazilian Jazz, Latin Jazz, World Fusion
Nana Vasconcelos is one of the cluster of endlessly inventive Brazilian percussionists who were changing the direction and sounds of Brazilian jazz in the post-bossa nova 1970s. Vasconcelos is an especially inventive virtuoso of the berimbau, the weird yet expressive instrument shaped like an archer's bow, and he is also adept at the odd-numbered meters (5/4, 7/4) that were used frequently in the north of Brazil but not in the South. As the son of a guitarist, Vasconcelos got his start in his father's band at age 12 playing bongos and maracas. Taking on a drum kit as part of his arsenal, he moved to Rio de Janeiro in the mid-1960s and caught on with the young Milton Nascimento, picking up several other Brazilian percussion instruments in the process. Gato Barbieri heard him and snatched him up. In 1976, he made a remarkable duo album with Brazilian guitarist/wood flute player Egberto Gismonti, *Danca Das Cabecas*, the first of several dates as a leader or sideman on the ECM label. With Collin Walcott, he formed Codona, a trio that played a fusion of music from four continents until Walcott's death in 1984. *—Richard S. Ginell*

● **Saudades** / Mar. ??, 1979 / ECM ✦✦✦✦✦
This 1979 recording is probably Afro-experimentalist Vasconcelos's finest. It presents his various facets—berimbao playing, intricate overlain vocals, fine percussion, even gorgeous guitar—simply and almost overwhelmingly. This is one of those performances that remind one to never let natural dogmatism get too out of hand. *—John Storm Roberts, Original Music*

Lester / Dec. 9, 1985-Dec. 10, 1985 / Brass Star ✦✦✦✦

Bush Dance / 1986 / Antilles ✦✦✦✦✦

Joe Venuti (Giuseppi Venuti)

b. Sep. 16, 1903, Philadelphia, PA, **d.** Aug. 14, 1978, Seattle, WA
Violin / Classic Jazz, Swing, Dixieland
Joe Venuti's was improvised music's first great violinist. He was a boyhood friend of Eddie Lang (jazz's first great guitarist) and the duo teamed up in a countless number of settings during the second half of the 1920s, including recording influential duets. Venuti moved to New York in 1925 and immediately he and Lang were greatly in demand for jazz recordings, studio work and club appearances. Venuti seemed to play with every top White jazz musician during the segregated era and in 1929 he and Lang joined Paul Whiteman's Orchestra. Lang's premature death in 1933 was a major blow to Venuti who gradually faded away from the spotlight. In 1935 after visiting Europe, the violinist formed a big band and, although it survived quite awhile and helped introduce both singer Kay Starr and drummer Barrett Deems, it was a minor-league orchestra that only recorded four songs. The 1936-66 period was the Dark Ages for Venuti as he drifted into alcoholism and was largely forgotten by the jazz world. However in 1967 he began a major comeback, playing at the peak of his powers. *—Scott Yanow*

Stringin' the Blues [Topaz] / Nov. 8, 1926-May 8, 1933 / Sony Special Products ✦✦✦✦✦
This two-LP set (long overdue to be reissued on CD) contains a definitive cross-section of the recordings of violinist Joe Venuti and guitarist Eddie Lang. The 32 performances include everything from duets and a few of Lang's meetings with fellow guitarist Lonnie Johnson to examples of Venuti's Blue Four and guest appearances with singer Annette Hanshaw, Clarence Williams, Tommy Dorsey (on trumpet) and Bing Crosby (on a hot "Some of These Days"). Virtually all of these recordings are superb, with solos also heard from bass saxophonist Adrian Rollini, Don Murray (on clarinet and baritone), cornetist King Oliver, the C-melody sax of Frankie Trumbauer, and Jimmy Dorsey (switching between clarinet, alto and cornet). Highly recommended for all collections. *—Scott Yanow*

Joe Venuti with Eddie Lang, Vols. 1 & 2 / 1926-1927 / JSP ✦✦✦✦✦
1926-1927. The early duos and Blue Four sessions (in chronological order). *Volume 1* is essential; *Vol. 2* is also recommended. *—Richard Lieberson*

Violin Jazz 1927-1934 / Jun. 28, 1927-Sep. 20, 1934 / Yazoo ✦✦✦✦
This hodgepodge sampler contains 14 of violinist Joe Venuti's better recordings from the 1927-34 period, many of them also featuring guitarist Eddie Lang. The performances are mostly drawn from sessions by Venuti's Blue Four with some of the soloists including Jimmy Dorsey (switching between clarinet, alto, trumpet and baritone), Frankie Trumbauer (on C-melody sax and bassoon), bass-saxophonist Adrian Rollini and, on "Sweet Lorraine," clarinetist Benny Goodman. The music is consistently exciting although serious collectors will want to acquire releases from the more complete European series instead. *—Scott Yanow*

Joe Venuti and Zoot Sims / May 1974-May 1975 / Chiaroscuro ✦✦✦✦✦
Violinist Joe Venuti's three recordings with tenorman Zoot Sims are all quite joyful and exciting. This Chiaroscuro recording matches the pair with pianist John Bunch, bassist Milt Hinton, drummer Bobby Rosengarden and, on "Don't Take Your Love from Me," trombonist Spiegel Willcox who was then 73. The small-group swing performances have plenty of life and more often than not are hard-swinging. *—Scott Yanow*

Gems / Aug. 1975 / Concord Jazz ✦✦✦✦✦
This matchup between violinist Joe Venuti and guitarist George Barnes works quite well. With fine accompaniment from rhythm guitarist Bob Gibbons, bassist Herb Mickman and drummer Jake Hanna, the lead voices are free to romp on the ten standards. There are many high points, including "I Want to Be Happy," "Oh Baby," "Hindustan" and "Lady Be Good." *—Scott Yanow*

Alone at the Palace / Apr. 27, 1977-Apr. 28, 1977 / Chiaroscuro ✦✦✦✦✦
For one of violinist Joe Venuti's final recording sessions, he engages in a set of duets with the talented swing pianist Dave McKenna. The original LP had a dozen performances and the reissue CD adds seven more. In addition to the usual standards, there are several Dixieland

tunes (including three versions of "At the Jazz Band Ball") and four Venuti originals. McKenna (with his rolling basslines) was a perfect partner for the violinist, making this set one of the best of Venuti's later years. *—Scott Yanow*

- **The Essential Joe Venuti** / 1971-1974 / Vanguard ✦✦✦✦

Stringing the Blues [Koch] / Mar. 28, 2000 / Koch ✦✦✦✦
A two-disc, 32-track set of early classic jazz covering the years 1927 to 1933. Besides the incomparable work of Venuti and Lang, these sides are peppered with jazz notables like Jimmy Dorsey, Tommy Dorsey (heard here on trumpet!), King Oliver, Frankie Trumbauer, Clarence Williams, and Adrian Rollini (on six different instruments), plus Lang's duets with bluesman Lonnie Johnson. With nary a bum track, this is a top-notch set for fans of early jazz, especially fans of early Django Reinhardt sides. *—Cub Koda*

Harold Vick

b. Apr. 3, 1936, Rocky Mount, NC, **d.** Nov. 13, 1987, New York, NY
Sax (Tenor), Sax (Soprano), Flute / Hard Bop, Soul-Jazz
An excellent thick-toned tenor, Harold Vick sounded quite at home in hard bop and soul jazz settings. His uncle Prince Robinson (a reed player from the 1920s) gave him a clarinet when he was 13 and three years later Vick switched to tenor. He rose to prominence playing with organ combos in the mid-'60s, recording and performing with Jack McDuff, Jimmy McGriff and Big John Patton among others. He started recording as a leader in 1966 and among his other associations were Jack DeJohnette's unusual group Compost (1972), Shirley Scott in the mid-'70s and Abbey Lincoln with whom he recorded two Billie Holiday tributes for Enja just a short time before his death. *—Scott Yanow*

- **Steppin' Out** / May 21, 1963 / Blue Note ✦✦✦✦✦
This soul jazz outing by tenor-saxophonist Harold Vick (his recording debut as a leader) casts him in a role that was often occupied by Stanley Turrentine. Vick, with a quintet that also includes trumpeter Blue Mitchell, guitarist Grant Green, organist John Patton and drummer Ben Dixon, performs four blues, a slightly trickier original (five of the six songs are his) plus the ballad "Laura" on this CD reissue. There are no real surprises but no disappointments either on what would be Harold Vick's only chance to lead a Blue Note date; at 27 he was already a fine player. *—Scott Yanow*

Eddie "Cleanhead" Vinson

b. Dec. 18, 1917, Houston, TX, **d.** Jul. 2, 1988, Los Angeles, CA
Vocals, Sax (Alto) / New York Blues, Jump Blues, Bop, West Coast Blues, R&B
An advanced stylist on alto saxophone who vacillated throughout his career between jump blues and jazz, bald-pated Eddie "Cleanhead" Vinson (he lost his hair early on after a botched bout with a lye-based hair-straightener) also possessed a playfully distinctive vocal delivery that stood him in good stead with blues fans. Vinson joined the Cootie Williams Orchestra from 1942 to 1945. His vocals on trumpeter Williams's renditions of "Cherry Red" and "Somebody's Got to Go" were in large part responsible for their wartime hit status. Vinson struck out on his own in 1945, forming his own large band, signing with Mercury, and enjoying a double-sided smash in 1947 with his romping R&B chart-topper "Old Maid Boogie" and the song that would prove his signature number, "Kidney Stew Blues." A 1949-52 stint at King Records produced only one hit, the amusing sequel "Somebody Done Stole My Cherry Red," along with the classic blues "Person to Person." Vinson's jazz leanings were probably heightened during 1952-53, when his band included a young John Coltrane. Somewhere along about here, Vinson wrote two Miles Davis classics, "Tune Up" and "Four." Vinson steadfastly kept one foot in the blues camp and the other in jazz, waxing jumping R&B for Mercury (in 1954) and Bethlehem (1957), jazz for Riverside in 1961 (with Cannonball Adderly), and blues for Blues Time and ABC-BluesWay. *—Bill Dahl*

- **Cherry Red Blues** / Aug. 10, 1949-Jul. 7, 1952 / King/Gusto ✦✦✦✦✦
Somehow, amidst all the CD reissues from the King Records vaults unleashed by Charly, Ace, Rhino, and King's current ownership, this versatile alto saxist has fallen through the cracks. Thus, this two-LP collection, boasting all but a handful of his jumping 1949-1952 outings for King, remains your best introduction to the Cleanheaded one's R&B output (along with the 1945-1947 sides he waxed for Mercury, which grace the seven-disc anthology *Blues, Boogie, & Bop: The 1940s Mercury Sessions*). *—Bill Dahl*

Eddie Cleanhead Vinson Sings / Sep. 1957 / Charly ✦✦✦✦✦
One of only two albums that altoist/singer Eddie "Cleanhead" Vinson led during 1956-1966, this infectious set finds him performing some of his best known tunes. With assistance by a medium-size group that plays in a Count Basie groove (including such Basie-ites as trumpeter Joe Newman, trombonist Henry Coker, either Frank Foster or Paul Quinichette on tenor, and pianist Nat Pierce), Cleanhead makes such songs as "Kidney Stew," "Caldonia," "Cherry Red," "Is You Is or Is You Ain't My Baby," and "Hold It Right There" sound full of joy. This CD reissue adds three alternate takes that were originally recorded in stereo. A good sampling of the great Cleanhead. *—Scott Yanow*

Old Kidney Stew Is Fine / Mar. 26, 1969-Mar. 28, 1969 / Delmark ✦✦✦✦✦
Although its programming has been juggled a bit, and the CD has been given liner notes, this Delmark release is a straight reissue of the original LP. Clocking in at around 38 minutes, the relatively brief set is the only recording that exists of Vinson, pianist Jay McShann, and guitarist T-Bone Walker playing together; the sextet is rounded out by the fine tenor Hal Singer, bassist Jackie Sampson, and drummer Paul Gunther. Vinson, whether singing "Plese Send Me Somebody to Love," "Just a Dream," and "Juice Head Baby" or taking boppish alto solos, is the main star throughout this album (originally on Black & Blue), a date that helped launch Vinson's commercial comeback. *—Scott Yanow*

Hold It Right There! / Aug. 25, 1978-Aug. 26, 1978 / Muse ✦✦✦✦✦
After years of neglect, Eddie "Cleanhead" Vinson was finally receiving long overdue recognition at the time of this live session—one of six albums recorded during a week at Sandy's Jazz Revival. Two of these albums featured tenors Arnett Cobb and Buddy Tate in lead roles. While Vinson has fine blues vocals on "Cherry Red" and "Hold It," it is his boppish alto solos on "Cherokee," "Now's the Time" and "Take the 'A' Train" (the latter also having spots for Cobb and Tate) that make this set recommended to blues and bop fans alike. *—Scott Yanow*

I Want a Little Girl / Feb. 10, 1981 / Pablo/OJC ✦✦✦✦✦
Eddie "Cleanhead" Vinson, 64 at the time of this Pablo recording, is in superior form on the blues-oriented material. With Art Hillery (on piano and organ) and guitarist Cal Green leading the rhythm section, and trumpeter Martin Banks and the tenor of Rashid Ali offering contrasting solo voices, this is a particularly strong release. It is true that Vinson had sung such songs as "I Want a Little Girl," "Somebody's Got to Go," and "Stormy Monday" a countless number of times previously but he still infuses these versions with enthusiasm and spirit, making this set a good example of Cleanhead's talents in his later years. *—Scott Yanow*

Eddie Cleanhead Vinson & Roomful of Blues / Jan. 27, 1982 / Muse ✦✦✦✦✦
If there were justice in the world, Eddie "Cleanhead" Vinson would have been able to tour with this type of group throughout much of his career. Roomful of Blues, a popular five-horn nonet, has rarely sounded more exciting than on this musical meeting with the legendary singer/altoist. Vinson himself is exuberant on some of the selections, particularly "House of Joy," one of five instrumentals among the eight selections. Whether one calls it blues, bebop, or early R&B, this accessible music is very enjoyable and deserves to be more widely heard. Among the supporting players, tenorman Greg Piccolo, trumpeter Bob Enos, and guitarist Ronnie Earl (in one of his earliest recordings) win honors. *—Scott Yanow*

Alexander von Schlippenbach

b. Apr. 7, 1938, Berlin, Germany
Piano / Orchestral Jazz, Avant-Garde Jazz, Early Creative, Progressive Big Band, Modern Creative
One of Europe's premier free jazz bandleaders, pianist Alexander von Schlippenbach's music mixes free and contemporary classical elements, with his slashing solos often the link between the two in his compositions. Schlippenbach formed The Globe Unity Orchestra in 1966 to perform the piece "Globe Unity," which had been commissioned by the Berliner Jazztage. He remained involved with the orchestra into the '80s, with the exception of one period from 1971 to 1972. Schlippenbach began taking lessons at eight, and studied at the Staatliche Hochschule for Musik in Cologne with composers Bernd Alois Zimmermann and Rudolf Petzold. He played with Gunther Hampel in 1963, and was in Manfred Schoof's quintet from 1964 to 1967. Schlippenbach began heading various bands after 1967, among them a 1970 trio with Evan Parker and Paul Lovens (both were also in his quartet along with bassist Peter Kowald), and a duo with drummer/vocalist Sven-Ake Johansson which they coformed in 1976. Schlippenbach has also given many solos performances. In the late '80s, he formed the Berlin Contemporary Jazz Orchestra, which has featured a number of esteemed European avant-garde jazz musicians including Evan Parker, Paul Lovens, and, as the orchestra's second pianist, Misha Mengelberg, then Aki Takase. Alexander von Schlippenbach has most frequently recorded for FMP, although Japo, Saba, and Po Torch have also released some of his work. In 2000, the Atavistic label was added to this list with their reissue of the Schlippenbach Quartet's 1975 album *Hunting the Snake*. *—Ron Wynn & Joslyn Layne*

- **Globe Unity** / 1966 / Saba ✦✦✦✦✦

Digger's Harvest / Nov. 5, 1998-Nov. 8, 1997 / FMP ✦✦✦✦✦
One of the few of the intense avant-garde jazz pianists to develop a style largely free of Cecil Taylor's influence, von Schlippenbach has mellowed only slightly with age. These seven duos with drummer Tony Oxley find both of these marvelous musicians in fine form, the energy level rarely abating. Von Schlippenbach is far from all crash and burn, however, as he slips in clips from bygone eras along his journeys. He can be introspective, too, when he focuses on sound and timbre. Oxley's extensive experience interacting with Taylor pays off, as he follows von Schlippenbach closely, never letting him stray too far. As usual, the drummer gives a lesson, if not a live seminar in his art, both as accompanist and as soloist. Unobtrusive, yet continuously creative, Oxley is the Max Roach of free jazz. When paired with von Schlippenbach, the results can be—as they are here—a successful integration of continuous invention and refined sensibility. *—Steven Loewy*

Hunting the Snake 1975 / Sep. 10, 1975 / Atavistic ✦✦✦

Mal Waldron

b. Aug. 16, 1926, New York, NY
Piano / Hard Bop, Post-Bop
A pianist with a brooding, rhythmic, introverted style, Mal Waldron's playing has long been flexible enough to fit into both hard bop and freer settings. Influenced by Thelonious Monk's use of space, Waldron has had his own distinctive chord voicings nearly from the start. He freelanced around New York in the early '50s with Ike Quebec (for whom he made his recording debut), Big Nick Nicholas and a variety of R&B-ish groups. Waldron frequently worked with Charles Mingus from 1954-56 and was Billie Holiday's regular accompanist during her last two years (1957-59). Often hired by Prestige to supervise recording sessions, Waldron contributed many originals (including "Soul Eyes," which became a standard) and basic arrangements that prevented spontaneous dates from becoming overly loose jam sessions. He has mostly led his own groups since Holiday's death, although he was part of the Eric Dolphy Booker Little Quintet that was recorded extensively at the Five Spot in 1961, and also worked with Abbey Lincoln for a time during the era. *—Scott Yanow*

Mal-1 / Nov. 9, 1956 / Prestige/OJC ✦✦✦✦

- **One and Two** / Nov. 9, 1956-May 17, 1957 / Prestige ✦✦✦✦✦
Two of pianist Mal Waldron's first three albums as a leader are combined on this two-LP set. Waldron is heard in a quintet with trumpeter Idrees Sulieman and altoist Gigi Gryce, leading a sextet with trumpeter Bill Hardman, altoist Jackie McLean, and tenor-saxophonist John Coltrane and with a different sextet that also stars Sulieman, Coltrane, and altoist Sahib Shi-

hab. Many of the Prestige sessions from the era were essentially jam sessions but Waldron's dates were better organized and had more challenging material. Five of the pianist's originals are among the dozen selections on this two-fer which also includes five standards and two obscurities. These hard bop performances are among Coltrane's lesser known recordings and show that, even in his early days, Mal Waldron had his style. *—Scott Yanow*

Mal/4 Trio / Sep. 26, 1958 / New Jazz/OJC ✦✦✦✦✦
It seems strange that this, pianist Mal Waldron's seventh session as a leader, was his first with a group as small as his trio. With the assistance of bassist Addison Farmer and drummer Kenny Dennis, Waldron performs four standards and three of his moody originals. His sometimes-brooding style was already quite recognizable and his inventive use of repetition was quite impressive. This recording gives listeners a definitive look at the early style of Mal Waldron. *—Scott Yanow*

Impressions / Mar. 20, 1959 / New Jazz/OJC ✦✦✦✦
This CD reissue brings back one of pianist Mal Waldron's lesser-known sessions from the 1950's. Teamed up in a trio with bassist Addison Farmer and drummer Al "Tootie" Heath, Waldron performs three originals from what he called his "Overseas Suite" along with a fine song by his wife ("All About Us") and three standards. Waldron's brooding Monk-influenced style is heard in its early prime on this excellent release. *—Scott Yanow*

The Quest / Jun. 27, 1961 / New Jazz/OJC ✦✦✦✦
Although often reissued under Eric Dolphy's name, this CD reissue gives the leadership back to pianist Mal Waldron. The seven originals not only feature altoist Dolphy (who makes a rare appearance on clarinet during "Warm Canto") but tenor-saxophonist Booker Ervin, Ron Carter (on cello) and Waldron. With bassist Joe Benjamin and drummer Charlie Persip giving alert support, the complex music (which falls between hard bop and the avant-garde) is successfully interpreted. Worth checking out. *—Scott Yanow*

Up Popped the Devil / Dec. 28, 1973 / Enja ✦✦✦✦✦
Pianist Mal Waldron's music is characterized by a heavily-brooding rhythmic quality, with the left hand usually carrying the theme at one repetitious tempo while the right hammers away in juxtaposition with a counter tempo (usually faster). Such was the case with "Up Popped the Devil," "Snake Out" and "Changachangachang," three very Waldronian pieces in both structure and execution, the latter deriving its melody from the whole-tone scale. Aside from Waldron, the record's strongest points were bassist Reggie Workman and drummer Billy Higgins, their work being sensitive and supportive throughout. *—Bob Rusch, Downbeat*

Hard Talk / May 4, 1974 / Enja ✦✦✦✦✦
This stimulating session (reissued on CD by Enja) features the masterful avant-garde cornetist Manfred Schoof (whose surprising jumps into the upper-register recall Kenny Wheeler), Steve Lacy on soprano, pianist Mal Waldron, bassist Isla Eckinger, and drummer Allen Blairman. They explore four of Waldron's advanced pieces, and it is interesting to hear how Lacy's playing a couple decades ago (with its piercing high notes and very abstract combination of notes) differs from his present-day lyrical approach. Waldron's percussive style is a logical progression from his hard bop playing of the 1950s, and the rhythm section is both alert and tight on these three romps and the ballad "Russian Melody." This is a strong live set that successfully combines together some distinctive musical personalities; Schoof often steals solo honors. *—Scott Yanow*

One-Upmanship / Feb. 12, 1977-May 8, 1978 / Enja ✦✦✦✦

One Entrance, Many Exits / Jan. 4, 1982 / Palo Alto ✦✦✦✦✦
It is a pity that this album is long out-of-print for the combination of musicians works quite well. Pianist Mal Waldron has an inside/outside post bop style that matches perfectly with tenor-saxophonist Joe Henderson, bassist David Friesen and drummer Billy Higgins. On five Waldron originals plus the standard "How Deep Is The Ocean," Henderson and the pianist are heard soloing in top form. Highlgihts include "Chazz Jazz" (dedicated to Charles Mingus), "Golden Golson" (which is purposely in the style of Benny Golson) and an ad-lib blues for the trio "Blues In 4 By 3." *—Scott Yanow*

Songs of Love and Regret / Nov. 9, 1985-Nov. 10, 1985 / Freelance ✦✦✦✦✦

Sempre Amore / Feb. 17, 1986 / Soul Note ✦✦✦✦
Pianist Mal Waldron and soprano-saxophonist Steve Lacy have collaborated on many occasions (on an irregular basis) starting in the 1980's. Both masterful musicians are expatriates whose styles developed after they made their initial impact in the 1950's. On this likable set, they perform eight songs composed by Duke Ellington and/or Billy Strayhorn. Although adventurous in spots, their intepretations of such pieces as "Johnny Come Lately," "Prelude To A Kiss" and "Smada" are quite respectful and keep the strong melodies in mind. Recommended. *—Scott Yanow*

Update / Mar. 10, 1986 / Soul Note ✦✦✦✦✦
This solo set by pianist Mal Waldron serves as a perfect introduction to his unique style during the more recent part of his career. Waldron performs four standards (including "Night In Tunisia" and "I Should Care") which show off his roots, but most significant are his lengthy "Free For C.T." and "Variations On A Theme By Cecil Taylor." It is always very interesting to hear musicians who started out in straightforward hard bop stretching themselves and playing quite freely. This recording rewards repeated listenings. *—Scott Yanow*

Left Alone '86 / Sep. 1, 1986 / Evidence ✦✦✦✦✦
Although he cannot maintain the same nonstop pace he had in the early '60s, Jackie McLean still plays magnificently. He demonstrated that repeatedly on this 1986 duo date with pianist Mal Waldron, whose lovely countermelodies, complementary solos, darting phrases, and supporting accompaniment proved a perfect contrast to McLean's forays. He is lyrical and engaging on some tracks; his explosive side emerges on others, where The McLean whose alto seemed ready to disintegrate on such sets as *Action* or *A Fickle Sonance* charges to the fore, hitting upper register home runs and ripping through the notes. It's good to know that McLean could still summon that drive. *—Ron Wynn*

Seagulls of Kristiansundi: Live at the Village Vanguard / Sep. 16, 1986 / Soul Note ✦✦✦✦✦

No More Tears (For Lady Day) / Nov. 1, 1988-Nov. 3, 1988 / Timeless ✦✦✦✦
Not to be confused with the trio session recorded in the early '70s, *Blues for Lady Day*, this recording takes the same familiar trio format to revisit several tunes associated with Billie Holiday, as well as a few written in her memory by Waldron. The pianist is in a somber mood, perhaps because of the theme, though his performance is up to his usually high standards. A master of understatement, Waldron favors lingering chords that hang laconically even with the faster tempos. He rarely inserts an unneeded note, but instead concentrates on total sound. Drummer John Betsch brings out the best in each tune, pushing Waldron when appropriate. Bassist Paulo Cardoso makes little impression, particularly as a soloist, where he sometimes appears trapped by the structures of the songs. He is more successful as an accompanist. The delightful ambience of the trio results in a laid-back atmosphere that soothes and calms. A fine antidote to a stressful world and a lovely tribute to Lady Day. *—Steven Loewy*

Bennie Wallace (Bennie Lee Wallace, Jr.)

b. Nov. 18, 1946, Chattanooga, TN
Sax (Tenor) / Post-Bop
Bennie Wallace has long had his own unique style, combining together the rapsy tone of Ben Webster with the frequent wide interval jumps of Eric Dolphy. He has an explorative style that soundwise looks back towards the swing era. Wallace started on clarinet when he was 12 and a few years later switched to tenor. He graduated from the University of Tennessee in 1968 and in 1971 moved to New York where he debuted with Monty Alexander. Wallace gigged with Sheila Jordan, played with many avant-garde musicians, was in George Gruntz's Concert Jazz Band in 1979 and led his own trio/quartet on-and-off throughout the 1970s and '80s. He recorded frequently prior to 1985 for Enja but his mid-to-late-'80s Blue Note recordings are more memorable for they find him infusing his appealing sound with touches of New Orleans R&B and a healthy dose of humor. In recent times Wallace has been writing music for films including *White Men Can't Jump*. *—Scott Yanow*

The Fourteen Bar Blues / Jan. 23, 1978 / Inner City ✦✦✦✦
Tenor-saxophonist Bennie Wallace's debut as a leader features the adventurous tenor in a trio with bassist Eddie Gomez and drummer Eddie Moore. This Lp (long overdue to be reissued on CD) has six Wallace originals (including the title cut and "Yard 'N Newk" which borrows aspects of Charlie Parker and Sonny Rollins) plus melodic interpretations of "Chelsea Bridge" and "Trinkle Tinkle" and a warm rendition of "Flamingo." Even at the near-start of his career, Bennie Wallace's sound, style and approach were fully formed. *—Scott Yanow*

Plays Monk / Mar. 4, 1981-Mar. 5, 1981 / Enja ✦✦✦✦✦
Recorded a year before pianist/composer Thelonious Monk's death, this tribute by Bennie Wallace features the dynamic tenor in trios with bassist Eddie Gomez and drummer Dannie Richmond plus three quartets with the addition of trombonist Jimmy Knepper. Wallace's eccentric interval jumps and very expressive sound (along with his advanced harmonic knowledge) made him a natural to explore Monk's music and he pours plenty of passion into these improvisations. In addition to seven of Monk's compositions, Wallace contributes his own "Prelude"; the CD reissue adds a second version of "'Round Midnight" to the original program. This colorful and chancetaking session can act as an introduction to both Bennie Wallace and Monk's music. *—Scott Yanow*

Big Jim's Tango / Nov. 30, 1982-Dec. 1, 1982 / Enja ✦✦✦✦✦

Sweeping Through the City / Mar. 1984-Apr. 1984 / Enja ✦✦✦✦
Tenor-saxophonist Bennie Wallace's first six recordings as a leader (all for Enja during 1978-82) featured his large tone and advanced solos with sparse rhythm sections. *Sweeping Through The City* was a transitional record that looked toward his upcoming Blue Note dates. Wallace is teamed with the rambunctious trombonist Ray Anderson, guitarist John Scofield, bass, drums and the four-voice gospel group "The Wings Of Song." Although the music looks toward the roots of black music, Wallace and Anderson's consistently wild solos keep the results from ever being predictable. Recommended. *—Scott Yanow*

• **Twilight Time** / 1985 / Blue Note ✦✦✦✦✦
This Blue Note album is a classic. Although tenor-saxophonist Bennie Wallace was originally thought of as an avant-gardist, his large tone (in the tradition of Ben Webster) and roots in Southern music always made him stand out from the crowd. On this inspired project, Wallace, trombonist Ray Anderson, and guitarist John Scofield are well-showcased in R&Bish and funky settings with such musicians as pianist Dr. John, Bob Cranshaw, or Eddie Gomez on bass, Jack DeJohnette, Chris Parker, or Bernard Purdie on drums, and (during two numbers) blues guitar legend Stevie Ray Vaughan. To hear the lead voices rocking out on "Is It True What They Say About Dixie," "Tennessee Waltz," and "Trouble in Mind" is a unique experience, and Wallace's lively cadenza on "Twilight Time" steals the show. Highly recommended. *—Scott Yanow*

Old Songs / Jan. 18, 1993-Jan. 20, 1993 / JVC ✦✦✦✦
Much of this date features Bennie Wallace's distinctive tenor in a pianoless trio with bassist Bill Hunington and drummer Alvin Queen. Although it could be said that Wallace combines the sound of Ben Webster with the interval jumps of Eric Dolphy (a very potent combination), he has had his own style for over a decade. These eight standards (along with an original blues "At Lulu White's") are taken at a variety of tempos and Wallace really digs into these fertile chord changes after showing respect for the melodies. *—Scott Yanow*

Bennie Wallace / Apr. 29, 1998-Apr. 30, 1998 / AudioQuest ✦✦✦✦
For this mostly relaxed date, tenor saxophonist Bennie Wallace (who plays pretty melodically throughout much of the session) is teamed with veteran pianist Tommy Flanagan, bassist Eddie Gomez and drummer Alvin Queen. Wallace does his best to temper some of his wilder interval jumps but it is such an integral part of his style that he does let loose in spots. The rhythm section is tight and tasteful and the quartet explores seven standards, plus an original apiece by Wallace ("Little Surprises") and Flanagan ("Beyond the Bluebird"). Other high-

lights include Duke Ellington's rarely played "Serenade to Sweden," "Moon Song" and "So in Love." *— Scott Yanow*

Fats Waller (Thomas Wright Waller)

b. May 21, 1904, New York, NY, **d.** Dec. 15, 1943, Kansas City, MO
Vocals, Piano, Organ, Composer / Jive, Classic Jazz, Stride, Swing
Not only was Fats Waller one of the greatest pianists jazz has ever known, he was also one of its most exuberantly funny entertainers—and as so often happens, one facet tends to obscure the other. His extraordinarily light and flexible touch belied his ample physical girth; he could swing as hard as any pianist alive or dead in his classic James P. Johnson-derived stride manner, with a powerful left hand delivering the octaves and tenths in a tireless, rapid, seamless stream. Waller also pioneered the use of the pipe organ and Hammond organ in jazz—he called the pipe organ the "God box"—adapting his irresistible sense of swing to the pedals and a staccato right hand while making imaginative changes of the registration. As a composer and improviser, his melodic invention rarely flagged, and he contributed fistfuls of joyous yet paradoxically winsome songs like "Honeysuckle Rose," "Ain't Misbehavin,'" "Keepin' Out of Mischief Now," "Blue Turning Grey Over You" and the extraordinary "Jitterbug Waltz" to the jazz repertoire. During his lifetime and afterwards, though, Fats Waller was best known to the world for his outsized comic personality and sly vocals, where he would send up trashy tunes that Victor Records made him record with his nifty combo, Fats Waller and his Rhythm. Yet on virtually any of his records, whether the song is an evergreen standard or the most trite bit of doggerel that a Tin Pan Alley hack could serve up, you will hear a winning combination of good knockabout humor, foot-tapping rhythm and fantastic piano playing. *—Richard S. Ginell*

☆ **Piano Masterworks, Vol. 1** / Oct. 21, 1922-Sep. 24, 1929 / EPM Musique ♦♦♦♦♦
Although he would become well-known in the '30s for his comic vocals and memorable personality, Fats Waller was always first and foremost a pianist. During the '20s he was purely an instrumentalist, one of the greatest and most powerful stride pianists of all time. This CD has all of Waller's early piano solos, including every one of the alternate takes (two versions of many titles and a very rare third take of "I've Got a Feeling I'm Falling"). With the exception of his initial two sides from 1922 and 1927's "Blue Black Bottom," all of these titles are from 1929, including the original version of "Ain't Misbehavin'." *— Scott Yanow*

Classic Jazz from Rare Piano Rolls / Mar. ??, 1923-Jan. ??, 1929 / Biograph ♦♦♦
During 1922-1927 Waller made 19 piano rolls, solos that could be reproduced by running marked paper through player pianos. Eleven of these are on this CD, along with a duet with his teacher James P. Johnson ("If I Could Be With You") and a version of Waller's "Ain't Misbehavin'" from 1929 by J. Lawrence Cook. Piano rolls always come a distant second to recorded piano solos since the unchanging tempos and steady rhythms generally come across as mechanical. His piano rolls are as rollicking and swinging as it is possible to get, and this interesting CD gives listeners versions of several tunes that Waller never did record. *— Scott Yanow*

☆ **Turn on the Heat: The Fats Waller Piano Solos** / Feb. 16, 1927-May 13, 1941 / Bluebird/RCA ♦♦♦♦♦
With the exception of a third take of "I've Got a Feeling I'm Falling" and his two earliest records from 1922, all of Fats Waller's recorded piano solos are on this superior double-CD set. Over half of these recordings are from 1929, but fortunately he also cut three sessions of piano solos after he became much more famous as a comedy personality with his Rhythm sides. Highlights include the virtuosic "Handful of Keys," the earliest version of "Ain't Misbehavin'," "Clothes Line Ballet," "I Ain't Got Nobody" and "Honeysuckle Rose." A special bonus is a pair of piano duets with Bennie Payne ("St. Louis Blues" and "After You've Gone"). Classic music. *— Scott Yanow*

☆ **Fats Waller and His Buddies** / May 20, 1927-Dec. 18, 1929 / Bluebird/RCA ♦♦♦♦♦
This CD has most of Fats Waller's best band recordings of the '20s, including eight selections by his "Buddies" (highlighted by "The Minor Drag" and "Harlem Fuss"), six (counting two alternate takes) from The Louisiana Sugar Babes (an odd quartet featuring Waller's organ and James P. Johnson's piano) and seven selections on which Waller sits in with cornetist Thomas Morris's Hot Babies in 1927. Surprisingly, other than his scat vocal on "Red Hot Dan," Fats Waller is heard strictly as a pianist but his talents were so giant as an instrumentalist that one never minds. With trombonists Charlie Irvis and Jack Teagarden and trumpeters Red Allen and Jabbo Smith among the strong supporting cast, the one word for this superior CD is hot. *— Scott Yanow*

Breakin' the Ice: The Early Years, Pt. 1 / May 16, 1934-May 6, 1935 / Bluebird/RCA ♦♦♦♦♦
This two-CD set has the first 42 recordings of Fats Waller with his Rhythm. The brilliant stride pianist/vocalist/ composer/personality became very popular due to these 1934-35 recordings which feature either Herman Autrey or Bill Coleman on trumpet, Gene Sedric, Ben Whitted, Mezz Mezzrow or Rudy Powell on reeds, guitarist Al Casey and a rhythm section. All of Waller's Victor recordings have been reissued on CD and this two-fer (which includes such memorable numbers as "A Porter's Love Song to a Chambermaid," "Serenade for a Wealthy Widow," "How Can You Face Me," "Honeysuckle Rose," "Believe It, Beloved," "I Ain't Got Nobody," "Oh Suzannah Dust Off That Old Pianna" and "You've Been Taking Lessons in Love") is a perfect place to start. *— Scott Yanow*

I'm Gonna Sit Right Down: The Early Years, Part 2 / May 8, 1935-Feb. 1, 1936 / Bluebird/RCA ♦♦♦♦♦
The second in a series of five CD packages that reissue all of Fats Waller's Victor recordings with his Rhythm, this two-CD set traces the pianist/composer/ vocalist/personality's career during a nine-month period. Among the sidemen are trumpeter Herman Autrey and either Rudy Powell or Gene Sedric on reeds; highlights include the hit version of "I'm Gonna Sit Right Down and Write Myself a Letter," a rambunctious "There'll Be Some Changes Made," "Truckin '," "Got a Bran' New Suit" and four performances from a big-band session. All of the Waller Victor recordings are full of joy and infectious swing. *— Scott Yanow*

1935-1936 / Nov. 29, 1935-Apr. 8, 1936 / Classics ♦♦♦♦
By the time of this ninth volume of French label Classics' chronological series, Fats Waller was among the most popular recording artists in the U.S., and the 24 selections here, drawn from sessions recorded in November and December 1935 and February and April 1936, reflect both that popularity and the kind of material necessary to maintain it. Nearly all the performances feature Waller vocals, and there are a lot of pop songs, most of which are not of the highest quality. The better compositions include Jimmy McHugh and Ted Koehler's "Spreadin' Rhythm Around," and the Gershwins' "I Got Rhythm," and Leon Berry and Andy Razaf's "Christopher Columbus." Of course, Waller personalizes the songs no matter how good they are on paper, and he scored a series of hits from these sessions, including the chart-toppers "A Little Bit Independent" and "All My Life." Waller is accompanied throughout by the quintet His Rhythm, and soloing sidemen trumpeter Herman Autrey and clarinetist/saxophonist Sedric get plenty of playing time. The tracks, doubtlessly mastered from records, are often scratchy-sounding, but overall sound quality is good. *— William Ruhlmann*

Fractious Fingering: Early Years, Vol. 3 (1936) / Apr. 8, 1936-Nov. 29, 1936 / RCA ♦♦♦♦
With the release of this two-CD set in 1997, it became possible for the first time ever to easily acquire all of pianist/composer/vocalist Fats Waller's Rhythm recordings of 1934-43. They are available in their entirety on three double-disc and three triple-disc sets, 15 discs in all. The 41 selections on this set feature Waller with trumpeter Herman Autrey, Gene Sedric on clarinet and tenor, guitarist Al Casey, bassist Charles Turner and either Yank Porter or Slick Jones on drums. The rarest performance ("Stay") has Elizabeth Handy (W.C.'s daughter) joining Fats for a duet vocal, and there are also five alternate takes (all previously released) of various tunes. This hard-swinging music is quite enjoyable (especially in small doses), with the most memorable selections including "All My Life," "Christopher Columbus" (with its hilarious lyrics), "Black Raspberry Jam," "Fractious Fingering," two run-throughs on "The Curse of an Aching Heart," the jubilant "Floatin' Down to Cotton Town," and two classic versions of "Swingin' Them Jingle Bells." This music is impossible not to like, and, as is always true of Fats Waller, it is touched with genius. *— Scott Yanow*

Fats Waller and His Rhythm: The Middle Years, Pt. 1 (1936-1938) / Dec. 24, 1936-Apr. 12, 1938 / Bluebird/RCA ♦♦♦♦♦
Part of Bluebird's very admirable reissue of all of Fats Waller's 1934-42 Victor recordings, this three-CD set has the pianist-vocalist's 70 studio performances from a busy 16-month period. Most selections are with his sextet that generally includes trumpeter Herman Autrey, Gene Sedric on clarinet and tenor, and guitarist Al Casey plus there are eight songs with Fats' occasional big band in 1938. Among the many highpoints are "I'm Sorry I Made You Cry," "Nero," "Beat It Out," "The Joint Is Jumpin'" (the original hit record), "The Sheik Of Araby" and instrumental versions of "Honeysuckle Rose" and "Blue, Turning Grey Over You." Highly recommended. *— Scott Yanow*

A Good Man is Hard to Find: The Middle Years, Part II / Apr. 12, 1938-Jan. 12, 1940 / Bluebird/RCA ♦♦♦♦♦
Subtitled "The Middle Years, Part 2," athis three-CD set contains all of pianist/vocalist Fats Waller's Victor recordings from a nearly two-year period including all of the alternate takes. In fact the first five selections (the only ones contained here from his short-lived big band) are all alternate takes to the selections that close "The Middle Years, Part 1." Otherwise these performances are by Waller's septet with either Herman Autrey or John Hamilton on trumpet and Gene Sedric (who doubled on tenor and clarinet); Chauncey Graham filled in for Sedric on one date. Waller's great popularity resulted in the large number of recordings from this era (68 are on this set) and they range from hits ("Two Sleepy People," "Yacht Club Swing," an amazing version of "Hold Tight," "Your Feet's Too Big" and a new rendition of "Squeeze Me") and fresh originals and novelties to trash that Waller did his best (often through satirization) to uplift. Nearly every selection has a liberal dose of his classic piano and taken as a whole these much-maligned recordings are quite listenable, enjoyable and historical. *— Scott Yanow*

1938-1939 / Dec. 7, 1938-Apr. 2, 1939 / Classics ♦♦♦♦

The Last Years (1940-1943) / Apr. 11, 1940-Jan. 23, 1943 / Bluebird/RCA ♦♦♦♦♦
Since all of the previous Fats Waller Rhythm reissue series start off in 1934 and get discontinued before reaching the '40s, this time around the newest program has started out with Waller's last recordings and is working its way backwards. This essential three-CD set contains the pianist/vocalist/composer's last 63 studio recordings. Some of the titles are quite laughable ("Little Curly Hair in a High Chair," "You're a Square from Delaware," "Abercrombie Had a Zombie" and "Come Down to Earth My Angel") but Waller manages to either satirize or save virtually all of the somewhat dubious material. There are some out-and-out classics included on this set too, including "Fats Waller's Original E Flat Blues," "All That Meat and No Potatoes" and "The Jitterbug Waltz"; this wonderful set of spirited music concludes with "Ain't Misbehavin'" from the soundtrack of *Stormy Weather*. *— Scott Yanow*

★ **The Very Best of Fats Waller** / Sep. 12, 2000 / Collectors' Choice Music ♦♦♦♦♦

George Wallington (Giacinto Figlia)

b. Oct. 27, 1924, Palmero, Sicily, Italy, **d.** Feb. 15, 1993, New York, NY
Piano / Bop
George Wallington was one of the first and best bop pianists, ranking up there with Al Haig just below Bud Powell. He was also the composer of two bop standards that caught on for a time: "Lemon Drop" and "Godchild." Born in Sicily, Wallington and his family moved to the U.S. in 1925. He arrived in New York in the early '40s and was a member of the first bop group to play on 52nd Street, Dizzy Gillespie's combo of 1943-44. After spending a year with Joe Marsala's band, Wallington played with the who's who of bop during 1946-52 including Charlie Parker, Serge Chaloff, Allan Eager, Kai Winding, Terry Gibbs, Brew Moore, Al Cohn, Gerry Mulligan, Zoot Sims and Red Rodney. He toured Europe with Lionel Hampton's ill-fated big band of 1953 and during 1954-60 he led groups in New York that included among its up-and-coming sidemen Donald Byrd and Jackie McLean (the latter succeeded by Phil

Woods). Then in 1960 Wallington gave up on the music business altogether and retired to work in his family's air-conditioning company. Twenty-four years later he re-emerged, recording three albums of original material before time ran out. *—Scott Yanow*

• **The George Wallington Trios** / Sep. 4, 1952-May 25, 1953 / Prestige/OJC ✦✦✦✦✦
Originally released as a pair of ten-inch Prestige albums, this CD reissue features the talented bop-oriented pianist George Wallington in trios with either Charles Mingus, Oscar Pettiford or Curly Russell on bass plus drummer Max Roach; guitarist Chuck Wayne sits in on mandola on "Love Beat." The 15 songs include concise interpretations of ten of Wallington's originals and it seems strange that latter-day jazz musicians have yet to really explore his inventive tunes. This is one of the best showcases ever of Wallington's playing and writing talents. *—Scott Yanow*

George Wallington Quintet Live at Cafe Bohemia / Sep. 9, 1955 / Prestige/OJC ✦✦✦✦✦
This live set, although led by pianist George Wallington, is most significant for giving listeners early examples of the playing of trumpeter Donald Byrd and altoist Jackie McLean; bassist Paul Chambers and drummer Art Taylor complete the quintet. The music, although comprised mostly of group originals (other than "Johnny One Note" and Oscar Pettiford's "Bohemia After Dark"), is essentially a bebop jam and it is particularly interesting to hear just how much McLean was influenced by Charlie Parker at this point (although his sound was already quickly recognizable). This was a solid if short-lived group and their brand of hard bop will be enjoyed by straightahead jazz fans. The CD reissue adds a second version of "Minor March" to the original program. *—Scott Yanow*

Jazz for the Carriage Trade / Jan. 20, 1956 / Prestige/OJC ✦✦✦✦
During 1956-57 trumpeter Donald Byrd and altoist Phil Woods (both important up-and-coming players) were regular members of pianist George Wallington's quintet. For this CD reissue, bassist Teddy Kotick and drummer Art Taylor complete the group on a program that includes three standards ("Our Delight," "Our Love Is Here to Stay" and "What's New"), a pair of Woods originals ("Together We Wail" and "But George") and Frank Foster's "Foster Dulles." The music falls between bebop and hard bop with Woods sounding quite strong while Byrd comes across as a promising (but not yet mature) youngster. A fine example of this somewhat forgotten but talented group, easily recommended to bop collectors. *—Scott Yanow*

Knight Music / Sep. 4, 1956-Sep. 5, 1956 / Koch International ✦✦✦✦
The fine bop pianist George Wallington hasn't received the recognition he deserved, possibly because of a two-dozen year gap from 1960-1984 when he was entirely out of the music business. This first-rate trio date for Atlantic has finally come out on CD and should help gain him some posthumous attention. One of his two greatest compositions, "Godchild" (which appears on the classic Miles Davis release *The Birth of the Cool*), opens the disc with a flourish, but there are many strong originals present. The lively stair-stepping "Serendipity" and the furious "Up Jumped the Devil" are worthy of comparison to Bud Powell. Wallington also covers several standards such as "Will You Still Be Mine?" and "It's All Right With Me" with finesse and imagination. *—Ken Dryden*

The New York Scene / Mar. 1, 1957 / New Jazz/OJC ✦✦✦✦✦
Before he retired from music in 1960, pianist George Wallington led a series of excellent bop-based quintet albums. For this particular CD (a reissue of a date originally put out by New Jazz), Wallington heads a group featuring altoist Phil Woods, trumpeter Donald Byrd, bassist Teddy Kotick and drummer Nick Stabulas. With the exception of the standard "Indian Summer," the repertoire is pretty obscure (with now-forgotten originals by Byrd, Woods and Mose Allison in addition to "Graduation Day") but of a consistent high quality. The emphasis is on hard-swinging and this set should greatly please straightahead jazz fans. *—Scott Yanow*

The Pleasure of a Jazz Inspiration / Aug. 19, 1985 / VSOP ✦✦✦✦
Pianist George Wallington, who retired from jazz in 1960, returned in the mid-'80s and recorded three solo albums; he passed away in 1993. This CD, which contains eight originals (which are subtitled *A Jazz Tone Poem*), is not as adventurous as one might think. Actually a lot of the songs are based on fairly common chord changes. Wallington plays quite well (mixing in his dominant Bud Powell influence with touches of Teddy Wilson), making one regret that the important bop-based pianist took so many years off. At least his final efforts were impressive, and this CD offers some fine examples of his playing after his "comeback." *—Scott Yanow*

Cedar Walton

b. Jan. 17, 1934, Dallas, TX
Piano, Composer / Hard Bop
One of the most valued of all hard bop accompanists, Cedar Walton is a versatile pianist whose funky touch and cogent melodic sense has graced the recordings of many of jazz's greatest players. He is also one of the music's more underrated composers; although he has always been a first-rate interpreter of standards, Walton wrote a number of excellent tunes ("Mosaic," "Ugetsu," and "Bolivia," to name a few) that found their way into Art Blakey's book during the pianist's early-'60s stint with the Jazz Messengers. He joined Blakey in 1961, with whom he remained until '64. This was perhaps Blakey's most influential group, with Freddie Hubbard and Wayne Shorter. Walton served time as Abbey Lincoln's accompanist from 1965-66 and made records with Lee Morgan from 1966-68; from 1967-69, he served as a sideman on many Prestige albums as well. Walton played in a band with Hank Mobley in the early '70s and returned to Blakey for a 1973 tour of Japan. Walton's own band of the period was called Eastern Rebellion, and was comprised of a rotating cast that included saxophonists Clifford Jordan, George Coleman and Bob Berg, bassist Sam Jones and drummer Billy Higgins. *—Chris Kelsey*

Plays Cedar Walton / Jul. 10, 1967-Jan. 14, 1969 / Prestige/OJC ✦✦✦✦✦
Still as criminally overlooked as he was in the hard-bop era, pianist Cedar Walton represents the cream of jazz composers and soloists dating back to the late '50s. He first gained notoriety as a solid sidemen for Art Blakey's early-'60s Jazz Messengers, contributing gems like "Ugetsu" and complimenting the talents of trumpeter Freddie Hubbard and tenor saxophonist Wayne Shorter. After stints with trumpeter Lee Morgan and singer Abbey Lincoln, Walton began his long solo career in 1967 with Prestige. Over the course of the next three years, Walton would showcase his very original writing skills and feature a host of top players from the period. This installment in the label's introductory sampler series finds Walton working through an exclusively original set within trio, quartet, and quintet formats. Joining the pianist are trumpeters Kenny Dorham and Blue Mitchell, tenor saxophonists Junior Cook and Clifford Jordan, bassists Leroy Vinnegar and Bob Cranshaw, and drummers Mickey Roker and Billy Higgins (a longtime Walton associate). Everyone is in top form throughout. Song highlights include "Head and Shoulders," "Spectrum," and a trio reading of "Ugetsu." Save for 1969's underrated *Soul Cycle* album (another victim of jazz purists unable to deal with electric pianos and Stevie Wonder covers), this overview nicely covers Walton's late '60s stay with Prestige and qualifies as a first-disc choice for newcomers. *—Stephen Cook*

★ **Breakthrough** / Feb. 22, 1972 / Muse ✦✦✦✦✦
As strong as pianist Cedar Walton plays on his session, the main honors are taken by two of his sidemen. Tenor-saxophonist Hank Mobley, whose career was about to go into a complete eclipse, is in brilliant form, showing how much he had grown since his earlier days. Baritonist Charles Davis, who too often through the years has been used as merely a section player, keeps up with Mobley and engages in a particularly memorable tradeoff on the lengthy title cut. Mobley is well-showcased on "Summertime," Davis switches successfully to soprano on "Early Morning Stroll," and Walton (with the trio) somehow turns the "Theme From Love Story" into jazz. Highly recommended. *—Scott Yanow*

A Night at Boomer's, Vol. 1 / Jan. 4, 1973 / Muse ✦✦✦✦✦

A Night at Boomer's, Vol. 2 / Jan. 4, 1973 / Muse ✦✦✦✦✦

Eastern Rebellion, Vol. 1 / Dec. 10, 1975 / Timeless ✦✦✦✦✦
This CD reissue brings back a classic set featuring four giants of the modern mainstream: pianist/leader Cedar Walton, tenor-saxophonist George Coleman, bassist Sam Jones and drummer Billy Higgins. All five performances are noteworthy, particularly a definitive version of Walton's most famous composition "Bolivia," Coleman's tricky "5/4 Thing" and Jones's boppish "Bittersweet." The veteran musicians all sound quite inspired on this advanced straightahead set. A gem. *—Scott Yanow*

Among Friends / Jul. 1982 / Evidence ✦✦✦✦
The music on this release was actually performed at San Francisco's Keystone Korner during a recorded engagement by the Bobby Hutcherson sextet. Pianist Cedar Walton opened each set with a few numbers and he was playing so well that in 1990 it was decided to release his material as a seperate CD. Walton performs three songs ("Ruby My Dear," "My Old Flame" and "I've Grown Accustomed to Her Face") solo, interprets four other pieces (three standards plus his own "Midnight Waltz") in a trio with bassist Buster Williams and drummer Billy Higgins, and Hutcherson himself makes the group a quartet on "My Foolish Heart." Excellent hard bop-based music from the talented pianist. *—Scott Yanow*

The Trio, Vol. 1 / Mar. 28, 1985 / Red ✦✦✦✦
There have been many Cedar Walton records put out through the years and the three that he and his trio made during a Bologna concert in 1985 rank with his best. Joined by bassist David Williams and drummer Billy Higgins, Walton stretches out on four standards (highlighted by "My Ship") and a pair of originals ("Holy Land" and "Voices Deep Within Me") during this first volume; all are easily recommended to straightahead jazz collectors. *—Scott Yanow*

The Trio, Vol. 2 / Mar. 28, 1985 / Red ✦✦✦✦
The second of three albums recorded by pianist Cedar Walton, bassist David Williams and drummer Billy Higgins during a single concert in Bologna, Italy is (like the other two) an excellent example of Walton's distinctive approach to hard bop. The trio stretches out on "Theme for Ernie," "For All We Know," Thelonious Monk's "Off Minor," Sonny Red's "Bluesville" and a couple of lesser-known Walton originals. *—Scott Yanow*

Bluesville Time / Apr. 21, 1985 / Criss Cross ✦✦✦✦

Blues for Myself / Feb. 1986 / Red ✦✦✦✦✦
Cedar Walton's second set of unaccompanied solos (following his little-known Clean Cuts release *Piano Solos* by five years) features the talented veteran pianist exploring six standards (including "Without a Song" and "Just in Time") plus four of his originals. Although always a hard bop stylist, Walton was never just a one-handed pianist and this superior release does not find him or listeners missing a bassist or drummer. Recommended. *—Scott Yanow*

Cedar Walton Plays / Sep. 29, 1986-Sep. 30, 1986 / Delos ✦✦✦✦✦
Pianist Cedar Walton heads a medium-size group on this 1986 Delos CD, a rhythm section with bassist Ron Carter and drummer Billy Higgins plus a five piece horn section: trumpeter Don Sickler, altoist Kenny Garrett, the obscure tenor Lou Orensteen, baritonist Charles Davis and trombonist Steve Turre. Unfortunately the horns mostly stick to ensemblework (except for an extended version of Benny Golson's "Out of the Past") but Walton and his trio are in top form on such numbers as Bud Powell's "Halluncinations," a lengthy rendition of Cole Porter's "So in Love," Nellie Lutcher's "He's a Real Gone Guy" and the leader's "Something in Common." *—Scott Yanow*

Live at Maybeck Recital Hall Series, Vol. 25 / Aug. 9, 1992 / Concord Jazz ✦✦✦✦
Although this is hardly Cedar Walton's first attempt to go completely solo, his fans still know him primarily from his ensemble work and will no doubt be surprised and pleased with this album, No. 25 in the Maybeck Recital Hall series. After warming up with an intricate self-composed workout, "The Maybeck Blues," Walton veers into some standards ("Stella By Starlight," "Sweet Lorraine") with the polystylistic twists and turns of an Art Tatum. Walton's other composition "Bremond's Blues" is somehow generated by the changes from "Giant Steps"—a neat trick. Beyond the strong Tatum influence, Walton remains a strong hard bopper with his right hand, a manner that takes very well to the characteristically bright, crisp tone of the hall's Yamaha pianos; but he also displays as fully equipped a harmonic arsenal

as that of anyone. The CD concludes with a technical tour de force on "Just One of Those Things," which almost, but not quite, ties itself in knots. *—Richard S. Ginell*

Manhattan Afternoon / Dec. 26, 1992 / Criss Cross ♦♦♦♦

David S. Ware

b. Nov. 7, 1949, Plainfield, NJ

Sax (Tenor) / Avant-Garde Jazz, Free Jazz

The critical buzz aroused by David S. Ware's work with Andrew Cyrille and Cecil Taylor in the '70s had, by the late '90s, turned into a consonant roar. New York's collective jazz press—always on the lookout for the music's next messiah—crowned Ware the "King of Free Jazz" on the basis of his energetic quartet albums from the mid-'90s. His saxophone technique is total; unlike a good many free players, Ware does not base his style on any particular technical shortcoming or theoretical misunderstanding. He's learned both the music and the horn up and down, inside and out, from the bottom up. In this respect, he's a true heir to Coltrane, who also based his free work on a comprehensive knowledge of his materials. Indeed, Ware's typical manner of performance—modal/free, rubato, high-energy collective improvisation—stems directly from *Meditations*-era Coltrane.

During the 1970s, Ware played with drummer Andrew Cyrille's group, in a trio with trumpeter Raphe Malik and with bop pianist Barry Harris' band (the two also recorded a duo album). He began his solo career with a pair of releases on the Silkheart label—1988's *Passage to Music* and 1990's *Great Bliss, Vol. 1.* His 1991 release, *Flight of i,* was recorded for the Japanese label DIW and distributed by Columbia. The late '90s had Ware recording with his quartet for a number of independent companies, though he signed to Columbia for 1998's *Go See the World,* and issued *Third Ear Recitation* on DIW/Koch later that same year. *—Chris Kelsey*

Passage to Music / Apr. 4, 1988-Apr. 5, 1988 / Silkheart ♦♦♦♦

A fiery avant-garde tenor saxophonist, David Ware had recorded two early sets for Hat Hut and Palm during 1977-78; a decade later he had his third opportunity to lead a record session. Joined by bassist William Parker and drummer Marc Edwards, Ware performs five of his free jazz originals, mostly on tenor but also playing one song apiece on saxello and stritch. Not for the weak-of-heart, David Ware's searching improvisations reward repeated listenings by open-eared listeners. *—Scott Yanow*

• **Flight of I** / Dec. 10, 1991Dec. 11, 1991 / Columbia ♦♦♦♦♦

Third Ear Recitation / Oct. 14, 1992Oct. 15, 1992 / DIW ♦♦♦♦

Cryptology / Dec. 2, 1994 / Homestead ♦♦♦♦♦

Earthquation / May 4, 1994-May 5, 1994 / DIW ♦♦♦♦

Godspelized / May 2, 1996May 3, 1996 / DIW ♦♦♦

Go See the World / Dec. 11, 1997-Dec. 12, 1997 / Columbia ♦♦♦

Surrendered / Oct. 20, 1999Oct. 21, 1999 / Columbia ♦♦♦

David S. Ware's second Columbia release is characteristically aggressive and anguished, but it is not atonal. The album features four Ware originals, all of which possess clear compositional form and harmonic structure. Ware's solos may be filled with squawks and wails—hallmarks of free jazz—but he is making the chord changes. "Peace Celestial," "Theme of Ages," and "Surrendered" are based on rubato statements of fairly simple chordal and/or melodic motifs. Ware and pianist Matthew Shipp play solos while bassist William Parker and drummer Guillermo E. Brown react in sturdy and empathic fashion. As these tracks play, one envisions landscapes dramatic and vast yet rocky and imposing. "Glorified Calypso," in contrast, bounces along with a buoyancy different in mood from the other cuts.

Two of the tracks are non-originals. Beaver Harris's "African Drums" begins with a 6/8 figure that resembles the vamp of Coltrane's "My Favorite Things"; an off-kilter and rather ugly harmonic shift occurs in the middle four bars of the form. "Sweet Georgia Bright" by Charles Lloyd begins with a medium swing feel and goes in and out of double-time for the solos. It's as straight-ahead an arrangement as Ware will ever play, but as the entire album reveals, Ware's music contains more conventional harmony, melody, and rhythm than is often supposed. *—David R. Adler*

Grover Washington, Jr.

b. Dec. 12, 1943, Buffalo, NY, **d.** Dec. 17, 1999

Sax (Tenor), Sax (Soprano), Sax (Alto) / Quiet Storm, Crossover Jazz, Soul-Jazz

One of the most popular saxophonists of all time (even his off records have impressive sales), Grover Washington, Jr. has long been the pacesetter in his field. His roots are in R&B and soul-jazz organ combos, but he also fares very well on the infrequent occasions when he plays straight-ahead jazz. A highly influential player, Washington has sometimes been blamed for the faults of his followers; Kenny G. largely based his soprano sound on Grover's tone. However, most of the time (except when relying on long hit medleys), Washington pushes himself with the spontaneity and chance-taking of a masterful jazz musician. His biggest break occurred in 1971, when Hank Crawford could not make it to a recording date; Washington was picked as his replacement, and the result was *Inner City Blues,* a big seller. From then on he became a major name, particularly after recording 1975's *Mister Magic* and 1980s *Winelight;* the latter included the Bill Withers hit "Just the Two of Us." Although some of his recordings since then find him coasting a bit, Washington usually stretches himself in concert, being almost overqualified for the R&B-ish music that he performs. He has developed his own personal voices on soprano, tenor, alto and even his infrequently used baritone. *—Scott Yanow*

Inner City Blues / Sep. 1971 / Motown Jazz ♦♦♦♦♦

Grover Washington Jr's debut as a leader is a classic of its kind. Straddling the boundary between soul jazz and r*bish crossover, $Washington* on alto and tenor (under the direction of Creed Taylor and utilizing the arrangements of Bob James) puts plenty of feeling into his soulful versions of "Mercy Mercy Me," "Ain't No Sunshine," "Georgia On My Mind" and "I Loves You Porgy." It is obvious from listening to this music alone that he was destined to be a star. *—Scott Yanow*

Mister Magic / Nov. 1974 / MoJazz ♦♦♦♦♦

This is one of Grover Washington Jr.'s best-loved recordings and considered a classic of r*bish jazz. All four songs (which includes $Billy Strayhorn's* "Passion Flower") are quite enjoyable but it is "Mister Magic" that really caught on as a major hit. Bob James provided the colorful if somewhat commercial arrangements, there are spots for guitarist Eric Gale, and Washington (mostly on tenor and soprano) is heard in particularly creative form. Highly recommended. *—Scott Yanow*

Live at the Bijou / May 1977 / Motown ♦♦♦

Winelight / Jun. 1980-Jul. 1980 / Elektra ♦♦♦♦♦

Grover Washington, Jr., has long been one of the leaders in what could be called rhythm & jazz, essentially R&B-influenced jazz. *Winelight* is one of his finest albums, and not primarily because of the Bill Withers hit "Just the Two of Us." It is the five instrumentals that find Washington (on soprano, alto and tenor) really stretching out. If he had been only interested in sales, Washington's solos could have been half as long and he would have stuck closely to the melody. Instead he really pushes himself on some of these selections, particularly the title cut. A memorable set of high-quality and danceable soul jazz. *—Scott Yanow*

Then and Now / 1988 / Columbia ♦♦♦♦

This is one of Grover Washington, Jr.'s occasional strays away from R&B-oriented jazz to play in a more straightahead setting. Switching between soprano, alto and tenor, Grover is accompanied by either Tommy Flanagan or Herbie Hancock on piano during five of the eight selections and he performs such numbers as Ron Carter's "Blues for D.P.," "Stolen Moments" and "Stella by Starlight" with swing and taste. Tenor-saxophonist Igor Butman also helps out on three songs. Worth acquiring. *—Scott Yanow*

• **Ultimate Collection** / Nov. 2, 1999 / Uptown/Universal ♦♦♦♦

Grover Washington Jr.'s *Ultimate Collection* collects 11 of the saxophonist's greatest hits, including "Just The Two Of Us" with Bill Withers, "Bright Moments, " "Black Frost" and his interpretation of Marvin Gaye's "Inner City Blues." "Mister Magic" and "Summer Song" are also featured on this concise collection of Washington's jazz/soul/pop performances. *—Heather Phares*

Sadao Watanabe

b. Feb. 1, 1933, Utsunomiya, Japan

Sax (Alto) / Jazz-Pop, Neo-Bop

Sadao Watanabe has long had a split musical personality. He alternates excellent bebop dates with weak pop albums that pale next to the leaders of the idiom (such as Grover Washington, Jr. and David Sanborn). Watanabe learned clarinet and alto in high school and in the 1950s he moved to Tokyo, joining Toshiko Akiyoshi's bop-oriented group in 1953. When the pianist moved to the U.S. in 1956, Watanabe took over the band. He attended Berklee during 1962-65 and had the opportunity to work with Gary McFarland, Chico Hamilton and Gabor Szabo. However Watanabe has remained mostly based in Japan throughout his career where he is a major influence on younger players. He has recorded steadily through the years, most notably with Chick Corea in New York (1970) and with the Galaxy All-Stars (1978). Watanabe's bop records are inspired by Charlie Parker but his Brazilian-flavored pop dates are instantly forgettable. *—Scott Yanow*

• **Round Trip** / Jul. 15, 1974 / Vanguard ♦♦♦♦♦

Sadao Watanabe has been disappointing on more than a few occasions. In fact, some of his more commercial, radio-oriented efforts have been quite forgettable. But when he's playing from the heart instead of pandering to commercial radio, Watanabe can be captivating. An adventurous "inside/outside" post-bop date employing Chick Corea (acoustic & electric piano), Miroslav Vitous (upright bass), and Jack De Johnette (drums), *Round Trip* is one of his finest accomplishments. There's nothing even remotely predictable about this CD, which ranges from the Celtic-influenced, Weather Report-ish "Pastoral" to the contemplative "Nostalgia" to the insistent, 20-minute "Round Trip: Going and Coming." Best known for his Charlie Parker-influenced alto playing, an especially inspired Watanabe sticks to the soprano sax and flute this time. *—Alex Henderson*

Birds of Passage / May 4, 1977 / Elektra ♦♦♦♦♦

Altoist Sadao Watanabe is considered one of Japan's top jazzmen. Some of his recordings are quite commercial but this particular one finds him paying tribute to Charlie Parker with what was called "the great jazz trio:" pianist Hank Jones, bassist Ron Carter and drummer Tony Williams. The seven selections (four Bird compositions and three standards often played by Parker) are all given strong treatment by the quartet. Watanabe's true love is bebop and his solos here are very much in that tradition yet displaying a personality of his own. This LP will be difficult to find. *—Scott Yanow*

Go Straight Ahead 'n Make a Left / 1997 / Verve ♦♦♦

Go Straight Ahead 'N Make A Left actually sounds like its title—Watanabe takes straight-ahead bebop around a left corner, courtesy of funky rhythm arrangements piloted by his longtime keyboardist, Bernard Wright. Together, they illustrate that there are still some new variations on the saxophonist's modern-day Charlie Parker-styled bop improvisations. Occasionally, the music dips into dangerously smooth territory, but Watanabe's strong playing keeps things on course and makes the record a pleasurable listen. (Watanabe is supported by Wright, bassist Stephen Teele, percussionist Steve Thornton and drummers Mike Flythe, Hassan Flythe and Charley Drayton on *Go Straight Ahead.*) *—Stephen Thomas Erlewine*

Remembrance / Jan. 24, 1999-Jan. 27, 1999 / Verve ♦♦♦♦

It's always an amazing thing when a popular musician is given the opportunity to follow his or her musical muse freely and, if so moved, can so effortlessly switch off between two forms of music whose fans tend to polarize. The famed Japanese saxman has had his handful of smooth jazz successes over the years (including a classic duet with Patti Austin) in the genre's early days called "Any Other Fool"), but here returns to his bop-influenced roots. With his place in jazz history secure and not having to prove too much chops wise, Watanabe often seems content here to blend in with his amazing band, dueting on lead melodies and giving ample solo time to each of his troop members. Who can blame him, though, with cats like flugelhornist Nicholas Payton (who matches the saxman's alto note for note on the swinging, percussive melody of the opening tune "Smokin' Section"), pianist Cyrus Chestnut, bassist Christian McBride, and drummer Billy Drummond— At a time in his life when he could just lay back and play some standards, Watanabe marks his return with all original material (a feat in itself) that's also very eclectic. In the 1990s, it's rare to hear trombone in settings other than a horn section, but Watanabe gives Robin Eubanks' trombone equal billing on the gentle blues ballad "Where You At." Eubanks also plays a key role on the densely percussive "Forest Song," an almost avante garde type piece that finds the trombone and sax in a race to determine which can be more wacky. Watanabe enjoys mood-swinging immensely, following that type of tune with the dreamy waltz-flavored title cut and then ending the set with a snazzy jam session like "Aquarian Groove." *—Jonathan Widran*

Bobby Watson

b. Aug. 23, 1953, Lawrence, KS
Sax (Alto) / Contemporary Jazz, Hard Bop, Post-Bop
Bobby Watson has long been one of the top altoists in jazz, a flexible player able to play swing (he once recorded a tribute to Johnny Hodges), hard bop and free jazz. He started playing the alto when he was 13 and was soon arranging and composing for his school bands. After graduating from the University of Miami in 1975 Watson moved to New York, hitting the big time by joining (and soon becoming the musical director of) Art Blakey's Jazz Messengers during 1977-81, participating in what were Wynton Marsalis' first recordings. In the 1980s Watson co-led groups with Curtis Lundy (with whom he formed the New Note label) and played with the George Coleman Octet, Charlie Persip's big band, Louis Hayes, Sam Rivers, Dameronia, the 29th Street Saxophone Quartet and the Savoy Sultans; quite a wide range of jazz styles! Watson also began leading his own regular bands in the mid-'80s and the following decade he headed a regular hard bop quintet known as Horizon. His many recordings (for Enja, Red, New Note, Blue Note, Evidence, Columbia and Kokopelli) are always stimulating and worth investigating. *—Scott Yanow*

Jewel / Apr. 1983 / Evidence ✦✦✦✦
Bobby Watson had not inked a major label recording pact and was not a finished improviser when he cut these songs in 1983. What he did not lack was intensity, passion, and drive, and those served him well. His solos and playing are spirited, and he builds and completes ideas impressively. Likewise, pianist Mulgrew Miller and vibist Steve Nelson were also growing young players and sometimes tried to cram too much into their solos. Drummer Marvin "Smitty" Smith, on the other hand, capably held things together rhythmically, along with bassist Curtis Lundy and percussionist Dom Um Romao. This was a pivotal session for Watson; he established his identity in the post-Blakey era and went on to become the star everyone felt he would be when they initially heard him in The Messengers. *—Ron Wynn*

Gumbo / Dec. 27, 1983 / Evidence ✦✦✦✦
At the time of this recording, Watson was still building his reputation, playing in a group co-led by bassist Curtis Lundy. This was an outstanding band bolstered by the booming baritone sax of Hamiett Bluiett and featuring a strong rhythm section with pianist Mulgrew Miller and drummer Marvin "Smitty" Smith alongside Lundy. Special guest trumpeter Melton Mustafa provided sparkling lines and fiery solos, interacting smoothly with Watson and Bluiett in a solid frontline. Watson has since recorded more impressively engineered and mastered dates, but few have been musically superior to this early-'80s session. *—Ron Wynn*

Advance / Aug. 8, 1984 / Enja ✦✦✦✦
1991 reissue that heralded arrival of former Jazz Messenger Bobby Watson as major figure in 1984. *—Ron Wynn*

Round Trip / Feb. 6, 1985 / Red ✦✦✦✦✦
Recorded the day after *Appointment in Milano* and with the same Italian trio (pianist Piero Bassini, bassist Attilio Zanchi and drummer Giampiero Prina), this quartet set by altoist Bobby Watson has plenty of variety. Watson performs an explorative version of Ornette Coleman's "Round Trip," a pair of sophisticated ballads ("Blue in Green" and the jazz waltz "Sweet Dreams"), fresh versions of two standards ("There Is No Greater Love" and a faster-than-usual rendition of Lee Morgan's "Ceora") and an original ("All the Things of Jo Maka") that is based on "All the Things You Are." Watson's music swings yet he was adapting elements of avant-garde innovations to his style; the results are quite stimulating. *—Scott Yanow*

The Year of the Rabbit / Feb. 7, 1987 / Evidence ✦✦✦✦✦
This CD is a surprise success for it features the modern altoist Bobby Watson paying tribute to the great Johnny Hodges. Watson performs his own brief "Blues for Alto" plus nine ballads, blues and swing stomps associated with Hodges, using a group that mixes together his usual sidemen of the period (pianist Mulgrew Miller, bassist Curtis Lundy and drummer Kenny Washington), a few veterans (trumpeter Irv Stokes, trombonist Art Baron and guitarist Lawrence Lucie) and younger but compatible players (Bill Easley on tenor and clarinet plus baritonist Jim Hartog). Watson modifies his own style and, although not too closely imitative of Hodges, improvises close to his style. Highlights of the memorable set include "The Jeep Is Jumpin," "Jeep's Blues," "Honey Bunny" and "Things Ain't What They Used to Be." *—Scott Yanow*

This Little Light of Mine / 1991 / Red ✦✦✦✦

● **Present Tense** / Dec. 9, 1991-Dec. 11, 1991 / Columbia ✦✦✦✦✦
After a period of time, Bobby Watson's Horizon became one of the top hard bop-oriented regular bands of the early '90s. Comprised of the leader on alto and occasional soprano, trumpeter Terell Stafford, pianist Edward Simon, bassist Essiet Essiet and drummer Victor Lewis, Horizon performs "I Got It Bad," "Minority" and ten originals by group members including Watson's "Monk He See, Monk He Do." All of the talented young musicians (Watson himself was only 38 at the time) are well-featured and heard throughout their definitive release in top form. *—Scott Yanow*

Post-Motown Bop / Sep. 17, 1980-Sep. 18, 1980 / Blue Note ✦✦✦✦✦
After dropping the synthesizers and reformatting his group Horizon in 1990, alto saxophonist Bobby Watson recorded one of the most memorable CDs of his career. His opener "The Punjab of Java Po'" is a powerful hard bop number with elements of East Indian and Brazilian influences, while its catchy bass vamp supports strong solos by pianist Ed Simon, trumpeter Melton Mustafa, and the leader. Drummer Victor Lewis proves to be as gifted a composer as Watson. He wrote two vehicles for Watson's soprano sax: "Big Girls" and the tense uptempo "7th Avenue." The arrangement of standards such as "Falling in Love With Love" and "In a Sentimental Mood" are also worth noting. A very commendable, but now out-of-print release. *—Ken Dryden*

Lu Watters (Lucious Watters)

b. Dec. 19, 1911, Santa Cruz, CA, **d.** Nov. 5, 1989, Santa Rosa, CA
Trumpet / Dixieland
It would be difficult to overestimate the importance of Lu Watters in the Dixieland revival movement. When he organized the two-trumpet Yerba Buena Jazz Band in late 1939, the New Orleans jazz of King Oliver and Jelly Roll Morton was not only considered old hat but worthy of extinction. Over 55 years later there are a countless number of trad bands patterned after the two-beat Watters group, which like its predecessor King Olivers' Creole Jazz Band is now considered classic. Lu Watters formed his first jazz band in 1925 but he spent most of the 1930s playing in San Francisco in his own big band. By 1939 (at the height of the swing era) he had met fellow trumpeter Bob Scobey, trombonist Turk Murphy and pianist Wally Rose and was planning to bring back the music of the 1920s which had been largely neglected for quite a few years. In December 1939 his new band started playing regularly at the Dawn Club and by 1941 when they made their first recordings, the Yerba Buena Jazz Band was building up a large following in San Francisco. The records kept the band's legacy alive when some of their members were drafted; the eventual departure of Scobey and Murphy (who would soon lead important groups of their own) weakened the Yerba Buena Band slightly but the vocals of its banjoist Clancy Hayes were a crowd-pleaser and the band remained a powerful force. *—Scott Yanow*

☆ **The Complete Good Time Jazz Recordings** / Dec. 19, 1941-Aug. 16, 1947 / Good Time Jazz ✦✦✦✦✦
Lu Watters's Yerba Buena Jazz Band was one of the most influential Dixieland groups of all time. With Watters and Bob Scobey on trumpets, trombonist Turk Murphy, clarinetist Bob Helm, pianist Wally Rose, banjo, tuba (or bass) and drums, this band had a lot of power and enthusiasm. At a time when swing dominated jazz and bebop was ready to take over, Watters's successful extension of 1920s jazz was a major force in fueling the Dixieland revival movement. This four-CD set has all of the group's studio recordings plus live broadcasts from 1946-47 and six rare performances by the wartime version of The YBJB featuring the talented but ill-fated trumpeter Benny Strickler. This reissue is absolutely essential for all traditional jazz fans and historians. The heated ensembles and joyous solos are great fun to hear. *—Scott Yanow*

Originals & Ragtime: San Francisco Style, Vol. 2 / Dec. 19, 1941-Jun. ??, 1946 / Good Time Jazz ✦✦✦✦✦
With the exception of an alternate take of pianist Wally Rose's feature on "Black and White Rag" (which is from 1941), this second of three CD volumes (an otherwise straight reissue of the earlier Good Time Jazz Lp) is taken from May-June 1946 when Lu Watters' Yerba Buena Jazz Band had their first postwar sessions. For the particularly strong set, the program is divided between memorable originals by the leader (highlighted by "Big Bear Stomp" and "Emperor Norton's Hunch") and rags (including Turk Murphy's "Trombone Rag," "Harlem Rag" and "That's A Plenty"). The two- trumpet frontline of Watters and Bob Scobey set the standard for dixieland bands of the next 20 years. All of this music (plus lots more) is also available in Watters' highly essential four-CD Good Time Jazz box set. *—Scott Yanow*

Stomps, Etc. and the Blues: San Francisco Style, Vol. 3 / Aug. ??, 1942-Jun. ??, 1946 / Good Time Jazz ✦✦✦✦✦
In addition to the dozen titles on the original Lp (which are taken from the very fruitful 1946 sessions of the reunited Lu Watters Yerba Buena Jazz Band), this CD reissue also includes the six titles recorded by trumpeter Benny Strickler (his only recordings) with the wartime edition of the group. While Strickler was a fine lyrical player, it is for the two-trumpet frontline of 1946 (which features Watters and Bob Scobey) that this third of three volumes is recommended; highpoints include spirited renditions of "South," "Chattanooga Stomp," "Copenhagen," "Panama" and "Weary Blues." The highly enjoyable music is also included in Lu Watters' four-CD "Complete on Good Time Jazz" box set. *—Scott Yanow*

● **Dawn Club Favorites: San Francisco Style, Vol. 1** / May ??, 1946-Jun. ??, 1946 / Good Time Jazz ✦✦✦✦✦
This is the first of three CD's reissued by the Good Time Jazz label that has all of the recordings from the first sessions by Lu Watters' Yerba Buena Jazz Band when they reunited after World War II. Two selections ("You Can't Shush Katie The Gabbiest Girl In Town" and "Maple Leaf Rag") are added to the original Lp program. With trumpeters Lu Watters and Bob Scobey, trombonist Turk Murphy and clarinetist Bob Helm forming an imposing frontline, the Yerba Buena Jazz Band practically defined revivalist jazz. Highlights include "Minstrels Of Annie Street," "Jazzin' Babies Blues," "Ostrich Walk" and "Ory's Creole Trombone." True Lu Watters fans will want to pick up his four-CD Good Time Jazz box set instead of these individual releases. *—Scott Yanow*

Blues over Bodega / 1963 / Good Time Jazz ✦✦✦✦
Nearly 14 years after he retired from music, trumpeter Lu Watters came out of retirement to musically protest the proposed building of a nuclear power plant on the San Andreas Fault. In addition to a few concerts with his former trombonist Turk Murphy, Watters recorded this

lone Fantasy LP. After the nuclear project was shelved, Watters went back into permanent retirement. Surprisingly he is heard in prime form throughout this excellent set, leading a septet that also includes trombonist Bob Mielke, clarinetist Bob Helm, and pianist Wally Rose through such numbers as "Some of These Days," "Emperor Norton's Hunch," and his new pieces "San Andreas Fault" and "Blues Over Bodega." Blues singer Barbara Dane helps out a couple of songs. *—Scott Yanow*

Bunk and Lu / 1988 / Good Time Jazz ✦✦✦✦✦

Ernie Watts

b. Oct. 23, 1945, Norfolk, VA

Sax (Tenor), Sax (Alto), Flute / Crossover Jazz, Jazz-Pop, Post-Bop, Bossa Nova

Because he was involved in many commercial recording projects from the mid-'70s through the early '80s and on an occasional basis ever since, some observers wrote Ernie Watts off prematurely as a pop/R&B tenorman. Actually Watts' main hero has always been John Coltrane and his more recent work reveals him to be an intense and masterful jazz improviser who has developed his own sheets of sound approach along with a distinctive and soulful sound. After attending Berklee, he had an important stint with Buddy Rich's big band (1966-68) before moving to Los Angeles. Watts worked in the big bands of Oliver Nelson and Gerald Wilson, recorded with Jean-Luc Ponty in 1969 and became a staff musician for NBC, performing with the Tonight Show Band on a regular basis. His own records of the 1970s and early '80s were generally poppish (1982's *Chariots of Fire* was a big seller) and Watts played frequently with Lee Ritenour and Stanley Clarke in addition to recording with Cannonball Adderley (one of his idols) in 1972. However Ernie Watts' work became much more interesting from a jazz standpoint starting in the mid-'80s when he joined Charlie Haden's Quartet West and started recording no-nonsense quartet dates for JVC. Ernie Watts has developed into one of the most powerful of tenormen with complete control over his horn and the ability to bring intensity and passion (plus taste) to any musical situation. *—Scott Yanow*

Ernie Watts Quartet: World Class / Dec. 14, 1987-Dec. 15, 1987 / JVC ✦✦✦✦✦

After years of being heard primarily in commercial settings, Ernie Watts finally had an opportunity to record exactly what he wanted as a leader on this JVC CD. Watts, in a quartet with pianist Pat Coil, bassist Joel DiBartolo and drummer Bob Leatherbarrow, features his Coltrane-influenced tenor and a bit of alto and soprano on some group originals and standards (including "My One and Only Love" "Skylark" and "Body and Soul"). One of his finest recordings to date. *—Scott Yanow*

● **Reaching Up** / Oct. 7, 1993-Oct. 8, 1993 / JVC ✦✦✦✦✦

For this quartet set with pianist Mulgrew Miller, bassist Charles Fambrough and drummer Jack DeJohnette, Ernie Watts definitely came to play. Virtually all of his solos are high-powered and even his ballad statements are filled with clusters of passionate notes. Trumpeter Arturo Sandval has two appearances and makes the music even more hyper. In addition, the rhythm section keeps the proceedings consistently stimulating. The main focus on these standards and originals is generally on Watts's tenor and, even though there isn't all that much variety, this CD is a strong example of his jazz talents. *—Scott Yanow*

Unity / Dec. 13, 1994-Dec. 14, 1994 / JVC ✦✦✦✦✦

The most unusual aspect to Ernie Watts's latest recording is that the great tenor is joined by a two-bass quartet. Eddie Gomez on acoustic and Steve Swallow on electric blend together quite well, are featured in a delightful version of Oscar Pettiford's "Tricotism" and (with pianist Geri Allen and drummer Jack Dejohnette) keep the accompaniment consistently stimulating. Ernie Watts is in top form throughout this fine modern mainstream date, playing with both passion and lyricism on a variety of standards and originals (which, in addition to four songs from the leader, include one apiece from DeJohnette and Swallow). There is just enough variety to keep the proceedings from ever getting predictable, making this one of Watts's finest sessions. *—Scott Yanow*

Classic Moods / Dec. 21, 1997Dec. 22, 1997 / JVC ✦✦✦✦

Classic Moods refers to a number of things—classic songs, the classic small hard-bop group, the classic sound of jazz ballads. It's clear that Ernie Watts was out to recapture the spirit of his hero John Coltrane's exquisite *Ballads*, and what's surprising is how close he comes to fulfilling his goal. Working with pianist Mulgrew Miller, bassist George Mraz and drummer Jimmy Cobb, Watts recaptures the classic sound of '50s small combos without ever sounding like a stodgy revivalist. That's because he's too concerned with feeling and fresh, vital improvisations to devote himself to painstaking re-creations of the past. Every musician in the group plays with passion, even during subtle interludes, and that is what brings such standards as "In a Sentimental Mood," "Green Dolphin Street" and "'Round Midnight" to life. You may have heard these songs countless times, but they're worth hearing again in this setting. *—Stephen Thomas Erlewine*

Weather Report

f. 1970, **db.** 1985

Group / Fusion

Weather Report practically defined the state of the jazz-rock art throughout almost all of its 15-year run, also anticipating and contributing to the North American interest in world music rhythms and structures, prodded by keyboardist/co-founder Joe Zawinul. Original members Zawinul, tenor saxophonist Wayne Shorter and percussionist Airto Moreira all had experience playing in and influencing the electric bands of Miles Davis. At first, the group was a direct extension of Miles' *In a Silent Way/Bitches Brew* period, with free-floating collective improvisation and interplay, combining elements of jazz, rock, funk, Latin and other ethnic musics. With the release of *Sweetnighter* in 1972, Zawinul's influence upon the band's direction began to deepen; the groove became more important, structures were imposed upon the material. When the innovative bassist Jaco Pastorius joined in 1976, WR entered its most popular phase, with Pastorius becoming a flamboyant third lead voice, Shorter's sax receding into more epigrammatic form, and Zawinul rediscovering his commercial touch and sharpening his electronic sophistication. The best-selling *Heavy Weather* (1977) actually served up a hit song that became a jazz standard ("Birdland"). Contrary to accepted wisdom, the departure of Pastorius in 1982 led to a recharging of WR's batteries, deepening Zawinul's inclinations for Third World rhythms, sounds and textures. After Shorter left the group in 1985 though, Weather Report issued one final album (*This Is This!*) and broke up. *—Richard S. Ginell*

★ **Weather Report** / Feb. 16, 1971-Mar. 17, 1971 / Columbia ✦✦✦✦✦

Here we have the free-floating, abstract beginnings of Weather Report, which would define the state of the electronic jazz/rock art from its first note almost to its last. Their first album is a direct extension of the Miles Davis *In a Silent Way/Bitches Brew* period, more fluid in sound and more volatile in interplay. Joe Zawinul ruminates in a delicate, liquid manner on Rhodes electric piano; at this early stage, he used a ring modulator to create weird synthesizer-like effects. Wayne Shorter's soprano sax shines like a beacon amidst the swirling ensemble work of co-founding bassist Miroslav Vitous, percussionist Airto Moreira, and drummer Alphonse Mouzon. Zawinul's most memorable theme is "Orange Lady" (previously recorded, though uncredited, by Davis on *Big Fun*), while Shorter scores on "Tears" and "Eurydice." One of the most impressive debuts of all time by a jazz group. *—Richard S. Ginell*

I Sing the Body Electric / Nov. 1971-Jan. 13, 1972 / Columbia ✦✦✦✦

Like the weather itself, this band would assume a new shape with virtually every release—and this album, half recorded in the studio and half live in Tokyo, set the pattern of change. Exit Airto Moreira and Alphonse Mouzon; enter percussionist Dom Um Romao, drummer Eric Gravatt, and a slew of cameo guests like guitarist Ralph Towner, flutist Hubert Laws, and others. The studio tracks are more biting, more ethnically diverse in influence, and more laden with electronic effects and grandiose structural complexities than before. The live material (heard in full on the import *Live in Tokyo*) is even fiercer and showcases for the first time some of the tremendous drive WR was capable of, though it doesn't give you much of an idea of its stream of consciousness nature. *—Richard S. Ginell*

Live in Tokyo / Jan. 13, 1972 / Columbia ✦✦✦✦✦

While side 2 of *I Sing the Body Electric* gives us heavily edited glimpses of Weather Report as heard live in Tokyo, this two-disc Japanese import contains entire group ensembles from that concert—and as such, it is a revelation. Now we can follow the wild stream-of-consciousness evolution of early Weather Report workouts, taking us into all kinds of stylistic territory from Joe Zawinul's lone acoustic piano to dissonant freeform and electronic explosions, with lots of adjustments of tempo and texture. The pulse of jazz is more evident in their work here than on the American albums, and the example of Miles Davis circa the Fillmore concerts directs the fierce interplay. In his subsequent recordings with WR and as a leader, Wayne Shorter would rarely equal the manic intensity he displayed in Tokyo. All of the music is encapsuled in five lengthy "medleys" of WR repertoire, three of which contain elongated versions of themes from WR's debut album. This would be the radical apogee of WR on records, though they could retain this level of fire in concert for years to come. *—Richard S. Ginell*

Sweetnighter / Feb. 3, 1973-Feb. 7, 1973 / Columbia ✦✦✦✦

Right from the start, a vastly different Weather Report emerges here, one that reflects co-leader Joe Zawinul's developing obsession with the groove. It is the groove that rules this mesmerizing album, leading off with the irresistible 3/4 marathon deceptively tagged as the "Boogie Woogie Waltz" and proceeding through a variety of Latin-grounded hip-shakers. It is a record of discovery for Zawinul, who augments his Rhodes electric piano with a funky wah-wah pedal, unveils the ARP synthesizer as a melodic instrument and sound-effects device, and often coasts along on one chord. The once fiery Wayne Shorter has been tamed, for he now contributes mostly sustained ethereal tunes on soprano sax, his tone sometimes doubled for a pleasing octave effect. The wane of freewheeling ensemble interplay is more than offset by the big increase in rhythmic push; bassist Miroslav Vitous, drummer Eric Gravatt, and percussionist Dom Um Romao are now cogs in one of jazz's great swinging machines. *—Richard S. Ginell*

Mysterious Traveller / 1973-1974 / Columbia ✦✦✦✦✦

Weather Report's fourth recording finds Wayne Shorter (on soprano and tenor) taking a lesser role as Joe Zawinul begins to really dominate the group's sound. Most selections also include bassist Alphonso Johnson and drummer Ishmael Wilburn although the personnel shifts from track to track. "Nubian Sundance" adds several vocalists while "Blackthorn Rose" is a Shorter-Zawinul duet. Overall the music is pretty stimulating and sometimes adventurous; high-quality fusion from 1974. *—Scott Yanow*

Tale Spinnin' / Feb. 1975-Apr. 4, 1975 / Columbia ✦✦✦✦

Weather Report's ever-changing lineup shifts again, with the somewhat heavier funk-oriented Leon "Ndugu" Chancler dropping into the drummer's chair and Alyrio Lima taking over the percussion table. As a result, *Tale Spinnin'* has a weightier feel than *Mysterious Traveller,* while continuing the latter's explorations in Latin-spiced electric jazz/funk. Zawinul's pioneering interest in what we now call world music is more in evidence with the African percussion, wordless vocals, and sandy sound effects of "Badia," and his synthesizer sophistication is growing along with the available technology. Wayne Shorter's work on soprano sax is more animated than on the previous two albums and Alphonso Johnson puts his melodic bass more to the fore. While not quite as inventive as its two predecessors, this remains an absorbing extension of WR's mid-'70s direction. *—Richard S. Ginell*

Black Market / 1976 / Columbia ✦✦✦✦✦

The shifts in Weather Report's personnel come fast and furious now, with Narada Michael Walden and Chester Thompson as the drummers, Alex Acuna and Don Alias at the percussion table, and Alphonso Johnson giving way to the mighty, martyred Jaco Pastorius. It is interesting to hear Pastorius expanding the bass role only incrementally over what the more funk-oriented Johnson was doing at this early point—that is, until "Barbary Coast," where suddenly Jaco leaps athletically forward into the spotlight. Joe Zawinul or just Zawinul, as he preferred to be billed—contributed all of side one's compositions, mostly Third World-flavored workouts except for "Cannon Ball," a touching tribute to his ex-boss Cannonball Adderley (who had died the year before). Shorter, Pastorius, and Johnson split the remainder of the tracks, with Shorter now set in a long-limbed compositional mode for electric bands that would serve him into the 1990s. While it goes without saying that most Weather Report albums are transition albums, this diverse record is even more transient than most, paving the way for WR's most popular period while retaining the old sense of adventure. *—Richard S. Ginell*

☆ **Heavy Weather** / 1977 / Columbia/Legacy ✦✦✦✦✦
Weather Report's biggest-selling album is that ideal thing, a popular and artistic success—and for the same reasons. For one thing, Joe Zawinul revealed an unexpectedly potent commercial streak for the first time since his Cannonball Adderley days, contributing what has become a perennial hit, "Birdland." Indeed, "Birdland" is a remarkable bit of record-making, a unified, ever-developing piece of music that evokes, without in any way imitating, a joyous evening on 52nd St. with a big band. The other factor is the full emergence of Jaco Pastorius as a co-leader; his dancing, staccato bass lifting itself out of the bass range as a third melodic voice, completely dominating his own ingenious "Teen Town" (where he also plays drums!). By now, Zawinul has become WR's de facto commander in the studio; his colorful synthesizers dictate the textures, his conceptions are carefully planned, with little of the free-wheeling improvisation of only five years before. Wayne Shorter's saxophones are now reticent, if always eloquent, beams of light in Zawinul's general scheme while Alex Acuna shifts ably over to the drums and Manolo Badrena handles the percussion. Released just as the jazz-rock movement began to run out of steam, this landmark album proved that there was plenty of creative life left in the idiom. *—Richard S. Ginell*

8:30 / Dec. 1979 / Columbia ✦✦✦✦✦
This double album gives one a fine retrospective of Weather Report from the vantage point of 1979 with the first three sides being taken up with live performances. There are remakes of such memorable selections as "Black Market," "Teen Town," "A Remark You Made" and Weather Report's big hit "Birdland." Not everything works (Wayne Shorter's unaccompanied tenor solo on "Thanks for the Memory" is merely odd) and the new studio recordings on side four is not at the same level but in general the music throughout this twofer is quite rewarding. Keyboardist Joe Zawinul, Shorter, bassist Jaco Pastorius and drummer Peter Erskine are all in top form. *—Scott Yanow*

Night Passage / 1980 / Columbia ✦✦✦✦
All things being relative, this is Weather Report's straightahead album, where the elaborate production layers of the late-'70s gave way to sparer textures and more unadorned solo improvisation in the jazz tradition, electric instruments and all. The flaw of this album is the shortage of really memorable compositions; it is more of a vehicle for the virtuosic feats of what is considered by some to be the classic WR lineup—Joe Zawinul, Wayne Shorter, Jaco Pastorius, Robert Thomas, Jr. and Peter Erskine. For Erskine, this is is first full studio album and he amply demonstrates his terrific sense of forward drive unique among the other superb drummers in WR annals. "Port of Entry" is a tour de force for Jaco, who knocks off several of those unbelievably slippery, pointed runs that have made him a posthumous legend. There is also a tremendously fun retro trip to Duke Ellington's "Rockin' in Rhythm," everybody swinging their heads and hands off. *—Richard S. Ginell*

Chick Webb (William Henry Webb)

b. Feb. 10, 1909, Baltimore, MD, **d.** Jun. 16, 1939, Baltimore, MD
Drums / Swing, Big Band
Chick Webb represented the triumph of the human spirit in jazz and life. Hunchbacked, small in stature, almost a dwarf with a large face and broad shoulders, Webb fought off congenital tuberculosis of the spine in order to become one of the most competitive drummers and bandleaders of the big band era. Perched high upon a platform, he used a wide variety of percussion instruments to create thundering solos of a complexity and energy that paved the way for Buddy Rich and Louie Bellson. Webb's band was oddly short on major soloists during its heyday from the mid-'30s onward, but made up for it with a crisp ensemble sound, the leader's disciplined, ferociously driving drum pyrotechnics, trumpeter Taft Jordan's impressions of Louis Armstrong, and most of all, a series of strong compositions and charts by Edgar Sampson. In 1935, Webb hired the teenaged Ella Fitzgerald and rebuilt his show around the singer, who provided him with his biggest hit record, "A Tisket-A-Tasket," in 1938. Though the band's fame continued to grow, Webb's precarious health gave way soon after and he died after a major operation in Baltimore. Fitzgerald fronted the the band until it finally broke up in 1942. *—Richard S. Ginell*

★ **1929-1934** / Jun. 14, 1929-Nov. 19, 1934 / Classics ✦✦✦✦✦
The perfect way to acquire drummer Chick Webb's recordings are to get his two Classics CD's which contain all of his performances as a leader other than Ella Fitzgerald's features (which are in a separate Ella series) and a few numbers from Webb's final dates. On the first of the CD's, Webb leads a pickup band in 1929 (for "Dog Bottom" and "Jungle Mama"), an early orchestra in 1931 (highlighted by the first version ever of Benny Carter's "Blues In My Heart"), two numbers from 1933 and all of his classic swing sides of 1934. With arranger-altoist Edgar Sampson providing such compositions as "When Dreams Come True," "Don't Be That Way," "Blue Lou" and "Stompin' At The Savoy" (all of which would become better-known for their slightly later Benny Goodman recordings), trumpeter Taft Jordan taking some vocals purposely influenced by Louis Armstrong, Jordan, trombonist Sandy Williams and tenor-saxophonist Elmer Williams coming up with consistently hot solos, and the drummer-leader driving the orchestra, this was one of the top jazz big bands of the era. Highly recommended as is Classics' *1935-1938* Chick Webb volume. *—Scott Yanow*

Spinnin' the Web / Jun. 14, 1929-Feb. 17, 1939 / Decca/GRP ✦✦✦✦✦
Drummer Chick Webb led one of the finest swing bands of the 1930s but ironically his orchestra is today best-remembered for backing singer Ella Fitzgerald in her early days. This CD consists of 20 instrumentals (other than a Louis Bacon vocal on "Blues in My Heart" and Ward Pinkett's scatting on "Dog Bottom") and allows one to hear how strong a big band Webb's ensemble could be. Although one regrets that only one of the four recordings by Chick Webb's Little Chicks was included (this small group featured the pioneering jazz flutist Wayman Carver), there are many enjoyable performances on this single disc. Highlights include "Don't Be That Way," "Blue Lou," "Clap Hands! Here Comes Charlie," and "Liza." The soloists (including Taft Jordan and Bobby Stark on trumpets, trombonist Sandy Williams and Elmer Williams on tenor) are excellent but it is the Edgar Sampson arrangements and the leader's drumming that really gave this band its own personality. *—Scott Yanow*

☆ **1935-1938** / Jun. 12, 1935-May 3, 1938 / Classics ✦✦✦✦✦
To a large extent the Chick Webb big band is now chiefly remembered as the launching pad for Ella Fitzgerald, but during its peak years it was one of the top swing bands. This 25-song CD from the European Classics label reissues all of the band's recordings from a three-year period that did not feature Fitzgerald as a solo singer; she does make a brief appearance on "Wake up and Live." Although there are nine vocals on this set (including three from a young Louis Jordan), the emphasis is very much on the band's instrumental talents. Such soloists as trumpeters Taft Jordan and Bobby Stark, trombonist Sandy Williams, Elmer Williams and Ted McRae on tenors and altoist Edgar Sampson are heard from while the drummer/leader propels the ensembles. A special highlight are the four numbers by Chick Webb's Little Chicks, an unusual quintet featuring the pioneering jazz flutist Wayman Carver and clarinetist Chauncey Haughton. This CD is highly recommended to swing fans. *—Scott Yanow*

Ella Swings the Band (1936-1939) / 1936-1939 / MCA ✦✦✦✦✦

Ben Webster

b. Mar. 27, 1909, Kansas City, MO, **d.** Sep. 20, 1973, Amsterdam, The Netherlands
Sax (Tenor) / Traditional Pop, Swing
Ben Webster was considered one of the "big three" swing tenors along with Coleman Hawkins and Lester Young. He had a tough, raspy and brutal tone on stomps (with his own distinctive growls) yet on ballads he would turn into a pussy cat and play with warmth and sentiment. He had stints with Jap Allen and Blanche Calloway (making his recording debut with the latter) before joining Bennie Moten's Orchestra in time to be one of the stars on a classic session in 1932. In 1940, Webster became Duke Ellington's first major tenor soloist. During the next three years he was on many famous recordings including "Cotton Tail" and "All Too Soon." After leaving Ellington in 1943 (he would return for a time in 1948-49), Webster worked on 52nd Street, recorded frequently as both a leader and a sideman, had short periods with Raymond Scott, John Kirby and Sid Catlett, and toured with Jazz at the Philharmonic during several seasons in the 1950s. Although his sound was considered out-of-style by that decade, Webster's work on ballads became quite popular and Norman Granz recorded him on many memorable sessions. *—Scott Yanow*

King of the Tenors / May 21, 1953Dec. 8, 1953 / Verve ✦✦✦✦
This 1953 date matched Webster with such peers as alto saxophonist Benny Carter, trumpeter Harry Edison, and pianist Oscar Peterson for a series of elegant yet soulful and exuberant small group dates. With no cut longer than four and a half minutes, the players didn't have time for excess statements or overkill; they had to quickly get to the heart of the matter in their solos, make their points, and return to the head. The original session has been enlarged by the addition of two previously unissued tracks, plus an alternate version of "That's All" that was later issued as a single. Label head Norman Granz excelled in producing swing-oriented, crisply played mainstream dates. Although this date is more than four decades old, Ben Webster's solos have a freshness and vitality that make them quite relevant to contemporary events. *—Ron Wynn*

The Soul of Ben Webster / Mar. 5, 1957-Jul. 1958 / Verve ✦✦✦✦
Although tenor saxophonist Ben Webster gets top billing, this two-CD set actually contains an LP apiece by Webster, trumpeter Harry "Sweets" Edison and altoist Johnny Hodges. Webster is on all of the recordings, but really only stars on the first date, a septet outing with trumpeter Art Farmer and fellow tenor Harold Ashby. The great tenor is at his best on a beautiful version of "Chelsea Bridge" and "When I Fall in Love." The Edison session is a sextet outing with Webster, the Oscar Peterson Trio and drummer Alvin Stoller mixing blues and swing standards; Edison's usually muted trumpet is quite effective. The final set puts the focus on altoist Hodges, who sounds beautiful on "Don't Take Your Love from Me," although the many blues performances also give solo space to trumpeter Roy Eldridge (literally explosive on "Honey Hill") and trombonist Vic Dickenson. A total of three previously unissued performances have been added to the program, and all three of these sessions had been long out of print; they add to the legacy of Norman Granz's Verve label, showing that many top swing all-stars were actually at their prime in the 1950s. Recommended. *—Scott Yanow*

★ **Soulville** / Oct. 15, 1957 / Verve ✦✦✦✦✦
The veteran tenor-saxophonist Ben Webster met up with the Oscar Peterson trio on this CD. Other than two fairly basic originals, the great tenor is showcased on durable standards and the ballads in particular are quite memorable. Peterson, bassist Ray Brown, guitarist Herb Ellis and drummer Stan Levey are superior in support of the masterful saxophonist. *—Scott Yanow*

Tenor Giants / Oct. 16, 1957-Apr. 9, 1959 / Verve ✦✦✦✦✦
Coleman Hawkins was always Ben Webster's idol. They finally shared a record date on October 16, 1957, and it was reissued as half of this two-LP set. With the backing of the Oscar Peterson Trio plus drummer Alvin Stoller, Webster and Hawk match wits and ideas on seven standards and two of Hawkins's originals. Webster was really no match for the elder tenor (and he knew it), particularly harmonically (Hawk was a master of chords), but he had the advantage of a huge emotional tone. Although Hawkins wins honors, it is not a runaway. The second album also features the two tenor greats plus the tenor of Budd Johnson, trumpeter Roy Eldridge, and a four-piece rhythm section. Webster wrote three songs for the date (including tributes to Hawk and Budd), and there is a 20-minute version of "In a Mellow Tone" to wrap up the proceedings. The results are a deadheat except on "Time After Time" where Webster's beautiful sound is well-featured. Recommended, but it will take a search to locate this two-fer. *—Scott Yanow*

Ben Webster and Associates / Apr. 9, 1959 / Verve ✦✦✦✦✦
Ben Webster and Associates is a 1959 session that took full advantage of the long-playing LP format. Highlighted by the 20-minute version of Ellington's "In a Mellow Tone" in which tenor titans Ben Webster, Coleman Hawkins, and Budd Johnson plus trumpeter Roy Eldridge stretch out, not so much in a cutting contest as a laid-back jam session amongst friends. This summit meeting turned out to be a tribute to another tenor master of the same generation, Lester Young, who had died less than four weeks before this session. The chosen rhythm section of Jimmy Jones on piano, Les Spann on guitar, Ray Brown on bass, and Jo Jones on drums equally matches the performance of the featured horns. Also tackled for this session were three Webster originals: "De-Dar," "Young Bean," and "Budd Johnson" and the standard "Time After Time." Unfortunately no bonus tracks are included (if they even exist) but the excellent sound restoration more than makes up for it. *—Al Campbell*

Meets Gerry Mulligan / Nov. 3, 1959 / Verve ✦✦✦✦✦

Ben Webster Meets Oscar Peterson / Nov. 1959 / Verve ✦✦✦✦

At the Renaissance / Oct. 14, 1960 / Contemporary/OJC ✦✦✦✦
This live set features tenor great Ben Webster playing with pianist Jimmy Rowles, guitarist Jim Hall, bassist Red Mitchell and drummer Frank Butler in a club and the music is consistently wonderful. Whether showing warmth and sentimentality on "Georgia on My Mind" and "Stardust" or growling and roaring on "Caravan" and "Ole Miss Blues," Webster (who was then somewhat taken for granted) is in superior and creative form. Recommended. *—Scott Yanow*

Ben and Sweets / Jun. 6, 1962Jun. 7, 1962 / Columbia ✦✦✦✦
Tenor-saxophonist Ben Webster and trumpeter Harry "Sweets" Edison, both veterans of the swing era (although associated with different orchestras), had long wanted to record a full album together. The results, a swinging quintet set with pianist Hank Jones, bassist George Duvivier and drummer Clarence Johnston, are quite rewarding. There are two ballad features for the tenor ("How Long Has This Been Going on" and a beautiful version of "My Romance") and one for Edison ("Embraceable You") along with three medium-tempo collaborations. Nothing unexpected occurs but the melodic music is quite enjoyable. *—Scott Yanow*

Soulmates / Sep. 20, 1963Oct. 14, 1963 / Riverside/OJC ✦✦✦✦
This is some of Zawinul's (k) best playing outside of his work in Miles bands, Weather Report, or his days with the Adderleys. *—Ron Wynn*

☆ **See You at the Fair** / Mar. 11, 1964-Nov. 10, 1964 / GRP ✦✦✦✦✦
Ben Webster's final American recording was one of his greatest. At 55, the tenor-saxophonist was still very much in his prime but considered out of style in the U.S. He would soon permanently move to Europe where he was better appreciated. This CD has the nine selections originally included on the LP of the same name, a quartet set with either Hank Jones or Roger Kellaway on piano, bassist Richard Davis and drummer Osie Johnson. Webster's tone has rarely sounded more beautiful than on "Someone to Watch over Me" and "Our Love Is Here to Stay." In addition one song from the same session (but originally released on a sampler) and two tunes featuring Webster on an Oliver Nelson date (*More Blues and the Abstract Truth*) wrap up this definitive CD. *—Scott Yanow*

Stormy Weather / Jan. 30, 1965 / 1201 Music ✦✦✦✦✦
Recorded around a month after the veteran tenor Ben Webster moved to Europe, this high-quality set with pianist Kenny Drew, bassist Neils Pederson and drummer Alex Riel features Webster stretching out on the traditional "Londonderry Air," two originals and seven familiar but fresh standards. Webster, although neglected in the U.S., was still in peak form in the mid-'60s as witness this and his other Black Lion CDs covering the period. *—Scott Yanow*

There Is No Greater Love / Sep. 5, 1965 / 1201 Music ✦✦✦✦
Ben Webster was one of the great swing-era saxophonists, a player whose tone was a bit rougher than that of his contemporaries Lester Young and Coleman Hawkins, but who shared with them a robust, broad-toned attack that fell out of favor during the bebop years. This session was recorded in Copenhagen in 1965 and features pianist Kenny Drew, bassist Niels-Henning Orsted Pedersen and drummer Alex Riel backing Webster on a program of standards. Webster blows sublimely throughout, delivering beautiful versions of "Easy to Love," "Stardust," "I Got It Bad (And That Ain't Good)" and, especially, "Autumn Leaves." But sloppy production is an irritant throughout; the rhythm section is poorly miked, and Webster's tenor saxophone is distorted in several places. Fans and completists shouldn't hesitate, but this album is not the best introduction to Webster's art. *—Rick Anderson*

Plays Ballads / Jul. 14, 1967-Nov. 22, 1971 / Storyville ✦✦✦✦
Ben Webster had a perfect tone for playing ballads, full of sentiment and emotion. On this Storyville release he caresses seven timeless melodies in a variety of settings including trios with either Teddy Wilson, Ole Kock Hansen or Kenny Drew on piano, backing by The Danish Radio Big Band (on "Cry Me a River") or a version of "Greensleeves" with a string orchestra. Although largely forgotten in the United States (he had moved to Europe in 1965), Ben Webster was still in fine form this late in his career. *—Scott Yanow*

Plays Duke Ellington / Jul. 14, 1967-Nov. 22, 1971 / Storyville ✦✦✦✦✦
Although he was only a member of Duke Ellington's Orchestra for three years, tenor-saxophonist Ben Webster was linked with Duke Ellington throughout his career. This Storyville release features the great tenor playing nine songs associated with Ellington. The music is drawn from five separate sessions including trio gigs with pianists Kenny Drew and Teddy Wilson and three with The Danish Radio Band. The emphasis is on uptempo pieces such as "Perdido," "Rockin' in Rhythm" and "Stompy Jones;" a special highlight are the two very different versions of "Cottontail." *—Scott Yanow*

Dick Wellstood

b. Nov. 25, 1927, Greenwich, CT, **d.** Jul. 24, 1987, Palo Alto, CA
Piano / Classic Jazz, Stride, Ragtime
One of the two great stride pianists (along with Ralph Sutton) to emerge during the 1940s when members of their generation were generally playing bebop, Wellstood kept an open mind towards later styles (he loved Monk) while sounding at his best playing classic jazz. A little more subtle than Sutton, Wellstood was also a powerful pianist who was a superb interpreter of the music of James P. Johnson and his contemporaries. He came to New York with Bob Wilber's Wildcats in 1946 and caught on in the trad jazz scene quickly. By 1947 he was playing with Sidney Bechet and in the 1950s he mostly worked with veteran players including trumpeters Roy Eldridge, Rex Stewart and Charlie Shavers and the Eddie Condon gang. He was in the intermission band at Condon's starting in 1956 and later was house pianist at the Metropole and Nick's. After a period with Gene Krupa's quartet, he toured with the World's Greatest Jazz Band. Wellstood remained active througout his all-too-short life, playing solo concerts, performing at jazz parties and recording quite a few memorable albums. *—Scott Yanow*

★ **Dick Wellstood and His All-Star Orchestra Featuring Kenny Davern Plus The Blue Three** / Dec. 1973-1981 / Chiaroscuro ✦✦✦✦✦
This is the Dick Wellstood CD to get. Two former LPs (*Dick Wellstood And His Famous Orchestra Featuring Kenny Davern* and *The Blue Three At Hanratty's*) have been reissued in full on this single-CD which contains 78 minutes of music. The first eight selections (from 1973) feature Wellstood with soprano-saxophonist Kenny Davern in a set of stirring duets while the final nine songs have a trio comprised of Wellstood, Davern (sticking to clarinet) and drummer Bobby Rosengarden. Wellstood and Davern make a perfectly compatible team whether on surprising versions of dixieland standards (such as "Original Dixieland One Step," "Tiger Rag" and "Indiana") or obscurities such as Eddie Condon's (not George Gershwin's) "Liza" and "Oh Peter"; the opening number is an original simply titled "Fast As A Bastard!" A highly recommended set of brilliant prebop hot jazz. *—Scott Yanow*

This Is the One . . . Dig! / Oct. 12, 1975 / Solo Art ✦✦✦✦✦
This was the great pianist Dick Wellstood's personal favorite record and one can understand why. The music is very well recorded and Wellstood sounds quite inspired throughout the solo set. For the 1994 CD reissue, the original eight songs are joined by eight additional (and previously unreleased) performances and the quality stays consistently high. Wellstood, who had an open mind toward more modern styles of jazz while keeping his stride piano style undiluted, performs surprising versions of "You Are The Sunshine Of My Life" and John Coltrane's "Giant Steps" in addition to some swing standards and classics associated with James P. Johnson, Fats Waller and Earl Hines. Among the highpoints are "Snowy Morning Blues," "If Dreams Come True," "Rosetta" and a piece based on a classical work ("Paganini's Thing"). This is an essential acquisition for classic jazz collectors. *—Scott Yanow*

Live at Hanratty's / 1981 / Chiaroscuro ✦✦✦✦✦
It is ironic that this double-LP, one of pianist Dick Wellstood's finest recordings, has been out of print almost since its 1981 release by the short-lived Chaz Jazz label. Wellstood's lengthy solo recital finds him interpreting a particularly eclectic repertoire that includes "Jingle Bells," a medley of tunes associated with Cole Porter and Bessie Smith, Sidney Bechet's obscure "Quincy Street Stomp," his own "Cha Cha for Charlie," and Louis Armstrong's famous "Cornet Chop Suey" among others. Wellstood is heard at the top of his form throughout, making one wish that some enterprising record producer would lease or purchase the valuable Chaz Jazz catalog and reissue all of the valuable music. *—Scott Yanow*

Live at the Sticky Wicket / Nov. 9, 1986 / Arbors ✦✦✦✦
The Big Three of post-World War II stride piano were Ralph Sutton, Dick Hyman and the late Dick Wellstood, who passed away in 1987. This double CD from 1997, recorded just 8Ω months before Wellstood's death, contains all of the music performed by the pianist during an informal club appearance and recorded privately with his permission; it was released here for the first time. Although a masterful stride player, Wellstood was not unaware of later developments in jazz (he always liked Thelonious Monk), and his extensive program even features a striding version of "Giant Steps," which he turns into a bit of a joke. An expert at interpreting James P. Johnson tunes, Wellstood also includes a variety of swing standards, Duke Ellington numbers and selections by Fats Waller, Jelly Roll Morton and George Gershwin, among many others. He informally talks to the audience about the music between most of the songs, answers a few requests and cracks some jokes. Although the talking may seem a bit tiresome by the third listen, Wellstood's piano playing is heard throughout in prime form and is filled with many exciting moments. Highly recommended to lovers of stride piano. *—Scott Yanow*

Randy Weston

b. Apr. 6, 1926, Brooklyn, NY
Piano, Composer / Hard Bop, Post-Bop
Placing Randy Weston into narrow bop-derived categories only tells part of the story of this restless musician. Starting with the gospel of bop according to Thelonious Monk, Weston has gradually absorbed the letter and spirit of African and Caribbean rhythms and tunes, welding everything together into a searching, energizing, often celebratory blend. His piano work ranges across a profusion of styles from boogie-woogie through bop into dissonance, marking by a stabbing quality reminiscent of, but not totally indebted to, Monk. Weston began working professionally in R&B bands in the late 1940s before playing in the bebop outfits of Payne and Kenny Dorham. After signing with Riverside in 1954, he led his own trios and quartets and attained a prominent reputation as a composer, contributing jazz standards like "Hi-Fly" and "Little Niles" to the repertoire. Weston's interest in his roots was stimulated by extended stays in Africa; he remained fascinated with the music and spiritual values of the continent ever since. In the 1970s, Weston made recordings for Arista-Freedom, Polydor and CTI while maintaining a peripatetic touring existence—mostly in Europe—returning to Morocco in the mid-'80s. However, starting in the late '80s, after a long recording drought, Weston's visibility in the U.S. skyrocketed with an extraordinarily productive period in the studios for Antilles and Verve. *—Richard S. Ginell*

Get Happy / Aug. 29, 1955-Aug. 31, 1955 / Riverside ✦✦✦✦

Jazz á la Bohemia / Oct. 14, 1956 / Riverside/OJC ✦✦✦✦✦

Randy Weston, who was more under Thelonious Monk's influence back in 1956 then he would be in the near future, is in top form during this live set. His quartet features the rarely heard but talented baritonist Cecil Payne, bassist Ahmed Abdul-Malik and drummer Al Dreares. Highpoints of the straightahead set (which has been reissued on CD) include the calypso "Hold 'Em Joe" (recorded almost a decade before Sonny Rollins), "It's All Right with Me" (one of two trio tracks) and the lone Weston original on the date, the stimulating "Chessman's Delight." *—Scott Yanow*

★ **Uhuru Africa/Highlife** / Nov. 1960-Apr. 1963 / Roulette ✦✦✦✦✦
A couple of pianist Randy Weston's most significant albums are combined on this single CD. 1960's *Uhuru Afrika* is one of the finest (and earliest) combinations of African rhythms with advanced jazz and it features Weston utilizing a 24-piece big band that includes 14 horns, one guitar, two bassists, three drummers, and three percussionists; Martha Flowers and Brock Peters take vocals on "African Lady," the best known of the four movements. Melba Liston was responsible for not only those charts but the *Highlife* session which has Weston showcased in a stripped-down 12-piece ensemble. Highly recommended, these sessions are among the recorded highpoints of Randy Weston's productive career. *—Scott Yanow*

Monterey '66 / Sep. 18, 1966 / Verve ✦✦✦✦✦
The 1966 farewell concert of pianist Randy Weston's sextet was recorded at the *Monterey Jazz Festival,* but for some reason languished unreleased until 1993. Weston has cited this group—featuring trumpeter Ray Copeland, baritone saxophonist Cecil Payne, bassist Bill Wood, drummer Lenny McBrowne, and conga player Big Black—as his best, but it only remained together for three years. Tenor saxophonist Booker Ervin, a crucial element in the original band, was listed as special guest, only because he had already formed his own new group. All compositions are Weston originals and feature a strong African thematic influence. The 25-minute heated finale is the percussion laden "African Cookbook," in which everyone contributes strong and inspired soloing. *—Al Campbell*

African Cookbook / Oct. 1964 / Koch Jazz ✦✦✦✦
When this set was recorded in 1964, pianist Randy Weston had no luck interesting any label to release the music, so he came out with it independently on his tiny Bakton company. In 1972, Atlantic released the performances and they are finally available on CD in 1999. It is surprising that no company in the mid-1960s signed Weston up because "Willie's Tune" from the set had the potential to catch on, "Berkshire Blues" is somewhat known and the mixture of accessible bop with African rhythms overall is appealing. Trumpeter Ray Copeland was responsible for the arrangements while Weston contributed all but one of the songs. Copeland and the great tenor Booker Ervin have their share of solo space, bassist Vishnu Wood and drummer Lenny McBrowne are fine in support, and on three numbers the percussion of Big Black and Sir Harold Murray are added; Big Black also sings on "Congolese Children." An excellent outing. *—Scott Yanow*

Tanjah / May 21, 1973-May 22, 1973 / Verve ✦✦✦✦✦
Originally on the Polydor label, this lesser-known classic (reissued on CD) teams together pianist/composer Randy Weston and arranger Melba Liston (his musical soulmate) on seven of Weston's originals. The fairly large band is filled with distinctive soloists including trumpeter Jon Faddis (19 at the time), trombonist Al Grey, Billy Harper on tenor, altoist Norris Turney (heard on three versions of "Sweet Meat," two of which were previously unreleased) and several percussionists among others. The weak points are Weston's use of the Fender Rhodes on a few songs (it waters down his personality) and Candido's chanting during an otherwise exciting version of "Hi-Fly," but those are easily compensated for by the infectious calypso "Jamaican East" and Liston's inventive reworking of "Little Niles." Recommended. *—Scott Yanow*

The Spirits of Our Ancestors / May 20, 1991-May 22, 1991 / Verve ✦✦✦✦✦
Pianist Randy Weston and arranger Melba Liston had a musical reunion on this special double-CD, their first joint project since 1973's *Tanjah.* Liston's charts for the pianist's ten originals perfectly fit Weston's adventurous style and the twelve-piece group (which includes three percussionists) is filled with highly individual voices including the tenors of Billy Harper and Dewey Redman. With trumpeter Dizzy Gillespie and tenor-saxophonist Pharoah Sanders making guest appearances and Randy Weston heard at the peak of his powers, this is a highly recommended set. *—Scott Yanow*

Marrakech in the Cool of the Evening / Sep. 28, 1992 / Verve ✦✦✦✦✦

Volcano Blues / Feb. 5, 1993-Feb. 6, 1993 / Antilles ✦✦✦✦✦
Pianist Randy Weston and trombonist/arranger Melba Liston have collaborated successfully for many years. This pairing was on a series of blues numbers, with Weston doubling as session producer and pianist while giving Liston almost total arranging control, except for three numbers. The results were an intriguing twist on standard 12-bar blues, as Weston's muscular piano lead the way through rigorous performances of Count Basie's "Volcano" and his own "Blues For Strayhorn," "Sad Beauty Blues" and "In Memory Of." Liston's arrangements required disciplined solos, and Weston's steady hand generated impressive cohesion and interaction during the unison segments. A superb example of the African/African-American musical continuum. *—Ron Wynn*

Saga / Apr. 14, 1995-Apr. 17, 1995 / Verve ✦✦✦✦

Khepara / Feb. 23, 1998-Feb. 25, 1998 / Verve ✦✦✦✦
The team of Randy Weston, composer/pianist, and Melba Liston, arranger, returns triumphantly to the territory carved out by *The Spirits of Our Ancestors*?only not at quite such length (just one CD) and with a new thrust, exploring ancient connections between African and Chinese cultures. The CD opens with a mighty building crash of percussion and continues in a kind of freeform depiction of creation, with Pharaoh Sanders—in thrilling form throughout much of the album—honking and evoking ancient spirits. A tragic grandeur sets in, the Chinese elements are evoked, and then midway through the record, the concept loses its train of thought; the rest of the album becomes a series of disconnected pieces (the theme of "Niger Mambo" threatens to break into "Puttin' On the Ritz" at any moment). The Chinese aspects of the music, signaled by the use of Min Xiao Fen's pipa (a Chinese lute) on a couple of tracks, are heavily outweighed by the thundering African percussion, so the ramifications of such a fusion aren't explored too thoroughly. However, Weston's impressions are almost always compelling anyway, with lots of mesmerizing vamps and passages that sometimes evoke John Coltrane's feelers into African music on *Kulu Se Mama.* Liston only has three wind voices to work with this time—Sanders, Benny Powell on trombone and Talib Kibawe on reeds—and she makes subtle use of them. This is, in any case, a powerful, even visionary piece of work for any musician, let alone one in his early 70s. *—Richard S. Ginell*

Kirk Whalum

b. Memphis, TN
Sax (Tenor) / Smooth Jazz, Crossover Jazz, Contemporary Jazz, Jazz-Pop
From the jazz purist standpoint, Kirk Whalum's career has thus far been a consistent disappointment. Although obviously a talented player, he has thus far been satisfied to make a good living by performing R&B and pop music while keeping well hidden any individuality that he might possess. Whalum debuted on record for Columbia in 1984 (on a Bob James record) and has been a popular attraction ever since. His album roster includes *And You Know That!* (1988), *Cache* (1993), *Colors* (1997), and *Joy Intersound* (1999). *Unconditional* was released on Warner Brothers in fall 2000. *—Scott Yanow*

And You Know That! / 1988 / Columbia ✦✦✦✦

The Promise / 1989 / Columbia ✦✦✦✦
Bob James gets the credit for discovering the passionate, soulful sax of Whalum in 1984. But you just know that a talent this size would have emerged on its own sooner or later. Between then and this release at the end of the decade, Whalum established himself as a major force on the contemporary scene, playing alongside the likes of James, Luther Vandross, Al Jarreau, and Larry Carlton, and releasing two powerful solo discs, 1985's *Floppy Disk* and 1988's *And You Know That.* But this third effort was his strongest outing to date, displaying a versatility which ranges from spiritual ("The Promise") to Brazilian (the tropical flavored "Desperately") to straight ahead rock & roll (the Larry Carlton tribute "LC's Back," which features the fancy licks of the guitarist himself). As producer, James gives his protégé's horn some fanciful grooves to work in and out of, most notably on the catchy, pop-like "Out a Hand." James also has a good time soloing on "Desperately" and the bass oriented "Don't Even Look." There are a lot of possible favorites in this collection, but the Carlton tribute is the one that hooks you from the very beginning. With this album, Whalum delivered in spades upon his early promise. *—Jonathan Widran*

● **Cache** / 1993 / Columbia ✦✦✦✦

Unconditional / Oct. 17, 2000 / Warner Brothers ✦✦✦✦✦
No doubt the title of *Unconditional* applies to the love of God that pervades his music and life, but like most of Whalum's efforts, this collection can be enjoyed by a wide audience. The centerpiece title song isn't blatantly gospel, but Whalum's textured multiple tenor lines rise powerfully towards the heavens like a soaring choir after making their main melodic hook statements. At one point, Whalum improvises crisply over Greg Phillinganes' simmering Rhodes as Luis Conte's percussion dances around him. "Now Till Forever" begins with a more meditative, smoky approach before Whalum, backed by John Stoddart's soulful wordless vocals, puts a little more oomph in the chorus. On "Playing With Fire," Whalum's soaring lines are answered and expounded upon by the balmy acoustic guitar breezes of Peter White; late in the tune, Whalum textures his sax to sound like a horn section, weaving that around White's sly lines. Gregg Karukas' moody keyboards and some colorful handclap effects help Whalum find some church in 'N Sync's "God Must Have Spent a Little More Time on You"; Tim Heintz's shimmering organ harmonies have the same gospel effect on a percussive cover of Macy Gray's "I Try," whose hook is also played as a one-man horn section. Whalum stretches out the slammin' funk and heartfelt meditations to over seven minutes on the cleverly titled "Groverworked and Underpaid," bouncing gleefully over Phillinganes' throbbing Rhodes and Paul Jackson Jr.'s plucky electric guitar, before improvising liberally. This kind of track represents a true risk for a smooth jazz album, but it seems Whalum was more concerned with portraying his feelings about the recently departed Grover Washington Jr. and his inspiration honestly. *—Jonathan Widran*

Kenny Wheeler

b. Jan. 14, 1930, Toronto, Ontario, Canada
Flugelhorn, Trumpet / Avant-Garde Jazz, Post-Bop
Kenny Wheeler has long been one of the most technically proficient of the avant-garde trumpeters. He started on cornet when he was 12, studied at the Toronto Conservatory and then in 1952 moved to England. He worked in many big bands during the next decade (including with John Dankworth during 1959-65) and became an excellent bop-based soloist. However by the mid-'60s his musical curiosity led him to freer forms of jazz and he did important work with John Stevens' Spontaneous Music Ensemble, Tony Oxley's sextet, the Mike Gibbs Orchestra, the Globe Unity Orchestra (starting in 1972), Anthony Braxton's Quartet and Azimuth. Wheeler has been a regular on ECM since the mid-'70s and during 1983-87 he was with the Dave Holland quintet. A thoughtful trumpeter with a wide range, Wheeler's playing is always stimulating yet generally introspective. *—Scott Yanow*

● **Gnu High** / Jun. 1975 / ECM ✦✦✦✦✦
Trumpeter Kenny Wheeler's debut as a leader for ECM is a memorable quartet set with pianist Keith Jarrett (one of his best recordings as a sideman), bassist Dave Holland and drummer Jack DeJohnette. The group plays three of Wheeler's originals (including the 21Ω-minute "Heyoke") and each of the musicians sound quite inspired. Wheeler's wide range, beautiful tone and searching style match particularly well with Jarrett's rhythmic and bluish accompaniment. Highly recommended. *—Scott Yanow*

Double, Double You / May 1983 / ECM ✦✦✦✦✦
Kenny Wheeler's string of ECM recordings are all quite rewarding, generally avoiding the ECM stereotype of introspective long tones and silence. A fiery but thoughtful trumpeter

whose style can range from advanced swinging to sound explorations, Wheeler is joined on this excellent set by tenor saxophonist Michael Brecker, pianist John Taylor, bassist Dave Holland and drummer Jack DeJohnette. They perform a set of Wheeler's originals and each of the world class musicians has an opportunity to be featured. A generally memorable outing. *—Scott Yanow*

All the More / Oct. 31, 1993Nov. 1, 1993 / Soul Note ♦♦♦♦
These 1993 recordings (released on a 1997 CD) are an excellent showcase for trumpeter Kenny Wheeler. Six of the eight compositions are his (all but drummer Pat Labarbera's "Kind of Bill" and the closing standard "Summer Night"); Wheeler's mostly mellow-toned trumpet matches very well with the lyrical piano of John Taylor (who has worked with Wheeler on and off for 20 years), bassist Furio Di Castri and Labarbera. Wheeler can sound so peaceful and wistful that it is always a surprise when he displays his wide range and hits some impressive high notes, as he does in spots throughout the set. His originals are complex yet friendly, unpredictable but logical, always seeming to develop gradually until their conclusion. He is also very democratic in allocating solo space. Well worth picking up. *—Scott Yanow*

Paul Whiteman

b. Mar. 28, 1890, Denver, CO, **d.** Dec. 29, 1967, Doylestown, PA
Violin, Bandleader / Classic Jazz
Because press agents dubbed him "The King of Jazz" in the 1920s, Paul Whiteman has always been considered a controversial figure in jazz history. Actually his orchestra was the most popular during the era and at times (despite its size) it did play very good jazz; perhaps "King of the Jazz Age" would have been a better title. Leader of a San Francisco dance band during 1918, Whiteman settled in New York two years later and became a household name thanks to big-selling recordings like "Japanese Sandman" and "Whispering." His superior dance band used some of the most technically skilled musicians of the era in a versatile show that included everything from pop tunes and waltzes to semi-classical works and jazz. Though Whiteman's symphonic jazz did not always swing, he made history in 1924 by introducing "Rhapsody in Blue" (with its composer George Gershwin on piano). In 1927, the addition of Bix Beiderbecke, Frankie Trumbauer and Bing Crosby finally gave him an important jazz band. Joe Venuti and Eddie Lang soon joined up and many of Whiteman's recordings of 1927-30 are among his finest. The Depression forced the bandleader to cut back on his personnel and Whiteman's music was considered old hat by the time of the swing era. He essentially retired by the early '40s, except for special appearances. *—Scott Yanow*

The King of Jazz / Aug. 9, 1920-Jun. 26, 1936 / ASV/Living Era ♦♦♦♦♦
ASV's Whiteman compilation covers the years 1920-36, which means that it partly overlaps with Collectors' Choice's 20-song RCA-Victor compilation of Whiteman's work. What makes this disc worth owning is that while many of the songs overlap, these are not the same tracks in many instances—several are later re-recordings (Whiteman was already re-cutting his hits in the middle and late 1920s, with the advent of electrical recording). So "Whispering" and "Rhapsody In Blue" are the 1922 and 1927 Victor cuts available elsewhere, but "Wang Wang Blues" is the 1920 version, not the 1927 version, and "Ol' Man River" from March 1928 features Paul Robeson, not Bing Crosby; similarly, "Three O'Clock In the Morning" is the 1926, not the 1922 version. And there are some non-overlapping numbers—the Whiteman band's 1925 recording of the "Charleston," "Whiteman Stomp" from 1927, "Darktown Strutters' Ball" featuring Jack Teagarden as singer and trombonist, and a pair of medleys from 1932, "A Night With Paul Whiteman," parts one and two. Mildred Bailey shows up on "When It's Sleepy Time Down South"; Bix Beiderbecke is featured on "Louisiana" and "You Took Advantage of Me"; and Bing Crosby and violinist Joe Venuti turn up on "Happy Feet." The sound is fair to good, with some surface noise—the quality doesn't match that of the Collectors' Choice disc, but so little of this repeats that it's not wholly fair to compare them. So one needn't be a Whiteman completist to enjoy this disc. *—Bruce Eder*

• **Jazz a La King (1920-1936)** / Aug. 23, 1920-Jun. 2, 1936 / RCA ♦♦♦♦♦
This definitive two-LP set traces the recording career of bandleader Paul Whiteman, who was given the unfortunate title of "The King of Jazz." Whiteman did lead the most popular jazz-influenced orchestra of the 1920s, and his oversized ensemble sometimes played fine jazz. The orchestra was at its creative peak during 1927-1929 when cornetist Bix Beiderbecke was its top soloist, but since those performances are readily available elsewhere, Bix is only heard on three of the 33 recordings reissued on this very interesting two-fer. Starting with 1920's "Wang Wang Blues" and "Whispering" and ending with the 1936 edition which sometimes featured trombonist Jack Teagarden, many of the jazz highpoints of Whiteman's career are on the set, programmed in chronological order. Highlights include "Hot Lips," "Charleston," "Milenberg Joys," "St. Louis Blues," "Whiteman Stomp," "Sensation," "From Monday On," "G. Blues," and "Nobody's Sweetheart." Thus far this release is superior to any Paul Whiteman collection reissued on CD. *—Scott Yanow*

Bix 'N' Bing / 1927-1930 / ASV/Living Era ♦♦♦♦♦
The focus of this 20-song CD is the work of the Paul Whiteman Orchestra featuring Bix Beiderbecke and Bing Crosby, a period covering 1927 through 1929, up through their recording of "Waiting at the End of the Road," and includes releases on both RCA-Victor and Columbia. Crosby is part of the Rhythm Boys on much of the material here, though he always gets at least a little solo spot. Four of the titles here—"Sunshine," "Mississippi Mud," "Do I Hear You Saying," and "You Took Advantage of Me"—never got out originally. Among the other curiosities before us, "Oh Miss Hannah" was only issued outside of the United States. The material is all first-rate, easily among the liveliest and most sophisticated material in the band's output, and among its most enduring today—Bix Beiderbecke is featured prominently throughout, so the value for his fans is a given, but one shouldn't forget Whiteman and the rest of the band, or some of the dazzling textures of their arrangements (especially those by Ferde Grofe). What's more, the group was still at its peak as a popular jazz ensemble when these sides were cut, so even listeners who are disinclined to appreciate vocal numbers may want to check this disc out—it's worth owning for "Mississippi Mud" alone, even though Crosby isn't half as prominent as Irene Taylor. Some of these cuts appear elsewhere, even on other ASV releases, but since Columbia's Crosby-Beiderbecke collection is out of print, this is the only way to get that end of the band's output on CD. The sound is generally good to very good, although few tracks such as "High Water" are marred by excess surface noise from their sources. *—Bruce Eder*

Victor Masters / Columbia/Legacy ♦♦♦♦♦
Some fine sessions. Regardless of anyone's feeling about whether or not he was overrated due to racial politics, Whiteman's music was very influential on a certain level. *—Ron Wynn*

Clarence Williams

b. Oct. 8, 1893, Plaquemine, LA, **d.** Nov. 6, 1965, New York, NY
Vocals, Piano, Composer / Classic Jazz
Although he was quite spirited playing jug, Clarence Williams was only a decent pianist and a likable but limited vocalist. However, he was also a talented composer, writing or co-writing dozens of memorable songs like "Everybody Loves My Baby," "West End Blues" and "Tain't Nobody's Business If I Do," and he was also a masterful organizer, responsible for scores of hot recordings issued under his name in the 1920s and '30s. After moving to New Orleans in 1906, Williams played piano in Storyville, worked with a minstrel show, and ran his own cabaret as well as a small publishing company. After the company became successful, he moved to Chicago and then New York, where he had great success composing songs and putting together all-star groups (which included dozens of major jazz heroes) to record them. Starting in 1923, he also worked as an A&R man for Okeh Records. At the height of his power in the early '30s, Clarence Williams' importance waned as the decade continued and swing took over. After 1937, he began concentrating on the business side of music. In 1943, he sold his company to Decca and became a shop owner in Harlem. Williams was seriously injured when hit by a taxi in 1956 and passed away in 1965. *—Scott Yanow*

1921-1924 / Oct. 11, 1921-Nov. 6, 1924 / Classics ♦♦♦♦♦

1924-1926 / Dec. 17, 1924-Feb. 1926 / Classics ♦♦♦♦♦

1926-1927 / Mar. 7, 1926-Jan. 29, 1927 / Classics ♦♦♦♦♦

1927 / Mar. 8, 1927-Sep. 23, 1927 / Classics ♦♦♦♦♦

1927-1928 / Oct. 1927-Aug. 1, 1928 / Classics ♦♦♦♦♦

1928-1929 / Aug. 1928-Jan. 1929 / Classics ♦♦♦♦♦

• **1929** / Jan. 1929-May 28, 1929 / Classics ♦♦♦♦♦
The seventh volume in the European Classics label's complete reissuance of bandleader Clarence Williams's very valuable recordings documents his music during a four-month period. Included are two Williams piano solos, his sessions leading The Barrelhouse Five Orchestra, Jazz Kings and The Memphis Jazzers, and quite a bit of superior small-group jazz. Among the sidemen are cornetist Ed Allen, trombonist Ed Cuffee, Arville Harris and Albert Socarras on reeds, banjoist Leroy Harris, pianist James P. Johnson (on two songs), the exuberant tuba of Cyrus St. Clair, Floyd Casey on drums and washboard and Williams himself on piano and occasional vocals. Highlights include "Endurance Stomp," "If You Like Me like I Like You," "Steamboat Days," "Baby, Won't You Please Come Home," "In Our Cottage of Love" and the original version of "Breeze." All of the CDs in this enjoyable series are easily recommended to 1920s collectors. *—Scott Yanow*

1929-1930 / Jun. 21, 1929-Apr. 23, 1930 / Classics ♦♦♦♦♦
The eighth CD in the European Classics series which is reissuing complete and in chronological order all of the recordings led by pianist/composer Clarence Williams documents his activity from a ten-month period. During this era Williams varied his personnel and instrumentation from session to session and the results are quite varied yet consistently hot. Williams's groups feature such sidemen as cornetist Ed Allen, trumpeter Charlie Gaines, the reeds of Arville Harris and Russell Procope, the enthusiastic tuba of Cyrus St. Clair, Floyd Casey on drums and washboard, two excellent vocals apiece by Margaret Webster (her "You've Got to Give Me Some" is a near-classic) and Eva Taylor and, on eight selections, the masterful pianist James P. Johnson. The highpoints are "How Could I Be Blue—" and "I've Found a New Baby," performances taken as piano duets by Johnson and Williams that include some humorous conversation. All of the CDs in this very valuable series are highly recommended to collectors of 1920s jazz. *—Scott Yanow*

1930-1931 / May 22, 1930-Feb. 19, 1931 / Classics ♦♦♦♦♦
This CD is the ninth in an extensive series that reissues all of the recordings led by pianist/composer Clarence Williams. Since Williams headed a wide variety of exciting small groups in the 1920s and '30s that utilized the playing of many top jazz players, all of the CDs are worth acquiring by collectors of classic jazz. The 22 selections on this particular CD range from novelty Williams solo performances to groups featuring trumpeters Red Allen and Ed Allen, Albert Socarras on several reeds (including flute), clarinetists Buster Bailey and Cecil Scott, Prince Robinson doubling on clarinet and tenor, pianist Herman Chittison, Ikey Robinson on banjo, the great tuba player Cyrus St. Clair, singer Eva Taylor, Floyd Casey on washboard, the Bingie Madison big band and Williams himself on vocals, piano and jug. Highlights of this spirited program include "You're Bound to Look like a Monkey When You Get Old," "High Society Blues," "Hot Lovin," "" "Baby, Won't You Please Come Home" and four different versions of "Shout Sister Shout." *—Scott Yanow*

1933 / May 15, 1933-Sep. 1, 1933 / Classics ♦♦♦♦

1933-1934 / Dec. 6, 1933-Jun. 28, 1934 / Classics ♦♦♦♦

1934-1937 / Sep. 11, 1934-Apr. 8, 1937 / Classics ♦♦♦♦

Cootie Williams (Charles Melvin Williams)

b. Jun. 24, 1910, Mobile, AL, **d.** Sep. 14, 1985, New York, NY
Trumpet / New York Blues, Jump Blues, Swing
Cootie Williams, one of the finest trumpeters of the 1930s, expanded upon the role originally

formed by Bubber Miley with Duke Ellington's Orchestra. Renowned for his work with the plunger mute, Cootie was also a fine soloist when playing open. He played for a short time with the orchestras of Chick Webb and Fletcher Henderson (recording with the latter) before joining Duke Ellington as Miley's replacement in February 1929. He was a fixture with Duke's band during the next 11 years, not only recording many classics with Ellington but leading some of his own sessions and recording with Lionel Hampton, Teddy Wilson and Billie Holiday. His decision to leave Ellington and join Benny Goodman's Orchestra in 1940 was considered a major event in the jazz world. Williams then headed his own orchestra which at times in the 1940s featured such up-and-coming players as pianist Bud Powell, tenorman Eddie "Lockjaw" Davis, altoist-singer Eddie "Cleanhead" Vinson and even Charlie Parker. Playing R&B-oriented music, he worked steadily at the Savoy but by the 1950s was drifting into obscurity. However in 1962, after a 22-year absence, Cootie Williams rejoined Ellington, staying even beyond Duke's death in 1974 as a featured soloist. By then his solos were much simpler and more primitive than earlier but Cootie remained the master with the plunger mute. *—Scott Yanow*

Echoes of Harlem / Jan. 4, 1944-Aug. 22, 1944 / Affinity ✦✦✦✦✦
The little known big band that trumpeter Cootie Williams led in 1944 had some rather notable sidemen: pianist Bud Powell (in his first recordings), altoist-vocalist Eddie "Cleanhead" Vinson, and tenor saxophonist Eddie "Lockjaw" Davis. This superior English LP from Affinity has all 16 recordings by Williams from that year, eight songs apiece from his sextet and his big band. In addition to the other soloists, a young Pearl Bailey has two vocals and future R&B tenor star Sam "The Man" Taylor gets in a few licks. Among the many highlights of this historic program are "Echoes of Harlem," "Honeysuckle Rose," "Cherry Red Blues," "Blue Garden Blues," and the earliest recording ever of Thelonious Monk's "'Round Midnight." *—Scott Yanow*

● **The Big Challenge** / Apr. 30, 1957May 7, 1957 / Fresh Sound ✦✦✦✦✦
This CD reissue from the Spanish Fresh Sound label brings back a fun and unusual Jazztone session. Six distinctive and very different veterans were teamed together: trumpeter Cootie Williams, cornetist Rex Stewart, trombonists Lawrence Brown and J.C. Higginbotham and the tenors of Coleman Hawkins and Bud Freeman. With pianist Hank Jones, guitarist Billy Bauer, bassist Milt Hinton and drummer Gus Johnson providing solid backup and Ernie Wilkins sketching out some arrangements, the unique matchups are very successful. Each of the musicians have opportunities to be featured and the tradeoffs are quite memorable. A colorful gem. *—Scott Yanow*

Cootie Williams in Hi Fi / Mar. 25, 1958-Apr. 8, 1958 / RCA ✦✦✦✦✦
When Cootie Williams recorded *Cootie Williams in Hi Fi* in 1958, he wasn't generally regarded at the peak of his form. He had spent several years leading his own orchestra in the '40s, gradually moving toward R&B-oriented music by the end of that decade. That's why *In Hi Fi* came as a bit of a surprise. It found Williams returning to big-band music, which is where he made his name. As a matter of fact, he even embraces tunes from former employers Benny Goodman and Duke Ellington. Returning to big-band swing and blues revitalized Williams—he sounds relaxed and invigorated, playing with a considerable dose of good humor. It's not just Williams who sounds lively; his supporting band (technically, there are three different groups, but they share many of the same members) is equally loose, and, as a result, this return to big band is surprisingly fresh and boundlessly enjoyable. *Cootie Williams in Hi Fi* is a minor treasure, proving that he still had "it," four years before his official comeback. The CD reissues of *In Hi Fi* (the 1999 RCA Victor issue sounds superb, thanks to 24-bit remastering) contain 11 bonus tracks recorded in 1957. All 11 songs are R&B numbers, complete with hard-driving guitars and jiving horn sections. There are also five vocal selections—two featuring Larry Dale, two featuring Wini Brown, and one duet between the two. These are all fine R&B recordings, but a little generic. As such, they only make *Cootie Williams in Hi Fi* sound all the more special. *—Stephen Thomas Erlewine*

1946-1949 / Sep. 11, 1946-Sep. 20, 1959 / Melodie Jazz Classics ✦✦✦✦
Classics picks up the story of former Ellington trumpeter Cootie Williams as the leader of his own orchestra from 1946 through 1949 on sides he recorded for Capitol, Majestic, and Mercury. Vocalists Bob Merrill, Billy Matthews, and Eddie Mack are heavily featured on these 22 cuts. The R&B jump music of Louis Jordan and Wynonie Harris were big draws in the nightclubs and jukeboxes of the time and much of this material lends itself to that style. "Inflation Blues" is a takeoff of the "Let the Good Times Roll" theme, while "Save the Bones for Henry Jones," "I Should O' Been Thinking Instead of Drinkin," "Gator Tail" (parts one and two), and "Doin' the Gator Tail" are enjoyable mixtures of novelty lyrics and stompin' R&B instrumentals. While Williams favored this commercial recipe during these years, he did manage to wax a few ballads, such as "I Can't Get Started" and "I Want to Be Loved," and orchestra numbers like "Rhapsody in Bass"; "Sound Track" leans toward the Ellingtonesque style he was an earlier participant in. *—Al Campbell*

Mary Lou Williams (Scruggs, Mary Elfrieda)

b. May 8, 1910, Atlanta, GA, **d.** May 28, 1981, Durham, NC
Piano, Arranger / Stride, Post-Bop, Swing, Bop
Although for decades Mary Lou Williams was often called jazz's greatest female musician, she would have been considered a major artist no matter what her sex. The fact that Williams and Duke Ellington were virtually the only stride pianists to modernize their style through the years would have been enough to guarantee her a place in jazz history books. Mary Lou managed to always sound modern during her half-century career, without forgetting her roots or how to play in older styles. Born Mary Elfrieda Scruggs, she taught herself the piano by ear and was playing in public at the age of six. When she was 13, she started working in vaudeville, and three years later married saxophonist John Williams, who joined Andy Kirk's Orchestra in 1929. Mary Lou wrote arrangements for the band, filled in for an absent pianist on Kirk's first recording session, and eventually became a member of the orchestra herself. Her arrangements were largely responsible for the band's distinctive sound and eventual success. Williams was soon recognized as Kirk's top soloist; in addition, she contributed hit songs and arrangements to other big bands, including those of Benny Goodman, Earl Hines, and Tommy Dorsey. Williams gradually modernized her style and by the early to mid-'40s was actively encouraging the young modernists who would lead the bebop revolution. Williams lived in Europe from 1952-54 and then retired from music for a few years before appearing as a guest with Dizzy Gillespie's Orchestra at the 1957 Newport Jazz Festival. Williams returned to jazz and by the early '70s sounded more like a young modal player than a survivor of the 1920s. By the time she passed away at the age of 71, she had a list of accomplishments that could have filled three lifetimes. *—Scott Yanow*

The Chronological Mary Lou Williams (1927-1940) / Jan. 1927-Nov. 1940 / Classics ✦✦✦✦✦
This CD features the great pianist Mary Lou Williams during her earliest period. She is heard in 1927 on six selections with The Synco Jazzers (a small group that included her then-husband John Williams on alto) and then on the first 19 selections ever recorded under her own name. Performed during the long period when she was the regular pianist with Andy Kirk's 12 Clouds of Joy, Williams is featured on two hot stride solos in 1930, leading trios in 1936 and 1938, playing "Little Joe from Chicago" unaccompanied in 1939 and heading septets in 1940; among her sidemen were trumpeter Harold "Shorty" Baker and the legendary tenor Dick Wilson. Many of the compositions were written by Williams including "Night Life," "New Froggy Bottom," "Mary's special," and "Scratchin' the Gravel;" her version of Jelly Roll Morton's "The Pearls" is a highpoint. *—Scott Yanow*

Asch Recordings, 1944-1947 / Mar. 12, 1944-1947 / Smithsonian/Folkways ✦✦✦✦✦
Mary Lou Williams recorded exclusively for Asch during this period, and most of her performances are included on this two-LP boxed set. Williams's style was in a state of transition as she was gradually discarding stride piano and developing a much more boppish approach. She is heard here in a wide variety of settings ranging from piano solos to small groups and even a big band. Among her sidemen are trumpeters Frankie Newton, Dick Vance, Bill Coleman (who is well-featured), and Kenny Dorham, clarinetist Edmund Hall, trombonist Vic Dickenson, and tenors Don Byas and Coleman Hawkins. This very valuable set is well-worth an extensive search. *—Scott Yanow*

Town Hall (1945): The Zodiac Suite / Dec. 31, 1945 / Smithsonian/Folkways ✦✦✦✦
Mary Lou Williams's *Zodiac Suite*, a 12-piece work with a different theme made for each of the signs of the zodiac (and keeping in mind the personalities of a few jazz musicians born during each period), was composed and first recorded in 1945. With the assistance of bassist Al Lucas and drummer Jack "The Bear" Parker, pianist Williams performs these moody and often introspective (but occasionally playful) sketches in a forward-looking swing style. Five alternate takes have been added to the original program on this CD reissue which, although not quite essential, has its interesting moments. *—Scott Yanow*

Zoning / Jan. 1974-Mar. 1974 / Smithsonian/Folkways ✦✦✦✦
Mary Lou Williams emerged in the early '70s after a long period in which she worked in the Catholic church to resume her always-stimulating career as a jazz pianist. On this CD reissue, one of her finest recordings of her later years has been brought back and augmented by two previously unissued performances. Williams performs in duos and trios with bassist Bob Cranshaw and drummer Mickey Roker, uses Zita Carno on second piano during a couple of the more avant-garde pieces, and also performs some trios with bassist Milton Suggs and Tony Waters on congas. Rather than sounding like a veteran of the 1920s, Mary Lou Williams sounds 40 years younger, shows the influence of McCoy Tyner and hints at free jazz in spots. An often-surprising set of modern jazz. *—Scott Yanow*

● **Live at the Cookery** / Nov. 1975 / Chiaroscuro ✦✦✦✦✦
This CD gives one a definitive look at the talented pianist Mary Lou Williams in her later years. In these duets with bassist Brian Torff, Williams essentially takes listeners on a trip through the history of jazz from hymns and blues to stride, swing and bop (including "All Blues"). The CD reissue adds three fine performances to the original program. Recommended. *—Scott Yanow*

Nite Life/From the Past / May 1971-Oct. 22, 1971 / Chiaroscuro ✦✦✦✦
The great pianist, Mary Lou Williams, is heard solo throughout this two-CD set. The first 11 selections were originally issued as the LP *From the Heart*. This two-fer also has nine additional performances (some of which are very different alternate takes) from the same studio dates. Sixty-one at the time, Williams was at the peak of her powers and her program ranges from a remake of her early stride classic "Nite Life" and versions of her compositions "What's Your Story Morning Glory" and "Little Joe from Chicago" to some more modern and impressionistic pieces. In addition, the set has a fascinating 32-and-a-half minute monologue by Williams in which she talks about her life story up to the late '30s, her days with Andy Kirk and her marriage to John Williams; plus, there is an intriguing set that the pianist performed at a Scott Joplin tribute concert. Because she did not care for the very straight performances of the classically-trained ragtime pianists who preceded her, Mary Lou Williams surprised the crowd by improvising on three Joplin pieces, throwing in stride, a bit of the blues and plenty of swing. All in all, this is a highly recommended set of great interest. *—Scott Yanow*

Tony Williams

b. Dec. 12, 1945, Chicago, IL, **d.** Feb. 23, 1997, Daly City, CA
Drums / Hard Bop, Post-Bop, Fusion
Tony Williams' death in 1997 of a heart attack after routine gall bladder surgery was a major shock to the jazz world. Just 51, Williams (who could be a very loud drummer) seemed so youthful, healthy and ageless even though he had been a major drummer for nearly 35 years. The open style that he created while with the Miles Davis Quintet in the mid-to-late '60s remains quite influential and he had a long list of accomplishments during the past couple of decades. During 1959-60 Williams often played with Sam Rivers and in December 1962 (when he was barely 17), the drummer moved to New York and played regularly with Jackie McLean. Within a few months he joined Miles Davis where his ability to imply the beat while playing quite freely influenced and inspired the other musicians; together with

Herbie Hancock and Ron Carter he was part of one of the great rhythm sections. Williams, who was 18 when he appeared on Eric Dolphy's classic *Out to Lunch* album, stayed with Davis into 1969, leading his own occasional sessions and becoming a household name in the jazz world. In addition to his interest in avant-garde jazz, Tony Williams was a fan of rock music and when he left Miles he formed the fusion band Lifetime, a trio with Larry Young and John McLaughlin. *—Scott Yanow*

Life Time / Aug. 21, 1964-Aug. 24, 1964 / Blue Note ♦♦♦♦♦
Drummer Tony Williams' first recording as a leader (made when he was 18 and still billed as Anthony Williams) gave him an opportunity to utilize an advanced group of musicians: tenor saxophonist Sam Rivers, vibraphonist Bobby Hutcherson, pianist Herbie Hancock, and both Richard Davis and Gary Peacock on bass. Williams wrote all four of the pieces and has a different combination of players on each song. The freely improvised "Memory" features Hutcherson, Hancock, and Williams in some colorful and at times spacy interplay; "Barb's Song to the Wizard" is a Hancock-Ron Carter duet; "Tomorrow Afternoon" has Rivers, Peacock and Williams in a trio; and all of the musicians (except Hutcherson) are on the side-long "2 Pieces of One." The unpredictable music holds one's interest; a very strong debut for the masterful drummer. *—Scott Yanow*

Spring / Aug. 12, 1965 / Blue Note ♦♦♦
Considering the extraordinary talent assembled for Tony Williams' second Blue Note date as a leader, this could have been a landmark session. Unfortunately, it's not. *Spring* isn't totally forgettable; on the contrary, the fire expected by members of the Miles Davis Quintet (Williams, Herbie Hancock and Wayne Shorter), all thoroughly influenced by "the new thing," were unleashed completely from Miles' tight rein. Add tenor saxophonist Sam Rivers and Albert Ayler bassist Gary Peacock into this mix and that influence thrived. However, the five Tony Williams compositions (including the drum only "Echo") often failed to provoke the musicians into reaching crucial unity, making *Spring* haphazard, falling short of the expected goal. Following *Spring*, Williams would not release another solo date for four years, returning on the Polydor label with the groundbreaking \electric rock trio recording *Emergency!* *—Al Campbell*

☆ **Emergency!** / May 26, 1969-May 28, 1969 / Polydor ♦♦♦♦♦
Tony Williams' *Emergency* was one of the first and most influential albums in late-'60s fusion, a record that shattered the boundaries between jazz and rock. Working with guitarist John McLaughlin and organist Larry Young, Williams pushed into new territory, creating dense, adventurous, unpredictable soundscapes. With *Emergency,* Tony Williams helped create the foundation of the style and sound of fusion. It's a seminal release, originally released on two albums and now available on one CD. *—Leo Stanley*

★ **Spectrum: The Anthology** / May 26, 1969-1972 / Verve ♦♦♦♦♦
Spectrum: Anthology is a double-disc, 25-track compilation that traces the evolution of Tony Williams' early '70s jazz-fusion combo, Lifetime. Over the course of their career, Lifetime featured a number of top jazz and rock players, including John McLaughlin, Ron Carter, Alan Holdsworth, Larry Young and Jack Bruce, with many of the musicians turning in edgy, exciting performances. In fact, *Spectrum* is a better way to get acquainted with Lifetime than the actual albums, since it condenses the cream of the crop down to one illuminating anthology. *—Leo Stanley*

Turn It Over / Jan. 17, 1970 / Polydor ♦♦♦♦
The addition of former Cream bassist Jack Bruce to Tony Williams' Lifetime not only gave the fusion group a harder rock edge, but it helped push the band toward both bluesier and more adventurous territory. While the end result wasn't as consistently impressive as *Emergency!, Turn It Over* was still unpredictable, challenging music that helped establish Williams as an influential bandleader in his own right. *—Leo Stanley*

Ego / Feb. 1971-Mar. 1971 / Polydor ♦♦♦

Lifetime: The Collection / Jul. 1975-Jun. 1976 / Columbia/Legacy ♦♦♦♦♦
This CD has all of the music from drummer Tony Williams' *Believe It* and *Million Dollar Legs* LPs. The best-known version of Williams' Lifetime is the trio he led during 1969-1970 with guitarist John McLaughlin and organist Larry Young. There are times (particularly on the first half of this reissue) that this later edition of Lifetime approaches the power and creativity of the original group. Key among the sidemen is guitarist Allan Holdsworth, a very underrated and creative musician whose style falls between rock and jazz and who often improvises more like a keyboardist than a guitarist. Alan Pasqua on electric piano and bassist Tony Newton (who also takes a few forgettable vocals) complete the group; background brass and strings are added to some of the songs in the later date. Although not flawless (some of the music has dated), these long-overlooked performances are worth exploring by fusion collectors, especially for Holdsworth's fiery yet thoughtful solos. *—Scott Yanow*

The Story of Neptune / Nov. 29, 1991-Dec. 1, 1991 / Blue Note ♦♦♦♦♦
The Tony Williams Quintet has two obvious assets that put it ahead of most acoustic jazz bands: Williams's powerful and consistently creative drumming and his compositional talents. On this group's fifth Blue Note recording, the drummer contributed the three-part "Neptune," essentially a feature for his drums, a more memorable original, "Crime Scene" and arrangements of three standards. *—Scott Yanow, Cadence*

☆ **Tokyo Live** / Mar. 2, 1992-Mar. 8, 1992 / Blue Note ♦♦♦♦♦
This live two-CD set, one of the last recordings by the Tony Williams Quintet before it disbanded, is a fine retrospective of the group's music. All but the Beatles' "Blackbird" are originals by the drummer/leader, and the 11 lengthy performances (only two songs clock in at less than nine minues and 51 seconds) give one a strong idea as to how the quintet sounded during a typical club performance. Trumpeter Wallace Roney and the versatile Bill Pierce (on tenor and soprano) have their spots, and pianist Mulgrew Miller is well-featured on the thoughtful "Citadel" while bassist Ira Coleman is heard purely in a supportive role. There is never any doubt who the leader is, for Tony Williams dominates the ensembles, taking several five-minute drum solos and being quite prominent in the mix. *—Scott Yanow*

Young at Heart / Sep. 24, 1996-Sep. 25, 1996 / Columbia ♦♦♦♦
This would be the drummer's last recording, cut six months before he died. It shows Williams in a more conciliatory mood, sublimating his huge chops and bombastic style for subtler shadings and support for pianist Mulgrew Miller and bassist Ira Coleman, while lessening none of his indefatigable swing. This was also the last band Williams toured with, indicating he was committed to and comfortable with the acoustic piano-bass-drums format. It's a setting he had never really fully exploited over his years of leadership, no doubt inspired by the Herbie Hancock-Ron Carter partnership within the Miles Davis quintet of the mid-'60s. On the six standards present, Miller shines like a million facet diamond, his ultra-bright ideas swimming happily in this cauldron of crackling rhythms. The pianist peculiarly reharmonizes—perhaps even shifts keys—on six bars of the first line of the ballad "Body and Soul" and hits the kicker, his composition "Promethean," hard and strong, ripping off boppish melodic and harmonic phrases as if child's play. Williams trades fours on "Promethean" and the bass-led feature for Coleman during "You and the Night and the Music"; he also busts out with his typical triplet and quadruplet fury for the solidly swinging, slightly reharmonized "On Green Dolphin Street." The trio also recapitulates the previously larger-ensemble Williams original "Neptune" in a more pensive, poised, Aquarian mode than the caravan processional of the earlier recording. Miller's extraordinary modal chord extrapolations at the end are stunningly beautiful. Although this might not be viewed by fans as typical of Tony Williams, it is a logical conclusion to a brilliant career in jazz, and holds up high the lofty improvisational values he kept close to his vest, but near to our hearts. Recommended. *—Michael G. Nastos*

Reuben Wilson

b. Apr. 9, 1935, Mounds, OK
Organ (Hammond), Keyboards, Organ / Hard Bop, Fusion, Soul-Jazz, Jazz-Funk
Reuben Wilson was one of only a handful of new soul-jazz organists to be signed to Blue Note in the late '60s. By that point in the label's history, most of their artists were concentrating on accessible soul-jazz, and Wilson more or less followed their rule. Between 1968 and 1971, he recorded five sessions for the label which didn't receive much acknowledgment at the time, but were later rediscovered by a new generation of soul-jazz and acid-jazz fans. A native of Mounds, Oklahoma, Wilson began performing professionally in 1962. In December 1966, Wilson relocated from L.A. to New York and landed a contract with Blue Note based on a demo. *On Broadway,* Wilson's first album, was recorded in October 1968; it was followed in March 1969 by *Love Bug.* His third album, *Blue Mode,* was cut in December 1969 and offered some of his hottest playing. 1970's *A Groovy Situation* moved in a commercial direction; July 1971's *Set Us Free* was his final album for the label. Wilson moved to Groove Merchant, where he released three albums during the mid-'70s. He also played on sessions by funk, soul and jazz artists, but eventually retired from music in the early '80s. By the late '80s, Wilson's sampled licks were appearing on dance floors throughout England and parts of New York; no longer dismissed as commercial fluff, his late-'60s and '70s records became cornerstones in the newly emerging acid-jazz and jazz-rap genres. Wilson decided to return to performing, and he toured with Guru's Jazzamatazz revue in 1995. He also began writing new material, and made the first of several new recordings in 1996. *—Stephen Thomas Erlewine*

Love Bug / Mar. 21, 1969-Oct. 31, 1969 / Blue Note ♦♦♦♦
Love Bug was an attempt to establish Reuben Wilson as an organist with either the vision of Larry Young or the fiery style of John Patton, and while it comes up short on both accounts, it nevertheless remains quite enjoyable. Working with an impressive backing band of guitarist Grant Green, trumpeter Lee Morgan, tenor saxophonist George Coleman and drummer Idris Muhammad, Wilson leads his band through a number of soul-jazz workouts, none of which ever really catch fire. Instead of working tight, funky grooves, the quintet tends to spiral off into vaguely experimental territory, which loses sight of the spirit of the song. Still, Green has a number of shining moments, as does Morgan and Coleman—in fact, they tend to overshadow Wilson, who nevertheless turns in a fine performance. Nevertheless, there are flashes on *Love Bug,* particularly on "Hot Rod" and the bonus track "Hold On, I'm Comin,'" that demonstrate the organist coming into his own. *—Stephen Thomas Erlewine*

● **Blue Mode** / Dec. 12, 1969 / Blue Note ♦♦♦♦♦
If *Love Bug* skirted the edges of free jazz and Black power, *Blue Mode* embraces soul-jazz and Memphis funk in no uncertain terms. Opening with the cinematic, stuttering "Bambu" and running through a set of relaxed, funky grooves, including covers of Eddie Floyd's "Knock on Wood" and Edwin Starr's "Twenty-Five Miles," *Blue Mode* isn't strictly a jazz album, but its gritty, jazzy vamps and urban soul-blues make it highly enjoyable. Reuben Wilson has a laid-back, friendly style, and his supporting band—tenor saxophonist John Manning, guitarist Melvin Sparks and drummer Tommy Derrick—demonstrating a similarly warm sense of tone. While none of them break through with any improvisations that would satiate hardcore jazz purists, they know how to work a groove, and that's what makes *Blue Mode* a winner. *—Stephen Thomas Erlewine*

Down with It / Jul. 14, 1998 / Cannonball ♦♦♦
Reuben Wilson's 30-year musical influence on the modern music scene is readily apparent on *Down With It.* Released in 1998 on the ultra-funky Cannonball label, Wilson's legend status is well deserved. Revered around the world as one of the pioneers of the Hammond B-3 organ sound, the "Godfather of Funk and Soul Jazz" continues to transplant his groove into the acid jazz movement. Unlike the previously released *Organ Donor,* Wilson does not revisit his classics "Hot Rod" and "Got to Get Your Own," but has written four new tunes on the set, including "One 2 Four," which reunites him with soul-jazz guitar pioneer Melvin Sparks. Pop and funk are taken to new heights on the title track, "Down With It," while Wilson's slow blues signature is stamped on "Speakin' With the Deacon." Wilson's mastery of the Hammond B-3 is in the pocket as the maestro continues to enjoy its renaissance and down-home funk. *—Paula Edelstein*

when he was 12. He had short stints with the orchestras of Alvino Rey and Sonny Dunham and played in a service band in the Coast Guard for three years. Winding's first burst of fame occured during his year with Stan Kenton's Orchestra (1946-47) during which his phrasing influenced and was adopted by the other trombonists, leading to a permanent change in the Kenton sound. He also participated in some early bop sessions, played with Tadd Dameron (1948-49) and was on one of the Miles Davis' nonet's famous recording sessions. After playing with the big bands of Charlie Ventura and Benny Goodman, he formed a quintet with J.J. Johnson (1954-56); the two trombonists (who sounded nearly identical at the time) had occasional reunions after going their separate ways. Winding led a four-trombone septet off and on through the latter half of the 1950s and into the '60s, was music director for the Playboy clubs in New York and during 1971-72 worked with the Giants of Jazz (an all-star group with Dizzy Gillespie, Sonny Stitt and Thelonious Monk). Although he recorded frequently both as a leader and a sideman throughout his career, most of Winding's sessions are not currently available on CD. *—Scott Yanow*

★ **Kai Winding, Jay Jay Johnson and Bennie Green with Strings** / May 13, 1952-Dec. 3, 1954 / Prestige/OJC ✦✦✦✦✦
Two unrelated session are combined on this CD reissue of an LP. Trombonist Bennie Green is heard on four ballads from 1952 while backed by a rhythm section and six strings. However the more significant selections are eight songs that for the first time matched together trombonists J.J. Johnson and Kai Winding in a quintet. The J.J. and Kai group would be quite popular during the next two years and, listening to the colorful and melodic versions of such tunes as "How Long Has This Been Going On," "Dinner for One" and "We'll Be Together Again," it is easy to see why. *—Scott Yanow*

Great Kai and J.J. / Nov. 9, 1960 / Impulse! ✦✦✦✦✦

The Incredible Kai Winding Trombones / Nov. 17, 1960-Dec. 13, 1960 / Impulse! ✦✦✦✦
After the J.J. Johnson-Kai Winding Quintet broke up in 1956, Kai Winding formed a four-trombone septet of his own which he led on a fairly regular basis through 1967. This long out-of-print Impulse LP was probably the group's best-known recording. Seven standards (including "Speak Low," "Doodlin'" and "Bye Bye Blackbird") and three of Winding's basic originals are played by the band with solos allocated not only to Kai but pianists Ross Tompkins and Bill Evans along with guest conga player Olatunji. Fine straightahead music obviously most enjoyed by listeners who like the sound of trombones. *—Scott Yanow*

Lionel Hampton Presents Kai Winding / Sep. 1, 1977 / Who's Who In Jazz ✦✦✦✦✦
Trombonist Kai Winding made relatively few quartet sessions throughout his career but this was his fourth of the 1974-1977 period. One of the few Who's Who LPs that did not have a guest appearance by vibraphonist Lionel Hampton, this outing by Winding features him in fine form with pianist Frank Strazzeri, bassist Kevin Brandon, and drummer Ted Hawke. Together they perform one original apiece by Winding and Strazzeri, plus six standards (highlighted by "Crazy She Calls Me," "Yardbird Suite," and "If I Didn't Care"). If this album was more widely available, it could serve as a strong introduction to Kai Winding's talents. *—Scott Yanow*

Phil Woods (Philip Wells Woods)

b. Nov. 2, 1931, Springfield, MA
Sax (Alto), Clarinet / Hard Bop, Bop
One of the true masters of the bop vocabulary, Phil Woods has had his own sound since the mid-1950s and stuck to his musical guns throughout a remarkably productive career. There has never been a doubt that he is one of the top alto saxophonists alive, and he has lost neither his enthusiasm nor his creativity through the years. Woods studied with Lennie Tristano, at the Manhattan School of Music, and at Juilliard, where he majored in clarinet. He worked with Charlie Barnet (1954), Jimmy Raney (1955), George Wallington, the Dizzy Gillespie Orchestra, Buddy Rich (1958-59), Quincy Jones (1959-61) and Benny Goodman (for BG's famous 1962 tour of the Soviet Union), but has mostly headed his own groups since 1955, including co-leadership of a combo with fellow altoist Gene Quill in the '50s logically known as "Phil & Quill." Woods was sometimes thought of as "the new Bird" due to his brilliance in bop settings, but he never really sounded like a copy of Charlie Parker. Discouraged with the jazz scene in the U.S., he moved to France in 1968. For the next few years, Woods led a very advanced group, The European Rhythm Machine, which leaned towards the avant-garde and included pianist George Gruntz. In 1972, he returned to the U.S. and tried unsuccessfully to lead an electronic group. In 1973, Woods formed a quintet with pianist Mike Melillo, bassist Steve Gilmore, drummer Bill Goodwin and guitarist Harry Leahey that had much greater success. Their recording *Live at the Showboat* officially launched the band which today, after a few personnel changes, still tours the world. *—Scott Yanow*

Early Quintets / Aug. 11, 1954-Mar. 3, 1959 / Prestige/OJC ✦✦✦✦
A pair of formerly rare quintet sets featuring altoist Phil Woods are combined on this CD reissue from the *OJC* series. One session was actually led by guitarist Jimmy Raney in 1954 (and also includes trumpeter John Wilson, bassist Bill Crow and drummer Joe Morello) while the other group (with trumpeter Howard McGhee, bassist Teddy Kotick and drummer Roy Haynes) was headed by pianist Dick Hyman in 1959. Both bop-oriented dates have their moments, with the edge going to Hyman's session. *—Scott Yanow*

Pairing Off / Jun. 15, 1956 / Prestige/OJC ✦✦✦✦
The title of this excellent CD reissue comes from the fact that the featured septet consists of two altos (Phil Woods and Gene Quill) and two trumpets (Donald Byrd and Kenny Dorham) in addition to a rhythm section (pianist Tommy Flanagan, bassist Doug Watkins and drummer Philly Joe Jones). Of the pairings, Woods and Dorham were more distinctive in 1956, but both Quill and Byrd get in some good licks. The full group stretches out on four lengthy numbers: three Woods originals and the ballad "Suddenly It's Spring." *—Scott Yanow*

The Young Bloods / Nov. 2, 1956 / Prestige/OJC ✦✦✦✦
For this early hard bop date, altoist Phil Woods and trumpeter Donald Byrd were co-leaders. In fact, the music had at one point earlier on been released with Byrd getting first billing. Since the spirited altoist contributed four of the six tunes (including "House of Chan" and "In Walked George") and consistently takes solo honors, it is only right that the date has finally been reissued on CD under Woods' name. With pianist Al Haig (who did not record that extensively during this period), bassist Teddy Kotick and drummer Charlie Persip offering stimulating accompaniment, this is an easily recommended release (despite its brief LP length) for straight-ahead jazz collectors. *—Scott Yanow*

Phil and Quill with Prestige / Mar. 29, 1957 / Prestige/OJC ✦✦✦✦
Altoists Phil Woods and Gene Quill always made for a mutually inspiring team. Both of the similar-sounding musicians were competitive, influenced by (but not imitative of) Charlie Parker, and really knew bebop. This CD reissue (which adds two selections from the same session that were originally part of the sampler *Bird Feathers*) features the two altoists in top form on six of Woods' obscure originals, plus "Airegin" and "Solar." The rhythm section (pianist George Syran, bassist Teddy Kotick and drummer Nick Stabulas) is tasteful and quietly supportive. *—Scott Yanow*

Sugan / Jul. 19, 1957 / New Jazz/OJC ✦✦✦✦
This CD from Fantasy's Original Jazz Classics series is essentially a bebop jam session. The quintet (altoist Phil Woods, trumpeter Ray Copeland, pianist Red Garland, bassist Teddy Kotick and drummer Nick Stabulas) performs three Charlie Parker compositions and three originals by Woods, but the melodies are quickly discarded in favor of heated solos. Woods and the greatly underrated Copeland work together very well, and Garland is a major asset both as a soloist and as an accompanist to the horns. This little-known date is quite enjoyable. *—Scott Yanow*

★ **Rights of Swing** / Jan. 26, 1960 / Candid ✦✦✦✦✦
This Candid recording is such a major success that it is surprising that altoist Phil Woods has rarely recorded in this context. The all-star octet not only features the altoist/leader but trumpeter Benny Bailey, trombonist Curtis Fuller, baritone saxophonist Sahib Shihab, the innovative French horn player Julius Watkins (a major factor in this music), pianist Tommy Flanagan, bassist Buddy Catlett, and drummer Osie Johnson. This set (reissued by Black Lion on CD) consists entirely of Woods' five-part "Rights of Swing" suite, which clocks in around 38 minutes. The colorful arrangements use the distinctive horns in inventive fashion and the music (which leaves room for many concise solos) holds one's interest throughout. One of Phil Woods' finest recordings, it's a true gem. *—Scott Yanow*

At the Montreux Jazz Festival / Jun. 18, 1969-Jun. 22, 1969 / Verve ✦✦✦✦

Musique Du Bois / Jan. 14, 1974 / 32 Jazz ✦✦✦✦✦
On *Musique Du Bois,* things start with a chorded bass-alto workout in the intro of "Samba du Bois", actually more a hard bop than Brazilian excursion, with Phil Woods' alto frying on the edges. The most inventive juxtaposition of "All Blues" welded to "Willow Weep for Me" works perfectly over ten-plus minutes, in a steady but quick waltz tempo. This is a tour-de-force reading, Woods wafting over Jaki Byard's blue-green chords. During his solo, the pianist goes light blue in cascading, flowing phrases that tumble out of the 88 keys. "Nefertiti" is vastly different than the Miles Davis-Wayne Shorter original; where that one was haunting, sparse, swelling and free, Woods interprets this as an easy swinger, anchored on terra firma with Byard's scurrying solo and funky R&B coda a listener's delight. The band goes through definite time shifts, from easy bluesy groove to funk and hard bop during "The Last Page"; they swing "Airegin" pretty well; and during "The Summer Knows," the altoist confirms what many have long since known—that he is an unsurpassed master when interpreting a standard in ballad form. A lilting alternate take of "Samba du Bois" is the more Latin-oriented one, same tempo but with drums and the trio introing and playing all the way through. This CD is a widely acknowledged modern jazz masterpiece, a classic in the discography of Woods, easily amongst the best five recordings of his long and storied career—and a must-buy. *—Michael G. Nastos*

European Tour Live / Nov. 12, 1980 / Red ✦✦✦✦✦
In one of the last performances by the Phil Woods Quartet before the departure of pianist Mike Melillo, this 1Ω-hour-plus concert finds the group at a creative peak. Woods isn't shy about stretching tunes out to explore every possibility with several long tracks; Lars Gullin's "Silhouette," a piece not likely familiar to many jazz fans, is a brilliant melancholy piece, with Woods' alto sax occasionally mimicking an accordion. "Rain Go Away" is a cheerful uptempo original by the leader, while his version of Joe Henderson's "Isotope" features a long introduction by drummer Bill Goodwin that sets the band afire. The only predictable part of the program is the almost obligatory beg-off performance of "Phil's Theme" (aka "How's Your Mama—"); listeners are then rewarded with an encore of Alec Wilder's delightful (but not often heard) "Trouble Is a Man." An enjoyable evening of hard bop by one of its true masters. *—Ken Dryden*

Phil Woods / Lew Tabackin / Dec. 10, 1980 / Evidence ✦✦✦✦✦
This album has such a logical matchup, it's surprising that it has not happened since. Altoist Phil Woods and tenor saxophonist Lew Tabackin (along with pianist Jimmy Rowles, bassist Michael Moore and drummer Bill Goodwin) are quite explosive on "Limehouse Blues," and display their ability to caress a ballad on a lengthy "Sweet And Lovely," and cook on Tadd Dameron's "Theme Of No Repeat" and three Woods originals. "Petite Chanson" finds Tabackin switching to flute while Woods brings out his clarinet. Everything on this recording works. *—Scott Yanow*

● **Bop Stew** / Nov. 1987 / Concord Jazz ✦✦✦✦✦
Phil Woods is in particularly inventive form throughout this live set from the 1987 *Fujitsu-Concord Jazz Festival.* Joined by his longtime quintet (with trumpeter Tom Harrell, pianist Hal Galper, bassist Steve Gilmore and drummer Bill Goodwin), the altoist stretches out on five selections, including a clarinet feature on "Poor Butterfly," and two of his originals. Galper's "Bop Stew" (which quotes several bop-era songs) is a highlight. Virtually every Phil Woods recording is easily recommended to modern mainstream jazz fans (he is one of the most consistent of all jazzmen), but this one seems even a touch more inspired than usual. *—Scott Yanow*

Teddy Wilson (Theodore Shaw Wilson)

b. Nov. 24, 1912, Austin, TX, **d.** Jul. 31, 1986, New Britain, CT
Piano / Swing

Teddy Wilson was the definitive swing pianist, a solid and impeccable soloist whose smooth and steady style was more accessible to the general public than Earl Hines or Art Tatum. He picked up early experience playing with Speed Webb in 1929 and appearing on some Louis Armstrong recordings in 1933. Discovered by John Hammond, Willie joined Benny Carter's band and recorded with the Chocolate Dandies later that year. In 1935 he began leading a series of classic small-group recordings with swing all-stars which on many occasions featured Billie Holiday. That was also the year that an informal jam session with Benny Goodman and Gene Krupa resulted in the formation of the Benny Goodman Trio (Lionel Hampton made the group a quartet the following year.) Although he was a special added attraction rather than a regular member of the orchestra, Wilson's public appearances with Goodman broke important ground in the long struggle against segregation. Between his own dates, many recordings with Benny Goodman's small groups and a series of piano solos, Teddy Wilson recorded a large number of gems during the second half of the 1930s. He left BG in 1939 to form his own big band but, despite some fine records, it folded in 1940. Wilson's style never changed and he played very similar in 1985 to how he sounded in 1935; no matter, the enthusiasm and solid sense of swing were present up until the end. *—Scott Yanow*

1934-1935 / May 22, 1934-Nov. 22, 1935 / Classics ♦♦♦♦♦
There have been several overlapping reissue programs covering the material in the Classics series, especially the many Teddy Wilson recordings in which the pianist accompanied Billie Holiday. This particular CD has Wilson's first five sessions as a leader. He is heard on four fairly rare piano solos from 1934 (a year before he became a member of the Benny Goodman Trio), six other solos from October 7 and November 22, 1935 and on two band dates that resulted in nine numbers (including seven Billie Holiday vocals); the sidemen include trumpeter Roy Eldridge, tenorman Ben Webster and (on three songs) clarinetist Benny Goodman. Lady Day's "What a Little Moonlight Can Do" and "I Wished on the Moon" are famous classics. *—Scott Yanow*

1935-1936 / Dec. 3, 1935-Aug. 24, 1936 / Classics ♦♦♦♦♦
The second CD in Classics' Teddy Wilson series features the definitive swing pianist on two piano solos and leading all-star groups. There are seven generally familiar Billie Holiday vocals (including classic renditions of "I Cried for You" and "These Foolish Things"), a pair from Ella Fitzgerald (her first recordings outside of the Chick Webb Orchestra), two rare ones from Helen Ward, a vocal by Roy Eldridge on a heated "Mary Had a Little Lamb" and seven instrumentals. The strong supporting cast includes such players as altoist Johnny Hodges, trumpeters Frankie Newton, Jonah Jones and Eldridge, trombonist Benny Morton, clarinetist Buster Bailey, tenorman Chu Berry and baritonist Harry Carney; Benny Goodman makes guest appearances on the two Helen Ward titles. Classic music although most of it is also easily available elsewhere. *—Scott Yanow*

1936-1937 / Aug. 24, 1936-Mar. 31, 1937 / Classics ♦♦♦♦♦
Swing collectors may very well find the Teddy Wilson series on Classics to be a bit troubling for, although it logically reissues all of the great swing pianist's recordings as a leader in order (skipping the alternate takes), many of the sides (those featuring Billie Holiday) are also available on Columbia's complete Lady Day program. This particular CD not only has 16 Holiday vocals (including "The Way You Look Tonight," "Pennies from Heaven," a version of "I Can't Give You Anything but Love" in which she shows off the influence of Louis Armstrong, and four wonderful titles from her first recorded meeting with tenor saxophonist Lester Young) but also three instrumentals and two rarities apiece from singers Red Harper and Midge Williams which are sure to frustrate completists. *—Scott Yanow*

☆ **And His All-Stars** / 1936-1940 / Columbia ♦♦♦♦♦
Pianist Teddy Wilson's most famous recordings of the 1930s as a leader are the ones in which he is joined by Billie Holiday, so it is a pleasure to have a double LP dominated by the lesser known—but often quite exciting—instrumentals performed by his all-star groups. Holiday is heard on six of these selections and Ella Fitzgerald on two others, but otherwise, the emphasis is on the hot soloing of such major swing stars as trumpeters Cootie Williams, Roy Eldridge, Jonah Jones, Frankie Newton, Buck Clayton, Harry James (heard at his best on "Just a Mood" and "Honeysuckle Rose"), and Bill Coleman, clarinetists Benny Goodman, Buster Bailey, and Pee Wee Russell, altoist Johnny Hodges, baritonist Harry Carney, and the tenors of Ben Webster and Chu Berry among others. This two-fer is well worth searching for. *—Scott Yanow*

1937 / Mar. 31, 1937-Aug. 29, 1937 / Classics ♦♦♦♦♦
For this Classics CD (one in a series of Teddy Wilson releases that reissue all of the pianist's early recordings as a leader), Billie Holiday is featured on nine of the titles including "I'll Get By," "Mean to Me," "Foolin' Myself" and "Easy Living"; all of those gems also feature tenor saxophonist Lester Young. Much rarer are three songs with singer Helen Ward, a vocal by Frances Hunt ("Big Apple"), three by the forgotten vocalist Boots Castle and five instrumentals. It is a pity that the selections without Holiday were not reissued separately since the Lady Day performances are generally quite common. Such immortal sidemen are heard from as Young, trumpeters Cootie Williams, Harry James and Buck Clayton, altoist Johnny Hodges, baritonist Harry Carney and clarinetists Buster Bailey and Benny Goodman; this music is essential in one form or another. *—Scott Yanow*

1937-1938 / Sep. 5, 1937-Apr. 28, 1938 / Classics ♦♦♦♦♦
This Classics CD traces pianist Teddy Wilson's recordings during a seven-month period. He backs singer Billie Holiday on eight memorable performances (including "My Man," "Can't Help Lovin' Dat Man," "When You're Smiling" and "I Can't Believe That You're in Love with Me"), is showcased on a pair of piano solos, accompanies singer Sally Gooding on four songs that were not initially released until the 1980s, and is heard on four almost-as-rare numbers with vocalist Nan Wynn. Most significant among the occasional instrumentals are a few tunes (including the two part "Just a Mood" and "Honeysuckle Rose") that Wilson performs in an exquisite quartet with trumpeter Harry James, xylophonist Red Norvo and bassist John Simmons. Among the other sidemen heard on this valuable CD are trumpeters Buck Clayton, Hot Lips Page and Bobby Hackett, clarinetist Pee Wee Russell, the tenors of Chu Berry and Lester Young and altoist Tab Smith. *—Scott Yanow*

And His Orchestra (1939) / Jan. 27, 1939-Sep. 12, 1939 / Classics ♦♦♦♦♦
This CD has quite a bit of variety. Teddy Wilson is featured on four of his better piano solos, backs Billie Holiday on one session (which resulted in superior versions of "More than You Know" and "Sugar" and has some fine solo space for altoist Benny Carter and trumpeter Roy Eldridge) and is heard on 13 selections with his new (and unfortunately short-lived) big band. The Teddy Wilson Orchestra was impeccable, tasteful and swinging (just like its leader) but, despite the presence of such soloists as trumpeter Harold "Shorty" Baker and tenor saxophonist Ben Webster, it never really stood a chance in the competitive swing world of 1939; the orchestra would only record eight additional titles. However the music on this CD is quite enjoyable and not as common as most of the recordings reissued by the Classics label. *—Scott Yanow*

★ **Central Avenue Blues** / 1948 / Vintage Jazz Classic ♦♦♦♦♦
Teddy Wilson was the definitive swing pianist, an influential stylist still best known for his association with Benny Goodman; however, Wilson had a long career after his years with Goodman. This CD mostly features him with his brilliant sextet of 1944-1945 which also includes trumpeter Charlie Shavers and vibraphonist Red Norvo playing concise versions of swing standards. Much of this music had previously been issued but never as complete as on this worthy set. Also here are three Wilson performances from a V-Disc session that features trumpeter $Joe Thomas *and clarinetist Edmund Hall and two other numbers in which the pianist is backed by a radio orchestra.* —Scott Yanow

The Complete Verve Recordings of the Teddy Wilson Trio / Dec. 16, 1952-Aug. 12, 1957 / Mosaic ♦♦♦♦
By 1952, Teddy Wilson's flawless swing style had already been fully formed for at least 17 years, and it would not change at all during the remaining three decades of his life. Wilson's performances were predictably excellent, but predictable nonetheless. This limited-edition five-CD set has all of the pianist's Verve trio recordings, which includes six-and-a-half former LPs (the half was an appearance at the 1957 *Newport Jazz Festival*), a set only released previously in Japan, and a live date that had never come out before. Wilson is teamed with bassists John Simmons, Aaron Bell, Arvell Shaw, Milt Hinton, Geme Ramey, and Al Lucas; and Buddy Rich, Denzil Best, J.C. Heard, Stick Evans, Jo Jones, Specs Powell, Roy Burnes, and Bert Dahlander in the drum slot. A version of "Sweet Georgia Brown" from *the Newport Festival* adds baritonist Gerry Mulligan. No real surprises occur, and the music, although quite pleasing, is best heard in small doses. *—Scott Yanow*

I Got Rhythm / Mar. 1956 / Verve ♦♦♦♦♦

Teddy Wilson & Gerry Mulligan at Newport / Jul. 6, 1957 / Verve ♦♦♦♦♦
Although in 1957 some listeners considered swing and cool jazz to be at the extreme poles of the jazz world, this LP, recorded at that year's *Newport Jazz Festival,* shows just how similar the two idioms were. The Teddy Wilson Trio (with bassist Milt Hinton and drummer Specs Powell) plays lightly swinging versions of four swing era standards and welcomes baritonist Gerry Mulligan to sit in on a spirited rendition of "Sweet Georgia Brown," and then Jeru's quartet (with trombonist Bob Brookmeyer, bassist Joe Benjamin, and drummer Dave Bailey) plays cooly exciting versions of "My Funny Valentine" and "Utter Chaos"; one could easily imagine Wilson helping out on those two songs. Strangely enough, this LP reissue of the original set also contains three standards by the Don Elliott Quartet with pianist Bill Evans, but never lists the full personnel (mellophonist Elliott, bassist Ernie Furtado, and drummer Al Beldini) or acknowledges the music in the liner notes. Worth acquiring anyway. *—Scott Yanow*

Masters of Jazz, Vol. 11 / Dec. 14, 1968-Jun. 15, 1980 / Storyville ♦♦♦♦♦
Storyville's *Masters of Jazz* series (which has since been reissued on CD) features swing stars playing material that has sometimes been released as part of other sets. In the case of Teddy Wilson, the two sessions that are included here are not on other releases. Wilson's swing piano style was unchanged through the years (at least since the mid-'30s) so these two dates (both recorded in Copenhagen) are equally rewarding, with fine backup from either Jesper Lundgaard or Niels Pedersen on bass and Ed Thigpen or Biarne Rostvold on drums. *—Scott Yanow*

☆ **With Billie in Mind** / May 1972 / Chiaroscuro ♦♦♦♦♦
The concept seemed so logical that it was surprising that no one else had thought of it earlier. Producer Hank O'Neal suggested to the veteran swing pianist Teddy Wilson that he record a set of Billie Holiday tunes since Lady Day had cut many of her greatest sides with Wilson in the 1930s. This solo CD, which was originally a 14-song LP, has been expanded with the release of six other solos cut at the same sessions. Wilson, who is in peak form, clearly enjoyed playing several tunes that he had not performed in years, and he is heard at the top of his game. Classic swing music. *—Scott Yanow*

● **The Best of Teddy Wilson & His Orchestra** / Oct. 7, 1935-Jul. 31, 1942 / Collectors' Choice Music ♦♦♦♦♦
The majority of the tracks on *Best of Teddy Wilson and His Orchestra* are actually recordings of Teddy Wilson's performances while he was in Benny Goodman's band. Nevertheless, it's an enjoyable selection of swing music from a great big band, half of which feature such all-but-forgotten vocalists as Nan Wynn and Boots Castle. The songs on this collection were all recorded for the Brunswick and Columbia labels between 1935 and 1942. *—Joslyn Layne*

Kai Winding

b. May 18, 1922, Aarhus, Denmark, **d.** May 6, 1983, Yonkers, NY
Trombone / Bop

One of the finest trombonists to emerge from the bebop era, Kai Winding was always to an extent overshadowed by J.J. Johnson although they co-led one of the most popular jazz groups of the mid-'50s. Born in Denmark, Winding emigrated to the U.S. with his family

Evolution / May 1988 / Concord Jazz ✦✦✦✦✦
This release is somewhat special for the Phil Woods Quintet (consisting of the altoist/leader, trumpeter Tom Harrell, pianist Hal Galper, bassist Steve Gilmore and drummer Bill Goodwin) is joined by trombonist Hal Crook (who would take Harrell's place in the near future), baritonist Nick Brignola and tenor saxophonist Nelson Hill to form the "Phil Woods Little Big Band." Woods contributed five of the eight songs (which are played along with selections from Crook, Jerry Dodgion and Miles Davis) and, since the chatty liner notes make no mention of it, chances are that he also wrote the colorful arrangements. The consistently inventive horn solos (which are often concise) and the telepathic communication by the rhythm section (which had been together for years) makes this a particularly notable release even among the dozens of excellent Phil Woods recordings. *—Scott Yanow*

Here's to My Lady / Dec. 20, 1988-Dec. 21, 1988 / Chesky ✦✦✦✦

All Bird's Children / Jun. 1990 / Concord Jazz ✦✦✦✦

Flowers for Hodges / 1991 / Concord Jazz ✦✦✦✦

Elsa / Jul. 31, 1991 / Philology ✦✦✦✦✦
Phil Woods' prolific recordings for the Italian label Philology (which is named in his honor) are always enjoyable; this duo concert with pianist Enrico Pieranunzi is no exception. The creativity of both men during a jaunty "Have You Met Miss Jones—" would be a difficult standard for any group to match during a live performance, yet the duo does just that, seemingly without effort. A very lyrical take of "September Song," followed by "Someday My Prince Will Come" (with a particularly dreamy introduction), Phil's well-known gritty arrangement of "Willow Weep for Me," and a spacy take of the classic "You and the Night and the Music" all prove to be equally compelling. The alto saxophonist also revisits "Goodbye Mr. Evans," his touching elegy to pianist Bill Evans. Pieranunzi contributes two memorable numbers: "Night Bird," a piece also featured on Phil Woods & the Space Jazz Trio's earlier Philology CD *Phil's Mood*, and "Chet," a moody yet warm tribute to Chet Baker (with whom he recorded on Baker's final studio album). Hopefully, there will be many more collaborations involving these two greats. *—Ken Dryden*

The Rev and I / Jan. 10, 1998-Jan. 11, 1998 / Blue Note ✦✦✦✦✦

Reggie Workman (Reginald Workman)

b. Jun. 26, 1937, Philadelphia, PA
Bass / Avant-Garde Jazz, Hard Bop
Reggie Workman has long been one of the most technically gifted of all bassists, a brilliant player whose versatile style fits into both hard bop and very avant-garde settings. He played piano, tuba and euphonium early on but settled on bass in the mid-'50s. After working regularly with Gigi Gryce (1958), Red Garland and Roy Haynes, he was a member of the John Coltrane Quartet for much of 1961, participating in several important recordings and even appearing with Coltrane and Eric Dolphy on a half-hour West German television show that is currently available on video (*The Coltrane Legacy*). After Jimmy Garrison took his place with Coltrane, Workman became a member of Art Blakey's Jazz Messengers (1962-64) and was in the groups of Yusef Lateef (1964-65), Herbie Mann and Thelonious Monk (1967). He recorded frequently in the 1960s (including many Blue Note dates and Archie Shepp's classic *Four for Trane*).

Since that time Workman has been both an educator (serving on the faculty of music schools including the University of Michigan) and a working musician, and has played with numerous legendary jazz musicians including Max Roach, Art Farmer, Mal Waldron, David Murray, Sam Rivers and Andrew Hill (Rivers and Hill joined Workman for the 1993 session, *Summit Conference*). In the 1980s, Workman began leading his own group, the Reggie Workman Ensemble. He also began a collaboration with pianist Marilyn Crispell that lasted into the next decade (the two acclaimed musicians reunited for a festival performance in 2000). During the '90s, Workman was not only active with his own ensemble, but also in Trio Three with Andrew Cyrille and Oliver Lake and Reggie Workman's Grooveship and Extravaganza.

In recognition of Reggie Workman's international performances and recordings spanning over 40 years, he was named a Living Legend by the African-American Historical and Cultural Museum in his hometown of Philadelphia; he is also a recipient of the Eubie Blake Award. *—Scott Yanow & Joslyn Layne*

Synthesis / Jan. 31, 1989-Jul. 1989 / Leo ✦✦✦

Summit Conference / Dec. 5, 1993-Dec. 6, 1993 / Postcards ✦✦✦✦✦
For this inspired 1994 date, veteran bassist Reggie Workman assembled four fellow avant-garde luminaries: pianist Andrew Hill, saxophonist Sam Rivers, trombonist Julian Priester, and drummer Pheeroan akLaff. By the usual standards of these highly adventurous players, the record is relatively accessible, but it does makes for challenging listening. The quintet opens with "Encounter," a busy and bold selection by the late John Carter. Overall, only Workman's "Summit Conference" and Priester's "Breath" feature sustained periods of cacophony, yet even these freer pieces are built around a defined melody and structure. Sonelius Smith's "Conversation" and Rivers' "Solace" bump along with Latin rhythms; Priester shines on both tracks. The trombonist is also the dominant voice on Rivers' fast-swinging "Meteor." Rivers plays soprano sax on Workman's "Estelle's Theme" and flute on Hill's "Gone," the latter a duet with Hill that closes the session on an austere yet calming note. *—David R. Adler*

● **Cerebral Caverns** / Apr. 27, 1995-Apr. 28, 1995 / Postcards ✦✦✦✦✦

Altered Spaces / Feb. 1992 / Leo ✦✦✦✦

World Saxophone Quartet

f. 1977
Group / Avant-Garde Jazz, Free Jazz, Avant-Garde
Probably the first of several saxophone-only ensembles that proliferated in jazz after 1975, the WSQ is unquestionably the most commercially (and, arguably, the most creatively) successful. Of course, commercial success is a relative thing in jazz, especially when you're speaking of an avant-garde group. But unlike most free jazz artists, the WSQ managed to attract an audience of significant size; the band did it on merit, too, with only a hint of compromise (manifested mainly by albums of R&B and Duke Ellington covers). By the time of its first record for Elektra/Musician in 1986, the band had evolved from its fire-breathing, free-improvising, ad-hoc beginnings into a smooth-playing, compositionally-minded, well-rehearsed band. All of the group's original members (Julius Hemphill, Oliver Lake, David Murray, Hamiet Bluiett) were estimable composers as well as improvisers.

Founded in 1976, after the four original members (all of them well-established solo artists) accepted an offer to conduct a series of clinics and performances. In 1977, the band recorded its first album, an almost completely improvised effort called *Point of No Return*. Later releases on Black Saint document the band's increasing interest in composition. The membership stayed constant until Hemphill's departure in 1989. Arthur Blythe was the first of Hemphill's several replacements (he was replaced by James Spaulding, Eric Person and later, John Purcell). After 1986's *Rhythm & Blues*, the WSQ began using other musicians on its recordings and performances, though in adding other musicians, the band sacrificed something of its distinctiveness. By the end of the '90s, the WSQ had lost its major-label deal and its much of its identity. *—Chris Kelsey*

Steppin' With / Dec. 1978 / Black Saint ✦✦✦✦✦
The second recording by The World Saxophone Quartet (which follows by a year their Moers Music release *Point of No Return*) gives one a well-rounded look at this powerful group. Comprised of altoist Julius Hemphill (who contributes four of the six group originals), altoist Oliver Lake, tenorman David Murray and baritonist Hamiet Bluiett, the explorative yet rhythmic group is heard in their early prime on this stimulating release. *—Scott Yanow*

W.S.Q. / Mar. 1980 / Black Saint ✦✦✦✦
There is plenty of variety to the third album by the unique World Saxophone Quartet. The music ranges from nearly free improvisations to the four-part "Suite Music," which was almost completely written out. Rather than being a screamfest for the four innovative saxophonists (baritonist Hamiet Bluiett, altoists Julius Hemphill and Oliver Lake and tenor saxophonist David Murray, all of whom double on other reeds), this is a well constructed and sometimes surprisingly accessible (although always explorative) program. *—Scott Yanow*

Live in Zurich / Nov. 6, 1981 / Black Saint ✦✦✦✦✦
By 1981, after four years of existence, it was obvious that the most talented writer in the World Saxophone Quartet was altoist Julius Hemphill. This Black Saint release finds Hemphill contributing six of the eight pieces (the other two are by Hamiet Bluiett), including the hard-swinging "Bordertown," the colorful "Steppin" and a vivid feature for David Murray's tenor on "My First Winter." A particularly strong release by a classic and innovative group. *—Scott Yanow*

★ **Plays Duke Ellington** / Apr. 1986 / Elektra/Nonesuch ✦✦✦✦✦
On their first six recordings, the World Saxophone Quartet (comprised of altoists Oliver Lake and Julius Hemphill, tenor saxophonist David Murray and baritonist Hamiet Bluiett) stuck exclusively to group originals. This 1986 release was a major departure, for the innovative group performed fresh and generally unpredictable versions of five songs by Duke Ellington and two (including two renditions of "Take the 'A' Train") by Billy Strayhorn. Although the tunes (which include "Lush Life," "Sophisticated Lady" and "In a Sentimental Mood") are familiar, the interpretations are certainly unusual, showing respect for the original melodies and then coming up with new directions. This is thought-provoking music that serves as the perfect introduction to the unique World Saxophone Quartet. *—Scott Yanow*

Rhythm & Blues / Nov. 1988 / Elektra ✦✦✦✦✦
With tunes such as "Let's Get It On," "(Sittin' On) The Dock of the Bay," "Try a Little Tenderness" and "Night Train" being included, this CD certainly qualifies as one of the most unusual of all the World Saxophone Quartet recordings. Far from being a sellout to commercialism, this set features the WSQ (altoists Julius Hemphill and Oliver Lake, tenor saxophonist David Murray and baritonist Hamiet Bluiett) meeting the six soul and R&B tunes (which are joined by three complementary originals) head on. The WSQ was always open to playing rhythmically and was not allergic to strong melodies while including solo and group improvisations that were quite advanced. The combination works quite well on this surprising success. *—Scott Yanow*

Moving Right Along / Oct. 18, 1993-Oct. 19, 1993 / Black Saint ✦✦✦✦✦
This title applies to The World Saxophone Quartet's personnel as well as its music. Charter residents David Murray, Oliver Lake and Hamiett Bluiett were joined by special guest James Spaulding on two tracks, making it a quintet, and throughout by new member Eric Person. Person's composition "Antithesis," like several other selections, represented a change in the group's approach. Instead of their hallmark collectively improvised unison passages, most numbers had one or two featured soloists, with the others operating as harmony/contrast players. The WSQ did its usual array of material, from bubbling R&B and funk-tempered numbers to hard bop and swing-oriented tunes, plus two stirring renditions of "Amazing Grace." *—Ron Wynn*

Breath of Life / Apr. 1992-Sep. 1992 / Elektra/Nonesuch ✦✦✦✦
This is the second World Saxophone Quartet disc to feature alto saxophonist Arthur Blythe (who replaced Julius Hemphill) and the first to feature a full rhythm section including bass, piano, and organ. Going a step further from the previous year's experiment with African drums on *Metamorphosis*, *Breath of Life* continues to find the sax quartet stretching the boundaries associated with its a cappella approach of the past. Included on its final release for the Elektra Nonesuch label are rhythm & blues-influenced originals by David Murray, Oliver Lake, and Hamiet Bluiett. The Quartet also pays tribute to Ray Charles, Little Willie John, and James Brown on "You Don't Know Me" and "Suffering With the Blues," featuring gospel-inspired performances by Fontella Bass (vocals), Donald Smith (organ), and Amina Claudine Myers (piano and organ). *—Al Campbell*

Selim Sevad: A Tribute to Miles Davis / Mar. 2, 1998-Mar. 3, 1998 / Justin Time ✦✦✦✦

M'Bizo / Nov. 10, 1997-Jun. 18, 1998 / Justin Time ✦✦✦✦

This is an unusual recording for the World Saxophone Quartet. Famous for being an *a cappella* saxophone band (which at the time consisted of David Murray on tenor and bass clarinet, Hamiet Bluiett on baritone, bass sax and contrabass clarinet, altoist Oliver Lake and John Purcell on saxello), the famous band is joined on this tribute to South Africa by a couple of different rhythm sections, many percussionists and quite a few singers in a vocal ensemble. Despite all of the extra musicians and vocalists, the WSQ does not get lost in the crowd. The music (the three part "M-Bizo Suite," "Snapapo" and "Matshidiso"), which was composed by *Murray,* is often jubilant and celebratory. The singers and percussionists add to the party atmosphere which even when remembering the dark days of apartheid, sounds quite hopeful and optimistic. Well worth exploring. *—Scott Yanow*

Requiem for Julius / 1999 / Justin Time ✦✦✦✦

Though much of the World Saxophone Quartet's music has been mindful of the contributions of founding member Julius Hemphill, it is on *Requiem for Julius* where that debt is acknowledged formally. There are the obligatory R&B, straight blues, or bebop lines here and there, but it's mainly the collective improvisational expertise of John Purcell, David Murray, Oliver Lake, and Hamiet Bluiett pushing the envelope of structure, rhythm, and tonal timbres. Alto saxophonist Lake's sour sound is as much his own as it is influenced by Hemphill, and he composed three selections that reflect this sonority. "Le Sport Suite" displays loose, scattershot improvisation and a unison strut in the middle. "Potato Vamp" is buoyed by Murray's bass clarinet, and is very tunefully contained. "Tone Poem" perfectly reflects the cadence of spoken word, with its spatially organized phrases arranged in chamber fashion. Purcell's "All Praise" carries a more sedate, patient, even reverent, improvisational mood. The Bluiett-penned "Free & Independent Thought" is exactly as the title states, but in a lower-keyed stance. Murray composed two numbers. The title track, supported by a processional framework replete with Hemphill's sweet/sour signature, is led by Purcell's soprano sax, sporting a very melodic center with a stretched harmonic edge. The 11-minute "Hurricane Floyd" is furiously intense, as the quartet tosses in several distinct melody lines throughout. Also revisited is Jack DeJohnette's "Ebony," with its familiar pussycat traipsing/moaning and juggernaut triple-melody lines. A long-overdue official farewell for Hemphill, *Requiem for Julius* not only harkens back to the sound of WSQ's initial recordings, but indicates that they have plenty of original music left in the tank. *—Michael G. Nastos*

The Yellowjackets

f. 1981

Group / Smooth Jazz, Crossover Jazz, Fusion

Although sometimes grouped with Spyro Gyra, the Yellowjackets are actually one of the most creative regular groups in the "rhythm and jazz" genre. Founded in 1981 as an R&B-oriented band that starred guitarist Robben Ford, the group took a giant step forward when after Ford's departure, altoist Marc Russo took his place. With original members Russell Ferrante on keyboards and electric bassist Jimmy Haslip in addition to drummer William Kennedy, the band found its own R&Bish sound, sometimes playing original compositions that sounded like Joe Zawinul at his most melodic. In recent times Russo chose to go out on his own and his replacement Bob Mintzer (on tenor and bass clarient) has added more jazz credibility to the group's music. Through the years the Yellowjackets have continued to evolve, sacrificing their popularity a bit by refusing to be overly predictable. They have recorded for Warner Brothers, MCA, GRP and Warner Bros. *—Scott Yanow*

Four Corners / 1987 / MCA ✦✦✦✦✦

Like a River / Apr. 1992 / GRP ✦✦✦✦✦

Other than the easy-listening pieces that appear near the beginning of the program, this is one of The Yellowjackets' strongest jazz dates. Bob Mintzer's creative reeds (switching between tenor, bass clarinet, soprano and the EWI) keep the music stimulating and keyboardist Russell Ferrante has come a long way as both an improviser (where he is most influenced by Herbie Hancock) and as the band's main composer. With bassist Jimmy Haslip and drummer William Kennedy in strong supporting roles, the ensemble plays intelligent funk grooves, some mood music and occasional sections of straightahead jamming. The inclusion of the Miles Davis-influenced trumpeter Tim Hagans on half of the selections adds variety to a particularly enjoyable set. *—Scott Yanow*

Run for Your Life / 1993 / GRP ✦✦✦✦✦

This is one of The Yellowjackets' most jazz-oriented sets. Roughly half of the music uses funky rhtyhyms while the remainder is straightahead. "Jacket Town" sounds like it could have come from a good Eddie Harris record, Bob Mintzer's tenor is heard on a rapid run-through of rhythm changes on "Runferyerlife," keyboardist Russell Ferrante hints strongly at Chick Corea's acoustic playing on "Muhammed" and Mintzer's ballad "Sage" is memorable. This fine release is recommended both to The Yellowjackets' longtime fans and those listeners who mistakenly think that this popular group is a mundane fusion band. *—Scott Yanow*

Dreamland / 1994 / Warner Brothers ✦✦✦✦✦

Perhaps the finest recording of this quartet's illustrious career, *Dreamland* captures Yellowjackets at the peak of their compositional and performing craft. This band has moved far beyond its peers with this release. The music here is simply intoxicating, full of gorgeous melodies, deceptively intricate changes, subtle rhythmic and harmonic nuances, and flawless playing. Because of the consistency of the music, it is impossible to point out high spots. Bobby McFerrin has never sounded better than on his guest appearance on "Summer Song," but it's the high level maintained by the four Jackets throughout the disc that especially entrances the listener here. This is a *Dreamland* where any connoisseur of quality music will find delight and quiet satisfaction. *—Jim Newsom*

● **The Best of Yellowjackets** / Dec. 14, 1999 / Warner Brothers ✦✦✦✦

Larry Young (Khalid Yasin Abdul Aziz)

b. Oct. 7, 1940, Newark, NJ, **d.** Mar. 30, 1978, New York, NY

Organ (Hammond), Organ / Hard Bop, Post-Bop, Fusion, Soul-Jazz

If Jimmy Smith was "the Charlie Parker of the organ," Larry Young was its John Coltrane, fashioning a distinctive modal approach to the Hammond B-3 at a time when Smith's earthy, blues-drenched soul-jazz style was the instrument's dominant voice. After playing with various R&B bands in the 1950s and being featured as a sideman with tenor saxman Jimmy Forrest in 1960, Young debuted as a leader that year with *Testifying,* which, like his subsequent soul-jazz efforts for Prestige, *Young Blues* (1960) and *Groove Street,* (1962), left no doubt that Smith was his primary inspiration. But when Young went to BlueNote in 1964, he was well on his way to becoming a major innovator. Coltrane's post-bop influence asserted itself more and more in Young's playing and composing, and his work grew much more cerebral and exploratory. *Unity,* recorded in 1965, remains his best-known album. Quick to embrace fusion, Young played with Miles Davis in 1969, John McLaughlin in 1970 and Tony Williams' groundbreaking Lifetime in the early 1970s. Unfortunately, his work turned uneven and erratic as the '70s progressed. Young was only 38 when, in 1978, he checked into the hospital suffering from stomach pains, and died from untreated pneumonia. *—Alex Henderson*

Testifying / Aug. 2, 1960 / New Jazz/OJC ✦✦✦

Organist Larry Young was 19 when he made this, his debut recording. Although he would become innovative later on, Young at this early stage was still influenced by Jimmy Smith, even if he had a lighter tone; the fact that he used Smith's former guitarist, Thornel Schwartz, and a drummer whose name was coincidentally Jimmie Smith kept the connection strong. R&B-ish tenor Joe Holiday helps out on two songs, and the music (standards, blues and ballads) always swings. Easily recommended to fans of the jazz organ. *—Scott Yanow*

Young Blues / Sep. 30, 1960 / New Jazz/OJC ✦✦✦✦✦

Organist Larry Young's second recording (cut shortly before he turned 20) is the best from his early period before he completely shook off the influence of Jimmy Smith. With guitarist Thornel Schwartz in top form, and bassist Wendell Marshall and drummer Jimmie Smith excellent in support, Young swings hard on a few recent jazz originals, some blues and two standards ("Little White Lies" and "Nica's Dream"). Recommended as a good example of his pre-Blue Note work. *—Scott Yanow*

Groove Street / Feb. 27, 1962 / Prestige/OJC ✦✦✦

Larry Young's third and final Prestige recording (reissued in the *OJC* series on CD) concludes his early period; he would next record as a leader two and a half years later on Blue Note, by which time his style would be much more original. For his 1962 outing, Young is joined by the obscure tenor Bill Leslie, guitarist Thornel Schwartz and drummer Jimmie Smith for some original blues and two standards ("I Found a New Baby" and "Sweet Lorraine"). Nothing all that substantial occurs, but fans of Jimmy Smith will enjoy the similar style that Larry Young had at the time. *—Scott Yanow*

☆ **Complete Blue Note Recordings** / Sep. 11, 1964-Feb. 7, 1969 / Mosaic ✦✦✦✦✦

Larry Young, one of the most significant jazz organists to emerge after the rise of Jimmy Smith, is heard on this limited-edition six-CD set at the peak of his creativity. Formerly available as nine LPs, the set includes the original Larry Young albums *Into Somethin', Unity, Of Love and Peace, Contrasts, Heaven on Earth,* and *Mother Ship,* while drawing from the compilations *40 Years of Jazz, The History of Blue Note* (Dutch), *The World of Jazz Organ* (Japanese), and *The Blue Note 50th Anniversary Collection Volume Two: The Jazz Message,* and also including guitarist Grant Green's *Talkin' About, Street of Dreams,* and *I Want to Hold Your Hand.* Young was still very much under Smith's influence on the first four sessions released as *Talkin' About, Into Somethin', Street of Dreams,* and *I Want to Hold Your Hand* (all featuring a trio with Green and drummer Elvin Jones plus guests Sam Rivers or Hank Mobley on tenor and vibraphonist Bobby Hutcherson). However, starting with the monumental *Unity* session (a quartet outing with Joe Henderson on tenor, trumpeter Woody Shaw, and Jones), Young emerged as a very advanced and original stylist in his own right. Young's final four dates (*Of Love and Peace, Contrasts, Heaven on Earth,* and *Mother Ship*) are generally pretty explorative and feature such notable sidemen as altoist James Spaulding and Byard Lancaster, guitarist George Benson, and trumpeter Lee Morgan along with some forgotten local players. This definitive Larry Young set is highly recommended. *—Scott Yanow*

Into Somethin' / Nov. 12, 1964 / Blue Note ✦✦✦✦✦

Larry Young, who like most organists originally sounded close to Jimmy Smith, took a big step away from the organ's dominant influence on this adventurous and colorful set, which was his debut as a leader for Blue Note. Performing with a quartet also including tenor saxophonist Sam Rivers, guitarist Grant Green and drummer Elvin Jones, Young performs four of his originals plus Green's "Plaza De Toros." Other than the blues "Backup," the music is fairly complex, grooving in its own fashion and showing that Young was quite aware of John Coltrane's modal excursions. *—Scott Yanow*

★ **Unity** / Nov. 10, 1965 / Blue Note ✦✦✦✦✦

This is a classic album, the finest of organist Larry Young's career. On this date (a quartet outing with trumpeter Woody Shaw, tenor saxophonist Joe Henderson, and drummer Elvin Jones), Young emerged as the first original voice on the organ since Jimmy Smith. Young keeps up with his illustrious sidemen on three Shaw originals (best known is "The Moontrane"), Henderson's "If," "Monk's Dream," and the standard "Softly As in a Morning Sunrise." The performances grow in interest with each listen and find all of the musicians inspired by each other and by the high-quality material. A gem. *—Scott Yanow*

Lester Young

b. Aug. 27, 1909, Woodville, MS, **d.** Mar. 15, 1959, New York, NY

Sax (Tenor), Clarinet / Mainstream Jazz, Swing, Cool

Lester Young was one of the true jazz giants, a tenor saxophonist who came up with a completely different conception in which to play his horn, floating over bar lines with a light tone rather than adopting Coleman Hawkins' then-dominant forceful approach. A nonconformist, Young (nicknamed "Pres" by Billie Holiday) had the ironic experience in the 1950s of hearing many young tenors try to sound exactly like him. Pres first made history during his years with Count Basie, not only participating on Count's record dates but starring with Billie Holiday and Teddy Wilson on a series of classic small group sessions. In addition on his rare recordings on clarinet with Basie and the Kansas City Six, Young displayed a very original cool sound that almost sounded like altoist Paul Desmond in the 1950s. After leaving Count in 1940, Young's career became a bit aimless, not capitalizing on his fame in the jazz world. He co-led a low-profile band with his brother drummer Lee Young in Los Angeles until rejoining Basie in December 1943. Young had a happy nine months back with the band, recorded a memorable quartet session with bassist Slam Stewart and starred in the short film *Jammin' the Blues* before he was drafted. His experiences dealing with racism in the military were horrifying, affecting his mental state of mind for the remainder of his life. Although many critics have written that Lester Young never sounded as good after getting out of the military, despite erratic health he actually was at his prime in the mid-to-late '40s. Nearly 40 years after his death, Pres is still considered (along with Coleman Hawkins and John Coltrane) one of the three most important tenor saxophonists of all time. *— Scott Yanow*

☆ **The Complete Aladdin Sessions** / Jul. 15, 1942-Dec. 29, 1948 / Blue Note ♦♦♦♦♦
Although it has often been written that the cool-toned tenor saxophonist Lester Young's experiences with racism in the military during 1944-1945 so scarred him that he never played at the same musical level as he had previously, the music on this essential two-CD reissue disproves that theory. It is true that his attitude toward life was affected and Young became somewhat self-destructive, but his postwar solos rank with the greatest work of his career. This two-fer, which has four selections from 1942 in which Young is heard in a trio with pianist Nat "King" Cole and bassist Red Callender and a rare 1945 session headed by singer Helen Humes (including a previously unknown instrumental "Riffin' Without Helen"), is mostly taken up with Young's very enjoyable 1945-1948 small-group dates. Highlights include "D.B. Blues," "Jumpin' With Symphony Sid" (which was a minor hit), "Sunday," and "New Lester Leaps In," among many others. Minor errors aside (trumpeter Snooky Young is left out of the personnel listing for the Humes date and Young's final Aladdin session is from 1948, not 1947), this is a well-conceived and brilliant set filled with exciting performances by one of the true greats of jazz. *— Scott Yanow*

☆ **The Complete Lester Young on Keynote** / Dec. 28, 1943-Mar. 22, 1944 / Verve ♦♦♦♦♦
This CD has two classic sessions featuring the great tenor saxophonist Lester Young. He is heard with the Kansas City Seven, a small group taken from the Count Basie Orchestra (which he had recently rejoined) and consisting of trumpeter Buck Clayton, trombonist Dicky Wells, pianist Basie, guitarist Freddie Green, bassist Rodney Richardson and drummer Jo Jones. The full group plays three jump pieces (plus three alternate takes), but the high point of the session is Prez's romp with the rhythm section, trading off with Basie on "Lester Leaps Again." However, that date is actually overshadowed by the four numbers (plus four alternate takes) that Young performed with pianist Johnny Guarnieri, bassist Slam Stewart and drummer Sid Catlett on Dec. 28, 1943. "I Never Knew" and "Afternoon of a Basie-ite" are heated jams, and "Just You, Just Me" is definitive, but it is "Sometimes I'm Happy" (especially the originally released version) that is truly memorable. The charming Slam Stewart solo (singing along with his bass) is only surpassed by Prez's absolutely perfect improvisation, which has been quoted many times by later jazz musicians. Highly recommended. *— Scott Yanow*

Master Takes / Apr. 18, 1944-Jun. 28, 1949 / Savoy ♦♦♦♦♦
Lester Young recorded for Savoy three separate times in four different settings. On Apr. 18, 1944 he performed as part of the Count Basie Orchestra (although Basie himself was absent) for three numbers and then cut four more songs with a septet that included trumpeter Billy Butterfield and pianist Johnny Guarnieri. A few weeks later he was featured on four selections in front of the Count Basie rhythm section. Prez made his final Savoy appearance in 1949, fronting a young sextet that also included pianist Junior Mance and drummer Roy Haynes. All of those performances are included on this CD minus the many alternate takes which can be heard (along with this entire program) on *The Complete Savoy Recordings*. *— Scott Yanow*

Lester Swings / Dec. 1945-Mar. 8, 1951 / Verve ♦♦♦♦♦
In selecting a little over an hour's worth of excerpts from the eight-CD box set *The Complete Lester Young Studio Sessions on Verve* for this highlights disc, the compilers have resisted the urge to stick with only a collection of Young's more accomplished early works and included a few examples of his deteriorated, but still moving, later work. They have hedged their bets somewhat, however, by not sequencing things chronologically, so that the album closes with a 1949 recording of the pop song "Polka Dots and Moonbeams" rather than, say, "Waldorf Blues" from 1958. Early or late, Young's playing is readily identifiable, if only for the chances it takes, whether on the up-tempo "It Don't Mean a Thing (If It Ain't Got That Swing)" or the strikingly excessive introductory blowing on the opening phrases of "Love Is Here to Stay." Young's associates on the tracks constitute a who's who of his contemporaries, including Ray Brown, Nat "King" Cole, Hary "Sweets" Edison, Roy Eldridge, Herb Ellis, Hank Jones, Jo Jones, Connie Kay, John Lewis, Oscar Peterson, Buddy Rich, and Teddy Wilson. While it takes more than an hour to get a full sense of Young's work on Verve (hence the box set), this is an intelligently constructed sampler. *— William Ruhlmann*

● **Prez Conferences (1946-1958)** / Mar. 20, 1946-1958 / Jass ♦♦♦♦♦
The great tenor Lester Young is heard in a variety of different settings on this CD, chiefly taken from radio and television broadcasts. The best performances find Prez playing two songs with the Nat "King" Cole Trio and drummer Buddy Rich in 1946, jamming three standards with trumpeter Buck Clayton and fellow tenor Coleman Hawkins, sitting in with the Count Basie Orchestra in 1952, and performing three numbers with the Bill Potts Trio in 1956. Throughout this very interesting set, Lester Young is in excellent form, making this an excellent introductory CD for listeners not already familiar with Prez's music, and a bonus for collectors who will probably not already have most of these rare performances. *— Scott Yanow*

Compact Jazz: Lester Young & the Piano Giants / Mar. 1946-Jan. 12, 1956 / Verve ♦♦♦

☆ **Pres and Teddy and Oscar** / Aug. 4, 1952-Jan. 13, 1956 / Verve ♦♦♦♦♦
It has been said so often that Lester Young's playing declined after his terrible experience in the Army during World War II that it has almost become unanimously accepted as fact. Only trouble is that many of his recordings dispute that theory. In reality, although Young's health declined gradually throughout the 1950s (until his death in 1959), his solos were often at a high level. This two-LP set contains two of the great tenor's finest recordings, a set with the Oscar Peterson Quartet in 1952 and a reunion with Teddy Wilson in a trio in 1956. Young's performances of "All of Me," "Prisoner of Love," "Just You, Just Me," and melodic renditions of seven straight ballads (the latter from the date with Oscar Peterson) rank with some of the finest work of his career. Essential music for all jazz collections. *— Scott Yanow*

★ **With the Oscar Peterson Trio** / Aug. 4, 1952 / Verve ♦♦♦♦♦
Defying what has become conventional wisdom, tenor saxophonist Lester Young (when he was reasonably healthy) actually cut some of his greatest recordings in the 1950s. On this wonderful effort with pianist Oscar Peterson, guitarist Barney Kessel, bassist Ray Brown and drummer J.C. Heard, Prez performs definitive versions of "Just You Just Me" and "Tea for Two" and plays a string of concise but memorable ballad renditions: "On the Sunny Side of the Street," "Almost Like Being in Love," "I Can't Give You Anything but Love," "There Will Never Be Another You" and "Confessin'." The 1997 CD reissue augments the original dozen songs with a version of the good-humored "It Takes Two to Tango" (which feature Young's only recorded vocals) and has a rather unnecessary false start ("I Can't Get Started") along with some studio chatter. Essential music. *— Scott Yanow*

Blue Lester / Apr. 18, 1944-Jun. 28, 1949 / Savoy Jazz ♦♦♦♦♦

☆ **The Jazz Giants '56** / Jan. 12, 1956 / Verve ♦♦♦♦♦
Even critics who feel (against the recorded evidence to the contrary) that little of tenor-saxophonist Lester Young's postwar playing is at the level of his earlier performances make an exception for this session. Young was clearly inspired by the other musicians (trumpeter Roy Eldridge, trombonist Vic Dickenson, pianist Teddy Wilson, guitarist Freddie Green, bassist Gene Ramey and drummer Jo Jones), which together made for a very potent band of swing all-stars. The five songs on this album include some memorable renditions of ballads and a fine version of "You Can Depend on Me," but it is the explosive joy of the fiery "Gigantic Blues" that takes honors. This set, a real gem, is highly recommended. *— Scott Yanow*

☆ **Pres and Teddy** / Jan. 13, 1956 / Verve ♦♦♦♦♦
Although it has been written much too often that Lester Young declined rapidly from the mid-'40s on, the truth is that when he was healthy, Young played at his very best during the 1950s, adding an emotional intensity to his sound that had not been present during the more carefree days of the '30s. This classic session, a reunion with pianist Teddy Wilson and drummer Jo Jones (bassist Gene Ramey completes the quartet), finds the great tenor in particularly expressive form. His rendition of "Prisoner of Love" is quite haunting, the version of "All of Me" is also memorable and all of the swing standards (which are joined by his original "Pres Returns") are well worth hearing. This date (which has been reissued on CD) was recorded the day after Young's other classic from his late-period, *Jazz Giants '56*. *— Scott Yanow*

Lester Young in Washington, D.C., 1956, Vol. 2 / Dec. 3, 1956-Dec. 9, 1956 / Pablo/OJC ♦♦♦♦♦
The second installment of four projected volumes, this once again captures latter-day Lester Young in top form, relaxed and playing with impeccable phrasing and swing. Ably backed by the Bill Potts Trio during his week-long stand at Olivia's Patio Lounge in Washington, these live tapes put the lie to the longstanding jazz myth that Young was well past his prime in the final decade of his life.

If anything, this second volume captures even more adventurous playing by Prez, with fast paced takes on his "Jumpin' With Symphony Sid" and "Lester Leaps In." But, as always, Young positively shines on midtempo and ballad material like "Three Little Words," "I'm Confessin' (That I Love You)," "These Foolish Things" and "Almost Like Being In Love." Lester shares much of the soloing space with all three members of the trio, and his swapping of four-bar phrases with drummer Jim Lucht can get a little wearing on repeated listens, but the group provides such a comfortable cushion for him to relax and stretch out that it's a minor niggle at best. This also includes Young's only known full-length treatment of "Lullaby of Birdland," almost worth the price of admission alone. Nobody could swing like Lester Young, and given the right setting and circumstances like he was on these dates, he was evidently swinging right to the end. *— Cub Koda*

Lester Young in Washington, D.C., 1956, Vol. 3 / Dec. 3, 1956-Dec. 9, 1956 / Pablo/OJC ♦♦♦♦♦
This third volume furthers explores the marvelous cache of tapes that have surfaced from Lester Young's 1956 engagement at *Olivia's Patio Lounge* in Washington, D.C. With the swinging but unobtrusive Bill Potts Trio, he provides the same empathetic support heard on the other volumes in this set, always playing the right changes without overt bop embellishments just for the sake of embroidery. Potts soloing is always in the pocket and his comping behind drummer Jim Lucht and bassist Norman Williams is equally fine and telling in what it leaves out. By laying down a simple beat with simple chord changes, you can actually hear Prez loosen up with each chorus, digging in and finding fresh ideas even in tunes that he had played hundreds of times over. This volume features swinging, finger-snapping versions of "Just You, Just Me," "Sometimes I'm Happy," and the bluesy "G's, If You Please," which sports the same intro as "Up 'n' Adam" until Lester comes in and starts taking it into new territory. A blazingly fast take of "Indiana" rounds out this excellent package. *— Cub Koda*

Lester Young in Washington, D.C., 1956, Vol. 4 / Dec. 3, 1956-Dec. 9, 1956 / Pablo/OJC ♦♦♦♦♦
The final volume of this four-volume chronicling of Prez' stand at *Olivia's Patio Lounge* in 1956 is no less fine than its preceding three volumes. Everything here is stretched out to a comfortable length, everybody is taking their time, giving the music plenty of room to breathe and most importantly, giving Young all the time he needs to get deep inside the mu-

sic itself. Nice readings of the ballad "I Cover the Waterfront," "Talk of the Town" and a swinging "Pennies from Heaven" are the big tickets here, imbued with an economy from Bill Potts' Trio that perfectly frames Young's flights of fancy. Fine alternate performances of "I'm Confessin' That I Love You," "Almost Like Being In Love," "G's, If You Please" and "D.B. Blues" (Lester's blues with a bridge that King Pleasure put words to) complete the set, a series that every jazz fan should have in their collection and one that no Lester Young fan can afford to be without. *—Cub Koda*

Laughin' to Keep from Cryin' / Feb. 8, 1958 / Verve ♦♦♦♦
One of tenor-saxophonist Lester Young's final studio sessions (he died a year later), this date apparently had a lot of difficulties but the recorded results are excellent. Prez was joined by two great swing trumpeters (Roy Eldridge and Harry "Sweets" Edison) and a fine rhythm section for two standards, two originals and the ballad "Gypsy in My Soul." Young takes rare clarinet solos on two of the selections with his emotional statement on "They Can't Take That Away from Me" being one of the highpoints of his career. Recommended. *—Scott Yanow*

☆ **The Kansas City Sessions** / Mar. 16, 1938-Mar. 27, 1944 / GRP ♦♦♦♦♦
This is a CD overflowing with classic performances. The great Lester Young is heard with the 1938 version of the Kansas City Six, a group also including trumpeter Buck Clayton (in prime form), Eddie Durham on electric guitar (where he preceded Charlie Christian) and trombone, the rhythm guitar of Freddie Green, bassist Walter Page and drummer Jo Jones The four selections (all of which are joined by an alternate take apiece) are most notable for Young's switching to clarinet on some of the pieces. His clarinet solo on "I Want a Little Girl" sounds eerily like Paul Desmond's alto of 15 years later. These classic cool jazz performances have delightful interplay between the two horns. The second part of the reissue features the 1944 Kansas City Six in which Young (sticking to tenor) and trumpeter Bill Coleman are joined by a three-piece rhythm section and trombonist Dickie Wells. Wells, who takes some very colorful and nearly riotous solos, rarely sounded better, and the four selections are highlighted by three equally rewarding versions of "I Got Rhythm" and two of "Three Little Words." The CD concludes with the four titles by 1938's Kansas City Five, which was essentially the early Kansas City Six without Young. Clayton is once again in top form, and Durham's guitar solos were among the first worthwhile examples of the electric guitar on record. This gem is highly recommended for all jazz collections. *—Scott Yanow*

Joe Zawinul

b. Jul. 7, 1932, Vienna, Austria
Piano (Electric), Keyboards, Piano / Hard Bop, Fusion, Soul-Jazz, World Fusion
Joe Zawinul belongs in a category unto himself—a European from the heartland of the classical music tradition (Vienna) who learned to swing as freely as any American jazzer, and whose appetite for growth and change remains insatiable. Zawinul's curiosity and openness to all kinds of sounds made him one of the driving forces behind the electronic jazz-rock revolution of the late '60s and '70s—and later, he would be almost alone in exploring fusions between jazz-rock and ethnic music from all over the globe. He is one of a bare handful of synthesizer players who actually learned how to play the instrument, to make it an expressive, swinging part of his arsenal. Prior to the invention of the portable synthesizer, Zawinul's example helped bring the Wurlitzer and Fender-Rhodes electric pianos into the jazz mainstream. Zawinul also has become a significant composer, ranging (like his idol Duke Ellington) from soulful hit tunes to large-scale symphonic-jazz canvases. Yet despite his classical background, he now prefers to improvise compositions spontaneously onto tape, not writing them out on paper. *—Richard S. Ginell*

● **The Rise & Fall of the Third Stream** / 1965 / Vortex ♦♦♦♦♦
The Rise & Fall Of The Third Stream featured Zawinul on acoustic and electric piano, where his funky, gospel and blues-drenched solos provided welcome relief in a setting where the large orchestra's arrangements were often ponderous and overly dense. *—Ron Wynn*

The Rise & Fall of the Third Stream/Money in the Pocket / 1965-Dec. 12, 1967 / Rhino ♦♦♦♦♦
Two of keyboardist Joe Zawinul's finest recordings as a leader were reissued on this single CD. The *Money in the Pocket* album from 1965 features Zawinul on acoustic piano in a sextet with trumpeter Blue Mitchell, tenor saxophonist Joe Henderson, and baritone saxophonist Pepper Adams playing superior hard bop, highlighted by the funky title cut, "If," and "My One and Only Love." The other session utilizes a string quartet, trumpeter Jimmy Owens, and the tenor and arrangements of William Fischer. Its diverse music hints at fusion (Zawinul doubles on electric piano) and has many colorful moments. This gem of a CD is highly recommended. *—Scott Yanow*

Zawinul / Aug. 6, 1970-Aug. 12, 1970 / Atlantic ♦♦♦♦
Conceptually, sonically, this is really the first Weather Report album in all but name, confirming that Joe Zawinul was the primary creative engine behind the group from the beginning. It is also the link between WR and Miles Davis' keyboard-laden experiments on *In a Silent Way;* indeed, the tune "In a Silent Way" is redone in the more complex form in which Zawinul envisioned it, and Miles even contributes a brief, generous tribute to Joe on the liner. Two keyboardists—Zawinul and the formidable Herbie Hancock—form the underpinning of this stately, probing album, garnishing their work with the galactic sound effects of the Echoplex and ring modulator. Earl Turbinton provides the Wayne Shorter-like beams of light on the soprano sax, spelled by Wayne himself on "Double Image." The third founder of WR, Miroslav Vitous, checks in on bass, and hard-bopping trumpeter Woody Shaw proves to be perfectly adept at the jazz-rock game. Two short-lived standards of the jazz-rock era, the aforementioned "Double Image" and "Doctor Honoris Causa," are introduced here, yet it is mood pieces like "His Last Journey" and "Arrival in New York" that with the help of tape-speed manipulation, establish the lasting, murky, reflective ambience of this CD. *—Richard S. Ginell*

★ **Dialects** / Jun. 1986 / Columbia ♦♦♦♦♦
If Joe Zawinul was out to prove that he didn't need Weather Report anymore, he succeeded spectacularly in this virtual one-man show. Zawinul recorded many of the vocals (assisted now and then by Bobby McFerrin and a vocal trio) and all of the synthesizers and rhythm machine tracks himself in his Pasadena home studio, yet the results are anything but mechanical. Zawinul in fact achieves a rare thing; he manages to get his stacks of electronics to swing like mad in these pan-global grooves that pick up where WR was about to leave off. "Waiting for the Rain" generates a ribbon of tension and anticipation, while "Zeebop" is a noisy rush of pure adrenaline. And "Carnivalito" is a total gas, a percolating, outrageously joyous evocation of a carnival that would put the world's best percussion players out of business if Zawinul's swinging talent could be bottled and sold. This is an important, overlooked album because it proves that electronic instruments can reach your emotions and shake your body when played by someone who has bothered to learn how to master them. *—Richard S. Ginell*

Lost Tribes / 1992 / Columbia ♦♦♦♦
Now reduced in size to a quintet (dropping the extra percussionist), Zawinul's Syndicate delivers its most overtly political album—or shall we say, its most anti-political album with its forget-our-differences, one-world tone poems. If *Lost Tribes* sounds more like a Weather Report album than its Syndicate predecessors, it may be because the CD is loaded with Zawinul's uncanny impersonations of Wayne Shorter on his Pepe synthesizer. Yet the album also cuts down on the pop and straight jazz strains of yore as it explores the sounds and grooves of world music, and Zawinul also resumes using introductory sound collages that produce effects not unlike twisting a short-wave radio dial. The record begins powerfully with the circulating, tense "Patriots"—depicting, oddly enough, the role of black soldiers in the Persian Gulf War—and segues into the relaxed, swinging "South Africa," a celebratory sequel to "Black Water" with vocals by Perri. Bass player Gerald Veasley contributes a track called "San Sebastian" which comes very close to pure flamenco. This CD ranks above the other Syndicate Columbias because it is emotionally deeper; Zawinul allows himself to brood and ponder as well as party. *—Richard S. Ginell*

My People / 1992-1996 / Escapade Music ♦♦♦♦♦
If one must indulge in categories, *My People,* featuring the Zawinul Syndicate and a United Nations coterie of guests, probably belongs on the vast world music shelf, the links to so-called jazz now so tenuous as to be nearly, but not quite, invisible. On the percolating "Slivovitz Trail," "Orient Express," "Many Churches," and the Caribbean-tinged cleverly-titled "In an Island Way," the music does suggest earlier versions of the Syndicate and Zawinul's nostalgic evocations of Wayne Shorter on the Korg Pepe reach back even further. Otherwise, Zawinul is looking entirely toward ethnic cultures for musical sustenance. The musical structures are linear, the rhythms full of intricacies welded to Zawinul's love affair with the groove, the synthesizer textures usually sparer than ever. There are vocals in several languages by Zawinul's longtime colleague Salif Keita (for whom Zawinul produced a great album in 1991), Syndicate percussionist Arto Tuncboyaciyan, a throat vocal specialist from South Siberia named Bolot, Thania Sanchez, Zawinul himself and several others. When translated, the lyrics speak of joy and unity among the cultures, and there isn't any doubt that Zawinul's bubbling music feeds the message of uplift. Hear it; you purists may be jiggling along in spite of yourselves. *—Richard S. Ginell*

World Tour / May 17, 1997-Nov. 13, 1997 / Zebra ♦♦♦♦♦
This version of The Zawinul Syndicate could swing harder than any Zawinul-led unit since the heyday of Weather Report, as this two-CD set—taken from three concerts in Berlin and Trier, Germany—triumphantly illustrates. Small wonder, for the lineup of the Syndicate looks almost like a Weather Report alumni gathering, with Zawinul, the brilliant percussionist Manolo Badrena from the 1977 *Heavy Weather* band, and bassist Victor Bailey, from the great '80s global-funk edition forming a quorum, with Paco Sery on drums and Gary Poulson on guitar filling out the ranks. Zawinul remains a marvel at 65, always in touch with the idea and feel of the groove, weaving spare, enigmatic electronic comments and spangled layers of synthesizers into the mix, creating a touching dialogue in "Zansa II" with Sery's kalimba. Some of the material stems from the early years of the Syndicate, and "Indiscretions" and "Two Lines" date all the way back to Weather Report. Among the greatest groovathons—at last presented in full glorious concert length on CD—are "Indiscretions," which gets the voodoo going in an insinuating manner, and "N'awlins," which manages to evoke the Crescent City R&B feeling in a swingingly original way. The set's two anomalies are "When There Was Royalty," a curious intermezzo consisting of Joe's polystylistic solo piano musings poorly recorded in his home studio on a Walkman; and "Success," a spoken poem by Erich Fried set against the stunning blend of Berlin church bells and electronics. For a souvenir of the state of Zawinul's art in the 1990s, this is the album to get. *—Richard S. Ginell*

John Zorn

b. Sep. 2, 1953, New York, NY
Sax (Alto), / Improvisation,, Jewish Music, , Avant-Garde Jazz,, Film Music,, Soundtracks,, Free Jazz, , 20th Century Classical/Modern Composition, , Post-Bop,, Avant-Garde,,
[See John Zorn's main entry in the Avant Garde section]

Yankees / 1984 / Charly ♦♦♦♦

● **The Big Gundown: John Zorn Plays the Music of Ennio Morricone** / Sep. 1984-Sep. 1985 / Tzadik ♦♦♦♦♦
On this intriguing concept album, altoist John Zorn (who also "sings" and plays harpsichord, game calls, piano, and musical saw) utilizes an odd assortment of open-minded avant-garde players (with a couple of ringers) on nine themes originally written for Italian films by Ennio Morricone, plus his own "Tre Nel 5000." These often-radical interpretations (which Morricone endorsed) keep the melodies in mind while getting very adventurous. Among the musicians heard on the colorful and very eccentric set (which utilizes different personnel and instrumentation on each track) are guitarists Bill Frisell and Vernon Reid, percussionist Bobby Previte, keyboardist Anthony Coleman, altoist Tim Berne, pianist Wayne Horvitz, organist Big John Patton, and even Toots Thielemans on harmonica and whistling among many others. There are certainly no dull moments on this often-riotous program. *—Scott Yanow*

Voodoo: The Music of Sonny Clark / Nov. 25, 1985-Nov. 26, 1985 / Black Saint ♦♦♦♦♦
This unusual album is an unlikely success. Altoist John Zorn, who is best-known for his avant-garde flights and rather eccentric concept albums, here plays it fairly straight. He interprets seven compositions (all fairly obscure) by the somewhat forgotten hard bop pianist Sonny Clark including "Cool Struttin'," "Voodoo" and "Sonny's Crib." With alert support from pianist Wayne Horvitz, bassist Ray Drummond and drummer Bobby Previte, Zorn creates fairly boppish solos with occasional hints at more advanced improvising techniques. Worth checking out. *—Scott Yanow*

Classic Guide to Strategy / 1985 / Tzadik ♦♦♦
The Classic Guide to Strategy, Volumes One & Two presents two Zorn albums from the mid-'80s which have long been out of print. Featuring a variety of manipulated saxophones, clarinets, and duck calls, the album plays at the edges of sounds traditionally associated with reed instruments. The album is not entirely accessible, especially *Volume One*?if it were produced by a college student sowing his experimental oats after a giddy term at *BAM*, it would probably be labeled a failure for its eccentricity, abruptness, and lack of a coherent theme. However, when a line is drawn through Zorn's previous work, it ends up here—the playfulness of sound, the variety of textures, the use of silence and space as part of the composition—if the listener approaches this album expecting to find musical genius, he or she will not have to look too far. Zorn manufactures the sounds of animals, voices, squeaks, scraps of melodic lines, drowning (or at least dampened) beasts, and cartoon worlds with his reeds, paying homage to the work of Carl Stalling, as well as the sounds of Anthony Braxton and Evan Parker. The first two tracks on this collection represent the original volume one; the last five belonged to the original volume two. Stylistically, they are similar, with the second volume containing less spacial breaks between the musical bursts and each song paying tribute to avant-garde Japanese artists like Mori Ikue, Enoken, Kondo Toshinori, Katsumi Shigeru, Aoyama Michi, and Togawa Jun. *—Stacia Proefrock*

☆ **News for Lulu** / Aug. 30, 1987 / hatHUT ♦♦♦♦♦
Avant-garde altoist John Zorn teams up with trombonist George Lewis and guitarist Bill Frisell to form a unique trio. Without the benefit of piano, bass, or drums, they interpret the hard bop compositions of Kenny Dorham, Hank Mobley, Sonny Clark, and Freddie Redd, generally not even the better-known ones. The performances are quite concise (Dorham's "Windmill" is covered in 40 seconds), respectful to the melodies, and unpredictable. There are hints of the avant-garde here and there, but also plenty of swinging, bop-oriented solos and coherent ensembles. Very intriguing music that is highly recommended to a wide audience of jazz and general listeners. *—Scott Yanow*

More News for Lulu / Jan. 18, 1989-Jan. 19, 1989 / hatART ♦♦♦♦♦

● **Torture Garden** / 1989-1990 / Shimmy Disc ♦♦♦♦
From the violent cover art to the Japanese text inside the album, at first glance one might mistake *Torture Garden* for a fetishist soundtrack. But jazz madman John Zorn and Boredoms frontman Yamatsuka Eye assembled another group of open-minded musicians to carry on their vision of grindcore and jazz uniting. Distinguished musicians Wayne Horovitz and Bill Frisell help Zorn and Eye take this from a curious side project to a fantastic metal band. Songs blur together but never get boring, no lyrics are actually sung, and few songs last longer than a minute. It also never takes itself seriously, a nice relief from Zorn's heavy-handed ambient collaborations. This would make a great introduction to the noise/jazz efforts that this group of musicians pioneered in the early '90s. *—Bradley Torreano*

Black Box: Torture Garden/Leng Tch'e / 1992 / Tzadik ♦♦♦♦

Kristallnacht / 1993 / Tzadik ♦♦♦♦♦
This release documents an intense musical representation of *Kristallnacht*, or the Night of Broken Glass, a coordinated attack on Jews throughout the German Reich that occurred on November 9, 1938, during which Nazis, SS members, and Hitler youth broke into Jewish homes and businesses, assaulting the people and their property. The official German report tallied 7,500 businesses destroyed, 267 synagogues burned (with 177 totally destroyed), and 91 Jews killed. John Zorn has created a musical work that powerfully represents the different stages of this historical event. "Shtetl (Ghetto Life)" is beautiful yet apprehensive klezmer, interspersed with sound bites of German rallies and speeches that become more frequent, increasingly crowding the life from the music. This segues into "Never Again," which, Zorn warns in the liner notes, "contains high frequency extremes at the limits of human hearing and beyond, which may cause nausea, headaches and ringing in the ears." While nearly unbearable, it is a fitting sound representation of *Kristallnacht*, as thousands of layers of shattering glass assault the ears. "Never Again" is both effective and affecting, if you can listen. This onslaught is followed by the loud silence and emptiness of "Gahelet (Embers)", a walk through the immediate aftermath of wind, darkness, and destruction. Alley echoes are heard as sound is overwhelmed by a dread and horror beyond expressing, and no words can contain what might begin to form in the midst of shock. This is a heavy silence. Strings have gone haggard on the next composition, and from this point the album becomes less literal and explicit, moving away from poignancy and focus into more chaos. Zorn's forceful undertaking is realized through the expert and passionate musicianship of violinist Mark Feldman, guitarist Marc Ribot, keyboardist Anthony Coleman, bassist Mark Dresser, and percussionist William Winant, as well as guest trumpeter Frank London and clarinetist David Krakauer. *—Joslyn Layne*

● **Execution Ground** / Nov. 15, 1994 / Subharmonic [Ltd. Edition] ♦♦♦♦♦
A trio consisting of alto saxophonist John Zorn, bassist Bill Laswell,and drummer Mick Harris, Painkiller was a novel blend of free improv, jazz, dub, and death metal. Although the lineup occasionally expanded to include the uniquely gifted Japanese vocalist Yamantaka Eye and other guests, *Execution Ground* is an investigation of the power and range of the core trio. The first disc of this inventive and unsettling two-disc set features three long improvisations that show off the band's dub influence. The second disc, subtitled "Ambient Dub," is a rethinking/remix of the third and first improvs on the first disc. Overall less thrashy than some Painkiller excursions, the improvisations here are striking for their greater sonic space without sacrificing any of the heaviness. At times, the band rests, making way for ominous breathing and distant sustained screams, which recur throughout. The transitions from silence to groove to noise and back are relentless and dramatic. Harris proves to be an astonishingly inventive drummer, consistently varying the foundation in surprising ways. Laswell's tone varies from the brightness of flanged round-wound strings scraping the frets to a clean, menacing low-frequency pulse, and sticks mostly to elemental, non-flashy lines that keep the mood deep and dark. Zorn's playing is excellent here, varying between extremely overblown piercing tones (perhaps the best way of being heard over such a rhythm section) and nearly conventional jazzy lines that confidently ride atop the din. An occasional microtonal chorus effect warps his playing, and the effect is so disturbing that it's surprising he soon abandoned this technique. *—Maurice Rickard*

Masada, Vol. 3: Gimel / Mar. 28, 1995 / DIW ♦♦♦♦♦

Elegy / Oct. 1995 / Tzadik ♦♦♦♦♦
A mysterious, elegant, exotic tone poem built around Jean Genet's image relating flowers and prisoners. There are four parts entitled *Blue, Yellow, Pink* and *Black*. A constantly changing soundscape of images—sweet, tortured, folk ceremony, hellishly cosmic, dungeon sounds of chains and locks, breathing and much more—highlighted by silences. Brilliantly evocative. With Barbara Chaffe, alto and bass flutes, David Abel, viola, Scummy, guitar, David Shea, turntables, David Slusser, sound effects, William Winant, percussion, and Mike Patton, voice. —"Blue" Gene Tyranny

Masada, Vol. 5: Hei / Nov. 21, 1995 / DIW ♦♦♦♦

Bar Kokhba / Aug. 20, 1996 / Tzadik ♦♦♦♦♦
Bar Kokhba encompasses the wealth of material John Zorn has composed with his eminent quartet Masada. The album is a collection of Masada songs that have been rearranged for chamber ensembles. For this effort, Zorn enlists some of New York's finest musicians: John Medeski, Marc Ribot, Anthony Coleman, and Erik Freedlander, among others. The compositions range from groups of four to solo performances by Ribot, Medeski, and Coleman. While some compositions retain their original structure and sound, some are expanded and probed by Zorn's arrangements, and resemble avant-garde classical music more than jazz. But this is the beauty of the album; the ensembles provide a forum for Zorn to expand his compositions. The album consistently impresses, and the highlights include "Gevurah," "Paran," and "Mochin." Zorn's genius as both songwriter and arranger are evidenced, and the recording sits well among the traditional Masada material. *—Marc Gilman*

Film Works, Vol. 5: Tears of Ecstasy / Nov. 19, 1996 / Tzadik ♦♦♦

● **Film Works, Vol. 3** / Mar. 18, 1997 / Tzadik ♦♦♦♦
The third volume cataloguing John Zorn's film scores is a quality release that offers the scores from two films, a rare piece of music cues that would lead to *Cynical Hysterie Hour*, and music spots for commercials. First comes the 1993 score for *Thieves Quartet*, which is warm, solid, smoky jazz written with Miles Davis' *Escalator to the Scaffold* soundtrack in mind. This score also marks the first recording of the quartet that would later be known as Masada. Combining musicians of the highest caliber and compatibility, this strong first outing gives full indication of the rapport between bassist Greg Cohen, trumpeter Dave Douglas, drummer Joey Baron and Zorn. Guitarist Robert Quine also guests on the closer, "End Titles." The track of music sketches for Japanese cartoonist Kiriko Kubo, "Music for Tsunta (nine cues)," separates the two film scores. Following this track is the score from 1994, for L.A. filmmaker Mei-Juin Chen's *Hollywood Hotel*. This recording joins a long, impressive list of Zorn's sax collaborations with electric guitarists that includes Eugene Chadbourne, Henry Kaiser, Derek Bailey, and Keiji Haino. Here is his saxophone duo with exemplary guitarist Marc Ribot; Ribot most often provides fabric and rhythm for Zorn's solos, in addition to his crucial role in a few atmospheric and a few splurtey pieces. The remaining 31 tracks on the album are shorts composed for a commercial advertising firm with which Zorn had an excellent and open working relationship. The musicianship and stylistic range found here is commendable. The reed and brass-less instrumentation varies between tracks, as guitarists Arto Lindsay, Quine, and Ribot provide a strong front, seamlessly relaxed in southwestern and surf. *—Joslyn Layne*

Film Works, Vol. 7: Cynical Hysterie Hour / Aug. 19, 1997 / Tzadik ♦♦♦
Cynical Hysterie Hour is John Zorn's music for four animated shorts by Japanese cartoonist Kiriko Kubo. Bursts of TV rock, synth whistles & barks, banjo licks, and sound effects intensify the caffeinated jumping through genre hoops of this slick and cinematically silly music. Clocking in at 25 minutes, this CD's value lies in that (1) it is Zorn's first venture into cartoon music, which he has long revered, and (2) it was in print on Sony for merely months in 1990, before being yanked out of print, making it the most sought-after rarity of Zorn's recordings. In late 1996, Zorn finally attained the rights for his music, and remastered and rereleased the album on his own label, Tzadik. *—Joslyn Layne*

Film Works, Vol. 4: S&M / 1997 / Tzadik ♦♦♦

Film Works, Vol. 8 / Feb. 17, 1998 / Tzadik ♦♦♦♦♦
Film Works 8 contains the scores for two films. First is music for *The Port of Last Resort*, a documentary about the Jewish refugees who fled to Shanghai from 1930s Nazi Germany. The music is a continuation of the Masada Chamber project, elegant klezmer jazz of as high a worth as *Bar Kokhba* or *Circle Maker* (the other two releases drawing from the Masada songbook that are not performed by the quartet). The Masada String Trio—violinist Mark Feldman, cellist Erik Friedlander, and bassist Greg Cohen—is joined by guitarist Marc Ribot, pianist Anthony Coleman, and pipa virtuoso Min Xiao Fen. The second half of this release is film music for *Latin Boys Go to Hell*, whose final edit, incidentally, barely used the music heard here. The low-key music of this score, with wind chime trances and pieces with a subtle tribal low-end, is performed entirely by the excellent percussionists Cyro Baptista and Kenny Wolleson. The sophisticated music of *Film Works 8* stands apart for its cosmopolitan assuredness, high level of musicianship, and beauty. *—Joslyn Layne*

★ **Circle Maker** / Mar. 17, 1998 / Tzadik ♦♦♦♦♦
This two-disc release captures beautiful and refined music that makes full use of the en-

sembles' extraordinary musicianship. Drawing from John Zorn's *Masada* songbook are the Masada String Trio and the Bar Khokba Sextet. Each ensemble fills one CD with beautiful chamber jazz woven around a heart of Jewish melodies. Superb and elegant music, Zorn skeptics will find the music on *Circlemaker* surprisingly stable and accessible. This is a fitting successor to the other *Masada* works that Zorn doesn't actually perform on—the first *Masada* chamber project, *Bar Khokba*, and *Film Works, Vol. 8*, whose recording session wrapped up weeks before this weekend date of December 1997. Issachar is the name of the disc on which bassist Greg Cohen, cellist Erik Friedlander, and violinist Mark Feldman perform. Zevulun is the *Bar Khokba* sextet: the Masada String Trio plus drummer Joey Baron, percussionist Cyro Baptista, and guitarist Marc Ribot. All of these musicians are accomplished in jazz and improvised music, and have performed extensively in world and/or classical settings, as well. *Circlemaker* is a very necessary recording for all appreciaters of chamber jazz, new Jewish music, or any of these stellar musicians. *—Joslyn Layne*

Bribe / Sep. 15, 1998 / Tzadik ✦✦✦✦✦
John Zorn's *Bribe* is a continuation and extension of his album *Spillane*. Like its predecessor, this album features almost the same line-up of extraordinary NYC improvisers including pianist Anthony Coleman, drummer Bobby Previte, organist Wayne Horvitz, turntablist Christian Marclay, and harpists Zeena Parkins and Carol Emanuel. Unlike the fast-spliced pace of *Spillane*, which functioned as its own narrative, the music on *Bribe* is allowed to stretch and develop because it was composed as a background for the dialogue in three 30-minute radio plays by Terry O'Reilly (it was later adapted to a stage production). O'Reilly described his creation as "low art; " along the lines of little respected categories such as pulp fiction and B-movies. Zorn then constructed appropriate music, continually switching styles and filling it with pop references. The overall mood of *Bribe* is also different from *Spillane* and much of Zorn's work (excluding *Film Works, Vol. 7*), in that it maintains a light-hearted approach, weaving music box chimes and carnival sounds into the music. A nicer mood pervades this release, yet given its kaleidoscopic and slightly demented tone, it certainly can't be described as relaxed. Then again, maybe "relaxed" isn't too far off, after all—perhaps by playing a supporting role to the production's cast instead of driving the concept, the musicians were able to enjoy themselves a little more. *—Joslyn Layne*

Masada: Live in Jerusalem / Apr. 20, 1999 / Tzadik ✦✦✦✦✦

★ **Godard/Spillane** / Jul. 20, 1999 / Tzadik ✦✦✦✦✦
"Godard" and "Spillane" were the two first (and purest) examples of the "file card" composition technique developed by John Zorn and inspired by theater director Richard Foreman. The compositions were constructed from independent scraps of music inscribed on file cards; the two principal works here called for assembly of the cards ("Spillane" used 60 cards within roughly 25 minutes) to create compositions within the conceptual frame of work by *Mickey Spillane* and Jean-Luc Godard. The goal was to translate imagery from Godard's films and *Spillane's* crime novels (and probably the films based on those novels) into unified compositions. Bits of text weave through musical fragments including gentle lounge piano, spacy electronic music, violent sonic crashes, and dive-bar jazz. Ironically, "Godard" and "Spillane" both work as unified compositions because they are made of fragments. The ideas of the filmmaker and the writer would have been too complex to be tackled by an overblown, operatic score; such a work could only scratch the surface of a few of their ideas without seeming disjointed. But Zorn's file card snippets bounce around like thoughts, overlapping and intruding on each other, reversing direction like a changed mind. Careful selection and arrangement make all the snippets seem essential and irreplaceable, despite their remarkable diversity. This album's execution is aided by a truly impressive cast of supporting musicians, whose close relationships with Zorn made it possible for the musical nuances to be communicated through interpersonal interaction. As a result, every piece sounds like a pure fragment of its genre instead of mere imitation. Perhaps most impressive were the contributions of Anthony Coleman and Bill Frisell, both of whom wrenched an amazing variety of sounds from their instruments. This collection, issued by Tzadik in 1999, also contains a delightful Christmas song, "Blues Noël," which applies the file card method in a much shorter, but charming, piece. *—Stacia Proefrock*

The String Quartets / Jul. 20, 1999 / Tzadik ✦✦✦✦
This fine CD from Tzadik includes all four of John Zorn's works for string quartet. The first piece was composed and recorded in 1988, while the rest were recorded for the first time in 1999, specifically for this release. Zorn describes *Cat O'Nine Tails* as being "about the visual." Full of humor and musical games, this fun composition is subtitled "Tex Avery Meets the Marquis de Sade," and includes beauty, dynamism, strain, and melodrama. *The Dead Man* (1990) is the "sensual" piece that Zorn considers—as he does *Torture Garden*?a soundtrack to S*M scenes. Appropriately, the strings portray the pulling of taut wires and painful screeching throughout the piece's13 sections, each less than two minutes long. &Memento Mori*, from two years later, is the CD's "emotional" work, dedicated to Ikue Mori. Listening to the strings' wavering, plummeting, dipping, and plucking is a journey toward inner depths. With its 29-minute length and unique approach, *Memento Mori* requires special attention; Zorn refers to it as a "complexly hermetic work." The final string quartet is the "spiritual" piece, *Kol Nidre* (1996), related in name (and spirit) to the song of the same name that opens Yom Kippur services. The holy day is a time for forgiveness and reflection; according to the Torah, it is a time to afflict your soul. The composition is a weeper with a slow sway of bowed drones beneath unfurling meditative melodies. Maybe Zorn's genius isn't that he creates entirely unique music, but he certainly has an ear for great musical ideas, gleaned from his years of deep listening. And so, while these compositions may not be landmarks among string quartet works, they are exceedingly well done. *—Joslyn Layne*

• **Masada: Live in Sevilla 2000** / Jul. 25, 2000 / Tzadik ✦✦✦✦✦
Live in Sevilla, recorded and released in the year 2000, is arguably the finest document in this extremely prolific jazz quartet's catalog. If there's anyone who still believes that John Zorn is nothing more than an avant-garde screamer, look no further. The interplay between Zorn's alto and the trumpet of Dave Douglas is nothing short of amazing, and each one's soloing is focused and intense. Joey Baron and Greg Cohen are a fantastic rhythm section; Cohen acts as anchor while Baron playfully dances around the beat, simultaneously supplying a driving pulse. Even when Zorn and Douglas enter the realm of extended techniques (as on the end of "Ne'eman"), Cohen and Baron keep things firmly grounded. Of course, the real stars of the show are Zorn and Douglas; their solos are never less than dazzling, and each has an utterly unique style. Zorn's trademark alto wails are delightful and Dave Douglas has a warm and buttery tone all his own. This might also be the best recorded of the live Masada releases, making it a real jewel in an already glittering discography. *Live in Sevilla* proves that Masada is one of the most exciting jazz ensembles in the world, bar none. *—Sean Westergaard*

Parachute Years, 1977-1980 / Tzadik ✦✦✦✦
The Parachute Years is a seven-CD box of John Zorn's first self-produced recordings, including his systems for structured improvisation based on games (namely "Lacrosse," "Hockey," "Pool," and "Archery"), as well as over two hours of previously unreleased outtakes, rehearsals, etc. Zorn first began developing his game-based ideas in 1974, inspired by the works of such modern composers as Braxton, Kagel, Stockhausen, and Wolff. Two discs worth of "Lacrosse" are here: the first (from June 1978) offers six takes ranging from six to 20 minutes in length performed by Zorn, Mark Abbott, Polly Bradfield, Eugene Chadbourne, and LaDonna Smith; the second presents the original "Lacrosse" recording (from one year earlier) featuring Zorn, Chadbourne, Henry Kaiser, and Bruce Ackley. Next comes a single disc of "Hockey." Two lineups offer their interpretations: first, there are four electric takes (1978) by Chadbourne, Wayne Horvitz, and Bob Ostertag; these are followed by 13 acoustic interpretations by Bradfield, Zorn, and Mark E. Miller. "Pool" was written in March 1979, and the recording included here took place one year later with musicians Zorn, Bradfield, Ostertag, Miller, and Charles K. Noyes, with prompter Lesli Dalaba. The three CDs of "Archery" (one of which is all rehearsals) document a 12-piece ensemble organized in 1981 and consisting of Robert Dick, George Lewis, Anthony Coleman, Kramer, Bill Laswell, Tom Cora, David Moss, Wayne and Bill Horvitz, Chadbourne, Bradfield, and Zorn. This box set is for dedicated fans already intrigued by the early annals of Zorn and his musical game theories. However, Zorn skeptics and listeners with less patience for theory (or history) should definitely avoid *The Parachute Years*. This set will not win anyone over; nor will the theories become more clear upon listening. The recordings in *The Parachute Years* helped the participants—inspired and creative musicians, all—to grow, but they also have more historical value than listening interest. *—Joslyn Layne*

Various Artists

Atlantic Jazz: Classics / Nov. 20, 1956-Jun. 21, 1969 / Rhino ✦✦✦✦
Released to celebrate Atlantic's 50th anniversary, *Atlantic Jazz Classics is a budget-priced, 13-track collection that culls highlights from the Atlantic vaults. The collection spans from the '40s to the '70s and features cuts by $Ray Charles* ("Sweet Sixteen Bars"), the Modern Jazz Quartet ("The Golden Striker"), Art Blakey & Thelonious Monk ("In Walked Bud"), David "Fathead" Newman ("Hard Times"), Charles Mingus ("Wednesday Night Prayer Meeting"), Ornette Coleman ("Ramblin'"), John Coltrane ("My Favorite Things"), Mose Allison ("Your Mind Is On Vacation"), Roland Kirk ("The Inflated Tear") and Les McCann & Eddie Harris' ("Compared to What"). Although it isn't a comprehensive overview, the disc is nevertheless a strong sampler showcasing the finest singers on Atlantic, making it a nice budget-priced introduction to the label for curious listeners on a budget. *—Stephen Thomas Erlewine*

The Bebop Singers / Sep. 16, 1950-Mar. 27, 1973 / Prestige ✦✦✦✦
Drawing almost entirely upon the Prestige archives, with one detour to the Hifijazz label, Fantasy has managed to touch most of the bases of early-'50s vocalese on one invaluable disc. Inevitably, attention clusters around a handful of singers—King Pleasure, Eddie Jefferson, Annie Ross, Jon Hendricks, Irv Taylor, and Joe Carroll—but there are also cameo appearances by the irrepressible Dizzy Gillespie ("She's Gone Again"), a young Betty Carter (with King Pleasure), and Blossom Dearie (also with Pleasure). A number of original landmarks are here: Pleasure's "I'm in the Mood for Love" and "Jumpin' With Symphony Sid," and Ross' still-freshly minted "Twisted." Contrary to the upbeat vocalese image, one is struck here by the quantity of despairing lyrics sung to happy music; Jefferson seems especially prone to depression. The disc does jump outside its period to take in some fine Hendricks remakes of "Moanin'" and "Along Came Betty" with Art Blakey & the Jazz Messengers; without looking at the dates, you can guess the era from Cedar Walton's swinging electric piano on "Moanin'." For collectors, eight of the 23 tracks are new to CD, all tracks from a Prestige LP anthology of the same name; no unreleased goodies, though. Anyone who wants to evoke the feeling of the jazz ethos of the '50s will probably flip over this reissue. *—Richard S. Ginell*

The Best Of Ken Burns Jazz / Sep. 21, 1926-Oct. 10, 1992 / Columbia/Legacy ✦✦✦✦✦

Best of Smooth Jazz / Oct. 28, 1997 / Warner Brothers ✦✦✦✦

The Best of the Swing Bands / 1979 / Vanguard ✦✦✦✦✦

Blue Break Beats, Vol. 1 / Jun. 17, 1964-Jun. 8, 1973 / Blue Note ✦✦✦✦
Blue Note released the two volume *Blue Break Beats* compilation in the early '90s. The music on *Blue Break Beats* dates from the late '60s and early '70s, when a large portion of Blue Note's soul-jazz artists began experimenting with funk and rock, creating dense electric fusions that concentrated on rhythm, not improvisation. None of this music has ever received much critical praise from jazz purists, but in the late '80s and early '90s, scores of hip-hop and dance DJs discovered these old records and began sampling the original tracks to use in new rap and dance songs. By the early '90s, this jazz/rap/funk fusion had become hip and profitable, which led Blue Note to assemble the *Blue Break Beats* compilations. All of the tracks on the two discs are rare tracks from out-of-print late '60s and early '70s albums, featuring multi-layered percussion, organs, and guitars. Every song on the two discs—which are sold seperately—is hot, with a deep funky groove, and there are no dull spots on the albums.

Though it's designed to appeal to fans of contemporary funk and rap, fans of rock-influenced soul-jazz will find *Blue Break Beats* a necessary purchase. *—Stephen Thomas Erlewine*

The Blue Note Years 1939-1999 / Jan. 6, 1939-May 1997 / Blue Note ✦✦✦✦✦

There have been many jazz labels as diverse and musically satisfying as Blue Note, but few have carried the same mystique as Alfred Lion's label, since they not only had the sound, they had the style. Like any label, it had its up and downs, but decades after its inception, the label remained beloved by almost all jazz aficionados. So, when the label's 60th anniversary rolled around in 1998/1999, it made sense that they decided to celebrate in grand style. Not only did they reissue many of their classic albums with glorious remastered sound and restored artwork, they compiled the gargantuan box set *The Blue Note Years: 1939-1999,* which contained no less than seven separate double-disc sets spotlighting different genres and eras in Blue Note's history (with the noticeable omission of anything recorded between 1968-1974, when $Alfred Lion left the label and the new owners instigated pop-jazz, funk, groove and fusion recordings). Certainly, a 14-disc box set isn't for casual fans, but anyone curious about digging deep into the label's past will be thrilled with the set. Each volume—for the record, they are Boogie, Blues & Bop, The Jazz Message, Organ and Soul, Hard Bop and Beyond, Avant Garde, New Era and Blue Note Now as Then—stands as its own little mini-history, covering the major players with representative songs. Sometimes the choices are familiar, sometimes they're not, but they're almost always revelatory, especially when taken in conjunction with the songs that surround them. True, the box is a lot to digest at once (perhaps that's why Blue Note later released all seven volumes individually), but anyone willing to devote the time and money to this set will be richly rewarded. *—Stephen Thomas Erlewine*

Blues, Boogie, and Bop: The Best of the 1940's Mercury Sessions / Apr. 8, 1946-Sep. 20, 1949 / Verve ✦✦✦✦✦

If the exquisitely packaged—the box is shaped like an old-time radio—limited-edition. The 1940s Mercury Sessions is too extravagantly priced or simply unobtainable, this single-disc sampler is the next best thing. For all of the diverse backgrounds and destinations of Mercury's artists, the music on this CD has a distinct identity, conjuring a forgotten time when swing and bop mixed easily with emerging rhythm & blues in bite-sized, under-three-minute slices suitable for every jukebox in every juke joint in the land. The CD leads off with a sampling of the supercharged Albert Ammons piano boogie sessions with a tight little rhythm section (there are more madly swinging choices than these, but you'll get the idea). We hear a pair of Helen Humes blues cuts with loose Buck Clayton-led backup groups, a neat Jay McShann sextet with vintage blues shouting by Jimmy Witherspoon, Eddie "Cleanhead" Vinson's exuberantly bright blues vocals and alto sax, Professor Longhair's early blues-drenched incarnation as plain old Roy Byrd, and Cootie Williams leading a hot jump sextet with tenor Willis Jackson blowin' his fool head off. Only the ornery Buddy Rich defies the Mercury jump-blues sound with two unrepentant sides of big-band swing. Above all, this is a most entertaining souvenir of a time when jazz was still a form of popular music. *—Richard S. Ginell*

Central Avenue Sounds: Jazz in Los Angeles 1921-1956 / Aug. 31, 1999 / Rhino ✦✦✦✦

A companion piece to Steven Isoardi's oral history of jazz of the same name, Rhino's four-disc box *Central Avenue Sounds: Jazz in Los Angeles (1921-1956)* is an ambitious attempt to chronicle the history of the music in the city prior to the cool revolution of the mid-'50s. It does its job well, beginning with Kid Ory and ending with the Gerald Wiggins Trio, and featuring such heavy hitters as Jelly Roll Morton, Louis Armstrong, Art Tatum, Lionel Hampton, Duke Ellington, Joe Turner, Lester Young, T-Bone Walker, Nat "King" Cole, Joe Liggins, Ernie Andrews, Roy Milton, Charlie Parker, Lucky Thompson, Howard McGhee, Jimmy Witherspoon, Charles Mingus, and Charles Brown along the way. That list, no matter how impressive it may be, points out the problem of the collection; it focuses on music recorded in Los Angeles, not music that is identified with Los Angeles. Technically, this is a correct approach; it mirrors the book, which focuses on how Los Angelino jazz came to be. But the approach doesn't quite work as a listening experience, since it feels as if a number of different styles—New Orleans jazz, East Coast jump blues and bop, even Texas blues—have been thrown in a blender. So, even if Central Avenue Sounds fulfills its goal of presenting a history and even if it contains some great, great music, as a listen, the sum is less than its individual parts. *—Stephen Thomas Erlewine*

Chiaroscuro Songbook, Vol. 1 / Mar. 1964-Aug. 8, 1992 / Chiaroscuro ✦✦✦✦

CIMPhonia 1998, Part 2 / May 26, 1998-May 27, 1998 / CIMP ✦✦✦✦✦

Like its predecessor, this is a who's who of some of the leading jazz artists from the CIMP label in a fascinating and wholly successful set of original, mostly improvised compositions. Highlights abound, with different combinations of instruments on each cut. Paul Smoker plays a deadly trumpet with Jay Rosen on drums on the invigorating "Standard," while bassists Dominic Duval and Peter Kowald open with a stunning duo on "Endorpher." Other players include the amazing Joe McPhee on soprano saxophone and pocket trumpet; Mark Whitecage on soprano sax, clarinets and clarisax (!); and Davis Prentice on violin. The two longest pieces, "Wow Wow II" and "Fractals5," feature all seven musicians with some of the best free improvisations on disk. This CD, along with its earlier companion, offer about as good an introduction to these aces of the avant garde as you are likely to find. *—Steve Loewy*

● **Columbia Jazz: The Best of the 50's and 60's** / 1999 / Columbia Jazz ✦✦✦✦✦

Columbia Jazz has been releasing music since 1917 and the label has featured some of the biggest names in jazz over the years. In the 1950s and '60s the label had some of the world's best and greatest jazz artists recording what were to become classic songs. To date, Columbia Jazz has never released a compilation of songs in one package—until this collection. *The Best of the 50's and 60's* is just what the title implies: a four-CD box set that captures the essence of the label during those two decades. This set is only available in Canada at a budget price and contains 47 tracks of incredible jazz classics. It includes an informative 20-page booklet featuring information on each artist and an overview by noted Canadian broadcaster and writer Ross Porter from the CBC. With classic performances by such artists as Louis Armstrong, Miles Davis, Dave Brubeck, Sarah Vaughan, Art Blakey, Aretha Franklin, Dexter Gordon, Billy Holiday and many more, it is easy to see why this is one of the most anticipated jazz releases of 1999. For the casual listener or jazz aficionado, there is something on this set for everyone, and it makes a great companion piece to similar styled jazz boxes released previously by the Verve and Mercury labels. *—Keith Pettipas*

The Commodore Story / Jan. 17, 1938-Apr. 27, 1950 / GRP ✦✦✦✦✦

★ **Complete Commodore Jazz Recordings, Vol. 1** / Apr. 1929-Dec. 21, 1943 / Mosaic ✦✦✦✦✦

The punchline for this 23-LP limited-edition box set is in its title, *Vol. 1.* On a total of 66 albums, Mosaic has reissued the entire jazz output of Milt Gabler's Commodore label, one of the most important jazz record companies of all time. There is an incredible amount of music included on this first set (the most essential of the three). After five early titles that Commodore acquired from other labels (featuring Cow Cow Davenport, Fletcher Henderson, and Django Reinhardt), one hears the birth of Commodore with the exciting January 17, 1938, outing by Eddie Condon. In addition to a lot more of Condon's freewheeling sessions (much of his best work was for Commodore), there are dates led by Bud Freeman, the Kansas City Five and Six (with Lester Young), Teddy Wilson, Jess Stacy, Chu Berry, Willie the Lion Smith, Billie Holiday, Stuff Smith, Jelly Roll Morton, Jack Teagarden, Art Hodes, Joe Marsala, Joe Bushkin, Coleman Hawkins, Lee Wiley, Pee Wee Russell, Bunk Johnson, Mel Powell (with Benny Goodman), Wild Bill Davison, George Brunies, and Edmond Hall. There are many previously unissued performances (not just alternate takes) and literally dozens of classics. Fans of Chicago jazz and small-group swing should bid as much as necessary to acquire this out of print box (along with the other two volumes). *—Scott Yanow*

Complete Jazz at Philharmonic on Verve 1944-1949 / Jul. 2, 1944-Mar. 1952 / Verve ✦✦✦✦✦

Starting in 1944 and continuing for 13 years, producer Norman Granz put on a series of touring all-star jam sessions that frequently matched together many of the top swing and bop musicians on standards and ballads. Critics of the period called the music exhibitionistic and did not think much of the howling audiences, but in reality, the performances were often quite rewarding and consistently exciting. This miraculous ten-CD set has every existing JATP performance from the 1944-49 period, including plenty of unissued performances. The highlights are many including a Nat King Cole/Les Paul tradeoff on "Blues," some screaming Illinois Jacquet solos, Flip Phillips' masterful use of repetition on "Perdido," Charlie Parker creating remarkable solos (particularly on "Lady Be Good" and "Embraceable You"), Ella Fitzgerald holding her own with the very best players of the day, etc. In addition to the jams, there are individual features for Slim Gaillard (the humorous "Groove Juice Symphony"), Meade Lux Lewis, Billie Holiday, the Gene Krupa Trio (including a mini-set from 1952 that was originally included as part of a late-'40s album), Coleman Hawkins, Ken Kersey, Slam Stewart, and Lester Young, among others. A special bit of history is included: Oscar Peterson's first performance in America, which is played to a visibly impressed audience. Among the other all-stars heard from are Roy Eldridge, Buck Clayton, Dizzy Gillespie, Howard McGhee, Bill Harris, J.J. Johnson, Trummy Young, Willie Smith, Hank Jones, Ray Brown, and Buddy Rich, among many others. In addition, on the final disc, there are a few numbers from a Leonard Feather-sponsored concert in 1947 that used similar personnel (including a showboating Charlie Shavers). Every true jazz fanatic has to own this set, which has extensive liner notes and is housed in an attractive box. Get it while you can! *—Scott Yanow*

David X. Young's Jazz Loft: 1954-1965 / 1954-Apr. 1965 / Jazz Magnet ✦✦✦✦✦

Painter/photographer David X. Young utilized his artist loft in New York City's Flower District as a forum and meeting place for many jazz musicians to stretch their wares, amid other extracurricular activities, during the mid-1950s up until 1965. With this sharply dressed 2000 two-CD release, the folks at Jazz Magnet offer the listener over two hours of previously unreleased jam material spanning 1957 through 1965, featuring tenor sax legend Zoot Sims, trombonist Bob Brookmeyer, pianist Dave McKenna, bassist Steve Swallow, and many others of note. Young originally recorded these performances on his Webcor tape machine, and the sonic characteristics are perhaps no less inferior than some of those dearly beloved Charlie Parker LPs that have subsequently been reissued on CD format. Essentially, these various small group ensembles swing into the late night hours, covering such material as Dizzy Gillespie's "Groovin High," Duke Ellington's "It Don't Mean a Thing If It Ain't Got That Swing," along with other standards and originals. And to augment these historic recordings, there is a very appealing 42-page booklet, complete with introductory liner notes by jazz journalist Howard Mandel, candid recollections from bassist Bill Crow, Brookmeyer, and others, along with a sampling of Young's illustrations and paintings. This compilation also includes a poster that is suitable for framing. Overall, the producers have assembled an appealing yet thoroughly contemporary synopsis of a very complex and altogether curiously interesting period in American jazz music. *—Glenn Astarita*

● **The Debut Records Story** / 1952-1957 / Debut ✦✦✦✦✦

In its brief history, Debut Records managed to record a galaxy of bop and progressive-minded jazzers of the time, and this four-CD box set is a great way to get a taste of almost all of the label's releases. A handful of tracks predate the label; they are mostly poorly recorded live snapshots of Charlie Parker, but the sound quality picks up considerably thereafter. The selections go through some quirky Charles Mingus and Max Roach-led sessions that simply reek of the hip early-'50s bop underground, before sampling the famous 1953 Massey Hall concert with Bud Powell, Dizzy Gillespie, Parker, Mingus, and Roach, the records that put Debut on the map. Some of the exciting four-trombone bop sessions with J.J. Johnson, Kai Winding, Bennie Green, and Willie Dennis are here, as are three downcast excerpts from Miles Davis' sole Debut LP *Blue Moods. Besides $Roach,* we hear trumpeters Kenny Dorham and Thad Jones, pianists Paul Bley and Alonzo Levister, trombonist Jimmy Knepper, singer Ada Moore, clarinetist Sam Most, and saxophonist John LaPorta in their debuts as leaders. In a curious jumping-of-the-gun, a description of some Teo Macero Quintet tracks is left in the booklet, even though Fantasy couldn't obtain the rights to the music. By and large, the set is dominated by first-rate bebop, with sprinklings of avant-garde experiments like some really odd, dissonant stuff from the Mingus Octet & Orchestra and LaPorta's offbeat group concepts. Ultimately, The Debut Records Story paints a compelling picture of a quirky yet courageously uncompromising label that catered to what amounted to a small dissident sect in a conformist decade. *— Richard S. Ginell*

★ **From Spirituals to Swing: Carnegie Hall Concerts, 1938-1939** / 1938-1939 / Vanguard ✦✦✦✦✦

From Spirituals to Swing: The Legendary 1938 & 1939 Carnegie Hall Concerts Produced by John Hammond is a three-CD box set which makes good on Hammond's claim that three LP sides' worth of material had gone unreleased after his initial Carnegie Hall Concert releases on Vanguard Records. The studio recordings Hammond surreptitiously added to the original LPs have been retained and documented; tracks that had been edited have been extended; and 23 previously unreleased tracks, most of them from the first concert, have been included. A 44-page booklet repeats notes from earlier editions and adds useful technical notes by reissue producer Steve Buckingham. Also included is a reproduction of the program from the first concert that conveys the political context of a show featuring African-American performers, many of whom had never previously appeared before a white audience, at such a prestigious venue as ~Carnegie Hall. Though extensive sound improvement has been performed, these are still primitive recordings from a period when live recording was almost unknown, and allowances must be made for sound quality. Nevertheless, the power of the performances comes through. The "From Spirituals to Swing" concerts were assembled with a historical, even scholarly intent, but they also brought some amazing music into the concert hall that continues to impress 60 years later. Now, they are not merely historical, but historic, having recorded a high-water mark in American popular music while also accurately tracing the path to that peak. *— William Ruhlmann*

Good Time Jazz Story / Nov. 1938-Oct. 6, 1993 / Good Time Jazz ✦✦✦✦✦

The Good Time Jazz label was formed in 1949 to record the Firehouse Five Plus Two and during its 20 years (particularly during 1949-59) it was one of the top Dixieland labels. It has been revived in the 1990s, most of its releases have been reissued on CD and there have even been a few new recordings. This four-CD box set is a definitive overview of the label. There is no previously unreleased material included but virtually every group that recorded for GTJ is represented: Jelly Roll Morton (1938 solos acquired years later), Burt Bales, Paul Lingle, Luckey Roberts, Willie "The Lion" Smith, Wally Rose, the Banjo Kings, Jesse Fuller, Bunk Johnson, Kid Ory, George Lewis, Johnny Wiggs, Eddie Pierson, Santo Pecora, Armand Hug, Sharkey Bonano, Paul Barbarin, Bill Matthews, George Girard, the Silver Leaf Jazz Band, Scott Black's Hot Horns, Lu Watters, Benny Strickler, Turk Murphy, Bob Scobey, the Bay City Jazz Band, Don Ewell, Clancy Hayes, Pete Daily, Kid Ory, the Castle Jazz Band and the Firehouse Five Plus Two. Although completists will prefer to get the full sessions (except for some of the Banjo Kings titles, virtually all of the selections are available elsewhere on CD) but the very attractive 60-page booklet and the definitive nature of the box will make it a tempting purchase. *— Scott Yanow*

● **Ken Burns' Jazz: The Story of American Music** / Nov. 14, 2000 / Columbia/Legacy ✦✦✦✦✦

In conjunction with documentary filmmaker Ken Burns' ten-part 2000 PBS special, Columbia/Legacy and Verve teamed up to issue a special series of reissues covering much of the history of 20th century jazz. The central release of this program is the five-CD box set Ken Burns Jazz: The Story of America's Music, its 94 selections covering the history of 20th century jazz, from 1917 to the mid-'90s. Chronologically, the set is very skewed toward the first 50 years of that time span; there is only just under a CD's worth of music dating from after the mid-'60s. What's here is a very good range of classic jazz from throughout the decades, touching upon performances, many acknowledged classics, from many of the music's giants: Louis Armstrong, Duke Ellington, Benny Goodman, Billie Holiday, Dizzy Gillespie, Charlie Parker, Thelonious Monk, John Coltrane, Miles Davis, Ornette Coleman, and up to Wynton Marsalis and Cassandra Wilson. There are just a few dubious inclusions (Grover Washington Jr.'s "Mister Magic," for instance), and as music it's nearly wall-to-wall excellence. As far as core classics of the jazz repertoire, there are quite a few: Armstrong's "West End Blues," Goodman's "Sing, Sing, Sing (With a Swing)," Count Basie's "Lester Leaps In," Holiday's "Strange Fruit," Ellington's "Take the 'A' Train," Gillespie's "Salt Peanuts," Monk's "Straight, No Chaser," Davis' "So What," Dave Brubeck's "Take Five," Coltrane's "Giant Steps," Weather Report's "Birdland," and Hancock's "Rockit." As education, if you didn't know much about jazz before hearing this box, you'll have been exposed to a good deal of its major touchstones after digesting it. Just don't be under the impression that it covers all of the main mileposts, or even that it gives you all of the key launching pads from which to explore further. *— Richie Unterberger*

Latino Blue / Jan. 25, 2000 / Blue Note ✦✦✦✦✦

Legends of Acid Jazz: Hammond Heroes / Oct. 12, 1958-Feb. 21, 1967 / Prestige ✦✦✦✦✦

Legends of Acid Jazz: Tenor Titans / Mar. 10, 1969-Aug. 1974 / Prestige ✦✦✦✦✦

The Lost Grooves / 1967-1970 / Blue Note ✦✦✦✦✦

Monterey Jazz Festival: 40 Legendary Years / Oct. 3, 1958-Sep. 22, 1996 / Malapaso/Warner Brothers ✦✦✦✦

This fascinating three-CD set has 28 performances (all but the Billie Holiday number were previously unreleased) taken from the Monterey Jazz Festival and programmed in chronological order. Starting with Dizzy Gillespie playing an unaccompanied version of "The Star Spangled Banner" that opened the very first festival and progressing up until the 1996 edition, there are many memorable selections. Billie Holiday is assisted by Gerry Mulligan on "Fine and Mellow." Mulligan and Art Farmer team up for an excellent version of "Blueport" that almost but not quite reaches the heights of Jeru's 1960 big-band version. Thelonious Monk is heard in 1964 playing "Straight No Chaser" with a workshop group; there are solos by his longtime tenor Charlie Rouse and altoist Buddy Collette, and a long one by trumpeter Bobby Bryant. In one of their earliest meetings, Dizzy Gillespie (still in his prime in 1973) teams up with 20-year-old trumpeter Jon Faddis on "Manteca." Count Basie's band (with trombonist Al Grey) sounds inspired on "I Needs to Be Bee'd With," as does Joe Williams, who sings the full-length version of "Goin' to Chicago." Wynton Marsalis in 1983 reinvents Thelonious Monk's "Think of One," while Sarah Vaughan sounds typically miraculous on "If You Could See Me Now." The colorful release ends with four outstanding tenor solos: Sonny Rollins on the cooking blues "Keep Hold of Yourself," Bob Berg taking a strong cadenza on "I Loves You, Porgy" with Chick Corea, Joshua Redman having a good time on "Home Fries," and Craig Handy emerging as the main voice on Herbie Hancock's "Cantaloupe Island." Recommended. *— Scott Yanow*

The New Wave in Jazz / Mar. 28, 1965 / Impulse! ✦✦✦✦

Nova Bossa: Red Hot on Verve / 1959-1996 / Verve ✦✦✦✦✦

Pioneers of the Jazz Guitar / Nov. 17, 1928-Aug. 26, 1937 / Yazoo ✦✦✦✦✦

● **The Riverside Records Story** / Jan. 25, 1955-Sep. 20, 1963 / Riverside ✦✦✦✦

The Riverside Records Story is essentially Orrin Keepnews' baby—and why not, for the grizzled jazz producer/journalist co-founded the label, ran it from day one in 1952 until it suddenly went bankrupt in 1964, and produced almost all of the original sessions. Riverside's current custodians at Fantasy had Keepnews select and sequence four CDs' worth of the label's output, which over the span of less than nine years made a big splash in the cloistered world of hard bop. Keepnews also writes a voluminous set of notes that settles old scores, crows about What Went Right, offers often self-deprecating analyses of What Went Wrong, and generally keeps the reader riveted to the pages. The box is loosely organized around four topics instead of the usual chronological rundown; indeed, the earliest track, Randy Weston's "Zulu," comes last. And Keepnews devotes lots of time to four major figures whose extensive recordings for Riverside form the cornerstones of their reputations: Cannonball Adderley, Bill Evans, Thelonious Monk, and Wes Montgomery. There are some imaginative sequences that give the collection extra star power—like Monk performing his standards with Coleman Hawkins, John Coltrane, Gerry Mulligan, and Clark Terry, respectively—and there is a welcome touch of the bizarre, too, like Philly Joe Jones' hammy "Blues for Dracula." Moreover, gratefully defying some of his holier-than-thou pronouncements elsewhere, Keepnews does not shy away from his own ventures into the commercial sphere, including Montgomery with strings on "Tune Up," Charlie Byrd likewise on "Meditation," Mongo Santamaria's Top Ten hit "Watermelon Man," and some soul-jazz singles. The first two discs by and large are consistently strong, while some of the lesser tracks on the remaining discs may be there more to represent the artist than to thrill the listener. *— Richard S. Ginell*

The Savoy Story, Vol. 1: Jazz / Sep. 21, 1999 / Savoy Jazz ✦✦✦✦

The old Savoy catalog gets bounced around from one distributor to the next like an unwanted foster child, with everyone starting from scratch once they get a hold of it. By 1999, it was Atlantic's turn and, hot on the heels of other label retrospectives, they have compiled a very good three-CD anthology of Savoy's jazz activities over 15 years in the middle of the 20th century. Decently remastered, the set opens around the tail end of the swing era (capturing some major figures in small-combo jazz like Ben Webster, Lester Young, Illinois Jacquet) and moves on to a detailed portrait of the emergence of bop just after the war. While rarely sticking with artists for very long to track their progress, Savoy (and the labels it absorbed) was a hugely important player in the early days of bop, managing to capture some of the earliest work of Charlie Parker, Dizzy Gillespie, Miles Davis, Fats Navarro, Stan Getz, George Shearing, and Dexter Gordon. The set also tracks mid- to late-'50s hard bop, including numbers by Milt Jackson, Cannonball Adderley, Charlie Byrd, Donald Byrd, Herbie Mann, and other major figures. There are no unreleased goodies—not much that truly ventures out beyond hard bop—and only after the opening of disc three does the canvas of each track expand beyond the length of a single. The set comes in a compact, laminated mini-box with mid-century-style cover art. *— Richard S. Ginell*

● **Swing Time! The Fabulous Big Band Era 1925-1955** / May 14, 1925-Feb. 15, 1955 / Columbia/Legacy ✦✦✦✦✦

This three-CD box set does an excellent job of covering the big-band era through 66 recordings (by almost as many orchestras) owned by Columbia. The selections (programmed in chronological order), although emphasizing the 1934-45 era, also include 18 earlier and six later recordings. The 60 Columbia/Okeh sides, which include the real rarities, are spiced with six tracks (Tommy Dorsey's "Marie," and Jimmy Dorsey's "Green Eyes," Glenn Miller's "In the Mood," Duke Ellington's "Take the 'A' Train," Bob Crosby's "South Rampart Street Parade," and Stan Kenton's "The Peanut Vendor") licensed from RCA, MCA etc., which cover some familiar bases for the benefit of beginners. The accompanying booklet is also excellent. *— Scott Yanow & Bruce Eder*

Texas Tenors / 1946-Aug. 11, 1969 / Prestige ✦✦✦✦✦

Texas isn't the only place that's known for big-toned, hard-blowing tenor saxophonists—Chicago is equally famous in that area—but it's certainly one of the first places that comes to mind when the subject of tenor playing comes up. Whether they are from Dallas/Ft. Worth, Houston, Austin or elsewhere—whether their forte is hard bop, soul-jazz, post-bop or swing—Texas' tenor players have been known for having fat tones and swinging aggressively. Spanning 1946-1969, this good to excellent compilation spotlights over a dozen tenor men who had some connection to the Lone Star State. They might not have spent their entire lives in Texas, but some type of Lone Star connection was there. Tenor fans will recognize most of the saxmen, who range from Arnett Cobb, King Curtis, and Illinois Jacquet, to Booker Ervin, Budd Johnson, and Don Wilkerson. James Clay and David "Fathead" Newman form a two-tenor front line for a 1960 interpretation of Babs Gonzales' "Wide Open Spaces," while Clifford Scott is featured on bluesman Jimmy Witherspoon's "Cane River" from the same year. And Wilton Felder of Crusaders fame is in fine form on organist Charles Kynard's 1969 number "Stomp" (which boasts Joe Pass on guitar). No, *Texas Tenors* isn't the last word on tenor men from the Lone Star State; but it's a rewarding collection that's well worth picking up. *— Alex Henderson*

Trumpet Legacy / May 14, 1997-Apr. 15, 1997 / Milestone ✦✦✦✦✦

Viva Cubop! Jazz the Afro-Cuban Way / Nov. 2, 1999 / Cubop ✦✦✦✦✦

★ **Wildflowers: The New York Loft Jazz Sessions—*Complete* / *May 14, 1976-May 23, 1976 / Knitting Factory*** ✦✦✦✦✦

Originally released as five separate albums under the title Wildflowers: The New York Loft

Sessions on Casablanca records in 1976, this single disc compilation contains ten tracks from those monumental sessions reissued by Knit Classics. Recorded May 14 through 23, 1976, at Sam Rivers' studio/loft/home Rivbea, featuring a collective of free jazz players who were having a hard time getting paying gigs. The entire disc is highlighted by a roster of legends including Hamiet Bluiett, Dave Burrell, Kalaparusha Maurice McIntyre, Sunny Murray, Randy Weston, Byard Lancaster, David Murray, Anthony Braxton, Julius Hemphill, and Ken Mcintyre. Listening to these recordings years after their initial release proves that while these musicians were certainly experimental, they were also obviously steeped in musical traditions like blues and gospel, which was lost on a jazz public turned off by their flashes of unhinged energy. *—Al Campbell*

Index

A

B

C

D

E

G

H

I

J

L

N

O

P

Q

R

S

T

U

V

W

The All Music Guide Series

All Music Guide

"The best overall guide–really the only one in its league." –The Beat

"The definitive reference book for the eclectic music consumer." –Los Angeles Daily News

"...delivers on the promise of every reference tool: It makes you delirious with knowledge." –Entertainment Weekly

"Highly recommended references for discriminating music buyers." –Reviewer's Bookwatch

"Although the AMG was developed specifically to help record buyers decide what to spend their music money on, we find it a powerful informational tool–very condensed and rarely wishy-washy...Such succint summings-up, along with terse chronologies of career phases, and those discussions of genre styles, make the book a true bargain." –Puncture

"Without peer." –Publishers Weekly

"The most useful single volume your money can buy." –Mojo

"A record buyer's bible. Four stars." –Q

"Indispensable.... A major publishing event." –San Francisco Examiner

All Music Guide to Rock

"Best rock guide of the year." –Seattle Times

"...a music lover's dream and a rock journalist's best friend." –Music Connection

"... the information here is sweeping, thorough, memory-jarring, and addictive." –The Arizona Republic

"Simply the best work in the field" –Reference & Research Book News

All Music Guide to Jazz

"Should be on every jazz enthusiast's bookshelf.... Most of the discs are reviewed and rated by the remarkable, indefatigable Scott Yanow." –Philip Elwood, San Francisco Examiner

"This is simply the best single-volume jazz reference book available." –American Reference Books Annual

"Towers over the rest...these vignettes elegantly note the virtues [of each recording] and unflinchingly articulate the flaws..." –Chicago Tribune

"An indispensable resource for any jazz record collector." –Los Angeles Times

"...an excellent and unique jazz reference book. This book is especially good for someone just starting to explore jazz, but it's valuable for everyone interested in the genre. Even the most avid fan will spend hours looking through it. Because it contains so much more than just reviews, the All Music Guide to Jazz is a crash course in jazz culture for the newcomer and a necessary addition to every jazz lover's shelf." –See Magazine